Principal Abbreviations used in the Dictionary

Flem.	Flemish
foll.	followed, following
form.	formation
Fr.	French
Frank.	Frankish
frequent.	frequentative(ly)
G	German
Gael.	Gaelic
gen.	general
genit.	genitive
Geog.	Geography
Geol.	Geology
Geom.	Geometry
Ger.	German
Gk	Greek
Gmc	Germanic
Goth.	Gothic
Gram.	Grammar
Heb.	Hebrew
Hind.	Hindustani
Hist.	History
hist.	with historical reference
Horol.	Horology
Hort.	Horticulture
Hung.	Hungarian
Icel.	Icelandic
IE	Indo-European
illit.	illiterate
imit.	imitative
immed.	immediate(ly)
imper.	imperative
impers.	impersonal
incept.	inceptive
incl.	including; inclusive
Ind.	of the subcontinent comprising India, Pakistan, and Bangladesh
ind.	indirect
indecl.	indeclinable
indef.	indefinite
infin.	infinitive
infl.	influence(d)
instr.	instrumental (case)
int.	interjection
interrog.	interrogative(ly)
intr.	intransitive
Ir.	Irish (language or usage)
iron.	ironical(ly)
irreg.	irregular(ly)
It.	Italian
Jap.	Japan, Japanese
Jav.	Javanese
joc.	jocular(ly)
L	Latin
lang.	language
LG	Low German
lit.	literal(ly)
LL	Late Latin
M	Middle (with languages)
masc.	masculine
Math.	Mathematics
ME	Middle English
Mech.	Mechanics
Med.	Medicine
med.	medieval
med.L	medieval Latin
metaph.	metaphorical
metath.	metathesis
Meteorol.	Meteorology
Mex.	Mexican
Mil.	Military
Mineral.	Mineralogy
mistransl.	mistranslation
mod.	modern
mod.L	modern Latin
Mus.	Music
Mythol.	Mythology
n.	noun
N.Amer.	North America, North American
Nat.	National
Naut.	Nautical
neg.	negative(ly)
N.Engl.	North of England
neut.	neuter
Norm.	Norman
north.	northern
Norw.	Norwegian
n.pl.	noun plural
num.	numeral
NZ	New Zealand
O	Old (with languages)
obj.	object; objective
obs.	obsolete
Obstet.	Obstetrics
occas.	occasional(ly)
OE	Old English
OF	Old French
offens.	offensive
ON	Old Norse
opp.	(as) opposed (to); opposite (of)
orig.	origin; original(ly)
Ornithol.	Ornithology
Palaeog.	Palaeography
Parl.	Parliament; Parliamentary
part.	participle
past part.	past participle
Pathol.	Pathology
pejor.	pejorative
perf.	perfect (tense)

(continued on back endpaper)

THE
CONCISE OXFORD
DICTIONARY

The CONCISE OXFORD DICTIONARY of Current English

FIRST EDITED BY
H. W. Fowler and F. G. Fowler

EIGHTH EDITION
EDITED BY R. E. ALLEN

CLARENDON PRESS · OXFORD

1990

Oxford University Press, Walton Street, Oxford OX2 6DP

Oxford New York Toronto
Delhi Bombay Calcutta Madras Karachi
Petaling Jaya Singapore Hong Kong Tokyo
Nairobi Dar es Salaam Cape Town
Melbourne Auckland
and associated companies in
Berlin Ibadan

Oxford is a trade mark of Oxford University Press

© Oxford University Press 1964, 1976, 1982, 1990

Published in the United States by
Oxford University Press, New York

First edition 1911
New edition (revised) 1929
Third edition (with Addenda) 1934
Fourth edition 1951
Fifth edition 1964
Sixth edition 1976
Seventh edition 1982
Eighth edition 1990

British Library Cataloguing Data
The concise Oxford dictionary of current English.—8th ed.
1. English language—Dictionaries
I. Allen, R. E. (Robert Edward), 1944–423
ISBN 0-19-861243-5 thumb index
ISBN 0-19-861200-1 plain

Library of Congress Cataloging Data
The Concise Oxford dictionary of current English.—8th ed./edited by R. E. Allen.
p. cm.
'First edited by H. W. Fowler and F. G. Fowler.'
ISBN 0-19-861200-1: £10.95.—ISBN 0-19-861243-5 (thumb index)
1. English language—Dictionaries. I. Allen, R. E. II. Fowler,
H. W. (Henry Watson), 1858–1933. III. Fowler, F. G. (Francis
George), 1870–1918.
PE1628.C68 1990
423—dc20 89-72114 CIP

Printed in the United States of America

Contents

Contents

Preface

THE *Concise Oxford Dictionary* is among the most famous books of the world. It is probably the best-known household dictionary despite the appearance in recent years of several rivals. In its previous seven editions, it has reached millions of users in many walks of life, who look to it for comprehensiveness and authority. It is even cited in lawsuits (though usually from old editions). It is, in fact, an institution. When I and my colleagues began the work of writing this edition we were faced, essentially, with the task of producing a dictionary for the 1990s without making it totally unrecognizable as the *Concise*. The result is a completely redesigned edition with clarity and ease of use as the paramount aims, yet retaining and enhancing the authority and thoroughness on which its reputation depends.

We have made very profound changes, especially to the structure and layout of the articles. These now have a systematic numbering of individual definitions (arranged in order of comparative familiarity), separate sections of idioms and phrases, and a greatly increased number of derivatives (routine formations in *-ly*, *-ness*, *-able*, and so on). A main entry is assigned to every defined item that is spelt as one word, and 'nesting' of items has been considerably reduced. Special conventions and abbreviations have been reduced to a minimum, and the swung dash (~) of the last four editions has been discarded. Grammatical information and collocation of words (such as the many constructions with *get* and *take*) are given as accompanying explanations and are no longer embedded in the definitions. A great deal of extra information is given on inflection (*taxis*, *budgeted*, and so on) even where this is arguably 'regular'; and a minimum is left implied, and therefore dependent on explanations given in the Introduction. The definitions have been rewritten in clear continuous prose without dictionary 'telegraphese'. The accounts of word origins (etymologies) have been recast to eliminate speculative and postulated material and to give the user a clearer path to the ultimate sources.

Of great importance is the use of the International Phonetic Alphabet (IPA: see the *User's Guide* at 2.1), newly adopted in this edition (as in the latest editions of the smaller *Pocket* and *Little Oxford Dictionaries*) in the interests of greater precision and consistency and to enable the guidance on pronunciation to be relevant internationally. At the same time the freeing of every headword from special marks and signs further enhances the straightforwardness of presentation which underlies all the changes introduced in this edition.

The choice of vocabulary has been reconsidered and extensively revised. The criterion of currency has been rigorously applied with regard both to individual words and to idiom, so that in general only uses that are well attested in current English are included and uses that are archaic or obsolete are included only when of special interest either because of their importance in literature (as with *e'er* and *forsooth*) or because they are sometimes still used for special effect. A great deal of new vocabulary has been added (several thousand items in all), and this falls broadly into four main areas, with considerable overlap between them.

The first is idiomatic colloquial English, as ever highly productive under many influences. This has been generously treated with the copious use of illustrative examples. The second is what may be loosely termed international English, the varieties of English in use in America, Africa, Australia, and other parts of the world (as more fully explained on p. xix). Thirdly, there are many new words adopted, often along with the things they designate, from other languages and cultures: for example, many terms from international cuisines, such as *nacho* and *tzatziki*, terms for political concepts, such as *glasnost*, and terms for religious ideas and concepts, such as *atman* and *fatwa*.

There is, finally, the vocabulary of science and technology, a growth area commensurate with the expansion of knowledge in the subjects concerned. Two subjects in particular call for mention: information technology (where, however, the new technical vocabulary surprisingly shows little sign of influencing or extending into general idiom), and environmental studies (where our growing awareness of the conditions around us compels us to take note of many new items of fundamental concern: *acid rain*, *CFC*, *global warming*, and so on). More generally, account has been taken of IUPAC nomenclature and other International Systems, such as the SI units. Formal binomial classification of plants and animals is given to support the definitions and to give them an international status.

Spelling and hyphenation have been extensively revised. Because English is a language that has an exceptional tolerance of variations in spelling (*enquire* and *inquire*, *generalize* and *generalise*, and so on) these are areas of particular difficulty to the users of a dictionary. The spellings have been revised in accordance with a critical evaluation of the evidence, which shows, for example, that *jail* is preferred to *gaol*, *inflection* prevails over *inflexion*, and *cooperate* is very widely spelt without a hyphen. With the hyphenation of compounds matters are not so straightforward. Some eighty years ago H. W. and F. G. Fowler, the editors of the original *Concise Oxford Dictionary*, complained that 'after trying hard at an early stage to arrive at some principle that should teach us when to separate, when to hyphen, and when to unite the parts of compound words, we had to abandon the attempt as hopeless, and welter in the prevailing chaos'. Although usage is still often chaotic with individual collocations spelt in any of the three ways (*race course*, *race-course*, or *racecourse*) there are discernible tendencies in more recent usage which make guidance more realistic. The wide use of computer technology in printing (especially in journalism) and in word-processing at all levels is perhaps one important reason for the diminished use of the permanent hyphen in straightforward compounds, and there is now a marked tendency to combine into one word, especially when the elements are both of single syllables. (For further consideration of the hyphen in compounds, see Appendix VIII, § 13.) Among the many changes are *benchmark*, *birdsong*, *breadwinner*, *coalface*, *eardrum*, *figurehead*, *lawbreaker*, *nationwide*, *playgroup*, and *scriptwriter*. This is a welcome tendency, because the hitherto much overused hyphen can now enjoy an enhanced role as a syntactic link to avoid ambiguity (as in *twenty-odd people*, *a third-world conflict*, words such as *re-form* (= form again), and so on).

The need for guidance in these respects is complemented by that relating to areas of disputed and controversial usage and sensitive and offensive vocabulary. Correspondence from users of dictionaries, together with market research, shows that this is an important consideration, and we have given it much attention in the preparation of this edition. Difficulties of linguistic and grammatical usage are dealt with by a system of brief usage notes, supplemented by the designation *disp.* (= disputed) when a use is well attested but controversial. Notes are also included to give additional information not readily contained in the definitions, for example to explain the status of *broker* and *dealer* since the London Stock Exchange reforms of 1986, the change in legal terminology relating to *burglary* and *housebreaking*, and the disappearance in the UK of inland telegrams.

Far greater difficulty attends the treatment of vocabulary that is or can be offensive, either generally or to particular groups of people. All languages contain such words, and no dictionary that claims to treat the language in current use can exclude them. In this edition we have added the label *offens.* to words and uses that are offensive either directly because they offend the people they refer to or by indirect reference or association, often by historical stereotypes. Linguistic usage in such stereotypes is seldom concerned with historical truth but the use, once established, has to be explained, and I hope that by explaining them with appropriate historical comment and a clear indication of the offensiveness involved, a better awareness of their inherent distastefulness may be generated. There are of course terms that vary in the offence they cause with the manner and context in which they are used, and some (such as *pommy* and *mick*) can range in effect from the jocular or even affectionate all the way to the downright offensive. We have tried to take account of these circumstances in the individual dictionary articles, and the user should be aware of them as a general underlying factor.

Users of the *Concise* in the past have often enquired about how the dictionary is written. I have added a brief account of the book's history and the way this edition has been compiled and produced. I have also written a short article on the way English has evolved over many centuries, especially as this affects the circumstances and difficulties that attend its use today.

Acknowledgements

THE most important acknowledgement, by far, is to colleagues who have worked on the dictionary with me. My senior editor, Dr Della Thompson, has made a considerable contribution, to which these few lines can hardly do justice; her intellectual vigour and generously given support have been invaluable. Dr Alexandra Clayton has been largely responsible for the revision of the scientific (especially biochemical and biological) vocabulary, and she has made many important and imaginative improvements. Mr Andrew Hodgson and Ms Fiona Mullan have also made a significant contribution in the preparation and revision of many entries. Ms Julia Swannell contributed to work in the early part of the alphabet. I must also thank, for substantial freelance support, Dr Cyprian Blamires, Mrs Barbara Burge, Mr David Edmonds, Ms Susan Folkins, Mrs Anna Howes, Ms Louise Jones, Mrs F. McDonald, Mrs Jane Reynard, and Ms Kate Stevenson; in scientific subjects, Dr Andrew Baker, Mrs Jane Bowen, Mr Peter Gilliver, Mr Michael Mabe, and Ms Alice Meadows; and, for help with proofreading, Mrs Deirdre Arnold, Mr Morris Carmichael, Mrs Jessica Harrison, Mr Keith Harrison, Ms Georgia Hole, Ms Helen Kemp, Ms E. McIlvanney, Dr Bernadette Paton, Mr Gerard O'Reilly, Dr Freda Thornton, Mr Anthony Toyne, and Mr George Tulloch. Others mentioned elsewhere also contributed to this task.

A central feature of the preparation of this edition has been the in-house computer-keyboarding of the text. Mrs Anne Whear, who has been involved with the *Concise* for some years and worked on materials for the sixth and seventh editions, undertook the management of the data-capture, and has performed a remarkable service which has been crucial to the production of the text; by her sharp vigilance and keen awareness of problems she has indeed contributed substantially to its quality. I am deeply indebted to her, and also to Dr Kate Mertes, who has given invaluable assistance in keyboarding and in organizing the distribution of materials in the proofreading and consultancy stages, and to Mrs Alison Allen, who has also contributed to the keyboarding.

For provision of an excellent computer program and support service I must acknowledge Compulexis Ltd., and in particular Mr Henning Madsen, its managing director; Mr Jerry Freestone; and Mr Simon Mills. They not only provided us with first-class materials, but stimulated a lively reconsideration of many aspects of the editorial work that has been of great benefit to the eventual text. It is a pleasure to be able to record at last my appreciation of their most important role. I must also thank Mr Ronald McIntosh, who put his considerable experience and wisdom at our disposal in the early stages. The work of setting and producing the dictionary was done by the Oxford Text System, and I should like to thank all those involved in this, especially Mr Graham Roberts.

Many people inside and outside the Oxford Dictionaries Department have provided critical advice of various kinds. Dr I. Grafe and Mr M. W. Grose both read the entire text and suggested many important additions and improvements. For help in special areas of knowledge I must thank the following: Mr Jonathan Bowen, Dr Humphrey Bowen, Mrs Barbara Burge, Mr Julian Clayton, Mrs Alana Dickinson, Ms Pamela Ferris, Dr D. Hall, Professor Anthony Hallam, Mr Ian Kingston, Dr Anne Lackie, Dr Ghislaine Lawrence, Dr Julius Lipner, Mr E. Luard, Mr Gerard O'Reilly, Mrs Jane Reynard, Dr Paul Singleton, and Dr William Trumble.

I should also like to thank the many correspondents who have sent in criticisms and other material, often in large quantities and over several years. I am especially indebted in this regard to Mr J. W. Gardner, Lord Kilbracken, Mr R. Lindsay, and Mr E. Trehern (who has corresponded with editors of the *Concise* since the 1930s).

I owe a very special debt to my predecessor, Dr J. B. Sykes, editor of the sixth and seventh editions of the *Concise*. Despite the many changes and additions introduced in the eighth edition, it continues to benefit from his scholarship and his profound understanding of language. I am also much indebted to Dr R. W. Burchfield, formerly Chief Editor of the Oxford English Dictionaries, for his continued interest in the work of this dictionary.

R.E.A.

February 1990

English over Fifteen Centuries

1. Fifteen centuries of English cannot easily be summarized in about the same number of paragraphs, and this account is intended to pick out features on the landscape of language rather than to describe the scene in detail. This may afford some perspective to the information given in the dictionary, and help to make more sense of the strange and often unpredictable ways in which words seem to behave.

Origins

2.1 English belongs to the Indo-European family of languages, a vast group with many branches, thought to be derived from a common ancestor-language called Proto-Indo-European. The words we use in English are derived from a wide range of sources, mostly within this family. The earliest sources are Germanic, Norse, and Romanic; later, they are the languages of Europe more generally; and most recently, with the growth and decline of the British Empire and the rapid development of communications, they have been worldwide.

2.2 It is difficult to be sure exactly what we mean by an 'English' word. Most obviously, words are English if they can be traced back to the Anglo-Saxons, Germanic peoples who settled in Britain from the fifth century and eventually established several kingdoms together corresponding roughly to present-day England. From this time are derived many common words such as *eat*, *drink*, *speak*, *work*, *house*, *door*, *man*, *woman*, *husband*, *wife*. They displaced the Celtic peoples, whose speech survives in Scottish and Irish Gaelic, in Welsh, and in the local languages of two extremities of the British Isles, Manx (in the Isle of Man) and Cornish. Little Celtic influence remains in English, except in names of places such as *Brecon*, *Carlisle*, and *London*, and in many river names, such as *Avon*, *Thames*, and *Trent*. This fact may be attributed to a lack of cultural interaction, the Celts being forced back into the fringes of the British Isles by the Anglo-Saxon invaders, although there must have been some social integration.

3. Anglo-Saxon Britain continued to have contact with the Roman Empire, of which Britain had formerly been a part, and with Latin, which was the official language throughout the Empire and survived as a language of ritual (and for a time also of learning and communication) in the Western Christian Church. Christianity was brought to England with the mission of St Augustine in AD 597. The Christianized Anglo-Saxons built churches and monasteries, and there were considerable advances in

art and learning. At this time English was enriched by many words from Latin, some of which are still in use, such as *angel*, *disciple*, *martyr*, and *shrine*. Other words were derived from Latin via the Germanic languages, for example *copper*, *mint* (in the sense of coinage), *pound*, *sack*, and *tile*, and others were ultimately of oriental origin, for example *camel* and *pepper*.

4.1 The next important influence on the vocabulary of English came from the Danish and other Scandinavian invaders of the ninth and tenth centuries, collectively called Vikings. They occupied much of the east side of England, and under Cnut (Canute) ruled the whole country for a time. The Danes had much more contact with the Anglo-Saxons than did the Celts, and their period of occupation has left its mark in the number of Scandinavian (Old Norse) words taken into English. Because Old Norse was also a Germanic language (of a different branch from English) many words were similar to the Anglo-Saxon ones, and it is difficult to establish the extent of the Old Norse influence. However, a number of Norse words are identifiable and are still in use, such as *call*, *take*, and *law*, names of parts of the body such as *leg*, and other basic words such as *egg*, *root*, and *window*. Many more Norse words are preserved in some dialects of the east side of England, in place-names such as those ending in *-thwaite* and *-thorpe* (both meaning 'settlement') and in *-by* (*Grimsby*, *Rugby*, *Whitby*, and so on), and in street-names ending in *-gate* (from the Old Norse *gata* meaning 'street') such as *Coppergate* in York.

4.2 In the Saxon kingdom of Wessex, King Alfred (871–99) and his successors did much to keep English alive by using it (rather than Latin) as the language of education and learning; by the tenth century there was a considerable amount of English prose and verse literature. Saxon and Danish kingdoms existed side by side for several generations, and there was much linguistic interaction. One very important effect on English was the gradual disappearance of many word-endings, or inflections, leading to a simpler grammar. This was partly because the stems of English and Norse words were often very close in form (for example, *stān* and *steinn*, meaning 'stone'), and only the inflections differed as an impediment to mutual understanding. So forms such as *stāne*, *stānes*, etc., began to be simplified and, eventually, eliminated. The process continued for hundreds of years into Middle English (see below).

The Norman Conquest

5. In 1066 William of Normandy defeated the English king, Harold, at the Battle of Hastings; he was crowned King of England on Christmas Day. The arrival of the French-speaking Normans as a ruling nobility brought a transforming Romance influence on the language. The Romance languages (chiefly French, Italian, Spanish, Portuguese, and Romanian) have their roots in the spoken or 'vulgar' Latin that continued in use

until about AD 600. For two hundred years after the Norman Conquest, French (in its regional Norman form) was the language of the aristocracy, the lawcourts, and the Church hierarchy in England. Gradually the Normans were integrated into English society (for example, by inter-marriage), and by the reign of Henry II (1154-89) many of the aristocracy spoke English. During these years many French words were adopted into English. Some were connected with law and government, such as *justice*, *council*, and *tax*, and some were abstract terms such as *liberty*, *charity*, and *conflict*. The Normans also had an important effect on the spelling of English words. The combination of letters *cw-*, for example, was standardized in the Norman manner to *qu-*, so that *cwēn* became *queen* and *cwic* became *quik* (later *quick*).

6. This mixture of conquering peoples and their languages—Germanic, Scandinavian, and Romance—has had a decisive effect on the forms of words in modern English. The three elements make up the basic stock of English vocabulary, and different practices of putting sounds into writing are reflected in each. The different grammatical characteristics of each element can be seen in the structure and endings of many words. Many of the variable endings such as *-ant* and *-ent*, *-er* and *-or*, *-able* and *-ible* exist because the Latin words on which they are based belonged to different classes of verbs and nouns, each of which had a different ending. For example, *important* comes from the Latin verb *portare*, meaning 'to carry' (which belongs to one class or conjugation) while *repellent* comes from the Latin verb *pellere*, meaning 'to drive' (which belongs to another). *Capable* comes from a Latin word ending in *-abilis*, while *sensible* comes from one ending in *-ibilis*, and so on.

Middle English

7. Middle English, as the English of *c.*1100-1500 is called, emerged as the spoken and written form of the language under these influences. The use of French diminished, especially after King John (1199-1216) lost possession of Normandy in 1204, severing an important Anglo-French link. Many Anglo-Saxon words continued in use, while others disappeared altogether: for example, *niman* was replaced by the Old Norse (Scan-dinavian) *taka* (meaning 'take'), and the Old English *sige* was replaced by a word derived from Old French, *victory*. Other Old English words that disappeared are *ādl* (disease), *lof* (praise), and *lyft* (air: compare German *Luft*). Sometimes new and old words continued in use side by side, in some cases on a roughly equal footing, and in others with a distinction in meaning (as with *doom* and *judgement*, and *stench* and *smell*). This has produced pairs of words which are both in use today, such as *shut* and *close*, and *buy* and *purchase*, in which the second word of each pair is Romance in origin. Sometimes an even larger overlap was produced, as when *commence* (from the French) was added to the existing Old English

begin and *start*. (The original meaning of *start* was 'leap', 'move suddenly', which is still current though no longer the main sense.)

8. Hundreds of the Romance words were short simple words that would now be distinguished with difficulty from Old English words if their origin were not known: for example, *bar*, *cry*, *fool*, *mean*, *pity*, *stuff*, *touch*, and *tender*. Others, such as *commence* and *purchase*, have more formal connotations. The result was a mixture of types of words, which is a feature especially of modern English. For many meanings we now have a choice of less and more formal words, and the more formal ones in some cases are used only in very specific circumstances. For example, the word *vendor* is used instead of *seller* only in the context of buying or selling property. Many technical words derived from or ultimately from Latin, such as *estop* and *usucaption*, survive only in legal contexts, to the great confusion of the layman. These levels of formality are reflected in the dictionary's identification of usage level in particular cases as colloquial, formal, and so on, more fully explained in the *Guide to the Use of the Dictionary* at 9.3.

Printing

9. There was much regional variation in the spelling and pronunciation of Middle English, although a good measure of uniformity was imposed by the development of printing from the fifteenth century. This uniformity was based as much on practical considerations of the printing process as on what seemed most 'correct' or suitable. It became common practice, for example, to add a final *e* to words to fill a line of print. The printers—many of whom were foreign—used rules from their own languages, especially Dutch and Flemish, when setting English into type. William Caxton, the first English printer (1422-91), exercised an important but not always beneficial influence. The unnecessary insertion of *h* in *ghost*, for example, is due to Caxton (who learned the business of printing on the Continent), and the change had its effect on other words such as *ghastly* and (perhaps) *ghetto*. In general, Caxton used the form of English prevalent in the south-east of England, although the East Midland dialect was the more extensive. This choice, together with the growing importance of London as the English capital, gave the dialect of the South-East a special importance that survives to the present day.

Pronunciation

10. At roughly the same time as the early development of printing, the pronunciation of English was also undergoing major changes. The main change, which began in the fourteenth century during the lifetime of the poet Chaucer, was in the pronunciation of vowel sounds. The so-called 'great vowel shift' resulted in the reduction of the number of long vowels (for example, in *deed* as distinct from *dead*) from seven to the five which

we know today (discernible in the words *bean*, *barn*, *born*, *boon*, and *burn*). It also affected the pronunciation of other vowels: the word *life*, for example, was once pronounced as we now pronounce *leaf*, and *name* was pronounced as two syllables to rhyme with *farmer*. In many cases, as with *name*, the form of the word did not change; and this accounts for many of the 'silent' vowels at the ends of words. The result of these developments was a growing difference between what was spoken and what was written.

The Renaissance

11.   The rediscovery in Europe of the culture and history of the ancient Greek and Roman worlds exercised a further Romanizing influence on English. This began at the end of the Middle Ages and blossomed in the European Renaissance of the fifteenth to seventeenth centuries. Scholarship flourished, and the language used by scholars and writers was Latin. During the Renaissance words such as *arena*, *dexterity*, *excision*, *genius*, *habitual*, *malignant*, *specimen*, and *stimulus* came into use in English. They are familiar and useful words but their Latin origins sometimes make them awkward to handle, as, for example, when we use *arena*, *genius*, and *stimulus* in the plural. There was also a tendency in the Renaissance to try to emphasize the Greek or Latin origins of words when writing them. This accounts for the *b* in *debt* (the earlier English word was *det*; in Latin it is *debitum*), the *l* in *fault* (earlier *faut*; the Latin source is *fallere* fail), the *s* in *isle* (earlier *ile*; *insula* in Latin), and the *p* in *receipt* (earlier *receit*; *recepta* in Latin). Some words that had gone out of use were reintroduced, usually with changed meanings, for example *artificial*, *disc* (originally the same as *dish*), and *fastidious*.

Later influences

12.   The development of machines and technology in Britain from the eighteenth century onwards, followed by the electronic revolution of our own times, has also played a part in continuing the influence of Latin. New technical terms have come into use, and they have often been formed on Latin or Greek source-words because these can convey precise ideas in easily combinable forms, for example *bacteriology*, *microscope*, *radioactive*, and *semiconductor*. Combinations of Germanic elements are also used, as in *software*, *splashdown*, and *take-off*. This process has sometimes produced odd mixtures, such as *television*, which is half Greek and half Latin, and *microchip*, which is half Greek and half Germanic.

13.1   In recent times English speakers have come into contact with people from other parts of the world, through trade, the growth of the British Empire, and improved communications generally. This contact has produced a rich supply of new words that are often strange in form. India, where the British first had major dealings in the seventeenth century, is the source of words such as *bungalow, jodhpurs*, and *khaki*. Usually these words have been altered or assimilated to make them look more natural in English (e.g. *bungalow* from Gujarati *bangalo*). Examples from other parts of the world are *harem* and *mufti* (from Arabic), *bazaar* (from Persian), *kiosk* (from Turkish), and *anorak* (from Eskimo). From European countries we have acquired *balcony* (from Italian), *envelope* (from French), and *yacht* (from Dutch).

13.2 Thousands of such words, though not English in the Germanic sense, are regarded as fully absorbed into English. In addition, there are many unnaturalized words and phrases that are used in English contexts but are generally regarded as 'foreign', and are conventionally printed in italics to distinguish them when used in an English context. Very many of these are French, for example *accouchement* (childbirth), *bagarre* (a scuffle), *bonhomie* (geniality), *flânerie* (idleness), and *rangé* (domesticated), but other languages are represented, as with *echt* (genuine) and *machtpolitik* (power politics) from German, and *mañana* (tomorrow) from Spanish.

14.1 Usage often recognizes the difficulties of absorbing words from various sources by assimilating them into forms that are already familiar. The word *picturesque*, which came into use in the eighteenth century, is a compromise between its French source *pittoresque* and the existing Middle English word *picture*, to which it is obviously related. The English word *cockroach* is a conversion of its Spanish source-word *cucaracha* into a pair of familiar words *cock* (a bird) and *roach* (a fish). Cockroaches have nothing to do with cocks or roaches, and the association is simply a matter of linguistic convenience.

14.2 Problems of inflection arise with words taken from other languages. The ending *-i* in particular is very unnatural in English, and usage varies between *-is* and *-ies* in the plural. A similar difficulty occurs with the many adopted nouns ending in *-o*, some of which come from the Italian (*solo*), some from Spanish (*armadillo*), and some from Latin (*hero*); here usage varies between *-os* and *-oes*. Verbs often need special treatment, as for example *bivouac* (from French, and before that probably from Swiss German) which needs a *k* in the past tense (*bivouacked*, not *bivouaced* which might be mispronounced), and *ski* (from Norwegian) where usage allows both *ski'd* and *skied* as past forms (though neither is satisfactory). In this dictionary extensive help is given with these and other difficulties of inflection.

Dictionaries

15.1 One obvious consequence of the development of printing in the fifteenth century was that it allowed the language to be recorded in glossaries and dictionaries, and this might be expected to have had a considerable effect on the way words were used and spelt. However, listing all the words in the language systematically in alphabetical order with their spellings and meanings is a relatively recent idea. There was nothing of the sort in Shakespeare's time, for example. In 1580, when Shakespeare was sixteen, a schoolmaster named William Bullokar published a manual for the 'ease, speed, and perfect reading and writing of English', and he called for the writing of an English dictionary. Such a dictionary, the work of Robert Cawdrey (another schoolmaster), was not published until 1604. Like the dictionaries that followed in quick succession (including Bullokar's own *English Expositor*), its purpose was described as being for the understanding of 'hard words'. It was not until the eighteenth century that dictionaries systematically listed all the words in general use at the time regardless of how 'easy' or 'hard' they were; the most notable of these were compiled by Nathaniel Bailey (1721) and, especially, Samuel Johnson (1755). They were partly a response to a call, expressed by Swift, Pope, Addison, and other writers, for the language to be fixed and stabilized, and for the establishment of an English Academy to monitor it. None of these hopes as such were realized, but the dictionaries played an important role in settling the form and senses of English words.

15.2 The systematic investigation and recording of words in all their aspects and on a historical basis is first and exclusively represented in the *Oxford English Dictionary*, begun by the Scottish schoolmaster James A. H. Murray in 1879. This describes historically the spelling, inflection, origin, and meaning of words, and is supported by citations from printed literature and other sources as evidence from Old English to the present day. To take account of more recent changes and developments in the language, a four-volume *Supplement* was added to the work from 1972 to 1986, and a new edition integrating the original dictionary and its *Supplement* appeared in 1989. Because of its depth of scholarship, the *Oxford English Dictionary* forms a major basis of all English dictionaries produced since. Smaller concise and other household dictionaries that aim at recording the main vocabulary in current use began to appear early this century and in recent years the number has grown remarkably.

15.3 Dictionaries of current English, as distinct from historical dictionaries, generally record the language as it is being used at the time, and with usage constantly changing the distinction between 'right' and 'wrong' is sometimes difficult to establish. Unlike French, which is guided by the rulings of the *Académie Française*, English is not monitored by any single authority; established usage is the principal criterion. One result of this is that English tolerates many more alternative spellings than other languages. The alternatives are based on certain patterns of word formation and variation in the different languages through which they have passed before reaching ours.

15.4 It should also be remembered that the smaller dictionaries, such as this one, provide a selection, based on currency, of a recorded stock of over half a million words; that is to say, they represent about 15–20 per cent of what is attested to exist by printed sources and other materials. Dictionaries therefore differ in the selection they make, beyond the core of vocabulary and idiom that can be expected to be found in any dictionary.

Dialect

16. Within the British Isles, regional forms and dialects, with varying accents and usage, have continued to exist since the Middle Ages, although in recent times, especially with the emergence of mass communications, they have been in decline. A special feature of a dialect is its vocabulary of words (often for everyday things) that are understood only locally. It is not possible in a small dictionary to treat this kind of vocabulary in any detail, but its influence can be seen in the origins of words that have achieved a more general currency, for example *boss-eyed* (from a dialect word *boss* meaning 'miss', 'bungle'), *fad*, *scrounge* (from dialect *scrunge* meaning 'steal'), and *shoddy*. Far more information on dialect words is available in *The English Dialect Dictionary* (ed. J. Wright, London, 1898–1905), in the *Oxford English Dictionary*, and in numerous glossaries published by dialect societies.

English Worldwide

17.1 Usage in modern times is greatly influenced by rapid worldwide communications, by newspapers and, in particular, by television and radio. Speakers of British English are brought into daily contact with alternative forms of the language, especially American English. This influence is often regarded as unsettling or harmful but it has had a considerable effect on the vocabulary, idiom, and spelling of British English, and continues to do so. Among the many words and idioms in use in British English, usually without any awareness of or concern about their American origin, are *OK*, *to fall for*, *to fly off the handle*, *round trip*, and *to snoop*. American English often has more regular spellings, for example the substitution of *-er* for *-re* in words such as *theatre*, the standardization of *-or* and *-our* to *-or* in words such as *harbour*, and the use of *-se* in forms such as *defense* and *license*, where British English either has *-ce* only or both forms (for example, a *practice* but to *practise*).

17.2 English is now used all over the world; as a result, there are many varieties of English, with varying accents, vocabulary, and usage. In addition to British and American English there are varieties in use in Southern Africa, India, Australia, New Zealand, Canada, and elsewhere. These varieties have an equal claim to be regarded as 'English' and, although learners of English may look to British English as the centre of an English-speaking world, or British and American English as the two poles of such a world, it is very important that dictionaries should take account of English overseas, especially as it affects that in use in Britain. The process is a strengthening and enriching one, and is the mark of a living and flourishing language.

Further reading

18. This survey has had to be brief, and restricted to those aspects of English that are of immediate concern to the users of a dictionary. Those who are interested in exploring further will find a host of books on the history and development of English. Good general accounts are A. C. Baugh and T. Cable, *A History of the English Language* (3rd edn., New Jersey and London, 1978) and B. M. H. Strang, *A History of English* (London, 1970). At a more popular level, and more up to date on recent trends, are R. W. Burchfield, *The English Language* (Oxford, 1985) and R. McCrum *et al.*, *The Story of English* (London, 1986). *The Oxford Companion to the English Language* (ed. T. McArthur, Oxford, forthcoming) contains much that will interest those who want to know more about the English of today and its place among the languages of the world.

Eighty Years of the *Concise Oxford Dictionary*

THE *Concise Oxford Dictionary* (COD) was one of the first small dictionaries of current English, though not the very first (*Chambers's Twentieth Century Dictionary*, for example, preceded it by ten years). It was published in 1911, in the wake of the colossal task of recording the language in the *New* (later *Oxford*) *English Dictionary* (OED), which at that stage had been issued up to the letter R. The first editors of the *Concise* were H. W. and F. G. Fowler, who had written a prescriptive manual of grammar, *The King's English*, published by the Clarendon Press in 1906. H. W. Fowler was later to write an even more famous book, *A Dictionary of Modern English Usage*, which was published in 1926. The Fowlers took five years to write the *Concise*, and the last part (from S to Z) was written without sight of the corresponding section of the OED. They worked at home on Guernsey, and lacked the extensive resources of data about language that are available to the modern dictionary-compiler.

They described the editorial approach as follows, in the preface to the first edition:

The book is designed as a dictionary, and not as an encyclopaedia; that is, the uses of words and phrases as such are its subject-matter, and it is concerned with giving information about the things for which those words and phrases stand only so far as correct use of the words depends upon knowledge of the things. The degree of this dependence varies greatly with the kind of word treated, the difference between cyclopaedic and dictionary treatment varies with it, and the line of distinction is accordingly a fluctuating and dubious one. It is to the endeavour to discern and keep to this line that we attribute whatever peculiarities we are conscious of in this dictionary as compared with others of the same size. One of these peculiarities is the large amount of space given to the common words that no one goes through the day without using scores or hundreds of times, often disposed of in a line or two on the ground that they are plain and simple and that every one knows all about them by the light of nature, but in fact entangled with other words in so many alliances and antipathies during their perpetual knocking about the world that the idiomatic use of them is far from easy; chief among such words are the prepositions, the conjunctions, the pronouns, and such 'simple' nouns and verbs as *hand* and *way*, go and *put*. Another peculiarity is the use, copious for so small a dictionary, of illustrative sentences as a necessary supplement to definition when a word has different senses between which the distinction is fine, or when a definition is obscure and unconvincing until exemplified; these sentences often are, but still more often are not, quotations from standard authors; they are meant to establish the sense of the definition by appeal not to external authority, but to the reader's own consciousness, and therefore their source, even when authoritative, is not named. A third and a fourth peculiarity are the direct results of the preceding ones; if common words are to be treated at length, and their uses to be copiously illustrated, space must be saved both by the curtest possible treatment of all that are either uncommon or fitter for the encyclopaedia than the dictionary, and by the severest economy of expression—amounting to the adoption of telegraphese—that readers can be expected to put up with.

H. W. Fowler added the following in the preface to the second edition:

The object we set before us, hinted at by the word *current* on our title-page, was to present as vivid a picture as the small dictionary could be made to give of the English that was being spoken and written at the time. The vividness was to be secured by allotting space to words more nearly in proportion to the frequency and variety of their use, and consequently to their practical value, than had been the custom; and further by an unprecedented abundance of illustrative quotation; define, and your reader gets a silhouette; illustrate, and he has it 'in the round'. That at least was our belief; and we hailed as confirmation of it one or two letters from persons unknown congratulating us on having 'produced a live dictionary', or 'treating English at last as a living language'.

It was a great achievement, assembling vast amounts of information in a small compass and in an ingeniously devised (some might now say idiosyncratic) style incorporating many special conventions and a complex use of typography. The dictionary articles examined the meanings of words in minute detail and explored the byways of idiom and grammar on the way, scattering phrases and compounds through the articles as they went. This basic approach remained intact in successive editions: the second (by H. W. Fowler, 1929), the third (by H. G. Le Mesurier, 1934), and the fourth and fifth (by E. McIntosh, 1951 and 1964). The sixth edition (by J. B. Sykes, 1976) was a far more extensive revision, with changes of presentation and the addition of much new vocabulary derived from work on the new *Supplement to the Oxford English Dictionary*, the second volume of which (H–N) was published in the same year. A seventh edition, also by J. B. Sykes, appeared in 1982.[1]

The following, from the Introduction to the sixth edition, remains fundamental:

The general aims of the dictionary have remained as they were specified by the original editors. The words, phrases, and meanings given are those current in the English of the present day—either in living use, or familiar through their occurrence in frequently quoted literature of the past. The attitude taken, however, is now essentially descriptive rather that prescriptive: that is, the dictionary seeks to record what is found to exist in the educated use of modern English.

Indeed, some of the vocabulary and usage contained in the present edition may not be regarded as particularly 'educated'; this too must have its place (appropriately identified) in the record.

---

[1] I have written a much fuller account of the history of the COD in *The History of Lexicography* (*Papers from the Dictionary Research Centre Seminar at Exeter, March 1986*), ed. R. R. K. Hartmann (Amsterdam Studies in the Theory and History of Linguistic Science, 1986), 1–11.

With this eighth edition the COD has entered the computer age. The text was initially assembled as a computer database, with some forty or so types of information (headword, pronunciation, part of speech, idiom, etc.) separately identified and electronically tagged. This database will continue to exist as a flexible and readily updated store of information; from it a printing tape has been derived to produce the pages of the text. The dictionary articles have a completely new structure, and the result is a text very different in appearance from that of its predecessors.

The content has been assembled from a number of sources. The ultimate source of everything in the dictionary is evidence of words in use. Nowadays this evidence includes computer databases as well as material on paper, and it is assembled from a large and varied body of extensively read printed sources, ranging from newspapers and popular literature to specialist journals, textbooks, and other technical matter. This forms the raw material from which the new vocabulary has been drawn and also informs the treatment of the inner core of vocabulary, which has been revised, and in large part rewritten, from the material in the previous edition.

In the present edition the distinction emphasized, with reservations, by the Fowlers between what is appropriate to a dictionary and what to an encyclopaedia is rather less strictly maintained, partly because of the substantial growth of technical vocabulary of a kind that requires more elaborate explanation of the things the words stand for. The 'economy of expression' is much less severe; and the 'telegraphese', as explained elsewhere, is abandoned. The result is a larger book. Dictionaries, like the language, are changing and developing. The COD has been an institution for eighty years and has always been, in style and content, a product of its age. With this edition, and with those that come after it, it will continue to be so.

Guide to the Use of the Dictionary

1. Use of conventions

1.1 In this edition, a great deal of the information given in the dictionary entries is self-explanatory, and the use of special conventions has been kept to a minimum. The following pages are meant to explain the editorial approach and to assist the user by explaining the principles involved in assembling the information.

2. Headword

2.1 The headword is printed in bold roman type, or in bold italic type if the word is not naturalized in English and is usually found in italics in printed matter:

> **saddle** /'sæd(ə)l/ n. & v. —n. **1** a seat of leather etc., usu. raised at the front and rear, fastened on a horse etc. for riding. **2** a seat for the rider of a bicycle etc. **3** a joint of meat consisting of the two loins. **4** a ridge rising to a summit at each end. **5** the part of a

2.2.1 Variant spellings are given before the definition; in all such cases the form given as the headword is the preferred form. Variant forms are also given at their own places in the dictionary when these are three or more entries away from the main form:

> **saguaro** /sæ'gwɑːrəʊ/ n. (also **sahuaro** /sæ'wɑːrəʊ/) (pl. **-os**) a giant cactus, *Carnegiea gigantea*, of the SW United States and Mexico. [Mex. Sp.]

2.2.2 Variant spellings given at the beginning of an entry normally apply to the whole entry, including any phrases and undefined derivatives (see below, 10–12).

2.2.3 When variants apply only to certain functions or senses of a word, these are given in brackets at the relevant point in the entry.

2.2.4 Words that are normally spelt with a capital initial are given in this form as the headword; when they are in some senses spelt with a small initial and in others with a capital initial this is indicated by repetition of the full word in the appropriate form within the entry.

2.2.5 Variant American spellings are indicated by the designation *US*. These variants are often found in American use in addition to the main forms given:

> **sabre** /'seɪbə(r)/ n. & v. (*US* **saber**) —n. **1** a cavalry sword with a curved blade. **2** a cavalry soldier and horse. **3** a light fencing-sword with a tapering blade. —v.tr. cut down or wound with a sabre.

2.2.6 Pronunciation of variants is given when this differs significantly from the pronunciation of the headword.

2.3 Words that are different but spelt the same way (homographs) are distinguished by superior numerals:

> **bat**[1] /bæt/ *n. & v.* —*n.* **1** an implement with a handle, usu. of wood and with a flat or curved surface, used for hitting balls in games. **2** a turn at using this. **3** a batsman, esp. in cricket, usu. described in some way (*an excellent bat*). **4** (usu. in *pl.*) an object like a table-tennis bat used to guide aircraft when taxiing. —*v.* (**batted, batting**) **1** *tr.* hit with or as with a bat. **2** *intr.* take a turn at batting. □**bat around 1** *sl.* potter aimlessly. **2** *US* discuss (an idea or proposal). **off one's own bat** unprompted, unaided. **right off the bat** *US* immediately. [ME f. OE *batt* club, perh. partly f. OF *batte* club f. *battre* strike]
> **bat**[2] /bæt/ *n.* any mouselike nocturnal mammal of the order Chiroptera, capable of flight by means of membranous wings extending from its forelimbs. □**have bats in the belfry** be eccentric or crazy. **like a bat out of hell** very fast. [16th c., alt. of ME *bakke* f. Scand.]
> **bat**[3] /bæt/ *v.tr.* (**batted, batting**) wink (one's eyelid) (now usu. in phr.). □**not** (or **never**) **bat an eyelid** *colloq.* show no reaction or emotion. [var. of obs. *bate* flutter]

3. Pronunciation

3.1.1 Guidance on pronunciation follows the system of the International Phonetic Alphabet (IPA), and is based on the pronunciation associated especially with southern England (sometimes called 'Received Pronunciation').

3.1.2 It is not possible in a dictionary of this size to show the many variations heard in educated speech in other parts of the English-speaking world.

3.2 The symbols used, with their values, are as follows:

3.2.1 *Consonants*:

b, d, f, h, k, l, m, n, p, r, s, t, v, w, and *z* have their usual English values. Other symbols are used as follows:

g	(get)	x	(loch)	ð	(this)	j	(yes)
tʃ	(chip)	ŋ	(ring)	ʃ	(she)		
dʒ	(jar)	θ	(thin)	ʒ	(decision)		

3.2.2 *Vowels*:

short vowels		long vowels		diphthongs	
æ	(cat)	ɑː	(arm)	eɪ	(day)
e	(bed)	iː	(see)	aɪ	(my)

short vowels	long vowels	diphthongs
ə (*ago*)	ɔ: (*saw*)	ɔɪ (b*oy*)
ɪ (s*it*)	ɜ: (h*er*)	əʊ (*no*)
ɒ (h*ot*)	u: (*too*)	aʊ (h*ow*)
ʌ (r*u*n)		ɪə (*near*)
ʊ (p*u*t)		eə (h*air*)
		ʊə (p*oor*)
		aɪə (*fire*)
		aʊə (s*our*)

3.2.3.1 (ə) signifies the indeterminate sound as in gard*e*n, carn*a*l, and rhyth*m*.

3.2.3.2 (r) at the end of a word indicates an r that is sounded when a word beginning with a vowel follows, as in *clutter up* and *an acre of land*.

3.2.4 The mark ˜ indicates a nasalized sound, as in the following sounds that are not natural in English:

æ̃ (t*i*mbre)
ɑ̃ (él*a*n)
ɔ̃ (garç*o*n)

3.2.5 The main or primary stress of a word is shown by ' preceding the relevant syllable; any secondary stress in words of three or more syllables is shown by ˌ preceding the relevant syllable.

3.3 With headwords consisting of two or more unhyphened words, the pronunciation is given only of the words that do not appear individually elsewhere in the dictionary.

3.4 Pronunciation of derivatives listed at the end of the entries is only given when there is a change of stress (as with many words in -*ation*) or some other significant change.

3.5 For the pronunciation of inflected forms, see below, 5.1.3.

3.6 For the pronunciation of prefixes, suffixes, and combining forms, see below, 14.3.

4. Part of speech

4.1 The grammatical identity of words as *noun*, *verb*, *adjective*, and so on, is given for all headwords and derivatives, and for compounds and phrases when necessary to aid clarity. The same part-of-speech label is used of groups of more than one word when the group has the function of that part of speech, e.g. **ad hoc**, **Parthian shot**.

4.2 When a headword has more than one part of speech, a list is given at the beginning of the entry, and the treatment of the successive parts of speech (in the same order as the list) is introduced by a bold dash in each case:

> **safe** /seɪf/ *adj. & n.* —*adj.* **1 a** free of danger or injury. **b** (often foll. by *from*) out of or not exposed to danger (*safe from their enemies*). **2** affording security or not involving danger or risk (*put it in a safe place*). **3** reliable, certain; that can be reckoned on (*a safe catch; a safe method; is safe to win*). **4** prevented from escaping or doing harm (*have got him safe*). **5** (also **safe and sound**) uninjured; with no harm done. **6** cautious and unenterprising; consistently moderate. —*n.* **1** a strong lockable cabinet etc. for valuables. **2** = *meat safe*.

4.3 The standard part-of-speech names are used, and the following additional explanations should be noted:

4.3.1 Nouns used attributively are designated *attrib.* when their function is not fully adjectival (e.g. **model** in *a model student*; *the student is very model* is not acceptable usage).

4.3.2.1 Adjectives are labelled *attrib.* (= attributive) when they are placed before the word they modify (as in *a blue car*), and *predic.* (= predicative) when they occur (usually after a verb) in the predicate of a sentence (as in *the car is blue*).

4.3.2.2 Some adjectives are restricted in such use: for example **aware** is normally used predicatively and **undue** is normally used attributively.

4.3.3 The designation *absol.* (= absolute) refers to uses of transitive verbs with an object implied but not stated (as in *smoking kills* and *let me explain*).

4.3.4 The designation 'in *comb.*' (= in combination), or 'also in *comb.*', refers to uses of words (especially adjectives) as an element joined by a hyphen with another word, as with **crested**, which often appears in forms such as *red-crested*, *large-crested*, and so on.

5. Inflection

5.1.1 Inflection of words (i.e. plurals, past tenses, etc.) is given after the part of speech concerned:

> **safari** /səˈfɑːrɪ/ *n.* (*pl.* **safaris**) **1** a hunting or scientific expedition, esp. in E. Africa (*go on safari*). **2** a sightseeing trip to see African animals in their natural habitat.

> **sag** /sæg/ *v. & n.* —*v.intr.* (**sagged, sagging**) **1** sink or subside under weight or pressure, esp. unevenly. **2** have a downward bulge or curve in the middle. **3** fall in price. **4** (of a ship) drift from its course, esp. to leeward.

5.1.2 The forms given are normally those in use in British English. Variant American forms are identified by the label *US*; these variants are often found in American use in addition to the main forms given.

5.1.3 Pronunciation of inflected forms is given when this differs significantly from the pronunciation of the headword. The designation 'pronunc. same' denotes that the pronunciation, despite a change of form, is the same as that of the headword.

5.2 In general, the inflection of nouns, verbs, adjectives, and adverbs is given when it is irregular (as described further below) or when, though regular, it causes difficulty (as with forms such as **budgeted**, **coos**, and **taxis**).

5.3 *Plurals of nouns*: nouns that form their plural regularly by adding -s (or -es when they end in -s, -x, -z, -sh, or soft -ch) receive no comment. Other plural forms are given, notably:

5.3.1 nouns ending in -i or -o.

5.3.2 nouns ending in -y.

5.3.3 nouns ending in Latinate forms such as -a and -um.

5.3.4 nouns with more than one plural form, e.g. **fish** and **aquarium**.

5.3.5 nouns with plurals involving a change in the stem, e.g. **foot, feet**.

5.3.6 nouns with a plural form identical to the singular form, e.g. **sheep**.

5.3.7 nouns in -ful, e.g. **handful**.

5.4 *Forms of verbs*:

The following forms are regarded as regular:

5.4.1 third person singular present forms adding -s to the stem (or -es to stems ending in -s, -x, -z, -sh, or soft -ch).

5.4.2 past tenses and past participles adding -ed to the stem, dropping a final silent e (e.g. **changed, danced**).

5.4.3 present participles adding -ing to the stem, dropping a final silent e (e.g. **changing, dancing**).

5.4.4 Other forms are given, notably:

5.4.4.1 doubling of a final consonant, e.g. **bat, batted, batting**.

5.4.4.2 strong and irregular forms involving a change in the stem, e.g. **come, came, come**, and **go, went, gone**.

5.5 *Comparative and Superlative of Adjectives and Adverbs*:

5.5.1 Words of one syllable adding -er or -est, those ending in silent e dropping the e (e.g. **braver, bravest**) are regarded as regular. Most one-syllable words have these forms, but participial adjectives (e.g. **pleased**) do not.

5.5.2 Those that double a final consonant (e.g. **hot, hotter, hottest**) are given, as are two-syllable words that have comparative and superlative forms in *-er* and *-est* (of which very many are forms ending in *-y*, e.g. **happy, happier, happiest**), and their negative forms (e.g. **unhappier, unhappiest**).

5.5.3 It should be noted that specification of these forms indicates only that they are available; it is usually also possible to form comparatives with *more* and superlatives with *most* (as in *more happy, most unhappy*), which is the standard way of proceeding with adjectives and adverbs that do not admit of inflection.

5.6 *Adjectives in* -able *formed from Transitive Verbs*:

These are given as derivatives when there is sufficient evidence of their currency; in general they are formed as follows:

5.6.1 Verbs drop silent final *-e* except after *c* and *g* (e.g. **movable** but **changeable**).

5.6.2 Verbs of more than one syllable ending in *-y* (preceded by a consonant or *qu*) change *y* to *i* (e.g. **enviable, undeniable**).

5.6.3 A final consonant is often doubled as in normal inflection (e.g. **conferrable, regrettable**).

6. Definition

6.1 Definitions are listed in a numbered sequence in order of comparative familiarity and importance, with the most current and important senses first:

> **sail** /seɪl/ *n. & v.* —*n.* **1** a piece of material (orig. canvas, now usu. nylon etc.) extended on rigging to catch the wind and propel a boat or ship. **2** a ship's sails collectively. **3 a** a voyage or excursion in a sailing-ship. **b** a voyage of specified duration. **4** a ship, esp. as discerned from its sails. **5** (*collect.*) ships in a squadron or company (*a fleet of twenty sail*). **6** (in *pl.*) *Naut.* **a** *sl.* a maker or repairer of sails. **b** *hist.* a chief petty officer in charge of rigging. **7** a wind-catching apparatus, usu. a set of boards, attached to the arm of a windmill. **8 a** the dorsal fin of a sailfish. **b** the tentacle of a nautilus. **c** the float of a Portuguese man-of-war. —*v.* **1** *intr.* travel on water by the use of sails or engine-power. **2** *tr.* **a** navigate (a ship etc.). **b** travel on (a sea). **3** *tr.* set (a toy boat) afloat. **4** *intr.* glide or move smoothly or in a stately manner. **5** *intr.* (often foll. by *through*) *colloq.* succeed easily (*sailed through the exams*).

6.2 They are subdivided into lettered senses (**a, b,** etc.) when these are closely related or call for collective treatment.

7. Illustrative examples

Many examples of words in use are given to support, and in some cases supplement, the definitions. These appear in italics in brackets. They are meant to amplify meaning and (especially when following a grammatical point) illustrate how the word is used in context, as in the following sense of **saint**:

> a very virtuous person; a person of great real or affected holiness (*would try the patience of a saint*).

8. Grammatical information

8.1 Definitions are often accompanied by explanations in brackets of how the word or phrase in question is used in context. Often, the comment refers to words that usually follow (foll. by) or precede (prec. by) the word being explained. For example, at **sack**[1]:

> **sack**[1] /sæk/ n. & v. —n. **1 a** a large strong bag, usu. made of hessian, paper, or plastic, for storing or conveying goods. **b** (usu. foll. by *of*) this with its contents (*a sack of potatoes*). **c** a quantity contained in a sack. **2** (prec. by *the*) *colloq.* dismissal from employment. **3** (prec. by *the*) *US sl.* bed. **4 a** a woman's short loose dress with a sacklike appearance. **b** *archaic* or *hist.* a woman's loose gown, or a silk train attached to the shoulders of this. **5** a man's or woman's loose-hanging coat not shaped to the back. —v.tr. **1** put into a sack or sacks. **2** *colloq.* dismiss from employment. □**sack race** a race between competitors in sacks up to the waist or neck. □□ **sackful** n. (pl. **-fuls**). **sacklike** adj. [OE *sacc* f. L *saccus* f. Gk *sakkos*, of Semitic orig.]

sense 1b usually appears as *a sack of* (something), as the example further shows; and senses 2 and 3 always appear as *the sack*.

8.2 With verbs, the fact that a sense is transitive or intransitive can affect the construction. In the examples given below, **prevail** is intransitive (and the construction is *prevail on a person*) and **urge** is transitive (and the construction is *urge a person on*).

> **prevail** /prɪ'veɪl/ v.intr. **1** (often foll. by *against, over*) be victorious or gain mastery. **2** be the more usual or predominant. **3** exist or occur in general use or experience; be current. **4** (foll. by *on, upon*) persuade.

> **urge** /ɜːdʒ/ v. & n. —v.tr. **1** (often foll. by *on*) drive forcibly; impel; hasten (*urged them on; urged the horses forward*). **2** (often foll. by *to* + infin. or *that* + clause) encourage or entreat earnestly or persistently (*urged them to go; urged them to action; urged that they should go*).

8.3 The formula (foll. by *to* + infin.) means that the word is followed by a normal infinitive with *to*, as in *want to leave* and *eager to learn*.

8.4 The formula (foll. by *that* + clause) indicates the routine addition of a clause with *that*, as in *said that it was late*. (For the omission of *that*, as in *said it was late*, see the usage note in the entry for **that**.)

8.5 'pres. part.' and 'verbal noun' denote verbal forms in -*ing* that function as adjectives and nouns respectively, as in *set him laughing* and *tired of asking*.

9. Usage

9.1 If the use of a word is restricted in any way, this is indicated by any of various labels printed in italics, as follows:

9.2 *Geographical*

9.2.1 *Brit.* indicates that the use is found chiefly in British English (and often also in Australian and New Zealand English, and in other parts of the Commonwealth) but not in American English.

9.2.2 *US* indicates that the use is found chiefly in American English (often including Canada and also in Australian and New Zealand English) but not in British English except as a conscious Americanism.

9.2.3 Other geographical designations (e.g. *Austral.*, *NZ*, *S.Afr.*) restrict uses to the areas named.

9.2.4 These usage labels should be distinguished from comments of the type '(in the UK)' or '(in the US)' preceding definitions, which denote that the thing defined is associated with the country named. For example, **Pentagon** is a US institution, but the term is not restricted to American English.

9.3 *Register*

9.3.1 Levels of usage, or *registers*, are indicated as follows:

9.3.2 *formal* indicates uses that are normally restricted to formal (esp. written) English, e.g. **commence**.

9.3.3 *colloq.* (= colloquial) indicates a use that is normally restricted to informal (esp. spoken) English.

9.3.4 *sl.* (= slang) indicates a use of the most informal kind, unsuited to written English and often restricted to a particular social group.

9.3.5 *archaic* indicates a word that is restricted to special contexts such as legal or religious use, or is used for special effect.

9.3.6 *literary* indicates a word or use that is found chiefly in literature.

9.3.7 *poet.* (= poetic) indicates uses confined to poetry or other contexts with romantic connotations.

9.3.8 *joc.* (= jocular) indicates uses that are intended to be humorous or playful.

9.3.9 *derog.* (= derogatory) denotes uses that are intentionally disparaging.

9.3.10 *offens.* (= offensive) denotes uses that cause offence, whether intentionally or not.

9.3.11 *disp.* (= disputed) indicates a use that is disputed or controversial. Often this is enough to alert the user to a danger or difficulty; when further explanation is needed a usage note (see below) is used as well or instead.

9.3.12 *hist.* (= historical) denotes a word or use that is confined to historical reference, normally because the thing referred to no longer exists.

9.3.13 *propr.* (= proprietary) denotes a term that has the status of a trade mark (see the Note on Proprietary Status, p. xxxix).

9.4 *Subject*

The many subject labels, e.g. *Law, Math., Naut.*, show that a word or sense is current only in a particular field of activity, and is not in general use.

9.5 *Usage Notes*

These are added to give extra information not central to the definition, and to explain points of grammar and usage. They are introduced by the symbol ¶. The purpose of these notes is not to prescribe usage but to alert the user to a difficulty or controversy attached to particular uses.

10. Phrases and idioms

10.1 These are listed (together with compounds) in alphabetical order after the treatment of the main senses, introduced by the symbol □. The words *a, the, one,* and *person* do not count for purposes of alphabetical order:

> □ **on the safe side** with a margin of security against risks. **safe bet** a bet that is certain to succeed. **safe-breaker** (or **-blower** or **-cracker**) a person who breaks open and robs safes. **safe conduct 1** a privilege of immunity from arrest or harm, esp. on a particular occasion. **2** a document securing this. **safe deposit** a building containing strongrooms and safes let separately. **safe house** a place of refuge or rendezvous for spies etc. **safe keeping** preservation in a safe place. **safe light** *Photog.* a filtered light for use in a darkroom. **safe period** the time during and near the menstrual period when conception is least likely. **safe seat** a seat in Parliament etc. that is usually won with a large margin by a particular party. □

10.2 They are normally defined under the earliest important word in the phrase, except when a later word is more clearly the key word or is the common word in a phrase with variants (in which case a cross-reference often appears at the entry for the earliest word):

> **make do 1** manage with the limited or inadequate means available. **2** (foll. by *with*) manage with (something) as an inferior substitute. **make an example of** punish as a warning to others. **make a fool of** see FOOL[1]. **make for 1** tend to result in (happiness etc.). **2** proceed towards (a place). **3** assault; attack. **4** confirm (an opinion). **make friends** (often foll. by *with*) become friendly. **make fun of** see FUN. **make good** see GOOD. **make a habit of** see HABIT. **make a hash of** see HASH[1]. **make hay** see HAY[1]. **make head or tail of** see HEAD. **make a House** *Polit.* secure the presence of enough members for a quorum or support in the House of Commons. **make it** *colloq.* **1** succeed in reaching, esp. in time. **2** be successful. **3** (usu. foll. by *with*) *sl.* have sexual intercourse (with). **make it up 1** be reconciled, esp. after a quarrel. **2** fill in a deficit. **make it up to** remedy negligence, an injury, etc. to (a person). **make light of** see LIGHT[2]. **make love** see LOVE. **make a meal of** see MEAL[1]. **make merry** see MERRY.

11. Compounds

11.1 Compound terms forming one word (e.g. **bathroom**, **newspaper**) are listed as main entries; those consisting of two or more words (e.g. **chain reaction**) or joined by a hyphen (e.g. **chain-gang**) are given under the first element or occasionally as main entries.

11.2 A hyphen in an item printed in bold occurring at the end of a line is always a permanent feature of the spelling, and not an end-of-line hyphen.

12. Derivatives

12.1 Words formed by adding a suffix to another word are in many cases listed at the end of the entry for the main word, introduced by the symbol □□. In this position they are not defined since they can be understood from the sense of the main word and that given at the suffix concerned:

> □□ **saintdom** *n.* **sainthood** *n.* **saintlike** *adj.* **saintling** *n.* **saintship** *n.*

When further definition is called for they are given main entries in their own right (e.g. **changeable**).

12.2 For derivative words used in combination (e.g. **-crested** in *red-crested*), see 4.3.4 above.

13. Etymology

13.1 The user is also referred to the section headed *English over Fifteen Centuries*, pp. xii-xx.

13.2 A brief account of the etymology, or origin, of words is given in square brackets at the end of entries. It is not given for compound words of obvious formation (such as **bathroom** and **jellyfish**), for routinely formed derivatives (such as **changeable, muddy,** and **seller**), or for words consisting of clearly identified elements already explained (such as **Anglo-Saxon, overrun,** and many words in *in-, re-, un-,* etc.). It is also not always given for every word of a set sharing the same basic origin (such as the group from **proprietary** to **propriety**). Noteworthy features, such as an origin in Old English, are however always given.

13.3 More detailed information can be found in the *Oxford Dictionary of English Etymology* (ed. C. T. Onions *et al.,* 1966) and the *Concise Oxford Dictionary of English Etymology* (ed. T. F. Hoad, 1986).

13.4 The immediate source language is given first. Forms in other languages are not given if they are exactly or nearly the same as the English form given in the headword.

13.5 Words of Germanic origin are described as 'f. Gmc' or 'f. WG' (West Germanic) as appropriate; unrecorded or postulated forms are not normally given.

13.6 OE (Old English) is used for words that are known to have been used before AD 1150, and ME (Middle English) for words traceable to the period 1150–1500 (no distinction being made between early and late Middle English).

13.7 Words of Romance origin are referred to their immediate source, usually F (French) or OF (Old French before 1400), and then to earlier sources when known.

13.7.1 AF (Anglo-French) denotes the variety of French current in England in the Middle Ages after the Norman Conquest.

13.7.2 Rmc (Romanic) denotes the vernacular descendants of Latin that are the source of French, Spanish, Italian, etc. Romanic forms are almost always of the 'unrecorded' or 'postulated' kind, and are not specified except to clarify a significant change of form. Often the formula 'ult. f. L' etc. (ultimately from Latin, etc.) is used to indicate that the route from Latin is via Romanic forms.

13.7.3 L (Latin) denotes classical Latin up to about AD 200; OL (Old Latin) Latin before about 75 BC; LL (Late Latin) Latin of about 200–600; med.L (medieval Latin) Latin of about 600–1500; mod.L (modern Latin) Latin in use (mainly for technical purposes) since about 1500.

13.7.4 Similar divisions for 'late', 'medieval', and 'modern' are made for Greek.

13.8 Many English words have corresponding forms in both French and Latin, and it cannot always be established which was the immediate source. In such cases the formula 'F or L' is used (e.g. **section** ... F *section* or L *sectio*); in these cases the Latin form is the source of the French word and (either directly or indirectly) of the English word.

13.9 Some words are derived from languages which are not in wide enough use for them to be included as entries in the dictionary. These languages are listed below by regions; further information about them can be found in encyclopaedias and other reference books.

13.9.1 Those spoken in America are Aleutian (related to Eskimo), Surinam Negro (a Creole based on English), and the following American Indian languages: Abnaki, Araucan, Aymará, Chinook, Creek, Dakota, Fox, Galibi, Hopi, Miskito, Narragansett, Nootka, Ojibwa, Paiute, Penobscot, Renape, and Taino.

13.9.2 Those spoken in Africa are Bangi, Fiot, Foulah, Khoisan, Kongo, Lingala, Mandingo, Mbuba, Mende, Nguni, Temne, and Twi.

13.9.3 Those spoken in Asia are Ambonese (spoken in Indonesia), Assamese (in India), Batti (in Tibet), Maldive (in the Maldive Islands), Mishmi (in India), Sundanese (in Indonesia), and Tungus (in Siberia).

13.9.4 Tongan is a Polynesian language.

13.10 When the origin of a word cannot be reliably established, the forms 'orig. unkn.' (= origin unknown) and 'orig. uncert.' (= origin uncertain) are used, even if frequently canvassed speculative derivations exist (as with **gremlin** and **pommy**). In these cases the century of the first recorded occurrence of the word in English is given.

13.11 An equals sign (=) precedes words in other languages that are parallel formations from a common source (cognates) rather than sources of the English word.

14. Prefixes, Suffixes, and Combining Forms

14.1 A large selection of these is given in the main body of the text; prefixes are given in the form **ex-**, **re-**, etc., and suffixes in the form **-ion**, **-ness**, etc. These entries should be consulted to explain the many routinely formed derivatives given at the end of entries (see above, 12).

14.2 Combining forms (e.g. **bio-**, **-graphy**) are semantically significant elements that can be attached to words or elements as explained in the usage note at the entry for **combine**.

14.3 The pronunciation given for a prefix, suffix, or combining form is an approximate one for purposes of articulating and (in some cases) identifying the headword; pronunciation and stress may change considerably when they form part of a word.

15. Cross-references

15.1 These are introduced by any of a number of reference types, as follows:

15.1.1 '=' denotes that the meaning of the item at which the cross-reference occurs is the same as that of the item referred to.

15.1.2 'see' indicates that the information sought will be found at the point referred to, and is widely used in the idiom sections of entries to deal with items that can be located at any of a number of words included in the idiom (see also above, 10.2).

15.1.3 'see also' indicates that further information can be found at the point referred to.

15.1.4 'cf.' denotes an item related or relevant to the one being consulted, and the reference often completes or clarifies the exact meaning of the item being treated.

15.1.5 'opp.' refers to a word or sense that is opposite to the one being treated, and again often completes or clarifies the sense.

15.1.6 References of the kind *'pl.* of' (= plural of), *'past* of' (= past tense of), etc., are given at entries for inflections and other related forms.

15.2 Cross-references preceded by any of these reference types appear in small capitals if the reference is to a main headword, and in italics if the reference is to a compound or idiom within an entry.

15.3 References in italics to compounds and defined phrases are to the entry for the first word unless another is specified.

Abbreviations used in the Dictionary

SOME abbreviations (especially of language-names) occur only in etymologies. Others may appear in italics. Abbreviations in general use (such as etc., i.e., and those for books of the Bible) are explained in the dictionary itself.

abbr.	abbreviation
ablat.	ablative
absol.	absolute(ly)
acc.	according
accus.	accusative
adj.	adjective
adv.	adverb
Aeron.	Aeronautics
AF	Anglo-French
Afr.	Africa, African
Afrik.	Afrikaans
Akkad.	Akkadian
AL	Anglo-Latin
alt.	alteration
Amer.	America, American
Anat.	Anatomy
anc.	ancient
Anglo-Ind.	Anglo-Indian
Anthropol.	Anthropology
Antiq.	Antiquities, Antiquity
app.	apparently
Arab.	Arabic
Aram.	Aramaic
arbitr.	arbitrary, arbitrarily
Archaeol.	Archaeology
Archit.	Architecture
Arith.	Arithmetic
assim.	assimilated
assoc.	associated, association
Assyr.	Assyrian
Astrol.	Astrology
Astron.	Astronomy
Astronaut.	Astronautics
attrib.	attributive(ly)
attrib.adj.	attributive adjective
augment.	augmentative
Austral.	Australia, Australian
aux.	auxiliary
back-form.	back-formation
Bibl.	Biblical
Bibliog.	Bibliography
Biochem.	Biochemistry
Biol.	Biology
Bot.	Botany

Braz.	Brazil, Brazilian
Bret.	Breton
Brit.	British, in British use
Bulg.	Bulgarian
Burm.	Burmese
Byz.	Byzantine
c.	century
c.	*circa*
Can.	Canada, Canadian
Cat.	Catalan
Celt.	Celtic
Ch.	Church
Chem.	Chemistry
Chin.	Chinese
Cinematog.	Cinematography
class.	classical
coarse sl.	coarse slang
cogn.	cognate
collect.	collective(ly)
colloq.	colloquial(ly)
comb.	combination; combining
compar.	comparative
compl.	complement
Conchol.	Conchology
conj.	conjunction
conn.	connected
constr.	construction
contr.	contraction
Corn.	Cornish
corresp.	corresponding
corrupt.	corruption
Criminol.	Criminology
Crystallog.	Crystallography
Da.	Danish
decl.	declension
def.	definite
Demog.	Demography
demons.	demonstrative
demons.adj.	demonstrative adjective
demons.pron.	demonstrative pronoun
deriv.	derivative
derog.	derogatory
dial.	dialect
different.	differentiated

dimin.	diminutive
disp.	disputed (use)
dissim.	dissimilated
distrib.	distributive
Du.	Dutch
E	English
Eccl.	Ecclesiastical
Ecol.	Ecology
Econ.	Economics
EFris.	East Frisian
Egypt.	Egyptian
E.Ind.	East Indian, of the East Indies
Electr.	Electricity
elem.	elementary
ellipt.	elliptical(ly)
emphat.	emphatic(ally)
Engin.	Engineering
Engl.	England; English
Entomol.	Entomology
erron.	erroneous(ly)
esp.	especial(ly)
etym.	etymology
euphem.	euphemism
Eur.	Europe, European
ex.	example
exc.	except
exclam.	exclamation
F	French
f.	from
fam.	familiar
fem.	feminine
fig.	figurative(ly)
Finn.	Finnish
Flem.	Flemish
foll.	followed, following
form.	formation
Fr.	French
Frank.	Frankish
frequent.	frequentative(ly)
G	German
Gael.	Gaelic
Gallo-Rom.	Gallo-Roman
gen.	general
genit.	genitive
Geog.	Geography

Geol.	Geology	M	Middle (with	OHG	Old High German
Geom.	Geometry		languages)	OIcel.	Old Icelandic
Ger.	German	masc.	masculine	OIr.	Old Irish
Gk	Greek	Math.	Mathematics	OIt.	Old Italian
Gk Hist.	Greek History	MDa.	Middle Danish	OL	Old Latin
Gmc	Germanic	MDu.	Middle Dutch	OLG	Old Low German
Goth.	Gothic	ME	Middle English	ON	Old Norse
Gram.	Grammar	Mech.	Mechanics	ONF	Old Northern
		Med.	Medicine		French
Heb.	Hebrew	med.	medieval	ONorw.	Old Norwegian
Hind.	Hindustani	med.L	medieval Latin	OPers.	Old Persian
Hist.	History	metaph.	metaphorical	OPort.	Old Portuguese
hist.	with historical	metath.	metathesis	opp.	(as) opposed (to);
	reference	Meteorol.	Meteorology		opposite (of)
Horol.	Horology	Mex.	Mexican	OProv.	Old Provençal
Hort.	Horticulture	MFlem.	Middle Flemish	orig.	origin; original(ly)
Hung.	Hungarian	MHG	Middle High	Ornithol.	Ornithology
			German	OS	Old Saxon
		Mil.	Military	OScand.	Old Scandinavian
Icel.	Icelandic	Mineral.	Mineralogy	OSlav.	Old Slavonic
IE	Indo-European	mistransl.	mistranslation	OSp.	Old Spanish
illit.	illiterate	MLG	Middle Low	OSw.	Old Swedish
imit.	imitative		German		
immed.	immediate(ly)	mod.	modern		
imper.	imperative	mod.L	modern Latin	Palaeog.	Palaeography
impers.	impersonal	MSw.	Middle Swedish	Parl.	Parliament;
incept.	inceptive	Mus.	Music		Parliamentary
incl.	including; inclusive	Mythol.	Mythology	part.	participle
Ind.	of the subcontinent			past part.	past participle
	comprising India,	n.	noun	Pathol.	Pathology
	Pakistan, and	N.Amer.	North America,	pejor.	pejorative
	Bangladesh		North American	perf.	perfect (tense)
ind.	indirect	Nat.	National	perh.	perhaps
indecl.	indeclinable	Naut.	Nautical	Pers.	Persian
indef.	indefinite	neg.	negative(ly)	pers.	person(al)
infin.	infinitive	N.Engl.	North of England	Peruv.	Peruvian
infl.	influence(d)	neut.	neuter	Pharm.	Pharmacy;
instr.	instrumental (case)	Norm.	Norman		Pharmacology
int.	interjection	north.	northern	Philol.	Philology
interrog.	interrogative(ly)	Norw.	Norwegian	Philos.	Philosophy
interrog.adj.	interrogative	n.pl.	noun plural	Phoen.	Phoenician
	adjective	num.	numeral	Phonet.	Phonetics
interrog.pron.	interrogative	NZ	New Zealand	Photog.	Photography
	pronoun			phr.	phrase
intr.	intransitive	O	Old (with	Phrenol.	Phrenology
Ir.	Irish (language or		languages)	Physiol.	Physiology
	usage)	obj.	object; objective	pl.	plural
iron.	ironical(ly)	OBret.	Old Breton	poet.	poetical
irreg.	irregular(ly)	OBrit.	Old British	Pol.	Polish
It.	Italian	obs.	obsolete	Polit.	Politics
		Obstet.	Obstetrics	pop.	popular, not
Jap.	Japan, Japanese	OBulg.	Old Bulgarian		technical
Jav.	Javanese	occas.	occasional(ly)	pop.L	popular Latin,
joc.	jocular(ly)	OCelt.	Old Celtic		informal spoken
		ODa.	Old Danish		Latin
		ODu.	Old Dutch	Port.	Portuguese
L	Latin	OE	Old English	poss.	possessive
lang.	language	OF	Old French	poss.pron.	possessive
LG	Low German	offens.	offensive		pronoun
LHeb.	Late Hebrew	OFrank.	Old Frankish	prec.	preceded, preceding
lit.	literal(ly)	OFris.	Old Frisian	predic.	predicate;
LL	Late Latin	OGael.	Old Gaelic		predicative(ly)

predic.adj.	predicative adjective		South American	Typog.	Typography
prep.	preposition	Sc.	Scottish	ult.	ultimate(ly)
pres.part.	present participle	Scand.	Scandinavia, Scandinavian	uncert.	uncertain
prob.	probable, probably	Sci.	Science	unexpl.	unexplained
pron.	pronoun	Shakesp.	Shakespeare	univ.	university
pronunc.	pronunciation	sing.	singular	unkn.	unknown
propr.	proprietary term	Sinh.	Sinhalese	US	American, in American use
Prov.	Provençal	Skr.	Sanskrit	usu.	usual(ly)
Psychol.	Psychology	sl.	slang		
		Slav.	Slavonic	v.	verb
RC Ch.	Roman Catholic Church	Sociol.	Sociology	var.	variant(s)
redupl.	reduplicated	Sp.	Spanish	v.aux.	auxiliary verb
ref.	reference	spec.	special(ly)	Vet.	Veterinary
refl.	reflexive(ly)	Stock Exch.	Stock Exchange	v.intr.	intransitive verb
rel.	related; relative	subj.	subject; subjunctive	voc.	vocative
rel.adj.	relative adjective	superl.	superlative	v.refl.	reflexive verb
Relig.	Religion	Sw.	Swedish	v.tr.	transitive verb
rel.pron.	relative pronoun	syll.	syllable		
repr.	representing	symb.	symbol	WFris.	West Frisian
Rhet.	Rhetoric	syn.	synonym	WG	West Germanic
rhet.	rhetorical(ly)			W.Ind.	West Indian, of the West Indies
Rmc	Romanic	techn.	technical(ly)		
Rom.	Roman	Telev.	Television	WS	West Saxon
Rom.Hist.	Roman History	Teut.	Teutonic	WSlav.	West Slavonic
Russ.	Russian	Theatr.	Theatre, Theatrical		
		Theol.	Theology	Zool.	Zoology
S.Afr.	South Africa, South African	tr.	transitive		
		transf.	in transferred sense		
S.Amer.	South America,	transl.	translation		
		Turk.	Turkish		

Note on Proprietary Status

THIS dictionary includes some words which are, or are asserted to be, proprietary names or trade marks. Their inclusion does not imply that they have acquired for legal purposes a non-proprietary or general significance, nor is any other judgement implied concerning their legal status. In cases where the editor has some evidence that a word is used as a proprietary name or trade mark this is indicated by the designation *propr.*, but no judgement concerning the legal status of such words is made or implied thereby.

A

A¹ /eɪ/ n. (also **a**) (pl. **As** or **A's**) **1** the first letter of the alphabet. **2** Mus. the sixth note of the diatonic scale of C major. **3** the first hypothetical person or example. **4** the highest class or category (of roads, academic marks, etc.). **5** (usu. **a**) Algebra the first known quantity. **6** a human blood type of the ABO system. □**A1** /eɪ 'wʌn/ **1** Naut. **a** a first-class vessel in Lloyd's Register of Shipping. **b** first-class. **2** colloq. excellent, first-rate. **A1**, **A2**, etc. the standard paper sizes, each half the previous one, e.g. A4 = 297 × 210 mm, A5 = 210 × 148 mm. **from A to B** from one place to another (a means of getting from A to B). **from A to Z** over the entire range, completely.

A² /eɪ/ abbr. (also **A.**) **1** Brit. (of films) classified as suitable for an adult audience but not necessarily for children. ¶ Now replaced by PG. **2** = A LEVEL. **3** ampere(s). **4** answer. **5** Associate of. **6** atomic (energy etc.).

a¹ /ə, eɪ/ adj. (also **an** before a vowel) (called the indefinite article) **1** (as an unemphatic substitute) one, some, any. **2** one like (a Judas). **3** one single (not a thing in sight). **4** the same (all of a size). **5** in, to, or for each (twice a year; £20 a man; seven a side). [weakening of OE ān one; sense 5 orig. = A²]

a² /ə/ prep. (usu. as prefix) **1** to, towards (ashore; aside). **2** (with verb in pres. part. or infin.) in the process of; in a specified state (a-hunting; a-wandering; abuzz; aflutter). **3** on (afire; afoot). **4** in (nowadays). [weakening of OE prep. an, on (see ON)]

a³ abbr. atto-.

Å abbr. ångström(s).

a-¹ /eɪ, æ/ prefix not, without (amoral; agnostic; apetalous). [Gk a-, or L f. Gk, or F f. L f. Gk]

a-² /ə/ prefix implying motion onward or away, adding intensity to verbs of motion (arise; awake). [OE a-, orig. ar-]

a-³ /ə/ prefix to, at, or into a state (adroit; agree; amass; avenge). [ME a- (= OF prefix a-), (f. F) f. L ad- to, at]

a-⁴ /ə/ prefix **1** from, away (abridge). **2** of (akin; anew). **3** out, utterly (abash; affray). **4** in, on, engaged in, etc. (see A²). [sense 1 f. ME a-, OF a-, f. L ab; sense 2 f. ME a- f. OE of prep.; sense 3 f. ME, AF a- = OF e-, es- f. L ex]

a-⁵ /ə, æ/ prefix assim. form of AD- before sc, sp, st.

-a¹ /ə/ suffix forming nouns from Greek, Latin, and Romanic feminine singular, esp.: **1** ancient or Latinized modern names of animals and plants (amoeba; campanula). **2** oxides (alumina). **3** geographical names (Africa). **4** ancient or Latinized modern feminine names (Lydia; Hilda).

-a² /ə/ suffix forming plural nouns from Greek and Latin neuter plural, esp. names (often from modern Latin) of zoological groups (phenomena; Carnivora).

-a³ /ə/ suffix colloq. sl. **1** of (kinda; coupla). **2** have (mighta; coulda). **3** to (oughta).

AA abbr. **1** Automobile Association. **2** Alcoholics Anonymous. **3** Mil. anti-aircraft. **4** Brit. (of films) classified as suitable for persons of over 14 years. ¶ Now replaced by PG.

AAA abbr. **1** (in the UK) Amateur Athletic Association. **2** American Automobile Association. **3** Australian Automobile Association.

A. & M. abbr. (Hymns) Ancient and Modern.

A. & R. abbr. **1** artists and recording. **2** artists and repertoire.

aardvark /'ɑːdvɑːk/ n. a nocturnal mammal of southern Africa, Orycteropus afer, with a tubular snout and a long extendible tongue, that feeds on termites. Also called ant-bear, earth-hog. [Afrik. f. aarde earth + vark pig]

aardwolf /'ɑːdwʊlf/ n. (pl. **aardwolves** /-wʊlvz/) an African mammal, Proteles cristatus, of the hyena family, with grey fur and black stripes, that feeds on insects. [Afrik. f. aarde earth + wolf wolf]

Aaron's beard /'eərənz/ n. any of several plants, esp. rose of Sharon (Hypericum calycinum). [ref. to Ps. 133:2]

Aaron's rod /'eərənz/ n. any of several tall plants, esp. the great mullein (Verbascum thapsus). [ref. to Num. 17:8]

A'asia abbr. Australasia.

aasvogel /'ɑːsˌfəʊɡ(ə)l/ n. a vulture. [Afrik. f. aas carrion + vogel bird]

AAU abbr. US Amateur Athletic Union.

AB¹ /eɪ'biː/ n. a human blood type of the ABO system.

AB² abbr. **1** able rating or seaman. **2** US Bachelor of Arts. [sense 1 f. able-bodied; sense 2 f. L Artium Baccalaureus]

ab- /əb, æb/ prefix off, away, from (abduct; abnormal; abuse). [F or L]

aba /'æbə/ n. (also **abba**, **abaya** /ə'beɪjə/) a sleeveless outer garment worn by Arabs. [Arab. 'abā']

abaca /'æbəkə/ n. **1** Manila hemp. **2** the plant, Musa textilis, yielding this. [Sp. abacá]

aback /ə'bæk/ adv. **1** archaic backwards, behind. **2** Naut. (of a sail) pressed against the mast by a head wind. □**take aback 1** surprise, disconcert (your request took me aback; I was greatly taken aback by the news). **2** (as **taken aback**) (of a ship) with the sails pressed against the mast by a head wind. [OE on bæc (as A², BACK)]

abacus /'æbəkəs/ n. (pl. **abacuses**) **1** an oblong frame with rows of wires or grooves along which beads are slid, used for calculating. **2** Archit. the flat slab on top of a capital, supporting the architrave. [L f. Gk abax abakos slab, drawing-board, f. Heb. 'āḇāḳ dust]

Abaddon /ə'bæd(ə)n/ n. **1** hell. **2** the Devil (Rev. 9: 11). [Heb., = destruction]

abaft /ə'bɑːft/ adv. & prep. Naut. —adv. in the stern half of a ship. —prep. nearer the stern than; aft of. [A² + -baft f. OE beæftan f. be BY + æftan behind]

abalone /ˌæbə'ləʊnɪ/ n. any mollusc of the genus Haliotis, with a shallow ear-shaped shell having respiratory holes, and lined with mother-of-pearl, e.g. the ormer. [Amer. Sp. abulón]

abandon /ə'bænd(ə)n/ v. & n. —v.tr. **1** give up completely or before completion (abandoned hope; abandoned the game). **2 a** forsake or desert (a person or a post of responsibility). **b** leave or desert (a motor vehicle or ship). **3 a** give up to another's control or mercy. **b** refl. yield oneself completely to a passion or impulse. —n. lack of inhibition or restraint; reckless freedom of manner. □□ **abandoner** n. **abandonment** n. [ME f. OF abandoner f. à bandon under control ult. f. LL bannus, -um BAN]

abandoned /ə'bænd(ə)nd/ adj. **1 a** (of a person) deserted, forsaken (an abandoned child). **b** (of a building, vehicle, etc.) left empty or unused (an abandoned cottage; an abandoned ship). **2** (of a person or behaviour) unrestrained, profligate.

abase /ə'beɪs/ v.tr. & refl. humiliate or degrade (another person or oneself). □□ **abasement** n. [ME f. OF abaissier (as A-³, baissier to lower ult. f. LL bassus short of stature): infl. by BASE²]

abash /ə'bæʃ/ v.tr. (usu. as **abashed** adj.) embarrass, disconcert. □□ **abashment** n. [ME f. OF esbaïr (es- = A-⁴ 3, baïr astound or baer yawn)]

abate /ə'beɪt/ v. **1** tr. & intr. make or become less

strong, severe, intense, etc. **2** *tr. Law* **a** quash (a writ or action). **b** put an end to (a nuisance). □□ **abatement** *n.* [ME f. OF *abatre* f. Rmc (as A-³, L *batt(u)ere* beat)]

abatis /'æbətɪs/ *n.* (also **abattis** /ə'bætɪs/) (*pl.* same /-tɪːz/; **abatises, abattises**) *hist.* a defence made of felled trees with the boughs pointing outwards. □□ **abatised** *adj.* [F f. *abatre* fell: see ABATE]

abattoir /'æbə,twɑ:(r)/ *n.* a slaughterhouse. [F (as ABATIS, -ORY¹)]

abaxial /æb'æksɪəl/ *adj. Bot.* facing away from the stem of a plant, esp. of the lower surface of a leaf (cf. ADAXIAL). [AB- + AXIAL]

abaya (also **abba**) var. of ABA.

abbacy /'æbəsɪ/ *n.* (*pl.* **-ies**) the office, jurisdiction, or period of office of an abbot or abbess. [ME f. eccl.L *abbacia* f. *abbat-* ABBOT]

Abbasid /ə'bæsɪd/ *n. & adj.* —*n.* a member of a dynasty of caliphs ruling in Baghdad 750–1258. —*adj.* of this dynasty. [*Abbas*, Muhammad's uncle d. 652]

abbatial /ə'beɪʃ(ə)l/ *adj.* of an abbey, abbot, or abbess. [F *abbatial* or med.L *abbatialis* (as ABBOT)]

abbé /'æbeɪ/ *n.* (in France) an abbot; a male entitled to wear ecclesiastical dress. [F f. eccl.L *abbas abbatis* ABBOT]

abbess /'æbɪs/ *n.* a woman who is the head of certain communities of nuns. [ME f. OF *abbesse* f. eccl.L *abbatissa* (as ABBOT)]

Abbevillian /æb'vɪlɪən/ *n. & adj.* —*n.* the culture of the earliest palaeolithic period in Europe. —*adj.* of this culture. [F *Abbevillien* f. *Abbeville* in N. France]

abbey /'æbɪ/ *n.* (*pl.* **-eys**) **1** the building(s) occupied by a community of monks or nuns. **2** the community itself. **3** a church or house that was once an abbey. [ME f. OF *abbeie* etc. f. med.L *abbatia* ABBACY]

abbot /'æbət/ *n.* a man who is the head of an abbey of monks. □□ **abbotship** *n.* [OE *abbod* f. eccl.L *abbas -atis* f. Gk *abbas* father f. Aram. *'abbā*]

abbreviate /ə'bri:vɪ,eɪt/ *v.tr.* shorten, esp. represent (a word etc.) by a part of it. [ME f. LL *abbreviare* shorten f. *brevis* short: cf. ABRIDGE]

abbreviation /ə,bri:vɪ'eɪʃ(ə)n/ *n.* **1** an abbreviated form, esp. a shortened form of a word or phrase. **2** the process of abbreviating.

ABC¹ /,eɪbi:'si:/ *n.* **1** the alphabet. **2** the rudiments of any subject. **3** an alphabetical guide.

ABC² *abbr.* **1** Australian Broadcasting Corporation. **2** American Broadcasting Company.

abdicate /'æbdɪ,keɪt/ *v.tr.* **1** (usu. *absol.*) give up or renounce (the throne). **2** renounce (a responsibility, duty, etc.). □□ **abdication** /,æbdɪ'keɪʃ(ə)n/ *n.* **abdicator** *n.* [L *abdicare abdicat-* (as AB-, *dicare* declare)]

abdomen /'æbdəmən/ *n.* **1** the part of the body containing the stomach, bowels, reproductive organs, etc. **2** *Zool.* the hinder part of an insect, crustacean, spider, etc. □□ **abdominal** /æb'dɒmɪn(ə)l/ *adj.* **abdominally** /æb'dɒmɪnəlɪ/ *adv.* [L]

abduct /əb'dʌkt/ *v.tr.* **1** carry off or kidnap (a person) illegally by force or deception. **2** (of a muscle etc.) draw (a limb etc.) away from the middle line of the body. □□ **abduction** *n.* **abductor** *n.* [L *abducere abduct-* (as AB-, *ducere* draw)]

abeam /ə'bi:m/ *adv.* **1** on a line at right angles to a ship's or an aircraft's length. **2** (foll. by *of*) opposite the middle of (a ship etc.). [A² + BEAM]

abed /ə'bed/ *adv. archaic* in bed. [OE (as A², BED)]

abele /ə'bi:l, 'eɪb(ə)l/ *n.* the white poplar, *Populus alba*. [Du. *abeel* f. OF *abel*, *aubel* ult. f. L *albus* white]

Aberdeen Angus /,æbədi:n 'æŋgəs/ *n.* **1** an animal of a Scottish breed of hornless black beef cattle. **2** this breed. [*Aberdeen* in Scotland, *Angus* Scottish county]

Aberdonian /,æbə'dəʊnɪən/ *adj. & n.* —*adj.* of Aberdeen. —*n.* a native or citizen of Aberdeen. [med.L *Aberdonia*]

aberrant /ə'berənt/ *adj.* **1** esp. *Biol.* diverging from the normal type. **2** departing from an accepted standard. □□ **aberrance** *n.* **aberrancy** *n.* [L *aberrare aberrant-* (as AB-, *errare* stray)]

aberration /,æbə'reɪʃ(ə)n/ *n.* **1** a departure from what is normal or accepted or regarded as right. **2** a moral or mental lapse. **3** *Biol.* deviation from a normal type. **4** *Optics* the failure of rays to converge at one focus because of a defect in a lens or mirror. **5** *Astron.* the apparent displacement of a celestial body, meteor, etc., caused by the observer's velocity. [L *aberratio* (as ABERRANT)]

abet /ə'bet/ *v.tr.* (**abetted, abetting**) (usu. in **aid and abet**) encourage or assist (an offender or offence). □□ **abetment** *n.* [ME f. OF *abeter* f. *à* to + *beter* BAIT¹]

abetter /ə'betə(r)/ *n.* (also **abettor**) one who abets.

abeyance /ə'beɪəns/ *n.* (usu. prec. by *in, into*) a state of temporary disuse or suspension. □□ **abeyant** *adj.* [AF *abeiance* f. OF *abeer* f. *à* to + *beer* f. med.L *batare* gape]

abhor /əb'hɔː(r)/ *v.tr.* (**abhorred, abhorring**) detest; regard with disgust and hatred. [ME f. F *abhorrer* or f. L *abhorrēre* (as AB-, *horrēre* shudder)]

abhorrence /əb'hɒrəns/ *n.* **1** disgust; detestation. **2** a detested thing.

abhorrent /əb'hɒrənt/ *adj.* **1** (often foll. by *to*) (of conduct etc.) inspiring disgust, repugnant; hateful, detestable. **2** (foll. by *to*) not in accordance with; strongly conflicting with (*abhorrent to the spirit of the law*). **3** (foll. by *from*) inconsistent with. □□ **abhorrer** *n.*

abide /ə'baɪd/ *v.* (*past* **abided** or rarely **abode** /ə'bəʊd/) **1** *tr.* (usu. in *neg.* or *interrog.*) tolerate, endure (*can't abide him*). **2** *intr.* (foll. by *by*) **a** act in accordance with (*abide by the rules*). **b** remain faithful to (a promise). **3** *intr. archaic* **a** remain, continue. **b** dwell. **4** *tr. archaic* sustain, endure. □□ **abidance** *n.* [OE *ābīdan* (as A-², *bidan* BIDE)]

abiding /ə'baɪdɪŋ/ *adj.* enduring, permanent (*an abiding sense of loss*). □□ **abidingly** *adv.*

ability /ə'bɪlɪtɪ/ *n.* (*pl.* **-ies**) **1** (often foll. by *to* + *infin.*) capacity or power (*has the ability to write songs*). **2** cleverness, talent; mental power (*a person of great ability; has many abilities*). [ME f. OF *ablete* f. L *habilitas -tatis* f. *habilis* able]

-ability /ə'bɪlɪtɪ/ *suffix* forming nouns of quality from, or corresponding to, adjectives in *-able* (*capability, vulnerability*). [F *-abilité* or L *-abilitas*: cf. -ITY]

ab initio /,æb ɪ'nɪʃɪəʊ/ *adv.* from the beginning. [L]

abiogenesis /,eɪbaɪəʊ'dʒenɪsɪs/ *n.* **1** the formation of living organisms from non-living substances. **2** the supposed spontaneous generation of living organisms. □□ **abiogenic** *adj.* [A-¹ + Gk *bios* life + GENESIS]

abject /'æbdʒekt/ *adj.* **1** miserable, wretched. **2** degraded, self-abasing, humble. **3** despicable. □□ **abjectly** *adv.* **abjectness** *n.* [ME f. L *abjectus* past part. of *abicere* (as AB-, *jacere* throw)]

abjection /əb'dʒekʃ(ə)n/ *n.* a state of misery or degradation. [ME f. OF *abjection* or L *abjectio* (as ABJECT)]

abjure /əb'dʒʊə(r)/ *v.tr.* **1** renounce on oath (an opinion, cause, claim, etc.). **2** swear perpetual absence from (one's country etc.). □□ **abjuration** /,æbdʒʊ'reɪʃ(ə)n/ *n.* [L *abjurare* (as AB-, *jurare* swear)]

ablation /æb'leɪʃ(ə)n/ *n.* **1** the surgical removal of body tissue. **2** *Geol.* the wasting or erosion of a glacier, iceberg, or rock by melting or the action of water. **3** *Astronaut.* the evaporation or melting of part of the outer surface of a spacecraft through heating by friction with the atmosphere. □□ **ablate** *v.tr.* [F *ablation* or LL *ablatio* f. L *ablat-* (as AB-, *lat-* past part. stem of *ferre* carry)]

ablative /'æblətɪv/ *n. & adj. Gram.* —*n.* the case (esp. in Latin) of nouns and pronouns (and words in grammatical agreement with them) indicating an agent, instrument, or location. —*adj.* of or in the ablative. □**ablative absolute** an absolute con-struction in Latin with a noun and participle or adjective in the ablative case (see ABSOLUTE). [ME f. OF *ablatif -ive* or L *ablativus* (as ABLATION)]

ablaut /'æblaʊt/ *n.* a change of vowel in related words or forms, esp. in Indo-European languages, arising from differences of accent and stress in the parent language, e.g. in *sing, sang, sung.* [G]

ablaze /ə'bleɪz/ *predic.adj.* & *adv.* **1** on fire (*set it ablaze; the house was ablaze*). **2** (often foll. by *with*) glittering, glowing. **3** (often foll. by *with*) greatly excited.

able /'eɪb(ə)l/ *adj.* (**abler, ablest**) **1** (often foll. by *to* + infin.; used esp. in *is able, will be able, was able,* etc., replacing tenses of *can*) having the capacity or power (*was not able to come*). **2** having great abil-ity; clever, skilful. □**able-bodied** fit, healthy. **able-bodied rating** (or **seaman**) *Naut.* one able to perform all duties. [ME f. OF *hable, able* f. L *habilis* handy f. *habēre* to hold]

-able /əb(ə)l/ *suffix* forming adjectives meaning: **1** that may or must be (*eatable; forgiveable; payable*). **2** that can be made the subject of (*dutiable; ob-jectionable*). **3** that is relevant to or in accordance with (*fashionable; seasonable*). **4** (with active sense, in earlier word-formations) that may (*comfortable; suitable*). [F *-able* or L *-abilis* forming verbal ad-jectives f. verbs of first conjugation]

abloom /ə'bluːm/ *predic.adj.* blooming; in flower.

ablush /ə'blʌʃ/ *predic.adj.* blushing.

ablution /ə'bluːʃ(ə)n/ *n.* (usu. in *pl.*) **1** the ceremonial washing of parts of the body or sacred vessels etc. **2** *colloq.* the ordinary washing of the body. **3** a building containing washing-places etc. in a camp, ship, etc. □□**ablutionary** *adj.* [ME f. OF *ablution* or L *ablutio* (as AB-, *lutio* f. *luere lut-* wash)]

ably /'eɪblɪ/ *adv.* capably, cleverly, competently.

-ably /əblɪ/ *suffix* forming adverbs corresponding to adjectives in *-able.*

ABM *abbr.* anti-ballistic missile.

abnegate /'æbnɪɡeɪt/ *v.tr.* **1** give up or deny oneself (a pleasure etc.). **2** renounce or reject (a right or belief). □□**abnegator** *n.* [L *abnegare abnegat-* (as AB-, *negare* deny)]

abnegation /ˌæbnɪ'ɡeɪʃ(ə)n/ *n.* **1** denial; the rejection or renunciation of a doctrine. **2** = SELF-ABNEGATION. [OF *abnegation* or LL *abnegatio* (as ABNEGATE)]

abnormal /æb'nɔːm(ə)l/ *adj.* **1** deviating from what is normal or usual; exceptional. **2** relating to or dealing with what is abnormal (*abnormal psychology*). □□**abnormally** *adv.* [earlier and F *anormal, anomal* f. Gk *anōmalos* ANOMALOUS, assoc. with L *abnormis*: see ABNORMITY]

abnormality /ˌæbnɔː'mælɪtɪ/ *n.* (*pl.* **-ies**) **1 a** an abnormal quality, occurrence, etc. **b** the state of being abnormal. **2** a physical irregularity.

abnormity /æb'nɔːmɪtɪ/ *n.* (*pl.* **-ies**) **1** an abnormality or irregularity. **2** a monstrosity. [L *abnormis* (as AB-, *normis* f. *norma* rule)]

Abo /'æbəʊ/ *n.* & *adj.* (also **abo**) *Austral. sl.* usu. *offens.* —*n.* (*pl.* **Abos**) an Aboriginal. —*adj.* Ab-original. [abbr.]

aboard /ə'bɔːd/ *adv.* & *prep.* **1** on or into (a ship, aircraft, train, etc.). **2** alongside. □**all aboard!** a call that warns of the imminent departure of a ship, train, etc. [ME f. A² + BOARD & F *à bord*]

abode¹ /ə'bəʊd/ *n.* **1** a dwelling-place; one's home. **2** *archaic* a stay or sojourn. [verbal noun of ABIDE: cf. *ride, rode, road*]

abode² *past of* ABIDE.

abolish /ə'bɒlɪʃ/ *v.tr.* put an end to the existence or practice of (esp. a custom or institution). □□ **abolishable** *adj.* **abolisher** *n.* **abolishment** *n.* [ME f. F *abolir* f. L *abolēre* destroy]

abolition /ˌæbə'lɪʃ(ə)n/ *n.* **1** the act or process of abolishing or being abolished. **2** an instance of this. [F *abolition* or L *abolitio* (as ABOLISH)]

abolitionist /ˌæbə'lɪʃənɪst/ *n.* one who favours the

abolition of a practice or institution, esp. of capital punishment or (formerly) of Negro slavery. □□ **abolitionism** *n.*

abomasum /ˌæbə'meɪs(ə)m/ *n.* (*pl.* **abomasa** /-sə/) the fourth stomach of a ruminant. [mod.L f. AB- + OMASUM]

A-bomb /'eɪbɒm/ *n.* = *atomic bomb.* [A (for ATOMIC) + BOMB]

abominable /ə'bɒmɪnəb(ə)l/ *adj.* **1** detestable; loath-some; morally reprehensible. **2** *colloq.* very bad or unpleasant (*abominable weather*). □**Abominable Snowman** an unidentified manlike or bearlike an-imal said to exist in the Himalayas; a yeti. □□ **abominably** *adv.* [ME f. OF f. L *abominabilis* f. *abominari* deprecate (as AB-, *ominari* f. OMEN)]

abominate /ə'bɒmɪˌneɪt/ *v.tr.* detest, loathe. □□ **abominator** *n.* [L *abominari* (as ABOMINABLE)]

abomination /əˌbɒmɪ'neɪʃ(ə)n/ *n.* **1** loathing. **2** an odious or degrading habit or act. **3** (often foll. by *to*) an object of disgust. [ME f. OF (as ABOMINATE)]

aboral /æb'ɔːr(ə)l/ *adj.* away from or opposite the mouth. [AB- + ORAL]

aboriginal /ˌæbə'rɪdʒɪn(ə)l/ *adj.* & *n.* —*adj.* **1** (of races and natural phenomena) inhabiting or existing in a land from the earliest times or from before the arrival of colonists. **2** (usu. **Aboriginal**) of the Australian Aboriginals. —*n.* **1** an aboriginal in-habitant. **2** (usu. **Aboriginal**) an aboriginal in-habitant of Australia. □□**aboriginally** *adv.* [as ABORIGINE + -AL]

aborigine /ˌæbə'rɪdʒɪnɪ/ *n.* (usu. in *pl.*) **1** an ab-original inhabitant. **2** (usu. **Aborigine**) an aboriginal inhabitant of Australia. ¶ *Aboriginal* is preferred, esp. in the singular. **3** an aboriginal plant or animal. [back-form. f. pl. *aborigines* f. L, prob. f. phr. *ab origine* from the beginning]

abort /ə'bɔːt/ *v.* & *n.* —*v.* **1** *intr.* **a** (of a woman) undergo abortion; miscarry. **b** (of a foetus) suffer abortion. **2** *tr.* **a** effect the abortion of (a foetus). **b** effect abortion in (a mother). **3 a** *tr.* cause to end fruitlessly or prematurely; stop in the early stages. **b** *intr.* end unsuccessfully or prematurely. **4 a** *tr.* abandon or terminate (a space flight or other technical project) before its completion, usu. because of a fault. **b** *intr.* terminate or fail to complete such an undertaking. **5** *Biol.* **a** *intr.* (of an organism) remain undeveloped; shrink away. **b** *tr.* cause to do this. —*n.* **1** a prematurely terminated space flight or other undertaking. **2** the termination of such an undertaking. [L *aboriri* miscarry (as AB-, *oriri ort-* be born)]

abortifacient /əˌbɔːtɪ'feɪʃ(ə)nt/ *adj.* & *n.* —*adj.* effecting abortion. —*n.* a drug or other agent that effects abortion.

abortion /ə'bɔːʃ(ə)n/ *n.* **1** the expulsion of a foetus (naturally or esp. by medical induction) from the womb before it is able to survive independently, esp. in the first 28 weeks of a human pregnancy. **2** a stunted or deformed creature or thing. **3** the failure of a project or an action. **4** *Biol.* the arrest of the development of an organ. [L *abortio* (as ABORT)]

abortionist /ə'bɔːʃənɪst/ *n.* **1** a person who carries out abortions, esp. illegally. **2** a person who favours the legalization of abortion.

abortive /ə'bɔːtɪv/ *adj.* **1** fruitless, unsuccessful, unfinished. **2** resulting in abortion. **3** *Biol.* (of an organ etc.) rudimentary; arrested in development. □□**abortively** *adv.* [ME f. OF *abortif -ive* f. L *abor-tivus* (as ABORT)]

ABO system /eɪbiː'əʊ/ *n.* a system of four types (A, AB, B, and O) by which human blood may be classified, based on the presence or absence of certain inherited antigens.

aboulia /ə'buːlɪə/ *n.* (also **abulia**) the loss of will-power as a mental disorder. □□**aboulic** *adj.* [Gk *a-* not + *boulē* will]

abound /ə'baʊnd/ *v.intr.* **1** be plentiful. **2** (foll. by *in, with*) be rich; teem or be infested. [ME f. OF *abunder* etc. f. L *abundare* overflow (as AB-, *undare* f. *unda* wave)]

about /ə'baʊt/ *prep. & adv.* —*prep.* **1 a** on the subject of; in connection with (*a book about birds*; *what are you talking about?*; *argued about money*). **b** relating to (*something funny about this*). **c** in relation to (*symmetry about a plane*). **d** so as to affect (*can do nothing about it*; *what are you going to do about it?*). **2** at a time near to (*come about four*). **3 a** in, round, surrounding (*wandered about the town*; *a scarf about her neck*). **b** all round from a centre (*look about you*). **4** here and there in; at points throughout (*toys lying about the house*). **5** at a point or points near to (*fighting going on about us*). **6** carried with (*have no money about me*). **7** occupied with (*what are you about?*). —*adv.* **1 a** approximately (*costs about a pound*; *is about right*). **b** *colloq.* used to indicate understatement (*just about had enough*; *it's about time they came*). **2** here and there; at points nearby (*a lot of flu about*; *I've seen him about recently*). **3** all round; in every direction (*look about*). **4** on the move; in action (*out and about*). **5** in partial rotation or alteration from a given position (*the wrong way about*). **6** in rotation or succession (*turn and turn about*). **7** *Naut.* on or to the opposite tack (*go about*; *put about*). □**be about to** be on the point of (doing something) (*was about to laugh*). [OE *onbūtan* (on = A², *būtan* BUT¹)]

about-face /-'feɪs/ *n.*, *v.*, & *int.* —*n.* & *v.intr.* = ABOUT-TURN *n.* & *v.* —*int.* = ABOUT TURN *int.*

about-turn /əbaʊt'tɜːn/ *n.*, *v.*, & *int.* —*n.* **1** a turn made so as to face the opposite direction. **2** a change of opinion or policy etc. —*v.intr.* make an about-turn. —*int.* (**about turn**) *Mil.* a command to make an about-turn. [orig. as int.]

above /ə'bʌv/ *prep.*, *adv.*, *adj.*, & *n.* —*prep.* **1** over; on the top of; higher (vertically, up a slope or stream etc.) than; over the surface of (*head above water*; *above the din*). **2** more than (*above twenty people*; *above average*). **3** higher in rank, position, importance, etc., than (*above all*). **4 a** too great or good for (*above one's station*; *is not above cheating at cards*). **b** beyond the reach of; not affected by (*above my understanding*; *above suspicion*). **5** *archaic* to an earlier time than (*not traced above the third century*). —*adv.* **1** at or to a higher point; overhead (*the floor above*; *the clouds above*). **2 a** upstairs (*lives above*). **b** upstream. **3** (of a text reference) further back on a page or in a book (*as noted above*). **4** on the upper side (*looks similar above and below*). **5** in addition (*over and above*). **6** *rhet.* in heaven (*Lord above!*). —*adj.* mentioned earlier; preceding (*the above argument*). —*n.* (prec. by *the*) what is mentioned above (*the above shows*). □**above-board** *adj. & adv.* without concealment; fair or fairly; open or openly. **above ground** alive. **above one's head** see HEAD. **above oneself** conceited, arrogant. [A² + OE *bufan* f. *be* = BY + *ufan* above]

ab ovo /æb 'əʊvəʊ/ *adv.* from the very beginning. [L, = from the egg]

Abp. *abbr.* Archbishop.

abracadabra /ˌæbrəkə'dæbrə/ *int.* & *n.* —*int.* a supposedly magic word used by conjurors in performing a trick. —*n.* **1** a spell or charm. **2** jargon or gibberish. [a mystical word engraved and used as a charm: L f. Gk]

abrade /ə'breɪd/ *v.tr.* scrape or wear away (skin, rock, etc.) by rubbing. □□**abrader** *n.* [L f. *radere ras-* scrape]

abrasion /ə'breɪʒ(ə)n/ *n.* **1** the scraping or wearing away (of skin, rock, etc.). **2** a damaged area resulting from this. [L *abrasio* (as ABRADE)]

abrasive /ə'breɪsɪv/ *adj.* & *n.* —*adj.* **1 a** tending to rub or graze. **b** capable of polishing by rubbing or grinding. **2** harsh or hurtful in manner. —*n.* an abrasive substance. [as ABRADE + -IVE]

abreact /ˌæbrɪ'ækt/ *v.tr. Psychol.* release (an emotion) by abreaction. [back-form. f. ABREACTION]

abreaction /ˌæbrɪ'ækʃ(ə)n/ *n. Psychol.* the free expression and consequent release of a previously repressed emotion. □□**abreactive** *adj.* [AB- + REACTION after G *Abreagierung*]

abreast /ə'brest/ *adv.* **1** side by side and facing the same way. **2 a** (often foll. by *with*) up to date. **b** (foll. by *of*) well-informed (*abreast of all the changes*). [ME f. A² + BREAST]

abridge /ə'brɪdʒ/ *v.tr.* **1** shorten (a book, film, etc.) by using fewer words or making deletions. **2** curtail (liberty). □□**abridgable** *adj.* **abridger** *n.* [ME f. OF *abreg(i)er* f. LL *abbreviare* ABBREVIATE]

abridgement /ə'brɪdʒmənt/ *n.* (also **abridgment**) **1 a** a shortened version, esp. of a book; an abstract. **b** the process of producing this. **2** a curtailment (of rights). [F *abrégement* (as ABRIDGE)]

abroad /ə'brɔːd/ *adv.* **1** in or to a foreign country or countries. **2** over a wide area; in different directions; everywhere (*scatter abroad*). **3** at large; freely moving about; in circulation (*there is a rumour abroad*). **4** *archaic* in or into the open; out of doors. **5** *archaic* wide of the mark; erring. □**from abroad** from another country. [ME f. A² + BROAD]

abrogate /'æbrəɡeɪt/ *v.tr.* repeal, annul, abolish (a law or custom). □□**abrogation** /ˌæbrə'ɡeɪʃ(ə)n/ *n.* **abrogator** *n.* [L *abrogare* (as AB-, *rogare* propose a law)]

abrupt /ə'brʌpt/ *adj.* **1** sudden and unexpected; hasty (*his abrupt departure*). **2** (of speech, manner, etc.) uneven; lacking continuity; curt. **3** steep, precipitous. **4** *Bot.* truncated. **5** *Geol.* (of strata) suddenly appearing at the surface. □□**abruptly** *adv.* **abruptness** *n.* [L *abruptus* past part. of *abrumpere* (as AB-, *rumpere* break)]

abs- /əbs, æbs/ *prefix* = AB-. [var. of L *ab-* used before *c, q, t*]

abscess /'æbsɪs/ *n.* a swollen area accumulating pus within a body tissue. □□**abscessed** *adj.* [L *abscessus* a going away (as AB-, *cedere cess-* go)]

abscisic acid /æb'saɪzɪk/ *n.* a plant hormone which promotes leaf detachment and bud dormancy and inhibits germination. [L *abscis-* past part. stem of *abscindere* (as AB-, *scindere* to cut)]

abscissa /əb'sɪsə/ *n.* (*pl.* **abscissae** /-siː/ or **abscissas**) *Math.* **1** (in a system of coordinates) the shortest distance from a point to the vertical or *y*-axis, measured parallel to the horizontal or *x*-axis; the Cartesian *x*-coordinate of a point (cf. ORDINATE). **2** the part of a line between a fixed point on it and an ordinate drawn to it from any other point. [mod.L *abscissa (linea)* fem. past part. of *abscindere absciss-* (as AB-, *scindere* cut)]

abscission /əb'sɪʒ(ə)n/ *n.* **1** the act or an instance of cutting off. **2** *Bot.* the natural detachment of leaves, branches, flowers, etc. [L *abscissio* (as ABSCISSA)]

abscond /əb'skɒnd/ *v.intr.* depart hurriedly and furtively, esp. unlawfully or to avoid arrest. □□**absconder** *n.* [L *abscondere* (as AB-, *condere* stow)]

abseil /'æbseɪl, -zɪl/ *v.* & *n. Mountaineering* —*v.intr.* descend a steep rock-face by using a doubled rope coiled round the body and fixed at a higher point. —*n.* a descent made by abseiling. [G *abseilen* f. *ab* down + *Seil* rope]

absence /'æbs(ə)ns/ *n.* **1** the state of being away from a place or person. **2** the time or duration of being away. **3** (foll. by *of*) the non-existence or lack of. □**absence of mind** inattentiveness. [ME f. OF f. L *absentia* (as ABSENT)]

absent *adj.* & *v.* —*adj.* /'æbs(ə)nt/ **1 a** not present. **b** (foll. by *from*) not present at or in. **2** not existing. **3** inattentive to the matter in hand. —*v.refl.* /əb'sent/ **1** stay away. **2** withdraw. □□**absently** *adv.* (in sense 3 of *adj.*). [ME ult. f. L *absent-* pres. part. of *abesse* be absent]

absentee /ˌæbsən'tiː/ *n.* a person not present, esp. one who is absent from work or school. □**absentee landlord** a landlord who lets a property while living elsewhere.

absenteeism /ˌæbsən'tiːɪz(ə)m/ *n.* the practice of absenting oneself from work or school etc., esp. frequently or illicitly.

absent-minded /ˌæbs(ə)nt'maɪndɪd/ *adj.* habitually forgetful or inattentive; with one's mind on other things.   □□ **absent-mindedly** *adv.*   **absent-mindedness** *n.*

absinth /'æbsɪnθ/ *n.* **1** a shrubby plant, *Atemisia absinthium*, or its essence. Also called WORMWOOD. **2** (usu. **absinthe**) a green aniseed-flavoured potent liqueur based on wormwood and turning milky when water is added. [F *absinthe* f. L *absinthium* f. Gk *apsinthion*]

absit omen /ˌæbsɪt 'əʊmen/ *int.* may what is threatened not become fact. [L, = may this (evil) omen be absent]

absolute /'æbsəˌluːt, -ˌljuːt/ *adj.* & *n.* —*adj.* **1** complete, utter, perfect (*an absolute fool*; *absolute bliss*). **2** unconditional, unlimited (*absolute authority*). **3** despotic; ruling arbitrarily or with unrestricted power (*an absolute monarch*). **4** (of a standard or other concept) universally valid; not admitting exceptions; not relative or comparative. **5** *Gram.* **a** (of a construction) syntactically independent of the rest of the sentence, as in *dinner being over, we left the table*; *let us toss for it, loser to pay*. **b** (of an adjective or transitive verb) used or usable without an expressed noun or object (e.g. *the deaf, guns kill*). **6** (of a legal decree etc.) final. —*n. Philos.* **1** a value, standard, etc., which is objective and universally valid, not subjective or relative. **2** (prec. by *the*) **a** *Philos.* that which can exist without being related to anything else. **b** *Theol.* ultimate reality; God. □**absolute alcohol** *Chem.* ethanol free from water or other impurities. **absolute magnitude** the magnitude, i.e. brightness, of a celestial body as seen at a standard distance of 10 parsecs (opp. *apparent magnitude*). **absolute majority 1** a majority over all others combined. **2** more than half. **absolute pitch** *Mus.* **1** the ability to recognize the pitch of a note or produce any given note. **2** a fixed standard of pitch defined by the rate of vibration. **absolute temperature** one measured from absolute zero. **absolute zero** a theoretical lowest possible temperature, at which the particles whose motion constitutes heat would be minimal, calculated as −273.15 °C (or 0 °K). □□ **absoluteness** *n.* [ME f. L *absolutus* past part.: see ABSOLVE]

absolutely /'æbsəˌluːtlɪ, -ˌljuːtlɪ/ *adv.* **1** completely, utterly, perfectly (*absolutely marvellous*; *he absolutely denies it*). **2** independently; in an absolute sense (*God exists absolutely*). **3** (foll. by *neg.*) (no or none) at all (*absolutely no chance of winning*; *absolutely nowhere*). **4** *colloq.* in actual fact; positively (*it absolutely exploded*). **5** *Gram.* in an absolute way, esp. (of a verb) without a stated object. **6** /-'luːtlɪ, -'ljuːtlɪ/ *colloq.* (used in reply) quite so; yes.

absolution /ˌæbsə'luːʃ(ə)n, -'ljuːʃ(ə)n/ *n.* **1** a formal release from guilt, obligation, or punishment. **2** an ecclesiastical declaration of forgiveness of sins. **3** a remission of penance. **4** forgiveness. [ME f. OF f. L *absolutio -onis* (as ABSOLVE)]

absolutism /'æbsəˌluːˌtɪz(ə)m, -ˌljuːˌtɪz(ə)m/ *n.* the acceptance of or belief in absolute principles in political, philosophical, ethical, or theological matters. □□ **absolutist** *n.* & *adj.*

absolve /əb'zɒlv/ *v.tr.* **1** (often foll. by *from*, *of*) **a** set or pronounce free from blame or obligation etc. **b** acquit; pronounce not guilty. **2** pardon or give absolution for (a sin etc.). □□ **absolver** *n.* [L *absolvere* (as AB-, *solvere solut-* loosen)]

absorb /əb'sɔːb, -'zɔːb/ *v.tr.* **1** include or incorporate as part of itself or oneself (*the country successfully absorbed its immigrants*). **2** take in; suck up (liquid, heat, knowledge, etc.) (*she quickly absorbed all she was taught*). **3** reduce the effect or intensity of; deal easily with (an impact, sound, difficulty, etc.). **4** consume (income, time, resources, etc.) (*his debts absorbed half his income*). **5** engross the attention of (*television absorbs them completely*). □□ **absorbable** *adj.* **absorbability** /-'bɪlɪtɪ/ *n.* **absorber** *n.* [ME f. F *absorber* or L *absorbēre absorpt-* (as AB-, *sorbēre* suck in)]

absorbed /əb'sɔːbd, -'zɔːbd/ *adj.* intensely engaged or interested (*he was absorbed in his work*). □□ **absorbedly** /-bɪdlɪ/ *adv.*

absorbent /əb'sɔːbənt, -'zɔːbənt/ *adj.* & *n.* —*adj.* having a tendency to absorb (esp. liquids). —*n.* **1** an absorbent substance. **2** any of the vessels in plants and animals (e.g. root tips) that absorb nutriment. □□ **absorbency** *n.* [L *absorbent-* f. *absorbēre* ABSORB]

absorbing /əb'sɔːbɪŋ, -'zɔːbɪŋ/ *adj.* engrossing; intensely interesting. □□ **absorbingly** *adv.*

absorption /əb'sɔːpʃ(ə)n, -'zɔːpʃ(ə)n/ *n.* **1** the process or action of absorbing or being absorbed. **2** disappearance through incorporation into something else. **3** mental engrossment. □□ **absorptive** *adj.* [L *absorptio* (as ABSORB)]

abstain /əb'steɪn/ *v.intr.* **1** (usu. foll. by *from*) restrain oneself; refrain from indulging in (*abstained from cakes and sweets*; *abstained from mentioning it*). **b** refrain from drinking alcohol. **2** formally decline to use one's vote. □□ **abstainer** *n.* [ME f. AF *astener* f. OF *abstenir* f. L *abstinēre abstent-* (as AB-, *tenēre* hold)]

abstemious /æb'stiːmɪəs/ *adj.* (of a person, habit, etc.) moderate, not self-indulgent, esp. in eating and drinking. □□ **abstemiously** *adv.* **abstemiousness** *n.* [L *abstemius* (as AB-, *temetum* strong drink)]

abstention /əb'stenʃ(ə)n/ *n.* the act or an instance of abstaining, esp. from voting. [F *abstention* or LL *abstentio -onis* (as ABSTAIN)]

abstinence /'æbstɪnəns/ *n.* **1** the act of abstaining, esp. from food or alcohol. **2** the habit of abstaining from pleasure, food, etc. [ME f. OF f. L *abstinentia* (as ABSTINENT)]

abstinent /'æbstɪnənt/ *adj.* practising abstinence. □□ **abstinently** *adv.* [ME f. OF f. L (as ABSTAIN)]

abstract *adj., v.,* & *n.* —*adj.* /'æbstrækt/ **1 a** to do with or existing in thought rather than matter, or in theory rather than practice; not tangible or concrete (*abstract questions rarely concerned him*). **b** (of a word, esp. a noun) denoting a quality or condition or intangible thing rather than a concrete object. **2** (of art) achieving its effect by grouping shapes and colours in satisfying patterns rather than by the recognizable representation of physical reality. —*v.* /əb'strækt/ **1** *tr.* (often foll. by *from*) take out of; extract; remove. **2 a** *tr.* summarize (an article, book, etc.). **b** *intr.* do this as an occupation. **3** *tr.* & *refl.* (often foll. by *from*) disengage (a person's attention etc.); distract. **4** *tr.* (foll. by *from*) consider abstractly or separately from something else. **5** *tr. euphem.* steal. —*n.* /'æbstrækt/ **1** a summary or statement of the contents of a book etc. **2** an abstract work of art. **3** an abstraction or abstract term. □**abstract expressionism** a development of abstract art which aims at a subjective emotional expression of an ideal rather than a picture of a physical object. **in the abstract** in theory rather than in practice. □□ **abstractly** /'æbstræktlɪ/ *adv.* **abstractor** /əb'stræktə(r)/ *n.* (in sense 2 of *v.*). [ME f. OF *abstract* or L *abstractus* past part. of *abstrahere* (as AB-, *trahere* draw)]

abstracted /əb'stræktɪd/ *adj.* inattentive to the matter in hand; preoccupied. □□ **abstractedly** *adv.*

abstraction /əb'strækʃ(ə)n/ *n.* **1** the act or an instance of abstracting or taking away. **2 a** an abstract or visionary idea. **b** the formation of abstract ideas. **3 a** abstract qualities (esp. in art). **b** an abstract work of art. **4** abstract-mindedness. [F *abstraction* or L *abstractio* (as ABSTRACT)]

abstractionism /əb'strækʃəˌnɪz(ə)m/ *n.* **1** the principles and practice of abstract art. **2** the pursuit or cult of abstract ideas. □□ **abstractionist** *n.*

abstruse /əb'stru:s/ adj. hard to understand; obscure; profound. □□ **abstrusely** adv. **abstruseness** n. [F abstruse or L abstrusus (as AB-, trusus past part. of trudere push)]

absurd /əb'sɜ:d/ adj. **1** (of an idea, suggestion, etc.) wildly unreasonable, illogical, or inappropriate. **2** (of a person) unreasonable or ridiculous in manner. **3** (of a thing) ludicrous, incongruous (an absurd hat; the situation was becoming absurd). □□ **absurdly** adv. **absurdness** n. [F absurde or L absurdus (as AB-, surdus deaf, dull)]

absurdity /əb'sɜ:dɪtɪ/ n. (pl. -ies) **1** wild inappropriateness or incongruity. **2** extreme unreasonableness. **3** an absurd statement or act. [F absurdité or LL absurditas (as ABSURD)]

ABTA /'æbtə/ abbr. Association of British Travel Agents.

abulia var. of ABOULIA.

abundance /ə'bʌnd(ə)ns/ n. **1** a very great quantity, usu. considered to be more than enough. **2** wealth, affluence. **3** wealth of emotion (abundance of heart). **4** a call in solo whist undertaking to make nine tricks. [ME f. OF abundance f. L abundantia (as ABUNDANT)]

abundant /ə'bʌnd(ə)nt/ adj. **1** existing or available in large quantities; plentiful. **2** (foll. by in) having an abundance of (a country abundant in fruit). □□ **abundantly** adv. [ME f. L (as ABOUND)]

abuse v. & n. —v.tr. /ə'bju:z/ **1** use to bad effect or for a bad purpose; misuse (abused his position of power). **2** insult verbally. **3** maltreat. —n. /ə'bju:s/ **1 a** incorrect or improper use (the abuse of power). **b** an instance of this. **2** insulting language (a torrent of abuse). **3** unjust or corrupt practice. **4** maltreatment of a person (child abuse). □□ **abuser** /ə'bju:zə(r)/ n. [ME f. OF abus (n.), abuser (v.) f. L abusus, abuti (as AB-, uti us- USE)]

abusive /ə'bju:sɪv/ adj. **1** using or containing insulting language. **2** (of language) insulting. □□ **abusively** adv. **abusiveness** n.

abut /ə'bʌt/ v. (abutted, abutting) **1** intr. (foll. by on) (of estates, countries, etc.) adjoin (another). **2** intr. (foll. by on, against) (of part of a building) touch or lean upon (another) with a projecting end or point (the shed abutted on the side of the house). **3** tr. abut on. [OF abouter (BUTT¹) and AL abuttare f. OF but end]

abutment /ə'bʌtmənt/ n. **1** the lateral supporting structure of a bridge, arch, etc. **2** the point of junction between such a support and the thing supported.

abutter /ə'bʌtə(r)/ n. Law the owner of an adjoining property.

abuzz /ə'bʌz/ adv. & adj. in a 'buzz' (see BUZZ n. 3); in a state of excitement or activity.

abysmal /ə'bɪzm(ə)l/ adj. **1** colloq. extremely bad (abysmal weather; the standard is abysmal). **2** profound, utter (abysmal ignorance). □□ **abysmally** adv. [archaic or poet. abysm = ABYSS, f. OF abi(s)me f. med.L abysmus]

abyss /ə'bɪs/ n. **1** a deep or seemingly bottomless chasm. **2 a** an immeasurable depth (abyss of despair). **b** a catastrophic situation as contemplated or feared (his loss brought him a step nearer the abyss). **3** (prec. by the) primal chaos, hell. [ME f. LL abyssus f. Gk abussos bottomless (as A-¹, bussos depth)]

abyssal /ə'bɪs(ə)l/ adj. **1** at or of the ocean depths or floor. **2** Geol. plutonic.

AC abbr. **1** (also **ac**) alternating current. **2** Brit. aircraftman. **3** before Christ. **4** Companion of the Order of Australia. [sense 3 f. L ante Christum]

Ac symb. Chem. the element actinium.

ac- /ək/ prefix assim. form of AD- before c, k, q.

a/c abbr. account. [account current: see ACCOUNT n. 2, 3]

-ac /æk/ suffix forming adjectives which are often also (or only) used as nouns (cardiac; maniac) (see also -ACAL). [F -aque or L -acus or Gk -akos adj. suffix]

acacia /ə'keɪʃə/ n. **1** any tree of the genus Acacia, with yellow or white flowers, esp. A. senegal yielding gum arabic. **2** (also **false acacia**) the locust tree, Robinia pseudoacacia, grown for ornament. [L f. Gk akakia]

academe /'ækə,di:m/ n. **1 a** the world of learning. **b** universities collectively. **2** literary a college or university. □**grove** (or **groves**) **of Academe** a university environment. [Gk Akadēmos (see ACADEMY): used by Shakesp. (Love's Labour's Lost I. i. 13) and Milton (Paradise Regained iv. 244)]

academia /,ækə'di:mɪə/ n. the academic world; scholastic life. [mod.L: see ACADEMY]

academic /,ækə'demɪk/ adj. & n. —adj. **1 a** scholarly; to do with learning. **b** of or relating to a scholarly institution (academic dress). **2** abstract; theoretical; not of practical relevance. **3** Art conventional, overformal. **4 a** of or concerning Plato's philosophy. **b** sceptical. —n. a teacher or scholar in a university or institute of higher education. □**academic year** a period of nearly a year reckoned from the time of the main student intake, usu. from the beginning of the autumn term to the end of the summer term. □□ **academically** adv. [F académique or L academicus (as ACADEMY)]

academical /,ækə'demɪk(ə)l/ adj. & n. —adj. belonging to a college or university. —n. (in pl.) university costume.

academician /ə,kædə'mɪʃ(ə)n/ n. a member of an Academy, esp. of the Royal Academy of Arts, the Académie française, or the USSR Academy of Sciences. [F académicien (as ACADEMIC)]

academicism /,ækə'demɪ,sɪz(ə)m/ n. (also **academism** /ə'kædə,mɪz(ə)m/) academic principles or their application in art.

academy /ə'kædəmɪ/ n. (pl. -ies) **1 a** a place of study or training in a special field (military academy; academy of dance). **b** hist. a place of study. **2** (usu. Academy) a society or institution of distinguished scholars, artists, scientists, etc. (Royal Academy). **3** Sc. a secondary school. **4 a** Plato's followers or philosophical system. **b** the garden near Athens where Plato taught. [F académie or L academia f. Gk akadēmeia f. Akadēmos the hero after whom Plato's garden was named]

Acadian /ə'keɪdɪən/ n. & adj. —n. **1** a native or inhabitant of Acadia in Nova Scotia, esp. a French-speaking descendant of the early French settlers in Canada. **2** a descendant of French-speaking Nova Scotian immigrants in Louisiana. —adj. of or relating to Acadians. [F Acadie Nova Scotia]

-acal /ək(ə)l/ suffix forming adjectives, often used to distinguish them from nouns in -ac (heliacal; maniacal).

acanthus /ə'kænθəs/ n. **1** any herbaceous plant or shrub of the genus Acanthus, with spiny leaves. **2** Archit. a conventionalized representation of an acanthus leaf, used esp. as a decoration for Corinthian column capitals. [L f. Gk akanthos f. akantha thorn perh. f. akē sharp point]

a cappella /,ɑː kə'pelə, ,æ kə'pelə/ adj. & adv. (also **alla cappella** /,ælə/) Mus. (of choral music) unaccompanied. [It., = in church style]

acaricide /ə'kærɪ,saɪd/ n. a preparation for destroying mites.

acarid /'ækərɪd/ n. any small arachnid of the order Acarina, including mites and ticks. [mod.L acarida f. acarus f. Gk akari mite]

acarpous /ə'kɑːpəs/ adj. Bot. (of a plant etc.) without fruit or that does not produce fruit. [A-¹ + Gk karpos fruit]

ACAS /'eɪkæs/ abbr. (in the UK) Advisory, Conciliation, and Arbitration Service.

Accadian var. of AKKADIAN.

accede /æk'si:d/ v.intr. (often foll. by to) **1** take office, esp. become monarch. **2** assent or agree (acceded to the proposal). **3** (foll. by to) formally subscribe to a treaty or other agreement. [ME f. L *accedere* (as AC-, *cedere cess-* go)]

accelerando /ək,selə'rændəʊ, ə,tʃel-/ *adv., adj., & n. Mus.* —*adj. & adv.* with a gradual increase of speed. —*n.* (*pl.* **accelerandos** or **accelerandi** /-dɪ/) a passage performed accelerando. [It.]

accelerate /ək'seləˌreɪt/ *v.* **1** *intr.* **a** (of a moving body, esp. a vehicle) move or begin to move more quickly; increase speed. **b** (of a process) happen or reach completion more quickly. **2** *tr.* **a** cause to increase speed. **b** cause (a process) to happen more quickly. [L *accelerare* (as AC-, *celerare* f. *celer* swift)]

acceleration /ək,selə'reɪʃ(ə)n/ *n.* **1** the process or act of accelerating or being accelerated. **2** an instance of this. **3** (of a vehicle etc.) the capacity to gain speed (*the car has good acceleration*). **4** *Physics* the rate of change of velocity measured in terms of a unit of time. [F *accélération* or L *acceleratio* (as ACCELERATE)]

accelerative /ək'selərətɪv/ *adj.* tending to increase speed; quickening.

accelerator /ək'seləˌreɪtə(r)/ *n.* **1** a device for increasing speed, esp. the pedal that controls the speed of a vehicle's engine. **2** *Physics* an apparatus for imparting high speeds to charged particles. **3** *Chem.* a substance that speeds up a chemical reaction.

accelerometer /ək,selə'rɒmɪtə(r)/ *n.* an instrument for measuring acceleration esp. of rockets. [ACCELERATE + -METER]

accent *n. & v.* —*n.* /'æks(ə)nt, -sent/ **1** a particular mode of pronunciation, esp. one associated with a particular region or group (*Liverpool accent*; *German accent*; *upper-class accent*). **2** prominence given to a syllable by stress or pitch. **3** a mark on a letter or word to indicate pitch, stress, or the quality of a vowel. **4** a distinctive feature or emphasis (*an accent on comfort*). **5** *Mus.* emphasis on a particular note or chord. —*v.tr.* /ək'sent/ **1** pronounce with an accent; emphasize (a word or syllable). **2** write or print accents on (words etc.). **3** accentuate. **4** *Mus.* play a note etc.) with an accent. □□ **accentual** /ək'sentjʊəl/ *adj.* [L *accentus* (as AC-, *cantus* song) repr. Gk *prosōidia* (PROSODY), or through F *accent, accenter*]

accentor /ək'sentə(r)/ *n.* any bird of the genus *Prunella*, e.g. the hedge sparrow. [med.L *accentor* f. L *ad* to + *cantor* singer]

accentuate /æk'sentjʊˌeɪt/ *v.tr.* emphasize; make prominent. □□ **accentuation** /æk,sentjʊ'eɪʃ(ə)n/ *n.* [med.L *accentuare accentuat-* (as ACCENT)]

accept /ək'sept/ *v.tr.* **1** (also *absol.*) consent to receive (a thing offered). **2** (also *absol.*) give an affirmative answer to (an offer or proposal). **3** regard favourably; treat as welcome (*her mother-in-law never accepted her*). **4 a** believe, receive (an opinion, explanation, etc.) as adequate or valid. **b** be prepared to subscribe to (a belief, philosophy, etc.). **5** receive as suitable (*the hotel accepts traveller's cheques*; *the machine only accepts tokens*). **6 a** tolerate; submit to (*accepted the umpire's decision*). **b** (often foll. by *that* + clause) be willing to believe (*we accept that you meant well*). **7** undertake (an office or responsibility). **8** agree to meet (a draft or bill of exchange). □ **accepted opinion** one generally held to be correct. □□ **accepter** *n.* [ME f. OF *accepter* or L *acceptare* f. *accipere* (as AC-, *capere* take)]

acceptable /ək'septəb(ə)l/ *adj.* **1 a** worthy of being accepted. **b** pleasing, welcome. **2** adequate, satisfactory. **3** tolerable (*an acceptable risk*). □□ **acceptability** /ək,septə'bɪlɪtɪ/ *n.* **acceptableness** *n.* **acceptably** *adv.* [ME f. OF f. LL *acceptabilis* (as ACCEPT)]

acceptance /ək'sept(ə)ns/ *n.* **1** willingness to receive (a gift, payment, duty, etc.). **2** an affirmative answer to an invitation or proposal. **3** (often foll. by *of*) a willingness to accept (conditions, a circumstance, etc.). **4 a** approval, belief (*found wide acceptance*). **b** willingness or ability to tolerate. **5 a** agreement to meet a bill of exchange. **b** a bill so accepted. [F f. *accepter* (as ACCEPT)]

acceptant /ək'sept(ə)nt/ *adj.* (foll. by *of*) willingly accepting. [F (as ACCEPTANCE)]

acceptation /,æksep'teɪʃ(ə)n/ *n.* a particular sense, or the generally recognized meaning, of a word or phrase. [ME f. OF f. med.L *acceptatio* (as ACCEPT)]

acceptor /ək'septə(r)/ *n.* **1** *Commerce* a person who accepts a bill. **2** *Physics* an atom or molecule able to receive an extra electron, esp. an impurity in a semiconductor. **3** *Chem.* a molecule or ion etc. to which electrons are donated in the formation of a bond. **4** *Electr.* a circuit able to accept a given frequency.

access /'ækses/ *n. & v.* —*n.* **1** a way of approaching or reaching or entering (*a building with rear access*). **2 a** (often foll. by *to*) the right or opportunity to reach or use or visit; admittance (*has access to secret files*; *was granted access to the prisoner*). **b** the condition of being readily approached; accessibility. **3** (often foll. by *of*) an attack or outburst (*an access of anger*). **4** (*attrib.*) *Brit.* (of broadcasting) allowed to minority or special-interest groups to undertake (*access television*). —*v.tr.* **1** *Computing* gain access to (data, a file, etc.). **2** accession. □ **access road** a road giving access only to the properties along it. **access time** *Computing* the time taken to retrieve data from storage. [ME f. OF *acces* or L *accessus* f. *accedere* (as AC-, *cedere cess-* go)]

accessary var. of ACCESSORY.

accessible /ək'sesɪb(ə)l/ *adj.* (often foll. by *to*) **1** that can readily be reached, entered, or used. **2** (of a person) readily available (esp. to subordinates). **3** (in a form) easy to understand. □□ **accessibility** /ək,sesɪ'bɪlɪtɪ/ *n.* **accessibly** *adv.* [F *accessible* or LL *accessibilis* (as ACCEDE)]

accession /ək'seʃ(ə)n/ *n. & v.* —*n.* **1** entering upon an office (esp. the throne) or a condition (as manhood). **2** (often foll. by *to*) a thing added (e.g. a book to a library); increase, addition. **3** *Law* the incorporation of one item of property in another. **4** assent; the formal acceptance of a treaty etc. —*v.tr.* record the addition of (a new item) to a library or museum. [F *accession* or L *accessio -onis* (as ACCEDE)]

accessorize /ək'sesəˌraɪz/ *v.tr.* provide (a costume etc.) with accessories.

accessory /ək'sesərɪ/ *n. & adj.* (also **accessary**) —*n.* (*pl.* **-ies**) **1** an additional or extra thing. **2** (usu. in *pl.*) **a** a small attachment or fitting. **b** a small item of (esp. a woman's) dress (e.g. shoes, gloves, handbag). **3** (often foll. by *to*) a person who helps in or knows the details of an (esp. illegal) act, without taking part in it. —*adj.* additional; contributing or aiding in a minor way; dispensable. □ **accessory before** (or **after**) **the fact** a person who incites (or assists) another to commit a crime. □□ **accessorial** /,ækse'sɔːrɪəl/ *adj.* [med.L *accessorius* (as ACCEDE)]

acciaccatura /ə,tʃækə'tʊərə/ *n. Mus.* a grace-note performed as quickly as possible before an essential note of a melody. [It.]

accidence /'æksɪd(ə)ns/ *n.* the part of grammar that deals with the variable parts or inflections of words. [med.L sense of L *accidentia* (transl. Gk *parepomena*) neut. pl. of *accidens* (as ACCIDENT)]

accident /'æksɪd(ə)nt/ *n.* **1** an event that is without apparent cause, or is unexpected (*their early arrival was just an accident*). **2** an unfortunate event, esp. one causing physical harm or damage, brought about unintentionally. **3** occurrence of things by chance; the working of fortune (*accident accounts for much in life*). **4** *colloq.* an occurrence of involuntary urination or defecation. **5** an irregularity in structure. □ **accident-prone** (of a person) subject to frequent accidents. **by accident** unintentionally. [ME f. OF f. LL *accidens* f. L *accidere* (as AC-, *cadere* fall)]

accidental /,æksɪ'dent(ə)l/ *adj. & n.* —*adj.* **1** happening by chance, unintentionally, or unexpectedly. **2** not essential to a conception; subsidiary. —*n.* **1** *Mus.* a sign indicating a momentary departure from the key signature by raising or lowering a note. **2** something not essential to a conception. □□ **accidentally** *adv.* [ME f. LL *accidentalis* (as ACCIDENT)]

accidie /'æksɪˌdiː/ *n.* laziness, sloth, apathy. [ME f. AF *accidie* f. OF *accide* f. med.L *accidia*]

acclaim /ə'kleɪm/ *v. & n.* —*v.tr.* **1** welcome or applaud enthusiastically; praise publicly. **2** (foll. by compl.) hail as (*acclaimed him king*; *was acclaimed the winner*). —*n.* **1** applause; welcome; public praise. **2** a shout of acclaim. □□ **acclaimer** *n.* [ME f. L *acclamare* (as AC-, *clamare* shout: spelling assim. to *claim*)]

acclamation /ˌæklə'meɪʃ(ə)n/ *n.* **1** loud and eager assent to a proposal. **2** (usu. in *pl.*) shouting in a person's honour. **3** the act or process of acclaiming. □**by acclamation** *US Polit.* (elected) unanimously and without ballot. [L *acclamatio* (as ACCLAIM)]

acclimate /'æklɪˌmeɪt, ə'klaɪ-/ *v.tr. US* acclimatize. [F *acclimater* f. *à* to + *climat* CLIMATE]

acclimation /ˌæklaɪ'meɪʃ(ə)n/ *n.* acclimatization. [irreg. f. ACCLIMATE]

acclimatize /ə'klaɪməˌtaɪz/ *v.* (also **-ise**) **1** *tr.* accustom to a new climate or to new conditions. **2** *intr.* become acclimatized. □□ **acclimatization** /-'zeɪʃ(ə)n/ *n.* [F *acclimater*: see ACCLIMATE]

acclivity /ə'klɪvɪtɪ/ *n.* (*pl.* **-ies**) an upward slope. □□ **acclivitous** *adj.* [L *acclivitas* f. *acclivis* (as AC-, *clivis* f. *clivus* slope)]

accolade /'ækəˌleɪd, -'leɪd/ *n.* **1** the awarding of praise; an acknowledgement of merit. **2** a touch made with a sword at the bestowing of a knighthood. [F f. Prov. *acolada* (as AC-, L *collum* neck)]

accommodate /ə'kɒməˌdeɪt/ *v.tr.* **1** provide lodging or room for (*the flat accommodates three people*). **2** adapt, harmonize, reconcile (*must accommodate ourselves to new surroundings*; *cannot accommodate your needs to mine*). **3 a** do service or favour to; oblige (a person). **b** (foll. by *with*) supply (a person) with. [L *accommodare* (as AC-, *commodus* fitting)]

accommodating /ə'kɒməˌdeɪtɪŋ/ *adj.* obliging, compliant. □□ **accommodatingly** *adv.*

accommodation /əˌkɒmə'deɪʃ(ə)n/ *n.* **1** (in *sing.* or *US* in *pl.*) lodgings; a place to live. **2** an adjustment or adaptation to suit a special or different purpose. **3** a convenient arrangement; a settlement or compromise. **4** (in *pl.*) *US* a seat in a vehicle etc. □**accommodation address** an address used on letters to a person who is unable or unwilling to give a permanent address. **accommodation bill** a bill to raise money on credit. **accommodation ladder** a ladder up the side of a ship from a small boat. **accommodation road** a road for access to a place not on a public road. [F *accommodation* or L *accommodatio -onis* (as ACCOMMODATE)]

accompaniment /ə'kʌmpənɪmənt/ *n.* **1** *Mus.* an instrumental or orchestral part supporting or partnering a solo instrument, voice, or group. **2** an accompanying thing; an appendage. [F *accompagnement* (as ACCOMPANY)]

accompanist /ə'kʌmpənɪst/ *n.* (also **accompanyist** /-nɪɪst/) a person who provides a musical accompaniment.

accompany /ə'kʌmpənɪ/ *v.tr.* (**-ies**, **-ied**) **1** go with; escort, attend. **2** (usu. in *passive*; foll. by *with*, *by*) **a** be done or found with; supplement (*speech accompanied with gestures*). **b** have as a result (*pills accompanied by side effects*). **3** *Mus.* support or partner with accompaniment. [ME f. F *accompagner* f. *à* to + OF *compaing* COMPANION[1]: assim. to COMPANY]

accomplice /ə'kʌmplɪs, -'kɒm-/ *n.* a partner in a crime or wrongdoing. [ME and F *complice* (prob. by assoc. with ACCOMPANY), f. LL *complex complicis* confederate: cf. COMPLICATE]

accomplish /ə'kʌmplɪʃ, ə'kɒm-/ *v.tr.* perform; complete; succeed in doing. [ME f. OF *acomplir* f. L *complēre* COMPLETE]

accomplished /ə'kʌmplɪʃd, ə'kɒm-/ *adj.* clever, skilled; well trained or educated.

accomplishment /ə'kʌmplɪʃmənt/ *n.* **1** the fulfilment or completion (of a task etc.). **2** an acquired skill, esp. a social one. **3** a thing done or achieved.

accord /ə'kɔːd/ *v. & n.* —*v.* **1** *intr.* (often foll. by *with*) (esp. of a thing) be in harmony; be consistent. **2** *tr.* **a** grant (permission, a request, etc.). **b** give (a welcome etc.). —*n.* **1** agreement, consent. **2** harmony or harmonious correspondence in pitch, tone, colour, etc. □**of one's own accord** on one's own initiative; voluntarily. **with one accord** unanimously; in a united way. [ME f. OF *acord, acorder* f. L *cor cordis* heart]

accordance /ə'kɔːd(ə)ns/ *n.* harmony, agreement. □**in accordance with** in a manner corresponding to (*we acted in accordance with your wishes*). [ME f. OF *acordance* (as ACCORD)]

accordant /ə'kɔːd(ə)nt/ *adj.* (often foll. by *with*) in tune; agreeing. □□ **accordantly** *adv.* [ME f. OF *acordant* (as ACCORD)]

according /ə'kɔːdɪŋ/ *adv.* **1** (foll. by *to*) **a** as stated by or in (*according to my sister*; *according to their statement*). **b** in a manner corresponding to; in proportion to (*he lives according to his principles*). **2** (foll. by *as* + clause) in a manner or to a degree that varies as (*he pays according as he is able*).

accordingly /ə'kɔːdɪŋlɪ/ *adv.* **1** as suggested or required by the (stated) circumstances (*silence is vital so please act accordingly*). **2** consequently, therefore (*accordingly, he left the room*).

accordion /ə'kɔːdɪən/ *n.* a portable musical instrument with reeds blown by bellows and played by means of keys and buttons. □**accordion pleat, wall,** etc. one folding like the bellows of an accordion. □□ **accordionist** *n.* [G *Akkordion* f. It. *accordare* to tune]

accost /ə'kɒst/ *v.tr.* **1** approach and address (a person), esp. boldly. **2** (of a prostitute) solicit. [F *accoster* f. It. *accostare* ult. f. L *costa* rib: see COAST]

accouchement /ˌækuː'ʃmɑ̃/ *n.* **1** childbirth. **2** the period of childbirth. [F f. *accoucher* act as midwife]

accoucheur /ˌækuː'ʃɜː(r)/ *n.* a male midwife. [F (as ACCOUCHEMENT)]

account /ə'kaunt/ *n. & v.* —*n.* **1** a narration or description (*gave a long account of the ordeal*). **2 a** an arrangement or facility at a bank or building society etc. for commercial or financial transactions, esp. for depositing and withdrawing money (*opened an account*). **b** the assets credited by such an arrangement (*has a large account*; *paid the money into her account*). **c** an arrangement at a shop for buying goods on credit (*has an account at the newsagent's*). **3 a** (often in *pl.*) a record or statement of money, goods, or services received or expended, with the balance (*firms must keep detailed accounts*). **b** (in *pl.*) the practice of accounting or reckoning (*is good at accounts*). **4** a statement of the administration of money in trust (*demand an account*). **5** the period during which transactions take place on a stock exchange; the period from one account day to the next. **6** counting, reckoning. —*v.tr.* (foll. by *to be* or compl.) consider, regard as (*account it a misfortune*; *account him wise*; *account him to be guilty*). ¶ Use with *as* (*we accounted him as wise*) is considered incorrect. □**account day** a day of periodic settlement of stock exchange accounts. **account for 1** serve as or provide an explanation or reason for (*that accounts for their misbehaviour*). **2 a** give a reckoning of or answer for (money etc. entrusted). **b** answer for (one's conduct). **3** succeed in killing, destroying, disposing of, or defeating. **4** supply or make up a specified amount or proportion of (*rent accounts for 50% of expenditure*). **account rendered** a bill which has been sent but is not yet paid. **by all accounts** in everyone's opinion. **call to account** require an explanation from (a person). **give a good** (or **bad)**

account of oneself make a favourable (or unfavourable) impression; be successful (or unsuccessful). **keep account of** keep a record of; follow closely. **leave out of account** fail or decline to consider. **money of account** denominations of money used in reckoning, but not current as coins. **of no account** unimportant. **of some account** important. **on account 1** (of goods) to be paid for later. **2** (of money) in part payment. **on account of** because of. **on no account** under no circumstances; certainly not. **on one's own account** for one's own purposes; at one's own risk. **settle** (or **square**) **accounts with 1** receive or pay money etc. owed to. **2** have revenge on. **take account of** (or **take into account**) consider along with other factors (*took their age into account*). **turn to account** (or **good account**) turn to one's advantage. [ME f. OF *acont*, *aconter* (as AC-, *conter* COUNT¹)]

accountable /əˈkaʊntəb(ə)l/ *adj.* **1** responsible; required to account for one's conduct (*accountable for one's actions*). **2** explicable, understandable. □□ **accountability** /-ˈbɪlɪtɪ/ *n.* **accountably** *adv.*

accountancy /əˈkaʊntənsɪ/ *n.* the profession or duties of an accountant.

accountant /əˈkaʊnt(ə)nt/ *n.* a professional keeper or inspector of accounts. [legal F f. pres. part. of OF *aconter* ACCOUNT]

accounting /əˈkaʊntɪŋ/ *n.* **1** the process of or skill in keeping and verifying accounts. **2** in senses of ACCOUNT *v.*

accoutre /əˈkuːtə(r)/ *v.tr.* (*US* **accouter**) (usu. as **accoutred** *adj.*) attire, equip, esp. with a special costume. [F *accoutrer* f. OF *acoustrer* (as A-³, *cousture* sewing: cf. SUTURE)]

accoutrement /əˈkuːtrəmənt, -təmənt/ *n.* (*US* **accouterment** /-təmənt/) (usu. in *pl.*) **1** equipment, trappings. **2** *Mil.* a soldier's outfit other than weapons and garments. [F (as ACCOUTRE)]

accredit /əˈkrɛdɪt/ *v.tr.* (**accredited**, **accrediting**) **1** (foll. by *to*) attribute (a saying etc.) to (a person). **2** (foll. by *with*) credit (a person) with (a saying etc.). **3** (usu. foll. by *to* or *at*) send (an ambassador etc.) with credentials; recommend by documents as an envoy (*was accredited to the sovereign*). **4** gain belief or influence for or make credible (an adviser, a statement, etc.). □□ **accreditation** /-ˈteɪʃ(ə)n/ *n.* [F *accréditer* (as AC-, *crédit* CREDIT)]

accredited /əˈkrɛdɪtɪd/ *adj.* **1** (of a person or organization) officially recognized. **2** (of a belief) generally accepted; orthodox. **3** (of cattle, milk, etc.) having guaranteed quality.

accrete /əˈkriːt/ *v.* **1** *intr.* grow together or into one. **2** *intr.* (often foll. by *to*) form round or on, as round a nucleus. **3** *tr.* attract (such additions). [L *accrescere* (as AC-, *crescere cret-* grow)]

accretion /əˈkriːʃ(ə)n/ *n.* **1** growth by organic enlargement. **2 a** the growing of separate things into one. **b** the product of such growing. **3 a** extraneous matter added to anything. **b** the adhesion of this. **4** *Law* **a** = ACCESSION. **b** the increase of a legacy etc. by the share of a failing co-legatee. □□ **accretive** *adj.* [L *accretio* (as ACCRETE)]

accrue /əˈkruː/ *v.intr.* (**accrues**, **accrued**, **accruing**) (often foll. by *to*) come as a natural increase or advantage, esp. financial. □□ **accrual** *n.* **accrued** *adj.* [ME f. AF *acru(e)*, past part. of *acreistre* increase f. L *accrescere* ACCRETE]

acculturate /əˈkʌltʃəreɪt/ *v.* **1** *intr.* adapt to or adopt a different culture. **2** *tr.* cause to do this. □□ **acculturation** /-ˈreɪʃ(ə)n/ *n.* **acculturative** /-rətɪv/ *adj.*

accumulate /əˈkjuːmjʊleɪt/ *v.* **1** *tr.* **a** acquire an increasing number or quantity of; heap up. **b** produce or acquire (a resulting whole) in this way. **2** *intr.* grow numerous or considerable; form an increasing mass or quantity. [L *accumulare* (as AC-, *cumulus* heap)]

accumulation /əˌkjuːmjʊˈleɪʃ(ə)n/ *n.* **1** the act or process of accumulating or being accumulated. **2** an accumulated mass. **3** the growth of capital by continued interest. [L *accumulatio* (as ACCUMULATE)]

accumulative /əˈkjuːmjʊlətɪv/ *adj.* **1** arising from accumulation; cumulative (*accumulative evidence*). **2** arranged so as to accumulate. **3** acquisitive; given to hoarding. □□ **accumulatively** *adv.*

accumulator /əˈkjuːmjʊˌleɪtə(r)/ *n.* **1** *Brit.* a rechargeable electric cell. **2** a bet placed on a sequence of events, the winnings and stake from each being placed on the next. **3** a register in a computer used to contain the results of an operation. **4** a person who accumulates things.

accuracy /ˈækjʊrəsɪ/ *n.* exactness or precision, esp. arising from careful effort.

accurate /ˈækjʊrət/ *adj.* **1** careful, precise; lacking errors. **2** conforming exactly with the truth or with a given standard. □□ **accurately** *adv.* [L *accuratus* done carefully, past part. of *accurare* (as AC-, *cura* care)]

accursed /əˈkɜːsɪd, əˈkɜːst/ *adj.* (*archaic* **accurst** /əˈkɜːst/) **1** lying under a curse; ill-fated. **2** *colloq.* detestable, annoying. [past part. of *accurse*, f. A-² + CURSE]

accusal /əˈkjuːz(ə)l/ *n.* accusation.

accusation /ˌækjuːˈzeɪʃ(ə)n/ *n.* **1** the act or process of accusing or being accused. **2** a statement charging a person with an offence or crime. [ME f. OF f. L *accusatio -onis* (as ACCUSE)]

accusative /əˈkjuːzətɪv/ *n.* & *adj. Gram.* —*n.* the case of nouns, pronouns, and adjectives, expressing the object of an action or the goal of motion. —*adj.* of or in this case. □□ **accusatival** /-ˈtaɪv(ə)l/ *adj.* **accusatively** *adv.* [ME f. OF *accusatif -ive* or L (*casus*) *accusativus*, transl. Gk (*ptōsis*) *aitiatikē*]

accusatorial /əˌkjuːzəˈtɔːrɪəl/ *adj. Law* (of proceedings) involving accusation by a prosecutor and a verdict reached by an impartial judge or jury (opp. INQUISITORIAL). [L *accusatorius* (as ACCUSE)]

accusatory /əˈkjuːzətərɪ/ *adj.* (of language, manner, etc.) of or implying accusation.

accuse /əˈkjuːz/ *v.tr.* **1** (foll. by *of*) charge (a person etc.) with a fault or crime; indict (*accused them of murder*; *was accused of stealing a car*). **2** lay the blame on. □ **the accused** the person charged with a crime. □□ **accuser** *n.* **accusingly** *adv.* [ME *acuse* f. OF *ac(c)user* f. L *accusare* (as AC-, CAUSE)]

accustom /əˈkʌstəm/ *v.tr.* & *refl.* (foll. by *to*) make (a person or thing or oneself) used to (*the army accustomed him to discipline*; *was accustomed to their strange ways*). [ME f. OF *acostumer* (as AD-, *costume* CUSTOM)]

accustomed /əˈkʌstəmd/ *adj.* **1** (usu. foll. by *to*) used to (*accustomed to hard work*). **2** customary, usual.

ace /eɪs/ *n.* & *adj.* —*n.* **1 a** a playing-card, domino, etc., with a single spot and generally having the value 'one' or in card-games the highest value in each suit. **b** a single spot on a playing-card etc. **2 a** a person who excels in some activity. **b** *Aeron.* a pilot who has shot down many enemy aircraft. **3 a** (in lawn tennis) a stroke (esp. a service) too good for the opponent to return. **b** a point scored in this way. —*adj. sl.* excellent. □ **ace up one's sleeve** (*US* **in the hole**) something effective kept in reserve. **play one's ace** use one's best resource. **within an ace of** on the verge of. [ME f. OF f. L *as* unity, AS²]

-acea /ˈeɪʃə/ *suffix* forming the plural names of orders and classes of animals (*Crustacea*) (cf. -ACEAN). [neut. pl. of L adj. suffix *-aceus* of the nature of]

-aceae /ˈeɪsɪiː/ *suffix* forming the plural names of families of plants (*Rosaceae*). [fem. pl. of L adj. suffix *-aceus* of the nature of]

-acean /ˈeɪʃ(ə)n/ *suffix* **1** forming adjectives, = -ACEOUS. **2** forming nouns as the sing. of names in *-acea* (*crustacean*). [L *-aceus*: see -ACEA]

acedia /əˈsiːdɪə/ *n.* = ACCIDIE. [LL *acedia* f. Gk *akēdia* listlessness]

acellular /eɪˈseljʊlə(r)/ *adj. Biol.* **1** having no cells;

not consisting of cells. **2** (esp. of protozoa) consisting of one cell only; unicellular.

-aceous /'eɪʃəs/ *suffix* forming adjectives, esp. from nouns in *-acea*, *-aceae* (*herbaceous*; *rosaceous*). [L *-aceus*: see -ACEA]

acephalous /ə'sefələs, ə'ke-/ *adj.* **1** headless. **2** having no chief. **3** *Zool.* having no part of the body specially organized as a head. **4** *Bot.* with a head aborted or cut off. **5** *Prosody* lacking a syllable or syllables in the first foot. [med.L *acephalus* f. Gk *akephalos* headless (as A-[1], *kephalē* head)]

acerbic /ə'sɜːbɪk/ *adj.* **1** astringently sour; harsh-tasting. **2** bitter in speech, manner, or temper. □□ **acerbically** *adv.* **acerbity** *n.* (*pl.* -ies). [L *acerbus* sour-tasting]

acetabulum /ˌæsɪ'tæbjʊləm/ *n.* (*pl.* **acetabula** /-lə/) *Zool.* **1** the socket for the head of the thigh-bone, or of the leg in insects. **2** a cup-shaped sucker of various organisms, including tapeworms and cuttlefish. [ME f. L, = vinegar cup f. *acetum* vinegar + *-abulum* dimin. of *-abrum* holder]

acetal /'æsɪˌtæl/ *n. Chem.* any of a class of organic compounds formed by the condensation of two alcohol molecules with an aldehyde molecule. [as ACETIC + -AL]

acetaldehyde /ˌæsɪ'tældɪˌhaɪd/ *n.* a colourless volatile liquid aldehyde. Also called ETHANAL. ¶ Chem. formula: CH_3CHO. [ACETIC + ALDEHYDE]

acetate /'æsɪˌteɪt/ *n.* **1** a salt or ester of acetic acid, esp. the cellulose ester used to make textiles, gramophone records, etc. Also called ETHANOATE. **2** a fabric made from cellulose acetate. □ **acetate fibre** (or **silk**) fibre (or silk) made artificially from cellulose acetate. [ACETIC + -ATE[1] 2]

acetic /ə'siːtɪk/ *adj.* of or like vinegar. □ **acetic acid** the clear liquid acid that gives vinegar its characteristic taste: also called ETHANOATE. ¶ Chem. formula: CH_3COOH. [F *acétique* f. L *acetum* vinegar]

aceto- /'æsɪtəʊ/ *comb. form Chem.* acetic, acetyl.

acetone /'æsɪˌtəʊn/ *n.* a colourless volatile liquid ketone valuable as a solvent of organic compounds esp. paints, varnishes, etc. Also called PROPANONE. ¶ Chem. formula: CH_3COCH_3. [ACETO- + -ONE]

acetous /'æsɪtəs/ *adj.* **1** having the qualities of vinegar. **2** producing vinegar. **3** sour. [LL *acetosus* sour (as ACETIC)]

acetyl /'æsɪtɪl, -ˌtaɪl/ *n. Chem.* the univalent radical of acetic acid. ¶ Chem. formula: CH_3CO-. □ **acetyl silk** = acetate silk. [ACETIC + -YL]

acetylcholine /ˌæsɪtɪl'kəʊliːn, ˌæsɪtaɪl-/ *n.* a compound serving to transmit impulses from nerve fibres. [ACETYL + CHOLINE]

acetylene /ə'setɪˌliːn/ *n.* a colourless hydrocarbon gas, burning with a bright flame, used esp. in welding and formerly in lighting. Also called ETHYNE. ¶ Chem. formula: C_2H_2. [ACETIC + -YL + -ENE]

acetylide /ə'setɪˌlaɪd/ *n.* any of a class of salts formed from acetylene and a metal.

acetylsalicylic acid /ˌæsɪtaɪlˌsælɪ'sɪlɪk/ *n.* = ASPIRIN. [ACETYL + SALICYLIC ACID]

Achaean /ə'kiːən/ *adj. & n.* **1** of or relating to Achaea in ancient Greece. **2** *literary* (esp. in Homeric contexts) Greek. —*n.* **1** an inhabitant of Achaea. **2** *literary* (usu. in *pl.*) a Greek. [L *Achaeus* f. Gk *Akhaios*]

Achaemenid /ə'kiːmənɪd/ *adj. & n.* (also **Achaemenian** /ˌækɪ'miːnɪən/) —*adj.* of or relating to the dynasty ruling in Persia from Cyrus I to Darius III (553–330 BC). —*n.* a member of this dynasty. [L *Achaemenius* f. Gk *Akhaimenēs*, ancestor of dynasty]

acharnement /ˌæʃɑːn'mɑ̃/ *n.* **1** bloodthirsty fury; ferocity. **2** gusto. [F]

ache /eɪk/ *n. & v.* —*n.* **1** a continuous or prolonged dull pain. **2** mental distress. —*v.intr.* **1** suffer from or be the source of an ache (*I ached all over; my left leg ached*). **2** (foll. by *to* + infin.) desire greatly (*we ached to be at home again*). □□ **achingly** *adv.* [ME f. OE *æce, acan*]

achene /ə'kiːn/ *n. Bot.* a small dry one-seeded fruit that does not open to liberate the seed (e.g. a strawberry pip). [mod.L *achaenium* (as A-[1], Gk *khainō* gape)]

Acheulian /ə'ʃuːlɪən/ *adj. & n.* (also **Acheulean**) —*adj.* of the palaeolithic period in Europe etc. following the Abbevillian and preceding the Mousterian. —*n.* the culture of this period. [F *acheuléen* f. St-*Acheul* in N. France, where remains of it were found]

achieve /ə'tʃiːv/ *v.tr.* **1 a** reach or attain by effort (*achieved victory*). **b** acquire, gain, earn (*achieved notoriety*). **2** accomplish or carry out (a feat or task). **3** *absol.* be successful; attain a desired level of performance. □□ **achievable** *adj.* **achiever** *n.* [ME f. OF *achever* f. *a chief* to a head]

achievement /ə'tʃiːvmənt/ *n.* **1** something achieved. **2 a** the act of achieving. **b** an instance of this. **3** *Psychol.* performance in a standardized test. **4** *Heraldry* **a** an escutcheon with adjuncts, or bearing, esp. in memory of a distinguished feat. **b** = HATCHMENT.

achillea /ˌækɪ'liːə/ *n.* any plant of the genus *Achillea*, comprising hardy perennial, usu. aromatic plants with flower-heads (often white or yellow) usu. in corymbs. [L f. Gk *Akhilleios* a plant supposed to have been used medicinally by Achilles]

Achilles' heel /ə'kɪliːz/ *n.* a person's weak or vulnerable point. [L *Achilles* f. Gk *Akhilleus*, a hero in the *Iliad*, invulnerable except in the heel]

Achilles' tendon /ə'kɪliːz/ *n.* the tendon connecting the heel with the calf muscles.

achiral /eɪ'kaɪər(ə)l/ *adj. Chem.* (of a crystal or molecule) not chiral.

achromat /'ækrəʊˌmæt/ *n.* a lens made achromatic by correction.

achromatic /ˌækrəʊ'mætɪk/ *adj. Optics* **1** that transmits light without separating it into constituent colours (*achromatic lens*). **2** without colour (*achromatic fringe*). □□ **achromatically** *adv.* **achromaticity** /əˌkrəʊmə'tɪsɪtɪ/ *n.* **achromatism** /ə'krəʊməˌtɪz(ə)m/ *n.* [F *achromatique* f. Gk *akhromatos* (as A-[1], CHROMATIC)]

achy /'eɪkɪ/ *adj.* (**achier, achiest**) full of or suffering from aches.

acid /'æsɪd/ *n. & adj.* —*n.* **1** *Chem.* **a** any of a class of substances that liberate hydrogen ions in water, are usu. sour and corrosive, turn litmus red, and have a pH of less than 7. **b** any compound or atom donating protons. **2** (in general use) any sour substance. **3** *sl.* the drug LSD. —*adj.* **1** sharp-tasting, sour. **2** biting, sharp (*an acid wit*). **3** *Chem.* having the essential properties of an acid. **4** *Geol.* containing much silica. **5** (of a colour) intense, bright. □ **acid drop** *Brit.* a kind of sweet with a sharp taste. **acid-head** *sl.* a user of the drug LSD. **acid house** a kind of synthesized music with a simple repetitive beat, often associated with the taking of hallucinogenic drugs. **acid radical** one formed by the removal of hydrogen ions from an acid. **acid rain** acid formed in the atmosphere esp. from industrial waste gases and falling with rain. **acid test 1** a severe or conclusive test. **2** a test in which acid is used to test for gold etc. **put the acid on** *Austral. sl.* seek to extract a loan or favour etc. from. □□ **acidic** /ə'sɪdɪk/ *adj.* **acidimeter** /ˌæsɪ'dɪmɪtə(r)/ *n.* **acidimetry** /ˌæsɪ'dɪmɪtrɪ/ *n.* **acidly** *adv.* **acidness** *n.* [F *acide* or L *acidus* f. *acēre* be sour]

acidify /ə'sɪdɪˌfaɪ/ *v.tr. & intr.* (-**ies**, -**ied**) make or become acid. □□ **acidification** /-fɪ'keɪʃ(ə)n/ *n.*

acidity /ə'sɪdɪtɪ/ *n.* (*pl.* -**ies**) an acid quality or state, esp. an excessively acid condition of the stomach.

acidosis /ˌæsɪ'dəʊsɪs/ *n.* an over-acid condition of the body fluids or tissues. □□ **acidotic** /-'dɒtɪk/ *adj.*

acidulate /ə'sɪdjʊˌleɪt/ *v.tr.* make somewhat acid. □□

æ cat ɑː arm e bed ɜː her ɪ sit iː see ɒ hot ɔː saw ʌ run ʊ put uː too ə ago aɪ my

acidulation /-'leɪʃ(ə)n/ n. [L acidulus dimin. of acidus sour]

acidulous /ə'sɪdjʊləs/ adj. somewhat acid.

acinus /'æsɪnəs/ n. (pl. **acini** /-ˌnaɪ/) **1** any of the small elements that make up a compound fruit of the blackberry, raspberry, etc. **2** the seed of a grape or berry. **3** Anat. **a** any multicellular gland with saclike secreting ducts. **b** the terminus of a duct in such a gland. [L, = berry, kernel]

-acious /'eɪʃəs/ suffix forming adjectives meaning 'inclined to, full of' (vivacious; pugnacious; voracious; capacious). [L -ax -acis, added chiefly to verbal stems to form adjectives + -ous]

-acity /'æsɪtɪ/ suffix forming nouns of quality or state corresponding to adjectives in -acious. [F -acité or L -acitas -tatis]

ack-ack /æ'kæk/ adj. & n. colloq. —adj. anti-aircraft. —n. an anti-aircraft gun etc. [formerly signallers' name for the letters AA]

ackee /'æki:/ n. (also **akee**) **1** a tropical tree, Blighia sapida. **2** its fruit, edible when cooked. [Kru ākee]

ack emma /æk 'emə/ adv. & n. Brit. colloq. = A.M. [formerly signallers' name for the letters AM]

acknowledge /ək'nɒlɪdʒ/ v.tr. **1 a** recognize; accept; admit the truth of (acknowledged the failure of the plan). **b** (often foll. by to be + compl.) recognize as (acknowledged it to be a great success). **c** (often foll. by that + clause or to + infin.) admit that something is so (acknowledged that he was wrong; acknowledged him to be wrong). **2** confirm the receipt of (acknowledged her letter). **3 a** show that one has noticed (acknowledged my arrival with a grunt). **b** express appreciation of (a service etc.). **4** own; recognize the validity of (the acknowledged king). □□ **acknowledgeable** adj. [obs. KNOWLEDGE v. after obs. acknow (as A-⁴, KNOW), or f. obs. noun acknowledge]

acknowledgement /ək'nɒlɪdʒmənt/ n. (also **acknowledgment**) **1** the act or an instance of acknowledging. **2 a** a thing given or done in return for a service etc. **b** a letter confirming receipt of something. **3** (usu. in pl.) an author's statement of indebtedness to others.

aclinic line /ə'klɪnɪk/ n. = magnetic equator. [Gk aklinēs (as A-¹, klinō bend)]

acme /'ækmɪ/ n. the highest point or period (of achievement, success, etc.); the peak of perfection (displayed the acme of good taste). [Gk, = highest point]

acne /'æknɪ/ n. a skin condition, usu. of the face, characterized by red pimples. □□ **acned** adj. [mod.L f. erron. Gk aknas for akmas accus. pl. of akmē facial eruption: cf. ACME]

acolyte /'ækəˌlaɪt/ n. **1** a person assisting a priest in a service or procession. **2** an assistant; a beginner. [ME f. OF acolyt or eccl.L acolytus f. Gk akolouthos follower]

aconite /'ækəˌnaɪt/ n. **1 a** any poisonous plant of the genus Aconitum, esp. monkshood or wolfsbane. **b** the drug obtained from this. Also called ACONITINE. **2** (in full **winter aconite**) any ranunculaceous plant of the genus Eranthis, with yellow flowers. □□ **aconitic** /ˌækə'nɪtɪk/ adj. Chem. [F aconit or L aconitum f. Gk akoniton]

aconitine /ə'kɒnɪˌtiːn/ n. Pharm. a poisonous alkaloid obtained from the aconite plant.

acorn /'eɪkɔːn/ n. the fruit of the oak, with a smooth nut in a rough cuplike base. □ **acorn barnacle** a multivalve marine cirriped, Balanus balanoides, living on rocks. **acorn worm** any marine wormlike animal of the phylum Hemichordata, having a proboscis and gill slits, and inhabiting seashores. [OE æcern, rel. to æcer ACRE, later assoc. with OAK and CORN¹]

acotyledon /əˌkɒtɪ'liːd(ə)n/ n. a plant with no distinct seed-leaves. □□ **acotyledonous** adj. [mod.L acotyledones pl. (as A-¹, COTYLEDON)]

acoustic /ə'kuːstɪk/ adj. & n. —adj. **1** relating to sound or the sense of hearing. **2** (of a musical instrument, gramophone, or recording) not having electrical amplification (acoustic guitar). **3** (of building materials) used for soundproofing or modifying sound. **4** Mil. (of a mine) that can be exploded by sound waves transmitted under water. —n. **1** (usu. in pl.) the properties or qualities (esp. of a room or hall etc.) in transmitting sound (good acoustics; a poor acoustic). **2** (in pl.; usu. treated as sing.) the science of sound (acoustics is not widely taught). □ **acoustic coupler** Computing a modem which converts digital signals into audible signals and vice versa, so that the former can be transmitted and received over telephone lines. □□ **acoustical** adj. **acoustically** adv. [Gk akoustikos f. akouō hear]

acoustician /ˌækuː'stɪʃ(ə)n/ n. an expert in acoustics.

acquaint /ə'kweɪnt/ v.tr. & refl. (usu. foll. by with) make (a person or oneself) aware of or familiar with (acquaint me with the facts). □ **be acquainted with** have personal knowledge of (a person or thing). [ME f. OF acointier f. LL accognitare (as AC-, cognoscere cognit- come to know)]

acquaintance /ə'kweɪnt(ə)ns/ n. **1** (usu. foll. by with) slight knowledge (of a person or thing). **2** the fact or process of being acquainted (our acquaintance lasted a year). **3** a person one knows slightly. □ **make one's acquaintance** first meet or introduce oneself to another person. **make the acquaintance of** come to know. □□ **acquaintanceship** n. [ME f. OF acointance (as ACQUAINT)]

acquiesce /ˌækwɪ'es/ v.intr. **1** agree, esp. tacitly. **2** raise no objection. **3** (foll. by in) accept (an arrangement etc.). □□ **acquiescence** n. **acquiescent** adj. [L acquiescere (as AC-, quiescere rest)]

acquire /ə'kwaɪə(r)/ v.tr. **1** gain by and for oneself; obtain. **2** come into possession of (acquired fame; acquired much property). □ **acquired characteristic** Biol. a characteristic caused by the environment, not inherited. **acquired immune deficiency syndrome** Med. see AIDS. **acquired taste 1** a liking gained by experience. **2** the object of such a liking. □□ **acquirable** adj. [ME f. OF aquerre ult. f. L acquirere (as AC-, quaerere seek)]

acquirement /ə'kwaɪəmənt/ n. **1** something acquired, esp. a mental attainment. **2** the act or an instance of acquiring.

acquisition /ˌækwɪ'zɪʃ(ə)n/ n. **1** something acquired, esp. if regarded as useful. **2** the act or an instance of acquiring. [L acquisitio (as ACQUIRE)]

acquisitive /ə'kwɪzɪtɪv/ adj. keen to acquire things; avaricious; materialistic. □□ **acquisitively** adv. **acquisitiveness** n. [F acquisitive or LL acquisitivus (as ACQUIRE)]

acquit /ə'kwɪt/ v. (**acquitted**, **acquitting**) **1** tr. (often foll. by of) declare (a person) not guilty (were acquitted of the offence). **2** refl. **a** conduct oneself or perform in a specified way (we acquitted ourselves well). **b** (foll. by of) discharge (a duty or responsibility). [ME f. OF aquiter f. med.L acquitare pay a debt (as AC-, QUIT)]

acquittal /ə'kwɪt(ə)l/ n. **1** the process of freeing or being freed from a charge, esp. by a judgement of not guilty. **2** performance of a duty.

acquittance /ə'kwɪt(ə)ns/ n. **1** payment of or release from a debt. **2** a written receipt attesting settlement of a debt. [ME f. OF aquitance (as ACQUIT)]

acre /'eɪkə(r)/ n. **1** a measure of land, 4,840 sq. yds., 0.405 ha. **2** a piece of land; a field. **3** (in pl.) a large area. □□ **acred** adj. (also in comb.). [OE æcer f. Gmc]

acreage /'eɪkərɪdʒ/ n. **1** a number of acres. **2** an extent of land.

acrid /'ækrɪd/ adj. (**acrider**, **acridest**) **1** bitterly pungent; irritating; corrosive. **2** bitter in temper or manner. □□ **acridity** /ə'krɪdɪtɪ/ n. **acridly** adv. [irreg. f. L acer acris keen + -ID¹, prob. after acid]

acridine /'ækrɪˌdiːn/ n. a colourless crystalline compound used in the manufacture of dyes and drugs. [ACRID + -INE⁴]

acriflavine /ˌækrɪˈfleɪvɪn, -viːn/ *n.* a reddish powder used as an antiseptic. [irreg. f. ACRIDINE + FLAVINE]

acrimonious /ˌækrɪˈməʊnɪəs/ *adj.* bitter in manner or temper. ▫▫ **acrimoniously** *adv.* [F *acrimonieux, -euse* f. med.L *acrimoniosus* f. L *acrimonia* ACRIMONY]

acrimony /ˈækrɪmənɪ/ *n.* (*pl.* -**ies**) bitterness of temper or manner; ill feeling. [F *acrimonie* or L *acrimonia* pungency (as ACRID)]

acrobat /ˈækrəˌbæt/ *n.* **1** a performer of spectacular gymnastic feats. **2** a person noted for constant change of mind, allegiance, etc. ▫▫ **acrobatic** /ˌækrəˈbætɪk/ *adj.* **acrobatically** /ˌækrəˈbætɪkəlɪ/ *adv.* [F *acrobate* f. Gk *akrobatēs* f. *akron* summit + *bainō* walk]

acrobatics /ˌækrəˈbætɪks/ *n.pl.* **1** acrobatic feats. **2** (as *sing.*) the art of performing these. **3** a skill requiring ingenuity (*mental acrobatics*).

acrogen /ˈækrədʒ(ə)n/ *n. Bot.* any non-flowering plant having a perennial stem with the growing point at its apex, e.g. a fern or moss. ▫▫ **acrogenous** /əˈkrɒdʒɪnəs/ *adj.* [Gk *akron* tip + -GEN]

acromegaly /ˌækrəˈmegəlɪ/ *n. Med.* the abnormal growth of the hands, feet, and face, caused by excessive activity of the pituitary gland. ▫▫ **acromegalic** /-mɪˈgælɪk/ *adj.* [F *acromégalie* f. Gk *akron* extremity + *megas megal-* great]

acronym /ˈækrənɪm/ *n.* a word, usu. pronounced as such, formed from the initial letters of other words (e.g. *Ernie, laser, Nato*). [Gk *akron* end + -*onum-* = *onoma* name]

acropetal /əˈkrɒpɪt(ə)l/ *adj. Bot.* developing from below upwards. ▫▫ **acropetally** *adv.* [Gk *akron* tip + L *petere* seek]

acrophobia /ˌækrəˈfəʊbɪə/ *n. Psychol.* an abnormal dread of heights. ▫▫ **acrophobic** *adj.* [Gk *akron* peak + -PHOBIA]

acropolis /əˈkrɒpəlɪs/ *n.* **1** a citadel or upper fortified part of an ancient Greek city. **2** (**Acropolis**) the ancient citadel at Athens. [Gk *akropolis* f. *akron* summit + *polis* city]

across /əˈkrɒs/ *prep.* & *adv.* —*prep.* **1** to or on the other side of (*walked across the road; lives across the river*). **2** from one side to another side of (*the cover stretched across the opening; a bridge across the river*). **3** at or forming an angle (esp. a right angle) with (*deep cuts across his legs*). —*adv.* **1** to or on the other side (*ran across; shall soon be across*). **2** from one side to another (*a blanket stretched across*). **3** forming a cross (*with cuts across*). **4** (of a crossword clue or answer) read horizontally (*cannot do nine across*). ▫ **across the board** general; generally; applying to all. [ME f. OF *a croix, en croix*, later regarded as f. A² + CROSS]

acrostic /əˈkrɒstɪk/ *n.* **1** a poem or other composition in which certain letters in each line form a word or words. **2** a word-puzzle constructed in this way. ▫ **double acrostic** one using the first and last letters of each line. **single acrostic** one using the first letter only. **triple acrostic** one using the first, middle, and last letters. [F *acrostiche* or Gk *akrostikhis* f. *akron* end + *stikhos* row, line of verse, assim. to -IC]

acrylic /əˈkrɪlɪk/ *adj.* & *n.* —*adj.* **1** of material made with a synthetic polymer derived from acrylic acid. **2** *Chem.* of or derived from acrylic acid. —*n.* an acrylic fibre. ▫ **acrylic acid** a pungent liquid organic acid. ¶ Chem. formula: $C_3H_4O_2$. **acrylic resin** any of various transparent colourless polymers of acrylic acid. [*acrolein* f. L *acer acris* pungent + *olēre* to smell + -IN + -YL + -IC]

ACT *abbr.* Australian Capital Territory.

act /ækt/ *n.* & *v.* —*n.* **1** something done; a deed; an action. **2** the process of doing something (*caught in the act*). **3 a** a piece of entertainment, usu. one of a series in a programme. **b** the performer(s) of this. **4** a pretence; behaviour intended to deceive or impress (*it was all an act*). **5** a main division of a play or opera. **6 a** a written ordinance of a parliament or other legislative body. **b** a document attesting a legal transaction. **7** (often in *pl.*) the recorded decisions or proceedings of a committee, an academic body, etc. **8** (**Acts**) (in full **Acts of the Apostles**) the New Testament book relating the growth of the early Church. —*v.* **1** *intr.* behave (*see how they act under stress*). **2** *intr.* perform actions or functions; operate effectively; take action (*act as referee; the brakes failed to act; we must act quickly*). **3** *intr.* (also foll. by *on*) exert energy or influence (*the medicine soon began to act; alcohol acts on the brain*). **4** *intr.* **a** perform a part in a play, film, etc. **b** pretend. **5** *tr.* **a** perform the part of (*acted Othello; acts the fool*). **b** perform (a play etc.). **c** portray (an incident) by actions. **d** feign (*we acted indifference*). ▫ **act for** be the (esp. legal) representative of. **act of God** the operation of uncontrollable natural forces. **act of grace** a privilege or concession that cannot be claimed as a right. **act on** (or **upon**) perform or carry out; put into operation (*acted on my advice*). **act out 1** translate (ideas etc.) into action. **2** *Psychol.* represent (one's subconscious desires etc.) in action. **act up** *colloq.* misbehave; give trouble (*my car is acting up again*). **get one's act together** *sl.* become properly organized; make preparations for an undertaking etc. **get into the act** *sl.* become a participant (esp. for profit). **put on an act** *colloq.* carry out a pretence. ▫▫ **actable** *adj.* (in sense 5 of *v.*). **actability** /-ˈbɪlɪtɪ/ *n.* (in sense 5 of *v.*). [ME ult. f. L *agere act-* do]

ACTH *abbr.* adrenocorticotrophic hormone.

acting /ˈæktɪŋ/ *n.* & *attrib. adj.* —*n.* **1** the art or occupation of performing parts in plays, films, etc. **2** in senses of ACT *v.* —*attrib.adj.* serving temporarily or on behalf of another or others (*acting manager; Acting Captain*).

actinia /ækˈtɪnɪə/ *n.* (*pl.* **actiniae** /-nɪˌiː/) any sea anemone, esp. of the genus *Actinia*. [mod.L f. Gk *aktis -inos* ray]

actinide /ˈæktɪˌnaɪd/ *n.* (also **actinoid** /ˈæktɪˌnɔɪd/) *Chem.* any of the series of 15 radioactive elements having increasing atomic numbers from actinium to lawrencium. ▫ **actinide series** this series of elements. [ACTINIUM + -IDE as in *lanthanide*]

actinism /ˈæktɪˌnɪz(ə)m/ *n.* the property of short-wave radiation that produces chemical changes, as in photography. ▫▫ **actinic** /ækˈtɪnɪk/ *adj.* [Gk *aktis -inos* ray]

actinium /ækˈtɪnɪəm/ *n. Chem.* a radioactive metallic element of the actinide series, occurring naturally in pitchblende. ¶ Symb.: **Ac**.

actinoid var. of ACTINIDE.

actinometer /ˌæktɪˈnɒmɪtə(r)/ *n.* an instrument for measuring the intensity of radiation, esp. ultraviolet radiation. [Gk *aktis -tinos* ray + -METER]

actinomorphic /ˌæktɪnəˈmɔːfɪk/ *adj. Biol.* radially symmetrical. [as ACTINOMETER + Gk *morphē* form]

actinomycete /ˌæktɪnəʊmaɪˈsiːt/ *n.* any of the usu. non-motile filamentous anaerobic bacteria of the order Actinomycetales. [as ACTINOMORPHIC + -*mycetes* f. Gk *mukēs -ētos* mushroom]

action /ˈækʃ(ə)n/ *n.* & *v.* —*n.* **1** the fact or process of doing or acting (*demanded action; put ideas into action*). **2** forcefulness or energy as a characteristic (*a woman of action*). **3** the exertion of energy or influence (*the action of acid on metal*). **4** something done; a deed or act (*not aware of his own actions*). **5 a** a series of events represented in a story, play, etc. **b** *sl.* exciting activity (*arrived late and missed the action; want some action*). **6 a** armed conflict; fighting (*killed in action*). **b** an occurrence of this, esp. a minor military engagement. **7 a** the way in which a machine, instrument, etc. works (*explain the action of an air pump*). **b** the mechanism that makes a machine, instrument, etc. (e.g. a musical instrument, a gun, etc.) work. **c** the mode or style of movement of an animal or human (usu. described in some way) (*a runner with good action*). **8** a legal process; a lawsuit (*bring an action*). **9** (in *imper.*) a word of command to begin, esp. used by a film director etc. —*v.tr.* bring a legal action against. □**action committee** (or **group** etc.) a body formed to take active steps, esp. in politics. **action-packed** *colloq.* full of action or excitement. **action painting** an aspect of abstract expressionism with paint applied by the artist's random or spontaneous gestures. **action point** a proposal for action, esp. arising from a discussion etc. **action replay** a playback of part of a television broadcast, esp. a sporting event, often in slow motion. **action stations** positions taken up by troops etc. ready for battle. **go into action** start work. **out of action** not working. **take action** begin to act (esp. energetically in protest). [ME f. OF f. L *actio -onis* (as ACT)]

actionable /ˈækʃənəb(ə)l/ *adj.* giving cause for legal action. □□**actionably** *adv.*

activate /ˈæktɪˌveɪt/ *v.tr.* **1** make active; bring into action. **2** *Chem.* cause reaction in; excite (a substance, molecules, etc.). **3** *Physics* make radioactive. □**activated carbon** carbon, esp. charcoal, treated to increase its adsorptive power. **activated sludge** aerated sewage containing aerobic bacteria. □□ **activation** /-ˈveɪʃ(ə)n/ *n.* **activator** *n.*

active /ˈæktɪv/ *adj. & n.* —*adj.* **1 a** consisting in or marked by action; energetic; diligent (*leads an active life*; *an active helper*). **b** able to move about or accomplish practical tasks (*infirmity made him less active*). **2** working, operative (*an active volcano*). **3** originating action; not merely passive or inert (*active support*; *active ingredients*). **4** radioactive. **5** *Gram.* designating the voice that attributes the action of a verb to the person or thing from which it logically proceeds (e.g. of the verbs in *guns kill*; *we saw him*). —*n. Gram.* the active form or voice of a verb. □**active carbon** = *activated carbon* (see ACTIVATE). **active list** *Mil.* a list of officers available for service. **active service** full-time service in the armed forces. □□ **actively** *adv.* **activeness** *n.* [ME f. OF *actif -ive* or L *activus* (as ACT *v.*)]

activism /ˈæktɪˌvɪz(ə)m/ *n.* a policy of vigorous action in a cause, esp. in politics. □□ **activist** *n.*

activity /ækˈtɪvɪtɪ/ *n.* (*pl.* **-ies**) **1 a** the condition of being active or moving about. **b** the exertion of energy; vigorous action. **2** (often in *pl.*) a particular occupation or pursuit (*outdoor activities*). **3** = RADIOACTIVITY. [F *activité* or LL *activitas* (as ACTIVE)]

actor /ˈæktə(r)/ *n.* **1** the performer of a part in a play, film, etc. **2** a person whose profession is performing such parts. [L, = doer, actor (as ACT, -OR¹)]

actress /ˈæktrɪs/ *n.* a female actor.

actual /ˈæktʃʊəl, ˈæktjʊəl/ *adj.* (usu. *attrib.*) **1** existing in fact; real (often as distinct from ideal). **2** existing now; current. ¶ Redundant use, as in *tell me the actual facts*, is *disp.*, but common. □□ **actualize** *v.tr.* (also **-ise**). **actualization** /-ˈzeɪʃ(ə)n/ *n.* [ME f. OF *actuel* f. LL *actualis* f. *agere* ACT]

actuality /ˌæktʃʊˈælɪtɪ, ˌæktjʊ-/ *n.* (*pl.* **-ies**) **1** reality; what is the case. **2** (in *pl.*) existing conditions. [ME f. OF *actualité* entity or med.L *actualitas* (as ACTUAL)]

actually /ˈæktʃʊəlɪ/ *adv.* **1** as a fact, really (*I asked for ten, but actually got nine*). **2** as a matter of fact, even (strange as it may seem) (*he actually refused!*). **3** at present; for the time being.

actuary /ˈæktʃʊərɪ/ *n.* (*pl.* **-ies**) an expert in statistics, esp. one who calculates insurance risks and premiums. □□ **actuarial** /-ˈeərɪəl/ *adj.* **actuarially** /-ˈeərɪəlɪ/ *adv.* [L *actuarius* bookkeeper f. *actus* past part. of *agere* ACT]

actuate /ˈæktʃʊˌeɪt/ *v.tr.* **1** communicate motion to (a machine etc.). **2** cause the operation of (an electrical device etc.). **3** cause (a person) to act. □□ **actuation** /-ˈeɪʃ(ə)n/ *n.* **actuator** *n.* [med.L *actuare* f. L *actus*: see ACTUAL]

acuity /əˈkjuːɪtɪ/ *n.* sharpness, acuteness (of a needle, senses, understanding). [F *acuité* or med.L *acuitas* f. *acuere* sharpen: see ACUTE]

aculeate /əˈkjuːlɪət/ *n.* **1** *Zool.* having a sting. **2** *Bot.*

prickly. **3** pointed, incisive. [L *aculeatus* f. *aculeus* sting, dimin. of *acus* needle]

acumen /ˈækjʊmən, əˈkjuːmən/ *n.* keen insight or discernment, penetration. [L *acumen -minis* anything sharp f. *acuere* sharpen: see ACUTE]

acuminate /əˈkjuːmɪnət/ *adj. Biol.* tapering to a point. [L *acuminatus* pointed (as ACUMEN)]

acupuncture /ˈækjuːˌpʌŋktʃə(r)/ *n.* a method (orig. Chinese) of treating various conditions by pricking the skin or tissues with needles. □□ **acupuncturist** *n.* [L *acu* with a needle + PUNCTURE]

acushla /əˈkʊʃlə/ *n. Ir.* darling. [Ir. *a cuisle* O pulse (of my heart)!]

acute /əˈkjuːt/ *adj. & n.* —*adj.* (**acuter**, **acutest**) **1** (of sensation or senses) keen, penetrating. **2** shrewd, perceptive (*an acute critic*). **3** (of a disease) coming sharply to a crisis; severe, not chronic. **4** (of a difficulty or controversy) critical, serious. **5 a** (of an angle) less than 90°. **b** sharp, pointed. **6** (of a sound) high, shrill. —*n.* = *acute accent*. □**acute accent** a mark (´) placed over letters in some languages to show quality, vowel length, pronunciation (e.g. *maté*), and (of an angle) acute. **acute rheumatism** *Med.* = *rheumatic fever*. □□ **acutely** *adv.* **acuteness** *n.* [L *acutus* past part. of *acuere* sharpen f. *acus* needle]

ACW *abbr. Brit.* (preceding a name) Aircraftwoman.

-acy /əsɪ/ *suffix* forming nouns of state or quality (*accuracy*; *piracy*; *supremacy*), or an instance of it (*conspiracy*; *fallacy*) (see also -CRACY). [a branch of the suffix -CY from or after F *-acie* or L *-acia* or *-atia* or Gk *-ateia*]

acyl /ˈæsɪl, -aɪl/ *n. Chem.* the univalent radical of an organic acid. [G (as ACID, -YL)]

AD *abbr.* (of a date) of the Christian era. ¶ Strictly, AD should precede a date (e.g. AD 410), but uses such as *the tenth century AD* are well established. [*Anno Domini* 'in the year of the Lord']

ad /æd/ *n. colloq.* an advertisement. [abbr.]

ad- /əd, æd/ *prefix* (also **a-** before *sc, sp, st*, **ac-** before *c, k, q*, **af-** before *f*, **ag-** before *g*, **al-** before *l*, **an-** before *n*, **ap-** before *p*, **ar-** before *r*, **as-** before *s*, **at-** before *t*) **1** with the sense of motion or direction to, reduction or change into, addition, adherence, increase, or intensification. **2** formed by assimilation of other prefixes (*accurse*; *admiral*; *advance*; *affray*). [(sense 1) (through OF *a-*) f. L *ad* to: (sense 2) *a-* repr. various prefixes other than *ad-*]

-ad¹ /əd, æd/ *suffix* forming nouns: **1** in collective numerals (*myriad*; *triad*). **2** in fem. patronymics (*Dryad*). **3** in names of poems and similar compositions (*Iliad*; *Dunciad*; *jeremiad*). [Gk *-as -ada*]

-ad² /əd/ *suffix* forming nouns (*ballad*; *salad*) (cf. -ADE¹). [F *-ade*]

adage /ˈædɪdʒ/ *n.* a traditional maxim, a proverb. [F f. L *adagium* (as AD-, root of *aio* say)]

adagio /əˈdɑːʒɪəʊ/ *adv., adj., & n. Mus.* —*adv. & adj.* in slow time. —*n.* (*pl.* **-os**) an adagio movement or passage. [It.]

Adam¹ /ˈædəm/ *n.* the first man, in the Biblical and Koranic traditions. □**Adam's ale** water. **Adam's apple** a projection of the thyroid cartilage of the larynx, esp. as prominent in men. **not know a person from Adam** be unable to recognize the person in question. [Heb. *'ādām* man]

Adam² /ˈædəm/ *adj.* of the style of architecture, furniture, and design created by the Scottish brothers Robert and James Adam (18th c.).

adamant /ˈædəmənt/ *adj. & n.* —*adj.* stubbornly resolute; resistant to persuasion. —*n.* archaic diamond or other hard substance. □□ **adamance** *n.* **adamantine** /-ˈmæntaɪn/ *adj.* **adamantly** *adv.* [OF *adamaunt* f. L *adamas adamant-* untameable f. Gk (as A-¹, *damaō* to tame)]

adapt /əˈdæpt/ *v.* **1** *tr.* **a** (foll. by *to*) fit, adjust (one thing to another). **b** (foll. by *to, for*) make suitable for a purpose. **c** alter or modify (esp. a text). **d** arrange for broadcasting etc. **2** *intr. & refl.* (usu. foll. by *to*) become adjusted to new conditions. □□

adaptive *adj.* **adaptively** *adv.* [F *adapter* f. L *adaptare* (as AD-, *aptare* f. *aptus* fit)]

adaptable /ə'dæptəb(ə)l/ *adj.* **1** able to adapt oneself to new conditions. **2** that can be adapted. □□ **adaptability** /-'bɪlɪtɪ/ *n.* **adaptably** *adv.*

adaptation /ˌædæp'teɪʃ(ə)n/ *n.* **1** the act or process of adapting or being adapted. **2** a thing that has been adapted. **3** *Biol.* the process by which an organism or species becomes suited to its environment. [F f. LL *adaptatio -onis* (as ADAPT)]

adaptor /ə'dæptə(r)/ *n.* (also **adapter**) **1** a device for making equipment compatible. **2** a device for connecting several electrical plugs to one socket. **3** a person who adapts.

adaxial /æd'æksɪəl/ *adj. Bot.* facing toward the stem of a plant, esp. of the upper side of a leaf (cf. ABAXIAL). [AD- + AXIAL]

ADC *abbr.* **1** aide-de-camp. **2** analogue-digital converter.

add /æd/ *v.tr.* **1** join (one thing to another) as an increase or supplement (*add your efforts to mine*; *add insult to injury*). **2** put together (two or more numbers) to find a number denoting their combined value. **3** say in addition (*added a remark*; *added that I was wrong*). □ **add in** include. **add-on** something added to an existing object or quantity. **add to** increase; be a further item among (*this adds to our difficulties*). **add up 1** find the total of. **2** (foll. by *to*) amount to; constitute (*adds up to a disaster*). **3** *colloq.* make sense; be understandable. □□ **added** *adj.* [ME f. L *addere* (as AD-, *dare* put)]

addax /'ædæks/ *n.* a large antelope, *Addax nasomaculatus*, of North Africa, with twisted horns. [L f. an African word]

addendum /ə'dendəm/ *n.* (*pl.* **addenda** /-də/) **1** a thing (usu. something omitted) to be added, esp. (in *pl.*) as additional matter at the end of a book. **2** an appendix; an addition. [L, gerundive of *addere* ADD]

adder /'ædə(r)/ *n.* any of various small venomous snakes, esp. the common viper, *Vipera berus*, the only poisonous snake in Great Britain. **adder's tongue** any fern of the genus *Ophioglossum*. [OE *nædre*: *n* lost in ME by wrong division of *a naddre*: cf. APRON, AUGER, UMPIRE]

addict *v.* & *n.* —*v.tr.* & *refl.* /ə'dɪkt/ (usu. foll. by *to*) devote or apply habitually or compulsively; make addicted. —*n.* /'ædɪkt/ a person addicted to a habit, esp. one dependent on a (specified) drug (*drug addict*; *heroin addict*). **2** *colloq.* an enthusiastic devotee of a sport or pastime (*film addict*). [L *addicere* assign (as AD-, *dicere* dict- say)]

addicted /ə'dɪktɪd/ *adj.* (foll. by *to*) **1** dependent on as a habit; unable to do without (*addicted to heroin*; *addicted to smoking*). **2** devoted (*addicted to football*).

addiction /ə'dɪkʃ(ə)n/ *n.* the fact or process of being addicted, esp. the condition of taking a drug habitually and being unable to give it up without incurring adverse effects. [L *addictio*: see ADDICT]

addictive /ə'dɪktɪv/ *adj.* (of a drug, habit, etc.) causing addiction or dependence.

Addison's disease /'ædɪs(ə)nz/ *n.* a disease characterized by progressive anaemia and debility and brown discoloration of the skin. [T. *Addison*, Engl. physician d. 1860, who first recognized it]

addition /ə'dɪʃ(ə)n/ *n.* **1** the act or process of adding or being added. **2** a person or thing added (*a useful addition to the team*). □ **in addition** (often foll. by *to*) as something added. [ME f. OF *addition* or f. L *additio* (as ADD)]

additional /ə'dɪʃən(ə)l/ *adj.* added, extra, supplementary. □□ **additionally** *adv.*

additive /'ædɪtɪv/ *n.* & *adj.* —*n.* a thing added, esp. a substance added to another so as to give it specific qualities (*food additive*). —*adj.* **1** characterized by addition (*additive process*). **2** to be added. [LL *additivus* (as ADD)]

addle /'æd(ə)l/ *v.* & *adj.* —*v.* **1** *tr.* muddle, confuse. **2** *intr.* (of an egg) become addled. —*adj.* **1** muddled, unsound (*addle-brained*; *addle-head*). **2** empty, vain. **3** (of an egg) addled. [OE *adela* filth, used as adj., then as verb]

addled /'æd(ə)ld/ *adj.* **1** (of an egg) rotten, producing no chick. **2** muddled. [ADDLE *adj.*, assim. to past part. form]

address /ə'dres/ *n.* & *v.* —*n.* **1 a** the place where a person lives or an organization is situated. **b** particulars of this, esp. for postal purposes. **c** *Computing* the location of an item of stored information. **2** a discourse delivered to an audience. **3** skill, dexterity, readiness. **4** (in *pl.*) a courteous approach, courtship (*pay one's addresses to*). **5** *archaic* manner in conversation. —*v.tr.* **1** write directions for delivery (esp. the name and address of the intended recipient) on (an envelope, packet, etc.). **2** direct in speech or writing (remarks, a protest, etc.). **3** speak or write to, esp. formally (*addressed the audience*; *asked me how to address a duke*). **4** direct one's attention to. **5** *Golf* take aim at or prepare to hit (the ball). □ **address oneself to 1** speak or write to. **2** attend to. □□ **addresser** *n.* [ME f. OF *adresser* ult. f. L (as AD-, *directus* DIRECT): (n.) perh. f. F *adresse*]

addressee /ˌædre'siː/ *n.* the person to whom something (esp. a letter) is addressed.

Addressograph /ə'dresəʊˌɡrɑːf/ *n. propr.* a machine for printing addresses on envelopes.

adduce /ə'djuːs/ *v.tr.* cite as an instance or as proof or evidence. □□ **adducible** *adj.* [L *adducere* adduct- (as AD-, *ducere* lead)]

adduct /ə'dʌkt/ *v.tr.* draw towards a middle line, esp. draw (a limb) towards the middle line of the body. □□ **adduction** *n.*

adductor /ə'dʌktə(r)/ *n.* (in full **adductor muscle**) any muscle that moves one part of the body towards another or towards the middle line of the body.

-ade[1] /eɪd/ *suffix* forming nouns: **1** an action done (*blockade*; *tirade*). **2** the body concerned in an action or process (*cavalcade*). **3** the product or result of a material or action (*arcade*; *lemonade*; *masquerade*). [from or after F *-ade* f. Prov., Sp., or Port. *-ada* or It. *-ata* f. L *-ata* fem. sing. past part. of verbs in *-are*]

-ade[2] /eɪd/ *suffix* forming nouns (*decade*) (cf. -AD[1]). [F *-ade* f. Gk *-as -ada*]

-ade[3] /eɪd/ *suffix* forming nouns: **1** = -ADE[1] (*brocade*). **2** a person concerned (*renegade*). [Sp. or Port. *-ado*, masc. form of *-ada*: see -ADE[1]]

adenine /'ædəˌniːn/ *n.* a purine derivative found in all living tissue as a component base of DNA or RNA. [G *Adenin* formed as ADENOIDS: see -INE[4]]

adenoids /'ædɪˌnɔɪdz/ *n.pl. Med.* a mass of enlarged lymphatic tissue between the back of the nose and the throat, often hindering speaking and breathing in the young. □□ **adenoidal** /-'nɔɪd(ə)l/ *adj.* **adenoidally** /-'nɔɪdəlɪ/ *adv.* [Gk *adēn -enos* gland + -OID]

adenoma /ˌædɪ'nəʊmə/ *n.* (*pl.* **adenomas** or **adenomata** /-mətə/) a glandlike benign tumour. [mod.L f. Gk *adēn* gland + -OMA]

adenosine /ə'denəˌsiːn/ *n.* a nucleoside of adenine and ribose present in all living tissue in a combined form (see AMP, ADP, ATP). [ADENINE + RIBOSE]

adept /'ædept, ə'dept/ *adj.* & *n.* —*adj.* (foll. by *at, in*) thoroughly proficient. —*n.* a skilled performer; an expert. □□ **adeptly** *adv.* **adeptness** *n.* [L *adeptus* past part. of *adipisci* attain]

adequate /'ædɪkwət/ *adj.* **1** sufficient, satisfactory (often with the implication of being barely so). **2** (foll. by *to*) proportionate. **3** barely sufficient. □□ **adequacy** *n.* **adequately** *adv.* [L *adaequatus* past part. of *adaequare* make equal (as AD-, *aequus* equal)]

à deux /ɑː 'dɜː/ *adv.* & *adj.* **1** for two. **2** between two. [F]

ad fin. /æd 'fɪn/ *abbr.* at or near the end. [L *ad finem*]

adhere /əd'hɪə(r)/ *v.intr.* **1** (usu. foll. by *to*) (of a substance) stick fast to a surface, another substance, etc. **2** (foll. by *to*) behave according to; follow in detail (*adhered to our plan*). **3** (foll. by *to*) give support or allegiance. [F *adhérer* or L *adhaerēre* (as AD-, *haerēre haes-* stick)]

adherent /əd'hɪərənt/ *n. & adj. —n.* **1** a supporter of a party, person, etc. **2** a devotee of an activity. *—adj.* **1** (foll. by *to*) faithfully observing a rule etc. **2** (often foll. by *to*) (of a substance) sticking fast. □□ **adherence** *n.* [F *adhérent* (as ADHERE)]

adhesion /əd'hiːʒ(ə)n/ *n.* **1** the act or process of adhering. **2** the capacity of a substance to stick fast. **3** *Med.* an unnatural union of surfaces due to inflammation. **4** the maintenance of contact between the wheels of a vehicle and the road. **5** the giving of support or allegiance. ¶ More common in physical senses (e.g. *the glue has good adhesion*), with *adherence* used in abstract senses (e.g. *adherence to principles*). [F *adhésion* or L *adhaesio* (as ADHERE)]

adhesive /əd'hiːsɪv/ *adj. & n. —adj.* sticky, enabling surfaces or substances to adhere to one another. *—n.* an adhesive substance, esp. one used to stick other substances together. □□ **adhesively** *adv.* **adhesiveness** *n.* [F *adhésif -ive* (as ADHERE)]

adhibit /əd'hɪbɪt/ *v.tr.* (**adhibited, adhibiting**) **1** affix. **2** apply or administer (a remedy). □□ **adhibition** /ˌædhɪ'bɪʃ(ə)n/ *n.* [L *adhibēre adhibit-* (as AD-, *habēre* have)]

ad hoc /æd 'hɒk/ *adv. & adj.* for a particular (usu. exclusive) purpose (*an ad hoc appointment*). [L, = to this]

ad hominem /æd 'hɒmɪˌnem/ *adv. & adj.* **1** relating to or associated with a particular person. **2** (of an argument) appealing to the emotions and not to reason. [L, = to the person]

adiabatic /ˌeɪdaɪə'bætɪk/ *adj. & n. Physics —adj.* **1** impassable to heat. **2** occurring without heat entering or leaving the system. *—n.* a curve or formula for adiabatic phenomena. □□ **adiabatically** *adv.* [Gk *adiabatos* impassable (as A-[1], *diabainō* pass)]

adiantum /ˌædɪ'æntəm/ *n.* **1** any fern of the genus *Adiantum*, e.g. maidenhair. **2** (in general use) a spleenwort. [L f. Gk *adianton* maidenhair (as A-[1], *diantos* wettable)]

adieu /ə'djuː/ *int. & n. —int.* goodbye. *—n.* (*pl.* **adieus** or **adieux** /ə'djuːz/) a goodbye. [ME f. OF f. *à* to + *Dieu* God]

ad infinitum /æd ˌɪnfɪ'naɪtəm/ *adv.* without limit; for ever. [L]

ad interim /æd 'ɪntərɪm/ *adv. & adj.* for the meantime. [L]

adios /ˌædɪ'ɒs/ *int.* goodbye. [Sp. *adiós* f. *a* to + *Dios* God]

adipocere /'ædɪpəˌsɪə(r)/ *n.* a greyish fatty or soapy substance generated in dead bodies subjected to moisture. [F *adipocire* f. L *adeps adipis* fat + F *cire* wax f. L *cera*]

adipose /'ædɪˌpəʊz/ *adj.* of or characterized by fat; fatty. □ **adipose tissue** fatty connective tissue in animals. □□ **adiposity** /-'pɒsɪtɪ/ *n.* [mod.L *adiposus* f. *adeps adipis* fat]

adit /'ædɪt/ *n.* **1** a horizontal entrance or passage in a mine. **2** a means of approach. [L *aditus* (as AD-, *itus* f. *ire it-* go)]

Adivasi /ˌædɪ'vɑːsɪ/ *n.* (*pl.* **Adivasis**) a member of the aboriginal tribal peoples of India. [Hindi *adinivāsī* original inhabitant]

Adj. *abbr.* (preceding a name) Adjutant.

adjacent /ə'dʒeɪs(ə)nt/ *adj.* (often foll. by *to*) lying near or adjoining. □□ **adjacency** *n.* [ME f. L *adjacēre* (as AD-, *jacēre* lie)]

adjective /'ædʒɪktɪv/ *n. & adj. —n.* a word or phrase naming an attribute, added to or grammatically related to a noun to modify it or describe it. *—adj.* additional; not standing by itself; dependent. □□ **adjectival** /ˌædʒɪk'taɪv(ə)l/ *adj.* **adjectivally** /ˌædʒɪk'taɪvəlɪ/ *adv.* [ME f. OF *adjectif -ive* ult. f. L *adjicere adject-* (as AD-, *jacere* throw)]

adjoin /ə'dʒɔɪn/ *v.tr.* **1** be next to and joined with. **2** *archaic* = ADD 1. [ME f. OF *ajoindre, ajoign-* f. L *adjungere adjunct-* (as AD-, *jungere* join)]

adjourn /ə'dʒɜːn/ *v.* **1** *tr.* **a** put off; postpone. **b** break off (a meeting, discussion, etc.) with the intention of resuming later. **2** *intr.* of persons at a meeting: **a** break off proceedings and disperse. **b** (foll. by *to*) transfer the meeting to another place. [ME f. OF *ajorner* (as AD-, *jorn* day ult. f. L *diurnus* DIURNAL): cf. JOURNAL, JOURNEY]

adjournment /ə'dʒɜːnmənt/ *n.* adjourning or being adjourned. □ **adjournment debate** a debate in the House of Commons on the motion that the House be adjourned, used as an opportunity for raising various matters.

adjudge /ə'dʒʌdʒ/ *v.tr.* **1** adjudicate (a matter). **2** (often foll. by *that* + clause, or *to* + infin.) pronounce judicially. **3** (foll. by *to*) award judicially. **4** *archaic* condemn. □□ **adjudgement** *n.* (also **adjudgment**). [ME f. OF *ajuger* f. L *adjudicare*: see ADJUDICATE]

adjudicate /ə'dʒuːdɪˌkeɪt/ *v.* **1** *intr.* act as judge in a competition, court, tribunal, etc. **2** *tr.* **a** decide judicially regarding (a claim etc.). **b** (foll. by *to be* + compl.) pronounce (*was adjudicated to be bankrupt*). □□ **adjudication** /-'keɪʃ(ə)n/ *n.* **adjudicative** *adj.* **adjudicator** *n.* [L *adjudicare* (as AD-, *judicare* f. *judex -icis* judge)]

adjunct /'ædʒʌŋkt/ *n.* **1** (foll. by *to, of*) a subordinate or incidental thing. **2** an assistant; a subordinate person, esp. one with temporary appointment only. **3** *Gram.* a word or phrase used to explain or amplify the predicate, subject, etc. □□ **adjunctive** /ə'dʒʌŋktɪv/ *adj.* **adjunctively** /ə'dʒʌŋktɪvlɪ/ *adv.* [L *adjunctus*: see ADJOIN]

adjure /ə'dʒʊə(r)/ *v.tr.* (usu. foll. by *to* + infin.) charge or request (a person) solemnly or earnestly, esp. under oath. □□ **adjuration** /ˌædʒʊə'reɪʃ(ə)n/ *n.* **adjuratory** /-rətərɪ/ *adj.* [ME f. L *adjurare* (as AD-, *jurare* swear) in LL sense 'put a person to an oath']

adjust /ə'dʒʌst/ *v.* **1** *tr.* **a** arrange; put in the correct order or position. **b** regulate, esp. by a small amount. **2** *tr.* (usu. foll. by *to*) make suitable. **3** *tr.* harmonize (discrepancies). **4** *tr.* assess (loss or damages). **5** *intr.* (usu. foll. by *to*) make oneself suited to; become familiar with (*adjust to one's surroundings*). □□ **adjustable** *adj.* **adjustability** /-'bɪlɪtɪ/ *n.* **adjuster** *n.* **adjustment** *n.* [F *adjuster* f. OF *ajoster* ult. f. L *juxta* near]

adjutant /'ædʒʊt(ə)nt/ *n.* **1** **a** *Mil.* an officer who assists superior officers by communicating orders, conducting correspondence, etc. **b** an assistant. **2** (in full **adjutant bird**) a giant Indian stork. □ **Adjutant-General** a high-ranking Army administrative officer. □□ **adjutancy** *n.* [L *adjutare* frequent. of *adjuvare*: see ADJUVANT]

adjuvant /'ædʒʊv(ə)nt/ *adj. & n. —adj.* helpful, auxiliary. *—n.* an adjuvant person or thing. [F *adjuvant* or L *adjuvare* (as AD-, *juvare jut-* help)]

Adlerian /æd'lɪərɪən/ *adj.* of or relating to A. Adler, Austrian psychologist d. 1937, or his system of psychology.

ad lib /æd 'lɪb/ *v., adj., adv., & n. —v.intr.* (**ad libbed, ad libbing**) speak or perform without formal preparation; improvise. *—adj.* improvised. *—adv.* as one pleases, to any desired extent. *—n.* something spoken or played extempore. [abbr. of AD LIBITUM]

ad libitum /æd 'lɪbɪtəm/ *adv.* = AD LIB *adv.* [L, = according to pleasure]

ad litem /æd 'laɪtem/ *adj.* (of a guardian etc.) appointed for a lawsuit. [L]

Adm. *abbr.* (preceding a name) Admiral.

adman /'ædmæn/ *n.* (*pl.* **admen**) *colloq.* a person who produces advertisements commercially.

admass /'ædmæs/ *n.* esp. *Brit.* the section of the community that is regarded as readily influenced by advertising and mass communication.

admeasure /əd'meʒə(r)/ *v.tr.* apportion; assign in due shares. □□ **admeasurement** *n.* [ME f. OF *amesurer* f. med.L *admensurare* (as AD-, MEASURE)]

admin /'ædmɪn/ *n. colloq.* administration. [abbr.]

adminicle /əd'mɪnɪk(ə)l/ *n.* **1** a thing that helps. **2**

(in Scottish law) collateral evidence of the contents of a missing document. □□ **adminicular** /ˌædmɪ'nɪkjʊlə(r)/ *adj.* [L *adminiculum* prop]

administer /əd'mɪnɪstə(r)/ *v.* **1** *tr.* attend to the running of (business affairs etc.); manage. **2** *tr.* **a** be responsible for the implementation of (the law, justice, punishment, etc.). **b** *Eccl.* give out, or perform the rites of (a sacrament). **c** (usu. foll. by *to*) direct the taking of (an oath). **3** *tr.* **a** provide, apply (a remedy). **b** give, deliver (a rebuke). **4** *intr.* act as administrator. □□ **administrable** *adj.* [ME f. OF *aministrer* f. L *administrare* (as AD-, MINISTER)]

administrate /əd'mɪnɪˌstreɪt/ *v.tr.* & *intr.* administer (esp. business affairs); act as an administrator. [L *administrare* (as ADMINISTER)]

administration /ədˌmɪnɪ'streɪʃ(ə)n/ *n.* **1** management of a business. **2** the management of public affairs; government. **3** the government in power; the ministry. **4** *US* a President's period of office. **5** *Law* the management of another person's estate. **6** (foll. by *of*) **a** the administering of justice, an oath, etc. **b** application of remedies. [ME f. OF *administration* or L *administratio* (as ADMINISTRATE)]

administrative /əd'mɪnɪstrətɪv/ *adj.* concerning or relating to the management of affairs. □□ **administratively** *adv.* [F *administratif -ive* or L *administrativus* (as ADMINISTRATE)]

administrator /əd'mɪnɪˌstreɪtə(r)/ *n.* **1** a person who administers a business or public affairs. **2** a person capable of organizing (*is no administrator*). **3** *Law* a person appointed to manage the estate of a person who has died intestate. **4** a person who performs official duties in some sphere, e.g. in religion or justice. □□ **administratorship** *n.* **administratrix** *n.* [L (as ADMINISTER)]

admirable /'ædmərəb(ə)l/ *adj.* **1** deserving admiration. **2** excellent. □□ **admirably** *adv.* [F f. L *admirabilis* (as ADMIRE)]

admiral /'ædmər(ə)l/ *n.* **1 a** the commander-in-chief of a country's navy. **b** a naval officer of high rank, the commander of a fleet or squadron. **c** (**Admiral**) an admiral of the second grade. **2** any of various butterflies (*red admiral*; *white admiral*). □ **Admiral of the Fleet** an admiral of the first grade. **Fleet Admiral** *US* = *Admiral of the Fleet*. □□ **admiralship** *n.* [ME f. OF *a(d)mira(i)l* etc. f. med.L *a(d)miralis* etc., f. Arab. *'amīr* commander (cf. AMIR), assoc. with ADMIRABLE]

Admiralty /'ædmərəltɪ/ *n.* (*pl.* -**ies**) **1** (*hist.* except in titles) (in the UK) the department administering the Royal Navy. **2** (**admiralty**) *Law* trial and decision of maritime questions and offences. □ **Admiralty Board** *hist.* a committee of the Ministry of Defence superintending the Royal Navy. [ME f. OF *admiral(i)té*]

admiration /ˌædmɪ'reɪʃ(ə)n/ *n.* **1** pleased contemplation. **2** respect, warm approval. **3** an object of this (*was the admiration of the whole town*). [F *admiration* or L *admiratio* (as ADMIRE)]

admire /əd'maɪə(r)/ *v.tr.* **1** regard with approval, respect, or satisfaction. **2** express one's admiration of. [F *admirer* or L *admirari* (as AD-, *mirari* wonder at)]

admirer /əd'maɪərə(r)/ *n.* **1** a woman's suitor. **2** a person who admires, esp. a devotee of an able or famous person.

admiring /əd'maɪrɪŋ/ *adj.* showing or feeling admiration (*an admiring follower*; *admiring glances*). □□ **admiringly** *adv.*

admissible /əd'mɪsɪb(ə)l/ *adj.* **1** (of an idea or plan) worth accepting or considering. **2** *Law* allowable as evidence. **3** (foll. by *to*) capable of being admitted. □□ **admissibility** /-'bɪlɪtɪ/ *n.* [F *admissible* or med.L *admissibilis* (as ADMIT)]

admission /əd'mɪʃ(ə)n/ *n.* **1** an acknowledgement (*admission of error*; *admission that he was wrong*). **2 a** the process or right of entering. **b** a charge for this (*admission is £5*). **3** a person admitted to a hospital.

¶ Has more general application in senses of ADMIT than *admittance*. [ME f. L *admissio* (as ADMIT)]

admit /əd'mɪt/ *v.* (**admitted**, **admitting**) **1** *tr.* **a** (often foll. by *to be*, or *that* + clause) acknowledge; recognize as true. **b** accept as valid or true. **2** *intr.* (foll. by *to*) acknowledge responsibility for a deed, fault, etc. **3** *tr.* **a** allow (a person) entrance or access. **b** allow (a person) to be a member of (a class, group, etc.) or to share in (a privilege etc.). **c** (of a hospital etc.) bring in (a person) for residential treatment. **4** *tr.* (of an enclosed space) have room for; accommodate. **5** *intr.* (foll. by *of*) allow as possible. [ME f. L *admittere admiss-* (as AD-, *mittere* send)]

admittance /əd'mɪt(ə)ns/ *n.* **1** the right or process of admitting or being admitted, usu. to a place (*no admittance except on business*). **2** *Electr.* the reciprocal of impedance. ¶ A more formal and technical word than *admission*.

admittedly /əd'mɪtɪdlɪ/ *adv.* as an acknowledged fact (*admittedly there are problems*).

admix /æd'mɪks/ *v.* **1** *tr.* & *intr.* (foll. by *with*) mingle. **2** *tr.* add as an ingredient.

admixture /æd'mɪkstʃə(r)/ *n.* **1** a thing added, esp. a minor ingredient. **2** the act of adding this. [L *admixtus* past part. of *admiscēre* (as AD-, *miscēre* mix)]

admonish /əd'mɒnɪʃ/ *v.tr.* **1** reprove. **2** (foll. by *to* + infin., or *that* + clause) urge. **3** give advice to. **4** (foll. by *of*) warn. □□ **admonishment** *n.* **admonition** /ˌædmə'nɪʃ(ə)n/ *n.* **admonitory** *adj.* [ME f. OF *amonester* ult. f. L *admonēre* (as AD-, *monēre monit-* warn)]

ad nauseam /æd 'nɔːzɪˌæm, 'nɔːsɪˌæm/ *adv.* to an excessive or disgusting degree. [L, = to sickness]

adnominal /æd'nɒmɪn(ə)l/ *adj. Gram.* attached to a noun. [L *adnomen -minis* (added name)]

ado /ə'duː/ *n.* (*pl.* **ados**) fuss, busy activity; trouble, difficulty. □ **without more ado** immediately. [orig. in *much ado* = much to do, f. north. ME *at do* (= to do) f. ON *at* AT as sign of infin. + DO[1]]

-ado /'ɑːdəʊ/ *suffix* forming nouns (*desperado*) (cf. -ADE[3]). [Sp. or Port. *-ado* f. L *-atus* past part. of verbs in *-are*]

adobe /ə'dəʊbɪ, ə'dəʊb/ *n.* **1** an unburnt sun-dried brick. **2** the clay used for making such bricks. [Sp. f. Arab.]

adolescent /ˌædə'les(ə)nt/ *adj.* & *n.* —*adj.* between childhood and adulthood. —*n.* an adolescent person. □□ **adolescence** *n.* [ME f. OF f. L *adolescere* grow up]

Adonis /ə'dəʊnɪs/ *n.* a handsome young man. □ **Adonis blue** a kind of butterfly, *Lysandra bellargus*. [the name of a youth loved by Venus: L f. Gk f. Phoen. *adōn* lord]

adopt /ə'dɒpt/ *v.tr.* **1** take (a person) into a relationship, esp. another's child as one's own. **2** choose to follow (a course of action etc.). **3** take over (an idea etc.) from another person. **4** choose as a candidate for office. **5** *Brit.* (of a local authority) accept responsibility for the maintenance of (a road etc.). **6** accept; formally approve (a report, accounts, etc.). □□ **adoption** *n.* [F *adopter* or L *adoptare* (as AD-, *optare* choose)]

adoptive /ə'dɒptɪv/ *adj.* due to adoption (*adoptive son*; *adoptive father*). □□ **adoptively** *adv.* [ME f. OF *adoptif -ive* f. L *adoptivus* (as ADOPT)]

adorable /ə'dɔːrəb(ə)l/ *adj.* **1** deserving adoration. **2** *colloq.* delightful, charming. □□ **adorably** *adv.* [F f. L *adorabilis* (as ADORE)]

adore /ə'dɔː(r)/ *v.tr.* **1** regard with honour and deep affection. **2 a** worship as divine. **b** *RC Ch.* offer reverence to (the Host etc.). **3** *colloq.* like very much. □□ **adoration** /ˌædə'reɪʃ(ə)n/ *n.* **adoring** *adj.* **adoringly** *adv.* [ME f. OF *aourer* f. L *adorare* worship (as AD-, *orare* speak, pray)]

adorer /ə'dɔːrə(r)/ *n.* **1** a worshipper. **2** an ardent admirer.

adorn /ə'dɔːn/ *v.tr.* **1** add beauty or lustre to; be an ornament to. **2** furnish with ornaments; decorate.

□□ **adornment** *n.* [ME f. OF *ao(u)rner* f. L *adornare* (as AD-, *ornare* furnish, deck)]

ADP *abbr.* **1** adenosine diphosphate. **2** automatic data processing.

ad personam /ˌæd pəˈsəʊnæm/ *adv.* & *adj.* —*adv.* to the person. —*adj.* personal. [L]

ad rem /æd ˈrem/ *adv.* & *adj.* to the point; to the purpose. [L, = to the matter]

adrenal /əˈdriːn(ə)l/ *adj.* & *n.* —*adj.* **1** at or near the kidneys. **2** of the adrenal glands. —*n.* (in full **adrenal gland**) either of two ductless glands above the kidneys, secreting adrenalin. [AD- + RENAL]

adrenalin /əˈdrenəlɪn/ *n.* (also **adrenaline**) **1** a hormone secreted by the adrenal glands, affecting circulation and muscular action, and causing excitement and stimulation. **2** the same substance obtained from animals or by synthesis, used as a stimulant.

adrenocorticotrophic hormone /əˌdriːnəˌkɔːtɪkə ˈtrɒfɪk/ *n.* (also **adrenocorticotropic** /-ˈtrɒpɪk/) a hormone secreted by the pituitary gland and stimulating the adrenal glands. ¶ Abbr.: **ACTH**. [ADRENAL + CORTEX + -TROPHIC, -TROPIC]

adrenocorticotrophin /əˌdriːnəˌkɔːtɪkəˈtrɒfɪn/ *n.* = ADRENOCORTICOTROPHIC HORMONE. [ADRENOCORTICO-TROPHIC (HORMONE) + -IN]

adrift /əˈdrɪft/ *adv.* & *predic.adj.* **1** drifting. **2** at the mercy of circumstances. **3** *colloq.* **a** unfastened. **b** out of touch. **c** absent without leave. **d** (often foll. by *of*) failing to reach a target. **e** out of order. **f** ill-informed. [A² + DRIFT]

adroit /əˈdrɔɪt/ *adj.* dextrous, skilful. □□ **adroitly** *adv.* **adroitness** *n.* [F f. *à droit* according to right]

adsorb /ədˈsɔːb/ *v.tr.* (usu. of a solid) hold (molecules of a gas or liquid or solute) to its surface, causing a thin film to form. □□ **adsorbable** *adj.* **adsorbent** *adj.* & *n.* **adsorption** *n.* (also **adsorbtion**). [AD-, after ABSORB]

adsorbate /ædˈsɔːbeɪt/ *n.* a substance adsorbed.

adsuki var. of ADZUKI.

adulate /ˈædjʊleɪt/ *v.tr.* flatter obsequiously. □□ **adulation** /-ˈleɪʃ(ə)n/ *n.* **adulator** *n.* **adulatory** *adj.* [L *adulari adulat-* fawn on]

adult /ˈædʌlt, əˈdʌlt/ *adj.* & *n.* —*adj.* **1** mature, grown-up. **2 a** of or for adults (*adult education*). **b** *euphem.* sexually explicit; indecent (*adult films*). —*n.* **1** an adult person. **2** *Law* a person who has reached the age of majority. □□ **adulthood** *n.* **adultly** *adv.* [L *adultus* past part. of *adolescere* grow up: cf. ADOLESCENT]

adulterant /əˈdʌltərənt/ *adj.* & *n.* —*adj.* used in adulterating. —*n.* an adulterant substance.

adulterate *v.* & *adj.* —*v.tr.* /əˈdʌltəˌreɪt/ debase (esp. foods) by adding other or inferior substances. —*adj.* /əˈdʌltərət/ spurious, debased, counterfeit. □□ **adulteration** /-ˈreɪʃ(ə)n/ *n.* **adulterator** *n.* [L *adulterare adulterat-* corrupt]

adulterer /əˈdʌltərə(r)/ *n.* (*fem.* **adulteress** /-ərɪs/) a person who commits adultery. [obs. *adulter* (v.) f. OF *avoutrer* f. L *adulterare*: see ADULTERATE]

adulterine /əˈdʌltəˌraɪn/ *adj.* **1** illegal, unlicensed. **2** spurious. **3** born of adultery. [L *adulterinus* f. *adulter*: see ADULTERY]

adulterous /əˈdʌltərəs/ *adj.* of or involved in adultery. □□ **adulterously** *adv.* [ME f. *adulter*: see ADULTERER]

adultery /əˈdʌltərɪ/ *n.* voluntary sexual intercourse between a married person and a person (married or not) other than his or her spouse. [ME f. OF *avoutrie* etc. f. *avoutre* adulterer f. L *adulter*, assim. to L *adulterium*]

adumbrate /ˈædʌmˌbreɪt/ *v.tr.* **1** indicate faintly. **2** represent in outline. **3** foreshadow, typify. **4** overshadow. □□ **adumbration** /-ˈbreɪʃ(ə)n/ *n.* **adumbrative** /əˈdʌmbrətɪv/ *adj.* [L *adumbrare* (as AD-, *umbrare* f. *umbra* shade)]

ad valorem /ˌæd vəˈlɔːrem/ *adv.* & *adj.* (of taxes) in proportion to the estimated value of the goods concerned. [L, = according to the value]

advance /ədˈvɑːns/ *v.*, *n.*, & *adj.* —*v.* **1** *tr.* & *intr.* move or put forward. **2** *intr.* make progress. **3** *tr.* **a** pay (money) before it is due. **b** lend (money). **4** *tr.* give active support to; promote (a person, cause, or plan). **5** *tr.* put forward (a claim or suggestion). **6** *tr.* cause (an event) to occur at an earlier date (*advanced the meeting three hours*). **7** *tr.* raise (a price). **8** *intr.* rise (in price). **9** *tr.* (as **advanced** *adj.*) **a** far on in progress (*the work is well advanced*). **b** ahead of the times (*advanced ideas*). —*n.* **1** an act of going forward. **2** progress. **3** a payment made before the due time. **4** a loan. **5** (esp. in *pl.*; often foll. by *to*) an amorous or friendly approach. **6** a rise in price. —*attrib.adj.* done or supplied beforehand (*advance warning*; *advance copy*). □ **advanced** (or **advanced supplementary**) **level** (in the UK) a GCE examination of a standard higher than ordinary level and GCSE. **advance guard** a body of soldiers preceding the main body of an army. **advance on** approach threateningly. **in advance** ahead in place or time. □□ **advancer** *n.* [ME f. OF *avancer* f. LL *abante* in front f. L *ab* away + *ante* before: (n.) partly through F *avance*]

advancement /ədˈvɑːnsmənt/ *n.* the promotion of a person, cause, or plan. [ME f. F *avancement* f. *avancer* (as ADVANCE)]

advantage /ədˈvɑːntɪdʒ/ *n.* & *v.* —*n.* **1** a beneficial feature; a favourable circumstance. **2** benefit, profit (*is not to your advantage*). **3** (often foll. by *over*) a better position; superiority in a particular respect. **4** (in lawn tennis) the next point won after deuce. —*v.tr.* **1** be beneficial or favourable to. **2** further, promote. □ **have the advantage of** be in a better position in some respect than. **take advantage of 1** make good use of (a favourable circumstance). **2** exploit or outwit (a person), esp. unfairly. **3** *euphem.* seduce. **to advantage** in a way which exhibits the merits (*was seen to advantage*). **turn to advantage** benefit from. □□ **advantageous** /ˌædvənˈteɪdʒəs/ *adj.* **advantageously** /ˌædvənˈteɪdʒəslɪ/ *adv.* [ME f. OF *avantage*, *avantager* f. *avant* in front f. LL *abante*: see ADVANCE]

advection /ədˈvekʃ(ə)n/ *n.* *Meteorol.* transfer of heat by the horizontal flow of air. □□ **advective** *adj.* [L *advectio* f. *advehere* (as AD-, *vehere vect-* carry)]

Advent /ˈædvent/ *n.* **1** the season before Christmas, including the four preceding Sundays. **2** the coming or second coming of Christ. **3** (**advent**) the arrival of esp. an important person or thing. □ **Advent calendar** *Brit.* a calendar for Advent, usu. of card with flaps to open each day revealing a picture or scene. **Advent Sunday** the first Sunday in Advent. [OE f. OF *advent*, *auvent* f. L *adventus* arrival f. *advenire* (as AD-, *venire vent-* come)]

Adventist /ˈædventɪst/ *n.* a member of a Christian sect that believes in the imminent second coming of Christ. □□ **Adventism** *n.*

adventitious /ˌædvenˈtɪʃəs/ *adj.* **1** accidental, casual. **2** added from outside. **3** *Biol.* formed accidentally or under unusual conditions. **4** *Law* (of property) coming from a stranger or by collateral succession rather than directly. □□ **adventitiously** *adv.* [L *adventicius* (as ADVENT)]

adventure /ədˈventʃə(r)/ *n.* & *v.* —*n.* **1** an unusual and exciting experience. **2** a daring enterprise; a hazardous activity. **3** enterprise (*the spirit of adventure*). **4** a commercial speculation. —*v.intr.* **1** (often foll. by *into*, *upon*) dare to go or come. **2** (foll. by *on*, *upon*) dare to undertake. **3** incur risk; engage in adventure. □ **adventure playground** a playground where children are provided with functional materials for climbing on, building with, etc. □□ **adventuresome** *adj.* [ME f. OF *aventure*, *aventurer* f. L *adventurus* about to happen (as ADVENT)]

adventurer /ədˈventʃərə(r)/ *n.* (*fem.* **adventuress** /-ərɪs/) **1** a person who seeks adventure, esp. for personal gain or enjoyment. **2** a financial speculator. [F *aventurier* (as ADVENTURE)]

adventurism /əd'ventʃə,rɪz(ə)m/ *n.* a tendency to take risks, esp. in foreign policy. □□ **adventurist** *n.*

adventurous /əd'ventʃərəs/ *adj.* **1** rash, venturesome; enterprising. **2** characterized by adventures. □□ **adventurously** *adv.* **adventurousness** *n.* [ME f. OF *aventuros* (as ADVENTURE)]

adverb /'ædvɜːb/ *n.* a word or phrase that modifies or qualifies another word (esp. an adjective, verb, or other adverb) or a word-group, expressing a relation of place, time, circumstance, manner, cause, degree, etc. (e.g. *gently, quite, then, there*). □□ **adverbial** /əd'vɜːbɪəl/ *adj.* [F *adverbe* or L *adverbium* (as AD-, VERB)]

adversarial /,ædvə'seərɪəl/ *adj.* **1** involving conflict or opposition. **2** opposed, hostile. [ADVERSARY + -IAL]

adversary /'ædvəsərɪ/ *n.* (*pl.* **-ies**) **1** an enemy. **2** an opponent in a sport or game; an antagonist. [ME f. OF *adversarie* f. L *adversarius* f. *adversus*: see ADVERSE]

adversative /əd'vɜːsətɪv/ *adj.* (of words etc.) expressing opposition or antithesis. □□ **adversatively** *adv.* [F *adversatif -ive* or LL *adversativus* f. *adversari* oppose f. *adversus*: see ADVERSE]

adverse /'ædvɜːs/ *adj.* (often foll. by *to*) **1** contrary, hostile. **2** hurtful, injurious. □□ **adversely** *adv.* **adverseness** *n.* [ME f. OF *advers* f. L *adversus* past part. of *advertere* (as AD-, *vertere vers-* turn)]

adversity /əd'vɜːsɪtɪ/ *n.* (*pl.* **-ies**) the condition of adverse fortune. **2** a misfortune. [ME f. OF *adversité* f. L *adversitas -tatis* (as ADVERSE)]

advert¹ /'ædvɜːt/ *n. Brit. colloq.* an advertisement. [abbr.]

advert² /əd'vɜːt/ *v.intr.* (foll. by *to*) *literary* refer in speaking or writing. [ME f. OF *avertir* f. L *advertere*: see ADVERSE]

advertise /'ædvə,taɪz/ *v.* **1** *tr.* draw attention to or describe favourably (goods or services) in a public medium to promote sales. **2** *tr.* make generally or publicly known. **3** *intr.* (foll. by *for*) seek by public notice, esp. in a newspaper. **4** *tr.* (usu. foll. by *of*, or *that* + clause) notify. □□ **advertiser** *n.* [ME f. OF *avertir* (stem *advertiss-*): see ADVERT²]

advertisement /əd'vɜːtɪsmənt, -tɪzmənt/ *n.* **1** a public notice or announcement, esp. one advertising goods or services in newspapers, on posters, or in broadcasts. **2** the act or process of advertising. **3** *archaic* a notice to readers in a book etc. [earlier *avert*- f. F *avertissement* (as ADVERTISE)]

advice /əd'vaɪs/ *n.* **1** words given or offered as an opinion or recommendation about future action or behaviour. **2** information given; news. **3** formal notice of a transaction. **4** (in *pl.*) communications from a distance. □ **take advice 1** obtain advice, esp. from an expert. **2** act according to advice given. [ME f. OF *avis* f. L *ad* to + *visum* past part. of *vidēre* see]

advisable /əd'vaɪzəb(ə)l/ *adj.* **1** (of a course of action etc.) to be recommended. **2** expedient. □□ **advisability** /-'bɪlɪtɪ/ *n.* **advisably** *adv.*

advise /əd'vaɪz/ *v.* **1** *tr.* (also *absol.*) give advice to. **2** *tr.* recommend; offer as advice (*they advise caution; advised me to rest*). **3** *tr.* (usu. foll. by *of*, or *that* + clause) inform, notify. **4** *intr.* (foll. by *with*) *US* consult. [ME f. OF *aviser* f. L *ad* to + *visare* frequent. of *vidēre* see]

advised /əd'vaɪzd/ *adj.* **1** judicious (*well-advised*). **2** deliberate, considered. □□ **advisedly** /-zɪdlɪ/ *adv.*

adviser /əd'vaɪzə(r)/ *n.* (also *disp.* **advisor**) **1** a person who advises, esp. one appointed to do so and regularly consulted. **2** *US* a person who advises students on education, careers, etc. ¶ The disputed form *advisor* is prob. influenced by the adj. *advisory*.

advisory /əd'vaɪzərɪ/ *adj. & n.* —*adj.* **1** giving advice; constituted to give advice (*an advisory body*). **2** consisting in giving advice. —*n.* (*pl.* **-ies**) *US* an advisory statement, esp. a bulletin about bad weather.

advocaat /,ædvə'kɑːt/ *n.* a liqueur of eggs, sugar, and brandy. [Du., = ADVOCATE (being orig. an advocate's drink)]

advocacy /'ædvəkəsɪ/ *n.* **1** (usu. foll. by *of*) verbal support or argument for a cause, policy, etc. **2** the function of an advocate. [ME f. OF *a(d)vocacie* f. med.L *advocatia* (as ADVOCATE)]

advocate *n. & v.* —*n.* /'ædvəkət/ **1** (foll. by *of*) a person who supports or speaks in favour. **2** a person who pleads for another. **3 a** a professional pleader in a court of justice. **b** *Sc.* a barrister. —*v.tr.* /'ædvə,keɪt/ **1** recommend or support by argument (a cause, policy, etc.). **2** plead for, defend. □□ **advocateship** *n.* **advocatory** /'ædvə,keɪtərɪ/ *adj.* [ME f. OF *avocat* f. L *advocatus* past part. of *advocare* (as AD-, *vocare* call)]

advowson /əd'vauz(ə)n/ *n. Brit. Eccl.* (in ecclesiastical law) the right of recommending a member of the clergy for a vacant benefice, or of making the appointment. [ME f. AF *a(d)voweson* f. OF *avoeson* f. L *advocatio -onis* (as ADVOCATE)]

advt. *abbr.* advertisement.

adytum /'ædɪtəm/ *n.* (*pl.* **adyta** /-tə/) the innermost part of an ancient temple. [L f. Gk *aduton* neut. of *adutos* impenetrable (as A-¹, *duō* enter)]

adze /ædz/ *n. & v.* (*US* **adz**) —*n.* a tool for cutting away the surface of wood, like an axe with an arched blade at right angles to the handle. —*v.tr.* dress or cut with an adze. [OE *adesa*]

adzuki /əd'zuːkɪ/ *n.* (also **adsuki, azuki**) **1** an annual leguminous plant, *Vigna angularis*, native to China and Japan. **2** the small round red edible bean of this plant. [Jap. *azuki*]

-ae /iː/ *suffix* forming plural nouns, used in names of animal and plant families, tribes, etc. (*Felidae*; *Rosaceae*) and instead of *-as* in the plural of many non-naturalized or unfamiliar nouns in *-a* derived from Latin or Greek (*larvae*; *actiniae*). [pl. *-ae* of L nouns in *-a* or pl. *-ai* of some Gk nouns]

aedile /'iːdaɪl/ *n.* either of a pair of Roman magistrates who administered public works, maintenance of roads, public games, the corn-supply, etc. □□ **aedileship** *n.* [L *aedilis* concerned with buildings f. *aedes* building]

aegis /'iːdʒɪs/ *n.* a protection; an impregnable defence. □ **under the aegis of** under the auspices of. [L f. Gk *aigis* mythical shield of Zeus or Athene]

aegrotat /'iːgrəʊˌtæt/ *n. Brit.* **1** a certificate that a university student is too ill to attend an examination. **2** an examination pass awarded in such circumstances. [L, = is sick f. *aeger* sick]

-aemia /'iːmɪə/ *comb. form* (also **-haemia** /'hiːmɪə/, *US* **-emia, -hemia** /'hiːmɪə/) forming nouns denoting that a substance is (esp. excessively) present in the blood (*bacteriaemia*; *pyaemia*). [mod.L f. Gk *-aimia* f. *haima* blood]

aeolian /iːˈəʊlɪən/ *adj.* (*US* **eolian**) wind-borne. □ **aeolian harp** a stringed instrument or toy that produces musical sounds when the wind passes through it. [L *Aeolius* f. *Aeolus* god of the winds f. Gk *Aiolos*]

Aeolian mode /iːˈəʊlɪən/ *n. Mus.* the mode represented by the natural diatonic scale A-A. [L *Aeolius* f. *Aeolis* in Asia Minor f. Gk *Aiolis*]

aeon /'iːɒn/ *n.* (also **eon**) **1** a very long or indefinite period. **2** an age of the universe. **3** *Astron.* a thousand million years. **4** an eternity. **5** *Philos.* (in Neoplatonism, Platonism, and Gnosticism) a power existing from eternity, an emanation or phase of the supreme deity. [eccl.L f. Gk *aiōn* age]

aerate /'eəreɪt/ *v.tr.* **1** charge (a liquid) with a gas, esp. carbon dioxide, e.g. to produce effervescence. **2** expose to the mechanical or chemical action of the air. □□ **aeration** /-'reɪʃ(ə)n/ *n.* **aerator** *n.* [L *aer* AIR + -ATE³, after F *aérer*]

aerenchyma /,æərən'kaɪmə/ *n. Bot.* a soft plant tissue containing air spaces found esp. in many aquatic plants. [Gk *aēr* air + *egkhuma* infusion]

aerial /'eərɪəl/ n. & adj. —n. a metal rod, wire, or other structure by which signals are transmitted or received as part of a radio transmission or receiving system. —adj. **1** by or from or involving aircraft (*aerial navigation; aerial photography*). **2 a** existing, moving, or happening in the air. **b** of or in the atmosphere, atmospheric. **3 a** thin as air, ethereal. **b** immaterial, imaginary. **c** of air, gaseous. □□ **aeriality** /-'ælɪtɪ/ n. **aerially** adv. [L *aerius* f. Gk *aerios* f. *aēr* air]

aerialist /'eərɪəlɪst/ n. a high-wire or trapeze artist.

aerie var. of EYRIE.

aeriform /'eərɪˌfɔːm/ adj. **1** of the form of air; gaseous. **2** unsubstantial, unreal. [L *aer* AIR + -FORM]

aero- /'eərəʊ/ comb. form **1** air. **2** aircraft. [Gk *aero-* f. *aēr* air]

aerobatics /ˌeərə'bætɪks/ n.pl. **1** feats of expert and usu. spectacular flying and manœuvring of aircraft. **2** (as *sing.*) a performance of these. [AERO- + ACROBATICS]

aerobe /'eərəʊb/ n. a micro-organism usu. growing in the presence of air, or needing air for growth. [F *aérobie* (as AERO-, Gk *bios* life)]

aerobic /eə'rəʊbɪk, eə'rɒb-/ adj. **1** of or relating to aerobics. **2** of or relating to aerobes.

aerobics /eə'rəʊbɪks/ n.pl. vigorous exercises designed to increase the body's oxygen intake.

aerobiology /ˌeərəbaɪ'ɒlədʒɪ/ n. the study of airborne micro-organisms, pollen, spores, etc., esp. as agents of infection.

aerodrome /'eərəˌdrəʊm/ n. Brit. a small airport or airfield. ¶ Now largely replaced by *airfield* and *airport*.

aerodynamics /ˌeərəʊdaɪ'næmɪks/ n.pl. (usu. treated as *sing.*) the study of the interaction between the air and solid bodies moving through it. □□ **aerodynamic** adj. **aerodynamically** adv. **aerodynamicist** n.

aero-engine /'eərəʊˌendʒɪn/ n. an engine used to power an aircraft.

aerofoil /'eərəˌfɔɪl/ n. Brit. a structure with curved surfaces (e.g. a wing, fin, or tailplane) designed to give lift in flight.

aerogramme /'eərəˌgræm/ n. (also **aerogram**) an air letter in the form of a single sheet that is folded and sealed.

aerolite /'eərəˌlaɪt/ n. a stony meteorite.

aerology /eə'rɒlədʒɪ/ n. the study of the upper levels of the atmosphere. □□ **aerological** /-ə'lɒdʒɪk(ə)l/ adj.

aeronautics /ˌeərəʊ'nɔːtɪks/ n.pl. (usu. treated as *sing.*) the science or practice of motion or travel in the air. □□ **aeronautic** adj. **aeronautical** adj. [mod.L *aeronautica* (as AERO-, NAUTICAL)]

aeronomy /eə'rɒnəmɪ/ n. the science of the upper atmosphere.

aeroplane /'eərəˌpleɪn/ n. esp. Brit. a powered heavier-than-air flying vehicle with fixed wings. [F *aéroplane* (as AERO-, PLANE¹)]

aerosol /'eərəˌsɒl/ n. **1 a** a container used to hold a substance packed under pressure with a device for releasing it as a fine spray. **b** the releasing device. **c** the substance contained in an aerosol. **2** a system of colloidal particles dispersed in a gas (e.g. fog or smoke). [AERO- + SOL²]

aerospace /'eərəʊˌspeɪs/ n. **1** the earth's atmosphere and outer space. **2** the technology of aviation in this region.

aerotrain /'eərəʊˌtreɪn/ n. a train that is supported on an air-cushion and guided by a track. [F *aérotrain* (as AERO-, TRAIN)]

aeruginous /ɪə'ruːdʒɪnəs/ adj. of the nature or colour of verdigris. [L *aeruginosus* f. *aerugo -inis* verdigris f. *aes aeris* bronze]

Aesculapian /ˌiːskjʊ'leɪpɪən/ adj. of or relating to medicine or physicians. [L *Aesculapius* f. Gk *Asklēpios* god of medicine]

aesthete /'iːsθiːt/ n. (US **esthete**) a person who has

or professes to have a special appreciation of beauty. [Gk *aisthētēs* one who perceives, or f. AESTHETIC]

aesthetic /iːs'θetɪk/ adj. & n. (US **esthetic**) —adj. **1** concerned with beauty or the appreciation of beauty. **2** having such appreciation; sensitive to beauty. **3** in accordance with the principles of good taste. —n. **1** (in *pl.*) the philosophy of the beautiful, esp. in art. **2** a set of principles of good taste and the appreciation of beauty. □□ **aesthetically** adv. **aestheticism** /-ˌsɪz(ə)m/ n. [Gk *aisthētikos* f. *aisthanomai* perceive]

aestival /'estɪv(ə)l, e'staɪv(ə)l, iː'staɪv(ə)l/ adj. (US **estival**) formal belonging to or appearing in summer. [ME f. OF *estival* f. L *aestivalis* f. *aestivus* f. *aestus* heat]

aestivate /'estɪˌveɪt, 'iːs-/ v.intr. (US **estivate**) **1** Zool. spend the summer or dry season in a state of torpor. **2** formal pass the summer. [L *aestivare aestivat-*]

aestivation /ˌestɪ'veɪʃ(ə)n, ˌiːs-/ n. (US **estivation**) **1** Bot. the arrangement of petals in a flower-bud before it opens (cf. VERNATION). **2** Zool. spending the summer or dry season in a state of torpor.

aet. abbr. (also **aetat.**) *aetatis*.

aetatis /iː'tɑːtɪs, aɪ-/ adj. of or at the age of.

aether var. of ETHER 2, 3.

aetiology /ˌiːtɪ'ɒlədʒɪ/ n. (US **etiology**) **1** the assignment of a cause or reason. **2** the philosophy of causation. **3** Med. the science of the causes of disease. □□ **aetiologic** /-ə'lɒdʒɪk/ adj. **aetiological** /-ə'lɒdʒɪk(ə)l/ adj. **aetiologically** /-ə'lɒdʒɪkəlɪ/ adv. [LL *aetiologia* f. Gk *aitiologia* f. *aitia* cause]

AEU abbr. (in the UK) Amalgamated Engineering Union.

AEU(TASS) abbr. Technical, Administrative, and Supervisory Section of the AEU.

AF abbr. audio frequency.

af- /əf/ prefix assim. form of AD- before *f*.

afar /ə'fɑː(r)/ adv. at or to a distance. □**from afar** from a distance. [ME f. A-², A-⁴ + FAR]

AFC abbr. **1** (in the UK) Air Force Cross. **2** Association Football Club.

AFDCS abbr. (in the UK) Association of First Division Civil Servants (cf. FDA).

affable /'æfəb(ə)l/ adj. **1** (of a person) approachable and friendly. **2** kind and courteous, esp. to inferiors. □□ **affability** /-'bɪlɪtɪ/ n. **affably** adv. [F f. L *affabilis* f. *affari* (as AD-, *fari* speak)]

affair /ə'feə(r)/ n. **1** a concern; a business; a matter to be attended to (*that is my affair*). **2 a** a celebrated or notorious happening or sequence of events. **b** colloq. a noteworthy thing or event (*was a puzzling affair*). **3** = *love affair*. **4** (in *pl.*) **a** ordinary pursuits of life. **b** business dealings. **c** public matters (*current affairs*). [ME f. AF *afere* f. OF *afaire* f. *à faire* to do: cf. ADO]

affaire /æ'feə(r)/ n. (also **affaire de cœur** /æˌfeə də 'kɜː(r)/) a love affair. [F]

affairé /æ'feəreɪ/ adj. busy; involved. [F]

affect¹ /ə'fekt/ v.tr. **1 a** produce an effect on. **b** (of a disease etc.) attack (*his liver is affected*). **2** move; touch the feelings of (*affected me deeply*). ¶ Often confused with *effect*, which as a verb means 'bring about; accomplish'. □□ **affecting** adj. **affectingly** adv. [F *affecter* or L *afficere affect-* influence (as AD-, *facere* do)]

affect² /ə'fekt/ v.tr. **1** pretend to have or feel (*affected indifference*). **2** (foll. by *to* + infin.) pretend. **3** assume the character or manner of; pose as (*affect the freethinker*). **4** make a show of liking or using (*she affects fancy hats*). [F *affecter* or L *affectare* aim at, frequent. of *afficere* (as AFFECT¹)]

affect³ /'æfekt/ n. Psychol. a feeling, emotion, or desire, esp. as leading to action. [G *Affekt* f. L *affectus* disposition f. *afficere* (as AFFECT¹)]

affectation /ˌæfek'teɪʃ(ə)n/ n. **1** an assumed or contrived manner of behaviour, esp. in order to impress. **2** (foll. by *of*) a studied display. **3** pretence. [F *affectation* or L *affectatio* (as AFFECT²)]

affected /ə'fektɪd/ adj. **1** in senses of AFFECT¹,

AFFECT². **2** artificially assumed or displayed; pretended (*an affected air of innocence*). **3** (of a person) full of affectation; artificial. **4** (prec. by adv.; often foll. by *towards*) disposed, inclined. □□ **affectedly** *adv.*

affection /ə'fekʃ(ə)n/ *n.* **1** (often foll. by *for, towards*) goodwill; fond or kindly feeling. **2** a disease; a diseased condition. **3** a mental state; an emotion. **4** a mental disposition. **5** the act or process of affecting or being affected. □□ **affectional** *adj.* (in sense 3). **affectionally** *adv.* [ME f. OF f. L *affectio -onis* (as AFFECT¹)]

affectionate /ə'fekʃənət/ *adj.* loving, fond; showing love or tenderness. □□ **affectionately** *adv.* [F *affectionné* or med.L *affectionatus* (as AFFECTION)]

affective /ə'fektɪv/ *adj.* **1** concerning the affections; emotional. **2** *Psychol.* relating to affects. □□ **affectivity** /ˌæfek'tɪvɪtɪ/ *n.* [F *affectif -ive* f. LL *affectivus* (as AFFECT¹)]

affenpinscher /'æfənˌpɪnʃə(r)/ *n.* **1** a dog of a small breed resembling the griffon. **2** this breed. [G f. *Affe* monkey + *Pinscher* terrier]

afferent /'æfərənt/ *adj. Physiol.* conducting inwards or towards (*afferent nerves; afferent vessels*) (opp. EFFERENT). [L *afferre* (as AD-, *ferre* bring)]

affiance /ə'faɪəns/ *v.tr.* (usu. in *passive*) *literary* promise solemnly to give (a person) in marriage. [ME f. OF *afiancer* f. med.L *affidare* (as AD-, *fidus* trusty)]

affidavit /ˌæfɪ'deɪvɪt/ *n.* a written statement confirmed by oath, for use as evidence in court. [med.L, = has stated on oath, f. *affidare*: see AFFIANCE]

affiliate *v. & n.* —*v.* /ə'fɪlɪˌeɪt/ **1** *tr.* (usu. in *passive*; foll. by *to, with*) attach or connect (a person or society) with a larger organization. **2** *tr.* (of an institution) adopt (persons as members, societies as branches). **3** *intr.* **a** (foll. by *to*) associate oneself with a society. **b** (foll. by *with*) associate oneself with a political party. —*n.* /ə'fɪlɪˌeɪt, -lɪɪt/ an affiliated person or organization. [med.L *affiliare* adopt (as AD-, *filius* son)]

affiliation /əˌfɪlɪ'eɪʃ(ə)n/ *n.* the act or process of affiliating or being affiliated. □ **affiliation order** *Brit.* a legal order that the man judged to be the father of an illegitimate child must help to support it. [F f. med.L *affiliatio* f. *affiliare*: see AFFILIATE]

affined /ə'faɪnd/ *adj.* related, connected. [*affine* (adj.) f. L *affinis* related: see AFFINITY]

affinity /ə'fɪnɪtɪ/ *n.* (*pl.* -ies) **1** (often foll. by *between*, or *disp. to, for*) a spontaneous or natural liking for or attraction to a person or thing. **2** relationship, esp. by marriage. **3** resemblance in structure between animals, plants, or languages. **4** a similarity of characters suggesting a relationship. **5** *Chem.* the tendency of certain substances to combine with others. [ME f. OF *afinité* f. L *affinitas -tatis* f. *affinis* related, lit. bordering on (as AD- + *finis* border)]

affirm /ə'fɜːm/ *v.* **1** *tr.* assert strongly; state as a fact. **2** *intr.* **a** *Law* make an affirmation. **b** make a formal declaration. **3** *tr. Law* confirm, ratify (a judgement). □□ **affirmatory** *adj.* **affirmer** *n.* [ME f. OF *afermer* f. L *affirmare* (as AD-, *firmus* strong)]

affirmation /ˌæfə'meɪʃ(ə)n/ *n.* **1** the act or process of affirming or being affirmed. **2** *Law* a solemn declaration by a person who conscientiously declines to take an oath. [F *affirmation* or L *affirmatio* (as AFFIRM)]

affirmative /ə'fɜːmətɪv/ *adj. & n.* —*adj.* **1** affirming; asserting that a thing is so. **2** (of a vote) expressing approval. —*n.* **1** an affirmative statement, reply, or word. **2** (prec. by *the*) a positive or affirming position. □ **affirmative action** esp. *US* action favouring those who often suffer from discrimination. **in the affirmative** with affirmative effect; so as to accept or agree to a proposal; yes (*the answer was in the affirmative*). □□ **affirmatively** *adv.* [ME f. OF *affirmatif -ive* f. LL *affirmativus* (as AFFIRM)]

affix *v. & n.* —*v.tr.* /ə'fɪks/ **1** (usu. foll. by *to, on*) attach, fasten. **2** add in writing (a signature or postscript). **3** impress (a seal or stamp). —*n.* /'æfɪks/ **1** an appendage; an addition. **2** *Gram.* an addition or element placed at the beginning (*prefix*) or end (*suffix*) of a root, stem, or word, or in the body of a word (*infix*), to modify its meaning. □□ **affixture** /ə'fɪkstʃə(r)/ *n.* [F *affixer, affixe* or med.L *affixare* frequent. of L *affigere* (as AD-, *figere fix-* fix)]

afflatus /ə'fleɪtəs/ *n.* a divine creative impulse; inspiration. [L f. *afflare* (as AD-, *flare flat-* to blow)]

afflict /ə'flɪkt/ *v.tr.* inflict bodily or mental suffering on. □ **afflicted with** suffering from. □□ **afflictive** *adj.* [ME f. L *afflictare*, or *afflict-* past part. stem of *affligere* (as AD-, *fligere flict-* dash)]

affliction /ə'flɪkʃ(ə)n/ *n.* **1** physical or mental distress, esp. pain or illness. **2** a cause of this. [ME f. OF f. L *afflictio -onis* (as AFFLICT)]

affluence /'æflʊəns/ *n.* an abundant supply of money, commodities, etc.; wealth. [ME f. F f. L *affluentia* f. *affluere*: see AFFLUENT]

affluent /'æflʊənt/ *adj. & n.* —*adj.* **1** wealthy, rich. **2** abundant. **3** flowing freely or copiously. —*n.* a tributary stream. □ **affluent society** a society in which material wealth is widely distributed. □□ **affluently** *adv.* [ME f. OF f. L *affluere* (as AD-, *fluere flux-* flow)]

afflux /'æflʌks/ *n.* a flow towards a point; an influx. [med.L *affluxus* f. L *affluere*: see AFFLUENT]

afford /ə'fɔːd/ *v.tr.* **1** (prec. by *can* or *be able to*; often foll. by *to* + infin.) **a** have enough money, means, time, etc., for; be able to spare (*can afford £50; could not afford a holiday; can we afford to buy a new television?*). **b** be in a position to do something (esp. without risk of adverse consequences) (*can't afford to let him think so*). **2** yield a supply of. **3** provide (*affords a view of the sea*). □□ **affordable** *adj.* **affordability** /-'bɪlɪtɪ/ *n.* [ME f. OE *geforthian* promote (as Y-, FORTH), assim. to words in AF-]

afforest /ə'fɒrɪst, æ-/ *v.tr.* **1** convert into forest. **2** plant with trees. □□ **afforestation** /-'steɪʃ(ə)n/ *n.* [med.L *afforestare* (as AD-, *foresta* FOREST)]

affranchise /ə'fræntʃaɪz/ *v.tr.* release from servitude or an obligation. [OF *afranchir* (as ENFRANCHISE, with prefix A-³)]

affray /ə'freɪ/ *n.* a breach of the peace by fighting or rioting in public. [ME f. AF *afrayer* (v.) f. OF *esfreer* f. Rmc]

affricate /'æfrɪkət/ *n. Phonet.* a combination of a plosive with an immediately following fricative or spirant, e.g. *ch*. [L *africare* (as AD-, *fricare* rub)]

affront /ə'frʌnt/ *n. & v.* —*n.* an open insult (*feel it an affront; offer an affront to*). —*v.tr.* **1** insult openly. **2** offend the modesty or self-respect of. **3** face, confront. [ME f. OF *afronter* slap in the face, insult, ult. f. L *frons frontis* face]

Afghan /'æfgæn/ *n. & adj.* —*n.* **1 a** a native or national of Afghanistan. **b** a person of Afghan descent. **2** the official language of Afghanistan (also called PASHTO). **3** (**afghan**) a knitted and sewn woollen blanket or shawl. **4** (in full **Afghan coat**) a kind of sheepskin coat with the skin outside and usu. with a shaggy border. —*adj.* of or relating to Afghanistan or its people or language. □ **Afghan hound** a tall hunting dog with long silky hair. [Pashto *afghānī*]

Afghani /æf'gɑːnɪ/ *n.* (*pl.* **Afghanis**) the chief monetary unit of Afghanistan. [Pashto]

aficionado /əˌfɪsjə'nɑːdəʊ/ *n.* (*pl.* -os) a devotee of a sport or pastime (orig. of bullfighting). [Sp.]

afield /ə'fiːld/ *adv.* **1** away from home; to or at a distance (esp. *far afield*). **2** in the field. [OE (as A², FIELD)]

afire /ə'faɪə(r)/ *adv. & predic.adj.* **1** on fire. **2** intensely roused or excited.

aflame /ə'fleɪm/ *adv. & predic.adj.* **1** in flames. **2** = AFIRE 2.

aflatoxin /'æfləˌtɒksɪn/ *n. Chem.* any of several related toxic compounds produced by the fungus

Aspergillus flavus, which cause tissue damage and cancer. [Aspergillus + *flavus* + TOXIN]

afloat /ə'fləʊt/ *adv. & predic.adj.* **1** floating in water or air. **2** at sea; on board ship. **3** out of debt or difficulty. **4** in general circulation; current. **5** full of or covered with a liquid. **6** in full swing. [OE (as A², FLOAT)]

AFM *abbr.* (in the UK) Air Force Medal.

afoot /ə'fʊt/ *adv. & predic.adj.* **1** in operation; progressing. **2** astir; on the move.

afore /ə'fɔː(r)/ *prep. & adv. archaic* before; previously; in front (of). [OE *onforan* (as A², FORE)]

afore- /ə'fɔː(r)/ *comb. form* before, previously (*aforementioned*; *aforesaid*).

aforethought /ə'fɔːθɔːt/ *adj.* premeditated (following a noun: *malice aforethought*).

a fortiori /ˌeɪ fɔːtɪ'ɔːraɪ/ *adv. & adj.* with a yet stronger reason (than a conclusion already accepted); more conclusively. [L]

afraid /ə'freɪd/ *predic.adj.* **1** (often foll. by *of*, or *that* or *lest* + clause) alarmed, frightened. **2** (foll. by *to* + infin.) unwilling or reluctant for fear of the consequences (*was afraid to go in*). □ **be afraid** (foll. by *that* + clause) *colloq.* admit or declare with (real or politely simulated) regret (*I'm afraid there's none left*). [ME, past part. of obs. *affray* (v.) f. AF *afrayer* f. OF *esfreer*]

afreet /'æfriːt/ *n.* (also **afrit**) a demon in Muslim mythology. [Arab. *'ifrīt*]

afresh /ə'freʃ/ *adv.* anew; with a fresh beginning. [A-² + FRESH]

African /'æfrɪkən/ *n. & adj.* —*n.* **1** a native of Africa (esp. a dark-skinned person). **2** a person of African descent. —*adj.* of or relating to Africa. □ **African American** an American citizen of African origin or descent. **African elephant** the elephant, *Loxodonta africana*, of Africa, which is larger than the Indian elephant. **African violet** a saintpaulia, *Saintpaulia ionantha*, with heart-shaped velvety leaves and blue, purple, or pink flowers. [L *Africanus*]

Africana /ˌæfrɪ'kɑːnə/ *n.pl.* things connected with Africa.

Africander /ˌæfrɪ'kændə(r)/ *n.* (also **Afrikander**) one of a S. African breed of sheep or longhorn cattle. [Afrik. *Afrikaander* alt. of Du. *Afrikaner* after *Hollander* etc.]

Afrikaans /ˌæfrɪ'kɑːns/ *n.* the language of the Afrikaner people developed from Cape Dutch, an official language of the Republic of South Africa. [Du., = African]

Afrikaner /ˌæfrɪ'kɑːnə(r)/ *n.* **1** an Afrikaans-speaking White person in S. Africa, esp. one of Dutch descent. **2** *Bot.* a S. African species of *Gladiolus* or *Homoglossum*. [Afrik., formed as AFRICANDER]

afrit var. of AFREET.

Afro /'æfrəʊ/ *adj. & n.* —*adj.* (of a hairstyle) long and bushy, as naturally grown by some Blacks. —*n.* (*pl.* **-os**) an Afro hairstyle. [AFRO-, or abbr. of AFRICAN]

Afro- /'æfrəʊ/ *comb. form* African (*Afro-Asian*). [L *Afer Afr-* African]

Afro-American /ˌæfrəʊə'merɪkən/ *adj. & n.* —*adj.* of or relating to American Blacks or their culture. —*n.* an American Black.

Afro-Caribbean /ˌæfrəʊˌkærɪ'biːən, -kə'rɪbɪən/ *n. & adj.* —*n.* a person of African descent in or from the Caribbean. —*adj.* of or relating to the Afro-Caribbeans or their culture.

afrormosia /ˌæfrɔː'məʊzɪə/ *n.* **1** an African tree, *Pericopsis* (formerly *Afrormosia*) *elata*, yielding a hard wood resembling teak and used for furniture. **2** this wood. [mod.L f. AFRO- + *Ormosia* genus of trees]

aft /ɑːft/ *adv. Naut. & Aeron.* at or towards the stern or tail. [prob. f. ME *baft*: see ABAFT]

after /'ɑːftə(r)/ *prep., conj., adv., & adj.* —*prep.* **1** following in time; later than (*after six months*; *after midnight*; *day after day*). **b** *US* in specifying time (*a quarter after eight*). **2** (with causal force) in view of (something that happened shortly before) (*after your behaviour tonight what do you expect?*). **3** (with concessive force) in spite of (*after all my efforts I'm no better off*). **4** behind (*shut the door after you*). **5** in pursuit or quest of (*run after them*; *inquire after him*; *hanker after it*; *is after a job*). **6** about, concerning (*asked after her*; *asked after her health*). **7** in allusion to (*named him William after the prince*). **8** in imitation of (a person, word, etc.) (*a painting after Rubens*; '*aesthete*' *is formed after* '*athlete*'). **9** next in importance to (*the best book on the subject after mine*). **10** according to (*after a fashion*). —*conj.* in or at a time later than that when (*left after they arrived*). —*adv.* **1** later in time (*soon after*; *a week after*). **2** behind in place (*followed on after*; *look before and after*). —*adj.* **1** later, following (*in after years*). **2** *Naut.* nearer the stern (*after cabins*; *after mast*; *after-peak*). □ **after all** **1** in spite of all that has happened or has been said etc. (*after all, what does it matter?*). **2** in spite of one's exertions, expectations, etc. (*they tried for an hour and failed after all*; *so you have come after all!*).

after-care care of a patient after a stay in hospital or of a person on release from prison. **after-damp** choking gas left after an explosion of firedamp in a mine. **after-effect** an effect that follows after an interval or after the primary action of something. **after-image** an image retained by a sense-organ, esp. the eye, and producing a sensation after the cessation of the stimulus. **after one's own heart** see HEART. **after-taste** a taste remaining or recurring after eating or drinking. **after you** a formula used in offering precedence. [OE *æfter* f. Gmc]

afterbirth /'ɑːftə,bɜːθ/ *n. Med.* the placenta and foetal membranes discharged from the womb after childbirth.

afterburner /'ɑːftə,bɜːnə(r)/ *n.* an auxiliary burner in a jet engine to increase thrust.

afterglow /'ɑːftə,gləʊ/ *n.* a light or radiance remaining after its source has disappeared or been removed.

afterlife /'ɑːftə,laɪf/ *n.* **1** *Relig.* life after death. **2** life at a later time.

aftermarket /'ɑːftə,mɑːkɪt/ *n.* **1** a market in spare parts and components. **2** *US Stock Exch.* a market in shares after their original issue.

aftermath /'ɑːftə,mæθ, -,mɑːθ/ *n.* **1** consequences; after-effects (*the aftermath of war*). **2** new grass growing after mowing or after a harvest. [AFTER *adj.* + *math* mowing f. OE *mæth* f. Gmc]

aftermost /'ɑːftə,məʊst/ *adj.* **1** last. **2** *Naut.* furthest aft. [AFTER *adj.* + -MOST]

afternoon /ˌɑːftə'nuːn, *attrib.* 'ɑːft-/ *n. & int.* —*n.* **1** the time from noon or lunch-time to evening (*this afternoon*; *during the afternoon*; *afternoon tea*). **2** this time spent in a particular way (*had a lazy afternoon*). **3** a time compared with this, esp. the later part of something (*the afternoon of life*). —*int.* = *good afternoon* (see GOOD *adj.* 14).

afterpains /'ɑːftə,peɪnz/ *n.pl.* pains caused by contraction of the womb after childbirth.

afters /'ɑːftəz/ *n.pl. Brit. colloq.* the course following the main course of a meal.

aftershave /'ɑːftə,ʃeɪv/ *n.* an astringent lotion for use after shaving.

afterthought /'ɑːftə,θɔːt/ *n.* an item or thing that is thought of or added later.

afterwards /'ɑːftəwədz/ *adv.* (*US* **afterward**) later, subsequently. [OE *æftanwearde* adj. f. *æftan* AFT + -WARD]

afterword /'ɑːftə,wɜːd/ *n.* concluding remarks in a book, esp. by a person other than its author.

Ag *symb. Chem.* the element silver. [L *argentum*]

ag- /əg/ *prefix* assim. form of AD- before g.

Aga /'ɑːgə/ *n. propr.* a type of large cooking stove or range burning solid fuel or powered by gas, oil, or electricity. [Sw. f. Svenska Aktienbolaget *Ga*sackumulator (Swedish Gas Accumulator Company), the original manufacturer]

aga /'ɑːgə/ n. (in Muslim countries, esp. under the Ottoman Empire) a commander, a chief. □ **Aga Khan** the spiritual leader of the Ismaili Muslims. [Turk. *aǧa* master]

again /ə'geɪn, ə'gen/ adv. **1** another time; once more. **2** as in a previous position or condition (*back again*; *home again*; *quite well again*). **3** in addition (*as much again*; *half as many again*). **4** further, besides (*again, what about the children?*). **5** on the other hand (*I might, and again I might not*). □ **again and again** repeatedly. [orig. a northern form of ME *ayen* etc., f. OE *ongēan*, *ongægn*, etc., f. Gmc]

against /ə'geɪnst, ə'genst/ prep. **1** in opposition to (*fight against the invaders*; *am against hanging*; *arson is against the law*). **2** into collision or in contact with (*ran against a rock*; *lean against the wall*; *up against a problem*). **3** to the disadvantage of (*his age is against him*). **4** in contrast to (*against a dark background*; *99 as against 102 yesterday*). **5** in anticipation of or preparation for (*against his coming*; *against a rainy day*; *protected against the cold*; *warned against pickpockets*). **6** as a compensating factor to (*income against expenditure*). **7** in return for (*issued against payment of the fee*). □ **against the clock** see CLOCK[1] 3. **against the grain** see GRAIN. **against time** see TIME. [ME *ayenes* etc. f. *ayen* AGAIN + *-t* as in *amongst*: see AMONG]

agama /'ægəmə/ n. any Old World lizard of the genus *Agama*. [Carib]

agamic /ə'gæmɪk/ adj. characterized by the absence of sexual reproduction. [as AGAMOUS + -IC]

agamogenesis /,ægəmə'dʒenɪsɪs/ n. Biol. asexual reproduction. □□ **agamogenetic** /-dʒɪ'netɪk/ adj. [as AGAMOUS + Gk *genesis* birth]

agamous /'ægəməs/ adj. Biol. without (distinguishable) sexual organs. [LL *agamus* f. Gk *agamos* (as A-[1], *gamos* marriage)]

agapanthus /,ægə'pænθəs/ n. any African plant of the genus *Agapanthus*, esp. the ornamental African lily, with blue or white flowers. [mod.L f. Gk *agapē* love + *anthos* flower]

agape[1] /ə'geɪp/ adv. & predic.adj. gaping, open-mouthed, esp. with wonder or expectation.

agape[2] /'ægəpeɪ/ n. **1** a Christian feast in token of fellowship, esp. one held by early Christians in commemoration of the Last Supper. **2** Theol. Christian fellowship, esp. as distinct from erotic love. [Gk, = brotherly love]

agar /'eɪgɑː(r)/ n. (also **agar-agar** /,eɪgɑː'eɪgɑː(r)/) a gelatinous substance obtained from any of various kinds of red seaweed and used in food, microbiological media, etc. [Malay]

agaric /'ægərɪk/ n. any fungus of the family Agaricaceae, with cap and stalk, including the common edible mushroom. [L *agaricum* f. Gk *agarikon*]

agate /'ægət/ n. **1** any of several varieties of hard usu. streaked chalcedony. **2** a coloured toy marble resembling this. [F *agate*, *-the*, f. L *achates* f. Gk *akhatēs*]

agave /ə'geɪvɪ/ n. any plant of the genus *Agave*, with rosettes of narrow spiny leaves, and tall inflorescences, e.g. the American aloe. [L f. Gk *Agauē*, proper name in myth f. *agauos* illustrious]

agaze /ə'geɪz/ adv. gazing.

age /eɪdʒ/ n. & v. —n. **1 a** the length of time that a person or thing has existed or is likely to exist. **b** a particular point in or part of one's life, often as a qualification (*old age*; *voting age*). **2 a** colloq. (often in pl.) a long time (*took an age to answer*; *have been waiting for ages*). **b** a distinct period of the past (*golden age*; *Bronze age*; *Middle Ages*). **c** Geol. a period of time. **d** a generation. **3** the latter part of life; old age (*the peevishness of age*). —v. (*pres. part.* **ageing**, **aging**) **1** intr. show signs of advancing age (*has aged a lot recently*). **2** intr. grow old. **3** intr. mature. **4** tr. cause or allow to age. □ **age-long** lasting for a very long time. **age of consent** see CONSENT. **age of discretion** see DISCRETION. **age-old** having

existed for a very long time. **come of age** reach adult status (esp. in Law at 18, formerly 21). **over age 1** old enough. **2** too old. **under age** not old enough, esp. not yet of adult status. [ME f. OF ult. f. L *aetas -atis* age]

-age /ɪdʒ/ suffix forming nouns denoting: **1** an action (*breakage*; *spillage*). **2** a condition or function (*bondage*; *a peerage*). **3** an aggregate or number of (*coverage*; *the peerage*; *acreage*). **4** fees payable for; the cost of using (*postage*). **5** the product of an action (*dosage*; *wreckage*). **6** a place; an abode (*anchorage*; *orphanage*; *parsonage*). [OF ult. f. L *-aticum* neut. of adj. suffix *-aticus* -ATIC]

aged adj. **1** /eɪdʒd/ **a** of the age of (*aged ten*). **b** that has been subjected to ageing. **c** (of a horse) over six years old. **2** /'eɪdʒɪd/ having lived long; old.

ageing /'eɪdʒɪŋ/ n. (also **aging**) **1** growing old. **2** giving the appearance of advancing age. **3** a change of properties occurring in some metals after heat treatment or cold working.

ageism /'eɪdʒɪz(ə)m/ n. (also **agism**) prejudice or discrimination on the grounds of age. □□ **ageist** adj. & n. (also **agist**).

ageless /'eɪdʒlɪs/ adj. **1** never growing or appearing old or outmoded. **2** eternal, timeless.

agency /'eɪdʒənsɪ/ n. (pl. **-ies**) **1 a** the business or establishment of an agent (*employment agency*). **b** the function of an agent. **2 a** active operation; action (*free agency*). **b** intervening action (*fertilized by the agency of insects*). **c** action personified (*an invisible agency*). **3** a specialized department of the United Nations. [med.L *agentia* f. L *agere* do]

agenda /ə'dʒendə/ n. **1** (pl. **agendas**) **a** a list of items of business to be considered at a meeting. **b** a series of things to be done. **2** (as pl.) **a** items to be considered. **b** things to be done. ¶ Now very common as a countable noun in sense 1 (cf. DATA, MEDIA). [L, neut. pl. of gerundive of *agere* do]

agent /'eɪdʒ(ə)nt/ n. **1 a** a person who acts for another in business, politics, etc. (*estate agent*; *insurance agent*). **b** a spy. **2 a** a person or thing that exerts power or produces an effect. **b** the cause of a natural force or effect on matter (*oxidizing agent*). **c** such a force or effect. □ **agent-general** a representative of an Australian State or Canadian province, usu. in London. □□ **agential** /ə'dʒenʃ(ə)l/ adj. [L *agent-* part. stem of *agere* do]

agent provocateur /,ɑːʒɒ̃ prə,vɒkɑː'tɜː(r)/ n. (pl. *agents provocateurs* pronunc. same) a person employed to detect suspected offenders by tempting them to overt self-incriminating action. [F, = provocative agent]

agglomerate v., n., & adj. —v.tr. & intr. /ə'glɒmə,reɪt/ **1** collect into a mass. **2** accumulate in a disorderly way. —n. /ə'glɒmərət/ **1** a mass or collection of things. **2** Geol. a mass of large volcanic fragments bonded under heat (cf. CONGLOMERATE). —adj. /ə'glɒmərət/ collected into a mass. □□ **agglomeration** /-'reɪʃ(ə)n/ n. **agglomerative** /ə'glɒmərətɪv/ adj. [L *agglomerare* (as AD-, *glomerare* f. *glomus -meris* ball)]

agglutinate /ə'gluːtɪ,neɪt/ v. **1** tr. unite as with glue. **2** tr. & intr. Biol. cause or undergo adhesion (of bacteria, erythrocytes, etc.). **3** tr. (of language) combine (simple words) without change of form to express compound ideas. □□ **agglutination** /-'neɪʃ(ə)n/ n. **agglutinative** /ə'gluːtɪnətɪv/ adj. [L *agglutinare* (as AD-, *glutinare* f. *gluten -tinis* glue)]

agglutinin /ə'gluːtɪnɪn/ n. Biol. a substance or antibody causing agglutination. [AGGLUTINATE + -IN]

aggrandize /ə'grændaɪz/ v.tr. (also **-ise**) **1** increase the power, rank, or wealth of (a person or State). **2** cause to appear greater than is the case. □□ **aggrandizement** /-dɪzmənt/ n. **aggrandizer** n. [F *agrandir* (stem *agrandiss-*), prob. f. It. *aggrandire* f. L *grandis* large: assim. to verbs in -IZE]

aggravate /'ægrə,veɪt/ v.tr. **1** increase the gravity of (an illness, offence, etc.). **2** disp. annoy, exasperate (a person). □□ **aggravation** /-'veɪʃ(ə)n/ n. [L aggravare aggravat- make heavy f. gravis heavy]

aggregate n., adj., & v. —n. /'ægrɪgət/ **1** a collection of, or the total of, disparate elements. **2** pieces of crushed stone, gravel, etc. used in making concrete. **3 a** Geol. a mass of minerals formed into solid rock. **b** a mass of particles. —adj. /'ægrɪgət/ **1** (of disparate elements) collected into one mass. **2** constituted by the collection of many units into one body. **3** Bot. **a** (of fruit) formed from several carpels derived from the same flower (e.g. raspberry). **b** (of a species) closely related. —v. /'ægrɪ,geɪt/ **1** tr. & intr. collect together; combine into one mass. **2** tr. colloq. amount to (a specified total). **3** tr. unite (was aggregated to the group). □**in the aggregate** as a whole. □□ **aggregation** /-'geɪʃ(ə)n/ n. **aggregative** /'ægrɪ,geɪtɪv/ adj. [L aggregare aggregat- herd together (as AD-, grex gregis flock)]

aggression /ə'greʃ(ə)n/ n. **1** the act or practice of attacking without provocation, esp. beginning a quarrel or war. **2** an unprovoked attack. **3** self-assertiveness; forcefulness. **4** Psychol. hostile or destructive tendency or behaviour. [F agression or L aggressio attack f. aggredi aggress- (as AD-, gradi walk)]

aggressive /ə'gresɪv/ adj. **1** of a person: **a** given to aggression; openly hostile. **b** forceful; self-assertive. **2** (of an act) offensive, hostile. **3** of aggression. □□ **aggressively** adv. **aggressiveness** n.

aggressor /ə'gresə(r)/ n. a person who attacks without provocation. [L (as AGGRESSION)]

aggrieved /ə'griːvd/ adj. having a grievance. □□ **aggrievedly** /-vɪdlɪ/ adv. [ME, past part. of aggrieve f. OF agrever make heavier (as AD-, GRIEVE¹)]

aggro /'ægrəʊ/ n. sl. **1** aggressive troublemaking. **2** trouble, difficulty. [abbr. of AGGRAVATION (see AGGRAVATE) or AGGRESSION]

aghast /ə'gɑːst/ adj. (usu. predic.; often foll. by at) filled with dismay or consternation. [ME, past part. of obs. agast, gast frighten: see GHASTLY]

agile /'ædʒaɪl/ adj. quick-moving, nimble, active. □□ **agilely** adv. **agility** /ə'dʒɪlɪtɪ/ n. [F f. L agilis f. agere do]

agin /ə'gɪn/ prep. colloq. or dial. against. [corrupt. of AGAINST or synonymous again obs. prep.]

aging var. of AGEING.

agio /'ædʒɪəʊ/ n. (pl. **agios**) **1** the percentage charged on the exchange of one currency, or one form of money, into another more valuable. **2** the excess value of one currency over another. **3** money-exchange business. [It. aggio]

agism var. of AGEISM.

agitate /'ædʒɪ,teɪt/ v. **1** tr. disturb or excite (a person or feelings). **2** intr. (often foll. by for, against) stir up interest or concern, esp. publicly (agitated for tax reform). **3** tr. shake or move, esp. briskly. □□ **agitatedly** adv. [L agitare agitat- frequent. of agere drive]

agitation /,ædʒɪ'teɪʃ(ə)n/ n. **1** the act or process of agitating or being agitated. **2** mental anxiety or concern. [F agitation or L agitatio (as AGITATE)]

agitato /,ædʒɪ'tɑːtəʊ/ adv. & adj. Mus. in an agitated manner. [It.]

agitator /'ædʒɪ,teɪtə(r)/ n. **1** a person who agitates, esp. publicly for a cause etc. **2** an apparatus for shaking or mixing liquid etc. [L (as AGITATE)]

agitprop /'ædʒɪt,prɒp, 'æg-/ n. the dissemination of Communist political propaganda, esp. in plays, films, books, etc. [Russ. (as AGITATION, PROPAGANDA)]

aglet /'æglɪt/ n. **1** a metal tag attached to each end of a shoelace etc. **2** = AIGUILLETTE. [ME f. F aiguillette small needle, ult. f. L acus needle]

agley /ə'gleɪ, -'liː/ adv. Sc. askew, awry. [A² + Sc. gley squint]

aglow /ə'gləʊ/ adv. & adj. —adv. glowingly. —predic.adj. glowing.

AGM abbr. annual general meeting.

agma /'ægmə/ n. **1** the sound represented by the symbol /ŋ/. **2** this symbol. [Gk, lit. 'fragment']

agnail /'ægneɪl/ n. **1** a piece of torn skin at the root of a fingernail. **2** the soreness resulting from this. [OE angnægl f. nægl NAIL n. 1: cf. HANGNAIL]

agnate /'ægneɪt/ adj. & n. —adj. **1** descended esp. by male line from the same male ancestor (cf. COGNATE). **2** descended from the same forefather; of the same clan or nation. **3** of the same nature; akin. —n. one who is descended esp. by male line from the same male ancestor. □□ **agnatic** /-'nætɪk/ adj. **agnation** /-'neɪʃ(ə)n/ n. [L agnatus f. ad to + gnasci be born f. stem gen- beget]

agnosia /æg'nəʊsɪə/ n. Med. the loss of the ability to interpret sensations. [mod.L f. Gk agnōsia ignorance]

agnostic /æg'nɒstɪk/ n. & adj. —n. a person who believes that nothing is known, or can be known, of the existence or nature of God or of anything beyond material phenomena. —adj. of or relating to agnostics. □□ **agnosticism** n. [A-¹ + GNOSTIC]

Agnus Dei /,ægnʊs 'deɪiː/ n. **1** a figure of a lamb bearing a cross or flag, as an emblem of Christ. **2** the part of the Roman Catholic mass beginning with the words 'Lamb of God'. [L, = lamb of God]

ago /ə'gəʊ/ adv. earlier, before the present (ten years ago; long ago). ¶ Note the construction it is 10 years ago that (not since) I saw them. [ME (ago, agone), past part. of obs. ago (v.) (as A-², GO¹)]

agog /ə'gɒg/ adv. & adj. —adv. eagerly, expectantly. —predic.adj. eager, expectant. [F en gogues f. en in + pl. of gogue fun]

à gogo /ə'gəʊgəʊ/ adv. in abundance (whisky à gogo). [F]

agonic /ə'gɒnɪk/ adj. having or forming no angle. □**agonic line** a line passing through the two poles, along which a magnetic needle points directly north or south. [Gk agōnios without angle (as A-¹, gōnia angle)]

agonistic /,ægə'nɪstɪk/ adj. polemical, combative. □□ **agonistically** adv. [LL agonisticus f. Gk agōnistikos f. agōnistēs contestant f. agōn contest]

agonize /'ægə,naɪz/ v. (also **-ise**) **1** intr. (often foll. by over) undergo (esp. mental) anguish; suffer agony. **2** tr. cause agony to. **3** tr. (as **agonized** adj.) expressing agony (an agonized look). **4** intr. struggle, contend. □□ **agonizingly** adv. [F agoniser or LL agonizare f. Gk agōnizomai contend f. agōn contest]

agony /'ægənɪ/ n. (pl. **-ies**) **1** extreme mental or physical suffering. **2** a severe struggle. □**agony aunt** colloq. a person (esp. a woman) who answers letters in an agony column. **agony column** colloq. **1** a column in a newspaper or magazine offering personal advice to readers who write in. **2** = personal column. [ME f. OF agonie or LL f. Gk agōnia f. agōn contest]

agoraphobe /'ægərə,fəʊb/ n. a person who suffers from agoraphobia.

agoraphobia /,ægərə'fəʊbɪə/ n. Psychol. an abnormal fear of open spaces or public places. □□ **agoraphobic** adj. & n. [mod.L f. Gk agora place of assembly, market-place + -PHOBIA]

agouti /ə'guːtɪ/ n. (also **aguti**) (pl. **agoutis**) any burrowing rodent of the genus Dasyprocta or Myoprocta of Central and S. America, related to the guinea-pig. [F agouti or Sp. aguti f. Tupi aguti]

AGR abbr. advanced gas-cooled (nuclear) reactor.

agrarian /ə'greərɪən/ adj. & n. —adj. **1** of or relating to the land or its cultivation. **2** relating to landed property. —n. a person who advocates a redistribution of landed property. [L agrarius f. ager agri field]

agree /ə'griː/ v. (**agrees**, **agreed**, **agreeing**) **1** intr. hold a similar opinion (I agree with you about that; they agreed that it would rain). **2** intr. (often foll. by to, or to + infin.) consent (agreed to the arrangement; agreed to go). **3** intr. (often foll. by with) **a** become or be in harmony. **b** suit; be good for (caviar didn't agree with him). **c** Gram. have the same number, gender, case, or person as. **4** *tr.* reach agreement about (*agreed a price*). **5** *tr.* consent to or approve of (terms, a proposal, etc.). **6** *tr.* bring (things, esp. accounts) into harmony. **7** *intr.* (foll. by *on*) decide by mutual consent (*agreed on a compromise*). □**agree to differ** leave a difference of opinion etc. unresolved. **be agreed** have reached the same opinion. [ME f. OF *agreer* ult. f. L *gratus* pleasing]

agreeable /ə'griːəb(ə)l/ *adj.* **1** (often foll. by *to*) pleasing. **2** (often foll. by *to*) (of a person) willing to agree (*was agreeable to going*). **3** (foll. by *to*) conformable. □□ **agreeableness** *n.* **agreeably** *adv.* [ME f. OF *agreable* f. *agreer* AGREE]

agreement /ə'griːmənt/ *n.* **1** the act of agreeing; the holding of the same opinion (*reached agreement*). **2** mutual understanding. **3** an arrangement between parties as to a course of action etc. **4** *Gram.* having the same number, gender, case, or person. **5** a state of being harmonious. [ME f. OF (as AGREE)]

agribusiness /'ægrɪ,bɪznɪs/ *n.* **1** agriculture conducted on strictly commercial principles, esp. using advanced technology. **2** an organization engaged in this. **3** the group of industries dealing with the produce of, and services to, farming. □□ **agribusinessman** /-'bɪznɪsmən/ *n.* (*pl.* -**men**). [AGRICULTURE + BUSINESS]

agriculture /'ægrɪ,kʌltʃə(r)/ *n.* the science or practice of cultivating the soil and rearing animals. □□ **agricultural** /-'kʌltʃər(ə)l/ *adj.* **agriculturalist** /-'kʌltʃərəlɪst/ *n.* **agriculturally** /-'kʌltʃərəlɪ/ *adv.* **agriculturist** /-'kʌltʃərɪst/ *n.* [F *agriculture* or L *agricultura* f. *ager agri* field + *cultura* CULTURE]

agrimony /'ægrɪmənɪ/ *n.* (*pl.* -**ies**) any perennial plant of the genus *Agrimonia*, esp. *A. eupatoria* with small yellow flowers. [ME f. OF *aigremoine* f. L *agrimonia* alt. of *argemonia* f. Gk *argemōnē* poppy]

agro- /'ægrəʊ/ *comb. form* agricultural (*agro-climatic*; *agro-ecological*). [Gk *agros* field]

agrochemical /,ægrəʊ'kemɪk(ə)l/ *n.* a chemical used in agriculture.

agronomy /ə'grɒnəmɪ/ *n.* the science of soil management and crop production. □□ **agronomic** /,ægrə'nɒmɪk/ *adj.* **agronomical** /,ægrə'nɒmɪk(ə)l/ *adj.* **agronomically** /,ægrə'nɒmɪkəlɪ/ *adv.* **agronomist** *n.* [F *agronomie* f. *agronome* agriculturist f. Gk *agros* field + *-nomos* f. *nemō* arrange]

aground /ə'graʊnd/ *predic.adj.* & *adv.* (of a ship) on or on to the bottom of shallow water (*be aground*; *run aground*). [ME f. A² + GROUND¹]

ague /'eɪgjuː/ *n.* **1** *hist.* a malarial fever, with cold, hot, and sweating stages. **2** a shivering fit. □□ **agued** *adj.* **aguish** *adj.* [ME f. OF f. med.L *acuta* (*febris*) acute (fever)]

aguti var. of AGOUTI.

AH *abbr.* in the year of the Hegira (AD 622); of the Muslim era. [L *anno Hegirae*]

ah /ɑː/ *int.* expressing surprise, pleasure, sudden realization, resignation, etc. ¶ The sense depends much on intonation. [ME f. OF *a*]

aha /ɑː'hɑː, ə'hɑː/ *int.* expressing surprise, triumph, mockery, irony, etc. ¶ The sense depends much on intonation. [ME f. AH + HA]

ahead /ə'hed/ *adv.* **1** further forward in space or time. **2** in the lead; further advanced (*ahead on points*). **3** in the line of one's forward motion (*roadworks ahead*). **4** straight forwards. □**ahead of** **1** further forward or advanced than. **2** in the line of the forward motion of. [orig. *Naut.*, f. A² + HEAD]

ahem /ə'həm, ə'hem/ *(not usu. clearly articulated) int.* used to attract attention, gain time, or express disapproval. [lengthened form of HEM²]

ahimsa /ə'hɪmsɑː/ *n.* (in the Hindu, Buddhist, and Jainist tradition) respect for all living things and avoidance of violence towards others both in thought and deed. [Skr. f. *a* without + *himsa* injury]

ahoy /ə'hɔɪ/ *int. Naut.* a call used in hailing. [AH + HOY¹]

à huis clos /ɑː wiː 'kləʊ/ *adv.* in private. [F, = with closed doors]

AI *abbr.* artificial insemination.

ai /'ɑːɪ/ *n.* (*pl.* **ais**) the three-toed sloth of S. America, of the genus *Bradypus*. [Tupi *ai*, repr. its cry]

AID *abbr.* artificial insemination by donor.

aid /eɪd/ *n.* & *v.* —*n.* **1** help. **2** financial or material help, esp. given by one country to another. **3** a material source of help (*teaching aid*). **4** a person or thing that helps. **5** *hist.* a grant of subsidy or tax to a king. —*v.tr.* **1** (often foll. by *to* + infin.) help. **2** promote or encourage (*sleep will aid recovery*). □**in aid of** in support of. **what's this** (or **all this**) **in aid of?** *colloq.* what is the purpose of this? [ME f. OF *aïde*, *aïdier*, ult. f. L *adjuvare* (as AD-, *juvare* *jut*-help)]

-aid /eɪd/ *comb. form* denoting an organization or event that raises money for charity (*school aid*). [20th c.: orig. in *Band Aid*, rock musicians campaigning for famine relief]

aide /eɪd/ *n.* **1** an aide-de-camp. **2** esp. *US* an assistant. **3** an unqualified assistant to a social worker. [abbr.]

aide-de-camp /,eɪd də 'kɑ̃/ *n.* (*pl.* **aides-de-camp** *pronunc.* same) an officer acting as a confidential assistant to a senior officer. [F]

aide-mémoire /,eɪdme'mwɑː(r)/ *n.* (*pl.* **aides-mémoire** *pronunc.* same) **1 a** an aid to the memory. **b** a book or document meant to aid the memory. **2** *Diplomacy* a memorandum. [F f. *aider* to help + *mémoire* memory]

Aids /eɪdz/ *n.* (also **AIDS**) acquired immune deficiency syndrome, an often fatal syndrome caused by a virus transmitted in the blood, marked by severe loss of resistance to infection. □**Aids-related complex** the symptoms of a person affected with the Aids virus without necessarily developing the disease. [abbr.]

aigrette /'eɪgret, eɪ'gret/ *n.* **1** an egret. **2** its white plume. **3** a tuft of feathers or hair. **4** a spray of gems or similar ornament. [F]

aiguille /eɪ'gwiːl/ *n.* a sharp peak of rock, esp. in the Alps. [F: see AGLET]

aiguillette /,eɪgwɪ'let/ *n.* a tagged point hanging from the shoulder on the breast of some uniforms. [F: see AGLET]

AIH *abbr.* artificial insemination by husband.

aikido /'aɪkɪ,dəʊ/ *n.* a Japanese form of self-defence making use of the attacker's own movements without causing injury. [Jap. f. *ai* mutual + *ki* mind + *dō* way]

ail /eɪl/ *v.* **1** *tr. archaic* (only in 3rd person interrog. or indefinite constructions) trouble or afflict in mind or body (*what ails him?*). **2** *intr.* (usu. **be ailing**) be ill. [OE *egl(i)an* f. *egle* troublesome]

ailanthus /eɪ'lænθəs/ *n.* a tall deciduous tree of the genus *Ailanthus*, esp. *A. altissima*, native to China and Australasia. [mod.L *ailantus* f. Ambonese *aylanto*]

aileron /'eɪlə,rɒn/ *n.* a hinged surface in the trailing edge of an aeroplane wing, used to control lateral balance. [F, dimin. of *aile* wing f. L *ala*]

ailing /'eɪlɪŋ/ *adj.* **1** ill, esp. chronically. **2** in poor condition.

ailment /'eɪlmənt/ *n.* an illness, esp. a minor one.

aim /eɪm/ *v.* & *n.* —*v.* **1** *intr.* (foll. by *at* + verbal noun, or *to* + infin.) intend or try (*aim at winning*; *aim to win*). **2** *tr.* (usu. foll. by *at*) direct or point (a weapon, remark, etc.). **3** *intr.* take aim. **4** *intr.* (foll. by *at, for*) seek to attain or achieve. —*n.* **1** a purpose, a design, an object aimed at. **2** the directing of a weapon, missile, etc., at an object. □**take aim** direct a weapon etc. at an object. [ME f. OF ult. f. L *aestimare* reckon]

aimless /'eɪmlɪs/ *adj.* without aim or purpose. □□ **aimlessly** *adv.* **aimlessness** *n.*

ain't /eɪnt/ *contr. colloq.* **1** am not; are not; is not (*you ain't doing it right*; *she ain't nice*). **2** has not; have not (*we ain't seen him*). ¶ Usually regarded as an uneducated use, and unacceptable in spoken and written English, except to represent dialect speech. [contr. of *are not*]

air /eə(r)/ *n. & v.* —*n.* **1** an invisible gaseous substance surrounding the earth, a mixture mainly of oxygen and nitrogen. **2 a** the earth's atmosphere. **b** the free or unconfined space in the atmosphere (*birds of the air; in the open air*). **c** the atmosphere as a place where aircraft operate. **3 a** a distinctive impression or characteristic (*an air of absurdity*). **b** one's manner or bearing, esp. a confident one (*with a triumphant air; does things with an air*). **c** (esp. in *pl.*) an affected manner; pretentiousness (*gave himself airs; airs and graces*). **4** *Mus.* a tune or melody; a melodious composition. **5** a breeze or light wind. —*v.tr.* **1** warm (washed laundry) to remove damp, esp. at a fire or in a heated cupboard. **2** expose (a room etc.) to the open air; ventilate. **3** express publicly (an opinion, grievance, etc.). **4** parade; show ostentatiously (esp. qualities). **5** *refl.* go out in the fresh air. □**air bag** a safety device that fills with air on impact to protect the occupants of a vehicle in a collision. **air-bed** an inflatable mattress. **air-bladder** a bladder or sac filled with air in fish or some plants (cf. *swim-bladder*). **air brake 1** a brake worked by air pressure. **2** a movable flap or other device on an aircraft to reduce its speed. **air-brick** a brick perforated with small holes for ventilation. **air-bridge** a portable bridge or walkway put against an aircraft door. **Air Chief Marshal** an RAF officer of high rank, below Marshal of the RAF and above Air Marshal. **Air Commodore** an RAF officer next above Group Captain. **air-conditioned** (of a room, building, etc.) equipped with air-conditioning. **air-conditioner** an air-conditioning apparatus. **air-conditioning 1** a system for regulating the humidity, ventilation, and temperature in a building. **2** the apparatus for this. **air-cooled** cooled by means of a current of air. **air corridor** = CORRIDOR 4. **air-cushion 1** an inflatable cushion. **2** the layer of air supporting a hovercraft or similar vehicle. **air force** a branch of the armed forces concerned with fighting or defence in the air. **air-hostess** a stewardess in a passenger aircraft. **air lane** a path or course regularly used by aircraft (cf. LANE 4). **air letter** a sheet of light paper forming a letter for sending by airmail. **air line** a pipe supplying air, esp. to a diver. **Air Marshal** an RAF officer of high rank, below Air Chief Marshal and above Air Vice-Marshal. **Air Officer** any RAF officer above the rank of Group Captain. **air plant** a plant growing naturally without soil. **air pocket** an apparent vacuum in the air causing an aircraft to drop suddenly. **air power** the ability to defend and attack by means of aircraft, missiles, etc. **air pump** a device for pumping air into or out of a vessel. **air raid** an attack by aircraft. **air rifle** a rifle using compressed air to propel pellets. **air sac** an extension of the lungs in birds or the tracheae in insects. **air-sea rescue** rescue from the sea by aircraft. **air speed** the speed of an aircraft relative to the air through which it is moving. **air terminal** a building in a city or town to which passengers report and which serves as a base for transport to and from an airport. **air time** time allotted for a broadcast. **air-to-air** from one aircraft to another in flight. **air traffic controller** an airport official who controls air traffic by giving radio instructions to pilots concerning route, altitude, take-off, and landing. **Air Vice-Marshal** an RAF officer of high rank, just below Air Marshal. **air waves** *colloq.* radio waves used in broadcasting. **by air** by aircraft; in an aircraft. **in the air 1** (of opinions or feelings) prevalent; gaining currency. **2** (of projects etc.) uncertain, not decided. **on** (or **off**) **the air** in (or not in) the process of broadcasting. **take the air** go out of doors. **tread** (or **walk**) **on air** feel elated. [ME f. F and L f. Gk *aēr*]

airbase /'eəbeɪs/ *n.* a base for the operation of military aircraft.

airborne /'eəbɔːn/ *adj.* **1** transported by air. **2** (of aircraft) in the air after taking off.

airbrush /'eəbrʌʃ/ *n. & v.* —*n.* an artist's device for spraying paint by means of compressed air. —*v.tr.* paint with an airbrush.

Airbus /'eəbʌs/ *n. propr.* a passenger aircraft serving routes of relatively short distance.

aircraft /'eəkrɑːft/ *n.* (*pl.* **aircraft**) a machine capable of flight, esp. an aeroplane or helicopter. □**aircraft-carrier** a warship that carries and serves as a base for aeroplanes.

aircraftman /'eəˌkrɑːftmən/ *n.* (*pl.* **-men**) the lowest rank in the RAF.

aircraftwoman /'eəkrɑːftˌwʊmən/ *n.* (*pl.* **-women**) the lowest rank in the WRAF.

aircrew /'eəkruː/ *n.* **1** the crew manning an aircraft. **2** (*pl.* **aircrew**) a member of such a crew.

Airedale /'eədeɪl/ *n.* **1** a large terrier of a rough-coated breed. **2** this breed. [*Airedale* in Yorkshire]

airer /'eərə(r)/ *n.* a frame or stand for airing or drying clothes etc.

airfield /'eəfiːld/ *n.* an area of land where aircraft take off and land, are maintained, etc.

airfoil /'eəfɔɪl/ *n.* US = AEROFOIL. [AIR + FOIL²]

airframe /'eəfreɪm/ *n.* the body of an aircraft as distinct from its engine(s).

airglow /'eəgləʊ/ *n.* radiation from the upper atmosphere, detectable at night.

airgun /'eəgʌn/ *n.* a gun using compressed air to propel pellets.

airhead /'eəhed/ *n.* **1** *Mil.* a forward base for aircraft in enemy territory. **2** esp. *US sl.* a silly or foolish person.

airing /'eərɪŋ/ *n.* **1** exposure to fresh air, esp. for exercise or an excursion. **2** exposure (of laundry etc.) to warm air. **3** public expression of an opinion etc. (*the idea will get an airing at tomorrow's meeting*).

airless /'eəlɪs/ *adj.* **1** stuffy; not ventilated. **2** without wind or breeze; still. □□ **airlessness** *n.*

airlift /'eəlɪft/ *n. & v.* —*n.* the transport of troops and supplies by air, esp. in a blockade or other emergency. —*v.tr.* transport in this way.

airline /'eəlaɪn/ *n.* an organization providing a regular public service of air transport on one or more routes.

airliner /'eəˌlaɪnə(r)/ *n.* a large passenger aircraft.

airlock /'eəlɒk/ *n.* **1** a stoppage of the flow in a pump or pipe, caused by an air bubble. **2** a compartment with controlled pressure and parallel sets of doors, to permit movement between areas at different pressures.

airmail /'eəmeɪl/ *n. & v.* —*n.* **1** a system of transporting mail by air. **2** mail carried by air. —*v.tr.* send by airmail.

airman /'eəmən/ *n.* (*pl.* **-men**) **1** a pilot or member of the crew of an aircraft, esp. in an air force. **2** a member of the RAF below commissioned rank.

airmiss /'eəmɪs/ *n.* a circumstance in which two or more aircraft in flight on different routes are less than a prescribed distance apart.

airmobile /eə'məʊbaɪl/ *adj.* (of troops) that can be moved about by air.

airplane /'eəpleɪn/ *n.* US = AEROPLANE.

airplay /'eəpleɪ/ *n.* broadcasting (of recorded music).

airport /'eəpɔːt/ *n.* a complex of runways and buildings for the take-off, landing, and maintenance of civil aircraft, with facilities for passengers.

airscrew /'eəskruː/ *n.* Brit. an aircraft propeller.

airship /'eəʃɪp/ *n.* a power-driven aircraft that is lighter than air.

airsick /'eəsɪk/ *adj.* affected with nausea due to travel in an aircraft. □□ **airsickness** *n.*

airspace /'eəspeɪs/ *n.* the air available to aircraft to fly in, esp. the part subject to the jurisdiction of a particular country.

airstrip /ˈeəstrɪp/ n. a strip of ground suitable for the take-off and landing of aircraft.

airtight /ˈeətaɪt/ adj. not allowing air to pass through.

airway /ˈeəweɪ/ n. **1 a** a recognized route followed by aircraft. **b** (often in pl.) = AIRLINE. **2** a ventilating passage in a mine.

airwoman /ˈeəˌwʊmən/ n. (pl. -women) **1** a woman pilot or member of the crew of an aircraft, esp. in an air force. **2** a member of the WRAF below commissioned rank.

airworthy /ˈeəˌwɜːðɪ/ adj. (of an aircraft) fit to fly.

airy /ˈeərɪ/ adj. (**airier**, **airiest**) **1** well-ventilated, breezy. **2** flippant, superficial. **3 a** light as air. **b** graceful, delicate. **4** insubstantial, ethereal, immaterial. □ **airy-fairy** colloq. unrealistic, impractical, foolishly idealistic. □□ **airily** adv. **airiness** n.

aisle /aɪl/ n. **1** part of a church, esp. one parallel to and divided by pillars from the nave, choir, or transept. **2** a passage between rows of pews, seats, etc. □□ **aisled** adj. [ME ele, ile f. OF ele f. L ala wing: confused with island and F aile wing]

ait /eɪt/ n. (also **eyot**) Brit. a small island, esp. in a river. [OE iggath etc. f. īeg ISLAND + dimin. suffix]

aitch /eɪtʃ/ n. the name of the letter H. □ **drop one's aitches** fail to pronounce the initial h in words. [ME f. OF ache]

aitchbone /ˈeɪtʃbəʊn/ n. **1** the buttock or rump bone. **2** a cut of beef lying over this. [ME nage-, nache-bone buttock, ult. f. L natis, -es buttock(s): for loss of n cf. ADDER, APRON]

ajar[1] /əˈdʒɑː(r)/ adv. & predic.adj. (of a door) slightly open. [A² + obs. char f. OE cerr a turn]

ajar[2] /əˈdʒɑː(r)/ adv. out of harmony. [A² + JAR²]

ajutage var. of ADJUTAGE.

AK abbr. US Alaska (in official postal use).

a.k.a. abbr. also known as.

akee var. of ACKEE.

akela /ɑːˈkeɪlə/ n. the adult leader of a group of Cub Scouts. [name of the leader of a wolf-pack in Kipling's Jungle Book]

akimbo /əˈkɪmbəʊ/ adv. (of the arms) with hands on the hips and elbows turned outwards. [ME in kenebowe, prob. f. ON]

akin /əˈkɪn/ predic.adj. **1** related by blood. **2** of similar or kindred character. [A-¹ + KIN]

Akkadian /əˈkeɪdɪən/ (also **Accadian**) adj. & n. hist. —adj. of Akkad in ancient Babylonia. —n. **1** the Semitic language of Akkad. **2** an inhabitant of Akkad.

akvavit var. of AQUAVIT.

AL abbr. US Alabama (in official postal use).

Al symb. Chem. the element aluminium.

al- /æl, əl/ prefix assim. form of AD- before l.

-al /əl/ suffix **1** forming adjectives meaning 'relating to, of the kind of': **a** from Latin or Greek words (central; regimental; colossal; tropical) (cf. -IAL, -ICAL). **b** from English nouns (tidal). **2** forming nouns, esp. of verbal action (animal; rival; arrival; proposal; trial). [sense 1 f. F -el or L -alis adj. suffix rel. to -aris (-AR¹); sense 2 f. F -aille or f. (or after) L -alis etc. used as noun]

Ala. abbr. Alabama.

à la /ˈɑː lɑː/ prep. after the manner of (à la russe). [F, f. À LA MODE]

alabaster /ˈæləˌbɑːstə(r), -ˌbæstə(r), ˌæləˈb-/ n. & adj. —n. a translucent usu. white form of gypsum, often carved into ornaments. —adj. **1** of alabaster. **2** like alabaster in whiteness or smoothness. □□ **alabastrine** /-ˈbɑːstrɪn, -ˈbæstrɪn, -aɪn/ adj. [ME f. OF alabastre f. L alabaster, -trum, f. Gk alabast(r)os]

à la carte /ˈɑː lɑː ˈkɑːt/ adv. & adj. ordered as separately priced item(s) from a menu, not as part of a set meal. [F]

alack /əˈlæk/ int. (also **alack-a-day** /əˈlækəˌdeɪ/) archaic an expression of regret or surprise. [prob. f. AH + LACK]

alacrity /əˈlækrɪtɪ/ n. briskness or cheerful readiness. [L alacritas f. alacer brisk]

Aladdin's cave /əˈlædɪnz/ n. a place of great riches. [Aladdin in the Arabian Nights' Entertainments]

Aladdin's lamp /əˈlædɪnz/ n. a talisman enabling its holder to gratify any wish.

à la mode /ˌɑː lɑː ˈməʊd/ adv. & adj. **1** in fashion; fashionable. **2 a** (of beef) braised in wine. **b** US served with ice-cream. [F, = in the fashion]

alar /ˈeɪlə(r)/ adj. **1** relating to wings. **2** winglike or wing-shaped. **3** axillary. [L alaris f. ala wing]

alarm /əˈlɑːm/ n. & v. —n. **1** a warning of danger etc. (gave the alarm). **2 a** a warning sound or device (the burglar alarm was set off accidentally). **b** = alarm clock. **3** frightened expectation of danger or difficulty (were filled with alarm). —v.tr. **1** frighten or disturb. **2** arouse to a sense of danger. □ **alarm clock** a clock with a device that can be made to sound at the time set in advance. [ME f. OF alarme f. It. allarme f. all'arme! to arms]

alarming /əˈlɑːmɪŋ/ adj. disturbing, frightening. □□ **alarmingly** adv.

alarmist /əˈlɑːmɪst/ n. & adj. —n. a person given to spreading needless alarm. —adj. creating needless alarm. □□ **alarmism** n.

alarum /əˈlɑːrəm/ n. archaic = ALARM. □ **alarums and excursions** joc. confused noise and bustle.

Alas. abbr. Alaska.

alas /əˈlæs, əˈlɑːs/ int. an expression of grief, pity, or concern. [ME f. OF a las(se) f. a ah + las(se) f. L lassus weary]

Alaska /əˈlæskə/ n. □ **baked Alaska** sponge cake and ice-cream in a meringue covering. [name of a State of the US]

alate /ˈeɪleɪt/ adj. having wings or winglike appendages. [L alatus f. ala wing]

alb /ælb/ n. a white vestment reaching to the feet, worn by some Christian priests at church ceremonies. [OE albe f. eccl.L alba fem. of L albus white]

albacore /ˈælbəˌkɔː(r)/ n. **1** a long-finned tunny, Thunnus alalunga. Also called GERMON. **2** any of various other related fish. [Port. albacor, -cora, f. Arab. al the + bakr young camel or bakūr premature, precocious]

Albanian /ælˈbeɪnɪən/ n. & adj. —n. **1 a** a native or national of Albania in SE Europe. **b** a person of Albanian descent. **2** the language of Albania. —adj. of or relating to Albania or its people or language.

albata /ælˈbɑːtə/ n. German silver; an alloy of nickel, copper, and zinc. [L albata whitened f. albus white]

albatross /ˈælbəˌtrɒs/ n. **1 a** any long-winged stout-bodied bird of the family Diomedeidae related to petrels, inhabiting the Pacific and Southern Oceans. **b** a source of frustration or guilt; an encumbrance. **2** Brit. Golf a score of three strokes under par at any hole. [alt. (after L albus white) of 17th-c. alcatras, applied to various sea-birds, f. Sp. and Port. alcatraz, var. of Port. alcatruz f. Arab. alḳādūs the pitcher]

albedo /ælˈbiːdəʊ/ n. (pl. -os) the proportion of light or radiation reflected by a surface, esp. of a planet or moon. [eccl.L, = whiteness, f. L albus white]

albeit /ɔːlˈbiːɪt/ conj. literary though (he tried, albeit without success).

albert /ˈælbət/ n. a watch-chain with a bar at one end for attaching to a buttonhole. [Prince Albert, consort of Queen Victoria, d. 1861]

albescent /ælˈbesənt/ adj. growing or shading into white. [L albescere albescent- f. albus white]

Albigenses /ˌælbɪˈdʒensiːz/ n.pl. the members of a heretic sect in S. France in the 12th–13th c. □□ **Albigensian** adj. [L f. Albi in S. France]

albino /ælˈbiːnəʊ/ n. (pl. -os) **1** a person or animal having a congenital absence of pigment in the skin and hair (which are white), and the eyes (which are usu. pink). **2** a plant lacking normal colouring. □□ **albinism** /ˈælbɪˌnɪzəm/ n. **albinotic** /ˌælbɪˈnɒtɪk/ adj. [Sp. & Port. (orig. of White Negroes) f. albo L f. albus white + -ino = -INE¹]

Albion /ˈælbɪən/ n. (also **perfidious Albion**) Britain or England. [OE f. L f. Celt. Albio (unrecorded): F la *perfide Albion* with ref. to alleged treachery to other nations]

albite /'ælbaɪt/ *n. Mineral.* a feldspar, usu. white, rich in sodium. [L *albus* white + -ITE[1]]

album /'ælbəm/ *n.* **1** a blank book for the insertion of photographs, stamps, etc. **2 a** a long-playing gramophone record. **b** a set of these. [L, = a blank tablet, neut. of *albus* white]

albumen /'ælbjʊmɪn/ *n.* **1** egg-white. **2** *Bot.* the substance found between the skin and germ of many seeds, usu. the edible part; = ENDOSPERM. [L *albumen -minis* white of egg f. *albus* white]

albumin /'ælbjʊmɪn/ *n.* any of a class of water-soluble proteins found in egg-white, milk, blood, etc. ▫▫ **albuminous** /æl'bju:mɪnəs/ *adj.* [F *albumine* f. L *albumin-*: see ALBUMEN]

albuminoid /æl'bju:mɪˌnɔɪd/ *n.* = SCLERO-PROTEIN.

albuminuria /ˌælbju:mɪˈnjʊərɪə/ *n.* the presence of albumin in the urine, usu. as a symptom of kidney disease.

alburnum /æl'bɜ:nəm/ *n.* = SAPWOOD. [L f. *albus* white]

alcahest var. of ALKAHEST.

alcaic /æl'keɪɪk/ *adj. & n. —adj.* of the verse metre invented by Alcaeus, lyric poet of Mytilene *c.*600 BC, occurring in four-line stanzas. *—n.* (in *pl.*) alcaic verses. [LL *alcaicus* f. Gk *alkaikos* f. *Alkaios* Alcaeus]

alcalde /ɑːlˈkɑːldeɪ/ *n.* a magistrate or mayor in a Spanish, Portuguese, or Latin American town. [Sp. f. Arab. *al-ḳāḍī* the judge: see CADI]

alchemy /'ælkəmɪ/ *n.* (*pl.* **-ies**) **1** the medieval forerunner of chemistry, esp. seeking to turn base metals into gold or silver. **2** a miraculous trans-formation or the means of achieving this. ▫▫ **alchemic** /æl'kemɪk/ *adj.* **alchemical** /æl 'kemɪk(ə)l/ *adj.* **alchemist** *n.* **alchemize** *v.tr.* (also **-ise**). [ME f. OF *alkemie, alkamie* f. med.L *al-chimia, -emia,* f. Arab. *alkīmiyā'* f. *al* the + *kīmiyā'* f. Gk *khēmia, -meia* art of transmuting metals]

alcheringa /ˌæltʃəˈrɪŋɡə/ *n.* (in the mythology of some Australian Aboriginals) the 'golden age' when the first ancestors were created. [Aboriginal, = dream-time]

alcohol /'ælkəˌhɒl/ *n.* **1** (in full **ethyl alcohol**) a colourless volatile inflammable liquid forming the intoxicating element in wine, beer, spirits, etc., and also used as a solvent, as fuel, etc. Also called ETHANOL. ¶ Chem. formula: C_2H_5OH. **2** any liquor containing this. **3** *Chem.* any of a large class of organic compounds that contain one or more hy-droxyl groups attached to carbon atoms. [F or med.L f. Arab. *al-kuḥl* f. *al* the + *kuḥl* KOHL]

alcoholic /ˌælkəˈhɒlɪk/ *adj. & n. —adj.* of, relating to, containing, or caused by alcohol. *—n.* a person suffering from alcoholism.

alcoholism /'ælkəhɒˌlɪz(ə)m/ *n.* **1** an addiction to the consumption of alcoholic liquor. **2** the diseased condition resulting from this. [mod.L *alcoholismus* (as ALCOHOL)]

alcoholometer /ˌælkəhɒˈlɒmɪtə(r)/ *n.* an instrument for measuring alcoholic concentration. ▫▫ **alcoholometry** *n.*

alcove /'ælkəʊv/ *n.* a recess, esp. in the wall of a room or of a garden. [F f. Sp. *alcoba* f. Arab. *al-ḳubba* f. *al* the + *ḳubba* vault]

aldehyde /'ældɪˌhaɪd/ *n. Chem.* any of a class of compounds formed by the oxidation of alcohols (and containing the group −CHO). ▫▫ **aldehydic** /ˌældɪ 'hɪdɪk/ *adj.* [abbr. of mod.L *alcohol dehydrogenatum* alcohol deprived of hydrogen]

al dente /æl 'dentɪ/ *adj.* (of pasta etc.) cooked so as to be still firm when bitten. [It., lit. 'to the tooth']

alder /'ɔ:ldə(r)/ *n.* any tree of the genus *Alnus,* related to the birch, with catkins and toothed leaves. ▫ **alder buckthorn** a shrub, *Frangula alnus,* related to the buckthorn. [OE *alor, aler,* rel. to L *alnus,* with euphonic *d*]

alderman /'ɔ:ldəmən/ *n.* (*pl.* **-men**) **1** esp. *hist.* a co-opted member of an English county or borough council, next in dignity to the Mayor. **2** *US & Austral.* the elected governor of a city. ▫▫ **aldermanic** /-'mænɪk/ *adj.* **aldermanship** *n.* [OE *aldor* patriarch f. *ald* old + MAN]

Aldis lamp /'ɔ:ldɪs/ *n.* a hand lamp for signalling in Morse code. [A. C. W. *Aldis,* its inventor]

aldrin /'ældrɪn/ *n.* a white crystalline chlorinated hydrocarbon used as an insecticide. [K. *Alder,* Ger. chemist d. 1958 + -IN]

ale /eɪl/ *n.* beer (usu. as a trade word). [OE *alu,* = ON *öl*]

aleatoric /ˌeɪlɪəˈtɒrɪk/ *adj.* **1** depending on the throw of a die or on chance. **2** *Mus. & Art* involving random choice by a performer or artist. [L *aleatorius aleator* dice-player f. *alea* die]

aleatory /'eɪlɪətərɪ/ *adj.* = ALEATORIC. [as ALEATORIC]

alec /'ælɪk/ *n.* (also **aleck**) *Austral. sl.* a stupid person. [shortening of SMART ALEC]

alee /əˈliː/ *adv. & predic.adj.* **1** on the lee or sheltered side of a ship. **2** to leeward. [ME, f. A[2] + LEE]

alehouse /'eɪlhaʊs/ *n. hist.* a tavern.

alembic /əˈlembɪk/ *n.* **1** *hist.* an apparatus formerly used in distilling. **2** a means of refining or extracting. [ME f. OF f. med.L *alembicus* f. Arab. *al-'anbīḳ* f. *al* the + *'anbīḳ* still f. Gk *ambix, -ikos* cup, cap of a still]

aleph /'ɑ:lef/ *n.* the first letter of the Hebrew alphabet. [Heb. *'ālep,* lit. 'ox']

alert /ə'lɜ:t/ *adj., n., & v. —adj.* **1** watchful or vigilant; ready to take action. **2** nimble (esp. of mental faculties); attentive. *—n.* **1** a warning call or alarm. **2 a** warning of an air raid. **b** the duration of this. *—v.tr.* (often foll. by *to*) make alert; warn (*were alerted to the danger*). ▫ **on the alert** on the lookout against danger or attack. ▫▫ **alertly** *adv.* **alertness** *n.* [F *alerte* f. It. *all' erta* to the watch-tower]

-ales /'eɪliz/ *suffix* forming the plural names of orders of plants (*Rosales*). [pl. of L adj. suffix *-alis*: see -AL]

aleuron /ə'ljʊərən/ *n.* (also **aleurone** /-rəʊn/) *Biochem.* a protein found as granules in the seeds of plants etc. [Gk *aleuron* flour]

A level /eɪ/ *n. Brit.* = *advanced level* (see ADVANCE).

alewife /'eɪlwaɪf/ *n.* (*pl.* **alewives**) *US* any of several species of fish allied to the herring. [corrupt. of 17th-c. *aloofe*: orig. uncert.]

alexanders /ˌælɪɡ'zɑːndəz/ *n.* an umbelliferous plant, *Smyrnium olusatrum,* formerly used in salads but superseded by celery. [OE f. med.L *alexandrum*]

Alexander technique /ˌælɪɡ'zɑːndə(r)/ *n.* a tech-nique for controlling posture as an aid to improved well-being. [F. M. *Alexander,* physiotherapist d. 1955]

Alexandrian /ˌælɪɡ'zɑːndrɪən/ *adj.* **1** of or char-acteristic of Alexandria in Egypt. **2 a** belonging to or akin to the schools of literature and philosophy of Alexandria. **b** (of a writer) derivative or imitative; fond of recondite learning.

alexandrine /ˌælɪɡ'zændraɪn/ *adj. & n. —adj.* (of a line of verse) having six iambic feet. *—n.* an alexandrine line. [F *alexandrin* f. *Alexandre* Al-exander (the Great), the subject of an Old French poem in this metre]

alexandrite /ˌælɪɡ'zɑːndraɪt/ *n. Mineral.* a green variety of chrysoberyl. [Tsar *Alexander* I of Russia + -ITE[1]]

alexia /ə'leksɪə/ *n.* the inability to see words or to read, caused by a condition of the brain. [mod.L, A-[1] + Gk *lexis* speech f. *legein* to speak, confused with L *legere* to read]

alfalfa /æl'fælfə/ *n.* a leguminous plant, *Medicago sativa,* with clover-like leaves and flowers used for fodder. Also called LUCERNE. [Sp. f. Arab. *al-faṣfaṣa,* a green fodder]

alfresco /æl'freskəʊ/ *adv. & adj.* in the open air (*we lunched alfresco; an alfresco lunch*). [It. *al fresco* in the fresh (air)]

alga /'ælɡə/ *n.* (*pl.* **algae** /'ældʒiː, 'ælɡiː/) (usu. in *pl.*) a non-flowering stemless water-plant, esp. seaweed and phytoplankton. □□ **algal** *adj.* **algoid** *adj.* [L]

algebra /'ældʒɪbrə/ *n.* **1** the branch of mathematics that uses letters and other general symbols to represent numbers and quantities in formulae and equations. **2** a system of this based on given axioms (*linear algebra*; *the algebra of logic*). □□ **algebraic** /ˌældʒɪ'breɪɪk/ *adj.* **algebraical** /ˌældʒɪ'breɪɪkəl/ *adj.* **algebraically** /ˌældʒɪ'breɪɪkəlɪ/ *adv.* **algebraist** /ˌældʒɪ'breɪɪst/ *n.* [It. & Sp. & med.L, f. Arab. *al-jabr* f. *al* the + *jabr* reunion of broken parts f. *jabara* reunite]

-algia /'ældʒə/ *comb. form Med.* denoting pain in a part specified by the first element (*neuralgia*). □□ **-algic** *comb. form* forming adjectives. [Gk f. *algos* pain]

algicide /'ældʒɪˌsaɪd/ *n.* a preparation for destroying algae.

algid /'ældʒɪd/ *adj. Med.* cold, chilly. □□ **algidity** /æl'dʒɪdɪtɪ/ *n.* [L *algidus* f. *algēre* be cold]

alginate /'ældʒɪˌneɪt/ *n.* a salt or ester of alginic acid. [ALGA + -IN + -ATE[1]]

alginic acid /æl'dʒɪnɪk/ *n.* an insoluble carbohydrate found (chiefly as salts) in many brown seaweeds. [ALGA + -IN + -IC]

algoid see ALGA.

Algol /'ælgɒl/ *n.* a high-level computer programming language. [ALGORITHMIC (see ALGORITHM) + LANGUAGE]

algolagnia /ˌælgə'lægnɪə/ *n.* sexual pleasure got from inflicting pain on oneself or others; masochism or sadism. □□ **algolagnic** *adj.* & *n.* [mod.L f. G *Algolagnie* f. Gk *algos* pain + *lagneia* lust]

algology /æl'gɒlədʒɪ/ *n.* the study of algae. □□ **algological** /-'lɒdʒɪk(ə)l/ *adj.* **algologist** *n.*

Algonquian /æl'gɒŋkwɪən/ *adj.* & *n.* (also **Algonkian** /-kɪən/) —*adj.* of or relating to a large group of N. American Indian tribes. —*n.* **1** a member of any of these tribes. **2** any of the languages or dialects used by them. [*Algonquin* people + -IAN]

algorithm /'ælgəˌrɪð(ə)m/ *n.* (also **algorism** /'ælgəˌrɪz(ə)m/) **1** *Math.* a process or set of rules used for calculation or problem-solving, esp. with a computer. **2** the Arabic or decimal notation of numbers. □□ **algorithmic** /ˌælgə'rɪðmɪk/ *adj.* [*algorism* ME ult. f. Pers. *al-Ḵuwārizmī* 9th-c. mathematician: *algorithm* infl. by Gk *arithmos* number (cf. F *algorithme*)]

alguacil /ˌælgwə'sɪl, 'ælgwəsɪl/ *n.* (also **alguazil** /ˌælgwə'zɪl, 'ælgwəzɪl/) **1** a mounted official at a bullfight. **2** a constable or an officer of justice in Spain or Spanish-speaking countries. [Sp. f. Arab. *al-wazīr* f. *al* the + *wazir*: see VIZIER]

alias /'eɪlɪəs/ *adv.* & *n.* —*adv.* also named or known as. —*n.* a false or assumed name. [L, = at another time, otherwise]

alibi /'ælɪˌbaɪ/ *n.* & *v.* —*n.* **1** a claim, or the evidence supporting it, that when an alleged act took place one was elsewhere. **2** *disp.* an excuse of any kind; a pretext or justification. —*v.* (**alibis, alibied, alibiing**) *colloq.* **1** *tr.* provide an alibi or offer an excuse for (a person). **2** *intr.* provide an alibi. [L, = elsewhere]

alicyclic /ˌælɪ'saɪklɪk/ *adj. Chem.* of, denoting, or relating to organic compounds combining a cyclic structure with aliphatic properties, e.g. cyclohexane. [G *alicyclisch* (as ALIPHATIC, CYCLIC)]

alidade /'ælɪˌdeɪd/ *n. Surveying* & *Astron.* an instrument for determining directions or measuring angles. [F f. med.L f. Arab. *al-'idāda* the revolving radius f. *'aḍud* upper arm]

alien /'eɪlɪən/ *adj.* & *n.* —*adj.* **1 a** (often foll. by *to*) unfamiliar; not in accordance or harmony; unfriendly; hostile; unacceptable or repugnant (*army discipline was alien to him*; *struck an alien note*). **b** (often foll. by *from*) different or separated. **2** foreign; from a foreign country (*help from alien powers*). **3** of or relating to beings supposedly from other worlds.

4 *Bot.* (of a plant) introduced from elsewhere and naturalized in its new home. —*n.* **1** a foreigner, esp. one who is not a naturalized citizen of the country where he or she is living. **2** a being from another world. **3** *Bot.* an alien plant. □□ **alienness** *n.* [ME f. OF f. L *alienus* belonging to another (*alius*)]

alienable /'eɪlɪənəb(ə)l/ *adj. Law* able to be transferred to new ownership. □□ **alienability** /-'bɪlɪtɪ/ *n.*

alienage /'eɪlɪənɪdʒ/ *n.* the state or condition of being an alien.

alienate /'eɪlɪəˌneɪt/ *v.tr.* **1 a** cause (a person) to become unfriendly or hostile. **b** (often foll. by *from*) cause (a person) to feel isolated or estranged from (friends, society, etc.). **2** transfer ownership of (property) to another person etc. □□ **alienator** *n.* [ME f. L *alienare alienat-* (as ALIEN)]

alienation /ˌeɪlɪə'neɪʃ(ə)n/ *n.* **1** the act or result of alienating. **2** (*Theatr.* **alienation effect**) a dramatic effect whereby an audience remains objective, not identifying with the characters or action of a play.

alienist /'eɪlɪənɪst/ *n. US* a psychiatrist, esp. a legal adviser on psychiatric problems. [F *aliéniste* (as ALIEN)]

aliform /'eɪlɪˌfɔːm/ *adj.* wing-shaped. [mod.L *aliformis* f. L *ala* wing: see -FORM]

alight[1] /ə'laɪt/ *v.intr.* **1 a** (often foll. by *from*) descend from a vehicle. **b** dismount from a horse. **2** descend and settle; come to earth from the air. **3** (foll. by *on*) find by chance; notice. [OE *ālīhtan* (as A-[2], *līhtan* LIGHT[2] *v.*)]

alight[2] /ə'laɪt/ *predic.adj.* **1** on fire; burning (*they set the old shed alight*; *is the fire still alight?*). **2** lighted up; excited (*eyes alight with expectation*). [ME, prob. f. phr. *on a light* (= lighted) *fire*]

align /ə'laɪn/ *v.tr.* **1** put in a straight line or bring into line (*three books were neatly aligned on the shelf*). **2** esp. *Polit.* (usu. foll. by *with*) bring (oneself etc.) into agreement or alliance with (a cause, policy, political party, etc.). □□ **alignment** *n.* [F *aligner* f. phr. *à ligne* into line: see LINE[1]]

alike /ə'laɪk/ *adj.* & *adv.* —*adj.* (usu. *predic.*) similar, like one another; indistinguishable. —*adv.* in a similar way or manner (*all were treated alike*). [ME f. OE *gelīc* and ON *glíkr* (LIKE[1])]

aliment /'ælɪmənt/ *n. formal* **1** food. **2** support or mental sustenance. □□ **alimental** /ˌælɪ'ment(ə)l/ *adj.* [ME f. F *aliment* or L *alimentum* f. *alere* nourish]

alimentary /ˌælɪ'mentərɪ/ *adj.* of, relating to, or providing nourishment or sustenance. □ **alimentary canal** *Anat.* the passage along which food is passed from the mouth to the anus during digestion. [L *alimentarius* (as ALIMENT)]

alimentation /ˌælɪmen'teɪʃ(ə)n/ *n.* **1** nourishment; feeding. **2** maintenance, support; supplying with the necessities of life. [F *alimentation* or med.L *alimentatio* f. *alimentare* (as ALIMENT)]

alimony /'ælɪmənɪ/ *n.* the money payable by a man to his wife or former wife or by a woman to her husband or former husband after they are separated or divorced. ¶ In UK use replaced by *maintenance*. [L *alimonia* nutriment f. *alere* nourish]

A-line /'eɪlaɪn/ *adj.* (of a garment) having a narrow waist or shoulders and somewhat flared skirt.

aliphatic /ˌælɪ'fætɪk/ *adj. Chem.* of, denoting, or relating to organic compounds in which carbon atoms form open chains, not aromatic rings. [Gk *aleiphar -atos* fat]

aliquot /'ælɪˌkwɒt/ *adj.* & *n.* —*adj.* (of a part or portion) contained by the whole an integral or whole number of times (*4 is an aliquot part of 12*). —*n.* **1** an aliquot part; an integral factor. **2** (in general use) any known fraction of a whole; a sample. [F *aliquote* f. L *aliquot* some, so many]

alive /ə'laɪv/ *adj.* (usu. *predic.*) **1** (of a person, animal, plant, etc.) living, not dead. **2 a** (of a thing) existing; continuing; in operation or action (*kept his interest alive*). **b** under discussion; provoking interest (*the topic is still very much alive today*). **3** (of a person or animal) lively, active. **4** charged with an electric current; connected to a source of electricity. **5** (foll. by *to*) aware of; alert or responsive to. **6** (foll. by *with*) **a** swarming or teeming with. **b** full of. □**alive and kicking** *colloq.* very active; lively. **alive and well** still alive or active (esp. despite contrary assumptions or rumours). □□**aliveness** *n.* [OE *on life* (as A², LIFE)]

alizarin /ə'lɪzərɪn/ *n.* **1** the red colouring matter of madder root, used in dyeing. **2** (*attrib.*) (of a dye) derived from or similar to this pigment. [F *alizarine* f. *alizari* madder f. Arab. *al-'iṣara* pressed juice f. *'aṣara* to press fruit]

alkahest /'ælkə,hest/ *n.* (also **alcahest**) the universal solvent sought by alchemists. [sham Arab., prob. invented by Paracelsus]

alkali /'ælkə,laɪ/ *n.* (*pl.* **alkalis**). **1 a** any of a class of substances that liberate hydroxide ions in water, usu. form caustic or corrosive solutions, turn litmus blue, and have a pH of more than 7, e.g. caustic soda. **b** any other substance with similar but weaker properties, e.g. sodium carbonate. **2** *Chem.* any substance that reacts with or neutralizes hydrogen ions. □**alkali metals** any of the univalent group of metals, lithium, sodium, potassium, rubidium, and caesium, whose hydroxides are alkalis. □□ **alkalimeter** /,ælkə'lɪmɪtə(r)/ *n.* **alkalimetry** /,ælkə'lɪmɪtrɪ/ *n.* [ME f. med.L, f. Arab. *al-ḳalī* calcined ashes f. *ḳala* fry]

alkaline /'ælkə,laɪn/ *adj.* of, relating to, or having the nature of an alkali; rich in alkali. □**alkaline earth 1** any of the bivalent group of metals, beryllium, magnesium, calcium, strontium, barium, and radium. **2** an oxide of the lime group. □□ **alkalinity** /,ælkə'lɪnɪtɪ/ *n.*

alkaloid /'ælkə,lɔɪd/ *n.* any of a series of nitrogenous organic compounds of plant origin, many of which are used as drugs, e.g. morphine, quinine. [G (as ALKALI)]

alkalosis /,ælkə'ləʊsɪs/ *n.* *Med.* an excessive alkaline condition of the body fluids or tissues.

alkane /'ælkeɪn/ *n.* *Chem.* any of a series of saturated aliphatic hydrocarbons having the general formula C_nH_{2n+2}, including methane, ethane, and propane. [ALKYL + -ANE²]

alkanet /'ælkə,net/ *n.* **1 a** any plant of the genus *Alkanna*, esp. *A. tinctoria*, yielding a red dye from its roots. **b** the dye itself. **2** any of various similar plants. [ME f. Sp. *alcaneta* dimin. of *alcana* f. Arab. *al-ḥinnā'* the henna shrub]

alkene /'ælkiːn/ *n.* *Chem.* any of a series of unsaturated aliphatic hydrocarbons containing a double bond and having the general formula C_nH_{2n}, including ethylene and propene. [ALKYL + -ENE]

alkyd /'ælkɪd/ *n.* any of the group of synthetic resins derived from various alcohols and acids. [ALKYL + ACID]

alkyl /'ælkaɪl, 'ælkɪl/ *n.* (in full **alkyl radical**) *Chem.* any radical derived from an alkane by the removal of a hydrogen atom. [G *Alkohol* ALCOHOL + -YL]

alkylate /'ælkɪ,leɪt/ *v.tr.* *Chem.* introduce an alkyl radical into (a compound).

alkyne /'ælkaɪn/ *n.* *Chem.* any of a series of unsaturated aliphatic hydrocarbons containing a triple bond and having the general formula C_nH_{2n-2}, including acetylene. [ALKYL + -YNE]

all /ɔːl/ *adj.*, *n.*, & *adv.* —*adj.* **1 a** the whole amount, quantity, or extent of (*waited all day*; *all his life*; *we all know why*; *take it all*). **b** (with *pl.*) the entire number of (*all the others left*; *all ten men*; *the children are all boys*; *film stars all*). **2** any whatever (*beyond all doubt*). **3** greatest possible (*with all speed*). —*n.* **1 a** all the persons or things concerned (*all were present*; *all were thrown away*). **b** everything (*all is lost*; *that is all*). **2** (foll. by *of*) **a** the whole of (*take all of it*). **b** every one of (*all of us*). **c** *colloq.* as much as (*all of six feet tall*). **d** *colloq.* affected by; in a state of (*all of a dither*). **3** one's whole strength or resources

(prec. by *my*, *your*, etc.). **4** (in games) on both sides (*two goals all*). ¶ Widely used with *of* in sense 2a, b, esp. when followed by a pronoun or by a noun implying a number of persons or things, as in *all of the children are here*. However, use with mass nouns (as in *all of the bread*) is often avoided. —*adv.* **1 a** entirely, quite (*dressed all in black*; *all round the room*; *the all-important thing*). **b** as an intensifier (*a book all about ships*; *stop all this grumbling*). **2** *colloq.* very (*went all shy*). **3** (foll. by *the* + compar.) **a** by so much; to that extent (*if they go, all the better*). **b** in the full degree to be expected (*that makes it all the worse*). □**all along** all the time (*he was joking all along*). **all-American 1** representing the whole of (or only) America or the US. **2** truly American (*all-American boy*). **all and sundry** everyone. **all-around** *US = all-round*. **All Blacks** *colloq.* the New Zealand international Rugby Union football team. **all but** very nearly (*it was all but impossible*; *he was all but drowned*). **all-clear** a signal that danger or difficulty is over. **All Fools' Day** 1 April. **all for** *colloq.* strongly in favour of. **All Hallows** see HALLOW. **all-important** crucial; vitally important. **all in** *colloq.* exhausted. **all-in** (*attrib.*) inclusive of all. **all in all** everything considered. **all-in wrestling** wrestling with few or no restrictions. **all manner of** see MANNER. **all of a sudden** see SUDDEN. **all one** (or **the same**) (usu. foll. by *to*) a matter of indifference (*it's all one to me*). **all out** involving all one's strength; at full speed (also (with hyphen) *attrib.*: *an all-out effort*). **all over 1** completely finished. **2** in or on all parts of (esp. the body) (*went hot and cold all over*; *mud all over the carpet*). **3** *colloq.* typically (*that is you all over*). **4** *sl.* effusively attentive to (a person). **all-purpose** suitable for many uses. **all right** (*predic.*) **1** satisfactory; safe and sound; in good condition. **2** satisfactorily, as desired (*it worked out all right*). **3 a** an interjection expressing consent or assent to a proposal or order. **b** as an intensifier (*that's the one all right*). **all-right** *attrib.adj.* *colloq.* fine, acceptable (*an all-right guy*). **all round 1** in all respects (*a good performance all round*). **2** for each person (*he bought drinks all round*). **all-round** (*attrib.*) (of a person) versatile. **all-rounder** *Brit.* a versatile person. **All Saints' Day** 1 Nov. **all the same** nevertheless, in spite of this (*he was innocent but was punished all the same*). **all set** *colloq.* ready to start. **All Souls' Day** 2 Nov. **all there** *colloq.* mentally alert. **all-time** (of a record etc.) hitherto unsurpassed. **all the time** see TIME. **all together** all at once; all in one place or in a group (*they came all together*) (cf. ALTOGETHER). **all told** in all. **all-up weight** the total weight of an aircraft with passengers, cargo, etc., when airborne. **all very well** *colloq.* an expression used to reject or to imply scepticism about a favourable or consoling remark. **all the way** the whole distance; completely. **at all** (with *neg.* or *interrog.*) in any way; to any extent (*did not swim at all*; *did you like it at all?*). **be all up with** see UP. **in all** in total number; altogether (*there were 10 people in all*). **on all fours** see FOUR. **one and all** everyone. [OE *all*, *eall*, prob. f. Gmc]

alla breve /,ælə 'breɪveɪ/ *n.* *Mus.* a time signature indicating 2 or 4 minim beats in a bar. [It., = at the BREVE]

alla cappella var. of A CAPPELLA.

Allah /'ælə/ *n.* the name of God among Arabs and Muslims. [Arab. *'allāh* contr. of *al-'ilāh* f. *al* the + *ilāh* god]

allantois /ə'læntəʊɪs/ *n.* (*pl.* **allantoides** /-ɪ,diːz/) *Zool.* one of several membranes that develop in embryonic reptiles, birds, or mammals. □□ **allantoic** /,ælən'təʊɪk/ *adj.* [mod.L f. Gk *allantoeidēs* sausage-shaped]

allay /ə'leɪ/ *v.tr.* **1** diminish (fear, suspicion, etc.). **2** relieve or alleviate (pain, hunger, etc.). [OE *ālecgan* (as A⁻², LAY¹)]

allegation /,ælɪ'geɪʃ(ə)n/ *n.* **1** an assertion, esp. an unproved one. **2** the act or an instance of alleging. [ME f. F *allégation* or L *allegatio* f. *allegare* allege]

allege /ə'ledʒ/ *v.tr.* **1** (often foll. by *that* + clause, or *to* + infin.) declare to be the case, esp. without proof. **2** advance as an argument or excuse. □□ **alleged** *adj.* [ME f. AF *allege* OF *esligier* clear at law; confused in sense with L *allegare*: see ALLEGATION]

allegedly /ə'ledʒɪdlɪ/ *adv.* as is alleged or said to be the case.

allegiance /ə'liːdʒ(ə)ns/ *n.* **1** loyalty (to a person or cause etc.). **2** the duty of a subject to his or her sovereign or government. [ME f. AF f. OF *ligeance* (as LIEGE): perh. assoc. with ALLIANCE]

allegorical /ˌælɪ'gɒrɪk(ə)l/ *adj.* (also **allegoric** /-rɪk/) consisting of or relating to allegory; by means of allegory. □□ **allegorically** *adv.*

allegorize /'ælɪgəˌraɪz/ *v.tr.* (also **-ise**) treat as or by means of an allegory. □□ **allegorization** /-'zeɪʃ(ə)n/ *n.*

allegory /'ælɪgərɪ/ *n.* (*pl.* **-ies**) **1** a story, play, poem, picture, etc., in which the meaning or message is represented symbolically. **2** the use of such symbols. **3** a symbol. □□ **allegorist** *n.* [ME f. OF *allegorie* f. L *allegoria* f. Gk *allēgoria* f. *allos* other + *-agoria* speaking]

allegretto /ˌælɪ'gretəʊ/ *adv., adj.,* & *n. Mus.* —*adv.* & *adj.* in a fairly brisk tempo. —*n.* (*pl.* **-os**) an allegretto passage or movement. [It., dimin. of ALLEGRO]

allegro /ə'leɪgrəʊ, ə'leg-/ *adv., adj.,* & *n. Mus.* —*adv.* & *adj.* in a brisk tempo. —*n.* (*pl.* **-os**) an allegro passage or movement. [It., = lively, gay]

allele /'æliːl/ *n.* (also **allel** /'ælel/) one of the (usu. two) alternative forms of a gene. □□ **allelic** /ə'liːlɪk/ *adj.* [G *Allel*, abbr. of ALLELOMORPH]

allelomorph /ə'liːləˌmɔːf/ *n.* = ALLELE. □□ **allelomorphic** /-'mɔːfɪk/ *adj.* [Gk *allēl-* one another + *morphē* form]

alleluia /ˌælɪ'luːjə/ *int.* & *n.* (also **alleluya, hallelujah** /hæl-/) —*int.* God be praised. —*n.* **1** praise to God. **2** a song of praise to God. **3** *RC Ch.* the part of the mass including this. [ME f. eccl.L f. (Septuagint) Gk *allēlouia* f. Heb. *hallˇlūyāh* praise ye the Lord]

allemande /'ælmɑːnd/ *n.* **1 a** the name of several German dances. **b** the music for any of these, esp. as a movement of a suite. **2** a figure in a country dance. [F, = German (dance)]

Allen key /'ælən/ *n. propr.* a spanner designed to fit into and turn an Allen screw. [*Allen*, name of the US manufacturer]

Allen screw /'ælən/ *n. propr.* a screw with a hexagonal socket in the head.

allergen /'ælədʒ(ə)n/ *n.* any substance that causes an allergic reaction. □□ **allergenic** /ˌælə'dʒenɪk/ *adj.* [ALLERGY + -GEN]

allergic /ə'lɜːdʒɪk/ *adj.* **1** (foll. by *to*) **a** having an allergy to. **b** *colloq.* having a strong dislike for (a person or thing). **2** caused by or relating to an allergy.

allergy /'ælədʒɪ/ *n.* (*pl.* **-ies**) **1** *Med.* a condition of reacting adversely to certain substances, esp. particular foods, pollen, fur, or dust. **2** *colloq.* an antipathy. □□ **allergist** *n.* [G *Allergie*, after *Energie* ENERGY, f. Gk *allos* other]

alleviate /ə'liːvɪˌeɪt/ *v.tr.* lessen or make less severe (pain, suffering, etc.). □□ **alleviation** /-'eɪʃ(ə)n/ *n.* **alleviative** /ə'liːvɪətɪv/ *adj.* **alleviator** *n.* **alleviatory** /ə'liːvɪətərɪ/ *adj.* [LL *alleviare* lighten f. L *allevare* (as AD-, *levare* raise)]

alley¹ /'ælɪ/ *n.* (*pl.* **-eys**) **1** (also **alley-way**) **a** a narrow street. **b** a narrow passageway, esp. between or behind buildings. **2** a path or walk in a park or garden. **3** an enclosure for skittles, bowling, etc. **4** (in lawn tennis) either of the two side strips of a doubles court. □ **alley cat** a stray town cat often mangy or half wild. [ME f. OF *alee* walking, passage f. *aler* go f. L *ambulare* walk]

alley² var. of ALLY².

alliaceous /ˌælɪ'eɪʃəs/ *adj.* **1** of or relating to the genus *Allium.* **2** tasting or smelling like onion or garlic. [mod.L *alliaceus* f. L *allium* garlic]

alliance /ə'laɪəns/ *n.* **1 a** union or agreement to cooperate, esp. of States by treaty or families by marriage. **b** the parties involved. **2** (**Alliance**) a political party formed by the allying of separate parties. **3** a relationship resulting from an affinity in nature or qualities etc. (*the old alliance between logic and metaphysics*). **4** *Bot.* a group of allied families. [ME f. OF *aliance* (as ALLY¹)]

allied /'ælaɪd/ *adj.* **1 a** united or associated in an alliance. **b** (**Allied**) of or relating to Britain and her allies in the wars of 1914–18 or 1939–45. **2** connected or related (*studied medicine and allied subjects*).

alligator /'ælɪˌgeɪtə(r)/ *n.* **1** a large reptile of the crocodile family native to S. America and China, with upper teeth that lie outside the lower teeth and a head broader and shorter than that of the crocodile. **2** (in general use) any of several large members of the crocodile family. **3 a** the skin of such an animal or material resembling it. **b** (in *pl.*) shoes of this. □ **alligator clip** a clip with teeth for gripping. **alligator pear** an avocado. **alligator tortoise** a large freshwater snapping turtle. [Sp. *el lagarto* the lizard f. L *lacerta*]

alliterate /ə'lɪtəˌreɪt/ *v.* **1** *intr.* **a** contain alliteration. **b** use alliteration in speech or writing. **2** *tr.* **a** construct (a phrase etc.) with alliteration. **b** speak or pronounce with alliteration. □□ **alliterative** /ə'lɪtərətɪv/ *adj.* [back-form. f. ALLITERATION]

alliteration /əˌlɪtə'reɪʃ(ə)n/ *n.* the occurrence of the same letter or sound at the beginning of adjacent or closely connected words (e.g. *cool, calm, and collected*). [mod.L *alliteratio* (as AD-, *littera* letter)]

allium /'ælɪəm/ *n.* any plant of the genus *Allium,* usu. bulbous and strong smelling, e.g. onion and garlic. [L, = garlic]

allo- /'æləʊ, ə'lɒ/ *comb. form* other (*allophone*; *allogamy*). [Gk *allos* other]

allocate /'æləˌkeɪt/ *v.tr.* (usu. foll. by *to*) assign or devote to (a purpose, person, or place). □□ **allocable** /'æləkəb(ə)l/ *adj.* **allocation** /ˌælə'keɪʃ(ə)n/ *n.* **allocator** *n.* [med.L *allocare* f. *locus* place]

allocution /ˌælə'kjuːʃ(ə)n/ *n.* formal or hortatory speech or manner of address. [L *allocutio* f. *alloqui allocut-* speak to]

allogamy /ə'lɒgəmɪ/ *n. Bot.* cross-fertilization in plants. [ALLO- + Gk *-gamia* f. *gamos* marriage]

allomorph /'æləˌmɔːf/ *n. Linguistics* any of two or more alternative forms of a morpheme. □□ **allomorphic** /ˌælə'mɔːfɪk/ *adj.* [ALLO- + MORPHEME]

allopath /'æləˌpæθ/ *n.* one who practises allopathy. [F *allopathe* back-form. f. *allopathie* = ALLOPATHY]

allopathy /ə'lɒpəθɪ/ *n.* the treatment of disease by conventional means, i.e. with drugs having opposite effects to the symptoms (cf. HOMOEOPATHY). □□ **allopathic** /ˌælə'pæθɪk/ *adj.* **allopathist** *n.* [G *Allopathie* (as ALLO-, -PATHY)]

allophone /'æləˌfəʊn/ *n. Linguistics* any of the variant sounds forming a single phoneme. □□ **allophonic** /ˌælə'fɒnɪk/ *adj.* [ALLO- + PHONEME]

allot /ə'lɒt/ *v.tr.* (**allotted, allotting**) **1** give or apportion to (a person) as a share or task; distribute officially to (*they allotted us each a pair of boots*; *the men were allotted duties*). **2** (foll. by *to*) give or distribute officially to (*a sum was allotted to each charity*). [OF *aloter* f. *a* to + LOT]

allotment /ə'lɒtmənt/ *n.* **1** a small piece of land rented (usu. from a local authority) for cultivation. **2** a share allotted. **3** the action of allotting.

allotrope /'æləˌtrəʊp/ *n.* any of two or more different physical forms in which an element can exist (*graphite, charcoal, and diamond are all allotropes of carbon*). [back-form. f. ALLOTROPY]

allotropy /ə'lɒtrəpɪ/ *n.* the existence of two or more different physical forms of a chemical element. □□

allotropic /ˌælə'trɒprɪk/ *adj.* **allotropical** /ˌælə'trɒpɪk(ə)l/ *adj.* [Gk *allotropos* of another form f. *allos* different + *tropos* manner f. *trepō* to turn]

allottee /əlɒ'tiː/ *n.* a person to whom something is allotted.

allow /ə'laʊ/ *v.* **1** *tr.* permit (a practice, a person to do something, a thing to happen, etc.) (*smoking is not allowed*; *we allowed them to speak*). **2** *tr.* give or provide; permit (a person) to have (a limited quantity or sum) (*we were allowed £500 a year*). **3** *tr.* provide or set aside for a purpose; add or deduct in consideration of something (*allow 10% for inflation*). **4** *tr.* **a** admit, agree, concede (*he allowed that it was so*; '*You know best,*' *he allowed*). **b** *US* state; be of the opinion. **5** *refl.* permit oneself, indulge oneself in (conduct) (*allowed herself to be persuaded*; *allowed myself a few angry words*). **6** *intr.* (foll. by *of*) admit of. **7** *intr.* (foll. by *for*) take into consideration or account; make addition or deduction corresponding to (*allowing for wastage*). □□ **allowable** *adj.* **allowably** *adv.* [ME, orig. = 'praise', f. OF *alouer* f. L *allaudare* to praise, and med.L *allocare* to place]

allowance /ə'laʊəns/ *n.* & *v.* —*n.* **1** an amount or sum allowed to a person, esp. regularly for a stated purpose. **2** an amount allowed in reckoning. **3** a deduction or discount (*an allowance on your old cooker*). **4** (foll. by *of*) tolerance of. —*v.tr.* **1** make an allowance to (a person). **2** supply in limited quantities. □ **make allowances** (often foll. by *for*) **1** take into consideration (mitigating circumstances) (*made allowances for his demented state*). **2** look with tolerance upon, make excuses for (a person, bad behaviour, etc.). [ME f. OF *alouance* (as ALLOW)]

allowedly /ə'laʊɪdlɪ/ *adv.* as is generally allowed or acknowledged.

alloy /'ælɔɪ, ə'lɔɪ/ *n.* & *v.* —*n.* **1** a mixture of two or more metals, e.g. brass (a mixture of copper and zinc). **2** an inferior metal mixed esp. with gold or silver. —*v.tr.* **1** mix (metals). **2** debase (a pure substance) by admixture. **3** moderate. [F *aloi* (n.), *aloyer* (v.) f. OF *aloier*, *aleier* combine f. L *alligare* bind]

allseed /'ɔːlsiːd/ *n.* any of various plants producing much seed, esp. *Radiola linoides.*

allspice /'ɔːlspaɪs/ *n.* **1** the aromatic spice obtained from the ground berry of the pimento plant, *Pimenta dioica.* **2** the berry of this plant. **3** any of various other aromatic shrubs.

allude /ə'luːd, ə'ljuːd/ *v.intr.* (foll. by *to*) **1** refer, esp. indirectly, covertly, or briefly to. **2** *disp.* mention. [L *alludere* (as AD-, *ludere lus-* play)]

allure /ə'ljʊə(r)/ *v.* & *n.* —*v.tr.* attract, charm, or fascinate. —*n.* attractiveness, personal charm, fascination. □□ **allurement** *n.* [ME f. OF *alurer* attract (as AD-, *luere* LURE 1)]

allusion /ə'luːʒ(ə)n, ə'ljuː-/ *n.* (often foll. by *to*) a reference, esp. a covert, passing, or indirect one. ¶ Often confused with *illusion.* [F *allusion* or LL *allusio* (as ALLUDE)]

allusive /ə'luːsɪv, ə'ljuː-/ *adj.* **1** (often foll. by *to*) containing an allusion. **2** containing many allusions. □□ **allusively** *adv.* **allusiveness** *n.*

alluvial /ə'luːvɪəl/ *adj.* & *n.* —*adj.* of or relating to alluvium. —*n.* alluvium, esp. containing a precious metal.

alluvion /ə'luːvɪən/ *n.* **1** the wash of the sea against the shore, or of a river against its banks. **2 a** a large overflow of water. **b** matter deposited by this, esp. alluvium. **3** the formation of new land by the movement of the sea or of a river. [F f. L *alluvio -onis* f. *luere* wash]

alluvium /ə'luːvɪəm/ *n.* (*pl.* **alluvia** /-vɪə/ or **alluviums**) a deposit of usu. fine fertile soil left during a time of flood, esp. in a river valley or delta. [L neut. of *alluvius* adj. f. *luere* wash]

ally[1] /'ælaɪ/ *n.* & *v.* —*n.* (*pl.* **-ies**) **1** a State formally cooperating or united with another for a special purpose, esp. by a treaty. **2** a person or organization

that cooperates with or helps another. —*v.tr.* /also ə'laɪ/ (**-ies**, **-ied**) (often foll. by *with*) combine or unite in alliance. [ME f. OF *al(e)ier* f. L *alligare* bind: cf. ALLOY]

ally[2] /'ælɪ/ *n.* (also **alley**) (*pl.* **-ies** or **-eys**) a choice playing-marble made of marble, alabaster, or glass. [perh. dimin. of ALABASTER]

-ally /əlɪ/ *suffix* forming adverbs from adjectives in *-al* (cf. -AL, -LY[2], -ICALLY).

allyl /'ælɪl, -laɪl/ *n. Chem.* the unsaturated univalent radical $CH_2 = CH - CH_2$. [L *allium* garlic + -YL]

almacantar var. of ALMUCANTAR.

Alma Mater /ˌælmə 'mɑːtə(r), 'meɪtə(r)/ *n.* the university, school, or college one attends or attended. [L, = bounteous mother]

almanac /'ɔːlmənæk, 'ɒl-/ *n.* (also **almanack**) an annual calendar of months and days, usu. with astronomical data and other information. [ME f. med.L *almanac(h)* f. Gk *almenikhiaka*]

almandine /'ælmən,diːn, -,daɪn/ *n.* a kind of garnet with a violet tint. [F, alt. of obs. *alabandine* f. med.L *alabandina* f. *Alabanda*, ancient city in Asia Minor]

almighty /ɔːl'maɪtɪ/ *adj.* & *adj.* —*adj.* **1** having complete power; omnipotent. **2** (**the Almighty**) God. **3** *sl.* very great (*an almighty crash*). —*adv. sl.* extremely; very much. [OE *ælmihtig* (as ALL, MIGHTY)]

almond /'ɑːmənd/ *n.* **1** the oval nutlike seed (kernel) of the stone-fruit from the tree *Prunus dulcis*, of which there are sweet and bitter varieties. **2** the tree itself, of the rose family and allied to the peach and plum. □ **almond eyes** narrow almond-shaped eyes. **almond oil** the oil expressed from the seed (esp. the bitter variety), used for toilet preparations, flavouring, and medicinal purposes. **almond paste** = MARZIPAN. [ME f. OF *alemande* etc. f. med.L *amandula* f. L *amygdala* f. Gk *amugdalē*: assoc. with words in AL-]

almoner /'ɑːmənə(r)/ *n.* **1** *Brit.* a social worker attached to a hospital and seeing to the after-care of patients. ¶ Now usu. called *medical social worker.* **2** *hist.* an official distributor of alms. [ME f. AF *aumoner*, OF *aumonier*, ult. f. med.L *eleēmosynarius* (as ALMS)]

almost /'ɔːlməʊst/ *adv.* all but; very nearly. [OE *ælmǽst* for the most part (as ALL, MOST)]

alms /ɑːmz/ *n.pl. hist.* the charitable donation of money or food to the poor. [OE *ælmysse, -messe,* f. Gmc ult. f. Gk *eleēmosunē* compassionateness f. *eleēmōn* (adj.) f. *eleos* compassion]

almshouse /'ɑːmzhaʊs/ *n. hist.* a house founded by charity for the poor.

almucantar /ˌælmə'kæntə(r)/ *n.* (also **almacantar**) *Astron.* a line of constant altitude above the horizon. [ME f. med.L *almucantarath* or F *almucantara* etc., f. Arab. *almuḳanṭarāt* sundial f. *ḳanṭara* arch]

aloe /'æləʊ/ *n.* **1** any plant of the genus *Aloe*, usu. having toothed fleshy leaves. **2** (in *pl.*) (in full **bitter aloes**) a strong laxative obtained from the bitter juice of various species of aloe. **3** (also **American aloe**) an agave native to Central America. [OE *al(e)we* f. L *aloē* f. Gk]

aloetic /ˌæləʊ'etɪk/ *adj.* & *n.* —*adj.* of or relating to an aloe. —*n.* a medicine containing aloes. [Gk *aloē* aloe, on the false analogy of *diuretic* etc.]

aloft /ə'lɒft/ *predic.adj.* & *adv.* **1** high up; overhead. **2** upwards. [ME f. ON *á lopt(i)* f. *á* in, on, to + *lopt* air: cf. LIFT, LOFT]

alogical /eɪ'lɒdʒɪk(ə)l/ *adj.* **1** not logical. **2** opposed to logic.

alone /ə'ləʊn/ *adj.* & *adv.* —*predic.adj.* **1 a** without others present (*they wanted to be alone*; *the tree stood alone*). **b** without others' help (*succeeded alone*). **c** lonely and wretched (*felt alone*). **2** (often foll. by *in*) standing by oneself in an opinion etc. (*was alone in thinking this*). —*adv.* only, exclusively (*you alone can help me*). □ **go it alone** act by oneself without assistance. □□ **aloneness** *n.* [ME f. ALL + ONE]

along /ə'lɒŋ/ *prep.* & *adv.* —*prep.* **1** from one end to the other end of (*a handkerchief with lace along the edge*). **2** on or through any part of the length of (*was walking along the road*). **3** beside or through the length of (*shelves stood along the wall*). —*adv.* **1** onward; into a more advanced state (*come along; getting along nicely*). **2** at or to a particular place; arriving (*I'll be along soon*). **3** in company with a person, esp. oneself (*bring a book along*). **4** beside or through part or the whole length of a thing. □**along with** in addition to; together with. [OE *andlang* f. WG, rel. to LONG¹]

alongshore /əlɒŋˈʃɔː(r)/ *adv.* along or by the shore.

alongside /əlɒŋˈsaɪd/ *adv. & prep.* —*adv.* at or to the side (of a ship, pier, etc.). —*prep.* close to the side of; next to. □**alongside of** side by side with; together or simultaneously with.

aloof /əˈluːf/ *adj. & adv.* —*adj.* distant, unsympathetic. —*adv.* away, apart (*he kept aloof from his colleagues*). □□ **aloofly** *adv.* **aloofness** *n.* [orig. Naut., f. A² + LUFF]

alopecia /ˌæləˈpiːʃə/ *n. Med.* the absence (complete or partial) of hair from areas of the body where it normally grows; baldness. [L f. Gk *alōpekia* fox-mange f. *alōpēx* fox]

aloud /əˈlaʊd/ *adv.* **1** audibly; not silently or in a whisper. **2** *archaic* loudly. [A² + LOUD]

alow /əˈləʊ/ *adv. & predic.adj. Naut.* in or into the lower part of a ship. [A² + LOW¹]

alp /ælp/ *n.* **1 a** a high mountain. **b** (**the Alps**) the high range of mountains in Switzerland and adjoining countries. **2** (in Switzerland) pasture-land on a mountainside. [orig. pl., f. F f. L *Alpes* f. Gk *Alpeis*]

alpaca /ælˈpækə/ *n.* **1** a S. American mammal, *Lama pacos*, related to the llama, with long shaggy hair. **2** the wool from the animal. **3** fabric made from the wool, with or without other fibres. [Sp. f. Aymará or Quechua]

alpargata /ˌælpɑːˈɡɑːtə/ *n.* a light canvas shoe with a plaited fibre sole; an espadrille. [Sp.]

alpenhorn /ˈælpənˌhɔːn/ *n.* a long wooden horn used by Alpine herdsmen to call their cattle. [G, = Alp-horn]

alpenstock /ˈælpənˌstɒk/ *n.* a long iron-tipped staff used in hillwalking. [G, = Alp-stick]

alpha /ˈælfə/ *n.* **1** the first letter of the Greek alphabet (A, α). **2** a first-class mark given for a piece of work or in an examination. **3** *Astron.* the chief star in a constellation. □**alpha and omega** the beginning and the end; the most important features. **alpha particle** (or **ray**) a helium nucleus emitted by a radioactive substance, orig. regarded as a ray. [ME f. L f. Gk]

alphabet /ˈælfəˌbet/ *n.* **1** the set of letters used in writing a language (*the Russian alphabet*). **2** a set of symbols or signs representing letters. [LL *alphabetum* f. Gk *alpha*, *bēta*, the first two letters of the alphabet]

alphabetical /ˌælfəˈbetɪk(ə)l/ *adj.* (also **alphabetic** /-ˈbetɪk/) **1** of or relating to an alphabet. **2** in the order of the letters of the alphabet. □□ **alphabetically** *adv.*

alphabetize /ˈælfəbəˌtaɪz/ *v.tr.* (also **-ise**) arrange (words, names, etc.) in alphabetical order. □□ **alphabetization** /-ˈzeɪʃ(ə)n/ *n.*

alphanumeric /ˌælfənjuːˈmerɪk/ *adj.* (also **alphameric** /ˌælfəˈmerɪk/, **alphanumerical**) containing both alphabetical and numerical symbols. [ALPHABETIC (see ALPHABETICAL) + NUMERICAL]

alpine /ˈælpaɪn/ *adj. & n.* —*adj.* **1 a** of or relating to high mountains. **b** growing or found on high mountains. **2** (**Alpine**) of or relating to the Alps. —*n.* a plant native or suited to mountain districts. [L *Alpinus*: see ALP]

Alpinist /ˈælpɪnɪst/ *n.* (also **alpinist**) a climber of high mountains, esp. the Alps. [F *alpiniste* (as ALPINE; see -IST)]

already /ɔːlˈredɪ/ *adv.* **1** before the time in question (*I knew that already*). **2** as early or as soon as this (*already at the age of six*). [ALL *adv.* + READY]

alright /ɔːlˈraɪt/ *adv. disp.* = *all right*.

Alsatian /ælˈseɪʃ(ə)n/ *n.* **1 a** a large dog of a breed of wolfhound. **b** this breed (also called *German shepherd dog*). **2** a native of Alsace, a region of E. France. [*Alsatia* (= Alsace) + -AN]

alsike /ˈælsɪk/ *n.* a species of clover, *Trifolium hybridum*. [*Alsike* in Sweden]

also /ˈɔːlsəʊ/ *adv.* in addition; likewise; besides. □**also-ran** **1** a horse or dog etc. not among the winners in a race. **2** an undistinguished person. [OE *alswā* (as ALL *adv.*, SO¹)]

Alta. *abbr.* Alberta.

altar /ˈɔːltə(r), ˈɒl-/ *n.* **1** a table or flat-topped block, often of stone, for sacrifice or offering to a deity. **2** a Communion-table. □**altar boy** a boy who serves as a priest's assistant in a service. **lead to the altar** marry (a woman). [OE *altar -er*, Gmc adoption of LL *altar*, *altarium* f. L *altaria* (pl.) burnt offerings, altar, prob. rel. to *adolēre* burn in sacrifice]

altarpiece /ˈɔːltəˌpiːs, ˈɒl-/ *n.* a piece of art, esp. a painting, set above or behind an altar.

altazimuth /ælˈtæzɪməθ/ *n.* an instrument for measuring the altitude and azimuth of celestial bodies. [ALTITUDE + AZIMUTH]

alter /ˈɔːltə(r), ˈɒl-/ *v.* **1** *tr. & intr.* make or become different; change. **2** *tr. US & Austral.* castrate or spay. □□ **alterable** *adj.* **alteration** /-ˈreɪʃ(ə)n/ *n.* [ME f. OF *alterer* f. LL *alterare* f. L *alter* other]

alterative /ˈɔːltərətɪv, ˈɒl-/ *adj. & n.* —*adj.* **1** tending to alter. **2** (of a medicine) that alters bodily processes. —*n.* an alterative medicine or treatment. [ME f. med.L *alterativus* (as ALTER)]

altercate /ˈɔːltəˌkeɪt, ˈɒl-/ *v.intr.* (often foll. by *with*) dispute hotly; wrangle. □□ **altercation** /-ˈkeɪʃ(ə)n/ *n.* [L *altercari altercat-*]

alter ego /ˌæltər ˈiːɡəʊ, ˈeɡəʊ/ *n.* (*pl.* *alter egos*) **1** an intimate and trusted friend. **2** a person's secondary or alternative personality. [L, = other self]

alternate *v., adj., & n.* —*v.* /ˈɔːltəˌneɪt, ˈɒl-/ **1** *intr.* (often foll. by *with*) (of two things) succeed each other by turns (*rain and sunshine alternated; elation alternated with depression*). **2** *intr.* (foll. by *between*) change repeatedly (between two conditions) (*the patient alternated between hot and cold fevers*). **3** *tr.* (often foll. by *with*) cause (two things) to succeed each other by turns (*the band alternated fast and slow tunes*; *we alternated criticism with reassurance*). —*adj.* /ɔːlˈtɜːnət, ɒl-/ **1** (with noun in *pl.*) every other (*comes on alternate days*). **2** (of things of two kinds) each following and succeeded by one of the other kind (*alternate joy and misery*). **3** (of a sequence etc.) consisting of alternate things. **4** *Bot.* (of leaves etc.) placed alternately on the two sides of the stem. **5** = ALTERNATIVE. —*n.* /ɔːlˈtɜːnət, ɒl-/ esp. *US* a deputy or substitute. □**alternate angles** two angles, not adjoining one another, that are formed on opposite sides of a line that intersects two other lines. **alternating current** an electric current that reverses its direction at regular intervals. □□ **alternately** /ɔːlˈtɜːnətlɪ, ɒl-/ *adv.* [L *alternatus* past part. of *alternare* do things by turns f. *alternus* every other f. *alter* other]

alternation /ˌɔːltəˈneɪʃ(ə)n, ˌɒl-/ *n.* the action or result of alternating. □**alternation of generations** reproduction by alternate processes, e.g. sexual and asexual.

alternative /ɔːlˈtɜːnətɪv, ɒl-/ *adj. & n.* —*adj.* **1** (of one or more things) available or usable instead of another (*an alternative route*). ¶ Use with reference to more than two options (e.g. *many alternative methods*) is common, and acceptable. **2** (of two things) mutually exclusive. **3** of or relating to practices that offer a substitute for the conventional ones (*alternative medicine; alternative theatre*). —*n.* **1** any of two or more possibilities. **2** the freedom or opportunity to choose between two or more things (*I* *had no alternative but to go).* □**the alternative society** a group of people dissociating themselves from conventional society and its values. □□ **alternatively** *adv.* [F *alternatif -ive* or med.L *alternativus* (as ALTERNATE)]

alternator /'ɔːltəˌneɪtə(r), 'ɒl-/ *n.* a dynamo that generates an alternating current.

althorn /'ælthɔːn/ *n. Mus.* an instrument of the saxhorn family, esp. the alto or tenor saxhorn in E flat. [G f. *alt* high f. L *altus* + HORN]

although /ɔːl'ðəʊ/ *conj.* = THOUGH *conj.* 1-3. [ME f. ALL *adv.* + THOUGH]

altimeter /'æltɪˌmiːtə(r)/ *n.* an instrument for showing height above sea or ground level, esp. one fitted to an aircraft. [L *altus* high + -METER]

altitude /'æltɪˌtjuːd/ *n.* **1** the height of an object in relation to a given point, esp. sea level or the horizon. **2** *Geom.* the length of the perpendicular from a vertex to the opposite side of a figure. **3** a high or exalted position (*a social altitude*). □**altitude sickness** a sickness experienced at high altitudes. □□ **altitudinal** /ˌæltɪ'tjuːdɪn(ə)l/ *adj.* [ME f. L *altitudo* f. *altus* high]

alto /'æltəʊ/ *n.* (*pl.* -os) **1** = CONTRALTO. **2 a** the highest adult male singing-voice, above tenor. **b** a singer with this voice. **c** a part written for it. **3 a** (*attrib.*) denoting the member of a family of instruments pitched second- or third-highest. **b** an alto instrument, esp. an alto saxophone. □**alto clef** a clef placing middle C on the middle line of the staff, used chiefly for viola music. [It. *alto* (*canto*) high (singing)]

altocumulus /ˌæltəʊ'kjuːmjʊləs/ *n.* (*pl.* altocumuli /-ˌlaɪ/) *Meteorol.* a cloud formation at medium altitude consisting of rounded masses with a level base. [mod.L f. L *altus* high + CUMULUS]

altogether /ˌɔːltə'geðə(r)/ *adv.* **1** totally, completely (*you are altogether wrong*). **2** on the whole (*altogether it had been a good day*). **3** in total (*there are six bedrooms altogether*). ¶ Note that *all together* is used to mean 'all at once' or 'all in one place', as in *there are six bedrooms all together.* □**in the altogether** *colloq.* naked. [ME f. ALL + TOGETHER]

alto-relievo /ˌæltəʊrɪ'liːvəʊ/ *n.* (*pl.* -os) *Sculpture* **1** a form of relief in which the sculptured shapes stand out from the background to at least half their actual depth. **2** a sculpture characterized by this. [ALTO + RELIEVO]

altostratus /ˌæltəʊ'streɪtəs, -'strɑːtəs/ *n.* (*pl.* altostrati /-tɪ/) a continuous and uniformly flat cloud formation at medium altitude. [mod.L f. L *altus* high + STRATUS]

altricial /æl'trɪʃ(ə)l/ *adj. & n.* —*adj.* (of a bird) whose young require care and feeding by the parents after hatching. —*n.* an altricial bird (cf. PRAECOCIAL). [L *altrix altricis* (fem.) nourisher f. *altor* f. *alere altus* nourish]

altruism /'æltruːˌɪz(ə)m/ *n.* **1** regard for others as a principle of action. **2** unselfishness; concern for other people. □□ **altruist** *n.* **altruistic** /ˌæltruː'ɪstɪk/ *adj.* **altruistically** /ˌæltruː'ɪstɪkəli/ *adv.* [F *altruisme* f. It. *altrui* somebody else (infl. by L *alter* other)]

alum /'æləm/ *n.* **1** a double sulphate of aluminium and potassium. **2** any of a group of compounds of double sulphates of a monovalent metal (or group) and a trivalent metal. [ME f. OF f. L *alumen aluminis*]

alumina /ə'luːmɪnə/ *n.* the compound oxide occurring naturally as corundum and emery. [L *alumen* alum, after *soda* etc.]

aluminium /ˌæljʊ'mɪnɪəm/ *n.* (*US* aluminum /ə'luːmɪnəm/) a silvery light and malleable metallic element resistant to tarnishing by air. ¶ Symb.: Al. □**aluminium bronze** an alloy of copper and aluminium. [*aluminium*, alt. (after *sodium* etc.) f. *aluminum*, earlier *alumium* f. ALUM + -IUM]

aluminize /ə'luːmɪˌnaɪz/ *v.tr.* (also -ise) coat with aluminium. □□ **aluminization** /-'zeɪʃ(ə)n/ *n.*

alumnus /ə'lʌmnəs/ *n.* (*pl.* alumni /-nɪ/; *fem.*

alumna, *pl.* **alumnae** /-nɪ/) a former pupil or student. [L, = nursling, pupil f. *alere* nourish]

alveolar /æl'vɪələ(r), ˌælvɪ'əʊlə(r)/ *adj.* **1** of an alveolus. **2** *Phonet.* (of a consonant) pronounced with the tip of the tongue in contact with the ridge of the upper teeth, e.g. *n, s, t.* [ALVEOLUS + -AR[1]]

alveolus /æl'vɪələs, ˌælvɪ'əʊləs/ *n.* (*pl.* **alveoli** /-laɪ, -lɪ/) **1** a small cavity, pit, or hollow. **2** any of the many tiny air sacs of the lungs which allow for rapid gaseous exchange. **3** the bony socket for the root of a tooth. **4** the cell of a honeycomb. □□ **alveolate** *adj.* [L dimin. of *alveus* cavity]

always /'ɔːlweɪz/ *adv.* **1** at all times; on all occasions (*they are always late*). **2** whatever the circumstances (*I can always sleep on the floor*). **3** repeatedly; often (*they are always complaining*). [ME, prob. distrib. genit. f. ALL + WAY + -'S[1]]

alyssum /'ælɪsəm/ *n.* any plant of the genus *Alyssum*, widely cultivated and usu. having yellow or white flowers. [L f. Gk *alusson*]

Alzheimer's disease /'ælts,haɪməz/ *n.* a serious disorder of the brain manifesting itself in premature senility. [A. *Alzheimer*, Ger. neurologist d. 1915]

AM *abbr.* **1** amplitude modulation. **2** *US* Master of Arts. **3** Member of the Order of Australia. [(sense 2) L *artium Magister*]

Am *symb. Chem.* the element americium.

am *1st person sing. present of* BE.

a.m. *abbr.* before noon. [L *ante meridiem*]

amadavat /ˌæmədə'væt/ *n.* (also **avadavat** /ˌævə-/) either of two small brightly coloured S. Asian waxbills, the green *Amandava formosa* or esp. the red *A. amandava.* [*Ahmadabad* in India]

amadou /'æməˌduː/ *n.* a spongy and combustible tinder prepared from dry fungi. [F f. mod.Prov., lit. = lover (because quickly kindled) f. L (as AMATEUR)]

amah /'ɑːmə/ *n.* (in the Far East and India) a nursemaid or maid. [Port. *ama* nurse]

amalgam /ə'mælgəm/ *n.* **1** a mixture or blend. **2** an alloy of mercury with one or more other metals, used esp. in dentistry. [ME f. F *amalgame* or med.L *amalgama* f. Gk *malagma* an emollient]

amalgamate /ə'mælgəˌmeɪt/ *v.* **1** *tr. & intr.* combine or unite to form one structure, organization, etc. **2** *intr.* (of metals) alloy with mercury. □□ **amalgamation** /-'meɪʃ(ə)n/ *n.* [med.L *amalgamare amalgamat-* (as AMALGAM)]

amanuensis /əˌmænju'ensɪs/ *n.* (*pl.* **amanuenses** /-siːz/) **1** a person who writes from dictation or copies manuscripts. **2** a literary assistant. [L f. (*servus*) *a manu* secretary + -*ensis* belonging to]

amaranth /'æməˌrænθ/ *n.* **1** any plant of the genus *Amaranthus*, usu. having small green, red, or purple tinted flowers, e.g. prince's feather and pigweed. **2** an imaginary flower that never fades. **3** a purple colour. □□ **amaranthine** /ˌæmə'rænθaɪn/ *adj.* [F *amarante* or mod.L *amaranthus* f. L f. Gk *amarantos* everlasting f. *a-* not + *marainō* wither, alt. after *polyanthus* etc.]

amaryllis /ˌæmə'rɪlɪs/ *n.* **1** a plant genus with a single species, *Amaryllis belladonna*, a bulbous lily-like plant native to S. Africa with white or rose-pink flowers (also called *belladonna lily*). **2** any of various related plants formerly of this genus now transferred to other genera, notably *Hippeastrum*. [L f. Gk *Amaryllis*, name of a country girl]

amass /ə'mæs/ *v.tr.* **1** gather or heap together. **2** accumulate (esp. riches). □□ **amasser** *n.* [F *amasser* or med.L *amassare* ult. f. L *massa* MASS[1]]

amateur /'æmətə(r)/ *n.* **1** a person who engages in a pursuit (e.g. an art or sport) as a pastime rather than a profession. **2** (*attrib.*) for or done by amateurs (*amateur athletics*). **3** (foll. by *of*) a person who is fond of (a thing). □□ **amateurism** *n.* [F f. It. *amatore* f. L *amator -oris* lover f. *amare* love]

amateurish /'æmətərɪʃ/ *adj.* characteristic of an amateur, esp. unskilful or inexperienced. □□ **amateurishly** *adv.* **amateurishness** *n.*

amatory /'æmətərɪ/ *adj.* of or relating to sexual love or desire. [L *amatorius* f. *amare* love]

amaurosis /ˌæmɔː'rəʊsɪs/ *n.* the partial or total loss of sight, from disease of the optic nerve, retina, spinal cord, or brain. □□ **amaurotic** /-'rɒtɪk/ *adj.* [mod.L f. Gk f. *amauroō* darken f. *amauros* dim]

amaze /ə'meɪz/ *v.tr.* (often foll. by *at*, or *that* + clause, or *to* + infin.) surprise greatly; overwhelm with wonder (*am amazed at your indifference*; *was amazed to find them alive*). □□ **amazement** *n.* **amazing** *adj.* **amazingly** *adv.* **amazingness** *n.* [ME f. OE *āmasod* past part. of *āmasian*, of uncert. orig.]

Amazon /'æməz(ə)n/ *n.* **1** a member of a mythical race of female warriors in Scythia and elsewhere. **2** (**amazon**) a very tall, strong, or athletic woman. □□ **Amazonian** /ˌæmə'zəʊnɪən/ *adj.* [ME f. L f. Gk: expl. by the Greeks as 'breastless' (as if A-[1] + *mazos* breast), but prob. of foreign orig.]

ambassador /æm'bæsədə(r)/ *n.* **1** an accredited diplomat sent by a State on a mission to, or as its permanent representative in, a foreign country. **2** a representative or promoter of a specified thing (*an ambassador of peace*). □**ambassador-at-large** *US* an ambassador with special duties, not appointed to a particular country. □□ **ambassadorial** /ˌæmbæsə'dɔːrɪəl/ *adj.* **ambassadorship** *n.* [ME f. F *ambassadeur* f. It. *ambasciator*, ult. f. L *ambactus* servant]

ambassadress /æm'bæsədrɪs/ *n.* **1** a female ambassador. **2** an ambassador's wife.

ambatch /'æmbætʃ/ *n.* an African tree, *Aeschynomene elaphroxylon*, with very light spongy wood. [Ethiopic]

amber /'æmbə(r)/ *n.* & *adj.* —*n.* **1 a** a yellowish translucent fossilized resin deriving from extinct (esp. coniferous) trees and used in jewellery. **b** the honey-yellow colour of this. **2** a yellow traffic-light meaning caution, showing between red for 'stop' and green for 'go'. —*adj.* made of or coloured like amber. [ME f. OF *ambre* f. Arab. *'anbar* ambergris, amber]

ambergris /'æmbəgrɪs, -ˌgriːs/ *n.* a strong-smelling waxlike secretion of the intestine of the sperm whale, found floating in tropical seas and used in perfume manufacture. [ME f. OF *ambre gris* grey AMBER]

amberjack /'æmbəˌdʒæk/ *n.* *US* any large brightly-coloured marine fish of the genus *Seriola* found in tropical and subtropical Atlantic waters.

ambiance var. of AMBIENCE.

ambidextrous /ˌæmbɪ'dekstrəs/ *adj.* (also **ambidexterous**) **1** able to use the right and left hands equally well. **2** working skilfully in more than one medium. □□ **ambidexterity** /-'sterɪtɪ/ *n.* **ambidextrously** *adv.* **ambidextrousness** *n.* [LL *ambidexter* f. *ambi-* on both sides + *dexter* right-handed]

ambience /'æmbɪəns/ *n.* (also **ambiance**) the surroundings or atmosphere of a place. [AMBIENT + -ENCE or F *ambiance*]

ambient /'æmbɪənt/ *adj.* surrounding. [F *ambiant* or L *ambiens -entis* pres. part. of *ambire* go round]

ambiguity /ˌæmbɪ'gjuːɪtɪ/ *n.* (*pl.* -**ies**) **1 a** a double meaning which is either deliberate or caused by inexactness of expression. **b** an example of this. **2** an expression able to be interpreted in more than one way (e.g. *dogs must be carried*). [ME f. OF *ambiguité* or L *ambiguitas* (as AMBIGUOUS)]

ambiguous /æm'bɪgjʊəs/ *adj.* **1** having an obscure or double meaning. **2** difficult to classify. □□ **ambiguously** *adv.* **ambiguousness** *n.* [L *ambiguus* doubtful f. *ambigere* f. *ambi-* both ways + *agere* drive]

ambisonics /ˌæmbɪ'sɒnɪks/ *n.pl.* a system of high-fidelity sound reproduction designed to reproduce the directional and acoustic properties of the sound source using two or more channels. [L *ambi-* on both sides + SONIC]

ambit /'æmbɪt/ *n.* **1** the scope, extent, or bounds of something. **2** precincts or environs. [ME f. L *ambitus* circuit f. *ambire*: see AMBIENT]

ambition /æm'bɪʃ(ə)n/ *n.* **1** (often foll. by *to* + infin.) the determination to achieve success or distinction, usu. in a chosen field. **2** the object of this determination. [ME f. OF f. L *ambitio -onis* f. *ambire ambit-* canvass for votes: see AMBIENT]

ambitious /æm'bɪʃəs/ *adj.* **1 a** full of ambition. **b** showing ambition (*an ambitious attempt*). **2** (foll. by *of*, or *to* + infin.) strongly determined. □□ **ambitiously** *adv.* **ambitiousness** *n.* [ME f. OF *ambitieux* f. L *ambitiosus* (as AMBITION)]

ambivalence /æm'bɪvələns/ *n.* (also **ambivalency** /-ənsɪ/) the coexistence in one person's mind of opposing feelings, esp. love and hate, in a single context. □□ **ambivalent** *adj.* **ambivalently** *adv.* [G *Ambivalenz* f. L *ambo* both, after *equivalence, -ency*]

ambivert /'æmbɪˌvɜːt/ *n.* *Psychol.* a person who fluctuates between being an introvert and an extrovert. □□ **ambiversion** /ˌæmbɪ'vɜːʃ(ə)n/ *n.* [L *ambi-* on both sides + *-vert* f. L *vertere* to turn, after EXTROVERT, INTROVERT]

amble /'æmb(ə)l/ *v.* & *n.* —*v.intr.* **1** move at an easy pace, in a way suggesting an ambling horse. **2** (of a horse etc.) move by lifting the two feet on one side together. **3** ride an ambling horse; ride at an easy pace. —*n.* an easy pace; the gait of an ambling horse. [ME f. OF *ambler* f. L *ambulare* walk]

amblyopia /ˌæmblɪ'əʊpɪə/ *n.* dimness of vision without obvious defect or change in the eye. □□ **amblyopic** /-'ɒpɪk/ *adj.* [Gk f. *ambluōpos* (adj.) f. *amblus* dull + *ōps, ōpos* eye]

ambo /'æmbəʊ/ *n.* (*pl.* -**os** or **ambones** /-'bəʊniːz/) a stand for reading lessons in an early Christian church etc. [med.L f. Gk *ambōn* rim (in med.Gk = pulpit)]

amboyna /æm'bɔɪnə/ *n.* the decorative wood of the SE Asian tree *Pterocarpus indicus*. [*Amboyna* Island in Indonesia]

ambrosia /æm'brəʊzɪə, -ʒə/ *n.* **1** (in Greek and Roman mythology) the food of the gods; the elixir of life. **2** anything very pleasing to taste or smell. **3** the food of certain bees and beetles. □□ **ambrosial** *adj.* **ambrosian** *adj.* [L f. Gk, = elixir of life f. *ambrotos* immortal]

ambry var. of AUMBRY.

ambulance /'æmbjʊləns/ *n.* **1** a vehicle specially equipped for conveying the sick or injured to and from hospital, esp. in emergencies. **2** a mobile hospital following an army. [F (as AMBULANT)]

ambulant /'æmbjʊlənt/ *adj.* *Med.* **1** (of a patient) able to walk about; not confined to bed. **2** (of treatment) not confining a patient to bed. [L *ambulare ambulant-* walk]

ambulatory /'æmbjʊlətərɪ/ *adj.* & *n.* —*adj.* **1** = AMBULANT. **2** of or adapted for walking. **3 a** movable. **b** not permanent. —*n.* (*pl.* -**ies**) a place for walking, esp. an aisle or cloister in a church or monastery. [L *ambulatorius* f. *ambulare* walk]

ambuscade /ˌæmbə'skeɪd/ *n.* & *v.* —*n.* an ambush. —*v.* **1** *tr.* attack by means of an ambush. **2** *intr.* lie in ambush. **3** *tr.* conceal in an ambush. [F *embuscade* f. It. *imboscata* or Sp. *emboscada* f. L *imboscare*: see AMBUSH, -ADE[1]]

ambush /'æmbʊʃ/ *n.* & *v.* —*n.* **1** a surprise attack by persons (e.g. troops) in a concealed position. **2 a** the concealment of troops etc. to make such an attack. **b** the place where they are concealed. **c** the troops etc. concealed. —*v.tr.* **1** attack by means of an ambush. **2** lie in wait for. [ME f. OF *embusche, embuschier*, f. a Rmc form = 'put in a wood': rel. to BUSH[1]]

ameba *US* var. of AMOEBA.

ameer var. of AMIR.

ameliorate /ə'miːlɪəˌreɪt/ *v.tr.* & *intr. formal* make or become better; improve. □□ **amelioration** /əˌmiːlɪə'reɪʃ(ə)n/ *n.* **ameliorative** *adj.* **ameliorator** *n.* [alt. of MELIORATE after F *améliorer*]

amen /ɑː'men, eɪ-/ *int.* & *n.* —*int.* **1** uttered at the end of a prayer or hymn etc., meaning 'so be it'. **2** (foll. by *to*) expressing agreement or assent (*amen to that*). —*n.* an utterance of 'amen' (sense 1). [ME f. eccl.L f. Gk f. Heb. *'āmēn* certainly]

amenable /əˈmiːnəb(ə)l/ *adj.* **1** responsive, tractable. **2** (often foll. by *to*) (of a person) responsible to law. **3** (foll. by *to*) (of a thing) subject or liable. □□ **amenability** /-ˈbɪlɪtɪ/ *n.* **amenableness** *n.* **amenably** *adv.* [AF (Law) f. F *amener* bring to f. *a*-to + *mener* bring f. LL *minare* drive animals f. L *minari* threaten]

amend /əˈmend/ *v.tr.* **1** make minor improvements in (a text or a written proposal). **2** correct an error or errors in (a document). **3** make better; improve. ¶ Often confused with *emend*, a more technical word used in the context of textual correction. □□ **amendable** *adj.* **amender** *n.* [ME f. OF *amender* ult. f. L *emendare* EMEND]

amende honorable /əˌmɑ̃d ɒnɒˈrɑːb(ə)l/ *n.* (*pl.* *amendes honorables pronunc.* same) a public or open apology, often with some form of reparation. [F, = honourable reparation]

amendment /əˈmendmənt/ *n.* **1** a minor improvement in a document (esp. a legal or statutory one). **2** an article added to the US Constitution. [AMEND + -MENT]

amends /əˈmendz/ *n.* □ **make amends** (often foll. by *for*) compensate or make up (for). [ME f. OF *amendes* penalties, fine, pl. of *amende* reparation f. *amender* AMEND]

amenity /əˈmiːnɪtɪ, əˈmenɪtɪ/ *n.* (*pl.* -**ies**) **1** (usu. in *pl.*) a pleasant or useful feature. **2** pleasantness (of a place, person, etc.). □ **amenity-bed** *Brit.* a bed available in a hospital to give more privacy for a small payment. [ME f. OF *amenité* or L *amoenitas* f. *amoenus* pleasant]

amenorrhoea /eɪˌmenəˈrɪə/ *n.* (*US* **amenorrhea**) *Med.* an abnormal absence of menstruation. [A-¹ + MENO- + Gk *-rrhoia* f. *rheō* flow]

ament /əˈment/ *n.* (also **amentum** /-təm/) (*pl.* **aments** or **amenta** /-tə/) a catkin. [L, = thong]

amentia /əˈmenʃə/ *n. Med.* severe congenital mental deficiency. [L f. *amens ament*- mad (as A-¹, *mens* mind)]

amerce /əˈmɜːs/ *v.tr.* **1** *Law* punish by fine. **2** punish arbitrarily. □□ **amercement** *n.* **amerciable** /-sɪəb(ə)l/ *adj.* [ME *amercy* f. AF *amercier* f. *a* at + *merci* MERCY]

American /əˈmerɪkən/ *adj. & n.* —*adj.* **1** of, relating to, or characteristic of the United States or its inhabitants. **2** (usu. in *comb.*) of or relating to the continents of America (*Latin-American*). —*n.* **1** a native or citizen of the United States. **2** (usu. in *comb.*) a native or inhabitant of the continents of America (*North Americans*). **3** the English language as it is used in the United States. □ **American dream** the traditional ideals of the American people, such as equality, democracy, and material prosperity. **American football** a kind of football played with an oval ball, evolved from Rugby football. **American Indian** see INDIAN. [mod.L *Americanus* f. *America* f. Latinized name of *Amerigo* Vespucci, It. navigator d. 1512]

Americana /əˌmerɪˈkɑːnə/ *n.pl.* things connected with America, esp. with the United States.

Americanism /əˈmerɪkəˌnɪz(ə)m/ *n.* **1 a** a word, sense, or phrase peculiar to or originating from the United States. **b** a thing or feature characteristic of or peculiar to the United States. **2** attachment to or sympathy for the United States.

Americanize /əˈmerɪkəˌnaɪz/ *v.* (also **-ise**) **1** *tr.* **a** make American in character. **b** naturalize as an American. **2** *intr.* become American in character. □□ **Americanization** /-ˈzeɪʃ(ə)n/ *n.*

americium /ˌæməˈrɪsɪəm, -ˈʃɪəm/ *n. Chem.* an artificially made transuranic radioactive metallic element. ¶ Symb.: **Am**. [*America* (where first made) + -IUM]

Amerind /ˈæmərɪnd/ *adj. & n.* (also **Amerindian** /ˌæməˈrɪndɪən/) = *American Indian* (see INDIAN). □□ **Amerindic** /-ˈrɪndɪk/ *adj.* [portmanteau word]

amethyst /ˈæmɪθɪst/ *n.* a precious stone of a violet or purple variety of quartz. □□ **amethystine** /-ˈθɪstiːn/ *adj.* [ME f. OF *ametiste* f. L *amethystus* f. Gk *amethustos* not drunken, the stone being supposed to prevent intoxication]

Amharic /æmˈhærɪk/ *adj. & n.* —*n.* the official and commercial language of Ethiopia. —*adj.* of this language. [*Amhara*, Ethiopian province + -IC]

amiable /ˈeɪmɪəb(ə)l/ *adj.* friendly and pleasant in temperament; likeable. □□ **amiability** /ˌeɪmɪəˈbɪlɪtɪ/ *n.* **amiableness** *n.* **amiably** *adv.* [ME f. OF f. LL *amicabilis* amicable: confused with F *aimable* lovable]

amianthus /ˌæmɪˈænθəs/ *n.* (also **amiantus** /-təs/) any fine silky-fibred variety of asbestos. [L f. Gk *amiantos* undefiled f. *a*- not + *miainō* defile, i.e. purified by fire, being incombustible: for *-h-* cf. AMARANTH]

amicable /ˈæmɪkəb(ə)l/ *adj.* showing or done in a friendly spirit (*an amicable meeting*). □□ **amicability** /ˌæmɪkəˈbɪlɪtɪ/ *n.* **amicableness** *n.* **amicably** *adv.* [LL *amicabilis* f. *amicus* friend]

amice¹ /ˈæmɪs/ *n.* a white linen cloth worn on the neck and shoulders by a priest celebrating the Eucharist. [ME f. med.L *amicia*, *-sia* (earlier *amit* f. OF), f. L *amictus* outer garment]

amice² /ˈæmɪs/ *n.* a cap, hood, or cape worn by members of certain religious orders. [ME f. OF *aumusse* f. med.L *almucia* etc., of unkn. orig.]

amicus curiae /æˌmiːkʊs ˈkjʊərɪˌiː/ *n.* (*pl.* *amici curiae* /-sɪ/) *Law* an impartial adviser in a court of law. [mod.L, = friend of the court]

amid /əˈmɪd/ *prep.* (also **amidst** /əˈmɪdst/) **1** in the middle of. **2** in the course of. [ME *amidde(s)* f. OE *on* ON + MID¹]

amide /ˈeɪmaɪd, ˈæm-/ *n. Chem.* a compound formed from ammonia by replacement of one (or sometimes more than one) hydrogen atom by a metal or an acyl radical. [AMMONIA + -IDE]

amidships /əˈmɪdʃɪps/ *adv.* (*US* **amidship**) in or into the middle of a ship. [MIDSHIP after AMID]

amidst var. of AMID.

amigo /æˈmiːgəʊ/ *n.* (*pl.* -**os**) esp. *US colloq.* (often as a form of address) a friend or comrade, esp. in Spanish-speaking areas. [Sp.]

amine /ˈeɪmiːn, ˈæm-/ *n. Chem.* a compound formed from ammonia by replacement of one or more hydrogen atoms by an organic radical or radicals. [AMMONIA + -INE⁴]

amino /əˈmiːnəʊ/ *n.* (*attrib.*) *Chem.* of, relating to, or containing the monovalent group -NH₂. [AMINE]

amino acid /əˈmiːnəʊ/ *n. Biochem.* any of a group of organic compounds containing both the carboxyl (COOH) and amino (NH₂) group, occurring naturally in plant and animal tissues and forming the basic constituents of proteins. [AMINE + ACID]

amir /əˈmɪə(r)/ *n.* (also **ameer**) the title of some Arab rulers. [Arab. *'amīr* commander f. *amara* command: cf. EMIR]

Amish /ˈɑːmɪʃ, ˈeɪ-/ *adj.* belonging to a strict US Mennonite sect. [prob. f. G *Amisch* f. J. *Amen* 17th-c. Swiss preacher]

amiss /əˈmɪs/ *predic.adj. & adv.* —*predic.adj.* wrong; out of order; faulty (*knew something was amiss*). —*adv.* wrong; wrongly; inappropriately (*everything went amiss*). □ **take amiss** be offended by (*took my words amiss*). [ME prob. f. ON *à mis* so as to miss f. *à* on + *mis* rel. to MISS¹]

amitosis /ˌæmɪˈtəʊsɪs/ *n. Biol.* a form of nuclear division that does not involve mitosis. [A-¹ + MITOSIS]

amitriptyline /ˌæmɪˈtrɪptɪˌliːn/ *n. Pharm.* an antidepressant drug that has a mild tranquillizing action. [AMINE + TRI- + *heptyl* (see HEPTANE) + -INE⁴]

amity /ˈæmɪtɪ/ *n.* friendship; friendly relations. [ME f. OF *amitié* ult. f. L *amicus* friend]

ammeter /'æmɪtə(r)/ n. an instrument for measuring electric current in amperes. [AMPERE + -METER]

ammo /'æməʊ/ n. colloq. ammunition. [abbr.]

ammonia /ə'məʊnɪə/ n. **1** a colourless strongly alkaline gas with a characteristic pungent smell. ¶ Chem. formula: NH_3. **2** (in full **ammonia water**) (in general use) a solution of ammonia gas in water. [mod.L f. SAL AMMONIAC]

ammoniacal /ˌæmə'naɪək(ə)l/ adj. of, relating to, or containing ammonia or sal ammoniac. [ME ammoniac f. OF (arm-, amm-) f. L f. Gk ammōniakos of Ammon (cf. SAL AMMONIAC) + -AL]

ammoniated /ə'məʊnɪˌeɪtɪd/ adj. combined or treated with ammonia.

ammonite /'æməˌnaɪt/ n. any extinct cephalopod mollusc of the order Ammonoidea, with a flat coiled spiral shell found as a fossil. [mod.L ammonites, after med.L cornu Ammonis, = L Ammonis cornu (Pliny), horn of (Jupiter) Ammon]

ammonium /ə'məʊnɪəm/ n. the univalent ion NH_4+, formed from ammonia. [mod.L (as AMMONIA)]

ammunition /ˌæmjʊ'nɪʃ(ə)n/ n. **1** a supply of projectiles (esp. bullets, shells, and grenades). **2** points used or usable to advantage in an argument. [obs. F amunition, corrupt. of (la) munition (the) MUNITION]

amnesia /æm'niːzɪə/ n. a partial or total loss of memory. □□ **amnesiac** /-zɪˌæk/ n. **amnesic** adj. & n. [mod.L f. Gk, = forgetfulness]

amnesty /'æmnɪstɪ/ n. & v. —n. (pl. -ies) a general pardon, esp. for political offences. —v.tr. (-ies, -ied) grant an amnesty to. □ **Amnesty International** an independent international organization in support of human rights, esp. for prisoners of conscience. [F amnestie or L f. Gk amnēstia oblivion]

amniocentesis /ˌæmnɪəʊsen'tiːsɪs/ n. (pl. **amniocenteses** /-siːz/) Med. the sampling of amniotic fluid by insertion of a hollow needle to determine the condition of an embryo. [AMNION + Gk kentēsis pricking f. kenteō to prick]

amnion /'æmnɪən/ n. (pl. **amnia**) Zool. & Physiol. the innermost membrane that encloses the embryo of a reptile, bird, or mammal. □□ **amniotic** /ˌæmnɪ'ɒtɪk/ adj. [Gk, = caul (dimin. of amnos lamb)]

amoeba /ə'miːbə/ n. (US **ameba**) (pl. **amoebas** or **amoebae** /-biː/) any usu. aquatic protozoan of the genus Amoeba, esp. A. proteus, capable of changing shape. □□ **amoebic** adj. **amoeboid** adj. [mod.L f. Gk amoibē change]

amok /ə'mɒk/ adv. (also **amuck** /ə'mʌk/) □ **run amok** run about wildly in an uncontrollable violent rage. [Malay amok rushing in a frenzy]

among /ə'mʌŋ/ prep. (also **amongst** /ə'mʌŋst/) **1** surrounded by; in the company of (lived among the trees; be among friends). **2** in the number of (among us were those who disagreed). **3** an example of; in the class or category of (is among the richest men alive). **4 a** between; within the limits of (collectively or distributively); shared by (had £5 among us; divide it among you). **b** by the joint action or from the joint resources of (among us we can manage it). **5** with one another; by the reciprocal action of (was decided among the participants; talked among themselves). **6** as distinguished from; preeminent in the category of (she is one among many). [OE ongemang f. on ON + gemang assemblage (cf. MINGLE): -st = adverbial genitive -s + -t as in AGAINST]

amontillado /əˌmɒntɪ'lɑːdəʊ/ n. (pl. -os) a medium dry sherry. [Sp. f. Montilla in Spain + -ado = -ATE²]

amoral /eɪ'mɒr(ə)l/ adj. **1** not concerned with or outside the scope of morality (cf. IMMORAL). **2** having no moral principles. □□ **amoralism** n. **amoralist** n. **amorality** /-'rælɪtɪ/ n.

amoretto /ˌæmɔ:'retəʊ/ n. (pl. **amoretti** /-tiː/) a Cupid. [It., dimin. of amore love f. L (as AMOUR)]

amorist /'æmərɪst/ n. a person who professes or writes of (esp. sexual) love. [L amor or F amour + -IST]

amoroso¹ /ˌæmə'rəʊsəʊ/ adv. & adj. Mus. in a loving or tender manner. [It.]

amoroso² /ˌæmə'rəʊsəʊ/ n. (pl. -os) a full rich type of sherry. [Sp., = amorous]

amorous /'æmərəs/ adj. **1** showing, feeling, or inclined to sexual love. **2** of or relating to sexual love. □□ **amorously** adv. **amorousness** n. [ME f. OF f. med.L amorosus f. L amor love]

amorphous /ə'mɔːfəs/ adj. **1** shapeless. **2** vague, ill-organized. **3** Mineral. & Chem. non-crystalline; having neither definite form nor structure. □□ **amorphously** adv. **amorphousness** n. [med.L amorphus f. Gk amorphos shapeless f. a- not + morphē form]

amortize /ə'mɔːtaɪz/ v.tr. (also -ise) Commerce **1** gradually extinguish (a debt) by money regularly put aside. **2** gradually write off the initial cost of (assets). **3** transfer (land) to a corporation in mortmain. □□ **amortization** /-'zeɪʃ(ə)n/ n. [ME f. OF amortir (stem amortiss-) ult. f. L ad to + mors mort- death]

amount /ə'maʊnt/ n. & v. —n. **1** a quantity, esp. the total of a thing or things in number, size, value, extent, etc. (a large amount of money; came to a considerable amount). **2** the full effect or significance. —v.intr. (foll. by to) be equivalent to in number, size, significance, etc. (amounted to £100; amounted to a disaster). □ **any amount** of a great deal of. **no amount of** not even the greatest possible amount of. [ME f. OF amunter f. amont upward, lit. uphill, f. L ad montem]

amour /ə'mʊə(r)/ n. a love affair, esp. a secret one. [F, = love, f. L amor amoris]

amour propre /æˌmʊə 'prɒpr/ n. self-respect. [F]

AMP abbr. adenosine monophosphate.

amp¹ /æmp/ n. Electr. an ampere. [abbr.]

amp² /æmp/ n. colloq. an amplifier. [abbr.]

ampelopsis /ˌæmpɪ'lɒpsɪs/ n. any plant of the genus Ampelopsis or Parthenocissus, usu. a climber supporting itself by twining tendrils, e.g. Virginia creeper. [mod.L f. Gk ampelos vine + opsis appearance]

amperage /'æmpərɪdʒ/ n. Electr. the strength of an electric current in amperes.

ampere /'æmpeə(r)/ n. Electr. the SI base unit of electric current. ¶ Symb.: A. [A. M. Ampère, Fr. physicist d. 1836]

ampersand /'æmpəˌsænd/ n. the sign & (= and). [corrupt. of and per se and ('&' by itself is 'and')]

amphetamine /æm'fetəmɪn, -ˌmiːn/ n. a synthetic drug used esp. as a stimulant. [abbr. of chemical name alpha-methyl phenethylamine]

amphi- /'æmfɪ/ comb. form **1** both. **2** of both kinds. **3** on both sides. **4** around. [Gk]

amphibian /æm'fɪbɪən/ adj. & n. —adj. **1** living both on land and in water. **2** Zool. of or relating to the class Amphibia. **3** (of a vehicle) able to operate on land and water. —n. **1** Zool. any vertebrate of the class Amphibia, with a life history of an aquatic gill-breathing larval stage followed by a terrestrial lung-breathing adult stage, including frogs, toads, newts, and salamanders. **2** (in general use) a creature living both on land and in water. **3** an amphibian vehicle.

amphibious /æm'fɪbɪəs/ adj. **1** living both on land and in water. **2** of or relating to or suited for both land and water. **3** Mil. **a** (of a military operation) involving forces landed from the sea. **b** (of forces) trained for such operations. **4** having a twofold nature; occupying two positions. □□ **amphibiously** adv.

amphibology /ˌæmfɪ'bɒlədʒɪ/ n. (pl. -ies) **1** a quibble. **2** an ambiguous wording. [ME f. OF amphibologie f. LL amphibologia for L f. Gk amphibolia ambiguity]

amphimixis /ˌæmfɪ'mɪksɪs/ n. Biol. true sexual reproduction with the fusion of gametes from two individuals (cf. APOMIXIS). □□ **amphimictic** adj. [mod.L, formed as AMPHI- + Gk mixis mingling]

amphioxus /ˌæmfɪˈɒksəs/ n. any lancelet of the genus *Branchiostoma* (formerly *Amphioxus*). [mod.L, formed as AMPHI- + Gk *oxus* sharp]

amphipathic /ˌæmfɪˈpæθɪk/ adj. Chem. **1** of a substance or molecule that has both a hydrophilic and a hydrophobic part. **2** consisting of such parts. [AMPHI- + Gk *pathikos* (as PATHOS)]

amphipod /ˈæmfɪˌpɒd/ n. any crustacean of the largely marine order Amphipoda, having a laterally compressed abdomen with two kinds of limb, e.g. the freshwater shrimp (*Gammarus pulex*). [AMPHI- + Gk *pous podos* foot]

amphiprostyle /æmˈfɪprəˌstaɪl/ n. & adj. —n. a classical building with a portico at each end. —adj. of or in this style. [L *amphiprostylus* f. Gk *amphiprostulos* (as AMPHI-, *prostulos* PROSTYLE)]

amphisbaena /ˌæmfɪsˈbiːnə/ n. **1** Mythol. & poet. a fabulous serpent with a head at each end. **2** Zool. any burrowing wormlike lizard of the family Amphisbaena, having no apparent division of head from body making both ends look similar. [ME f. L f. Gk *amphisbaina* f. *amphis* both ways + *bainō* go]

amphitheatre /ˈæmfɪˌθɪətə(r)/ n. (US **amphitheater**) **1** a round, usu. unroofed building with tiers of seats surrounding a central space. **2** a semicircular gallery in a theatre. **3** a large circular hollow. **4** the scene of a contest. [L *amphitheatrum* f. Gk *amphitheatron* (as AMPHI-, THEATRE)]

amphora /ˈæmfərə/ n. (pl. **amphorae** /-ˌriː/ or **amphoras**) a Greek or Roman vessel with two handles and a narrow neck. [L f. Gk *amphoreus*]

amphoteric /ˌæmfəˈterɪk/ adj. Chem. able to react as a base and an acid. [Gk *amphoteros* compar. of *amphō* both]

ampicillin /ˌæmpɪˈsɪlɪn/ n. Pharm. a semi-synthetic penicillin used esp. in treating infections of the urinary and respiratory tracts. [*amino* + *penicillin*]

ample /ˈæmp(ə)l/ adj. (**ampler**, **amplest**) **1 a** plentiful, abundant, extensive. **b** euphem. (esp. of a person) large, stout. **2** enough or more than enough. □□ **ampleness** n. **amply** adv. [F f. L *amplus*]

amplifier /ˈæmplɪˌfaɪə(r)/ n. an electronic device for increasing the strength of electrical signals, esp. for conversion into sound in radio etc. equipment.

amplify /ˈæmplɪˌfaɪ/ v. (**-ies**, **-ied**) **1** tr. increase the volume or strength of (sound, electrical signals, etc.). **2** tr. enlarge upon or add detail to (a story etc.). **3** intr. expand what is said or written. □□ **amplification** /-fɪˈkeɪʃ(ə)n/ n. [ME f. OF *amplifier* f. L *amplificare* (as AMPLE, -FY)]

amplitude /ˈæmplɪˌtjuːd/ n. **1 a** Physics the maximum extent of a vibration or oscillation from the position of equilibrium. **b** Electr. the maximum departure of the value of an alternating current or wave from the average value. **2 a** spaciousness, breadth; wide range. **b** abundance. □ **amplitude modulation** Electr. **1** the modulation of a wave by variation of its amplitude. **2** the system using such modulation. [F *amplitude* or L *amplitudo* (as AMPLE)]

ampoule /ˈæmpuːl/ n. a small capsule in which measured quantities of liquids or solids, esp. for injecting, are sealed ready for use. [F f. L AMPULLA]

ampulla /æmˈpʊlə/ n. (pl. **ampullae** /-liː/) **1 a** a Roman globular flask with two handles. **b** a vessel for sacred uses. **2** Anat. the dilated end of a vessel or duct. [L]

amputate /ˈæmpjʊˌteɪt/ v.tr. cut off by surgical operation (a part of the body, esp. a limb), usu. because of injury or disease. □□ **amputation** /-ˈteɪʃ(ə)n/ n. **amputator** n. [L *amputare* f. *amb*-about + *putare* prune]

amputee /ˌæmpjʊˈtiː/ n. a person who has lost a limb etc. by amputation.

amtrac /ˈæmtræk/ n. (also **amtrak**) US an amphibious tracked vehicle used for landing assault troops on a shore. [*amphibious* + *tractor*]

amu abbr. atomic mass unit.

amuck var. of AMOK.

amulet /ˈæmjʊlɪt/ n. **1** an ornament or small piece of jewellery worn as a charm against evil. **2** something which is thought to give such protection. [L *amuletum*, of unkn. orig.]

amuse /əˈmjuːz/ v. **1** tr. cause (a person) to laugh or smile. **2** tr. & refl. (often foll. by *with*, *by*) interest or occupy; keep (a person) entertained. □□ **amusing** adj. **amusingly** adv. [ME f. OF *amuser* cause to muse (see MUSE[2]) f. causal *a* to + *muser* stare]

amusement /əˈmjuːzmənt/ n. **1** something that amuses, esp. a pleasant diversion, game, or pastime. **2 a** the state of being amused. **b** the act of amusing. **3** a mechanical device (e.g. a roundabout) for entertainment at a fairground etc. □ **amusement arcade** Brit. an indoor area for entertainment with automatic game-machines. [F f. *amuser*: see AMUSE, -MENT]

amygdaloid /əˈmɪɡdəˌlɔɪd/ adj. shaped like an almond. □ **amygdaloid nucleus** a roughly almond-shaped mass of grey matter deep inside each cerebral hemisphere, associated with the sense of smell. [L *amygdala* f. Gk *amugdalē* almond]

amyl /ˈeɪmaɪl, ˈæmɪl/ n. (used attrib.) Chem. the monovalent group C_5H_{11}-, derived from pentane. Also called PENTYL. [L *amylum* starch, from which oil containing it was distilled]

amylase /ˈæmɪˌleɪz/ n. Biochem. any of several enzymes that convert starch and glycogen into simple sugars. [AMYL + -ASE]

amylopsin /ˌæmɪˈlɒpsɪn/ n. Biochem. an enzyme of the pancreas that converts starch into maltose. [AMYL after *pepsin*]

Amytal /ˈæmɪˌtæl/ n. propr. a name for amylo-barbitone, a barbiturate drug used as a sedative and a hypnotic. [chem. name *amylethyl barbituric acid*]

an /æn, ən/ adj. the form of the indefinite article (see A[1]) used before words beginning with a vowel sound (*an egg*; *an hour*; *an MP*). ¶ Now less often used before aspirated words beginning with *h* and stressed on a syllable other than the first (so *a hotel*, not *an hotel*).

an-[1] /ən, æn/ prefix not, without (*anarchy*) (cf. A-[1]). [Gk *an-*]

an-[2] /ən, æn/ assim. form of AD- before *n*.

-an /ən/ suffix (also **-ean**, **-ian**) forming adjectives and nouns, esp. from names of places, systems, zoological classes or orders, and founders (*Mexican*; *Anglican*; *crustacean*; *European*; *Lutheran*; *Georgian*; *theologian*). [ult. f. L adj. endings *-(i)anus*, *-aeus*: cf. Gk *-aios*, *-eios*]

ana /ˈɑːnə/ n. **1** (as pl.) anecdotes or literary gossip about a person. **2** (as sing.) a collection of a person's memorable sayings. [= -ANA]

ana- /ˈænə/ prefix (usu. **an-** before a vowel) **1** up (*anadromous*). **2** back (*anamnesis*). **3** again (*anabaptism*). [Gk *ana* up]

-ana /ˈɑːnə/ suffix forming plural nouns meaning 'things associated with' (*Victoriana*; *Americana*). [neut. pl. of L adj. ending *-anus*]

Anabaptism /ˌænəˈbæptɪz(ə)m/ n. the doctrine that baptism should only be administered to believing adults. □□ **Anabaptist** n. [eccl.L *anabaptismus* f. Gk *anabaptismos* (as ANA-, BAPTISM)]

anabas /ˈænəˌbæs/ n. any of the freshwater fish of the climbing perch family native to Asia and Africa, esp. the genus *Anabas*, able to breathe air and move on land. [mod.L f. Gk past part. of *anabainō* walk up]

anabasis /əˈnæbəsɪs/ n. (pl. **anabases** /-ˌsiːz/) **1** the march of the younger Cyrus into Asia in 401 BC as narrated by Xenophon in his work *Anabasis*. **2** a military up-country march. [Gk, = ascent f. *anabainō* (as ANA-, *bainō* go)]

anabatic /ˌænəˈbætɪk/ adj. Meteorol. (of a wind) caused by air flowing upwards (cf. KATABATIC). [Gk *anabatikos* ascending (as ANABASIS)]

anabiosis /ˌænəbaɪˈəʊsɪs/ n. (pl. **anabioses** /-siːz/)

revival after apparent death. □□ **anabiotic** /-'ɒtɪk/ *adj.* [med.L f. Gk *anabiōsis* f. *anabioō* return to life]

anabolic /ˌænə'bɒlɪk/ *adj. Biochem.* of or relating to anabolism. □ **anabolic steroid** any of a group of synthetic steroid hormones used to increase muscle size.

anabolism /ə'næbəˌlɪz(ə)m/ *n. Biochem.* the synthesis of complex molecules in living organisms from simpler ones together with the storage of energy; constructive metabolism (opp. CATABOLISM). [Gk *anabolē* ascent (as ANA-, *ballō* throw)]

anabranch /'ænəˌbrɑːntʃ/ *n.* esp. *Austral.* a stream that leaves a river and re-enters it lower down. [ANASTOMOSE + BRANCH]

anachronic /ˌænə'krɒnɪk/ *adj.* **1** out of date. **2** involving anachronism. [ANACHRONISM after *synchronic* etc.]

anachronism /ə'nækrəˌnɪz(ə)m/ *n.* **1 a** the attribution of a custom, event, etc., to a period to which it does not belong. **b** a thing attributed in this way. **2 a** anything out of harmony with its period. **b** an old-fashioned or out-of-date person or thing. □□ **anachronistic** /-'nɪstɪk/ *adj.* **anachronistically** /-'nɪstɪkəlɪ/ *adv.* [F *anachronisme* or Gk *anakhronismos* (as ANA-, *khronos* time)]

anacoluthon /ˌænəkə'luːθɒn/ *n.* (*pl.* **anacolutha** /-'luːθə/) a sentence or construction which lacks grammatical sequence (e.g. *while in the garden the door banged shut*). □□ **anacoluthic** *adj.* [LL f. Gk *anakolouthon* (as AN-¹, *akolouthos* following)]

anaconda /ˌænə'kɒndə/ *n.* a large non-poisonous snake living mainly in water or in trees that kills its prey by constriction. [alt. of *anacondaia* f. Sinh. *henakandayā* whip-snake f. *hena* lightning + *kanda* stem: orig. of a snake in Sri Lanka]

anacreontic /əˌnækrɪ'ɒntɪk/ *n. & adj.* —*n.* a poem written after the manner of Anacreon, a Greek lyric poet (d. 478 BC). —*adj.* **1** after the manner of Anacreon. **2** convivial and amatory in tone. [LL *anacreonticus* f. Gk *Anakreōn*]

anacrusis /ˌænə'kruːsɪs/ *n.* (*pl.* **anacruses** /-siːz/) **1** (in poetry) an unstressed syllable at the beginning of a verse. **2** *Mus.* an unstressed note or notes before the first bar-line. [Gk *anakrousis* (as ANA-, *krousis* f. *krouō* strike)]

anadromous /ə'nædrəmʊs/ *adj.* (of a fish, e.g. the salmon) that swims up a river from the sea to spawn (opp. CATADROMOUS). [Gk *anadromos* (as ANA-, *dromos* -running)]

anaemia /ə'niːmɪə/ *n.* (*US* **anemia**) a deficiency in the blood, usu. of red cells or their haemoglobin, resulting in pallor and weariness. □ **pernicious anaemia** a defective formation of red blood cells through a lack of vitamin B₁₂ or folic acid. [mod.L f. Gk *anaimia* (as AN-¹, -AEMIA)]

anaemic /ə'niːmɪk/ *adj.* (*US* **anemic**) **1** relating to or suffering from anaemia. **2** pale; lacking in vitality.

anaerobe /'ænəˌrəʊb, ə'neərəʊb/ *n.* an organism that grows without air, or requires oxygen-free conditions to live. □□ **anaerobic** /ˌæneə'rəʊbɪk/ *adj.* [F *anaérobie* formed as AN-¹ + AEROBE]

anaesthesia /ˌænɪs'θiːzɪə/ *n.* (*US* **anesthesia**) the absence of sensation, esp. artificially induced insensitivity to pain usu. achieved by the administration of gases or the injection of drugs. □□ **anaesthesiology** /-'blədʒɪ/ *n.* [mod.L f. Gk *anaisthēsia* (as AN-¹, *aisthēsis* sensation)]

anaesthetic /ˌænɪs'θetɪk/ *adj. & n.* (*US* **anesthetic**) —*n.* a substance that produces insensibility to pain etc. —*adj.* producing partial or complete insensibility to pain etc. □ **general anaesthetic** an anaesthetic that affects the whole body, usu. with loss of consciousness. **local anaesthetic** an anaesthetic that affects a restricted area of the body. [Gk *anaisthētos* insensible (as ANAESTHESIA)]

anaesthetist /ə'niːsθətɪst/ *n.* a specialist in the administration of anaesthetics.

anaesthetize /ə'niːsθəˌtaɪz/ *v.tr.* (also **-ise**, *US*

anesthetize) **1** administer an anaesthetic to. **2** deprive of physical or mental sensation. □□ **anaesthetization** /-'zeɪʃ(ə)n/ *n.*

anaglyph /'ænəglɪf/ *n.* **1** *Photog.* a composite stereoscopic photograph printed in superimposed complementary colours. **2** an embossed object cut in low relief. □□ **anaglyphic** /-'glɪfɪk/ *adj.* [Gk *anagluphē* (as ANA-, *gluphē* f. *gluphō* carve)]

anaglypta /ˌænə'glɪptə/ *n.* a type of thick embossed wallpaper, usu. for painting over. [L *anaglypta* work in bas-relief: cf. ANAGLYPH]

anagram /'ænəˌgræm/ *n.* a word or phrase formed by transposing the letters of another word or phrase. □□ **anagrammatic** /-grə'mætɪk/ *adj.* **anagrammatical** /-grə'mætɪk(ə)l/ *adj.* **anagrammatize** /-'græməˌtaɪz/ *v.tr.* (also **-ise**). [F *anagramme* or mod.L *anagramma* f. Gk ANA- + *gramma -atos* letter: cf. -GRAM]

anal /'eɪn(ə)l/ *adj.* relating to or situated near the anus. □ **anal retentive** (of a person) excessively orderly and fussy (supposedly owing to aspects of toilet-training in infancy). □□ **anally** *adv.* [mod.L *analis* (as ANUS)]

analects /'ænəˌlekts/ *n.pl.* (also **analecta** /ˌænə'lektə/) a collection of short literary extracts. [L f. Gk *analekta* things gathered f. *analegō* pick up]

analeptic /ˌænə'leptɪk/ *adj. & n.* —*adj.* (of a drug etc.) restorative. —*n.* a restorative medicine or drug. [Gk *analēptikos* f. *analambanō* take back]

analgesia /ˌænæl'dʒiːzɪə, -sɪə/ *n.* the absence or relief of pain. [mod.L f. Gk, = painlessness]

analgesic /ˌænæl'dʒiːsɪk, -zɪk/ *adj. & n.* —*adj.* relieving pain. —*n.* an analgesic drug.

analog *US* var. of ANALOGUE.

analogize /ə'næləˌdʒaɪz/ *v.* (also **-ise**) **1** *tr.* represent or explain by analogy. **2** *intr.* use analogy.

analogous /ə'næləgəs/ *adj.* (usu. foll. by *to*) partially similar or parallel; showing analogy. □□ **analogously** *adv.* [L *analogus* f. Gk *analogos* proportionate]

analogue /'ænəˌlɒg/ *n.* (*US* **analog**) **1** an analogous or parallel thing. **2** (*attrib.*) (usu. **analog**) (of a computer or electronic process) using physical variables, e.g. voltage, weight, or length, to represent numbers (cf. DIGITAL). [F f. Gk *analogon* neut. adj.: see ANALOGOUS]

analogy /ə'nælədʒɪ/ *n.* (*pl.* **-ies**) **1** (usu. foll. by *to, with, between*) correspondence or partial similarity. **2** *Logic* a process of arguing from similarity in known respects to similarity in other respects. **3** *Philol.* the imitation of existing words in forming inflections or constructions of others, without the existence of corresponding intermediate stages. **4** *Biol.* the resemblance of function between organs essentially different. **5** an analogue. □□ **analogical** /ˌænə'lɒdʒɪk(ə)l/ *adj.* **analogically** /ˌænə'lɒdʒɪkəlɪ/ *adv.* [F *analogie* or L *analogia* proportion f. Gk (as ANALOGOUS)]

analysand /ə'nælɪˌsænd/ *n.* a person undergoing psychoanalysis.

analyse /'ænəˌlaɪz/ *v.tr.* (*US* **analyze**) **1** examine in detail the constitution or structure of. **2** *Chem.* ascertain the constituents of (a sample of a mixture or compound). **3** find or show the essence or structure of (a book, music, etc.). **4** *Gram.* resolve (a sentence) into its grammatical elements. **5** psychoanalyse. □□ **analysable** *adj.* **analyser** *n.* [obs. *analyse* (n.) or F *analyser* f. *analyse* (n.) f. med.L ANALYSIS]

analysis /ə'nælɪsɪs/ *n.* (*pl.* **analyses** /-ˌsiːz/) **1 a** a detailed examination of the elements or structure of a substance etc. **b** a statement of the result of this. **2** *Chem.* the determination of the constituent parts of a mixture or compound. **3** psychoanalysis. **4** *Math.* the use of algebra and calculus in problem-solving. **5** *Cricket* a statement of the performance of a bowler, usu. giving the numbers of overs and maiden overs bowled, runs conceded, and wickets taken. □ **in the final** (or **last** or **ultimate**) **analysis** after all due consideration; in the end. [med.L f. Gk *analusis* (as ANA-, *luō* set free)]

analyst /ˈænəlɪst/ *n.* **1** a person skilled in (esp. chemical) analysis. **2** a psychoanalyst. [F *analyste*]

analytic /ˌænəˈlɪtɪk/ *adj.* **1** of or relating to analysis. **2** *Philol.* analytical. **3** *Logic* (of a statement etc.) such that its denial is self-contradictory; true by definition (see SYNTHETIC). [LL f. Gk *analutikos* (as ANALYSIS)]

analytical /ˌænəˈlɪtɪk(ə)l/ *adj.* **1** using analytic methods. **2** *Philol.* using separate words instead of inflections (cf. SYNTHETIC). □**analytical geometry** geometry using coordinates. □□**analytically** *adv.*

analyze *US* var. of ANALYSE.

anamnesis /ˌænæmˈniːsɪs/ *n.* (*pl.* **anamneses** /-siːz/) **1** recollection (esp. of a supposed previous existence). **2** a patient's account of his or her medical history. **3** *Eccl.* the part of the anaphora recalling the Passion, Resurrection, and Ascension of Christ. [Gk, = remembrance]

anandrous /əˈnændrəs/ *adj. Bot.* having no stamens. [Gk *anandros* without males f. *an-* not + *anēr andros* male]

anapaest /ˈænəˌpiːst/ *n.* (*US* **anapest**) *Prosody* a foot consisting of two short or unstressed syllables followed by one long or stressed syllable. □□ **anapaestic** /-ˈpiːstɪk/ *adj.* [L *anapaestus* f. Gk *anapaistos* reversed (because the reverse of a dactyl)]

anaphase /ˈænəˌfeɪz/ *n. Biol.* the stage of meiotic or mitotic cell division when the chromosomes move away from one another towards opposite poles of the spindle. [ANA- + PHASE]

anaphora /əˈnæfərə/ *n.* **1** *Rhet.* the repetition of a word or phrase at the beginning of successive clauses. **2** *Gram.* the use of a word referring to or replacing a word used earlier in a sentence, to avoid repetition (e.g. *do* in *I like it and so do they*). **3** *Eccl.* the part of the Eucharist which contains the consecration, anamnesis, and communion. □□ **anaphoric** /ˌænəˈfɒrɪk/ *adj.* [L f. Gk, = repetition (as ANA-, *pherō* to bear)]

anaphrodisiac /ænˌæfrəˈdɪzɪˌæk/ *adj. & n.* —*adj.* tending to reduce sexual desire. —*n.* an anaphrodisiac drug.

anaphylaxis /ˌænəfɪˈlæksɪs/ *n.* (*pl.* **anaphylaxes** /-ksiːz/) *Med.* hypersensitivity of tissues to a dose of antigen, as a reaction against a previous dose. □□ **anaphylactic** *adj.* [mod.L f. F *anaphylaxie* (as ANA- + Gk *phulaxis* guarding)]

anaptyxis /ˌænəpˈtɪksɪs/ *n.* (*pl.* **anaptyxes** /-siːz/) *Phonet.* the insertion of a vowel between two consonants to aid pronunciation (as in *went thataway*). □□ **anaptyctic** *adj.* [mod.L f. Gk *anaptuxis* (as ANA-, *ptussō* fold)]

anarchism /ˈænəˌkɪz(ə)m/ *n.* the doctrine that all government should be abolished. [F *anarchisme* (as ANARCHY)]

anarchist /ˈænəkɪst/ *n.* an advocate of anarchism or of political disorder. □□ **anarchistic** /-ˈkɪstɪk/ *adj.* [F *anarchiste* (as ANARCHY)]

anarchy /ˈænəkɪ/ *n.* **1** disorder, esp. political or social. **2** lack of government in a society. □□ **anarchic** /əˈnɑːkɪk/ *adj.* **anarchical** /əˈnɑːkɪk(ə)l/ *adj.* **anarchically** /əˈnɑːkɪkəlɪ/ *adv.* [med.L *anarkhia* (as AN-[1], *arkhē* rule)]

anastigmat /əˈnæstɪɡˌmæt/ *n.* a lens or lens-system made free from astigmatism by correction. [G f. *anastigmatisch* ANASTIGMATIC]

anastigmatic /ˌænəstɪɡˈmætɪk/ *adj.* free from astigmatism.

anastomose /əˈnæstəˌməʊz/ *v.intr.* link by anastomosis. [F *anastomoser* (as ANASTOMOSIS)]

anastomosis /əˌnæstəˈməʊsɪs/ *n.* (*pl.* **anastomoses** /-siːz/) a cross-connection of arteries, branches, rivers, etc. [mod.L f. Gk f. *anastomoō* furnish with a mouth (as ANA-, *stoma* mouth)]

anastrophe /əˈnæstrəfɪ/ *n. Rhet.* the inversion of the usual order of words or clauses. [Gk *anastrophē* turning back (as ANA-, *strephō* to turn)]

anathema /əˈnæθəmə/ *n.* (*pl.* **anathemas**) **1** a detested thing or person (*is anathema to me*). **2 a** a curse of the Church, excommunicating a person or denouncing a doctrine. **b** a cursed thing or person. **c** a strong curse. [eccl.L, = excommunicated person, excommunication, f. Gk *anathema* thing devoted, (later) accursed thing, f. *anatithēmi* set up]

anathematize /əˈnæθəməˌtaɪz/ *v.tr. & intr.* (also -ise) curse. [F *anathématiser* f. L *anathematīzāre* f. Gk *anathematizo* (as ANATHEMA)]

anatomical /ˌænəˈtɒmɪk(ə)l/ *adj.* **1** of or relating to anatomy. **2** structural. □□ **anatomically** *adv.* [F *anatomique* or LL *anatomicus* (as ANATOMY)]

anatomist /əˈnætəmɪst/ *n.* a person skilled in anatomy. [F *anatomiste* or med.L *anatomista* (as ANATOMIZE)]

anatomize /əˈnætəˌmaɪz/ *v.tr.* (also -ise) **1** examine in detail. **2** dissect. [F *anatomiser* or med.L *anatomizare* f. *anatomia* (as ANATOMY)]

anatomy /əˈnætəmɪ/ *n.* (*pl.* -ies) **1** the science of the bodily structure of animals and plants. **2** this structure. **3** *colloq.* a human body. **4** analysis. **5** the dissection of the human body, animals, or plants. [F *anatomie* or LL *anatomia* f. Gk (as ANA-, -TOMY)]

anatta (also **anatto**) var. of ANNATTO.

ANC *abbr.* African National Congress.

-ance /əns/ *suffix* forming nouns expressing: **1** a quality or state or an instance of one (*arrogance*; *protuberance*; *relevance*; *resemblance*). **2** an action (*assistance*; *furtherance*; *penance*). [from or after F *-ance* f. L *-antia*, *-entia* (cf. -ENCE) f. pres. part. stem *-ant-*, *-ent-*]

ancestor /ˈænsestə(r)/ *n.* (*fem.* **ancestress** /-strɪs/) **1** any (esp. remote) person from whom one is descended. **2** an early type of animal or plant from which others have evolved. **3** an early prototype or forerunner (*ancestor of the computer*). [ME f. OF *ancestre* f. L *antecessor -oris* f. *antecedere* (as ANTE-, *cedere cess-* go)]

ancestral /ænˈsestr(ə)l/ *adj.* belonging to or inherited from one's ancestors. [F *ancestrel* (as ANCESTOR)]

ancestry /ˈænsestrɪ/ *n.* (*pl.* -ies) **1** one's (esp. remote) family descent. **2** one's ancestors collectively. [ME alt. of OF *ancesserie* (as ANCESTOR)]

anchor /ˈæŋkə(r)/ *n. & v.* —*n.* **1** a heavy metal weight used to moor a ship to the sea-bottom or a balloon to the ground. **2** a thing affording stability. **3** a source of confidence. —*v.* **1** *tr.* secure (a ship or balloon) by means of an anchor. **2** *tr.* fix firmly. **3** *intr.* cast anchor. **4** *intr.* be moored by means of an anchor. □**anchor-plate** a heavy piece of timber or metal, e.g. as support for suspension-bridge cables. **at anchor** moored by means of an anchor. **cast (or come to) anchor** let the anchor down. **weigh anchor** take the anchor up. [OE *ancor* f. L *anchora* f. Gk *agkura*]

anchorage /ˈæŋkərɪdʒ/ *n.* **1** a place where a ship may be anchored. **2** the act of anchoring or lying at anchor. **3** anything dependable.

anchorite /ˈæŋkəˌraɪt/ *n.* (also **anchoret** /-rɪt/) (*fem.* **anchoress** /-rɪs/) **1** a hermit; a religious recluse. **2** a person of secluded habits. □□ **anchoretic** /-ˈretɪk/ *adj.* **anchoritic** /-ˈrɪtɪk/ *adj.* [ME f. med.L *anc(h)orita* f. eccl.L *anchoreta* f. eccl.Gk *anakhōrētēs* f. *anakhōreō* retire]

anchorman /ˈæŋkəmən/ *n.* (*pl.* -men) **1** a person who coordinates activities, esp. as compère in a broadcast. **2** a person who plays a crucial part, esp. at the back of a tug-of-war team or as the last runner in a relay race.

anchoveta /ˌæntʃəˈvetə/ *n.* a small Pacific anchovy caught for use as bait or to make fish-meal. [Sp., dimin. of *anchova*: cf. ANCHOVY]

anchovy /ˈæntʃəvɪ, ænˈtʃəʊvɪ/ *n.* (*pl.* -ies) any of various small silvery fish of the herring family usu. preserved in salt and oil and having a strong taste. □**anchovy pear** a W. Indian fruit like a mango.

anchovy toast toast spread with paste made from anchovies. [Sp. & Port. *ancho(v)a*, of uncert. orig.]

anchusa /æn'kjuːzə, æn'tʃuːzə/ *n.* any plant of the genus *Anchusa*, akin to borage. [L f. Gk *agkhousa*]

anchylose var. of ANKYLOSE.

anchylosis var. of ANKYLOSIS.

ancien régime /ɑ̃ˌsjæ re'ʒiːm/ *n.* (*pl.* **anciens régimes** *pronunc.* same) **1** the political and social system in France before the Revolution of 1789. **2** any superseded regime. [F, = old rule]

ancient[1] /'eɪnʃ(ə)nt/ *adj.* & *n.* —*adj.* **1** of long ago. **2** having lived or existed long. —*n.* archaic an old man. □**ancient history 1** the history of the ancient civilizations of the Mediterranean area and the Near East before the fall of the Western Roman Empire in 476. **2** something already long familiar. **ancient lights** a window that a neighbour may not deprive of light by building. **ancient monument** *Brit.* an old building etc. preserved usu. under Government control. **the ancients** the people of ancient times, esp. the Greeks and Romans. □□ **ancientness** *n.* [ME f. AF *auncien* f. OF *ancien*, ult. f. L *ante* before]

ancient[2] /'eɪnʃ(ə)nt/ *n.* archaic = ENSIGN. [corrupt. of form *ensyne* etc. by assoc. with *ancien* = ANCIENT[1]]

anciently /'eɪnʃəntlɪ/ *adv.* long ago.

ancillary /æn'sɪlərɪ/ *adj.* & *n.* —*adj.* **1** (of a person, activity, or service) providing essential support to a central service or industry, esp. the medical service. **2** (often foll. by *to*) subordinate, subservient. —*n.* (*pl.* -**ies**) **1** an ancillary worker. **2** something which is ancillary; an auxiliary or accessory. [L *ancillaris* f. *ancilla* maidservant]

ancon /'æŋkən/ *n.* (*pl.* -**es** /æŋ'kəʊniːz/) *Archit.* **1** a console, usu. of two volutes, supporting or appearing to support a cornice. **2** each of a pair of projections on either side of a block of stone etc. for lifting or repositioning. [L f. Gk *agkōn* elbow]

-ancy /ənsɪ/ *suffix* forming nouns denoting a quality (*constancy*; *relevancy*) or state (*expectancy*; *infancy*) (cf. -ANCE). [from or after L -*antia*: cf. -ENCY]

and /ænd, ənd/ *conj.* **1 a** connecting words, clauses, or sentences, that are to be taken jointly (*cakes and buns*; *white and brown bread*; *buy and sell*; *two hundred and forty*). **b** implying progression (*better and better*). **c** implying causation (*do that and I'll hit you*; *she hit him and he cried*). **d** implying great duration (*he cried and cried*). **e** implying a great number (*miles and miles*). **f** implying addition (*two and two are four*). **g** implying variety (*there are books and books*). **h** implying succession (*walking two and two*). **2** *colloq.* to (*try and open it*). **3** in relation to (*Britain and the EEC*). □**and/or** either or both of two stated possibilities (usually restricted to legal and commercial use). [OE *and*]

-and /ænd/ *suffix* forming nouns meaning 'a person or thing to be treated in a specified way' (*ordinand*). [L gerundive ending -*andus*]

andante /æn'dæntɪ/ *adv.*, *adj.*, & *n.* *Mus.* —*adv.* & *adj.* in a moderately slow tempo. —*n.* an andante passage or movement. [It., part. of *andare* go]

andantino /ˌændæn'tiːnəʊ/ *adv.*, *adj.*, & *n.* *Mus.* —*adv.* & *adj.* rather quicker (orig. slower) than andante. —*n.* (*pl.* -**os**) an andantino passage or movement. [It., dimin. of ANDANTE]

andesite /'ændɪˌzaɪt/ *n.* a fine-grained brown or greyish intermediate volcanic rock. [*Andes* mountain chain in S. America + -ITE[1]]

andiron /'ændˌaɪən/ *n.* a metal stand (usu. one of a pair) for supporting burning wood in a fireplace; a firedog. [ME f. OF *andier* of unkn. orig.: assim. to IRON]

androecium /æn'driːsɪəm/ *n.* (*pl.* **androecia** /-sɪə/) *Bot.* the stamens taken collectively. [mod.L f. Gk *andro-* male + *oikion* house]

androgen /'ændrədʒ(ə)n/ *n.* a male sex hormone or other substance capable of developing and maintaining certain male sexual characteristics. □□ **androgenic** /-'dʒenɪk/ *adj.* [Gk *andro-* male + -GEN]

androgyne /'ændrəˌdʒaɪn/ *adj.* & *n.* —*adj.* hermaphrodite. —*n.* a hermaphrodite person. [OF *androgyne* or L *androgynus* f. Gk *androgunos* (*anēr andros* male, *gunē* woman)]

androgynous /æn'drɒdʒɪnəs/ *adj.* **1** hermaphrodite. **2** *Bot.* with stamens and pistils in the same flower or inflorescence.

androgyny /æn'drɒdʒɪnɪ/ *n.* hermaphroditism.

android /'ændrɔɪd/ *n.* a robot with a human appearance. [Gk *andro-* male, man + -OID]

-androus /ændrəs/ *comb. form Bot.* forming adjectives meaning 'having specified male organs or stamens' (*monandrous*). [mod.L f. Gk -*andros* f. *anēr andros* male + -OUS]

-ane[1] /eɪn/ *suffix* var. of -AN; usu. with distinction of sense (*germane*; *humane*; *urbane*) but sometimes with no corresponding form in -*an* (*mundane*).

-ane[2] /eɪn/ *suffix Chem.* forming names of paraffins and other saturated hydrocarbons (*methane*; *propane*). [after -*ene*, -*ine*, etc.]

anecdotage /'ænɪkˌdəʊtɪdʒ/ *n.* **1** *joc.* garrulous old age. **2** anecdotes. [ANECDOTE + -AGE: sense 1 after DOTAGE]

anecdote /'ænɪkˌdəʊt/ *n.* a short account (or painting etc.) of an entertaining or interesting incident. □□ **anecdotal** /-'dəʊt(ə)l/ *adj.* **anecdotalist** /-'dəʊtəlɪst/ *n.* **anecdotic** /-'dɒtɪk/ *adj.* **anecdotist** *n.* [F *anecdote* or mod.L f. Gk *anekdota* things unpublished (as AN-[1], *ekdotos* f. *ekdidōmi* publish)]

anechoic /ˌænɪ'kəʊɪk/ *adj.* free from echo.

anele /ə'niːl/ *v.tr.* archaic anoint, esp. in extreme unction. [ME f. AN-[1] + *elien* f. OE *ele* f. L *oleum* oil]

anemia *US* var. of ANAEMIA.

anemic *US* var. of ANAEMIC.

anemograph /ə'neməˌgrɑːf/ *n.* an instrument for recording on paper the direction and force of the wind. □□ **anemographic** /-'græfɪk/ *adj.* [Gk *anemos* wind + -GRAPH[1]]

anemometer /ˌænɪ'mɒmɪtə(r)/ *n.* an instrument for measuring the force of the wind. [Gk *anemos* wind + -METER]

anemometry /ˌænɪ'mɒmɪtrɪ/ *n.* the measurement of the force of the wind. □□ **anemometric** /-mə'metrɪk/ *adj.* [Gk *anemos* wind + -METRY]

anemone /ə'nemənɪ/ *n.* **1** any plant of the genus *Anemone*, akin to the buttercup, with flowers of various vivid colours. **2** = PASQUE-FLOWER. [L f. Gk *anemōnē* wind-flower f. *anemos* wind]

anemophilous /ˌænɪ'mɒfɪləs/ *adj.* wind-pollinated. [Gk *anemos* wind + -*philous* (see -PHILIA)]

anent /ə'nent/ *prep.* archaic or *Sc.* concerning. [OE *on efen* on a level with]

-aneous /'eɪnɪəs/ *suffix* forming adjectives (*cutaneous*; *miscellaneous*). [L -*aneus* + -OUS]

aneroid /'ænəˌrɔɪd/ *adj.* & *n.* —*adj.* (of a barometer) that measures air-pressure by its action on the elastic lid of an evacuated box, not by the height of a column of fluid. —*n.* an aneroid barometer. [F *anéroïde* f. Gk *a-* not + *nēros* water]

anesthesia etc. *US* var. of ANAESTHESIA etc.

aneurin /ə'njʊərɪn, 'æn-/ *n.* = THIAMINE. [*anti-* + *poly*neuritis + vitamin]

aneurysm /'ænjʊˌrɪz(ə)m/ *n.* (also **aneurism**) an excessive localized enlargement of an artery. □□ **aneurysmal** /-'rɪzm(ə)l/ *adj.* (also **aneurismal**). [Gk *aneurusma* f. *aneurunō* widen out f. *eurus* wide]

anew /ə'njuː/ *adv.* **1** again. **2** in a different way. [ME, f. A-[4] + NEW]

anfractuosity /ˌænfræktjʊ'ɒsɪtɪ/ *n.* **1** circuitousness. **2** intricacy. [F *anfractuosité* f. LL *anfractuosus* f. L *anfractus* a bending]

angary /'æŋgərɪ/ *n.* *Law* the right of a belligerent (subject to compensation for loss) to seize or destroy neutral property under military necessity. [F *angarie* ult. f. Gk *aggareia* f. *aggaros* courier]

angel /'eɪndʒ(ə)l/ *n.* **1 a** an attendant or messenger of God. **b** a conventional representation of this in human form with wings. **c** an attendant spirit (*evil* *angel; guardian angel).* **d** a member of the lowest order of the ninefold celestial hierarchy (see ORDER). **2 a** a very virtuous person. **b** an obliging person (*be an angel and answer the door*). **3** an old English coin bearing the figure of the archangel Michael piercing the dragon. **4** *sl.* a financial backer of an enterprise, esp. in the theatre. **5** an unexplained radar echo. □**angel cake** a very light sponge cake. **angel-fish** any of various fish, esp. *Pterophyllum scalare*, with large dorsal and ventral fins. **angel-shark** = MONKFISH 2. **angels-on-horseback** a savoury of oysters wrapped in slices of bacon. [ME f. OF *angele* f. eccl.L *angelus* f. Gk *aggelos* messenger]

angelic /æn'dʒelɪk/ *adj.* **1** like or relating to angels. **2** having characteristics attributed to angels, esp. sublime beauty or innocence. □□**angelical** *adj.* **angelically** *adv.* [ME f. F *angélique* or LL *angelicus* f. Gk *aggelikos* (as ANGEL)]

angelica /æn'dʒelɪkə/ *n.* **1** an aromatic umbelliferous plant, *Angelica archangelica*, used in cooking and medicine. **2** its candied stalks. [med.L (*herba*) *angelica* angelic herb]

angelus /'ændʒɪləs/ *n.* **1** a Roman Catholic devotion commemorating the Incarnation, said at morning, noon, and sunset. **2** a bell rung to announce this. [opening words *Angelus domini* (L, = the angel of the Lord)]

anger /'æŋgə(r)/ *n.* & *v.* —*n.* extreme or passionate displeasure. —*v.tr.* make angry; enrage. [ME f. ON *angr* grief, *angra* vex]

Angevin /'ændʒɪvɪn/ *n.* & *adj.* —*n.* **1** a native or inhabitant of Anjou. **2** a Plantagenet, esp. any of the English kings from Henry II to John. —*adj.* **1** of Anjou. **2** of the Plantagenets. [F]

angina /æn'dʒaɪnə/ *n.* **1** an attack of intense constricting pain often causing suffocation. **2** (in full **angina pectoris** /'pektərɪs/) pain in the chest brought on by exertion, owing to an inadequate blood supply to the heart. [L, = spasm of the chest f. *angina* quinsy f. Gk *agkhonē* strangling]

angioma /ændʒɪ'əʊmə/ *n.* (*pl.* **angiomata** /-mətə/) a tumour produced by the dilatation or new formation of blood-vessels. [mod.L f. Gk *aggeion* vessel]

angiosperm /'ændʒɪə,spɜːm/ *n.* any plant producing flowers and reproducing by seeds enclosed within a carpel, including herbaceous plants, herbs, shrubs, grasses and most trees (opp. GYMNOSPERM). □□ **angiospermous** /ˌændʒɪə'spɜːməs/ *adj.* [Gk *aggeion* vessel + *sperma* seed]

Angle /'æŋg(ə)l/ *n.* (usu. in *pl.*) a member of a tribe from Schleswig that settled in Eastern Britain in the 5th c. □□ **Anglian** *adj.* [L *Anglus* f. Gmc (OE *Engle*: cf. ENGLISH) f. *Angul* a district of Schleswig (now in N. Germany) (as ANGLE²)]

angle¹ /'æŋg(ə)l/ *n.* & *v.* —*n.* **1 a** the space between two meeting lines or surfaces. **b** the inclination of two lines or surfaces to each other. **2 a** a corner. **b** a sharp projection. **3 a** the direction from which a photograph etc. is taken. **b** the aspect from which a matter is considered. —*v.* **1** *tr.* & *intr.* move or place obliquely. **2** *tr.* present (information) from a particular point of view (*was angled in favour of the victim*). □**angle brackets** brackets in the form < > (see BRACKET *n.* 3). **angle-iron** a piece of iron or steel with an L-shaped cross-section, used to strengthen a framework. **angle of repose** the angle beyond which an inclined body will not support another on its surface by friction. [ME f. OF *angle* or f. L *angulus*]

angle² /'æŋg(ə)l/ *v.* & *n.* —*v.intr.* **1** (often foll. by *for*) fish with hook and line. **2** (foll. by *for*) seek an objective by devious or calculated means (*angled for a pay rise*). —*n.* archaic a fish-hook. [OE *angul*]

angled /'æŋg(ə)ld/ *adj.* **1** placed at an angle to something else. **2** presented to suit a particular point of view. **3** having an angle.

angler /'æŋglə(r)/ *n.* **1** a person who fishes with a hook and line. **2** = *angler-fish*. □**angler-fish** any of various fishes that prey upon small fish, attracting

them by filaments arising from the dorsal fin: also called *frog-fish* (see FROG¹).

Anglican /'æŋglɪkən/ *adj.* & *n.* —*adj.* of or relating to the Church of England or any Church in communion with it. —*n.* a member of an Anglican Church. □□ **Anglicanism** *n.* [med.L *Anglicanus* (Magna Carta) f. *Anglicus* (Bede) f. *Anglus* ANGLE]

anglice /'æŋglɪsɪ/ *adv.* in English. [med.L]

Anglicism /'æŋglɪ,sɪz(ə)m/ *n.* **1** a peculiarly English word or custom. **2** Englishness. **3** preference for what is English. [L *Anglicus* (see ANGLICAN) + -ISM]

Anglicize /'æŋglɪ,saɪz/ *v.tr.* (also **-ise**) make English in form or character.

Anglist /'æŋglɪst/ *n.* a student of or scholar in English language or literature. □□ **Anglistics** /-'glɪstɪks/ *n.* [G f. L *Anglus* English]

Anglo /'æŋgləʊ/ *n.* (*pl.* **-os**) *US* a person of British or northern-European origin. [abbr. of ANGLO-SAXON]

Anglo- /'æŋgləʊ/ *comb. form* **1** English (*Anglo-Catholic*). **2** of English origin (*an Anglo-American*). **3** English or British and (*an Anglo-American agreement*). [f. mod.L f. L *Anglus* English]

Anglo-Catholic /ˌæŋgləʊˈkæθəlɪk/ *adj.* & *n.* —*adj.* of a High Church Anglican group which emphasizes its Catholic tradition. —*n.* a member of this group.

Anglocentric /ˌæŋgləʊ'sentrɪk/ *adj.* centred on or considered in terms of England.

Anglo-French /ˌæŋgləʊˈfrentʃ/ *adj.* & *n.* —*adj.* **1** English (or British) and French. **2** of Anglo-French. —*n.* the French language as retained and separately developed in England after the Norman Conquest.

Anglo-Indian /ˌæŋgləʊ'ɪndɪən/ *adj.* & *n.* —*adj.* **1** of or relating to England and India. **2 a** of British descent or birth but living or having lived long in India. **b** of mixed British and Indian parentage. **3** (of a word) adopted into English from an Indian language. —*n.* an Anglo-Indian person.

Anglo-Latin /ˌæŋgləʊˈlætɪn/ *adj.* & *n.* —*adj.* of Latin as used in medieval England. —*n.* this form of Latin.

Anglomania /ˌæŋgləʊ'meɪnɪə/ *n.* excessive admiration of English customs.

Anglo-Norman /ˌæŋgləʊ'nɔːmən/ *adj.* & *n.* —*adj.* **1** English and Norman. **2** of the Normans in England after the Norman Conquest. **3** of the dialect of French used by them. —*n.* the Anglo-Norman dialect.

Anglophile /'æŋgləʊ,faɪl/ *n.* & *adj.* (also **Anglophil** /-fɪl/) —*n.* a person who is fond of or greatly admires England or the English. —*adj.* being or characteristic of an Anglophile.

Anglophobe /'æŋgləʊ,fəʊb/ *n.* & *adj.* —*n.* a person who greatly hates or fears England or the English. —*adj.* being or characteristic of an Anglophobe.

Anglophobia /ˌæŋgləʊ'fəʊbɪə/ *n.* intense hatred or fear of England or the English.

anglophone /'æŋgləʊ,fəʊn/ *adj.* & *n.* —*adj.* English-speaking. —*n.* an English-speaking person. [ANGLO-, after FRANCOPHONE]

Anglo-Saxon /ˌæŋgləʊ'sæks(ə)n/ *adj.* & *n.* —*adj.* **1** of the English Saxons (as distinct from the Old Saxons of the continent, and from the Angles) before the Norman Conquest. **2** of the Old English people as a whole before the Norman Conquest. **3** of English descent. —*n.* **1** an Anglo-Saxon person. **2** the Old English language. **3 a** *colloq.* plain (esp. crude) English. **b** *US* the modern English language. [mod.L *Anglo-Saxones*, med.L *Angli Saxones* after OE *Angulseaxe, -an*]

angora /æŋ'gɔːrə/ *n.* **1** a fabric made from the hair of the angora goat or rabbit. **2** a long-haired variety of cat, goat, or rabbit. □**angora wool** a mixture of sheep's wool and angora rabbit hair. [*Angora* (Ankara) in Turkey]

angostura /ˌæŋgə'stjʊərə/ *n.* (in full **angostura bark**) an aromatic bitter bark used as a flavouring, and formerly used as a tonic and to reduce fever. □**Angostura Bitters** *propr.* a kind of tonic first made in Angostura. [*Angostura*, a town in Venezuela on the Orinoco, now Ciudad Bolívar]

angry /'æŋgrɪ/ adj. (**angrier, angriest**) **1** feeling or showing anger; extremely displeased or resentful. **2** (of a wound, sore, etc.) inflamed, painful. **3** suggesting or seeming to show anger (*an angry sky*). □□ **angrily** adv. [ME, f. ANGER + -Y¹]

angst /æŋst/ n. **1** anxiety. **2** a feeling of guilt or remorse. [G]

angstrom /'æŋstrəm/ n. (also **ångström** /'ɒŋstrɜːm/) a unit of length equal to 10⁻¹⁰ metre. ¶ Symb.: Å. [A.J. *Ångström*, Swedish physicist d. 1874]

anguine /'æŋgwɪn/ adj. of or resembling a snake. [L *anguinus* f. *anguis* snake]

anguish /'æŋgwɪʃ/ n. severe misery or mental suffering. [ME f. OF *anguisse* choking f. L *angustia* tightness f. *angustus* narrow]

anguished /'æŋgwɪʃt/ adj. suffering or expressing anguish. [past part. of *anguish* (v.) f. OF *anguissier* f. eccl.L *angustiare* to distress, formed as ANGUISH]

angular /'æŋgjʊlə(r)/ adj. **1 a** having angles or sharp corners. **b** (of a person) having sharp features; lean and bony. **c** awkward in manner. **2** forming an angle. **3** measured by angle (*angular distance*). □ **angular momentum** the quantity of rotation of a body, the product of its moment of inertia and angular velocity. **angular velocity** the rate of change of angular position of a rotating body. □□ **angularity** /-'lærɪtɪ/ n. **angularly** adv. [L *angularis* f. *angulus* ANGLE¹]

anhedral /æn'hiːdr(ə)l/ n. & adj. Aeron. —n. the angle between wing and horizontal when the wing is inclined downwards. —adj. of or having an anhedral. [AN-¹ + -hedral (see -HEDRON)]

anhydride /æn'haɪdraɪd/ n. Chem. a substance obtained by removing the elements of water from a compound, esp. from an acid. [as ANHYDROUS + -IDE]

anhydrite /æn'haɪdraɪt/ n. a naturally occurring, usu. rock-forming anhydrous mineral form of calcium sulphate. [as ANHYDROUS + -ITE¹ 2]

anhydrous /æn'haɪdrəs/ adj. Chem. without water, esp. water of crystallization. [Gk *anudros* (as AN-¹, *hudōr* water)]

aniline /'ænɪˌliːn, -lɪn, -ˌlaɪn/ n. a colourless oily liquid, used in the manufacture of dyes, drugs, and plastics. □ **aniline dye 1** any of numerous dyes made from aniline. **2** any synthetic dye. [G *Anilin* f. *Anil* indigo (from which it was orig. obtained), ult. f. Arab. *an-nīl*]

anima /'ænɪmə/ n. Psychol. **1** the inner personality (opp. PERSONA). **2** Jung's term for the feminine part of a man's personality (opp. ANIMUS). [L, = mind, soul]

animadvert /ˌænɪmæd'vɜːt/ v.intr. (foll. by *on*) criticize, censure (conduct, a fault, etc.). □□ **animadversion** n. [L *animadvertere* f. *animus* mind + *advertere* (as AD-, *vertere* vers- turn)]

animal /'ænɪm(ə)l/ n. & adj. —n. **1** a living organism which feeds on organic matter, usu. one with specialized sense-organs and nervous system, and able to respond rapidly to stimuli. **2** such an organism other than man. **3** a brutish or uncivilized person. **4** colloq. a person or thing of any kind (*there is no such animal*). —adj. **1** characteristic of animals. **2** of animals as distinct from vegetables (*animal charcoal*). **3** characteristic of the physical needs of animals; carnal, sensual. □ **animal husbandry** the science of breeding and caring for farm animals. **animal magnetism** hist. mesmerism. **animal spirits** natural exuberance. [L f. *animale* neut. of *animalis* having breath f. *anima* breath]

animalcule /ˌænɪ'mælkjuːl/ n. archaic a microscopic animal. □□ **animalcular** adj. [mod.L *animalculum* (as ANIMAL, -CULE)]

animalism /'ænɪməˌlɪz(ə)m/ n. **1** the nature and activity of animals. **2** the belief that humans are not superior to other animals. **3** concern with physical matters; sensuality.

animality /ˌænɪ'mælɪtɪ/ n. **1** the animal world. **2** the nature or behaviour of animals. [F *animalité* f. *animal* (adj.)]

animalize /'ænɪməˌlaɪz/ v.tr. (also -**ise**) **1** make (a person) bestial; sensualize. **2** convert to animal substance. □□ **animalization** /-'zeɪʃ(ə)n/ n.

animate adj. & v. —adj. /'ænɪmət/ **1** having life. **2** lively. —v.tr. /'ænɪˌmeɪt/ **1** enliven, make lively. **2** give life to. **3** inspire, actuate. **4** encourage. [L *animatus* past part. of *animare* give life to f. *anima* life, soul]

animated /'ænɪˌmeɪtɪd/ adj. **1** lively, vigorous. **2** having life. **3** (of a film etc.) using techniques of animation. □□ **animatedly** adv. **animator** n. (in sense 3).

animation /ˌænɪ'meɪʃ(ə)n/ n. **1** vivacity, ardour. **2** the state of being alive. **3** Cinematog. the technique of filming successive drawings or positions of puppets to create an illusion of movement when the film is shown as a sequence.

animé /'ænɪˌmeɪ/ n. any of various resins, esp. a W. Indian resin used in making varnish. [F, of uncert. orig.]

animism /'ænɪˌmɪz(ə)m/ n. **1** the attribution of a living soul to plants, inanimate objects, and natural phenomena. **2** the belief in a supernatural power that organizes and animates the material universe. □□ **animist** n. **animistic** /-'mɪstɪk/ adj. [L *anima* life, soul + -ISM]

animosity /ˌænɪ'mɒsɪtɪ/ n. (pl. -**ies**) a spirit or feeling of strong hostility. [ME f. OF *animosité* or LL *animositas* f. *animosus* spirited, formed as ANIMUS]

animus /'ænɪməs/ n. **1** a display of animosity. **2** ill feeling. **3** a motivating spirit or feeling. **4** Psychol. Jung's term for the masculine part of a woman's personality (opp. ANIMA). [L, = spirit, mind]

anion /'ænˌaɪən/ n. a negatively charged ion; an ion that is attracted to the anode in electrolysis (opp. CATION). [ANA- + ION]

anionic /ˌænaɪ'ɒnɪk/ adj. **1** of an anion or anions. **2** having an active anion.

anise /'ænɪs/ n. an umbelliferous plant, *Pimpinella anisum*, having aromatic seeds (see ANISEED). [ME f. OF *anis* f. L f. Gk *anison* anise, dill]

aniseed /'ænɪˌsiːd/ n. the seed of the anise, used to flavour liqueurs and sweets. [ME f. ANISE + SEED]

anisette /ˌænɪ'zet/ n. a liqueur flavoured with aniseed. [F, dimin. of *anis* ANISE]

anisotropic /ˌænaɪsə'trɒpɪk/ adj. having physical properties that are different in different directions, e.g. the strength of wood along the grain differing from that across the grain (opp. ISOTROPIC). □□ **anisotropically** adv. **anisotropy** /-'sɒtrəpɪ/ n. [AN-¹ + ISOTROPIC]

ankh /æŋk/ n. a device consisting of a looped bar with a shorter crossbar, used in ancient Egypt as a symbol of life. [Egypt., = life, soul]

ankle /'æŋk(ə)l/ n. & v. —n. **1** the joint connecting the foot with the leg. **2** the part of the leg between this and the calf. —v.intr. sl. walk. □ **ankle-bone** a bone forming the ankle. **ankle sock** a short sock just covering the ankle. [ME f. ON *ankul*- (unrecorded) f. Gmc: rel. to ANGLE¹]

anklet /'æŋklɪt/ n. an ornament or fetter worn round the ankle. [ANKLE + -LET, after BRACELET]

ankylose /'æŋkɪˌləʊz/ v.tr. & intr. (also **anchylose**) (of bones or a joint) stiffen or unite by ankylosis. [back-form. f. ANKYLOSIS after *anastomose* etc.]

ankylosis /ˌæŋkɪ'ləʊsɪs/ n. (also **anchylosis**) **1** the abnormal stiffening and immobility of a joint by fusion of the bones. **2** such fusion. □□ **ankylotic** adj. [mod.L f. Gk *agkulōsis* f. *agkuloō* crook]

anna /'ænə/ n. a former monetary unit of India and Pakistan, one-sixteenth of a rupee. [Hind. *ānā*]

annal /'æn(ə)l/ n. **1** the annals of one year. **2** a record of one item in a chronicle. [back-form. f. ANNALS]

annalist /'ænəlɪst/ n. a writer of annals. □□ **annalistic** /-'lɪstɪk/ adj. **annalistically** /-'lɪstɪkəlɪ/ adv.

annals /'æn(ə)lz/ n.pl. **1** a narrative of events year by year. **2** historical records. [F *annales* or L *annales* (*libri*) yearly (books) f. *annus* year]

annates /'æneɪts/ *n.pl. RC Ch.* the first year's revenue of a see or benefice, paid to the Pope. [F *annate* f. med.L *annata* year's proceeds f. *annus* year]

annatto /ə'nætəʊ/ *n.* (also **anatta** /-tə/, **anatto**) an orange-red dye from the pulp of a tropical fruit, used for colouring foods. [Carib name of the fruit-tree]

anneal /ə'niːl/ *v.* & *n.* —*v.tr.* **1** heat (metal or glass) and allow it to cool slowly, esp. to toughen it. **2** toughen. —*n.* treatment by annealing. □□ **annealer** *n.* [OE *onǣlan* f. *on* + *ǣlan* burn, bake f. *āl* fire]

annectent /ə'nekt(ə)nt/ *adj. Biol.* connecting (*annectent link*). [L *annectere annectent-* bind (as ANNEX)]

annelid /'ænəlɪd/ *n.* any segmented worm of the phylum Annelida, e.g. earthworms, lugworms, etc. [F *annélide* or mod.L *annelida* (pl.) f. F *annelés* ringed animals f. OF *anel* ring f. L *anellus* dimin. of *anulus* ring]

annelidan /ə'nelɪd(ə)n/ *adj.* & *n.* —*adj.* of the annelids. —*n.* an annelid.

annex /æ'neks, ə'n-/ *v.tr.* **1 a** add as a subordinate part. **b** (often foll. by *to*) append to a book etc. **2** incorporate (territory of another) into one's own. **3** add as a condition or consequence. **4** *colloq.* take without right. □□ **annexation** /-'seɪʃ(ə)n/ *n.* [ME f. OF *annexer* f. L *annectere* (as AN-², *nectere nex-* bind)]

annexe /'æneks/ *n.* (also **annex**) **1** a separate or added building, esp. for extra accommodation. **2** an addition to a document. [F *annexe* f. L *annexum* past part. of *annectere* bind: see ANNEX]

annihilate /ə'naɪə‚leɪt, ə'naɪɪl-/ *v.tr.* **1** completely destroy. **2** defeat utterly; make insignificant or powerless. □□ **annihilator** *n.* [LL *annihilare* (as AN-², *nihil* nothing)]

annihilation /ə‚naɪə'leɪʃ(ə)n, ə‚naɪɪl-/ *n.* **1** the act or process of annihilating. **2** *Physics* the conversion of a particle and an antiparticle into radiation. [F *annihilation* or LL *annihilatio* (as ANNIHILATE)]

anniversary /‚ænɪ'vɜːsərɪ/ *n.* (*pl.* -**ies**) **1** the date on which an event took place in a previous year. **2** the celebration of this. [ME f. L *anniversarius* f. *annus* year + *versus* turned]

Anno Domini /‚ænəʊ 'dɒmɪ‚naɪ/ *adv.* & *n.* —*adv.* in the year of our Lord, in the year of the Christian era. —*n. colloq.* advancing age (*suffering from Anno Domini*). [L, = in the year of the Lord]

annotate /'ænə‚teɪt, 'ænə‚teɪt/ *v.tr.* add explanatory notes to (a book, document, etc.). □□ **annotatable** *adj.* **annotation** /-'teɪʃ(ə)n/ *n.* **annotative** *adj.* **annotator** *n.* [L *annotare* (as AD-, *nota* mark)]

announce /ə'naʊns/ *v.tr.* **1** (often foll. by *that*) make publicly known. **2** make known the arrival or imminence of (a guest, dinner, etc.). **3** make known (without words) to the senses or the mind; be a sign of. □□ **announcement** *n.* [ME f. OF *annoncer* f. L *annuntiare* (as AD-, *nuntius* messenger)]

announcer /ə'naʊnsə(r)/ *n.* a person who announces, esp. introducing programmes in broadcasting.

annoy /ə'nɔɪ/ *v.tr.* **1** cause slight anger or mental distress to. **2** (in *passive*) be somewhat angry (*am annoyed with you*; *was annoyed at my remarks*). **3** molest; harass repeatedly. □□ **annoyance** *n.* **annoyer** *n.* [ME f. OF *anuier*, *anui*, *anoi*, etc., ult. f. L *in odio* hateful]

annual /'ænjʊəl/ *adj.* & *n.* —*adj.* **1** reckoned by the year. **2** occurring every year. **3** living or lasting for one year. —*n.* **1** a book etc. published once a year; a yearbook. **2** a plant that lives only for a year or less. □**annual general meeting** a yearly meeting of members or shareholders, esp. for holding elections and reporting on the year's events. **annual ring** a ring in the cross-section of a plant, esp. a tree, produced by one year's growth. □□ **annually** *adv.* [ME f. OF *annuel* f. LL *annualis* f. L *annalis* f. *annus* year]

annualized /'ænjʊə‚laɪzd/ *adj.* (of rates of interest,

inflation, etc.) calculated on an annual basis, as a projection from figures obtained for a shorter period.

annuitant /ə'njuːɪt(ə)nt/ *n.* a person who holds or receives an annuity. [ANNUITY + -ANT, by assim. to *accountant* etc.]

annuity /ə'njuːɪtɪ/ *n.* (*pl.* -**ies**) **1** a yearly grant or allowance. **2** an investment of money entitling the investor to a series of equal annual sums. **3** a sum payable in respect of a particular year. [ME f. F *annuité* f. med.L *annuitas -tatis* f. L *annuus* yearly (as ANNUAL)]

annul /ə'nʌl/ *v.tr.* (**annulled**, **annulling**) **1** declare (a marriage etc.) invalid. **2** cancel, abolish. □□ **annulment** *n.* [ME f. OF *anuller* f. LL *annullare* (as AD-, *nullus* none)]

annular /'ænjʊlə(r)/ *adj.* ring-shaped; forming a ring. □**annular eclipse** an eclipse of the sun in which the moon leaves a ring of sunlight visible round it. □□ **annularly** *adv.* [F *annulaire* or L *annularis* f. *an(n)ulus* ring]

annulate /'ænjʊlət/ *adj.* having rings; marked with or formed of rings. □□ **annulation** /-'leɪʃ(ə)n/ *n.* [L *annulatus* (as ANNULUS)]

annulet /'ænjʊlɪt/ *n.* **1** *Archit.* a small fillet or band encircling a column. **2** a small ring. [L *annulus* ring + -ET¹]

annulus /'ænjʊləs/ *n.* (*pl.* **annuli** /-laɪ/) esp. *Math.* & *Biol.* a ring. [L *an(n)ulus*]

annunciate /ə'nʌnʃɪ‚eɪt/ *v.tr.* **1** proclaim. **2** indicate as coming or ready. [LL *annunciare* f. L *annuntiare annuntiat-* announce]

annunciation /ə‚nʌnsɪ'eɪʃ(ə)n/ *n.* **1** (**Annunciation**) **a** the announcing of the Incarnation, made by the angel Gabriel to Mary, related in Luke 1:26–38. **b** the festival commemorating this (Lady Day) on 25 March. **2 a** the act or process of announcing. **b** an announcement. [ME f. OF *annonciation* f. LL *annuntiatio -onis* (as ANNUNCIATE)]

annunciator /ə'nʌnʃɪ‚eɪtə(r)/ *n.* **1** a device giving an audible or visible indication of which of several electrical circuits has been activated, of the position of a train, etc. **2** an announcer. [LL *annuntiator* (as ANNUNCIATE)]

annus mirabilis /‚ænəs mɪ'rɑːbɪlɪs/ *n.* a remarkable or auspicious year. [mod.L, = wonderful year]

anoa /ə'nəʊə/ *n.* any of several small deerlike water buffalo of the genus *Bubalus*, native to Sulawesi. [name in Sulawesi]

anode /'ænəʊd/ *n. Electr.* **1** the positive electrode in an electrolytic cell or electronic valve or tube. **2** the negative terminal of a primary cell such as a battery (opp. CATHODE). □**anode ray** a beam of particles emitted from the anode of a high-vacuum tube. □□ **anodal** *adj.* **anodic** /ə'nɒdɪk/ *adj.* [Gk *anodos* way up f. *ana* up + *hodos* way]

anodize /'ænə‚daɪz/ *v.tr.* (also **-ise**) coat (a metal, esp. aluminium) with a protective oxide layer by electrolysis. □□ **anodizer** *n.* [ANODE + -IZE]

anodyne /'ænə‚daɪn/ *adj.* & *n.* —*adj.* **1** able to relieve pain. **2** mentally soothing. —*n.* an anodyne drug or medicine. [L *anodynus* f. Gk *anōdunos* painless (as AN-¹, *odunē* pain)]

anoesis /‚ænəʊ'iːsɪs/ *n. Psychol.* consciousness with sensation but without thought. □□ **anoetic** /-'etɪk/ *adj.* [A-¹ + Gk *noēsis* understanding]

anoint /ə'nɔɪnt/ *v.tr.* **1** apply oil or ointment to, esp. as a religious ceremony (e.g. at baptism, or the consecration of a priest or king, or in ministering to the sick). **2** (usu. foll. by *with*) smear, rub. □□ **anointer** *n.* [ME f. AF *anoint* (adj.) f. OF *enoint* past part. of *enoindre* f. L *inungere* (as IN-², *ungere unct-* smear with oil)]

anomalistic /ə‚nɒmə'lɪstɪk/ *adj. Astron.* of the anomaly or angular distance of a planet from its perihelion. □**anomalistic month** a month measured between successive perigees of the moon. **anomalistic year** a year measured between successive perihelia of the earth.

anomalous /ə'nɒmələs/ adj. having an irregular or deviant feature; abnormal. □□ **anomalously** adv. **anomalousness** n. [LL anomalus f. Gk anōmalos (as AN-[1], homalos even)]

anomalure /ə'nɒmə,ljʊə(r)/ n. any of the squirrel-like rodents of the family Anomaluridae, having tails with rough overlapping scales on the underside. [mod.L anomalurus f. Gk anōmalos ANOMALOUS + oura tail]

anomaly /ə'nɒməlɪ/ n. (pl. -ies) 1 an anomalous circumstance or thing; an irregularity. 2 irregularity of motion, behaviour, etc. 3 Astron. the angular distance of a planet or satellite from its last perihelion or perigee. [L f. Gk anōmalia f. anōmalos ANOMALOUS]

anomy /'ænəmɪ/ n. (also **anomie**) lack of the usual social or ethical standards in an individual or group. □□ **anomic** /ə'nɒmɪk/ adj. [Gk anomia f. anomos lawless: -ie f. F]

anon /ə'nɒn/ adv. archaic or literary soon, shortly (will say more of this anon). [OE on ān into one, on āne in one]

anon. /ə'nɒn/ abbr. anonymous; an anonymous author.

anonym /'ænənɪm/ n. 1 an anonymous person or publication. 2 a pseudonym. [F anonyme f. Gk anōnumos: see ANONYMOUS]

anonymous /ə'nɒnɪməs/ adj. 1 of unknown name. 2 of unknown or undeclared source or authorship. 3 without character; featureless, impersonal. □□ **anonymity** /,ænə'nɪmɪtɪ/ n. **anonymously** adv. [LL anonymus f. Gk anōnumos nameless (as AN-[1], onoma name)]

anopheles /ə'nɒfɪ,liːz/ n. any of various mosquitoes of the genus Anopheles, many of which are carriers of the malarial parasite. [mod.L f. Gk anōphelēs unprofitable]

anorak /'ænə,ræk/ n. a waterproof jacket of cloth or plastic, usu. with a hood, of a kind orig. used in polar regions. [Greenland Eskimo anoraq]

anorectic /,ænə'rektɪk/ adj. & n. (also **anorexic** /-'reksɪk/) —adj. involving, producing, or characterized by a lack of appetite, esp. in anorexia nervosa. —n. 1 an anorectic agent. 2 a person with anorexia. [Gk anorektos without appetite (as ANOREXIA): anorexic f. F anoréxique]

anorexia /,ænə'reksɪə/ n. 1 a lack or loss of appetite for food. 2 (in full **anorexia nervosa** /nɜː'vəʊsə/) a psychological illness, esp. in young women, characterized by an obsessive desire to lose weight by refusing to eat. [LL f. Gk f. an- not + orexis appetite]

anosmia /æ'nɒzmɪə/ n. the loss of the sense of smell. □□ **anosmic** adj. [LL f. Gk f. an- not + osmē smell]

another /ə'nʌðə(r)/ adj. & pron. —adj. 1 an additional; one more (have another cake; after another six months). 2 a person like or comparable to (another Callas). 3 a different (quite another matter). 4 some or any other (will not do another man's work). —pron. 1 an additional one (have another). 2 a different one (take this book away and bring me another). 3 some or any other one (I love another). 4 Brit. an unnamed additional party to a legal action (X versus Y and another). 5 (also **A. N. Other** /,eɪ en 'ʌðə(r)/) a player unnamed or not yet selected. □ **another place** Brit. the other House of Parliament (used in the Commons to refer to the Lords, and vice versa). **such another** another of the same sort. [ME f. AN + OTHER]

anovulant /æ'nɒvjʊlənt/ n. & adj. Pharm. —n. a drug preventing ovulation. —adj. preventing ovulation. [AN-[1] + ovulation (see OVULATE) + -ANT]

anoxia /ə'nɒksɪə/ n. Med. an absence or deficiency of oxygen reaching the tissues; severe hypoxia. □□ **anoxic** adj. [mod.L, formed as AN-[1] + OXYGEN + -IA[1]]

anschluss /'ænʃlʊs/ n. a unification, esp. the annexation of Austria by Germany in 1938. [G f. anschliessen join]

anserine /'ænsə,raɪn/ adj. 1 of or like a goose. 2 silly. [L anserinus f. anser goose]

answer /'ɑːnsə(r)/ n. & v. —n. 1 something said or done to deal with or in reaction to a question, statement, or circumstance. 2 the solution to a problem. —v. 1 tr. make an answer to (answer me; answer my question). 2 intr. (often foll. by to) make an answer. 3 tr. respond to the summons or signal of (answer the door; answer the telephone). 4 tr. be satisfactory for (a purpose or need). 5 intr. (foll. by for, to) be responsible (you will answer to me for your conduct). 6 intr. (foll. by to) correspond, esp. to a description. 7 intr. be satisfactory or successful. □ **answer back** answer a rebuke etc. impudently. **answering machine** a tape recorder which supplies a recorded answer to a telephone call. **answering service** a business that receives and answers telephone calls for its clients. **answer to the name of** be called. [OE andswaru, andswarian f. Gmc, = swear against (charge)]

answerable /'ɑːnsərəb(ə)l/ adj. 1 (usu. foll. by to, for) responsible (answerable to them for any accident). 2 that can be answered.

answerphone /'ɑːnsə,fəʊn/ n. a telephone answering machine.

ant /ænt/ n. any small insect of a widely distributed hymenopterous family, living in complex social colonies, wingless (except for males in the mating season), and proverbial for industry. □ **ant-bear** = AARDVARK. **ant** (or **ant's**) **eggs** pupae of ants. **ant-lion** any of various dragonfly-like insects. **white ant** = TERMITE. [OE ǣmet(t)e, ēmete (see EMMET) f. WG]

ant- /ænt/ assim. form of ANTI- before a vowel or h (Antarctic).

-ant /ənt/ suffix 1 forming adjectives denoting attribution of an action (pendant; repentant) or state (arrogant; expectant). 2 forming nouns denoting an agent (assistant; celebrant; deodorant). [F -ant or L -ant-, -ent-, pres. part. stem of verbs: cf. -ENT]

antacid /ænt'æsɪd/ n. & adj. —n. a substance that prevents or corrects acidity esp. in the stomach. —adj. having these properties.

antagonism /æn'tægə,nɪz(ə)m/ n. active opposition or hostility. [F antagonisme (as ANTAGONIST)]

antagonist /æn'tægənɪst/ n. 1 an opponent or adversary. 2 Biol. a substance or organ that partially or completely opposes the action of another. □□ **antagonistic** /-'nɪstɪk/ adj. **antagonistically** /-'nɪstɪkəlɪ/ adv. [F antagoniste or LL antagonista f. Gk antagōnistēs (as ANTAGONIZE)]

antagonize /æn'tægə,naɪz/ v.tr. (also **-ise**) 1 evoke hostility or opposition or enmity in. 2 (of one force etc.) counteract or tend to neutralize (another). □□ **antagonization** /-'zeɪʃ(ə)n/ n. [Gk antagōnizomai (as ANTI-, agōnizomai f. agōn contest)]

antalkali /ænt'ælkəlaɪ/ n. (pl. **antalkalis**) any substance that counteracts an alkali.

Antarctic /ænt'ɑːktɪk/ adj. & n. —adj. of the south polar regions. —n. this region. □ **Antarctic Circle** the parallel of latitude 66° 32' S., forming an imaginary line round this region. [ME f. OF antartique or L antarcticus f. Gk antarktikos (as ANTI-, arktikos ARCTIC)]

ante /'æntɪ/ n. & v. —n. 1 a stake put up by a player in poker etc. before receiving cards. 2 an amount to be paid in advance. —v.tr. (**antes, anted**) 1 put up as an ante. 2 US a bet, stake. b (foll. by up) pay. [L, = before]

ante- /'æntɪ/ prefix forming nouns and adjectives meaning 'before, preceding' (ante-room; antenatal; ante-post). [L ante (prep. & adv.), = before]

anteater /'ænt,iːtə(r)/ n. any of various mammals feeding on ants and termites, e.g. a tamandua.

ante-bellum /,æntɪ'beləm/ adj. occurring or existing before a particular war, esp. the US Civil War. [L f. ante before + bellum war]

antecedent /,æntɪ'siːd(ə)nt/ n. & adj. —n. 1 a preceding thing or circumstance. 2 Gram. a word, phrase, clause, or sentence, to which another word

b but d dog f few g get h he j yes k cat l leg m man n no p pen r red s sit t top v voice

(esp. a relative pronoun, usu. following) refers. **3** (in *pl.*) past history, esp. of a person. **4** *Logic* the statement contained in the 'if' clause of a conditional proposition. —*adj.* **1** (often foll. by *to*) previous. **2** presumptive, a priori. □□ **antecedence** *n.* **antecedently** *adv.* [ME f. F *antecedent* or L *antecedere* (as ANTE-, *cedere* go)]

antechamber /'æntɪ,tʃeɪmbə(r)/ *n.* a small room leading to a main one. [earlier *anti*-, f. F *antichambre* f. It. *anticamera* (as ANTE-, CHAMBER)]

antechapel /'æntɪ,tʃæp(ə)l/ *n.* the outer part at the west end of a college chapel.

antedate *v. & n.* —*v.tr.* /,æntɪ'deɪt/ **1** exist or occur at a date earlier than. **2** assign an earlier date to (a document, event, etc.), esp. one earlier than its actual date. —*n.* /'æntɪ,deɪt/ a date earlier than the actual one.

antediluvian /,æntɪdɪ'lu:vɪən, -'lju:vɪən/ *adj.* **1** of or belonging to the time before the Biblical Flood. **2** *colloq.* very old or out of date. [ANTE- + L *diluvium* DELUGE + -AN]

antelope /'æntɪ,ləʊp/ *n.* (*pl.* same or **antelopes**) **1** any of various deerlike ruminants of the family Bovidae, esp. abundant in Africa and typically tall, slender, graceful, and swift-moving with smooth hair and upward-pointing horns, e.g. gazelles, gnus, kudus, and impala. **2** leather made from the skin of any of these. [ME f. OF *antelop* or f. med.L *ant(h)alopus* f. late Gk *antholops*, of unkn. orig.]

antenatal /,æntɪ'neɪt(ə)l/ *adj.* **1** existing or occurring before birth. **2** relating to the period of pregnancy.

antenna /æn'tenə/ *n.* (*pl.* **antennae** /-ni:/) **1** *Zool.* one of a pair of mobile appendages on the heads of insects, crustaceans, etc., sensitive to touch and taste; a feeler. **2** (*pl.* **antennas**) = AERIAL *n.* □□ **antennal** *adj.* (in sense 1). **antennary** *adj.* (in sense 1). [L, = sail-yard]

antenuptial /,æntɪ'nʌpʃ(ə)l/ *adj.* existing or occurring before marriage. □ **antenuptial contract** *S.Afr.* a contract between two persons intending to marry each other, setting out the terms and conditions of their marriage. [LL *antenuptialis* (as ANTE-, NUPTIAL)]

antependium /,æntɪ'pendɪəm/ *n.* (*pl.* **antependia** /-dɪə/) a veil or hanging for the front of an altar. [med.L (as ANTE-, *pendēre* hang)]

antepenult /,æntɪpɪ'nʌlt/ *n.* the last syllable but two in a word. [abbr. of LL *antepaenultimus* (as ANTE-, *paenultimus* PENULT)]

antepenultimate /,æntɪpɪ'nʌltɪmət/ *adj. & n.* —*adj.* last but two. —*n.* anything that is last but two.

ante-post /,æntɪ'pəʊst/ *adj.* *Brit.* (of betting) done at odds determined at the time of betting, in advance of the event concerned. [ANTE- + POST[1]]

anterior /æn'tɪərɪə(r)/ *adj.* **1** nearer the front. **2** (often foll. by *to*) earlier, prior. □□ **anteriority** /-rɪ'ɒrɪtɪ/ *n.* **anteriorly** *adv.* [F *antérieur* or L *anterior* f. *ante* before]

ante-room /'æntɪ,ru:m, -,rʊm/ *n.* **1** a small room leading to a main one. **2** *Mil.* a sitting-room in an officers' mess.

antheap /'ænthi:p/ *n.* = ANTHILL.

anthelion /æn'θi:lɪən/ *n.* (*pl.* **anthelia** /-lɪə/) a luminous halo projected on a cloud or fog-bank opposite to the sun. [Gk, neut. of *anthēlios* opposite to the sun (as ANTI-, *hēlios* sun)]

anthelmintic /,ænθel'mɪntɪk/ (also **anthelminthic** /-θɪk/) *n. & adj.* —*n.* any drug or agent used to destroy parasitic, esp. intestinal, worms, e.g. tapeworms, roundworms, and flukes. —*adj.* having the power to eliminate or destroy parasitic worms. [ANTI- + Gk *helmins helminthos* worm]

anthem /'ænθəm/ *n.* **1** an elaborate choral composition usu. based on a passage of scripture for (esp. Anglican) church use. **2** a solemn hymn of praise etc., esp. = *national anthem*. **3** a composition sung

antiphonally. [OE *antefn*, *antifne* f. LL *antiphona* ANTIPHON]

anthemion /æn'θi:mɪən/ *n.* (*pl.* **anthemia** /-mɪə/) a flower-like ornament used in art. [Gk, = flower]

anther /'ænθə(r)/ *n.* *Bot.* the apical portion of a stamen containing pollen. □□ **antheral** *adj.* [F *anthère* or mod.L *anthera*, in L 'medicine extracted from flowers' f. Gk *anthēra* flowery, fem. adj. f. *anthos* flower]

antheridium /,ænθə'rɪdɪəm/ *n.* (*pl.* **antheridia** /-dɪə/) *Bot.* the male sex organ of algae, mosses, ferns, etc. [mod.L f. *anthera* (as ANTHER) + Gk -*idion* dimin. suffix]

anthill /'ænthɪl/ *n.* **1** a moundlike nest built by ants or termites. **2** a community teeming with people.

anthologize /æn'θɒlə,dʒaɪz/ *v.tr. & intr.* (also -**ise**) compile or include in an anthology.

anthology /æn'θɒlədʒɪ/ *n.* (*pl.* -**ies**) a published collection of passages from literature (esp. poems), songs, reproductions of paintings, etc. □□ **anthologist** *n.* [F *anthologie* or med.L f. Gk *anthologia* f. *anthos* flower + -*logia* collection f. *legō* gather]

anthozoan /,ænθə'zəʊən/ *n. & adj.* —*n.* any of the sessile marine coelenterates of the class Anthozoa, including sea anemones and corals. —*adj.* of or relating to this class. [mod.L *Anthozoa* f. Gk *anthos* flower + *zōia* animals]

anthracene /'ænθrə,si:n/ *n.* a colourless crystalline aromatic hydrocarbon obtained by the distillation of crude oils and used in the manufacture of chemicals. [Gk *anthrax -akos* coal + -ENE]

anthracite /'ænθrə,saɪt/ *n.* coal of a hard variety burning with little flame and smoke. □□ **anthracitic** /-'sɪtɪk/ *adj.* [Gk *anthrakitis* a kind of coal (as ANTHRACENE)]

anthrax /'ænθræks/ *n.* a disease of sheep and cattle transmissible to humans. [LL f. Gk, = carbuncle]

anthropo- /'ænθrəpəʊ/ *comb. form* human, mankind. [Gk *anthrōpos* human being]

anthropocentric /,ænθrəpəʊ'sentrɪk/ *adj.* regarding mankind as the centre of existence. □□ **anthropocentrically** *adv.* **anthropocentrism** *n.*

anthropogenesis /,ænθrəpəʊ'dʒenɪsɪs/ *n.* = ANTHROPOGENY.

anthropogeny /,ænθrə'pɒdʒɪnɪ/ *n.* the study of the origin of man. □□ **anthropogenic** /,ænθrəpəʊ'dʒenɪk/ *adj.*

anthropoid /'ænθrə,pɔɪd/ *adj. & n.* —*adj.* **1** resembling a human being in form. **2** *colloq.* (of a person) apelike. —*n.* a being that is human in form only, esp. an anthropoid ape. [Gk *anthrōpoeidēs* (as ANTHROPO-, -OID)]

anthropology /,ænθrə'pɒlədʒɪ/ *n.* **1** the study of mankind, esp. of its societies and customs. **2** the study of the structure and evolution of man as an animal. □□ **anthropological** /-pə'lɒdʒɪk(ə)l/ *adj.* **anthropologist** *n.*

anthropometry /,ænθrə'pɒmɪtrɪ/ *n.* the scientific study of the measurements of the human body. □□ **anthropometric** /-pə'metrɪk/ *adj.*

anthropomorphic /,ænθrəpə'mɔ:fɪk/ *adj.* of or characterized by anthropomorphism. □□ **anthropomorphically** *adv.* [as ANTHROPOMORPHOUS + -IC]

anthropomorphism /,ænθrəpə'mɔ:fɪz(ə)m/ *n.* the attribution of a human form or personality to a god, animal, or thing. □□ **anthropomorphize** *v.tr.*

anthropomorphous /,ænθrəpə'mɔ:fəs/ *adj.* human in form. [Gk *anthrōpomorphos* (as ANTHROPO-, *morphē* form)]

anthroponymy /,ænθrə'pɒnɪmɪ/ *n.* the study of personal names. [ANTHROPO- + Gk *ōnumia* f. *onoma* name: cf. TOPONYMY]

anthropophagy /,ænθrə'pɒfədʒɪ/ *n.* cannibalism. □□ **anthropophagous** *adj.* [Gk *anthrōpophagia* (as ANTHROPO-, *phagō* eat)]

anti /'æntɪ/ *prep. & n.* —*prep.* (also *absol.*) opposed to (*is anti everything*; *seems to be rather anti*). —*n.* (*pl.* **antis**) a person opposed to a particular policy etc. [ANTI-]

anti- /'ænti/ *prefix* (also **ant-** before a vowel or *h*) forming nouns and adjectives meaning: **1** opposed to; against (*antivivisectionism*). **2** preventing (*antiscorbutic*). **3** the opposite of (*anticlimax*). **4** rival (*antipope*). **5** unlike the conventional form (*anti-hero*; *anti-novel*). **6** *Physics* the antiparticle of a specified particle (*antineutrino*; *antiproton*). [from or after Gk *anti-* against]

anti-aircraft /ˌænti'eəkrɑːft/ *adj.* (of a gun, missile, etc.) used to attack enemy aircraft.

antiar /'ænti,ɑː(r)/ *n.* = UPAS 1a, 2. [Jav. *antjar*]

antibiosis /ˌæntibaɪ'əʊsɪs/ *n.* an antagonistic association between two organisms (esp. micro-organisms), in which one is adversely affected (cf. SYMBIOSIS). [mod.L f. F *antibiose* (as ANTI-, SYMBIOSIS)]

antibiotic /ˌæntibaɪ'ɒtɪk/ *n.* & *adj.* *Pharm.* —*n.* any of various substances (e.g. penicillin) produced by micro-organisms or made synthetically, that can inhibit or destroy susceptible micro-organisms. —*adj.* functioning as an antibiotic. [F *antibiotique* (as ANTI-, Gk *biōtikos* fit for life f. *bios* life)]

antibody /'ænti,bɒdi/ *n.* (*pl.* **-ies**) any of various blood proteins produced in response to and then counteracting antigens. [transl. of G *Antikörper* (as ANTI-, *Körper* body)]

antic /'æntik/ *n.* & *adj.* —*n.* **1** (usu. in *pl.*) absurd or foolish behaviour. **2** an absurd or silly action. —*adj.* *archaic* grotesque, bizarre. [It. *antico* ANTIQUE, used as = grotesque]

anticathode /ˌænti'kæθəʊd/ *n.* the target (or anode) of an X-ray tube on which the electrons from the cathode impinge and from which X-rays are emitted.

Antichrist /'ænti,kraɪst/ *n.* **1** an arch-enemy of Christ. **2** a postulated personal opponent of Christ expected by the early Church to appear before the end of the world. [ME f. OF *antecrist* f. eccl.L *antichristus* f. Gk *antikhristos* (as ANTI-, *Khristos* CHRIST)]

antichristian /ˌænti'krɪstjən, -tiən/ *adj.* **1** opposed to Christianity. **2** concerning the Antichrist.

anticipate /æn'tɪsɪ,peɪt/ *v.tr.* **1** deal with or use before the proper time. **2** *disp.* expect, foresee; regard as probable (*did not anticipate any difficulty*). **3** forestall (a person or thing). **4** look forward to. □□ **anticipative** *adj.* **anticipator** *n.* **anticipatory** *adj.* [L *anticipare* f. *anti-* for ANTE- + *-cipare* f. *capere* take]

anticipation /æn,tɪsɪ'peɪʃ(ə)n/ *n.* **1** the act or process of anticipating. **2** *Mus.* the introduction beforehand of part of a chord which is about to follow. [F *anticipation* or L *anticipatio* (as ANTICIPATE)]

anticlerical /ˌænti'klerɪk(ə)l/ *adj.* & *n.* —*adj.* opposed to the influence of the clergy, esp. in politics. —*n.* an anticlerical person. □□ **anticlericalism** *n.*

anticlimax /ˌænti'klaɪmæks/ *n.* a trivial conclusion to something significant or impressive, esp. where a climax was expected. □□ **anticlimactic** /-'mæktɪk/ *adj.* **anticlimactically** /-'mæktɪkəli/ *adv.*

anticline /'ænti,klaɪn/ *n.* *Geol.* a ridge or fold of stratified rock in which the strata slope down from the crest (opp. SYNCLINE). □□ **anticlinal** /-'klaɪn(ə)l/ *adj.* [ANTI- + Gk *klinō* lean, after INCLINE]

anticlockwise /ˌænti'klɒkwaɪz/ *adv.* & *adj.* —*adv.* in a curve opposite in direction to the movement of the hands of a clock. —*adj.* moving anticlockwise.

anticoagulant /ˌæntikəʊ'ægjʊlənt/ *n.* & *adj.* —*n.* any drug or agent that retards or inhibits coagulation, esp. of the blood. —*adj.* retarding or inhibiting coagulation.

anticodon /ˌænti'kəʊdɒn/ *n.* *Biochem.* a sequence of three nucleotides forming a unit of genetic code in a transfer RNA molecule that corresponds to a complementary codon in messenger RNA.

anticonvulsant /ˌæntikən'vʌls(ə)nt/ *n.* & *adj.* —*n.* any drug or agent that prevents or reduces the

severity of convulsions, esp. epileptic fits. —*adj.* preventing or reducing convulsions.

anticyclone /ˌænti'saɪkləʊn/ *n.* a system of winds rotating outwards from an area of high barometric pressure, producing fine weather. □□ **anticyclonic** /-'klɒnɪk/ *adj.*

antidepressant /ˌæntidɪ'pres(ə)nt/ *n.* & *adj.* —*n.* any drug or agent that alleviates depression. —*adj.* alleviating depression.

antidiuretic hormone /ˌænti,daɪjʊ'retɪk/ *n.* = VASOPRESSIN. [ANTI- + DIURETIC]

antidote /'ænti,dəʊt/ *n.* **1** a medicine etc. taken or given to counteract poison. **2** anything that counteracts something unpleasant or evil. □□ **antidotal** *adj.* [F *antidote* or L *antidotum* f. Gk *antidoton* neut. of *antidotos* given against (as ANTI- + stem of *didonai* give)]

antifreeze /'ænti,friːz/ *n.* a substance (usu. ethylene glycol) added to water to lower its freezing-point, esp. in the radiator of a motor vehicle.

anti-g /ˌænti'dʒiː/ *adj.* (of clothing for an astronaut etc.) designed to counteract the effects of high acceleration. [ANTI- + *g* symb. for acceleration due to gravity]

antigen /'æntidʒ(ə)n/ *n.* a foreign substance (e.g. toxin) which causes the body to produce antibodies. □□ **antigenic** /-'dʒenɪk/ *adj.* [G (as ANTIBODY, -GEN)]

anti-gravity /ˌænti'grævɪti/ *n.* *Physics* a hypothetical force opposing gravity.

anti-hero /'ænti,hɪərəʊ/ *n.* (*pl.* **-oes**) a central character in a story or drama who noticeably lacks conventional heroic attributes.

antihistamine /ˌænti'hɪstəmɪn, -ˌmiːn/ *n.* a substance that counteracts the effects of histamine, used esp. in the treatment of allergies.

antiknock /'ænti,nɒk/ *n.* a substance added to motor fuel to prevent premature combustion.

antilog /'ænti,lɒg/ *n.* *colloq.* = ANTILOGARITHM. [abbr.]

antilogarithm /ˌænti'lɒgə,rɪð(ə)m/ *n.* the number to which a logarithm belongs (*100 is the common antilogarithm of 2*).

antilogy /æn'tɪlədʒi/ *n.* (*pl.* **-ies**) a contradiction in terms. [F *antilogie* f. Gk *antilogia* (as ANTI-, -LOGY)]

antimacassar /ˌæntimə'kæsə(r)/ *n.* a covering put over furniture, esp. over the back of a chair, as a protection from grease in the hair or as an ornament. [ANTI- + MACASSAR]

antimatter /'ænti,mætə(r)/ *n.* *Physics* matter composed solely of antiparticles.

antimetabolite /ˌæntimɪ'tæbə,laɪt/ *n.* *Pharm.* a drug that interferes with the normal metabolic processes within cells, usu. by combining with enzymes.

antimony /'æntiməni/ *n.* *Chem.* a brittle silvery-white metallic element used esp. in alloys. ¶ Symb.: **Sb**. □□ **antimonial** /-'məʊniəl/ *adj.* **antimonic** /-'məʊnɪk/ *adj.* **antimonious** /-'məʊniəs/ *adj.* [ME f. med.L *antimonium* (11th c.), of unkn. orig.]

antinode /'ænti,nəʊd/ *n.* *Physics* the position of maximum displacement in a standing wave system.

antinomian /ˌænti'nəʊmiən/ *adj.* & *n.* —*adj.* of or relating to the view that Christians are released from the obligation of observing the moral law. —*n.* (**Antinomian**) *hist.* a person who holds this view. □□ **antinomianism** *n.* [med.L *Antinomi*, name of a sect in Germany (1535) alleged to hold this view (as ANTI-, Gk *nomos* law)]

antinomy /æn'tɪnəmi/ *n.* (*pl.* **-ies**) **1** a contradiction between two beliefs or conclusions that are in themselves reasonable; a paradox. **2** a conflict between two laws or authorities. [L *antinomia* f. Gk (as ANTI-, *nomos* law)]

antinovel /'ænti,nɒv(ə)l/ *n.* a novel in which the conventions of the form are studiously avoided.

anti-nuclear /ˌænti'njuːklɪə(r)/ *adj.* opposed to the development of nuclear weapons or nuclear power.

æ *cat* ɑː *arm* e *bed* ɜː *her* ɪ *sit* iː *see* ɒ *hot* ɔː *saw* ʌ *run* ʊ *put* uː *too* ə *ago* aɪ *my*

antioxidant /ˌæntɪˈɒksɪd(ə)nt/ n. an agent that inhibits oxidation, esp. used to reduce deterioration of products stored in air.

antiparticle /ˈæntɪˌpɑːtɪk(ə)l/ n. Physics an elementary particle having the same mass as a given particle but opposite electric or magnetic properties.

antipasto /ˌæntɪˈpɑːstəʊ, -ˈpæstəʊ/ n. (pl. -os or antipasti /-tɪ/) an hors d'œuvre, esp. in an Italian meal. [It.]

antipathetic /ˌæntɪpəˈθetɪk/ adj. (usu. foll. by to) having a strong aversion or natural opposition. □□ antipathetical adj. antipathetically adv. [as ANTIPATHY after PATHETIC]

antipathic /ˌæntɪˈpæθɪk/ adj. of a contrary nature or character.

antipathy /ænˈtɪpəθɪ/ n. (pl. -ies) (often foll. by to, for, between) a strong or deep-seated aversion or dislike. [F antipathie or L antipathia f. Gk antipatheia f. antipathēs opposed in feeling (as ANTI-, pathos -eos feeling)]

anti-personnel /ˌæntɪˌpɜːsəˈnel/ adj. (of a bomb, mine, etc.) designed to kill or injure people rather than to damage buildings or equipment.

antiperspirant /ˌæntɪˈpɜːspɪrənt/ n. & adj. —n. a substance applied to the skin to prevent or reduce perspiration. —adj. that acts as an antiperspirant.

antiphlogistic /ˌæntɪfləˈdʒɪstɪk/ n. & adj. —n. any drug or agent that alleviates or reduces inflammation. —adj. alleviating or reducing inflammation.

antiphon /ˈæntɪf(ə)n/ n. 1 a hymn or psalm, the parts of which are sung or recited alternately by two groups. 2 a versicle or phrase from this. 3 a sentence sung or recited before or after a psalm or canticle. 4 a response. [eccl.L antiphona f. Gk (as ANTI-, phōnē sound)]

antiphonal /ænˈtɪfən(ə)l/ adj. & n. —adj. 1 sung or recited alternately by two groups. 2 responsive, answering. —n. a collection of antiphons. □□ antiphonally adv.

antiphonary /ænˈtɪfənərɪ/ n. (pl. -ies) a book of antiphons. [eccl.L antiphonarium (as ANTIPHON)]

antiphony /ænˈtɪfənɪ/ n. (pl. -ies) 1 antiphonal singing or chanting. 2 a response or echo.

antipode /ˈæntɪˌpəʊd/ n. (usu. foll. by of, to) the exact opposite. [see ANTIPODES]

antipodes /ænˈtɪpəˌdiːz/ n.pl. 1 a (also Antipodes) a place diametrically opposite to another, esp. Australasia as the region on the opposite side of the earth to Europe. b places diametrically opposite to each other. 2 (usu. foll. by of, to) the exact opposite. □□ antipodal adj. antipodean /-ˈdiːən/ adj. & n. [F or LL f. Gk antipodes having the feet opposite (as ANTI-, pous podos foot)]

antipole /ˈæntɪˌpəʊl/ n. 1 the direct opposite. 2 the opposite pole.

antipope /ˈæntɪˌpəʊp/ n. a person set up as pope in opposition to one (held by others to be) canonically chosen. [F antipape f. med.L antipapa, assim. to POPE[1]]

antiproton /ˌæntɪˈprəʊtɒn/ n. Physics the negatively charged antiparticle of a proton.

antipruritic /ˌæntɪprʊəˈrɪtɪk/ adj. & n. —adj. relieving itching. —n. an antipruritic drug or agent. [ANTI- + PRURITUS + -IC]

antipyretic /ˌæntɪpaɪˈretɪk/ adj. & n. —adj. preventing or reducing fever. —n. an antipyretic drug or agent.

antiquarian /ˌæntɪˈkweərɪən/ adj. & n. —adj. 1 of or dealing in antiques or rare books. 2 of the study of antiquities. —n. an antiquary. □□ antiquarianism n. [see ANTIQUARY]

antiquary /ˈæntɪkwərɪ/ n. (pl. -ies) a student or collector of antiques or antiquities. [L antiquarius f. antiquus ancient]

antiquated /ˈæntɪˌkweɪtɪd/ adj. old-fashioned; out of date. [eccl.L antiquare antiquat- make old]

antique /ænˈtiːk/ n., adj., & v. —n. an object of considerable age, esp. an item of furniture or the decorative arts having a high value. —adj. 1 of or existing from an early date. 2 old-fashioned, archaic. 3 of ancient times. —v.tr. (antiques, antiqued, antiquing) give an antique appearance to (furniture etc.) by artificial means. [F antique or L antiquus, anticus former, ancient f. ante before]

antiquity /ænˈtɪkwɪtɪ/ n. (pl. -ies) 1 ancient times, esp. the period before the Middle Ages. 2 great age (a city of great antiquity). 3 (usu. in pl.) physical remains or relics from ancient times, esp. buildings and works of art. 4 (in pl.) customs, events, etc., of ancient times. 5 the people of ancient times regarded collectively. [ME f. OF antiquité f. L antiquitas -tatis f. antiquus: see ANTIQUE]

antiracism /ˌæntɪˈreɪsɪz(ə)m/ n. the policy or practice of opposing racism and promoting racial tolerance. □□ antiracist n. & adj.

antirrhinum /ˌæntɪˈraɪnəm/ n. any plant of the genus Antirrhinum, esp. the snapdragon. [L f. Gk antirrhinon f. anti counterfeiting + rhis rhinos nose, from the resemblance of the flower to an animal's snout)]

antiscorbutic /ˌæntɪskɔːˈbjuːtɪk/ adj. & n. —adj. preventing or curing scurvy. —n. an antiscorbutic agent or drug.

anti-Semite /ˌæntɪˈsiːmaɪt, -ˈsemaɪt/ n. a person hostile to or prejudiced against Jews. □□ anti-Semitic /-sɪˈmɪtɪk/ adj. anti-Semitism /-ˈsemɪˌtɪz(ə)m/ n.

antisepsis /ˌæntɪˈsepsɪs/ n. the process of using antiseptics to eliminate undesirable micro-organisms such as bacteria, viruses, and fungi that cause disease. [mod.L (as ANTI-, SEPSIS)]

antiseptic /ˌæntɪˈseptɪk/ adj. & n. —adj. 1 counteracting sepsis esp. by preventing the growth of disease-causing micro-organisms. 2 sterile or free from contamination. 3 lacking character. —n. an antiseptic agent. □□ antiseptically adv.

antiserum /ˈæntɪˌsɪərəm/ n. (pl. antisera /-rə/) a blood serum containing antibodies against specific antigens, injected to treat or protect against specific diseases.

antisocial /ˌæntɪˈsəʊʃ(ə)l/ adj. 1 opposed or contrary to normal social instincts or practices. 2 not sociable. 3 opposed or harmful to the existing social order.

antistatic /ˌæntɪˈstætɪk/ adj. that counteracts the effects of static electricity.

antistrophe /ænˈtɪstrəfɪ/ n. the second section of an ancient Greek choral ode or of one division of it (see STROPHE). [LL f. Gk antistrophē f. antistrephō turn against]

antitetanus /ˌæntɪˈtetənəs/ adj. effective against tetanus.

antithesis /ænˈtɪθɪsɪs/ n. (pl. antitheses /-ˌsiːz/) 1 (foll. by of, to) the direct opposite. 2 (usu. foll. by of, between) contrast or opposition between two things. 3 a contrast of ideas expressed by parallelism of strongly contrasted words. [LL f. Gk antitithēmi set against (as ANTI-, tithēmi place)]

antithetical /ˌæntɪˈθetɪk(ə)l/ adj. (also antithetic) 1 contrasted, opposite. 2 connected with, containing, or using antithesis. □□ antithetically adv. [Gk antithetikos (as ANTITHESIS)]

antitoxin /ˌæntɪˈtɒksɪn/ n. an antibody that counteracts a toxin. □□ antitoxic adj.

antitrades /ˌæntɪˈtreɪdz, ˈæntɪ-/ n.pl. winds that blow in the opposite direction to (and usu. above) a trade wind.

antitrust /ˌæntɪˈtrʌst/ adj. US (of a law etc.) opposed to or controlling trusts or other monopolies.

antitype /ˈæntɪˌtaɪp/ n. 1 that which is represented by a type or symbol. 2 a person or thing of the opposite type. □□ antitypical /-ˈtɪpɪk(ə)l/ adj. [Gk antitupos corresponding as an impression to the die (as ANTI-, tupos stamp)]

antivenene /ˌæntɪvɪˈniːn/ n. (also antivenin /-ˈvenɪn/) an antiserum containing antibodies against specific poisons in the venom of esp. snakes, spiders, scorpions, etc. [ANTI- + L *venenum* poison + -ENE, -IN]

antiviral /ˌæntɪ'vaɪər(ə)l/ *adj.* effective against viruses.

antivivisectionism /ˌæntɪ'vɪvɪ'sekʃ(ə)nɪz(ə)m/ *n.* opposition to vivisection. □□ **antivivisectionist** *n.*

antler /'æntlə(r)/ *n.* **1** each of the branched horns of a stag or other (usu. male) deer. **2** a branch of this. □□ **antlered** *adj.* [ME f. AF, var. of OF *antoillier*, of unkn. orig.]

antonomasia /ˌæntənə'meɪzɪə/ *n.* **1** the substitution of an epithet or title etc. for a proper name (e.g. *the Maid of Orleans* for Joan of Arc, *his Grace* for an archbishop). **2** the use of a proper name to express a general idea (e.g. *a Scrooge* for a miser). [L f. Gk f. *antonomazō* name instead (as ANTI-, + *onoma* name)]

antonym /'æntənɪm/ *n.* a word opposite in meaning to another in the same language (e.g. *bad* and *good*) (opp. SYNONYM). □□ **antonymous** /æn'tɒnɪməs/ *adj.* [F *antonyme* (as ANTI-, SYNONYM)]

antrum /'æntrəm/ *n.* (*pl.* **antra** /-trə/) *Anat.* a natural chamber or cavity in the body, esp. in a bone. □□ **antral** *adj.* [L f. Gk *antron* cave]

anuran /ə'njʊərən, æ-/ *n. & adj.* —*n.* any tailless amphibian of the order Anura, including frogs and toads. —*adj.* of or relating to this order. [mod.L *Anura* (AN-¹ + Gk *oura* tail)]

anus /'eɪnəs/ *n. Anat.* the excretory opening at the end of the alimentary canal. [L]

anvil /'ænvɪl/ *n.* **1** a block (usu. of iron) with a flat top, concave sides, and often a pointed end, on which metals are worked in forging. **2** *Anat.* a bone of the ear; the incus. [OE *anfilte* etc.]

anxiety /æŋ'zaɪətɪ/ *n.* (*pl.* -**ies**) **1** the state of being anxious. **2** concern about an imminent danger, difficulty, etc. **3** (foll. by *for*, or *to* + infin.) anxious desire. **4** a thing that causes anxiety (*my greatest anxiety is that I shall fall ill*). **5** *Psychol.* a nervous disorder characterized by a state of excessive uneasiness. [F *anxiété* or L *anxietas* -*tatis* (as ANXIOUS)]

anxious /'æŋkʃəs/ *adj.* **1** troubled; uneasy in the mind. **2** causing or marked by anxiety (*an anxious moment*). **3** (foll. by *for*, or *to* + infin.) earnestly or uneasily wanting or trying (*anxious to please*; *anxious for you to succeed*). □□ **anxiously** *adv.* **anxiousness** *n.* [L *anxius* f. *angere* choke]

any /'enɪ/ *adj., pron., & adv.* —*adj.* **1** (with *interrog.*, *neg.*, or conditional expressed or implied) **a** one, no matter which, of several (*cannot find any answer*). **b** some, no matter how much or many or of what sort (*if any books arrive*; *have you any sugar?*). **2** a minimal amount of (*hardly any difference*). **3** whichever is chosen (*any fool knows that*). **4 a** an appreciable or significant (*did not stay for any length of time*). **b** a very large (*has any amount of money*). —*pron.* **1** any one (*did not know any of them*). **2** any number (*are any of them yours?*). **3** any amount (*is there any left?*). —*adv.* (usu. with *neg.* or *interrog.*) at all, in some degree (*is that any good?*; *do not make it any larger*; *without being any the wiser*). □ **any more** to any further extent (*don't like you any more*). **any time** *colloq.* at any time. **any time** (or **day** or **minute** etc.) **now** *colloq.* at any time in the near future. **not having any** *colloq.* unwilling to participate. [OE *ænig* f. Gmc (as ONE, -Y¹)]

anybody /'enɪˌbɒdɪ/ *n. & pron.* **1 a** a person, no matter who. **b** a person of any kind. **c** whatever person is chosen. **2** a person of importance (*are you anybody?*). □ **anybody's** (of a contest) evenly balanced (*it was anybody's game*). **anybody's guess** see GUESS.

anyhow /'enɪˌhaʊ/ *adv.* **1** anyway. **2** in a disorderly manner or state (*does his work anyhow*; *things are all anyhow*).

anyone /'enɪˌwʌn/ *pron.* anybody. ¶ Written as two words to imply a numerical sense, as in *any one of us can do it*.

anyplace /'enɪˌpleɪs/ *adv. US* anywhere.

anything /'enɪθɪŋ/ *pron.* **1** a thing, no matter which. **2** a thing of any kind. **3** whatever thing is chosen. □ **anything but** not at all (*was anything but honest*). **like anything** *colloq.* with great vigour, intensity, etc.

anyway /'enɪˌweɪ/ *adv.* **1** in any way or manner. **2** at any rate. **3** in any case. **4** to resume (*anyway, as I was saying*).

anywhere /'enɪˌweə(r)/ *adv. & pron.* —*adv.* in or to any place. —*pron.* any place (*anywhere will do*).

anywise /'enɪˌwaɪz/ *adv. archaic* in any manner. [OE *on ænige wīsan* in any wise]

Anzac /'ænzæk/ *n.* **1** a soldier in the Australian and New Zealand Army Corps (1914–18). **2** any person, esp. a member of the armed services, from Australia or New Zealand. □ **Anzac Day** 25 April, commemorating the Anzac landing at Gallipoli in 1915. [acronym]

Anzus /'ænzəs/ *n.* (also **ANZUS**) Australia, New Zealand, and the US, as an alliance for the Pacific area.

AO *abbr.* Officer of the Order of Australia.

AOB *abbr.* any other business.

A-OK *abbr. US colloq.* excellent; in good order. [*all systems OK*]

aorist /'eərɪst/ *n. & adj. Gram.* —*n.* an unqualified past tense of a verb (esp. in Greek), without reference to duration or completion. —*adj.* of or designating this tense. □□ **aoristic** /eə'rɪstɪk/ *adj.* [Gk *aoristos* indefinite f. *a*- not + *horizō* define, limit]

aorta /eɪ'ɔːtə/ *n.* (*pl.* **aortas**) the main artery, giving rise to the arterial network through which oxygenated blood is supplied to the body from the heart. □□ **aortic** *adj.* [Gk *aortē* f. *a(e)irō* raise]

à outrance /ɑ ˈuːtrɑ̃s/ *adv.* **1** to the death. **2** to the bitter end. [F, = to the utmost]

ap-¹ /æp/ *prefix* assim. form of AD- before *p*.

ap-² /æp/ *prefix* assim. form of APO- before a vowel or *h*.

apace /ə'peɪs/ *adv. literary* swiftly, quickly. [OF *à pas* at (a considerable) pace]

Apache /ə'pætʃɪ/ *n.* **1** a member of a N. American Indian tribe. **2** (**apache**) (/ə'pæʃ/) a violent street ruffian, orig. in Paris. [Mex. Sp.]

apanage var. of APPANAGE.

apart /ə'pɑːt/ *adv.* **1** separately; not together (*keep your feet apart*). **2** into pieces (*came apart in my hands*). **3 a** to or on one side. **b** out of consideration (*placed after noun: joking apart*). **4** to or at a distance. □ **apart from 1** excepting; not considering. **2** in addition to (*apart from roses we grow irises*). [ME f. OF f. *à* to + *part* side]

apartheid /ə'pɑːteɪt/ *n.* **1** (esp. in S. Africa) a policy or system of segregation or discrimination on grounds of race. **2** segregation in other contexts. [Afrik. (as APART, -HOOD)]

apartment /ə'pɑːtmənt/ *n.* **1** (in *pl.*) a suite of rooms, usu. furnished and rented. **2** a single room in a house. **3** *US* a flat. □ **apartment house** *US* a block of flats. [F *appartement* f. It. *appartamento* f. *appartare* to separate f. *a parte* apart]

apathetic /ˌæpə'θetɪk/ *adj.* having or showing no emotion or interest. □□ **apathetically** *adv.* [APATHY, after PATHETIC]

apathy /'æpəθɪ/ *n.* (often foll. by *towards*) lack of interest or feeling; indifference. [F *apathie* f. L *apathia* f. Gk *apatheia* f. *apathēs* without feeling f. *a*-not + *pathos* suffering]

apatite /'æpəˌtaɪt/ *n.* a naturally occurring crystalline mineral of calcium phosphate and fluoride, used in the manufacture of fertilizers. [G *Apatit* f. Gk *apatē* deceit (from its deceptive forms)]

ape /eɪp/ *n. & v.* —*n.* **1** any of the various primates of the family Pongidae characterized by the absence of a tail, e.g. the gorilla, chimpanzee, orang-utan, or gibbon. **2** (in general use) any monkey. **3 a** an imitator. **b** an apelike person. —*v.tr.* imitate, mimic.

□**ape-man** (*pl.* **-men**) any of various apelike primates held to be forerunners of present-day man. **go ape** *sl.* become crazy. **naked ape** present-day man. [OE *apa* f. Gmc]

aperçu /ˌæpɜːˈsjuː/ *n.* **1** a summary or survey. **2** an insight. [F, past part. of *apercevoir* perceive]

aperient /əˈpɪərɪənt/ *adj. & n.* —*adj.* laxative. —*n.* a laxative medicine. [L *aperire aperient-* to open]

aperiodic /ˌeɪpɪərɪˈɒdɪk/ *adj.* **1** not periodic; irregular. **2** *Physics* (of a potentially oscillating or vibrating system, e.g. an instrument with a pointer) that is adequately damped to prevent oscillation or vibration. **3** (of an oscillation or vibration) without a regular period. □□**aperiodicity** /-rɪəˈdɪsɪtɪ/ *n.*

aperitif /əˌperɪˈtiːf, əˈpe-/ *n.* an alcoholic drink taken before a meal to stimulate the appetite. [F *apéritif* f. med.L *aperitivus* f. L *aperire* to open]

aperture /ˈæpəˌtjʊə(r)/ *n.* **1** an opening; a gap. **2** a space through which light passes in an optical or photographic instrument, esp. a variable space in a camera. [L *apertura* (as APERITIF)]

apery /ˈeɪpərɪ/ *n.* (*pl.* **-ies**) **1** mimicry. **2** an ape-house.

apetalous /eɪˈpetələs/ *adj. Bot.* (of flowers) having no petals. [mod.L *apetalus* f. Gk *apetalos* leafless f. *a*- not + *petalon* leaf]

APEX /ˈeɪpeks/ *abbr.* Association of Professional, Executive, Clerical, and Computer Staff.

Apex /ˈeɪpeks/ *n.* (also **APEX**) (often *attrib.*) a system of reduced fares for scheduled airline flights when paid for before a certain period in advance of departure. [*Advance Purchase Excursion*]

apex /ˈeɪpeks/ *n.* (*pl.* **apexes** or **apices** /ˈeɪpɪˌsiːz/) **1** the highest point. **2** a climax; a high point of achievement etc. **3** the vertex of a triangle or cone. **4** a tip or pointed end. [L, = peak, tip]

apfelstrudel /ˈæpfəlˌstruːd(ə)l/ *n.* a confection of flaky pastry filled with spiced apple. [G f. *Apfel* apple + STRUDEL]

aphaeresis /əˈfɪərɪsɪs/ *n.* (*pl.* **aphaereses** /-ˌsiːz/) the omission of a letter or syllable at the beginning of a word as a morphological development (e.g. in the derivation of *adder*). [LL f. Gk *aphairesis* (as APO-, *haireō* take)]

aphasia /əˈfeɪzɪə/ *n. Med.* the loss of ability to understand or express speech, owing to brain damage. □□**aphasic** *adj. & n.* [mod.L f. Gk f. *aphatos* speechless f. *a*- not + *pha-* speak]

aphelion /æpˈhiːlɪən, əˈfiːlɪən/ (*pl.* **aphelia** /-lɪə/) the point in a body's orbit where it is furthest from the sun (opp. PERIHELION). ¶ Symb.: **Q**. [Graecized f. mod.L *aphelium* f. Gk *aph' hēliou* from the sun]

aphesis /ˈæfɪsɪs/ *n.* (*pl.* **apheses** /-ˌsiːz/) the gradual loss of an unstressed vowel at the beginning of a word (e.g. of *e* from *esquire* to form *squire*). □□ **aphetic** /əˈfetɪk/ *adj.* **aphetically** /əˈfetɪkəlɪ/ *adv.* [Gk, = letting go (as APO-, *hiēmi* send)]

aphid /ˈeɪfɪd/ *n.* any small homopterous insect which feeds by sucking sap from leaves, stems, or roots of plants; a plant-louse. [back-form. f. *aphides*: see APHIS]

aphis /ˈeɪfɪs/ *n.* (*pl.* **aphides** /-ˌdiːz/) an aphid, esp. of the genus *Aphis* including the greenfly. [mod.L (Linnaeus) f. Gk (1523), perh. a misreading of *koris* bug]

aphonia /əˈfəʊnɪə/ *n.* (also **aphony** /ˈæfənɪ/) *Med.* the loss or absence of the voice through a disease of the larynx or mouth. [mod.L *aphonia* f. Gk f. *aphōnos* voiceless f. *a*- not + *phōnē* voice]

aphorism /ˈæfəˌrɪz(ə)m/ *n.* **1** a short pithy maxim. **2** a brief statement of a principle. □□**aphorist** *n.* **aphoristic** /-ˈrɪstɪk/ *adj.* **aphoristically** /-ˈrɪstɪkəlɪ/ *adv.* **aphorize** *v.intr.* (also **-ise**). [F *aphorisme* or LL f. Gk *aphorismos* definition f. *aphorizō* (as APO-, *horos* boundary)]

aphrodisiac /ˌæfrəˈdɪzɪˌæk/ *adj. & n.* —*adj.* that arouses sexual desire. —*n.* an aphrodisiac drug. [Gk *aphrodisiakos* f. *aphrodisios* f. *Aphroditē* Gk goddess of love]

aphyllous /əˈfɪləs/ *adj. Bot.* (of plants) having no leaves. [mod.L f. Gk *aphullos* f. *a*- not + *phullon* leaf]

apian /ˈeɪpɪən/ *adj.* of or relating to bees. [L *apianus* f. *apis* bee]

apiary /ˈeɪpɪərɪ/ *n.* (*pl.* **-ies**) a place where bees are kept. □□ **apiarist** *n.* [L *apiarium* f. *apis* bee]

apical /ˈeɪpɪk(ə)l, ˈæp-/ *adj.* of, at, or forming an apex. □□ **apically** *adv.* [L *apex apicis*: see APEX]

apices *pl.* of APEX.

apiculture /ˈeɪpɪˌkʌltʃə(r)/ *n.* bee-keeping. □□ **apicultural** /-ˈkʌltʃər(ə)l/ *adj.* **apiculturist** /-ˈkʌltʃərɪst/ *n.* [L *apis* bee, after AGRICULTURE]

apiece /əˈpiːs/ *adv.* for each one; severally (*had five pounds apiece*). [A² + PIECE]

apish /ˈeɪpɪʃ/ *adj.* **1** of or like an ape. **2** silly, affected. □□ **apishly** *adv.* **apishness** *n.*

aplanat /ˈæpləˌnæt/ *n.* a reflecting or refracting surface made aplanatic by correction. [G]

aplanatic /ˌæpləˈnætɪk/ *adj.* (of a reflecting or refracting surface) free from spherical aberration. [Gk *aplanētos* free from error f. *a*- not + *planaō* wander]

aplasia /əˈpleɪzɪə/ *n. Med.* total or partial failure of development of an organ or tissue. □□ **aplastic** /əˈplæstɪk/ *adj.* [mod.L f. Gk f. *a*- not + *plasis* formation]

aplenty /əˈplentɪ/ *adv.* in plenty.

aplomb /əˈplɒm/ *n.* assurance; self-confidence. [F, = perpendicularity, f. *à plomb* according to a plummet]

apnoea /æpˈniːə/ *n.* (*US* **apnea**) *Med.* a temporary cessation of breathing. [mod.L f. Gk *apnoia* f. *apnous* breathless]

apo- /ˈæpə/ *prefix* **1** away from (*apogee*). **2** separate (*apocarpous*). [Gk *apo* from, away, un-, quite]

Apoc. *abbr.* **1** Apocalypse (New Testament). **2** Apocrypha.

apocalypse /əˈpɒkəlɪps/ *n.* **1** (**the Apocalypse**) Revelation, the last book of the New Testament, recounting a divine revelation to St John. **2** a revelation, esp. of the end of the world. **3** a grand or violent event resembling those described in the Apocalypse. [ME f. OF ult. f. Gk *apokalupsis* f. *apokaluptō* uncover, reveal]

apocalyptic /əˌpɒkəˈlɪptɪk/ *adj.* **1** of or resembling the Apocalypse. **2** revelatory, prophetic. □□ **apocalyptically** *adv.* [Gk *apokaluptikos* (as APOCALYPSE)]

apocarpous /ˌæpəˈkɑːpəs/ *adj. Bot.* (of ovaries) having distinct carpels not joined together (opp. SYNCARPOUS). [APO- + Gk *karpos* fruit]

apochromat /ˈæpəkrəˌmæt/ *n.* a lens or lens-system that reduces spherical and chromatic aberrations. □□ **apochromatic** /-krəˈmætɪk/ *adj.* [APO- + CHROMATIC]

apocope /əˈpɒkəpɪ/ *n.* the omission of a letter or letters at the end of a word as a morphological development (e.g. in the derivation of *curio*). [LL f. Gk *apokopē* (as APO-, *koptō* cut)]

Apocr. *abbr.* Apocrypha.

apocrine /ˈæpəˌkraɪn, -krɪn/ *adj. Biol.* (of a multicellular gland, e.g. the mammary gland) releasing some cytoplasm when secreting. [APO- + Gk *krinō* to separate]

Apocrypha /əˈpɒkrɪfə/ *n.pl.* **1** the books included in the Septuagint and Vulgate versions of the Old Testament but not in the Hebrew Bible. ¶ Modern Bibles sometimes include them in the Old Testament or as an appendix, and sometimes omit them. **2** (**apocrypha**) writings or reports not considered genuine. [ME f. eccl.L *apocrypha (scripta)* hidden writings f. Gk *apokruphos* f. *apokruptō* hide away]

apocryphal /əˈpɒkrɪf(ə)l/ *adj.* **1** of doubtful authenticity (orig. of some early Christian texts resembling those of the New Testament). **2** invented, mythical (*an apocryphal story*). **3** of or belonging to the Apocrypha.

apodal /ˈæpəd(ə)l/ *adj.* **1** without (or with undeveloped) feet. **2** (of fish) without ventral fins. [*apod*

---

w *we*   z *zoo*   ʃ *she*   ʒ *decision*   θ *thin*   ð *this*   ŋ *ring*   x *loch*   tʃ *chip*   dʒ *jar*   (*see over for vowels*)

apodal creature f. Gk *apous* footless f. *a-* not + *pous podos* foot]

apodictic /ˌæpəˈdɪktɪk/ *adj.* (also **apodeictic** /-ˈdaɪktɪk/) **1** clearly established. **2** of clear demonstration. [L *apodicticus* f. Gk *apodeiktikos* (as APO-, *deiknumi* show)]

apodosis /əˈpɒdəsɪs/ *n.* (*pl.* **apodoses** /-ˌsiːz/) the main (consequent) clause of a conditional sentence (e.g. *I would agree* in *if you asked me I would agree*). [LL f. Gk f. *apodidōmi* give back (as APO-, *didōmi* give)]

apogee /ˈæpəˌdʒiː/ *n.* **1** the point in a celestial body's orbit where it is furthest from the earth (opp. PERIGEE). **2** the most distant or highest point. □□ **apogean** /ˌæpəˈdʒiːən/ *adj.* [F *apogée* or mod.L *apogaeum* f. Gk *apogeion* away from earth (as APO-, *gē* earth)]

apolitical /ˌeɪpəˈlɪtɪk(ə)l/ *adj.* not interested in or concerned with politics.

Apollonian /ˌæpəˈləʊnɪən/ *adj.* **1** of or relating to Apollo, the Greek and Roman sun-god, patron of music and poetry. **2** orderly, rational, self-disciplined. [L *Apollonius* f. Gk *Apollōnios*]

apologetic /əˌpɒləˈdʒetɪk/ *adj.* & *n.* —*adj.* **1** regretfully acknowledging or excusing an offence or failure. **2** diffident. **3** of reasoned defence or vindication. —*n.* (usu. in *pl.*) a reasoned defence, esp. of Christianity. □□ **apologetically** *adv.* [F *apologétique* f. LL *apologeticus* f. Gk *apologētikos* f. *apologeomai* speak in defence]

apologia /ˌæpəˈləʊdʒɪə/ *n.* a formal defence of one's opinions or conduct. [L: see APOLOGY]

apologist /əˈpɒlədʒɪst/ *n.* a person who defends something by argument. [F *apologiste* f. Gk *apologizomai* render account f. *apologos* account]

apologize /əˈpɒləˌdʒaɪz/ *v.intr.* (also **-ise**) make an apology; express regret. [Gk *apologizomai*: see APOLOGIST]

apologue /ˈæpəˌlɒg/ *n.* a moral fable. [F *apologue* or L *apologus* f. Gk *apologos* story (as APO-, *logos* discourse)]

apology /əˈpɒlədʒɪ/ *n.* (*pl.* **-ies**) **1** a regretful acknowledgement of an offence or failure. **2** an assurance that no offence was intended. **3** an explanation or defence. **4** (foll. by *for*) a poor or scanty specimen of (*this apology for a letter*). [F *apologie* or LL *apologia* f. Gk (as APOLOGETIC)]

apolune /ˈæpəˌluːn, -ˌljuːn/ *n.* the point in a body's lunar orbit where it is furthest from the moon's centre (opp. PERILUNE). [APO- + L *luna* moon, after *apogee*]

apomixis /ˌæpəˈmɪksɪs/ *n.* (*pl.* **apomixes** /-siːz/) *Biol.* a form of asexual reproduction (cf. AMPHIMIXIS). □□ **apomictic** *adj.* [mod.L, formed as APO- + Gk *mixis* mingling]

apophthegm /ˈæpəˌθem, ˈæpəfˌθem/ *n.* (*US* **apothegm**) a terse saying or maxim, an aphorism. □□ **apophthegmatic** /-θegˈmætɪk/ *adj.* [F *apophthegme* or mod.L *apothegma* f. Gk *apophthegma -matos* f. *apophtheggomai* speak out]

apoplectic /ˌæpəˈplektɪk/ *adj.* **1** of, causing, suffering, or liable to apoplexy. **2** *colloq.* enraged. □□ **apoplectically** *adv.* [F *apoplectique* or LL *apoplecticus* f. Gk *apoplēktikos* f. *apoplēssō* strike completely (as APO-, *plēssō* strike)]

apoplexy /ˈæpəˌpleksɪ/ *n.* a sudden loss of consciousness, voluntary movement, and sensation caused by blockage or rupture of a brain artery; a stroke. [ME f. OF *apoplexie* f. LL *apoplexia* f. Gk *apoplēxia* (as APOPLECTIC)]

aposematic /ˌæpəsɪˈmætɪk/ *adj.* *Zool.* (of coloration, markings, etc.) serving to warn or repel. [APO- + Gk *sēma sēmatos* sign]

apostasy /əˈpɒstəsɪ/ *n.* (*pl.* **-ies**) **1** renunciation of a belief or faith, esp. religious. **2** abandonment of principles or of a party. **3** an instance of apostasy. [ME f. eccl.L f. NT Gk *apostasia* f. *apostasis* defection (as APO-, *stat-* stand)]

apostate /əˈpɒsteɪt/ *n.* & *adj.* —*n.* a person who renounces a former belief, adherence, etc. —*adj.* engaged in apostasy. □□ **apostatical** /ˌæpəˈstætɪk(ə)l/ *adj.* [ME f. OF *apostate* or eccl.L *apostata* f. Gk *apostatēs* deserter (as APOSTASY)]

apostatize /əˈpɒstəˌtaɪz/ *v.intr.* (also **-ise**) renounce a former belief, adherence, etc. [med.L *apostatizare* f. *apostata*: see APOSTATE]

a posteriori /ˌeɪ pɒˌsterɪˈɔːraɪ/ *adj.* & *adv.* —*adj.* (of reasoning) inductive, empirical; proceeding from effects to causes. —*adv.* inductively, empirically; from effects to causes (opp. A PRIORI). [L, = from what comes after]

apostle /əˈpɒs(ə)l/ *n.* **1** (**Apostle**) **a** any of the chosen twelve sent out to preach the Christian Gospel. **b** the first successful Christian missionary in a country or to a people. **2** a leader or outstanding figure, esp. of a reform movement (*apostle of temperance*). **3** a messenger or representative. □ **apostle-bird** any of various Australian birds, forming flocks of about a dozen. **Apostles' Creed** an early form of the Christian creed, ascribed to the Apostles. □□ **apostleship** *n.* [OE *apostol* f. eccl.L *apostolus* f. Gk *apostolos* messenger (as APO-, *stellō* send forth)]

apostolate /əˈpɒstələt/ *n.* **1** the position or authority of an Apostle. **2** leadership in reform. [eccl.L *apostolatus* (as APOSTLE)]

apostolic /ˌæpəˈstɒlɪk/ *adj.* **1** of or relating to the Apostles. **2** of the Pope regarded as the successor of St Peter. **3** of the character of an Apostle. □ **Apostolic Fathers** the Christian leaders immediately succeeding the Apostles. **apostolic succession** the uninterrupted transmission of spiritual authority from the Apostles through successive popes and bishops. [F *apostolique* or eccl.L *apostolicus* f. Gk *apostolikos* (as APOSTLE)]

apostrophe¹ /əˈpɒstrəfɪ/ *n.* a punctuation mark used to indicate: **1** the omission of letters or numbers (e.g. *can't*; *he's*; *1 Jan. '92*). **2** the possessive case (e.g. *Harry's book*; *boys' coats*). [F *apostrophe* or LL *apostrophus* f. Gk *apostrophos* accent of elision f. *apostrephō* turn away (as APO-, *strephō* turn)]

apostrophe² /əˈpɒstrəfɪ/ *n.* an exclamatory passage in a speech or poem, addressed to a person (often dead or absent) or thing (often personified). □□ **apostrophize** *v.tr.* & *intr.* (also **-ise**). [L f. Gk, lit. 'turning away' (as APOSTROPHE¹)]

apothecary /əˈpɒθəkərɪ/ *n.* (*pl.* **-ies**) *archaic* a chemist licensed to dispense medicines and drugs. □ **apothecaries' measure** (or **weight**) *Brit.* units of weight and liquid volume formerly used in pharmacy. ¶ 12 ounces = one pound; 20 fluid ounces = one pint. [ME f. OF *apotecaire* f. LL *apothecarius* f. L *apotheca* f. Gk *apothēkē* storehouse]

apothegm *US* var. of APOPHTHEGM.

apothem /ˈæpəˌθem/ *n.* *Geom.* a line from the centre of a regular polygon at right angles to any of its sides. [Gk *apotithēmi* put aside (as APO-, *tithēmi* place)]

apotheosis /əˌpɒθɪˈəʊsɪs/ *n.* (*pl.* **apotheoses** /-siːz/) **1** elevation to divine status; deification. **2** a glorification of a thing; a sublime example (*apotheosis of the dance*). **3** a deified ideal. [eccl.L f. Gk *apotheoō* make a god of (as APO-, *theos* god)]

apotheosize /əˈpɒθɪəˌsaɪz/ *v.tr.* (also **-ise**) **1** make divine; deify. **2** idealize, glorify.

apotropaic /ˌæpətrəˈpeɪɪk/ *adj.* supposedly having the power to avert an evil influence or bad luck. [Gk *apotropaios* (as APO-, *trepō* turn)]

appal /əˈpɔːl/ *v.tr.* (*US* **appall**) (**appalled**, **appalling**) **1** greatly dismay or horrify. **2** (as **appalling** *adj.*) *colloq.* shocking, unpleasant; bad. □□ **appallingly** *adv.* [ME f. OF *apalir* grow pale]

Appaloosa /ˌæpəˈluːsə/ *n.* **1** a horse of a N. American breed having dark spots on a light background. **2** this breed. [*Opelousa* in Louisiana, or *Palouse*, a river in Idaho]

appanage /ˈæpənɪdʒ/ *n.* (also **apanage**) **1** provision for the maintenance of the younger children of kings etc. **2** a perquisite. **3** a natural accompaniment or attribute. [F ult. f. med.L *appanare* endow with the means of subsistence (as APO-, *panis* bread)]

apparat /ˌæpəˈrɑːt/ *n.* the administrative system of a Communist party, esp. in a Communist country. [Russ. f. G, = apparatus]

apparatchik /ˌæpəˈrɑːtʃɪk/ *n.* (*pl.* **apparatchiks** or **apparatchiki** /-ˌkiː/) **1 a** a member of a Communist *apparat*. **b** a Communist agent or spy. **2 a** a member of a political party in any country who executes policy; a jealous functionary. **b** an official of a public or private organization. [Russ.: see APPARAT]

apparatus /ˌæpəˈreɪtəs, ˈæp-/ *n.* **1** the equipment needed for a particular purpose or function, esp. scientific or technical. **2** a political or other complex organization. **3** *Anat.* the organs used to perform a particular process. **4** (in full **apparatus criticus**) a collection of variants and annotations accompanying a printed text and usu. appearing below it. [L f. *apparare apparat-* make ready for]

apparel /əˈpær(ə)l/ *n. & v.* —*n.* **1** *formal* clothing, dress. **2** embroidered ornamentation on some ecclesiastical vestments. —*v.tr.* (**apparelled**, **apparelling**; *US* **appareled**, **appareling**) *archaic* clothe. [ME *aparailen* (v.) f. OF *apareillier* f. Rmc *appariculare* (unrecorded) make equal or fit, ult. f. L *par* equal]

apparent /əˈpærənt/ *adj.* **1** readily visible or perceivable. **2** seeming. □**apparent horizon** see HORIZON 1b. **apparent magnitude** the magnitude, i.e. brightness, of a celestial body as seen from the earth (opp. *absolute magnitude*). **apparent time** solar time (see SOLAR *adj.*). □□**apparently** *adv.* [ME f. OF *aparant* f. L (as APPEAR)]

apparition /ˌæpəˈrɪʃ(ə)n/ *n.* a sudden or dramatic appearance, esp. of a ghost or phantom; a visible ghost. [ME f. F *apparition* or f. L *apparitio* attendance (as APPEAR)]

appeal /əˈpiːl/ *v. & n.* —*v.* **1** *intr.* make an earnest or formal request; plead (*appealed for calm*; *appealed to us not to leave*). **2** *intr.* (usu. foll. by *to*) be attractive or of interest; be pleasing. **3** *intr.* (foll. by *to*) resort to or cite for support. **4** *Law* **a** (often foll. by *to*) apply (to a higher court) for a reconsideration of the decision of a lower court. **b** *tr.* refer to a higher court to review (a case). **c** *intr.* (foll. by *against*) apply to a higher court to reconsider (a verdict or sentence). **5** *intr. Cricket* call on the umpire for a decision on whether a batsman is out. —*n.* **1** the act or an instance of appealing. **2** a formal or urgent request for public support, esp. financial, for a cause. **3** *Law* the referral of a case to a higher court. **4** attractiveness; appealing quality (*sex appeal*). □□ **appealer** *n.* [ME f. OF *apel, apeler* f. L *appellare* to address]

appealable /əˈpiːləb(ə)l/ *adj. Law* (of a case) that can be referred to a higher court for review.

appealing /əˈpiːlɪŋ/ *adj.* attractive, likeable. □□ **appealingly** *adv.*

appear /əˈpɪə(r)/ *v.intr.* **1** become or be visible. **2** be evident (*a new problem then appeared*). **3** seem; have the appearance of being (*appeared unwell*; *you appear to be right*). **4** present oneself publicly or formally, esp. on stage or as the accused or counsel in a lawcourt. **5** be published (*it appeared in the papers*; *a new edition will appear*). [ME f. OF *apareir* f. L *apparēre apparit-* come in sight]

appearance /əˈpɪərəns/ *n.* **1** the act or an instance of appearing. **2** an outward form as perceived (whether correctly or not), esp. visually (*has an appearance of prosperity*; *gives the appearance of trying hard*). **3** a semblance. □**keep up appearances** maintain an impression or pretence of virtue, affluence, etc. **make** (or **put in**) **an appearance** be present, esp. briefly. **to all appearances** as far as can be seen; apparently. [ME f. OF *aparance, -ence* f. LL *apparentia* (as APPEAR, -ENCE)]

appease /əˈpiːz/ *v.tr.* **1** make calm or quiet, esp. conciliate (a potential aggressor) by making concessions. **2** satisfy (an appetite, scruples). □□ **appeasement** *n.* **appeaser** *n.* [ME f. AF *apeser*, OF *apaisier* f. *à* to + *pais* PEACE]

appellant /əˈpelənt/ *n. Law* a person who appeals to a higher court. [ME f. F (as APPEAL, -ANT)]

appellate /əˈpelət/ *adj. Law* (esp. of a court) concerned with or dealing with appeals. [L *appellatus* (as APPEAL, -ATE²)]

appellation /ˌæpəˈleɪʃ(ə)n/ *n. formal* a name or title; nomenclature. [ME f. OF f. L *appellatio -onis* (as APPEAL, -ATION)]

appellative /əˈpelətɪv/ *adj.* **1** naming. **2** *Gram.* (of a noun) that designates a class; common. [LL *appellativus* (as APPEAL, -ATIVE)]

append /əˈpend/ *v.tr.* (usu. foll. by *to*) attach, affix, add, esp. to a written document etc. [L *appendere* hang]

appendage /əˈpendɪdʒ/ *n.* **1** something attached; an addition. **2** *Zool.* a leg or other projecting part of an arthropod.

appendant /əˈpend(ə)nt/ *adj. & n.* —*adj.* (usu. foll. by *to*) attached in a subordinate capacity. —*n.* an appendant person or thing. [OF *apendant* f. *apendre* formed as APPEND, -ANT]

appendectomy /ˌæpenˈdektəmɪ/ *n.* (also **appendicectomy** /-dɪˈsektəmɪ/) (*pl.* **-ies**) the surgical removal of the appendix. [APPENDIX + -ECTOMY]

appendicitis /əˌpendɪˈsaɪtɪs/ *n.* inflammation of the appendix. [APPENDIX + -ITIS]

appendix /əˈpendɪks/ *n.* (*pl.* **appendices** /-ˌsiːz/; **appendixes**) **1** (in full **vermiform appendix**) *Anat.* a small outgrowth of tissue forming a tube-shaped sac attached to the lower end of the large intestine. **2** subsidiary matter at the end of a book or document. [L *appendix -icis* f. *appendere* APPEND]

apperceive /ˌæpəˈsiːv/ *v.tr.* **1** be conscious of perceiving. **2** *Psychol.* compare (a perception) to previously held ideas so as to extract meaning from it. □□ **apperception** /-ˈsepʃ(ə)n/ *n.* **apperceptive** /-ˈseptɪv/ *adj.* [ME (in obs. sense 'observe') f. OF *aperceveir* ult. f. L *percipere* PERCEIVE]

appertain /ˌæpəˈteɪn/ *v.intr.* (foll. by *to*) **1** relate. **2** belong as a possession or right. **3** be appropriate. [ME f. OF *apertenir* f. LL *appertinēre* f. *pertinēre* PERTAIN]

appetence /ˈæpɪt(ə)ns/ *n.* (also **appetency** /-sɪ/) (foll. by *for*) longing or desire. [F *appétence* or L *appetentia* f. *appetere* seek after]

appetite /ˈæpɪˌtaɪt/ *n.* **1** a natural desire to satisfy bodily needs, esp. for food or sexual activity. **2** (usu. foll. by *for*) an inclination or desire. □□ **appetitive** /əˈpetɪtɪv/ *adj.* [ME f. OF *apetit* f. L *appetitus* f. *appetere* seek after]

appetizer /ˈæpɪˌtaɪzə(r)/ *n.* (also **-iser**) a small amount, esp. of food or drink, to stimulate an appetite. [*appetize* (back-form. f. APPETIZING)]

appetizing /ˈæpɪˌtaɪzɪŋ/ *adj.* (also **-ising**) stimulating an appetite, esp. for food. □□ **appetizingly** *adv.* [F *appétissant* irreg. f. *appétit*, formed as APPETITE]

applaud /əˈplɔːd/ *v.* **1** *intr.* express strong approval or praise, esp. by clapping. **2** *tr.* express approval of (a person or action). [L *applaudere applaus-* clap hands]

applause /əˈplɔːz/ *n.* **1** an expression of approbation, esp. from an audience etc. by clapping. **2** emphatic approval. [med.L *applausus* (as APPLAUD)]

apple /ˈæp(ə)l/ *n.* **1** the fruit of a tree of the genus *Malus*, rounded in form and with a crisp flesh. **2** the tree bearing this. □**apple of one's eye** a cherished person or thing. **apple-pie bed** a bed made (as a joke) with the sheets folded short, so that the legs cannot be accommodated. **apple-pie order** perfect order; extreme neatness. **she's apple** *Austral. sl.* everything is fine. **upset the apple-cart** spoil careful plans. [OE *æppel* f. Gmc]

applejack /ˈæp(ə)lˌdʒæk/ n. US a spirit distilled from fermented apple juice. [APPLE + JACK¹]

appliance /əˈplaɪəns/ n. a device or piece of equipment used for a specific task. [APPLY + -ANCE]

applicable /ˈæplɪkəb(ə)l, əˈplɪkəb(ə)l/ adj. (often foll. by to) 1 that may be applied. 2 having reference; appropriate. □□ **applicability** /-ˈbɪlɪtɪ/ n. **applicably** adv. [OF applicable or med.L applicabilis (as APPLY, -ABLE)]

applicant /ˈæplɪkənt/ n. a person who applies for something, esp. a post. [APPLICATION + -ANT]

application /ˌæplɪˈkeɪʃ(ə)n/ n. 1 the act of applying, esp. medicinal ointment to the skin. 2 a formal request, usu. in writing, for employment, membership, etc. 3 a relevance. b the use to which something can or should be put. 4 sustained or concentrated effort; diligence. [ME f. F f. L applicatio -onis (as APPLY, -ATION)]

applicator /ˈæplɪˌkeɪtə(r)/ n. a device for applying a substance to a surface, esp. the skin. [APPLICATION + -OR¹]

applied /əˈplaɪd/ adj. (of a subject of study) put to practical use as opposed to being theoretical (cf. PURE adj. 9). □ **applied mathematics** see MATHEMATICS.

appliqué /æˈpliːkeɪ/ n., adj., & v. —n. ornamental work in which fabric is cut out and attached, usu. sewn, to the surface of another fabric to form pictures or patterns. —adj. executed in appliqué. —v.tr. (**appliqués, appliquéd, appliquéing**) decorate with appliqué; make using appliqué technique. [F, past part. of appliquer apply f. L applicare: see APPLY]

apply /əˈplaɪ/ v. (-ies, -ied) 1 intr. (often foll. by for, to, or to + infin.) make a formal request for something to be done, given, etc. (apply for a job; apply for help to the governors; applied to be sent overseas). 2 intr. have relevance (does not apply in this case). 3 tr. a make use of as relevant or suitable; employ (apply the rules). b operate (apply the handbrake). 4 tr. (often foll. by to) a put or spread on (applied the ointment to the cut). b administer (applied the remedy; applied common sense to the problem). 5 refl. (often foll. by to) devote oneself (applied myself to the task). □□ **applier** n. [ME f. OF aplier f. L applicare fold, fasten to]

appoggiatura /əˌpɒdʒəˈtʊərə/ n. Mus. a grace-note performed before an essential note of a melody and normally taking half its time-value. [It.]

appoint /əˈpɔɪnt/ v.tr. 1 assign a post or office to (appoint him governor; appoint him to govern; appointed to the post). 2 (often foll. by for) fix, decide on (a time, place, etc.) (Wednesday was appointed for the meeting; 8.30 was the appointed time). 3 prescribe; ordain (Holy Writ appointed by the Church). 4 Law a (also absol.) declare the destination of (property etc.). b declare (a person) as having an interest in property etc. (Jones was appointed in the will). 5 (as **appointed** adj.) equipped, furnished (a badly appointed hotel). □□ **appointee** /-ˈtiː/ n. **appointer** n. **appointive** adj. US [ME f. OF apointer f. à point to a point]

appointment /əˈpɔɪntmənt/ n. 1 an arrangement to meet at a specific time and place. 2 a a post or office available for applicants, or recently filled (took up the appointment on Monday). b a person appointed. 3 (usu. in pl.) a furniture, fittings. b equipment. [ME f. OF apointement (as APPOINT, -MENT)]

apport /əˈpɔːt/ n. 1 the production of material objects by supposedly occult means at a seance. 2 an object so produced. [ME (in obs. senses), f. OF aport f. aporter f. à to + porter bring]

apportion /əˈpɔːʃ(ə)n/ v.tr. (often foll. by to) share out; assign as a share. □□ **apportionable** adj.

apportionment n. [F apportionner or f. med.L apportionare (as AD-, PORTION)]

apposite /ˈæpəzɪt/ adj. (often foll. by to) 1 apt; well chosen. 2 well expressed. □□ **appositely** adv. **appositeness** n. [L appositus past part. of apponere (as AD-, ponere put)]

apposition /ˌæpəˈzɪʃ(ə)n/ n. 1 placing side by side;

juxtaposition. 2 Gram. the placing of a word next to another, esp. the addition of one noun to another, in order to qualify or explain the first (e.g. William the Conqueror; my friend Sue). □□ **appositional** adj. [ME f. F apposition or f. LL appositio (as APPOSITE, -ITION)]

appraisal /əˈpreɪz(ə)l/ n. the act or an instance of appraising.

appraise /əˈpreɪz/ v.tr. 1 estimate the value or quality of (appraised her skills). 2 (esp. of an official valuer) set a price on; value. □□ **appraisable** adj. **appraiser** n. **appraisive** adj. [APPRIZE by assim. to PRAISE]

appreciable /əˈpriːʃəb(ə)l/ adj. large enough to be noticed; significant; considerable (appreciable progress has been made). □□ **appreciably** adv. [F f. apprécier (as APPRECIATE)]

appreciate /əˈpriːʃɪˌeɪt, -sɪˌeɪt/ v. 1 tr. a esteem highly; value. b be grateful for (we appreciate your sympathy). c be sensitive to (appreciate the nuances). 2 tr. (often foll. by that + clause) understand; recognize (I appreciate that I may be wrong). 3 a intr. (of property etc.) rise in value. b tr. raise in value. □□ **appreciative** /-ʃətɪv/ adj. **appreciatively** /-ʃətɪvlɪ/ adv. **appreciativeness** /-ʃətɪvnɪs/ n. **appreciator** n. **appreciatory** /-ʃɪətərɪ/ adj. [LL appretiare appraise (as AD-, pretium price)]

appreciation /əˌpriːʃɪˈeɪʃ(ə)n, əˌpriːsɪ-/ n. 1 favourable or grateful recognition. 2 an estimation or judgement; a sensitive understanding or reaction (a quick appreciation of the problem). 3 an increase in value. 4 a (usu. favourable) review of a book, film, etc. [F f. LL appretiatio -onis (as APPRECIATE, -ATION)]

apprehend /ˌæprɪˈhend/ v.tr. 1 understand, perceive (apprehend your meaning). 2 seize, arrest (apprehended the criminal). 3 anticipate with uneasiness or fear (apprehending the results). [F appréhender or L apprehendere (as AD-, prehendere prehens- lay hold of)]

apprehensible /ˌæprɪˈhensɪb(ə)l/ adj. capable of being apprehended by the senses or the intellect (an apprehensible theory; an apprehensible change in her expression). □□ **apprehensibility** /-ˈbɪlɪtɪ/ n. [LL apprehensibilis (as APPREHEND, -IBLE)]

apprehension /ˌæprɪˈhenʃ(ə)n/ n. 1 uneasiness; dread. 2 understanding, grasp. 3 arrest, capture (apprehension of the suspect). 4 an idea; a conception. [F appréhension or LL apprehensio (as APPREHEND, -ION)]

apprehensive /ˌæprɪˈhensɪv/ adj. 1 (often foll. by of, for) uneasily fearful; dreading. 2 relating to perception by the senses or the intellect. 3 archaic perceptive; intelligent. □□ **apprehensively** adv. **apprehensiveness** n. [F appréhensif or med.L apprehensivus (as APPREHEND, -IVE)]

apprentice /əˈprentɪs/ n. & v. —n. 1 a person who is learning a trade by being employed in it for an agreed period at low wages. 2 a beginner; a novice. —v.tr. (usu. foll. by to) engage or bind as an apprentice (was apprenticed to a builder). □□ **apprenticeship** n. [ME f. OF aprentis f. apprendre learn (as APPREHEND), after words in -tis, -tif, f. L -tivus: see -IVE]

apprise /əˈpraɪz/ v.tr. inform. □ **be apprised of** be aware of. [F appris -ise past part. of apprendre learn, teach (as APPREHEND)]

apprize /əˈpraɪz/ v.tr. archaic 1 esteem highly. 2 appraise. [ME f. OF aprisier f. à to + pris PRICE]

appro /ˈæprəʊ/ n. Brit. colloq. □ **on appro** = on approval (see APPROVAL). [abbr. of approval or approbation]

approach /əˈprəʊtʃ/ v. & n. —v. 1 tr. come near or nearer to (a place or time). 2 intr. come near or nearer in space or time (the hour approaches). 3 tr. make a tentative proposal or suggestion to (approached me about a loan). 4 tr. a be similar in character, quality, etc., to (doesn't approach her for artistic skill). b approximate to (a population approaching 5 million). 5 tr. attempt to influence or bribe. **6** *tr.* set about (a task etc.). **7** *intr. Golf* play an approach shot. **8** *intr. Aeron.* prepare to land. **9** *tr. archaic* bring near. —*n.* **1** an act or means of approaching (*made an approach*; *an approach lined with trees*). **2** an approximation (*an approach to an apology*). **3** a way of dealing with a person or thing (*needs a new approach*). **4** (usu. in *pl.*) a sexual advance. **5** *Golf* a stroke from the fairway to the green. **6** *Aeron.* the final part of a flight before landing. **7** *Bridge* a bidding method with a gradual advance to a final contract. □ **approach road** *Brit.* a road by which traffic enters a motorway. [ME f. OF *aproch(i)er* f. eccl.L *appropiare* draw near (as AD-, *propius* compar. of *prope* near)]

approachable /əˈprəʊtʃəb(ə)l/ *adj.* **1** friendly; easy to talk to. **2** able to be approached. □□ **approachability** /-ˈbɪlɪtɪ/ *n.*

approbate /ˈæprəˌbeɪt/ *v.tr. US* approve formally; sanction. [ME f. L *approbare* (as AD-, *probare* test f. *probus* good)]

approbation /ˌæprəˈbeɪʃ(ə)n/ *n.* approval, consent. □□ **approbative** /ˈæprəˌbeɪtɪv/ *adj.* **approbatory** *adj.* [ME f. OF f. L *approbatio -onis* (as APPROBATE, -ATION)]

appropriate *adj. & v.* —*adj.* /əˈprəʊprɪət/ (often foll. by *to, for*) **1** suitable or proper. **2** *formal* belonging or particular. —*v.tr.* /əˈprəʊprɪˌeɪt/ **1** take possession of, esp. without authority. **2** devote (money etc.) to special purposes. □□ **appropriately** *adv.* **appropriateness** *n.* **appropriation** /əˌprəʊprɪˈeɪʃ(ə)n/ *n.* **appropriator** /-ˌeɪtə(r)/ *n.* [LL *appropriatus* past part. of *appropriare* (as AD-, *proprius* own)]

approval /əˈpruːv(ə)l/ *n.* **1** the act of approving. **2** an instance of this; consent; a favourable opinion (*with your approval*; *looked at him with approval*). □ **on approval** (of goods supplied) to be returned if not satisfactory.

approve /əˈpruːv/ *v.* **1** *tr.* confirm; sanction (*approved his application*). **2** *intr.* give or have a favourable opinion. **3** *tr.* commend (*approved the new hat*). **4** *tr. archaic* (usu. *refl.*) demonstrate oneself to be (*approved himself a coward*). □ **approved school** *hist.* a residential place of training for young offenders. **approve of 1** pronounce or consider good or satisfactory; commend. **2** agree to. □□ **approvingly** *adv.* [ME f. OF *aprover* f. L (as APPROBATE)]

approx. *abbr.* **1** approximate. **2** approximately.

approximate *adj. & v.* —*adj.* /əˈprɒksɪmət/ **1** fairly correct or accurate; near to the actual (*the approximate time of arrival*; *an approximate guess*). **2** near or next (*your approximate neighbour*). —*v.tr. & intr.* /əˈprɒksɪˌmeɪt/ (often foll. by *to*) bring or come near (esp. in quality, number, etc.), but not exactly (*approximates to the truth*; *approximates the amount required*). □□ **approximately** /-mətlɪ/ *adv.* **approximation** /-ˈmeɪʃ(ə)n/ *n.* [LL *approximatus* past part. of *approximare* (as AD-, *proximus* very near)]

appurtenance /əˈpɜːtɪnəns/ *n.* (usu. in *pl.*) a belonging; an appendage; an accessory. [ME f. AF *apurtenaunce*, OF *apertenance* (as APPERTAIN, -ANCE)]

appurtenant /əˈpɜːtɪnənt/ *adj.* (often foll. by *to*) belonging or appertaining; pertinent. [ME f. OF *apartenant* pres. part. (as APPERTAIN)]

APR *abbr.* annual or annualized percentage rate (esp. of interest on loans or credit).

Apr. *abbr.* April.

après-ski /ˌæpreɪˈskiː/ *n. & adj.* —*n.* the evening, esp. its social activities, following a day's skiing. —*attrib.adj.* (of clothes, drinks, etc.) appropriate to social activities following skiing. [F]

apricot /ˈeɪprɪˌkɒt/ *n. & adj.* —*n.* **1 a** a juicy soft fruit, smaller than a peach, of an orange-yellow colour. **b** the tree, *Prunus armeniaca*, bearing it. **2** the ripe fruit's orange-yellow colour. —*adj.* orange-yellow (*apricot dress*). [Port. *albricoque* or Sp. *al-baricoque* f. Arab. *al* the + *barḳuḳ* f. late Gk *praikokion* f. L *praecoquum* var. of *praecox* early-ripe: *apri-* after L *apricus* ripe, *-cot* by assim. to F *abricot*]

April /ˈeɪprɪl, ˈeɪpr(ə)l/ *n.* the fourth month of the year. □ **April Fool** a person successfully tricked on 1 April. **April Fool's** (or **Fools'**) **Day** 1 April. [ME f. L *Aprilis*]

a priori /ˌeɪ praɪˈɔːraɪ/ *adj. & adv.* —*adj.* **1** (of reasoning) deductive; proceeding from causes to effects (opp. A POSTERIORI). **2** (of concepts, knowledge, etc.) logically independent of experience; not derived from experience (opp. EMPIRICAL). **3** not submitted to critical investigation (*an a priori conjecture*). —*adv.* **1** in an a priori manner. **2** as far as one knows; presumptively. □□ **apriorism** /eɪˈpraɪəˌrɪz(ə)m/ *n.* [L, = from what is before]

apron /ˈeɪprən/ *n.* **1 a** a garment covering and protecting the front of a person's clothes, either from chest or waist level, and tied at the back. **b** official clothing of this kind (*bishop's apron*). **c** anything resembling an apron in shape or function. **2** *Theatr.* the part of a stage in front of the curtain. **3** the hard-surfaced area on an airfield used for manœuvring or loading aircraft. **4** an endless conveyor belt. □ **tied to a person's apron-strings** dominated by or dependent on that person (usu. a woman). □□ **aproned** *adj.* **apronful** *n.* (*pl.* **-fuls**). [ME *naperon* etc. f. OF dimin. of *nape* table-cloth f. L *mappa*: for loss of *n* cf. ADDER]

apropos /ˈæprəˌpəʊ, -ˈpəʊ/ *adj. & adv.* —*adj.* **1** to the point or purpose; appropriate (*his comment was apropos*). **2** *colloq.* (often foll. by *of*) in respect of; concerning (*apropos the meeting*; *apropos of the talk*). —*adv.* **1** appropriately (*spoke apropos*). **2** (*absol.*) by the way; incidentally (*apropos, she's not going*). [F *à propos* f. *à* to + *propos* PURPOSE]

apse /æps/ *n.* **1** a large semicircular or polygonal recess, arched or with a domed roof, esp. at the eastern end of a church. **2** = APSIS. □□ **apsidal** /ˈæpsɪd(ə)l/ *adj.* [L APSIS]

apsis /ˈæpsɪs/ *n.* (*pl.* **apsides** /-ˌdiːz/) either of two points on the orbit of a planet or satellite that are nearest to or furthest from the body round which it moves. □□ **apsidal** *adj.* [L f. Gk *(h)apsis, -idos* arch, vault]

APT *abbr.* (in the UK) Advanced Passenger Train.

apt /æpt/ *adj.* **1** appropriate, suitable. **2** (foll. by *to* + infin.) having a tendency (*apt to lose his temper*). **3** clever; quick to learn (*an apt pupil*; *apt at the work*). □□ **aptly** *adv.* **aptness** *n.* [ME f. L *aptus* fitted, past part. of *apere* fasten]

apterous /ˈæptərəs/ *adj.* **1** *Zool.* (of insects) without wings. **2** *Bot.* (of seeds or fruits) having no winglike expansions. [Gk *apteros* f. *a-* not + *pteron* wing]

apteryx /ˈæptərɪks/ *n.* = KIWI. [mod.L f. Gk *a-* not + *pterux* wing]

aptitude /ˈæptɪˌtjuːd/ *n.* **1** a natural propensity or talent (*shows an aptitude for drawing*). **2** ability or fitness, esp. to acquire a particular skill. [F f. LL *aptitudo -inis* (as APT, -TUDE)]

aqua /ˈækwə/ *n.* the colour aquamarine. [abbr.]

aquaculture /ˈækwəˌkʌltʃə(r), -ˌkʌltjə(r)/ *n.* the cultivation or rearing of aquatic plants or animals. [L *aqua* water + CULTURE, after *agriculture*]

aqua fortis /ˌækwə ˈfɔːtɪs/ *n. Chem.* nitric acid. [L, = strong water]

aqualung /ˈækwəˌlʌŋ/ *n. & v.* —*n.* a portable breathing-apparatus for divers, consisting of cylinders of compressed air strapped on the back, feeding air automatically through a mask or mouthpiece. —*v.intr.* use an aqualung. [L *aqua* water + LUNG]

aquamarine /ˌækwəməˈriːn/ *n.* **1** a light bluish-green beryl. **2** its colour. [L *aqua marina* sea water]

aquanaut /ˈækwəˌnɔːt/ *n.* an underwater swimmer or explorer. [L *aqua* water + Gk *nautēs* sailor]

aquaplane /'ækwə,pleɪn/ n. & v. —n. a board for riding on the water, pulled by a speedboat. —v.intr. **1** ride on an aquaplane. **2** (of a vehicle) glide uncontrollably on the wet surface of a road. [L aqua water + PLANE¹]

aqua regia /,ækwə 'riːdʒɪə/ n. Chem. a mixture of concentrated nitric and hydrochloric acids, a highly corrosive liquid attacking many substances unaffected by other reagents. [L, = royal water]

aquarelle /,ækwə'rel/ n. a painting in thin, usu. transparent water-colours. [F f. It. acquarella watercolour, dimin. of acqua f. L aqua water]

aquarium /ə'kweərɪəm/ n. (pl. **aquariums** or **aquaria** /-rɪə/) an artificial environment designed for keeping live aquatic plants and animals for study or exhibition, esp. a tank of water with transparent sides. [neut. of L aquarius of water (aqua) after vivarium]

Aquarius /ə'kweərɪəs/ n. **1** a constellation, traditionally regarded as contained in the figure of a water-carrier. **2 a** the eleventh sign of the zodiac (the Water-carrier). **b** a person born when the sun is in this sign. □□ **Aquarian** adj. & n. [ME f. L (as AQUARIUM)]

aquatic /ə'kwætɪk/ adj. & n. —adj. **1** growing or living in or near water. **2** (of a sport) played in or on water. —n. **1** an aquatic plant or animal. **2** (in pl.) aquatic sports. [ME f. F aquatique or L aquaticus f. aqua water]

aquatint /'ækwətɪnt/ n. **1** a print resembling a water-colour, produced from a copper plate etched with nitric acid. **2** the process of producing this. [F aquatinte f. It. acqua tinta coloured water]

aquavit /'ækwəvɪt, -,viːt/ (also **akvavit** /'ækvə-/) n. an alcoholic spirit made from potatoes etc. [Scand.]

aqua vitae /,ækwə 'viːtaɪ/ n. a strong alcoholic spirit, esp. brandy. [L = water of life]

aqueduct /'ækwɪ,dʌkt/ n. **1** an artificial channel for conveying water, esp. in the form of a bridge supported by tall columns across a valley. **2** Physiol. a small canal, esp. in the head of mammals. [L aquae ductus conduit f. aqua water + ducere duct- to lead]

aqueous /'eɪkwɪəs/ adj. **1** of, containing, or like water. **2** Geol. produced by water (aqueous rocks). □ **aqueous humour** Anat. the clear fluid in the eye between the lens and the cornea. [med.L aqueus f. L aqua water]

aquifer /'ækwɪfə(r)/ n. Geol. a layer of rock or soil able to hold or transmit much water. [L aqui- f. aqua water + -fer bearing f. ferre bear]

aquilegia /,ækwɪ'liːdʒə/ n. any (often blue-flowered) plant of the genus Aquilegia. Also called COLUMBINE. [mod. use of a med.L word: orig. unkn.]

aquiline /'ækwɪ,laɪn/ adj. **1** of or like an eagle. **2** (of a nose) curved like an eagle's beak. [L aquilinus f. aquila eagle]

AR abbr. US Arkansas (in official postal use).

Ar symb. Chem. the element argon.

ar- /ə(r)/ prefix assim. form of AD- before r.

-ar¹ /ə(r)/ suffix **1** forming adjectives (angular; linear; nuclear; titular). **2** forming nouns (scholar). [OF -aire or -ier or L -aris]

-ar² /ə(r)/ suffix forming nouns (pillar). [F -er or L -ar, -are, neut. of -aris]

-ar³ /ə(r)/ suffix forming nouns (bursar; exemplar; mortar; vicar). [OF -aire or -ier or L -arius, -arium]

-ar⁴ /ə(r)/ suffix assim. form of -ER¹, -OR¹ (liar; pedlar).

ARA abbr. Associate of the Royal Academy.

Arab /'ærəb/ n. & adj. —n. **1** a member of a Semitic people inhabiting originally Saudi Arabia and the neighbouring countries, now the Middle East generally. **2** a horse of a breed orig. native to Arabia. —adj. of Arabia or the Arabs (esp. with ethnic reference). [F Arabe f. L Arabs Arabis f. Gk Araps -abos f. Arab. 'arab]

arabesque /,ærə'besk/ n. **1** Ballet a posture with one leg extended horizontally backwards, torso extended forwards, and arms outstretched. **2** a design of

intertwined leaves, scrolls, etc. **3** Mus. a florid melodic section or composition. [F f. It. arabesco f. arabo Arab]

Arabian /ə'reɪbɪən/ adj. & n. —adj. of or relating to Arabia (esp. with geographical reference) (the Arabian desert). —n. a native of Arabia. ¶ Now less common than Arab in this sense. □ **Arabian camel** a domesticated camel, Camelus dromedarius, native to the deserts of N. Africa and the Near East, with one hump: also called DROMEDARY. [ME f. OF arabi prob. f. Arab. 'arabī, or f. L Arabus, Arabius f. Gk Arabios]

Arabic /'ærəbɪk/ n. & adj. —n. the Semitic language of the Arabs, now spoken in much of N. Africa and the Middle East. —adj. of or relating to Arabia (esp. with reference to language or literature). □ **arabic numeral** any of the numerals 0, 1, 2, 3, 4, 5, 6, 7, 8, and 9 (cf. roman numeral). [ME f. OF arabic f. L arabicus f. Gk arabikos]

arabis /'ærəbɪs/ n. any plant of the genus Arabis, low-growing or mat-forming with toothed leaves and usu. white flowers. Also called rock cress (see ROCK¹), wall cress. [med.L f. Gk, = Arabian]

Arabist /'ærəbɪst/ n. a student of Arabic civilization, language, etc.

arable /'ærəb(ə)l/ adj. & n. —adj. **1** (of land) ploughed, or suitable for ploughing and crop production. **2** (of crops) that can be grown on arable land. —n. arable land or crops. [F arable or L arabilis f. arare to plough]

Araby /'ærəbɪ/ n. poet. Arabia. [OF Arabie f. L Arabia f. Gk]

arachnid /ə'ræknɪd/ n. any arthropod of the class Arachnida, having four pairs of walking legs and characterized by simple eyes, e.g. scorpions, spiders, mites, and ticks. □□ **arachnidan** adj. & n. [F arachnide or mod.L arachnida f. Gk arakhnē spider]

arachnoid /ə'ræknɔɪd/ n. & adj. —n. Anat. (in full **arachnoid membrane**) one of the three membranes (see MENINX) that surround the brain and spinal cord of vertebrates. —adj. Bot. covered with long cobweb-like hairs. [mod.L arachnoides f. Gk arakhnoeidēs like a cobweb f. arakhnē: see ARACHNID]

arak var. of ARRACK.

Araldite /'ærəl,daɪt/ n. propr. an epoxy resin used as a strong heatproof cement to mend china, plastic, etc. [20th c.: orig. uncert.]

Aramaic /,ærə'meɪɪk/ n. & adj. —n. a branch of the Semitic family of languages, esp. the language of Syria used as a lingua franca in the Near East from the sixth century BC, later dividing into varieties one of which included Syriac and Mandaean. —adj. of or in Aramaic. [L Aramaeus f. Gk Aramaios of Aram (bibl. name of Syria)]

arational /eɪ'ræʃən(ə)l/ adj. that does not purport to be rational.

araucaria /,ærɔː'keərɪə/ n. any evergreen conifer of the genus Araucaria, e.g. the monkey-puzzle tree. [mod.L f. Arauco, name of a province in Chile]

arbalest /'ɑːbə,lest/ n. (also **arblast** /'ɑːblɑːst/) hist. a crossbow with a mechanism for drawing the string. [OE arblast f. OF arbaleste f. LL arcubalista f. arcus bow + BALLISTA]

arbiter /'ɑːbɪtə(r)/ n. (fem. **arbitress** /-trɪs/) **1 a** an arbitrator in a dispute. **b** a judge; an authority (arbiter of taste). **2** (often foll. by of) a person who has entire control of something. □ **arbiter elegantiarum** (or **elegantiae**) /,ele,gænti'ɑːrəm, ,ele'gænʃɪ,iː/ a judge of artistic taste and etiquette. [L]

arbitrage /'ɑːbɪ,trɑːʒ, -trɪdʒ/ n. the buying and selling of stocks or bills of exchange to take advantage of varying prices in different markets. [F f. arbitrer (as ARBITRATE)]

arbitrageur /,ɑːbɪtrɑː'ʒɜː(r)/ n. (also **arbitrager** /'ɑːbɪtrɪdʒə(r)/) a person who engages in arbitrage. [F]

arbitral /'ɑːbɪtr(ə)l/ adj. concerning arbitration. [F arbitral or LL arbitralis: see ARBITER]

arbitrament /ɑːˈbɪtrəmənt/ n. **1** the deciding of a dispute by an arbiter. **2** an authoritative decision made by an arbiter. [ME f. OF *arbitrement* f. med.L *arbitramentum* (as ARBITRATE, -MENT)]

arbitrary /ˈɑːbɪtrərɪ/ adj. **1** based on or derived from uninformed opinion or random choice; capricious. **2** despotic. □□ **arbitrarily** adv. **arbitrariness** n. [L *arbitrarius* or F *arbitraire* (as ARBITER, -ARY¹)]

arbitrate /ˈɑːbɪˌtreɪt/ v.tr. & intr. decide by arbitration. [L *arbitrari* judge]

arbitration /ˌɑːbɪˈtreɪʃ(ə)n/ n. the settlement of a dispute by an arbitrator. [ME f. OF f. L *arbitratio -onis* (as ARBITER, -ATION)]

arbitrator /ˈɑːbɪˌtreɪtə(r)/ n. a person appointed to settle a dispute; an arbiter. □□ **arbitratorship** n. [ME f. LL (as ARBITRATION, -OR¹)]

arbitress see ARBITER.

arblast var. of ARBALEST.

arbor¹ /ˈɑːbə(r)/ n. **1** an axle or spindle on which something revolves. **2** US a device holding a tool in a lathe etc. [F *arbre* tree, axis, f. L *arbor*: refashioned on L]

arbor² US var. of ARBOUR.

arboraceous /ˌɑːbəˈreɪʃəs/ adj. **1** treelike. **2** wooded. [L *arbor* tree + -ACEOUS]

Arbor Day /ˈɑːbə/ n. a day dedicated annually to public tree-planting in the US, Australia, and other countries. [L *arbor* tree]

arboreal /ɑːˈbɔːrɪəl/ adj. of, living in, or connected with trees. [L *arboreus* f. *arbor* tree]

arboreous /ɑːˈbɔːrɪəs/ adj. **1** wooded. **2** arboreal.

arborescent /ˌɑːbəˈres(ə)nt/ adj. treelike in growth or general appearance. □□ **arborescence** n. [L *arborescere* grow into a tree (*arbor*)]

arboretum /ˌɑːbəˈriːtəm/ n. (pl. **arboretums** or **arboreta** /-tə/) a botanical garden devoted to trees. [L f. *arbor* tree]

arboriculture /ˈɑːbərɪˌkʌltʃə(r)/ n. the cultivation of trees and shrubs. □□ **arboricultural** /-ˈkʌltʃər(ə)l/ adj. **arboriculturist** /-ˈkʌltʃərɪst/ n. [L *arbor -oris* tree, after *agriculture*]

arborization /ˌɑːbəraɪˈzeɪʃ(ə)n/ n. (also **-isation**) a treelike arrangement esp. in anatomy.

arbor vitae /ˌɑːbə ˈviːtaɪ, ˈvaɪtɪ/ n. any of the evergreen conifers of the genus *Thuja*, native to N. Asia and N. America, usu. of pyramidal habit with flattened shoots bearing scale leaves. [L, = tree of life]

arbour /ˈɑːbə(r)/ n. (US **arbor**) a shady garden alcove with the sides and roof formed by trees or climbing plants; a bower. □□ **arboured** adj. [ME f. AF *erber* f. OF *erbier* f. *erbe* herb f. L *herba*: phonetic change to *ar-* assisted by assoc. with L *arbor* tree]

arbutus /ɑːˈbjuːtəs/ n. any evergreen ericaceous tree or shrub of the genus *Arbutus*, having white or pink clusters of flowers and strawberry-like berries. Also called *strawberry-tree*. □**trailing arbutus** US the mayflower, *Epigaea repens*. [L]

ARC abbr. **1** (in the UK) Agricultural Research Council. **2** Aids-related complex.

arc /ɑːk/ n. & v. —n. **1** part of the circumference of a circle or any other curve. **2** *Electr.* a luminous discharge between two electrodes. —v.intr. (**arced** /ɑːkt/; **arcing** /ˈɑːkɪŋ/) form an arc. □**arc lamp** (or **light**) a light source using an electric arc. **arc welding** a method of using an electric arc to melt metals to be welded. [ME f. OF f. L *arcus* bow, curve]

arcade /ɑːˈkeɪd/ n. **1** a passage with an arched roof. **2** any covered walk, esp. with shops along one or both along a wall. **3** *Archit.* a series of arches supporting or set along a wall. □□ **arcaded** adj. [F f. Prov. *arcada* or It. *arcata* f. Rmc: rel. to ARCH¹]

Arcadian /ɑːˈkeɪdɪən/ n. & adj. —n. an idealized peasant or country dweller, esp. in poetry. —adj. simple and poetically rural. □□ **Arcadianism** n. [L *Arcadius* f. Gk *Arkadia* mountain district in Peloponnese]

Arcady /ˈɑːkədɪ/ n. poet. an ideal rustic paradise. [Gk *Arkadia*: see ARCADIAN]

arcane /ɑːˈkeɪn/ adj. mysterious, secret; understood by few. □□ **arcanely** adv. [F *arcane* or L *arcanus* f. *arcēre* shut up f. *arca* chest]

arcanum /ɑːˈkeɪnəm/ n. (pl. **arcana** /-nə/) (usu. in pl.) a mystery; a profound secret. [L neut. of *arcanus*: see ARCANE]

arch¹ /ɑːtʃ/ n. & v. —n. **1 a** a curved structure as an opening or a support for a bridge, roof, floor, etc. **b** an arch used in building as an ornament. **2** any arch-shaped curve, e.g. as on the inner side of the foot, the eyebrows, etc. —v. **1** tr. provide with or form into an arch. **2** tr. span like an arch. **3** intr. form an arch. [ME f. OF *arche* ult. f. L *arcus* arc]

arch² /ɑːtʃ/ adj. self-consciously or affectedly playful or teasing. □□ **archly** adv. **archness** n. [ARCH-, orig. in *arch rogue* etc.]

arch- /ɑːtʃ/ comb. form **1** chief, superior (*archbishop*; *archdiocese*; *archduke*). **2** pre-eminent of its kind (esp. in unfavourable senses) (*arch-enemy*). [OE *arce-* or OF *arche-*, ult. f. Gk *arkhos* chief]

Archaean /ɑːˈkiːən/ adj. & n. (US **Archean**) —adj. of or relating to the earlier part of the Precambrian era. —n. this time. [Gk *arkhaios* ancient f. *arkhē* beginning]

archaeology /ˌɑːkɪˈɒlədʒɪ/ n. (US **archeology**) the study of human history and prehistory through the excavation of sites and the analysis of physical remains. □□ **archaeologic** /-ˈlɒdʒɪk/ adj. **archaeological** /-ˈlɒdʒɪk(ə)l/ adj. **archaeologist** n. **archaeologize** v.intr. (also **-ise**). [mod.L *archaeologia* f. Gk *arkhaiologia* ancient history (as ARCHAEAN, -LOGY)]

archaeopteryx /ˌɑːkɪˈɒptərɪks/ n. the oldest known fossil bird, *Archaeopteryx lithographica*, with teeth, feathers, and a reptilian tail. [Gk *arkhaios* ancient + *pterux* wing]

archaic /ɑːˈkeɪɪk/ adj. **1 a** antiquated. **b** (of a word etc.) no longer in ordinary use, though retained for special purposes. **2** primitive. **3** of an early period of art or culture, esp. the 7th-6th c. BC in Greece. □□ **archaically** adv. [F *archaïque* f. Gk *arkhaïkos* (as ARCHAEAN)]

archaism /ˈɑːkeɪˌɪz(ə)m/ n. **1** the retention or imitation of the old or obsolete, esp. in language or art. **2** an archaic word or expression. □□ **archaist** n. **archaistic** /-ˈɪstɪk/ adj. [mod.L f. Gk *arkhaïsmos* f. *arkhaïzō* (as ARCHAIZE, -ISM)]

archaize /ˈɑːkeɪˌaɪz/ v. (also **-ise**) **1** intr. imitate the archaic. **2** tr. make (a work of art, literature, etc.) imitate the archaic. [Gk *arkhaïzō* be old-fashioned f. *arkhaios* ancient]

archangel /ˈɑːkˌeɪndʒ(ə)l/ n. **1** an angel of the highest rank. **2** a member of the eighth order of the nine ranks of heavenly beings (see ORDER). □□ **archangelic** /-ænˈdʒelɪk/ adj. [OE f. AF *archangele* f. eccl.L *archangelus* f. eccl.Gk *arkhaggelos* (as ARCH-, ANGEL)]

archbishop /ɑːtʃˈbɪʃəp/ n. the chief bishop of a province. [OE (as ARCH-, BISHOP)]

archbishopric /ɑːtʃˈbɪʃəprɪk/ n. the office or diocese of an archbishop. [OE (as ARCH-, BISHOPRIC)]

archdeacon /ɑːtʃˈdiːkən/ n. **1** an Anglican cleric ranking below a bishop. **2** a member of the clergy of similar rank in other Churches. □□ **archdeaconry** n. (pl. **-ies**). **archdeaconship** n. [OE *arce-, ercediacon*, f. eccl.L *archidiaconus* f. eccl.Gk *arkhidiakonos* (as ARCH-, DEACON)]

archdiocese /ɑːtʃˈdaɪəsɪs/ n. the diocese of an archbishop. □□ **archdiocesan** /ˌɑːtʃdaɪˈɒsɪs(ə)n/ adj.

archduke /ɑːtʃˈdjuːk/ n. (fem. **archduchess** /-ˈdʌtʃɪs/) hist. the chief duke (esp. as the title of a son of the Emperor of Austria). □□ **archducal** adj. **archduchy** /-ˈdʌtʃɪ/ n. (pl. **-ies**). [OF *archeduc* f. med.L *archidux -ducis* (as ARCH-, DUKE)]

Archean US var. of ARCHAEAN.

archegonium /ˌɑːkɪˈɡəʊnɪəm/ n. (pl. **archegonia**

/-ɪə/) *Bot.* the female sex organ in mosses, ferns, conifers, etc. [L, dimin. of Gk *arkhegonos* f. *arkhe-* chief + *gonos* race]

arch-enemy /ɑːtʃˈenəmɪ/ *n.* (*pl.* **-ies**) **1** a chief enemy. **2** the Devil.

archeology *US* var. of ARCHAEOLOGY.

archer /ˈɑːtʃə(r)/ *n.* **1** a person who shoots with a bow and arrows. **2** (**the Archer**) the zodiacal sign or constellation Sagittarius. □**archer-fish** a SE Asian fish that catches flying insects by shooting water at them from its mouth. [AF f. OF *archier* ult. f. L *arcus* bow]

archery /ˈɑːtʃərɪ/ *n.* shooting with a bow and arrows, esp. as a sport. [OF *archerie* f. *archier* (as ARCHER, -ERY)]

archetype /ˈɑːkɪˌtaɪp/ *n.* **1 a** an original model; a prototype. **b** a typical specimen. **2** (in Jungian psychology) a primitive mental image inherited from man's earliest ancestors, and supposed to be present in the collective unconscious. **3** a recurrent symbol or motif in literature, art, etc. □□ **archetypal** /-ˈtaɪp(ə)l/ *adj.* **archetypical** /-ˈtɪpɪk(ə)l/ *adj.* [L *archetypum* f. Gk *arkhetupon* (as ARCH-, *tupos* stamp)]

archidiaconal /ˌɑːkɪdaɪˈækən(ə)l/ *adj.* of or relating to an archdeacon. □□ **archidiaconate** /-nət, -ˌneɪt/ *n.* [med.L *archidiaconalis* (as ARCH-, DIACONAL)]

archiepiscopal /ˌɑːkɪɪˈpɪskəp(ə)l/ *adj.* of or relating to an archbishop. □□ **archiepiscopate** /-pət, -ˌpeɪt/ *n.* [eccl.L *archiepiscopus* f. Gk *arkhiepiskopos* archbishop]

archil var. of ORCHIL.

archimandrite /ˌɑːkɪˈmændraɪt/ *n.* **1** the superior of a large monastery or group of monasteries in the Orthodox Church. **2** an honorary title given to a monastic priest. [F *archimandrite* or eccl.L *archimandrita* f. eccl. Gk *arkhimandrites* (as ARCH-, *mandra* monastery)]

Archimedean /ˌɑːkɪˈmiːdɪən/ *adj.* of or associated with the Greek mathematician Archimedes (d. 212 BC). □**Archimedean screw** a device of ancient origin for raising water by means of a spiral tube.

Archimedes' principle /ˌɑːkɪˈmiːdiːz/ *n.* the law that a body totally or partially immersed in a fluid is subject to an upward force equal in magnitude to the weight of fluid it displaces.

archipelago /ˌɑːkɪˈpeləˌgəʊ/ *n.* (*pl.* **-os** or **-oes**) **1** a group of islands. **2** a sea with many islands. [It. *arcipelago* f. Gk *arkhi-* chief + *pelagos* sea (orig. = the Aegean Sea)]

architect /ˈɑːkɪˌtekt/ *n.* **1** a designer who prepares plans for buildings, ships, etc., and supervises their construction. **2** (foll. by *of*) a person who brings about a specified thing (*the architect of his own fortune*). [F *architecte* f. It. *architetto*, or L *architectus* f. Gk *arkhitektōn* (as ARCH-, *tektōn* builder)]

architectonic /ˌɑːkɪtekˈtɒnɪk/ *adj.* & *n.* —*adj.* **1** of or relating to architecture or architects. **2** of or relating to the systematization of knowledge. —*n.* (in *pl.*; usu. treated as *sing.*) **1** the scientific study of architecture. **2** the study of the systematization of knowledge. [L *architectonicus* f. Gk *arkhitektonikos* (as ARCHITECT)]

architecture /ˈɑːkɪˌtektʃə(r)/ *n.* **1** the art or science of designing and constructing buildings. **2** the style of a building as regards design and construction. **3** buildings or other structures collectively. □□ **architectural** /-ˈtektʃər(ə)l/ *adj.* **architecturally** /-ˈtektʃərəlɪ/ *adv.* [F *architecture* or L *architectura* f. *architectus* ARCHITECT)]

architrave /ˈɑːkɪˌtreɪv/ *n.* **1** (in classical architecture) a main beam resting across the tops of columns. **2** the moulded frame around a doorway or window. **3** a moulding round the exterior of an arch. [F f. It. (as ARCH-, *trave* f. L *trabs trabis* beam)]

archive /ˈɑːkaɪv/ *n.* & *v.* —*n.* (usu. in *pl.*) **1** a collection of esp. public or corporate documents or records. **2** the place where these are kept. —*v.tr.* **1** place or store in an archive. **2** *Computing* transfer

(data) to a less frequently used file, e.g. from disc to tape. □□ **archival** /ɑːˈkaɪv(ə)l/ *adj.* [F *archives* (pl.) f. L *archi(v)a* f. Gk *arkheia* public records f. *arkhē* government]

archivist /ˈɑːkɪvɪst/ *n.* a person who maintains and is in charge of archives.

archivolt /ˈɑːkɪˌvəʊlt/ *n.* **1** a band of mouldings round the lower curve of an arch. **2** the lower curve itself from impost to impost of the columns. [F *archivolte* or It. *archivolto* (as ARC, VAULT)]

archlute /ˈɑːtʃluːt, -ˌljuːt/ *n.* a bass lute with an extended neck and unstopped bass strings. [F *archiluth* (as ARCH-, LUTE[1])]

archon /ˈɑːkən, ˈɑːkɒn/ *n.* each of the nine chief magistrates in ancient Athens. □□ **archonship** *n.* [Gk *arkhōn* ruler, = pres. part. of *arkhō* rule]

archway /ˈɑːtʃweɪ/ *n.* **1** a vaulted passage. **2** an arched entrance.

Arctic /ˈɑːktɪk/ *adj.* & *n.* —*adj.* **1** of the north polar regions. **2** (**arctic**) *colloq.* (esp. of weather) very cold. —*n.* **1** the Arctic regions. **2** (**arctic**) *US* a thick waterproof overshoe. □**Arctic Circle** the parallel of latitude 66° 33′ N, forming an imaginary line round this region. [ME f. OF *artique* f. L *ar(c)ticus* f. Gk *arktikos* f. *arktos* bear, Ursa Major]

arcuate /ˈɑːkjʊət/ *adj.* shaped like a bow; curved. [L *arcuatus* past part. of *arcuare* curve f. *arcus* bow, curve]

arcus senilis /ˌɑːkʊs seˈniːlɪs/ *n.* a narrow opaque band commonly encircling the cornea in old age. [L, lit. 'senile bow']

-ard /əd/ *suffix* **1** forming nouns in depreciatory senses (*drunkard*; *sluggard*). **2** forming nouns in other senses (*bollard*; *Spaniard*; *wizard*). [ME & OF f. G *-hard* hardy (in proper names)]

ardent /ˈɑːd(ə)nt/ *adj.* **1** eager, zealous; (of persons or feelings) fervent, passionate. **2** burning. □□ **ardency** *n.* **ardently** *adv.* [ME f. OF *ardant* f. L *ardens -entis* f. *ardēre* burn]

ardour /ˈɑːdə(r)/ *n.* (*US* **ardor**) zeal, burning enthusiasm, passion. [ME f. OF f. L *ardor -oris* f. *ardēre* burn]

arduous /ˈɑːdjuːəs/ *adj.* **1** hard to achieve or overcome; laborious, strenuous. **2** steep, difficult (*an arduous path*). □□ **arduously** *adv.* **arduousness** *n.* [L *arduus* steep, difficult]

are[1] *2nd sing. present* & *1st, 2nd, 3rd pl. present* of BE.

are[2] /ɑː(r)/ *n.* a metric unit of measure, equal to 100 square metres. [F f. L *area*]

area /ˈeərɪə/ *n.* **1** the extent or measure of a surface (*over a large area*; *3 acres in area*; *the area of a triangle*). **2** a region or tract (*the southern area*). **3** a space allocated for a specific purpose (*dining area*; *camping area*). **4** the scope or range of an activity or study. **5** *US* a space below ground level in front of the basement of a building. **6** (prec. by *the*) *Football* = *penalty area*. □□ **areal** *adj.* [L, = vacant piece of level ground]

areaway /ˈeərɪəˌweɪ/ *n.* *US* = AREA 5.

areca /ˈærɪkə, əˈriːkə/ *n.* any tropical palm of the genus *Areca*, native to Asia. □**areca nut** the astringent seed of a species of areca, *A. catechu*: also called *betel-nut*. [Port. f. Malayalam *áḍekka*]

areg pl. of ERG[2].

arena /əˈriːnə/ *n.* **1** the central part of an amphitheatre etc., where contests take place. **2** a scene of conflict; a sphere of action or discussion. □**arena stage** a stage situated with the audience all round it. [L (*h*)*arena* sand, sand-strewn place of combat]

arenaceous /ˌærɪˈneɪʃəs/ *adj.* **1** (of rocks) containing sand; having a sandy texture. **2** sandlike. **3** (of plants) growing in sand. [L *arenaceus* (as ARENA, -ACEOUS)]

aren't /ɑːnt/ *contr.* **1** are not. **2** (in *interrog.*) am not (*aren't I coming too?*).

areola /æˈrɪələ/ *n.* (*pl.* **areolae** /-liː/) **1** *Anat.* a circular pigmented area, esp. that surrounding a nipple. **2** any of the spaces between lines on a surface, e.g. of a

---

b *but*   d *dog*   f *few*   g *get*   h *he*   j *yes*   k *cat*   l *leg*   m *man*   n *no*   p *pen*   r *red*   s *sit*   t *top*   v *voice*

leaf or an insect's wing. □□ **areolar** *adj.* [L, dimin. of *area* AREA]

arête /æ'ret/ *n.* a sharp mountain ridge. [F f. L *arista* ear of corn, fishbone, spine]

argali /'ɑːgəli/ *n.* (*pl.* same) a large Asiatic wild sheep, *Ovis ammon*, with massive horns. [Mongol]

argent /'ɑːdʒ(ə)nt/ *n.* & *adj.* Heraldry silver; silvery white. [F f. L *argentum*]

argentiferous /ˌɑːdʒən'tɪfərəs/ *adj.* containing natural deposits of silver. [L *argentum* + -FEROUS]

Argentine /'ɑːdʒən,taɪn, -ˌtiːn/ *adj.* & *n.* (also **Argentinian** /-'tɪnɪən/) —*adj.* of or relating to Argentina in S. America. —*n.* **1** a native or national of Argentina. **2** a person of Argentine descent. □ **the Argentine** Argentina. [Sp. *Argentina* (as ARGENTINE)]

argentine /'ɑːdʒən,taɪn/ *adj.* of silver; silvery. [F *argentin* f. *argent* silver]

argil /'ɑːdʒɪl/ *n.* clay, esp. that used in pottery. □□ **argillaceous** *adj.* [F *argille* f. L *argilla* f. Gk *argillos* f. *argos* white]

arginine /'ɑːdʒɪ,niːn, -ˌnaɪn/ *n.* an amino acid present in many animal proteins and an essential nutrient in the vertebrate diet. [G *Arginin*, of uncert. orig.]

Argive /'ɑːgaɪv/ *adj.* & *n.* —*adj.* **1** of Argos in ancient Greece. **2** *literary* (esp. in Homeric contexts) Greek. —*n.* **1** a citizen of Argos. **2** *literary* (usu. in *pl.*) a Greek. [L *Argivus* f. Gk *Argeios*]

argol /'ɑːgɒl/ *n.* crude potassium hydrogen tartrate. [ME f. AF *argoile*, of unkn. orig.]

argon /'ɑːgɒn/ *n. Chem.* an inert gaseous element, of the noble gas group and forming almost 1% of the earth's atmosphere. ¶ Symb.: **Ar**. [Gk, neut. of *argos* idle f. *a*- not + *ergon* work]

argosy /'ɑːgəsi/ *n.* (*pl.* -ies) *poet.* a large merchant ship, orig. esp. from Ragusa (now Dubrovnik) or Venice. [prob. It. *Ragusea* (*nave*) Ragusan (vessel)]

argot /'ɑːgəʊ/ *n.* the jargon of a group or class, formerly esp. of criminals. [F: orig. unkn.]

arguable /'ɑːgjʊəb(ə)l/ *adj.* **1** that may be argued or reasonably proposed. **2** reasonable; supported by argument. □□ **arguably** *adv.*

argue /'ɑːgjuː/ *v.* (**argues**, **argued**, **arguing**) **1** *intr.* (often foll. by *with*, *about*, etc.) exchange views or opinions, especially heatedly or contentiously (with a person). **2** *tr.* & *intr.* (often foll. by *that* + clause) indicate; maintain by reasoning. **3** *intr.* (foll. by *for*, *against*) reason (*argued against joining*). **4** *tr.* treat by reasoning (*argue the point*). **5** *tr.* (foll. by *into*, *out of*) persuade (*argued me into going*). □ **argue the toss** *colloq.* dispute a decision or choice already made. □□ **arguer** *n.* [ME f. OF *arguer* f. L *argutari* prattle, frequent. of *arguere* make clear, prove, accuse]

argufy /'ɑːgjʊ,faɪ/ *v.intr.* (-ies, -ied) *colloq.* argue excessively or tediously. [fanciful f. ARGUE: cf. SPEECHIFY]

argument /'ɑːgjʊmənt/ *n.* **1** an exchange of views, esp. a contentious or prolonged one. **2** (often foll. by *for*, *against*) a reason advanced; a reasoning process (*an argument for abolition*). **3** a summary of the subject-matter or line of reasoning of a book. **4** *Math.* an independent variable determining the value of a function. [ME f. OF f. L *argumentum* f. *arguere* (as ARGUE, -MENT)]

argumentation /ˌɑːgjʊmen'teɪʃ(ə)n/ *n.* **1** methodical reasoning. **2** debate or argument. [F f. L *argumentatio* f. *argumentari* (as ARGUMENT, -ATION)]

argumentative /ˌɑːgjʊ'mentətɪv/ *adj.* **1** fond of arguing; quarrelsome. **2** using methodical reasoning. □□ **argumentatively** *adv.* **argumentativeness** *n.* [F *argumentatif* -*ive* or LL *argumentativus* (as ARGUMENT, -ATIVE)]

Argus /'ɑːgəs/ *n.* **1** a watchful guardian. **2** an Asiatic pheasant having markings on its tail resembling eyes. **3** a butterfly having markings resembling eyes. □ **Argus-eyed** vigilant. [ME f. L f. Gk *Argos* mythical person with a hundred eyes]

argute /ɑː'gjuːt/ *adj. literary* **1** sharp or shrewd. **2** (of sounds) shrill. □□ **argutely** *adv.* [ME f. L *argutus* past part. of *arguere*: see ARGUE]

argy-bargy /ˌɑːdʒɪ'bɑːdʒɪ/ *n.* & *v. joc.* —*n.* (*pl.* -ies) a dispute or wrangle. —*v.intr.* (-ies, -ied) quarrel, esp. loudly. [orig. Sc.]

aria /'ɑːrɪə/ *n. Mus.* a long accompanied song for solo voice in an opera, oratorio, etc. [It.]

Arian /'eərɪən/ *n.* & *adj.* —*n.* an adherent of the doctrine of Arius of Alexandria (4th c.), who denied the divinity of Christ. —*adj.* of or concerning this doctrine. □□ **Arianism** *n.*

-arian /'eərɪən/ *suffix* forming adjectives and nouns meaning '(one) concerned with or believing in' (*agrarian*; *antiquarian*; *humanitarian*; *vegetarian*). [L -*arius* (see -ARY[1])]

arid /'ærɪd/ *adj.* **1 a** (of ground, climate, etc.) dry, parched. **b** too dry to support vegetation; barren. **2** uninteresting (*arid verse*). □□ **aridity** /ə'rɪdɪtɪ/ *n.* **aridly** *adv.* **aridness** *n.* [F *aride* or L *aridus* f. *arēre* be dry]

Aries /'eəriːz/ *n.* (*pl.* same) **1** a constellation, traditionally regarded as contained in the figure of a ram. **2 a** the first sign of the zodiac (the Ram). **b** a person born when the sun is in this sign. □□ **Arian** /-rɪən/ *adj.* & *n.* [ME f. L, = ram]

aright /ə'raɪt/ *adv.* rightly. [OE (as A[2], RIGHT)]

aril /'ærɪl/ *n. Bot.* an extra seed-covering, often coloured and hairy or fleshy, e.g. the red fleshy cup around a yew seed. □□ **arillate** *adj.* [mod.L *arillus*: cf. med.L *arilli* dried grape-stones]

-arious /'eərɪəs/ *suffix* forming adjectives (*gregarious*; *vicarious*). [L -*arius* (see -ARY[1]) + -OUS]

arise /ə'raɪz/ *v.intr.* (*past* **arose** /ə'rəʊz/; *past part.* **arisen** /ə'rɪz(ə)n/) **1** begin to exist; originate. **2** (usu. foll. by *from*, *out of*) result (*accidents can arise from carelessness*). **3** come to one's notice; emerge (*the question of payment arose*). **4** rise, esp. from the dead. [OE *ārīsan* (as A-[2], RISE)]

arisings /ə'raɪzɪŋz/ *n.pl.* materials forming the secondary or waste products of industrial operations.

aristocracy /ˌærɪ'stɒkrəsi/ *n.* (*pl.* -ies) **1 a** the highest class in society; the nobility. **b** the nobility as a ruling class. **2 a** government by the nobility or a privileged group. **b** a State governed in this way. **3** (often foll. by *of*) the best representatives or upper echelons (*aristocracy of intellect*; *aristocracy of labour*). [F *aristocratie* f. Gk *aristokratia* f. *aristos* best + *kratia* (as -CRACY)]

aristocrat /'ærɪstə,kræt/ *n.* a member of the nobility. [F *aristocrate* (as ARISTOCRATIC)]

aristocratic /ˌærɪstə'krætɪk/ *adj.* **1** of or relating to the aristocracy. **2 a** distinguished in manners or bearing. **b** grand; stylish. □□ **aristocratically** *adv.* [F *aristocratique* f. Gk *aristokratikos* (as ARISTO-CRACY)]

Aristotelian /ˌærɪstə'tiːlɪən/ *n.* & *adj.* —*n.* a disciple or student of the Greek philosopher Aristotle (d. 322 BC). —*adj.* of or concerning Aristotle or his ideas.

Arita /ə'riːtə/ *n.* (usu. *attrib.*) a type of Japanese porcelain characterized by asymmetric decoration. [*Arita* in Japan]

arithmetic *n.* & *adj.* —*n.* /ə'rɪθmətɪk/ **1 a** the science of numbers. **b** one's knowledge of this (*have improved my arithmetic*). **2** the use of numbers; computation (*a problem involving arithmetic*). —*adj.* /ˌærɪθ'metɪk/ (also **arithmetical** /-'metɪk(ə)l/) of or concerning arithmetic. □ **arithmetic mean** the central number in an arithmetic progression. **arithmetic progression 1** an increase or decrease by a constant quantity (e.g. 1, 2, 3, 4, etc., 9, 7, 5, 3, etc.). **2** a sequence of numbers showing this. □□ **arithmetician** /əˌrɪθmə'tɪʃ(ə)n/ *n.* [ME f. OF *arismetique* f. L *arithmetica* f. Gk *arithmētikē* (*tekhnē*) art of counting f. *arithmos* number]

-arium /'eərɪəm/ *suffix* forming nouns usu. denoting a place (*aquarium*; *planetarium*). [L, neut. of adjs. in -*arius*: see -ARY[1]]

Ariz. *abbr.* Arizona.

Ark. *abbr.* Arkansas.

ark /ɑːk/ *n.* **1** = NOAH'S ARK 1. **2** *archaic* a chest or box. □**Ark of the Covenant** (or **Testimony**) a chest or cupboard containing the scrolls or tables of Jewish Law. **out of the ark** *colloq.* very antiquated. [OE ærc f. L *arca* chest]

arm[1] /ɑːm/ *n.* **1** each of the two upper limbs of the human body from the shoulder to the hand. **2 a** the forelimb of an animal. **b** the flexible limb of an invertebrate animal (e.g. an octopus). **3 a** the sleeve of a garment. **b** the side part of a chair etc., used to support a sitter's arm. **c** a thing resembling an arm in branching from a main stem (*an arm of the sea*). **d** a large branch of a tree. **4** a control; a means of reaching (*arm of the law*). □**an arm and a leg** a large sum of money. **arm in arm** (of two or more persons) with arms linked. **arm-wrestling** a trial of strength in which each party tries to force the other's arm down on to a table on which their elbows rest. **as long as your** (or **my**) **arm** *colloq.* very long. **at arm's length 1** as far as an arm can reach. **2** far enough to avoid undue familiarity. **in arms** (of a baby)ˈ too young to walk. **in a person's arms** embraced. **on one's arm** supported by one's arm. **under one's arm** between the arm and the body. **within arm's reach** reachable without moving one's position. **with open arms** cordially. □□**armful** *n.* (*pl.* -**fuls**). **armless** *adj.* [OE f. Gmc]

arm[2] /ɑːm/ *n.* & *v.* —*n.* **1** (usu. in *pl.*) **a** a weapon. **b** = FIREARM. **2** (in *pl.*) the military profession. **3** a branch of the military (e.g. infantry, cavalry, artillery, etc.). **4** (in *pl.*) heraldic devices (*coat of arms*). —*v.tr.* & *refl.* **1** (also *absol.*) supply with weapons. **2** supply with tools or other requisites or advantages (*armed with the truth*). **3** make (a bomb etc.) able to explode. □**arms control** international disarmament or arms limitation, esp. by mutual agreement. **arms race** a contest for superiority in nuclear weapons, esp. between East and West. **in arms** armed. **lay down one's arms** cease fighting. **take up arms** begin fighting. **under arms** ready for war or battle. **up in arms** (usu. foll. by *against*, *about*) actively rebelling. □□**armless** *adj.* [ME f. OF *armes* (pl.), *armer*, f. L *arma* arms, fittings]

armada /ɑːˈmɑːdə/ *n.* a fleet of warships, esp. that sent by Spain against England in 1588. [Sp. f. Rmc *armata* army]

armadillo /ˌɑːməˈdɪləʊ/ *n.* (*pl.* -**os**) any nocturnal insect-eating mammal of the family Dasypodidae, native to Central and S. America, with large claws for digging and a body covered in bony plates, often rolling itself into a ball when threatened. [Sp. dimin. of *armado* armed man f. L *armatus* past part. of *armare* ARM[2]]

Armageddon /ˌɑːməˈged(ə)n/ *n.* **1 a** (in the New Testament) the last battle between good and evil before the Day of Judgement. **b** the place where this will be fought. **2** a bloody battle or struggle on a huge scale. [Gk f. Heb. *har megiddōn* hill of Megiddo: see Rev. 16:16]

armament /ˈɑːməmənt/ *n.* **1** (often in *pl.*) military weapons and equipment, esp. guns on a warship. **2** the process of equipping for war. **3** a force equipped for war. [L *armamentum* (as ARM[2], -MENT)]

armamentarium /ˌɑːməmenˈteərɪəm/ *n.* (*pl.* **armamentaria** /-rɪə/) **1** a set of medical equipment or drugs. **2** the resources available to a person engaged in a task. [L, = arsenal]

armature /ˈɑːməˌtjʊə(r)/ *n.* **1 a** the rotating coil or coils of a dynamo or electric motor. **b** any moving part of an electrical machine in which a voltage is induced by a magnetic field. **2** a piece of soft iron placed in contact with the poles of a horseshoe magnet to preserve its power. Also called KEEPER. **3** *Biol.* the protective covering of an animal or plant. **4** a metal framework on which a sculpture is moulded with clay or similar material. **5** *archaic* arms; armour. [F f. L *armatura* armour (as ARM[2], -URE)]

armband /ˈɑːmbænd/ *n.* a band worn around the upper arm to hold up a shirtsleeve or as a form of identification etc.

armchair /ɑːmˈtʃeə(r), ˈɑːm-/ *n.* **1** a comfortable, usu. upholstered, chair with side supports for the arms. **2** (*attrib.*) theoretical rather than active or practical (*an armchair critic*).

Armenian /ɑːˈmiːnɪən/ *n.* & *adj.* —*n.* **1 a** a native of Armenia, an ancient kingdom corresponding to an area in modern Turkey, Iran, and the USSR. **b** a person of Armenian descent. **2** the language of Armenia. —*adj.* of or relating to Armenia, its language, or the Christian Church established there *c.*300.

armhole /ˈɑːmhəʊl/ *n.* each of two holes in a garment through which the arms are put, usu. into a sleeve.

armiger /ˈɑːmɪdʒə(r)/ *n.* a person entitled to heraldic arms. □□**armigerous** /-ˈmɪdʒərəs/ *adj.* [L, = bearing arms, f. *arma* arms + *gerere* bear]

armillary /ɑːˈmɪlərɪ/ *adj.* relating to bracelets. □**armillary sphere** *hist.* a representation of the celestial globe constructed from metal rings and showing the equator, the tropics, etc. [mod.L *armillaris* f. L *armilla* bracelet]

Arminian /ɑːˈmɪnɪən/ *adj.* & *n.* —*adj.* relating to the doctrine of Arminius, a Dutch Protestant theologian (d. 1609), who opposed the views of Calvin, esp. on predestination. —*n.* an adherent of this doctrine. □□**Arminianism** *n.*

armistice /ˈɑːmɪstɪs/ *n.* a stopping of hostilities by common agreement of the opposing sides; a truce. □**Armistice Day** the anniversary of the armistice of 11 Nov. 1918 (cf. *Remembrance Sunday*). [F *armistice* or mod.L *armistitium*, f. *arma* arms (ARM[2]) + -*stitium* stoppage]

armlet /ˈɑːmlɪt/ *n.* **1** a band worn round the arm. **2** a small inlet of the sea, or branch of a river.

armor *US* var. of ARMOUR.

armorer *US* var. of ARMOURER.

armory[1] /ˈɑːmərɪ/ *n.* (*pl.* -**ies**) heraldry. □□**armorial** /ɑːˈmɔːrɪəl/ *adj.* [OF *armoierie*: see ARMOURY]

armory[2] *US* var. of ARMOURY.

armour /ˈɑːmə(r)/ *n.* & *v.* (*US* **armor**) —*n.* **1** a defensive covering, usu. of metal, formerly worn to protect the body in fighting. **2 a** (in full **armour-plate**) a protective metal covering for an armed vehicle, ship, etc. **b** armoured fighting vehicles collectively. **3** a protective covering or shell on certain animals and plants. **4** heraldic devices. —*v.tr.* (usu. as **armoured** *adj.*) provide with a protective covering, and often with guns (*armoured car*; *armoured train*). [ME f. OF *armure* f. L *armatura*: see ARMATURE]

armourer /ˈɑːmərə(r)/ *n.* (*US* **armorer**) **1** a maker or repairer of arms or armour. **2** an official in charge of a ship's or a regiment's arms. [AF *armurer*, OF -*urier* (as ARMOUR, -ER[5])]

armoury /ˈɑːmərɪ/ *n.* (*US* **armory**) (*pl.* -**ies**) **1** a place where arms are kept; an arsenal. **2** an array of weapons, defensive resources, usable material, etc. **3** *US* a place where arms are manufactured. [ME f. OF *armoirie*, *armoierie* f. *armoier* to blazon f. *arme* ARM[2]: assim. to ARMOUR]

armpit /ˈɑːmpɪt/ *n.* **1** the hollow under the arm at the shoulder. **2** *US colloq.* a place or part considered disgusting or contemptible (*the armpit of the world*).

armrest /ˈɑːmrest/ *n.* = ARM[1] 3b.

army /ˈɑːmɪ/ *n.* (*pl.* -**ies**) **1** an organized force armed for fighting on land. **2** (prec. by *the*) the military profession. **3** (often foll. by *of*) a very large number (*an army of locusts*; *an army of helpers*). **4** an organized body regarded as fighting for a particular cause (*Salvation Army*). □**army ant** any ant of the subfamily Dorylinae, foraging in large groups. **Army List** *Brit.* an official list of commissioned officers. **army worm** any of various moth or fly larvae occurring in destructive swarms. [ME f. OF *armee* f. Rmc *armata* fem. past part. of *armare* arm]

arnica /'ɑːnɪkə/ *n.* **1** any composite plant of the genus *Arnica*, having erect stems bearing yellow daisy-like flower heads, e.g. mountain tobacco. **2** a medicine prepared from this, used for bruises etc. [mod.L: orig. unkn.]

aroid /'eərɔɪd/ *adj.* of or relating to the family Araceae, including arums. [ARUM + -OID]

aroma /ə'rəʊmə/ *n.* **1** a fragrance; a distinctive and pleasing smell, often of food. **2** a subtle pervasive quality. [L f. Gk *arōma -atos* spice]

aromatherapy /ə,rəʊmə'θerəpɪ/ *n.* the use of plant extracts and essential oils in massage. □□ **aromatherapeutic** /-'pjuːtɪk/ *adj.* **aromatherapist** *n.*

aromatic /,ærə'mætɪk/ *adj. & n.* —*adj.* **1** fragrant, spicy; (of a smell) pleasantly pungent. **2** *Chem.* of organic compounds having an unsaturated ring, esp. containing a benzene ring. —*n.* an aromatic substance. □□ **aromatically** *adv.* **aromaticity** /,ærəmə'tɪsɪtɪ/ *n.* [ME f. OF *aromatique* f. LL *aromaticus* f. Gk *arōmatikos* (as AROMA, -IC)]

aromatize /ə'rəʊmə,taɪz/ *v.tr. Chem.* convert (a compound) into an aromatic structure. □□ **aromatization** /-'zeɪʃ(ə)n/ *n.*

arose *past* of ARISE.

around /ə'raʊnd/ *adv. & prep.* —*adv.* **1** on every side; all round; round about. **2** in various places; here and there; at random (*fool around*; *shop around*). **3** *colloq.* **a** in existence; available (*has been around for weeks*). **b** near at hand (*it's good to have you around*). —*prep.* **1** on or along the circuit of. **2** on every side of; enveloping. **3** here and there in or near (*chairs around the room*). **4** *US* (and increasingly *Brit.*) a round (*the church around the corner*). **b** approximately at; at a time near to (*come around four o'clock*; *happened around June*). □**have been around** *colloq.* be widely experienced. [A² + ROUND]

arouse /ə'raʊz/ *v.tr.* **1** induce; call into existence (esp. a feeling, emotion, etc.). **2** awake from sleep. **3** stir into activity. **4** stimulate sexually. □□ **arousable** *adj.* **arousal** *n.* **arouser** *n.* [A-² + ROUSE]

arpeggio /ɑː'pedʒɪəʊ/ *n.* (*pl.* **-os**) *Mus.* the notes of a chord played in succession, either ascending or descending. [It. f. *arpeggiare* play the harp f. *arpa* harp]

arquebus var. of HARQUEBUS.

arr. *abbr.* **1** *Mus.* arranged by. **2** arrives.

arrack /'ærək/ *n.* (also **arak** /ə'ræk/) an alcoholic spirit, esp. distilled from coco sap or rice. [Arab. *'araḳ* sweat, alcoholic spirit from grapes or dates]

arraign /ə'reɪn/ *v.tr.* **1** indict before a tribunal; accuse. **2** find fault with; call into question (an action or statement). □□ **arraignment** *n.* [ME f. AF *arainer* f. OF *araisnier* (ult. as AD-, L *ratio -onis* reason, discourse)]

arrange /ə'reɪndʒ/ *v.* **1** *tr.* put into the required order; classify. **2** *tr.* plan or provide for; cause to occur (*arranged a meeting*). **3** *tr.* settle beforehand the order or manner of. **4** *intr.* take measures; form plans; give instructions (*arrange to be there at eight*; *arranged for a taxi to come*; *will you arrange about the cake?*). **5** *intr.* come to an agreement (*arranged with her to meet later*). **6** *tr.* **a** *Mus.* adapt (a composition) for performance with instruments or voices other than those originally specified. **b** adapt (a play etc.) for broadcasting. **7** *tr.* settle (a dispute etc.). □□ **arrangeable** *adj.* **arranger** *n.* (esp. in sense 6). [ME f. OF *arangier* f. *à* to + *rangier* RANGE]

arrangement /ə'reɪndʒmənt/ *n.* **1** the act or process of arranging or being arranged. **2** the condition of being arranged; the manner in which a thing is arranged. **3** something arranged. **4** (in *pl.*) plans, measures (*make your own arrangements*). **5** *Mus.* a composition arranged for performance by different instruments or voices (see ARRANGE 6a). **6** settlement of a dispute etc. [F (as ARRANGE, -MENT)]

arrant /'ærənt/ *adj.* downright, utter, notorious (*arrant liar*; *arrant nonsense*). □□ **arrantly** *adv.* [ME,

var. of ERRANT, orig. in phrases like *arrant* (= outlawed, roving) *thief*]

arras /'ærəs/ *n. hist.* a rich tapestry, often hung on the walls of a room, or to conceal an alcove. [*Arras*, a town in NE France famous for the fabric]

array /ə'reɪ/ *n. & v.* —*n.* **1** an imposing or well-ordered series or display. **2** an ordered arrangement, esp. of troops (*battle array*). **3** *poet.* an outfit or dress (*in fine array*). **4 a** *Math.* an arrangement of quantities or symbols in rows and columns; a matrix. **b** *Computing* an ordered set of related elements. **5** *Law* a list of jurors empanelled. —*v.tr.* **1** deck, adorn. **2** set in order; marshal (forces). **3** *Law* empanel (a jury). [ME f. AF *araier*, OF *areer* ult. f. a Gmc root, = prepare]

arrears /ə'rɪəz/ *n.pl.* an amount still outstanding or uncompleted, esp. work undone or a debt unpaid. □**in arrears** (or **arrear**) behindhand, esp. in payment. □□ **arrearage** *n.* [ME (orig. as adv.) f. OF *arere* f. med.L *adretro* (as AD-, *retro* backwards): first used in phr. *in arrear*]

arrest /ə'rest/ *v. & n.* —*v.tr.* **1 a** seize (a person) and take into custody, esp. by legal authority. **b** seize (a ship) by legal authority. **2** stop or check (esp. a process or moving thing). **3 a** attract (a person's attention). **b** attract the attention of (a person). —*n.* **1** the act of arresting or being arrested, esp. the legal seizure of a person. **2** a stoppage or check (*cardiac arrest*). □**arrest of judgement** *Law* the staying of proceedings, notwithstanding a verdict, on the grounds of a material irregularity in the course of the trial. □□ **arrestingly** *adv.* [ME f. OF *arester* ult. f. L *restare* remain, stop]

arrestable /ə'restəb(ə)l/ *adj.* **1** susceptible of arrest. **2** *Law* (esp. of an offence) such that the offender may be arrested without a warrant.

arrester /ə'restə(r)/ *n.* (also **arrestor**) a device, esp. on an aircraft carrier, for slowing an aircraft by means of a hook and cable after landing.

arrestment /ə'restmənt/ *n.* esp. *Sc.* attachment of property for the satisfaction of a debt.

arrière-pensée /,ærjerpɑ̃'seɪ/ *n.* **1** an undisclosed motive. **2** a mental reservation. [F, = behind thought]

arris /'ærɪs/ *n. Archit.* a sharp edge formed by the meeting of two flat or curved surfaces. [corrupt. f. F *areste*, mod. ARÊTE]

arrival /ə'raɪv(ə)l/ *n.* **1 a** the act of arriving. **b** an appearance on the scene. **2** a person or thing that has arrived. □**new arrival** *colloq.* a newborn child. [ME f. AF *arrivaille* (as ARRIVE, -AL)]

arrive /ə'raɪv/ *v.intr.* (often foll. by *at, in*) **1** reach a destination; come to the end of a journey or a specified part of a journey (*arrived in Tibet*; *arrived at the station*; *arrived late*). **2** (foll. by *at*) reach (a conclusion, decision, etc.). **3** *colloq.* establish one's reputation or position. **4** *colloq.* (of a child) be born. **5** (of a thing) be brought (*the flowers have arrived*). **6** (of a time) come (*her birthday arrived at last*). [ME f. OF *ariver*, ult. as AD- + L *ripa* shore]

arriviste /,æri'viːst/ *n.* an ambitious or ruthlessly self-seeking person. [F *arriver* f. OF (as ARRIVE, -IST)]

arrogant /'ærəgənt/ *adj.* (of a person, attitude, etc.) aggressively assertive or presumptuous; over-bearing. □□ **arrogance** *n.* **arrogantly** *adv.* [ME f. OF (as ARROGATE, -ANT)]

arrogate /'ærə,geɪt/ *v.tr.* **1** (often foll. by *to* oneself) claim (power, responsibility, etc.) without justification. **2** (often foll. by *to*) attribute unjustly (to a person). □□ **arrogation** /-'geɪʃ(ə)n/ *n.* [L *arrogare arrogat-* (as AD-, *rogare* ask)]

arrondissement /æ,rɔ̃diːs'mɑ̃/ *n.* **1** a subdivision of a French department, for local government administration purposes. **2** an administrative district of a large city, esp. Paris. [F]

arrow /'ærəʊ/ *n.* **1** a sharp pointed wooden or metal stick shot from a bow as a weapon. **2** a drawn or printed etc. representation of an arrow indicating a direction; a pointer. □**arrow-grass** a marsh plant of the genus *Triglochin*. **arrow worm** = CHAETOGNATH. **broad arrow** *Brit.* a mark formerly used on British prison clothing and other Government stores. □□ **arrowy** *adj*. [OE *ar(e)we* f. ON *ör* f. Gmc]

arrowhead /ˈærəʊˌhed/ *n*. **1** the pointed end of an arrow. **2** a water-plant, *Sagittaria sagittaria*, with arrow-shaped leaves. **3** a decorative device resembling an arrowhead.

arrowroot /ˈærəʊˌruːt/ *n*. a plant of the family Marantaceae from which a starch is prepared and used for nutritional and medicinal purposes.

arroyo /əˈrɔɪəʊ/ *n*. (*pl.* -os) *US* **1** a brook or stream. **2** a gully. [Sp.]

arse /ɑːs/ *n*. & *v*. (*US* **ass** /æs/) *coarse sl.* —*n*. the buttocks. —*v.intr*. (usu. foll. by *about, around*) play the fool. □**arse-hole 1** the anus. **2** *offens*. a term of contempt for a person. **arse-licking** obsequiousness for the purpose of gaining favour; toadying. ¶ Usually considered a taboo word. [OE *ærs*]

arsenal /ˈɑːsən(ə)l/ *n*. **1** a store of weapons. **2** a government establishment for the storage and manufacture of weapons and ammunition. **3** resources of anything compared with weapons (e.g. abuse), regarded collectively. [obs. F *arsenal* or It. *arzanale* f. Arab. *dārṣinā'a* f. *dār* house + *sinā'a* art, industry f. *ṣana'a* fabricate]

arsenic *n*. & *adj*. —*n*. /ˈɑːsənɪk/ **1** a non-scientific name for arsenic trioxide, a highly poisonous white powdery substance used in weed-killers, rat poison, etc. **2** *Chem*. a brittle semi-metallic element, used in semiconductors and alloys. ¶ Symb.: **As**. —*adj*. /ɑːˈsenɪk/ **1** of or concerning arsenic. **2** *Chem*. containing arsenic with a valency of five. □**red arsenic** = REALGAR. **white arsenic** = sense 1. □□ **arsenious** /ɑːˈsiːnɪəs/ *adj*. [ME f. OF f. L *arsenicum* f. Gk *arsenikon* yellow orpiment, identified with *arsenikos* male, but in fact f. Arab. *al-zarnīk* f. *al* the + *zarnīk* orpiment f. Pers. f. *zar* gold]

arsenical /ɑːˈsenɪk(ə)l/ *adj*. & *n*. —*adj*. of or containing arsenic. —*n*. a drug containing arsenic.

arsine /ˈɑːsiːn/ *n*. *Chem*. arsenic trihydride, a colourless poisonous gas smelling slightly of garlic. [ARSENIC after *amine*]

arsis /ˈɑːsɪs/ *n*. (*pl.* **arses** /-siːz/) a stressed syllable or part of a metrical foot in Greek or Latin verse (opp. THESIS). [ME f. LL f. Gk, = lifting f. *airō* raise]

arson /ˈɑːs(ə)n/ *n*. the act of maliciously setting fire to property. □□**arsonist** *n*. [legal AF, OF, f. med.L *arsio -onis* f. L *ardēre ars-* burn]

arsphenamine /ɑːsˈfenəmɪn, -ˌmiːn/ *n*. a drug formerly used in the treatment of syphilis and parasitic diseases. [ARSENIC + PHENYL + AMINE]

art[1] /ɑːt/ *n*. **1 a** human creative skill or its application. **b** work exhibiting this. **2 a** (in *pl*.; prec. by *the*) the various branches of creative activity concerned with the production of imaginative designs, sounds, or ideas, e.g. painting, music, writing, considered collectively. **b** any one of these branches. **3** creative activity, esp. painting and drawing, resulting in visual representation (*interested in music but not art*). **4** human skill or workmanship as opposed to the work of nature (*art and nature had combined to make her a great beauty*). **5** (often foll. by *of*) a skill, aptitude, or knack (*the art of writing clearly; keeping people happy is quite an art*). **6** (in *pl*.; usu. prec. by *the*) those branches of learning (esp. languages, literature, and history) associated with creative skill as opposed to scientific, technical, or vocational skills. □**art and mystery** any of the special skills or techniques in a specified area. **art deco** /ˈdekəʊ/ the predominant decorative art style of the period 1910-30, characterized by precise and boldly delineated geometric motifs, shapes, and strong colours. **art form 1** any medium of artistic expression. **2** an established form of composition (e.g. the novel,

sonata, sonnet, etc.). **art nouveau** /ˌɑː nuːˈvəʊ/ a European art style of the late 19th century characterized by flowing lines and natural organic forms. **art paper** smooth-coated high quality paper. **arts and crafts** decorative design and handicraft. [ME f. OF f. L *ars artis*]

art[2] /ɑːt/ *archaic* or *dial. 2nd sing. present* of BE.

art. /ɑːt/ *abbr.* article.

artefact /ˈɑːtɪˌfækt/ *n*. (also **artifact**) **1** a product of human art and workmanship. **2** *Archaeol.* a product of prehistoric or aboriginal workmanship as distinguished from a similar object naturally produced. **3** *Biol.* etc. a feature not naturally present, introduced during preparation or investigation (e.g. as in the preparation of a slide). □□**artefactual** *adj*. (in senses 1 and 2). [L *arte* (ablat. of *ars* art) + *factum* (neut. past part. of *facere* make)]

artel /ɑːˈtel/ *n*. an association of craftsmen, peasants, etc., in the USSR. [Russ.]

arterial /ɑːˈtɪərɪəl/ *adj*. **1** of or relating to an artery (*arterial blood*). **2** (esp. of a road) main, important, esp. linking large cities or towns. [F *artériel* f. *artère* artery]

arterialize /ɑːˈtɪərɪəˌlaɪz/ *v.tr*. (also **-ise**) **1** convert venous into arterial (blood) by reoxygenation esp. in the lungs. **2** provide with an arterial system. □□ **arterialization** /-ˈzeɪʃ(ə)n/ *n*.

arteriole /ɑːˈtɪərɪˌəʊl/ *n*. a small branch of an artery leading into capillaries. [F *artériole*, dimin. of *artère* ARTERY]

arteriosclerosis /ɑːˌtɪərɪəʊsklɪəˈrəʊsɪs/ *n*. the loss of elasticity and thickening of the walls of the arteries, esp. in old age; hardening of the arteries. □□ **arteriosclerotic** /-ˈrɒtɪk/ *adj*. [ARTERY + SCLEROSIS]

artery /ˈɑːtərɪ/ *n*. (*pl.* -ies) **1** any of the muscular-walled tubes forming part of the blood circulation system of the body, carrying oxygen-enriched blood from the heart (cf. VEIN). **2** a main road or railway line. □□**arteritis** /-ˈraɪtɪs/ *n*. [ME f. L *arteria* f. Gk *artēria* prob. f. *airō* raise]

artesian well /ɑːˈtiːzɪən, -ʒ(ə)n/ *n*. a well bored perpendicularly, esp. through rock, into water-bearing strata lying at an angle, so that natural pressure produces a constant supply of water with little or no pumping. [F *artésien* f. *Artois*, an old French province]

artful /ˈɑːtfʊl/ *adj*. (of a person or action) crafty, deceitful. □□**artfully** *adv*. **artfulness** *n*.

arthritis /ɑːˈθraɪtɪs/ *n*. inflammation of a joint or joints. □□**arthritic** /-ˈθrɪtɪk/ *adj*. & *n*. [L f. Gk f. *arthron* joint]

arthropod /ˈɑːθrəˌpɒd/ *n*. *Zool.* any invertebrate animal of the phylum Arthropoda, with a segmented body, jointed limbs, and an external skeleton, e.g. an insect, spider, or crustacean. [Gk *arthron* joint + *pous podos* foot]

Arthurian /ɑːˈθjʊərɪən/ *adj*. relating to or associated with King Arthur, the legendary British ruler, or his court.

artichoke /ˈɑːtɪˌtʃəʊk/ *n*. **1** a European plant, *Cynara scolymus*, allied to the thistle. **2** (in full **globe artichoke**) the flower-head of the artichoke, the bracts of which have edible bases (see also JERUSALEM ARTICHOKE). [It. *articiocco* f. Arab. *al-karṣūfa*]

article /ˈɑːtɪk(ə)l/ *n*. & *v*. —*n*. **1** (often in *pl*.) an item or commodity, usu. not further distinguished (*a collection of odd articles*). **2** a non-fictional essay, esp. one included with others in a newspaper, magazine, journal, etc. **3 a** a particular part (*an article of faith*). **b** a separate clause or portion of any document (*articles of apprenticeship*). **4** *Gram.* the definite or indefinite article. —*v.tr.* bind by articles of apprenticeship. □**definite article** *Gram.* the word (*the* in English) preceding a noun and implying a specific or known instance (as in *the book on the table; the art of government; the famous public school in Berkshire*). **indefinite article** *Gram.* the word (e.g. *a, an, some* in English) preceding a noun and implying lack of specificity (as in *bought me a book*; *government is an art*; *went to a public school*). **the Thirty-nine Articles** a set of beliefs affirmed by the ministers of the Church of England. [ME f. OF f. L *articulus* dimin. of *artus* joint]

articular /ɑːˈtɪkjʊlə(r)/ *adj.* of or relating to the joints. [ME f. L *articularis* (as ARTICLE, -AR[1])]

articulate *adj. & v.* —*adj.* /ɑːˈtɪkjʊlət/ **1** able to speak fluently and coherently. **2** (of sound or speech) having clearly distinguishable parts. **3** having joints. —*v.* /ɑːˈtɪkjʊˌleɪt/ **1** *tr.* **a** pronounce (words, syllables, etc.) clearly and distinctly. **b** express (an idea etc.) coherently. **2** *intr.* speak distinctly (*was quite unable to articulate*). **3** *tr.* (usu. in *passive*) connect by joints. **4** *tr.* mark with apparent joints. **5** *intr.* (often foll. by *with*) form a joint. □**articulated lorry** *Brit.* a lorry consisting of two or more sections connected by a flexible joint. □□**articulacy** *n.* **articulately** *adv.* **articulateness** *n.* **articulator** *n.* [L *articulatus* (as ARTICLE, -ATE[2])]

articulation /ɑːˌtɪkjʊˈleɪʃ(ə)n/ *n.* **1 a** the act of speaking. **b** articulate utterance; speech. **2 a** the act or a mode of jointing. **b** a joint. [F *articulation* or L *articulatio* f. *articulare* joint (as ARTICLE, -ATION)]

artifact var. of ARTEFACT.

artifice /ˈɑːtɪfɪs/ *n.* **1** a clever device; a contrivance. **2 a** cunning. **b** an instance of this. **3** skill, dexterity. [F f. L *artificium* f. *ars artis* art, -*ficium* making f. *facere* make]

artificer /ɑːˈtɪfɪsə(r)/ *n.* **1** an inventor. **2** a craftsman. **3** a skilled mechanic in the armed forces. [ME f. AF, prob. alt. of OF *artificien*]

artificial /ˌɑːtɪˈfɪʃ(ə)l/ *adj.* **1** produced by human art or effort rather than originating naturally (*an artificial lake*). **2** formed in imitation of something natural (*artificial flowers*). **3** affected, insincere (*an artificial smile*). □**artificial insemination** the injection of semen into the vagina or uterus other than by sexual intercourse. **artificial intelligence** the application of computers to areas normally regarded as requiring human intelligence. **artificial kidney** an apparatus that performs the functions of the human kidney (outside the body), when one or both organs are damaged. **artificial respiration** the restoration or initiation of breathing by manual or mechanical or mouth-to-mouth methods. **artificial silk** rayon. □□**artificiality** /-ʃɪˈælɪtɪ/ *n.* **artificially** *adv.* [ME f. OF *artificiel* or L *artificialis* (as ARTIFICE, -AL)]

artillery /ɑːˈtɪlərɪ/ *n.* (*pl.* -**ies**) **1** large-calibre guns used in warfare on land. **2** a branch of the armed forces that uses these. □□**artillerist** *n.* [ME f. OF *artillerie* f. *artiller* alt. of *atillier*, *atirier* equip, arm]

artilleryman /ɑːˈtɪlərɪˌmæn/ *n.* (*pl.* -**men**) a member of the artillery.

artisan /ˌɑːtɪˈzæn, ˈɑː-/ *n.* **1** a skilled (esp. manual) worker. **2** a mechanic. [F f. It. *artigiano*, ult. f. L *artitus* past part. of *artire* instruct in the arts]

artist /ˈɑːtɪst/ *n.* **1** a painter. **2** a person who practises any of the arts. **3** an artiste. **4** a person who works with the dedication and attributes associated with an artist (*an artist in crime*). **5** *colloq.* a devotee; a habitual practiser of a specified (usu. reprehensible) activity (*con artist*). □□**artistry** *n.* [F *artiste* f. It. *artista* (as ART[1], -IST)]

artiste /ɑːˈtiːst/ *n.* a professional performer, esp. a singer or dancer. [F: see ARTIST]

artistic /ɑːˈtɪstɪk/ *adj.* **1** having natural skill in art. **2** made or done with art. **3** of art or artists. □□**artistically** *adv.*

artless /ˈɑːtlɪs/ *adj.* **1** guileless, ingenuous. **2** not resulting from or displaying art. **3** clumsy. □□**artlessly** *adv.*

artwork /ˈɑːtwɜːk/ *n.* the illustrations in a printed work.

arty /ˈɑːtɪ/ *adj.* (**artier**, **artiest**) *colloq.* pretentiously or affectedly artistic. □**arty-crafty** quaintly artistic;

(of furniture etc.) seeking stylistic effect rather than usefulness or comfort. □□**artiness** *n.*

arum /ˈeərəm/ *n.* any plant of the genus *Arum*, usu. stemless with arrow-shaped leaves, e.g. lords and ladies. □**arum lily** a tall lily-like plant, *Zantedeschia aethiopica*, with white spathe and spadix. [L f. Gk *aron*]

arvo /ˈɑːvəʊ/ *n. Austral. sl.* afternoon. [abbr.]

-ary[1] /ərɪ/ *suffix* **1** forming adjectives (*budgetary*; *contrary*; *primary*; *unitary*). **2** forming nouns (*dictionary*; *fritillary*; *granary*; *January*). [F -*aire* or L -*arius* 'connected with']

-ary[2] /ərɪ/ *suffix* forming adjectives (*military*). [F -*aire* or f. L -*aris* 'belonging to']

Aryan /ˈeərɪən/ *n. & adj.* —*n.* **1** a member of the peoples speaking any of the languages of the Indo-European (esp. Indo-Iranian) family. **2** the parent language of this family. **3** *improperly* (in Nazi ideology) a Caucasian not of Jewish descent. —*adj.* of or relating to Aryan or the Aryans. [Skr. *āryas* noble]

aryl /ˈæraɪl, ˈærɪl/ *n. Chem.* any radical derived from or related to an aromatic hydrocarbon by removal of a hydrogen atom. [G *Aryl* (as AROMATIC, -YL)]

AS *abbr.* Anglo-Saxon.

As *symb. Chem.* the element arsenic.

as[1] /æz, unstressed əz/ *adv., conj., & pron.* —*adv. & conj.* (*adv.* as antecedent in main sentence; *conj.* in relative clause expressed or implied) ... to the extent to which ... is or does etc. (*I am as tall as he*; *am as tall as he is*; *am not so tall as he*; (*colloq.*) *am as tall as him*; *as many as six*; *as recently as last week*; *it is not as easy as you think*). —*conj.* (with relative clause expressed or implied) **1** (with antecedent *so*) expressing result or purpose (*came early so as to meet us*; *we so arranged matters as to avoid a long wait*; *so good as to exceed all hopes*). **2** (with antecedent adverb omitted) having concessive force (*good as it is* = although it is good; *try as he might* = although he might try). **3** (without antecedent adverb) **a** in the manner in which (*do as you like*; *was regarded as a mistake*; *they rose as one man*). **b** in the capacity or form of (*I speak as your friend*; *Olivier as Hamlet*; *as a matter of fact*). **c** during or at the time that (*came up as I was speaking*; *fell just as I reached the door*). **d** for the reason that; seeing that (*as you are here, we can talk*). **e** for instance (*cathedral cities, as York*). —*rel.pron.* (with verb of relative clause expressed or implied) **1** that, who, which (*I had the same trouble as you*; *he is a writer, as is his wife*; *such money as you have*; *such countries as France*). **2** (with sentence as antecedent) a fact that (*he lost, as you know*). □**as and when** to the extent and at the time that (*I'll do it as and when I want to*). **as for** with regard to (*as for you, I think you are wrong*). **as from** on and after (a specified date). **as if** (or **though**) as would be the case if (*acts as if he were in charge*; *as if you didn't know!*; *looks as though we've won*). **as it is** (or **as is**) in the existing circumstances or state. **as it were** in a way; to a certain extent (*he is, as it were, infatuated*). **as long as** see LONG[1]. **as much** see MUCH. **as of 1** = *as from*. **2** as at (a specified time). **as per** see PER. **as regards** see REGARD. **as soon as** see SOON. **as such** see SUCH. **as though** see *as if*. **as to** with respect to; concerning (*said nothing as to money*; *as to you, I think you are wrong*). **as was** in the previously existing circumstances or state. **as well** see WELL[1]. **as yet** until now or a particular time in the past (usu. with *neg.* and with implied reserve about the future: *have received no news as yet*). [reduced form of OE *alswā* ALSO]

as[2] /æs/ *n.* (*pl.* **asses**) a Roman copper coin. [L]

as- /əs/ *prefix* assim. form of AD- before *s*.

ASA *abbr.* **1** Amateur Swimming Association. **2** American Standards Association.

asafoetida /ˌæsəˈfiːtɪdə, -ˈfetɪdə/ *n.* (*US* **asafetida**) a resinous plant gum with a fetid ammoniac smell, formerly used in medicine, now as a herbal remedy and in Indian cooking. [ME f. med.L f. *asa* f. Pers. *azā* mastic + *fetida* (as FETID)]

a.s.a.p. *abbr.* as soon as possible.

asbestos /æz'bɛstɒs, æs-/ *n.* **1** a fibrous silicate mineral that is incombustible. **2** this used as a heat-resistant or insulating material. □□ **asbestine** /-tɪn/ *adj.* [ME f. OF *albeston*, ult. f. Gk *asbestos* unquenchable f. *a-* not + *sbestos* f. *sbennumi* quench]

asbestosis /ˌæzbɛ'stəʊsɪs, ˌæs-/ *n.* a lung disease resulting from the inhalation of asbestos particles.

ascarid /'æskərɪd/ *n.* (also **ascaris** /-rɪs/) a parasitic nematode worm of the genus *Ascaris*, e.g. the intestinal roundworm of mankind and other vertebrates. [mod.L *ascaris* f. Gk *askaris*]

ascend /ə'sɛnd/ *v.* **1** *intr.* move upwards; rise. **2** *intr.* **a** slope upwards. **b** lie along an ascending slope. **3** *tr.* climb; go up. **4** *intr.* rise in rank or status. **5** *tr.* mount upon. **6** *intr.* (of sound) rise in pitch. **7** *tr.* go along (a river) to its source. **8** *intr. Printing* (of a letter) have part projecting upwards. □ **ascend the throne** become king or queen. [ME f. L *ascendere* (as AD-, *scandere* climb)]

ascendancy /ə'sɛnd(ə)nsɪ/ *n.* (also **ascendency**) (often foll. by *over*) a superior or dominant condition or position.

ascendant /ə'sɛnd(ə)nt/ *adj. & n.* —*adj.* **1** rising. **2** *Astron.* rising towards the zenith. **3** *Astrol.* just above the eastern horizon. **4** predominant. —*n. Astrol.* the point of the sun's apparent path that is ascendant at a given time (*Aries in the ascendant*). □ **in the ascendant 1** supreme or dominating. **2** rising; gaining power or authority. [ME f. OF f. L (as ASCEND, -ANT)]

ascender /ə'sɛndə(r)/ *n.* **1 a** a part of a letter that extends above the main part (as in *b* and *d*). **b** a letter having this. **2** a person or thing that ascends.

ascension /ə'sɛnʃ(ə)n/ *n.* **1** the act or an instance of ascending. **2** (**Ascension**) the ascent of Christ into heaven on the fortieth day after the Resurrection. □ **Ascension Day** the Thursday on which this is celebrated annually. **right ascension** *Astron.* longitude measured along the celestial equator. □□ **ascensional** *adj.* [ME f. OF f. L *ascensio -onis* (as ASCEND, -ION)]

Ascensiontide /ə'sɛnʃ(ə)n,taɪd/ *n.* the period of ten days from Ascension Day to Whitsun Eve.

ascent /ə'sɛnt/ *n.* **1** the act or an instance of ascending. **2 a** an upward movement or rise. **b** advancement or progress (*the ascent of man*). **3** a way by which one may ascend; an upward slope. [ASCEND, after *descent*]

ascertain /ˌæsə'teɪn/ *v.tr.* **1** find out as a definite fact. **2** get to know. □□ **ascertainable** *adj.* **ascertainment** *n.* [ME f. OF *acertener*, stem *acertain-* f. *à* to + CERTAIN]

ascesis /ə'siːsɪs/ *n.* the practice of self-discipline. [Gk *askēsis* training f. *askeō* exercise]

ascetic /ə'sɛtɪk/ *n. & adj.* —*n.* a person who practises severe self-discipline and abstains from all forms of pleasure, esp. for religious or spiritual reasons. —*adj.* relating to or characteristic of ascetics or asceticism; abstaining from pleasure. □□ **ascetically** *adv.* **asceticism** /-tɪ,sɪz(ə)m/ *n.* [med.L *asceticus* or Gk *askētikos* f. *askētēs* monk f. *askeō* exercise]

ascidian /ə'sɪdɪən/ *n. Zool.* any tunicate animal of the class Ascidiacea, often found in colonies, the adults sedentary on rocks or seaweeds, e.g. the sea squirt. [mod.L *Ascidia* f. Gk *askidion* dimin. of *askos* wineskin]

ASCII /'æskɪ/ *abbr. Computing* American Standard Code for Information Interchange.

ascites /ə'saɪtiːz/ *n.* (*pl.* same) *Med.* the accumulation of fluid in the abdominal cavity causing swelling. [ME f. LL f. Gk f. *askitēs* f. *askos* wineskin]

ascorbic acid /ə'skɔːbɪk/ *n.* a vitamin found in citrus fruits and green vegetables, essential in maintaining healthy connective tissue, a deficiency of which results in scurvy. Also called *vitamin C*.

ascribe /ə'skraɪb/ *v.tr.* (usu. foll. by *to*) **1** attribute or impute (*ascribes his well-being to a sound constitution*). **2** regard as belonging. □□ **ascribable** *adj.* [ME f. L *ascribere* (as AD-, *scribere script-* write)]

ascription /ə'skrɪpʃ(ə)n/ *n.* **1** the act or an instance of ascribing. **2** a preacher's words ascribing praise to God at the end of a sermon. [L *ascriptio -onis* as ASCRIBE)]

asdic /'æzdɪk/ *n.* an early form of echo-sounder. [initials of *A*llied *S*ubmarine *D*etection *I*nvestigation *C*ommittee]

-ase /eɪz/ *suffix Biochem.* forming the name of an enzyme (*amylase*). [DIASTASE]

ASEAN /'æsɪən/ *abbr.* Association of South East Asian Nations.

asepsis /eɪ'sɛpsɪs, ə-/ *n.* **1** the absence of harmful bacteria, viruses, or other micro-organisms. **2** a method of achieving asepsis in surgery.

aseptic /eɪ'sɛptɪk/ *adj.* **1** free from contamination caused by harmful bacteria, viruses, or other micro-organisms. **2** (of a wound, instrument, or dressing) surgically sterile or sterilized. **3** (of a surgical method etc.) aiming at the elimination of harmful micro-organisms, rather than counteraction (cf. ANTISEPTIC).

asexual /eɪ'sɛksjʊəl, æ-/ *adj. Biol.* **1** without sex or sexual organs. **2** (of reproduction) not involving the fusion of gametes. **3** without sexuality. □□ **asexuality** /-'ælɪtɪ/ *n.* **asexually** *adv.*

ASH /æʃ/ *abbr.* Action on Smoking and Health.

ash[1] /æʃ/ *n.* **1** (often in *pl.*) the powdery residue left after the burning of any substance. **2** (*pl.*) the remains of the human body after cremation or disintegration. **3** (**the Ashes**) *Cricket* a trophy competed for regularly by Australia and England. **4** ashlike material thrown out by a volcano. □ **ash blonde 1** a very pale blonde colour. **2** a person with hair of this colour. **Ash Wednesday** the first day of Lent (from the custom of marking the foreheads of penitents with ashes on that day). [OE *æsce*]

ash[2] /æʃ/ *n.* **1** any forest-tree of the genus *Fraxinus*, with silver-grey bark, compound leaves, and hard, tough, pale wood. **2** its wood. **3** an Old English runic letter, = æ (named from a word of which it was the first letter). □ **ash-key** the winged seed of the ash-tree, growing in clusters resembling keys. **ash-plant** a sapling from an ash-tree, used as a walking-stick etc. [OE *æsc* f. Gmc]

ashamed /ə'ʃeɪmd/ *adj.* (usu. *predic.*) **1** (often foll. by *of* (= with regard to), *for* (= on account of), or *to* + infin.) embarrassed or disconcerted by shame (*ashamed of his aunt*; *ashamed of having lied*; *ashamed for you*; *ashamed to be seen with him*). **2** (foll. by *to* + infin.) hesitant, reluctant (but usu. not actually refusing or declining) (*am ashamed to admit that I was wrong*). □□ **ashamedly** /-mɪdlɪ/ *adv.* [OE *āscamod* past part. of *āscamian* feel shame (as A-[2], SHAME)]

ashbin /'æʃbɪn/ *n.* a receptacle for the disposal of ashes.

ashcan /'æʃkæn/ *n. US* a dustbin.

ashen[1] /'æʃ(ə)n/ *adj.* **1** of or resembling ashes. **2** ash-coloured; grey or pale.

ashen[2] /'æʃ(ə)n/ *adj.* **1** of or relating to the ash-tree. **2** *archaic* made of ash wood.

ashet /'æʃɪt/ *n. Sc. & NZ* a large plate or dish. [F *assiette*]

Ashkenazi /ˌæʃkə'nɑːzɪ/ *n.* (*pl.* **Ashkenazim** /-zɪm/) **1** an East European Jew. **2** a Jew of East European ancestry (cf. SEPHARDI). □□ **Ashkenazic** *adj.* [mod.Heb., f. *Ashkenaz* (Gen. 10:3)]

ashlar /'æʃlə(r)/ *n.* **1** a large square-cut stone used in building. **2** masonry made of ashlars. **3** such masonry used as a facing on a rough rubble or brick wall. [ME f. OF *aisselier* f. L *axilla* dimin. of *axis* board]

ashlaring /'æʃlərɪŋ/ *n.* **1** ashlar masonry. **2** the short upright boarding in a garret which cuts off the acute angle between the roof and the floor.

æ *cat* ɑ: *arm* e *bed* ɜ: *her* ɪ *sit* iː *see* ɒ *hot* ɔ: *saw* ʌ *run* ʊ *put* uː *too* ə *ago* aɪ *my*

ashore /əˈʃɔː(r)/ *adv.* towards or on the shore or land (*sailed ashore; stayed ashore*).

ashpan /ˈæʃpæn/ *n.* a tray under a grate to catch the ash.

ashram /ˈæʃrəm/ *n. Ind.* a place of religious retreat for Hindus; a hermitage. [Skr. *āshrama* hermitage]

ashtray /ˈæʃtreɪ/ *n.* a small receptacle for cigarette ash, stubs, etc.

ashy /ˈæʃɪ/ *adj.* (**ashier, ashiest**) **1** = ASHEN¹. **2** covered with ashes.

Asian /ˈeɪʃ(ə)n, -ʒ(ə)n/ *n. & adj.* —*n.* **1** a native of Asia. **2** a person of Asian descent. —*adj.* of or relating to Asia or its people, customs, or languages. [L *Asianus* f. Gk *Asianos* f. *Asia*]

Asiatic /ˌeɪʃɪˈætɪk, ˌeɪz-/ *n. & adj.* —*n. offens.* an Asian. —*adj.* Asian. [L *Asiaticus* f. Gk *Asiatikos*]

aside /əˈsaɪd/ *adv. & n.* —*adv.* **1** to or on one side; away. **2** out of consideration (placed after noun: *joking aside*). —*n.* **1** words spoken in a play for the audience to hear, but supposed not to be heard by the other characters. **2** an incidental remark. □**aside from** *US* apart from. **set aside 1** put to one side. **2** keep for a special purpose or future use. **3** reject or disregard. **4** annul. **5** remove (land) from agricultural production to fallow, forestry, or other use. **take aside** engage (a person) esp. for a private conversation. [orig. *on side*: see A²]

A-side /ˈeɪsaɪd/ *n.* the side of a gramophone record regarded as the main one.

asinine /ˈæsɪˌnaɪn/ *adj.* **1** stupid. **2** of or concerning asses; like an ass. □□**asininity** /-ˈnɪnɪtɪ/ *n.* [L *asininus* f. *asinus* ass]

-asis /əsɪs/ *suffix* (usu. as **-iasis**) forming the names of diseases (*psoriasis; satyriasis*). [L f. Gk *-asis* in nouns of state f. verbs in *-aō*]

ask /ɑːsk/ *v.* **1** *tr.* call for an answer to or about (*ask her about it; ask him his name; ask a question of him*). **2** *tr.* seek to obtain from another person (*ask a favour of; ask to be allowed*). **3** *tr.* (usu. foll. by *out* or *over*, or *to* (a function etc.)) invite; request the company of (*must ask them over; asked her to dinner*). **4** *intr.* (foll. by *for*) seek to obtain, meet, or be directed to (*ask for a donation; ask for the post office; asking for you*). **5** *tr. archaic* require (a thing). □**ask after** inquire about (esp. a person). **ask for it** *sl.* invite trouble. **asking price** the price of an object set by the seller. **ask me another** *colloq.* I do not know. **for the asking** (obtainable) for nothing. **I ask you!** an exclamation of disgust, surprise, etc. **if you ask me** *colloq.* in my opinion. □□**asker** *n.* [OE *āscian* etc. f. WG]

askance /əˈskæns, -ˈskɑːns/ *adv.* (also **askant** /-ˈskænt, -ˈskɑːnt/) sideways or squinting. □**look askance at** regard with suspicion or disapproval. [16th c.: orig. unkn.]

askari /æˈskɑːrɪ/ *n.* (*pl.* same or **askaris**) an East African soldier or policeman. [Arab. *'askarī* soldier]

askew /əˈskjuː/ *adv. & predic.adj.* —*adv.* obliquely; awry. —*predic.adj.* oblique; awry. [A² + SKEW]

aslant /əˈslɑːnt/ *adv. & prep.* —*adv.* obliquely or at a slant. —*prep.* obliquely across (*lay aslant the path*).

asleep /əˈsliːp/ *predic.adj. & adv.* **1 a** in or into a state of sleep (*he fell asleep*). **b** inactive, inattentive (*the nation is asleep*). **2** (of a limb etc.) numb. **3** *euphem.* dead.

Aslef /ˈæzlɛf/ *abbr.* (in the UK) Associated Society of Locomotive Engineers and Firemen.

aslope /əˈsləʊp/ *adv. & predic.adj.* sloping; crosswise. [ME: orig. uncert.]

ASM *abbr.* air-to-surface missile.

asocial /eɪˈsəʊʃ(ə)l/ *adj.* **1** not social; antisocial. **2** *colloq.* inconsiderate of or hostile to others.

asp /æsp/ *n.* **1** a small viper, *Vipera aspis*, native to Southern Europe, resembling the adder. **2** a small venomous snake, *Naja haje*, native to North Africa and Arabia. [ME f. OF *aspe* or L *aspis* f. Gk]

asparagus /əˈspærəgəs/ *n.* **1** any plant of the genus *Asparagus*. **2** one species of this, *A. officinalis*, with edible young shoots and leaves; this as food. □**asparagus fern** a decorative plant, *Asparagus setaceus*. [L f. Gk *asparagos*]

aspartame /əˈspɑːteɪm/ *n.* a very sweet low-calorie substance used as a sweetener instead of sugar or saccharin. [contr. of the chem. name *1-methyl N-L-aspartyl-L-phenylalanine*, f. *aspartic acid* (invented name)]

aspect /ˈæspɛkt/ *n.* **1 a** a particular component or feature of a matter (*only one aspect of the problem*). **b** a particular way in which a matter may be considered. **2 a** a facial expression; a look (*a cheerful aspect*). **b** the appearance of a person or thing, esp. as presented to the mind of the viewer (*has a frightening aspect*). **3** the side of a building or location facing a particular direction (*southern aspect*). **4** *Gram.* a verbal category or form expressing inception, duration, or completion. **5** *Astrol.* the relative position of planets etc. measured by angular distance. □**aspect ratio 1** *Aeron.* the ratio of the span to the mean chord of an aerofoil. **2** *Telev.* the ratio of picture width to height. □□**aspectual** /æˈspɛktjʊəl/ *adj.* (in sense 4). [ME f. L *aspectus* f. *adspicere adspect-* look at (as AD-, *specere* look)]

aspen /ˈæspən/ *n.* a poplar tree, *Populus tremula*, with especially tremulous leaves. [earlier name *asp* f. OE *æspe* + -EN² forming adj. taken as noun]

asperity /əˈspɛrɪtɪ/ *n.* (*pl.* **-ies**) **1** harshness or sharpness of temper or tone. **2** roughness. **3** a rough excrescence. [ME f. OF *asperité* or L *asperitas* f. *asper* rough]

asperse /əˈspɜːs/ *v.tr.* (often foll. by *with*) attack the reputation of; calumniate. [ME, = besprinkle, f. L *aspergere aspers-* (as AD-, *spargere* sprinkle)]

aspersion /əˈspɜːʃ(ə)n/ *n.* □**cast aspersions on** attack the reputation or integrity of. [L *aspersio* (as ASPERSE, -ION)]

asphalt /ˈæsfælt/ *n. & v.* —*n.* **1** a dark bituminous pitch occurring naturally or made from petroleum. **2** a mixture of this with sand, gravel, etc., for surfacing roads etc. —*v.tr.* surface with asphalt. □□ **asphalter** *n.* **asphaltic** /-ˈfæltɪk/ *adj.* [ME, ult. f. LL *asphalton, -um,* f. Gk *asphalton*]

asphodel /ˈæsfəˌdɛl/ *n.* **1** any plant of the genus *Asphodelus*, of the lily family. **2** *poet.* an immortal flower growing in Elysium. [L *asphodelus* f. Gk *asphodelos*: cf. DAFFODIL]

asphyxia /æsˈfɪksɪə/ *n.* a lack of oxygen in the blood, causing unconsciousness or death; suffocation. □□ **asphyxial** *adj.* **asphyxiant** *adj. & n.* [mod.L f. Gk *asphuxia* f. *a-* not + *sphuxis* pulse]

asphyxiate /æsˈfɪksɪeɪt/ *v.tr.* cause (a person) to have asphyxia; suffocate. □□**asphyxiation** /-ˈeɪʃ(ə)n/ *n.* **asphyxiator** *n.*

aspic /ˈæspɪk/ *n.* a savoury meat jelly used as a garnish or to contain game, eggs, etc. [F, = ASP, from the colours of the jelly (compared to those of the asp)]

aspidistra /ˌæspɪˈdɪstrə/ *n.* a foliage plant of the genus *Aspidistra*, with broad tapering leaves, often grown as a house-plant. [mod.L f. Gk *aspis -idos* shield (from the shape of the leaves)]

aspirant /ˈæspɪrənt, əˈspaɪərənt/ *adj. & n.* (usu. foll. by *to, after, for*) —*adj.* aspiring. —*n.* a person who aspires. [F *aspirant* or f. L *aspirant-* (as ASPIRE, -ANT)]

aspirate /ˈæspərət/ *adj., n., & v. Phonet.* —*adj.* **1** pronounced with an exhalation of breath. **2** blended with the sound of *h*. —*n.* **1** a consonant pronounced in this way. **2** the sound of *h*. —*v.* /-ˌreɪt/ **1 a** *tr.* pronounce with a breath. **b** *intr.* make the sound of *h*. **2** *tr.* draw (fluid) by suction from a vessel or cavity. [L *aspiratus* part. of *aspirare*: see ASPIRE]

aspiration /ˌæspɪˈreɪʃ(ə)n/ *n.* **1** a strong desire to achieve an end; an ambition. **2** the act or process of drawing breath. **3** the action of aspirating. [ME f. OF *aspiration* or L *aspiratio* (as ASPIRE, -ATION)]

aspirator /ˈæspɪˌreɪtə(r)/ *n.* an apparatus for aspirating fluid. [L *aspirare* (as ASPIRATE, -OR¹)]

aspire /ə'spaɪə(r)/ v.intr. (usu. foll. by to or after, or to + infin.) **1** have ambition or strong desire. **2** poet. rise high. [ME f. F aspirer or L aspirare f. ad to + spirare breathe]

aspirin /'æsprɪn/ n. (pl. same or **aspirins**) **1** a white powder, acetylsalicylic acid, used to relieve pain and reduce fever. **2** a tablet of this. [G, formed as ACETYL + spiraeic (= salicylic) acid + -IN]

asquint /ə'skwɪnt/ predic.adj. & adv. (usu. look asquint). **1** to one side; out of the corner of an eye. **2** with a squint. [ME perh. f. Du. schuinte slant]

ass[1] /æs/ n. & v. —n. **1 a** either of two kinds of four-legged long-eared mammal of the horse genus Equus, E. africana of Africa and E. hemionus of Asia. **b** (in general use) a donkey. **2** a stupid person. —v.intr. sl. (foll. by about, around) act the fool. □**asses' bridge** = PONS ASINORUM. **make an ass of** make (a person) look absurd or foolish. [OE assa through OCelt. f. L asinus]

ass[2] US var. of ARSE.

assagai var. of ASSEGAI.

assai /æ'saɪ/ adv. Mus. very (adagio assai). [It.]

assail /ə'seɪl/ v.tr. **1** make a strong or concerted attack on. **2** make a resolute start on (a task). **3** make a strong or constant verbal attack on (was assailed with angry questions). □□**assailable** adj. [ME f. OF asaill- stressed stem of asalir f. med.L assalire f. L assilire (as AD-, salire salt- leap)]

assailant /ə'seɪlənt/ n. a person who attacks another physically or verbally. [F (as ASSAIL)]

assassin /ə'sæsɪn/ n. **1** a killer, esp. of a political or religious leader. **2** hist. any of a group of Muslim fanatics sent on murder missions in the time of the Crusades. [F assassin or f. med.L assassinus f. Arab. ḥaššāš hashish-eater]

assassinate /ə'sæsɪˌneɪt/ v.tr. kill (esp. a political or religious leader) for political or religious motives. □□**assassination** /-'neɪʃ(ə)n/ n. **assassinator** n. [med.L assassinare f. assassinus: see ASSASSIN]

assault /ə'sɔːlt, ə'sɒlt/ n. & v. —n. **1** a violent physical or verbal attack. **2 a** Law an act that threatens physical harm to a person (whether or not actual harm is done). **b** euphem. an act of rape. **3** (attrib.) relating to or used in an assault (assault craft; assault troops). **4** a vigorous start made to a lengthy or difficult task. **5** a final rush on a fortified place, esp. at the end of a prolonged attack. —v.tr. **1** make an assault on. **2** euphem. rape. □**assault and battery** Law a threatening act that results in physical harm done to a person. **assault course** an obstacle course used in training soldiers etc. □□**assaulter** n. **assaultive** adj. [ME f. OF asaut, assauter ult. f. L (salire salt- leap)]

assay /ə'seɪ, 'æseɪ/ n. & v. —n. **1** the testing of a metal or ore to determine its ingredients and quality. **2** Chem. etc. the determination of the content or strength of a substance. —v. **1** tr. make an assay of (a metal or ore). **2** tr. Chem. etc. perform a concentration on (a substance). **3** tr. show (content) on being assayed. **4** intr. make an assay. **5** tr. archaic attempt. □**Assay Office** an establishment which awards hallmarks. □□**assayer** n. [ME f. OF assaier, assai, var. of essayer, essai: see ESSAY]

assegai /'æsɪˌɡaɪ/ n. (also **assagai** /'æsəˌɡaɪ/) a slender iron-tipped spear of hard wood, esp. as used by S. African peoples. [obs. F azagaie or Port. azagaia f. Arab. az-zaġāyah f. al the + zaġāyah spear]

assemblage /ə'semblɪdʒ/ n. **1** the act or an instance of bringing or coming together. **2** a collection of things or gathering of people. **3 a** the act or an instance of fitting together. **b** an object made of pieces fitted together. **4** a work of art made by grouping found or unrelated objects.

assemble /ə'semb(ə)l/ v. **1** tr. & intr. gather together; collect. **2** tr. arrange in order. **3** tr. esp. Mech. fit together the parts of. [ME f. OF asembler ult. f. L ad to + simul together]

assembler /ə'semblə(r)/ n. a person who assembles

a machine or its parts. **2** Computing **a** a program for converting instructions written in low-level symbolic code into machine code. **b** the low-level symbolic code itself; an assembly language.

assembly /ə'semblɪ/ n. (pl. -ies) **1** the act or an instance of assembling or gathering together. **2 a** a group of persons gathered together, esp. as a deliberative body or a legislative council. **b** a gathering of the entire members of a school. **3** the assembling of a machine or structure or its parts. **4** Mil. a call to assemble, given by drum or bugle. □**assembly language** Computing the low-level symbolic code converted by an assembler. **assembly line** machinery arranged in stages by which a product is progressively assembled. **assembly room** (or **shop**) a place where a machine or its components are assembled. **assembly rooms** public rooms in which meetings or social functions are held. [ME f. OF asemblee fem. past part. of asembler: see ASSEMBLE]

assent /ə'sent/ v. & n. —v.intr. (usu. foll. by to) **1** express agreement (assented to my view). **2** consent (assented to my request). —n. **1** mental or inward acceptance or agreement (a nod of assent). **2** consent or sanction, esp. official. □**royal assent** assent of the sovereign to a bill passed by Parliament. □□**assenter** n. (also **assentor**). [ME f. OF asenter, as(s)ente ult. f. L assentari (ad to, sentire think)]

assentient /ə'senʃ(ə)nt, -ʃɪənt/ adj. & n. —adj. assenting. —n. a person who assents. [L assentire (as ASSENT, -ENT)]

assert /ə'sɜːt/ v. **1** tr. declare; state clearly (assert one's beliefs; assert that it is so). **2** refl. insist on one's rights or opinions; demand recognition. **3** tr. vindicate a claim to (assert one's rights). □□**assertor** n. [L asserere (as AD-, serere sert- join)]

assertion /ə'sɜːʃ(ə)n/ n. **1** a declaration; a forthright statement. **2** the act or an instance of asserting. **3** (also **self-assertion**) insistence on the recognition of one's rights or claims. [ME f. F assertion or L assertio (as ASSERT, -ION)]

assertive /ə'sɜːtɪv/ adj. **1** tending to assert oneself; forthright, positive. **2** dogmatic. □□**assertively** adv. **assertiveness** n.

asses pl. of AS[2], ASS[1], ASS[2].

assess /ə'ses/ v.tr. **1 a** estimate the size or quality of. **b** estimate the value of (a property) for taxation. **2 a** (usu. foll. by on) fix the amount of (a tax etc.) and impose it on a person or community. **b** (usu. foll. by in, at) fine or tax (a person, community, etc.) in or at a specific amount (assessed them at £100). □□**assessable** adj. **assessment** n. [ME f. F assesser f. L assidēre (as AD-, sedēre sit)]

assessor /ə'sesə(r)/ n. **1** a person who assesses taxes or estimates the value of property for taxation or insurance purposes. **2** a person called upon to advise a judge, committee of inquiry, etc., on technical questions. □□**assessorial** /ˌæse'sɔːrɪəl/ adj. [ME f. OF assessour f. L assessor -oris assistant-judge (as ASSESS, -OR[1]): sense 1 f. med.L]

asset /'æset/ n. **1 a** a useful or valuable quality. **b** a person or thing possessing such a quality or qualities (is an asset to the firm). **2** (usu. in pl.) **a** property and possessions, esp. regarded as having value in meeting debts, commitments, etc. **b** any possession having value. □**asset-stripping** Commerce the practice of taking over a company and selling off its assets to make a profit. [assets (taken as pl.), f. AF asetz f. OF asez enough, ult. f. L ad to + satis enough]

asseverate /ə'sevəˌreɪt/ v.tr. declare solemnly. □□**asseveration** /-'reɪʃ(ə)n/ n. [L asseverare (as AD-, severus serious)]

assibilate /ə'sɪbɪˌleɪt/ v.tr. Phonet. **1** pronounce (a sound) as a sibilant or affricate ending in a sibilant. **2** alter (a syllable) to become this. □□**assibilation** /-'leɪʃ(ə)n/ n. [L assibilare (as AD-, sibilare hiss)]

assiduity /ˌæsɪ'djuːɪtɪ/ n. (pl. -ies) **1** constant or close attention to what one is doing. **2** (usu. in pl.) constant attentions to another person. [L *assiduitas* (as AS-SIDUOUS, -ITY)]

assiduous /əˈsɪdjʊəs/ *adj.* **1** persevering, hard-working. **2** attending closely. □□ **assiduously** *adv.* **assiduousness** *n.* [L *assiduus* (as ASSESS)]

assign /əˈsaɪn/ *v. & n.* —*v.tr.* **1** (usu. foll. by *to*) **a** allot as a share or responsibility. **b** appoint to a position, task, etc. **2** fix (a time, place, etc.) for a specific purpose. **3** (foll. by *to*) ascribe or refer to (a reason, date, etc.) (*assigned the manuscript to 1832*). **4** (foll. by *to*) transfer formally (esp. personal property) to (another). —*n.* a person to whom property or rights are legally transferred. □□ **assignable** *adj.* **assigner** *n.* **assignor** *n.* (in sense 4 of *v.*). [ME f. OF *asi(g)ner* f. L *assignare* mark out to (as AD-, *signum* sign)]

assignation /ˌæsɪgˈneɪʃ(ə)n/ *n.* **1 a** an appointment to meet. **b** a secret appointment, esp. between illicit lovers. **2** the act or an instance of assigning or being assigned. [ME f. OF f. L *assignatio -onis* (as ASSIGN, -ATION)]

assignee /ˌæsaɪˈniː/ *n.* **1** a person appointed to act for another. **2** an assign. [ME f. OF *assigné* past part. of *assigner* ASSIGN]

assignment /əˈsaɪnmənt/ *n.* **1** something assigned, esp. a task allotted to a person. **2** the act or an instance of assigning or being assigned. **3 a** a legal transfer. **b** the document effecting this. [ME f. OF *assignement* f. med.L *assignamentum* (as ASSIGN, -MENT)]

assimilate /əˈsɪmɪˌleɪt/ *v.* **1** *tr.* **a** absorb and digest (food etc.) into the body. **b** absorb (information etc.) into the mind. **c** absorb (people) into a larger group. **2** *tr.* (usu. foll. by *to*, *with*) make like; cause to resemble. **3** *tr. Phonet.* make (a sound) more like another in the same or next word. **4** *intr.* be absorbed into the body, mind, or a larger group. □□ **assimilable** *adj.* **assimilation** /-ˈleɪʃ(ə)n/ *n.* **assimilative** *adj.* **assimilator** *n.* **assimilatory** /-lətəri/ *adj.* [ME f. L *assimilare* (as AD-, *similis* like)]

assist /əˈsɪst/ *v. & n.* —*v.* **1** *tr.* (often foll. by *in* + verbal noun) help (a person, process, etc.) (*assisted them in running the playgroup*). **2** *intr.* (often foll. by *in*, *at*) take part or be present (*assisted in the ceremony*). —*n. US* **1** help; an act of helping. **2** *Baseball* etc. a player's action of helping to put out an opponent, score a goal, etc. □□ **assistance** *n.* **assister** *n.* [ME f. F *assister* f. L *assistere* take one's stand by (as AD-, *sistere* take one's stand)]

assistant /əˈsɪst(ə)nt/ *n.* **1** a helper. **2** (often *attrib.*) a person who assists, esp. as a subordinate in a particular job or role. **3** = *shop assistant*. [ME *assistent* f. med.L *assistens assistent-* present (as ASSIST, -ANT, -ENT)]

assize /əˈsaɪz/ *n.* (usu. in *pl.*) *hist.* a court sitting at intervals in each county of England and Wales to administer the civil and criminal law. ¶ In 1972 the civil jurisdiction of assizes was transferred to the High Court and the criminal jurisdiction to the Crown Court. [ME f. OF *as(s)ise*, fem. past part. of *aseeir* sit at, f. L *assidēre*: cf. ASSESS]

Assoc. *abbr.* (as part of a title) Association.

associable /əˈsəʊʃəb(ə)l/ *adj.* (usu. foll. by *with*) capable of being connected in thought. □□ **associability** /-ˈbɪlɪtɪ/ *n.* [F f. *associer* (as ASSOCIATE, -ABLE)]

associate *v., n., & adj.* —*v.* /əˈsəʊʃɪˌeɪt, -sɪˌeɪt/ **1** *tr.* connect in the mind (*associate holly with Christmas*). **2** *tr.* join or combine. **3** *refl.* make oneself a partner; declare oneself in agreement (*associate myself in your endeavour; did not want to associate ourselves with the plan*). **4** *intr.* combine for a common purpose. **5** *intr.* (usu. foll. by *with*) meet frequently or have dealings. —*n.* /əˈsəʊʃɪət, -sɪət/ **1** a business partner or colleague. **2** a friend or companion. **3** a subordinate member of a body, institute, etc. **4** a thing connected with another. —*adj.* /əˈsəʊʃɪət, -sɪət/ **1** joined in companionship, function, or dignity. **2** allied; in the

same group or category. **3** of less than full status (*associate member*). □□ **associateship** /əˈsəʊʃɪətʃɪp, əˈsəʊs-/ *n.* **associator** /əˈsəʊʃɪˌeɪtə(r), əˈsəʊs-/ *n.* **associatory** /əˈsəʊʃɪətəri, əˈsəʊs-/ *adj.* [E f. L *associatus* past part. of *associare* (as AD-, *socius* sharing, allied)]

association /əˌsəʊsɪˈeɪʃ(ə)n/ *n.* **1** a group of people organized for a joint purpose; a society. **2** the act or an instance of associating. **3** fellowship or companionship. **4** a mental connection between ideas. **5** *Chem.* a loose aggregation of molecules. **6** *Ecol.* a group of associated plants. □**Association Football** *Brit.* football played by sides of 11 with a round ball which may not be handled during play except by the goalkeepers. □□ **associational** *adj.* [F *association* or med.L *associatio* (as ASSOCIATE, -ATION)]

associative /əˈsəʊʃɪətɪv, əˈsəʊs-/ *adj.* **1** of or involving association. **2** *Math. & Computing* involving the condition that a group of quantities connected by operators (see OPERATOR 4) gives the same result whatever their grouping, as long as their order remains the same, e.g. $(a \times b) \times c = a \times (b \times c)$.

assonance /ˈæsənəns/ *n.* the resemblance of sound between two syllables in nearby words, arising from the rhyming of two or more accented vowels, but not consonants, or the use of identical consonants with different vowels, e.g. *sonnet*, *porridge*, and *killed*, *cold*, *culled*. □□ **assonant** *adj.* **assonate** /-ˌneɪt/ *v.intr.* [F f. L *assonare* respond to (as AD-, *sonus* sound)]

assort /əˈsɔːt/ *v.* **1** *tr.* (usu. foll. by *with*) classify or arrange in groups. **2** *intr.* suit; fit into; harmonize with (usu. *assort ill* or *well with*). [OF *assorter* f. *à* to + *sorte* SORT]

assortative /əˈsɔːtətɪv/ *adj.* assorting. □**assortative mating** *Biol.* selective mating based on the similarity of the partners' characteristics etc.

assorted /əˈsɔːtɪd/ *adj.* **1** of various sorts put together; miscellaneous. **2** sorted into groups. **3** matched (*ill-assorted; poorly assorted*).

assortment /əˈsɔːtmənt/ *n.* a set of various sorts of things or people put together; a mixed collection.

ASSR *abbr.* Autonomous Soviet Socialist Republic.

Asst. *abbr.* Assistant.

assuage /əˈsweɪdʒ/ *v.tr.* **1** calm or soothe (a person, pain, etc.). **2** appease or relieve (an appetite or desire). □□ **assuagement** *n.* **assuager** *n.* [ME f. OF *as(s)ouagier* ult. f. L *suavis* sweet]

assume /əˈsjuːm/ *v.tr.* **1** (usu. foll. by *that* + clause) take or accept as being true, without proof, for the purpose of argument or action. **2** simulate or pretend (ignorance etc.). **3** undertake (an office or duty). **4** take or put on oneself or itself (an aspect, attribute, etc.) (*the problem assumed immense proportions*). **5** (usu. foll. by *to*) arrogate, usurp, or seize (credit, power, etc.) (*assumed to himself the right of veto*). □□ **assumable** *adj.* **assumedly** /-mɪdlɪ/ *adv.* [ME f. L *assumere* (as AD-, *sumere sumpt-* take)]

assuming /əˈsjuːmɪŋ/ *adj.* (of a person) taking too much for granted; arrogant, presumptuous.

assumption /əˈsʌmpʃ(ə)n/ *n.* **1** the act or an instance of assuming. **2 a** the act or an instance of accepting without proof. **b** a thing assumed in this way. **3** arrogance. **4** (**Assumption**) **a** the reception of the Virgin Mary bodily into heaven, according to Roman Catholic doctrine. **b** the feast in honour of this (15 August). [ME f. OF *asompsion* or L *assumptio* (as ASSUME, -ION)]

assumptive /əˈsʌmptɪv/ *adj.* **1** taken for granted. **2** arrogant. [L *assumptivus* (as ASSUME, -IVE)]

assurance /əˈʃʊərəns/ *n.* **1** a positive declaration that a thing is true. **2** a solemn promise or guarantee. **3** insurance, esp. life insurance. **4** certainty. **5 a** self-confidence. **b** impudence. [ME f. OF *aseürance* f. *aseürer* (as ASSURE, -ANCE)]

assure /əˈʃʊə(r)/ *v.tr.* **1** (often foll. by *of*) **a** make (a person) sure; convince (*assured him of my sincerity*). **b** tell (a person) confidently (*assured him the bus* *went to Westminster*). **2 a** make certain of; ensure the happening etc. of (*will assure her success*). **b** make safe (against overthrow etc.). **3** insure (esp. a life). **4** (as **assured** *adj.*) **a** guaranteed. **b** self-confident. □**rest assured** remain confident. □□ **assurable** *adj.* **assurer** *n.* [ME f. OF *aseürer* ult. f. L *securus* safe, SECURE]

assuredly /əˈʃʊərɪdlɪ/ *adv.* certainly.

Assyrian /əˈsɪrɪən/ *n. & adj. hist.* —*n.* **1** an inhabitant of Assyria, an ancient kingdom in Mesopotamia. **2** the Semitic language of Assyria. —*adj.* of or relating to Assyria. [L *Assyrius* f. Gk *Assurios* of Assyria]

Assyriology /əˌsɪrɪˈɒlədʒɪ/ *n.* the study of the language, history, and antiquities of Assyria. □□ **Assyriologist** *n.*

AST *abbr.* Atlantic Standard Time.

astable /eɪˈsteɪb(ə)l/ *adj.* **1** not stable. **2** *Electr.* of or relating to a circuit which oscillates spontaneously between unstable states.

astatic /eɪˈstætɪk, ə-/ *adj.* **1** not static; unstable or unsteady. **2** *Physics* not tending to keep one position or direction. □**astatic galvanometer** one in which the effect of the earth's magnetic field on the meter needle is greatly reduced. [Gk *astatos* unstable f. *a-* not + *sta-* stand]

astatine /ˈæstəˌtiːn/ *n. Chem.* a radioactive element, the heaviest of the halogens, which occurs naturally and can be artificially made by nuclear bombardment of bismuth. ¶ Symb: **At**. [formed as ASTATIC + -INE⁴]

aster /ˈæstə(r)/ *n.* any composite plant of the genus *Aster*, with bright daisy-like flowers, e.g. the Michaelmas daisy. □**China aster** a related plant, *Callistephus chinensis*, cultivated for its bright and showy flowers. [L f. Gk *astēr* star]

-aster /ˈæstə(r)/ *suffix* **1** forming nouns denoting poor quality (*criticaster*; *poetaster*). **2** *Bot.* denoting incomplete resemblance (*oleaster*; *pinaster*). [L]

asterisk /ˈæstərɪsk/ *n. & v.* —*n.* a symbol (*) used in printing and writing to mark words etc. for reference, to stand for omitted matter, etc. —*v.tr.* mark with an asterisk. [ME f. LL *asteriscus* f. Gk *asteriskos* dimin. (as ASTER)]

asterism /ˈæstəˌrɪz(ə)m/ *n.* **1** a cluster of stars. **2** a group of three asterisks (✱) calling attention to following text. [Gk *asterismos* (as ASTER, -ISM)]

astern /əˈstɜːn/ *adv. Naut. & Aeron.* (often foll. by *of*) **1** aft; away to the rear. **2** backwards. [A² + STERN²]

asteroid /ˈæstəˌrɔɪd/ *n.* **1** any of the minor planets revolving round the sun, mainly between the orbits of Mars and Jupiter. **2** *Zool.* a starfish. □□ **asteroidal** /ˌæstəˈrɔɪd(ə)l/ *adj.* [Gk *asteroeidēs* (as ASTER, -OID)]

asthenia /æsˈθiːnɪə/ *n. Med.* loss of strength; debility. [mod.L f. Gk *astheneia* f. *asthenēs* weak]

asthenic /æsˈθenɪk/ *adj. & n.* —*adj.* **1** of lean or long-limbed build. **2** *Med.* of or characterized by asthenia. —*n.* a lean long-limbed person.

asthma /ˈæsmə/ *n.* a usu. allergic respiratory disease, often with paroxysms of difficult breathing. [ME f. Gk *asthma -matos* f. *azō* breathe hard]

asthmatic /æsˈmætɪk/ *adj. & n.* —*adj.* relating to or suffering from asthma. —*n.* a person suffering from asthma. □□ **asthmatically** *adv.* [L *asthmaticus* f. Gk *asthmatikos* (as ASTHMA, -IC)]

Asti /ˈæstɪ/ *n.* (*pl.* **Astis**) an Italian white wine. □**Asti spumante** /spuːˈmæntɪ/ a sparkling form of this. [*Asti* in Piedmont]

astigmatism /əˈstɪgməˌtɪz(ə)m/ *n.* a defect in the eye or in a lens resulting in distorted images, as light rays are prevented from meeting at a common focus. □□ **astigmatic** /ˌæstɪgˈmætɪk/ *adj.* [A-¹ + Gk *stigma -matos* point]

astilbe /əˈstɪlbɪ/ *n.* any plant of the genus *Astilbe*, with plumelike heads of tiny white or red flowers. [mod.L f. Gk *a-* not + *stilbē* fem. of *stilbos* glittering, from the inconspicuous (individual) flowers]

astir /əˈstɜː(r)/ *predic.adj. & adv.* **1** in motion. **2** awake and out of bed (*astir early*; *already astir*). **3** excited. [A² + STIR¹ *n.*]

astonish /əˈstɒnɪʃ/ *v.tr.* amaze; surprise greatly. □□ **astonishing** *adj.* **astonishingly** *adv.* **astonishment** *n.* [obs. *astone* f. OF *estoner* f. Gallo-Roman: see -ISH²]

astound /əˈstaʊnd/ *v.tr.* shock with alarm or surprise; amaze. □□ **astounding** *adj.* **astoundingly** *adv.* [obs. *astound* (adj.) = *astoned* past part. of obs. *astone*: see ASTONISH]

astraddle /əˈstræd(ə)l/ *adv. & predic.adj.* in a straddling position.

astragal /ˈæstrəg(ə)l/ *n. Archit.* a small semicircular moulding round the top or bottom of a column. [ASTRAGALUS]

astragalus /əˈstrægələs/ *n.* (*pl.* **-li** /-ˌlaɪ/) **1** *Anat.* = TALUS¹. **2** *Bot.* a leguminous plant of the genus *Astragalus*, e.g. the milk-vetch. [L f. Gk *astragalos* ankle-bone, moulding, a plant]

astrakhan /ˌæstrəˈkæn/ *n.* **1** the dark curly fleece of young lambs from Astrakhan. **2** a cloth imitating astrakhan. [*Astrakhan* in the USSR]

astral /ˈæstr(ə)l/ *adj.* **1** of or connected with the stars. **2** consisting of stars; starry. **3** *Theosophy* relating to or arising from a supposed ethereal existence, esp. of a counterpart of the body, associated with oneself in life and surviving after death. [LL *astralis* f. *astrum* star]

astray /əˈstreɪ/ *adv. & predic.adj.* **1** in or into error or sin (esp. *lead astray*). **2** out of the right way. □**go astray** be lost or mislaid. [ME f. OF *estraié* past part. of *estraier* ult. f. L *extra* out of bounds + *vagari* wander]

astride /əˈstraɪd/ *adv. & prep.* —*adv.* **1** (often foll. by *of*) with a leg on each side. **2** with legs apart. —*prep.* with a leg on each side of; extending across.

astringent /əˈstrɪndʒ(ə)nt/ *adj. & n.* —*adj.* **1** causing the contraction of body tissues. **2** checking bleeding. **3** severe, austere. —*n.* an astringent substance or drug. □□ **astringency** *n.* **astringently** *adv.* [F f. L *astringere* (as AD-, *stringere* bind)]

astro- /ˈæstrəʊ/ *comb. form* **1** relating to the stars or celestial bodies. **2** relating to outer space. [Gk f. *astron* star]

astrochemistry /ˌæstrəʊˈkemɪstrɪ/ *n.* the study of molecules and radicals in interstellar space.

astrodome /ˈæstrəˌdəʊm/ *n.* a domed window in an aircraft for astronomical observations.

astrohatch /ˈæstrəˌhætʃ/ *n.* = ASTRODOME.

astrolabe /ˈæstrəˌleɪb/ *n.* an instrument, usu. consisting of a disc and pointer, formerly used to make astronomical measurements, esp. of the altitudes of celestial bodies, and as an aid in navigation. [ME f. OF *astrelabe* f. med.L *astrolabium* f. Gk *astrolabon*, neut. of *astrolabos* star-taking]

astrology /əˈstrɒlədʒɪ/ *n.* the study of the movements and relative positions of celestial bodies interpreted as an influence on human affairs. □□ **astrologer** *n.* **astrological** /ˌæstrəˈlɒdʒɪk(ə)l/ *adj.* **astrologist** *n.* [ME f. OF *astrologie* f. L *astrologia* f. Gk (as ASTRO-, -LOGY)]

astronaut /ˈæstrəˌnɔːt/ *n.* a person who is trained to travel in a spacecraft. □□ **astronautical** /ˌæstrəˈnɔːtɪk(ə)l/ *adj.* [ASTRO-, after *aeronaut*]

astronautics /ˌæstrəˈnɔːtɪks/ *n.* the science of space travel.

astronomical /ˌæstrəˈnɒmɪk(ə)l/ *adj.* (also **astronomic**) **1** of or relating to astronomy. **2** extremely large; too large to contemplate. □**astronomical unit** a unit of measurement in astronomy equal to the mean distance from the centre of the earth to the centre of the sun, 1.495×10^{11} metres or 92.9 million miles. **astronomical year** see YEAR *n.* 1. □□ **astronomically** *adv.* [L *astronomicus* f. Gk *astronomikos*]

astronomy /əˈstrɒnəmɪ/ *n.* the scientific study of celestial bodies. □□ **astronomer** *n.* [ME f. OF *astronomie* f. L f. Gk *astronomia* f. *astronomos* (adj.) star-arranging f. *nemō* arrange]

astrophysics /ˌæstrəʊˈfɪzɪks/ *n.* a branch of astronomy concerned with the physics and chemistry of celestial bodies. □□**astrophysical** *adj.* **astrophysicist** /-sɪst/ *n.*

Astroturf /ˈæstrəʊˌtɜːf/ *n. propr.* an artificial grass surface, esp. for sports fields. [*Astro*dome, name of a sports stadium in Texas where it was first used, + TURF]

astute /əˈstjuːt/ *adj.* **1** shrewd; sagacious. **2** crafty. □□**astutely** *adv.* **astuteness** *n.* [obs. F *astut* or L *astutus* f. *astus* craft]

asunder /əˈsʌndə(r)/ *adv. literary* apart. [OE *on sundran* into pieces: cf. SUNDER]

asylum /əˈsaɪləm/ *n.* **1** sanctuary; protection, esp. for those pursued by the law (*seek asylum*). **2** *hist.* any of various kinds of institution offering shelter and support to distressed or destitute individuals, esp. the mentally ill. □**political asylum** protection given by a State to a political refugee from another country. [ME f. L f. Gk *asulon* refuge f. *a*- not + *sulon* right of seizure]

asymmetry /eɪˈsɪmɪtrɪ, æ'sɪmɪtrɪ/ *n.* lack of symmetry. □□**asymmetric** /-ˈmetrɪk/ *adj.* **asymmetrical** /-ˈmetrɪk(ə)l/ *adj.* **asymmetrically** /-ˈmetrɪkəlɪ/ *adv.* [Gk *asummetria* (as A-¹, SYMMETRY)]

asymptomatic /eɪˌsɪmptəˈmætɪk/ *adj.* producing or showing no symptoms.

asymptote /ˈæsɪmpˌtəʊt, ˈæsɪmˌtəʊt/ *n.* a line that continually approaches a given curve but does not meet it at a finite distance. □□**asymptotic** /ˌæsɪmpˈtɒtɪk/ *adj.* **asymptotically** /ˌæsɪmpˈtɒtɪkəlɪ/ *adv.* [mod.L *asymptota* (*linea* line) f. Gk *asumptōtos* not falling together f. *a*- not + *sun* together + *ptōtos* falling f. *piptō* fall]

asynchronous /eɪˈsɪŋkrənəs/ *adj.* not synchronous. □□**asynchronously** *adv.*

asyndeton /əˈsɪndɪt(ə)n/ *n.* (*pl.* **asyndeta** /-tə/) the omission of a conjunction. □□**asyndetic** /ˌæsɪnˈdetɪk/ *adj.* [mod.L f. Gk *asundeton* (neut. adj.) f. *a*- not + *sundetos* bound together]

At *symb. Chem.* the element astatine.

at /æt, *unstressed* ət/ *prep.* **1** expressing position, exact or approximate (*wait at the corner*; *at the top of the hill*; *met at Bath*; *is at school*; *at a distance*). **2** expressing a point in time (*see you at three*; *went at dawn*). **3** expressing a point in a scale or range (*at boiling-point*; *at his best*). **4** expressing engagement or concern in a state or activity (*at war*; *at work*; *at odds*). **5** expressing a value or rate (*sell at £10 each*). **6 a** with or with reference to; in terms of (*at a disadvantage*; *annoyed at losing*; *good at cricket*; *play at fighting*; *sick at heart*; *came at a run*; *at short notice*; *work at it*). **b** by means of (*starts at a touch*; *drank it at a gulp*). **7** expressing: **a** motion towards (*arrived at the station*; *went at them*). **b** aim towards or pursuit of (physically or conceptually) (*aim at the target*; *work at a solution*; *guess at the truth*; *laughed at us*; *has been at the milk again*). □**at all** see ALL. **at hand** see HAND. **at home** see HOME. **at it 1** engaged in an activity; working hard. **2** *colloq.* repeating a habitual (usu. disapproved of) activity (*found them at it again*). **at once** see ONCE. **at that** moreover (*found one, and a good one at that*). **at times** see TIME. **where it's at** *sl.* the fashionable scene or activity. [OE *æt*, rel. to L *ad* to]

at- /ət/ *prefix* assim. form of AD- before *t.*

Atabrine var. of ATEBRIN.

ataractic /ˌætəˈræktɪk/ *adj. & n.* (also **ataraxic** /-ˈræksɪk/) —*adj.* calming or tranquillizing. —*n.* a tranquillizing drug. [Gk *ataraktos* calm: cf. ATARAXY]

ataraxy /ˈætəˌræksɪ/ *n.* (also **ataraxia** /ˌætəˈræksɪə/) calmness or tranquillity; imperturbability. [F *ataraxie* f. Gk *ataraxia* impassiveness]

atavism /ˈætəˌvɪz(ə)m/ *n.* **1** a resemblance to remote ancestors rather than to parents in plants or animals. **2** reversion to an earlier type. □□**atavistic** /-ˈvɪstɪk/ *adj.* **atavistically** /-ˈvɪstɪkəlɪ/ *adv.* [F *atavisme* f. L *atavus* great-grandfather's grandfather]

ataxy /əˈtæksɪ/ *n.* (also **ataxia** /-sɪə/) *Med.* the loss of full control of bodily movements. □□**ataxic** *adj.* [mod.L *ataxia* f. Gk f. *a*- not + *taxis* order]

ATC *abbr. Brit.* **1** air traffic control. **2** Air Training Corps.

ate *past* of EAT.

-ate¹ /ət, eɪt/ *suffix* **1** forming nouns denoting: **a** status or office (*doctorate*; *episcopate*). **b** state or function (*curate*; *magistrate*; *mandate*). **2** *Chem.* forming nouns denoting the salt of an acid with a corresponding name ending in -*ic* (*chlorate*; *nitrate*). **3** forming nouns denoting a group (*electorate*). **4** *Chem.* forming nouns denoting a product (*condensate*; *filtrate*). [from or after OF -*at* or *é*(*e*) or f. L -*atus* noun or past part.: cf. -ATE²]

-ate² /ət, eɪt/ *suffix* **1** forming adjectives and nouns (*associate*; *delegate*; *duplicate*; *separate*). **2** forming adjectives from Latin or English nouns and adjectives (*cordate*; *insensate*; *Italianate*). [from or after (F -*é* f.) L -*atus* past part. of verbs in -*are*]

-ate³ /eɪt/ *suffix* forming verbs (*associate*; *duplicate*; *fascinate*; *hyphenate*; *separate*). [from or after (F -*er* f.) L -*are* (past part. -*atus*): cf. -ATE²]

Atebrin /ˈætəbrɪn/ *n.* (also **Atabrine** /-ˌbriːn/) *propr.* = QUINACRINE. [-ATE¹ 2 + BRINE]

atelier /əˈtelɪˌeɪ, ˈætəˌljeɪ/ *n.* a workshop or studio, esp. of an artist or designer. [F]

a tempo /ɑː ˈtempəʊ/ *adv. Mus.* in the previous tempo. [It., lit. 'in time']

Athanasian Creed /ˌæθəˈneɪʃ(ə)n/ *n.* an affirmation of Christian faith formerly thought to have been drawn up by Athanasius, bishop of Alexandria d. 373.

atheism /ˈeɪθɪˌɪz(ə)m/ *n.* the theory or belief that God does not exist. □□**atheist** *n.* **atheistic** /-ˈɪstɪk/ *adj.* **atheistical** /-ˈɪstɪk(ə)l/ *adj.* [F *athéisme* f. Gk *atheos* without God f. *a*- not + *theos* god]

atheling /ˈæθəlɪŋ/ *n. hist.* a prince or lord in Anglo-Saxon England. [OE *ætheling* = OHG *ediling* f. WG: see -ING³]

athematic /ˌæθɪˈmætɪk, ˌeɪ-/ *adj.* **1** *Mus.* not based on the use of themes. **2** *Gram.* (of a verb-form) having a suffix attached to the stem without a correcting (thematic) vowel.

athenaeum /ˌæθɪˈniːəm/ *n.* (*US* **atheneum**) **1** an institution for literary or scientific study. **2** a library. [LL *Athenaeum* f. Gk *Athēnaion* temple of Athene (used as a place of teaching)]

Athenian /əˈθiːnɪən/ *n. & adj.* —*n.* a native or inhabitant of ancient or modern Athens. —*adj.* of or relating to Athens. [L *Atheniensis* f. *Athenae* f. Gk *Athēnai* Athens, principal city of Greece]

atherosclerosis /ˌæθərəʊsklɪəˈrəʊsɪs/ *n.* a form of arteriosclerosis characterized by the degeneration of the arteries because of the build-up of fatty deposits. □□**atherosclerotic** /-ˈrɒtɪk/ *adj.* [G *Athero-sklerose* f. Gk *athērē* groats + SCLEROSIS]

athirst /əˈθɜːst/ *predic.adj. poet.* **1** (usu. foll. by *for*) eager (*athirst for knowledge*). **2** thirsty. [OE *ofthyrst* for *ofthyrsted* past part. of *ofthyrstan* be thirsty]

athlete /ˈæθliːt/ *n.* **1** a skilled performer in physical exercises, esp. in track and field events. **2** a healthy person with natural athletic ability. □**athlete's foot** a fungal foot condition affecting esp. the skin between the toes. [L *athleta* f. Gk *athlētēs* f. *athleō* contend for a prize (*athlon*)]

athletic /æθˈletɪk/ *adj.* **1** of or relating to athletes or athletics (*an athletic competition*). **2** muscular or physically powerful. □□**athletically** *adv.* **athleticism** /-ˈletɪˌsɪz(ə)m/ *n.* [F *athlétique* or L *athleticus* f. Gk *athlētikos* (as ATHLETE, -IC)]

athletics /æθˈletɪks/ *n.pl.* (usu. treated as *sing.*) **1 a** physical exercises, esp. track and field events. **b** the practice of these. **2** *US* physical sports and games of any kind.

athwart /əˈθwɔːt/ *adv. & prep.* —*adv.* **1** across from side to side (usu. obliquely). **2** perversely or in opposition. —*prep.* **1** from side to side of. **2** in opposition to. [A² + THWART]

-atic /ˈætɪk/ *suffix* forming adjectives and nouns (*aquatic*; *fanatic*; *idiomatic*). [F -*atique* or L -*aticus*, often ult. f. Gk -*atikos*]

atilt /əˈtɪlt/ *adv.* tilted and nearly falling. [A² + TILT]

-ation /ˈeɪʃ(ə)n/ *suffix* **1** forming nouns denoting an action or an instance of it (*alteration*; *flirtation*; *hesitation*). **2** forming nouns denoting a result or product of action (*plantation*; *starvation*; *vexation*) (see also -FICATION). [from or after F -*ation* or L -*atio* -*ationis* f. verbs in -*are*: see -ION]

-ative /ətɪv, eɪtɪv/ *suffix* forming adjectives denoting a characteristic or propensity (*authoritative*; *imitative*; *pejorative*; *qualitative*; *talkative*). [from or after F -*atif* -*ative* or f. L -*ativus* f. past part. stem -*at*- of verbs in -*are* + -*ivus* (see -IVE): cf. -ATIC]

Atlantean /ætˈlæntɪən/ *adj. literary* of or like Atlas, esp. in physical strength. [L *Atlanteus* (as ATLAS)]

atlantes /ətˈlæntiːz/ *n.pl. Archit.* male figures carved in stone and used as columns to support the entablature of a Greek or Greek-style building. [Gk, pl. of *Atlas*: see ATLAS]

Atlantic /ətˈlæntɪk/ *n. & adj.* —*n.* the ocean between Europe and Africa to the east, and America to the west. —*adj.* of or adjoining the Atlantic. □**Atlantic Time** the standard time used in the most eastern parts of Canada and Central America. [ME f. L *Atlanticus* f. Gk *Atlantikos* (as ATLAS, -IC): orig. of the Atlas Mountains, then of the sea near the W. African coast]

atlas /ˈætləs/ *n.* **1** a book of maps or charts. **2** *Anat.* the cervical vertebra of the backbone articulating with the skull at the neck. [L f. Gk *Atlas* -*antos* a Titan who held up the pillars of the universe, whose picture appeared at the beginning of early atlases]

atm *abbr. Physics* atmosphere(s).

atman /ˈɑːtmæn/ *n. Hinduism & Buddhism* **1** the real self. **2** the supreme spiritual principle. [Skr. *ātmán* essence, breath]

atmosphere /ˈætməsˌfɪə(r)/ *n.* **1 a** the envelope of gases surrounding the earth, any other planet, or any substance. **b** the air in any particular place, esp. if unpleasant. **2 a** the pervading tone or mood of a place or situation, esp. with reference to the feelings or emotions evoked. **b** the feelings or emotions evoked by a work of art, a piece of music, etc. **3** *Physics* a unit of pressure equal to mean atmospheric pressure at sea level, 101,325 pascals. ¶ Abbr.: **atm.** □□ **atmospheric** /-ˈferɪk/ *adj.* **atmospherical** /-ˈferɪk(ə)l/ *adj.* **atmospherically** /-ˈferɪkəlɪ/ *adv.* [mod.L *atmosphaera* f. Gk *atmos* vapour: see SPHERE]

atmospherics /ˌætməsˈferɪks/ *n.pl.* **1** electrical disturbance in the atmosphere, esp. caused by lightning. **2** interference with telecommunications caused by this.

atoll /ˈætɒl/ *n.* a ring-shaped coral reef enclosing a lagoon. [Maldive *atolu*]

atom /ˈætəm/ *n.* **1 a** the smallest particle of a chemical element that can take part in a chemical reaction. **b** this particle as a source of nuclear energy. **2** (usu. with *neg.*) the least portion of a thing or quality (*not an atom of pity*). □**atom bomb** a bomb involving the release of energy by nuclear fission = *fission bomb*. **atom-smasher** *colloq.* = ACCELERATOR 2. [ME f. OF *atome* f. L *atomus* f. Gk *atomos* indivisible]

atomic /əˈtɒmɪk/ *adj.* **1** concerned with or using atomic energy or atomic bombs. **2** of or relating to an atom or atoms. □**atomic bomb** = *atom bomb*. **atomic clock** a clock in which the periodic process (time scale) is regulated by the vibrations of an atomic or molecular system, such as caesium or ammonia. **atomic energy** nuclear energy. **atomic mass** the mass of an atom measured in atomic mass units. **atomic mass unit** a unit of mass used to express atomic and molecular weights that is equal to one twelfth of the mass of an atom of carbon-12. ¶ Abbr.: **amu**. **atomic number** the number of protons

in the nucleus of an atom, which is characteristic of a chemical element and determines its place in the periodic table. ¶ Symb.: Z. **atomic particle** any one of the particles of which an atom is constituted. **atomic philosophy** atomism. **atomic physics** the branch of physics concerned with the structure of the atom and the characteristics of the elementary particles of which it is composed. **atomic pile** a nuclear reactor. **atomic power** nuclear power. **atomic spectrum** the emission or absorption spectrum arising from electron transitions inside an atom and characteristic of the element. **atomic structure** the structure of an atom as being a central positively charged nucleus surrounded by negatively charged orbiting electrons. **atomic theory 1** the concept of an atom as being composed of elementary particles. **2** the theory that all matter is made up of small indivisible particles called atoms, and that the atoms of any one element are identical in all respects but differ from those of other elements and only unite to form compounds in fixed proportions. **3** *Philos.* atomism. **atomic warfare** warfare involving the use of atom bombs. **atomic weight** = *relative atomic mass*. □□ **atomically** *adv.* [mod.L *atomicus* (as ATOM, -IC)]

atomicity /ˌætəˈmɪsɪtɪ/ *n.* **1** the number of atoms in the molecules of an element. **2** the state or fact of being composed of atoms.

atomism /ˈætəˌmɪz(ə)m/ *n. Philos.* **1** the theory that all matter consists of tiny individual particles. **2** *Psychol.* the theory that mental states are made up of elementary units. □□ **atomist** *n.* **atomistic** /-ˈmɪstɪk/ *adj.*

atomize /ˌætəˈmaɪz/ *v.tr.* (also **-ise**) reduce to atoms or fine particles. □□ **atomization** /-ˈzeɪʃ(ə)n/ *n.*

atomizer /ˈætəˌmaɪzə(r)/ *n.* (also **-iser**) an instrument for emitting liquids as a fine spray.

atomy /ˈætəmɪ/ *n.* (*pl.* **-ies**) *archaic* **1** a skeleton. **2** an emaciated body. [ANATOMY taken as *an atomy*]

atonal /eɪˈtəʊn(ə)l, ə-/ *adj. Mus.* not written in any key or mode. □□ **atonality** /-ˈnælɪtɪ/ *n.*

atone /əˈtəʊn/ *v.intr.* (usu. foll. by *for*) make amends; expiate (for a wrong). [back-form. f. ATONEMENT]

atonement /əˈtəʊnmənt/ *n.* **1** expiation; reparation for a wrong or injury. **2** the reconciliation of God and man. □**the Atonement** the expiation by Christ of mankind's sin. **Day of Atonement** the most solemn religious fast of the Jewish year, eight days after the Jewish New Year. [*at one* + -MENT, after med.L *adunamentum* and earlier *onement* f. obs. *one* (v.) unite]

atonic /əˈtɒnɪk/ *adj.* **1** without accent or stress. **2** *Med.* lacking bodily tone. □□ **atony** /ˈætənɪ/ *n.*

atop /əˈtɒp/ *adv. & prep.* —*adv.* (often foll. by *of*) on the top. —*prep.* on the top of.

-ator /ˈeɪtə(r)/ *suffix* forming agent nouns, usu. from Latin words (sometimes via French) (*agitator*; *creator*; *equator*; *escalator*). See also -OR¹. [L -*ator*]

-atory /ətərɪ/ *suffix* forming adjectives meaning 'relating to or involving (a verbal action)' (*amatory*; *explanatory*; *predatory*). See also -ORY². [L -*atorius*]

ATP *abbr.* adenosine triphosphate.

atrabilious /ˌætrəˈbɪljəs/ *adj. literary* melancholy; ill-tempered. [L *atra bilis* black bile, transl. Gk *melagkholia* MELANCHOLY]

atrium /ˈeɪtrɪəm/ *n.* (*pl.* **atriums** or **atria** /-trɪə/) **1 a** the central court of an ancient Roman house. **b** a usu. skylit central court rising through several storeys with galleries and rooms opening off at each level. **c** esp. *US* (in a modern house) a central hall or glazed court with rooms opening off it. **2** *Anat.* a cavity in the body, esp. one of the two upper cavities of the heart, receiving blood from the veins. □□ **atrial** *adj.* [L]

atrocious /əˈtrəʊʃəs/ *adj.* **1** very bad or unpleasant (*atrocious weather*; *their manners were atrocious*). **2** extremely savage or wicked (*atrocious cruelty*). □□

atrociously *adv.* **atrociousness** *n.* [L *atrox -ocis* cruel]

atrocity /ə'trɒsɪtɪ/ *n.* (*pl.* **-ies**) **1** an extremely wicked or cruel act, esp. one involving physical violence or injury. **2** extreme wickedness. [F *atrocité* or L *atrocitas* (as ATROCIOUS, -ITY)]

atrophy /'ætrəfɪ/ *v. & n.* —*v.* (**-ies, -ied**) **1** *intr.* waste away through undernourishment, ageing, or lack of use; become emaciated. **2** *tr.* cause to atrophy. —*n.* the process of atrophying; emaciation. [F *atrophie* or LL *atrophia* f. Gk f. *a-* not + *trophē* food]

atropine /'ætrəˌpiːn, -pɪn/ *n.* a poisonous alkaloid found in deadly nightshade, used in medicine to treat renal and biliary colic etc. [mod.L *Atropa belladonna* deadly nightshade f. Gk *Atropos* inflexible, the name of one of the Fates]

attach /ə'tætʃ/ *v.* **1** *tr.* fasten, affix, join. **2** *tr.* (in *passive*; foll. by *to*) be very fond of or devoted to (*am deeply attached to her*). **3** *tr.* attribute, assign (some function, quality, or characteristic) (*can you attach a name to it?; attaches great importance to it*). **4 a** *tr.* accompany; form part of (*no conditions are attached*). **b** *intr.* (foll. by *to*) be an attribute or characteristic (*great prestige attaches to the job*). **5** *refl.* (usu. foll. by *to*) take part in; join (*attached themselves to the expedition*). **6** *tr.* appoint for special or temporary duties. **7** *tr. Law* seize (a person or property) by legal authority. □□ **attachable** *adj.* **attacher** *n.* [ME f. OF *estachier* fasten f. Gmc: in Law sense through OF *atachier*]

attaché /ə'tæʃeɪ/ *n.* a person appointed to an ambassador's staff, usu. with a special sphere of activity (*military attaché; press attaché*). □ **attaché case** a small flat rectangular case for carrying documents etc. [F, past part. of *attacher*: see ATTACH]

attachment /ə'tætʃmənt/ *n.* **1** a thing attached or to be attached, esp. to a machine, device, etc., for a special function. **2** affection, devotion. **3** a means of attaching. **4** the act of attaching or the state of being attached. **5** legal seizure. **6** a temporary position in, or secondment to, an organization. [ME f. F *attachement* f. *attacher* (as ATTACH, -MENT)]

attack /ə'tæk/ *v. & n.* —*v.* **1** *tr.* act against with (esp. armed) force. **2** *tr.* seek to hurt or defeat. **3** *tr.* criticize adversely. **4** *tr.* act harmfully upon (*a virus attacking the nervous system*). **5** *tr.* vigorously apply oneself to; begin work on (*attacked his meal with gusto*). **6** *intr.* make an attack. **7** *intr.* be in a mode of attack. —*n.* **1** the act or process of attacking. **2** an offensive operation or mode of behaviour. **3** *Mus.* the action or manner of beginning a piece, passage, etc. **4** gusto, vigour. **5** a sudden occurrence of an illness. **6** a player or players seeking to score goals etc. □□ **attacker** *n.* [F *attaque, attaquer* f. It. *attacco* attack, *attaccare* ATTACH]

attain /ə'teɪn/ *v.* **1** *tr.* arrive at; reach (a goal etc.). **2** *tr.* gain, accomplish (an aim, distinction, etc.). **3** *intr.* (foll. by *to*) arrive at by conscious development or effort. □□ **attainable** *adj.* **attainability** /-'bɪlɪtɪ/ *n.* **attainableness** *n.* [ME f. AF *atain-, atein-*, OF *ataign-* stem of *ataindre* f. L *attingere* (as AD-, *tangere* touch)]

attainder /ə'teɪndə(r)/ *n. hist.* the forfeiture of land and civil rights suffered as a consequence of a sentence of death for treason or felony. □ **act** (or **bill**) **of attainder** an item of legislation inflicting attainder without judicial process. [ME f. AF, = OF *ateindre* ATTAIN used as noun: see -ER⁶]

attainment /ə'teɪnmənt/ *n.* **1** (often in *pl.*) something attained or achieved; an accomplishment. **2** the act or an instance of attaining.

attaint /ə'teɪnt/ *v.tr.* **1** *hist.* subject to attainder. **2 a** (of disease etc.) strike, affect. **b** taint. [ME f. obs. *attaint* (adj.) f. OF *ataint, ateint* past part. formed as ATTAIN: confused in meaning with TAINT]

attar /'ætɑː(r)/ *n.* (also **otto** /'ɒtəʊ/) a fragrant essential oil, esp. from rose-petals. [Pers. *'atar* f. Arab. f. *'iṭr* perfume]

attempt /ə'tempt/ *v. & n.* —*v.tr.* **1** (often foll. by *to* + infin.) seek to achieve or complete (a task or action) (*attempted the exercise; attempted to explain*). **2** seek to climb or master (a mountain etc.). —*n.* (often foll. by *at, on,* or *to* + infin.) an act of attempting; an endeavour (*made an attempt at winning; an attempt to succeed; an attempt on his life*). □ **attempt the life of** *archaic* try to kill. □□ **attemptable** *adj.* [OF *attempter* f. L *attemptare* (as AD-, *temptare* TEMPT)]

attend /ə'tend/ *v.* **1** *tr.* **a** be present at (*attended the meeting*). **b** go regularly to (*attends the local school*). **2** *intr.* **a** be present (*many members failed to attend*). **b** be present in a serving capacity; wait. **3 a** *tr.* escort, accompany (*the king was attended by soldiers*). **b** *intr.* (foll. by *on*) wait on; serve. **4** *intr.* **a** (usu. foll. by *to*) turn or apply one's mind; focus one's attention (*attend to what I am saying; was not attending*). **b** (foll. by *to*) deal with (*shall attend to the matter myself*). **5** *tr.* (usu. in *passive*) follow as a result from (*the error was attended by serious consequences*). □□ **attender** *n.* [ME f. OF *atendre* f. L *attendere* (as AD-, *tendere tent-* stretch)]

attendance /ə'tend(ə)ns/ *n.* **1** the act of attending or being present. **2** the number of people present (*a high attendance*). □ **attendance allowance** (in the UK) a State benefit paid to disabled people in need of constant care at home. **attendance centre** *Brit.* a place where young offenders report by order of a court as a minor penalty. [ME f. OF *atendance* (as ATTEND, -ANCE)]

attendant /ə'tend(ə)nt/ *n. & adj.* —*n.* a person employed to wait on others or provide a service (*cloakroom attendant; museum attendant*). —*adj.* **1** accompanying (*attendant circumstances*). **2** waiting on; serving (*ladies attendant on the queen*). [ME f. OF (as ATTEND, -ANT)]

attendee /ˌæten'diː/ *n.* a person who attends (a meeting etc.).

attention /ə'tenʃ(ə)n/ *n. & int.* —*n.* **1** the act or faculty of applying one's mind (*give me your attention; attract his attention*). **2 a** consideration (*give attention to the problem*). **b** care (*give special attention to your handwriting*). **3** (in *pl.*) **a** ceremonious politeness (*he paid his attentions to her*). **b** wooing, courting (*she was the subject of his attentions*). **4** *Mil.* an erect attitude of readiness (*stand at attention*). —*int.* (in full **stand at attention!**) an order to assume an attitude of attention. [ME f. L *attentio* (as ATTEND, -ION)]

attentive /ə'tentɪv/ *adj.* **1** concentrating; paying attention. **2** assiduously polite. **3** heedful. □□ **attentively** *adv.* **attentiveness** *n.* [ME f. F *attentif -ive* f. *attente*, OF *atente*, fem. past part. of *atendre* ATTEND]

attenuate *v. & adj.* —*v.tr.* /ə'tenjʊˌeɪt/ **1** make thin. **2** reduce in force, value, or virulence. **3** *Electr.* reduce the amplitude of (a signal or current). —*adj.* /ə'tenjʊət/ **1** slender. **2** tapering gradually. **3** rarefied. □□ **attenuated** *adj.* **attenuation** /-'eɪʃ(ə)n/ *n.* **attenuator** *n.* [L *attenuare* (as AD-, *tenuis* thin)]

attest /ə'test/ *v.* **1** *tr.* certify the validity of. **2** *tr.* enrol (a recruit) for military service. **3** *intr.* (foll. by *to*) bear witness to. **4** *intr.* enrol oneself for military service. □□ **attestable** *adj.* **attestor** *n.* [F *attester* f. L *attestari* (as AD-, *testis* witness)]

attestation /ˌæte'steɪʃ(ə)n/ *n.* **1** the act of attesting. **2** a testimony. [F *attestation* or LL *attestatio* (as ATTEST, -ATION)]

Attic /'ætɪk/ *adj. & n.* —*adj.* of ancient Athens or Attica, or the form of Greek spoken there. —*n.* the form of Greek used by the ancient Athenians. □ **Attic salt** (or **wit**) refined wit. [L *Atticus* f. Gk *Attikos*]

attic /'ætɪk/ *n.* **1** the uppermost storey in a house, usu. under the roof. **2** a room in the attic area. [F *attique*, as ATTIC: orig. (Archit.) a small order above a taller one]

atticism /'ætɪˌsɪz(ə)m/ *n.* **1** extreme elegance of

speech. **2** an instance of this. [Gk *Attikismos* (as ATTIC, -ISM)]

attire /ə'taɪə(r)/ *v. & n. formal* —*v.tr.* dress, esp. in fine clothes or formal wear. —*n.* clothes, esp. fine or formal. [ME f. OF *atir(i)er* equip f. *à tire* in order, of unkn. orig.]

attitude /'ætɪˌtjuːd/ *n.* **1 a** a settled opinion or way of thinking. **b** behaviour reflecting this (*I don't like his attitude*). **2 a** a bodily posture. **b** a pose adopted in a painting or a play, esp. for dramatic effect (*strike an attitude*). **3** the position of an aircraft, spacecraft, etc., in relation to specified directions. □ **attitude of mind** a settled way of thinking. □□ **attitudinal** /ˌætɪ'tjuːdɪn(ə)l/ *adj.* [F f. It. *attitudine* fitness, posture, f. LL *aptitudo -dinis* f. *aptus* fit]

attitudinize /ˌætɪ'tjuːdɪˌnaɪz/ *v.intr.* (also -**ise**) **1** practise or adopt attitudes, esp. for effect. **2** speak, write, or behave affectedly. [It. *attitudine* f. LL (as ATTITUDE) + -IZE]

attn. *abbr.* **1** attention. **2** for the attention of.

atto- /'ætəʊ/ *comb. form Math.* denoting a factor of 10^{-18} (*attometre*). [Da. or Norw. *atten* eighteen + -o-]

attorney /ə'tɜːnɪ/ *n.* (*pl.* -**eys**) **1** a person, esp. a lawyer, appointed to act for another in business or legal matters. **2** *US* a qualified lawyer, esp. one representing a client in a lawcourt. □ **Attorney General** the chief legal officer in England, the US, and other countries. **District Attorney** see DISTRICT. **power of attorney** the authority to act for another person in legal or financial matters. □□ **attorneyship** *n.* [ME f. OF *atorné* past part. of *atorner* assign f. *à* to + *torner* turn]

attract /ə'trækt/ *v.tr.* **1** (also *absol.*) draw or bring to oneself or itself (*attracts many admirers*; *attracts attention*). **2** be attractive to; fascinate. **3** (of a magnet, gravity, etc.) exert a pull on (an object). □□ **attractable** *adj.* **attractor** *n.* [L *attrahere* (as AD-, *trahere tract-* draw)]

attractant /ə'trækt(ə)nt/ *n. & adj.* —*n.* a substance which attracts (esp. insects). —*adj.* attracting.

attraction /ə'trækʃ(ə)n/ *n.* **1 a** the act or power of attracting (*the attraction of foreign travel*). **b** a person or thing that attracts by arousing interest (*the fair is a big attraction*). **2** *Physics* the force by which bodies attract or approach each other (opp. REPULSION). **3** *Gram.* the influence exerted by one word on another which causes it to change to an incorrect form, e.g. *the wages of sin is death*. [F *attraction* or L *attractio* (as ATTRACT, -ION)]

attractive /ə'træktɪv/ *adj.* **1** attracting or capable of attracting; interesting (*an attractive proposition*). **2** aesthetically pleasing or appealing. □□ **attractively** *adv.* **attractiveness** *n.* [F *attractif -ive* f. LL *attractivus* (as ATTRACT, -IVE)]

attribute *v. & n.* —*v.tr.* /ə'trɪbjuːt/ (usu. foll. by *to*) **1** regard as belonging or appropriate to (*a poem attributed to Shakespeare*). **2** ascribe to; regard as the effect of a stated cause (*the delays were attributed to the heavy traffic*). —*n.* /'ætrɪˌbjuːt/ **1 a** a quality ascribed to a person or thing. **b** a characteristic quality. **2** a material object recognized as appropriate to a person, office, or status (*a large car is an attribute of seniority*). **3** *Gram.* an attributive adjective or noun. □□ **attributable** /ə'trɪbjʊtəb(ə)l/ *adj.* **attribution** /ˌætrɪ'bjuːʃ(ə)n/ *n.* [ME f. L *attribuere attribut-* (as AD-, *tribuere* assign): (n.) f. OF *attribut* or L *attributum*]

attributive /ə'trɪbjʊtɪv/ *adj. Gram.* (of an adjective or noun) preceding the word described and expressing an attribute, as *old* in *the old dog* (but not in *the dog is old*) and *expiry* in *expiry date* (opp. PREDICATIVE). □□ **attributively** *adv.* [F *attributif -ive* (as ATTRIBUTE, -IVE)]

attrition /ə'trɪʃ(ə)n/ *n.* **1 a** the act or process of gradually wearing out, esp. by friction. **b** abrasion. **2** *Theol.* sorrow for sin, falling short of contrition. □ **war of attrition** a war in which one side wins by gradually wearing the other down with repeated attacks etc. □□ **attritional** *adj.* [ME f. LL *attritio* f. *atterere attrit-* rub]

attune /ə'tjuːn/ *v.tr.* **1** (usu. foll. by *to*) adjust (a person or thing) to a situation. **2** bring (an orchestra, instrument, etc.) into musical accord. [AT- + TUNE]

Atty. *abbr.* Attorney.

atypical /eɪ'tɪpɪk(ə)l/ *adj.* not typical; not conforming to a type. □□ **atypically** *adv.*

AU *abbr.* **1** (also **au.**) astronomical unit. **2** ångström unit.

Au *symb. Chem.* the element gold. [L *aurum*]

aubade /əʊ'bɑːd/ *n.* a poem or piece of music appropriate to the dawn or early morning. [F f. Sp. *albada* f. *alba* dawn]

auberge /əʊ'beəʒ/ *n.* an inn. [F]

aubergine /'əʊbəˌʒiːn/ *n.* **1** a tropical plant, *Solanum melongena*, having erect or spreading branches bearing white or purple egg-shaped fruit. **2** this fruit eaten as a vegetable. Also called EGGPLANT. **3** the dark purple colour of this fruit. [F f. Cat. *alberginia* f. Arab. *al-bādinjān* f. Pers. *bādingān* f. Skr. *vātiṃgaṇa*]

aubrietia /ɔː'briːʃə/ *n.* (also **aubretia**) any dwarf perennial rock-plant of the genus *Aubrieta*, having purple or pink flowers in spring. [mod.L f. Claude *Aubriet*, Fr. botanist d. 1743]

auburn /'ɔːbən/ *adj.* reddish brown (usu. of a person's hair). [ME, orig. yellowish white, f. OF *auborne*, *alborne*, f. L *alburnus* whitish f. *albus* white]

AUC *abbr.* (of a date) from the foundation of the city (of Rome). [L *ab urbe condita*]

au courant /ˌəʊ kuː'rɑ̃/ *predic.adj.* (usu. foll. by *with*, *of*) knowing what is going on; well-informed. [F, = in the (regular) course]

auction /'ɔːkʃ(ə)n/ *n. & v.* —*n.* a sale of goods, usu. in public, in which articles are sold to the highest bidder. —*v.tr.* sell by auction. □ **auction bridge 1** a form of bridge in which players bid for the right to name trumps. **2** the sequence of bids made at bridge. **Dutch auction** a sale, usu. public, of goods in which the price is reduced by the auctioneer until a buyer is found. [L *auctio* increase, auction f. *augēre auct-* increase]

auctioneer /ˌɔːkʃə'nɪə(r)/ *n.* a person who conducts auctions professionally, by calling for bids and declaring goods sold. □□ **auctioneering** *n.*

audacious /ɔː'deɪʃəs/ *adj.* **1** daring, bold. **2** impudent. □□ **audaciously** *adv.* **audaciousness** *n.* **audacity** /ɔː'dæsɪtɪ/ *n.* [L *audax -acis* bold f. *audēre* dare]

audible /'ɔːdɪb(ə)l/ *adj.* capable of being heard. □□ **audibility** /-'bɪlɪtɪ/ *n.* **audibleness** *n.* **audibly** *adv.* [LL *audibilis* f. *audire* hear]

audience /'ɔːdɪəns/ *n.* **1 a** the assembled listeners or spectators at an event, esp. a stage performance, concert, etc. **b** the people addressed by a film, book, play, etc. **2** a formal interview with a person in authority. **3** *archaic* a hearing (*give audience to my plea*). [ME f. OF f. L *audientia* f. *audire* hear]

audile /'ɔːdaɪl/ *adj.* of or referring to the sense of hearing. [irreg. f. L *audire* hear, after *tactile*]

audio /'ɔːdɪəʊ/ *n.* (usu. *attrib.*) sound or the reproduction of sound. □ **audio frequency** a frequency capable of being perceived by the human ear. **audio typist** a person who types direct from a recording. [AUDIO-]

audio- /'ɔːdɪəʊ/ *comb. form* hearing or sound. [L *audire* hear + -o-]

audiology /ˌɔːdɪ'ɒlədʒɪ/ *n.* the science of hearing. □□ **audiologist** *n.*

audiometer /ˌɔːdɪ'ɒmɪtə(r)/ *n.* an instrument for testing hearing.

audiophile /'ɔːdɪəʊˌfaɪl/ *n.* a hi-fi enthusiast.

audiotape /'ɔːdɪəʊˌteɪp/ *n. & v.* —*n.* **1 a** magnetic tape on which sound can be recorded. **b** a length of this. **2** a sound recording on tape. —*v.tr.* record (sound, speech, etc.) on tape.

audiovisual /ˌɔːdɪəʊ'vɪʒʊəl/ *adj.* (esp. of teaching methods) using both sight and sound.

æ *cat* ɑː *arm* e *bed* ɜː *her* ɪ *sit* iː *see* ɒ *hot* ɔː *saw* ʌ *run* ʊ *put* uː *too* ə *ago* aɪ *my*

audit /'ɔːdɪt/ n. & v. —n. an official examination of accounts. —v.tr. (**audited, auditing**) **1** conduct an audit of. **2** US attend (a class) informally, without working for credits. [ME f. L *auditus* hearing f. *audire* audit- hear]

audition /ɔː'dɪʃ(ə)n/ n. & v. —n. **1** an interview for a role as a singer, actor, dancer, etc., consisting of a practical demonstration of suitability. **2** the power of hearing or listening. —v. **1** tr. interview (a candidate at an audition). **2** intr. be interviewed at an audition. [F *audition* or L *auditio* f. *audire* audit- hear]

auditive /'ɔːdɪtɪv/ adj. concerned with hearing. [F *auditif* -*ive* (as AUDITION, -IVE)]

auditor /'ɔːdɪtə(r)/ n. **1** a person who audits accounts. **2** a listener. □□ **auditorial** /-'tɔːrɪəl/ adj. [ME f. AF *auditour* f. L *auditor* -*oris* (as AUDITIVE, -OR¹)]

auditorium /ˌɔːdɪ'tɔːrɪəm/ n. (pl. **auditoriums** or **auditoria** /-rɪə/) the part of a theatre etc. in which the audience sits. [L neut. of *auditorius* (adj.): see AUDITORY, -ORIUM]

auditory /'ɔːdɪtərɪ/ adj. **1** concerned with hearing. **2** received by the ear. [L *auditorius* (as AUDITOR, -ORY²)]

AUEW abbr. (in the UK) Amalgamated Union of Engineering Workers.

au fait /əʊ 'feɪ/ predic.adj. (usu. foll. by *with*) having current knowledge; conversant (*fully au fait with the arrangements*). □ **put** (or **make**) *au fait* **with** instruct in. [F]

au fond /əʊ 'fɔ̃/ adv. basically; at bottom. [F]

Aug. abbr. August.

Augean /ɔː'dʒiːən/ adj. filthy; extremely dirty. [L *Augeas* f. Gk *Augeias* (in Gk mythology, the owner of stables cleaned by Hercules by diverting a river through them)]

auger /'ɔːgə(r)/ n. **1** a tool resembling a large corkscrew, for boring holes in wood. **2** a similar larger tool for boring holes in the ground. [OE *nafogār* f. *nafu* NAVE², + *gār* pierce: for loss of *n* cf. ADDER]

aught¹ /ɔːt/ n. (also **ought**) archaic (usu. implying neg.) anything at all. [OE *āwiht* f. Gmc]

aught² var. of OUGHT².

augite /'ɔːdʒaɪt/ n. Mineral. a complex calcium magnesium aluminous silicate occurring in many igneous rocks. [L *augites* f. Gk *augitēs* f. *augē* lustre]

augment v. & n. —v.tr. & intr. /ɔːg'ment/ make or become greater; increase. —n. /'ɔːgment/ Gram. a vowel prefixed to the past tenses in the older Indo-European languages. □ **augmented interval** Mus. a perfect or major interval that is increased by a semitone. □□ **augmenter** n. [ME f. OF *augment* (n.), F *augmenter* (v.), or LL *augmentum, augmentare* f. L *augēre* increase]

augmentation /ˌɔːgmen'teɪʃ(ə)n/ n. **1** enlargement; growth; increase. **2** Mus. the lengthening of the time-values of notes in melodic parts. [ME f. F f. LL *augmentatio -onis* f. *augmentare* (as AUGMENT)]

augmentative /ɔːg'mentətɪv/ adj. **1** having the property of increasing. **2** Gram. (of an affix or derived word) reinforcing the idea of the original word. [F *augmentatif -ive* or med.L *augmentativus* (as AUGMENT)]

au gratin /ˌəʊ græ'tæ̃/ adj. Cookery cooked with a crisp brown crust usu. of breadcrumbs or melted cheese. [F f. *gratter*, = by grating, f. GRATE¹]

augur /'ɔːgə(r)/ v. & n. —v. **1** tr. **a** (of an event, circumstance, etc.) suggest a specified outcome (usu. *augur well* or *ill*). **b** portend, bode (*all augured well for our success*). **2** tr. **a** foresee, predict. **b** portend. —n. a Roman religious official who observed natural signs, esp. the behaviour of birds, interpreting these as an indication of divine approval or disapproval of a proposed action. □□ **augural** adj. [L]

augury /'ɔːgjərɪ/ n. (pl. **-ies**) **1** an omen; a portent. **2** the work of an augur; the interpretation of omens. [ME f. OF *augurie* or L *augurium* f. AUGUR]

August /'ɔːgəst/ n. the eighth month of the year. [OE f. L *Augustus* Caesar, the first Roman emperor]

august /ɔː'gʌst/ adj. inspiring reverence and admiration; venerable; impressive. □□ **augustly** adv. **augustness** n. [F *auguste* or L *augustus* consecrated, venerable]

Augustan /ɔː'gʌst(ə)n/ adj. & n. —adj. **1** connected with, occurring during, or influenced by the reign of the Roman emperor Augustus, esp. as an outstanding period of Latin literature. **2** (of a nation's literature) refined and classical in style (in England of the literature of the 17th-18th c.). —n. a writer of the Augustan age of any literature. [L *Augustanus* f. *Augustus*]

Augustine /ɔː'gʌstiːn/ n. an Augustinian friar. [ME f. OF *augustin* f. L *Augustinus*: see AUGUSTINIAN]

Augustinian /ˌɔːgə'stɪnɪən/ adj. & n. —adj. **1** of or relating to St Augustine, a Doctor of the Church (d. 430), or his doctrines. **2** belonging to a religious order observing a rule derived from St Augustine's writings. —n. **1** an adherent of the doctrines of St Augustine. **2** one of the order of Augustinian friars. [L *Augustinus* Augustine]

auk /ɔːk/ n. any sea diving-bird of the family Alcidae, with heavy body, short wings, and black and white plumage, e.g. the guillemot, puffin, and razorbill. □ **great auk** an extinct flightless auk, *Alca impennis*. **little auk** a small arctic auk, *Plautus alle*. [ON *álka*]

auld /ɔːld/ adj. Sc. old. [OE *ald*, Anglian form of OLD]

auld lang syne /ˌɔːld læŋ 'saɪn/ n. times long past. [Sc., = old long since: also as the title and refrain of a song]

aumbry /'ɔːmbrɪ/ n. (also **ambry** /'æmbrɪ/) (pl. **-ies**) **1** a small recess in the wall of a church. **2** hist. a small cupboard. [ME f. OF *almarie, armarie* f. L *armarium* closet, chest f. *arma* utensils]

au naturel /ˌəʊ nætjə'rel, -tju:'rel/ predic.adj. & adv. Cookery uncooked; (cooked) in the most natural or simplest way. [F, = in the natural state]

aunt /ɑːnt/ n. **1** the sister of one's father or mother. **2** an uncle's wife. **3** colloq. an unrelated woman friend of a child or children. □ **Aunt Sally 1** a game in which players throw sticks or balls at a wooden dummy. **2** the object of an unreasonable attack. **my** (or **my sainted** etc.) **aunt** sl. an exclamation of surprise, disbelief, etc. [ME f. AF *aunte*, OF *ante*, f. L *amita*]

auntie /'ɑːntɪ/ n. (also **aunty**) (pl. **-ies**) colloq. **1** = AUNT. **2** (**Auntie**) an institution considered to be conservative or cautious, esp. the BBC.

au pair /əʊ 'peə(r)/ n. a young foreign person, esp. a woman, helping with housework etc. in exchange for room, board, and pocket money, esp. as a means of learning a language. [F]

aura /'ɔːrə/ n. (pl. **aurae** /-riː/ or **auras**) **1** the distinctive atmosphere diffused by or attending a person, place, etc. **2** (in mystic or spiritualistic use) a supposed subtle emanation, visible as a sphere of white or coloured light, surrounding the body of a living creature. **3** a subtle emanation or aroma from flowers etc. **4** Med. premonitory symptom(s) in epilepsy etc. □□ **aural** adj. **auric** adj. [ME f. L f. Gk, = breeze, breath]

aural /'ɔːr(ə)l/ adj. of or relating to or received by the ear. □□ **aurally** adv. [L *auris* ear]

aureate /'ɔːrɪət/ adj. **1** golden, gold-coloured. **2** resplendent. **3** (of a language) highly ornamented. [ME f. LL *aureatus* f. L *aureus* golden f. *aurum* gold]

aureole /'ɔːrɪˌəʊl/ n. (also **aureola** /ɔː'rɪələ/) **1** a halo or circle of light, esp. round the head or body of a portrayed religious figure. **2** a corona round the sun or moon. [ME f. L *aureola* (*corona*), = golden (crown), fem. of *aureolus* f. *aureus* f. *aurum* gold: *aureole* f. OF f. L *aureola*]

aureomycin /ˌɔːrɪəʊ'maɪsɪn/ n. an antibiotic used esp. in lung diseases. [L *aureus* golden + Gk *mukēs* fungus + -IN]

au revoir /əʊ rə'vwɑː(r)/ int. & n. goodbye (until we meet again). [F]

auric /'ɔːrɪk/ *adj.* of or relating to trivalent gold. [L *aurum* gold]

auricle /'ɔːrɪk(ə)l/ *n. Anat.* **1 a** a small muscular pouch on the surface of each atrium of the heart. **b** the atrium itself. **2** the external ear of animals. Also called PINNA. **3** an appendage shaped like the ear. [AURICULA]

auricula /ɔːˈrɪkjʊlə/ *n.* a primula, *Primula auricula*, with leaves shaped like bears' ears. [L, dimin. of *auris* ear]

auricular /ɔːˈrɪkjʊlə(r)/ *adj.* **1** of or relating to the ear or hearing. **2** of or relating to the auricle of the heart. **3** shaped like an auricle. □□ **auricularly** *adv.* [LL *auricularis* (as AURICULA)]

auriculate /ɔːˈrɪkjʊlət/ *adj.* having one or more auricles or ear-shaped appendages. [L]

auriferous /ɔːˈrɪfərəs/ *adj.* naturally bearing gold. [L *aurifer* f. *aurum* gold]

Aurignacian /ˌɔːrɪgˈneɪʃ(ə)n/ *n. & adj.* —*n.* a flint culture of the palaeolithic period in Europe following the Mousterian and preceding the Solutrean. —*adj.* of this culture. [F *Aurignacien* f. *Aurignac* in SW France, where remains of it were found]

aurochs /'ɔːrɒks, 'aʊrɒks/ *n.* (*pl.* same) an extinct wild ox, *Bos primigenius*, ancestor of domestic cattle and formerly native to many parts of the world. Also called URUS. [G f. OHG *ūrohso* f. *ūr*- urus + *ohso* ox]

aurora /ɔːˈrɔːrə/ *n.* (*pl.* **auroras** or **aurorae** /-riː/) **1 a** luminous electrical atmospheric phenomenon, usu. of streamers of light in the sky above the northern or southern magnetic pole. **2** *poet.* the dawn. □**aurora australis** /ɔːˈstreɪlɪs/ a southern occurrence of aurora. **aurora borealis** /ˌbɒrɪˈeɪlɪs/ a northern occurrence of aurora. □□ **auroral** *adj.* [L, = dawn, goddess of dawn]

auscultation /ˌɔːskəlˈteɪʃ(ə)n/ *n.* the act of listening, esp. to sounds from the heart, lungs, etc., as a part of medical diagnosis. □□ **auscultatory** /-ˈkʌltətəri/ *adj.* [L *auscultatio* f. *auscultare* listen to]

auspice /'ɔːspɪs/ *n.* **1** (in *pl.*) patronage (esp. *under the auspices of*). **2** a forecast. [orig. 'observation of bird-flight in divination': F *auspice* or L *auspicium* f. *auspex* observer of birds f. *avis* bird]

auspicious /ɔːˈspɪʃəs/ *adj.* **1** of good omen; favourable. **2** prosperous. □□ **auspiciously** *adv.* **auspiciousness** *n.* [AUSPICE + -OUS]

Aussie /'ɒzɪ, 'ɒsɪ/ *n. & adj.* (also **Ossie, Ozzie**) *colloq.* —*n.* **1** an Australian. **2** Australia. —*adj.* Australian. [abbr.]

austere /ɒˈstɪə(r), ɔːˈstɪə(r)/ *adj.* (**austerer, austerest**) **1** severely simple. **2** morally strict. **3** harsh, stern. □□ **austerely** *adv.* [ME f. OF f. L *austerus* f. Gk *austēros* severe]

austerity /ɒˈsterɪtɪ, ɔːˈsterɪtɪ/ *n.* (*pl.* **-ies**) **1** sternness; moral severity. **2** severe simplicity, e.g. of nationwide economies. **3** (esp. in *pl.*) an austere practice (*the austerities of a monk's life*).

Austin /'ɒstɪn, 'ɔːstɪn/ *n.* = AUGUSTINIAN. [contr. of AUGUSTINE]

austral /'ɔːstr(ə)l, 'ɒstr(ə)l/ *adj.* **1** southern. **2** (**Austral**) of Australia or Australasia (*Austral English*). [ME f. L *australis* f. *Auster* south wind]

Australasian /ˌɒstrəˈleɪʒ(ə)n, -ʃ(ə)n/ *adj.* of or relating to Australasia, a region consisting of Australia and islands of the SW Pacific. [*Australasia* f. F *Australasie*, formed as *Australia* + *Asia*]

Australian /ɒˈstreɪlɪən/ *n. & adj.* —*n.* **1** a native or national of Australia. **2** a person of Australian descent. —*adj.* of or relating to Australia. □ **Australian bear** a koala bear. **Australian Rules** a form of football played with a Rugby ball by teams of 18. **Australian terrier** a wire-haired Australian breed of terrier. □□ **Australianism** *n.* [F *australien* f. L (as AUSTRAL)]

Australopithecus /ˌɒstrələʊˈpɪθɪkəs/ *n.* any extinct bipedal primate of the genus *Australopithecus* having apelike and human characteristics, or its fossilized remains. □□ **australopithecine** /-ɪˌsiːn/ *n. & adj.* [mod.L f. L *australis* southern + Gk *pithēkos* ape]

Austro- /'ɒstrəʊ/ *comb. form* Austrian; Austrian and (*Austro-Hungarian*).

AUT *abbr.* (in the UK) Association of University Teachers.

autarchy /'ɔːtɑːkɪ/ *n.* (*pl.* **-ies**) **1** absolute sovereignty. **2** despotism. **3** an autarchic country or society. □□ **autarchic** /ɔːˈtɑːkɪk/ *adj.* **autarchical** /ɔːˈtɑːkɪk(ə)l/ *adj.* [mod.L *autarchia* (as AUTO-, Gk *-arkhia* f. *arkhō* rule)]

autarky /'ɔːtɑːkɪ/ *n.* (*pl.* **-ies**) **1** self-sufficiency, esp. as an economic system. **2** a state etc. run according to such a system. □□ **autarkic** /ɔːˈtɑːkɪk/ *adj.* **autarkical** /ɔːˈtɑːkɪk(ə)l/ *adj.* **autarkist** *n.* [Gk *autarkeia* (as AUTO-, *arkeō* suffice)]

authentic /ɔːˈθentɪk/ *adj.* **1 a** of undisputed origin; genuine. **b** reliable or trustworthy. **2** *Mus.* (of a mode) containing notes between the final and an octave higher (cf. PLAGAL). □□ **authentically** *adv.* **authenticity** /ˌɔːθenˈtɪsɪtɪ/ *n.* [ME f. OF *autentique* f. LL *authenticus* f. Gk *authentikos* principal, genuine]

authenticate /ɔːˈθentɪkeɪt/ *v.tr.* **1** establish the truth or genuineness of. **2** validate. □□ **authentication** /-ˈkeɪʃ(ə)n/ *n.* **authenticator** *n.* [med.L *authenticare* f. LL *authenticus*: see AUTHENTIC]

author /'ɔːθə(r)/ *n. & v.* —*n.* (*fem.* **authoress** /'ɔːθrɪs, ˌɔːθəˈres/) **1** a writer, esp. of books. **2** the originator of an event, a condition, etc. (*the author of all my woes*). —*v.tr. disp.* be the author of (a book, the universe, a child, etc.). □□ **authorial** /ɔːˈθɔːrɪəl/ *adj.* [ME f. AF *autour*, OF *autor* f. L *auctor* f. *augēre auct*- increase, originate, promote]

authoritarian /ɔːˌθɒrɪˈteərɪən/ *adj. & n.* —*adj.* **1** favouring, encouraging, or enforcing strict obedience to authority, as opposed to individual freedom. **2** tyrannical or domineering. —*n.* a person favouring absolute obedience to a constituted authority. □□ **authoritarianism** *n.*

authoritative /ɔːˈθɒrɪtətɪv/ *adj.* **1** being recognized as true or dependable. **2** (of a person, behaviour, etc.) commanding or self-confident. **3** official; supported by authority (*an authoritative document*). □□ **authoritatively** *adv.* **authoritativeness** *n.*

authority /ɔːˈθɒrɪtɪ/ *n.* (*pl.* **-ies**) **1 a** the power or right to enforce obedience. **b** (often foll. by *for*, or *to* + infin.) delegated power. **2** (esp. in *pl.*) a person or body having authority, esp. political or administrative. **3 a** an influence exerted on opinion because of recognized knowledge or expertise. **b** such an influence expressed in a book, quotation, etc. (*an authority on vintage cars*). **c** a person whose opinion is accepted, esp. an expert in a subject. **4** the weight of evidence. [ME f. OF *autorité* f. L *auctoritas* f. *auctor*: see AUTHOR]

authorize /'ɔːθəˌraɪz/ *v.tr.* (also **-ise**) **1** sanction. **2** (foll. by *to* + infin.) **a** give authority. **b** commission (a person or body) (*authorized to trade*). □ **Authorized Version** an English translation of the Bible made in 1611 and traditionally used in Anglican worship. □□ **authorization** /ˌɔːθəraɪˈzeɪʃ(ə)n/ *n.* [ME f. OF *autoriser* f. med.L *auctorizare* f. *auctor*: see AUTHOR]

authorship /'ɔːθəʃɪp/ *n.* **1** the origin of a book or other written work (*of unknown authorship*). **2** the occupation of writing.

autism /'ɔːtɪz(ə)m/ *n. Psychol.* a mental condition, usu. present from childhood, characterized by complete self-absorption and a reduced ability to respond to or communicate with the outside world. □□ **autistic** /ɔːˈtɪstɪk/ *adj.* [mod.L *autismus* (as AUTO-, -ISM)]

auto /'ɔːtəʊ/ *n.* (*pl.* **-os**) *US colloq.* a motor car. [abbr. of AUTOMOBILE]

auto- /'ɔːtəʊ/ *comb. form* (usu. **aut-** before a vowel) **1** self (*autism*). **2** one's own (*autobiography*). **3** by oneself or spontaneous (*auto-suggestion*). **4** by itself or automatic (*automobile*). [from or after Gk *auto-* f. *autos* self]

autobahn /'ɔːtəʊˌbɑːn/ n. (pl. **autobahns** or **autobahnen** /-nən/) a German, Austrian, or Swiss motorway. [G f. *Auto* motor car + *Bahn* path, road]

autobiography /ˌɔːtəʊbaɪ'ɒɡrəfɪ/ n. (pl. **-ies**) 1 a personal account of one's own life, esp. for publication. 2 this as a process or literary form. □□ **autobiographer** n. **autobiographic** /ˌɔːtəʊˌbaɪə'ɡræfɪk/ adj. **autobiographical** /-'ɡræfɪk(ə)l/ adj.

autocade /'ɔːtəʊˌkeɪd/ n. US a motorcade. ¶ *Motorcade* is more usual. [AUTOMOBILE + CAVALCADE]

autocar /'ɔːtəʊˌkɑː(r)/ n. archaic a motor vehicle.

autocephalous /ˌɔːtəʊ'sefələs/ adj. 1 (esp. of an Eastern Church) appointing its own head. 2 (of a bishop, Church, etc.) independent. [Gk *autokephalos* (as AUTO-, *kephalē* head)]

autochthon /ɔː'tɒkθ(ə)n/ n. (pl. **autochthons** or **autochthones** /-θəˌniːz/) (in pl.) the original or earliest known inhabitants of a country; aboriginals. □□ **autochthonal** adj. **autochthonic** /-'θɒnɪk/ adj. **autochthonous** adj. [Gk, = sprung from the earth (as AUTO-, *khthōn*, *-onos* earth)]

autoclave /'ɔːtəˌkleɪv/ n. 1 a strong vessel used for chemical reactions at high pressures and temperatures. 2 a sterilizer using high-pressure steam. [AUTO- + L *clavus* nail or *clavis* key]

autocracy /ɔː'tɒkrəsɪ/ n. (pl. **-ies**) 1 absolute government by one person. 2 the power exercised by such a person. 3 an autocratic country or society. [Gk *autokrateia* (as AUTOCRAT)]

autocrat /'ɔːtəˌkræt/ n. 1 an absolute ruler. 2 a dictatorial person. □□ **autocratic** /-'krætɪk/ adj. **autocratically** /-'krætɪkəlɪ/ adv. [F *autocrate* f. Gk *autokratēs* (as AUTO-, *kratos* power)]

autocross /'ɔːtəʊˌkrɒs/ n. motor-racing across country or on unmade roads. [AUTOMOBILE + CROSS- 1]

Autocue /'ɔːtəʊˌkjuː/ n. propr. a device, unseen by the audience, displaying a television script to a speaker or performer as an aid to memory (cf. TELE-PROMPTER).

auto-da-fé /ˌɔːtəʊdɑː'feɪ/ n. (pl. **autos-da-fé** /ˌɔːtəʊz-/ 1 a sentence of punishment by the Spanish Inquisition. 2 the execution of such a sentence, esp. the burning of a heretic. [Port., = act of the faith]

autodidact /'ɔːtəʊˌdaɪdækt/ n. a self-taught person. □□ **autodidactic** /-'dæktɪk/ adj. [AUTO- + *didact* as DIDACTIC]

auto-erotism /ˌɔːtəʊ'erəˌtɪz(ə)m/ n. (also **auto-eroticism** /-ɪ'rɒtɪˌsɪz(ə)m/) Psychol. sexual excitement generated by stimulating one's own body; masturbation. □□ **auto-erotic** /-ɪ'rɒtɪk/ adj.

autofocus /'ɔːtəʊˌfəʊkəs/ n. a device for focusing a camera etc. automatically.

autogamy /ɔː'tɒɡəmɪ/ n. Bot. self-fertilization in plants. □□ **autogamous** adj. [AUTO- + Gk *-gamia* f. *gamos* marriage]

autogenous /ɔː'tɒdʒɪnəs/ adj. self-produced. □ **autogenous welding** a process of joining metal by melting the edges together, without adding material.

autogiro /ˌɔːtəʊ'dʒaɪərəʊ/ n. (also **autogyro**) (pl. **-os**) an early form of helicopter with freely rotating horizontal vanes and a propeller. [Sp. (as AUTO-, *giro* gyration)]

autograft /'ɔːtəˌɡrɑːft/ n. Surgery a graft of tissue from one point to another of the same person's body.

autograph /'ɔːtəˌɡrɑːf/ n. & v. —n. 1 a a signature, esp. that of a celebrity. b handwriting. 2 a manuscript in an author's own handwriting. 3 a document signed by its author. —v.tr. 1 sign (a photograph, autograph album, etc.). 2 write (a letter etc.) by hand. [F *autographe* or LL *autographum* f. Gk *autographon* neut. of *autographos* (as AUTO-, -GRAPH)]

autography /ɔː'tɒɡrəfɪ/ n. 1 writing done with one's own hand. 2 the facsimile reproduction of writing or illustration. □□ **autographic** /-'ɡræfɪk/ adj.

autogyro var. of AUTOGIRO.

autoharp /'ɔːtəˌhɑːp/ n. a kind of zither with a mechanical device to allow the playing of chords.

autoimmune /ˌɔːtəʊɪ'mjuːn/ adj. Med. (of a disease) caused by antibodies produced against substances naturally present in the body. □□ **autoimmunity** n.

autointoxication /ˌɔːtəʊɪnˌtɒksɪ'keɪʃ(ə)n/ n. Med. poisoning by a toxin formed within the body itself.

autolysis /ɔː'tɒlɪsɪs/ n. the destruction of cells by their own enzymes. □□ **autolytic** /ˌɔːtə'lɪtɪk/ adj. [G *Autolyse* (as AUTO-, -LYSIS)]

automat /'ɔːtəˌmæt/ n. US 1 a slot-machine that dispenses goods. 2 a cafeteria containing slot-machines dispensing food and drink. [G f. F *automate*, formed as AUTOMATION]

automate /'ɔːtəˌmeɪt/ v.tr. convert to or operate by automation (*the ticket office has been automated*). [back-form. f. AUTOMATION]

automatic /ˌɔːtə'mætɪk/ adj. & n. —adj. 1 (of a machine, device, etc., or its function) working by itself, without direct human intervention. 2 a done spontaneously, without conscious thought or intention (*an automatic reaction*). b necessary and inevitable (*an automatic penalty*). 3 Psychol. performed unconsciously or subconsciously. 4 (of a firearm) that continues firing until the ammunition is exhausted or the pressure on the trigger is released. 5 (of a motor vehicle or its transmission) using gears that change automatically according to speed and acceleration. —n. 1 an automatic device, esp. a gun or transmission. 2 colloq. a vehicle with automatic transmission. □ **automatic pilot** a device for keeping an aircraft on a set course. □□ **automatically** adv.

automaticity /ˌɔːtəmə'tɪsɪtɪ/ n. [formed as AUTOMATON + -IC]

automation /ˌɔːtə'meɪʃ(ə)n/ n. 1 the use of automatic equipment to save mental and manual labour. 2 the automatic control of the manufacture of a product through its successive stages. [irreg. f. AUTOMATIC + -ATION]

automatism /ɔː'tɒmə,tɪz(ə)m/ n. 1 Psychol. the performance of actions unconsciously or subconsciously; such action. 2 involuntary action. 3 unthinking routine. [F *automatisme* f. *automate* AUTOMATON]

automatize /ɔː'tɒmə,taɪz/ v.tr. (also **-ise**) 1 make (a process etc.) automatic. 2 subject (a business, enterprise, etc.) to automation. □□ **automatization** /-'zeɪʃ(ə)n/ n. [AUTOMATIC + -IZE]

automaton /ɔː'tɒmət(ə)n/ n. (pl. **automata** /-tə/ or **automatons**) 1 a piece of mechanism with concealed motive power. 2 a person who behaves mechanically, like an automaton. [L f. Gk, neut. of *automatos* acting of itself: see AUTO-]

automobile /'ɔːtəmə,biːl/ n. US a motor car. [F (as AUTO-, MOBILE)]

automotive /ˌɔːtə'məʊtɪv/ adj. concerned with motor vehicles.

autonomic /ˌɔːtə'nɒmɪk/ adj. esp. Physiol. functioning involuntarily. □ **autonomic nervous system** the part of the nervous system responsible for control of the bodily functions not consciously directed, e.g. heartbeat. [AUTONOMY + -IC]

autonomous /ɔː'tɒnəməs/ adj. 1 having self-government. 2 acting independently or having the freedom to do so. □□ **autonomously** adv. [Gk *autonomos* (as AUTONOMY)]

autonomy /ɔː'tɒnəmɪ/ n. (pl. **-ies**) 1 the right of self-government. 2 personal freedom. 3 freedom of the will. 4 a self-governing community. □□ **autonomist** n. [Gk *autonomia* f. *autos* self + *nomos* law]

autopilot /'ɔːtəʊˌpaɪlət/ n. an automatic pilot. [abbr.]

autopista /'aʊtəʊˌpɪstə/ n. a Spanish motorway. [Sp. (as AUTOMOBILE, *pista* track)]

autopsy /'ɔːtɒpsɪ, ɔː'tɒpsɪ/ n. (pl. **-ies**) 1 a post-mortem examination. 2 any critical analysis. 3 a personal inspection. [F *autopsie* or mod.L *autopsia* f. Gk f. *autoptēs* eye-witness]

autoradiograph /ˌɔːtə'reɪdɪəˌɡrɑːf/ n. a photograph of an object, produced by radiation from radioactive material in the object. □□ **autoradiographic**

/ˌɔːtəˌreɪdɪəˈgræfɪk/ *adj.* **autoradiography** /ˌɔːtə
ˌreɪdɪˈɒgrəfɪ/ *n.*

autoroute /ˈɔːtəʊˌruːt/ *n.* a French motorway. [F (as
AUTOMOBILE, ROUTE)]

autostrada /ˈɔːtəʊˌstrɑːdə/ *n.* (*pl.* **autostradas** or *auto-
strade* /-deɪ/) an Italian motorway. [It. (as AUTO-
MOBILE, *strada* road)]

auto-suggestion /ˌɔːtəʊsəˈdʒestʃ(ə)n/ *n.* a hypnotic
or subconscious suggestion made by a person to
himself or herself and affecting behaviour.

autotelic /ˌɔːtəˈtelɪk/ *adj.* having or being a purpose
in itself. [AUTO- + Gk *telos* end]

autotomy /ɔːˈtɒtəmɪ/ *n. Zool.* the casting off of a part
of the body when threatened, e.g. the tail of a lizard.

autotoxin /ˌɔːtəˈtɒksɪn/ *n.* a poisonous substance
originating within an organism. □□ **autotoxic** *adj.*

autotrophic /ˌɔːtəˈtrɒfɪk/ *adj. Biol.* able to form
complex nutritional organic substances from simple
inorganic substances such as carbon dioxide (cf.
HETEROTROPHIC). [AUTO- + Gk *trophos* feeder]

autotype /ˈɔːtəˌtaɪp/ *n.* **1** a facsimile. **2 a** a photographic printing process for monochrome reproduction. **b** a print made by this process.

autoxidation /ɔːˌtɒksɪˈdeɪʃ(ə)n/ *n. Chem.* oxidation
by exposure to air at room temperature.

autumn /ˈɔːtəm/ *n.* **1** the third season of the year,
when crops and fruits are gathered, and leaves fall,
in the N. hemisphere from September to November
and in the S. hemisphere from March to May. **2**
Astron. the period from the autumnal equinox to the
winter solstice. **3** a time of maturity or incipient
decay. □ **autumn crocus** any plant of the genus
Colchicum, esp. meadow saffron, of the lily family
and unrelated to the true crocus. [ME f. OF *autompne*
f. L *autumnus*]

autumnal /ɔːˈtʌmn(ə)l/ *adj.* **1** of, characteristic of,
or appropriate to autumn (*autumnal colours*). **2**
occurring in autumn (*autumnal equinox*). **3** maturing
or blooming in autumn. **4** past the prime of life. [L
autumnalis (as AUTUMN, -AL)]

auxanometer /ˌɔːksəˈnɒmɪtə(r)/ *n.* an instrument for
measuring the linear growth of plants. [Gk *auxanō*
increase + -METER]

auxiliary /ɔːgˈzɪljərɪ/ *adj. & n.* —*adj.* **1** (of a person
or thing) that gives help. **2** (of services or equipment)
subsidiary, additional. —*n.* (*pl.* **-ies**) **1** an auxiliary
person or thing. **2** (in *pl.*) *Mil.* auxiliary troops. **3**
Gram. an auxiliary verb. □ **auxiliary troops** *Mil.*
foreign or allied troops in a belligerent nation's
service. **auxiliary verb** *Gram.* one used in forming
tenses, moods, and voices of other verbs. [L *aux-
iliarius* f. *auxilium* help]

auxin /ˈɔːksɪn/ *n.* a plant hormone that regulates
growth. [G f. Gk *auxō* increase + -IN]

AV *abbr.* **1** audiovisual (teaching aids etc.). **2** Authorized Version (of the Bible).

avadavat var. of AMADAVAT.

avail /əˈveɪl/ *v. & n.* —*v.* **1** *tr.* help, benefit. **2** *refl.*
(foll. by *of*) profit by; take advantage of. **3** *intr.* **a**
provide help. **b** be of use, value, or profit. —*n.* (usu.
in *neg.* or *interrog.* phrases) use, profit (*of no avail*;
without avail; *of what avail?*). [ME f. obs. *vail* (v.) f.
OF *valoir* be worth f. L *valēre*]

available /əˈveɪləb(ə)l/ *adj.* (often foll. by *to, for*) **1**
capable of being used; at one's disposal. **2** within one's
reach. □□ **availability** /-ˈbɪlɪtɪ/ *n.* **availableness** *n.*
availably *adv.* [ME f. AVAIL + -ABLE]

avalanche /ˈævəˌlɑːnʃ/ *n. & v.* —*n.* **1** a mass of snow
and ice, tumbling rapidly down a mountain. **2** a
sudden appearance or arrival of anything in large
quantities (*faced with an avalanche of work*). —*v.* **1**
intr. descend like an avalanche. **2** *tr.* carry down
like an avalanche. [F, alt. of dial. *lavanche* after
avaler descend]

avant-garde /ˌævɑ̃ˈgɑːd/ *n. & adj.* —*n.* pioneers or
innovators esp. in art and literature. —*adj.* (of
ideas etc.) new, progressive. □□ **avant-gardism** *n.*
avant-gardist *n.* [F, = vanguard]

avarice /ˈævərɪs/ *n.* extreme greed for money or
gain; cupidity. □□ **avaricious** /ˌævəˈrɪʃəs/ *adj.*
avariciously /-ˈrɪʃəslɪ/ *adv.* **avariciousness**
/-ˈrɪʃəsnɪs/ *n.* [ME f. OF f. L *avaritia* f. *avarus* greedy]

avast /əˈvɑːst/ *int. Naut.* stop, cease. [Du. *houd vast*
hold fast]

avatar /ˈævəˌtɑː(r)/ *n.* **1** (in Hindu mythology) the
descent of a deity or released soul to earth in bodily
form. **2** incarnation; manifestation. **3** a manifestation
or phase. [Skr. *avatāra* descent f. *áva* down + *tṛ-*
pass over]

avaunt /əˈvɔːnt/ *int. archaic* begone. [ME f. AF f. OF
avant ult. f. L *ab* from + *ante* before]

Ave. *abbr.* Avenue.

ave /ˈɑːveɪ, ˈɑːvɪ/ *int. & n.* —*int.* **1** welcome. **2** farewell.
—*n.* **1** (in full **Ave Maria**) a prayer to the Virgin
Mary, the opening line from Luke 1:28. Also called
Hail Mary. **2** a shout of welcome or farewell. [ME f.
L, 2nd sing. imper. of *avēre* fare well]

avenge /əˈvendʒ/ *v.tr.* **1** inflict retribution on behalf
of (a person, a violated right, etc.). **2** take vengeance
for (an injury). □ **be avenged** avenge oneself. □□
avenger *n.* [ME f. OF *avengier* f. *à* to + *vengier* f. L
vindicare vindicate]

avens /ˈæv(ə)nz/ *n.* any of various plants of the genus
Geum. □ **mountain avens** a related plant (*Dryas
octopetala*). [ME f. OF *avence* (med.L *avencia*), of
unkn. orig.]

aventurine /əˈventjʊˌriːn/ *n. Mineral.* **1** brownish
glass or mineral containing sparkling gold-coloured
particles usu. of copper or gold. **2** a variety of
spangled quartz resembling this. [F f. It. *avventurino*
f. *avventura* chance (because of its accidental
discovery)]

avenue /ˈævəˌnjuː/ *n.* **1 a** a broad road or street, often
with trees at regular intervals along its sides. **b** a
tree-lined approach to a country house. **2** a way of
approaching or dealing with something (*explored
every avenue to find an answer*). [F, fem. past part. of
avenir f. L *advenire* come to]

aver /əˈvɜː(r)/ *v.tr.* (**averred**, **averring**) assert,
affirm. [ME f. OF *averer* (as AD-, L *verus* true)]

average /ˈævərɪdʒ/ *n., adj., & v.* —*n.* **1 a** the usual
amount, extent, or rate. **b** the ordinary standard. **2**
an amount obtained by dividing the total of given
amounts by the number of amounts in the set. **3**
Law the distribution of loss resulting from damage
to a ship or cargo. —*adj.* **1** usual, ordinary. **2**
estimated or calculated by average. —*v.tr.* **1** amount
on average to (*the sale of the product averaged one
hundred a day*). **2** do on average (*averages six hours'
work a day*). **3 a** estimate the average of. **b** estimate
the general standard of. □ **average adjustment** *Law*
the apportionment of average. **average out** result
in an average. **average out at** result in an average
of. **batting average 1** *Cricket* a batsman's runs
scored per completed innings. **2** *Baseball* a batter's
safe hits per time at bat. **bowling average** *Cricket* a
bowler's conceded runs per wicket taken. **law of
averages** the principle that if one of two extremes
occurs the other will also tend to so as to maintain
the normal average. **on** (or **on an**) **average** as an
average rate or estimate. □□ **averagely** *adv.* [F
avarie damage to ship or cargo (see sense 3), f. It.
avaria f. Arab. *ʿawārīya* damaged goods f. *ʿawār*
damage at sea, loss: *-age* after *damage*]

averment /əˈvɜːmənt/ *n.* a positive statement; an
affirmation, esp. *Law* one with an offer of proof. [ME
f. AF, OF *aver(r)ement* (as AVER, -MENT)]

averse /əˈvɜːs/ *predic.adj.* (often foll. by *to, from*)
opposed, disinclined (*was not averse to helping me*).
¶ Construction with *to* is now more common. [L
aversus (as AVERT)]

aversion /əˈvɜːʃ(ə)n/ *n.* **1** (usu. foll. by *to, from, for*) a
dislike or unwillingness (*has an aversion to hard
work*). **2** an object of dislike (*my pet aversion*).
□ **aversion therapy** therapy designed to make a

subject averse to an existing habit. [F *aversion* or L *aversio* (as AVERT, -ION)]

avert /ə'vɜːt/ *v.tr.* (often foll. by *from*) **1** turn away (one's eyes or thoughts). **2** prevent or ward off (an undesirable occurrence). □□ **avertable** *adj.* **avertible** *adj.* [ME f. L *avertere* (as AB-, *vertere* versturn): partly f. OF *avertir* f. Rmc]

Avesta /ə'vestə/ *n.* (usu. prec. by *the*) the sacred writings of Zoroastrianism (cf. ZEND). [Pers.]

Avestan /ə'vest(ə)n/ *adj.* & *n.* —*adj.* of or relating to the Avesta. —*n.* the ancient Iranian language of the Avesta.

avian /'eɪvɪən/ *adj.* of or relating to birds. [L *avis* bird]

aviary /'eɪvɪərɪ/ *n.* (*pl.* -**ies**) a large enclosure or building for keeping birds. [L *aviarium* (as AVIAN, -ARY¹)]

aviate /'eɪvɪ,eɪt/ *v.* **1** *intr.* fly in an aeroplane. **2** *tr.* pilot (an aeroplane). [back-form. f. AVIATION]

aviation /,eɪvɪ'eɪʃ(ə)n/ *n.* **1** the skill or practice of operating aircraft. **2** aircraft manufacture. [F f. L *avis* bird]

aviator /'eɪvɪ,eɪtə(r)/ *n.* (*fem.* **aviatrix** /'eɪvɪətrɪks/) an airman or airwoman. [F *aviateur* f. L *avis* bird]

aviculture /'eɪvɪ,kʌltʃə(r)/ *n.* the rearing and keeping of birds. □□ **aviculturist** /-'kʌltʃərɪst/ *n.* [L *avis* bird, after AGRICULTURE]

avid /'ævɪd/ *adj.* (usu. foll. by *of, for*) eager, greedy. □□ **avidity** /ə'vɪdɪtɪ/ *n.* **avidly** *adv.* [F *avide* or L *avidus* f. *avēre* crave]

avifauna /'eɪvɪ,fɔːnə/ *n.* birds of a region or country collectively. [L *avis* bird + FAUNA]

avionics /,eɪvɪ'ɒnɪks/ *n.* electronics as applied to aviation.

avitaminosis /eɪ,vɪtəmɪ'nəʊsɪs/ *n.* *Med.* a condition resulting from a deficiency of one or more vitamins.

avizandum /,ævɪ'zændəm/ *n. Sc. Law* a period of time for further consideration of a judgement. [med.L, gerund of *avizare* consider (as ADVISE)]

avocado /,ævə'kɑːdəʊ/ *n.* (*pl.* -**os**) **1** (in full **avocado pear**) a pear-shaped fruit with rough leathery skin, a smooth oily edible flesh, and a large stone. **2** the tropical evergreen tree, *Persea americana*, native to Central America, bearing this fruit. Also called *alligator pear.* **3** the light green colour of the flesh of this fruit. [Sp., = advocate (substituted for Aztec *ahuacatl*)]

avocation /,ævə'keɪʃ(ə)n/ *n.* **1** a minor occupation. **2** *colloq.* a vocation or calling. [L *avocatio* f. *avocare* call away]

avocet /'ævə,set/ *n.* any wading bird of the genus *Recurvirostra* with long legs and a long slender upward-curved bill and usu. black and white plumage. [F *avocette* f. It. *avosetta*]

Avogadro's constant /,ævə'gɑːdrəʊz/ *n.* (also **Avogadro's number**) *Physics* the number of atoms or molecules in one mole of a substance. [A. *Avogadro*, It. physicist d. 1856]

Avogadro's law /,ævə'gɑːdrəʊz/ *n. Physics* the law that equal volumes of all gases at the same temperature and pressure contain the same number of molecules.

avoid /ə'vɔɪd/ *v.tr.* **1** keep away or refrain from (a thing, person, or action). **2** escape; evade. **3** *Law* **a** nullify (a decree or contract). **b** quash (a sentence). □□ **avoidable** *adj.* **avoidably** *adv.* **avoidance** *n.* **avoider** *n.* [AF *avoider*, OF *evuider* clear out, get quit of, f. *vuide* empty, VOID]

avoirdupois /,ævədə'pɔɪz/ *n.* (in full **avoirdupois weight**) a system of weights based on a pound of 16 ounces or 7,000 grains. [ME f. OF *aveir de peis* goods of weight f. *aveir* f. L *habēre* have + *peis* (see POISE¹)]

avouch /ə'vaʊtʃ/ *v.tr.* & *intr. archaic* or *rhet.* guarantee, affirm, confess. □□ **avouchment** *n.* [ME f. OF *avochier* f. L *advocare* (as AD-, *vocare* call)]

avow /ə'vaʊ/ *v.tr.* **1** admit, confess. **2 a** *refl.* admit that one is (*avowed himself the author*). **b** (as **avowed** *adj.*) admitted (*the avowed author*). □□ **avowal** *n.*

avowedly /ə'vaʊɪdlɪ/ *adv.* [ME f. OF *avouer* acknowledge f. L *advocare* (as AD-, *vocare* call)]

avulsion /ə'vʌlʃ(ə)n/ *n.* **1** a tearing away. **2** *Law* a sudden removal of land by a flood etc. to another person's estate. [F *avulsion* or L *avulsio* f. *avellere avuls-* pluck away]

avuncular /ə'vʌnkjʊlə(r)/ *adj.* like or of an uncle; kind and friendly, esp. towards a younger person. [L *avunculus* maternal uncle, dimin. of *avus* grandfather]

AWACS /'eɪwæks/ *n.* a long-range radar system for detecting enemy aircraft. [abbr. of *airborne warning and control system*]

await /ə'weɪt/ *v.tr.* **1** wait for. **2** (of an event or thing) be in store for (*a surprise awaits you*). [ME f. AF *awaitier*, OF *aguaitier* (as AD-, *waitier* WAIT)]

awake /ə'weɪk/ *v.* & *adj.* —*v.* (*past* **awoke** /ə'wəʊk/; *past part.* **awoken** /ə'wəʊkən/) **1** *intr.* **a** cease to sleep. **b** become active. **2** *intr.* (foll. by *to*) become aware of. **3** *tr.* rouse from sleep. —*predic.adj.* **1 a** not asleep. **b** vigilant. **2** (foll. by *to*) aware of. [OE *āwæcnan*, *āwacian* (as A-², WAKE¹)]

awaken /ə'weɪkən/ *v.tr.* & *intr.* **1** = AWAKE *v.* **2** *tr.* (often foll. by *to*) make aware. [OE *onwæcnan* etc. (as A-², WAKEN)]

award /ə'wɔːd/ *v.* & *n.* —*v.tr.* **1** give or order to be given as a payment, penalty, or prize (*awarded him a knighthood; was awarded damages*). **2** grant, assign. —*n.* **1** a payment, penalty, or prize awarded. **2** a judicial decision. □□ **awarder** *n.* [ME f. AF *awarder*, ult. f. Gmc: see WARD]

aware /ə'weə(r)/ *predic.adj.* **1** (often foll. by *of*, or *that* + clause) conscious; not ignorant; having knowledge. **2** well-informed. ¶ Also found in *attrib.* use in sense 2, as in *a very aware person*; this is *disp.* □□ **awareness** *n.* [OE *gewær*]

awash /ə'wɒʃ/ *predic.adj.* **1** level with the surface of water, so that it just washes over. **2** carried or washed by the waves; flooded.

away /ə'weɪ/ *adv.*, *adj.*, & *n.* —*adv.* **1** to or at a distance from the place, person, or thing in question (*go away; give away; look away; they are away; 5 miles away*). **2** towards or into non-existence (*sounds die away; explain it away; idled their time away*). **3** constantly, persistently, continuously (*work away; laugh away*). **4** without delay (*ask away*). —*adj. Sport* played on an opponent's ground etc. (*away match; away win*). —*n. Sport* an away match or win. □ **away with** (as *imper.*) take away; let us be rid of. [OE *onweg*, *aweg* on one's way f. A² + WAY]

awe /ɔː/ *n.* & *v.* —*n.* reverential fear or wonder (*stand in awe of*). —*v.tr.* inspire with awe. □ **awe-inspiring** causing awe or wonder; amazing, magnificent. [ME *age* f. ON *agi* f. Gmc]

aweary /ə'wɪərɪ/ *predic.adj. poet.* (often foll. by *of*) weary. [aphetic *a* + WEARY]

aweigh /ə'weɪ/ *predic.adj. Naut.* (of an anchor) clear of the sea or river bed; hanging. [A² + WEIGH¹]

awesome /'ɔːsəm/ *adj.* inspiring awe; dreaded. □□ **awesomely** *adv.* **awesomeness** *n.* [AWE + -SOME¹]

awestricken /'ɔː,strɪkən/ *adj.* (also **awestruck** /-strʌk/) struck or afflicted with awe.

awful /'ɔːfʊl/ *adj.* **1** *colloq.* **a** unpleasant or horrible (*awful weather*). **b** poor in quality; very bad (*has awful writing*). **c** (*attrib.*) excessive; large (*an awful lot of money*). **2** *poet.* inspiring awe. □□ **awfulness** *n.* [AWE + -FUL]

awfully /'ɔːfəlɪ, -flɪ/ *adv.* **1** in an unpleasant, bad, or horrible way (*he played awfully*). **2** *colloq.* very (*she's awfully pleased; thanks awfully*). **3** *poet.* reverently.

awhile /ə'waɪl/ *adv.* for a short time. [OE *āne hwīle* a while]

awkward /'ɔːkwəd/ *adj.* **1** ill-adapted for use; causing difficulty in use. **2** clumsy or bungling. **3 a** embarrassed (*felt awkward about it*). **b** embarrassing (*an awkward situation*). **4** difficult to deal with (*an awkward customer*). □ **the awkward age** adolescence. □□ **awkwardly** *adv.* **awkwardness** *n.*

aʊ *how*   eɪ *day*   əʊ *no*   eə *hair*   ɪə *near*   ɔɪ *boy*   ʊə *poor*   aɪə *fire*   aʊə *sour*   (*see over for consonants*)

[obs. *awk* backhanded, untoward (ME f. ON *afugr* turned the wrong way) + -WARD]

awl /ɔːl/ *n.* a small pointed tool used for piercing holes, esp. in leather. [OE *æl*]

awn /ɔːn/ *n.* a stiff bristle growing from the grain-sheath of grasses, or terminating a leaf etc. □□ **awned** *adj.* [ME f. ON *ögn*]

awning /ˈɔːnɪŋ/ *n.* a sheet of canvas or similar material stretched on a frame and used to shade a shop window, doorway, ship's deck, or other area from the sun or rain. [17th c. (Naut.): orig. uncert.]

awoke *past* of AWAKE.

awoken *past part.* of AWAKE.

AWOL /ˈeɪwɒl/ *abbr. colloq.* absent without leave.

awry /əˈraɪ/ *adv. & adj.* —*adv.* **1** crookedly or askew. **2** improperly or amiss. —*predic.adj.* crooked; deviant or unsound (*his theory is awry*). □**go awry** go or do wrong. [ME f. A[2] + WRY]

axe /æks/ *n. & v.* (*US* **ax**) —*n.* **1** a chopping-tool, usu. of iron with a steel edge and wooden handle. **2** the drastic cutting or elimination of expenditure, staff, etc. —*v.tr.* (**axing**) **1** cut (esp. costs or services) drastically. **2** remove or dismiss. □**axe-breaker** a hard-wooded Australian tree. **an axe to grind** private ends to serve. [OE *æx* f. Gmc]

axel /ˈæks(ə)l/ *n.* a jumping movement in skating, similar to a loop (see LOOP *n.* 7) but from one foot to the other. [*Axel* R. Paulsen, Norw. skater d. 1938]

axes *pl.* of AXIS[1].

axial /ˈæksɪəl/ *adj.* **1** forming or belonging to an axis. **2** round an axis (*axial rotation; axial symmetry*). □□ **axiality** (/ˌæksɪˈælɪtɪ/) *n.* **axially** *adv.*

axil /ˈæksɪl/ *n.* the upper angle between a leaf and the stem it springs from, or between a branch and the trunk. [L *axilla*: see AXILLA]

axilla /ækˈsɪlə/ *n.* (*pl.* **axillae** /-liː/) **1** *Anat.* the armpit. **2** an axil. [L, = armpit, dimin. of *ala* wing]

axillary /ækˈsɪlərɪ/ *adj.* **1** *Anat.* of or relating to the armpit. **2** *Bot.* in or growing from the axil.

axiom /ˈæksɪəm/ *n.* **1** an established or widely accepted principle. **2** esp. *Geom.* a self-evident truth. [F *axiome* or L *axioma* f. Gk *axiōma axiōmat-* f. *axios* worthy]

axiomatic /ˌæksɪəˈmætɪk/ *adj.* **1** self-evident. **2** relating to or containing axioms. □□ **axiomatically** *adv.* [Gk *axiōmatikos* (as AXIOM)]

axis[1] /ˈæksɪs/ *n.* (*pl.* **axes** /-siːz/) **1 a** an imaginary line about which a body rotates or about which a plane figure is conceived as generating a solid. **b** a line which divides a regular figure symmetrically. **2** *Math.* a fixed reference line for the measurement of coordinates etc. **3** *Bot.* the central column of an inflorescence or other growth. **4** *Anat.* the second cervical vertebra. **5** *Physiol.* the central part of an organ or organism. **6 a** an agreement or alliance between two or more countries forming a centre for an eventual larger grouping of nations sharing an ideal or objective. **b** (**the Axis**) the alliance of Germany and Italy formed before and during the war of 1939–45, later extended to include Japan and other countries; these countries as a group. [L, = axle, pivot]

axis[2] /ˈæksɪs/ *n.* a white spotted deer, *Cervus axis*, of S. Asia. Also called CHITAL. [L]

axle /ˈæks(ə)l/ *n.* a rod or spindle (either fixed or rotating) on which a wheel or group of wheels is fixed. [orig. *axle-tree* f. ME *axel-tre* f. ON *öxull-trē*]

Axminster /ˈæksˌmɪnstə(r)/ *n.* (in full **Axminster carpet**) a kind of machine-woven patterned carpet with a cut pile. [*Axminster* in S. England]

axolotl /ˈæksəˌlɒt(ə)l/ *n.* an aquatic newtlike salamander, *Ambystoma mexicanum*, from Mexico, which in natural conditions retains its larval form for life but in time is able to breed. [Nahuatl f. *atl* water + *xolotl* servant]

axon /ˈæksɒn/ *n. Anat. & Zool.* a long threadlike part of a nerve cell, conducting impulses from the cell body. [mod.L f. Gk *axōn* axis]

ay var. of AYE[1].

ayah /ˈaɪə/ *n.* a native nurse or maidservant, esp. in India and other former British territories abroad. [Anglo-Ind. f. Port. *aia* nurse]

ayatollah /ˌaɪəˈtɒlə/ *n.* a Shiite religious leader in Iran. [Pers. f. Arab., = token of God]

aye[1] /aɪ/ *adv. & n.* (also **ay**) —*adv.* **1** *archaic* or *dial.* yes. **2** (in voting) I assent. **3** (as **aye aye**) *Naut.* a response accepting an order. —*n.* an affirmative answer or assent, esp. in voting. □**the ayes have it** the affirmative votes are in the majority. [16th c.: prob. f. first pers. personal pron. expressing assent]

aye[2] /eɪ/ *adv. archaic* ever, always. □**for aye** for ever. [ME f. ON *ei, ey* f. Gmc]

aye-aye /ˈaɪaɪ/ *n.* an arboreal nocturnal lemur, *Daubentonia madagascariensis*, native to Madagascar. [F f. Malagasy *aiay*]

Aylesbury /ˈeɪlzbərɪ/ *n.* (*pl.* **Aylesburys**) **1** a bird of a breed of large white domestic ducks. **2** this breed. [*Aylesbury* in S. England]

Ayrshire /ˈeəʃə(r)/ *n.* **1** an animal of a mainly white breed of dairy cattle. **2** this breed. [name of a former Scottish county]

AZ *abbr. US* Arizona (in official postal use).

azalea /əˈzeɪlɪə/ *n.* any of various flowering deciduous shrubs of the genus *Rhododendron*, with large pink, purple, white, or yellow flowers. [mod.L f. Gk, fem. of *azaleos* dry (from the dry soil in which it was believed to flourish)]

azeotrope /əˈziːəˌtrəʊp/ *n. Chem.* a mixture of liquids in which the boiling-point remains constant during distillation, at a given pressure, without change in composition. □□ **azeotropic** /əˌziːəˈtrɒpɪk/ *adj.* [A-[1] + Gk *zeō* boil + *tropos* turning]

azide /ˈeɪzaɪd/ *n. Chem.* any compound containing the radical N_3–.

Azilian /əˈzɪlɪən/ *n. & adj. Geol.* —*n.* the transitional period between the palaeolithic and neolithic ages in Europe. —*adj.* of or relating to this period. [Mas d'*Azil* in the French Pyrenees, where remains of it were found]

azimuth /ˈæzɪməθ/ *n.* **1** the angular distance from a north or south point of the horizon to the intersection with the horizon of a vertical circle passing through a given celestial body. **2** the horizontal angle or direction of a compass bearing. □□ **azimuthal** /-ˈmjuːθ(ə)l/ *adj.* [ME f. OF *azimut* f. Arab. *as-sumūt* f. *al* the + *sumūt* pl. of *samt* way, direction]

azine /ˈeɪziːn/ *n. Chem.* any organic compound with two or more nitrogen atoms in a six-atom ring. [AZO- + -INE[4]]

azo- /ˈæzəʊ, ˈeɪ-/ *prefix Chem.* containing two adjacent nitrogen atoms between carbon atoms. [F *azote* nitrogen f. Gk *azōos* without life]

azoic /əˈzəʊɪk/ *adj.* **1** having no trace of life. **2** *Geol.* (of an age etc.) having left no organic remains. [Gk *azōos* without life]

AZT /ˌerzed'tiː/ *n.* a drug intended for use against the Aids virus. [chem. name *azidothymidine*]

Aztec /ˈæztek/ *n. & adj.* —*n.* **1** a member of the native people dominant in Mexico before the Spanish conquest of the 16th century. **2** the language of the Aztecs. —*adj.* of the Aztecs or their language (see also NAHUATL). [F *Aztèque* or Sp. *Azteca* f. Nahuatl *aztecatl* men of the north]

azuki var. of ADZUKI.

azure /ˈæʒə(r), -zjə(r), ˈeɪ-/ *n. & adj.* —*n.* **1 a** a deep sky-blue colour. **b** *Heraldry* blue. **2** *poet.* the clear sky. —*adj.* **1 a** of the colour azure. **b** *Heraldry* blue. **2** serene, untroubled. [ME f. OF *asur, azur,* f. med.L *azzurum, azolum* f. Arab. *al* the + *lāzaward* f. Pers. *lāžward* lapis lazuli]

azygous /ˈæzɪgəs/ *adj. & n. Anat.* —*adj.* (of any organic structure) single, not existing in pairs. —*n.* an organic structure occurring singly. [Gk *azugos* unyoked f. *a*- not + *zugon* yoke]

B

B¹ /biː/ *n.* (also **b**) (*pl.* **Bs** or **B's**) **1** the second letter of the alphabet. **2** *Mus.* the seventh note of the diatonic scale of C major. **3** the second hypothetical person or example. **4** the second highest class or category (of roads, academic marks, etc.). **5** *Algebra* (usu. **b**) the second known quantity. **6** a human blood type of the ABO system. □**B film** a supporting film in a cinema programme.

B² *symb.* **1** *Chem.* the element boron. **2** *Physics* magnetic flux density.

B³ *abbr.* (also **B.**) **1** Bachelor. **2** bel(s). **3** bishop. **4** black (pencil-lead). **5** Blessed.

b *symb. Physics* barn.

b. *abbr.* **1** born. **2** *Cricket* **a** bowled by. **b** bye. **3** billion.

BA *abbr.* **1** Bachelor of Arts. **2** British Academy. **3** British Airways. **4** British Association.

Ba *symb. Chem.* the element barium.

BAA *abbr.* British Airports Authority.

baa /baː/ *v. & n.* —*v.intr.* (**baas**, **baaed** or **baa'd**) (esp. of a sheep) bleat. —*n.* (*pl.* **baas**) the cry of a sheep or lamb. [imit.]

baas /baːs/ *n. S.Afr.* boss, master (often as a form of address). [Du.: cf. BOSS¹]

baasskap /ˈbaːskaːp/ *n. S.Afr.* domination, esp. of non-Whites by Whites. [Afrik. f. *baas* master + -*skap* condition]

baba /ˈbaːbaː/ *n.* (in full **rum baba**) a small rich sponge cake, usu. soaked in rum-flavoured syrup. [F f. Pol.]

babacoote /ˈbaːbəˌkuːt/ *n.* = INDRI. [Malagasy *babakoto*]

Babbitt¹ /ˈbæbɪt/ *n.* **1** (in full **Babbitt metal**) any of a group of soft alloys of tin, antimony, copper, and usu. lead, used for lining bearings etc., to diminish friction. **2** (**babbitt**) a bearing-lining made of this. [I. *Babbitt*, Amer. inventor d. 1862]

Babbitt² /ˈbæbɪt/ *n.* a materialistic, complacent businessman. □□**Babbittry** *n.* [George *Babbitt*, a character in the novel *Babbitt* (1922) by S. Lewis]

babble /ˈbæb(ə)l/ *v. & n.* —*v.* **1** *intr.* **a** talk in an inarticulate or incoherent manner. **b** chatter excessively or irrelevantly. **c** (of a stream etc.) murmur, trickle. **2** *tr.* repeat foolishly; divulge through chatter. —*n.* **1 a** incoherent speech. **b** foolish, idle, or childish talk. **2** the murmur of voices, water, etc. **3** *Telephony* background disturbance caused by interference from conversations on other lines. □□**babblement** *n.* [ME f. MLG *babbelen*, or imit.]

babbler /ˈbæbl(ə)r/ *n.* **1** a chatterer. **2** a person who reveals secrets. **3** any of a large group of passerine birds with loud chattering voices.

babe /beɪb/ *n.* **1** *literary* a baby. **2** an innocent or helpless person (*babes and sucklings*; *babes in the wood*). **3** *US sl.* a young woman (often as a form of address). [ME: imit. of child's *ba, ba*]

babel /ˈbeɪb(ə)l/ *n.* **1** a confused noise, esp. of voices. **2** a noisy assembly. **3** a scene of confusion. □**Tower of Babel** a visionary or unrealistic plan. [ME f. Heb. *Bāḇel* Babylon f. Akkad. *bab ili* gate of god (with ref. to the biblical account of the tower that was built to reach heaven but ended in chaos when Jehovah confused the builders' speech: see Gen. 11)]

Babis /ˈbæbɪs/ *n.* a member of a Persian eclectic sect founded in 1844 whose doctrine includes Muslim, Christian, Jewish, and Zoroastrian elements. □□ **Babism** *n.* [Pers. *Bab*-ed-Din, gate (= intermediary) of the Faith]

baboon /bəˈbuːn/ *n.* **1** any of various large Old World monkeys of the genus *Papio*, having a long doglike snout, large teeth, and naked callosities on the buttocks. **2** an ugly or uncouth person. [ME f. OF *babuin* or med.L *babewynus*, of unkn. orig.]

babu /ˈbaːbuː/ *n.* (also **baboo**) *Ind.* **1** a title of respect, esp. to Hindus. **2** *derog.* formerly, an English-writing Indian clerk. [Hindi *bābū*]

babushka /bəˈbuːʃkə/ *n.* a headscarf tied under the chin. [Russ., = grandmother]

baby /ˈbeɪbɪ/ *n. & v.* —*n.* (*pl.* -**ies**) **1** a very young child or infant, esp. one not yet able to walk. **2** an unduly childish person (*is a baby about injections*). **3** the youngest member of a family, team, etc. **4** (often *attrib.*) **a** a young or newly born animal. **b** a thing that is small of its kind (*baby car*; *baby rose*). **5** *sl.* a young woman; a sweetheart (often as a form of address). **6** *sl.* a person or thing regarded with affection or familiarity. **7** one's own responsibility, invention, concern, achievement, etc., regarded in a personal way. —*v.tr.* (-**ies**, -**ied**) **1** treat like a baby. **2** pamper. □**baby boom** *colloq.* a temporary marked increase in the birthrate. **baby boomer** a person born during a baby boom, esp. after the war of 1939–45. **baby-bouncer** *Brit.* a frame supported by elastic or springs, into which a child is harnessed to exercise its limbs. **Baby Buggy** (*pl.* -**ies**) *Brit. propr.* a kind of child's collapsible pushchair. **baby carriage** *US* a pram. **baby grand** the smallest size of grand piano. **baby-snatcher** *colloq.* **1** a person who kidnaps babies. **2** = *cradle-snatcher*. **baby-talk** childish talk used by or to young children. **baby-walker** a wheeled frame in which a baby learns to walk. **carry** (or **hold**) **the baby** bear unwelcome responsibility. **throw away the baby with the bath-water** reject the essential with the inessential. □□**babyhood** *n.* [ME, formed as BABE, -Y²]

Babygro /ˈbeɪbɪˌɡrəʊ/ *n.* (*pl.* -**os**) *propr.* a kind of all-in-one stretch garment for babies. [BABY + GROW]

babyish /ˈbeɪbɪɪʃ/ *adj.* **1** childish, simple. **2** immature. □□**babyishly** *adv.* **babyishness** *n.*

Babylonian /ˌbæbɪˈləʊnɪən/ *n. & adj.* —*n.* an inhabitant of Babylon, an ancient city and kingdom in Mesopotamia. —*adj.* of or relating to Babylon. [L *Babylonius* f. Gk *Babulonios* f. *Babulon* f. Heb. *Bāḇel*]

babysit /ˈbeɪbɪsɪt/ *v.intr.* (-**sitting**; *past* and *past part.* -**sat**) look after a child or children while the parents are out. □□**babysitter** *n.*

Bacardi /bəˈkaːdɪ/ *n.* (*pl.* **Bacardis**) *propr.* a West Indian rum produced orig. in Cuba. [name of the company producing it]

baccalaureate /ˌbækəˈlɔːrɪət/ *n.* **1** the university degree of bachelor. **2** an examination intended to qualify successful candidates for higher education. [F *baccalauréat* or med.L *baccalaureatus* f. *baccalaureus* bachelor]

baccarat /ˈbækəˌraː/ *n.* a gambling card-game played by punters in turn against the banker. [F]

baccate /ˈbækeɪt/ *adj. Bot.* **1** bearing berries. **2** of or like a berry. [L *baccatus* berried f. *bacca* berry]

bacchanal /ˈbækən(ə)l/ *n. & adj.* —*n.* **1** a wild and drunken revelry. **2** a drunken reveller. **3** a priest, worshipper, or follower of Bacchus. —*adj.* **1** of or like Bacchus, the Greek or Roman god of wine, or his rites. **2** riotous, roistering. [L *bacchanalis* f. *Bacchus* god of wine f. Gk *Bakkhos*]

Bacchanalia /ˌbækəˈneɪlɪə/ *n.pl.* **1** the Roman festival of Bacchus. **2** (**bacchanalia**) a drunken revelry. □□**Bacchanalian** *adj. & n.* [L, neut. pl. of *bacchanalis*: see BACCHANAL]

bacchant /ˈbækənt/ *n. & adj.* —*n.* (*pl.* **bacchants** or

---

w *we*   z *zoo*   ʃ *she*   ʒ *decision*   θ *thin*   ð *this*   ŋ *ring*   x *loch*   tʃ *chip*   dʒ *jar*   (*see over for vowels*)

bacchantes /bə'kæntiːz/; *fem.* **bacchante** /bə'kænti/) **1** a priest, worshipper, or follower of Bacchus. **2** a drunken reveller. —*adj.* **1** of or like Bacchus or his rites. **2** riotous, roistering. ▫▫ **bacchantic** /bə'kæntɪk/ *adj.* [F *bacchante* f. L *bacchari* celebrate Bacchanal rites]

Bacchic /'bækɪk/ *adj.* = BACCHANAL *adj.* [L *bacchicus* f. Gk *bakkhikos* of Bacchus]

baccy /'bæki/ *n.* (*pl.* -ies) *Brit. colloq.* tobacco. [abbr.]

bachelor /'bætʃələ(r)/ *n.* **1** an unmarried man. **2** a man or woman who has taken the degree of Bachelor of Arts or Science etc. **3** *hist.* a young knight serving under another's banner. ▫ **bachelor girl** an independent unmarried young woman. **bachelor's buttons** any of various button-like flowers, esp. the double buttercup. ▫▫ **bachelorhood** *n.*

bachelorship *n.* [ME & OF *bacheler* aspirant to knighthood, of uncert. orig.]

bacillary /bə'sɪlərɪ/ *adj.* relating to or caused by bacilli.

bacilliform /bə'sɪlɪˌfɔːm/ *adj.* rod-shaped.

bacillus /bə'sɪləs/ *n.* (*pl.* **bacilli** /-laɪ/) **1** any rod-shaped bacterium. **2** (usu. in *pl.*) any pathogenic bacterium. [LL, dimin. of L *baculus* stick]

back /bæk/ *n., adv., v.,* & *adj.* —*n.* **1 a** the rear surface of the human body from the shoulders to the hips. **b** the corresponding upper surface of an animal's body. **c** the spine (*fell and broke his back*). **d** the keel of a ship. **2 a** any surface regarded as corresponding to the human back, e.g. of the head or hand, or of a chair. **b** the part of a garment that covers the back. **3 a** the less active or visible or important part of something functional, e.g. of a knife or a piece of paper (*write it on the back*). **b** the side or part normally away from the spectator or the direction of motion or attention, e.g. of a car, house, or room (*stood at the back*). **4 a** a defensive player in field games. **b** this position. **5** (**the Backs**) the grounds of Cambridge colleges which back on to the River Cam. —*adv.* **1** to the rear; away from what is considered to be the front (*go back a bit*; *ran off without looking back*). **2 a** in or into an earlier or normal position or condition (*came back late*; *went back home*; *ran back to the car*; *put it back on the shelf*). **b** in return (*pay back*). **3** in or into the past (*back in June*; *three years back*). **4** at a distance (*stand back from the road*). **5** in check (*hold him back*). **6** (foll. by *of*) *US* behind (*was back of the house*). —*v.* **1** *tr.* **a** help with moral or financial support. **b** bet on the success of (a horse etc.). **2** *tr.* & *intr.* move, or cause (a vehicle etc.) to move, backwards. **3** *tr.* **a** put or serve as a back, background, or support to. **b** *Mus.* accompany. **4** *tr.* lie at the back of (*a beach backed by steep cliffs*). **5** *intr.* (of the wind) move round in an anticlockwise direction. —*adj.* **1** situated behind, esp. as remote or subsidiary (*backstreet*; *back teeth*). **2** of or relating to the past; not current (*back pay*; *back issue*). **3** reversed (*back flow*). ▫ **at a person's back** in pursuit or support. **at the back of one's mind** remembered but not consciously thought of. **back and forth** to and fro. **back bench** a back-bencher's seat in the House of Commons. **back-bencher** a member of Parliament not holding a senior office. **back-boiler** *Brit.* a boiler behind and integral with a domestic fire. **back-breaking** (esp. of manual work) extremely hard. **back country** esp. *Austral.* & *NZ* an area away from settled districts. **back-crawl** = BACKSTROKE. **back-cross** *Biol.* **1** cross a hybrid with one of its parents. **2** an instance or the product of this. **back door** a secret or ingenious means of gaining an objective. **back-door** *adj.* (of an activity) clandestine, underhand (*a back-door deal*). **back down** withdraw one's claim or point of view etc.; concede defeat in an argument etc. **back-down** *n.* an instance of backing down. **back-fill** refill an excavated hole with the material dug out of it. **back-formation 1** the formation of a word from its seeming derivative (e.g.

laze from *lazy*). **2** a word formed in this way. **back number 1** an issue of a periodical earlier than the current one. **2** *sl.* an out-of-date person or thing. **the back of beyond** a very remote or inaccessible place. **back off 1** draw back, retreat. **2** abandon one's intention, stand, etc. **back on to** have its back adjacent to (*the house backs on to a field*). **back out** (often foll. by *of*) withdraw from a commitment. **back passage** *colloq.* the rectum. **back-pedal** (**-pedalled**, **-pedalling**; *US* **-pedaled**, **-pedaling**) **1** pedal backwards on a bicycle etc. **2** reverse one's previous action or opinion. **back-projection** the projection of a picture from behind a translucent screen for viewing or filming. **back room** (often with hyphen) *attrib.*) a place where secret work is done. **back-scattering** the scattering of radiation in a reverse direction. **back seat** an inferior position or status. **back-seat driver** a person who is eager to advise without responsibility (orig. of a passenger in a car etc.). **back slang** slang using words spelt backwards (e.g. *yob*). **back-stop** = LONGSTOP. **back talk** *US* = BACKCHAT. **back to back** with backs adjacent and opposite each other (*we stood back to back*). **back-to-back** *adj.* esp. *Brit.* (of houses) with a party wall at the rear. **back to front 1** with the back at the front and the front at the back. **2** in disorder. **back-to-nature** (usu. *attrib.*) applied to a movement or enthusiast for the reversion to a simpler way of life. **back up 1** give (esp. moral) support to. **2** *Computing* make a spare copy of (data, a disk, etc.). **3** (of running water) accumulate behind an obstruction. **4** reverse (a vehicle) into a desired position. **5** *US* form a queue of vehicles etc., esp. in congested traffic. **back water** reverse a boat's forward motion using oars. **get** (or **put**) **a person's back up** annoy or anger a person. **get off a person's back** stop troubling a person. **go back on** fail to honour (a promise or commitment). **know like the back of one's hand** be entirely familiar with. **on one's back** injured or ill in bed. **on the back burner** see BURNER. **put one's back into** approach (a task etc.) with vigour. **see the back of** see SEE¹. **turn one's back on 1** abandon. **2** ignore. **with one's back to** (or **up against**) **the wall** in a desperate situation; hard-pressed. ▫▫ **backer** *n.* (in sense 1 of *v.*). **backless** *adj.* [OE *bæc* f. Gmc]

backache /'bækeɪk/ *n.* a (usu. prolonged) pain in one's back.

backbite /'bækbaɪt/ *v.tr.* slander; speak badly of. ▫▫ **backbiter** *n.*

backblocks /'bækblɒks/ *n.pl. Austral.* & *NZ* land in the remote and sparsely inhabited interior.

backboard /'bækbɔːd/ *n.* **1** a board worn to support or straighten the back. **2** a board placed at or forming the back of anything.

backbone /'bækbəʊn/ *n.* **1** the spine. **2** the main support of a structure. **3** firmness of character. **4** *US* the spine of a book.

backchat /'bæktʃæt/ *n. Brit. colloq.* the practice of replying rudely or impudently.

backcloth /'bækklɒθ/ *n. Brit. Theatr.* a painted cloth at the back of the stage as a main part of the scenery.

backcomb /'bækkəʊm/ *v.tr.* comb (the hair) towards the scalp to make it look thicker.

backdate /bæk'deɪt/ *v.tr.* **1** put an earlier date to (an agreement etc.) than the actual one. **2** make retrospectively valid.

backdrop /'bækdrɒp/ *n.* = BACKCLOTH.

backfire *v.* & *n.* —*v.intr.* /bæk'faɪə(r)/ **1** undergo a mistimed explosion in the cylinder or exhaust of an internal-combustion engine. **2** (of a plan etc.) rebound adversely on the originator; have the opposite effect to what was intended. —*n.* /'bækfaɪə(r)/ an instance of backfiring.

backgammon /'bækˌgæmən, bæk'gæmən/ *n.* **1** a game for two played on a board with pieces moved according to throws of the dice. **2** the most complete form of win in this. [BACK + GAMMON²]

background /'bækgraʊnd/ n. **1** part of a scene, picture, or description, that serves as a setting to the chief figures or objects and foreground. **2** an inconspicuous or obscure position (*kept in the background*). **3** a person's education, knowledge, or social circumstances. **4** explanatory or contributory information or circumstances. **5** *Physics* low-intensity ambient radiation from radioisotopes present in the natural environment. **6** *Electronics* unwanted signals, such as noise in the reception or recording of sound. □**background music** music intended as an unobtrusive accompaniment to some activity, or to provide atmosphere in a film etc.

backhand /'bækhænd/ n. *Tennis* etc. **1** a stroke played with the back of the hand turned towards the opponent. **2** (*attrib.*) of or made with a backhand (*backhand volley*).

backhanded /bæk'hændɪd/ adj. **1** (of a blow etc.) delivered with the back of the hand, or in a direction opposite to the usual one. **2** indirect; ambiguous (*a backhanded compliment*). **3** = BACKHAND adj.

backhander /'bæk,hændə(r)/ n. **1 a** a backhand stroke. **b** a backhanded blow. **2** *colloq.* an indirect attack. **3** *Brit. sl.* a bribe.

backing /'bækɪŋ/ n. **1 a** support. **b** a body of supporters. **c** material used to form a back or support. **2** musical accompaniment, esp. to a singer.

backlash /'bæklæʃ/ n. **1** an excessive or marked adverse reaction. **2 a** a sudden recoil or reaction between parts of a mechanism. **b** excessive play between such parts.

backlist /'bæklɪst/ n. a publisher's list of books published before the current season and still in print.

backlit /'bæklɪt/ adj. (esp. in photography) illuminated from behind.

backlog /'bæklɒg/ n. **1** arrears of uncompleted work etc. **2** a reserve; reserves (*a backlog of goodwill*).

backmarker /'bæk,mɑːkə(r)/ n. *Brit.* a competitor who has the least favourable handicap in a race etc.

backmost /'bækmoʊst/ adj. furthest back.

backpack /'bækpæk/ n. & v. —n. a rucksack. —v.intr. travel or hike with a backpack. □□ **backpacker** n.

backrest /'bækrest/ n. a support for the back.

backscratcher /'bæk,skrætʃə(r)/ n. **1** a rod terminating in a clawed hand for scratching one's own back. **2** a person who performs mutual services with another for gain.

backsheesh var. of BAKSHEESH.

backside /bæk'saɪd, 'bæk-/ n. *colloq.* the buttocks.

backsight /'bæksaɪt/ n. **1** the sight of a rifle etc. that is nearer the stock. **2** *Surveying* a sight or reading taken backwards or towards the point of starting.

backslapping /'bæk,slæpɪŋ/ adj. vigorously hearty.

backslash /'bækslæʃ/ n. a backward-sloping diagonal line; a reverse solidus (\).

backslide /'bækslaɪd/ v.intr. (*past* -slid; *past part.* -slid or -slidden) relapse into bad ways or error. □□ **backslider** n.

backspace /'bækspeɪs/ v.intr. move a typewriter carriage etc. back one or more spaces.

backspin /'bækspɪn/ n. a backward spin imparted to a ball causing it to fly off at an angle on hitting a surface.

backstage /bæk'steɪdʒ/ adv. & adj. —adv. **1** *Theatr.* out of view of the audience, esp. in the wings or dressing-rooms. **2** not known to the public. —adj. /also 'bæk-/ that is backstage; concealed.

backstairs /'bæksteəz/ n.pl. **1** stairs at the back or side of a building. **2** (also **backstair**) (*attrib.*) denoting underhand or clandestine activity.

backstay /'bæksteɪ/ n. a rope etc. leading downwards and aft from the top of a mast.

backstitch /'bækstɪtʃ/ n. & v. —n. sewing with overlapping stitches. —v.tr. & intr. sew using backstitch.

backstreet /'bækstriːt/ n. **1** a street in a quiet part of a town, away from the main streets. **2** (*attrib.*) denoting illicit or illegal activity (*a backstreet abortion*).

backstroke /'bækstroʊk/ n. a swimming stroke performed on the back with the arms lifted alternately out of the water in a backward circular motion and the legs extended in a kicking action.

backtrack /'bæktræk/ v.intr. **1** retrace one's steps. **2** reverse one's previous action or opinion.

backup /'bækʌp/ n. **1** moral or technical support (*called for extra backup*). **2** a reserve. **3** *Computing* (often *attrib.*) **a** the procedure for making security copies of data (*backup facilities*). **b** the copy itself (*made a backup*). **4** *US* a queue of vehicles etc., esp. in congested traffic. □**backup light** *US* a reversing light.

backveld /'bækvelt/ n. *S.Afr.* remote country districts, esp. those strongly conservative. □□ **backvelder** n.

backward /'bækwəd/ adv. & adj. —adv. = BACKWARDS. ¶ *Backwards* is now more common, esp. in literal senses. —adj. **1** directed to the rear or starting-point (*a backward look*). **2** reversed. **3** mentally retarded or slow. **4** reluctant, shy, unassertive. □□ **backwardness** n. [earlier *abackward*, assoc. with BACK]

backwardation /,bækwə'deɪʃ(ə)n/ n. esp. *Brit. Stock Exch.* the percentage paid by a person selling stock for the right of delaying the delivery of it (cf. CONTANGO).

backwards /'bækwədz/ adv. **1** away from one's front (*lean backwards*; *look backwards*). **2 a** with the back foremost (*walk backwards*). **b** in reverse of the usual way (*count backwards*; *spell backwards*). **3 a** into a worse state (*new policies are taking us backwards*). **b** into the past (*looked backwards over the years*). **c** (of a thing's motion) back towards the starting-point (*rolled backwards*). □**backwards and forwards** in both directions alternately; to and fro. **bend** (or **fall** or **lean**) **over backwards** (often foll. by *to* + infin.) *colloq.* make every effort, esp. to be fair or helpful. **know backwards** be entirely familiar with.

backwash /'bækwɒʃ/ n. **1 a** receding waves created by the motion of a ship etc. **b** a backward current of air created by a moving aircraft. **2** repercussions.

backwater /'bæk,wɔːtə(r)/ n. **1** a place or condition remote from the centre of activity or thought. **2** stagnant water fed from a stream.

backwoods /'bækwʊdz/ n.pl. **1** remote uncleared forest land. **2** any remote or sparsely inhabited region.

backwoodsman /'bæk,wʊdzmən/ n. (*pl.* -men) **1** an inhabitant of backwoods. **2** an uncouth person.

backyard /bæk'jɑːd/ n. a yard at the back of a house etc. □**in one's own backyard** *colloq.* near at hand.

baclava var. of BAKLAVA.

bacon /'beɪkən/ n. cured meat from the back or sides of a pig. □**bring home the bacon** *colloq.* **1** succeed in one's undertaking. **2** supply material provision or support. [ME f. OF f. Frank. *bako* = OHG *bahho* ham, flitch]

Baconian /beɪ'koʊnɪən/ adj. & n. —adj. of or relating to the English philosopher Sir Francis Bacon (d. 1626), or to his inductive method of reasoning and philosophy. —n. **1** a supporter of the view that Bacon was the author of Shakespeare's plays. **2** a follower of Bacon.

bacteria pl. of BACTERIUM.

bactericide /bæk'tɪərɪ,saɪd/ n. a substance capable of destroying bacteria. □□ **bactericidal** /-'saɪd(ə)l/ adj.

bacteriology /,bæktɪərɪ'ɒlədʒɪ/ n. the study of bacteria. □□ **bacteriological** /-ə'lɒdʒɪk(ə)l/ adj. **bacteriologically** /-ə'lɒdʒɪkəlɪ/ adv. **bacteriologist** n.

bacteriolysis /bæk,tɪərɪ'blɪsɪs/ n. the rupture of bacterial cells.

bacteriolytic /bæk,tɪərɪə'lɪtɪk/ adj. capable of lysing bacteria.

bacteriophage /bæk'tɪərɪəʊˌfeɪdʒ, -ˌfɑːʒ/ *n.* a virus parasitic on a bacterium, by infecting it and reproducing inside it. [BACTERIUM + Gk *phagein* eat]

bacteriostasis /bækˌtɪərɪəʊ'steɪsɪs/ *n.* the inhibition of the growth of bacteria without destroying them. □□ **bacteriostatic** /-'stætɪk/ *adj.*

bacterium /bæk'tɪərɪəm/ *n.* (*pl.* **bacteria** /-rɪə/) a member of a large group of unicellular microorganisms lacking organelles and an organized nucleus, some of which can cause disease. □□ **bacterial** *adj.* [mod.L f. Gk *baktērion* dimin. of *baktron* stick]

Bactrian /'bæktrɪən/ *adj.* of or relating to Bactria in central Asia. □ **Bactrian camel** a camel, *Camelus bactrianus*, native to central Asia, with two humps. [L *Bactrianus* f. Gk *Baktrianos*]

bad /bæd/ *adj., n.,* & *adv.* —*adj.* (**worse** /wɜːs/; **worst** /wɜːst/) **1** inferior, inadequate, defective (*bad work*; *a bad driver*; *bad light*). **2 a** unpleasant, unwelcome (*bad weather*; *bad news*). **b** unsatisfactory, unfortunate (*a bad business*). **3** harmful (*is bad for you*). **4** (of food) decayed, putrid. **5** *colloq.* ill, injured (*am feeling bad today*; *a bad leg*). **6** *colloq.* regretful, guilty, ashamed (*feels bad about it*). **7** (of an unwelcome thing) serious, severe (*a bad headache*; *a bad mistake*). **8 a** morally wicked or offensive (*a bad man*; *bad language*). **b** naughty; badly behaved (*a bad child*). **9** worthless; not valid (*a bad cheque*). **10** (**badder, baddest**) esp. *US sl.* good, excellent. —*n.* **1 a** ill fortune (*take the bad with the good*). **b** ruin; a degenerate condition (*go to the bad*). **2** the debit side of an account (*£500 to the bad*). **3** (as *pl.*; prec. by *the*) bad or wicked people. —*adv. US colloq.* badly (*took it bad*). □ **bad blood** ill feeling. **bad books** see BOOK. **bad breath** unpleasant-smelling breath. **bad debt** a debt that is not recoverable. **bad egg** see EGG[1]. **bad faith** see FAITH. **bad form** see FORM. **a bad job** *colloq.* an unfortunate state of affairs. **bad mouth** *US* malicious gossip or criticism. **bad-mouth** *v.tr. US* subject to malicious gossip or criticism. **bad news** *colloq.* an unpleasant or troublesome person or thing. **from bad to worse** into an even worse state. **in a bad way** ill; in trouble (*looked in a bad way*). **not** (or **not so**) **bad** *colloq.* fairly good. **too bad** *colloq.* (of circumstances etc.) regrettable but now beyond retrieval. □□ **baddish** *adj.* **badness** *n.* [ME, perh. f. OE *bæddel* hermaphrodite, womanish man: for loss of *l* cf. MUCH, WENCH]

baddy /'bædɪ/ *n.* (*pl.* **-ies**) *colloq.* a villain or criminal, esp. in a story, film, etc.

bade see BID.

badge /bædʒ/ *n.* **1** a distinctive emblem worn as a mark of office, membership, achievement, licensed employment, etc. **2** any feature or sign which reveals a characteristic condition or quality. [ME: orig. unkn.]

badger /'bædʒə(r)/ *n.* & *v.* —*n.* **1** an omnivorous grey-coated nocturnal mammal of the family Mustelidae with a white stripe flanked by black stripes on its head, which lives in sets. **2** a fishing-fly, brush, etc., made of its hair. —*v.tr.* pester, harass, tease. [16th c.: perh. f. BADGE, with ref. to its white forehead mark]

badinage /'bædɪˌnɑːʒ/ *n.* humorous or playful ridicule. [F f. *badiner* to joke]

badlands /'bædlændz/ *n.* extensive uncultivable eroded tracts in arid areas. [transl. F *mauvaises terres*]

badly /'bædlɪ/ *adv.* (**worse** /wɜːs/; **worst** /wɜːst/) **1** in a bad manner (*works badly*). **2** *colloq.* very much (*wants it badly*). **3** severely (*was badly defeated*).

badminton /'bædmɪnt(ə)n/ *n.* **1** a game with rackets in which a shuttlecock is played back and forth across a net. **2** a summer drink of claret, soda, and sugar. [*Badminton* in S. England]

bad-tempered /bæd'tempəd/ *adj.* having a bad temper; irritable; easily annoyed. □□ **bad-temperedly** *adv.*

Baedeker /'beɪdɪkə(r)/ *n.* any of various travel guidebooks published by the firm founded by the German Karl *Baedeker* (d. 1859).

baffle /'bæf(ə)l/ *v.* & *n.* —*v.tr.* **1** confuse or perplex (a person, one's faculties, etc.). **2 a** frustrate or hinder (plans etc.). **b** restrain or regulate the progress of (fluids, sounds, etc.). —*n.* (also **baffle-plate**) a device used to restrain the flow of fluid, gas, etc., through an opening, often found in microphones etc. to regulate the emission of sound. □ **baffle-board** a device to prevent sound from spreading in different directions, esp. round a loudspeaker cone. □□ **bafflement** *n.* **baffling** *adj.* **bafflingly** *adv.* [perh. rel. to F *bafouer* ridicule, OF *beffer* mock]

baffler /'bæflə(r)/ *n.* = BAFFLE *n.*

BAFTA *abbr.* British Association of Film and Television Arts.

bag /bæg/ *n.* & *v.* —*n.* **1** a receptacle of flexible material with an opening at the top. **2 a** (usu. in *pl.*) a piece of luggage (*put the bags in the boot*). **b** a woman's handbag. **3** (in *pl.*; usu. foll. by *of*) *colloq.* a large amount; plenty (*bags of time*). **4** (in *pl.*) *Brit. colloq.* trousers. **5** *sl. derog.* a woman, esp. regarded as unattractive or unpleasant. **6** an animal's sac containing poison, honey, etc. **7** an amount of game shot by a sportsman. **8** (usu. in *pl.*) baggy folds of skin under the eyes. **9** *sl.* a person's particular interest or preoccupation, esp. in a distinctive style or category of music (*his bag is Indian music*). —*v.* (**bagged, bagging**) **1** *tr.* put in a bag. **2** *tr. colloq.* **a** secure; get hold of (*bagged the best seat*). **b** *colloq.* steal. **c** shoot (game). **d** (often in phr. **bags I**) *Brit. colloq.* claim on grounds of being the first to do so (*bagged first go*; *bags I go first*). **3** *intr.* hang loosely; bulge; swell. **b** *tr.* cause to do this. **4** *tr. Austral. sl.* criticize, disparage. □ **bag and baggage** with all one's belongings. **bag lady** *US* a homeless woman who carries her possessions around in shopping bags. **bag** (or **whole bag**) **of tricks** *colloq.* everything; the whole lot. **in the bag** *colloq.* achieved; as good as secured. □□ **bagful** *n.* (*pl.* **-fuls**). [ME, perh. f. ON *baggi*]

bagarre /bɑː'gɑː(r)/ *n.* a scuffle or brawl. [F]

bagasse /bə'gæs/ *n.* the dry pulpy residue left after the extraction of juice from sugar cane, usable as fuel or to make paper etc. [F f. Sp. *bagazo*]

bagatelle /ˌbægə'tel/ *n.* **1** a game in which small balls are struck into numbered holes on a board, with pins as obstructions. **2** a mere trifle; a negligible amount. **3** *Mus.* a short piece of music, esp. for the piano. [F f. It. *bagatella* dimin., perh. f. *baga* BAGGAGE]

bagel /'beɪg(ə)l/ *n.* (also **beigel**) *US* a hard bread roll in the shape of a ring. [Yiddish *beygel*]

baggage /'bægɪdʒ/ *n.* **1** everyday belongings packed up in suitcases etc. for travelling; luggage. **2** the portable equipment of an army. **3** *joc.* or *derog.* a girl or woman. □ **baggage check** *US* a luggage ticket. [ME f. OF *bagage* f. *baguer* tie up or *bagues* bundles: perh. rel. to BAG]

baggy /'bægɪ/ *adj.* (**baggier, baggiest**) **1** hanging in loose folds. **2** puffed out. □□ **baggily** *adv.* **bagginess** *n.*

bagman /'bægmən/ *n.* (*pl.* **-men**) **1** *Brit. sl.* a travelling salesman. **2** *Austral.* a tramp. **3** *US sl.* an agent who collects or distributes money for illicit purposes.

bagnio /'bɑːnjəʊ/ *n.* (*pl.* **-os**) **1** a brothel. **2** an Oriental prison. [It. *bagno* f. L *balneum* bath]

bagpipe /'bægpaɪp/ *n.* (usu. in *pl.*) a musical instrument consisting of a windbag connected to two kinds of reeded pipes: drone pipes which produce single sustained notes and a fingered melody pipe or 'chanter'. □□ **bagpiper** *n.*

baguette /bæ'get/ *n.* **1** a long narrow French loaf. **2** a gem cut in a long rectangular shape. **3** *Archit.* a small moulding, semicircular in section. [F f. It. *bacchetto* dimin. of *bacchio* f. L *baculum* staff]

bah /bɑː/ *int.* an expression of contempt or disbelief. [prob. F]

Baha'i /bəˈhɑːɪ/ *n.* (*pl.* **Baha'is**) a member of a monotheistic religion founded in 1863 as a branch of Babism (see BABIS), emphasizing religious unity and world peace. □□ **Baha'ism** *n.* [Pers. *bahá* splendour]

Bahamian /bəˈheɪmɪən/ *n. & adj.* —*n.* **1** a native or national of the Bahamas in the W. Indies. **2** a person of Bahamian descent. —*adj.* of or relating to the Bahamas.

Bahasa Indonesia /bɑːˌhɑːsə ˌɪndəˈniːsɪə/ *n.* the official language of Indonesia. [Indonesian *bahasa* language f. Skr. *bhāṣā* f. *bhāṣate* he speaks: see INDONESIAN]

bail¹ /beɪl/ *n. & v.* —*n.* **1** money etc. required as security against the temporary release of a prisoner pending trial. **2** a person or persons giving such security. —*v.tr.* (usu. foll. by *out*) **1** release or secure the release of (a prisoner) on payment of bail. **2** (also **bale** by assoc. with *bale out* 1: see BALE¹) release from a difficulty; come to the rescue of. □**forfeit** (*colloq.* **jump**) **bail** fail to appear for trial after being released on bail. **go** (or **stand**) **bail** (often foll. by *for*) act as surety (for an accused person). □□ **bailable** *adj.* [ME f. OF *bail* custody, *bailler* take charge of, f. L *bajulare* bear a burden]

bail² /beɪl/ *n. & v.* —*n.* **1** *Cricket* either of the two crosspieces bridging the stumps. **2** the bar on a typewriter holding the paper against the platen. **3** a bar separating horses in an open stable. **4** *Austral. & NZ* a framework for securing the head of a cow during milking. —*v. Austral. & NZ* (usu. foll. by *up*) **1** *tr.* secure (a cow) during milking. **2 a** *tr.* make (a person) hold up his or her arms to be robbed. **b** *intr.* surrender by throwing up one's arms. **c** *tr.* buttonhole (a person). [ME f. OF *bail(e)*, perh. f. *bailler* enclose]

bail³ /beɪl/ *v.tr.* (also **bale**) **1** (usu. foll. by *out*) scoop water out of (a boat etc.). **2** scoop (water etc.) out. □**bail out** var. of *bale out* 1 (see BALE¹). □□ **bailer** *n.* [obs. *bail* (n.) bucket f. F *baille* ult. f. L *bajulus* carrier]

bailee /beɪˈliː/ *n. Law* a person or party to whom goods are committed for a purpose, e.g. custody or repair, without transfer of ownership. [BAIL¹ + -EE]

bailey /ˈbeɪlɪ/ *n.* (*pl.* **-eys**) **1** the outer wall of a castle. **2** a court enclosed by it. [ME, var. of BAIL²]

Bailey bridge /ˈbeɪlɪ/ *n.* a temporary bridge of lattice steel designed for rapid assembly from pre-fabricated standard parts, used esp. in military operations. [Sir D. *Bailey* (d. 1985), its designer]

bailie /ˈbeɪlɪ/ *n.* esp. *hist.* a municipal officer and magistrate in Scotland. [ME, f. OF *bailli(s)* BAILIFF]

bailiff /ˈbeɪlɪf/ *n.* **1** a sheriff's officer who executes writs and processes and carries out distraints and arrests. **2** *Brit.* the agent or steward of a landlord. **3** *US* an official in a court of law who keeps order, looks after prisoners, etc. **4** *Brit.* (*hist.* except in formal titles) the sovereign's representative in a district, esp. the chief officer of a hundred. **5** the first civil officer in the Channel Islands. [ME f. OF *baillif* ult. f. L *bajulus* carrier, manager]

bailiwick /ˈbeɪlɪwɪk/ *n.* **1** *Law* the district or jurisdiction of a bailie or bailiff. **2** *joc.* a person's sphere of operations or particular area of interest. [BAILIE + WICK²]

bailment /ˈbeɪlmənt/ *n.* the act of delivering goods etc. for a (usu. specified) purpose.

bailor /ˈbeɪlə(r)/ *n. Law* a person or party that entrusts goods to a bailee. [BAIL¹ + -OR]

bailsman /ˈbeɪlzmən/ *n.* (*pl.* **-men**) a person who stands bail for another. [BAIL¹ + MAN]

bain-marie /ˌbæ̃mæˈriː/ *n.* (*pl.* **bains-marie** *pronunc.* same) a cooking utensil consisting of a vessel of hot water in which a receptacle containing a sauce etc. can be slowly and gently heated; a double boiler. [F, transl. med.L *balneum Mariae* bath of Maria (an alleged Jewish alchemist)]

Bairam /baɪˈræm, ˈbaɪræm/ *n.* either of two annual Muslim festivals. □**Greater Bairam** at the end of the Islamic year. **Lesser Bairam** at the end of Ramadan. [Turk. & Pers.]

bairn /beən/ *n. Sc. & N.Engl.* a child. [OE *bearn*]

bait¹ /beɪt/ *n. & v.* —*n.* **1** food used to entice a prey, esp. a fish or an animal. **2** an allurement; something intended to tempt or entice. **3** *archaic* a halt on a journey for refreshment or a rest. **4** = BATE. —*v.* **1** *tr.* **a** harass or annoy (a person). **b** torment (a chained animal). **2** *tr.* put bait on (a hook, trap, etc.) to entice a prey. **3** *archaic* **a** *tr.* give food to (horses on a journey). **b** *intr.* stop on a journey to take food or a rest. [ME f. ON *beita* hunt or chase]

bait² var. of BATE.

baize /beɪz/ *n.* a coarse usu. green woollen material resembling felt used as a covering or lining, esp. on the tops of billiard- and card-tables. [F *baies* (pl.) fem. of *bai* chestnut-coloured (BAY⁴), treated as sing.: cf. BODICE]

bajra /ˈbɑːdʒrə/ *n. Ind.* pearl millet or similar grain. [Hindi]

bake /beɪk/ *v. & n.* —*v.* **1 a** *tr.* cook (food) by dry heat in an oven or on a hot surface, without direct exposure to a flame. **b** *intr.* undergo the process of being baked. **2** *intr. colloq.* **a** (usu. as **be baking**) (of weather etc.) be very hot. **b** (of a person) become hot. **3 a** *tr.* harden (clay etc.) by heat. **b** *intr.* (of clay etc.) be hardened by heat. **4 a** *tr.* (of the sun) affect by its heat, e.g. ripen (fruit). **b** *intr.* (e.g. of fruit) be affected by the sun's heat. —*n.* **1** the act or an instance of baking. **2** a batch of baking. **3** *US* a social gathering at which baked food is eaten. □**baked Alaska** see ALASKA. **baked beans** baked haricot beans, usu. tinned in tomato sauce. **baking-powder** a mixture of sodium bicarbonate, cream of tartar, etc., used instead of yeast in baking. **baking-soda** sodium bicarbonate. [OE *bacan*]

bakehouse /ˈbeɪkhaʊs/ *n.* = BAKERY.

Bakelite /ˈbeɪkəˌlaɪt/ *n. propr.* any of various thermosetting resins or plastics made from formaldehyde and phenol and used for cables, buttons, plates, etc. [G *Bakelit* f. L.H. *Baekeland* its Belgian-born inventor d. 1944]

baker /ˈbeɪkə(r)/ *n.* a person who bakes and sells bread, cakes, etc., esp. professionally. □**baker's dozen** thirteen (so called from the former bakers' custom of adding an extra loaf to a dozen sold; the exact reason for this is unclear). [OE *bæcere*]

bakery /ˈbeɪkərɪ/ *n.* (*pl.* **-ies**) a place where bread and cakes are made or sold.

Bakewell tart /ˈbeɪkwel/ *n.* a baked open pie consisting of a pastry case lined with jam and filled with a rich almond paste. [*Bakewell* in Derbyshire]

baklava /ˈbækləvə, ˌbækləˈvɑː/ *n.* (also **baclava**) a rich sweetmeat of flaky pastry, honey, and nuts. [Turk.]

baksheesh /ˈbækʃiːʃ/ *n.* (also **backsheesh**) (in some oriental countries) a small sum of money given as a gratuity or as alms. [ult. f. Pers. *bakšīš* f. *bakšīdan* give]

Balaclava /ˌbæləˈklɑːvə/ *n.* (in full **Balaclava helmet**) a tight woollen garment covering the whole head and neck except for parts of the face, worn orig. by soldiers on active service in the Crimean War. [*Balaclava* in the Crimea, the site of a battle in 1854]

balalaika /ˌbæləˈlaɪkə/ *n.* a guitar-like musical instrument having a triangular body and 2-4 strings, popular in Russia and other Slav countries. [Russ.]

balance /ˈbæləns/ *n. & v.* —*n.* **1** an apparatus for weighing, esp. one with a central pivot, beam, and two scales. **2 a** a counteracting weight or force. **b** (in full **balance-wheel**) the regulating device in a clock etc. **3 a** an even distribution of weight or amount. **b** stability of body or mind (*regained his balance*). **4** a preponderating weight or amount (*the balance of opinion*). **5 a** an agreement between or the difference between credits and debits in an account. **b** the difference between an amount due and an amount paid (*will pay the balance next week*). **c** an amount left over; the rest. **6 a** *Art* harmony of design and proportion. **b** *Mus.* the relative volume of various sources of sound (*bad balance between violins and trumpets*). **7** (**the Balance**) the zodiacal sign or constellation Libra. —*v.* **1** *tr.* (foll. by *with, against*) offset or compare (one thing) with another (*must balance the advantages with the disadvantages*). **2** *tr.* counteract, equal, or neutralize the weight or importance of. **3 a** *tr.* bring into or keep in equilibrium (*balanced a book on her head*). **b** *intr.* be in equilibrium (*balanced on one leg*). **4** *tr.* (usu. as **balanced** *adj.*) establish equal or appropriate proportions of elements in (*a balanced diet; balanced opinion*). **5** *tr.* weigh (arguments etc.) against each other. **6 a** *tr.* compare and esp. equalize debits and credits of (an account). **b** *intr.* (of an account) have credits and debits equal. □ **balance of payments** the difference in value between payments into and out of a country. **balance of power 1** a situation in which the chief States of the world have roughly equal power. **2** the power held by a small group when larger groups are of equal strength. **balance of trade** the difference in value between imports and exports. **balance sheet** a statement giving the balance of an account. **in the balance** uncertain; at a critical stage. **on balance** all things considered. **strike a balance** choose a moderate course or compromise. □□ **balanceable** *adj.* **balancer** *n.* [ME f. OF, ult. f. LL (*libra*) *bilanx bilancis* two-scaled (balance)]

balata /ˈbælətə/ *n.* **1** any of several latex-yielding trees of Central America, esp. *Manilkara bidentata*. **2** the dried sap of this used as a substitute for gutta-percha. [ult. f. Carib]

Balbriggan /bælˈbrɪgən/ *n.* a knitted cotton fabric used for underwear etc. [*Balbriggan* in Ireland, where it was orig. made]

balcony /ˈbælkənɪ/ *n.* (*pl.* -ies) **1** a usu. balustraded platform on the outside of a building, with access from an upper-floor window or door. **2 a** the tier of seats in a theatre above the dress circle. **b** the upstairs seats in a cinema etc. **c** *US* the dress circle in a theatre. □□ **balconied** *adj.* [It. *balcone*]

bald /bɔːld/ *adj.* **1** (of a person) with the scalp wholly or partly lacking hair. **2** (of an animal, plant, etc.) not covered by the usual hair, feathers, leaves, etc. **3** *colloq.* with the surface worn away (*a bald tyre*). **4 a** blunt, unelaborated (*a bald statement*). **b** undisguised (*the bald effrontery*). **5** meagre or dull (*a bald style*). **6** marked with white, esp. on the face (*a bald horse*). □ **bald eagle** a white-headed eagle (*Haliaeetus leucocephalus*), used as the emblem of the United States. □□ **balding** *adj.* (in senses 1–3). **baldish** *adj.* **baldly** *adv.* (in sense 4). **baldness** *n.* [ME *ballede*, orig. 'having a white blaze', prob. f. an OE root *ball-* 'white patch']

baldachin /ˈbɔːldəkɪn/ *n.* (also **baldaquin**) **1** a ceremonial canopy over an altar, throne, etc. **2** a rich brocade. [It. *baldacchino* f. *Baldacco* Baghdad, its place of origin]

balderdash /ˈbɔːldədæʃ/ *n.* senseless talk or writing; nonsense. [earlier = 'mixture of drinks': orig. unkn.]

baldhead /ˈbɔːldhɛd/ *n.* a person with a bald head.

baldmoney /ˈbɔːldˌmʌnɪ/ *n.* (*pl.* -eys) an aromatic white-flowered umbelliferous mountain plant *Meum athamanticum*. [ME in sense 'gentian': orig. unkn.]

baldric /ˈbɔːldrɪk/ *n. hist.* a belt for a sword, bugle, etc., hung from the shoulder across the body to the opposite hip. [ME *baudry* f. OF *baudrei*: cf. MHG *balderich*, of unkn. orig.]

bale[1] /beɪl/ *n. & v.* —*n.* **1** a bundle of merchandise or hay etc. tightly wrapped and bound with cords or hoops. **2** the quantity in a bale as a measure, esp. *US* 500 lb. of cotton. —*v.tr.* make up into bales. □ **bale** (or **bail**) **out 1** (of an airman) make an emergency parachute descent from an aircraft (cf. BAIL[3]). **2** =

BAIL[1] *v.* 2. [ME prob. f. MDu., ult. identical with BALL[1]]

bale[2] /beɪl/ *n. archaic* or *poet.* evil, destruction, woe, pain, misery. [OE *b(e)alu*]

bale[3] var. of BAIL[3].

baleen /bəˈliːn/ *n.* whalebone. □ **baleen whale** any of various whales of the suborder Mysticeti, having plates of baleen fringed with bristles for straining plankton from the water. [ME f. OF *baleine* f. L *balaena* whale]

baleful /ˈbeɪlfʊl/ *adj.* **1** (esp. of a manner, look, etc.) gloomy, menacing. **2** harmful, malignant, destructive. □□ **balefully** *adv.* **balefulness** *n.* [BALE[2] + -FUL]

baler /ˈbeɪlə(r)/ *n.* a machine for making bales of hay, straw, metal, etc.

Balinese /ˌbɑːlɪˈniːz/ *n. & adj.* —*n.* (*pl.* same) **1** a native of Bali, an island in Indonesia. **2** the language of Bali. —*adj.* of or relating to Bali or its people or language.

balk var. of BAULK.

Balkan /ˈbɔːlkən/ *adj. & n.* —*adj.* **1** of or relating to the region of SE Europe bounded by the Adriatic, the Aegean, and the Black Sea. **2** of or relating to its peoples or countries. —*n.* (**the Balkans**) the Balkan countries. [Turk.]

balky var. of BAULKY.

ball[1] /bɔːl/ *n. & v.* —*n.* **1** a solid or hollow sphere, esp. for use in a game. **2 a** a ball-shaped object; material forming the shape of a ball (*ball of snow; ball of wool; rolled himself into a ball*). **b** a rounded part of the body (*ball of the foot*). **3** a solid non-explosive missile for a cannon etc. **4** a single delivery of a ball in cricket, baseball, etc., or passing of a ball in football. **5** (in *pl.*) *coarse sl.* **a** the testicles. **b** (usu. as an exclam. of contempt) nonsense, rubbish. **c** = *balls-up.* **d** courage, 'guts'. ¶ Sense 5 is usually considered a taboo use. —*v.* **1** *tr.* squeeze or wind into a ball. **2** *intr.* form or gather into a ball or balls. □ **ball-and-socket joint** *Anat.* a joint in which a rounded end lies in a concave cup or socket, allowing freedom of movement. **ball-bearing 1** a bearing in which the two halves are separated by a ring of small metal balls which reduce friction. **2** one of these balls. **ball game 1 a** any game played with a ball. *US* a game of baseball. **2** esp. *US colloq.* a particular affair or concern (*a whole new ball game*). **the ball is in your** etc. **court** you etc. must be next to act. **ball lightning** a rare globular form of lightning. **ball-point (pen)** a pen with a tiny ball as its writing point. **balls** (or **ball**) **up** *coarse sl.* bungle; make a mess of. **balls-up** *n. coarse sl.* a mess; a confused or bungled situation. **have the ball at one's feet** have one's best opportunity. **keep the ball rolling** maintain the momentum of an activity. **on the ball** *colloq.* alert. **play ball** *colloq.* cooperate. **start** etc. **the ball rolling** set an activity in motion; make a start. [ME f. ON *böllr* f. Gmc]

ball[2] /bɔːl/ *n.* **1** a formal social gathering for dancing. **2** *sl.* an enjoyable time (esp. *have a ball*). [F *bal* f. LL *ballare* to dance]

ballad /ˈbæləd/ *n.* **1** a poem or song narrating a popular story. **2** a slow sentimental or romantic song. □ **ballad metre** = *common metre.* [ME f. OF *balade* f. Prov. *balada* dancing-song f. *balar* to dance]

ballade /bæˈlɑːd/ *n.* **1** a poem of one or more triplets of stanzas with a repeated refrain and an envoy. **2** *Mus.* a short lyrical piece, esp. for piano. [earlier spelling and pronunc. of BALLAD]

balladeer /ˌbæləˈdɪə(r)/ *n.* a singer or composer of ballads.

balladry /ˈbælədrɪ/ *n.* ballad poetry.

ballast /ˈbæləst/ *n. & v.* —*n.* **1** any heavy material placed in a ship or the car of a balloon etc. to secure stability. **2** coarse stone etc. used to form the bed of a railway track or road. **3** *Electr.* any device used to stabilize the current in a circuit. **4** anything that affords stability or permanence. —*v.tr.* **1** provide with ballast. **2** afford stability or weight to. [16th c.: f. LG or Scand., of uncert. orig.]

ballboy /ˈbɔːlbɔɪ/ *n.* (*fem.* **ballgirl** /-gɜːl/) (in lawn tennis) a boy or girl who retrieves balls that go out of play during a game.

ballcock /ˈbɔːlkɒk/ *n.* a floating ball on a hinged arm, whose movement up and down controls the water level in a cistern.

ballerina /ˌbæləˈriːnə/ *n.* a female ballet-dancer. [It., fem. of *ballerino* dancing-master f. *ballare* dance f. LL: see BALL²]

ballet /ˈbæleɪ/ *n.* **1 a** a dramatic or representational style of dancing and mime, using set steps and techniques and usu. (esp. in classical ballet) accompanied by music. **b** a particular piece or performance of ballet. **c** the music for this. **2** a company performing ballet. □**ballet-dancer** a dancer who specializes in ballet. □□ **balletic** /bəˈletɪk/ *adj.* [F f. It. *balletto* dimin. of *ballo* BALL²]

balletomane /ˈbælɪtəʊˌmeɪn/ *n.* a devotee of ballet. □□ **balletomania** /-ˈmeɪnɪə/ *n.*

ballista /bəˈlɪstə/ *n.* (*pl.* **ballistae** /-stiː/) a catapult used in ancient warfare for hurling large stones etc. [L f. Gk *ballō* throw]

ballistic /bəˈlɪstɪk/ *adj.* **1** of or relating to projectiles. **2** moving under the force of gravity only. □**ballistic missile** a missile which is initially powered and guided but falls under gravity on its target. □□ **ballistically** *adv.* [BALLISTA + -IC]

ballistics /bəˈlɪstɪks/ *n.pl.* (usu. treated as *sing.*) the science of projectiles and firearms.

ballocks var. of BOLLOCKS.

ballon d'essai /bæˌlɔ̃ deˈseɪ/ *n.* (*pl.* **ballons d'essai** *pronunc.* same) an experiment to see how a new policy etc. will be received. [F, = trial balloon]

balloon /bəˈluːn/ *n.* & *v.* —*n.* **1** a small inflatable rubber pouch with a neck, used as a child's toy or as decoration. **2** a large usu. round bag inflatable with hot air or gas to make it rise in the air, often carrying a basket for passengers. **3** *colloq.* a balloon shape enclosing the words or thoughts of characters in a comic strip or cartoon. **4** a large globular drinking glass, usu. for brandy. —*v.* **1** *intr.* & *tr.* swell out or cause to swell out like a balloon. **2** *intr.* travel by balloon. **3** *tr. Brit.* hit or kick (a ball etc.) high in the air. □□ **balloonist** *n.* [F *ballon* or It. *ballone* large ball]

ballot /ˈbælət/ *n.* & *v.* —*n.* **1** a process of voting, in writing and usu. secret. **2** the total of votes recorded in a ballot. **3** the drawing of lots. **4** a paper or ticket etc. used in voting. —*v.* (**balloted, balloting**) **1** *intr.* (usu. foll. by *for*) **a** hold a ballot; give a vote. **b** draw lots for precedence etc. **2** *tr.* take a ballot of (*the union balloted its members*). □**ballot-box** a sealed box into which voters put completed ballot-papers. **ballot-paper** a slip of paper used to register a vote. [It. *ballotta* dimin. of *balla* BALL¹]

ballpark /ˈbɔːlpɑːk/ *n. US* **1** a baseball ground. **2** (*attrib.*) *colloq.* approximate, rough (*a ballpark figure*). □**in the right ballpark** *colloq.* close to one's objective; approximately correct.

ballroom /ˈbɔːlruːm, -rʊm/ *n.* a large room or hall for dancing. □**ballroom dancing** formal social dancing as a recreation.

bally /ˈbælɪ/ *adj.* & *adv. Brit. sl.* a mild form of *bloody* (see BLOODY *adj.* 3) (*took the bally lot*). [alt. of BLOODY]

ballyhoo /ˌbælɪˈhuː/ *n.* **1** a loud noise or fuss; a confused state or commotion. **2** extravagant or sensational publicity. [19th or 20th c., orig. US (in sense 2): orig. unkn.]

ballyrag /ˈbælɪˌræg/ *v.tr.* (also **bullyrag** /ˈbʊl-/) (**-ragged, -ragging**) *sl.* play tricks on; scold, harass. [18th c.: orig. unkn.]

balm /bɑːm/ *n.* **1** an aromatic ointment for anointing, soothing, or healing. **2** a fragrant and medicinal exudation from certain trees and plants. **3** a healing or soothing influence or consolation. **4** an Asian and N. African tree yielding balm. **5** any aromatic herb,

esp. one of the genus *Melissa.* **6** a pleasant perfume or fragrance. □**balm of Gilead** (cf. Jer. 8:22) **1 a** a fragrant resin formerly much used as an unguent. **b** a plant of the genus *Commiphora* yielding such resin. **2** the balsam fir or poplar. [ME f. OF *ba(s)me* f. L *balsamum* BALSAM]

balmoral /bælˈmɒr(ə)l/ *n.* **1** a type of brimless boat-shaped cocked hat with a cockade or ribbons attached, usu. worn by certain Scottish regiments. **2** a heavy leather walking-boot with laces up the front. [*Balmoral* Castle in Scotland]

balmy /ˈbɑːmɪ/ *adj.* (**balmier, balmiest**) **1** mild and fragrant; soothing. **2** yielding balm. **3** *sl.* = BARMY. □□ **balmily** *adv.* **balminess** *n.*

balneology /ˌbælnɪˈɒlədʒɪ/ *n.* the scientific study of bathing and medicinal springs. □□ **balneological** /-nɪəˈlɒdʒɪk(ə)l/ *adj.* **balneologist** *n.* [L *balneum* bath + -LOGY]

baloney var. of BOLONEY.

BALPA *abbr.* British Air Line Pilots' Association.

balsa /ˈbɒlsə, ˈbɔːl-/ *n.* **1** (in full **balsa-wood**) a type of tough lightweight wood used for making models etc. **2** the tropical American tree, *Ochroma lagopus*, from which it comes. [Sp., = raft]

balsam /ˈbɒlsəm, ˈbɔːl-/ *n.* **1** any of several aromatic resinous exudations, such as balm, obtained from various trees and shrubs and used as a base for certain fragrances and medical preparations. **2** an ointment, esp. one composed of a substance dissolved in oil or turpentine. **3** any of various trees or shrubs which yield balsam. **4** any of several flowering plants of the genus *Impatiens.* **5** a healing or soothing agency. □**balsam apple** any of various gourdlike plants of the genus *Momordica*, having warted orange-yellow fruits. **balsam fir** a N. American tree (*Abies balsamea*) which yields balsam. **balsam poplar** any of various N. American poplars, esp. *Populus balsamifera*, yielding balsam. □□ **balsamic** /-ˈsæmɪk/ *adj.* [OE f. L *balsamum*]

Baltic /ˈbɔːltɪk, ˈbɒl-/ *n.* & *adj.* —*n.* **1** (**the Baltic**) **a** an almost land-locked sea of NE Europe. **b** the States bordering this sea. **2** an Indo-European branch of languages including Old Prussian, Lithuanian, Latvian, and Lettish. —*adj.* of or relating to the Baltic or the branch of languages called *Baltic.* [med.L *Balticus* f. LL *Balthae* dwellers near the Baltic Sea]

baluster /ˈbæləstə(r)/ *n.* each of a series of often ornamental short posts or pillars supporting a rail or coping etc. ¶ Often confused with *banister.* [F *balustre* f. It. *balaustro* f. L f. Gk *balaustion* wild-pomegranate flower]

balustrade /ˌbæləˈstreɪd/ *n.* a railing supported by balusters, esp. forming an ornamental parapet to a balcony, bridge, or terrace. [F (as BALUSTER)]

bambino /bæmˈbiːnəʊ/ *n.* (*pl.* **bambini** /-nɪ/) *colloq.* a young (esp. Italian) child. [It., dimin. of *bambo* silly]

bamboo /bæmˈbuː/ *n.* **1** a mainly tropical giant woody grass of the subfamily Bambusidae. **2** its hollow jointed stem, used as a stick or to make furniture etc. [Du. *bamboes* f. Port. *mambu* f. Malay]

bamboozle /bæmˈbuːz(ə)l/ *v.tr. colloq.* cheat, hoax, mystify. □□ **bamboozlement** *n.* **bamboozler** *n.* [c.1700: prob. of cant orig.]

ban /bæn/ *v.* & *n.* —*v.tr.* (**banned, banning**) forbid, prohibit, esp. formally. —*n.* **1** a formal or authoritative prohibition (*a ban on smoking*). **2** a tacit prohibition by public opinion. **3** a sentence of outlawry. **4** *archaic* a curse or execration. [OE *bannan* summon f. Gmc]

banal /bəˈnɑːl/ *adj.* trite, feeble, commonplace. □□ **banality** /-ˈnælɪtɪ/ *n.* (*pl.* **-ies**). **banally** *adv.* [orig. in sense 'compulsory', hence 'common to all', f. F f. *ban* (as BAN)]

banana /bəˈnɑːnə/ *n.* **1** a long curved fruit with soft pulpy flesh and yellow skin when ripe, growing in clusters. **2** (in full **banana-tree**) the tropical and subtropical treelike plant, *Musa sapientum*, bearing this. □**banana republic** *derog.* a small State, esp. in Central America, dependent on the influx of foreign capital. **banana skin 1** the skin of a banana. **2** a cause of upset or humiliation; a blunder. **banana split** a sweet dish made with split bananas, ice-cream, sauce, etc. **go bananas** *sl.* become crazy or angry. [Port. or Sp., f. a name in Guinea]

banausic /bə'nɔːsɪk/ *adj. derog.* **1 a** uncultivated. **b** materialistic. **2** suitable only for artisans. [Gk *banausikos* for artisans]

Banbury cake /'bænbəri/ *n.* a flat pastry with a spicy currant filling. [*Banbury* in S. England, where it was orig. made]

banc /bæŋk/ *n.* □**in banc** *Law* sitting as a full court. [AF (= bench) f. med.L (as BANK²)]

band¹ /bænd/ *n. & v.* —*n.* **1** a flat, thin strip or loop of material (e.g. paper, metal, or cloth) put round something esp. to hold it together or decorate it (*headband*). **2 a** a strip of material forming part of a garment (*hatband*; *waistband*). **b** a stripe of a differ-ent colour or material on an object. **3 a** a range of frequencies or wavelengths in a spectrum (esp. of radio frequencies). **b** a range of values within a series. **4** *Mech.* a belt connecting wheels or pulleys. **5** (in *pl.*) a collar having two hanging strips, worn by some lawyers, ministers, and academics in formal dress. **6** *archaic* a thing that restrains, binds, connects, or unites; a bond. —*v.tr.* **1** put a band on. **2 a** mark with stripes. **b** (as **banded** *adj.*) *Bot. & Zool.* marked with coloured bands or stripes. □**band-saw** a mechanical saw with a blade formed by an endless toothed band. [ME f. OF *bande*, *bende* (sense 6 f. ON *band*) f. Gmc]

band² /bænd/ *n. & v.* —*n.* **1** an organized group of people having a common object, esp. of a criminal nature (*band of cutthroats*). **2 a** a group of musicians, esp. playing wind instruments (*brass band*; *military band*). **b** a group of musicians playing jazz, pop, or dance music. **c** *colloq.* an orchestra. **3** *US* a herd or flock. —*v.tr. & intr.* form into a group for a purpose (*band together for mutual protection*). □**Band of Hope** an association promoting total abstinence from alcohol. [ME f. OF *bande*, *bander*, med.L *banda*, prob. of Gmc orig.]

bandage /'bændɪdʒ/ *n. & v.* —*n.* **1** a strip of material for binding up a wound etc. **2** a piece of material used as a blindfold. —*v.tr.* bind (a wound etc.) with a bandage. [F f. *bande* (as BAND¹)]

bandanna /bæn'dænə/ *n.* a large coloured hand-kerchief or neckerchief, usu. of silk or cotton, and often having white spots. [prob. Port. f. Hindi]

b. & b. *abbr.* bed and breakfast.

bandbox /'bændbɒks/ *n.* a usu. circular cardboard box for carrying hats. □**out of a bandbox** extremely neat. [BAND¹ + BOX¹]

bandeau /'bændəʊ, -'dəʊ/ *n.* (*pl.* **bandeaux** /-dəʊz/) a narrow band worn round the head. [F]

banderilla /ˌbændə'rɪljə/ *n.* a decorated dart thrust into a bull's neck or shoulders during a bullfight. [Sp.]

banderole /ˌbændə'rəʊl/ *n.* (also **banderol**) **1 a** a long narrow flag with a cleft end, flown at a masthead. **b** an ornamental streamer on a knight's lance. **2 a** a ribbon-like scroll. **b** a stone band resembling a banderole, bearing an inscription. [F *banderole* f. It. *banderuola* dimin. of *bandiera* BANNER]

bandicoot /'bændɪˌkuːt/ *n.* **1** any of the insect- and plant-eating marsupials of the family *Peramelidae*. **2** (in full **bandicoot rat**) *Ind.* a destructive rat, *Bandicota benegalensis*. [Telugu *pandikokku* pig-rat]

bandit /'bændɪt/ *n.* (*pl.* **bandits** or **banditti** /-'dɪti/) **1** a robber or murderer, esp. a member of a gang; a gangster. **2** an outlaw. □□**banditry** *n.* [It. *bandito* (pl. *-iti*), past part. of *bandire* ban, = med.L *bannire* proclaim: see BANISH]

bandmaster /'bændˌmɑːstə(r)/ *n.* the conductor of a (esp. military or brass) band. [BAND² + MASTER]

bandolier /ˌbændə'lɪə(r)/ *n.* (also **bandoleer**) a shoulder belt with loops or pockets for cartridges. [Du. *bandelier* or F *bandoulière*, prob. formed as BANDEROLE]

bandsman /'bændzmən/ *n.* (*pl.* **-men**) a player in a (esp. military or brass) band.

bandstand /'bændstænd/ *n.* a covered outdoor plat-form for a band to play on, usu. in a park.

bandwagon /'bændˌwægən/ *n. US* a wagon used for carrying a band in a parade etc. □**climb** (or **jump**) **on the bandwagon** join a party, cause, or group that seems likely to succeed.

bandwidth /'bændwɪtθ, -wɪdθ/ *n.* the range of fre-quencies within a given band (see BAND¹ *n.* 3a).

bandy¹ /'bændi/ *adj.* (**bandier, bandiest**) **1** (of the legs) curved so as to be wide apart at the knees. **2** (also **bandy-legged**) (of a person) having bandy legs. [perh. f. obs. *bandy* curved stick]

bandy² /'bændi/ *v.tr.* (**-ies, -ied**) **1** (often foll. by *about*) **a** pass (a story, rumour, etc.) to and fro. **b** throw or pass (a ball etc.) to and fro. **2** (often foll. by *about*) discuss disparagingly (*bandied her name about*). **3** (often foll. by *with*) exchange (blows, insults, etc.) (*don't bandy words with me*). [perh. f. F *bander* take sides f. *bande* BAND²]

bane /beɪn/ *n.* **1** the cause of ruin or trouble; the curse (esp. *the bane of one's life*). **2** *poet.* ruin; woe. **3** *archaic* (except in *comb.*) poison (*ratsbane*). □□ **baneful** *adj.* **banefully** *adv.* [OE *bana* f. Gmc]

baneberry /'beɪnbəri/ *n.* (*pl.* **-ies**) **1** a plant of the genus *Actaea*. **2** the bitter poisonous berry of this plant.

bang /bæŋ/ *n., v., & adv.* —*n.* **1 a** a loud short sound. **b** an explosion. **c** the report of a gun. **2 a** a sharp blow. **b** the sound of this. **3** esp. *US* a fringe of hair cut straight across the forehead. **4** *coarse sl.* an act of sexual intercourse. **5** *sl.* a drug injection (cf. BHANG). —*v.* **1** *tr. & intr.* strike or shut noisily (*banged the door shut*; *banged on the table*). **2** *tr. & intr.* make or cause to make the sound of a blow or an explosion. **3** *tr.* esp. *US* cut (hair) in a bang. **4** *coarse sl.* **a** *intr.* have sexual intercourse. **b** *tr.* have sexual intercourse with. —*adv.* **1** with a bang or sudden impact. **2** *colloq.* exactly (*bang in the middle*). □**bang off** *Brit. sl.* immediately. **bang on** *Brit. colloq.* exactly right. **bang-up** *US sl.* first-class, excellent (esp. *bang-up job*). **go bang 1** (of a door etc.) shut noisily. **2** explode. **3** *colloq.* be suddenly destroyed (*bang went their chances*). **go with a bang** go successfully. [16th c.: perh. f. Scand.]

banger /'bæŋə(r)/ *n. Brit.* **1** *sl.* a sausage. **2** *sl.* an old car, esp. a noisy one. **3** a loud firework.

bangle /'bæŋg(ə)l/ *n.* a rigid ornamental band worn round the arm or occas. the ankle. [Hindi *bangri* glass bracelet]

bangtail /'bæŋteɪl/ *n.* a horse, esp. with its tail cut straight across. □**bangtail muster** *Austral.* the counting of cattle involving cutting across the tufts at the tail-ends as each is counted.

banian var. of BANYAN.

banish /'bænɪʃ/ *v.tr.* **1** formally expel (a person), esp. from a country. **2** dismiss from one's presence or mind. □□ **banishment** *n.* [ME f. OE *banir* ult. f. Gmc]

banister /'bænɪstə(r)/ *n.* (also **bannister**) **1** (in *pl.*) the uprights and handrail at the side of a staircase. **2** (usu. in *pl.*) an upright supporting a handrail. ¶ Often confused with *baluster*. [earlier *barrister*, corrupt. of BALUSTER]

banjo /'bændʒəʊ/ *n.* (*pl.* **-os** or **-oes**) a stringed musical instrument with a neck and head like a guitar and an open-backed body consisting of parchment stretched over a metal hoop. □□ **banjoist** *n.* [US southern corrupt. of earlier *bandore* ult. f. Gk *pandoura* three-stringed lute]

bank¹ /bæŋk/ *n. & v.* —*n.* **1 a** the sloping edge of land by a river. **b** the area of ground alongside a river (*had a picnic on the bank*). **2** a raised shelf of ground; a slope. **3** an elevation in the sea or a river bed. **4** the artificial slope of a road etc., enabling vehicles to maintain speed round a curve. **5** a mass of cloud, fog, snow, etc. **6** the edge of a hollow place (e.g. the top of a mine-shaft). —*v.* **1** *tr.* & *intr.* (often foll. by *up*) heap or rise into banks. **2** *tr.* heap up (a fire) tightly so that it burns slowly. **3 a** *intr.* (of a vehicle or aircraft or its occupant) travel with one side higher than the other in rounding a curve. **b** *tr.* cause (a vehicle or aircraft) to do this. **4** *tr.* contain or confine within a bank or banks. **5** *tr.* build (a road etc.) higher at the outer edge of a bend to enable fast cornering. [ME f. Gmc f. ON *banki* (unrecorded: cf. OIcel. *bakki*): rel. to BENCH]

bank² /bæŋk/ *n.* & *v.* —*n.* **1 a** a financial establishment which uses money deposited by customers for investment, pays it out when required, makes loans at interest, exchanges currency, etc. **b** a building in which this business takes place. **2** = *piggy bank.* **3 a** the money or tokens held by the banker in some gambling games. **b** the banker in such games. **4** a place for storing anything for future use (*blood bank*; *data bank*). —*v.* **1** *tr.* deposit (money or valuables) in a bank. **2** *intr.* engage in business as a banker. **3** *intr.* (often foll. by *at, with*) keep money (at a bank). **4** *intr.* act as banker in some gambling games. □**bank balance** the amount of money held in a bank account at a given moment. **bank-bill 1** *Brit.* a bill drawn by one bank on another. **2** *US* = BANKNOTE. **bank-book** = PASSBOOK. **bank card** = *cheque card.* **bank holiday** a day on which banks are officially closed, (in the UK) usu. kept as a public holiday. **bank manager** a person in charge of a local branch of a bank. **the Bank of England** the central bank of England and Wales, issuing banknotes and having the Government as its main customer. **bank on** rely on (*I'm banking on your help*). **bank statement** a printed statement of transactions and balance issued periodically to the holder of a bank account. [F *banque* or It. *banca* f. med.L *banca, bancus*, f. Gmc: rel. to BANK¹]

bank³ /bæŋk/ *n.* **1** a row of similar objects, esp. of keys, lights, or switches. **2** a tier of oars. [ME f. OF *banc* f. Gmc: rel. to BANK¹, BENCH]

bankable /'bæŋkəb(ə)l/ *adj.* **1** acceptable at a bank. **2** reliable (*a bankable reputation*).

banker¹ /'bæŋkə(r)/ *n.* **1** a person who manages or owns a bank or group of banks. **2 a** a keeper of the bank or dealer in some gambling games. **b** a card-game involving gambling. **3** *Brit.* a result forecast identically (while other forecasts differ) on several football-pool entries on one coupon. □**banker's card** = *cheque card.* **banker's order** an instruction to a bank to pay money or deliver property, signed by the owner or the owner's agent. [F *banquier* f. *banque* BANK²]

banker² /'bæŋkə(r)/ *n.* **1 a** a fishing boat off Newfoundland. **b** a Newfoundland fisherman. **2** *Austral. colloq.* a river flooded to the top of its banks. [BANK¹ + -ER¹]

banking /'bæŋkɪŋ/ *n.* the business transactions of a bank.

banknote /'bæŋknəʊt/ *n.* a banker's promissory note, esp. from a central bank, payable to the bearer on demand, and serving as money.

bankroll /'bæŋkrəʊl/ *n.* & *v. US* —*n.* **1** a roll of banknotes. **2** funds. —*v.tr. colloq.* support financially.

bankrupt /'bæŋkrʌpt/ *adj., n., & v.* —*adj.* **1 a** insolvent; declared in law unable to pay debts. **b** undergoing the legal process resulting from this. **2** (often foll. by *of*) exhausted or drained (of some quality etc.); deficient, lacking. —*n.* **1 a** an insolvent person whose estate is administered and disposed of for the benefit of the creditors. **b** an insolvent debtor. **2** a person exhausted of or deficient in a certain attribute (*a moral bankrupt*). —*v.tr.* make bankrupt. □□**bankruptcy** /-,rʌptsɪ/ *n.* (*pl.* -ies). [16th c.: f. It *banca rotta* broken bench (as BANK², L *rumpere rupt-* break), assim. to L]

banksia /'bæŋksɪə/ *n.* any evergreen flowering shrub of the genus *Banksia*, native to Australia. □**banksia rose** a Chinese climbing rose with small flowers. [Sir J. *Banks*, Engl. naturalist d. 1820]

banner /'bænə(r)/ *n.* **1 a** a large rectangular sign bearing a slogan or design and usu. carried on two side-poles or a crossbar in a demonstration or procession. **b** a long strip of cloth etc. hung across a street or along the front of a building etc. and bearing a slogan. **2** a slogan or phrase used to represent a belief or principle. **3** a flag on a pole used as the standard of a king, knight, etc., esp. in battle. **4** (*attrib.*) *US* excellent, outstanding (*a banner year in sales*). □**banner headline** a large newspaper headline, esp. one across the top of the front page. **join** (or **follow**) **the banner of** adhere to the cause of. □□**bannered** *adj.* [ME f. AF *banere*, OF *baniere* f. Rmc ult. f. Gmc]

banneret /'bænərɪt/ *n. hist.* **1** a knight who commanded his own troops in battle under his own banner. **2** a knighthood given on the battlefield for courage. [ME & OF *baneret* f. *baniere* BANNER + -*et* as -ATE¹]

bannister var. of BANISTER.

bannock /'bænək/ *n. Sc.* & *N.Engl.* a round flat loaf, usu. unleavened. [OE *bannuc*, perh. f. Celt.]

banns /bænz/ *n.pl.* a notice read out on three successive Sundays in a parish church, announcing an intended marriage and giving the opportunity for objections. □**forbid the banns** raise an objection to an intended marriage, esp. in church following the reading of the banns. [pl. of BAN]

banquet /'bæŋkwɪt/ *n.* & *v.* —*n.* **1** an elaborate usu. extensive feast. **2** a dinner for many people followed by speeches in favour of a cause or in celebration of an event. —*v.* (**banqueted, banqueting**) **1** *intr.* hold a banquet; feast. **2** *tr.* entertain with a banquet. □□**banqueter** *n.* [F, dimin. of *banc* bench, BANK²]

banquette /bæŋ'ket/ *n.* **1** an upholstered bench along a wall, esp. in a restaurant or bar. **2** a raised step behind a rampart. [F f. It. *banchetta* dimin. of *banca* bench, BANK²]

banshee /'bænʃiː, -'ʃiː/ *n. Ir.* & *Sc.* a female spirit whose wailing warns of a death in a house. [Ir. *bean sídhe* f. *ben síde* woman of the fairies]

bantam /'bæntəm/ *n.* **1** any of several small breeds of domestic fowl, of which the cock is very aggressive. **2** a small but aggressive person. [app. f. *Bāntān* in Java, although the fowl is not native there]

bantamweight /'bæntəm,weɪt/ *n.* **1** a weight in certain sports intermediate between flyweight and featherweight, in the amateur boxing scale 51-4 kg but differing for professional boxers, wrestlers, and weightlifters. **2** a sportsman of this weight.

banter /'bæntə(r)/ *n.* & *v.* —*n.* good-humoured teasing. —*v.* **1** *tr.* ridicule in a good-humoured way. **2** *intr.* talk humorously or teasingly. □□**banterer** *n.* [17th c.: orig. unkn.]

Bantu /bæn'tuː/ *n.* & *adj.* —*n.* (*pl.* same or **Bantus**) **1** often *offens.* **a** a large group of Negroid peoples of central and southern Africa. **b** a member of any of these peoples. **2** the group of languages spoken by them. —*adj.* of or relating to these peoples or languages. [Bantu, = people]

Bantustan /,bæntu:'stɑːn/ *n. S.Afr.* often *offens.* any of several partially self-governing areas reserved for Black South Africans (see also HOMELAND). [BANTU + -*stan* as in *Hindustan*]

banyan /'bænɪən, -jən/ *n.* (also **banian**) **1** an Indian fig tree, *Ficus benghalensis*, the branches of which hang down and root themselves. **2** a Hindu trader. **3** a loose flannel jacket, shirt, or gown worn in India. [Port. *banian* f. Gujarati *vāṇiyo* man of trading caste, f. Skr.: applied orig. to one such tree under which banyans had built a pagoda]

banzai /bɑːn'zaɪ/ *int.* **1** a Japanese battle cry. **2** a form of greeting used to the Japanese emperor. [Jap., = ten thousand years (of life to you)]

baobab /'beɪəʊˌbæb/ n. an African tree, *Adansonia digitata*, with an enormously thick trunk and large fruit containing edible pulp. [L (1592), prob. f. an Afr. lang.]

BAOR abbr. British Army of the Rhine.

bap /bæp/ n. *Brit*. a soft flattish bread roll. [16th c.: orig. unkn.]

baptism /'bæptɪz(ə)m/ n. **1 a** the religious rite, symbolizing admission to the Christian Church, of sprinkling the forehead with water, or (usu. only with adults) by immersion, generally accompanied by name-giving. **b** the act of baptizing or being baptized. **2** an initiation, e.g. into battle. **3** the naming of ships, church bells, etc. □**baptism of fire 1** initiation into battle. **2** a painful new undertaking or experience. □□ **baptismal** /-'tɪzm(ə)l/ adj. [ME f. OF ba(p)te(s)me f. eccl.L baptismus f. eccl.Gk baptismos f. baptizō BAPTIZE]

baptist /'bæptɪst/ n. **1** a person who baptizes, esp. John the Baptist. **2** (**Baptist**) a Christian advocating baptism by total immersion, esp. of adults, as a symbol of membership of and initiation into the Church. [ME f. OF baptiste f. eccl.L baptista f. eccl.Gk baptistēs f. baptizō BAPTIZE]

baptistery /'bæptɪstərɪ/ n. (also **baptistry** /-trɪ/) (pl. -ies) **1 a** the part of a church used for baptism. **b** hist. a building next to a church, used for baptism. **2** (in a Baptist chapel) a sunken receptacle used for total immersion. [ME f. OF baptisterie f. eccl.L baptisterium f. eccl.Gk baptistērion bathing-place f. baptizō BAPTIZE]

baptize /bæp'taɪz/ v.tr. (also **-ise**) **1** (also absol.) administer baptism to. **2** give a name or nickname to; christen. [ME f. OF baptiser f. eccl.L baptizare f. Gk baptizō immerse, baptize]

bar[1] /bɑː(r)/ n., v., & prep. —n. **1** a long rod or piece of rigid wood, metal, etc., esp. used as an obstruction, confinement, fastening, weapon, etc. **2 a** something resembling a bar in being (thought of as) straight, narrow, and rigid (*bar of soap*; *bar of chocolate*). **b** a band of colour or light, esp. on a flat surface. **c** the heating element of an electric fire. **d** = CROSSBAR. **e** *Brit.* a metal strip below the clasp of a medal, awarded as an extra distinction. **f** a sandbank or shoal at the mouth of a harbour or an estuary. **g** *Brit.* a rail marking the end of each chamber in the Houses of Parliament. **h** *Heraldry* a narrow horizontal stripe across a shield. **3 a** a barrier of any shape. **b** a restriction (*colour bar*; *a bar to promotion*). **4 a** a counter in a public house, restaurant, or café across which alcohol or refreshments are served. **b** a room in a public house in which customers may sit and drink. **c** *US* a public house. **d** a small shop or stall serving refreshments (*snack bar*). **e** a specialized department in a large store (*heel bar*). **5 a** an enclosure in which a prisoner stands in a lawcourt. **b** a public standard of acceptability, before which a person is said to be tried (*bar of conscience*). **c** a plea arresting an action or claim in a law case. **d** a particular court of law. **6** *Mus.* **a** any of the sections of usu. equal time-value into which a musical composition is divided by vertical lines across the staff. **b** = *bar-line*. **7** (**the Bar**) *Law* **a** barristers collectively. **b** the profession of barrister. —v.tr. (**barred**, **barring**) **1 a** fasten (a door, window, etc.) with a bar or bars. **b** (usu. foll. by in, out) shut or keep in or out (*barred him in*). **2** obstruct, prevent (*bar his progress*). **3 a** (usu. foll. by from) prohibit, exclude (*bar them from attending*). **b** exclude from consideration (cf. BARRING). **4** mark with stripes. **5** *Law* prevent or delay (an action) by objection. —prep. **1** except (*all were there bar a few*). **2** *Racing* except (the horses indicated: used in stating the odds, indicating the number of horses excluded) (*33–1 bar three*). □**bar billiards** a form of billiards in which balls are knocked into holes in the table. **bar chart** a chart using bars to represent quantity. **bar-code** a machine-readable code in the form of a pattern of stripes printed on and identifying a commodity, used esp. for stock-control. **bar-line** *Mus.* a vertical line used to mark divisions between bars. **bar none** with no exceptions. **bar person** a barmaid or barman. **bar sinister** = *bend sinister* (see BEND[2]). **bar tracery** tracery with strips of stone across an aperture. **be called to the Bar** *Brit.* be admitted as a barrister. **be called within the Bar** *Brit.* be appointed a Queen's Counsel. **behind bars** in prison. **the outer Bar** barristers who are not Queen's Counsels. [ME f. OF barre, barrer, f. Rmc]

bar[2] /bɑː(r)/ n. esp. *Meteorol.* a unit of pressure, 10^5 newton per square metre, approx. one atmosphere. [Gk baros weight]

barathea /ˌbærə'θɪə/ n. a fine woollen cloth, sometimes mixed with silk or cotton, used esp. for coats, suits, etc. [19th c.: orig. unkn.]

barb /bɑːb/ n. & v. —n. **1** a secondary backward-facing projection from an arrow, fish-hook, etc., angled to make extraction difficult. **2** a deliberately hurtful remark. **3** a beardlike filament at the mouth of some fish, e.g. barbel and catfish. **4** any one of the fine hairlike filaments growing from the shaft of a feather, forming the vane. —v.tr. **1** provide (an arrow, a fish-hook, etc.) with a barb or barbs. **2** (as **barbed** adj.) (of a remark etc.) deliberately hurtful. □**barbed wire** wire bearing sharp pointed spikes close together and used in fencing, or in warfare as an obstruction. [ME f. OF barbe f. L barba beard]

Barbadian /bɑː'beɪdɪən/ n. & adj. —n. **1** a native or national of Barbados in the W. Indies. **2** a person of Barbadian descent. —adj. of or relating to Barbados or its people.

barbarian /bɑː'beərɪən/ n. & adj. —n. **1** an uncultured or brutish person; a lout. **2** a member of a primitive community or tribe. —adj. **1** rough and uncultured. **2** uncivilized. [orig. of any foreigner with a different language or customs: F barbarien f. barbare (as BARBAROUS)]

barbaric /bɑː'bærɪk/ adj. **1** brutal; cruel (*flogging is a barbaric punishment*). **2** rough and uncultured; unrestrained. **3** of or like barbarians and their art or taste; primitive. □□ **barbarically** adv. [ME f. OF barbarique or L barbaricus f. Gk barbarikos f. barbaros foreign]

barbarism /'bɑːbəˌrɪz(ə)m/ n. **1 a** the absence of culture and civilized standards; ignorance and rudeness. **b** an example of this. **2** a word or expression not considered correct; a solecism. **3** anything considered to be in bad taste. [F barbarisme f. L barbarismus f. Gk barbarismos f. barbarizō speak like a foreigner f. barbaros foreign]

barbarity /bɑː'bærɪtɪ/ n. (pl. -ies) **1** savage cruelty. **2** an example of this.

barbarize /'bɑːbəˌraɪz/ v.tr. & intr. (also **-ise**) make or become barbarous. □□ **barbarization** /-'zeɪʃ(ə)n/ n.

barbarous /'bɑːbərəs/ adj. **1** uncivilized. **2** cruel. **3** coarse and unrefined. □□ **barbarously** adv. **barbarousness** n. [orig. of any foreign language or people: f. L f. Gk barbaros foreign]

Barbary ape /'bɑːbərɪ/ n. a macaque, *Macaca sylvana*, of N. Africa and Gibraltar. [*Barbary*, an old name of the western part of N. Africa, ult. f. Arab. barbar BERBER]

barbecue /'bɑːbɪˌkjuː/ n. & v. —n. **1 a** a meal cooked on an open fire out of doors, esp. meat grilled on a metal appliance. **b** a party at which such a meal is cooked and eaten. **2 a** the metal appliance used for the preparation of a barbecue. **b** a fireplace, usu. of brick, containing such an appliance. —v.tr. (**barbecues, barbecued, barbecuing**) cook (esp. meat) on a barbecue. □**barbecue sauce** a highly seasoned sauce, usu. containing chillies, in which meat etc. may be cooked. [Sp. barbacòa f. Haitian barbaca wooden frame on posts]

barbel /'bɑːb(ə)l/ n. **1** any large European freshwater fish of the genus *Barbus*, with fleshy filaments hanging from its mouth. **2** such a filament growing from the mouth of any fish. [ME f. OF f. LL *barbellus* dimin. of *barbus* barbel f. *barba* beard]

barbell /'bɑːbel/ *n.* an iron bar with a series of graded discs at each end, used for weightlifting exercises. [BAR¹ + BELL¹]

barber /'bɑːbə(r)/ *n. & v.* —*n.* a person who cuts men's hair and shaves or trims beards as an occupation; a men's hairdresser. —*v.tr.* **1** cut the hair, shave or trim the beard of. **2** cut or trim closely (*barbered the grass*). □**barber-shop** (or **barber-shop quartet**) *US colloq.* a popular style of close harmony singing for four male voices. **barber's pole** a spirally painted striped red and white pole hung outside barbers' shops as a business sign. [ME & AF f. OF *barbeor* f. med.L *barbator -oris* f. *barba* beard]

barberry /'bɑːbərɪ/ *n.* (*pl.* **-ies**) **1** any shrub of the genus *Berberis*, with spiny shoots, yellow flowers, and ovoid red berries, often grown as hedges. **2** its berry. [ME f. OF *berberis*, of unkn. orig.: assim. to BERRY]

barbet /'bɑːbɪt/ *n.* any small brightly coloured tropical bird of the family Capitonidae, with bristles at the base of its beak. [F f. *barbe* beard]

barbette /bɑː'bet/ *n.* a platform in a fort or ship from which guns can be fired over a parapet etc. without an embrasure. [F, dimin. of *barbe* beard]

barbican /'bɑːbɪkən/ *n.* the outer defence of a city, castle, etc., esp. a double tower above a gate or drawbridge. [ME f. OF *barbacane*, of unkn. orig.]

barbitone /'bɑːbɪˌtəʊn/ *n.* (*US* **barbital** /'bɑːbɪt(ə)l/) a sedative drug. [as BARBITURIC ACID + -ONE, -*al* as in *veronal*]

barbiturate /bɑː'bɪtjʊrət, -ˌreɪt/ *n.* any derivative of barbituric acid used in the preparation of sedative and sleep-inducing drugs. [BARBITURIC + -ATE¹]

barbituric acid /ˌbɑːbɪ'tjʊərɪk/ *n. Chem.* an organic acid from which various sedatives and sleep-inducing drugs are derived. [F *barbiturique* f. G *Barbitursäure* (*Säure* acid) f. the name *Barbara*]

barbola /bɑː'bəʊlə/ *n.* (in full **barbola work**) **1** the craft of making small models of fruit, flowers, etc. from a plastic paste. **2** articles, e.g. mirrors, decorated with such models. [arbitr. f. *barbotine* clay slip for ornamenting pottery]

barbule /'bɑːbjuːl/ *n.* a minute filament projecting from the barb of a feather. [L *barbula*, dimin. of *barba* beard]

barbwire /'bɑːbˌwaɪə(r)/ *n. US* = *barbed wire* (see BARB).

barcarole /'bɑːkəˌrəʊl/ *n.* (also **barcarolle** /-ˌrɒl/) **1** a song sung by Venetian gondoliers. **2** music in imitation of this. [F *barcarolle* f. Venetian It. *barcarola* boatman's song f. *barca* boat]

bard¹ /bɑːd/ *n.* **1 a** *hist.* a Celtic minstrel. **b** the winner of a prize for Welsh verse at an Eisteddfod. **2** *poet.* a poet, esp. one treating heroic themes. □**the Bard** (or **the Bard of Avon**) Shakespeare. □□ **bardic** *adj.* [Gael. & Ir. *bárd*, Welsh *bardd*, f. OCelt.]

bard² /bɑːd/ *n. & v.* —*n.* a rasher of fat bacon placed on meat or game before roasting. —*v.tr.* cover (meat etc.) with bards. [F *barde*, orig. = horse's breastplate, ult. f. Arab.]

bardy /'bɑːdɪ/ *n.* (*pl.* **-ies**) *Austral.* an edible wood-boring grub. [Aboriginal]

bare /beə(r)/ *adj. & v.* —*adj.* **1** (esp. of part of the body) unclothed or uncovered (*with bare head*). **2** without appropriate covering or contents: **a** (of a tree) leafless. **b** unfurnished; empty (*bare rooms*; *the cupboard was bare*). **c** (of a floor) uncarpeted. **3 a** undisguised (*the bare truth*). **b** unadorned (*bare facts*). **4** (*attrib.*) **a** scanty (*a bare majority*). **b** mere (*bare necessities*). —*v.tr.* **1** uncover, unsheathe (*bared his teeth*). **2** reveal (*bared his soul*). □**bare contract** *Law* a contract lacking a consideration and therefore void unless under seal. **bare of** without. **with one's**

bare hands without using tools or weapons. □□ **bareness** *n.* [OE *bær*, *barian* f. Gmc]

bareback /'beəbæk/ *adj. & adv.* on an unsaddled horse, donkey, etc.

barefaced /'beəfeɪst/ *adj.* undisguised; impudent (*barefaced cheek*). □□ **barefacedly** /-'feɪsɪdlɪ/ *adv.* **barefacedness** *n.*

barefoot /'beəfʊt/ *adj. & adv.* (also **barefooted** /-'fʊtɪd/) with nothing on the feet. □**barefoot doctor** a paramedical worker with basic medical training, esp. in China.

barège /bə'reɪʒ/ *n.* a silky gauze made from wool or other material. [F f. *Barèges* in SW France, where it was orig. made]

bareheaded /beə'hedɪd/ *adj. & adv.* without a covering for the head.

barely /'beəlɪ/ *adv.* **1** only just; scarcely (*barely escaped*). **2** scantily (*barely furnished*). **3** *archaic* openly, explicitly.

barf /bɑːf/ *v. & n. sl.* —*v.intr.* vomit or retch. —*n.* an attack of vomiting. [20th c.: orig. unkn.]

barfly /'bɑːflaɪ/ *n.* (*pl.* **-flies**) *colloq.* a person who frequents bars.

bargain /'bɑːgɪn/ *n. & v.* —*n.* **1 a** an agreement on the terms of a transaction or sale. **b** this seen from the buyer's viewpoint (*a bad bargain*). **2** something acquired or offered cheaply. —*v.intr.* (often foll. by *with, for*) discuss the terms of a transaction (*expected him to bargain, but he paid up*; *bargained with her*; *bargained for the table*). □**bargain away** part with for something worthless (*had bargained away the estate*). **bargain basement** the basement of a shop where bargains are displayed. **bargain for** (or *colloq.* **on**) (usu. with *neg.* actual or implied) be prepared for; expect (*didn't bargain for bad weather*; *more than I bargained for*). **bargain on** rely on. **drive a hard bargain** pursue one's own profit in a transaction keenly. **into** (*US* **in**) **the bargain** moreover; in addition to what was expected. **make** (or **strike**) **a bargain** agree a transaction. □□ **bargainer** *n.* [ME f. OF *bargaine*, *bargaignier*, prob. f. Gmc]

barge /bɑːdʒ/ *n. & v.* —*n.* **1** a long flat-bottomed boat for carrying freight on canals, rivers, etc. **2** a long ornamental boat used for pleasure or ceremony. **3** a boat used by the chief officers of a man-of-war. —*v.intr.* **1** (often foll. by *around*) lurch or rush clumsily about. **2** (foll. by *in, into*) **a** intrude or interrupt rudely or awkwardly (*barged in while we were kissing*). **b** collide with (*barged into her*). [ME f. OF perh. f. med.L *barica* f. Gk *baris* Egyptian boat]

bargeboard /'bɑːdʒbɔːd/ *n.* a board (often ornamental) fixed to the gable-end of a roof to hide the ends of the roof timbers. [perh. f. med.L *bargus* gallows]

bargee /bɑː'dʒiː/ *n. Brit.* a person in charge of or working on a barge.

bargepole /'bɑːdʒpəʊl/ *n.* a long pole used for punting barges etc. and for fending off obstacles. □**would not touch with a bargepole** refuse to be associated or concerned with (a person or thing).

barilla /bə'rɪlə/ *n.* **1** any plant of the genus *Salsola* found chiefly in Spain and Sicily. **2** an impure alkali made by burning either this or kelp. [Sp.]

barite /'beəraɪt/ *n. US* = BARYTES.

baritone /'bærɪˌtəʊn/ *n. & adj.* —*n.* **1 a** the second-lowest adult male singing voice. **b** a singer with this voice. **c** a part written for it. **2 a** an instrument that is second-lowest in pitch in its family. **b** its player. —*adj.* of the second-lowest range. [It. *baritono* f. Gk *barutonos* f. *barus* heavy + *tonos* TONE]

barium /'beərɪəm/ *n. Chem.* a white reactive soft metallic element of the alkaline earth group. ¶ Symb.: **Ba**. □**barium meal** a mixture of barium sulphate and water, which is opaque to X-rays, and is given to patients requiring radiological examination of the stomach and intestines. [BARYTA + -IUM]

bark¹ /bɑːk/ *n. & v.* —*n.* **1** the sharp explosive cry of a dog, fox, etc. **2** a sound resembling this cry. —*v.* **1** *intr.* (of a dog, fox, etc.) give a bark. **2** *tr.* & *intr.* speak or utter sharply or brusquely. **3** *intr.* cough fiercely. **4** *tr.* *US* sell or advertise publicly by calling out. □**one's bark is worse than one's bite** one is not as ferocious as one appears. **bark up the wrong tree** be on the wrong track; make an effort in the wrong direction. [OE *beorcan*]

bark[2] /baːk/ *n.* & *v.* —*n.* **1** the tough protective outer sheath of the trunks, branches, and twigs of trees or woody shrubs. **2** this material used for tanning leather or dyeing material. —*v.tr.* **1** graze or scrape (one's shin etc.). **2** strip bark from (a tree etc.). **3** tan or dye (leather etc.) using the tannins found in bark. [ME f. OIcel. *börkr bark-*: perh. rel. to BIRCH]

bark[3] /baːk/ *n. poet.* a ship or boat. [= BARQUE]

barkeeper /ˈbaːˌkiːpə(r)/ *n.* (also **barkeep**) *US* a person serving drinks in a bar.

barkentine esp. *US* var. of BARQUENTINE.

barker /ˈbaːkə(r)/ *n.* a tout at an auction, sideshow, etc., who calls out for custom to passers-by. [BARK[1] + -ER[1]]

barley /ˈbaːlɪ/ *n.* **1** any of various hardy awned cereals of the genus *Hordeum* widely used as food and in malt liquors and spirits such as whisky. **2** the grain produced from this (cf. *pearl barley*). □**barley sugar** an amber-coloured sweet made of boiled sugar, traditionally shaped as a twisted stick. **barley water** a drink made from water and a boiled barley mixture. [OE *bærlic* (adj.) f. *bære, bere* barley]

barleycorn /ˈbaːlɪˌkɔːn/ *n.* **1** the grain of barley. **2** a former unit of measure (about a third of an inch) based on the length of a grain of barley.

barleymow /ˈbaːlɪˌməʊ/ *n. Brit.* a stack of barley.

barm /baːm/ *n.* **1** the froth on fermenting malt liquor. **2** *archaic* or *dial.* yeast or leaven. [OE *beorma*]

barmaid /ˈbaːmeɪd/ *n.* a woman serving behind the bar of a public house, hotel, etc.

barman /ˈbaːmən/ *n.* (*pl.* **-men**) a man serving behind the bar of a public house, hotel, etc.

barmbrack /ˈbaːmbræk/ *n.* (also **barnbrack** /ˈbaːn-/) *Ir.* soft spicy bread with currants etc. [Ir. *bairigen breac* speckled cake]

Barmecide /ˈbaːmɪˌsaɪd/ *adj.* & *n.* —*adj.* illusory, imaginary; such as to disappoint. —*n.* a giver of benefits that are illusory or disappointing. [the name of a wealthy man in the *Arabian Nights' Entertainments* who gave a beggar a feast consisting of ornate but empty dishes]

bar mitzvah /baː ˈmɪtzvə/ *n.* **1** the religious initiation ceremony of a Jewish boy who has reached the age of 13. **2** the boy undergoing this ceremony. [Heb., = 'son of the commandment']

barmy /ˈbaːmɪ/ *adj.* (**barmier, barmiest**) esp. *Brit. sl.* crazy, stupid. □□**barmily** *adv.* **barminess** *n.* [earlier = frothy, f. BARM]

barn[1] /baːn/ *n.* **1** a large farm building for storing grain etc. **2** *derog.* a large plain or unattractive building. **3** *US* a large shed for storing road or railway vehicles. □**barn dance 1** an informal social gathering for country dancing, orig. in a barn. **2** a dance for a number of couples forming a line or circle, with couples moving along it in turn. **barn-owl** a kind of owl, *Tyto alba*, frequenting barns. [OE *bern, beren* f. *bere* barley + *ern, ærn* house]

barn[2] /baːn/ *n. Physics* a unit of area, 10^{-28} square metres, used esp. in particle physics. ¶ Symb.: **b**. [perh. f. phrase 'as big as a barn']

barnacle /ˈbaːnək(ə)l/ *n.* **1** any of various species of small marine crustaceans of the class Cirripedia which in adult form cling to rocks, ships' bottoms, etc. **2** a tenacious attendant or follower who cannot easily be shaken off. □**barnacle goose** an Arctic goose, *Branta leucopsis*, which visits Britain in winter. □□**barnacled** *adj.* [ME *bernak* (= med.L *bernaca*), of unkn. orig.]

barnbrack var. of BARMBRACK.

barney /ˈbaːnɪ/ *n.* (*pl.* **-eys**) *Brit. colloq.* a noisy quarrel. [perh. dial.]

barnstorm /ˈbaːnstɔːm/ *v.intr.* **1** tour rural districts giving theatrical performances (formerly often in barns). **2** *US* make a rapid tour holding political meetings. **3** *US Aeron.* give informal flying exhibitions; do stunt flying. □□**barnstormer** *n.*

barnyard /ˈbaːnjaːd/ *n.* the area around a barn; a farmyard.

barograph /ˈbærəˌgraːf/ *n.* a barometer equipped to record its readings. [Gk *baros* weight + -GRAPH]

barometer /bəˈrɒmɪtə(r)/ *n.* **1** an instrument measuring atmospheric pressure, esp. in forecasting the weather and determining altitude. **2** anything which reflects changes in circumstances, opinions, etc. □□**barometric** /ˌbærəʊˈmetrɪk/ *adj.* **barometrical** /ˌbærəʊˈmetrɪk(ə)l/ *adj.* **barometry** *n.*

baron /ˈbærən/ *n.* **1 a** a member of the lowest order of the British nobility. **b** a similar member of a foreign nobility. **2** an important businessman or other powerful or influential person (*sugar baron*; *newspaper baron*). **3** *hist.* a person who held lands or property from the sovereign or a powerful overlord. □**baron of beef** an undivided double sirloin. [ME f. AF *barun*, OF *baron* f. med.L *baro, -onis* man, of unkn. orig.]

baronage /ˈbærənɪdʒ/ *n.* **1** barons or nobles collectively. **2** an annotated list of barons or peers. [ME f. OF *barnage* (as BARON)]

baroness /ˈbærənɪs/ *n.* **1** a woman holding the rank of baron either as a life peerage or as a hereditary rank. **2** the wife or widow of a baron. [ME f. OF *baronesse* (as BARON)]

baronet /ˈbærənɪt/ *n.* a member of the lowest hereditary order of the British nobility. [ME f. AL *baronettus* (as BARON)]

baronetage /ˈbærənɪtɪdʒ/ *n.* **1** baronets collectively. **2** an annotated list of baronets.

baronetcy /ˈbærənɪtsɪ/ *n.* (*pl.* **-ies**) the domain, rank, or tenure of a baronet.

baronial /bəˈrəʊnɪəl/ *adj.* of, relating to, or befitting barons.

barony /ˈbærənɪ/ *n.* (*pl.* **-ies**) **1** the domain, rank, or tenure of a baron. **2** (in Ireland) a division of a county. **3** (in Scotland) a large manor or estate. [ME f. OF *baronie* (as BARON)]

baroque /bəˈrɒk/ *adj.* & *n.* —*adj.* **1** highly ornate and extravagant in style, esp. of European art, architecture, and music of the 17th and 18th c. **2** of or relating to this period. —*n.* **1** the baroque style. **2** baroque art collectively. [F (orig. = 'irregular pearl') f. Port. *barroco*, of unkn. orig.]

barouche /bəˈruːʃ/ *n.* a horse-drawn carriage with four wheels and a collapsible hood over the rear half, used esp. in the 19th c. [G (dial.) *Barutsche* f. It. *baroccio* ult. f. L *birotus* two-wheeled]

barque /baːk/ *n.* **1** a sailing-ship with the rear mast fore-and-aft-rigged and the remaining (usu. two) masts square-rigged. **2** *poet.* any boat. [ME f. F prob. f. Prov. *barca* f. L *barca* ship's boat]

barquentine /ˈbaːkənˌtiːn/ *n.* (also **barkentine, barquantine**) a sailing ship with the foremast square-rigged and the remaining (usu. two) masts fore-and-aft-rigged. [BARQUE after *brigantine*]

barrack[1] /ˈbærək/ *n.* & *v.* —*n.* (usu. in *pl.*, often treated as *sing.*) **1** a building or building complex used to house soldiers. **2** any building used to accommodate large numbers of people. **3** a large building of a bleak or plain appearance. —*v.tr.* place (soldiers etc.) in barracks. □**barrack-room lawyer** *Brit.* a pompously argumentative person. **barrack-square** a drill-ground near a barracks. [F *baraque* f. It. *baracca* or Sp. *barraca* soldier's tent, of unkn. orig.]

barrack[2] /ˈbærək/ *v. Brit.* **1** *tr.* shout or jeer at (players in a game, a performer, speaker, etc.). **2** *intr.* (of spectators at games etc.) shout or jeer. [app. f. BORAK]

---

b *but* d *dog* f *few* g *get* h *he* j *yes* k *cat* l *leg* m *man* n *no* p *pen* r *red* s *sit* t *top* v *voice*

barracouta /ˌbærəˈkuːtə/ n. (pl. same or **barracoutas**) **1** a long slender fish, *Thyrsites atun*, usu. found in southern oceans. **2** *NZ* a small narrow loaf of bread. [var. of BARRACUDA]

barracuda /ˌbærəˈkuːdə/ n. (pl. same or **barracudas**) a large and voracious tropical marine fish of the family Sphyraenidae. [Amer. Sp. *barracuda*]

barrage /ˈbærɑːʒ/ n. **1** a concentrated artillery bombardment over a wide area. **2** a rapid succession of questions or criticisms. **3** an artificial barrier, esp. in a river. **4** a heat or deciding event in fencing, show jumping, etc. □**barrage balloon** a large anchored balloon, often with netting suspended from it, used (usu. as one of a series) as a defence against low-flying aircraft. [F f. *barrer* (as BAR¹)]

barramundi /ˌbærəˈmʌndɪ/ n. (pl. same or **barramundis**) any of various Australian freshwater fishes, esp. *Lates calcarifer*, used as food. [Aboriginal]

barrator /ˈbærətə(r)/ n. **1** a malicious person causing discord. **2** *hist.* a vexatious litigant. [ME f. AF *baratour*, OF *barateor* trickster, f. *barat* deceit]

barratry /ˈbærətrɪ/ n. **1** fraud or gross negligence of a ship's master or crew at the expense of its owners or users. **2** *hist.* vexatious litigation or incitement to it. **3** *hist.* trade in the sale of Church or State appointments. □□**barratrous** adj. [ME f. OF *baraterie* (as BARRATOR)]

barre /bɑː(r)/ n. a horizontal bar at waist level used in dance exercises. [F]

barré /ˈbæreɪ/ n. *Mus.* a method of playing a chord on the guitar etc. with a finger laid across the strings at a particular fret, raising their pitch. [F, past part. of *barrer* bar]

barrel /ˈbær(ə)l/ n. & v. —n. **1** a cylindrical container usu. bulging out in the middle, traditionally made of wooden staves with metal hoops round them. **2** the contents of this. **3** a measure of capacity, usu. varying from 30 to 40 gallons. **4** a cylindrical tube forming part of an object such as a gun or a pen. **5** the belly and loins of a four-legged animal, e.g. a horse. —v. (**barrelled**, **barrelling**; *US* **barreled**, **barreling**) **1** tr. put into a barrel or barrels. **2** intr. *US sl.* drive fast. □**barrel-chested** having a large rounded chest. **barrel-organ** a mechanical musical instrument in which a rotating pin-studded cylinder acts on a series of pipe-valves, strings, or metal tongues. **barrel roll** an aerobatic manœuvre in which an aircraft follows a single turn of a spiral while rolling once about its longitudinal axis. **barrel vault** *Archit.* a vault forming a half cylinder. **over a barrel** *colloq.* in a helpless position; at a person's mercy. [ME f. OF *baril* perh. f. Rmc.: rel to BAR¹]

barren /ˈbærən/ adj. & n. —adj. (**barrener**, **barrenest**) **1 a** unable to bear young. **b** unable to produce fruit or vegetation. **2** meagre, unprofitable. **3** dull, unstimulating. **4** (foll. by *of*) lacking in (*barren of wit*). —n. a barren tract or tracts of land esp. (in *pl.*) in N. America. □□**barrenly** adv. **barrenness** n. [ME f. AF *barai(g)ne*, OF *barhaine* etc., of unkn. orig.]

barricade /ˌbærɪˈkeɪd/ n. & v. —n. a barrier, esp. one improvised across a street etc. —v.tr. block or defend with a barricade. [F f. *barrique* cask f. Sp. *barrica*, rel. to BARREL]

barrier /ˈbærɪə(r)/ n. **1** a fence or other obstacle that bars advance or access. **2** an obstacle or circumstance that keeps people or things apart, or prevents communication (*class barriers*; *a language barrier*). **3** anything that prevents progress or success. **4** a gate at a car park, railway station, etc., that controls access. **5** *colloq.* = sound barrier. □**barrier cream** a cream used to protect the skin from damage or infection. **barrier reef** a coral reef separated from the shore by a broad deep channel. [ME f. AF *barrere*, OF *barriere*]

barring /ˈbɑːrɪŋ/ prep. except, not including. [BAR¹ + -ING²]

barrio /ˈbɑːrɪəʊ/ n. (pl. **-os**) (in the US) the Spanish-speaking quarter of a town or city. [Sp., = district of a town]

barrister /ˈbærɪstə(r)/ n. (in full **barrister-at-law**) **1** *Brit.* a person called to the bar and entitled to practise as an advocate in the higher courts. **2** *US* a lawyer. [16th c.: f. BAR¹, perh. after *minister*]

barrow¹ /ˈbærəʊ/ n. **1** *Brit.* a two-wheeled handcart used esp. by street vendors. **2** = WHEELBARROW. **3** a metal frame with two wheels used for transporting luggage etc. □**barrow boy** *Brit.* a boy who sells wares from a barrow. [OE *bearwe* f. Gmc]

barrow² /ˈbærəʊ/ n. *Archaeol.* an ancient grave-mound or tumulus. [OE *beorg* f. Gmc]

Bart. /bɑːt/ abbr. Baronet.

bartender /ˈbɑːˌtendə(r)/ n. a person serving behind the bar of a public house.

barter /ˈbɑːtə(r)/ v. & n. —v. **1** tr. exchange (goods or services) without using money. **2** intr. make such an exchange. —n. trade by exchange of goods. □□ **barterer** n. [prob. OF *barater*: see BARRATOR]

bartizan /ˈbɑːtɪz(ə)n, ˌbɑːtɪˈzæn/ n. *Archit.* a battle-mented parapet or an overhanging corner turret at the top of a castle or church tower. □□ **bartizaned** adj. [var. of *bertisene*, erron. spelling of *bratticing*: see BRATTICE]

baryon /ˈbærɪˌɒn/ n. *Physics* an elementary particle that is of equal mass to or greater mass than a proton (i.e. is a nucleon or a hyperon). □□ **baryonic** /-ˈɒnɪk/ adj. [Gk *barus* heavy + -ON]

barysphere /ˈbærɪˌsfɪə(r)/ n. the dense interior of the earth, including the mantle and core, enclosed by the lithosphere. [Gk *barus* heavy + *sphaira* sphere]

baryta /bəˈraɪtə/ n. barium oxide or hydroxide. □□ **barytic** /-ˈrɪtɪk/ adj. [BARYTES, after *soda* etc.]

barytes /bəˈraɪtiːz/ n. a mineral form of barium sulphate. [Gk *barus* heavy, partly assim. to mineral names in *-ites*]

basal /ˈbeɪs(ə)l/ adj. **1** of, at, or forming a base. **2** fundamental. □**basal metabolism** the chemical processes occurring in an organism at complete rest. [BASE¹ + -AL]

basalt /ˈbæsɔːlt/ n. **1** a dark basic volcanic rock whose strata sometimes form columns. **2** a kind of black stoneware resembling basalt. □□ **basaltic** /bəˈsɔːltɪk/ adj. [L *basaltes* var. of *basanites* f. Gk f. *basanos* touchstone]

bascule bridge /ˈbæskjuːl/ n. a type of drawbridge which is raised and lowered using counterweights. [F, earlier *bacule* see-saw f. *battre* bump + *cul* buttocks]

base¹ /beɪs/ n. & v. —n. **1 a** a part that supports from beneath or serves as a foundation for an object or structure. **b** a notional structure or entity on which something draws or depends (*power base*). **2** a principle or starting-point; a basis. **3** esp. *Mil.* a place from which an operation or activity is directed. **4 a** a main or important ingredient of a mixture. **b** a substance, e.g. water, in combination with which pigment forms paint etc. **5** a substance used as a foundation for make-up. **6** *Chem.* a substance capable of combining with an acid to form a salt and water and usu. producing hydroxide ions when dissolved in water. **7** *Math.* a number in terms of which other numbers or logarithms are expressed (see RADIX). **8** *Archit.* the part of a column between the shaft and pedestal or pavement. **9** *Geom.* a line or surface on which a figure is regarded as standing. **10** *Surveying* a known line used as a geometrical base for trigonometry. **11** *Electronics* the middle part of a transistor separating the emitter from the collector. **12** *Linguistics* a root or stem as the origin of a word or a derivative. **13** *Baseball* etc. one of the four stations that must be reached in turn when scoring a run. **14** *Bot.* & *Zool.* the end at which an organ is attached to the trunk. **15** *Heraldry* the lowest part of a shield. —v.tr. **1** (usu. foll. by *on*, *upon*) found or establish (*a theory based on speculation*; *his opinion was soundly based*). **2** (foll. by *at*, *in*, etc.) station (*troops were based in Malta*). □**base hospital** esp. *Austral.* a hospital in a rural area, or (in warfare) removed from the field of action. **base pairing** *Biochem.* complementary binding by means of hydrogen bonds of a purine to a pyrimidine base in opposite strands of nucleic acids. **base rate** *Brit.* the interest rate set by the Bank of England, used as the basis for other banks' rates. **base unit** a unit that is defined arbitrarily and not by combinations of other units. [F *base* or L *basis* stepping f. Gk]

base² /beɪs/ *adj.* **1** lacking moral worth; cowardly, despicable. **2** menial. **3** not pure; alloyed (*base coin*). **4** (of a metal) low in value (opp. NOBLE, PRECIOUS). □□ **basely** *adv.* **baseness** *n.* [ME in sense 'of small height', f. F *bas* f. med.L *bassus* short (in L as a cognomen)]

baseball /ˈbeɪsbɔːl/ *n.* **1** a game played esp. in the US with teams of nine, a bat and ball, and a circuit of four bases which the batsman must complete. **2** the ball used in this game.

baseboard /ˈbeɪsbɔːd/ *n.* *US* a skirting-board.

baseless /ˈbeɪslɪs/ *adj.* unfounded, groundless. □□ **baselessly** *adv.* **baselessness** *n.*

baseline /ˈbeɪslaɪn/ *n.* **1** a line used as a base or starting-point. **2** (in lawn tennis) the line marking each end of a court.

baseload /ˈbeɪsləʊd/ *n.* *Electr.* the permanent load on power supplies etc.

baseman /ˈbeɪsmən/ *n.* (*pl.* **-men**) *Baseball* a fielder stationed near a base.

basement /ˈbeɪsmənt/ *n.* the lowest floor of a building, usu. at least partly below ground level. [prob. Du., perh. f. It. *basamento* column-base]

bases *pl.* of BASE¹, BASIS.

bash /bæʃ/ *v.* & *n.* —*v.* **1** *tr.* **a** strike bluntly or heavily. **b** (often foll. by *up*) *colloq.* attack violently. **c** (often foll. by *down*, *in*, etc.) damage or break by striking forcibly. **2** *intr.* (foll. by *into*) collide with. —*n.* **1** a heavy blow. **2** *sl.* an attempt (*had a bash at painting*). **3** *sl.* a party or social event. [imit., perh. f. *bang*, *smash*, *dash*, etc.]

bashful /ˈbæʃfʊl/ *adj.* **1** shy, diffident, self-conscious. **2** sheepish. □□ **bashfully** *adv.* **bashfulness** *n.* [obs. *bash* (v.), = ABASH]

BASIC /ˈbeɪsɪk/ *n.* a computer programming language using familiar English words, designed for beginners and widely used on microcomputers. [*Beginner's All-purpose Symbolic Instruction Code*]

basic /ˈbeɪsɪk/ *adj.* & *n.* —*adj.* **1** forming or serving as a base. **2** fundamental. **3 a** simplest or lowest in level (*basic pay*; *basic requirements*). **b** vulgar (*basic humour*). **4** *Chem.* having the properties of or containing a base. **5** *Geol.* (of volcanic rocks etc.) having less than 50 per cent silica. **6** *Metallurgy* of or produced in a furnace etc. which is made of a basic material. —*n.* (usu. in *pl.*) the fundamental facts or principles. □**basic dye** a dye consisting of salts of organic bases. **Basic English** a simplified form of English limited to 850 selected words intended for international communication. **basic industry** an industry of fundamental economic importance. **basic slag** fertilizer containing phosphates formed as a by-product during steel manufacture. **basic wage** *Austral.* & *NZ* the minimum living wage, fixed by industrial tribunal. □□ **basically** *adv.* [BASE¹ + -IC]

basicity /beɪˈsɪsɪtɪ/ *n.* *Chem.* the number of protons with which a base will combine.

basidium /bəˈsɪdɪəm/ *n.* (*pl.* **basidia** /-dɪə/) a microscopic spore-bearing structure produced by certain fungi. [mod.L f. Gk *basidion* dimin. of BASIS]

basil /ˈbæz(ə)l/ *n.* an aromatic herb of the genus *Ocimum*, esp. *O. basilicum* (in full **sweet basil**), whose leaves are used as a flavouring in savoury dishes. [ME f. OF *basile* f. med.L *basilicus* f. Gk *basilikos* royal]

basilar /ˈbæzɪlə(r)/ *adj.* of or at the base (esp. of the skull). [mod.L *basilaris* (as BASIS)]

basilica /bəˈzɪlɪkə/ *n.* **1** an ancient Roman public hall with an apse and colonnades, used as a lawcourt and place of assembly. **2** a similar building used as a Christian church. **3** a church having special privileges from the Pope. □□ **basilican** *adj.* [L f. Gk *basilikē* (*oikia*, *stoa*) royal (house, portico) f. *basileus* king]

basilisk /ˈbæzɪlɪsk/ *n.* **1** a mythical reptile with a lethal breath and look. **2** any small American lizard of the genus *Basiliscus*, with a crest from its back to its tail. **3** *Heraldry* a cockatrice. [ME f. L *basiliscus* f. Gk *basiliskos* kinglet, serpent]

basin /ˈbeɪs(ə)n/ *n.* **1** a wide shallow open container, esp. a fixed one for holding water. **2** a hollow rounded depression. **3** any sheltered area of water where boats can moor safely. **4** a round valley. **5** an area drained by rivers and tributaries. **6** *Geol.* **a** a rock formation where the strata dip towards the centre. **b** an accumulation of rock strata formed in this dip as a result of subsidence and sedimentation. □□ **basinful** *n.* (*pl.* **-fuls**). [ME f. OF *bacin* f. med.L *ba(s)cinus*, perh. f. Gaulish]

basipetal /beɪˈsɪpɪt(ə)l/ *adj.* *Bot.* (of each new part produced) developing nearer the base than the previous one did. □□ **basipetally** *adv.* [BASIS + L *petere* seek]

basis /ˈbeɪsɪs/ *n.* (*pl.* **bases** /-siːz/) **1** the foundation or support of something, esp. an idea or argument. **2** the main or determining principle or ingredient (*on a purely friendly basis*). **3** the starting-point for a discussion etc. [L f. Gk, = BASE¹]

bask /bɑːsk/ *v.intr.* **1** sit or lie back lazily in warmth and light (*basking in the sun*). **2** (foll. by *in*) derive great pleasure (from) (*basking in glory*). □**basking shark** a very large shark, *Cetorhinus maximus*, which often lies near the surface. [ME, app. f. ON: rel. to BATHE]

basket /ˈbɑːskɪt/ *n.* **1** a container made of interwoven cane etc. **2** a container resembling this. **3** the amount held by a basket. **4** the goal in basketball, or a goal scored. **5** *Econ.* a group or range (of currencies). **6** *euphem.* *colloq.* bastard. □**basket weave** a weave resembling that of a basket. □□ **basketful** *n.* (*pl.* **-fuls**). [AF & OF *basket*, AL *baskettum*, of unkn. orig.]

basketball /ˈbɑːskɪtbɔːl/ *n.* **1** a game between two teams of five or six, in which goals are scored by making the ball drop through hooped nets fixed high up at each end of the court. **2** the ball used in this game.

basketry /ˈbɑːskɪtrɪ/ *n.* **1** the art of making baskets. **2** baskets collectively.

basketwork /ˈbɑːskɪtwɜːk/ *n.* **1** material woven in the style of a basket. **2** the art of making this.

basmati /bæzˈmɑːtɪ/ *n.* (in full **basmati rice**) a superior kind of Indian rice. [Hindi, = fragrant]

Basque /bæsk, bɑːsk/ *n.* & *adj.* —*n.* **1** a member of a people of the Western Pyrenees. **2** the language of this people. —*adj.* of or relating to the Basques or their language. [F f. L *Vasco -onis*]

basque /bæsk/ *n.* a close-fitting bodice extending from the shoulders to the waist and often with a short continuation below waist level. [BASQUE]

bas-relief /ˈbæsrɪˌliːf/ *n.* sculpture or carving in which the figures project slightly from the background. [earlier *basse relieve* f. It. *basso rilievo* low relief: later altered to F form]

bass¹ /beɪs/ *n.* & *adj.* —*n.* **1 a** the lowest adult male singing voice. **b** a singer with this voice. **c** a part written for it. **2** the lowest part in harmonized music. **3 a** an instrument that is the lowest in pitch in its family. **b** its player. **4** *colloq.* **a** a bass guitar or double-bass. **b** its player. **5** the low-frequency output of a radio, record-player, etc., corresponding to the bass in music. —*adj.* **1** lowest in musical pitch. **2** deep-sounding. □**bass clef** a clef placing F below middle C on the second highest line of the staff. **bass viol 1 a** a viola da gamba. **b** its player. **2** *US* a double-bass. □□**bassist** *n.* (in sense 4). [alt. of BASE² after It. *basso*]

bass² /bæs/ *n.* (*pl.* same or **basses**) **1** the common perch. **2 a** a marine fish of the family Serranidae, with spiny fins. **b** a similar N. American marine fish, *Morone saxatilis*. **3** any of various American freshwater fish, esp. *Micropterus salmoides*. [earlier *barse* f. OE *bærs*]

bass³ /bæs/ *n.* = BAST. [alt. f. BAST]

basset /'bæsɪt/ *n.* (in full **basset-hound**) **1** a sturdy hunting-dog of a breed with a long body, short legs, and big ears. **2** this breed. [F, dimin. of *bas basse* low: see BASE²]

basset-horn /'bæsɪt,hɔːn/ *n.* an alto clarinet in F, with a dark tone. [G, transl. of F *cor de bassette* f. It. *corno di bassetto* f. *corno* horn + *bassetto* dimin. of *basso* BASE²]

bassinet /,bæsɪ'net/ *n.* a child's wicker cradle, usu. with a hood. [F, dimin. of *bassin* BASIN]

basso /'bæsəʊ/ *n.* (*pl.* **-os** or **bassi** /-sɪ/) a singer with a bass voice. □**basso profondo** a bass singer with an exceptionally low range. [It., = BASS¹; *profondo* deep]

bassoon /bə'suːn/ *n.* **1 a** a bass instrument of the oboe family, with a double reed. **b** its player. **2** an organ stop with the quality of a bassoon. □□ **bassoonist** *n.* (in sense 1). [F *basson* f. *bas* BASS¹]

basso-rilievo /,bæsəʊrɪ'ljeɪvəʊ/ *n.* (*pl.* **-os**) = BAS-RELIEF. [It.]

basswood /'bæswʊd/ *n.* **1** the American lime, *Tilia americana*. **2** the wood of this tree. [BASS³ + WOOD]

bast /bæst/ *n.* the inner bark of lime, or other flexible fibrous bark, used as a fibre in matting etc. [OE *bæst* f. Gmc]

bastard /'bɑːstəd, 'bæ-/ *n.* & *adj.* —*n.* **1** a person born of parents not married to each other. **2** *sl.* **a** an unpleasant or despicable person. **b** a person of a specified kind (*poor bastard*; *rotten bastard*; *lucky bastard*). **3** *sl.* a difficult or awkward thing, undertaking, etc. —*adj.* **1** born of parents not married to each other; illegitimate. **2** (of things): **a** unauthorized, counterfeit. **b** hybrid. □□ **bastardy** *n.* (in sense 1 of *n.*). [ME f. OF f. med.L *bastardus*, perh. f. *bastum* pack-saddle]

bastardize /'bɑːstə,daɪz/ *v.tr.* (also **-ise**) **1** declare (a person) illegitimate. **2** corrupt, debase. □□ **bastardization** /-'zeɪʃ(ə)n/ *n.*

baste¹ /beɪst/ *v.tr.* moisten (meat) with gravy or melted fat during cooking. [16th c.: orig. unkn.]

baste² /beɪst/ *v.tr.* stitch loosely together in preparation for sewing; tack. [ME f. OF *bastir* sew lightly, ult. f. Gmc]

baste³ /beɪst/ *v.tr.* beat soundly; thrash. [perh. figurative use of BASTE¹]

bastille /bæ'stiːl/ *n. hist.* a fortress or prison. [ME f. OF *bastille* f. Prov. *bastir* build: orig. of the fortress and prison in Paris, destroyed in 1789]

bastinado /,bæstɪ'neɪdəʊ/ *n.* & *v.* —*n.* punishment by beating with a stick on the soles of the feet. —*v.tr.* (**-oes**, **-oed**) punish (a person) in this way. [Sp. *bastonada* f. *baston* BATON]

bastion /'bæstɪən/ *n.* **1** a projecting part of a fortification built at an angle of, or against the line of, a wall. **2** a thing regarded as protecting (*bastion of freedom*). **3** a natural rock formation resembling a bastion. [F f. It. *bastione* f. *bastire* build]

bat¹ /bæt/ *n.* & *v.* —*n.* **1** an implement with a handle, usu. of wood and with a flat or curved surface, used for hitting balls in games. **2** a turn at using this. **3** a batsman, esp. in cricket, usu. described in some way (*an excellent bat*). **4** (usu. in *pl.*) an object like a table-tennis bat used to guide aircraft when taxiing. —*v.* (**batted**, **batting**) **1** *tr.* hit with or as with a bat. **2** *intr.* take a turn at batting. □**bat around 1** *sl.* potter aimlessly. **2** *US* discuss (an idea or proposal). **off one's own bat** unprompted, unaided. **right off**

the bat *US* immediately. [ME f. OE *batt* club, perh. partly f. OF *batte* club f. *battre* strike]

bat² /bæt/ *n.* any mouselike nocturnal mammal of the order Chiroptera, capable of flight by means of membranous wings extending from its forelimbs. □**have bats in the belfry** be eccentric or crazy. **like a bat out of hell** very fast. [16th c., alt. of ME *bakke* f. Scand.]

bat³ /bæt/ *v.tr.* (**batted**, **batting**) wink (one's eyelid) (now usu. in phr.). □**not** (or **never**) **bat an eyelid** *colloq.* show no reaction or emotion. [var. of obs. *bate* flutter]

batch /bætʃ/ *n.* & *v.* —*n.* **1** a number of things or persons forming a group or dealt with together. **2** an instalment (*have sent off the latest batch*). **3** the loaves produced at one baking. **4** (*attrib.*) using or dealt with in batches, not as a continuous flow (*batch production*). **5** *Computing* a group of records processed as a single unit. —*v.tr.* arrange or deal with in batches. [ME f. OE *bæcce* f. *bacan* BAKE]

bate /beɪt/ *n.* (also **bait**) *Brit. sl.* a rage; a cross mood (*is in an awful bate*). [BAIT¹ = state of baited person]

bateau /'bætəʊ/ *n.* (*pl.* **bateaux** /-əʊz/) a light riverboat, esp. of the flat-bottomed kind used in Canada. [F, = boat]

bated /'beɪtɪd/ *adj.* □**with bated breath** very anxiously. [past part. of obs. *bate* (v.) restrain, f. ABATE]

bateleur /'bætə,lɜ:(r)/ *n.* a short-tailed African eagle, *Terathopius ecaudatus*. [F, = juggler]

bath /bɑ:θ/ *n.* & *v.* —*n.* (*pl.* **baths** /bɑ:ðz/) **1 a** (in full **bath-tub**) a container for liquid, usu. water, used for immersing and washing the body. **b** this with its contents (*your bath is ready*). **2** the act or process of immersing the body for washing or therapy (*have a bath*; *take a bath*). **3 a** a vessel containing liquid in which something is immersed, e.g. a film for developing, for controlling temperature, etc. **b** this with its contents. **4** (usu. in *pl.*) a building with baths or a swimming pool, usu. open to the public. —*v.* *Brit.* **1** *tr.* wash (esp. a person) in a bath. **2** *intr.* take a bath. □**bath cube** a cube of compacted bath salts. **bath salts** soluble salts used for softening or scenting bath-water. [OE *bæth* f. Gmc]

Bath bun /bɑ:θ/ *n. Brit.* a round spiced kind of bun with currants, often iced. [*Bath* in S. England, named from its hot springs]

Bath chair /bɑ:θ/ *n.* a wheelchair for invalids.

Bath chap see CHAP³.

bathe /beɪð/ *v.* & *n.* —*v.* **1** *intr.* immerse oneself in water, esp. to swim or esp. *US* wash oneself. **2** *tr.* immerse in or wash or treat with liquid esp. for cleansing or medicinal purposes. **3** *tr.* (of sunlight etc.) envelop. —*n. Brit.* immersion in liquid, esp. to swim. □**bathing-costume** (or **-suit**) a garment worn for swimming. [OE *bathian* f. Gmc]

bather /'beɪðə(r)/ *n.* **1** a person who bathes. **2** (in *pl.*) *Austral.* a bathing-suit.

bathhouse /'bɑ:θhaʊs/ *n.* a building with baths for public use.

batholith /'bæθəlɪθ/ *n.* a dome of igneous rock extending inwards to an unknown depth. [G f. Gk *bathos* depth + -LITH]

Bath Oliver /,bɑ:θ 'blɪvə(r)/ *n. Brit. propr.* a kind of savoury biscuit. [Dr W. *Oliver* of *Bath* d. 1764, who invented it]

bathometer /bə'θɒmɪtə(r)/ *n.* an instrument used to measure the depth of water. [Gk *bathos* depth + -METER]

bathos /'beɪθɒs/ *n.* an unintentional lapse in mood from the sublime to the absurd or trivial; a commonplace or ridiculous feature offsetting an otherwise sublime situation; an anticlimax. □□ **bathetic** /bə'θetɪk/ *adj.* **bathotic** /bə'θɒtɪk/ *adj.* [Gk, = depth]

bathrobe /'bɑ:θrəʊb/ *n. US* a loose coat usu. of towelling worn before and after taking a bath.

bathroom /'bɑ:θru:m, -rʊm/ *n.* **1** a room containing a bath and usu. other washing facilities. **2** esp. *US* a room containing a lavatory.

bathyscaphe /'bæθɪ,skæf/ n. a manned vessel for deep-sea diving. [Gk *bathus* deep + *skaphos* ship]

bathysphere /'bæθɪ,sfɪə(r)/ n. a spherical vessel for deep-sea observation. [Gk *bathus* deep + SPHERE]

batik /bə'ti:k, 'bætɪk/ n. a method (orig. used in Java) of producing coloured designs on textiles by applying wax to the parts to be left uncoloured; a piece of cloth treated in this way. [Jav., = painted]

batiste /bæ'ti:st/ n. & adj. —n. a fine linen or cotton cloth. —adj. made of batiste. [F (earlier *batiche*), perh. rel. to *battre* BATTER¹]

batman /'bætmən/ n. (pl. -men) Mil. an attendant serving an officer. [OF *bat*, *bast* f. med.L *bastum* pack-saddle + MAN]

baton /'bæt(ə)n/ n. 1 a thin stick used by a conductor to direct an orchestra, choir, etc. 2 *Athletics* a short stick or tube carried and passed on by the runners in a relay race. 3 a long stick carried and twirled by a drum major. 4 a staff of office or authority, esp. a Field Marshal's. 5 a policeman's truncheon. 6 *Heraldry* a narrow truncated bend. 7 *Horol.* a short bar replacing some figures on dials. □**baton round** a rubber or plastic bullet. [F *bâton*, *baston* ult. f. LL *bastum* stick]

batrachian /bə'treɪkɪən/ n. & adj. —n. any of the amphibians that discard gills and tails, esp. the frog and toad. —adj. of or relating to the batrachians. [Gk *batrakhos* frog]

bats /bæts/ predic.adj. sl. crazy. [f. phr. (*have*) *bats in the belfry*: see BAT²]

batsman /'bætsmən/ n. (pl. -men) 1 a person who bats or is batting, esp. in cricket. 2 a signaller using bats to guide aircraft on the ground. □□ **batsmanship** n. (in sense 1).

battalion /bə'tælɪən/ n. 1 a large body of men ready for battle, esp. an infantry unit forming part of a brigade. 2 a large group of people pursuing a common aim or sharing a major undertaking. [F *battaillon* f. It. *battaglione* f. *battaglia* BATTLE]

battels /'bæt(ə)lz/ n.pl. Brit. an Oxford college account for expenses, esp. for board and the supply of provisions. [perh. f. obs. *battle* (v.) fatten f. obs. *battle* (adj.) nutritious: cf. BATTEN²]

batten¹ /'bæt(ə)n/ n. & v. —n. 1 a long flat strip of squared timber or metal, esp. used to hold something in place or as a fastening against a wall etc. 2 a strip of wood used for clamping the boards of a door etc. 3 *Naut.* a strip of wood or metal for securing a tarpaulin over a ship's hatchway. —v.tr. strengthen or fasten with battens. □**batten down the hatches 1** *Naut.* secure a ship's tarpaulins. 2 prepare for a difficulty or crisis. [OF *batant* part. of *batre* beat f. L *battuere*]

batten² /'bæt(ə)n/ v.intr. (foll. by *on*) thrive or prosper at another's expense. [ON *batna* get better f. *bati* advantage]

Battenberg /'bæt(ə)n,bɜːg/ n. a kind of oblong cake, usu. of two colours of sponge and covered with marzipan. [*Battenberg* in Germany]

batter¹ /'bætə(r)/ v. 1 a tr. strike repeatedly with hard blows, esp. so as to cause visible damage. b intr. (often foll. by *against*, *at*, etc.) strike repeated blows; pound heavily and insistently (*batter at the door*). 2 tr. (often in *passive*) a handle roughly, esp. over a long period. b censure or criticize severely. □**battered baby** an infant that has suffered repeated violence from adults, esp. its parents. **battered wife** a wife subjected to repeated violence by her husband. **battering-ram** hist. a heavy beam, orig. with an end in the form of a carved ram's head, used in breaching fortifications. □□ **batterer** n. [ME f. AF *baterer* f. OF *batre* beat f. L *battuere*]

batter² /'bætə(r)/ n. 1 a fluid mixture of flour, egg, and milk or water, used in cooking, esp. for pancakes and for coating food before frying. 2 *Printing* an area of damaged type. [ME f. AF *batour* f. OF *bateüre* f. *batre*: see BATTER¹]

batter³ /'bætə(r)/ n. Sport a player batting, esp. in baseball.

batter⁴ /'bætə(r)/ n. & v. —n. 1 a wall etc. with a sloping face. 2 a receding slope. —v.intr. have a receding slope. [ME: orig. unkn.]

battered /'bætəd/ adj. (esp. of fish) coated in batter and deep-fried.

battery /'bætərɪ/ n. (pl. -ies) 1 a usu. portable container of a cell or cells carrying an electric charge, as a source of current. 2 (often *attrib.*) esp. *Brit.* a series of cages for the intensive breeding and rearing of poultry or cattle. 3 a set of similar units of equipment, esp. connected. 4 a series of tests, esp. psychological. 5 a a fortified emplacement for heavy guns. b an artillery unit of guns, men, and vehicles. 6 *Law* an act inflicting unlawful personal violence on another (see ASSAULT). 7 *Baseball* the pitcher and the catcher. [F *batterie* f. *batre*, *battre* strike f. L *battuere*]

batting /'bætɪŋ/ n. 1 the action of hitting with a bat. 2 cotton wadding prepared in sheets for use in quilts etc. □**batting order** the order in which people act or take their turn, esp. of batsmen in cricket.

battle /'bæt(ə)l/ n. & v. —n. 1 a prolonged fight between large organized armed forces. 2 a contest; a prolonged or difficult struggle (*life is a constant battle*; *a battle of wits*). —v. 1 intr. struggle; fight persistently (*battled against the elements*; *battled for women's rights*). 2 tr. fight (one's way etc.). 3 tr. US engage in battle with. □**battle-cruiser** hist. a heavy-gunned ship faster and more lightly armoured than a battleship. **battle-cry** a cry or slogan of participants in a battle or contest. **battle fatigue** = *combat fatigue*. **battle royal 1** a battle in which several combatants or all available forces engage; a free fight. 2 a heated argument. **half the battle** the key to the success of an undertaking. □□ **battler** n. [ME f. OF *bataille* ult. f. LL *battualia* gladiatorial exercises f. L *battuere* beat]

battleaxe /'bæt(ə)l,æks/ n. 1 a large axe used in ancient warfare. 2 *colloq.* a formidable or domineering older woman.

battledore /'bæt(ə)l,dɔː(r)/ n. hist. 1 a (in full **battledore and shuttlecock**) a game played with a shuttlecock and rackets. b the racket used in this. 2 a kind of wooden utensil like a paddle, formerly used in washing, baking, etc. [15th c., perh. f. Prov. *batedor* beater f. *batre* beat]

battledress /'bæt(ə)l,dres/ n. the everyday uniform of a soldier.

battlefield /'bæt(ə)l,fiːld/ n. (also **battleground** /-,graund/) the piece of ground on which a battle is or was fought.

battlement /'bæt(ə)lmənt/ n. (usu. in pl.) 1 a parapet with recesses along the top of a wall, as part of a fortification. 2 a section of roof enclosed by this (*walking on the battlements*). □□ **battlemented** adj. [OF *bataillier* furnish with ramparts + -MENT]

battleship /'bæt(ə)l,ʃɪp/ n. a warship with the heaviest armour and the largest guns.

battue /bæ'tjuː, bæ'tuː/ n. 1 a the driving of game towards hunters by beaters. b a shooting-party arranged in this way. 2 wholesale slaughter. [F, fem. past part. of *battre* beat f. L *battuere*]

batty /'bætɪ/ adj. (**battier**, **battiest**) sl. crazy. □□ **battily** adv. **battiness** n. [BAT² + -Y¹]

batwing /'bætwɪŋ/ adj. (esp. of a sleeve or a flame) shaped like the wing of a bat.

batwoman /'bæt,wumən/ n. (pl. -women) a female attendant serving an officer in the women's services. [as BATMAN + WOMAN]

bauble /'bɔːb(ə)l/ n. 1 a showy trinket or toy of little value. 2 a baton formerly used as an emblem by jesters. [ME f. OF *ba(u)bel* child's toy, of unkn. orig.]

baud /bɔːd, bəʊd/ n. (pl. same or **bauds**) *Computing* etc. 1 a unit used to express the speed of electronic code signals, corresponding to one information unit per second. 2 (loosely) a unit of data-transmission speed of one bit per second. [J. M. E. *Baudot*, Fr. engineer d. 1903]

b *but* d *dog* f *few* g *get* h *he* j *yes* k *cat* l *leg* m *man* n *no* p *pen* r *red* s *sit* t *top* v *voice*

Bauhaus /'bauhaus/ n. **1** a German school of architectural design (1919–33). **2** its principles, based on functionalism and development of existing skills. [G f. *Bau* building + *Haus* house]

baulk /bɔːlk, bɔːk/ v. & n. (also **balk**) —v. **1** intr. **a** refuse to go on. **b** (often foll. by *at*) hesitate. **2** tr. **a** thwart, hinder. **b** disappoint. **3** tr. **a** miss, let slip (a chance etc.). **b** ignore, shirk. —n. **1** a hindrance; a stumbling-block. **2 a** a roughly-squared timber beam. **b** a tie-beam of a house. **3** *Billiards* etc. the area on a billiard-table from which a player begins a game. **4** *Baseball* an illegal action made by a pitcher. **5** a ridge left unploughed between furrows. □□ **baulker** n. [OE *balc* f. ON *bálkr* f. Gmc]

baulky /'bɔːlkɪ/ adj. (also **balky**) (-ier, -iest) reluctant, perverse. □□ **baulkiness** n. [BAULK + -Y¹]

bauxite /'bɔːksaɪt/ n. a claylike mineral containing varying proportions of alumina, the chief source of aluminium. □□ **bauxitic** /-'sɪtɪk/ adj. [F f. *Les Baux* near Arles in S. France + -ITE¹]

bawd /bɔːd/ n. a woman who runs a brothel. [ME *bawdstrot* f. OF *baudetrot*, *baudestroyt* procuress]

bawdy /'bɔːdɪ/ adj. & n. —adj. (**bawdier**, **bawdiest**) humorously indecent. —n. bawdy talk or writing. □ **bawdy-house** a brothel. □□ **bawdily** adv. **bawdiness** n. [BAWD + -Y¹]

bawl /bɔːl/ v. **1** tr. speak or call out noisily. **2** intr. weep loudly. □ **bawl out** colloq. reprimand angrily. □□ **bawler** n. [imit.: cf. med.L *baulare* bark, Icel. *baula* (Sw. *böla*) to low]

bay¹ /beɪ/ n. **1** a broad inlet of the sea where the land curves inwards. **2** a recess in a mountain range. □ **Bay State** US Massachusetts. [ME f. OF *baie* f. OSp. *bahia*]

bay² /beɪ/ n. **1** (in full **bay laurel**) a laurel, *Laurus nobilis*, having deep green leaves and purple berries. Also called SWEET BAY. **2** (in *pl.*) a wreath made of bay-leaves, for a victor or poet. □ **bay-leaf** the aromatic (usu. dried) leaf of the bay-tree, used in cooking. **bay rum** a perfume, esp. for the hair, distilled orig. from bayberry leaves in rum. [OF *baie* f. L *baca* berry]

bay³ /beɪ/ n. **1** a space created by a window-line projecting outwards from a wall. **2** a recess; a section of wall between buttresses or columns, esp. in the nave of a church etc. **3** a compartment (*bomb bay*). **4** an area specially allocated or marked off (*sick bay*; *loading bay*). **5** *Brit.* the terminus of a branch line at a railway station also having through lines, usu. at the side of an outer platform. □ **bay window** a window built into a bay. [ME f. OF *baie* f. *ba(y)er* gape f. med.L *batare*]

bay⁴ /beɪ/ adj. & n. —adj. (esp. of a horse) dark reddish-brown. —n. a bay horse with a black mane and tail. [OF *bai* f. L *badius*]

bay⁵ /beɪ/ v. & n. —v. **1** intr. (esp. of a large dog) bark or howl loudly and plaintively. **2** tr. bay at. —n. the sound of baying, esp. in chorus from hounds in close pursuit. □ **at bay 1** cornered, apparently unable to escape. **2** in a desperate situation. **bring to bay** gain on in pursuit; trap. **hold** (or **keep**) **at bay** hold off (a pursuer). **stand at bay** turn to face one's pursuers. [ME f. OF *bai*, *baiier* bark f. It. *baiare*, of imit. orig.]

bayberry /'beɪbərɪ/ n. (*pl.* -ies) any of various N. American plants of the genus *Myrica*, having aromatic leaves and bearing berries covered in a wax coating. [BAY² + BERRY]

bayonet /'beɪənet/ n. & v. —n. **1** a stabbing blade attachable to the muzzle of a rifle. **2** an electrical or other fitting engaged by being pushed into a socket and twisted. —v.tr. (**bayoneted**, **bayoneting**) stab with a bayonet. [F *baïonnette*, perh. f. *Bayonne* in SW France, where they were first made]

bayou /'baɪuː/ n. a marshy offshoot of a river etc. in the southern US. [Amer. F: cf. Choctaw *bayuk*]

bazaar /bə'zɑː(r)/ n. **1** a market in an oriental country. **2** a fund-raising sale of goods, esp. for

charity. **3** a large shop selling fancy goods etc. [Pers. *bāzār*, prob. through Turk. and It.]

bazooka /bə'zuːkə/ n. **1** a tubular short-range rocket-launcher used against tanks. **2** a crude trombone-like musical instrument. [app. f. *bazoo* mouth, of unkn. orig.]

BB abbr. double-black (pencil-lead).

BBC abbr. British Broadcasting Corporation. □ **BBC English** English as supposedly pronounced by BBC announcers.

bbl. abbr. barrels (esp. of oil).

BC abbr. British Columbia.

BC abbr. (of a date) before Christ.

BCD /ˌbiːsiː'diː/ n. *Computing* a code representing decimal numbers as a string of binary digits. [abbr. for *binary coded decimal*]

BCE abbr. before the Common Era.

BCG Bacillus Calmette-Guérin, an anti-tuberculosis vaccine.

BD abbr. Bachelor of Divinity.

Bde abbr. Brigade.

bdellium /'delɪəm/ n. **1** any of various trees, esp. of the genus *Commiphora*, yielding resin. **2** this fragrant resin used in perfumes. [L f. Gk *bdellion* f. Heb. *bᵉdhōlaḥ*]

Bdr. abbr. (before a name) Bombardier.

BDS abbr. Bachelor of Dental Surgery.

BE abbr. **1** Bachelor of Education. **2** Bachelor of Engineering. **3** bill of exchange.

Be symb. *Chem.* the element beryllium.

be /biː, bɪ/ v. & v.aux. (sing. present **am** /æm, əm/; **are** /ɑː(r), ə(r)/; **is** /ɪz/; pl. present **are**; 1st and 3rd sing. past **was** /wɒz, wəz/; 2nd sing. past and pl. past **were** /wɜː(r), wə(r)/; present subj. **be**; past subj. **were**; pres. part. **being**; past part. **been** /biːn, bɪn/) —v.intr. **1** (often prec. by *there*) exist, live (*I think, therefore I am*; *there is a house on the corner*; *there is no God*). **2 a** occur; take place (*dinner is at eight*). **b** occupy a position in space (*he is in the garden*; *she is from abroad*; *have you been to Paris?*). **3** remain, continue (*let it be*). **4** linking subject and predicate, expressing: **a** identity (*she is the person*; *today is Thursday*). **b** condition (*he is ill today*). **c** state or quality (*he is very kind*; *they are my friends*). **d** opinion (*I am against hanging*). **e** total (*two and two are four*). **f** cost or significance (*it is £5 to enter*; *it is nothing to me*). —v.aux. **1** with a past participle to form the passive mood (*it was done*; *it is said*; *we shall be helped*). **2** with a present participle to form continuous tenses (*we are coming*; *it is being cleaned*). **3** with an infinitive to express duty or commitment, intention, possibility, destiny, or hypothesis (*I am to tell you*; *we are to wait here*; *he is to come at four*; *it was not to be found*; *they were never to meet again*; *if I were to die*). **4** archaic with the past participle of intransitive verbs to form perfect tenses (*the sun is set*; *Babylon is fallen*). □ **be about** occupy oneself with (*is about his business*). **be-all and end-all** colloq. (often foll. by *of*) the whole being or essence. **be at** occupy oneself with (*what is he at?*; *mice have been at the food*). **been** (or **been and gone**) and sl. an expression of protest or surprise (*he's been and taken my car!*). **be off** colloq. go away; leave. **be that as it may** see MAY. **-to-be** of the future (in comb.: *bride-to-be*). [OE *beo(m)*, (e)am, is, (e)aron; past f. OE *wæs* f. *wesan* to be; there are numerous Gmc cognates]

be- /bɪ/ prefix forming verbs: **1** (from transitive verbs) **a** all over; all round (*beset*; *besmear*). **b** thoroughly, excessively (*begrudge*; *belabour*). **2** (from intransitive verbs) expressing transitive action (*bemoan*; *bestride*). **3** (from adjectives and nouns) expressing transitive action (*befool*; *befoul*). **4** (from nouns) **a** affect with (*befog*). **b** treat as (*befriend*). **c** (forming adjectives in *-ed*) having; covered with (*bejewelled*; *bespectacled*). [OE *be-*, weak form of *bī* BY as in *bygone*, *byword*, etc.]

BEA abbr. British Epilepsy Association.

beach /biːtʃ/ n. & v. —n. a pebbly or sandy shore

esp. of the sea between high- and low-water marks. —*v.tr.* run or haul up (a boat etc.) on to a beach. □ **beach-ball** a large inflated ball for games on the beach. **beach buggy** a low wide-wheeled motor vehicle for recreational driving on sand. **beach plum 1** a maritime N. American shrub, *Prunus maritima.* **2** its edible fruit. [16th c.: orig. unkn.]

beachcomber /'biːtʃˌkəʊmə(r)/ *n.* **1** a vagrant who lives by searching beaches for articles of value. **2** a long wave rolling in from the sea.

beachhead /'biːtʃhed/ *n. Mil.* a fortified position established on a beach by landing forces. [after *bridgehead*]

Beach-la-mar /ˌbiːtʃləˈmɑː(r)/ *n. Brit.* = BISLAMA. [corrupt. f. Port. *bicho do mar* BÊCHE-DE-MER]

beacon /'biːkən/ *n.* **1 a** a fire or light set up in a high or prominent position as a warning etc. **b** *Brit.* (now often in place-names) a hill suitable for this. **2** a visible warning or guiding point or device (e.g. a lighthouse, navigation buoy, etc.). **3** a radio transmitter whose signal helps fix the position of a ship or aircraft. **4** *Brit.* = BELISHA BEACON. [OE *bēacn* f. WG]

bead /biːd/ *n. & v.* —*n.* **1 a** a small usu. rounded and perforated piece of glass, stone, etc., for threading with others to make jewellery, or sewing on to fabric, etc. **b** (in *pl.*) a string of beads; a rosary. **2** a drop of liquid; a bubble. **3** a small knob in the foresight of a gun. **4** the inner edge of a pneumatic tyre that grips the rim of the wheel. **5** *Archit.* **a** a moulding like a series of beads. **b** a narrow moulding with a semicircular cross-section. —*v.* **1** *tr.* furnish or decorate with beads. **2** *tr.* string together. **3** *intr.* form or grow into beads. □ **draw a bead on** take aim at. **tell one's beads** use the beads of a rosary etc. in counting prayers. □□ **beaded** *adj.* [orig. = 'prayer' (for which the earliest use of beads arose): OE *gebed* f. Gmc, rel. to BID]

beading /'biːdɪŋ/ *n.* **1** decoration in the form of or resembling a row of beads, esp. lacelike looped edging. **2** *Archit.* a bead moulding. **3** the bead of a tyre.

beadle /'biːd(ə)l/ *n.* **1** *Brit.* a ceremonial officer of a church, college, etc. **2** *Sc.* a church officer attending on the minister. **3** *Brit. hist.* a minor parish officer dealing with petty offenders etc. □□ **beadleship** *n.* [ME f. OF *bedel* ult. f. Gmc]

beadsman /'biːdzmən/ *n.* (*pl.* **-men**) *hist.* **1** a pensioner provided for by a benefactor in return for prayers. **2** an inmate of an almshouse.

beady /'biːdɪ/ *adj.* (**beadier, beadiest**) **1** (of the eyes) small, round, and bright. **2** covered with beads or drops. □ **beady-eyed** with beady eyes. □□ **beadily** *adv.* **beadiness** *n.*

beagle /'biːg(ə)l/ *n. & v.* —*n.* **1 a** a small hound of a breed with a short coat, used for hunting hares. **b** this breed. **2** *hist.* an informer or spy; a constable. —*v.intr.* (often as **beagling** *n.*) hunt with beagles. □□ **beagler** *n.* [ME f. OF *beegueule* noisy person, prob. f. *beer* open wide + *gueule* throat]

beak[1] /biːk/ *n.* **1 a** a bird's horny projecting jaws; a bill. **b** the similar projecting jaw of other animals, e.g. a turtle. **2** *sl.* a hooked nose. **3** *Naut. hist.* the projection at the prow of a warship. **4** a spout. □□ **beaked** *adj.* **beaky** *adj.* [ME f. OF *bec* f. L *beccus*, of Celt. orig.]

beak[2] /biːk/ *n. Brit. sl.* **1** a magistrate. **2** a schoolmaster. [19th c.: prob. f. thieves' cant]

beaker /'biːkə(r)/ *n.* **1** a tall drinking-vessel, usu. of plastic and tumbler-shaped. **2** a lipped cylindrical glass vessel for scientific experiments. **3** *archaic* or *literary* a large drinking-vessel with a wide mouth. □ **Beaker Folk** *Archaeol.* a people thought to have come to Britain from Central Europe in the early Bronze Age, named after beaker-shaped pottery found in their graves. [ME f. ON *bikarr*, perh. f. Gk *bikos* drinking-bowl]

beam /biːm/ *n. & v.* —*n.* **1** a long sturdy piece of

squared timber or metal spanning an opening or room, usu. to support the structure above. **2 a** a ray or shaft of light. **b** a directional flow of particles or radiation. **3** a bright look or smile. **4 a** a series of radio or radar signals as a guide to a ship or aircraft. **b** the course indicated by this (*off beam*). **5** the crossbar of a balance. **6 a** a ship's breadth at its widest point. **b** the width of a person's hips (esp. *broad in the beam*). **7** (in *pl.*) the horizontal cross-timbers of a ship supporting the deck and joining the sides. **8** the side of a ship (*land on the port beam*). **9** the chief timber of a plough. **10** the cylinder in a loom on which the warp or cloth is wound. **11** the main stem of a stag's antlers. **12** the lever in an engine connecting the piston-rod and crank. **13** the shank of an anchor. —*v.* **1** *tr.* emit or direct (light, radio waves, etc.). **2** *intr.* **a** shine. **b** look or smile radiantly. □ **beam-compass** (or **-compasses**) compasses with a beam connecting sliding sockets, used for large circles. **a beam in one's eye** a fault that is greater in oneself than in the person one is finding fault with (see Matt. 7:3). **off beam** *colloq.* mistaken. **on the beam** *colloq.* on the right track. **on the beam-ends** (of a ship) on its side; almost capsizing. **on one's beam-ends** near the end of one's resources. [OE *bēam* tree f. WG]

beamer /'biːmə(r)/ *n. Cricket colloq.* a ball bowled at a batsman's head.

beamy /'biːmɪ/ *adj.* (of a ship) broad-beamed.

bean /biːn/ *n. & v.* —*n.* **1 a** any kind of leguminous plant with edible usu. kidney-shaped seeds in long pods. **b** one of these seeds. **2** a similar seed of coffee and other plants. **3** *US sl.* the head. **4** (in *pl.*; with *neg.*) *US sl.* anything at all (*doesn't know beans about it*). —*v.tr. US sl.* hit on the head. □ **bean curd** jelly or paste made from beans, used esp. in Asian cookery. **bean sprout** a sprout of a bean seed, esp. of the mung bean, used as food. **full of beans** *colloq.* lively; in high spirits. **not a bean** *Brit. sl.* no money. **old bean** *Brit. sl.* a friendly form of address, usu. to a man. [OE *bēan* f. Gmc]

beanbag /'biːnbæg/ *n.* **1** a small bag filled with dried beans and used esp. in children's games. **2** a large cushion filled usu. with polystyrene beads and used as a seat.

beanery /'biːnərɪ/ *n.* (*pl.* **-ies**) *US sl.* a cheap restaurant.

beanfeast /'biːnfiːst/ *n.* **1** *Brit. colloq.* a celebration; a merry time. **2** an employer's annual dinner given to employees. [BEAN + FEAST, beans and bacon being regarded as an indispensable dish]

beanie /'biːnɪ/ *n.* a small close-fitting hat worn on the back of the head. [perh. f. BEAN 'head' + -IE]

beano /'biːnəʊ/ *n.* (*pl.* **-os**) *Brit. sl.* a celebration; a party. [abbr. of BEANFEAST]

beanpole /'biːnpəʊl/ *n.* **1** a stick for supporting bean plants. **2** *colloq.* a tall thin person.

beanstalk /'biːnstɔːk/ *n.* the stem of a bean plant.

bear[1] /beə(r)/ *v.* (*past* **bore** /bɔː(r)/; *past part.* **borne, born** /bɔːn/) ¶ In the passive *born* is used with reference to birth (e.g. *was born in July*), except for *borne by* foll. by the name of the mother (e.g. *was borne by Sarah*). **1** *tr.* carry, bring, or take (esp. visibly) (*bear gifts*). **2** *tr.* show; be marked by; have as an attribute or characteristic (*bear marks of violence; bears no relation to the case; bore no name*). **3** *tr.* **a** produce, yield (fruit etc.). **b** give birth to (*has borne a son; was born last week*). **4** *tr.* **a** sustain (weight, responsibility, cost, etc.). **b** stand, endure (an ordeal, difficulty, etc.). **5** *tr.* (usu. with *neg.* or *interrog.*) **a** tolerate; put up with (*can't bear him; how can you bear it?*). **b** admit of; be fit for (*does not bear thinking about*). **6** *tr.* carry in thought or memory (*bear a grudge*). **7** *intr.* veer in a given direction (*bear left*). **8** *tr.* bring or provide (something needed) (*bear him company*). **9** *refl.* behave (in a certain way). □ **bear arms 1** carry weapons; serve as a soldier. **2** wear or display heraldic devices. **bear**

away (or **off**) win (a prize etc.). **bear down** exert downward pressure. **bear down on** approach rapidly or purposefully. **bear fruit** have results. **bear a hand** help. **bear hard on** oppress. **bear in mind** take into account having remembered. **bear on** (or **upon**) be relevant to. **bear out** support or confirm (an account or the person giving it). **bear repeating** be worth repetition. **bear up** raise one's spirits; not despair. **bear with** treat forbearingly; tolerate patiently. **bear witness** testify. [OE *beran* f. Gmc]

bear² /beə(r)/ *n. & v.* —*n.* **1** any large heavy mammal of the family Ursidae, having thick fur and walking on its soles. **2** a rough, unmannerly, or uncouth person. **3** *Stock Exch.* a person who sells shares hoping to buy them back later at a lower price. **4** = TEDDY. **5** (**the Bear**) *colloq.* Russia. —*v. Stock Exch.* **1** *intr.* speculate for a fall in price. **2** *tr.* produce a fall in the price of (stocks etc.). □**bear-baiting** *hist.* an entertainment involving setting dogs to attack a captive bear. **bear-hug** a tight embrace. **bear market** *Stock Exch.* a market with falling prices. **bear's breech** a kind of acanthus, *Acanthus mollis.* **bear's ear** auricula. **bear's foot** a hellebore, *Helleborus fetidus.* **the Great Bear, the Little Bear** two constellations near the North Pole. **like a bear with a sore head** *Brit. colloq.* very irritable. [OE *bera* f. WG]

bearable /'beərəb(ə)l/ *adj.* that may be endured or tolerated. □□ **bearability** /-'bɪlɪtɪ/ *n.* **bearableness** *n.* **bearably** *adv.*

beard /'bɪəd/ *n. & v.* —*n.* **1** hair growing on the chin and lower cheeks of the face. **2** a similar tuft or part on an animal (esp. a goat). **3** the awn of a grass, sheath of barley, etc. —*v.tr.* oppose openly; defy. □□ **bearded** *adj.* **beardless** *adj.* [OE f. WG]

beardie /'bɪədɪ/ *n. Brit. colloq.* a bearded man.

bearer /'beərə(r)/ *n.* **1** a person or thing that bears, carries, or brings. **2** a carrier of equipment on an expedition etc. **3** a person who presents a cheque or other order to pay money. **4** (*attrib.*) payable to the possessor (*bearer stock*). **5** *hist.* (in India etc.) a personal servant.

beargarden /'beəga:d(ə)n/ *n.* a rowdy or noisy scene.

bearing /'beərɪŋ/ *n.* **1** a person's bodily attitude or outward behaviour. **2** (foll. by *on, upon*) relation or relevance to (*his comments have no bearing on the subject*). **3** endurability (*beyond bearing*). **4** a part of a machine that supports a rotating or other moving part. **5** direction or position relative to a fixed point, measured esp. in degrees. **6** (in *pl.*) **a** one's position relative to one's surroundings. **b** awareness of this; a sense of one's orientation (*get one's bearings; lose one's bearings*). **7** *Heraldry* a device or charge. **8** = *ball-bearing* (see BALL¹). □**bearing-rein** a fixed rein from bit to saddle that forces a horse to arch its neck.

bearish /'beərɪʃ/ *adj.* **1** like a bear, esp. in temper. **2** *Stock Exch.* causing or associated with a fall in prices.

Béarnaise sauce /ˌbeɪa:'neɪz/ *n.* a rich sauce thickened with egg yolks and flavoured with tarragon. [F, fem. of *béarnais* of *Béarn* in SW France]

bearskin /'beəskɪn/ *n.* **1 a** the skin of a bear. **b** a wrap etc. made of this. **2** a tall furry hat worn ceremonially by some regiments.

beast /bi:st/ *n.* **1** an animal other than a human being, esp. a wild quadruped. **2 a** a brutal person. **b** *colloq.* an objectionable or unpleasant person or thing (*he's a beast for not inviting her; a beast of a problem*). **3** (prec. by *the*) a human being's brutish or uncivilized characteristics (*saw the beast in him*). □**beast of burden** an animal, e.g. an ox, used for carrying loads. **beast of prey** see PREY. [ME f. OF *beste* f. Rmc *besta* f. L *bestia*]

beastie /'bi:stɪ/ *n. Sc.* or *joc.* a small animal.

beastly /'bi:stlɪ/ *adj. & adv.* —*adj.* (**beastlier, beastliest**) **1** *colloq.* objectionable, unpleasant. **2** like a beast; brutal. —*adv. colloq.* very, extremely. □□ **beastliness** *n.*

beat /bi:t/ *v., n., & adj.* —*v.* (*past* **beat**; *past part.* **beaten** /'bi:t(ə)n/) **1** *tr.* **a** strike (a person or animal) persistently or repeatedly, esp. to harm or punish. **b** strike (a thing) repeatedly, e.g. to remove dust from (a carpet etc.), to sound (a drum etc.). **2** *intr.* (foll. by *against, at, on*, etc.) **a** pound or knock repeatedly (*waves beat against the shore; beat at the door*). **b** = *beat down* 3. **3** *tr.* **a** overcome; surpass; win a victory over. **b** complete an activity before (another person etc.). **c** be too hard for; perplex. **4** *tr.* (often foll. by *up*) stir (eggs etc.) vigorously into a frothy mixture. **5** *tr.* (often foll. by *out*) fashion or shape (metal etc.) by blows. **6** *intr.* (of the heart, a drum, etc.) pulsate rhythmically. **7** *tr.* (often foll. by *out*) **a** indicate (a tempo or rhythm) by gestures, tapping, etc. **b** sound (a signal etc.) by striking a drum or other means (*beat a tattoo*). **8 a** *intr.* (of a bird's wings) move up and down. **b** *tr.* cause (wings) to move in this way. **9** *tr.* make (a path etc.) by trampling. **10** *tr.* strike (bushes etc.) to rouse game. **11** *intr. Naut.* sail in the direction from which the wind is blowing. —*n.* **1 a** a main accent or rhythmic unit in music or verse (*three beats to the bar; missed a beat and came in early*). **b** the indication of rhythm by a conductor's movements (*watch the beat*). **c** (in popular music) a strong rhythm. **d** (*attrib.*) characterized by a strong rhythm (*beat music*). **2 a** a stroke or blow (e.g. on a drum). **b** a measured sequence of strokes (*the beat of the waves on the rocks*). **c** a throbbing movement or sound (*the beat of his heart*). **3 a** a route or area allocated to a police officer etc. **b** a person's habitual round. **4** *Physics* a pulsation due to the combination of two sounds or electric currents of similar but not equivalent frequencies. **5** *colloq.* = BEATNIK. —*adj.* **1** (*predic.*) *sl.* exhausted, tired out. **2** (*attrib.*) of the beat generation or its philosophy. □**beat about** (often foll. by *for*) search (for an excuse etc.). **beat about the bush** discuss a matter without coming to the point. **beat the bounds** *Brit.* mark parish boundaries by striking certain points with rods. **beat one's breast** strike one's chest in anguish or sorrow. **beat the clock** complete a task within a stated time. **beat down 1 a** bargain with (a seller) to lower the price. **b** cause a seller to lower (the price). **2** strike (a resisting object) until it falls (*beat the door down*). **3** (of the sun, rain, etc.) radiate heat or fall continuously and vigorously. **beat the drum for** publicize, promote. **beaten at the post** defeated at the last moment. **beat generation** the members of a movement of young people esp. in the 1950s who rejected conventional society in their dress, habits, and beliefs. **beat in** crush. **beat it** *sl.* go away. **beat off** drive back (an attack etc.). **beat a retreat** withdraw; abandon an undertaking. **beat time** indicate or follow a musical tempo with a baton or other means. **beat a person to it** arrive or achieve something before another person. **beat up** give a beating to, esp. with punches and kicks. **beat-up** *adj. colloq.* dilapidated; in a state of disrepair. **it beats me** I do not understand (it). □□ **beatable** *adj.* [OE *bēatan* f. Gmc]

beaten /'bi:t(ə)n/ *adj.* **1** outwitted; defeated. **2** exhausted; dejected. **3** (of gold or any other metal) shaped by a hammer. **4** (of a path etc.) well-trodden, much-used. □**off the beaten track 1** in or into an isolated place. **2** unusual. [past part. of BEAT]

beater /'bi:tə(r)/ *n.* **1** a person employed to rouse game for shooting. **2** an implement used for beating (esp. a carpet or eggs). **3** a person who beats metal.

beatific /ˌbi:ə'tɪfɪk/ *adj.* **1** *colloq.* blissful (*a beatific smile*). **2 a** of or relating to blessedness. **b** making blessed. □□ **beatifically** *adv.* [F *béatifique* or L *beatificus* f. *beatus* blessed]

beatification /bi:ˌætɪfɪ'keɪʃ(ə)n/ *n.* **1** *RC Ch.* the act of formally declaring a dead person 'blessed', often a step towards canonization. **2** making or being blessed. [F *béatification* or eccl.L *beatificatio* (as BEATIFY)]

beatify /bɪ'ætɪˌfaɪ/ v.tr. (-ies, -ied) 1 RC Ch. announce the beatification of. 2 make happy. [F béatifier or eccl.L beatificare f. L beatus blessed]

beating /'biːtɪŋ/ n. 1 a physical punishment or assault. 2 a defeat. □take some (or a lot of) beating be difficult to surpass.

beatitude /biː'ætɪˌtjuːd/ n. 1 blessedness. 2 (in pl.) the declarations of blessedness in Matt. 5:3-11. 3 a title given to patriarchs in the Orthodox Church. [F béatitude or L beatitudo f. beatus blessed]

beatnik /'biːtnɪk/ n. a member of the beat generation (see BEAT). [BEAT + -nik after sputnik, perh. infl. by US use of Yiddish -nik agent-suffix]

beau /bəʊ/ n. (pl. beaux or beaus /bəʊz, bəʊ/) 1 esp. US an admirer; a boyfriend. 2 a fop; a dandy. [F, = handsome, f. L bellus]

Beaufort scale /'bəʊfət/ n. a scale of wind speed ranging from 0 (calm) to 12 (hurricane). [Sir F. Beaufort, Engl. admiral d. 1857]

beau geste /bəʊ 'ʒest/ n. (pl. beaux gestes pronunc. same) a generous or gracious act. [F, = splendid gesture]

beau ideal /ˌbəʊ iːdeɪˈæl/ n. (pl. beaux ideals /ˌbəʊz iːdeɪˈæl/) the highest type of excellence or beauty. [F beau idéal = ideal beauty: see BEAU, IDEAL]

Beaujolais /'bəʊʒəˌleɪ/ n. a red or white burgundy wine from the Beaujolais district of France.

beau monde /bəʊ 'mɒnd/ n. fashionable society. [F]

beaut /bjuːt/ n. & adj. Austral. & NZ sl. —n. an excellent or beautiful person or thing. —adj. excellent; beautiful. [abbr. of BEAUTY]

beauteous /'bjuːtɪəs/ adj. poet. beautiful. [ME f. BEAUTY + -OUS, after bounteous, plenteous]

beautician /bjuːˈtɪʃ(ə)n/ n. 1 a person who gives beauty treatment. 2 a person who runs or owns a beauty salon.

beautiful /'bjuːtɪˌfʊl/ adj. 1 delighting the aesthetic senses (a beautiful voice). 2 pleasant, enjoyable (had a beautiful time). 3 excellent (a beautiful specimen). □□beautifully adv.

beautify /'bjuːtɪˌfaɪ/ v.tr. (-ies, -ied) make beautiful; adorn. □□beautification /-fɪˈkeɪʃ(ə)n/ n. beautifier /-ˌfaɪə(r)/ n.

beauty /'bjuːtɪ/ n. (pl. -ies) 1 a a combination of qualities such as shape, colour, etc., that pleases the aesthetic senses, esp. the sight. b a combination of qualities that pleases the intellect or moral sense (the beauty of the argument). 2 colloq. a an excellent specimen (what a beauty!). b an attractive feature; an advantage (that's the beauty of it!). 3 a beautiful woman. □beauty is only skin-deep a pleasing appearance is not a guide to character. beauty parlour (or salon) an establishment in which massage, manicure, hairdressing, make-up, etc., are offered to women. beauty queen the woman judged most beautiful in a competition. beauty sleep sleep before midnight, supposed to be health-giving. beauty spot 1 a place known for its beauty. 2 a small natural or artificial mark such as a mole on the face, considered to enhance another feature. beauty treatment cosmetic treatment received in a beauty parlour. [ME f. AF beuté, OF bealté, beauté, ult. f. L (as BEAU)]

beaux pl. of BEAU.

beaux arts /bəʊˈzɑː/ n.pl. 1 fine arts. 2 (attrib.) relating to the rules and conventions of the École des Beaux-Arts in Paris (later called Académie des Beaux Arts). [F beaux-arts]

beaver[1] /'biːvə(r)/ n. & v. —n. (pl. same or beavers) 1 a any large amphibious broad-tailed rodent of the genus Castor, native to N. America, Europe, and Asia, and able to cut down trees and build dams. b its soft light-brown fur. c a hat of this. 2 (in full beaver cloth) a heavy woollen cloth like beaver fur. 3 (Beaver) a boy aged six or seven who is an affiliate member of the Scout Association. —v.intr. colloq. (usu. foll. by away) work hard. □beaver lamb lamb's wool made to look like beaver fur. eager

beaver colloq. an over-zealous person. [OE be(o)for f. Gmc]

beaver[2] /'biːvə(r)/ n. hist. the lower face-guard of a helmet. [OF baviere bib f. baver slaver f. beve saliva f. Rmc]

beaver[3] /'biːvə(r)/ n. sl. a bearded man. [20th c.: orig. uncert.]

Beaverboard /'biːvəˌbɔːd/ n. propr. a kind of fibreboard. [BEAVER[1] + BOARD]

bebop /'biːbɒp/ n. a type of jazz originating in the 1940s and characterized by complex harmony and rhythms. □□bebopper n. [imit. of the typical rhythm]

becalm /bɪˈkɑːm/ v.tr. (usu. in passive) deprive (a ship) of wind.

became past of BECOME.

because /bɪˈkɒz/ conj. for the reason that; since. □because of on account of; by reason of. [ME f. BY prep. + CAUSE, after OF par cause de by reason of]

béchamel /'beʃəˌmel/ n. a kind of thick white sauce. [invented by the Marquis de Béchamel, Fr. courtier d. 1703]

bêche-de-mer /ˌbeʃ də 'meə(r)/ n. (pl. same or bêches-de-mer pronunc. same) 1 a kind of sea cucumber eaten in China usu. in long dried strips. 2 = BEACH-LA-MAR. [F, alt. of biche de mer f. Port. bicho do mar sea-worm]

beck[1] /bek/ n. N.Engl. a brook; a mountain stream. [ME f. ON bekkr f. Gmc]

beck[2] /bek/ n. poet. a gesture requesting attention, e.g. a nod, wave, etc. □at a person's beck and call having constantly to obey a person's orders. [beck (v.) f. BECKON]

becket /'bekɪt/ n. Naut. a contrivance such as a hook, bracket, or rope-loop, for securing loose ropes, tackle, or spars. [18th c.: orig. unkn.]

beckon /'bekən/ v. 1 tr. attract the attention of; summon by gesture. 2 intr. (usu. foll. by to) make a signal to attract a person's attention; summon a person by doing this. [OE bíecnan, bécnan ult. f. WG baukna BEACON]

becloud /bɪˈklaʊd/ v.tr. 1 obscure (becloud the argument). 2 cover with clouds.

become /bɪˈkʌm/ v. (past became /bɪˈkeɪm/; past part. become) 1 intr. (foll. by compl.) begin to be (became president; will become famous). 2 tr. a look well on; suit (blue becomes him). b befit (it ill becomes you to complain). 3 intr. (as becoming adj.) a flattering the appearance. b suitable; decorous. □become of happen to (what will become of me?). □□becomingly adv. becomingness n. [OE becuman f. Gmc: cf. BE-, COME]

becquerel /'bekəˌrel/ n. Physics the SI unit of radioactivity, corresponding to one disintegration per second. [A. H. Becquerel, Fr. physicist d. 1908]

bed /bed/ n. & v. —n. 1 a a piece of furniture used for sleeping on, usu. a framework with a mattress and coverings. b such a mattress, with or without coverings. 2 any place used by a person or animal for sleep or rest; a litter. 3 a a garden plot, esp. one used for planting flowers. b a place where other things may be grown (osier bed). 4 the use of a bed: a colloq. for sexual intercourse (only thinks of bed). b for rest (needs his bed). 5 something flat, forming a support or base as in: a the bottom of the sea or a river. b the foundations of a road or railway. c the slates etc. on a billiard-table. 6 a stratum, such as a layer of oysters etc. —v. (bedded, bedding) 1 tr. & intr. (usu. foll. by down) put or go to bed. 2 tr. colloq. have sexual intercourse with. 3 tr. (usu. foll. by out) plant in a garden bed. 4 tr. cover up or fix firmly in something. 5 a tr. arrange as a layer. b intr. be or form a layer. □bed and board 1 lodging and food. 2 marital relations. bed and breakfast 1 one night's lodging and breakfast in a hotel etc. 2 an establishment that provides this. bed of roses a life of ease. brought to bed (often foll. by of) delivered of a child. get out of bed on the wrong side be bad-tempered all day long. **go to bed 1** retire for the night. **2** have sexual intercourse. **3** (of a newspaper) go to press. **keep one's bed** stay in bed because of illness. **make the bed** tidy and arrange the bed for use. **make one's bed and lie in it** accept the consequences of one's acts. **put to bed 1** cause to go to bed. **2** make (a newspaper) ready for press. **take to one's bed** stay in bed because of illness. [OE *bed(d), beddian* f. Gmc]

B.Ed. *abbr.* Bachelor of Education.

bedabble /bɪ'dæb(ə)l/ *v.tr.* stain or splash with dirty liquid, blood, etc.

bedad /bɪ'dæd/ *int. Ir.* by God! [corrupt.: cf. GAD²]

bedaub /bɪ'dɔːb/ *v.tr.* smear or daub with paint etc.; decorate gaudily.

bedazzle /bɪ'dæz(ə)l/ *v.tr.* **1** dazzle. **2** confuse (a person). ▫▫ **bedazzlement** *n.*

bedbug /'bedbʌg/ *n.* either of two flat, wingless, evil-smelling insects of the genus *Cimex* infesting beds and unclean houses and sucking blood.

bedchamber /'bed,tʃeɪmbə(r)/ *n.* **1** *archaic* a bedroom. **2 (Bedchamber)** part of the title of some of the sovereign's attendants (*Lady of the Bedchamber*).

bedclothes /'bedkləʊðz/ *n.pl.* coverings for a bed, such as sheets, blankets, etc.

beddable /'bedəb(ə)l/ *adj. colloq.* sexually attractive. [BED + -ABLE]

bedder /'bedə(r)/ *n.* **1** a plant suitable for a garden bed. **2** *Brit. colloq.* a college bedmaker.

bedding /'bedɪŋ/ *n.* **1** a mattress and bedclothes. **2** a litter for cattle, horses, etc. **3** a bottom layer. **4** *Geol.* the stratification of rocks, esp. when clearly visible. ▫ **bedding plant** a plant suitable for a garden bed.

bedeck /bɪ'dek/ *v.tr.* adorn.

bedeguar /'bedɪ,gɑː(r)/ *n.* a mosslike growth on rose-bushes produced by a gall wasp. [F *bédegar* f. Pers. *bād-āwar* wind-brought]

bedel /'biːd(ə)l, bɪ'del/ *n.* (also **bedell**) *Brit.* a university official with chiefly processional duties. [= BEADLE]

bedevil /bɪ'dev(ə)l/ *v.tr.* (**bedevilled, bedevilling;** *US* **bedeviled, bedeviling**) **1** plague; afflict. **2** confound; confuse. **3** possess as if with a devil; bewitch. **4** treat with diabolical violence or abuse. ▫▫ **bedevilment** *n.*

bedew /bɪ'djuː/ *v.tr.* **1** cover or sprinkle with dew or drops of water. **2** *poet.* sprinkle with tears.

bedfellow /'bed,feləʊ/ *n.* **1** a person who shares a bed. **2** an associate.

Bedford cord /'bedfəd/ *n.* a tough woven fabric having prominent ridges, similar to corduroy. [*Bedford* in S. England]

bedight /bɪ'daɪt/ *adj. archaic* arrayed; adorned. [ME past part. of *bedight* (v.) (as BE-, DIGHT)]

bedim /bɪ'dɪm/ *v.tr.* (**bedimmed, bedimming**) *poet.* make (the eyes, mind, etc.) dim.

bedizen /bɪ'daɪz(ə)n, -'dɪz(ə)n/ *v.tr. poet.* deck out gaudily. [BE- + obs. *dizen* deck out]

bedjacket /'bed,dʒækɪt/ *n.* a jacket worn when sitting up in bed.

bedlam /'bedləm/ *n.* **1** a scene of uproar and confusion (*the traffic was bedlam*). **2** *archaic* a madhouse; an asylum. [hospital of St Mary of *Bethlehem* in London]

bedlinen /'bed,lɪnɪn/ *n.* sheets and pillowcases.

Bedlington terrier /'bedlɪŋt(ə)n/ *n.* **1** a terrier of a breed with narrow head, long legs, and curly grey hair. **2** this breed. [*Bedlington* in Northumberland]

bedmaker /'bed,meɪkə(r)/ *n. Brit.* a person employed to clean and tidy students' rooms in a college.

Bedouin /'beduɪn/ *n. & adj.* (also **Beduin**) (*pl.* same) —*n.* **1** a nomadic Arab of the desert. **2** a wanderer; a nomad. —*adj.* **1** of or relating to the Bedouin. **2** wandering; nomadic. [ME f. OF *beduin* ult. f. Arab. *badwiyyīn* (oblique case) dwellers in the desert f. *badw* desert]

bedpan /'bedpæn/ *n.* a receptacle used by a bedridden patient for urine and faeces.

bedplate /'bedpleɪt/ *n.* a metal plate forming the base of a machine.

bedpost /'bedpəʊst/ *n.* any of the four upright supports of a bedstead. ▫ **between you and me and the bedpost** *colloq.* in strict confidence.

bedraggle /bɪ'dræg(ə)l/ *v.tr.* **1** wet (a dress etc.) by trailing it, or so that it hangs limp. **2** (as **bedraggled** *adj.*) untidy; dishevelled. [BE- + DRAGGLE]

bedrest /'bedrest/ *n.* confinement of an invalid to bed.

bedridden /'bed,rɪd(ə)n/ *adj.* **1** confined to bed by infirmity. **2** decrepit. [OE *bedreda* f. *ridan* ride]

bedrock /'bedrɒk/ *n.* **1** solid rock underlying alluvial deposits etc. **2** the underlying principles or facts of a theory, character, etc.

bedroll /'bedrəʊl/ *n.* esp. *US* portable bedding rolled into a bundle, esp. a sleeping-bag.

bedroom /'bedruːm, -rʊm/ *n.* **1** a room for sleeping in. **2** (*attrib.*) of or referring to sexual relations (*bedroom comedy*).

Beds. *abbr.* Bedfordshire.

bedside /'bedsaɪd/ *n.* **1** the space beside esp. a patient's bed. **2** (*attrib.*) of or relating to the side of a bed (*bedside lamp*). ▫ **bedside manner** (of a doctor) an approach or attitude to a patient.

bedsitter /bed'sɪtə(r)/ *n.* (also **bedsit**) *colloq.* = BEDSITTING ROOM. [contr.]

bedsitting room /bed'sɪtɪŋ/ *n. Brit.* a one-roomed unit of accommodation usu. consisting of combined bedroom and sitting-room with cooking facilities.

bedsock /'bedsɒk/ *n.* each of a pair of thick socks worn in bed.

bedsore /'bedsɔː(r)/ *n.* a sore developed by an invalid because of pressure caused by lying in bed.

bedspread /'bedspred/ *n.* an often decorative cloth used to cover a bed when not in use.

bedstead /'bedsted/ *n.* the framework of a bed.

bedstraw /'bedstrɔː/ *n.* **1** any herbaceous plant of the genus *Galium*, once used as straw for bedding. **2** (in full **Our Lady's bedstraw**) a bedstraw, *G. verum*, with yellow flowers.

bedtable /'bed,teɪb(ə)l/ *n.* a portable table or tray with legs used by a person sitting up in bed.

bedtime /'bedtaɪm/ *n.* **1** the usual time for going to bed. **2** (*attrib.*) of or relating to bedtime (*bedtime drink*).

Beduin var. of BEDOUIN.

bedwetting /'bed,wetɪŋ/ *n.* involuntary urination during the night.

bee /biː/ *n.* **1** any four-winged insect of the superfamily Apoidea which collects nectar and pollen, produces wax and honey, and lives in large communities. **2** any insect of a similar type. **3** (usu. **busy bee**) a busy person. **4** esp. *US* a meeting for communal work or amusement. ▫ **bee-bread** honey or pollen used as food by bees. **bee dance** a dance performed by worker bees to inform the colony of the location of food. **bee-eater** any bright-plumaged insect-eating bird of the family Meropidae with a long slender curved bill. **a bee in one's bonnet** an obsession. **bee-keeper** a keeper of bees. **bee-keeping** the occupation of keeping bees. **bee-master** a bee-keeper. **bee orchid** a kind of European orchid, *Ophrys apifera*, with bee-shaped flowers. **the bee's knees** *sl.* something outstandingly good (*thinks he's the bee's knees*). [OE *bēo* f. Gmc]

Beeb /biːb/ *n.* (prec. by *the*) *Brit. colloq.* the BBC. [abbr.]

beech /biːtʃ/ *n.* **1** any large forest tree of the genus *Fagus*, having smooth grey bark and glossy leaves. **2** (also **beechwood**) its wood. **3** *Austral.* any of various similar trees in Australia. ▫ **beech-fern** a fern, *Thelypteris phagopteris*, found in damp woods. **beech-marten** a white-breasted marten, *Martes foina*, of S. Europe and Asia. ▫▫ **beechy** *adj.* [OE *bēce* f. Gmc]

beechmast /'biːtʃmɑːst/ n. (pl. same) the small rough-skinned fruit of the beech tree. [BEECH + MAST²]

beef /biːf/ n. & v. —n. 1 the flesh of the ox, bull, or esp. the cow, for eating. 2 colloq. well-developed male muscle. 3 (pl. **beeves** /biːvz/ or US **beefs**) a cow, bull, or ox fattened for beef; its carcass. 4 (pl. **beefs**) sl. a complaint; a protest. —v.intr. sl. complain. □**beef tea** stewed extract of beef, given to invalids. **beef up** sl. strengthen, reinforce, augment. **beef-wood** 1 any of various Australian and W. Indian hardwood trees. 2 the close-grained red timber of these. [ME f. AF, OF boef f. L bos bovis ox]

beefburger /'biːfˌbɜːgə(r)/ n. = HAMBURGER.

beefcake /'biːfkeɪk/ n. esp. US sl. well-developed male muscles, esp. when displayed for admiration.

beefeater /'biːfˌiːtə(r)/ n. a warder in the Tower of London; a Yeoman of the Guard. [f. obs. sense 'well-fed menial']

beefsteak /biːfˈsteɪk, ˈbiːf-/ n. a thick slice of lean beef, esp. from the rump, usu. for grilling or frying. □**beefsteak fungus** a red edible fungus, Fistulina hepatica, resembling beef.

beefy /'biːfɪ/ adj. (**beefier**, **beefiest**) 1 like beef. 2 solid; muscular. □□ **beefily** adv. **beefiness** n.

beehive /'biːhaɪv/ n. 1 an artificial habitation for bees. 2 a busy place. 3 anything resembling a wicker beehive in being domed.

beeline /'biːlaɪn/ n. a straight line between two places. □**make a beeline for** hurry directly to.

Beelzebub /biːˈelzɪˌbʌb/ n. the Devil. [OE f. L f. Gk beelzeboub & Heb. baʿal zᵉḇūḇ lord of the flies, name of a Philistine god]

been past part. of BE.

beep /biːp/ n. & v. —n. 1 the sound of a motor-car horn. 2 any similar high-pitched noise. —v.intr. emit a beep. □□ **beeper** n. [imit.]

beer /bɪə(r)/ n. 1 a an alcoholic drink made from yeast-fermented malt etc., flavoured with hops. b a glass of this, esp. a pint or half-pint. 2 any of several other fermented drinks, e.g. ginger beer. □**beer and skittles** amusement (life is not all beer and skittles). **beer-cellar** 1 an underground room for storing beer. 2 a basement or cellar for selling or drinking beer. **beer-engine** Brit. a machine that draws up beer from a barrel in a cellar. **beer garden** a garden where beer is sold and drunk. **beer hall** a large room where beer is sold and drunk. **beer-mat** a small table-mat for a beer-glass. **beer pump** US = beer-engine. [OE bēor f. LL biber drink f. L bibere]

beerhouse /'bɪəhaʊs/ n. Brit. a public house licensed to sell beer but not spirits.

beery /'bɪərɪ/ adj. (**beerier**, **beeriest**) 1 showing the influence of drink in one's appearance or behaviour. 2 smelling or tasting of beer. □□ **beerily** adv. **beeriness** n.

beestings /'biːstɪŋz/ n.pl. (also treated as sing.) the first milk (esp. of a cow) after giving birth. [OE bēsting (implied by bēost), of unkn. orig.]

beeswax /'biːzwæks/ n. & v. —n. 1 the wax secreted by bees to make honeycombs. 2 this wax refined and used to polish wood. —v.tr. polish (furniture etc.) with beeswax.

beeswing /'biːzwɪŋ/ n. a filmy second crust on old port.

beet /biːt/ n. any plant of the genus Beta with an edible root (see BEETROOT, sugar beet). [OE bēte f. L beta, perh. of Celt. orig.]

beetle¹ /'biːt(ə)l/ n. & v. —n. 1 any insect of the order Coleoptera, with modified front wings forming hard protective cases closing over the back wings. 2 colloq. any similar, usu. black, insect. 3 sl. a type of compact rounded Volkswagen saloon car. 4 a dice game in which a beetle is drawn or assembled. —v.intr. colloq. (foll. by about, away, etc.) Brit. hurry, scurry. □**beetle-crusher** Brit. colloq. a large boot or foot. [OE bitula biter f. bītan BITE]

beetle² /'biːt(ə)l/ n. & v. —n. 1 a tool with a heavy

head and a handle, used for ramming, crushing, driving wedges, etc. 2 a machine used for heightening the lustre of cloth by pressure from rollers. —v.tr. 1 ram, crush, drive, etc., with a beetle. 2 finish (cloth) with a beetle. [OE bētel f. Gmc]

beetle³ /'biːt(ə)l/ adj. & v. —adj. (esp. of the eyebrows) projecting, shaggy, scowling. —v.intr. (usu. as **beetling** adj.) (of brows, cliffs, etc.) projecting; overhanging threateningly. □**beetle-browed** with shaggy, projecting, or scowling eyebrows. [ME: orig. unkn.]

beetroot /'biːtruːt/ n. esp. Brit. 1 a beet, Beta vulgaris, with an edible spherical dark red root. 2 this root used as a vegetable.

beeves pl. of BEEF.

BEF abbr. hist. British Expeditionary Force.

befall /bɪˈfɔːl/ v. (past **befell** /bɪˈfel/; past part. **befallen** /bɪˈfɔːlən/) poet. 1 intr. happen (so it befell). 2 tr. happen to (a person etc.) (what has befallen her?). [OE befeallan (as BE-, feallan FALL)]

befit /bɪˈfɪt/ v.tr. (**befitted**, **befitting**) 1 be fitted or appropriate for; suit. 2 be incumbent on. □□ **befitting** adj. **befittingly** adv.

befog /bɪˈfɒg/ v.tr. (**befogged**, **befogging**) 1 confuse; obscure. 2 envelop in fog.

befool /bɪˈfuːl/ v.tr. make a fool of; delude.

before /bɪˈfɔː(r)/ conj., prep., & adv. —conj. 1 earlier than the time when (crawled before he walked). 2 rather than that (would starve before he stole). —prep. 1 a in front of (before her in the queue). b ahead of (crossed the line before him). c under the impulse of (recoil before the attack). d awaiting (the future before them). 2 earlier than; preceding (Lent comes before Easter). 3 rather than (death before dishonour). 4 a in the presence of (appear before the judge). b for the attention of (a plan put before the committee). —adv. 1 a earlier than the time in question; already (heard it before). b in the past (happened long before). 2 ahead (go before). 3 on the front (hit before and behind). □**Before Christ** (of a date) reckoned backwards from the birth of Christ. **before God** a solemn oath meaning 'as God sees me'. **before time** see TIME. [OE beforan f. Gmc]

beforehand /bɪˈfɔːhænd/ adv. in anticipation; in advance; in readiness (had prepared the meal beforehand). □**be beforehand with** anticipate; forestall. [ME f. BEFORE + AF avant main]

befoul /bɪˈfaʊl/ v.tr. poet. 1 make foul or dirty. 2 degrade; defile (befouled her name).

befriend /bɪˈfrend/ v.tr. act as a friend to; help.

befuddle /bɪˈfʌd(ə)l/ v.tr. 1 make drunk. 2 confuse. □□ **befuddlement** n.

beg /beg/ v. (**begged**, **begging**) 1 a intr. (usu. foll. by for) ask for (esp. food, money, etc.) (begged for alms). b tr. ask for (food, money, etc.) as a gift. c intr. live by begging. 2 tr. & intr. (usu. foll. by for, or to + infin.) ask earnestly or humbly (begged for forgiveness; begged to be allowed out; please, I beg of you; beg your indulgence for a time). 3 tr. ask formally for (beg leave). 4 intr. (of a dog etc.) sit up with the front paws raised expectantly. 5 tr. take or ask leave (to do something) (I beg to differ; beg to enclose). □**beg one's bread** live by begging. **begging bowl** 1 a bowl etc. held out for food or alms. 2 an earnest appeal for help. **beg off** 1 decline to take part in or attend. 2 get (a person) excused a penalty etc. **beg pardon** see PARDON. **beg the question** 1 assume the truth of an argument or proposition to be proved, without arguing it. 2 disp. pose the question. 3 colloq. evade a difficulty. **go begging** (or **a-begging**) (of a chance or a thing) not be taken; be unwanted. [ME prob. f. OE bedecian f. Gmc: rel. to BID]

begad /bɪˈgæd/ int. archaic colloq. by God! [corrupt.: cf. GAD²]

began past of BEGIN.

begat archaic past of BEGET.

beget /bɪˈget/ v.tr. (**begetting**; past **begot** /bɪˈgɒt/; archaic **begat** /bɪˈgæt/; past part. **begotten**

/brɪˈgɒt(ə)n/ *literary* **1** (usu. of a father, sometimes of a father and mother) procreate. **2** give rise to; cause (*beget strife*). □□ **begetter** *n*. [OE *begietan*, formed as BE- + GET = procreate]

beggar /ˈbegə(r)/ *n*. & *v*. —*n*. **1** a person who begs, esp. one who lives by begging. **2** a poor person. **3** *colloq*. a person; a fellow (*poor beggar*). —*v.tr*. **1** reduce to poverty. **2** outshine. **3** exhaust the resources of (*beggar description*). □ **beggar-my-neighbour** **1** a card-game in which a player seeks to capture an opponent's cards. **2** (*attrib*.) (esp. of national policy) self-aggrandizing at the expense of competitors. **beggars cannot** (or **must not**) **be choosers** those without other resources must take what is offered. [ME f. BEG + -AR³]

beggarly /ˈbegəlɪ/ *adj*. **1** poverty-stricken; needy. **2** intellectually poor. **3** mean; sordid. **4** ungenerous. □□ **beggarliness** *n*.

beggary /ˈbegərɪ/ *n*. extreme poverty.

begin /brˈgɪn/ *v*. (**beginning**; *past* **began** /brˈgæn/; *past part.* **begun** /brˈgʌn/) **1** *tr*. perform the first part of; start (*begin work*; *begin crying*; *begin to understand*). **2** *intr*. come into being; arise: **a** in time (*war began in 1939*). **b** in space (*Wales begins beyond the river*). **3** *tr*. (usu. foll. by *to* + infin.) start at a certain time (*then began to feel ill*). **4** *intr*. be begun (*the meeting will begin at 7*). **5** *intr*. **a** start speaking ('*No,' he began*). **b** take the first step; be the first to do something (*who wants to begin?*). **6** *intr*. *colloq*. (usu. with *neg*.) show any attempt or likelihood (*can't begin to compete*). □ **begin at** start from. **begin on** (or **upon**) set to work at. **begin school** attend school for the first time. **begin with** take (a subject, task, etc.) first or as a starting-point. **to begin with** in the first place; as the first thing. [OE *beginnan* f. Gmc]

beginner /brˈgɪnə(r)/ *n*. a person just beginning to learn a skill etc. □ **beginner's luck** good luck supposed to attend a beginner at games etc.

beginning /brˈgɪnɪŋ/ *n*. **1** the time or place at which anything begins. **2** a source or origin. **3** the first part. □ **the beginning of the end** the first clear sign of a final result.

begone /brˈgɒn/ *int. poet.* go away at once!

begonia /brˈgəʊnjə/ *n*. any plant of the genus *Begonia* with brightly coloured sepals and no petals, and often having brilliant glossy foliage. [M. *Bégon*, Fr. patron of science d. 1710]

begorra /brˈgɒrə/ *int. Ir.* by God! [corrupt.]

begot *past* of BEGET.

begotten *past part.* of BEGET.

begrime /brˈgraɪm/ *v.tr.* make grimy.

begrudge /brˈgrʌdʒ/ *v.tr.* **1** resent; be dissatisfied at. **2** envy (a person) the possession of. □□ **begrudgingly** *adv*.

beguile /brˈgaɪl/ *v.tr.* **1** charm; amuse. **2** divert attention pleasantly from (toil etc.). **3** (usu. foll. by *of, out of,* or *into* + verbal noun) delude; cheat (*beguiled him into paying*). □□ **beguilement** *n*. **beguiler** *n*. **beguiling** *adj*. **beguilingly** *adv*. [BE- + obs. *guile* to deceive]

beguine /brˈgiːn/ *n*. **1** a popular dance of W. Indian origin. **2** its rhythm. [Amer. F f. F *béguin* infatuation]

begum /ˈbeɪgəm/ *n*. in the Indian subcontinent: **1** a Muslim lady of high rank. **2** (**Begum**) the title of a married Muslim woman, equivalent to Mrs. [Urdu *begam* f. E.Turk. *bīgam* princess, fem. of *big* prince: cf. BEY]

begun *past part.* of BEGIN.

behalf /brˈhɑːf/ *n*. □ **on** (*US* **in**) **behalf of** (or **on a person's behalf**) **1** in the interests of (a person, principle, etc.). **2** as representative of (*acting on behalf of my client*). [mixture of earlier phrases *on his halve* and *bihalve him*, both = on his side: see BY, HALF]

behave /brˈheɪv/ *v*. **1** *intr*. **a** act or react (in a specified way) (*behaved well*). **b** (esp. to or of a child) conduct oneself properly. **c** (of a machine etc.) work well (or in a specified way) (*the computer is not*

behaving today). **2** *refl*. (esp. of or to a child) show good manners (*behaved herself*). □ **behave towards** treat (in a specified way). **ill-behaved** having bad manners or conduct. **well-behaved** having good manners or conduct. [BE- + HAVE]

behaviour /brˈheɪvjə(r)/ *n*. (*US* **behavior**) **1 a** the way one conducts oneself; manners. **b** the treatment of others; moral conduct. **2** the way in which a ship, machine, chemical substance, etc., acts or works. **3** *Psychol*. the response (of a person, animal, etc.) to a stimulus. □ **behaviour therapy** the treatment of neurotic symptoms by training the patient's reactions (see BEHAVIOURISM). **be on one's good** (or **best**) **behaviour** behave well when being observed. [BEHAVE after *demeanour* and obs. *haviour* f. *have*]

behavioural /brˈheɪvjər(ə)l/ *adj*. (*US* **behavioral**) of or relating to behaviour. □ **behavioural science** the scientific study of human behaviour (see BEHAVIOURISM). □□ **behaviouralist** *n*.

behaviourism /brˈheɪvjəˌrɪz(ə)m/ *n*. (*US* **behaviorism**) *Psychol*. **1** the theory that human behaviour is determined by conditioning rather than by thoughts or feelings, and that psychological disorders are best treated by altering behaviour patterns. **2** such study and treatment in practice. □□ **behaviourist** *n*. **behaviouristic** /-ˈrɪstɪk/ *adj*.

behead /brˈhed/ *v.tr.* **1** cut off the head of (a person), esp. as a form of execution. **2** kill by beheading. [OE *behēafdian* (as BE-, *hēafod* HEAD)]

beheld *past* and *past part.* of BEHOLD.

behemoth /brˈhiːmɒθ/ *n*. an enormous creature or thing. [ME f. Heb. *bᵉhēmōṯ* intensive pl. of *bᵉhēmāh* beast, perh. f. Egyptian *p-ehe-mau* water-ox]

behest /brˈhest/ *n. literary* a command; an entreaty (*went at his behest*). [OE *behǣs* f. Gmc]

behind /brˈhaɪnd/ *prep., adv.,* & *n*. —*prep*. **1 a** in, towards, or to the rear of. **b** on the further side of (*behind the bush*). **c** hidden by (*something behind that remark*). **2 a** in the past in relation to (*trouble is behind me now*). **b** late in relation to (*behind schedule*). **3** inferior to; weaker than (*rather behind the others in his maths*). **4 a** in support of (*she's right behind us*). **b** responsible for; giving rise to (*the man behind the project; the reasons behind his resignation*). **5** in the tracks of; following. —*adv*. **1 a** in or to or towards the rear; further back (*the street behind*; *glance behind*). **b** on the further side (*a high wall with a field behind*). **2** remaining after departure (*leave behind; stay behind*). **3** (usu. foll. by *with*) **a** in arrears (*behind with the rent*). **b** late in accomplishing a task etc. (*working too slowly and getting behind*). **4** in a weak position; backward (*behind in Latin*). **5** following (*his dog running behind*). —*n*. **1** *colloq*. the buttocks. **2** (in Australian Rules) a kick etc. scoring one point. □ **behind a person's back** without a person's knowledge. **behind the scenes** see SCENE. **behind time** late. **behind the times** antiquated. **come from behind** win after lagging. **fall** (or **lag**) **behind** not keep up. **put behind one 1** refuse to consider. **2** get over (an unhappy experience etc.). [OE *behindan, bihindan* f. *bi* BY + *hindan* from behind, *hinder* below]

behindhand /brˈhaɪndhænd/ *adv.* & *predic.adj.* **1** (usu. foll. by *with, in*) late (in discharging a duty, paying a debt, etc.). **2** out of date; behind time. [BEHIND + HAND: cf. BEFOREHAND]

behold /brˈhəʊld/ *v.tr.* (*past* & *past part.* **beheld** /brˈheld/) *literary* (esp. in *imper.*) see, observe. □□ **beholder** *n*. [OE *bihaldan* (as BE-, *haldan* hold)]

beholden /brˈhəʊld(ə)n/ *predic.adj.* (usu. foll. by *to*) under obligation. [past part. (obs. except in this use) of BEHOLD, = bound]

behoof /brˈhuːf/ *n. archaic* (prec. by *to, for, on*; foll. by *of*) benefit; advantage. [OE *behōf*]

behove /brˈhəʊv/ *v.tr.* (*US* **behoove** /-ˈhuːv/) *formal* (prec. by *it* as subject; foll. by *to* + infin.) **1** be incumbent on. **2** (usu. with *neg*.) befit (*ill behoves him to protest*). [OE *behōfian* f. *behōf*: see BEHOOF]

beige /beɪʒ/ *n. & adj.* —*n.* a pale sandy fawn colour. —*adj.* of this colour. [F: orig. unkn.]

beigel var. of BAGEL.

being /'biːɪŋ/ *n.* **1** existence. **2** the nature or essence (of a person etc.) (*his whole being revolted*). **3** a human being. **4** anything that exists or is imagined. □in being existing.

bejabers /bɪ'dʒeɪbəz/ *int.* (also **bejabbers** /-'dʒæbəz/) *Ir.* by Jesus! [corrupt.]

bejewelled /bɪ'dʒuːəld/ *adj.* (*US* **bejeweled**) adorned with jewels.

bel /bel/ *n.* a unit used in the comparison of power levels in electrical communication or intensities of sound, corresponding to an intensity ratio of 10 to 1 (cf. DECIBEL). [A. G. *Bell*, Amer. inventor of telephone d. 1922]

belabour /bɪ'leɪbə(r)/ *v.tr.* (*US* **belabor**) **1 a** thrash; beat. **b** attack verbally. **2** argue or elaborate (a subject) in excessive detail. [BE- + LABOUR = exert one's strength]

belated /bɪ'leɪtɪd/ *adj.* **1** coming late or too late. **2** overtaken by darkness. □□**belatedly** *adv.* **belatedness** *n.* [past part. of obs. *belate* delay (as BE-, LATE)]

belay /bɪ'leɪ/ *v. & n.* —*v.* **1** *tr.* fix (a running rope) round a cleat, pin, rock, etc., to secure it. **2** *tr. & intr.* (usu. in *imper.*) *Naut. sl.* stop; enough! (esp. *belay there!*). —*n.* **1** an act of belaying. **2** a spike of rock etc. used for belaying. □**belaying-pin** a fixed wooden or iron pin used for fastening a rope round. [Du. *beleggen*]

bel canto /bel 'kæntəʊ/ *n.* **1** a lyrical style of operatic singing using a full rich broad tone and smooth phrasing. **2** (*attrib.*) (of a type of aria or voice) characterized by this type of singing. [It., = fine song]

belch /beltʃ/ *v. & n.* —*v.* **1** *intr.* emit wind noisily from the stomach through the mouth. **2** *tr.* **a** (of a chimney, volcano, gun, etc.) send (smoke etc.) out or up. **b** utter forcibly. —*n.* an act of belching. [OE *belcettan*]

beldam /'beldəm/ *n.* (also **beldame**) *archaic* **1** an old woman; a hag. **2** a virago. [ME & OF *bel* beautiful + DAM², DAME]

beleaguer /bɪ'liːɡə(r)/ *v.tr.* **1** besiege. **2** vex; harass. [Du. *belegeren* camp round (as BE-, *leger* a camp)]

belemnite /'beləm,naɪt/ *n.* any extinct cephalopod of the order Belemnoidea, having a bullet-shaped internal shell often found in fossilized form. [mod.L *belemnites* f. Gk *belemnon* dart + -ITE¹]

bel esprit /,bel e'spriː/ *n.* (*pl.* ***beaux esprits*** /,bəʊz e'spriː/) a witty person. [F, lit. fine mind]

belfry /'belfrɪ/ *n.* (*pl.* **-ies**) **1** a bell tower or steeple housing bells, esp. forming part of a church. **2** a space for hanging bells in a church tower. □**bats in the belfry** see BAT². [ME f. OF *berfrei* f. Frank.: altered by assoc. with *bell*]

Belgian /'beldʒ(ə)n/ *n. & adj.* —*n.* **1** a native or national of Belgium in W. Europe. **2** a person of Belgian descent. —*adj.* of or relating to Belgium. □**Belgian hare** a dark-red long-eared breed of domestic rabbit.

Belgic /'beldʒɪk/ *adj.* **1** of the ancient Belgae of N. Gaul. **2** of the Low Countries. [L *Belgicus* f. *Belgae*]

Belial /'biːlɪəl/ *n.* the Devil. [Heb. *bᵉliyya'al* worthless]

belie /bɪ'laɪ/ *v.tr.* (**belying**) **1** give a false notion of; fail to corroborate (*its appearance belies its age*). **2 a** fail to fulfil (a promise etc.). **b** fail to justify (a hope etc.). [OE *belēogan* (as BE-, *lēogan* LIE²)]

belief /bɪ'liːf/ *n.* **1 a** a person's religion; religious conviction (*has no belief*). **b** a firm opinion (*my belief is that he did it*). **c** an acceptance (of a thing, fact, statement, etc.) (*belief in the afterlife*). **2** (usu. foll. by *in*) trust or confidence. □**beyond belief** incredible. **to the best of my belief** in my genuine opinion. [ME f. OE *gelēafa* (as BELIEVE)]

believe /bɪ'liːv/ *v.* **1** *tr.* accept as true or as conveying the truth (*I believe it; don't believe him; believes what*

he is told). **2** *tr.* think, suppose (*I believe it's raining*; *Mr Smith, I believe?*). **3** *intr.* (foll. by *in*) **a** have faith in the existence of (*believes in God*). **b** have confidence in (a remedy, a person, etc.) (*believes in alternative medicine*). **c** have trust in the advisability of (*believes in telling the truth*). **4** *intr.* have (esp. religious) faith. □**believe one's ears** (or **eyes**) accept that what one apparently hears or sees etc. is true. **believe it or not** *colloq.* it is true though surprising. **make believe** (often foll. by *that* + clause, or *to* + infin.) pretend (*let's make believe that we're young again*). **would you believe it?** *colloq.* = *believe it or not*. □□ **believable** *adj.* **believability** /-,liːvə'bɪlɪtɪ/ *n.* [OE *belfan*, *belēfan*, with change of prefix f. *gelēfan* f. Gmc: rel. to LIEF]

believer /bɪ'liːvə(r)/ *n.* **1** an adherent of a specified religion. **2** a person who believes, esp. in the efficacy of something (*a great believer in exercise*).

Belisha beacon /bə'liːʃə/ *n. Brit.* a flashing orange ball surmounted on a striped post, marking some pedestrian crossings. [L. Hore-*Belisha* d. 1957, Minister of Transport 1934]

belittle /bɪ'lɪt(ə)l/ *v.tr.* **1** depreciate. **2** make small; dwarf. □□ **belittlement** *n.* **belittler** *n.* **belittlingly** *adv.*

bell¹ /bel/ *n. & v.* —*n.* **1 a** a hollow usu. metal object in the shape of a deep upturned cup usu. widening at the lip, made to sound a clear musical note when struck (either externally or by means of a clapper inside). **2 a** a sound or stroke of a bell, esp. as a signal. **b** (prec. by a numeral) *Naut.* the time as indicated every half-hour of a watch by the striking of the ship's bell one to eight times. **3** anything that sounds like or functions as a bell, esp. an electronic device that rings etc. as a signal. **4 a** any bell-shaped object or part, e.g. of a musical instrument. **b** the corolla of a flower when bell-shaped. **5** (in *pl.*) *Mus.* a set of cylindrical metal tubes of different lengths, suspended in a frame and played by being struck with a hammer. —*v.tr.* **1** provide with a bell or bells; attach a bell to. **2** (foll. by *out*) form into the shape of the lip of a bell. □**bell-bottom 1** a marked flare below the knee (of a trouser-leg). **2** (in *pl.*) trousers with bell-bottoms. **bell-bottomed** having bell-bottoms. **bell-buoy** a buoy equipped with a warning bell rung by the motion of the sea. **bell-founder** a person who casts large bells in a foundry. **bell-glass** a bell-shaped glass cover for plants. **bell-jar** a bell-shaped glass cover or container for use in a laboratory. **bell-metal** an alloy of copper and tin for making bells (the tin content being greater than in bronze). **bell-pull** a cord or handle which rings a bell when pulled. **bell-push** a button that operates an electric bell when pushed. **bell-ringer** a person who rings church bells or handbells. **bell-ringing** this as an activity. **bell-tent** a cone-shaped tent supported by a central pole. **bell-wether 1** the leading sheep of a flock, with a bell on its neck. **2** a ringleader. **clear** (or **sound**) **as a bell** perfectly clear or sound. **ring a bell** *colloq.* revive a distant recollection; sound familiar. [OE *belle*: perh. rel. to BELL²]

bell² /bel/ *n. & v.* —*n.* the cry of a stag or buck at rutting-time. —*v.intr.* make this cry. [OE *bellan* bark, bellow]

belladonna /,belə'dɒnə/ *n.* **1** *Bot.* a poisonous plant, *Atropa belladonna*, with purple flowers and purple-black berries. Also called *deadly nightshade*. **2** *Med.* a drug prepared from this. □**belladonna lily** a S. African amaryllis with white or pink flowers, *Amaryllis belladonna*. [mod.L f. It., = fair lady, perh. from its use as a cosmetic]

bellbird /'belbɜːd/ *n.* any of various birds with a bell-like song, esp. any Central or S. American bird of the genus *Procnias*, a New Zealand honey-eater, *Anthornis melanura*, and an Australian bird, *Oreoica gutturalis*.

bellboy /'belbɔɪ/ *n.* esp. *US* a page in a hotel or club.

belle /bel/ *n.* **1** a beautiful woman. **2** a woman recognized as the most beautiful (*the belle of the ball*). [F f. L *bella* fem. of *bellus* beautiful]

belle époque /ˌbel eˈppk/ *n.* the period of settled and comfortable life preceding the war of 1914–18. [F, = fine period]

belle laide /bel ˈleɪd/ *n.* (*pl.* **belles laides** pronunc. same) a fascinatingly ugly woman. [F f. *belle* beautiful + *laide* ugly]

belles-lettres /bel ˈletr/ *n.pl.* (also treated as *sing.*) writings or studies of a literary nature, esp. essays and criticisms. ◻◻ **belletrism** /beˈletrɪz(ə)m/ *n.* **belletrist** /beˈletrɪst/ *n.* **belletristic** /ˌbeləˈtrɪstɪk/ *adj.* [F, = fine letters]

bellflower /ˈbelˌflaʊə(r)/ *n.* = CAMPANULA.

bellicose /ˈbelɪˌkəʊz/ *adj.* eager to fight; warlike. ◻◻ **bellicosity** /-ˈkɒsɪtɪ/ *n.* [ME f. L *bellicosus* f. *bellum* war]

belligerence /bɪˈlɪdʒərəns/ *n.* (also **belligerency** /-rənsɪ/) **1** aggressive or warlike behaviour. **2** the status of a belligerent.

belligerent /bɪˈlɪdʒərənt/ *adj. & n.* —*adj.* **1** engaged in war or conflict. **2** given to constant fighting; pugnacious. —*n.* a nation or person engaged in war or conflict. ◻◻ **belligerently** *adv.* [L *belligerare* wage war f. *bellum* war + *gerere* wage]

bellman /ˈbelmən/ *n.* (*pl.* -**men**) *hist.* a town crier.

bellow /ˈbeləʊ/ *v. & n.* —*v.* **1** *intr.* **a** emit a deep loud roar. **b** cry or shout with pain. **2** *tr.* utter loudly and usu. angrily. —*n.* a bellowing sound. [ME: perh. rel. to BELL²]

bellows /ˈbeləʊz/ *n.pl.* (also treated as *sing.*) **1** a device with an air bag that emits a stream of air when squeezed, esp.: **a** (in full **pair of bellows**) a kind with two handles used for blowing air on to a fire. **b** a kind used in a harmonium or small organ. **2** an expandable component, e.g. joining the lens to the body of a camera. [ME prob. f. OE *belga* pl. of *belig* belly]

belly /ˈbelɪ/ *n. & v.* —*n.* (*pl.* -**ies**) **1** the part of the human body below the chest, containing the stomach and bowels. **2** the stomach, esp. representing the body's need for food. **3** the front of the body from the waist to the groin. **4** the underside of a four-legged animal. **5 a** a cavity or bulging part of anything. **b** the surface of an instrument of the violin family, across which the strings are placed. —*v.tr. & intr.* (-**ies**, -**ied**) (often foll. by *out*) swell or cause to swell; bulge. ◻ **belly button** *colloq.* the navel. **belly-dance** an oriental dance performed by a woman, involving voluptuous movements of the belly. **belly-dancer** a woman who performs belly-dances, esp. professionally. **belly-dancing** the performance of belly-dances. **belly-landing** a crash-landing of an aircraft on the underside of the fuselage, without lowering the undercarriage. **belly-laugh** a loud unrestrained laugh. [OE *belig* (orig. = bag) f. Gmc]

bellyache /ˈbelɪˌeɪk/ *n. & v.* —*n. colloq.* a stomach pain. —*v.intr. sl.* complain noisily or persistently. ◻◻ **bellyacher** *n.*

bellyband /ˈbelɪˌbænd/ *n.* a band placed round a horse's belly, holding the shafts of a cart etc.

bellyflop /ˈbelɪˌflɒp/ *n. & v. colloq.* —*n.* a dive into water in which the body lands with the belly flat on the water. —*v.intr.* (-**flopped**, -**flopping**) perform this dive.

bellyful /ˈbelɪˌfʊl/ *n.* (*pl.* -**fuls**) **1** enough to eat. **2** *colloq.* enough or more than enough of anything (esp. unwelcome).

belong /bɪˈlɒŋ/ *v.intr.* **1** (foll. by *to*) **a** be the property of. **b** be rightly assigned to as a duty, right, part, member, characteristic, etc. **c** be a member of (a club, family, group, etc.). **2** have the right personal or social qualities to be a member of a particular group (*he's nice but just doesn't belong*); (foll. by *in*, *under*). **a** be rightly placed or classified. **b** fit a particular environment. ◻◻ **belongingness** *n.* [ME

f. intensive BE- + *longen* belong f. OE *langian* (*gelang* at hand)]

belongings /bɪˈlɒŋɪŋz/ *n.pl.* one's movable possessions or luggage.

Belorussian /ˌbeləʊˈrʌʃ(ə)n/ *n. & adj.* (also **Byelorussian** /ˌbjeləʊ-/) —*n.* **1** a native of Belorussia in the western USSR. **2** the language of Belorussia. —*adj.* of or relating to Belorussia or its people or language. [Russ. *Belorussiya* f. *belyi* white + *Russiya* Russia]

beloved /bɪˈlʌvɪd, *predic.* also -lʌvd/ *adj. & n.* —*adj.* much loved. —*n.* a much loved person. [obs. *belove* (v.)]

below /bɪˈləʊ/ *prep. & adv.* —*prep.* **1** lower in position (vertically, down a slope or stream, etc.) than. **2** beneath the surface of; at or to a greater depth than (*head below water*; *below 500 feet*). **3** lower or less than in amount or degree (*below freezing-point*; *temperature is 20 below*). **4** lower in rank, position, or importance than. **5** unworthy of. —*adv.* **1** at or to a lower point or level. **2 a** downstairs (*lives below*). **b** downstream. **3** (of a text reference) further forward on a page or in a book (*as noted below*). **4** on the lower side (*looks similar above and below*). **5** *rhet.* on earth; in hell. ◻ **below stairs** in the basement of a house esp. as the part occupied by servants. [BE- + LOW¹]

Bel Paese /ˌbel pɑːˈeɪzeɪ/ *n. propr.* a rich white mild creamy cheese of a kind orig. made in Italy. [It., = fair country]

belt /belt/ *n. & v.* —*n.* **1** a strip of leather or other material worn round the waist or across the chest, esp. to retain or support clothes or to carry weapons or as a safety-belt. **2** a belt worn as a sign of rank or achievement. **3 a** a circular band of material used as a driving medium in machinery. **b** a conveyor belt. **c** a flexible strip carrying machine-gun cartridges. **4** a strip of colour or texture etc. differing from that on each side. **5** a distinct region or extent (*cotton belt*; *commuter belt*; *a belt of rain*). **6** *sl.* a heavy blow. —*v.* **1** *tr.* put a belt round. **2** *tr.* (often foll. by *on*) fasten with a belt. **3** *tr.* **a** beat with a belt. **b** *sl.* hit hard. **4** *intr. sl.* rush, hurry (usu. with compl.: *belted along*; *belted home*). ◻ **below the belt** unfair or unfairly; disregarding the rules. **belt and braces** (of a policy etc.) of twofold security. **belt out** *sl.* sing or utter loudly and forcibly. **belt up** *Brit.* **1** *sl.* be quiet. **2** *colloq.* put on a seat belt. **tighten one's belt** live more frugally. **under one's belt 1** (of food) eaten. **2** securely acquired (*has a degree under her belt*). ◻◻ **belter** *n.* (esp. in sense of *belt out*). [OE f. Gmc f. L *balteus*]

Beltane /ˈbelteɪn/ *n.* an ancient Celtic festival celebrated on May Day. [Gael. *bealltainn*]

beltman /ˈbeltmæn/ *n.* (*pl.* -**men**) *Austral.* a member of a life-saving team of surfers.

beluga /bəˈluːgə/ *n.* **1 a** a large kind of sturgeon, *Huso huso*. **b** caviare obtained from it. **2** a white whale. [Russ. *beluga* f. *belyi* white]

belvedere /ˈbelvɪˌdɪə(r)/ *n.* a summer-house or open-sided gallery usu. at rooftop level. [It. f. *bel* beautiful + *vedere* see]

belying *pres. part.* of BELIE.

BEM *abbr.* British Empire Medal.

bemire /bɪˈmaɪə(r)/ *v.tr.* **1** cover or stain with mud. **2** (in *passive*) be stuck in mud. [BE- + MIRE]

bemoan /bɪˈməʊn/ *v.tr.* **1** express regret or sorrow over; lament. **2** complain about. [BE- + MOAN]

bemuse /bɪˈmjuːz/ *v.tr.* stupefy or bewilder (a person). ◻◻ **bemusedly** /-zɪdlɪ/ *adv.* **bemusement** *n.* [BE- + MUSE²]

ben¹ /ben/ *n. Sc.* a high mountain or mountain peak, esp. in names (*Ben Nevis*). [Gael. *beann*]

ben² /ben/ *n. Sc.* an inner room, esp. of a two-roomed cottage. [ellipt. use of *ben* (adv.), = within (OE *binnan*)]

bench /bentʃ/ *n. & v.* —*n.* **1** a long seat of wood or stone for seating several people. **2** a working-table, e.g. for a carpenter, mechanic, or scientist. **3** (prec. by *the*) **a** the office of judge or magistrate. **b** a judge's seat in a lawcourt. **c** a lawcourt. **d** judges and magistrates collectively. **4** (often in *pl.*) *Sport* an area to the side of a pitch, with seating where coaches and players not taking part can watch the game. **5** *Brit. Parl.* a seat appropriated as specified (*front bench*). **6** a level ledge in masonry or an earthwork, on a hill-slope, etc. —*v.tr.* **1** exhibit (a dog) at a show. **2** *Sport US* withdraw (a player) from the pitch to the benches. □**bench test** esp. *Computing n.* a test made by benchmarking. —*v.tr.* run a series of tests on (a computer etc.) before its use. **King's (or Queen's) Bench** (in the UK) a division of the High Court of Justice. **on the bench** appointed a judge or magistrate. [OE *benc* f. Gmc]

bencher /ˈbentʃə(r)/ *n. Brit.* **1** *Law* a senior member of any of the Inns of Court. **2** (in *comb.*) *Parl.* an occupant of a specified bench (*backbencher*).

benchmark /ˈbentʃmɑːk/ *n. & v.* —*n.* **1** a surveyor's mark cut in a wall, pillar, building, etc., used as a reference point in measuring altitudes. **2** a standard or point of reference. **3** a means of testing a computer, usu. by a set of programs run on a series of different machines. —*v.tr.* evaluate (a computer) by a benchmark. □**benchmark test** a test using a benchmark.

bend[1] /bend/ *v. & n.* —*v.* (*past* **bent**; *past part.* **bent** exc. in *bended knee*) **1 a** *tr.* force or adapt (something straight) into a curve or angle. **b** *intr.* (of an object) be altered in this way. **2** *intr.* move or stretch in a curved course (*the road bends to the left*). **3** *intr. & tr.* (often foll. by *down*, *over*, etc.) incline or cause to incline from the vertical (*bent down to pick it up*). **4** *tr.* interpret or modify (a rule) to suit oneself. **5** *tr. & refl.* (foll. by *to*, *on*) direct or devote (oneself or one's attention, energies, etc.). **6** *tr.* turn (one's steps or eyes) in a new direction. **7** *tr.* (in *passive*; foll. by *on*) have firmly decided; be determined (*was bent on selling*; *on pleasure bent*). **8 a** *intr.* stoop or submit (*bent before his master*). **b** *tr.* force to submit. **9** *tr. Naut.* attach (a sail or cable) with a knot. —*n.* **1** a curve in a road or other course. **2** a departure from a straight course. **3** a bent part of anything. **4** (in *pl.*; prec. by *the*) *colloq.* sickness due to too rapid decompression underwater. □**bend over backwards** see BACKWARDS. **round the bend** *colloq.* crazy, insane. □□ **bendable** *adj.* [OE *bendan* f. Gmc]

bend[2] /bend/ *n.* **1** *Naut.* any of various knots for tying ropes (*fisherman's bend*). **2** *Heraldry* **a** a diagonal stripe from top right to bottom left of a shield. **b** (**bend sinister**) a diagonal stripe from top left to bottom right, as a sign of bastardy. [OE *bend* band, bond f. Gmc]

bender /ˈbendə(r)/ *n. sl.* a wild drinking-spree. [BEND[1] + -ER[1]]

bendy /ˈbendɪ/ *adj.* (**bendier**, **bendiest**) *colloq.* capable of bending; soft and flexible. □□ **bendiness** *n.*

beneath /bɪˈniːθ/ *prep. & adv.* —*prep.* **1** not worthy of; too demeaning for (*it was beneath him to reply*). **2** below, under. —*adv.* below, under, underneath. □**beneath contempt** see CONTEMPT. [OE *binithan*, *bineothan* f. *bi* BY + *nithan* etc. below f. Gmc]

benedicite /ˌbenɪˈdaɪsɪtɪ/ *n.* a blessing, esp. a grace said at table in religious communities. [ME f. L, = bless ye: see BENEDICTION]

Benedictine /ˌbenɪˈdɪktɪn/ *n.*, (in sense 2) -ˌtiːn/ *n. & adj.* —*n.* **1** a monk or nun of an order following the rule of St Benedict established *c.*540. **2** *propr.* a liqueur based on brandy, orig. made by Benedictines in France. —*adj.* of St Benedict or his order. [F *bénédictine* or mod.L *benedictinus* f. *Benedictus* Benedict]

benediction /ˌbenɪˈdɪkʃ(ə)n/ *n.* **1** the utterance of a blessing, esp. at the end of a religious service or as a special Roman Catholic service. **2** the state of being blessed. [ME f. OF f. L *benedictio -onis* f. *benedicere -dict-* bless]

benedictory /ˌbenɪˈdɪktərɪ/ *adj.* of or expressing benediction. [L *benedictorius* (as BENEDICTION)]

Benedictus /ˌbenɪˈdɪktəs/ *n.* **1** the section of the Roman Catholic Mass beginning *Benedictus qui venit in nomine Domini* (Blessed is he who comes in the name of the Lord). **2** a canticle beginning *Benedictus Dominus Deus* (Blessed be the Lord God) from Luke 1:68–79. [L, = blessed: see BENEDICTION]

benefaction /ˌbenɪˈfækʃ(ə)n/ *n.* **1** a donation or gift. **2** an act of giving or doing good. [LL *benefactio* (as BENEFIT)]

benefactor /ˈbenɪˌfæktə(r)/ *n.* (*fem.* **benefactress** /-trɪs/) a person who gives support (esp. financial) to a person or cause. [ME f. LL (as BENEFIT)]

benefice /ˈbenɪfɪs/ *n.* **1** a living from a church office. **2** the property attached to a church office, esp. that bestowed on a rector or vicar. □□ **beneficed** *adj.* [ME f. OF f. L *beneficium* favour f. *bene* well + *facere* do]

beneficent /bɪˈnefɪs(ə)nt/ *adj.* doing good; generous, actively kind. □□ **beneficence** *n.* **beneficently** *adv.* [L *beneficent-* (as BENEFICE)]

beneficial /ˌbenɪˈfɪʃ(ə)l/ *adj.* **1** advantageous; having benefits. **2** *Law* relating to the use or benefit of property; having rights to this use or benefit. □□ **beneficially** *adv.* [ME f. F *bénéficial* or LL *beneficialis* (as BENEFICE)]

beneficiary /ˌbenɪˈfɪʃərɪ/ *n.* (*pl.* -ies) **1** a person who receives benefits, esp. under a person's will. **2** a holder of a church living. [L *beneficiarius* (as BENEFICE)]

benefit /ˈbenɪfɪt/ *n. & v.* —*n.* **1** a favourable or helpful factor or circumstance; advantage, profit. **2** (often in *pl.*) payment made under insurance or social security (*sickness benefit*). **3** a public performance or game of which the proceeds go to a particular player or company or charitable cause. —*v.* (**benefited**, **benefiting**; *US* **benefitted**, **benefitting**) **1** *tr.* do good to; bring advantage to. **2** *intr.* (often foll. by *from*, *by*) receive an advantage or gain. □**benefit of clergy 1** *hist.* exemption of the English tonsured clergy and nuns from the jurisdiction of the ordinary civil courts. **2** ecclesiastical sanction or approval (*marriage without benefit of clergy*). **the benefit of the doubt** a concession that a person is innocent, correct, etc., although doubt exists. **benefit society** a society for mutual insurance against illness or the effects of old age. [ME f. AF *benfet*, OF *bienfet*, f. L *benefactum* f. *bene facere* do well]

Benelux /ˈbenɪˌlʌks/ *n.* Belgium, the Netherlands, and Luxembourg in association as a regional economic group. [*Bel*gium + *Ne*therlands + *Lux*emburg]

benevolent /bɪˈnevələnt/ *adj.* **1** wishing to do good; actively friendly and helpful. **2** charitable (*benevolent fund*; *benevolent society*). □□ **benevolence** *n.* **benevolently** *adv.* [ME f. OF *benivolent* f. L *bene volens -entis* well wishing f. *velle* wish]

B.Eng. *abbr.* Bachelor of Engineering.

Bengali /beŋˈɡɔːlɪ/ *n. & adj.* —*n.* **1** a native of Bengal, a former Indian province now consisting of Bangladesh and the Indian State of W. Bengal. **2** the language of this people. —*adj.* of or relating to Bengal or its people or language.

Bengal light /beŋˈɡɔːl/ *n.* a kind of firework giving off a blue flame, used for signals.

benighted /bɪˈnaɪtɪd/ *adj.* **1** intellectually or morally ignorant. **2** overtaken by darkness. □□ **benightedness** *n.* [obs. *benight* (v.)]

benign /bɪˈnaɪn/ *adj.* **1** gentle, mild, kindly. **2** fortunate, salutary. **3** (of the climate, soil, etc.) mild, favourable. **4** *Med.* (of a disease, tumour, etc.) not malignant. □□ **benignly** *adv.* [ME f. OF *benigne* f. L *benignus* f. *bene* well + *-genus* born]

benignant /bɪˈrɪɡnənt/ *adj.* **1** kindly, esp. to inferiors. **2** salutary, beneficial. **3** *Med.* = BENIGN. □□ **benignancy** *n.* **benignantly** *adv.* [f. BENIGN or L *benignus*, after *malignant*]

benignity /bɪˈnɪɡnɪtɪ/ *n.* (*pl.* -ies) **1** kindliness. **2** an act of kindness. [ME f. OF *benignité* or L *benignitas* (as BENIGN)]

benison /'benɪz(ə)n/ *n. archaic* a blessing. [ME f. OF *beneiçun* f. L *benedictio -onis*]

bent[1] /bent/ *past* and *past part.* of BEND[1] *v.* —*adj.* **1** curved or having an angle. **2** *sl.* dishonest, illicit. **3** *sl.* sexually deviant. **4** (foll. by *on*) determined to do or have. —*n.* **1** an inclination or bias. **2** (foll. by *for*) a talent for something specified (*a bent for mimicry*).

bent[2] /bent/ *n.* **1 a** any stiff grass of the genus *Agrostis.* **b** any of various grasslike reeds, rushes, or sedges. **2** a stiff stalk of a grass usu. with a flexible base. **3** *archaic* or *dial.* a heath or unenclosed pasture. [ME repr. OE *beonet-* (in place-names), f. Gmc]

Benthamism /'benθəmɪz(ə)m/ *n.* the utilitarian philosophy of Jeremy Bentham, Engl. philosopher d. 1832. □□ **Benthamite** *n.* & *adj.*

benthos /'benθɒs/ *n.* the flora and fauna found at the bottom of a sea or lake. □□ **benthic** *adj.* [Gk, = depth of the sea]

bentonite /'bentə,naɪt/ *n.* a kind of absorbent clay used esp. as a filler. [Fort *Benton* in Montana, US]

ben trovato /,ben trəʊˈvɑːtəʊ/ *adj.* **1** well invented. **2** characteristic if not true. [It., = well found]

bentwood /'bentwʊd/ *n.* wood that is artificially shaped for use in making furniture.

benumb /bɪˈnʌm/ *v.tr.* **1** make numb; deaden. **2** paralyse (the mind or feelings). [orig. = deprived, as past part. of ME *benimen* f. OE *beniman* (as BE-, *niman* take)]

Benzedrine /'benzɪ,driːn/ *n. propr.* amphetamine. [BENZOIC + EPHEDRINE]

benzene /'benziːn/ *n.* a colourless carcinogenic volatile liquid found in coal tar, petroleum, etc., and used as a solvent and in the manufacture of plastics etc. ¶ Chem. formula: C_6H_6. □ **benzene ring** the hexagonal unsaturated ring of six carbon atoms in the benzene molecule. □□ **benzenoid** *adj.* [BENZOIC + -ENE]

benzine /'benziːn/ *n.* (also **benzin** /-zɪn/) a mixture of liquid hydrocarbons obtained from petroleum. [BENZOIN + -INE[4]]

benzoic /ben'zəʊɪk/ *adj.* containing or derived from benzoin or benzoic acid. □ **benzoic acid** a white crystalline substance used as a food preservative. ¶ Chem. formula: $C_7H_6O_2$. [BENZOIN + -IC]

benzoin /'benzəʊɪn/ *n.* **1** a fragrant gum resin obtained from various E. Asian trees of the genus *Styrax,* and used in the manufacture of perfumes and incense. **2** the white crystalline constituent of this. Also called *gum benjamin.* [earlier *benjoin* ult. f. Arab. *lubān jāwī* incense of Java]

benzol /'benzɒl/ *n.* (also **benzole** /-zəʊl/) benzene, esp. unrefined and used as a fuel.

benzoyl /'benzəʊɪl/ *n.* (usu. *attrib.*) *Chem.* the radical C_6H_5CO.

benzyl /'benzaɪl, -zɪl/ *n.* (usu. *attrib.*) *Chem.* the radical $C_6H_5CH_2$.

bequeath /bɪˈkwiːð/ *v.tr.* **1** leave (a personal estate) to a person by a will. **2** hand down to posterity. □□ **bequeathal** *n.* **bequeather** *n.* [OE *becwethan* (as BE-, *cwethan* say: cf. QUOTH)]

bequest /bɪˈkwest/ *n.* **1** the act or an instance of bequeathing. **2** a thing bequeathed. [ME f. BE- + obs. *quiste* f. OE *-cwiss, cwide* saying]

berate /bɪˈreɪt/ *v.tr.* scold, rebuke. [BE- + RATE[2]]

Berber /'bɜːbə(r)/ *n.* & *adj.* —*n.* **1** a member of the indigenous mainly Muslim Caucasian peoples of N. Africa. **2** the language of these peoples. —*adj.* of the Berbers or their language. [Arab. *barbar*]

berberis /'bɜːbərɪs/ *n.* = BARBERRY. [med.L & OF, of unkn. orig.]

berceuse /,beəˈsɜːz/ *n.* (*pl.* **berceuses** *pronunc.* same) **1** a lullaby. **2** an instrumental piece in the style of a lullaby. [F]

bereave /bɪˈriːv/ *v.tr.* (esp. as **bereaved** *adj.*) (foll. by *of*) deprive of a relation, friend, etc., esp. by death. □□ **bereavement** *n.* [OE *berēafian* (as BE-, REAVE)]

bereft /bɪˈreft/ *adj.* (foll. by *of*) deprived (esp. of a non-material asset) (*bereft of hope*). [past part. of BEREAVE]

beret /'bereɪ/ *n.* a round flattish cap of felt or cloth. [F *béret* Basque cap f. Prov. *berret*]

berg[1] /bɜːg/ *n.* = ICEBERG. [abbr.]

berg[2] /bɜːg/ *n. S.Afr.* a mountain or hill. □ **berg wind** a hot dry northerly wind blowing from the interior to coastal districts. [Afrik. f. Du.]

bergamot[1] /'bɜːgə,mɒt/ *n.* **1** an aromatic herb, esp. *Mentha citrata.* **2** an oily perfume extracted from the rind of the fruit of the citrus tree *Citrus bergamia,* a dwarf variety of the Seville orange tree. **3** the tree itself. [*Bergamo* in N. Italy]

bergamot[2] /'bɜːgə,mɒt/ *n.* a variety of fine pear. [F *bergamotte* f. It. *bergamotta* f. Turk. *begarmūdi* prince's pear f. *beg* prince + *armudi* pear]

bergschrund /'beəkʃrʊnt/ *n.* a crevasse or gap at the head of a glacier or névé. [G]

beriberi /,berɪˈberɪ/ *n.* a disease causing inflammation of the nerves due to a deficiency of vitamin B_1. [Sinh., f. *beri* weakness]

berk /bɜːk/ *n.* (also **burk**) *Brit. sl.* a fool; a stupid person. ¶ Usu. not considered *offens.* despite the etymology. [abbr. of *Berkeley* or *Berkshire Hunt,* rhyming sl. for *cunt*]

berkelium /bɜːˈkiːlɪəm, 'bɜːklɪəm/ *n. Chem.* a transuranic radioactive metallic element produced by bombardment of americium. ¶ Symb.: **Bk.** [mod.L f. *Berkeley* in California (where first made) + -IUM]

Berks. /bɑːks/ *abbr.* Berkshire.

Berliner /bɜːˈlɪnə(r)/ *n.* **1** a native or citizen of Berlin in Germany. **2** a lightly fried yeast bun with jam filling and vanilla icing. [G]

berm /bɜːm/ *n.* **1** a narrow path or grass strip beside a road, canal, etc. **2** a narrow ledge, esp. in a fortification between a ditch and the base of a parapet. [F *berme* f. Du. *berm*]

Bermuda shorts /bəˈmjuːdə/ *n.pl.* (also **Bermudas**) close-fitting shorts reaching the knees. [*Bermuda* in the W. Atlantic]

Bermuda triangle /bəˈmjuːdə/ *n.* an area of the western Atlantic where ships and aircraft are reported to have disappeared without trace.

berry /'berɪ/ *n.* & *v.* —*n.* (*pl.* -ies) **1** any small roundish juicy fruit without a stone. **2** *Bot.* a fruit with its seeds enclosed in a pulp (e.g. a banana, tomato, etc.). **3** any of various kernels or seeds (e.g. coffee bean etc.). **4** a fish egg or roe of a lobster etc. —*v.intr.* (-ies, -ied) **1** (usu. as **berrying** *n.*) go gathering berries. **2** form a berry; bear berries. □□ **berried** *adj.* (also in *comb.*). [OE *berie* f. Gmc]

berserk /bəˈsɜːk, -ˈzɜːk/ *adj.* & *n.* —*adj.* (esp. in **go berserk**) wild, frenzied; in a violent rage. —*n.* (also **berserker** /-kə(r)/) an ancient Norse warrior who fought with a wild frenzy. [Icel. *berserkr* (n.) prob. f. *bern-* BEAR[2] + *serkr* coat]

berth /bɜːθ/ *n.* & *v.* —*n.* **1** a fixed bunk on a ship, train, etc., for sleeping in. **2** a ship's place at a wharf. **3** room for a ship to swing at anchor. **4** adequate sea room. **5** *colloq.* a situation or appointment. **6** the proper place for anything. —*v.* **1** *tr.* moor (a ship) in its berth. **2** *tr.* provide a sleeping place for. **3** *intr.* (of a ship) come to its mooring-place. □ **give a wide berth** to stay away from. [prob. f. naut. use of BEAR[1] + -TH[2]]

bertha /'bɜːθə/ *n.* **1** a deep falling collar often of lace. **2** a small cape on a dress. [F *berthe* f. *Berthe* Bertha (the name)]

beryl /'berɪl/ *n.* **1** a kind of transparent precious stone, esp. pale green, blue, or yellow, and consisting of beryllium aluminium silicate in a hexagonal form. **2** a mineral species which includes this, emerald, and aquamarine. [ME f. OF f. L *beryllus* f. Gk *bērullos*]

beryllium /bəˈrɪlɪəm/ *n. Chem.* a hard white metallic

element used in the manufacture of light corrosion-resistant alloys. ¶ Symb.: **Be**. [BERYL + -IUM]

beseech /bɪˈsiːtʃ/ v.tr. (past and past part. **besought** /-ˈsɔːt/ or **beseeched**) **1** (foll. by for, or to + infin.) entreat. **2** ask earnestly for. □□ **beseeching** adj. [ME f. BE- + secan SEEK]

beset /bɪˈset/ v.tr. (**besetting**; past and past part. **beset**) **1** attack or harass persistently (beset by worries). **2** surround or hem in (a person etc.). **3** archaic cover round with (beset with pearls). □ **besetting sin** the sin that especially or most frequently tempts one. □□ **besetment** n. [OE besettan f. Gmc]

beside /bɪˈsaɪd/ prep. **1** at the side of; near. **2** compared with. **3** irrelevant to (beside the point). □ **beside oneself** overcome with worry, anger, etc. [OE be sīdan (as BY, SIDE)]

besides /bɪˈsaɪdz/ prep. & adv. —prep. in addition to; apart from. —adv. also; as well; moreover.

besiege /bɪˈsiːdʒ/ v.tr. **1** lay siege to. **2** crowd round oppressively. **3** harass with requests. □□ **besieger** n. [ME f. assiege by substitution of BE-, f. OF asegier f. Rmc]

besmear /bɪˈsmɪə(r)/ v.tr. **1** smear with greasy or sticky stuff. **2** sully (a reputation etc.). [OE bismierwan (as BE-, SMEAR)]

besmirch /bɪˈsmɜːtʃ/ v.tr. **1** soil, discolour. **2** dishonour; sully the reputation or name of. [BE- + SMIRCH]

besom /ˈbiːz(ə)m/ n. **1** a broom made of twigs tied round a stick. **2** esp. N.Engl. derog. or joc. a woman. [OE besema]

besotted /bɪˈsɒtɪd/ adj. **1** infatuated. **2** foolish, confused. **3** intoxicated, stupefied. [besot (v.) (as BE-, SOT)]

besought past and past part. of BESEECH.

bespangle /bɪˈspæŋg(ə)l/ v.tr. adorn with spangles.

bespatter /bɪˈspætə(r)/ v.tr. **1** spatter (an object) all over. **2** spatter (liquid etc.) about. **3** overwhelm with abuse etc.

bespeak /bɪˈspiːk/ v.tr. (past **bespoke** /-ˈspəʊk/; past part. **bespoken** /-ˈspəʊkən/ or as adj. **bespoke**) **1** engage in advance. **2** order (goods). **3** suggest; be evidence of (his gift bespeaks a kind heart). **4** literary speak to. [OE bisprecan (as BE-, SPEAK)]

bespectacled /bɪˈspektək(ə)ld/ adj. wearing spectacles.

bespoke past and past part. of BESPEAK. —adj. **1** (of goods, esp. clothing) made to order. **2** (of a tradesman) making goods to order.

bespoken past part. of BESPEAK.

besprinkle /bɪˈsprɪŋk(ə)l/ v.tr. **1** sprinkle or strew all over with liquid etc. **2** sprinkle (liquid etc.) over. [ME f. BE- + sprengen in the same sense]

Bessemer converter /ˈbesɪmə(r)/ n. a special furnace used to purify pig-iron using the Bessemer process. [Sir H. Bessemer, Engl. engineer d. 1898]

Bessemer process /ˈbesɪmə(r)/ n. a process once widely used, in which air is blown through molten pig-iron to remove carbon, silicon, and other impurities in order to render it suitable for making steel.

best /best/ adj., adv., n., & v. —adj. (superl. of GOOD) of the most excellent or outstanding or desirable kind (my best work; the best solution; the best thing to do would be to confess). —adv. (superl. of WELL¹). **1** in the best manner (does it best). **2** to the greatest degree (like it best). **3** most usefully (is best ignored). —n. **1** that which is best (the best is yet to come). **2** the chief merit or advantage (brings out the best in him). **3** (foll. by of) a winning majority of (a certain number of games etc. played) (the best of five). **4** = Sunday best. —v.tr. colloq. defeat, outwit, outbid, etc. □ **all the best** an expression used to wish a person good fortune. **as best one can** (or **may**) as effectively as possible under the circumstances. **at best** on the most optimistic view. **at one's best** in peak condition etc. **at the best of times** even in the

most favourable circumstances. **be for** (or **all for**) **the best** be desirable in the end. **best end of neck** the rib end of a neck of lamb etc. for cooking. **best man** the bridegroom's chief attendant at a wedding. **the best part of** most of. **best seller 1** a book or other item that has sold in large numbers. **2** the author of such a book. **do one's best** do all one can. **get the best of** defeat, outwit. **give a person the best** admit the superiority of that person. **had best** would find it wisest to. **make the best of** derive what limited advantage one can from (something unsatisfactory or unwelcome); put up with. **to the best of one's ability, knowledge**, etc. as far as one can do, know, etc. **with the best of them** as well as anyone. [OE betest (adj.), bet(o)st (adv.), f. Gmc]

bestial /ˈbestɪəl/ adj. **1** brutish, cruel, savage. **2** sexually depraved; lustful. **3** of or like a beast. □□ **bestialize** v.tr. (also -**ise**). **bestially** adv. [ME f. OF f. LL bestialis f. bestia beast]

bestiality /ˌbestɪˈælɪtɪ/ n. (pl. -**ies**) **1** bestial behaviour or an instance of this. **2** sexual intercourse between a person and an animal. [F bestialité (as BESTIAL)]

bestiary /ˈbestɪərɪ/ n. (pl. -**ies**) a moralizing medieval treatise on real and imaginary beasts. [med.L bestiarium f. L bestia beast]

bestir /bɪˈstɜː(r)/ v.refl. (**bestirred**, **bestirring**) exert or rouse (oneself).

bestow /bɪˈstəʊ/ v.tr. **1** (foll. by on, upon) confer (a gift, right, etc.). **2** deposit. □□ **bestowal** n. [ME f. BE- + OE stow a place]

bestrew /bɪˈstruː/ v.tr. (past part. **bestrewed** or **bestrewn** /-ˈstruːn/) **1** (foll. by with) cover or partly cover (a surface). **2** scatter (things) about. **3** lie scattered over. [OE bestrēowian (as BE-, STREW)]

bestride /bɪˈstraɪd/ v.tr. (past **bestrode** /-ˈstrəʊd/; past part. **bestridden** /-ˈstrɪd(ə)n/) **1** sit astride on. **2** stand astride over. [OE bestrīdan]

bet /bet/ v. & n. —v. (**betting**; past and past part. **bet** or **betted**) **1** intr. (foll. by on or against with ref. to the outcome) risk a sum of money etc. against another's on the basis of the outcome of an unpredictable event (esp. the result of a race, game, etc., or the outcome in a game of chance). **2** tr. risk (an amount) on such an outcome or result (bet £10 on a horse). **3** tr. risk a sum of money against (a person). **4** tr. colloq. feel sure (bet they've forgotten it). —n. **1** the act of betting (make a bet). **2** the money etc. staked (put a bet on). **3** colloq. an opinion, esp. a quickly formed or spontaneous one (my bet is that he won't come). **4** colloq. a choice or course of action (she's our best bet). □ **you bet** you may be sure. [16th c.: perh. a shortened form of ABET]

beta /ˈbiːtə/ n. **1** the second letter of the Greek alphabet (B, β). **2** a second-class mark given for a piece of work or in an examination. **3** Astron. the second brightest star in a constellation. **4** the second member of a series. □ **beta-blocker** Pharm. a drug that prevents the stimulation of increased cardiac action, used to treat angina and reduce high blood pressure. **beta particle** (or **ray**) a fast-moving electron emitted by radioactive decay of substances (orig. regarded as rays). [ME f. L f. Gk]

betake /bɪˈteɪk/ v.refl. (past **betook** /bɪˈtʊk/; past part. **betaken** /bɪˈteɪkən/) (foll. by to) go to (a place or person).

betatron /ˈbiːtətrɒn/ n. Physics an apparatus for accelerating electrons in a circular path by magnetic induction. [BETA + -TRON]

betel /ˈbiːt(ə)l/ n. the leaf of the Asian evergreen climbing plant Piper betle, chewed in the East with parings of the areca nut. □ **betel-nut** the areca nut. [Port. f. Malayalam veṭṭila]

bête noire /beɪt ˈnwɑː(r)/ n. (pl. **bêtes noires** pronunc. same) a person or thing one particularly dislikes or fears. [F, = black beast]

bethink /bɪˈθɪŋk/ v.refl. (past and past part. **bethought** /-ˈθɔːt/) (foll. by of, how, or that + clause) *formal* **1** reflect; stop to think. **2** be reminded by reflection. [OE *bithencan* f. Gmc (as BE-, THINK)]

betide /bɪ'taɪd/ *v.* (only in infin. and 3rd sing. subj.) **1** *tr.* happen to (*woe betide him*). **2** *intr.* happen (*whate'er may betide*). [ME f. obs. *tide* befall f. OE *tīdan*]

betimes /bɪ'taɪmz/ *adv. literary* early; in good time. [ME f. obs. *betime* (as BY, TIME)]

bêtise /beɪ'tiːz/ *n.* **1** a foolish or ill-timed remark or action. **2** a piece of folly. [F]

betoken /bɪ'təʊkən/ *v.tr.* **1** be a sign of; indicate. **2** augur. [OE (as BE-, *tācnian* signify: see TOKEN)]

betony /'betənɪ/ *n.* **1** a purple-flowered plant, *Stachys officinalis.* **2** any of various similar plants. [ME f. OF *betoine* f. L *betonica*]

betook *past* of BETAKE.

betray /bɪ'treɪ/ *v.tr.* **1** place (a person, one's country, etc.) in the hands or power of an enemy. **2** be disloyal to (another person, a person's trust, etc.). **3** reveal involuntarily or treacherously; be evidence of (*his shaking hand betrayed his fear*). **4** lead astray or into error. □□ **betrayal** *n.* **betrayer** *n.* [ME f. obs. *tray*, ult. f. L *tradere* hand over]

betroth /bɪ'trəʊð/ *v.tr.* (usu. as **betrothed** *adj.*) bind with a promise to marry. □□ **betrothal** *n.* [ME f. BE- + *trouthe*, *treuthe* TRUTH, later assim. to TROTH]

better[1] /'betə(r)/ *adj., adv., n., & v.* —*adj.* (*compar.* of GOOD). **1** of a more excellent or outstanding or desirable kind (*a better product; it would be better to go home*). **2** partly or fully recovered from illness (*feeling better*). —*adv.* (*compar.* of WELL[1]). **1** in a better manner (*she sings better*). **2** to a greater degree (*like it better*). **3** more usefully or advantageously (*is better forgotten*). —*n.* **1** that which is better (*the better of the two*). **2** (usu. in *pl.*; prec. by *my* etc.) one's superior in ability or rank (*take notice of your betters*). —*v.* **1** *tr.* improve on; surpass (*I can better his offer*). **2** *tr.* make better; improve. **3** *refl.* improve one's position etc. **4** *intr.* become better; improve. □ **better feelings** one's conscience. **better half** *colloq.* one's wife or husband. **better off** in a better (esp. financial) position. **the better part of** most of. **for better or for worse** on terms accepting all results; whatever the outcome. **get the better of** defeat, outwit; win an advantage over. **go one better 1** outbid etc. by one. **2** outdo another person. **had better** would find it wiser to. [OE *betera* f. Gmc]

better[2] /'betə(r)/ *n.* (also **bettor**) a person who bets.

betterment /'betəmənt/ *n.* **1** making better; improvement. **2** *Econ.* enhanced value (of real property) arising from local improvements.

betting /'betɪŋ/ *n.* **1** gambling by risking money on an unpredictable outcome. **2** the odds offered in this. □ **betting-shop** *Brit.* a bookmaker's shop or office. **what's the betting?** *colloq.* it is likely or to be expected (*what's the betting he'll be late?*).

bettor var. of BETTER[2].

between /bɪ'twiːn/ *prep. & adv.* —*prep.* **1 a** at or to a point in the area or interval bounded by two or more other points in space, time, etc. (*broke down between London and Dover; we must meet between now and Friday*). **b** along the extent of such an area or interval (*there are five shops between here and the main road; works best between five and six; the numbers between 10 and 20*). **2** separating, physically or conceptually (*the distance between here and Leeds; the difference between right and wrong*). **3 a** by combining the resources of (*great potential between them; between us we could afford it*). **b** shared by; as the joint resources of (*£5 between them*). **c** by joint or reciprocal action (*an agreement between us; sorted it out between themselves*). ¶ Use in sense 3 with reference to more than two people or things is established and acceptable (e.g. *relations between Britain, France, and Germany*). **4** to and from (*runs between London and Sheffield*). **5** taking one and rejecting the other (*decide between eating here and going out*). —*adv.* (also **in between**) at a point or in the area bounded

by two or more other points in space, time, sequence, etc. (*not fat or thin but in between*). □ **between ourselves** (or **you and me**) in confidence. **between times** (or **whiles**) in the intervals between other actions; occasionally. [OE *betwēonum* f. Gmc (as BY, TWO)]

betwixt /bɪ'twɪkst/ *prep. & adv. archaic* between. □ **betwixt and between** *colloq.* neither one thing nor the other. [ME f. OE *betwēox* f. Gmc: cf. AGAINST]

BeV *abbr.* a billion (=10⁹) electron-volts. Also called GeV.

bevatron /'bevə,trɒn/ *n.* a synchrotron used to accelerate protons to energies in the billion electronvolt range. [BeV + -TRON]

bevel /'bev(ə)l/ *n. & v.* —*n.* **1** a slope from the horizontal or vertical in carpentry and stonework; a sloping surface or edge. **2** (in full **bevel square**) a tool for marking angles in carpentry and stonework. —*v.* (**bevelled, bevelling;** *US* **beveled, beveling**) **1** *tr.* reduce (a square edge) to a sloping edge. **2** *intr.* slope at an angle; slant. □ **bevel gear** a gear working another gear at an angle to it by means of bevel wheels. **bevel wheel** a toothed wheel whose working face is oblique to the axis. [OF *bevel* (unrecorded) f. *baïf* f. *baer* gape]

beverage /'bevərɪdʒ/ *n. formal* a drink (*hot beverage; alcoholic beverage*). [ME f. OF *be(u)vrage*, ult. f. L *bibere* drink]

bevy /'bevɪ/ *n.* (*pl.* **-ies**) **1** a flock of quails or larks. **2** a company or group (orig. of women). [15th c.: orig. unkn.]

bewail /bɪ'weɪl/ *v.tr.* **1** greatly regret or lament. **2** wail over; mourn for. □□ **bewailer** *n.*

beware /bɪ'weə(r)/ *v.* (only in *imper.* or *infin.*) **1** *intr.* (often foll. by *of*, or *that*, *lest*, etc. + clause) be cautious, take heed (*beware of the dog; told us to beware; beware that you don't fall*). **2** *tr.* be cautious of (*beware the Ides of March*). [BE + WARE[3]]

bewilder /bɪ'wɪldə(r)/ *v.tr.* utterly perplex or confuse. □□ **bewilderedly** *adv.* **bewildering** *adj.* **bewilderingly** *adv.* **bewilderment** *n.* [BE- + obs. *wilder* lose one's way]

bewitch /bɪ'wɪtʃ/ *v.tr.* **1** enchant; greatly delight. **2** cast a spell on. □□ **bewitching** *adj.* **bewitchingly** *adv.* [ME f. BE- + OE *wiccian* enchant f. *wicca* WITCH]

bey /beɪ/ *n. hist.* (in the Ottoman Empire) the title of a governor of a province. [Turk.]

beyond /bɪ'jɒnd/ *prep., adv., & n.* —*prep.* **1** at or to the further side of (*beyond the river*). **2** outside the scope, range, or understanding of (*beyond repair; beyond a joke; it is beyond me*). **3** more than. —*adv.* **1** at or to the further side. **2** further on. —*n.* (prec. by *the*) the unknown after death. □ **the back of beyond** see BACK. [OE *beg(e)ondan* (as BY, YON, YONDER)]

bezant /'bez(ə)nt, bɪ'zænt/ *n.* **1** *hist.* a gold or silver coin orig. minted at Byzantium. **2** *Heraldry* a gold roundel. [ME f. OF *besanz -ant* f. L *Byzantius* Byzantine]

bezel /'bez(ə)l/ *n.* **1** the sloped edge of a chisel. **2** the oblique faces of a cut gem. **3 a** a groove holding a watch-glass or gem. **b** a rim holding a glass etc. cover. [OF *besel* (unrecorded: cf. F *béseau*, *bizeau*) of unkn. orig.]

bezique /bɪ'ziːk/ *n.* **1** a card-game for two with a double pack of 64 cards, including the ace to seven only in each suit. **2** a combination of the queen of spades and the jack of diamonds in this game. [F *bésigue*, perh. f. Pers. *bāzīgar* juggler]

bezoar /'biːzɔː(r), 'bezəʊ,ɑː(r)/ *n.* a small stone which may form in the stomachs of certain animals, esp. ruminants, and which was once used as an antidote for various ills. [ult. f. Pers. *pādzahr* antidote, Arab. *bāzahr*]

b.f. *abbr.* **1** *Brit. colloq.* bloody fool. **2** brought forward. **3** *Printing* bold face.

bhang /bæŋ/ *n.* the leaves and flower-tops of Indian

hemp used as a narcotic. [Port. *bangue*, Pers. *bang*, & Urdu etc. *bhāng* f. Skr. *bhaṅgā*]

bharal /'bʌr(ə)l/ *n.* (also **burhel**) a Himalayan wild sheep, *Pseudois nayaur*, with blue-black coat and horns curved rearward. [Hindi]

b.h.p. *abbr.* brake horsepower.

Bi *symb. Chem.* the element bismuth.

bi- /baɪ/ *comb. form* (often **bin-** before a vowel) forming nouns and adjectives meaning: **1** having two; a thing having two (*bilateral*; *binaural*; *biplane*). **2 a** occurring twice in every one or once in every two (*bi-weekly*). **b** lasting for two (*biennial*). **3** doubly; in two ways (*biconcave*). **4** *Chem.* a substance having a double proportion of the acid etc. indicated by the simple word (*bicarbonate*). **5** *Bot.* & *Zool.* (of division and subdivision) twice over (*bipinnate*). [L]

biannual /baɪ'ænjʊəl/ *adj.* occurring, appearing, etc., twice a year (cf. BIENNIAL). □□ **biannually** *adv.*

bias /'baɪəs/ *n.* & *v.* —*n.* **1** (often foll. by *towards*, *against*) a predisposition or prejudice. **2** *Statistics* a systematic distortion of a statistical result due to a factor not allowed for in its derivation. **3** an edge cut obliquely across the weave of a fabric. **4** *Sport* **a** the irregular shape given to a bowl. **b** the oblique course this causes it to run. **5** *Electr.* a steady voltage, magnetic field, etc., applied to an electronic system or device. —*v.tr.* (**biased**, **biasing**; **biassed**, **biassing**) **1** (esp. as **biased** *adj.*) influence (usu. unfairly); prejudice. **2** give a bias to. □ **bias binding** a strip of fabric cut obliquely and used to bind edges. **on the bias** obliquely, diagonally. [F *biais*, of unkn. orig.]

biathlon /baɪ'æθlən/ *n. Sport* an athletic contest in skiing and shooting. □□ **biathlete** *n.* [BI-, after PENTATHLON]

biaxial /baɪ'æksɪəl/ *adj.* (esp. of crystals) having two axes along which polarized light travels with equal velocity.

bib[1] /bɪb/ *n.* **1** a piece of cloth or plastic fastened round a child's neck to keep the clothes clean while eating. **2** the top front part of an apron, dungarees, etc. **3** the edible marine fish *Trisopterus luscus* of the cod family. Also called POUT[2]. □ **best bib and tucker** best clothes. **stick** (or **poke** etc.) **one's bib in** *Austral. sl.* interfere. [perh. f. BIB[2]]

bib[2] /bɪb/ *v.intr.* (**bibbed**, **bibbing**) *archaic* drink much or often. □□ **bibber** *n.* [ME, perh. f. L *bibere* drink]

bib-cock /'bɪbkɒk/ *n.* a tap with a bent nozzle fixed at the end of a pipe. [perh. f. BIB[1] + COCK[1]]

bibelot /'bi:bləʊ/ *n.* a small curio or artistic trinket. [F]

Bible /'baɪb(ə)l/ *n.* **1 a** the Christian scriptures consisting of the Old and New Testaments. **b** the Jewish scriptures. **c** (**bible**) any copy of these (*three bibles on the table*). **d** a particular edition of the Bible (*New English Bible*). **2** *colloq.* any authoritative book (*Wisden is his Bible*). **3** the scriptures of any non-Christian religion. □ **Bible-basher** (or **-thumper** etc.) a person given to Bible-bashing. **Bible-bashing** (or **-thumping** etc.) *sl.* aggressive fundamentalist preaching. **Bible belt** esp. *US* the reputedly puritanical area of the southern and central US. **Bible oath** a solemn oath taken on the Bible. [ME f. OF f. eccl.L *biblia* f. Gk *biblia* books (pl. of *biblion*), orig. dimin. of *biblos*, *bublos* papyrus]

biblical /'bɪblɪk(ə)l/ *adj.* **1** of, concerning, or contained in the Bible. **2** resembling the language of the Authorized Version of the Bible. □□ **biblically** *adv.*

biblio- /'bɪblɪəʊ/ *comb. form* denoting a book or books. [Gk f. *biblion* book]

bibliography /ˌbɪblɪ'ɒɡrəfɪ/ *n.* (*pl.* **-ies**) **1 a** a list of the books referred to in a scholarly work, usu. printed as an appendix. **b** a list of the books of a specific author or publisher, or on a specific subject, etc. **2 a** the history or description of books, including authors, editions, etc. **b** any book containing such information. □□ **bibliographer** *n.* **bibliographic**

/-ə'ɡræfɪk/ *adj.* **bibliographical** /-ə'ɡræfɪk(ə)l/ *adj.* **bibliographically** /-ə'ɡræfɪkəlɪ/ *adv.* **bibliographize** *v.tr.* (also **-ise**). [F *bibliographie* f. mod.L *bibliographia* f. Gk (as BIBLE, -GRAPHY)]

bibliomancy /'bɪblɪəʊˌmænsɪ/ *n.* foretelling the future by the analysis of a randomly chosen passage from a book, esp. the Bible.

bibliomania /ˌbɪblɪəʊ'meɪnɪə/ *n.* an extreme enthusiasm for collecting and possessing books. □□ **bibliomaniac** /-nɪˌæk/ *n.* & *adj.*

bibliophile /'bɪblɪəʊˌfaɪl/ *n.* (also **bibliophil** /-fɪl/) a person who collects or is fond of books. □□ **bibliophilic** /-'fɪlɪk/ *adj.* **bibliophily** /-'ɒfɪlɪ/ *n.* [F *bibliophile* (as BIBLIO-, -PHILE)]

bibliopole /'bɪblɪəʊˌpəʊl/ *n.* a seller of (esp. rare) books. □□ **bibliopoly** /-'ɒpəlɪ/ *n.* [L *bibliopola* f. Gk *bibliopōlēs* f. *biblion* book + *pōlēs* seller]

bibulous /'bɪbjʊləs/ *adj.* given to drinking alcoholic liquor. □□ **bibulously** *adv.* **bibulousness** *n.* [L *bibulus* freely drinking f. *bibere* drink]

bicameral /baɪ'kæmər(ə)l/ *adj.* (of a parliament or legislative body) having two chambers. □□ **bicameralism** *n.* [BI- + L *camera* chamber]

bicarb /'baɪkɑːb/ *n. colloq.* = BICARBONATE 2. [abbr.]

bicarbonate /baɪ'kɑːbənɪt/ *n.* **1** *Chem.* any acid salt of carbonic acid. **2** (in full **bicarbonate of soda**) sodium bicarbonate used as an antacid or in baking powder.

bice /baɪs/ *n.* **1** any of various pigments made from blue or green basic copper carbonate. **2** any similar pigment made from smalt. **3** a shade of blue or green given by these. □ **blue bice** a shade of blue between ultramarine and azure derived from smalt. **green bice** a yellowish green colour derived by adding yellow orpiment to smalt. [orig. = brownish grey, f. OF *bis* dark grey, of unkn. orig.]

bicentenary /ˌbaɪsen'tiːnərɪ/ *n.* & *adj.* —*n.* (*pl.* **-ies**) **1** a two-hundredth anniversary. **2** a celebration of this. —*adj.* of or concerning a bicentenary.

bicentennial /ˌbaɪsen'tenɪəl/ *n.* & *adj.* esp. *US* —*n.* a bicentenary. —*adj.* **1** lasting two hundred years or occurring every two hundred years. **2** of or concerning a bicentenary.

bicephalous /baɪ'sefələs/ *adj.* having two heads.

biceps /'baɪseps/ *n.* a muscle having two heads or attachments, esp. the one which bends the elbow. [L, = two-headed, formed as BI- + -*ceps* f. *caput* head]

bicker /'bɪkə(r)/ *v.intr.* **1** quarrel pettily; wrangle. **2** *poet.* **a** (of a stream, rain, etc.) patter (over stones etc.). **b** (of a flame, light, etc.) flash, flicker. □□ **bickerer** *n.* [ME *biker*, *beker*, of unkn. orig.]

bicolour /'baɪˌkʌlə(r)/ *adj.* & *n.* —*adj.* having two colours. —*n.* a bicolour blossom or animal.

biconcave /baɪ'kɒnkeɪv/ *adj.* (esp. of a lens) concave on both sides.

biconvex /baɪ'kɒnveks/ *adj.* (esp. of a lens) convex on both sides.

bicultural /baɪ'kʌltʃər(ə)l/ *adj.* having or combining two cultures.

bicuspid /baɪ'kʌspɪd/ *adj.* & *n.* —*adj.* having two cusps or points. —*n.* **1** the premolar tooth in humans. **2** a tooth with two cusps. □□ **bicuspidate** *adj.* [BI- + L *cuspis -idis* sharp point]

bicycle /'baɪsɪk(ə)l/ *n.* & *v.* —*n.* a vehicle of two wheels held in a frame one behind the other, propelled by pedals and steered with handlebars attached to the front wheel. —*v.intr.* ride a bicycle. □ **bicycle-chain** a chain transmitting power from the bicycle pedals to the wheels. **bicycle-clip** either of two metal clips used to confine a cyclist's trousers at the ankle. **bicycle-pump** a portable pump for inflating bicycle tyres. □□ **bicycler** *n.* **bicyclist** /-klɪst/ *n.* [F f. BI- + Gk *kuklos* wheel]

bid /bɪd/ *v.* & *n.* —*v.* (**bidding**; *past* **bid**, *archaic* **bade** /beɪd, bæd/; *past part.* **bid**, *archaic* **bidden** /'bɪd(ə)n/) **1** *tr.* & *intr.* (*past* and *past part.* **bid**) (often foll. by *for*, *against*) **a** (esp. at an auction) offer (a certain price) (*did not bid for the vase*; *bid against* *the dealer*; *bid £20*). **b** offer to do work etc. for a stated price. **2** *tr. archaic* or *literary* **a** command; order (*bid the soldiers shoot*). **b** invite (*bade her start*). **3** *tr. archaic* or *literary* **a** utter (greeting or farewell) to (*I bade him welcome*). **b** proclaim (defiance etc.). **4** (*past* and *past part*. **bid**) *Cards* **a** *intr*. state before play how many tricks one intends to make. **b** *tr*. state (one's intended number of tricks). —*n*. **1 a** (esp. at an auction) an offer (of a price) (*a bid of £5*). **b** an offer (to do work, supply goods, etc.) at a stated price; a tender. **2** *Cards* a statement of the number of tricks a player proposes to make. **3** *colloq*. an attempt; an effort (*a bid for power*). ▫**bid fair to** seem likely to. **make a bid for** try to gain (*made a bid for freedom*). ▫▫ **bidder** *n*. [OE *biddan* ask f. Gmc, & OE *bēodan* offer, command]

biddable /'bɪdəb(ə)l/ *adj*. **1** obedient. **2** *Cards* (of a hand or suit) suitable for being bid. ▫▫ **biddability** /-'bɪlɪtɪ/ *n*.

bidden *archaic past part*. of BID.

bidding /'bɪdɪŋ/ *n*. **1** the offers at an auction. **2** *Cards* the act of making a bid or bids. **3** a command, request, or invitation. ▫**bidding-prayer** one inviting the congregation to join in.

biddy /'bɪdɪ/ *n*. (*pl*. **-ies**) *sl. derog*. a woman (esp. *old biddy*). [pet-form of the name *Bridget*]

bide /baɪd/ *v.intr. archaic* or *dial*. remain; stay. ▫**bide one's time** await one's best opportunity. [OE *bīdan* f. Gmc]

bidet /'biːdeɪ/ *n*. a low oval basin used esp. for washing the genital area. [F, = pony]

Biedermeier /'biːdə,maɪə(r)/ *attrib.adj*. **1** (of styles, furnishings, etc.) characteristic of the period 1815–48 in Germany. **2** *derog*. conventional; bourgeois. [*Biedermaier* a fictitious German poet (1854)]

biennial /baɪ'enɪəl/ *adj. & n*. —*adj*. **1** lasting two years. **2** recurring every two years (cf. BIANNUAL). —*n*. **1** *Bot*. a plant that takes two years to grow from seed to fruition and die (cf. ANNUAL, PERENNIAL). **2** an event celebrated or taking place every two years. ▫▫ **biennially** *adv*. [L *biennis* (as BI-, *annus* year)]

biennium /baɪ'enɪəm/ *n*. (*pl*. **bienniums** or **biennia** /-nɪə/) a period of two years. [L (as BIENNIAL)]

bier /bɪə(r)/ *n*. a movable frame on which a coffin or a corpse is placed, or taken to a grave. [OE *bēr* f. Gmc]

biff /bɪf/ *n. & v. sl*. —*n*. a sharp blow (a person). [imit.] —*v.tr*. strike

biffin /'bɪfɪn/ *n. Brit*. a deep-red cooking-apple. [= *beefing* f. BEEF + -ING[1], with ref. to the colour]

bifid /'baɪfɪd/ *adj*. divided by a deep cleft into two parts. [L *bifidus* (as BI-, *fidus* f. stem of *findere* cleave)]

bifocal /baɪ'fəʊk(ə)l/ *adj. & n*. —*adj*. having two focuses, esp. of a lens with a part for distant vision and a part for near vision. —*n*. (in *pl*.) bifocal spectacles.

bifurcate /'baɪfə,keɪt/ *v. & adj*. —*v.tr. & intr*. divide into two branches; fork. —*adj*. forked; branched. [med.L *bifurcare* f. L *bifurcus* two-forked (as BI-, *furca* fork)]

bifurcation /,baɪfə'keɪʃ(ə)n/ *n*. **1 a** a division into two branches. **b** either or both of such branches. **2** the point of such a division.

big /bɪg/ *adj. & adv*. —*adj*. (**bigger**, **biggest**) **1 a** of considerable size, amount, intensity, etc. (*a big mistake*; *a big helping*). **b** of a large or the largest size (*big toe*; *big drum*). **2** important; significant; outstanding (*the big race*; *my big chance*). **3 a** grown up (*a big boy now*). **b** elder (*big sister*). **4** *colloq*. boastful (*big words*; *big mouth*). **b** often *iron*. generous (*big of him*). **c** ambitious (*big ideas*). **5** (usu. foll. by *with*) advanced in pregnancy; fecund (*big with child*; *big with consequences*). —*adv. colloq*. in a big manner, esp.: **1** effectively (*went over big*). **2** boastfully (*talk big*). **3** ambitiously (*think big*). ▫**Big Apple** *US sl*. New York City. **big band** a large jazz or pop orchestra. **big bang** *Stock Exch*. (in the UK) the introduction in 1986 of important changes in the

regulations and procedures for trading, esp. the widening of membership, the relaxation of rules for brokers, and the introduction of computerized communications. **big bang theory** the theory that the universe began with the explosion of dense matter. **Big Ben** the great clock tower of the Houses of Parliament and its bell. **Big Board** *US colloq*. the New York Stock Exchange. **Big Brother** an all-powerful supposedly benevolent dictator (as in Orwell's *1984*). **big bud** a plant disease caused by the gall-mite. **big bug** *sl*. = BIGWIG. **big business** large-scale financial dealings, esp. when sinister or exploitative. **Big Chief** (or **Daddy**) *sl*. = BIGWIG. **big deal!** *sl. iron*. I am not impressed. **big dipper 1** a fairground switchback. **2** *US* = *the Great Bear* (see BEAR[2]). **big end** (in a motor vehicle) the end of the connecting-rod that encircles the crankpin. **big game** large animals hunted for sport. **big gun** *sl*. = BIGWIG. **big-head** *colloq*. a conceited person. **big-headed** *colloq*. conceited. **big-headedness** *colloq*. conceitedness. **big-hearted** generous. **big house 1** the principal house in a village etc. **2** *sl*. a prison. **big idea** often *iron*. the important intention or scheme. **big money** large amounts; high profit; high pay. **big name** a famous person. **big noise** (or **pot** or **shot**) *colloq*. = BIGWIG. **big smoke** *Brit. sl*. **1** London. **2** any large town. **big stick** a display of force. **Big Three** (or **Four** etc.) the predominant few. **the big time** *sl*. success in a profession, esp. show business. **big-timer** *sl*. a person who achieves success. **big top** the main tent in a circus. **big tree** *US* a giant evergreen conifer, *Sequoiadendron giganteum*, usu. with a trunk of large girth. **big wheel 1** a Ferris wheel. **2** *US sl*. = BIGWIG. **come** (or **go**) **over big** make a great effect. **in a big way 1** on a large scale. **2** *colloq*. with great enthusiasm, display, etc. **look** (or **talk**) **big** boast. **think big** be ambitious. **too big for one's boots** (or **breeches**) *sl*. conceited. ▫▫ **biggish** *adj*. **bigness** *n*. [ME: orig. unkn.]

bigamy /'bɪgəmɪ/ *n*. (*pl*. **-ies**) the crime of marrying when one is lawfully married to another person. ▫▫ **bigamist** *n*. **bigamous** *adj*. [ME f. OF *bigamie* f. *bigame* bigamous f. LL *bigamus* (as BI-, Gk *gamos* marriage)]

bighorn /'bɪghɔːn/ *n*. an American sheep, *Ovis canadensis*, esp. native to the Rocky Mountains.

bight /baɪt/ *n*. **1** a curve or recess in a coastline, river, etc. **2** a loop of rope. [OE *byht*, MLG *bucht* f. Gmc: see BOW[2]]

bigot /'bɪgət/ *n*. an obstinate and intolerant believer in a religion, political theory, etc. ▫▫ **bigotry** *n*. [16th c. f. F: orig. unkn.]

bigoted /'bɪgətɪd/ *adj*. unreasonably prejudiced and intolerant.

bigwig /'bɪgwɪg/ *n. colloq*. an important person.

bijou /'biːʒuː/ *n. & adj*. —*n*. (*pl*. **bijoux** *pronunc*. same) a jewel; a trinket. —*attrib.adj*. (**bijou**) small and elegant. [F]

bijouterie /biː'ʒuːtərɪ/ *n*. jewellery; trinkets. [F (as BIJOU, -ERY)]

bike /baɪk/ *n. & v. colloq*. —*n*. a bicycle or motor cycle. —*v.intr*. ride a bicycle or motor cycle. [abbr.]

biker /'baɪkə(r)/ *n*. a cyclist, esp. a motor cyclist.

bikini /bɪ'kiːnɪ/ *n*. a two-piece swimsuit for women. ▫**bikini briefs** women's scanty briefs. [*Bikini*, an atoll in the Marshall Islands in the Pacific where an atomic bomb was exploded in 1946, from the supposed 'explosive' effect]

bilabial /baɪ'leɪbɪəl/ *adj. Phonet*. (of a sound etc.) made with closed or nearly closed lips.

bilateral /baɪ'lætər(ə)l/ *adj*. **1** of, on, or with two sides. **2** affecting or between two parties, countries, etc. (*bilateral negotiations*). ▫**bilateral symmetry** symmetry about a plane. ▫▫ **bilaterally** *adv*.

bilberry /'bɪlbərɪ/ *n*. (*pl*. **-ies**) **1** a hardy dwarf shrub, *Vaccinium myrtillus*, of N. Europe, growing on heaths and mountains, and having red drooping flowers and dark blue berries. **2** the small blue edible berry of this species. **3** any of various shrubs of the genus *Vaccinium* having dark blue berries. [orig. uncert.: cf. Da. *böllebær*]

bilbo /'bɪlbəʊ/ n. (pl. **-os** or **-oes**) hist. a sword noted for the temper and elasticity of its blade. [*Bilboa* = Bilbao in Spain]

bilboes /'bɪlbəʊz/ n.pl. hist. an iron bar with sliding shackles for a prisoner's ankles. [16th c.: orig. unkn.]

Bildungsroman /'bɪldʊŋzrəʊˌmɑːn/ n. a novel dealing with one person's early life and development. [G]

bile /baɪl/ n. **1** a bitter greenish-brown alkaline fluid which aids digestion and is secreted by the liver and stored in the gall-bladder. **2** bad temper; peevish anger. □**bile-duct** the duct which conveys bile from the liver and the gall-bladder to the duodenum. [F f. L *bilis*]

bilge /bɪldʒ/ n. & v. —n. **1 a** the almost flat part of a ship's bottom, inside or out. **b** (in full **bilge-water**) filthy water that collects inside the bilge. **2** sl. nonsense; rot (*don't talk bilge*). —v. **1** tr. stave in the bilge of (a ship). **2** intr. spring a leak in the bilge. **3** intr. swell out; bulge. □**bilge-keel** a plate or timber fastened under the bilge to prevent rolling. [prob. var. of BULGE]

bilharzia /bɪl'hɑːtsɪə/ n. **1** a tropical flatworm of the genus *Schistosoma* (formerly *Bilharzia*) which is parasitic in blood vessels in the human pelvic region. Also called SCHISTOSOME. **2** the chronic tropical disease produced by its presence. Also called BILHARZIASIS, SCHISTOSOMIASIS. [mod.L f. T. *Bilharz*, Ger. physician d. 1862]

bilharziasis /ˌbɪlhɑː'tsaɪəsɪs/ n. the disease of bilharzia. Also called SCHISTOSOMIASIS.

biliary /'bɪlɪərɪ/ adj. of the bile. [F *biliaire*: see BILE, -ARY²]

bilingual /baɪ'lɪŋgw(ə)l/ adj. & n. —adj. **1** able to speak two languages, esp. fluently. **2** spoken or written in two languages. —n. a bilingual person. □□ **bilingualism** n. [L *bilinguis* (as BI-, *lingua* tongue)]

bilious /'bɪljəs/ adj. **1** affected by a disorder of the bile. **2** bad-tempered. □□ **biliously** adv. **biliousness** n. [L *biliosus* f. *bilis* bile]

bilirubin /ˌbɪlɪ'ruːbɪn/ n. the orange-yellow pigment occurring in bile. [G f. L *bilis* BILE + *ruber* red]

bilk /bɪlk/ v.tr. sl. **1** cheat. **2** give the slip to. **3** avoid paying (a creditor or debt). □□ **bilker** n. [orig. uncert., perh. = BALK: earliest use (17th c.) in cribbage, = spoil one's opponent's score]

bill¹ /bɪl/ n. & v. —n. **1 a** a printed or written statement of charges for goods supplied or services rendered. **b** the amount owed (*ran up a bill of £300*). **2** a draft of a proposed law. **3 a** a poster; a placard. **b** = HANDBILL. **4 a** a printed list, esp. a theatre programme. **b** the entertainment itself (*top of the bill*). **5** US a banknote (*ten dollar bill*). —v.tr. **1** put in the programme; announce. **2** (foll. by *as*) advertise. **3** send a note of charges to (*billed him for the books*). □**bill of exchange** *Econ.* a written order to pay a sum of money on a given date to the drawer or to a named payee. **bill of fare 1** a menu. **2** a programme (for a theatrical event). **bill of health 1** *Naut.* a certificate regarding infectious disease on a ship or in a port at the time of sailing. **2** (**clean bill of health**) **a** such a certificate stating that there is no disease. **b** a declaration that a person or thing examined has been found to be free of illness or in good condition. **bill of indictment** *hist.* or *US* a written accusation as presented to a grand jury. **bill of lading** *Naut.* **1** a shipmaster's detailed list of the ship's cargo. **2** *US* = WAYBILL. **Bill of Rights 1** *Law* the English constitutional settlement of 1689. **2** *Law* (in the US) the constitutional amendments of 1791. **3** a statement of the rights of a class of people. **bill of sale** *Econ.* a certificate of transfer of personal property, esp. as a security against debt. □□ **billable** adj. [ME f. AF *bille*, AL *billa*, prob. alt. of med.L *bulla* seal, sealed documents, BULL²]

bill² /bɪl/ n. & v. —n. **1** the beak of a bird, esp. when

it is slender, flattened, or weak, or belongs to a web-footed bird or a bird of the pigeon family. **2** the muzzle of a platypus. **3** a narrow promontory. **4** the point of an anchor-fluke. —v.intr. (of doves etc.) stroke a bill with a bill. □**bill and coo** exchange caresses. □□ **billed** adj. (usu. in *comb.*). [OE *bile*, of unkn. orig.]

bill³ /bɪl/ n. **1** hist. a weapon like a halberd with a hook instead of a blade. **2** = BILLHOOK. [OE *bil*, ult. f. Gmc]

billabong /'bɪləˌbɒŋ/ n. Austral. a branch of a river forming a backwater or a stagnant pool. [Aboriginal *Billibang* Bell River f. *billa* water]

billboard /'bɪlbɔːd/ n. esp. US a large outdoor board for advertisements etc.

billet¹ /'bɪlɪt/ n. & v. —n. **1 a** a place where troops etc. are lodged, usu. with civilians. **b** a written order requiring a householder to lodge the bearer, usu. a soldier. **2** colloq. a situation; a job. —v.tr. (**billeted**, **billeting**) **1** (usu. foll. by *on*, *in*, *at*) quarter (soldiers etc.). **2** (of a householder) provide (a soldier etc.) with board and lodging. □□ **billetee** /-'tiː/ n. **billeter** n. [ME f. AF *billette*, AL *billetta*, dimin. of *billa* BILL¹]

billet² /'bɪlɪt/ n. **1** a thick piece of firewood. **2** a small metal bar. **3** *Archit.* each of a series of short rolls inserted at intervals in Norman decorative mouldings. [ME f. F *billette* small log, ult. prob. of Celtic orig.]

billet-doux /ˌbɪlɪ'duː/ n. (pl. **billets-doux** /-'duːz/) often *joc.* a love-letter. [F, = sweet note]

billfold /'bɪlfəʊld/ n. US a wallet for keeping banknotes.

billhead /'bɪlhed/ n. a printed account form.

billhook /'bɪlhʊk/ n. a sickle-shaped tool with a sharp inner edge, used for pruning, lopping, etc.

billiards /'bɪljədz/ n. **1** a game played on an oblong cloth-covered table, with three balls struck with cues into pockets round the edge of the table. **2** (**billiard**) (in *comb.*) used in billiards (*billiard-ball*; *billiard-table*). [orig. pl., f. F *billard* billiards, cue, dimin. of *bille* log: see BILLET²]

billion /'bɪljən/ n. & adj. —n. (pl. same or (in sense 3) **billions**) (in *sing.* prec. by *a* or *one*) **1 a** thousand million (1,000,000,000 or 10⁹). **2** (now less often, esp. *Brit.*) a million million (1,000,000,000,000 or 10¹²). **3** (in *pl.*) colloq. a very large number (*billions of years*). —adj. that amount to a billion. □□ **billionth** adj. & n. [F (as BI-, MILLION)]

billionaire /ˌbɪljə'neə(r)/ n. a person possessing over a billion pounds, dollars, etc. [after MILLIONAIRE]

billon /'bɪlən/ n. an alloy of gold or silver with a predominating admixture of a base metal. [F f. *bille* BILLET²]

billow /'bɪləʊ/ n. & v. —n. **1** a wave. **2** a soft upward-curving flow. **3** any large soft mass. —v.intr. move or build up in billows. □□ **billowy** adj. [ON *bylgja* f. Gmc]

billposter /'bɪlˌpəʊstə(r)/ n. (also **billsticker** /-ˌstɪkə(r)/) a person who pastes up advertisements on hoardings. □□ **billposting** n.

billy¹ /'bɪlɪ/ n. (pl. **-ies**) (in full **billycan**) (orig. Austral.) a tin or enamel cooking-pot with a lid and wire handle, for use out of doors. [perh. f. Abor. *billa* water]

billy² /'bɪlɪ/ n. (pl. **-ies**) = BILLY-GOAT.

billycan /'bɪlɪˌkæn/ n. = BILLY¹.

billy-goat /'bɪlɪˌgəʊt/ n. a male goat. [*Billy*, pet-form of the name *William*]

billy-oh /'bɪlɪəʊ/ n. □**like billy-oh** sl. very much, hard, strongly, etc. (*raining like billy-oh*). [19th c.: orig. unkn.]

bilobate /baɪ'ləʊbət/ adj. (also **bilobed** /-'ləʊbd/) having or consisting of two lobes.

biltong /'bɪltɒŋ/ n. S.Afr. boneless meat salted and dried in strips. [Afrik., of uncert. orig.]

BIM abbr. British Institute of Management.

bimanal /'bɪmən(ə)l/ adj. (also **bimanous** /-nəs/) having two hands. [BI- + L *manus* hand]

bimbo /'bɪmbəʊ/ n. (pl. -os or -oes) sl. usu. derog. **1** a person. **2** a woman, esp. a young empty-headed one. [It., = little child]

bimetallic /ˌbaɪmɪ'tælɪk/ adj. **1** made of two metals. **2** of or relating to bimetallism. □**bimetallic strip** a sensitive element in some thermostats made of two bands of different metals that expand at different rates when heated, causing the strip to bend. [F bimétallique (as BI-, METALLIC)]

bimetallism /baɪ'metəˌlɪz(ə)m/ n. a system of allowing the unrestricted currency of two metals (e.g. gold and silver) at a fixed ratio to each other, as coined money. □□ **bimetallist** n.

bimillenary /ˌbaɪmɪ'lenərɪ/ adj. & n. —adj. of or relating to a two-thousandth anniversary. —n. (pl. -ies) a bimillenary year or festival.

bimonthly /baɪ'mʌnθlɪ/ adj., adv., & n. —adj. occurring twice a month or every two months. —adv. twice a month or every two months. —n. (pl. -ies) a periodical produced bimonthly. ¶ Often avoided, because of the ambiguity of meaning, in favour of two-monthly and twice-monthly.

bin /bɪn/ n. & v. —n. **1** a large receptacle for storage or for depositing rubbish. —v.tr. colloq. (**binned**, **binning**) store or put in a bin. □ **bin end** one of the last bottles from a bin of wine, usu. sold at a reduced price. **bin-liner** a bag (usu. of plastic) for lining a rubbish bin. [OE bin(n), binne]

bin- /bɪn, baɪn/ prefix var. of BI- before a vowel.

binary /'baɪnərɪ/ adj. & n. —adj. **1 a** dual. **b** of or involving pairs. **2** of the arithmetical system using 2 as a base. —n. (pl. -ies) **1** something having two parts. **2** a binary number. **3** a binary star. □**binary code** Computing a coding system using the binary digits 0 and 1 to represent a letter, digit, or other character in a computer (see BCD). **binary compound** Chem. a compound having two elements or radicals. **binary fission** the division of a cell or organism into two parts. **binary number** (or **digit**) one of two digits (usu. 0 or 1) in a binary system of notation. **binary star** a system of two stars orbiting each other. **binary system** a system in which information can be expressed by combinations of the digits 0 and 1 (corresponding to 'off' and 'on' in computing). **binary tree** a data structure in which a record is branched to the left when greater and to the right when less than the previous record. [LL binarius f. bini two together]

binate /'baɪneɪt/ adj. Bot. **1** growing in pairs. **2** composed of two equal parts. [mod.L binatus f. L bini two together]

binaural /baɪ'nɔːr(ə)l/ adj. **1** of or used with both ears. **2** (of sound) recorded using two microphones and usu. transmitted separately to the two ears.

bind /baɪnd/ v. & n. —v. (past and past part. **bound** /baʊnd/) (see also BOUNDEN). **1** tr. (often foll. by to, on, together) tie or fasten tightly. **2** tr. **a** restrain; put in bonds. **b** (as **-bound** adj.) constricted, obstructed (snowbound). **3** tr. esp. Cookery cause (ingredients) to cohere using another ingredient. **4** tr. fasten or hold together as a single mass. **5** tr. compel; impose an obligation or duty on. **6** tr. **a** edge (fabric etc.) with braid etc. **b** fix together and fasten (the pages of a book) in a cover. **7** tr. constipate. **8** tr. ratify (a bargain, agreement, etc.). **9** tr. (in passive) be required by an obligation or duty (am bound to answer). **10** tr. (often foll. by up) **a** put a bandage or other covering round. **b** fix together with something put round (bound her hair). **11** tr. indenture as an apprentice. **12** intr. (of snow etc.) cohere, stick. **13** intr. be prevented from moving freely. **14** intr. sl. complain. —n. **1** colloq. a nuisance; a restriction. **2** = BINE. □**be bound up with** be closely associated with. **bind over** Law order (a person) to do something, esp. keep the peace. **bind up** bandage. **I'll be bound** a statement of assurance, or guaranteeing the truth of something. [OE bindan]

binder /'baɪndə(r)/ n. **1** a cover for sheets of paper,

for a book, etc. **2** a substance that acts cohesively. **3** a reaping-machine that binds grain into sheaves. **4** a bookbinder.

bindery /'baɪndərɪ/ n. (pl. -ies) a workshop or factory for binding books.

bindi-eye /'bɪndɪˌaɪ/ n. Austral. a small perennial Australian herb, Calotis cuneifolia, which has a burlike fruit. [20th c.: orig. unkn.]

binding /'baɪndɪŋ/ n. & adj. —n. something that binds, esp. the covers, glue, etc., of a book. —adj. (often foll. by on) obligatory.

bindweed /'baɪndwiːd/ n. **1** convolvulus. **2** any of various species of climbing plants such as honeysuckle.

bine /baɪn/ n. **1** the twisting stem of a climbing plant, esp. the hop. **2** a flexible shoot. [orig. a dial. form of BIND]

Binet–Simon test /'biːneɪˌsiːmɑ̃/ adj. (also **Binet test**) Psychol. a test used to measure intelligence, esp. of children. [A. Binet d. 1911 and T. Simon d. 1961, Fr. psychologists]

binge /bɪndʒ/ n. & v. sl. —n. a spree; a period of uncontrolled eating, drinking, etc. —v.intr. go on a spree; indulge in uncontrolled eating, drinking, etc. [prob. orig. dial., = soak]

bingo /'bɪŋgəʊ/ n. & int. —n. a game for any number of players, each having a card of squares with numbers, which are marked off as numbers are randomly drawn by a caller. —int. expressing sudden surprise, satisfaction, etc., as in winning at bingo. [prob. imit.: cf. dial. bing 'with a bang']

binman /'bɪnmæn/ n. (pl. -men) colloq. a dustman.

binnacle /'bɪnək(ə)l/ n. a built-in housing for a ship's compass. [earlier bittacle, ult. f. L habitaculum habitation f. habitare inhabit]

binocular /baɪ'nɒkjʊlə(r)/ adj. adapted for or using both eyes. [BIN- + L oculus eye]

binoculars /bɪ'nɒkjʊləz/ n.pl. an optical instrument with a lens for each eye, for viewing distant objects.

binomial /baɪ'nəʊmɪəl/ n. & adj. —n. **1** an algebraic expression of the sum or the difference of two terms. **2** a two-part name, esp. in taxonomy. —adj. consisting of two terms. □**binomial classification** a system of classification using two terms, the first one indicating the genus and the second the species. **binomial distribution** a frequency distribution of the possible number of successful outcomes in a given number of trials in each of which there is the same probability of success. **binomial theorem** a formula for finding any power of a binomial without multiplying at length. □□ **binomially** adv. [F binôme or mod.L binomium (as BI-, Gk nomos part, portion)]

binominal /baɪ'nɒmɪn(ə)l/ adj. = BINOMIAL. [L binominis (as BI-, nomen -inis name)]

bint /bɪnt/ n. sl. usu. offens. a girl or woman. [Arab., = daughter, girl]

binturong /'bɪntjʊˌrɒŋ/ n. a civet, Arctictis binturong, of S. Asia, with a shaggy black coat and a prehensile tail. [Malay]

bio- /'baɪəʊ/ comb. form **1** life (biography). **2** biological (biomathematics). **3** of living beings (biophysics). [Gk bios (course of) human life]

biochemistry /ˌbaɪəʊ'kemɪstrɪ/ n. the study of the chemical and physico-chemical processes of living organisms. □□ **biochemical** adj. **biochemist** n.

biocoenosis /ˌbaɪəʊsiː'nəʊsɪs/ n. (US **biocenosis**) (pl. -noses /-siːz/) **1** an association of different organisms forming a community. **2** the relationship existing between such organisms. □□ **biocoenology** /-'nɒlədʒɪ/ n. **biocoenotic** /-'nɒtɪk/ adj. [mod.L f. BIO- + Gk koinōsis sharing f. koinos common]

biodegradable /ˌbaɪəʊdɪ'greɪdəb(ə)l/ adj. capable of being decomposed by bacteria or other living organisms. □□ **biodegradability** /-'brɪlɪtɪ/ n. **biodegradation** /ˌbaɪəʊˌdegrə'deɪʃ(ə)n/ n.

bioengineering /ˌbaɪəʊˌendʒɪ'nɪərɪŋ/ n. **1** the application of engineering techniques to biological processes. **2** the use of artificial tissues, organs, or organ components to replace damaged or absent parts of the body, e.g. artificial limbs, heart pacemakers, etc. □□ **bioengineer** *n.* & *v.*

bioethics /ˌbaɪəʊˈeθɪks/ *n.pl.* (treated as *sing.*) the ethics of medical and biological research. □□ **bioethicist** *n.*

biofeedback /ˌbaɪəʊˈfiːdbæk/ *n.* the technique of using the feedback of a normally automatic bodily response to a stimulus, in order to acquire voluntary control of that response.

bioflavonoid /ˌbaɪəʊˈfleɪvənɔɪd/ *n.* = CITRIN. [BIO- + *flavonoid* f. FLAVINE + -OID]

biogenesis /ˌbaɪəʊˈdʒenɪsɪs/ *n.* **1** the synthesis of substances by living organisms. **2** the hypothesis that a living organism arises only from another similar living organism. □□ **biogenetic** /-dʒɪˈnetɪk/ *adj.*

biogenic /ˌbaɪəʊˈdʒenɪk/ *adj.* produced by living organisms.

biogeography /ˌbaɪəʊdʒɪˈɒɡrəfɪ/ *n.* the scientific study of the geographical distribution of plants and animals. □□ **biogeographical** /-dʒɪəˈɡræfɪk(ə)l/ *adj.*

biography /baɪˈɒɡrəfɪ/ *n.* (*pl.* **-ies**) **1 a** a written account of a person's life, usu. by another. **b** such writing as a branch of literature. **2** the course of a living (usu. human) being's life. □□ **biographer** *n.* **biographic** /ˌbaɪəˈɡræfɪk/ *adj.* **biographical** /ˌbaɪəˈɡræfɪk(ə)l/ *adj.* [F *biographie* or mod.L *biographia* f. med.Gk]

biological /ˌbaɪəˈlɒdʒɪk(ə)l/ *adj.* of or relating to biology or living organisms. □ **biological clock** an innate mechanism controlling the rhythmic physiological activities of an organism. **biological control** the control of a pest by the introduction of a natural enemy. **biological warfare** warfare involving the use of toxins or micro-organisms. □□ **biologically** *adv.*

biology /baɪˈɒlədʒɪ/ *n.* **1** the study of living organisms. **2** the plants and animals of a particular area. □□ **biologist** *n.* [F *biologie* f. G *Biologie* (as BIO-, -LOGY)]

bioluminescence /ˌbaɪəʊˌluːmɪˈnes(ə)ns/ *n.* the emission of light by living organisms such as the firefly and glow-worm. □□ **bioluminescent** *adj.*

biomass /ˈbaɪəʊˌmæs/ *n.* the total quantity or weight of organisms in a given area or volume. [BIO- + MASS[1]]

biomathematics /ˌbaɪəʊˌmæθɪˈmætɪks/ *n.* the science of the application of mathematics to biology.

biome /ˈbaɪəʊm/ *n.* **1** a large naturally occurring community of flora and fauna adapted to the particular conditions in which they occur, e.g. tundra. **2** the geographical region containing such a community. [BIO- + -OME]

biomechanics /ˌbaɪəʊmɪˈkænɪks/ *n.* the study of the mechanical laws relating to the movement or structure of living organisms.

biometry /baɪˈɒmɪtrɪ/ *n.* (also **biometrics** /ˌbaɪəʊˈmetrɪks/) the application of statistical analysis to biological data. □□ **biometric** /ˌbaɪəʊˈmetrɪk/ *adj.* **biometrical** /ˌbaɪəʊˈmetrɪk(ə)l/ *adj.* **biometrician** /ˌbaɪəʊmɪˈtrɪʃ(ə)n/ *n.*

biomorph /ˈbaɪəʊˌmɔːf/ *n.* a decorative form based on a living organism. □□ **biomorphic** /-ˈmɔːfɪk/ *adj.* [BIO- + Gk *morphē* form]

bionic /baɪˈɒnɪk/ *adj.* **1** having artificial body parts or the superhuman powers resulting from these. **2** relating to bionics. □□ **bionically** *adv.* [BIO- after ELECTRONIC]

bionics /baɪˈɒnɪks/ *n.pl.* (treated as *sing.*) the study of mechanical systems that function like living organisms or parts of living organisms.

bionomics /ˌbaɪəˈnɒmɪks/ *n.pl.* (treated as *sing.*) the study of the mode of life of organisms in their natural habitat and their adaptations to their surroundings. □□ **bionomic** *adj.* [BIO- after ECONOMICS]

biophysics /ˌbaɪəʊˈfɪzɪks/ *n.pl.* (treated as *sing.*) the science of the application of the laws of physics

to biological phenomena. □□ **biophysical** *adj.* **biophysicist** *n.*

biopsy /ˈbaɪɒpsɪ/ *n.* (*pl.* **-ies**) the examination of tissue removed from a living body to discover the presence, cause, or extent of a disease. [F *biopsie* f. Gk *bios* life + *opsis* sight, after *necropsy*]

biorhythm /ˈbaɪəʊˌrɪð(ə)m/ *n.* **1** any of the recurring cycles of biological processes thought to affect a person's emotional, intellectual, and physical activity. **2** any periodic change in the behaviour or physiology of an organism. □□ **biorhythmic** /-ˈrɪðmɪk/ *adj.* **biorhythmically** /-ˈrɪðmɪkəlɪ/ *adv.*

bioscope /ˈbaɪəˌskəʊp/ *n.* *S.Afr. sl.* a cinema.

biosphere /ˈbaɪəʊˌsfɪə(r)/ *n.* the regions of the earth's crust and atmosphere occupied by living organisms. [G *Biosphäre* (as BIO-, SPHERE)]

biosynthesis /ˌbaɪəʊˈsɪnθɪsɪs/ *n.* the production of organic molecules by living organisms. □□ **biosynthetic** /-ˈθetɪk/ *adj.*

biota /baɪˈəʊtə/ *n.* the animal and plant life of a region. [mod.L: cf. Gk *biotē* life]

biotechnology /ˌbaɪəʊtekˈnɒlədʒɪ/ *n.* the exploitation of biological processes for industrial and other purposes, esp. genetic manipulation of microorganisms (for the production of antibiotics, hormones, etc.).

biotic /baɪˈɒtɪk/ *adj.* **1** relating to life or to living things. **2** of biological origin. [F *biotique* or LL *bioticus* f. Gk *biōtikos* f. *bios* life]

biotin /ˈbaɪətɪn/ *n.* a vitamin of the B complex, found in egg yolk, liver, and yeast, and involved in the metabolism of carbohydrates, fats, and proteins. [G f. Gk *bios* life + -IN]

biotite /ˈbaɪəˌtaɪt/ *n.* *Mineral.* a black, dark brown, or green micaceous mineral occurring as a constituent of metamorphic and igneous rocks. [J. B. *Biot*, Fr. physicist d. 1862]

bipartisan /ˌbaɪpɑːtɪˈzæn, baɪˈpɑːtɪz(ə)n/ *adj.* of or involving two (esp. political) parties. □□ **bipartisanship** *n.*

bipartite /baɪˈpɑːtaɪt/ *adj.* **1** consisting of two parts. **2** shared by or involving two parties. **3** *Law* (of a contract, treaty, etc.) drawn up in two corresponding parts or between two parties. [L *bipartitus* f. *bipartire* (as BI-, *partire* PART)]

biped /ˈbaɪped/ *n.* & *adj.* —*n.* a two-footed animal. —*adj.* two-footed. □□ **bipedal** *adj.* [L *bipes* -*edis* (as BI-, *pes pedis* foot)]

bipinnate /baɪˈpɪneɪt/ *adj.* (of a pinnate leaf) having leaflets that are further subdivided in a pinnate arrangement.

biplane /ˈbaɪpleɪn/ *n.* an early type of aeroplane having two sets of wings, one above the other.

bipolar /baɪˈpəʊlə(r)/ *adj.* having two poles or extremities. □□ **bipolarity** /-ˈlærɪtɪ/ *n.*

birch /bɜːtʃ/ *n.* & *v.* —*n.* **1** any tree of the genus *Betula*, having thin peeling bark, bearing catkins, and found predominantly in northern temperate regions. **2** (in full **birchwood**) the hard fine-grained pale wood of these trees. **3** *NZ* any of various similar trees. **4** (in full **birch-rod**) a bundle of birch twigs used for flogging. —*v.tr.* beat with a birch (in sense 4). □ **birch-bark 1** the bark of *Betula papyrifera* used to make canoes. **2** *US* such a canoe. □□ **birchen** *adj.* [OE *bi(e)rce* f. Gmc]

bird /bɜːd/ *n.* **1** a feathered vertebrate with a beak, with two wings and two feet, egg-laying and usu. able to fly. **2** a game-bird. **3** *Brit. sl.* a young woman. **4** *colloq.* a person (*a wily old bird*). **5** *sl.* **a** a prison. **b** *rhyming sl.* a prison sentence (short for *birdlime* = time). □ **bird-bath** a basin in a garden etc. with water for birds to bathe in. **bird-call 1** a bird's natural call. **2** an instrument imitating this. **bird cherry** a wild cherry *Prunus padus*. **bird-fancier** a person who knows about, collects, breeds, or deals in, birds. **a bird in the hand** something secured or certain. **the bird is** (or **has**) **flown** the prisoner, quarry, etc., has escaped. **bird-** (or **birds'-**) **nesting**

hunting for birds' nests, usu. to get eggs. **bird of paradise** any bird of the family Paradiseidae found chiefly in New Guinea, the males having very beautiful brilliantly coloured plumage. **bird of passage 1** a migrant. **2** any transient visitor. **bird of prey** see PREY. **bird sanctuary** an area where birds are protected and encouraged to breed. **the birds and the bees** *euphem.* sexual activity and reproduction. **bird's-eye** —*n.* **1** any of several plants having small bright round flowers, such as the germander speedwell. **2** a pattern with many small spots. —*adj.* of or having small bright round flowers (*bird's-eye primrose*). **bird's-eye view** a general view from above. **bird's-foot** (*pl.* **bird's-foots**) any plant like the foot of a bird, esp. of the genus *Lotus*, having claw-shaped pods. **bird's nest soup** soup made (esp. in Chinese cookery) from the dried gelatinous coating of the nests of swifts and other birds. **birds of a feather** people of like character. **bird-strike** a collision between a bird and an aircraft. **bird table** a raised platform on which food for birds is placed. **bird-watcher** a person who observes birds in their natural surroundings. **bird-watching** this occupation. **for** (or **strictly for**) **the birds** *colloq.* trivial, uninteresting. **get the bird** *sl.* **1** be dismissed. **2** be hissed at or booed. **like a bird** without difficulty or hesitation. **a little bird** an unnamed informant. [OE *brid*, of unkn. orig.]

birdbrain /'bɜːdbreɪn/ *n. colloq.* a stupid or flighty person. □□ **birdbrained** *adj.*

birdcage /'bɜːdkeɪdʒ/ *n.* **1** a cage for birds usu. made of wire or cane. **2** an object of a similar design.

birder /'bɜːdə(r)/ *n. US* a bird-watcher. □□ **birding** *n.*

birdie /'bɜːdɪ/ *n. & v.* —*n.* **1** *colloq.* a little bird. **2** *Golf* a score of one stroke less than par at any hole. —*v.tr.* (**birdies**, **birdied**, **birdying**) *Golf* play (a hole) in a birdie.

birdlime /'bɜːdlaɪm/ *n.* sticky material painted on to twigs to trap small birds.

birdseed /'bɜːdsiːd/ *n.* a blend of seed for feeding birds, esp. ones which are caged.

birdsong /'bɜːdsɒŋ/ *n.* the musical cry of a bird or birds.

birefringent /ˌbaɪrɪˈfrɪndʒ(ə)nt/ *adj. Physics* having two different refractive indices. □□ **birefringence** *n.*

bireme /'baɪriːm/ *n. hist.* an ancient Greek warship, with two files of oarsmen on each side. [L *biremis* (as BI-, *remus* oar)]

biretta /bɪˈretə/ *n.* a square usu. black cap with three flat projections on top, worn by (esp. Roman Catholic) clergymen. [It. *berretta* or Sp. *birreta* f. LL *birrus* cape]

biriani /ˌbɪrɪˈɑːnɪ/ *n.* (also **biryani**) an orig. Indian dish with highly seasoned rice, and meat or fish etc. [Urdu]

Biro /'baɪərəʊ/ *n.* (*pl.* **-os**) *Brit. propr.* a kind of ball-point pen. [L. *Bíró*, Hung. inventor d. 1985]

birth /bɜːθ/ *n. & v.* —*n.* **1** the emergence of a (usu. fully developed) infant or other young from the body of its mother. **2** *rhet.* the beginning or coming into existence of something (*the birth of civilization*; *the birth of socialism*). **3 a** origin, descent, ancestry (*of noble birth*). **b** high or noble birth; inherited position. —*v.tr. US colloq.* **1** to give birth to. **2** to assist (a woman) to give birth. □ **birth certificate** an official document identifying a person by name, place, date of birth, and parentage. **birth control** the control of the number of children one conceives, esp. by contraception. **birth pill** the contraceptive pill. **birth rate** the number of live births per thousand of population per year. **give birth** bear a child etc. **give birth to 1** produce (young) from the womb. **2** cause to begin, found. [ME f. ON *byrth* f. Gmc: see BEAR[1], -TH[2]]

birthday /'bɜːθdeɪ/ *n.* **1** the day on which a person etc. was born. **2** the anniversary of this. □ **birthday honours** *Brit.* titles etc. given on a sovereign's official birthday. **in one's birthday suit** *joc.* naked.

birthmark /'bɜːθmɑːk/ *n.* an unusual brown or red mark on one's body at or from birth.

birthplace /'bɜːθpleɪs/ *n.* the place where a person was born.

birthright /'bɜːθraɪt/ *n.* a right of possession or privilege one has from birth, esp. as the eldest son.

birthstone /'bɜːθstəʊn/ *n.* a gemstone popularly associated with the month of one's birth.

biryani var. of BIRIANI.

biscuit /'bɪskɪt/ *n. & adj.* —*n.* **1** *Brit.* a small unleavened cake, usu. flat and crisp and often sweet. **2** fired unglazed pottery. **3** a light brown colour. —*adj.* biscuit-coloured. [ME f. OF *bescoit* etc. ult. f. L *bis* twice + *coctus* past part. of *coquere* cook]

bise /biːz/ *n.* a keen dry northerly wind in Switzerland, S. France, etc. [ME f. OF]

bisect /baɪˈsekt/ *v.tr.* divide into two (strictly, equal) parts. □□ **bisection** *n.* **bisector** *n.* [BI- + L *secare sect-* cut]

bisexual /baɪˈseksjʊəl/ *adj. & n.* —*adj.* **1** sexually attracted by persons of both sexes. **2** *Biol.* having characteristics of both sexes. **3** of or concerning both sexes. —*n.* a bisexual person. □□ **bisexuality** /-ˈælɪtɪ/ *n.*

bish /bɪʃ/ *n. sl.* a mistake. [20th c.: orig. uncert.]

bishop /'bɪʃəp/ *n.* **1** a senior member of the Christian clergy usu. in charge of a diocese, and empowered to confer holy orders. **2** a chess piece with the top sometimes shaped like a mitre. **3** mulled and spiced wine. [OE *biscop*, ult. f. Gk *episkopos* overseer (as EPI-, *-skopos* -looking)]

bishopric /'bɪʃəprɪk/ *n.* **1** the office of a bishop. **2** a diocese. [OE *bisceoprīce* (as BISHOP, *rīce* realm)]

bismuth /'bɪzməθ/ *n. Chem.* **1** a brittle reddish-white metallic element, occurring naturally and used in alloys. ¶ Symb.: **Bi**. **2** any compound of this element used medicinally. [mod.L *bisemutum*, Latinization of G *Wismut*, of unkn. orig.]

bison /'baɪs(ə)n/ *n.* (*pl.* same) either of two wild hump-backed shaggy-haired oxen of the genus *Bison*, native to N. America (*B. bison*) or Europe (*B. bonasus*). [ME f. L f. Gmc]

bisque[1] /bɪsk/ *n.* a rich shellfish soup, made esp. from lobster. [F]

bisque[2] /bɪsk/ *n. Tennis, Croquet, & Golf* an advantage of scoring one free point, or taking an extra turn or stroke. [F]

bisque[3] /bɪsk/ *n.* = BISCUIT 2.

bistable /baɪˈsteɪb(ə)l/ *adj.* (of an electrical circuit etc.) having two stable states.

bister var. of BISTRE.

bistort /'bɪstɔːt/ *n.* a herb, *Polygonum bistorta*, with a twisted root and a terminal spike of flesh-coloured flowers. [F *bistorte* or med.L *bistorta* f. *bis* twice + *torta* fem. past part. of *torquēre* twist]

bistoury /'bɪstərɪ/ *n.* (*pl.* **-ies**) a surgical scalpel. [F *bistouri*, *bistorie*, orig. = dagger, of unkn. orig.]

bistre /'bɪstə(r)/ *n. & adj.* (*US* **bister**) —*n.* **1** a brownish pigment made from the soot of burnt wood. **2** the brownish colour of this. —*adj.* of this colour. [F, of unkn. orig.]

bistro /'biːstrəʊ/ *n.* (*pl.* **-os**) a small restaurant. [F]

bisulphate /baɪˈsʌlfeɪt/ *n.* (*US* **bisulfate**) *Chem.* a salt or ester of sulphuric acid.

bit[1] /bɪt/ *n.* **1** a small piece or quantity (*a bit of cheese*; *give me another bit*; *that bit is too small*). **2** (prec. by *a*) **a** a fair amount (*sold quite a bit*; *needed a bit of persuading*). **b** *colloq.* somewhat (*am a bit tired*). **c** (foll. by *of*) *colloq.* rather (*a bit of an idiot*). **d** (foll. by *of*) *colloq.* only a little; a mere (*a bit of a boy*). **3** a short time or distance (*wait a bit*; *move up a bit*). **4** *US sl.* a unit of 12½ cents (used only in even multiples). □ **bit by bit** gradually. **bit of all right** *sl.* a pleasing person or thing, esp. a woman. **bit of fluff** (or **skirt** or **stuff**) see FLUFF, SKIRT, STUFF. **bit on the side** *sl.* an extramarital sexual relationship. **bit part** a minor part in a play or a film. **bits and pieces** (or **bobs**) an assortment of small items. **do one's bit** *colloq.* make a useful contribution to an effort or cause. **every bit** as see EVERY. **not a bit** (or **not a bit of it**) not at all. **to bits** into pieces. [OE *bita* f. Gmc, rel. to BITE]

bit[2] *past* of BITE.

bit[3] /bɪt/ *n. & v.* —*n.* **1** a metal mouthpiece on a bridle, used to control a horse. **2** a (usu. metal) tool or piece for boring or drilling. **3** the cutting or gripping part of a plane, pincers, etc. **4** the part of a key that engages with the lock-lever. **5** the copper head of a soldering-iron. —*v.tr.* **1** put a bit into the mouth of (a horse). **2** restrain. □**take the bit between one's teeth 1** take decisive personal action. **2** escape from control. [OE *bite* f. Gmc, rel. to BITE]

bit[4] /bɪt/ *n. Computing* a unit of information expressed as a choice between two possibilities; a 0 or 1 in binary notation. [BINARY + DIGIT]

bitch /bɪtʃ/ *n. & v.* —*n.* **1** a female dog or other canine animal. **2** *sl. offens.* a malicious or spiteful woman. **3** *sl.* a very unpleasant or difficult thing or situation. —*v.* **1** *intr.* (often foll. by *about*) **a** speak scathingly. **b** complain. **2** *tr.* be spiteful or unfair to. [OE *bicce*]

bitchy /ˈbɪtʃɪ/ *adj.* (**bitchier, bitchiest**) *sl.* spiteful; bad-tempered. □□ **bitchily** *adv.* **bitchiness** *n.*

bite /baɪt/ *v. & n.* —*v.* (*past* **bit** /bɪt/; *past part.* **bitten** /ˈbɪt(ə)n/) **1** *tr.* cut or puncture using the teeth. **2** *tr.* (foll. by *off, away*, etc.) detach with the teeth. **3** *tr.* (of an insect, snake, etc.) wound with a sting, fangs, etc. **4** *intr.* (of a wheel, screw, etc.) grip, penetrate. **5** *intr.* accept bait or an inducement. **6** *intr.* have a (desired) adverse effect. **7** *tr.* (in *passive*) **a** take in; swindle. **b** (foll. by *by, with*, etc.) be infected by (enthusiasm etc.). **8** *tr.* (as **bitten** *adj.*) cause a glowing or smarting pain to (*frostbitten*). **9** *intr.* (foll. by *at*) snap at. —*n.* **1** an act of biting. **2** a wound or sore made by biting. **3 a** a mouthful of food. **b** a snack or light meal. **4** the taking of bait by a fish. **5** pungency (esp. of flavour). **6** incisiveness, sharpness. **7** = OCCLUSION 3. □**bite back** restrain (one's speech etc.) by or as if by biting the lips. **bite** (or **bite on**) **the bullet** *sl.* behave bravely or stoically. **bite the dust** *sl.* **1** die. **2** fail; break down. **bite the hand that feeds one** hurt or offend a benefactor. **bite a person's head off** *colloq.* respond fiercely or angrily. **bite one's lip** see LIP. **bite off more than one can chew** take on a commitment one cannot fulfil. **once bitten twice shy** an unpleasant experience induces caution. **put the bite on** *US sl.* borrow or extort money from. **what's biting you?** *sl.* what is worrying you? □□ **biter** *n.* [OE *bītan* f. Gmc]

biting /ˈbaɪtɪŋ/ *adj.* **1** stinging; intensely cold (*a biting wind*). **2** sharp; effective (*biting wit; biting sarcasm*). □□ **bitingly** *adv.*

bitten *past part.* of BITE.

bitter /ˈbɪtə(r)/ *adj. & n.* —*adj.* **1** having a sharp pungent taste; not sweet. **2 a** caused by or showing mental pain or resentment (*bitter memories; bitter rejoinder*). **b** painful or difficult to accept (*bitter disappointment*). **3 a** harsh; virulent (*bitter animosity*). **b** piercingly cold. —*n.* **1** *Brit.* beer strongly flavoured with hops and having a bitter taste. **2** (in *pl.*) liquor with a bitter flavour (esp. of wormwood) used as an additive in cocktails. □**bitter-apple** = COLOCYNTH. **bitter orange** = SEVILLE ORANGE. **bitter pill** something unpleasant that has to be accepted. **bitter-sweet** *adj.* **1** sweet with a bitter after-taste. **2** arousing pleasure tinged with pain or sorrow. —*n.* **1 a** a sweetness with a bitter after-taste. **b** pleasure tinged with pain or sorrow. **2** = *woody nightshade* (see NIGHTSHADE). **to the bitter end** to the very end in spite of difficulties. □□ **bitterly** *adv.* **bitterness** *n.* [OE *biter* prob. f. Gmc: *to the bitter end* may be assoc. with a Naut. word *bitter* = 'last part of a cable': see BITTS]

bitterling /ˈbɪtəlɪŋ/ *n.* a small brightly coloured freshwater fish, *Rhodeus amarus*, from Central Europe. [BITTER + -LING[1]]

bittern /ˈbɪt(ə)n/ *n.* **1** any of a group of wading birds of the heron family, esp. of the genus *Botaurus* with a distinctive booming call. **2** *Chem.* the liquid remaining after the crystallization of common salt from sea water. [ME f. OF *butor* ult. f. L *butio* bittern + *taurus* bull; -*n* perh. f. assoc. with HERON]

bitts /bɪts/ *n.pl. Naut.* a pair of posts on the deck of a ship, for fastening cables etc. [ME prob. f. LG: cf. LG & Du. *beting*]

bitty /ˈbɪtɪ/ *adj.* (**bittier, bittiest**) made up of unrelated bits; scrappy. □□ **bittily** *adv.* **bittiness** *n.*

bitumen /ˈbɪtjʊmɪn/ *n.* **1** any of various tarlike mixtures of hydrocarbons derived from petroleum naturally or by distillation and used for road surfacing and roofing. **2** *Austral. colloq.* a tarred road. [L *bitumen* -*minis*]

bituminize /bɪˈtjuːmɪˌnaɪz/ *v.tr.* (also -**ise**) convert into, impregnate with, or cover with bitumen. □□ **bituminization** /-ˈzeɪʃ(ə)n/ *n.*

bituminous /bɪˈtjuːmɪnəs/ *adj.* of, relating to, or containing bitumen. □**bituminous coal** a form of coal burning with a smoky flame.

bivalent /baɪˈveɪlənt/ *adj. & n.* —*adj.* **1** *Chem.* having a valency of two. **2** *Biol.* (of homologous chromosomes) associated in pairs. —*n. Biol.* any pair of homologous chromosomes. □□ **bivalency** *n.* [BI- + *valent-* pres. part. stem formed as VALENCE[1]]

bivalve /ˈbaɪvælv/ *n. & adj.* —*n.* any of a group of aquatic molluscs of the class Bivalvia, with laterally compressed bodies enclosed within two hinged shells, e.g. oysters, mussels, etc. —*adj.* **1** with a hinged double shell. **2** *Biol.* having two valves, e.g. of a pea-pod.

bivouac /ˈbɪvʊˌæk/ *n. & v.* —*n.* a temporary open encampment without tents, esp. of soldiers. —*v.intr.* (**bivouacked, bivouacking**) camp in a bivouac, esp. overnight. [F, prob. f. Swiss G *Beiwacht* additional guard at night]

biweekly /baɪˈwiːklɪ/ *adv., adj., & n.* —*adv.* **1** every two weeks. **2** twice a week. —*adj.* produced or occurring biweekly. —*n.* (*pl.* -**ies**) a biweekly periodical. ¶ See the note at *bimonthly.*

biyearly /baɪˈjɪəlɪ/ *adv. & adj.* —*adv.* **1** every two years. **2** twice a year. —*adj.* produced or occurring biyearly. ¶ See the note at *bimonthly.*

biz /bɪz/ *n. colloq.* business. [abbr.]

bizarre /bɪˈzɑː(r)/ *adj.* strange in appearance or effect; eccentric; grotesque. □□ **bizarrely** *adv.* **bizarreness** *n.* [F, = handsome, brave, f. Sp. & Port. *bizarro* f. Basque *bizarra* beard]

bizarrerie /bɪˈzɑːrərɪ/ *n.* a bizarre quality; bizarreness. [F]

Bk *symb. Chem.* the element berkelium.

bk. *abbr.* book.

BL *abbr.* **1** *Sc. & Ir.* Bachelor of Law. **2** British Library. **3** *hist.* British Leyland. **4** bill of lading.

bl. *abbr.* **1** barrel. **2** black.

blab /blæb/ *v. & n.* —*v.* (**blabbed, blabbing**) **1** *intr.* **a** talk foolishly or indiscreetly. **b** reveal secrets. **2** *tr.* reveal (a secret etc.) by indiscreet talk. —*n.* a person who blabs. [ME prob. f. Gmc]

blabber /ˈblæbə(r)/ *n. & v.* —*n.* (also **blabbermouth** /ˈblæbəˌmaʊθ/) a person who blabs. —*v.intr.* (often foll. by *on*) talk foolishly or inconsequentially, esp. at length.

black /blæk/ *adj., n., & v.* —*adj.* **1** very dark, having no colour from the absorption of all or nearly all incident light (like coal or soot). **2** completely dark from the absence of a source of light (*black night*). **3** (**Black**) **a** of the human group having dark-coloured skin, esp. of African or Aboriginal descent. **b** of or relating to Black people (*Black rights*). **4** (of the sky, a cloud, etc.) dusky; heavily overcast. **5** angry, threatening (*a black look*). **6** implying disgrace or condemnation (*in his black books*). **7** wicked, sinister, deadly (*black-hearted*). **8** gloomy, depressed, sullen (*a black mood*). **9** portending trouble or difficulty (*things looked black*). **10** (of hands, clothes, etc.)

dirty, soiled. **11** (of humour or its representation) with sinister or macabre, as well as comic, import (*black comedy*). **12** (of tea or coffee) without milk. **13** *Brit.* **a** (of industrial labour or its products) boycotted, esp. by a trade union, in an industrial dispute. **b** (of a person) doing work or handling goods that have been boycotted. **14** dark in colour as distinguished from a lighter variety (*black bear; black pine*). —*n.* **1** a black colour or pigment. **2** black clothes or material (*dressed in black*). **3 a** (in a game or sport) a black piece, ball, etc. **b** the player using such pieces. **4** the credit side of an account (*in the black*). **5** (**Black**) a member of a dark-skinned race, esp. a Negro or Aboriginal. —*v.tr.* **1** make black (*blacked his face*). **2** polish with blacking. **3** *Brit.* declare (goods etc.) 'black'. □**Black Africa** the area of Africa, generally south of the Sahara, where Blacks predominate. **black and blue** discoloured by bruises. **Black and Tans** an armed force recruited to fight Sinn Fein in Ireland in 1921, wearing a mixture of military and constabulary uniforms. **black and white 1** recorded in writing or print (*down in black and white*). **2** (of film etc.) not in colour. **3** consisting of extremes only, oversimplified (*interpreted the problem in black and white terms*). **the black art** = *black magic*. **black beetle** the common cockroach, *Blatta orientalis*. **black belt 1** a black belt worn by an expert in judo, karate, etc. **2** a person qualified to wear this. **black body** *Physics* a hypothetical perfect absorber and radiator of energy, with no reflecting power. **black box 1** a flight-recorder in an aircraft. **2** any complex piece of equipment, usu. a unit in an electronic system, with contents which are mysterious to the user. **black bread** a coarse dark-coloured type of rye bread. **black bryony** a rooted climber, *Tamus communis*, with clusters of red berries. **Black Country** (usu. prec. by *the*) a district of the Midlands with heavy industry. **black damp** = *choke-damp*. **Black Death** (usu. prec. by *the*) a widespread epidemic of bubonic plague in Europe in the 14th c. **black diamond** (in *pl.*) coal. **black disc** a long-playing gramophone record, as distinct from a compact disc. **black earth** = CHERNOZEM. **black economy** unofficial economic activity. **Black English** the form of English spoken by many Blacks, esp. as an urban dialect of the US. **black eye** bruised skin around the eye resulting from a blow. **black-eyed** (or **black-eye**) **bean** a variety of bean, *Vigna sinensis*, with seeds often dried and stored prior to eating (so called from its black hilum). **black-eyed Susan** any of several flowers, esp. of the genus *Rudbeckia*, with yellow-coloured petals and a dark centre. **black-face 1** a variety of sheep with a black face. **2** the make-up used by a non-Black performer playing a Negro role. **black flag** see FLAG¹. **black forest gateau** a chocolate sponge with layers of morello cherries or cherry jam and whipped cream and topped with chocolate icing, orig. from S. Germany. **Black Friar** a Dominican friar. **black frost** see FROST. **black game** (or **grouse**) a European grouse, *Lyrurus tetrix*. **black hole 1** a region of space possessing a strong gravitational field from which matter and radiation cannot escape: also called COLLAPSAR. **2** a place of confinement for punishment, esp. in the armed services. **black ice** thin hard transparent ice, esp. on a road surface. **black in the face** livid with strangulation, exertion, or passion. **black lead** graphite. **black leopard** = PANTHER. **black letter** an old heavy style of type. **black light** *Physics* the invisible ultraviolet or infrared radiations of the electromagnetic spectrum. **black magic** magic involving supposed invocation of evil spirits. **Black Maria** *sl.* a police vehicle for transporting prisoners. **black mark** a mark of discredit. **black market** an illicit traffic in officially controlled or scarce commodities. **black marketeer** a person who engages in a black market. **Black Mass** a travesty of

the Roman Catholic Mass in worship of Satan. **Black Monk** a Benedictine monk. **Black Muslim** *US* a member of an exclusively Black Islamic sect proposing a separate Black community. **Black Nationalism** advocacy of the national civil rights of US (and occas. other) Blacks. **black nightshade** see NIGHTSHADE. **black out 1 a** effect a blackout on. **b** undergo a blackout. **2** obscure windows etc. or extinguish all lights for protection esp. against an air attack. **Black Panther** *US* one of a group of extremist fighters for Blacks' rights. **black pepper** pepper made by grinding the whole dried berry, including the husk, of the pepper plant. **Black Power** a movement in support of rights and political power for Blacks. **black pudding** a black sausage containing pork, dried pig's blood, suet, etc. **Black Rod** *Brit.* the principal usher of the Lord Chamberlain's department, House of Lords, etc. **black sheep** *colloq.* an unsatisfactory member of a family, group, etc.; a scoundrel. **black spot** a place of danger or difficulty, esp. on a road (*an accident black spot*). **black swan 1** something extremely rare. **2** an Australian swan, *Cygnus atratus*, with black plumage. **black tea** tea that is fully fermented before drying. **black tie 1** a black bow-tie worn with a dinner jacket. **2** *colloq.* formal evening dress. **black tracker** *Austral.* an Aboriginal employed to help find persons lost or hiding in the bush. **black velvet** a drink of stout and champagne. **Black Watch** (usu. prec. by *the*) the Royal Highland Regiment (so called from its dark tartan uniform). **black-water fever** a complication of malaria, in which blood cells are rapidly destroyed, resulting in dark urine. **black widow** a venomous spider, *Latrodectus mactans*, of which the female devours the male. □□ **blackish** *adj.* **blackly** *adv.* **blackness** *n.* [OE *blæc*]

blackamoor /'blækəˌmʊə(r), -ˌmɔː(r)/ *n. archaic* a dark-skinned person, esp. a Negro. [BLACK + MOOR²]

blackball /'blækbɔːl/ *v.tr.* reject (a candidate) in a ballot (orig. by voting with a black ball).

blackberry /'blækbərɪ/ *n. & v.* (*pl.* **-ies**) **1** a climbing thorny rosaceous shrub, *Rubus fruticosus*, bearing white or pink flowers. Also called BRAMBLE. **2** a black fleshy edible fruit of this plant. —*v.intr.* (**-ies, -ied**) gather blackberries.

blackbird /'blækbɜːd/ *n.* **1** a common thrush, *Turdus merula*, of which the male is black with an orange beak. **2** *US* any of various birds, esp. a grackle, with black plumage. **3** *hist.* a kidnapped Negro or Polynesian on a slave-ship.

blackboard /'blækbɔːd/ *n.* a board with a smooth usu. dark surface for writing on with chalk.

blackboy /'blækbɔɪ/ *n.* any tree of the genus *Xanthorrhea*, native to Australia, with a thick dark trunk and a head of grasslike leaves. Also called *grass tree*.

blackbuck /'blækbʌk/ *n.* a small Indian gazelle, *Antilope cervicapra*, with a black back and white underbelly. Also called SASIN.

blackcap /'blækkæp/ *n.* a small warbler, *Sylvia atricapilla*, the male of which has a black-topped head.

blackcock /'blækkɒk/ *n.* the male of the black grouse (cf. *grey-hen*).

blackcurrant /blæk'kʌrənt/ *n.* **1** a widely cultivated shrub, *Ribes nigrum*, bearing flowers in racemes. **2** the small dark edible berry of this plant.

blacken /'blækən/ *v.* **1** *tr. & intr.* make or become black or dark. **2** *tr.* speak evil of, defame (*blacken someone's character*).

blackfellow /'blækˌfeləʊ/ *n. hist.* an Australian Aboriginal.

blackfish /'blækfɪʃ/ *n.* **1** any of several species of dark-coloured fish. **2** a salmon at spawning.

blackfly /'blækflaɪ/ *n.* (*pl.* **-flies**) any of various thrips or aphids, esp. *Aphis fabae*, infesting plants.

blackguard /'blægɑːd, -gəd/ *n. & v.* —*n.* a villain; a scoundrel; an unscrupulous, unprincipled person. —*v.tr.* abuse scurrilously. □□ **blackguardly** *adj.*

[BLACK + GUARD: orig. applied collectively to menials etc.]

blackhead /'blækhed/ n. a black-topped pimple on the skin.

blacking /'blækɪŋ/ n. any black paste or polish, esp. for shoes.

blackjack[1] /'blækdʒæk/ n. **1** the card-game pontoon. **2** US a flexible leaded bludgeon. [BLACK + JACK[1]]

blackjack[2] /'blækdʒæk/ n. a pirates' black flag. [BLACK + JACK[1]]

blackjack[3] /'blækdʒæk/ n. a tarred-leather vessel for alcoholic liquor. [BLACK + JACK[2]]

blacklead /'blæk'led/ n. & v. —n. graphite. —v.tr. polish with graphite.

blackleg /'blækleg/ n. & v. —n. (often attrib.) Brit. derog. a person who fails or declines to take part in industrial action. —v.intr. (**-legged, -legging**) act as a blackleg.

blacklist /'blæklɪst/ n. & v. —n. a list of persons under suspicion, in disfavour, etc. —v.tr. put the name of (a person) on a blacklist.

blackmail /'blækmeɪl/ n. & v. —n. **1 a** an extortion of payment in return for not disclosing discreditable information, a secret, etc. **b** any payment extorted in this way. **2** the use of threats or moral pressure. —v.tr. **1** extort or try to extort money etc. from (a person) by blackmail. **2** threaten, coerce. □□ **blackmailer** n. [BLACK + obs. mail rent, OE māl f. ON mál agreement]

blackout /'blækaʊt/ n. **1** a temporary or complete loss of vision, consciousness, or memory. **2** a loss of power, radio reception, etc. **3** a compulsory period of darkness as a precaution against air raids. **4** a temporary suppression of the release of information, esp. from police or government sources. **5** a sudden darkening of a theatre stage.

blackshirt /'blækʃɜːt/ n. a member of a Fascist organization. [f. the colour of the It. Fascist uniform]

blacksmith /'blæksmɪθ/ n. a smith who works in iron.

blackthorn /'blækθɔːn/ n. **1** a thorny rosaceous shrub, Prunus spinosa, bearing white-petalled flowers before small blue-black fruits. Also called SLOE. **2** a cudgel or walking-stick made from its wood. □ **blackthorn winter** the time when the plant flowers, usu. marked by cold NE winds.

blacktop /'blæktɒp/ n. US a type of road-surfacing material.

bladder /'blædə(r)/ n. **1 a** any of various membranous sacs in some animals, containing urine (**urinary bladder**), bile (**gall-bladder**), or air (**swim-bladder**). **b** this or part of it or a similar object prepared for various uses. **2** an inflated pericarp or vesicle in various plants. **3** anything inflated and hollow. [OE blǣdre f. Gmc]

bladderwort /'blædə,wɜːt/ n. any insect-consuming aquatic plant of the genus Utricularia, with leaves having small bladders for trapping insects.

bladderwrack /'blædə,ræk/ n. a common brown seaweed, Fucus vesiculosus, with fronds containing air-bladders which give buoyancy to the plant.

blade /bleɪd/ n. **1 a** the flat part of a knife, chisel, etc., that forms the cutting edge. **b** = razor-blade. **2** the flattened functional part of an oar, spade, propeller, bat, skate, etc. **3 a** the flat, narrow, usu. pointed leaf of grass and cereals. **b** the whole of such plants before the ear is formed (in the blade). **c** Bot. the broad thin part of a leaf apart from the petiole. **4** (in full **blade-bone**) a flat bone, e.g. in the shoulder. **5** Archaeol. a long narrow flake (see FLAKE[1] 3). **6** poet. a sword. **7** colloq. (usu. archaic) a carefree young fellow. □□ **bladed** adj. (also in comb.). [OE blǣd f. Gmc]

blaeberry /'bleɪbərɪ/ n. (pl. **-ies**) Brit. = BILBERRY. [ME f. blae (Sc. and N.Engl. dial. f. ME blo f. ON blár f. Gmc: see BLUE[1]) + BERRY]

blag /blæg/ n. & v. sl. —n. robbery, esp. with violence; theft. —v.tr. & intr. (**blagged, blagging**) rob (esp.

with violence); steal. □□ **blagger** n. [19th c.: orig. unkn.]

blague /blɑːg/ n. humbug, claptrap. [F]

blagueur /blɑː'gɜː(r)/ n. a pretentious talker. [F]

blah /blɑː/ n. (also **blah-blah**) colloq. pretentious nonsense. [imit.]

blain /bleɪn/ n. an inflamed swelling or sore on the skin. [OE blegen f. WG]

blakey /'bleɪkɪ/ n. (also **Blakey**) (pl. **-eys**) a metal cap on the heel or toe of a shoe or boot. [Blakey, name of the manufacturer]

blame /bleɪm/ v. & n. —v.tr. **1** assign fault or responsibility to. **2** (foll. by on) assign the responsibility for (an error or wrong) to a person etc. (blamed his death on a poor diet). —n. **1** responsibility for a bad result; culpability (shared the blame equally; put the blame on the bad weather). **2** the act of blaming or attributing responsibility; censure (she got all the blame). □ **be to blame** (often foll. by for) be responsible; deserve censure (she is not to blame for the accident). **have only oneself to blame** be solely responsible (for something one suffers). **I don't blame you** etc. I think your etc. action was justifiable. □□ **blameable** adj. [ME f. OF bla(s)mer (v.), blame (n.) f. pop.L blastemare f. eccl.L blasphemare reproach f. Gk blasphēmeō blaspheme]

blameful /'bleɪmfʊl/ adj. deserving blame; guilty. □□ **blamefully** adv.

blameless /'bleɪmlɪs/ adj. innocent; free from blame. □□ **blamelessly** adv. **blamelessness** n.

blameworthy /'bleɪm,wɜːðɪ/ adj. deserving blame. □□ **blameworthiness** n.

blanch /blɑːntʃ/ v. **1** tr. make white or pale by extracting colour. **2** intr. & tr. grow or make pale from shock, fear, etc. **3** tr. Cookery **a** peel (almonds etc.) by scalding. **b** immerse (vegetables or meat) briefly in boiling water. **4** tr. whiten (a plant) by depriving it of light. □ **blanch over** give a deceptively good impression of (a fault etc.) by misrepresentation. [ME f. OF blanchir f. blanc white, BLANK]

blancmange /blə'mɒndʒ/ n. a sweet opaque gelatinous dessert made with flavoured cornflour and milk. [ME f. OF blancmanger f. blanc white, BLANK + manger eat f. L manducare MANDUCATE]

blanco /'blæŋkəʊ/ n. & v. Mil. —n. **1** a white substance for whitening belts etc. **2** a similar coloured substance. —v.tr. (**-oes, -oed**) treat with blanco. [F blanc white, BLANK]

bland /blænd/ adj. **1 a** mild, not irritating. **b** tasteless, unstimulating, insipid. **2** gentle in manner; suave. □□ **blandly** adv. **blandness** n. [L blandus soft, smooth]

blandish /'blændɪʃ/ v.tr. flatter; coax, cajole. [ME f. OF blandir (-ISH[2]) f. L blandiri f. blandus soft, smooth]

blandishment /'blændɪʃmənt/ n. (usu. in pl.) flattery; cajolery.

blank /blæŋk/ adj., n., & v. —adj. **1 a** (of paper) not written or printed on. **b** (of a document) with spaces left for a signature or details. **2 a** not filled; empty (a blank space). **b** unrelieved; sheer (a blank wall). **3 a** having or showing no interest or expression (a blank face). **b** void of incident or result. **c** puzzled, nonplussed. **d** having (temporarily) no knowledge or understanding (my mind went blank). **4** (with neg. import) complete, downright (a blank refusal; blank despair). **5** euphem. used in place of an adjective regarded as coarse or abusive. —n. **1 a** a space left to be filled in a document. **b** a document having blank spaces to be filled. **2** (in full **blank cartridge**) a cartridge containing gunpowder but no bullet, used for training, etc. **3** an empty space or period of time. **4 a** a coin-disc before stamping. **b** a metal or wooden block before final shaping. **5 a** a dash written instead of a word or letter, esp. instead of an obscenity. **b** euphem. used in place of a noun regarded as coarse. **6** a domino with one or both halves blank. **7** a lottery ticket that gains no prize. **8** the white centre of the target in archery etc. —v.tr. **1** (usu. foll. by off, out) screen, obscure (*clouds blanked out the sun*). **2** (usu. foll. by *out*) cut (a metal blank). **3** *US* defeat without allowing to score. □**blank cheque 1** a cheque with the amount left for the payee to fill in. **2** *colloq.* unlimited freedom of action (cf. CARTE BLANCHE). **blank test** *Chem.* a scientific test done without a specimen, to verify the absence of the effects of reagents etc. **blank verse** unrhymed verse, esp. iambic pentameters. **draw a blank** elicit no response; fail. □□ **blankly** *adv.* **blankness** *n.* [ME f. OF *blanc* white, ult. f. Gmc]

blanket /ˈblæŋkɪt/ *n., adj.,* & *v.* —*n.* **1** a large piece of woollen or other material used esp. as a bed-covering or to wrap up a person or an animal for warmth. **2** (usu. foll. by *of*) a thick mass or layer that covers something (*blanket of fog*; *blanket of silence*). **3** *Printing* a rubber surface transferring an impression from a plate to paper etc. in offset printing. —*adj.* covering all cases or classes; inclusive (*blanket condemnation*; *blanket agreement*). —*v.tr.* (**blanketed, blanketing**) **1** cover with or as if with a blanket (*snow blanketed the land*). **2** stifle; keep quiet (*blanketed all discussion*). **3** *Naut.* take wind from the sails of (another craft) by passing to windward. □**blanket bath** a body wash given to a bedridden patient. **blanket stitch** a stitch used to neaten the edges of a blanket or other material. **born on the wrong side of the blanket** illegitimate. **electric blanket** an electrically-wired blanket used for heating a bed. **wet blanket** *colloq.* a gloomy person preventing the enjoyment of others. [ME f. OF *blancquet, blanchet* f. *blanc* white, BLANK]

blankety /ˈblæŋkəti/ *adj.* & *n.* (also **blanky** /ˈblæŋki/) *Brit. colloq.* = BLANK *adj.* 5.

blanky var. of BLANKETY.

blanquette /blɑ̃ˈket/ *n. Cookery* a dish consisting of white meat, e.g. veal, in a white sauce. [F (as BLANKET)]

blare /bleə(r)/ *v.* & *n.* —*v.* **1** *tr.* & *intr.* sound or utter loudly. **2** *intr.* make the sound of a trumpet. —*n.* a loud sound resembling that of a trumpet. [ME f. MDu. *blaren, bleren,* imit.]

blarney /ˈblɑːni/ *n.* & *v.* —*n.* **1** cajoling talk; flattery. **2** nonsense. —*v.* (**-eys, -eyed**) **1** *tr.* flatter (a person) with blarney. **2** *intr.* talk flatteringly. [*Blarney,* an Irish castle near Cork with a stone said to confer a cajoling tongue on whoever kisses it]

blasé /ˈblɑːzeɪ/ *adj.* **1** unimpressed or indifferent because of over-familiarity. **2** tired of pleasure; surfeited. [F]

blaspheme /blæsˈfiːm/ *v.* **1** *intr.* talk profanely, making use of religious names, etc. **2** *tr.* talk profanely about; revile. □□ **blasphemer** *n.* [ME f. OF *blasfemer* f. eccl.L *blasphemare* f. Gk *blasphēmeō*: cf. BLAME]

blasphemy /ˈblæsfəmi/ *n.* (*pl.* **-ies**) **1** profane talk. **2** an instance of this. □□ **blasphemous** *adj.* **blasphemously** *adv.* [ME f. OF *blasfemie* f. eccl.L f. Gk *blasphēmia* slander, blasphemy]

blast /blɑːst/ *n., v.,* & *int.* —*n.* **1** a strong gust of wind. **2 a** a destructive wave of highly compressed air spreading outwards from an explosion. **b** such an explosion. **3** the single loud note of a wind instrument, car horn, whistle, etc. **4** *colloq.* a severe reprimand. **5** a strong current of air used in smelting etc. —*v.* **1** *tr.* blow up (rocks etc.) with explosives. **2** *tr.* **a** wither, shrivel, or blight (a plant, animal, limb, etc.) (*blasted oak*). **b** destroy, ruin (*blasted her hopes*). **c** strike with divine anger; curse. **3** *intr.* & *tr.* make or cause to make a loud or explosive noise (*blasted away on his trumpet*). **4** *tr. colloq.* reprimand severely. **5** *colloq.* **a** *tr.* shoot; shoot at. **b** *intr.* shoot. —*int.* expressing annoyance. □**at full blast** *colloq.* working at maximum speed etc. **blast-furnace** a smelting furnace into which compressed hot air is driven. **blast-hole** a hole containing an explosive charge for blasting. **blast off** (of a rocket etc.) take off from a launching site. **blast-off** *n.* **1** the launching

of a rocket etc. **2** the initial thrust for this. [OE *blæst* f. Gmc]

-blast /blɑːst/ *comb. form Biol.* **1** an embryonic cell (*erythroblast*) (cf. -CYTE). **2** a germ layer of an embryo (*epiblast*). [Gk *blastos* sprout]

blasted /ˈblɑːstɪd/ *adj.* & *adv.* —*attrib.adj.* damned; annoying (*that blasted dog!*). —*adv. colloq.* damned; extremely (*it's blasted cold*).

blaster /ˈblɑːstə(r)/ *n.* **1** in senses of BLAST *v.* **2** *Golf* a heavy lofted club for playing from a bunker.

blastula /ˈblæstjʊlə/ *n.* (*pl.* **blastulae** /-ˌliː/ or *US* **blastulas**) *Biol.* an animal embryo at an early stage of development when it is a hollow ball of cells. [mod.L f. Gk *blastos* sprout]

blatant /ˈbleɪt(ə)nt/ *adj.* **1** flagrant, unashamed (*blatant attempt to steal*). **2** offensively noisy or obtrusive. □□ **blatancy** *n.* **blatantly** *adv.* [a word used by Spenser (1596), perh. after Sc. *blatand* = bleating]

blather /ˈblæðə(r)/ *n.* & *v.* (also **blether** /ˈbleðə(r)/) —*n.* foolish chatter. —*v.intr.* chatter foolishly. [ME *blather,* Sc. *blether,* f. ON *blathra* talk nonsense f. *blathr* nonsense]

blatherskite /ˈblæðəˌskaɪt/ (also **bletherskate** /ˈbleðəˌskeɪt/) *n.* **1** a person who blathers. **2** = BLATHER *n.* [BLATHER + *skite,* corrupt. of derog. use of SKATE²]

blaze¹ /bleɪz/ *n.* & *v.* —*n.* **1 a** a bright flame or fire. **2 a** a bright glaring light; the sun set in a blaze of orange. **b** a full light (*a blaze of publicity*). **3** a violent outburst (of passion etc.) (*a blaze of patriotic fervour*). **4 a** a glow of colour (*roses were a blaze of scarlet*). **b** a bright display (*a blaze of glory*). —*v.intr.* **1** burn with a bright flame. **2** be brilliantly lighted. **3** be consumed with anger, excitement, etc. **4 a** show bright colours (*blazing with jewels*). **b** emit light (*stars blazing*). □**blaze away** (often foll. by *at*) **1** fire continuously with rifles etc. **2** work enthusiastically. **blaze up 1** burst into flame. **2** burst out in anger. **like blazes** *sl.* **1** with great energy. **2** very fast. **what the blazes!** *sl.* what the hell! □□ **blazingly** *adv.* [OE *blæse* torch, f. Gmc: ult. rel. to BLAZE²]

blaze² /bleɪz/ *n.* & *v.* —*n.* **1** a white mark on an animal's face. **2** a mark made on a tree by slashing the bark esp. to mark a route. —*v.tr.* mark (a tree or a path) by chipping bark. □**blaze a trail 1** mark out a path or route. **2** be the first to do, invent, or study something; pioneer. [17th c.: ult. rel. to BLAZE¹]

blaze³ /bleɪz/ *v.tr.* proclaim as with a trumpet. □**blaze abroad** spread (news) about. [ME f. LG or Du. *blāzen* blow, f. Gmc *blāsan*]

blazer /ˈbleɪzə(r)/ *n.* **1** a coloured, often striped, summer jacket worn by schoolchildren, sportsmen, etc., esp. as part of a uniform. **2** a man's plain jacket, often dark blue, not worn with matching trousers. [BLAZE¹ + -ER¹]

blazon /ˈbleɪz(ə)n/ *v.* & *n.* —*v.tr.* **1** proclaim (esp. *blazon abroad*). **2** *Heraldry* **a** describe or paint (arms). **b** inscribe or paint (an object) with arms, names, etc. —*n.* **1** *Heraldry* **a** a shield, coat of arms, bearings, or a banner. **b** a correct description of these. **2** a record or description, esp. of virtues, etc. □□ **blazoner** *n.* **blazonment** *n.* [ME f. OF *blason* shield, of unkn. orig.; verb also f. BLAZE³]

blazonry /ˈbleɪzənri/ *n. Heraldry* **1 a** the art of describing or painting heraldic devices or armorial bearings. **b** such devices or bearings. **2** brightly coloured display.

bleach /bliːtʃ/ *v.* & *n.* —*v.tr.* & *intr.* whiten by exposure to sunlight or by a chemical process. —*n.* **1** a bleaching substance. **2** the process of bleaching. □**bleaching-powder** calcium hypochlorite used esp. to remove colour from materials. [OE *blǣcan* f. Gmc]

bleacher /ˈbliːtʃə(r)/ *n.* **1 a** a person who bleaches (esp. textiles). **b** a vessel or chemical used in bleaching. **2** (usu. in *pl.*) esp. *US* an outdoor uncovered bench-seat at a sports ground, arranged in tiers and very cheap.

bleak¹ /bliːk/ *adj.* **1** bare, exposed; windswept. **2** unpromising; dreary (*bleak prospects*). □□ **bleakly** *adv.* **bleakness** *n.* [16th c.: rel. to obs. adjs. *bleach*, *blake* (f. ON *bleikr*) pale, ult. f. Gmc: cf. BLEACH]

bleak² /bliːk/ *n.* any of various species of small river-fish, esp. *Alburnus alburnus.* [ME prob. f. ON *bleikja*, OHG *bleicha* f. Gmc]

blear /blɪə(r)/ *adj. & v. archaic* —*adj.* **1** (of the eyes or the mind) dim, dull, filmy. **2** indistinct. —*v.tr.* make dim or obscure; blur. [ME, of uncert. orig.]

bleary /ˈblɪərɪ/ *adj.* (**blearier, bleariest**) **1** (of the eyes or mind) dim; blurred. **2** indistinct. □ **bleary-eyed** having dim sight or wits. □□ **blearily** *adv.* **bleariness** *n.*

bleat /bliːt/ *v. & n.* —*v.* **1** *intr.* (of a sheep, goat, or calf) make a weak, wavering cry. **2** *intr. & tr.* (often foll. by *out*) speak or say feebly, foolishly, or plaintively. —*n.* **1** the sound made by a sheep, goat, etc. **2** a weak, plaintive, or foolish cry. □□ **bleater** *n.* **bleatingly** *adv.* [OE *blǣtan* (imit.)]

bleb /bleb/ *n.* **1** esp. *Med.* a small blister on the skin. **2** a small bubble in glass or on water. [var. of BLOB]

bleed /bliːd/ *v. & n.* —*v.* (*past* and *past part.* **bled** /bled/) **1** *intr.* emit blood. **2** *tr.* draw blood from surgically. **3 a** *tr.* extort money from. **b** *intr.* part with money lavishly; suffer extortion. **4** *intr.* (often foll. by *for*) suffer wounds or violent death (*bled for the Revolution*). **5** *intr.* **a** (of a plant) emit sap. **b** (of dye) come out in water. **6** *tr.* **a** allow (fluid or gas) to escape from a closed system through a valve etc. **b** treat (such a system) in this way. **7** *Printing* **a** *intr.* (of a printed area) be cut into when pages are trimmed. **b** *tr.* cut into the printed area of when trimming. **c** *tr.* extend (an illustration) to the cut edge of a page. —*n.* an act of bleeding (cf. NOSEBLEED). □ **one's heart bleeds** usu. *iron.* one is very sorrowful. [OE *blēdan* f. Gmc]

bleeder /ˈbliːdə(r)/ *n.* **1** *coarse sl.* a person (esp. as a term of contempt or disrespect) (*you bleeder; lucky bleeder*). **2** *colloq.* a haemophiliac.

bleeding /ˈbliːdɪŋ/ *adj. & adv. Brit. coarse sl.* expressing annoyance or antipathy (*a bleeding nuisance*). □ **bleeding heart 1** *colloq.* a dangerously soft-hearted person. **2** any of various plants, esp. *Dicentra spectabilis* having heart-shaped crimson flowers hanging from an arched stem.

bleep /bliːp/ *n. & v.* —*n.* an intermittent high-pitched sound made electronically. —*v.intr. & tr.* make or cause to make such a sound, esp. as a signal. [imit.]

bleeper /ˈbliːpə(r)/ *n.* a small portable electronic device which emits a bleep when the wearer is contacted.

blemish /ˈblemɪʃ/ *n. & v.* —*n.* a physical or moral defect; a stain; a flaw (*not a blemish on his character*). —*v.tr.* spoil the beauty or perfection of; stain (*spots blemished her complexion*). [ME f. OF *ble(s)mir* (-ISH²)]

blench /blentʃ/ *v.intr.* flinch; quail. [ME f. OE *blencan*, ult. f. Gmc]

blend /blend/ *v. & n.* —*v.* **1** *tr.* **a** mix (esp. sorts of tea, spirits, tobacco, etc.) together to produce a desired flavour etc. **b** produce by this method (*blended whisky*). **2** *intr.* form a harmonious compound; become one. **3 a** *tr. & intr.* (often foll. by *with*) mingle or be mingled (*truth blended with lies; blends well with the locals*). **b** *tr.* (often foll. by *in, with*) mix thoroughly. **4** *intr.* (esp. of colours): **a** pass imperceptibly into each other. **b** go well together; harmonize. —*n.* **1 a** a mixture, esp. of various sorts of tea, spirits, tobacco, fibre, etc. **b** a combination (of different abstract or personal qualities). **2** a portmanteau word. [ME prob. f. ON *blanda* mix]

blende /blend/ *n.* any naturally occurring metal sulphide, esp. zinc blende. [G f. *blenden* deceive, so called because while often resembling galena it yielded no lead]

blender /ˈblendə(r)/ *n.* **1** a mixing machine used in food preparation for liquidizing, chopping, or

puréeing. **2 a** a thing that blends. **b** a person who blends.

Blenheim /ˈblenɪm/ *n.* **1** a small spaniel of a red and white breed. **2** this breed. [the Duke of Marlborough's seat at Woodstock in S. England, named after his victory at Blenheim in Bavaria (1704)]

Blenheim Orange /ˈblenɪm/ *n.* a golden-coloured apple which ripens late in the season.

blenny /ˈblenɪ/ *n.* (*pl.* -**ies**) any of a family of small spiny-finned marine fish, esp. of the genus *Blennius*, having scaleless skins. [L *blennius* f. Gk *blennos* mucus, with reference to its mucous coating]

blent /blent/ *poet. past* and *past part.* of BLEND.

blepharitis /ˌblefəˈraɪtɪs/ *n.* inflammation of the eyelids. [Gk *blepharon* eyelid + -ITIS]

blesbok /ˈblesbɒk/ *n.* (also **blesbuck** /-bʌk/) a subspecies of bontebok, native to southern Africa, having small lyre-shaped horns. [Afrik. f. *bles* BLAZE², (from the white mark on its forehead) + *bok* goat]

bless /bles/ *v.tr.* (*past* and *past part.* **blessed**, *poet.* **blest** /blest/) **1** (of a priest etc.) pronounce words, esp. in a religious rite, asking for divine favour; ask God to look favourably on (*bless this house*). **2 a** consecrate (esp. bread and wine). **b** sanctify by the sign of the cross. **3** call (God) holy; adore. **4** attribute one's good fortune to (an auspicious time, one's fate, etc.); thank (*bless the day I met her; bless my stars*). **5** (usu. in *passive*; often foll. by *with*) make happy or successful (*blessed with children; they were truly blessed*). **6** *euphem.* curse; damn (*bless the boy!*). □ **(God) bless me** (or **my soul**) an exclamation of surprise, pleasure, indignation, etc. **(God) bless you! 1** an exclamation of endearment, gratitude, etc. **2** an exclamation made to a person who has just sneezed. **I'm** (or **well, I'm**) **blessed** (or **blest**) an exclamation of surprise etc. **not have a penny to bless oneself with** be impoverished. [OE *blēdsian, blētsian*, f. *blōd* blood (hence mark with blood, consecrate): meaning infl. by its use at the conversion of the English to translate L *benedicare* praise]

blessed /ˈblesɪd, blest/ *adj.* (also *poet.* **blest**) **1 a** consecrated (*Blessed Sacrament*). **b** revered. **2** /blest/ (usu. foll. by *with*) often *iron.* fortunate (in the possession of) (*blessed with good health; blessed with children*). **3** *euphem.* cursed; damned (*blessed nuisance!*). **4 a** in paradise. **b** *RC Ch.* a title given to a dead person as an acknowledgement of his or her holy life; beatified. **5** bringing happiness; blissful (*blessed ignorance*). □□ **blessedly** *adv.*

blessedness /ˈblesɪdnɪs/ *n.* **1** happiness. **2** the enjoyment of divine favour. □ **single blessedness** *joc.* the state of being unmarried (perversion of Shakesp. *Midsummer Night's Dream* I. i. 78).

blessing /ˈblesɪŋ/ *n.* **1** the act of declaring, seeking, or bestowing (esp. divine) favour (*sought God's blessing; mother gave them her blessing*). **2** grace said before or after a meal. **3** a gift of God, nature, etc.; a thing one is glad of (*what a blessing he brought it!*). □ **blessing in disguise** an apparent misfortune that eventually has good results.

blest /blest/ *poet.* var. of BLESSED.

blether var. of BLATHER.

bletherskate var. of BLATHERSKITE.

blew *past* of BLOW¹, BLOW³.

blewits /ˈbluːɪts/ *n.* any fungus of the genus *Tricholoma*, with edible lilac-stemmed mushrooms. [prob. f. BLUE¹]

blight /blaɪt/ *n. & v.* —*n.* **1** any plant disease caused by mildews, rusts, smuts, fungi, or insects. **2** any insect or parasite causing such a disease. **3** any obscure force which is harmful or destructive. **4** an unsightly or neglected urban area. —*v.tr.* **1** affect with blight. **2** harm, destroy. **3** spoil. [17th c.: orig. unkn.]

blighter /ˈblaɪtə(r)/ *n. Brit. colloq.* a person (esp. as a term of contempt or disparagement). [BLIGHT + -ER¹]

Blighty /'blaɪtɪ/ n. (pl. -ies) sl. (used by soldiers, esp. during the war of 1914-18) England; home. [Anglo-Ind. corrupt. of Hind. bilāyatī, wilāyatī foreign, European]

blimey /'blaɪmɪ/ int. (also **cor blimey** /kɔː/) Brit. coarse sl. an expression of surprise, contempt, etc. [corrupt. of (God) blind me!]

blimp /blɪmp/ n. **1** (also (**Colonel**) **Blimp**) a proponent of reactionary establishment opinions. **2 a** a small non-rigid airship. **b** a barrage balloon. **3** a soundproof cover for a cine-camera. ▭▭ **blimpery** n. **blimpish** adj. [20th. c., of uncert. orig.: in sense 1, a pompous, obese, elderly character invented by cartoonist David Low (d. 1963), and used in anti-German or anti-Government drawings before and during the war of 1939-45]

blind /blaɪnd/ adj., v., n., & adv. —adj. **1** lacking the power of sight. **2 a** without foresight, discernment, intellectual perception, or adequate information (blind effort). **b** (often foll. by to) unwilling or unable to appreciate (a factor, circumstance, etc.) (blind to argument). **3** not governed by purpose or reason (blind forces). **4** reckless (blind hitting). **5 a** concealed (blind ditch). **b** (of a door, window, etc.) walled up. **c** closed at one end. **6** Aeron. (of flying) without direct observation, using instruments only. **7** Cookery (of a flan case, pie base, etc.) baked without a filling. **8** sl. drunk. —v. **1** tr. deprive of sight, permanently or temporarily (blinded by tears). **2** tr. (often foll. by to) rob of judgement; deceive (blinded them to the danger). **3** intr. sl. go very fast and dangerously, esp. in a motor vehicle. —n. **1 a** a screen for a window, esp. on a roller, or with slats (roller blind; Venetian blind). **b** an awning over a shop window. **2 a** something designed or used to hide the truth; a pretext. **b** a legitimate business concealing a criminal enterprise (he's a spy, and his job is just a blind). **3** any obstruction to sight or light. **4** Brit. sl. a heavy drinking-bout. **5** Cards a stake put up by a poker player before the cards dealt are seen. **6** US = HIDE¹ n. —adv. blindly (fly blind; bake it blind). ▭**blind alley 1** a cul-de-sac. **2** a course of action leading nowhere. **blind as a bat** completely blind. **blind coal** coal burning without a flame. **blind corner** a corner round which a motorist etc. cannot see. **blind date 1** a social engagement between a man and a woman who have not previously met. **2** either of the couple on a blind date. **blind drunk** extremely drunk. **blind gut** the caecum. **blind man's buff** a game in which a blindfold player tries to catch others while being pushed about by them. **blind side** a direction in which one cannot see the approach of danger etc. **blind spot 1** Anat. the point of entry of the optic nerve on the retina, insensitive to light. **2** an area in which a person lacks understanding or impartiality. **3** a point of unusually weak radio reception. **blind stamping** (or **tooling**) embossing a book cover without the use of colour or gold leaf. **blind-stitch** n. sewing visible on one side only. —v.tr. & intr. sew with this stitch. **blind to** incapable of appreciating. **blind with science** overawe with a display of (often spurious) knowledge. **go it blind** act recklessly or without proper consideration. **not a blind bit of** (or **not a blind**) sl. not the slightest; not a single (took not a blind bit of notice; not a blind word out of him). **turn a** (or **one's**) **blind eye to** pretend not to notice. ▭▭ **blindly** adv. **blindness** n. [OE f. Gmc]

blinder /'blaɪndə(r)/ n. colloq. **1** an excellent piece of play in a game. **2** (in pl.) US blinkers.

blindfold /'blaɪndfəʊld/ v., n., adj., & adv. —v.tr. **1** deprive (a person) of sight by covering the eyes, esp. with a tied cloth. **2** deprive of understanding; hoodwink. —n. **1** a bandage or cloth used to blindfold. **2** any obstruction to understanding. —adj. & adv. **1** with eyes bandaged. **2** without care or

circumspection (went into it blindfold). **3** Chess without sight of board and men. [replacing (by assoc. with FOLD¹) ME blindfellen, past part. blindfelled (FELL¹) strike blind]

blinding /'blaɪndɪŋ/ n. **1** the process of covering a newly made road etc. with grit to fill cracks. **2** such grit.

blindworm /'blaɪndwɜːm/ n. = SLOW-WORM.

blink /blɪŋk/ v. & n. —v. **1** intr. shut and open the eyes quickly and usu. involuntarily. **2** intr. (often foll. by at) look with eyes opening and shutting. **3** tr. **a** (often foll. by back) prevent (tears) by blinking. **b** (often foll. by away, from) clear (dust etc.) from the eyes by blinking. **4** tr. & (foll. by at) intr. shirk consideration of; ignore; condone. **5** intr. **a** shine with an unsteady or intermittent light. **b** cast a momentary gleam. **6** tr. blink with (eyes). —n. **1** an act of blinking. **2** a momentary gleam or glimpse. **3** = ICEBLINK. ▭**on the blink** sl. out of order, esp. intermittently. [partly var. of blenk = BLENCH, partly f. MDu. blinken shine]

blinker /'blɪŋkə(r)/ n. & v. —n. **1** (usu. in pl.) either of a pair of screens attached to a horse's bridle to prevent it from seeing sideways. **2** a device that blinks, esp. a vehicle's indicator. —v.tr. **1** obscure with blinkers. **2** (as **blinkered** adj.) having narrow and prejudiced views.

blinking /'blɪŋkɪŋ/ adj. & adv. Brit. sl. an intensive, esp. expressing disapproval (a blinking idiot; a blinking awful time). [BLINK + -ING² (euphem. for BLOODY)]

blip /blɪp/ n. & v. —n. **1** a quick popping sound, as of dripping water or an electronic device. **2** a small image of an object on a radar screen. —v. (**blipped**, **blipping**) **1** intr. make a blip. **2** tr. strike briskly. [imit.]

bliss /blɪs/ n. **1 a** a perfect joy or happiness. **b** enjoyment; gladness. **2 a** being in heaven. **b** a state of blessedness. [OE blīths, bliss f. Gmc blīthsjō f. blīthiz BLITHE: sense infl. by BLESS]

blissful /'blɪsfʊl/ adj. perfectly happy; joyful. ▭**blissful ignorance** fortunate unawareness of something unpleasant. ▭▭ **blissfully** adv. **blissfulness** n.

blister /'blɪstə(r)/ n. & v. —n. **1** a small bubble on the skin filled with serum and caused by friction, burning, etc. **2** a similar swelling on any other surface. **3** Med. anything applied to raise a blister. **4** sl. an annoying person. —v. **1** tr. raise a blister on. **2** intr. come up in a blister or blisters. **3** tr. attack sharply (blistered them with his criticisms). ▭**blister copper** copper which is almost pure. **blister gas** a poison gas causing blisters on the skin. **blister pack** a bubble pack. ▭▭ **blistery** adj. [ME perh. f. OF blestre, blo(u)stre swelling, pimple]

blithe /blaɪð/ adj. **1** poet. gay, joyous. **2** careless, casual (with blithe indifference). ▭▭ **blithely** adv. **blitheness** n. **blithesome** /-səm/ adj. [OE blīthe f. Gmc]

blithering /'blɪðərɪŋ/ adj. colloq. **1** senselessly talkative. **2 a** (attrib.) utter; hopeless (blithering idiot). **b** contemptible. [blither, var. of BLATHER + -ING²]

B.Litt. abbr. Bachelor of Letters. [L Baccalaureus Litterarum]

blitz /blɪts/ n. & v. colloq. —n. **1 a** an intensive or sudden (esp. aerial) attack. **b** an energetic intensive attack, usu. on a specific task (must have a blitz on this room). **2** (**the Blitz**) the German air raids on London in 1940. —v.tr. attack, damage, or destroy by a blitz. [abbr. of BLITZKRIEG]

blitzkrieg /'blɪtskriːg/ n. an intense military campaign intended to bring about a swift victory. [G, = lightning war]

blizzard /'blɪzəd/ n. a severe snowstorm with high winds. [US 'violent blow' (1829), 'snowstorm' (1859), perh. imit.]

bloat /bləʊt/ v. **1** tr. & intr. inflate, swell (wind bloated the sheets; bloated with gas). **2** tr. (as **bloated** adj.) **a** swollen, puffed. **b** puffed up with pride or excessive wealth (*bloated plutocrat*). **3** *tr.* cure (a herring) by salting and smoking lightly. [obs. *bloat* swollen, soft and wet, perh. f. ON *blautr* soaked, flabby]

bloater /'bləʊtə(r)/ *n.* a herring cured by bloating.

blob /blɒb/ *n.* **1** a small roundish mass; a drop of matter. **2** a drop of liquid. **3** a spot of colour. **4** *Cricket sl.* a score of 0. [imit.: cf. BLEB]

bloc /blɒk/ *n.* a combination of parties, governments, groups, etc. sharing a common purpose. □ **bloc vote** = *block vote*. [F, = block]

block /blɒk/ *n.*, *v.*, & *adj.* —*n.* **1** a solid hewn or unhewn piece of hard material, esp. of rock, stone, or wood (*block of ice*). **2** a flat-topped block used as a base for chopping, beheading, standing something on, hammering on, or for mounting a horse from. **3 a** a large building, esp. when subdivided (*block of flats*). **b** a compact mass of buildings bounded by (usu. four) streets. **4** an obstruction; anything preventing progress or normal working (*a block in the pipe*). **5** a chock for stopping the motion of a wheel etc. **6** a pulley or system of pulleys mounted in a case. **7** (in *pl.*) any of a set of solid cubes etc., used as a child's toy. **8** *Printing* a piece of wood or metal engraved for printing on paper or fabric. **9** a head-shaped mould used for shaping hats or wigs. **10** *sl.* the head (*knock his block off*). **11** *US* **a** the area between streets in a town or suburb. **b** the length of such an area, esp. as a measure of distance (*lives three blocks away*). **12** a stolid, unimaginative, or hard-hearted person. **13** a large quantity or allocation of things treated as a unit, esp. shares, seats in a theatre, etc. **14** a set of sheets of paper used for writing, or esp. drawing, glued along one edge. **15** *Cricket* a spot on which a batsman blocks the ball before the wicket, and rests the bat before playing. **16** *Athletics* = *starting-block*. **17** *Amer. Football* a blocking action. **18** *Austral.* **a** a tract of land offered to an individual settler by a government. **b** a large area of land. —*v.tr.* **1 a** (often foll. by *up*) obstruct (a passage etc.) (*the road was blocked; you are blocking my view*). **b** put obstacles in the way of (progress etc.). **2** restrict the use or conversion of (currency or any other asset). **3** use a block for making (a hat, wig, etc.). **4** emboss or impress a design on (a book cover). **5** *Cricket* stop (a ball) with a bat defensively. **6** *Amer. Football* intercept (an opponent) with one's body. —*attrib.adj.* treating (many similar things) as one unit (*block booking*). □ **block and tackle** a system of pulleys and ropes, esp. for lifting. **block capitals** (or **letters**) letters printed without serifs, or written with each letter separate and in capitals. **block diagram** a diagram showing the general arrangement of parts of an apparatus. **block in 1** sketch roughly; plan. **2** confine. **block mountain** *Geol.* a mountain formed by natural faults. **block out 1 a** shut out (light, noise, etc.). **b** exclude from memory, as being too painful. **2** sketch roughly; plan. **block-ship** *Naut.* a ship used to block a channel. **block system** a system by which no railway train may enter a section that is not clear. **block tin** refined tin cast in ingots. **block up 1** confine; shut (a person etc.) in. **2** infill (a window, doorway, etc.) with bricks etc. **block vote** a vote proportional in power to the number of people a delegate represents. **mental** (or **psychological**) **block** a particular mental inability due to subconscious emotional factors. **on the block** *US* being auctioned. **put the blocks on** prevent from proceeding. □□ **blocker** *n.* [ME f. OF *bloc, bloquer* f. MDu. *blok*, of unkn. orig.]

blockade /blɒ'keɪd/ *n.* & *v.* —*n.* **1** the surrounding or blocking of a place, esp. a port, by an enemy to prevent entry and exit of supplies etc. **2** anything that prevents access or progress. **3** *US* an obstruction by snow etc. —*v.tr.* **1** subject to a blockade. **2** obstruct (a passage, a view, etc.). □ **blockade-runner 1** a vessel which runs or attempts to run into a

blockaded port. **2** the owner, master, or one of the crew of such a vessel. **run a blockade** enter or leave a blockaded port by evading the blockading force. □□ **blockader** *n.* [BLOCK + -ADE¹, prob. after *ambuscade*]

blockage /'blɒkɪdʒ/ *n.* **1** an obstruction. **2** a blocked state.

blockboard /'blɒkbɔːd/ *n.* a plywood board with a core of wooden strips.

blockbuster /'blɒk,bʌstə(r)/ *n. sl.* **1** something of great power or size, esp. an epic film or a book. **2** a huge bomb capable of destroying a whole block of buildings.

blockhead /'blɒkhed/ *n.* a stupid person. □□ **blockheaded** *adj.*

blockhouse /'blɒkhaʊs/ *n.* **1** a reinforced concrete shelter used as an observation point etc. **2** *hist.* a one-storeyed timber building with loopholes, used as a fort. **3** a house made of squared logs.

blockish /'blɒkɪʃ/ *adj.* **1** resembling a block. **2** excessively dull; stupid, obtuse. **3** clumsy, rude, roughly hewn. □□ **blockishly** *adv.* **blockishness** *n.*

bloke /bləʊk/ *n. Brit. sl.* a man, a fellow. [Shelta]

blond /blɒnd/ *adj.* & *n.* —*adj.* **1** (of hair) light-coloured; fair. **2** (of the complexion, esp. as an indication of race) light-coloured. —*n.* a person, esp. a man, with fair hair and skin. □□ **blondish** *adj.* **blondness** *n.* [ME f. F f. med.L *blondus, blundus* yellow, perh. of Gmc orig.]

blonde /blɒnd/ *adj.* & *n.* —*adj.* (of a woman or a woman's hair) blond. —*n.* a blond-haired woman. [F fem. of *blond*; see BLOND]

blood /blʌd/ *n.* & *v.* —*n.* **1** a liquid, usually red and circulating in the arteries and veins of vertebrates, that carries oxygen to and carbon dioxide from the tissues of the body. **2** a corresponding fluid in invertebrates. **3** bloodshed, esp. killing. **4** passion, temperament. **5** race, descent, parentage (*of the same blood*). **6** a relationship; relations (*own flesh and blood; blood is thicker than water*). **7** a dandy; a man of fashion. —*v.tr.* **1** give (a hound) a first taste of blood. **2** initiate (a person) by experience. □ **bad blood** ill feeling. **blood-and-thunder** (*attrib.*) *colloq.* sensational, melodramatic. **blood bank** a place where supplies of blood or plasma for transfusion are stored. **blood bath** a massacre. **blood-brother** a brother by birth or by the ceremonial mingling of blood. **blood count 1** the counting of the number of corpuscles in a specific amount of blood. **2** the number itself. **blood-curdling** horrifying. **blood donor** one who gives blood for transfusion. **blood feud** a feud between families involving killing or injury. **blood group** any one of the various types of human blood determining compatibility in transfusion. **blood-heat** the normal body temperature of a healthy human being, about 37 °C and 98.4 °F. **blood horse** a thoroughbred. **one's blood is up** one is in a fighting mood. **blood-letting 1** the surgical removal of some of a patient's blood. **2** *joc.* bloodshed. **blood-lust** the desire for shedding blood. **blood-money 1** money paid to the next of kin of a person who has been killed. **2** money paid to a hired murderer. **3** money paid for information about a murder or murderer. **blood orange** an orange with red or red-streaked pulp. **blood-poisoning** a diseased state caused by the presence of micro-organisms in the blood. **blood pressure** the pressure of the blood in the circulatory system, often measured for diagnosis since it is closely related to the force and rate of the heartbeat and the diameter and elasticity of the arterial walls. **blood-red** red as blood. **blood relation** (or **relative**) a relative by blood, not by marriage. **blood royal** the royal family. **blood serum** see SERUM. **blood sport** sport involving the wounding or killing of animals, esp. hunting. **blood sugar** the amount of glucose in the blood. **blood test** a scientific examination of blood, esp. for diagnosis. **blood transfusion** the injection of a volume of blood, previously taken from a healthy person, into a patient. **blood-vessel** a vein, artery, or capillary carrying blood. **blood-wort** any of various plants having red roots or leaves, esp. the red-veined dock. **first blood 1** the first shedding of blood, esp. in boxing. **2** the first point gained in a contest etc. **in one's blood** inherent in one's character. **make one's blood boil** infuriate one. **make one's blood run cold** horrify one. **new** (or **fresh**) **blood** new members admitted to a group, esp. as an invigorating force. **of the blood** royal. **out for a person's blood** set on getting revenge. **taste blood** be stimulated by an early success. **young blood 1** a younger member or members of a group. **2** a rake or fashionable young man. [OE *blōd* f. Gmc]

blooded /'blʌdɪd/ *adj.* **1** (of horses etc.) of good pedigree. **2** (in *comb.*) having blood or a disposition of a specified kind (*cold-blooded*; *red-blooded*).

bloodhound /'blʌdhaʊnd/ *n.* **1** a large hound of a breed used in tracking and having a very keen sense of smell. **2** this breed.

bloodless /'blʌdlɪs/ *adj.* **1** without blood. **2** unemotional; cold. **3** pale. **4** without bloodshed (*a bloodless coup*). **5** feeble; lifeless. □□ **bloodlessly** *adv.* **bloodlessness** *n.*

bloodshed /'blʌdʃed/ *n.* **1** the spilling of blood. **2** slaughter.

bloodshot /'blʌdʃɒt/ *adj.* (of an eyeball) inflamed, tinged with blood.

bloodstain /'blʌdsteɪn/ *n.* a discoloration caused by blood.

bloodstained /'blʌdsteɪnd/ *adj.* **1** stained with blood. **2** guilty of bloodshed.

bloodstock /'blʌdstɒk/ *n.* thoroughbred horses.

bloodstone /'blʌdstəʊn/ *n.* a type of green chalcedony spotted or streaked with red, often used as a gemstone.

bloodstream /'blʌdstriːm/ *n.* blood in circulation.

bloodsucker /'blʌdˌsʌkə(r)/ *n.* **1** an animal or insect that sucks blood, esp. a leech. **2** an extortioner. □□ **bloodsucking** *adj.*

bloodthirsty /'blʌdˌθɜːstɪ/ *adj.* (**bloodthirstier**, **bloodthirstiest**) eager for bloodshed. □□ **bloodthirstily** *adv.* **bloodthirstiness** *n.*

bloodworm /'blʌdwɜːm/ *n.* **1** any of a variety of bright-red midge-larvae. **2** a small tubifex worm used as food for aquarium fish.

bloody /'blʌdɪ/ *adj.*, *adv.*, & *v.* —*adj.* (**bloodier**, **bloodiest**) **1 a** of or like blood. **b** running or smeared with blood (*bloody bandage*). **2 a** involving, loving, or resulting from bloodshed (*bloody battle*). **b** sanguinary; cruel (*bloody butcher*). **3** *coarse sl.* expressing annoyance or antipathy, or as an intensive (*a bloody shame*; *a bloody sight better*; *not a bloody chocolate left*). **4** red. —*adv. coarse sl.* as an intensive (*a bloody good job*; *I'll bloody thump him*). —*v.tr.* (-ies, -ied) make bloody; stain with blood. □ **bloody hand** *Heraldry* the armorial device of a baronet. **Bloody Mary** a drink composed of vodka and tomato juice. **bloody-minded** *colloq.* deliberately uncooperative. **bloody-mindedly** *colloq.* in a perverse or uncooperative manner. **bloody-mindedness** *colloq.* perversity, contrariness. □□ **bloodily** *adv.* **bloodiness** *n.* [OE *blōdig* (as BLOOD, -Y¹)]

bloom¹ /bluːm/ *n.* & *v.* —*n.* **1 a** a flower, esp. one cultivated for its beauty. **b** the state of flowering (*in bloom*). **2** a state of perfection or loveliness; the prime (*in full bloom*). **3 a** (of the complexion) a flush; a glow. **b** a delicate powdery surface deposit on plums, grapes, leaves, etc., indicating freshness. **c** a cloudiness on a shiny surface. —*v.* **1** *intr.* bear flowers; be in flower. **2** *intr.* **a** come into, or remain in, full beauty. **b** flourish; be in a healthy, vigorous state. **3** *tr. Photog.* coat (a lens) so as to reduce reflection from its surface. □ **take the bloom off** make stale. **water-bloom** scum formed by algae on the surface of standing water. [ME f. ON *blóm*, *blómi* etc. f. Gmc: cf. BLOSSOM]

bloom² /bluːm/ *n.* & *v.* —*n.* a mass of puddled iron hammered or squeezed into a thick bar. —*v.tr.* make into bloom. [OE *blōma*]

bloomer¹ /'bluːmə(r)/ *n. sl.* a blunder. [= BLOOMING error]

bloomer² /'bluːmə(r)/ *n. Brit.* an oblong loaf with a rounded diagonally slashed top. [20th c.: orig. uncert.]

bloomer³ /'bluːmə(r)/ *n.* a plant that blooms (in a specified way) (*early autumn bloomer*).

bloomers /'bluːməz/ *n.pl.* **1** women's loose-fitting almost knee-length knickers. **2** *colloq.* any women's knickers. **3** *hist.* women's loose-fitting trousers, gathered at the knee or (orig.) the ankle. [Mrs A. *Bloomer*, Amer. social reformer d. 1894, who advocated a similar costume]

bloomery /'bluːmərɪ/ *n.* (*pl.* -**ies**) a factory that makes puddled iron into blooms.

blooming /'bluːmɪŋ/ *adj.* & *adv.* —*adj.* **1** flourishing; healthy. **2** *Brit. sl.* an intensive (*a blooming miracle*). —*adv. Brit. sl.* an intensive (*was blooming difficult*). [BLOOM¹ + -ING²: euphem. for BLOODY]

Bloomsbury /'bluːmzbərɪ, -brɪ/ *n.* & *adj.* —*n.* (in full **Bloomsbury Group**) a group of writers, artists, and philosophers living in or associated with Bloomsbury in London in the early 20th c. —*adj.* **1** associated with or similar to the Bloomsbury Group. **2** intellectual; highbrow.

blooper /'bluːpə(r)/ *n.* esp. *US colloq.* an embarrassing error. [imit. *bloop* + -ER¹]

blossom /'blɒsəm/ *n.* & *v.* —*n.* **1** a flower or a mass of flowers, esp. of a fruit-tree. **2** the stage or time of flowering (*the cherry tree in blossom*). **3** a promising stage (*the blossom of youth*). —*v.intr.* **1** open into flower. **2** reach a promising stage; mature, thrive. □□ **blossomy** *adj.* [OE *blōstm(a)* prob. formed as BLOOM¹]

blot /blɒt/ *n.* & *v.* —*n.* **1** a spot or stain of ink etc. **2** a moral defect in an otherwise good character; a disgraceful act or quality. **3** any disfigurement or blemish. —*v.* (**blotted**, **blotting**) **1 a** *tr.* spot or stain with ink; smudge. **b** *intr.* (of a pen, ink, etc.) make blots. **2** *tr.* **a** use blotting-paper or other absorbent material to absorb excess ink. **b** (of blotting-paper etc.) soak up (esp. ink). **3** *tr.* disgrace (*blotted his reputation*). □ **blot one's copybook** damage one's reputation. **blot on the escutcheon** a disgrace to the family name. **blot out 1 a** obliterate (writing). **b** obscure (a view, sound, etc.). **2** obliterate (from the memory) as too painful. **3** destroy. **blotting-paper** unglazed absorbent paper used for soaking up excess ink. [ME prob. f. Scand.: cf. Icel. *blettr* spot, stain]

blotch /blɒtʃ/ *n.* & *v.* —*n.* **1** a discoloured or inflamed patch on the skin. **2** an irregular patch of ink or colour. —*v.tr.* cover with blotches. □□ **blotchy** *adj.* (**blotchier**, **blotchiest**). [17th c.: f. obs. *plotch* and BLOT]

blotter /'blɒtə(r)/ *n.* **1** a sheet or sheets of blotting-paper, usu. inserted into a frame. **2** *US* a temporary recording-book, esp. a police charge-sheet.

blotto /'blɒtəʊ/ *adj. sl.* very drunk, esp. unconscious from drinking. [20th c.: perh. f. BLOT]

blouse /blaʊz/ *n.* & *v.* —*n.* **1 a** a woman's loose, usu. lightweight, upper garment, usu. buttoned and collared. **b** the upper part of a soldier's or airman's battledress. **2** a workman's or peasant's loose linen or cotton garment, usu. belted at the waist. —*v.tr.* make (a bodice etc.) loose like a blouse. [F, of unkn. orig.]

blouson /'bluːzɒn/ *n.* a short blouse-shaped jacket. [F]

blow¹ /bləʊ/ *v.* & *n.* —*v.* (*past* **blew** /bluː/; *past part.* **blown** /bləʊn/) **1 a** *intr.* (of the wind or air, or impersonally) move along; act as an air-current (*it was blowing hard*). **b** *intr.* be driven by an air-current (*waste paper blew along the gutter*). **c** *tr.* drive with an air-current (*blew the door open*). **2 a** *tr.* send out (esp. air) by breathing (*blew cigarette smoke; blew a bubble*). **b** *intr.* send a directed air-current from the mouth. **3** *tr.* & *intr.* sound or be sounded by blowing (*the whistle blew; they blew the trumpets*). **4** *tr.* **a** direct an air-current at (*blew the embers*). **b** (foll. by *off, away*, etc.) clear of by means of an air-current (*blew the dust off*). **5** *tr.* (*past part.* **blowed**) *sl.* (esp. in *imper.*) curse, confound (*blow it!; I'll be blowed!; let's take a taxi and blow the expense*). **6** *tr.* **a** clear (the nose) of mucus by blowing. **b** remove contents from (an egg) by blowing through it. **7 a** *intr.* puff, pant. **b** *tr.* (esp. in *passive*) exhaust of breath. **8** *sl.* **a** *tr.* depart suddenly from (*blew the town yesterday*). **b** *intr.* depart suddenly. **9** *tr.* shatter or send flying by an explosion (*the bomb blew the tiles off the roof; blew them to smithereens*). **10** *tr.* make or shape (glass or a bubble) by blowing air in. **11** *tr.* & *intr.* melt or cause to melt from overloading (*the fuse has blown*). **12** *intr.* (of a whale) eject air and water through a blow-hole. **13** *tr.* break into (a safe etc.) with explosives. **14** *tr. sl.* **a** squander, spend recklessly (*blew £20 on a meal*). **b** spoil, bungle (an opportunity etc.) (*he's blown his chances of winning*). **c** reveal (a secret etc.). **15** *intr.* (of a food-tin etc.) swell and eventually burst from internal gas pressure. **16** *tr.* work the bellows of (an organ). **17** *tr.* (of flies) deposit eggs in. **18** *intr. US & Austral. colloq.* boast. —*n.* **1 a** an act of blowing (e.g. one's nose, a wind instrument). **b** *colloq.* a turn or spell of playing jazz (on any instrument); a musical session. **2 a** a gust of wind or air. **b** exposure to fresh air. **3** = *fly-blow* (see FLY²). **4** *US* a boaster. □ **be blowed if one will** *sl.* be unwilling to. **blow-ball** the globular seed-head of a dandelion etc. **blow-dry** arrange (the hair) while drying it with a hand-held drier. **blow-drier** (or **-dryer**) a drier used for this. **blow the gaff** reveal a secret inadvertently. **blow-hole 1** the nostril of a whale, on the top of its head. **2** a hole (esp. in ice) for breathing or fishing through. **3** a vent for air, smoke, etc., in a tunnel etc. **blow hot and cold** *colloq.* vacillate. **blow in 1** break inwards by an explosion. **2** *colloq.* arrive unexpectedly. **blow-job** *coarse sl.* fellatio; cunnilingus. **blow a kiss** kiss one's hand and wave it to a distant person. **blow a person's mind** *sl.* cause a person to have drug-induced hallucinations or a similar experience. **blow off 1** escape or allow (steam etc.) to escape forcibly. **2** *sl.* break wind noisily. **blow on** (or **upon**) make stale; discredit. **blow out 1 a** extinguish by blowing. **b** send outwards by an explosion. **2** (of a tyre) burst. **3** (of a fuse etc.) melt. **blow-out** *n. colloq.* **1** a burst tyre. **2** a melted fuse. **3** a huge meal. **blow over** (of trouble etc.) fade away without serious consequences. **blow one's own trumpet** praise oneself. **blow one's top** (*US* **stack**) *colloq.* explode in rage. **blow up 1 a** shatter or destroy by an explosion. **b** explode, erupt. **2** *colloq.* rebuke strongly. **3** inflate (a tyre etc.). **4** *colloq.* **a** enlarge (a photograph). **b** exaggerate. **5** *colloq.* come to notice; arise. **6** *colloq.* lose one's temper. **blow-up** *n.* **1** *colloq.* an enlargement (of a photograph etc.). **2** an explosion. **blow the whistle on** see WHISTLE. [OE *blāwan* f. Gmc]

blow² /bləʊ/ *n.* **1** a hard stroke with a hand or weapon. **2** a sudden shock or misfortune. □ **at one blow** by a single stroke; in one operation. **blow-by-blow** (of a description etc.) giving all the details in sequence. **come to blows** end up fighting. **strike a blow for** (or **against**) help (or oppose). [15th c.: orig. unkn.]

blow³ /bləʊ/ *v.* & *n. archaic* —*v.intr.* (*past* **blew** /bluː/; *past part.* **blown** /bləʊn/) burst into or be in flower. —*n.* blossoming, bloom (*in full blow*). [OE *blōwan* f. Gmc]

blower /ˈbləʊə(r)/ *n.* **1** in senses of BLOW¹ *v.* **2** a device for creating a current of air. **3** *colloq.* a telephone.

blowfish /ˈbləʊfɪʃ/ *n.* any of several kinds of fish able to inflate their bodies when frightened etc.

blowfly /ˈbləʊflaɪ/ *n.* (*pl.* **-flies**) a meat-fly, a bluebottle.

blowgun /ˈbləʊgʌn/ *n. US* = BLOWPIPE.

blowhard /ˈbləʊhɑːd/ *n. & adj. colloq.* —*n.* a boastful person. —*adj.* boastful; blustering.

blowlamp /ˈbləʊlæmp/ *n.* a portable device with a very hot flame used for burning off paint, soldering, etc.

blown *past part.* of BLOW¹, BLOW³.

blowpipe /ˈbləʊpaɪp/ *n.* **1** a tube used esp. by primitive peoples for propelling arrows or darts by blowing. **2** a tube used to intensify the heat of a flame by blowing air or other gas through it at high pressure. **3** a tube used in glass-blowing.

blowtorch /ˈbləʊtɔːtʃ/ *n. US* = BLOWLAMP.

blowy /ˈbləʊɪ/ *adj.* (**blowier**, **blowiest**) windy, windswept. □□ **blowiness** *n.*

blowzy /ˈblaʊzɪ/ *adj.* (**blowzier**, **blowziest**) **1** coarse-looking; red-faced. **2** dishevelled, slovenly. □□ **blowzily** *adv.* **blowziness** *n.* [obs. *blowze* beggar's wench, of unkn. orig.]

blub /blʌb/ *v.intr.* (**blubbed**, **blubbing**) *sl.* sob. [abbr. of BLUBBER¹]

blubber¹ /ˈblʌbə(r)/ *n.* & *v.* —*n.* **1** whale fat. **2** a spell of weeping. —*v.* **1** *intr.* sob loudly. **2** *tr.* sob out (words). □□ **blubberer** *n.* **blubberingly** *adv.* **blubbery** *adj.* [ME perh. imit. (obs. meanings 'foaming, bubble')]

blubber² /ˈblʌbə(r)/ *adj.* (of the lips) swollen, protruding. [earlier *blabber*, *blobber*, imit.]

bluchers /ˈbluːkəz/ *n.pl. hist.* strong leather half-boots or high shoes. [G. L. von *Blücher*, Prussian general d. 1819]

bludge /blʌdʒ/ *v.* & *n. Austral. & NZ sl.* —*v.intr.* avoid work. —*n.* an easy job or assignment. □ **bludge on** impose on. [back-form. f. BLUDGER]

bludgeon /ˈblʌdʒ(ə)n/ *n.* & *v.* —*n.* a club with a heavy end. —*v.tr.* **1** beat with a bludgeon. **2** coerce. [18th c.: orig. unkn.]

bludger /ˈblʌdʒə(r)/ *n. Austral. & NZ sl.* **1** a hanger-on. **2** a loafer. [orig. E sl., = pimp, f. obs. *bludgeoner* f. BLUDGEON]

blue¹ /bluː/ *adj., n., & v.* —*adj.* **1** having a colour like that of a clear sky. **2** sad, depressed; (of a state of affairs) gloomy, dismal (*feel blue; blue times*). **3** indecent, pornographic (*a blue film*). **4** with bluish skin through cold, fear, anger, etc. **5** *Brit.* politically conservative. **6** having blue as a distinguishing colour (*blue jay*). —*n.* **1** a blue colour or pigment. **2** blue clothes or material (*dressed in blue*). **3** *Brit.* **a** a person who has represented a university in a sport, esp. Oxford or Cambridge. **b** this distinction. **4** *Brit.* a supporter of the Conservative party. **5** any of various small blue-coloured butterflies of the family Lycaenidae. **6** blue powder used to whiten laundry. **7** *Austral. sl.* **a** an argument or row. **b** (as a nickname) a red-headed person. **8** a blue ball, piece, etc. in a game or sport. **9** (prec. by *the*) the clear sky. —*v.tr.* (**blues**, **blued**, **bluing** or **blueing**) **1** make blue. **2** treat with laundering blue. □ **blue baby** a baby with a blue complexion from lack of oxygen in the blood due to a congenital defect of the heart or great vessels. **blue bag** a lawyer's brief-bag. **blue blood** noble birth. **blue-blooded** of noble birth. **Blue Book** a report issued by Parliament or the Privy Council. **blue cheese** cheese produced with veins of blue mould, e.g. Stilton and Danish Blue. **blue-chip** (*attrib.*) of shares of reliable investment, though less secure than gilt-edged stock. **blue-collar** (*attrib.*) of manual or unskilled work. **blue dahlia** something rare or impossible. **blue ensign** see ENSIGN. **blue-eyed boy** esp. *Brit. colloq.* usu. *derog.* a favoured person; a favourite. **blue funk** esp. *Brit. colloq.* a state of great terror or panic. **blue-green alga** = CYANOBACTERIUM. **blue ground** = KIMBERLITE. **blue in the face** in a state of extreme anger or exasperation. **blue metal** broken blue stone used for road-making. **blue mould** a bluish fungus growing on food and other organic matter. **blue-pencil** (**-pencilled**, **-pencilling**; *US* **-penciled**, **-penciling**) censor or make cuts in (a manuscript, film, etc.). **Blue Peter** a blue flag with a white square raised on board a ship leaving port. **blue ribbon 1** a high honour. **2** *Brit.* the ribbon of the Order of the Garter. **blue rinse** a preparation for tinting grey hair. **blue roan** see ROAN[1]. **blue rock** = *rock-dove* (see ROCK[1]). **blue stone** (or **vitriol**) copper sulphate crystals. **blue tit** a common tit, *Parus caeruleus*, with a distinct blue crest on a black and white head. **blue water** open sea. **blue whale** a rorqual, *Balaenoptera musculus*, the largest known living mammal. **once in a blue moon** very rarely. **out of the blue** unexpectedly. □□ **blueness** *n.* [ME f. OF *bleu* f. Gmc]

blue[2] /bluː/ *v.tr.* (**blues**, **blued**, **bluing** or **blueing**) *sl.* squander (money). [perh. var. of BLOW[1]]

Bluebeard /'bluːbɪəd/ *n.* **1** a man who murders his wives. **2** a person with a horrible secret. [a character in a fairy-tale told orig. in F (*Barbe-Bleue*) by Perrault]

bluebell /'bluːbel/ *n.* **1** a liliaceous plant, *Hyacinthoides nonscripta*, with clusters of bell-shaped blue flowers on a stem arising from a rhizome. Also called *wild hyacinth*, *wood hyacinth* (see HYACINTH). **2** *Sc.* a plant, *Campanula rotundifolia*, with solitary bell-shaped blue flowers on long stalks. Also called HAREBELL. **3** any of several plants with blue bell-shaped flowers.

blueberry /'bluːbərɪ/ *n.* (*pl.* **-ies**) **1** any of several plants of the genus *Vaccinium*, cultivated for their edible fruit. **2** the small blue-black fruit of these plants.

bluebird /'bluːbɜːd/ *n.* any of various N. American songbirds of the thrush family, esp. of the genus *Sialia*, with distinctive blue plumage usu. on the back or head.

bluebottle /'bluːˌbɒt(ə)l/ *n.* **1** a large buzzing fly, *Calliphora vomitoria*, with a metallic-blue body. Also called BLOWFLY. **2** *Austral.* a Portuguese man-of-war. **3** a dark blue cornflower. **4** *Brit. colloq.* a policeman.

bluefish /'bluːfɪʃ/ *n.* a voracious marine fish, *Pomatomus saltatrix*, inhabiting tropical waters and popular as a game-fish.

bluegrass /'bluːgrɑːs/ *n. US* **1** any of several bluish-green grasses, esp. of Kentucky. **2** a kind of instrumental country-and-western music characterized by virtuosic playing of banjos, guitars, etc.

bluegum /'bluːgʌm/ *n.* any tree of the genus *Eucalyptus*, esp. *E. regnans* with blue-green aromatic leaves.

bluejacket /'bluːˌdʒækɪt/ *n.* a seaman in the Navy.

Bluemantle /'bluːˌmænt(ə)l/ *n.* one of four pursuivants of the English College of Arms.

blueprint /'bluːprɪnt/ *n. & v.* —*n.* **1** a photographic print of the final stage of engineering or other plans in white on a blue background. **2** a detailed plan, esp. in the early stages of a project or idea. —*v.tr. US* work out (a programme, plan, etc.).

blues /bluːz/ *n.pl.* **1** (prec. by *the*) a bout of depression (*had a fit of the blues*). **2 a** (prec. by *the*; often treated as *sing.*) melancholic music of Black American folk origin, often in a twelve-bar sequence (*always singing the blues*). **b** (*pl.* same) (as *sing.*) a piece of such music (*the band played a blues*). □□ **bluesy** *adj.* (in sense 2).

bluestocking /'bluːˌstɒkɪŋ/ *n.* usu. *derog.* an intellectual or literary woman. [from the (less formal) blue stockings worn by one man at a literary society meeting *c*.1750]

bluet /'bluːɪt/ *n. US* a blue-flowered plant of the genus *Houstonia*.

bluey /'bluːɪ/ *n.* (*pl.* **-eys**) *Austral. colloq.* **1** a bundle carried by a bushman. **2** = BLUE *n.* 7b.

bluff[1] /blʌf/ *v. & n.* —*v.* **1** *intr.* make a pretence of strength or confidence to gain an advantage. **2** *tr.*

mislead by bluffing. —*n.* an act of bluffing; a show of confidence or assertiveness intended to deceive. □ **call a person's bluff** challenge a person thought to be bluffing. □□ **bluffer** *n.* [19th c. (orig. in poker) f. Du. *bluffen* brag]

bluff[2] /blʌf/ *adj. & n.* —*adj.* **1** (of a cliff, or a ship's bows) having a vertical or steep broad front. **2** (of a person or manner) blunt, frank, hearty. —*n.* a steep cliff or headland. □□ **bluffly** *adv.* (in sense 2 of *adj.*). **bluffness** *n.* (in sense 2 of *adj.*). [17th-c. Naut. word: orig. unkn.]

bluish /'bluːɪʃ/ *adj.* somewhat blue.

blunder /'blʌndə(r)/ *n. & v.* —*n.* a clumsy or foolish mistake, esp. an important one. —*v.* **1** *intr.* make a blunder; act clumsily or ineptly. **2** *tr.* deal incompetently with; mismanage. **3** *intr.* move about blindly or clumsily; stumble. □□ **blunderer** *n.* **blunderingly** *adv.* [ME prob. f. Scand.: cf. MSw *blundra* shut the eyes]

blunderbuss /'blʌndəˌbʌs/ *n. hist.* a short large-bored gun firing balls or slugs. [alt. of Du. *donderbus* thunder gun, assoc. with BLUNDER]

blunge /blʌndʒ/ *v.tr.* (in ceramics etc.) mix (clay etc.) with water. □□ **blunger** *n.* [after *plunge*, *blend*]

blunt /blʌnt/ *adj. & v.* —*adj.* **1** (of a knife, pencil, etc.) lacking in sharpness; having a worn-down point or edge. **2** (of a person or manner) direct, uncompromising, outspoken. —*v.tr.* make blunt or less sharp. □□ **bluntly** *adv.* (in sense 2 of *adj.*). **bluntness** *n.* [ME perh. f. Scand.: cf. ON *blunda* shut the eyes]

blur /blɜː(r)/ *v. & n.* —*v.* (**blurred**, **blurring**) **1** *tr. & intr.* make or become unclear or less distinct. **2** *tr.* smear; partially efface. **3** *tr.* make (one's memory, perception, etc.) dim or less clear. —*n.* something that appears or sounds indistinct or unclear. □□ **blurry** *adj.* (**blurrier**, **blurriest**). [16th c.: perh. rel. to BLEAR]

blurb /blɜːb/ *n.* a (usu. eulogistic) description of a book, esp. printed on its jacket, as promotion by its publishers. [coined by G. Burgess, Amer. humorist d. 1951]

blurt /blɜːt/ *v.tr.* (usu. foll. by *out*) utter abruptly, thoughtlessly, or tactlessly. [prob. imit.]

blush /blʌʃ/ *v. & n.* —*v.intr.* **1 a** develop a pink tinge in the face from embarrassment or shame. **b** (of the face) redden in this way. **2** feel embarrassed or ashamed. **3** be or become red or pink. —*n.* **1** the act of blushing. **2** a pink tinge. □ **at first blush** on the first glimpse or impression. **spare a person's blushes** refrain from causing embarrassment esp. by praise. [ME f. OE *blyscan*]

blusher /'blʌʃə(r)/ *n.* a cosmetic used to give a warmth of colour to the face.

bluster /'blʌstə(r)/ *v. & n.* —*v.intr.* **1** behave pompously and boisterously; utter empty threats. **2** (of the wind etc.) blow fiercely. —*n.* **1** noisily self-assertive talk. **2** empty threats. □□ **blusterer** *n.* **blustery** *adj.* [16th c.: ult. imit.]

BM *abbr.* **1** British Museum. **2** Bachelor of Medicine.

BMA *abbr.* British Medical Association.

B.Mus. *abbr.* Bachelor of Music.

BMX /ˌbiːemˈeks/ *n.* **1** organized bicycle-racing on a dirt-track, esp. for youngsters. **2** a kind of bicycle used for this. **3** (*attrib.*) of or related to such racing or the equipment used (*BMX gloves*). [abbr. of bicycle *moto-cross*]

Bn. *abbr.* Battalion.

bn. *abbr.* billion.

BO *abbr. colloq.* body odour.

bo[1] /bəʊ/ *int.* = BOO. [imit.]

bo[2] /bəʊ/ *n. US colloq.* (as a form of address) pal; old chap. [19th c.: perh. f. BOY]

boa /'bəʊə/ *n.* **1** any large non-poisonous snake from tropical America esp. of the genus *Boa*, which kills its prey by crushing and suffocating it in its coils. **2** any snake which is similar in appearance, such as Old World pythons. **3** a long thin stole made of feathers or fur. □**boa constrictor** a large snake, *Boa constrictor*, native to tropical America and the West Indies, which crushes its prey. [L]

boar /bɔː(r)/ *n*. **1** (in full **wild boar**) the tusked wild pig, *Sus scrofa*, from which domestic pigs are descended. **2** an uncastrated male pig. **3** its flesh. **4** a male guinea-pig etc. [OE *bār* f. WG]

board /bɔːd/ *n*. & *v*. —*n*. **1 a** a flat thin piece of sawn timber, usu. long and narrow. **b** a piece of material resembling this, made from compressed fibres. **c** a thin slab of wood or a similar substance, often with a covering, used for any of various purposes (*chessboard*; *ironing-board*; *notice-board*). **d** thick stiff card used in bookbinding. **2** the provision of regular meals, usu. with accommodation, for payment. **3** *archaic* a table spread for a meal. **4** the directors of a company; any other specially constituted administrative body, e.g. a committee or group of councillors, examiners, etc. **5** (in *pl*.) the stage of a theatre (cf. *tread the boards*). **6** *Naut*. the side of a ship. —*v*. **1** *tr*. **a** go on board (a ship, train, aircraft, etc.). **b** force one's way on board (a ship etc.) in attack. **2 a** *intr*. receive regular meals, or (esp. of a schoolchild) meals and lodging, for payment. **b** *tr*. (often foll. by *out*) arrange accommodation away from home for (esp. a child). **c** *tr*. provide (a lodger etc.) with regular meals. **3** *tr*. (usu. foll. by *up*) cover with boards; seal or close. □**board-game** a game played on a board. **board of trade** *US* a chamber of commerce. **go by the board** be neglected, omitted, or discarded. **on board** on or on to a ship, aircraft, oil rig, etc. **take on board** consider (a new idea etc.). [OE *bord* f. Gmc]

boarder /ˈbɔːdə(r)/ *n*. **1** a person who boards (see BOARD *v*. 2a), esp. a pupil at a boarding-school. **2** a person who boards a ship, esp. an enemy.

boarding-house /ˈbɔːdɪŋhaʊs/ *n*. an unlicensed establishment providing board and lodging, esp. to holiday-makers.

boarding-school /ˈbɔːdɪŋskuːl/ *n*. a school where pupils are resident in term-time.

boardroom /ˈbɔːdruːm, -rʊm/ *n*. a room in which a board of directors etc. meets regularly.

boardsailing /ˈbɔːdˌseɪlɪŋ/ *n*. = WINDSURFING. □□ **boardsailor** *n*. (also **boardsailer**).

boardwalk /ˈbɔːdwɔːk/ *n*. *US* **1** a wooden walkway across sand, marsh, etc. **2** a promenade along a beach.

boart var. of BORT.

boast /bəʊst/ *v*. & *n*. —*v*. **1** *intr*. declare one's achievements, possessions, or abilities with indulgent pride and satisfaction. **2** *tr*. own or have as something praiseworthy etc. (*the hotel boasts magnificent views*). —*n*. **1** an act of boasting. **2** something one is proud of. □□ **boaster** *n*. **boastingly** *adv*. [ME f. AF *bost*, of unkn. orig.]

boastful /ˈbəʊstfʊl/ *adj*. **1** given to boasting. **2** characterized by boasting (*boastful talk*). □□ **boastfully** *adv*. **boastfulness** *n*.

boat /bəʊt/ *n*. & *v*. —*n*. **1** a small vessel propelled on water by an engine, oars, or sails. **2** (in general use) a ship of any size. **3** an elongated boat-shaped jug used for holding sauce etc. —*v*.*intr*. travel or go in a boat, esp. for pleasure. □**boat-hook** a long pole with a hook and a spike at one end, for moving boats. **boat-house** a shed at the edge of a river, lake, etc., for housing boats. **boat people** refugees who have left a country by sea. **boat race** a race between rowing crews, esp. (**Boat Race**) the one between Oxford and Cambridge. **boat-train** a train scheduled to meet or go on a boat. **in the same boat** sharing the same adverse circumstances. **push the boat out** *colloq*. celebrate lavishly. □□ **boatful** *n*. (*pl*. -**fuls**). [OE *bāt* f. Gmc]

boatel var. of BOTEL.

boater /ˈbəʊtə(r)/ *n*. a flat-topped hardened straw hat with a brim.

boating /ˈbəʊtɪŋ/ *n*. rowing or sailing in boats as a sport or form of recreation.

boatload /ˈbəʊtləʊd/ *n*. **1** enough to fill a boat. **2** *colloq*. a large number of people.

boatman /ˈbəʊtmən/ *n*. (*pl*. -**men**) a person who hires out boats or provides transport by boat.

boatswain /ˈbəʊs(ə)n/ *n*. (also **bo'sun**, **bosun**, **bo's'n**) a ship's officer in charge of equipment and the crew. □**boatswain's chair** a seat suspended from ropes for work on the side of a ship or building. [OE *bātswegen* (as BOAT, SWAIN)]

bob[1] /bɒb/ *v*. & *n*. —*v*.*intr*. (**bobbed**, **bobbing**) **1** move quickly up and down; dance. **2** (usu. foll. by *back*, *up*) **a** bounce buoyantly. **b** emerge suddenly; become active or conspicuous again after a defeat etc. **3** curtsy. **4** (foll. by *for*) try to catch with the mouth alone (fruit etc. floating or hanging). —*n*. **1** a jerking or bouncing movement, esp. upward. **2** a curtsy. **3** one of several kinds of change in long peals in bell-ringing. [14th c.: prob. imit.]

bob[2] /bɒb/ *n*. & *v*. —*n*. **1** a short hairstyle for women and children. **2** a weight on a pendulum, plumb-line, or kite-tail. **3** = BOB-SLEIGH. **4** a horse's docked tail. **5** a short line at or towards the end of a stanza. **6** a knot of hair; a tassel-shaped curl. —*v*. (**bobbed**, **bobbing**) **1** *tr*. cut (a woman's or child's hair) so that it hangs clear of the shoulders. **2** *intr*. ride on a bob-sleigh. [ME: orig. unkn.]

bob[3] /bɒb/ *n*. (*pl*. same) *Brit*. *sl*. a former shilling (now = 5 decimal pence). [19th c.: orig. unkn.]

bob[4] /bɒb/ *n*. □**bob's your uncle** *Brit*. *sl*. an expression of completion or satisfaction. [pet-form of the name *Robert*]

bobbin /ˈbɒbɪn/ *n*. **1 a** a cylinder or cone holding thread, yarn, wire, etc., used esp. in weaving and machine sewing. **b** a spool or reel. **2** a small bar and string for raising a door-latch. □**bobbin-lace** lace made by hand with thread wound on bobbins. [F *bobine*]

bobbinet /ˈbɒbɪˌnet/ *n*. machine-made cotton net (imitating lace made with bobbins on a pillow). [BOBBIN + NET[1]]

bobble /ˈbɒb(ə)l/ *n*. a small woolly or tufted ball as a decoration or trimming. [dimin. of BOB[2]]

bobby[1] /ˈbɒbɪ/ *n*. (*pl*. -**ies**) *Brit*. *colloq*. a policeman. [Sir *Robert* Peel, Engl. statesman d. 1850, founder of the metropolitan police force]

bobby[2] /ˈbɒbɪ/ *n*. (*pl*. -**ies**) (in full **bobby calf**) *Austral*. & *NZ* an unweaned calf slaughtered for veal. [Eng. dial.]

bobby-dazzler /ˈbɒbɪˌdæzlə(r)/ *n*. *colloq*. a remarkable or excellent person or thing. [dial., rel. to DAZZLE]

bobby-pin /ˈbɒbɪpɪn/ *n*. *US*, *Austral*., & *NZ* a flat hairpin. [BOB[2] + -Y[2]]

bobby socks /ˈbɒbɪ ˌsɒks/ *n.pl*. esp. *US* short socks reaching just above the ankle.

bobcat /ˈbɒbkæt/ *n*. a small N. American lynx, *Felix rufus*, with a spotted reddish-brown coat and a short tail. [BOB[2] + CAT]

bobolink /ˈbɒbəlɪŋk/ *n*. a N. American oriole, *Dolichonyx oryzivorus*. [orig. *Bob* (o') *Lincoln*: imit. of its call]

bob-sled /ˈbɒbsled/ *n*. *US* = BOB-SLEIGH.

bob-sleigh /ˈbɒbsleɪ/ *n*. & *v*. —*n*. a mechanically-steered and -braked sledge used for racing down a steep ice-covered run. —*v*.*intr*. race in a bob-sleigh. [BOB[2] + SLEIGH]

bobstay /ˈbɒbsteɪ/ *n*. the chain or rope holding down a ship's bowsprit. [prob. BOB[1] + STAY[2]]

bobtail /ˈbɒbteɪl/ *n*. a docked tail; a horse or a dog with a bobtail. [BOB[2] + TAIL[1]]

bocage /bəˈkɑːʒ/ *n*. the representation of silvan scenery in ceramics. [F f. OF *boscage*: see BOSCAGE]

Boche /bɒʃ/ *n*. & *adj*. *sl*. *derog*. —*n*. **1** a German, esp. a soldier. **2** (prec. by *the*) Germans, esp. German soldiers, collectively. —*adj*. German. [F *sl*., orig. = rascal: applied to Germans in the war of 1914–18]

æ cat ɑː arm e bed ɜː her ɪ sit iː see ɒ hot ɔː saw ʌ run ʊ put uː too ə ago aɪ my

bock /bɒk/ n. a strong dark German beer. [F f. G abbr. of *Eimbockbier* f. *Einbeck* in Hanover]

BOD abbr. biochemical oxygen demand.

bod /bɒd/ n. *Brit. colloq.* a person. [abbr. of BODY]

bode /bəʊd/ v. 1 tr. portend, foreshow. 2 tr. foresee, foretell (evil). □ **bode well** (or **ill**) show good (or bad) signs for the future. □□ **boding** n. [OE *bodian* f. *boda* messenger]

bodega /bəʊˈdiːgə/ n. a cellar or shop selling wine and food, esp. in a Spanish-speaking country. [Sp. f. L *apotheca* f. Gk *apothēkē* storehouse]

bodge var. of BOTCH.

Bodhisattva /ˌbəʊdɪˈsætvə/ n. in Mahayana Buddhism, one who is able to reach nirvana but delays doing so through compassion for suffering beings. [Skr., = one whose essence is perfect knowledge]

bodice /ˈbɒdɪs/ n. 1 the part of a woman's dress (excluding sleeves) which is above the waist. 2 a woman's undergarment, like a vest, for the same part of the body. [orig. *pair of bodies* = stays, corsets]

bodiless /ˈbɒdɪlɪs/ adj. 1 lacking a body. 2 incorporeal, insubstantial.

bodily /ˈbɒdɪlɪ/ adj. & adv. —adj. of or concerning the body. —adv. 1 with the whole bulk; as a whole (*threw them bodily*). 2 in the body; as a person.

bodkin /ˈbɒdkɪn/ n. 1 a blunt thick needle with a large eye used esp. for drawing tape etc. through a hem. 2 a long pin for fastening hair. 3 a small pointed instrument for piercing cloth, removing a piece of type for correction, etc. [ME perh. f. Celt.]

body /ˈbɒdɪ/ n. & v. —n. (pl. **-ies**) 1 the physical structure, including the bones, flesh, and organs, of a person or an animal, whether dead or alive. 2 the trunk apart from the head and the limbs. 3 a the main or central part of a thing (*body of the car*; *body of the attack*). b the bulk or majority; the aggregate (*body of opinion*). 4 a a group of persons regarded collectively, esp. as having a corporate function (*governing body*). b (usu. foll. by *of*) a collection (*body of facts*). 5 a quantity (*body of water*). 6 a piece of matter (*heavenly body*). 7 *colloq.* a person. 8 a full or substantial quality of flavour, tone, etc., e.g. in wine, musical sounds, etc. —v.tr. (**-ies, -ied**) (usu. foll. by *forth*) give body or substance to. □ **body-blow** a severe setback. **body-building** the practice of strengthening the body, esp. shaping and enlarging the muscles, by exercise. **body-colour** an opaque pigment. **body language** the process of communicating through conscious or unconscious gestures and poses. **body-line bowling** *Cricket* persistent fast bowling on the leg side threatening the batsman's body. **body odour** the smell of the human body, esp. when unpleasant. **body politic** the nation or State as a corporate body. **body scanner** a scanning X-ray machine for taking tomograms of the whole body. **body shop** a workshop where repairs to the bodywork of vehicles are carried out. **body stocking** a woman's undergarment, usually made of knitted nylon, which covers the torso. **body warmer** a sleeveless quilted or padded jacket worn as an outdoor garment. **in a body** all together. **keep body and soul together** keep alive, esp. barely. **over my dead body** *colloq.* entirely without my assent. □□ **-bodied** adj. (in *comb.*) (*able-bodied*). [OE *bodig*, of unkn. orig.]

body-check /ˈbɒdɪˌtʃek/ n. & v. *Sport* —n. a deliberate obstruction of one player by another. —v.tr. obstruct in this way.

bodyguard /ˈbɒdɪˌgɑːd/ n. a person or group of persons escorting and protecting another person (esp. a dignitary).

bodywork /ˈbɒdɪˌwɜːk/ n. the outer shell of a vehicle.

Boer /ˈbəʊə(r), bʊə(r)/ n. & adj. —n. a South African of Dutch descent. —adj. of or relating to the Boers. [Du.: see BOOR]

boffin /ˈbɒfɪn/ n. esp. *Brit. colloq.* a person engaged in scientific (esp. military) research. [20th c.: orig. unkn.]

Bofors gun /ˈbəʊfəz/ n. a type of light anti-aircraft gun. [*Bofors* in Sweden]

bog /bɒg/ n. & v. —n. 1 a wet spongy ground. b a stretch of such ground. 2 *Brit. sl.* a lavatory. —v.tr. (**bogged, bogging**) (foll. by *down*; usu. in *passive*) impede (*was bogged down by difficulties*). □ **bog-bean** = BUCKBEAN. **bog myrtle** a deciduous shrub, *Myrica gale*, which grows in damp open places and has short upright catkins and aromatic grey-green leaves: also called *sweet-gale* (see GALE²). **bog oak** an ancient oak which has been preserved in a black state in peat. **bog spavin** see SPAVIN. **bog-trotter** *sl. derog.* an Irishman. □□ **boggy** adj. (**boggier, boggiest**). **bogginess** n. [Ir. or Gael. *bogach* f. *bog* soft]

bogey¹ /ˈbəʊgɪ/ n. & v. *Golf* —n. (pl. **-eys**) 1 a score of one stroke more than par at any hole. 2 (formerly) a score that a good player should do a hole or course in; par. —v.tr. (**-eys, -eyed**) play (a hole) in one stroke more than par. [perh. f. *Bogey* as an imaginary player]

bogey² /ˈbəʊgɪ/ n. (also **bogy**) (pl. **-eys** or **-ies**) 1 an evil or mischievous spirit; a devil. 2 an awkward thing or circumstance. 3 *sl.* a piece of dried nasal mucus. [19th c., orig. as a proper name: cf. BOGLE]

bogeyman /ˈbəʊgɪˌmæn/ n. (also **bogyman**) (pl. **-men**) a person (real or imaginary) causing fear or difficulty.

boggle /ˈbɒg(ə)l/ v.intr. *colloq.* 1 be startled or baffled (esp. *the mind boggles*). 2 (usu. foll. by *about*, *at*) hesitate, demur. [prob. f. dial. *boggle* BOGEY²]

bogie /ˈbəʊgɪ/ n. esp. *Brit.* 1 a wheeled undercarriage pivoted below the end of a rail vehicle. 2 a small truck used for carrying coal, rubble, etc. [19th-c. north. dial. word: orig. unkn.]

bogle /ˈbəʊg(ə)l/ n. 1 = BOGEY². 2 a phantom. 3 a scarecrow. [orig. Sc. (16th c.), prob. rel. to BOGEY]

bogus /ˈbəʊgəs/ adj. sham, fictitious, spurious. □□ **bogusly** adv. **bogusness** n. [19th-c. US word: orig. unkn.]

bogy var. of BOGEY².

bogyman var. of BOGEYMAN.

bohea /bəʊˈhiː/ n. a black China tea, the last crop of the season and usu. regarded as of low quality. [*Bu-i* (Wuyi) Hills in China]

Bohemian /bəʊˈhiːmɪən/ n. & adj. —n. 1 a native of Bohemia, a former kingdom in central Europe corresponding to part of modern Czechoslovakia; Czech. 2 (also **bohemian**) a socially unconventional person, esp. an artist or writer. —adj. 1 of, relating to, or characteristic of Bohemia or its people. 2 socially unconventional. □□ **bohemianism** n. (in sense 2). [*Bohemia* + -AN: sense 2 f. F *bohémien* gypsy]

boil¹ /bɔɪl/ v. & n. —v. 1 intr. a (of a liquid) start to bubble up and turn into vapour; reach a temperature at which this happens. b (of a vessel) contain boiling liquid (*the kettle is boiling*). 2 a tr. bring (a liquid or vessel) to a temperature at which it boils. b tr. cook (food) by boiling. c intr. (of food) be cooked by boiling. d tr. subject to the heat of boiling water, e.g. to clean. 3 intr. a (of the sea etc.) undulate or seethe like boiling water. b (of a person or feelings) be greatly agitated, esp. by anger. —n. the act or process of boiling; boiling-point (*on the boil*; *bring to the boil*). □ **boil down** 1 reduce volume by boiling. 2 reduce to essentials. 3 (foll. by *to*) amount to; signify basically. **boiled shirt** a dress shirt with a starched front. **boiled sweet** *Brit.* a sweet made of boiled sugar. **boil over** 1 spill over in boiling. 2 lose one's temper; become over-excited. **make one's blood boil** see BLOOD. [ME f. AF *boiller*, OF *boillir*, f. L *bullire* to bubble f. *bulla* bubble]

boil² /bɔɪl/ n. an inflamed pus-filled swelling caused by infection of a hair follicle etc. [OE *bȳl(e)* f. WG]

boiler /ˈbɔɪlə(r)/ n. 1 a fuel-burning apparatus for heating a hot-water supply. 2 a tank for heating water, esp. for turning it to steam under pressure. 3 a metal tub for boiling laundry etc. 4 a fowl, vegetable, etc., suitable for cooking only by boiling. □**boiler-room** a room with a boiler and other heating equipment, esp. in the basement of a large building. **boiler suit** a one-piece suit worn as overalls for heavy manual work.

boiling /ˈbɔɪlɪŋ/ *adj.* (also **boiling hot**) *colloq.* very hot.

boiling-point /ˈbɔɪlɪŋ/ *n.* **1** the temperature at which a liquid starts to boil. **2** high excitement (*feelings reached boiling-point*).

boisterous /ˈbɔɪstərəs/ *adj.* **1** (of a person) rough; noisily exuberant. **2** (of the sea, weather, etc.) stormy, rough. □□ **boisterously** *adv.* **boisterousness** *n.* [var. of ME *boist(u)ous*, of unkn. orig.]

bolas /ˈbəʊləs/ *n.* (as *sing.* or *pl.*) (esp. in S. America) a missile consisting of a number of balls connected by strong cord, which when thrown entangles the limbs of the quarry. [Sp. & Port., pl. of *bola* ball]

bold /bəʊld/ *adj.* **1** confidently assertive; adventurous, courageous. **2** forthright, impudent. **3** vivid, distinct, well-marked (*bold colours; a bold imagination*). **4** *Printing* (in full **bold-face** or **-faced**) printed in a thick black typeface. □**as bold as brass** excessively bold or self-assured. **make** (or **be**) **so bold as to** presume to; venture to. □□ **boldly** *adv.* **boldness** *n.* [OE *bald* dangerous f. Gmc]

bole[1] /bəʊl/ *n.* the stem or trunk of a tree. [ME f. ON *bolr*, perh. rel. to BALK[1]]

bole[2] /bəʊl/ *n.* fine compact earthy clay. [LL BOLUS]

bolero /bəˈleərəʊ/ *n.* (*pl.* **-os**) **1 a** a Spanish dance in simple triple time. **b** music for or in the time of a bolero. **2** /also ˈbɒlərəʊ/ a woman's short open jacket. [Sp.]

boll /bəʊl/ *n.* a rounded capsule containing seeds, esp. flax or cotton. □**boll-weevil** a small American or Mexican weevil, *Anthonomus grandis*, whose larvae destroy cotton bolls. [ME f. MDu. *bolle*: see BOWL[1]]

bollard /ˈbɒlɑːd/ *n.* **1** *Brit.* a short metal, concrete, or plastic post in the road, esp. as part of a traffic island. **2** a short post on a quay or ship for securing a rope. [ME perh. f. ON *bolr* BOLE[1] + -ARD]

bollocking /ˈbɒləkɪŋ/ *n.* *coarse sl.* a severe reprimand.

bollocks /ˈbɒləks/ *n.* (also **ballocks**) *coarse sl.* ¶ Usually considered a taboo word. **1** the testicles. **2** (usu. as an exclam. of contempt) nonsense, rubbish. [OE *bealluc*, rel. to BALL[1]]

bologna /bəˈləʊnjə/ *n.* *US* = BOLOGNA SAUSAGE.

Bologna sausage /bəˈləʊnjə/ *n.* *US* a large smoked sausage made of bacon, veal, pork-suet, and other meats, and sold ready for eating. [*Bologna* in Italy]

bolometer /bəˈlɒmɪtə(r)/ *n.* a sensitive electrical instrument for measuring radiant energy. □□ **bolometry** *n.* **bolometric** /ˌbəʊləˈmetrɪk/ *adj.* [Gk *bolē* ray + -METER]

boloney /bəˈləʊnɪ/ *n.* (also **baloney**) (*pl.* **-eys**) *sl.* **1** humbug, nonsense. **2** = BOLOGNA SAUSAGE. [20th c.: orig. uncert.]

Bolshevik /ˈbɒlʃəvɪk/ *n.* & *adj.* —*n.* **1** *hist.* a member of the radical faction of the Russian socialist party, which became the communist party in 1918. **2** a Russian communist. **3** (in general use) any revolutionary socialist. —*adj.* **1** of, relating to, or characteristic of the Bolsheviks. **2** communist. □□ **Bolshevism** *n.* **Bolshevist** *n.* [Russ., = a member of the majority, one who (in 1903) favoured extreme measures, f. *bol'she* greater]

Bolshie /ˈbɒlʃɪ/ *adj.* & *n.* (also **Bolshy**) *sl.* —*adj.* (usu. **bolshie**) **1** uncooperative, rebellious, awkward; bad-tempered. **2** left-wing, socialist. —*n.* (*pl.* **-ies**) a Bolshevik. □□ **bolshiness** *n.* (in sense 1 of *adj.*). [abbr.]

bolster[1] /ˈbəʊlstə(r)/ *n.* & *v.* —*n.* **1** a long thick pillow. **2** a pad or support, esp. in a machine. **3** *Building* a short timber cap over a post to increase the bearing of the beams it supports. —*v.tr.* (usu. foll. by *up*) **1** encourage, reinforce (*bolstered our*

morale). **2** support with a bolster; prop up. □□ **bolsterer** *n.* [OE f. Gmc]

bolster[2] /ˈbəʊlstə(r)/ *n.* a chisel for cutting bricks. [20th c.: orig. uncert.]

bolt[1] /bəʊlt/ *n., v.,* & *adv.* —*n.* **1** a sliding bar and socket used to fasten or lock a door, gate, etc. **2** a large usu. metal pin with a head, usu. riveted or used with a nut, to hold things together. **3** a discharge of lightning. **4** an act of bolting (cf. sense 4 of *v.*); a sudden escape or dash for freedom. **5** *hist.* an arrow for shooting from a crossbow. **6** a roll of fabric (orig. as a measure). —*v.* **1** *tr.* fasten or lock with a bolt. **2** *tr.* (foll. by *in, out*) keep (a person etc.) from leaving or entering by bolting a door. **3** *tr.* fasten together with bolts. **4** *intr.* **a** dash suddenly away, esp. to escape. **b** (of a horse) suddenly gallop out of control. **5** *tr.* gulp down (food) unchewed; eat hurriedly. **6** *intr.* (of a plant) run to seed. —*adv.* (usu. in **bolt upright**) rigidly, stiffly. □**a bolt from the blue** a complete surprise. **bolt-hole 1** a means of escape. **2** a secret refuge. **shoot one's bolt** do all that is in one's power. □□ **bolter** *n.* (in sense 4 of *v.*). [OE *bolt* arrow]

bolt[2] /bəʊlt/ *v.tr.* (also **boult**) sift (flour etc.). □□ **bolter** *n.* [ME f. OF *bulter, buleter,* of unkn. orig.]

bolus /ˈbəʊləs/ *n.* (*pl.* **boluses**) **1** a soft ball, esp. of chewed food. **2** a large pill. [LL f. Gk *bōlos* clod]

bomb /bɒm/ *n.* & *v.* —*n.* **1 a** a container with explosive, incendiary material, smoke, or gas etc., designed to explode on impact or by means of a time-mechanism or remote-control device. **b** an ordinary object fitted with an explosive device (*letter-bomb*). **2** (prec. by *the*) the atomic or hydrogen bomb considered as a weapon with supreme destructive power. **3** *Brit. sl.* a large sum of money (*cost a bomb*). **4** a mass of solidified lava thrown from a volcano. **5** *US colloq.* bad failure (esp. a theatrical one). **6** *sl.* a drugged cigarette. **7** *Med.* = *radium bomb.* —*v.* **1** *tr.* attack with bombs; drop bombs on. **2** *tr.* (foll. by *out*) drive (a person etc.) out of a building or refuge by using bombs. **3** *intr.* throw or drop bombs. **4** *intr.* esp. *US sl.* fail badly. **5** *intr. colloq.* (usu. foll. by *along, off*) move or go very quickly. **6** *tr. US sl.* criticize fiercely. □**bomb-bay** a compartment in an aircraft used to hold bombs. **bomb-disposal** the defusing or removal and detonation of an unexploded bomb. **bomb-sight** a device in an aircraft for aiming bombs. **bomb-site** an area where buildings have been destroyed by bombs. **go down a bomb** *colloq.*, often *iron.* be very well received. **like a bomb** *Brit. colloq.* **1** often *iron.* very successfully. **2** very fast. [F *bombe* f. It. *bomba* f. L *bombus* f. Gk *bombos* hum]

bombard /bɒmˈbɑːd/ *v.tr.* **1** attack with a number of heavy guns or bombs. **2** (often foll. by *with*) subject to persistent questioning, abuse, etc. **3** *Physics* direct a stream of high-speed particles at (a substance). □□ **bombardment** *n.* [F *bombarder* f. *bombarde* f. med.L *bombarda* a stone-throwing engine: see BOMB]

bombardier /ˌbɒmbəˈdɪə(r)/ *n.* **1** *Brit.* a non-commissioned officer in the artillery. **2** *US* a member of a bomber crew responsible for sighting and releasing bombs. [F (as BOMBARD)]

bombardon /bɒmˈbɑːd(ə)n, ˈbɒmbəd(ə)n/ *n. Mus.* **1** a type of valved bass tuba. **2** an organ stop imitating this. [It. *bombardone* f. *bombardo* bassoon]

bombasine var. of BOMBAZINE.

bombast /ˈbɒmbæst/ *n.* pompous or extravagant language. □□ **bombastic** /-ˈbæstɪk/ *adj.* **bombastically** /-ˈbæstɪkəlɪ/ *adv.* [earlier *bombace* cotton wool f. F f. med.L *bombax -acis* alt. f. *bombyx*; see BOMBAZINE]

Bombay duck /bɒmˈbeɪ dʌk/ *n.* a dried fish, esp. bummalo, usu. eaten with curried dishes. [corrupt. of *bombil*: see BUMMALO]

bombazine /ˈbɒmbəˌziːn, -ˈziːn/ (also **bombasine**) *n.* a twilled dress-material of worsted with or without an admixture of silk or cotton, esp., when black, formerly used for mourning. [F *bombasin* f. med.L *bombacinum* f. LL *bombycinus* silken f. *bombyx -ycis* silk or silkworm f. Gk *bombux*]

bombe /bɔ̃b/ *n. Cookery* a dome-shaped dish or confection, freq. frozen. [F, = BOMB]

bomber /ˈbɒmə(r)/ *n.* **1** an aircraft equipped to carry and drop bombs. **2** a person using bombs, esp. illegally. □**bomber jacket** a short leather or cloth jacket tightly gathered at the waist and cuffs.

bombora /bɒmˈbɔːrə/ *n. Austral.* a dangerous sea area where waves break over a submerged reef. [Aboriginal]

bombproof /ˈbɒmpruːf/ *adj.* strong enough to resist the effects of blast from a bomb.

bombshell /ˈbɒmʃel/ *n.* **1** an overwhelming surprise or disappointment. **2** an artillery bomb. **3** *sl.* a very attractive woman (*blonde bombshell*).

bona fide /ˌbəʊnə ˈfaɪdɪ/ *adj. & adv.* —*adj.* genuine; sincere. —*adv.* genuinely; sincerely. [L, ablat. sing. of BONA FIDES]

bona fides /ˌbəʊnə ˈfaɪdiːz/ *n.* **1** esp. *Law* an honest intention; sincerity. **2** (as *pl.*) *colloq.* documentary evidence of acceptability (*his bona fides are in order*). [L, = good faith]

bonanza /bəˈnænzə/ *n. & adj.* —*n.* **1** a source of wealth or prosperity. **2** a large output (esp. of a mine). **3 a** prosperity; good luck. **b** a run of good luck. —*adj.* greatly prospering or productive. [orig. US f. Sp., = fair weather, f. L *bonus* good]

bona vacantia /ˌbəʊnə vəˈkæntɪə/ *n. Law* goods without an apparent owner. [L, = ownerless goods]

bon-bon /ˈbɒnbɒn/ *n.* a piece of confectionery; a sweet. [F f. *bon* good f. L *bonus*]

bonce /bɒns/ *n. Brit.* **1** *sl.* the head. **2** a large playing-marble. [19th c.: orig. unkn.]

bond /bɒnd/ *n. & v.* —*n.* **1 a** a thing that ties another down or together. **b** (usu. in *pl.*) a thing restraining bodily freedom (*broke his bonds*). **2** (often in *pl.*) **a** a uniting force (*sisterly bond*). **b** a restraint; a responsibility (*bonds of duty*). **3** a binding engagement; an agreement (*his word is his bond*). **4** *Commerce* a certificate issued by a government or a public company promising to repay borrowed money at a fixed rate of interest at a specified time; a debenture. **5** adhesiveness. **6** *Law* a deed by which a person is bound to make payment to another. **7** *Chem.* linkage between atoms in a molecule or a solid. **8** *Building* the laying of bricks in one of various patterns in a wall in order to ensure strength (*English bond*; *Flemish bond*). —*v.* **1** *tr.* **a** lay (bricks) overlapping. **b** bind together (resin with fibres, etc.). **2** *intr.* adhere; hold together. **3** *tr.* connect with a bond. **4** *tr.* place (goods) in bond. **5** *intr.* become emotionally attached. □**bond paper** high-quality writing-paper. **bond-washing** dividend-stripping. **in bond** (of goods) stored in a bonded warehouse until the importer pays the duty owing (see BONDED). [ME var. of BAND[1]]

bondage /ˈbɒndɪdʒ/ *n.* **1** serfdom; slavery. **2** subjection to constraint, influence, obligation, etc. **3** sado-masochistic practices, including the use of physical restraints or mental enslavement. [ME f. AL *bondagium*: infl. by BOND]

bonded /ˈbɒndɪd/ *adj.* **1** (of goods) placed in bond. **2** (of material) reinforced by or cemented to another. **3** (of a debt) secured by bonds. □**bonded warehouse** a Customs-controlled warehouse for the retention of imported goods until the duty owed is paid.

bondsman /ˈbɒndzmən/ *n.* (*pl.* **-men**) **1** a slave. **2** a person in thrall to another. [var. of *bondman* (f. archaic *bond* in serfdom or slavery) as though f. *bond*'s genitive of BOND[1]]

bone /bəʊn/ *n. & v.* —*n.* **1** any of the pieces of hard tissue making up the skeleton in vertebrates. **2** (in *pl.*) **a** the skeleton, esp. as remains after death. **b** the body, esp. as a seat of intuitive feeling (*felt it in my bones*). **3 a** the material of which bones consist. **b** a similar substance such as ivory, dentine, or whalebone. **4** a thing made of bone. **5** (in *pl.*) the essential

part of a thing (*the bare bones*). **6** (in *pl.*) **a** dice. **b** castanets. **7** a strip of stiffening in a corset etc. —*v.* **1** *tr.* take out the bones from (meat or fish). **2** *tr.* stiffen (a garment) with bone etc. **3** *tr. Brit. sl.* steal. □**bone china** fine china made of clay mixed with the ash from bones. **bone-dry** quite dry. **bone idle** (or **lazy**) utterly idle or lazy. **bone-meal** crushed or ground bones used esp. as a fertilizer. **bone of contention** a source or ground of dispute. **bone-setter** a person who sets broken or dislocated bones, esp. without being a qualified surgeon. **bone spavin** see SPAVIN. **bone up** (often foll. by *on*) *colloq.* study (a subject) intensively. **close to** (or **near**) **the bone 1** tactless to the point of offensiveness. **2** destitute; hard up. **have a bone to pick** (usu. foll. by *with*) have a cause for dispute (with another person). **make no bones about 1** admit or allow without fuss. **2** not hesitate or scruple. **point the bone** (usu. foll. by *at*) *Austral.* **1** wish bad luck on. **2** cast a spell on in order to kill. **to the bone 1** to the bare minimum. **2** penetratingly. **work one's fingers to the bone** work very hard, esp. thanklessly. □□ **boneless** *adj.* [OE *bān* f. Gmc]

bonefish /ˈbəʊnfɪʃ/ *n. US* any of several species of large game-fish, esp. *Albula vulpes*, having many small bones.

bonehead /ˈbəʊnhed/ *n. sl.* a stupid person. □□ **boneheaded** *adj.*

boner /ˈbəʊnə(r)/ *n. sl.* a stupid mistake. [BONE + -ER[1]]

boneshaker /ˈbəʊnˌʃeɪkə(r)/ *n.* **1** a decrepit or uncomfortable old vehicle. **2** an old type of bicycle with solid tyres.

bonfire /ˈbɒnˌfaɪə(r)/ *n.* a large open-air fire for burning rubbish, as part of a celebration, or as a signal. □**Bonfire Night** *Brit.* 5 Nov., on which fireworks are displayed and an effigy of Guy Fawkes burnt (see GUY[1]). **make a bonfire of** destroy by burning. [earlier *bonefire* f. BONE (bones being the chief material formerly used) + FIRE]

bongo[1] /ˈbɒŋgəʊ/ *n.* (*pl.* **-os** or **-oes**) either of a pair of small long-bodied drums usu. held between the knees and played with the fingers. [Amer. Sp. *bongó*]

bongo[2] /ˈbɒŋgəʊ/ *n.* (*pl.* same or **-os**) a rare antelope, *Tragelaphus euryceros*, native to the forests of central Africa, having spiralled horns and a chestnut-red coat with narrow white vertical stripes. [cf. Bangi *mbangani*, Lingala *mongu*]

bonhomie /ˌbɒnɒˈmiː/ *n.* geniality; good-natured friendliness. [F f. *bonhomme* good fellow]

bonhomous /ˈbɒnəməs/ *adj.* full of *bonhomie.*

bonito /bəˈniːtəʊ/ *n.* (*pl.* **-os**) any of several tunny-like fish which are striped like mackerel and are common in tropical seas. [Sp.]

bonk /bɒŋk/ *v. & n.* —*v.* **1** *tr.* hit resoundingly. **2** *intr.* bang; bump. **3** *coarse sl.* **a** *intr.* have sexual intercourse. **b** *tr.* have sexual intercourse with. —*n.* an instance of bonking (*a bonk on the head*). □□ **bonker** *n.* [imit.: cf. BANG, BUMP[1], CONK[2]]

bonkers /ˈbɒŋkəz/ *adj. sl.* crazy. [20th c.: orig. unkn.]

bon mot /bɔ̃ ˈməʊ, bɒn-/ *n.* (*pl.* **bons mots** pronunc. same or /-məʊz/) a witty saying. [F]

bonne bouche /bɒn ˈbuːʃ/ *n.* (*pl.* **bonne bouches** or **bonnes bouches** pronunc. same) a titbit, esp. to end a meal with. [F f. *bonne* fem. good + *bouche* mouth]

bonnet /ˈbɒnɪt/ *n.* **1 a** a woman's or child's hat tied under the chin and usu. with a brim framing the face. **b** a soft round brimless hat like a beret worn by men and boys in Scotland (cf. TAM-O'-SHANTER). **c** *colloq.* any hat. **2** *Brit.* a hinged cover over the engine of a motor vehicle. **3** the ceremonial feathered head-dress of an American Indian. **4** the cowl of a chimney etc. **5** a protective cap in various machines. **6** *Naut.* additional canvas laced to the foot of a sail. □**bonnet monkey** an Indian macaque, *Macaca radiata*, with a bonnet-like tuft of hair. □□ **bonneted** *adj.* [ME f. OF *bonet* short for *chapel de bonet* cap of some kind of material (med.L *bonetus*)]

bonnethead /ˈbɒnɪtˌhed/ n. = SHOVELHEAD.

bonny /ˈbɒnɪ/ adj. (**bonnier**, **bonniest**) esp. Sc. & N.Engl. **1 a** physically attractive. **b** healthy-looking. **2** good, fine, pleasant. □□ **bonnily** adv. **bonniness** n. [16th c.: perh. f. F bon good]

bonsai /ˈbɒnsaɪ/ n. (pl. same) **1** the art of cultivating ornamental artificially dwarfed varieties of trees and shrubs. **2** a tree or shrub grown by this method. [Jap.]

bonspiel /ˈbɒnspiːl/ n. esp. Sc. a curling-match (usu. between two clubs). [16th c.: perh. f. LG]

bontebok /ˈbɒntɪˌbʌk/ n. (also **bontbok** /ˈbɒntbʌk/) (pl. same or **-boks**) a large chestnut antelope, Damaliscus dorcas, native to southern Africa, having a white tail and a white patch on its head and rump. [Afrik. f. bont spotted + bok BUCK[1]]

bonus /ˈbəʊnəs/ n. **1** an unsought or unexpected extra benefit. **2 a** a usu. seasonal gratuity to employees beyond their normal pay. **b** an extra dividend or issue paid to the shareholders of a company. **c** a distribution of profits to holders of an insurance policy. [L bonus, bonum good (thing)]

bon vivant /ˌbɒ̃ viːˈvɑ̃/ n. (pl. **bon vivants** or **bons vivants** pronunc. same) a person indulging in good living; a gourmand. [F, lit. good liver f. vivre to live]

bon viveur /ˌbɒ̃ viːˈvɜː(r)/ n. (pl. **bon viveurs** or **bons viveurs** pronunc. same) = BON VIVANT. [pseudo-F]

bon voyage /ˌbɒ̃ vwaːˈjɑːʒ, vɔɪˈjɑːʒ/ int. & n. an expression of good wishes to a departing traveller. [F]

bony /ˈbəʊnɪ/ adj. (**bonier**, **boniest**) **1** (of a person) thin with prominent bones. **2** having many bones. **3** of or like bone. **4** (of a fish) having bones rather than cartilage. □□ **boniness** n.

bonze /bɒnz/ n. a Japanese or Chinese Buddhist priest. [F bonze or Port. bonzo perh. f. Jap. bonzō f. Chin. fanseng religious person, or f. Jap. bō-zi f. Chin. fasi teacher of the law]

bonzer /ˈbɒnzə(r)/ adj. Austral. sl. excellent, first-rate. [perh. f. BONANZA]

boo /buː/ int., n., & v. —int. **1** an expression of disapproval or contempt. **2** a sound, made esp. to a child, intended to surprise. —n. an utterance of boo, esp. as an expression of disapproval or contempt made to a performer etc. —v. (**boos**, **booed**) **1** intr. utter a boo or boos. **2** tr. jeer at (a performer etc.) by booing. □ **can't** (or **wouldn't**) **say boo to a goose** is very shy or timid. [imit.]

boob[1] /buːb/ n. & v. sl. —n. **1** Brit. an embarrassing mistake. **2** a simpleton. —v.intr. Brit. make an embarrassing mistake. [abbr. of BOOBY]

boob[2] /buːb/ n. sl. a woman's breast. □ **boob tube** sl. **1** a woman's low-cut close-fitting usu. strapless top. **2** (usu. prec. by the) US television; one's television set. [earlier bubby, booby, of uncert. orig.]

booboo /ˈbuːbuː/ n. sl. a mistake. [BOOB[1]]

boobook /ˈbuːbʊk, ˈbʊəbʊək/ n. Austral. a brown spotted owl, Ninox novae-seelandiae, native to Australia and New Zealand. [imit. of its call]

booby /ˈbuːbɪ/ n. (pl. **-ies**) **1** a stupid or childish person. **2** a small gannet of the genus Sula. □ **booby-hatch** esp. US sl. a mental hospital. **booby prize** a prize given to the least successful competitor in any contest. **booby trap 1** a trap intended as a practical joke, e.g. an object placed on top of a door ajar. **2** Mil. an apparently harmless explosive device intended to kill or injure anyone touching it. **booby-trap** v.tr. place a booby trap or traps in or on. [prob. f. Sp. bobo (in both senses) f. L balbus stammering]

boodle /ˈbuːd(ə)l/ n. sl. money, esp. when gained or used dishonestly, e.g. as a bribe. [Du. boedel possessions]

boogie /ˈbuːgɪ/ v. & n. —v.intr. (**boogies**, **boogied**, **boogying**) sl. dance enthusiastically to pop music. —n. **1** = BOOGIE-WOOGIE. **2** sl. a dance to pop music. [BOOGIE-WOOGIE]

boogie-woogie /ˌbuːgɪˈwuːgɪ/ n. a style of playing blues or jazz on the piano, marked by a persistent bass rhythm. [20th c.: orig. unkn.]

book /bʊk/ n. & v. —n. **1 a** a written or printed work consisting of pages glued or sewn together along one side and bound in covers. **b** a literary composition intended for publication (is working on her book). **2** a bound set of blank sheets for writing or keeping records in. **3** a set of tickets, stamps, matches, cheques, samples of cloth, etc., bound up together. **4** (in pl.) a set of records or accounts. **5** a main division of a literary work, or of the Bible (the Book of Deuteronomy). **6** (in full **book of words**) a libretto, script of a play, etc. **7** colloq. a magazine. **8** a telephone directory (his number's in the book). **9** a record of bets made and money paid out at a race meeting by a bookmaker. **10** a set of six tricks collected together in a card-game. **11** an imaginary record or list (the book of life). —v. **1** tr. **a** engage (a seat etc.) in advance; make a reservation of. **b** engage (a guest, supporter, etc.) for some occasion. **2** tr. **a** take the personal details of (an offender or rule-breaker). **b** enter in a book or list. **3** tr. issue a railway etc. ticket to. **4** intr. make a reservation (no need to book). □ **book club** a society which sells its members selected books on special terms. **book-end** a usu. ornamental prop used to keep a row of books upright. **book in** esp. Brit. register one's arrival at a hotel etc. **book learning** mere theory. **book-plate** a decorative label stuck in the front of a book bearing the owner's name. **book-rest** an adjustable support for an open book on a table. **book token** Brit. a voucher which can be exchanged for books to a specified value. **book up 1** buy tickets in advance for a theatre, concert, holiday, etc. **2** (as **booked up**) with all places reserved. **book value** the value of a commodity as entered in a firm's books (opp. market value). **bring to book** call to account. **closed** (or **sealed**) **book** a subject of which one is ignorant. **go by the book** proceed according to the rules. **the good Book** the Bible. **in a person's bad** (or good) **books** in disfavour (or favour) with a person. **in my book** in my opinion. **make a book** take bets and pay out winnings at a race meeting. **not in the book** disallowed. **on the books** contained in a list of members etc. **suits my book** is convenient to me. **take a leaf out of a person's book** imitate a person. **throw the book at** colloq. charge or punish to the utmost. [OE bōc, bōcian, f. Gmc, usu. taken to be rel. to BEECH (the bark of which was used for writing on)]

bookbinder /ˈbʊkˌbaɪndə(r)/ n. a person who binds books professionally. □□ **bookbinding** n.

bookcase /ˈbʊkkeɪs/ n. a set of shelves for books in the form of a cabinet.

bookie /ˈbʊkɪ/ n. colloq. = BOOKMAKER.

booking /ˈbʊkɪŋ/ n. the act or an instance of booking or reserving a seat, a room in a hotel, etc.; a reservation (see BOOK v. 1). □ **booking-clerk** an official selling tickets at a railway station. **booking-hall** (or **-office**) Brit. a room or area at a railway station in which tickets are sold.

bookish /ˈbʊkɪʃ/ adj. **1** studious; fond of reading. **2** acquiring knowledge from books rather than practical experience. **3** (of a word, language, etc.) literary; not colloquial. □□ **bookishly** adv. **bookishness** n.

bookkeeper /ˈbʊkˌkiːpə(r)/ n. a person who keeps accounts for a trader, a public office, etc. □□ **bookkeeping** n.

bookland /ˈbʊklænd/ n. hist. an area of common land granted by charter to a private owner.

booklet /ˈbʊklɪt/ n. a small book consisting of a few sheets usu. with paper covers.

bookmaker /ˈbʊkˌmeɪkə(r)/ n. a person who takes bets, esp. on horse-races, calculates odds, and pays out winnings. □□ **bookmaking** n.

bookman /ˈbʊkmən/ n. (pl. **-men**) a literary man, esp. a reviewer.

bookmark /ˈbʊkmɑːk/ n. (also **bookmarker**) a strip

of leather, card, etc., used to mark one's place in a book.

bookmobile /ˈbʊkməˌbiːl/ n. US a mobile library. [after AUTOMOBILE]

bookseller /ˈbʊkˌselə(r)/ n. a dealer in books.

bookshop /ˈbʊkʃɒp/ n. a shop where books are sold.

bookstall /ˈbʊkstɔːl/ n. a stand for selling books, newspapers, etc., esp. out of doors or at a station.

bookstore /ˈbʊkstɔː(r)/ n. US = BOOKSHOP.

booksy /ˈbʊksɪ/ adj. colloq. having literary or bookish pretensions.

bookwork /ˈbʊkwɜːk/ n. the study of books (as opposed to practical work).

bookworm /ˈbʊkwɜːm/ n. 1 colloq. a person devoted to reading. 2 the larva of a moth or beetle which feeds on the paper and glue used in books.

Boolean /ˈbuːlɪən/ adj. denoting a system of algebraic notation to represent logical propositions. □**Boolean logic** the use of the logical operators 'and', 'or', and 'not' in retrieving information from a computer database. [G. *Boole*, Engl. mathematician d. 1864]

boom[1] /buːm/ n. & v. —n. a deep resonant sound. —v.intr. make or speak with a boom. [imit.]

boom[2] /buːm/ n. & v. —n. a period of prosperity or sudden activity in commerce. —v.intr. (esp. of commercial ventures) be suddenly prosperous or successful. □**boom town** a town undergoing sudden growth due to a boom. □□**boomlet** n. [19th-c. US word, perhaps f. BOOM[1] (cf. *make things hum*)]

boom[3] /buːm/ n. 1 Naut. a pivoted spar to which the foot of a sail is attached, allowing the angle of the sail to be changed. 2 a long pole over a film or television set, carrying microphones and other equipment. 3 a floating barrier across the mouth of a harbour or river. [Du., = BEAM n.]

boomer /ˈbuːmə(r)/ n. 1 a large male kangaroo. 2 a N. American mountain beaver, *Aplodontia rufa*. 3 a large wave.

boomerang /ˈbuːməˌræŋ/ n. & v. —n. 1 a curved flat hardwood missile used by Australian Aboriginals to kill prey, and often of a kind able to return in flight to the thrower. 2 a plan or scheme that recoils on its originator. —v.intr. 1 act as a boomerang. 2 (of a plan or action) backfire. [Aboriginal name, perh. modified]

boomslang /ˈbuːmslæŋ/ n. a large venomous tree-snake, *Dispholidus typus*, native to southern Africa. [Afrik. f. *boom* tree + *slang* snake]

boon[1] /buːn/ n. 1 an advantage; a blessing. 2 archaic a a thing asked for; a request. b a gift; a favour. [ME, orig. = prayer, f. ON *bón* f. Gmc]

boon[2] /buːn/ adj. close, intimate, favourite (usu. *boon companion*). [ME (orig. = jolly, congenial) f. OF *bon* f. L *bonus* good]

boondock /ˈbuːndɒk/ n. (usu. in *pl.*) US sl. rough or isolated country. [Tagalog *bundok* mountain]

boor /ˈbʊə(r)/ n. 1 a rude, ill-mannered person. 2 a clumsy person. □□**boorish** adj. **boorishly** adv. **boorishness** n. [LG *būr* or Du. *boer* farmer: cf. BOWER[3]]

boost /buːst/ v. & n. colloq. —v.tr. 1 a promote or increase the reputation of (a person, scheme, commodity, etc.) by praise or advertising; push; increase or assist (*boosted his spirits*; *boost sales*). b push from below; assist (*boosted me up the tree*). 2 a raise the voltage in (an electric circuit etc.). b amplify (a radio signal). —n. 1 an act, process, or result of boosting; a push (*asked for a boost up the hill*). 2 a an advertisement campaign. b the resulting advance in value, reputation, etc. [19th-c. US word: orig. unkn.]

booster /ˈbuːstə(r)/ n. 1 a device for increasing electrical power or voltage. 2 an auxiliary engine or rocket used to give initial acceleration. 3 Med. a dose of an immunizing agent increasing or renewing the effect of an earlier one. 4 a person who boosts by helping or encouraging.

boot[1] /buːt/ n. & v. —n. 1 an outer covering for the foot, esp. of leather, reaching above the ankle, often

to the knee. 2 Brit. the luggage compartment of a motor car, usu. at the rear. 3 colloq. a firm kick. 4 (prec. by *the*) colloq. dismissal, esp. from employment (*gave them the boot*). 5 a covering to protect the lower part of a horse's leg. 6 hist. an instrument of torture encasing and crushing the foot. —v.tr. 1 kick, esp. hard. 2 (often foll. by *out*) dismiss (a person) forcefully. 3 (usu. foll. by *up*) put (a computer) in a state of readiness (cf. BOOTSTRAP 2). □**the boot is on the other foot** (or **leg**) the truth or responsibility is the other way round. **die with one's boots on** (of a soldier etc.) die fighting. **put the boot in** 1 kick brutally. 2 act aggressively against a person. **you bet your boots** sl. it is quite certain. □□**booted** adj. [ME f. ON *bóti* or f. OF *bote*, of unkn. orig.]

boot[2] /buːt/ n. □**to boot** as well; to the good; in addition. [orig. = 'advantage': OE *bōt* f. Gmc]

bootblack /ˈbuːtblæk/ n. US a person who polishes boots and shoes.

bootee /buːˈtiː/ n. 1 a soft shoe, esp. a woollen one, worn by a baby. 2 a woman's short boot.

booth /buːð, buːθ/ n. 1 a small temporary roofed structure of canvas, wood, etc., used esp. as a market stall, for puppet shows, etc. 2 an enclosure or compartment for various purposes, e.g. telephoning or voting. 3 a set of a table and benches in a restaurant or bar. [ME f. Scand.]

bootjack /ˈbuːtdʒæk/ n. a device for holding a boot by the heel to ease withdrawal of the leg.

bootlace /ˈbuːtleɪs/ n. a cord or leather thong for lacing boots.

bootleg /ˈbuːtleg/ adj. & v. —adj. (esp. of liquor) smuggled; illicitly sold. —v.tr. (**-legged**, **-legging**) make, distribute, or smuggle illicit goods (esp. alcohol). □□**bootlegger** n. [f. the smugglers' practice of concealing bottles in their boots]

bootless /ˈbuːtlɪs/ adj. archaic unavailing, useless. [OE *bōtlēas* (as BOOT[2], LESS)]

bootlicker /ˈbuːtˌlɪkə(r)/ n. colloq. a person who behaves obsequiously or servilely; a toady.

boots /buːts/ n. Brit. a hotel servant who cleans boots and shoes, carries luggage. etc.

bootstrap /ˈbuːtstræp/ n. 1 a loop at the back of a boot used to pull it on. 2 Computing a technique of loading a program into a computer by means of a few initial instructions which enable the introduction of the rest of the program from an input device. □**pull oneself up by one's bootstraps** better oneself by one's own efforts.

booty /ˈbuːtɪ/ n. 1 plunder gained esp. in war or by piracy. 2 colloq. something gained or won. [ME f. MLG *būte*, *buite* exchange, of uncert. orig.]

booze /buːz/ n. & v. colloq. —n. 1 alcoholic drink. 2 the drinking of this (*on the booze*). —v.intr. drink alcoholic liquor, esp. excessively or habitually. □**booze-up** sl. a drinking bout. [earlier *bouse*, *bowse*, f. MDu. *būsen* drink to excess]

boozer /ˈbuːzə(r)/ n. colloq. 1 a person who drinks alcohol, esp. to excess. 2 Brit. a public house.

boozy /ˈbuːzɪ/ adj. (**boozier**, **booziest**) colloq. intoxicated; addicted to drink. □□**boozily** adv. **booziness** n.

bop[1] /bɒp/ n. & v. colloq. —n. 1 = BEBOP. 2 a a spell of dancing, esp. to pop music. b an organized social occasion for this. —v.intr. (**bopped**, **bopping**) dance, esp. to pop music. □□**bopper** n. [abbr. of BEBOP]

bop[2] /bɒp/ v. & n. colloq. —v.tr. (**bopped**, **bopping**) hit, punch lightly. —n. a light blow or hit. [imit.]

bo-peep /bəʊˈpiːp/ n. a game of hiding and suddenly reappearing, played with a young child. [BO[1] + PEEP[1]]

bora[1] /ˈbɔːrə/ n. a strong cold dry NE wind blowing in the upper Adriatic. [It. dial. f. L *boreas* north wind: see BOREAL]

bora[2] /ˈbɔːrə/ n. Austral. an Aboriginal rite in which boys are initiated into manhood. [Aboriginal]

boracic /bəˈræsɪk/ adj. of borax; containing boron. □**boracic acid** = *boric acid*. [med.L *borax -acis*]

borage /ˈbɒrɪdʒ/ n. any plant of the genus *Borago*,

aʊ h**ow** eɪ d**ay** əʊ n**o** eə h**air** ɪə n**ear** ɔɪ b**oy** ʊə p**oor** aɪə f**ire** aʊə s**our** (*see over for consonants*)

esp. *Borago officinalis* with bright blue flowers and leaves used as flavouring. [OF *bourrache* f. med.L *borrago* f. Arab. *'abu 'āraḳ* father of sweat (from its use as a diaphoretic)]

borak /ˈbɔːræk/ *n. Austral. & NZ sl.* banter, ridicule. [Aboriginal Austral.]

borane /ˈbɔːreɪn/ *n. Chem.* any hydride of boron.

borate /ˈbɔːreɪt/ *n.* a salt or ester of boric acid.

borax /ˈbɔːræks/ *n.* **1** the mineral salt sodium borate, occurring in alkaline deposits as an efflorescence or as crystals. **2** the purified form of this salt, used in making glass and china, and as an antiseptic. [ME f. OF *boras* f. med.L *borax* f. Arab. *būraḳ* f. Pers. *būrah*]

borazon /ˈbɔːrəˌzɒn/ *n.* a hard form of boron nitride, resistant to oxidation. [BORON + AZO- nitrogen + -*on*]

borborygmus /ˌbɔːbəˈrɪɡməs/ *n.* (*pl.* **borborygmi** /-maɪ/) a rumbling of gas in the intestines. □□ **borborygmic** *adj.* [mod.L f. Gk]

Bordeaux /bɔːˈdəʊ/ *n.* (*pl.* same /-ˈdəʊz/) any of various red, white, or rosé wines from the district of Bordeaux in SW France. □ **Bordeaux mixture** a fungicide for vines, fruit-trees, etc., composed of equal quantities of copper sulphate and calcium oxide in water.

bordello /bɔːˈdeləʊ/ *n.* (*pl.* **-os**) esp. *US* a brothel. [ME (f. It. *bordello*) f. OF *bordel* small farm, dimin. of *borde* ult. f. Frank.: see BOARD]

border /ˈbɔːdə(r)/ *n. & v.* —*n.* **1** the edge or boundary of anything, or the part near it. **2 a** the line separating two political or geographical areas, esp. countries. **b** the district on each side of this. **c (the Border)** a particular boundary and its adjoining districts, esp. between Scotland and England (usu. **the Borders**), or N. Ireland and the Irish Republic. **3** a distinct edging round anything, esp. for strength or decoration. **4** a long narrow bed of flowers or shrubs in a garden (*herbaceous border*). —*v.* **1** *tr.* be a border to. **2** *tr.* provide with a border. **3** *intr.* (usu. foll. by *on*, *upon*) **a** adjoin; come close to being. **b** approximate, resemble. □ **Border collie** a common working sheepdog of the North Country. **Border terrier 1** a small terrier of a breed with rough hair. **2** this breed. [ME f. OF *bordure*: cf. BOARD]

borderer /ˈbɔːdərə(r)/ *n.* a person who lives near a border, esp. that between Scotland and England.

borderland /ˈbɔːdəˌlænd/ *n.* **1** the district near a border. **2** an intermediate condition between two extremes. **3** an area for debate.

borderline /ˈbɔːdəˌlaɪn/ *n. & adj.* —*n.* **1** the line dividing two (often extreme) conditions. **2** a line marking a boundary. —*adj.* **1** on the borderline. **2** verging on an extreme condition; only just acceptable.

bordure /ˈbɔːdjʊə(r)/ *n. Heraldry* a border round the edge of a shield. [ME form of BORDER]

bore[1] /bɔː(r)/ *v. & n.* —*v.* **1** *tr.* make a hole in, esp. with a revolving tool. **2** *tr.* hollow out (a tube etc.). **3** *tr.* **a** make (a hole) by boring or excavation. **b** make (one's way) through a crowd etc. **4** *intr.* (of an athlete, racehorse, etc.) push another competitor out of the way. **5** *intr.* drill a well (for oil etc.). —*n.* **1** the hollow of a firearm barrel or of a cylinder in an internal-combustion engine. **2** the diameter of this; the calibre. **3** = BOREHOLE. [OE *borian* f. Gmc]

bore[2] /bɔː(r)/ *n. & v.* —*n.* a tiresome or dull person or thing. —*v.tr.* weary by tedious talk or dullness. □ **bore a person to tears** weary (a person) in the extreme. [18th c.: orig. unkn.]

bore[3] /bɔː(r)/ *n.* a high tidal wave rushing up a narrow estuary. Also called EAGRE. [ME, perh. f. ON *bára* wave]

bore[4] *past* of BEAR[1].

boreal /ˈbɔːrɪəl/ *adj.* **1** of the North or northern regions. **2** of the north wind. [ME f. F *boréal* or LL *borealis* f. L *Boreas* f. Gk *Boreas* god of the north wind]

boredom /ˈbɔːdəm/ *n.* the state of being bored; ennui.

borehole /ˈbɔːhəʊl/ *n.* **1** a deep narrow hole, esp. one made in the earth to find water, oil, etc. **2** *Austral.* a water-hole for cattle.

borer /ˈbɔːrə(r)/ *n.* **1** any of several worms, molluscs, insects, or insect larvae which bore into wood, other plant material, and rock. **2** a tool for boring.

boric /ˈbɔːrɪk/ *adj.* of or containing boron. □ **boric acid** an acid derived from borax, used as a mild antiseptic and in the manufacture of heat-resistant glass and enamels.

boring /ˈbɔːrɪŋ/ *adj.* that makes one bored; uninteresting, tedious, dull. □□ **boringly** *adv.* **boringness** *n.*

born /bɔːn/ *adj.* **1** existing as a result of birth. **2 a** being such or likely to become such by natural ability or quality (*a born leader*). **b** (usu. foll. by *to* + infin.) having a specified destiny or prospect (*born lucky; born to be king; born to lead men*). **3** (in *comb.*) of a certain status by birth (*French-born; well-born*). □ **born-again** (*attrib.*) converted (esp. to fundamentalist Christianity). **born and bred** by birth and upbringing. **in all one's born days** *colloq.* in one's life so far. **not born yesterday** *colloq.* not stupid; shrewd. [past part. of BEAR[1]]

borne /bɔːn/ **1** *past part.* of BEAR[1]. **2** (in *comb.*) carried or transported by (*airborne*).

borné /ˈbɔːneɪ/ *adj.* **1** narrow-minded; of limited ideas. **2** having limitations. [F]

Bornholm's disease /ˈbɔːnhəʊmz/ *n.* a viral infection with fever and pain in the muscles of the ribs. [*Bornholm* in Denmark]

boro- /ˈbɔːrəʊ/ *comb. form* indicating salts containing boron.

boron /ˈbɔːrɒn/ *n. Chem.* a non-metallic yellow crystalline or brown amorphous element extracted from borax and boracic acid and mainly used for hardening steel. ¶ Symb.: **B**. [BORAX + -*on* f. *carbon* (which it resembles in some respects)]

boronia /bəˈrəʊnɪə/ *n. Austral.* any sweet-scented shrub of the genus *Boronia*. [F. *Borone*, It. botanist d. 1794]

borosilicate /ˌbɔːrəʊˈsɪlɪˌkeɪt/ *n.* any of many substances containing boron, silicon, and oxygen generally used in glazes and enamels and in the production of glass.

borough /ˈbʌrə/ *n.* **1** *Brit.* **a** a town represented in the House of Commons. **b** a town or district granted the status of a borough. **2** *Brit. hist.* a town with a municipal corporation and privileges conferred by a royal charter. **3** *US* a municipal corporation in certain States. **4** *US* each of five divisions of New York City. **5** *US* (in Alaska) a county. [OE *burg*, *burh* f. Gmc: cf. BURGH]

borrow /ˈbɒrəʊ/ *v.* **1 a** *tr.* acquire temporarily with the promise or intention of returning. **b** *intr.* obtain money in this way. **2** *tr.* use (an idea, invention, etc.) originated by another; plagiarize. **3** *intr. Golf* **a** play the ball uphill so that it rolls back towards the hole. **b** allow for the wind or a slope. □ **borrowed time** an unexpected extension esp. of life. □□ **borrower** *n.* **borrowing** *n.* [OE *borgian* give a pledge]

borsch var. of BORTSCH.

Borstal /ˈbɔːst(ə)l/ *n. Brit. hist.* an institution for reforming and training young offenders. ¶ Now replaced by *detention centre* and *youth custody centre*. [*Borstal* in S. England, where the first of these was established]

bort /bɔːt/ *n.* (also **boart**) **1** an inferior or malformed diamond, used for cutting. **2** fragments of diamonds produced in cutting. [Du. *boort*]

bortsch /bɔːtʃ/ *n.* (also **borsch** /bɔːʃ/) a highly seasoned Russian or Polish soup with various ingredients including beetroot and cabbage and served with sour cream. [Russ. *borshch*]

borzoi /ˈbɔːzɔɪ/ *n.* **1** a large Russian wolfhound of a breed with a narrow head and silky, usu. white, coat. **2** this breed. [Russ. f. *borzyi* swift]

boscage /ˈbɒskɪdʒ/ *n.* (also **boskage**) **1** masses of trees or shrubs. **2** wooded scenery. [ME f. OF *boscage* f. Gmc: cf. BUSH¹]

bosh /bɒʃ/ *n. & int. sl.* nonsense; foolish talk. [Turk. *boş* empty]

bosky /'bɒskɪ/ *adj.* (**boskier, boskiest**) *literary* wooded, bushy. [ME *bosk* thicket]

bo's'n var. of BOATSWAIN.

bosom /'bʊz(ə)m/ *n.* **1 a** a person's breast or chest, esp. a woman's. **b** *colloq.* each of a woman's breasts. **c** the enclosure formed by a person's breast and arms. **2** an emotional centre, esp. as the source of an enfolding relationship (*in the bosom of one's family*). **3** the part of a woman's dress covering the breast. □**bosom friend** a very close or intimate friend. [OE *bōsm* f. Gmc]

bosomy /'bʊzəmɪ/ *adj.* (of a woman) having large breasts.

boson /'bəʊzɒn/ *n. Physics* any of several elementary particles obeying the relations stated by Bose and Einstein, with a zero or integral spin, e.g. photons (cf. FERMION). [S. N. *Bose*, Ind. physicist d. 1974]

boss¹ /bɒs/ *n. & v. colloq.* —*n.* **1** a person in charge; an employer, manager, or overseer. **2** *US* a person who controls or dominates a political organization. —*v.tr.* **1** (usu. foll. by *about, around*) treat domineeringly; give constant peremptory orders to. **2** be the master or manager of. [orig. US: f. Du. *baas* master]

boss² /bɒs/ *n.* **1** a round knob, stud, or other protuberance, esp. on the centre of a shield or in ornamental work. **2** *Archit.* a piece of ornamental carving etc. covering the point where the ribs in a vault or ceiling cross. **3** *Geol.* a large mass of igneous rock. **4** *Mech.* an enlarged part of a shaft. [ME f. OF *boce* f. Rmc]

bossa nova /,bɒsə 'nəʊvə/ *n.* **1** a dance like the samba, originating in Brazil. **2** a piece of music for this or in its rhythm. [Port., = new flair]

boss-eyed /'bɒsaɪd/ *adj. Brit. colloq.* **1** having only one good eye; cross-eyed. **2** crooked; out of true. [dial. *boss* miss, bungle]

boss-shot /'bɒsʃɒt/ *n. Brit. dial. & sl.* **1** a bad shot or aim. **2** an unsuccessful attempt. [as BOSS-EYED]

bossy /'bɒsɪ/ *adj.* (**bossier, bossiest**) *colloq.* domineering; tending to boss. □**bossy-boots** *colloq.* a domineering person. □□**bossily** *adv.* **bossiness** *n.*

bosun (also **bo'sun**) var. of BOATSWAIN.

bot /bɒt/ *n.* (also **bott**) any of various parasitic larvae of flies of the family Oestridae, infesting horses, sheep, etc. □**bot-fly** (*pl.* **-flies**) any dipterous fly of the genus *Oestrus*, with stout hairy bodies. [prob. of LG orig.]

bot. *abbr.* **1** bottle. **2** botanic; botanical; botany. **3** bought.

botanize /'bɒtənaɪz/ *v.intr.* (also **-ise**) study plants, esp. in their habitat.

Botany /'bɒtənɪ/ *n.* (in full **Botany wool**) merino wool, esp. from Australia. [*Botany Bay*, New S. Wales, named from the variety of its flora]

botany /'bɒtənɪ/ *n.* **1** the study of the physiology, structure, genetics, ecology, distribution, classification, and economic importance of plants. **2** the plant life of a particular area or time. □□ **botanic** /bə'tænɪk/ *adj.* **botanical** /bə'tænɪk(ə)l/ *adj.* **botanically** /bə'tænɪkəlɪ/ *adv.* **botanist** *n.* [*botanic* f. F *botanique* or LL *botanicus* f. Gk *botanikos* f. *botanē* plant]

botch /bɒtʃ/ *v. & n.* (also **bodge**) —*v.tr.* **1** bungle; do badly. **2** patch or repair clumsily. —*n.* bungled or spoilt work (*made a botch of it*). □□ **botcher** *n.* [ME: orig. unkn.]

botel /bəʊ'tel/ *n.* (also **boatel**) a waterside hotel with facilities for mooring boats. [blend of BOAT and HOTEL]

both /bəʊθ/ *adj., pron., & adv.* —*adj. & pron.* the two, not only one (*both boys; both the boys; both of the boys; the boys are both here*). ¶ Widely used with *of*, esp. when followed by a pronoun (e.g. *both of us*) or a noun implying separate rather than collective consideration, e.g. *both of the boys* suggests *each boy* rather than the two together. —*adv.* with equal truth in two cases (*both the boy and his sister are here; are both here and hungry*). □**both ways** = *each way*. **have it both ways** alternate between two incompatible points of view to suit the needs of the moment. [ME f. ON *báthir*]

bother /'bɒðə(r)/ *v., n., & int.* —*v.* **1** *tr.* **a** give trouble to; worry, disturb. **b** *refl.* (often foll. by *about*) be anxious or concerned. **2** *intr.* **a** (often foll. by *about*, or *to* + infin.) worry or trouble oneself (*don't bother about that; didn't bother to tell me*). **b** (foll. by *with*) be concerned. —*n.* **1 a** a person or thing that bothers or causes worry. **b** a minor nuisance. **2** trouble, worry, fuss. —*int. esp. Brit.* expressing annoyance or impatience. □**cannot be bothered** will not make the effort needed. [Ir. *bodhraim* deafen]

botheration /,bɒðə'reɪʃ(ə)n/ *n. & int. colloq.* = BOTHER *n., int.*

bothersome /'bɒðəsəm/ *adj.* causing bother; troublesome.

bothy /'bɒθɪ/ *n.* (also **bothie**) (*pl.* **-ies**) *Sc.* a small hut or cottage, esp. one for housing labourers. [18th c.: orig. unkn.: perh. rel. to BOOTH]

bo-tree /'bəʊtriː/ *n.* the Indian fig-tree, *Ficus religiosa*, regarded as sacred by Buddhists. Also called PIPAL or PEEPUL. [repr. Sinh. *bogaha* tree of knowledge (Buddha's enlightenment having occurred beneath such a tree)]

bott var. of BOT.

bottle /'bɒt(ə)l/ *n. & v.* —*n.* **1** a container, usu. of glass or plastic and with a narrow neck, for storing liquid. **2** the amount that will fill a bottle. **3** a baby's feeding-bottle. **4** = *hot-water bottle*. **5** a metal cylinder for liquefied gas. **6** *Brit. sl.* courage, confidence. —*v.tr.* **1** put into bottles or jars. **2** preserve (fruit etc.) in jars. **3** (foll. by *up*) **a** conceal or restrain for a time (esp. a feeling). **b** keep (an enemy force etc.) contained or entrapped. **4** (as **bottled** *adj.*) *sl.* drunk. □ **bottle bank** a place where used bottles may be deposited for recycling. **bottle-brush 1** a cylindrical brush for cleaning inside bottles. **2** any of various plants with a flower of this shape. **bottle-green** a dark shade of green. **bottle party** a party to which guests bring bottles of drink. **bottle tree** any of various Australian trees of the genus *Brachychiton* with a swollen bottle-shaped trunk. **hit the bottle** *sl.* drink heavily. **on the bottle** *sl.* drinking (alcoholic drink) heavily. □□ **bottleful** *n.* (*pl.* **-fuls**). [ME f. OF *botele*, *botaille* f. med.L *butticula* dimin. of LL *buttis* BUTT⁴]

bottle-feed /'bɒt(ə)l,fiːd/ *v.tr.* (*past* and *past part.* **-fed**) feed (a baby) with milk by means of a bottle.

bottleneck /'bɒt(ə)l,nek/ *n.* **1** a point at which the flow of traffic, production, etc., is constricted. **2** a narrow place causing constriction.

bottlenose /'bɒt(ə)l,nəʊz/ *n.* (also **bottlenosed**) a swollen nose. □**bottlenose dolphin** a dolphin, *Tursiops truncatus*, with a bottle-shaped snout.

bottler /'bɒtlə(r)/ *n.* **1** a person who bottles drinks etc. **2** *Austral. & NZ sl.* an excellent person or thing.

bottom /'bɒtəm/ *n., adj., & v.* —*n.* **1 a** the lowest point or part (*bottom of the stairs*). **b** the part on which a thing rests (*bottom of a saucepan*). **c** the underneath part (*scraped the bottom of the car*). **d** the furthest or inmost part (*bottom of the garden*). **2** *colloq.* **a** the buttocks. **b** the seat of a chair etc. **3 a** the less honourable, important, or successful end of a table, a class, etc. (*at the bottom of the list of requirements*). **b** a person occupying this place (*he's always bottom of the class*). **4** the ground under the water of a lake, a river, etc. (*swam until he touched the bottom*). **5** the basis; the origin (*he's at the bottom of it*). **6** the essential character; reality. **7** *Naut.* **a** the keel or hull of a ship. **b** a ship, esp. as a cargo-carrier. **8** staying power; endurance. —*adj.* **1** lowest (*bottom button*). **2** last (*got the bottom score*). —*v.* **1** *tr.* put a bottom to (a chair, saucepan, etc.). **2** *intr.* (of a ship) reach or touch the bottom. **3** *tr.* find the extent or real nature of; work out. **4** *tr.* (usu. foll. by *on*) base (an argument etc.) (*reasoning bottomed on logic*). **5** *tr.* touch the bottom or lowest point of. □**at bottom** basically, essentially. **be at the bottom of** have caused. **bet one's bottom dollar** *sl.* stake all. **bottom dog** = UNDERDOG. **bottom drawer** *Brit.* linen etc. stored by a woman in preparation for her marriage. **bottom falls out** collapse occurs. **bottom gear** see GEAR. **bottom line** *colloq.* the underlying or ultimate truth; the ultimate, esp. financial, criterion. **bottom out** reach the lowest level. **bottoms up!** a call to drain one's glass. **bottom up** upside-down. **get to the bottom of** fully investigate and explain. **knock the bottom out of** prove (a thing) worthless. □□ **bottommost** /'bɒtəm,məʊst/ *adj.* [OE *botm* f. Gmc]

bottomless /'bɒtəmlɪs/ *adj.* **1** without a bottom. **2** (of a supply etc.) inexhaustible.

bottomry /'bɒtəmrɪ/ *n. & v. Naut.* —*n.* a system of using a ship as security against a loan to finance a voyage, the lender losing his or her money if the ship sinks. —*v.tr.* (-ies, -ied) pledge (a ship) in this way. [BOTTOM = ship + -RY, after Du. *bodemerij*]

botulism /'bɒtjʊ,lɪz(ə)m/ *n.* poisoning caused by a toxin produced by the bacillus *Clostridium botulinum* growing in poorly preserved food. [G *Botulismus* f. L *botulus* sausage]

bouclé /'buːkleɪ/ *n.* **1** a looped or curled yarn (esp. wool). **2** a fabric, esp. knitted, made of this. [F, = buckled, curled]

boudoir /'buːdwɑː(r)/ *n.* a woman's small private room or bedroom. [F, lit. sulking-place f. *bouder* sulk]

bouffant /'buːfɑ̃/ *adj.* (of a dress, hair, etc.) puffed out. [F]

bougainvillaea /,buːgən'vɪlɪə/ *n.* any tropical widely cultivated plant of the genus *Bougainvillaea*, with large coloured bracts (usu. purple, red, or white) almost concealing the inconspicuous flowers. [L. A. de *Bougainville*, Fr. navigator d. 1811]

bough /baʊ/ *n.* a branch of a tree, esp. a main one. [OE *bōg, bōh* f. Gmc]

bought *past* and *past part.* of BUY.

boughten /'bɔːt(ə)n/ *adj. US* or *dial.* bought at a shop, not home-made. [var. of past part. of BUY]

bougie /'buːʒiː/ *n.* **1** *Med.* a thin flexible surgical instrument for exploring, dilating, etc. the passages of the body. **2** a wax candle. [F f. Arab. *Bujiya* Algerian town with a wax trade]

bouillabaisse /,buːjə'bes/ *n. Cookery* a rich, spicy fish-stew, orig. from Provence. [F]

bouilli /buː'jiː/ *n. Cookery* stewed or boiled meat. [F, = boiled]

bouillon /buː'jõ, 'buːjɒn/ *n.* thin soup; broth. [F f. *bouillir* to boil]

boulder /'bəʊldə(r)/ *n.* a large stone worn smooth by erosion. □ **boulder-clay** *Geol.* a mixture of boulders etc. formed by deposition from massive bodies of melting ice, to give distinctive glacial formations. [short for *boulderstone*, ME f. Scand.]

boule[1] /buːl/ *n.* (also **boules** *pronunc.* same) a French form of bowls, played on rough ground with usu. metal balls. [F, = BOWL[2]]

boule[2] /'buːliː/ *n.* a legislative body of an ancient Greek city or of modern Greece. [Gk *boulē* senate]

boule[3] var. of BUHL.

boules var. of BOULE[1].

boulevard /'buːlə,vɑːd, 'buːlvɑː(r)/ *n.* **1** a broad tree-lined avenue. **2** esp. *US* a broad main road. [F f. G *Bollwerk* BULWARK, orig. of a promenade on a demolished fortification]

boulle var. of BUHL.

boult var. of BOLT[2].

bounce /baʊns/ *v. & n.* —*v.* **1 a** *intr.* (of a ball etc.) rebound. **b** *tr.* cause to rebound. **c** *tr. & intr.* bounce repeatedly. **2** *intr. sl.* (of a cheque) be returned by a bank when there are insufficient funds to meet it. **3**

intr. **a** (foll. by *about, up*) (of a person, dog, etc.) jump or spring energetically. **b** (foll. by *in, out*, etc.) rush noisily, angrily, enthusiastically, etc. (*bounced into the room; bounced out in a temper*). **4** *tr. colloq.* (usu. foll. by *into* + verbal noun) hustle, persuade (*bounced him into signing*). **5** *intr. colloq.* talk boastfully. **6** *tr. sl.* eject forcibly (from a dancehall, club, etc.). —*n.* **1 a** rebound. **b** the power of rebounding (*this ball has a good bounce*). **2** *colloq.* **a** swagger, self-confidence (*has a lot of bounce*). **b** liveliness. **3** *sl.* an ejection. □**bounce back** regain one's good health, spirits, prosperity, etc. [ME *bunsen* beat, thump, (perh. imit.), or f. LG *bunsen*, Du. *bons* thump]

bouncer /'baʊnsə(r)/ *n.* **1** *sl.* a person employed to eject troublemakers from a dancehall, club, etc. **2** *Cricket* = BUMPER.

bouncing /'baʊnsɪŋ/ *adj.* **1** (esp. of a baby) big and healthy. **2** boisterous.

bouncy /'baʊnsɪ/ *adj.* (**bouncier, bounciest**) **1** (of a ball etc.) that bounces well. **2** cheerful and lively. **3** resilient, springy (*a bouncy sofa*). □□ **bouncily** *adv.* **bounciness** *n.*

bound[1] /baʊnd/ *v. & n.* —*v.intr.* **1 a** spring, leap (*bounded out of bed*). **b** walk or run with leaping strides. **2** (of a ball etc.) recoil from a wall or the ground; bounce. —*n.* **1** a springy movement upwards or outwards; a leap. **2 a** bounce. □**by leaps and bounds** see LEAP. [F *bond, bondir* (orig. of sound) f. LL *bombitare* f. L *bombus* hum]

bound[2] /baʊnd/ *n. & v.* —*n.* (usu. in *pl.*) **1** a limitation; a restriction (*beyond the bounds of possibility*). **2** a border of a territory; a boundary. —*v.tr.* **1** (esp. in passive; foll. by *by*) set bounds to; limit (*views bounded by prejudice*). **2** be the boundary of. □**out of bounds** **1** outside the part of a school etc. in which one is allowed to be. **2** beyond what is acceptable; forbidden. [ME f. AF *bounde*, OF *bonde* etc., f. med.L *bodina*, earlier *butina*, of unkn. orig.]

bound[3] /baʊnd/ *adj.* **1** (usu. foll. by *for*) ready to start or having started (*bound for stardom*). **2** (in *comb.*) moving in a specified direction (*northbound; outward bound*). [ME f. ON *búinn* past part. of *búa* get ready: -d euphonic, or partly after BIND[1]]

bound[4] /baʊnd/ *past* and *past part.* of BIND. □**bound to** certain to (*he's bound to come*).

boundary /'baʊndərɪ, -drɪ/ *n.* (*pl.* **-ies**) **1** a line marking the limits of an area, territory, etc. (*the fence is the boundary; boundary between liberty and licence*). **2** *Cricket* a hit crossing the limits of the field, scoring 4 or 6 runs. □**boundary layer** the fluid immediately surrounding an object that is immersed and moving. **boundary rider** *Austral. & NZ* a person employed to ride round the fences etc. of a cattle or sheep station and keep them in good order. **boundary umpire** (in Australian Rules) an umpire on the sidelines who signals when the ball is out. [dial. *bounder* f. BOUND[2] + -ER[1] perh. after *limitary*]

bounden /'baʊnd(ə)n/ *adj. archaic* obligatory. □ **bounden duty** solemn responsibility. [archaic past part. of BIND]

bounder /'baʊndə(r)/ *n. colloq.* or *joc.* a cad; an ill-bred person.

boundless /'baʊndlɪs/ *adj.* unlimited; immense (*boundless enthusiasm*). □□ **boundlessly** *adv.* **boundlessness** *n.*

bounteous /'baʊntɪəs/ *adj. poet.* **1** generous, liberal. **2** freely given (*bounteous affection*). □□ **bounteously** *adv.* **bounteousness** *n.* [ME f. OF *bontif* f. *bonté* BOUNTY after *plenteous*]

bountiful /'baʊntɪ,fʊl/ *adj.* **1** = BOUNTEOUS. **2** ample. □**Lady Bountiful** a charitable but patronizing lady of a neighbourhood (after a character in Farquhar's *Beaux' Stratagem*, 1707). □□ **bountifully** *adv.* [BOUNTY + -FUL]

bounty /'baʊntɪ/ *n.* (*pl.* **-ies**) **1** liberality; generosity. **2** a gift or reward, made usu. by the State, esp.: **a** a sum paid for a valiant act. **b** a sum paid to encourage a trading enterprise etc. **c** a sum paid to army or navy recruits on enlistment. □**bounty-hunter** a person who pursues a criminal or seeks an achievement for the sake of the reward. **King's** (or **Queen's) bounty** *hist.* a grant made to a mother of triplets. [ME f. OF *bonté* f. L *bonitas -tatis* f. *bonus* good]

bouquet /buːˈkeɪ, bəʊ-/ *n.* **1** a bunch of flowers, esp. for carrying at a wedding or other ceremony. **2** the scent of wine etc. **3** a favourable comment; a compliment. □**bouquet garni** /ˈgɑːniː/ *Cookery* a bunch of herbs used for flavouring stews etc. [F f. dial. var. of OF *bos, bois* wood]

Bourbon /ˈbʊəbən, ˈbʊəbɔ̃/ *n.* **1** a chocolate-flavoured biscuit with chocolate-cream filling. **2** *US* a reactionary. [the Bourbon family, whose descendants founded dynasties in France and Spain]

bourbon /ˈbɜːbən, ˈbʊə-/ *n. US* whisky distilled from maize and rye. [*Bourbon* County, Kentucky, where it was first made]

bourdon /ˈbʊəd(ə)n/ *n. Mus.* **1** a low-pitched stop in an organ or harmonium. **2** the lowest bell in a peal of bells. **3** the drone pipe of a bagpipe. [F, = bagpipe-drone, f. Rmc, imit.]

bourgeois /ˈbʊəʒwɑː/ *adj. & n.* often *derog.* —*adj.* **1 a** conventionally middle-class. **b** humdrum, unimaginative. **c** selfishly materialistic. **2** upholding the interests of the capitalist class; non-communist. —*n.* a bourgeois person. [F: see BURGESS]

bourgeoisie /ˌbʊəʒwɑːˈziː/ *n.* **1** the capitalist class. **2** the middle class. [F]

bourn[1] /bɔːn, bʊən/ *n.* a small stream. [ME: S. Engl. var. of BURN[2]]

bourn[2] /bɔːn, bʊən/ *n.* (also **bourne**) *archaic* **1** a goal; a destination. **2** a limit. [F *borne* f. OF *bodne* BOUND[2]]

bourrée /ˈbʊəreɪ/ *n.* **1** a lively French dance like a gavotte. **2** the music for this dance. [F]

bourse /bʊəs/ *n.* **1** (**Bourse**) the Paris equivalent of the Stock Exchange. **2** a money-market. [F, = purse, f. med.L *bursa*: cf. PURSE[1]]

boustrophedon /ˌbaʊstrəˈfiːd(ə)n, ˌbuː-/ *adj. & adv.* (of written words) from right to left and from left to right in alternate lines. [Gk (adv.) = as an ox turns in ploughing f. *bous* ox + *-strophos* turning]

bout /baʊt/ *n.* (often foll. by *of*) **1 a** a limited period of intensive work or exercise. **b** a drinking session. **c** a period (of illness) (*a bout of flu*). **2 a** a wrestling- or boxing-match. **b** a trial of strength. [16th c.: app. the same as obs. *bought* bending]

boutique /buːˈtiːk/ *n.* a small shop or department of a store, selling (esp. fashionable) clothes or accessories. [F, = small shop, f. L (as BODEGA)]

boutonnière /ˌbuːtɒnɪˈeə(r)/ *n.* a spray of flowers worn in a buttonhole. [F]

bouzouki /buːˈzuːkɪ/ *n.* a Greek form of mandolin. [mod. Gk]

bovate /ˈbəʊveɪt/ *n. hist.* a measure of land, as much as one ox could plough in a year, varying from 10 to 18 acres. [med.L *bovata* f. L *bos bovis* ox]

bovine /ˈbəʊvaɪn/ *adj.* **1** of or relating to cattle. **2** stupid, dull. □□ **bovinely** *adv.* [LL *bovinus* f. L *bos bovis* ox]

Bovril /ˈbɒvrɪl/ *n. propr.* a concentrated essence of beef diluted with hot water to make a drink. [L *bos bovis* ox, cow]

bovver /ˈbɒvə(r)/ *n. Brit. sl.* deliberate troublemaking. □**bovver boot** a heavy laced boot worn typically by skinheads. **bovver boy** a violent hooligan. [cockney pronunc. of BOTHER]

bow[1] /bəʊ/ *n. & v.* —*n.* **1 a** a slip-knot with a double loop. **b** a ribbon, shoelace, etc., tied with this. **c** a decoration (on clothing, or painted etc.) in the form of a bow. **2** a device for shooting arrows with a taut string joining the ends of a curved piece of wood etc. **3 a** a rod with horsehair stretched along its length, used for playing the violin, cello, etc. **b** a single stroke of a bow over strings. **4 a** a shallow curve or bend. **b** a rainbow. **5** = *saddle-bow*. **6** a metal ring forming the handle of scissors, a key, etc. **7** *US* the side-piece of a spectacle-frame. **8** *Archery* =

BOWMAN[1]. —*v.tr.* (also *absol.*) use a bow on (a violin etc.) (*he bowed vigorously*). □**bow-compass** (or **-compasses**) compasses with jointed legs. **bow-legged** having bandy legs. **bow-legs** bandy legs. **bow-saw** *Carpentry* a narrow saw stretched like a bowstring on a light frame. **bow-tie** a necktie in the form of a bow (sense 1). **bow-window** a curved bay window. **two strings to one's bow** a twofold resource. [OE *boga* f. Gmc: cf. BOW[2]]

bow[2] /baʊ/ *v. & n.* —*v.* **1** *intr.* incline the head or trunk, esp. in greeting or assent or acknowledgement of applause. **2** *intr.* submit (*bowed to the inevitable*). **3** *tr.* cause to incline (*bowed his head*; *bowed his will to hers*). **4** *tr.* express (thanks, assent, etc.) by bowing (*bowed agreement to the plan*). **5** *tr.* (foll. by *in*, *out*) usher or escort obsequiously (*bowed us out of the restaurant*). —*n.* an inclining of the head or body in greeting, assent, or in the acknowledgement of applause, etc. □**bow and scrape** be obsequious; fawn. **bow down 1** bend or kneel in submission or reverence (*bowed down before the king*). **2** (usu. in *passive*) make stoop; crush (*was bowed down by care*). **bowing acquaintance** a person one acknowledges but does not know well enough to speak to. **bow out 1** make one's exit (esp. formally). **2** retreat, withdraw; retire gracefully. **make one's bow** make a formal exit or entrance. **take a bow** acknowledge applause. [OE *būgan*, f. Gmc: cf. BOW[1]]

bow[3] /baʊ/ *n. Naut.* **1** (often in *pl.*) the fore-end of a boat or a ship. **2** = BOWMAN[2]. □**bow wave** a wave set up at the bows of a moving ship or in front of a body moving in air. **on the bow** within 45° of the point directly ahead. **shot across the bows** a warning. [LG *boog*, Du. *boeg*, ship's bow, orig. shoulder: see BOUGH]

bowdlerize /ˈbaʊdləˌraɪz/ *v.tr.* (also **-ise**) expurgate (a book etc.). □□ **bowdlerism** *n.* **bowdlerization** /-ˈzeɪʃ(ə)n/ *n.* [T. *Bowdler* (d. 1825), expurgator of Shakesp.]

bowel /ˈbaʊəl/ *n.* **1 a** the part of the alimentary canal below the stomach. **b** the intestine. **2** (in *pl.*) the depths; the innermost parts (*the bowels of the earth*). □**bowel movement 1** discharge from the bowels; defecation. **2** the faeces discharged from the body. [ME f. OF *buel* f. L *botellus* little sausage]

bower[1] /ˈbaʊə(r)/ *n. & v.* —*n.* **1 a** a secluded place, esp. in a garden, enclosed by foliage; an arbour. **b** a summer-house. **2** *poet.* an inner room; a boudoir. —*v. tr. poet.* embower. □□ **bowery** *adj.* [OE *būr* f. Gmc]

bower[2] /ˈbaʊə(r)/ *n.* (in full **bower-anchor**) either of two anchors carried at a ship's bow. □**best bower** the starboard bower. **bower-cable** the cable attached to a bower-anchor. **small bower** the port bower. [BOW[3] + -ER[1]]

bower[3] /ˈbaʊə(r)/ *n.* either of two cards at euchre and similar games. □**left bower** the jack of the same colour as the right bower. **right bower** the jack of trumps. [G *Bauer* peasant, jack at cards, rel. to Du. *boer*: see BOOR]

bowerbird /ˈbaʊəˌbɜːd/ *n.* **1** any of various birds of the Ptilonorhynchidae family, native to Australia and New Guinea, the males of which construct elaborate bowers of feathers, grasses, shells, etc. during courtship. **2** a person who collects bric-à-brac.

bowery /ˈbaʊərɪ/ *n.* (also **Bowery**) (*pl.* **-ies**) *US* a district known as a resort of drunks and down-and-outs. [orig. the Bowery, a street in New York City, f. Du. *bouwerij* farm]

bowfin /ˈbəʊfɪn/ *n.* a voracious American freshwater fish, *Amia calva*. [BOW[1] + FIN]

bowhead /ˈbəʊhed/ *n.* an Arctic whale, *Balaena mysticetus*.

bowie /ˈbəʊɪ/ *n.* (in full **bowie knife**) a long knife with a blade double-edged at the point, used as a weapon by American pioneers. [J. *Bowie*, Amer. soldier d. 1836]

bowl[1] /bəʊl/ *n.* **1 a** a usu. round deep basin used for food or liquid. **b** the quantity (of soup etc.) a bowl holds. **c** the contents of a bowl. **2 a** any deep-sided container shaped like a bowl (*lavatory bowl*). **b** the bowl-shaped part of a tobacco-pipe, spoon, balance, etc. **3** esp. *US* a bowl-shaped region or building, esp. an amphitheatre (*Hollywood Bowl*). □□ **bowlful** *n.* (*pl.* **-fuls**). [OE *bolle*, *bolla*, f. Gmc]

bowl[2] /bəʊl/ *n. & v.* —*n.* **1 a** a wooden or hard rubber ball, slightly asymmetrical so that it runs on a curved course, used in the game of bowls. **b** a wooden ball or disc used in playing skittles. **c** a large ball with indents for gripping, used in tenpin bowling. **2** (in *pl.*; usu. treated as *sing.*) **a** a game played with bowls (sense 1a) on grass. **b** tenpin bowling. **c** skittles. **3 a** spell or turn of bowling in cricket. —*v.* **1 a** *tr.* roll (a ball, a hoop, etc.) along the ground. **b** *intr.* play bowls or skittles. **2** *tr.* (also *absol.*) *Cricket* etc. **a** deliver (a ball, an over, etc.) (*bowled six overs*; *bowled well*). **b** (often foll. by *out*) dismiss (a batsman) by knocking down the wicket with a ball (*soon bowled him out*). **c** (often foll. by *down*) knock (a wicket) over. **3** *intr.* (often foll. by *along*) go along rapidly by revolving, esp. on wheels (*the cart bowled along the road*). □ **bowl out** *Cricket* dismiss (a batsman or a side). **bowl over 1** knock down. **2** *colloq.* **a** impress greatly. **b** overwhelm (*bowled over by her energy*). [ME & F *boule* f. L *bulla* bubble]

bowler[1] /ˈbəʊlə(r)/ *n.* **1** *Cricket* etc. a member of the fielding side who bowls or is bowling. **2** a player at bowls.

bowler[2] /ˈbəʊlə(r)/ *n.* (in full **bowler hat**) a man's hard felt hat with a round dome-shaped crown. □ **bowler-hat** (**-hatted**, **-hatting**) *sl.* retire (a person) from the army etc. (*he's been bowler-hatted*). [*Bowler*, a hatter, who designed it in 1850]

bowline /ˈbəʊlɪn/ *n. Naut.* **1** a rope attaching the weather side of a square sail to the bow. **2** a simple knot for forming a non-slipping loop at the end of a rope. [ME f. MLG *bōlīne* (as BOW[3], LINE[1])]

bowling /ˈbəʊlɪŋ/ *n.* the game of bowls as a sport or recreation. □ **bowling-alley 1** a long enclosure for skittles or tenpin bowling. **2** a building containing these. **bowling-crease** *Cricket* the line from behind which a bowler delivers the ball. **bowling-green** a lawn for playing bowls.

bowman[1] /ˈbəʊmən/ *n.* (*pl.* **-men**) an archer.

bowman[2] /ˈbaʊmən/ *n.* (*pl.* **-men**) the rower nearest the bow of esp. a racing boat.

bowser /ˈbaʊzə(r)/ *n.* **1** a tanker used for fuelling aircraft etc. **2** *Austral. & NZ* a petrol pump. [trade name, orig. propr.]

bowshot /ˈbəʊʃɒt/ *n.* the distance to which a bow can send an arrow.

bowsprit /ˈbəʊsprɪt/ *n. Naut.* a spar running out from a ship's bow to which the forestays are fastened. [ME f. Gmc (as BOW[3], SPRIT)]

Bow Street runner /ˈbəʊ/ *n.* (also **Bow Street officer**) *hist.* a London policeman. [*Bow Street* in London, containing the chief metropolitan police-court]

bowstring /ˈbəʊstrɪŋ/ *n. & v.* —*n.* the string of an archer's bow. —*v.tr.* strangle with a bowstring (a former Turkish method of execution).

bow-wow /ˈbaʊwaʊ, -ˈwaʊ/ *int. & n.* —*int.* an imitation of a dog's bark. —*n.* **1** *colloq.* a dog. **2 a** dog's bark. [imit.]

bowyang /ˈbəʊjæŋ/ *n. Austral. & NZ* either of a pair of bands or straps worn round the trouser-legs below the knee. [dial. *bowy-yangs* etc.]

bowyer /ˈbəʊjə(r)/ *n.* a maker or seller of archers' bows.

box[1] /bɒks/ *n. & v.* —*n.* **1** a container, usu. with flat sides and of firm material such as wood or card, esp. for holding solids. **2 a** the amount that will fill a box. **b** *Brit.* a gift of a kind formerly given to tradesmen etc. at Christmas. **3** a separate compartment for any of various purposes, e.g. for a small group in a theatre, for witnesses in a lawcourt, for horses in a stable or vehicle. **4** an enclosure or receptacle for a

special purpose (often in *comb.*: *money box*; *telephone box*). **5** a facility at a newspaper office for receiving replies to an advertisement. **6** (prec. by *the*) *colloq.* television; one's television set (*what's on the box?*). **7** an enclosed area or space. **8** a space or area of print on a page, enclosed by a border. **9** *Brit.* a small country house for use when shooting, fishing, or for other sporting activity. **10** a protective casing for a piece of mechanism. **11** a light shield for protecting the genitals in sport, esp. in cricket. **12** (prec. by *the*) *Football colloq.* the penalty area. **13** *Baseball* the area occupied by the batter or the pitcher. **14** a coachman's seat. —*v.tr.* **1** put in or provide with a box. **2** (foll. by *in*, *up*) confine; restrain from movement. **3** (foll. by *up*) *Austral. & NZ* mix up (different flocks of sheep). □ **box camera** a simple box-shaped hand camera. **box the compass** *Naut.* recite the points of the compass in the correct order. **box girder** a hollow girder square in cross-section. **box junction** *Brit.* a road area at a junction marked with a yellow grid, which a vehicle should enter only if its exit from it is clear. **box kite** a kite in the form of a long box open at each end. **box number** a number by which replies are made to a private advertisement in a newspaper. **box office 1** an office for booking seats and buying tickets at a theatre, cinema, etc. **2** the commercial aspect of the arts and entertainment (often *attrib.*: *a box-office failure*). **box pleat** a pleat consisting of two parallel creases forming a raised band. **box spanner** a spanner with a box-shaped end fitting over the head of a nut. **box spring** each of a set of vertical springs housed in a frame, e.g. in a mattress. □□ **boxful** *n.* (*pl.* **-fuls**). **boxlike** *adj.* [OE f. LL *buxis* f. L PYXIS]

box[2] /bɒks/ *v. & n.* —*v.* **1 a** *tr.* fight (an opponent) at boxing. **b** *intr.* practise boxing. **2** slap (esp. a person's ears). —*n.* a slap with the hand, esp. on the ears. □ **box clever** *colloq.* act in a clever or effective way. [ME: orig. unkn.]

box[3] /bɒks/ *n.* **1** any small evergreen tree or shrub of the genus *Buxus*, esp. *B. sempervirens*, a slow-growing tree with glossy dark green leaves which is often used in hedging. **2** its wood, used for carving, turning, engraving, etc. **3** any of various trees in Australasia which have similar wood or foliage, esp. those of several species of *Eucalyptus*. **4** = BOXWOOD. □ **box elder** the American ash-leaved maple, *Acer negundo*. [OE f. L *buxus*, Gk *puxos*]

Box and Cox /ˌbɒks ənd ˈkɒks/ *n. & v.* —*n.* (often *attrib.*) two persons sharing accommodation etc., and using it at different times. —*v.intr.* share accommodation, duties, etc. by a strictly timed arrangement. [the names of characters in a play (1847) by J. M. Morton]

boxcar /ˈbɒkskɑː(r)/ *n. US* an enclosed railway goods wagon, usu. with sliding doors on the sides.

Boxer /ˈbɒksə(r)/ *n. hist.* a member of a fiercely nationalist Chinese secret society that flourished in the 19th c. [transl. of Chin. *i ho chuan*, lit. 'righteous harmony fists']

boxer /ˈbɒksə(r)/ *n.* **1** a person who practises boxing, esp. for sport. **2 a** a medium-size dog of a breed with a smooth brown coat and puglike face. **b** this breed. □ **boxer shorts** men's underpants similar to shorts worn in boxing, with a shallow curved slit at each side.

boxing /ˈbɒksɪŋ/ *n.* the practice of fighting with the fists, esp. in padded gloves as a sport. □ **boxing glove** each of a pair of heavily padded gloves used in boxing. **boxing weight** each of a series of fixed weight-ranges at which boxers are matched.

Boxing Day /ˈbɒksɪŋ/ *n.* the first weekday after Christmas. [from the custom of giving tradesmen gifts or money: see BOX[1] *n.* 2b]

boxroom /ˈbɒksruːm, -rʊm/ *n. Brit.* a room or large cupboard for storing boxes, cases, etc.

boxwood /ˈbɒkswʊd/ *n.* **1** the wood of the box used

esp. by engravers for the fineness of its grain and for its hardness. **2** = BOX[3] 1.

boxy /'bɒksɪ/ *adj.* (**boxier, boxiest**) reminiscent of a box; (of a room or space) very cramped.

boy /bɔɪ/ *n.* & *int.* —*n.* **1** a male child or youth. **2** a young man, esp. regarded as not yet mature. **3** a male servant, attendant, etc. **4** (**the boys**) *colloq.* a group of men mixing socially. —*int.* expressing pleasure, surprise, etc. □**boy scout** = SCOUT[1] 4. **boys in blue** *Brit.* policemen. □□ **boyhood** *n.* **boyish** *adj.* **boyishly** *adv.* **boyishness** *n.* [ME = servant, perh. ult. f. L *boia* fetter]

boyar /bəʊ'jɑ:(r)/ *n. hist.* a member of the old aristocracy in Russia. [Russ. *boyarin* grandee]

boycott /'bɔɪkɒt/ *v.* & *n.* —*v.tr.* **1** combine in refusing social or commercial relations with (a person, group, country, etc.) usu. as punishment or coercion. **2** refuse to handle (goods) to this end. —*n.* such a refusal. [Capt. C. C. *Boycott*, Irish land-agent d. 1897, so treated from 1880]

boyfriend /'bɔɪfrend/ *n.* a person's regular male companion or lover.

Boyle's law /bɔɪlz/ *n.* the law that the pressure of a given mass of gas is inversely proportional to its volume at a constant temperature. [Robert *Boyle*, Irish scientist d. 1691]

boyo /'bɔɪəʊ/ *n.* (*pl.* **-os**) *Welsh* & *Ir. colloq.* boy, fellow (esp. as a form of address).

boysenberry /'bɔɪzənberɪ/ *n.* (*pl.* **-ies**) **1** a hybrid of several species of bramble. **2** the large red edible fruit of this plant. [R. *Boysen*, 20th-c. Amer. horticulturalist]

BP *abbr.* **1** boiling-point. **2** blood pressure. **3** before the present (era). **4** British Petroleum. **5** British Pharmacopoeia.

Bp. *abbr.* Bishop.

BPC *abbr.* British Pharmaceutical Codex.

B.Phil. *abbr.* Bachelor of Philosophy.

Bq *abbr.* becquerel.

BR *abbr.* British Rail.

Br *symb. Chem.* the element bromine.

Br. *abbr.* **1** British. **2** Brother.

bra /brɑ:/ *n.* (*pl.* **bras**) *colloq.* = BRASSIÈRE. [abbr.]

brace /breɪs/ *n.* & *v.* —*n.* **1** a device that clamps or fastens tightly. **2** (in *pl.*) *Brit.* straps supporting trousers from the shoulders. **3** a wire device for straightening the teeth. **4** (*pl.* same) a pair (esp. of game). **5** a rope attached to the yard of a ship for trimming the sail. **6 a** a connecting mark { or } used in printing. **b** *Mus.* a similar mark connecting staves to be performed at the same time. —*v.tr.* **1** fasten tightly, give firmness to. **2** make steady by supporting. **3** (esp. as **bracing** *adj.*) invigorate, refresh. **4** (often *refl.*) prepare for a difficulty, shock, etc. □**brace and bit** a revolving tool with a D-shaped central handle for boring. □□ **bracingly** *adv.* **bracingness** *n.* [ME f. OF *brace* two arms, *bracier* embrace, f. L *bra(c)chia* arms]

bracelet /'breɪslɪt/ *n.* **1** an ornamental band, hoop, or chain worn on the wrist or arm. **2** *sl.* a handcuff. [ME f. OF, dimin. of *bracel* f. L *bracchiale* f. *bra(c)chium* arm]

bracer /'breɪsə(r)/ *n. colloq.* a tonic.

brachial /'breɪkɪəl/ *adj.* **1** of or relating to the arm (*brachial artery*). **2** like an arm. [L *brachialis* f. *bra(c)chium* arm]

brachiate /'breɪkɪeɪt/ *v.* & *adj.* —*v.intr.* (of certain apes and monkeys) move by using the arms to swing from branch to branch. —*adj. Biol.* **1** having arms. **2** having paired branches on alternate sides. □□ **brachiation** /-'eɪʃ(ə)n/ *n.* **brachiator** *n.* [L *bra(c)chium* arm]

brachiopod /'breɪkɪəʊˌpɒd, 'bræk-/ *n.* any marine invertebrate of the phylum Brachiopoda (esp. a fossil one) having a two-valved chalky shell and a ciliated feeding arm. [mod.L f. Gk *brakhiōn* arm + *pous podos* foot]

brachiosaurus /ˌbreɪkɪə'sɔ:rəs, ˌbræk-/ *n.* any huge

plant-eating dinosaur of the genus *Brachiosaurus* with forelegs longer than its hind legs. [mod.L f. Gk *brakhiōn* arm + *sauros* lizard]

brachistochrone /bræ'kɪstəˌkrəʊn/ *n.* a curve between two points along which a body can move in a shorter time than for any other curve. [Gk *brakhistos* shortest + *khronos* time]

brachy- /'brækɪ/ *comb. form* short. [Gk *brakhus* short]

brachycephalic /ˌbrækɪsɪ'fælɪk/ *adj.* having a broad short head. □□ **brachycephalous** /ˌbrækɪ'sefələs/ *adj.* [BRACHY- + Gk *kephalē* head]

brachylogy /brə'kɪlədʒɪ/ *n.* (*pl.* **-ies**) **1** overconciseness of expression. **2** an instance of this.

brack /bræk/ *n. Ir.* cake or bread containing dried fruit etc. [abbr. of BARMBRACK]

bracken /'brækən/ *n.* **1** any large coarse fern, esp. *Pteridium aquilinum*, abundant on heaths and moorlands, and in woods. **2** a mass of such ferns. Also called BRAKE[5]. [north. ME f. ON]

bracket /'brækɪt/ *n.* & *v.* —*n.* **1** a right-angled or other support attached to and projecting from a vertical surface. **2** a shelf fixed with such a support to a wall. **3** each of a pair of marks () [] {} used to enclose words or figures. **4** a group classified as containing similar elements or falling between given limits (*income bracket*). **5** *Mil.* the distance between two artillery shots fired either side of the target to establish range. —*v.tr.* (**bracketed, bracketing**) **1 a** couple (names etc.) with a brace. **b** imply a connection or equality between. **2 a** enclose in brackets as parenthetic or spurious. **b** *Math.* enclose in brackets as having specific relations to what precedes or follows. **3** *Mil.* establish the range of (a target) by firing two preliminary shots one short of and the other beyond it. [F *braguette* or Sp. *bragueta* codpiece, dimin. of F *brague* f. Prov. *braga* f. L *braca*, pl. *bracae* breeches]

brackish /'brækɪʃ/ *adj.* (of water etc.) slightly salty. □□ **brackishness** *n.* [obs. *brack* (adj.) f. MLG, MDu. *brac*]

bract /brækt/ *n.* a modified and often brightly coloured leaf, with a flower or an inflorescence in its axil. □□ **bracteal** *adj.* **bracteate** /-tɪɪt/ *adj.* [L *bractea* thin plate, gold-leaf]

brad /bræd/ *n.* a thin flat nail with a head in the form of slight enlargement at the top. [var. of ME *brod* goad, pointed instrument, f. ON *broddr* spike]

bradawl /'brædɔ:l/ *n.* a small tool with a pointed end for boring holes by hand. [BRAD + AWL]

bradycardia /ˌbrædɪ'kɑ:dɪə/ *n. Med.* abnormally slow heart-action. [Gk *bradus* slow + *kardia* heart]

brae /breɪ/ *n. Sc.* a steep bank or hillside. [ME f. ON *brá* eyelash]

brag /bræg/ *v.* & *n.* —*v.* (**bragged, bragging**) **1** *intr.* talk boastfully. **2** *tr.* boast about. —*n.* **1** a card-game like poker. **2** a boastful statement; boastful talk. □□ **bragger** *n.* **braggingly** *adv.* [ME, orig. adj., = spirited, boastful: orig. unkn.]

braggadocio /ˌbrægə'dəʊtʃɪəʊ, -'dəʊʃɪəʊ/ *n.* empty boasting; a boastful manner of speech and behaviour. [*Braggadochio*, a braggart in Spenser's *Faerie Queene*, f. BRAG or BRAGGART + It. augment. suffix *-occio*]

braggart /'brægət/ *n.* & *adj.* —*n.* a person given to bragging. —*adj.* boastful. [F *bragard* f. *braguer* BRAG]

Brahma /'brɑ:mə/ *n.* **1** the Hindu Creator. **2** the supreme divine reality in Hindu belief. [Skr., = creator]

Brahman /'brɑ:mən/ *n.* (also **brahman**) (*pl.* **-mans**) **1** a member of the highest Hindu caste, whose members are traditionally eligible for the priesthood. **2** = BRAHMA 2. □□ **Brahmanic** /-'mænɪk/ *adj.* **Brahmanical** /-'mænɪk(ə)l/ *adj.* **Brahmanism** *n.* [Skr. *brāhmaṇas* f. *brahman* priest]

brahmaputra /ˌbrɑ:mə'pu:trə/ *n.* (also **brahma**) **1** any bird of a large Asian breed of domestic fowl. **2**

this breed. [river *Brahmaputra* in India, from where it was brought]

Brahmin /'brɑːmɪn/ *n.* **1** = BRAHMAN. **2** *US* a socially or intellectually superior person. [var. of BRAHMAN]

braid /breɪd/ *n. & v.* —*n.* **1** a woven band of silk or thread used for edging or trimming. **2** a length of entwined hair. —*v.tr.* **1** plait or intertwine (hair or thread). **2** trim or decorate with braid. □□ **braider** *n.* [OE *bregdan* f. Gmc]

braiding /'breɪdɪŋ/ *n.* **1** various types of braid collectively. **2** braided work.

Braille /breɪl/ *n. & v.* —*n.* a system of writing and printing for the blind, in which characters are represented by patterns of raised dots. —*v.tr.* print or transcribe in Braille. [L. *Braille*, Fr. teacher d. 1852, its inventor]

brain /breɪn/ *n. & v.* —*n.* **1** an organ of soft nervous tissue contained in the skull of vertebrates, functioning as the coordinating centre of sensation, and of intellectual and nervous activity. **2** (in *pl.*) the substance of the brain, esp. as food. **3 a** a person's intellectual capacity (*has a poor brain*). **b** (often in *pl.*) intelligence; high intellectual capacity (*has a brain*; *has brains*). **4** (in *pl.*; prec. by *the*) *colloq.* **a** the cleverest person in a group. **b** a person who originates a complex plan or idea (*the brains behind the robbery*). **5** an electronic device with functions comparable to those of a brain. —*v.tr.* **1** dash out the brains of. **2** strike hard on the head. □ **brain-dead** suffering from brain death. **brain death** irreversible brain damage causing the end of independent respiration, regarded as indicative of death. **brain drain** *colloq.* the loss of skilled personnel by emigration. **brain fever** inflammation of the brain. **brain-pan** *colloq.* the skull. **brain stem** the central trunk of the brain, upon which the cerebrum and cerebellum are set, and which continues downwards to form the spinal cord. **brains** (*US* **brain**) **trust** a group of experts who give impromptu answers to questions, usu. publicly. **brain-teaser** (or **-twister**) *colloq.* a puzzle or problem. **brain trust** *US* a group of expert advisers. **on the brain** *colloq.* obsessively in one's thoughts. [OE *brægen* f. WG]

brainchild /'breɪntʃaɪld/ *n.* (*pl.* **-children**) *colloq.* an idea, plan, or invention regarded as the result of a person's mental effort.

brainless /'breɪnlɪs/ *adj.* stupid, foolish.

brainpower /'breɪn,paʊə(r)/ *n.* mental ability or intelligence.

brainstorm /'breɪnstɔːm/ *n.* **1** a violent or excited outburst often as a result of a sudden mental disturbance. **2** *colloq.* mental confusion. **3** *US* a brain-wave. **4** a concerted intellectual treatment of a problem by discussing spontaneous ideas about it. □□ **brainstorming** *n.* (in sense 4).

brainwash /'breɪnwɒʃ/ *v.tr.* subject (a person) to a prolonged process by which ideas other than and at variance with those already held are implanted in the mind. □□ **brainwashing** *n.*

brainwave /'breɪnweɪv/ *n.* **1** (usu. in *pl.*) an electrical impulse in the brain. **2** *colloq.* a sudden bright idea.

brainy /'breɪnɪ/ *adj.* (**brainier**, **brainiest**) intellectually clever or active. □□ **brainily** *adv.* **braininess** *n.*

braise /breɪz/ *v.tr.* fry lightly and then stew slowly with a little liquid in a closed container. [F *braiser* f. *braise* live coals]

brake[1] /breɪk/ *n. & v.* —*n.* **1** (often in *pl.*) a device for checking the motion of a mechanism, esp. a wheel or vehicle, or for keeping it at rest. **2** anything that has the effect of hindering or impeding (*shortage of money was a brake on their enthusiasm*). —*v.* **1** *intr.* apply a brake. **2** *tr.* retard or stop with a brake. □ **brake block** a block used to hold a brake shoe. **brake drum** a cylinder attached to a wheel on which the brake shoe presses to brake. **brake fluid** fluid used in a hydraulic brake system. **brake**

horsepower the power of an engine reckoned in terms of the force needed to brake it. **brake lining** a strip of fabric which increases the friction of the brake shoe. **brake shoe** a long curved block which presses on the brake drum to brake. **brake van** *Brit.* a railway coach or vehicle from which the train's brakes can be controlled. □□ **brakeless** *adj.* [prob. obs. *brake* in sense 'machine-handle, bridle']

brake[2] /breɪk/ *n.* a large estate car. [var. of BREAK[2]]

brake[3] /breɪk/ *n. & v.* —*n.* **1** a toothed instrument used for crushing flax and hemp. **2** (in full **brake harrow**) a heavy kind of harrow for breaking up large lumps of earth. —*v.tr.* crush (flax or hemp) by beating it. [ME, rel. to BREAK[1]]

brake[4] /breɪk/ *n.* **1** a thicket. **2** brushwood. [ME f. OF *bracu*, MLG *brake* branch, stump]

brake[5] /breɪk/ *n.* bracken. [ME, perh. shortened f. BRACKEN, *-en* being taken as a pl. ending]

brake[6] *archaic past* of BREAK[1].

brakeman /'breɪkmən/ *n.* (*pl.* **-men**) **1** *US* an official on a train, responsible for maintenance on a journey. **2** a person in charge of brakes. [BRAKE[1] + MAN]

brakesman /'breɪksmən/ *n.* (*pl.* **-men**) *Brit.* = BRAKEMAN 2.

bramble /'bræmb(ə)l/ *n.* **1** any of various thorny shrubs bearing fleshy red or black berries, esp. the blackberry bush, *Rubus fruticosus.* **2** the edible berry of these shrubs. **3** any of various other rosaceous shrubs with similar foliage, esp. the dog rose (*Rosa canina*). □□ **brambly** *adj.* [OE *brǣmbel* (earlier *brǣmel*): see BROOM]

brambling /'bræmblɪŋ/ *n.* the speckled finch, *Fringilla montifringilla*, native to northern Eurasia, the male having a distinctive red breast. [G *Brämling* f. WG (cf. BRAMBLE)]

Bramley /'bræmlɪ/ *n.* (*pl.* **-eys**) (in full **Bramley's seedling**) a large green variety of cooking apple. [M. *Bramley*, Engl. butcher in whose garden it may have first grown *c.*1850]

bran /bræn/ *n.* grain husks separated from the flour. □ **bran-tub** *Brit.* a lucky dip with prizes concealed in bran. [ME f. OF, of unkn. orig.]

branch /brɑːntʃ/ *n. & v.* —*n.* **1** a limb extending from a tree or bough. **2** a lateral extension or subdivision, esp. of a river, road, or railway. **3** a conceptual extension or subdivision, as of a family, knowledge, etc. **4** a local division or office etc. of a large business, as of a bank, library, etc. —*v.intr.* (often foll. by *off*) **1** diverge from the main part. **2** divide into branches. □ **branch out** extend one's field of interest. □□ **branched** *adj.* **branchlet** *n.* **branchlike** *adj.* **branchy** *adj.* [ME f. OF *branche* f. LL *branca* paw]

branchia /'bræŋkɪə/ *n.pl.* (also **branchiae** /-kɪ,iː/) gills. □□ **branchial** *adj.* **branchiate** /-kɪ,eɪt/ *adj.* [L *branchia*, pl. *-ae*, f. Gk *bragkhia* pl.]

brand /brænd/ *n. & v.* —*n.* **1 a** a particular make of goods. **b** an identifying trade mark, label, etc. **2** (usu. foll. by *of*) a special or characteristic kind (*brand of humour*). **3** an identifying mark burned on livestock or (formerly) prisoners etc. with a hot iron. **4** an iron used for this. **5** a piece of burning, smouldering, or charred wood. **6** a stigma; a mark of disgrace. **7** *poet.* **a** a torch. **b** a sword. **8** a kind of blight, leaving leaves with a burnt appearance. —*v.tr.* **1** mark with a hot iron. **2** stigmatize; mark with disgrace (*they branded him a liar*; *was branded for life*). **3** impress unforgettably on one's mind. **4** assign a trademark or label to. □ **brand-new** completely or obviously new. □□ **brander** *n.* [OE f. Gmc]

brandish /'brændɪʃ/ *v.tr.* wave or flourish as a threat or in display. □□ **brandisher** *n.* [OF *brandir* ult. f. Gmc, rel. to BRAND]

brandling /'brændlɪŋ/ *n.* a red earthworm, *Eisenia foetida*, with rings of a brighter colour, which is often found in manure and used as bait. [BRAND + -LING[1]]

brandy /'brændɪ/ *n.* (*pl.* **-ies**) a strong alcoholic spirit distilled from wine or fermented fruit juice.

▫**brandy-ball** *Brit.* a kind of brandy-flavoured sweet. **brandy butter** a rich sweet hard sauce made with brandy, butter, and sugar. **brandy-snap** a crisp rolled gingerbread wafer usu. filled with cream. [earlier *brand(e)wine* f. Du. *brandewijn* burnt (distilled) wine]

brank-ursine /bræŋkˈɜːsaɪn/ *n.* the plant *Acanthus mollis* or *A. spinosus*, with three-lobed flowers and spiny leaves, used as a motif for the Corinthian capital. Also called *bear's breech* (see BEAR²). [F *branche ursine*, med.L *branca ursina* bear's claw: see BRANCH, URSINE]

brant *US* var. of BRENT.

brash¹ /bræʃ/ *adj.* **1** vulgarly or ostentatiously self-assertive. **2** hasty, rash. **3** impudent. ▫▫ **brashly** *adv.* **brashness** *n.* [orig. dial., perh. f. RASH¹]

brash² /bræʃ/ *n.* **1** loose broken rock or ice. **2** clippings from hedges, shrubs, etc. [18th c.: orig. unkn.]

brash³ /bræʃ/ *n.* an eruption of fluid from the stomach. [16th c., perh. imit.]

brass /brɑːs/ *n. & adj.* —*n.* **1** a yellow alloy of copper and zinc. **2 a** an ornament or other decorated piece of brass. **b** brass objects collectively. **3** *Mus.* brass wind instruments (including trumpet, horn, trombone) forming a band or a section of an orchestra. **4** *Brit. sl.* money. **5** (in full **horse-brass**) a round flat brass ornament for the harness of a draught-horse. **6** (in full **top brass**) *colloq.* persons in authority or of high (esp. military) rank. **7** an inscribed or engraved memorial tablet of brass. **8** *colloq.* effrontery (*then had the brass to demand money*). **9** a brass block or die used for making a design on a book binding. —*adj.* made of brass. **brass band** a group of musicians playing brass instruments, sometimes also with percussion. **brassed off** *sl.* fed up. **brass hat** *Brit. colloq.* an officer of high rank, usu. one with gold braid on the cap. **brass monkey** *coarse sl.* used in various phrases to indicate extreme cold. **brass-rubbing 1** the rubbing of heelball etc. over paper laid on an engraved brass to take an impression of its design. **2** the impression obtained by this. **brass tacks** *sl.* actual details; real business (*get down to brass tacks*). **not a brass farthing** *colloq.* no money or assets at all. [OE *bræs*, of unkn. orig.]

brassard /ˈbræsɑːd/ *n.* a band worn on the sleeve, esp. with a uniform. [F *bras* arm + -ARD]

brasserie /ˈbræsərɪ/ *n.* a restaurant, orig. one serving beer with food. [F, = brewery]

brassica /ˈbræsɪkə/ *n.* any cruciferous plant of the genus *Brassica*, having tap roots and erect branched stems, including cabbage, swede, brussel sprout, mustard, rape, cauliflower, kohlrabi, calabrese, kale, and turnip. [L, = cabbage]

brassie /ˈbræsɪ/ *n.* (also **brassy**) (*pl.* -ies) a wooden-headed golf club with a brass sole.

brassière /ˈbræzɪə(r), -sɪˌeə(r)/ *n.* an undergarment worn by women to support the breasts. [F, = child's vest]

brassy¹ /ˈbrɑːsɪ/ *adj.* (**brassier**, **brassiest**) **1** impudent. **2** pretentious, showy. **3** loud and blaring. **4** of or like brass. ▫▫ **brassily** *adv.* **brassiness** *n.*

brassy² var. of BRASSIE.

brat /bræt/ *n.* usu. *derog.* a child, esp. an ill-behaved one. ▫▫ **bratty** *adj.* [perh. abbr. of Sc. *bratchart* hound, or f. *brat* rough garment]

brattice /ˈbrætɪs/ *n.* a wooden partition or shaft-lining in a coalmine. [ME ult. f. OE *brittisc* BRITISH]

bratwurst /ˈbrætvʊəst, -vɜːst/ *n.* a type of small German pork sausage. [G f. *braten* fry, roast + *Wurst* sausage]

bravado /brəˈvɑːdəʊ/ *n.* a bold manner or a show of boldness intended to impress. [Sp. *bravata* f. *bravo*: cf. BRAVE, -ADO]

brave /breɪv/ *adj., n., & v.* —*adj.* **1** able or ready to face and endure danger or pain. **2** *formal* splendid, spectacular (*make a brave show*). —*n.* an American Indian warrior. —*v.tr.* defy; encounter bravely.

▫**brave it out** behave defiantly under suspicion or blame. ▫▫ **bravely** *adv.* **braveness** *n.* [ME f. F, ult. f. L *barbarus* BARBAROUS]

bravery /ˈbreɪvərɪ/ *n.* **1** brave conduct. **2** a brave nature. [F *braverie* or It. *braveria* (as BRAVE)]

bravo¹ /brɑːˈvəʊ/ *int. & n.* —*int.* expressing approval of a performer etc. —*n.* (*pl.* -os) a cry of bravo. [F f. It.]

bravo² /ˈbrɑːvəʊ/ *n.* (*pl.* -oes or -os) a hired ruffian or killer. [It.: see BRAVE]

bravura /brəˈvʊərə, -ˈvjʊərə/ *n.* (often *attrib.*) **1** a brilliant or ambitious action or display. **2 a** a style of (esp. vocal) music requiring exceptional ability. **b** a passage of this kind. **3** bravado. [It.]

braw /brɔː/ *adj.* Sc. fine, good. [var. of *brawf* BRAVE]

brawl /brɔːl/ *n. & v.* —*n.* a noisy quarrel or fight. —*v.intr.* **1** quarrel noisily or roughly. **2** (of a stream) run noisily. ▫▫ **brawler** *n.* [ME f. OProv., rel. to BRAY¹]

brawn /brɔːn/ *n.* **1** muscular strength. **2** muscle; lean flesh. **3** *Brit.* a jellied preparation of the chopped meat from a boiled pig's head. [ME f. AF *braun*, OF *braon* f. Gmc]

brawny /ˈbrɔːnɪ/ *adj.* (**brawnier**, **brawniest**) muscular, strong. ▫▫ **brawniness** *n.*

bray¹ /breɪ/ *n. & v.* —*n.* **a** the cry of a donkey. **b** a sound like this cry, e.g. that of a harshly-played brass instrument, a laugh, etc. —*v.* **1** *intr.* make a braying sound. **2** *tr.* utter harshly. [ME f. OF *braire*, perh. ult. f. Celt.]

bray² /breɪ/ *v.tr. archaic* pound or crush to small pieces, esp. with a pestle and mortar. [ME f. AF *braier*, OF *breier* f. Gmc]

braze¹ /breɪz/ *v. & n.* —*v.tr.* solder with an alloy of brass and zinc at a high temperature. —*n.* **1** a brazed joint. **2** the alloy used for brazing. [F *braser* solder f. *braise* live coals]

braze² /breɪz/ *v.tr.* **1 a** make of brass. **b** cover or ornament with brass. **2** make hard like brass. [OE *bræsen* f. *bræs* BRASS]

brazen /ˈbreɪz(ə)n/ *adj. & v.* —*adj.* **1** (also **brazen-faced**) flagrant and shameless; insolent. **2** made of brass. **3** of or like brass, esp. in colour or sound. —*v.tr.* (foll. by *out*) face or undergo defiantly. ▫**brazen it out** be defiantly unrepentant under censure. ▫▫ **brazenly** *adv.* **brazenness** /ˈbreɪzənnɪs/ *n.* [OE *bræsen* f. *bræs* brass]

brazier¹ /ˈbreɪzɪə(r), -ʒə(r)/ *n.* a portable heater consisting of a pan or stand for holding lighted coals. [F *brasier* f. *braise* hot coals]

brazier² /ˈbreɪzɪə(r), -ʒə(r)/ *n.* a worker in brass. ▫▫ **braziery** *n.* [ME prob. f. BRASS + -IER, after *glass*, *glazier*]

Brazil /brəˈzɪl/ *n.* **1 a** a lofty tree, *Bertholletia excelsa*, forming large forests in S. America. **b** (in full **Brazil nut**) a large three-sided nut with an edible kernel from this tree. **2** (in full **Brazil-wood**) a hard red wood from any tropical tree of the genus *Caesalpina*, that yields dyes. [the name of a S.Amer. country, named from *Brazil-wood*, ult. f. med.L *brasilium*]

BRCS *abbr.* British Red Cross Society.

breach /briːtʃ/ *n. & v.* —*n.* **1** (often foll. by *of*) the breaking of or failure to observe a law, contract, etc. **2 a** a breaking of relations; an estrangement. **b** a quarrel. **3 a** a broken state. **b** a gap, esp. one made by artillery in fortifications. —*v.tr.* **1** break through; make a gap in. **2** break (a law, contract, etc.). ▫**breach of the peace** an infringement or violation of the public peace by any disturbance or riot etc. **breach of promise** the breaking of a promise, esp. a promise to marry. **stand in the breach** bear the brunt of an attack. **step into the breach** give help in a crisis, esp. by replacing someone who has dropped out. [ME f. OF *breche*, ult. f. Gmc]

bread /bred/ *n. & v.* —*n.* **1** baked dough made of flour usu. leavened with yeast and moistened, eaten as a staple food. **2** a necessary food. **b** (also **daily bread**) one's livelihood. **3** *sl.* money. —*v.tr.* coat with breadcrumbs for cooking. □**bread and butter 1** bread spread with butter. **2 a** one's livelihood. **b** routine work to ensure an income. **bread-and-butter letter** a letter of thanks for hospitality. **bread and circuses** the public provision of subsistence and entertainment. **bread and wine** the Eucharist. **bread basket 1** a basket for bread or rolls. **2** *sl.* the stomach. **bread bin** a container for keeping bread in. **bread sauce** a white sauce thickened with breadcrumbs. **cast one's bread upon the waters** do good without expecting gratitude or reward. **know which side one's bread is buttered** know where one's advantage lies. **take the bread out of a person's mouth** take away a person's living, esp. by competition etc. [OE *brēad* f. Gmc]

breadboard /ˈbredbɔːd/ *n.* **1** a board for cutting bread on. **2** a board for making an experimental model of an electric circuit.

breadcrumb /ˈbredkrʌm/ *n.* **1** a small fragment of bread. **2** (in *pl.*) bread crumbled for use in cooking.

breadfruit /ˈbredfruːt/ *n.* **1** a tropical evergreen tree, *Artocarpus altilis*, bearing edible usu. seedless fruit. **2** the fruit of this tree which when roasted becomes soft like new bread.

breadline /ˈbredlaɪn/ *n.* **1** subsistence level (esp. *on the breadline*). **2** *US* a queue of people waiting to receive free food.

breadth /bredθ/ *n.* **1** the distance or measurement from side to side of a thing; broadness. **2** a piece (of cloth etc.) of standard or full breadth. **3** extent, distance, room. **4** (usu. foll. by *of*) capacity to respect other opinions; freedom from prejudice or intolerance (esp. *breadth of mind* or *view*). **5** *Art* unity of the whole, achieved by the disregard of unnecessary details. □□**breadthways** *adv.* **breadthwise** *adv.* [obs. *brede*, OE *brǣdu*, f. Gmc, rel. to BROAD]

breadwinner /ˈbred,wɪnə(r)/ *n.* a person who earns the money to support a family.

break[1] /breɪk/ *v. & n.* —*v.* (*past* **broke** /brəʊk/ or *archaic* **brake** /breɪk/; *past part.* **broken** /ˈbrəʊkən/ or *archaic* **broke**) **1** *tr. & intr.* **a** separate into pieces under a blow or strain; shatter. **b** make or become inoperative, esp. from damage (*the toaster has broken*). **c** break a bone in or dislocate (part of the body). **d** break the skin of (the head or crown). **2 a** *tr.* cause or effect an interruption in (*broke our journey*; *the spell was broken*; *broke the silence*). **b** *intr.* have an interval between spells of work (*let's break now*; *we broke for tea*). **3** *tr.* fail to observe or keep (a law, promise, etc.). **4 a** *tr. & intr.* make or become subdued or weakened; yield or cause to yield (*broke his spirit*; *he broke under the strain*). **b** *tr.* weaken the effect of (a fall, blow, etc.). **c** *tr.* = *break in* 3c. **d** *tr.* defeat, destroy (*broke the enemy's power*). **e** *tr.* defeat the object of (a strike, e.g. by engaging other personnel). **5** *tr.* surpass (a record). **6** *intr.* (foll. by *with*) quarrel or cease association with (another person etc.). **7** *tr.* **a** be no longer subject to (a habit). **b** (foll. by *of*) cause (a person) to be free of a habit (*broke them of their addiction*). **8** *tr. & intr.* reveal or be revealed; (cause to) become known (*broke the news*; *the story broke on Friday*). **9** *intr.* **a** (of the weather) change suddenly, esp. after a fine spell. **b** (of waves) curl over and dissolve into foam. **c** (of the day) dawn. **d** (of clouds) move apart; show a gap. **e** (of a storm) begin violently. **10** *tr. Electr.* disconnect (a circuit). **11** *intr.* **a** (of the voice) change with emotion. **b** (of a boy's voice) change in register etc. at puberty. **12** *tr.* **a** (often foll. by *up*) divide (a set etc.) into parts, e.g. by selling to different buyers. **b** change (a banknote etc.) for coins. **13** *tr.* ruin (an individual or institution) financially (see also BROKE *adj.*). **14** *tr.* penetrate (e.g. a safe) by force. **15** *tr.* decipher (a code). **16** *tr.* make (a way, path, etc.) by separating obstacles. **17** *intr.* burst forth (*the sun broke through the clouds*). **18** *Mil.* **a** *intr.* (of troops)

disperse in confusion. **b** *tr.* make a rupture in (ranks). **19 a** *intr.* (usu. foll. by *free, loose, out,* etc.) escape from constraint by a sudden effort. **b** *tr.* escape or emerge from (prison, bounds, cover, etc.). **20** *tr. Tennis etc.* win a game against (an opponent's service). **21** *intr. Boxing* etc. (of two fighters, usu. at the referee's command) come out of a clinch. **22** *Mil.* *tr.* demote (an officer). **23** *intr.* esp. *Stock Exch.* (of prices) fall sharply. **24** *intr. Cricket* (of a bowled ball) change direction on bouncing. **25** *intr. Billiards* etc. disperse the balls at the beginning of a game. **26** *tr.* unfurl (a flag etc.). **27** *tr. Phonet.* subject (a vowel) to fracture. **28** *tr.* fail to rejoin (one's ship) after absence on leave. **29** *tr.* disprove (an alibi). —*n.* **1** an act or instance of breaking. **b** a point where something is broken; a gap. **2** an interval, an interruption; a pause in work. **3** a sudden dash (esp. to escape). **4** *colloq.* **a** a piece of good luck; a fair chance. **b** (also **bad break**) an unfortunate remark or action, a blunder. **5** *Cricket* a change in direction of a bowled ball on bouncing. **6** *Billiards* etc. **a** a series of points scored during one turn. **b** the opening shot that disperses the balls. **7** *Mus.* (in jazz) a short unaccompanied passage for a soloist, usu. improvised. **8** *Electr.* a discontinuity in a circuit. □**bad break** *colloq.* **1** a piece of bad luck. **2** a mistake or blunder. **break away** make or become free or separate (see also BREAKAWAY). **break the back of 1** do the hardest or greatest part of. **2** overburden (a person). **break bulk** see BULK. **break crop** a crop grown to avoid the continual growing of cereals. **break-dancing** an energetic style of street-dancing, developed by US Blacks. **break down 1 a** fail in mechanical action; cease to function. **b** (of human relationships etc.) fail, collapse. **c** fail in (esp. mental) health. **d** be overcome by emotion; collapse in tears. **2 a** demolish, destroy. **b** suppress (resistance). **c** force (a person) to yield under pressure. **3** analyse into components (see also BREAKDOWN). **break even** emerge from a transaction etc. with neither profit nor loss. **break a person's heart** see HEART. **break the ice 1** begin to overcome formality or shyness, esp. between strangers. **2** make a start. **break in 1** enter premises by force, esp. with criminal intent. **2** interrupt. **3 a** accustom to a habit etc. **b** wear etc. until comfortable. **c** tame or discipline (an animal); accustom (a horse) to saddle and bridle etc. **4** *Austral. & NZ* bring (virgin land) into cultivation. **break-in** *n.* an illegal forced entry into premises, esp. with criminal intent. **breaking and entering** (formerly) the illegal entering of a building with intent to commit a felony. **breaking-point** the point of greatest strain, at which a thing breaks or a person gives way. **break in on** disturb; interrupt. **break into 1** enter forcibly or violently. **2 a** suddenly begin, burst forth with (a song, laughter, etc.). **b** suddenly change one's pace for (a faster one) (*broke into a gallop*). **3** interrupt. **break-line** *Printing* the last line of a paragraph (usu. not of full length). **break of day** dawn. **break off 1** detach by breaking. **2** bring to an end. **3** cease talking etc. **break open** open forcibly. **break out 1** escape by force, esp. from prison. **2** begin suddenly; burst forth (*then violence broke out*). **3** (foll. by *in*) become covered in (a rash etc.). **4** exclaim. **5** release (a run-up flag). **6** *US* **a** open up (a receptacle) and remove its contents. **b** remove (articles) from a place of storage. **break-out** *n.* a forcible escape. **break point 1** a place or time at which an interruption or change is made. **2** *Computing* (usu. **breakpoint**) a place in a computer program where the sequence of instructions is interrupted, esp. by another program. **3 a** (in lawn tennis) a point which would win the game for the player(s) receiving service. **b** the situation at which the receiver(s) may break service by winning such a point. **4** = *breaking-point*. **break step** get out of step. **break up 1** break into small pieces. **2** disperse; disband. **3** end the school term. **4 a** terminate a relationship; disband. **b** cause to do this. **5** (of the weather) change suddenly (esp. after a fine spell). **6** esp. *US* **a** upset or be upset. **b** excite or be excited. **c** convulse or be convulsed (see also BREAKUP). **break wind** release gas from the anus. **break one's word** see WORD. [OE *brecan* f. Gmc]

break[2] /breɪk/ *n.* **1** a carriage-frame without a body, for breaking in young horses. **2** = BRAKE[2]. [perh. = *brake* framework: 17th c., of unkn. orig.]

breakable /ˈbreɪkəb(ə)l/ *adj. & n.* —*adj.* that may or is apt to be broken easily. —*n.* (esp. in *pl.*) a breakable thing.

breakage /ˈbreɪkɪdʒ/ *n.* **1 a** a broken thing. **b** damage caused by breaking. **2** an act or instance of breaking.

breakaway /ˈbreɪkəˌweɪ/ *n.* **1** the act or an instance of breaking away or seceding. **2** (*attrib.*) that breaks away or has broken away; separate. **3** *Austral.* a stampede, esp. at the sight or smell of water. **4** a false start in a race. **5** *Rugby Football* an outside second-row forward.

breakdown /ˈbreɪkdaʊn/ *n.* **1 a** a mechanical failure. **b** a loss of (esp. mental) health and strength. **2** a collapse or disintegration (*breakdown of communication*). **3** a detailed analysis (of statistics etc.).

breaker /ˈbreɪkə(r)/ *n.* **1** a person or thing that breaks something, esp. disused machinery. **2** a person who breaks in a horse. **3** a heavy wave that breaks.

breakfast /ˈbrekfəst/ *n. & v.* —*n.* the first meal of the day. —*v.intr.* have breakfast. □□ **breakfaster** *n.* [BREAK[1] interrupt + FAST[2]]

breakneck /ˈbreɪknek/ *adj.* (of speed) dangerously fast.

breakthrough /ˈbreɪkθruː/ *n.* **1** a major advance or discovery. **2** an act of breaking through an obstacle etc.

breakup /ˈbreɪkʌp/ *n.* **1** disintegration, collapse. **2** dispersal.

breakwater /ˈbreɪkˌwɔːtə(r)/ *n.* a barrier built out into the sea to break the force of waves.

bream[1] /briːm/ *n.* (*pl.* same) **1** a yellowish arch-backed freshwater fish, *Abramis brama.* **2** (in full **sea bream**) a similarly shaped marine fish of the family Sparidae. [ME f. OF *bre(s)me* f. WG]

bream[2] /briːm/ *v.tr. Naut. hist.* clean (a ship's bottom) by burning and scraping. [prob. f. LG: rel. to BROOM]

breast /brest/ *n. & v.* —*n.* **1 a** either of two milk-secreting organs on the upper front of a woman's body. **b** the corresponding usu. rudimentary part of a man's body. **2 a** the upper front part of a human body; the chest. **b** the corresponding part of an animal. **3** the part of a garment that covers the breast. **4** the breast as a source of nourishment or emotion. —*v.tr.* **1** face, meet in full opposition (*breast the wind*). **2** contend with (*breast it out against difficulties*). **3** reach the top of (a hill). □ **breast-feed** (*past* and *past part.* **-fed**) feed (a baby) from the breast. **breast-high** as high as the breast; submerged to the breast. **breast-pin** a brooch etc. worn on the breast. **breast-stroke** a stroke made while swimming on the breast by extending arms forward and sweeping them back in unison. **breast the tape** see TAPE. **make a clean breast of** confess fully. □□ **breasted** *adj.* (also in *comb.*). **breastless** *adj.* [OE *brēost* f. Gmc]

breastbone /ˈbrestbəʊn/ *n.* a thin flat vertical bone and cartilage in the chest connecting the ribs.

breastplate /ˈbrestpleɪt/ *n.* a piece of armour covering the breast.

breastsummer /ˈbresəmə(r)/ *n. Archit.* a beam across a broad opening, sustaining a superstructure. [BREAST + SUMMER[2]]

breastwork /ˈbrestwɜːk/ *n.* a low temporary defence or parapet.

breath /breθ/ *n.* **1 a** the air taken into or expelled from the lungs. **b** one respiration of air. **c** an exhalation of air that can be seen, smelt, or heard (*breath steamed in the cold air; bad breath*). **2 a** a slight movement of air; a breeze. **b** a whiff of perfume

etc. **3** a whisper, a murmur (esp. of a scandalous nature). **4** the power of breathing; life (*is there breath in him?*). □ **below** (or **under**) **one's breath** in a whisper. **breath of fresh air 1** a small amount of or a brief time in the fresh air. **2** a refreshing change. **breath of life** a necessity. **breath test** *Brit.* a test of a person's alcohol consumption, using a breathalyser. **catch one's breath 1** cease breathing momentarily in surprise, suspense, etc. **2** rest after exercise to restore normal breathing. **draw breath** breathe; live. **hold one's breath** cease breathing temporarily. **in the same breath** (esp. of saying two contradictory things) within a short time. **out of breath** gasping for air, esp. after exercise. **take breath** pause for rest. **take one's breath away** astound; surprise; awe; delight. **waste one's breath** talk or give advice without effect. [OE *brǣth* f. Gmc]

Breathalyser /ˈbreθəˌlaɪzə(r)/ *n.* (also **Breathalyzer**) *Brit. propr.* an instrument for measuring the amount of alcohol in the breath (and hence in the blood) of a driver. □□ **breathalyse** *v.tr.* (also **-lyze**). [BREATH + ANALYSE + -ER[1]]

breathe /briːð/ *v.* **1** *intr.* take air into and expel it from the lungs. **2** *intr.* be or seem alive (*is she breathing?*). **3** *tr.* **a** utter; say (esp. quietly) (*breathed her forgiveness*). **b** express; display (*breathed defiance*). **4** *intr.* take breath, pause. **5** *tr.* send out or take in (as if) with breathed air (*breathed new life into them; breathed whisky*). **6** *intr.* (of wine, fabric, etc.) be exposed to fresh air. **7** *intr.* **a** sound, speak (esp. quietly). **b** (of wind) blow softly. **8** *tr.* allow (a horse etc.) to breathe; give rest after exertion. □ **breathe again** (or **freely**) recover from a shock, fear, etc., and be at ease. **breathe down a person's neck** follow or check up on a person, esp. menacingly. **breathe one's last** die. **breathe upon** tarnish, taint. **not breathe a word of** keep quite secret. [ME f. BREATH]

breather /ˈbriːðə(r)/ *n.* **1** *colloq.* **a** a brief pause for rest. **b** a short spell of exercise. **2** a safety-vent in the crankcase of a motor vehicle etc.

breathing /ˈbriːðɪŋ/ *n. Phonet.* **1** the process of taking air into and expelling it from the lungs. **2** a sign in Greek indicating that an initial vowel or rho is aspirated (**rough breathing**) or not aspirated (**smooth breathing**). □ **breathing-space** time to breathe; a pause.

breathless /ˈbreθlɪs/ *adj.* **1** panting, out of breath. **2** holding the breath because of excitement, suspense, etc. (*a state of breathless expectancy*). **3** unstirred by wind; still. □□ **breathlessly** *adv.* **breathlessness** *n.*

breathtaking /ˈbreθˌteɪkɪŋ/ *adj.* astounding; awe-inspiring. □□ **breathtakingly** *adv.*

breathy /ˈbreθɪ/ *adj.* (**breathier**, **breathiest**) (of a singing-voice etc.) containing the sound of breathing. □□ **breathily** *adv.* **breathiness** *n.*

breccia /ˈbretʃɪə/ *n. & v.* —*n.* a rock of angular stones etc. cemented by finer material. —*v.tr.* form into breccia. □□ **brecciate** *v.tr.* **brecciation** /-ˈeɪʃ(ə)n/ *n.* [It., = gravel, f. Gmc, rel. to BREAK[1]]

bred /bred/ *past* and *past part.* of BREED.

breech /briːtʃ/ *n. & v.* —*n.* **1 a** the part of a cannon behind the bore. **b** the back part of a rifle or gun barrel. **2** *archaic* the buttocks. —*v.tr. archaic* put (a boy) into breeches after being in petticoats since birth. □ **breech birth** (or **delivery**) the delivery of a baby with the buttocks or feet foremost. **breech-block** a metal block which closes the breech aperture in a gun. **breech-loader** a gun loaded at the breech, not through the muzzle. **breech-loading** (of a gun) loaded at the breech, not through the muzzle. [OE *brōc*, pl. *brēc* (treated as sing. in ME), f. Gmc]

breeches /ˈbrɪtʃɪz/ *n.pl.* (also **pair of breeches** *sing.*) **1** short trousers, esp. fastened below the knee, now used esp. for riding or in court costume. **2** *colloq.* any trousers, knickerbockers, or underpants. □ **Breeches Bible** the Geneva Bible of 1560 with *breeches* for *aprons* in Gen. 3:7. **breeches buoy** a lifebuoy suspended from a rope which has canvas breeches for the user's legs. [pl. of BREECH]

breed /briːd/ v. & n. —v. (past and past part. **bred** /bred/) **1** tr. & intr. bear, generate (offspring). **2** tr. & intr. propagate or cause to propagate; raise (livestock). **3** tr. **a** yield, produce; result in (war breeds famine). **b** spread (discontent bred by rumour). **4** intr. arise; spread (disease breeds in the Tropics). **5** tr. bring up; train (bred to the law; Hollywood breeds stars). **6** tr. Physics create (fissile material) by nuclear reaction. —n. **1** a stock of animals or plants within a species, having a similar appearance, and usu. developed by deliberate selection. **2** a race; a lineage. **3** a sort, a kind. □**bred and born** = born and bred. **bred in the bone** hereditary. **breeder reactor** a nuclear reactor that can create more fissile material than it consumes. **breed in** mate with or marry near relations. □□ **breeder** n. [OE brēdan: rel. to BROOD]

breeding /ˈbriːdɪŋ/ n. **1** the process of developing or propagating (animals, plants, etc.). **2** generation; childbearing. **3** the result of training or education; behaviour. **4** good manners (as produced by an aristocratic heredity) (has no breeding).

breeks /briːks/ n.pl. Sc. var. of BREECHES.

breeze¹ /briːz/ n. & v. —n. **1** a gentle wind. **2** Meteorol. a wind of 4–31 m.p.h. and between force 2 and force 6 on the Beaufort scale. **3** a wind blowing from land at night or sea during the day. **4** esp. Brit. colloq. a quarrel or display of temper. **5** esp. US colloq. an easy task. —v.intr. (foll. by in, out, along, etc.) colloq. come or go in a casual or lighthearted manner. [prob. f. OSp. & Port. briza NE wind]

breeze² /briːz/ n. small cinders. □**breeze-block** any lightweight building block, esp. one made from breeze mixed with sand and cement. [F braise live coals]

breeze³ /briːz/ n. a gadfly or cleg. [OE briosa, of unkn. orig.]

breezy /ˈbriːzɪ/ adj. (**breezier**, **breeziest**) **1 a** windswept. **b** pleasantly windy. **2** colloq. lively; jovial. **3** colloq. careless (with breezy indifference). □□ **breezily** adv. **breeziness** n.

bremsstrahlung /ˈbremzˌʃtraːlʊŋ/ n. Physics the electromagnetic radiation produced by the acceleration or esp. the deceleration of a charged particle after passing through the electric and magnetic fields of a nucleus. [G, = braking radiation]

Bren /bren/ n. (in full **Bren gun**) a lightweight quick-firing machine-gun. [Brno in Czechoslovakia (where orig. made) + Enfield in England (where later made)]

brent /brent/ n. (US **brant**) (in full **brent-goose**) a small migratory goose, Branta bernicla. [16th c.: orig. unkn.]

brethren see BROTHER.

Breton /ˈbretən, brəˈtɔ̃/ n. & adj. —n. **1** a native of Brittany. **2** the Celtic language of Brittany. —adj. of or relating to Brittany or its people or language. [OF, = BRITON]

bretzel var. of PRETZEL.

breve /briːv/ n. **1** Mus. a note, now rarely used, having the time value of two semibreves. **2** a written or printed mark (˘) indicating a short or unstressed vowel. **3** hist. an authoritative letter from a sovereign or pope. [ME var. of BRIEF]

brevet /ˈbrevɪt/ n. & v. —n. (often attrib.) a document conferring a privilege from a sovereign or government, esp. a rank in the army, without the appropriate pay (was promoted by brevet; brevet major). —v.tr. (**breveted**, **breveting** or **brevetted**, **brevetting**) confer brevet rank on. [ME f. OF dimin. of bref BRIEF]

breviary /ˈbriːvɪərɪ/ n. (pl. **-ies**) RC Ch. a book containing the service for each day, to be recited by those in orders. [L breviarium summary f. breviare abridge: see ABBREVIATE]

brevity /ˈbrevɪtɪ/ n. **1** economy of expression; conciseness. **2** shortness (of time etc.) (the brevity of happiness). [AF breveté, OF brieveté f. bref BRIEF]

brew /bruː/ v. & n. —v. **1** tr. **a** make (beer etc.) by infusion, boiling, and fermentation. **b** make (tea etc.) by infusion or (punch etc.) by mixture. **2** intr. undergo either of these processes (the tea is brewing). **3** intr. (of trouble, a storm, etc.) gather force; threaten (mischief was brewing). **4** tr. bring about; set in train; concoct (brewed their fiendish scheme). —n. **1** an amount (of beer etc.) brewed at one time (this year's brew). **2** what is brewed (esp. with regard to its quality) (a good strong brew). **3** the action or process of brewing. □**brew up** make tea. **brew-up** n. an instance of making tea. □□ **brewer** n. [OE brēowan f. Gmc]

brewery /ˈbruːərɪ/ n. (pl. **-ies**) a place where beer etc. is brewed commercially.

briar¹ var. of BRIER¹.

briar² var. of BRIER².

bribe /braɪb/ v. & n. —v.tr. (often foll. by to + infin.) persuade (a person etc.) to act improperly in one's favour by a gift of money, services, etc. (bribed the guard to release the suspect). —n. money or services offered in the process of bribing. □□ **bribable** adj. **briber** n. **bribery** n. [ME f. OF briber, brimber beg, of unkn. orig.]

bric-à-brac /ˈbriːkəˌbræk/ n. (also **bric-a-brac**, **bricabrac**) miscellaneous, often old, ornaments, trinkets, furniture, etc., of no great value. [F f. obs. à bric à brac at random]

brick /brɪk/ n., v., & adj. —n. **1 a** a small, usu. rectangular, block of fired or sun-dried clay, used in building. **b** the material used to make these. **c** a similar block of concrete etc. **2** Brit. a child's toy building-block. **3** a brick-shaped solid object (a brick of ice-cream). **4** sl. a generous or loyal person. —v.tr. (foll. by in, up) close or block with brickwork. —adj. **1** built of brick (brick wall). **2** of a dull red colour. □**bang** (or **knock** or **run**) **one's head against a brick wall** attempt the impossible. **brick-field** a place at which bricks are made. **brick-red** the colour of bricks. **like a load** (or **ton**) **of bricks** colloq. with crushing weight, force, or authority. **see through a brick wall** have miraculous insight. □□ **bricky** adj. [ME f. MLG, MDu. bri(c)ke, of unkn. orig.]

brickbat /ˈbrɪkbæt/ n. **1** a piece of brick, esp. when used as a missile. **2** an uncomplimentary remark.

brickfielder /ˈbrɪkˌfiːldə(r)/ n. Austral. a hot, dry north wind.

brickie /ˈbrɪkɪ/ n. sl. a bricklayer.

bricklayer /ˈbrɪkˌleɪə(r)/ n. a worker who builds with bricks. □□ **bricklaying** n.

brickwork /ˈbrɪkwɜːk/ n. **1** building in brick. **2** a wall, building, etc. made of brick.

brickyard /ˈbrɪkjɑːd/ n. a place where bricks are made.

bridal /ˈbraɪd(ə)l/ adj. of or concerning a bride or a wedding. □□ **bridally** adv. [orig. as noun, = wedding-feast, f. OE brȳd-ealu f. brȳd BRIDE + ealu ale-drinking]

bride /braɪd/ n. a woman on her wedding day and for some time before and after it. □**bride-cake** a wedding cake. **bride-price** money or goods given to a bride's family esp. in primitive societies. [OE brȳd f. Gmc]

bridegroom /ˈbraɪdgruːm, -grʊm/ n. a man on his wedding day and for some time before and after it. [OE brȳdguma (as BRIDE, guma man, assim. to GROOM)]

bridesmaid /ˈbraɪdzmeɪd/ n. a girl or unmarried woman attending a bride on her wedding day. [earlier bridemaid, f. BRIDE + MAID]

bridewell /ˈbraɪdw(ə)l, -wel/ n. archaic a prison; a reformatory. [St Bride's Well in London, near which such a building stood]

bridge¹ /brɪdʒ/ n. & v. —n. **1 a** a structure carrying a road, path, railway, etc., across a stream, ravine,

æ cat ɑː arm e bed ɜː her ɪ sit iː see ɒ hot ɔː saw ʌ run ʊ put uː too ə ago aɪ my

road, railway, etc. **b** anything providing a connection between different things (*English is a bridge between nations*). **2** the superstructure on a ship from which the captain and officers direct operations. **3** the upper bony part of the nose. **4** *Mus.* an upright piece of wood on a violin etc. over which the strings are stretched. **5** = BRIDGEWORK. **6** *Billiards* etc. **a** a long stick with a structure at the end which is used to support a cue for a difficult shot. **b** a support for a cue formed by a raised hand. **7** = *land-bridge.* —*v.tr.* **1 a** be a bridge over (*a fallen tree bridges the stream*). **b** make a bridge over; span. **2** span as if with a bridge (*bridged their differences with understanding*). □ **bridge of asses** = *pons asinorum.* **bridge of boats** a bridge formed by mooring boats together abreast across a river etc. **bridge passage** *Mus.* a transitional piece between main themes. **bridging loan** a loan from a bank etc. to cover the short interval between buying a house etc. and selling another. **cross a** (or **that**) **bridge when one comes to it** deal with a problem when and if it arises. □□ **bridgeable** *adj.* [OE *brycg* f. Gmc]

bridge² /brɪdʒ/ *n.* a card-game derived from whist, in which one player's cards are exposed and are played by his or her partner (cf. *auction bridge, contract bridge*). □ **bridge roll** a small soft bread roll. [19th c.: orig. unkn.]

bridgehead /'brɪdʒhed/ *n. Mil.* a fortified position held on the enemy's side of a river or other obstacle.

bridgework /'brɪdʒwɜːk/ *n. Dentistry* a dental structure used to cover a gap, joined to and supported by the teeth on either side.

bridle /'braɪd(ə)l/ *n. & v.* —*n.* **1 a** the headgear used to control a horse, consisting of buckled leather straps, a metal bit, and reins. **b** a restraining thing or influence (*put a bridle on your tongue*). **2** *Naut.* a mooring-cable. **3** *Physiol.* a ligament checking the motion of a part. —*v.* **1** *tr.* put a bridle on (a horse etc.). **2** *tr.* bring under control; curb. **3** *intr.* (often foll. by *up*) express offence, resentment, etc., esp. by throwing up the head and drawing in the chin. □ **bridle-path** (or **-road** or **-way**) a rough path or road fit only for riders or walkers, not vehicles. [OE *brīdel*]

bridoon /brɪ'duːn/ *n.* the snaffle and rein of a military bridle. [F *bridon* f. *bride* bridle]

Brie /briː/ *n.* a kind of soft cheese. [*Brie* in N. France]

brief /briːf/ *adj., n., & v.* —*adj.* **1** of short duration. **2** concise in expression. **3** abrupt, brusque (*was rather brief with me*). **4** scanty; lacking in substance (*wearing a brief skirt*). —*n.* **1** (in *pl.*) **a** women's brief pants. **b** men's brief underpants. **2** *Law* **a** a summary of the facts and legal points of a case drawn up for counsel. **b** a piece of work for a barrister. **3** instructions given for a task, operation, etc. (orig. a bombing plan given to an aircrew). **4** *RC Ch.* a letter from the Pope to a person or community on a matter of discipline. —*v.tr.* **1** *Brit. Law* instruct (a barrister) by brief. **2** instruct (an employee, a participant, etc.) in preparation for a task; inform or instruct thoroughly in advance (*briefed him for the interview*) (cf. DEBRIEF). □ **be brief** use few words. **hold a brief for** **1** argue in favour of. **2** be retained as counsel for. **in brief** in short. **watching brief** **1** a brief held by a barrister following a case for a client not directly involved. **2** a state of interest maintained in a proceeding not directly or immediately concerning one. □□ **briefly** *adv.* **briefness** *n.* [ME f. AF *bref*, OF *brief*, f. L *brevis* short]

briefcase /'briːfkeɪs/ *n.* a flat rectangular case for carrying documents etc.

briefing /'briːfɪŋ/ *n.* **1** a meeting for giving information or instructions. **2** the information or instructions given; a brief. **3** the action of informing or instructing.

briefless /'briːflɪs/ *adj. Law* (of a barrister) having no clients.

brier¹ /'braɪə(r)/ *n.* (also **briar**) any prickly bush esp.

of a wild rose. □ **brier-rose** dog-rose. **sweet-brier** a wild rose, *Rosa eglanteria*, with small fragrant leaves and flowers. □□ **briery** *adj.* [OE *brǣr*, *brēr*, of unkn. orig.]

brier² /'braɪə(r)/ *n.* (also **briar**) **1** a white heath, *Erica arborea*, native to S. Europe. **2** a tobacco pipe made from its root. [19th-c. *bruyer* f. F *bruyère* heath]

Brig. *abbr.* Brigadier.

brig¹ /brɪg/ *n.* **1** a two-masted square-rigged ship, with an additional lower fore-and-aft sail on the gaff and a boom to the mainmast. **2** *US* a prison, esp. on a warship. [abbr. of BRIGANTINE]

brig² /brɪg/ *n. Sc. & N.Engl.* var. of BRIDGE¹.

brigade /brɪ'geɪd/ *n. & v.* —*n.* **1** *Mil.* **a** a subdivision of an army. **b** a British infantry unit consisting usu. of 3 battalions and forming part of a division. **c** a corresponding armoured unit. **2** an organized or uniformed band of workers (*fire brigade*). **3** *colloq.* any group of people with a characteristic in common (*the couldn't-care-less brigade*). —*v.tr.* form into a brigade. [F f. It. *brigata* company f. *brigare* be busy with f. *briga* strife]

brigadier /ˌbrɪgə'dɪə(r)/ *n. Mil.* **1** an officer commanding a brigade. **2 a** a staff officer of similar standing, above a colonel and below a major-general. **b** the titular rank granted to such an officer. □ **brigadier general** *US* an officer ranking next above colonel. [F (as BRIGADE, -IER)]

brigalow /'brɪgə,ləʊ/ *n. Austral.* any of various acacia trees, esp. *Acacia harpophylla*. [Aboriginal]

brigand /'brɪgənd/ *n.* a member of a robber band living by pillage and ransom, usu. in wild terrain. □□ **brigandage** *n.* **brigandish** *adj.* **brigandism** *n.* **brigandry** *n.* [ME f. OF f. It. *brigante* f. *brigare*: see BRIGADE]

brigantine /'brɪgən,tiːn/ *n.* a two-masted sailing-ship with a square-rigged foremast and a fore-and-aft rigged mainmast. [OF *brigandine* or It. *brigantino* f. *brigante* BRIGAND]

bright /braɪt/ *adj. & adv.* —*adj.* **1** emitting or reflecting much light; shining. **2** (of colour) intense, vivid. **3** clever, talented, quick-witted (*a bright idea; a bright child*). **4** cheerful, vivacious. —*adv.* esp. *poet.* brightly (*the moon shone bright*). □ **bright and early** very early in the morning. **bright-eyed and bushy-tailed** *colloq.* alert and sprightly. **the bright lights** the glamour and excitement of the city. **look on the bright side** be optimistic. □□ **brightish** *adj.* **brightly** *adv.* **brightness** *n.* [OE *beorht*, (adv.) *beorhte*, f. Gmc]

brighten /'braɪt(ə)n/ *v.tr. & intr.* **1** make or become brighter. **2** make or become more cheerful.

Bright's disease /braɪts/ *n.* inflammation of the kidney from any of various causes; nephritis. [R. Bright, Engl. physician d. 1858]

brill¹ /brɪl/ *n.* a European flat-fish, *Scophthalmus rhombus*, resembling a turbot. [15th c.: orig. unkn.]

brill² /brɪl/ *adj. colloq.* = BRILLIANT *adj.* 4. [abbr.]

brilliance /'brɪlɪəns/ *n.* (also **brilliancy** /-ənsɪ/) **1** great brightness; sparkling or radiant quality. **2** outstanding talent or intelligence.

brilliancy var. of BRILLIANCE.

brilliant /'brɪlɪənt/ *adj. & n.* —*adj.* **1** very bright; sparkling. **2** outstandingly talented or intelligent. **3** showy; outwardly impressive. **4** *colloq.* excellent, superb. —*n.* a diamond of the finest cut with many facets. □□ **brilliantly** *adv.* [F *brillant* part. of *briller* shine f. It. *brillare*, of unkn. orig.]

brilliantine /'brɪljən,tiːn/ *n.* **1** an oily liquid dressing for making the hair glossy. **2** *US* a lustrous dress fabric. [F *brillantine* (as BRILLIANT)]

brim /brɪm/ *n. & v.* —*n.* **1** the edge or lip of a cup or other vessel, or of a hollow. **2** the projecting edge of a hat. —*v.tr. & intr.* (**brimmed**, **brimming**) fill or be full to the brim. □ **brim over** overflow. □□ **brimless** *adj.* **brimmed** *adj.* (usu. in *comb.*). [ME *brimme*, of unkn. orig.]

brim-full /ˈbrɪmˈfʊl/ adj. (also **brimful**) (often foll. by of) filled to the brim.

brimstone /ˈbrɪmstəʊn/ n. 1 archaic the element sulphur. 2 a butterfly, *Gonepteryx rhamni*, or moth, *Opisthograptis luteolata*, having yellow wings. [ME prob. f. OE *bryne* burning + STONE]

brindled /ˈbrɪnd(ə)ld/ adj. (also **brindle**) brownish or tawny with streaks of other colour (esp. of domestic animals). [earlier *brinded, brended* f. *brend*, perh. of Scand. orig.]

brine /braɪn/ n. & v. —n. 1 water saturated or strongly impregnated with salt. 2 sea water. —v.tr. soak in or saturate with brine. [OE *brīne*, of unkn. orig.]

bring /brɪŋ/ v.tr. (past and past part. **brought** /brɔːt/) 1 a come conveying esp. by carrying or leading. b come with. 2 cause to come or be present (*what brings you here?*). 3 cause or result in (*war brings misery*). 4 be sold for; produce as income. 5 a prefer (a charge). b initiate (legal action). 6 cause to become or to reach a particular state (*brings me alive; brought them to their senses; cannot bring myself to agree*). 7 adduce (evidence, an argument, etc.). □**bring about** 1 cause to happen. 2 turn (a ship) around. **bring-and-buy sale** Brit. a kind of charity sale at which participants bring items for sale and buy what is brought by others. **bring back** call to mind. **bring down** 1 cause to fall. 2 lower (a price). 3 sl. make unhappy or less happy. 4 colloq. damage the reputation of; demean. **bring forth** 1 give birth to. 2 produce, emit, cause. **bring forward** 1 move to an earlier date or time. 2 transfer from the previous page or account. 3 draw attention to; adduce. **bring home to** cause to realize fully (*brought home to me that I was wrong*). **bring the house down** receive rapturous applause. **bring in** 1 introduce (legislation, a custom, fashion, topic, etc.). 2 yield as income or profit. **bring into play** cause to operate; activate. **bring low** overcome. **bring off** achieve successfully. **bring on** 1 cause to happen or appear. 2 accelerate the progress of. **bring out** 1 emphasize; make evident. 2 publish. **bring over** convert to one's own side. **bring round** 1 restore to consciousness. 2 persuade. **bring through** aid (a person) through adversity, esp. illness. **bring to** 1 restore to consciousness (*brought him to*). 2 check the motion of. **bring to bear** (usu. foll. by on) direct and concentrate (forces). **bring to mind** recall; cause one to remember. **bring to pass** cause to happen. **bring under** subdue. **bring up** 1 rear (a child). 2 vomit, regurgitate. 3 call attention to. 4 (absol.) stop suddenly. **bring upon oneself** be responsible for (something one suffers). □□ **bringer** n. [OE *bringan* f. Gmc]

brinjal /ˈbrɪndʒ(ə)l/ n. (in India and Africa) an aubergine. [ult. Port. *berinjela* formed as AUBERGINE]

brink /brɪŋk/ n. 1 the extreme edge of land before a precipice, river, etc., esp. when a sudden drop follows. 2 the furthest point before something dangerous or exciting is discovered. □**on the brink of** about to experience or suffer; in imminent danger of. [ME f. ON: orig. unkn.]

brinkmanship /ˈbrɪŋkmənʃɪp/ n. the art or policy of pursuing a dangerous course to the brink of catastrophe before desisting.

briny /ˈbraɪnɪ/ adj. & n. —adj. (**brinier, briniest**) of brine or the sea; salty. —n. (prec. by the) Brit. sl. the sea. □□ **brininess** n.

brio /ˈbriːəʊ/ n. dash, vigour, vivacity. [It.]

brioche /ˈbriːɒʃ/ n. a small rounded sweet roll made with a light yeast dough. [F]

briquette /brɪˈket/ n. (also **briquet**) a block of compressed coal dust used as fuel. [F *briquette*, dimin. of *brique* brick]

brisk /brɪsk/ adj. & v. —adj. 1 quick, lively, keen (*a brisk pace; brisk trade*). 2 enlivening (*a brisk wind*). —v.tr. & intr. (often foll. by up) make or grow brisk.

brisken v.tr. & intr. **briskly** adv. **briskness** n. [prob. F *brusque* BRUSQUE]

brisket /ˈbrɪskɪt/ n. an animal's breast, esp. as a joint of meat. [AF f. OF *bruschet*, perh. f. ON]

brisling /ˈbrɪzlɪŋ, ˈbrɪs-/ n. a small herring or sprat. [Norw. & Da., = sprat]

bristle /ˈbrɪs(ə)l/ n. & v. —n. 1 a short stiff hair, esp. one of those on an animal's back. 2 this, or a man-made substitute, set in clumps to make a brush. —v. 1 a intr. (of the hair) stand upright, esp. in anger or pride. b tr. make (the hair) do this. 2 intr. show irritation or defensiveness. 3 intr. (usu. foll. by with) be covered or abundant (in). [ME *bristel, brestel* f. OE *byrst*]

bristletail /ˈbrɪs(ə)lˌteɪl/ n. = SILVERFISH.

bristly /ˈbrɪslɪ/ adj. (**bristlier, bristliest**) full of bristles; rough, prickly.

Bristol board /ˈbrɪst(ə)l/ n. a kind of fine smooth pasteboard for drawing on. [*Bristol* in S. England]

Bristol fashion /ˈbrɪst(ə)l/ n. (functioning as *predic.adj.*) (in full **shipshape and Bristol fashion**) orig. Naut. with all in good order.

bristols /ˈbrɪst(ə)lz/ n.pl. Brit. sl. a woman's breasts. [rhyming sl. f. *Bristol cities* = *titties*]

Brit /brɪt/ n. colloq. a British person. [abbr.]

Brit. abbr. 1 British. 2 Britain.

Britannia /brɪˈtænjə/ n. the personification of Britain, esp. as a helmeted woman with shield and trident. □**Britannia metal** a silvery alloy of tin, antimony, and copper. [L f. Gk *Brettania* f. *Brettanoi* Britons]

Britannic /brɪˈtænɪk/ adj. (esp. in **His** or **Her Britannic Majesty**) of Britain. [L *Britannicus* (as BRITANNIA)]

Briticism /ˈbrɪtɪˌsɪz(ə)m/ n. (also **Britishism** /-ˌʃɪz(ə)m/) an idiom used in Britain but not in other English-speaking countries. [BRITISH, after GALLICISM]

British /ˈbrɪtɪʃ/ adj. & n. —adj. 1 of or relating to Great Britain or the United Kingdom, or to its people or language. 2 of the British Commonwealth or (formerly) the British Empire (*British subject*). —n. 1 (prec. by the; treated as pl.) the British people. 2 US = British English. □**British English** English as used in Great Britain, as distinct from that used elsewhere. **British Legion** = *Royal British Legion*. **British summer time** = *summer time* (see SUMMER[1]). **British thermal unit** see THERMAL. □□ **Britishness** n. [OE *Brettisc* etc. f. *Bret* f. L *Britto* or OCelt.]

Britisher /ˈbrɪtɪʃə(r)/ n. a British subject, esp. of British descent. ¶ Not used in British English.

Britishism var. of BRITICISM.

Briton /ˈbrɪt(ə)n/ n. 1 one of the people of S. Britain before the Roman conquest. 2 a native or inhabitant of Great Britain or (formerly) of the British Empire. [ME & OF *Breton* f. L *Britto -onis* f. OCelt.]

brittle /ˈbrɪt(ə)l/ adj. & n. —adj. hard and fragile; apt to break. —n. a brittle sweet made from nuts and set melted sugar. □**brittle-bone disease** = OSTEOPOROSIS. **brittle-star** an echinoderm of the class Ophiuroidea, with long brittle arms radiating from a small central body. □□ **brittlely** adv. **brittleness** n. **brittly** adv. [ME ult. f. a Gmc root rel. to OE *brēotan* break up]

bro. abbr. brother.

broach /brəʊtʃ/ v. & n. —v.tr. 1 raise (a subject) for discussion. 2 pierce (a cask) to draw liquor. 3 open and start using contents of (a box, bale, bottle, etc.). 4 begin drawing (liquor). —n. 1 a bit for boring. 2 a roasting-spit. □**broach spire** an octagonal church spire rising from a square tower without a parapet. [ME f. OF *broche* (n.), *brocher* (v.) ult. f. L *brocc(h)us* projecting]

broad /brɔːd/ adj. & n. —adj. 1 large in extent from one side to the other; wide. 2 (following a measurement) in breadth (*2 metres broad*). 3 spacious or extensive (*broad acres; a broad plain*). 4 full and clear (*broad daylight*). **5** explicit, unmistakable (*broad hint*). **6** general; not taking account of detail (*broad intentions*; *a broad inquiry*; *in the broadest sense of the word*). **7** chief or principal (*the broad facts*). **8** tolerant, liberal (*take a broad view*). **9** somewhat coarse (*broad humour*). **10** (of speech) markedly regional (*broad Scots*). —*n.* **1** the broad part of something (*broad of the back*). **2** *US sl.* a young woman. **3** (**the Broads**) large areas of fresh water in E. Anglia, formed where rivers widen. □**broad arrow** see ARROW. **broad bean 1** a kind of bean, *Vicia faba*, with pods containing large edible flat seeds. **2** one of these seeds. **Broad Church** a group within the Anglican Church favouring a liberal interpretation of doctrine. **broad gauge** a railway track with a gauge wider than the standard one. **broad-leaved** (of a tree) deciduous and hard-timbered. **broad pennant** a short swallow-tailed pennant distinguishing the commodore's ship in a squadron. **broad spectrum** (of a medicinal substance) effective against a large variety of micro-organisms. □□**broadness** *n.* **broadways** *adv.* **broadwise** *adv.* [OE *brād* f. Gmc]

broadcast /ˈbrɔːdkɑːst/ *v.*, *n.*, *adj.*, & *adv.* —*v.* (past **broadcast** or **broadcasted**; past part. **broadcast**) **1** *tr.* transmit (programmes or information) by radio or television. **2** *intr.* undertake or take part in a radio or television transmission. **3** *tr.* scatter (seed etc.) over a large area, esp. by hand. —*n.* a radio or television programme or transmission. —*adj.* **1** transmitted by radio or television. **2 a** scattered widely. **b** (of information etc.) widely disseminated. —*adv.* over a large area. □□**broadcaster** *n.* **broadcasting** *n.* [BROAD + CAST past part.]

broadcloth /ˈbrɔːdklɒθ/ *n.* a fine cloth of wool, cotton, or silk. [orig. with ref. to width and quality]

broaden /ˈbrɔːd(ə)n/ *v.tr.* & *intr.* make or become broader.

broadloom /ˈbrɔːdluːm/ *adj.* (esp. of carpet) woven in broad widths.

broadly /ˈbrɔːdlɪ/ *adv.* in a broad manner; widely (*grinned broadly*). □**broadly speaking** disregarding minor exceptions.

broad-minded /brɔːdˈmaɪndɪd/ *adj.* tolerant or liberal in one's views. □□**broad-mindedly** *adv.* **broad-mindedness** *n.*

broadsheet /ˈbrɔːdʃiːt/ *n.* a large sheet of paper printed on one side only, esp. with information.

broadside /ˈbrɔːdsaɪd/ *n.* **1** the firing of all guns from one side of a ship. **2** a vigorous verbal onslaught. **3** the side of a ship above the water between the bow and quarter. □**broadside on** sideways on.

broadsword /ˈbrɔːdsɔːd/ *n.* a sword with a broad blade, for cutting rather than thrusting.

broadtail /ˈbrɔːdteɪl/ *n.* **1** the karacul sheep. **2** the fleece or wool from its lamb.

broadway /ˈbrɔːdweɪ/ *n.* a large open or main road.

brocade /brəˈkeɪd, brəʊ-/ *n.* & *v.* —*n.* a rich fabric with a silky finish woven with a raised pattern, and often with gold or silver thread. —*v.tr.* weave with this design. [Sp. & Port. *brocado* f. It. *broccato* f. *brocco* twisted thread]

broccoli /ˈbrɒkəlɪ/ *n.* **1** a variety of cabbage, similar to the cauliflower, with a loose cluster of greenish flower buds. **2** the flower-stalk and head used as a vegetable. [It., pl. of *broccolo* dimin. of *brocco* sprout]

broch /brɒk, brɒx/ *n.* (in Scotland) a prehistoric circular stone tower. [ON *borg* castle]

brochette /brɒˈʃet, brəˈʃet/ *n.* a skewer on which chunks of meat are cooked, esp. over an open fire. [F, dimin. of *broche* BROACH]

brochure /ˈbrəʊʃə(r), brəʊˈʃjʊə(r)/ *n.* a pamphlet or leaflet, esp. one giving descriptive information. [F, lit. 'stitching', f. *brocher* stitch]

brock /brɒk/ *n.* (dial. or esp. in rural use) a badger. [OE *broc(c)* f. OBrit. *brokkos*]

brocket /ˈbrɒkɪt/ *n.* any small deer of the genus *Mazama*, native to Central and S. America, having

short straight antlers. [ME f. AF *broque* (= *broche* BROACH)]

broderie anglaise /ˌbrəʊdərɪ ɑ̃ˈgleɪz/ *n.* open embroidery on white linen or cambric, esp. in floral patterns. [F, = English embroidery]

brogue[1] /brəʊg/ *n.* **1** a strong outdoor shoe with ornamental perforated bands. **2** a rough shoe of untanned leather. [Gael. & Ir. *brōg* f. ON *brók*]

brogue[2] /brəʊg/ *n.* a marked accent, esp. Irish. [18th c.: orig. unkn.: perh. allusively f. BROGUE[1]]

broil[1] /brɔɪl/ *v.* esp. *US* **1** *tr.* cook (meat) on a rack or a gridiron. **2** *tr.* & *intr.* make or become very hot, esp. from the sun. [ME f. OF *bruler* burn f. Rmc]

broil[2] /brɔɪl/ *n.* a row; a tumult. [obs. *broil* to muddle: cf. EMBROIL]

broiler /ˈbrɔɪlə(r)/ *n.* **1** a young chicken raised for broiling or roasting. **2** a gridiron etc. for broiling. **3** *colloq.* a very hot day. □**broiler house** a building for rearing broiler chickens in close confinement.

broke /brəʊk/ past of BREAK[1]. —*predic.adj. colloq.* having no money; financially ruined. □**go for broke** *sl.* risk everything in a strenuous effort. [(adj.) archaic past part. of BREAK[1]]

broken /ˈbrəʊkən/ past part. of BREAK[1]. —*adj.* **1** that has been broken; out of order. **2** (of a person) reduced to despair; beaten. **3** (of a language or of speech) spoken falteringly and with many mistakes, as by a foreigner (*broken English*). **4** disturbed, interrupted (*broken time*). **5** uneven (*broken ground*). □**broken chord** *Mus.* a chord in which the notes are played successively. **broken-down 1** worn out by age, use, or ill-treatment. **2** out of order. **broken-hearted** overwhelmed with sorrow or grief. **broken-heartedness** grief. **broken home** a family in which the parents are divorced or separated. **broken reed** a person who has become unreliable or ineffective. **broken wind** heaves (see HEAVE *n.* 3). **broken-winded** (of a horse) disabled by ruptured air-cells in the lungs. □□**brokenly** *adv.* **brokenness** *n.*

broker /ˈbrəʊkə(r)/ *n.* **1** an agent who buys and sells for others; a middleman. **2** a member of the Stock Exchange dealing in stocks and shares. ¶ In the UK from Oct. 1986 officially called **broker-dealer** and entitled to act as agent and principal in share dealings. **3** *Brit.* an official appointed to sell or appraise distrained goods. [ME f. AF *brocour*, of unkn. orig.]

brokerage /ˈbrəʊkərɪdʒ/ *n.* a broker's fee or commission.

broking /ˈbrəʊkɪŋ/ *n.* the trade or business of a broker.

brolga /ˈbrɒlgə/ *n.* *Austral.* a large Australian crane, *Grus rubicunda*, with a booming call. [Aboriginal]

brolly /ˈbrɒlɪ/ *n.* (pl. **-ies**) *Brit.* **1** *colloq.* an umbrella. **2** *sl.* a parachute. [abbr.]

bromate /ˈbrəʊmeɪt/ *n.* *Chem.* a salt or ester of bromic acid.

brome /brəʊm/ *n.* any oatlike grass of the genus *Bromus*, having slender stems with flowering spikes. [mod.L *Bromus* f. Gk *bromos* oat]

bromelia /brəʊˈmiːlɪə/ *n.* (also **bromeliad** /-lɪad/) any plant of the family Bromeliaceae (esp. of the genus *Bromelia*), native to the New World, having short stems with rosettes of stiff usu. spiny leaves, e.g. pineapple. [O. *Bromel*, Sw. botanist d. 1705]

bromic /ˈbrəʊmɪk/ *adj.* *Chem.* of or containing bromine. □**bromic acid** a strong acid used as an oxidizing agent.

bromide /ˈbrəʊmaɪd/ *n.* **1** *Chem.* any binary compound of bromine. **2** *Pharm.* a preparation of usu. potassium bromide, used as a sedative. **3** a trite remark. □**bromide paper** a photographic printing paper coated with silver bromide emulsion.

bromine /ˈbrəʊmiːn/ *n.* *Chem.* a dark fuming liquid element with a choking irritating smell, extracted from bittern and used in the manufacture of chemicals for photography and medicine. ¶ Symb.: **Br**. □□ **bromism** *n.* [F *brome* f. Gk *brōmos* stink]

bromo- /'brəʊməʊ/ comb. form Chem. bromine.
bronc /brɒŋk/ n. US colloq. = BRONCO. [abbr.]
bronchi pl. of BRONCHUS.
bronchial /'brɒŋkɪəl/ adj. of or relating to the bronchi or bronchioles. □**bronchial tree** the branching system of bronchi and bronchioles conducting air from the windpipe to the lungs.
bronchiole /'brɒŋkɪ,əʊl/ n. any of the minute divisions of a bronchus. □□ **bronchiolar** /-'əʊlə(r)/ adj.
bronchitis /brɒŋ'kaɪtɪs/ n. inflammation of the mucous membrane in the bronchial tubes. □□ **bronchitic** /-'kɪtɪk/ adj. & n.
broncho- /'brɒŋkəʊ/ comb. form bronchi.
bronchocele /'brɒŋkə,si:l/ n. a goitre.
bronchopneumonia /,brɒŋkəʊnju:'məʊnɪə/ n. inflammation of the lungs, arising in the bronchi or bronchioles.
bronchoscope /'brɒŋkə,skəʊp/ n. a usu. fibre-optic instrument for inspecting the bronchi. □□ **bronchoscopy** /-'kɒskəpɪ/ n.
bronchus /'brɒŋkəs/ n. (pl. **bronchi** /-kaɪ/) any of the major air passages of the lungs, esp. either of the two main divisions of the windpipe. [LL f. Gk brogkhos windpipe]
bronco /'brɒŋkəʊ/ n. (pl. **-os**) a wild or half-tamed horse of the western US. □**bronco-buster** US sl. a person who breaks in horses. [Sp., = rough]
brontosaurus /,brɒntə'sɔːrəs/ n. (also **brontosaur** /'brɒntə,sɔː(r)/) a large plant-eating dinosaur of the genus Brontosaurus, with a long whiplike tail and trunk-like legs. [Gk brontē thunder + sauros lizard]
bronze /brɒnz/ n., adj., & v. —n. 1 any alloy of copper and tin. 2 its brownish colour. 3 a thing made of bronze, esp. as a work of art. —adj. made of or coloured like bronze. —v. 1 tr. give a bronzelike surface to. 2 tr. & intr. make or become brown; tan. □**Bronze Age** Archaeol. the period preceding the Iron Age, when weapons and tools were usu. made of bronze. **bronze medal** a medal usu. awarded to a competitor who comes third (esp. in sport). □□ **bronzy** adj. [F f. It. bronzo, prob. f. Pers. birinj copper]
brooch /brəʊtʃ/ n. an ornament fastened to clothing with a hinged pin. [ME broche = BROACH n.]
brood /bru:d/ n. & v. —n. 1 the young of an animal (esp. a bird) produced at one hatching or birth. 2 colloq. the children in a family. 3 a group of related things. 4 bee or wasp larvae. 5 (attrib.) kept for breeding (brood-mare). —v. 1 intr. (often foll. by on, over, etc.) worry or ponder (esp. resentfully). 2 a intr. sit as a hen on eggs to hatch them. b tr. sit on (eggs) to hatch them. 3 intr. (usu. foll. by over) (of silence, a storm, etc.) hang or hover closely. □□ **broodingly** adv. [OE brōd f. Gmc]
brooder /'bru:də(r)/ n. 1 a heated house for chicks, piglets, etc. 2 a person who broods.
broody /'bru:dɪ/ adj. (**broodier**, **broodiest**) 1 (of a hen) wanting to brood. 2 sullenly thoughtful or depressed. 3 colloq. (of a woman) wanting to have a baby. □□ **broodily** adv. **broodiness** n.
brook¹ /brʊk/ n. a small stream. □□ **brooklet** /-lɪt/ n. [OE brōc, of unkn. orig.]
brook² /brʊk/ v.tr. (usu. with neg.) literary tolerate, allow. [OE brūcan f. Gmc]
brooklime /'brʊklaɪm/ n. a kind of speedwell, Veronica beccabunga, growing in wet areas.
brookweed /'brʊkwi:d/ n. a small herb, Samolus valerandi, having slender stems with tiny white flowers and growing in wet places.
broom /bru:m/ n. 1 a long-handled brush of bristles, twigs, etc. for sweeping (orig. one made of twigs of broom). 2 any of various shrubs, esp. Cytisus scoparius bearing bright yellow flowers. □**new broom** a newly appointed person eager to make changes. [OE brōm]
broomrape /'bru:mreɪp/ n. any parasitic plant of the genus Orobanche, with tubular flowers on a leafless brown stem, and living on the roots of broom and similar plants. [BROOM + L rapum tuber]
broomstick /'bru:mstɪk/ n. the handle of a broom, esp. as allegedly ridden on through the air by witches.
Bros. abbr. Brothers (esp. in the name of a firm).
brose /brəʊz/ n. esp. Sc. Cookery a dish of oatmeal with boiling water or milk poured on it. [Sc. form of brewis broth: ME f. OF bro(u)ez, ult. f. Gmc]
broth /brɒθ/ n. 1 Cookery a a thin soup of meat or fish stock. b unclarified meat or fish stock. 2 Biol. meat stock as a nutrient medium for bacteria. [OE f. Gmc: rel. to BREW]
brothel /'brɒθ(ə)l/ n. a house etc. where prostitution takes place. [orig. brothel-house f. ME brothel worthless man, prostitute, f. OE brēothan go to ruin]
brother /'brʌðə(r)/ n. 1 a man or boy in relation to other sons and daughters of his parents. 2 a (often as a form of address) a close male friend or associate. b a male fellow member of a trade union etc. 3 (pl. also **brethren** /'breðrɪn/) a a member of a male religious order, esp. a monk. b a fellow member of the Christian Church, a religion, or (formerly) a guild etc. 4 a fellow human being. □**brother german** see GERMAN. **brother-in-law** (pl. **brothers-in-law**) 1 the brother of one's wife or husband. 2 the husband of one's sister. 3 the husband of one's sister-in-law. **brother uterine** see UTERINE 2. □□ **brotherless** adj. **brotherly** adj. & adv. **brotherliness** n. [OE brōthor f. Gmc]
brotherhood /'brʌðə,hʊd/ n. 1 a the relationship between brothers. b brotherly friendliness; companionship. 2 a an association, society, or community of people linked by a common interest, religion, trade, etc. b its members collectively. 3 US a trade union. 4 community of feeling between all human beings. [ME alt. f. brotherrede f. OE brōthor-rǣden (cf. KINDRED) after words in -HOOD, -HEAD]
brougham /'bru:əm, bru:m/ n. hist. 1 a horse-drawn closed carriage with a driver perched outside in front. 2 a motor car with an open driver's seat. [Lord Brougham, d. 1868]
brought past and past part. of BRING.
brouhaha /'bru:ha:,ha:/ n. commotion, sensation; hubbub, uproar. [F]
brow /braʊ/ n. 1 the forehead. 2 (usu. in pl.) an eyebrow. 3 the summit of a hill or pass. 4 the edge of a cliff etc. 5 colloq. intellectual level. □□ **browed** adj. [OE brū f. Gmc]
browbeat /'braʊbi:t/ v.tr. (past **-beat**; past part. **-beaten**) intimidate with stern looks and words. □□ **browbeater** n.
brown /braʊn/ adj., n., & v. —adj. 1 having the colour produced by mixing red, yellow, and black, as of dark wood or rich soil. 2 dark-skinned or suntanned. 3 (of bread) made from a dark flour as wholemeal or wheatmeal. 4 (of species or varieties) distinguished by brown coloration. —n. 1 a brown colour or pigment. 2 brown clothes or material (dressed in brown). 3 (in a game or sport) a brown ball, piece, etc. 4 (prec. by the) Brit. a brown mass of flying game-birds. —v.tr. & intr. make or become brown by cooking, sunburn, etc. □**brown ale** a dark, mild, bottled beer. **brown bear** a large N. American brown bear, Ursus arctos. **brown coal** = LIGNITE. **browned off** Brit. sl. fed up, disheartened. **brown fat** a dark-coloured adipose tissue with a rich supply of blood vessels. **brown holland** see HOLLAND. **brown owl** 1 any of various owls, esp. the tawny owl. 2 (**Brown Owl**) an adult leader of a Brownie Guides pack. **brown rice** unpolished rice with only the husk of the grain removed. **Brown-shirt** a Nazi; a member of a fascist organization. **brown sugar** unrefined or partially refined sugar. **in a brown study** see STUDY. □□ **brownish** adj. **brownness** n. **browny** adj. [OE brūn f. Gmc]
Brownian movement /'braʊnɪən/ n. (also **Brownian motion**) Physics the erratic random movement of microscopic particles in a liquid, gas,

etc., as a result of continuous bombardment from molecules of the surrounding medium. [R. *Brown*, Sc. botanist d. 1858]

Brownie /'braʊnɪ/ *n.* **1** (in full **Brownie Guide**) a member of the junior branch of the Guides. **2** (**brownie**) *Cookery* **a** a small square of rich, usu. chocolate, cake with nuts. **b** *Austral. & NZ* a sweet currant-bread. **3** (**brownie**) a benevolent elf said to haunt houses and do household work secretly. □**Brownie point** *colloq.* a notional credit for something done to please or win favour.

browning /'braʊnɪŋ/ *n.* *Brit. Cookery* browned flour or any other additive to colour gravy.

brownstone /'braʊnstəʊn/ *n. US* **1** a kind of reddish-brown sandstone used for building. **2** a building faced with this.

browse /braʊz/ *v. & n.* —*v.* **1** *intr. & tr.* read desultorily. **2** *intr.* (often foll. by *on*) feed (on leaves, twigs, or scanty vegetation). **3** *tr.* crop and eat. —*n.* **1** twigs, young shoots, etc., as fodder for cattle. **2** an act of browsing. □□ **browser** *n.* [(n.) f. earlier *brouse* f. OF *brost* young shoot, prob. f. Gmc; (v.) f. F *broster*]

BRS *abbr.* British Road Services.

brucellosis /ˌbruːsəˈləʊsɪs/ *n.* a disease caused by bacteria of the genus *Brucella*, affecting esp. cattle and causing undulant fever in humans. [*Brucella* f. Sir D. *Bruce*, Sc. physician d. 1931 + -OSIS]

brucite /'bruːsaɪt/ *n.* a mineral form of magnesium hydroxide. [A. *Bruce*, US mineralogist d. 1818]

Bruin /'bruːɪn/ *n.* a personal name used for a bear. [ME f. Du., = BROWN: used as a name in *Reynard the Fox*]

bruise /bruːz/ *n. & v.* —*n.* **1** an injury appearing as an area of discoloured skin on a human or animal body, caused by a blow or impact. **2** a similar area of damage on a fruit etc. —*v.* **1** *tr.* **a** inflict a bruise on. **b** hurt mentally. **2** *intr.* be susceptible to bruising. **3** *tr.* crush or pound. [ME f. OE *brȳsan* crush, reinforced by AF *bruser*, OF *bruisier* break]

bruiser /'bruːzə(r)/ *n. colloq.* **1** a large tough-looking person. **2** a professional boxer.

bruit /bruːt/ *v. & n.* —*v.tr.* (often foll. by *abroad*, *about*) spread (a report or rumour). —*n. archaic* a report or rumour. [F, = noise f. *bruire* roar]

Brum /brʌm/ *n. colloq.* Birmingham (in England). [abbr. of BRUMMAGEM]

brumby /'brʌmbɪ/ *n.* (*pl.* -ies) *Austral.* a wild or unbroken horse. [19th c.: orig. unkn.]

brume /bruːm/ *n. literary* mist, fog. [F f. L *bruma* winter]

Brummagem /'brʌmədʒəm/ *adj.* **1** cheap and showy (*Brummagem goods*). **2** counterfeit. [dial. form of *Birmingham*, England, with ref. to counterfeit coins and plated goods once made there]

Brummie /'brʌmɪ/ *n. & adj.* (also **Brummy**) *colloq.* —*n.* (*pl.* -ies) a native of Birmingham. —*adj.* of or characteristic of a Brummie (*a Brummie accent*). [BRUM]

brunch /brʌntʃ/ *n. & v.* —*n.* a late-morning meal eaten as the first meal of the day. —*v.intr.* eat brunch. [BR(EAKFAST) + (L)UNCH]

brunette /bruːˈnet/ *n. & adj.* —*n.* a woman with dark brown hair. —*adj.* (of a woman) having dark brown hair. [F, fem. of *brunet*, dimin. of *brun* BROWN]

brunt /brʌnt/ *n.* the chief or initial impact of an attack, task, etc. (esp. *bear the brunt of*). [ME: orig. unkn.]

brush /brʌʃ/ *n. & v.* —*n.* **1** an implement with bristles, wire, etc. varying in firmness set into a block or projecting from the end of a handle, for any of various purposes, esp. cleaning or scrubbing, painting, arranging the hair, etc. **2** the application of a brush; brushing. **3 a** (usu. foll. by *with*) a short esp. unpleasant encounter (*a brush with the law*). **b** a skirmish. **4 a** the bushy tail of a fox. **b** a brushlike tuft. **5** *Electr.* **a** a piece of carbon or metal serving as an electrical contact esp. with a moving part. **b** (in full **brush discharge**) a brushlike discharge of

sparks. **6** esp. *US & Austral.* **a** undergrowth, thicket; small trees and shrubs. **b** *US* such wood cut in faggots. **c** land covered with brush. **d** *Austral.* dense forest. **7** *Austral. & NZ sl.* a girl or young woman. —*v.* **1** *tr.* **a** sweep or scrub or put in order with a brush. **b** treat (a surface) with a brush so as to change its nature or appearance. **2** *tr.* **a** remove (dust etc.) with a brush. **b** apply (a liquid preparation) to a surface with a brush. **3** *tr. & intr.* graze or touch in passing. **4** *intr.* perform a brushing action or motion. □**brush aside** dismiss or dispose of (a person, idea, etc.) curtly or lightly. **brushed aluminium** aluminium with a lustreless surface. **brushed fabric** fabric brushed so as to raise the nap. **brush off** rebuff; dismiss abruptly. **brush-off** *n.* a rebuff; an abrupt dismissal. **brush over** paint lightly. **brush turkey** *Austral.* a large mound-building bird, *Alectura lathami*. **brush up 1** clean up or smarten. **2** revive one's former knowledge of (a subject). **brush-up** *n.* the process of cleaning up. □□ **brushlike** *adj.* **brushy** *adj.* [ME f. OF *brosse*]

brushless /'brʌʃlɪs/ *adj.* not requiring the use of a brush.

brushwood /'brʌʃwʊd/ *n.* **1** cut or broken twigs etc. **2** undergrowth; a thicket.

brushwork /'brʌʃwɜːk/ *n.* **1** manipulation of the brush in painting. **2** a painter's style in this.

brusque /brʊsk, bruːsk, brʌsk/ *adj.* abrupt or offhand in manner or speech. □□ **brusquely** *adv.* **brusqueness** *n.* **brusquerie** /'brʊskəˌriː/ *n.* [F f. It. *brusco* sour]

Brussels carpet /'brʌs(ə)lz/ *n.* a carpet with a wool pile and a stout linen back. [*Brussels* in Belgium]

Brussels lace /'brʌs(ə)lz/ *n.* an elaborate needlepoint or pillow lace.

Brussels sprout /'brʌs(ə)lz/ *n.* **1** a variety of cabbage with small compact cabbage-like buds borne close together along a tall single stem. **2** any of these buds used as a vegetable.

brut /bruːt/ *adj.* (of wine) unsweetened. [F]

brutal /'bruːt(ə)l/ *adj.* **1** savagely or coarsely cruel. **2** harsh, merciless. □□ **brutality** /-ˈtælɪtɪ/ *n.* (*pl.* -ies). **brutally** *adv.* [F *brutal* or med.L *brutalis* f. *brutus* BRUTE]

brutalism /'bruːtəˌlɪz(ə)m/ *n.* **1** brutality. **2** a heavy plain style of architecture etc.

brutalize /'bruːtəˌlaɪz/ *v.tr.* (also -ise) **1** make brutal. **2** treat brutally. □□ **brutalization** /-ˈzeɪʃ(ə)n/ *n.*

brute /bruːt/ *n. & adj.* —*n.* **1 a** a brutal or violent person or animal. **b** *colloq.* an unpleasant person. **2** an animal as opposed to a human being. —*adj.* **1** not possessing the capacity to reason. **2 a** animal-like, cruel. **b** stupid, sensual. **3** unthinking, merely material (*brute force; brute matter*). □□ **brutehood** *n.* **brutish** *adj.* **brutishly** *adv.* **brutishness** *n.* [F f. L *brutus* stupid]

bruxism /'brʌksɪz(ə)m/ *n.* the involuntary or habitual grinding or clenching of the teeth. [Gk *brukhein* gnash the teeth]

bryology /braɪˈɒlədʒɪ/ *n.* the study of bryophytes. □□ **bryological** /-əˈlɒdʒɪk(ə)l/ *adj.* **bryologist** *n.* [Gk *bruon* moss]

bryony /'braɪənɪ/ *n.* (*pl.* -ies) any climbing plant of the genus *Bryonia*, esp. *B. dioica* bearing greenish-white flowers and red berries. □**black bryony** a similar unrelated plant, *Tamus communis*, bearing poisonous berries. [L *bryonia* f. Gk *bruōnia*]

bryophyte /'braɪəˌfaɪt/ *n.* any plant of the phylum Bryophyta, including mosses and liverworts. □□ **bryophytic** /-ˈfɪtɪk/ *adj.* [mod.L *Bryophyta* f. Gk *bruon* moss + *phuton* plant]

bryozoan /ˌbraɪəˈzəʊən/ *n. & adj.* —*n.* any aquatic invertebrate animal of the phylum Bryozoa, forming colonies attached to rocks, seaweeds, etc. Also called POLYZOAN. —*adj.* of or relating to the phylum Bryozoa. □□ **bryozoology** /-ˈzəʊɒlədʒɪ/ *n.* [Gk *bruon* moss + *zōia* animals]

Brythonic /brɪˈθɒnɪk/ *n. & adj.* —*n.* the language

of the Celts of southern Britain and Brittany. —*adj.* of or relating to this people or their language. [W *Brython* Britons f. OCelt.]

BS *abbr.* **1** *US* Bachelor of Science. **2** Bachelor of Surgery. **3** Blessed Sacrament. **4** British Standard(s).

B.Sc. *abbr.* Bachelor of Science.

BSE *abbr.* bovine spongiform encephalopathy, a usu. fatal disease of cattle involving the central nervous system and causing extreme agitation.

BSI *abbr.* British Standards Institution.

B-side /'biːsaɪd/ *n.* the side of a gramophone record regarded as less important.

BST *abbr.* **1** British Summer Time. **2** British Standard Time (in use 1968-71). **3** bovine somatotrophin, a growth hormone found naturally in cows and introduced into cattle-feed to boost milk production.

BT *abbr.* British Telecom.

Bt. *abbr.* Baronet.

B.th.u. *abbr.* (also **B.t.u.**, **BTU**, **B.Th.U.**) British thermal unit(s).

bu. *abbr.* bushel(s).

bub /bʌb/ *n.* *US colloq.* a boy or a man, often used as a form of address. [earlier *bubby*, perh. a childish form of BROTHER or f. G *Bube* boy]

bubal /'bjuːb(ə)l/ *n.* = HARTEBEEST. [L *bubalus* f. Gk *boubalos* oxlike antelope]

bubble /'bʌb(ə)l/ *n.* & *v.* —*n.* **1 a** a thin sphere of liquid enclosing air etc. **b** an air-filled cavity in a liquid or a solidified liquid such as glass or amber. **2** the sound or appearance of boiling. **3** a transparent domed cavity. **4** a visionary or unrealistic project or enterprise (*the South Sea Bubble*). —*v.intr.* **1** rise in or send up bubbles. **2** make the sound of boiling. □**bubble and squeak** *Brit.* cooked cabbage fried with cooked potatoes or meat. **bubble bath 1** a preparation for adding to bath water to make it foam. **2** a bath with this added. **bubble car** *Brit.* a small motor car with a transparent dome. **bubble chamber** *Physics* an apparatus designed to make the tracks of ionizing particles visible as a row of bubbles in a liquid. **bubble gum** chewing-gum that can be blown into bubbles. **bubble memory** *Computing* a type of memory which stores data as a pattern of magnetized regions in a thin layer of magnetic material. **bubble over** (often foll. by *with*) be exuberant with laughter, excitement, anger, etc. **bubble pack** a small package enclosing goods in a transparent material on a backing. [ME: prob. imit.]

bubbly /'bʌblɪ/ *adj.* & *n.* —*adj.* (**bubblier**, **bubbliest**) **1** having or resembling bubbles. **2** exuberant. —*n. colloq.* champagne. □**bubbly-jock** *Sc.* a turkeycock.

bubo /'bjuːbəʊ/ *n.* (*pl.* **-oes**) a swollen inflamed lymph node in the armpit or groin. [med.L *bubo -onis* swelling f. Gk *boubōn* groin]

bubonic /bjuːˈbɒnɪk/ *adj.* relating to or characterized by buboes. □**bubonic plague** a contagious bacterial disease characterized by fever, delirium, and the formation of buboes.

buccal /'bʌk(ə)l/ *adj.* **1** of or relating to the cheek. **2** of or in the mouth. [L *bucca* cheek]

buccaneer /ˌbʌkəˈnɪə(r)/ *n.* & *v.* —*n.* **1** a pirate, orig. off the Spanish-American coasts. **2** an unscrupulous adventurer. —*v.intr.* be a buccaneer. □□ **buccaneering** *n.* & *adj.* **buccaneerish** *adj.* [F *boucanier* f. *boucaner* cure meat on a barbecue f. *boucan* f. Tupi *mukem*]

buccinator /'bʌksɪ,neɪtə(r)/ *n.* a flat thin cheek muscle. [L f. *buccinare* blow a trumpet (*buccina*)]

buck¹ /bʌk/ *n.* & *v.* —*n.* **1** the male of various animals, esp. the deer, hare, or rabbit. **2** *archaic* a fashionable young man. **3** (*attrib.*) **a** *sl.* male (*buck antelope*). **b** *US Mil.* of the lowest rank (*buck private*). —*v.* **1** *intr.* (of a horse) jump upwards with back arched and feet drawn together. **2** *tr.* **a** (usu. foll. by *off*) throw (a rider or burden) in this way. **b** *US* oppose, resist. **3** *tr.* & *intr.* (usu. foll. by *up*) *colloq.* a

make or become more cheerful. **b** hurry. **4** *tr.* (as **bucked** *adj.*) *colloq.* encouraged, elated. □**buck fever** *US* nervousness when called on to act. **buck-horn** horn of buck as a material for knife-handles etc. **buck-hound** a small kind of staghound. **buck rarebit** Welsh rarebit with a poached egg on top. **buck-tooth** an upper tooth that projects. □□**bucker** *n.* [OE *buc* male deer, *bucca* male goat, f. ON]

buck² /bʌk/ *n.* *US etc. sl.* a dollar. □**a fast buck** easy money. [19th c.: orig. unkn.]

buck³ /bʌk/ *n.* *sl.* an article placed as a reminder before a player whose turn it is to deal at poker. □**pass the buck** *colloq.* shift responsibility (to another). [19th c.: orig. unkn.]

buck⁴ /bʌk/ *n.* **1** *US* a saw-horse. **2** a vaulting-horse. [Du. (*zaag*)*boc*]

buck⁵ /bʌk/ *n.* the body of a cart. [perh. f. obs. *bouk* belly, f. OE *būc* f. Gmc]

buck⁶ /bʌk/ *n.* conversation; boastful talk. [Hindi *buk buk*]

buckbean /'bʌkbiːn/ *n.* a bog plant, *Menyanthes trifoliata*, with white or pinkish hairy flowers. Also called *bog-bean*.

buckboard /'bʌkbɔːd/ *n.* *US* a horse-drawn vehicle with the body formed by a plank fixed to the axles. [BUCK⁵ + BOARD]

bucket /'bʌkɪt/ *n.* & *v.* —*n.* **1 a** a roughly cylindrical open container, esp. of metal, with a handle, used for carrying, drawing, or holding water etc. **b** the amount contained in this (*need three buckets to fill the bath*). **2** (in *pl.*) large quantities of liquid, esp. rain or tears (*wept buckets*). **3** a compartment on the outer edge of a water wheel. **4** the scoop of a dredger or a grain-elevator. —*v.* (**bucketed**, **bucketing**) **1** *intr.* & *tr.* (often foll. by *along*) *Brit.* move or drive jerkily or bumpily. **2** *intr.* (often foll. by *down*) (of liquid, esp. rain) pour heavily. □**bucket seat** a seat with a rounded back to fit one person, esp. in a car. **bucket-shop 1** an office for gambling in stocks, speculating on markets, etc. **2** *colloq.* a travel agency specializing in cheap air tickets. □□ **bucketful** *n.* (*pl.* **-fuls**). [ME & AF *buket*, *buquet*, perh. f. OE *būc* pitcher]

buckeye /'bʌkaɪ/ *n.* **a** any shrub of the genus *Aesculus*, with large sticky buds and showy red or white flowers. **b** the shiny brown fruit of this plant.

buckle /'bʌk(ə)l/ *n.* & *v.* —*n.* **1** a flat often rectangular frame with a hinged pin, used for joining the ends of a belt, strap, etc. **2** a similarly shaped ornament, esp. on a shoe. —*v.* **1** *tr.* (often foll. by *up*, *on*, etc.) fasten with a buckle. **2** *tr.* & *intr.* (often foll. by *up*) give way or cause to give way under longitudinal pressure; crumple up. □**buckle down** make a determined effort. **buckle to** (or **down to**) prepare for, set about (work etc.). **buckle to** get to work, make a vigorous start. [ME f. OF *boucle* f. L *buccula* cheek-strap of a helmet f. *bucca* cheek: sense 2 of *v.* f. F *boucler* bulge]

buckler /'bʌklə(r)/ *n.* **1** *hist.* a small round shield held by a handle. **2** *Bot.* any of several ferns of the genus *Dryopteris*, having buckler-shaped indusia. Also called *shield-fern*. [ME f. OF *bocler* lit. 'having a boss' f. *boucle* BOSS²]

Buckley's /'bʌklɪz/ *n.* (in full **Buckley's chance**) *Austral.* & *NZ colloq.* little or no chance. [19th c.: orig. uncert.]

buckling /'bʌklɪŋ/ *n.* a smoked herring. [G *Bückling* bloater]

bucko /'bʌkəʊ/ *n.* & *adj.* *Naut. sl.* —*n.* (*pl.* **-oes**) a swaggering or domineering fellow. —*adj.* blustering, swaggering, bullying. [BUCK¹ + -O]

buckram /'bʌkrəm/ *n.* & *adj.* —*n.* **1** a coarse linen or other cloth stiffened with gum or paste, and used as interfacing or in bookbinding. **2** *archaic* stiffness in manner. —*adj.* *archaic* starchy; formal. □**men in buckram** a figment (Shakesp. *1 Henry IV* II. iv. 210-

50). [ME f. AF *bukeram*, OF *boquerant*, perh. f. *Bokhara* in central Asia]

Bucks. /bʌks/ *abbr.* Buckinghamshire.

Buck's Fizz /bʌks/ *n.* a cocktail of champagne or sparkling white wine and orange juice. [*Buck's* Club in London + FIZZ]

buckshee /bʌkˈʃiː/ *adj. & adv. Brit. sl.* free of charge. [corrupt. of BAKSHEESH]

buckshot /ˈbʌkʃɒt/ *n.* coarse lead shot.

buckskin /ˈbʌkskɪn/ *n.* **1 a** the skin of a buck. **b** leather made from a buck's skin. **2** a thick smooth cotton or woollen cloth.

buckthorn /ˈbʌkθɔːn/ *n.* any thorny shrub of the genus *Rhamnus*, esp. *R. cathartica* with berries formerly used as a cathartic.

buckwheat /ˈbʌkwiːt/ *n.* any cereal plant of the genus *Fagopyrum*, esp. *F. esculentum* with seeds used for fodder and for flour to make bread and pancakes. [MDu. *boecweite* beech wheat, its grains being shaped like beechmast]

bucolic /bjuːˈkɒlɪk/ *adj. & n.* —*adj.* of or concerning shepherds, the pastoral life, etc.; rural. —*n.* **1** (usu. in *pl.*) a pastoral poem or poetry. **2** a peasant. □□ **bucolically** *adv.* [L *bucolicus* f. Gk *boukolikos* f. *boukolos* herdsman f. *bous* ox]

bud¹ /bʌd/ *n. & v.* —*n.* **1 a** an immature knoblike shoot from which a stem, leaf, or flower develops. **b** a flower or leaf that is not fully open. **2** *Biol.* an asexual outgrowth from a parent organism that separates to form a new individual. **3** anything still undeveloped. —*v.* (**budded, budding**) **1** *intr. Bot. & Zool.* form a bud. **2** *intr.* begin to grow or develop (*a budding cricketer*). **3** *tr. Hort.* graft a bud (of a plant) on to another plant. □ **in bud** having newly formed buds. [ME: orig. unkn.]

bud² /bʌd/ *n. US colloq.* (as a form of address) = BUDDY. [abbr.]

Buddha /ˈbʊdə/ *n.* **1** a title given to successive teachers of Buddhism, esp. to its founder, Gautama. **2** a statue or picture of the Buddha. [Skr., = enlightened, past part. of *budh* know]

Buddhism /ˈbʊdɪz(ə)m/ *n.* a widespread Asian religion or philosophy, founded by Gautama Buddha in India in the 5th c. BC, which teaches that elimination of the self and earthly desires is the highest goal (cf. NIRVANA). □□ **Buddhist** *n. & adj.* **Buddhistic** /-ˈdɪstɪk/ *adj.* **Buddhistical** /-ˈdɪstɪk(ə)l/ *adj.*

buddleia /ˈbʌdlɪə/ *n.* any shrub of the genus *Buddleia*, with fragrant lilac, yellow, or white flowers attractive to butterflies. [A. *Buddle*, Engl. botanist d. 1715]

buddy /ˈbʌdɪ/ *n. & v. esp. US colloq.* —*n.* (*pl.* -ies) (often as a form of address) a close friend or mate. —*v.intr.* (-ies, -ied) (often foll. by *up*) become friendly. [perh. corrupt. of *brother*, or var. of BUTTY¹]

budge /bʌdʒ/ *v.* (usu. with *neg.*) **1** *intr.* **a** make the slightest movement. **b** change one's opinion (*he's stubborn, he won't budge*). **2** *tr.* cause or compel to budge (*nothing will budge him*). □ **budge up** (or **over**) make room for another person by moving. [F *bouger* stir ult. f. L *bullire* boil]

budgerigar /ˈbʌdʒərɪˌgɑː(r)/ *n.* a small green parrot, *Melopsittacus undulatus*, native to Australia, and bred in coloured varieties which are often kept as cage-birds. [Aboriginal, = good cockatoo]

budget /ˈbʌdʒɪt/ *n. & v.* —*n.* **1** the amount of money needed or available (for a specific item etc.) (*a budget of £200; mustn't exceed the budget*). **2 a** (**the Budget**) *Brit.* the usu. annual estimate of national revenue and expenditure. **b** an estimate or plan of expenditure in relation to income. **c** a private person's or family's similar estimate. **3** (*attrib.*) cheap. **4** *archaic* a quantity of material etc., esp. written or printed. —*v.tr. & intr.* (**budgeted, budgeting**) (often foll. by *for*) allow or arrange for in a budget (*have budgeted for a new car; can budget £60*). □ **budget account** (or **plan**) a bank account, or account with a store, into which one makes regular, usu. monthly, payments

to cover bills. **on a budget** avoiding expense; cheap. □□ **budgetary** *adj.* [ME = pouch, f. OF *bougette* dimin. of *bouge* leather bag f. L *bulga* (f. Gaulish) knapsack: cf. BULGE]

budgie /ˈbʌdʒɪ/ *n. colloq.* = BUDGERIGAR. [abbr.]

buff /bʌf/ *adj., n., & v.* —*adj.* of a yellowish beige colour (*buff envelope*). —*n.* **1** a yellowish beige colour. **2** *colloq.* an enthusiast, esp. for a particular hobby (*railway buff*). **3** *colloq.* the human skin unclothed. **4 a** a velvety dull-yellow ox-leather. **b** (*attrib.*) (of a garment etc.) made of this (*buff gloves*). **5** (**the Buffs**) the former East Kent Regiment (from the colour of its uniform facings). —*v.tr.* **1** polish (metal, fingernails, etc.). **2** make (leather) velvety like buff, by removing the surface. □ **buff-stick** a stick covered with buff and used for polishing. **in the buff** *colloq.* naked. [orig. sense 'buffalo', prob. f. F *buffle*; sense 2 of *n.* orig. f. buff uniforms formerly worn by New York volunteer firemen, applied to enthusiastic fire-watchers]

buffalo /ˈbʌfəˌləʊ/ *n. & v.* —*n.* (*pl.* same or -oes) **1** either of two species of ox, *Synceros caffer*, native to Africa, or *Bubalus arnee*, native to Asia with heavy backswept horns. **2** a N. American bison, *Bison bison*. —*v.tr.* (-oes, -oed) *US sl.* overawe, outwit. □ **buffalo grass 1** a grass, *Buchloe dactyloides*, of the N. American plains. **2** a grass, *Stenotaphrum secundatum*, of Australia and New Zealand. [prob. f. Port. *bufalo* f. LL *bufalus* f. L *bubalus* f. Gk *boubalos* antelope, wild ox]

buffer¹ /ˈbʌfə(r)/ *n. & v.* —*n.* **1 a** a device that protects against or reduces the effect of an impact. **b** *Brit.* such a device (usu. one of a pair) on the front and rear of a railway vehicle or at the end of a track. **2** *Biochem.* a substance that maintains the hydrogen ion concentration of a solution when an acid or alkali is added. **3** *Computing* a temporary memory area or queue for data to aid its transfer between devices or programs operating at different speeds etc. —*v.tr.* **1** act as a buffer to. **2** *Biochem.* treat with a buffer. □ **buffer State** a small State situated between two larger ones potentially hostile to one another and regarded as reducing the likelihood of open hostilities. **buffer stock** a reserve of commodity to offset price fluctuations. [prob. f. obs. *buff* (v.), imit. of the sound of a soft body struck]

buffer² /ˈbʌfə(r)/ *n. Brit. sl.* a silly or incompetent old man (esp. *old buffer*). [18th c.: prob. formed as BUFFER¹ or with the sense 'stutterer']

buffet¹ /ˈbʊfeɪ, ˈbʌfeɪ/ *n.* **1** a room or counter where light meals or snacks may be bought (*station buffet*). **2** a meal consisting of several dishes set out from which guests serve themselves (*buffet lunch*). **3** /also ˈbʌfɪt/ a sideboard or recessed cupboard for china etc. □ **buffet car** *Brit.* a railway coach serving light meals or snacks. [F f. OF *bufet* stool, of unkn. orig.]

buffet² /ˈbʌfɪt/ *v. & n.* —*v.* (**buffeted, buffeting**) **1** *tr.* **a** strike or knock repeatedly (*wind buffeted the trees*). **b** strike, esp. repeatedly, with the hand or fist. **2** *tr.* (of fate etc.) treat badly; plague (*cheerful though buffeted by misfortune*). **3 a** *intr.* struggle; fight one's way (through difficulties etc.). **b** *tr.* contend with (waves etc.). —*n.* **1** a blow, esp. of the hand or fist. **2** a shock. [ME f. OF dimin. of *bufe* blow]

buffeting /ˈbʌfɪtɪŋ/ *n.* **1** a beating; repeated blows. **2** *Aeron.* an irregular oscillation, caused by air eddies, of any part of an aircraft.

bufflehead /ˈbʌf(ə)lˌhed/ *n.* a duck, *Bucephala albeola*, native to N. America, with a head that appears over-large. [obs. *buffle* buffalo + HEAD]

buffo /ˈbʊfəʊ/ *n. & adj.* —*n.* (*pl.* -os) a comic actor, esp. in Italian opera. —*adj.* comic, burlesque. [It.]

buffoon /bəˈfuːn/ *n.* **1** a jester; a mocker. **2** a stupid person. □□ **buffoonery** *n.* **buffoonish** *adj.* [F *bouffon* f. It. *buffone* f. med.L *buffo* clown f. Rmc]

bug /bʌg/ *n. & v.* —*n.* **1 a** any of various hemipterous insects with oval flattened bodies and mouthparts modified for piercing and sucking. **b** *US* any small insect. **2** *sl.* a micro-organism, esp. a bacterium, or a disease caused by it. **3** a concealed microphone. **4** *sl.* an error in a computer program or system etc. **5** *sl.* an obsession, enthusiasm, etc. —*v.* (**bugged**, **bugging**) **1** *tr. sl.* conceal a microphone in (esp. a building or room). **2** *tr. sl.* annoy, bother. **3** *intr.* (often foll. by *out*) *US sl.* leave quickly. □**bug-eyed** with bulging eyes. [17th c.: orig. unkn.]

bugaboo /ˈbʌgəˌbuː/ *n.* a bogey (see BOGEY[2]) or bugbear. [prob. of dial. orig.: cf. Welsh *bwcibo* the Devil, *bwci* hobgoblin]

bugbear /ˈbʌgbeə(r)/ *n.* **1** a cause of annoyance or anger; a *bête noire.* **2** an object of baseless fear. **3** *archaic* a sort of hobgoblin or any being invoked to intimidate children. [obs. *bug* + BEAR[2]]

bugger /ˈbʌgə(r)/ *n., v., & int. coarse sl.* (except in sense 2 of *n.* and 3 of *v.*) ❡ Usually considered a taboo word. —*n.* **1 a** an unpleasant or awkward person or thing (*the bugger won't fit*). **b** a person of a specified kind (*he's a miserable bugger; you clever bugger!*). **2** a person who commits buggery. —*v.tr.* **1** as an exclamation of annoyance (*bugger the thing!*). **2** (often foll. by *up*) *Brit.* **a** ruin; spoil (*really buggered it up; no good, its buggered*). **b** exhaust, tire out. **3** commit buggery with. —*int.* expressing annoyance. □**bugger about** (or **around**) (often foll. by *with*) **1** mess about. **2** mislead; persecute. **bugger-all** nothing. **bugger off** (often in *imper.*) go away. [ME f. MDu. f. OF *bougre,* orig. 'heretic' f. med.L *Bulgarus* Bulgarian (member of the Greek Church)]

buggery /ˈbʌgərɪ/ *n.* **1** anal intercourse. **2** = BESTIALITY 2. [ME f. MDu. *buggerie* f. OF *bougerie*: see BUGGER]

buggy[1] /ˈbʌgɪ/ *n.* (*pl.* **-ies**) **1** a light, horse-drawn, esp. two-wheeled, vehicle for one or two people. **2** a small, sturdy, esp. open, motor vehicle (*beach buggy; dune buggy*). **3** *US* a pram. [18th c.: orig. unkn.]

buggy[2] /ˈbʌgɪ/ *adj.* (**buggier, buggiest**) infested with bugs.

bugle[1] /ˈbjuːg(ə)l/ *n. & v.* —*n.* (also **bugle-horn**) a brass instrument like a small trumpet, used esp. by huntsmen and for military signals. —*v.* **1** *intr.* sound a bugle. **2** *tr.* sound (a note, a call, etc.) on a bugle. □□**bugler** /ˈbjuːglə(r)/ *n.* **buglet** /ˈbjuːglɪt/ *n.* [ME, orig. = 'buffalo', f. OF f. L *buculus* dimin. of *bos* ox]

bugle[2] /ˈbjuːg(ə)l/ *n.* a blue-flowered mat-forming plant, *Ajuga reptans.* [ME f. LL *bugula*]

bugle[3] /ˈbjuːg(ə)l/ *n.* a tube-shaped bead sewn on a dress etc. for ornament. [16th c.: orig. unkn.]

bugloss /ˈbjuːglɒs/ *n.* **1** any of various bristly plants related to borage, esp. of the genus *Anchusa* with bright blue tubular flowers. **2** = *viper's bugloss* (see VIPER). [F *buglosse* or L *buglossus* f. Gk *bouglōssos* ox-tongued]

buhl /buːl/ *n.* (also **boule, boulle**) **1** pieces of brass, tortoiseshell, etc., cut to make a pattern and used as decorative inlays esp. on furniture. **2** work inlaid with buhl. **3** (*attrib.*) inlaid with buhl. [(*buhl* Germanized) f. A. C. *Boule,* Fr. wood-carver d. 1732]

build /bɪld/ *v. & n.* —*v.tr.* (*past* and *past. part.* **built** /bɪlt/) **1 a** construct (a house, vehicle, fire, road, model, etc.) by putting parts or material together. **b** commission, finance, and oversee the building of (*the council has built two new schools*). **2** (often foll. by *up*) establish, develop, make, or accumulate gradually (*built the business up from nothing*); (often foll. by *on*); base (hopes, theories, etc.) (*ideas built on a false foundation*). **3** (as **built** *adj.*) having a specified build (*sturdily built; brick-built*). —*n.* **1** the proportions of esp. the human body (*a slim build*). **2** a style of construction; a make (*build of his suit was pre-war*). □**build in** incorporate as part of a structure. **build in** (or **round** or **up**) surround with houses etc.; block up. **build on** add (an extension etc.). **build up 1** increase in size or strength. **2** praise; boost. **3** gradually become established. **build-up** *n.* **1** a favourable description in advance; publicity. **2** a gradual approach to a climax or

maximum (*the build-up was slow but sure*). **built-in 1** forming an integral part of a structure. **2** forming an integral part of a person's character (*built-in integrity*). **built on sand** unstable. **built-up 1** (of a locality) densely covered by houses etc. **2** increased in height etc. by the addition of parts. **3** composed of separately prepared parts. [OE *byldan* f. *bold* dwelling f. Gmc: cf. BOWER[1], BOOTH]

builder /ˈbɪldə(r)/ *n.* **1** a contractor for building houses etc.; a master builder. **2** a person engaged as a bricklayer etc. on a building site.

building /ˈbɪldɪŋ/ *n.* **1** a permanent fixed structure forming an enclosure and providing protection from the elements etc. (e.g. a house, school, factory, or stable). **2** the constructing of such structures. □**building line** a limit or boundary between a house and a street beyond which the owner may not build. **building site** an area before or during the construction of a house etc. **building society** *Brit.* a public finance company which accepts investments at interest and lends capital for mortgages on houses etc.

built *past* and *past part.* of BUILD.

bulb /bʌlb/ *n.* **1 a** an underground fleshy-leaved storage organ of some plants (e.g. lily, onion) sending roots downwards and leaves upwards. **b** a plant grown from this, e.g. a daffodil. **2** = *light-bulb* (see LIGHT[1]). **3** any object or part shaped like a bulb. [L *bulbus* f. Gk *bolbos* onion]

bulbous /ˈbʌlbəs/ *adj.* **1** shaped like a bulb; fat or bulging. **2** having a bulb or bulbs. **3** (of a plant) growing from a bulb.

bulbul /ˈbʊlbʊl/ *n.* **1** any songbird of the family Pycnonotidae, of dull plumage with contrasting bright patches. **2** a singer or poet. [Pers. f. Arab., of imit. orig.]

Bulgar /ˈbʌlgɑː(r)/ *n.* **1** a member of a tribe who settled in what is now Bulgaria in the 7th c. **2** a Bulgarian. [med.L *Bulgarus* f. OBulg. *Blŭgarinŭ*]

bulgar var. of BULGUR.

Bulgarian /bʌlˈgeərɪən/ *n. & adj.* —*n.* **1 a** a native or national of Bulgaria. **b** a person of Bulgarian descent. **2** the language of Bulgaria. —*adj.* of or relating to Bulgaria or its people or language. [med.L *Bulgaria* f. *Bulgarus*: see BULGAR]

bulge /bʌldʒ/ *n. & v.* —*n.* **1 a** a convex part of an otherwise flat or flatter surface. **b** an irregular swelling; a lump. **2** *colloq.* a temporary increase in quantity or number (*baby bulge*). **3** *Naut.* the bilge of a ship. **4** *Mil.* a salient. —*v.* **1** *intr.* swell outwards. **2** *intr.* be full or replete. **3** *tr.* swell (a bag, cheeks, etc.) by stuffing. □**have** (or **get**) **the bulge on** *sl.* have or get an advantage over. □□**bulgingly** *adv.* **bulgy** *adj.* [ME f. OF *boulge, bouge* f. L *bulga*: see BUDGET]

bulgur /ˈbʌlgə(r)/ *n.* (also **bulgar, bulghur**) a cereal food of whole wheat partially boiled then dried, eaten esp. in Turkey. [Turk.]

bulimarexia /bjuːˌlɪməˈreksɪə/ *n.* esp. *US* = BULIMIA 2. □□**bulimarexic** *adj. & n.* [BULIMIA + ANOREXIA]

bulimia /bjuːˈlɪmɪə/ *n. Med.* **1** insatiable overeating. **2** (in full **bulimia nervosa**) an emotional disorder in which bouts of extreme overeating are followed by depression and self-induced vomiting, purging, or fasting. □□**bulimic** *adj. & n.* [mod.L f. Gk *boulimia* f. *bous* ox + *limos* hunger]

bulk /bʌlk/ *n. & v.* —*n.* **1 a** size; magnitude (esp. large). **b** a large mass, body, or person. **c** a large quantity. **2** a large shape, body, or person (*jacket barely covered his bulk*). **3** (usu. prec. by *the*; treated as *pl.*) the greater part or number (*the bulk of the applicants are women*). **4** roughage. **5** *Naut.* cargo, esp. unpackaged. —*v.* **1** *intr.* seem in respect of size or importance (*bulks large in his reckoning*). **2** *tr.* make (a book, a textile yarn, etc.) seem thicker by suitable treatment (*bulked it with irrelevant stories*). **3** *tr.* combine (consignments etc.). □**break bulk** begin unloading (cargo). **bulk-buying 1** buying in large amounts at a discount. **2** the purchase by one buyer of all or most of a producer's output. **in bulk 1** in large quantities. **2** (of a cargo) loose, not packaged. [sense 'cargo' f. OIcel. *búlki*; sense 'mass' etc. perh. alt. f. obs. *bouk* (cf. BUCK³)]

bulkhead /'bʌlkhed/ *n.* an upright partition separating the compartments in a ship, aircraft, vehicle, etc. [*bulk* stall f. ON *bálkr* + HEAD]

bulky /'bʌlkɪ/ *adj.* (**bulkier, bulkiest**) **1** taking up much space, large. **2** awkwardly large, unwieldy. □□ **bulkily** *adv.* **bulkiness** *n.*

bull¹ /bʊl/ *n.*, *adj.*, & *v.* —*n.* **1 a** an uncastrated male bovine animal. **b** a male of the whale, elephant, and other large animals. **2 (the Bull)** the zodiacal sign or constellation Taurus. **3** *Brit.* the bull's-eye of a target. **4** *Stock Exch.* a person who buys shares hoping to sell them at a higher price later (cf. BEAR²). —*adj.* like that of a bull (*bull neck*). —*v.* **1** *tr.* & *intr.* act or treat violently. **2** *Stock Exch.* speculate for a rise. **b** *tr.* raise price of (stocks, etc.). □ **bull ant** *Austral.* = **bulldog ant. bull at a gate** a hasty or rash person. **bull-fiddle** *US colloq.* a double-bass. **bull-horn** a megaphone. **bull in a china shop** a reckless or clumsy person. **bull market** a market with shares rising in price. **bull-nose** (or **-nosed**) with rounded end. **bull session** *US* an informal group discussion. **bull's-eye 1** the centre of a target. **2** a large hard peppermint-flavoured sweet. **3** a hemisphere or thick disc of glass in a ship's deck or side to admit light. **4** a small circular window. **5 a** a hemispherical lens. **b** a lantern fitted with this. **6** a boss of glass at the centre of a blown glass sheet. **bull-terrier 1** a short-haired dog of a breed that is a cross between a bulldog and a terrier. **2** this breed. **take the bull by the horns** face danger or challenge boldly. □□ **bullish** *adj.* [ME f. ON *boli* = MLG, MDu. *bulle*]

bull² /bʊl/ *n.* a papal edict. [ME f. OF *bulle* f. L *bulla* rounded object, in med.L 'seal']

bull³ /bʊl/ *n.* **1** (also **Irish bull**) an expression containing a contradiction in terms or implying ludicrous inconsistency. **2** *sl.* **a** unnecessary routine tasks or discipline. **b** nonsense. **c** trivial or insincere talk or writing. **d** *US* a bad blunder (cf. BULLSHIT). [17th c.: orig. unkn.]

bullace /'bʊlɪs/ *n.* a thorny shrub, *Prunus insititia*, bearing globular yellow or purple-black fruits, of which the damson is the cultivated form. [ME f. OF *buloce, beloce*]

bulldog /'bʊldɒg/ *n.* **1 a** a dog of a sturdy powerful breed with a large head and smooth hair. **b** this breed. **2** a tenacious and courageous person. □ **bulldog ant** *Austral.* a large ant with a powerful sting. **bulldog clip** a strong sprung clip for papers.

bulldoze /'bʊldəʊz/ *v.tr.* **1** clear with a bulldozer. **2** *colloq.* **a** intimidate. **b** make (one's way) forcibly.

bulldozer /'bʊl,dəʊzə(r)/ *n.* **1** a powerful tractor with a broad curved vertical blade at the front for clearing ground. **2** a forceful and domineering person. [*bulldose* (or *-doze*) *US* = intimidate, f. BULL¹: second element uncert.]

bullet /'bʊlɪt/ *n.* a small round or cylindrical missile with a pointed end, fired from a rifle, revolver, etc. □ **bullet-headed** having a round head. [F *boulet, boulette* dimin. of *boule* ball f. L *bulla* bubble]

bulletin /'bʊlɪtɪn/ *n.* **1** a short official statement of news. **2** a regular list of information etc. issued by an organization or society. □ **bulletin-board** *US* a notice-board. [F f. It. *bullettino* dimin. of *bulletta* passport, dimin. of *bulla* seal, BULL²]

bulletproof /'bʊlɪt,pruːf/ *adj.* & *v.* —*adj.* (of a material) designed to resist the penetration of bullets. —*v.tr.* make bulletproof.

bullfight /'bʊlfaɪt/ *n.* a sport of baiting and (usu.) killing bulls as a public spectacle, esp. in Spain. □□ **bullfighter** *n.* **bullfighting** *n.*

bullfinch /'bʊlfɪntʃ/ *n.* a finch, *Pyrrhula pyrrhula*, with a short stout beak and bright plumage.

bullfrog /'bʊlfrɒg/ *n.* a large frog, *Rana catesbiana*, native to N. America, with a bellowing croak.

bullhead /'bʊlhed/ *n.* any of various marine fishes with large flattened heads.

bull-headed /bʊl'hedɪd/ *adj.* obstinate; impetuous; blundering. □□ **bull-headedly** *adv.* **bull-headedness** *n.*

bullion /'bʊlɪən/ *n.* a metal (esp. gold or silver) in bulk before coining, or valued by weight. [AF = mint, var. of OF *bouillon* ult. f. L *bullire* boil]

bullish /'bʊlɪʃ/ *adj.* **1** like a bull, esp. in temper. **2** *Stock Exch.* causing or associated with a rise in prices.

bullock /'bʊlək/ *n.* & *v.* —*n.* a castrated bull. —*v.intr.* (often foll. by *at*) *Austral. colloq.* work very hard. [OE *bulluc*, dimin. of BULL¹]

bullocky /'bʊləkɪ/ *n.* *Austral.* & *NZ colloq.* a bullock-driver.

bullring /'bʊlrɪŋ/ *n.* an arena for bullfights.

bullshit /'bʊlʃɪt/ *n.* & *v. coarse sl.* —*n.* **1** (often as *int.*) nonsense, rubbish. **2** trivial or insincere talk or writing. —*v.intr.* (**-shitted, -shitting**) talk nonsense; bluff. □□ **bullshitter** *n.* [BULL³ + SHIT]

bulltrout /'bʊltraʊt/ *n.* *Brit.* a salmon trout.

bully¹ /'bʊlɪ/ *n.* & *v.* —*n.* (*pl.* **-ies**) a person who uses strength or power to coerce others by fear. —*v.tr.* (**-ies, -ied**) **1** persecute or oppress by force or threats. **2** (foll. by *into* + verbal noun) pressure or coerce (a person) to do something (*bullied him into agreeing*). □ **bully-boy** a hired ruffian. [orig. as a term of endearment, prob. f. MDu. *boele* lover]

bully² /'bʊlɪ/ *adj.* & *int. colloq.* —*adj.* very good; first-rate. —*int.* (foll. by *for*) expressing admiration or approval, or iron. (*bully for them!*). [perh. f BULLY¹]

bully³ /'bʊlɪ/ *n.* & *v.* (in full **bully off**) —*n.* (*pl.* **-ies**) the start of play in hockey in which two opponents strike each other's sticks three times and then go for the ball. —*v.intr.* (**-ies, -ied**) start play in this way. [19th c.: perh. f. *bully* scrum in Eton football, of unkn. orig.]

bully⁴ /'bʊlɪ/ *n.* (in full **bully beef**) corned beef. [F *bouilli* boiled beef f. *bouillir* BOIL¹]

bullyrag var. of BALLYRAG.

bully tree /'bʊlɪ/ *n.* = BALATA. [corrupt.]

bulrush /'bʊlrʌʃ/ *n.* **1** = reed-mace (see REED¹). **2** a rushlike water-plant, *Scirpus lacustris*, used for weaving. **3** *Bibl.* a papyrus plant. [perh. f. BULL¹ = large, coarse, as in *bullfrog, bulltrout*, etc.]

bulwark /'bʊlwək/ *n.* **1** a defensive wall, esp. of earth; a rampart; a mole or breakwater. **2** a person, principle, etc., that acts as a defence. **3** (usu. in *pl.*) a ship's side above deck. [ME f. MLG, MDu. *bolwerk*: see BOLE¹, WORK]

bum¹ /bʌm/ *n.* *Brit. sl.* the buttocks. □ **bum-bailiff** *hist.* a bailiff empowered to collect debts or arrest debtors for non-payment. **bum-boat** any small boat plying with provisions etc. for ships. **bum-sucker** *sl.* a toady. **bum-sucking** toadying. [ME *bom*, of unkn. orig.]

bum² /bʌm/ *n.*, *v.*, & *adj. US sl.* —*n.* a habitual loafer or tramp; a lazy dissolute person. —*v.* (**bummed, bumming**) **1** *intr.* (often foll. by *about, around*) loaf or wander around; be a bum. **2** *tr.* get by begging; cadge. —*attrib.adj.* of poor quality. □ **bum rap** imprisonment on a false charge. **bum's rush** forcible ejection. **bum steer** false information. **on the bum** vagrant, begging. [prob. abbr. or back-form. f. BUMMER]

bumble /'bʌmb(ə)l/ *v.intr.* **1** (foll. by *on*) speak in a rambling incoherent way. **2** (often as **bumbling** *adj.*) move or act ineptly; blunder. **3** make a buzz or hum. □□ **bumbler** *n.* [BOOM¹ + -LE⁴: partly f. *bumble* = blunderer]

bumble-bee /'bʌmb(ə)l,biː/ *n.* any large loud humming bee of the genus *Bombus*. [as BUMBLE]

bumf /bʌmf/ *n.* (also **bumph**) *Brit. colloq.* **1** usu. *derog.* papers, documents. **2** lavatory paper. [abbr. of *bum-fodder*]

bummalo /'bʌmə,ləʊ/ *n.* (*pl.* same) a small fish, *Harpodon nehereus*, of S. Asian coasts, dried and used as food (see BOMBAY DUCK). [perh. f. Marathi *bombīl(a)*]

bummer /'bʌmə(r)/ *n. US sl.* **1** an idler; a loafer. **2** an unpleasant occurrence. [19th c.: perh. f. G *Bummler*]

bump /bʌmp/ *n., v.,* & *adv.* —*n.* **1** a dull-sounding blow or collision. **2** a swelling or dent caused by this. **3** an uneven patch on a road, field, etc. **4** *Phrenol.* any of various prominences on the skull thought to indicate different mental faculties. **5** (in narrow-river races where boats make a spaced start one behind another) the point at which a boat begins to overtake (and usu. touches) the boat ahead, thereby defeating it. **6** *Aeron.* **a** an irregularity in an aircraft's motion. **b** a rising air current causing this. —*v.* **1 a** *tr.* hit or come against with a bump. **b** *intr.* (of two objects) collide. **2** *intr.* (foll. by *against, into*) hit with a bump; collide with. **3** *tr.* (often foll. by *against, on*) hurt or damage by striking (*bumped my head on the ceiling*; *bumped the car while parking*). **4** *intr.* (usu. foll. by *along*) move or travel with much jolting (*we bumped along the road*). **5** *tr.* (in a boat-race) gain a bump against. **6** *tr. US* displace, esp. by seniority. —*adv.* with a bump; suddenly; violently. □**bump into** *colloq.* meet by chance. **bump off** *sl.* murder. **bump up** *colloq.* increase (prices etc.). [16th c., imit.: perh. f. Scand.]

bumper /'bʌmpə(r)/ *n.* **1** a horizontal bar or strip fixed across the front or back of a motor vehicle to reduce damage in a collision or as a trim. **2** (usu. *attrib.*) an unusually large or fine example (*a bumper crop*). **3** *Cricket* a ball rising high after pitching. **4** a brim-full glass of wine etc. □**bumper car** = DODGEM.

bumph var. of BUMF.

bumpkin /'bʌmpkɪn/ *n.* a rustic or socially inept person. [perh. Du. *boomken* little tree or MDu. *bommekijn* little barrel]

bumptious /'bʌmpʃəs/ *adj.* offensively self-assertive or conceited. □□**bumptiously** *adv.* **bumptiousness** *n.* [BUMP, after FRACTIOUS]

bumpy /'bʌmpɪ/ *adj.* (**bumpier, bumpiest**) **1** having many bumps (*a bumpy road*). **2** affected by bumps (*a bumpy ride*). □□**bumpily** *adv.* **bumpiness** *n.*

bun /bʌn/ *n.* **1** a small usu. sweetened bread roll or cake, often with dried fruit. **2** *Sc.* a rich fruit cake or currant bread. **3** hair worn in the shape of a bun. □**bun fight** *Brit. sl.* a tea party. **have a bun in the oven** *sl.* be pregnant. **hot cross bun** a bun marked with a cross, traditionally eaten on Good Friday. [ME: orig. unkn.]

buna /'bjuːnə, 'buːnə/ *n.* a synthetic rubber made by polymerization of butadiene. [G (as BUTADIENE, *natrium* sodium)]

bunch /bʌntʃ/ *n.* & *v.* —*n.* **1** a cluster of things growing or fastened together (*bunch of grapes*; *bunch of keys*). **2** a collection; a set or lot (*best of the bunch*). **3** *colloq.* a group; a gang. —*v.* **1** *tr.* make into a bunch or bunches; gather into close folds. **2** *intr.* form into a group or crowd. □**bunch grass** a N. American grass that grows in clumps. **bunch of fives** *sl.* a fist. □□**bunchy** *adj.* [ME: orig. unkn.]

bunco /'bʊŋkəʊ/ *n.* & *v. US sl.* —*n.* (*pl.* **-os**) a swindle, esp. by card-sharping or a confidence trick. —*v.tr.* (**-oes, -oed**) swindle, cheat. [perh. f. Sp. *banca* a card-game]

buncombe var. of BUNKUM.

Bundesrat /'bʊndəs,raːt/ *n.* the Upper House of Parliament in the Federal Republic of Germany or in Austria. [G f. *Bund* federation + *Rat* council]

Bundestag /'bʊndəs,taːg/ *n.* the Lower House of Parliament in the Federal Republic of Germany. [G f. *Bund* federation + *tagen* confer]

bundle /'bʌnd(ə)l/ *n.* & *v.* —*n.* **1** a collection of things tied or fastened together. **2** a set of nerve fibres etc. banded together. **3** *sl.* a large amount of money. —*v.* **1** *tr.* (usu. foll. by *up*) tie in or make into a bundle

(*bundled up my squash kit*). **2** *tr.* (usu. foll. by *into*) throw or push, esp. quickly or confusedly (*bundled the papers into the drawer*). **3** *tr.* (usu. foll. by *out, off, away*, etc.) send (esp. a person) away hurriedly or unceremoniously (*bundled them off the premises*). **4** *intr.* sleep clothed with another person, esp. a fiancé(e), as a local custom. □**be a bundle of nerves** (or **prejudices** etc.) be extremely nervous (or prejudiced etc.). **bundle up** dress warmly or cumbersomely. **go a bundle on** *sl.* be very fond of. □□**bundler** *n.* [ME, perh. f. OE *byndelle* a binding, but also f. LG, Du *bundel*]

bung[1] /bʌŋ/ *n.* & *v.* —*n.* **1** a stopper for closing a hole in a container, esp. a cask. —*v.tr.* **1** stop with a bung. **2** *Brit. sl.* throw, toss. □**bunged up** closed, blocked. **bung-hole** a hole for filling or emptying a cask etc. [MDu. *bonghe*]

bung[2] /bʌŋ/ *adj. Austral.* & *NZ sl.* dead; ruined, useless. □**go bung 1** die. **2** fail; go bankrupt. [Aboriginal]

bungalow /'bʌŋgə,ləʊ/ *n.* a one-storeyed house. [Gujarati *bangalo* f. Hind. *banglā* belonging to Bengal]

bungle /'bʌŋg(ə)l/ *v.* & *n.* —*v.* **1** *tr.* blunder over, mismanage, or fail at (a task). **2** *intr.* work badly or clumsily. —*n.* a bungled attempt; bungled work. □□**bungler** *n.* [imit.: cf. BUMBLE]

bunion /'bʌnjən/ *n.* a swelling on the foot, esp. at the first joint of the big toe. [OF *buignon* f. *buigne* bump on the head]

bunk[1] /bʌŋk/ *n.* a sleeping-berth, esp. a shelflike bed against a wall, e.g. in a ship. □**bunk-bed** each of two or more beds one above the other, forming a unit. **bunk-house** a house where workmen etc. are lodged. [18th c.: orig. unkn.]

bunk[2] /bʌŋk/ *n.* □**do a bunk** *Brit. sl.* leave or abscond hurriedly. [19th c.: orig. unkn.]

bunk[3] /bʌŋk/ *n. sl.* nonsense, humbug. [abbr. of BUNKUM]

bunker /'bʌŋkə(r)/ *n.* & *v.* —*n.* **1** a large container or compartment for storing fuel. **2** a reinforced underground shelter, esp. for use in wartime. **3** a hollow filled with sand, used as an obstacle in a golf-course. —*v.tr.* **1** fill the fuel bunkers of (a ship etc.). **2** (usu. in *passive*) **a** trap in a bunker (in sense 3). **b** bring into difficulties. [19th c.: orig. unkn.]

bunkum /'bʌŋkəm/ *n.* (also **buncombe**) nonsense; humbug. [orig. *buncombe* f. *Buncombe* County in N. Carolina, mentioned in a nonsense speech by its Congressman, *c.*1820]

bunny /'bʌnɪ/ *n.* (*pl.* **-ies**) **1** a child's name for a rabbit. **2** *Austral. sl.* a victim or dupe. **3** (in full **bunny girl**) a club hostess, waitress, etc., wearing a skimpy costume with ears and a tail suggestive of a rabbit. [dial. *bun* rabbit]

Bunsen burner /'bʌns(ə)n/ *n.* a small adjustable gas burner used in scientific work as a source of great heat. [R. W. *Bunsen*, Ger. chemist d. 1899]

bunt[1] /bʌnt/ *n.* the baggy centre of a fishing-net, sail, etc. [16th c.: orig. unkn.]

bunt[2] /bʌnt/ *n.* a disease of wheat caused by the fungus *Tilletia caries*. [18th c.: orig. unkn.]

bunt[3] /bʌnt/ *v.* & *intr.* **1** *tr.* push with the head or horns; butt. **2** *tr. US Baseball* stop (a ball) with the bat without swinging. —*n.* an act of bunting. [19th c.: cf. BUTT[1]]

buntal /'bʌnt(ə)l/ *n.* the straw from a talipot palm. [Tagalog]

bunting[1] /'bʌntɪŋ/ *n.* any of numerous seed-eating birds of the family Emberizidae, related to the finches and sparrows. [ME: orig. unkn.]

bunting[2] /'bʌntɪŋ/ *n.* **1** flags and other decorations. **2** a loosely-woven fabric used for these. [18th c.: orig. unkn.]

buntline /'bʌntlaɪn/ *n.* a line for confining the bunt (see BUNT[1]) when furling a sail.

bunya /'bʌnjə/ *n.* (also **bunya bunya** /'bʌnjə,bʌnjə/) *Austral.* a tall coniferous tree, *Araucaria bidwillii*, bearing large nutritious cones. [Aboriginal]

---

b *but*　d *dog*　f *few*　g *get*　h *he*　j *yes*　k *cat*　l *leg*　m *man*　n *no*　p *pen*　r *red*　s *sit*　t *top*　v *voice*

bunyip /ˈbʌnjɪp/ *n. Austral.* **1** a fabulous monster inhabiting swamps and lagoons. **2** an imposter. [Aboriginal]

buoy /bɔɪ/ *n. & v.* —*n.* **1** an anchored float serving as a navigation mark or to show reefs etc. **2** a lifebuoy. —*v.tr.* **1** (usu. foll. by *up*) **a** keep afloat. **b** sustain the courage or spirits of (a person etc.); uplift, encourage. **2** (often foll. by *out*) mark with a buoy or buoys. [ME prob. f. MDu. *bo(e)ye*, ult. f. L *boia* collar f. Gk *boeiai* ox-hides]

buoyancy /ˈbɔɪənsɪ/ *n.* **1** the capacity to be or remain buoyant. **2** resilience; recuperative power. **3** cheerfulness.

buoyant /ˈbɔɪənt/ *adj.* **1 a** able or apt to keep afloat or rise to the top of a liquid or gas. **b** (of a liquid or gas) able to keep something afloat. **2** light-hearted. □□ **buoyantly** *adv.* [F *buoyant* or Sp. *boyante* part. of *boyar* float f. *boya* BUOY]

bur /bɜː(r)/ *n.* (also **burr**) **1 a** a prickly clinging seed-case or flower-head. **b** any plant producing these. **2** a person hard to shake off. **3** = BURR *n.* 2. □**bur oak** a N. American oak, *Quercus macrocarpa* with large fringed acorn-cups. [ME: cf. Da. *burre* bur, burdock, Sw. *kard-borre* burdock]

burble /ˈbɜːb(ə)l/ *v. & n.* —*v.intr.* **1** speak ramblingly; make a murmuring noise. **2** *Aeron.* (of an air-flow) break up into turbulence. —*n.* **1** a murmuring noise. **2** rambling speech. □□ **burbler** *n.* [19th c.: imit.]

burbot /ˈbɜːbət/ *n.* an eel-like flat-headed bearded freshwater fish, *Lota lota*. [ME: cf. OF *barbote*]

burden /ˈbɜːd(ə)n/ *n. & v.* —*n.* **1** a load, esp. a heavy one. **2** an oppressive duty, obligation, expense, emotion, etc. **3** the bearing of loads (*beast of burden*). **4** (also *archaic* **burthen** /ˈbɜːð(ə)n/) a ship's carrying-capacity, tonnage. **5 a** the refrain or chorus of a song. **b** the chief theme or gist of a speech, book, poem, etc. —*v.tr.* load with a burden; encumber, oppress. □**burden of proof** the obligation to prove one's case. □□ **burdensome** *adj.* [OE *byrthen*: rel. to BIRTH]

burdock /ˈbɜːdɒk/ *n.* any plant of the genus *Arctium*, with prickly flowers and docklike leaves. [BUR + DOCK³]

bureau /ˈbjʊərəʊ, -ˈrəʊ/ *n.* (*pl.* **bureaux** or **bureaus** /-rəʊz/) **1 a** *Brit.* a writing-desk with drawers and usu. an angled top opening downwards to form a writing surface. **b** *US* a chest of drawers. **2 a** an office or department for transacting specific business. **b** a government department. [F, = desk, orig. its baize covering, f. OF *burel* f. *bure, buire* dark brown ult. f. Gk *purros* red]

bureaucracy /bjʊəˈrɒkrəsɪ/ *n.* (*pl.* **-ies**) **1 a** government by central administration. **b** a State or organization so governed. **2** the officials of such a government, esp. regarded as oppressive and inflexible. **3** conduct typical of such officials. [F *bureaucratie*: see BUREAU]

bureaucrat /ˈbjʊərəˌkræt, -rəʊˌkræt/ *n.* **1** an official in a bureaucracy. **2** an inflexible or insensitive administrator. □□ **bureaucratic** /-ˈkrætɪk/ *adj.* **bureaucratically** /-ˈkrætɪkəlɪ/ *adv.* [F *bureaucrate* (as BUREAUCRACY)]

bureaucratize /bjʊəˈrɒkrəˌtaɪz/ *v.tr.* (also **-ise**) govern by or transform into a bureaucratic system. □□ **bureaucratization** /-ˈzeɪʃ(ə)n/ *n.*

burette /bjʊəˈret/ *n.* (*US* **buret**) a graduated glass tube with an end-tap for measuring small volumes of liquid in chemical analysis. [F]

burg /bɜːg/ *n. US colloq.* a town or city. [see BOROUGH]

burgage /ˈbɜːgɪdʒ/ *n. hist.* (in England and Scotland) tenure of land in a town on a yearly rent. [ME f. med.L *burgagium* f. *burgus* BOROUGH]

burgee /bɜːˈdʒiː/ *n.* a triangular or swallow-tailed flag bearing the colours or emblem of a sailing-club. [18th c.: perh. = (ship)owner, ult. F *bourgeois*: see BURGESS]

burgeon /ˈbɜːdʒ(ə)n/ *v. & n. literary* —*v.intr.* **1** begin to grow rapidly; flourish. **2** put forth young shoots;

bud. —*n.* a bud or young shoot. [ME f. OF *bor-, burjon* ult. f. LL *burra* wool]

burger /ˈbɜːgə(r)/ *n.* **1** *colloq.* a hamburger. **2** (in *comb.*) a certain kind of hamburger or variation of it (*beefburger; nutburger*). [abbr.]

burgess /ˈbɜːdʒɪs/ *n.* **1** *Brit.* an inhabitant of a town or borough, esp. of one with full municipal rights. **2** *Brit. hist.* a Member of Parliament for a borough, corporate town, or university. **3** *US* a borough magistrate or governor. [ME f. OF *burgeis* ult. f. LL *burgus* BOROUGH]

burgh /ˈbʌrə/ *n. hist.* a Scottish borough or chartered town. ¶ This status was abolished in 1975. □□ **burghal** /ˈbɜːg(ə)l/ *adj.* [Sc. form of BOROUGH]

burgher /ˈbɜːgə(r)/ *n.* **1** a citizen or freeman, esp. of a Continental town. **2** *S.Afr. hist.* a citizen of a Boer republic. **3** a descendant of a Dutch or Portuguese colonist in Sri Lanka. [G *Burger* or Du. *burger* f. *Burg, burg* BOROUGH]

burglar /ˈbɜːglə(r)/ *n.* a person who commits burglary. □□ **burglarious** /-ˈgleərɪəs/ *adj.* [legal AF *burgler*, rel. to OF *burgier* pillage]

burglarize /ˈbɜːgləˌraɪz/ *v.tr. & intr.* (also **-ise**) *US* = BURGLE.

burglary /ˈbɜːglərɪ/ *n.* (*pl.* **-ies**) **1** entry into a building illegally with intent to commit theft, do bodily harm, or do damage. **2** an instance of this. ¶ Before 1968 in English law a crime under statute and in common law; after 1968 a statutory crime only (cf. HOUSEBREAKING). [legal AF *burglarie*: see BURGLAR]

burgle /ˈbɜːg(ə)l/ *v.* **1** *tr.* commit burglary on (a building or person). **2** *intr.* commit burglary. [back-form. f BURGLAR]

burgomaster /ˈbɜːgəˌmɑːstə(r)/ *n.* the mayor of a Dutch or Flemish town. [Du. *burgemeester* f. *burg* BOROUGH: assim. to MASTER]

burgrave /ˈbɜːgreɪv/ *n. hist.* the ruler of a town or castle. [G *Burggraf* f. *Burg* BOROUGH + *Graf* COUNT²]

burgundy /ˈbɜːgəndɪ/ *n.* (*pl.* **-ies**) **1 a** the wine (usu. red) of Burgundy in E. France. **b** a similar wine from another place. **2** the red colour of Burgundy wine.

burhel var. of BHARAL.

burial /ˈberɪəl/ *n.* **1 a** the burying of a dead body. **b** a funeral. **2** *Archaeol.* a grave or its remains. □**burial-ground** a cemetery. [ME, erron. formed as sing. of OE *byrgels* f. Gmc: rel. to BURY]

burin /ˈbjʊərɪn/ *n.* **1** a steel tool for engraving on copper or wood. **2** *Archaeol.* a flint tool with a chisel point. [F]

burk var. of BERK.

burka /ˈbɜːkə/ *n.* a long enveloping garment worn in public by Muslim women. [Hind. f. Arab. *burḳa'*]

Burkitt's lymphoma /ˈbɜːkɪts/ *n. Med.* a malignant tumour of the lymphatic system, esp. affecting children of Central Africa. [D. P. *Burkitt*, Brit. surgeon b. 1911]

burl /bɜːl/ *n.* **1** a knot or lump in wool or cloth. **2** *US* a flattened knotty growth on a tree. [ME f. OF *bourle* tuft of wool, dimin. of *bourre* coarse wool f. LL *burra* wool]

burlap /ˈbɜːlæp/ *n.* **1** coarse canvas esp. of jute used for sacking etc. **2** a similar lighter material for use in dressmaking or furnishing. [17th c.: orig. unkn.]

burlesque /bɜːˈlesk/ *n., adj., & v.* —*n.* **1 a** comic imitation, esp. in parody of a dramatic or literary work. **b** a performance or work of this kind. **c** bombast, mock-seriousness. **2** *US* a variety show, often including striptease. —*adj.* of or in the nature of burlesque. —*v.tr.* (**burlesques, burlesqued, burlesquing**) make or give a burlesque of. □□ **burlesquer** *n.* [F f. It. *burlesco* f. *burla* mockery]

burly /ˈbɜːlɪ/ *adj.* (**burlier, burliest**) of stout sturdy build; big and strong. □□ **burliness** *n.* [ME *borli* prob. f. an OE form = 'fit for the bower' (BOWER¹)]

Burman /ˈbɜːmən/ *adj. & n.* (*pl.* **Burmans**) = BURMESE.

Burmese /bɜːˈmiːz/ *n. & adj.* —*n.* (*pl.* same) **1 a** a native or national of Burma (now Myanmar) in SE Asia. **b** a person of Burmese descent. **2** a member of the largest ethnic group of Burma. **3** the language of this group. —*adj.* of or relating to Burma or its people or language.

burn[1] /bɜːn/ *v. & n.* —*v.* (*past* and *past part.* **burnt** or **burned**) **1** *tr. & intr.* be or cause to be consumed or destroyed by fire. **2** *intr.* **a** blaze or glow with fire. **b** be in the state characteristic of fire. **3** *tr. & intr.* be or cause to be injured or damaged by fire or great heat or by radiation. **4** *tr. & intr.* use or be used as a source of heat, light, or other energy. **5** *tr. & intr.* char or scorch in cooking (*burned the vegetables*; *the vegetables are burning*). **6** *tr.* produce (a hole, a mark, etc.) by fire or heat. **7** *tr.* **a** subject (clay, chalk, etc.) to heat for a purpose. **b** harden (bricks) by fire. **c** make (lime or charcoal) by heat. **8** *tr.* colour, tan, or parch with heat or light (*we were burnt brown by the sun*). **9** *tr. & intr.* put or be put to death by fire. **10** *tr.* **a** cauterize, brand. **b** (foll. by *in*) imprint by burning. **11** *tr. & intr.* make or be hot, give or feel a sensation or pain of or like heat. **12** *tr. & intr.* (often foll. by *with*) make or be passionate; feel or cause to feel great emotion (*burn with shame*). **13** *intr. sl.* drive fast. **14** *tr. US sl.* anger, infuriate. **15** *intr.* (foll. by *into*) (of acid etc.) gradually penetrate (into) causing disintegration. —*n.* **1** a mark or injury caused by burning. **2** the ignition of a rocket engine in flight, giving extra thrust. **3** *US, Austral., & NZ* a forest area cleared by burning. **4** *sl.* a cigarette. **5** *sl.* a car race. □**burn one's boats** (or **bridges**) commit oneself irrevocably. **burn the candle at both ends** exhaust one's strength or resources by undertaking too much. **burn down 1 a** destroy (a building) by burning. **b** (of a building) be destroyed by fire. **2** burn less vigorously as fuel fails. **burn one's fingers** suffer for meddling or rashness. **burn a hole in one's pocket** (of money) be quickly spent. **burning-glass** a lens for concentrating the sun's rays on an object to burn it. **burn low** (of fire) be nearly out. **burn the midnight oil** read or work late into the night. **burn out 1** be reduced to nothing by burning. **2** fail or cause to fail by burning. **3** (usu. *refl.*) esp. *US* suffer physical or emotional exhaustion. **4** consume the contents of by burning. **5** make (a person) homeless by burning his or her house. **burn-out** *n. US* **1** physical or emotional exhaustion, esp. caused by stress. **2** depression, disillusionment. **burnt ochre** (or **sienna** or **umber**) a pigment darkened by burning. **burnt offering 1** an offering burnt on an altar as a sacrifice. **2** *joc.* overcooked food. **burnt-out** physically or emotionally exhausted. **burn up 1** get rid of by fire. **2** begin to blaze. **3** *US sl.* be or make furious. **have money to burn** have more money than one needs. [OE *birnan*, *bærnan* f. Gmc]

burn[2] /bɜːn/ *n. Sc.* a small stream. [OE *burna* etc. f. Gmc]

burner /ˈbɜːnə(r)/ *n.* the part of a gas cooker, lamp, etc. that emits and shapes the flame. □**on the back** (or **front**) **burner** *colloq.* receiving little (or much) attention.

burnet /ˈbɜːnɪt/ *n.* **1** any rosaceous plant of the genus *Sanguisorba*, with pink or red flowers. **2** any of several diurnal moths of the family Zygaenidae, with crimson spots on greenish-black wings. [obs. *burnet* (adj.) dark brown f. OF *burnete*]

burning /ˈbɜːnɪŋ/ *adj.* **1** ardent, intense (*burning desire*). **2** hotly discussed, exciting (*burning question*). **3** flagrant (*burning shame*). □**burning bush 1** any of various shrubs with red fruits or red autumn leaves (with ref. to Exod. 3:2). **2** fraxinella. □□ **burningly** *adv.*

burnish /ˈbɜːnɪʃ/ *v.tr.* polish by rubbing. □□ **burnisher** *n.* [ME f. OF *burnir* = *brunir* f. *brun* BROWN]

burnous /bɜːˈnuːs/ *n.* an Arab or Moorish hooded cloak. [F f. Arab. *burnus* f. Gk *birros* cloak]

burnt see BURN[1].

burp /bɜːp/ *v. & n. colloq.* —*v.* **1** *intr.* belch. **2** *tr.* make (a baby) belch, usu. by patting its back. —*n.* a belch. □**burp gun** *US sl.* an automatic pistol. [imit.]

burr /bɜː(r)/ *n. & v.* —*n.* **1 a** a whirring sound. **b** a rough sounding of the letter *r*. **2** (also **bur**) **a** a rough edge left on cut or punched metal or paper. **b** a surgeon's or dentist's small drill. **3 a** a siliceous rock used for millstones. **b** a whetstone. **4** = BUR 1, 2. **5** the coronet of a deer's antler. —*v.* **1** *tr.* pronounce with a burr. **2** *intr.* speak indistinctly. **3** *intr.* make a whirring sound. [var. of BUR]

burrawang /ˈbʌrəˌwæŋ/ *n. Austral.* **1** any palmlike tree of the genus *Macrozamia*. **2** the nut produced by this tree. [Mount *Budawang* in New South Wales]

burrito /bəˈriːtəʊ/ *n.* (*pl.* **-os**) *US* a tortilla rolled round a savoury filling. [Amer. Sp., dimin. of *burro* BURRO]

burro /ˈbʌrəʊ/ *n.* (*pl.* **-os**) *US* a small donkey used as a pack-animal. [Sp.]

burrow /ˈbʌrəʊ/ *n. & v.* —*n.* **a** a hole or tunnel dug by a small animal, esp. a rabbit, as a dwelling. —*v.* **1** *intr.* make or live in a burrow. **2** *tr.* make (a hole etc.) by digging. **3** *intr.* hide oneself. **4** *intr.* (foll. by *into*) investigate, search. □□ **burrower** *n.* [ME, app. var. of BOROUGH]

bursa /ˈbɜːsə/ *n.* (*pl.* **bursae** /-siː/ or **bursas**) *Anat.* a fluid-filled sac or saclike cavity to lessen friction. □□ **bursal** *adj.* [med.L = bag: cf. PURSE]

bursar /ˈbɜːsə(r)/ *n.* **1** a treasurer, esp. the person in charge of the funds and other property of a college. **2** the holder of a bursary. □□ **bursarship** *n.* [F *boursier* or (in sense 1) med.L *bursarius* f. *bursa* bag]

bursary /ˈbɜːsərɪ/ *n.* (*pl.* **-ies**) **1** a grant, esp. a scholarship. **2** the post or room of a bursar. □□ **bursarial** /-ˈseərɪəl/ *adj.* [med.L *bursaria* (as BURSAR)]

bursitis /bɜːˈsaɪtɪs/ *n.* inflammation of a bursa.

burst /bɜːst/ *v. & n.* —*v.* (*past* and *past part.* **burst**) **1 a** *intr.* break suddenly and violently apart by expansion of contents or internal pressure. **b** *tr.* cause to do this. **c** *tr.* send (a container etc.) violently apart. **2 a** *tr.* open forcibly. **b** *intr.* come open or be opened forcibly. **3 a** *intr.* (usu. foll. by *in*, *out*) make one's way suddenly, dramatically, or by force. **b** *tr.* break away from or through (*the river burst its banks*). **4** *tr. & intr.* fill or be full to overflowing. **5** *intr.* appear or come suddenly (*burst into flame*; *burst upon the view*; *sun burst out*). **6** *intr.* (foll. by *into*) suddenly begin to shed or utter (esp. *burst into tears* or *laughter* or *song*). **7** *intr.* be as if about to burst because of effort, excitement, etc. **8** *tr.* suffer bursting of (*burst a blood-vessel*). **9** *tr.* separate (continuous stationery) into single sheets. —*n.* **1** the act of or an instance of bursting; a split. **2** a sudden issuing forth (*burst of flame*). **3** a sudden outbreak (*burst of applause*). **4 a** a short sudden effort; a spurt. **b** a gallop. **5** an explosion. □**burst out 1** suddenly begin (*burst out laughing*). **2** exclaim. [OE *berstan* f. Gmc]

burstproof /ˈbɜːstpruːf/ *adj.* (of a door lock) able to withstand a violent impact.

burthen *archaic* var. of BURDEN *n.* 4.

burton[1] /ˈbɜːt(ə)n/ *n.* □**go for a burton** *Brit. sl.* be lost or destroyed or killed. [20th c.: perh. *Burton* ale f. *Burton-on-Trent* in England]

burton[2] /ˈbɜːt(ə)n/ *n.* a light two-block tackle for hoisting. [ME *Breton tackles*: see BRETON]

bury /ˈberɪ/ *v.tr.* (**-ies**, **-ied**) **1** place (a dead body) in the earth, in a tomb, or in the sea. **2** lose by death (*has buried three husbands*). **3 a** put under ground (*bury alive*). **b** hide (treasure, a bone, etc.) in the earth. **c** cover up; submerge. **4 a** put out of sight (*buried his face in his hands*). **b** consign to obscurity (*the idea was buried after brief discussion*). **c** put away; forget. **5** involve deeply (*buried himself in his work*; *was buried in a book*). □**bury the hatchet** cease to quarrel. **burying-beetle** a sexton beetle. **burying-ground** (or **-place**) a cemetery. [OE *byrgan* f. WG: cf. BURIAL]

bus /bʌs/ n. & v. —n. (pl. **buses** or US **busses**) 1 a large passenger vehicle, esp. one serving the public on a fixed route. 2 colloq. a motor car, aeroplane, etc. 3 Computing a defined set of conductors carrying data and control signals within a computer. —v. (**buses** or **busses**, **bussed**, **bussing**) 1 intr. go by bus. 2 tr. US transport by bus, esp. to promote racial integration. □**bus lane** a part of a road's length marked off mainly for use by buses. **bus shelter** a shelter from rain etc. beside a bus stop. **bus station** a centre, esp. in a town, where (esp. long-distance) buses depart and arrive. **bus-stop** 1 a regular stopping-place of a bus. 2 a sign marking this. [abbr. of OMNIBUS]

busbar /'bʌsbɑː(r)/ n. Electr. a system of conductors in a generating or receiving station on which power is concentrated for distribution.

busby /'bʌzbɪ/ n. (pl. **-ies**) (not in official use) a tall fur hat worn by hussars etc. [18th c.: orig. unkn.]

bush[1] /bʊʃ/ n. 1 a shrub or clump of shrubs with stems of moderate length. 2 a thing resembling this, esp. a clump of hair or fur. 3 (esp. in Australia and Africa) a wild uncultivated district; woodland or forest. 4 hist. a bunch of ivy as a vintner's sign. □**bush-baby** (pl. **-ies**) a small African tree-climbing lemur; a galago. **bush basil** a culinary herb, Ocimum minimum. **bush jacket** a light cotton jacket with a belt. **bush lawyer** 1 Austral. & NZ a person claiming legal knowledge without qualifications for it. 2 NZ a bramble. **bush-ranger** hist. an Australian outlaw living in the bush. **bush sickness** a disease of animals due to a lack of cobalt in the soil. **bush telegraph** rapid spreading of information, a rumour, etc. **go bush** Austral. leave one's usual surroundings; run wild. [ME f. OE & ON, ult. f. Gmc]

bush[2] /bʊʃ/ n. & v. —n. 1 a metal lining for a round hole enclosing a revolving shaft etc. 2 a sleeve providing electrical insulation. —v.tr. provide with a bush. [MDu. busse BOX[1]]

bushbuck /'bʊʃbʌk/ n. a small antelope, Tragelaphus scriptus, of southern Africa, having a chestnut coat with white stripes. [BUSH[1] + BUCK[1], after Du. boschbok f. bosch bush]

bushed /bʊʃt/ adj. colloq. 1 Austral. & NZ **a** lost in the bush. **b** bewildered. 2 US tired out.

bushel /'bʊʃ(ə)l/ n. a measure of capacity for corn, fruit, liquids, etc. (Brit. 8 gallons, or 36.4 litres; US 64 US pints). □□ **bushelful** n. (pl. **-fuls**). [ME f. OF buissiel etc., perh. of Gaulish orig.]

bushfire /'bʊʃfaɪə(r)/ n. a fire in a forest or in scrub often spreading widely.

bushido /buˈʃiːdəʊ/ n. the code of honour and morals evolved by the Japanese samurai. [Jap., = military knight's way]

bushing /'bʊʃɪŋ/ n. = BUSH[2] n.

bushman /'bʊʃmən/ n. (pl. **-men**) 1 a person who lives or travels in the Australian bush. 2 (**Bushman**) **a** a member of an aboriginal people in S. Africa. **b** the language of this people. [BUSH[1] + MAN: sense 2 after Du. boschjesman f. bosch bush]

bushmaster /'bʊʃmɑːstə(r)/ n. a venomous viper, Lachesis muta, of Central and S. America. [perh. f. Du. boschmeester]

bushveld /'bʊʃfelt/ n. open country consisting largely of bush. [BUSH[1] + VELD, after Afrik. bosveld]

bushwhack /'bʊʃwæk/ v. 1 intr. US, Austral., & NZ **a** clear woods and bush country. **b** live or travel in bush country. 2 tr. US ambush.

bushwhacker /'bʊʃwækə(r)/ n. 1 US, Austral., & NZ **a** a person who clears woods and bush country. **b** a person who lives or travels in bush country. 2 US a guerrilla fighter (orig. in the American Civil War).

bushy[1] /'bʊʃɪ/ adj. (**bushier**, **bushiest**) 1 growing thickly like a bush. 2 having many bushes. 3 covered with bush. □□ **bushily** adv. **bushiness** n.

bushy[2] /'bʊʃɪ/ n. (pl. **-ies**) Austral. & NZ colloq. a person who lives in the bush (as distinct from in a town).

busily /'bɪzɪlɪ/ adv. in a busy manner.

business /'bɪznɪs/ n. 1 one's regular occupation, profession, or trade. 2 a thing that is one's concern. 3 **a** a task or duty. **b** a reason for coming (what is your business?). 4 serious work or activity (get down to business). 5 derog. **a** an affair, a matter (sick of the whole business). **b** a structure (a lath-and-plaster business). 6 a thing or series of things needing to be dealt with (the business of the day). 7 buying and selling; trade (good stroke of business). 8 a commercial house or firm. 9 Theatr. action on stage. 10 a difficult matter (what a business it is!; made a great business of it). □**business card** a card printed with one's name and professional details. **the business end** colloq. the functional part of a tool or device. **business park** an area designed to accommodate businesses and light industry. **business person** a businessman or businesswoman. **business studies** training in economics, management, etc. **has no business to** has no right to. **in business** 1 trading or dealing. 2 able to begin operations. **in the business of** 1 engaged in. 2 intending to (we are not in the business of surrendering). **like nobody's business** colloq. extraordinarily. **make it one's business to** undertake to. **mind one's own business** not meddle. **on business** with a definite purpose, esp. one relating to one's regular occupation. **send a person about his** or her **business** dismiss a person; send a person away. [OE bisignis (as BUSY, -NESS)]

businesslike /'bɪznɪs,laɪk/ adj. efficient, systematic, practical.

businessman /'bɪznɪsmən/ n. (pl. **-men**; fem. **businesswoman**, pl. **-women**) a man or woman engaged in trade or commerce, esp. at a senior level (see also business person).

busk /bʌsk/ v.intr. perform (esp. music) for voluntary donations, usu. in the street or in subways. □□ **busker** n. **busking** n. [busk peddle etc. (perh. f. obs. F busquer seek)]

buskin /'bʌskɪn/ n. 1 either of a pair of thick-soled laced boots worn by an ancient Athenian tragic actor to gain height. 2 (usu. prec. by the) tragic drama; its style or spirit. 3 hist. either of a pair of calf- or knee-high boots of cloth or leather worn in the Middle Ages. □□ **buskined** adj. [prob. f. OF bouzequin, var. of bro(u)sequin, of unkn. orig.]

busman /'bʌsmən/ n. (pl. **-men**) the driver of a bus. □**busman's holiday** leisure time spent in an activity similar to one's regular work.

buss /bʌs/ n. & v. archaic or US colloq. —n. a kiss. —v.tr. kiss. [earlier bass (n. & v.): cf. F baiser f. L basiare]

bust[1] /bʌst/ n. 1 **a** the human chest, esp. that of a woman; the bosom. **b** the circumference of the body at bust level (a 36-inch bust). 2 a sculpture of a person's head, shoulders, and chest. [F buste f. It. busto, of unkn. orig.]

bust[2] /bʌst/ v., n., & adj. —v. (past and past part. **busted** or **bust**) colloq. 1 tr. & intr. burst, break. 2 tr. esp. US reduce (a soldier etc.) to a lower rank; dismiss. 3 tr. esp. US **a** raid, search. **b** arrest. —n. 1 a sudden failure; a bankruptcy. 2 a police raid. 3 a drinking-bout. 4 esp. US a punch; a hit. 5 a worthless thing. 6 a bad hand at cards. —adj. (also **busted**) 1 broken, burst, collapsed. 2 bankrupt. □**bust up** 1 bring or come to collapse; explode. 2 (of esp. a married couple) separate. **bust-up** n. 1 a quarrel. 2 a collapse; an explosion. **go bust** become bankrupt; fail. [orig. a (dial.) pronunc. of BURST]

bustard /'bʌstəd/ n. any large terrestrial bird of the family Otididae, with long neck, long legs, and stout tapering body. [ME f. OF bistarde f. L avis tarda slow bird (? = slow on the ground; but possibly a perversion of a foreign word)]

bustee /'bʌstiː/ n. Ind. a shanty town; a slum. [Hind. bastī dwelling]

buster /'bʌstə(r)/ n. **1** esp. US sl. mate; fellow (used esp. as a disrespectful form of address). **2** a violent gale.

bustier /'bʌstɪˌeɪ/ n. a strapless close-fitting bodice, usu. boned. [F]

bustle[1] /'bʌs(ə)l/ v. & n. —v. **1** intr. (often foll. by about) **a** work etc. showily, energetically, and officiously. **b** hasten (bustled about the kitchen banging saucepans). **2** tr. make (a person) hurry or work hard (bustled him into his overcoat). **3** intr. (as **bustling** adj.) colloq. full of activity. —n. excited activity; a fuss. □□ **bustler** n. [perh. f. buskle frequent. of busk prepare]

bustle[2] /'bʌs(ə)l/ n. hist. a pad or frame worn under a skirt and puffing it out behind. [18th c.: orig. unkn.]

busty /'bʌstɪ/ adj. (**bustier**, **bustiest**) (of a woman) having a prominent bust. □□ **bustiness** n.

busy /'bɪzɪ/ adj., v., & n. —adj. (**busier**, **busiest**) **1** (often foll. by in, with, at, or pres. part.) occupied or engaged in work etc. with the attention concentrated (busy at their needlework; he was busy packing). **2** full of activity or detail; fussy (a busy evening; a picture busy with detail). **3** employed continuously; unresting (busy as a bee). **4** meddlesome; prying. **5** esp. US (of a telephone line) engaged. —v.tr. (**-ies**, **-ied**) (often refl.) keep busy; occupy (the work busied him for many hours; busied herself with the accounts). —n. (pl. **-ies**) sl. a detective; a policeman. □ **busy Lizzie** a house-plant, Impatiens Walleriana, with usu. toothed leaves and pendulous flowers. □□ **busily** /'bɪzɪlɪ/ adv. **busyness** /'bɪzɪnɪs/ n. (cf. BUSINESS). [OE bisig]

busybody /'bɪzɪˌbɒdɪ/ n. (pl. **-ies**) **1** a meddlesome person. **2** a mischief-maker.

but[1] /bʌt, bət/ conj., prep., adv., pron., n., & v. —conj. **1 a** nevertheless, however (tried hard but did not succeed; I am old, but I am not weak). **b** on the other hand; on the contrary (I am old but you are young). **2** (prec. by can etc.; in neg. or interrog.) except, other than, otherwise than (cannot choose but do it; what could we do but run?). **3** without the result that (it never rains but it pours). **4** prefixing an interruption to the speaker's train of thought (the weather is ideal—but is that a cloud on the horizon?). —prep. except; apart from; other than (everyone went but me; nothing but trouble). —adv. **1** only; no more than; only just (we can but try; is but a child; had but arrived; did it but once). **2** introducing emphatic repetition; definitely (wanted to see nobody, but nobody). **3** Austral. & NZ though, however (didn't like it, but). —rel.pron. who not; that not (there is not a man but feels pity). —n. an objection (ifs and buts). —v.tr. (in phr. **but me no buts**) do not raise objections. □ **but for** without the help or hindrance etc. of (but for you I'd be rich by now). **but one** (or **two** etc.) excluding one (or two etc.) from the number (next door but one; last but one). **but that** (prec. by neg.) that (I don't deny but that it's true). **but that** (or colloq. **what**) other than that; except that (who knows but that it is true?). **but then** (or **yet**) however, on the other hand (I won, but then the others were beginners). [OE be-ūtan, būtan, būta outside, without]

but[2] /bʌt/ n. Sc. □ **but and ben** the outer and inner rooms of a two-roomed house (see BEN[2]). [BUT[1] = outside]

butadiene /ˌbjuːtəˈdaɪiːn/ n. Chem. a colourless gaseous hydrocarbon used in the manufacture of synthetic rubbers. ¶ Chem. formula: C_4H_6. [BUTANE + DI-[2] + -ENE: cf. BUNA]

butane /'bjuːteɪn, bjuːˈteɪn/ n. Chem. a gaseous hydrocarbon of the alkane series used in liquefied form as fuel. ¶ Chem. formula: C_4H_8. [BUTYL + -ANE]

butch /bʊtʃ/ adj. & n. sl. —adj. masculine; tough-looking. —n. **1** (often attrib.) **a** a mannish woman. **b** a mannish lesbian. **2** a tough, usu. muscular, youth or man. [perh. abbr. of BUTCHER]

butcher /'bʊtʃə(r)/ n. & v. —n. **1 a** a person whose trade is dealing in meat. **b** a person who slaughters animals for food. **2** a person who kills or has people killed indiscriminately or brutally. —v.tr. **1** slaughter or cut up (an animal) for food. **2** kill (people) wantonly or cruelly. **3** ruin (esp. a job or a musical composition) through incompetence. □ **the butcher, the baker, the candlestick-maker** people of all kinds or trades. **butcher-bird** a shrike of the genus Lanius, native to Australia and New Guinea, with a long hook-tipped bill for catching prey. **butcher's** rhyming sl. a look (short for butcher's hook). **butcher's-broom** a low spiny-leaved evergreen shrub, Ruscus aculeatus. **butcher's meat** slaughtered fresh meat excluding game, poultry, and bacon. □□ **butcherly** adv. [ME f. OF bo(u)chier f. boc BUCK[1]]

butchery /'bʊtʃərɪ/ n. (pl. **-ies**) **1** needless or cruel slaughter (of people). **2** the butcher's trade. **3** a slaughterhouse. [ME f. OF boucherie (as BUTCHER)]

butle var. of BUTTLE.

butler /'bʌtlə(r)/ n. the principal manservant of a household, usu. in charge of the wine cellar, pantry, etc. [ME f. AF buteler, OF bouteillier: see BOTTLE]

butt[1] /bʌt/ v. & n. —v. **1** tr. & intr. push with the head or horns. **2 a** intr. (usu. foll. by against, upon) come with one end flat against, meet end to end with, abut. **b** tr. (usu. foll. by against) place (timber etc.) with the end flat against a wall etc. —n. **1** a push with the head. **2** a join of two edges. □ **butt in** interrupt, meddle. [ME f. AF buter, OF boter f. Gmc: infl. by BUTT[2] and ABUT]

butt[2] /bʌt/ n. **1** (often foll. by of) an object (of ridicule etc.) (the butt of his jokes; made him their butt). **2 a** a mound behind a target. **b** (in pl.) a shooting-range. **c** a target. **3** a grouse-shooter's stand screened by low turf or a stone wall. [ME f. OF but goal, of unkn. orig.]

butt[3] /bʌt/ n. **1** (also **butt-end**) the thicker end, esp. of a tool or a weapon (gun butt). **2 a** the stub of a cigar or a cigarette. **b** (also **butt-end**) a remnant (the butt of the evening). **3** esp. US sl. the buttocks. **4** (also **butt-end**) the square end of a plank meeting a similar end. **5** the trunk of a tree, esp. the part just above the ground. □ **butt weld** a weld in which the pieces are joined end to end. [Du. bot stumpy]

butt[4] /bʌt/ n. a cask, esp. as a measure of wine or ale. [AL butta, bota, AF but, f. OF bo(u)t f. LL buttis]

butt[5] /bʌt/ n. a flat-fish (e.g. a sole, plaice, or turbot). [MLG, MDu. but flat-fish]

butte /bjuːt/ n. US a high isolated steep-sided hill. [F, = mound]

butter /'bʌtə(r)/ n. & v. —n. **1 a** a pale yellow edible fatty substance made by churning cream and used as a spread or in cooking. **b** a substance of a similar consistency or appearance (peanut butter). **2** excessive flattery. —v.tr. spread, cook, or serve with butter (butter the bread; buttered carrots). □ **butter-and-eggs** any of several plants having two shades of yellow in the flower, e.g. toadflax. **butter-bean 1** the flat, dried, white lima bean. **2** a yellow-podded bean. **butter-cream** (or **-icing**) a mixture of butter, icing sugar, etc. used as a filling or a topping for a cake. **butter-fingers** colloq. a clumsy person prone to drop things. **butter-knife** a blunt knife used for cutting butter at table. **butter muslin** a thin, loosely-woven cloth with a fine mesh, orig. for wrapping butter. **butter-nut 1** a N. American tree, Juglans cinerea. **2** the oily nut of this tree. **butter up** colloq. flatter excessively. **look as if butter wouldn't melt in one's mouth** seem demure or innocent, probably deceptively. [OE butere f. L butyrum f. Gk bouturon]

butterball /'bʌtəˌbɔːl/ n. **1** a piece of butter shaped into a ball. **2** US = BUFFLEHEAD (because it is very fat in autumn). **3** US sl. a fat person.

butterbur /'bʌtəˌbɜː(r)/ n. any of several plants of

the genus *Petasites* with large soft leaves, formerly used to wrap butter.

buttercup /'bʌtəˌkʌp/ *n.* any common yellow-flowered plant of the genus *Ranunculus*.

butterfat /'bʌtəˌfæt/ *n.* the essential fats of pure butter.

butterfish /'bʌtəˌfɪʃ/ *n.* = GUNNEL[1].

butterfly /'bʌtəˌflaɪ/ *n.* (*pl.* **-flies**) **1** any diurnal insect of the order Lepidoptera, with knobbed antennae, a long thin body, and four usu. brightly coloured wings erect when at rest. **2** a showy or frivolous person. **3** (in *pl.*) *colloq.* a nervous sensation felt in the stomach. □**butterfly net** a fine net on a ring attached to a pole, used for catching butterflies. **butterfly nut** a kind of wing-nut. **butterfly stroke** a stroke in swimming, with both arms raised and lifted forwards together. **butterfly valve** a valve with hinged semi-circular plates. [OE *buttor-flēoge* (as BUTTER, FLY[2])]

buttermilk /'bʌtəmɪlk/ *n.* a slightly acid liquid left after churning butter.

butterscotch /'bʌtəˌskɒtʃ/ *n.* a brittle sweet made from butter, brown sugar, etc. [SCOTCH]

butterwort /'bʌtəˌwɜːt/ *n.* any bog plant of the genus *Pinguicula*, esp. *P. vulgaris* with violet-like flowers and fleshy leaves that secrete a fluid to trap small insects for nutrient.

buttery[1] /'bʌtərɪ/ *n.* (*pl.* **-ies**) a room, esp. in a college, where provisions are kept and supplied to students etc. [ME f. AF *boterie* butt-store (as BUTT[4])]

buttery[2] /'bʌtərɪ/ *adj.* like, containing, or spread with butter. □□ **butteriness** *n.*

buttle /'bʌt(ə)l/ *v.intr.* (also **butle**) *joc.* work as a butler. [back-form. f. BUTLER]

buttock /'bʌtək/ *n.* (usu. in *pl.*) **1** each of two fleshy protuberances on the lower rear part of the human body. **2** the corresponding part of an animal. [*butt* ridge + -OCK]

button /'bʌt(ə)n/ *n. & v.* —*n.* **1** a small disc or knob sewn on to a garment, either to fasten it by being pushed through a buttonhole, or as an ornament or badge. **2** a knob on a piece of esp. electronic equipment which is pressed to operate it. **3 a** a small round object (*chocolate buttons*). **b** (*attrib.*) anything resembling a button (*button nose*). **4 a** a bud. **b** a button mushroom. **5** *Fencing* a terminal knob on a foil making it harmless. —*v.* **1** *tr. & intr.* = *button up* 1. **2** *tr.* supply with buttons. □**buttonball tree** (or **button wood**) *US* a plane-tree, *Platanus occidentalis*. **button chrysanthemum** a variety of chrysanthemum with small spherical flowers. **buttoned up** *colloq.* **1** formal and inhibited in manner. **2** silent. **button one's lip** esp. *US sl.* remain silent. **button mushroom** a young unopened mushroom. **button-through** (of a dress) fastened with buttons from neck to hem like a coat. **button up 1** fasten with buttons. **2** *colloq.* complete (a task etc.) satisfactorily. **3** *colloq.* become silent. **not worth a button** worthless. **on the button** esp. *US sl.* precisely. □□ **buttoned** *adj.* **buttonless** *adj.* **buttony** *adj.* [ME f. OF *bouton*, ult. f. Gmc]

buttonhole /'bʌt(ə)nˌhəʊl/ *n. & v.* —*n.* **1** a slit made in a garment to receive a button for fastening. **2** a flower or spray worn in a lapel buttonhole. —*v.tr.* **1** *colloq.* accost and detain (a reluctant listener). **2** make buttonholes in. □**buttonhole stitch** a looped stitch used for making buttonholes.

buttonhook /'bʌt(ə)nˌhʊk/ *n.* a hook formerly used esp. for pulling the buttons on tight boots into place for fastening.

buttons /'bʌt(ə)nz/ *n. colloq.* a liveried page-boy. [from the rows of buttons on his jacket]

buttress /'bʌtrɪs/ *n. & v.* —*n.* **1 a** a projecting support of stone or brick etc. built against a wall. **b** a source of help or encouragement (*she was a buttress to him in his trouble*). **2** a projecting portion of a hill or mountain. —*v.tr.* (often foll. by *up*) **1** support with a buttress. **2** support by argument etc. (*claim buttressed by facts*). [ME f. OF (*ars*) *bouterez* thrusting (arch) f. *bouteret* f. *bouter* BUTT[1]]

butty[1] /'bʌtɪ/ *n.* (*pl.* **-ies**) **1** *colloq.* or *dial.* a mate; a companion. **2** *hist.* a middleman negotiating between a mine-owner and the miners. **3** a barge or other craft towed by another. □**butty-gang** a gang of men contracted to work on a large job and sharing the profits equally. [19th c.: perh. f. BOOTY in phr. *play booty* join in sharing plunder]

butty[2] /'bʌtɪ/ *n.* (*pl.* **-ies**) *N.Engl.* **1** a sandwich (*bacon butty*). **2** a slice of bread and butter. [BUTTER + -Y[2]]

butyl /'bjuːtaɪl/ *n. Chem.* the univalent alkyl radical C_4H_9. □**butyl rubber** a synthetic rubber used in the manufacture of tyre inner tubes. [BUTYRIC (ACID) + -YL]

butyric acid /bjuː'tɪrɪk/ *n. Chem.* either of two colourless syrupy liquid organic acids found in rancid butter or arnica oil. □□ **butyrate** /'bjuːtɪˌreɪt/ *n.* [L *butyrum* BUTTER + -IC]

buxom /'bʌksəm/ *adj.* (esp. of a woman) plump and healthy-looking; large and shapely; busty. □□ **buxomly** *adv.* **buxomness** *n.* [earlier sense *pliant*: ME f. stem of OE *būgan* BOW[2] + -SOME[1]]

buy /baɪ/ *v. & n.* —*v.* (**buys**, **buying**; *past* and *past part.* **bought** /bɔːt/) **1** *tr.* **a** obtain in exchange for money etc. **b** (usu. in *neg.*) serve to obtain (*money can't buy happiness*). **2** *tr.* procure (the loyalty etc.) of a person by bribery, promises, etc. **b** win over (a person) in this way. **3** *tr.* get by sacrifice, great effort, etc. (*dearly bought; bought with our sweat*). **4** *tr. sl.* accept, believe in, approve of (*it's a good scheme, I'll buy it; he bought it, he's so gullible*). **5** *absol.* be a buyer for a store etc. (*buys for Selfridges; are you buying or selling?*). —*n. colloq.* a purchase (*that sofa was a good buy*). □**best buy** the purchase giving the best value in proportion to its price; a bargain. **buy in 1** buy a stock of. **2** withdraw (an item) at auction because of failure to reach the reserve price. **buy into** obtain a share in (an enterprise) by payment. **buy it** (usu. in *past*) *sl.* be killed. **buy off** get rid of (a claim, a claimant, a blackmailer) by payment. **buy oneself out** obtain one's release (esp. from the armed services) by payment. **buy out** pay (a person) to give up an ownership, interest, etc. **buy-out** *n.* the purchase of a controlling share in a company etc. **buy over** bribe. **buy time** delay an event, conclusion, etc., temporarily. **buy up 1** buy as much as possible of. **2** absorb (another firm etc.) by purchase. [OE *bycgan* f. Gmc]

buyer /'baɪə(r)/ *n.* **1** a person employed to select and purchase stock for a large store etc. **2** a purchaser, a customer. □**buyer's** (or **buyers'**) **market** an economic position in which goods are plentiful and cheap and buyers have the advantage.

buzz /bʌz/ *n. & v.* —*n.* **1** the hum of a bee etc. **2** the sound of a buzzer. **3 a** a confused low sound as of people talking; a murmur. **b** a stir; hurried activity (*a buzz of excitement*). **c** *colloq.* a rumour. **4** *sl.* a telephone call. **5** *sl.* a thrill; a euphoric sensation. —*v.* **1** *intr.* make a humming sound. **2 a** *tr. & intr.* signal or signal to with a buzzer. **b** *tr.* telephone. **3** *intr.* **a** (often foll. by *about*) move or hover busily. **b** (of a place) have an air of excitement or purposeful activity. **4** *tr. colloq.* throw hard. **5** *tr. Aeron. colloq.* fly fast and very close to (another aircraft). □**buzz off** *sl.* go or hurry away. **buzz-saw** *US* a circular saw. **buzz-word** *sl.* **1** a fashionable piece of esp. technical or computer jargon. **2** a catchword; a slogan. [imit.]

buzzard /'bʌzəd/ *n.* **1** any of a group of predatory birds of the hawk family, esp. of the genus *Butea*, with broad wings well adapted for soaring flight. **2** *US* a turkey buzzard. [ME f. OF *busard*, *buson* f. L *buteo -onis* falcon]

buzzer /'bʌzə(r)/ *n.* **1** an electrical device, similar to a bell, that makes a buzzing noise. **2** a whistle or hooter.

BVM *abbr.* Blessed Virgin Mary.

bwana /'bwɑːnə/ n. Afr. master, sir. [Swahili]

BWI abbr. hist. British West Indies.

BWR abbr. boiling-water (nuclear) reactor.

by /baɪ/ prep., adv., & n. —prep. **1** near, beside, in the region of (stand by the door; sit by me; path by the river). **2** through the agency, means, instrumentality, or causation of (by proxy; bought by a millionaire; a poem by Donne; went by bus; succeeded by persisting; divide four by two). **3** not later than; as soon as (by next week; by now; by the time he arrives). **4 a** past, beyond (drove by the church; came by us). **b** passing through; via (went by Paris). **5** in the circumstances of (by day; by daylight). **6** to the extent of (missed by a foot; better by far). **7** according to; using as a standard or unit (judge by appearances; paid by the hour). **8** with the succession of (worse by the minute; day by day; one by one). **9** concerning; in respect of (did our duty by them; Smith by name; all right by me). **10** used in mild oaths (orig. = as surely as one believes in) (by God; by gum; swear by all that is sacred). **11** placed between specified lengths in two directions (three feet by two). **12** avoiding, ignoring (pass by him; passed us by). **13** inclining to (north by north-west). —adv. **1** near (sat by, watching; lives close by). **2** aside; in reserve (put £5 by). **3** past (they marched by). —n. = BYE. □**by and by** before long; eventually. **by and large** on the whole, everything considered. **by the by** (or **bye**) incidentally, parenthetically. **by oneself 1 a** unaided. **b** without prompting. **2** alone; without company. [OE bī, bi, be f. Gmc]

by- /baɪ/ prefix (also **bye-**) subordinate, incidental, secondary (by-effect; by-road).

by-blow /'baɪbləʊ/ n. **1** a side-blow not at the main target. **2** an illegitimate child.

bye[1] /baɪ/ n. **1** Cricket a run scored from a ball that passes the batsman without being hit. **2** the status of an unpaired competitor in a sport, who proceeds to the next round as if having won. **3** Golf one or more holes remaining unplayed after the match has been decided. □**by the bye** = by the by. **leg-bye** Cricket a run scored from a ball that touches the batsman. [BY as noun]

bye[2] /baɪ/ int. colloq. = GOODBYE. [abbr.]

bye- prefix var. of BY-.

bye-bye[1] /'baɪbaɪ, bə'baɪ/ int. colloq. = GOODBYE. [childish corrupt.]

bye-bye[2] /'baɪbaɪ/ n. (also **bye-byes** /-baɪz/) (a child's word for) sleep. [ME, f. the sound used in lullabies]

by-election /'baɪ,lekʃ(ə)n/ n. the election of an MP in a single constituency to fill a vacancy arising during a government's term of office.

Byelorussian var. of BELORUSSIAN.

by-form /'baɪfɔːm/ n. a collateral form of a word etc.

bygone /'baɪgɒn/ adj. & n. —adj. past, antiquated (bygone years). —n. (in pl.) past offences (let bygones be bygones).

by-law /'baɪlɔː/ n. (also **bye-law**) **1** Brit. a regulation made by a local authority or corporation. **2** a rule made by a company or society for its members. [ME prob. f. obs. byrlaw local custom (ON býjar genitive sing. of býr town, but assoc. with BY)]

byline /'baɪlaɪn/ n. **1** a line in a newspaper etc. naming the writer of an article. **2** a secondary line of work. **3** a goal-line or touch-line.

byname /'baɪneɪm/ n. a sobriquet; a nickname.

bypass /'baɪpɑːs/ n. & v. —n. **1** a road passing round a town or its centre to provide an alternative route for through traffic. **2 a** a secondary channel or pipe etc. to allow a flow when the main one is closed or blocked. **b** an alternative passage for the circulation of blood during a surgical operation on the heart. —v.tr. **1** avoid; go round. **2** provide with a bypass.

bypath /'baɪpɑːθ/ n. **1** a secluded path. **2** a minor or obscure branch of a subject.

byplay /'baɪpleɪ/ n. a secondary action or sequence of events, esp. in a play.

by-product /'baɪ,prɒdʌkt/ n. **1** an incidental or secondary product made in the manufacture of something else. **2** a secondary result.

byre /'baɪə(r)/ n. a cowshed. [OE býre: perh. rel. to BOWER]

byroad /'baɪrəʊd/ n. a minor road.

Byronic /baɪ'rɒnɪk/ adj. **1** characteristic of Lord Byron, English poet d. 1824, or his romantic poetry. **2** (of a man) handsomely dark, mysterious, or moody.

byssinosis /,bɪsɪ'nəʊsɪs/ n. Med. a lung disease caused by prolonged inhalation of textile fibre dust. [mod.L f. Gk bussinos made of byssus + -OSIS]

byssus /'bɪsəs/ n. hist. (pl. **byssuses** or **byssi** /-saɪ/) **1** hist. a fine textile fibre and fabric of flax. **2** a tuft of tough silky filaments by which some molluscs adhere to rocks etc. [ME f. L f. Gk bussos]

bystander /'baɪ,stændə(r)/ n. a person who stands by but does not take part; a mere spectator.

byte /baɪt/ n. Computing a group of eight binary digits, often used to represent one character. [20th c.: perh. based on BIT[4] and BITE]

byway /'baɪweɪ/ n. **1** a byroad or bypath. **2** a minor activity.

byword /'baɪwɜːd/ n. **1** a person or thing cited as a notable example (is a byword for luxury). **2** a familiar saying; a proverb.

Byzantine /bɪ'zæntaɪn, baɪ-, 'bɪzən,tiːn, 'bɪzən,taɪn/ adj. & n. —adj. **1** of Byzantium or the E. Roman Empire. **2** (of a political situation etc.): **a** extremely complicated. **b** inflexible. **c** carried on by underhand methods. **3** Archit. & Painting of a highly decorated style developed in the Eastern Empire. —n. a citizen of Byzantium or the E. Roman Empire. □□ **Byzantinism** n. **Byzantinist** n. [F byzantin or L Byzantinus f. Byzantium, later Constantinople and now Istanbul]

C

C¹ /siː/ n. (also **c**) (pl. **Cs** or **C's**) **1** the third letter of the alphabet. **2** *Mus.* the first note of the diatonic scale of C major (the major scale having no sharps or flats). **3** the third hypothetical person or example. **4** the third highest class or category (of academic marks etc.). **5** *Algebra* (usu. **c**) the third known quantity. **6** (as a Roman numeral) 100. **7** (c) the speed of light in a vacuum. **8** (also ©) copyright.

C² *symb. Chem.* the element carbon.

C³ *abbr.* (also **C.**) **1** Cape. **2** Conservative. **3** Command Paper (second series, 1870–99). **4** Celsius, Centigrade. **5** coulomb(s), capacitance.

c. *abbr.* **1** century; centuries. **2** chapter. **3** cent(s). **4** cold. **5** cubic. **6** colt. **7** *Cricket* caught by. **8** centi-.

c. *abbr. circa*, about.

c/- *abbr. Austral. & NZ* care of.

CA *abbr.* **1** *US* California (in official postal use). **2** *Sc. & Can.* chartered accountant.

Ca *symb. Chem.* the element calcium.

ca. *abbr. circa*, about.

CAA *abbr.* (in the UK) Civil Aviation Authority.

Caaba var. of KAABA.

CAB *abbr.* **1** Citizens' Advice Bureau. **2** *US* Civil Aeronautics Board.

cab /kæb/ n. **1** a taxi. **2** the driver's compartment in a lorry, train, or crane. **3** *hist.* a hackney carriage. [abbr. of CABRIOLET]

cabal /kə'bæl/ n. **1** a secret intrigue. **2** a political clique or faction. **3** *hist.* a committee of five ministers under Charles II, whose surnames happened to begin with C, A, B, A, and L. [F *cabale* f. med.L *cabala*, CABBALA]

cabala var. of CABBALA.

caballero /ˌkæbə'ljeərəʊ/ n. (pl. **-os**) a Spanish gentleman. [Sp.: see CAVALIER]

cabana /kə'bɑːnə/ n. *US* a hut or shelter at a beach or swimming-pool. [Sp. *cabaña* f. LL (as CABIN)]

cabaret /'kæbə,reɪ/ n. **1** an entertainment in a nightclub or restaurant while guests eat or drink at tables. **2** such a nightclub etc. [F, = wooden structure, tavern]

cabbage /'kæbɪdʒ/ n. **1 a** any of several cultivated varieties of *Brassica oleracea*, with thick green or purple leaves forming a round heart or head. **b** this head usu. eaten as vegetable. **2** *colloq. derog.* a person who is inactive or lacks interest. □ **cabbage palm** a palm tree, *Cordyline australis*, with edible cabbage-like terminal buds. **cabbage rose** a double rose with a large round compact flower. **cabbage tree** = *cabbage palm*. **cabbage white** a butterfly, *Pieris brassicae*, whose caterpillars feed on cabbage leaves. □□ **cabbagy** adj. [earlier *cabache*, *-oche* f. OF (Picard) *caboche* head, OF *caboce*, of unkn. orig.]

cabbala /kə'bɑːlə, 'kæbələ/ n. (also **cabala**, **kabbala**) **1** the Jewish mystical tradition. **2** mystic interpretation; any esoteric doctrine or occult lore. □□ **cabbalism** n. **cabbalist** n. **cabbalistic** /-'lɪstɪk/ adj. [med.L f. Rabbinical Heb. *ḳabbālā* tradition]

cabby /'kæbɪ/ n. (also **cabbie**) (pl. **-ies**) *colloq.* a taxi-driver. [CAB + -Y²]

caber /'keɪbə(r)/ n. a roughly trimmed tree-trunk used in the Scottish Highland sport of tossing the caber. [Gael. *cabar* pole]

cabin /'kæbɪn/ n. & v. —n. **1** a small shelter or house, esp. of wood. **2** a room or compartment in an aircraft or ship for passengers or crew. **3** a driver's cab. —v.tr. (**cabined**, **cabining**) confine in a small place, cramp. □ **cabin-boy** a boy who waits on a ship's officers or passengers. **cabin class** the intermediate class of accommodation in a ship. **cabin crew** the crew members on an aeroplane attending to passengers and cargo. **cabin cruiser** a large motor boat with living accommodation. [ME f. OF *cabane* f. Prov. *cabana* f. LL *capanna*, *cavanna*]

cabinet /'kæbɪnɪt/ n. **1 a** a cupboard or case with drawers, shelves, etc., for storing or displaying articles. **b** a piece of furniture housing a radio or television set etc. **2** (**Cabinet**) the committee of senior ministers responsible for controlling government policy. **3** *archaic* a small private room. □ **cabinet-maker** a skilled joiner. **Cabinet Minister** *Brit.* a member of the Cabinet. **cabinet photograph** one of about 6 by 4 inches. **cabinet pudding** a steamed pudding with dried fruit. [CABIN + -ET¹, infl. by F *cabinet*]

cable /'keɪb(ə)l/ n. & v. —n. **1** a thick rope of wire or hemp. **2** an encased group of insulated wires for transmitting electricity or electrical signals. **3** a cablegram. **4 a** *Naut.* the chain of an anchor. **b** a measure of 200 yards. **5** (in full **cable stitch**) a knitted stitch resembling twisted rope. **6** *Archit.* a rope-shaped ornament. —v. **1 a** *tr.* transmit (a message) by cablegram. **b** *tr.* inform (a person) by cablegram. **c** *intr.* send a cablegram. **2** *tr.* furnish or fasten with a cable or cables. **3** *Archit. tr.* furnish with cables. □ **cable-car 1** a small cabin (often one of a series) suspended on an endless cable and drawn up and down a mountainside etc. by an engine at one end. **2** a carriage drawn along a cable railway. **cable-laid** (of rope) having three triple strands. **cable railway** a railway along which carriages are drawn by an endless cable. **cable television** a broadcasting system with signals transmitted by cable to subscribers' sets. [ME f. OF *chable*, ult. f. LL *capulum* halter f. Arab. *ḥabl*]

cablegram /'keɪb(ə)l,græm/ n. a telegraph message sent by undersea cable etc.

cableway /'keɪb(ə)l,weɪ/ n. a transporting system with a usu. elevated cable.

cabman /'kæbmən/ n. (pl. **-men**) the driver of a cab.

cabochon /'kæbə,ʃɒn/ n. a gem polished but not faceted. □ **en cabochon** (of a gem) treated in this way. [F dimin. of *caboche*: see CABBAGE]

caboodle /kə'buːd(ə)l/ n. □ **the whole caboodle** *sl.* the whole lot (of persons or things). [19th c. US: perh. f. phr. *kit and boodle*]

caboose /kə'buːs/ n. **1** a kitchen on a ship's deck. **2** *US* a guard's van; a car on a freight train for workmen etc. [Du. *cabūse*, of unkn. orig.]

cabotage /'kæbə,tɑːʒ, -tɪdʒ/ n. **1** *Naut.* coastal navigation and trade. **2** esp. *Aeron.* the reservation to a country of (esp. air) traffic operation within its territory. [F f. *caboter* to coast, perh. f. Sp. *cabo* CAPE²]

cabotin /ˌkɑːbə'tæ̃/ n. (fem. **cabotine** /-'tiːn/) a second-rate actor; a strolling player. [F, = strolling player, perh. formed as CABOTAGE, from the resemblance to vessels travelling from port to port]

cabriole /'kæbrɪ,əʊl/ n. a kind of curved leg characteristic of Queen Anne and Chippendale furniture. [F f. *cabrioler*, *caprioler* f. It. *capriolare* to leap in the air; from the resemblance to a leaping animal's foreleg: see CAPRIOLE]

cabriolet /ˌkæbrɪəʊ'leɪ/ n. **1** a light two-wheeled carriage with a hood, drawn by one horse. **2** a motor car with a folding top. [F f. *cabriole* goat's leap (cf. CAPRIOLE), applied to its motion]

ca'canny /kɑː'kænɪ/ n. **1** the practice of 'going slow' at work; a trade union policy of limiting output. **2**

---

extreme caution. [Sc., = proceed warily: see CALL v. 16, CANNY]

cacao /kə'kɑːəʊ, -'keɪəʊ/ n. (pl. -os) **1** a seed pod from which cocoa and chocolate are made. **2** a small widely cultivated evergreen tree, *Theobroma cacao*, bearing these. [Sp. f. Nahuatl *cacauatl* (*uatl* tree)]

cachalot /'kæʃəˌlɒt, -ˌləʊt/ n. a sperm whale. [F f. Sp. & Port. *cachalote*, of unkn. orig.]

cache /kæʃ/ n. & v. —n. **1** a hiding-place for treasure, provisions, ammunition, etc. **2** what is hidden in a cache. —v.tr. put in a cache. [F f. *cacher* to hide]

cachectic /kə'kektɪk/ adj. relating to or having the symptoms of cachexia.

cachet /'kæʃeɪ/ n. **1** a distinguishing mark or seal. **2** prestige. **3** *Med.* a flat capsule enclosing a dose of unpleasant-tasting medicine. [F f. *cacher* press ult. f. L *coactare* constrain]

cachexia /kə'keksɪə/ n. (also **cachexy** /-ksɪ/) a condition of weakness of body or mind associated with chronic disease. [F *cachexie* or LL *cachexia* f. Gk *kakhexia* f. *kakos* bad + *hexis* habit]

cachinnate /'kækɪˌneɪt/ v.intr. *literary* laugh loudly. □□ **cachinnation** /-'neɪʃ(ə)n/ n. **cachinnatory** /-'neɪtərɪ/ adj. [L *cachinnare cachinnat-*]

cacholong /'kæʃəˌlɒŋ/ n. a kind of opal. [F f. Mongolian *kashchilon* beautiful stone]

cachou /'kæʃuː/ n. **1** a lozenge to sweeten the breath. **2** var. of CATECHU. [F f. Port. *cachu* f. Malay *kāchu*: cf. CATECHU]

cachucha /kə'tʃuːtʃə/ n. a Spanish solo dance. [Sp.]

cacique /kə'siːk/ n. **1** a W. Indian or American Indian native chief. **2** a political boss in Spain or Latin America. [Sp., of Carib orig.]

cack-handed /kæk'hændɪd/ adj. *colloq.* **1** awkward, clumsy. **2** left-handed. □□ **cack-handedly** adv. **cack-handedness** n. [dial. *cack* excrement]

cackle /'kæk(ə)l/ n. & v. —n. **1** a clucking sound as of a hen or a goose. **2** a loud silly laugh. **3** noisy inconsequential talk. —v. **1** intr. emit a cackle. **2** intr. talk noisily and inconsequentially. **3** tr. utter or express with a cackle. □ **cut the cackle** *colloq.* stop talking aimlessly and come to the point. [ME prob. f. MLG, MDu. *kākelen* (imit.)]

cacodemon /ˌkækə'diːmən/ n. (also **cacodaemon**) **1** an evil spirit. **2** a malignant person. [Gk *kakodaimōn* f. *kakos* bad + *daimōn* spirit]

cacodyl /'kækəˌdaɪl/ n. a malodorous, toxic, spontaneously flammable liquid, tetramethyldiarsine. □□ **cacodylic** /-'daɪlɪk/ adj. [Gk *kakōdēs* stinking f. *kakos* bad]

cacoethes /ˌkækəʊ'iːθiːz/ n. an urge to do something inadvisable. [L f. Gk *kakoēthes* neut. adj. f. *kakos* bad + *ēthos* disposition]

cacography /kə'kɒɡrəfɪ/ n. **1** bad handwriting. **2** bad spelling. □□ **cacographer** n. **cacographic** /ˌkækə'ɡræfɪk/ adj. **cacographical** /ˌkækə'ɡræfɪk(ə)l/ adj. [Gk *kakos* bad, after *orthography*]

cacology /kə'kɒlədʒɪ/ n. **1** bad choice of words. **2** bad pronunciation. [LL *cacologia* f. Gk *kakologia* vituperation f. *kakos* bad]

cacomistle /'kækəˌmɪs(ə)l/ n. any racoon-like animal of several species of the genus *Bassariscus*, native to Central America, having a dark-ringed tail. [Amer. Sp. *cacomixtle* f. Nahuatl *tlacomiztli*]

cacophony /kə'kɒfənɪ/ n. (pl. -ies) **1** a harsh discordant mixture of sound. **2** dissonance; discord. □□ **cacophonous** adj. [F *cacophonie* f. Gk *kakophōnia* f. *kakophōnos* f. *kakos* bad + *phōnē* sound]

cactus /'kæktəs/ n. (pl. **cacti** /-taɪ/ or **cactuses**) any succulent plant of the family Cactaceae, with a thick fleshy stem, usu. spines but no leaves, and brilliantly coloured flowers. □ **cactus dahlia** any kind of dahlia with quilled petals resembling a cactus flower. □□ **cactaceous** /-'teɪʃəs/ adj. [L f. Gk *kaktos* cardoon]

cacuminal /kæ'kjuːmɪn(ə)l/ adj. *Phonet.* pronounced with the tongue-tip curled up towards the hard palate. [L *cacuminare* make pointed f. *cacumen -minis* tree-top]

CAD abbr. computer-aided design.

cad /kæd/ n. a person (esp. a man) who behaves dishonourably. □□ **caddish** adj. **caddishly** adv. **caddishness** n. [abbr. of CADDIE in sense 'odd-job man']

cadastral /kə'dæstr(ə)l/ adj. of or showing the extent, value, and ownership, of land for taxation. [F f. *cadastre* register of property f. Prov. *cadastro* f. It. *catast(r)o*, earlier *catastico* f. late Gk *katastikhon* list, register f. *kata stikhon* line by line]

cadaver /kə'deɪvə(r), -'dɑːvə(r)/ n. esp. *Med.* a corpse. □□ **cadaveric** /-'dævərɪk/ adj. [ME f. L f. *cadere* fall]

cadaverous /kə'dævərəs/ adj. **1** corpselike. **2** deathly pale. [L *cadaverosus* (as CADAVER)]

caddie /'kædɪ/ n. & v. (also **caddy**) —n. (pl. -ies) a person who assists a golfer during a match, by carrying clubs etc. —v.intr. (**caddies**, **caddied**, **caddying**) act as caddie. □ **caddie car** (or **cart**) a light two-wheeled trolley for transporting golf clubs during a game. [orig. Sc. f. F CADET]

caddis-fly /'kædɪs/ n. (pl. -flies) any small hairy-winged nocturnal insect of the order Trichoptera, living near water. [17th c.: orig. unkn.]

caddish see CAD.

caddis-worm /'kædɪs/ n. (also **caddis**) a larva of the caddis-fly, living in water and making protective cylindrical cases of sticks, leaves, etc., and used as fishing-bait. [as CADDIS-FLY]

caddy¹ /'kædɪ/ n. (pl. -ies) a small container, esp. a box for holding tea. [earlier *catty* weight of 1⅓ lb., f. Malay *kātī*]

caddy² var. of CADDIE.

cadence /'keɪd(ə)ns/ n. **1** a fall in pitch of the voice, esp. at the end of a phrase or sentence. **2** intonation, tonal inflection. **3** *Mus.* the close of a musical phrase. **4** rhythm; the measure or beat of sound or movement. □□ **cadenced** adj. [ME f. OF f. It. *cadenza*, ult. f. L *cadere* fall]

cadential /kə'denʃ(ə)l/ adj. of a cadence or cadenza.

cadenza /kə'denzə/ n. *Mus.* a virtuosic passage for a solo instrument or voice, usu. near the close of a movement of a concerto, sometimes improvised. [It.: see CADENCE]

cadet /kə'det/ n. **1** a young trainee in the armed services or police force. **2** *NZ* an apprentice in sheep-farming. **3** a younger son. □□ **cadetship** n. [F f. Gascon dial. *capdet*, ult. f. L *caput* head]

cadge /kædʒ/ v. **1** tr. get or seek by begging. **2** intr. beg. □□ **cadger** n. [19th c., earlier = ? bind, carry: orig. unkn.]

cadi /'kɑːdɪ, 'keɪdɪ/ n. (also **kadi**) (pl. -is) a judge in a Muslim country. [Arab. *ḳāḍī* f. *ḳaḍā* to judge]

Cadmean victory /kæd'miːən/ n. = *pyrrhic victory* (see PYRRHIC¹). [L *Cadmeus* f. Gk *Kadmeios* f. *Kadmos* Cadmus: see CADMIUM]

cadmium /'kædmɪəm/ n. a soft bluish-white metallic element occurring naturally with zinc ores, and used in the manufacture of solders and in electroplating. ¶ Symb.: **Cd**. □ **cadmium cell** *Electr.* a standard primary cell. **cadmium yellow** an intense yellow pigment containing cadmium sulphide and used in paints etc. [obs. *cadmia* calamine f. L *cadmia* f. Gk *kadm(e)ia* (*gē*) Cadmean (earth), f. *Cadmus* legendary founder of Thebes: see -IUM]

cadre /'kɑːdə(r), 'kɑːdrə/ n. **1** a basic unit, esp. of servicemen, forming a nucleus for expansion when necessary. **2** /also 'keɪdə(r)/ **a** a group of activists in a communist or any revolutionary party. **b** a member of such a group. [F f. It. *quadro* f. L *quadrus* square]

caduceus /kə'djuːsɪəs/ n. (pl. **caducei** /-sɪˌaɪ/) an Ancient Greek or Roman herald's wand, esp. as carried by the messenger-god Hermes or Mercury. [L f. Doric Gk *karuk(e)ion* f. *kērux* herald]

caducous /kə'djuːkəs/ adj. *Biol.* (of organs and parts) easily detached or shed at an early stage. □□ **caducity** /-sɪtɪ/ n. [L *caducus* falling f. *cadere* fall]

caecilian /si:'sɪlɪən/ n. (also **coecilian**) any burrowing wormlike amphibian of the order Gymnophiona, having poorly developed eyes and no limbs. [L *caecilia* kind of lizard]

caecitis /sɪ'kaɪtɪs/ n. (US **cecitis**) inflammation of the caecum.

caecum /'si:kəm/ n. (US **cecum**) (pl. **-ca** /-kə/) a blind-ended pouch at the junction of the small and large intestines. □□ **caecal** adj. [L for *intestinum caecum* f. *caecus* blind, transl. of Gk *tuphlon enteron*]

Caenozoic var. of CENOZOIC.

Caerns. abbr. Caernarvonshire (a former county in Wales).

Caerphilly /keə'fɪlɪ, kə-/ n. a kind of mild white cheese orig. made in Caerphilly in Wales.

Caesar /'si:zə(r)/ n. **1** the title of the Roman emperors, esp. from Augustus to Hadrian. **2** an autocrat. **3** Med. sl. a Caesarean section; a case of this. □ **Caesar's wife** a person required to be above suspicion. [L, family name of Gaius Julius *Caesar*, Roman statesman d. 44 BC]

Caesarean /sɪ'zeərɪən/ adj. & n. (also **Caesarian**, US **Ces-**) —adj. **1** of Caesar or the Caesars. **2** (of a birth) effected by Caesarean section. —n. a Caesarean section. □ **Caesarean section** an operation for delivering a child by cutting through the wall of the abdomen (Julius Caesar supposedly having been born this way). [L *Caesarianus*]

caesious /'si:zɪəs/ adj. Bot. bluish or lavender. [L *caesius*]

caesium /'si:zɪəm/ n. (US **cesium**) a soft silver-white element of the alkali metal group, occurring naturally in a number of minerals, used in photoelectric cells. ¶ Symb.: **Cs**. □ **caesium clock** an atomic clock that uses caesium. [as CAESIOUS (from its spectrum lines)]

caesura /sɪ'zjʊərə/ n. (pl. **caesuras**) Prosody **1** (in Greek and Latin verse) a break between words within a metrical foot. **2** (in modern verse) a pause near the middle of a line. □□ **caesural** adj. [L f. *caedere caes-* cut]

CAF abbr. US cost and freight.

cafard /ka:'fɑ:(r)/ n. melancholia. [F, = cockroach, hypocrite]

café /'kæfeɪ, 'kæfɪ/ n. (also **cafe** /also joc. kæf, keɪf/) **1** a small coffee-house or teashop; a simple restaurant. **2** US a bar. □ **café au lait** /əʊ 'leɪ/ **1** coffee with milk. **2** the colour of this. **café noir** /'nwɑ:(r)/ black coffee. **café society** the regular patrons of fashionable restaurants and nightclubs. [F, = coffee, coffee-house]

cafeteria /ˌkæfɪ'tɪərɪə/ n. a restaurant in which customers collect their meals on trays at a counter and usu. pay before sitting down to eat. [Amer. Sp. *cafetería* coffee-shop]

caff /kæf/ n. Brit. sl. = CAFÉ. [abbr.]

caffeine /'kæfi:n/ n. an alkaloid drug with stimulant action found in tea leaves and coffee beans. [F *caféine* f. *café* coffee]

caftan /'kæftæn/ n. (also **kaftan**) **1** a long usu. belted tunic worn by men in countries of the Near East. **2 a** a woman's long loose dress. **b** a loose shirt or top. [Turk. *kaftān*, partly through F *cafetan*]

cage /keɪdʒ/ n. & v. —n. **1** a structure of bars or wires, esp. for confining animals or birds. **2** any similar open framework, esp. an enclosed platform or lift in a mine or the compartment for passengers in a lift. **3** colloq. a camp for prisoners of war. —v.tr. place or keep in a cage. □ **cage-bird** a bird of the kind customarily kept in a cage. [ME f. OF f. L *cavea*]

cagey /'keɪdʒɪ/ adj. (also **cagy**) (**cagier**, **cagiest**) colloq. cautious and uncommunicative; wary. □□ **cagily** adv. **caginess** n. (also **cageyness**). [20th-c. US: orig. unkn.]

cagoule /kə'gu:l/ n. a hooded thin windproof garment worn in mountaineering etc. [F]

cahoots /kə'hu:ts/ n.pl. □ **in cahoots** (often foll. by *with*) sl. in collusion. [19th c.: orig. uncert.]

CAI abbr. computer-assisted (or -aided) instruction.

caiman var. of CAYMAN.

Cain /keɪn/ n. □ **raise Cain** colloq. make a disturbance; create trouble. [*Cain*, eldest son of Adam (Gen. 4)]

Cainozoic var. of CENOZOIC.

caique /kaɪ'i:k/ n. **1** a light rowing-boat on the Bosporus. **2** a Levantine sailing-ship. [F f. It. *caicco* f. Turk. *kayık*]

cairn /keən/ n. **1** a mound of rough stones as a monument or landmark. **2** (in full **cairn terrier**) **a** a small terrier of a breed with short legs, a longish body, and a shaggy coat (perhaps so called from its being used to hunt among cairns). **b** this breed. [Gael. *carn*]

cairngorm /'keəngɔ:m/ n. a yellow or wine-coloured semi-precious form of quartz. [found on *Cairngorm*, a mountain in Scotland f. Gael. *carn gorm* blue cairn]

caisson /'keɪs(ə)n, kə'su:n/ n. **1** a watertight chamber in which underwater construction work can be done. **2** a floating vessel used as a floodgate in docks. **3** an ammunition chest or wagon. □ **caisson disease** = decompression sickness. [F (f. It. *cassone*) assim. to *caisse* CASE²]

caitiff /'keɪtɪf/ n. & adj. poet. or archaic —n. a base or despicable person; a coward. —adj. base, despicable, cowardly. [ME f. OF *caitif, chaitif* ult. f. L *captivus* CAPTIVE]

cajole /kə'dʒəʊl/ v.tr. (often foll. by *into, out of*) persuade by flattery, deceit, etc. □□ **cajolement** n. **cajoler** n. **cajolery** n. [F *cajoler*]

cake /keɪk/ n. & v. —n. **1 a** a mixture of flour, butter, eggs, sugar, etc., baked in the oven. **b** a quantity of this baked in a flat round or ornamental shape and often iced and decorated. **2 a** other food in a flat round shape (*fish cake*). **b** = cattle-cake. **3** a flattish compact mass (*a cake of soap*). **4** Sc. & N.Engl. thin oaten bread. —v. **1** tr. & intr. form into a compact mass. **2** tr. (usu. foll. by *with*) cover (with a hard or sticky mass) (*boots caked with mud*). □ **cakes and ale** merrymaking. **have one's cake and eat it** colloq. enjoy both of two mutually exclusive alternatives. **like hot cakes** rapidly or successfully. **a piece of cake** colloq. something easily achieved. **a slice of the cake** participation in benefits. [ME f. ON *kaka*]

cakewalk /'keɪkwɔ:k/ n. **1** a dance developed from an American Black contest in graceful walking with a cake as a prize. **2** colloq. an easy task. **3** a form of fairground entertainment consisting of a promenade moved by machinery.

CAL abbr. computer-assisted learning.

Cal abbr. large calorie(s).

Cal. abbr. California.

cal abbr. small calorie(s).

Calabar bean /'kæləˌbɑ:(r)/ n. a poisonous seed of the tropical African climbing plant *Physostigma venosum*, yielding a medicinal extract. [*Calabar* in Nigeria]

calabash /'kæləˌbæʃ/ n. **1 a** an evergreen tree, *Crescentia cujete*, native to tropical America, bearing fruit in the form of large gourds. **b** a gourd from this tree. **2** the shell of this or a similar gourd used as a vessel for water, to make a tobacco pipe, etc. [F *calebasse* f. Sp. *calabaza* perh. f. Pers. *karbuz* melon]

calaboose /ˌkælə'bu:s/ n. US a prison. [Black F *calabouse* f. Sp. *calabozo* dungeon]

calabrese /ˌkælə'bri:z, ˌkælə'breɪseɪ/ n. a large succulent variety of sprouting broccoli. [It., = Calabrian]

calamanco /ˌkælə'mæŋkəʊ/ n. (pl. **-oes**) hist. a glossy woollen cloth chequered on one side. [16th c.: orig. unkn.]

calamander /'kæləˌmændə(r)/ n. a fine-grained red-brown ebony streaked with black, from the Asian tree *Diospyros qualsita*, used in furniture. [19th c.: orig. unkn.: perh. conn. with Sinh. word for the tree *kalu-madīriya*]

calamary /'kæləmərɪ/ n. (pl. **-ies**) any cephalopod

mollusc with a long tapering penlike horny internal shell, esp. a squid of the genus *Loligo*. [med.L *calamarium* pen-case f. L *calamus* pen]

calamine /'kælə,maɪn/ *n.* **1** a pink powder consisting of zinc carbonate and ferric oxide used as a lotion or ointment. **2** a zinc mineral usu. zinc carbonate. [ME f. F f. med.L *calamina* alt. f. L *cadmia*: see CADMIUM]

calamint /'kæləmɪnt/ *n.* any aromatic herb or shrub of the genus *Calamintha*, esp. *C. officinalis* with purple or lilac flowers. [ME f. OF *calament* f. med.L *calamentum* f. LL *calaminthe* f. Gk *kalaminthē*]

calamity /kə'læmɪtɪ/ *n.* (*pl.* **-ies**) **1** a disaster, a great misfortune. **2 a** adversity. **b** deep distress. □**Calamity Jane** a prophet of disaster. □□ **calamitous** *adj.* **calamitously** *adv.* [ME f. F *calamité* f. L *calamitas -tatis*]

calando /kæ'lændə/ *adv. Mus.* gradually decreasing in speed and volume. [It., = slackening]

calash /kə'læʃ/ *n. hist.* **1 a** a light low-wheeled carriage with a removable folding hood. **b** the folding hood itself. **2** *Can.* a two-wheeled horse-drawn vehicle. **3** a woman's hooped silk hood. [F *calèche* f. G *Kalesche* f. Pol. *kolaska* or Czech *kolesa*]

calc- /kælk/ *comb. form* lime or calcium. [G *Kalk* f. L CALX]

calcaneus /kæl'keɪnɪəs/ *n.* (also **calcaneum** /-nɪəm/) (*pl.* **calcanei** /-nɪ,aɪ/ or **calcanea** /-nɪə/) the bone forming the heel. [L]

calcareous /kæl'keərɪəs/ *adj.* (also **calcarious**) of or containing calcium carbonate; chalky. [L *calcarius* (as CALX)]

calceolaria /,kælsɪə'leərɪə/ *n. Bot.* any plant of the genus *Calceolaria*, native to S. America, with slipper-shaped flowers. [mod.L f. L *calceolus* dimin. of *calceus* shoe + *-aria* fem. = -ARY¹]

calceolate /'kælsɪə,leɪt/ *adj. Bot.* slipper-shaped.

calces *pl.* of CALX.

calciferol /kæl'sɪfə,rɒl/ *n.* one of the D vitamins, routinely added to dairy products, essential for the deposition of calcium in bones. Also called ERGOCALCIFEROL, *vitamin D₂*. [CALCIFEROUS + -OL¹]

calciferous /kæl'sɪfərəs/ *adj.* yielding calcium salts, esp. calcium carbonate. [L CALX lime + -FEROUS]

calcify /'kælsɪ,faɪ/ *v.tr.* & *intr.* (**-ies**, **-ied**) **1** harden or become hardened by deposition of calcium salts; petrify. **2** convert or be converted to calcium carbonate. □□ **calcific** /-'sɪfɪk/ *adj.* **calcification** /-fɪ'keɪʃ(ə)n/ *n.*

calcine /'kælsɪn, -saɪn/ *v.* **1** *tr.* **a** reduce, oxidize, or desiccate by strong heat. **b** burn to ashes; consume by fire; roast. **c** reduce to calcium oxide by roasting or burning. **2** *tr.* consume or purify as if by fire. **3** *intr.* undergo any of these. □□ **calcination** /-'neɪʃ(ə)n/ *n.* [ME f. OF *calciner* or med.L *calcinare* f. LL *calcina* lime f. L CALX]

calcite /'kælsaɪt/ *n.* natural crystalline calcium carbonate. [G *Calcit* f. L CALX lime]

calcium /'kælsɪəm/ *n.* a soft grey metallic element of the alkaline earth group occurring naturally in limestone, marble, chalk, etc., that is important in industry and essential for normal growth in living organisms. ¶ Symb.: Ca. □**calcium carbide** a greyish solid used in the production of acetylene. **calcium carbonate** a white insoluble solid occurring naturally as chalk, limestone, marble, and calcite, and used in the manufacture of lime and cement. **calcium hydroxide** a white crystalline powder used in the manufacture of plaster and cement; slaked lime. **calcium oxide** a white crystalline solid from which many calcium compounds are manufactured: also called QUICKLIME, CALX. **calcium phosphate** the main constituent of animal bones, used as bone ash fertilizer. **calcium sulphate** a white crystalline solid occurring as anhydrite and gypsum. [L CALX lime + -IUM]

calcrete /'kælkriːt/ *n. Geol.* a conglomerate formed by the cementation of sand and gravel with calcium carbonate. [L *calc* lime + *concrete*]

calcspar /'kælkspɑː(r)/ *n.* = CALCITE. [CALC- + SPAR³]

calculable /'kælkjʊləb(ə)l/ *adj.* able to be calculated or estimated. □□ **calculability** /-'bɪlɪtɪ/ *n.* **calculably** *adv.*

calculate /'kælkjʊ,leɪt/ *v.* **1** *tr.* ascertain or determine beforehand, esp. by mathematics or by reckoning. **2** *tr.* plan deliberately. **3** *intr.* (foll. by *on*, *upon*) rely on; make an essential part of one's reckoning (*calculated on a quick response*). **4** *tr.* US *colloq.* suppose, believe. □□ **calculative** /-lətɪv/ *adj.* [LL *calculare* (as CALCULUS)]

calculated /'kælkjʊ,leɪtɪd/ *adj.* **1** (of an action) done with awareness of the likely consequences. **2** (foll. by *to* + infin.) designed or suitable; intended. □□ **calculatedly** *adv.*

calculating /'kælkjʊ,leɪtɪŋ/ *adj.* (of a person) shrewd, scheming. □□ **calculatingly** *adv.*

calculation /,kælkjʊ'leɪʃ(ə)n/ *n.* **1** the act or process of calculating. **2** a result got by calculating. **3** a reckoning or forecast. [ME f. OF f. LL *calculatio* (as CALCULATE)]

calculator /'kælkjʊ,leɪtə(r)/ *n.* **1** a device (esp. a small electronic one) used for making mathematical calculations. **2** a person or thing that calculates. **3** a set of tables used in calculation. [ME f. L (as CALCULATE)]

calculus /'kælkjʊləs/ *n.* (*pl.* **calculuses** or **calculi** /-,laɪ/) **1** *Math.* **a** a particular method of calculation or reasoning (*calculus of probabilities*). **b** the infinitesimal calculuses of integration or differentiation (see *integral calculus*, *differential calculus*). **2** *Med.* a stone or concretion of minerals formed within the body. □□ **calculous** *adj.* (in sense 2). [L, = small stone used in reckoning on an abacus]

caldera /kɑː'deərə/ *n.* a large volcanic depression. [Sp. f. LL *caldaria* boiling-pot]

caldron var. of CAULDRON.

Caledonian /,kælɪ'dəʊnɪən/ *adj.* & *n.* —*adj.* **1** of or relating to Scotland. **2** *Geol.* of a mountain-forming period in Europe in the Palaeozoic era. —*n.* a Scotsman. [L *Caledonia* northern Britain]

calefacient /,kælɪ'feɪʃ(ə)nt/ *n.* & *adj. Med.* —*n.* a substance producing or causing a sensation of warmth. —*adj.* of this substance. [L *calefacere* f. *calēre* be warm + *facere* make]

calendar /'kælɪndə(r)/ *n.* & *v.* —*n.* **1** a system by which the beginning, length, and subdivisions of the year are fixed. **2** a chart or series of pages showing the days, weeks, and months of a particular year, or giving special seasonal information. **3** a timetable or programme of appointments, special events, etc. —*v.tr.* register or enter in a calendar or timetable etc. □**calendar month** (or **year**) see MONTH, YEAR. □□ **calendric** /-'lendrɪk/ *adj.* **calendrical** /-'lendrɪk(ə)l/ *adj.* [ME f. AF *calender*, OF *calendier* f. L *calendarium* account-book (as CALENDS)]

calender /'kælɪndə(r)/ *n.* & *v.* —*n.* a machine in which cloth, paper, etc., is pressed by rollers to glaze or smooth it. —*v.tr.* press in a calender. [F *calendre(r)*, of unkn. orig.]

calends /'kælendz/ *n.pl.* (also **kalends**) the first of the month in the ancient Roman calendar. [ME f. OF *calendes* f. L *kalendae*]

calendula /kə'lendjʊlə/ *n.* any plant of the genus *Calendula*, with large yellow or orange flowers, e.g. marigold. [mod.L dimin. of *calendae* (as CALENDS), perh. = little clock]

calenture /'kælentʃə(r)/ *n. hist.* a tropical delirium of sailors, who think the sea is green fields. [F f. Sp. *calentura* fever f. *calentar* be hot ult. f. L *calēre* be warm]

calf¹ /kɑːf/ *n.* (*pl.* **calves** /kɑːvz/) **1** a young bovine animal, used esp. of domestic cattle. **2** the young of other animals, e.g. elephant, deer, and whale. **3** *Naut.* a floating piece of ice detached from an iceberg. □**calf-love** romantic attachment or affection between adolescents. **in** (or **with**) **calf** (of a cow) pregnant. □□ **calfhood** *n.* **calfish** *adj.* **calflike** *adj.* [OE *cælf* f. WG]

calf² /kɑːf/ *n.* (*pl.* **calves** /kɑːvz/) the fleshy hind part of the human leg below the knee. □□ **-calved** /kɑːvd/ *adj.* (in *comb.*). [ME f. ON *kálfi*, of unkn. orig.]

calfskin /'kɑːfskɪn/ *n.* calf-leather, esp. in bookbinding and shoemaking.

calibrate /'kælɪˌbreɪt/ *v.tr.* **1** mark (a gauge) with a standard scale of readings. **2** correlate the readings of (an instrument) with a standard. **3** determine the calibre of (a gun). **4** determine the correct capacity or value of. □□ **calibration** /-'breɪʃ(ə)n/ *n.* **calibrator** *n.* [CALIBRE + -ATE³]

calibre /'kælɪbə(r)/ *n.* (*US* **caliber**) **1 a** the internal diameter of a gun or tube. **b** the diameter of a bullet or shell. **2** strength or quality of character; ability, importance (*we need someone of your calibre*). □□ **calibred** *adj.* (also in *comb.*). [F *calibre* or It. *calibro*, f. Arab. *ḳālib* mould]

caliche /kə'liːtʃɪ/ *n.* **1** a mineral deposit of gravel, sand, and nitrates, esp. Chile saltpetre, found in dry areas of America. **2** = CALCRETE. [Amer. Sp.]

calico /'kælɪkəʊ/ *n. & adj.* —*n.* (*pl.* **-oes** or *US* **-os**) **1** a cotton cloth, esp. plain white or unbleached. **2** *US* a printed cotton fabric. —*adj.* **1** made of calico. **2** *US* multicoloured, piebald. [earlier *calicut* f. *Calicut* in India]

Calif. *abbr.* California.

californium /ˌkælɪ'fɔːnɪəm/ *n. Chem.* a transuranic radioactive metallic element produced artificially from curium. ¶ Symb.: **Cf**. [*California* (where it was first made) + -IUM]

caliper var. of CALLIPER.

caliph /'keɪlɪf, 'kæl-/ *n.* esp. *hist.* the chief Muslim civil and religious ruler, regarded as the successor of Muhammad. □□ **caliphate** *n.* [ME f. OF *caliphe* f. Arab. *Ḳalīfa* successor]

calisthenics var. of CALLISTHENICS.

calk *US* var. of CAULK.

call /kɔːl/ *v. & n.* —*v.* **1** *intr.* **a** (often foll. by *out*) cry, shout; speak loudly. **b** (of a bird or animal) emit its characteristic note or cry. **2** *tr.* communicate or converse with by telephone or radio. **3** *tr.* **a** bring to one's presence by calling; summon (*will you call the children?*). **b** arrange for (a person or thing) to come or be present (*called a taxi*). **4** *intr.* (often foll. by *at*, *in*, *on*) pay a brief visit (*called at the house; called in to see you; come and call on me*). **5** *tr.* **a** order to take place; fix a time for (*called a meeting*). **b** direct to happen; announce (*call a halt*). **6 a** *intr.* require one's attention or consideration (*duty calls*). **b** *tr.* urge, invite, nominate (*call to the bar*). **7** *tr.* name; describe as (*call her Della*). **8** *tr.* consider; regard or estimate as (*I call that silly*). **9** *tr.* rouse from sleep (*call me at 8*). **10** *intr.* guess the outcome of tossing a coin etc. **11** *intr.* (foll. by *for*) order, require, demand (*called for silence*). **12** *tr.* (foll. by *over*) read out (a list of names to determine those present). **13** *intr.* (foll. by *on*, *upon*) invoke; appeal to; request or require (*called on us to be quiet*). **14** *tr. Cricket* (of an umpire) disallow a ball from (a bowler). **15** *tr. Cards* specify (a suit or contract) in bidding. **16** *tr. Sc.* drive (an animal, vehicle, etc.). —*n.* **1** a shout or cry; an act of calling. **2 a** the characteristic cry of a bird or animal. **b** an imitation of this. **c** an instrument for imitating it. **3** a brief visit (*paid them a call*). **4 a** an act of telephoning. **b** a telephone conversation. **5 a** an invitation or summons to appear or be present. **b** an appeal or invitation (from a specific source or discerned by a person's conscience etc.) to follow a certain profession, set of principles, etc. **6** (foll. by *for*, or *to* + infin.) a duty, need, or occasion (*no call to be rude; no call for violence*). **7** (foll. by *for*, *on*) a demand (*not much call for it these days; a call on one's time*). **8** a signal on a bugle etc.; a signalling-whistle. **9** *Stock Exch.* an option of buying stock at a fixed price at a given date. **10** *Cards* **a** a player's right or turn to make a bid. **b** a bid made. □ **at call** = *on call*. **call**

away divert, distract. **call-box** a public telephone box or kiosk. **call-boy** a theatre attendant who summons actors when needed on stage. **call down 1** invoke. **2** reprimand. **call forth** elicit. **call-girl** a prostitute who accepts appointments by telephone. **call in** *tr.* **1** withdraw from circulation. **2** seek the advice or services of. **calling-card** *US* = *visiting-card*. **call in** (or **into**) **question** dispute; doubt the validity of. **call into play** give scope for; make use of. **call a person names** abuse a person verbally. **call off 1** cancel (an arrangement etc.). **2** order (an attacker or pursuer) to desist. **call of nature** a need to urinate or defecate. **call out 1** summon (troops etc.) to action. **2** order (workers) to strike. **call-over 1** a roll-call. **2** reading aloud of a list of betting prices. **call the shots** (or **tune**) be in control; take the initiative. **call-sign** (or **-signal**) a broadcast signal identifying the radio transmitter used. **call to account** see ACCOUNT. **call to mind** recollect; cause one to remember. **call to order 1** request to be orderly. **2** declare (a meeting) open. **call up 1** reach by telephone. **2** imagine, recollect. **3** summon, esp. to serve in the army. **call-up** *n.* the act or process of calling up (sense 3). **on call 1** (of a doctor etc.) available if required but not formally on duty. **2** (of money lent) repayable on demand. **within call** near enough to be summoned by calling. [OE *ceallian* f. ON *kalla*]

calla /'kælə/ *n.* **1** (in full **calla lily**) = *arum lily*. **2** an aquatic plant, *Calla palustris*. [mod.L]

caller /'kɔːlə(r)/ *n.* **1** a person who calls, esp. one who pays a visit or makes a telephone call. **2** *Austral.* a racing commentator.

calligraphy /kə'lɪgrəfɪ/ *n.* **1** handwriting, esp. when fine or pleasing. **2** the art of handwriting. □□ **calligrapher** *n.* **calligraphic** /-'græfɪk/ *adj.* **calligraphist** *n.* [Gk *kalligraphia* f. *kallos* beauty]

calling /'kɔːlɪŋ/ *n.* **1** a profession or occupation. **2** an inwardly felt call or summons; a vocation.

calliope /kə'laɪəpɪ/ *n. US* a keyboard instrument resembling an organ, with a set of steam whistles producing musical notes. [Gk *Kalliopē* muse of epic poetry (lit. 'beautiful-voiced')]

calliper /'kælɪpə(r)/ *n. & v.* (also **caliper**) —*n.* **1** (in *pl.*) (also **calliper compasses**) compasses with bowed legs for measuring the diameter of convex bodies, or with out-turned points for measuring internal dimensions. **2** (in full **calliper splint**) a metal splint to support the leg. —*v.tr.* measure with callipers. [app. var. of CALIBRE]

callisthenics /ˌkælɪs'θenɪks/ *n.pl.* (also **calisthenics**) gymnastic exercises to achieve bodily fitness and grace of movement. □□ **callisthenic** *adj.* [Gk *kallos* beauty + *sthenos* strength]

callop /'kæləp/ *n. Austral.* a gold-coloured freshwater fish, *Plectroplites ambiguus*, used as food. Also called *golden perch*. [Aboriginal]

callosity /kə'lɒsɪtɪ/ *n.* (*pl.* **-ies**) a hard thick area of skin usu. occurring in parts of the body subject to pressure or friction. [F *callosité* or L *callositas* (as CALLOUS)]

callous /'kæləs/ *adj. & n.* —*adj.* **1** unfeeling, insensitive. **2** (of skin) hardened or hard. —*n.* = CALLUS 1. □□ **callously** *adv.* (in sense 1 of *adj.*). **callousness** *n.* [ME f. L *callosus* (as CALLUS) or F *calleux*]

callow /'kæləʊ/ *adj.* inexperienced, immature. □□ **callowly** *adv.* **callowness** *n.* [OE *calu*]

calluna /kə'luːnə/ *n.* any common heather of the genus *Calluna*, native to Europe and N. Africa. [mod.L f. Gk *kallunō* beautify f. *kallos* beauty]

callus /'kæləs/ *n.* **1** a hard thick area of skin or tissue. **2** a hard tissue formed round bone ends after a fracture. **3** *Bot.* a new protective tissue formed over a wound. [L]

calm /kɑːm/ *adj., n., & v.* —*adj.* **1** tranquil, quiet, windless (*a calm sea; a calm night*). **2** (of a person or disposition) settled; not agitated (*remained calm throughout the ordeal*). **3** self-assured, confident (*his* calm assumption that we would wait). —n. **1** a state of being calm; stillness, serenity. **2** a period without wind or storm. —v.tr. by down) make or become calm. □□ **calmly** adv. **calmness** n. [ME ult. f. LL cauma f. Gk kauma heat]

calmative /'kælmətɪv, 'kɑːm-/ adj. & n. Med. —adj. tending to calm or sedate. —n. a calmative drug etc.

calomel /'kælə,mel/ n. a compound of mercury, esp. when used medicinally as a cathartic. [mod.L perh. f. Gk kalos beautiful + melas black]

Calor gas /'kælə/ n. propr. liquefied butane gas stored under pressure in containers for domestic use and used as a substitute for mains gas. [L calor heat]

caloric /'kælərɪk/ adj. & n. —adj. of heat or calories. —n. hist. a supposed material form or cause of heat. [F calorique f. L calor heat]

calorie /'kælərɪ/ n. (also **calory**) (pl. -ies) a unit of quantity of heat: **1** (in full **small calorie**) the amount needed to raise the temperature of 1 gram of water through 1 °C. ¶ Abbr.: **cal**. **2** (in full **large calorie**) the amount needed to raise the temperature of 1 kilogram of water through 1 °C, often used to measure the energy value of foods. ¶ Abbr.: **Cal**. [F, arbitr. f. L calor heat + -ie]

calorific /ˌkælə'rɪfɪk/ adj. producing heat. □ **calorific value** the amount of heat produced by a specified quantity of fuel, food, etc. □□ **calorifically** adv. [L calorificus f. calor heat]

calorimeter /ˌkælə'rɪmɪtə(r)/ n. any of various instruments for measuring quantity of heat, esp. to find calorific values. □□ **calorimetric** /-'metrɪk/ adj. **calorimetry** n. [L calor heat + -METER]

calory var. of CALORIE.

calque /kælk/ n. Philol. = loan-translation. [F, = copy, tracing f. calquer trace ult. f. L calcare tread]

caltrop /'kæltrəp/ n. (also **caltrap**) **1** hist. a four-spiked iron ball thrown on the ground to impede cavalry horses. **2** Heraldry a representation of this. **3** any creeping plant of the genus Tribulus, with woody carpels usu. having hard spines. [(sense 3) OE calcatrippe f. med.L calcatrippa: (senses 1-2) ME f. OF chauchetrape f. chauchier tread, trappe trap: ult. the same word]

calumet /'kæljʊ,met/ n. a N. American Indian peace-pipe. [F, ult. f. L calamus reed]

calumniate /kə'lʌmnɪ,eɪt/ v.tr. slander. □□ **calumniation** /-'eɪʃ(ə)n/ n. **calumniator** n. **calumniatory** adj. [L calumniari]

calumny /'kæləmnɪ/ n. & v. (pl. -ies) **1** slander; malicious representation. **2** an instance of this. —v.tr. (-ies, -ied) slander. □□ **calumnious** adj. [L calumnia]

calvados /'kælvə,dɒs/ n. an apple brandy. [Calvados in France]

Calvary /'kælvərɪ/ n. the place where Christ was crucified. [ME f. LL calvaria skull, transl. Gk golgotha, Aram. gûlgûltâ (Matt. 27:33)]

calve /kɑːv/ v. **1 a** intr. give birth to a calf. **b** tr. (esp. in passive) give birth to (a calf). **2** tr. (also absol.) (of an iceberg) break off or shed (a mass of ice). [OE calfian]

calves pl. of CALF[1], CALF[2].

Calvinism /'kælvɪ,nɪz(ə)m/ n. the theology of the French theologian J. Calvin (d. 1564) or his followers, in which predestination and justification by faith are important elements. □□ **Calvinist** n. **Calvinistic** /-'nɪstɪk/ adj. **Calvinistical** /-'nɪstɪk(ə)l/ adj. [F calvinisme or mod.L calvinismus]

calx /kælks/ n. (pl. **calces** /'kælsiːz/) **1** a powdery metallic oxide formed when an ore or mineral has been heated. **2** calcium oxide. [L calx calcis lime prob. f. Gk khalix pebble, limestone]

calypso /kə'lɪpsəʊ/ n. (pl. -os) a W. Indian song in African rhythm, usu. improvised on a topical theme. [20th c.: orig. unkn.]

calyx /'keɪlɪks, 'kæl-/ n. (also **calix**) (pl. **calyces** /-lɪ,siːz/ or **calyxes**) **1** Bot. the sepals collectively, forming the protective layer of a flower in bud. **2**

Biol. any cuplike cavity or structure. [L f. Gk kalux case of bud, husk: cf. kaluptō hide]

cam /kæm/ n. a projection on a rotating part in machinery, shaped to impart reciprocal or variable motion to the part in contact with it. [Du. kam comb: cf. Du. kamrad cog-wheel]

camaraderie /ˌkæmə'rɑːdərɪ/ n. mutual trust and sociability among friends. [F]

camarilla /ˌkæmə'rɪlə/ n. a cabal or clique. [Sp., dimin. of camara chamber]

Camb. abbr. Cambridge.

camber /'kæmbə(r)/ n. & v. —n. **1** the slightly convex or arched shape of the surface of a road, ship's deck, aircraft wing, etc. **2** the slight sideways inclination of the front wheel of a motor vehicle. —v. **1** intr. (of a surface) have a camber. **2** tr. give a camber to; build with a camber. [F cambre arched f. L camurus curved inwards]

Camberwell Beauty /'kæmbə,wel/ n. a deep purple butterfly, Nymphalis antiopa, with yellow-bordered wings. [Camberwell in London]

cambium /'kæmbɪəm/ n. (pl. **cambia** /-bɪə/ or **cambiums**) Bot. a cellular plant tissue responsible for the increase in girth of stems and roots. □□ **cambial** adj. [med.L, = change, exchange]

Cambodian /kæm'bəʊdɪən/ n. & adj. —n. **1 a** a native or national of Cambodia (Kampuchea) in SE Asia. **b** a person of Cambodian descent. **2** the language of Cambodia. —adj. of or relating to Cambodia or its people or language. Also called KAMPUCHEAN.

Cambrian /'kæmbrɪən/ adj. & n. —adj. **1** Welsh. **2** Geol. of or relating to the first period in the Palaeozoic era, marked by the occurrence of many forms of invertebrate life (including trilobites and brachiopods). ¶ Cf. Appendix II. —n. this period or system. [L Cambria var. of Cumbria f. Welsh Cymry Welshman or Cymru Wales]

cambric /'kæmbrɪk/ n. a fine white linen or cotton fabric. [Kamerijk, Flem. form of Cambrai in N. France, where it was orig. made]

Cambridge blue /'keɪmbrɪdʒ/ n. & adj. a pale blue. [Cambridge in S. England]

Cambs. abbr. Cambridgeshire.

camcorder /'kæm,kɔːdə(r)/ n. a combined video camera and sound recorder. [camera + recorder]

came past of COME.

camel /'kæm(ə)l/ n. **1** either of two kinds of large cud-chewing mammals having slender cushion-footed legs and one hump (**Arabian camel**, Camelus dromedarius) or two humps (**Bactrian camel**, Camelus bactrianus). **2** a fawn colour. **3** an apparatus for providing additional buoyancy to ships etc. □ **camel** (or **camel's**) -**hair 1** the hair of a camel. **2 a** a fine soft hair used in artists' brushes. **b** a fabric made of this. [OE f. L camelus f. Gk kamēlos, of Semitic orig.]

cameleer /ˌkæmə'lɪə(r)/ n. a camel-driver.

camellia /kə'miːlɪə/ n. any evergreen shrub of the genus Camellia, native to E. Asia, with shiny leaves and showy flowers. [J. Camellus or Kamel, 17th-c. Jesuit botanist]

camelopard /'kæmələ,pɑːd, kə'mel-/ n. archaic a giraffe. [L camelopardus f. Gk kamēlopardalis (as CAMEL, PARD)]

camelry /'kæməlrɪ/ n. (pl. -ies) troops mounted on camels.

Camembert /'kæməm,beə(r)/ n. a kind of soft creamy cheese, usu. with a strong flavour. [Camembert in N. France, where it was orig. made]

cameo /'kæmɪ,əʊ/ n. (pl. -os) **1 a** a small piece of onyx or other hard stone carved in relief with a background of a different colour. **b** a similar relief design using other materials. **2 a** a short descriptive literary sketch or acted scene. **b** a small character part in a play or film, usu. brief and played by a distinguished actor. [ME f. OF camahieu and med.L cammaeus]

camera /'kæmrə, -ərə/ n. **1** an apparatus for taking photographs, consisting of a lightproof box to hold light-sensitive film, a lens, and a shutter mechanism, either for still photographs or for motion-picture film. **2** *Telev.* a piece of equipment which forms an optical image and converts it into electrical impulses for transmission or storage. □**camera obscura** /ɒb'skjʊərə/ an internally darkened box with an aperture for projecting the image of an external object on a screen inside it. **camera-ready** *Printing* (of copy) in a form suitable for immediate photographic reproduction. **in camera 1** *Law* in a judge's private room. **2** privately; not in public. **on camera** (esp. of an actor or actress) being filmed or televised at a particular moment. [orig. = chamber f. L *camera* f. Gk *kamara* vault etc.]

cameraman /'kæmrəmən/ n. (pl. **-men**) a person who operates a camera professionally, esp. in film-making or television.

camiknickers /'kæmɪˌnɪkəz/ n.pl. *Brit.* a one-piece close-fitting undergarment formerly worn by women. [CAMISOLE + KNICKERS]

camisole /'kæmɪˌsəʊl/ n. an under-bodice, usu. embroidered. [F f. It. *camiciola* or Sp. *camisola*: see CHEMISE]

camomile /'kæməˌmaɪl/ n. (also **chamomile**) any aromatic plant of the genus *Anthemis* or *Matricaria*, with daisy-like flowers. □**camomile tea** an infusion of its dried flowers used as a tonic. [ME f. OF *camomille* f. LL *camomilla* or *chamomilla* f. Gk *khamaimēlon* earth-apple (from the apple-smell of its flowers)]

camouflage /'kæməˌflɑːʒ/ n. & v. —n. **1 a** the disguising of military vehicles, aircraft, ships, artillery, and installations by painting them or covering them to make them blend with their surroundings. **b** such a disguise. **2** the natural colouring of an animal which enables it to blend in with its surroundings. **3** a misleading or evasive precaution or expedient. —v.tr. hide or disguise by means of camouflage. [F f. *camoufler* disguise f. It. *camuffare* disguise, deceive]

camp[1] /kæmp/ n. & v. —n. **1 a** a place where troops are lodged or trained. **b** the military life (*court and camp*). **2** temporary overnight lodging in tents etc. in the open. **3 a** temporary accommodation of various kinds, usu. consisting of huts or tents, for detainees, homeless persons, and other emergency use. **b** a complex of buildings for holiday accommodation, usu. with extensive recreational facilities. **4** an ancient fortified site or its remains. **5** the adherents of a particular party or doctrine regarded collectively (*the Labour camp was jubilant*). **6** *S.Afr.* a portion of veld fenced off for pasture on farms. **7** *Austral. & NZ* an assembly place of sheep or cattle. —v.intr. **1** set up or spend time in a camp (in senses 1 and 2 of n.). **2** (often foll. by *out*) lodge in temporary quarters or in the open. **3** *Austral. & NZ* (of sheep or cattle) flock together esp. for rest. □**camp-bed** a folding portable bed of a kind used in camping. **camp-fire** an open-air fire in a camp etc. **camp-follower 1** a civilian worker in a military camp. **2** a disciple or adherent. **camp-site** a place for camping. □□**camping** n. [F f. It. *campo* f. L *campus* level ground]

camp[2] /kæmp/ adj., n., & v. colloq. —adj. **1** affected, effeminate. **2** homosexual. **3** done in an exaggerated way for effect. —n. a camp manner or style. —v.intr. & tr. behave or do in a camp way. □**camp it up** overact; behave affectedly. □□**campy** adj. (**campier, campiest**). **campily** adv. **campiness** n. [20th c.: orig. uncert.]

campaign /kæm'peɪn/ n. & v. —n. **1** an organized course of action for a particular purpose, esp. to arouse public interest (e.g. before a political election). **2 a** a series of military operations in a definite area or to achieve a particular objective. **b** military service in the field (*on campaign*). —v.intr. conduct or take part in a campaign. □□**campaigner** n.

[F *campagne* open country f. It. *campagna* f. LL *campania*]

campanile /ˌkæmpə'niːlɪ/ n. a bell-tower (usu. free-standing), esp. in Italy. [It. f. *campana* bell]

campanology /ˌkæmpə'nɒlədʒɪ/ n. **1** the study of bells. **2** the art or practice of bell-ringing. □□ **campanologer** n. **campanological** /-nə'lɒdʒɪk(ə)l/ adj. **campanologist** n. [mod.L *campanologia* f. LL *campana* bell]

campanula /kæm'pænjʊlə/ n. any plant of the genus *Campanula*, with bell-shaped usu. blue, purple, or white flowers. Also called BELLFLOWER. [mod.L dimin. of L *campana* bell]

campanulate /kæm'pænjʊlət/ adj. *Bot. & Zool.* bell-shaped.

Campeachy wood /kæm'piːtʃɪ/ n. = LOGWOOD. [*Campeche* in Mexico, from where it was first exported]

camper /'kæmpə(r)/ n. **1** a person who camps out or lives temporarily in a tent, hut, etc., esp. on holiday. **2** a large motor vehicle with accommodation for camping out.

camphor /'kæmfə(r)/ n. a white translucent crystalline volatile substance with aromatic smell and bitter taste, used to make celluloid and in medicine. □□ **camphoric** /-'fɒrɪk/ adj. [ME f. OF *camphore* or med.L *camphora* f. Arab. *kāfūr* f. Skr. *karpūram*]

camphorate /'kæmfəˌreɪt/ v.tr. impregnate or treat with camphor.

campion /'kæmpɪən/ n. **1** any plant of the genus *Silene*, with usu. pink or white notched flowers. **2** any of several similar cultivated plants of the genus *Lychnis*. [perh. f. obs. *campion* f. OF, = CHAMPION: transl. of Gk *lukhnis stephanōmatikē* a plant used for (champions') garlands]

campus /'kæmpəs/ n. (pl. **campuses**) **1** the grounds of a university or college. **2** esp. *US* a university, esp. as a teaching institution. [L, = field]

CAMRA /'kæmrə/ abbr. Campaign for Real Ale.

camshaft /'kæmʃɑːft/ n. a shaft with one or more cams attached to it.

camwood /'kæmwʊd/ n. a hard red wood from a tree *Pterocarpus soyauxii*, native to W. Africa. [perh. f. Temne]

can[1] /kæn, kən/ v.aux. (*3rd sing. present* can; *past* could /kʊd/) (foll. by infin. without *to*, or absol.; present and past only in use) **1 a** be able to; know how to (*I can run fast; can he?; can you speak German?*). **b** be potentially capable of (*you can do it if you try*). **2** be permitted to (*can we go to the party?*). [OE *cunnan* know]

can[2] /kæn/ n. & v. —n. **1** a metal vessel for liquid. **2** a tin container in which food or drink is hermetically sealed to enable storage over long periods. **3** (prec. by *the*) *sl.* **a** prison (*sent to the can*). **b** *US* lavatory. —v.tr. (**canned, canning**) **1** put or preserve in a can. **2** record on film or tape for future use. □**can of worms** colloq. a complicated problem. **can-opener** a device for opening cans (in sense 2 of n.). **in the can** colloq. completed, ready (orig. of filmed or recorded material). □□ **canner** n. [OE *canne*]

Can. abbr. Canada; Canadian.

Canaan /'keɪnən/ n. **1** a promised land (orig. that west of the River Jordan, the Promised Land of the Israelites). **2** heaven. [eccl.L f. eccl.Gk *Khanaan* f. Heb. *kᵉna'an*]

Canada balsam /'kænədə/ n. *Biol.* a yellow resin obtained from the balsam fir and used for mounting preparations on microscope slides (its refractive index being similar to that of glass).

Canada goose /'kænədə/ n. a wild goose, *Branta canadensis*, of N. America, with a brownish-grey body and white cheeks and breast.

canaille /kə'nɑːɪ/ n. the rabble; the populace. [F f. It. *canaglia* pack of dogs f. *cane* dog]

canal /kə'næl/ n. **1** an artificial waterway for inland navigation or irrigation. **2** any of various tubular ducts in a plant or animal, for carrying food, liquid, or air. **3** *Astron.* any of a network of apparent linear markings on the planet Mars, which are observed from earth but not at close range. □**canal boat** a long narrow boat for use on canals. **canal ray** a beam of positive ions moving through a bored hole in the cathode of a high-vacuum tube. [ME f. OF (earlier *chanel*) f. L *canalis* or It. *canale*]

canalize /ˈkænəˌlaɪz/ *v.tr.* (also **-ise**) **1** make a canal through. **2** convert (a river) into a canal. **3** provide with canals. **4** give the desired direction or purpose to. □□ **canalization** /-ˈzeɪʃ(ə)n/ *n.* [F *canaliser*: see CANAL]

canapé /ˈkænəpɪ/ *n.* **1** a small piece of bread or pastry with a savoury on top, often served as an hors-d'œuvre. **2** a sofa. [F]

canard /kəˈnɑːd, ˈkænɑːd/ *n.* **1** an unfounded rumour or story. **2** an extra surface attached to an aeroplane forward of the main lifting surface, for extra stability or control. [F, = duck]

Canarese var. of KANARESE.

canary /kəˈneərɪ/ *n.* (*pl.* **-ies**) **1** any of various small finches of the genus *Serinus*, esp. *S. canaria*, a songbird native to the Canary Islands, with mainly yellow plumage. **2** *hist.* a sweet wine from the Canary Islands. □**canary-coloured** coloured canary yellow. **canary creeper** a climbing plant, *Tropaeolum peregrinum*, with flowers of bright yellow deeply toothed petals which give the appearance of a small bird in flight. **canary grass** a Mediterranean plant *Phalaris canariensis*, grown as a crop plant for bird seed. **canary yellow** bright yellow. [*Canary* Islands f. F *Canarie* f. Sp. & L *Canaria* f. *canis* dog, one of the islands being noted in Roman times for large dogs]

canasta /kəˈnæstə/ *n.* **1** a card-game using two packs and resembling rummy, the aim being to collect sets (or melds) of cards. **2** a set of seven cards in this game. [Sp., = basket]

canaster /kəˈnæstə(r)/ *n.* tobacco made from coarsely broken dried leaves. [orig. the container: Sp. *canastro* ult. f. Gk *kanastron*]

cancan /ˈkænkæn/ *n.* a lively stage-dance with high kicking, performed by women in long skirts and petticoats. [F]

cancel /ˈkæns(ə)l/ *v. & n.* —*v.* (**cancelled**, **cancelling**; *US* **canceled, canceling**) **1** *tr.* **a** withdraw or revoke (a previous arrangement). **b** discontinue (an arrangement in progress). **2** *tr.* obliterate or delete (writing etc.). **3** *tr.* mark or pierce (a ticket, stamp, etc.) to invalidate it. **4** *tr.* annul; make void; abolish. **5** (often foll. by *out*) **a** *tr.* (of one factor or circumstance) neutralize or counterbalance (another). **b** *intr.* (of two factors or circumstances) neutralize each other. **6** *tr. Math.* strike out (an equal factor) on each side of an equation or from the numerator and denominator of a fraction. —*n.* **1** a countermand. **2** the cancellation of a postage stamp. **3** *Printing* a new page or section inserted in a book to replace the original text, usu. to correct an error. **4** *Mus. US* a natural-sign. □□ **canceller** *n.* [ME f. F *canceller* f. L *cancellare* f. *cancelli* crossbars, lattice]

cancellate /ˈkænsɪlət/ *adj.* (also **cancellated** /-ˌleɪtɪd/) *Biol.* marked with crossing lines. [L *cancelli* lattice]

cancellation /ˌkænsəˈleɪʃ(ə)n/ *n.* **1** the act or an instance of cancelling or being cancelled. **2** something that has been cancelled, esp. a booking or reservation. [L *cancellatio* (as CANCEL)]

cancellous /ˈkænsɪləs/ *adj.* (of a bone) with pores. [L *cancelli* lattice]

cancer /ˈkænsə(r)/ *n.* **1 a** any malignant growth or tumour from an abnormal and uncontrolled division of body cells. **b** a disease caused by this. **2** an evil influence or corruption spreading uncontrollably. **3** (**Cancer**) **a** a constellation, traditionally regarded as contained in the figure of a crab. **b** the fourth sign of the zodiac (the Crab). **c** a person born when the sun is in this sign. □**cancer stick** *sl.* a cigarette. □□

Cancerian /-ˈsɪərɪən/ *n. & adj.* (in sense 3).
cancerous *adj.* [ME f. L, = crab, cancer, after Gk *karkinos*]

cancroid /ˈkæŋkrɔɪd/ *adj. & n.* —*adj.* **1** crablike. **2** resembling cancer. —*n.* a disease resembling cancer.

candela /kænˈdiːlə, -ˈdeɪlə/ *n.* the SI unit of luminous intensity. ¶ Abbr.: **cd.** [L, = candle]

candelabrum /ˌkændɪˈlɑːbrəm/ *n.* (also **candelabra** /-brə/) (*pl.* **candelabra**, *US* **candelabrums**, **candelabras**) a large branched candlestick or lamp-holder. □**candelabrum tree** a tropical E. African tree, *Euphorbia candelabrum*, with foliage shaped like a candelabrum. [L f. *candela* CANDLE]

candescent /kænˈdes(ə)nt/ *adj.* glowing with or as with white heat. □□ **candescence** *n.* [L *candēre* be white]

candid /ˈkændɪd/ *adj.* **1** frank; not hiding one's thoughts. **2** (of a photograph) taken informally, usu. without the subject's knowledge. □**candid camera** a small camera for taking candid photographs. □□ **candidly** *adv.* **candidness** *n.* [F *candide* or L *candidus* white]

candida /ˈkændɪdə/ *n.* any yeastlike parasitic fungus of the genus *Candida*, esp. *C. albicans* causing thrush. [mod.L fem. of L *candidus*: see CANDID]

candidate /ˈkændɪdət, -ˌdeɪt/ *n.* **1** a person who seeks or is nominated for an office, award, etc. **2** a person or thing likely to gain some distinction or position. **3** a person entered for an examination. □□ **candidacy** *n.* **candidature** *n. Brit.* [F *candidat* or L *candidatus* white-robed (Roman candidates wearing white)]

candle /ˈkænd(ə)l/ *n. & v.* —*n.* **1** a cylinder or block of wax or tallow with a central wick, for giving light when burning. **2** = CANDLEPOWER. —*v.tr.* test (an egg) for freshness by holding it to the light. □**cannot hold a candle to** cannot be compared with; is much inferior to. **not worth the candle** not justifying the cost or trouble. □□ **candler** *n.* [OE *candel* f. L *candela* f. *candēre* shine]

candlelight /ˈkænd(ə)lˌlaɪt/ *n.* **1** light provided by candles. **2** dusk.

Candlemas /ˈkænd(ə)lməs, -ˌmæs/ *n.* a feast with blessing of candles (2 Feb.), commemorating the Purification of the Virgin Mary and the presentation of Christ in the Temple. [OE *Candelmæsse* (as CANDLE, MASS[2])]

candlepower /ˈkænd(ə)lˌpaʊə(r)/ *n.* a unit of luminous intensity.

candlestick /ˈkænd(ə)lstɪk/ *n.* a holder for one or more candles.

candlewick /ˈkænd(ə)lwɪk/ *n.* **1** a thick soft cotton yarn. **2** material made from this, usu. with a tufted pattern.

candour /ˈkændə(r)/ *n.* (*US* **candor**) candid behaviour or action; frankness. [F *candeur* or L *candor* whiteness]

C. & W. *abbr.* country-and-western.

candy /ˈkændɪ/ *n. & v.* —*n.* (*pl.* **-ies**) **1** (in full **sugar-candy**) sugar crystallized by repeated boiling and slow evaporation. **2** *US* sweets; a sweet. —*v.tr.* (**-ies, -ied**) (usu. as **candied** *adj.*) preserve by coating and impregnating with a sugar syrup (*candied fruit*). [F *sucre candi* candied sugar f. Arab. *ḳand* sugar]

candyfloss /ˈkændɪˌflɒs/ *n. Brit.* a fluffy mass of spun sugar wrapped round a stick.

candystripe /ˈkændɪˌstraɪp/ *n.* a pattern consisting of alternate stripes of white and a colour (usu. pink). □□ **candystriped** *adj.*

candytuft /ˈkændɪˌtʌft/ *n.* any of various plants of the genus *Iberis*, native to W. Europe, with white, pink, or purple flowers in tufts. [obs. *Candy* (Candia Crete) + TUFT]

cane /keɪn/ *n. & v.* —*n.* **1 a** the hollow jointed stem of giant reeds or grasses (*bamboo cane*). **b** the solid stem of slender palms (*malacca cane*). **2** = *sugar cane*. **3** a raspberry-cane. **4** material of cane used for wickerwork etc. **5 a** a cane used as a walking-stick or a support for a plant or an instrument of punishment. **b** any slender walking-stick. —*v.tr.* **1** beat with a cane. **2** weave cane into (a chair etc.). □**cane-brake** *US* a tract of land overgrown with canes. **cane chair** a chair with a seat made of woven cane strips. **cane-sugar** sugar obtained from sugar-cane. **cane-trash** see TRASH. □□ **caner** *n.* (in sense 2 of *v.*). **caning** *n.* [ME f. OF f. L *canna* f. Gk *kanna*]

canine /'keɪnaɪn, 'kæn-/ *adj.* & *n.* —*adj.* **1** of a dog or dogs. **2** of or belonging to the family Canidae, including dogs, wolves, foxes, etc. —*n.* **1** a dog. **2** (in full **canine tooth**) a pointed tooth between the incisors and premolars. [ME f. *canin -ine* or f. L *caninus* f. *canis* dog]

canister /'kænɪstə(r)/ *n.* **1** a small container, usu. of metal and cylindrical, for storing tea etc. **2 a** a cylinder shot, tear-gas, etc., that explodes on impact. **b** such cylinders collectively. [L *canistrum* f. Gk f. *kanna* CANE]

canker /'kæŋkə(r)/ *n.* & *v.* —*n.* **1 a** a destructive fungus disease of trees and plants. **b** an open wound in the stem of a tree or plant. **2** *Zool.* an ulcerous ear disease of animals esp. cats and dogs. **3** *Med.* an ulceration esp. of the lips. **4** a corrupting influence. —*v.tr.* **1** consume with canker. **2** corrupt. **3** (as **cankered** *adj.*) soured, malignant, crabbed. □ **canker-worm** any caterpillar of various wingless moths which consume the buds and leaves of shade and fruit trees in N. America. □□ **cankerous** *adj.* [OE *cancer* & ONF *cancre*, OF *chancre* f. L *cancer* crab]

canna /'kænə/ *n.* any tropical plant of the genus *Canna* with bright flowers and ornamental leaves. [L: see CANE]

cannabis /'kænəbɪs/ *n.* **1** any hemp plant of the genus *Cannabis*, esp. Indian hemp. **2** a preparation of parts of this used as an intoxicant or hallucinogen. □**cannabis resin** a sticky product, esp. from the flowering tops of the female cannabis plant. [L f. Gk]

canned /kænd/ *adj.* **1** pre-recorded (*canned laughter; canned music*). **2** supplied in a can (*canned beer*). **3** *sl.* drunk.

cannel /'kæn(ə)l/ *n.* (in full **cannel coal**) a bituminous coal burning with a bright flame. [16th c.: orig. N.Engl.]

cannelloni /ˌkænə'ləʊnɪ/ *n.pl.* tubes or rolls of pasta stuffed with meat or a vegetable mixture. [It. f. *cannello* stalk]

cannelure /'kænəljʊə(r)/ *n.* the groove round a bullet etc. [F f. *canneler* f. *canne* reed, CANE]

cannery /'kænərɪ/ *n.* (*pl.* -ies) a factory where food is canned.

cannibal /'kænɪb(ə)l/ *n.* & *adj.* —*n.* **1** a person who eats human flesh. **2** an animal that feeds on flesh of its own species. —*adj.* of or like a cannibal. □□ **cannibalism** *n.* **cannibalistic** /-bə'lɪstɪk/ *adj.* **cannibalistically** /-bə'lɪstɪkəlɪ/ *adv.* [orig. pl. *Canibales* f. Sp.: var. of *Caribes* name of a W.Ind. nation]

cannibalize /'kænɪbəˌlaɪz/ *v.tr.* (also **-ise**) use (a machine etc.) as a source of spare parts for others. □□ **cannibalization** /-'zeɪʃ(ə)n/ *n.*

cannikin /'kænɪkɪn/ *n.* a small can. [Du. *kanneken* (as CAN², -KIN)]

cannon /'kænən/ *n.* & *v.* —*n.* **1** *hist.* (*pl.* same) a large heavy gun installed on a carriage or mounting. **2** an automatic aircraft gun firing shells. **3** *Billiards* the hitting of two balls successively by the cue-ball. **4** *Mech.* a hollow cylinder moving independently on a shaft. **5** (in full **cannon-bit**) a smooth round bit for a horse. —*v.intr.* **1** (usu. foll. by *against, into*) collide heavily or obliquely. **2** *Billiards* make a cannon shot. □**cannon-ball** *hist.* a large usu. metal ball fired by a cannon. **cannon-bone** the tube-shaped bone between the hock and fetlock of a horse. **cannon-fodder** soldiers regarded merely as material to be expended in war. [F *canon* f. It. *cannone*

large tube f. *canna* CANE: in Billiards sense f. older CAROM]

cannonade /ˌkænə'neɪd/ *n.* & *v.* —*n.* a period of continuous heavy gunfire. —*v.tr.* bombard with a cannonade. [F f. It. *cannonata*]

cannot /'kænɒt, kæ'nɒt/ *v.aux.* can not.

cannula /'kænjʊlə/ *n.* (*pl.* **cannulae** /-liː/ or **cannulas**) *Surgery* a small tube for inserting into the body to allow fluid to enter or escape. [L, dimin. of *canna* cane]

cannulate /'kænjʊˌleɪt/ *v.tr. Surgery* introduce a cannula into.

canny /'kænɪ/ *adj.* (**cannier**, **canniest**) **1 a** shrewd, worldly-wise. **b** thrifty. **c** circumspect. **2** sly, drily humorous. **3** *Sc.* & *N.Engl.* pleasant, agreeable. □□ **cannily** *adv.* **canniness** *n.* [CAN¹ (in sense 'know') + -Y¹]

canoe /kə'nuː/ *n.* & *v.* —*n.* a small narrow boat with pointed ends usu. propelled by paddling. —*v.intr.* (**canoes, canoed, canoeing**) travel in a canoe. □□ **canoeist** *n.* [Sp. and Haitian *canoa*]

canon /'kænən/ *n.* **1 a** a general law, rule, principle, or criterion. **b** a church decree or law. **2** (*fem.* **canoness**) **a** a member of a cathedral chapter. **b** a member of certain RC orders. **3 a** a collection or list of sacred books etc. accepted as genuine. **b** the recognized genuine works of a particular author; a list of these. **4** the part of the Roman Catholic Mass containing the words of consecration. **5** *Mus.* a piece with different parts taking up the same theme successively, either at the same or at a different pitch. □**canon law** ecclesiastical law. **canon regular** (or **regular canon**) see REGULAR *adj.* 9b. [OE f. L f. Gk *kanōn*, in ME also f. AF & OF *canun, -on*; in sense 2 ME f. OF *canonie* f. eccl.L *canonicus*: cf. CANONICAL]

cañon var. of CANYON.

canonic /kə'nɒnɪk/ *adj.* = CANONICAL *adj.* [OE f. OF *canonique* or L *canonicus* f. L *canonikos* (as CANON)]

canonical /kə'nɒnɪk(ə)l/ *adj.* & *n.* —*adj.* **1 a** according to or ordered by canon law. **b** included in the canon of Scripture. **2** authoritative, standard, accepted. **3** of a cathedral chapter or a member of it. **4** *Mus.* in canon form. —*n.* (in *pl.*) the canonical dress of the clergy. □**canonical hours** *Eccl.* the times fixed for a formal set of prayers or for the celebration of marriage. □□ **canonically** *adv.* [med.L *canonicalis* (as CANONIC)]

canonicate /kə'nɒnɪkət/ *n.* = CANONRY.

canonicity /ˌkænə'nɪsɪtɪ/ *n.* the status of being canonical. [L *canonicus* canonical]

canonist /'kænənɪst/ *n.* an expert in canon law. [ME f. F *canoniste* or f. med.L *canonista*: see CANON]

canonize /'kænəˌnaɪz/ *v.tr.* (also **-ise**) **1 a** declare officially to be a saint, usu. with a ceremony. **b** regard as a saint. **2** admit to the canon of Scripture. **3** sanction by Church authority. □□ **canonization** /-'zeɪʃ(ə)n/ *n.* [ME f. med.L *canonizare*: see CANON]

canonry /'kænənrɪ/ *n.* (*pl.* -ies) the office or benefice of a canon.

canoodle /kə'nuːd(ə)l/ *v.intr. colloq.* kiss and cuddle amorously. [19th-c. US: orig. unkn.]

Canopic /kə'nəʊpɪk/ *adj.* □**Canopic jar** (or **vase**) an urn used for holding the entrails of an embalmed body in an ancient Egyptian burial. [L *Canopicus* f. *Canopus* in ancient Egypt]

canopy /'kænəpɪ/ *n.* & *v.* —*n.* (*pl.* -ies) **1 a** a covering hung or held up over a throne, bed, person, etc. **b** the sky. **c** an overhanging shelter. **2** *Archit.* a rooflike projection over a niche etc. in a forest. **3** the uppermost layers of foliage etc. in a forest. **4 a** the expanding part of a parachute. **b** the cover of an aircraft's cockpit. —*v.tr.* (-ies, -ied) supply or be a canopy to. [ME f. med.L *canopeum* f. L *conopeum* f. Gk *kōnōpeion* couch with mosquito-curtains f. *kōnōps* gnat]

canorous /kə'nɔːrəs/ *adj.* melodious, resonant. [L *canorus* f. *canere* sing]

canst /kænst/ *archaic 2nd person sing.* of CAN¹.

cant¹ /kænt/ *n.* & *v.* —*n.* **1** insincere pious or moral talk. **2** ephemeral or fashionable catchwords. **3** language peculiar to a class, profession, sect, etc.; jargon. —*v.intr.* use cant. □**canting arms** *Heraldry* arms containing an allusion to the name of the bearer. [earlier of musical sound, of intonation, and of beggars' whining; perh. from the singing of religious mendicants: prob. f. L *canere* sing]

cant² /kænt/ *n.* & *v.* —*n.* **1 a** a slanting surface, e.g. of a bank. **b** a bevel of a crystal etc. **2** an oblique push or movement that upsets or partly upsets something. **3** a tilted or sloping position. —*v.* **1** *tr.* push or pitch out of level; tilt. **2** *intr.* take or lie in a slanting position. **3** *tr.* impart a bevel to. **4** *intr. Naut.* swing round. □**cant-dog** (or **-hook**) an iron hook at the end of a long handle, used for rolling logs. [ME f. MLG *kant, kante*, MDu. *cant*, point, side, edge, ult. f. L *cant(h)us* iron tire]

can't /kɑːnt/ *contr.* can not.

Cant. *abbr.* Canticles (Old Testament).

Cantab. /'kæntæb/ *abbr.* of Cambridge University. [L *Cantabrigiensis*]

cantabile /kæn'tɑːbɪlɪ/ *adv., adj.,* & *n. Mus.* —*adv.* & *adj.* in a smooth singing style. —*n.* a cantabile passage or movement. [It., = singable]

Cantabrigian /ˌkæntə'brɪdʒɪən/ *adj.* & *n.* —*adj.* of Cambridge or Cambridge University. —*n.* **1** a member of Cambridge University. **2** a native of Cambridge. [L *Cantabrigia* Cambridge]

cantal /'kænt(ə)l/ *n.* a type of hard strong French cheese. [name of a department of Auvergne, France]

cantaloup /'kæntə,luːp/ *n.* (also **cantaloupe**) a small round ribbed variety of melon with orange flesh. [F *cantaloup* f. *Cantaluppi* near Rome, where it was first grown in Europe]

cantankerous /kæn'tæŋkərəs/ *adj.* bad-tempered, quarrelsome. □□**cantankerously** *adv.* **cantankerousness** *n.* [perh. f. Ir. *cant* outbidding + *rancorous*]

cantata /kæn'tɑːtə/ *n. Mus.* a short narrative or descriptive composition with vocal solos and usu. chorus and orchestral accompaniment. [It. *cantata* (*aria*) sung (air) f. *cantare* sing]

canteen /kæn'tiːn/ *n.* **1 a** a restaurant for employees in an office or factory etc. **b** a shop selling provisions or liquor in a barracks or camp. **2** a case or box of cutlery. **3** a soldier's or camper's water-flask or set of eating or drinking utensils. [F *cantine* f. It. *cantina* cellar]

canter /'kæntə(r)/ *n.* & *v.* —*n.* a gentle gallop. —*v.* **1** *intr.* (of a horse or its rider) go at a canter. **2** *tr.* make (a horse) canter. □**in a canter** easily (*win in a canter*). [short for *Canterbury pace*, from the supposed easy pace of medieval pilgrims to Canterbury]

canterbury /'kæntəbərɪ/ *n.* (*pl.* **-ies**) a piece of furniture with partitions for holding music etc. [*Canterbury* in Kent]

Canterbury bell /'kæntəbərɪ/ *n.* a cultivated campanula with large flowers. [after the bells of Canterbury pilgrims' horses: see CANTER]

cantharides /kæn'θærɪˌdiːz/ *n.pl.* a preparation made from dried bodies of a beetle *Lytta vesicatoria*, causing blistering of the skin and formerly used in medicine and as an aphrodisiac. Also called *Spanish fly.* [L f. Gk *kantharis* Spanish fly]

canthus /'kænθəs/ *n.* (*pl.* **canthi** /-θaɪ/) the outer or inner corner of the eye, where the upper and lower lids meet. [L f. Gk *kanthos*]

canticle /'kæntɪk(ə)l/ *n.* **1** a song or chant with a Biblical text. **2** (also **Canticle of Canticles**) the Song of Solomon. [ME f. OF *canticle* (var. of *cantique*) or L *canticulum* dimin. of *canticum* f. *canere* sing]

cantilena /ˌkæntɪ'liːnə/ *n. Mus.* a simple or sustained melody. [It.]

cantilever /'kæntɪˌliːvə(r)/ *n.* & *v.* —*n.* **1** a long bracket or beam etc. projecting from a wall to support a balcony etc. **2** a beam or girder fixed at only one end. —*v.intr.* **1** project as a cantilever. **2** be supported by cantilevers. □**cantilever bridge** a bridge made

of cantilevers projecting from the piers and connected by girders. [17th c.: orig. unkn.]

cantillate /'kæntɪˌleɪt/ *v.tr.* & *intr.* chant or recite with musical tones. □□**cantillation** /-'leɪʃ(ə)n/ *n.* [L *cantillare* sing low: see CHANT]

cantina /kæn'tiːnə/ *n.* a bar-room or wine-shop. [Sp. & It.]

canto /'kæntəʊ/ *n.* (*pl.* **-os**) a division of a long poem. [It., = song, f. L *cantus*]

canton *n.* & *v.* —*n.* **1** /'kæntɒn/ **a** a subdivision of a country. **b** a State of the Swiss confederation. **2** /'kænt(ə)n/ *Heraldry* a square division, less than a quarter, in the upper (usu. dexter) corner of a shield. —*v.tr.* **1** /kæn'tuːn/ put (troops) into quarters. **2** /kæn'tɒn/ divide into cantons. □□**cantonal** /'kæntən(ə)l, kæn'tɒn(ə)l/ *adj.* [OF, = corner (see CANT²): (v.) also partly f. F *cantonner*]

Cantonese /ˌkæntə'niːz/ *adj.* & *n.* —*adj.* of Canton or the Cantonese dialect of Chinese. —*n.* (*pl.* same) **1** a native of Canton. **2** the dialect of Chinese spoken in SE China and Hong Kong. [*Canton* in China]

cantonment /kæn'tuːnmənt/ *n.* **1** a lodging assigned to troops. **2** a permanent military station in India. [F *cantonnement*: see CANTON]

cantor /'kæntɔː(r)/ *n.* **1** the leader of the singing in church; a precentor. **2** the precentor in a synagogue. [L, = singer f. *canere* sing]

cantorial /kæn'tɔːrɪəl/ *adj.* **1** of or relating to the cantor. **2** of the north side of the choir in a church (cf. DECANAL).

cantoris /kæn'tɔːrɪs/ *adj. Mus.* to be sung by the cantorial side of the choir in antiphonal singing (cf. DECANI). [L, genit. of CANTOR precentor]

cantrail /'kæntreɪl/ *n. Brit.* a timber etc. support for the roof of a railway carriage. [CANT² + RAIL]

cantrip /'kæntrɪp/ *n. Sc.* **1** a witch's trick. **2** a piece of mischief; a playful act. [18th c.: orig. unkn.]

Canuck /kə'nʌk/ *n.* & *adj. US sl.* usu. *derog.* —*n.* **1** a Canadian, esp. a French Canadian. **2** a Canadian horse or pony. —*adj.* Canadian, esp. French Canadian. [app. f. *Canada*]

canvas /'kænvəs/ *n.* & *v.* —*n.* **1 a** a strong coarse kind of cloth made from hemp or flax or other coarse yarn and used for sails and tents etc. and as a surface for oil-painting. **b** a piece of this. **2** a painting on canvas, esp. in oils. **3** an open kind of canvas used as a basis for tapestry and embroidery. **4** *sl.* the floor of a boxing or wrestling ring. **5** a racing-boat's covered end. —*v.tr.* (**canvassed, canvassing**; *US* **canvased, canvasing**) cover with canvas. □**by a canvas** (in boat-racing) by a small margin (*win by a canvas*). **canvas-back** a wild duck *Aythya valisineria*, of N. America, with back feathers the colour of unbleached canvas. **under canvas 1** in a tent or tents. **2** with sails spread. [ME & ONF *canevas*, ult. f. L *cannabis* hemp]

canvass /'kænvəs/ *v.* & *n.* —*v.* **1 a** *intr.* solicit votes. **b** *tr.* solicit votes from (electors in a constituency). **2** *tr.* **a** ascertain opinions of. **b** seek custom from. **c** discuss thoroughly. **3** *tr. Brit.* propose (an idea or plan etc.). **4** *intr. US* check the validity of votes. —*n.* the process of or an instance of canvassing, esp. of electors. □□**canvasser** *n.* [orig. = toss in a sheet, agitate, f. CANVAS]

canyon /'kænjən/ *n.* (also **cañon**) a deep gorge, often with a stream or river. [Sp. *cañón* tube, ult. f. L *canna* CANE]

canzonetta /ˌkænzə'netə/ *n.* (also **canzonet** /-'net/) **1** a short light song. **2** a kind of madrigal. [It., dimin. of *canzone* song f. L *cantio -onis* f. *canere* sing]

caoutchouc /'kaʊtʃʊk/ *n.* raw rubber. [F f. Carib *cahuchu*]

CAP *abbr.* Common Agricultural Policy (of the EEC).

cap /kæp/ *n.* & *v.* —*n.* **1 a** a soft brimless head-covering, usu. with a peak. **b** a head-covering worn in a particular profession (*nurse's cap*). **c** esp. *Brit.* a cap awarded as a sign of membership of a sports team. **d** an academic mortarboard or soft hat. **e a**

special hat as part of Highland costume. **2 a** a cover like a cap in shape or position (*knee cap*; *toecap*). **b** a device to seal a bottle or protect the point of a pen, lens of a camera, etc. **3 a** = *Dutch cap.* **b** = *percussion cap.* **4** = CROWN *n.* 9b. —*v.tr.* (**capped, capping**) **1 a** put a cap on. **b** cover the top or end of. **c** set a limit to (*rate-capping*). **2 a** esp. *Brit.* award a sports cap to. **b** *Sc.* & *NZ* confer a university degree on. **3 a** lie on top of; form the cap of. **b** surpass, excel. **c** improve on (a story, quotation, etc.) esp. by producing a better or more apposite one. □**cap in hand** humbly. **cap of maintenance** a cap or hat worn as a symbol of official dignity or carried before the sovereign etc. **cap rock** a hard rock or stratum overlying a deposit of oil, gas, coal, etc. **cap sleeve** a sleeve extending only a short distance from the shoulder. **if the cap fits** (said of a generalized comment) it seems to be true (of a particular person). **set one's cap at** try to attract as a suitor. □□**capful** *n.* (*pl.* **-fuls**). **capping** *n.* [OE *cæppe* f. LL *cappa*, perh. f. L *caput* head]

cap. *abbr.* **1** capital. **2** capital letter. **3** chapter. [L *capitulum* or *caput*]

capability /ˌkeɪpəˈbɪlɪtɪ/ *n.* (*pl.* **-ies**) **1** (often foll. by *of, for, to*) ability, power; the condition of being capable. **2** an undeveloped or unused faculty.

capable /ˈkeɪpəb(ə)l/ *adj.* **1** competent, able, gifted. **2** (foll. by *of*) having the ability or fitness or necessary quality for. **b** susceptible or admitting of (explanation or improvement etc.). □□**capably** *adv.* [F f. LL *capabilis* f. L *capere* hold]

capacious /kəˈpeɪʃəs/ *adj.* roomy; able to hold much. □□**capaciously** *adv.* **capaciousness** *n.* [L *capax -acis* f. *capere* hold]

capacitance /kəˈpæsɪt(ə)ns/ *n.* *Electr.* **1** the ability of a system to store an electric charge. **2** the ratio of the change in an electric charge in a system to the corresponding change in its electric potential. ¶ Symb.: **C**. [CAPACITY + -ANCE]

capacitate /kəˈpæsɪˌteɪt/ *v.tr.* **1** (usu. foll. by *for*, or *to* + infin.) render capable. **2** make legally competent.

capacitor /kəˈpæsɪtə(r)/ *n.* *Electr.* a device of one or more pairs of conductors separated by insulators used to store an electric charge.

capacity /kəˈpæsɪtɪ/ *n.* (*pl.* **-ies**) **1 a** the power of containing, receiving, experiencing, or producing (*capacity for heat, pain*, etc.). **b** the maximum amount that can be contained or produced etc. **c** the volume, e.g. of the cylinders in an internal-combustion engine. **d** (*attrib.*) fully occupying the available space, resources, etc. (*a capacity audience*). **2 a** mental power. **b** a faculty or talent. **3** a position or function (*in a civil capacity*; *in my capacity as a critic*). **4** legal competence. **5** *Electr.* capacitance. □**measure of capacity** a measure used for vessels and liquids or grains etc. **to capacity** fully; using all resources (*working to capacity*). □□**capacitative** /-tətɪv/ *adj.* (also **capacitive**) (in sense 5). [ME f. F f. L *capacitas -tatis* (as CAPACIOUS)]

caparison /kəˈpærɪs(ə)n/ *n.* & *v.* —*n.* **1** (usu. in *pl.*) a horse's trappings. **2** equipment, finery. —*v.tr.* put caparisons on; adorn richly. [obs. F *caparasson* f. Sp. *caparazón* saddle-cloth f. *capa* CAPE¹]

cape¹ /keɪp/ *n.* **1** a sleeveless cloak. **2** a short sleeveless cloak as a fixed or detachable part of a longer cloak or coat. [F f. Prov. *capa* f. LL *cappa* CAP]

cape² /keɪp/ *n.* **1** a headland or promontory. **2** (**the Cape**) **a** the Cape of Good Hope. **b** the S. African province containing it. □**Cape Coloured** *adj.* *S.Afr.* of the Coloured (see COLOURED 2) population of Cape Province. —*n.* a member of this population. **Cape doctor** *S.Afr.* *colloq.* a strong SE wind. **Cape Dutch** *archaic* Afrikaans. **Cape gooseberry 1** an edible soft roundish yellow berry enclosed in a lantern-like husk. **2** the plant, *Physalis peruviana*, bearing these. [ME f. OF *cap* f. Prov. *cap* ult. f. L *caput* head]

capelin /ˈkæplɪn/ *n.* (also **caplin**) a small smeltlike fish, *Mallotus villosus*, of the N. Atlantic, used as

food and as bait for catching cod etc. [F f. Prov. *capelan*: see CHAPLAIN]

caper¹ /ˈkeɪpə(r)/ *v.* & *n.* —*v.intr.* jump or run about playfully. —*n.* **1** a playful jump or leap. **2 a** a fantastic proceeding; a prank. **b** *sl.* any activity or occupation. □**cut a caper** (or **capers**) act friskily. □□**caperer** *n.* [abbr. of CAPRIOLE]

caper² /ˈkeɪpə(r)/ *n.* **1** a bramble-like S. European shrub, *Capparis spinosa*. **2** (in *pl.*) its flower buds cooked and pickled for use as flavouring esp. for a savoury sauce. [ME *capres* & F *câpres* f. L *capparis* f. Gk *kapparis*, treated as pl.: cf. CHERRY, PEA]

capercaillie /ˌkæpəˈkeɪlɪ/ *n.* (also **capercailzie** /-lzɪ/) a large European grouse, *Tetrao urogallus*. [Gael. *capull coille* horse of the wood]

capeskin /ˈkeɪpskɪn/ *n.* a soft leather made from S. African sheepskin.

capias /ˈkeɪpɪˌæs, ˈkeɪp-/ *n.* *Law* a writ ordering the arrest of the person named. [L, = you are to seize, f. *capere* take]

capillarity /ˌkæpɪˈlærɪtɪ/ *n.* a phenomenon at liquid boundaries resulting in the rise or depression of liquids in narrow tubes. Also called *capillary action.* [F *capillarité* (as CAPILLARY)]

capillary /kəˈpɪlərɪ/ *adj.* & *n.* —*adj.* **1** of or like a hair. **2** (of a tube) of hairlike internal diameter. **3** of one of the delicate ramified blood vessels intervening between arteries and veins. —*n.* (*pl.* **-ies**) **1** a capillary tube. **2** a capillary blood vessel. □**capillary action** = CAPILLARITY. [L *capillaris* f. *capillus* hair]

capital¹ /ˈkæpɪt(ə)l/ *n., adj.,* & *int.* —*n.* **1** the most important town or city of a country or region, usu. its seat of government and administrative centre. **2 a** the money or other assets with which a company starts in business. **b** accumulated wealth, esp. as used in further production. **c** money invested or lent at interest. **3** capitalists generally. **4** a capital letter. —*adj.* **1 a** principal; most important; leading. **b** *colloq.* excellent, first-rate. **2 a** involving or punishable by death (*capital punishment*; *a capital offence*). **b** (of an error etc.) vitally harmful; fatal. **3** (of letters of the alphabet) large in size and of the form used to begin sentences and names etc. —*int.* expressing approval or satisfaction. □**capital gain** a profit from the sale of investments or property. **capital goods** goods, esp. machinery, plant, etc., used or to be used in producing commodities (opp. *consumer goods*). **capital levy 1** the appropriation by the State of a fixed proportion of the wealth in the country. **2** a wealth tax. **capital sum** a lump sum of money, esp. payable to an insured person. **capital territory** a territory containing the capital city of a country. **capital transfer tax** *hist.* (in the UK) a tax levied on the transfer of capital by gift or bequest etc. ¶ Replaced in 1986 by *inheritance tax.* **make capital out of** use to one's advantage. **with a capital** — emphatically such (*art with a capital A*). □□**capitally** *adv.* [ME f. OF f. L *capitalis* f. *caput -itis* head]

capital² /ˈkæpɪt(ə)l/ *n.* *Archit.* the head or cornice of a pillar or column. [ME f. OF *capitel* f. LL *capitellum* dimin. of L *caput* head]

capitalism /ˈkæpɪtəˌlɪz(ə)m/ *n.* **1 a** an economic system in which the production and distribution of goods depend on invested private capital and profit-making. **b** the possession of capital or wealth. **2** *Polit.* the dominance of private owners of capital and production for profit.

capitalist /ˈkæpɪtəlɪst/ *n.* & *adj.* —*n.* **1** a person using or possessing capital; a rich person. **2** an advocate of capitalism. —*adj.* of or favouring capitalism. □□**capitalistic** /-ˈlɪstɪk/ *adj.* **capitalistically** /-ˈlɪstɪkəlɪ/ *adv.*

capitalize /ˈkæpɪtəˌlaɪz/ *v.* (also **-ise**) **1** *tr.* **a** convert into or provide with capital. **b** calculate or realize the present value of an income. **c** reckon (the value of an asset) by setting future benefits against the cost of maintenance. **2** *tr.* **a** write (a letter of the alphabet) as a capital. **b** begin (a word) with a capital letter. **3** *intr.* (foll. by *on*) use to one's advantage; profit from. □□ **capitalization** /-'zeɪʃ(ə)n/ *n.* [F *capitaliser* (as CAPITAL[1])]

capitation /ˌkæpɪ'teɪʃ(ə)n/ *n.* **1** a tax or fee at a set rate per person. **2** the levying of such a tax or fee. □ **capitation grant** a grant of a sum calculated from the number of people to be catered for, esp. in education. [F *capitation* or LL *capitatio* poll-tax f. *caput* head]

capitular /kə'pɪtjʊlə(r)/ *adj.* **1** of or relating to a cathedral chapter. **2** *Anat.* of or relating to a terminal protuberance of a bone. [LL *capitularis* f. L *capitulum* CHAPTER]

capitulary /kə'pɪtjʊlərɪ/ *n.* (*pl.* **-ies**) a collection of ordinances, esp. of the Frankish kings. [LL *capitularius* (as CAPITULAR)]

capitulate /kə'pɪtjʊˌleɪt/ *v.intr.* surrender, esp. on stated conditions. □□ **capitulator** *n.* **capitulatory** /-lətərɪ/ *adj.* [med.L *capitulare* draw up under headings f. L *caput* head]

capitulation /kəˌpɪtjʊ'leɪʃ(ə)n/ *n.* **1** the act of capitulating; surrender. **2** a statement of the main divisions of a subject. **3** an agreement or set of conditions.

capitulum /kə'pɪtjʊləm/ *n.* (*pl.* **capitula** /-lə/) *Bot.* an inflorescence with flowers clustered together like a head, as in the daisy family. [L, dimin. of *caput* head]

caplin var. of CAPELIN.

cap'n /kæpn/ *n. sl.* captain. [contr.]

capo /'kæpəʊ/ *n.* (in full **capo tasto** /'tæstəʊ/) (*pl.* **capos** or **capo tastos**) *Mus.* a device secured across the neck of a fretted instrument to raise equally the tuning of all strings by the required amount. [It. *capo tasto* head stop]

capon /'keɪpən/ *n.* a domestic cock castrated and fattened for eating. □□ **caponize** *v.tr.* (also **-ise**). [OE f. AF *capun*, OF *capon*, ult. f. L *capo -onis*]

caponier /ˌkæpə'nɪə(r)/ *n.* a covered passage across a ditch round a fort. [Sp. *caponera*, lit. 'capon-pen']

capot /kə'pɒt/ *n. & v.* —*n.* (in piquet) the winning of all the tricks by one player. —*v.tr.* (**capotted**, **capotting**) score a capot against (an opponent). [F]

capote /kə'pəʊt/ *n. hist.* a long cloak with a hood, formerly worn by soldiers and travellers etc. [F, dimin. of *cape* CAPE[1]]

cappuccino /ˌkæpʊ'tʃiːnəʊ/ *n.* (*pl.* **-os**) coffee with milk made frothy with pressurized steam. [It., = CAPUCHIN]

capriccio /kə'prɪtʃɪəʊ/ *n.* (*pl.* **-os**) **1** a lively and usu. short musical composition. **2** a painting etc. representing a fantasy or a mixture of real and imaginary features. [It., = sudden start, orig. 'horror']

capriccioso /kəˌprɪtʃɪ'əʊsəʊ/ *adv., adj., & n. Mus.* —*adv. & adj.* in a free and impulsive style. —*n.* (*pl.* **-os**) a capriccioso passage or movement. [It., = capricious]

caprice /kə'priːs/ *n.* **1 a** an unaccountable or whimsical change of mind or conduct. **b** a tendency to this. **2** a work of lively fancy in painting, drawing, or music; a capriccio. [F f. It. CAPRICCIO]

capricious /kə'prɪʃəs/ *adj.* **1** guided by or given to caprice. **2** irregular, unpredictable. □□ **capriciously** *adv.* **capriciousness** *n.* [F *capricieux* f. It. CAPRICCIOSO]

Capricorn /'kæprɪˌkɔːn/ *n.* (also **Capricornus** /-'kɔːnəs/) **1** a constellation, traditionally regarded as contained in the figure of a goat's horns. **2 a** the tenth sign of the zodiac (the Goat). **b** a person born when the sun is in this sign. □□ **Capricornian** *n. & adj.* [ME f. OF *capricorne* f. L *capricornus* f. *caper -pri* goat + *cornu* horn]

caprine /'kæpraɪn/ *adj.* of or like a goat. [ME f. L *caprinus* f. *caper -pri* goat]

capriole /'kæprɪˌəʊl/ *n. & v.* —*n.* **1** a leap or caper. **2** a trained horse's high leap and kick without advancing. —*v.* **1** *intr.* (of a horse or its rider) perform a capriole. **2** *tr.* make (a horse) capriole. [F f. It. *capriola* leap, ult. f. *caper -pri* goat]

Capris /kə'priːz/ *n.pl.* (also **Capri pants**) women's close-fitting tapered trousers. [*Capri*, an island in the bay of Naples]

caps. *abbr.* capital letters.

Capsian /'kæpsɪən/ *adj. & n.* —*adj.* of or relating to a palaeolithic culture of N. Africa and S. Europe. —*n.* this culture. [L *Capsa* = Gafsa in Tunisia]

capsicum /'kæpsɪkəm/ *n.* **1** any plant of the genus *Capsicum*, having edible capsular fruits containing many seeds, esp. *C. annuum* yielding several varieties of pepper. **2** the fruit of any of these plants, which vary in size, colour, and pungency. [mod.L, perh. f. L *capsa* box]

capsid[1] /'kæpsɪd/ *n.* any bug of the family Capsidae, esp. one that feeds on plants. [mod.L *Capsus* a genus of them]

capsid[2] /'kæpsɪd/ *n.* the protein coat or shell of a virus. [F *capside* f. L *capsa* box]

capsize /kæp'saɪz/ *v.* **1** *tr.* upset or overturn (a boat). **2** *intr.* be capsized. □□ **capsizal** *n.* [*cap-* as in Prov. *capvirar*, F *chavirer*: *-size* unexpl.]

capstan /'kæpst(ə)n/ *n.* **1** a thick revolving cylinder with a vertical axis, for winding an anchor cable or a halyard etc. **2** a revolving spindle on a tape recorder, that guides the tape past the head. □ **capstan lathe** a lathe with a revolving tool-holder. [Prov. *cabestan*, ult. f. L *capistrum* halter f. *capere* seize]

capstone /'kæpstəʊn/ *n.* coping; a coping-stone.

capsule /'kæpsjuːl/ *n.* **1** a small soluble case of gelatine enclosing a dose of medicine and swallowed with it. **2** a detachable compartment of a spacecraft or nose-cone of a rocket. **3** an enclosing membrane in the body. **4 a** a dry fruit that releases its seeds when ripe. **b** the spore-producing part of mosses and liverworts. **5** *Biol.* an enveloping layer surrounding certain bacteria. **6** (*attrib.*) concise; highly condensed (*a capsule history of jazz*). □□ **capsular** *adj.* **capsulate** *adj.* [F f. L *capsula* f. *capsa* CASE[2]]

capsulize /'kæpsjʊˌlaɪz/ *v.tr.* (also **-ise**) put (information etc.) in compact form.

Capt. *abbr.* Captain.

captain /'kæptɪn/ *n. & v.* —*n.* **1 a** a chief or leader. **b** the leader of a team, esp. in sports. **c** a powerful or influential person (*captain of industry*). **2 a** the person in command of a merchant or passenger ship. **b** the pilot of a civil aircraft. **3** (as a title **Captain**) **a** an army or *US* Air Force officer next above lieutenant. **b** a Navy officer in command of a warship; one ranking below commodore or rear admiral and above commander. **c** *US* a police officer in charge of a precinct, ranking below Chief Officer. **4 a** a foreman. **b** a head boy or girl in a school. **c** *US* a supervisor of waiters or bellboys. **5 a** a great soldier or strategist. **b** an experienced commander. —*v.tr.* be captain of; lead. □ **captain-general** an honorary officer, esp. of artillery. **Captain of the Fleet** *Brit.* a Navy staff officer in charge of maintenance. □□ **captaincy** *n.* (*pl.* **-ies**). **captainship** *n.* [ME & OF *capitain* f. LL *capitaneus* chief f. L *caput capit-* head]

caption /'kæpʃ(ə)n/ *n. & v.* —*n.* **1** a title or brief explanation appended to an illustration, cartoon, etc. **2** wording appearing on a cinema or television screen as part of a film or broadcast. **3** the heading of a chapter or article etc. **4** *Law* a certificate attached to or written on a document. —*v.tr.* provide with a caption. [ME f. L *captio* f. *capere capt-* take]

captious /'kæpʃəs/ *adj.* given to finding fault or raising petty objections. □□ **captiously** *adv.* **captiousness** *n.* [ME f. OF *captieux* or L *captiosus* (as CAPTION)]

captivate /'kæptɪˌveɪt/ *v.tr.* **1** overwhelm with charm or affection. **2** fascinate. □□ **captivatingly** *adv.*

captivation /-'veɪʃ(ə)n/ *n.* [LL *captivare* take captive (as CAPTIVE)]

captive /ˈkæptɪv/ n. & adj. —n. a person or animal that has been taken prisoner or confined. —adj. **1 a** taken prisoner. **b** kept in confinement or under restraint. **2 a** unable to escape. **b** in a position of having to comply (captive audience; captive market). **3** of or like a prisoner (captive state). □**captive balloon** a balloon held by a rope from the ground. [ME f. L captivus f. capere capt- take]

captivity /kæpˈtɪvɪtɪ/ n. (pl. -ies) **1 a** the condition or circumstances of being a captive. **b** a period of captivity. **2 (the Captivity)** the captivity of the Jews in Babylon in the 6th c. BC.

captor /ˈkæptə(r), -tɔː(r)/ n. a person who captures (a person, place, etc.). [L (as CAPTIVE)]

capture /ˈkæptʃə(r)/ v. & n. —v.tr. **1 a** take prisoner; seize as a prize. **b** obtain by force or trickery. **2** portray in permanent form (could not capture the likeness). **3** Physics absorb (a subatomic particle). **4** (in board games) make a move that secures the removal of (an opposing piece) from the board. **5** (of a stream) divert the upper course of (another stream) by encroaching on its basin. **6** cause (data) to be stored in a computer. —n. **1** the act of capturing. **2** a thing or person captured. □□**capturer** n. [F f. L captura f. capere capt- take]

Capuchin /ˈkæpjuːtʃɪn/ n. **1** a Franciscan friar of the new rule of 1529. **2** a cloak and hood formerly worn by women. **3 (capuchin) a** any monkey of the genus Cebus of S. America, with cowl-like head hair. **b** a variety of pigeon with head and neck feathers resembling a cowl. [F f. It. cappuccino f. cappuccio cowl f. cappa CAPE¹]

capybara /ˌkæpɪˈbɑːrə/ n. a very large semi-aquatic rodent, Hydrochoerus hydrochaeris, native to S. America. [Tupi]

car /kɑː(r)/ n. **1** (in full **motor car**) a road vehicle with an enclosed passenger compartment, powered by an internal-combustion engine. **2** (in comb.) **a** a wheeled vehicle, esp. of a specified kind (tramcar). **b** a railway carriage of a specified type (dining-car). **3** US any railway carriage or van. **4** the passenger compartment of a lift, cableway, balloon, etc. **5** poet. a wheeled vehicle; a chariot. □**car bomb** a terrorist bomb concealed in or under a parked car. **car-boot sale** an outdoor sale at which participants sell unwanted possessions from the boots of their cars. **car coat** a short coat designed esp. for car drivers. **car park** an area for parking cars. **car phone** a radio-telephone for use in a motor vehicle. □□**carful** n. (pl. -fuls). [ME f. AF & ONF carre ult. f. L carrum, carrus, of OCelt. orig.]

carabineer /ˌkærəbɪˈnɪə(r)/ n. (also **carabinier**) hist. **1** a soldier whose principal weapon is a carbine. **2 (the Carabineers)** the Royal Scots Dragoon Guards. [F carabinier f. carabine CARBINE]

carabiniere /ˌkærəbɪnˈjeərɪ/ n. (pl. **carabinieri** pronunc. same) an Italian gendarme. [It.]

caracal /ˈkærəkæl/ n. a lynx, Felis caracal, native to N. Africa and SW Asia. [F or Sp. f. Turk. karakulak f. kara black + kulak ear]

caracole /ˈkærəkəʊl/ n. & v. —n. a horse's half-turn to the right or left. —v. **1** intr. (of a horse or its rider) perform a caracole. **2** tr. make (a horse) caracole. [F]

caracul var. of KARAKUL.

carafe /kəˈræf, -rɑːf/ n. a glass container for water or wine, esp. at a table or bedside. [F f. It. caraffa, ult. f. Arab. ġarrāfa drinking vessel]

carambola /ˌkærəmˈbəʊlə/ n. **1** a small tree, Averrhoa carambola, native to SE Asia, bearing golden-yellow ribbed fruit. **2** this fruit. Also called star fruit. [Port., prob. of Indian or E. Indian orig.]

caramel /ˈkærəmel/ n. **1 a** a sugar or syrup heated until it turns brown, then used as a flavouring or to colour spirits etc. **b** a kind of soft toffee made with sugar, butter, etc., melted and further heated. **2** the light-brown colour of caramel. [F f. Sp. caramelo]

caramelize /ˈkærəməlaɪz/ v. (also **-ise**) **1 a** tr.

convert (sugar or syrup) into caramel. **b** intr. (of sugar or syrup) be converted into caramel. **2** tr. coat or cook (food) with caramelized sugar or syrup. □□ **caramelization** /-ˈzeɪʃ(ə)n/ n.

carapace /ˈkærəˌpeɪs/ n. the hard upper shell of a tortoise or a crustacean. [F f. Sp. carapacho]

carat /ˈkærət/ n. **1** a unit of weight for precious stones, now equivalent to 200 milligrams. **2** (US **karat**) a measure of purity of gold, pure gold being 24 carats. [F f. It. carato f. Arab. ḳīrāṭ weight of four grains, f. Gk keration fruit of the carob (dimin. of keras horn)]

caravan /ˈkærəˌvæn/ n. & v. —n. **1 a** Brit. a vehicle equipped for living in and usu. towed by a motor vehicle or a horse. **b** US a covered motor vehicle equipped for living in. **2** a company of merchants or pilgrims etc. travelling together, esp. across a desert in Asia or N. Africa. **3** a covered cart or carriage. —v.intr. (**caravanned**, **caravanning**) travel or live in a caravan. □**caravan site** (or **park**) a place where caravans are parked as dwellings, often with special amenities. □□ **caravanner** n. [F caravane f. Pers. kārwān]

caravanette /ˌkærəvæˈnet/ n. a motor vehicle with a caravan-like rear compartment for eating, sleeping, etc.

caravanserai /ˌkærəˈvænsəraɪ, -ˌraɪ/ n. an Eastern inn with a central court where caravans (see CARAVAN 2) may rest. [Pers. kārwānsarāy f. sarāy palace]

caravel /ˈkærəˌvel/ n. (also **carvel** /ˈkɑːv(ə)l/) hist. a small light fast ship, chiefly Spanish and Portuguese of the 15th-17th c. [F caravelle f. Port. caravela f. Gk karabos horned beetle, light ship]

caraway /ˈkærəˌweɪ/ n. an umbelliferous plant, Carum carvi, bearing clusters of tiny white flowers. □**caraway seed** its fruit used as flavouring and as a source of oil. [prob. OSp. alcarahueya f. Arab. alkarāwiyā, perh. f. Gk karon, kareon cumin]

carb /kɑːb/ n. colloq. a carburettor. [abbr.]

carbamate /ˈkɑːbəˌmeɪt/ n. Chem. a salt or ester of an amide of carbonic acid. [CARBONIC + AMIDE]

carbide /ˈkɑːbaɪd/ n. Chem. **1** a binary compound of carbon. **2** = calcium carbide.

carbine /ˈkɑːbaɪn/ n. a short firearm, usu. a rifle, orig. for cavalry use. [F carabine (this form also earlier in Engl.), weapon of the carabin mounted musketeer]

carbo- /ˈkɑːbəʊ/ comb. form carbon (carbohydrate; carbolic; carboxyl).

carbohydrate /ˌkɑːbəˈhaɪdreɪt/ n. Biochem. any of a large group of energy-producing organic compounds containing carbon, hydrogen, and oxygen, e.g. starch, glucose, and other sugars.

carbolic /kɑːˈbɒlɪk/ n. (in full **carbolic acid**) phenol, esp. when used as a disinfectant. □**carbolic soap** soap containing this. [CARBO- + -OL¹ + -IC]

carbon /ˈkɑːbən/ n. **1** a non-metallic element occurring naturally as diamond, graphite, and charcoal, and in all organic compounds. ¶ Symb.: **C**. **2 a** = carbon copy. **b** = carbon paper. **3** a rod of carbon in an arc lamp. □**carbon black** a fine carbon powder made by burning hydrocarbons in insufficient air. **carbon copy 1** a copy made with carbon paper. **2** a person or thing identical or similar to another (is a carbon copy of his father). **carbon cycle** Biol. the cycle in which carbon compounds are interconverted, usu. by living organisms. **carbon dating** the determination of the age of an organic object from the ratio of isotopes which changes as carbon-14 decays. **carbon dioxide** a colourless odourless gas occurring naturally in the atmosphere and formed by respiration. ¶ Chem. formula: CO_2. **carbon disulphide** a colourless liquid used as a solvent. ¶ Chem. formula: CS_2. **carbon fibre** a thin strong crystalline filament of carbon used as strengthening material in resins, ceramics, etc. **carbon-14** a long-lived radioactive carbon isotope of mass 14, used in radiocarbon dating, and as a tracer in biochemistry.

carbon monoxide a colourless odourless toxic gas formed by the incomplete burning of carbon. ¶ Chem. formula: CO. **carbon paper** a thin carbon-coated paper used for making (esp. typed) copies. **carbon steel** a steel with properties dependent on the percentage of carbon present. **carbon tetrachloride** a colourless volatile liquid used as a solvent. ¶ Chem. formula: CCl₄. **carbon-12** a carbon isotope of mass 12, used in calculations of atomic mass units. [F *carbone* f. L *carbo -onis* charcoal]

carbonaceous /ˌkɑːbəˈneɪʃəs/ *adj.* **1** consisting of or containing carbon. **2** of or like coal or charcoal.

carbonade /ˌkɑːbəˈneɪd/ *n.* a rich beef stew made with onions and beer. [F]

carbonado /ˌkɑːbəˈneɪdəʊ/ *n.* (*pl.* **-os**) a dark opaque or impure kind of diamond used as an abrasive, for drills etc. [Port.]

carbonate /ˈkɑːbəˌneɪt/ *n. & v.* — *n. Chem.* a salt of carbonic acid. — *v.tr.* **1** impregnate with carbon dioxide; aerate. **2** convert into a carbonate. □□ **carbonation** /-ˈneɪʃ(ə)n/ *n.* [F *carbonat* f. mod.L *carbonatum* (as CARBON)]

carbonic /kɑːˈbɒnɪk/ *adj. Chem.* containing carbon. □**carbonic acid** a very weak acid formed from carbon dioxide dissolved in water. **carbonic acid gas** *archaic* carbon dioxide.

carboniferous /ˌkɑːbəˈnɪfərəs/ *adj. & n.* — *adj.* **1** producing coal. **2** (**Carboniferous**) *Geol.* of or relating to the fifth period in the Palaeozoic era, with evidence of the first reptiles and extensive coal-forming swamp forests. ¶ Cf. Appendix II. — *n.* (**Carboniferous**) *Geol.* this period or system.

carbonize /ˈkɑːbəˌnaɪz/ *v.tr.* (also **-ise**) **1** convert into carbon by heating. **2** reduce to charcoal or coke. **3** coat with carbon. □□ **carbonization** /-ˈzeɪʃ(ə)n/ *n.*

carbonyl /ˈkɑːbəˌnaɪl/ *n.* (used *attrib.*) *Chem.* the divalent radical CO.

carborundum /ˌkɑːbəˈrʌndəm/ *n.* a compound of carbon and silicon used esp. as an abrasive. [CARBON + CORUNDUM]

carboxyl /kɑːˈbɒksɪl/ *n. Chem.* the univalent acid radical (– COOH), present in most organic acids. □□ **carboxylic** *adj.* [CARBON + OXYGEN + -YL]

carboy /ˈkɑːbɔɪ/ *n.* a large globular glass bottle usu. protected by a frame, for containing liquids. [Pers. *ḳarāba* large glass flagon]

carbuncle /ˈkɑːbʌŋk(ə)l/ *n.* **1** a severe abscess in the skin. **2** a bright red gem. □□ **carbuncular** /-ˈbʌŋkjʊlə(r)/ *adj.* [ME f. OF *charbucle* etc. f. L *carbunculus* small coal f. *carbo* coal]

carburation /ˌkɑːbjʊˈreɪʃ(ə)n/ *n.* the process of charging air with a spray of liquid hydrocarbon fuel, esp. in an internal-combustion engine. [as CARBURET]

carburet /ˌkɑːbjʊˈret/ *v.tr.* (**carburetted**, **carburetting**; *US* **carbureted**, **carbureting**) combine (a gas etc.) with carbon. [earlier *carbure* f. F f. L *carbo* (as CARBON)]

carburettor /ˌkɑːbjʊˈretə(r), ˌkɑːbə-/ *n.* (also **carburetter**; *US* **carburetor**) an apparatus for carburation of petrol and air in an internal-combustion engine. [as CARBURET + -OR¹]

carcajou /ˈkɑːkəˌdʒuː:, -kəˌʒuː/ *n. US* = WOLVERINE. [F, app. of Amer. Ind. orig.]

carcass /ˈkɑːkəs/ *n.* (also **carcase**) **1** the dead body of an animal, esp. a trunk for cutting up as meat. **2** the bones of a cooked bird. **3** *derog.* the human body, living or dead. **4** the skeleton, framework of a building, ship, etc. **5** worthless remains. □**carcass meat** raw meat, not preserved. [ME f. AF *carcois* (OF *charcois*) & f. F *carcasse*: ult. orig. unkn.]

carcinogen /kɑːˈsɪnədʒ(ə)n/ *n.* any substance that produces cancer. [as CARCINOMA + -GEN]

carcinogenesis /ˌkɑːsɪnəˈdʒenɪsɪs/ *n.* the production of cancer.

carcinogenic /ˌkɑːsɪnəˈdʒenɪk/ *adj.* producing cancer. □□ **carcinogenicity** /-ˈnɪsɪtɪ/ *n.*

carcinoma /ˌkɑːsɪˈnəʊmə/ *n.* (*pl.* **carcinomata** /-tə/

or **carcinomas**) a cancer, esp. one arising in epithelial tissue. □□ **carcinomatous** *adj.* [L f. Gk *karkinōma* f. *karkinos* crab]

card¹ /kɑːd/ *n. & v.* — *n.* **1** thick stiff paper or thin pasteboard. **2 a** a flat piece of this, esp. for writing or printing on. **b** = POSTCARD. **c** a card used to send greetings, issue an invitation, etc. (*birthday card*). **d** = *visiting-card*. **e** = *business card*. **f** a ticket of admission or membership. **3 a** = PLAYING-CARD. **b** a similar card in a set designed for particular games, e.g. happy families. **c** (in *pl.*) card-playing; a card-game. **4** (in *pl.*) *colloq.* an employee's documents, esp. for tax and national insurance, held by the employer. **5 a** a programme of events at a race-meeting etc. **b** *Cricket* a score-card. **c** a list of holes on a golf course, on which a player's scores are entered. **6** *colloq.* a person, esp. an odd or amusing one (*what a card!*; *a knowing card*). **7** a plan or expedient (*sure card*). **8** a printed or written notice, set of rules, etc., for display. **9** a small rectangular piece of plastic issued by a bank, building society, etc., with personal (often machine-readable) data on it, chiefly to obtain cash or credit (*cheque card*; *credit card*; *do you have a card?*). — *v.tr.* **1** fix to a card. **2** write on a card, esp. for indexing. □**ask for** (or **get**) **one's cards** ask (or be told) to leave one's employment. **card-carrying** being a registered member of an organization, esp. a political party or trade union. **card-game** a game in which playing-cards are used. **card index** an index in which each item is entered on a separate card. **card-index** *v.tr.* make a card index of. **card-playing** the playing of card-games. **card-sharp** (or **-sharper**) a swindler at card-games. **card-table** a table for card-playing, esp. a folding one. **card up one's sleeve** a plan in reserve. **card vote** *US* a block vote, esp. in trade-union meetings. **on** (*US* **in**) **the cards** possible or likely. **put** (or **lay**) **one's cards on the table** reveal one's resources, intentions, etc. [ME f. OF *carte* f. L *charta* f. Gk *khartēs* papyrus-leaf]

card² /kɑːd/ *n. & v.* — *n.* a toothed instrument, wire brush, etc., for raising a nap on cloth or for disentangling fibres before spinning. — *v.tr.* brush, comb, cleanse, or scratch with a card. □**carding-wool** short-stapled wool. □□ **carder** *n.* [ME f. OF *carde* f. Prov. *carda* f. *cardar* tease, comb, ult. f. L *carere* card]

Card. *abbr.* Cardinal.

cardamom /ˈkɑːdəməm/ *n.* (also **cardamum**) **1** an aromatic SE Asian plant, *Elettaria cardamomum*. **2** the seed-capsules of this used as a spice. [L *cardamomum* or F *cardamome* f. Gk *kardamōmon* f. *kardamon* cress + *amōmon* a spice plant]

cardan joint /ˈkɑːd(ə)n/ *n. Engin.* a universal joint. [G. *Cardano*, It. mathematician d. 1576]

cardan shaft /ˈkɑːd(ə)n/ *n. Engin.* a shaft with a universal joint at one or both ends.

cardboard /ˈkɑːdbɔːd/ *n. & adj.* — *n.* pasteboard or stiff paper, esp. for making cards or boxes. — *adj.* **1** made of cardboard. **2** flimsy, insubstantial.

cardiac /ˈkɑːdɪˌæk/ *adj. & n.* — *adj.* **1** of or relating to the heart. **2** of or relating to the part of the stomach nearest the oesophagus. — *n.* a person with heart disease. [F *cardiaque* or L *cardiacus* f. Gk *kardiakos* f. *kardia* heart]

cardie var. of CARDY.

cardigan /ˈkɑːdɪgən/ *n.* a knitted jacket fastening down the front, usu. with long sleeves. [named after the 7th Earl of *Cardigan* d. 1868]

cardinal /ˈkɑːdɪn(ə)l/ *n. & adj.* — *n.* **1** (as a title **Cardinal**) a leading dignitary of the RC Church, one of the college electing the Pope. **2** any small American songbird of the genus *Richmondena*, the males of which have scarlet plumage. **3** *hist.* a woman's cloak, orig. of scarlet cloth with a hood. — *adj.* **1** chief, fundamental; on which something hinges. **2** of deep scarlet (like a cardinal's cassock). □**cardinal-flower** the scarlet lobelia. **cardinal humour** see HUMOUR.

cardinal numbers those denoting quantity (one, two, three, etc.), as opposed to ordinal numbers (first, second, third, etc.). **cardinal points** the four main points of the compass (N., S., E., W.). **cardinal virtues** the chief moral attributes: justice, prudence, temperance, and fortitude. □□ **cardinalate** /-ˌleɪt/ n. (in sense 1 of n.). **cardinally** adv. **cardinalship** n. (in sense 1 of n.). [ME f. OF f. L cardinalis f. cardo -inis hinge: in Eng. first applied to the four virtues on which conduct 'hinges']

cardio- /ˈkɑːdɪəʊ/ comb. form heart (cardiogram; cardiology). [Gk kardia heart]

cardiogram /ˈkɑːdɪəʊˌgræm/ n. a record of muscle activity within the heart, made by a cardiograph.

cardiograph /ˈkɑːdɪəʊˌgrɑːf/ n. an instrument for recording heart muscle activity. □□ **cardiographer** /-ˈɒgrəfə(r)/ n. **cardiography** /-ˈɒgrəfɪ/ n.

cardiology /ˌkɑːdɪˈɒlədʒɪ/ n. the branch of medicine concerned with diseases and abnormalities of the heart. □□ **cardiologist** n.

cardiovascular /ˌkɑːdɪəʊˈvæskjʊlə(r)/ adj. of or relating to the heart and blood vessels.

cardoon /kɑːˈduːn/ n. a thistle-like plant, Cynara cardunculus, allied to the globe artichoke, with leaves used as a vegetable. [F cardon ult. f. L cardu(u)s thistle]

cardphone /ˈkɑːdfəʊn/ n. a public telephone operated by the insertion of a prepaid plastic machine-readable card instead of money.

cardy /ˈkɑːdɪ/ n. (also **cardie**) (pl. -ies) colloq. a cardigan. [abbr.]

care /keə(r)/ n. & v. —n. **1** worry, anxiety. **2** an occasion for this. **3** serious attention; heed, caution, pains (assembled with care; handle with care). **4** a protection, charge. **b** Brit. = child care. **5** a thing to be done or seen to. —v.intr. **1** (usu. foll. by about, for, whether) feel concern or interest. **2** (usu. foll. by for, about, and with neg. expressed or implied) feel liking, affection, regard, or deference (don't care for jazz). **3** (foll. by to + infin.) wish or be willing (should not care to be seen with him; would you care to join them?). □ **care for** provide for; look after. **care-label** a label attached to clothing, with instructions for washing etc. **care of** at the address of (sent it care of his sister). **for all one cares** colloq. denoting uninterest or unconcern (for all I care they can leave tomorrow; I could be dying for all you care). **have a care** take care; be careful. **I** (etc.) **couldn't** (US **could**) **care less** colloq. an expression of complete indifference. **in care** Brit. (of a child) taken into the care of a local authority. **take care 1** be careful. **2** (foll. by to + infin.) not fail or neglect. **take care of 1** look after; keep safe. **2** deal with. **3** dispose of. [OE caru, carian, f. Gmc]

careen /kəˈriːn/ v. **1** tr. turn (a ship) on one side for cleaning, caulking, or repair. **2 a** intr. tilt; lean over. **b** tr. cause to do this. **3** intr. US swerve about; career. ¶ Sense 3 is infl. by career (v.). □□ **careenage** n. [earlier as noun, = careened position of ship, f. F carène f. It. carena f. L carina keel]

career /kəˈrɪə(r)/ n. & v. —n. **1 a** one's advancement through life, esp. in a profession. **b** the progress through history of a group or institution. **2 a** profession or occupation, esp. as offering advancement. **3** (attrib.) a pursuing or wishing to pursue a career (career woman). **b** working permanently in a specified profession (career diplomat). **4** swift course; impetus (in full career). —v.intr. **1** move or swerve about wildly. **2** go swiftly. [F carrière f. It. carriera ult. f. L carrus CAR]

careerist /kəˈrɪərɪst/ n. a person predominantly concerned with personal advancement.

carefree /ˈkeəfriː/ adj. free from anxiety or responsibility; light-hearted. □□ **carefreeness** n.

careful /ˈkeəfʊl/ adj. **1** painstaking, thorough. **2** cautious. **3** done with care and attention. **4** (usu. foll. by that + clause, or to + infin.) taking care; not neglecting. **5** (foll. by for, of) concerned for; taking

care of. □□ **carefully** adv. **carefulness** n. [OE carful (as CARE, -FUL)]

careless /ˈkeəlɪs/ adj. **1** not taking care or paying attention. **2** unthinking, insensitive. **3** done without care; inaccurate. **4** light-hearted. **5** (foll. by of) not concerned about; taking no heed of. **6** effortless. □□ **carelessly** adv. **carelessness** n. [OE carlēas (as CARE, -LESS)]

carer /ˈkeərə(r)/ n. a person who cares for a sick or elderly person.

caress /kəˈres/ v. & n. —v.tr. **1** touch or stroke gently or lovingly; kiss. **2** treat fondly or kindly. —n. a loving or gentle touch or kiss. [F caresse (n.), caresser (v.), f. It. carezza ult. f. L carus dear]

caret /ˈkærət/ n. a mark (∧, ⋏) indicating a proposed insertion in printing or writing. [L, = is lacking]

caretaker /ˈkeəˌteɪkə(r)/ n. **1** a person employed to look after something, esp. a house in the owner's absence, or Brit. a public building. **2** (attrib.) exercising temporary authority (caretaker government).

careworn /ˈkeəwɔːn/ adj. showing the effects of prolonged worry.

carfare /ˈkɑːfeə(r)/ n. US a passenger's fare to travel by bus.

cargo /ˈkɑːgəʊ/ n. (pl. -oes or -os) **1** goods carried on a ship or aircraft. **2** US goods carried in a motor vehicle. □ **cargo cult** (orig. in the Pacific Islands) a belief in the forthcoming arrival of ancestral spirits bringing cargoes of food and other goods. [Sp. (as CHARGE)]

carhop /ˈkɑːhɒp/ n. US colloq. a waiter at a drive-in restaurant.

cariama var. of SERIEMA.

Carib /ˈkærɪb/ n. & adj. —n. **1** an aboriginal inhabitant of the southern W. Indies or the adjacent coasts. **2** the language of this people. —adj. of or relating to this people. [Sp. Caribe f. Haitian]

Caribbean /ˌkærɪˈbiːən, kəˈrɪbɪən/ n. & adj. —n. the part of the Atlantic between the southern W. Indies and Central America. —adj. **1** of or relating to this region. **2** of the Caribs or their language or culture.

caribou /ˈkærɪˌbuː/ n. (pl. same) a N. American reindeer. [Can. F, prob. f. Amer. Ind.]

caricature /ˈkærɪkətjʊə(r)/ n. & v. —n. **1** a grotesque usu. comic representation of a person by exaggeration of characteristic traits, in a picture, writing, or mime. **2** a ridiculously poor or absurd imitation or version. —v.tr. make or give a caricature of. □□ **caricatural** adj. **caricaturist** n. [F f. It. caricatura f. caricare load, exaggerate: see CHARGE]

caries /ˈkeərɪːz, -rɪˌiːz/ n. (pl. same) decay and crumbling of a tooth or bone. [L]

carillon /kəˈrɪljən, ˈkærɪljən/ n. **1** a set of bells sounded either from a keyboard or mechanically. **2** a tune played on bells. **3** an organ-stop imitating a peal of bells. [F f. OF quarregnon peal of four bells, alt. of Rmc quaternio f. L quattuor four]

carina /kəˈriːnə/ n. Biol. a keel-shaped structure, esp. the ridge of a bird's breastbone. □□ **carinal** adj. [L, = keel]

carinate /ˈkærɪˌneɪt/ adj. (of a bird) having a keeled breastbone (opp. RATITE). [L carinatus keeled f. carina keel]

caring /ˈkeərɪŋ/ adj. compassionate, esp. with reference to the professional care of the sick or elderly.

carioca /ˌkærɪˈəʊkə/ n. **1 a** a Brazilian dance like the samba. **b** the music for this. **2** a native of Rio de Janeiro. [Port.]

cariogenic /ˌkeərɪəʊˈdʒenɪk/ adj. causing caries.

carious /ˈkeərɪəs/ adj. (of bones or teeth) decayed. [L cariosus]

carking /ˈkɑːkɪŋ/ adj. archaic burdensome (carking care). [part. f. obs. cark (v.) f. ONF carkier f. Rmc, rel. to CHARGE]

carl /kɑːl/ n. Sc. a man; a fellow. [OE f. ON karl, rel. to CHURL]

carline /ˈkɑːlɪn/ n. any plant of the genus Carlina,

esp. the thistle-like *C. vulgaris*. [F f. med.L *carlina* perh. for *cardina* (L *carduus* thistle), assoc. with *Carolus Magnus* Charlemagne]

carload /'kɑːləʊd/ *n.* **1 a** quantity that can be carried in a car. **2** *US* the minimum quantity of goods for which a lower rate is charged for transport.

Carlovingian var. of CAROLINGIAN.

carman /'kɑːmæn/ *n.* *US* **1** the driver of a van. **2** a carrier.

Carmelite /'kɑːmɪˌlaɪt/ *n. & adj.* —*n.* **1** a friar of the Order of Our Lady of Mount Carmel, following a rule of extreme asceticism. **2** a nun of a similar order. —*adj.* of or relating to the Carmelites. [F *Carmelite* or med.L *carmelita* f. Mt. *Carmel* in Palestine, where the order was founded in the 12th c.]

carminative /'kɑːmɪnətɪv/ *adj. & n.* —*adj.* relieving flatulence. —*n.* a carminative drug. [F *carminatif* -*ive* or med.L *carminare* heal (by incantation): see CHARM]

carmine /'kɑːmaɪn/ *adj. & n.* —*adj.* of a vivid crimson colour. —*n.* **1** this colour. **2** a vivid crimson pigment made from cochineal. [F *carmin* or med.L *carminium* perh. f. *carmesinum* crimson + *minium* cinnabar]

carnage /'kɑːnɪdʒ/ *n.* great slaughter, esp. of human beings in battle. [F f. It. *carnaggio* f. med.L *carnaticum* f. L *caro carnis* flesh]

carnal /'kɑːn(ə)l/ *adj.* **1** of the body or flesh; worldly. **2** sensual, sexual. ▫**carnal knowledge** *Law* sexual intercourse. ▫▫**carnality** /-'nælɪtɪ/ *n.* **carnalize** *v.tr.* (also -**ise**). **carnally** *adv.* [ME f. LL *carnalis* f. *caro carnis* flesh]

carnassial /kɑː'næsɪəl/ *adj. & n.* —*adj.* (of a carnivore's upper premolar and lower molar teeth) adapted for shearing flesh. —*n.* such a tooth. Also called SECTORIAL. [F *carnassier* carnivorous]

carnation[1] /kɑː'neɪʃ(ə)n/ *n.* **1** any of several cultivated varieties of clove-scented pink, with variously coloured showy flowers (see also CLOVE[1] 2). **2** this flower. [orig. uncert.: in early use varying with *coronation*]

carnation[2] /kɑː'neɪʃ(ə)n/ *n. & adj.* —*n.* a rosy pink colour. —*adj.* of this colour. [F f. It. *carnagione* ult. f. L *caro carnis* flesh]

carnauba /kɑː'naʊbə, -'nɔːbə, -'naʊbə/ *n.* **1** a fan palm, *Copernicia cerifera*, native to NE Brazil. **2** (in full **carnauba wax**) the yellowish leaf-wax of this tree used as a polish etc. [Port.]

carnelian var. of CORNELIAN.

carnet /'kɑːneɪ/ *n.* **1** a customs permit to take a motor vehicle across a frontier for a limited period. **2** a permit allowing use of a camp-site. [F, = notebook]

carnival /'kɑːnɪv(ə)l/ *n.* **1 a** the festivities usual during the period before Lent in Roman Catholic countries. **b** any festivities, esp. those occurring at a regular date. **2** merrymaking, revelry. **3** *US* a travelling funfair or circus. [It. *carne-*, *carnovale* f. med.L *carnelevarium* etc. Shrovetide f. L *caro carnis* flesh + *levare* put away]

carnivore /'kɑːnɪˌvɔː(r)/ *n.* **1 a** any mammal of the order Carnivora, with powerful jaws and teeth adapted for stabbing, tearing, and eating flesh, including cats, dogs, and bears. **b** any other flesh-eating mammal. **2** any flesh-eating plant.

carnivorous /kɑː'nɪvərəs/ *adj.* **1** (of an animal) feeding on flesh. **2** (of a plant) digesting trapped insects or other animal substances. **3** of or relating to the order Carnivora. ▫▫**carnivorously** *adv.* **carnivorousness** *n.* [L *carnivorus* f. *caro carnis* flesh + -VOROUS]

carob /'kærəb/ *n.* **1** (in full **carob-tree**) an evergreen tree, *Ceratonia siliqua*, native to the Mediterranean, bearing edible pods. **2** its bean-shaped edible seed pod sometimes used as a substitute for chocolate. [obs. F *carobe* f. med.L *carrubia*, -*um* f. Arab. *ḳarrūba*]

carol /'kær(ə)l/ *n. & v.* —*n.* a joyous song, esp. a

Christmas hymn. —*v.* (**carolled, carolling**; *US* **caroled, caroling**) **1** *intr.* sing carols, esp. outdoors at Christmas. **2** *tr. & intr.* sing joyfully. ▫▫**caroler** *n.* (also **caroller**). [ME f. OF *carole, caroler*, of unkn. orig.]

Caroline /'kærəˌlaɪn/ *adj.* **1** (also **Carolean** /-'liːən/) of the time of Charles I or II of England. **2** = CAROLINGIAN *adj.* 2. [L *Carolus* Charles]

Carolingian /ˌkærə'lɪndʒɪən/ *adj. & n.* (also **Carlovingian** /ˌkɑːlə'vɪndʒɪən/) —*adj.* **1** of or relating to the second Frankish dynasty, founded by Charlemagne (d. 814). **2** of a style of script developed in France at the time of the Charlemagne. —*n.* **1** a member of the Carolingian dynasty. **2** the Carolingian style of script. [F *carlovingien* f. *Karl* Charles after *mérovingien* (see MEROVINGIAN): reformed after L *Carolus*]

carom /'kærəm/ *n. & v.* *US Billiards* —*n.* a cannon. —*v.intr.* **1** make a carom. **2** (usu. foll. by *off*) strike and rebound. [abbr. of *carambole* f. Sp. *carambola*]

carotene /'kærəˌtiːn/ *n.* any of several orange-coloured plant pigments found in carrots, tomatoes, etc., acting as a source of vitamin A. [G *Carotin* f. L *carota* CARROT]

carotenoid /kə'rɒtɪˌnɔɪd/ *n.* any of a group of yellow, orange, or brown pigments giving characteristic colour to plant organs, e.g. ripe tomatoes, carrots, autumn leaves, etc.

carotid /kə'rɒtɪd/ *n. & adj.* —*n.* each of the two main arteries carrying blood to the head and neck. —*adj.* of or relating to either of these arteries. [F *carotide* or mod.L *carotides* f. Gk *karōtides* (pl.) f. *karoō* stupefy (compression of these arteries being thought to cause stupor)]

carouse /kə'raʊz/ *v. & n.* —*v.intr.* **1** have a noisy or lively drinking-party. **2** drink heavily. —*n.* a noisy or lively drinking-party. ▫▫**carousal** *n.* **carouser** *n.* [orig. as adv. = right out, in phr. *drink carouse* f. G *gar aus trinken*]

carousel /ˌkærə'sel, -'zel/ *n.* (*US* **carrousel**) **1** *US* a merry-go-round or roundabout. **2** a rotating delivery or conveyor system, esp. for passengers' luggage at an airport. **3** *hist.* a kind of equestrian tournament. [F *carrousel* f. It. *carosello*]

carp[1] /kɑːp/ *n.* (*pl.* same) any freshwater fish of the family Cyprinidae, esp. *Cyprinus carpio*, often bred for use as food. [ME f. OF *carpe* f. Prov. or f. LL *carpa*]

carp[2] /kɑːp/ *v.intr.* (usu. foll. by *at*) find fault; complain pettily. ▫▫**carper** *n.* [obs. ME senses 'talk, say, sing' f. ON *karpa* to brag: mod. sense (16th c.) from or infl. by L *carpere* pluck at, slander]

carpal /'kɑːp(ə)l/ *adj. & n.* —*adj.* of or relating to the bones in the wrist. —*n.* any of the bones forming the wrist. [CARPUS + -AL]

carpel /'kɑːp(ə)l/ *n.* *Bot.* the female reproductive organ of a flower, consisting of a stigma, style, and ovary. ▫▫**carpellary** *adj.* [F *carpelle* or mod.L *carpellum* f. Gk *karpos* fruit]

carpenter /'kɑːpɪntə(r)/ *n. & v.* —*n.* a person skilled in woodwork, esp. of a structural kind (cf. JOINER). —*v.* **1** *intr.* do carpentry. **2** *tr.* make by means of carpentry. **3** *tr.* (often foll. by *together*) construct; fit together. ▫**carpenter ant** any large ant of the genus *Camponotus*, boring into wood to nest. **carpenter bee** any of various solitary bees, which bore into wood. [ME & AF; OF *carpentier* f. LL *carpentarius* f. *carpentum* wagon f. Gaulish]

carpentry /'kɑːpɪntrɪ/ *n.* **1** the work or occupation of a carpenter. **2** timber-work constructed by a carpenter. [ME f. OF *carpenterie* f. L *carpentaria*: see CARPENTER]

carpet /'kɑːpɪt/ *n. & v.* —*n.* **1 a** thick fabric for covering a floor or stairs. **b** a piece of this fabric. **2** an expanse or layer resembling a carpet in being smooth, soft, bright, or thick (*carpet of snow*). —*v.tr.* (**carpeted, carpeting**) **1** cover with or as with a carpet. **2** *colloq.* reprimand, reprove. ▫**carpet-bag** a travelling-bag of a kind orig. made of carpet-like material. **carpet-bagger 1** esp. *US* a political candidate in an area where the candidate has no local connections (orig. a northerner in the southern US after the Civil War). **2** an unscrupulous opportunist. **carpet bombing** intensive bombing. **carpet slipper** a kind of slipper with the upper made orig. of carpet-like material. **carpet-sweeper** a household implement with a revolving brush or brushes for sweeping carpets. **on the carpet 1** *colloq.* being reprimanded. **2** under consideration. **sweep under the carpet** conceal (a problem or difficulty) in the hope that it will be forgotten. [ME f. OF *carpite* or med.L *carpita*, f. obs. It. *carpita* woollen counterpane, ult. f. L *carpere* pluck, pull to pieces]

carpeting /ˈkɑːpɪtɪŋ/ *n.* **1** material for carpets. **2** carpets collectively.

carpology /kɑːˈpɒlədʒɪ/ *n.* the study of the structure of fruit and seeds. [Gk *karpos* fruit]

carport /ˈkɑːpɔːt/ *n.* a shelter with a roof and open sides for a car, usu. beside a house.

carpus /ˈkɑːpəs/ *n.* (*pl.* **carpi** /-paɪ/) the small bones between the forelimb and metacarpus in terrestrial vertebrates, forming the wrist in humans. [mod.L f. Gk *karpos* wrist]

carrack /ˈkærək/ *n. hist.* a large armed merchantship. [ME f. F *caraque* f. Sp. *carraca* f. Arab. *ḳarāḳir*]

carrageen /ˈkærəˌgiːn/ *n.* (also **carragheen**) an edible red seaweed, *Chondrus crispus*, of the N. hemisphere. Also called *Irish moss*. [orig. uncert.: perh. f. Ir. *cosáinín carraige* carrageen, lit. 'little stem of the rock']

carrel /ˈkær(ə)l/ *n.* **1** a small cubicle for a reader in a library. **2** *hist.* a small enclosure or study in a cloister. [OF *carole*, med.L *carola*, of unkn. orig.]

carriage /ˈkærɪdʒ/ *n.* **1** *Brit.* a railway passenger vehicle. **2** a wheeled passenger vehicle, esp. one with four wheels and pulled by horses. **3 a** the conveying of goods. **b** the cost of this (*carriage paid*). **4** the part of a machine (e.g. a typewriter) that carries other parts into the required position. **5** a gun-carriage. **6** a manner of carrying oneself; one's bearing or deportment. □**carriage and pair** a carriage with two horses pulling it. **carriage clock** a portable clock in a rectangular case with a handle on top. **carriage-dog** a dalmatian. [ME f. ONF *cariage* f. *carier* CARRY]

carriageway /ˈkærɪdʒweɪ/ *n. Brit.* the part of a road intended for vehicles.

carrick bend /ˈkærɪk/ *n. Naut.* a kind of knot used to join ropes. [BEND² : *carrick* perh. f. CARRACK]

carrier /ˈkærɪə(r)/ *n.* **1** a person or thing that carries. **2** a person or company undertaking to convey goods or passengers for payment. **3** = *carrier bag*. **4** a part of a bicycle etc. for carrying luggage or a passenger. **5** a person or animal that may transmit a disease or a hereditary characteristic without suffering from or displaying it. **6** = *aircraft-carrier*. **7** a substance used to support or convey a pigment, a catalyst, radioactive material, etc. **8** *Physics* a mobile electron or hole that carries a charge in a semiconductor. □**carrier bag** *Brit.* a disposable plastic or paper bag with handles. **carrier pigeon** a pigeon trained to carry messages tied to its neck or leg. **carrier wave** a high-frequency electromagnetic wave modulated in amplitude or frequency to convey a signal.

carriole /ˈkærɪˌəʊl/ *n.* **1** a small open carriage for one. **2** a covered light cart. **3** a Canadian sledge. [F f. It. *carriuola*, dimin. of *carro* CAR]

carrion /ˈkærɪən/ *n. & adj.* —*n.* **1** dead putrefying flesh. **2** something vile or filthy. —*adj.* rotten, loathsome. □**carrion crow** a black crow, *Corvus corone*, native to Europe, feeding mainly on carrion. **carrion flower** = STAPELIA. [ME f. AF & ONF *caroine*, -*oigne*, OF *charoigne* ult. f. L *caro* flesh]

carrot /ˈkærət/ *n.* **1 a** an umbelliferous plant, *Daucus carota*, with a tapering orange-coloured root. **b** this root as a vegetable. **2** a means of enticement or

persuasion. **3** (in *pl.*) *sl.* a red-haired person. □□ **carroty** *adj.* [F *carotte* f. L *carota* f. Gk *karōton*]

carrousel *US* var. of CAROUSEL.

carry /ˈkærɪ/ *v. & n.* —*v.* (**-ies, -ied**) **1** *tr.* support or hold up, esp. while moving. **2** *tr.* convey with one from one place to another. **3** *tr.* have on one's person (*carry a watch*). **4** *tr.* conduct or transmit (*pipe carries water*; *wire carries electric current*). **5** *tr.* take (a process etc.) to a specified point (*carry into effect*; *carry a joke too far*). **6** *tr.* (foll. by *to*) continue or prolong (*carry modesty to excess*). **7** *tr.* involve, imply; have as a feature or consequence (*carries a two-year guarantee*; *principles carry consequences*). **8** *tr.* (in reckoning) transfer (a figure) to a column of higher value. **9** *tr.* hold in a specified way (*carry oneself erect*). **10** *tr.* **a** (of a newspaper or magazine) publish; include in its contents, esp. regularly. **b** (of a radio or television station) broadcast, esp. regularly. **11** *tr.* (of a retailing outlet) keep a regular stock of (particular goods for sale) (*have stopped carrying that brand*). **12** *intr.* **a** (of sound, esp. a voice) be audible at a distance. **b** (of a missile) travel, penetrate. **13** *tr.* (of a gun etc.) propel to a specified distance. **14** *tr.* **a** win victory or acceptance for (a proposal etc.). **b** win acceptance from (*carried the audience with them*). **c** win, capture (a prize, a fortress, etc.). **d** *US* gain (a State or district) in an election. **e** *Golf* cause the ball to pass beyond (a bunker etc.). **15** *tr.* **a** endure the weight of; support (*columns carry the dome*). **b** be the chief cause of the effectiveness of; be the driving force in (*you carry the sales department*). **16** *tr.* be pregnant with (*is carrying twins*). **17** *tr.* **a** (of a motive, money, etc.) cause or enable (a person) to go to a specified place. **b** (of a journey) bring (a person) to a specified point. —*n.* (*pl.* **-ies**) **1** an act of carrying. **2** *Golf* the distance a ball travels before reaching the ground. **3** a portage between rivers etc. **4** the range of a gun etc. □**carry-all 1** a light carriage (cf. CARRIOLE). **2** *US* a car with seats placed sideways. **3** *US* a large bag or case. **carry all before one** succeed; overcome all opposition. **carry away 1** remove. **2** inspire; affect emotionally or spiritually. **3** deprive of self-control (*got carried away*). **4** *Naut.* **a** lose (a mast etc.) by breakage. **b** break off or away. **carry back** take (a person) back in thought to a past time. **carry one's bat** *Cricket* be not out at the end of a side's completed innings. **carry the can** *colloq.* bear the responsibility or blame. **carry conviction** be convincing. **carry-cot** a portable cot for a baby. **carry the day** be victorious or successful. **carry forward** transfer to a new page or account. **carrying-on** (or **carryings-on**) = *carry-on*. **carrying-trade** the conveying of goods from one country to another by water or air as a business. **carry it off** (or **carry it off well**) do well under difficulties. **carry off 1** take away, esp. by force. **2** win (a prize). **3** (esp. of a disease) kill. **4** render acceptable or passable. **carry on 1** continue (*carry on eating*; *carry on, don't mind me*). **2** engage in (a conversation or a business). **3** *colloq.* behave strangely or excitedly. **4** (often foll. by *with*) *colloq.* flirt or have a love affair. **5** advance (a process) by a stage. **carry-on** *n. Brit. sl.* **1** a state of excitement or fuss. **2** a questionable piece of behaviour. **3** a flirtation or love affair. **carry out** put (ideas, instructions, etc.) into practice. **carry-out** *attrib.adj. & n.* esp. *Sc. & US* = *take-away*. **carry over 1** = *carry forward*. **2** postpone (work etc.). **3** *Stock Exch.* keep over to the next settling-day. **carry-over** *n.* something carried over. **2** *Stock Exch.* postponement to the next settling-day. **carry through 1** complete successfully. **2** bring safely out of difficulties. **carry weight** be influential or important. **carry with one** bear in mind. [ME f. AF & ONF *carier* (as CAR)]

carse /kɑːs/ *n. Sc.* fertile lowland beside a river. [ME, perh. f. *carrs* swamps]

carsick /ˈkɑːsɪk/ *adj.* affected with nausea caused by the motion of a car. □□ **carsickness** *n.*

cart /kɑːt/ n. & v. —n. **1** a strong vehicle with two or four wheels for carrying loads, usu. drawn by a horse. **2** a light vehicle for pulling by hand. **3** a light vehicle with two wheels for driving in, drawn by a single horse. —v.tr. **1** convey in or as in a cart. **2** sl. carry (esp. a cumbersome thing) with difficulty or over a long distance (carted it all the way home). □cart-horse a thickset horse suitable for heavy work. cart-load **1** an amount filling a cart. **2** a large quantity of anything. cart off remove, esp. by force. cart-track (or -road) a track or road too rough for ordinary vehicles. cart-wright a maker of carts. in the cart sl. in trouble or difficulty. put the cart before the horse **1** reverse the proper order or procedure. **2** take an effect for a cause. □□ carter n. cartful n. (pl. -fuls). [ME f. ON kartr cart & OE cræt, prob. infl. by AF & ONF carete dimin. of carre CAR]

cartage /'kɑːtɪdʒ/ n. the price paid for carting.

carte var. of QUART 4.

carte blanche /kɑːt 'blɑ̃ʃ/ n. full discretionary power given to a person. [F, = blank paper]

cartel /kɑː'tel/ n. **1** an informal association of manufacturers or suppliers to maintain prices at a high level, and control production, marketing arrangements, etc. **2** a political combination between parties. □□ cartelize /'kɑːtəˌlaɪz/ v.tr. & intr. (also -ise). [G Kartell f. F cartel f. It. cartello dimin. of carta CARD¹]

Cartesian /kɑː'tiːzjən, -ʒ(ə)n/ adj. & n. —adj. of or relating to R. Descartes, 17th-c. French philosopher and mathematician. —n. a follower of Descartes. □Cartesian coordinates a system for locating a point by reference to its distance from two or three axes intersecting at right angles. □□ Cartesianism n. [mod.L Cartesianus f. Cartesius, name of Descartes]

Carthusian /kɑː'θjuːzjən/ n. & adj. —n. a monk of a contemplative order founded by St Bruno in 1084. —adj. of or relating to this order. [med.L Carthusianus f. L Cart(h)usia Chartreuse, near Grenoble]

cartilage /'kɑːtɪlɪdʒ/ n. gristle, a firm flexible connective tissue forming the infant skeleton, which is mainly replaced by bone in adulthood. □□ cartilaginoid /-'lædʒɪˌnɔɪd/ adj. cartilaginous /-'lædʒɪnəs/ adj. [F f. L cartilago -ginis]

cartogram /'kɑːtəˌgræm/ n. a map with diagrammatic statistical information. [F cartogramme f. carte map, card]

cartography /kɑː'tɒgrəfɪ/ n. the science or practice of map-drawing. □□ cartographer n. cartographic /-tə'græfɪk/ adj. cartographical /-tə'græfɪk(ə)l/ adj. [F cartographie f. carte map, card]

cartomancy /'kɑːtəˌmænsɪ/ n. fortune-telling by interpreting a random selection of playing-cards. [F cartomancie f. carte CARD¹]

carton /'kɑːt(ə)n/ n. a light box or container, esp. one made of cardboard. [F (as CARTOON)]

cartoon /kɑː'tuːn/ n. & v. —n. **1** a humorous drawing in a newspaper, magazine, etc., esp. as a topical comment. **2** a sequence of drawings, often with speech indicated, telling a story (strip cartoon). **3** a filmed sequence of drawings using the technique of animation. **4** a full-size drawing on stout paper as an artist's preliminary design for a painting, tapestry, mosaic, etc. —v. **1** tr. draw a cartoon of. **2** intr. draw cartoons. □□ cartoonist n. [It. cartone f. carta CARD¹]

cartouche /kɑː'tuːʃ/ n. **1 a** Archit. a scroll-like ornament, e.g. the volute of an Ionic capital. **b** a tablet imitating, or a drawing of, a scroll with rolled-up ends, used ornamentally or bearing an inscription. **c** an ornate frame. **2** Archaeol. an oval ring enclosing Egyptian hieroglyphs, usu. representing the name and title of a king. [F, = cartridge, f. It. cartoccio f. carta CARD¹]

cartridge /'kɑːtrɪdʒ/ n. **1** a case containing a charge of propelling explosive for firearms or blasting, with a bullet or shot if for small arms. **2** a spool of film, magnetic tape, etc., in a sealed container ready for

insertion. **3** a component carrying the stylus on the pick-up head of a record-player. **4** an ink-container for insertion in a pen. □cartridge-belt a belt with pockets or loops for cartridges (in sense 1). cartridge paper thick rough paper used for cartridges, for drawing, and for strong envelopes. [corrupt. of CARTOUCHE (but recorded earlier)]

cartwheel /'kɑːtwiːl/ n. **1** the (usu. spoked) wheel of a cart. **2** a circular sideways handspring with the arms and legs extended.

caruncle /'kærəŋk(ə)l, kə'rʌŋk(ə)l/ n. **1** Zool. a fleshy excrescence, e.g. a turkeycock's wattles or the red prominence at the inner angle of the eye. **2** Bot. an outgrowth from a seed near the micropyle. □□ caruncular /-kjʊlə(r)/ adj. [obs. F f. L caruncula f. caro carnis flesh]

carve /kɑːv/ v. **1** tr. produce or shape (a statue, representation in relief, etc.) by cutting into a hard material (carved a figure out of rock; carved it in wood). **2** tr. **a** cut patterns, designs, letters, etc. in (hard material). **b** (foll. by into) form a pattern, design, etc., from (carved it into a bust). **c** (foll. by with) cover or decorate (material) with figures or designs cut in it. **3** tr. (absol.) cut (meat etc.) into slices for eating. □carve out **1** take from a larger whole. **2** establish (a career etc.) purposefully (carved out a name for themselves). carve up divide into several pieces; subdivide (territory etc.). carve-up n. sl. a sharing-out, esp. of spoils. carving knife a knife with a long blade, for carving meat. [OE ceorfan cut f. WG]

carvel /'kɑːv(ə)l/ n. var. of CARAVEL. □carvel-built (of a boat) made with planks flush, not overlapping (cf. CLINKER-BUILT). [as CARAVEL]

carven /'kɑːv(ə)n/ archaic past part. of CARVE.

Carver /'kɑːvə(r)/ n. US a chair with arms, a rush seat, and a back having horizontal and vertical spindles. [J. Carver, first governor of Plymouth Colony, d. 1621, for whom a prototype was allegedly made]

carver /'kɑːvə(r)/ n. **1** a person who carves. **2 a** carving knife. **b** (in pl.) a knife and fork for carving. **3** Brit. the principal chair, with arms, in a set of dining-chairs, intended for the person who carves. ¶ To be distinguished (in sense 3) from Carver.

carvery /'kɑːvərɪ/ n. (pl. -ies) a buffet or restaurant with joints displayed, and carved as required, in front of customers.

carving /'kɑːvɪŋ/ n. a carved object, esp. as a work of art.

caryatid /ˌkærɪ'ætɪd/ n. (pl. caryatides /-ˌdiːz/ or caryatids) Archit. a pillar in the form of a draped female figure, supporting an entablature. [F caryatide f. It. cariatide or L f. Gk karuatis -idos priestess at Caryae (Karuai) in Laconia]

caryopsis /ˌkærɪ'ɒpsɪs/ n. (pl. caryopses /-siːz/) Bot. a dry one-seeded indehiscent fruit, as in wheat and maize. [mod.L f. Gk karuon nut + opsis appearance]

Casanova /ˌkæsə'nəʊvə/ n. a man notorious for seducing women. [G. J. Casanova de Seingalt, It. adventurer d. 1798]

casbah var. of KASBAH.

cascade /kæs'keɪd/ n. & v. —n. **1** a small waterfall, esp. forming one in a series or part of a large broken waterfall. **2** a succession of electrical devices or stages in a process. **3** a quantity of material etc. draped in descending folds. **4** a process of disseminating information from senior to junior levels in an organization. —v.intr. fall in or like a cascade. [F f. It. cascata f. cascare to fall ult. f. L casus: see CASE¹]

cascara /kæs'kɑːrə/ n. (in full cascara sagrada /səg'rɑːdə/) the bark of a Californian buckthorn, Rhamnus purshiana, used as a purgative. [Sp., = sacred bark]

case¹ /keɪs/ n. **1** an instance of something occurring. **2** a state of affairs, hypothetical or actual. **3 a** an instance of a person receiving professional guidance, e.g. from a doctor or social worker. **b** this person or the circumstances involved. **4** a matter under official investigation, esp. by the police. **5** *Law* **a** a cause or suit for trial. **b** a statement of the facts in a cause *sub judice*, drawn up for a higher court's consideration (*judge states a case*). **c** a cause that has been decided and may be cited (*leading case*). **6 a** the sum of the arguments on one side, esp. in a lawsuit (*that is our case*). **b** a set of arguments, esp. in relation to persuasiveness (*have a good case*; *have a weak case*). **c** a valid set of arguments (*have no case*). **7** *Gram.* **a** the relation of a word to other words in a sentence. **b** a form of a noun, adjective, or pronoun expressing this. **8** *colloq.* a comical person. **9** the position or circumstances in which one is. □**as the case may be** according to the situation. **case history** information about a person for use in professional treatment, e.g. by a doctor. **case-law** the law as established by the outcome of former cases (cf. *common law, statute law*). **case-load** the cases with which a doctor etc. is concerned at one time. **case-study 1** an attempt to understand a person, institution, etc., from collected information. **2** a record of such an attempt. **3** the use of a particular instance as an exemplar of general principles. **in any case** whatever the truth is; whatever may happen. **in case 1** in the event that; if. **2** lest; in provision against a stated or implied possibility (*take an umbrella in case it rains*; *took it in case*). **in case of** in the event of. **in the case of** as regards. **in no case** under no circumstances. **in that case** if that is true; should that happen. **is** (or **is not**) **the case** is (or is not) so. [ME f. OF *cas* f. L *casus* fall f. *cadere cas-* to fall]

case² /keɪs/ *n. & v.* —*n.* **1** a container or covering serving to enclose or contain. **2** a container with its contents. **3** the outer protective covering of a watch, book, seed-vessel, sausage, etc. **4** an item of luggage, esp. a suitcase. **5** *Printing* a partitioned receptacle for type. **6** a glass box for showing specimens, curiosities, etc. —*v.tr.* **1** enclose in a case. **2** (foll. by *with*) surround. **3** *sl.* reconnoitre (a house etc.) esp. with a view to robbery. □**case-bound** (of a book) in a hard cover. **case-harden 1** harden the surface of, esp. give a steel surface to (iron) by carbonizing. **2** make callous. **case-knife** a knife carried in a sheath. **case-shot 1** bullets in an iron case fired from a cannon. **2** shrapnel. **lower case** small letters. **upper case** capitals. [ME f. OF *casse, chasse,* f. L *capsa* f. *capere* hold]

casebook /ˈkeɪsbʊk/ *n.* a book containing a record of legal or medical cases.

casein /ˈkeɪsɪɪn, ˈkeɪsiːn/ *n.* the main protein in milk, esp. in coagulated form as in cheese. [L *caseus* cheese]

caseinogen /keɪˈsɪnədʒ(ə)n/ *n.* the soluble form of casein as it occurs in milk.

casemate /ˈkeɪsmeɪt/ *n.* **1** a chamber in the thickness of the wall of a fortress, with embrasures. **2** an armoured enclosure for guns on a warship. [F *casemate* & It. *casamatta* or Sp. *-mata,* f. *camata,* perh. f. Gk *khasma -atos* gap]

casement /ˈkeɪsmənt/ *n.* **1** a window or part of a window hinged vertically to open like a door. **2** *poet.* a window. [ME f. AL *cassimentum* f. *cassa* CASE²]

casework /ˈkeɪswɜːk/ *n.* social work concerned with individuals, esp. involving understanding of the client's family and background. □□**caseworker** *n.*

cash¹ /kæʃ/ *n. & v.* —*n.* **1** money in coins or notes, as distinct from cheques or orders. **2** (also **cash down**) money paid as full payment at the time of purchase, as distinct from credit. **3** *colloq.* wealth. —*v.tr.* give or obtain cash for (a note, cheque, etc.). □**cash and carry 1** a system of wholesaling in which goods are paid for in cash and taken away by the purchaser. **2** a store where this system operates. **cash-book** a book in which receipts and payments of cash are recorded. **cash crop** a crop produced for sale, not

for use as food etc. **cash desk** a counter or compartment in a shop where goods are paid for. **cash dispenser** an automatic machine from which customers of a bank etc. may withdraw cash, esp. by using a cashcard. **cash flow** the movement of money into and out of a business, as a measure of profitability, or as affecting liquidity. **cash in 1** obtain cash for. **2** *colloq.* (usu. foll. by *on*) profit (from); take advantage (of). **3** pay into a bank etc. **4** (in full **cash in one's checks**) *colloq.* die. **cash on delivery** a system of paying the carrier for goods when they are delivered. **cash register** a machine in a shop etc. with a drawer for money, recording the amount of each sale, totalling receipts, etc. **cash up** *Brit.* count and check cash takings at the end of a day's trading. □□**cashable** *adj.* **cashless** *adj.* [obs. F *casse* box or It. *cassa* f. L *capsa* CASE²]

cash² /kæʃ/ *n.* (*pl.* same) *hist.* any of various small coins of China or the E. Indies. [ult. f. Port. *ca(i)xa* f. Tamil *kāsu* f. Skr. *karsha*]

cashcard /ˈkæʃkɑːd/ *n.* a plastic card (see CARD¹ *n.* 9) which enables the holder to draw money from a cash dispenser.

cashew /ˈkæʃuː, kæˈʃuː/ *n.* **1** a bushy evergreen tree, *Anacardium occidentale,* native to Central and S. America, bearing kidney-shaped nuts attached to fleshy fruits. **2** (in full **cashew nut**) the edible nut of this tree. □**cashew apple** the edible fleshy fruit of this tree. [Port. f. Tupi *(a)caju*]

cashier¹ /kæˈʃɪə(r)/ *n.* a person dealing with cash transactions in a shop, bank, etc. [Du. *cassier* or F *caissier* (as CASH¹)]

cashier² /kæˈʃɪə(r)/ *v.tr.* dismiss from service, esp. from the armed forces with disgrace. [Flem. *kasseren* disband, revoke, f. F *casser* f. L *quassare* QUASH]

cashmere /ˈkæʃmɪə(r)/ *n.* **1** a fine soft wool, esp. that of a Kashmir goat. **2** a material made from this. [*Kashmir* in Asia]

cashpoint /ˈkæʃpɔɪnt/ *n.* = *cash dispenser.*

casing /ˈkeɪsɪŋ/ *n.* **1** a protective or enclosing cover or shell. **2** the material for this.

casino /kəˈsiːnəʊ/ *n.* (*pl.* **-os**) a public room or building for gambling. [It., dimin. of *casa* house f. L *casa* cottage]

cask /kɑːsk/ *n.* **1** a large barrel-like container made of wood, metal, or plastic, esp. one for alcoholic liquor. **2** its contents. **3** its capacity. [F *casque* or Sp. *casco* helmet]

casket /ˈkɑːskɪt/ *n.* **1** a small often ornamental box or chest for jewels, letters, etc. **2 a** a small wooden box for cremated ashes. **b** *US* a coffin, esp. a rectangular one. [perh. f. AF form of OF *cassette* f. It. *cassetta* dimin. of *cassa* f. L *capsa* CASE²]

casque /kæsk/ *n.* **1** *hist.* or *poet.* a helmet. **2** *Zool.* a helmet-like structure, e.g. the process on the bill of the cassowary. [F f. Sp. *casco*]

Cassandra /kəˈsændrə/ *n.* a prophet of disaster, esp. one who is disregarded. [L f. Gk *Kassandra,* daughter of Priam King of Troy: she was condemned by Apollo to prophesy correctly but not be believed]

cassata /kəˈsɑːtə/ *n.* a type of ice-cream containing candied or dried fruit and nuts. [It.]

cassation /kəˈseɪʃ(ə)n/ *n. Mus.* an informal instrumental composition of the 18th c., similar to a divertimento and orig. often for outdoor performance. [It. *cassazione*]

cassava /kəˈsɑːvə/ *n.* **1 a** any plant of the genus *Manihot,* esp. the cultivated varieties *M. esculenta* (**bitter cassava**) and *M. dulcis* (**sweet cassava**), having starchy tuberous roots. **b** the roots themselves. **2** a starch or flour obtained from these roots. Also called TAPIOCA, MANIOC. [earlier *cas(s)avi* etc., f. Taino *casavi,* infl. by F *cassave*]

casserole /ˈkæsəˌrəʊl/ *n. & v.* —*n.* **1** a covered dish, usu. of earthenware or glass, in which food is cooked, esp. slowly in the oven. **2** food cooked in a casserole. —*v.tr.* cook in a casserole. [F f. *cassole* dimin. of *casse* f. Prov. *casa* f. LL *cattia* ladle, pan f. Gk *kuathion* dimin. of *kuathos* cup]

cassette /kæˈset, kə-/ *n.* a sealed case containing a length of tape, ribbon, etc., ready for insertion in a machine, esp.: **1** a length of magnetic tape wound on to spools, ready for insertion in a tape recorder. **2** a length of photographic film, ready for insertion in a camera. [F, dimin. of *casse* CASE²]

cassia /ˈkæsɪə, ˈkæʃə/ *n.* **1** any tree of the genus *Cassia*, bearing leaves from which senna is extracted. **2** the cinnamon-like bark of this tree used as a spice. [L f. Gk *kasia* f. Heb. *ḳeṣiʿāh* bark like cinnamon]

cassis /kæˈsiːs/ *n.* a syrupy usu. alcoholic black-currant flavouring for drinks etc. [F, = blackcurrant]

cassiterite /kəˈsɪtəˌraɪt/ *n.* a naturally occurring ore of tin dioxide, from which tin is extracted. Also called TINSTONE. [Gk *kassiteros* tin]

cassock /ˈkæsək/ *n.* a long close-fitting usu. black or red garment worn by clergy, members of choirs, etc. □□ **cassocked** *adj.* [F *casaque* long coat f. It. *casacca* horseman's coat, prob. f. Turkic: cf. COSSACK]

cassoulet /ˈkæsuˌleɪ/ *n.* a ragout of meat and beans. [F, dimin. of dial. *cassolo* stew-pan]

cassowary /ˈkæsəˌweərɪ/ *n.* (*pl.* **-ies**) any large flightless Australasian bird of the genus *Casuarius*, with heavy body, stout legs, a wattled neck, and a bony crest on its forehead. [Malay *kasuārī, kasavārī*]

cast /kɑːst/ *v. & n.* —*v.* (*past* and *past part.* **cast**) **1** *tr.* throw, esp. deliberately or forcefully. **2** *tr.* (often foll. by *on, over*) **a** direct or cause to fall (one's eyes, a glance, light, a shadow, a spell, etc.). **b** express (doubts, aspersions, etc.). **3** *tr.* throw out (a fishing-line) into the water. **4** *tr.* let down (an anchor or sounding-lead). **5** *tr.* **a** throw off, get rid of. **b** shed (skin etc.) esp. in the process of growth. **c** (of a horse) lose (a shoe). **6** *tr.* record, register, or give (a vote). **7** *tr.* **a** shape (molten metal or plastic material) in a mould. **b** make (a product) in this way. **8** *tr. Printing* make (type). **9** *tr.* **a** (usu. foll. by *as*) assign (an actor) to play a particular character. **b** allocate roles in (a play, film, etc.). **10** *tr.* (foll. by *in, into*) arrange or formulate (facts etc.) in a specified form. **11** *tr. & intr.* reckon, add up, calculate (accounts or figures). **12** *tr.* calculate and record details of (a horoscope). —*n.* **1 a** the throwing of a missile etc. **b** the distance reached by this. **2** a throw or a number thrown at dice. **3** a throw of a net, sounding-lead, or fishing-line. **4** *Fishing* **a** that which is cast, esp. the gut with hook and fly. **b** a place for casting (*a good cast*). **5 a** an object of metal, clay, etc., made in a mould. **b** a moulded mass of solidified material, esp. plaster protecting a broken limb. **6** the actors taking part in a play, film, etc. **7** form, type, or quality (*cast of features; cast of mind*). **8** a tinge or shade of colour. **9 a** (in full **cast in the eye**) a slight squint. **b** a twist or inclination. **10 a** a mass of earth excreted by a worm. **b** a mass of indigestible food thrown up by a hawk, owl, etc. **11** the form into which any work is thrown or arranged. **12 a** a wide area covered by a dog or pack to find a trail. **b** *Austral. & NZ* a wide sweep made by a sheepdog in mustering sheep. □ **cast about** (or **around** or **round**) make an extensive search (actually or mentally) (*cast about for a solution*). **cast adrift** leave to drift. **cast ashore** (of waves etc.) throw to the shore. **cast aside** give up using; abandon. **cast away 1** reject. **2** (in *passive*) be shipwrecked (cf. CASTAWAY). **cast one's bread upon the waters** see BREAD. **cast down** depress, deject (cf. DOWNCAST). **casting vote** a deciding vote usu. given by the chairperson when the votes on two sides are equal. ¶ From an obsolete sense of *cast* = turn the scale. **cast iron** a hard alloy of iron, carbon, and silicon cast in a mould. **cast-iron** *adj.* **1** made of cast iron. **2** hard, unchallengeable, unchangeable. **cast loose** detach; detach oneself. **cast lots** see LOT. **cast-net** a net thrown out and immediately drawn in. **cast off 1** abandon. **2** *Knitting* take the stitches off the needle by looping each over the next to finish

the edge. **3** *Naut.* **a** set a ship free from a quay etc. **b** loosen and throw off (rope etc.). **4** *Printing* estimate the space that will be taken in print by manuscript copy. **cast-off** *adj.* abandoned, discarded. —*n.* a cast-off thing, esp. a garment. **cast on** *Knitting* make the first row of loops on the needle. **cast out** expel. **cast up 1** (of the sea) deposit on the shore. **2** add up (figures etc.). [ME f. ON *kasta*]

castanet /ˌkæstəˈnet/ *n.* (usu. in *pl.*) a small concave piece of hardwood, ivory, etc., in pairs held in the hands and clicked together by the fingers as a rhythmic accompaniment, esp. by Spanish dancers. [Sp. *castañeta* dimin. of *castaña* f. L *castanea* chestnut]

castaway /ˈkɑːstəˌweɪ/ *n. & adj.* —*n.* a shipwrecked person. —*adj.* **1** shipwrecked. **2** cast aside; rejected.

caste /kɑːst/ *n.* **1** any of the Hindu hereditary classes whose members have no social contact with other classes, but are socially equal with one another and often follow the same occupations. **2** a more or less exclusive social class. **3** a system of such classes. **4** the position it confers. **5** *Zool.* a form of social insect having a particular function. □ **caste mark** a symbol on the forehead denoting a person's caste. **lose caste** descend in the social order. [Sp. and Port. *casta* lineage, race, breed, fem. of *casto* pure, CHASTE]

casteism /ˈkɑːstɪz(ə)m/ *n.* often *derog.* the caste system.

castellan /ˈkæstələn/ *n. hist.* the governor of a castle. [ME f. ONF *castelain* f. med.L *castellanus*: see CASTLE]

castellated /ˈkæstəˌleɪtɪd/ *adj.* **1** having battlements. **2** castle-like. □□ **castellation** /-ˈleɪʃ(ə)n/ *n.* [med.L *castellatus*: see CASTLE]

caster /ˈkɑːstə(r)/ *n.* **1** var. of CASTOR¹. **2** a person who casts. **3** a machine for casting type.

castigate /ˈkæstɪˌgeɪt/ *v.tr.* rebuke or punish severely. □□ **castigation** /-ˈgeɪʃ(ə)n/ *n.* **castigator** *n.* **castigatory** *adj.* [L *castigare* reprove f. *castus* pure]

Castile soap /kæˈstiːl/ *n.* a fine hard white or mottled soap made with olive oil and soda. [as CASTILIAN]

Castilian /kæˈstɪlɪən/ *n. & adj.* —*n.* **1** a native of Castile in Spain. **2** the language of Castile, standard spoken and literary Spanish. —*adj.* of or relating to Castile.

casting /ˈkɑːstɪŋ/ *n.* an object made by casting, esp. of molten metal.

castle /ˈkɑːs(ə)l/ *n. & v.* —*n.* **1 a** a large fortified building or group of buildings; a stronghold. **b** a formerly fortified mansion. **2** *Chess* = ROOK². —*v.* *Chess* **1** *intr.* make a special move (once only in a game on each side) in which the king is moved two squares along the back rank and the nearer rook is moved to the square passed over by the king. **2** *tr.* move (the king) by castling. □ **castles in the air** (or **in Spain**) a visionary unattainable scheme; a day-dream. □□ **castled** *adj.* [AF & ONF *castel, chastel* f. L *castellum* dimin. of *castrum* fort]

castor¹ /ˈkɑːstə(r)/ *n.* (also **caster**) **1** a small swivelled wheel (often one of a set) fixed to a leg (or the underside) of a piece of furniture. **2** a small container with holes in the top for sprinkling the contents. □ **castor action** swivelling of vehicle wheels to ensure stability. **castor sugar** finely granulated white sugar. [orig. a var. of CASTER (in the general sense)]

castor² /ˈkɑːstə(r)/ *n.* an oily substance secreted by beavers and used in medicine and perfumes. [F or L f. Gk *kastōr* beaver]

castor oil /ˈkɑːstə(r)/ *n.* **1** an oil from the seeds of a plant, *Ricinus communis*, used as a purgative and lubricant. **2** (in full **castor oil plant**) this plant. □ **castor oil bean** (or **castor bean**) a seed of the castor oil plant. [18th c.: orig. uncert.: perh. so called as having succeeded CASTOR² in the medical sense]

castrate /kæˈstreɪt/ *v.tr.* **1** remove the testicles of; geld. **2** deprive of vigour. □□ **castration** *n.* **castrator** *n.* [L *castrare*]

castrato /kæˈstrɑːtəʊ/ *n.* (*pl.* **castrati** /-tɪ/) *hist.* a male singer castrated in boyhood so as to retain a soprano or alto voice. [It., past part. of *castrare*: see CASTRATE]

casual /'kæʒʊəl, -ʒʊəl/ *adj.* & *n.* —*adj.* 1 accidental; due to chance. 2 not regular or permanent; temporary, occasional (*casual work*; *a casual affair*). 3 a unconcerned, uninterested (*was very casual about it*). b made or done without great care or thought (*a casual remark*). c acting carelessly or unmethodically. 4 (of clothes) informal. —*n.* 1 a casual worker. 2 (usu. in *pl.*) casual clothes or shoes. □□ **casually** *adv.* **casualness** *n.* [ME f. OF *casuel* & L *casualis* f. *casus* CASE¹]

casualty /'kæʒʊəltɪ, 'kæʒjʊ-/ *n.* (*pl.* -ies) 1 a person killed or injured in a war or accident. 2 a thing lost or destroyed. 3 = *casualty department*. 4 an accident, mishap, or disaster. □ **casualty department** (or **ward**) the part of a hospital where casualties are treated. [ME f. med.L *casualitas* (as CASUAL), after ROYALTY etc.]

casuarina /ˌkæsjʊ'riːnə/ *n.* any tree of the genus *Casuarina*, native to Australia and SE Asia, having tiny scale leaves on slender jointed branches, resembling gigantic horsetails. [mod.L *casuarius* cassowary (from the resemblance between branches and feathers)]

casuist /'kæʒjuːɪst, 'kæʒʊɪst/ *n.* 1 a person, esp. a theologian, who resolves problems of conscience, duty, etc., often with clever but false reasoning. 2 a sophist or quibbler. □□ **casuistic** /-'ɪstɪk/ *adj.* **casuistical** /-'ɪstɪk(ə)l/ *adj.* **casuistically** /-'ɪstɪkəlɪ/ *adv.* **casuistry** *n.* [F *casuiste* f. Sp. *casuista* f. L *casus* CASE¹]

casus belli /ˌkɑːzəs 'belɪ, ˌkeɪsəs/ *n.* an act or situation provoking or justifying war. [L]

CAT *abbr.* 1 computer-assisted (or -aided) testing. 2 *Med.* computerized axial tomography.

cat /kæt/ *n.* & *v.* —*n.* 1 a small soft-furred four-legged domesticated animal, *Felis catus*. 2 a any wild animal of the genus *Felis*, e.g. a lion, tiger, or leopard. b = *wild cat*. 3 a catlike animal of any other species (*civet cat*). 4 *colloq.* a malicious or spiteful woman. 5 *sl.* a jazz enthusiast. 6 *Naut.* = CATHEAD. 7 = *cat-o'-nine-tails*. 8 a short tapered stick in the game of tipcat. —*v.tr.* (also *absol.*) (**catted, catting**) *Naut.* raise (an anchor) from the surface of the water to the cathead. □ **cat-and-dog** (of a relationship etc.) full of quarrels. **cat burglar** a burglar who enters by climbing to an upper storey. **cat flap** (or **door**) a small swinging flap in an outer door, for a cat to pass in and out. **cat-ice** thin ice unsupported by water. **cat-o'-nine-tails** *hist.* a rope whip with nine knotted lashes for flogging sailors, soldiers, or criminals. **cat's cradle** a child's game in which a loop of string is held between the fingers and patterns are formed. **Cat's-eye** *Brit. propr.* one of a series of reflector studs set into a road. **cat's-eye** a precious stone of Sri Lanka and Malabar. **cat's-foot** any small plant of the genus *Antennaria*, having soft woolly leaves and growing on the surface of the ground. **cat's-paw** 1 a person used as a tool by another. 2 a slight breeze rippling the surface of the water. **cat's-tail** = *reed-mace* (see REED¹). **cat's whiskers** (or **pyjamas**) *sl.* an excellent person or thing. **let the cat out of the bag** reveal a secret, esp. involuntarily. **like a cat on hot bricks** (or **on a hot tin roof**) very agitated or agitatedly. **put** (or **set**) **the cat among the pigeons** cause trouble. **rain cats and dogs** rain very hard. [OE *catt(e)* f. LL *cattus*]

cata- /'kætə/ *prefix* (usu. **cat-** before a vowel or *h*) 1 down, downwards (*catadromous*). 2 wrongly, badly (*catachresis*). [Gk *kata* down]

catabolism /kə'tæbəˌlɪz(ə)m/ *n.* (also **katabolism**) *Biochem.* the breakdown of complex molecules in living organisms to form simpler ones with the release of energy; destructive metabolism (opp. ANABOLISM). □□ **catabolic** /ˌkætə'bɒlɪk/ *adj.* [Gk *katabolē* descent f. *kata* down + *bolē* f. *ballō* throw]

catachresis /ˌkætə'kriːsɪs/ *n.* (*pl.* **catachreses** /-siːz/) an incorrect use of words. □□ **catachrestic** /-'kriːstɪk, -'krestɪk/ *adj.* [L f. Gk *katakhrēsis* f. *khraomai* use]

cataclasis /ˌkætə'kleɪsɪs/ *n.* (*pl.* **cataclases** /-siːz/) *Geol.* the natural process of fracture, shearing, or breaking up of rocks. □□ **cataclastic** /-'klæstɪk/ *adj.* [mod.L f. Gk *kataklasis* breaking down]

cataclasm /'kætəˌklæz(ə)m/ *n.* a violent break; a disruption. [Gk *kataklasma* (as CATA-, *klaō* to break)]

cataclysm /'kætəˌklɪz(ə)m/ *n.* 1 a a violent, esp. social or political, upheaval or disaster. b a great change. 2 a great flood or deluge. □□ **cataclysmal** /-'klɪzm(ə)l/ *adj.* **cataclysmic** /-'klɪzmɪk/ *adj.* **cataclysmically** /-'klɪzmɪkəlɪ/ *adv.* [F *cataclysme* f. L *cataclysmus* f. Gk *kataklusmos* f. *klusmos* flood f. *kluzō* wash]

catacomb /'kætəˌkuːm, -ˌkəʊm/ *n.* (often in *pl.*) 1 an underground cemetery, esp. a Roman subterranean gallery with recesses for tombs. 2 a similar underground construction; a cellar. [F *catacombes* f. LL *catacumbas* (name given in the 5th c. to the cemetery of St Sebastian near Rome), of unkn. orig.]

catadromous /kə'tædrəməs/ *adj.* (of a fish, e.g. the eel) that swims down rivers to the sea to spawn (cf. ANADROMOUS). [Gk *katadromos* f. *kata* down + *dromos* running]

catafalque /'kætəˌfælk/ *n.* a decorated wooden framework for supporting the coffin of a distinguished person during a funeral or while lying in state. [F f. It. *catafalco*, of unkn. orig.: cf. SCAFFOLD]

Catalan /'kætəlæn/ *n.* & *adj.* —*n.* 1 a native of Catalonia in Spain. 2 the language of Catalonia. —*adj.* of or relating to Catalonia or its people or language. [F f. Sp.]

catalase /'kætəˌleɪz/ *n.* *Biochem.* an enzyme that catalyses the reduction of hydrogen peroxide. [CATALYSIS]

catalepsy /'kætəˌlepsɪ/ *n.* a state of trance or seizure with loss of sensation and consciousness accompanied by rigidity of the body. □□ **cataleptic** /-'leptɪk/ *adj.* & *n.* [F *catalepsie* or LL *catalepsia* f. Gk *katalēpsis* (as CATA-, *lēpsis* seizure)]

catalogue /'kætəˌlɒg/ *n.* & *v.* (US **catalog**) —*n.* 1 a complete list of items (e.g. articles for sale, books held by a library), usu. in alphabetical or other systematic order and often with a description of each. 2 an extensive list (*a catalogue of crimes*). 3 *US* a university course-list etc. —*v.tr.* (**catalogues, catalogued, cataloguing**; *US* **catalogs, cataloged, cataloging**) 1 make a catalogue of. 2 enter in a catalogue. □□ **cataloguer** *n.* (US **cataloger**). [F f. LL *catalogus* f. Gk *katalogos* f. *katalegō* enrol (as CATA-, *legō* choose)]

catalogue raisonné /'kætəˌlɒg 'reɪzɒ'neɪ/ *n.* a descriptive catalogue with explanations or comments. [F, = explained catalogue]

catalpa /kə'tælpə/ *n.* any tree of the genus *Catalpa*, with heart-shaped leaves, trumpet-shaped flowers, and long pods. [Amer. Ind. (Creek)]

catalyse /'kætəˌlaɪz/ *v.tr.* (US **catalyze**) *Chem.* produce (a reaction) by catalysis. [as CATALYSIS after *analyse*]

catalysis /kə'tælɪsɪs/ *n.* (*pl.* **catalyses** /-ˌsiːz/) *Chem.* & *Biochem.* the acceleration of a chemical or biochemical reaction by a catalyst. [Gk *katalusis* dissolution (as CATA-, *luō* set free)]

catalyst /'kætəlɪst/ *n.* 1 *Chem.* a substance that, without itself undergoing any permanent chemical change, increases the rate of a reaction. 2 a person or thing that precipitates a change. [as CATALYSIS after *analyst*]

catalytic /ˌkætə'lɪtɪk/ *adj.* *Chem.* relating to or involving catalysis. □ **catalytic converter** a device incorporated in the exhaust system of a motor vehicle, with a catalyst for converting pollutant gases into harmless products. **catalytic cracker** a device for cracking (see CRACK *v.* 9) petroleum oils by catalysis.

catalyze *US* var. of CATALYSE.

catamaran /ˌkætəməˈræn/ *n.* **1** a boat with twin hulls in parallel. **2** a raft of yoked logs or boats. **3** *colloq.* a quarrelsome woman. [Tamil *kaṭṭumaram* tied wood]

catamite /ˈkætəˌmaɪt/ *n.* **1** a boy kept for homosexual practices. **2** the passive partner in sodomy. [L *catamitus* through Etruscan f. Gk *Ganumēdēs* Ganymede, cupbearer of Zeus]

catamountain /ˈkætəˌmaʊntɪn/ *n.* **1** a lynx, leopard, puma, or other tiger-cat. **2** a wild quarrelsome person. [ME f. *cat of the mountain*]

catananche /ˌkætəˈnæŋkɪ/ *n.* any composite plant of the genus *Catananche*, with blue or yellow flowers. [mod.L f. L *catanancē* plant used in love-potions f. Gk *katanagkē* (as CATA-, *anagkē* compulsion)]

cataplexy /ˈkætəˌpleksɪ/ *n.* sudden temporary paralysis due to fright etc. □□ **cataplectic** /-ˈplektɪk/ *adj.* [Gk *kataplēxis* stupefaction]

catapult /ˈkætəˌpʌlt/ *n. & v.* —*n.* **1** a forked stick etc. with elastic for shooting stones. **2** *hist.* a military machine worked by a lever and ropes for hurling large stones etc. **3** a mechanical device for launching a glider, an aircraft from the deck of a ship, etc. —*v.* **1** *tr.* **a** hurl from or launch with a catapult. **b** fling forcibly. **2** *intr.* leap or be hurled forcibly. [F *catapulte* or L *catapulta* f. Gk *katapeltēs* (as CATA-, *pallō* hurl)]

cataract /ˈkætəˌrækt/ *n.* **1 a** a large waterfall or cascade. **b** a downpour; a rush of water. **2** *Med.* a condition in which the eye-lens becomes progressively opaque resulting in blurred vision. [L *cataracta* f. Gk *katarrhaktēs* down-rushing; in med. sense prob. f. obs. sense 'portcullis']

catarrh /kəˈtɑː(r)/ *n.* **1** inflammation of the mucous membrane of the nose, air passages, etc. **2** a watery discharge in the nose or throat due to this. □□ **catarrhal** *adj.* [F *catarrhe* f. LL *catarrhus* f. Gk *katarrhous* f. *katarrheō* flow down]

catarrhine /ˈkætəˌraɪn/ *adj. & n. Zool.* —*adj.* (of primates) having nostrils close together, and directed downwards, e.g. a baboon, chimpanzee, or human. —*n.* such an animal (cf. PLATYRRHINE). [CATA- + *rhis rhinos* nose]

catastrophe /kəˈtæstrəfɪ/ *n.* **1** a great and usu. sudden disaster. **2** the denouement of a drama. **3** a disastrous end; ruin. **4** an event producing a subversion of the order of things. □□ **catastrophic** /-ˈstrɒfɪk/ *adj.* **catastrophically** /-ˈstrɒfɪkəlɪ/ *adv.* [L *catastropha* f. Gk *katastrophē* (as CATA-, *strophē* turning f. *strephō* turn)]

catastrophism /kəˈtæstrəˌfɪz(ə)m/ *n. Geol.* the theory that changes in the earth's crust have occurred in sudden violent and unusual events. □□ **catastrophist** *n.*

catatonia /ˌkætəˈtəʊnɪə/ *n.* **1** schizophrenia with intervals of catalepsy and sometimes violence. **2** catalepsy. □□ **catatonic** /-ˈtɒnɪk/ *adj. & n.* [G *Katatonie* (as CATA-, TONE)]

catawba /kəˈtɔːbə/ *n.* **1** a US variety of grape. **2** a white wine made from it. [River *Catawba* in S. Carolina]

catboat /ˈkætbəʊt/ *n.* a sailing-boat with a single mast placed well forward and carrying only one sail. [perh. f. *cat* a former type of coaler in NE England, + BOAT]

catcall /ˈkætkɔːl/ *n. & v.* —*n.* a shrill whistle of disapproval made at meetings etc. —*v.* **1** *intr.* make a catcall. **2** *tr.* make a catcall at.

catch /kætʃ/ *v. & n.* —*v.* (*past* and *past part.* **caught** /kɔːt/) **1** *tr.* **a** lay hold of so as to restrain or prevent from escaping; capture in a trap, in one's hands, etc. **b** (also **catch hold of**) get into one's hands so as to retain, operate, etc. (*caught hold of the handle*). **2** *tr.* detect or surprise (a person, esp. in a wrongful or embarrassing act) (*caught me in the act; caught him smoking*). **3** *tr.* **a** intercept and hold (a moving thing) in the hands etc. (*failed to catch the ball; a bowl to catch the drips*). **b** *Cricket* dismiss (a batsman) by catching the ball before it reaches the ground. **4** *tr.*

a contract (a disease) by infection or contagion. **b** acquire (a quality or feeling) from another's example (*caught her enthusiasm*). **5** *tr.* **a** reach in time and board (a train, bus, etc.). **b** be in time to see etc. (a person or thing about to leave or finish) (*if you hurry you'll catch them; caught the end of the performance*). **6** *tr.* **a** apprehend with the senses or the mind (esp. a thing occurring quickly or briefly) (*didn't catch what he said*). **b** (of an artist etc.) reproduce faithfully. **7 a** *intr.* become fixed or entangled; be checked (*the bolt began to catch*). **b** *tr.* cause to do this (*caught her tights on a nail*). **c** *tr.* (often foll. by *on*) hit, deal a blow to (*caught him on the nose; caught his elbow on the table*). **8** *tr.* draw the attention of; captivate (*caught his eye; caught her fancy*). **9** *intr.* begin to burn. **10** *tr.* (often foll. by *up*) reach or overtake (a person etc. ahead). **11** *tr.* check suddenly (*caught his breath*). **12** *tr.* (foll. by *at*) grasp or try to grasp. —*n.* **1 a** an act of catching. **b** *Cricket* a chance or act of catching the ball. **2 a** an amount of a thing caught, esp. of fish. **b** a thing or person caught or worth catching, esp. in marriage. **3 a** a question, trick, etc., intended to deceive, incriminate, etc. **b** an unexpected or hidden difficulty or disadvantage. **4** a device for fastening a door or window etc. **5** *Mus.* a round, esp. with words arranged to produce a humorous effect. □ **catch-all** (often *attrib.*) a thing designed to be all-inclusive. **catch-as-catch-can** a style of wrestling with few holds barred. **catch at a straw** see STRAW. **catch crop** a crop grown between two staple crops (in position or time). **catch one's death** see DEATH. **catch fire** see FIRE. **catch it** *sl.* be punished or in trouble. **catch me!** etc. (often foll. by *pres. part.*) *colloq.* you may be sure I etc. shall not. **catch on** *colloq.* **1** (of a practice, fashion, etc.) become popular. **2** (of a person) understand what is meant. **catch out 1** detect in a mistake etc. **2** take unawares; cause to be bewildered or confused. **3** = sense 3b of *v.* **catch-phrase** a phrase in frequent use. **catch the sun 1** be in a sunny position. **2** become sunburnt. **catch up 1 a** (often foll. by *with*) reach a person etc. ahead (*he caught up in the end; he caught us up; he caught up with us*). **b** (often foll. by *with, on*) make up arrears (of work etc.) (*must catch up with my correspondence*). **2** snatch or pick up hurriedly. **3** (often in *passive*) **a** involve; entangle (*caught up in suspicious dealings*). **b** fasten up (*hair caught up in a ribbon*). □□ **catchable** *adj.* [ME f. AF & ONF *cachier*, OF *chacier*, ult. f. L *captare* try to catch]

catcher /ˈkætʃə(r)/ *n.* **1** a person or thing that catches. **2** *Baseball* a fielder who stands behind the batter.

catchfly /ˈkætʃflaɪ/ *n.* (*pl.* **-ies**) any plant of the genus *Silene* or *Lychnis* with a sticky stem.

catching /ˈkætʃɪŋ/ *adj.* **1 a** (of a disease) infectious. **b** (of a practice, habit, etc.) likely to be imitated. **2** attractive; captivating.

catchline /ˈkætʃlaɪn/ *n. Printing* a short line of type esp. at the head of copy or as a running headline.

catchment /ˈkætʃmənt/ *n.* the collection of rainfall. □ **catchment area 1** the area from which rainfall flows into a river etc. **2** the area served by a school, hospital, etc.

catchpenny /ˈkætʃˌpenɪ/ *adj.* intended merely to sell quickly; superficially attractive.

catch-22 /ˌkætʃˌtwentɪˈtuː/ *n.* (often *attrib.*) *colloq.* a dilemma or circumstance from which there is no escape because of mutually conflicting or dependent conditions. [title of a novel by J. Heller (1961) featuring a dilemma of this kind]

catchup var. of KETCHUP.

catchweight /ˈkætʃweɪt/ *adj. & n.* —*adj.* unrestricted as regards weight. —*n.* unrestricted weight, as a weight category in sports.

catchword /ˈkætʃwɜːd/ *n.* **1** a word or phrase in common (often temporary) use; a topical slogan. **2** a word so placed as to draw attention. **3** *Theatr.* an actor's cue. **4** *Printing* the first word of a page given at the foot of the previous one.

---

b *but* d *dog* f *few* g *get* h *he* j *yes* k *cat* l *leg* m *man* n *no* p *pen* r *red* s *sit* t *top* v *voice*

catchy /'kætʃɪ/ adj. (**catchier**, **catchiest**) **1** (of a tune) easy to remember; attractive. **2** that snares or entraps; deceptive. **3** (of the wind etc.) fitful, spasmodic. □□ **catchily** adv. **catchiness** n. [CATCH + -Y[1]]

cate /keɪt/ n. archaic (usu. in pl.) choice food, delicacies. [obs. acate purchase f. AF acat, OF achat f. acater, achater buy: see CATER]

catechetical /,kætɪ'ketɪk(ə)l/ adj. (also **catechetic**) **1** of or by oral teaching. **2** according to the catechism of a Church. **3** consisting of or proceeding by question and answer. □□ **catechetically** adv. **catechetics** n. [eccl.Gk katēkhētikos f. katēkhētēs oral teacher: see CATECHIZE]

catechism /'kætɪ,kɪz(ə)m/ n. **1 a** a summary of the principles of a religion in the form of questions and answers. **b** a book containing this. **2** a series of questions put to anyone. □□ **catechismal** /-'kɪzm(ə)l/ adj. [eccl.L catechismus (as CATECHIZE)]

catechist /'kætɪkɪst/ n. a religious teacher, esp. one using a catechism.

catechize /'kætɪ,kaɪz/ v.tr. (also **-ise**) **1** instruct by means of question and answer, esp. from a catechism. **2** put questions to; examine. □□ **catechizer** n. [LL catechizare f. eccl.Gk katēkhizō f. katēkheō make hear (as CATA-, ēkheō sound)]

catechu /'kætɪ,tʃuː/ n. (also **cachou** /'kæʃuː/) gambier or similar vegetable extract, containing tannin. [mod.L f. Malay kachu]

catechumen /,kætɪ'kjuːmən/ n. a Christian convert under instruction before baptism. [ME f. OF catechumene or eccl.L catechumenus f. Gk katēkheō: see CATECHIZE]

categorical /,kætɪ'gɒrɪk(ə)l/ adj. unconditional, absolute; explicit, direct (a categorical refusal). □ **categorical imperative** Ethics an unconditional moral obligation derived from pure reason; the bidding of conscience as ultimate moral law. □□ **categorically** adv. [F catégorique or LL categoricus f. Gk katēgorikos: see CATEGORY]

categorize /'kætɪgə,raɪz/ v.tr. (also **-ise**) place in a category or categories. □□ **categorization** /-'zeɪʃ(ə)n/ n.

category /'kætɪgərɪ/ n. (pl. **-ies**) **1** a class or division. **2** Philos. **a** one of a possibly exhaustive set of classes among which all things might be distributed. **b** one of the a priori conceptions applied by the mind to sense-impressions. **c** any relatively fundamental philosophical concept. □□ **categorial** /-'gɔːrɪəl/ adj. [F catégorie or LL categoria f. Gk katēgoria statement f. katēgoros accuser]

catena /kə'tiːnə/ n. (pl. **catenae** /-niː/ or **catenas**) **1** a connected series of patristic comments on Scripture. **2** a series or chain. [L, = chain: orig. catena patrum chain of the Fathers (of the Church)]

catenary /kə'tiːnərɪ/ n. & adj. —n. (pl. **-ies**) a curve formed by a uniform chain hanging freely from two points not in the same vertical line. —adj. of or resembling such a curve. □ **catenary bridge** a suspension bridge hung from such chains. [L catenarius f. catena chain]

catenate /'kætɪ,neɪt/ v.tr. connect like links of a chain. □□ **catenation** /-'neɪʃ(ə)n/ n. [L catenare catenat- (as CATENARY)]

cater /'keɪtə(r)/ v.intr. **1** supply food. **2** (foll. by for) **a** provide meals for. **b** provide entertainment for. **3** (foll. by to) pander to (evil inclinations). [obs. noun cater (now caterer), f. acater f. AF acatour buyer f. acater buy f. Rmc]

cateran /'kætərən/ n. Sc. a Highland irregular fighting man; a marauder. [ME f. med.L cateranus & Gael. ceathairne peasantry]

cater-cornered /'kætə,kɔːnəd/ adj. & adv. (also **cater-corner**, **catty-cornered** /'kætɪ-/) US —adj. placed or situated diagonally. —adv. diagonally. [dial. adv. cater diagonally (cf. obs. cater the four on dice f. F quatre f. L quattuor four)]

caterer /'keɪtərə(r)/ n. a person who supplies food for social events, esp. professionally.

catering /'keɪtərɪŋ/ n. the profession or work of a caterer.

caterpillar /'kætə,pɪlə(r)/ n. **1 a** the larva of a butterfly or moth. **b** (in general use) any similar larva of various insects. **2** (**Caterpillar**) **a** (in full **Caterpillar track** or **tread**) propr. a steel band passing round the wheels of a tractor etc. for travel on rough ground. **b** a vehicle with these tracks, e.g. a tractor or tank. [perh. AF var. of OF chatepelose lit. hairy cat, infl. by obs. piller ravager]

caterwaul /'kætə,wɔːl/ v. & n. —v.intr. make the shrill howl of a cat. —n. a caterwauling noise. [ME f. CAT + -waul etc. imit.]

catfish /'kætfɪʃ/ n. any of various esp. freshwater fish, usu. having whisker-like barbels round the mouth.

catgut /'kætgʌt/ n. a material used for the strings of musical instruments and surgical sutures, made of the twisted intestines of the sheep, horse, or ass (but not the cat).

Cath. abbr. **1** Cathedral. **2** Catholic.

Cathar /'kæθə(r)/ n. (pl. **Cathars** or **Cathari** /-rɪ/) a member of a medieval sect which sought to achieve great spiritual purity. □□ **Catharism** n. **Catharist** n. [med.L Cathari (pl.) f. Gk katharoi pure]

catharsis /kə'θɑːsɪs/ n. (pl. **catharses** /-,siːz/) **1** an emotional release in drama or art. **2** Psychol. the process of freeing repressed emotion by association with the cause, and elimination by abreaction. **3** Med. purgation. [mod.L f. Gk katharsis f. kathairō cleanse: sense 1 f. Aristotle's Poetics]

cathartic /kə'θɑːtɪk/ adj. & n. —adj. **1** effecting catharsis. **2** purgative. —n. a cathartic drug. □□ **cathartically** adv. [LL catharticus f. Gk kathartikos (as CATHARSIS)]

Cathay /kæ'θeɪ/ n. archaic or poet. the country China. [med.L Cataya]

cathead /'kæthed/ n. Naut. a horizontal beam from each side of a ship's bow for raising and carrying the anchor.

cathectic see CATHEXIS.

cathedral /kə'θiːdr(ə)l/ n. the principal church of a diocese, containing the bishop's throne. □ **cathedral city** a city in which there is a cathedral. [ME (as adj.) f. OF cathedral or f. LL cathedralis f. L f. Gk kathedra seat]

Catherine wheel /'kæθrɪn/ n. **1** a firework in the form of a flat coil which spins when fixed and lit. **2** a circular window with radial divisions. [mod.L Catharina f. Gk Aikaterina name of a saint martyred on a spiked wheel]

catheter /'kæθɪtə(r)/ n. Med. a tube for insertion into a body cavity for introducing or removing fluid. [LL f. Gk kathetēr f. kathiēmi send down]

catheterize /'kæθɪtə,raɪz/ v.tr. (also **-ise**) Med. insert a catheter into.

cathetometer /,kæθɪ'tɒmɪtə(r)/ n. a telescope mounted on a graduated scale along which it can slide, used for accurate measurement of small vertical distances. [L cathetus f. Gk kathetos perpendicular line (as CATHETER + -METER)]

cathexis /kə'θeksɪs/ n. (pl. **cathexes** /-siːz/) Psychol. concentration of mental energy in one channel. □□ **cathectic** adj. [Gk kathexis retention]

cathode /'kæθəʊd/ n. (also **kathode**) Electr. **1** the negative electrode in an electrolytic cell or electronic valve or tube. **2** the positive terminal of a primary cell such as a battery (opp. ANODE). □ **cathode ray** a beam of electrons emitted from the cathode of a high-vacuum tube. **cathode-ray tube** a high-vacuum tube in which cathode rays produce a luminous image on a fluorescent screen. ¶ Abbr.: **CRT**. □□ **cathodal** adj. **cathodic** /kə'θɒdɪk/ adj. [Gk kathodos descent f. kata down + hodos way]

catholic /'kæθəlɪk, 'kæθlɪk/ adj. & n. —adj. **1** of interest or use to all; universal. **2** all-embracing; of wide sympathies or interests (*has catholic tastes*). **3** (**Catholic**) **a** of the Roman Catholic religion. **b** including all Christians. **c** including all of the Western Church. —*n.* (**Catholic**) a Roman Catholic. □□**catholically** *adv.* **Catholicism** /kəˈθɒlɪˌsɪz(ə)m/ *n.* **catholicity** /ˌkæθəˈlɪsɪtɪ/ *n.* **catholicly** *adv.* OF *catholique* or LL *catholicus* f. Gk *katholikos* universal f. *kata* in respect of + *holos* whole]

catholicize /kəˈθɒlɪˌsaɪz/ *v.tr.* & *intr.* (also **-ise**) **1** make or become catholic. **2** (**Catholicize**) make or become a Roman Catholic.

cation /ˈkætˌaɪən/ *n.* a positively charged ion; an ion that is attracted to the cathode in electrolysis (opp. ANION). [CATA- + ION]

cationic /ˌkætaɪˈɒnɪk/ *adj.* **1** of a cation or cations. **2** having an active cation.

catkin /ˈkætkɪn/ *n.* a spike of usu. downy or silky male or female flowers hanging from a willow, hazel, etc. [obs. Du. *katteken* kitten]

catlick /ˈkætlɪk/ *n. colloq.* a perfunctory wash.

catlike /ˈkætlaɪk/ *adj.* **1** like a cat. **2** stealthy.

catmint /ˈkætmɪnt/ *n.* a white-flowered plant, *Nepeta cataria*, having a pungent smell attractive to cats. Also called CATNIP.

catnap /ˈkætnæp/ *n.* & *v.* —*n.* a short sleep. —*v.intr.* (**-napped**, **-napping**) have a catnap.

catnip /ˈkætnɪp/ *n.* = CATMINT. [CAT + dial. *nip* catmint, var. of dial. *nep*]

catoptric /kəˈtɒptrɪk/ *adj.* of or relating to a mirror, a reflector, or reflection. □□**catoptrics** *n.* [Gk *katoptrikos* f. *katoptron* mirror]

catsuit /ˈkætsuːt, -sjuːt/ *n.* a close-fitting garment with trouser legs, covering the body from neck to feet.

catsup /ˈkætsəp/ *esp. US* var. of KETCHUP.

cattery /ˈkætərɪ/ *n.* (*pl.* **-ies**) a place where cats are boarded or bred.

cattish /ˈkætɪʃ/ *adj.* = CATTY. □□**cattishly** *adv.* **cattishness** *n.*

cattle /ˈkæt(ə)l/ *n.pl.* **1** any bison, buffalo, yak, or domesticated bovine animal, esp. of the genus *Bos*. **2** *archaic* livestock. □**cattle-cake** *Brit.* a concentrated food for cattle, in cake form. **cattle-grid** *Brit.* a grid covering a ditch, allowing vehicles to pass over but not cattle, sheep, etc. **cattle-guard** *US* = *cattle-grid*. **cattle-plague** rinderpest. **cattle-stop** *NZ* = *cattle-grid*. [ME & AF *catel* f. OF *chatel* CHATTEL]

cattleman /ˈkæt(ə)lmən/ *n.* (*pl.* **-men**) *US* a person who tends or rears cattle.

cattleya /ˈkætlɪə/ *n.* any epiphytic orchid of the genus *Cattleya*, with handsome violet, pink, or yellow flowers. [mod.L f. W. *Cattley*, Engl. patron of botany d. 1832]

catty /ˈkætɪ/ *adj.* (**cattier**, **cattiest**) **1** sly, spiteful; deliberately hurtful in speech. **2** catlike. □□**cattily** *adv.* **cattiness** *n.*

catty-cornered var. of CATER-CORNERED.

catwalk /ˈkætwɔːk/ *n.* **1** a narrow footway along a bridge, above a theatre stage, etc. **2** a narrow platform or gangway used in fashion shows etc.

Caucasian /kɔːˈkeɪʒ(ə)n, -ˈkeɪzɪən/ *adj.* & *n.* —*adj.* **1** of or relating to the White or light-skinned division of mankind. **2** of or relating to the Caucasus. —*n.* a Caucasian person. [*Caucasus*, mountains in the USSR, its supposed place of origin]

Caucasoid /ˈkɔːkəˌsɔɪd/ *adj.* of or relating to the Caucasian division of mankind.

caucus /ˈkɔːkəs/ *n.* **1** *US* **a** a meeting of the members of a political party, esp. in the Senate etc., to decide policy. **b** a bloc of such members. **c** this system as a political force. **2** often *derog.* (esp. in the UK) **a** a usu. secret meeting of a group within a larger organization or party. **b** such a group. [18th-c. US, perh. f. Algonquin *cau'-cau-as'u* adviser]

caudal /ˈkɔːd(ə)l/ *adj.* **1** of or like a tail. **2** of the posterior part of the body. □□**caudally** *adv.* [mod.L *caudalis* f. L *cauda* tail]

caudate /ˈkɔːdeɪt/ *adj.* having a tail. [see CAUDAL]

caudillo /kaʊˈdiːljəʊ/ *n.* (*pl.* **-os**) (in Spanish-speaking countries) a military or political leader. [Sp. f. LL *capitellum* dimin. of *caput* head]

caught *past* and *past part.* of CATCH.

caul /kɔːl/ *n.* **1 a** the inner membrane enclosing a foetus. **b** part of this occasionally found on a child's head at birth, thought to bring good luck. **2** *hist.* **a** a woman's close-fitting indoor head-dress. **b** the plain back part of a woman's indoor head-dress. **3** the omentum. [ME perh. f. OF *cale* small cap]

cauldron /ˈkɔːldrən/ *n.* (also **caldron**) a large deep bowl-shaped vessel for boiling over an open fire; an ornamental vessel resembling this. [ME f. AF & ONF *caudron*, ult. f. L *caldarium* hot bath f. *calidus* hot]

cauliflower /ˈkɒlɪˌflaʊə(r)/ *n.* **1** a variety of cabbage with a large immature flower-head of small usu. creamy-white flower-buds. **2** the flower-head eaten as a vegetable. □**cauliflower cheese** a savoury dish of cauliflower in a cheese sauce. **cauliflower ear** an ear thickened by repeated blows, esp. in boxing. [earlier *cole-florie* etc. f. obs. F *chou fleuri* flowered cabbage, assim. to COLE and FLOWER]

caulk /kɔːk/ *v.tr.* (*US* **calk**) **1** stop up (the seams of a boat etc.) with oakum etc. and waterproofing material, or by driving plate-junctions together. **2** make (esp. a boat) watertight by this method. □□**caulker** *n.* [OF dial. *cauquer* tread, press with force, f. L *calcare* tread f. *calx* heel]

causal /ˈkɔːz(ə)l/ *adj.* **1** of, forming, or expressing a cause or causes. **2** relating to, or of the nature of, cause and effect. □□**causally** *adv.* [LL *causalis*: see CAUSE]

causality /kɔːˈzælɪtɪ/ *n.* **1** the relation of cause and effect. **2** the principle that everything has a cause.

causation /kɔːˈzeɪʃ(ə)n/ *n.* **1** the act of causing or producing an effect. **2** = CAUSALITY. [F *causation* or L *causatio* pretext etc., in med.L the action of causing, f. *causare* CAUSE]

causative /ˈkɔːzətɪv/ *adj.* **1** acting as cause. **2** (foll. by *of*) producing; having as effect. **3** *Gram.* expressing cause. □□**causatively** *adv.* [ME f. OF *causatif* or f. LL *causativus*: see CAUSATION]

cause /kɔːz/ *n.* & *v.* —*n.* **1 a** that which produces an effect, or gives rise to an action, phenomenon, or condition. **b** a person or thing that occasions something. **c** a reason or motive; a ground that may be held to justify something (*no cause for complaint*). **2** a reason adjudged adequate (*show cause*). **3 a** principle, belief, or purpose which is advocated or supported (*faithful to the cause*). **4 a** a matter to be settled at law. **b** an individual's case offered at law (*plead a cause*). **5** the side taken by any party in a dispute. —*v.tr.* **1** be the cause of, produce, make happen (*caused a commotion*). **2** (foll. by *to* + infin.) induce (*caused me to smile*; *caused it to be done*). □**in the cause of** to maintain, defend, or support (*in the cause of justice*). **make common cause with** join the side of. □□**causable** *adj.* **causeless** *adj.* **causer** *n.* [ME f. OF f. L *causa*]

'cause /kɒz/ *conj.* & *adv. colloq.* = BECAUSE. [abbr.]

cause célèbre /ˌkɔːz seˈlebr/ *n.* (*pl.* **causes célèbres** *pronunc.* same) a lawsuit that attracts much attention. [F]

causerie /ˈkəʊzərɪ/ *n.* (*pl.* **causeries** *pronunc.* same) an informal article or talk, esp. on a literary subject. [F f. *causer* talk]

causeway /ˈkɔːzweɪ/ *n.* **1** a raised road or track across low or wet ground or a stretch of water. **2** a raised path by a road. [earlier *cauce*, *cauceway* f. ONF *caucié* ult. f. L CALX lime, limestone]

causey /ˈkɔːzɪ/ *n. archaic* or *dial.* = CAUSEWAY.

caustic /ˈkɔːstɪk/ *adj.* & *n.* —*adj.* **1** that burns or corrodes organic tissue. **2** sarcastic, biting. **3** *Chem.* strongly alkaline. **4** *Physics* formed by the intersection of reflected or refracted parallel rays from a curved surface. —*n.* **1** a caustic substance. **2** *Physics* a caustic surface or curve. □**caustic potash** potassium hydroxide. **caustic soda** sodium hydroxide. □□**caustically** *adv.* **causticity** /-ˈtɪsɪtɪ/

n. [L *causticus* f. Gk *kaustikos* f. *kaustos* burnt f. *kaiō* burn]

cauterize /'kɔːtəˌraɪz/ *v.tr.* (also **-ise**) *Med.* burn or coagulate (tissue) with a heated instrument or caustic substance, esp. to stop bleeding. □□ **cauterization** /-'zeɪʃ(ə)n/ *n.* [F *cautériser* f. LL *cauterizare* f. Gk *kautēriazō* f. *kautērion* branding-iron f. *kaiō* burn]

cautery /'kɔːtərɪ/ *n.* (*pl.* **-ies**) *Med.* 1 an instrument or caustic for cauterizing. 2 the operation of cauterizing. [L *cauterium* f. Gk *kautērion*: see CAUTERIZE]

caution /'kɔːʃ(ə)n/ *n. & v.* —*n.* 1 attention to safety; prudence, carefulness. 2 **a** esp. *Brit.* a warning, esp. a formal one in law. **b** a formal warning and reprimand. 3 *colloq.* an amusing or surprising person or thing. —*v.tr.* 1 (often foll. by *against*, or *to* + infin.) warn or admonish. 2 esp. *Brit.* issue a caution to. □ **caution money** *Brit.* a sum deposited as security for good conduct. [ME f. OF f. L *cautio -onis* f. *cavēre caut-* take heed]

cautionary /'kɔːʃənərɪ/ *adj.* that gives or serves as a warning (*a cautionary tale*).

cautious /'kɔːʃəs/ *adj.* careful, prudent; attentive to safety. □□ **cautiously** *adv.* **cautiousness** *n.* [ME f. OF f. L: see CAUTION]

cavalcade /ˌkævəl'keɪd/ *n.* a procession or formal company of riders, motor vehicles, etc. [F f. It. *cavalcata* f. *cavalcare* ride ult. f. L *caballus* pack-horse]

cavalier /ˌkævə'lɪə(r)/ *n. & adj.* —*n.* 1 *hist.* (**Cavalier**) a supporter of Charles I in the Civil War. 2 a courtly gentleman, esp. as a lady's escort. 3 *archaic* a horseman. —*adj.* offhand, supercilious, blasé. □□ **cavalierly** *adv.* [F f. It. *cavaliere*: see CHEVALIER]

cavalry /'kævəlrɪ/ *n.* (*pl.* **-ies**) (usu. treated as *pl.*) soldiers on horseback or in armoured vehicles. □ **cavalry twill** a strong fabric in a double twill. [F *cavallerie* f. It. *cavalleria* f. *cavallo* horse f. L *caballus*]

cavalryman /'kævəlrɪmən/ *n.* (*pl.* **-men**) a soldier of a cavalry regiment.

cavatina /ˌkævə'tiːnə/ *n.* 1 a short simple song. 2 a similar piece of instrumental music, usu. slow and emotional. [It.]

cave[1] /keɪv/ *n. & v.* —*n.* 1 a large hollow in the side of a cliff, hill, etc., or underground. 2 *Brit. hist.* a dissident political group. —*v.intr.* explore caves, esp. interconnecting or underground. □ **cave-bear** an extinct kind of large bear, whose bones have been found in caves. **cave-dweller** = CAVEMAN. **cave in 1 a** (of a wall, earth over a hollow, etc.) subside, collapse. **b** cause (a wall, earth, etc.) to do this. 2 yield or submit under pressure; give up. **cave-in** *n.* a collapse, submission, etc. □□ **cavelike** *adj.* **caver** *n.* [ME f. OF f. L *cava* f. *cavus* hollow: *cave in* prob. f. E. Anglian dial. *calve in*]

cave[2] /'keɪvɪ/ *int. Brit. school sl.* look out! (as a warning cry). □ **keep cave** act as lookout. [L, = beware]

caveat /'kævɪˌæt/ *n.* 1 a warning or proviso. 2 *Law* a process in court to suspend proceedings. [L, = let a person beware]

caveat emptor /'kævɪˌæt 'emptɔː(r)/ *n.* the principle that the buyer alone is responsible if dissatisfied. [L, = let the buyer beware]

caveman /'keɪvmæn/ *n.* (*pl.* **-men**) 1 a prehistoric man living in a cave. 2 a primitive or crude person.

cavern /'kæv(ə)n/ *n.* 1 a cave, esp. a large or dark one. 2 a dark cavelike place, e.g. a room. □□ **cavernous** *adj.* **cavernously** *adv.* [ME f. OF *caverne* or f. L *caverna* f. *cavus* hollow]

caviare /'kævɪˌɑː(r), ˌkævɪ'ɑː(r)/ *n.* (*US* **caviar**) the pickled roe of sturgeon or other large fish, eaten as a delicacy. [early forms repr. It. *caviale*, Fr. *caviar*, prob. f. med.Gk *khaviari*]

cavil /'kævɪl/ *v. & n.* —*v.intr.* (**cavilled**, **cavilling**; *US* **caviled**, **caviling**) (usu. foll. by *at*, *about*) make petty objections; carp. —*n.* a trivial objection. □□ **caviller** *n.* [F *caviller* f. L *cavillari* f. *cavilla* mockery]

caving /'keɪvɪŋ/ *n.* exploring caves as a sport or pastime.

cavitation /ˌkævɪ'teɪʃ(ə)n/ *n.* 1 the formation of a cavity in a structure. 2 the formation of bubbles, or of a vacuum, in a liquid.

cavity /'kævɪtɪ/ *n.* (*pl.* **-ies**) 1 a hollow within a solid body. 2 a decayed part of a tooth. □ **cavity wall** a wall formed from two skins of brick or blockwork with a space between. [F *cavité* or LL *cavitas* f. L *cavus* hollow]

cavort /kə'vɔːt/ *v.intr.* caper excitedly; gambol; prance. [US, perh. f. CURVET]

cavy /'keɪvɪ/ *n.* (*pl.* **-ies**) any small rodent of the family Caviidae, native to S. America and having a sturdy body and vestigial tail, including guinea pigs. [mod.L *cavia* f. Galibi *cabiai*]

caw /kɔː/ *n. & v.* —*n.* the harsh cry of a rook, crow, etc. —*v.intr.* utter this cry. [imit.]

cay /keɪ/ *n.* a low insular bank or reef of coral, sand, etc. (cf. KEY[2]). [Sp. *cayo* shoal, reef f. F *quai*: see QUAY]

cayenne /keɪ'en/ *n.* (in full **cayenne pepper**) a pungent red powder obtained from various plants of the genus *Capsicum* and used for seasoning. [Tupi *kyynha* assim. to *Cayenne* capital of French Guiana]

cayman /'keɪmən/ *n.* (also **caiman**) any of various S. American alligator-like reptilians, esp. of the genus *Caiman*. [Sp. & Port. *caiman*, f. Carib *acayuman*]

CB *abbr.* 1 citizens' band. 2 (in the UK) Companion of the Order of the Bath.

Cb *symb. US Chem.* the element columbium.

CBC *abbr.* Canadian Broadcasting Corporation.

CBE *abbr.* Commander of the Order of the British Empire.

CBI *abbr.* (in the UK) Confederation of British Industry.

CBS *abbr. US* Columbia Broadcasting System.

CC *abbr.* 1 *Brit.* **a** City Council. **b** County Council. **c** County Councillor. 2 Cricket Club. 3 Companion of the Order of Canada.

cc *abbr.* (also **c.c.**) 1 cubic centimetre(s). 2 carbon copy.

CD *abbr.* 1 compact disc. 2 Civil Defence. 3 *Corps Diplomatique.*

Cd *symb. Chem.* the element cadmium.

Cd. *abbr.* Command Paper (1900-18).

cd *abbr.* candela.

Cdr. *abbr. Mil.* Commander.

Cdre. *abbr.* Commodore.

CD-ROM /ˌsiːdiː'rɒm/ *abbr.* compact disc read-only memory (for retrieval of text or data on a VDU screen).

CDT *abbr. US* Central Daylight Time.

CD-video /ˌsiːdiː 'vɪdɪəʊ/ *n.* a system of simultaneously reproducing high-quality sound and video pictures from a compact disc.

CE *abbr.* 1 Church of England. 2 civil engineer. 3 Common Era.

Ce *symb. Chem.* the element cerium.

ceanothus /ˌsiːə'nəʊθəs/ *n.* any shrub of the genus *Ceanothus*, with small blue or white flowers. [mod.L f. Gk *keanōthos* kind of thistle]

cease /siːs/ *v. & n.* —*v.tr. & intr.* stop; bring or come to an end (*ceased breathing*). —*n.* (in **without cease**) unending. □ **cease fire** *Mil.* stop firing. **cease-fire** *n.* 1 the order to do this. 2 a period of truce; a suspension of hostilities. [ME f. OF *cesser*, L *cessare* frequent. of *cedere cess-* yield]

ceaseless /'siːslɪs/ *adj.* without end; not ceasing. □□ **ceaselessly** *adv.*

cecitis *US* var. of CAECITIS.

cecum *US* var. of CAECUM.

cedar /'siːdə(r)/ *n.* 1 any spreading evergreen conifer of the genus *Cedrus*, bearing tufts of small needles and cones of papery scales. 2 any of various similar conifers yielding timber. 3 (in full **cedar wood**) the

fragrant durable wood of any cedar tree. □□ **cedarn**
adj. poet. [ME f. OF *cedre* f. L *cedrus* f. Gk *kedros*]

cede /siːd/ *v.tr.* give up one's rights to or possession
of. [F *céder* or L *cedere* yield]

cedilla /sɪˈdɪlə/ *n.* **1** a mark written under the letter
c, esp. in French, to show that it is sibilant (as in
façade). **2** a similar mark under *s* in Turkish and
other oriental languages. [Sp. *cedilla* dimin. of *zeda*
f. Gk *zēta* letter Z]

Ceefax /ˈsiːfæks/ *n. Brit. propr.* a teletext service
provided by the BBC.

CEGB *abbr.* (in the UK) Central Electricity Generating Board.

ceilidh /ˈkeɪlɪ/ *n.* orig. *Ir.* & *Sc.* an informal gathering
for conversation, music, dancing, songs, and stories.
[Gael.]

ceiling /ˈsiːlɪŋ/ *n.* **1 a** the upper interior surface of a
room or other similar compartment. **b** the material
forming this. **2** an upper limit on prices, wages,
performance, etc. **3** *Aeron.* the maximum altitude a
given aircraft can reach. **4** *Naut.* the inside planking
of a ship's bottom and sides. [ME *celynge*, *siling*,
perh. ult. f. L *caelum* heaven or *celare* hide]

celadon /ˈselədɒn/ *n.* & *adj.* —*n.* **1** a willow-green
colour. **2** a grey-green glaze used on some pottery. **3**
Chinese pottery glazed in this way. —*adj.* of a
grey-green colour. [F, f. the name of a character in
d'Urfé's *L'Astrée* (1607–27)]

celandine /ˈseləndaɪn/ *n.* either of two yellow-
flowered plants, the greater celandine, *Chelidonium
majus*, and the lesser celandine, *Ranunculus ficaria*.
[ME and OF *celidoine* ult. f. Gk *khelidōn* swallow:
the flowering of the plant was associated with the
arrival of swallows]

-cele /siːl/ *comb. form* (also **-coele**) *Med.* swelling,
hernia (*gastrocele*). [Gk *kēlē* tumour]

celebrant /ˈselɪbrənt/ *n.* a person who performs a
rite, esp. a priest at the Eucharist. [F *célébrant* or L
celebrare celebrant-: see CELEBRATE]

celebrate /ˈselɪbreɪt/ *v.* **1** *tr.* mark (a festival or
special event) with festivities etc. **2** *tr.* perform
publicly and duly (a religious ceremony etc.). **3 a** *tr.*
officiate at (the Eucharist). **b** *intr.* officiate, esp. at
the Eucharist. **4** *intr.* engage in festivities, usu. after
a special event etc. **5** *tr.* (as **celebrated** *adj.*) publicly
honoured, widely known. □□ **celebration**
/-ˈbreɪʃ(ə)n/ *n.* **celebrator** *n.* **celebratory** *adj.* [L
celebrare f. *celeber* -*bris* frequented, honoured]

celebrity /sɪˈlebrɪtɪ/ *n.* (*pl.* **-ies**) **1** a well-known
person. **2** fame. [F *célébrité* or L *celebritas* f. *celeber*:
see CELEBRATE]

celeriac /sɪˈlerɪˌæk/ *n.* a variety of celery with a
swollen turnip-like stem-base used as a vegetable.
[CELERY: -*ac* is unexplained]

celerity /sɪˈlerɪtɪ/ *n. archaic* or *literary* swiftness
(esp. of a living creature). [ME f. F *célérité* f. L
celeritas -*tatis* f. *celer* swift]

celery /ˈselərɪ/ *n.* an umbelliferous plant, *Apium
graveolens*, with closely packed succulent leaf-stalks
used as a vegetable. □ **celery pine** an Australasian
tree, *Phyllocladus trichomanoides*, with branchlets
like celery leaves. [F *céleri* f. It. dial. *selleri* f. L
selinum f. Gk *selinon* parsley]

celesta /sɪˈlestə/ *n. Mus.* a small keyboard instrument resembling a glockenspiel, with hammers
striking steel plates suspended over wooden resonators, giving an ethereal bell-like sound. [pseudo-L
f. F *céleste*: see CELESTE]

celeste /sɪˈlest/ *n. Mus.* **1** an organ and harmonium
stop with a soft tremulous tone. **2** = CELESTA. [F
céleste heavenly f. L *caelestis* f. *caelum* heaven]

celestial /sɪˈlestɪəl/ *adj.* **1** heavenly; divinely good
or beautiful; sublime. **2 a** of the sky; of the part of
the sky commonly observed in astronomy etc. **b** of
heavenly bodies. □ **celestial equator** the great circle
of the sky in the plane perpendicular to the earth's
axis. **celestial horizon** see HORIZON 1c. **celestial
navigation** navigation by the stars etc. □□

celestially *adv.* [ME f. OF f. med.L *caelestialis* f. L
caelestis: see CELESTE]

celiac *US* var. of COELIAC.

celibate /ˈselɪbət/ *adj.* & *n.* —*adj.* **1** committed to
abstention from sexual relations and from marriage,
esp. for religious reasons. **2** abstaining from sexual
relations. —*n.* a celibate person. □□ **celibacy** *n.* [F
célibat or L *caelibatus* unmarried state f. *caelebs* -*ibis*
unmarried]

cell /sel/ *n.* **1** a small room, esp. in a prison
or monastery. **2** a small compartment, e.g. in a
honeycomb. **3** a small group as a nucleus of political
activity, esp. of a subversive kind. **4** *hist.* a small
monastery or nunnery dependent on a larger one. **5**
Biol. **a** the structural and functional usu. microscopic
unit of an organism, consisting of cytoplasm and a
nucleus enclosed in a membrane. **b** an enclosed
cavity in an organism etc. **6** *Electr.* a vessel for
containing electrodes within an electrolyte for
current-generation or electrolysis. □□ **celled** *adj.*
(also in *comb.*). [ME f. OF *celle* or f. L *cella* storeroom
etc.]

cellar /ˈselə(r)/ *n.* & *v.* —*n.* **1** a room below ground
level in a house, used for storage, esp. of wine or
coal. **2** a stock of wine in a cellar (*has a good cellar*).
—*v.tr.* store or put in a cellar. [ME f. AF *celer*, OF
celier f. LL *cellarium* storehouse]

cellarage /ˈselərɪdʒ/ *n.* **1** cellar accommodation. **2**
the charge for the use of a cellar or storehouse.

cellarer /ˈselərə(r)/ *n.* a monastic officer in charge of
wine.

cellaret /ˌseləˈret/ *n.* a case or sideboard for holding
wine bottles in a dining-room.

cello /ˈtʃeləʊ/ *n.* (*pl.* **-os**) a bass instrument of the
violin family, held upright on the floor between the
legs of the seated player. □□ **cellist** *n.* [abbr. of
VIOLONCELLO]

Cellophane /ˈseləˌfeɪn/ *n. propr.* a thin transparent
wrapping material made from viscose. [CELLULOSE +
-*phane* (cf. DIAPHANOUS)]

cellphone /ˈselfəʊn/ *n.* a small portable radio-
telephone having access to a cellular radio system.

cellular /ˈseljʊlə(r)/ *adj.* **1** of or having small compartments or cavities. **2** of open texture; porous. **3**
Physiol. of or consisting of cells. □ **cellular blanket**
a blanket of open texture. **cellular plant** a plant
with no distinct stem, leaves, etc. **cellular radio** a
system of mobile radio-telephone transmission with
an area divided into 'cells' each served by its own
small transmitter. □□ **cellularity** /-ˈlærɪtɪ/ *n.*
cellulate *adj.* **cellulation** /-ˈleɪʃ(ə)n/ *n.* **cellulous**
adj. [F *cellulaire* f. mod.L *cellularis*: see CELLULE]

cellule /ˈselˌjuːl/ *n. Biol.* a small cell or cavity. [F
cellule or L *cellula* dimin. of *cella* CELL]

cellulite /ˈseljʊˌlaɪt/ *n.* a lumpy form of fat, esp. on
the hips and thighs of women, causing puckering of
the skin. [F (as CELLULE)]

cellulitis /ˌseljʊˈlaɪtɪs/ *n.* inflammation of cellular
tissue.

celluloid /ˈseljʊˌlɔɪd/ *n.* **1** a transparent flammable
plastic made from camphor and cellulose nitrate. **2**
cinema film. [irreg. f. CELLULOSE]

cellulose /ˈseljʊˌləʊz, -ˌləʊs/ *n.* **1** *Biochem.* a carbohydrate forming the main constituent of plant-cell
walls, used in the production of textile fibres. **2** (in
general use) a paint or lacquer consisting of esp.
cellulose acetate or nitrate in solution. □□ **cellulosic**
/-ˈləʊsɪk/ *adj.* [F (as CELLULE)]

celom *US* var. of COELOM.

Celsius /ˈselsɪəs/ *adj.* of or denoting a temperature
on the Celsius scale. □ **Celsius scale** a scale of
temperature on which water freezes at 0° and boils
at 100° under standard conditions. [A. *Celsius*, Sw.
astronomer d. 1744]

Celt /kelt, selt/ *n.* (also **Kelt**) a member of a group
of W. European peoples, including the pre-Roman
of W. European peoples, including the pre-Roman
inhabitants of Britain and Gaul and their descendants, esp. in Ireland, Wales, Scotland, Cornwall,

b *but* d *dog* f *few* g *get* h *he* j *yes* k *cat* l *leg* m *man* n *no* p *pen* r *red* s *sit* t *top* v *voice*

Brittany, and the Isle of Man. [L *Celtae* (pl.) f. Gk *Keltoi*]

celt /kelt/ *n.* Archaeol. a stone or metal prehistoric implement with a chisel edge. [med.L *celtes* chisel]

Celtic /'keltɪk, 'seltɪk/ *adj.* & *n.* —*adj.* of or relating to the Celts. —*n.* a group of languages spoken by Celtic peoples, including Gaelic, Welsh, Cornish, and Breton. □**Celtic cross** a Latin cross with a circle round the centre. □□**Celticism** /-ˌsɪz(ə)m/ *n.* [L *celticus* (as CELT) or F *celtique*]

cembalo /'tʃembəˌləʊ/ *n.* (*pl.* **-os**) a harpsichord. [abbr. of CLAVICEMBALO]

cement /sɪ'ment/ *n.* & *v.* —*n.* **1** a powdery substance made by calcining lime and clay, mixed with water to form mortar or used in concrete (see also *Portland cement*). **2** any similar substance that hardens and fastens on setting. **3** a uniting factor or principle. **4** a substance for filling cavities in teeth. **5** (also **cementum**) *Anat.* a thin layer of bony material that fixes teeth to the jaw. —*v.tr.* **1 a** unite with or as with cement. **b** establish or strengthen (a friendship etc.). **2** apply cement to. **3** line or cover with cement. □**cement-mixer** a machine (usu. with a revolving drum) for mixing cement with water. □□**cementer** *n.* [ME f. OF *ciment* f. L *caementum* quarry stone f. *caedere* hew]

cementation /ˌsiːmen'teɪʃ(ə)n/ *n.* **1** the act or process of cementing or being cemented. **2** the heating of iron with charcoal powder to form steel.

cemetery /'semɪtərɪ/ *n.* (*pl.* **-ies**) a burial ground, esp. one not in a churchyard. [LL *coemeterium* f. Gk *koimētērion* dormitory f. *koimaō* put to sleep]

C.Eng. *abbr. Brit.* chartered engineer.

cenobite *US* var. of COENOBITE.

cenotaph /'senəˌtɑːf/ *n.* a tomblike monument, esp. a war memorial, to a person whose body is elsewhere. [F *cénotaphe* f. LL *cenotaphium* f. Gk *kenos* empty + *taphos* tomb]

Cenozoic /ˌsiːnə'zəʊɪk/ (also **Cainozoic** /ˌkaɪnə-/, **Caenozoic** /ˌsiːn-/) *adj.* & *n. Geol.* —*adj.* of or relating to the most recent era of geological time, marked by the evolution and development of mammals, birds, and flowers. ¶ Cf. Appendix II. —*n.* this era (cf. MESOZOIC, PALAEOZOIC). [Gk *kainos* new + *zōion* animal]

censer /'sensə(r)/ *n.* a vessel in which incense is burnt, esp. during a religious procession or ceremony. [ME f. AF *censer*, OF *censier* aphetic of *encensier* f. *encens* INCENSE[1]]

censor /'sensə(r)/ *n.* & *v.* —*n.* **1** an official authorized to examine printed matter, films, news, etc., before public release, and to suppress any parts on the grounds of obscenity, a threat to security, etc. **2** *Rom.Hist.* either of two annual magistrates responsible for holding censuses and empowered to supervise public morals. **3** *Psychol.* an impulse which is said to prevent certain ideas and memories from emerging into consciousness. —*v.tr.* **1** act as a censor of. **2** make deletions or changes in. ¶ As a verb, often confused with *censure*. □□**censorial** /-'sɔːrɪəl/ *adj.*

censorship *n.* [L f. *censēre* assess: in sense 3 mistransl. of G *Zensur* censorship]

censorious /sen'sɔːrɪəs/ *adj.* severely critical; faultfinding; quick or eager to criticize. □□**censoriously** *adv.* **censoriousness** *n.* [L *censorius*: see CENSOR]

censure /'senʃə(r)/ *v.* & *n.* —*v.tr.* criticize harshly; reprove. ¶ Often confused with *censor*. —*n.* harsh criticism; expression of disapproval. □□**censurable** *adj.* [ME f. OF f. L *censura* f. *censēre* assess]

census /'sensəs/ *n.* (*pl.* **censuses**) the official count of a population or of a class of things, often with various statistics noted. [L f. *censēre* assess]

cent /sent/ *n.* **1 a** a monetary unit valued at one-hundredth of a dollar or other metric unit. **b** a coin of this value. **2** *colloq.* a very small sum of money. **3** see PER CENT. [F *cent* or It. *cento* or L *centum* hundred]

cent. *abbr.* century.

centaur /'sentɔː(r)/ *n.* a creature in Greek mythology with the head, arms, and torso of a man and the body and legs of a horse. [ME f. L *centaurus* f. Gk *kentauros*, of unkn. orig.]

centaury /'sentɔːrɪ/ *n.* (*pl.* **-ies**) any plant of the genus *Centaurium*, esp. *C. erythraea*, formerly used in medicine. [LL *centaurea* ult. f. Gk *kentauros* CENTAUR: from the legend that it was discovered by the centaur Chiron]

centavo /sen'tɑːvəʊ/ *n.* a small coin of Spain, Portugal, and some Latin American countries, worth one-hundredth of the standard unit. [Sp. f. L *centum* hundred]

centenarian /ˌsentɪ'neərɪən/ *n.* & *adj.* —*n.* a person a hundred or more years old. —*adj.* a hundred or more years old.

centenary /sen'tiːnərɪ/ *n.* & *adj.* —*n.* (*pl.* **-ies**) **1** a hundredth anniversary. **2** a celebration of this. —*adj.* **1** of or relating to a centenary. **2** occurring every hundred years. [L *centenarius* f. *centeni* a hundred each f. *centum* a hundred]

centennial /sen'tenɪəl/ *adj.* & *n.* —*adj.* **1** lasting for a hundred years. **2** occurring every hundred years. —*n. US* = CENTENARY *n.* [L *centum* a hundred, after BIENNIAL]

center *US* var. of CENTRE.

centerboard *US* var. of CENTREBOARD.

centerfold *US* var. of CENTREFOLD.

centering *US* var. of CENTRING.

centesimal /sen'tesɪm(ə)l/ *adj.* reckoning or reckoned by hundredths. □□**centesimally** *adv.* [L *centesimus* hundredth f. *centum* hundred]

centi- /'sentɪ/ *comb. form* **1** one-hundredth, esp. of a unit in the metric system (*centigram*; *centilitre*). **2** hundred. ¶ Abbr.: **c.** [L *centum* hundred]

centigrade /'sentɪˌɡreɪd/ *adj.* **1** = CELSIUS. **2** having a scale of a hundred degrees. ¶ In sense 1 *Celsius* is usually preferred in technical use. [F f. L *centum* hundred + *gradus* step]

centigram /'sentɪˌɡræm/ *n.* (also **centigramme**) a metric unit of mass, equal to one-hundredth of a gram.

centilitre /'sentɪˌliːtə(r)/ *n.* (*US* **centiliter**) a metric unit of capacity, equal to one-hundredth of a litre.

centime /'sɒtiːm/ *n.* **1** a monetary unit valued at one-hundredth of a franc. **2** a coin of this value. [F f. L *centum* a hundred]

centimetre /'sentɪˌmiːtə(r)/ *n.* (*US* **centimeter**) a metric unit of length, equal to one-hundredth of a metre. □**centimetre-gram-second system** the system using these as basic units of length, mass, and time. ¶ Abbr.: **cgs system**.

centipede /'sentɪˌpiːd/ *n.* any arthropod of the class Chilopoda, with a wormlike body of many segments each with a pair of legs. [F *centipède* or L *centipeda* f. *centum* hundred + *pes pedis* foot]

cento /'sentəʊ/ *n.* (*pl.* **-os**) a composition made up of quotations from other authors. [L, = patchwork garment]

central /'sentr(ə)l/ *adj.* **1** of, at, or forming the centre. **2** from the centre. **3** chief, essential, most important. □**Central America** the isthmus joining North and South America. **central bank** a national bank issuing currency etc. **central heating** a method of warming a building by pipes, radiators, etc., fed from a central source of heat. **central nervous system** *Anat.* the complex of nerve tissues that controls the activities of the body, in vertebrates the brain and spinal cord. **central processor** (or **processing unit**) the principal operating part of a computer. □□**centrality** /-'trælɪtɪ/ *n.* **centrally** *adv.* [F *central* or L *centralis* f. *centrum* CENTRE]

centralism /'sentrəˌlɪz(ə)m/ *n.* a system that centralizes (esp. an administration) (see also *democratic centralism*). □□**centralist** *n.*

centralize /'sentrəˌlaɪz/ *v.* (also **-ise**) **1** *tr.* & *intr.* bring or come to a centre. **2** *tr.* **a** concentrate (administration) at a single centre. **b** subject (a State) to this system. □□**centralization** /-'zeɪʃ(ə)n/ *n.*

centre /'sentə(r)/ n. & v. (US **center**) —n. **1** the middle point, esp. of a line, circle, or sphere, equidistant from the ends or from any point on the circumference or surface. **2** a pivot or axis of rotation. **3 a** a place or group of buildings forming a central point in a district, city, etc., or a main area for an activity (*shopping centre; town centre*). **b** (with preceding word) a piece or set of equipment for a number of connected functions (*music centre*). **4** a point of concentration or dispersion; a nucleus or source. **5** a political party or group holding moderate opinions. **6** the filling in a chocolate etc. **7** *Sport* **a** the middle player in a line or group in some field games. **b** a kick or hit from the side to the centre of the pitch. **8** (in a lathe etc.) a conical adjustable support for the workpiece. **9** (*attrib.*) of or at the centre. —v. **1** *intr.* (foll. by *in, on; disp.* foll. by *round*) have as its main centre. **2** *tr.* place in the centre. **3** *tr.* mark with a centre. **4** *tr.* (foll. by *in* etc.) concentrate. **5** *tr. Sport* kick or hit (the ball) from the side to the centre of the pitch. □ **centre-bit** a boring tool with a centre point and side cutters. **centre forward** *Sport* the middle player or position in a forward line. **centre half** *Sport* the middle player or position in a half-back line. **centre of attention 1** a person or thing that draws general attention. **2** *Physics* the point to which bodies tend by gravity. **centre of gravity** (or **mass**) the point at which the weight of a body may be considered to act. **centre-piece 1** an ornament for the middle of a table. **2** a principal item. **centre spread** the two facing middle pages of a newspaper etc. □□ **centred** adj. (often in *comb.*). **centremost** adj. **centric** adj. **centrical** adj. **centricity** /-'trɪsɪtɪ/ n. [ME f. OF *centre* or L *centrum* f. Gk *kentron* sharp point]

centreboard /'sentə,bɔːd/ n. (US **centerboard**) a board for lowering through a boat's keel to prevent leeway.

centrefold /'sentə,fəʊld/ n. (US **centerfold**) a printed and usu. illustrated sheet folded to form the centre spread of a magazine etc.

centreing var. of CENTRING.

-centric /'sentrɪk/ comb. form forming adjectives with the sense 'having a (specified) centre' (*anthropocentric; eccentric*). [after *concentric* etc. f. Gk *kentrikos*: see CENTRE]

centrifugal /,sentrɪ'fjuːg(ə)l, sen'trɪfjʊg(ə)l/ adj. moving or tending to move from a centre (cf. CENTRIPETAL). □ **centrifugal force** an apparent force that acts outwards on a body moving about a centre. □□ **centrifugally** adv. [mod.L *centrifugus* f. L *centrum* centre + *fugere* flee]

centrifuge /'sentrɪ,fjuːdʒ/ n. & v. —n. a machine with a rapidly rotating device designed to separate liquids from solids or other liquids (e.g. cream from milk). —v.tr. **1** subject to the action of a centrifuge. **2** separate by centrifuge. □□ **centrifugation** /-fjʊ'geɪʃ(ə)n/ n.

centring /'sentrɪŋ/ (also **centreing** /'sentərɪŋ/, US **centering** /'sentərɪŋ/) n. a temporary frame used to support an arch, dome, etc., while under construction.

centriole /'sentrɪ,əʊl/ n. Biol. a minute organelle usu. within a centrosome involved esp. in the development of spindles in cell division. [med.L *centriolum* dimin. of *centrum* centre]

centripetal /sen'trɪpɪt(ə)l/ adj. moving or tending to move towards a centre (cf. CENTRIFUGAL). □ **centripetal force** the force acting on a body causing it to move about a centre. □□ **centripetally** adv. [mod.L *centripetus* f. L *centrum* centre + *petere* seek]

centrist /'sentrɪst/ n. Polit. often derog. a person who holds moderate views. □□ **centrism** n.

centromere /'sentrəmɪə(r)/ n. Biol. the point on a chromosome to which the spindle is attached during cell division. [L *centrum* centre + Gk *meros* part]

centrosome /'sentrə,səʊm/ n. Biol. a distinct part of the cytoplasm in a cell, usu. near the nucleus, that contains the centriole. [G *Centrosoma* f. L *centrum* centre + Gk *sōma* body]

centuple /'sentjʊp(ə)l/ n., adj., & v. —n. a hundredfold amount. —adj. increased a hundredfold. —v.tr. multiply by a hundred; increase a hundredfold. [F *centuple* or eccl.L *centuplus, centuplex* f. L *centum* hundred]

centurion /sen'tjʊərɪən/ n. the commander of a century in the ancient Roman army. [ME f. L *centurio -onis* (as CENTURY)]

century /'sentʃərɪ, -tjʊrɪ/ n. (pl. **-ies**) **1 a** a period of one hundred years. **b** any of the centuries reckoned from the birth of Christ (*twentieth century* = 1901-2000; *fifth century* BC = 500-401 BC). ¶ In modern use often reckoned as (e.g.) 1900-1999. **2 a** a score etc. of a hundred in a sporting event, esp. a hundred runs by one batsman in cricket. **b** a group of a hundred things. **3 a** a company in the ancient Roman army, orig. of 100 men. **b** an ancient Roman political division for voting. □ **century plant** a plant, *Agave americana*, flowering once in many years and yielding sap from which tequila is distilled: also called American aloe (see ALOE). [L *centuria* f. *centum* hundred]

cep /sep/ n. an edible mushroom, *Boletus edulis*, with a stout stalk and brown smooth cap. [F *cèpe* f. Gascon *cep* f. L *cippus* stake]

cephalic /sɪ'fælɪk, ke-/ adj. of or in the head. □ **cephalic index** Anthropol. a number expressing the ratio of a head's greatest breadth and length. [F *céphalique* f. L *cephalicus* f. Gk *kephalikos* f. *kephalē* head]

-cephalic /sɪ'fælɪk/ comb. form = -CEPHALOUS.

cephalopod /'sefələ,pɒd/ n. any mollusc of the class Cephalopoda, having a distinct tentacled head, e.g. octopus, squid, and cuttlefish. [Gk *kephalē* head + *pous podos* foot]

cephalothorax /,sefələʊ'θɔːræks/ n. (pl. **-thoraces** /-rə,siːz/ or **-thoraxes**) Anat. the fused head and thorax of a spider, crab, or other arthropod.

-cephalous /'sefələs/ comb. form -headed (*brachycephalous; dolichocephalic*). [Gk *kephalē* head]

cepheid /'siːfiɪd, 'sefiɪd/ n. (in full **cepheid variable**) Astron. any of a class of variable stars with a regular cycle of brightness that can be used to measure distances. [L *Cepheus* f. Gk *Kēpheus*, a mythical king whose name was given to a constellation]

ceramic /sɪ'ræmɪk, kɪ-/ adj. & n. —adj. **1** made of (esp.) clay and permanently hardened by heat (a *ceramic bowl*). **2** of or relating to ceramics (*the ceramic arts*). —n. **1** a ceramic article or product. **2** a substance, esp. clay, used to make ceramic articles. [Gk *keramikos* f. *keramos* pottery]

ceramics /sɪ'ræmɪks, kɪ-/ n.pl. **1** ceramic products collectively (*exhibition of ceramics*). **2** (usu. treated as sing.) the art of making ceramic articles.

ceramist /'serəmɪst/ n. a person who makes ceramics.

cerastes /sɪ'ræstiːz/ n. any viper of the genus *Cerastes*, esp. *C. cerastes* having a sharp upright spike over each eye and moving forward in a lateral motion. [L f. Gk *kerastēs* f. *keras* horn]

cerastium /sɪ'ræstɪəm/ n. any plant of the genus *Cerastium*, with white flowers and often horn-shaped capsules. [mod.L f. Gk *kerastes* horned f. *keras* horn]

cere /sɪə(r)/ n. a waxy fleshy covering at the base of the upper beak in some birds. [L *cera* wax]

cereal /'sɪərɪəl/ n. & adj —n. **1** (usu. in pl.) **a** any kind of grain used for food. **b** any grass producing this, e.g. wheat, maize, rye, etc. **2** a breakfast food made from a cereal and requiring no cooking. —adj. of edible grain or products of it. [L *cerealis* f. *Ceres* goddess of agriculture]

cerebellum /,serɪ'beləm/ n. (pl. **cerebellums** or **cerebella** /-lə/) the part of the brain at the back of the skull in vertebrates, which coordinates and regulates muscular activity. □□ **cerebellar** *adj.* [L dimin. of CEREBRUM]

cerebral /'serɪbr(ə)l/ *adj.* **1** of the brain. **2** intellectual rather than emotional. **3** = CACUMINAL. □**cerebral hemisphere** each of the two halves of the vertebrate cerebrum. **cerebral palsy** *Med.* spastic paralysis from brain damage before or at birth, with jerky or uncontrolled movements. □□ **cerebrally** *adv.* [L *cerebrum* brain]

cerebration /ˌserɪ'breɪʃ(ə)n/ *n.* working of the brain. □**unconscious cerebration** action of the brain with results reached without conscious thought. □□ **cerebrate** /'serɪˌbreɪt/ *v.intr.*

cerebro- /'serɪbrəʊ/ *comb. form* brain (*cerebrospinal*).

cerebrospinal /ˌserɪbrəʊ'spaɪn(ə)l/ *adj.* of the brain and spine.

cerebrovascular /ˌserɪbrəʊ'væskjʊlə(r)/ *adj.* of the brain and its blood vessels.

cerebrum /'serɪbrəm/ *n.* (*pl.* **cerebra** /-brə/) the principal part of the brain in vertebrates, located in the front area of the skull, which integrates complex sensory and neural functions. [L, = brain]

cerecloth /'sɪəklɒθ/ *n. hist.* waxed cloth used as a waterproof covering or (esp.) as a shroud. [earlier *cered cloth* f. *cere* to wax f. L *cerare* f. *cera* wax]

cerement /'sɪəmənt/ *n.* (usu. in *pl.*) *literary* grave-clothes; cerecloth. [first used by Shakesp. in *Hamlet* (1602): app. f. CERECLOTH]

ceremonial /ˌserɪ'məʊnɪəl/ *adj. & n.* —*adj.* **1** with or concerning ritual or ceremony. **2** formal (*a ceremonial bow*). —*n.* **1** a system of rites etc. to be used esp. at a formal or religious occasion. **2** the formalities or behaviour proper to any occasion (*with all due ceremonial*). **3** *RC Ch.* a book containing an order of ritual. □□ **ceremonialism** *n.* **ceremonialist** *n.* **ceremonially** *adv.* [LL *caerimonialis* (as CEREMONY)]

ceremonious /ˌserɪ'məʊnɪəs/ *adj.* **1** excessively polite; punctilious. **2** having or showing a fondness for ritualistic observance or formality. □□ **ceremoniously** *adv.* **ceremoniousness** *n.* [F *cérémonieux* or LL *caerimoniosus* (as CEREMONY)]

ceremony /'serɪmənɪ/ *n.* (*pl.* **-ies**) **1** a formal religious or public occasion, esp. celebrating a particular event or anniversary. **2** formalities, esp. of an empty or ritualistic kind (*ceremony of exchanging compliments*). **3** excessively polite behaviour (*bowed low with great ceremony*). □**Master of Ceremonies 1** (also **MC**) a person introducing speakers at a banquet, or entertainers in a variety show. **2** a person in charge of ceremonies at a state or public occasion. **stand on ceremony** insist on the observance of formalities. **without ceremony** informally. [ME f. OF *ceremonie* or L *caerimonia* religious worship]

Cerenkov radiation /tʃe'renkɒf/ *n.* (also **Cherenkov**) the electromagnetic radiation emitted by particles moving in a medium at speeds faster than that of light in the same medium. [P. A. *Cherenkov*, Russian physicist b. 1904]

ceresin /'serɪsɪn/ *n.* a hard whitish wax used with or instead of beeswax. [mod.L *ceres* f. L *cera* wax + -IN]

cerise /sə'riːz, -'riːs/ *adj. & n.* —*adj.* of a light clear red. —*n.* this colour. [F, = CHERRY]

cerium /'sɪərɪəm/ *n. Chem.* a silvery metallic element of the lanthanide series occurring naturally in various minerals and used in the manufacture of lighter flints. ¶ Symb.: **Ce**. [named after the asteroid *Ceres*, discovered (1801) about the same time as this]

cermet /'sɜːmet/ *n.* a heat-resistant material made of ceramic and sintered metal. [*ceramic* + *metal*]

CERN /sɜːn/ *abbr.* European Organization for Nuclear Research. [F *Conseil Européen pour la Recherche Nucléaire*, its former title]

cero- /'sɪərəʊ/ *comb. form* wax (cf. CEROGRAPHY, CEROPLASTIC). [L *cera* or Gk *kēros* wax]

cerography /sɪə'rɒgrəfɪ/ *n.* the technique of engraving or designing on or with wax.

ceroplastic /ˌsɪərəʊ'plæstɪk/ *adj.* **1** modelled in wax. **2** of or concerning wax-modelling.

cert /sɜːt/ *n. sl.* (esp. **dead cert**) **1** an event or result regarded as certain to happen. **2** a horse strongly tipped to win. [abbr. of CERTAIN, CERTAINTY]

cert. /sɜːt/ *abbr.* **1** a certificate. **2** certified.

certain /'sɜːt(ə)n, -tɪn/ *adj. & pron.* —*adj.* **1 a** (often foll. by *of*, or *that* + clause) confident, convinced (*certain that I put it here*). **b** (often foll. by *that* + clause) indisputable; known for sure (*it is certain that he is guilty*). **2** (often foll. by *to* + infin.) **a** that may be relied on to happen (*it is certain to rain*). **b** destined (*certain to become a star*). **3** definite, unfailing, reliable (*a certain indication of the coming storm; his touch is certain*). **4** (of a person, place, etc.) that might be specified, but is not (*a certain lady; of a certain age*). **5** some though not much (*a certain reluctance*). **6** (of a person, place, etc.) existing, though probably unknown to the reader or hearer (*a certain John Smith*). —*pron.* (as *pl.*) some but not all (*certain of them were wounded*). □**for certain** without doubt. **make certain** = *make sure* (see SURE). [ME f. OF ult. f. L *certus* settled]

certainly /'sɜːtənlɪ, -tɪnlɪ/ *adv.* **1** undoubtedly, definitely. **2** confidently. **3** in affirmative answer to a question or command) yes; by all means.

certainty /'sɜːtəntɪ, -tɪntɪ/ *n.* (*pl.* **-ies**) **1 a** an undoubted fact. **b** a certain prospect (*his return is a certainty*). **2** (often foll. by *of*, or *that* + clause) an absolute conviction (*has a certainty of his own worth*). **3** (often foll. by *to* + infin.) a thing or person that may be relied on (*a certainty to win the Derby*). □**for a certainty** beyond the possibility of doubt. [ME f. AF *certainté*, OF *-eté* (as CERTAIN)]

Cert. Ed. *abbr.* (in the UK) Certificate in Education.

certifiable /ˌsɜːtɪ'faɪəb(ə)l, 'sɜːt-/ *adj.* **1** able or needing to be certified. **2** *colloq.* insane.

certificate *n. & v.* /sə'tɪfɪkət/ —*n.* a formal document attesting a fact, esp. birth, marriage, or death, a medical condition, a level of achievement, a fulfilment of requirements, ownership of shares, etc. —*v.tr.* /-ˌkeɪt/ (esp. as **certificated** *adj.*) provide with or license or attest by a certificate. □**Certificate of Secondary Education** *hist.* **1** an examination set for secondary-school pupils in England and Wales. **2** the certificate gained by passing it. ¶ Replaced in 1988 by the General Certificate of Secondary Education. □□ **certification** /ˌsɜːtɪfɪ'keɪʃ(ə)n/ *n.* [F *certificat* or med.L *certificatum* f. *certificare*: see CERTIFY]

certify /'sɜːtɪˌfaɪ/ *v.tr.* (**-ies**, **-ied**) **1** make a formal statement of; attest; attest to (*certified that he had witnessed the crime*). **2** declare by certificate (that a person is qualified or competent) (*certified as a trained bookkeeper*). **3** officially declare insane (*he should be certified*). □**certified cheque** a cheque the validity of which is guaranteed by a bank. **certified mail** *US* = *recorded delivery* (see RECORD). **certified milk** milk guaranteed free from the tuberculosis bacillus. [ME f. OF *certifier* f. med.L *certificare* f. L *certus* certain]

certiorari /ˌsɜːtɪɔː'reəraɪ/ *n. Law* a writ from a higher court requesting the records of a case tried in a lower court. [LL passive of *certiorare* inform f. *certior* compar. of *certus* certain]

certitude /'sɜːtɪˌtjuːd/ *n.* a feeling of absolute certainty or conviction. [ME f. LL *certitudo* f. *certus* certain]

cerulean /sə'ruːlɪən/ *adj. & n. literary* —*adj.* deep blue like a clear sky. —*n.* this colour. [L *caeruleus* sky-blue f. *caelum* sky]

cerumen /sə'ruːmen/ *n.* the yellow waxy substance in the outer ear. □□ **ceruminous** *adj.* [mod.L f. L *cera* wax]

ceruse /'sɪəruːs, sɪ'ruːs/ *n.* white lead. [ME f. OF f. L *cerussa*, perh. f. Gk *kēros* wax]

cervelat /'sɜ:və,lɑ:, -,læt/ n. a kind of smoked pork sausage. [obs. F f. It. *cervellata*]

cervical /sɜ:'vaɪk(ə)l, 'sɜ:vɪk(ə)l/ adj. Anat. **1** of or relating to the neck (*cervical vertebrae*). **2** of or relating to the cervix. □**cervical screening** examination of a large number of apparently healthy women for cervical cancer. **cervical smear** a specimen of cellular material from the neck of the womb for detection of cancer. [F *cervical* or mod.L *cervicalis* f. L *cervix -icis* neck]

cervine /'sɜ:vaɪn/ adj. of or like a deer. [L *cervinus* f. *cervus* deer]

cervix /'sɜ:vɪks/ n. (pl. **cervices** /-,si:z/) Anat. **1** the neck. **2** any necklike structure, esp. the neck of the womb. [L]

Cesarean (also **Cesarian**) US var. of CAESAREAN.

cesarevitch /sɪ'zærɪvɪtʃ/ n. (also **cesarewitch** /-wɪtʃ/) **1** hist. the eldest son of the emperor of Russia (cf. TSAREVICH). **2** (**Cesarewitch**) a horse-race run annually at Newmarket. [Russ. *tsesarevich*]

cesium US var. of CAESIUM.

cess[1] /ses/ n. (also **sess**) Sc., Ir., & Ind. etc. a tax, a levy. [properly *sess* for obs. *assess* n.: see ASSESS]

cess[2] /ses/ n. Ir. □**bad cess to** may evil befall (*bad cess to their clan*). [perh. f. CESS[1]]

cessation /se'seɪʃ(ə)n/ n. **1** a ceasing (*cessation of the truce*). **2** a pause (*resumed fighting after the cessation*). [ME f. L *cessatio* f. *cessare* CEASE]

cesser /'sesə(r)/ n. Law a coming to an end; a cessation (of a term, a liability, etc.). [AF & OF, = CEASE]

cession /'seʃ(ə)n/ n. **1** (often foll. by *of*) the ceding or giving up (of rights, property, and esp. of territory by a State). **2** the territory etc. so ceded. [ME f. OF *cession* or L *cessio* f. *cedere cess-* go away]

cessionary /'seʃənəri/ n. (pl. **-ies**) Law = ASSIGN n.

cesspit /'sespɪt/ n. **1** a pit for the disposal of refuse. **2** = CESSPOOL. [*cess* in CESSPOOL + PIT[1]]

cesspool /'sespu:l/ n. **1** an underground container for the temporary storage of liquid waste or sewage. **2** a centre of corruption, depravity, etc. [perh. alt., after POOL[1], f. earlier *cesperalle*, f. *suspiral* vent, water-pipe, f. OF *souspirail* air-hole f. L *suspirare* breathe up, sigh (as SUB-, *spirare* breathe)]

cestode /'sestəʊd/ n. (also **cestoid** /'sestɔɪd/) any flatworm of the class Cestoda, including tapeworms. [L *cestus* f. Gk *kestos* girdle]

CET abbr. Central European Time.

cetacean /sɪ'teɪʃ(ə)n/ n. & adj. —n. any marine mammal of the order Cetacea with streamlined hairless body and dorsal blowhole for breathing, including whales, dolphins, and porpoises. —adj. of cetaceans. □□**cetaceous** adj. [mod.L *Cetacea* f. L *cetus* f. Gk *kētos* whale]

cetane /'si:teɪn/ n. Chem. a colourless liquid hydrocarbon of the alkane series used in standardizing ratings of diesel fuel. □**cetane number** a measure of the ignition properties of diesel fuel. [f. SPERMACETI after *methane* etc.]

ceteris paribus /,setərɪs 'pærɪ,bʊs/ adv. other things being equal. [L]

Ceylon moss /sɪ'lɒn/ n. a red seaweed, *Gracilaria lichenoides*, from E. India. [*Ceylon*, now Sri Lanka]

CF abbr. Brit. Chaplain to the Forces.

Cf symb. Chem. the element californium.

cf. abbr. compare. [L *confer* imper. of *conferre* compare]

c.f. abbr. carried forward.

CFC abbr. Chem. chloro-fluorocarbon, any of various usu. gaseous compounds of carbon, hydrogen, chlorine, and fluorine, used in refrigerants, aerosol propellants, etc., and thought to be harmful to the ozone layer in the earth's atmosphere.

CFE abbr. College of Further Education.

cg abbr. centigram(s).

CGS abbr. Chief of General Staff.

cgs abbr. centimetre-gram-second.

CH abbr. (in the UK) Companion of Honour.

ch. abbr. **1** church. **2** chapter. **3** chestnut.

cha var. of CHAR[3].

Chablis /'ʃæbli/ n. (pl. same /-li:z/) a dry white burgundy wine. [*Chablis* in E. France]

cha-cha /'tʃɑ:tʃɑ:/ (also **cha-cha-cha** /,tʃɑ:tʃɑ:'tʃɑ:/) n. & v. —n. **1** a ballroom dance with a Latin-American rhythm. **2** music for or in the rhythm of a cha-cha. —v.intr. (**cha-chas**, **cha-chaed** /-tʃɑ:d/ or **cha-cha'd**, **cha-chaing** /-tʃɑ:ɪŋ/) dance the cha-cha. [Amer. Sp.]

chaconne /ʃə'kɒn/ n. Mus. **1 a** a musical form consisting of variations on a ground bass. **b** a musical composition in this style. **2** hist. a dance performed to this music. [F f. Sp. *chacona*]

chador /'tʃʌdə(r)/ n. (also **chadar**, **chuddar**) a large piece of cloth worn in some countries by Muslim women, wrapped around the body to leave only the face exposed. [Pers. *chador*, Hindi *chador*]

chaetognath /'ki:təg,næθ/ n. any dart-shaped worm of the phylum Chaetognatha, usu. living among marine plankton, and having a head with external thorny teeth. [mod.L *Chaetognatha* f. Gk *khaitē* long hair + *gnathos* jaw]

chafe /tʃeɪf/ v. & n. —v. **1** tr. & intr. make or become sore or damaged by rubbing. **2** tr. rub (esp. the skin to restore warmth or sensation). **3** tr. & intr. make or become annoyed; fret (*was chafed by the delay*). —n. **1 a** an act of chafing. **b** a sore resulting from this. **2** a state of annoyance. [ME f. OF *chaufer* ult. f. L *calefacere* f. *calēre* be hot + *facere* make]

chafer /'tʃeɪfə(r)/ n. any of various large slow-moving beetles of the family Scarabeidae, esp. the cockchafer. [OE *ceafor*, *cefer* f. Gmc]

chaff /tʃɑ:f/ n. & v. —n. **1** the husks of corn or other seed separated by winnowing or threshing. **2** chopped hay and straw used as fodder. **3** light-hearted joking; banter. **4** worthless things; rubbish. **5** strips of metal foil released in the atmosphere to obstruct radar detection. —v. **1** tr. & intr. tease; banter. **2** tr. chop (straw etc.). □**chaff-cutter** a machine for chopping fodder. **separate the wheat from the chaff** distinguish good from bad. □□**chaffy** adj. [OE *ceaf*, *cæf* prob. f. Gmc: sense 3 of n. & 1 of v. perh. f. CHAFE]

chaffer /'tʃæfə(r)/ v. & n. —v.intr. haggle; bargain. —n. bargaining; haggling. □□**chafferer** n. [ME f. OE *ceapfaru* f. *ceap* bargain + *faru* journey]

chaffinch /'tʃæfɪntʃ/ n. Brit. a common European finch, *Fringilla coelebs*, the male of which has a blue-grey head with pinkish cheeks. [OE *ceaffinc*: see CHAFF, FINCH]

chafing-dish /'tʃeɪfɪŋ/ n. **1** a cooking pot with an outer pan of hot water, used for keeping food warm. **2** a dish with a spirit-lamp etc. for cooking at table. [obs. sense of CHAFE = warm]

Chagas' disease /'tʃɑ:gəs/ (also **Chagas's disease**) n. a kind of sleeping sickness caused by a protozoan transmitted by blood-sucking bugs. [C. *Chagas*, Braz. physician d. 1934]

chagrin /'ʃægrɪn, ʃə'gri:n/ n. & v. —n. acute vexation or mortification. —v.tr. affect with chagrin. [F *chagrin(er)*, of uncert. orig.]

chain /tʃeɪn/ n. & v. —n. **1 a** a connected flexible series of esp. metal links as decoration or for a practical purpose. **b** something resembling this (*formed a human chain*). **2** (in pl.) **a** fetters used to confine prisoners. **b** any restraining force. **3** a sequence, series, or set (*chain of events*; *mountain chain*). **4** a group of associated hotels, shops, newspapers, etc. **5** a badge of office in the form of a chain worn round the neck (*mayoral chain*). **6 a** a jointed measuring-line consisting of linked metal rods. **b** its length (66 ft.). **7** Chem. a group of (esp. carbon) atoms bonded in sequence in a molecule. **8** a figure in a quadrille or similar dance. **9** (in pl.) Naut. channels (see CHANNEL[2]). **10** (also **chain-shot**) hist. two cannon-balls or half balls joined by a chain and used in sea battles for bringing down a mast etc. —v.tr. **1** (often foll. by *up*) secure or confine with a chain. **2** confine or restrict (a person) (*is chained to the office*).

□**chain-armour** armour made of interlaced rings. **chain bridge** a suspension bridge on chains. **chain drive** a system of transmission by endless chains. **chain-gang** a team of convicts chained together and forced to work in the open air. **chain-gear** a gear transmitting motion by means of an endless chain. **chain-letter** one of a sequence of letters the recipient of which is requested to send copies to a specific number of other people. **chain-link** made of wire in a diamond-shaped mesh (*chain-link fencing*). **chain-mail** = chain-armour. **chain reaction** 1 *Physics* a self-sustaining nuclear reaction, esp. one in which a neutron from a fission reaction initiates a series of these reactions. 2 *Chem.* a self-sustaining molecular reaction in which intermediate products initiate further reactions. 3 a series of events, each caused by the previous one. **chain-saw** a motor-driven saw with teeth on an endless chain. **chain-smoker** a person who smokes continually, esp. one who lights a cigarette etc. from the stub of the last one smoked. **chain-stitch** an ornamental embroidery or crochet stitch resembling chains. **chain store** one of a series of shops owned by one firm and selling the same sort of goods. **chain-wale** = CHANNEL². **chain-wheel** a wheel transmitting power by a chain fitted to its edges. [ME f. OF cha(e)ine f. L catena]

chair /tʃeə(r)/ n. & v. —n. 1 a separate seat for one person, of various forms, usu. having a back and four legs. 2 a a professorship (*offered the chair in physics*). b a seat of authority, esp. on a board of directors. c a mayoralty. 3 a a chairperson. b the seat or office of a chairperson (*will you take the chair?; I'm in the chair*). 4 US = electric chair. 5 an iron or steel socket holding a railway rail in place. 6 hist. = sedan chair. —v.tr. 1 act as chairperson of or preside over (a meeting). 2 Brit. carry (a person) aloft in a chair or in a sitting position, in triumph. 3 install in a chair, esp. as a position of authority. □**chair-bed** a chair that unfolds into a bed. **chair-borne** colloq. (of an administrator) not active. **chair-car** a railway carriage with chairs instead of long seats; a parlour car. **chair-lift** a series of chairs on an endless cable for carrying passengers up and down a mountain etc. **take a chair** sit down. [ME f. AF chaere, OF chaiere f. L cathedra f. Gk kathedra: see CATHEDRAL]

chairlady /'tʃeə,leɪdɪ/ n. (pl. -ies) = CHAIRWOMAN.

chairman /'tʃeəmən/ n. (pl. -men; fem. **chairwoman**, pl. -women) 1 a person chosen to preside over a meeting. 2 the permanent president of a committee, a board of directors, a firm, etc. 3 the master of ceremonies at an entertainment etc. 4 hist. either of two sedan-bearers. □□**chairmanship** n.

chairperson /'tʃeə,pɜːs(ə)n/ n. a chairman or chairwoman (used as a neutral alternative).

chaise /ʃeɪz/ n. 1 esp. hist. a horse-drawn carriage for one or two persons, esp. one with an open top and two wheels. 2 = post-chaise (see POST²). [F var. of chaire, formed as CHAIR]

chaise longue /ʃeɪz 'lɒŋɡ/ n. a sofa with only one arm rest. [F, lit. long chair]

chalaza /kə'leɪzə/ n. (pl. **chalazae** /-ziː/) each of two twisted membranous strips joining the yolk to the ends of an egg. [mod.L f. Gk, = hailstone]

chalcedony /kæl'sedənɪ/ n. a type of quartz occurring in several different forms, e.g. onyx, agate, tiger's eye, etc. □□**chalcedonic** /,kælsɪ'dɒnɪk/ adj. [ME f. L c(h)alcedonius f. Gk khalkēdōn]

chalcolithic /,kælkə'lɪθɪk/ adj. Archaeol. of a prehistoric period in which both stone and bronze implements were used. [Gk khalkos copper + lithos stone]

chalcopyrite /,kælkə'paɪraɪt/ n. a yellow mineral of copper-iron sulphide, which is the principal ore of copper. [Gk khalkos copper + PYRITE]

Chaldean /kæl'diːən/ n. & adj. —n. 1 a a native of

ancient Chaldea or Babylonia. b the language of the Chaldeans. 2 an astrologer. 3 a member of the Uniat (formerly Nestorian) sect in Iran etc. —adj. 1 of or relating to ancient Chaldea or its people or language. 2 of or relating to astrology. 3 of or relating to the Uniat sect. [L Chaldaeus f. Gk Khaldaios f. Assyr. Kaldu]

Chaldee /kæl'diː/ n. 1 the language of the Chaldeans. 2 a native of ancient Chaldea. 3 the Aramaic language as used in Old Testament books. [ME, repr. L Chaldaei (pl.) (as CHALDEAN)]

chalet /'ʃæleɪ/ n. 1 a small suburban house or bungalow, esp. with an overhanging roof. 2 a small, usu. wooden, hut or house on a beach or in a holiday camp. 3 a Swiss cowherd's hut, or wooden cottage, with overhanging eaves. [Swiss F]

chalice /'tʃælɪs/ n. 1 literary a goblet. 2 a wine-cup used in the Communion service. [ME f. OF f. L calix -icis cup]

chalk /tʃɔːk/ n. & v. —n. 1 a white soft earthy limestone (calcium carbonate) formed from the skeletal remains of sea creatures. 2 a a similar substance (calcium sulphate), sometimes coloured, used for writing or drawing. b a piece of this (*a box of chalks*). 3 a series of strata consisting mainly of chalk. 4 = French chalk. —v.tr. 1 rub, mark, draw, or write with chalk. 2 (foll. by up) a write or record with chalk. b register (a success etc.). c charge (to an account). □**as different as chalk and** (or from) **cheese** fundamentally different. **by a long chalk** Brit. by far (from the use of chalk to mark the score in games). **chalk and talk** traditional teaching (employing blackboard, chalk, and interlocution). **chalk out** sketch or plan a thing to be accomplished. **chalk-pit** a quarry in which chalk is dug. **chalk-stone** a concretion of urates like chalk in tissues and joints esp. of hands and feet. **chalk-stripe** a pattern of thin white stripes on a dark background. **chalk-striped** having chalk-stripes. [OE cealc ult. f. WG f. L CALX]

chalkboard /'tʃɔːkbɔːd/ n. US = BLACKBOARD.

chalky /'tʃɔːkɪ/ adj. (**chalkier**, **chalkiest**) 1 a abounding in chalk. b white as chalk. 2 like or containing chalk stones. □□**chalkiness** n.

challenge /'tʃælɪndʒ/ n. & v. —n. 1 a a summons to take part in a contest or a trial of strength etc., esp. to a duel. b a summons to prove or justify something. 2 a demanding or difficult task (*rose to the challenge of the new job*). 3 Law an objection made to a jury member. 4 a call to respond, esp. a sentry's call for a password etc. 5 an invitation to a sporting contest, esp. one issued to a reigning champion. 6 Med. a test of immunity after immunization treatment. —v.tr. 1 (often foll. by to + infin.) a invite to take part in a contest, game, debate, duel, etc. b invite to prove or justify something. 2 dispute, deny (*I challenge that remark*). 3 a stretch, stimulate (*challenges him to produce his best*). b (as **challenging** adj.) demanding; stimulatingly difficult. 4 (of a sentry) call to respond. 5 claim (attention, etc.). 6 Law object to (a jury member, evidence, etc.). 7 Med. test by a challenge. □□**challengeable** /-dʒəb(ə)l/ adj. **challenger** n. [ME f. OF c(h)alenge, c(h)alenger f. L calumnia calumniari calumny]

challis /'ʃælɪs, 'ʃælɪ/ n. a lightweight soft clothing fabric. [perh. f. a surname]

chalybeate /kə'lɪbɪət/ adj. (of mineral water etc.) impregnated with iron salts. [mod.L chalybeatus f. L chalybs f. Gk khalups -ubos steel]

chamaephyte /'kæmɪ,faɪt/ n. a plant whose buds are on or near the ground. [Gk khamai on the ground + -PHYTE]

chamber /'tʃeɪmbə(r)/ n. 1 a a hall used by a legislative or judicial body. b the body that meets in it. c any of the houses of a parliament (*Chamber of Deputies; second chamber*). 2 (in pl.) Brit. Law a rooms used by a barrister or group of barristers, esp. in the Inns of Court. b a judge's room used for hearing cases not needing to be taken in court. **3** *poet.* or *archaic* a room, esp. a bedroom. **4** *Mus.* (*attrib.*) of or for a small group of instruments (*chamber orchestra*; *chamber music*). **5** an enclosed space in machinery etc. (esp. the part of a gun-bore that contains the charge). **6 a** a cavity in a plant or in the body of an animal. **b** a compartment in a structure. **7** = *chamber-pot*. □**Chamber of Commerce** an association to promote local commercial interests. **chamber-pot** a receptacle for urine etc., used in a bedroom. [ME f. OF *chambre* f. L CAMERA]

chambered /ˈtʃeɪmbəd/ *adj.* (of a tomb) containing a burial chamber.

chamberlain /ˈtʃeɪmbəlɪn/ *n.* **1** an officer managing the household of a sovereign or a great noble. **2** the treasurer of a corporation etc. □**Lord Chamberlain (of the Household)** the official in charge of the Royal Household, formerly the licenser of plays. **Lord Great Chamberlain of England** the hereditary holder of a ceremonial office. □□**chamberlainship** *n.* [ME f. OF *chamberlain* etc. f. Frank. f. L *camera* CAMERA]

chambermaid /ˈtʃeɪmbəˌmeɪd/ *n.* **1** a housemaid at a hotel etc. **2** *US* a housemaid.

Chambertin /ˈʃɑ̃bəˌtæ̃/ *n.* a high-quality dry red burgundy wine. [*Gevrey Chambertin* region in E. France]

chambray /ˈʃæmbreɪ/ *n.* a linen-finished gingham cloth with a white weft and a coloured warp. [irreg. f. *Cambrai*: see CAMBRIC]

chambré /ˈʃɑ̃breɪ/ *adj.* (of red wine) brought to room temperature. [F, past part. of *chambrer* f. *chambre* room: see CHAMBER]

chameleon /kəˈmiːlɪən/ *n.* **1** any of a family of small lizards having grasping tails, long tongues, protruding eyes, and the power of changing colour. **2** a variable or inconstant person. □□**chameleonic** /-ˈɒnɪk/ *adj.* [ME f. L f. Gk *khamaileōn* f. *khamai* on the ground + *leōn* lion]

chamfer /ˈtʃæmfə(r)/ *v. & n.* —*v.tr.* bevel symmetrically (a right-angled edge or corner). —*n.* a bevelled surface at an edge or corner. [back-form. f. *chamfering* f. F *chamfrain* f. *chant* edge (CANT²) + *fraint* broken f. OF *fraindre* break f. L *frangere*]

chamois /ˈʃæmwɑː/ *n.* (*pl.* same /-wɑːz/) **1** an agile goat antelope, *Rupicapra rupicapra*, native to the mountains of Europe and Asia. **2** /ˈʃæmɪ, ˈʃæmwɑː/ (in full **chamois leather**) **a** a soft pliable leather from sheep, goats, deer, etc. **b** a piece of this for polishing etc. [F: cf. Gallo-Roman *camox*]

chamomile var. of CAMOMILE.

champ¹ /tʃæmp/ *v. & n.* —*v.* **1** *tr. & intr.* munch or chew noisily. **2** *tr.* (of a horse etc.) work (the bit) noisily between the teeth. **3** *intr.* fret with impatience (*is champing to be away*). —*n.* a chewing noise or motion. □**champ at the bit** be restlessly impatient. [prob. imit.]

champ² /tʃæmp/ *n. sl.* a champion. [abbr.]

champagne /ʃæmˈpeɪn/ *n.* **1 a** a white sparkling wine from Champagne. **b** (loosely) a similar wine from elsewhere. ¶ Use in sense b is strictly incorrect. **2** a pale cream or straw colour. [*Champagne*, former province in E. France]

champaign /ʃæmˈpeɪn/ *n. literary* **1** open country. **2** an expanse of open country. [ME f. OF *champagne* f. LL *campania*: cf. CAMPAIGN]

champers /ˈʃæmpəz/ *n. sl.* champagne.

champerty /ˈtʃæmpətɪ/ *n.* (*pl.* **-ies**) *Law* an illegal agreement in which a person not naturally interested in a lawsuit finances it with a view to sharing the disputed property. □□**champertous** *adj.* [ME f. AF *champartie* f. OF *champart* feudal lord's share of produce, f. L *campus* field + *pars* part]

champion /ˈtʃæmpɪən/ *n., v., adj., & adv.* —*n.* **1** (often *attrib.*) a person (esp. in a sport or game), an animal, plant, etc., that has defeated or surpassed all rivals in a competition etc. **2 a** a person who fights or argues for a cause or on behalf of another person. **b** *hist.* a knight etc. who fought in single combat on behalf of a king etc. —*v.tr.* support the cause of, defend, argue in favour of. —*adj. colloq.* or *dial.* first-class, splendid. —*adv. colloq.* or *dial.* splendidly, well. □**Champion of England** (or **King's** or **Queen's Champion**) a hereditary official at coronations. [ME f. OF f. med.L *campio -onis* fighter f. L *campus* field]

championship /ˈtʃæmpɪənʃɪp/ *n.* **1** (often in *pl.*) a contest for the position of champion in a sport etc. **2** the position of champion over all rivals. **3** the advocacy or defence (of a cause etc.).

champlevé /ˌʃɑ̃ləˈveɪ/ *n. & adj.* —*n.* a type of enamelwork in which hollows made in a metal surface are filled with coloured enamels. —*adj.* of or relating to champlevé (cf. CLOISONNÉ). [F, = raised field]

chance /tʃɑːns/ *n., adj., & v.* —*n.* **1 a** a possibility (*just a chance we will catch the train*). **b** (often in *pl.*) probability (*the chances are against it*). **2** a risk (*have to take a chance*). **3 a** an undesigned occurrence (*just a chance that they met*). **b** the absence of design or discoverable cause (*here merely because of chance*). **4** an opportunity (*didn't have a chance to speak to him*). **5** the way things happen; fortune; luck (*we'll just leave it to chance*). **6** (often **Chance**) the course of events regarded as a power; fate (*blind Chance rules the universe*). **7** *Cricket* an opportunity for dismissing a batsman. —*adj.* fortuitous, accidental (*a chance meeting*). —*v.* **1** *tr. colloq.* risk (*we'll chance it and go*). **2** *intr.* (often foll. by *that* + clause, or *to* + infin.) happen without intention (*it chanced that I found it*; *I chanced to find it*). □**by any chance** as it happens; perhaps. **by chance** without design; unintentionally. **chance one's arm** make an attempt though unlikely to succeed. **chance on** (or **upon**) happen to find, meet, etc. **game of chance** a game decided by luck, not skill. **the off chance** the slight possibility. **on the chance** (often foll. by *of*, or *that* + clause) in view of the possibility. **stand a chance** have a prospect of success etc. **take a chance** (or **chances**) behave riskily; risk failure. **take a** (or **one's**) **chance on** (or **with**) consent to take the consequences of; trust to luck. [ME f. AF *ch(e)aunce*, OF *chěance chěoir* fall ult. f. L *cadere*]

chancel /ˈtʃɑːns(ə)l/ *n.* the part of a church near the altar, reserved for the clergy, the choir, etc., usu. enclosed by a screen or separated from the nave by steps. [ME f. OF f. L *cancelli* lattice]

chancellery /ˈtʃɑːnsələrɪ/ *n.* (*pl.* **-ies**) **1 a** the position, office, staff, department, etc., of a chancellor. **b** the official residence of a chancellor. **2** *US* an office attached to an embassy or consulate. [ME f. OF *chancellerie* (as CHANCELLOR)]

chancellor /ˈtʃɑːnsələ(r)/ *n.* **1** a State or legal official of various kinds. **2** the head of the government in some European countries, e.g. W. Germany. **3** the non-resident honorary head of a university. **4** a bishop's law officer. **5** *US* the president of a chancery court. □**Chancellor of the Duchy of Lancaster** a member of the government legally representing the Queen as Duke of Lancaster, often a Cabinet Minister employed on non-departmental work. **Chancellor of the Exchequer** the finance minister of the United Kingdom. **Chancellor of the Garter** etc. a government officer who seals commissions etc. **Lord** (or **Lord High**) **Chancellor** an officer presiding in the House of Lords, the Chancery Division, or the Court of Appeal. □□**chancellorship** *n.* [OE f. AF *c(h)anceler*, OF *-ier* f. LL *cancellarius* porter, secretary, f. *cancelli* lattice]

chance-medley /ˌtʃɑːnsˈmedlɪ/ *n.* (*pl.* **-eys**) **1** *Law* a fight, esp. homicidal, beginning unintentionally. **2** inadvertency. [AF *chance medlee* (see MEDDLE) mixed chance]

chancery /ˈtʃɑːnsərɪ/ *n.* (*pl.* **-ies**) **1** *Law* (**Chancery**) the Lord Chancellor's court, a division of the High Court of Justice. **2** *hist.* the records office of an order of knighthood. **3** *hist.* the court of a bishop's chancellor. **4** an office attached to an embassy or consulate. **5** a public record office. **6** *US* a court of equity. □**in chancery** *sl.* (of a boxer or wrestler) with the head held under the opponent's arm and being pummelled. [ME, contracted f. CHANCELLERY]

chancre /ˈʃæŋkə(r)/ *n.* a painless ulcer developing in venereal disease etc. [F f. L CANCER]

chancroid /ˈʃæŋkrɔɪd/ *n.* ulceration of lymph nodes in the groin, from venereal disease.

chancy /ˈtʃɑːnsɪ/ *adj.* (**chancier**, **chanciest**) subject to chance; uncertain; risky. □□**chancily** *adv.* **chanciness** *n.*

chandelier /ˌʃændɪˈlɪə(r)/ *n.* an ornamental branched hanging support for several candles or electric light bulbs. [F (*chandelle* f. as CANDLE)]

chandler /ˈtʃɑːndlə(r)/ *n.* a dealer in candles, oil, soap, paint, groceries, etc. □**corn chandler** a dealer in corn. **ship** (or **ship's**) **chandler** a dealer in cordage, canvas, etc. [ME f. AF *chaundeler*, OF *chandelier* (as CANDLE)]

chandlery /ˈtʃɑːndlərɪ/ *n.* the goods sold by a chandler.

change /tʃeɪndʒ/ *n. & v.* —*n.* **1 a** the act or an instance of making or becoming different. **b** an alteration or modification (*the change in her expression*). **2 a** money given in exchange for money in larger units or a different currency. **b** money returned as the balance of that given in payment. **c** = *small change*. **3** a new experience; variety (*fancied a change; for a change*). **4 a** the substitution of one thing for another; an exchange (*change of scene*). **b** a set of clothes etc. put on in place of another. **5** (in full **change of life**) *colloq.* the menopause. **6** (usu. in *pl.*) the different orders in which a peal of bells can be rung. **7** (**Change**) (also **'Change**) *hist.* a place where merchants etc. met to do business. **8** (of the moon) arrival at a fresh phase, esp. at the new moon. —*v.* **1** *tr. & intr.* undergo, show, or subject to change; make or become different (*the wig changed his appearance*; *changed from an introvert into an extrovert*). **2** *tr.* a take or use another instead of; go from one to another (*change one's socks; changed his doctor; changed trains*). **b** (usu. foll. by *for*) give up or get rid of in exchange (*changed the car for a van*). **3** *tr.* **a** give or get change in smaller denominations for (*can you change a ten-pound note?*). **b** (foll. by *for*) exchange (a sum of money) for (*changed his dollars for pounds*). **4** *tr. & intr.* put fresh clothes or coverings on (*changed the baby as he was wet; changed into something loose*). **5** *tr.* (often foll. by *with*) give and receive, exchange (*changed places with him*; *we changed places*). **6** *intr.* change trains etc. (*changed at Crewe*). **7** *intr.* (of the moon) arrive at a fresh phase, esp. become new. □**change colour** blanch or flush. **change down** engage a lower gear in a vehicle. **change gear** engage a different gear in a vehicle. **change hands 1** pass to a different owner. **2** substitute one hand for another. **change one's mind** adopt a different opinion or plan. **change of air** a different climate; variety. **change of heart** a conversion to a different view. **change over** change from one system or situation to another. **change-over** *n.* such a change. **change step** begin to keep step with the opposite leg when marching etc. **change the subject** begin talking of something different, esp. to avoid embarrassment. **change one's tune 1** voice a different opinion from that expressed previously. **2** change one's style of language or manner, esp. from an insolent to a respectful tone. **change up** engage a higher gear in a vehicle. **get no change out of** *sl.* **1** fail to get information from. **2** fail to get the better of (in business etc.). **ring the changes (on)** vary the ways of expressing, arranging, or doing something. □□**changeful** *adj.* **changer** *n.* [ME f. AF *chaunge*, OF *change*, *changer* f. LL *cambiare*, L *cambire* barter, prob. of Celt. orig.]

changeable /ˈtʃeɪndʒəb(ə)l/ *adj.* **1** irregular, inconstant. **2** that can change or be changed. □□ **changeability** /-ˈbɪlɪtɪ/ *n.* **changeableness** *n.* **changeably** *adv.* [ME f. OF, formed as CHANGE]

changeless /ˈtʃeɪndʒlɪs/ *adj.* unchanging. □□ **changelessly** *adv.* **changelessness** *n.*

changeling /ˈtʃeɪndʒlɪŋ/ *n.* a child believed to be substituted for another by stealth, esp. an elf-child left by fairies.

channel[1] /ˈtʃæn(ə)l/ *n. & v.* —*n.* **1 a** a length of water wider than a strait, joining two larger areas, esp. seas. **b** (**the Channel**) the English Channel between Britain and France. **2** a medium of communication; an agency for conveying information (*through the usual channels*). **3** *Broadcasting* **a** a band of frequencies used in radio and television transmission, esp. as used by a particular station. **b** a service or station using this. **4** the course in which anything moves; a direction. **5 a** a natural or artificial hollow bed of water. **b** the navigable part of a waterway. **6** a tubular passage for liquid. **7** *Electronics* a lengthwise strip on recording tape etc. **8** a groove or a flute, esp. in a column. —*v.tr.* (**channelled**, **channelling**; *US* **channeled**, **channeling**) **1** guide, direct (*channelled them through customs*). **2** form channels in; groove. [ME f. OF *chanel* f. L *canalis* CANAL]

channel[2] /ˈtʃæn(ə)l/ *n. Naut.* any of the broad thick planks projecting horizontally from a ship's side abreast of the masts, used to widen the basis for the shrouds. [for *chain-wale*: cf. *gunnel* for *gunwale*]

channelize /ˈtʃænəˌlaɪz/ *v.tr.* (also **-ise**) convey in, or as if in, a channel; guide.

chanson de geste /ˈʃɑ̃sɔ̃ də ˈʒest/ *n.* (*pl.* **chansons** *pronunc.* same) any of a group of medieval French epic poems. [F, = song of heroic deeds]

chant /tʃɑːnt/ *n. & v.* —*n.* **1 a** a spoken singsong phrase, esp. one performed in unison by a crowd etc. **b** a repetitious singsong way of speaking. **2** *Mus.* **a** a short musical passage in two or more phrases used for singing unmetrical words, e.g. psalms, canticles. **b** the psalm or canticle so sung. **c** a song, esp. monotonous or repetitive. **3** a musical recitation, esp. of poetry. —*v.tr. & intr.* **1** talk or repeat monotonously (*a crowd chanting slogans*). **2** sing or intone (a psalm etc.). [ME (orig. as verb) f. OF *chanter* sing f. L *cantare* frequent. of *canere* cant- sing]

chanter /ˈtʃɑːntə(r)/ *n. Mus.* the melody-pipe, with finger-holes, of a bagpipe.

chanterelle /ˌtʃæntəˈrel/ *n.* an edible fungus, *Cantharellus cibarius*, with a yellow funnel-shaped cap and smelling of apricots. [F f. mod.L *cantharellus* dimin. of *cantharus* f. Gk *kantharos* a kind of drinking vessel]

chanteuse /ʃɑːnˈtɜːz/ *n.* a female singer of popular songs. [F]

chanticleer /ˌtʃæntɪˈklɪə(r), ˌtʃɑːn-, ˌʃæn-, ˌʃɑːn-/ *n. literary* a name given to a domestic cock, esp. in fairy tales etc. [ME f. OF *chantecler* (as CHANT, CLEAR), a name in *Reynard the Fox*]

Chantilly /ʃænˈtɪlɪ, ʃɑːtiːˈjiː/ *n.* **1** a delicate kind of bobbin-lace. **2** sweetened or flavoured whipped cream. [*Chantilly* near Paris]

chantry /ˈtʃɑːntrɪ/ *n.* (*pl.* **-ies**) **1** an endowment for a priest or priests to celebrate masses for the founder's soul. **2** the priests, chapel, altar, etc., endowed. [ME f. AF *chaunterie*, OF *chanterie* f. *chanter* CHANT]

chanty var. of SHANTY[2].

Chanukkah var. of HANUKKAH.

chaos /ˈkeɪɒs/ *n.* **1** utter confusion. **2** the formless matter supposed to have existed before the creation of the universe. □□**chaotic** /keɪˈɒtɪk/ *adj.* **chaotically** /-ˈɒtɪkəlɪ/ *adv.* [F or L f. Gk *khaos*: *-otic* after *erotic* etc.]

chap[1] /tʃæp/ *v. & n.* —*v.* (**chapped**, **chapping**) **1** *intr.* (esp. of the skin; also of dry ground etc.) crack in fissures, esp. because of exposure and dryness. **2** *tr.* (of the wind, cold, etc.) cause to chap. —*n.* (usu.

in *pl.*) **1** a crack in the skin. **2** an open seam. [ME, perh. rel. to MLG, MDu. *kappen* chop off]

chap² /tʃæp/ *n. colloq.* a man; a boy; a fellow. [abbr. of CHAPMAN.

chap³ /tʃæp/ *n.* the lower jaw or half of the cheek, esp. of a pig as food. □**chap-fallen** dispirited, dejected (with the lower jaw hanging). [16th c.: var. of CHOP², of unkn. orig.]

chap. *abbr.* chapter.

chaparejos /ˌʃæpəˈreɪəʊs, ˌtʃæp-/ *n.pl. US* a cowboy's leather protection for the front of the legs. [Mex. Sp.]

chaparral /ˌtʃæpəˈræl, ˌʃæp-/ *n. US* dense tangled brushwood; undergrowth. □**chaparral cock** = ROADRUNNER. [Sp. f. *chaparra* evergreen oak]

chapatti /tʃəˈpɑːti, -ˈpæti/ *n.* (also **chapati**, **chupatty**) (*pl.* **-is** or **chupatties**) *Ind.* a flat thin cake of unleavened wholemeal bread. [Hindi *capāti*]

chap-book /ˈtʃæpbʊk/ *n. hist.* a small pamphlet containing tales, ballads, tracts, etc., hawked by chapmen. [19th c.: see CHAPMAN]

chape /tʃeɪp/ *n.* **1** the metal cap of a scabbard-point. **2** the back-piece of a buckle attaching it to a strap etc. **3** a sliding loop on a belt or strap. [ME f. OF, = cope, hood, formed as CAP]

chapeau-bras /ˌʃæpəʊˈbrɑː/ *n.* (*pl.* **chapeaux-bras** *pronunc.* same) a three-cornered flat silk hat often carried under the arm. [F f. *chapeau* hat + *bras* arm]

chapel /ˈtʃæp(ə)l/ *n.* **1 a** a place for private Christian worship in a large church or esp. a cathedral, with its own altar and dedication (*Lady chapel*). **b** a place of Christian worship attached to a private house or institution. **2** *Brit.* **a** a place of worship for nonconformist bodies. **b** (*predic.*) an attender at or believer in nonconformist worship (*they are strictly chapel*). **c** a chapel service. **d** attendance at a chapel. **3** an Anglican church subordinate to a parish church. **4** *Printing* **a** the members or branch of a printers' trade union at a specific place of work. **b** a meeting of them. □**chapel of ease** an Anglican chapel for the convenience of remote parishioners. **chapel of rest** an undertaker's mortuary. **chapel royal** a chapel in a royal palace. **father of chapel** (or **the chapel**) the shop steward of a printers' chapel. [ME f. OF *chapele* f. med.L *cappella* dimin. of *cappa* cloak: the first chapel was a sanctuary in which St Martin's sacred cloak (*cappella*) was preserved]

chapelry /ˈtʃæpəlri/ *n.* (*pl.* **-ies**) a district served by an Anglican chapel.

chaperon /ˈʃæpəˌrəʊn/ *n. & v.* (also **chaperone**) —*n.* **1** a person, esp. an older woman, who ensures propriety by accompanying a young unmarried woman on social occasions. **2** a person who takes charge of esp. young people in public. —*v.tr.* act as a chaperon to. □□ **chaperonage** /ˈʃæpərənɪdʒ/ *n.* [F, = hood, chaperon, dimin. of *chape* cope, formed as CAP]

chaplain /ˈtʃæplɪn/ *n.* a member of the clergy attached to a private chapel, institution, ship, regiment, etc. □□ **chaplaincy** *n.* (*pl.* **-ies**). [ME f. AF & OF *c(h)apelain* f. med.L *cappellanus*, orig. custodian of the cloak of St Martin: see CHAPEL]

chaplet /ˈtʃæplɪt/ *n.* **1** a garland or circlet for the head. **2** a string of 55 beads (one-third of the rosary number) for counting prayers, or as a necklace. **3** a bead-moulding. □□ **chapleted** *adj.* [ME f. OF *chapelet*, ult. f. LL *cappa* CAP]

chapman /ˈtʃæpmən/ *n.* (*pl.* **-men**) *hist.* a pedlar. [OE *cēapman* f. *cēap* barter]

chappal /ˈtʃæp(ə)l/ *n.* an Indian sandal, usu. of leather. [Hindi]

chappie /ˈtʃæpɪ/ *n. colloq.* = CHAP².

chappy /ˈtʃæpɪ/ *adj.* full of chaps; chapped (*chappy knuckles*).

chaps /tʃæps, ʃæps/ *n.* = CHAPAREJOS. [abbr.]

chapstick /ˈtʃæpstɪk/ *n. US* a cylinder of a cosmetic substance used to prevent chapping of the lips.

chapter /ˈtʃæptə(r)/ *n.* **1** a main division of a book. **2** a period of time (in a person's life, a nation's history,

etc.). **3** a series or sequence (*a chapter of misfortunes*). **4 a** the canons of a cathedral or other religious community or knightly order. **b** a meeting of these. **5** an Act of Parliament numbered as part of a session's proceedings. **6** *US* a local branch of a society. □**chapter and verse** an exact reference or authority. **chapter house 1** a building used for the meetings of a chapter. **2** *US* the place where a college fraternity or sorority meets. [ME f. OF *chapitre* f. L *capitulum* dimin. of *caput -itis* head]

char¹ /tʃɑː(r)/ *v.tr. & intr.* (**charred**, **charring**) **1** make or become black by burning; scorch. **2** burn or be burnt to charcoal. [app. back-form. f. CHARCOAL]

char² /tʃɑː(r)/ *n. & v. Brit. colloq.* —*n.* = CHARWOMAN. —*v.intr.* (**charred**, **charring**) work as a charwoman. [earlier *chare* f. OE *cerr* a turn, *cierran* to turn]

char³ /tʃɑː(r)/ *n.* (also **cha** /tʃɑː/) *Brit. sl.* tea. [Chin. *cha*]

char⁴ /tʃɑː(r)/ *n.* (also **charr**) (*pl.* same) any small troutlike fish of the genus *Salvelinus*. [17th c.: orig. unkn.]

charabanc /ˈʃærəˌbæŋ/ *n. Brit. hist.* an early form of motor coach. [F *char à bancs* seated carriage]

character /ˈkærɪktə(r)/ *n. & v.* —*n.* **1** the collective qualities or characteristics, esp. mental and moral, that distinguish a person or thing. **2 a** moral strength (*has a weak character*). **b** reputation, esp. good reputation. **3 a** a person in a novel, play, etc. **b** a part played by an actor; a role. **4** *colloq.* a person, esp. an eccentric or outstanding individual (*he's a real character*). **5 a** a printed or written letter, symbol, or distinctive mark (*Chinese characters*). **b** *Computing* any of a group of symbols representing a letter etc. **6** a written description of a person's qualities; a testimonial. **7** a characteristic (esp. of a biological species). —*v.tr. archaic* inscribe; describe. □**character actor** an actor who specializes in playing eccentric or unusual persons. **character assassination** a malicious attempt to harm or destroy a person's good reputation. **in** (or **out of**) **character** consistent (or inconsistent) with a person's character. □□ **characterful** *adj.* **characterfully** *adv.* **characterless** *adj.* [ME f. OF *caractere* f. L *character* f. Gk *kharaktēr* stamp, impress]

characteristic /ˌkærɪktəˈrɪstɪk/ *adj. & n.* —*adj.* typical, distinctive (*with characteristic expertise*). —*n.* **1** a characteristic feature or quality. **2** *Math.* the whole number or integral part of a logarithm. □**characteristic curve** a graph showing the relationship between two variable but interdependent quantities. **characteristic radiation** radiation the wavelengths of which are peculiar to the element which emits them. □□ **characteristically** *adv.* [F *caractéristique* or med.L *characterizare* f. Gk *kharaktērizō*]

characterize /ˈkærɪktəˌraɪz/ *v.tr.* (also **-ise**) **1 a** describe the character of. **b** (foll. by *as*) describe as. **2** be characteristic of. **3** impart character to. □□ **characterization** /-ˈzeɪʃ(ə)n/ *n.* [F *caractériser* or med.L *characterizare* f. Gk *kharaktērizō*]

charade /ʃəˈrɑːd/ *n.* **1 a** (usu. in *pl.*, treated as *sing.*) a game of guessing a word from a written or acted clue given for each syllable and for the whole. **b** one such clue. **2** an absurd pretence. [F f. mod.Prov. *charrado* conversation f. *charra* chatter]

charas /ˈtʃɑːrəs/ *n.* a narcotic resin from the flower-heads of hemp; cannabis resin. [Hindi]

charcoal /ˈtʃɑːkəʊl/ *n.* **1 a** an amorphous form of carbon consisting of a porous black residue from partially burnt wood, bones, etc. **b** (usu. in *pl.*) a piece of this used for drawing. **2** a drawing in charcoal. **3** (in full **charcoal grey**) a dark grey colour. □**charcoal biscuit** a biscuit containing wood-charcoal to aid digestion. [ME COAL = charcoal: first element perh. *chare* turn (cf. CHAR¹, CHAR²)]

chard /tʃɑːd/ *n.* a kind of beet, *Beta vulgaris*, with edible broad white leaf-stalks and green blades. Also called *seakale beet*. [F *carde*, and *chardon* thistle: cf. CARDOON]

Chardonnay /'ʃɑːdɒˌneɪ/ *n*. **1** a variety of white grape used for making champagne and other wines. **2** the vine on which this grape grows. **3** a wine made from Chardonnay grapes. [F]

charge /tʃɑːdʒ/ *v. & n.* —*v.* **1** *tr.* **a** ask (an amount) as a price (*charges £5 a ticket*). **b** ask (a person) for an amount as a price (*you forgot to charge me*). **2** *tr.* **a** (foll. by *to*, *up to*) debit the cost of to (a person or account) (*charge it to my account; charge it up to me*). **b** debit (a person or an account) (*bought a new car and charged the company*). **3** *tr.* **a** (often foll. by *with*) accuse (of an offence) (*charged him with theft*). **b** (foll. by *that* + clause) make an accusation that. **4** *tr.* (foll. by *to* + infin.) instruct or urge. **5** (foll. by *with*) **a** *tr.* entrust with. **b** *refl.* undertake. **6** a *intr.* make a rushing attack; rush headlong. **b** *tr.* make a rushing attack on; throw oneself against. **7** *tr.* (often foll. by *up*) **a** give an electric charge to (a body). **b** store energy in (a battery). **8** *tr.* (often foll. by *with*) load or fill (a vessel, gun, etc.) to the full or proper extent. **9** *tr.* (usu. as **charged** *adj.*) **a** (foll. by *with*) saturated with (*air charged with vapour*). **b** (usu. foll. by *with*) pervaded (with strong feelings etc.) (*atmosphere charged with emotion; a charged atmosphere*). —*n.* **1 a** a price asked for goods or services. **b** a financial liability or commitment. **2** an accusation, esp. against a prisoner brought to trial. **3 a** a task, duty, or commission. **b** care, custody, responsible possession. **c** a person or thing entrusted; a minister's congregation. **4 a** an impetuous rush or attack, esp. in a battle. **b** the signal for this. **5** the appropriate amount of material to be put into a receptacle, mechanism, etc. at one time, esp. of explosive for a gun. **6 a** a property of matter that is a consequence of the interaction between its constituent particles and exists in a positive or negative form, causing electrical phenomena. **b** the quantity of this carried by a body. **c** energy stored chemically for conversion into electricity. **d** the process of charging a battery. **7** an exhortation; directions, orders. **8** a burden or load. **9** *Heraldry* a device; a bearing. □**charge account** *US* a credit account at a shop etc. **charge card** a credit card for which the account must be paid in full when a statement is issued. **charge-hand** *Brit.* a worker, ranking below a foreman, in charge of others on a particular job. **charge-nurse** *Brit.* a nurse in charge of a ward etc. **charge-sheet** *Brit.* a record of cases and charges made at a police station. **free of charge** gratis. **give a person in charge** hand a person over to the police. **in charge** having command. **lay to a person's charge** accuse a person of. **put a person on a charge** charge a person with a specified offence. **return to the charge** begin again, esp. in argument. **take charge** (often foll. by *of*) assume control or direction. □□**chargeable** *adj.* [ME f. OF *charger* f. LL *car(ri)care* load f. L *carrus* CAR]

chargé d'affaires /ˌʃɑːʒeɪ dæˈfeə(r)/ *n.* (also **chargé**) (*pl.* **chargés** *pronunc.* same) **1** an ambassador's deputy. **2** an envoy to a minor country. [F, = in charge (of affairs)]

charger[1] /'tʃɑːdʒə(r)/ *n.* **1 a** a cavalry horse. **b** *poet.* any horse. **2** an apparatus for charging a battery. **3** a person or thing that charges.

charger[2] /'tʃɑːdʒə(r)/ *n. archaic* a large flat dish. [ME f. AF *chargeour*]

chariot /'tʃærɪət/ *n. & v.* —*n.* **1** *hist.* **a** a two-wheeled vehicle drawn by horses, used in ancient warfare and racing. **b** a four-wheeled carriage with back seats only. **2** *poet.* a stately or triumphal vehicle. —*v.tr. literary* convey in or as in a chariot. [ME f. OF, augment. of *char* CAR]

charioteer /ˌtʃærɪəˈtɪə(r)/ *n.* a chariot-driver.

charisma /kəˈrɪzmə/ *n.* (*pl.* **charismata** /kəˈrɪzmətə/) **1 a** the ability to inspire followers with devotion and enthusiasm. **b** an attractive aura; great

charm. **2** a divinely conferred power or talent. [eccl.L f. Gk *kharisma* f. *kharis* favour, grace]

charismatic /ˌkærɪzˈmætɪk/ *adj.* **1** having charisma; inspiring enthusiasm. **2** (of Christian worship) characterized by spontaneity, ecstatic utterances, etc. □**charismatic movement** a neo-pentecostal movement affecting Roman Catholic, Anglican, and other Christian Churches. □□**charismatically** *adv.*

charitable /'tʃærɪtəb(ə)l/ *adj.* **1** generous in giving to those in need. **2** of, relating to, or connected with a charity or charities. **3** apt to judge favourably of persons, acts, and motives. □□**charitableness** *n.* **charitably** *adv.* [ME f. OF f. *charité* CHARITY]

charity /'tʃærɪtɪ/ *n.* (*pl.* -**ies**) **1 a** giving voluntarily to those in need; alms-giving. **b** the help, esp. money, so given. **2** an institution or organization for helping those in need. **3 a** kindness, benevolence. **b** tolerance in judging others. **c** love of one's fellow men. □**Charity Commission** (in the UK) a board established to control charitable trusts. [OE f. OF *charité* f. L *caritas -tatis* f. *carus* dear]

charivari /ˌʃɑːrɪˈvɑːrɪ/ *n.* (also **shivaree** /ˌʃɪvəˈriː/) **1** a serenade of banging saucepans etc. to a newly-married couple. **2** a medley of sounds; a hubbub. [F, = serenade with pans, trays, etc., to an unpopular person]

charlady /'tʃɑːˌleɪdɪ/ *n.* (*pl.* -**ies**) = CHARWOMAN.

charlatan /'ʃɑːlət(ə)n/ *n.* a person falsely claiming a special knowledge or skill. □□**charlatanism** *n.* **charlatanry** *n.* [F f. It. *ciarlatano* f. *ciarlare* babble]

Charles' Law /'tʃɑːlz/ (also **Charles's Law** /'tʃɑːlzɪz/) *n. Chem.* the law stating that the volume of an ideal gas at constant pressure is directly proportional to the absolute temperature. [J. A. C. *Charles*, Fr. scientist d. 1823]

Charles's Wain /ˌtʃɑːlzɪz 'weɪn/ *n.* the constellation Ursa Major or its seven bright stars. Also called PLOUGH. [OE *Carles wægn* the wain of Carl (Charles the Great, Charlemagne), perh. by assoc. of the star Arcturus with legends of King Arthur and Charlemagne]

charleston /'tʃɑːlst(ə)n/ *n. & v.* (also **Charleston**) —*n.* a lively American dance of the 1920s with side-kicks from the knee. —*v.intr.* dance the charleston. [*Charleston* in S. Carolina, US]

charley horse /'tʃɑːlɪ/ *n. US sl.* stiffness or cramp in an arm or leg. [19th c.: orig. uncert.]

charlie /'tʃɑːlɪ/ *n. Brit. sl.* **1** a fool. **2** (in *pl.*) a woman's breasts. [dimin. of the name *Charles*]

charlock /'tʃɑːlɒk/ *n.* a wild mustard, *Sinapis arvensis*, with yellow flowers. Also called *field mustard*. [OE *cerlic*, of unkn. orig.]

charlotte /'ʃɑːlɒt/ *n.* a pudding made of stewed fruit with a casing or layers or covering of bread, sponge cake, biscuits, or breadcrumbs (*apple charlotte*). □**charlotte russe** /'ruːs/ custard etc. enclosed in sponge cake or a casing of sponge fingers. [F]

charm /tʃɑːm/ *n. & v.* —*n.* **1 a** the power or quality of giving delight or arousing admiration. **b** fascination, attractiveness. **c** (usu. in *pl.*) an attractive or enticing quality. **2** a trinket on a bracelet etc. **3 a** an object, act, or word(s) supposedly having occult or magic power; a spell. **b** a thing worn to avert evil etc.; an amulet. **4** *Physics* a property of matter manifested by some elementary particles. —*v.tr.* **1** delight, captivate (*charmed by the performance*). **2** influence or protect as if by magic (*leads a charmed life*). **3 a** gain by charm (*charmed agreement out of him*). **b** influence by charm (*charmed her into consenting*). **4** cast a spell on, bewitch. □**charm-bracelet** a bracelet hung with small trinkets. **like a charm** perfectly, wonderfully. □□**charmer** *n.* [ME f. OF *charme, charmer* f. L *carmen* song]

charmeuse /ʃɑːˈmɜːz/ *n.* a soft smooth silky dress-fabric. [F, fem. of *charmeur* (as CHARM)]

charming /'tʃɑːmɪŋ/ *adj.* **1** delightful, attractive, pleasing. **2** (often as *int.*) *iron.* expressing displeasure or disapproval. □□ **charmingly** *adv.*

charmless /ˈtʃɑːmlɪs/ *adj.* lacking charm; unattractive. □□ **charmlessly** *adv.* **charmlessness** *n.*

charnel-house /ˈtʃɑːn(ə)lˌhaʊs/ *n.* a house or vault in which dead bodies or bones are piled. [ME & OF *charnel* burying-place f. med.L *carnale* f. LL *carnalis* CARNAL]

Charollais /ˈʃærəˌleɪ/ *n.* (also **Charolais**) (*pl.* same) **1** an animal of a breed of large white beef-cattle. **2** this breed. [Monts du *Charollais* in E. France]

charpoy /ˈtʃɑːpɔɪ/ *n.* *Ind.* a light bedstead. [Hind. *chārpāi*]

charr var. of CHAR⁴.

chart /tʃɑːt/ *n.* & *v.* —*n.* **1** a geographical map or plan, esp. for navigation by sea or air. **2** a sheet of information in the form of a table, graph, or diagram. **3** (usu. in *pl.*) *colloq.* a listing of the currently most popular gramophone records. —*v.tr.* make a chart of, map. [F *charte* f. L *charta* CARD¹]

chartbuster /ˈtʃɑːtˌbʌstə(r)/ *n.* *colloq.* a best-selling popular song, record, etc.

charter /ˈtʃɑːtə(r)/ *n.* & *v.* —*n.* **1 a** a written grant of rights, by the sovereign or legislature, esp. the creation of a borough, company, university, etc. **b** a written constitution or description of an organization's functions etc. **2** a contract to hire an aircraft, ship, etc., for a special purpose. **3** = CHARTER-PARTY. —*v.tr.* **1** grant a charter to. **2** hire (an aircraft, ship, etc.). □ **chartered accountant, engineer, librarian, surveyor,** etc. *Brit.* a member of a professional body that has a royal charter. **chartered libertine** a person allowed to do as he or she pleases. **charter flight** a flight by a chartered aircraft. **charter-member** an original member of a society, corporation, etc. **Great Charter** = MAGNA CARTA. □□ **charterer** *n.* [ME f. OF *chartre* f. L *chartula* dimin. of *charta* CARD¹]

charter-party /ˈtʃɑːtəˌpɑːtɪ/ *n.* (*pl.* -**ies**) a deed between a ship-owner and a merchant for the hire of a ship and the delivery of cargo. [F *charte partie* f. med.L *charta partita* divided charter, indenture]

Chartism /ˈtʃɑːtɪz(ə)m/ *n.* *hist.* the principles of the UK Parliamentary reform movement of 1837–48. □□ **Chartist** *n.* [L *charta* charter + -ISM: name taken from the manifesto 'People's Charter']

chartreuse /ʃɑːˈtrɜːz/ *n.* **1** a pale green or yellow liqueur of brandy and aromatic herbs etc. **2** the pale yellow or pale green colour of this. **3** a dish of fruit enclosed in jelly etc. [La Grande *Chartreuse* (Carthusian monastery near Grenoble)]

charwoman /ˈtʃɑːˌwʊmən/ *n.* (*pl.* -**women**) a woman employed as a cleaner in houses or offices.

chary /ˈtʃeərɪ/ *adj.* (**charier, chariest**) **1** cautious, wary (*chary of employing such people*). **2** sparing; ungenerous (*chary of giving praise*). **3** shy. □□ **charily** *adv.* **chariness** *n.* [OE *cearig*]

Charybdis see SCYLLA AND CHARYBDIS.

Chas. *abbr.* Charles.

chase¹ /tʃeɪs/ *v.* & *n.* —*v.* **1** *tr.* pursue in order to catch. **2** *tr.* (foll. by *from, out of, to,* etc.) drive. **3** *intr.* **a** (foll. by *after*) hurry in pursuit of (a person). **b** (foll. by *round* etc.) *colloq.* act or move about hurriedly. **4** *tr.* (usu. foll. by *up*) *colloq.* pursue (overdue work, payment, etc. or the person responsible for it). **5** *tr.* *colloq.* **a** try to attain. **b** court persistently and openly. —*n.* **1** pursuit. **2** unenclosed hunting-land. **3** (prec. by *the*) hunting, esp. as a sport. **4** an animal etc. that is pursued. **5** = STEEPLECHASE. □ **go and chase oneself** (usu. in *imper.*) *colloq.* depart. [ME f. OF *chace chacier,* ult. f. L *capere* take]

chase² /tʃeɪs/ *v.tr.* emboss or engrave (metal). [app. f. earlier *enchase* f. F *enchâsser* (as EN-¹, CASE²)]

chase³ /tʃeɪs/ *n.* *Printing* a metal frame holding composed type. [F *châsse* f. L *capsa* CASE²]

chase⁴ /tʃeɪs/ *n.* **1** the part of a gun enclosing the bore. **2** a trench or groove cut to receive a pipe etc.

[F *chas* enclosed space f. Prov. *ca(u)s* f. med.L *capsum* thorax]

chaser /ˈtʃeɪsə(r)/ *n.* **1** a person or thing that chases. **2** a horse for steeplechasing. **3** *colloq.* a drink taken after another of a different kind, e.g. beer after spirits. **4** *US colloq.* an amorous pursuer of women.

chasm /ˈkæz(ə)m/ *n.* **1** a deep fissure or opening in the earth, rock, etc. **2** a wide difference of feeling, interests, etc.; a gulf. **3** *archaic* a hiatus. □□ **chasmic** *adj.* [L *chasma* f. Gk *khasma* gaping hollow]

chasse /ʃɑːs/ *n.* a liqueur taken after coffee etc. [F f. *chasser* CHASE¹]

chassé /ˈʃæseɪ/ *n.* & *v.* —*n.* a gliding step in dancing. —*v.intr.* (**chasséd; chasséing**) make this step. [F, = chasing]

chassis /ˈʃæsɪ/ *n.* (*pl.* same /-sɪz/) **1** the base-frame of a motor vehicle, carriage, etc. **2** a frame to carry radio etc. components. [F *châssis* ult. f. L *capsa* CASE²]

chaste /tʃeɪst/ *adj.* **1** abstaining from extramarital, or from all, sexual intercourse. **2** (of behaviour, speech, etc.) pure, virtuous, decent. **3** (of artistic etc. style) simple, unadorned. □ **chaste-tree** an ornamental shrub, *Vitex agnus-castus*, with blue or white flowers. □□ **chastely** *adv.* **chasteness** *n.* [ME f. OF f. L *castus*]

chasten /ˈtʃeɪs(ə)n/ *v.tr.* **1** (esp. as **chastening, chastened** *adjs.*) subdue, restrain (*a chastening experience; chastened by his failure*). **2** discipline, punish. **3** moderate. □□ **chastener** *n.* [obs. *chaste* (v.) f. OF *chastier* f. L *castigare* CASTIGATE]

chastise /tʃæsˈtaɪz/ *v.tr.* **1** rebuke or reprimand severely. **2** punish, esp. by beating. □□ **chastisement** *n.* **chastiser** *n.* [ME, app. irreg. formed f. obs. verbs *chaste, chasty:* see CHASTEN]

chastity /ˈtʃæstɪtɪ/ *n.* **1** being chaste. **2** sexual abstinence; virginity. **3** simplicity of style or taste. □ **chastity belt** *hist.* a garment designed to prevent a woman from having sexual intercourse. [ME f. OF *chasteté* f. L *castitas -tatis* f. *castus* CHASTE]

chasuble /ˈtʃæzjʊb(ə)l/ *n.* a loose sleeveless usu. ornate outer vestment worn by a priest celebrating Mass or the Eucharist. [ME f. OF *chesible*, later -*uble*, ult. f. L *casula* hooded cloak, little cottage, dimin. of *casa* cottage]

chat¹ /tʃæt/ *v.* & *n.* —*v.intr.* (**chatted, chatting**) talk in a light familiar way. —*n.* **1** informal conversation or talk. **2** an instance of this. □ **chat show** *Brit.* a television or radio programme in which celebrities are interviewed informally. **chat up** *Brit.* *colloq.* chat to, esp. flirtatiously or with an ulterior motive. [ME: shortening of CHATTER]

chat² /tʃæt/ *n.* any of various small birds with harsh calls, esp. a stonechat or whinchat or any of certain American or Australian warblers. [prob. imit.]

château /ˈʃætəʊ/ *n.* (*pl.* **châteaux** /-təʊz/) a large French country house or castle, often giving its name to wine made in its neighbourhood. [F f. OF *chastel* CASTLE]

chateaubriand /ˌʃætəʊˈbriːɑ̃/ *n.* a thick fillet of beef steak. [Vicomte de *Chateaubriand* (d. 1848), Fr. writer and statesman]

chatelaine /ˈʃætəˌleɪn/ *n.* **1** the mistress of a large house. **2** *hist.* a set of short chains attached to a woman's belt, for carrying keys etc. [F *châtelaine*, fem. of -*ain* lord of a castle, f. med.L *castellanus* CASTELLAN]

chattel /ˈtʃæt(ə)l/ *n.* (usu. in *pl.*) a moveable possession; any possession or piece of property other than real estate or a freehold. □ **chattel mortgage** *US* the conveyance of chattels by mortgage as security for a debt. **goods and chattels** personal possessions. [ME f. OF *chatel:* see CATTLE]

chatter /ˈtʃætə(r)/ *v.* & *n.* —*v.intr.* **1** talk quickly, incessantly, trivially, or indiscreetly. **2** (of a bird) emit short quick notes. **3** (of the teeth) click repeatedly together (usu. from cold). **4** (of a tool) clatter from vibration. —*n.* **1** chattering talk or sounds. **2**

the vibration of a tool. □□ **chatterer** *n.* **chattery** *adj.* [ME: imit.]

chatterbox /'tʃætəˌbɒks/ *n.* a talkative person.

chatty /'tʃætɪ/ *adj.* (**chattier, chattiest**) **1** fond of chatting; talkative. **2** resembling chat; informal and lively (*a chatty letter*). □□ **chattily** *adv.* **chattiness** *n.*

Chaucerian /tʃɔːˈsɪərɪən/ *adj.* & *n.* —*adj.* of or relating to the English poet Chaucer (d. 1400) or his style. —*n.* a student of Chaucer.

chaud-froid /ʃəʊˈfrwɑː/ *n.* a dish of cold cooked meat or fish in jelly or sauce. [F f. *chaud* hot + *froid* cold]

chauffeur /'ʃəʊfə(r), -ˈfɜː(r)/ *n.* & *v.* —*n.* (*fem.* **chauffeuse** /-ˈfɜːz/) a person employed to drive a private or hired motor car. —*v.tr.* drive (a car or a person) as a chauffeur. [F, = stoker]

chaulmoogra /tʃɔːlˈmuːɡrə/ *n.* any tree of the genus *Hydnocarpus*, esp. *H. wightiana*, with seeds yielding an oil formerly used in the treatment of leprosy. [Bengali]

chautauqua /tʃɔːˈtɔːkwə, ʃɔː-/ *n.* US a summer school or similar educational course. [*Chautauqua* in New York State]

chauvinism /'ʃəʊvɪˌnɪz(ə)m/ *n.* **1** exaggerated or aggressive patriotism. **2** excessive or prejudiced support or loyalty for one's cause or group or sex (*male chauvinism*). [*Chauvin*, a Napoleonic veteran in the Cogniards' *Cocarde Tricolore* (1831)]

chauvinist /'ʃəʊvɪnɪst/ *n.* **1** a person exhibiting chauvinism. **2** (in full **male chauvinist**) a man showing excessive loyalty to men and prejudice against women. □□ **chauvinistic** /-ˈnɪstɪk/ *adj.* **chauvinistically** /-ˈnɪstɪkəlɪ/ *adv.*

Ch.B. *abbr.* Bachelor of Surgery. [L *Chirurgiae Baccalaureus*]

cheap /tʃiːp/ *adj.* & *adv.* —*adj.* **1** low in price; worth more than its cost (*a cheap holiday*; *cheap labour*). **2** charging low prices; offering good value (*a cheap restaurant*). **3** of poor quality; inferior (*cheap housing*). **4 a** costing little effort or acquired by discreditable means and hence of little worth (*cheap popularity*; *a cheap joke*). **b** contemptible; despicable (*a cheap criminal*). —*adv.* cheaply (*got it cheap*). □ **cheap and nasty** of low cost and bad quality. **dirt cheap** very cheap. **feel cheap** feel ashamed or contemptible. **on the cheap** cheaply. □□ **cheapish** *adj.* **cheaply** *adv.* **cheapness** *n.* [obs. phr. *good cheap* f. *cheap* a bargain f. OE *cēap* barter, ult. f. L *caupo* innkeeper]

cheapen /'tʃiːpən/ *v.tr.* & *intr.* make or become cheap or cheaper; depreciate, degrade.

cheapjack /'tʃiːpdʒæk/ *n.* & *adj.* —*n.* a seller of inferior goods at low prices. —*adj.* inferior, shoddy. [CHEAP + JACK[1]]

cheapo /'tʃiːpəʊ/ *attrib.adj. sl.* cheap.

cheapskate /'tʃiːpskeɪt/ *n.* esp. *US colloq.* a mean or contemptible person.

cheat /tʃiːt/ *v.* & *n.* —*v.* **1** *tr.* **a** (often foll. by *into, out of*) deceive or trick (*cheated into parting with his savings*). **b** (foll. by *of*) deprive of (*cheated of a chance to reply*). **2** *intr.* gain unfair advantage by deception or breaking rules, esp. in a game or examination. **3** *tr.* avoid (something undesirable) by luck or skill (*cheated the bad weather*). **4** *tr. archaic* divert attention from, beguile (time, tedium, etc.). —*n.* **1** a person who cheats. **2** a trick, fraud, or deception. **3** an act of cheating. □ **cheat on** *colloq.* be sexually unfaithful to. □□ **cheatingly** *adv.* [ME *chete* f. *achete*, var. of ESCHEAT]

cheater /'tʃiːtə(r)/ *n.* **1** a person who cheats. **2** (in *pl.*) *US sl.* spectacles.

check¹ /tʃek/ *v., n.,* & *int.* —*v.* **1** *tr.* (also *absol.*) **a** examine the accuracy, quality, or condition of. **b** (often foll. by *that* + clause) make sure; verify; establish to one's satisfaction (*checked that the doors were locked*; *checked the train times*). **2** *tr.* **a** stop or slow the motion of; curb, restrain (*progress was checked by bad weather*). **b** *colloq.* find fault with;

rebuke. **3** *tr. Chess* move a piece into a position that directly threatens (the opposing king). **4** *intr.* US agree or correspond when compared. **5** *tr.* US mark with a tick etc. **6** *tr.* US deposit (luggage etc.) for storage or dispatch. **7** *intr.* (of hounds) pause to ensure or regain scent. —*n.* **1** a means or act of testing or ensuring accuracy, quality, satisfactory condition, etc. **2 a** a stopping or slowing of motion; a restraint on action. **b** a rebuff or rebuke. **c** a person or thing that restrains. **3** *Chess* (also as *int.*) **a** the exposure of a king to direct attack from an opposing piece. **b** an announcement of this by the attacking player. **4** US a bill in a restaurant. **5** esp. US a token of identification for left luggage etc. **6** US *Cards* a counter used in various games. **7** a temporary loss of the scent in hunting. **8** a crack or flaw in timber. —*int.* US expressing assent or agreement. □ **check in 1** arrive or register at a hotel, airport, etc. **2** record the arrival of. **check-in** *n.* the act or place of checking in. **check into** register one's arrival at (a hotel etc.). **check-list** a list for reference and verification. **check-nut** = *lock-nut*. **check off** mark on a list etc. as having been examined or dealt with. **check on** examine carefully or in detail; ascertain the truth about; keep a watch on (a person, work done, etc.). **check out 1** (often foll. by *of*) leave a hotel etc. with due formalities. **2** US investigate; examine for authenticity or suitability. **check over** examine for errors; verify. **check-rein** a rein attaching one horse's rein to another's bit, or preventing a horse from lowering its head. **check through** inspect or examine exhaustively; verify successive items of. **check up** ascertain, verify, make sure. **check-up** *n.* a thorough (esp. medical) examination. **check up on** = *check on*. **check-valve** a valve allowing flow in one direction only. **in check** under control, restrained. □□ **checkable** *adj.* [ME f. OF *eschequier* play chess, give check to, and OF *eschec*, ult. f. Pers. *šāh* king]

check² /tʃek/ *n.* **1** a pattern of small squares. **2** fabric having this pattern. [ME, prob. f. CHEQUER]

check³ US var. of CHEQUE.

checked /tʃekt/ *adj.* having a check pattern.

checker¹ /'tʃekə(r)/ *n.* **1** a person or thing that verifies or examines, esp. in a factory etc. **2** US a cashier in a supermarket etc.

checker² /'tʃekə(r)/ *n.* **1** var. of CHEQUER. **2** US **a** (in *pl.*, usu. treated as *sing.*) the game of draughts. **b** = CHECKERMAN.

checkerberry /'tʃekəbərɪ/ *n.* (*pl.* **-ies**) **1** a wintergreen, *Gaultheria procumbens*. **2** the fruit of this plant. [*checkers* berries of service-tree]

checkerboard /'tʃekəbɔːd/ *n.* US = DRAUGHTBOARD.

checkerman /'tʃekəˌmæn/ *n.* (*pl.* **-men**) each of the 'men' in a game of draughts.

checking account /'tʃekɪŋ/ *n.* US a current account at a bank. [CHECK³]

checkmate /'tʃekmeɪt/ *n.* & *v.* —*n.* **1** (also as *int.*) *Chess* **a** check from which a king cannot escape. **b** an announcement of this. **2** a final defeat or deadlock. —*v.tr.* **1** *Chess* put into checkmate. **2** defeat; frustrate. [ME f. OF *eschec mat* f. Pers. *šāh māt* the king is dead]

checkout /'tʃekaʊt/ *n.* **1** an act of checking out. **2** a point at which goods are paid for in a supermarket etc.

checkpoint /'tʃekpɔɪnt/ *n.* a place, esp. a barrier or manned entrance, where documents, vehicles, etc., are inspected.

checkroom /'tʃekruːm, -rʊm/ *n.* US **1** a cloakroom in a hotel or theatre. **2** an office for left luggage etc.

Cheddar /'tʃedə(r)/ *n.* a kind of firm smooth cheese orig. made in Cheddar in S. England.

cheek /tʃiːk/ *n.* & *v.* —*n.* **1 a** the side of the face below the eye. **b** the side-wall of the mouth. **2 a** impertinent speech. **b** impertinence; cool confidence (*had the cheek to ask for more*). **3** *sl.* either buttock. **4 a** either of the side-posts of a door etc. **b** either of the jaws of a vice. **c** either of the side-pieces of various parts of machines arranged in lateral pairs. —*v.tr.* speak impertinently to. □**cheek-bone** the bone below the eye. **cheek by jowl** close together; intimate. **turn the other cheek** accept attack etc. meekly; refuse to retaliate. [OE *cē(a)ce, cēoce*]

cheeky /'tʃiːkɪ/ adj. (**cheekier, cheekiest**) impertinent, impudent. □□**cheekily** adv. **cheekiness** n.

cheep /tʃiːp/ n. & v. —n. the weak shrill cry of a young bird. —*v.intr.* make such a cry. [imit.: cf. PEEP²]

cheer /'tʃɪə(r)/ n. & v. —n. **1** a shout of encouragement or applause. **2** mood, disposition (*full of good cheer*). **3** (in *pl.*; as *int.*) *Brit. colloq.* **a** expressing good wishes on parting or before drinking. **b** expressing gratitude. —v. **1** tr. **a** applaud with shouts. **b** (usu. foll. by *on*) urge or encourage with shouts. **2** *intr.* shout for joy. **3** *tr.* gladden; comfort. □**cheer-leader** a person who leads cheers of applause etc. **cheer up** make or become less depressed. **three cheers** three successive hurrahs for a person or thing honoured. [ME f. AF *chere* face etc., OF *chiere* f. LL *cara* face f. Gk *kara* head]

cheerful /'tʃɪəfʊl/ adj. **1** in good spirits, noticeably happy (*a cheerful disposition*). **2** bright, pleasant (*a cheerful room*). **3** willing, not reluctant. □□ **cheerfully** adv. **cheerfulness** n.

cheerio /ˌtʃɪrɪ'əʊ/ int. Brit. colloq. expressing good wishes on parting or before drinking.

cheerless /'tʃɪəlɪs/ adj. gloomy, dreary, miserable. □□**cheerlessly** adv. **cheerlessness** n.

cheerly /'tʃɪəlɪ/ adv. & adj. —adv. esp. Naut. heartily, with a will. —adj. archaic cheerful.

cheery /'tʃɪərɪ/ adj. (**cheerier, cheeriest**) lively; in good spirits; genial, cheering. □□**cheerily** adv. **cheeriness** n.

cheese¹ /tʃiːz/ n. **1 a** a food made from the pressed curds of milk. **b** a complete cake of this with rind. **2** a conserve having the consistency of soft cheese (*lemon cheese*). **3** a round flat object, e.g. the heavy flat wooden disc used in skittles. □**cheese-cutter 1** a knife with a broad curved blade. **2** a device for cutting cheese by pulling a wire through it. **cheese-fly** (*pl.* **-flies**) a small black fly, *Piophila casei*, breeding in cheese. **cheese-head** the squat cylindrical head of a screw etc. **cheese-mite** any mite of the genus *Tyroglyphus* feeding on cheese. **cheese-paring** adj. stingy. —n. stinginess. **cheese plant** = *Swiss cheese plant*. **cheese-skipper** = *cheese-fly*. **cheese straw** a thin cheese-flavoured strip of pastry. **hard cheese** *sl.* bad luck. [OE *cēse* etc. ult. f. L *caseus*]

cheese² /tʃiːz/ v.tr. Brit. sl. (as **cheesed** adj.) (often foll. by *off*) bored, fed up. □**cheese it** stop it, leave off. [19th c.: orig. unkn.]

cheese³ /tʃiːz/ n. (also **big cheese**) sl. an important person. [perh. f. Hind. *chīz* thing]

cheeseboard /'tʃiːzbɔːd/ n. **1** a board from which cheese is served. **2** a selection of cheeses.

cheeseburger /'tʃiːzˌbɜːgə(r)/ n. a hamburger with cheese in or on it.

cheesecake /'tʃiːzkeɪk/ n. **1** a tart filled with sweetened curds etc. **2** *sl.* the portrayal of women in a sexually attractive manner.

cheesecloth /'tʃiːzklɒθ/ n. thin loosely woven cloth, used orig. for wrapping cheese.

cheesemonger /'tʃiːzˌmʌŋgə(r)/ n. a dealer in cheese, butter, etc.

cheesewood /'tʃiːzwʊd/ n. **1** an Australian tree of the genus *Pittosporum*. **2** its hard yellowish wood.

cheesy /'tʃiːzɪ/ adj. (**cheesier, cheesiest**) **1** like cheese in taste, smell, appearance, etc. **2** *sl.* inferior; cheap and nasty. □□**cheesiness** n.

cheetah /'tʃiːtə/ n. a swift-running feline, *Acinonyx jubatus*, with a leopard-like spotted coat. [Hindi *cītā*, perh. f. Skr. *citraka* speckled]

chef /ʃef/ n. a (usu. male) cook, esp. the chief cook in a restaurant etc. [F, = head]

chef-d'œuvre /ʃer'dɜːvr/ n. (pl. **chefs-d'œuvre** pronunc. same) a masterpiece. [F]

cheiro- comb. form var. of CHIRO-.

chela¹ /'kiːlə/ n. (pl. **chelae** /-liː/) a prehensile claw of crabs, lobsters, scorpions, etc. [mod.L f. L *chele*, or Gk *khēlē* claw]

chela² /'tʃeɪlə/ n. **1** (in esoteric Buddhism) a novice qualifying for initiation. **2** a disciple; a pupil. [Hindi, = servant]

chelate /'kiːleɪt/ n., adj., & v. —n. Chem. a usu. organometallic compound containing a bonded ring of atoms including a metal atom. —adj. **1** Chem. of a chelate. **2** Zool. & Anat. of or having chelae. —*v.intr.* Chem. form a chelate. □□ **chelation** /-'leɪʃ(ə)n/ n.

Chellean /'ʃelən/ adj. Archaeol. = ABBEVILLIAN. [F *chelléen* f. *Chelles* near Paris]

chelonian /kɪ'ləʊnɪən/ n. & adj. —n. any reptile of the order Chelonia, including turtles, terrapins, and tortoises, having a shell of bony plates covered with horny scales. —adj. of or relating to this order. [mod.L *Chelonia* f. Gk *khelōnē* tortoise]

Chelsea bun /'tʃelsɪ/ n. a kind of currant bun in the form of a flat spiral. [*Chelsea* in London]

Chelsea pensioner /'tʃelsɪ/ n. an inmate of the Chelsea Royal Hospital for old or disabled soldiers.

Chelsea ware /'tʃelsɪ/ n. any of various soft-paste porcelains made at Chelsea in the 18th c.

chemi- comb. form var. of CHEMO-.

chemical /'kemɪk(ə)l/ adj. & n. —adj. of, made by, or employing chemistry or chemicals. —n. a substance obtained or used in chemistry. □**chemical bond** the force holding atoms together in a molecule or crystal. **chemical engineer** one engaged in chemical engineering, esp. professionally. **chemical engineering** the design, manufacture, and operation of industrial chemical plants. **chemical reaction** a process that involves change in the structure of atoms, molecules, or ions. **chemical warfare** warfare using poison gas and other chemicals. **fine chemicals** chemicals of high purity usu. used in small amounts. **heavy chemicals** bulk chemicals used in industry and agriculture. □□ **chemically** adv. [*chemic* alchemic f. F *chimique* or mod.L *chimicus, chymicus,* f. med.L *alchymicus*: see ALCHEMY]

chemico- /'kemɪkəʊ/ comb. form chemical; chemical and (*chemico-physical*).

chemiluminescence /ˌkemɪˌluːmɪ'nes(ə)ns, -ˌljuːmɪ 'nes(ə)ns/ n. the emission of light during a chemical reaction. □□ **chemiluminescent** adj. [G *Chemilumineszenz* (as CHEMI-, LUMINESCENCE)]

chemin de fer /ʃəˌmæ̃ də 'feə(r)/ n. a form of baccarat. [F, = railway, lit. road of iron]

chemise /ʃə'miːz/ n. hist. a woman's loose-fitting under-garment or dress hanging straight from the shoulders. [ME f. OF f. LL *camisia* shirt]

chemisorption /ˌkemɪ'sɔːpʃ(ə)n/ n. adsorption by chemical bonding. [CHEMI- + ADSORPTION (see ADSORB)]

chemist /'kemɪst/ n. **1** Brit. **a** a dealer in medicinal drugs, usu. also selling other medical goods and toiletries. **b** an authorized dispenser of medicines. **2** a person practising or trained in chemistry. [earlier *chymist* f. F *chimiste* f. mod.L *chimista* f. *alchimista* ALCHEMIST (see ALCHEMY)]

chemistry /'kemɪstrɪ/ n. (pl. **-ies**) **1** the study of the elements and the compounds they form and the reactions they undergo. **2** any complex (esp. emotional) change or process (*the chemistry of fear*). **3** colloq. a person's personality or temperament.

chemo- /'kiːməʊ/ comb. form (also **chemi-** /'kemɪ/) chemical.

chemosynthesis /ˌkiːmə'sɪnθɪsɪs/ n. the synthesis of organic compounds by energy derived from chemical reactions.

chemotherapy /ˌkiːmə'θerəpɪ/ n. the treatment of

disease, esp. cancer, by use of chemical substances. □□ **chemotherapist** *n.*

chemurgy /'kemɜ:dʒɪ/ *n.* *US* the chemical and industrial use of organic raw materials. □□ **chemurgic** /-'mɜ:dʒɪk/ *adj.* [CHEMO-, after *metallurgy*]

chenille /ʃə'ni:l/ *n.* **1** a tufty velvety cord or yarn, used in trimming furniture etc. **2** fabric made from this. [F, = hairy caterpillar f. L *canicula* dimin. of *canis* dog]

cheongsam /tʃɪɒŋ'sæm/ *n.* a Chinese woman's garment with a high neck and slit skirt. [Chin.]

cheque /tʃek/ *n.* (*US* **check**) **1** a written order to a bank to pay the stated sum from the drawer's account. **2** the printed form on which such an order is written. □ **cheque-book** a book of forms for writing cheques. **cheque-book journalism** the payment of large sums for exclusive rights to material for (esp. personal) newspaper stories. **cheque card** a card issued by a bank to guarantee the honouring of cheques up to a stated amount. [special use of CHECK[1] to mean 'device for checking the amount of an item']

chequer /'tʃekə(r)/ *n. & v.* (also **checker**) —*n.* **1** (often in *pl.*) a pattern of squares often alternately coloured. **2** (in *pl.*) (usu. as **checkers**) *US* the game of draughts. —*v.tr.* **1** mark with chequers. **2** variegate; break the uniformity of. **3** (as **chequered** *adj.*) with varied fortunes (a *chequered career*). □ **chequer-board 1** a chessboard. **2** a pattern resembling it. [ME f. EXCHEQUER]

Cherenkov radiation var. of CERENKOV RADIATION.

cherish /'tʃerɪʃ/ *v.tr.* **1** protect or tend (a child, plant, etc.) lovingly. **2** hold dear, cling to (hopes, feelings, etc.). [ME f. OF *cherir* f. *cher* f. L *carus* dear]

chernozem /'tʃɜ:nəʊˌzem/ *n.* a fertile black soil rich in humus, found in temperate regions, esp. S. Russia. Also called *black earth*. [Russ. f. *chernyĭ* black + *zemlya* earth]

Cherokee /'tʃerəkɪ/ *n. & adj.* —*n.* **1 a** an American Indian tribe formerly inhabiting much of the southern US. **b** a member of this tribe. **2** the language of this tribe. —*adj.* of or relating to the Cherokees or their language. □ **Cherokee rose** a fragrant white rose, *Rosa laevigata*, of the southern US. [Cherokee *Tsálăgĭ*]

cheroot /ʃə'ru:t/ *n.* a cigar with both ends open. [F *cheroute* f. Tamil *shuruṭṭu* roll]

cherry /'tʃerɪ/ *n. & adj.* —*n.* (*pl.* **-ies**) **1 a** a small soft round stone-fruit. **b** any of several trees of the genus *Prunus* bearing this or grown for its ornamental flowers. **2** (in full **cherry wood**) the wood of a cherry. **3** *US sl.* **a** virginity. **b** a virgin. —*adj.* of a light red colour. □ **cherry brandy** a dark-red liqueur of brandy in which cherries have been steeped. **cherry-laurel** *Brit.* a small evergreen tree, *Prunus laurocerasus*, with white flowers and cherry-like fruits. **cherry-picker** *colloq.* a crane for raising and lowering people. **cherry-pie 1** a pie made with cherries. **2** a garden heliotrope. **cherry plum 1** a tree, *Prunus cerasifera*, native to SW Asia, with solitary white flowers and red fruits. **2** the fruit of this tree. **cherry tomato** a miniature tomato with a strong flavour. [ME f. ONF *cherise* (taken as pl.: cf. PEA) f. med.L *ceresia* perh. f. L f. Gk *kerasos*]

chersonese /'kɜ:sə,ni:s/ *n.* a peninsula, esp. the Thracian peninsula view of the Hellespont. [L *chersonesus* f. Gk *khersonēsos* f. *khersos* dry + *nēsos* island]

chert /tʃɜ:t/ *n.* a flintlike form of quartz composed of chalcedony. □□ **cherty** *adj.* [17th c.: orig. unkn.]

cherub /'tʃerəb/ *n.* **1** (*pl.* **cherubim** /-bɪm/) an angelic being of the second order of the celestial hierarchy. **2 a** a representation of a winged child or the head of a winged child. **b** a beautiful or innocent child. □□ **cherubic** /tʃɪ'ru:bɪk/ *adj.* **cherubically** /tʃɪ'ru:bɪkəlɪ/ *adv.* [ME f. OE *cherubin* and f. Heb. *kᵉrūḇ*, pl. *kᵉrūḇim*]

chervil /'tʃɜ:vɪl/ *n.* an umbelliferous plant, *Anthriscus cerefolium*, with small white flowers, used as a herb for flavouring soup, salads, etc. [OE *cerfille* f. L *chaerephylla* f. Gk *khairephullon*]

Ches. *abbr.* Cheshire.

Cheshire /'tʃeʃə(r)/ *n.* a kind of firm crumbly cheese, orig. made in Cheshire. □ **like a Cheshire cat** with a broad fixed grin. [*Cheshire*, a county in England]

chess /tʃes/ *n.* a game for two with 16 men each, played on a chessboard. [ME f. OF *esches* pl. of *eschec* CHECK[1]]

chessboard /'tʃesbɔ:d/ *n.* a chequered board of 64 squares on which chess and draughts are played.

chessman /'tʃesmæn/ *n.* (*pl.* **-men**) any of the 32 pieces and pawns with which chess is played.

chest /tʃest/ *n.* **1** a large strong box, esp. for storage or transport e.g. of blankets, tea, etc. **2 a** the part of a human or animal body enclosed by the ribs. **b** the front surface of the body from neck to waist. **3** a small cabinet for medicines etc. **4 a** the treasury or financial resources of an institution. **b** the money available from it. □ **chest of drawers** a piece of furniture consisting of a set of drawers in a frame. **chest-voice** the lowest register of the voice in singing or speaking. **get a thing off one's chest** *colloq.* disclose a fact, secret, etc., to relieve one's anxiety about it. **play** (one's cards, a thing, etc.) **close to one's chest** *colloq.* be cautious or secretive about. □□ **-chested** *adj.* (in *comb.*). [OE *cest, cyst* f. Gmc f. L f. Gk *kistē*]

chesterfield /'tʃestə,fi:ld/ *n.* **1** a sofa with arms and back of the same height and curved outwards at the top. **2** a man's plain overcoat usu. with a velvet collar. [19th-c. Earl of *Chesterfield*]

chestnut /'tʃesnʌt/ *n. & adj.* —*n.* **1 a** a glossy hard brown edible nut. **b** the tree *Castanea sativa*, bearing flowers in catkins and nuts enclosed in a spiny fruit. Also called *Spanish chestnut* or *sweet chestnut*. **2** any other tree of the genus *Castanea*. **3** = *horse chestnut*. **4** (in full **chestnut-wood**) the heavy wood of any chestnut tree. **5** a horse of a reddish-brown or yellowish-brown colour. **6** *colloq.* a stale joke or anecdote. **7** a small hard patch on a horse's leg. **8** a reddish-brown colour. —*adj.* of the colour chestnut. □ **liver chestnut** a dark kind of chestnut horse. [obs. *chesten* f. OF *chastaine* f. L *castanea* f. Gk *kastanea*]

chesty /'tʃestɪ/ *adj.* (**chestier**, **chestiest**) **1** *Brit. colloq.* inclined to or symptomatic of chest disease. **2** *colloq.* having a large chest or prominent breasts. **3** *US sl.* arrogant. □□ **chestily** *adv.* **chestiness** *n.*

chetnik /'tʃetnɪk/ *n. hist.* a member of a guerrilla force in the Balkans, esp. during the wars of 1914–18 and 1939–45. [Serbian *četnik* f. *četa* band, troop]

cheval-glass /ʃə'væl/ *n.* a tall mirror swung on an upright frame. [F *cheval* horse, frame]

chevalier /ʃe'væliə(r)/ *n.* **1 a** a member of certain orders of knighthood, and of modern French orders, as the Legion of Honour. **b** *archaic* or *hist.* a knight. **2** *hist.* the title of the Old and Young Pretenders. **3** a chivalrous man; a cavalier. [ME f. AF *chevaler*, OF *chevalier* f. med.L *caballarius* f. L *caballus* horse]

chevet /ʃə'veɪ/ *n.* the apsidal end of a church, sometimes with an attached group of apses. [F, = pillow, f. L *capitium* f. *caput* head]

Cheviot /'tʃeviət, 'tʃi:v-/ *n.* **1 a** a large sheep of a breed with short thick wool. **b** this breed. **2** (**cheviot**) the wool or cloth obtained from this breed. [*Cheviot* Hills in N. England and Scotland]

chèvre /ʃevr/ *n.* a variety of goat's-milk cheese. [F, = goat, she-goat]

chevron /'ʃevrən/ *n.* **1** a badge in a V shape on the sleeve of a uniform indicating rank or length of service. **2** *Heraldry & Archit.* a bent bar of an inverted V shape. **3** any V-shaped line or stripe. [ME f. OF ult. f. L *caper* goat: cf. L *capreoli* pair of rafters]

chevrotain /'ʃevrə,teɪn/ *n.* (also **chevrotin** /-tɪn/) *n.* any small deerlike animal of the family Tragulidae, native to Africa and SE Asia, having small tusks.

---

w *we* z *zoo* ʃ *she* ʒ *decision* θ *thin* ð *this* ŋ *ring* x *loch* tʃ *chip* dʒ *jar* (*see over for vowels*)

Also called *mouse deer*. [F, dimin. of OF *chevrot* dimin. of *chèvre* goat]

chevy var. of CHIVVY.

chew /tʃuː/ v. & n. —v.tr. (also *absol.*) work (food etc.) between the teeth; crush or indent with the teeth. —n. 1 an act of chewing. 2 something for chewing, esp. a chewy sweet. □**chew the cud** reflect, ruminate. **chew the fat** (or **rag**) *sl.* 1 chat. 2 grumble. **chewing-gum** flavoured gum, esp. chicle, for chewing. **chew on** 1 work continuously between the teeth (*chewed on a piece of string*). 2 think about; meditate on. **chew out** *US colloq.* reprimand. **chew over** 1 discuss, talk over. 2 think about; meditate on. □□**chewable** adj. **chewer** n. [OE *cēowan*]

chewy /tʃuːɪ/ adj. (**chewier, chewiest**) 1 needing much chewing. 2 suitable for chewing. □□**chewiness** n.

Cheyenne /ʃaɪˈæn/ n. & adj. —n. 1 a an American Indian tribe formerly living between the Missouri and Arkansas rivers. b a member of this tribe. 2 the language of this tribe. —adj. of or relating to the Cheyennes or their language. [Canadian F f. Dakota *Sahiyena*]

Cheyne–Stokes respiration /tʃeɪnˈstəʊks/ adj. *Med.* (of a breathing cycle) with a gradual decrease of movement to a complete stop, followed by a gradual increase. [J. *Cheyne*, Sc. physician d. 1836, and W. *Stokes*, Ir. physician d. 1878]

chez /ʃeɪ/ prep. at the house or home of. [F f. OF *chiese* f. L *casa* cottage]

chi /kaɪ/ n. the twenty-second letter of the Greek alphabet (Χ, χ). □**chi-rho** a monogram of chi and rho as the first two letters of Greek *Khristos* Christ. **chi-square test** a method of comparing observed and theoretical values in statistics. [ME f. Gk *khi*]

Chianti /kɪˈæntɪ/ n. (pl. **Chiantis**) a dry red Italian wine. [*Chianti*, an area in Tuscany, Italy]

chiaroscuro /kɪˌɑːrəˈskʊərəʊ/ n. 1 the treatment of light and shade in drawing and painting. 2 the use of contrast in literature etc. 3 (*attrib.*) half-revealed. [It. f. *chiaro* CLEAR + *oscuro* dark, OBSCURE]

chiasma /kaɪˈæzmə/ n. (pl. **chiasmata** /-tə/) *Biol.* the point at which paired chromosomes remain in contact after crossing over during meiosis. [mod.L f. Gk *chiasma* a cross-shaped mark]

chiasmus /kaɪˈæzməs/ n. inversion in the second of two parallel phrases of the order followed in the first (e.g. *to stop too fearful and too faint to go*). □□**chiastic** adj. [mod.L f. Gk *khiasmos* crosswise arrangement f. *khiazō* mark with letter CHI]

chibouk /tʃɪˈbuːk/ n. (also **chibouque**) a long Turkish tobacco-pipe. [Turk. *çubuk* tube]

chic /ʃiːk/ adj. & n. —adj. (**chic-er, chic-est**) stylish, elegant (in dress or appearance). —n. stylishness, elegance. □□**chicly** adv. [F]

chicane /ʃɪˈkeɪn/ n. & v. —n. 1 chicanery. 2 an artificial barrier or obstacle on a motor racecourse. 3 *Bridge* a hand without trumps, or without cards of one suit. —v. *archaic* 1 intr. use chicanery. 2 tr. (usu. foll. by *into, out of*, etc.) cheat (a person). [F *chicane(r)* quibble]

chicanery /ʃɪˈkeɪnərɪ/ n. (pl. **-ies**) 1 clever but misleading talk; a false argument. 2 trickery, deception. [F *chicanerie* (as CHICANE)]

chicano /tʃɪˈkɑːnəʊ/ n. (pl. **-os**) *US* an American of Mexican origin. [Sp. *mejicano* Mexican]

chichi /ˈʃiːʃiː/ adj. & n. —adj. 1 (of a thing) frilly, showy. 2 (of a person or behaviour) fussy, affected. —n. 1 over-refinement, pretentiousness, fussiness. 2 a frilly, showy, or pretentious object. [F]

chick[1] /tʃɪk/ n. 1 a young bird, esp. one newly hatched. 2 *sl.* a a young woman. b a child. [ME: shortening of CHICKEN]

chick[2] /tʃɪk/ n. *Ind.* a screen for a doorway etc., made from split bamboo and twine. [Hindi *chik*]

chickadee /ˈtʃɪkəˌdiː/ n. *US* any of various small birds of the tit family, esp. *Parus atricapillus* with a distinctive dark-crowned head. [imit.]

chicken /ˈtʃɪkɪn/ n., adj., & v. —n. (pl. same or **chickens**) 1 a young bird of a domestic fowl. 2 a a domestic fowl prepared as food. b its flesh. 3 a youthful person (usu. with *neg.: is no chicken*). 4 *colloq.* a children's pastime testing courage, usu. recklessly. —adj. *colloq.* cowardly. —v.intr. (foll. by *out*) *colloq.* withdraw from or fail in some activity through fear or lack of nerve. □**chicken-and-egg problem** (or **dilemma** etc.) the unresolved question as to which of two things caused the other. **chicken brick** an earthenware container in two halves for roasting a chicken in its own juices. **chicken cholera** see CHOLERA. **chicken-feed** 1 food for poultry. 2 *colloq.* an unimportant amount, esp. of money. **chicken-hearted** (or **-livered**) easily frightened; lacking nerve or courage. **chicken-wire** a light wire netting with a hexagonal mesh. [OE *cicen, cȳcen* f. Gmc]

chickenpox /ˈtʃɪkɪnˌpɒks/ n. an infectious disease, esp. of children, with a rash of small blisters. Also called VARICELLA.

chick-pea /ˈtʃɪkpiː/ n. 1 a leguminous plant, *Cicer arietinum*, with short swollen pods containing yellow beaked seeds. 2 this seed used as a vegetable. [orig. *ciche pease* f. L *cicer*: see PEASE]

chickweed /ˈtʃɪkwiːd/ n. any of numerous small plants, esp. *Stellaria media*, a garden weed with slender stems and tiny white flowers.

chicle /ˈtʃɪk(ə)l, ˈtʃiːkliː/ n. the milky juice of the sapodilla tree, used in the manufacture of chewing-gum. [Amer. Sp. f. Nahuatl *tzictli*]

chicory /ˈtʃɪkərɪ/ n. (pl. **-ies**) 1 a blue flowered plant, *Cichorium intybus*, cultivated for its salad leaves and its root. 2 its root, roasted and ground for use with or instead of coffee. 3 *US* = ENDIVE. [ME f. obs. F *cicorée* endive f. med.L *cic(h)orea* f. L *cichorium* f. Gk *kikhorion* SUCCORY]

chide /tʃaɪd/ v.tr. & intr. (past **chided** or **chid** /tʃɪd/; past part. **chided** or **chidden** /ˈtʃɪd(ə)n/) *archaic* or *literary* scold, rebuke. □□**chider** n. **chidingly** adv. [OE *cīdan*, of unkn. orig.]

chief /tʃiːf/ n. & adj. —n. 1 a a leader or ruler. b the head of a tribe, clan, etc. 2 the head of a department; the highest official. 3 *Heraldry* the upper third of a shield. —adj. (usu. *attrib.*) 1 first in position, importance, influence, etc. (*chief engineer*). 2 prominent, leading. □**Chief of Staff** the senior staff officer of a service or command. **-in-Chief** supreme (*Commander-in-Chief*). □□**chiefdom** n. [ME f. OF *ch(i)ef* ult. f. L *caput* head]

chiefly /ˈtʃiːflɪ/ adv. above all; mainly but not exclusively.

chieftain /ˈtʃiːft(ə)n/ n. (fem. **chieftainess** /-nɪs/) the leader of a tribe, clan, etc. □□**chieftaincy** /-sɪ/ n. (pl. **-ies**). **chieftainship** n. [ME f. OF *chevetaine* f. LL *capitaneus* CAPTAIN: assim. to CHIEF]

chiffchaff /ˈtʃɪftʃæf/ n. a small European bird, *Phylloscopus collybita*, of the warbler family. [imit.]

chiffon /ˈʃɪfɒn/ n. & adj. —n. a light diaphanous fabric of silk, nylon, etc. —adj. 1 made of chiffon. 2 (of a pie-filling, dessert, etc.) light-textured. [F f. *chiffe* rag]

chiffonier /ˌʃɪfəˈnɪə(r)/ n. a movable low cupboard with a sideboard top. [F *chiffonnier, -ière* rag-picker, chest of drawers for odds and ends]

chigger /ˈtʃɪgə(r)/ n. 1 = CHIGOE. 2 any harvest mite of the genus *Leptotrombidium* with parasitic larvae. [var. of CHIGOE]

chignon /ˈʃiːnjɒ̃/ n. a coil or mass of hair at the back of a woman's head. [F, orig. = nape of the neck]

chigoe /ˈtʃɪgəʊ/ n. a tropical flea, *Tunga penetrans*, the females of which burrow beneath the skin causing painful sores. Also called CHIGGER. [Carib]

chihuahua /tʃɪˈwɑːwə/ n. 1 a very small dog of a smooth-haired large-eyed breed originating in Mexico. 2 this breed. [*Chihuahua* State and city in Mexico]

chilblain /ˈtʃɪlbleɪn/ n. a painful itching swelling of

æ *cat* ɑː *arm* e *bed* ɜː *her* ɪ *sit* iː *see* ɒ *hot* ɔː *saw* ʌ *run* ʊ *put* uː *too* ə *ago* aɪ *my*

the skin usu. on a hand, foot, etc., caused by exposure to cold and by poor circulation. □□ **chilblained** adj. [CHILL + BLAIN]

child /tʃaɪld/ n. (pl. **children** /'tʃɪldrən/) **1 a** a young human being below the age of puberty. **b** an unborn or newborn human being. **2** one's son or daughter (at any age). **3** (foll. by of) a descendant, follower, adherent, or product of (children of Israel; child of God; child of nature). **4** a childish person. □**child abuse** maltreatment of a child, esp. by physical violence or sexual interference. **child benefit** (in the UK) regular payment by the State to the parents of a child up to a certain age. **child care** the care of children, esp. by a local authority. **child-minder** a person who looks after children for payment. **child's play** an easy task. □□ **childless** adj. **childlessness** n. [OE cild]

childbed /'tʃaɪldbed/ n. archaic = CHILDBIRTH.

childbirth /'tʃaɪldbɜːθ/ n. the act of giving birth to a child.

Childe /tʃaɪld/ n. archaic a youth of noble birth (Childe Harold). [var. of CHILD]

Childermas /'tʃɪldə,mæs/ n. archaic the feast of the Holy Innocents, 28 Dec. [OE cildramæsse f. cildra genit. pl. of cild CHILD + mæsse MASS²]

childhood /'tʃaɪldhʊd/ n. the state or period of being a child. □**second childhood** a person's dotage. [OE cildhād]

childish /'tʃaɪldɪʃ/ adj. **1** of, like, or proper to a child. **2** immature, silly. □□ **childishly** adv. **childishness** n.

childlike /'tʃaɪldlaɪk/ adj. having the good qualities of a child as innocence, frankness, etc.

childproof /'tʃaɪldpruːf/ adj. that cannot be damaged or operated by a child.

children pl. of CHILD.

Chilean /'tʃɪlɪən/ n. & adj. —n. **1** a native or national of Chile in S. America. **2** a person of Chilean descent. —adj. of or relating to Chile.

Chile pine /'tʃɪlɪ/ n. a monkey-puzzle tree.

Chile saltpetre /'tʃɪlɪ/ n. (also **Chile nitre**) naturally occurring sodium nitrate.

chili var. of CHILLI.

chiliad /'kɪlɪ,æd/ n. **1** a thousand. **2** a thousand years. [LL chilias chiliad- f. Gk khilias -ados]

chiliasm /'kɪlɪ,æz(ə)m/ n. the doctrine of or belief in Christ's prophesied reign of 1000 years on earth (see MILLENNIUM). [Gk khiliasmos: see CHILIAD]

chiliast /'kɪlɪ,æst/ n. a believer in chiliasm. □□ **chiliastic** /-'æstɪk/ adj. [LL chiliastes: see CHILIAD, CHILIASM]

chill /tʃɪl/ n., v., & adj. —n. **1 a** an unpleasant cold sensation; lowered body temperature. **b** a feverish cold (catch a chill). **2** unpleasant coldness (of air, water, etc.). **3 a** a depressing influence (cast a chill over). **b** a feeling of fear or dread accompanied by coldness. **4** coldness of manner. —v. **1** tr. & intr. make or become cold. **2** tr. depress, dispirit. **3** tr. cool (food or drink); preserve by cooling. **4** tr. harden (molten metal) by contact with cold material. —adj. literary chilly. □**take the chill off** warm slightly. □□ **chiller** n. **chillingly** adv. **chillness** n. **chillsome** adj. literary. [OE cele, ciele, etc.: in mod. use the verb is the oldest (ME), and is of obscure orig.]

chilli /'tʃɪlɪ/ n. (pl. **-ies**) (also US **chili**) a small hot-tasting dried red pod of a capsicum, Capsicum frutescens, used as seasoning and in curry powder, cayenne pepper, etc. □**chilli con carne** /kɒn 'kɑːnɪ/ a stew of chilli-flavoured minced beef and beans. **chilli sauce** a hot sauce made with tomatoes, chillies, and spices. [Sp. chile, chili, f. Aztec chilli]

chilly /'tʃɪlɪ/ adj. (**chillier, chilliest**) **1** (of the weather or an object) somewhat cold. **2** (of a person or animal) feeling somewhat cold; sensitive to the cold. **3** unfriendly; unemotional. □□ **chilliness** n.

Chiltern Hundreds /'tʃɪlt(ə)n/ n.pl. a Crown manor, whose administration is a nominal office for which an MP applies as a way of resigning from the House of Commons. [Chiltern Hills in S. England]

chimaera var. of CHIMERA.

chime¹ /tʃaɪm/ n. & v. —n. **1 a** a set of attuned bells. **b** the series of sounds given by this. **c** (usu. in pl.) a set of attuned bells as a door bell. **2** agreement, correspondence, harmony. —v. **1 a** intr. (of bells) ring. **b** tr. sound (a bell or chime) by striking. **2** tr. show (the hour) by chiming. **3** intr. (usu. foll. by together, with) be in agreement, harmonize. □**chime in 1** interject a remark. **2** join in harmoniously. **3** (foll. by with) agree with. □□ **chimer** n. [ME, prob. f. chym(b)e bell f. OE cimbal f. L cymbalum f. Gk kumbalon CYMBAL]

chime² /tʃaɪm/ n. (also **chimb**) the projecting rim at the end of a cask. [ME: cf. MDu., MLG kimme]

chimera /kaɪ'mɪərə, kɪ-/ (also **chimaera**) n. **1** (in Greek mythology) a fire-breathing female monster with a lion's head, a goat's body, and a serpent's tail. **2** a fantastic or grotesque product of the imagination; a bogey. **3** any fabulous beast with parts taken from various animals. **4** Biol. **a** an organism containing genetically different tissues, formed by grafting, mutation, etc. **b** a nucleic acid formed by laboratory manipulation. **5** any cartilaginous fish of the family Chimaeridae, usu. having a long tapering caudal fin. □□ **chimeric** /-'merɪk/ adj. **chimerical** /-'merɪk(ə)l/ adj. **chimerically** /-'merɪkəlɪ/ adv. [L f. Gk khimaira she-goat, chimera]

chimney /'tʃɪmnɪ/ n. (pl. **-eys**) **1** a vertical channel conducting smoke or combustion gases etc. up and away from a fire, furnace, engine, etc. **2** the part of this which projects above a roof. **3** a glass tube protecting the flame of a lamp. **4** a narrow vertical crack in a rock-face, often used by mountaineers to ascend. □**chimney-breast** a projecting interior wall surrounding a chimney. **chimney-piece** an ornamental structure around an open fireplace; a mantelpiece. **chimney-pot** an earthenware or metal pipe at the top of a chimney, narrowing the aperture and increasing the up draught. **chimney-stack 1** a number of chimneys grouped in one structure. **2** = sense 2. **chimney-sweep** a person whose job is removing soot from inside chimneys. [ME f. OF cheminée f. LL caminata having a fire-place, f. L caminus f. Gk kaminos oven]

chimp /tʃɪmp/ n. colloq. = CHIMPANZEE.

chimpanzee /,tʃɪmpən'ziː/ n. a small African anthropoid ape, Pan troglodytes. [F chimpanzé f. Kongo]

chin /tʃɪn/ n. the front of the lower jaw. □**chin-strap** a strap for fastening a hat etc. under the chin. **chin up** colloq. cheer up. **chin-wag** sl. n. a talk or chat. —v.intr. (**-wagged, -wagging**) have a gossip. **keep one's chin up** colloq. remain cheerful, esp. in adversity. **take on the chin 1** suffer a severe blow from (a misfortune etc.). **2** endure courageously. □□ **-chinned** adj. (in comb.). [OE cin(n) f. Gmc]

china /'tʃaɪnə/ n. & adj. —n. **1** a kind of fine white or translucent ceramic ware, porcelain, etc. **2** things made from ceramic, esp. household tableware. **3** rhyming sl. one's 'mate', i.e. husband or wife (short for china plate). —adj. made of china. □**china clay** kaolin. **China tea** smoke-cured tea from a small-leaved tea plant grown in China. [orig. China ware (from China in Asia): name f. Pers. chīnī]

Chinagraph /'tʃaɪnə,grɑːf/ n. propr. a waxy coloured pencil used to write on china, glass, etc.

Chinaman /'tʃaɪnəmən/ n. (pl. **-men**) **1** archaic or derog. (now usu. offens.) a native of China. **2** Cricket a ball bowled by a left-handed bowler that spins from off to leg.

Chinatown /'tʃaɪnə,taʊn/ n. a district of any non-Chinese town, esp. a city or seaport, in which the population is predominantly Chinese.

chinch /tʃɪntʃ/ n. (in full **chinch-bug**) US **1** a small insect, Blissus leucopterus, that destroys the shoots of grasses and grains. **2** a bedbug. [Sp. chinche f. L cimex -icis]

chincherinchee /ˌtʃɪntʃərɪnˈtʃiː/ n. a white-flowered bulbous plant, *Ornithogalum thyrsoides*, native to S. Africa. [imit. of the squeaky rubbing of its stalks]

chinchilla /tʃɪnˈtʃɪlə/ n. **1 a** any small rodent of the genus *Chinchilla*, native to S. America, having soft silver-grey fur and a bushy tail. **b** its highly valued fur. **2** a breed of cat or rabbit. [Sp. prob. f. S. Amer. native name]

chin-chin /tʃɪnˈtʃɪn/ int. Brit. colloq. a toast; a greeting or farewell. [Chin. *qingqing* (pr. ch-)]

Chindit /ˈtʃɪndɪt/ n. hist. a member of the Allied forces behind the Japanese lines in Burma (now Myanmar) in 1943-5. [Burm. *chinthé*, a mythical creature]

chine[1] /tʃaɪn/ n. & v. —n. **1 a** a backbone, esp. of an animal. **b** a joint of meat containing all or part of this. **2** a ridge or arête. —v.tr. cut (meat) across or along the backbone. [ME f. OF *eschine* f. L *spina* SPINE]

chine[2] /tʃaɪn/ n. a deep narrow ravine in the Isle of Wight or Dorset. [OE *cinu* chink etc. f. Gmc]

chine[3] /tʃaɪn/ n. the join between the side and the bottom of a ship etc. [var. of CHIME[2]]

Chinese /tʃaɪˈniːz/ adj. & n. —adj. **a** of or relating to China. **b** of Chinese descent. —n. **1** the Chinese language. **2** (pl. same) **a** a native or national of China. **b** a person of Chinese descent. □**Chinese cabbage** = *Chinese leaf*. **Chinese gooseberry** = *kiwi fruit*. **Chinese lantern 1** a collapsible paper lantern. **2** a solanaceous plant, *Physalis alkekengi*, bearing white flowers and globular orange fruits enclosed in an orange-red papery calyx. **Chinese leaf** a lettuce-like cabbage, *Brassica chinensis*. **Chinese puzzle** a very intricate puzzle or problem. **Chinese water chestnut** see *water chestnut* 2. **Chinese white** zinc oxide as a white pigment.

chink[1] /tʃɪŋk/ n. **1** an unintended crack that admits light or allows an attack. **2** a narrow opening; a slit. [16th c.: rel. to CHINE[2]]

chink[2] /tʃɪŋk/ v. & n. —v. **1** intr. make a slight ringing sound, as of glasses or coins striking together. **2** tr. cause to make this sound. —n. this sound. [imit.]

Chink /tʃɪŋk/ n. sl. offens. a Chinese. □□ **Chinky** adj. [abbr.]

chinless /ˈtʃɪnlɪs/ adj. colloq. weak or feeble in character. □**chinless wonder** Brit. an ineffectual esp. upper class person.

Chino- /ˈtʃaɪnəʊ/ comb. form = SINO-.

chino /ˈtʃiːnəʊ/ n. US (pl. -os) **1** a cotton twill fabric, usu. khaki-coloured. **2** (in pl.) a garment, esp. trousers, made from this. [Amer. Sp., = toasted]

chinoiserie /ʃiːnˈwɑːzərɪ/ n. **1** the imitation of Chinese motifs and techniques in painting and in decorating furniture. **2** an object or objects in this style. [F]

chinook /ʃəˈnʊk, tʃə-, -ˈnuːk/ n. **1** a warm dry wind which blows east of the Rocky Mountains. **2** a warm wet southerly wind west of the Rocky Mountains. □**chinook salmon** a large salmon, *Oncorhynchus tshawytscha*, of the N. Pacific. [Amer. Ind. name of a tribe]

chintz /tʃɪnts/ n. & adj. —n. a printed multicoloured cotton fabric with a glazed finish. —adj. made from or upholstered with this fabric. [earlier *chints* (pl.) f. Hindi *chīṇṭ* f. Skr. *citra* variegated]

chintzy /ˈtʃɪntsɪ/ adj. (**chintzier, chintziest**) **1** like chintz. **2** gaudy, cheap. **3** characteristic of the décor associated with chintz soft furnishings. □□ **chintzily** adv. **chintziness** n.

chionodoxa /ˌkaɪənəˈdɒksə/ n. any liliaceous plant of the genus *Chionodoxa*, having early-blooming blue flowers. Also called *glory-of-the-snow*. [mod.L f. Gk *khiōn* snow + *doxa* glory]

chip /tʃɪp/ n. & v. —n. **1** a small piece removed by or in the course of chopping, cutting, or breaking, esp. from hard material such as wood or stone. **2** the place where such a chip has been made. **3 a** (usu. in pl.) a strip of potato, deep fried. **b** (in pl.) US potato crisps. **4** a counter used in some gambling games to represent money. **5** Electronics = MICROCHIP. **6 a** a thin strip of wood, straw, etc., used for weaving hats, baskets, etc. **b** a basket made from these. **7** Football etc. & Golf a short shot, kick, or pass with the ball describing an arc. —v. (**chipped, chipping**) **1** tr. (often foll. by off, away) cut or break (a piece) from a hard material. **2** intr. (often foll. by at, away at) cut pieces off (a hard material) to alter its shape, break it up, etc. **3** intr. (of stone, china, etc.) be susceptible to being chipped; be apt to break at the edge (will chip easily). **4** tr. (also absol.) Football etc. & Golf strike or kick (the ball) with a chip (cf. sense 7 of n.). **5** tr. (usu. as **chipped** adj.) cut (potatoes) into chips. □**chip heater** Austral. & NZ a domestic water-heater that burns wood chips. **chip in** colloq. **1** interrupt or contribute abruptly to a conversation (chipped in with a reminiscence). **2** contribute (money or resources). **a chip off the old block** a child who resembles a parent, esp. in character. **a chip on one's shoulder** colloq. a disposition or inclination to feel resentful or aggrieved. **chip shot** = sense 7 of n. **have had one's chips** Brit. colloq. be unable to avoid defeat, punishment, etc. **when the chips are down** colloq. when it comes to the point. [ME f. OF *cipp, cyp* beam]

chipboard /ˈtʃɪpbɔːd/ n. a rigid sheet or panel made from compressed wood chips and resin.

chipmunk /ˈtʃɪpmʌŋk/ n. any ground squirrel of the genus *Tamias* or *Eutamias*, having alternate light and dark stripes running down the body. [Algonquian]

chipolata /ˌtʃɪpəˈlɑːtə/ n. Brit. a small thin sausage. [F f. It. *cipollata* a dish of onions f. *cipolla* onion]

Chippendale /ˈtʃɪpəndeɪl/ adj. **1** (of furniture) designed or made by the English cabinet-maker Thomas Chippendale (d. 1779). **2** in the ornately elegant style of Chippendale's furniture.

chipper /ˈtʃɪpə(r)/ adj. esp. US colloq. **1** cheerful. **2** smartly dressed. [perh. f. N.Engl. dial. *kipper* lively]

chippie var. of CHIPPY.

chipping /ˈtʃɪpɪŋ/ n. **1** a small fragment of stone, wood, etc. **2** (in pl.) these used as a surface for roads, roofs, etc.

chippy /ˈtʃɪpɪ/ n. (also **chippie**) (pl. **-ies**) Brit. colloq. **1** a fish-and-chip shop. **2** a carpenter.

Chips /tʃɪps/ n. Naut. sl. a ship's carpenter.

chiral /ˈkaɪər(ə)l/ adj. Chem. (of a crystal etc.) not superposable on its mirror image. □□ **chirality** /-ˈrælɪtɪ/ n. [Gk *kheir* hand]

chiro- /ˈkaɪərəʊ/ (also **cheiro-**) comb. form of the hand. [Gk *kheir* hand]

chirography /kaɪəˈrɒgrəfɪ/ n. handwriting, calligraphy.

chiromancy /ˈkaɪərəʊˌmænsɪ/ n. palmistry.

chiropody /kɪˈrɒpədɪ/ n. the treatment of the feet and their ailments. □□ **chiropodist** n. [CHIRO- + Gk *pous podos* foot]

chiropractic /ˌkaɪərəʊˈpræktɪk/ n. the diagnosis and manipulative treatment of mechanical disorders of the joints, esp. of the spinal column. □□ **chiropractor** /ˈkaɪərəʊ-/ n. [CHIRO- + Gk *praktikos*: see PRACTICAL]

chiropteran /ˌkaɪəˈrɒptərən/ n. any member of the order Chiroptera, with membraned limbs serving as wings, including bats and flying foxes. □□ **chiropterous** adj. [CHIRO- + Gk *pteron* wing]

chirp /tʃɜːp/ v. & n. —v. **1** intr. (usu. of small birds, grasshoppers, etc.) utter a short sharp high-pitched note. **2** tr. & intr. (esp. of a child) speak or utter in a lively or jolly way. —n. a chirping sound. □□ **chirper** n. [ME, earlier *chirk, chirt*: imit.]

chirpy /ˈtʃɜːpɪ/ adj. colloq. (**chirpier, chirpiest**) cheerful, lively. □□ **chirpily** adv. **chirpiness** n.

chirr /tʃɜː(r)/ v. & n. (also **churr**) —v.intr. (esp. of insects) make a prolonged low trilling sound. —n. this sound. [imit.]

chirrup /ˈtʃɪrəp/ v. & n. —v.intr. (**chirruped,**

chirruping) (esp. of small birds) chirp, esp. repeatedly; twitter. —*n.* a chirruping sound. □□ **chirrupy** *adj.* [trilled form of CHIRP]

chisel /'tʃɪz(ə)l/ *n.* & *v.* —*n.* a hand tool with a squared bevelled blade for shaping wood, stone, or metal. —*v.* **1** *tr.* (**chiselled, chiselling**; US **chiseled, chiseling**) cut or shape with a chisel. **2** *tr.* (as **chiselled** *adj.*) (of facial features) clear-cut, fine. **3** *tr.* & *intr. sl.* cheat, swindle. □□ **chiseller** *n.* [ME f. ONF ult. f. LL *cisorium* f. L *caedere caes-* cut]

chit[1] /tʃɪt/ *n.* **1** *derog.* or *joc.* a young, small, or frail girl or woman (esp. *a chit of a girl*). **2** a young child. [ME, = whelp, cub, kitten, perh. = dial. *chit* sprout]

chit[2] /tʃɪt/ *n.* **1** a note of requisition; a note of a sum owed, esp. for food or drink. **2** esp. *Brit.* a note or memorandum. [earlier *chitty*: Anglo-Ind. f. Hindi *ciṭṭhī* pass f. Skr. *citra* mark]

chital /'tʃiːt(ə)l/ *n.* = AXIS[2]. [Hindi *cītal*]

chit-chat /'tʃɪttʃæt/ *n.* & *v. colloq.* —*n.* light conversation; gossip. —*v.intr.* (**-chatted, -chatting**) talk informally; gossip. [redupl. of CHAT[1]]

chitin /'kaɪtɪn/ *n. Chem.* a polysaccharide forming the major constituent in the exoskeleton of arthropods and in the cell walls of fungi. □□ **chitinous** *adj.* [F *chitine* irreg. f. Gk *khitōn*: see CHITON]

chiton /'kaɪt(ə)n/ *n.* **1** a long woollen tunic worn by ancient Greeks. **2** any marine mollusc of the class Amphineura, having a shell of overlapping plates. [Gk *khitōn* tunic]

chitterling /'tʃɪtəlɪŋ/ *n.* (usu. in *pl.*) the smaller intestines of pigs etc., esp. as cooked for food. [ME: orig. uncert.]

chivalrous /'ʃɪvəlrəs/ *adj.* **1** (usu. of a male) gallant, honourable, courteous. **2** involving or showing chivalry. □□ **chivalrously** *adv.* [ME f. OF *chevalerous*: see CHEVALIER]

chivalry /'ʃɪvəlrɪ/ *n.* **1** the medieval knightly system with its religious, moral, and social code. **2** the combination of qualities expected of an ideal knight, esp. courage, honour, courtesy, justice, and readiness to help the weak. **3** a man's courteous behaviour, esp. towards women. **4** *archaic* knights, noblemen, and horsemen collectively. □□ **chivalric** *adj.* [ME f. OF *chevalerie* etc. f. med.L *caballerius* for LL *caballarius* horseman: see CAVALIER]

chive /tʃaɪv/ *n.* a small alliaceous plant, *Allium schoenoprasum*, having purple-pink flowers and dense tufts of long tubular leaves which are used as a herb. [ME f. OF *cive* f. L *cepa* onion]

chivvy /'tʃɪvɪ/ *v.tr.* (**-ies, -ied**) (also **chivy, chevy** /'tʃevɪ/) harass, nag; pursue. [*chevy* (n. & v.), prob. f. the ballad of *Chevy Chase*, a place on the Scottish border]

chlamydia /klə'mɪdɪə/ *n.* (*pl.* **chlamydiae** /-dɪˌiː/) any parasitic bacterium of the genus *Chlamydia*, some of which cause diseases such as trachoma, psittacosis, and nonspecific urethritis. [mod.L f. Gk *khlamus -udos* cloak]

chlamydomonas /ˌklæmɪdə'məʊnəs/ *n.* any unicellular green freshwater alga of the genus *Chlamydomonas*. [mod.L (as CHLAMYDIA)]

chlor- var. of CHLORO-.

chloral /'klɔːr(ə)l/ *n.* **1** a colourless liquid aldehyde used in making DDT. **2** (in full **chloral hydrate**) *Pharm.* a colourless crystalline solid made from chloral and used as a sedative. [F f. *chlore* chlorine + *alcool* alcohol]

chloramphenicol /ˌklɔːræm'fenɪˌkɒl/ *n. Pharm.* an antibiotic prepared from *Streptomyces venezuelae* or produced synthetically and used esp. against typhoid fever. [CHLORO- + AMIDE + PHENO- + NITRO- + GLYCOL]

chlorate /'klɔːreɪt/ *n. Chem.* any salt of chloric acid.

chlorella /klɔː'relə/ *n.* any non-motile unicellular green alga of the genus *Chlorella*. [mod.L, dimin. of Gk *khlōros* green]

chloric acid /'klɔːrɪk/ *n. Chem.* a colourless liquid acid with strong oxidizing properties. [CHLORO- + -IC]

chloride /'klɔːraɪd/ *n. Chem.* **1** any compound of chlorine with another element or group. **2** any bleaching agent containing chloride. [CHLORO- + -IDE]

chlorinate /'klɔːrɪˌneɪt/ *v.tr.* **1** impregnate or treat with chlorine. **2** *Chem.* cause to react or combine with chlorine. □□ **chlorinator** *n.*

chlorination /ˌklɔːrɪ'neɪʃ(ə)n/ *n.* **1** the treatment of water with chlorine to disinfect it. **2** *Chem.* a reaction in which chlorine is introduced into a compound.

chlorine /'klɔːriːn/ *n. Chem.* a poisonous greenish-yellow gaseous element of the halogen group occurring naturally in salt, sea-water, rock-salt, etc., and used for purifying water, bleaching, and the manufacture of many organic chemicals. ¶ Symb.: Cl. [Gk *khlōros* green + -INE[4]]

chlorite /'klɔːraɪt/ *n. Chem.* any salt of chlorous acid. □□ **chloritic** /-'rɪtɪk/ *adj.*

chloro- /'klɔːrəʊ/ *comb. form* (also **chlor-** esp. before a vowel) **1** *Bot.* & *Mineral.* green. **2** *Chem.* chlorine. [Gk *khlōros* green: in sense 2 f. CHLORINE]

chloro-fluorocarbon see CFC.

chloroform /'klɒrəˌfɔːm, 'klɔːrə-/ *n.* & *v.* —*n.* a colourless volatile sweet-smelling liquid used as a solvent and formerly used as a general anaesthetic. ¶ Chem. formula: CHCl$_3$. —*v.tr.* render (a person) unconscious with this. [F *chloroforme* formed as CHLORO- + *formyle*: see FORMIC (acid)]

Chloromycetin /ˌklɔːrəʊmaɪ'siːtɪn/ *n. propr.* = CHLORAMPHENICOL. [CHLORO- + Gk *mukēs -ētos* fungus]

chlorophyll /'klɒrəfɪl/ *n.* the green pigment found in most plants, responsible for light absorption to provide energy for photosynthesis. □□ **chlorophyllous** /-'fɪləs/ *adj.* [F *chlorophylle* f. Gk *phullon* leaf: see CHLORO-]

chloroplast /'klɔːrəʊˌplæst/ *n.* a plastid containing chlorophyll, found in plant cells undergoing photosynthesis. [G: (as CHLORO-, PLASTID)]

chlorosis /klə'rəʊsɪs, klɔː-/ *n.* **1** *hist.* a severe form of anaemia from iron deficiency esp. in young women, causing a greenish complexion (cf. GREENSICK). **2** *Bot.* a reduction or loss of the normal green coloration of plants. □□ **chlorotic** *adj.* [CHLORO- + -OSIS]

chlorous acid /'klɔːrəs/ *n. Chem.* a pale yellow liquid acid with oxidizing properties. ¶ Chem. formula: HClO$_2$. [CHLORO- + -OUS]

chlorpromazine /klɔː'prɒməˌziːn/ *n. Pharm.* a drug used as a sedative and to control nausea and vomiting. [F (as CHLORO-, PROMETHAZINE)]

Ch.M. *abbr.* Master of Surgery. [L *Chirurgiae Magister*]

choc /tʃɒk/ *n.* & *adj. colloq.* chocolate. □**choc-ice** a bar of ice-cream covered with a thin coating of chocolate. [abbr.]

chocho /'tʃəʊtʃəʊ/ *n.* (*pl.* **-os**) *W.Ind.* = CHOKO.

chock /tʃɒk/ *n.*, *v.*, & *adv.* —*n.* a block or wedge of wood to check motion, esp. of a cask or a wheel. —*v.tr.* **1** fit or make fast with chocks. **2** (usu. foll. by *up*) *Brit.* cram full. —*adv.* as closely or tightly as possible. [prob. f. OF *çouche, çoche,* of unkn. orig.]

chock-a-block /'tʃɒkə,blɒk/ *adj.* & *adv.* crammed close together; crammed full (a *street chock-a-block with cars*). [orig. Naut., with ref. to tackle with the two blocks run close together]

chocker /'tʃɒkə(r)/ *adj. Brit. sl.* fed up, disgusted. [CHOCK-A-BLOCK]

chock-full /'tʃɒkfʊl, -'fʊl/ *adj.* & *adv.* = CHOCK-A-BLOCK (*chock-full of rubbish*). [CHOCK + FULL[1]: ME *chokkefulle* (rel. to CHOKE[1]) is doubtful]

chocolate /'tʃɒkələt, 'tʃɒklət/ *n.* & *adj.* —*n.* **1 a** a food preparation in the form of a paste or solid block made from roasted and ground cacao seeds, usually sweetened. **b** a sweet made of or coated with this. **c** a drink made with chocolate. **2** a deep brown colour. —*adj.* **1** made from or of chocolate. **2** chocolate-coloured. □**chocolate-box 1** a decorated box filled with chocolates. **2** (*attrib.*) stereotypically pretty or romantic. □□ **chocolatey** *adj.* (also

chocolaty). [F *chocolat* or Sp. *chocolate* f. Aztec *chocolatl*]

Choctaw /'tʃɒktɔ:/ *n.* (*pl.* same or **Choctaws**) **1 a** a member of a N. American people orig. from Alabama. **b** the language of this people. **2** (in skating) a step from one edge of a skate to the other edge of the other skate in the opposite direction. [native name]

choice /tʃɔɪs/ *n.* & *adj.* —*n.* **1 a** the act or an instance of choosing. **b** a thing or person chosen (*not a good choice*). **2** a range from which to choose. **3** (usu. foll. by *of*) the élite, the best. **4** the power or opportunity to choose (*what choice have I?*). —*adj.* of superior quality; carefully chosen. □□**choicely** *adv.* **choiceness** *n.* [ME f. OF *chois* f. *choisir* CHOOSE]

choir /'kwaɪə(r)/ *n.* **1** a regular group of singers, esp. taking part in church services. **2** the part of a cathedral or large church between the altar and the nave, used by the choir and clergy. **3** a company of singers, birds, angels etc. (*a heavenly choir*). **4** *Mus.* a group of instruments of one family playing together. □**choir organ** the softest of three parts making up a large organ having its row of keys the lowest of the three. **choir-stall** = STALL¹ *n.* 3a. [ME f. OF *quer* f. L *chorus*: see CHORUS]

choirboy /'kwaɪə,bɔɪ/ *n.* a boy who sings in a church or cathedral choir.

choke¹ /tʃəʊk/ *v.* & *n.* —*v.* **1** *tr.* hinder or impede the breathing of (a person or animal) esp. by constricting the windpipe or (of gas, smoke, etc.) by being unbreathable. **2** *intr.* suffer a hindrance or stoppage of breath. **3** *tr.* & *intr.* make or become speechless from emotion. **4** *tr.* retard the growth of or kill (esp. plants) by the deprivation of light, air, nourishment, etc. **5** *tr.* (often foll. by *back*) suppress (feelings) with difficulty. **6** *tr.* block or clog (a passage, tube, etc.). **7** *tr.* (as **choked** *adj.*) *colloq.* disgusted, disappointed. **8** *tr.* enrich the fuel mixture in (an internal-combustion engine) by reducing the intake of air. —*n.* **1** the valve in the carburettor of an internal-combustion engine that controls the intake of air, esp. to enrich the fuel mixture. **2** *Electr.* an inductance coil used to smooth the variations of an alternating current or to alter its phase. □**choke-chain** a chain looped round a dog's neck to exert control by pressure on its windpipe when the dog pulls. **choke-cherry** (*pl.* **-cherries**) an astringent N. American cherry, *Prunus virginiana.* **choke-damp** carbon dioxide in mines, wells, etc. **choke down** swallow with difficulty. **choke up** block (a channel etc.). [ME f. OE *ācēocian* f. *cēoce, cēce* CHEEK]

choke² /tʃəʊk/ *n.* the centre part of an artichoke. [prob. confusion of the ending of *artichoke* with CHOKE¹]

chokeberry /'tʃəʊkbərɪ/ *n.* (*pl.* **-ies**) *Bot.* **1** any rosaceous shrub of the genus *Aronia.* **2** its scarlet berry-like fruit.

choker /'tʃəʊkə(r)/ *n.* **1** a close-fitting necklace or ornamental neckband. **2** a clerical or other high collar.

choko /'tʃəʊkəʊ/ *n.* (*pl.* **-os**) *Austral.* & *NZ* a succulent green pear-shaped vegetable like a cucumber in flavour. [Braz. Ind. *chocho*]

choky¹ /'tʃəʊkɪ/ *n.* (also **chokey**) (*pl.* **-ies** or **-eys**) *Brit. sl.* prison. [orig. Anglo-Ind., f. Hindi *caukī* shed]

choky² /'tʃəʊkɪ/ *adj.* (**chokier, chokiest**) tending to choke or to cause choking.

cholangiography /,kɒlændʒɪ'ɒɡrəfɪ/ *n.* *Med.* X-ray examination of the bile ducts, used to find the site and nature of any obstruction. [CHOLE- + Gk *aggeion* vessel + -GRAPHY]

chole- /'kɒlɪ/ *comb. form* (also **chol-** esp. before a vowel) *Med.* & *Chem.* bile. [Gk *kholē* gall, bile]

cholecalciferol /,kɒlɪkæl'sɪfə,rɒl/ *n.* one of the D vitamins, produced by the action of sunlight on a cholesterol derivative widely distributed in the skin, a deficiency of which results in rickets in children and osteomalacia in adults. Also called *vitamin D₃.* [CHOLE- + CALCIFEROL]

cholecystography /,kɒlɪsɪs'tɒɡrəfɪ/ *n.* *Med.* X-ray examination of the gall-bladder, esp. used to detect the presence of any gallstones. [CHOLE- + CYSTO- + -GRAPHY]

choler /'kɒlə(r)/ *n.* **1** *hist.* one of the four humours, bile. **2** *poet.* or *archaic* anger, irascibility. [ME f. OF *colere* bile, anger f. L *cholera* f. Gk *kholera* diarrhoea, in LL = bile, anger, f. Gk *kholē* bile]

cholera /'kɒlərə/ *n.* *Med.* an infectious and often fatal disease of the small intestine caused by the bacterium *Vibrio cholerae,* resulting in severe vomiting and diarrhoea. □**chicken** (or **fowl**) **cholera** an infectious disease of fowls. □□**choleraic** /-'reɪɪk/ *adj.* [ME f. L f. Gk *cholera:* see CHOLER]

choleric /'kɒlərɪk/ *adj.* irascible, angry. □□ **cholerically** *adv.* [ME f. OF *cholerique* f. L *cholericus* f. Gk *kholerikos:* see CHOLER]

cholesterol /kə'lestə,rɒl/ *n.* *Biochem.* a sterol found in most body tissues, including the blood, where high concentrations promote arteriosclerosis. [*cholesterin* f. Gk *kholē* bile + *stereos* stiff]

choli /'tʃəʊlɪ/ *n.* (*pl.* **cholis**) a type of short-sleeved bodice worn by Indian women. [Hindi *colī*]

choliamb /'kəʊlɪ,æmb/ *n.* *Prosody* = SCAZON. □□ **choliambic** /kəʊlɪ'æmbɪk/ *adj.* [LL *choliambus* f. Gk *khōliambos* f. *khōlos* lame: see IAMBUS]

choline /'kəʊliːn, -lɪn/ *n.* *Biochem.* a basic nitrogenous organic compound occurring widely in living matter. [G *Cholin* f. Gk *kholē* bile]

chomp /tʃɒmp/ *v.tr.* = CHAMP¹. [imit.]

chondrite /'kɒndraɪt/ *n.* a stony meteorite containing small mineral granules. [G *Chondrit* f. Gk *khondros* granule]

chondrocranium /,kɒndrəʊ'kreɪnɪəm/ *n.* *Anat.* the embryonic skull composed of cartilage and later replaced by bone. [Gk *khondros* grain, cartilage]

choo-choo /'tʃuː,tʃuː/ *n.* *colloq.* (esp. as a child's word) a railway train or locomotive, esp. a steam engine. [imit.]

chook /tʃʊk/ *n.* (also **chookie**) *Austral.* & *NZ colloq.* **1** a chicken or fowl. **2** *sl.* an older woman. [E dial. *chuck* chicken]

choose /tʃuːz/ *v.* (*past* **chose** /tʃəʊz/; *past part.* **chosen** /'tʃəʊz(ə)n/) **1** *tr.* select out of a greater number. **2** *intr.* (usu. foll. by *between, from*) take or select one or another. **3** *tr.* (usu. foll. by *to* + infin.) decide, be determined (*chose to stay behind*). **4** *tr.* (foll. by complement) select as (*was chosen king*). **5** *tr. Theol.* (esp. as **chosen** *adj.*) destine to be saved (*God's chosen people*). □**cannot choose but** *archaic* must. **nothing** (or **little**) **to choose between them** they are equivalent. □□**chooser** *n.* [OE *cēosan* f. Gmc]

choosy /'tʃuːzɪ/ *adj.* (**choosier, choosiest**) *colloq.* fastidious. □□**choosily** *adv.* **choosiness** *n.*

chop¹ /tʃɒp/ *v.* & *n.* —*v.tr.* (**chopped, chopping**) **1** (usu. foll. by *off, down,* etc.) cut or fell by a blow, usu. with an axe. **2** (often foll. by *up*) cut (esp. meat or vegetables) into small pieces. **3** strike (esp. a ball) with a short heavy edgewise blow. **4** *Brit. colloq.* dispense with; shorten or curtail. —*n.* **1** a cutting blow, esp. with an axe. **2** a thick slice of meat (esp. pork or lamb) usu. including a rib. **3** a short heavy edgewise stroke or blow in tennis, cricket, boxing, etc. **4** the broken motion of water, usu. owing to the action of the wind against the tide. **5** (prec. by *the*) *Brit. sl.* **a** dismissal from employment. **b** the action of killing or being killed. □**chop logic** argue pedantically. [ME, var. of CHAP¹]

chop² /tʃɒp/ *n.* (usu. in *pl.*) the jaw of an animal etc. [16th-c. var. (occurring earlier) of CHAP³, of unkn. orig.]

chop³ /tʃɒp/ *v.intr.* (**chopped, chopping**) □**chop and change** vacillate; change direction frequently. [ME, perh. rel. to *chap* f. OE *cēapian* (as CHEAP)]

chop⁴ /tʃɒp/ *n.* *Brit. archaic* a trade mark; a brand of goods. □**not much chop** esp. *Austral.* & *NZ* no good. [orig. in India & China, f. Hindi *chāp* stamp]

chop-chop /ˈtʃɒpˈtʃɒp/ adv. & int. (pidgin English) quickly, quick. [f. Chin. dial. k'wâi-k'wâi]

chopper /ˈtʃɒpə(r)/ n. **1 a** Brit. a short axe with a large blade. **b** a butcher's cleaver. **2** colloq. a helicopter. **3** a device for regularly interrupting an electric current or light-beam. **4** colloq. a type of bicycle or motor cycle with high handlebars. **5** (in pl.) Brit. sl. teeth. **6** US sl. a machine-gun.

choppy /ˈtʃɒpɪ/ adj. (**choppier, choppiest**) (of the sea, the weather, etc.) fairly rough. □□ **choppily** adv. **choppiness** n. [CHOP¹ + -Y¹]

chopstick /ˈtʃɒpstɪk/ n. each of a pair of small thin sticks of wood or ivory etc., held both in one hand as eating utensils by the Chinese, Japanese, etc. [pidgin Engl. f. chop = quick + STICK¹ equivalent of Cantonese k'wâi-tsze nimble ones]

chopsuey /tʃɒpˈsuːɪ/ n. (pl. -eys) a Chinese-style dish of meat stewed and fried with bean sprouts, bamboo shoots, onions, and served with rice. [Cantonese shap sui mixed bits]

choral /ˈkɔːr(ə)l/ adj. of, for, or sung by a choir or chorus. □ **choral society** a group which meets regularly to sing choral music. □□ **chorally** adv. [med.L choralis f. L chorus: see CHORUS]

chorale /kɒˈrɑːl/ n. (also **choral**) **1** a stately and simple hymn tune; a harmonized version of this. **2** esp. US a choir or choral society. [G Choral(gesang) f. med.L cantus choralis]

chord¹ /kɔːd/ n. Mus. a group of (usu. three or more) notes sounded together, as a basis of harmony. □□ **chordal** adj. [orig. cord f. ACCORD: later confused with CHORD²]

chord² /kɔːd/ n. **1** Math. & Aeron. etc. a straight line joining the ends of an arc, the wings of an aeroplane, etc. **2** Anat. = CORD. **3** poet. the string of a harp etc. **4** Engin. one of the two principal members, usu. horizontal, of a truss. □ **strike a chord 1** recall something to a person's memory. **2** elicit sympathy. **touch the right chord** appeal skilfully to the emotions. □□ **chordal** adj. [16th-c. refashioning of CORD after L chorda]

chordate /ˈkɔːdeɪt/ n. & adj. —n. any animal of the phylum Chordata, possessing a notochord at some stage during its development. —adj. of or relating to the chordates. [mod.L chordata f. L chorda CHORD² after Vertebrata etc.]

chore /tʃɔː(r)/ n. a tedious or routine task, esp. domestic. [orig. dial. & US form of CHAR²]

chorea /kɒˈrɪə/ n. Med. a disorder characterized by jerky involuntary movements affecting esp. the shoulders, hips, and face. □ **Huntington's chorea** chorea accompanied by a progressive dementia. **Sydenham's chorea** chorea esp. in children as one of the manifestations of rheumatic fever: also called ST VITUS'S DANCE. [L f. Gk khoreia (as CHORUS)]

choreograph /ˈkɒrɪəˌɡrɑːf/ v.tr. compose the choreography for (a ballet etc.). □□ **choreographer** /-ɪˈɒɡrəfə(r)/ n. [back-form. f. CHOREOGRAPHY]

choreography /ˌkɒrɪˈɒɡrəfɪ/ n. **1** the design or arrangement of a ballet or other staged dance. **2** the sequence of steps and movements in dance. **3** the written notation for this. □□ **choreographic** /ˌkɒrɪəˈɡræfɪk/ adj. **choreographically** /ˌkɒrɪəˈɡræfɪkəlɪ/ adv. [Gk khoreia dance + -GRAPHY]

choreology /ˌkɒrɪˈɒlədʒɪ/ n. the study and description of the movements of dancing. □□ **choreologist** n.

choriambus /ˌkɒrɪˈæmbəs/ n. (pl. **choriambi** /-baɪ/) Prosody a metrical foot consisting of two short (unstressed) syllables between two long (stressed) ones. □□ **choriambic** adj. [LL Gk khoriambos f. khoreios of the dance + IAMBUS]

choric /ˈkɔːrɪk/ adj. of, like, or for a chorus in drama or recitation. [LL choricus f. Gk khorikos (as CHORUS)]

chorine /ˈkɔːriːn/ n. US a chorus girl. [CHORUS + -INE³]

chorion /ˈkɔːrɪən/ n. the outermost membrane surrounding an embryo of a reptile, bird, or mammal. □□ **chorionic** /-ˈɒnɪk/ adj. [Gk khorion]

chorister /ˈkɒrɪstə(r)/ n. **1** a member of a choir, esp. a choirboy. **2** US the leader of a church choir. [ME, ult. f. OF cueriste f. quer CHOIR]

chorography /kəˈrɒɡrəfɪ/ n. the systematic description of regions or districts. □□ **chorographer** n. **chorographic** /ˌkɒrəˈɡræfɪk/ adj. [F chorographie or L f. Gk khōrographia f. khōra region]

choroid /ˈkɔːrɔɪd/ adj. & n. —adj. like a chorion in shape or vascularity. —n. (in full **choroid coat** or **membrane**) a layer of the eyeball between the retina and the sclera. [Gk khoroeidēs for khorioeidēs: see CHORION]

chorology /kəˈrɒlədʒɪ/ n. the study of the geographical distribution of animals and plants. □□ **chorological** /ˌkɒrəˈlɒdʒɪk(ə)l/ adj. **chorologist** n. [Gk khōra region + -LOGY]

chortle /ˈtʃɔːt(ə)l/ v. & n. —v.intr. colloq. chuckle gleefully. —n. a gleeful chuckle. [portmanteau word coined by Lewis Carroll, prob. f. CHUCKLE + SNORT]

chorus /ˈkɔːrəs/ n. & v. —n. (pl. **choruses**) **1** a group (esp. a large one) of singers; a choir. **2** a piece of music composed for a choir. **3** the refrain or the main part of a popular song, in which a chorus participates. **4** any simultaneous utterance by many persons etc. (a chorus of disapproval followed). **5** a group of singers and dancers performing in concert in a musical comedy, opera, etc. **6** Gk Antiq. **a** in Greek tragedy, a group of performers who comment together in voice and movement on the main action. **b** an utterance of the chorus. **7** esp. in Elizabethan drama, a character who speaks the prologue and other linking parts of the play. **8** the part spoken by this character. —v.tr. & intr. (of a group) speak or utter simultaneously. □ **chorus girl** a young woman who sings or dances in the chorus of a musical comedy etc. **in chorus** (uttered) together; in unison. [L f. Gk khoros]

chose past of CHOOSE.

chosen past part. of CHOOSE.

chough /tʃʌf/ n. any corvine bird of the genus Pyrrhocorax, with a glossy blue-black plumage and red legs. [ME, prob. orig. imit.]

choux pastry /ʃuː/ n. very light pastry enriched with eggs. [F, pl. of chou cabbage, rosette]

chow /tʃaʊ/ n. **1** sl. food. **2** offens. a Chinese. **3 a** a dog of a Chinese breed with long hair and bluish-black tongue. **b** this breed. [shortened f. CHOW-CHOW]

chow-chow /ˈtʃaʊtʃaʊ/ n. **1** = CHOW. **2** a Chinese preserve of ginger, orange-peel, etc., in syrup. **3** a mixed vegetable pickle. [pidgin Engl.]

chowder /ˈtʃaʊdə(r)/ n. US a soup or stew usu. of fresh fish, clams, or corn with bacon, onions, etc. [perh. F chaudière pot: see CAULDRON]

chow mein /tʃaʊ ˈmeɪn/ n. a Chinese-style dish of fried noodles with shredded meat or shrimps etc. and vegetables. [Chin. chao mian fried flour]

Chr. abbr. Chronicles (Old Testament).

chrestomathy /kresˈtɒməθɪ/ n. (pl. **-ies**) a selection of passages used esp. to help in learning a language. [F chrestomathie or Gk khrēstomatheia f. khrēstos useful + -matheia learning]

chrism /ˈkrɪz(ə)m/ n. a consecrated oil or unguent used esp. for anointing in Catholic and Greek Orthodox rites. [OE crisma f. eccl.L f. Gk khrisma anointing]

chrisom /ˈkrɪz(ə)m/ n. **1** = CHRISM. **2** (in full **chrisom-cloth**) hist. a white robe put on a child at baptism, and used as its shroud if it died within the month. [ME, as pop. pronunc. of CHRISM]

Christ /kraɪst/ n. & int. —n. **1** the title, also now treated as a name, given to Jesus of Nazareth, believed by Christians to have fulfilled the Old Testament prophecies of a coming Messiah. **2** the Messiah as prophesied in the Old Testament. **3** an image or picture of Jesus. —int. sl. expressing surprise, anger, etc. □□ **Christhood** n. **Christlike** adj. **Christly** adj. [OE Crīst f. L Christus f. Gk khristos anointed one f. khriō anoint: transl. of Heb. māšiah MESSIAH]

Christadelphian /ˌkrɪstəˈdelfɪən/ n. & adj. —n. a member of a Christian sect rejecting the doctrine of the Trinity and expecting a second coming of Christ on earth. —adj. of or adhering to this sect and its beliefs. [CHRIST + Gk adelphos brother]

christen /ˈkrɪs(ə)n/ v.tr. **1** give a Christian name to at baptism as a sign of admission to a Christian Church. **2** give a name to anything, esp. formally or with a ceremony. **3** colloq. use for the first time. □□ **christener** n. **christening** n. [OE crīstnian make Christian]

Christendom /ˈkrɪsəndəm/ n. Christians worldwide, regarded as a collective body. [OE crīstendōm f. cristen CHRISTIAN + -DOM]

Christian /ˈkrɪstɪən, ˈkrɪstʃ(ə)n/ adj. & n. —adj. **1** of Christ's teaching or religion. **2** believing in or following the religion of Jesus Christ. **3** showing the qualities associated with Christ's teaching. **4** colloq. (of a person) kind, fair, decent. —n. **1 a** a person who has received Christian baptism. **b** an adherent of Christ's teaching. **2** a person exhibiting Christian qualities. □ **Christian era** the era reckoned from the traditional date of Christ's birth. **Christian name** a forename, esp. as given at baptism. **Christian Science** a Christian sect believing in the power of healing by prayer alone. **Christian Scientist** an adherent of Christian Science. □□ **Christianize** v.tr. & intr. (also -ise). **Christianization** /ˌkrɪstɪənaɪˈzeɪʃ(ə)n/ n. **Christianly** adv. [Christianus f. Christus CHRIST]

Christianity /ˌkrɪstɪˈænɪtɪ/ n. **1** the Christian religion; its beliefs and practices. **2** being a Christian; Christian quality or character. **3** = CHRISTENDOM. [ME cristianite f. OF crestienté f. crestien CHRISTIAN]

Christie /ˈkrɪstɪ/ n. (also **Christy**) (pl. -ies) Skiing a sudden turn in which the skis are kept parallel, used for changing direction fast or stopping short. [abbr. of Christiania (now Oslo) in Norway]

Christingle /ˈkrɪstɪŋ(ə)l/ n. a lighted candle symbolizing Christ as the light of the world, held by children esp. at Advent services. [perh. f. G Christkindl dimin. of Christkind Christ child]

Christmas /ˈkrɪsməs/ n. & int. —n. (pl. **Christmases**) **1** (also **Christmas Day**) the annual festival of Christ's birth, celebrated on 25 Dec. **2** the season in which this occurs; the time immediately before and after 25 Dec. —int. sl. expressing surprise, dismay, etc. □ **Christmas-box** a present or gratuity given at Christmas esp. to tradesmen and employees. **Christmas cake** Brit. a rich fruit cake usu. covered with marzipan and icing and eaten at Christmas. **Christmas card** a card sent with greetings at Christmas. **Christmas Eve** the day or the evening before Christmas Day. **Christmas pudding** Brit. a rich boiled pudding eaten at Christmas, made with flour, suet, dried fruit, etc. **Christmas rose** a white-flowered winter-blooming evergreen, Helleborus niger. **Christmas tree** an evergreen (usu. spruce) or artificial tree set up with decorations at Christmas. □□ **Christmassy** adj. [OE Crīstes mæsse (MASS²)]

Christo- /ˈkrɪstəʊ/ comb. form Christ.

Christology /krɪsˈtɒlədʒɪ/ n. the branch of theology relating to Christ.

Christy var. of CHRISTIE. [abbr.]

chroma /ˈkrəʊmə/ n. purity or intensity of colour. [Gk khrōma colour]

chromate /ˈkrəʊmeɪt/ n. Chem. a salt or ester of chromic acid.

chromatic /krəˈmætɪk/ adj. **1** of or produced by colour; in (esp. bright) colours. **2** Mus. **a** of or having notes not belonging to a diatonic scale. **b** (of a scale) ascending or descending by semitones. □□ **chromatic aberration** Optics the failure of different wavelengths of electromagnetic radiation to come to the

same focus after refraction. **chromatic semitone** Mus. an interval between a note and its flat or sharp. □□ **chromatically** adv. **chromaticism** /-tɪˌsɪz(ə)m/ n. [F chromatique or L chromaticus f. Gk khrōmatikos f. khrōma -atos colour]

chromaticity /ˌkrəʊməˈtɪsɪtɪ/ n. the quality of colour regarded independently of brightness.

chromatid /ˈkrəʊmətɪd/ n. either of two threadlike strands into which a chromosome divides longitudinally during cell division. [Gk khrōma -atos colour + -ID²]

chromatin /ˈkrəʊmətɪn/ n. the material in a cell nucleus that stains with basic dyes and consists of protein, RNA, and DNA, of which eukaryotic chromosomes are composed. [G: see CHROMATID]

chromato- /ˈkrəʊmətəʊ/ comb. form (also **chromo-** /ˈkrəʊməʊ/) colour (chromatopsia). [Gk khrōma -atos colour]

chromatography /ˌkrəʊməˈtɒgrəfɪ/ n. Chem. the separation of the components of a mixture by slow passage through or over a material which adsorbs them differently. □□ **chromatograph** /-ˈmætəˌgrɑːf/ n. **chromatographic** /-mætəʊˈgræfɪk/ adj. [G Chromatographie (as CHROMATO-, -GRAPHY)]

chromatopsia /ˌkrəʊməˈtɒpsɪə/ n. Med. abnormally coloured vision. [CHROMATO- + Gk -opsia seeing]

chrome /krəʊm/ n. **1** chromium, esp. as plating. **2** (in full **chrome yellow**) a yellow pigment obtained from lead chromate. □ **chrome leather** leather tanned with chromium salts. **chrome-nickel** (of stainless steel) containing chromium and nickel. **chrome steel** a hard fine-grained steel containing much chromium and used for tools etc. [F, = chromium, f. Gk khrōma colour]

chromic /ˈkrəʊmɪk/ adj. Chem. of or containing trivalent chromium. □ **chromic acid** an acid that exists only in solution or in the form of chromate salts.

chromite /ˈkrəʊmaɪt/ n. **1** Mineral. a black mineral of chromium and iron oxides, which is the principal ore of chromium. **2** Chem. a salt of bivalent chromium.

chromium /ˈkrəʊmɪəm/ n. Chem. a hard white metallic transition element, occurring naturally as chromite and used as a shiny decorative electroplated coating. ¶ Symb.: **Cr**. □ **chromium steel** = chrome steel. [mod.L f. F CHROME]

chromium-plate /ˌkrəʊmɪəmˈpleɪt/ n. & v. —n. an electrolytically deposited protective coating of chromium. —v.tr. **1** coat with this. **2** (as **chromium-plated** adj.) pretentiously decorative.

chromo-¹ /ˈkrəʊməʊ/ comb. form Chem. chromium.

chromo-² comb. form var. of CHROMATO-.

chromolithograph /ˌkrəʊməʊˈlɪθəˌgrɑːf/ n. & v. —n. a coloured picture printed by lithography. —v.tr. print or produce by this process. □□ **chromolithographer** /-ˈθɒgrəfə(r)/ n. **chromolithographic** /-ˌlɪθəˈgræfɪk/ adj. **chromolithography** /-lɪˈθɒgrəfɪ/ n.

chromosome /ˈkrəʊməˌsəʊm/ n. Biochem. one of the threadlike structures, usu. found in the cell nucleus, that carry the genetic information in the form of genes. □ **chromosome map** a plan showing the relative positions of genes along the length of a chromosome. □□ **chromosomal** adj. [G Chromosom (as CHROMO-², -SOME³)]

chromosphere /ˈkrəʊməˌsfɪə(r)/ n. a gaseous layer of the sun's atmosphere between the photosphere and the corona. □□ **chromospheric** /-ˈsferɪk/ adj. [CHROMO-² + SPHERE]

Chron. abbr. Chronicles (Old Testament).

chronic /ˈkrɒnɪk/ adj. **1** persisting for a long time (usu. of an illness or a personal or social problem). **2** having a chronic complaint. **3** colloq. disp. habitual, inveterate (a chronic liar). **4** Brit. colloq. very bad; intense, severe. □□ **chronically** adv. **chronicity** /krɒˈnɪsɪtɪ/ n. [F chronique f. L chronicus (in LL of disease) f. Gk khronikos f. khronos time]

chronicle /ˈkrɒnɪk(ə)l/ n. & v. —n. 1 a register of events in order of their occurrence. 2 a narrative, a full account. 3 (**Chronicles**) the name of two of the historical books of the Old Testament or Hebrew bible. —v.tr. record (events) in the order of their occurrence. □□ **chronicler** n. [ME f. AF cronicle ult. f. L chronica f. Gk khronika annals: see CHRONIC]

chrono- /ˈkrəʊnəʊ/ comb. form time. [Gk khronos time]

chronograph /ˈkrɒnəˌɡrɑːf, ˈkrəʊnə-, -ˌɡræf/ n. 1 an instrument for recording time with extreme accuracy. 2 a stopwatch. □□ **chronographic** /-ˈɡræfɪk/ adj.

chronological /ˌkrɒnəˈlɒdʒɪk(ə)l/ adj. 1 (of a number of events) arranged or regarded in the order of their occurrence. 2 of or relating to chronology. □□ **chronologically** adv.

chronology /krəˈnɒlədʒɪ/ n. (pl. -ies) 1 the study of historical records to establish the dates of past events. 2 a the arrangement of events, dates, etc. in the order of their occurrence. b a table or document displaying this. □□ **chronologist** n. **chronologize** v.tr. (also -ise). [mod.L chronologia (as CHRONO-, -LOGY)]

chronometer /krəˈnɒmɪtə(r)/ n. a time-measuring instrument, esp. one keeping accurate time at all temperatures and used in navigation.

chronometry /krəˈnɒmɪtrɪ/ n. the science of accurate time-measurement. □□ **chronometric** /ˌkrɒnəˈmetrɪk/ adj. **chronometrical** /ˌkrɒnəˈmetrɪk(ə)l/ adj. **chronometrically** /ˌkrɒnəˈmetrɪkəlɪ/ adv.

chrysalis /ˈkrɪsəlɪs/ n. (pl. **chrysalises** or **chrysalides** /krɪˈsælɪˌdiːz/) 1 a a quiescent pupa of a butterfly or moth. b the hard outer case enclosing it. 2 a preparatory or transitional state. [L f. Gk khrusallis -idos f. khrusos gold]

chrysanth /krɪˈsænθ/ n. colloq. any of the autumn-blooming cultivated varieties of chrysanthemum. [abbr.]

chrysanthemum /krɪˈsænθəməm/ n. any composite plant of the genus Chrysanthemum, having brightly coloured flowers. [L f. Gk khrusanthemon f. khrusos gold + anthemon flower]

chryselephantine /ˌkrɪselɪˈfæntaɪn/ adj. (of ancient Greek sculpture) overlaid with gold and ivory. [Gk khruselephantinos f. khrusos gold + elephas ivory]

chrysoberyl /ˈkrɪsəˌberɪl/ n. a yellowish-green gem consisting of a beryllium salt. [L chrysoberyllus f. Gk khrusos gold + bērullos beryl]

chrysolite /ˈkrɪsəˌlaɪt/ n. a precious stone, a yellowish-green or brownish variety of olivine. [ME f. OF crisolite f. med.L crisolitus f. L chrysolithus f. Gk khrusolithos f. khrusos gold + lithos stone]

chrysoprase /ˈkrɪsəˌpreɪz/ n. 1 an apple-green variety of chalcedony containing nickel and used as a gem. 2 (in the New Testament) prob. a golden-green variety of beryl. [ME f. OF crisopace f. L chrysopassus var. of L chrysoprasus f. Gk khrusoprasos f. khrusos gold + prason leek]

chthonic /ˈkθɒnɪk, ˈθɒnɪk/ (also **chthonian** /ˈkθəʊnɪən, ˈθəʊ-/) adj. of, relating to, or inhabiting the underworld. [Gk khthōn earth]

chub /tʃʌb/ n. a thick-bodied coarse-fleshed river fish, Leuciscus cephalus. [15th c.: orig. unkn.]

chubby /ˈtʃʌbɪ/ adj. (**chubbier**, **chubbiest**) plump and rounded (esp. of a person or a part of the body). □□ **chubbily** adv. **chubbiness** n. [CHUB]

chuck[1] /tʃʌk/ v. & n. —v.tr. 1 colloq. fling or throw carelessly or with indifference. 2 colloq. (often foll. by in, up) give up; reject (chucked in my job). 3 touch playfully, esp. under the chin. —n. a playful touch under the chin. □the chuck sl. dismissal (he got the chuck). **chucker-out** colloq. a person employed to expel troublesome people from a gathering etc. **chuck it** sl. stop, desist. **chuck out** colloq. 1 expel (a person) from a gathering etc. 2 get rid of, discard. [16th c., perh. f. F chuquer, choquer to knock]

chuck[2] /tʃʌk/ n. & v. —n. 1 a cut of beef between the neck and the ribs. 2 a device for holding a workpiece in a lathe or a tool in a drill. —v.tr. fix (wood, a tool, etc.) to a chuck. [var. of CHOCK]

chuck[3] /tʃʌk/ n. US colloq. food. □chuck-wagon 1 a provision-cart on a ranch etc. 2 a roadside eating-place. [19th c.: perh. f. CHUCK[2]]

chuckle /ˈtʃʌk(ə)l/ v. & n. —v.intr. laugh quietly or inwardly. —n. a quiet or suppressed laugh. □□ **chuckler** n. [chuck cluck]

chucklehead /ˈtʃʌkəlˌhed/ n. colloq. a stupid person. □□ **chuckleheaded** adj. [chuckle clumsy, prob. rel. to CHUCK[2]]

chuddar var. of CHADOR.

chuff /tʃʌf/ v.intr. (of a steam engine etc.) work with a regular sharp puffing sound. [imit.]

chuffed /tʃʌft/ adj. Brit. sl. delighted. [dial. chuff pleased]

chug /tʃʌɡ/ v. & n. —v.intr. (**chugged**, **chugging**) 1 emit a regular muffled explosive sound, as of an engine running slowly. 2 move with this sound. —n. a chugging sound. [imit.]

chukar /tʃʌˈkɑː(r)/ n. a red-legged partridge, Alectoris chukar, native to India. [Hindi cakor]

chukker /ˈtʃʌkə(r)/ n. (also **chukka**) each of the periods of play into which a game of polo is divided. □chukka boot an ankle-high leather boot as worn for polo. [Hindi cakkar f. Skr. cakra wheel]

chum[1] /tʃʌm/ n. & v. —n. colloq. (esp. among schoolchildren) a close friend. —v.intr. (often foll. by with) share rooms. □chum up (often foll. by with) become a close friend (of). □□ **chummy** adj. (**chummier**, **chummiest**). **chummily** adv. **chumminess** n. [17th c.: prob. short for chamber-fellow]

chum[2] /tʃʌm/ n. & v. US —n. 1 refuse from fish. 2 chopped fish used as bait. —v. 1 intr. fish using chum. 2 tr. bait (a fishing place) using chum. [19th c.: orig. unkn.]

chump /tʃʌmp/ n. 1 colloq. a foolish person. 2 Brit. the thick end, esp. of a loin of lamb or mutton (chump chop). 3 a short thick block of wood. 4 Brit. sl. the head. □off one's chump Brit. sl. crazy. [18th c.: blend of CHUNK and LUMP[1]]

chunder /ˈtʃʌndə(r)/ v.intr. & n. Austral. sl. vomit. [20th c.: orig. unkn.]

chunk /tʃʌŋk/ n. 1 a thick solid slice or piece of something firm or hard. 2 a substantial amount or piece. [prob. var. of CHUCK[2]]

chunky /ˈtʃʌŋkɪ/ adj. (**chunkier**, **chunkiest**) 1 containing or consisting of chunks. 2 short and thick; small and sturdy. 3 (of clothes) made of a thick material. □□ **chunkiness** n.

Chunnel /ˈtʃʌn(ə)l/ n. colloq. a projected tunnel under the English Channel linking England and France. [portmanteau word f. Channel tunnel]

chunter /ˈtʃʌntə(r)/ v.intr. Brit. colloq. mutter, grumble. [prob. imit.]

chupatty var. of CHAPATTI.

church /tʃɜːtʃ/ n. & v. —n. 1 a building for public (usu. Christian) worship. 2 a meeting for public worship in such a building (go to church; met after church). 3 (**Church**) the body of all Christians. 4 (**Church**) the clergy or clerical profession (went into the Church). 5 (**Church**) an organized Christian group or society of any time, country, or distinct principles of worship (the primitive Church; Church of Scotland; High Church). 6 (**Church**) institutionalized religion as a political or social force (Church and State). —v.tr. bring (esp. a woman after childbirth) to church for a service of thanksgiving. □Church Army an organization of the Church of England concerned with social welfare. **Church Commissioners** a body managing the finances of the Church of England. **Church of England** the English Church, recognized by the State and having the sovereign as its head. **church school** a school founded by or associated with the Church of England.

[OE *cirice*, *circe*, etc. f. med. Gk *kurikon* f. Gk *kuriakon* (*dōma*) Lord's (house) f. *kurios* Lord: cf. KIRK]

churchgoer /ˈtʃɜːtʃˌgəʊə(r)/ n. a person who goes to church, esp. regularly. □□ **churchgoing** n. & adj.

churchman /ˈtʃɜːtʃmən/ n. (pl. **-men**) 1 a member of the clergy or of a church. 2 a supporter of the church.

churchwarden /tʃɜːtʃˈwɔːd(ə)n/ n. 1 either of two elected lay representatives of a parish, assisting with routine administration. 2 a long-stemmed clay pipe.

churchwoman /ˈtʃɜːtʃˌwʊmən/ n. (pl. **-women**) 1 a woman member of the clergy or of a church. 2 a woman supporter of the Church.

churchy /ˈtʃɜːtʃɪ/ adj. 1 obtrusively or intolerantly devoted to the Church or opposed to religious dissent. 2 like a church. □□ **churchiness** n.

churchyard /ˈtʃɜːtʃjɑːd/ n. the enclosed ground around a church, esp. as used for burials.

churinga /tʃʌˈrɪŋgə/ n. (pl. same or **churingas**) a sacred object, esp. an amulet, among the Australian Aboriginals. [Aboriginal]

churl /tʃɜːl/ n. 1 an ill-bred person. 2 *archaic* a peasant; a person of low birth. 3 *archaic* a surly or mean person. [OE *ceorl* f. a WG root, = man]

churlish /ˈtʃɜːlɪʃ/ adj. surly; mean. □□ **churlishly** adv. **churlishness** n. [OE *cierlisc*, *ceorlisc* f. *ceorl* CHURL]

churn /tʃɜːn/ n. & v. —n. 1 *Brit.* a large milk-can. 2 a machine for making butter by agitating milk or cream. —v. 1 tr. agitate (milk or cream) in a churn. 2 tr. produce (butter) in this way. 3 tr. (usu. foll. by *up*) cause distress to; upset, agitate. 4 intr. (of a liquid) seethe, foam violently (*the churning sea*). 5 tr. agitate or move (liquid) vigorously, causing it to foam. □ **churn out** produce routinely or mechanically, esp. in large quantities. [OE *cyrin* f. Gmc]

churr var. of CHIRR.

chute[1] /ʃuːt/ n. 1 a sloping channel or slide, with or without water, for conveying things to a lower level. 2 a slide into a swimming-pool. [F *chute* fall (of water etc.), f. OF *cheoite* fem. past part. of *cheoir* fall f. L *cadere*; in some senses = SHOOT]

chute[2] /ʃuːt/ n. *colloq.* parachute. □□ **chutist** n. [abbr.]

chutney /ˈtʃʌtnɪ/ n. (pl. **-eys**) a pungent orig. Indian condiment made of fruits or vegetables, vinegar, spices, sugar, etc. [Hindi *caṭnī*]

chutzpah /ˈxʊtzpə/ n. *sl.* shameless audacity; cheek. [Yiddish]

chyle /kaɪl/ n. a milky fluid consisting of lymph and absorbed food materials from the intestine after digestion. □□ **chylous** adj. [LL *chylus* f. Gk *khulos* juice]

chyme /kaɪm/ n. the acidic semisolid and partly digested food produced by the action of gastric secretion. □□ **chymous** adj. [LL *chymus* f. Gk *khumos* juice]

chypre /ˈʃiːpr/ n. a heavy perfume made from sandalwood. [F, = Cyprus, perh. where it was first made]

CI abbr. 1 Channel Islands. 2 *hist.* Order of the Crown of India.

Ci abbr. curie.

CIA abbr. (in the US) Central Intelligence Agency.

ciao /tʃaʊ/ int. *colloq.* 1 goodbye. 2 hello. [It.]

ciborium /sɪˈbɔːrɪəm/ n. (pl. **ciboria** /-rɪə/) 1 a vessel with an arched cover used to hold the Eucharist. 2 *Archit.* a a canopy. b a shrine with a canopy. [med.L f. Gk *kibōrion* seed-vessel of the water-lily, a cup made from it]

cicada /sɪˈkɑːdə, -ˈkeɪdə/ n. (also **cicala** /sɪˈkɑːlə/) any transparent-winged large insect of the family Cicadidae, the males of which make a loud rhythmic chirping sound. [L *cicada*, It. f. L *cicala*, It. *cigala*]

cicatrice /ˈsɪkətrɪs/ n. (also **cicatrix** /ˈsɪkətrɪks/) (pl. **cicatrices** /ˌsɪkəˈtraɪsiːz/) 1 any mark left by a healed wound; a scar. 2 *Bot.* a a mark on a stem etc. left when a leaf or other part becomes detached. b a scar

on the bark of a tree. □□ **cicatricial** /ˌsɪkəˈtrɪʃ(ə)l/ adj. [ME f. OF *cicatrice* or L *cicatrix -icis*]

cicatrize /ˈsɪkətraɪz/ v. (also **-ise**) 1 tr. heal (a wound) by scar formation. 2 intr. (of a wound) heal by scar formation. □□ **cicatrization** /-ˈzeɪʃ(ə)n/ n. [F *cicatriser*: see CICATRICE]

cicely /ˈsɪsəlɪ/ n. (pl. **-ies**) any of various umbelliferous plants, esp. sweet cicely (see SWEET). [app. f. L *seselis* f. Gk, assim. to the woman's Christian name]

cicerone /ˌtʃɪtʃəˈrəʊnɪ, ˌsɪsəˈrəʊnɪ/ n. (pl. **ciceroni** pronunc. same) a guide who gives information about antiquities, places of interest, etc. to sightseers. [It.: see CICERONIAN]

Ciceronian /ˌsɪsəˈrəʊnɪən/ adj. (of language) eloquent, classical, or rhythmical, in the style of Cicero. [L *Ciceronianus* f. *Cicero -onis* Roman statesman and orator d. 43 BC]

cichlid /ˈsɪklɪd/ n. any tropical freshwater fish of the family Cichlidae, esp. the kinds kept in aquariums. [mod.L *Cichlidae* f. Gk *kikhlē* a kind of fish]

CID abbr. (in the UK) Criminal Investigation Department.

-cide /saɪd/ suffix forming nouns meaning: 1 a person or substance that kills (*regicide; insecticide*). 2 the killing of (*infanticide; suicide*). [F f. L *-cida* (sense 1), *-cidium* (sense 2), *caedere* kill]

cider /ˈsaɪdə(r)/ n. (also **cyder**) 1 *Brit.* an alcoholic drink made from fermented apple-juice. 2 *US* an unfermented drink made from apple-juice. □ **cider-press** a press for crushing apples to make cider. [ME f. OF *sidre*, ult. f. Heb. *šēkār* strong drink]

ci-devant /ˌsiːdəˈvɑ̃/ adj. & adv. that has been (with person's earlier name or status); former or formerly. [F, = heretofore]

CIE abbr. *hist.* Companion (of the Order) of the Indian Empire.

c.i.f. abbr. cost, insurance, freight (as being included in a price).

cig /sɪg/ n. *colloq.* cigarette, cigar. [abbr.]

cigala /sɪˈgɑːlə/ n. = CICADA. [F *cigale*, It. & Prov. *cigala* f. L *cicada*]

cigar /sɪˈgɑː(r)/ n. a cylinder of tobacco rolled in tobacco leaves for smoking. [F *cigare* or Sp. *cigarro*]

cigarette /ˌsɪgəˈret/ n. (*US* also **cigaret**) 1 a thin cylinder of finely-cut tobacco rolled in paper for smoking. 2 a similar cylinder containing a narcotic or medicated substance. □ **cigarette card** a small picture card of a kind formerly included in a packet of cigarettes. **cigarette-end** the unsmoked remainder of a cigarette. [F, dimin. of *cigare* CIGAR]

cigarillo /ˌsɪgəˈrɪləʊ/ n. (pl. **-os**) a small cigar. [Sp., dimin. of *cigarro* CIGAR]

ciggy /ˈsɪgɪ/ n. (pl. **-ies**) *colloq.* cigarette. [abbr.]

CIGS abbr. *hist.* Chief of the Imperial General Staff.

cilice /ˈsɪlɪs/ n. 1 haircloth. 2 a garment of this. [F f. L *cilicium* f. Gk *kilikion* f. *Kilikia* Cilicia in Asia Minor]

cilium /ˈsɪlɪəm/ n. (pl. **cilia** /-lɪə/) 1 a short minute hairlike vibrating structure on the surface of some cells, causing currents in the surrounding fluid. 2 an eyelash. □□ **ciliary** adj. **ciliate** /-ˌeɪt, -ət/ adj. **ciliated** adj. **ciliation** /-ˈeɪʃ(ə)n/ n. [L, = eyelash]

cill var. of SILL.

cimbalom /ˈsɪmbələm/ n. a dulcimer. [Magyar f. It. *cembalo*]

C.-in-C. abbr. Commander-in-Chief.

cinch /sɪntʃ/ n. & v. —n. 1 *colloq.* a a sure thing; a certainty. b an easy task. 2 *US* a firm hold. 3 esp. *US* a girth for a saddle or pack. —v.tr. 1 a tighten as with a cinch (*cinched at the waist with a belt*). b secure a grip on. 2 *sl.* make certain of. 3 esp. *US* put a cinch (sense 3) on. [Sp. *cincha*]

cinchona /sɪŋˈkəʊnə/ n. 1 a any evergreen tree or shrub of the genus *Cinchona*, native to S. America, with fragrant flowers and yielding cinchona bark. b the bark of this tree, containing quinine. 2 any drug from this bark formerly used as a tonic and to stimulate the appetite. □□ **cinchonic** /-'kɒnɪk/ *adj.*

cinchonine /'sɪŋkə,niːn/ *n.* [mod.L f. Countess of Chinchón d. 1641, introducer of drug into Spain]

cincture /'sɪŋktʃə(r)/ *n.* **1** *literary* a girdle, belt, or border. **2** *Archit.* a ring at either end of a column-shaft. [L *cinctura* f. *cingere cinct-* gird]

cinder /'sɪndə(r)/ *n.* **a** the residue of coal or wood etc. that has stopped giving off flames but still has combustible matter in it. **b** slag. **c** (in *pl.*) ashes. □**burnt to a cinder** made useless by burning. □□ **cindery** *adj.* [OE *sinder*, assim. to the unconnected F *cendre* and L *cinis* ashes]

Cinderella /,sɪndə'relə/ *n.* **1** a person or thing of unrecognized or disregarded merit or beauty. **2** a neglected or despised member of a group. [the name of a girl in a fairy-tale]

cine- /'sɪnɪ/ *comb. form* cinematographic (*cine-camera*; *cinephotography*). [abbr.]

cineaste /'sɪnɪ,æst/ *n.* (also **cineast**) a cinema enthusiast. [F *cinéaste* (as CINE-): cf. ENTHUSIAST]

cinema /'sɪnɪ,mɑː, -mə/ *n.* **1** *Brit.* a theatre where motion-picture films (see FILM *n.* 3) are shown. **2** films collectively. **b** the production of films as an art or industry; cinematography. □**cinema organ** *Mus.* a kind of organ with extra stops and special effects. [F *cinéma*: see CINEMATOGRAPH]

cinematheque /'sɪnɪmə,tek/ *n.* **1** a film library or archive. **2** a small cinema. [F]

cinematic /,sɪnɪ'mætɪk/ *adj.* **1** having the qualities characteristic of the cinema. **2** of or relating to the cinema. □□ **cinematically** *adv.*

cinematograph /,sɪnɪ'mætə,grɑːf/ (also **kinematograph** /,kɪn-/) *n.* an apparatus for showing motion-picture films. [F *cinématographe* f. Gk *kinēma -atos* movement f. *kineō* move]

cinematography /,sɪnɪmə'tɒgrəfɪ/ *n.* the art of making motion-picture films. □□ **cinematographer** *n.* **cinematographic** /-,mætə'græfɪk/ *adj.* **cinematographically** /-,mætə'græfɪkəlɪ/ *adv.*

cinéma-vérité /,sɪne,mɑː verɪ'teɪ/ *n. Cinematog.* **1** the art or process of making realistic (esp. documentary) films which avoid artificiality and artistic effect. **2** such films collectively. [F, = cinema truth]

cineraria /,sɪnə'reərɪə/ *n.* any of several varieties of the composite plant, *Cineraria cruentus*, having bright flowers and ash-coloured down on its leaves. [mod.L, fem. of L *cinerarius* of ashes f. *cinis -eris* ashes, from the ash-coloured down on the leaves]

cinerarium /,sɪnə'reərɪəm/ *n.* (*pl.* **cinerariums**) a place where a cinerary urn is deposited. [LL, neut. of *cinerarius*: see CINERARIA]

cinerary /'sɪnərərɪ/ *adj.* of ashes. □**cinerary urn** an urn for holding the ashes after cremation. [L *cinerarius*: see CINERARIA]

cinereous /sɪ'nɪərɪəs/ *adj.* (esp. of a bird or plumage) ash-grey. [L *cinereus* f. *cinis -eris* ashes]

ciné-vérité /'sɪnɪ,verɪ,teɪ/ *n. Cinematog.* = CINÉMA-VÉRITÉ.

Cingalese /,sɪŋgə'liːz/ *adj. & n.* (*pl.* same) *archaic* Sinhalese. [F *cing(h)alais*: see SINHALESE]

cingulum /'sɪŋgjʊləm/ *n.* (*pl.* **cingula** /-lə/) *Anat.* a girdle, belt, or analogous structure, esp. a ridge surrounding the base of the crown of a tooth. [L, = belt]

cinnabar /'sɪnə,bɑː(r)/ *n.* **1** a bright red mineral form of mercuric sulphide from which mercury is obtained. **2** vermilion. **3** a moth (*Callimorpha jacobaeae*) with reddish marked wings. [ME f. L *cinnabaris* f. Gk *kinnabari*, of oriental orig.]

cinnamon /'sɪnəmən/ *n.* **1** an aromatic spice from the peeled, dried, and rolled bark of a SE Asian tree. **2** any tree of the genus *Cinnamomum*, esp. *C. zeylanicum* yielding the spice. **3** yellowish-brown. [ME f. OF *cinnamome* f. L *cinnamomum* f. Gk *kinnamōmon*, and L *cinnamon* f. Gk *kinnamon*, f. Semitic (cf. Heb. *ḳinnāmôn*)]

cinque /sɪŋk/ *n.* (also **cinq**) the five on dice. [ME f. OF *cinc*, *cink*, f. L *quinque* five]

cinquecento /,tʃɪŋkwɪ'tʃentəʊ/ *n.* the style of Italian art and literature of the 16th c., with a reversion to classical forms. □□ **cinquecentoist** /-təʊɪst/ *n.* [It., = 500, used with ref. to the years 1500-99]

cinquefoil /'sɪŋkfɔɪl/ *n.* **1** any plant of the genus *Potentilla*, with compound leaves of five leaflets. **2** *Archit.* a five-cusped ornament in a circle or arch. [ME f. L *quinquefolium* f. *quinque* five + *folium* leaf]

Cinque Ports /sɪŋk 'pɔːts/ *n.pl.* a group of ports (orig. five only) on the SE coast of England with ancient privileges. [ME f. OF *cink porz*, L *quinque portus* five ports]

cion *US* var. of SCION 1.

cipher /'saɪfə(r)/ *n. & v.* (also **cypher**) —*n.* **1 a** a secret or disguised way of writing. **b** a thing written in this way. **c** the key to it. **2** the arithmetical symbol (0) denoting no amount but used to occupy a vacant place in decimal etc. numeration (as in 12.05). **3** a person or thing of no importance. **4** the interlaced initials of a person or company etc.; a monogram. **5** any Arabic numeral. **6** continuous sounding of an organ-pipe, caused by a mechanical defect. —*v.* **1** *tr.* put into secret writing, encipher. **2 a** *tr.* (usu. foll. by *out*) work out by arithmetic, calculate. **b** *intr. archaic* do arithmetic. [ME, f. OF *cif(f)re*, ult. f. Arab *ṣifr* ZERO]

cipolin /'sɪpəlɪn/ *n.* an Italian white-and-green marble. [F *cipolin* or It. *cipollino* f. *cipolla* onion]

circa /'sɜːkə/ *prep.* (preceding a date) about. [L]

circadian /sɜː'keɪdɪən/ *adj. Physiol.* occurring or recurring about once per day. [irreg. f. L *circa* about + *dies* day]

circinate /'sɜːsɪ,neɪt/ *adj. Bot. & Zool.* rolled up with the apex in the centre, e.g. of young fronds of ferns. [L *circinatus* past part. of *circinare* make round f. *circinus* pair of compasses]

circle /'sɜːk(ə)l/ *n. & v.* —*n.* **1 a** a round plane figure whose circumference is everywhere equidistant from its centre. **b** the line enclosing a circle. **2** a roundish enclosure or structure. **3** a ring. **4** a curved upper tier of seats in a theatre etc. (*dress circle*). **5** a circular route. **6** *Archaeol.* a group of (usu. large embedded) stones arranged in a circle. **7** *Hockey* = *striking-circle*. **8** persons grouped round a centre of interest. **9** a set or class or restricted group (*literary circles*; *not done in the best circles*). **10** a period or cycle (*the circle of the year*). **11** (in full **vicious circle**) **a** an unbroken sequence of reciprocal cause and effect. **b** an action and reaction that intensify each other (cf. *virtuous circle*). **c** the fallacy of proving a proposition from another which depends on the first for its own proof. —*v.* **1** *intr.* (often foll. by *round*, *about*) move in a circle. **2** *tr.* **a** revolve round. **b** form a circle round. □**circle back** move in a wide loop towards the starting-point. **come full circle** return to the starting-point. **go round in circles** make no progress despite effort. **great** (or **small**) **circle** a circle on the surface of a sphere whose plane passes (or does not pass) through the sphere's centre. **run round in circles** *colloq.* be fussily busy with little result. □□ **circler** *n.* [ME f. OF *cercle* f. L *circulus* dimin. of *circus* ring]

circlet /'sɜːklɪt/ *n.* **1** a small circle. **2** a circular band, esp. of gold or jewelled etc., as an ornament.

circs /sɜːks/ *n.pl. colloq.* circumstances. [abbr.]

circuit /'sɜːkɪt/ *n.* **1 a** a line or course enclosing an area; the distance round. **b** the area enclosed. **2** *Electr.* **a** the path of a current. **b** the apparatus through which a current passes. **3 a** the journey of a judge in a particular district to hold courts. **b** this district. **c** the lawyers following a circuit. **4 a** chain of theatres or cinemas etc. under a single management. **5** *Brit.* a motor-racing track. **6 a** a sequence of sporting events (*the US tennis circuit*). **b** a sequence of athletic exercises. **7** a roundabout journey. **8 a** a group of local Methodist churches forming a minor administrative unit. **b** the journey of an itinerant minister within this. □**circuit-breaker** an automatic device for stopping the flow of current in an electrical circuit. [ME f. OF, f. L *circuitus* f. CIRCUM- + *ire it-* go]

circuitous /sɜːˈkjuːɪtəs/ *adj.* **1** indirect (and usu. long). **2** going a long way round. □□**circuitously** *adv.* **circuitousness** *n.* [med.L *circuitosus* f. *circuitus* CIRCUIT]

circuitry /ˈsɜːkɪtrɪ/ *n.* (*pl.* -**ies**) **1** a system of electric circuits. **2** the equipment forming this.

circular /ˈsɜːkjʊlə(r)/ *adj.* & *n.* —*adj.* **1 a** having the form of a circle. **b** moving or taking place along a circle (*circular tour*). **2** *Logic* (of reasoning) depending on a vicious circle. **3** (of a letter or advertisement etc.) printed for distribution to a large number of people. —*n.* a circular letter, leaflet, etc. □**circular saw** a power saw with a rapidly rotating toothed disc. □□**circularity** /-ˈlærɪtɪ/ *n.* **circularly** *adv.* [ME f. AF *circuler*, OF *circulier*, *cerclier* f. LL *circularis* f. L *circulus* CIRCLE]

circularize /ˈsɜːkjʊləˌraɪz/ *v.tr.* (also -**ise**) **1** distribute circulars to. **2** *US* seek opinions of (people) by means of a questionnaire. □□**circularization** /-ˈzeɪʃ(ə)n/ *n.*

circulate /ˈsɜːkjʊleɪt/ *v.* **1** *intr.* go round from one place or person etc. to the next and so on; be in circulation. **2** *tr.* **a** cause to go round; put into circulation. **b** give currency to (a report etc.). **c** circularize. **3** *intr.* be actively sociable at a party, gathering, etc. □**circulating library** a small library with books lent to a group of subscribers in turn. **circulating** medium notes or gold etc. used in exchange. □□**circulative** *adj.* **circulator** *n.* [L *circulare circulat-* f. *circulus* CIRCLE]

circulation /ˌsɜːkjʊˈleɪʃ(ə)n/ *n.* **1 a** movement to and fro, or from and back to a starting point, esp. of a fluid in a confined area or circuit. **b** the movement of blood from and to the heart. **c** a similar movement of sap etc. **2 a** the transmission or distribution (of news or information or books etc.). **b** the number of copies sold, esp. of journals and newspapers. **3 a** currency, coin, etc. **b** the movement or exchange of this in a country etc. □**in** (or **out of**) **circulation** participating (or not participating) in activities etc. [F *circulation* or L *circulatio* f. *circulare* CIRCULATE]

circulatory /ˌsɜːkjʊˈleɪtərɪ, ˈsɜːkjʊlətərɪ/ *adj.* of or relating to the circulation of blood or sap.

circum- /ˈsɜːkəm/ *comb. form* round, about, around, used: **1** adverbially (*circumambient*; *circumfuse*). **2** prepositionally (*circumlunar*; *circumocular*). [from or after L *circum* prep. = round, about]

circumambient /ˌsɜːkəmˈæmbɪənt/ *adj.* (esp. of air or another fluid) surrounding. □□**circumambience** *n.* **circumambiency** *n.*

circumambulate /ˌsɜːkəmˈæmbjʊˌleɪt/ *v.tr.* & *intr.* *formal* walk round or about. □□**circumambulation** /-ˈleɪʃ(ə)n/ *n.* **circumambulatory** *adj.* [CIRCUM- + *ambulate* f. L *ambulare* walk]

circumcircle /ˈsɜːkəmˌsɜːk(ə)l/ *n.* *Geom.* a circle touching all the vertices of a triangle or polygon.

circumcise /ˈsɜːkəmˌsaɪz/ *v.tr.* **1** cut off the foreskin, as a Jewish or Muslim rite or a surgical operation. **2** cut off the clitoris (and sometimes the labia), usu. as a religious rite. **3** *Bibl.* purify (the heart etc.). [ME f. OF f. L *circumcidere circumcis-* (as CIRCUM-, *caedere* cut)]

circumcision /ˌsɜːkəmˈsɪʒ(ə)n/ *n.* **1** the act or rite of circumcising or being circumcised. **2** (**Circumcision**) *Eccl.* the feast of the Circumcision of Christ, 1 Jan. [ME f. OF *circoncision* f. LL *circumcisio -onis* (as CIRCUMCISE)]

circumference /sɜːˈkʌmfərəns/ *n.* **1** the enclosing boundary, esp. of a circle or other figure enclosed by a curve. **2** the distance round. □□**circumferential** /ˌsɜːkəmfəˈrenʃ(ə)l/ *adj.* **circumferentially** /ˌsɜːkəmfəˈrenʃəlɪ/ *adv.* [ME f. OF *circonference* f. L *circumferentia* (as CIRCUM-, *ferre* bear)]

circumflex /ˈsɜːkəmˌfleks/ *n.* & *adj.* —*n.* (in full

circumflex accent) a mark (ˆ or ˜) placed over a vowel in some languages to indicate a contraction, length, or a special quality. —*adj.* *Anat.* curved, bending round something else (*circumflex nerve*). [L *circumflexus* (as CIRCUM-, *flectere flex-* bend), transl. of Gk *perispōmenos* drawn around]

circumfluent /səˈkʌmflʊənt/ *adj.* flowing round, surrounding. □□**circumfluence** *n.* [L *circumfluere* (as CIRCUM-, *fluere* flow)]

circumfuse /ˌsɜːkəmˈfjuːz/ *v.tr.* pour round or about. [CIRCUM- + L *fundere fus-* pour]

circumjacent /ˌsɜːkəmˈdʒeɪs(ə)nt/ *adj.* situated around. [L *circumjacēre* (as CIRCUM-, *jaceō* lie)]

circumlocution /ˌsɜːkəmləˈkjuːʃ(ə)n/ *n.* **1 a** a roundabout expression. **b** evasive talk. **2** the use of many words where fewer would do; verbosity. □□**circumlocutional** *adj.* **circumlocutionary** *adj.* **circumlocutionist** *n.* **circumlocutory** /-ˈlɒkjʊtərɪ/ *adj.* [ME f. F *circumlocution* or L *circumlocutio* (as CIRCUM-, LOCUTION), transl. of Gk PERIPHRASIS]

circumlunar /ˌsɜːkəmˈluːnə(r), -ˈljuːnə(r)/ *adj.* moving or situated around the moon.

circumnavigate /ˌsɜːkəmˈnævɪˌgeɪt/ *v.tr.* sail round (esp. the world). □□**circumnavigation** /-ˈgeɪʃ(ə)n/ *n.* **circumnavigator** *n.* [L *circumnavigare* (as CIRCUM-, NAVIGATE)]

circumpolar /ˌsɜːkəmˈpəʊlə(r)/ *adj.* **1** *Geog.* around or near one of the earth's poles. **2** *Astron.* (of a star or motion etc.) above the horizon at all times in a given latitude.

circumscribe /ˈsɜːkəmˌskraɪb/ *v.tr.* **1** (of a line etc.) enclose or outline. **2** lay down the limits of; confine, restrict. **3** *Geom.* draw (a figure) round another, touching it at points but not cutting it (cf. INSCRIBE). □□**circumscribable** /-ˈskraɪbəb(ə)l/ *adj.* **circumscription** *n.* **circumscriptive** /-ˈskrɪpʃ(ə)n/ *n.* [L *circumscribere* (as CIRCUM-, *scribere script-* write)]

circumsolar /ˌsɜːkəmˈsəʊlə(r)/ *adj.* moving or situated around or near the sun.

circumspect /ˈsɜːkəmˌspekt/ *adj.* wary, cautious; taking everything into account. □□**circumspection** /-ˈspekʃ(ə)n/ *n.* **circumspectly** *adv.* [ME f. L *circumspicere circumspect-* (as CIRCUM-, *specere spect-* look)]

circumstance /ˈsɜːkəmstəns/ *n.* **1 a** a fact, occurrence, or condition, esp. (in *pl.*) the time, place, manner, cause, occasion etc., or surroundings of an act or event. **b** (in *pl.*) the external conditions that affect or might affect an action. **2** (often foll. by *that* + clause) an incident, occurrence, or fact, as needing consideration (*the circumstance that he left early*). **3** (in *pl.*) one's state of financial or material welfare (*in reduced circumstances*). **4** ceremony, fuss (*pomp and circumstance*). **5** full detail in a narrative (*told it with much circumstance*). □**in** (or **under**) **the** (or **these**) **circumstances** the state of affairs being what it is. **in** (or **under**) **no circumstances** not at all; never. □□**circumstanced** *adj.* [ME f. OF *circonstance* or L *circumstantia* (as CIRCUM-, *stantia* f. *sto* stand)]

circumstantial /ˌsɜːkəmˈstænʃ(ə)l/ *adj.* **1** given in full detail (*a circumstantial account*). **2** (of evidence, a legal case, etc.) tending to establish a conclusion by inference from known facts hard to explain otherwise. **3 a** depending on circumstances. **b** adventitious, incidental. □□**circumstantiality** /-ʃɪˈælɪtɪ/ *n.* **circumstantially** *adv.* [L *circumstantia*: see CIRCUMSTANCE]

circumterrestrial /ˌsɜːkəmtəˈrestrɪəl/ *adj.* moving or situated around the earth.

circumvallate /ˌsɜːkəmˈvæleɪt/ *v.tr.* surround with or as with a rampart. [L *circumvallare circumvallat-* (as CIRCUM-, *vallare* f. *vallum* rampart)]

circumvent /ˌsɜːkəmˈvent/ *v.tr.* **1 a** evade (a difficulty); find a way round. **b** baffle, outwit. **2** entrap (an enemy) by surrounding. □□**circumvention** *n.* [L *circumvenire circumvent-* (as CIRCUM-, *venire* come)]

circumvolution /ˌsɜːkəmvəˈljuːʃ(ə)n/ *n.* **1** rotation. **2** the winding of one thing round another. **3** a sinuous movement. [ME f. L *circumvolvere circumvolut-* (as CIRCUM-, *volvere* roll)]

circus /'sɜːkəs/ *n.* (*pl.* **circuses**) **1** a travelling show of performing animals, acrobats, clowns, etc. **2** *colloq.* **a** a scene of lively action; a disturbance. **b** a group of people in a common activity, esp. sport. **3** *Brit.* an open space in a town, where several streets converge (*Piccadilly Circus*). **4** a circular hollow surrounded by hills. **5** *Rom. Antiq.* **a** a rounded or oval arena with tiers of seats, for equestrian and other sports and games. **b** a performance given there (*bread and circuses*). [L, = ring]

ciré /'sɪəreɪ/ *n.* & *adj.* —*n.* a fabric with a smooth shiny surface obtained esp. by waxing and heating. —*adj.* having such a surface. [F, = waxed]

cire perdue /ˌsɪə pɜː'djuː/ *n.* a method of bronze-casting using a clay core and a wax coating placed in a mould: the wax is melted in the mould and bronze poured into the space left, producing a hollow bronze figure when the core is discarded. [F, = lost wax]

cirque /sɜːk/ *n.* **1** *Geol.* a deep bowl-shaped hollow at the head of a valley or on a mountainside. **2** *poet.* **a** a ring. **b** an amphitheatre or arena. [F f. L CIRCUS]

cirrhosis /sɪ'rəʊsɪs/ *n.* a chronic disease of the liver marked by the degeneration of cells and the thickening of surrounding tissues, as a result of alcoholism, hepatitis, etc. □□ **cirrhotic** /sɪ'rɒtɪk/ *adj.* [mod.L f. Gk *kirrhos* tawny]

cirriped /'sɪrɪˌped/ *n.* (also **cirripede** /'sɪrɪˌpiːd/) any marine crustacean of the class Cirripedia, having a valved shell and usu. sessile when adult, e.g. a barnacle. [mod.L Cirripedia f. L *cirrus* curl (from the form of the legs) + *pes pedis* foot]

cirro- /'sɪrəʊ/ *comb. form* cirrus (cloud).

cirrus /'sɪrəs/ *n.* (*pl.* **cirri** /-raɪ/) **1** *Meteorol.* a form of white wispy cloud, esp. at high altitude. **2** *Bot.* a tendril. **3** *Zool.* a long slender appendage or filament. □□ **cirrose** *adj.* **cirrous** *adj.* [L, = curl]

cis- /sɪs/ *prefix* (opp. TRANS- or ULTRA-). **1** on this side of; on the side nearer to the speaker or writer (*cisatlantic*). **2** *Rom. Antiq.* on the Roman side of (*cisalpine*). **3** (of time) closer to the present (*cis-Elizabethan*). **4** *Chem.* (of an isomer) having two atoms or groups on the same side of a given plane in the molecule. [L *cis* on this side of]

cisalpine /sɪs'ælpaɪn/ *adj.* on the southern side of the Alps.

cisatlantic /ˌsɪsət'læntɪk/ *adj.* on this side of the Atlantic.

cisco /'sɪskəʊ/ *n.* (*pl.* **-oes**) any of various freshwater whitefish of the genus *Coregonus*, native to N. America. [19th c.: orig. unkn.]

cislunar /sɪs'luːnə(r)/ *adj.* between the earth and the moon.

cispontine /sɪs'pɒntaɪn/ *adj.* on the north side of the Thames in London. [CIS- (orig. the better-known side) + L *pons pont-* bridge]

cissy var. of SISSY.

cist[1] /sɪst, kɪst/ *n.* (also **kist** /kɪst/) *Archaeol.* a coffin or burial-chamber made from stone or a hollowed tree. [Welsh, = CHEST]

cist[2] /sɪst/ *n.* Gk *Antiq.* a box used for sacred utensils. [L *cista* f. Gk *kistē* box]

Cistercian /sɪ'stɜːʃ(ə)n/ *n.* & *adj.* —*n.* a monk or nun of an order founded in 1098 as a stricter branch of the Benedictines. —*adj.* of the Cistercians. [F *cistercien* f. L *Cistercium* Cîteaux near Dijon in France, where the order was founded]

cistern /'sɪst(ə)n/ *n.* **1** a tank for storing water, esp. one in a roof-space supplying taps or as part of a flushing lavatory. **2** an underground reservoir for rainwater. [ME f. OF *cisterne* f. L *cisterna* (as CIST[2])]

cistus /'sɪstəs/ *n.* any shrub of the genus *Cistus*, with large white or red flowers. Also called *rock rose*. [mod.L f. Gk *kistos*]

citadel /'sɪtəd(ə)l, -ˌdel/ *n.* **1** a fortress, usu. on high ground protecting or dominating a city. **2** a

meeting-hall of the Salvation Army. [F *citadelle* or It. *citadella*, ult. f. L *civitas -tatis* city]

citation /saɪ'teɪʃ(ə)n/ *n.* **1** the citing of a book or other source; a passage cited. **2** a mention in an official dispatch. **3** a note accompanying an award, describing the reasons for it.

cite /saɪt/ *v.tr.* **1** adduce as an instance. **2** quote (a passage, book, or author) in support of an argument etc. **3** mention in an official dispatch. **4** summon to appear in a lawcourt. □□ **citable** *adj.* [ME f. F f. L *citare* f. *ciēre* set moving]

citified /'sɪtɪˌfaɪd/ *adj.* (also **cityfied**) usu. *derog.* city-like or urban in appearance or behaviour.

citizen /'sɪtɪz(ə)n/ *n.* **1** a member of a State or Commonwealth, either native or naturalized (*British citizen*). **2** (usu. foll. by *of*) **a** an inhabitant of a city. **b** a freeman of a city. **3** *US* a civilian. □**citizen of the world** a person who is at home anywhere; a cosmopolitan. **Citizens' Advice Bureau** (in the UK) an office at which the public can receive free advice and information on civil matters. **citizen's arrest** an arrest by an ordinary person without a warrant, allowable in certain cases. **citizen's band** a system of local intercommunication by individuals on special radio frequencies. □□ **citizenhood** *n.* **citizenry** *n.* **citizenship** *n.* [ME f. AF *citesein*, OF *citeain* ult. f. L *civitas -tatis* city: cf. DENIZEN]

citole /sɪ'təʊl/ *n.* a small cittern. [ME f. OF: rel. to CITTERN with dimin. suffix]

citric /'sɪtrɪk/ *adj.* derived from citrus fruit. □**citric acid** a sharp-tasting water-soluble organic acid found in the juice of lemons and other sour fruits. □□ **citrate** *n.* [F *citrique* f. L *citrus* citron]

citrin /'sɪtrɪn/ *n.* a group of substances occurring mainly in citrus fruits and blackcurrants, and formerly thought to be a vitamin. Also called BIOFLAVONOID.

citrine /'sɪtrɪn/ *adj.* & *n.* —*adj.* lemon-coloured. —*n.* a transparent yellow variety of quartz. Also called *false topaz*. [ME f. OF *citrin* (as CITRUS)]

citron /'sɪtrən/ *n.* **1** a shrubby tree, *Citrus medica*, bearing large lemon-like fruits with thick fragrant peel. **2** this fruit. [F f. L CITRUS, after *limon* lemon]

citronella /ˌsɪtrə'nelə/ *n.* **1** any fragrant grass of the genus *Cymbopogon*, native to S. Asia. **2** the scented oil from these, used in insect repellent, and perfume and soap manufacture. [mod.L, formed as CITRON + dimin. suffix]

citrus /'sɪtrəs/ *n.* **1** any tree of the genus *Citrus*, including citron, lemon, lime, orange, and grapefruit. **2** (in full **citrus fruit**) a fruit from such a tree. □□ **citrous** *adj.* [L, = citron-tree or thuja]

cittern /'sɪt(ə)n/ *n.* *hist.* a wire-stringed lutelike instrument usu. played with a plectrum. [L *cithara*, Gk *kithara* a kind of harp, assim. to GITTERN]

city /'sɪtɪ/ *n.* (*pl.* **-ies**) **1 a** a large town. **b** *Brit.* (strictly) a town created a city by charter and containing a cathedral. **c** *US* a municipal corporation occupying a definite area. **2** (**the City**) **a** the part of London governed by the Lord Mayor and the Corporation. **b** the business part of this. **c** commercial circles; high finance. **3** (*attrib.*) of a city or the City. □**City Company** a corporation descended from an ancient trade-guild. **city desk** a department of a newspaper dealing with business news or *US* with local news. **City editor 1** the editor dealing with financial news in a newspaper or magazine. **2** (**city editor**) *US* the editor dealing with local news. **city father** (usu. in *pl.*) a person concerned with or experienced in the administration of a city. **city hall** *US* municipal offices or officers. **city manager** *US* an official directing the administration of a city. **city page** *Brit.* the part of a newspaper or magazine dealing with the financial and business news. **city slicker** usu. *derog.* **1** a smart and sophisticated city-dweller. **2** a plausible rogue as found in cities. **city-state** esp. *hist.* a city that with its surrounding territory forms an independent state. □□ **cityward**

adj. & *adv.* **citywards** *adv.* [ME f. OF *cité* f. L *civitas -tatis* f. *civis* citizen]

cityfied var. of CITIFIED.

cityscape /ˈsɪtɪˌskeɪp/ *n.* **1** a view of a city (actual or depicted). **2** city scenery.

civet /ˈsɪvɪt/ *n.* **1** (in full **civet-cat**) any catlike animal of the mongoose family, esp. *Civettictis civetta* of Central Africa, having well developed anal scent glands. **2** a strong musky perfume obtained from the secretions of these scent glands. [F *civette* f. It. *zibetto* f. med.L *zibethum* f. Arab. *azzabād* f. *al* the + *zabād* this perfume]

civic /ˈsɪvɪk/ *adj.* **1** of a city; municipal. **2** of or proper to citizens (*civic virtues*). **3** of citizenship, civil. □ **civic centre** *Brit.* the area where municipal offices and other public buildings are situated; the buildings themselves. □□ **civically** *adv.* [F *civique* or L *civicus* f. *civis* citizen]

civics /ˈsɪvɪks/ *n.pl.* (usu. treated as *sing.*) the study of the rights and duties of citizenship.

civil /ˈsɪv(ə)l, -ɪl/ *adj.* **1** of or belonging to citizens. **2** of ordinary citizens and their concerns, as distinct from military or naval or ecclesiastical matters. **3** polite, obliging, not rude. **4** *Law* relating to civil law (see below), not criminal or political matters (*civil court; civil lawyer*). **5** (of the length of a day, year, etc.) fixed by custom or law, not natural or astronomical. □ **civil aviation** non-military, esp. commercial aviation. **civil commotion** a riot or similar disturbance. **civil defence** the organization and training of civilians for the protection of lives and property during and after attacks in wartime. **civil disobedience** the refusal to comply with certain laws or to pay taxes etc. as a peaceful form of political protest. **civil engineer** an engineer who designs or maintains roads, bridges, dams, etc. **civil engineering** this work. **civil law 1** law concerning private rights (opp. *criminal law*). **2** *hist.* Roman or non-ecclesiastical law. **civil libertarian** an advocate of increased civil liberty. **civil liberty** (often in *pl.*) freedom of action and speech subject to the law. **civil list** (in the UK) an annual allowance voted by Parliament for the royal family's household expenses. **civil marriage** a marriage solemnized as a civil contract without religious ceremony. **civil rights** the rights of citizens to political and social freedom and equality. **civil servant** a member of the civil service. **civil service** the permanent professional branches of State administration, excluding military and judicial branches and elected politicians. **civil state** being single or married or divorced etc. **civil war** a war between citizens of the same country. **civil year** see YEAR 2. □□ **civilly** *adv.* [ME f. OF f. L *civilis* f. *civis* citizen]

civilian /sɪˈvɪlɪən/ *n.* & *adj.* —*n.* a person not in the armed services or the police force. —*adj.* of or for civilians.

civilianize /sɪˈvɪlɪəˌnaɪz/ *v.tr.* (also **-ise**) make civilian in character or function. □□ **civilianization** /-ˈzeɪʃ(ə)n/ *n.*

civility /sɪˈvɪlɪtɪ/ *n.* (*pl.* **-ies**) **1** politeness. **2** an act of politeness. [ME f. OF *civilité* f. L *civilitas -tatis* (as CIVIL)]

civilization /ˌsɪvɪlaɪˈzeɪʃ(ə)n, ˌsɪvɪlɪ-/ *n.* (also **-isation**) **1** an advanced stage or system of social development. **2** those peoples of the world regarded as having this. **3** a people or nation (esp. of the past) regarded as an element of social evolution (*ancient civilizations; the Inca civilization*). **4** making or becoming civilized.

civilize /ˈsɪvɪˌlaɪz/ *v.tr.* (also **-ise**) **1** bring out of a barbarous or primitive stage of society. **2** enlighten; refine and educate. □□ **civilizable** *adj.* **civilizer** *n.* [F *civiliser* (as CIVIL)]

civvies /ˈsɪvɪz/ *n.pl. sl.* civilian clothes. [abbr.]

Civvy Street /ˈsɪvɪ/ *n. sl.* civilian life. [abbr.]

CJ *abbr.* Chief Justice.

Cl *symb. Chem.* the element chlorine.

cl *abbr.* **1** centilitre(s). **2** class.

clack /klæk/ *v.* & *n.* —*v.intr.* **1** make a sharp sound as of boards struck together. **2** chatter, esp. loudly. —*n.* **1** a clacking sound. **2** clacking talk. □□ **clacker** *n.* [ME, = to chatter, prob. f. ON *klaka*, of imit. orig.]

clad[1] /klæd/ *adj.* **1** clothed. **2** provided with cladding. [past part. of CLOTHE]

clad[2] /klæd/ *v.tr.* (**cladding**; *past* and *past part.* **cladded** or **clad**) provide with cladding. [app. f. CLAD[1]]

cladding /ˈklædɪŋ/ *n.* a covering or coating on a structure or material etc.

clade /kleɪd/ *n. Biol.* a group of organisms evolved from a common ancestor. [Gk *klados* branch]

cladistics /kləˈdɪstɪks/ *n.pl.* (usu. treated as *sing.*) *Biol.* a method of classification of animals and plants on the basis of shared characteristics, which are assumed to indicate common ancestry. □□ **cladism** /ˈklædɪz(ə)m/ *n.* [as CLADE + -IST + -ICS]

cladode /ˈkleɪdəʊd/ *n.* a flattened leaflike stem. [Gk *kladōdēs* many-shooted f. *klados* shoot]

claim /kleɪm/ *v.* & *n.* —*v.tr.* **1 a** (often foll. by *that* + clause) demand as one's due or property. **b** (usu. *absol.*) submit a request for payment under an insurance policy. **2 a** represent oneself as having or achieving (*claim victory; claim accuracy*). **b** (foll. by *to* + infin.) profess (*claimed to be the owner*). **c** assert, contend (*claim that one knows*). **3** have as an achievement or a consequence (*could then claim five wins; the fire claimed many victims*). **4** (of a thing) deserve (one's attention etc.). —*n.* **1 a** a demand or request for something considered one's due (*lay claim to; put in a claim*). **b** an application for compensation under the terms of an insurance policy. **2** (foll. by *to, on*) a right or title to a thing (*his only claim to fame; have many claims on my time*). **3** a contention or assertion. **4** a thing claimed. **5** a statement of the novel features in a patent. **6** *Mining* a piece of land allotted or taken. □ **no claim** (or **claims**) **bonus** a reduction of an insurance premium after an agreed period without a claim under the terms of the policy. □□ **claimable** *adj.* **claimer** *n.* [ME f. OF *claime* f. *clamer* call out f. L *clamare*]

claimant /ˈkleɪmənt/ *n.* a person making a claim, esp. in a lawsuit or for a State benefit.

clairaudience /kleəˈrɔːdɪəns/ *n.* the supposed faculty of perceiving, as if by hearing, what is inaudible. □□ **clairaudient** *adj.* & *n.* [F *clair* CLEAR, + AUDIENCE, after CLAIRVOYANCE]

clairvoyance /kleəˈvɔɪəns/ *n.* **1** the supposed faculty of perceiving things or events in the future or beyond normal sensual contact. **2** exceptional insight. [F *clairvoyance* f. *clair* CLEAR + *voir voy-* see]

clairvoyant /kleəˈvɔɪənt/ *n.* & *adj.* —*n.* (*fem.* **clairvoyante**) a person having clairvoyance. —*adj.* having clairvoyance. □□ **clairvoyantly** *adv.*

clam /klæm/ *n.* & *v.* —*n.* **1** any bivalve mollusc, esp. the edible N. American hard or round clam (*Mercenaria mercenaria*) or the soft or long clam (*Mya arenaria*). **2** *colloq.* a shy or withdrawn person. —*v.intr.* (**clammed, clamming**) **1** dig for clams. **2** (foll. by *up*) *colloq.* refuse to talk. [16th c.: app. f. *clam* a clamp]

clamant /ˈkleɪmənt/ *adj. literary* noisy; insistent, urgent. □□ **clamantly** *adv.* [L *clamare clamant-* cry out]

clamber /ˈklæmbə(r)/ *v.* & *n.* —*v.intr.* climb with hands and feet, esp. with difficulty or laboriously. —*n.* a difficult climb. [ME, prob. f. *clamb*, obs. past tense of CLIMB]

clammy /ˈklæmɪ/ *adj.* (**clammier, clammiest**) **1** unpleasantly damp and sticky or slimy. **2** (of weather) cold and damp. □□ **clammily** *adv.* **clamminess** *n.* [ME f. *clam* to daub]

clamour /ˈklæmə(r)/ *n.* & *v.* (*US* **clamor**) —*n.* **1** loud or vehement shouting or noise. **2** a protest or complaint; an appeal or demand. —*v.* **1** *intr.* make a clamour. **2** *tr.* utter with a clamour. □□ **clamorous**

æ *cat* ɑː *arm* e *bed* ɜː *her* ɪ *sit* iː *see* ɒ *hot* ɔː *saw* ʌ *run* ʊ *put* uː *too* ə *ago* aɪ *my*

adj. **clamorously** *adv.* **clamorousness** *n.* [ME f. OF f. L *clamor -oris* f. *clamare* cry out]

clamp[1] /klæmp/ *n. & v.* —*n.* **1** a device, esp. a brace or band of iron etc., for strengthening other materials or holding things together. **2** a device for immobilizing an illegally parked car. —*v.tr.* **1** strengthen or fasten with a clamp. **2** place or hold firmly. **3** immobilize (an illegally parked car) by fixing a clamp to one of its wheels. □**clamp down 1** (often foll. by *on*) be rigid in enforcing a rule etc. **2** (foll. by *on*) try to suppress. **clamp-down** *n.* severe restriction or suppression. [ME prob. f. MDu., MLG *klamp(e)*]

clamp[2] /klæmp/ *n.* **1** a heap of potatoes or other root vegetables stored under straw or earth. **2** a pile of bricks for burning. **3** a pile of turf or peat or garden rubbish etc. [16th c.: prob. f. Du. *klamp* heap (in sense 2 related to CLUMP)]

clan /klæn/ *n.* **1** a group of people with a common ancestor, esp. in the Scottish Highlands. **2** a large family as a social group. **3** a group with a strong common interest. **4 a** a genus, species, or class. **b** a family or group of animals, e.g. elephants. [ME f. Gael. *clann* f. L *planta* sprout]

clandestine /klæn'destɪn/ *adj.* surreptitious, secret. □□**clandestinely** *adv.* **clandestinity** /-'tɪnɪtɪ/ *n.* [F *clandestin* or L *clandestinus* f. *clam* secretly]

clang /klæŋ/ *n. & v.* —*n.* a loud resonant metallic sound as of a bell or hammer etc. —*v.* **1** *intr.* make a clang. **2** *tr.* cause to clang. [imit.: infl. by L *clangere* resound]

clanger /'klæŋə(r)/ *n. sl.* a mistake or blunder. □**drop a clanger** commit a conspicuous indiscretion.

clangour /'klæŋgə(r)/ *n.* (*US* **clangor**) **1** a prolonged or repeated clanging noise. **2** an uproar or commotion. □□**clangorous** *adj.* **clangorously** *adv.* [L *clangor* noise of trumpets etc.]

clank /klæŋk/ *n. & v.* —*n.* a sound as of heavy pieces of metal meeting or a chain rattling. —*v.* **1** *intr.* make a clanking sound. **2** *tr.* cause to clank. □□ **clankingly** *adv.* [imit.: cf. CLANG, CLINK[1], Du. *klank*]

clannish /'klænɪʃ/ *adj.* usu. *derog.* **1** (of a family or group) tending to hold together. **2** of or like a clan. □□**clannishly** *adv.* **clannishness** *n.*

clanship /'klænʃɪp/ *n.* **1** a patriarchal system of clans. **2** loyalty to one's clan.

clansman /'klænzmən/ *n.* (*pl.* **-men**; *fem.* **clanswoman**, *pl.* **-women**) a member or fellow-member of a clan.

clap[1] /klæp/ *v. & n.* —*v.* (**clapped, clapping**) **1 a** *intr.* strike the palms of one's hands together as a signal or repeatedly as applause. **b** *tr.* strike (the hands) together in this way. **2** *tr.* applaud or show one's approval of (esp. a person) in this way. **3** *tr.* (of a bird) flap (its wings) audibly. **4** *tr.* put or place quickly or with determination (*clapped him in prison*; *clap a tax on whisky*). —*n.* **1** the act of clapping, esp. as applause. **2** an explosive sound, esp. of thunder. **3** a slap, a pat. □**clap eyes on** *colloq.* see. **clap on the back** = *slap on the back*. **clapped out** *Brit. sl.* worn out (esp. of machinery etc.); exhausted. [OE *clappian* throb, beat, of imit. orig.]

clap[2] /klæp/ *n. coarse sl.* venereal disease, esp. gonorrhoea. [OF *clapoir* venereal bubo]

clapboard /'klæpbɔːd, 'klæbəd/ *n. US* = WEATHER-BOARD. [Anglicized f. LG *klappholt* cask-stave]

clapper /'klæpə(r)/ *n.* the tongue or striker of a bell. □**like the clappers** *Brit. sl.* very fast or hard.

clapperboard /'klæpə,bɔːd/ *n. Cinematog.* a device of hinged boards struck together to synchronize the starting of picture and sound machinery in filming.

claptrap /'klæptræp/ *n.* **1** insincere or pretentious talk, nonsense. **2** language used or feelings expressed only to gain applause. [CLAP[1] + TRAP[1]]

claque /klæk, klɑːk/ *n.* a group of people hired to applaud in a theatre etc. [F f. *claquer* to clap]

claqueur /klæ'kɜː(r), klɑː-/ *n.* a member of a claque. [F (as CLAQUE)]

clarabella /'klærə,belə, 'klɑː-/ *n.* an organ-stop of flute quality. [fem. forms of L *clarus* clear and *bellus* pretty]

clarence /'klærəns/ *n. hist.* a four-wheeled closed carriage with seats for four inside and two on the box. [Duke of *Clarence*, afterwards William IV]

Clarenceux /'klærən,sjuː/ *n. Heraldry* (in the UK) the title given to the second King of Arms, with jurisdiction south of the Trent (cf. NORROY, *King of Arms*). [ME f. AF f. Duke of *Clarence* f. *Clare* in Suffolk]

claret /'klærət/ *n. & adj.* —*n.* **1** red wine, esp. from Bordeaux. **2** a deep purplish-red. **3** *archaic sl.* blood. —*adj.* claret-coloured. [ME f. OF (*vin*) *claret* f. med.L *claratum* (*vinum*) f. L *clarus* clear]

clarify /'klærɪ,faɪ/ *v.* (**-ies, -ied**) **1** *tr. & intr.* make or become clearer. **2** *tr.* **a** free (liquid, butter, etc.) from impurities. **b** make transparent. **c** purify. □□**clarification** /-fɪ'keɪʃ(ə)n/ *n.* **clarificatory** /-fɪ'keɪtərɪ/ *n.* **clarifier** *n.* [ME f. OF *clarifier* f. L *clarus* clear]

clarinet /,klærɪ'net/ *n.* **1 a** a woodwind instrument with a single-reed mouthpiece, a cylindrical tube with a flared end, holes, and keys. **b** its player. **2** an organ-stop with a quality resembling a clarinet. □□ **clarinettist** *n.* (*US* **clarinetist**). [F *clarinette*, dimin. of *clarine* a kind of bell]

clarion /'klærɪən/ *n. & adj.* —*n.* **1** a clear rousing sound. **2** *hist.* a shrill narrow-tubed war trumpet. **3** an organ-stop with the quality of a clarion. —*adj.* clear and loud. [ME f. med.L *clario -onis* f. L *clarus* clear]

clarity /'klærɪtɪ/ *n.* the state or quality of being clear, esp. of sound or expression. [ME f. L *claritas* f. *clarus* clear]

clarkia /'klɑːkɪə/ *n.* any plant of the genus *Clarkia*, with showy white, pink, or purple flowers. [mod.L f. W. *Clark*, US explorer d. 1838]

clary /'kleərɪ/ *n.* (*pl.* **-ies**) any of various aromatic herbs of the genus *Salvia*. [ME f. obs. F *clarie* repr. med.L *sclarea*]

clash /klæʃ/ *n. & v.* —*n.* **1 a** a loud jarring sound as of metal objects being struck together. **b** a collision, esp. with force. **2 a** a conflict or disagreement. **b** a discord of colours etc. —*v.* **1 a** *intr.* make a clashing sound. **b** *tr.* cause to clash. **2** *intr.* collide; coincide awkwardly. **3** *intr.* (often foll. by *with*) **a** come into conflict or be at variance. **b** (of colours) be discordant. □□**clasher** *n.* [imit.: cf. *clack, clang, crack, crash*]

clasp /klɑːsp/ *n. & v.* —*n.* **1 a** a device with interlocking parts for fastening. **b** a buckle or brooch. **c** a metal fastening on a book-cover. **2 a** an embrace; a person's reach. **b** a grasp or handshake. **3** a bar of silver on a medal-ribbon with the name of the battle etc. at which the wearer was present. —*v.* **1** *tr.* fasten with or as with a clasp. **2** *tr.* grasp, hold closely. **b** embrace, encircle. **3** *intr.* fasten a clasp. □**clasp hands** shake hands with fervour or affection. **clasp one's hands** interlace one's fingers. **clasp-knife** a folding knife, usu. with a catch holding the blade when open. □□ **clasper** *n.* [ME: orig. unkn.]

clasper /'klɑːspə(r)/ *n.* (in *pl.*) the appendages of some male fish and insects used to hold the female in copulation.

class /klɑːs/ *n. & v.* —*n.* **1** any set of persons or things grouped together, or graded or differentiated from others esp. by quality (*first class*; *economy class*). **2 a** a division or order of society (*upper class*; *professional classes*). **b** a caste system, a system of social classes. **c** (**the classes**) *archaic* the rich or educated. **3** *colloq.* distinction or high quality in appearance, behaviour, etc.; stylishness. **4 a** a group of students or pupils taught together. **b** the occasion when they meet. **c** their course of instruction. **5** *US* all the college or school students of the same standing or graduating in a given year (*the class of 1990*). **6** (in conscripted armies) all the recruits of a given year (*the 1950 class*). **7** *Brit.* a division of candidates according to merit in an examination. **8** *Biol.* a grouping of organisms, the next major rank below a division or phylum. —*v.tr.* assign to a class or category. □**class-conscious** aware of and reacting to social divisions or one's place in a system of social class. **class-consciousness** this awareness. **class-list** *Brit.* a list of candidates in an examination with the class achieved by each. **class war** conflict between social classes. **in a class of** (or **on**) **its** (or **one's**) **own** unequalled. **no class** *colloq.* lacking quality or distinction. [L *classis* assembly]

classic /'klæsɪk/ *adj.* & *n.* —*adj.* **1 a** of the first class; of acknowledged excellence. **b** remarkably typical; outstandingly important (*a classic case*). **2 a** of ancient Greek and Latin literature, art, or culture. **b** (of style in art, music, etc.) simple, harmonious, well-proportioned; in accordance with established forms (cf. ROMANTIC). **3** having literary or historic associations (*classic ground*). **4** (of clothes) made in a simple elegant style not much affected by changes in fashion. —*n.* **1** a classic writer, artist, work, or example. **2 a** an ancient Greek or Latin writer. **b** (in *pl.*) the study of ancient Greek and Latin literature and history. **c** *archaic* a scholar of ancient Greek and Latin. **3** a follower of classic models (cf. ROMANTIC). **4** a garment in classic style. **5** (in *pl.*) *Brit.* the classic races. □**classic races** *Brit.* the five main flat races, namely the Two Thousand and the One Thousand Guineas, the Derby, the Oaks, and the St Leger. [F *classique* or L *classicus* f. *classis* class]

classical /'klæsɪk(ə)l/ *adj.* **1 a** of ancient Greek or Latin literature or art. **b** (of language) having the form used by the ancient standard authors (*classical Latin; classical Hebrew*). **c** based on the study of ancient Greek and Latin (*a classical education*). **d** learned in classical studies. **2 a** (of music) serious or conventional; following traditional principles and intended to be of permanent rather than ephemeral value (cf. POPULAR, LIGHT). **b** of the period from *c.*1750–1800 (cf. ROMANTIC). **3 a** in or following the restrained style of classical antiquity (cf. ROMANTIC). **b** in or relating to a long-established style. **4** *Physics* relating to the concepts which preceded relativity and quantum theory. □□**classicalism** *n.* **classicalist** *n.* **classicality** /-'kælɪtɪ/ *n.* **classically** *adv.* [L *classicus* (as CLASSIC)]

classicism /'klæsɪsɪz(ə)m/ *n.* **1** the following of a classic style. **2 a** classical scholarship. **b** the advocacy of a classical education. **3** an ancient Greek or Latin idiom. □□**classicist** *n.*

classicize /'klæsɪsaɪz/ *v.* (also **-ise**) **1** *tr.* make classic. **2** *intr.* imitate a classical style.

classified /'klæsɪfaɪd/ *adj.* **1** arranged in classes or categories. **2** (of information etc.) designated as officially secret. **3** *Brit.* (of a road) assigned to a category according to its importance. **4** *Brit.* (of newspaper advertisements) arranged in columns according to various categories.

classify /'klæsɪfaɪ/ *v.tr.* (**-ies**, **-ied**) **1 a** arrange in classes or categories. **b** assign (a thing) to a class or category. **2** designate as officially secret or not for general disclosure. □□**classifiable** *adj.* **classification** /-fɪ'keɪʃ(ə)n/ *n.* **classificatory** /-'keɪtərɪ/ *adj.* **classifier** *n.* [back-form. f. *classification* f. F (as CLASS)]

classless /'klɑːslɪs/ *adj.* making or showing no distinction of classes (*classless society; classless accent*). □□**classlessness** *n.*

classmate /'klɑːsmeɪt/ *n.* a fellow-member of a class, esp. at school.

classroom /'klɑːsruːm, -rʊm/ *n.* a room in which a class of students is taught, esp. in a school.

classy /'klɑːsɪ/ *adj.* (**classier**, **classiest**) *colloq.* superior, stylish. □□**classily** *adv.* **classiness** *n.*

clastic /'klæstɪk/ *adj.* *Geol.* composed of broken pieces of older rocks. □**clastic rocks** conglomerates, sandstones, etc. [F *clastique* f. Gk *klastos* broken in pieces]

clathrate /'klæθreɪt/ *n.* *Chem.* a solid in which one component is enclosed in the structure of another. [L *clathratus* f. *clathri* lattice-bars f. Gk *klēthra*]

clatter /'klætə(r)/ *n.* & *v.* —*n.* **1** a rattling sound as of many hard objects struck together. **2** noisy talk. —*v.* **1** *intr.* make a clatter. **b** fall or move etc. with a clatter. **2** *tr.* cause (plates etc.) to clatter. [OE, of imit. orig.]

claudication /,klɔːdɪ'keɪʃ(ə)n/ *n.* *Med.* a cramping pain, esp. in the leg, caused by arterial obstruction; limping. [L *claudicare* limp f. *claudus* lame]

clause /klɔːz/ *n.* **1** *Gram.* a distinct part of a sentence, including a subject and predicate. **2** a single statement in a treaty, law, bill, or contract. □□**clausal** *adj.* [ME f. OF f. L *clausula* conclusion f. *claudere claus-* shut]

claustral /'klɔːstr(ə)l/ *adj.* **1** of or associated with the cloister; monastic. **2** narrow-minded. [ME f. LL *claustralis* f. *claustrum* CLOISTER]

claustrophobia /,klɔːstrə'fəʊbɪə/ *n.* an abnormal fear of confined places. □□**claustrophobe** /'klɔːstrəfəʊb/ *n.* [mod.L f. L *claustrum*: see CLOISTER]

claustrophobic /,klɔːstrə'fəʊbɪk/ *adj.* **1** suffering from claustrophobia. **2** inducing claustrophobia. □□**claustrophobically** *adv.*

clavate /'kleɪveɪt/ *adj.* *Bot.* club-shaped. [mod.L *clavatus* f. L *clava* club]

clave[1] /kleɪv, klɑːv/ *n.* *Mus.* a hardwood stick used in pairs to make a hollow sound when struck together. [Amer. Sp. f. Sp., = keystone, f. L *clavis* key]

clave[2] *past* of CLEAVE[2].

clavicembalo /,klævɪ'tʃembə,ləʊ/ *n.* (*pl.* **-os**) a harpsichord. [It.]

clavichord /'klævɪkɔːd/ *n.* a small keyboard instrument with a very soft tone. [ME f. med.L *clavichordium* f. L *clavis* key, *chorda* string: see CHORD[2]]

clavicle /'klævɪk(ə)l/ *n.* the collar-bone. □□**clavicular** /klə'vɪkjʊlə(r)/ *adj.* [L *clavicula* dimin. of *clavis* key (from its shape)]

clavier /klə'vɪə(r), 'klævɪə(r)/ *n.* *Mus.* **1** any keyboard instrument. **2** its keyboard. [F *clavier* or G *Klavier* f. med.L *claviarius*, orig. = key-bearer, f. L *clavis* key]

claviform /'klævɪfɔːm/ *adj.* club-shaped. [L *clava* club]

claw /klɔː/ *n.* & *v.* —*n.* **1 a** a pointed horny nail on an animal's or bird's foot. **b** a foot armed with claws. **2** the pincers of a shellfish. **3** a device for grappling, holding, etc. —*v.* **1** *tr.* & *intr.* scratch, maul, or pull (a person or thing) with claws. **2** *tr.* & *intr.* *Sc.* scratch gently. **3** *intr.* *Naut.* beat to windward. □**claw back 1** regain laboriously or gradually. **2** recover (money paid out) from another source (e.g. taxation). **claw-back** *n.* **1** the act of clawing back. **2** money recovered in this way. **claw-hammer** a hammer with one side of the head forked for extracting nails. □□**clawed** *adj.* (also in *comb.*). **clawer** *n.* **clawless** *adj.* [OE *clawu, clawian*]

clay /kleɪ/ *n.* **1** a stiff sticky earth, used for making bricks, pottery, ceramics, etc. **2** *poet.* the substance of the human body. **3** (in full **clay pipe**) a tobacco-pipe made of clay. □**clay-pan** *Austral.* a natural hollow in clay soil, retaining water after rain. **clay pigeon** a breakable disc thrown up from a trap as a target for shooting. □□**clayey** *adj.* **clayish** *adj.* **claylike** *adj.* [OE *clæg* f. WG]

claymore /'kleɪmɔː(r)/ *n.* **1** *hist.* **a** a Scottish two-edged broadsword. **b** a broadsword, often with a single edge, having a hilt with a basketwork design. **2** *US* a type of anti-personnel mine. [Gael. *claidheamh mór* great sword]

-cle /k(ə)l/ *suffix* forming (orig. diminutive) nouns (*article; particle*). [as -CULE]

clean /kliːn/ *adj., adv., v.,* & *n.* —*adj.* **1** (often foll. by *of*) free from dirt or contaminating matter, unsoiled. **2** clear; unused or unpolluted; preserving what is regarded as the original state (*clean air; clean page*). **3** free from obscenity or indecency. **4 a**

attentive to personal hygiene and cleanliness. **b** (of children and animals) toilet-trained or house-trained. **5** complete, clear-cut, unobstructed, even. **6 a** (of a ship, aircraft, or car) streamlined, smooth. **b** well-formed, slender and shapely (*clean-limbed*; *the car has clean lines*). **7** adroit, skilful (*clean fielding*). **8** (of a nuclear weapon) producing relatively little fallout. **9 a** free from ceremonial defilement or from disease. **b** (of food) not prohibited. **10 a** free from any record of a crime, offence, etc. (*a clean driving-licence*). **b** *sl.* free from suspicion; not carrying incriminating material. **11** (of a taste, smell, etc.) sharp, fresh, distinctive. **12** (of timber) free from knots. —*adv.* **1** completely, outright, simply (*clean bowled*; *cut clean through*; *clean forgot*). **2** in a clean manner. —*v.* **1** *tr.* (also foll. by *of*) *&* *intr.* make or become clean. **2** *tr.* eat all the food on (one's plate). **3** *tr. Cookery* remove the innards of (fish or fowl). **4** *intr.* make oneself clean. —*n.* the act or process of cleaning or being cleaned (*give it a clean*). □**clean bill of health** see BILL[1]. **clean break** a quick and final separation. **clean-cut** sharply outlined. **clean down** clean by brushing or wiping. **clean hands** freedom from guilt. **clean-living** of upright character. **clean out 1** clean thoroughly. **2** *sl.* empty or deprive (esp. of money). **clean-shaven** without beard, whiskers, moustache. **clean sheet** (or **slate**) freedom from commitments or imputations; the removal of these from one's record. **clean up 1 a** clear (a mess) away. **b** (also *absol.*) put (things) tidy. **c** make (oneself) clean. **2** restore order or morality to. **3** *sl.* **a** acquire as gain or profit. **b** make a gain or profit. **clean-up** *n.* an act of cleaning up. **come clean** *colloq.* own up; confess everything. **make a clean breast of** see BREAST. **make a clean job of** *colloq.* do thoroughly. **make a clean sweep of** see SWEEP. □□ **cleanable** *adj.* **cleanish** *adj.* **cleanness** *n.* [OE *clǣne* (adj. & adv.), *clēne* (adv.), f. WG]

cleaner /ˈkliːnə(r)/ *n.* **1** a person employed to clean the interior of a building. **2** (usu. in *pl.*) a commercial establishment for cleaning clothes. **3** a device or substance for cleaning. □**take to the cleaners** *sl.* **1** defraud or rob (a person) of all his or her money. **2** criticize severely.

cleanly[1] /ˈkliːnlɪ/ *adv.* **1** in a clean way. **2** efficiently; without difficulty. [OE *clǣnlīce*: see CLEAN, -LY[2]]

cleanly[2] /ˈklenlɪ/ *adj.* (**cleanlier, cleanliest**) habitually clean; with clean habits. □□ **cleanlily** *adv.* **cleanliness** *n.* [OE *clǣnlic*: see CLEAN, -LY[1]]

cleanse /klenz/ *v.tr.* **1** usu. *formal.* make clean. **2** (often foll. by *of*) purify from sin or guilt. **3** *archaic* cure (a leper etc.). □**cleansing cream** cream for removing unwanted matter from the face, hands, etc. **cleansing department** *Brit.* a local service of refuse collection etc. □□ **cleanser** *n.* [OE *clǣnsian* (see CLEAN)]

cleanskin /ˈkliːnskɪn/ *n. Austral.* **1** an unbranded animal. **2** *sl.* a person free from blame, without a police record, etc.

clear /klɪə(r)/ *adj., adv., & v.* —*adj.* **1** free from dirt or contamination. **2** (of weather, the sky, etc.) not dull or cloudy. **3** transparent. **b** lustrous, shining; free from obscurity. **4** (of soup) not containing solid ingredients. **5** (of a fire) burning with little smoke. **6 a** distinct, easily perceived by the senses. **b** unambiguous, easily understood (*make a thing clear*; *make oneself clear*). **c** manifest; not confused or doubtful (*clear evidence*). **7** that discerns or is able to discern readily and accurately (*clear thinking*; *clear-sighted*). **8** (usu. foll. by *about, on,* or *that* + clause) confident, convinced, certain. **9** (of a conscience) free from guilt. **10** (of a road etc.) unobstructed, open. **11 a** net, without deduction (*a clear £1000*). **b** complete (*three clear days*). **12** (often foll. by *of*) free, unhampered; unencumbered by debt, commitments, etc. **13** (foll. by *of*) not obstructed by. —*adv.* **1** clearly (*speak loud and clear*). **2** completely (*he got clear away*). **3** apart, out of contact (*keep*

clear; *stand clear of the doors*). **4** (foll. by *to*) *US* all the way. —*v.* **1** *tr. & intr.* make or become clear. **2 a** *tr.* (often foll. by *of*) free from prohibition or obstruction. **b** *tr. & intr.* make or become empty or unobstructed. **c** *tr.* free (land) for cultivation or building by cutting down trees etc. **d** *tr.* cause people to leave (a room etc.). **3** *tr.* (often foll. by *of*) show or declare (a person) to be innocent (*cleared them of complicity*). **4** *tr.* approve (a person) for special duty, access to information, etc. **5** *tr.* pass over or by safely or without touching, esp. by jumping. **6** *tr.* make (an amount of money) as a net gain or to balance expenses. **7** *tr.* pass (a cheque) through a clearing-house. **8** *tr.* pass through (a customs office etc.). **9** *tr.* remove (an obstruction, an unwanted object, etc.) (*clear them out of the way*). **10** *tr.* (also *absol.*) *Football* send (the ball) out of one's defensive zone. **11** *intr.* (often foll. by *away, up*) (of physical phenomena) disappear, gradually diminish (*mist cleared by lunch-time*; *my cold has cleared up*). **12** *tr.* (often foll. by *off*) discharge (a debt). □**clear the air 1** make the air less sultry. **2** disperse an atmosphere of suspicion, tension, etc. **clear away 1** remove completely. **2** remove the remains of a meal from the table. **clear-cut** sharply defined. **clear the decks** prepare for action, esp. fighting. **clear off 1** get rid of. **2** *colloq.* go away. **clear out 1** empty. **2** remove. **3** *colloq.* go away. **clear one's throat** cough slightly to make one's voice clear. **clear up 1** tidy up. **2** solve (a mystery etc.). **3** (of weather) become fine. **clear the way 1** remove obstacles. **2** stand aside. **clear a thing with** get approval or authorization for a thing from (a person). **in clear** not in cipher or code. **in the clear** free from suspicion or difficulty. **out of a clear sky** as a complete surprise. □□ **clearable** *adj.* **clearer** *n.* **clearly** *adv.* **clearness** *n.* [ME f. OF *cler* f. L *clarus*]

clearance /ˈklɪərəns/ *n.* **1** the removal of obstructions etc., esp. removal of buildings, persons, etc., so as to clear land. **2** clear space allowed for the passing of two objects or two parts in machinery etc. **3** special authorization or permission (esp. for an aircraft to take off or land, or for access to information etc.). **4 a** the clearing of a person, ship, etc., by customs. **b** a certificate showing this. **5** the clearing of cheques. **6** *Football* a kick sending the ball out of a defensive zone. **7** making clear. □**clearance order** an order for the demolition of buildings. **clearance sale** *Brit.* a sale to get rid of superfluous stock.

clearcole /ˈklɪəkəʊl/ *n. & v.* —*n.* a mixture of size and whiting or white lead, used as a primer for distemper. —*v.tr.* paint with clearcole. [F *claire colle* clear glue]

clearing /ˈklɪərɪŋ/ *n.* **1** in senses of CLEAR *v.* **2** an area in a forest cleared for cultivation. □**clearing bank** *Brit.* a bank which is a member of a clearing-house. **clearing-house 1** a bankers' establishment where cheques and bills from member banks are exchanged, so that only the balances need be paid in cash. **2** an agency for collecting and distributing information etc.

clearstory *US* var. of CLERESTORY.

clearway /ˈklɪəweɪ/ *n. Brit.* a main road (other than a motorway) on which vehicles are not normally permitted to stop.

cleat /kliːt/ *n.* **1** a piece of metal, wood, etc., bolted on for fastening ropes to, or to strengthen woodwork etc. **2** a projecting piece on a spar, gangway, boot, etc., to give footing or prevent a rope from slipping. **3** a wedge. [OE: cf. CLOT]

cleavage /ˈkliːvɪdʒ/ *n.* **1** the hollow between a woman's breasts, esp. as exposed by a low-cut garment. **2** a division or splitting. **3** the splitting of rocks, crystals, etc., in a preferred direction.

cleave[1] /kliːv/ *v.* (*past* **clove** /kləʊv/ or **cleft** /kleft/ or **cleaved**; *past part.* **cloven** /ˈkləʊv(ə)n/ or **cleft** or **cleaved**) *literary* **1 a** *tr.* chop or break apart, split, esp. along the grain or the line of cleavage. **b** *intr.* come apart in this way. **2** *tr.* make one's way through (air or water). □□ **cleavable** *adj.* [OE *clēofan* f. Gmc]

cleave² /kli:v/ *v.intr.* (*past* **cleaved** or **clave** /kleɪv/) (foll. by *to*) *literary* stick fast; adhere. [OE *cleofian*, *clifian* f. WG: cf. CLAY]

cleaver /ˈkli:və(r)/ *n.* **1** a tool for cleaving, esp. a heavy chopping tool used by butchers. **2** a person who cleaves.

cleavers /ˈkli:vəz/ *n.* (also **clivers** /ˈklɪvəz/) (treated as *sing.* or *pl.*) a plant, *Galium aparine*, having hooked bristles on its stem that catch on clothes etc. Also called GOOSEGRASS. [OE *clife*, formed as CLEAVER²]

clef /klef/ *n.* *Mus.* any of several symbols placed at the beginning of a staff, indicating the pitch of the notes written on it. [F f. L *clavis* key]

cleft¹ /kleft/ *adj.* split, partly divided. □ **cleft palate** a congenital split in the roof of the mouth. **in a cleft stick** in a difficult position, esp. one allowing neither retreat nor advance. [past part. of CLEAVE¹]

cleft² /kleft/ *n.* a split or fissure; a space or division made by cleaving. [OE (rel. to CLEAVE¹): assim. to CLEFT¹]

cleg /kleg/ *n.* *Brit.* a horsefly. [ON *kleggi*]

cleistogamic /ˌklaɪstəˈgæmɪk/ *adj.* *Bot.* (of a flower) permanently closed and self-fertilizing. [Gk *kleistos* closed + *gamos* marriage]

clematis /ˈklemətɪs, kləˈmeɪtɪs/ *n.* any erect or climbing plant of the genus *Clematis*, bearing white, pink, or purple flowers and feathery seeds, e.g. old man's beard. [L f. Gk *klēmatis* f. *klēma* vine branch]

clement /ˈklemənt/ *adj.* **1** mild (*clement weather*). **2** merciful. □□ **clemency** *n.* [ME f. L *clemens -entis*]

clementine /ˈklemən.ti:n, -.taɪn/ *n.* a small citrus fruit, thought to be a hybrid between a tangerine and sweet orange. [F *clémentine*]

clench /klentʃ/ *v.* & *n.* —*v.tr.* **1** close (the teeth or fingers) tightly. **2** grasp firmly. **3** = CLINCH *v.* 4. —*n.* **1** a clenching action. **2** a clenched state. [OE f. Gmc: cf. CLING]

clepsydra /ˈklepsɪdrə, -ˈsɪdrə/ *n.* an ancient time-measuring device worked by a flow of water. [L f. Gk *klepsudra* f. *kleptō* steal + *hudōr* water]

clerestory /ˈklɪəstərɪ, -ˌstɔ:rɪ/ *n.* (*US* **clearstory**) (*pl.* -ies) **1** an upper row of windows in a cathedral or large church, above the level of the aisle roofs. **2** *US* a raised section of the roof of a railway carriage, with windows or ventilators. [ME f. CLEAR + STOREY]

clergy /ˈklɜ:dʒɪ/ *n.* (*pl.* -ies) (usu. treated as *pl.*) **1** (usu. prec. by *the*) the body of all persons ordained for religious duties in the Christian churches. **2** a number of such persons (*ten clergy were present*). [ME, partly f. OF *clergé* f. eccl.L *clericatus*, partly f. OF *clergie* f. *clerc* CLERK]

clergyman /ˈklɜ:dʒɪmən/ *n.* (*pl.* -men) a member of the clergy, esp. of the Church of England.

cleric /ˈklerɪk/ *n.* a member of the clergy. [(orig. adj.) f. eccl.L f. Gk *klērikos* f. *klēros* lot, heritage, as in Acts 1:17]

clerical /ˈklerɪk(ə)l/ *adj.* **1** of the clergy or clergymen. **2** of or done by a clerk or clerks. □ **clerical collar** a stiff upright white collar fastening at the back, as worn by the clergy in some Churches. **clerical error** an error made in copying or writing out. □□ **clericalism** *n.* **clericalist** *n.* **clerically** *adv.* [eccl.L *clericalis* (as CLERIC)]

clerihew /ˈklerɪ.hju:/ *n.* a short comic or nonsensical verse, usu. in two rhyming couplets with lines of unequal length and referring to a famous person. [E. *Clerihew* Bentley, Engl. writer d. 1956, its inventor]

clerk /klɑ:k/ *n.* & *v.* —*n.* **1** a person employed in an office, bank, shop, etc., to keep records, accounts, etc. **2** a secretary, agent, or record-keeper of a local council (*town clerk*), court, etc. **3** a lay officer of a church (*parish clerk*), college chapel, etc. **4** a senior official in Parliament. **5** *US* an assistant in a shop or hotel. **6** *archaic* a clergyman. —*v.intr.* work as a clerk. □ **clerk in holy orders** *formal* a clergyman.

clerk of the course the judges' secretary etc. in horse or motor racing. **clerk of the works** (or **of works**) an overseer of building works etc. □□ **clerkdom** *n.* **clerkess** *n.* *Sc.* **clerkish** *adj.* **clerkly** *adj.* **clerkship** *n.* [OE *cleric*, *clerc*, & OF *clerc*, f. eccl.L *clericus* CLERIC]

clever /ˈklevə(r)/ *adj.* (**cleverer**, **cleverest**) **1** skilful, talented; quick to understand and learn. **2** adroit, dextrous. **3** (of the doer or the thing done) ingenious, cunning. □ **clever Dick** (or **clogs** etc.) *colloq.* a person who is or purports to be smart or knowing. **not too clever** *Austral. colloq.* unwell, indisposed. □□ **cleverly** *adv.* **cleverness** *n.* [ME, = adroit: perh. rel. to CLEAVE², with sense 'apt to seize']

clevis /ˈklevɪs/ *n.* **1** a U-shaped piece of metal at the end of a beam for attaching tackle etc. **2** a connection in which a bolt holds one part that fits between the forked ends of another. [16th c.: rel. to CLEAVE¹]

clew /klu:/ *n.* & *v.* —*n.* **1** *Naut.* **a** a lower or after corner of a sail. **b** a set of small cords suspending a hammock. **2** *archaic* **a** a ball of thread or yarn, esp. with reference to the legend of Theseus and the labyrinth. **b** = CLUE. —*v.tr.* *Naut.* **1** (foll. by *up*) draw the lower ends of (a sail) to the upper yard or the mast ready for furling. **2** (foll. by *down*) let down (a sail) by the clews in unfurling. [OE *cliwen*, *cleowen*]

clianthus /klɪˈænθəs/ *n.* any leguminous plant of the genus *Clianthus*, native to Australia and New Zealand, bearing drooping clusters of red pealike flowers. [mod.L, app. f. Gk *klei-*, *kleos* glory + *anthos* flower]

cliché /ˈkli:ʃeɪ/ *n.* **1** a hackneyed phrase or opinion. **2** *Brit.* a metal casting of a stereotype or electrotype. [F f. *clicher* to stereotype]

clichéd /ˈkli:ʃeɪd/ *adj.* (also **cliché'd**) hackneyed; full of clichés.

click /klɪk/ *n.* & *v.* —*n.* **1** a slight sharp sound as of a switch being operated. **2** a sharp non-vocal suction, used as a speech-sound in some languages. **3** a catch in machinery acting with a slight sharp sound. **4** (of a horse) an action causing a hind foot to touch the shoe of a fore foot. —*v.* **1 a** *intr.* make a click. **b** *tr.* cause (one's tongue, heels, etc.) to click. **2** *intr. colloq.* **a** become clear or understandable (often prec. by *it* as subject: *when I saw them it all clicked*). **b** be successful, secure one's object. **c** (foll. by *with*) become friendly, esp. with a person of the opposite sex. **d** come to an agreement. □ **click beetle** any of a family of beetles (Elateridae) that make a click in recovering from being overturned. □□ **clicker** *n.* [imit.: cf. Du. *klikken*, F *cliquer*]

client /ˈklaɪənt/ *n.* **1** a person using the services of a lawyer, architect, social worker, or other professional person. **2** a customer. **3** *Rom.Hist.* a plebeian under the protection of a patrician. **4** *archaic* a dependant or hanger-on. □□ **clientship** *n.* [ME f. L *cliens -entis* f. *cluere* hear, obey]

clientele /ˌkli:ɒnˈtel/ *n.* **1** clients collectively. **2** customers, esp. of a shop. **3** the patrons of a theatre etc. [L *clientela* clientship & F *clientèle*]

cliff /klɪf/ *n.* a steep rock-face, esp. at the edge of the sea. □ **cliff-hanger** a story etc. with a strong element of suspense; a suspenseful ending to an episode of a serial. **cliff-hanging** full of suspense. □□ **clifflike** *adj.* **cliffy** *adj.* [OE *clif* f. Gmc]

climacteric /klaɪˈmæktərɪk, ˌklaɪmækˈterɪk/ *n.* & *adj.* —*n.* **1** *Med.* the period of life when fertility and sexual activity are in decline. **2** a supposed critical period in life (esp. occurring at intervals of seven years). —*adj.* **1** *Med.* occurring at the climacteric. **2** constituting a crisis; critical. [F *climatérique* or L *climactericus* f. Gk *klimaktērikos* f. *klimaktēr* critical period f. *klimax -akos* ladder]

climactic /klaɪˈmæktɪk/ *adj.* of or forming a climax. □□ **climactically** *adv.* [CLIMAX + -IC, perh. after SYNTACTIC or CLIMACTERIC]

climate /ˈklaɪmɪt/ *n.* **1** the prevailing weather conditions of an area. **2** a region with particular weather conditions. **3** the prevailing trend of opinion or public feeling. □□ **climatic** /-'mætɪk/ *adj.* **climatical** /-'mætɪk(ə)l/ *adj.* **climatically** /-'mætɪkəlɪ/ *adv.* [ME f. OF *climat* or LL *clima climat-* f. Gk *klima* f. *klinō* slope]

climatology /ˌklaɪmə'tɒlədʒɪ/ *n.* the scientific study of climate. □□ **climatological** /-tə'lɒdʒɪk(ə)l/ *adj.* **climatologist** *n.*

climax /'klaɪmæks/ *n. & v.* —*n.* **1** the event or point of greatest intensity or interest; a culmination or apex. **2** a sexual orgasm. **3** *Rhet.* **a** a series arranged in order of increasing importance etc. **b** the last term in such a series. **4** *Ecol.* a state of equilibrium reached by a plant community. —*v.tr. & intr. colloq.* bring or come to a climax. [LL f. Gk *klimax -akos* ladder, climax]

climb /klaɪm/ *v. & n.* —*v.* **1** *tr. & intr.* (often foll. by *up*) ascend, mount, go or come up, esp. by using one's hands. **2** *intr.* (of a plant) grow up a wall, tree, trellis, etc. by clinging with tendrils or by twining. **3** *intr.* make progress from one's own efforts, esp. in social rank, intellectual or moral strength, etc. **4** *intr.* (of an aircraft, the sun, etc.) go upwards. **5** *intr.* slope upwards. —*n.* **1** an ascent by climbing. **2 a** a place, esp. a hill, climbed or to be climbed. **b** a recognized route up a mountain etc. □ **climb down 1** descend with the help of one's hands. **2** withdraw from a stance taken up in argument, negotiation, etc. **climb-down** *n.* such a withdrawal. **climbing-frame** a structure of joined bars etc. for children to climb on. **climbing-iron** a set of spikes attachable to a boot for climbing trees or ice slopes. □□ **climbable** *adj.* [OE *climban* f. WG, rel. to CLEAVE²]

climber /'klaɪmə(r)/ *n.* **1** a mountaineer. **2** a climbing plant. **3** a person with strong social etc. aspirations.

clime /klaɪm/ *n. literary* **1** a region. **2** a climate. [LL *clima*: see CLIMATE]

clinch /klɪntʃ/ *v. & n.* —*v.* **1** *tr.* confirm or settle (an argument, bargain, etc.) conclusively. **2** *intr. Boxing & Wrestling* (of participants) become too closely engaged. **3** *intr. colloq.* embrace. **4** *tr.* secure (a nail or rivet) by driving the point sideways when through. **5** *tr. Naut.* fasten (a rope) with a particular half hitch. —*n.* **1 a** a clinching action. **b** a clinched state. **2** *colloq.* an (esp. amorous) embrace. **3** *Boxing & Wrestling* an action or state in which participants become too closely engaged. [16th-c. var. of CLENCH]

clincher /'klɪntʃ(ə)r/ *n. colloq.* a remark or argument that settles a matter conclusively.

clincher-built var. of CLINKER-BUILT.

cline /klaɪn/ *n. Biol.* the graded sequence of differences within a species etc. □□ **clinal** *adj.* [Gk *klinō* to slope]

cling /klɪŋ/ *v. & n.* —*v.intr.* (*past* and *past part.* **clung** /klʌŋ/) **1** (foll. by *to*) adhere, stick, or hold on (by means of stickiness, suction, grasping, or embracing). **2** (foll. by *to*) remain persistently or stubbornly faithful (to a friend, habit, idea, etc.). **3** maintain one's grasp; keep hold; resist separation. —*n.* = CLINGSTONE. □ **cling film** a very thin clinging transparent plastic film, used as a covering esp. for food. **cling together** remain in one body or in contact. □□ **clinger** *n.* **clingingly** *adv.* [OE *clingan* f. Gmc: cf. CLENCH]

clingstone /'klɪŋstəʊn/ *n.* a variety of peach or nectarine in which the flesh adheres to the stone (cf. FREESTONE).

clingy /'klɪŋɪ/ *adj.* (**clingier**, **clingiest**) liable to cling. □□ **clinginess** *n.*

clinic /'klɪnɪk/ *n.* **1** *Brit.* a private or specialized hospital. **2** a place or occasion for giving specialist medical treatment or advice (*eye clinic*; *fertility clinic*). **3** a gathering at a hospital bedside for the teaching of medicine or surgery. **4** *US* a conference or short course on a particular subject (*golf clinic*). □□ **clinician** /klɪ'nɪʃ(ə)n/ *n.* [F *clinique* f. Gk *klinikē* (*tekhnē*) clinical, lit. bedside (art)]

clinical /'klɪnɪk(ə)l/ *adj.* **1** *Med.* **a** of or for the

treatment of patients. **b** taught or learnt at the hospital bedside. **2** dispassionate, coldly detached. □ **clinical death** death judged by observation of a person's condition. **clinical medicine** medicine dealing with the observation and treatment of patients. **clinical thermometer** a thermometer with a small range, for taking a person's temperature. □□ **clinically** *adv.* [L *clinicus* f. Gk *klinikos* f. *klinē* bed]

clink¹ /klɪŋk/ *n. & v.* —*n.* a sharp ringing sound. —*v.* **1** *intr.* make a clink. **2** *tr.* cause (glasses etc.) to clink. [ME, prob. f. MDu. *klinken*; cf. CLANG, CLANK]

clink² /klɪŋk/ *n.* (often prec. by *in*) *sl.* prison. [16th c.: orig. unkn.]

clinker¹ /'klɪŋkə(r)/ *n.* **1** a mass of slag or lava. **2** a stony residue from burnt coal. [earlier *clincard* etc. f. obs. Du. *klinkaerd* f. *klinken* CLINK¹]

clinker² /'klɪŋkə(r)/ *n.* **1** *Brit. sl.* something excellent or outstanding. **2** *US sl.* a mistake or blunder. [CLINK¹ + -ER¹]

clinker-built /'klɪŋkəˌbɪlt/ *adj.* (also **clincher-built** /'klɪntʃəˌbɪlt/) (of a boat) having external planks overlapping downwards and secured with clinched copper nails. [*clink* N.Engl. var. of CLINCH + -ER¹]

clinkstone /'klɪŋkstəʊn/ *n.* a kind of feldspar that rings like iron when struck.

clinometer /klaɪ'nɒmɪtə(r)/ *n. Surveying* an instrument for measuring slopes. [Gk *klinō* to slope + -METER]

cliometrics /ˌklaɪə'metrɪks/ *n.pl.* (usu. treated as *sing.*) a method of historical research making much use of statistical information and methods. [*Clio*, Muse of history + METRIC + -ICS]

clip¹ /klɪp/ *n. & v.* —*n.* **1** a device for holding things together or for attachment to an object as a marker, esp. a paper-clip or a device worked by a spring. **2** a piece of jewellery fastened by a clip. **3** a set of attached cartridges for a firearm. —*v.tr.* (**clipped**, **clipping**) **1** fix with a clip. **2** grip tightly. **3** surround closely. □ **clip-on** attached by a clip. [OE *clyppan* embrace f. WG]

clip² /klɪp/ *v. & n.* —*v.tr.* (**clipped**, **clipping**) **1** cut with shears or scissors, esp. cut short or trim (hair, wool, etc.). **2** trim or remove the hair or wool of (a person or animal). **3** *colloq.* hit smartly. **4 a** omit a letter etc. from a word. **b** omit letters or syllables of (words pronounced). **5** *Brit.* remove a small piece of (a ticket) to show that it has been used. **6** cut (an extract) from a newspaper etc. **7** *sl.* swindle, rob. **8** pare the edge of (a coin). —*n.* **1** an act of clipping, esp. shearing or hair-cutting. **2** *colloq.* a smart blow, esp. with the hand. **3** a short sequence from a motion picture. **4** the quantity of wool clipped from a sheep, flock, etc. **5** *colloq.* speed, esp. rapid. □ **clip-joint** *sl.* a club etc. charging exorbitant prices. **clip a person's wings** prevent a person from pursuing ambitions or acting effectively. □□ **clippable** *adj.* [ME f. ON *klippa*, prob. imit.]

clipboard /'klɪpbɔːd/ *n.* a small board with a spring clip for holding papers etc. and providing support for writing.

clip-clop /'klɪpklɒp/ *n. & v.* —*n.* a sound such as the beat of a horse's hooves. —*v.intr.* (**-clopped**, **-clopping**) make such a sound. [imit.]

clipper /'klɪpə(r)/ *n.* **1** (usu. in *pl.*) any of various instruments for clipping hair, fingernails, hedges, etc. **2** a fast sailing-ship, esp. one with raking bows and masts. **3** a fast horse.

clippie /'klɪpɪ/ *n. Brit. colloq.* a bus conductress.

clipping /'klɪpɪŋ/ *n.* a piece clipped or cut from something, esp. from a newspaper.

clique /kliːk/ *n.* a small exclusive group of people. □□ **cliquey** *adj.* (**cliquier**, **cliquiest**). **cliquish** *adj.* **cliquishness** *n.* **cliquism** *n.* [F f. *cliquer* CLICK]

C.Lit. *abbr. Brit.* Companion of Literature.

clitic /'klɪtɪk/ *n.* (often *attrib.*) an enclitic or proclitic. □□ **cliticization** /-tɪkaɪ'zeɪʃ(ə)n/ *n.*

clitoris /'klɪtərɪs, 'klaɪ-/ *n.* a small erectile part of

the female genitals at the upper end of the vulva. □□
clitoral *adj.* [mod.L f. Gk *kleitoris*]

clivers var. of CLEAVERS.

Cllr. *abbr. Brit.* Councillor.

cloaca /kləʊˈeɪkə/ *n.* (*pl.* **cloacae** /-siː/) **1** the genital and excretory cavity at the end of the intestinal canal in birds, reptiles, etc. **2** a sewer. □□ **cloacal** *adj.* [L, = sewer]

cloak /kləʊk/ *n. & v.* —*n.* **1** an outdoor over-garment, usu. sleeveless, hanging loosely from the shoulders. **2** a covering (*cloak of snow*). **3** (in *pl.*) = CLOAKROOM. —*v.tr.* **1** cover with a cloak. **2** conceal, disguise. □**cloak-and-dagger** involving intrigue and espionage. **under the cloak of** using as a pretext. [ME f. OF *cloke*, dial. var. of *cloche* bell, cloak (from its bell shape) f. med.L *clocca* bell: see CLOCK[1]]

cloakroom /ˈkləʊkruːm, -rʊm/ *n.* **1** a room where outdoor clothes or luggage may be left by visitors, clients, etc. **2** *Brit. euphem.* a lavatory.

clobber[1] /ˈklɒbə(r)/ *n. Brit. sl.* clothing or personal belongings. [19th c.: orig. unkn.]

clobber[2] /ˈklɒbə(r)/ *v.tr. sl.* **1** hit repeatedly; beat up. **2** defeat. **3** criticize severely. [20th c.: orig. unkn.]

cloche /klɒʃ, kləʊʃ/ *n.* **1** a small translucent cover for protecting or forcing outdoor plants. **2** (in full **cloche hat**) a woman's close-fitting bell-shaped hat. [F, = bell, f. med.L *clocca*: see CLOCK[1]]

clock[1] /klɒk/ *n. & v.* —*n.* **1** an instrument for measuring time, driven mechanically or electrically and indicating hours, minutes, etc., by hands on a dial or by displayed figures. **2 a** any measuring device resembling a clock. **b** *colloq.* a speedometer, taximeter, or stopwatch. **3** time taken as an element in competitive sports etc. (*ran against the clock*). **4** *Brit. sl.* a person's face. **5** a downy seed-head, esp. that of a dandelion. —*v.tr.* **1** *colloq.* **a** (often foll. by *up*) attain or register (a stated time, distance, or speed, esp. in a race). **b** time (a race) with a stopwatch. **2** *Brit. sl.* hit, esp. on the head. □**clock golf** a game in which a golf ball is putted into a hole from successive points in a circle. **clock in** (or **on**) register one's arrival at work, esp. by means of an automatic recording clock. **clock off** (or **out**) register one's departure similarly. **clock radio** a combined radio and alarm clock. **round the clock** all day and (usu.) night. **watch the clock** = CLOCK-WATCH. [ME f. MDu., MLG *klocke* f. med.L *clocca* bell, perh. f. Celt.]

clock[2] /klɒk/ *n.* an ornamental pattern on the side of a stocking or sock near the ankle. [16th c.: orig. unkn.]

clock-watch /ˈklɒkwɒtʃ/ *v.intr.* work over-anxiously to time, esp. so as not to exceed minimum working hours. □□ **clock-watcher** *n.* **clock-watching** *n.*

clockwise /ˈklɒkwaɪz/ *adj. & adv.* in a curve corresponding in direction to the movement of the hands of a clock.

clockwork /ˈklɒkwɜːk/ *n.* **1** a mechanism like that of a mechanical clock, with a spring and gears. **2** (*attrib.*) **a** driven by clockwork. **b** regular, mechanical. □**like clockwork** smoothly, regularly, automatically.

clod /klɒd/ *n.* **1** a lump of earth, clay, etc. **2** *sl.* a silly or foolish person. **3** meat cut from the neck of an ox. □□ **cloddy** *adj.* [ME: var. of CLOT]

cloddish /ˈklɒdɪʃ/ *adj.* loutish, foolish, clumsy. □□ **cloddishly** *adv.* **cloddishness** *n.*

clodhopper /ˈklɒdˌhɒpə(r)/ *n.* **1** (usu. in *pl.*) *colloq.* a large heavy shoe. **2** = CLOD 2.

clodhopping /ˈklɒdˌhɒpɪŋ/ *adj.* = CLODDISH.

clodpoll /ˈklɒdpɒl/ *n. sl.* = CLOD 2.

clog /klɒɡ/ *n. & v.* —*n.* **1** a shoe with a thick wooden sole. **2** *archaic* an encumbrance or impediment. **3** a block of wood to impede an animal's movement. —*v.* (**clogged**, **clogging**) **1** (often foll. by *up*) **a** *tr.* obstruct, esp. by accumulation of glutinous matter. **b** *intr.* become obstructed. **2** *tr.* impede, hamper. **3** *tr. & intr.* (often foll. by *up*) fill with glutinous or

choking matter. □**clog-dance** a dance performed in clogs. [ME: orig. unkn.]

cloggy /ˈklɒɡɪ/ *adj.* (**cloggier**, **cloggiest**) **1** lumpy, knotty. **2** sticky.

cloisonné /ˈklwɑːzɒˌneɪ/ *n. & adj.* —*n.* **1** an enamel finish produced by forming areas of different colours separated by strips of wire placed edgeways on a metal backing. **2** this process. —*adj.* (of enamel) made by this process. [F f. *cloison* compartment]

cloister /ˈklɔɪstə(r)/ *n. & v.* —*n.* **1** a covered walk, often with a wall on one side and a colonnade open to a quadrangle on the other, esp. in a convent, monastery, college, or cathedral. **2** monastic life or seclusion. **3** a convent or monastery. —*v.tr.* seclude or shut up usu. in a convent or monastery. □□ **cloistral** *adj.* [ME f. OF *cloistre* f. L *claustrum*, *clostrum* lock, enclosed place f. *claudere claus-* CLOSE[2]]

cloistered /ˈklɔɪstəd/ *adj.* **1** secluded, sheltered. **2** monastic.

clomp var. of CLUMP *v.* 2.

clone /kləʊn/ *n. & v.* —*n.* **1 a** a group of organisms produced asexually from one stock or ancestor. **b** one such organism. **2** a person or thing regarded as identical with another. —*v.tr.* propagate as a clone. □□ **clonal** *adj.* [Gk *klōn* twig, slip]

clonk /klɒŋk/ *n. & v.* —*n.* an abrupt heavy sound of impact. —*v.* **1** *intr.* make such a sound. **2** *tr. colloq.* hit. [imit.]

clonus /ˈkləʊnəs/ *n. Physiol.* a spasm with alternate muscular contractions and relaxations. □□ **clonic** *adj.* [Gk *klonos* turmoil]

clop /klɒp/ *n. & v.* —*n.* the sound made by a horse's hooves. —*v.intr.* (**clopped**, **clopping**) make this sound. [imit.]

cloqué /ˈklɒkeɪ/ *n.* a fabric with an irregularly raised surface. [F, = blistered]

close[1] /kləʊs/ *adj., adv., & n.* —*adj.* **1** (often foll. by *to*) situated at only a short distance or interval. **2 a** having a strong or immediate relation or connection (*close friend*; *close relative*). **b** in intimate friendship or association (*were very close*). **c** corresponding almost exactly (*close resemblance*). **d** fitting tightly (*close cap*). **e** (of hair etc.) short, near the surface. **3** in or almost in contact (*close combat*; *close proximity*). **4** dense, compact, with no or only slight intervals (*close texture*; *close writing*; *close formation*; *close thicket*). **5** in which competitors are almost equal (*close contest*; *close election*). **6** leaving no gaps or weaknesses, rigorous (*close reasoning*). **7** concentrated, searching (*close examination*; *close attention*). **8** (of air etc.) stuffy or humid. **9** closed, shut. **10** limited or restricted to certain persons etc. (*close corporation*; *close scholarship*). **11 a** hidden, secret, covered. **b** secretive. **12** (of a danger etc.) directly threatening, narrowly avoided (*that was close*). **13** niggardly. **14** (of a vowel) pronounced with a relatively narrow opening of the mouth. **15** narrow, confined, contracted. **16** under prohibition. —*adv.* (often foll. by *by*, *on*, *to*, *upon*) at only a short distance or interval (*they live close by*; *close to the church*). **2** closely, in a close manner (*shut close*). —*n.* **1** an enclosed space. **2** *Brit.* a street closed at one end. **3** *Brit.* the precinct of a cathedral. **4** *Brit.* a school playing-field or playground. **5** *Sc.* an entry from the street to a common stairway or to a court at the back. □**at close quarters** very close together. **close-fisted** niggardly. **close-fitting** (of a garment) fitting close to the body. **close-grained** without gaps between fibres etc. **close harmony** harmony in which the notes of the chord are close together. **close-hauled** (of a ship) with the sails hauled aft to sail close to the wind. **close-knit** tightly bound or interlocked; closely united in friendship. **close-mouthed** reticent. **close score** *Mus.* a score with more than one part on the same staff. **close season** *Brit.* the season when something, esp. the killing of game etc., is illegal. **close-set** separated

---

b *but* d *dog* f *few* ɡ *get* h *he* j *yes* k *cat* l *leg* m *man* n *no* p *pen* r *red* s *sit* t *top* v *voice*

only by a small interval or intervals. **close shave** *colloq.* a narrow escape. **close to the wind** see WIND¹. **close-up 1** a photograph etc. taken at close range and showing the subject on a large scale. **2** an intimate description. **go close** (of a racehorse) win or almost win. □□ **closely** *adv.* **closeness** *n.* **closish** *adj.* [ME f. OF *clos* f. L *clausum* enclosure & *clausus* past part. of *claudere* shut]

close² /kləʊz/ *v. & n.* —*v.* **1 a** *tr.* shut (a lid, box, door, room, house, etc.). **b** *intr.* be shut (*the door closed slowly*). **c** *tr.* block up. **2 a** *tr. & intr.* bring or come to an end. **b** *intr.* finish speaking (*closed with an expression of thanks*). **c** *tr.* settle (a bargain etc.). **3 a** *intr.* end the day's business. **b** *tr.* end the day's business at (a shop, office, etc.). **4** *tr. & intr.* bring or come closer or into contact (*close ranks*). **5** *tr.* make (an electric circuit etc.) continuous. **6** *intr.* (foll. by *with*) express agreement (with an offer, terms, or the person offering them). **7** *intr.* (often foll. by *with*) come within striking distance; grapple. **8** *intr.* (foll. by *on*) (of a hand, box, etc.) grasp or entrap. —*n.* **1** a conclusion, an end. **2** *Mus.* a cadence. □ **close down 1** (of a shop, factory, etc.) discontinue business, esp. permanently. **2** *Brit.* (of a broadcasting station) end transmission esp. until the next day. **close one's eyes 1** (foll. by *to*) pay no attention. **2** die. **close in 1** enclose. **2** come nearer. **3** (of days) get successively shorter with the approach of the winter solstice. **close out** *US* discontinue, terminate, dispose of (a business). **close up 1** (often foll. by *to*) move closer. **2** shut, esp. temporarily. **3** block up. **4** (of an aperture) grow smaller. **5** coalesce. **closing-time** the time at which a public house, shop, etc., ends business. □□ **closable** *adj.* **closer** *n.* [ME f. OF *clos-* stem of *clore* f. L *claudere* shut]

closed /kləʊzd/ *adj.* **1** not giving access; shut. **2** (of a shop etc.) having ceased business temporarily. **3** (of a society, system, etc.) self-contained; not communicating with others. **4** (of a sport etc.) restricted to specified competitors etc. □ **closed book** see BOOK. **closed-circuit** (of television) transmitted by wires to a restricted set of receivers. **closed-end** having a predetermined range of function (cf. *open-ended*). **closed season** *US* = *close season* (see CLOSE¹). **closed shop 1** a place of work etc. where all employees must belong to an agreed trade union. **2** this system. **closed syllable** a syllable ending in a consonant.

closet /ˈklɒzɪt/ *n. & v.* —*n.* **1** a small or private room. **2** a cupboard or recess. **3** = *water-closet*. **4** (*attrib.*) secret, covert (*closet homosexual*). —*v.tr.* (**closeted**, **closeting**) shut away, esp. in private conference or study. □ **Clerk of the Closet** (in the UK) the sovereign's principal chaplain. **closet play** a play to be read rather than acted. [ME f. OF, dimin. of *clos*: see CLOSE¹]

closure /ˈkləʊʒə(r)/ *n. & v.* —*n.* **1** the act or process of closing. **2** a closed condition. **3** something that closes or seals, e.g. a cap or tie. **4** a procedure for ending a debate and taking a vote, esp. in Parliament. —*v.tr.* apply the closure to (a motion, speakers, etc.). [ME f. OF f. LL *clausura* f. *claudere claus-* CLOSE²]

clot /klɒt/ *n. & v.* —*n.* **1 a** a thick mass of coagulated liquid, esp. of blood exposed to air. **b** a mass of material stuck together. **2** *Brit. colloq.* a silly or foolish person. —*v.tr. & intr.* (**clotted**, **clotting**) form into clots. □ **clotted cream** *Brit.* thick cream obtained by slow scalding. [OE *clot(t)* f. WG: cf. CLEAT]

cloth /klɒθ/ *n.* (*pl.* **cloths** /klɒθs, klɒðz/) **1** woven or felted material. **2** a piece of this. **3** a piece of cloth for a particular purpose; a tablecloth, dishcloth, etc. **4** woollen woven fabric as used for clothes. **5 a** profession or status, esp. of the clergy, as shown by clothes (*respect due to his cloth*). **b** (prec. by *the*) the clergy. □ **cloth-cap** relating to or associated with the working class. **cloth-eared** *colloq.* somewhat deaf. **cloth of gold** (or **silver**) tissue of gold (or silver)

threads interwoven with silk or wool. [OE *clāth*, of unkn. orig.]

clothe /kləʊð/ *v.tr.* (*past* and *past part.* **clothed** or *formal* **clad**) **1** put clothes on; provide with clothes. **2** cover as with clothes or a cloth. **3** (foll. by *with*) endue (with qualities etc.). [OE: rel. to CLOTH]

clothes /kləʊðz/ *n.pl.* **1** garments worn to cover the body and limbs. **2** bedclothes. □ **clothes-horse 1** a frame for airing washed clothes. **2** *colloq.* an affectedly fashionable person. **clothes-line** a rope or wire etc. on which washed clothes are hung to dry. **clothes-moth** any moth of the family Tineidae, with a larva destructive to wool, fur, etc. **clothes-peg** *Brit.* a clip or forked device for securing clothes to a clothes-line. **clothes-pin** *US* a clothes-peg. [OE *clāthas* pl. of *clāth* CLOTH]

clothier /ˈkləʊðɪə(r)/ *n.* a seller of men's clothes. [ME *clother* f. CLOTH]

clothing /ˈkləʊðɪŋ/ *n.* clothes collectively.

cloture /ˈkləʊtʃə(r), -tjʊə(r)/ *n. & v.* *US* —*n.* the closure of a debate. —*v.tr.* closure. [F *clôture* f. OF CLOSURE]

clou /kluː/ *n.* **1** the point of greatest interest; the chief attraction. **2** the central idea. [F, = nail]

cloud /klaʊd/ *n. & v.* —*n.* **1** a visible mass of condensed watery vapour floating in the atmosphere high above the general level of the ground. **2** a mass of smoke or dust. **3** (foll. by *of*) a great number of insects, birds, etc., moving together. **4 a** a state of gloom, trouble, or suspicion. **b** a frowning or depressed look (*a cloud on his brow*). **5** a local dimness or a vague patch of colour in or on a liquid or a transparent body. **6** an unsubstantial or fleeting thing. **7** obscurity. —*v.* **1** *tr.* cover or darken with clouds or gloom or trouble. **2** *intr.* (often foll. by *over, up*) become overcast or gloomy. **3** *tr.* make unclear. **4** *tr.* variegate with vague patches of colour. □ **cloud-castle** a daydream. **cloud chamber** a device containing vapour for tracking the paths of charged particles, X-rays, and gamma rays. **clouded leopard** a mottled arboreal S. Asian feline, *Neofelis nebulosa*. **cloud-hopping** movement of an aircraft from cloud to cloud esp. for concealment. **cloud-land** a utopia or fairyland. **in the clouds 1** unreal, imaginary, mystical. **2** (of a person) abstracted, inattentive. **on cloud nine** (or **seven**) *colloq.* extremely happy. **under a cloud** out of favour, discredited, under suspicion. **with one's head in the clouds** daydreaming, unrealistic. □□ **cloudless** *adj.* **cloudlessly** *adv.* **cloudlet** *n.* [OE *clūd* mass of rock or earth, prob. rel. to CLOD]

cloudberry /ˈklaʊdbərɪ/ *n.* (*pl.* **-ies**) a small mountain bramble, *Rubus chamaemorus*, with a white flower and an orange-coloured fruit.

cloudburst /ˈklaʊdbɜːst/ *n.* a sudden violent rainstorm.

cloud-cuckoo-land /klaʊdˈkʊkuːˌlænd/ *n.* a fanciful or ideal place. [transl. of Gk *Nephelokokkugia* f. *nephelē* cloud + *kokkux* cuckoo (in Aristophanes' *Birds*)]

cloudscape /ˈklaʊdskeɪp/ *n.* **1** a picturesque grouping of clouds. **2** a picture or view of clouds. [CLOUD *n.*, after *landscape*]

cloudy /ˈklaʊdɪ/ *adj.* (**cloudier**, **cloudiest**) **1 a** (of the sky) covered with clouds, overcast. **b** (of weather) characterized by clouds. **2** not transparent; unclear. □□ **cloudily** *adv.* **cloudiness** *n.*

clough /klʌf/ *n. dial.* a steep valley usu. with a torrent bed; a ravine. [OE *clōh* f. Gmc]

clout /klaʊt/ *n. & v.* —*n.* **1** a heavy blow. **2** *colloq.* influence, power of effective action esp. in politics or business. **3** *dial.* a piece of cloth or clothing (*cast not a clout*). **4** *Archery hist.* a piece of canvas on a frame, used as a mark. **5** a nail with a large flat head. **6** a patch. —*v.tr.* **1** hit hard. **2** mend with a patch. [OE *clūt*, rel. to CLEAT, CLOT]

clove¹ /kləʊv/ *n.* **1 a** a dried flower-bud of a tropical plant, *Eugenia aromatica*, used as a pungent aromatic spice. **b** this plant. **2** (in full **clove gillyflower** or **clove pink**) a clove-scented pink, *Dianthus caryophyllus*, the original of the carnation and other double pinks. [ME f. OF *clou (de girofle)* nail (of gillyflower), from its shape, GILLYFLOWER being orig. the name of the spice; later applied to the similarly scented pink]

clove² /kləʊv/ *n.* any of the small bulbs making up a compound bulb of garlic, shallot, etc. [OE *clufu*, rel. to CLEAVE¹]

clove³ *past* of CLEAVE¹.

clove hitch /kləʊv/ *n.* a knot by which a rope is secured by passing it twice round a spar or rope that it crosses at right angles. [old past part. of CLEAVE¹, as showing parallel separate lines]

cloven /ˈkləʊv(ə)n/ *adj.* split, partly divided. □**cloven hoof** (or **foot**) the divided hoof of ruminant quadrupeds (e.g. oxen, sheep, goats); also ascribed to the god Pan, and so to the Devil. **show the cloven hoof** reveal one's evil nature. □□ **cloven-footed** /-ˈfʊtɪd/ *adj.* **cloven-hoofed** /-ˈhuːfd/ *adj.* [past part. of CLEAVE¹]

clover /ˈkləʊvə(r)/ *n.* any leguminous fodder plant of the genus *Trifolium*, having dense flower heads and leaves each consisting of usu. three leaflets. □**clover leaf** a junction of roads intersecting at different levels with connecting sections forming the pattern of a four-leaved clover. **in clover** in ease and luxury. [OE *clǣfre* f. Gmc]

clown /klaʊn/ *n. & v.* —*n.* **1** a comic entertainer, esp. in a pantomime or circus, usu. with traditional costume and make-up. **2** a silly, foolish, or playful person. **3** *archaic* a rustic. —*v.* **1** *intr.* (often foll. by *about*, *around*) behave like a clown; act foolishly or playfully. **2** *tr.* perform (a part, an action, etc.) like a clown. □□**clownery** *n.* **clownish** *adj.* **clownishly** *adv.* **clownishness** *n.* [16th c.: perh. of LG orig.]

cloy /klɔɪ/ *v.tr.* (usu. foll. by *with*) satiate or sicken with an excess of sweetness, richness, etc. □□ **cloyingly** *adv.* [ME f. obs. *acloy* f. AF *acloyer*, OF *encloyer* f. Rmc: cf. ENCLAVE]

cloze /kləʊz/ *n.* the exercise of supplying a word that has been omitted from a passage as a test of readability or comprehension (usu. *attrib.: cloze test*). [CLOSURE]

club /klʌb/ *n. & v.* —*n.* **1** a heavy stick with a thick end, used as a weapon etc. **2** a stick used in a game, esp. a stick with a head used in golf. **3 a** a playing-card of a suit denoted by a black trefoil. **b** (in *pl.*) this suit. **4** an association of persons united by a common interest, usu. meeting periodically for a shared activity (*tennis club*; *yacht club*). **5** an organization or premises offering members social amenities, meals and temporary residence, etc. **6** an organization offering subscribers certain benefits (*book club*). **7** a group of persons, nations, etc., having something in common. **8** = CLUBHOUSE. **9** a structure or organ, esp. in a plant, with a knob at the end. —*v.* (**clubbed**, **clubbing**) **1** *tr.* beat with or as with a club. **2** *intr.* (foll. by *together*, *with*) combine for joint action, esp. making up a sum of money for a purpose. **3** *tr.* contribute (money etc.) to a common stock. □**club-class** a class of fare on aircraft etc. designed for the business traveller. **club-foot** a congenitally deformed foot. **club-footed** having a club-foot. **club-man** (*pl.* **-men**) a member of one or more clubs (in sense 5 of *n.*). **club-root** a disease of cabbages etc. with swelling at the base of the stem. **club sandwich** *US* a sandwich with two layers of filling between three slices of toast or bread. **in the club** *Brit. sl.* pregnant. **on the club** *colloq.* receiving relief from the funds of a benefit society. □□ **clubber** *n.* [ME f. ON *klubba* assim. form of *klumba* club, rel. to CLUMP]

clubbable /ˈklʌbəb(ə)l/ *adj.* sociable; fit for membership of a club. □□ **clubbability** /-ˈbɪlɪtɪ/ *n.* **clubbableness** *n.*

clubby /ˈklʌbɪ/ *adj.* (**clubbier, clubbiest**) esp. *US* sociable; friendly.

clubhouse /ˈklʌbhaʊs/ *n.* the premises used by a club.

clubland /ˈklʌblænd/ *n. Brit.* an area where many clubs are, esp. St James's in London.

clubmoss /ˈklʌbmɒs/ *n.* any pteridophyte of the family Lycopodiaceae, bearing upright spikes of spore-cases.

cluck /klʌk/ *n. & v.* —*n.* **1** a guttural cry like that of a hen. **2** *sl.* a silly or foolish person (*dumb cluck*). —*v.intr.* emit a cluck or clucks. [imit.]

clucky /ˈklʌkɪ/ *adj.* (of a hen) sitting on eggs.

clue /kluː/ *n. & v.* —*n.* **1** a fact or idea that serves as a guide, or suggests a line of inquiry, in a problem or investigation. **2** a piece of evidence etc. in the detection of a crime. **3** a verbal formula serving as a hint as to what is to be inserted in a crossword. **4 a** the thread of a story. **b** a train of thought. —*v.tr.* (**clues, clued, cluing** or **clueing**) provide a clue to. □**clue in** (or **up**) *sl.* inform. **not have a clue** *colloq.* be ignorant or incompetent. [var. of CLEW]

clueless /ˈkluːlɪs/ *adj. colloq.* ignorant, stupid. □□ **cluelessly** *adv.* **cluelessness** *n.*

clump /klʌmp/ *n. & v.* —*n.* **1** (foll. by *of*) a cluster of plants, esp. trees or shrubs. **2** an agglutinated mass of blood-cells etc. **3** a thick extra sole on a boot or shoe. —*v.* **1 a** *intr.* form a clump. **b** *tr.* heap or plant together. **2** *intr.* (also **clomp** /klɒmp/) walk with heavy tread. **3** *tr. colloq.* hit. □□**clumpy** *adj.* (**clumpier, clumpiest**). [MLG *klumpe*, MDu. *klompe*: see CLUB]

clumsy /ˈklʌmzɪ/ *adj.* (**clumsier, clumsiest**) **1** awkward in movement or shape; ungainly. **2** difficult to handle or use. **3** tactless. □□**clumsily** *adv.* **clumsiness** *n.* [obs. *clumse* be numb with cold (prob. f. Scand.)]

clung *past* and *past part.* of CLING.

clunk /klʌŋk/ *n. & v.* —*n.* a dull sound as of thick pieces of metal meeting. —*v.intr.* make such a sound. [imit.]

cluster /ˈklʌstə(r)/ *n. & v.* —*n.* **1** a close group or bunch of similar things growing together. **2** a close group or swarm of people, animals, faint stars, gems, etc. **3** a group of successive consonants or vowels. —*v.* **1** *tr.* bring into a cluster or clusters. **2** *intr.* be or come into a cluster or clusters. **3** *intr.* (foll. by *round*, *around*) gather, congregate. □**cluster bomb** an anti-personnel bomb spraying pellets on impact. **cluster pine** a Mediterranean pine *Pinus pinaster* with clustered cones: also called PINASTER. [OE *cluster*: cf. CLOT]

clustered /ˈklʌstəd/ *adj.* **1** growing in or brought into a cluster. **2** *Archit.* (of pillars, columns, or shafts) several close together, or disposed round or half detached from a pier.

clutch¹ /klʌtʃ/ *v. & n.* —*v.* **1** *tr.* seize eagerly; grasp tightly. **2** *intr.* (foll. by *at*) snatch suddenly. —*n.* **1** a tight grasp. **b** (foll. by *at*) grasping. **2** (in *pl.*) grasping hands, esp. as representing a cruel or relentless grasp or control. **3 a** (in a motor vehicle) a device for connecting and disconnecting the engine to the transmission. **b** the pedal operating this. **c** an arrangement for connecting or disconnecting working parts of a machine. □**clutch bag** a slim flat handbag without handles. [ME *clucche, clicche* f. OE *clyccan* crook, clench, f. Gmc]

clutch² /klʌtʃ/ *n.* **1** a set of eggs for hatching. **2** a brood of chickens. [18th c.: prob. S.Engl. var. of *cletch* f. *cleck* to hatch f. ON *klekja*, assoc. with CLUTCH¹]

clutter /ˈklʌtə(r)/ *n. & v.* —*n.* **1** a crowded and untidy collection of things. **2** an untidy state. —*v.tr.* (often foll. by *up*, *with*) crowd untidily, fill with clutter. [partly var. of *clotter* coagulate, partly assoc. with CLUSTER, CLATTER]

Clydesdale /ˈklaɪdzdeɪl/ *n.* **1 a** a horse of a heavy powerful breed, used as draught-horses. **b** this breed.

2 a kind of small terrier. [orig. bred near the river *Clyde* in Scotland: see DALE]

clypeus /'klɪpɪəs/ *n.* (*pl.* **clypei** /-pɪaɪ/) the hard protective area of an insect's head. □□ **clypeal** *adj.* **clypeate** *adj.* [L, = round shield]

clyster /'klɪstə(r)/ *n.* & *v. archaic* —*n.* an enema. —*v.tr.* treat with an enema. [ME f. OF *clystere* or f. L f. Gk *klustēr* syringe f. *kluzō* wash out]

CM *abbr.* Member of the Order of Canada.

Cm. *Brit.* Command Paper (1986-).

Cm *symb. Chem.* the element curium.

cm *abbr.* centimetre(s).

Cmd. *abbr. Brit.* Command Paper (1918–56).

Cmdr. *abbr.* Commander.

Cmdre. *abbr.* Commodore.

CMG *abbr.* (in the UK) Companion (of the Order) of St Michael and St George.

Cmnd. *abbr. Brit.* Command Paper (1956–86).

CNAA *abbr.* Council for National Academic Awards.

CND *abbr.* (in the UK) Campaign for Nuclear Disarmament.

cnr. *abbr.* corner.

CO *abbr.* **1** Commanding Officer. **2** conscientious objector. **3** *US* Colorado (in official postal use).

Co *symb. Chem.* the element cobalt.

Co. *abbr.* **1** company. **2** county. □ **and Co.** /kəʊ/ *colloq.* and the rest of them; and similar things.

co- /kəʊ/ *prefix* **1** added to: **a** nouns, with the sense 'joint, mutual, common' (*co-author*; *coequality*). **b** adjectives and adverbs, with the sense 'jointly, mutually' (*co-belligerent*; *coequal*; *coequally*). **c** verbs, with the sense 'together with another or others' (*cooperate*; *co-author*). **2** *Math.* **a** of the complement of an angle (*cosine*). **b** the complement of (*co-latitude*; *coset*). [orig. a form of COM-]

c/o *abbr.* care of.

coach /kəʊtʃ/ *n.* & *v.* —*n.* **1** a single-decker bus, usu. comfortably equipped for longer journeys. **2** a railway carriage. **3** a horse-drawn carriage, usu. closed, esp. a State carriage or a stagecoach. **4** **a** an instructor or trainer in sport. **b** a private tutor. **5** *US* economy-class seating in an aircraft. **6** *Austral.* a docile cow or bullock used as a decoy to attract wild cattle. —*v.* **1** *tr.* **a** train or teach (a pupil, sports team, etc.) as a coach. **b** give hints to; prime with facts. **2** *intr.* travel by stagecoach (*in the old coaching days*). □ **coach-built** (of motor-car bodies) individually built by craftsmen. **coach-house** an outhouse for carriages. **coach station** a stopping-place for a number of coaches, usu. with buildings and amenities. [F *coche* f. Magyar *kocsi* (adj.) f. *Kocs* in Hungary]

coachload /'kəʊtʃləʊd/ *n.* a number of people, esp. holiday-makers, taken by coach.

coachman /'kəʊtʃmən/ *n.* (*pl.* **-men**) the driver of a horse-drawn carriage.

coachwood /'kəʊtʃwʊd/ *n. Austral.* any tree esp. *Ceratopetalum apetalum* with close-grained wood suitable for cabinet-making.

coachwork /'kəʊtʃwɜːk/ *n.* the bodywork of a road or rail vehicle.

coadjutor /kəʊ'ædʒʊtə(r)/ *n.* an assistant, esp. an assistant bishop. [ME f. OF *coadjuteur* f. LL *coadjutor* (as co-, *adjutor* f. *adjuvare -jut-* help)]

coagulant /kəʊ'ægjʊlənt/ *n.* a substance that produces coagulation.

coagulate /kəʊ'ægjʊˌleɪt/ *v.tr.* & *intr.* **1** change from a fluid to a solid or semisolid state. **2** clot, curdle. **3** set, solidify. □□ **coagulable** *adj.* **coagulative** /-lətɪv/ *adj.* **coagulator** *n.* [ME f. L *coagulare* f. *coagulum* rennet]

coagulation /ˌkəʊægjʊ'leɪʃ(ə)n/ *n.* the process by which a liquid changes to a semisolid mass. [as COAGULATE]

coagulum /kəʊ'ægjʊləm/ *n.* (*pl.* **coagula** /-lə/) a mass of coagulated matter. [L: see COAGULATE]

coal /kəʊl/ *n.* & *v.* —*n.* **1** **a** a hard black or blackish rock, mainly carbonized plant matter, found in underground seams and used as a fuel and in the manufacture of gas, tar, etc. **b** *Brit.* a piece of this for burning. **2** a red-hot piece of coal, wood, etc. in a fire. —*v.* **1** *intr.* take in a supply of coal. **2** *tr.* put coal into (an engine, fire, etc.). □ **coal-bed** a stratum of coal. **coal-black** completely black. **coal-fired** heated or driven by coal. **coal gas** mixed gases extracted from coal and used for lighting and heating. **coal-hole** *Brit.* a compartment or small cellar for storing coal. **coal measures** a series of rocks formed by seams of coal with intervening strata. **coal oil** *US* petroleum or paraffin. **coal-sack 1** a sack for carrying coal. **2** a black patch in the Milky Way, esp. the one near the Southern Cross. **coal-scuttle** a container for coal to supply a domestic fire. **coal-seam** a stratum of coal suitable for mining. **coals to Newcastle** something brought or sent to a place where it is already plentiful. **coal tar** a thick black oily liquid distilled from coal and used as a source of benzene. **coal-tit** (or **cole-tit**) a small greyish bird, *Parus ater*, with a black head: also called COALMOUSE. **haul** (or **call**) **over the coals** reprimand. □□ **coaly** *adj.* [OE *col* f. Gmc]

coaler /'kəʊlə(r)/ *n.* a ship etc. transporting coal.

coalesce /ˌkəʊə'les/ *v.intr.* **1** come together and form one whole. **2** combine in a coalition. □□ **coalescence** *n.* **coalescent** *adj.* [L *coalescere* (as co-, *alescere* *alit-* grow f. *alere* nourish)]

coalface /'kəʊlfeɪs/ *n.* an exposed surface of coal in a mine.

coalfield /'kəʊlfiːld/ *n.* an extensive area with strata containing coal.

coalfish /'kəʊlfɪʃ/ *n.* = SAITHE.

coalition /ˌkəʊə'lɪʃ(ə)n/ *n.* **1** *Polit.* a temporary alliance for combined action, esp. of distinct parties forming a government, or of States. **2** fusion into one whole. □□ **coalitionist** *n.* [med.L *coalitio* (as COALESCE)]

coalman /'kəʊlmən/ *n.* (*pl.* **-men**) a man who carries or delivers coal.

coalmine /'kəʊlmaɪn/ *n.* a mine in which coal is dug. □□ **coalminer** *n.*

coalmouse /'kəʊlmaʊs/ *n.* (also **colemouse**) (*pl.* **-mice**) = *coal-tit.* [OE *colmāse* f. *col* COAL + *māse* as TITMOUSE]

coaming /'kəʊmɪŋ/ *n.* a raised border round the hatches etc. of a ship to keep out water. [17th c.: orig. unkn.]

coarse /kɔːs/ *adj.* **1** **a** rough or loose in texture or grain; made of large particles. **b** (of a person's features) rough or large. **2** lacking refinement or delicacy; crude, obscene (*coarse humour*). **3** rude, uncivil. **4** inferior, common. □ **coarse fish** *Brit.* any freshwater fish other than salmon and trout. □□ **coarsely** *adv.* **coarseness** *n.* **coarsish** *adj.* [ME: orig. unkn.]

coarsen /'kɔːs(ə)n/ *v.tr.* & *intr.* make or become coarse.

coast /kəʊst/ *n.* & *v.* —*n.* **1** **a** the border of the land near the sea; the seashore. **b** (**the Coast**) *US* the Pacific coast of the US. **2** **a** a run, usu. downhill, on a bicycle without pedalling or in a motor vehicle without using the engine. **b** *US* a toboggan slide or slope. —*v.intr.* **1** ride or move, usu. downhill, without use of power, free-wheel. **2** make progress without much effort. **3** *US* slide down a hill on a toboggan. **4** **a** sail along the coast. **b** trade between ports on the same coast. □ **the coast is clear** there is no danger of being observed or caught. **coast-to-coast** across an island or continent. □□ **coastal** *adj.* [ME f. OF *coste*, *costeier* f. L *costa* rib, flank, side]

coaster /'kəʊstə(r)/ *n.* **1** a ship that travels along the coast from port to port. **2** a small tray or mat for a bottle or glass. **3** *US* **a** a sledge for coasting. **b** a roller-coaster.

coastguard /'kəʊstɡɑːd/ *n.* **1** an organization keeping watch on the coasts and on local shipping to save life, prevent smuggling, etc. **2** a member of this.

coastline /ˈkəʊstlaɪn/ n. the line of the seashore, esp. with regard to its shape (a rugged coastline).

coastwise /ˈkəʊstwaɪz/ adj. & adv. along, following, or connected with the coast.

coat /kəʊt/ n. & v. —n. 1 an outer garment with sleeves and often extending below the hips; an overcoat or jacket. 2 a an animal's fur, hair, etc. b Physiol. a structure, esp. a membrane, enclosing or lining an organ. c a skin, rind, or husk. d a layer of a bulb etc. 3 a a layer or covering. b a covering of paint etc. laid on a surface at one time. —v.tr. 1 (usu. foll. by with, in) a apply a coat of paint etc. to; provide with a layer or covering. b (as coated adj.) covered with. 2 (of paint etc.) form a covering to. □coat armour coats of arms. coat dress a woman's tailored dress resembling a coat. coat-hanger see HANGER¹. coat of arms the heraldic bearings or shield of a person, family, or corporation. coat of mail a jacket of mail armour (see MAIL²). on a person's coat-tails undeservedly benefiting from another's success. □□ coated adj. (also in comb.). [ME f. OF cote f. Rmc f. Frank., of unkn. orig.]

coatee /kəʊˈtiː/ n. 1 a woman's or infant's short coat. 2 archaic a close-fitting short coat.

coati /kəʊˈɑːtɪ/ n. (pl. coatis) any racoon-like flesh-eating mammal of the genus Nasua, with a long flexible snout and a long usu. ringed tail. [Tupi f. cua belt + tim nose]

coatimundi /ˌkəʊɑːtɪˈmʌndɪ/ n. (pl. coatimundis) = COATI. [as COATI + Tupi mondi solitary]

coating /ˈkəʊtɪŋ/ n. 1 a thin layer or covering of paint etc. 2 material for making coats.

co-author /ˌkəʊˈɔːθə(r)/ n. & v. —n. a joint author. —v.tr. be a joint author of.

coax /kəʊks/ v.tr. 1 (usu. foll. by into, or to + infin.) persuade (a person) gradually or by flattery. 2 (foll. by out of) obtain (a thing from a person) by coaxing. 3 manipulate (a thing) carefully or slowly. □□ coaxer n. coaxingly adv. [16th c.: f. 'make a cokes of' f. obs. cokes simpleton, of unkn. orig.]

coaxial /kəʊˈæksɪəl/ adj. 1 having a common axis. 2 Electr. (of a cable or line) transmitting by means of two concentric conductors separated by an insulator. □□ coaxially adv.

cob¹ /kɒb/ n. 1 a roundish lump of coal etc. 2 Brit. a domed loaf of bread. 3 Brit. = corn-cob (see CORN¹). 4 (in full cob-nut) a large hazelnut. 5 a sturdy riding- or driving-horse with short legs. 6 a male swan. [ME: orig. unkn.]

cob² /kɒb/ n. a material for walls, made from compressed earth, clay, or chalk reinforced with straw. [17th c.: orig. unkn.]

cobalt /ˈkəʊbɔːlt, -bɒlt/ n. Chem. a silvery-white magnetic metallic element occurring naturally as a mineral in combination with sulphur and arsenic, and used in many alloys. ¶ Symb.: Co. □cobalt blue 1 a pigment containing a cobalt salt. 2 the deep-blue colour of this. □□ cobaltic /kəˈbɔːltɪk/ adj. cobaltous /kəˈbɔːltəs/ adj. [G Kobalt etc., prob. = KOBOLD in mines]

cobber /ˈkɒbə(r)/ n. Austral. & NZ colloq. a companion or friend. [19th c.: perh. rel. to E dial. cob take a liking to]

cobble¹ /ˈkɒb(ə)l/ n. & v. —n. 1 (in full cobblestone) a small rounded stone of a size used for paving. 2 (in pl.) Brit. coal in lumps of this size. —v.tr. pave with cobbles. [ME cobel(-ston), f. COB¹]

cobble² /ˈkɒb(ə)l/ v.tr. 1 mend or patch up (esp. shoes). 2 (often foll. by together) join or assemble roughly. [back-form. f. COBBLER]

cobbler /ˈkɒblə(r)/ n. 1 a person who mends shoes, esp. professionally. 2 an iced drink of wine etc., sugar, and lemon (sherry cobbler). 3 a a fruit pie topped with scones. b esp. US a fruit pie with a rich thick crust. 4 (in pl.) Brit. sl. nonsense. 5 Austral. & NZ sl. the last sheep to be shorn. □cobbler's wax a resinous substance used for waxing thread. [ME, of

unkn. orig.: sense 4 f. rhyming sl. cobbler's awls = balls: sense 5 with pun on LAST³]

co-belligerent /ˌkəʊbɪˈlɪdʒərənt/ n. & adj. —n. any of two or more nations engaged in war as allies. —adj. of or as a co-belligerent. □□ co-belligerence n. co-belligerency n.

coble /ˈkəʊb(ə)l/ n. a flat-bottomed fishing-boat in Scotland and NE England. [OE, perh. f. Celt.]

COBOL /ˈkəʊbɒl/ n. Computing a programming language designed for use in commerce. [common business oriented language]

cobra /ˈkəʊbrə, ˈkɒbrə/ n. any venomous snake of the genus Naja, native to Africa and Asia, with a neck dilated like a hood when excited. [Port. f. L colubra snake]

cobweb /ˈkɒbweb/ n. 1 a a fine network of threads spun by a spider from a liquid secreted by it, used to trap insects etc. b the thread of this. 2 anything compared with a cobweb, esp. in flimsiness of texture. 3 a trap or insidious entanglement. 4 (in pl.) a state of languishing; fustiness. □□ cobwebbed adj. cobwebby adj. [ME cop(pe)web f. obs. coppe spider]

coca /ˈkəʊkə/ n. 1 a a S. American shrub, Erythroxylum coca. b its dried leaves, chewed as a stimulant. [Sp. f. Quechua cuca]

Coca-Cola /ˌkəʊkəˈkəʊlə/ n. propr. an aerated non-alcoholic drink sometimes flavoured with cola seeds.

cocaine /kəˈkeɪn, kəʊ-/ n. a drug derived from coca or prepared synthetically, used as a local anaesthetic and as a stimulant. [COCA + -INE⁴]

coccidiosis /ˌkɒksɪdɪˈəʊsɪs/ n. a disease of birds and mammals caused by any of various parasitic protozoa, esp. of the genus Eimeria, affecting the intestine. [coccidium (mod.L f. Gk kokkis dimin. of kokkos berry) + -OSIS]

coccus /ˈkɒkəs/ n. (pl. cocci /-kɪ/) any spherical or roughly spherical bacterium. □□ coccal adj. coccoid adj. [mod.L f. Gk kokkos berry]

coccyx /ˈkɒksɪks/ n. (pl. coccyges /-ˌdʒiːz/ or coccyxes) the small triangular bone at the base of the spinal column in humans and some apes. □□ coccygeal /kɒkˈsɪdʒɪəl/ adj. [L f. Gk kokkux -ugos cuckoo (from being shaped like its bill)]

cochin /ˈkəʊtʃɪn/ n. (in full cochin-china) 1 a fowl of an Asian breed with feathery legs. 2 this breed. [Cochin China in Vietnam]

cochineal /ˈkɒtʃɪniːl, -ˈniːl/ n. 1 a scarlet dye used esp. for colouring food. 2 the dried bodies of the female of the Mexican insect, Dactylopius coccus, yielding this. [F cochenille or Sp. cochinilla f. L coccinus scarlet f. Gk kokkos berry]

cochlea /ˈkɒklɪə/ n. (pl. cochleae /-klɪˌiː/) the spiral cavity of the internal ear. □□ cochlear adj. [L, = snail-shell, f. Gk kokhlias]

cock¹ /kɒk/ n. & v. —n. 1 a a male bird, esp. of a domestic fowl. b a male lobster, crab, or salmon. c = WOODCOCK. 2 Brit. sl. (usu. old cock as a form of address) a friend; a fellow. 3 coarse sl. the penis. 4 Brit. sl. nonsense. ¶ In senses 3, 4 usually considered a taboo word. 5 a a firing lever in a gun which can be raised to be released by the trigger. b the cocked position of this (at full cock). 6 a tap or valve controlling flow. —v.tr. 1 raise or make upright or erect. 2 turn or move (the eye or ear) attentively or knowingly. 3 set aslant, or turn up the brim of (a hat). 4 raise the cock of (a gun). □at half cock only partly ready. cock-a-doodle-doo a cock's crow. cock-and-bull story an absurd or incredible account. cock crow dawn. cocked hat a brimless triangular hat pointed at the front, back, and top. cock-fight a fight between cocks as sport. cock-fighting this sport. cock-of-the-rock a S. American bird, Rupicola rupicola, having a crest and bright orange plumage. cock-of-the-walk a dominant or arrogant person. cock-of-the-wood 1 a capercaillie. 2 US a red-crested woodpecker. cock-shy 1 a target for throwing at with sticks, stones, etc. b a throw at this. 2 an object of ridicule or criticism. **cock a snook** see SNOOK[1]. **cock sparrow 1** a male sparrow. **2** a lively quarrelsome person. **cock up** *Brit. sl.* bungle; make a mess of. **cock-up** *n. Brit. sl.* a muddle or mistake. **knock into a cocked hat** defeat utterly. [OE *cocc* and OF *coq* prob. f. med.L *coccus*]

cock² /kɒk/ *n. & v.* —*n.* a small pile of hay, straw, etc. with vertical sides and a rounded top. —*v.tr.* pile into cocks. [ME, perh. of Scand. orig.]

cockade /kɒˈkeɪd/ *n.* a rosette etc. worn in a hat as a badge of office or party, or as part of a livery. □□ **cockaded** *adj.* [F *cocarde* orig. in *bonnet à la coquarde*, f. fem. of obs. *coquard* saucy f. *coq* COCK¹]

cock-a-hoop /ˌkɒkəˈhuːp/ *adj. & adv.* —*adj.* exultant; crowing boastfully. —*adv.* exultantly. [16th c.: orig. in phr. *set cock a hoop* denoting some action preliminary to hard drinking]

cock-a-leekie /ˌkɒkəˈliːkɪ/ *n.* (also **cocky-leeky** /ˌkɒkɪ-/) a soup traditionally made in Scotland with boiling fowl and leeks. [COCK¹ + LEEK]

cockalorum /ˌkɒkəˈlɔːrəm/ *n. colloq.* a self-important little man. [18th c.: arbitr. f. COCK¹]

cockatiel /ˌkɒkəˈtiːl/ *n.* (also **cockateel**) *Austral.* a small delicately coloured crested parrot, *Nymphicus hollandicus.* [Du. *kaketielje*]

cockatoo /ˌkɒkəˈtuː/ *n.* **1** any of several parrots of the family Cacatuinae, having powerful beaks and erectile crests. **2** *Austral. & NZ colloq.* a small farmer. [Du. *kaketoe* f. Malay *kakatua*, assim. to COCK¹]

cockatrice /ˈkɒkətrɪs, -ˌtraɪs/ *n.* **1** = BASILISK 1. **2** *Heraldry* a fabulous animal, a cock with a serpent's tail. [ME f. OF *cocatris* f. L *calcare* tread, track, rendering Gk *ikhneumōn* tracker: see ICHNEUMON]

cockboat /ˈkɒkbəʊt/ *n.* a small ship's-boat. [obs. *cock* small boat (f. OF *coque*) + BOAT]

cockchafer /ˈkɒkˌtʃeɪfə(r)/ *n.* a large nocturnal beetle, *Melolontha melolontha*, which feeds on leaves and whose larva feeds on roots of crops etc. Also called *May-bug*. [perh. f. COCK¹ as expressing size or vigour + CHAFER]

cocker /ˈkɒkə(r)/ *n.* (in full **cocker spaniel**) **1** a small spaniel of a breed with a silky coat. **2** this breed. [as COCK¹, from use in hunting woodcocks etc.]

cockerel /ˈkɒkər(ə)l/ *n.* a young cock. [ME: dimin. of COCK¹]

cock-eyed /ˈkɒkaɪd/ *adj. colloq.* **1** crooked, askew, not level. **2** (of a scheme etc.) absurd, not practical. **3** drunk. **4** squinting. [19th c.: app. f. COCK¹ + EYE]

cockle¹ /ˈkɒk(ə)l/ *n.* **1 a** any edible mollusc of the genus *Cardium*, having a chubby ribbed bivalve shell. **b** its shell. **2** (in full **cockle-shell**) a small shallow boat. □ **warm the cockles of one's heart** make one contented; be satisfying. [ME f. OF *coquille* shell ult. f. Gk *kogkhulion* f. *kogkhē* CONCH]

cockle² /ˈkɒk(ə)l/ *n.* **1** any of various plants, esp. the pink-flowered corn-cockle, *Agrostemma githago*, growing among corn, esp. wheat. **2** a disease of wheat that turns the grains black. [OE *coccul*, perh. ult. f. LL *coccus*]

cockle³ /ˈkɒk(ə)l/ *v. & n.* —*v.* **1** *intr.* pucker, wrinkle. **2** *tr.* cause to cockle. —*n.* a pucker or wrinkle in paper, glass, etc. [F *coquiller* blister (bread in cooking) f. *coquille*: see COCKLE¹]

cockney /ˈkɒknɪ/ *n. & adj.* —*n.* (pl. **-eys**) **1 a** a native of East London, esp. one born within hearing of Bow Bells. **b** the dialect or accent typical of this area. **2** *Austral.* a young snapper fish, *Chrysophrys auratus.* —*adj.* of or characteristic of cockneys or their dialect or accent. □□ **cockneyism** *n.* [ME *cokeney* cock's egg, later derog. for 'townsman']

cockpit /ˈkɒkpɪt/ *n.* **1 a** a compartment for the pilot (or the pilot and crew) of an aircraft or spacecraft. **b** a similar compartment for the driver in a racing car. **c** a space for the helmsman in some small yachts. **2** an arena of war or other conflict. **3** a place where cock-fights are held. [orig. in sense 3, f. COCK¹ + PIT¹]

cockroach /ˈkɒkrəʊtʃ/ *n.* any of various flat brown insects, esp. *Blatta orientalis*, infesting kitchens, bathrooms, etc. [Sp. *cucaracha*, assim. to COCK¹, ROACH¹]

cockscomb /ˈkɒkskəʊm/ *n.* **1** the crest or comb of a cock. **2** a garden plant *Celosia cristata*, with a terminal plume of tiny white or red flowers.

cocksfoot /ˈkɒksfʊt/ *n.* any pasture grass of the genus *Dactylis*, with broad leaves and green or purplish spikes.

cocksure /ˌkɒkˈʃʊə(r), -ˈʃɔː(r)/ *adj.* **1** presumptuously or arrogantly confident. **2** (foll. by *of, about*) absolutely sure. □□ **cocksurely** *adv.* **cocksureness** *n.* [*cock* = God + SURE]

cocktail /ˈkɒkteɪl/ *n.* **1** a usu. alcoholic drink made by mixing various spirits, fruit juices, etc. **2** a dish of mixed ingredients (*fruit cocktail*; *shellfish cocktail*). **3** any hybrid mixture. □ **cocktail dress** a usu. short evening dress suitable for wearing at a drinks party. **cocktail stick** a small pointed stick for serving an olive, cherry, small sausage, etc. [orig. unkn.: cf. earlier sense 'docked horse' f. COCK¹: the connection is unclear]

cocky¹ /ˈkɒkɪ/ *adj.* (**cockier, cockiest**) **1** conceited, arrogant. **2** saucy, impudent. □□ **cockily** *adv.* **cockiness** *n.* [COCK¹ + -Y¹]

cocky² /ˈkɒkɪ/ *n.* (pl. **-ies**) *Austral. & NZ colloq.* = COCKATOO 2. [abbr.]

cocky-leeky var. of COCK-A-LEEKIE.

coco /ˈkəʊkəʊ/ *n.* (also **cocoa**) (pl. **cocos** or **cocoas**) a tall tropical palm tree, *Cocos nucifera*, bearing coconuts. [Port. & Sp. *coco* grimace: the base of the shell resembles a face]

cocoa /ˈkəʊkəʊ/ *n.* **1** a powder made from crushed cacao seeds, often with other ingredients. **2** a drink made from this. □ **cocoa bean** a cacao seed. **cocoa butter** a fatty substance obtained from cocoa beans and used for confectionery, cosmetics, etc. [alt. of CACAO]

coco-de-mer /ˌkəʊkəʊ-de-ˈmeə(r)/ *n.* a tall palm-tree, *Lodoicea maldivica*, of the Seychelles. [F]

coconut /ˈkəʊkəˌnʌt/ *n.* (also **cocoanut**) **1 a** a large ovate brown seed of the coco, with a hard shell and edible white fleshy lining enclosing a milky juice. **b** = COCO. **c** the edible white fleshy lining of a coconut. **2** *sl.* the human head. □ **coconut butter** a solid oil obtained from the lining of the coconut, and used in soap, candles, ointment, etc. **coconut ice** a sweet of sugar and desiccated coconut. **coconut matting** a matting made of fibre from coconut husks. **coconut shy** a fairground sideshow where balls are thrown to dislodge coconuts. **double coconut** a very large nut of the coco-de-mer. [COCO + NUT]

cocoon /kəˈkuːn/ *n. & v.* —*n.* **1 a** a silky case spun by many insect larvae for protection as pupae. **b** a similar structure made by other animals. **2** a protective covering, esp. to prevent corrosion of metal equipment. —*v.* **1** *tr. & intr.* wrap in or form a cocoon. **2** *tr.* spray with a protective coating. [F *cocon* f. mod. Prov. *coucoun* dimin. of *coca* shell]

cocotte /kəˈkɒt/ *n.* **1 a** a small fireproof dish for cooking and serving an individual portion of food. **b** a deep cooking pot with a tight-fitting lid and handles. **2** *archaic* a fashionable prostitute. [F]

COD *abbr.* **1 a** cash on delivery. **b** *US* collect on delivery. **2** Concise Oxford Dictionary.

cod¹ /kɒd/ *n.* (pl. same) any large marine fish of the family Gadidae, used as food, esp. *Gadus morhua*. □ **cod-liver oil** an oil pressed from the fresh liver of cod, which is rich in vitamins D and A. [ME: orig. unkn.]

cod² /kɒd/ *n. & v. Brit. sl.* —*n.* **1** a parody. **2** a hoax. **3** (*attrib.*) = MOCK *adj.* —*v.* (**codded, codding**) **1 a** *intr.* perform a hoax. **b** *tr.* play a trick on; fool. **2** *tr.* parody. [19th c.: orig. unkn.]

cod³ /kɒd/ *n. sl.* nonsense. [abbr. of CODSWALLOP]

coda /ˈkəʊdə/ *n.* **1** *Mus.* the concluding passage of a piece or movement, usu. forming an addition to the basic structure. **2** *Ballet* the concluding section of a dance. **3** a concluding event or series of events. [It. f. L *cauda* tail]

coddle /'kɒd(ə)l/ *v.tr.* **1 a** treat as an invalid; protect attentively. **b** (foll. by *up*) strengthen by feeding. **2** cook (an egg) in water below boiling point. □□ **coddler** *n.* [prob. dial. var. of *caudle* invalids' gruel]

code /kəʊd/ *n. & v.* —*n.* **1** a system of words, letters, figures, or symbols, used to represent others for secrecy or brevity. **2** a system of prearranged signals, esp. used to ensure secrecy in transmitting messages. **3** *Computing* a piece of program text. **4 a** a systematic collection of statutes, a body of laws so arranged as to avoid inconsistency and overlapping. **b** a set of rules on any subject. **5 a** the prevailing morality of a society or class (*code of honour*). **b** a person's standard of moral behaviour. —*v.tr.* put (a message, program, etc.) into code. □**code-book** a list of symbols etc. used in a code. **code-name** (or **-number**) a word or symbol (or number) used for secrecy or convenience instead of the usual name. □□ **coder** *n.* [ME f. OF f. L CODEX]

codeine /'kəʊdiːn/ *n.* an alkaloid derived from morphine and used to relieve pain. [Gk *kōdeia* poppyhead + -INE[4]]

co-determination /ˌkəʊdɪˌtɜːmɪ'neɪʃ(ə)n/ *n.* cooperation between management and workers in decision-taking. [CO- + DETERMINATION, after G *Mitbestimmung*]

codex /'kəʊdeks/ *n.* (*pl.* **codices** /'kəʊdɪˌsiːz, 'kɒd-/) **1** an ancient manuscript text in book form. **2** a collection of pharmaceutical descriptions of drugs etc. [L, = block of wood, tablet, book]

codfish /'kɒdfɪʃ/ *n.* = COD[1].

codger /'kɒdʒə(r)/ *n.* (usu. in **old codger**) *colloq.* a person, esp. an old or strange one. [perh. var. of *cadger*: see CADGE]

codices *pl.* of CODEX.

codicil /'kəʊdɪsɪl, 'kɒd-/ *n.* an addition explaining, modifying, or revoking a will or part of one. □□ **codicillary** /ˌkɒdɪ'sɪləri/ *adj.* [L *codicillus*, dimin. of CODEX]

codicology /ˌkəʊdɪ'kɒlədʒɪ/ *n.* the study of manuscripts. □□ **codicological** /-kə'lɒdʒɪk(ə)l/ *adj.* **codicologically** /-kə'lɒdʒɪkəlɪ/ *adv.* [F *codicologie* f. L *codex codicis*: see CODEX]

codify /'kəʊdɪˌfaɪ, 'kɒd-/ *v.tr.* (**-ies, -ied**) arrange (laws etc.) systematically into a code. □□ **codification** /-fɪ'keɪʃ(ə)n/ *n.* **codifier** *n.*

codling[1] /'kɒdlɪŋ/ *n.* (also **codlin**) **1** any of several varieties of cooking-apple, having a long tapering shape. **2** a small moth, *Carpocapsa pomonella*, the larva of which feeds on apples. □**codlings-and-cream** the great willow-herb, *Epilobium angustifolium*. [ME f. AF *quer de lion* lion-heart]

codling[2] /'kɒdlɪŋ/ *n.* a small codfish.

codomain /'kəʊdəʊˌmeɪn/ *n. Math.* a set that includes all the possible expressions of a given function. [CO- 2 + DOMAIN]

codon /'kəʊdɒn/ *n. Biochem.* a sequence of three nucleotides, forming a unit of genetic code in a DNA or RNA molecule. [CODE + -ON]

codpiece /'kɒdpiːs/ *n. hist.* an appendage like a small bag or flap at the front of a man's breeches. [ME, f. *cod* scrotum + PIECE]

co-driver /kəʊ'draɪvə(r)/ *n.* a person who shares the driving of a vehicle with another, esp. in a race, rally, etc.

codswallop /'kɒdzˌwɒləp/ *n. Brit. sl.* nonsense. [20th c.: orig. unkn.]

coecilian var. of CAECILIAN.

coed /'kəʊed, kəʊ'ed/ *n. & adj. colloq.* —*n.* **1** a coeducational system or institution. **2** esp. *US* a female student at a coeducational institution. —*adj.* coeducational. [abbr.]

coeducation /ˌkəʊedjuː'keɪʃ(ə)n/ *n.* the education of pupils of both sexes together. □□ **coeducational** *adj.*

coefficient /ˌkəʊɪ'fɪʃ(ə)nt/ *n.* **1** *Math.* a quantity

placed before and multiplying an algebraic expression (e.g. *4* in $4x^y$). **2** *Physics* a multiplier or factor that measures some property (*coefficient of expansion*). [mod.L *coefficientes* (as CO-, EFFICIENT)]

coelacanth /'siːləˌkænθ/ *n.* a large bony marine fish, *Latimeria chalumnae*, formerly thought to be extinct, having a trilobed tail-fin and fleshy pectoral fins. [mod.L *Coelacanthus* f. Gk *koilos* hollow + *akantha* spine]

-coele *comb. form* var. of -CELE.

coelenterate /siː'lentəˌreɪt/ *n.* any marine animal of the phylum Coelenterata with a simple tube-shaped or cup-shaped body, e.g. jellyfish, corals, and sea anemones. [mod.L *Coelenterata* f. Gk *koilos* hollow + *enteron* intestine]

coeliac /'siːlɪˌæk/ *adj.* (*US* **celiac**) of or affecting the belly. □**coeliac disease** a digestive disease of the small intestine brought on by contact with dietary gluten. [L *coeliacus* f. Gk *koiliakos* f. *koilia* belly]

coelom /'siːləm, 'siːləʊm/ *n.* (*US* **celom**) (*pl.* **-oms** or **-omata** /-'ləʊmətə/) *Zool.* the principal body cavity in animals, between the intestinal canal and the body wall. □□ **coelomate** *adj. & n.* [Gk *koilōma* cavity]

coelostat /'siːləˌstæt/ *n. Astron.* an instrument with a rotating mirror that continuously reflects the light from the same area of sky allowing the path of a celestial body to be monitored. [L *caelum* sky + -STAT]

coenobite /'siːnəˌbaɪt/ *n.* (*US* **cenobite**) a member of a monastic community. □□ **coenobitic** /-'bɪtɪk/ *adj.* **coenobitical** /-'bɪtɪk(ə)l/ *adj.* [OF *cenobite* or eccl.L *coenobita* f. LL *coenobium* f. Gk *koinobion* convent f. *koinos* common + *bios* life]

coenzyme /'kəʊˌenzaɪm/ *n. Biochem.* a nonproteinaceous compound that assists in the action of an enzyme.

coequal /kəʊ'iːkw(ə)l/ *adj. & n. archaic or literary* —*adj.* equal with one another. —*n.* an equal. □□ **coequality** /ˌkəʊiː'kwɒlɪtɪ/ *n.* **coequally** *adv.* [ME f. L or eccl.L *coaequalis* (as CO-, EQUAL)]

coerce /kəʊ'ɜːs/ *v.tr.* (often foll. by *into*) persuade or restrain (an unwilling person) by force (*coerced you into signing*). □□ **coercible** *adj.* [ME f. L *coercēre* restrain (as CO-, *arcēre* restrain)]

coercion /kəʊ'ɜːʃ(ə)n/ *n.* **1** the act or process of coercing. **2** government by force. □□ **coercive** *adj.* **coercively** *adv.* **coerciveness** *n.* [OF *cohercion*, -*tion* f. L *coer(c)tio*, *coercitio* -*onis* (as COERCE)]

coeval /kəʊ'iːv(ə)l/ *adj. & n.* —*adj.* **1** having the same age or date of origin. **2** living or existing at the same epoch. **3** having the same duration. —*n.* a coeval person, a contemporary. □□ **coevality** /-'vælɪtɪ/ *n.* **coevally** *adv.* [LL *coaevus* (as CO-, L *aevum* age)]

coexist /ˌkəʊɪg'zɪst/ *v.intr.* (often foll. by *with*) **1** exist together (in time or place). **2** (esp. of nations) exist in mutual tolerance though professing different ideologies etc. □□ **coexistence** *n.* **coexistent** *adj.* [LL *coexistere* (as CO-, EXIST)]

coextensive /ˌkəʊɪk'stensɪv/ *adj.* extending over the same space or time.

C. of E. *abbr.* Church of England.

coffee /'kɒfɪ/ *n.* **1 a** a drink made from the roasted and ground beanlike seeds of a tropical shrub. **b** a cup of this. **2 a** any shrub of the genus *Coffea*, yielding berries containing one or more seeds. **b** these seeds raw, or roasted and ground. **3** a pale brown colour, of coffee mixed with milk. □**coffee bar** a bar or café serving coffee and light refreshments from a counter. **coffee bean** the beanlike seeds of the coffee shrub. **coffee-cup** a small cup for serving coffee. **coffee-essence** a concentrated extract of coffee usu. containing chicory. **coffee-house** a place serving coffee and other refreshments. **coffee-mill** a small machine for grinding roasted coffee beans. **coffee-morning** a morning gathering at which coffee is served, often in aid of charity. **coffee nibs** coffee beans removed from their shells. **coffee-shop** a small informal restaurant, esp. in a hotel or department store. **coffee-table** a small low table. **coffee-table book** a large lavishly illustrated book. [ult. f. Turk. *kahveh* f. Arab. *ḳahwa*, the drink]

coffer /'kɒfə(r)/ *n.* **1** a box, esp. a large strongbox for valuables. **2** (in *pl.*) a treasury or store of funds. **3** a sunken panel in a ceiling etc. □**coffer-dam** a watertight enclosure pumped dry to permit work below the waterline on building bridges etc., or for repairing a ship. □□ **coffered** *adj.* [ME f. OF *coffre* f. L *cophinus* f. Gk *kophinos* basket]

coffin /'kɒfɪn/ *n. & v.* —*n.* **1** a long narrow usu. wooden box in which a corpse is buried or cremated. **2** the part of a horse's hoof below the coronet. —*v.tr.* (**coffined**, **coffining**) put in a coffin. □**coffin-bone** a bone in a horse's hoof. **coffin corner** *US Football* the corner between the goal-line and sideline. **coffin-joint** the joint at the top of a horse's hoof. **coffin-nail** *sl.* a cigarette. [ME f. OF *cof(f)in* little basket etc. f. L *cophinus*: see COFFER]

coffle /'kɒf(ə)l/ *n.* a line of animals, slaves, etc., fastened together. [Arab. *ḳāfila* caravan]

cog /kɒg/ *n.* **1** each of a series of projections on the edge of a wheel or bar transferring motion by engaging with another series. **2** an unimportant member of an organization etc. □**cog-wheel** a wheel with cogs. □□ **cogged** *adj.* [ME: prob. f. Scand. orig.]

cogent /'kəʊdʒ(ə)nt/ *adj.* (of arguments, reasons, etc.) convincing, compelling. □□ **cogency** *n.* **cogently** *adv.* [L *cogere* compel (as CO-, *agere act-* drive)]

cogitable /'kɒdʒɪtəb(ə)l/ *adj.* able to be grasped by the mind; conceivable. [L *cogitabilis* (as COGITATE)]

cogitate /'kɒdʒɪ,teɪt/ *v.tr. & intr.* ponder, meditate. □□ **cogitation** /-'teɪʃ(ə)n/ *n.* **cogitative** /-'tətɪv/ *adj.* **cogitator** *n.* [L *cogitare* think (as CO-, AGITATE)]

cogito /'kəʊgɪ,təʊ/ *n. Philos.* the principle establishing the existence of a being from the fact of its thinking or awareness. [L, = I think, in Fr. philosopher Descartes's formula (1641) *cogito, ergo sum* I think, therefore I exist]

cognac /'kɒnjæk/ *n.* a high-quality brandy, properly that distilled in Cognac in W. France.

cognate /'kɒgneɪt/ *adj. & n.* —*adj.* **1** related to or descended from a common ancestor (cf. AGNATE). **2** *Philol.* (of a word) having the same linguistic family or derivation (as another); representing the same original word or root (e.g. English *father*, German *Vater*, Latin *pater*). —*n.* **1** a relative. **2** a cognate word. □**cognate object** *Gram.* an object that is related in origin and sense to the verb governing it (as in *live a good life*). □□ **cognately** *adv.* **cognateness** *n.* [L *cognatus* (as CO-, *natus* born)]

cognition /kɒg'nɪʃ(ə)n/ *n.* **1** *Philos.* knowing, perceiving, or conceiving as an act or faculty distinct from emotion and volition. **2** a result of this; a perception, sensation, notion, or intuition. □□ **cognitional** *adj.* **cognitive** /'kɒgnɪtɪv/ *adj.* [L *cognitio* (as CO-, *gnoscere gnit-* apprehend)]

cognizable /'kɒgnɪzəb(ə)l, 'kɒn-/ *adj.* (also **-isable**) **1** perceptible, recognizable; clearly identifiable. **2** within the jurisdiction of a court. □□ **cognizably** *adv.* [COGNIZANCE + -ABLE]

cognizance /'kɒgnɪz(ə)ns, 'kɒn-/ *n.* (also **cognisance** /-z(ə)ns/) **1** knowledge or awareness; perception, notice. **2** the sphere of one's observation or concern. **3** *Law* the right of a court to deal with a matter. **4** *Heraldry* a distinctive device or mark. □**have cognizance of** know, esp. officially. **take cognizance of** attend to; take account of. [ME f. OF *conoisance* ult. f. L *cognoscent-* f. *cognitio*: see COGNITION]

cognizant /'kɒgnɪz(ə)nt, 'kɒn-/ *adj.* (also **cognisant** /-z(ə)nt/) (foll. by *of*) having knowledge or being aware of.

cognomen /kɒg'nəʊmen/ *n.* **1** a nickname. **2** an ancient Roman's personal name or epithet, as in Marcus Tullius *Cicero*, Publius Cornelius Scipio *Africanus*. [L]

cognoscente /,kɒnjə'ʃentɪ/ *n.* (*pl.* **cognoscenti** /-tɪ/) (usu. in *pl.*) a connoisseur. [It., lit. one who knows]

cohabit /kəʊ'hæbɪt/ *v.intr.* (**cohabited**, **cohabiting**) live together, esp. as husband and wife without being married to one another. □□ **cohabitant** *n.* **cohabitation** /-'teɪʃ(ə)n/ *n.* **cohabitee** /-'tiː/ *n.* **cohabiter** *n.* [L *cohabitare* (as CO-, *habitare* dwell)]

cohere /kəʊ'hɪə(r)/ *v.intr.* **1** (of parts or a whole) stick together, remain united. **2** (of reasoning etc.) be logical or consistent. [L *cohaerēre cohaes-* (as CO-, *haerēre* stick)]

coherent /kəʊ'hɪərənt/ *adj.* **1** (of a person) able to speak intelligibly and articulately. **2** (of speech, an argument, etc.) logical and consistent; easily followed. **3** cohering; sticking together. **4** *Physics* (of waves) having a constant phase relationship. □□ **coherence** *n.* **coherency** *n.* **coherently** *adv.* [L *cohaerēre cohaerent-* (as COHERE)]

cohesion /kəʊ'hiːʒ(ə)n/ *n.* **1 a** the act or condition of sticking together. **b** a tendency to cohere. **2** *Chem.* the force with which molecules cohere. □□ **cohesive** /-sɪv/ *adj.* **cohesively** /-sɪvlɪ/ *adv.* **cohesiveness** /-sɪvnɪs/ *n.* [L *cohaes-* (see COHERE) after *adhesion*]

coho /'kəʊhəʊ/ *n.* (also **cohoe**) (*pl.* **-os** or **-oes**) a silver salmon, *Oncorhynchus kisutch*, of the N. Pacific. [19th c.: orig. unkn.]

cohort /'kəʊhɔːt/ *n.* **1** an ancient Roman military unit, equal to one-tenth of a legion. **2** a band of warriors. **3 a** persons banded or grouped together, esp. in a common cause. **b** a group of persons with a common statistical characteristic. **4** *US* a companion or colleague. [ME f. F *cohorte* or L *cohors cohort-* enclosure, company]

COHSE /'kəʊzɪ/ *abbr.* (in the UK) Confederation of Health Service Employees.

COI *abbr.* (in the UK) Central Office of Information.

coif /kɔɪf/ *n. hist.* **1** a close-fitting cap, esp. as worn by nuns under a veil. **2** a protective metal skullcap worn under armour. [ME f. OF *coife* f. LL *cofia* helmet]

coiffeur /kwɑːˈfɜː(r)/ *n.* (*fem.* **coiffeuse** /-ˈfɜːz/) a hairdresser. [F]

coiffure /kwɑːˈfjʊə(r)/ *n.* the way hair is arranged; a hairstyle. [F]

coign /kɔɪn/ *n.* □**coign of vantage** a favourable position for observation or action. [earlier spelling of COIN in the sense 'cornerstone']

coil[1] /kɔɪl/ *n. & v.* —*n.* **1** anything arranged in a joined sequence of concentric circles. **2** a length of rope, a spring, etc., arranged in this way. **3** a single turn of something coiled, e.g. a snake. **4** a lock of hair twisted and coiled. **5** an intra-uterine contraceptive device in the form of a coil. **6** *Electr.* a device consisting of a coiled wire for converting low voltage to high voltage, esp. for transmission to the sparking plugs of an internal-combustion engine. **7** a piece of wire, piping, etc., wound in circles or spirals. **8** a roll of postage stamps. —*v.* **1** *tr.* arrange in a series of concentric loops or rings. **2** *tr. & intr.* twist or be twisted into a circular or spiral shape. **3** *intr.* move sinuously. [OF *coillir* f. L *colligere* COLLECT[1]]

coil[2] /kɔɪl/ *n.* □**this mortal coil** the difficulties of earthly life (with ref. to Shakesp. *Hamlet* III. i. 67). [16th c.: orig. unkn.]

coin /kɔɪn/ *n. & v.* —*n.* **1** a piece of flat usu. round metal stamped and issued by authority as money. **2** (*collect.*) metal money. —*v.tr.* **1** make (coins) by stamping. **2** make (metal) into coins. **3** invent or devise (esp. a new word or phrase). □**coin-box 1** a telephone operated by inserting coins. **2** the receptacle for these. **coin money** make much money quickly. **coin-op** a launderette etc. with automatic machines operated by inserting coins. **to coin a phrase** *iron.* introducing a banal remark or cliché. [ME f. OF, = stamping-die, f. L *cuneus* wedge]

coinage /'kɔɪnɪdʒ/ *n.* **1** the act or process of coining

2 a coins collectively. **b** a system or type of coins in use (*decimal coinage*; *bronze coinage*). **3** an invention, esp. of a new word or phrase. [ME f. OF *coigniage*]

coincide /ˌkəʊɪnˈsaɪd/ *v.intr.* **1** occur at or during the same time. **2** occupy the same portion of space. **3** (often foll. by *with*) be in agreement; have the same view. [med.L *coincidere* (as CO-, INCIDENT)]

coincidence /kəʊˈɪnsɪd(ə)ns/ *n.* **1 a** occurring or being together. **b** an instance of this. **2** a remarkable concurrence of events or circumstances without apparent causal connection. **3** *Physics* the presence of ionizing particles etc. in two or more detectors simultaneously, or of two or more signals simultaneously in a circuit. [med.L *coincidentia* (as COINCIDE)]

coincident /kəʊˈɪnsɪd(ə)nt/ *adj.* **1** occurring together in space or time. **2** (foll. by *with*) in agreement; harmonious. □□ **coincidently** *adv.*

coincidental /kəʊˌɪnsɪˈdent(ə)l/ *adj.* **1** in the nature of or resulting from a coincidence. **2** happening or existing at the same time. □□ **coincidentally** *adv.*

coiner /ˈkɔɪnə(r)/ *n.* **1** a person who coins money, esp. *Brit.* the maker of counterfeit coin. **2** a person who invents or devises something (esp. a new word or phrase).

Cointreau /ˈkwɑːntrəʊ/ *n. propr.* a colourless orange-flavoured liqueur. [F]

coir /ˈkɔɪə(r)/ *n.* fibre from the outer husk of the coconut, used for ropes, matting, etc. [Malayalam *kāyar* cord f. *kāyaru* be twisted]

coition /kəʊˈɪʃ(ə)n/ *n. Med.* = COITUS. [L *coitio* f. *coire coit-* go together]

coitus /ˈkəʊɪtəs/ *n. Med.* sexual intercourse. □ **coitus interruptus** /ˌɪntəˈrʌptəs/ sexual intercourse in which the penis is withdrawn before ejaculation. □□ **coital** *adj.* [L (as COITION)]

Coke /kəʊk/ *n. propr.* Coca-Cola. [abbr.]

coke[1] /kəʊk/ *n. & v.* —*n.* **1** a solid substance left after the gases have been extracted from coal. **2** a residue left after the incomplete combustion of petrol etc. —*v.tr.* convert (coal) into coke. [prob. f. N.Engl. dial. *colk* core, of unkn. orig.]

coke[2] /kəʊk/ *n. sl.* cocaine. [abbr.]

Col. *abbr.* **1** Colonel. **2** Colossians (New Testament).

col /kɒl/ *n.* **1** a depression in the summit-line of a chain of mountains, generally affording a pass from one slope to another. **2** *Meteorol.* a low-pressure region between anticyclones. [F, = neck, f. L *collum*]

col. *abbr.* column.

col- /kɒl/ *prefix* assim. form of COM- before *l*.

cola /ˈkəʊlə/ *n.* (also **kola**) **1** any small tree of the genus *Cola*, native to W. Africa, bearing seeds containing caffeine. **2** a carbonated drink usu. flavoured with these seeds. □ **cola nut** a seed of the tree. [W.Afr.]

colander /ˈkʌləndə(r)/ *n.* a perforated vessel used to strain off liquid in cookery. [ME, ult. f. L *colare* strain]

co-latitude /kəʊˈlætɪˌtjuːd/ *n. Astron.* the complement of the latitude, the difference between it and 90°.

colchicine /ˈkɒltʃɪˌsiːn, ˈkɒlk-/ *n.* a yellow alkaloid obtained from colchicum, used in the treatment of gout.

colchicum /ˈkɒltʃɪkəm, ˈkɒlkɪ-/ *n.* **1** any liliaceous plant of the genus *Colchicum*, esp. meadow saffron. **2** its dried corm or seed. Also called *autumn crocus*. [L f. Gk *kolkhikon* of Kolkhis, a region east of the Black Sea]

cold /kəʊld/ *adj., n., & adv.* —*adj.* **1** of or at a low or relatively low temperature, esp. when compared with the human body. **2** not heated; cooled after being heated. **3** (of a person) feeling cold. **4** lacking ardour, friendliness, or affection; undemonstrative, apathetic. **5** depressing, dispiriting, uninteresting (*cold facts*). **6 a** dead. **b** *colloq.* unconscious. **7** *colloq.* at one's mercy (*had me cold*). **8** sexually frigid. **9** (of soil) slow to absorb heat. **10** (of a scent in hunting) having become weak. **11** (in children's games) far from finding or guessing what is sought. **12** without preparation or rehearsal. —*n.* **1 a** the prevalence of a low temperature, esp. in the atmosphere. **b** cold weather; a cold environment (*went out into the cold*). **2** an infection in which the mucous membrane of the nose and throat becomes inflamed, causing running at the nose, sneezing, sore throat, etc. —*adv.* esp. *US* completely, entirely (*was stopped cold mid-sentence*). □ **catch a cold 1** become infected with a cold. **2** encounter trouble or difficulties. **cold call** sell goods or services by making unsolicited calls on prospective customers by telephone or in person. **cold cathode** a cathode that emits electrons without being heated. **cold chisel** a chisel suitable for cutting metal. **cold comfort** poor or inadequate consolation. **cold cream** ointment for cleansing and softening the skin. **cold cuts** slices of cold cooked meats. **cold feet** *colloq.* loss of nerve or confidence. **cold frame** an unheated frame with a glass top for growing small plants. **cold front** the forward edge of an advancing mass of cold air. **cold fusion** nuclear fusion at room temperature esp. as a possible energy source. **cold shoulder** a show of intentional unfriendliness. **cold-shoulder** *v.tr.* be deliberately unfriendly to. **cold sore** inflammation and blisters in and around the mouth, caused by a virus infection. **cold storage 1** storage in a refrigerator or other cold place for preservation. **2** a state in which something (esp. an idea) is put aside temporarily. **cold sweat** a state of sweating induced by fear or illness. **cold table** a selection of dishes of cold food. **cold turkey** *US sl.* **1** a series of blunt statements or behaviour. **2** abrupt withdrawal from addictive drugs; the symptoms of this. **cold war** a state of hostility between nations without actual fighting. **cold wave 1** a temporary spell of cold weather over a wide area. **2** a kind of permanent wave for the hair using chemicals and without heat. **in cold blood** without feeling or passion; deliberately, ruthlessly. **out in the cold** ignored, neglected. **throw** (or **pour**) **cold water on** be discouraging or depreciatory about. □□ **coldish** *adj.* **coldly** *adv.* **coldness** *n.* [OE *cald* f. Gmc, rel. to L *gelu* frost]

cold-blooded /kəʊldˈblʌdɪd/ *adj.* **1** having a body temperature varying with that of the environment (e.g. of fish); poikilothermic. **2** callous; deliberately cruel. □□ **cold-bloodedly** *adv.* **cold-bloodedness** *n.*

cold-hearted /kəʊldˈhɑːtɪd/ *adj.* lacking affection or warmth; unfriendly. □□ **cold-heartedly** *adv.* **cold-heartedness** *n.*

cold-short /ˈkəʊldʃɔːt/ *adj.* (of a metal) brittle in its cold state. [Sw. *kallskör* f. *kall* cold + *skör* brittle: assim. to SHORT]

cole /kəʊl/ *n.* (usu. in *comb.*) **1** cabbage. **2** = RAPE[2]. [ME f. ON *kál* f. L *caulis* stem, cabbage]

colemouse var. of COALMOUSE.

coleopteron /ˌkɒlɪˈɒptəˌrɒn/ *n.* any insect of the order Coleoptera, with front wings modified into sheaths to protect the hinder wings, e.g. a beetle or weevil. □□ **coleopterist** *n.* **coleopterous** *adj.* [mod.L *Coleoptera* f. Gk *koleopteros* f. *koleon* sheath + *pteron* wing]

coleoptile /ˌkɒlɪˈɒptaɪl/ *n. Bot.* a sheath protecting a young shoot tip in grasses. [Gk *koleon* sheath + *ptilon* feather]

coleseed /ˈkəʊlsiːd/ *n.* = COLE 2.

coleslaw /ˈkəʊlslɔː/ *n.* a dressed salad of sliced raw cabbage, carrot, onion, etc. [Du. *koolsla*: see COLE, SLAW]

cole-tit var. of *coal-tit*.

coleus /ˈkəʊlɪəs/ *n.* any plant of the genus *Coleus*, having variegated coloured leaves. [mod.L f. Gk *koleon* sheath]

coley /ˈkəʊlɪ/ *n.* (*pl.* **-eys**) *Brit.* any of various fish used as food, esp. the saithe or rock-salmon. [perh. f. *coal-fish*]

colic /ˈkɒlɪk/ *n.* a severe spasmodic abdominal pain.

b *but* d *dog* f *few* g *get* h *he* j *yes* k *cat* l *leg* m *man* n *no* p *pen* r *red* s *sit* t *top* v *voice*

□□ **colicky** *adj.* [ME f. F *colique* f. LL *colicus*: see COLON²]

coliseum /ˌkɒlɪˈsiːəm/ *n. US* = COLOSSEUM.

colitis /kəˈlaɪtɪs/ *n.* inflammation of the lining of the colon.

Coll. *abbr.* College.

collaborate /kəˈlæbəˌreɪt/ *v.intr.* (often foll. by *with*) **1** work jointly, esp. in a literary or artistic production. **2** cooperate traitorously with an enemy. □□ **collaboration** /-ˈreɪʃ(ə)n/ *n.* **collaborationist** /-ˈreɪʃənɪst/ *n. & adj.* **collaborative** /-rətɪv/ *adj.* **collaborator** *n.* [L *collaborare collaborat-* (as COM-, *laborare* work)]

collage /ˈkɒlɑːʒ, kəˈlɑːʒ/ *n.* **1** a form of art in which various materials (e.g. photographs, pieces of paper, matchsticks) are arranged and glued to a backing. **2** a work of art done in this way. **3** a collection of unrelated things. □□ **collagist** *n.* [F, = gluing]

collagen /ˈkɒlədʒ(ə)n/ *n.* a protein found in animal connective tissue, yielding gelatin on boiling. [F *collagène* f. Gk *kolla* glue + *-gène* = -GEN]

collapsar /kɒˈlæpsɑː(r)/ *n. Astron.* = *black hole* 1.

collapse /kəˈlæps/ *n. & v.* —*n.* **1** the tumbling down or falling in of a structure; folding up; giving way. **2** a sudden failure of a plan, undertaking, etc. **3** a physical or mental breakdown. —*v.* **1 a** *intr.* undergo or experience a collapse. **b** *tr.* cause to collapse. **2** *intr. colloq.* lie or sit down and relax, esp. after prolonged effort (*collapsed into a chair*). **3 a** *intr.* (of furniture etc.) be foldable into a small space. **b** *tr.* fold (furniture) in this way. □□ **collapsible** *adj.* **collapsibility** /-ˈbɪlɪtɪ/ *n.* [L *collapsus* past part. of *collabi* (as COM-, *labi* slip)]

collar /ˈkɒlə(r)/ *n. & v.* —*n.* **1** the part of a shirt, dress, coat, etc., that goes round the neck, either upright or turned over. **2** a band of linen, lace, etc., completing the upper part of a costume. **3** a band of leather or other material put round an animal's (esp. a dog's) neck. **4** a restraining or connecting band, ring, or pipe in machinery. **5** a coloured marking resembling a collar round the neck of a bird or animal. **6** *Brit.* a piece of meat rolled up and tied. —*v.tr.* **1** seize (a person) by the collar or neck. **2** capture, apprehend. **3** *colloq.* accost. **4** *sl.* take, esp. illicitly. □**collar-beam** a horizontal beam connecting two rafters and forming with them an A-shaped roof-truss. **collar-bone** either of two bones joining the breastbone and the shoulder-blades. **collared dove** a dove, *Streptopelia decaoto*, having distinct neck-markings. □□ **collared** *adj.* (also in *comb.*). **collarless** *adj.* [ME f. AF *coler*, OF *colier*, f. L *collare* f. *collum* neck]

collate /kəˈleɪt/ *v.tr.* **1** analyse and compare (texts, statements, etc.) to identify points of agreement and difference. **2** *Bibliog.* verify the order of (sheets) by their signatures. **3** assemble (information) from different sources. **4** (often foll. by *to*) *Eccl.* appoint (a clergyman) to a benefice. □□ **collator** *n.* [L *collat-* past part. stem of *conferre* compare]

collateral /kəˈlætər(ə)l/ *n. & adj.* —*n.* **1** security pledged as a guarantee for repayment of a loan. **2** a person having the same descent as another but by a different line. —*adj.* **1** descended from the same stock but by a different line. **2** side by side; parallel. **3 a** additional but subordinate. **b** contributory. **c** connected but aside from the main subject, course, etc. □□ **collaterality** /-ˈrælɪtɪ/ *n.* **collaterally** *adv.* [ME f. med.L *collateralis* (as COM-, LATERAL)]

collation /kəˈleɪʃ(ə)n/ *n.* **1** the act or an instance of collating. **2** *RC Ch.* a light meal allowed during a fast. **3** a light informal meal. [ME f. OF f. L *collatio -onis* (see COLLATE): sense 2 f. Cassian's *Collationes Patrum* (= *Lives of the Fathers*) read by Benedictines and followed by a light meal]

colleague /ˈkɒliːg/ *n.* a fellow official or worker, esp. in a profession or business. [F *collègue* f. L *collega* (as COM-, *legare* depute)]

collect¹ /kəˈlekt/ *v., adj., & adv.* —*v.* **1** *tr. & intr.*

bring or come together; assemble, accumulate. **2** *tr.* systematically seek and acquire (books, stamps, etc.), esp. as a continuing hobby. **3 a** *tr.* obtain (taxes, contributions, etc.) from a number of people. **b** *intr. colloq.* receive money. **4** *tr.* call for; fetch (*went to collect the laundry*). **5 a** *refl.* regain control of oneself esp. after a shock. **b** *tr.* concentrate (one's energies, thoughts, etc.). **c** *tr.* (as **collected** *adj.*) calm and cool; not perturbed or distracted. **6** *tr.* infer, gather, conclude. —*adj. & adv. US* to be paid for by the receiver (of a telephone call, parcel, etc.). □□ **collectable** *adj.* **collectedly** *adv.* [F *collecter* or med.L *collectare* f. L *collectus* past part. of *colligere* (as COM-, *legere* pick)]

collect² /ˈkɒlekt, -ɪkt/ *n.* a short prayer of the Anglican and Roman Catholic Church, esp. one assigned to a particular day or season. [ME f. OF *collecte* f. L *collecta* fem. past part. of *colligere*: see COLLECT¹]

collectible /kəˈlektɪb(ə)l/ *adj. & n.* —*adj.* worth collecting. —*n.* an item sought by collectors.

collection /kəˈlekʃ(ə)n/ *n.* **1** the act or process of collecting or being collected. **2** a group of things collected together, esp. systematically. **3** (foll. by *of*) an accumulation; a mass or pile (*a collection of dust*). **4 a** the collecting of money, esp. in church or for a charitable cause. **b** the amount collected. **5** the regular removal of mail, esp. from a postbox, for dispatch. **6** (in *pl.*) *Brit.* college examinations held at the end of a term, esp. at Oxford University. [ME f. OF f. L *collectio -onis* (as COLLECT¹)]

collective /kəˈlektɪv/ *adj. & n.* —*adj.* **1** formed by or constituting a collection. **2** taken as a whole; aggregate (*our collective opinion*). **3** of or from several or many individuals; common. —*n.* **1 a** = *collective farm*. **b** any cooperative enterprise. **c** its members. **2** = *collective noun.* □**collective bargaining** negotiation of wages etc. by an organized body of employees. **collective farm** a jointly-operated esp. State-owned amalgamation of several smallholdings. **collective noun** *Gram.* a noun that is grammatically singular and denotes a collection or number of individuals (e.g. *assembly*, *family*, *troop*). **collective ownership** ownership of land, means of production, etc., by all for the benefit of all. **collective unconscious** *Psychol.* (in Jungian theory) the part of the unconscious mind derived from ancestral memory and experience common to all mankind, as distinct from the personal unconscious. □□ **collectively** *adv.* **collectiveness** *n.* **collectivity** /-ˈtɪvɪtɪ/ *n.* [F *collectif* or L *collectivus* (as COLLECT¹)]

collectivism /kəˈlektɪˌvɪz(ə)m/ *n.* the theory and practice of the collective ownership of land and the means of production. □□ **collectivist** *n.* **collectivistic** /-ˈvɪstɪk/ *adj.*

collectivize /kəˈlektɪˌvaɪz/ *v.tr.* (also **-ise**) organize on the basis of collective ownership. □□ **collectivization** /-ˈzeɪʃ(ə)n/ *n.*

collector /kəˈlektə(r)/ *n.* **1** a person who collects, esp. things of interest as a hobby. **2** a person who collects money etc. due (*tax-collector*; *ticket-collector*). **3** *Electronics* the region in a transistor that absorbs carriers of a charge. □**collector's item** (or **piece**) a valuable object, esp. one of interest to collectors. [ME f. AF *collectour* f. med.L *collector* (as COLLECT¹)]

colleen /kɒˈliːn/ *n. Ir.* a girl. [Ir. *cailín*, dimin. of *caile* country-woman]

college /ˈkɒlɪdʒ/ *n.* **1** an establishment for further or higher education, sometimes part of a university. **2** an establishment for specialized professional education (*business college*; *college of music*; *naval college*). **3** the buildings or premises of a college (*lived in college*). **4** the students and teachers in a college. **5** *Brit.* a public school. **6** an organized body of persons with shared functions and privileges (*College of Physicians*). □**College of Arms** (in the UK) a corporation recording lineage and granting arms. **college of education** *Brit.* a training college for schoolteachers. **college pudding** *Brit.* a small baked or steamed suet pudding with dried fruit. □□

collegial /kəˈliːdʒ(ə)l/ *adj.* [ME f. OF *college* or L *collegium* f. *collega* (as COLLEAGUE)]

collegian /kəˈliːdʒ(ə)n/ *n.* a member of a college. [med.L *collegianus* (as COLLEGE)]

collegiate /kəˈliːdʒət/ *adj.* constituted as or belonging to a college; corporate. □**collegiate church** 1 a church endowed for a chapter of canons but without a bishop's see. 2 *US & Sc.* a church or group of churches established under a joint pastorate. □□ **collegiately** *adv.* [LL *collegiatus* (as COLLEGE)]

collenchyma /kɒˈleŋkɪmə/ *n. Bot.* a tissue of cells with thick cellulose cell walls, strengthening young stems etc. [Gk *kolla* glue + *egkhuma* infusion]

Colles' fracture /ˈkɒlɪs/ *n.* a fracture of the lower end of the radius with a backward displacement of the hand. [A. *Colles*, Ir. surgeon d. 1843]

collet /ˈkɒlɪt/ *n.* 1 a flange or socket for setting a gem in jewellery. 2 *Engin.* a segmented band or sleeve put round a shaft or spindle and tightened to grip it. 3 *Horol.* a small collar to which the inner end of a balance spring is attached. [F, dimin. of COL]

collide /kəˈlaɪd/ *v.intr.* (often foll. by *with*) 1 come into abrupt or violent impact. 2 be in conflict. [L *collidere collis-* (as COM-, *laedere* strike, damage)]

collie /ˈkɒlɪ/ *n.* 1 a sheepdog orig. of a Scottish breed, with a long pointed nose and usu. dense long hair. 2 this breed. [perh. f. *coll* COAL (as being orig. black)]

collier /ˈkɒlɪə(r)/ *n.* 1 a coalminer. 2 a a coal-ship. b a member of its crew. [ME, f. COAL + -IER]

colliery /ˈkɒlɪərɪ/ *n.* (*pl.* -ies) a coalmine and its associated buildings.

colligate /ˈkɒlɪɡeɪt/ *v.tr.* bring into connection (esp. isolated facts by a generalization). □□ **colligation** /-ˈɡeɪʃ(ə)n/ *n.* [L *colligare colligat-* (as COM-, *ligare* bind)]

collimate /ˈkɒlɪmeɪt/ *v.tr.* 1 adjust the line of sight of (a telescope etc.). 2 make (telescopes or rays) accurately parallel. □□ **collimation** /-ˈmeɪʃ(ə)n/ *n.* [L *collimare*, erron. for *collineare* align (as COM-, *linea* line)]

collimator /ˈkɒlɪˌmeɪtə(r)/ *n.* 1 a device for producing a parallel beam of rays or radiation. 2 a small fixed telescope used for adjusting the line of sight of an astronomical telescope, etc.

collinear /kəˈlɪnɪə(r)/ *adj. Geom.* (of points) lying in the same straight line. □□ **collinearity** /-ˈærɪtɪ/ *n.* **collinearly** *adv.*

Collins /ˈkɒlɪnz/ *n.* an iced drink made of gin or whisky etc. with soda, lemon or lime juice, and sugar. [20th c.: orig. unkn.]

collision /kəˈlɪʒ(ə)n/ *n.* 1 a violent impact of a moving body, esp. a vehicle or ship, with another or with a fixed object. 2 the clashing of opposed interests or considerations. 3 *Physics* the action of particles striking or coming together. □**collision course** a course or action that is bound to cause a collision or conflict. □□ **collisional** *adj.* [ME f. LL *collisio* (as COLLIDE)]

collocate /ˈkɒləkeɪt/ *v.tr.* 1 place together or side by side. 2 arrange; set in a particular place. 3 (often foll. by *with*) *Linguistics* juxtapose (a word etc.) with another. □□ **collocation** /-ˈkeɪʃ(ə)n/ *n.* [L *collocare collocat-* (as COM-, *locare* to place)]

collocutor /ˈkɒləˌkjuːtə(r), kəˈlɒkjuːtə(r)/ *n.* a person who takes part in a conversation. [LL f. *colloqui* (as COM-, *loqui locut-* talk)]

collodion /kəˈləʊdɪən/ *n.* a syrupy solution of cellulose nitrate in a mixture of alcohol and ether, used in photography and surgery. [Gk *kollōdēs* gluelike f. *kolla* glue]

collogue /kəˈləʊɡ/ *v.intr.* (**collogues, collogued, colloguing**) (foll. by *with*) talk confidentially. [prob. alt. of obs. *colleague* conspire, by assoc. with L *colloqui* converse]

colloid /ˈkɒlɔɪd/ *n.* 1 *Chem.* a a substance consisting of ultramicroscopic particles. b a mixture of such a substance uniformly dispersed through a second substance esp. to form a viscous solution. 2 *Med.* a substance of a homogeneous gelatinous consistency. □□ **colloidal** /-ˈlɔɪd(ə)l/ *adj.* [Gk *kolla* glue + -OID]

collop /ˈkɒləp/ *n.* a slice, esp. of meat or bacon; an escalope. [ME, = fried bacon and eggs, of Scand. orig.]

colloquial /kəˈləʊkwɪəl/ *adj.* belonging to or proper to ordinary or familiar conversation, not formal or literary. □□ **colloquially** *adv.* [L *colloquium* COLLOQUY]

colloquialism /kəˈləʊkwɪəˌlɪz(ə)m/ *n.* 1 a colloquial word or phrase. 2 the use of colloquialisms.

colloquium /kəˈləʊkwɪəm/ *n.* (*pl.* **colloquiums** or **colloquia** /-kwɪə/) an academic conference or seminar. [L: see COLLOQUY]

colloquy /ˈkɒləkwɪ/ *n.* (*pl.* -quies) 1 the act of conversing. 2 a conversation. 3 *Eccl.* a gathering for discussion of theological questions. [L *colloquium* (as COM-, *loqui* speak)]

collotype /ˈkɒləˌtaɪp/ *n. Printing* 1 a thin sheet of gelatin exposed to light, treated with reagents, and used to make high quality prints by lithography. 2 a print made by this process. [Gk *kolla* glue + TYPE]

collude /kəˈluːd, -ˈljuːd/ *v.intr.* come to an understanding or conspire together, esp. for a fraudulent purpose. □□ **colluder** *n.* [L *colludere collus-* (as COM-, *ludere lus-* play)]

collusion /kəˈluːʒ(ə)n, -ˈljuːʒ(ə)n/ *n.* 1 a secret understanding, esp. for a fraudulent purpose. 2 *Law* such an understanding between ostensible opponents in a lawsuit. □□ **collusive** *adj.* **collusively** *adv.* [ME f. OF *collusion* or L *collusio* (as COLLUDE)]

collyrium /kəˈlɪrɪəm/ *n.* (*pl.* **collyria** /-rɪə/) a medicated eye-lotion. [L f. Gk *kollurion* poultice f. *kollura* coarse bread-roll]

collywobbles /ˈkɒlɪˌwɒb(ə)lz/ *n.pl. colloq.* 1 a rumbling or pain in the stomach. 2 a feeling of strong apprehension. [fanciful, f. COLIC + WOBBLE]

Colo. *abbr.* Colorado.

colobus /ˈkɒləbəs/ *n.* any leaf-eating monkey of the genus *Colobus*, native to Africa, having shortened thumbs. [mod.L f. Gk *kolobos* docked]

colocynth /ˈkɒləsɪnθ/ *n.* (also **coloquintida** /ˌkɒləˈkwɪntɪdə/) 1 a a plant of the gourd family, *Citrullus colocynthis*, bearing a pulpy fruit. b this fruit. 2 a bitter purgative drug obtained from the fruit. [L *colocynthis* f. Gk *kolokunthis*]

cologne /kəˈləʊn/ *n.* (in full **cologne water**) eau-de-Cologne or a similar scented toilet water. [abbr.]

colon[1] /ˈkəʊlən, -lɒn/ *n.* a punctuation mark (:), used esp. to introduce a quotation or a list of items or to separate clauses when the second expands or illustrates the first; also between numbers in a statement of proportion (as in 10:1) and in Biblical references (as in Exodus 3:2). [L f. Gk *kōlon* limb, clause]

colon[2] /ˈkəʊlən, -lɒn/ *n. Anat.* the lower and greater part of the large intestine, from the caecum to the rectum. □□ **colonic** /kəˈlɒnɪk/ *adj.* [ME, ult. f. Gk *kolon*]

colonel /ˈkɜːn(ə)l/ *n.* 1 an army officer in command of a regiment, immediately below a brigadier in rank. 2 *US* an officer of corresponding rank in the Air Force. 3 = *lieutenant-colonel.* □**Colonel Blimp** see BLIMP *n.* 1. □□ **colonelcy** *n.* (*pl.* -ies). [obs. F *coronel* f. It. *colonnello* f. *colonna* COLUMN]

colonial /kəˈləʊnɪəl/ *adj. & n.* —*adj.* 1 of, relating to, or characteristic of a colony or colonies, esp. of a British Crown Colony. 2 (esp. of architecture or furniture) built or designed in, or in a style characteristic of, the period of the British colonies in America before independence. —*n.* 1 a native or inhabitant of a colony. 2 a house built in colonial style. □**colonial goose** *Austral.* & *NZ* a boned and stuffed roast leg of mutton. □□ **colonially** *adv.*

colonialism /kəˈləʊnɪəˌlɪz(ə)m/ *n.* 1 a policy of acquiring or maintaining colonies. 2 *derog.* this policy regarded as the esp. economic exploitation of weak or backward peoples by a larger power. □□ **colonialist** n.

colonist /ˈkɒlənɪst/ n. a settler in or inhabitant of a colony.

colonize /ˈkɒləˌnaɪz/ v. (also **-ise**) **1** tr. **a** establish a colony or colonies in (a country or area). **b** settle as colonists. **2** intr. establish or join a colony. **3** tr. US Polit. plant voters in (a district) for party purposes. **4** tr. Biol. (of plants and animals) become established (in an area). □□ **colonization** /-ˈzeɪʃ(ə)n/ n. **colonizer** n.

colonnade /ˌkɒləˈneɪd/ n. a row of columns, esp. supporting an entablature or roof. □□ **colonnaded** adj. [F f. colonne COLUMN]

colony /ˈkɒlənɪ/ n. (pl. **-ies**) **1 a** a group of settlers in a new country (whether or not already inhabited) fully or partly subject to the mother country. **b** the settlement or its territory. **2 a** people of one nationality or race or occupation in a city, esp. if living more or less in isolation or in a special quarter. **b** a separate or segregated group (nudist colony). **3** Biol. a collection of animals, plants, etc., connected, in contact, or living close together. [ME f. L colonia f. colonus farmer f. colere cultivate]

colophon /ˈkɒləˌfɒn, -fən/ n. **1** a publisher's device or imprint, esp. on the title-page. **2** a tailpiece in a manuscript or book, often ornamental, giving the writer's or printer's name, the date, etc. [LL f. Gk kolophōn summit, finishing touch]

colophony /kəˈlɒfənɪ/ n. = ROSIN. [L colophonia (resin) from Colophon in Asia Minor]

coloquintida var. of COLOCYNTH.

color etc. US var. of COLOUR etc.

Colorado beetle /ˌkɒləˈrɑːdəʊ/ n. a yellow and black striped beetle, Leptinotarsa decemlineata, the larva of which is highly destructive to the potato plant. [Colorado in the US]

coloration /ˌkʌləˈreɪʃ(ə)n/ n. (also **colouration**) **1** colouring; a scheme or method of applying colour. **2** the natural (esp. variegated) colour of living things or animals. [F coloration or LL coloratio f. colorare COLOUR]

coloratura /ˌkɒlərəˈtʊərə/ n. **1** elaborate ornamentation of a vocal melody. **2** a singer (esp. a soprano) skilled in coloratura singing. [It. f. L colorare COLOUR]

colorific /ˌkɒləˈrɪfɪk, ˌkʌl-/ adj. **1** producing colour. **2** highly coloured. [F colorifique or mod.L colorificus (as COLOUR)]

colorimeter /ˌkɒləˈrɪmɪtə(r), ˌkʌl-/ n. an instrument for measuring the intensity of colour. □□ **colorimetric** /-ˈmetrɪk/ adj. **colorimetry** n. [L color COLOUR + -METER]

colossal /kəˈlɒs(ə)l/ adj. **1** of immense size; huge, gigantic. **2** colloq. remarkable, splendid. **3** Archit. (of an order) having more than one storey of columns. **4** Sculpture (of a statue) about twice life size. □□ **colossally** adv. [F f. colosse COLOSSUS]

colosseum /ˌkɒləˈsiːəm/ n. a large stadium or amphitheatre. [med.L, neut. of colosseus gigantic (as COLOSSUS)]

colossus /kəˈlɒsəs/ n. (pl. **colossi** /-saɪ/ or **colossuses**) **1** a statue much bigger than life size. **2** a gigantic person, animal, building, etc. **3** an imperial power personified. [L f. Gk kolossos]

colostomy /kəˈlɒstəmɪ/ n. (pl. **-ies**) Surgery an operation on the colon to make an opening in the abdominal wall to provide an artificial anus. [as COLON² + Gk stoma mouth]

colostrum /kəˈlɒstrəm/ n. the first secretion from the mammary glands occurring after giving birth. [L]

colotomy /kəˈlɒtəmɪ/ n. (pl. **-ies**) Surgery an incision in the colon. [as COLON² + -TOMY]

colour /ˈkʌlə(r)/ n. & v. (US **color**) —n. **1 a** the sensation produced on the eye by rays of light when resolved as by a prism, selective reflection, etc., into

different wavelengths. **b** perception of colour; a system of colours. **2** one, or any mixture, of the constituents into which light can be separated as in a spectrum or rainbow, sometimes including (loosely) black and white. **3** a colouring substance, esp. paint. **4** the use of all colours, not only black and white, as in photography and television. **5 a** pigmentation of the skin, esp. when dark. **b** this as a ground for prejudice or discrimination. **6** ruddiness of complexion (a healthy colour). **7** (in pl.) appearance or aspect (see things in their true colours). **8** (in pl.) Brit. a coloured ribbon or uniform etc. worn to signify membership of a school, club, team, etc. **b** the flag of a regiment or ship. **c** a national flag. **9** quality, mood, or variety in music, literature, speech, etc.; distinctive character or timbre. **10** a show of reason; a pretext (lend colour to; under colour of). —v. **1** tr. apply colour to, esp. by painting or dyeing or with coloured pens or pencils. **2** tr. influence (an attitude coloured by experience). **3** tr. misrepresent, exaggerate, esp. with spurious detail (a highly coloured account). **4** intr. take on colour; blush. □ **colour bar** the denial of services and facilities to non-White people. **colour-blind** unable to distinguish certain colours. **colour-blindness** the condition of being colour-blind. **colour code** use of colours as a standard means of identification. **colour-code** v.tr. identify by means of a colour code. **colour-fast** dyed in colours that will not fade or be washed out. **colour-fastness** the condition of being colour-fast. **colour scheme** an arrangement or planned combination of colours esp. in interior design. **colour-sergeant** the senior sergeant of an infantry company. **colour supplement** Brit. a magazine with coloured illustrations, issued as a supplement to a newspaper. **colour wash** coloured distemper. **colour-wash** v.tr. paint with coloured distemper. **Queen's** (or **King's** or **regimental**) **colour** a flag carried by a regiment. **show one's true colours** reveal one's true character or intentions. **under false colours** falsely, deceitfully. **with flying colours** see FLYING. [ME f. OF color, colorer f. L color, colorare]

colourable /ˈkʌlərəb(ə)l/ adj. (US **colorable**) **1** specious, plausible. **2** counterfeit. □□ **colourably** adv.

colourant /ˈkʌlərənt/ n. (US **colorant**) a colouring substance.

colouration var. of COLORATION.

coloured /ˈkʌləd/ adj. & n. (US **colored**) —adj. **1** having colour(s). **2** (**Coloured**) **a** wholly or partly of non-White descent. **b** S.Afr. of mixed White and non-White descent. **c** of or relating to Coloured people (a Coloured audience). —n. (**Coloured**) **1** a Coloured person. **2** S.Afr. a person of mixed descent speaking Afrikaans or English as the mother tongue.

colourful /ˈkʌləˌfʊl/ adj. (US **colorful**) **1** having much or varied colour; bright. **2** full of interest; vivid, lively. □□ **colourfully** adv. **colourfulness** n.

colouring /ˈkʌlərɪŋ/ n. (US **coloring**) **1** the process of or skill in using colour(s). **2** the style in which a thing is coloured, or in which an artist uses colour. **3** facial complexion.

colourist /ˈkʌlərɪst/ n. (US **colorist**) a person who uses colour, esp. in art.

colourless /ˈkʌlələs/ adj. (US **colorless**) **1** without colour. **2** lacking character or interest. **3** dull or pale in hue. **4** neutral, impartial, indifferent. □□ **colourlessly** adv.

coloury /ˈkʌlərɪ/ adj. US (**colory**) having a distinctive colour, esp. as indicating good quality.

colposcopy /ˌkɒlˈpɒskəpɪ/ n. examination of the vagina and the neck of the womb. □□ **colposcope** n. [Gk kolpos womb + -SCOPY]

colt /kəʊlt/ n. **1** a young uncastrated male horse, usu. less than four years old. **2** Sport a young or inexperienced player; a member of a junior team.

□□**colthood** *n.* **coltish** *adj.* **coltishly** *adv.*
coltishness *n.* [OE, = young ass or camel]

colter US var. of COULTER.

coltsfoot /ˈkəʊltsfʊt/ *n.* (*pl.* **coltsfoots**) a wild composite plant, *Tussilago farfara*, with large leaves and yellow flowers.

colubrine /ˈkɒljʊˌbraɪn/ *adj.* **1** snakelike. **2** of the subfamily Colubrinae of non-poisonous snakes. [L *colubrinus* f. *coluber* snake]

Columbine /ˈkɒləmˌbaɪn/ *n.* the partner of Harlequin in pantomime. [F *Colombine* f. It. *Colombina* f. *colombino* dovelike]

columbine /ˈkɒləmˌbaɪn/ *n.* any plant of the genus *Aquilegia*, esp. *A. vulgaris*, having purple-blue flowers. Also called AQUILEGIA. [ME f. OF *colombine* f. med.L *colombina herba* dovelike plant f. L *columba* dove (from the supposed resemblance of the flower to a cluster of 5 doves)]

columbite /kəˈlʌmbaɪt/ *n. US Chem.* an ore of iron and niobium found in America. [*Columbia*, a poetic name for America, + -ITE[1]]

columbium /kəˈlʌmbɪəm/ *n. US Chem.* = NIOBIUM.

column /ˈkɒləm/ *n.* **1** *Archit.* an upright cylindrical pillar often slightly tapering and usu. supporting an entablature or arch, or standing alone as a monument. **2** a structure or part shaped like a column. **3** a vertical cylindrical mass of liquid or vapour. **4 a** a vertical division of a page, chart, etc., containing a sequence of figures or words. **b** the figures or words themselves. **5** a part of a newspaper regularly devoted to a particular subject (*gossip column*). **6 a** *Mil.* an arrangement of troops in successive lines, with a narrow front. **b** *Naut.* a similar arrangement of ships. □**column-inch** a quantity of print (esp. newsprint) occupying a one-inch length of a column. **dodge the column** *colloq.* shirk one's duty; avoid work. □□**columnar** /kəˈlʌmnə(r)/ *adj.* **columned** *adj.* [ME f. OF *columpne* & L *columna* pillar]

columnist /ˈkɒləmnɪst, -mɪst/ *n.* a journalist contributing regularly to a newspaper.

colure /kəˈlʊə(r)/ *n. Astron.* either of two great circles intersecting at right angles at the celestial poles and passing through the ecliptic either the equinoxes or the solstices. [ME f. LL *colurus* f. Gk *kolouros* truncated]

colza /ˈkɒlzə/ *n.* = RAPE[2]. [F *kolza(t)* f. LG *kōlsāt* (as COLE, SEED)]

COM *abbr.* computer output on microfilm or microfiche.

com- /kɒm, kəm, kʌm/ *prefix* (also **co-**, **col-**, **con-**, **cor-**) with, together, jointly, altogether. ¶ *com-* is used before *b*, *m*, *p*, and occas. before vowels and *f*; *co-* esp. before vowels, *h*, and *gn*; *col-* before *l*, *cor-* before *r*, and *con-* before other consonants. [L *com-*, *cum* with]

coma[1] /ˈkəʊmə/ *n.* (*pl.* **comas**) a prolonged deep unconsciousness, caused esp. by severe injury or excessive use of drugs. [med.L f. Gk *kōma* deep sleep]

coma[2] /ˈkəʊmə/ *n.* (*pl.* **comae** /-miː/) **1** *Astron.* a cloud of gas and dust surrounding the nucleus of a comet. **2** *Bot.* a tuft of silky hairs at the end of some seeds. [L f. Gk *komē* hair of head]

comatose /ˈkəʊməˌtəʊz/ *adj.* **1** in a coma. **2** drowsy, sleepy, lethargic.

comb /kəʊm/ *n.* & *v.* —*n.* **1** a toothed strip of rigid material for tidying and arranging the hair, or for keeping it in place. **2** a part of a machine having a similar design or purpose. **3 a** the red fleshy crest of a fowl, esp. a cock. **b** an analogous growth in other birds. **4** a honeycomb. —*v.tr.* **1** arrange or tidy (the hair) by drawing a comb through. **2** curry (a horse). **3** dress (wool or flax) with a comb. **4** search (a place) thoroughly. □**comb out 1** tidy and arrange (hair) with a comb. **2** remove with a comb. **3** search or attack systematically. **4** search out and get rid of (anything unwanted). □□**combed** *adj.* [OE *camb* f. Gmc]

combat /ˈkɒmbæt, ˈkʌm-/ *n.* & *v.* —*n.* a fight, struggle, or contest. —*v.* (**combated**, **combating**) **1** *intr.* engage in combat. **2** *tr.* engage in combat with. **3** *tr.* oppose; strive against. □**combat fatigue** a mental disorder caused by stress in wartime combat. **single combat** a duel. [F *combat* f. *combattre* f. LL (as COM-, L *batuere* fight)]

combatant /ˈkɒmbət(ə)nt, ˈkʌm-/ *n.* & *adj.* —*n.* a person engaged in fighting. —*adj.* **1** fighting. **2** for fighting.

combative /ˈkɒmbətɪv, ˈkʌm-/ *adj.* ready or eager to fight; pugnacious. □□**combatively** *adv.* **combativeness** *n.*

combe var. of COOMB.

comber[1] /ˈkəʊmə(r)/ *n.* **1** a person or thing that combs, esp. a machine for combing cotton or wool very fine. **2** a long curling wave; a breaker.

comber[2] /ˈkəʊmə(r)/ *n. Brit.* a fish of the perch family, *Serranus cabrilla*. [18th c.: orig. unkn.]

combination /ˌkɒmbɪˈneɪʃ(ə)n/ *n.* **1** the act or an instance of combining; the process of being combined. **2** a combined state (*in combination with*). **3** a combined set of things or people. **4** a sequence of numbers or letters used to open a combination lock. **5** *Brit.* a motor cycle with side-car attached. **6** (in *pl.*) *Brit.* a single undergarment for the body and legs. **7** a group of things chosen from a larger number without regard to their arrangement. **8 a** united action. **b** *Chess* a coordinated and effective sequence of moves. **9** *Chem.* a union of substances in a compound with new properties. □**combination lock** a lock that can be opened only by a specific sequence of movements. □□**combinative** /ˈkɒmbɪnətɪv/ *adj.* **combinational** *adj.* **combinatory** /ˈkɒmbɪnətərɪ/ *adj.* [obs. F *combination* or LL *combinatio* (as COMBINE)]

combinatorial /ˌkɒmbɪnəˈtɔːrɪəl/ *adj. Math.* relating to combinations of items.

combine *v.* & *n.* —*v.* /kəmˈbaɪn/ **1** *tr.* & *intr.* join together; unite for a common purpose. **2** *tr.* possess (qualities usually distinct) together (*combines charm and authority*). **3 a** *intr.* coalesce in one substance. **b** *tr.* cause to do this. **c** *intr.* form a chemical compound. **4** *intr.* cooperate. **5** /ˈkɒmbaɪn/ *tr.* harvest (crops etc.) by means of a combine harvester. —*n.* /ˈkɒmbaɪn/ a combination of esp. commercial interests to control prices etc. □**combine harvester** a mobile machine that reaps and threshes in one operation. **combining form** *Gram.* a linguistic element used in combination with another element to form a word (e.g. *Anglo-* = English, *bio-* = life, *-graphy* writing). ¶ In this dictionary, *combining form* is used of an element that contributes to the particular sense of words (as with both elements of *biography*), as distinct from a prefix or suffix that adjusts the sense of or determines the function of words (as with *un-*, *-able*, and *-ation*). □□**combinable** *adj.* [ME f. OF *combiner* or LL *combinare* (as COM-, L *bini* two)]

combing /ˈkəʊmɪŋ/ *n.* (in *pl.*) hairs combed off. □**combing wool** long-stapled wool, suitable for combing and making into worsted.

combo /ˈkɒmbəʊ/ *n.* (*pl.* **-os**) *sl.* a small jazz or dance band. [abbr. of COMBINATION + -o]

combs /kɒmz/ *n.pl. colloq.* combinations (see COMBINATION 6).

combust /kəmˈbʌst/ *v.tr.* subject to combustion. [obs. *combust* (adj.) f. L *combustus* past part. (as COMBUSTION)]

combustible /kəmˈbʌstɪb(ə)l/ *adj.* & *n.* —*adj.* **1** capable of or used for burning. **2** excitable; easily irritated. —*n.* a combustible substance. □□**combustibility** /-ˈbɪlɪtɪ/ *n.* [F *combustible* or med.L *combustibilis* (as COMBUSTION)]

combustion /kəmˈbʌstʃ(ə)n/ *n.* **1** burning; consumption by fire. **2** *Chem.* the development of light and heat from the chemical combination of a substance with oxygen. □□**combustive** *adj.* [ME f.

F *combustion* or LL *combustio* f. L *comburere combust-* burn up]

come /kʌm/ *v. & n.* —*v.intr.* (*past* **came** /keɪm/; *past part.* **come**) **1** move, be brought towards, or reach a place thought of as near or familiar to the speaker or hearer (*come and see me*; *shall we come to your house?*; *the books have come*). **2** reach or be brought to a specified situation or result (*you'll come to no harm*; *have come to believe it*; *has come to be used wrongly*; *came into prominence*). **3** reach or extend to a specified point (*the road comes within a mile of us*). **4** traverse or accomplish (with compl.: *have come a long way*). **5** occur, happen; become present instead of future (*how did you come to break your leg?*). **6** take or occupy a specified position in space or time (*it comes on the third page*; *Nero came after Claudius*; *it does not come within the scope of the inquiry*). **7** become perceptible or known (*the church came into sight*; *the news comes as a surprise*; *it will come to me*). **8** be available (*the dress comes in three sizes*; *this model comes with optional features*). **9** become (with compl.: *the handle has come loose*). **10** (foll. by *of*) **a** be descended from (*comes of a rich family*). **b** be the result of (*that comes of complaining*). **11** *colloq.* play the part of; behave like (with compl.: *don't come the bully with me*). **12** *sl.* have a sexual orgasm. **13** (in *subj.*) *colloq.* when a specified time is reached (*come next month*). **14** (as *int.*) expressing caution or reserve (*come, it cannot be that bad*). —*n.* *sl.* semen ejaculated at a sexual orgasm. □**as ... as they come** typically or supremely so (*is as tough as they come*). **come about** happen; take place. **come across 1** be effective or understood. **2** (foll. by *with*) *sl.* hand over what is wanted. **3** meet or find by chance (*came across an old jacket*). **come again** *colloq.* **1** make a further effort. **2** (as *imper.*) what did you say? **come along 1** make progress; move forward. **2** (as *imper.*) hurry up. **come and go 1** pass to and fro; be transitory. **2** pay brief visits. **come apart** fall or break into pieces, disintegrate. **come at 1** reach, discover; get access to. **2** attack (*came at me with a knife*). **come-at-able** /-'ætəb(ə)l/ *adj.* reachable, accessible. **come away 1** become detached or broken off (*came away in my hands*). **2** (foll. by *with*) be left with a feeling, impression, etc. (*came away with many misgivings*). **come back 1** return. **2** recur to one's memory. **3** become fashionable or popular again. **4** *US* reply, retort. **come before 1** be dealt with by (a judge etc.). **come between 1** interfere with the relationship of a. **2** separate; prevent contact between. **come by 1** pass; go past. **2** call on a visit (*why not come by tomorrow?*). **3** acquire, obtain (*came by a new bicycle*). **come clean** see CLEAN. **come down 1** come to a place or position regarded as lower. **2** lose position or wealth (*has come down in the world*). **3** be handed down by tradition or inheritance. **4** be reduced; show a downward trend (*prices are coming down*). **5** (foll. by *against, in favour of*) reach a decision or recommendation (*the report came down against change*). **6** (foll. by *to*) signify or betoken basically; be dependent on (a factor) (*it comes down to who is willing to go*). **7** (foll. by *on*) criticize harshly; rebuke, punish. **8** (foll. by *with*) begin to suffer from (a disease). **come for 1** come to collect or receive. **2** attack (*came for me with a hammer*). **come forward 1** advance. **2** offer oneself for a task, post, etc. **come-hither** *attrib.adj. colloq.* (of a look or manner) enticing, flirtatious. **come in 1** enter a house or room. **2** take a specified position in a race etc. (*came in third*). **3** become fashionable or seasonable. **4 a** have a useful role or function. **b** (with compl.) prove to be (*came in very handy*). **c** have a part to play (*where do I come in?*). **5** be received (*more news has just come in*). **6** begin speaking, esp. in radio transmission. **7** be elected; come to power. **8** *Cricket* begin an innings. **9** (foll. by *for*) receive; be the object of (usu. something unwelcome) (*came in for much*

criticism). **10** (foll. by *on*) join (an enterprise etc.). **11** (of a tide) turn to high tide. **12** (of a train, ship, or aircraft) approach its destination. **come into 1** see senses 2, 7 of *v.* **2** receive, esp. as heir. **come near** see NEAR. **come of age** see AGE. **come off 1** *colloq.* (of an action) succeed; be accomplished. **2** (with compl.) fare; turn out (*came off badly*; *came off the winner*). **3** *coarse sl.* have a sexual orgasm. **4** be detached or detachable (from). **5** fall (from). **6** be reduced or subtracted from (*£5 came off the price*). **come off it** (as *imper.*) *colloq.* an expression of disbelief or refusal to accept another's opinion, behaviour, etc. **come on 1** continue to come. **2** advance, esp. to attack. **3** make progress; thrive (*is really coming on*). **4** (foll. by *to* + infin.) begin (*it came on to rain*). **5** appear on the stage, field of play, etc. **6** be heard or seen on television, on the telephone, etc. **7** arise to be discussed. **8** (as *imper.*) expressing encouragement. **9** = **come upon**. **come-on** *n. sl.* a lure or enticement. **come out 1** emerge; become known (*it came out that he had left*). **2** appear or be published (*comes out every Saturday*). **3 a** declare oneself; make a decision (*came out in favour of joining*). **b** openly declare that one is a homosexual. **4** *Brit.* go on strike. **5 a** be satisfactorily visible in a photograph etc., or present in a specified way (*the dog didn't come out*; *he came out badly*). **b** (of a photograph) be produced satisfactorily or in a specified way (*only three have come out*; *they all came out well*). **6** attain a specified result in an examination etc. **7** (of a stain etc.) be removed. **8** make one's début on stage or in society. **9** (foll. by *in*) be covered with (*came out in spots*). **10** (of a problem) be solved. **11** (foll. by *with*) declare openly; disclose. **come over 1** come from some distance or nearer to the speaker (*came over from Paris*; *come over here a moment*). **2** change sides or one's opinion. **3 a** (of a feeling etc.) overtake or affect (a person). **b** *colloq.* feel suddenly (*came over faint*). **4** appear or sound in a specified way (*you come over very well*; *the ideas came over clearly*). **5** affect or influence (*I don't know what came over me*). **come round 1** pay an informal visit. **2** recover consciousness. **3** be converted to another person's opinion. **4** (of a date or regular occurrence) recur; be imminent again. **come through 1** be successful; survive. **2** be received by telephone. **3** survive or overcome (a difficulty) (*came through the ordeal*). **come to 1** recover consciousness. **2** *Naut.* bring a vessel to a stop. **3** reach in total; amount to. **4** *refl.* **a** recover consciousness. **b** stop being foolish. **5** have as a destiny; reach (*what is the world coming to?*). **come to hand** become available; be recovered. **come to light** see LIGHT[1]. **come to nothing** have no useful result in the end; fail. **come to pass** happen, occur. **come to rest** cease moving. **come to one's senses** see SENSE. **come to that** *colloq.* in fact; if that is the case. **come under 1** be classified as or among. **2** be subject to (influence or authority). **come up 1** come to a place or position regarded as higher. **2** attain wealth or position (*come up in the world*). **3** (of an issue, problem, etc.) arise; present itself; be mentioned or discussed. **4** (often foll. by *to*) **a** approach a person, esp. to talk. **b** approach or draw near to a specified time, event, etc. (*is coming up to eight o'clock*). **5** (foll. by *to*) match (a standard etc.). **6** (foll. by *with*) produce (an idea etc.), esp. in response to a challenge. **7** (of a plant etc.) spring up out of the ground. **8** become brighter (e.g. with polishing); shine more brightly. **come up against** be faced with or opposed by. **come upon 1** meet or find by chance. **2** attack by surprise. **come what may** no matter what happens. **have it coming to one** *colloq.* be about to get one's deserts. **how come?** *colloq.* how did that happen? **if it comes to that** in that case. **to come** future; in the future (*the year to come*; *many problems were still to come*). [OE *cuman* f. Gmc]

comeback /'kʌmbæk/ *n.* **1** a return to a previous

(esp. successful) state. **2** *sl.* a retaliation or retort. **3** *Austral.* a sheep bred from crossbred and purebred parents for both wool and meat.

Comecon /ˈkɒmɪˌkɒn/ *n.* an economic association of Communist countries in E. Europe. [abbr. of *Council for Mutual Economic Assistance*]

comedian /kəˈmiːdɪən/ *n.* **1** a humorous entertainer on stage, television, etc. **2** an actor in comedy. [F *comédien* f. *comédie* COMEDY]

comedienne /kəˌmiːdɪˈen/ *n.* a female comedian. [F fem. (as COMEDIAN)]

comedist /ˈkɒmɪdɪst/ *n.* a writer of comedies.

comedo /ˈkɒmɪˌdəʊ/ *n.* (*pl.* **comedones** /-ˈdəʊniːz/) *Med.* a blackhead. [L, = glutton f. *comedere* eat up]

comedown /ˈkʌmdaʊn/ *n.* **1** a loss of status; decline or degradation. **2** a disappointment.

comedy /ˈkɒmɪdɪ/ *n.* (*pl.* **-ies**) **1 a** a play, film, etc., of an amusing or satirical character, usu. with a happy ending. **b** the dramatic genre consisting of works of this kind (*she excels in comedy*) (cf. TRAGEDY). **2** an amusing or farcical incident or series of incidents in everyday life. **3** humour, esp. in a work of art etc. □**comedy of manners** see MANNER. □□**comedic** /kəˈmiːdɪk/ *adj.* [ME f. OF *comedie* f. L *comoedia* f. Gk *kōmōidia* f. *kōmōidos* comic poet f. *kōmos* revel]

comely /ˈkʌmlɪ/ *adj.* (**comelier**, **comeliest**) (usu. of a woman) pleasant to look at. □□**comeliness** /ˈkʌmlɪnɪs/ *n.* [ME *cumelich*, *cumli* prob. f. *becumelich* f. BECOME]

comer /ˈkʌmə(r)/ *n.* **1** a person who comes, esp. as an applicant, participant, etc. (*offered the job to the first comer*). **2** *colloq.* a person likely to be a success. □**all comers** any applicants (with reference to a position, or esp. a challenge to a champion, that is unrestricted in entry).

comestible /kəˈmestɪb(ə)l/ *n.* (usu. in *pl.*) *formal* or *joc.* food. [ME f. F f. med.L *comestibilis* f. L *comedere comest-* eat up]

comet /ˈkɒmɪt/ *n.* a hazy object usu. with a nucleus of ice and dust surrounded by gas and with a tail pointing away from the sun, moving about the sun in an eccentric orbit. □□**cometary** *adj.* [ME f. OF *comete* f. L *cometa* f. Gk *komētes* long-haired (star)]

comeuppance /kʌmˈʌpəns/ *n. colloq.* one's deserved fate or punishment (*got his comeuppance*). [COME + UP + -ANCE]

comfit /ˈkʌmfɪt/ *n. archaic* a sweet consisting of a nut, seed, etc., coated in sugar. [ME f. OF *confit* f. L *confectum* past part. of *conficere* prepare: see CONFECTION]

comfort /ˈkʌmfət/ *n. & v.* —*n.* **1** consolation; relief in affliction. **2 a** a state of physical well-being; being comfortable (*live in comfort*). **b** (usu. in *pl.*) things that make life easy or pleasant (*has all the comforts*). **3** a cause of satisfaction (*a comfort to me that you are here*). **4** a person who consoles or helps one (*he's a comfort to her in her old age*). **5** *US* a warm quilt. —*v.tr.* **1** soothe in grief; console. **2** make comfortable (*comforted by the warmth of the fire*). □**comfort station** *US euphem.* a public lavatory. [ME f. OF *confort*(*er*) f. LL *confortare* strengthen (as COM-, L *fortis* strong)]

comfortable /ˈkʌmftəb(ə)l, -fətəb(ə)l/ *adj. & n.* —*adj.* **1** ministering to comfort; giving ease (*a comfortable pair of shoes*). **2** free from discomfort; at ease (*I'm quite comfortable thank you*). **3** *colloq.* having an adequate standard of living; free from financial worry. **4** having an easy conscience (*did not feel comfortable about refusing him*). **5** with a wide margin (*a comfortable win*). —*n.* *US* a warm quilt. □□**comfortableness** *n.* **comfortably** *adv.* [ME f. AF *confortable* (as COMFORT)]

comforter /ˈkʌmfətə(r)/ *n.* **1** a person who comforts. **2** a baby's dummy. **3** *archaic* a woollen scarf. **4** *US* a warm quilt. [ME f. AF *confortour*, OF *-eor* (as COMFORT)]

comfortless /ˈkʌmfətlɪs/ *adj.* **1** dreary, cheerless. **2** without comfort.

comfrey /ˈkʌmfrɪ/ *n.* (*pl.* **-eys**) any of various plants of the genus *Symphytum*, esp. *S. officinale* having large hairy leaves and clusters of usu. white or purple bell-shaped flowers. [ME f. AF *cumfrie*, ult. f. L *conferva* (as COM-, *fervēre* boil)]

comfy /ˈkʌmfɪ/ *adj.* (**comfier**, **comfiest**) *colloq.* comfortable. □□**comfily** *adv.* **comfiness** *n.* [abbr.]

comic /ˈkɒmɪk/ *adj. & n.* —*adj.* **1** (often *attrib.*) of, or in the style of, comedy (*a comic actor*; *comic opera*). **2** causing or meant to cause laughter; funny (*comic to see his struggles*). —*n.* **1** a professional comedian. **2 a** a children's periodical, mainly in the form of comic strips. **b** a similar publication intended for adults. □**comic opera 1** an opera with much spoken dialogue, usu. with humorous treatment. **2** this genre of opera. **comic strip** a horizontal series of drawings in a comic, newspaper, etc., telling a story. [L *comicus* f. Gk *kōmikos* f. *kōmos* revel]

comical /ˈkɒmɪk(ə)l/ *adj.* funny; causing laughter. □□**comicality** /-ˈkælɪtɪ/ *n.* **comically** *adv.* [COMIC]

coming /ˈkʌmɪŋ/ *adj. & n.* —*attrib.adj.* **1** approaching, next (*in the coming week*; *this coming Sunday*). **2** of potential importance (*a coming man*). —*n.* arrival; approach.

Comintern /ˈkɒmɪnˌtɜːn/ *n.* the Third International (see INTERNATIONAL *n.* 2), a communist organization (1919–43). [Russ. *Komintern* f. Russ. forms of *communist, international*]

comitadji /ˌkɒmɪˈtædʒɪ/ *n.* (also **komitadji**, **komitaji**) a member of an irregular band of soldiers in the Balkans. [Turk. *komitacı*, lit. 'member of a (revolutionary) committee']

comity /ˈkɒmɪtɪ/ *n.* (*pl.* **-ies**) **1** courtesy, civility; considerate behaviour towards others. **2 a** an association of nations etc. for mutual benefit. **b** (in full **comity of nations**) the mutual recognition by nations of the laws and customs of others. [L *comitas* f. *comis* courteous]

comma /ˈkɒmə/ *n.* **1** a punctuation mark (,) indicating a pause between parts of a sentence, or dividing items in a list, string of figures, etc. **2** *Mus.* a definite minute interval or difference of pitch. □**comma bacillus** a comma-shaped bacillus causing cholera. [L f. Gk *komma* clause]

command /kəˈmɑːnd/ *v. & n.* —*v.tr.* **1** (often foll. by *to* + infin., or *that* + clause) give formal order or instructions to (*commands us to obey*; *commands that it be done*). **2** (also *absol.*) have authority or control over. **3 a** (often *refl.*) restrain, master. **b** gain the use of; have at one's disposal or within reach (skill, resources, etc.) (*commands an extensive knowledge of history*; *commands a salary of £40,000*). **4** deserve and get (sympathy, respect, etc.). **5** *Mil.* dominate (a strategic position) from a superior height; look down over. —*n.* **1** an authoritative order; an instruction. **2** mastery, control, possession (*a good command of languages*; *has command of the resources*). **3** the exercise or tenure of authority, esp. naval or military (*has command of this ship*). **4** *Mil.* **a** a body of troops etc. (*Bomber Command*). **b** a district under a commander (*Western Command*). **5** *Computing* **a** an instruction causing a computer to perform one of its basic functions. **b** a signal initiating such an operation. □**at command** ready to be used at will. **at** (or **by**) **a person's command** in pursuance of a person's bidding. **command module** the control compartment in a spacecraft. **Command Paper** (in the UK) a paper laid before Parliament by command of the Crown. **command performance** (in the UK) a theatrical or film performance given by royal command. **command post** the headquarters of a military unit. **in command of** commanding; having under control. **under command of** commanded by. **word of command 1** *Mil.* an order for a movement in a drill etc. **2** a prearranged spoken signal for the start of an operation. [ME f. AF *comaunder*, OF *comander* f. LL *commandare* COMMEND]

commandant /ˌkɒmənˈdænt, -ˈdɑːnt, ˈkɒm-/ *n.* a

commanding officer, esp. of a particular force, military academy, etc. □**Commandant-in-Chief** the supreme commandant. □□**commandantship** *n.* [F *commandant*, or It. or Sp. *commandante* (as COMMAND)]

commandeer /ˌkɒmənˈdɪə(r)/ *v.tr.* **1** seize (men or goods) for military purposes. **2** take possession of without authority. [S.Afr. Du. *kommanderen* f. F *commander* COMMAND]

commander /kəˈmɑːndə(r)/ *n.* **1** a person who commands, esp.: **a** a naval officer next in rank below captain. **b** = *wing commander*. **2** an officer in charge of a London police district. **3** (in full **knight commander**) a member of a higher class in some orders of knighthood. **4** a large wooden mallet. □**commander-in-chief** the supreme commander, esp. of a nation's forces. **Commander of the Faithful** a title of a Caliph. □□**commandership** *n.* [ME f. OF *comandere*, -*ēor* f. Rmc (as COMMAND)]

commanding /kəˈmɑːndɪŋ/ *adj.* **1** dignified, exalted, impressive. **2** (of a hill or other high point) giving a wide view. **3** (of an advantage, a position, etc.) controlling; superior (*has a commanding lead*). □□ **commandingly** *adv.*

commandment /kəˈmɑːndmənt/ *n.* a divine command. □**the Ten Commandments** the divine rules of conduct given by God to Moses on Mount Sinai, according to Exod. 20:1–17. [ME f. OF *comandement* (as COMMAND)]

commando /kəˈmɑːndəʊ/ *n.* (*pl.* **-os**) *Mil.* **1 a** a unit of British amphibious shock troops. **b** a member of such a unit. **c** a similar unit or member of such a unit elsewhere. **2 a** a party of men called out for military service. **b** a body of troops. **3** (*attrib.*) of or concerning a commando (*a commando operation*). [Port. f. *commandar* COMMAND]

comme ci, comme ça /ˌkɒmˈsiː ˌkɒmˈsɑː/ *adv. & adj.* so so; middling or middlingly. [F, = like this, like that]

commedia dell'arte /kɒˈmeɪdɪə delˈɑːteɪ/ *n.* an improvised kind of popular comedy in Italian theatres in the 16th–18th c., based on stock characters. [It., = comedy of art]

comme il faut /ˌkɒm iːl ˈfəʊ/ *adj. & adv.* —*predic.adj.* (esp. of behaviour, etiquette, etc.) proper, correct. —*adv.* properly, correctly. [F, = as is necessary]

commemorate /kəˈmeməˌreɪt/ *v.tr.* **1** celebrate in speech or writing. **2 a** preserve in memory by some celebration. **b** (of a stone, plaque, etc.) be a memorial of. □□**commemorative** /kəˈmemərətɪv/ *adj.* **commemorator** *n.* [L *commemorare* (as COM-, *memorare* relate f. *memor* mindful)]

commemoration /kəˌmeməˈreɪʃ(ə)n/ *n.* **1** an act of commemorating. **2** a service or part of a service in memory of a person, an event, etc. [ME f. F *commemoration* or L *commemoratio* (as COMMEMORATE)]

commence /kəˈmens/ *v.tr. & intr. formal* begin. [ME f. OF *com(m)encier* f. Rmc (as COM-, L *initiare* INITIATE)]

commencement /kəˈmensmənt/ *n. formal* **1** a beginning. **2** esp. *US* a ceremony of degree conferment. [ME f. OF (as COMMENCE)]

commend /kəˈmend/ *v.tr.* **1** (often foll. by *to*) entrust, commit (*commends his soul to God*). **2** praise (*commends her singing voice*). **3** recommend (*method commends itself*). □**commend me to** *archaic* remember me kindly to. **highly commended** (of a competitor etc.) just missing the top places. [ME f. L *commendare* (as COM-, *mendare* = *mandare* entrust: see MANDATE)]

commendable /kəˈmendəb(ə)l/ *adj.* praiseworthy. □□ **commendably** *adv.* [ME f. OF f. L *commendabilis* (as COMMEND)]

commendation /ˌkɒmenˈdeɪʃ(ə)n/ *n.* **1** an act of commending or recommending (esp. a person to another's favour). **2** praise. [ME f. OF f. L *commendatio* (as COMMEND)]

commendatory /kəˈmendətərɪ/ *adj.* commending, recommending. [LL *commendatorius* (as COMMEND)]

commensal /kəˈmens(ə)l/ *adj. & n.* —*adj.* **1** *Biol.* of, relating to, or exhibiting commensalism. **2** (of a person) eating at the same table as another. —*n.* **1** *Biol.* a commensal organism. **2** one who eats at the same table as another. □□**commensality** /ˌkɒmənˈsælɪtɪ/ *n.* [ME f. F *commensal* or med.L *commensalis* (in sense 2) (as COM-, *mensa* table)]

commensalism /kəˈmensəˌlɪz(ə)m/ *n.* *Biol.* an association between two organisms in which one benefits and the other derives no benefit or harm.

commensurable /kəˈmenʃərəb(ə)l, -sjərəb(ə)l/ *adj.* **1** (often foll. by *with*, *to*) measurable by the same standard. **2** (foll. by *to*) proportionate to. **3** *Math.* (of numbers) in a ratio equal to the ratio of integers. □□ **commensurability** /-ˈbɪlɪtɪ/ *n.* **commensurably** *adv.* [LL *commensurabilis* (as COM-, MEASURE)]

commensurate /kəˈmenʃərət, -sjərət/ *adj.* **1** (usu. foll. by *with*) having the same size, duration, etc.; coextensive. **2** (often foll. by *to*, *with*) proportionate. □□**commensurately** *adv.* [LL *commensuratus* (as COM-, MEASURE)]

comment /ˈkɒment/ *n. & v.* —*n.* **1 a** a remark, esp. critical; an opinion (*passed a comment on her hat*). **b** commenting; criticism (*his behaviour aroused much comment*; *an hour of news and comment*). **2 a** an explanatory note (e.g. on a written text). **b** written criticism or explanation (e.g. of a text). **3** (of a play, book, etc.) a critical illustration; a parable (*his art is a comment on society*). —*v.intr.* **1** (often foll. by *on*, *upon*, or *that* + clause) make (esp. critical) remarks (*commented on her choice of friends*). **2** (often foll. by *on*, *upon*) write explanatory notes. □**no comment** *colloq.* I decline to answer your question. □□ **commenter** *n.* [ME f. L *commentum* contrivance (in LL also = interpretation), neut. past part. of *comminisci* devise, or F *commenter* (v.)]

commentary /ˈkɒməntərɪ/ *n.* (*pl.* **-ies**) **1** a set of explanatory or critical notes on a text etc. **2** a descriptive spoken account (esp. on radio or television) of an event or a performance as it happens. [L *commentarius*, -*ium* adj. used as noun (as COMMENT)]

commentate /ˈkɒmənˌteɪt/ *v.intr. disp.* act as a commentator. [back-form. f. COMMENTATOR]

commentator /ˈkɒmənˌteɪtə(r)/ *n.* **1** a person who provides a commentary on an event etc. **2** the writer of a commentary. **3** a person who writes or speaks on current events. [L f. *commentari* frequent. of *comminisci* devise]

commerce /ˈkɒmɜːs/ *n.* **1** financial transactions, esp. the buying and selling of merchandise, on a large scale. **2** social intercourse (*the daily commerce of gossip and opinion*). **3** *archaic* sexual intercourse. [F *commerce* or L *commercium* (as COM-, *mercium* f. *merx mercis* merchandise)]

commercial /kəˈmɜːʃ(ə)l/ *adj. & n.* —*adj.* **1** of, engaged in, or concerned with, commerce. **2** having profit as a primary aim rather than artistic etc. value; philistine. **3** (of chemicals) supplied in bulk more or less unpurified. —*n.* **1** a television or radio advertisement. **2** *archaic* a commercial traveller. □**commercial art** art used in advertising, selling, etc. **commercial broadcasting** television or radio broadcasting in which programmes are financed by advertisements. **commercial traveller** a firm's travelling salesman or saleswoman who visits shops to get orders. **commercial vehicle** a vehicle used for carrying goods or fare-paying passengers. □□ **commercialism** *n.* **commerciality** /-ʃɪˈælɪtɪ/ *n.* **commercially** *adv.*

commercialize /kəˈmɜːʃəˌlaɪz/ *v.tr.* (also **-ise**) **1** exploit or spoil for the purpose of gaining profit. **2** make commercial. □□**commercialization** /-ˈzeɪʃ(ə)n/ *n.*

commère /ˈkɒmeə(r)/ *n. Brit.* a female compère. [F, fem. of COMPÈRE]

Commie /ˈkɒmɪ/ *n. sl. derog.* a Communist. [abbr.]

commination /ˌkɒmɪˈneɪʃ(ə)n/ n. **1** the threatening of divine vengeance. **2 a** the recital of divine threats against sinners in the Anglican Liturgy for Ash Wednesday. **b** the service that includes this. [ME f. L *comminatio* f. *comminari* threaten]

comminatory /ˈkɒmɪnətəri/ adj. threatening, denunciatory. [med.L *comminatorius* (as COMMINATION)]

commingle /kəˈmɪŋg(ə)l/ v.tr. & intr. literary mingle together.

comminute /ˈkɒmɪˌnjuːt/ v.tr. **1** reduce to small fragments. **2** divide (property) into small portions. □ **comminuted fracture** a fracture producing multiple bone splinters. □□ **comminution** /-ˈnjuːʃ(ə)n/ n. [L *comminuere comminut-* (as COM-, *minuere* lessen)]

commis /ˈkɒmɪ, ˈkɒmɪs/ n. (pl. **commis** /ˈkɒmɪ, ˈkɒmɪz/) a junior waiter or chef. [orig. = deputy, clerk, f. F, past part. of *commettre* entrust (as COMMIT)]

commiserate /kəˈmɪzəˌreɪt/ v. **1** intr. (usu. foll. by *with*) express or feel pity. **2** tr. archaic express or feel pity for (*commiserate you on your loss*). □□ **commiseration** /-ˈreɪʃ(ə)n/ n. **commiserative** /-rətɪv/ adj. **commiserator** n. [L *commiserari* (as COM-, *miserari* pity f. *miser* wretched)]

commissar /ˈkɒmɪˌsɑː(r)/ n. **1** an official of the Soviet Communist Party responsible for political education and organization. **2** hist. the head of a government department in the USSR before 1946. [Russ. *komissar* f. F *commissaire* (as COMMISSARY)]

commissariat /ˌkɒmɪˈseərɪət, -ˈsærɪˌæt/ n. **1** esp. Mil. **a** a department for the supply of food etc. **b** the food supplied. **2** hist. a government department of the USSR before 1946. [F *commissariat* & med.L *commissariatus* (as COMMISSARY)]

commissary /ˈkɒmɪsəri, kəˈmɪs-/ n. (pl. **-ies**) **1** a deputy or delegate. **2** a representative or deputy of a bishop. **3** Mil. an officer responsible for the supply of food etc. to soldiers. **4** US **a** a restaurant in a film studio etc. **b** the food supplied. **5** US Mil. a store for the supply of food etc. to soldiers. □□ **commissarial** /-ˈseərɪəl/ adj. **commissaryship** n. [ME f. med.L *commissarius* person in charge (as COMMIT)]

commission /kəˈmɪʃ(ə)n/ n. & v. —n. **1 a** the authority to perform a task or certain duties. **b** a person or group entrusted esp. by a government with such authority (*set up a commission to look into it*). **c** an instruction, command, or duty given to such a group or person (*their commission was to simplify the procedure; my commission was to find him*). **2** an order for something, esp. a work of art, to be produced specially. **3** Mil. **a** a warrant conferring the rank of officer in the army, navy, or air force. **b** the rank so conferred. **4 a** the authority to act as agent for a company etc. in trade. **b** a percentage paid to the agent from the profits of goods etc. sold, or business obtained (*his wages are low, but he gets 20 per cent commission*). **c** the pay of a commissioned agent. **5** the act of committing (a crime, sin, etc.). **6** the office or department of a commissioner. —v.tr. **1** authorize or empower by a commission. **2 a** give (an artist etc.) a commission for a piece of work. **b** order (a work) to be written (*commissioned a new concerto*). **3** Naut. **a** give (an officer) the command of a ship. **b** prepare (a ship) for active service. **4** bring (a machine, equipment, etc.) into operation. □ **commission-agent** a bookmaker. **commission of the peace 1** Justices of the Peace. **2** the authority given to them. **in commission** (of a warship etc.) manned, armed, and ready for service. **out of commission** (esp. of a ship) not in service, not in working order. **Royal Commission** a commission of inquiry appointed by the Crown at the instance of the Government. **2** a committee so appointed. [ME f. OF f. L *commissio -onis* (as COMMIT)]

commissionaire /kəˌmɪʃəˈneə(r)/ n. esp. Brit. a uniformed door-attendant at a theatre, cinema, etc. [F (as COMMISSIONER)]

commissioner /kəˈmɪʃənə(r)/ n. **1** a person appointed by a commission to perform a specific task, e.g. the head of the London police, a delegate to the General Assembly of the Church of Scotland, etc. **2** a person appointed as a member of a government commission (*Charity Commissioner; Civil Service Commissioner*). **3** a representative of the supreme authority in a district, department, etc. □ **Commissioner for Oaths** a solicitor authorized to administer an oath to a person making an affidavit. **Lord** (or **Lord High**) **Commissioner** the representative of the Crown at the General Assembly of the Church of Scotland. [ME f. med.L *commissionarius* (as COMMISSION)]

commissure /ˈkɒmɪˌsjʊə(r)/ n. **1** a junction, joint, or seam. **2** Anat. **a** the joint between two bones. **b** a band of nerve tissue connecting the hemispheres of the brain, the two sides of the spinal cord, etc. **c** the line where the upper and lower lips, or eyelids, meet. **3** Bot. any of several joints etc. between different parts of a plant. □□ **commissural** /kəmɪˈsjʊərəl/ adj. [ME f. L *commissura* junction (as COMMIT)]

commit /kəˈmɪt/ v.tr. (**committed**, **committing**) **1** (usu. foll. by *to*) entrust or consign for: **a** safe keeping (*I commit him to your care*). **b** treatment, usu. destruction (*committed the book to the flames*). **2** perpetrate, do (esp. a crime, sin, or blunder). **3** pledge, involve, or bind (esp. oneself) to a certain course or policy (*does not like committing herself; committed by the vow he had made*). **4** (as **committed** adj.) (often foll. by *to*) **a** morally dedicated or politically aligned (*a committed Christian; committed to the cause; a committed socialist*). **b** obliged (to take certain action) (*felt committed to staying there*). **5** Polit. refer (a bill etc.) to a committee. □ **commit to memory** memorize. **commit to prison** consign officially to custody, esp. on remand. □□ **committable** adj. **committer** n. [ME f. L *committere* join, entrust (as COM-, *mittere miss-* send)]

commitment /kəˈmɪtmənt/ n. **1** an engagement or (esp. financial) obligation that restricts freedom of action. **2** the process or an instance of committing oneself; a pledge or undertaking.

committal /kəˈmɪt(ə)l/ n. **1** the act of committing a person to an institution, esp. prison or a mental hospital. **2** the burial of a dead body.

committee /kəˈmɪtɪ/ n. **1 a** a body of persons appointed for a specific function by, and usu. out of, a larger body. **b** such a body appointed by Parliament etc. to consider the details of proposed legislation. **c** (**Committee**) Brit. the whole House of Commons when sitting as a committee. **2** /ˌkɒmɪˈtiː/ Law a person entrusted with the charge of another person or another person's property. □ **committee-man** (pl. **-men**; fem. **committee-woman**, pl. **-women**) a member of a committee, esp. a habitual member of committees. **committee stage** Brit. the third of five stages of a bill's progress through Parliament when it may be considered in detail and amendments made. **select committee** a small parliamentary committee appointed for a special purpose. **standing committee** a committee that is permanent during the existence of the appointing body. [COMMIT + -EE]

commix /kəˈmɪks/ v.tr. & intr. archaic or poet. mix. □□ **commixture** n. [ME: back-form. f. *commixt* past part. f. L *commixtus* (as COM-, MIXED)]

commode /kəˈməʊd/ n. **1** a chest of drawers. **2** (also **night-commode**) **a** a bedside table with a cupboard containing a chamber-pot. **b** a chamber-pot concealed in a chair with a hinged cover. **3** = CHIFFONIER. [F, adj. (as noun) f. L *commodus* convenient (as COM-, *modus* measure)]

commodious /kəˈməʊdɪəs/ adj. **1** roomy and comfortable. **2** archaic convenient. □□ **commodiously** adv. **commodiousness** n. [F *commodieux* or f. med.L *commodiosus* f. L *commodus* (as COMMODE)]

commodity /kəˈmɒdɪtɪ/ n. (pl. **-ies**) **1** Commerce an article or raw material that can be bought and sold, esp. a product as opposed to a service. **2** a useful thing. [ME f. OF *commodité* or f. L *commoditas* (as COMMODE)]

commodore /ˈkɒmədɔː(r)/ *n.* **1** a naval officer above a captain and below a rear-admiral. **2** the commander of a squadron or other division of a fleet. **3** the president of a yacht-club. **4** the senior captain of a shipping line. **□Commodore-in-Chief** the supreme officer in the air force. [prob. f. Du. *komandeur* f. F *commandeur* COMMANDER]

common /ˈkɒmən/ *adj. & n.* —*adj.* (**commoner**, **commonest**) **1 a** occurring often (*a common mistake*). **b** ordinary; of ordinary qualities; without special rank or position (*no common mind; common soldier; the common people*). **2 a** shared by, coming from, or done by, more than one (*common knowledge; by common consent; our common benefit*). **b** belonging to, open to, or affecting, the whole community or the public (*common land*). **3** *derog.* low-class; vulgar; inferior (*a common little man*). **4** of the most familiar type (*common cold; common nightshade*). **5** *Math.* belonging to two or more quantities (*common denominator; common factor*). **6** *Gram.* (of gender) referring to individuals of either sex (e.g. *teacher*). **7** *Prosody* (of a syllable) that may be either short or long. **8** *Mus.* having two or four beats, esp. four crotchets, in a bar. **9** *Law* (of a crime) of lesser importance (cf. GRAND, PETTY). —*n.* **1** a piece of open public land, esp. in a village or town. **2** *sl.* = *common sense; (use your common)*. **3** *Eccl.* a service used for each of a group of occasions. **4** (in full **right of common**) *Law* a person's right over another's land, e.g. for pasturage. **□common carrier** a person or firm undertaking to transport any goods or person in a specified category. **common chord** *Mus.* any note with its major or minor third and perfect fifth. **common crier** see CRIER. **common denominator** see DENOMINATOR. **Common Era** the Christian era. **common ground** a point or argument accepted by both sides in a dispute. **common jury** a jury with members of no particular social standing (cf. *special jury*). **common law** law derived from custom and judicial precedent rather than statutes (cf. *case-law* (see CASE¹)). **common-law husband** (or **wife**) a partner in a marriage recognized by common law, esp. after a period of cohabitation. **Common Market** the European Economic Community. **common metre** a hymn stanza of four lines with 8, 6, 8, and 6 syllables. **common noun** (or **name**) *Gram.* a name denoting a class of objects or a concept as opposed to a particular individual (e.g. *boy, chocolate, beauty*). **common or garden** *colloq.* ordinary. **Common Prayer** the Church of England liturgy orig. set forth in the *Book of Common Prayer* of Edward VI (1549). **common-room 1** a room in some colleges, schools, etc., which members may use for relaxation or work. **2** the members who use this. **common salt** see SALT. **common seal** the official seal of a corporate body. **common sense** sound practical sense, esp. in everyday matters. **Common Serjeant** see SERJEANT. **common soldier** see SOLDIER. **common stock** *US* = *ordinary shares*. **common weal** public welfare. **common year** see YEAR 2. **in common 1** in joint use; shared. **2** of joint interest (*have little in common*). **in common with** in the same way as. **least** (or **lowest**) **common denominator**, **multiple** see DENOMINATOR, MULTIPLE. **out of the common** unusual. **□□ commonly** *adv.* **commonness** *n.* [ME f. OF *comun* f. L *communis*]

commonable /ˈkɒmənəb(ə)l/ *adj.* **1** (of an animal) that may be pastured on common land. **2** (of land) that may be held in common. [obs. *common* to exercise right of common + -ABLE]

commonage /ˈkɒmənɪdʒ/ *n.* **1** = *right of common* (see COMMON *n.* 4). **2** land held in common. **b** the state of being held in common. **3** the common people; commonalty.

commonality /ˌkɒməˈnælɪtɪ/ *n.* (*pl.* -**ies**) **1** the

sharing of an attribute. **2** a common occurrence. **3** = COMMONALTY. [var. of COMMONALTY]

commonalty /ˈkɒmənəltɪ/ *n.* (*pl.* -**ies**) **1** the common people. **2** the general body (esp. of mankind). **3** a corporate body. [ME f. OF *comunalté* f. med.L *communalitas -tatis* (as COMMON)]

commoner /ˈkɒmənə(r)/ *n.* **1** one of the common people, as opposed to the aristocracy. **2** a person who has the right of common. **3** a student at a British university who does not have a scholarship. [ME f. med.L *communarius* f. *communa* (as COMMUNE¹)]

commonplace /ˈkɒmənpleɪs/ *adj. & n.* —*adj.* lacking originality; trite. —*n.* **1 a** an everyday saying; a platitude (*uttered a commonplace about the weather*). **b** an ordinary topic of conversation. **2** anything usual or trite. **3** a notable passage in a book etc. copied into a commonplace-book. **□commonplace-book** a book into which notable extracts from other works are copied for personal use. **□□ commonplaceness** *n.* [transl. of L *locus communis* = Gk *koinos topos* general theme]

commons /ˈkɒmənz/ *n.pl.* **1** (**the Commons**) = *House of Commons*. **2 a** the common people. **b** (prec. by *the*) the common people regarded as a part of a political, esp. British, system. **3** provisions shared in common; daily fare. **□short commons** insufficient food. [ME pl. of COMMON]

commonsensical /ˌkɒmənˈsensɪk(ə)l/ *adj.* possessing or marked by common sense. [*common sense* (see COMMON)]

commonweal /ˈkɒmənˌwiːl/ *n. archaic* **1** = *common weal*. **2** = COMMONWEALTH.

commonwealth /ˈkɒmənˌwelθ/ *n.* **1 a** an independent State or community, esp. a democratic republic. **b** such a community or organization of shared interests in a non-political field (*the commonwealth of learning*). **2** (**the Commonwealth**) **a** (in full **the British Commonwealth of Nations**) an international association consisting of the UK together with States that were previously part of the British Empire. **b** the republican period of government in Britain 1649-60. **c** *US* a part of the title of some of the States of the US. **d** the title of the federated Australian States. **□Commonwealth Day** a day each year commemorating the British Commonwealth (formerly called *Empire Day*). [COMMON + WEALTH]

commotion /kəˈməʊʃ(ə)n/ *n.* **1 a** a confused and noisy disturbance or outburst. **b** loud and confusing noise. **2** a civil insurrection. [ME f. OF *commotion* or L *commotio* (as COM-, MOTION)]

communal /ˈkɒmjʊn(ə)l/ *adj.* **1** relating to or benefiting a community; for common use (*communal baths*). **2** of a commune, esp. the Paris Commune. **□□ communality** /-ˈnælɪtɪ/ *n.* **communally** *adv.* [F f. LL *communalis* (as COMMUNE¹)]

communalism /ˈkɒmjʊnəˌlɪz(ə)m/ *n.* **1** a principle of political organization based on federated communes. **2** the principle of communal ownership etc. **□□ communalist** *n.* **communalistic** /-ˈlɪstɪk/ *adj.*

communalize /ˈkɒmjʊnəˌlaɪz/ *v.tr.* (also -**ise**) make communal. **□□ communalization** /-ˈzeɪʃ(ə)n/ *n.*

communard /ˈkɒmjʊˌnɑːd/ *n.* **1** a member of a commune. **2** (also **Communard**) *hist.* a supporter of the Paris Commune. [F (as COMMUNE¹)]

commune¹ /ˈkɒmjuːn/ *n.* **1 a** a group of people, not necessarily related, sharing living accommodation, goods, etc., esp. as a political act. **b** a communal settlement esp. for the pursuit of shared interests. **2 a** the smallest French territorial division for administrative purposes. **b** a similar division elsewhere. **3** (**the Commune**) the communalistic government in Paris in 1871. [F f. med.L *communia* neut. pl. of L *communis* common]

commune² /kəˈmjuːn/ *v.intr.* **1** (usu. foll. by *with*) **a** speak confidentially and intimately (*communed together about their loss; communed with his heart*). **b** feel in close touch (with nature etc.) (*communed* *with the hills*). **2** *US* receive Holy Communion. [ME f. OF *comuner* share f. *comun* COMMON]

communicable /kə'mju:nɪkəb(ə)l/ *adj.* **1** (esp. of a disease) able to be passed on. **2** *archaic* communicative. □□ **communicability** /-'bɪlɪtɪ/ *n.* **communicably** *adv.* [ME f. OF *communicable* or LL *communicabilis* (as COMMUNICATE)]

communicant /kə'mju:nɪkənt/ *n.* **1** a person who receives Holy Communion, esp. regularly. **2** a person who imparts information. [L *communicare communicant-* (as COMMON)]

communicate /kə'mju:nɪ,keɪt/ *v.* **1** *tr.* **a** transmit or pass on by speaking or writing (*communicated his ideas*). **b** transmit (heat, motion, etc.). **c** pass on (an infectious illness). **d** impart (feelings etc.) non-verbally (*communicated his affection*). **2** *intr.* succeed in conveying information, evoking understanding etc. (*he communicates well*). **3** *intr.* (often foll. by *with*) share a feeling or understanding; relate socially. **4** *intr.* (often foll. by *with*) (of a room etc.) have a common door (*my room communicates with yours*). **5 a** *tr.* administer Holy Communion to. **b** *intr.* receive Holy Communion. □□ **communicator** *n.* **communicatory** *adj.* [L *communicare communicat-* (as COMMON)]

communication /kə,mju:nɪ'keɪʃ(ə)n/ *n.* **1 a** the act of imparting, esp. news. **b** an instance of this. **c** the information etc. communicated. **2** a means of connecting different places, such as a door, passage, road, or railway. **3** social intercourse (*it was difficult to maintain communication in the uproar*). **4** (in *pl.*) the science and practice of transmitting information esp. by electronic or mechanical means. **5** (in *pl.*) *Mil.* the means of transport between a base and the front. **6** a paper read to a learned society. □ **communication cord** *Brit.* a cord or chain in a railway carriage that may be pulled to stop the train in an emergency. **communication** (or **communications**) **satellite** an artificial satellite used to relay telephone circuits or broadcast programmes. **communication theory** the study of the principles and methods by which information is conveyed.

communicative /kə'mju:nɪkətɪv/ *adj.* **1** open, talk-ative, informative. **2** ready to communicate. □□ **communicatively** *adv.* [LL *communicativus* (as COMMUNICATE)]

communion /kə'mju:nɪən/ *n.* **1** a sharing, esp. of thoughts etc.; fellowship (*their minds were in communion*). **2** participation; a sharing in common (*communion of interests*). **3** (**Communion, Holy Communion**) **a** the Eucharist. **b** participation in the Communion service. **c** (*attrib.*) of or used in the Communion service (*Communion-table*; *Communion-cloth*; *Communion-rail*). **4** fellowship, esp. between branches of the Catholic Church. **5** a body or group within the Christian faith (*the Methodist communion*). □ **communion of saints** fellowship between Christians living and dead. [ME f. OF *communion* or L *communio* f. *communis* common]

communiqué /kə'mju:nɪ,keɪ/ *n.* an official communication, esp. a news report. [F, = communicated]

communism /'kɒmju,nɪz(ə)m/ *n.* **1** a political theory derived from Marx, advocating class war and leading to a society in which all property is publicly owned and each person is paid and works according to his or her needs and abilities. **2** (usu. **Communism**) **a** the communistic form of society established in the USSR and elsewhere. **b** any movement or political doctrine advocating communism. **3** = COMMUNALISM. [F *communisme* f. *commun* COMMON]

communist /'kɒmjʊnɪst/ *n.* & *adj.* —*n.* **1** a person advocating or practising communism. **2** (**Communist**) a member of a Communist Party. —*adj.* of or relating to communism (*a communist play*). □□ **communistic** /-'nɪstɪk/ *adj.* [COMMUNISM]

communitarian /kə,mju:nɪ'teərɪən/ *n.* & *adj.* —*n.* a member of a communistic community. —*adj.* of or

relating to such a community. [COMMUNITY + -ARIAN after *unitarian* etc.]

community /kə'mju:nɪtɪ/ *n.* (*pl.* **-ies**) **1 a** all the people living in a specific locality. **b** a specific locality, including its inhabitants. **2** a body of people having a religion, a profession, etc., in common (*the immigrant community*). **3** fellowship of interests etc.; similarity (*community of intellect*). **4** a monastic, socialistic, etc. body practising common ownership. **5** joint ownership or liability (*community of goods*). **6** (prec. by *the*) the public. **7** a body of nations unified by common interests. **8** *Ecol.* a group of animals or plants living or growing together in the same area. □ **community centre** a place providing social etc. facilities for a neighbourhood. **community charge** (in the UK) a tax levied locally on every adult in a community. **community chest** *US* a fund for charity and welfare work in a community. **community home** *Brit.* a centre for housing young offenders and other juveniles in need of custodial care. **community service order** an order for a convicted offender to perform a period of unpaid work in the community. **community singing** singing by a large crowd or group, esp. of old popular songs or hymns. **community spirit** a feeling of belonging to a community, expressed in mutual support etc. [ME f. OF *comuneté* f. L *communitas -tatis* (as COMMON)]

communize /'kɒmjʊ,naɪz/ *v.tr.* (also **-ise**) **1** make (land etc.) common property. **2** make (a person etc.) communistic. □□ **communization** /-'zeɪʃ(ə)n/ *n.* [L *communis* COMMON]

commutable /kə'mju:təb(ə)l/ *adj.* **1** convertible into money; exchangeable. **2** *Law* (of a punishment) able to be commuted. **3** within commuting distance. □□ **commutability** /-'bɪlɪtɪ/ *n.* [L *commutabilis* (as COMMUTE)]

commutate /'kɒmju:,teɪt/ *v.tr. Electr.* **1** regulate the direction of (an alternating current), esp. to make it a direct current. **2** reverse the direction of (an electric current). [L *commutare commutat-* (as COMMUTE)]

commutation /,kɒmju:'teɪʃ(ə)n/ *n.* **1** the act or process of commuting or being commuted (in legal and exchange senses). **2** *Electr.* the act or process of commutating or being commutated. **3** *Math.* the reversal of the order of two quantities. □ **commutation ticket** *US* a season ticket. [F *commutation* or L *commutatio* (as COMMUTE)]

commutative /kə'mju:tətɪv/ *adj.* **1** relating to or involving substitution. **2** *Math.* unchanged in result by the interchange of the order of quantities. [F *commutatif* or med.L *commutativus* (as COMMUTE)]

commutator /'kɒmju:,teɪtə(r)/ *n.* **1** *Electr.* a device for reversing electric current. **2** an attachment connected with the armature of a dynamo which directs and makes continuous the current produced.

commute /kə'mju:t/ *v.* **1** *intr.* travel to and from one's daily work, usu. in a city, esp. by car or train. **2** *tr. Law* (usu. foll. by *to*) change (a judicial sentence etc.) to another less severe. **3** *tr.* (often foll. by *into*, *for*) **a** change (one kind of payment) for another. **b** make a payment etc. to change (an obligation etc.) for another. **4** *tr.* **a** exchange; interchange (two things). **b** change (to another thing). **5** *tr. Electr.* commutate. **6** *intr. Math.* have a commutative relation. **7** *intr. US* buy and use a season ticket. [L *commutare commutat-* (as COM-, *mutare* change)]

commuter /kə'mju:tə(r)/ *n.* a person who travels some distance to work, esp. in a city, usu. by car or train.

comose /'kəʊməʊs/ *adj. Bot.* (of seeds etc.) having hairs, downy. [L *comosus* (as COMA²)]

comp /kɒmp/ *n.* & *v. colloq.* —*n.* **1** a competition. **2** *Printing* a compositor. **3** *Mus.* an accompaniment. —*v.* **1** *Mus.* **a** *tr.* accompany. **b** *intr.* play an accompaniment. **2** *Printing* **a** *intr.* work as a compositor. **b** *tr.* work as a compositor on. [abbr.]

compact¹ *adj.*, *v.*, & *n.* —*adj.* /kəm'pækt/ **1** closely or neatly packed together. **2** (of a piece of equipment, a room, etc.) well-fitted and practical though small. **3** (of style etc.) condensed; brief. **4** (esp. of the human body) small but well-proportioned. **5** (foll. by *of*) composed or made up of. —*v.tr.* /kəm'pækt/ **1** join or press firmly together. **2** condense. **3** (usu. foll. by *of*) compose; make up. —*n.* /'kɒmpækt/ **1** a small, flat, usu. decorated, case for face-powder, a mirror, etc. **2** an object formed by compacting powder. **3** *US* a medium-sized motor car. □**compact disc** /'kɒmpækt/ a disc on which information or sound is recorded digitally and reproduced by reflection of laser light. □□**compaction** *n.* **compactly** *adv.* **compactness** *n.* **compactor** *n.* [ME f. L *compingere compact-* (as COM-, *pangere* fasten)]

compact² /'kɒmpækt/ *n.* an agreement or contract between two or more parties. [L *compactum* f. *compacisci compact-* (as COM-, *pacisci* covenant): cf. PACT]

compages /kəm'peɪdʒiːz/ *n.* (*pl.* same) **1** a framework; a complex structure. **2** something resembling a compages in complexity etc. [L *compages* (as COM-, *pages* f. *pangere* fasten)]

companion¹ /kəm'pænjən/ *n.* & *v.* —*n.* **1 a** (often foll. by *in*, *of*) a person who accompanies, associates with, or shares with, another (*a companion in adversity*; *they were close companions*). **b** a person, esp. an unmarried or widowed woman, employed to live with and assist another. **2** a handbook or reference book on a particular subject (*A Companion to North Wales*). **3** a thing that matches another (*the companion of this book-end is over there*). **4** (**Companion**) a member of the lowest grade of some orders of knighthood (*Companion of the Bath*). **5** *Astron.* a star etc. that accompanies another. **6** equipment or a piece of equipment that combines several uses. —*v.* **1** *tr.* accompany. **2** *intr. literary* (often foll. by *with*) be a companion. □**companion in arms** a fellow-soldier. **Companion of Honour** (in the UK) a member of an order founded in 1917. **Companion of Literature** (in the UK) a member of an order founded in 1961. **companion-set** a set of fireside implements on a stand. [ME f. OF *compaignon* ult. f. L *panis* bread]

companion² /kəm'pænjən/ *n. Naut.* **1** a raised frame on a quarterdeck used for lighting the cabins etc. below. **2** = *companion-way*. □**companion-hatch** a wooden covering over a companion-way. **companion hatchway** an opening in a deck leading to a cabin. **companion ladder** a ladder from a deck to a cabin. **companion-way** a staircase to a cabin. [obs. Du. *kompanje* quarterdeck f. OF *compagne* f. It. (*camera della*) *compagna* pantry, prob. ult. rel. to COMPANION¹]

companionable /kəm'pænjənəb(ə)l/ *adj.* agreeable as a companion; sociable. □□**companionableness** *n.* **companionably** *adv.*

companionate /kəm'pænjənɪt/ *adj.* **1** well-suited; (of clothes) matching. **2** of or like a companion.

companionship /kəm'pænjənʃɪp/ *n.* good fellowship; friendship.

company /'kʌmpəni/ *n.* & *v.* —*n.* (*pl.* -**ies**) **1 a** a number of people assembled; a crowd; an audience (*addressed the company*). **b** guests or a guest (*am expecting company*). **2** a state of being a companion or fellow; companionship, esp. of a specific kind (*enjoys low company*; *do not care for his company*). **3 a** a commercial business. **b** (usu. **Co.**) the partner or partners not named in the title of a firm (*Smith and Co.*). **4** a troupe of actors or entertainers. **5** *Mil.* a subdivision of an infantry battalion usu. commanded by a major or a captain. **6** a group of Guides. —*v.* (-**ies**, -**ied**) **1** *tr. archaic* accompany. **2** *intr. literary* (often foll. by *with*) be a companion. □**company officer** a captain or a lower commissioned officer. **company Sergeant-major** see SERGEANT. **err** (or **be**) **in good company** discover that one's companions, or better people, have done the same as oneself. **good** (or **bad**) **company 1** a pleasant (or dull) companion. **2** a suitable (or unsuitable)

associate or group of friends. **in company** not alone. **in company with** together with. **keep company** (often foll. by *with*) associate habitually. **keep** (*archaic* **bear**) **a person company** accompany a person; be sociable. **part company** (often foll. by *with*) cease to associate. **ship's company** the entire crew. [ME f. AF *compainie*, OF *compai(g)nie* f. Rmc (as COMPANION¹)]

comparable /'kɒmpərəb(ə)l/ *adj.* **1** (often foll. by *with*) able to be compared. **2** (often foll. by *to*) fit to be compared; worth comparing. ¶ Use with *to* and *with* corresponds to the senses at *compare*; *to* is more common. □□**comparability** /-'bɪlɪti/ *n.* **comparableness** *n.* **comparably** *adv.* [ME f. OF f. L *comparabilis* (as COMPARE)]

comparative /kəm'pærətɪv/ *adj.* & *n.* —*adj.* **1** perceptible by comparison; relative (*in comparative comfort*). **2** estimated by comparison (*the comparative merits of the two ideas*). **3** of or involving comparison (esp. of sciences etc.). **4** *Gram.* (of an adjective or adverb) expressing a higher degree of a quality, but not the highest possible (e.g. *braver*, *more fiercely*) (cf. POSITIVE, SUPERLATIVE). —*n. Gram.* **1** the comparative expression or form of an adjective or adverb. **2** a word in the comparative. □□**comparatively** *adv.* [ME f. L *comparativus* (as COMPARE)]

comparator /kəm'pærətə(r)/ *n. Engin.* a device for comparing a product, an output, etc., with a standard, esp. an electronic circuit comparing two signals.

compare /kəm'peə(r)/ *v.* & *n.* —*v.* **1** *tr.* (usu. foll. by *to*) express similarities in; liken (*compared the landscape to a painting*). **2** *tr.* (often foll. by *to*, *with*) estimate the similarity or dissimilarity of; assess the relation between (*compared radio with television*; *that lacks quality compared to this*). ¶ In current use *to* and *with* are generally interchangeable, but *with* often implies a greater element of formal analysis, as in *compared my account with yours*. **3** *intr.* (often foll. by *with*) bear comparison (*compares favourably with the rest*). **4** *intr.* (often foll. by *with*) be equal or equivalent to. **5** *tr. Gram.* form the comparative and superlative degrees of (an adjective or an adverb). —*n. literary* comparison (*beyond compare*; *without compare*; *has no compare*). □**compare notes** exchange ideas or opinions. [ME f. OF *comparer* f. L *comparare* (as COM-, *parare* f. *par* equal)]

comparison /kəm'pærɪs(ə)n/ *n.* **1** the act or an instance of comparing. **2** a simile or semantic illustration. **3** capacity for being likened; similarity (*there's no comparison*). **4** (in full **degrees of comparison**) *Gram.* the positive, comparative, and superlative forms of adjectives and adverbs. □**bear** (or **stand**) **comparison** (often foll. by *with*) be able to be compared favourably. **beyond comparison 1** totally different in quality. **2** greatly superior; excellent. **in comparison with** compared to. [ME f. OF *comparesoun* f. L *comparatio -onis* (as COMPARE)]

compartment /kəm'pɑːtmənt/ *n.* & *v.* —*n.* **1** a space within a larger space, separated from the rest by partitions, e.g. in a railway carriage, wallet, desk, etc. **2** *Naut.* a watertight division of a ship. **3** an area of activity etc. kept apart from others in a person's mind. —*v.tr.* put into compartments. □□**compartmentation** /-'teɪʃ(ə)n/ *n.* [F *compartiment* f. It. *compartimento* f. LL *compartiri* (as COM-, *partiri* share)]

compartmental /ˌkɒmpɑːt'ment(ə)l/ *adj.* consisting of or relating to compartments or a compartment. □□**compartmentally** *adv.*

compartmentalize /ˌkɒmpɑːt'mentəˌlaɪz/ *v.tr.* (also -**ise**) divide into compartments or categories. □□**compartmentalization** /-'zeɪʃ(ə)n/ *n.*

compass /'kʌmpəs/ *n.* & *v.* —*n.* **1** (in full **magnetic compass**) an instrument showing the direction of magnetic north and bearings from it. **2** (usu. in *pl.*) an instrument for taking measurements and describing circles, with two arms connected at one end by a movable joint. **3** a circumference or boundary. **4** area, extent; scope (e.g. of knowledge or experience) (*beyond my compass*). **5** the range of tones of a voice or a musical instrument. —*v.tr.* *literary* **1** hem in. **2** grasp mentally. **3** contrive, accomplish. **4** go round. □**compass card** a circular rotating card showing the 32 principal bearings, forming the indicator of a magnetic compass. **compass rose** a circle of the principal directions marked on a chart. **compass-saw** a saw with a narrow blade, for cutting curves. **compass window** a bay window with a semicircular curve. □□ **compassable** *adj.* [ME f. OF *compas* ult. f. L *passus* PACE¹]

compassion /kəmˈpæʃ(ə)n/ *n.* pity inclining one to help or be merciful. [ME f. OF f. eccl.L *compassio* -*onis* f. *compati* (as COM-, *pati pass-* suffer)]

compassionate /kəmˈpæʃənət/ *adj.* sympathetic, pitying. □**compassionate leave** *Brit.* leave granted on grounds of bereavement etc. □□ **compassionately** *adv.* [obs. F *compassioné* f. *compassioner* feel pity (as COMPASSION)]

compatible /kəmˈpætəb(ə)l/ *adj.* **1** (often foll. by *with*) **a** able to coexist; well-suited; mutually tolerant (*a compatible couple*). **b** consistent (*their views are not compatible with their actions*). **2** (of equipment, machinery, etc.) capable of being used in combination. □□**compatibility** /-ˈbɪlɪtɪ/ *n.* **compatibly** *adv.* [F f. med.L *compatibilis* (as COMPASSION)]

compatriot /kəmˈpætrɪət/ *n.* a fellow-countryman. □□**compatriotic** /-ˈɒtɪk/ *adj.* [F *compatriote* f. LL *compatriota* (as COM-, *patriota* PATRIOT)]

compeer /ˈkɒmpɪə(r), -ˈpɪə(r)/ *n.* **1** an equal, a peer. **2** a comrade. [ME f. OF *comper* (as COM-, PEER²)]

compel /kəmˈpel/ *v.tr.* (**compelled, compelling**) **1** (usu. foll. by *to* + infin.) force, constrain (*compelled them to admit it*). **2** bring about (an action) by force (*compel submission*). **3** (as **compelling** *adj.*) rousing strong interest, attention, conviction, or admiration. **4** *archaic* drive forcibly. □□**compellable** *adj.* **compellingly** *adv.* [ME f. L *compellere compuls-* (as COM-, *pellere* drive)]

compendious /kəmˈpendɪəs/ *adj.* (esp. of a book etc.) comprehensive but fairly brief. □□ **compendiously** *adv.* **compendiousness** *n.* [ME f. OF *compendieux* f. L *compendiosus* brief (as COMPENDIUM)]

compendium /kəmˈpendəm/ *n.* (*pl.* **compendiums** or **compendia** /-dɪə/) **1** esp. *Brit.* a usu. one-volume handbook or encyclopaedia. **2 a** a summary or abstract of a larger work. **b** an abridgement. **3 a** a collection of games in a box. **b** any collection or mixture. **4** a package of writing paper, envelopes, etc. [L, = what is weighed together, f. *compendere* (as COM-, *pendere* weigh)]

compensate /ˈkɒmpən.seɪt/ *v.* **1** *tr.* (often foll. by *for*) recompense (a person) (*compensated him for his loss*). **2** *intr.* (usu. foll. by *for* a thing, *to* a person) make amends (*compensated for the insult; will compensate to her in full*). **3** *tr.* counterbalance. **4** *tr.* *Mech.* provide (a pendulum etc.) with extra or less weight etc. to neutralize the effects of temperature etc. **5** *intr. Psychol.* offset a disability or frustration by development in another direction. □□ **compensative** /-sətɪv/ *adj.* **compensator** *n.* **compensatory** /-ˈpensətərɪ, -ˈseɪtərɪ/ *adj.* [L *compensare* (as COM-, *pensare* frequent. of *pendere pens-* weigh)]

compensation /ˌkɒmpenˈseɪʃ(ə)n/ *n.* **1 a** the act of compensating. **b** the process of being compensated. **2** something, esp. money, given as a recompense. **3** *Psychol.* **a** an act of compensating. **b** the result of compensating. **4** *US* a salary or wages. □**compensation pendulum** *Physics* a pendulum designed to neutralize the effects of temperature variation. □□ **compensational** *adj.* [ME f. OF f. L *compensatio* (as COMPENSATE)]

compère /ˈkɒmpeə(r)/ *n. & v. Brit.* —*n.* a person who introduces and links the artistes in a variety show etc.; a master of ceremonies. —*v.* **1** *tr.* act as a compère to. **2** *intr.* act as compère. [F, = godfather f. Rmc (as COM-, L *pater* father)]

compete /kəmˈpiːt/ *v.intr.* **1** (often foll. by *with*, *against* a person, *for* a thing) strive for superiority or supremacy (*competed with his brother; compete against the Russians; compete for the victory*). **2** (often foll. by *in*) take part (in a contest etc.) (*competed in the hurdles*). [L *competere competit-*, in late sense 'strive after or contend for (something)' (as COM-, *petere* seek)]

competence /ˈkɒmpɪt(ə)ns/ *n.* (also **competency** /ˈkɒmpɪtənsɪ/) **1** (often foll. by *for*, or *to* + infin.) ability; the state of being competent. **2** an income large enough to live on, usu. unearned. **3** *Law* the legal capacity (of a court, a magistrate, etc.) to deal with a matter.

competent /ˈkɒmpɪt(ə)nt/ *adj.* **1 a** (usu. foll. by *to* + infin. or *for*) adequately qualified or capable (*not competent to drive*). **b** effective (*a competent batsman*). **2** *Law* (of a judge, court, or witness) legally qualified or qualifying. □□ **competently** *adv.* [ME f. OF *competent* or L *competent-* (as COMPETE)]

competition /ˌkɒmpəˈtɪʃ(ə)n/ *n.* **1** (often foll. by *for*) competing, esp. in an examination, in trade, etc. **2** an event or contest in which people compete. **3 a** the people competing against a person. **b** the opposition they represent. [LL *competitio* rivalry (as COMPETITIVE)]

competitive /kəmˈpetɪtɪv/ *adj.* **1** involving, offered for, or by competition (*competitive contest*). **2** (of prices etc.) low enough to compare well with those of rival traders. **3** (of a person) having a strong urge to win; keen to compete. □□ **competitively** *adv.* **competitiveness** *n.* [*competit-*, past part. stem of L *competere* COMPETE]

competitor /kəmˈpetɪtə(r)/ *n.* a person who competes; a rival, esp. in business or commerce. [F *compétiteur* or L *competitor* (as COMPETE)]

compilation /ˌkɒmpɪˈleɪʃ(ə)n/ *n.* **1 a** the act of compiling. **b** the process of being compiled. **2** something compiled, esp. a book etc. composed of separate articles, stories, etc. [ME f. OF f. L *compilatio -onis* (as COMPILE)]

compile /kəmˈpaɪl/ *v.tr.* **1 a** collect (material) into a list, volume, etc. **b** make up (a volume etc.) from such material. **2** accumulate (a large number of) (*compiled a score of 160*). **3** *Computing* produce (a machine-coded form of a high-level program). [ME f. OF *compiler* or its apparent source, L *compilare* plunder, plagiarize]

compiler /kəmˈpaɪlə(r)/ *n.* **1** *Computing* a program for translating a high-level programming language into machine code. **2** a person who compiles.

complacency /kəmˈpleɪsənsɪ/ *n.* (also **complacence**) **1** smug self-satisfaction. **2** tranquil pleasure. [med.L *complacentia* f. L *complacēre* (as COM-, *placēre* please)]

complacent /kəmˈpleɪs(ə)nt/ *adj.* **1** smugly self-satisfied. **2** calmly content. ¶ Often confused with *complaisant*. □□ **complacently** *adv.* [L *complacēre*: see COMPLACENCY]

complain /kəmˈpleɪn/ *v.intr.* **1** (often foll. by *about*, *at*, or *that* + clause) express dissatisfaction (*complained at the state of the room; is always complaining*). **2** (foll. by *of*) **a** announce that one is suffering from (an ailment) (*complained of a headache*). **b** state a grievance concerning (*complained of the delay*). **3** make a mournful sound; groan, creak under a strain. □□ **complainer** *n.* **complainingly** *adv.* [ME f. OF *complaindre* (stem *complaign-*) f. med.L *complangere* bewail (as COM-, *plangere planct-* lament)]

complainant /kəmˈpleɪnənt/ *n. Law* a plaintiff in certain lawsuits.

complaint /kəmˈpleɪnt/ *n.* **1** an act of complaining. **2** a grievance. **3** an ailment or illness. **4** *US Law* the plaintiff's case in a civil action. [ME f. OF *complainte* f. *complaint* past part. of *complaindre*: see COMPLAIN]

complaisant /kəm'pleɪz(ə)nt/ *adj.* **1** politely deferential. **2** willing to please; acquiescent. ¶ Often confused with *complacent*. □□ **complaisance** *n.* [F f. *complaire* (stem *complais-*) acquiesce to please, f. L *complacēre*: see COMPLACENCY]

compleat *archaic* var. of COMPLETE.

complement *n.* & *v.* —*n.*/'kɒmplɪmənt/ **1 a** something that completes. **b** one of a pair, or one of two things that go together. **2** (often **full complement**) the full number needed to man a ship, fill a conveyance, etc. **3** *Gram.* a word or phrase added to a verb to complete the predicate of a sentence. **4** *Biochem.* a group of proteins in the blood capable of lysing bacteria etc. **5** *Math.* any element not belonging to a specified set or class. **6** *Geom.* the amount by which an angle is less than 90° (cf. SUPPLEMENT). —*v.tr.* /'kɒmplɪˌment/ **1** complete. **2** form a complement to (*the scarf complements her dress*). □□ **complemental** /-'ment(ə)l/ *adj.* [ME f. L *complementum* (as COMPLETE)]

complementarity /ˌkɒmplɪmen'tærɪtɪ/ *n.* (*pl.* **-ies**) **1** a complementary relationship or situation. **2** *Physics* the concept that a single model may not be adequate to explain atomic systems in different experimental conditions.

complementary /ˌkɒmplɪ'mentərɪ/ *adj.* **1** completing; forming a complement. **2** (of two or more things) complementing each other. □ **complementary angle** either of two angles making up 90°. **complementary colour** a colour that combined with a given colour makes white or black. □□ **complementarily** *adv.* **complementariness** *n.*

complete /kəm'pli:t/ *adj.* & *v.* —*adj.* **1** having all its parts; entire (*the set is complete*). **2** finished (*my task is complete*). **3** of the maximum extent or degree (*a complete surprise; a complete stranger*). **4** (also **compleat** after Walton's *Compleat Angler*) *joc.* accomplished (*the complete horseman*). —*v.tr.* **1** finish. **2 a** make whole or perfect. **b** make up the amount of (*completes the quota*). **3** fill in the answers to (a questionnaire etc.). **4** (usu. *absol.*) *Law* conclude a sale of property. □ **complete with** having (as an important accessory) (*comes complete with instructions*). □□ **completely** *adv.* **completeness** *n.* **completion** /-'pli:ʃ(ə)n/ *n.* [ME f. OF *complet* or L *completus* past part. of *complēre* fill up]

complex /'kɒmpleks/ *n.* & *adj.* —*n.* **1** a building, a series of rooms, a network, etc. made up of related parts (*the arts complex*). **2** *Psychol.* a related group of usu. repressed feelings or thoughts which cause abnormal behaviour or mental states. **3** (in general use) a preoccupation or obsession (*has a complex about punctuality*). **4** *Chem.* a compound in which molecules or ions form coordinate bonds to a metal atom or ion. —*adj.* **1** consisting of related parts; composite. **2** complicated (*a complex problem*). **3** *Math.* containing real and imaginary parts (cf. IMAGINARY). □ **complex sentence** a sentence containing a subordinate clause or clauses. □□ **complexity** /kəm'pleksɪtɪ/ *n.* (*pl.* **-ies**). **complexly** *adv.* [F *complexe* or L *complexus* past part. of *complectere* embrace, assoc. with *complexus* plaited]

complexion /kəm'plekʃ(ə)n/ *n.* **1** the natural colour, texture, and appearance, of the skin, esp. of the face. **2** an aspect; a character (*puts a different complexion on the matter*). □□ **complexioned** *adj.* (also in *comb.*) [ME f. OF f. L *complexio -onis* (as COMPLEX): orig. = combination of supposed qualities determining the nature of a body]

complexionless /kəm'plekʃənlɪs/ *adj.* paleskinned.

compliance /kəm'plaɪəns/ *n.* **1** the act or an instance of complying; obedience to a request, command, etc. **2** *Mech.* **a** the capacity to yield under an applied force. **b** the degree of such yielding. **3** unworthy acquiescence. □ **in compliance with** according to (a wish, command, etc.).

compliant /kəm'plaɪənt/ *adj.* disposed to comply; yielding, obedient. □□ **compliantly** *adv.*

complicate /'kɒmplɪˌkeɪt/ *v.tr.* & *intr.* **1** (often foll. by *with*) make or become difficult, confused, or complex. **2** (as **complicated** *adj.*) complex; intricate. □□ **complicatedly** *adv.* **complicatedness** *n.* [L *complicare complicat-* (as COM-, *plicare* fold)]

complication /ˌkɒmplɪ'keɪʃ(ə)n/ *n.* **1 a** an involved or confused condition or state. **b** a complicating circumstance; a difficulty. **2** *Med.* a secondary disease or condition aggravating a previous one. [F *complication* or LL *complicatio* (as COMPLICATE)]

complicity /kəm'plɪsɪtɪ/ *n.* partnership in a crime or wrongdoing. [*complice* (see ACCOMPLICE) + -ITY]

compliment *n.* & *v.* —*n.* /'kɒmplɪmənt/ **1 a** spoken or written expression of praise. **b** an act or circumstance implying praise (*their success was a compliment to their efforts*). **2** (in *pl.*) **a** formal greetings, esp. as a written accompaniment to a gift etc. (*with the compliments of the management*). **b** praise (*my compliments to the cook*). —*v.tr.* /'kɒmplɪˌment/ **1** (often foll. by *on*) congratulate; praise (*complimented him on his roses*). **2** (often foll. by *with*) present as a mark of courtesy (*complimented her with his attention*). □ **compliments of the season** greetings appropriate to the time of year, esp. Christmas. **compliments slip** a printed slip of paper sent with a gift etc., esp. from a business firm. **pay a compliment to** praise. **return the compliment 1** give a compliment in return for another. **2** retaliate or recompense in kind. [F *complimenter* f. It. *complimento* ult. f. L (as COMPLEMENT)]

complimentary /ˌkɒmplɪ'mentərɪ/ *adj.* **1** expressing a compliment; praising. **2** (of a ticket for a play etc.) given free of charge, esp. as a mark of favour. □□ **complimentarily** *adv.*

compline /'kɒmplɪn, -plaɪn/ *n. Eccl.* **1** the last of the canonical hours of prayer. **2** the service taking place during this. [ME f. OF *complie*, fem. past part. of obs. *complir* complete, ult. f. L *complēre* fill up]

comply /kəm'plaɪ/ *v.intr.* (**-ies**, **-ied**) (often foll. by *with*) act in accordance (with a wish, command, etc.) (*complied with her expectation; had no choice but to comply*). [It. *complire* f. Cat. *complir*, Sp. *cumplir* f. L *complēre* fill up]

compo /'kɒmpəʊ/ *n.* & *adj.* —*n.* (*pl.* **-os**) a composition of plaster etc., e.g. stucco. —*adj.* = COMPOSITE. □ **compo rations** a large pack of food designed to last for several days. [abbr.]

component /kəm'pəʊnənt/ *n.* & *adj.* —*n.* **1** a part of a larger whole, esp. part of a motor vehicle. **2** *Math.* one of two or more vectors equivalent to a given vector. —*adj.* being part of a larger whole (*assembled the component parts*). □□ **componential** /ˌkɒmpə'nenʃ(ə)l/ *adj.* [L *componere component-* (as COM-, *ponere* put)]

comport /kəm'pɔ:t/ *v.refl. literary* **on**) conduct oneself; behave. □ **comport with** suit, befit. □□ **comportment** *n.* [L *comportare* (as COM-, *portare* carry)]

compos var. of COMPOS MENTIS.

compose /kəm'pəʊz/ *v.* **1 a** *tr.* construct or create (a work of art, esp. literature or music). **b** *intr.* compose music (*gave up composing in 1917*). **2** *tr.* constitute; make up (*six tribes which composed the German nation*). ¶ Preferred to *comprise* in this sense. **3** *tr.* put together to form a whole, esp. artistically; order; arrange (*composed the group for the photographer*). **4** *tr.* **a** (often *refl.*) calm; settle (*compose your expression; composed himself to wait*). **b** (as **composed** *adj.*) calm, settled. **5** *tr.* settle (a dispute etc.). **6** *tr. Printing* **a** set up (type) to form words and blocks of words. **b** set up (a manuscript etc.) in type. □ **composed of** made up of, consisting of (*a flock composed of sheep and goats*). □□ **composedly** /-zɪdlɪ/ *adv.* [F *composer*, f. L *componere* (as COM-, *ponere* put)]

composer /kəm'pəʊzə(r)/ *n.* a person who composes (esp. music).

composite /'kɒmpəzɪt, -ˌzaɪt/ *adj., n.,* & *v. —adj.* **1** made up of various parts; blended. **2** (esp. of a synthetic building material) made up of recognizable constituents. **3** *Archit.* of the fifth classical order of architecture, consisting of elements of the Ionic and Corinthian orders. **4** *Bot.* of the plant family Compositae. *—n.* **1** a thing made up of several parts or elements. **2** a synthetic building material. **3** *Bot.* any plant of the family Compositae, having a head of many small flowers forming one bloom, e.g. the daisy or the dandelion. **4** *Polit.* a resolution composed of two or more related resolutions. *—v.tr. Polit.* amalgamate (two or more similar resolutions). □□ **compositely** *adv.* **compositeness** *n.* [F f. L *compositus* past part. of *componere* (as COM-, *ponere* posit-put)]

composition /ˌkɒmpə'zɪʃ(ə)n/ *n.* **1 a** the act of putting together; formation or construction. **b** something so composed; a mixture. **c** the constitution of such a mixture; the nature of its ingredients (*the composition is two parts oil to one part vinegar*). **2 a** a literary or musical work. **b** the act or art of producing such a work. **c** an essay, esp. written by a schoolchild. **d** an artistic arrangement (of parts of a picture, subjects for a photograph, etc.). **3** mental constitution; character (*jealousy is not in his composition*). **4** (often *attrib.*) a compound artificial substance, esp. one serving the purpose of a natural one. **5** *Printing* the setting-up of type. **6** *Gram.* the formation of words into a compound word. **7** *Law* **a** a compromise, esp. a legal agreement to pay a sum in lieu of a larger sum, or other obligation (*made a composition with his creditors*). **b** a sum paid in this way. **8** *Math.* the combination of functions in a series. □□ **compositional** *adj.* **compositionally** *adv.* [ME f. OF, f. L *compositio -onis* (as COMPOSITE)]

compositor /kəm'pɒzɪtə(r)/ *n. Printing* a person who sets up type for printing. [ME f. AF *compositour* f. L *compositor* (as COMPOSITE)]

compos mentis /ˌkɒmpɒs 'mentɪs/ *adj.* (also *compos*) having control of one's mind; sane. [L]

compossible /kəm'pɒsɪb(ə)l/ *adj. formal* (often foll. by *with*) able to coexist. [OF f. med.L *compossibilis* (as COM-, POSSIBLE)]

compost /'kɒmpɒst/ *n.* & *v. —n.* **1 a** a mixed manure, esp. of organic origin. **b** a loam soil or other medium with added compost, used for growing plants. **2 a** mixture of ingredients (*a rich compost of lies and innuendo*). *—v.tr.* **1** treat (soil) with compost. **2** make (manure, vegetable matter, etc.) into compost. □ **compost heap** (or **pile**) a layered structure of garden refuse, soil, etc., which decays to become compost. [ME f. OF *composte* f. L *compos(i)tum* (as COMPOSITE)]

composure /kəm'pəʊʒə(r)/ *n.* a tranquil manner; calmness. [COMPOSE + -URE]

compote /'kɒmpəʊt, -pɒt/ *n.* fruit preserved or cooked in syrup. [F f. OF *composte* (as COMPOSITE)]

compound[1] /'kɒmpaʊnd/ *n., adj.,* & *v. —n.* **1** a mixture of two or more things, qualities, etc. **2** (also **compound word**) a word made up of two or more existing words. **3** *Chem.* a substance formed from two or more elements chemically united in fixed proportions. *—adj.* **1 a** made up of several ingredients. **b** consisting of several parts. **2** combined; collective. **3** *Zool.* consisting of individual organisms. **4** *Biol.* consisting of several or many parts. *—v.* /kəm'paʊnd/ **1** *tr.* mix or combine (ingredients, ideas, motives, etc.) (*grief compounded with fear*). **2** *tr.* increase or complicate (difficulties etc.) (*anxiety compounded by discomfort*). **3** *tr.* make up (a composite whole). **4** *tr.* (also *absol.*) settle (a debt, dispute, etc.) by concession or special arrangement. **5** *tr. Law* **a** condone (a liability or offence) in exchange for money etc. **b** forbear from prosecuting (a felony) from private motives. **6** *intr.* (usu. foll. by *with, for*) *Law* come to terms with a person, for forgoing a claim etc. for an offence. **7** *tr.* combine (words or elements) into a word. □ **compound eye** an eye consisting of numerous visual units, as found in insects and crustaceans. **compound fracture** a fracture complicated by a skin wound. **compound interest** interest payable on capital and its accumulated interest (cf. *simple interest*). **compound interval** *Mus.* an interval exceeding one octave. **compound leaf** a leaf consisting of several or many leaflets. **compound sentence** a sentence with more than one subject or predicate. **compound time** *Mus.* music having more than one group of simple-time units in each bar. □□ **compoundable** /kəm'paʊndəb(ə)l/ *adj.* [ME *compoun(e)* f. OF *compondre* f. L *componere* (as COM-, *ponere* put: *-d* as in *expound*)]

compound[2] /'kɒmpaʊnd/ *n.* **1** a large open enclosure for housing workers etc., esp. miners in S. Africa. **2** an enclosure, esp. in India, China, etc., in which a factory or a house stands (cf. KAMPONG). **3** a large enclosed space in a prison or prison camp. **4** = POUND[3]. [Port. *campon* or Du. *kampong* f. Malay]

comprador /ˌkɒmprə'dɔː(r)/ *n.* (also **compradore**) **1** *hist.* a Chinese business agent of a foreign company. **2** an agent of a foreign power. [Port. *comprador* buyer f. LL *comparator* f. L *comparare* purchase]

comprehend /ˌkɒmprɪ'hend/ *v.tr.* **1** grasp mentally; understand (a person or a thing). **2** include; take in. [ME f. OF *comprehender* or L *comprehendere comprehens-* (as COM-, *prehendere* grasp)]

comprehensible /ˌkɒmprɪ'hensɪb(ə)l/ *adj.* **1** that can be understood; intelligible. **2** that can be included or contained. □□ **comprehensibility** /-'bɪlɪtɪ/ *n.* **comprehensibly** *adv.* [F *compréhensible* or L *comprehensibilis* (as COMPREHEND)]

comprehension /ˌkɒmprɪ'henʃ(ə)n/ *n.* **1 a** the act or capability of understanding, esp. writing or speech. **b** an extract from a text set as an examination, with questions designed to test understanding of it. **2** inclusion. **3** *Eccl. hist.* the inclusion of Nonconformists in the Anglican Church. [F *compréhension* or L *comprehensio* (as COMPREHENSIBLE)]

comprehensive /ˌkɒmprɪ'hensɪv/ *adj.* & *n. —adj.* **1** complete; including all or nearly all elements, aspects, etc. (*a comprehensive grasp of the subject*). **2** of or relating to understanding (*the comprehensive faculty*). **3** (of motor-vehicle insurance) providing complete protection. *—n.* (in full **comprehensive school**) *Brit.* a secondary school catering for children of all abilities from a given area. □□ **comprehensively** *adv.* **comprehensiveness** *n.* [F *compréhensif -ive* or LL *comprehensivus* (as COMPREHENSIBLE)]

compress *v.* & *n. —v.tr.* /kəm'pres/ **1** squeeze together. **2** bring into a smaller space or shorter extent. *—n.* /'kɒmpres/ a pad of lint etc. pressed on to part of the body to relieve inflammation, stop bleeding, etc. □ **compressed air** air at more than atmospheric pressure. □□ **compressible** /kəm'presɪb(ə)l/ *adj.* **compressibility** /-'bɪlɪtɪ/ *n.* **compressive** /kəm'presɪv/ *adj.* [ME f. OF *compresser* or LL *compressare* frequent. of L *comprimere compress-* (as COM-, *premere* press)]

compression /kəm'preʃ(ə)n/ *n.* **1** the act of compressing or being compressed. **2** the reduction in volume (causing an increase in pressure) of the fuel mixture in an internal-combustion engine before ignition. [F f. L *compressio* (as COMPRESS)]

compressor /kəm'presə(r)/ *n.* an instrument or device for compressing, esp. a machine used for increasing the pressure of air or other gases.

comprise /kəm'praɪz/ *v.tr.* **1** include; comprehend. **2** consist of, be composed of (*the book comprises 350 pages*). **3** *disp.* make up, compose (*the essays comprise his total work*). □□ **comprisable** *adj.* [ME f. F, fem. past part. of *comprendre* COMPREHEND]

compromise /'kɒmprəˌmaɪz/ *n.* & *v. —n.* **1** the settlement of a dispute by mutual concession (*reached a compromise by bargaining*). **2** (often foll.

by *between*) an intermediate state between conflicting opinions, actions, etc., reached by mutual concession or modification (*a compromise between ideals and material necessity*). —*v.* **1** *a intr.* settle a dispute by mutual concession (*compromised over the terms*). **b** *tr. archaic* settle (a dispute) by mutual concession. **2** *tr.* bring into disrepute or danger esp. by indiscretion or folly. □□ **compromiser** *n.* **compromisingly** *adv.* [ME f. OF *compromis* f. LL *compromissum* neut. past part. of *compromittere* (as COM-, *promittere* PROMISE)]

compte rendu /ˌkɔ̃t rãˈdju:/ *n.* (*pl.* *comptes rendus* *pronunc.* same) a report; a review; a statement. [F]

Comptometer /kɒmpˈtɒmɪtə(r)/ *n. propr.* an early type of calculating-machine. [app. f. F *compte* COUNT¹ + -METER]

comptroller /kənˈtrəʊlə(r)/ *n.* a controller (used in the title of some financial officers) (*Comptroller and Auditor General*). [var. of CONTROLLER, by erron. assoc. with COUNT¹, L *computus*]

compulsion /kəmˈpʌlʃ(ə)n/ *n.* **1** a constraint; an obligation. **2** *Psychol.* an irresistible urge to a form of behaviour, esp. against one's conscious wishes. □ **under compulsion** because one is compelled. [ME f. F f. LL *compulsio -onis* (as COMPEL)]

compulsive /kəmˈpʌlsɪv/ *adj.* **1** compelling. **2** resulting or acting from, or as if from, compulsion (*a compulsive gambler*). **3** *Psychol.* resulting or acting from compulsion against one's conscious wishes. **4** irresistible (*compulsive entertainment*). □□ **compulsively** *adv.* **compulsiveness** *n.* [med.L *compulsivus* (as COMPEL)]

compulsory /kəmˈpʌlsəri/ *adj.* **1** required by law or a rule (*it is compulsory to keep dogs on leads*). **2** essential; necessary. □ **compulsory purchase** the enforced purchase of land or property by a local authority etc., for public use. □□ **compulsorily** *adv.* **compulsoriness** *n.* [med.L *compulsorius* (as COMPEL)]

compunction /kəmˈpʌŋkʃ(ə)n/ *n.* (usu. with *neg.*) **1** the pricking of the conscience. **2** a slight regret; a scruple (*without compunction; have no compunction in refusing him*). □□ **compunctious** /-ʃəs/ *adj.* **compunctiously** /-ʃəslɪ/ *adv.* [ME f. OF *componction* f. eccl.L *compunctio -onis* f. L *compungere compunct-* (as COM-, *pungere* prick)]

compurgation /ˌkɒmpɜːˈɡeɪʃ(ə)n/ *n. Law hist.* an acquittal from a charge or accusation obtained by the oaths of witnesses. □□ **compurgatory** /kəmˈpɜːɡətərɪ/ *adj.* [med.L *compurgatio* f. L *compurgare* (as COM-, *purgare* purify)]

compurgator /ˈkɒmpɜːˌɡeɪtə(r)/ *n. Law hist.* a witness who swore to the innocence or good character of an accused person.

compute /kəmˈpjuːt/ *v.* **1** *tr.* (often foll. by *that* + clause) reckon or calculate (a number, an amount, etc.). **2** *intr.* make a reckoning, esp. using a computer. □□ **computability** /-təˈbɪlɪtɪ/ *n.* **computable** /-ˈpjuːtəb(ə)l, ˈkɒm-/ *adj.* **computation** /ˌkɒmpjuːˈteɪʃ(ə)n/ *n.* [F *computer* or L *computare* (as COM-, *putare* reckon)]

computer /kəmˈpjuːtə(r)/ *n.* **1** a usu. electronic device for storing and processing data (usu. in binary form), according to instructions given to it in a variable program. **2** a person who computes or makes calculations. □ **computer-literate** able to use computers; familiar with the operation of computers. **computer science** the study of the principles and use of computers. **computer virus** a hidden code within a computer program intended to corrupt a system or destroy data stored in it.

computerize /kəmˈpjuːtəˌraɪz/ *v.tr.* (also **-ise**) **1** equip with a computer; install a computer in. **2** store, perform, or produce by computer. □□ **computerization** /-ˈzeɪʃ(ə)n/ *n.*

comrade /ˈkɒmreɪd, -rɪd/ *n.* **1** a (usu. of males) a workmate, friend, or companion. **b** (also **comrade-in-arms**) a fellow soldier etc. **2** *Polit.* a fellow socialist or communist (often as a form of address). □□ **comradely** *adj.* **comradeship** *n.* [earlier *cama- camerade* f. F *camerade, camarade* (orig. fem.) f. Sp. *camarada* room-mate (as CHAMBER)]

comsat /ˈkɒmsæt/ *n.* a communication satellite. [abbr.]

con¹ /kɒn/ *n. & v. sl.* —*n.* a confidence trick. —*v.tr.* (**conned, conning**) swindle; deceive (*conned him into thinking he had won*). □ **con man** = *confidence man.* [abbr.]

con² /kɒn/ *n., prep., & adv.* —*n.* (usu. in *pl.*) a reason against. —*prep. & adv.* against (cf. PRO²). [L *contra* against]

con³ /kɒn/ *n. sl.* a convict. [abbr.]

con⁴ /kɒn/ *v.tr.* (*US* **conn**) (**conned, conning**) *Naut.* direct the steering of (a ship). [app. weakened form of obs. *cond, condie,* f. F *conduire* f. L *conducere* CONDUCT]

con⁵ /kɒn/ *v.tr.* (**conned, conning**) *archaic* (often foll. by *over*) study, learn by heart (*conned his part well*). [ME *cunn-, con,* forms of CAN¹]

con- /kɒn, kən/ *prefix* assim. form of COM- before *c, d, f, g, j, n, q, s, t, v,* and sometimes before vowels.

conacre /ˈkɒnˌeɪkə(r)/ *n. Ir.* the letting by a tenant of small portions of land prepared for crops or grazing. [CORN¹ + ACRE]

con amore /ˌkɒn æˈmɔːrɪ/ *adv.* **1** with devotion or zeal. **2** (**con amore**) *Mus.* tenderly. [It., = with love]

conation /kəˈneɪʃ(ə)n/ *n. Philos. & Psychol.* **1** the desire to perform an action. **2** voluntary action; volition. □□ **conative** /ˈkɒnətɪv, ˈkəʊ-/ *adj.* [L *conatio* f. *conari* try]

con brio /kɒn ˈbriːəʊ/ *adv. Mus.* with vigour. [It.]

concatenate /kənˈkætɪˌneɪt/ *v. & adj.* —*v.tr.* link together (a chain of events, things, etc.). —*adj.* joined; linked. □□ **concatenation** /-ˈneɪʃ(ə)n/ *n.* [LL *concatenare* (as COM-, *catenare* f. *catena* chain)]

concave /ˈkɒnkeɪv/ *adj.* having an outline or surface curved like the interior of a circle or sphere (cf. CONVEX). □□ **concavely** *adv.* **concavity** /-ˈkævɪtɪ/ *n.* [L *concavus* (as COM-, *cavus* hollow), or through F *concave*]

conceal /kənˈsiːl/ *v.tr.* **1** (often foll. by *from*) keep secret (*concealed her motive from him*). **2** not allow to be seen; hide (*concealed the letter in her pocket*). □□ **concealer** *n.* **concealment** *n.* [ME f. OF *conceler* f. L *concelare* (as COM-, *celare* hide)]

concede /kənˈsiːd/ *v.tr.* **1** a (often foll. by *that* + clause) admit (a defeat etc.) to be true (*conceded that his work was inadequate*). **b** admit defeat in. **2** (often foll. by *to*) grant, yield, or surrender (a right, a privilege, points or a start in a game, etc.). **3** *Sport* allow an opponent to score (a goal) or to win (a match), etc. □□ **conceder** *n.* [F *concéder* or L *concedere concess-* (as COM-, *cedere* yield)]

conceit /kənˈsiːt/ *n.* **1** personal vanity; pride. **2** *literary* **a** a far-fetched comparison, esp. as a stylistic affectation; a convoluted or unlikely metaphor. **b** a fanciful notion. [ME f. CONCEIVE after *deceit, deceive,* etc.]

conceited /kənˈsiːtɪd/ *adj.* vain, proud. □□ **conceitedly** *adv.* **conceitedness** *n.*

conceivable /kənˈsiːvəb(ə)l/ *adj.* capable of being grasped or imagined; understandable. □□ **conceivability** /-ˈbɪlɪtɪ/ *n.* **conceivably** *adv.*

conceive /kənˈsiːv/ *v.* **1** *intr.* become pregnant. **2** *tr.* become pregnant with (a child). **3** *tr.* (often foll. by *that* + clause) **a** imagine, fancy, think (*can't conceive that he could be guilty*). **b** (usu. in *passive*) formulate, express (a belief, a plan, etc.). □ **conceive of** form in the mind; imagine. [ME f. OF *conceiv-* stressed stem of *concevoir* f. L *concipere concept-* (as COM-, *capere* take)]

concelebrate /kənˈselɪˌbreɪt/ *v.intr. RC Ch.* **1** (of two or more priests) celebrate the mass together. **2** (esp. of a newly ordained priest) celebrate the mass with the ordaining bishop. □□ **concelebrant** /-brənt/ *n.* **concelebration** /-ˈbreɪʃ(ə)n/ *n.* [L *concelebrare* (as COM-, *celebrare* CELEBRATE)]

concentrate /ˈkɒnsənˌtreɪt/ v. & n. —v. 1 intr. (often foll. by on, upon) focus all one's attention or mental ability. 2 tr. bring together (troops, power, attention, etc.) to one point; focus. 3 tr. increase the strength of (a liquid etc.) by removing water or any other diluting agent. 4 tr. (as **concentrated** adj.) (of hate etc.) intense, strong. —n. 1 a concentrated substance. 2 a concentrated form of esp. food. □□ **concentratedly** adv. **concentrative** adj. **concentrator** n. [after concentre f. F concentrer (as CON- + CENTRE)]

concentration /ˌkɒnsənˈtreɪʃ(ə)n/ n. 1 a the act or power of concentrating (needs to develop concentration). b an instance of this (interrupted my concentration). 2 something concentrated (a concentration of resources). 3 something brought together; a gathering. 4 the weight of substance in a given weight or volume of material. □ **concentration camp** a camp for the detention of political prisoners, internees, etc., esp. in Nazi Germany.

concentre /kənˈsentə(r)/ v.tr. & intr. (US **concenter**) bring or come to a common centre. [F concentrer: see CONCENTRATE]

concentric /kənˈsentrɪk/ adj. (often foll. by with) (esp. of circles) having a common centre (cf. ECCENTRIC). □□ **concentrically** adv. **concentricity** /ˌkɒnsenˈtrɪsɪti/ n. [ME f. OF concentrique or med.L concentricus (as COM-, centricus as CENTRE)]

concept /ˈkɒnsept/ n. 1 a general notion; an abstract idea (the concept of evolution). 2 colloq. an idea or invention to help sell or publicize a commodity (a new concept in swimwear). 3 Philos. an idea or mental picture of a group or class of objects formed by combining all their aspects. [LL conceptus f. concept-: see CONCEIVE]

conception /kənˈsepʃ(ə)n/ n. 1 the act or an instance of conceiving; the process of being conceived. 2 an idea or plan, esp. as being new or daring (the whole conception showed originality). 3 a general notion; an inability to imagine. □□ **conceptional** adj. [ME f. OF f. L conceptio -onis (as CONCEPT)]

conceptive /kənˈseptɪv/ adj. 1 conceiving mentally. 2 of conception. [L conceptivus (as CONCEPTION)]

conceptual /kənˈseptjʊəl/ adj. of mental conceptions or concepts. □□ **conceptually** adv. [med.L conceptualis (conceptus as CONCEPT)]

conceptualism /kənˈseptjʊəˌlɪz(ə)m/ n. Philos. the theory that universals exist, but only as concepts in the mind. □□ **conceptualist** n.

conceptualize /kənˈseptjʊəˌlaɪz/ v.tr. (also **-ise**) form a concept or idea of. □□ **conceptualization** /-ˈzeɪʃ(ə)n/ n.

concern /kənˈsɜːn/ v. & n. —v.tr. 1 a be relevant or important to (this concerns you). b relate to; be about. 2 (usu. refl.; often foll. by with, in, about, or to + infin.) interest or involve oneself (don't concern yourself with my problems). 3 worry, affect (it concerns me that he is always late). —n. 1 anxiety, worry (felt a deep concern). 2 a a matter of interest or importance to one (no concern of mine). b (usu. in pl.) affairs, private business (meddling in my concerns). 3 a business, a firm (quite a prosperous concern). 4 colloq. a complicated or awkward thing (have lost the whole concern). □ **have a concern in** have an interest or share in. **have no concern with** have nothing to do with. **to whom it may concern** to those who have a proper interest in the matter (as an address to the reader of a testimonial, reference, etc.). [F concerner or LL concernere (as COM-, cernere sift, discern)]

concerned /kənˈsɜːnd/ adj. 1 involved, interested (the people concerned; concerned with proving his innocence). 2 (often foll. by that, about, at, for, or to + infin.) troubled, anxious (concerned about him; concerned to hear that). □ **as** (or **so**) **far as I am concerned** as regards my interests. **be concerned** (often foll. by in) take part. **I am not concerned** it

is not my business. □□ **concernedly** /-ˈsɜːnɪdli/ adv. **concernedness** /-ˈsɜːnɪdnɪs/ n.

concerning /kənˈsɜːnɪŋ/ prep. about, regarding.

concernment /kənˈsɜːnmənt/ n. formal 1 an affair or business. 2 importance. 3 (often foll. by with) a state of being concerned; anxiety.

concert n. & v. —n. /ˈkɒnsət/ 1 a musical performance of usu. several separate compositions. 2 agreement, accordance, harmony. 3 a combination of voices or sounds. —v.tr. /kənˈsɜːt/ arrange (by mutual agreement or coordination). □ **concert-goer** a person who often goes to concerts. **concert grand** the largest size of grand piano, used for concerts. **concert-master** esp. US the leading first-violin player in some orchestras. **concert overture** Mus. a piece like an overture but intended for independent performance. **concert performance** Mus. a performance (of an opera etc.) without scenery, costumes, or action. **concert pitch 1** Mus. the pitch internationally agreed in 1960 whereby the A above middle C = 440 Hz. 2 a state of unusual readiness, efficiency, and keenness (for action etc.). **in concert 1** (often foll. by with) acting jointly and accordantly. 2 (predic.) (of a musician) in a performance. [F concert (n.), concerter (v.) f. It. concertare harmonize]

concerted /kənˈsɜːtɪd/ adj. 1 combined together; jointly arranged or planned (a concerted effort). 2 Mus. arranged in parts for voices or instruments.

concertina /ˌkɒnsəˈtiːnə/ n. & v. —n. a musical instrument held in the hands and stretched and squeezed like bellows, having reeds and a set of buttons at each end to control the valves. —v.tr. & intr. (**concertinas, concertinaed** /-nəd/ or **concertina'd, concertinaing**) compress or collapse in folds like those of a concertina (the car concertinaed into the bridge). [CONCERT + -INA]

concertino /ˌkɒntʃəˈtiːnəʊ/ n. (pl. **-os**) Mus. 1 a simple or short concerto. 2 a solo instrument or solo instruments playing in a concerto. [It., dimin. of CONCERTO]

concerto /kənˈtʃeətəʊ, -ˈtʃɜːtəʊ/ n. (pl. **-os** or **concerti** /-tɪ/) Mus. a composition for a solo instrument or instruments accompanied by an orchestra. □ **concerto grosso** /ˈɡrɒsəʊ, ˈɡrəʊ-/ (pl. **concerti grossi** /-sɪ/ or **concerto grossos**) a composition for a group of solo instruments accompanied by an orchestra. [It. (see CONCERT): grosso big]

concession /kənˈseʃ(ə)n/ n. 1 a the act or an instance of conceding (made the concession that we were right). b a thing conceded. 2 a reduction in price for a certain category of person. 3 a the right to use land or other property, granted esp. by a government or local authority, esp. for a specific use. b the right, given by a company, to sell goods, esp. in a particular territory. c the land or property used or given. □□ **concessionary** adj. (also **concessional**). [F concession f. L concessio (as CONCEDE)]

concessionaire /kənˌseʃəˈneə(r)/ n. (also **concessionnaire**) the holder of a concession or grant, esp. for the use of land or trading rights. [F concessionnaire (as CONCESSION)]

concessive /kənˈsesɪv/ adj. 1 of or tending to concession. 2 Gram. a (of a preposition or conjunction) introducing a phrase or clause which might be expected to preclude the action of the main clause, but does not (e.g. in spite of, although). b (of a phrase or clause) introduced by a concessive preposition or conjunction. [LL concessivus (as CONCEDE)]

conch /kɒŋk, kɒntʃ/ n. (pl. **conchs** /kɒŋks/ or **conches** /ˈkɒntʃɪz/) 1 a a thick heavy spiral shell, occasionally bearing long projections, of various marine gastropod molluscs of the family Strombidae. b any of these gastropods. 2 Archit. the domed roof of a semicircular apse. 3 = CONCHA. [L concha shell f. Gk kogkhē]

concha /ˈkɒŋkə/ n. (pl. **conchae** /-kiː/) Anat. any part resembling a shell, esp. the depression in the external ear leading to its central cavity. [L: see CONCH]

conchie /'kɒntʃɪ/ n. (also **conchy**) (pl. **-ies**) derog. sl. a conscientious objector. [abbr.]

conchoidal /kɒŋ'kɔɪd(ə)l/ adj. Mineral. (of a solid fracture etc.) resembling the surface of a bivalve shell.

conchology /kɒŋ'kɒlədʒɪ/ n. Zool. the scientific study of shells. □□ **conchological** /-kə'lɒdʒɪk(ə)l/ adj. **conchologist** n. [Gk kogkhē shell + -LOGY]

conchy var. of CONCHIE.

concierge /ˌkɔ̃sɪ'eəʒ, ˌkɒn-/ n. (esp. in France) a door-keeper or porter of a block of flats etc. [F, prob. ult. f. L conservus fellow slave]

conciliar /kən'sɪlɪə(r)/ adj. of or concerning a council, esp. an ecclesiastical council. [med.L consiliarius counsellor]

conciliate /kən'sɪlɪˌeɪt/ v.tr. 1 make calm and amenable; pacify. 2 gain (esteem or goodwill). 3 archaic reconcile, make compatible. □□ **conciliative** /-'sɪlɪətɪv/ adj. **conciliator** n. **conciliatory** /-'sɪlɪətərɪ/ adj. **conciliatoriness** /-'sɪlɪətərɪnɪs/ n. [L conciliare combine, gain (concilium COUNCIL)]

conciliation /kənˌsɪlɪ'eɪʃ(ə)n/ n. the use of conciliating measures; reconcilement. [L conciliatio (as CONCILIATE)]

concinnity /kən'sɪnɪtɪ/ n. elegance or neatness of literary style. □□ **concinnous** adj. [L concinnitas f. concinnus well-adjusted]

concise /kən'saɪs/ adj. (of speech, writing, style, or a person) brief but comprehensive in expression. □□ **concisely** adv. **conciseness** n. [F concis or L concisus past part. of concidere (as COM-, caedere cut)]

concision /kən'sɪʒ(ə)n/ n. (esp. of literary style) conciseness. [ME f. L concisio (as CONCISE)]

conclave /'kɒnkleɪv/ n. 1 a private meeting. 2 RC Ch. **a** the assembly of cardinals for the election of a pope. **b** the meeting-place for a conclave. [ME f. OF f. L conclave lockable room (as COM-, clavis key)]

conclude /kən'kluːd/ v. 1 tr. & intr. bring or come to an end. 2 tr. (often foll. by from, or that + clause) infer (from given premises) (what did you conclude?; concluded from the evidence that he had been mistaken). 3 tr. settle, arrange (a treaty etc.). 4 intr. (usu. foll. by to + infin.) esp. US decide. [ME f. L concludere (as COM-, claudere shut)]

conclusion /kən'kluːʒ(ə)n/ n. 1 a final result; a termination. 2 a judgement reached by reasoning. 3 the summing-up of an argument, article, book, etc. 4 a settling; an arrangement (the conclusion of peace). 5 Logic a proposition that is reached from given premises; the third and last part of a syllogism. □ **in conclusion** lastly, to conclude. **try conclusions with** engage in a trial of skill etc. with. [ME f. OF conclusion or L conclusio (as CONCLUDE)]

conclusive /kən'kluːsɪv/ adj. decisive, convincing. □□ **conclusively** adv. **conclusiveness** n. [LL conclusivus (as CONCLUSION)]

concoct /kən'kɒkt/ v.tr. 1 make by mixing ingredients (concocted a stew). 2 invent (a story, a lie, etc.). □□ **concocter** n. **concoction** /-'kɒkʃ(ə)n/ n. **concoctor** n. [L concoquere concoct- (as COM-, coquere cook)]

concomitance /kən'kɒmɪt(ə)ns/ n. (also **concomitancy**) 1 coexistence. 2 Theol. the doctrine of the coexistence of the body and blood of Christ both in the bread and in the wine of the Eucharist. [med.L concomitantia (as CONCOMITANT)]

concomitant /kən'kɒmɪt(ə)nt/ adj. & n. —adj. going together; associated (concomitant circumstances). —n. an accompanying thing. □□ **concomitantly** adv. [LL concomitari (as COM-, comitari f. L comes -mitis companion)]

concord /'kɒnkɔːd, 'kɒŋ-/ n. 1 agreement or harmony between people or things. 2 a treaty. 3 Mus. a chord that is pleasing or satisfactory in itself. 4 Gram. agreement between words in gender, number, etc.

[ME f. OF concorde f. L concordia f. concors of one mind (as COM-, cors f. cor cordis heart)]

concordance /kən'kɔːd(ə)ns, kən-/ n. 1 agreement. 2 a book containing an alphabetical list of the important words used in a book or by an author, usu. with citations of the passages concerned. [ME f. OF f. med.L concordantia (as CONCORDANT)]

concordant /kən'kɔːd(ə)nt/ adj. 1 (often foll. by with) agreeing, harmonious. 2 Mus. in harmony. □□ **concordantly** adv. [ME f. OF f. L concordare f. concors (as CONCORD)]

concordat /kən'kɔːdæt/ n. an agreement, esp. between the Roman Catholic Church and a State. [F concordat or L concordatum neut. past part. of concordare (as CONCORDANCE)]

concourse /'kɒnkɔːs, 'kɒŋ-/ n. 1 a crowd. 2 a coming together; a gathering (a concourse of ideas). 3 an open central area in a large public building, a railway station, etc. [ME f. OF concours f. L concursus (as CONCUR)]

concrescence /kən'kres(ə)ns/ n. Biol. coalescence; growing together. □□ **concrescent** adj. [CON-, after excrescence etc.]

concrete /'kɒnkriːt, 'kɒŋ-/ adj., n., & v. —adj. 1 **a** existing in a material form; real. **b** specific, definite (concrete evidence; a concrete proposal). 2 Gram. (of a noun) denoting a material object as opposed to an abstract quality, state, or action. —n. (often attrib.) a composition of gravel, sand, cement, and water, used for building. —v. 1 tr. **a** cover with concrete. **b** embed in concrete. 2 **a** tr. & intr. form into a mass; solidify. **b** tr. make concrete instead of abstract. □**concrete-mixer** a machine, usu. with a revolving drum, used for mixing concrete. **concrete music** music constructed by mixing recorded sounds. **concrete poetry** poetry using unusual typographical layout to enhance the effect on the page. **in the concrete** in reality or in practice. □□ **concretely** adv. **concreteness** n. [F concret or L concretus past part. of concrescere (as COM-, crescere cret- GROW)]

concretion /kən'kriːʃ(ə)n/ n. 1 a hard solid concreted mass. **b** the forming of this by coalescence. 2 Med. a stony mass formed within the body. 3 Geol. a small round mass of rock particles embedded in limestone or clay. □□ **concretionary** adj. [F f. L concretio (as CONCRETE)]

concretize /'kɒnkrɪˌtaɪz, 'kɒŋ-/ v.tr. (also **-ise**) make concrete instead of abstract. □□ **concretization** /-'zeɪʃ(ə)n/ n.

concubinage /kən'kjuːbɪnɪdʒ/ n. 1 the cohabitation of a man and a woman not married to each other. 2 the state of being or having a concubine. [ME f. F (as CONCUBINE)]

concubine /'kɒŋkjʊˌbaɪn/ n. 1 a woman who lives with a man as his wife. 2 (among polygamous peoples) a secondary wife. □□ **concubinary** /kən'kjuːbɪnərɪ/ adj. [ME f. OF f. L concubina (as COM-, cubina f. cubare lie)]

concupiscence /kən'kjuːpɪs(ə)ns/ n. formal sexual desire. □□ **concupiscent** adj. [ME f. OF f. LL concupiscentia f. L concupiscere begin to desire (as COM-, inceptive f. cupere desire)]

concur /kən'kɜː(r)/ v.intr. (concurred, concurring) 1 happen together; coincide. 2 (often foll. by with) **a** agree in opinion. **b** express agreement. 3 combine together for a cause; act in combination. [L concurrere (as COM-, currere run)]

concurrent /kən'kʌrənt/ adj. 1 (often foll. by with) **a** existing or in operation at the same time (served two concurrent sentences). **b** existing or acting together. 2 Geom. (of three or more lines) meeting at or tending towards one point. 3 agreeing, harmonious. □□ **concurrence** n. **concurrently** adv.

concuss /kən'kʌs/ v.tr. 1 subject to concussion. 2 shake violently. 3 archaic intimidate. [L concutere concuss- (as COM-, cutere = quatere shake)]

concussion /kən'kʌʃ(ə)n/ n. 1 Med. temporary unconsciousness or incapacity due to injury to the head. **2** violent shaking; shock. [L *concussio* (as CONCUSS)]

condemn /kən'dem/ *v.tr.* **1** express utter disapproval of; censure (*was condemned for his irresponsible behaviour*). **2 a** find guilty; convict. **b** (usu. foll. by *to*) sentence to (a punishment, esp. death). **c** bring about the conviction of (*his looks condemn him*). **3** pronounce (a building etc.) unfit for use or habitation. **4** (usu. foll. by *to*) doom or assign (to something unwelcome or painful) (*condemned to spending hours at the kitchen sink*). **5 a** declare (smuggled goods, property, etc.) to be forfeited. **b** pronounce incurable. □**condemned cell** a cell for a prisoner condemned to death. □□**condemnable** /-'demnəb(ə)l/ *adj.* **condemnation** /ˌkɒndem'neɪʃ(ə)n/ *n.* **condemnatory** /-'demnətərɪ/ *adj.* [ME f. OF *condem(p)ner* f. L *condemnare* (as COM-, *damnare* DAMN)]

condensate /kən'denseɪt, 'kɒndənˌseɪt/ *n.* a substance produced by condensation.

condensation /ˌkɒnden'seɪʃ(ə)n/ *n.* **1** the act of condensing. **2** any condensed material (esp. water on a cold surface). **3** an abridgement. **4** *Chem.* the combination of molecules with the elimination of water or other small molecules. □**condensation trail** = vapour trail. [LL *condensatio* (as CONDENSE)]

condense /kən'dens/ *v.* **1** *tr.* make denser or more concentrated. **2** *tr.* express in fewer words; make concise. **3** *tr.* & *intr.* reduce or be reduced from a gas or solid to a liquid. □**condensed milk** milk thickened by evaporation and sweetened. □□ **condensable** *adj.* [F *condenser* or L *condensare* (as COM-, *densus* thick)]

condenser /kən'densə(r)/ *n.* **1** an apparatus or vessel for condensing vapour. **2** *Electr.* = CAPACITOR. **3** a lens or system of lenses for concentrating light. **4** a person or thing that condenses.

condescend /ˌkɒndɪ'send/ *v.intr.* **1** (usu. foll. by *to* + infin.) be gracious enough (to do a thing) esp. while showing one's sense of dignity or superiority (*condescended to attend the meeting*). **2** (foll. by *to*) behave as if one is on equal terms with (an inferior), usu. while maintaining an attitude of superiority. **3** (as **condescending** *adj.*) patronizing; kind to inferiors. □□ **condescendingly** *adv.* [ME f. OF *condescendre* f. eccl.L *condescendere* (as COM-, DESCEND)]

condescension /ˌkɒndɪ'senʃ(ə)n/ *n.* **1** a patronizing manner. **2** affability towards inferiors. [obs. F f. eccl.L *condescensio* (as CONDESCEND)]

condign /kən'daɪn/ *adj.* (of a punishment etc.) severe and well-deserved. □□ **condignly** *adv.* [ME f. OF *condigne* f. L *condignus* (as COM-, *dignus* worthy)]

condiment /'kɒndɪmənt/ *n.* a seasoning or relish for food. [ME f. L *condimentum* f. *condire* pickle]

condition /kən'dɪʃ(ə)n/ *n.* & *v.* —*n.* **1** a stipulation; something upon the fulfilment of which something else depends. **2 a** the state of being or fitness of a person or thing (*arrived in bad condition; not in a condition to be used*). **b** an ailment or abnormality (*a heart condition*). **3** (in *pl.*) circumstances, esp. those affecting the functioning or existence of something (*working conditions are good*). **4** *archaic* social rank (*all sorts and conditions of men*). **5** *Gram.* a clause expressing a condition. **6** *US* a subject in which a student must pass an examination within a stated time to maintain a provisionally granted status. —*v.tr.* **1 a** bring into a good or desired state or condition. **b** make fit (esp. dogs or horses). **2** teach or accustom to adopt certain habits etc. (*conditioned by society*). **3** govern, determine (*his behaviour was conditioned by his drunkenness*). **4 a** impose conditions on. **b** be essential to (*the two things condition each other*). **5** test the condition of (textiles etc.). **6** *US* subject (a student) to re-examination. □**conditioned reflex** a reflex response to a non-natural stimulus, established by training. **in** (or **out of**) **condition** in good (or bad) condition. **in no condition to** certainly not fit to. **on condition that** with the stipulation that. [ME f. OF *condicion* (n.),

condicionner (v.) or med.L *condicionare* f. L *condicio* *-onis* f. *condicere* (as COM-, *dicere* say)]

conditional /kən'dɪʃən(ə)l/ *adj.* & *n.* —*adj.* **1** (often foll. by *on*) dependent; not absolute; containing a condition or stipulation (*a conditional offer*). **2** *Gram.* (of a clause, mood, etc.) expressing a condition. —*n.* *Gram.* **1** a conditional clause etc. **2** the conditional mood. □**conditional discharge** *Law* an order made by a criminal court whereby an offender will not be sentenced for an offence unless a further offence is committed within a stated period. □□ **conditionality** /-'nælɪtɪ/ *n.* **conditionally** *adv.* [ME f. OF *condicionel* or f. LL *conditionalis* (as CONDITION)]

conditioner /kən'dɪʃənə(r)/ *n.* an agent that brings something into good condition, esp. a substance applied to the hair.

condo /'kɒndəʊ/ *n.* (*pl.* **-os**) *US colloq.* a condominium. [abbr.]

condolatory /kən'dəʊlətərɪ/ *adj.* expressing condolence. [CONDOLE, after *consolatory* etc.]

condole /kən'dəʊl/ *v.intr.* (foll. by *with*) express sympathy with a person over a loss, grief, etc. ¶ Often confused with *console*. [LL *condolēre* (as COM-, *dolēre* suffer)]

condolence /kən'dəʊləns/ *n.* (often in *pl.*) an expression of sympathy (*sent my condolences*).

condom /'kɒndɒm/ *n.* a rubber sheath worn on the penis during sexual intercourse as a contraceptive or to prevent infection. [18th c.: orig. unkn.]

condominium /ˌkɒndə'mɪnɪəm/ *n.* **1** the joint control of a State's affairs by other States. **2** *US* a building containing flats which are individually owned. [mod.L (as COM-, *dominium* DOMINION)]

condone /kən'dəʊn/ *v.tr.* **1** forgive or overlook (an offence or wrongdoing). **2** approve or sanction, usu. reluctantly. **3** (of an action) atone for (an offence); make up for. □□ **condonation** /ˌkɒndə'neɪʃ(ə)n/ *n.* **condoner** *n.* [L *condonare* (as COM-, *donare* give)]

condor /'kɒndɔː(r)/ *n.* **1** (in full **Andean condor**) a large vulture, *Vultur gryphus*, of S. America, having black plumage with a white neck ruff and a fleshy wattle on the forehead. **2** (in full **California condor**) a small vulture, *Gymnogyps californianus*, of California. [Sp. f. Quechua *cuntur*]

condottiere /ˌkɒndɒtɪ'jeərɪ/ *n.* (*pl.* **condottieri** *pronunc.* same) *hist.* a leader or a member of a troop of mercenaries in Italy etc. [It. f. *condotto* troop under contract (*condotta*) (as CONDUCT)]

conduce /kən'djuːs/ *v.intr.* (foll. by *to*) (usu. of an event or attribute) lead or contribute to (a result). [L *conducere conduct-* (as COM-, *ducere duct-* lead)]

conducive /kən'djuːsɪv/ *adj.* `often foll. by *to*) contributing or helping (towards something) (*not a conducive atmosphere for negotiation; good health is conducive to happiness*).

conduct *n.* & *v.* —*n.* /'kɒndʌkt/ **1** behaviour (esp. in its moral aspect). **2** the action or manner of directing or managing (business, war, etc.). **3** *Art* mode of treatment, execution. **4** leading, guidance. —*v.* /kən'dʌkt/ **1** *tr.* lead or guide (a person or persons). **2** *tr.* direct or manage (business etc.). **3** *tr.* (also *absol.*) be the conductor of (an orchestra, choir, etc.). **4** *tr.* *Physics* transmit (heat, electricity, etc.) by conduction. **5** *refl.* behave (*conducted himself appropriately*). □**conducted tour** a tour led by a guide on a fixed itinerary. **conduct sheet** a record of a person's offences and punishments. □□ **conductible** /kən'dʌktɪb(ə)l/ *adj.* **conductibility** /kənˌdʌktɪ'bɪlɪtɪ/ *n.* [ME f. L *conductus* (as COM-, *ducere duct-* lead): (v.) f. OF *conduite* past part. of *conduire*]

conductance /kən'dʌkt(ə)ns/ *n.* *Physics* the power of a specified material to conduct electricity.

conduction /kən'dʌkʃ(ə)n/ *n.* **1 a** the transmission of heat through a substance from a region of higher temperature to a region of lower temperature. **b** the transmission of electricity through a substance by the application of an electric field. **2** the transmission of impulses along nerves. **3** the conducting of liquid through a pipe etc. [F *conduction* or L *conductio* (as CONDUCT)]

conductive /kən'dʌktɪv/ *adj.* having the property of conducting (esp. heat, electricity, etc.). □**conductive education** a system of education for children and adults with motor disorders. □□**conductively** *adv.*

conductivity /ˌkɒndʌk'tɪvɪtɪ/ *n.* the conducting power of a specified material.

conductor /kən'dʌktə(r)/ *n.* **1** a person who directs the performance of an orchestra or choir etc. **2** (*fem.* **conductress** /-trɪs/) **a** a person who collects fares in a bus etc. **b** *US* an official in charge of a train. **3** *Physics* **a** a thing that conducts or transmits heat or electricity, esp. regarded in terms of its capacity to do this (*a poor conductor*). **b** = *lightning-conductor*. **4** a guide or leader. **5** a manager or director. □**conductor rail** a rail transmitting current to an electric train etc. □□**conductorship** *n.* [ME f. F *conducteur* f. L *conductor* (as CONDUCT)]

conductus /kən'dʌktəs/ *n.* (*pl.* **conducti** /-taɪ/) a musical composition of the 12th–13th c., with Latin text. [med.L: see CONDUIT]

conduit /'kɒndɪt, -djʊɪt/ *n.* **1** a channel or pipe for conveying liquids. **2 a** a tube or trough for protecting insulated electric wires. **b** a length or stretch of this. [ME f. OF *conduit* f. med.L *conductus* CONDUCT *n.*]

condyle /'kɒndɪl/ *n. Anat.* a rounded process at the end of some bones, forming an articulation with another bone. □□**condylar** *adj.* **condyloid** *adj.* [F f. L *condylus* f. Gk *kondulos* knuckle]

cone /kəʊn/ *n. & v.* —*n.* **1** a solid figure with a circular (or other curved) plane base, tapering to a point. **2** a thing of a similar shape, solid or hollow, e.g. as used to mark off areas of roads. **3** the dry fruit of a conifer. **4** an ice-cream cornet. **5** any of the minute cone-shaped structures in the retina. **6** a conical mountain esp. of volcanic origin. **7** (in full **cone-shell**) any marine gastropod mollusc of the family Conidae. **8** *Pottery* a ceramic pyramid, melting at a known temperature, used to indicate the temperature of a kiln. —*v.tr.* **1** shape like a cone. **2** (foll. by *off*) *Brit.* mark off (a road etc.) with cones. [F *cône* f. L *conus* f. Gk *kōnos*]

coney var. of CONY.

confab /'kɒnfæb/ *n. & v. colloq.* —*n.* = CON-FABULATION (see CONFABULATE). —*v.intr.* (**confabbed, confabbing**) = CONFABULATE. [abbr.]

confabulate /kən'fæbjʊˌleɪt/ *v.intr.* **1** converse, chat. **2** *Psychol.* fabricate imaginary experiences as compensation for the loss of memory. □□**confabulation** /-'leɪʃ(ə)n/ *n.* **confabulatory** *adj.* [L *confabulari* (as COM-, *fabulari* f. *fabula* tale)]

confect /kən'fekt/ *v.tr. literary* make by putting together ingredients. [L *conficere confect-* put together (as COM-, *facere* make)]

confection /kən'fekʃ(ə)n/ *n.* **1** a dish or delicacy made with sweet ingredients. **2** mixing, compounding. **3** a fashionable or elaborate article of women's dress. □□**confectionary** *adj.* (in sense 1). [ME f. OF f. L *confectio -onis* (as CONFECT)]

confectioner /kən'fekʃənə(r)/ *n.* a maker or retailer of confectionery.

confectionery /kən'fekʃənərɪ/ *n.* sweets and other confections.

confederacy /kən'fedərəsɪ/ *n.* (*pl.* **-ies**) **1** a league or alliance, esp. of confederate States. **2** a league for an unlawful or evil purpose; a conspiracy. **3** the condition or fact of being confederate; alliance; conspiracy. [ME, AF, OF *confederacie* (as CONFEDERATE)]

confederate /kən'fedərət/ *adj., n., & v.* —*adj.* esp. *Polit.* allied; joined by an agreement or treaty. —*n.* **1** an ally, esp. (in a bad sense) an accomplice. **2** (**Confederate**) a supporter of the Confederate States. —*v.* /-ˌreɪt/ (often foll. by *with*) **1** *tr.* bring (a person, State, or oneself) into alliance. **2** *intr.* come into alliance. □**Confederate States** States which seceded

from the US in 1860–1. [LL *confoederatus* (as COM-, FEDERATE)]

confederation /kənˌfedə'reɪʃ(ə)n/ *n.* **1** a union or alliance of States etc. **2** the act or an instance of confederating; the state of being confederated. [F *confédération* (as CONFEDERATE)]

confer /kən'fɜː(r)/ *v.* (**conferred, conferring**) **1** *tr.* (often foll. by *on, upon*) grant or bestow (a title, degree, favour, etc.). **2** *intr.* (often foll. by *with*) converse, consult. □□**conferrable** *adj.* [L *conferre* (as COM-, *ferre* bring)]

conferee /ˌkɒnfə'riː/ *n.* **1** a person on whom something is conferred. **2** a participant in a conference.

conference /'kɒnfərəns/ *n.* **1** consultation, discussion. **2** a meeting for discussion, esp. a regular one held by an association or organization. **3** an annual assembly of the Methodist Church. **4** an association in commerce, sport, etc. **5** the linking of several telephones, computer terminals, etc., so that each user may communicate with the others simultaneously. □**in conference** engaged in discussion. □□**conferential** /ˌkɒnfə'renʃ(ə)l/ *adj.* [F *conférence* or med.L *conferentia* (as CONFER)]

conferment /kən'fɜːmənt/ *n.* **1** the conferring of a degree, honour, etc. **2** an instance of this.

conferral /kən'fɜːr(ə)l/ *n.* esp. *US* = CONFERMENT.

confess /kən'fes/ *v.* **1** *a tr.* (also *absol.*) acknowledge or admit (a fault, wrongdoing, etc.). **b** *intr.* (foll. by *to*) admit to (*confessed to having lied*). **2** *tr.* admit reluctantly (*confessed it would be difficult*). **3 a** *tr.* (also *absol.*) declare (one's sins) to a priest. **b** *tr.* (of a priest) hear the confession of. **c** *refl.* declare one's sins to a priest. [ME f. OF *confesser* f. Rmc f. L *confessus* past part. of *confitēri* (as COM-, *fatēri* declare, avow)]

confessant /kən'fes(ə)nt/ *n.* a person who confesses to a priest.

confessedly /kən'fesɪdlɪ/ *adv.* by one's own or general admission.

confession /kən'feʃ(ə)n/ *n.* **1 a** a confessing or acknowledgement of a fault, wrongdoing, a sin to a priest, etc. **b** an instance of this. **c** a thing confessed. **2** (in full **confession of faith**) **a** a declaration of one's religious beliefs. **b** a statement of one's principles. □□**confessionary** *adj.* [ME f. OF f. L *confessio -onis* (as CONFESS)]

confessional /kən'feʃən(ə)l/ *n. & adj.* —*n.* an enclosed stall in a church in which a priest hears confessions. —*adj.* **1** of or relating to confession. **2** denominational. [F f. It. *confessionale* f. med.L, neut. of *confessionalis* (as CONFESSION)]

confessor /kən'fesə(r)/ *n.* **1** a person who makes a confession. **2** (also 'kɒn-/ a priest who hears confessions and gives spiritual counsel. **3** a person who avows a religion in the face of its suppression, but does not suffer martyrdom. [ME f. AF *confessur*, OF *-our*, f. eccl.L *confessor* (as CONFESS)]

confetti /kən'fetɪ/ *n.* small bits of coloured paper thrown by wedding guests at the bride and groom. [It., = sweetmeats f. L (as COMFIT)]

confidant /ˌkɒnfɪ'dænt, 'kɒn-/ *n.* (*fem.* **confidante** *pronunc.* same) a person trusted with knowledge of one's private affairs. [18th-c. for earlier CONFIDENT *n.*, prob. to represent the pronunc. of F *confidente* (as CONFIDE)]

confide /kən'faɪd/ *v.* **1** *tr.* (usu. foll. by *to*) tell (a secret etc.) in confidence. **2** *tr.* (foll. by *to*) entrust (an object of care, a task, etc.) to. **3** *intr.* (foll. by *in*) **a** have trust or confidence in. **b** talk confidentially to. □□**confidingly** *adv.* [L *confidere* (as COM-, *fidere* trust)]

confidence /'kɒnfɪd(ə)ns/ *n.* **1** firm trust (*have confidence in his ability*). **2 a** a feeling of reliance or certainty. **b** a sense of self-reliance; boldness. **3 a** something told confidentially. **b** the telling of private matters with mutual trust. □**confidence man** a man who robs by means of a confidence trick. **confidence trick** (*US* **game**) a swindle in which the victim is persuaded to trust the swindler in some way. **in confidence** as a secret. **in a person's confidence** trusted with a person's secrets. **take into one's confidence** confide in. [ME f. L *confidentia* (as CONFIDE)]

confident /'kɒnfɪd(ə)nt/ *adj. & n.* —*adj.* 1 feeling or showing confidence; self-assured, bold (*spoke with a confident air*). 2 (often foll. by *of*, or *that* + clause) assured, trusting (*confident of your support*; *confident that he will come*). —*n. archaic* = CONFIDANT. □□ **confidently** *adv.* [F f. It. *confidente* (as CONFIDE)]

confidential /ˌkɒnfɪ'denʃ(ə)l/ *adj.* 1 spoken or written in confidence. 2 entrusted with secrets (*a confidential secretary*). 3 confiding. □□ **confidentiality** /-ʃɪ'ælɪtɪ/ *n.* **confidentially** *adv.*

configuration /kənˌfɪgjʊ'reɪʃ(ə)n, -gə'reɪʃ(ə)n/ *n.* 1 a an arrangement of parts or elements in a particular form or figure. b the form, shape, or figure resulting from such an arrangement. 2 *Astron. & Astrol.* the relative position of planets etc. 3 *Psychol.* = GESTALT. 4 *Physics* the distribution of electrons among the energy levels of an atom, or of nucleons among the energy levels of a nucleus, as specified by quantum numbers. 5 *Chem.* the fixed three-dimensional relationship of the atoms in a molecule. 6 *Computing* a the interrelating or interconnecting of a computer system or elements of it so that it will accommodate a particular specification. b an instance of this. □□ **configurational** *adj.* **configure** *v.tr.* (in senses 1, 2, 6). [LL *configuratio* f. L *configurare* (as COM-, *figurare* fashion)]

confine *v. & n.* —*v.tr.* /kən'faɪn/ (often foll. by *in*, *to*, *within*) 1 keep or restrict (within certain limits etc.). 2 hold captive; imprison. —*n.* /'kɒnfaɪn/ (usu. in *pl.*) a limit or boundary (*within the confines of the town*). □ **be confined** be in childbirth. [(v.) f. F *confiner*, (n.) ME f. F *confins* (pl.), f. L *confinia* (as COM-, *finia* neut. pl. f. *finis* end, limit)]

confinement /kən'faɪnmənt/ *n.* 1 the act or an instance of confining; the state of being confined. 2 the time of a woman's giving birth.

confirm /kən'fɜːm/ *v.tr.* 1 provide support for the truth or correctness of; make definitely valid (*confirmed my suspicions*; *confirmed his arrival time*). 2 (foll. by *in*) encourage (a person) in (an opinion etc.). 3 establish more firmly (power, possession, etc.). 4 ratify (a treaty, possession, title, etc.); make formally valid. 5 administer the religious rite of confirmation to. □□ **confirmative** *adj.* **confirmatory** *adj.* [ME f. OF *confermer* f. L *confirmare* (as COM-, FIRM[1])]

confirmand /'kɒnfəˌmænd/ *n. Eccl.* a person who is to be or has just been confirmed.

confirmation /ˌkɒnfə'meɪʃ(ə)n/ *n.* 1 a the act or an instance of confirming; the state of being confirmed. b an instance of this. 2 a a religious rite confirming a baptized person, esp. at the age of discretion, as a member of the Christian Church. b a ceremony of confirming persons of about this age in the Jewish faith. [ME f. OF f. L *confirmatio -onis* (as CONFIRM)]

confirmed /kən'fɜːmd/ *adj.* firmly settled in some habit or condition (*confirmed in his ways*; *a confirmed bachelor*).

confiscate /'kɒnfɪˌskeɪt/ *v.tr.* 1 take or seize by authority. 2 appropriate to the public treasury (by way of a penalty). □□ **confiscable** /kən'fɪskəb(ə)l/ *adj.* **confiscation** /-'skeɪʃ(ə)n/ *n.* **confiscator** *n.* **confiscatory** /kən'fɪskətərɪ/ *adj.* [L *confiscare* (as COM-, *fiscare* f. *fiscus* treasury)]

conflagration /ˌkɒnflə'greɪʃ(ə)n/ *n.* a great and destructive fire. [L *conflagratio* f. *conflagrare* (as COM-, *flagrare* blaze)]

conflate /kən'fleɪt/ *v.tr.* blend or fuse together (esp. two variant texts into one). □□ **conflation** /-'fleɪʃ(ə)n/ *n.* [L *conflare* (as COM-, *flare* blow)]

conflict *n. & v.* —*n.* /'kɒnflɪkt/ 1 a a state of opposition or hostilities. b a fight or struggle. 2 (often foll. by *of*) a the clashing of opposed principles etc. b an instance of this. 3 *Psychol.* a the opposition of incompatible wishes or needs in a person. b an instance of this. c the distress resulting from this. —*v.intr.* /kən'flɪkt/ 1 clash; be incompatible. 2 (often foll. by *with*) struggle or contend. 3 (as **conflicting** *adj.*) contradictory. □ **in conflict** conflicting. □□ **confliction** /kən'flɪkʃ(ə)n/ *n.* **conflictual** /kən'flɪktʃʊəl/ *adj.* [ME f. L *confligere conflict-* (as COM-, *fligere* strike)]

confluence /'kɒnflʊəns/ *n.* 1 a place where two rivers meet. 2 a a coming together. b a crowd of people. [L *confluere* (as COM-, *fluere* flow)]

confluent /'kɒnflʊənt/ *adj. & n.* —*adj.* flowing together, uniting. —*n.* a stream joining another.

conflux /'kɒnflʌks/ *n.* = CONFLUENCE. [LL *confluxus* (as CONFLUENCE)]

conform /kən'fɔːm/ *v.* 1 *intr.* comply with rules or general custom. 2 *intr. & tr.* (often foll. by *to*) be or make accordant or suitable. 3 *tr.* (often foll. by *to*) form according to a pattern; make similar. 4 *intr.* (foll. by *to*, *with*) comply with; be in accordance with. □□ **conformer** *n.* [ME f. OF *conformer* f. L *conformare* (as COM-, FORM)]

conformable /kən'fɔːməb(ə)l/ *adj.* 1 (often foll. by *to*) similar. 2 (often foll. by *with*) consistent. 3 (often foll. by *to*) adapted. 4 tractable, submissive. 5 *Geol.* (of strata in contact) lying in the same direction. □□ **conformability** /-'bɪlɪtɪ/ *n.* **conformably** *adv.* [med.L *conformabilis* (as CONFORM)]

conformal /kən'fɔːm(ə)l/ *adj.* (of a map) showing any small area in its correct shape. □□ **conformally** *adv.* [LL *conformalis* (as CONFORM)]

conformance /kən'fɔːməns/ *n.* (often foll. by *to*, *with*) = CONFORMITY 1, 2.

conformation /ˌkɒnfɔː'meɪʃ(ə)n/ *n.* 1 the way in which a thing is formed; shape, structure. 2 (often foll. by *to*) adjustment in form or character; adaptation. 3 *Chem.* any spatial arrangement of atoms in a molecule from the rotation of part of the molecule about a single bond. [L *conformatio* (as CONFORM)]

conformist /kən'fɔːmɪst/ *n. & adj.* —*n.* 1 a person who conforms to an established practice; a conventional person. 2 *Brit.* a person who conforms to the practices of the Church of England. —*adj.* (of a person) conforming to established practices; conventional. □□ **conformism** *n.*

conformity /kən'fɔːmɪtɪ/ *n.* 1 (often foll. by *to*, *with*) action or behaviour in accordance with established practice; compliance. 2 (often foll. by *to*, *with*) correspondence in form or manner; likeness, agreement. 3 *Brit.* compliance with the practices of the Church of England. [ME f. OF *conformité* or LL *conformitas* (as CONFORM)]

confound /kən'faʊnd/ *v. & int.* —*v.tr.* 1 throw into perplexity or confusion. 2 mix up; confuse (in one's mind). 3 *archaic* defeat, overthrow. —*int.* expressing annoyance (*confound you!*). [ME f. AF *conf(o)undre*, OF *confondre* f. L *confundere* mix up (as COM-, *fundere fus-* pour)]

confounded /kən'faʊndɪd/ *adj. colloq.* damned (*a confounded nuisance!*). □□ **confoundedly** *adv.*

confraternity /ˌkɒnfrə'tɜːnɪtɪ/ *n.* (*pl.* **-ies**) a brotherhood, esp. religious or charitable. [ME f. OF *confraternité* f. med.L *confraternitas* (as COM-, FRATERNITY)]

confrère /'kɒnfreə(r)/ *n.* a fellow member of a profession, scientific body, etc. [ME f. OF f. med.L *confrater* (as COM-, *frater* brother)]

confront /kən'frʌnt/ *v.tr.* 1 a face in hostility or defiance. b face up to and deal with (a problem, difficulty, etc.). 2 (of a difficulty etc.) present itself to (*countless obstacles confronted us*). 3 (foll. by *with*) a bring (a person) face to face with (a circumstance), esp. by way of accusation (*confronted them with the evidence*). b set (a thing) face to face with (another) for comparison. 4 meet or stand facing. □□ **confrontation** /ˌkɒnfrʌn'teɪʃ(ə)n/ *n.*

confrontational /ˌkɒnfrʌnˈteɪʃən(ə)l/ *adj.* [F *confronter* f. med.L *confrontare* (as COM-, *frontare* f. *frons frontis* face)]

Confucian /kənˈfjuːʃ(ə)n/ *adj. & n.* —*adj.* of or relating to Confucius, Chinese philosopher d. 479 BC, or his philosophy. —*n.* a follower of Confucius. □□ **Confucianism** *n.* **Confucianist** *n.* [*Confucius*, Latinization of *Kongfuze* Kong the master]

confusable /kənˈfjuːzəb(ə)l/ *adj.* that is able or liable to be confused. □□ **confusability** /-ˈbɪlɪtɪ/ *n.*

confuse /kənˈfjuːz/ *v.tr.* **1 a** disconcert, perplex, bewilder. **b** embarrass. **2** mix up in the mind; mistake (one for another). **3** make indistinct (*that point confuses the issue*). **4** (as **confused** *adj.*) mentally decrepit. **5** (often as **confused** *adj.*) throw into disorder (*a confused jumble of clothes*). □□ **confusedly** /kənˈfjuːzɪdlɪ/ *adv.* **confusing** *adj.* **confusingly** *adv.* [19th-c. back-form. f. *confused* (14th c.) f. OF *confus* f. L *confusus*: see CONFOUND]

confusion /kənˈfjuːʒ(ə)n/ *n.* **1 a** the act of confusing (*the confusion of fact and fiction*). **b** an instance of this; a misunderstanding (*confusions arise from a lack of communication*). **2 a** the result of confusing; a confused state; disorder (*thrown into confusion by his words; trampled in the confusion of battle*). **b** (foll. by *of*) a disorderly jumble (*a confusion of ideas*). **3 a** civil commotion (*confusion broke out at the announcement*). **b** an instance of this. [ME f. OF *confusion* or L *confusio* (as CONFUSE)]

confute /kənˈfjuːt/ *v.tr.* **1** prove (a person) to be in error. **2** prove (an argument) to be false. □□ **confutation** /ˌkɒnfjuːˈteɪʃ(ə)n/ *n.* [L *confutare* restrain]

conga /ˈkɒŋgə/ *n. & v.* —*n.* **1** a Latin-American dance of African origin, usu. with several persons in a single line, one behind the other. **2** (also **conga drum**) a tall, narrow, low-toned drum beaten with the hands. —*v.intr.* (**congas, congaed** /-gəd/ or **conga'd, congaing** /-gəɪŋ/) perform the conga. [Amer. Sp. f. Sp. *conga* (fem.) of the Congo]

congé /ˈkɔ̃ʒeɪ/ *n.* an unceremonious dismissal; leave-taking. [F: earlier *congee*, ME f. OF *congié* f. L *commeatus* leave of absence f. *commeare* go and come (as COM-, *meare* go): now usu. treated as mod. F]

congeal /kənˈdʒiːl/ *v.tr. & intr.* **1** make or become semi-solid by cooling. **2** (of blood etc.) coagulate. □□ **congealable** *adj.* **congealment** *n.* [ME f. OF *congeler* f. L *congelare* (as COM-, *gelare* f. *gelu* frost)]

congelation /ˌkɒndʒɪˈleɪʃ(ə)n/ *n.* **1** the process of congealing. **2** a congealed state. **3** a congealed substance. [ME f. OF *congelation* or L *congelatio* (as CONGEAL)]

congener /kənˈdʒiːnə(r)/ *n.* a thing or person of the same kind or category as another, esp. animals or plants of a specified genus (*the goldfinch is a congener of the canary*). [L (as CON-, GENUS)]

congeneric /ˌkɒndʒɪˈnerɪk/ *adj.* **1** of the same genus, kind, or race. **2** allied in nature or origin; akin. □□ **congenerous** /kənˈdʒenərəs/ *adj.*

congenial /kənˈdʒiːnɪəl/ *adj.* **1** (often foll. by *with*, *to*) (of a person, character, etc.) pleasant because akin to oneself in temperament or interests. **2** (often foll. by *to*) suited or agreeable. □□ **congeniality** /-ˈælɪtɪ/ *n.* **congenially** *adv.* [CON- + GENIAL[1]]

congenital /kənˈdʒenɪt(ə)l/ *adj.* **1** (esp. of a disease, defect, etc.) existing from birth. **2** that is (or as if) such from birth (*a congenital liar*). □□ **congenitally** *adv.* [L *congenitus* (as COM-, *genitus* past part. of *gigno* beget)]

conger /ˈkɒŋgə(r)/ *n.* (in full **conger eel**) any large marine eel of the family Congridae. [ME f. OF *congre* f. L *conger, congrus*, f. Gk *goggros*]

congeries /kənˈdʒɪəriːz, -ˈdʒerɪˌiːz/ *n.* (*pl.* same) a disorderly collection; a mass or heap. [L, formed as CONGEST]

congest /kənˈdʒest/ *v.tr.* (esp. as **congested** *adj.*) affect with congestion; obstruct, block (*congested*

streets; congested lungs*). □□ **congestive *adj.* [L *congerere congest-* (as COM-, *gerere* bring)]

congestion /kənˈdʒestʃ(ə)n/ *n.* abnormal accumulation, crowding, or obstruction, esp. of traffic etc. or of blood or mucus in a part of the body. [F f. L *congestio -onis* (as CONGEST)]

conglomerate /kənˈglɒmərət/ *adj., n., & v.* —*adj.* **1** gathered into a rounded mass. **2** *Geol.* (of rock) made up of small stones held together (cf. AGGLOMERATE). —*n.* **1** a number of things or parts forming a heterogeneous mass. **2** a group or corporation formed by the merging of separate and diverse firms. **3** *Geol.* conglomerate rock. —*v.tr. & intr.* /kənˈglɒməˌreɪt/ collect into a coherent mass. □□ **conglomeration** /kənˌglɒ8məˈreɪʃ(ə)n/ *n.* [L *conglomeratus* past part. of *conglomerare* (as COM-, *glomerare* f. *glomus -eris* ball)]

Congolese /ˌkɒŋgəˈliːz/ *adj. & n.* —*adj.* of or relating to the Republic of the Congo in Central Africa, or the region surrounding the Congo river. —*n.* a native of either of these regions. [F *congolais*]

congou /ˈkɒŋguː, -gəʊ/ *n.* a variety of black China tea. [Chin. dial. *kung hu tē* tea laboured for]

congrats /kənˈgræts/ *n.pl. & int. colloq.* congratulations. [abbr.]

congratulate /kənˈgrætjʊˌleɪt/ *v.tr. & refl.* (often foll. by *on, upon*) **1** *tr.* express pleasure at the happiness or good fortune or excellence of (a person) (*congratulated them on their success*). **2** *refl.* think oneself fortunate or clever. □□ **congratulant** *adj. & n.* **congratulator** *n.* **congratulatory** /-lətərɪ/ *adj.* [L *congratulari* (as COM-, *gratulari* show joy f. *gratus* pleasing)]

congratulation /kənˌgrætjʊˈleɪʃ(ə)n/ *n.* **1** congratulating. **2** (also as *int.*; usu. in *pl.*) an expression of this (*congratulations on winning!*). [L *congratulatio* (as CONGRATULATE)]

congregant /ˈkɒŋgrɪgənt/ *n.* a member of a congregation (esp. Jewish). [L *congregare* (as CONGREGATE)]

congregate /ˈkɒŋgrɪˌgeɪt/ *v.intr. & tr.* collect or gather into a crowd or mass. [ME f. L *congregare* (as COM-, *gregare* f. *grex gregis* flock)]

congregation /ˌkɒŋgrɪˈgeɪʃ(ə)n/ *n.* **1** the process of congregating; collection into a crowd or mass. **2** a crowd or mass gathered together. **3 a** a body assembled for religious worship. **b** a body of persons regularly attending a particular church etc. **c** *RC Ch.* a body of persons obeying a common religious rule. **d** *RC Ch.* any of several permanent committees of the Roman Catholic College of Cardinals. **4** (**Congregation**) *Brit.* (in some universities) a general assembly of resident senior members. [ME f. OF *congregation* or L *congregatio* (as CONGREGATE)]

congregational /ˌkɒŋgrɪˈgeɪʃən(ə)l/ *adj.* **1** of a congregation. **2** (**Congregational**) of or adhering to Congregationalism.

Congregationalism /ˌkɒŋgrɪˈgeɪʃənəˌlɪz(ə)m/ *n.* a system of ecclesiastical organization whereby individual churches are largely self-governing. □□ **Congregationalist** *n.* **Congregationalize** *v.tr.* (also **-ise**).

congress /ˈkɒŋgres/ *n.* **1** a formal meeting of delegates for discussion. **2** (**Congress**) a national legislative body, esp. that of the US. **3** a society or organization. **4** coming together, meeting. □□ **congressional** /kənˈgreʃən(ə)l/ *adj.* [L *congressus* f. *congredi* (as COM-, *gradi* walk)]

congressman /ˈkɒŋgresmən/ *n.* (*pl.* **-men**; *fem.* **congresswoman**, *pl.* **-women**) a member of the US Congress.

congruence /ˈkɒŋgruəns/ *n.* (also **congruency** /-ənsɪ/) **1** agreement, consistency. **2** *Geom.* the state of being congruent. [ME f. L *congruentia* (as CONGRUENT)]

congruent /ˈkɒŋgruənt/ *adj.* **1** (often foll. by *with*) suitable, agreeing. **2** *Geom.* (of figures) coinciding exactly when superimposed. □□ **congruently** *adv.* [ME f. L *congruere* agree]

w *we*   z *zoo*   ʃ *she*   ʒ *decision*   θ *thin*   ð *this*   ŋ *ring*   x *loch*   tʃ *chip*   dʒ *jar*   (*see over for vowels*)

congruous /ˈkɒŋgrʊəs/ *adj.* (often foll. by *with*) suitable, agreeing; fitting. □□ **congruity** /-ˈgruːɪtɪ/ *n.* **congruously** *adv.* [L *congruus* (as CONGRUENT)]

conic /ˈkɒnɪk/ *adj. & n.* —*adj.* of a cone. —*n.* **1** a conic section. **2** (in *pl.*) the study of conic sections. □**conic section** a figure formed by the intersection of a cone and a plane. [mod.L *conicus* f. Gk *kōnikos* (as CONE)]

conical /ˈkɒnɪk(ə)l/ *adj.* cone-shaped. □□ **conically** *adv.*

conidium /kəˈnɪdɪəm/ *n.* (*pl.* **conidia** /-dɪə/) a spore produced asexually by various fungi. [mod.L dimin. f. Gk *konis* dust]

conifer /ˈkɒnɪfə(r), ˈkəʊn-/ *n.* any evergreen tree of a group usu. bearing cones, including pines, yews, cedars, and redwoods. □□ **coniferous** /kəˈnɪfərəs/ *adj.* [L (as CONE, -FEROUS)]

coniform /ˈkəʊnɪfɔːm/ *adj.* cone-shaped. [L *conus* cone + -FORM]

coniine /ˈkəʊnɪiːn/ *n.* a poisonous alkaloid found in hemlock, that paralyses the nerves. [L *conium* f. Gk *kōneion* hemlock]

conjectural /kənˈdʒektʃər(ə)l/ *adj.* based on, involving, or given to conjecture. □□ **conjecturally** *adv.* [F f. L *conjecturalis* (as CONJECTURE)]

conjecture /kənˈdʒektʃə(r)/ *n. & v.* —*n.* **1 a** the formation of an opinion on incomplete information; guessing. **b** an opinion or conclusion reached in this way. **2 a** (in textual criticism) the guessing of a reading not in the text. **b** a proposed reading. —*v.* **1** *tr. & intr.* guess. **2** *tr.* (in textual criticism) propose (a reading). □□ **conjecturable** *adj.* [ME f. OF *conjecture* or L *conjectura* f. *conjicere* (as COM-, *jacere* throw)]

conjoin /kənˈdʒɔɪn/ *v.tr. & intr.* join, combine. [ME f. OF *conjoign-* pres. stem of *conjoindre* f. L *conjungere* (as COM-, *jungere junct-* join)]

conjoint /kənˈdʒɔɪnt/ *adj.* associated, conjoined. □□ **conjointly** *adv.* [ME f. OF, past part. (as CONJOIN)]

conjugal /ˈkɒndʒʊg(ə)l/ *adj.* of marriage or the relation between husband and wife. □**conjugal rights** those rights (esp. to sexual relations) regarded as exercisable in law by each partner in a marriage. □□ **conjugality** /-ˈgælɪtɪ/ *n.* **conjugally** *adv.* [L *conjugalis* f. *conjux* consort (as COM-, *-jux -jugis* f. root of *jungere* join)]

conjugate *v., adj., & n.* —*v.* /ˈkɒndʒʊgeɪt/ **1** *tr.* *Gram.* give the different forms of (a verb). **2** *intr.* **a** unite sexually. **b** (of gametes) become fused. **3** *intr. Chem.* (of protein) combine with non-protein. —*adj.* /ˈkɒndʒʊgət/ **1** joined together, esp. as a pair. **2** *Gram.* derived from the same root. **3** *Biol.* fused. **4** *Chem.* (of an acid or base) related by loss or gain of an electron. **5** *Math.* joined in a reciprocal relation, esp. having the same real parts, and equal magnitudes but opposite signs of imaginary parts. —*n.* /ˈkɒndʒʊgət/ a conjugate word or thing. □□ **conjugately** /ˈkɒndʒʊgətlɪ/ *adv.* [L *conjugare* yoke together (as COM-, *jugare* f. *jugum* yoke)]

conjugation /ˌkɒndʒʊˈgeɪʃ(ə)n/ *n.* **1** *Gram.* a system of verbal inflection. **2 a** the act or an instance of conjugating. **b** an instance of this. **3** *Biol.* the fusion of two gametes in reproduction. □□ **conjugational** *adj.* [L *conjugatio* (as CONJUGATE)]

conjunct /kənˈdʒʌŋkt/ *adj.* joined together; combined; associated. [ME f. L *conjunctus* (as CONJOIN)]

conjunction /kənˈdʒʌŋkʃ(ə)n/ *n.* **1 a** the action of joining; the condition of being joined. **b** an instance of this. **2** *Gram.* a word used to connect clauses or sentences or words in the same clause (e.g. *and*, *but*, *if*). **3 a** a combination (of events or circumstances). **b** a number of associated persons or things. **4** *Astron. & Astrol.* the alignment of two bodies in the solar system so that they have the same longitude as seen from the earth. □**in conjunction with** together with. □□ **conjunctional** *adj.* [ME f. OF *conjonction* f. L *conjunctio -onis* (as CONJUNCT)]

conjunctiva /ˌkɒndʒʌŋkˈtaɪvə, kənˈdʒʌŋktɪvə/ *n.* (*pl.*

conjunctivas) *Anat.* the mucous membrane that covers the front of the eye and lines the inside of the eyelids. □□ **conjunctival** *adj.* [med.L (*membrana*) *conjunctiva* (as CONJUNCTIVE)]

conjunctive /kənˈdʒʌŋktɪv/ *adj. & n.* —*adj.* serving to join; connective. **2** *Gram.* of the nature of a conjunction. —*n.* *Gram.* a conjunctive word. □□ **conjunctively** *adv.* [LL *conjunctivus* (as CONJOIN)]

conjunctivitis /kənˌdʒʌŋktɪˈvaɪtɪs/ *n.* inflammation of the conjunctiva.

conjuncture /kənˈdʒʌŋktʃə(r)/ *n.* a combination of events; a state of affairs. [obs. F f. It. *congiuntura* (as CONJOIN)]

conjuration /ˌkɒndʒʊˈreɪʃ(ə)n/ *n.* an incantation; a magic spell. [ME f. OF f. L *conjuratio -onis* (as CONJURE)]

conjure /ˈkʌndʒə(r)/ *v.* **1** *intr.* perform tricks which are seemingly magical, esp. by rapid movements of the hands. **2** *tr.* (usu. foll. by *out of*, *away*, *to*, etc.) cause to appear or disappear as if by magic (*conjured a rabbit out of a hat*; *conjured them to a desert island*; *his pain was conjured away*). **3** *tr.* call upon (a spirit) to appear. **4** *intr.* perform marvels. **5** *tr.* /kənˈdʒʊə(r)/ (often foll. by *to* + infin.) appeal solemnly to (a person). □**conjure up 1** bring into existence or cause to appear as if by magic. **2** cause to appear to the eye or mind; evoke. [ME f. OF *conjurer* plot, exorcise f. L *conjurare* band together by oath (as COM-, *jurare* swear)]

conjuror /ˈkʌndʒərə(r)/ *n.* (also **conjurer**) a performer of conjuring tricks. [CONJURE + -ER[1] & AF *conjurour* (OF *-eor*) f. med.L *conjurator* (as CONJURE)]

conk[1] /kɒŋk/ *v.intr.* (usu. foll. by *out*) *colloq.* **1** (of a machine etc.) break down. **2** (of a person) become exhausted and give up; faint; die. [20th c.: orig. unkn.]

conk[2] /kɒŋk/ *n. & v. sl.* —*n.* **1 a** the nose. **b** the head. **2 a** a punch on the nose or head. **b** a blow. —*v.tr.* punch on the nose; hit on the head etc. [19th c.: perh. = CONCH]

conker /ˈkɒŋkə(r)/ *n.* **1** the hard fruit of a horse chestnut. **2** (in *pl.*) *Brit.* a children's game played with conkers on strings, one hit against another to try to break it. [dial. *conker* snail-shell (orig. used in the game), assoc. with CONQUER]

con moto /kɒn ˈməʊtəʊ/ *adv. Mus.* with movement. [It., = with movement]

conn *US* var. of CON[4].

Conn. *abbr.* Connecticut.

connate /ˈkɒneɪt/ *adj.* **1** existing in a person or thing from birth; innate. **2** formed at the same time. **3** allied, congenial. **4** *Bot.* (of organs) congenitally united so as to form one part. **5** *Geol.* (of water) trapped in sedimentary rock during its deposition. [LL *connatus* past part. of *connasci* (as COM-, *nasci* be born)]

connatural /kəˈnætʃər(ə)l/ *adj.* **1** (often foll. by *to*) innate; belonging naturally. **2** of like nature. □□ **connaturally** *adv.* [LL *connaturalis* (as COM-, NATURAL)]

connect /kəˈnekt/ *v.* **1 a** *tr.* (often foll. by *to*, *with*) join (one thing with another) (*connected the hose to the tap*). **b** *tr.* join (two things) (*a track connected the two villages*). **c** *intr.* be joined or joinable (*the two parts do not connect*). **2** *tr.* (often foll. by *with*) associate mentally or practically (*did not connect the two ideas*; *never connected her with the theatre*). **3** *intr.* (foll. by *with*) (of a train etc.) be synchronized at its destination with another train etc., so that passengers can transfer (*the train connects with the boat*). **4** *tr.* put into communication by telephone. **5 a** *tr.* (usu. in *passive*; foll. by *with*) unite or associate with others in relationships etc. (*am connected with the royal family*). **b** *intr.* form a logical sequence; be meaningful. **6** *intr. colloq.* hit or strike effectively. □**connecting-rod** the rod between the piston and the crankpin etc. in an internal-combustion engine or between the wheels of a locomotive. □□ **connectable**

adj. **connector** *n.* [L *connectere connex-* (as COM-, *nectere* bind)]

connected /kə'nektɪd/ *adj.* **1** joined in sequence. **2** (of ideas etc.) coherent. **3** related or associated. □ **well-connected** associated, esp. by birth, with persons of good social position. □□ **connectedly** *adv.* **connectedness** *n.*

connection /kə'nekʃ(ə)n/ *n.* (also *Brit.* **connexion**) **1 a** the act of connecting; the state of being connected. **b** an instance of this. **2** the point at which two things are connected (*broke at the connection*). **3 a** a thing or person that connects; a link (*a radio formed the only connection with the outside world; cannot see the connection between the two ideas*). **b** a telephone link (*got a bad connection*). **4** arrangement or opportunity for catching a connecting train etc.; the train etc. itself (*missed the connection*). **5** *Electr.* **a** the linking up of an electric current by contact. **b** a device for effecting this. **6** (often in *pl.*) a relative or associate, esp. one with influence (*has connections in the Home Office; heard it through a business connection*). **7** a relation of ideas; a context (*in this connection I have to disagree*). **8** *sl.* a supplier of narcotics. **9** a religious body, esp. Methodist. □ **in connection with** with reference to. **in this** (or **that**) **connection** with reference to this (or that). □□ **connectional** *adj.* [L *connexio* (as CONNECT): spelling *-ct-* after CONNECT]

connective /kə'nektɪv/ *adj. & n.* —*adj.* serving or tending to connect. —*n.* something that connects. □ **connective tissue** *Anat.* a fibrous tissue that supports, binds, or separates more specialized tissue.

conning tower /'kɒnɪŋ/ *n.* **1** the superstructure of a submarine from which steering, firing, etc., are directed on or near the surface, and which contains the periscope. **2** the armoured pilot-house of a warship. [CON⁴ + -ING¹]

connivance /kə'naɪv(ə)ns/ *n.* **1** (often foll. by *at, in*) conniving (*connivance in the crime*). **2** tacit permission (*done with his connivance*). [F *connivence* or L *conniventia* (as CONNIVE)]

connive /kə'naɪv/ *v.intr.* **1** (foll. by *at*) disregard or tacitly consent to (a wrongdoing). **2** (usu. foll. by *with*) conspire. □□ **conniver** *n.* [F *conniver* or L *connivēre* shut the eyes (to)]

connoisseur /ˌkɒnə'sɜː(r)/ *n.* (often foll. by *of, in*) an expert judge in matters of taste (*a connoisseur of fine wine*). □□ **connoisseurship** *n.* [F, obs. spelling of *connaisseur* f. pres. stem of *connaître* know + *-eur* -OR¹: cf. *reconnoitre*]

connotation /ˌkɒnə'teɪʃ(ə)n/ *n.* **1** that which is implied by a word etc. in addition to its literal or primary meaning (*a letter with sinister connotations*). **2** the act of connoting or implying.

connote /kə'nəʊt/ *v.tr.* **1** (of a word etc.) imply in addition to the literal or primary meaning. **2** (of a fact) imply as a consequence or condition. **3** mean, signify. □□ **connotative** /'kɒnə,teɪtɪv, kə'nəʊtətɪv/ *adj.* [med.L *connotare* mark in addition (as COM-, *notare* f. *nota* mark)]

connubial /kə'njuːbɪəl/ *adj.* of or relating to marriage or the relationship of husband and wife. □□ **connubiality** /-bɪ'ælɪtɪ/ *n.* **connubially** *adv.* [L *connubialis* f. *connubium* (*nubium* f. *nubere* marry)]

conoid /'kəʊnɔɪd/ *adj. & n.* —*adj.* (also **conoidal** /-'nɔɪd(ə)l/) cone-shaped. —*n.* a cone-shaped object.

conquer /'kɒŋkə(r)/ *v.tr.* **1 a** overcome and control (an enemy or territory) by military force. **b** *absol.* be victorious. **2** overcome (a habit, emotion, disability, etc.) by effort (*conquered his fear*). **3** climb (a mountain) successfully. □□ **conquerable** *adj.* [ME f. OF *conquerre* f. Rmc f. L *conquirere* (as COM-, *quaerere* seek, get)]

conqueror /'kɒŋkərə(r)/ *n.* **1** a person who conquers. **2** *Brit.* = CONKER. [ME f. AF *conquerour* (OF *-eor*) f. *conquerre* (as CONQUER)]

conquest /'kɒŋkwest/ *n.* **1** the act or an instance of conquering; the state of being conquered. **2 a** conquered territory. **b** something won. **3** a person

whose affection or favour has been won. **4** (**the Conquest** or **Norman Conquest**) the conquest of England by William of Normandy in 1066. □ **make a conquest of** win the affections of. [ME f. OF *conquest(e)* f. Rmc (as CONQUER)]

conquistador /kɒn'kwɪstə,dɔː(r)/ *n.* (*pl.* **conquistadores** /-rez/ or **conquistadors**) a conqueror, esp. one of the Spanish conquerors of Mexico and Peru in the 16th c. [Sp.]

con-rod /'kɒnrɒd/ *n. colloq.* connecting-rod. [abbr.]

Cons. *abbr.* Conservative.

consanguineous /ˌkɒnsæŋ'gwɪnɪəs/ *adj.* descended from the same ancestor; akin. □□ **consanguinity** *n.* [L *consanguineus* (as COM-, *sanguis -inis* blood)]

conscience /'kɒnʃ(ə)ns/ *n.* **1** a moral sense of right and wrong esp. as felt by a person and affecting behaviour (*my conscience won't allow me to do that*). **2** an inner feeling as to the goodness or otherwise of one's behaviour (*my conscience is clear; has a guilty conscience*). □ **case of conscience** a matter in which one's conscience has to decide a conflict of principles. **conscience clause** a clause in a law, ensuring respect for the consciences of those affected. **conscience money** a sum paid to relieve one's conscience, esp. about a payment previously evaded. **conscience-stricken** (or **-struck**) made uneasy by a bad conscience. **for conscience** (or **conscience'**) **sake** to satisfy one's conscience. **freedom of conscience** a system allowing all citizens a free choice of religion. **in all conscience** *colloq.* by any reasonable standard; by all that is fair. **on one's conscience** causing one feelings of guilt. **prisoner of conscience** a person imprisoned by a State for holding political or religious views it does not tolerate. □□ **conscienceless** *adj.* [ME f. OF f. L *conscientia* f. *conscire* be privy to (as COM-, *scire* know)]

conscientious /ˌkɒnʃɪ'enʃəs/ *adj.* (of a person or conduct) diligent and scrupulous. □ **conscientious objector** a person who for reasons of conscience objects to conforming to a requirement, esp. that of military service. □□ **conscientiously** *adv.* **conscientiousness** *n.* [F *consciencieux* f. med.L *conscientiosus* (as CONSCIENCE)]

conscious /'kɒnʃəs/ *adj. & n.* —*adj.* **1** awake and aware of one's surroundings and identity. **2** (usu. foll. by *of*, or *that* + clause) aware, knowing (*conscious of his inferiority*). **3** (of actions, emotions, etc.) realized or recognized by the doer; intentional (*made a conscious effort not to laugh*). **4** (in *comb.*) aware of; concerned with (*appearance-conscious*). —*n.* (prec. by *the*) the conscious mind. □□ **consciously** *adv.* [L *conscius* knowing with others or in oneself f. *conscire* (as COM-, *scire* know)]

consciousness /'kɒnʃəsnɪs/ *n.* **1** the state of being conscious (*lost consciousness during the fight*). **2 a** awareness, perception (*had no consciousness of being ridiculed*). **b** (in *comb.*) awareness of (*class-consciousness*). **3** the totality of a person's thoughts and feelings, or of a class of these (*moral consciousness*). □ **consciousness-raising** the activity of increasing esp. social or political sensitivity or awareness.

conscribe /kən'skraɪb/ *v.tr.* = CONSCRIPT *v.* [L *conscribere* (as CONSCRIPTION)]

conscript *v. & n.* —*v.tr.* /kən'skrɪpt/ enlist by conscription. —*n.* /'kɒnskrɪpt/ a person enlisted by conscription. [(v.) back-form. f. CONSCRIPTION: (n.) f. F *conscrit* f. L *conscriptus* (as CONSCRIPTION)]

conscription /kən'skrɪpʃ(ə)n/ *n.* compulsory enlistment for State service, esp. military service. [F f. LL *conscriptio* levying of troops f. L *conscribere conscript-* enrol (as COM-, *scribere* write)]

consecrate /'kɒnsɪ,kreɪt/ *v.tr.* **1** make or declare sacred; dedicate formally to a religious or divine purpose. **2** (in Christian belief) make (bread and wine) into the body and blood of Christ. **3** (foll. by *to*) devote (one's life etc.) to (a purpose). **4** ordain (esp.

a bishop) to a sacred office. □□ **consecration** /-'kreɪʃ(ə)n/ *n.* **consecrator** *n.* **consecratory** *adj.* [ME f. L *consecrare* (as COM-, *secrare* = *sacrare* dedicate f. *sacer* sacred)]

consecution /ˌkɒnsɪ'kjuːʃ(ə)n/ *n.* **1** logical sequence (in argument or reasoning). **2** sequence, succession (of events etc.). [L *consecutio* f. *consequi consecut-* overtake (as COM-, *sequi* pursue)]

consecutive /kən'sekjʊtɪv/ *adj.* **1 a** following continuously. **b** in unbroken or logical order. **2** *Gram.* expressing consequence. □**consecutive intervals** *Mus.* intervals of the same kind (esp. fifths or octaves), occurring in succession between two voices or parts in harmony. □□ **consecutively** *adv.* **consecutiveness** *n.* [F *consécutif -ive* f. med.L *consecutivus* (as CONSECUTION)]

consensual /kən'sensjʊəl, -'senʃʊəl/ *adj.* of or by consent or consensus. □□ **consensually** *adv.* [L *consensus* (see CONSENSUS) + -AL]

consensus /kən'sensəs/ *n.* (often foll. by *of*) **1 a** general agreement (of opinion, testimony, etc.). **b** an instance of this. **2** (*attrib.*) majority view, collective opinion (*consensus politics*). [L, = agreement (as CONSENT)]

consent /kən'sent/ *v.* & *n.* —*v.intr.* (often foll. by *to*) express willingness, give permission, agree. —*n.* voluntary agreement, permission, compliance. □**age of consent** the age at which consent to sexual intercourse is valid in law. **consenting adult 1** an adult who consents to something, esp. a homosexual act. **2** a homosexual. [ME f. OF *consentir* f. L *consentire* (as COM-, *sentire sens-* feel)]

consentient /kən'senʃ(ə)nt/ *adj.* **1** agreeing, united in opinion. **2** concurrent. **3** (often foll. by *to*) consenting. [L *consentient-* (as CONSENT)]

consequence /'kɒnsɪkwəns/ *n.* **1** the result or effect of an action or condition. **2 a** importance (*it is of no consequence*). **b** social distinction (*persons of consequence*). **3** (in *pl.*) a game in which a narrative is made up by the players, each ignorant of what has already been contributed. □**in consequence** as a result. **take the consequences** accept the results of one's choice or action. [ME f. OF f. L *consequentia* (as CONSEQUENT)]

consequent /'kɒnsɪkwənt/ *adj.* & *n.* —*adj.* **1** (often foll. by *on, upon*) following as a result or consequence. **2** logically consistent. —*n.* **1** a thing that follows another. **2** *Logic* the second part of a conditional proposition, dependent on the antecedent. [ME f. OF f. L *consequi* (as CONSECUTION)]

consequential /ˌkɒnsɪ'kwenʃ(ə)l/ *adj.* **1** following as a result or consequence. **2** resulting indirectly (*consequential damage*). **3** (of a person) self-important. □□ **consequentiality** /-ʃɪ'ælɪtɪ/ *n.* **consequentially** *adv.* [L *consequentia*]

consequently /'kɒnsɪˌkwentlɪ/ *adv.* & *conj.* as a result; therefore.

conservancy /kən'sɜːvənsɪ/ *n.* (*pl.* -ies) **1** *Brit.* a commission etc. controlling a port, river, etc. (*Thames Conservancy*). **2** a body concerned with the preservation of natural resources (*Nature Conservancy*). **3** conservation; official preservation (of forests etc.). [18th-c. alt. of obs. *conservacy* f. AF *conservacie* f. AL *conservatia* f. L *conservatio* (as CONSERVE)]

conservation /ˌkɒnsə'veɪʃ(ə)n/ *n.* preservation, esp. of the natural environment. □**conservation area** an area containing a noteworthy environment and specially protected by law against undesirable changes. **conservation of energy** (or **mass** or **momentum** etc.) *Physics* the principle that the total quantity of energy etc. of any system not subject to external action remains constant. □□ **conservational** *adj.* [ME f. OF *conservation* or L *conservatio* (as CONSERVE)]

conservationist /ˌkɒnsə'veɪʃənɪst/ *n.* a supporter or advocate of environmental conservation.

conservative /kən'sɜːvətɪv/ *adj.* & *n.* —*adj.* **1 a** averse to rapid change. **b** (of views, taste, etc.) moderate, avoiding extremes (*conservative in his dress*). **2** (of an estimate etc.) purposely low; moderate, cautious. **3** (**Conservative**) of or characteristic of Conservatives or the Conservative Party. **4** tending to conserve. —*n.* **1** a conservative person. **2** (**Conservative**) a supporter or member of the Conservative Party. □**Conservative Judaism** Judaism allowing only minor changes in traditional ritual etc. **Conservative Party 1** a British political party promoting free enterprise and private ownership. **2** a similar party elsewhere. **conservative surgery** surgery that seeks to preserve tissues as far as possible. □□ **conservatism** *n.* **conservatively** *adv.* **conservativeness** *n.* [ME f. LL *conservativus* (as CONSERVE)]

conservatoire /kən'sɜːvəˌtwɑː(r)/ *n.* a (usu. European) school of music or other arts. [F f. It. *conservatorio* (as CONSERVATORY)]

conservator /'kɒnsəˌveɪtə(r), kən'sɜːvətə(r)/ *n.* a person who preserves something; an official custodian (of a museum etc.). [ME f. AF *conservatour*, OF *-ateur* f. L *conservator -oris* (as CONSERVE)]

conservatorium /kənˌsɜːvə'tɔːrɪəm/ *n.* *Austral.* = CONSERVATOIRE.

conservatory /kən'sɜːvətərɪ/ *n.* (*pl.* -ies) **1** a greenhouse for tender plants, esp. one attached to and communicating with a house. **2** esp. *US* = CONSERVATOIRE. [LL *conservatorium* (as CONSERVE): sense 2 through It. *conservatorio*]

conserve /kən'sɜːv/ *v.* & *n.* —*v.tr.* **1** store up; keep from harm or damage, esp. for later use. **2** *Physics* maintain a quantity of (heat etc.). **3** preserve (food, esp. fruit), usu. with sugar. —*n.* /also 'kɒnsɜːv/ fruit etc. preserved in sugar. **2** fresh fruit jam. [ME f. OF *conserver* f. L *conservare* (as COM-, *servare* keep)]

consider /kən'sɪdə(r)/ *v.tr.* (often *absol.*) **1** contemplate mentally, esp. in order to reach a conclusion. **2** examine the merits of (a course of action, a candidate, claim, etc.). **3** give attention to. **4** reckon with; take into account. **5** (foll. by *that* + clause) have the opinion. **6** (foll. by compl.) believe; regard as (*consider it to be genuine*; *consider it settled*). **7** (as **considered** *adj.*) formed after careful thought (*a considered opinion*). □**all things considered** taking everything into account. [ME f. OF *considerer* f. L *considerare* examine]

considerable /kən'sɪdərəb(ə)l/ *adj.* **1** enough in amount or extent to need consideration. **2** much; a lot of (*considerable pain*). **3** notable, important. □□ **considerably** *adv.*

considerate /kən'sɪdərət/ *adj.* **1** thoughtful towards other people; careful not to cause hurt or inconvenience. **2** *archaic* careful. □□ **considerately** *adv.*

consideration /kənˌsɪdə'reɪʃ(ə)n/ *n.* **1** the act of considering; careful thought. **2** thoughtfulness for others; being considerate. **3** a fact or a thing taken into account in deciding or judging something. **4** compensation; a payment or reward. **5** *Law* (in a contractual agreement) anything given or promised or forborne by one party in exchange for the promise or undertaking of another. **6** *archaic* importance or consequence. □**in consideration of** in return for; on account of. **take into consideration** include as a factor, reason, etc.; make allowance for. **under consideration** being considered. [ME f. OF f. L *consideratio -onis* (as CONSIDER)]

considering /kən'sɪdərɪŋ/ *prep.* **1** in view of; taking into consideration (*considering their youth*; *considering that it was snowing*). **2** (without compl.) *colloq.* all in all; taking everything into account (*not so bad, considering*).

consign /kən'saɪn/ *v.tr.* (often foll. by *to*) **1** hand over; deliver to a person's possession or trust. **2** assign; commit decisively or permanently (*consigned it to the dustbin*; *consigned to years of misery*). **3** transmit or send (goods), usu. by a public carrier.

□□ **consignee** /ˌkɒnsaɪˈniː/ n. **consignor** n. [ME f. F consigner or L consignare mark with a seal (as COM-, SIGN)]

consignment /kənˈsaɪnmənt/ n. **1** the act or an instance of consigning; the process of being consigned. **2** a batch of goods consigned.

consist /kənˈsɪst/ v.intr. **1** (foll. by of) be composed; have specified ingredients or elements. **2** (foll. by in, of) have its essential features as specified (its beauty consists in the use of colour). **3** (usu. foll. by with) harmonize; be consistent. [L consistere exist (as COM-, sistere stop)]

consistency /kənˈsɪstənsɪ/ n. (also **consistence**) (pl. -ies or -es) **1** the degree of density, firmness, or viscosity, esp. of thick liquids. **2** the state of being consistent; conformity with other or earlier attitudes, practice, etc. **3** the state or quality of holding or sticking together and retaining shape. [F consistence or LL consistentia (as CONSIST)]

consistent /kənˈsɪst(ə)nt/ adj. (usu. foll. by with) **1** compatible or in harmony; not contradictory. **2** (of a person) constant to the same principles of thought or action. □□ **consistently** adv. [L consistere (as CONSIST)]

consistory /kənˈsɪstərɪ/ n. (pl. -ies) **1** RC Ch. the council of cardinals (with or without the pope). **2** (in full **consistory court**) (in the Church of England) a court presided over by a bishop, for the administration of ecclesiastical law in a diocese. **3** (in other Churches) a local administrative body. □□ **consistorial** /ˌkɒnsɪˈstɔːrɪəl/ adj. [ME f. AF consistorie, OF -oire f. LL consistorium (as CONSIST)]

consociation /kənˌsəʊʃɪˈeɪʃ(ə)n, kənˌsəʊsɪˈeɪʃ(ə)n/ n. **1** close association, esp. of Churches or religious communities. **2** Ecol. a closely-related sub-group of plants having one dominant species. [L consociatio, -onis f. consociare (as COM-, socius fellow)]

consolation /ˌkɒnsəˈleɪʃ(ə)n/ n. **1** the act or an instance of consoling; the state of being consoled. **2** a consoling thing, person, or circumstance. □ **consolation prize** a prize given to a competitor who just fails to win a main prize. □□ **consolatory** /kənˈsɒlətərɪ/ adj. [ME f. OF f. L consolatio -onis (as CONSOLE[1])]

console[1] /kənˈsəʊl/ v.tr. comfort, esp. in grief or disappointment. ¶ Often confused with condole. □□ **consolable** adj. **consoler** n. **consolingly** adv. [F consoler f. L consolari]

console[2] /ˈkɒnsəʊl/ n. **1** a panel or unit accommodating a set of switches, controls, etc. **2** a cabinet for television or radio equipment etc. **3** Mus. a cabinet with the keyboards, stops, pedals, etc., of an organ. **4** an ornamented bracket supporting a shelf etc. □ **console table** a table supported by a bracket against a wall. [F, perh. f. consolider (as CONSOLIDATE)]

consolidate /kənˈsɒlɪˌdeɪt/ v. **1** tr. & intr. make or become strong or solid. **2** tr. reinforce or strengthen (one's position, power, etc.). **3** tr. combine (territories, companies, debts, etc.) into one whole. □ **consolidated fund** (or **annuities**) Brit. a Bank of England fund into which tax revenue is paid and from which payments not dependent on annual votes in Parliament are made. □□ **consolidation** /kənˌsɒlɪˈdeɪʃ(ə)n/ n. **consolidator** n. **consolidatory** adj. [L consolidare (as COM-, solidare f. solidus solid)]

consols /ˈkɒnsɒlz/ n.pl. British government securities without redemption date and with fixed annual interest. [abbr. of consolidated annuities]

consommé /kənˈsɒmeɪ/ n. a clear soup made with meat stock. [F, past part. of consommer f. L consummare (as CONSUMMATE)]

consonance /ˈkɒnsənəns/ n. **1** agreement, harmony. **2** Prosody a recurrence of similar-sounding consonants. **3** Mus. a harmonious combination of notes; a harmonious interval. [ME f. OF consonance or L consonantia (as CONSONANT)]

consonant /ˈkɒnsənənt/ n. & adj. —n. **1** a speech sound in which the breath is at least partly obstructed, and which to form a syllable must be combined with a vowel. **2** a letter or letters representing this. —adj. (foll. by with, to) **1** consistent; in agreement or harmony. **2** similar in sound. **3** Mus. making a concord. □□ **consonantal** /-ˈnænt(ə)l/ adj. **consonantly** adv. [ME f. F f. L consonare (as sonare sound f. sonus)]

con sordino /kɒn sɔːˈdiːnəʊ/ adv. Mus. with the use of a mute. [It.]

consort[1] n. & v. —n. /ˈkɒnsɔːt/ **1** a wife or husband, esp. of royalty (prince consort). **2** a ship sailing with another. —v. /kənˈsɔːt/ **1** intr. (usu. foll. by with, together) **a** keep company; associate. **b** harmonize. **2** tr. class or bring together. [ME f. F f. L consors sharer, comrade (as COM-, sors sortis lot, destiny)]

consort[2] /ˈkɒnsɔːt/ n. Mus. a group of players or instruments, esp. playing early music (recorder consort). [earlier form of CONCERT]

consortium /kənˈsɔːtɪəm/ n. (pl. **consortia** /-tɪə/ or **consortiums**) **1** an association, esp. of several business companies. **2** Law the right of association with a husband or wife (loss of consortium). [L, = partnership (as CONSORT[1])]

conspecific /ˌkɒnspɪˈsɪfɪk/ adj. Biol. of the same species.

conspectus /kənˈspektəs/ n. **1** a general or comprehensive survey. **2** a summary or synopsis. [L f. conspicere conspect- (as COM-, spicere look at)]

conspicuous /kənˈspɪkjʊəs/ adj. **1** clearly visible; striking to the eye; attracting notice. **2** remarkable of its kind (conspicuous extravagance). □□ **conspicuously** adv. **conspicuousness** n. [L conspicuus (as CONSPECTUS)]

conspiracy /kənˈspɪrəsɪ/ n. (pl. -ies) **1** a secret plan to commit a crime or do harm, often for political ends; a plot. **2** the act of conspiring. □ **conspiracy of silence** an agreement to say nothing. [ME f. AF conspiracie, alt. form of OF conspiration f. L conspiratio -onis (as CONSPIRE)]

conspirator /kənˈspɪrətə(r)/ n. a person who takes part in a conspiracy. □□ **conspiratorial** /-ˈtɔːrɪəl/ adj. **conspiratorially** /-ˈtɔːrɪəlɪ/ adv. [ME f. AF conspiratour, OF -teur (as CONSPIRE)]

conspire /kənˈspaɪə(r)/ v.intr. **1** combine secretly to plan and prepare an unlawful or harmful act. **2** (often foll. by against, or to + infin.) (of events or circumstances) seem to be working together, esp. disadvantageously. [ME f. OF conspirer f. L conspirare agree, plot (as COM-, spirare breathe)]

constable /ˈkʌnstəb(ə)l/ n. **1** Brit. **a** a policeman or policewoman. **b** (also **police constable**) a police officer of the lowest rank. **2** the governor of a royal castle. **3** hist. the principal officer in a royal household. □ **Chief Constable** the head of the police force of a county or other region. [ME f. OF conestable f. LL comes stabuli count of the stable]

constabulary /kənˈstæbjʊlərɪ/ n. & adj. —n. (pl. -ies) an organized body of police; a police force. —attrib.adj. of or concerning the police force. [med.L constabularius (as CONSTABLE)]

constancy /ˈkɒnstənsɪ/ n. **1** the quality of being unchanging and dependable; faithfulness. **2** firmness, endurance. [L constantia (as CONSTANT)]

constant /ˈkɒnst(ə)nt/ adj. & n. —adj. **1** continuous (needs constant attention). **2** occurring frequently (receive constant complaints). **3** (often foll. by to) unchanging, faithful, dependable. —n. **1** anything that does not vary. **2** Math. a component of a relationship between variables that does not change its value. **3** Physics **a** a number expressing a relation, property, etc., and remaining the same in all circumstances. **b** such a number that remains the same for a substance in the same conditions. □□ **constantly** adv. [ME f. OF f. L constare (as COM-, stare stand)]

constantan /ˈkɒnstənˌtæn/ n. an alloy of copper and

nickel used in electrical equipment. [CONSTANT + -AN]

constellate /ˈkɒnstəˌleɪt/ v.tr. **1** form into (or as if into) a constellation. **2** adorn as with stars.

constellation /ˌkɒnstəˈleɪʃ(ə)n/ n. **1** a group of fixed stars whose outline is traditionally regarded as forming a particular figure. **2** a group of associated persons, ideas, etc. [ME f. OF f. LL *constellatio -onis* (as COM-, *stella* star)]

consternate /ˈkɒnstəˌneɪt/ v.tr. (usu. in *passive*) dismay; fill with anxiety. [L *consternare* (as COM-, *sternere* throw down)]

consternation /ˌkɒnstəˈneɪʃ(ə)n/ n. anxiety or dismay causing mental confusion. [F *consternation* or L *consternatio* (as CONSTERNATE)]

constipate /ˈkɒnstɪˌpeɪt/ v.tr. (esp. as **constipated** adj.) affect with constipation. [L *constipare* (as COM-, *stipare* press)]

constipation /ˌkɒnstɪˈpeɪʃ(ə)n/ n. **1** a condition with hardened faeces and difficulty in emptying the bowels. **2** a restricted state. [ME f. OF *constipation* or LL *constipatio* (as CONSTIPATE)]

constituency /kənˈstɪtjʊənsɪ/ n. (pl. **-ies**) **1** a body of voters in a specified area who elect a representative member to a legislative body. **2** the area represented in this way. **3** a body of customers, supporters, etc.

constituent /kənˈstɪtjʊənt/ adj. & n. —adj. **1** composing or helping to make up a whole. **2** able to make or change a (political etc.) constitution (*constituent assembly*). **3** appointing or electing. —n. **1** a member of a constituency (esp. political). **2** a component part. **3** *Law* a person who appoints another as agent. [L *constituent-* partly through F *-ant* (as CONSTITUTE)]

constitute /ˈkɒnstɪˌtjuːt/ v.tr. **1** be the components or essence of; make up, form. **2 a** be equivalent or tantamount to (*this constitutes an official warning*). **b** formally establish (*does not constitute a precedent*). **3** give legal or constitutional form to; establish by law. □□ **constitutor** n. [L *constituere* (as COM-, *statuere* set up)]

constitution /ˌkɒnstɪˈtjuːʃ(ə)n/ n. **1** the act or method of constituting; the composition (of something). **2 a** the body of fundamental principles or established precedents according to which a State or other organization is acknowledged to be governed. **b** a (usu. written) record of this. **3** a person's physical state as regards vitality, health, strength, etc. **4** a person's mental or psychological make-up. **5** *hist.* a decree or ordinance. [ME f. OF *constitution* or L *constitutio* (as CONSTITUTE)]

constitutional /ˌkɒnstɪˈtjuːʃən(ə)l/ adj. & n. —adj. **1** of, consistent with, authorized by, or limited by a political constitution (*a constitutional monarchy*). **2** inherent in, stemming from, or affecting the physical or mental constitution. —n. a walk taken regularly to maintain or restore good health. □□ **constitutionality** /-ˈnælɪtɪ/ n. **constitutionalize** v.tr. (also **-ise**). **constitutionally** adv.

constitutionalism /ˌkɒnstɪˈtjuːʃənəˌlɪz(ə)m/ n. **1** a constitutional system of government. **2** the adherence to or advocacy of such a system. □□ **constitutionalist** n.

constitutive /ˈkɒnstɪˌtjuːtɪv/ adj. **1** able to form or appoint. **2** component. **3** essential. □□ **constitutively** adv. [LL *constitutivus* (as CONSTITUTE)]

constrain /kənˈstreɪn/ v.tr. **1** compel; urge irresistibly or by necessity. **2 a** confine forcibly; imprison. **b** restrict severely as regards action, behaviour, etc. **3** bring about by compulsion. **4** (as **constrained** adj.) forced, embarrassed (*a constrained voice*; *a constrained manner*). □□ **constrainedly** /kənˈstreɪnɪdlɪ/ adv. [ME f. OF *constraindre* f. L *constringere* (as COM-, *stringere* stricttie)]

constraint /kənˈstreɪnt/ n. **1** the act or result of constraining or being constrained; restriction of liberty. **2** something that constrains; a limitation on

motion or action. **3** the restraint of natural feelings or their expression; a constrained manner. [ME f. OF *constreinte*, fem. past part. (as CONSTRAIN)]

constrict /kənˈstrɪkt/ v.tr. **1** make narrow or tight; compress. **2** *Biol.* cause (organic tissue) to contract. □□ **constriction** n. **constrictive** adj. [L (as CONSTRAIN)]

constrictor /kənˈstrɪktə(r)/ n. **1** any snake (esp. a boa) that kills by coiling round its prey and compressing it. **2** *Anat.* any muscle that compresses or contracts an organ or part of the body. [mod.L (as CONSTRICT)]

construct v. & n. —v.tr. /kənˈstrʌkt/ **1** make by fitting parts together; build, form (something physical or abstract). **2** *Geom.* draw or delineate, esp. accurately to given conditions (*construct a triangle*). —n. /ˈkɒnstrʌkt/ **1** a thing constructed, esp. by the mind. **2** *Linguistics* a group of words forming a phrase. □□ **constructor** n. [L *construere construct-* (as COM-, *struere* pile, build)]

construction /kənˈstrʌkʃ(ə)n/ n. **1** the act or a mode of constructing. **2** a thing constructed. **3** an interpretation or explanation (*they put a generous construction on his act*). **4** *Gram.* an arrangement of words according to syntactical rules. □□ **constructional** adj. **constructionally** adv. [ME f. OF f. L *constructio -onis* (as CONSTRUCT)]

constructionism /kənˈstrʌkʃəˌnɪz(ə)m/ n. = CONSTRUCTIVISM.

constructive /kənˈstrʌktɪv/ adj. **1 a** of construction; tending to construct. **b** tending to form a basis for ideas (*constructive criticism*). **2** helpful, positive (*a constructive approach*). **3** derived by inference; not expressed (*constructive permission*). **4** belonging to the structure of a building. □□ **constructively** adv. **constructiveness** n. [LL *constructivus* (as CONSTRUCT)]

constructivism /kənˈstrʌktɪˌvɪz(ə)m/ n. *Art* a Russian movement in which assorted (usu. mechanical or industrial) objects are combined into nonrepresentational and mobile structural forms. □□ **constructivist** n. [Russ. *konstruktivizm* (as CONSTRUCT)]

construe /kənˈstruː/ v.tr. (**construes**, **construed**, **construing**) **1** interpret (words or actions) (*their decision can be construed in many ways*). **2** (often foll. by *with*) combine (words) grammatically ('*rely* is construed with '*on*'). **3** analyse the syntax of (a sentence). **4** translate word for word. □□ **construable** adj. **construal** n. [ME f. L *construere* CONSTRUCT]

consubstantial /ˌkɒnsəbˈstænʃ(ə)l/ adj. *Theol.* of the same substance (esp. of the three persons of the Trinity). □□ **consubstantiality** /-ʃɪˈælɪtɪ/ n. [ME f. eccl.L *consubstantialis*, transl. Gk *homoousios* (as COM-, SUBSTANTIAL)]

consubstantiation /ˌkɒnsəbˌstænʃɪˈeɪʃ(ə)n/ n. *Theol.* the real substantial presence of the body and blood of Christ together with the bread and wine in the Eucharist. [mod.L *consubstantiatio*, after *transubstantiatio* TRANSUBSTANTIATION]

consuetude /ˈkɒnswɪˌtjuːd/ n. a custom, esp. one having legal force in Scotland. □□ **consuetudinary** /ˌkɒnswɪˈtjuːdɪnərɪ/ adj. [ME f. OF *consuetude* or L *consuetudo -dinis* f. *consuetus* accustomed]

consul /ˈkɒns(ə)l/ n. **1** an official appointed by a State to live in a foreign city and protect the State's citizens and interests there. **2** *hist.* either of two annually elected chief magistrates in ancient Rome. **3** any of the three chief magistrates of the French republic (1799-1804). □□ **consular** /ˈkɒnsjʊlə(r)/ adj. **consulship** n. [ME f. L, rel. to *consulere* take counsel]

consulate /ˈkɒnsjʊlət/ n. **1** the building officially used by a consul. **2** the office, position, or period of office of consul. **3** *hist.* government by consuls. **4** *hist.* the period of office of a consul. **5** *hist.* (**Consulate**) the government of France by three consuls (1799-1804). [ME f. L *consulatus* (as CONSUL)]

consult /kənˈsʌlt/ v. **1** *tr.* seek information or advice from (a person, book, watch, etc.). **2** *intr.* (often foll. by *with*) refer to a person for advice, an opinion, etc. **3** *tr.* seek permission or approval from (a person) for a proposed action. **4** *tr.* take into account; consider (feelings, interests, etc.). □□ **consultative** /-'tətɪv/ *adj.* [F *consulter* f. L *consultare* frequent. of *consulere* *consult-* take counsel]

consultancy /kən'sʌltənsɪ/ *n.* (*pl.* **-ies**) the professional practice or position of a consultant.

consultant /kən'sʌlt(ə)nt/ *n.* **1** a person providing professional advice etc., esp. for a fee. **2** a senior specialist in a branch of medicine responsible for patients in a hospital. [prob. F (as CONSULT)]

consultation /ˌkɒnsəl'teɪʃ(ə)n/ *n.* **1** a meeting arranged to consult (esp. with a consultant). **2** the act or an instance of consulting. **3** a conference. [ME f. OF *consultation* or L *consultatio* (as CONSULTANT)]

consulting /kən'sʌltɪŋ/ *attrib.adj.* giving professional advice to others working in the same field or subject (*consulting physician*).

consumable /kən'sju:məb(ə)l/ *adj.* & *n.* —*adj.* that can be consumed; intended for consumption. —*n.* (usu. in *pl.*) a commodity that is eventually used up, worn out, or eaten.

consume /kən'sju:m/ *v.tr.* **1** eat or drink. **2** completely destroy; reduce to nothing or to tiny particles (*fire consumed the building*). **3** (as **consumed** *adj.*) possessed by or entirely taken up (foll. by *with*: *consumed with rage*). **4** use up (time, energy, etc.). □□ **consumingly** *adv.* [ME f. L *consumere* (as COM-, *sumere sumpt-* take up): partly through F *consumer*]

consumer /kən'sju:mə(r)/ *n.* **1** a person who consumes, esp. one who uses a product. **2** a purchaser of goods or services. □ **consumer durable** a household product with a relatively long useful life (e.g. a radio or washing-machine). **consumer goods** goods put to use by consumers, not used in producing other goods (opp. *capital goods* (see CAPITAL¹)). **consumer research** investigation of purchasers' needs and opinions. **consumer society** a society in which the marketing of goods and services is an important social and economic activity.

consumerism /kən'sju:məˌrɪz(ə)m/ *n.* the protection or promotion of consumers' interests in relation to the producer. □□ **consumerist** *adj.* & *n.*

consummate *v.* & *adj.* —*v.tr.* /'kɒnsəˌmeɪt/ **1** complete; make perfect. **2** complete (a marriage) by sexual intercourse. —*adj.* /kən'sʌmɪt, 'kɒnsəmɪt/ complete, perfect; fully skilled (*a consummate general*). □□ **consummately** *adv.* **consummative** *adj.* **consummator** /'kɒnsəˌmeɪtə(r)/ *n.* [L *consummare* (as COM-, *summare* complete f. *summus* utmost)]

consummation /ˌkɒnsə'meɪʃ(ə)n/ *n.* **1** completion, esp. of a marriage by sexual intercourse. **2** a desired end or goal; perfection. [ME f. OF *consommation* or L *consummatio* (as CONSUMMATE)]

consumption /kən'sʌmpʃ(ə)n/ *n.* **1** the act or an instance of consuming; the process of being consumed. **2** any disease causing wasting of tissues, esp. pulmonary tuberculosis. **3** an amount consumed. **4** the purchase and use of goods etc. [ME f. OF *consomption* f. L *consumptio* (as CONSUME)]

consumptive /kən'sʌmptɪv/ *adj.* & *n.* —*adj.* **1** of or tending to consumption. **2** tending to or affected with pulmonary tuberculosis. —*n.* a consumptive patient. □□ **consumptively** *adv.* [med.L *consumptivus* (as CONSUMPTION)]

cont. *abbr.* **1** contents. **2** continued.

contact /'kɒntækt/ *n.* & *v.* —*n.* **1** the state or condition of touching, meeting, or communicating. **2** a person who is or may be communicated with for information, supplies, assistance, etc. **3** *Electr.* **a** a connection for the passage of a current. **b** a device for providing this. **4** a person likely to carry a contagious disease through being associated with an infected person. **5** (usu. in *pl.*) *colloq.* a contact lens. —*v.tr.* /'kɒntækt, kən'tækt/ **1** get into communication

with (a person). **2** begin correspondence or personal dealings with. □ **contact lens** a small lens placed directly on the eyeball to correct the vision. **contact print** a photographic print made by placing a negative directly on sensitized paper etc. and illuminating it. **contact sport** a sport in which participants necessarily come into bodily contact with one another. □□ **contactable** *adj.* [L *contactus* f. *contingere* (as COM-, *tangere* touch)]

contagion /kən'teɪdʒ(ə)n/ *n.* **1 a** the communication of disease from one person to another by bodily contact. **b** a contagious disease. **2** a contagious or harmful influence. **3** moral corruption, esp. when tending to be widespread. [ME f. L *contagio* (as COM-, *tangere* touch)]

contagious /kən'teɪdʒəs/ *adj.* **1 a** (of a person) likely to transmit disease by contact. **b** (of a disease) transmitted in this way. **2** (of emotions, reactions, etc.) likely to affect others (*contagious enthusiasm*). □ **contagious abortion** brucellosis of cattle. □□ **contagiously** *adv.* **contagiousness** *n.* [ME f. LL *contagiosus* (as CONTAGION)]

contain /kən'teɪn/ *v.tr.* **1** hold or be capable of holding within itself; include, comprise. **2** (of measures) consist of or be equal to (*a gallon contains eight pints*). **3** prevent (an enemy, difficulty, etc.) from moving or extending. **4** control or restrain (oneself, one's feelings, etc.). **5** (of a number) be divisible by (a factor) without a remainder. □□ **containable** *adj.* [ME f. OF *contenir* f. L *continēre content-* (as COM-, *tenēre* hold)]

container /kən'teɪnə(r)/ *n.* **1** a vessel, box, etc., for holding particular things. **2** a large boxlike receptacle of standard design for the transport of goods, esp. one readily transferable from one form of transport to another (also *attrib.*: *container ship*).

containerize /kən'teɪnəˌraɪz/ *v.tr.* (also **-ise**) **1** pack in or transport by container. **2** adapt to transport by container. □□ **containerization** /-'zeɪʃ(ə)n/ *n.*

containment /kən'teɪnmənt/ *n.* the action or policy of preventing the expansion of a hostile country or influence.

contaminate /kən'tæmɪˌneɪt/ *v.tr.* **1** pollute, esp. with radioactivity. **2** infect. □□ **contaminant** *n.* **contamination** /-'neɪʃ(ə)n/ *n.* **contaminator** *n.* [L *contaminare* (as COM-, *tamen-* rel. to *tangere* touch)]

contango /kən'tæŋɡəʊ/ *n.* (*pl.* **-os**) *Brit. Stock Exch.* **1** the postponement of the transfer of stock from one account day to the next. **2** a percentage paid by the buyer for such a postponement. □ **contango day** the eighth day before settling day. [19th c.: prob. an arbitrary formation]

conte /kɒ̃t/ *n.* **1** a short story (as a form of literary composition). **2** a medieval narrative tale. [F]

contemn /kən'tem/ *v.tr. literary* despise; treat with disregard. □□ **contemner** /-'temə(r), -'temnə(r)/ *n.* [ME f. OF *contemner* or L *contemnere* (as COM-, *temnere tempt-* despise)]

contemplate /'kɒntəmˌpleɪt/ *v.* **1** *tr.* survey with the eyes or in the mind. **2** *tr.* regard (an event) as possible. **3** *tr.* intend; have as one's purpose (*we contemplate leaving tomorrow*). **4** *intr.* meditate. □□ **contemplation** /-'pleɪʃ(ə)n/ *n.* **contemplator** *n.* [L *contemplari* (as COM-, *templum* place for observations)]

contemplative /kən'templətɪv/ *adj.* & *n.* —*adj.* of or given to (esp. religious) contemplation; meditative. —*n.* a person whose life is devoted to religious contemplation. □□ **contemplatively** *adv.* [ME f. OF *contemplatif* -*ive*, or L *contemplativus* (as CONTEMPLATE)]

contemporaneous /kənˌtempə'reɪnɪəs/ *adj.* (usu. foll. by *with*) **1** existing or occurring at the same time. **2** of the same period. □□ **contemporaneity** /-'ni:ɪtɪ/ *n.* **contemporaneously** *adv.* **contemporaneousness** *n.* [L *contemporaneus* (as COM-, *temporaneus* f. *tempus -oris* time)]

contemporary /kən'tempərərɪ/ *adj.* & *n.* —*adj.* **1**

living or occurring at the same time. **2** approximately equal in age. **3** following modern ideas or fashion in style or design. —*n.* (*pl.* **-ies**) **1** a person or thing living or existing at the same time as another. **2** a person of roughly the same age as another. □□ **contemporarily** *adv.* **contemporariness** *n.* **contemporarize** *v.tr.* (also **-ise**). [med.L *contemporarius* (as CONTEMPORANEOUS)]

contempt /kən'tempt/ *n.* **1** a feeling that a person or a thing is beneath consideration or worthless, or deserving scorn or extreme reproach. **2** the condition of being held in contempt. **3** (in full **contempt of court**) disobedience to or disrespect for a court of law and its officers. □ **beneath contempt** utterly despicable. **hold in contempt** despise. [ME f. L *contemptus* (as CONTEMN)]

contemptible /kən'temptɪb(ə)l/ *adj.* deserving contempt; despicable. □□ **contemptibility** *n.* **contemptibly** *adv.* [ME f. OF or LL *contemptibilis* (as CONTEMN)]

contemptuous /kən'temptjʊəs/ *adj.* (often foll. by *of*) showing contempt, scornful; insolent. □□ **contemptuously** *adv.* [med.L *contemptuosus* f. L *contemptus* (as CONTEMPT)]

contend /kən'tend/ *v.* **1** *intr.* (usu. foll. by *with*) strive, fight. **2** *intr.* compete (*contending emotions*). **3** *tr.* (usu. foll. by *that* + clause) assert, maintain. □□ **contender** *n.* [OF *contendre* or L *contendere* (as COM-, *tendere tent-* stretch, strive)]

content[1] /kən'tent/ *adj.*, *v.*, & *n.* —*predic.adj.* **1** satisfied; adequately happy; in agreement. **2** (foll. by *to* + infin.) willing. —*v.tr.* make content; satisfy. —*n.* a contented state; satisfaction. □ **to one's heart's content** to the full extent of one's desires. [ME f. OF f. L *contentus* satisfied, past part. of *continēre* (as CONTAIN)]

content[2] /'kɒntent/ *n.* **1** (usu. in *pl.*) what is contained in something, esp. in a vessel, book, or house. **2** the amount of a constituent contained (*low sodium content*). **3** the substance or material dealt with (in a speech, work of art, etc.) as distinct from its form or style. **4** the capacity or volume of a thing. [ME f. med.L *contentum* (as CONTAIN)]

contented /kən'tentɪd/ *adj.* (often foll. by *with*, or *to* + infin.) **1** happy, satisfied. **2** (foll. by *with*) willing to be content (*was contented with the outcome*). □□ **contentedly** *adv.* **contentedness** *n.*

contention /kən'tenʃ(ə)n/ *n.* **1** a dispute or argument; rivalry. **2** a point contended for in an argument (*it is my contention that you are wrong*). □ **in contention** competing, esp. with a good chance of success. [ME f. OF *contention* or L *contentio* (as CONTEND)]

contentious /kən'tenʃəs/ *adj.* **1** argumentative, quarrelsome. **2** likely to cause an argument; disputed, controversial. □□ **contentiously** *adv.* **contentiousness** *n.* [ME f. OF *contentieux* f. L *contentiosus* (as CONTENTION)]

contentment /kən'tentmənt/ *n.* a satisfied state; tranquil happiness.

conterminous /kɒn'tɜːmɪnəs/ *adj.* (often foll. by *with*) **1** having a common boundary. **2** coextensive, coterminous. □□ **conterminously** *adv.* [L *conterminus* (as COM-, *terminus* boundary)]

contessa /kɒn'tesə/ *n.* an Italian countess. [It. f. LL *comitissa*: see COUNTESS]

contest *n.* & *v.* —*n.* /'kɒntest/ **1** a process of contending; a competition. **2** a dispute; a controversy. —*v.tr.* /kən'test/ **1** challenge or dispute (a decision etc.). **2** debate (a point, statement, etc.). **3** contend or compete for (a prize, parliamentary seat, etc.); compete in (an election). □□ **contestable** /kən'testəb(ə)l/ *adj.* **contester** /kən'testə(r)/ *n.* [L *contestari* (as COM-, *testis* witness)]

contestant /kən'test(ə)nt/ *n.* a person who takes part in a contest or competition.

contestation /ˌkɒntes'teɪʃ(ə)n/ *n.* **1** a disputation. **2** an assertion contended for. [L *contestatio* partly through F (as CONTEST)]

context /'kɒntekst/ *n.* **1** the parts of something written or spoken that immediately precede and follow a word or passage and clarify its meaning. **2** the circumstances relevant to something under consideration (*must be seen in context*). □ **out of context** without the surrounding words or circumstances and so not fully understandable. □□ **contextual** /kən'tekstjʊəl/ *adj.* **contextualize** /kən'tekstjʊəlaɪz/ *v.tr.* (also **-ise**). **contextualization** /kənˌtekstjʊəlaɪˌzeɪʃ(ə)n/ *n.* **contextually** /kən'tekstjʊəlɪ/ *adv.* [ME f. L *contextus* (as COM-, *texere text-* weave)]

contiguity /ˌkɒntɪ'gjuːɪtɪ/ *n.* **1** being contiguous; proximity; contact. **2** *Psychol.* the proximity of ideas or impressions in place or time, as a principle of association.

contiguous /kən'tɪgjʊəs/ *adj.* (usu. foll. by *with*, *to*) touching, esp. along a line; in contact. □□ **contiguously** *adv.* [L *contiguus* (as COM-, *tangere* touch)]

continent[1] /'kɒntɪnənt/ *n.* **1** any of the main continuous expanses of land (Europe, Asia, Africa, N. and S. America, Australia, Antarctica). **2** (the **Continent**) the mainland of Europe as distinct from the British Isles. **3** continuous land; a mainland. [L *terra continens* (see CONTAIN) continuous land]

continent[2] /'kɒntɪnənt/ *adj.* **1** able to control movements of the bowels and bladder. **2** exercising self-restraint, esp. sexually. □□ **continence** *n.* **continently** *adv.* [ME f. L (as CONTAIN)]

continental /ˌkɒntɪ'nent(ə)l/ *adj.* & *n.* —*adj.* **1** of or characteristic of a continent. **2** (**Continental**) *Brit.* of, relating to, or characteristic of mainland Europe. —*n.* an inhabitant of mainland Europe. □ **continental breakfast** a light breakfast of coffee, rolls, etc. **continental climate** a climate having wide variations of temperature. **continental drift** *Geol.* the hypothesis that the continents are moving slowly over the surface of the earth on a deep-lying plastic substratum. **continental quilt** *Brit.* a duvet. **continental shelf** an area of relatively shallow seabed between the shore of a continent and the deeper ocean. □□ **continentally** *adv.*

contingency /kən'tɪndʒənsɪ/ *n.* (*pl.* **-ies**) **1** a future event or circumstance regarded as likely to occur, or as influencing present action. **2** something dependent on another uncertain event or occurrence. **3** uncertainty of occurrence. **4 a** one thing incident to another. **b** an incidental expense etc. □ **contingency fund** a fund to cover incidental or unforeseen expenses. [earlier *contingence* f. LL *contingentia* (as CONTINGENT)]

contingent /kən'tɪndʒ(ə)nt/ *adj.* & *n.* —*adj.* **1** (usu. foll. by *on*, *upon*) conditional, dependent (on an uncertain event or circumstance). **2** associated. **3** (usu. foll. by *to*) incidental. **4 a** that may or may not occur. **b** fortuitous; occurring by chance. **5** true only under existing or specified conditions. —*n.* a body (esp. of troops, ships, etc.) forming part of a larger group. □□ **contingently** *adv.* [L *contingere* (as COM-, *tangere* touch)]

continual /kən'tɪnjʊəl/ *adj.* constantly or frequently recurring; always happening. □□ **continually** *adv.* [ME f. OF *continuel* f. *continuer* (as CONTINUE)]

continuance /kən'tɪnjʊəns/ *n.* **1** a state of continuing in existence or operation. **2** the duration of an event or action. **3** *US Law* an adjournment. [ME f. OF (as CONTINUE)]

continuant /kən'tɪnjʊənt/ *n.* & *adj.* *Phonet.* —*n.* a speech sound in which the vocal tract is only partly closed, allowing the breath to pass through and the sound to be prolonged (as with *f*, *r*, *s*, *v*). —*adj.* of or relating to such a sound. [F *continuant* and L *continuare* (as CONTINUE)]

continuation /kənˌtɪnjʊ'eɪʃ(ə)n/ *n.* **1** the act or an instance of continuing; the process of being

b *but* d *dog* f *few* g *get* h *he* j *yes* k *cat* l *leg* m *man* n *no* p *pen* r *red* s *sit* t *top* v *voice*

continued. **2** a part that continues something else. **3** *Brit. Stock Exch.* the carrying over of an account to the next settling day. □**continuation day** *Stock Exch.* = *contango day*. [ME f. OF f. L *continuatio -onis* (as CONTINUE)]

continuative /kən'tɪnjʊətɪv/ *adj.* tending or serving to continue. [LL *continuativus* (as CONTINUATION)]

continue /kən'tɪnju:/ *v.* (**continues**, **continued**, **continuing**) **1** *tr.* (often foll. by verbal noun, or *to* + infin.) persist in, maintain, not stop (an action etc.). **2 a** *tr.* (also *absol.*) resume or prolong (a narrative, journey, etc.). **b** *intr.* recommence after a pause (*the concert will continue shortly*). **3** *tr.* be a sequel to. **4** *intr.* **a** remain in existence or unchanged. **b** (with compl.) remain in a specified state (*the weather continued fine*). **5** *tr. US Law* adjourn (proceedings). □□**continuable** *adj.* **continuer** *n.* [ME f. OF *continuer* f. L *continuare* make or be CONTINUOUS]

continuity /,kɒntɪ'nju:ɪtɪ/ *n.* (*pl.* -**ies**) **1 a** the state of being continuous. **b** an unbroken succession. **c** a logical sequence. **2** the detailed and self-consistent scenario of a film or broadcast. **3** the linking of broadcast items. □**continuity girl** (or **man**) the person responsible for agreement of detail between different sessions of filming. [F *continuité* f. L *continuitas -tatis* (as CONTINUOUS)]

continuo /kən'tɪnjʊəʊ/ *n.* (*pl.* -**os**) *Mus.* an accompaniment providing a bass line and harmonies which are indicated by figures, usu. played on a keyboard instrument. [*basso continuo* (It., = continuous bass)]

continuous /kən'tɪnjʊəs/ *adj.* **1** unbroken, uninterrupted, connected throughout in space or time. **2** *Gram.* = PROGRESSIVE. □**continuous assessment** the evaluation of a pupil's progress throughout a course of study, as well as or instead of by examination. **continuous creation** the creation of the universe or the matter in it regarded as a continuous process. **continuous stationery** a continuous ream of paper, usu. perforated to form single sheets. □□**continuously** *adv.* **continuousness** *n.* [L *continuus* uninterrupted f. *continēre* (as COM-, *tenēre* hold)]

continuum /kən'tɪnjʊəm/ *n.* (*pl.* **continua** /-jʊə/) anything seen as having a continuous, not discrete, structure (*space-time continuum*). [L, neut. of *continuus*: see CONTINUOUS]

contort /kən'tɔ:t/ *v.tr.* twist or force out of normal shape. [L *contorquēre contort-* (as COM-, *torquēre* twist)]

contortion /kən'tɔ:ʃ(ə)n/ *n.* **1** the act or process of twisting. **2** a twisted state, esp. of the face or body. [L *contortio* (as CONTORT)]

contortionist /kən'tɔ:ʃənɪst/ *n.* an entertainer who adopts contorted postures.

contour /'kɒntʊə(r)/ *n. & v.* —*n.* **1** an outline, esp. representing or bounding the shape or form of something. **2** the outline of a natural feature, e.g. a coast or mountain mass. **3** a line separating differently coloured parts of a design. —*v.tr.* **1** mark with contour lines. **2** carry (a road or railway) round the side of a hill. □**contour line** a line on a map joining points of equal altitude. **contour map** a map marked with contour lines. **contour ploughing** ploughing along lines of constant altitude to minimize soil erosion. [F f. It. *contorno* f. *contornare* draw in outline (as COM-, *tornare* turn)]

contra /'kɒntrə/ *n.* (*pl.* **contras**) a member of a counter-revolutionary guerrilla force in Nicaragua. [abbr. of Sp. *contrarevolucionario* counter-revolutionary]

contra- /'kɒntrə/ *comb. form* **1** against, opposite (*contradict*). **2** *Mus.* (of instruments, organ-stops, etc.) pitched an octave below (*contra-bassoon*). [L *contra* against]

contraband /'kɒntrə,bænd/ *n. & adj.* —*n.* **1** goods that have been smuggled, or imported or exported illegally. **2** prohibited trade; smuggling. **3** (in full

contraband of war) goods forbidden to be supplied by neutrals to belligerents. —*adj.* **1** forbidden to be imported or exported (at all or without payment of duty). **2** concerning traffic in contraband (*contraband trade*). □□**contrabandist** *n.* [Sp. *contrabanda* f. It. (as CONTRA-, *bando* proclamation)]

contrabass /'kɒntrə,beɪs/ *n. Mus.* = *double-bass.* [It. (*basso* BASS[1])]

contraception /,kɒntrə'sepʃ(ə)n/ *n.* the intentional prevention of pregnancy; the use of contraceptives. [CONTRA- + CONCEPTION]

contraceptive /,kɒntrə'septɪv/ *adj. & n.* —*adj.* preventing pregnancy. —*n.* a contraceptive device or drug.

contract *n. & v.* —*n.* /'kɒntrækt/ **1** a written or spoken agreement between two or more parties, intended to be enforceable by law. **2** a document recording this. **3** marriage regarded as a binding commitment. **4** *Bridge* etc. an undertaking to win the number of tricks bid. —*v.* /kən'trækt/ **1** *tr. & intr.* make or become smaller. **2 a** *intr.* (usu. foll. by *with*) make a contract. **b** *intr.* (usu. foll. by *for*, or *to* + infin.) enter formally into a business or legal arrangement. **c** *tr.* (often foll. by *out*) arrange (work) to be done by contract. **3** *tr.* catch or develop (a disease). **4** *tr.* form or develop (a friendship, habit, etc.). **5** *tr.* enter into (marriage). **6** *tr.* incur (a debt etc.). **7** *tr.* shorten (a word) by combination or elision. **8** *tr.* draw (one's muscles, brow, etc.) together. □**contract bridge** the most common form of bridge, in which only tricks bid and won count towards the game. **contract in** (or **out**) (also *refl.*) *Brit.* choose to be involved in (or withdraw or remain out of) a scheme or commitment. □□**contractive** *adj.* [earlier as adj., = contracted: OF, f. L *contractus* (as COM-, *trahere tract-* draw)]

contractable /kən'træktəb(ə)l/ *adj.* (of a disease) that can be contracted.

contractible /kən'træktɪb(ə)l/ *adj.* that can be shrunk or drawn together.

contractile /kən'træktaɪl/ *adj.* capable of or producing contraction. □□**contractility** /,kɒntræk'tɪlɪtɪ/ *n.*

contraction /kən'trækʃ(ə)n/ *n.* **1** the act of contracting. **2** *Med.* (usu. in *pl.*) shortening of the uterine muscles during childbirth. **3** shrinking, diminution. **4 a** a shortening of a word by combination or elision. **b** a contracted word or group of words. [F f. L *contractio -onis* (as CONTRACT)]

contractor /kən'træktə(r)/ *n.* a person who undertakes a contract, esp. to provide materials, conduct building operations, etc. [LL (as CONTRACT)]

contractual /kən'træktjʊəl/ *adj.* of or in the nature of a contract. □□**contractually** *adv.*

contradict /,kɒntrə'dɪkt/ *v.tr.* **1** deny or express the opposite of (a statement). **2** deny or express the opposite of a statement made by (a person). **3** be in opposition to or in conflict with (*new evidence contradicted our theory*). □□**contradictor** *n.* [L *contradicere contradict-* (as CONTRA-, *dicere* say)]

contradiction /,kɒntrə'dɪkʃ(ə)n/ *n.* **1 a** statement of the opposite; denial. **b** an instance of this. **2** inconsistency. □**contradiction in terms** a self-contradictory statement or group of words. [ME f. OF f. L *contradictio -onis* (as CONTRADICT)]

contradictory /,kɒntrə'dɪktərɪ/ *adj.* **1** expressing a denial or opposite statement. **2** (of statements etc.) mutually opposed or inconsistent. **3** (of a person) inclined to contradict. **4** *Logic* (of two propositions) so related that one and only one must be true. □□**contradictorily** *adv.* **contradictoriness** *n.* [ME f. LL *contradictorius* (as CONTRADICT)]

contradistinction /,kɒntrədɪ'stɪŋkʃ(ə)n/ *n.* a distinction made by contrasting.

contradistinguish /,kɒntrədɪ'stɪŋgwɪʃ/ *v.tr.* (usu. foll. by *from*) distinguish two things by contrasting them.

contraflow /'kɒntrə,fləʊ/ *n. Brit.* a flow (esp. of road traffic) alongside, and in a direction opposite to, an established or usual flow, esp. as a temporary or emergency arrangement.

contrail /'kɒntreɪl/ n. a condensation trail, esp. from an aircraft. [abbr.]

contraindicate /ˌkɒntrəˈɪndɪˌkeɪt/ v.tr. Med. act as an indication against (the use of a particular substance or treatment). □□ **contraindication** /-ˈkeɪʃ(ə)n/ n.

contralto /kənˈtræltəʊ/ n. (pl. **-os**) **1 a** the lowest female singing-voice. **b** a singer with this voice. **2** a part written for contralto. [It. (as CONTRA-, ALTO)]

contraposition /ˌkɒntrəpəˈzɪʃ(ə)n/ n. **1** opposition or contrast. **2** Logic conversion of a proposition from all A is B to all not-B is not-A. □□ **contrapositive** /-ˈpɒzɪtɪv/ adj. & n. [LL contrapositio (as CONTRA-, ponere posit- place)]

contraption /kənˈtræpʃ(ə)n/ n. often derog. or joc. a machine or device, esp. a strange or cumbersome one. [19th c.: perh. f. CONTRIVE, INVENTION: assoc. with TRAP[1]]

contrapuntal /ˌkɒntrəˈpʌnt(ə)l/ adj. Mus. of or in counterpoint. □□ **contrapuntally** adv. **contrapuntist** n. [It. contrappunto counterpoint]

contrariety /ˌkɒntrəˈraɪɪtɪ/ n. **1** opposition in nature, quality, or action. **2** disagreement, inconsistency. [ME f. OF contrarieté f. LL contrarietas -tatis (as CONTRARY)]

contrariwise /kənˈtreərɪˌwaɪz/ adv. **1** on the other hand. **2** in the opposite way. **3** perversely. [ME f. CONTRARY + -WISE]

contrary /'kɒntrərɪ/ adj., n., & adv. —adj. **1** (usu. foll. by to) opposed in nature or tendency. **2** /kənˈtreərɪ/ colloq. perverse, self-willed. **3** (of a wind) unfavourable, impeding. **4** mutually opposed. **5** opposite in position or direction. —n. (pl. **-ies**) (prec. by the) the opposite. —adv. (foll. by to) in opposition or contrast (contrary to expectations it rained). □**on the contrary** intensifying a denial of what has just been implied or stated. **to the contrary** to the opposite effect (can find no indication to the contrary). □□ **contrarily** /'kɒntrərɪlɪ/ (/kənˈtreərɪlɪ/ in sense 2 of adj.) adv. **contrariness** /'kɒntrərɪnɪs/ (/kənˈtreərɪnɪs/ in sense 2 of adj.) n. [ME f. AF contrarie, OF contraire, f. L contrarius f. contra against]

contrast n. & v. —n. /'kɒntrɑːst/ **1 a** a juxtaposition or comparison showing striking differences. **b** a difference so revealed. **2** (often foll. by to) a thing or person having qualities noticeably different from another. **3 a** the degree of difference between tones in a television picture or a photograph. **b** the change of apparent brightness or colour of an object caused by the juxtaposition of other objects. —v. /kənˈtrɑːst/ (often foll. by with) **1** tr. distinguish or set together so as to reveal a contrast. **2** intr. have or show a contrast. □□ **contrastingly** /kənˈtrɑːstɪŋlɪ/ adv. **contrastive** /kənˈtrɑːstɪv/ adj. [F contraste, contraster, f. It. contrasto f. med.L contrastare (as CONTRA-, stare stand)]

contrasty /'kɒntrɑːstɪ/ adj. (of photographic negatives or prints or of a television picture) showing a high degree of contrast.

contra-suggestible /ˌkɒntrəsəˈdʒestɪb(ə)l/ adj. Psychol. tending to respond to a suggestion by believing or doing the contrary.

contrate wheel /'kɒntreɪt/ n. = crown wheel. [med.L & Rmc contrata: see COUNTRY]

contravene /ˌkɒntrəˈviːn/ v.tr. **1** infringe (a law or code of conduct). **2** (of things) conflict with. □□ **contravener** n. [LL contravenire (as CONTRA-, venire vent- come)]

contravention /ˌkɒntrəˈvenʃ(ə)n/ n. **1** infringement. **2** an instance of this. □**in contravention of** infringing, violating (a law etc.). [F f. med.L contraventio (as CONTRAVENE)]

contretemps /'kɔːntrəˌtɑ̃/ n. **1** an awkward or unfortunate occurrence. **2** an unexpected mishap. [F]

contribute /kənˈtrɪbjuːt, disp. 'kɒntrɪˌbjuːt/ v. (often foll. by to) **1** tr. give (money, an idea, help, etc.) towards a common purpose (contributed £5 to the fund). **2** intr. help to bring about a result etc. (contributed to their downfall). **3** tr. (also absol.) supply (an article etc.) for publication with others in a journal etc. □□ **contributive** /kənˈtrɪb-/ adj. [L contribuere contribut- (as COM-, tribuere bestow)]

contribution /ˌkɒntrɪˈbjuːʃ(ə)n/ n. **1** the act of contributing. **2** something contributed, esp. money. **3** an article etc. contributed to a publication. [ME f. OF contribution or LL contributio (as CONTRIBUTE)]

contributor /kənˈtrɪbjʊtə(r)/ n. a person who contributes (esp. an article or literary work).

contributory /kənˈtrɪbjʊtərɪ/ adj. & n. —adj. **1** that contributes. **2** operated by means of contributions (contributory pension scheme). —n. Brit. Law a person liable to contribute towards the payment of a wound-up company's debts. □**contributory negligence** Law negligence on the part of the injured party through failure to take precautions against an accident. [med.L contributorius (as CONTRIBUTE)]

contrite /'kɒntraɪt, kənˈtraɪt/ adj. **1** completely penitent. **2** feeling remorse or penitence; affected by guilt. **3** (of an action) showing a contrite spirit. □□ **contritely** adv. **contriteness** n. [ME f. OF contrit f. L contritus bruised (as COM-, terere trit- rub)]

contrition /kənˈtrɪʃ(ə)n/ n. the state of being contrite; thorough penitence. [ME f. OF f. LL contritio -onis (as CONTRITE)]

contrivance /kənˈtraɪv(ə)ns/ n. **1** something contrived, esp. a mechanical device or a plan. **2** an act of contriving, esp. deceitfully. **3** inventive capacity.

contrive /kənˈtraɪv/ v.tr. **1** devise; plan or make resourcefully or with skill. **2** (often foll. by to + infin.) manage (contrived to make matters worse). □□ **contrivable** adj. **contriver** n. [ME f. OF controver find, imagine f. med.L contropare compare]

contrived /kənˈtraɪvd/ adj. planned so carefully as to seem unnatural; artificial, forced (the plot seemed contrived).

control /kənˈtrəʊl/ n. & v. —n. **1** the power of directing, command (under the control of). **2** the power of restraining, esp. self-restraint. **3** a means of restraint; a check. **4** (usu. in pl.) a means of regulating prices etc. **5** (usu. in pl.) switches and other devices by which a machine, esp. an aircraft or vehicle, is controlled (also attrib.: control panel; control room). **6 a** a place where something is controlled or verified. **b** a person or group that controls something. **7** a standard of comparison for checking the results of a survey or experiment. —v.tr. (**controlled**, **controlling**) **1** have control or command of; dominate. **2** exert control over; regulate. **3** hold in check; restrain (told him to control himself). **4** serve as control to. **5** check, verify. □**controlling interest** a means of determining the policy of a business etc., esp. by ownership of a majority of the stock. **control rod** a rod of neutron-absorbing material used to vary the output power of a nuclear reactor. **control tower** a tall building at an airport etc. from which air traffic is controlled. **in control** (often foll. by of) directing an activity. **out of control** no longer subject to containment, restraint, or guidance. **under control** being controlled; in order. □□ **controllable** adj. **controllability** /-ˈbɪlɪtɪ/ n. **controllably** adv. [ME f. AF contreroller keep a copy of a roll of accounts, f. med.L contrarotulare (as CONTRA-, rotulus ROLL n.): (n.) partic. f. F contrôle]

controller /kənˈtrəʊlə(r)/ n. **1** a person or thing that controls. **2** a person in charge of expenditure, esp. a steward or comptroller. □□ **controllership** n. [ME counterroller f. AF contrerollour (as CONTROL)]

controversial /ˌkɒntrəˈvɜːʃ(ə)l/ adj. **1** causing or subject to controversy. **2** of controversy. **3** given to controversy. □□ **controversialism** n.

controversialist *n.* **controversially** *adv.* [LL *controversialis* (as CONTROVERSY)]

controversy /ˈkɒntrəˌvɜːsɪ, disp. kənˈtrɒvəsɪ/ *n.* (*pl.* **-ies**) a prolonged argument or dispute, esp. when conducted publicly. [ME f. L *controversia* (as CONTROVERT)]

controvert /ˈkɒntrəˌvɜːt, -ˈvɜːt/ *v.tr.* **1** dispute, deny. **2** argue about; discuss. □□ **controvertible** *adj.* [orig. past part.; f. F *controvers(e)* f. L *controversus* (as CONTRA-, *vertere* *vers-* turn)]

contumacious /ˌkɒntjuːˈmeɪʃəs/ *adj.* insubordinate; stubbornly or wilfully disobedient, esp. to a court order. □□ **contumaciously** *adv.* [L *contumax*, perh. rel. to *tumēre* swell]

contumacy /ˈkɒntjʊməsɪ/ *n.* stubborn refusal to obey or comply. [L *contumacia* f. *contumax*: see CONTUMACIOUS]

contumelious /ˌkɒntjuːˈmiːlɪəs/ *adj.* reproachful, insulting, or insolent. □□ **contumeliously** *adv.* [ME f. OF *contumelieus* f. L *contumeliosus* (as CONTUMELY)]

contumely /ˈkɒntjuːmlɪ/ *n.* **1** insolent or reproachful language or treatment. **2** disgrace. [ME f. OF *contumelie* f. L *contumelia* (as COM-, *tumēre* swell)]

contuse /kənˈtjuːz/ *v.tr.* injure without breaking the skin; bruise. □□ **contusion** *n.* [L *contundere contus-* (as COM-, *tundere* thump)]

conundrum /kəˈnʌndrəm/ *n.* **1** a riddle, esp. one with a pun in its answer. **2** a hard or puzzling question. [16th c.: orig. unkn.]

conurbation /ˌkɒnɜːˈbeɪʃ(ə)n/ *n.* an extended urban area, esp. one consisting of several towns and merging suburbs. [CON- + L *urbs urbis* city + -ATION]

conure /kɒˈnjʊə(r)/ *n.* any medium-sized parrot of the genus *Pyrrhura*, with mainly green plumage and a long gradated tail. [mod.L *conurus* f. Gk *kōnos* cone + *oura* tail]

convalesce /ˌkɒnvəˈles/ *v.intr.* recover one's health after illness or medical treatment. [ME f. L *convalescere* (as COM-, *valēre* be well)]

convalescent /ˌkɒnvəˈles(ə)nt/ *adj.* & *n.* —*adj.* recovering from an illness. —*n.* a convalescent person. □□ **convalescence** *n.*

convection /kənˈvekʃ(ə)n/ *n.* **1** transference of heat in a gas or liquid by upward movement of the heated and less dense medium. **2** *Meteorol.* the transfer of heat by the upward flow of hot air or downward flow of cold air. □**convection current** circulation that results from convection. □□ **convectional** *adj.* **convective** *adj.* [LL *convectio* f. L *convehere convect-* (as COM-, *vehere vect-* carry)]

convector /kənˈvektə(r)/ *n.* a heating appliance that circulates warm air by convection.

convenance /ˈkɔ̃vəˌnɑːs/ *n.* (usu. in *pl.*) conventional propriety. [F f. *convenir* be fitting (as CONVENE)]

convene /kənˈviːn/ *v.* **1** *tr.* summon or arrange (a meeting etc.). **2** *intr.* assemble. **3** *tr.* summon (a person) before a tribunal. □□ **convenable** *adj.* **convener** *n.* **convenor** *n.* [ME f. L *convenire convent-* assemble, agree, fit (as COM-, *venire* come)]

convenience /kənˈviːnɪəns/ *n.* **1** the quality of being convenient; suitability. **2** freedom from difficulty or trouble; material advantage (*for convenience*). **3** an advantage (*a great convenience*). **4** a useful thing, esp. an installation or piece of equipment. **5** *Brit.* a lavatory, esp. a public one. □**at one's convenience** at a time or place that suits one. **at one's earliest convenience** as soon as one can. **convenience food** food, esp. complete meals, sold in convenient form and requiring very little preparation. **convenience store** *US* a large shop with extended opening hours. **make a convenience of** take advantage of (a person) insensitively. [ME f. L *convenientia* (as CONVENE)]

convenient /kənˈviːnɪənt/ *adj.* **1** (often foll. by *for*, *to*) **a** serving one's comfort or interests; easily accessible. **b** suitable. **c** free of trouble or difficulty. **2** available or occurring at a suitable time or place (*will try to find a convenient moment*). **3** well situated

for some purpose (*convenient for the shops*). □□ **conveniently** *adv.* [ME (as CONVENE)]

convent /ˈkɒnv(ə)nt, -vent/ *n.* **1** a religious community, esp. of nuns, under vows. **2** the premises occupied by this. **3** (in full **convent school**) a school attached to and run by a convent. [ME f. AF *covent*, OF *convent* f. L *conventus* assembly (as CONVENE)]

conventicle /kənˈventɪk(ə)l/ *n.* esp. *hist.* **1** a secret or unlawful religious meeting, esp. of dissenters. **2** a building used for this. [ME f. L *conventiculum* (place of) assembly, dimin. of *conventus* (as CONVENE)]

convention /kənˈvenʃ(ə)n/ *n.* **1 a** general agreement, esp. agreement on social behaviour etc. by implicit consent of the majority. **b** a custom or customary practice, esp. an artificial or formal one. **2 a** a formal assembly or conference for a common purpose. **b** *US* an assembly of the delegates of a political party to select candidates for office. **c** *hist.* a meeting of Parliament without a summons from the sovereign. **3 a** a formal agreement. **b** an agreement between States, esp. one less formal than a treaty. **4** *Cards* an accepted method of play (in leading, bidding, etc.) used to convey information to a partner. **5** the act of convening. [ME f. OF f. L *conventio -onis* (as CONVENE)]

conventional /kənˈvenʃ(ə)n(ə)l/ *adj.* **1** depending on or according with convention. **2** (of a person) attentive to social conventions. **3** usual; of agreed significance. **4** not spontaneous or sincere or original. **5** (of weapons or power) non-nuclear. **6** *Art* following tradition rather than nature. □□ **conventionalism** *n.* **conventionalist** *n.* **conventionality** /-ˈnælɪtɪ/ *n.* **conventionalize** *v.tr.* (also -**ise**). **conventionally** *adv.* [F *conventionnel* or LL *conventionalis* (as CONVENTION)]

conventioneer /kənˌvenʃəˈnɪə(r)/ *n.* *US* a person attending a convention.

conventual /kənˈventjʊəl/ *adj.* & *n.* —*adj.* **1** of or belonging to a convent. **2** of the less strict branch of the Franciscans, living in large convents. —*n.* **1** a member or inmate of a convent. **2** a conventual Franciscan. [ME f. med.L *conventualis* (as CONVENT)]

converge /kənˈvɜːdʒ/ *v.intr.* **1** come together as if to meet or join. **2** (of lines) tend to meet at a point. **3** (foll. by *on*, *upon*) approach from different directions. **4** *Math.* (of a series) approximate in the sum of its terms towards a definite limit. [LL *convergere* (as COM-, *vergere* incline)]

convergent /kənˈvɜːdʒ(ə)nt/ *adj.* **1** converging. **2** *Biol.* (of unrelated organisms) having the tendency to become similar while adapting to the same environment. **3** *Psychol.* (of thought) tending to reach only the most rational result. □□ **convergence** *n.* **convergency** *n.*

conversant /kənˈvɜːs(ə)nt, ˈkɒnvəs(ə)nt/ *adj.* (foll. by *with*) well experienced or acquainted with a subject, person, etc. □□ **conversance** *n.* **conversancy** *n.* [ME f. OF, pres. part. of *converser* CONVERSE[1]]

conversation /ˌkɒnvəˈseɪʃ(ə)n/ *n.* **1** the informal exchange of ideas by spoken words. **2** an instance of this. □**conversation piece** **1** a small genre painting of a group of figures. **2** a thing that serves as a topic of conversation because of its unusualness etc. **conversation stopper** *colloq.* an unexpected remark, esp. one that cannot readily be answered. [ME f. OF f. L *conversatio -onis* (as CONVERSE[1])]

conversational /ˌkɒnvəˈseɪʃən(ə)l/ *adj.* **1** of or in conversation. **2** fond of or good at conversation. **3** colloquial. □□ **conversationally** *adv.*

conversationalist /ˌkɒnvəˈseɪʃənəlɪst/ *n.* one who is good at or fond of conversing.

conversazione /ˌkɒnvəˌsætsɪˈəʊnɪ/ *n.* (*pl.* **conversazioni** or **conversazioni** *pronunc.* same) a social gathering held by a learned or art society. [It. f. L (as CONVERSATION)]

converse[1] *v.* & *n.* —*v.intr.* /kənˈvɜːs/ (often foll. by *with*) engage in conversation (*conversed with him about various subjects*). —*n.* /ˈkɒnvɜːs/ *archaic* conversation. □□ **converser** /kən'vɜːsə(r)/ n. [ME f. OF converser f. L conversari keep company (with), frequent. of converse (CONVERSE)]

converse² /'kɒnvɜːs/ adj. & n. —adj. opposite, contrary, reversed. —n. **1** something that is opposite or contrary. **2** a statement formed from another statement by the transposition of certain words, e.g. some philosophers are men from some men are philosophers. **3** Math. a theorem whose hypothesis and conclusion are the conclusion and hypothesis of another. □□ **conversely** /'kɒnvɜːslɪ, kən'vɜːslɪ/ adv. [L conversus, past part. of convertere (CONVERT)]

conversion /kən'vɜːʃ(ə)n/ n. **1 a** the act or an instance of converting or the process of being converted, esp. in belief or religion. **b** an instance of this. **2 a** an adaptation of a building for new purposes. **b** a converted building. **3** transposition, inversion. **4** Theol. the turning of sinners to God. **5** the transformation of fertile into fissile material in a nuclear reactor. **6** Rugby Football the scoring of points by a successful kick at goal after scoring a try. **7** Psychol. the change of an unconscious conflict into a physical disorder or disease. [ME f. OF f. L conversio -onis (as CONVERT)]

convert v. & n. —v. /kən'vɜːt/ **1** tr. (usu. foll. by into) change in form, character, or function. **2** tr. cause (a person) to change beliefs, opinion, party, etc. **3** tr. change (moneys, stocks, units in which a quantity is expressed, etc.) into others of a different kind. **4** tr. make structural alterations in (a building) to serve a new purpose. **5** tr. (also absol.) **a** Rugby Football score extra points from (a try) by a successful kick at goal. **b** Amer. Football complete (a touchdown) by kicking a goal or crossing the goal-line. **6** intr. be converted or convertible (the sofa converts into a bed). **7** tr. Logic interchange the terms of (a proposition). —n. /'kɒnvɜːt/ (often foll. by to) a person who has been converted to a different belief, opinion, etc. □ **convert to one's own use** wrongly make use of (another's property). [ME f. OF convertir ult. f. L convertere convers- turn about (as COM-, vertere turn)]

converter /kən'vɜːtə(r)/ n. (also **convertor**) **1** a person or thing that converts. **2** Electr. **a** an electrical apparatus for the interconversion of alternating current and direct current. **b** Electronics an apparatus for converting a signal from one frequency to another. **3** a reaction vessel used in making steel. □ **converter reactor** a nuclear reactor that converts fertile material into fissile material.

convertible /kən'vɜːtɪb(ə)l/ adj. & n. —adj. **1** that may be converted. **2** (of currency etc.) that may be converted into other forms, esp. into gold or US dollars. **3** (of a car) having a folding or detachable roof. **4** (of terms) synonymous. —n. a car with a folding or detachable roof. □□ **convertibility** /-'bɪlɪtɪ/ n. **convertibly** adv. [OF f. L convertibilis (as CONVERT)]

convex /'kɒnveks/ adj. having an outline or surface curved like the exterior of a circle or sphere (cf. CONCAVE). □□ **convexity** /-'veksɪtɪ/ n. **convexly** adv. [L convexus vaulted, arched]

convey /kən'veɪ/ v.tr. **1** transport or carry (goods, passengers, etc.). **2** communicate (an idea, meaning, etc.). **3** Law transfer the title to (property). **4** transmit (sound, smell, etc.). □□ **conveyable** adj. [ME f. OF conveier f. med.L conviare (as COM-, L via way)]

conveyance /kən'veɪəns/ n. **1 a** the act or process of carrying. **b** the communication (of ideas etc.). **c** transmission. **2 a** a means of transport; a vehicle. **3** Law **a** the transfer of property from one owner to another. **b** a document effecting this. □□ **conveyancer** n. (in sense 3). **conveyancing** n. (in sense 3).

conveyor /kən'veɪə(r)/ n. (also **conveyer**) a person or thing that conveys. □ **conveyor belt** an endless moving belt for conveying articles or materials, esp. in a factory.

convict v. & n. —v.tr. /kən'vɪkt/ **1** (often foll. by of) prove to be guilty (of a crime etc.). **2** declare guilty by the verdict of a jury or the decision of a judge. —n. /'kɒnvɪkt/ **1** a person found guilty of a criminal offence. **2** chiefly hist. a person serving a prison sentence, esp. in a penal colony. [ME f. L convincere convict- (as COM-, vincere conquer): noun f. obs. convict convicted]

conviction /kən'vɪkʃ(ə)n/ n. **1 a** the act or process of proving or finding guilty. **b** an instance of this (has two previous convictions). **2 a** the action or resulting state of being convinced. **b** a firm belief or opinion. **c** an act of convincing. [L convictio (as CONVICT)]

convince /kən'vɪns/ v.tr. **1** (often foll. by of, or that + clause) persuade (a person) to believe or realize. **2** (as **convinced** adj.) firmly persuaded (a convinced pacifist). □□ **convincer** n. **convincible** adj. [L (as CONVICT)]

convincing /kən'vɪnsɪŋ/ adj. **1** able to or such as to convince. **2** leaving no margin of doubt, substantial (a convincing victory). □□ **convincingly** adv.

convivial /kən'vɪvɪəl/ adj. **1** fond of good company; sociable and lively. **2** festive (a convivial atmosphere). □□ **conviviality** /-'ælɪtɪ/ n. **convivially** adv. [L convivialis f. convivium feast (as COM-, vivere live)]

convocation /ˌkɒnvə'keɪʃ(ə)n/ n. **1** the act of calling together. **2** a large formal gathering of people, esp.: **a** Brit. a provincial synod of the Anglican clergy of Canterbury or York. **b** Brit. a legislative or deliberative assembly of a university. □□ **convocational** adj. [ME f. L convocatio (as CONVOKE)]

convoke /kən'vəʊk/ v.tr. formal call (people) together for a meeting etc.; summon to assemble. [L convocare convocat- (as COM-, vocare call)]

convoluted /'kɒnvəˌluːtɪd/ adj. **1** coiled, twisted. **2** complex, intricate. □□ **convolutedly** adv. [past part. of convolute f. L convolutus (as COM-, volvere volut- roll)]

convolution /ˌkɒnvə'luːʃ(ə)n/ n. **1** coiling, twisting. **2** a coil or twist. **3** complexity. **4** a sinuous fold in the surface of the brain. □□ **convolutional** adj. [med.L convolutio (as CONVOLUTED)]

convolve /kən'vɒlv/ v.tr. & intr. (esp. as **convolved** adj.) roll together; coil up. [L convolvere (as CONVOLUTED)]

convolvulus /kən'vɒlvjʊləs/ n. any twining plant of the genus Convolvulus, with trumpet-shaped flowers, e.g. bindweed. [L]

convoy /'kɒnvɔɪ/ n. & v. —n. **1** a group of ships travelling together or under escort. **2** a supply of provisions etc. under escort. **3** a group of vehicles travelling on land together or under escort. **4** the act of travelling or moving in a group or under escort. —v.tr. **1** (of a warship) escort (a merchant or passenger vessel). **2** escort, esp. with armed force. [OF convoyer var. of conveier CONVEY]

convulsant /kən'vʌls(ə)nt/ adj. & n. Pharm. —adj. producing convulsions. —n. a drug that may produce convulsions. [F f. convulser (as CONVULSE)]

convulse /kən'vʌls/ v.tr. **1** (usu. in passive) affect with convulsions. **2** cause to laugh uncontrollably. **3** shake violently; agitate; disturb. [L convellere convuls- (as COM-, vellere pull)]

convulsion /kən'vʌlʃ(ə)n/ n. **1** (usu. in pl.) violent irregular motion of a limb or limbs or the body caused by involuntary contraction of muscles, esp. as a disorder of infants. **2** a violent natural disturbance, esp. an earthquake. **3** violent social or political agitation. **4** (in pl.) uncontrollable laughter. □□ **convulsionary** adj. [F convulsion or L convulsio (as CONVULSE)]

convulsive /kən'vʌlsɪv/ adj. **1** characterized by or affected with convulsions. **2** producing convulsions. □□ **convulsively** adv.

cony /'kəʊnɪ/ n. (also **coney**) (pl. **-ies** or **-eys**) **1 a** a rabbit. **b** its fur. **2** Bibl. a hyrax. [ME cuning(g) f. AF coning, OF conin, f. L cuniculus]

coo /kuː/ n., v., & int. —n. a soft murmuring sound

like that of a dove or pigeon. —*v.* (**coos, cooed**) **1** *intr.* make the sound of a coo. **2** *intr.* & *tr.* talk or say in a soft or amorous voice. —*int. Brit. sl.* expressing surprise or incredulity. □□ **cooingly** *adv.* [imit.]

cooee /ˈkuːiː/ *n.*, *int.*, & *v. colloq.* —*n.* & *int.* a sound used to attract attention, esp. at a distance. —*v.intr.* (**cooees, cooeed, cooeeing**) make this sound. □**within cooee** (or **a cooee**) **of** *Austral.* & *NZ colloq.* very near to. [imit. of a signal used by Australian Aboriginals and copied by settlers]

cook /kʊk/ *v.* & *n.* —*v.* **1** *tr.* prepare (food) by heating it. **2** *intr.* (of food) undergo cooking. **3** *tr. colloq.* falsify (accounts etc.); alter to produce a desired result. **4** *tr. sl.* ruin, spoil. **5** *tr.* (esp. as **cooked** *adj.*) *Brit. sl.* fatigue, exhaust. **6** *tr.* & *intr. US colloq.* do or proceed successfully. **7** *intr.* (as **be cooking**) *colloq.* be happening or about to happen (*went to find out what was cooking*). —*n.* a person who cooks, esp. professionally or in a specified way (*a good cook*). □**cook-chill 1** the process of cooking and re-frigerating food ready for reheating at a later time. **2** (*attrib.*) (of food) prepared in this way. **cook a person's goose** ruin a person's chances. **cook up** *colloq.* invent or concoct (a story, excuse, etc.). □□ **cookable** *adj.* & *n.* [OE *cōc* f. pop.L *cocus* for L *coquus*]

cookbook /ˈkʊkbʊk/ *n. US* a cookery book.

cooker /ˈkʊkə(r)/ *n.* **1 a** a container or device for cooking food. **b** *Brit.* an appliance powered by gas, electricity, etc., for cooking food. **2** *Brit.* a fruit etc. (esp. an apple) that is more suitable for cooking than for eating raw.

cookery /ˈkʊkərɪ/ *n.* (*pl.* **-ies**) **1** the art or practice of cooking. **2** *US* a place or establishment for cooking. □**cookery book** *Brit.* a book containing recipes and other information about cooking.

cookhouse /ˈkʊkhaʊs/ *n.* **1** a camp kitchen. **2** an outdoor kitchen in warm countries. **3** a ship's galley.

cookie /ˈkʊkɪ/ *n.* **1** *US* a small sweet biscuit. **2** *US sl.* a person. **3** *Sc.* a plain bun. □**the way the cookie crumbles** *US colloq.* how things turn out; the un-alterable state of affairs. [Du. *koekje* dimin. of *koek* cake]

cooking /ˈkʊkɪŋ/ *n.* **1** the art or process by which food is cooked. **2** (*attrib.*) suitable for or used in cooking (*cooking apple*; *cooking utensils*).

cookout /ˈkʊkaʊt/ *n. US* a gathering with an open-air cooked meal; a barbecue.

cookshop /ˈkʊkʃɒp/ *n. NZ* the kitchen of a sheep-station.

cookware /ˈkʊkweə(r)/ *n.* utensils for cooking, esp. dishes, pans, etc.

cool /kuːl/ *adj.*, *n.*, & *v.* —*adj.* **1** of or at a fairly low temperature, fairly cold (*a cool day*; *a cool bath*). **2** suggesting or achieving coolness (*cool colours*; *cool clothes*). **3** calm, unexcited. **4** lacking zeal or enthu-siasm. **5** unfriendly; lacking cordiality (*got a cool reception*). **6** (of jazz playing) restrained, relaxed. **7** calmly audacious (*a cool customer*). **8** (prec. by *a*) *colloq.* at least; not less than (*cost me a cool thousand*). **9** *sl.* esp. *US* excellent, marvellous. —*n.* **1** coolness. **2** cool air; a cool place. **3** *sl.* calmness, composure (*keep one's cool*; *lose one's cool*). —*v.tr.* & *intr.* (often foll. by *down, off*) make or become cool. □**cool-bag** (or **-box**) an insulated container for keeping food cool. **cool-headed** not easily excited. **cool one's heels** see HEEL[1]. **cooling-off period** an interval to allow for a change of mind before commitment to action. **cooling tower** a tall struc-ture for cooling hot water before reuse, esp. in industry. **cool it** *sl.* relax, calm down. □□ **coolish** *adj.* **coolly** /ˈkuːllɪ/ *adv.* **coolness** *n.* [OE *cōl, cōlian*, f. Gmc: cf. COLD]

coolabah /ˈkuːlə,bɑː/ *n.* (also **coolibah** /-lɪ,bɑː/) *Aus-tral.* any of various gum-trees, esp. *Eucalyptus mi-crotheca*. [Aboriginal]

coolant /ˈkuːlənt/ *n.* **1** a cooling agent, esp. fluid, to remove heat from an engine, nuclear reactor, etc. **2** a fluid used to lessen the friction of a cutting tool. [COOL + -ANT after *lubricant*]

cooler /ˈkuːlə(r)/ *n.* **1** a vessel in which a thing is cooled. **2** *US* a refrigerator. **3** a long drink, esp. a spritzer. **4** *sl.* prison or a prison cell.

coolibah var. of COOLABAH.

coolie /ˈkuːlɪ/ *n.* (also **cooly**) (*pl.* **-ies**) an unskilled native labourer in Eastern countries. □**coolie hat** a broad conical hat as worn by coolies. [perh. f. *Kulī*, an aboriginal tribe of Gujarat, India]

coomb /kuːm/ *n.* (also **combe**) *Brit.* **1** a valley or hollow on the side of a hill. **2** a short valley running up from the coast. [OE *cumb*: cf. CWM]

coon /kuːn/ *n.* **1** *US* a racoon. **2** *sl. offens.* a Black. [abbr.]

coon-can /kuːnˈkæn/ *n.* a simple card-game like rummy (orig. Mexican). [Sp. *con quién* with whom?]

coonskin /ˈkuːnskɪn/ *n.* **1** the skin of a racoon. **2** a cap etc. made of this.

coop /kuːp/ *n.* & *v.* —*n.* **1** a cage placed over sitting or fattening fowls. **2** a fowl-run. **3** a small place of confinement, esp. a prison. **4** *Brit.* a basket used in catching fish. —*v.tr.* **1** put or keep (a fowl) in a coop. **2** (often foll. by *up, in*) confine (a person) in a small space. [ME *cupe* basket f. MDu., MLG *kūpe*, ult. f. L *cupa* cask]

co-op /ˈkəʊɒp/ *n. colloq.* **1** *Brit.* a cooperative society or shop. **2** a cooperative business or enterprise. [abbr.]

cooper /ˈkuːpə(r)/ *n.* & *v.* —*n.* a maker or repairer of casks, barrels, etc. —*v.tr.* make or repair (a cask). [ME f. MDu., MLG *kūper* f. *kūpe* COOP]

cooperage /ˈkuːpərɪdʒ/ *n.* **1** the work or es-tablishment of a cooper. **2** money payable for a cooper's work.

cooperate /kəʊˈɒpəˌreɪt/ *v.intr.* (also **co-operate**) **1** (often foll. by *with*) work or act together. **2** (of things) concur in producing an effect. □□ **cooperant** *adj.* **cooperator** *n.* [eccl.L *cooperari* (as CO-, *operari* f. *opus operis* work)]

cooperation /kəʊ,ɒpəˈreɪʃ(ə)n/ *n.* (also **co-operation**) **1** working together to the same end. **2** *Econ.* the formation and operation of cooperatives. [ME f. L *cooperatio* (as COOPERATE): partly through F *coopération*]

cooperative /kəʊˈɒpərətɪv/ *adj.* & *n.* (also **co-operative**) —*adj.* **1** of or affording cooperation. **2** willing to cooperate. **3** *Econ.* (of a farm, shop, or other business, or a society owning such businesses) owned and run jointly by its members, with profits shared among them. —*n.* a cooperative farm or society or business. □□ **cooperatively** *adv.* **cooperativeness** *n.* [LL *cooperativus* (as COOPERATE)]

co-opt /kəʊˈɒpt/ *v.tr.* appoint to membership of a body by invitation of the existing members. □□ **co-optation** /-ˈteɪʃ(ə)n/ *n.* **co-option** *n.* **co-optive** *adj.* [L *cooptare* (as CO-, *optare* choose)]

coordinate *v.*, *adj.*, & *n.* (also **co-ordinate**) —*v.* /kəʊˈɔːdɪˌneɪt/ **1** *tr.* bring (various parts, movements, etc.) into a proper or required relation to ensure harmony or effective operation etc. **2** *intr.* work or act together effectively. **3** *tr.* make coordinate. —*adj.* /kəʊˈɔːdɪnət/ **1** equal in rank or importance. **2** in which the parts are coordinated; involving co-ordination. **3** *Gram.* (of parts of a compound sen-tence) equal in status (cf. SUBORDINATE). **4** *Chem.* denoting a type of covalent bond in which one atom provides both the shared electrons. —*n.* /kəʊˈɔːdɪnət/ **1** *Math.* each of a system of magnitudes used to fix the position of a point, line, or plane. **2** a person or thing equal in rank or importance. **3** (in *pl.*) matching items of clothing. □□ **coordinately** /-nətlɪ/ *adv.* **coordination** /-ˈneɪʃ(ə)n/ *n.* **coordinative** /-,neɪtɪv/ *adj.* **coordinator** /-,neɪtə(r)/ *n.* [CO- + L *ordinare* *ordinat-* f. *ordo -inis* order]

coot /kuːt/ *n.* **1** any black aquatic bird of the genus *Fulica*, esp. *F. atra* with the upper mandible extended backwards to form a white plate on the forehead. **2** *colloq.* a stupid person. [ME, prob. f. LG]

cootie /'ku:tɪ/ *n. sl.* a body louse. [perh. f. Malay *kutu* a biting parasite]

cop¹ /kɒp/ *n. & v. sl.* —*n.* **1** a policeman. **2** *Brit.* a capture or arrest (*it's a fair cop*). —*v.tr.* (**copped, copping**) **1** catch or arrest (an offender). **2** receive, suffer. **3** take, seize. □**cop it 1** get into trouble; be punished. **2** be killed. **cop out 1** withdraw; give up an attempt. **2** go back on a promise. **3** escape. **cop-out** *n.* **1** a cowardly or feeble evasion. **2** an escape; a way of escape. **cop-shop** a police station. **not much** (or **no**) **cop** *Brit.* of little or no value or use. [perh. f. obs. *cap* arrest f. OF *caper* seize f. L *capere*: (n.) cf. COPPER²]

cop² /kɒp/ *n.* (in spinning) a conical ball of thread wound on a spindle. [OE *cop* summit]

copacetic /ˌkəʊpə'setɪk, -'si:tɪk/ *adj. US sl.* excellent; in good order. [20th c.: orig. unkn.]

copaiba /kə'paɪbə/ *n.* an aromatic oil or resin from any plant of the genus *Copaifera*, used in medicine and perfumery. [Sp. & Port. f. Guarani *cupauba*]

copal /'kəʊp(ə)l/ *n.* a resin from any of various tropical trees, used for varnish. [Sp. f. Aztec *copalli* incense]

copartner /kəʊ'pɑ:tnə(r)/ *n.* a partner or associate, esp. when sharing equally. □□**copartnership** *n.*

cope¹ /kəʊp/ *v.intr.* **1** (foll. by *with*) deal effectively or contend successfully with a person or task. **2** manage successfully; deal with a situation or problem (*found they could no longer cope*). [ME f. OF *coper, colper* f. *cop, colp* blow f. med.L *colpus* f. L *colaphus* f. Gk *kolaphos* blow with the fist]

cope² /kəʊp/ *n. & v.* —*n.* **1** *Eccl.* a long cloaklike vestment worn by a priest or bishop in ceremonies and processions. **2** esp. *poet.* a covering compared with a cope. —*v.tr.* cover with a cope or coping. [ME ult. f. LL *cappa* CAP, CAPE¹]

copeck /'kəʊpek, 'kɒpek/ *n.* (also **kopeck, kopek**) a Russian coin and monetary unit worth one-hundredth of a rouble. [Russ. *kopeĭka* dimin. of *kop'ë* lance (from the figure of Ivan IV bearing a lance instead of a sword in 1535)]

copepod /'kəʊpɪˌpɒd/ *n.* any small aquatic crustacean of the class Copepoda, many of which form the minute components of plankton. [Gk *kōpē* oar-handle + *pous podos* foot]

coper /'kəʊpə(r)/ *n.* a horse-dealer. [obs. *cope* buy, f. MDu., MLG *kōpen,* G *kaufen:* rel. to CHEAP]

Copernican system /kə'pɜ:nɪkən/ *n.* (also **Copernican theory**) *Astron.* the theory that the planets (including the earth) move round the sun (cf. *Ptolemaic system*). [*Copernicus* latinized f. M. *Kopernik,* Polish astronomer d. 1543]

copestone /'kəʊpstəʊn/ *n.* **1** = *coping-stone.* **2** a finishing touch. [COPE² + STONE]

copiable /'kɒpɪəb(ə)l/ *adj.* that can or may be copied.

copier /'kɒpɪə(r)/ *n.* a machine or person that copies (esp. documents).

copilot /'kəʊˌpaɪlət/ *n.* a second pilot in an aircraft.

coping /'kəʊpɪŋ/ *n.* the top (usu. sloping) course of masonry in a wall or parapet. □**coping-stone** a stone used in a coping.

coping saw /'kəʊpɪŋ/ *n.* a D-shaped saw for cutting curves in wood. [*cope* cut wood f. OF *coper:* see COPE¹]

copious /'kəʊpɪəs/ *adj.* **1** abundant, plentiful. **2** producing much. **3** providing much information. **4** profuse in speech. □□**copiously** *adv.* **copiousness** *n.* [ME f. OF *copieux* or f. L *copiosus* f. *copia* plenty]

copita /kə'pi:tə/ *n.* **1** a tulip-shaped sherry-glass. **2** a glass of sherry. [Sp., dimin. of *copa* cup]

coplanar /kəʊ'pleɪnə(r)/ *adj. Geom.* in the same plane. □□**coplanarity** /-plə'nærɪtɪ/ *n.*

copolymer /kəʊ'pɒlɪmə(r)/ *n. Chem.* a polymer with units of more than one kind. □□**copolymerize** *v.tr.* & *intr.* (also **-ise**).

copper¹ /'kɒpə(r)/ *n., adj., & v.* —*n.* **1** *Chem.* a

malleable red-brown metallic element of the transition series occurring naturally esp. in cuprite and malachite, and used esp. for electrical cables and apparatus. ¶ Symb.: **Cu**. **2** a bronze coin. **3** a large metal vessel for boiling esp. laundry. **4** any of various butterflies with copper-coloured wings. —*adj.* made of or coloured like copper. —*v.tr.* cover (a ship's bottom, a pan, etc.) with copper. □**copper beech** a variety of beech with copper-coloured leaves. **copper belt** a copper-mining area of Central Africa. **copper-bit** a soldering tool pointed with copper. **copper-bottomed 1** having a bottom sheathed with copper (esp. of a ship or pan). **2** genuine or reliable (esp. financially). **copper pyrites** a double sulphide of copper and iron: also called CHALCOPYRITE. **copper sulphate** a blue crystalline solid used in electroplating, textile dyeing, etc. **copper vitriol** copper sulphate. [OE *copor, coper,* ult. f. L *cyprium aes* Cyprus metal]

copper² /'kɒpə(r)/ *n. Brit. sl.* a policeman. [COP¹ + ER¹]

copperas /'kɒpərəs/ *n.* green iron-sulphate crystals. [ME *coperose* f. OF *couperose* f. med.L *cup(e)rosa:* perh. orig. *aqua cuprosa* copper water]

copperhead /'kɒpəˌhed/ *n.* **1** a venomous viper, *Agkistrodon contortrix,* native to N. America. **2** a venomous cobra, *Denisonia superba,* native to Australia.

copperplate /'kɒpəˌpleɪt/ *n. & adj.* —*n.* **1 a** a polished copper plate for engraving or etching. **b** a print made from this. **2** an ornate style of handwriting resembling that orig. used in engravings. —*adj.* of or in copperplate writing.

coppersmith /'kɒpəsmɪθ/ *n.* a person who works in copper.

coppery /'kɒpərɪ/ *adj.* of or like copper, esp. in colour.

coppice /'kɒpɪs/ *n. & v.* —*n.* an area of undergrowth and small trees, grown for periodic cutting. —*v.tr.* cut back (young trees) periodically to stimulate growth of shoots. □□**coppiced** *adj.* [OF *copeiz* ult. f. med.L *colpus* blow: see COPE¹]

copra /'kɒprə/ *n.* the dried kernels of the coconut. [Port. f. Malayalam *koppara* coconut]

co-precipitation /ˌkəʊprɪˌsɪpɪ'teɪʃ(ə)n/ *n. Chem.* the simultaneous precipitation of more than one compound from a solution.

copro- /'kɒprəʊ/ *comb. form* dung, faeces. [Gk *kopros* dung]

co-production /ˌkəʊprə'dʌkʃ(ə)n/ *n.* a production of a play, broadcast, etc., jointly by more than one company.

coprolite /'kɒprəˌlaɪt/ *n. Archaeol.* fossil dung or a piece of it.

coprophagous /kɒ'prɒfəgəs/ *adj. Zool.* dung-eating. [COPRO-]

coprophilia /ˌkɒprə'fɪlɪə/ *n.* an abnormal interest in faeces and defecation.

coprosma /kə'prɒzmə/ *n.* any small evergreen plant of the genus *Coprosma,* native to Australasia. [mod.L f. Gk *kopros* dung + *osmē* smell]

copse /kɒps/ *n.* **1** = COPPICE. **2** (in general use) a small wood. □□**copsy** *adj.* [shortened f. COPPICE]

copsewood /'kɒpswʊd/ *n.* undergrowth.

Copt /kɒpt/ *n.* **1** a native Egyptian in the Hellenistic and Roman periods. **2** a native Christian of the independent Egyptian Church. [F *Copte* or mod.L *Coptus* f. Arab. *al-ḳibṭ, al-ḳubṭ* Copts f. Coptic *Gyptios* f. Gk *Aiguptios* Egyptian]

Coptic /'kɒptɪk/ *n. & adj.* —*n.* the language of the Copts, now used only in the Coptic Church. —*adj.* of or relating to the Copts.

copula /'kɒpjʊlə/ *n.* (*pl.* **copulas**) *Logic & Gram.* a connecting word, esp. a part of the verb *be* connecting a subject and predicate. □□**copular** *adj.* [L (as CO-, *apere* fasten)]

copulate /'kɒpjʊˌleɪt/ *v.intr.* (often foll. by *with*) have sexual intercourse. □□ **copulatory** *adj*. [L *copulare* fasten together (as COPULA)]

copulation /ˌkɒpjʊˈleɪʃ(ə)n/ *n*. **1** sexual union. **2** a grammatical or logical connection. [ME f. OF f. L *copulatio* (as COPULATE)]

copulative /ˈkɒpjʊlətɪv/ *adj*. **1** serving to connect. **2** *Gram*. **a** (of a word) that connects words or clauses linked in sense (cf. DISJUNCTIVE). **b** connecting a subject and predicate. **3** relating to sexual union. □□ **copulatively** *adv*. [ME f. OF *copulatif -ive* or LL *copulativus* (as COPULATE)]

copy /ˈkɒpɪ/ *n. & v.* —*n*. (*pl*. **-ies**) **1** a thing made to imitate or be identical to another. **2** a single specimen of a publication or issue (*ordered twenty copies*). **3** a matter to be printed. **b** material for a newspaper or magazine article (*scandals make good copy*). **c** the text of an advertisement. **4 a** a model to be copied. **b** a page written after a model (of penmanship). —*v*. (**-ies, -ied**) **1** *tr*. **a** make a copy of. **b** (often foll. by *out*) transcribe. **2** *intr*. make a copy, esp. clandestinely. **3** *tr*. (foll. by *to*) send a copy of (a letter) to a third party. □ **copy-edit** edit (copy) for printing. **copy editor** a person who edits copy for printing. **copy-typist** a person who makes typewritten transcripts of documents. [ME f. OF *copie, copier*, ult. f. L *copia* abundance (in med.L = transcript)]

copybook /ˈkɒpɪˌbʊk/ *n*. **1** a book containing models of handwriting for learners to imitate. **2** (*attrib*.) **a** tritely conventional. **b** accurate, exemplary.

copycat /ˈkɒpɪˌkæt/ *n. colloq.* (esp. as a child's word) a person who copies another, esp. slavishly.

copydesk /ˈkɒpɪˌdesk/ *n*. the desk at which copy is edited for printing.

copyhold /ˈkɒpɪˌhəʊld/ *n. Brit. hist.* **1** tenure of land based on manorial records. **2** land held in this way. □□ **copyholder** *n*.

copyist /ˈkɒpɪɪst/ *n*. **1** a person who makes (esp. written) copies. **2** an imitator. [earlier *copist* f. F *copiste* or med.L *copista* (as COPY)]

copyreader /ˈkɒpɪˌriːdə(r)/ *n*. a person who reads and edits copy for a newspaper or book. □□ **copyread** *v.tr.*

copyright /ˈkɒpɪˌraɪt/ *n., adj., & v.* —*n*. the exclusive legal right granted for a specified period to an author, designer, etc., or another appointed person, to print, publish, perform, film, or record original literary, artistic, or musical material. —*adj*. (of such material) protected by copyright. —*v.tr*. secure copyright for (material). □ **copyright library** *Brit.* a library entitled to a free copy of each book published in the UK.

copywriter /ˈkɒpɪˌraɪtə(r)/ *n*. a person who writes or prepares copy (esp. of advertising material) for publication. □□ **copywriting** *n*.

coq au vin /ˌkɒk əʊ ˈvæ̃/ *n*. a casserole of chicken pieces cooked in wine. [F]

coquetry /ˈkɒkɪtrɪ, ˈkəʊk-/ *n*. (*pl*. **-ies**) **1** coquettish behaviour. **2** a coquettish act. **3** trifling with serious matters. [F *coquetterie* f. *coqueter* (as COQUETTE)]

coquette /kɒˈket, kəˈket/ *n*. **1** a woman who flirts. **2** any crested humming-bird of the genus *Lophornis*. □□ **coquettish** *adj*. **coquettishly** *adv*. **coquettishness** *n*. [F, fem. of *coquet* wanton, dimin. of *coq* cock]

coquina /kəˈkiːnə/ *n. US* a soft limestone of broken shells, used in road-making. [Sp., = cockle]

coquito /kəˈkiːtəʊ/ *n*. (*pl*. **-os**) a palm-tree, *Jubaea chilensis*, native to Chile, yielding honey from its sap, and fibre. [Sp., dimin. of *coco* coconut]

Cor. *abbr.* **1** Corinthians (New Testament). **2** *US* corner.

cor /kɔː(r)/ *int. Brit. sl.* expressing surprise, alarm, exasperation, etc. □ **cor blimey** see BLIMEY. [corrupt. of *God*]

cor- /kər/ *prefix* assim. form of COM- before *r*.

coracle /ˈkɒrək(ə)l/ *n. Brit.* a small boat of wickerwork covered with watertight material, used on Welsh and Irish lakes and rivers. [Welsh *corwgl* (*corwg* = Ir. *currach* boat: cf. CURRACH)]

coracoid /ˈkɒrəˌkɔɪd/ *n*. (in full **coracoid process**) a short projection from the shoulder-blade in vertebrates. [mod.L *coracoides* f. Gk *korakoeidēs* raven-like f. *korax -akos* raven]

coral /ˈkɒr(ə)l/ *n. & adj.* —*n*. **1 a** a hard red, pink, or white calcareous substance secreted by various marine polyps for support and habitation. **b** any of these usu. colonial organisms. **2** the unimpregnated roe of a lobster or scallop. —*adj*. **1** like coral, esp. in colour. **2** made of coral. □ **coral island** (or **reef**) one formed by the growth of coral. **coral rag** limestone containing beds of petrified corals. **coral-snake** any of various brightly coloured poisonous snakes, esp. *Micrurus nigrocinctus*, native to Central America. [ME f. OF f. L *corallum* f. Gk *korallion*, prob. of Semitic orig.]

coralline /ˈkɒrəˌlaɪn/ *n. & adj.* —*n*. **1** any seaweed of the genus *Corallina* having a calcareous jointed stem. **2** (in general use) the name of various plantlike compound organisms. —*adj*. **1** coral-red. **2** of or like coral. [F *corallin* & It. *corallina* f. LL *corallinus* (as CORAL)]

corallite /ˈkɒrəˌlaɪt/ *n*. **1** the coral skeleton of a marine polyp. **2** fossil coral. [L *corallum* CORAL]

coralloid /ˈkɒrəˌlɔɪd/ *adj. & n.* —*adj*. like or akin to coral. —*n*. a coralloid organism.

coram populo /ˌkɔːrəm ˈpɒpjʊˌləʊ/ *adv*. in public. [L, = in the presence of the people]

cor anglais /kɔːr ˈɒŋgleɪ, ɑ̃ˈgleɪ/ *n*. (*pl*. **cors anglais** *pronunc.* same) *Mus.* **1** an alto woodwind instrument of the oboe family. **2** its player. **3** an organ stop with the quality of a cor anglais. [F, = English horn]

corbel /ˈkɔːb(ə)l/ *n. & v. Archit.* —*n*. **1** a projection of stone, timber, etc., jutting out from a wall to support a weight. **2** a short timber laid longitudinally under a beam to help support it. —*v.tr. & intr.* (**corbelled**, **corbelling**; *US* **corbeled**, **corbeling**) (foll. by *out*, *off*) support or project on corbels. □ **corbel-table** a projecting course resting on corbels. [ME f. OF, dimin. of *corp*: see CORBIE]

corbie /ˈkɔːbɪ/ *n. Sc.* **1** a raven. **2** a carrion crow. □ **corbie-steps** the steplike projections on the sloping sides of a gable. [ME f. OF *corb, corp* f. L *corvus* crow]

cord /kɔːd/ *n. & v.* —*n*. **1 a** long thin flexible material made from several twisted strands. **b** a piece of this. **2** *Anat.* a structure in the body resembling a cord (*spinal cord*). **3 a** ribbed fabric, esp. corduroy. **b** (in *pl.*) corduroy trousers. **c** a cordlike rib on fabric. **4** an electric flex. **5** a measure of cut wood (usu. 128 cu.ft., 3.6 cubic metres). **6** a moral or emotional tie (*cords of affection; fourfold cord of evidence*). —*v.tr*. **1** fasten or bind with cord. **2** (as **corded** *adj*.) **a** (of cloth) ribbed. **b** provided with cords. **c** (of muscles) standing out like taut cords. □□ **cordlike** *adj*. [ME f. OF *corde* f. L *chorda* f. Gk *khordē* gut, string of musical instrument]

cordage /ˈkɔːdɪdʒ/ *n*. cords or ropes, esp. in the rigging of a ship. [ME f. F (as CORD)]

cordate /ˈkɔːdeɪt/ *adj*. heart-shaped. [mod.L *cordatus* f. L *cor cordis* heart]

cordelier /ˌkɔːdɪˈlɪə(r)/ *n*. a Franciscan friar of the strict rule (wearing a knotted cord round the waist). [ME f. OF f. *cordele* dimin. of *corde* CORD]

cordial /ˈkɔːdɪəl/ *adj. & n.* —*adj*. **1** heartfelt, sincere. **2** warm, friendly. —*n*. **1** a fruit-flavoured drink. **2** a comforting or pleasant-tasting medicine. □□ **cordiality** /-ˈælɪtɪ/ *n*. **cordially** *adv*. [ME f. med.L *cordialis* f. L *cor cordis* heart]

cordillera /ˌkɔːdɪˈljeərə/ *n*. a system or group of usu. parallel mountain ranges together with intervening plateaux etc., esp. of the Andes and in Central America and Mexico. [Sp. f. *cordilla* dimin. of *cuerda* CORD]

cordite /ˈkɔːdaɪt/ *n*. a smokeless explosive made from

cellulose nitrate and nitroglycerine. [CORD (from its appearance) + -ITE¹]

cordless /'kɔːdlɪs/ *adj.* (of an electrical appliance, telephone, etc.) working from an internal source of energy etc. (esp. a battery) and without a connection to a mains supply or central unit.

cordon /'kɔːd(ə)n/ *n. & v.* —*n.* 1 a line or circle of police, soldiers, guards, etc., esp. preventing access to or from an area. 2 a an ornamental cord or braid. b the ribbon of a knightly order. 3 a fruit-tree trained to grow as a single stem. 4 *Archit.* a string-course. —*v.tr.* (often foll. by *off*) enclose or separate with a cordon of police etc. [It. *cordone* augmentative of *corda* CORD, & F *cordon* (as CORD)]

cordon bleu /ˌkɔːdɒn 'bləː, ˌkɔːdɔ̃/ *adj. & n. Cookery* —*adj.* of the highest class. —*n.* a cook of this class. [F, = blue ribbon]

cordon sanitaire /ˌkɔːdɒn ˌsænɪ'teə(r)/ *n.* 1 a guarded line between infected and uninfected districts. 2 any measure designed to prevent communication or the spread of undesirable influences.

cordovan /'kɔːdəv(ə)n/ *n.* a kind of soft leather. [Sp. *cordovan* of Cordova (Cordoba) where it was orig. made]

corduroy /'kɔːdərɔɪ, -djʊrɔɪ/ *n.* 1 a thick cotton fabric with velvety ribs. 2 (in *pl.*) corduroy trousers. □**corduroy road** a road made of tree-trunks laid across a swamp. [18th c.: prob. f. CORD ribbed fabric + obs. *duroy* coarse woollen fabric]

cordwainer /'kɔːdˌweɪnə(r)/ *n. Brit. archaic* a shoe-maker (usu. in names of guilds etc.). [obs. *cordwain* CORDOVAN]

cordwood /'kɔːdwʊd/ *n.* wood that is or can easily be measured in cords.

CORE *abbr. US* Congress of Racial Equality.

core /kɔː(r)/ *n. & v.* —*n.* 1 the horny central part of various fruits, containing the seeds. 2 a the central or most important part of anything (also *attrib.*: *core curriculum*). b the central part, of different character from the surroundings. 3 the central region of the earth. 4 the central part of a nuclear reactor, containing the fissile material. 5 a magnetic structural unit in a computer, storing one bit of data (see BIT⁴). 6 the inner strand of an electric cable, rope, etc. 7 a piece of soft iron forming the centre of an electromagnet or an induction coil. 8 an internal mould filling a space to be left hollow in a casting. 9 the central part cut out (esp. of rock etc. in boring). 10 *Archaeol.* a piece of flint from which flakes or blades have been removed. —*v.tr.* remove the core from. □**core memory** *Computing* the memory of a computer consisting of many cores. **core time** (in a flexitime system) the central part of the working day, when all employees must be present. □□ **corer** *n.* [ME: orig. unkn.]

corelation var. of CORRELATION.

co-religionist /ˌkəʊrɪ'lɪdʒənɪst/ *n.* (*US* **coreligionist**) an adherent of the same religion.

corella /kə'relə/ *n. Austral.* either of two small white cockatoos, *Cacatua tenuirostris* or *C. sanguinea*. [app. Latinized f. Aboriginal *ca-rall*]

coreopsis /ˌkɒrɪ'ɒpsɪs/ *n.* any composite plant of the genus *Coreopsis*, having rayed usu. yellow flowers. [mod.L f. Gk *koris* bug + *opsis* appearance, with ref. to the shape of the seed]

co-respondent /ˌkəʊrɪ'spɒnd(ə)nt/ *n.* (*US* **corespondent**) a person cited in a divorce case as having committed adultery with the respondent.

corf /kɔːf/ *n.* (*pl.* **corves** /kɔːvz/) *Brit.* 1 a basket in which fish are kept alive in the water. 2 a small wagon, formerly a large basket, used in mining. [MDu., MLG *korf*, OHG *chorp*, *korb* f. L *corbis* basket]

corgi /'kɔːgɪ/ *n.* (*pl.* **corgis**) (in full **Welsh corgi**) 1 a dog of a short-legged breed with foxlike head. 2 this breed. [Welsh f. *cor* dwarf + *ci* dog]

coriaceous /ˌkɒrɪ'eɪʃəs/ *adj.* like leather; leathery. [LL *coriaceus* f. *corium* leather]

coriander /ˌkɒrɪ'ændə(r)/ *n.* 1 a plant, *Coriandrum*

sativum, with leaves used for flavouring and small round aromatic fruits. 2 (also **coriander seed**) the dried fruit used for flavouring curries etc. [ME f. OF *coriandre* f. L *coriandrum* f. Gk *koriannon*]

Corinthian /kə'rɪnθɪən/ *adj. & n.* —*adj.* 1 of ancient Corinth in southern Greece. 2 *Archit.* of an order characterized by ornate decoration and flared capitals with rows of acanthus leaves, used esp. by the Romans. 3 *archaic* profligate. —*n.* a native of Corinth. [L *Corinthius* f. Gk *Korinthios* + -AN]

Coriolis effect /ˌkɒrɪ'əʊlɪs/ *n.* a hypothetical force used to explain rotating systems, such that the movement of air or water over the surface of the rotating earth is directed clockwise in the northern hemisphere and anticlockwise in the southern hemisphere. [G. G. *Coriolis*, Fr. scientist d. 1843]

corium /'kɔːrɪəm/ *n. Anat.* the dermis. [L, = skin]

cork /kɔːk/ *n. & v.* —*n.* 1 the buoyant light-brown bark of the cork-oak. 2 a bottle-stopper of cork or other material. 3 a float of cork used in fishing etc. 4 *Bot.* a protective layer of dead cells immediately below the bark of woody plants. 5 (*attrib.*) made of cork. —*v.tr.* (often foll. by *up*) 1 stop or confine. 2 restrain (feelings etc.). 3 blacken with burnt cork. □**cork-oak** a S. European oak, *Quercus suber*. **cork-tipped** *Brit.* (of a cigarette) having a filter of corklike material. □□ **corklike** *adj.* [ME f. Du. & LG *kork* f. Sp. *alcorque* cork sole, perh. f. Arab.]

corkage /'kɔːkɪdʒ/ *n.* a charge made by a restaurant or hotel for serving wine etc. when brought in by customers.

corked /kɔːkt/ *adj.* 1 stopped with a cork. 2 (of wine) spoilt by a decayed cork. 3 blackened with burnt cork.

corker /'kɔːkə(r)/ *n. sl.* an excellent or astonishing person or thing.

corking /'kɔːkɪŋ/ *adj. sl.* strikingly large or splendid.

corkscrew /'kɔːkskruː/ *n. & v.* —*n.* 1 a spirally twisted steel device for extracting corks from bottles. 2 (often *attrib.*) a thing with a spiral shape. —*v.tr. & intr.* move spirally; twist.

corkwood /'kɔːkwʊd/ *n.* 1 any shrub of the genus *Duboisia*, yielding a light porous wood. 2 this wood.

corky /'kɔːkɪ/ *adj.* (**corkier**, **corkiest**) 1 corklike. 2 (of wine) corked.

corm /kɔːm/ *n. Bot.* an underground swollen stem base of some plants, e.g. crocus. [mod.L *cormus* f. Gk *kormos* trunk with boughs lopped off]

cormorant /'kɔːmərənt/ *n.* any diving sea bird of the family Phalacrocoracidae, esp. *Phalacrocorax carbo* having lustrous black plumage. [ME f. OF *cormaran* f. med.L *corvus marinus* sea-raven: for ending *-ant* cf. *peasant*, *tyrant*]

corn¹ /kɔːn/ *n. & v.* —*n.* 1 a any cereal before or after harvesting, esp. the chief crop of a region: wheat, oats, or (in the US and Australia) maize. b a grain or seed of a cereal plant. 2 *colloq.* something corny or trite. —*v.tr.* (as **corned** *adj.*) sprinkled or preserved with salt or brine (*corned beef*). □**corn-cob** the cylindrical centre of the maize ear to which rows of grains are attached. **corn-cob pipe** a tobacco-pipe made from a corn-cob. **corn-cockle** see COCKLE². **corn dolly** a symbolic or decorative figure made of plaited straw. **corn exchange** a place for trade in corn. **corn-factor** *Brit.* a dealer in corn. **corn marigold** a daisy-like yellow-flowered plant, *Chrysanthemum segetum*, growing amongst corn. **corn on the cob** maize cooked and eaten from the corn-cob. **corn-salad** = *lamb's lettuce* (see LAMB). **corn-spurry** see SPURRY. **corn-whiskey** *US* whisky distilled from maize. [OE f. Gmc: rel. to L *granum* grain]

corn² /kɔːn/ *n.* a small area of horny usu. tender skin esp. on the toes, extending into subcutaneous tissue. [ME f. AF f. L *cornu* horn]

cornbrash /'kɔːnbræʃ/ *n. Geol. Brit.* an earthy limestone layer of the Jurassic period. [CORN¹ + BRASH²]

corncrake /'kɔːnkreɪk/ n. a rail, *Crex crex*, inhabiting grassland and nesting on the ground.

cornea /'kɔːnɪə/ n. the transparent circular part of the front of the eyeball. □□ **corneal** adj. [med.L *cornea tela* horny tissue, f. L *corneus* horny f. *cornu* horn]

cornel /'kɔːn(ə)l/ n. any plant of the genus *Cornus*, esp. a dwarf kind, *C. suecica*. [ME f. L *cornus*]

cornelian /kɔːˈniːlɪən/ n. (also **carnelian** /kɑː-/) **1** a dull red or reddish-white variety of chalcedony. **2** this colour. [ME f. OF *corneline*; *car-* after L *caro carnis* flesh]

corneous /'kɔːnɪəs/ adj. hornlike, horny. [L *corneus* f. *cornu* horn]

corner /'kɔːnə(r)/ n. & v. —n. **1** a place where converging sides or edges meet. **2** a projecting angle, esp. where two streets meet. **3** the internal space or recess formed by the meeting of two sides, esp. of a room. **4** a difficult position, esp. one from which there is no escape (*driven into a corner*). **5** a secluded or remote place. **6** a region or quarter, esp. a remote one (*from the four corners of the earth*). **7** the action or result of buying or controlling the whole available stock of a commodity, thereby dominating the market. **8** *Boxing & Wrestling* **a** an angle of the ring, esp. one where a contestant rests between rounds. **b** a contestant's supporters offering assistance at the corner between rounds. **9** *Football & Hockey* a free kick or hit from a corner of the pitch after the ball has been kicked over the goal-line by a defending player. **10** a triangular cut of gammon or ham. —v. **1** tr. force (a person or animal) into a difficult or inescapable position. **2** tr. **a** establish a corner in (a commodity). **b** dominate (dealers or the market) in this way. **3** intr. (esp. of or in a vehicle) go round a corner. □ **corner shop** a small local shop, esp. at a street corner. **just round** (or **around**) **the corner** *colloq.* very near, imminent. [ME f. AF ult. f. L *cornu* horn]

cornerstone /'kɔːnəˌstəʊn/ n. **1 a** a stone in a projecting angle of a wall. **b** a foundation-stone. **2** an indispensable part or basis of something.

cornerwise /'kɔːnəˌwaɪz/ adv. diagonally.

cornet[1] /'kɔːnɪt/ n. **1** *Mus.* **a** a brass instrument resembling a trumpet but shorter and wider. **b** its player. **c** an organ stop with the quality of a cornet. **d** a cornetto. **2** *Brit.* a conical wafer for holding ice-cream. □□ **cornetist** /kɔːˈnetɪst, 'kɔːnɪtɪst/ n. **cornettist** /kɔːˈnetɪst/ n. [ME f. OF ult. f. L *cornu* horn]

cornet[2] /'kɔːnɪt/ n. *Brit. hist.* the fifth commissioned officer in a cavalry troop, who carried the colours. □□ **cornetcy** n. (pl. **-ies**). [earlier sense 'pennon, standard' f. F *cornette* dimin. of *corne* ult. f. L *cornua* horns]

cornett /'kɔːnɪt/ n. *Mus.* = CORNETTO. [var. of CORNET[1]]

cornetto /kɔːˈnetəʊ/ n. (pl. **cornetti** /-tiː/) *Mus.* an old woodwind instrument like a flageolet. [It., dimin. of *corno* horn (as CORNET[1])]

cornfield /'kɔːnfiːld/ n. a field in which corn is being grown.

cornflake /'kɔːnfleɪk/ n. **1** (in pl.) a breakfast cereal of toasted flakes made from maize flour. **2** a flake of this cereal.

cornflour /'kɔːnˌflaʊə(r)/ n. **1** a fine-ground maize flour. Also called CORNSTARCH. **2** a flour of rice or other grain.

cornflower /'kɔːnˌflaʊə(r)/ n. any plant of the genus *Centaurea* growing among corn, esp. *C. cyanus*, with deep-blue flowers.

cornice /'kɔːnɪs/ n. **1** *Archit.* **a** an ornamental moulding round the wall of a room just below the ceiling. **b** a horizontal moulded projection crowning a building or structure, esp. the uppermost member of the entablature of an order, surmounting the frieze. **2** *Mountaineering* an overhanging mass of hardened snow at the edge of a precipice. □□

corniced adj. [F *corniche* etc. f. It. *cornice*, perh. f. L *cornix -icis* crow]

corniche /'kɔːnɪʃ, kɔːˈniːʃ/ n. (in full **corniche road**) **1** a road cut into the edge of a cliff etc. **2** a coastal road with wide views. [F: see CORNICE]

Cornish /'kɔːnɪʃ/ adj. & n. —adj. of or relating to Cornwall in SW England. —n. the ancient Celtic language of Cornwall. □ **Cornish cream** clotted cream. **Cornish pasty** seasoned meat and vegetables baked in a pastry envelope.

cornstarch /'kɔːnstɑːtʃ/ n. = CORNFLOUR.

cornstone /'kɔːnstəʊn/ n. *Brit. Geol.* a mottled red and green limestone usu. formed under usu. arid conditions, esp. in the Devonian period.

cornucopia /ˌkɔːnjʊˈkəʊpɪə/ n. **1 a** a symbol of plenty consisting of a goat's horn overflowing with flowers, fruit, and corn. **b** an ornamental vessel shaped like this. **2** an abundant supply. □□ **cornucopian** adj. [LL f. L *cornu copiae* horn of plenty]

corny /'kɔːnɪ/ adj. (**cornier**, **corniest**) **1** *colloq.* **a** trite. **b** feebly humorous. **c** sentimental. **d** old-fashioned; out of date. **2** of or abounding in corn. □□ **cornily** adv. **corniness** n. [CORN[1] + -Y[1]: sense 1 f. sense 'rustic']

corolla /kəˈrɒlə/ n. *Bot.* a whorl or whorls of petals forming the inner envelope of a flower. [L, dimin. of *corona* crown]

corollary /kəˈrɒlərɪ/ n. & adj. —n. (pl. **-ies**) **1 a** a proposition that follows from (and is often appended to) one already proved. **b** an immediate deduction. **2** (often foll. by *of*) a natural consequence or result. —adj. **1** supplementary, associated. **2** (often foll. by *to*) forming a corollary. [ME f. L *corollarium* money paid for a garland, gratuity: neut. adj. f. COROLLA]

corona[1] /kəˈrəʊnə/ n. (pl. **coronae** /-niː/) **1 a** a small circle of light round the sun or moon. **b** the rarefied gaseous envelope of the sun, seen as an irregularly shaped area of light around the moon's disc during a total solar eclipse. **2** a circular chandelier hung from a roof. **3** *Anat.* a crown or crownlike structure. **4** *Bot.* a crownlike outgrowth from the inner side of a corolla. **5** *Archit.* a broad vertical face of a cornice, usu. of considerable projection. **6** *Electr.* the glow around a conductor at high potential. [L, = crown]

corona[2] /kəˈrəʊnə/ n. a long cigar with straight sides. [Sp. *La Corona* the crown]

coronach /'kɒrənək, -nəx/ n. *Sc. & Ir.* a funeral-song or dirge. [Ir. *coranach*, Gael. *corranach* f. *comh-* together + *rànach* outcry]

coronagraph /kəˈrəʊnəˌgrɑːf/ n. an instrument for observing the sun's corona, esp. other than during a solar eclipse.

coronal[1] /kəˈrəʊn(ə)l, 'kɒrən(ə)l/ adj. **1** *Astron. & Bot.* of a corona. **2** *Anat.* of the crown of the head. □ **coronal bone** the frontal bone of the skull. **coronal plane** an imaginary plane dividing the body into dorsal and ventral parts. **coronal suture** a transverse suture of the skull separating the frontal bone from the parietal bones. [F *coronal* or L *coronalis* (as CORONA[1])]

coronal[2] /'kɒrən(ə)l/ n. **1** a circlet (esp. of gold or gems) for the head. **2** a wreath or garland. [ME, app. f. AF f. *corone* CROWN]

coronary /'kɒrənərɪ/ adj. & n. —adj. *Anat.* resembling or encircling like a crown. —n. (pl. **-ies**) = coronary thrombosis. □ **coronary artery** an artery supplying blood to the heart. **coronary thrombosis** *Med.* a blockage of the blood flow caused by a blood clot in a coronary artery. [L *coronarius* f. *corona* crown]

coronation /ˌkɒrəˈneɪʃ(ə)n/ n. the ceremony of crowning a sovereign or a sovereign's consort. [ME f. OF f. med.L *coronatio -onis* f. *coronare* to crown f. CORONA[1]]

coroner /'kɒrənə(r)/ n. **1** an officer of a county, district, or municipality, holding inquests on deaths thought to be violent or accidental, and inquiries in cases of treasure trove. **2** *hist.* an officer charged with maintaining the rights of the private property of the Crown. □□ **coronership** n. [ME f. AF cor(o)uner f. coro(u)ne CROWN]

coronet /'kɒrənɪt, -ˌnet/ n. **1** a small crown (esp. as worn, or used as a heraldic device, by a peer or peeress). **2** a circlet of precious materials, esp. as a woman's head-dress or part of one. **3** a garland for the head. **4** the lowest part of a horse's pastern. **5** a ring of bone at the base of a deer's antler. □□ **coroneted** adj. [OF coronet(t)e dimin. of corone CROWN]

corozo /kə'rəʊzəʊ/ n. (pl. -os) Bot. any of various palm-trees native to S. America. □ **corozo-nut** a seed of one species of palm, Phytelephas macrocarpa, which when hardened forms vegetable ivory: also called ivory-nut. [Sp.]

Corp. abbr. **1** Corporal. **2** US Corporation.

corpora pl. of CORPUS.

corporal[1] /'kɔːpər(ə)l/ n. **1** a non-commissioned army or air-force officer ranking next below sergeant. **2** (in full **ship's corporal**) Brit. an officer under the master-at-arms, attending to police matters. **3** US a freshwater fallfish, Semotilus corporalis. [obs. F, var. of caporal f. It. caporale prob. f. L corporalis (as CORPORAL[2]), confused with It. capo head]

corporal[2] /'kɔːpər(ə)l/ adj. of or relating to the human body (cf. CORPOREAL). □ **corporal punishment** punishment inflicted on the body, esp. by beating. □□ **corporally** adv. [ME f. OF f. L corporalis f. corpus -oris body]

corporal[3] /'kɔːpər(ə)l/ n. a cloth on which the vessels containing the consecrated elements are placed during the celebration of the Eucharist. [OE f. OF corporal or med.L corporale pallium body cloth (as CORPORAL[2])]

corporality /ˌkɔːpə'rælɪtɪ/ n. (pl. -ies) **1** material existence. **2** a body. [ME f. LL corporalitas (as CORPORAL[2])]

corporate /'kɔːpərət/ adj. **1** forming a corporation (corporate body; body corporate). **2** forming one body of many individuals. **3** of or belonging to a corporation or group (corporate responsibility). **4** corporative. □□ **corporately** adv. **corporatism** n. [L corporare corporat- form into a body (corpus -oris)]

corporation /ˌkɔːpə'reɪʃ(ə)n/ n. **1** a group of people authorized to act as an individual and recognized in law as a single entity, esp. in business. **2** the municipal authorities of a borough, town, or city. **3** joc. a protruding stomach. [LL corporatio (as CORPORATE)]

corporative /'kɔːpərətɪv/ adj. **1** of a corporation. **2** governed by or organized in corporations, esp. of employers and employed. □□ **corporativism** n.

corporeal /kɔː'pɔːrɪəl/ adj. **1** bodily, physical, material, esp. as distinct from spiritual (cf. CORPOREAL). **2** Law consisting of material objects. □□ **corporeality** /-'ælɪtɪ/ n. **corporeally** adv. [LL corporealis f. L corporeus f. corpus -oris body]

corporeity /ˌkɔːpə'riːɪtɪ/ n. **1** the quality of being or having a material body. **2** bodily substance. [F corporéité or med.L corporeitas f. L corporeus (as CORPOREAL)]

corposant /'kɔːpəz(ə)nt/ n. a luminous electrical discharge sometimes seen on a ship or aircraft during a storm. [OSp., Port., It. corpo santo holy body]

corps /kɔː(r)/ n. (pl. **corps** /kɔːz/) **1** Mil. **a** a body of troops with special duties (intelligence corps; Royal Army Medical Corps). **b** a main subdivision of an army in the field, consisting of two or more divisions. **2** a body of people engaged in a special activity (diplomatic corps; press corps). [F (as CORPSE)]

corps de ballet /ˌkɔː də 'bæleɪ/ n. the company of ensemble dancers in a ballet. [F]

corps d'élite /ˌkɔː deɪ'liːt/ n. a select group. [F]

corps diplomatique /ˌkɔː dɪpləmæ'tiːk/ n. a diplomatic corps. [F]

corpse /kɔːps/ n. a dead (usu. human) body.

□ **corpse-candle 1** a lambent flame seen in a churchyard or over a grave, regarded as an omen of death. **2** a lighted candle placed beside a corpse before burial. [ME corps, var. spelling of cors (CORSE), f. OF cors f. L corpus body]

corpulent /'kɔːpjʊlənt/ adj. bulky in body, fat. □□ **corpulence** n. **corpulency** n. [ME f. L corpulentus f. corpus body]

corpus /'kɔːpəs/ n. (pl. **corpora** /'kɔːpərə/ or **corpuses**) **1** a body or collection of writings, texts, spoken material, etc. **2** Anat. a structure of a special character in the animal body. [ME f. L, = body]

Corpus Christi /ˌkɔːpəs 'krɪstɪ/ n. a feast commemorating the Eucharist, observed on the Thursday after Trinity Sunday. [ME f. L, = Body of Christ]

corpuscle /'kɔːpʌs(ə)l/ n. a minute body or cell in an organism, esp. (in pl.) the red or white cells in the blood of vertebrates. □□ **corpuscular** /kɔː'pʌskjʊlə(r)/ adj. [L corpusculum (as CORPUS)]

corpus delicti /ˌkɔːpəs dɪ'lɪktaɪ/ n. Law the facts and circumstances constituting a breach of a law. [L, = body of offence]

corpus luteum /ˌkɔːpəs 'luːtɪəm/ n. Anat. a body developed in the ovary after discharge of the ovum, remaining in existence only if pregnancy has begun. [mod.L f. CORPUS + luteus, -um yellow]

corral /kɒ'rɑːl/ n. & v. — n. **1** US a pen for cattle, horses, etc. **2** an enclosure for capturing wild animals. **3** esp. US hist. a defensive enclosure of wagons in an encampment. — v.tr. (**corralled**, **corralling**) **1** put or keep in a corral. **2** form (wagons) into a corral. **3** US colloq. acquire. [Sp. & OPort. (as KRAAL)]

corrasion /kə'reɪʒ(ə)n/ n. Geol. erosion of the earth's surface by rock material being carried over it by water, ice, etc. [L corradere corras- scrape together (as COM-, radere scrape)]

correct /kə'rekt/ adj. & v. — adj. **1** true, right, accurate. **2** (of conduct, manners, etc.) proper, right. **3** in accordance with good standards of taste etc. — v.tr. **1** set right; amend (an error, omission, etc., or the person responsible for it). **2** mark the errors in (written or printed work etc.). **3** substitute the right thing for (the wrong one). **4 a** admonish or rebuke (a person). **b** punish (a person or fault). **5** counteract (a harmful quality). **6** adjust (an instrument etc.) to function accurately or accord with a standard. □□ **correctly** adv. **correctness** n. [ME (adj. through F) f. L corrigere correct- (as COM-, regere guide)]

correction /kə'rekʃ(ə)n/ n. **1 a** the act or process of correcting. **b** an instance of this. **2** a thing substituted for what is wrong. **3** archaic punishment (house of correction). □□ **correctional** adj. [ME f. OF f. L correctio -onis (as CORRECT)]

correctitude /kə'rektɪˌtjuːd/ n. correctness, esp. conscious correctness of conduct. [19th c., f. CORRECT + RECTITUDE]

corrective /kə'rektɪv/ adj. & n. — adj. serving or tending to correct or counteract something undesired or harmful. — n. a corrective measure or thing. □□ **correctively** adv. [F correctif -ive or LL correctivus (as CORRECT)]

corrector /kə'rektə(r)/ n. a person who corrects or points out faults. [ME f. AF correctour f. L corrector (as CORRECT)]

correlate /'kɒrəˌleɪt, 'kɒrɪ-/ v. & n. — v. **1** intr. (foll. by with, to) have a mutual relation. **2** tr. (usu. foll. by with) bring into a mutual relation. — n. each of two related or complementary things (esp. so related that one implies the other). [back-form. f. COR- RELATION, CORRELATIVE]

correlation /ˌkɒrə'leɪʃ(ə)n, ˌkɒrɪ-/ n. (also **corelation** /ˌkəʊrɪ-/) **1** a mutual relation between two or more things. **2 a** interdependence of variable quantities. **b** a quantity measuring the extent of this. **3** the act of correlating. □□ **correlational** adj. [med.L correlatio (as CORRELATIVE)]

correlative /kɒ'relətɪv, kə-/ adj. & n. — adj. **1** (often foll. by *with*, *to*) having a mutual relation. **2** *Gram.* (of words) corresponding to each other and regularly used together (as *neither* and *nor*). —*n.* a correlative word or thing. □□ **correlatively** *adv.* **correlativity** /-'tıvıtı/ *n.* [med.L *correlativus* (as COM-, RELATIVE)]

correspond /ˌkɒrı'spɒnd/ *v.intr.* **1 a** (usu. foll. by *to*) be analogous or similar. **b** (usu. foll. by *to*) agree in amount, position, etc. **c** (usu. foll. by *with*, *to*) be in harmony or agreement. **2** (usu. foll. by *with*) communicate by interchange of letters. □ **corresponding member** an honorary member of a learned society etc. with no voice in the society's affairs. □□ **correspondingly** *adv.* [F *correspondre* f. med.L *correspondere* (as COM-, RESPOND)]

correspondence /ˌkɒrı'spɒnd(ə)ns/ *n.* **1** (usu. foll. by *with*, *to*, *between*) agreement, similarity, or harmony. **2 a** communication by letters. **b** letters sent or received. □ **correspondence college** (or **school**) a college conducting correspondence courses. **correspondence column** the part of a newspaper etc. that contains letters from readers. **correspondence course** a course of study conducted by post. [ME f. OF f. med.L *correspondentia* (as CORRESPOND)]

correspondent /ˌkɒrı'spɒnd(ə)nt/ *n.* & *adj.* —*n.* **1 a** person who writes letters to a person or a newspaper, esp. regularly. **2 a** person employed to contribute material for publication in a periodical or for broadcasting (*our chess correspondent; the BBC's Moscow correspondent*). **3** a person or firm having regular business relations with another, esp. in another country. —*adj.* (often foll. by *to*, *with*) *archaic* corresponding. □□ **correspondently** *adv.* [ME f. OF *correspondant* or med.L (as CORRESPOND)]

corrida /kɔ:'ri:də/ *n.* **1** a bullfight. **2** bullfighting. [Sp. *corrida de toros* running of bulls]

corridor /'kɒrıˌdɔ:(r)/ *n.* **1** a passage from which doors lead into rooms (orig. an outside passage connecting parts of a building, now usu. a main passage in a large building). **2** a passage in a railway carriage from which doors lead into compartments. **3** a strip of the territory of one State passing through that of another, esp. securing access to the sea. **4** a route to which aircraft are restricted, esp. over a foreign country. □ **corridors of power** places where covert influence is said to be exerted in government. [F f. It. *corridore* corridor for *corridojo* running-place f. *correre* run, by confusion with *corridore* runner]

corrie /'kɒrı/ *n.* *Sc.* a circular hollow on a mountainside; a cirque. [Gael. *coire* cauldron]

corrigendum /ˌkɒrı'gendəm, -'dʒendəm/ *n.* (*pl.* **corrigenda** /-də/) a thing to be corrected, esp. an error in a printed book. [L, neut. gerundive of *corrigere*: see CORRECT]

corrigible /'kɒrıdʒıb(ə)l/ *adj.* **1** capable of being corrected. **2** (of a person) submissive; open to correction. □□ **corrigibly** *adv.* [ME f. F f. med.L *corrigibilis* (as CORRECT)]

corroborate /kə'rɒbəˌreıt/ *v.tr.* confirm or give support to (a statement or belief, or the person holding it), esp. in relation to witnesses in a lawcourt. □□ **corroboration** /-'reıʃ(ə)n/ *n.* **corroborative** /-rətıv/ *adj.* **corroborator** *n.* **corroboratory** /-rətərı/ *adj.* [L *corroborare* strengthen (as COM-, *roborare* f. *robur -oris* strength)]

corroboree /kə'rɒbərı/ *n.* **1** a festive or warlike dance-drama with song of Australian Aboriginals. **2** a noisy party. [Aboriginal dial.]

corrode /kə'rəʊd/ *v.* **1 a** *tr.* wear away, esp. by chemical action. **b** *intr.* be worn away; decay. **2** *tr.* destroy gradually (*optimism corroded by recent misfortunes*). □□ **corrodible** *adj.* [ME f. L *corrodere corros-* (as COM-, *rodere* gnaw)]

corrosion /kə'rəʊʒ(ə)n/ *n.* **1** the process of corroding, esp. of a rusting metal. **2 a** damage caused by corroding. **b** a corroded area.

corrosive /kə'rəʊsıv/ *adj.* & *n.* —*adj.* tending to corrode or consume. —*n.* a corrosive substance.

□ **corrosive sublimate** mercuric chloride, a strong acid poison, used as a fungicide, antiseptic, etc. □□ **corrosively** *adv.* **corrosiveness** *n.* [ME f. OF *corosif -ive* (as CORRODE)]

corrugate /'kɒrʊˌgeıt/ *v.* **1** *tr.* (esp. as **corrugated** *adj.*) form into alternate ridges and grooves, esp. to strengthen (*corrugated iron*; *corrugated paper*). **2** *tr.* & *intr.* contract into wrinkles or folds. □□ **corrugation** /-'geıʃ(ə)n/ *n.* [L *corrugare* (as COM-, *rugare* f. *ruga* wrinkle)]

corrugator /'kɒrʊˌgeıtə(r)/ *n.* *Anat.* either of two muscles that contract the brow in frowning. [mod.L (as CORRUGATE)]

corrupt /kə'rʌpt/ *adj.* & *v.* —*adj.* **1** morally depraved; wicked. **2** influenced by or using bribery or fraudulent activity. **3** (of a text, language, etc.) harmed (esp. made suspect or unreliable) by errors or alterations. **4** rotten. —*v.* **1** *tr.* & *intr.* make or become corrupt or depraved. **2** *tr.* affect or harm by errors or alterations. **3** *tr.* infect, taint. □ **corrupt practices** fraudulent activity, esp. at elections. □□ **corruptible** *adj.* **corruptibility** /-'bılıtı/ *n.* **corruptive** *adj.* **corruptly** *adv.* **corruptness** *n.* [ME f. OF *corrupt* or L *corruptus* past part. of *corrumpere corrupt-* (as COM-, *rumpere* break)]

corruption /kə'rʌpʃ(ə)n/ *n.* **1** moral deterioration, esp. widespread. **2** use of corrupt practices, esp. bribery or fraud. **3 a** irregular alteration (of a text, language, etc.) from its original state. **b** an irregularly altered form of a word. **4** decomposition, esp. of a corpse or other organic matter. [ME f. OF *corruption* or L *corruptio* (as CORRUPT)]

corsac /'kɔ:sæk/ *n.* (also **corsak**) a fox, *Vulpes corsac*, of Central Asia. [Turki]

corsage /kɔ:'sɑ:ʒ/ *n.* **1** a small bouquet worn by a woman. **2** the bodice of a woman's dress. [ME f. OF f. *cors* body: see CORPSE]

corsair /'kɔ:seə(r)/ *n.* **1** a pirate ship. **2** a pirate. **3** *hist.* a privateer, esp. of the Barbary Coast. [F *corsaire* f. med.L *cursarius* f. *cursus* inroad f. *currere* run]

corsak var. of CORSAC.

corse /kɔ:s/ *n.* *archaic* a corpse. [var. of CORPSE]

corselet var. of CORSLET, CORSELETTE.

corselette /'kɔ:slıt, 'kɔ:səˌlet/ *n.* (also **corselet**) a woman's foundation garment combining corset and brassière.

corset /'kɔ:sıt/ *n.* & *v.* —*n.* **1** a closely-fitting undergarment worn by women to support the abdomen. **2** a similar garment worn by men and women because of injury, weakness, or deformity. —*v.tr.* (**corseted**, **corseting**) **1** provide with a corset. **2** control closely. □□ **corseted** *adj.* **corsetry** *n.* [ME f. OF, dimin. of *cors* body: see CORPSE]

corsetière /'kɔ:sıˌtjeə(r)/ *n.* a woman who makes or fits corsets. [F, fem. of *corsetier* (as CORSET, -IER)]

Corsican /'kɔ:sıkən/ *adj.* & *n.* —*adj.* of or relating to Corsica, an island in the Mediterranean under French rule. —*n.* **1** a native of Corsica. **2** the Italian dialect of Corsica.

corslet /'kɔ:slıt/ *n.* (also **corselet**) **1** a garment (usu. tight-fitting) covering the trunk but not the limbs. **2** *hist.* a piece of armour covering the trunk. [OF *corselet*, dimin. formed as CORSET]

cortège /kɔ:'teıʒ/ *n.* **1** a procession, esp. for a funeral. **2** a train of attendants. [F]

Cortes /'kɔ:tes, -tez/ *n.* the legislative assembly of Spain and formerly of Portugal. [Sp. & Port., pl. of *corte* COURT]

cortex /'kɔ:teks/ *n.* (*pl.* **cortices** /-tıˌsi:z/) **1** *Anat.* the outer part of an organ, esp. of the brain (**cerebral cortex**) or kidneys (**renal cortex**). **2** *Bot.* **a** an outer layer of tissue immediately below the epidermis. **b** bark. □□ **cortical** /'kɔ:tık(ə)l/ *adj.* [L *cortex, -icis* bark]

Corti /'kɔ:tı/ *n.* □ **organ of Corti** *Anat.* a structure in the inner ear of mammals, responsible for converting sound signals into nerve impulses. [A. *Corti*, It. anatomist d. 1876]

corticate /'kɔːtɪˌkeɪt/ adj. (also **corticated**) 1 having bark or rind. 2 barklike. [L corticatus (as CORTEX)]

corticotrophic hormone /ˌkɔːtɪkəʊ'trɒfɪk/ adj. (also **corticotropic**) = ADRENOCORTICOTROPHIC HORMONE.

corticotrophin /ˌkɔːtɪkəʊ'trəʊfɪn/ n. (also **corticotropin**) = ADRENOCORTICOTROPHIN.

cortisone /'kɔːtɪˌzəʊn/ n. Biochem. a steroid hormone produced by the adrenal cortex or synthetically, used medicinally esp. against inflammation and allergy. [Chem. name 17-hydroxy-11-dehydrocorticosterone]

corundum /kə'rʌndəm/ n. Mineral. extremely hard crystallized alumina, used esp. as an abrasive, and varieties of which, e.g. ruby and sapphire, are used for gemstones. [Tamil kurundam f. Skr. kuruvinda ruby]

coruscate /'kɒrəˌskeɪt/ v.intr. 1 give off flashing light; sparkle. 2 be showy or brilliant. □□ **coruscation** /-'skeɪʃ(ə)n/ n. [L coruscare glitter]

corvée /kɔː'veɪ/ n. 1 hist. a day's work of unpaid labour due to a lord from a vassal. 2 labour exacted in lieu of paying taxes. 3 an onerous task. [ME f. OF ult. f. L corrogare ask for, collect (as COM-, rogare ask)]

corves pl. of CORF.

corvette /kɔː'vet/ n. Naut. 1 a small naval escort-vessel. 2 hist. a flush-decked warship with one tier of guns. [F f. MDu. korf kind of ship + dimin. -ETTE]

corvine /'kɔːvaɪn/ adj. of or akin to the raven or crow. [L corvinus f. corvus raven]

corybantic /ˌkɒrɪ'bæntɪk/ adj. wild, frenzied. [Corybantes priests of Cybele performing wild dances (L f. Gk Korubantes)]

corymb /'kɒrɪmb/ n. Bot. a flat-topped cluster of flowers with the flower-stalks proportionally longer lower down the stem. □□ **corymbose** adj. [F corymbe or L corymbus f. Gk korumbos cluster]

coryphée /'kɒrɪˌfeɪ/ n. a leading dancer in a corps de ballet. [F f. Gk koruphaios leader of a chorus f. koruphē head]

coryza /kə'raɪzə/ n. 1 a catarrhal inflammation of the mucous membrane in the nose; a cold in the head. 2 any disease with this as a symptom. [L f. Gk koruza running at the nose]

cos[1] /kɒs/ n. a variety of lettuce with crisp narrow leaves forming a long upright head. [L f. Gk Kōs, island in the Aegean, where it originated]

cos[2] /kɒs, kɒz/ abbr. cosine.

cos[3] /kɒz/ conj. & adv. (also **'cos**) colloq. because. [abbr.]

Cosa Nostra /ˌkəʊzə 'nɒstrə/ n. a US criminal organization resembling and related to the Mafia. [It., = our affair]

cosec /'kəʊsek/ abbr. cosecant.

cosecant /kəʊ'siːkənt/ n. Math. the ratio of the hypotenuse (in a right-angled triangle) to the side opposite an acute angle; the reciprocal of sine. [mod.L cosecans and F cosécant (as CO-, SECANT)]

coseismal /kəʊ'saɪzm(ə)l/ adj. & n. —adj. of or relating to points of simultaneous arrival of an earthquake wave. —n. a straight line or a curve connecting these points. [CO- + SEISMAL (see SEISMIC)]

coset /'kəʊset/ n. Math. a set composed of all the products obtained by multiplying on the right or on the left each element of a subgroup in turn by one particular element of the group containing the subgroup. [CO- + SET[2]]

cosh[1] /kɒʃ/ n. & v. Brit. colloq. —n. a heavy blunt weapon. —v.tr. hit with a cosh. [19th c.: orig. unkn.]

cosh[2] /kɒʃ, kɒs'eɪtʃ/ abbr. Math. hyperbolic cosine.

co-signatory /kəʊ'sɪgnətərɪ/ n. & adj. (US **cosignatory**) —n. (pl. -ies) a person or State signing (a treaty etc.) jointly with others. —adj. signing jointly.

cosine /'kəʊsaɪn/ n. Math. the ratio of the side adjacent to an acute angle (in a right-angled triangle) to the hypotenuse. [mod.L cosinus (as CO-, SINE)]

cosmea /'kɒzmɪə/ n. = COSMOS[2]. [mod.L, formed as COSMOS[2]]

cosmetic /kɒz'metɪk/ adj. & n. —adj. 1 intended to adorn or beautify the body, esp. the face. 2 intended to improve only appearances; superficially improving or beneficial (a cosmetic change). 3 (of surgery or a prosthetic device) imitating, restoring, or enhancing the normal appearance. —n. a cosmetic preparation, esp. for the face. □□ **cosmetically** adv. [F cosmétique f. Gk kosmētikos f. kosmeō adorn f. kosmos order, adornment]

cosmic /'kɒzmɪk/ adj. 1 of the universe or cosmos, esp. as distinct from the earth. 2 of or for space travel. □**cosmic dust** small particles of matter distributed throughout space. **cosmic rays** (or **radiation**) radiations from space etc. that reach the earth from all directions, usu. with high energy and penetrative power. □□ **cosmical** adj. **cosmically** adv.

cosmogony /kɒz'mɒgənɪ/ n. (pl. -ies) 1 the origin of the universe. 2 a theory about this. □□ **cosmogonic** /-mə'gɒnɪk/ adj. **cosmogonical** /-mə'gɒnɪk(ə)l/ adj. **cosmogonist** n. [Gk kosmogonia f. kosmos world + -gonia -begetting]

cosmography /kɒz'mɒgrəfɪ/ n. (pl. -ies) a description or mapping of general features of the universe. □□ **cosmographer** n. **cosmographic** /-mə'græfɪk/ adj. **cosmographical** /-mə'græfɪk(ə)l/ adj. [ME f. F cosmographie or f. LL f. Gk kosmographia (as COSMOS[1], -GRAPHY)]

cosmology /kɒz'mɒlədʒɪ/ n. the science or theory of the universe. □□ **cosmological** /-mə'lɒdʒɪk(ə)l/ adj. **cosmologist** n. [F cosmologie or mod.L cosmologia (as COSMOS[1], -LOGY)]

cosmonaut /'kɒzməˌnɔːt/ n. a Soviet astronaut. [Russ. kosmonavt, as COSMOS[1], after astronaut]

cosmopolis /kɒz'mɒpəlɪs/ n. a cosmopolitan city. [Gk kosmos world + polis city]

cosmopolitan /ˌkɒzmə'pɒlɪt(ə)n/ adj. & n. —adj. 1 **a** of or from or knowing many parts of the world. **b** consisting of people from many or all parts. 2 free from national limitations or prejudices. 3 Ecol. (of a plant, animal, etc.) widely distributed. —n. 1 a cosmopolitan person. 2 Ecol. a widely distributed animal or plant. □□ **cosmopolitanism** n. **cosmopolitanize** v.tr. & intr. (also -ise). [COSMOPOLITE + -AN]

cosmopolite /kɒz'mɒpəˌlaɪt/ n. & adj. —n. 1 a cosmopolitan person. 2 Ecol. = COSMOPOLITAN n. 2. —adj. free from national attachments or prejudices. [F f. Gk kosmopolitēs f. kosmos world + politēs citizen]

cosmos[1] /'kɒzmɒs/ n. 1 the universe, esp. as a well-ordered whole. 2 **a** an ordered system of ideas etc. **b** a sum total of experience. [Gk kosmos]

cosmos[2] /'kɒzmɒs/ n. any composite plant of the genus Cosmos, bearing single dahlia-like blossoms of various colours. [mod.L f. Gk kosmos in sense 'ornament']

COSPAR abbr. Committee on Space Research.

Cossack /'kɒsæk/ n. & adj. —n. 1 a member of a people of southern Imperial Russia, orig. famous for their military skill. 2 a member of a Cossack military unit. —adj. of, relating to, or characteristic of the Cossacks. [F cosaque f. Russ. kazak f. Turki quzzāq nomad, adventurer]

cosset /'kɒsɪt/ v.tr. (**cosseted**, **cosseting**) pamper. [dial. cosset = pet lamb, prob. f. AF coscet, cozet f. OE cotsǣta cottager (as COT[2], SIT)]

cost /kɒst/ v. & n. —v. (past and past part. **cost**) 1 tr. be obtainable for (a sum of money); have as a price (what does it cost?; it cost me £50). 2 tr. involve as a loss or sacrifice (it cost them much effort; it cost him his life). 3 tr. (past and past part. **costed**) fix or estimate the cost or price of. 4 colloq. **a** tr. be costly to (it'll cost you). **b** intr. be costly. —n. 1 what a thing costs; the price paid or to be paid. 2 a loss or sacrifice; an expenditure of time, effort, etc. 3 (in pl.)

legal expenses, esp. those allowed in favour of the winning party or against the losing party in a suit. □**at all costs** (or **at any cost**) no matter what the cost or risk may be. **at cost** at the initial cost; at cost price. **at the cost of** at the expense of losing or sacrificing. **cost accountant** an accountant who records costs and (esp. overhead) expenses in a business concern. **cost-benefit** assessing the relation between the cost of an operation and the value of the resulting benefits (*cost-benefit analysis*). **cost** (or **costing**) **clerk** a clerk who records costs and expenses in a business concern. **cost a person dear** (or **dearly**) involve a person in a high cost or a heavy penalty. **cost-effective** effective or productive in relation to its cost. **cost of living** the level of prices esp. of the basic necessities of life. **cost-plus** calculated as the basic cost plus a profit factor. **cost price** the price paid for a thing by one who later sells it. **cost push** *Econ.* factors other than demand that cause inflation. **to a person's cost** at a person's expense; with loss or disadvantage to a person. [ME f. OF *coster, couster, coust* ult. f. L *constare* stand firm, stand at a price (as COM-, *stare* stand)]

costal /ˈkɒst(ə)l/ *adj.* of the ribs. [F f. mod.L *costalis* f. L *costa* rib]

co-star /ˈkəʊstɑː(r)/ *n. & v.* —*n.* a cinema or stage star appearing with another or others of equal importance. —*v.* (**-starred, -starring**) **1** *intr.* take part as a co-star. **2** *tr.* (of a production) include as a co-star.

costard /ˈkɒstəd/ *n. Brit.* **1** a large ribbed variety of apple. **2** *archaic joc.* the head. [ME f. AF f. *coste* rib f. L *costa*]

costate /ˈkɒsteɪt/ *adj.* ribbed; having ribs or ridges. [L *costatus* f. *costa* rib]

coster /ˈkɒstə(r)/ *n. Brit.* = COSTERMONGER. [abbr.]

costermonger /ˈkɒstəˌmʌŋgə(r)/ *n. Brit.* a person who sells fruit, vegetables, etc., in the street from a barrow. [COSTARD + MONGER]

costive /ˈkɒstɪv/ *adj.* **1** constipated. **2** niggardly. □□ **costively** *adv.* **costiveness** *n.* [ME f. OF *costivé* f. L *constipatus*: see CONSTIPATE]

costly /ˈkɒstlɪ/ *adj.* (**costlier, costliest**) **1** costing much; expensive. **2** of great value. □□ **costliness** *n.*

costmary /ˈkɒstˌmeərɪ/ *n.* (*pl.* **-ies**) an aromatic composite plant, *Balsamita major*, formerly used in medicine and for flavouring ale. [OE *cost* f. L *costum* f. Gk *kostos* f. Arab. *ḳusṭ* an aromatic plant + (*St*) *Mary* (with whom it was associated in medieval times)]

costume /ˈkɒstjuːm/ *n. & v.* —*n.* **1** a style or fashion of dress, esp. that of a particular place, time, or class. **2** a set of clothes. **3** clothing for a particular activity (*swimming-costume*). **4** an actor's clothes for a part. **5** a woman's matching jacket and skirt. —*v.tr.* provide with a costume. □**costume jewellery** artificial jewellery worn to adorn clothes. **costume play** (or **piece**) a play in which the actors wear historical costume. [F f. It. f. L *consuetudo* CUSTOM]

costumier /kɒˈstjuːmɪə(r)/ *n.* (also **costumer** /-mə(r)/) a person who makes or deals in costumes, esp. for theatrical use. [F *costumier* (as COSTUME)]

cosy /ˈkəʊzɪ/ *adj., n., & v.* (*US* **cozy**) —*adj.* (**cosier, cosiest**) **1** comfortable and warm; snug. **2** *derog.* complacent. **3** warm and friendly. —*n.* (*pl.* **-ies**) **1** a cover to keep something hot, esp. a teapot or a boiled egg. **2** a canopied corner seat for two. —*v.tr.* (**-ies, -ied**) (often foll. by *along*) *colloq.* reassure, esp. deceptively. □**cosy up to** *US colloq.* **1** ingratiate oneself with. **2** snuggle up to. □□ **cosily** *adv.* **cosiness** *n.* [18th c. f. Sc., of unkn. orig.]

cot[1] /kɒt/ *n.* **1** *Brit.* a small bed with high sides, esp. for a baby or very young child. **2** a hospital bed. **3** *US* a small folding bed. **4** *Ind.* a light bedstead. **5** *Naut.* a kind of swinging bed hung from deck beams, formerly used by officers. □**cot-case** a person too ill to leave his or her bed. **cot-death** the unexplained

death of a baby while sleeping. [Anglo-Ind., f. Hindi *khāṭ* bedstead, hammock]

cot[2] /kɒt/ *n. & v.* —*n.* **1** a small shelter; a cote (*bell-cot; sheep-cot*). **2** *poet.* a cottage. —*v.tr.* (**cotted, cotting**) put (sheep) in a cot. [OE f. Gmc, rel. to COTE]

cot[3] /kɒt/ *abbr. Math.* cotangent.

cotangent /kəʊˈtændʒ(ə)nt/ *n. Math.* the ratio of the side adjacent to an acute angle (in a right-angled triangle) to the opposite side.

cote /kəʊt/ *n.* a shelter, esp. for animals or birds; a shed or stall (*sheep-cote*). [OE f. Gmc, rel. to COT[2]]

coterie /ˈkəʊtərɪ/ *n.* **1** an exclusive group of people sharing interests. **2** a select circle in society. [F, orig. = association of tenants, ult. f. MLG *kote* COTE]

coterminous /kəʊˈtɜːmɪnəs/ *adj.* (often foll. by *with*) having the same boundaries or extent (in space, time, or meaning). [CO- + TERMINUS + -OUS]

coth /kɒθ/ *abbr. Math.* hyperbolic cotangent.

co-tidal line /kəʊˈtaɪd(ə)l/ *n.* a line on a map connecting points at which tidal levels (as high tide or low tide) occur simultaneously.

cotillion /kəˈtɪljən/ *n.* **1** any of various French dances with elaborate steps, figures, and ceremonial. **2** *US* **a** a ballroom dance resembling a quadrille. **b** a formal ball. [F *cotillon* petticoat, dimin. of *cotte* f. OF *cote* COAT]

cotoneaster /kəˌtəʊnɪˈæstə(r)/ *n.* any rosaceous shrub of the genus *Cotoneaster*, bearing usu. bright red berries. [mod.L f. L *cotoneum* QUINCE + -ASTER]

cotta /ˈkɒtə/ *n. Eccl.* a short surplice. [It., formed as COAT]

cottage /ˈkɒtɪdʒ/ *n.* **1** a small simple house, esp. in the country. **2** a dwelling forming part of a farm establishment, used by a worker. □**cottage cheese** soft white cheese made from curds of skimmed milk without pressing. **cottage hospital** *Brit.* a small hospital not having resident medical staff. **cottage industry** a business activity partly or wholly carried on at home. **cottage loaf** a loaf formed of two round masses, the smaller on top of the larger. **cottage pie** *Brit.* a dish of minced meat topped with browned mashed potato. □□ **cottagey** *adj.* [ME f. AF, formed as COT[2], COTE]

cottager /ˈkɒtɪdʒə(r)/ *n.* a person who lives in a cottage.

cottar /ˈkɒtə(r)/ *n.* (also **cotter**) **1** *Sc. & hist.* a farm-labourer or tenant occupying a cottage in return for labour as required. **2** *Ir. hist.* = COTTIER. [COT[2] + -ER[1] (Sc. -*ar*)]

cotter /ˈkɒtə(r)/ *n.* **1** a bolt or wedge for securing parts of machinery etc. **2** (in full **cotter pin**) a split pin that opens after passing through a hole. [17th c. (rel. to earlier *cotterel*): orig. unkn.]

cottier /ˈkɒtɪə(r)/ *n. Brit.* **1** a cottager. **2** *hist.* an Irish peasant under cottier tenure. □**cottier tenure** *hist.* the letting of land in small portions at a rent fixed by competition. [ME f. OF *cotier* f. med.L *cotarius*: see COTERIE]

cotton /ˈkɒt(ə)n/ *n. & v.* —*n.* **1** a soft white fibrous substance covering the seeds of certain plants. **2 a** (in full **cotton plant**) such a plant, esp. any of the genus *Gossypium*. **b** cotton-plants cultivated as a crop for the fibre or the seeds. **3** thread or cloth made from the fibre. **4** (*attrib.*) made of cotton. —*v.intr.* (foll. by *to*) be attracted by (a person). □**cotton-cake** compressed cotton seed used as food for cattle. **cotton candy** *US* candyfloss. **cotton-gin** a machine for separating cotton from its seeds. **cotton-grass** any grasslike plant of the genus *Eriophorum*, with long white silky hairs. **cotton on** (often foll. by *to*) *colloq.* begin to understand. **cotton-picking** *US sl.* unpleasant, wretched. **cotton waste** refuse yarn used to clean machinery etc. **cotton wool 1** esp. *Brit.* fluffy wadding of a kind orig. made from raw cotton. **2** *US* raw cotton. □□ **cottony** *adj.* [ME f. OF *coton* f. Arab. *ḳuṭn*]

cottontail /ˈkɒt(ə)nˌteɪl/ *n.* any rabbit of the genus

Sylvilagus, native to America, having a mainly white fluffy tail.

cottonwood /'kɒt(ə)n,wʊd/ *n.* **1** any of several poplars, native to N. America, having seeds covered in white cottony hairs. **2** any of several trees native to Australia, esp. a downy-leaved tree, *Bedfordia arborescens*.

cotyledon /,kɒtɪ'li:d(ə)n/ *n.* **1** an embryonic leaf in seed-bearing plants. **2** any succulent plant of the genus *Umbilicus*, e.g. pennywort. □□ **cotyledonary** *adj.* **cotyledonous** *adj.* [L, = pennywort, f. Gk *kotulēdōn* cup-shaped cavity f. *kotulē* cup]

coucal /'ku:kæl/ *n.* any ground-nesting bird of the genus *Centropus*, related to the cuckoos. [F, perh. f. *coucou* cuckoo + *alouette* lark]

couch[1] /kaʊtʃ/ *n. & v.* —*n.* **1** an upholstered piece of furniture for several people; a sofa. **2** a long padded seat with a headrest at one end, esp. one on which a psychiatrist's or doctor's patient reclines during examination. —*v.* **1** *tr.* (foll. by *in*) express in words of a specified kind (*couched in simple language*). **2** *tr.* lay on or as on a couch. **3** *intr.* **a** (of an animal) lie, esp. in its lair. **b** lie in ambush. **4** *tr.* lower (a spear etc.) to the position for attack. **5** *tr. Med.* treat (a cataract) by displacing the lens of the eye. □ **couch potato** *US sl.* a young person who likes lazing at home. [ME f. OF *couche, coucher* f. L *collocare* (as COM-, *locare* place)]

couch[2] /kuːtʃ, kaʊtʃ/ *n.* (in full **couch grass**) any of several grasses of the genus *Agropyron*, esp. *A. repens*, having long creeping roots. [var. of QUITCH]

couchant /'kaʊtʃ(ə)nt/ *adj.* (placed after noun) *Heraldry* (of an animal) lying with the body resting on the legs and the head raised. [F, pres. part. of *coucher*: see COUCH[1]]

couchette /kuː'ʃet/ *n.* **1** a railway carriage with seats convertible into sleeping-berths. **2** a berth in this. [F, = little bed, dimin. of *couche* COUCH[1]]

coudé /kuː'deɪ/ *adj. & n.* —*adj.* of or relating to a telescope in which rays are bent to a focus off the axis. —*n.* such a telescope. [F, past part. of *couder* bend at right angles f. *coude* elbow formed as CUBIT]

Couéism /'kuːeɪ,ɪz(ə)m/ *n.* a system of usu. optimistic auto-suggestion as psychotherapy. [E. *Coué*, Fr. psychologist d. 1926]

cougar /'kuːgə(r)/ *n. US* a puma. [F, repr. Guarani *guaçu ara*]

cough /kɒf/ *v. & n.* —*v.intr.* **1** expel air from the lungs with a sudden sharp sound produced by abrupt opening of the glottis, to remove an obstruction or congestion. **2** (of an engine, gun, etc.) make a similar sound. **3** *sl.* confess. —*n.* **1** an act of coughing. **2** a condition of the respiratory organs causing coughing. **3** a tendency to cough. □ **cough drop** (or **sweet**) a medicated lozenge to relieve a cough. **cough mixture** a liquid medicine to relieve a cough. **cough out 1** eject by coughing. **2** say with a cough. **cough up 1** = *cough out*. **2** *sl.* bring out or give (money or information) reluctantly. □□ **cougher** *n.* [ME *coghe, cowhe*, rel. to MDu. *kuchen*, MHG *kūchen*, of imit. orig.]

could *past* of CAN[1].

couldn't /'kʊd(ə)nt/ *contr.* could not.

coulée /'kuːleɪ, 'kuːlɪ/ *n. Geol.* **1** a solidified lava-flow. **2** *US* a deep ravine. [F, fem. past part. of *couler* flow, f. L *colare* strain, filter]

coulisse /kuː'liːs/ *n.* **1** (usu. in *pl.*) *Theatr.* a piece of side scenery or a space between two of these; the wings. **2** a place of informal discussion or negotiation. [F f. *coulis* sliding: see PORTCULLIS]

couloir /'kuːlwɑː(r)/ *n.* a steep narrow gully on a mountainside. [F f. *couler* glide: see COULÉE]

coulomb /'kuːlɒm/ *n. Electr.* the SI unit of electric charge, equal to the quantity of electricity conveyed in one second by a current of one ampere. ¶ Symb.: **C**. [C. A. de *Coulomb*, Fr. physicist d. 1806]

coulometry /kuː'lɒmɪtrɪ/ *n. Chem.* a method of chemical analysis by measurement of the number of coulombs used in electrolysis. □□ **coulometric** /,kuːlə'metrɪk/ *adj.*

coulter /'kəʊltə(r)/ *n.* (*US* **colter**) a vertical cutting blade fixed in front of a ploughshare. [OE f. L *culter*]

coumarin /'kuːmərɪn/ *n.* an aromatic substance found in many plants and formerly used for flavouring food. [F *coumarine* f. Tupi *cumarú* tonka bean]

coumarone /'kuːmə,rəʊn/ *n.* an organic liquid obtained from coal tar by synthesis and used in paints and varnishes. □ **coumarone resin** a thermoplastic resin formed by polymerization of coumarone. [COUMARIN + -ONE]

council /'kaʊns(ə)l/ *n.* **1 a** an advisory, deliberative, or administrative body of people formally constituted and meeting regularly. **b** a meeting of such a body. **2 a** the elected local administrative body of a parish, district, town, city, or administrative county and its paid officers and workforce. **b** (*attrib.*) (esp. of housing) provided by a local council (*council flat*; *council estate*). **3** a body of persons chosen as advisers (*Privy Council*). **4** an ecclesiastical assembly (*ecumenical council*). □ **council-chamber** a room in which a council meets. **council-house** a building in which a council meets. **council of war 1** an assembly of officers called in a special emergency. **2** any meeting held to plan a response to an emergency. **the Queen** (or **King**) **in Council** the Privy Council as issuing Orders in Council or receiving petitions etc. [ME f. AF *cuncile* f. L *concilium* convocation, assembly f. *calare* summon: cf. COUNSEL]

councillor /'kaʊnsələ(r)/ *n.* an elected member of a council, esp. a local one. □□ **councillorship** *n.* [ME, alt. of COUNSELLOR: assim. to COUNCIL]

councilman /'kaʊns(ə)lmən/ *n.* (*pl.* **-men**; *fem.* **councilwoman**, *pl.* **-women**) esp. *US* a member of a council; a councillor.

counsel /'kaʊns(ə)l/ *n. & v.* —*n.* **1** advice, esp. formally given. **2** consultation, esp. to seek or give advice. **3** (*pl.* same) a barrister or other legal adviser; a body of these advising in a case. **4** a plan of action. —*v.tr.* (**counselled**, **counselling**; *US* **counseled**, **counseling**) **1** (often foll. by *to* + infin.) advise (a person). **2 a** give advice to (a person) on social or personal problems, esp. professionally. **b** assist or guide (a person) in resolving personal difficulties. **3** (often foll. by *that*) recommend (a course of action). □ **counsel of despair** action to be taken when all else fails. **counsel of perfection 1** advice that is ideal but not feasible. **2** advice guiding towards moral perfection. **keep one's own counsel** not confide in others. **Queen's** (or **King's**) **Counsel** *Brit.* a counsel to the Crown, taking precedence over other barristers. **take counsel** (usu. foll. by *with*) consult. [ME f. OF *c(o)unseil, conseiller* f. L *consilium* consultation, advice]

counselling /'kaʊnsəlɪŋ/ *n.* (*US* **counseling**) **1** the act or process of giving counsel. **2** the process of assisting and guiding clients, esp. by a trained person on a professional basis, to resolve esp. personal, social, or psychological problems and difficulties (cf. COUNSEL *v.* 2b).

counsellor /'kaʊnsələ(r)/ *n.* (*US* **counselor**) **1** a person who gives counsel; an adviser. **2** a person trained to give guidance on personal, social, or psychological problems (*marriage guidance counsellor*). **3** a senior officer in the diplomatic service. **4 a** (also **counselor-at-law**) *US* a barrister. **b** (also **counselor-at-law**) *Ir.* an advising barrister. □ **Counsellor of State** *Brit.* a temporary regent during a sovereign's absence. [ME f. OF *conseiller* (f. L *consiliarius*), *conseillour*, *-eur* (f. L *consiliator*): see COUNSEL]

count[1] /kaʊnt/ *v. & n.* —*v.* **1** *tr.* determine the total number or amount of, esp. by assigning successive numbers (*count the stations*). **2** *intr.* repeat numbers in ascending order; conduct a reckoning. **3 a** *tr.* (often foll. by *in*) include in one's reckoning or plan (*you can count me in*; *fifteen people, counting the guide*). **b** *intr.* be included in a reckoning or plan. **4** *tr.* consider (a thing or a person) to be (lucky etc.) (*count no man happy until he is dead*). **5** *intr.* (often foll. by *for*) have value; matter (*his opinion counts for a great deal*). —*n.* **1 a** the act of counting; a reckoning (*after a count of fifty*). **b** the sum total of a reckoning (*blood count*; *pollen count*). **2** *Law* each charge in an indictment (*guilty on ten counts*). **3** a count of up to ten seconds by a referee when a boxer is knocked down. **4** *Polit.* the act of counting the votes after a general or local election. **5** one of several points under discussion. **6** the measure of the fineness of a yarn expressed as the weight of a given length or the length of a given weight. **7** *Physics* the number of ionizing particles detected by a counter. □**count against** be reckoned to the disadvantage of. **count one's blessings** be grateful for what one has. **count one's chickens** be over-optimistic or hasty in anticipating good fortune. **count the cost** consider the risks before taking action. **count the days** (or **hours** etc.) be impatient. **count down** recite numbers backwards to zero, esp. as part of a rocket-launching procedure. **counting-house** a place where accounts are kept. **count noun** a countable noun (see COUNTABLE 2). **count on** (or **upon**) depend on, rely on; expect confidently. **count out 1** count while taking from a stock. **2** complete a count of ten seconds over (a fallen boxer etc.), indicating defeat. **3** (in children's games) select (a player) for dismissal or a special role by use of a counting rhyme etc. **4** *colloq.* exclude from a plan or reckoning (*I'm too tired, count me out*). **5** *Brit. Polit.* procure the adjournment of (the House of Commons) when fewer than 40 members are present. **count up** find the sum of. **keep count** take note of how many there have been etc. **lose count** fail to take note of the number etc. **not counting** excluding from the reckoning. **out for the count 1** *Boxing* defeated by being unable to rise within ten seconds. **2 a** defeated or demoralized. **b** soundly asleep. **take the count** *Boxing* be defeated. [ME f. OF *co(u)nter, co(u)nte* f. LL *computus, computare* COMPUTE]

count² /kaʊnt/ *n.* a foreign noble corresponding to an earl. □**Count Palatine** *hist.* a high official of the Holy Roman Empire with royal authority within his domain. □□ **countship** *n.* [OF *conte* f. L *comes comitis* companion]

countable /ˈkaʊntəb(ə)l/ *adj.* **1** that can be counted. **2** *Gram.* (of a noun) that can form a plural or be used with the indefinite article (e.g. *book, kindness*).

countdown /ˈkaʊntdaʊn/ *n.* **1 a** the act of counting down, esp. at the launching of a rocket etc. **b** the procedures carried out during this time. **2** the final moments before any significant event.

countenance /ˈkaʊntɪnəns/ *n.* & *v.* —*n.* **1 a** the face. **b** the facial expression. **2** composure. **3** moral support. —*v.tr.* **1** give approval to (an act etc.) (*cannot countenance this breach of the rules*). **2** (often foll. by *in*) encourage (a person or a practice). □**change countenance** alter one's expression as an effect of emotion. **keep one's countenance** maintain composure, esp. by refraining from laughter. **keep a person in countenance** support or encourage a person. **lose countenance** become embarrassed. **out of countenance** disconcerted. [ME f. AF *c(o)untenance*, OF *contenance* bearing f. *contenir*: see CONTAIN]

counter¹ /ˈkaʊntə(r)/ *n.* **1 a** a long flat-topped fitment in a shop, bank, etc., across which business is conducted with customers. **b** a similar structure used for serving food etc. in a cafeteria or bar. **2 a** a small disc used for keeping the score etc. esp. in table-games. **b** a token representing a coin. **c** something used in bargaining; a pawn (*a counter in the struggle for power*). **3** an apparatus used for counting. **4** *Physics* an apparatus used for counting

individual ionizing particles etc. **5** a person or thing that counts. □**over the counter** by ordinary retail purchase. **under the counter** (esp. of the sale of scarce goods) surreptitiously, esp. illegally. [AF *count(e)our*, OF *conteo(i)r*, f. med.L *computatorium* (as COMPUTE)]

counter² /ˈkaʊntə(r)/ *v., adv., adj.,* & *n.* —*v.* **1** *tr.* a oppose, contradict (*countered our proposal with their own*). **b** meet by a countermove. **2** *intr.* **a** make a countermove. **b** make an opposing statement ('*I shall!*' *he countered*). **3** *intr. Boxing* give a return blow while parrying. —*adv.* **1** in the opposite direction (*ran counter to the fox*). **2** contrary (*his action was counter to my wishes*). —*adj.* **1** opposed; opposite. **2** duplicate; serving as a check. —*n.* **1 a** parry; a countermove. **2** something opposite or opposed. □**act** (or **go**) **counter to** disobey (instructions etc.). **go** (or **hunt** or **run**) **counter** run or ride against the direction taken by a quarry. **run counter to** act contrary to. [ME f. OF *countre* f. L *contra* against: see COUNTER-]

counter³ /ˈkaʊntə(r)/ *n.* **1** the part of a horse's breast between the shoulders and under the neck. **2** the curved part of the stern of a ship. **3** *Printing* a part of a printing-type etc. that is completely enclosed by an outline (e.g. the loop of P). [17th c.: orig. unkn.]

counter⁴ /ˈkaʊntə(r)/ *n.* the back part of a shoe or a boot round the heel. [abbr. of *counterfort* buttress]

counter- /ˈkaʊntə(r)/ *comb. form* denoting: **1** retaliation, opposition, or rivalry (*counter-threat; counter-cheers*). **2** opposite direction (*counter-current*). **3** correspondence, duplication, or substitution (*counterpart; countersign*). [from or after AF *countre-*, OF *contre* f. L *contra* against]

counteract /ˌkaʊntəˈrækt/ *v.tr.* **1** hinder or oppose by contrary action. **2** neutralize. □□ **counteraction** *n.* **counteractive** *adj.*

counter-attack /ˈkaʊntərəˌtæk/ *n.* & *v.* —*n.* an attack in reply to an attack by an enemy or opponent. —*v.tr.* & *intr.* attack in reply.

counter-attraction /ˈkaʊntərəˌtrækʃ(ə)n/ *n.* **1** a rival attraction. **2** the attraction of a contrary tendency.

counterbalance /ˈkaʊntəˌbæləns/ *n.* & *v.* —*n.* **1** a weight balancing another. **2** an argument, force, etc., balancing another. —*v.tr.* act as a counterbalance to.

counterblast /ˈkaʊntəˌblɑːst/ *n.* (often foll. by *to*) an energetic or violent verbal or written reply to an argument etc.

counterchange /ˈkaʊntəˌtʃeɪndʒ/ *v.* **1** *tr.* change (places or parts); interchange. **2** *tr. literary* chequer, esp. with contrasting colours etc. **3** *intr.* change places or parts. [F *contrechanger* (as COUNTER-, CHANGE)]

countercharge /ˈkaʊntəˌtʃɑːdʒ/ *n.* & *v.* —*n.* a charge or accusation in return for one received. —*v.tr.* make a countercharge against.

countercheck /ˈkaʊntəˌtʃek/ *n.* & *v.* —*n.* **1 a** a restraint that opposes something. **b** a restraint that operates against another. **2** a second check, esp. for security or accuracy. **3** *archaic* a retort. —*v.tr.* make a countercheck on.

counter-claim /ˈkaʊntəˌkleɪm/ *n.* & *v.* —*n.* **1** a claim made against another claim. **2** *Law* a claim made by a defendant in a suit against the plaintiff. —*v.tr.* & *intr.* make a counter-claim (for).

counter-clockwise /ˌkaʊntəˈklɒkwaɪz/ *adv.* & *adj.* *US* = ANTICLOCKWISE.

counter-culture /ˈkaʊntəˌkʌltʃə(r)/ *n.* a way of life etc. opposed to that usually considered normal.

counter-espionage /ˌkaʊntərˈespɪɑˌnɑːʒ, -ɪdʒ/ *n.* action taken to frustrate enemy spying.

counterfeit /ˈkaʊntəfɪt, -fiːt/ *adj., n.,* & *v.* —*adj.* **1** (of a coin, writing, etc.) made in imitation; not genuine; forged. **2** (of a claimant etc.) pretended. —*n.* a forgery; an imitation. —*v.tr.* **1 a** imitate fraudulently (a coin, handwriting, etc.); forge. **b**

make an imitation of. **2** simulate (feelings etc.) (*counterfeited interest*). **3** resemble closely. □□ **counterfeiter** *n*. [ME f. OF *countrefet, -fait*, past part. of *contrefaire* f. Rmc]

counterfoil /'kaʊntəˌfɔɪl/ *n*. the part of a cheque, receipt, etc., retained by the payer and containing details of the transaction.

counter-intelligence /ˌkaʊntərɪn'telɪdʒ(ə)ns/ *n*. = COUNTER-ESPIONAGE.

counterirritant /ˌkaʊntər'ɪrɪt(ə)nt/ *n*. **1** *Med*. something used to produce surface irritation of the skin, thereby counteracting more painful symptoms. **2** anything resembling a counterirritant in its effects. □□ **counterirritation** /-'teɪʃ(ə)n/ *n*.

countermand /ˌkaʊntə'mɑːnd/ *v*. & *n*. —*v.tr*. **1** *Mil*. **a** revoke (an order or command). **b** recall (forces etc.) by a contrary order. **2** cancel an order for (goods etc.). —*n*. an order revoking a previous one. [ME f. OF *contremander* f. med.L *contramandare* (as CONTRA-, *mandare* order)]

countermarch /ˌkaʊntə'mɑːtʃ/ *v*. & *n*. —*v.intr*. & *tr*. esp. *Mil*. march or cause to march in the opposite direction, e.g. with the front marchers turning and marching back through the ranks. —*n*. an act of countermarching.

countermeasure /'kaʊntəˌmeʒə(r)/ *n*. an action taken to counteract a danger, threat, etc.

countermine /'kaʊntəˌmaɪn/ *n*. & *v*. —*n*. **1** *Mil*. **a** a mine dug to intercept another dug by an enemy. **b** a submarine mine sunk to explode an enemy's mines. **2** a counterplot. —*v.tr*. make a countermine against.

countermove /'kaʊntəˌmuːv/ *n*. & *v*. —*n*. a move or action in opposition to another. —*v.intr*. make a countermove. □□ **countermovement** *n*.

counter-offensive /'kaʊntərəˌfensɪv/ *n*. **1** *Mil*. an attack made from a defensive position in order to effect an escape. **2** any attack made from a defensive position.

counterpane /'kaʊntəˌpeɪn/ *n*. a bedspread. [alt. (with assim. to *pane* in obs. sense 'cloth') f. obs. *counterpoint* f. OF *contrepointe* alt. f. *cou(l)tepointe* f. med.L *culcita puncta* quilted mattress]

counterpart /'kaʊntəˌpɑːt/ *n*. **1 a** a person or thing extremely like another. **b** a person or thing forming a natural complement or equivalent to another. **2** *Law* one of two copies of a legal document. □ **counterpart funds** *US* funds etc. in a local currency equivalent to goods etc. received from abroad.

counterplot /'kaʊntəˌplɒt/ *n*. & *v*. —*n*. a plot intended to defeat another plot. —*v*. (**-plotted, -plotting**) **1** *intr*. make a counterplot. **2** *tr*. make a counterplot against.

counterpoint /'kaʊntəˌpɔɪnt/ *n*. & *v*. —*n*. **1** *Mus*. **a** the art or technique of setting, writing, or playing a melody or melodies in conjunction with another, according to fixed rules. **b** a melody played in conjunction with another. **2** a contrasting argument, plot, idea, or literary theme, etc., used to set off the main element. —*v.tr*. **1** *Mus*. add counterpoint to. **2** set (an argument, plot, etc.) in contrast to (a main element). □ **strict counterpoint** an academic exercise in writing counterpoint, not necessarily intended as a composition. [OF *contrepoint* f. med.L *contrapunctum* pricked or marked opposite, i.e. to the original melody (as CONTRA-, *pungere punct-* prick)]

counterpoise /'kaʊntəˌpɔɪz/ *n*. & *v*. —*n*. **1** a force etc. equivalent to another on the opposite side. **2** a state of equilibrium. **3** a counterbalancing weight. —*v.tr*. **1** counterbalance. **2** compensate. **3** bring into or keep in equilibrium. [ME f. OF *contrepeis, -pois, contrepeser* (as COUNTER-, *peis, pois* f. L *pensum* weight: cf. POISE[1])]

counter-productive /ˌkaʊntəprə'dʌktɪv/ *adj*. having the opposite of the desired effect.

counter-reformation /ˌkaʊntəˌrefə'meɪʃ(ə)n/ *n*. **1** (**Counter-Reformation**) *hist*. the reform of the Church of Rome in the 16th and 17th centuries which

took place in response to the Protestant Reformation. **2** a reformation running counter to another.

counter-revolution /ˌkaʊntəˌrevə'luːʃ(ə)n/ *n*. a revolution opposing a former one or reversing its results. □□ **counter-revolutionary** *adj*. & *n*. (*pl*. **-ies**).

counterscarp /'kaʊntəˌskɑːp/ *n*. *Mil*. the outer wall or slope of a ditch in a fortification. [F *contrescarpe* f. It. *contrascarpa* (as CONTRA-, SCARP)]

countershaft /'kaʊntəˌʃɑːft/ *n*. **1** an intermediate shaft driven by a main shaft and transmitting motion to a particular machine etc. **2** *US* = LAYSHAFT.

countersign /'kaʊntəˌsaɪn/ *v*. & *n*. —*v.tr*. **1** add a signature to (a document already signed by another). **2** ratify. —*n*. **1** a watchword or password spoken to a person on guard (cf. PAROLE). **2** a mark used for identification etc. □□ **counter-signature** /-'sɪgnətʃə(r)/ *n*. [F *contresigner* (v.), *contresigne* (n.) f. It. *contrasegno* (as COUNTER-, SIGN)]

countersink /'kaʊntəˌsɪŋk/ *v.tr*. (*past* and *past part*. **-sunk**) **1** enlarge and bevel (the rim of a hole) so that a screw or bolt can be inserted flush with the surface. **2** sink (a screw etc.) in such a hole.

counterstroke /'kaʊntəˌstrəʊk/ *n*. a blow given in return for another.

counter-tenor /'kaʊntəˌtenə(r)/ *n*. *Mus*. **1 a** a male alto singing-voice. **b** a singer with this voice. **2 a** part written for counter-tenor. [ME f. F *contre-teneur* f. obs. It. *contratenore* (as CONTRA-, TENOR)]

countervail /ˌkaʊntə'veɪl, 'kaʊntə-/ *v*. **1** *tr*. counterbalance. **2** *tr*. & *intr*. (often foll. by *against*) oppose forcefully and usu. successfully. □ **countervailing duty** a tax put on imports to offset a subsidy in the exporting country or a tax on similar goods not from abroad. [ME f. AF *contrevaloir* f. L *contra valēre* be of worth against]

countervalue /'kaʊntəˌvælju:/ *n*. an equivalent value, esp. in military strategy.

counterweight /'kaʊntəˌweɪt/ *n*. a counterbalancing weight.

countess /'kaʊntɪs/ *n*. **1** the wife or widow of a count or an earl. **2** a woman holding the rank of count or earl. [ME f. OF *contesse, cuntesse*, f. LL *comitissa* fem. of *comes* COUNT[2]]

countless /'kaʊntlɪs/ *adj*. too many to be counted.

countrified /'kʌntrɪˌfaɪd/ *adj*. (also **countryfied**) often *derog*. rural or rustic, esp. of manners, appearance, etc. [past part. of *countrify* f. COUNTRY]

country /'kʌntrɪ/ *n*. (*pl*. **-ies**) **1 a** the territory of a nation with its own government; a State. **b** a territory possessing its own language, people, culture, etc. **2** (often *attrib*.) rural districts as opposed to towns or the capital (*a cottage in the country; a country town*). **3** the land of a person's birth or citizenship; a fatherland. **4 a** a territory, esp. an area of interest or knowledge. **b** a region associated with a particular person, esp. a writer (*Hardy country*). **5** *Brit*. a national population, esp. as voters (*the country won't stand for it*). □ **across country** not keeping to roads. **country-and-western** rural or cowboy songs originating in the US, and usu. accompanied by a guitar etc. **country club** a sporting and social club in a rural setting. **country cousin** often *derog*. a person with a countrified appearance or manners. **country dance** a traditional sort of dance, esp. English, with couples facing each other in long lines. **country gentleman** a gentleman with landed property. **country house** a usu. large house in the country, often the seat of a country gentleman. **country music** = *country-and-western*. **country party** a political party supporting agricultural interests. **country seat** a large country house belonging to an aristocratic family. **country-wide** extending throughout a nation. **go** (or **appeal**) **to the country** *Brit*. test public opinion by dissolving Parliament and holding a general election. **in the country** *Cricket sl*. far from the wickets; in the deep field. **line of country** a subject about which a person is knowledgeable. **unknown country** an unfamiliar place or topic. [ME f. OF *cuntree*, f. med.L *contrata* (*terra*) (land) lying opposite (CONTRA)]

countryfied var. of COUNTRIFIED.

countryman /'kʌntrɪmən/ *n.* (*pl.* **-men**; *fem.* **countrywoman**, *pl.* **-women**) **1** a person living in a rural area. **2 a** (also **fellow-countryman**) a person of one's own country or district. **b** (often in *comb.*) a person from a specified country or district (*north-countryman*).

countryside /'kʌntrɪ,saɪd/ *n.* **1 a** a rural area. **b** rural areas in general. **2** the inhabitants of a rural area.

county /'kaʊntɪ/ *n. & adj.* —*n.* (*pl.* **-ies**) **1 a** any of the territorial divisions of some countries, forming the chief unit of local administration. **b** US a political and administrative division of a State. **2** the people of a county, esp. the leading families. —*adj.* having the social status or characteristics of county families. □**county borough** *hist.* a large borough ranking as a county for administrative purposes. **county corporate** *hist.* a city or town ranking as an administrative county. **county council** the elected governing body of an administrative county. **county court** a judicial court for civil cases (in the US for civil and criminal cases). **county cricket** cricket matches between teams representing counties. **county family** an aristocratic family with an ancestral seat in a county. **County Palatine** the territory of a Count or Earl Palatine. **county town** (*US* **seat**) the administrative capital of a county. [ME f. AF *counté*, OF *conté*, *cunté*, f. L *comitatus* (as COUNT[2])]

coup /ku:/ *n.* (*pl.* **coups** /ku:z/) **1** a notable or successful stroke or move. **2** = COUP D'ÉTAT. **3** *Billiards* a direct pocketing of the ball. [F f. med.L *colpus* blow: see COPE[1]]

coup de grâce /,ku: də 'grɑːs/ *n.* a finishing stroke, esp. to kill a wounded animal or person. [F, lit. stroke of grace]

coup de main /,ku: də 'mæ̃/ *n.* a sudden vigorous attack. [F, lit. stroke of the hand]

coup d'état /,ku: deɪ'tɑ:/ *n.* a violent or illegal seizure of power. [F, lit. stroke of the State]

coup d'œil /ku: 'dɔɪ/ *n.* **1** a comprehensive glance. **2** a general view. [F, lit. stroke of the eye]

coupe /ku:p/ *n.* **1** a shallow glass or dish used for serving fruit, ice-cream, etc. **2** fruit, ice-cream, etc. served in this. [F, = goblet]

coupé /'ku:peɪ/ *n.* (*US* **coupe** /ku:p/) **1** a car with a hard roof, esp. one with two seats and a sloping rear. **2** *hist.* a four-wheeled enclosed carriage for two passengers and a driver. [F, past part. of *couper* cut (formed as COUP)]

couple /'kʌp(ə)l/ *n. & v.* —*n.* **1** (usu. foll. by *of*; often as *sing.*) **a** two (*a couple of girls*). **b** about two (*a couple of hours*). **2** (often as *sing.*) **a** a married or engaged pair. **b** a pair of partners in a dance, a game, etc. **c** a pair of rafters. **3** (*pl.* **couple**) a pair of hunting dogs (*six couple of hounds*). **4** (in *pl.*) a pair of joined collars used for holding hounds together. **5** *Mech.* a pair of equal and parallel forces acting in opposite directions, and tending to cause rotation about an axis perpendicular to the plane containing them. —*v.* **1** *tr.* fasten or link together; connect (esp. railway carriages). **2** *tr.* (often foll. by *together, with*) associate in thought or speech (*papers coupled their names*; *couple our congratulations with our best wishes*). **3** *intr.* copulate. **4** *tr. Physics* connect (oscillators) with a coupling. [ME f. OF *cople, cuple, copler, cupler* f. L *copulare*, L COPULA]

coupler /'kʌplə(r)/ *n.* **1** *Mus.* **a** a device in an organ for connecting two manuals, or a manual with pedals, so that they both sound when only one is played. **b** (also **octave coupler**) a similar device for connecting notes with their octaves above or below. **2** anything that connects two things, esp. a transformer used for connecting electric circuits.

couplet /'kʌplɪt/ *n. Prosody* two successive lines of verse, usu. rhyming and of the same length. [F dimin. of *couple*, formed as COUPLE]

coupling /'kʌplɪŋ/ *n.* **1 a** a link connecting railway carriages etc. **b** a device for connecting parts of machinery. **2** *Physics* a connection between two systems, causing one to oscillate when the other does so. **3** *Mus.* **a** the arrangement of items on a gramophone record. **b** each such item.

coupon /'ku:pɒn/ *n.* **1** a form etc. in a newspaper, magazine, etc., which may be filled in and sent as an application for a purchase, information, etc. **2** *Brit.* an entry form for a football pool or other competition. **3** a voucher given with a retail purchase, a certain number of which entitle the holder to a discount etc. **4 a** a detachable ticket entitling the holder to a ration of food, clothes, etc., esp. in wartime. **b** a similar ticket entitling the holder to payment, goods, services, etc. [F, = piece cut off f. *couper* cut: see COUPÉ]

courage /'kʌrɪdʒ/ *n.* the ability to disregard fear; bravery. □**courage of one's convictions** the courage to act on one's beliefs. **lose courage** become less brave. **pluck up** (or **take**) **courage** muster one's courage. **take one's courage in both hands** nerve oneself to a venture. [ME f. OF *corage*, f. L *cor* heart]

courageous /kə'reɪdʒəs/ *adj.* brave, fearless. □□ **courageously** *adv.* **courageousness** *n.* [ME f. AF *corageus*, OF *corageus* (as COURAGE)]

courante /kʊ'rɑːnt/ *n.* **1** *hist.* a running or gliding dance. **2** *Mus.* the music used for this, esp. as a movement of a suite. [F, fem. pres. part. (as noun) of *courir* run f. L *currere*]

courgette /kʊə'ʒet/ *n.* a small green variety of vegetable marrow. Also called ZUCCHINI. [F, dimin. of *courge* gourd]

courier /'kʊrɪə(r)/ *n.* **1** a person employed, usu. by a travel company, to guide and assist a group of tourists. **2** a special messenger. [ME f. obs. F, f. It. *corriere*, & f. OF *coreor*, both f. L *currere* run]

course /kɔːs/ *n. & v.* —*n.* **1** a continuous onward movement or progression. **2 a** a line along which a person or thing moves; a direction taken (*has changed course*; *the course of the winding river*). **b** a correct or intended direction or line of movement. **c** the direction taken by a ship or aircraft. **3 a** the ground on which a race (or other sport involving extensive linear movement) takes place. **b** a series of fences, hurdles, or other obstacles to be crossed in a race etc. **4 a** a series of lectures, lessons, etc., in a particular subject. **b** a book for such a course (*A Modern French Course*). **5** any of the successive parts of a meal. **6** *Med.* a sequence of medical treatment etc. (*prescribed a course of antibiotics*). **7** a line of conduct (*disappointed by the course he took*). **8** *Archit.* a continuous horizontal layer of brick, stone, etc., in a building. **9** a channel in which water flows. **10** the pursuit of game (esp. hares) with hounds, esp. greyhounds, by sight rather than scent. **11** *Naut.* a sail on a square-rigged ship (*fore course*; *main course*). —*v.* **1** *intr.* (esp. of liquid) run, esp. fast (*blood coursed through his veins*). **2** *tr.* (also *absol.*) **a** use (hounds) to hunt. **b** pursue (hares etc.) in hunting. □**the course of nature** ordinary events or procedure. **in course of** in the process of. **in the course of** during. **in the course of time** as time goes by; eventually. **a matter of course** the natural or expected thing. **of course** naturally; as is or was to be expected; admittedly. **on** (or **off**) **course** following (or deviating from) the desired direction or goal. **run** (or **take**) **its course** (esp. of an illness) complete its natural development. □□ **courser** *n.* (in sense 2 of *v.*). [ME f. OF *cours* f. L *cursus* f. *currere* *curs-* run]

courser[1] /'kɔːsə(r)/ *n. poet.* a swift horse. [ME f. OF *corsier* f. Rmc]

courser[2] /'kɔːsə(r)/ *n.* any fast-running plover-like bird of the genus *Cursorius*, native to Africa and

Asia, having long legs and a slender bill. [LL *cursorius* adapted for running]

court /kɔːt/ *n. & v.* —*n.* **1** (in full **court of law**) **a** an assembly of judges or other persons acting as a tribunal in civil and criminal cases. **b** = COURTROOM. **2 a** an enclosed quadrangular area for games, which may be open or covered (*tennis-court; squash-court*). **b** an area marked out for lawn tennis etc. (*hit the ball out of court*). **3 a** a small enclosed street in a town, having a yard surrounded by houses, and adjoining a larger street. **b** *Brit.* = COURTYARD. **c** (**Court**) the name of a large house, block of flats, street, etc. (*Grosvenor Court*). **d** (at Cambridge University) a college quadrangle. **e** a subdivision of a building, usu. a large hall extending to the ceiling with galleries and staircases. **4 a** the establishment, retinue, and courtiers of a sovereign. **b** a sovereign and his or her councillors, constituting a ruling power. **c** a sovereign's residence. **d** an assembly held by a sovereign; a State reception. **5** attention paid to a person whose favour, love, or interest is sought (*paid court to her*). **6 a** the qualified members of a company or a corporation. **b** (in some Friendly Societies) a local branch. **c** a meeting of a court. —*v.tr.* **1 a** try to win the affection or favour of (a person). **b** pay amorous attention to (*courting couples*). **2** seek to win (applause, fame, etc.). **3** invite (misfortune) by one's actions (*you are courting disaster*). □**court-card** a playing-card that is a king, queen, or jack (orig. *coat-card*). **court circular** *Brit.* a daily report of royal court affairs, published in some newspapers. **court dress** formal dress worn at a royal court. **court-house** a building in which a judicial court is held. **2** *US* a building containing the administrative offices of a county. **Court leet** see LEET[1]. **Court of Appeal** a court of law hearing appeals against judgements in the Crown Court, High Court, County Court, etc. **Court of Protection** *Brit.* the department of the Supreme Court attending to the affairs of the mentally unfit. **court of record** a court whose proceedings are recorded and available as evidence of fact. **Court of St James's** the British sovereign's court. **Court of Session** the supreme civil court in Scotland. **court of summary jurisdiction** a court having the authority to use summary proceedings and arrive at a judgement or conviction. **court order** a direction issued by a court or a judge, usu. requiring a person to do or not do something. **court plaster** *hist.* sticking-plaster for cuts etc. (formerly used by ladies at court for face-patches). **court roll** *hist.* a manorial-court register of holdings. **court shoe** a woman's light, usu. high-heeled, shoe with a low-cut upper. **court tennis** *US* real tennis. **go to court** take legal action. **in court** appearing as a party or an advocate in a court of law. **out of court 1** (of a plaintiff) not entitled to be heard. **2** (of a settlement) arranged before a hearing or judgement can take place. **3** not worthy of consideration (*that suggestion is out of court*). [ME f. AF *curt*, OF *cort*, ult. f. L *cohors, -hortis* yard, retinue: (v.) after OIt. *corteare*, OF *courtoyer*]

court bouillon /ˌkʊə(r) buˈjɔ̃/ *n.* stock usu. made from wine, vegetables, etc., often used in fish dishes. [F f. *court* short + BOUILLON]

courteous /ˈkɜːtɪəs/ *adj.* polite, kind, or considerate in manner; well-mannered. □□**courteously** *adv.* **courteousness** *n.* [ME f. OF *corteis, curteis* f. Rmc (as COURT): assim. to words in -OUS]

courtesan /ˌkɔːtɪˈzæn, ˈkɔːt-/ *n. literary* **1** a prostitute, esp. one with wealthy or upper-class clients. **2** the mistress of a wealthy man. [F *courtisane* f. It. *cortigiana*, fem. of *cortigiano* courtier f. *corte* COURT]

courtesy /ˈkɜːtɪsɪ/ *n.* (*pl.* -**ies**) **1** courteous behaviour; good manners. **2** a courteous act. **3** *archaic* = CURTSY. □**by courtesy** by favour, not by right. **by courtesy of** with the formal permission of (a person etc.). **courtesy light** a light in a car that is switched on by opening a door. **courtesy title** a title held by

courtesy, usu. having no legal validity, e.g. a title given to the heir of a duke etc. [ME f. OF *curtesie, co(u)rtesie* f. *curteis* etc. COURTEOUS]

courtier /ˈkɔːtɪə(r)/ *n.* a person who attends or frequents a sovereign's court. [ME f. AF *courte(i)our*, f. OF f. *cortoyer* be present at court]

courtly /ˈkɔːtlɪ/ *adj.* (**courtlier, courtliest**) **1** polished or refined in manners. **2** obsequious. **3** punctilious. □**courtly love** the conventional medieval tradition of knightly love for a lady, and the etiquette used in its (esp. literary) expression. □□ **courtliness** *n.* [COURT]

court martial /ˌkɔːt ˈmɑːʃ(ə)l/ *n. & v.* —*n.* (*pl.* **courts martial**) a judicial court for trying members of the armed services. —*v.tr.* (**court-martial**) (**-martialled, -martialling;** *US* **-martialed, -martialing**) try by a court martial.

courtroom /ˈkɔːtruːm, -rʊm/ *n.* the place or room in which a court of law meets.

courtship /ˈkɔːtʃɪp/ *n.* **1 a** courting with a view to marriage. **b** the courting behaviour of male animals, birds, etc. **c** a period of courting. **2** an attempt, often protracted, to gain advantage by flattery, attention, etc.

courtyard /ˈkɔːtjɑːd/ *n.* an area enclosed by walls or buildings, often opening off a street.

couscous /ˈkuːskuːs/ *n.* a N. African dish of wheat grain or coarse flour steamed over broth, often with meat or fruit added. [F f. Arab. *kuskus* f. *kaskasa* to pound]

cousin /ˈkʌz(ə)n/ *n.* **1** (also **first cousin, cousin-german**) the child of one's uncle or aunt. **2** (usu. in *pl.*) applied to the people of kindred races or nations (*our American cousins*). **3** *hist.* a title formerly used by a sovereign in addressing another sovereign or a noble of his or her own country. □**second cousin** a child of one's parent's first cousin. □□ **cousinhood** *n.* **cousinly** *adj.* **cousinship** *n.* [ME f. OF *cosin, cusin,* f. L *consobrinus* mother's sister's child]

couth /kuːθ/ *adj. joc.* cultured; well-mannered. [backform. as antonym of UNCOUTH]

couture /kuːˈtjʊə(r)/ *n.* the design and manufacture of fashionable clothes; = HAUTE COUTURE. [F, = sewing, dressmaking]

couturier /kuːˈtjʊərɪˌeɪ/ *n.* (*fem.* **couturière** /-rɪˈeə(r)/) a fashion designer or dressmaker. [F]

couvade /kuːˈvɑːd/ *n.* a custom by which a father appears to undergo labour and childbirth when his child is being born. [F f. *couver* hatch f. L *cubare* lie down]

couvert /kuːˈveə(r)/ *n.* = COVER *n.* 6. [F]

couverture /ˌkuːvəˈtjʊə(r)/ *n.* chocolate for covering sweets, cakes, etc. [F, = covering]

covalency /kəʊˈveɪlənsɪ/ *n. Chem.* **1** the linking of atoms by a covalent bond. **2** the number of pairs of electrons an atom can share with another.

covalent /kəʊˈveɪlənt/ *adj. Chem.* of, relating to, or characterized by covalency. □**covalent bond** *Chem.* a bond formed by sharing of electrons usu. in pairs by two atoms in a molecule. □□ **covalence** *n.* **covalently** *adv.* [co- + *valent*, after *trivalent* etc.]

cove[1] /kəʊv/ *n. & v.* —*n.* **1** a small, esp. sheltered, bay or creek. **2** a sheltered recess. **3** *Archit.* a concave arch or arched moulding, esp. one formed at the junction of a wall with a ceiling. —*v.tr. Archit.* **1** provide (a room, ceiling, etc.) with a cove. **2** slope (the sides of a fireplace) inwards. [OE *cofa* chamber f. Gmc]

cove[2] /kəʊv/ *n. Brit. sl. archaic* a fellow; a chap. [16th-c. cant: orig. unkn.]

coven /ˈkʌv(ə)n/ *n.* an assembly of witches. [var. of *covent*; see CONVENT]

covenant /ˈkʌvənənt/ *n. & v.* —*n.* **1** an agreement; a contract. **2** *Law* **a** a contract drawn up under a seal, esp. undertaking to make regular payments to a charity. **b** a clause of a covenant. **3** (**Covenant**) *Bibl.* the agreement between God and the Israelites (see

Ark of the Covenant). —*v.tr.* & *intr.* agree, esp. by legal covenant. □**land of the Covenant** Canaan. □□

covenantal /-ˈnænt(ə)l/ *adj.* **covenantor** *n.* [ME f. OF, pres. part. of *co(n)venir*, formed as CONVENE]

covenanted /ˈkʌvənəntɪd/ *adj.* bound by a covenant.

covenanter /ˈkʌvənəntə(r)/ *n.* **1** a person who covenants. **2** (**Covenanter**) *hist.* an adherent of the National Covenant of the Solemn League and Covenant in 17th-c. Scotland, in support of Presbyterianism.

Coventry /ˈkɒvəntrɪ/ *n.* □**send a person to Coventry** refuse to associate with or speak to a person. [*Coventry* in W. Midlands]

cover /ˈkʌvə(r)/ *v.* & *n.* —*v.tr.* **1** (often foll. by *with*) protect or conceal by means of a cloth, lid, etc. **2 a** extend over; occupy the whole surface of (*covered in dirt; covered with writing*). **b** (often foll. by *with*) strew thickly or thoroughly (*covered the floor with straw*). **c** lie over; be a covering to (*the blanket scarcely covered him*). **3 a** protect; clothe. **b** (as **covered** *adj.*) wearing a hat; having a roof. **4** include; comprise; deal with (*the talk covered recent discoveries*). **5** travel (a specified distance) (*covered sixty miles*). **6** *Journalism* **a** report (events, a meeting, etc.). **b** investigate as a reporter. **7** be enough to defray (expenses, a bill, etc.) (*£20 should cover it*). **8 a** *refl.* take precautionary measures so as to protect oneself (*had covered myself by saying I might be late*). **b** (*absol.*; foll. by *for*) deputize or stand in for (a colleague etc.) (*will you cover for me?*). **9** *Mil.* **a** aim a gun etc. at. **b** (of a fortress, guns, etc.) command (a territory). **c** stand behind (a person in the front rank). **d** protect (an exposed person etc.) by being able to return fire. **10 a** esp. *Cricket* stand behind (another player) to stop any missed balls. **b** (in team games) mark (a corresponding player of the other side). **11** (also *absol.*) (in some card-games) play a card higher than (one already played to the same trick). **12** (of a stallion, a bull, etc.) copulate with. —*n.* **1** something that covers or protects, esp.: **a** a lid. **b** the binding of a book. **c** either board of this. **d** an envelope or the wrapper of a parcel (*under separate cover*). **e** the outer case of a pneumatic tyre. **f** (in *pl.*) bedclothes. **2** a hiding-place; a shelter. **3** woods or undergrowth sheltering game or covering the ground (see COVERT). **4 a** a pretence; a screen (*under cover of humility*). **b** a spy's pretended identity or activity, intended as concealment. **c** *Mil.* a supporting force protecting an advance party from attack. **5 a** funds, esp. obtained by insurance, to meet a liability or secure against a contingent loss. **b** the state of being protected (*third-party cover*). **6** a place setting at table, esp. in a restaurant. **7** *Cricket* = *cover-point*. □**break cover** (of an animal, esp. game, or a hunted person) leave a place of shelter, esp. vegetation. **cover charge** an extra charge levied per head in a restaurant, nightclub, etc. **cover crop** a crop grown for the protection and enrichment of the soil. **cover-drive** *Cricket* a drive past cover-point. **cover girl** a female model whose picture appears on magazine covers etc. **cover in** provide with a roof etc. **covering letter** (or **note**) an explanatory letter sent with an enclosure. **cover note** *Brit.* a temporary certificate of current insurance. **cover-point** *Cricket* **1** a fielding position on the off side and halfway to the boundary. **2** a fielder at this position. **cover story** a news story in a magazine, that is illustrated or advertised on the front cover. **cover one's tracks** conceal evidence of what one has done. **cover up 1** completely cover or conceal. **2** conceal (circumstances etc., esp. illicitly) (also *absol.: refused to cover up for them*). **cover-up** *n.* an act of concealing circumstances, esp. illicitly. **from cover to cover** from beginning to end of a book etc. **take cover** use a natural or prepared shelter against an attack. □□ **coverable** *adj.* **coverer** *n.* [ME f. OF *covrir, cuvrir* f. L *cooperire* (as CO-, *operire opert-* cover)]

coverage /ˈkʌvərɪdʒ/ *n.* **1** an area or an amount covered. **2** *Journalism* the amount of press etc. publicity received by a particular story, person, etc. **3** a risk covered by an insurance policy. **4** an area reached by a particular broadcasting station or advertising medium.

coverall /ˈkʌvərɔːl/ *n.* & *adj.* esp. *US* —*n.* **1** something that covers entirely. **2** (usu. in *pl.*) a full-length protective outer garment often zipped up the front. —*attrib.adj.* covering entirely (*a coverall term*).

covering /ˈkʌvərɪŋ/ *n.* something that covers, esp. a bedspread, blanket, etc., or clothing.

coverlet /ˈkʌvəlɪt/ *n.* a bedspread. [ME f. AF *covrelet, -lit* f. OF *covrir* cover + *lit* bed]

covert /ˈkʌvət/ *adj.* & *n.* —*adj.* secret or disguised (*a covert glance; covert operations*). —*n.* **1** a shelter, esp. a thicket hiding game. **2** a feather covering the base of a bird's flight-feather. □**covert coat** a short, light, overcoat worn for shooting, riding, etc. □□ **covertly** *adv.* **covertness** *n.* [ME f. OF *covert* past part. of *covrir* COVER]

coverture /ˈkʌvətjʊə(r), -tʃə(r)/ *n.* **1** covering; shelter. **2** *Law hist.* the position of a married woman, considered to be under her husband's protection. [ME f. OF (as COVERT)]

covet /ˈkʌvɪt/ *v.tr.* (**coveted, coveting**) desire greatly (esp. something belonging to another person) (*coveted her friend's earrings*). □□ **covetable** *adj.* [ME f. OF *cu-, coveitier* f. Rmc]

covetous /ˈkʌvɪtəs/ *adj.* (usu. foll. by *of*) **1** greatly desirous (esp. of another person's property). **2** grasping, avaricious. □□ **covetously** *adv.* **covetousness** *n.* [ME f. OF *coveitous* f. Gallo-Roman]

covey /ˈkʌvɪ/ *n.* (*pl.* **-eys**) **1** a brood of partridges. **2** a small party or group of people or things. [ME f. OF *covee* f. Rmc f. L *cubare* lie]

covin /ˈkʌvɪn/ *n.* **1** *Law* a conspiracy to commit a crime etc. against a third party. **2** *archaic* fraud, deception. [ME f. OF *covin(e)* f. med.L *convenium -ia* f. *convenire*: see CONVENE]

coving *n.* = COVE[^1] *n.* 3.

cow[1] /kaʊ/ *n.* **1** a fully grown female of any bovine animal, esp. of the genus *Bos*, used as a source of milk and beef. **2** the female of other large animals, esp. the elephant, whale, and seal. **3** *derog. sl.* **a** a woman esp. a coarse or unpleasant one. **b** *Austral.* & *NZ* an unpleasant person, thing, situation, etc. □**cow-fish 1** any of several small plant-eating mammals, e.g. the manatee. **2** a marine fish, *Lactoria diaphana*, covered in hard bony plates and having hornlike spines over the eyes and on other parts of the body. **cow-heel** the foot of a cow or an ox stewed to a jelly. **cow-lick** a projecting lock of hair. **cow-parsley** a hedgerow plant *Anthriscus sylvestris*, having lacelike umbels of flowers: also called *Queen Anne's lace.* **cow-pat** a flat round piece of cow-dung. **cow-tree** a tree, *Brosimum galactodendron*, native to S. America, yielding a milklike juice which is used as a substitute for cow's milk. **cow-wheat** any plant of the genus *Melampyrum*, esp. *M. pratense* growing on heathland. **till the cows come home** *colloq.* an indefinitely long time. [OE *cū* f. Gmc, rel. to L *bos*, Gk *bous*]

cow[2] /kaʊ/ *v.tr.* (usu. in *passive*) intimidate or dispirit (*cowed by ill-treatment*). [prob. f. ON *kúga* oppress]

cowage /ˈkaʊɪdʒ/ *n.* (also **cowhage**) a climbing plant, *Mucuna pruritum*, having hairy pods which cause stinging and itching. [Hindi *kawãnch*]

coward /ˈkaʊəd/ *n.* & *adj.* —*n.* a person who is easily frightened or intimidated by danger or pain. —*adj.* *poet.* easily frightened. [ME f. OF *cuard, couard* ult. f. L *cauda* tail]

cowardice /ˈkaʊədɪs/ *n.* a lack of bravery. [ME f. OF *couardise* (as COWARD)]

cowardly /ˈkaʊədlɪ/ *adj.* & *adv.* —*adj.* **1** of or like a coward; lacking courage. **2** (of an action) done against one who cannot retaliate. —*adv.* *archaic* like a coward; with cowardice. □□ **cowardliness** *n.*

cowbane /ˈkaʊbeɪn/ *n.* = *water hemlock*.

cowbell /ˈkaʊbel/ n. **1** a bell worn round a cow's neck for easy location of the animal. **2** a similar bell used as a percussion instrument.

cowberry /ˈkaʊbəri/ n. (pl. **-ies**) **1** an evergreen shrub, *Vaccinium vitis-idaea*, bearing dark-red berries. **2** the berry of this plant.

cowboy /ˈkaʊbɔɪ/ n. **1** (fem. **cowgirl**) a person who herds and tends cattle, esp. in the western US. **2** this as a conventional figure in American folklore, esp. in films. **3** colloq. an unscrupulous or reckless person in business, esp. an unqualified one.

cowcatcher /ˈkaʊ͵kætʃə(r)/ n. US a peaked metal frame at the front of a locomotive for pushing aside obstacles on the line.

cower /ˈkaʊə(r)/ v.intr. **1** crouch or shrink back, esp. in fear; cringe. **2** stand or squat in a bent position. [ME f. MLG *kūren* lie in wait, of unkn. orig.]

cowhage var. of COWAGE.

cowherd /ˈkaʊhɜːd/ n. a person who tends cattle.

cowhide /ˈkaʊhaɪd/ n. **1 a** a cow's hide. **b** leather made from this. **2** a leather whip made from cowhide.

cowhouse /ˈkaʊhaʊs/ n. a shed or shelter for cows.

cowl /kaʊl/ n. **1 a** the hood of a monk's habit. **b** a loose hood. **c** a monk's hooded habit. **2** the hood-shaped covering of a chimney or ventilating shaft. **3** the removable cover of a vehicle or aircraft engine. □□ **cowled** adj. (in sense 1). [OE *cugele*, *cūle* f. eccl.L *cuculla* f. L *cucullus* hood of a cloak]

cowling /ˈkaʊlɪŋ/ n. = COWL 3.

cowman /ˈkaʊmən/ n. (pl. **-men**) **1** = COWHERD. **2** US a cattle-owner.

co-worker /kəʊˈwɜːkə(r)/ n. a person who works in collaboration with another.

cowpoke /ˈkaʊpəʊk/ n. US = COWBOY 1.

cowpox /ˈkaʊpɒks/ n. a disease of cows, of which the virus was formerly used in vaccination against smallpox.

cowpuncher /ˈkaʊ͵pʌntʃə(r)/ n. US = COWBOY 1.

cowrie /ˈkaʊri/ n. (also **cowry**) (pl. **-ies**) **1** any gastropod mollusc of the family Cypraeidae, having a smooth glossy and usu. brightly-coloured shell. **2** its shell, esp. used as money in parts of Africa and S. Asia. [Urdu & Hindi *kaurī*]

cowshed /ˈkaʊʃed/ n. **1** a shed for cattle that are not at pasture. **2** a milking-shed.

cowslip /ˈkaʊslɪp/ n. **1** a primula, *Primula veris*, with fragrant yellow flowers and growing in pastures. **2** US a marsh marigold. [OE *cūslyppe* f. *cū* COW[1] + *slyppe* slimy substance, i.e. cow-dung]

Cox /kɒks/ n. (in full **Cox's orange pippin**) a variety of eating-apple with a red-tinged green skin. [R. *Cox*, amateur Eng. fruit grower d. 1825]

cox /kɒks/ n. & v. —n. **1** a coxswain, esp. of a racing-boat. —v. **1** intr. act as a cox (*coxed for Cambridge*). **2** tr. act as cox for (*coxed the winning boat*). [abbr.]

coxa /ˈkɒksə/ n. (pl. **coxae** /-siː/) **1** Anat. the hip-bone or hip-joint. **2** Zool. the first segment of an insect's leg. □□ **coxal** adj. [L]

coxcomb /ˈkɒkskəʊm/ n. an ostentatiously conceited man; a dandy. □□ **coxcombry** /-kəmri/ n. (pl. **-ies**). [= *cock's comb* (see COCK[1]), orig. (a cap worn by) a jester]

coxswain /ˈkɒkswern, -s(ə)n/ n. & v. —n. **1** a person who steers, esp. in a rowing-boat. **2** the senior petty officer in a small ship. —v. **1** intr. act as a coxswain. **2** tr. act as a coxswain of. □□ **coxswainship** n. [ME f. *cock* (see COCKBOAT) + SWAIN: cf. BOATSWAIN]

Coy. abbr. esp. Mil. Company.

coy /kɔɪ/ adj. (**coyer**, **coyest**) **1** archly or affectedly shy. **2** irritatingly reticent (*always coy about her age*). **3** (esp. of a girl) modest or shy. □□ **coyly** adv. **coyness** n. [ME f. OF *coi*, *quei* f. L *quietus* QUIET]

coyote /kɔɪˈəʊti, ˈkɔɪəʊt/ n. (pl. same or **coyotes**) a wolflike wild dog, *Canis latrans*, native to N. America. [Mex. Sp. f. Aztec *coyotl*]

coypu /ˈkɔɪpuː/ n. (pl. **coypus**) an aquatic beaver-like rodent, *Myocastor coypus*, native to S. America and kept in captivity for its fur. [Araucan]

coz /kʌz/ n. archaic cousin. [abbr.]

cozen /ˈkʌz(ə)n/ v. literary **1** tr. (often foll. by *of*, *out of*) cheat, defraud. **2** tr. (often foll. by *into*) beguile; persuade. **3** intr. act deceitfully. □□ **cozenage** n. [16th-c. cant, perh. rel. to COUSIN]

cozy US var. of COSY.

CP abbr. **1** Cape Province. **2** Communist Party. **3** Austral. Country Party.

cp. abbr. compare.

c.p. abbr. candlepower.

Cpl. abbr. Corporal.

CPO abbr. Chief Petty Officer.

CPR abbr. Canadian Pacific Railway.

CPRE abbr. Council for the Protection of Rural England.

cps abbr. (also **c.p.s.**) **1** Computing characters per second. **2** cycles per second.

CPSA abbr. (in the UK) Civil and Public Services Association.

CPU abbr. Computing central processing unit.

CR abbr. Community of the Resurrection.

Cr symb. Chem. the element chromium.

Cr. abbr. **1** Councillor. **2** creditor.

crab[1] /kræb/ n. **1 a** any of numerous ten-footed crustaceans having the first pair of legs modified as pincers. **b** the flesh of a crab, esp. *Cancer pagurus*, as food. **2** (**the Crab**) the zodiacal sign or constellation Cancer. **3** (in full **crab-louse**) (often in pl.) a parasitic louse, *Phthirus pubis*, infesting hairy parts of the body and causing extreme irritation. **4** a machine for hoisting heavy weights. □ **catch a crab** Rowing effect a faulty stroke in which the oar is jammed under water or misses the water altogether. **crab-grass** US a creeping grass infesting lawns. **crab-pot** a wicker trap for crabs. □□ **crablike** adj. [OE *crabba*, rel. to ON *krafla* scratch]

crab[2] /kræb/ n. **1** (in full **crab-apple**) a small sour apple-like fruit. **2** (in full **crab tree** or **crab-apple tree**) any of several trees bearing this fruit. **3** a sour person. [ME, perh. alt. (after CRAB[1] or CRABBED) of earlier *scrab*, prob. of Scand. orig.]

crab[3] /kræb/ v. (**crabbed**, **crabbing**) colloq. **1** tr. & intr. criticize adversely or captiously; grumble. **2** tr. act so as to spoil (*the mistake crabbed his chances*). [orig. of hawks fighting, f. MLG *krabben*]

crabbed /ˈkræbɪd/ adj. **1** irritable or morose. **2** (of handwriting) ill-formed and hard to decipher. **3** perverse or cross-grained. **4** difficult to understand. □□ **crabbedly** adv. **crabbedness** n. [ME f. CRAB[1], assoc. with CRAB[2]]

crabby /ˈkræbɪ/ adj. (**crabbier**, **crabbiest**) = CRABBED 1,3. □□ **crabbily** adv. **crabbiness** n.

crabwise /ˈkræbwaɪz/ adv. & attrib.adj. (of movement) sideways or backwards like a crab.

crack /kræk/ n., v., & adj. —n. **1 a** a sudden sharp or explosive noise (*the crack of a whip; a rifle crack*). **b** (in a voice) a sudden harshness or change in pitch. **2** a sharp blow (*a crack on the head*). **3 a** a narrow opening formed by a break (*entered through a crack in the wall*). **b** a partial fracture, with the parts still joined (*the teacup has a crack in it*). **c** a chink (*looked through the crack formed by the door; a crack of light*). **4** colloq. a mischievous or malicious remark or aside (*a nasty crack about my age*). **5** colloq. an attempt (*I'll have a crack at it*). **6** the exact moment (*at the crack of noon; the crack of dawn*). **7** colloq. a first-rate player, horse, etc. **8** dial. colloq. conversation; good company; fun (*only went there for the crack*). **9** sl. a potent hard crystalline form of cocaine broken into small pieces and inhaled or smoked for its stimulating effect. —v. **1** tr. & intr. break without a complete separation of the parts (*cracked the window; the cup cracked on hitting the floor*). **2** intr. & tr. make or cause to make a sudden sharp or explosive sound. **3** intr. & tr. break or cause to break with a sudden sharp sound. **4** intr. & tr. give way or cause to give way (under torture etc.); yield. **5** *intr.* (of the voice, esp. of an adolescent boy or a person under strain) become dissonant; break. **6** *tr. colloq.* find a solution to (a problem, code, etc.). **7** *tr.* say (a joke etc.) in a jocular way. **8** *tr. colloq.* hit sharply or hard (*cracked her head on the ceiling*). **9** *tr. Chem.* decompose (heavy oils) by heat and pressure with or without a catalyst to produce lighter hydrocarbons (such as petrol). **10** *tr.* break (wheat) into coarse pieces. —*attrib.adj. colloq.* excellent; first-rate (*a crack regiment*; *a crack shot*). □**crack a bottle** open a bottle, esp. of wine, and drink it. **crack-brained** crazy. **crack a crib** *sl.* break into a house. **crack-down** *colloq.* severe measures (esp. against law-breakers etc.). **crack down on** *colloq.* take severe measures against. **crack-jaw** *colloq.* —*adj.* (of a word) difficult to pronounce. —*n.* such a word. **crack of doom** a thunder-peal announcing the Day of Judgement. **crack up** *colloq.* **1** collapse under strain. **2** praise. **crack-up** *n. colloq.* **1** a mental breakdown. **2** a car crash. **crack-willow** a species of willow, *Salix fragilis*, with brittle branches. **fair crack of the whip** *colloq.* a fair chance to participate etc. **get cracking** *colloq.* begin promptly and vigorously. **have a crack at** *colloq.* attempt. [OE *cracian* resound]

cracked /krækt/ *adj.* **1** having cracks. **2** (*predic.*) *sl.* crazy. □**cracked wheat** wheat that has been crushed into small pieces.

cracker /'krækə(r)/ *n.* **1** a paper cylinder both ends of which are pulled at Christmas etc. making a sharp noise and releasing a small toy etc. **2** a firework exploding with a sharp noise. **3** (usu. in *pl.*) an instrument for cracking (*nutcrackers*). **4** a thin dry biscuit often eaten with cheese. **5** *sl. Brit.* a notable or attractive person. **6** *US* a biscuit. **7** *US offens.* = *poor White*. □**cracker-barrel** *US* (of philosophy etc.) homespun; unsophisticated.

crackerjack /'krækə,dʒæk/ *adj.* & *n. US sl.* —*adj.* exceptionally fine or expert. —*n.* an exceptionally fine thing or person.

crackers /'krækəz/ *predic.adj. Brit. sl.* crazy.

cracking /'krækɪŋ/ *adj.* & *adv. sl.* —*adj.* **1** outstanding; very good (*a cracking performance*). **2** (*attrib.*) fast and exciting (*a cracking speed*). —*adv.* outstandingly (*a cracking good time*).

crackle /'kræk(ə)l/ *v.* & *n.* —*v.intr.* make a repeated slight cracking sound (*radio crackled*; *fire was crackling*). —*n.* **1** such a sound. **2 a** paintwork, china, or glass decorated with a pattern of minute surface cracks. **b** the smooth surface of such paintwork etc. □□ **crackly** *adj.* [CRACK + -LE⁴]

crackling /'kræklɪŋ/ *n.* **1** the crisp skin of roast pork. **2** *joc.* or *offens.* attractive women regarded collectively as objects of sexual desire. □**bit of crackling** *colloq.* an attractive woman.

cracknel /'kræk(ə)l/ *n.* a light crisp biscuit. [ME f. F *craquelin* f. MDu. *krākelinc* f. *krāken* CRACK]

crackpot /'krækpɒt/ *n.* & *adj. sl.* —*n.* an eccentric or impractical person. —*adj.* mad, unworkable (*a crackpot scheme*).

cracksman /'kræksmən/ *n.* (*pl.* -**men**) *sl.* a burglar, esp. a safe-breaker.

cracky /'krækɪ/ *adj.* covered with cracks. □□ **crackiness** *n.*

-cracy /krəsɪ/ *comb. form* denoting a particular form of government, rule, or influence (*aristocracy*; *bureaucracy*). [from or after F -*cratie* f. med.L -*cratia* f. Gk -*kratia* f. *kratos* strength, power]

cradle /'kreɪd(ə)l/ *n.* & *v.* —*n.* **1 a** a child's bed or cot, esp. one mounted on rockers. **b** a place in which a thing begins, esp. a civilization etc., or is nurtured in its infancy (*cradle of choral singing*; *cradle of democracy*). **2** a framework resembling a cradle, esp.: **a** that on which a ship, a boat, etc., rests during construction or repairs. **b** that on which a worker is suspended to work on a ceiling, a ship, the vertical side of a building, etc. **c** the part of a telephone on

which the receiver rests when not in use. —*v.tr.* **1** contain or shelter as if in a cradle (*cradled his head in her arms*). **2** place in a cradle. □**cradle-snatcher** *sl.* a person amorously attached to a much younger person. **cradle-song** a lullaby. **from the cradle** from infancy. **from the cradle to the grave** from infancy till death (esp. of State welfare). [OE *cradol*, perh. rel. to OHG *kratto* basket]

cradling /'kreɪdlɪŋ/ *n. Archit.* a wooden or iron framework, esp. one used as a structural support in a ceiling.

craft /krɑːft/ *n.* & *v.* —*n.* **1** skill, esp. in practical arts. **2 a** (esp. in *comb.*) a trade or an art (*statecraft*; *handicraft*; *priestcraft*; *the craft of pottery*). **b** the members of a craft. **3** (*pl.* **craft**) **a** a boat or vessel. **b** an aircraft or spacecraft. **4** cunning or deceit. **5** (**the Craft**) the brotherhood of Freemasons. —*v.tr.* make in a skilful way (*crafted a poem*; *a well-crafted piece of work*). □**craft-brother** a fellow worker in the same trade. **craft-guild** *hist.* a guild of workers of the same trade. [OE *cræft*]

craftsman /'krɑːftsmən/ *n.* (*pl.* -**men**; *fem.* **craftswoman**, *pl.* -**women**) **1** a skilled and usu. time-served worker. **2** a person who practises a handicraft. **3** a private soldier in the Royal Electrical and Mechanical Engineers. □□ **craftsmanship** *n.* [ME, orig. *craft's man*]

crafty /'krɑːftɪ/ *adj.* (**craftier, craftiest**) cunning, artful, wily. □□ **craftily** *adv.* **craftiness** *n.* [OE *cræftig*]

crag¹ /kræg/ *n. Brit.* a steep or rugged rock. [ME, of Celt. orig.]

crag² /kræg/ *n. Geol.* rock consisting of a shelly sand. [18th c.: perh. f. CRAG¹]

craggy /'krægɪ/ *adj.* (**craggier, craggiest**) **1** (esp. of a person's face) rugged; rough-textured. **2** (of a landscape) having crags. □□ **craggily** *adv.* **cragginess** *n.*

cragsman /'krægzmən/ *n.* (*pl.* -**men**) a skilled climber of crags.

crake /kreɪk/ *n.* **1** any rail (see RAIL³), esp. a corncrake. **2** the cry of a corncrake. [ME f. ON *kráka* (imit.): cf. CROAK]

cram /kræm/ *v.* (**crammed, cramming**) **1** *tr.* **a** fill to bursting; stuff (*the room was crammed*). **b** (foll. by *in, into*) force (a thing) into (*cram the sandwiches into the bag*). **2** *tr.* & *intr.* prepare for an examination by intensive study. **3** *tr.* (often foll. by *with*) feed (poultry etc.) to excess. **4** *tr.* & *intr. colloq.* eat greedily. □**cram-full** as full as possible. **cram in** push in to bursting point (*crammed in another five minutes' work*). [OE *crammian* f. Gmc]

crambo /'kræmbəʊ/ *n.* a game in which a player gives a word or verse-line to which each of the others must find a rhyme. [earlier *crambe*, app. allusive f. L *crambe repetita* cabbage served up again]

crammer /'kræmə(r)/ *n.* a person or institution that crams pupils for examinations.

cramp /kræmp/ *n.* & *v.* —*n.* **1 a** a painful involuntary contraction of a muscle or muscles from the cold, exertion, etc. **b** = *writer's cramp* (see WRITER). **2** (also **cramp-iron**) a metal bar with bent ends for holding masonry etc. together. **3** a portable tool for holding two planks etc. together; a clamp. **4** a restraint. —*v.tr.* **1** affect with cramp. **2** confine narrowly. **3** restrict (energies etc.). **4** (as **cramped** *adj.*) (of handwriting) small and difficult to read. **5** fasten with a cramp. □**cramp a person's style** prevent a person from acting freely or naturally. **cramp up** confine narrowly. [ME f. OF *crampe* f. MDu., MLG *krampe*, OHG *krampfo* f. adj. meaning 'bent': cf. CRIMP]

crampon /'kræmpən/ *n.* (*US* **crampoon** /-'puːn/) (usu. in *pl.*) **1** an iron plate with spikes fixed to a boot for walking on ice, climbing, etc. **2** a metal hook for lifting timber, rock, etc.; a grappling-iron. [ME f. F (as CRAMP)]

cran /kræn/ n. Sc. a measure for fresh herrings (37½ gallons). [= Gael. crann, of uncert. orig.]

cranage /'kreɪnɪdʒ/ n. **1** the use of a crane or cranes. **2** the money paid for this.

cranberry /'krænbəri/ n. (pl. -ies) **1** any evergreen shrub of the genus Vaccinium, esp. V. macrocarpon of America and V. oxycoccos of Europe, yielding small red acid berries. **2** a berry from this used for a sauce and in cooking. Also called fen-berry. [17th c.: named by Amer. colonists f. G Kranbeere, LG kranebere crane-berry]

crane /kreɪn/ n. & v. —n. **1** a machine for moving heavy objects, usu. by suspending them from a projecting arm or beam. **2** any tall wading bird of the family Gruidae, with long legs, long neck, and straight bill. **3** a moving platform supporting a television camera or cine-camera. —v.tr. **1** (also absol.) stretch out (one's neck) in order to see something. **2** tr. move (an object) by a crane. □**crane-fly** (pl. -flies) any fly of the family Tipulidae, having two wings and long legs: also called daddy-long-legs. [OE cran, rel. to L grus, Gk geranos]

cranesbill /'kreɪnzbɪl/ n. any of various plants of the genus Geranium, having beaked fruits.

cranial /'kreɪnɪəl/ adj. of or relating to the skull. □**cranial index** the ratio of the width and length of a skull. [CRANIUM + -AL]

craniate /'kreɪnɪət/ adj. & n. —adj. having a skull. —n. a craniate animal. [mod.L craniatus f. CRANIUM]

cranio- /'kreɪnɪəʊ/ comb. form cranium.

craniology /ˌkreɪnɪ'ɒlədʒɪ/ n. the scientific study of the shape and size of the human skull. □□ **craniological** /ˌkreɪnɪə'lɒdʒɪk(ə)l/ adj. **craniologist** n.

craniometry /ˌkreɪnɪ'ɒmɪtrɪ/ n. the scientific measurement of skulls. □□ **craniometric** /-nɪə'metrɪk/ adj.

craniotomy /ˌkreɪnɪ'ɒtəmɪ/ n. (pl. -ies) **1** surgical removal of a portion of the skull. **2** surgical perforation of the skull of a dead foetus to ease delivery.

cranium /'kreɪnɪəm/ n. (pl. **craniums** or **crania** /-nɪə/) **1** the skull. **2** the part of the skeleton that encloses the brain. [ME f. med.L f. Gk kranion skull]

crank[1] /kræŋk/ n. & v. —n. **1** part of an axle or shaft bent at right angles for interconverting reciprocal and circular motion. **2** an elbow-shaped connection in bell-hanging. —v.tr. **1** cause to move by means of a crank. **2 a** bend into a crank-shape. **b** furnish or fasten with a crank. □**crank up 1** start (a car engine) by turning a crank. **2** sl. increase (speed etc.) by intensive effort. [OE cranc, app. f. crincan, rel. to cringan fall in battle, orig. 'curl up']

crank[2] /kræŋk/ n. **1 a** an eccentric person, esp. one obsessed by a particular theory (health-food crank). **b** US a bad-tempered person. **2** literary a fanciful turn of speech (quips and cranks). [back-form. f. CRANKY]

crank[3] /kræŋk/ adj. Naut. liable to capsize. [perh. f. crank weak, shaky, or CRANK[1]]

crankcase /'kræŋkkeɪs/ n. a case enclosing a crankshaft.

crankpin /'kræŋkpɪn/ n. a pin by which a connecting-rod is attached to a crank.

crankshaft /'kræŋkʃɑːft/ n. a shaft driven by a crank (see CRANK[1] n. 1).

cranky /'kræŋkɪ/ adj. (**crankier, crankiest**) **1** colloq. eccentric, esp. obsessed with a particular theory (cranky ideas about women). **2** working badly; shaky. **3** esp. US ill-tempered or crotchety. □□ **crankily** adv. **crankiness** n. [perh. f. obs. crank rogue feigning sickness]

crannog /'krænəg/ n. an ancient lake-dwelling in Scotland or Ireland. [Ir. f. crann tree, beam]

cranny /'krænɪ/ n. (pl. -ies) a chink, a crevice, a crack. □□ **crannied** /-ɪd/ adj. [ME f. OF crané past part. of craner f. cran f. pop.L crena notch]

crap[1] /kræp/ n. & v. coarse sl. —n. **1** (often as int.) nonsense, rubbish (he talks crap). **2** faeces. —v.intr. (**crapped, crapping**) defecate. ¶ Usually considered a taboo word. □**crap out** US **1** be unsuccessful. **2** withdraw from a game etc. [earlier senses 'chaff, refuse from fat-boiling': ME f. Du. krappe]

crap[2] /kræp/ n. US a losing throw of 2, 3, or 12 in craps. □**crap game** a game of craps. [formed as CRAPS]

crape /kreɪp/ n. **1** crêpe, usu. of black silk or imitation silk, formerly used for mourning clothes. **2** a band of this formerly worn round a person's hat etc. as a sign of mourning. □**crape fern** a NZ fern, Leptopteris superba, with tall dark-green fronds. **crape hair** artificial hair used in stage make-up. □□ **crapy** adj. [earlier crispe, crespe f. F crespe CRÊPE]

crappy /'kræpɪ/ adj. (**crappier, crappiest**) coarse sl. **1** rubbishy, cheap. **2** disgusting.

craps /kræps/ n.pl. US a gambling game played with dice. □**shoot craps** play craps. [19th c.: perh. f. crab lowest throw at dice]

crapulent /'kræpjʊlənt/ adj. **1** given to indulging in alcohol. **2** resulting from drunkenness. **3 a** drunk. **b** suffering from the effects of drunkenness. □□ **crapulence** n. **crapulous** adj. [LL crapulentus very drunk f. L crapula inebriation f. Gk kraipalē drunken headache]

craquelure /'krækə‚ljʊə(r)/ n. a network of fine cracks in a painting or its varnish. [F]

crash[1] /kræʃ/ v., n., & adv. —v. **1** intr. & tr. make or cause to make a loud smashing noise (the cymbals crashed; crashed the plates together). **2** tr. & intr. throw, drive, move, or fall with a loud smashing noise. **3** intr. & tr. **a** collide or cause (a vehicle) to collide violently with another vehicle, obstacle, etc.; overturn at high speed. **b** fall or cause (an aircraft) to fall violently on to the land or the sea (crashed the plane; the airman crashed into the sea). **4** intr. (usu. foll. by into) collide violently (crashed into the window). **5** intr. undergo financial ruin. **6** tr. colloq. enter without permission (crashed the cocktail party). **7** intr. colloq. be heavily defeated (crashed to a 4-0 defeat). **8** intr. Computing (of a machine or system) fail suddenly. **9** tr. colloq. pass (a red traffic-light etc.). **10** intr. (often foll. by out) sl. sleep for a night, esp. in an improvised setting. —n. **1 a** a loud and sudden smashing noise (a thunder crash; the crash of crockery). **b** a breakage (esp. of crockery, glass, etc.). **2 a** a violent collision, esp. of one vehicle with another or with an object. **b** the violent fall of an aircraft on to the land or sea. **3** ruin, esp. financial. **4** Computing a sudden failure which puts a system out of action. **5** (attrib.) done rapidly or urgently (a crash course in first aid). —adv. with a crash (the window went crash). □**crash barrier** a barrier intended to prevent a car from leaving the road etc. **crash-dive** —v. **1** intr. **a** (of a submarine or its pilot) dive hastily and steeply in an emergency. **b** (of an aircraft or airman) dive and crash. **2** tr. cause to crash-dive. —n. such a dive. **crash-halt** a sudden stop by a vehicle. **crash-helmet** a helmet worn esp. by a motorcyclist to protect the head in a crash. **crash-land 1** intr. (of an aircraft or airman) land hurriedly with a crash, usu. without lowering the undercarriage. **2** tr. cause (an aircraft) to crash-land. **crash landing** a hurried landing with a crash. **crash pad** sl. a place to sleep, esp. in an emergency. **crash-stop** = crash-halt. **crash-tackle** Football a vigorous tackle. [ME: imit.]

crash[2] /kræʃ/ n. a coarse plain linen, cotton, etc., fabric. [Russ. krashenina coloured linen]

crashing /'kræʃɪŋ/ adj. colloq. overwhelming (a crashing bore).

crasis /'kreɪsɪs/ n. (pl. **crases** /-siːz/) the contraction of two adjacent vowels in ancient Greek into one long vowel or diphthong. [Gk krasis mixture]

crass /kræs/ adj. **1** grossly stupid (a crass idea). **2** gross (crass stupidity). **3** literary thick or gross. □□ **crassitude** n. **crassly** adv. **crassness** n. [L crassus solid, thick]

-crat /kræt/ comb. form a member or supporter of a

particular form of government or rule (*autocrat*; *democrat*). [from or after F *-crate*: see -CRACY]

cratch /krætʃ/ n. a rack used for holding food for farm animals out of doors. [ME f. OF *creche* f. Gmc: rel. to CRIB]

crate /kreɪt/ n. & v. —n. **1** a large wickerwork basket or slatted wooden case etc. for packing esp. fragile goods for transportation. **2** *sl.* an old aeroplane or other vehicle. —v.tr. pack in a crate. □□ **crateful** n. (pl. **-fuls**). [ME, perh. f. Du. *krat* basket etc.]

crater /'kreɪtə(r)/ n. & v. —n. **1** the mouth of a volcano. **2** a bowl-shaped cavity, esp. that made by the explosion of a shell or bomb. **3** *Astron.* a hollow with a raised rim on the surface of a planet or moon, caused by the impact of a meteorite. **4** *Antiq.* a large ancient Greek bowl, used for mixing wine. —v.tr. form a crater in. □□ **craterous** adj. [L f. Gk *kratēr* mixing-bowl: see CRASIS]

-cratic /'krætɪk/ comb. form (also **-cratical**) denoting a particular kind of government or rule (*autocratic*; *democratic*). □□ **-cratically** comb. form (adv.) [from or after F *-cratique*: see -CRACY]

cravat /krə'væt/ n. **1** a scarf worn by men inside an open-necked shirt. **2** *hist.* a necktie. □□ **cravatted** adj. [F *cravate* f. G *Krawat*, *Kroat* f. Serbo-Croatian *Hrvat* Croat]

crave /kreɪv/ v. **1** tr. **a** long for (*craved affection*). **b** beg for (*craves a blessing*). **2** intr. (foll. by *for*) long for; beg for (*craved for comfort*). □□ **craver** n. [OE *crafian*, rel. to ON *krefja*]

craven /'kreɪv(ə)n/ adj. & n. —adj. (of a person, behaviour, etc.) cowardly; abject. —n. a cowardly person. □□ **cravenly** adv. **cravenness** n. [ME *cravand* etc. perh. f. OF *cravanté* defeated, past part. of *cravanter* ult. f. L *crepare* burst; assim. to -EN³]

craving /'kreɪvɪŋ/ n. (usu. foll. by *for*) a strong desire or longing.

craw /krɔː/ n. *Zool.* the crop of a bird or insect. □ **stick in one's craw** be unacceptable. [ME, rel. to MDu. *crāghe*, MLG *krage*, MHG *krage* neck, throat]

crawfish /'krɔːfɪʃ/ n. & v. —n. (pl. same) a large marine spiny lobster. —v.intr. *US* retreat; back out. [var. of CRAYFISH]

crawl /krɔːl/ v. & n. —v.intr. **1** move slowly, esp. on hands and knees. **2** (of an insect, snake, etc.) move slowly with the body close to the ground etc. **3** walk or move slowly (*the train crawled into the station*). **4** (often foll. by *to*) *colloq.* behave obsequiously or ingratiatingly in the hope of advantage. **5** (often foll. by *with*) be covered or filled with crawling or moving things, or with people etc. compared to this. **6** (esp. of the skin) feel a creepy sensation. **7** swim with a crawl stroke. —n. **1** an act of crawling. **2** a slow rate of movement. **3** a high-speed swimming stroke with alternate overarm movements and rapid straight-legged kicks. **4 a** (usu. in *comb.*) *colloq.* a leisurely journey between places of interest (*church-crawl*). **b** = *pub-crawl*. □□ **crawlingly** adv. **crawly** adj. (in senses 5, 6 of v.). [ME: orig. unkn.: cf. Sw. *kravla*, Da. *kravle*]

crawler /'krɔːlə(r)/ n. **1** *sl.* a person who behaves obsequiously in the hope of advantage. **2** anything that crawls, esp. an insect. **3** a tractor moving on an endless chain. **4** (usu. in *pl.*) esp. *US* a baby's overall for crawling in; rompers.

cray /kreɪ/ n. *Austral.* & *NZ* = CRAYFISH.

crayfish /'kreɪfɪʃ/ n. (pl. same) **1** a small lobster-like freshwater crustacean. **2** a crawfish. [ME f. OF *crevice*, *crevis*, ult. f. OHG *krebiz* CRAB¹: assim. to FISH¹]

crayon /'kreɪən, -ɒn/ n. & v. —n. **1** a stick or pencil of coloured chalk, wax, etc. used for drawing. **2** a drawing made with this. —v.tr. draw with crayons. [F f. *craie* f. L *creta* chalk]

craze /kreɪz/ v. & n. —v. **1** tr. (usu. as **crazed** adj.) make insane (*crazed with grief*). **2 a** tr. produce fine surface cracks on (pottery glaze etc.). **b** intr. develop such cracks. —n. **1 a** a usu. temporary enthusiasm (*a craze for hula hoops*). **b** the object of this. **2** an insane fancy or condition. [ME, orig. = break, shatter, perh. f. ON]

crazy /'kreɪzɪ/ adj. (**crazier, craziest**) **1** *colloq.* (of a person, an action, etc.) insane or mad; foolish. **2** *colloq.* (usu. foll. by *about*) extremely enthusiastic. **3** *sl.* **a** exciting, unrestrained. **b** excellent. **4** (*attrib.*) (of paving, a quilt, etc.) made of irregular pieces fitted together. **5** *archaic* (of a ship, building, etc.) unsound, shaky. □ **crazy bone** *US* the funny bone. **like crazy** *colloq.* = *like mad* (see MAD). □□ **crazily** adv. **craziness** n.

creak /kriːk/ n. & v. —n. a harsh scraping or squeaking sound. —v.intr. **1** make a creak. **2 a** move with a creaking noise. **b** move stiffly and awkwardly. **c** show weakness or frailty under strain. □□ **creakingly** adv. [ME, imit.: cf. CRAKE, CROAK]

creaky /'kriːkɪ/ adj. (**creakier, creakiest**) **1** liable to creak. **2 a** stiff or frail (*creaky joints*). **b** (of a practice, institution, etc.) decrepit, dilapidated, outmoded. □□ **creakily** adv. **creakiness** n.

cream /kriːm/ n., v., & adj. —n. **1 a** the fatty content of milk which gathers at the top and can be made into butter by churning. **b** this eaten (often whipped) with a dessert, as a cake-filling, etc. (*strawberries and cream*; *cream gateau*). **2** the part of a liquid that gathers at the top. **3** (usu. prec. by *the*) the best or choicest part of something, esp.: **a** the point of an anecdote. **b** an élite group of people (*the cream of the nation*). **4** a creamlike preparation, esp. a cosmetic (*hand cream*). **5** a very pale yellow or off-white colour. **6 a** a dish or sweet like or made with cream. **b** a soup or sauce containing milk or cream. **c** a full-bodied mellow sweet sherry. **d** a biscuit with a creamy sandwich filling. **e** a chocolate-covered usu. fruit-flavoured fondant. —v. **1** tr. **a** take the cream from (milk). **b** take the best or a specified part from. **2** tr. work (butter etc.) to a creamy consistency. **3** tr. treat (the skin etc.) with cosmetic cream. **4** tr. add cream to (coffee etc.). **5** intr. (of milk or any other liquid) form a cream or scum. **6** tr. *US colloq.* defeat (esp. in a sporting contest). —adj. pale yellow; off-white. □ **cream bun** (or **cake**) a bun or cake filled or topped with cream. **cream cheese** a soft rich cheese made from unskimmed milk and cream. **cream-coloured** pale yellowish white. **cream cracker** *Brit.* a crisp dry unsweetened biscuit usu. eaten with cheese. **cream-laid** (or **-wove**) laid (or wove) cream-coloured paper. **cream off 1** take (the best or a specified part) from a whole (*creamed off the brightest pupils*). **2** = sense 1b of v. **cream of tartar** purified and crystallized potassium hydrogen tartrate, used in medicine, baking powder, etc. **cream puff 1** a cake made of puff pastry filled with cream. **2** an ineffectual or effeminate person. **cream soda** a carbonated vanilla-flavoured soft drink. **cream tea** afternoon tea with scones, jam, and cream. [ME f. OF *cre(s)me* f. LL *cramum* (perh. f. Gaulish) & eccl.L *chrisma* CHRISM]

creamer /'kriːmə(r)/ n. **1** a flat dish used for skimming the cream off milk. **2** a machine used for separating cream from milk. **3** *US* a jug for cream.

creamery /'kriːmərɪ/ n. (pl. **-ies**) **1** a factory producing butter and cheese. **2** a shop where milk, cream, etc., are sold; a dairy. [CREAM, after F *crémerie*]

creamy /'kriːmɪ/ adj. (**creamier, creamiest**) **1** like cream in consistency or colour. **2** rich in cream. □□ **creamily** adv. **creaminess** n.

crease¹ /kriːs/ n. & v. —n. **1 a** a line in paper etc. caused by folding. **b** a fold or wrinkle. **2** *Cricket* a line marking the position of the bowler or batsman (see POPPING-CREASE, *bowling-crease*). **3** an area near the goal in ice hockey or lacrosse into which the puck or the ball must precede the players. —v. **1** tr. make creases in (material). **2** intr. become creased (*linen creases badly*). **3** tr. & intr. *sl.* (often foll. by *up*) make or become incapable through laughter. **4**

tr. esp. *US sl.* **a** tire out. **b** stun or kill. [earlier *creast* = CREST ridge in material]

crease² var. of KRIS.

create /kriː'eɪt/ *v.* **1** *tr.* **a** (of natural or historical forces) bring into existence; cause (*poverty creates resentment*). **b** (of a person or persons) make or cause (*create a diversion; create a good impression*). **2** *tr.* originate (*an actor creates a part*). **3** *tr.* invest (a person) with a rank (*created him a lord*). **4** *intr. sl. Brit.* make a fuss; grumble. □□ **creatable** *adj.* [ME f. L *creare*]

creatine /'kriːətɪn/ *n.* a product of protein metabolism found in the muscles of vertebrates. [Gk *kreas* meat + -INE⁴]

creation /kriː'eɪʃ(ə)n/ *n.* **1 a** the act of creating. **b** an instance of this. **2 a** (usu. **the Creation**) the creating of the universe regarded as an act of God. **b** (usu. **Creation**) everything so created; the universe. **3 a** product of human intelligence, esp. of imaginative thought or artistic ability. **4 a** the act of investing with a title or rank. **b** an instance of this. [ME f. OF f. L *creatio -onis* (as CREATE)]

creationism /kriː'eɪʃə,nɪz(ə)m/ *n. Theol.* a theory attributing all matter, biological species, etc., to separate acts of creation, rather than to evolution. □□ **creationist** *n.*

creative /kriː'eɪtɪv/ *adj.* **1** inventive and imaginative. **2** creating or able to create. □□ **creatively** *adv.* **creativeness** *n.* **creativity** /-'tɪvɪtɪ/ *n.*

creator /kriː'eɪtə(r)/ *n.* **1** a person who creates. **2** (as **the Creator**) God. [ME f. OF *creat(o)ur* f. L *creator -oris* (as CREATE)]

creature /'kriːtʃə(r)/ *n.* **1 a** an animal, as distinct from a human being. **b** any living being (*we are all God's creatures*). **2** a person of a specified kind (*poor creature*). **3** a person owing status to and obsequiously subservient to another. **4** anything created; a creation. □ **creature comforts** material comforts such as good food, warmth, etc. **creature of habit** a person set in an unvarying routine. □□ **creaturely** *adj.* [ME f. OF f. LL *creatura* (as CREATE)]

crèche /kreʃ, kreɪʃ/ *n.* **1** a day nursery for babies and young children. **2** *US* a representation of a Nativity scene. [F (as CRATCH)]

credal see CREED.

credence /'kriːd(ə)ns/ *n.* **1** belief. **2** (in full **credence table**) a small side-table, shelf, or niche which holds the elements of the Eucharist before they are consecrated. □ **give credence to** believe. **letter of credence** a letter of introduction, esp. of an ambassador. [ME f. OF f. med.L *credentia* f. *credere* believe]

credential /krɪ'denʃ(ə)l/ *n.* (usu. in *pl.*) **1** evidence of a person's achievements or trustworthiness, usu. in the form of certificates, references, etc. **2** a letter or letters of introduction. [med.L *credentialis* (as CREDENCE)]

credenza /krɪ'denzə/ *n.* a sideboard or cupboard. [It. f. med.L (as CREDENCE)]

credibility /,kredɪ'bɪlɪtɪ/ *n.* **1** the condition of being credible or believable. **2** reputation, status. □ **credibility gap** an apparent difference between what is said and what is true.

credible /'kredɪb(ə)l/ *adj.* **1** (of a person or statement) believable or worthy of belief. **2** (of a threat etc.) convincing. □□ **credibly** *adv.* [ME f. L *credibilis* f. *credere* believe]

credit /'kredɪt/ *n. & v.* —*n.* **1** (usu. of a person) a source of honour, pride, etc. (*is a credit to the school*). **2** the acknowledgement of merit (*must give him credit for consistency*). **3** a good reputation (*his credit stands high*). **4 a** belief or trust (*I place credit in that*). **b** something believable or trustworthy (*that statement has credit*). **5 a** a person's financial standing; the sum of money at a person's disposal in a bank etc. **b** the power to obtain goods etc. before payment (based on the trust that payment will be made). **6** (usu. in *pl.*) an acknowledgement of a contributor's services

to a film, television programme, etc. **7** a grade above a pass in an examination. **8** a reputation for solvency and honesty in business. **9 a** (in bookkeeping) the acknowledgement of being paid by an entry on the credit side of an account. **b** the sum entered. **c** the credit side of an account. **10** *US* a certificate indicating that a student has completed a course. —*v.tr.* (**credited, crediting**) **1** believe (*cannot credit it*). **2** (usu. foll. by *to, with*) enter on the credit side of an account (*credited £20 to him; credited him with £20*). □ **credit account** *Brit.* an account with a shop etc. for obtaining goods or services before payment. **credit card** a card from a bank etc. authorizing the obtaining of goods on credit. **credit note** a note given by a shop etc. in return for goods returned, stating the value of goods owed to the customer. **credit rating** an estimate of a person's suitability to receive commercial credit. **credit sale** the sale of goods on credit. **credit title** a person's name appearing at the beginning or end of a film or broadcast etc. as an acknowledgement. **credit transfer** a transfer from one person's bank account to another's. **credit a person with** ascribe (a good quality) to a person. **do credit to** (or **do a person credit**) enhance the reputation of. **get credit for** be given credit for. **give a person credit for 1** enter (a sum) to a person's credit. **2** ascribe (a good quality) to a person. **give credit to** believe. **letter of credit** a letter from a banker authorizing a person to draw money up to a specified amount, usu. from another bank. **on credit** with an arrangement to pay later. **to one's credit** in one's praise, commendation, or defence (*to his credit, he refused the offer*). [F *crédit* f. It. *credito* or L *creditum* f. *credere credit-* believe, trust]

creditable /'kredɪtəb(ə)l/ *adj.* (often foll. by *to*) bringing credit or honour. □□ **creditability** /-'bɪlɪtɪ/ *n.* **creditably** *adv.*

creditor /'kredɪtə(r)/ *n.* **1** a person to whom a debt is owing. **2** a person or company that gives credit for money or goods (cf. DEBTOR). [ME f. AF *creditour* (OF *-eur*) f. L *creditor -oris* (as CREDIT)]

creditworthy /'kredɪt,wɜːðɪ/ *adj.* considered suitable to receive commercial credit. □□ **creditworthiness** *n.*

credo /'kreɪdəʊ, 'kriː-/ *n.* (*pl.* **-os**) **1** (**Credo**) a statement of belief; a creed, esp. the Apostles' or Nicene creed beginning with *credo*. **2** a musical setting of the Nicene Creed. [ME f. L, = I believe]

credulous /'kredjʊləs/ *adj.* **1** too ready to believe; gullible. **2** (of behaviour) showing such gullibility. □□ **credulity** /krɪ'djuːlɪtɪ/ *n.* **credulously** *adv.* **credulousness** *n.* [L *credulus* f. *credere* believe]

Cree /kriː/ *n. & adj.* —*n.* (*pl.* same or **Crees**) **1 a** an American Indian people of Central America. **b** a member of this people. **2** the language of this people. —*adj.* of or relating to the Crees or their language. [Canadian F *Cris* (earlier *Cristinaux*) f. Algonquian]

creed /kriːd/ *n.* **1** a set of principles or opinions, esp. as a philosophy of life (*his creed is moderation in everything*). **2 a** (often **the Creed**) = Apostles' Creed (see APOSTLE). **b** a brief formal summary of Christian doctrine (cf. NICENE CREED, Athanasian Creed). **c** the Creed as part of the Mass. □□ **credal** /'kriːd(ə)l/ *adj.* **creedal** *adj.* [OE *crēda* f. L CREDO]

creek /kriːk/ *n.* **1** *Brit.* **a** a small bay or harbour on a sea-coast. **b** a narrow inlet on a sea-coast or in a river-bank. **2** esp. *US* a tributary of a river; a stream. **3** *Austral.* & *NZ* a stream or brook. □ **up the creek** *sl.* **1** in difficulties or trouble. **2** crazy. [ME *crike* f. ON *kriki* nook (or partly f. OF *crique* f. ON), & ME *crēke* f. MDu. *krēke* (or f. *crike* by lengthening): ult. orig. unkn.]

creel /kriːl/ *n.* **1** a large wicker basket for fish. **2** an angler's fishing-basket. [ME, orig. Sc.: ult. orig. unkn.]

creep /kriːp/ *v. & n.* —*v.intr.* (*past* and *past part.* **crept** /krept/) **1** move with the body prone and close to the ground; crawl. **2** (often foll. by *in, out, up*, etc.) come, go, or move slowly and stealthily or timidly (*crept out without being seen*). **3** enter slowly (into a person's affections, life, awareness, etc.) (*a feeling crept over her; crept into her heart*). **4** *colloq.* act abjectly or obsequiously in the hope of advancement. **5** (of a plant) grow along the ground or up a wall by means of tendrils etc. **6** (as **creeping** *adj.*) developing slowly and steadily (*creeping inflation*). **7** (of the flesh) feel as if insects etc. were creeping over it, as a result of fear, horror, etc. **8** (of metals etc.) undergo creep. —*n.* **1 a** the act of creeping. **b** an instance of this. **2** (in *pl.*; prec. by *the*) *colloq.* a nervous feeling of revulsion or fear (*gives me the creeps*). **3** *sl.* an unpleasant person. **4** the gradual downward movement of disintegrated rock due to gravitational forces etc. **5** (of metals etc.) a gradual change of shape under stress. **6** a low arch under a railway embankment, road, etc. □**creeping barrage** a barrage moving ahead of advancing troops. **creeping Jenny** any of various creeping plants, esp. moneywort. **creeping Jesus** *sl.* an abject or hypocritical person. **creep up on** approach (a person) stealthily or unnoticed. [OE *crēopan* f. Gmc]

creeper /'kri:pə(r)/ *n.* **1** *Bot.* any climbing or creeping plant. **2** any bird that climbs, esp. a treecreeper. **3** *sl.* a soft-soled shoe.

creepy /'kri:pɪ/ *adj.* (**creepier, creepiest**) **1** *colloq.* having or producing a creeping of the flesh (*I feel creepy; a creepy film*). **2** given to creeping. □□ **creepily** *adv.* **creepiness** *n.* [CREEP]

creepy-crawly /ˌkri:pɪ'krɔ:lɪ/ *n.* & *adj. Brit. colloq.* —*n.* (*pl.* -**ies**) an insect, worm, etc. —*adj.* creeping and crawling.

creese var. of KRIS.

cremate /krɪ'meɪt/ *v.tr.* consume (a corpse etc.) by fire. □□ **cremation** /-'meɪʃ(ə)n/ *n.* **cremator** *n.* [L *cremare* burn]

crematorium /ˌkremə'tɔ:rɪəm/ *n.* (*pl.* **crematoria** or **crematoriums**) a place for cremating corpses in a furnace. [mod.L (as CREMATE, -ORY)]

crematory /'krematərɪ/ *adj.* & *n.* —*adj.* of or relating to cremation. —*n.* (*pl.* -**ies**) *US* = CREMATORIUM.

crème /krem/ *n.* **1** = CREAM *n.* 6a. **2** a name for various creamy liqueurs (*crème de cassis*). □**crème brûlée** /bru:'leɪ/ a pudding of cream or custard topped with caramelized sugar. **crème caramel** a custard coated with caramel. **crème de la crème** /ˌkrem də lɑ: 'krem/ the best part; the élite. **crème de menthe** /də 'mɑ̃t, 'mɒnt/ a peppermint-flavoured liqueur. [F, = cream]

crenate /'kri:neɪt/ *adj. Bot.* & *Zool.* having a notched edge or rounded teeth. □□ **crenated** *adj.* **crenation** /-'neɪʃ(ə)n/ *n.* **crenature** /'krenə,tjʊə(r), 'kri:-/ *n.* [mod.L *crenatus* f. pop.L *crena* notch]

crenel /'kren(ə)l/ *n.* (also **crenelle** /krɪ'nel/) an indentation or gap in the parapet of a tower, castle, etc., orig. for shooting through etc. [ME f. OF *crenel*, ult. f. pop.L *crena* notch]

crenellate /'krenə,leɪt/ *v.tr.* provide (a tower etc.) with battlements or loopholes. □□ **crenellation** /-'leɪʃ(ə)n/ *n.* [F *créneler* (as CRENEL)]

Creole /'kri:əʊl/ *n.* & *adj.* —*n.* **1 a** a descendant of European (esp. Spanish) settlers in the W. Indies or Central or S. America. **b** a White descendant of French settlers in the southern US. **c** a person of mixed European and Black descent. **2** a language formed from the contact of a European language (esp. English, French, or Portuguese) with another (esp. African) language. —*adj.* **1** of or relating to a Creole or Creoles. **2** (usu. **creole**) of Creole origin or production (*creole cooking*). [F *créole, criole* f. Sp. *criollo*, prob. f. Port. *crioulo* home-born slave f. *criar* breed f. L *creare* CREATE]

creolize /'kri:ə,laɪz/ *v.tr.* (also -**ise**) form a Creole from (another language). □□ **creolization** /-'zeɪʃ(ə)n/ *n.*

creosote /'kri:ə,səʊt/ *n.* & *v.* —*n.* **1** (in full **creosote**

oil) a dark-brown oil distilled from coal tar, used as a wood-preservative. **2** a colourless oily fluid distilled from wood tar, used as an antiseptic. —*v.tr.* treat with creosote. [G *Kreosote* f. Gk *kreas* flesh + *sōtēr* preserver, with ref. to its antiseptic properties]

crêpe /kreɪp/ *n.* **1** a fine often gauzelike fabric with a wrinkled surface. **2** a thin pancake, usu. with a savoury or sweet filling. **3** (also **crêpe rubber**) a very hard-wearing wrinkled sheet rubber used for the soles of shoes etc. □**crêpe de Chine** /də 'ʃi:n/ a fine silk crêpe. **crêpe paper** thin crinkled paper. **crêpe Suzette** /su:'zet/ a small dessert pancake flamed in alcohol at the table. □□ **crêpey** *adj.* **crêpy** *adj.* [F f. OF *crespe* curled f. L *crispus*]

crepitate /'krepɪ,teɪt/ *v.intr.* **1** make a crackling sound. **2** *Zool.* (of a beetle) eject pungent fluid with a sharp report. □□ **crepitant** *adj.* [L *crepitare* frequent. of *crepare* creak]

crepitation /ˌkrepɪ'teɪʃ(ə)n/ *n.* **1** *Med.* = CREPITUS. **2** the action or sound of crackling or rattling.

crepitus /'krepɪtəs/ *n. Med.* **1** a grating noise from the ends of a fractured bone rubbing together. **2** a similar sound heard from the chest in pneumonia etc. [L f. *crepare* rattle]

crept *past* and *past part.* of CREEP.

crepuscular /krɪ'pʌskjʊlə(r)/ *adj.* **1 a** of twilight. **b** dim. **2** *Zool.* appearing or active in twilight. [L *crepusculum* twilight]

Cres. *abbr.* Crescent.

cresc. *abbr.* (also **cres.**) *Mus.* = CRESCENDO.

crescendo /krɪ'ʃendəʊ/ *n., adv., adj.,* & *v.* —*n.* (*pl.* -**os**) **1** *Mus.* a passage gradually increasing in loudness. **2 a** progress towards a climax (*a crescendo of emotions*). **b** *disp.* a climax (*reached a crescendo then died away*). —*adv.* & *adj.* with a gradual increase in loudness. —*v.intr.* (-**oes, -oed**) increase gradually in loudness or intensity. [It., part. of *crescere* grow (as CRESCENT)]

crescent /'krez(ə)nt, 'kres-/ *n.* & *adj.* —*n.* **1** the curved sickle shape of the waxing or waning moon. **2** anything of this shape, esp. *Brit.* a street forming an arc. **3 a** the crescent-shaped emblem of Islam or Turkey. **b** (**the Crescent**) the world or power of Islam. —*adj.* **1** *poet.* increasing. **2** crescent-shaped. □□ **crescentic** /-'sentɪk/ *adj.* [ME f. AF *cressaunt*, OF *creissant*, f. L *crescere* grow]

cresol /'kri:sɒl/ *n.* any of three isomeric phenols present in creosote and used as disinfectants. □□ **cresyl** /'kri:sɪl/ *adj.* [CREOSOTE + -OL[2]]

cress /kres/ *n.* any of various cruciferous plants usu. with pungent edible leaves, e.g. watercress. [OE *cresse* f. WG]

cresset /'kresɪt/ *n. hist.* a metal container for oil, coal, etc., lighted and usu. mounted on a pole for illumination. [ME f. OF *cresset, craisset*, f. *craisse* = *graisse* GREASE]

crest /krest/ *n.* & *v.* —*n.* **1 a** a comb or tuft of feathers, fur, etc. on a bird's or animal's head. **b** something resembling this, esp. a plume of feathers on a helmet. **c** a helmet; the top of a helmet. **2** the top of something, esp. of a mountain, wave, roof, etc. **3** *Heraldry* **a** a device above the shield and helmet of a coat of arms. **b** such a device reproduced on writing paper or on a seal, signifying a family. **4 a** a line along the top of the neck of some animals. **b** the hair growing from this; a mane. **5** *Anat.* a ridge along the surface of a bone. —*v.* **1** *tr.* reach the crest of (a hill, wave, etc.). **2** *tr.* provide with a crest. **b** serve as a crest to. **3** *intr.* (of a wave) form into a crest. □**on the crest of a wave** at the most favourable moment in one's progress. □□ **crested** *adj.* (also in *comb.*). **crestless** *adj.* [ME f. OF *creste* f. L *crista* tuft]

crestfallen /'krest,fɔ:lən/ *adj.* **1** dejected, dispirited. **2** with a fallen or drooping crest.

cretaceous /krɪ'teɪʃəs/ *adj.* & *n.* —*adj.* **1** of the nature of chalk. **2** (**Cretaceous**) *Geol.* of or relating to the last period of the Mesozoic era, with evidence of the first flowering plants, the extinction of dinosaurs, and extensive deposits of chalk. ¶ Cf. Appendix II. —*n. Geol.* this era or system. [L *cretaceus* f. *creta* chalk]

Cretan /'kri:t(ə)n/ *n. & adj.* —*n.* a native of Crete, an island SE of the Greek mainland. —*adj.* of or relating to Crete or the Cretans. [L *Cretanus* f. *Creta* f. Gk *Krētē* Crete]

cretic /'kri:tɪk/ *n. Prosody* a foot containing one short or unstressed syllable between two long or stressed ones. [L *Creticus* f. Gk *Krētikos* (as CRETAN)]

cretin /'kretɪn/ *n.* **1** a person who is deformed and mentally retarded as the result of a thyroid deficiency. **2** *colloq.* a stupid person. □□ **cretinism** *n.* cretinize *v.tr.* (also -ise). cretinous *adj.* [F *crétin* f. Swiss F. *creitin*, *crestin* f. L *Christianus* CHRISTIAN]

cretonne /kre'tɒn, 'kre-/ *n.* (often *attrib.*) a heavy cotton fabric with a usu. floral pattern printed on one or both sides, used for upholstery. [F f. *Creton* in Normandy]

crevasse /krə'væs/ *n.* **1** a deep open crack, esp. in a glacier. **2** *US* a breach in a river levee. [F f. OF *crevace*: see CREVICE]

crevice /'krevɪs/ *n.* a narrow opening or fissure, esp. in a rock or building etc. [ME f. OF *crevace* f. *crever* burst f. L *crepare*]

crew[1] /kru:/ *n. & v.* —*n.* (often treated as *pl.*) **1 a** a body of people manning a ship, aircraft, train, etc. **b** such a body as distinguished from the captain or officers. **c** a body of people working together; a team. **2** *colloq.* a company of people; a gang (*a motley crew*). —*v.* **1** *tr.* supply or act as a crew or member of a crew for. **2** *intr.* act as a crew or member of a crew. □ **crew cut** an orig. man's haircut which is short all over the head. **crew neck** a close-fitting round neckline, esp. on a sweater. [ME f. OF *creüe* increase, fem. past part. of *croistre* grow f. L *crescere*]

crew[2] *past* of CROW[2].

crewel /'kru:əl/ *n.* a thin worsted yarn used for tapestry and embroidery. □ **crewel-work** a design worked in crewel on linen or cloth. [ME *crule* etc., of unkn. orig.]

crewman /'kru:mən/ *n.* (*pl.* **-men**) a member of a crew.

crib /krɪb/ *n. & v.* —*n.* **1 a** a child's bed with barred or latticed sides; a cot. **b** a model of the Nativity of Christ, with a manger as a bed. **2** a barred container or rack for animal fodder. **3** *colloq.* **a** a translation of a text for the (esp. surreptitious) use of students. **b** plagiarized work etc. **4** a small house or cottage. **5** a framework lining the shaft of a mine. **6** *colloq.* **a** cribbage. **b** a set of cards given to the dealer at cribbage by all the players. **7** heavy crossed timbers used in foundations in loose soil etc. **8** *sl.* a brothel. **9** *Austral. & NZ* a light meal; food. —*v.tr.* (also *absol.*) (**cribbed**, **cribbing**) **1** *colloq.* copy (another person's work) unfairly or without acknowledgement. **2** confine in a small space. **3** *colloq.* pilfer, steal. **4** *colloq.* grumble. □ **crib-biting** a horse's habit of biting the manger while noisily breathing in and swallowing. □□ **cribber** *n.* [OE *crib(b)*]

cribbage /'krɪbɪdʒ/ *n.* a card game for two, three, or four players, in which the dealer may score from the cards in the crib (see CRIB 6b). □ **cribbage-board** a board with pegs and holes used for scoring at cribbage. [17th c.: orig. unkn.]

cribo /'krɪbəʊ, 'kraɪbəʊ/ *n.* (*pl.* **-os**) a large harmless snake, *Drymarchon corais*, of tropical America. Also called *gopher snake* (see GOPHER[1]). [19th c.: orig. unkn.]

cribriform /'krɪbrɪˌfɔːm/ *adj. Anat. & Bot.* having numerous small holes. [L *cribrum* sieve + -FORM]

cribwork /'krɪbwɜːk/ *n.* = CRIB *n.* 7.

crick /krɪk/ *n. & v.* —*n.* a sudden painful stiffness in the neck or the back etc. —*v.tr.* produce a crick in (the neck etc.). [ME: orig. unkn.]

cricket[1] /'krɪkɪt/ *n. & v.* —*n.* a game played on a grass pitch with two teams of 11 players taking turns to bowl at a wicket defended by a batting player of

the other team. —*v.intr.* (**cricketed**, **cricketing**) play cricket. □ **cricket-bag** a long bag used for carrying a cricketer's bat etc. **not cricket** *Brit. colloq.* underhand or unfair behaviour. □□ **cricketer** *n.* [16th c.: orig. uncert.]

cricket[2] /'krɪkɪt/ *n.* any of various grasshopper-like insects of the order Orthoptera, the males of which produce a characteristic chirping sound. [ME f. OF *criquet* f. *criquer* creak etc. (imit.)]

cricoid /'kraɪkɔɪd/ *adj. & n.* —*adj.* ring-shaped. —*n.* (in full **cricoid cartilage**) *Anat.* the ring-shaped cartilage of the larynx. [mod.L *cricoides* f. Gk *krikoeidēs* f. *krikos* ring]

cri de cœur /ˌkriː də 'kɜː(r)/ *n.* (*pl.* **cris de cœur** pronunc. same) a passionate appeal, complaint, or protest. [F, = cry from the heart]

cried *past* and *past part.* of CRY.

crier /'kraɪə(r)/ *n.* (also **cryer**) **1** a person who cries. **2** an officer who makes public announcements in a court of justice. □ **town** (or **common**) **crier** *hist.* an officer employed by a town council etc. to make public announcements in the streets or market-place. [ME f. AF *criour*, OF *criere* f. *crier* CRY]

crikey /'kraɪkɪ/ *int. sl.* an expression of astonishment. [euphem. for CHRIST]

crim /krɪm/ *n. & adj. Austral. sl.* = CRIMINAL. [abbr.]

crime /kraɪm/ *n. & v.* —*n.* **1 a** an offence punishable by law. **b** illegal acts as a whole (*resorted to crime*). **2** an evil act (*a crime against humanity*). **3** *colloq.* a shameful act (*a crime to tease them*). **4** a soldier's offence against military regulations. —*v.tr. Mil.* etc. charge with or convict of an offence. □ **crime-sheet** *Mil.* a record of a defendant's offences. **crime wave** a sudden increase in crime. **crime-writer** a writer of detective fiction or thrillers. [ME f. OF f. L *crimen -minis* judgement, offence]

crime passionnel /ˌkriːm pæsjɒ'nel/ *n.* (*pl.* **crimes passionnels** pronunc. same) a crime, esp. murder, committed in a fit of sexual jealousy. [F, = crime of passion]

criminal /'krɪmɪn(ə)l/ *n. & adj.* —*n.* a person who has committed a crime or crimes. —*adj.* **1** of, involving, or concerning crime (*criminal records*). **2** having committed (and usu. been convicted of) a crime. **3** *Law* relating to or expert in criminal law rather than civil or political matters (*criminal code*; *criminal lawyer*). **4** *colloq.* scandalous, deplorable. □ **criminal law** law concerned with punishment of offenders (opp. *civil law*). **criminal libel** see LIBEL. □□ **criminality** /-'nælɪtɪ/ *n.* **criminally** *adv.* [ME f. LL *criminalis* (as CRIME)]

criminalistic /ˌkrɪmɪnə'lɪstɪk/ *adj.* relating to criminals or their habits.

criminalistics /ˌkrɪmɪnə'lɪstɪks/ *n.pl.* esp. *US* forensic science.

criminology /ˌkrɪmɪ'nɒlədʒɪ/ *n.* the scientific study of crime. □□ **criminological** /-nə'lɒdʒɪk(ə)l/ *adj.* **criminologist** *n.* [L *crimen -minis* CRIME + -OLOGY]

crimp /krɪmp/ *v. & n.* —*v.tr.* **1** compress into small folds or ridges; frill. **2** make narrow wrinkles or flutings in; corrugate. **3** make waves in (the hair) with a hot iron. —*n.* a crimped thing or form. □ **put a crimp in** *US sl.* thwart; interfere with. □□ **crimper** *n.* **crimpy** *adj.* **crimpily** *adv.* **crimpiness** *n.* [ME, prob. ult. f. OHG *krimphan*]

Crimplene /'krɪmpliːn/ *n. propr.* a synthetic crease-resistant fibre and fabric.

crimson /'krɪmz(ə)n/ *adj., n., & v.* —*adj.* of a rich deep red inclining to purple. —*n.* this colour. —*v.tr. & intr.* make or become crimson. [ME *cremesin*, *crimesin*, ult. f. Arab. *ḳirmizī* KERMES]

cringe /krɪndʒ/ *v. & n.* —*v.intr.* **1** shrink back in fear or apprehension; cower. **2** (often foll. by *to*) behave obsequiously. —*n.* the act or an instance of cringing. □□ **cringer** *n.* [ME *crenge*, *crenche*, OE *cringan*, *crincan*: see CRANK[1]]

cringle /'krɪŋɡ(ə)l/ *n. Naut.* an eye of rope containing a thimble for another rope to pass through. [LG *kringel* dimin. of *kring* ring f. root of CRANK[1]]

crinkle /'krɪŋk(ə)l/ *n.* & *v.* —*n.* a wrinkle or crease in paper, cloth, etc. —*v.* **1** *intr.* form crinkles. **2** *tr.* form crinkles in. □**crinkle-cut** (of vegetables) cut with wavy edges. □□ **crinkly** *adj.* [ME f. OE *crincan*: see CRANK[1]]

crinoid /'krɪnɔɪd/ *n.* & *adj.* —*n.* any echinoderm of the class Crinoidea, usu. sedentary with feathery arms, e.g. sea lilies and feather stars. —*adj.* lily-shaped. □□ **crinoidal** /-'nɔɪd(ə)l/ *adj.* [Gk *krinoeidēs* f. *krinon* lily]

crinoline /'krɪnəlɪn/ *n.* **1** a stiffened or hooped petticoat formerly worn to make a long skirt stand out. **2** a stiff fabric of horsehair etc. used for linings, hats, etc. [F f. L *crinis* hair + *linum* thread]

cripple /'krɪp(ə)l/ *n.* & *v.* —*n.* a person who is permanently lame. —*v.tr.* **1** make a cripple of; lame. **2** disable, impair. **3** weaken or damage (an institution, enterprise, etc.) seriously (*crippled by the loss of funding*). □□ **crippledom** *n.* **cripplehood** *n.* **crippler** *n.* [OE *crypel*, rel. to CREEP]

cris var. of KRIS.

crisis /'kraɪsɪs/ *n.* (*pl.* **crises** /-siːz/) **1 a** a decisive moment. **b** a time of danger or great difficulty. **2** the turning-point, esp. of a disease. [L f. Gk *krisis* decision f. *krinō* decide]

crisp /krɪsp/ *adj.*, *n.*, & *v.* —*adj.* **1** hard but brittle. **2 a** (of air) bracing. **b** (of a style or manner) lively, brisk and decisive. **c** (of features etc.) neat and clear-cut. **d** (of paper) stiff and crackling. **e** (of hair) closely curling. —*n.* **1** (in full **potato crisp**) *Brit.* a thin fried slice of potato sold in packets etc. and eaten as a snack or appetizer. **2** a thing overdone in roasting etc. (*burnt to a crisp*). —*v.tr.* & *intr.* **1** make or become crisp. **2** curl in short stiff folds or waves. □□ **crisply** *adv.* **crispness** *n.* [OE f. L *crispus* curled]

crispate /'krɪspeɪt/ *adj.* **1** crisped. **2** *Bot.* & *Zool.* having a wavy margin. [L *crispare* curl]

crispbread /'krɪspbred/ *n.* **1** a thin crisp biscuit of crushed rye etc. **2** these collectively (*a packet of crispbread*).

crisper /'krɪspə(r)/ *n.* a compartment in a refrigerator for storing fruit and vegetables.

crispy /'krɪspɪ/ *adj.* (**crispier**, **crispiest**) **1** crisp, brittle. **2** curly. **3** brisk. □□ **crispiness** *n.*

criss-cross /'krɪskrɒs/ *n.*, *adj.*, *adv.*, & *v.* —*n.* **1** a pattern of crossing lines. **2** the crossing of lines or currents etc. —*adj.* crossing; in cross lines (*criss-cross marking*). —*adv.* crosswise; at cross purposes. —*v.* **1** *intr.* **a** intersect repeatedly. **b** move crosswise. **2** *tr.* mark or make with a criss-cross pattern. [15th c., f. *Christ's cross*: later treated as redupl. of CROSS]

crista /'krɪstə/ *n.* (*pl.* **cristae** /-tiː/) **1** *Anat.* & *Zool.* a ridge or crest. **2** *Anat.* an infold of the inner membrane of a mitochondrion. □□ **cristate** *adj.* [L]

cristobalite /krɪ'stəʊbəˌlaɪt/ *n.* *Mineral.* a principal form of silica, occurring as opal. [G *Cristobalit* f. Cerro San *Cristóbal* in Mexico]

crit /krɪt/ *n.* *colloq.* **1** = CRITICISM 2. **2** = CRITIQUE. **3** *Physics* critical mass. [abbr.]

criterion /kraɪ'tɪərɪən/ *n.* (*pl.* **criteria** /-rɪə/) a principle or standard that a thing is judged by. □□ **criterial** *adj.* [Gk *kritērion* means of judging (cf. CRITIC)]

critic /'krɪtɪk/ *n.* **1** a person who censures. **2** a person who reviews or judges the merits of literary, artistic, or musical works etc., esp. regularly or professionally. **3** a person engaged in textual criticism. [L *criticus* f. Gk *kritikos* f. *kritēs* judge f. *krinō* judge, decide]

critical /'krɪtɪk(ə)l/ *adj.* **1 a** making or involving adverse or censorious comments or judgements. **b** expressing or involving criticism. **2** skilful at or engaged in criticism. **3** providing textual criticism (*a critical edition of Milton*). **4 a** of or at a crisis; involving risk or suspense (*in a critical condition*; *a* *critical operation*). **b** decisive, crucial (*of critical importance*; *at the critical moment*). **5 a** *Math.* & *Physics* marking transition from one state etc. to another (*critical angle*). **b** *Physics* (of a nuclear reactor) maintaining a self-sustaining chain reaction. □**critical apparatus** = APPARATUS 4. **critical mass** *Physics* the amount of fissile material needed to maintain a nuclear chain reaction. **critical path** the sequence of stages determining the minimum time needed for an operation. **critical temperature** *Chem.* the temperature above which a gas cannot be liquefied. □□ **criticality** /-'kælɪtɪ/ *n.* (in sense 5). **critically** *adv.* **criticalness** *n.* [L *criticus*: see CRITIC]

criticaster /ˌkrɪtɪ'kæstə(r), 'krɪt-/ *n.* a minor or inferior critic.

criticism /'krɪtɪˌsɪz(ə)m/ *n.* **1 a** finding fault; censure. **b** a statement or remark expressing this. **2 a** the work of a critic. **b** an article, essay, etc., expressing or containing an analytical evaluation of something. □**the higher criticism** criticism dealing with the origin and character etc. of texts, esp. of Biblical writings. **the lower criticism** textual criticism of the Bible. [CRITIC or L *criticus* + -ISM]

criticize /'krɪtɪˌsaɪz/ *v.tr.* (also **-ise**) (also *absol.*) **1** find fault with; censure. **2** discuss critically. □□ **criticizable** *adj.* **criticizer** *n.*

critique /krɪ'tiːk/ *n.* & *v.* —*n.* a critical essay or analysis; an instance or the process of formal criticism. —*v.tr.* (**critiques**, **critiqued**, **critiquing**) discuss critically. [F f. Gk *kritikē tekhnē* critical art]

critter /'krɪtə(r)/ *n.* **1** *dial.* or *joc.* a creature. **2** *derog.* a person. [var. of CREATURE]

croak /krəʊk/ *n.* & *v.* —*n.* **1** a deep hoarse sound as of a frog or a raven. **2** a sound resembling this. —*v.* **1 a** *intr.* utter a croak. **b** *tr.* utter with a croak or in a dismal manner. **2** *sl.* **a** *intr.* die. **b** *tr.* kill. [ME: imit.]

croaker /'krəʊkə(r)/ *n.* **1** an animal that croaks. **2** a prophet of evil.

croaky /'krəʊkɪ/ *adj.* (**croakier**, **croakiest**) (of a voice) croaking; hoarse. □□ **croakily** *adv.* **croakiness** *n.*

Croat /'krəʊæt/ *n.* & *adj.* —*n.* **1 a** a native of Croatia in Yugoslavia. **b** a person of Croatian descent. **2** the Slavonic dialect of the Croats (cf. SERBO-CROAT). —*adj.* of or relating to the Croats or their dialect. [mod.L *Croatae* f. Serbo-Croatian *Hrvat*]

Croatian /krəʊ'eɪʃ(ə)n/ *n.* & *adj.* = CROAT.

croc /krɒk/ *n.* *colloq.* a crocodile. [abbr.]

croceate /'krəʊsɪˌeɪt/ *adj.* saffron-coloured. [L *croceus* f. CROCUS]

crochet /'krəʊʃeɪ, -ʃɪ/ *n.* & *v.* —*n.* **1** a handicraft in which yarn is made up into a patterned fabric by means of a hooked needle. **2** work made in this way. —*v.* (**crocheted** /-ʃeɪd/; **crocheting** /-ʃeɪɪŋ/) **1** *tr.* make by crocheting. **2** *intr.* do crochet. □□ **crocheter** /'krəʊʃeɪə(r)/ *n.* [F, dimin. of *croc* hook]

crocidolite /krəʊ'sɪdəˌlaɪt/ *n.* a fibrous blue or green silicate of iron and sodium; blue asbestos. [Gk *krokis -idos* nap of cloth]

crock[1] /krɒk/ *n.* & *v.* *colloq.* —*n.* **1** an inefficient, broken-down, or worn-out person. **2** a worn-out vehicle, ship, etc. —*v.* **1** *intr.* (foll. by *up*) break down, collapse. **2** *tr.* (often foll. by *up*) disable, cause to collapse. [orig. Sc., perh. f. Flem.]

crock[2] /krɒk/ *n.* **1** an earthenware pot or jar. **2** a broken piece of earthenware. [OE *croc(ca)*]

crockery /'krɒkərɪ/ *n.* earthenware or china dishes, plates, etc. [obs. *crocker* potter: see CROCK[2]]

crocket /'krɒkɪt/ *n.* *Archit.* a small carved ornament (usu. a bud or curled leaf) on the inclined side of a pinnacle etc. [ME var. of OF *crochet*: see CROCHET]

crocodile /'krɒkəˌdaɪl/ *n.* **1 a** any large tropical amphibious reptile of the order Crocodilia, with thick scaly skin, long tail, and long jaws. **b** leather from its skin, used to make bags, shoes, etc. **2** *Brit.* *colloq.* a line of schoolchildren etc. walking in pairs. □**crocodile clip** a clip with teeth for gripping. **crocodile tears** insincere grief (from the belief that crocodiles wept while devouring or alluring their prey). □□ **crocodilian** /-'dılıən/ *adj.* [ME f. OF *co-codrille* f. med.L *cocodrillus* f. L *crocodilus* f. Gk *krokodilos* f. *krokē* pebble + *drilos* worm]

crocus /'krəʊkəs/ *n.* (*pl.* **crocuses**) any dwarf plant of the genus *Crocus*, growing from a corm and having brilliant usu. yellow or purple flowers. [ME, = saffron, f. L f. Gk *krokos* crocus, of Semitic orig.]

Croesus /'kriːsəs/ *n.* a person of great wealth. [name of a king of Lydia (6th c. BC)]

croft /krɒft/ *n. & v. Brit.* —*n.* **1** an enclosed piece of (usu. arable) land. **2** a small rented farm in Scotland or N. England. —*v.intr.* farm a croft; live as a crofter. [OE: orig. unkn.]

crofter /'krɒftə(r)/ *n. Brit.* a person who rents a smallholding, esp. a joint tenant of a divided farm in parts of Scotland.

croissant /'krwʌsɑ̃/ *n.* a crescent-shaped roll made of rich yeast pastry. [F, formed as CRESCENT]

Cro-Magnon /krəʊ'mænjɒn, -'mæɡnən/ *adj. Anthropol.* of a tall broad-faced European race of late palaeolithic times. [name of a hill in the Dordogne, France, where remains were found in 1868]

cromlech /'krɒmlek/ *n.* **1** a dolmen; a megalithic tomb. **2** a circle of upright prehistoric stones. [Welsh f. *crom* fem. of *crwm* bent + *llech* flat stone]

crone /krəʊn/ *n.* **1** a withered old woman. **2** an old ewe. [ME, ult. f. ONF *carogne* CARRION]

cronk /krɒŋk/ *adj. Austral. colloq.* **1** unsound; liable to collapse. **2** a fraudulent. **b** (of a horse) dishonestly run, unfit. [19th c.: cf. CRANK³]

crony /'krəʊnɪ/ *n.* (*pl.* **-ies**) a close friend or companion. [17th-c. *chrony*, university sl. f. Gk *khronios* long-standing f. *khronos* time]

crook /krʊk/ *n., v., & adj.* —*n.* **1** the hooked staff of a shepherd or bishop. **2 a** a bend, curve, or hook. **b** anything hooked or curved. **3** *colloq.* **a** a rogue; a swindler. **b** a professional criminal. —*v.tr. & intr.* bend, curve. —*adj.* **1** crooked. **2** *Austral. & NZ colloq.* **a** unsatisfactory, out of order; (of a person) unwell, injured. **b** unpleasant. **c** dishonest, unscrupulous. **d** bad-tempered, irritable, angry. □ **crook-back** a hunchback. **crook-backed** hunchbacked. **go crook** (usu. foll. by *at, on*) *Austral. & NZ colloq.* lose one's temper; become angry. □□ **crookery** *n.* [ME f. ON *krókr* hook]

crooked /'krʊkɪd/ *adj.* (**crookeder, crookedest**) **1 a** not straight or level; bent, curved, twisted. **b** deformed, bent with age. **2** *colloq.* not straightforward; dishonest. **3** /krʊkt/ *Austral. & NZ sl.* = CROOK *adj.* 2. **4** (foll. by *on*) *Austral. sl.* hostile to. □□ **crookedly** *adv.* **crookedness** *n.* [ME f. CROOK, prob. after ON *krókóttr*]

croon /kruːn/ *v. & n.* —*v.tr. & intr.* hum or sing in a low subdued voice, esp. in a sentimental manner. —*n.* such singing. □□ **crooner** *n.* [ME (orig. Sc. & N.Engl.) f. MDu. & MLG *krōnen* groan, lament]

crop /krɒp/ *n. & v.* —*n.* **1 a** the produce of cultivated plants, esp. cereals. **b** the season's total yield of this (*a good crop*). **2** a group or an amount produced or appearing at one time (*this year's crop of students*). **3** (in full **hunting crop**) the stock or handle of a whip. **4 a** a style of hair cut very short. **b** the cropping of hair. **5** *Zool.* **a** the pouch in a bird's gullet where food is prepared for digestion. **b** a similar organ in other animals. **6** the entire tanned hide of an animal. **7** a piece cut off or out of something. —*v.* (**cropped, cropping**) **1** *tr.* **a** cut off. **b** (of animals) bite off the tops of (plants). **2** *tr.* cut (hair, cloth, edges of a book, etc.) short. **3** *tr.* gather or reap (produce). **4** *tr.* (foll. by *with*) sow or plant (land) with a crop. **5** *intr.* (of land) bear a crop. □ **crop-dusting** the sprinkling of powdered insecticide or fertilizer on crops, esp. from the air. **crop-eared** having the ears (esp. of animals) or hair cut short. **crop-full** having a full crop or stomach. **crop out** *Geol.* appear at the surface. **crop-over** a W. Indian celebration marking the end of the sugar-cane harvest. **crop up** **1** (of a subject,

circumstance, etc.) appear or come to one's notice unexpectedly. **2** *Geol.* appear at the surface. [OE *crop(p)*]

cropper /'krɒpə(r)/ *n.* a crop-producing plant of specified quality (*a good cropper; a heavy cropper*). □ **come a cropper** *sl.* **1** fall heavily. **2** fail badly.

croquet /'krəʊkeɪ, -kɪ/ *n. & v.* —*n.* **1** a game played on a lawn, with wooden balls which are driven through a series of hoops with mallets. **2** the act of croqueting a ball. —*v.tr.* (**croqueted** /-keɪd/; **croqueting** /-keɪɪŋ/) drive away (one's opponent's ball in croquet) by placing one's own against it and striking one's own. [perh. dial. form of F CROCHET hook]

croquette /krə'ket/ *n.* a fried breaded roll or ball of mashed potato or minced meat etc. [F f. *croquer* crunch]

crore /krɔː(r)/ *n. Ind.* **1** ten million. **2** one hundred lakhs (of rupees, units of measurement, persons, etc.). [Hindi *k(a)rōr*, ult. f. Skr. *koṭi* apex]

crosier /'krəʊzɪə(r), -ʒə(r)/ *n.* (also **crozier**) **1** a hooked staff carried by a bishop as a symbol of pastoral office. **2** a crook. [orig. = bearer of a crook, f. OF *crocier* & OF *croisier* f. *crois* CROSS]

cross /krɒs/ *n., v., & adj.* —*n.* **1** an upright post with a transverse bar, as used in antiquity for crucifixion. **2 a** (**the Cross**) in Christianity, the cross on which Christ was crucified. **b** a representation of this as an emblem of Christianity. **c** = *sign of the cross.* **3** a staff surmounted by a cross and borne before an archbishop or in a religious procession. **4 a** a thing or mark shaped like a cross, esp. a figure made by two short intersecting lines (+ or ×). **b** a monument in the form of a cross, esp. one in the centre of a town or on a tomb. **5** a cross-shaped decoration indicating rank in some orders of knighthood or awarded for personal valour. **6 a** an intermixture of animal breeds or plant varieties. **b** an animal or plant resulting from this. **7** (foll. by *between*) a mixture or compromise of two things. **8 a** a crosswise movement, e.g. of an actor on stage. **b** *Football* etc. a pass of the ball across the direction of play. **c** *Boxing* a blow with a crosswise movement of the fist. **9** a trial or affliction; something to be endured (*bear one's crosses*). —*v.* **1** *tr.* (often foll. by *over*; also *absol.*) go across or to the other side of (a road, river, sea, etc.). **2 a** *intr.* intersect or be across one another (*the roads cross near the bridge*). **b** *tr.* cause to do this; place crosswise (*cross one's legs*). **3** *tr.* **a** draw a line or lines across. **b** *Brit.* mark (a cheque) with two parallel lines, and often an annotation, to indicate that it must be paid into a named bank account. **4** *tr.* (foll. by *off, out, through*) cancel or obliterate or remove from a list with lines drawn across. **5** *tr.* (often *refl.*) make the sign of the cross on or over. **6** *intr.* **a** pass in opposite or different directions. **b** (of letters between two correspondents) each be dispatched before receipt of the other. **c** (of telephone lines) become wrongly interconnected so that intrusive calls can be heard. **7** *tr.* a cause to interbreed. **b** cross-fertilize (plants). **8** *tr.* thwart or frustrate (*crossed in love*). **9** *tr. sl.* cheat. —*adj.* **1** (often foll. by *with*) peevish, angry. **2** (usu. *attrib.*) transverse; reaching from side to side. **3** (usu. *attrib.*) intersecting. **4** (usu. *attrib.*) contrary, opposed, reciprocal. □ **as cross as two sticks** extremely angry or peevish. **at cross purposes** misunderstanding or conflicting with one another. **cross one's fingers** (or **keep one's fingers crossed**) **1** put one finger across another as a sign of hoping for good luck. **2** trust in good luck. **cross the floor** join the opposing side in a debating-assembly. **cross one's heart** make a solemn pledge, esp. by crossing one's front. **cross one's mind** (of a thought etc.) occur to one, esp. transiently. **cross a person's palm** (usu. foll. by *with*) pay a person for a favour. **cross the path of 1** meet with (a person). **2** thwart. **cross swords** (often foll. by *with*) encounter in opposition; have an argument or dispute. **cross wires** (or **get one's wires crossed**) **1** become wrongly connected by telephone. **2** have a misunderstanding. **on the cross 1** diagonally. **2** *sl.* fraudulently, dishonestly. □□ **crossly** *adv.* **crossness** *n.* [OE *cros* f. ON *kross* f. OIr. *cros* f. L *crux cruc-*]

cross- /krɒs/ *comb. form* **1** denoting movement or position across something (*cross-channel*; *cross-country*). **2** denoting interaction (*cross-breed*; *cross-cultural*; *cross-fertilize*). **3 a** passing from side to side; transverse (*crossbar*; *cross-current*). **b** having a transverse part (*crossbow*). **4** describing the form or figure of a cross (*cross-keys*; *crossroads*).

crossbar /'krɒsbɑː(r)/ *n.* a horizontal bar, esp. held on a pivot or between two upright bars etc., e.g. of a bicycle or of a football goal.

cross-bedding /'krɒs,bedɪŋ/ *n.* *Geol.* lines of stratification crossing the main rock strata. Also called *false bedding*.

cross-bench /'krɒsbentʃ/ *n.* *Brit.* a seat in Parliament (now only the House of Lords) occupied by a member not taking the whip from a political party. □□ **cross-bencher** *n.*

cross-bill /'krɒsbɪl/ *n.* any stout finch of the genus *Loxia*, having a bill with crossed mandibles for opening pine cones.

crossbones /'krɒsbəʊnz/ *n.* a representation of two crossed thigh-bones (see SKULL).

crossbow /'krɒsbəʊ/ *n.* chiefly *hist.* a bow fixed across a wooden stock, with a groove for an arrow and a mechanism for drawing and releasing the string. □□ **crossbowman** *n.* (*pl.* **-men**)

cross-breed /'krɒsbriːd/ *n.* & *v.* —*n.* **1** a breed of animals or plants produced by crossing. **2** an individual animal or plant of a cross-breed. —*v.tr.* (*past* and *past part.* **-bred**) produce by crossing.

cross-check /'krɒstʃek/ *v.* & *n.* —*v.tr.* check by a second or alternative method, or by several methods. —*n.* an instance of cross-checking.

cross-country /krɒs'kʌntrɪ/ *adj.* & *adv.* **1** across fields or open country. **2** not keeping to main or direct roads.

cross-cut /'krɒskʌt/ *adj.* & *n.* —*adj.* cut across the main grain or axis. —*n.* a diagonal cut, path, etc. □ **cross-cut saw** a saw for cutting across the grain of wood.

cross-dating /'krɒs,deɪtɪŋ/ *n.* *Archaeol.* dating by correlation with another site or level.

crosse /krɒs/ *n.* a stick with a triangular net at the end for conveying the ball in lacrosse. [F f. OF *croce*, *croc* hook]

cross-examine /,krɒsɪg'zæmɪn/ *v.tr.* examine (esp. a witness in a lawcourt) to check or extend testimony already given. □□ **cross-examination** /-'neɪʃ(ə)n/ *n.* **cross-examiner** *n.*

cross-eyed /'krɒsaɪd/ *adj.* (as a disorder) having one or both eyes turned permanently inwards towards the nose.

cross-fade /'krɒsfeɪd/ *v.intr.* *Radio* etc. fade in one sound as another is faded out.

cross-fertilize /krɒs'fɜːtɪ,laɪz/ *v.tr.* (also **-ise**) **1** fertilize (an animal or plant) from one of a different species. **2** help by the interchange of ideas etc. □□ **cross-fertilization** /-'zeɪʃ(ə)n/ *n.*

crossfire /'krɒs,faɪə(r)/ *n.* **1** firing in two crossing directions simultaneously. **2 a** attack or criticism from several sources at once. **b** a lively or combative exchange of views etc.

cross-grain /'krɒsgreɪn/ *n.* a grain in timber, running across the regular grain.

cross-grained /'krɒsgreɪnd/ *adj.* **1** (of timber) having a cross-grain. **2** perverse, intractable.

cross-hair /'krɒsheə(r)/ *n.* a fine wire at the focus of an optical instrument for use in measurement.

cross-hatch /'krɒshætʃ/ *v.tr.* shade with intersecting sets of parallel lines.

cross-head /'krɒshed/ *n.* **1** a bar between the piston-rod and connecting-rod in a steam engine. **2** = CROSS-HEADING.

cross-heading /'krɒs,hedɪŋ/ *n.* a heading to a paragraph printed across a column in the body of an article in a newspaper etc.

crossing /'krɒsɪŋ/ *n.* **1** a place where things (esp. roads) cross. **2** a place at which one may cross a street etc. (*pedestrian crossing*). **3** a journey across water (*had a smooth crossing*). **4** the intersection of a church nave and transepts. **5** *Biol.* mating. □ **crossing over** *Biol.* an exchange of genes between homologous chromosomes (cf. RECOMBINATION).

cross-legged /krɒs'legd, -'legɪd, 'krɒs-/ *adj.* with one leg crossed over the other.

cross-link /'krɒslɪŋk/ *n.* (also **cross-linkage**) *Chem.* a bond between chains of atoms in a polymer etc.

crossmatch /krɒs'mætʃ/ *v.tr.* *Med.* test the compatibility of (a donor's and a recipient's blood). □□ **crossmatching** *n.*

crossover /'krɒs,əʊvə(r)/ *n.* & *adj.* —*n.* a point or place of crossing from one side to the other. —*adj.* having a crossover.

crosspatch /'krɒspætʃ/ *n.* *colloq.* a bad-tempered person. [CROSS *adj.* 1 + obs. *patch* fool, clown]

crosspiece /'krɒspiːs/ *n.* a transverse beam or other component of a structure etc.

cross-ply /'krɒsplaɪ/ *adj.* (of a tyre) having fabric layers with cords lying crosswise.

cross-pollinate /krɒs'pɒlɪ,neɪt/ *v.tr.* pollinate (a plant) from another. □□ **cross-pollination** /-'neɪʃ(ə)n/ *n.*

cross-question /krɒs'kwestʃ(ə)n/ *v.tr.* = CROSS-EXAMINE.

cross-refer /,krɒsrɪ'fɜː(r)/ *v.intr.* (**-referred**, **-referring**) refer from one part of a book, article, etc., to another.

cross-reference /'krɒs,refərəns/ *n.* & *v.* —*n.* a reference from one part of a book, article, etc., to another. —*v.tr.* provide with cross-references.

crossroad /'krɒsrəʊd/ *n.* **1** (usu. in *pl.*) an intersection of two or more roads. **2** *US* a road that crosses a main road or joins two main roads. □ **at the crossroads** at a critical point in one's life.

cross-ruff /'krɒsrʌf/ *n.* & *v.* *Bridge* etc. —*n.* the alternate trumping of partners' leads. —*v.intr.* play in this way.

cross-section /krɒs'sekʃ(ə)n/ *n.* **1 a** a cutting of a solid at right angles to an axis. **b** a plane surface produced in this way. **c** a representation of this. **2** a representative sample, esp. of people. **3** *Physics* a quantity expressing the probability of interaction between particles. □□ **cross-sectional** *adj.*

cross-stitch /'krɒsstɪtʃ/ *n.* **1** a stitch formed of two stitches crossing each other. **2** needlework done using this stitch.

crosstalk /'krɒstɔːk/ *n.* **1** unwanted transfer of signals between communication channels. **2** *Brit.* witty talk; repartee.

cross-trees /'krɒstriːz/ *n.pl.* *Naut.* a pair of horizontal timbers at the top of a lower mast, supporting the topmast.

cross-voting /'krɒs,vəʊtɪŋ/ *n.* voting for a party not one's own, or for more than one party.

crosswalk /'krɒswɔːk/ *n.* *US* a pedestrian crossing.

crossways /'krɒsweɪz/ *adv.* = CROSSWISE.

crosswind /'krɒswɪnd/ *n.* a wind blowing across one's direction of travel.

crosswise /'krɒswaɪz/ *adj.* & *adv.* **1** in the form of a cross; intersecting. **2** transverse or transversely.

crossword /'krɒswɜːd/ *n.* (also **crossword puzzle**) a puzzle of a grid of squares and blanks into which words crossing vertically and horizontally have to be filled from clues.

crotch /krɒtʃ/ *n.* a place where something forks, esp. the legs of the human body or a garment (cf. CRUTCH). [perh. = ME & OF *croc(he)* hook, formed as CROOK]

crotchet /'krɒtʃɪt/ *n.* **1** *Mus.* a note having the time value of a quarter of a semibreve and usu.

representing one beat, drawn as a large dot with a stem. Also called *quarter note*. **2** a whimsical fancy. **3** a hook. [ME f. OF *crochet* dimin. of *croc* hook (see CROTCH)]

crotchety /ˈkrɒtʃɪtɪ/ adj. peevish, irritable. □□ **crotchetiness** n. [CROTCHET + -Y¹]

croton /ˈkrəʊt(ə)n/ n. **1** any small tree or shrub of the genus *Croton*, producing a capsule-like fruit. **2** any small tree or shrub of the genus *Codiaeum*, esp. *C. variegatum*, with coloured ornamental leaves. □**croton oil** a powerful purgative obtained from the fruit of *Croton tiglium*. [mod.L f. Gk *krotōn* sheep-tick, croton (from the shape of its seeds)]

crouch /kraʊtʃ/ v. & n. —v.intr. lower the body with the limbs close to the chest, esp. for concealment, or (of an animal) before pouncing; be in this position. —n. an act of crouching; a crouching position. [ME, perh. f. OF *crochir* be bent f. *croc* hook: cf. CROOK]

croup¹ /kruːp/ n. an inflammation of the larynx and trachea in children, with a hard cough and difficulty in breathing. □□ **croupy** adj. [*croup* to croak (imit.)]

croup² /kruːp/ n. the rump or hindquarters esp. of a horse. [ME f. OF *croupe*, rel. to CROP]

croupier /ˈkruːpɪə(r), -ɪˌeɪ/ n. **1** the person in charge of a gaming-table, raking in and paying out money etc. **2** the assistant chairperson at a public dinner, seated at the foot of the table. [F, orig. = rider on the croup: see CROUP²]

croûton /ˈkruːtɒn/ n. a small piece of fried or toasted bread served with soup or used as a garnish. [F f. *croûte* CRUST]

crow¹ /krəʊ/ n. **1** any large black bird of the genus *Corvus*, having a powerful black beak. **2** any similar bird of the family Corvidae, e.g. the raven, rook, and jackdaw. **3** *sl. derog.* a woman, esp. an old or ugly one. □**as the crow flies** in a straight line. **crow-bill** forceps for extracting bullets etc. **crow's-foot** (pl. -feet) **1** (usu. in pl.) a wrinkle at the outer corner of a person's eye. **2** Mil. a caltrop. **crow's-nest** a barrel or platform fixed at the masthead of a sailing vessel as a shelter for a lookout man. **crow steps** corbie-steps. **crow-toe** *archaic* or *dial.* any of various flowers, esp. the bluebell or buttercup. **eat crow** US submit to humiliation. [OE *crāwe* ult. f. WG]

crow² /krəʊ/ v. & n. —v.intr. **1** (past **crowed** or **crew** /kruː/) (of a cock) utter its characteristic loud cry. **2** (of a baby) utter happy cries. **3** (usu. foll. by *over*) express unrestrained gleeful satisfaction. —n. **1** the cry of a cock. **2** a happy cry of a baby. [OE *crāwan*, of imit. orig.]

crowbar /ˈkrəʊbɑː(r)/ n. an iron bar with a flattened end, used as a lever.

crowberry /ˈkrəʊbərɪ/ n. (pl. -ies) **1 a** a heathlike evergreen shrub *Empetrum nigrum*, bearing black berries. **b** the flavourless edible berry of this plant. **2** US a cranberry.

crowd /kraʊd/ n. & v. —n. **1** a large number of people gathered together, usu. without orderly arrangement. **2** a mass of spectators; an audience. **3** *colloq.* a particular company or set of people (*met the crowd from the sales department*). **4** (prec. by *the*) the mass or multitude of people (*go along with the crowd*). **5** a large number (of things). **6** actors representing a crowd. —v. **1 a** intr. come together in a crowd. **b** tr. cause to do this. **c** intr. force one's way. **2** tr. **a** (foll. by *into*) force or compress into a confined space. **b** (often foll. by *with*; usu. in *passive*) fill or make abundant with (*was crowded with tourists*). **3** tr. **a** (of a number of people) come aggressively close to. **b** *colloq.* harass or pressure (a person). □**crowd out** exclude by crowding. □□ **crowdedness** n. [OE *crūdan* press, drive]

crowfoot /ˈkrəʊfʊt/ n. any of various aquatic plants of the genus *Ranunculus*, with white buttercup-like flowers held above the water.

crown /kraʊn/ n. & v. —n. **1** a monarch's ornamental and usu. jewelled head-dress. **2** (**the Crown**) **a** the monarch, esp. as head of State. **b** the power or

authority residing in the monarchy. **3 a** a wreath of leaves or flowers etc. worn on the head, esp. as an emblem of victory. **b** an award or distinction gained by a victory or achievement, esp. in sport. **4** a crown-shaped thing, esp. a device or ornament. **5** the top part of a thing, esp. of the head or a hat. **6 a** the highest or central part of an arched or curved thing (*crown of the road*). **b** a thing that completes or forms the summit. **7** the part of a plant just above and below the ground. **8** the upper part of a cut gem above the girdle. **9 a** the part of a tooth projecting from the gum. **b** an artificial replacement or covering for this. **10 a** a former British coin equal to five shillings (25p). **b** any of several foreign coins with a name meaning 'crown', esp. the krona or krone. **11** a former size of paper, 504 × 384 mm. —v.tr. **1** put a crown on (a person or a person's head). **2** invest (a person) with a royal crown or authority. **3** be a crown to; encircle or rest on the top of. **4 a** (often as **crowning** adj.) be or cause to be the consummation, reward, or finishing touch to (*the crowning glory*). **b** bring (efforts) to a happy issue. **5** fit a crown to (a tooth). **6** *sl.* hit on the head. □**crown cap** a cork-lined metal cap for a bottle. **Crown Colony** a British colony controlled by the Crown. **Crown Court** a court of criminal jurisdiction in England and Wales. **Crown Derby** a soft-paste porcelain made at Derby and often marked with a crown above the letter 'D'. **crown glass** glass made without lead or iron and orig. in a circular sheet; used formerly in windows, now as optical glass of low refractive index. **crown green** a kind of bowling-green rising towards the middle. **crown imperial** a tall fritillary, *Fritillaria imperialis*, with a flower-cluster at the top of the stalk. **crown jewels** the regalia and other jewellery worn by the sovereign on certain State occasions. **Crown Office** (in the UK) an office of the Supreme Court transacting common-law business of Chancery. **crown of thorns** any starfish of the genus *Acanthaster* feeding on coral. **Crown prince** a male heir to a sovereign throne. **Crown princess 1** the wife of a Crown prince. **2** a female heir to a sovereign throne. **crown roast** a roast of rib-pieces of pork or lamb arranged like a crown. **crown saw** a cylinder with a toothed edge for making a circular hole. **crown wheel** a wheel with teeth set at right angles to its plane, esp. in the gears of motor vehicles. [ME f. AF *corune*, OF *corone* f. L *corona*]

crozier var. of CROSIER.

CRT abbr. cathode-ray tube.

cru /kruː/ n. **1** a French vineyard or wine-producing region. **2** the grade of wine produced from it. [F f. *crû* grown]

cruces pl. of CRUX.

crucial /ˈkruːʃ(ə)l/ adj. **1** decisive, critical. **2** *disp.* very important. □□ **cruciality** /-ʃɪˈælɪtɪ/ n. (pl. -ies). **crucially** adv. [F f. L *crux crucis* cross]

crucian /ˈkruːʃ(ə)n/ n. a yellow cyprinoid fish, *Carassius carassius*, allied to the goldfish. [LG *karusse* etc.]

cruciate /ˈkruːʃɪˌeɪt/ adj. Zool. cross-shaped. [mod.L *cruciatus* f. L (as CRUCIBLE)]

crucible /ˈkruːsɪb(ə)l/ n. **1** a melting-pot for metals etc. **2** a severe test or trial. [ME f. med.L *crucibulum* night-lamp, crucible, f. L *crux crucis* cross]

crucifer /ˈkruːsɪfə(r)/ n. a cruciferous plant.

cruciferous /kruːˈsɪfərəs/ adj. Bot. of the family Cruciferae, having flowers with four petals arranged in a cross. [LL *crucifer* (as CRUCIAL, -FEROUS)]

crucifix /ˈkruːsɪfɪks/ n. a model or image of a cross with a figure of Christ on it. [ME f. OF f. eccl.L *crucifixus* f. L *cruci fixus* fixed to a cross]

crucifixion /ˌkruːsɪˈfɪkʃ(ə)n/ n. **1** a crucifying or being crucified. **b** an instance of this. **2** (**Crucifixion**) **a** the crucifixion of Christ. **b** a representation of this. [eccl.L *crucifixio* (as CRUCIFIX)]

cruciform /ˈkruːsɪˌfɔːm/ adj. cross-shaped (esp. of a church with transepts). [L *crux crucis* cross + -FORM]

crucify /ˈkruːsɪˌfaɪ/ v.tr. (-ies, -ied) **1** put to death by fastening to a cross. **2 a** cause extreme pain to. **b** persecute, torment. **c** sl. defeat thoroughly in an argument, match, etc. □□ **crucifier** n. [ME f. OF crucifier f. LL crucifigere (as CRUCIFIX)]

cruck /krʌk/ n. Brit. hist. either of a pair of curved timbers extending to the ground in the framework of a type of medieval house-roof. [var. of CROOK]

crud /krʌd/ n. sl. **1 a** a deposit of unwanted impurities, grease, etc. **b** a corrosive deposit in a nuclear reactor. **2** an unpleasant person. □□ **cruddy** adj. (**cruddier, cruddiest**). [var. of CURD]

crude /kruːd/ adj. & n. —adj. **1 a** in the natural or raw state; not refined. **b** rough, unpolished; lacking finish. **2 a** (of an action or statement or manners) rude, blunt. **b** offensive, indecent (a crude gesture). **3 a** Statistics (of figures) not adjusted or corrected. **b** rough (a crude estimate). —n. natural mineral oil. □□ **crudely** adv. **crudeness** n. **crudity** n. [ME f. L crudus raw, rough]

crudités /ˌkruːdɪˈteɪ/ n.pl. an hors d'œuvre of mixed raw vegetables often served with a sauce into which they are dipped. [F]

cruel /ˈkruːəl/ adj. & v. —adj. (**crueller, cruellest** or **crueler, cruelest**) **1** indifferent to or gratified by another's suffering. **2** causing pain or suffering, esp. deliberately. —v.tr. (**cruelled, cruelling**) Austral. sl. thwart, spoil. □□ **cruelly** adv. **cruelness** n. [ME f. OF f. L crudelis, rel. to crudus (as CRUDE)]

cruelty /ˈkruːəltɪ/ n. (pl. **-ies**) **1** a cruel act or attitude; indifference to another's suffering. **2** a succession of cruel acts; a continued cruel attitude (suffered much cruelty). **3** Law physical or mental harm inflicted (whether or not intentional), esp. as a ground for divorce. [ME f. OF cruelté ult. f. L crudelitas]

cruet /ˈkruːɪt/ n. **1** a small container for salt, pepper, oil, or vinegar for use at table. **2** (in full **cruet-stand**) a stand holding cruets. **3** Eccl. a small container for the wine and water in the celebration of the Eucharist. [ME through AF f. OF crue pot f. OS krūka: rel. to CROCK²]

cruise /kruːz/ v. & n. —v. **1** intr. make a journey by sea calling at a series of ports usu. according to a predetermined plan, esp. for pleasure. **2** intr. sail about without a precise destination. **3** intr. **a** (of a motor vehicle or aircraft) travel at a moderate or economical speed. **b** (of a vehicle or its driver) travel at random, esp. slowly. **4** intr. achieve an objective, win a race etc., with ease. **5** intr. & tr. sl. walk or drive about (the streets etc.) in search of a sexual (esp. homosexual) partner. —n. a cruising voyage, esp. as a holiday. □ **cruise missile** one able to fly at a low altitude and guide itself by reference to the features of the region it traverses. **cruising speed** a comfortable and economical speed for a motor vehicle, below its maximum speed. [prob. f. Du. kruisen f. kruis CROSS]

cruiser /ˈkruːzə(r)/ n. **1** a warship of high speed and medium armament. **2** = cabin cruiser. **3** US a police patrol car. [Du. (as CRUISE)]

cruiserweight /ˈkruːzəˌweɪt/ n. esp. Brit. = light heavyweight (see HEAVYWEIGHT).

cruller /ˈkrʌlə(r)/ n. US a small cake made of a rich dough twisted or curled and fried in fat. [prob. f. Du. krullen curl]

crumb /krʌm/ n. & v. —n. **1 a** a small fragment, esp. of bread. **b** a small particle (a crumb of comfort). **2** the soft inner part of a loaf of bread. **3** sl. an objectionable person. —v.tr. **1** cover with breadcrumbs. **2** break into crumbs. [OE cruma]

crumble /ˈkrʌmb(ə)l/ v. & n. —v. **1** tr. & intr. break or fall into crumbs or fragments. **2** intr. (of power, a reputation, etc.) gradually disintegrate. —n. **1** Brit. a mixture of flour and fat, rubbed to the texture of breadcrumbs and cooked as a topping for fruit etc. (apple crumble; vegetable crumble). **2** a crumbly or crumbled substance. [ME f. OE, formed as CRUMB]

crumbly /ˈkrʌmblɪ/ adj. (**crumblier, crumbliest**) consisting of, or apt to fall into, crumbs or fragments. □□ **crumbliness** n.

crumbs /krʌmz/ int. Brit. sl. expressing dismay or surprise. [euphem. for Christ]

crumby /ˈkrʌmɪ/ adj. (**crumbier, crumbiest**) **1** like or covered in crumbs. **2** = CRUMMY.

crumhorn var. of KRUMMHORN.

crummy /ˈkrʌmɪ/ adj. (**crummier, crummiest**) colloq. dirty, squalid; inferior, worthless. □□ **crummily** adv. **crumminess** n. [var. of CRUMBY]

crump /krʌmp/ n. & v. Mil. sl. —n. the sound of a bursting bomb or shell. —v.intr. make this sound. [imit.]

crumpet /ˈkrʌmpɪt/ n. **1** a soft flat cake of a yeast mixture cooked on a griddle and eaten toasted and buttered. **2** Brit. joc. or offens. **a** a sexually attractive person, esp. a woman. **b** women regarded collectively, esp. as objects of sexual desire. **3** archaic sl. the head. [17th c.: orig. uncert.]

crumple /ˈkrʌmp(ə)l/ v. & n. —v. **1** tr. & intr. (often foll. by up) **a** crush or become crushed into creases. **b** ruffle, wrinkle. **2** intr. (often foll. by up) collapse, give way. —n. a crease or wrinkle. □ **crumple zone** a part of a motor vehicle, esp. the extreme front and rear, designed to crumple easily in a crash and absorb impact. □□ **crumply** adj. [obs. crump (v. & adj.) (make or become) curved]

crunch /krʌntʃ/ v. & n. —v. **1** tr. **a** crush noisily with the teeth. **b** grind (gravel, dry snow, etc.) under foot, wheels, etc. **2** intr. (often foll. by up, through) make a crunching sound in walking, moving, etc. —n. **1** crunching; a crunching sound. **2** colloq. a decisive event or moment. [earlier cra(u)nch, assim. to munch]

crunchy /ˈkrʌntʃɪ/ adj. (**crunchier, crunchiest**) that can be or has been crunched or crushed into small pieces; hard and crispy. □□ **crunchily** adv. **crunchiness** n.

crupper /ˈkrʌpə(r)/ n. **1** a strap buckled to the back of a saddle and looped under the horse's tail to hold the harness back. **2** the hindquarters of a horse. [ME f. OF cropiere (cf. CROUP²)]

crural /ˈkrʊər(ə)l/ adj. Anat. of the leg. [F crural or L cruralis f. crus cruris leg]

crusade /kruːˈseɪd/ n. & v. —n. **1 a** any of several medieval military expeditions made by Europeans to recover the Holy Land from the Muslims. **b** a war instigated by the Church for alleged religious ends. **2** a vigorous campaign in favour of a cause. —v.intr. engage in a crusade. □□ **crusader** n. [earlier croisade (F f. croix cross) or crusado (Sp. f. cruz cross)]

cruse /kruːz/ n. archaic an earthenware pot or jar. [OE crūse, of unkn. orig.]

crush /krʌʃ/ v. & n. —v.tr. **1** compress with force or violence, so as to break, bruise, etc. **2** reduce to powder by pressure. **3** crease or crumple by rough handling. **4** defeat or subdue completely (crushed by my reply). —n. **1** an act of crushing. **2** a crowded mass of people. **3** a drink made from the juice of crushed fruit. **4** colloq. **a** (usu. foll. by on) a (usu. passing) infatuation. **b** the object of an infatuation (who's the latest crush?). □ **crush bar** a place in a theatre for audiences to buy drinks in the intervals. **crush barrier** a barrier, esp. a temporary one, for restraining a crowd. □□ **crushable** adj. **crusher** n. **crushingly** adv. [ME f. AF crussir, corussier, OF croissir, cruissir, gnash (teeth), crack, f. Rmc]

crust /krʌst/ n. & v. —n. **1 a** the hard outer part of a loaf of bread. **b** a piece of this with some soft bread attached. **c** a hard dry scrap of bread. **d** esp. Austral. sl. a livelihood (what do you do for a crust?). **2** the pastry covering of a pie. **3** a hard casing of a softer thing, e.g. a harder layer over soft snow. **4** Geol. the outer portion of the earth. **5 a** a coating or deposit on the surface of anything. **b** a hard dry formation on the skin, a scab. **6** a deposit of tartar formed in bottles of old wine. **7 a** sl. impudence (you have a crust!). **b** a superficial hardness of manner. —v.tr. &

intr. **1** cover or become covered with a crust. **2** form into a crust. □□ **crustal** *adj.* (in sense 4 of *n.*). [ME f. OF *crouste* f. L *crusta* rind, shell]

crustacean /krʌˈsteɪʃ(ə)n/ *n.* & *adj.* —*n.* any arthropod of the class Crustacea, having a hard shell and usu. aquatic, e.g. the crab, lobster, and shrimp. —*adj.* of or relating to crustaceans. □□ **crustaceology** /-ʃɪˈɒlədʒɪ/ *n.* **crustaceous** /-ʃəs/ *adj.* [mod.L *crustaceus* f. *crusta*: see CRUST]

crusted /ˈkrʌstɪd/ *adj.* **1 a** having a crust. **b** (of wine) having deposited a crust. **2** antiquated, venerable (*crusted prejudice*).

crusty /ˈkrʌstɪ/ *adj.* (**crustier, crustiest**) **1** having a crisp crust (*a crusty loaf*). **2** irritable, curt. **3** hard, crustlike. □□ **crustily** *adv.* **crustiness** *n.*

crutch /krʌtʃ/ *n.* **1** a support for a lame person, usu. with a crosspiece at the top fitting under the armpit (*pair of crutches*). **2** any support or prop. **3** the crotch of the human body or garment. [OE *cryc(c)* f. Gmc]

crux /krʌks/ *n.* (*pl.* **cruxes** or **cruces** /ˈkruːsiːz/) **1** the decisive point at issue. **2** a difficult matter; a puzzle. [L, = cross]

cruzado /kruːˈzɑːdəʊ/ *n.* (*pl.* **-os**) the chief monetary unit of Brazil from 1986. [Port. *cruzado, crusado,* = marked with the cross]

cruzeiro /kruːˈzeərəʊ/ *n.* (*pl.* **-os**) the former monetary unit of Brazil; from 1986 one-thousandth of a cruzado. [Port., = large cross]

cry /kraɪ/ *v.* & *n.* —*v.* (**cries, cried**) **1** *intr.* (often foll. by *out*) make a loud or shrill sound, esp. to express pain, grief, etc., or to appeal for help. **2 a** *intr.* shed tears; weep. **b** *tr.* shed (tears). **3** *tr.* (often foll. by *out*) say or exclaim loudly or excitedly. **4** *intr.* (of an animal, esp. a bird) make a loud call. **5** *tr.* (of a hawker etc.) proclaim (wares etc.) in the street. —*n.* (*pl.* **cries**) **1** a loud inarticulate utterance of grief, pain, fear, joy, etc. **2** a loud excited utterance of words. **3** an urgent appeal or entreaty. **4** a spell of weeping. **5 a** public demand; a strong movement of opinion. **b** a watchword or rallying call. **6** the natural utterance of an animal, esp. of hounds on the scent. **7** the street-call of a hawker etc. □ **cry-baby** a person, esp. a child, who sheds tears frequently. **cry down** disparage, belittle. **cry one's eyes** (or **heart**) **out** weep bitterly. **cry for the moon** ask for what is unattainable. **cry from the heart** a passionate appeal or protest. **cry off** *colloq.* withdraw from a promise or undertaking. **cry out for** demand as a self-evident requirement or solution. **cry over spilt milk** see MILK. **cry stinking fish** disparage one's own efforts, products, etc. **cry up** praise, extol. **cry wolf** see WOLF. **a far cry 1** a long way. **2** a very different thing. **for crying out loud** *colloq.* an exclamation of surprise or annoyance. **in full cry** (of hounds) in keen pursuit. [ME f. OF *crier, cri* f. L *quiritare* wail]

cryer var. of CRIER.

crying /ˈkraɪɪŋ/ *attrib.adj.* (of an injustice or other evil) flagrant, demanding redress (*a crying need; a crying shame*).

cryo- /ˈkraɪəʊ/ *comb. form* (extreme) cold. [Gk *kruos* frost]

cryobiology /ˌkraɪəʊbaɪˈɒlədʒɪ/ *n.* the biology of organisms below their normal temperatures. □□ **cryobiological** /-ˌbaɪəˈlɒdʒɪk(ə)l/ *adj.* **cryobiologist** *n.*

cryogen /ˈkraɪədʒ(ə)n/ *n.* a freezing-mixture; a substance used to produce very low temperatures.

cryogenics /ˌkraɪəʊˈdʒenɪks/ *n.* the branch of physics dealing with the production and effects of very low temperatures. □□ **cryogenic** *adj.*

cryolite /ˈkraɪəˌlaɪt/ *n. Mineral.* a lustrous mineral of sodium-aluminium fluoride, used in the manufacture of aluminium.

cryopump /ˈkraɪəʊˌpʌmp/ *n.* a vacuum pump using liquefied gases.

cryostat /ˈkraɪəʊˌstæt/ *n.* an apparatus for maintaining a very low temperature.

cryosurgery /ˌkraɪəʊˈsɜːdʒərɪ/ *n.* surgery using the local application of intense cold for anaesthesia or therapy.

crypt /krɪpt/ *n.* an underground room or vault, esp. one beneath a church, used usu. as a burial-place. [ME f. L *crypta* f. Gk *kruptē* f. *kruptos* hidden]

cryptanalysis /ˌkrɪptəˈnælɪsɪs/ *n.* the art or process of deciphering cryptograms by analysis. □□ **cryptanalyst** /-ˈænəlɪst/ *n.* **cryptanalytic** /-ˌænəˈlɪtɪk/ *adj.* **cryptanalytical** /-ænəˈlɪtɪk(ə)l/ *adj.* [CRYPTO- + ANALYSIS]

cryptic /ˈkrɪptɪk/ *adj.* **1 a** obscure in meaning. **b** (of a crossword clue etc.) indirect; indicating the solution in a way that is not obvious. **c** secret, mysterious, enigmatic. **2** *Zool.* (of coloration etc.) serving for concealment. □□ **cryptically** *adv.* [LL *crypticus* f. Gk *kruptikos* (as CRYPTO-)]

crypto /ˈkrɪptəʊ/ *n.* (*pl.* **-os**) *colloq.* a person having a secret allegiance to a political creed etc., esp. communism. [as CRYPTO-]

crypto- /ˈkrɪptəʊ/ *comb. form* concealed, secret (*crypto-communist*). [Gk *kruptos* hidden]

cryptocrystalline /ˌkrɪptəʊˈkrɪstəˌlaɪn/ *adj.* having a crystalline structure visible only when magnified.

cryptogam /ˈkrɪptəˌgæm/ *n.* a plant that has no true flowers or seeds, e.g. ferns, mosses, algae, and fungi. □□ **cryptogamic** /-ˈgæmɪk/ *adj.* **cryptogamous** /-ˈtɒgəməs/ *adj.* [F *cryptogame* f. mod.L *cryptogamae* (*plantae*) formed as CRYPTO- + Gk *gamos* marriage]

cryptogram /ˈkrɪptəˌgræm/ *n.* a text written in cipher.

cryptography /krɪpˈtɒgrəfɪ/ *n.* the art of writing or solving ciphers. □□ **cryptographer** *n.* **cryptographic** /-təˈgræfɪk/ *adj.* **cryptographically** /-təˈgræfɪkəlɪ/ *adv.*

cryptomeria /ˌkrɪptəˈmɪərɪə/ *n.* a tall evergreen tree, *Cryptomeria japonica*, native to China and Japan, with long curved spirally arranged leaves and short cones. Also called *Japanese cedar*. [CRYPTO- + Gk *meros* part (because the seeds are enclosed by scales)]

crystal /ˈkrɪst(ə)l/ *n.* & *adj.* —*n.* **1 a** a clear transparent mineral, esp. rock crystal. **b** a piece of this. **2** (in full **crystal glass**) a highly transparent glass; flint glass. **b** articles made of this. **3** the glass over a watch-face. **4** *Electronics* a crystalline piece of semiconductor. **5** *Chem.* **a** an aggregation of molecules with a definite internal structure and the external form of a solid enclosed by symmetrically arranged plane faces. **b** a solid whose constituent particles are symmetrically arranged. —*adj.* (usu. *attrib.*) made of, like, or clear as crystal. □ **crystal ball** a glass globe used in crystal-gazing. **crystal class** *Crystallog.* any of 32 categories of crystals classified according to their symmetry. **crystal clear** unclouded, transparent. **crystal-gazing** the process of concentrating one's gaze on a crystal ball supposedly in order to obtain a picture of future events etc. **crystal lattice** *Crystallog.* the regular repeating pattern of atoms, ions, or molecules in a crystalline substance. **crystal set** a simple early form of radio receiving apparatus with a crystal touching a metal wire as the rectifier. **crystal system** *Crystallog.* any of seven possible unique combinations of unit cells, crystal lattices, and symmetry elements of a crystal class. [OE f. OF *cristal* f. L *crystallum* f. Gk *krustallos* ice, crystal]

crystalline /ˈkrɪstəˌlaɪn/ *adj.* **1** of, like, or clear as crystal. **2** *Chem.* & *Mineral.* having the structure and form of a crystal. □ **crystalline lens** a transparent lens enclosed in a membranous capsule behind the iris of the eye. □□ **crystallinity** /-ˈlɪnɪtɪ/ *n.* [ME f. OF *cristallin* f. L *crystallinus* f. Gk *krustallinos* (as CRYSTAL)]

crystallite /ˈkrɪstəˌlaɪt/ *n.* **1** a small crystal. **2** an individual perfect crystal or grain in a metal etc. **3** *Bot.* a region of cellulose etc. with a crystal-like structure.

crystallize /ˈkrɪstəˌlaɪz/ v. (also **-ise**) **1** tr. & intr. form or cause to form crystals. **2** (often foll. by *out*) **a** intr. (of ideas or plans) become definite. **b** tr. make definite. **3** tr. & intr. coat or impregnate or become coated or impregnated with sugar (*crystallized fruit*). □□ **crystallizable** adj. **crystallization** /-ˈzeɪʃ(ə)n/ n.

crystallography /ˌkrɪstəˈlɒgrəfɪ/ n. the science of crystal form and structure. □□ **crystallographer** n. **crystallographic** /-ləˈgræfɪk/ adj.

crystalloid /ˈkrɪstəˌlɔɪd/ adj. & n. —adj. **1** crystal-like. **2** having a crystalline structure. —n. a substance that in solution is able to pass through a semipermeable membrane (cf. COLLOID).

CS abbr. **1** Civil Service. **2** chartered surveyor. **3** Court of Session.

Cs symb. Chem. the element caesium.

c/s abbr. cycles per second.

csardas /ˈtʃɑːdɑːʃ/ n. (also **czardas**) (pl. same) a Hungarian dance with a slow start and a quick wild finish. [Magyar *csárdás* f. *csárda* inn]

CSC abbr. **1** Civil Service Commission. **2** Conspicuous Service Cross.

CSE abbr. hist. (in the UK) Certificate of Secondary Education. ¶ Replaced in 1988 by GCSE.

CS gas /siːˈes/ n. a gas causing tears and choking, used to control riots etc. [B. B. *Corson* & R. W. *Stoughton*, Amer. chemists]

CSI abbr. Companion of the Order of the Star of India.

CSIRO abbr. Commonwealth Scientific and Industrial Research Organization.

CSM abbr. (in the UK) Company Sergeant-Major.

CST abbr. (in the US) Central Standard Time.

CSU abbr. (in the UK) Civil Service Union.

CT abbr. US Connecticut (in official postal use).

ct. abbr. **1** carat. **2** cent.

CTC abbr. **1** (in the UK) Cyclists' Touring Club. **2** (in the UK) City Technology College.

ctenoid /ˈtiːnɔɪd/ adj. Zool. (of fish scales) characterized by tiny toothlike processes (cf. PLACOID). [Gk *kteis ktenos* comb]

ctenophore /ˈtiːnəˌfɔː(r), ˈten-/ n. any marine animal of the phylum Ctenophora, having a jellyfish-like body bearing rows of cilia, e.g. sea gooseberries. [mod.L *ctenophorus* (as CTENOID)]

CU abbr. Cambridge University.

Cu symb. Chem. the element copper.

cu. abbr. cubic.

cub /kʌb/ n. & v. —n. **1** the young of a fox, bear, lion, etc. **2** an ill-mannered young man. **3** (**Cub**) (in full **Cub Scout**) a member of the junior branch of the Scout Association. **4** (in full **cub reporter**) colloq. a young or inexperienced newspaper reporter. **5** US an apprentice. —v.tr. (**cubbed, cubbing**) (also absol.) give birth to (cubs). □□ **cubhood** n. [16th c.: orig. unkn.]

Cuban /ˈkjuːbən/ adj. & n. —adj. of or relating to Cuba, an island republic in the Caribbean, or its people. —n. a native or national of Cuba. □ **Cuban heel** a moderately high straight heel of a man's or woman's shoe.

cubby /ˈkʌbɪ/ n. (pl. **-ies**) (in full **cubby-hole**) **1** a very small room. **2** a snug or confined space. [dial. *cub* stall, pen, of LG orig.]

cube /kjuːb/ n. & v. —n. **1** a solid contained by six equal squares. **2** a cube-shaped block. **3** Math. the product of a number multiplied by its square. —v.tr. **1** find the cube of (a number). **2** cut (food for cooking etc.) into small cubes. □ **cube root** the number which produces a given number when cubed. □□ **cuber** n. [F *cube* or L *cubus* f. Gk *kubos*]

cubeb /ˈkjuːbeb/ n. **1** a climbing plant, *Piper cubeba*, bearing pungent berries. **2** this berry crushed for use in medicated cigarettes. [ME f. OF *cubebe, quibibe* ult. f. Arab. *kobāba, kubāba*]

cubic /ˈkjuːbɪk/ adj. **1** cube-shaped. **2** of three dimensions. **3** involving the cube (and no higher power) of a number (*cubic equation*). **4** Crystallog.

having three equal axes at right angles. □ **cubic content** the volume of a solid expressed in cubic metres. **cubic metre** etc. the volume of a cube whose edge is one metre etc. [F *cubique* or L *cubicus* f. Gk *kubikos* (as CUBE)]

cubical /ˈkjuːbɪk(ə)l/ adj. cube-shaped. □□ **cubically** adv.

cubicle /ˈkjuːbɪk(ə)l/ n. **1** a small partitioned space, screened for privacy. **2** a small separate sleeping-compartment. [L *cubiculum* f. *cubare* lie down]

cubiform /ˈkjuːbɪˌfɔːm/ adj. cube-shaped.

cubism /ˈkjuːbɪz(ə)m/ n. a style and movement in art, esp. painting, in which objects are represented as an assemblage of geometrical forms. □□ **cubist** n. & adj. [F *cubisme* (as CUBE)]

cubit /ˈkjuːbɪt/ n. an ancient measure of length, approximately equal to the length of a forearm. [ME f. L *cubitum* elbow, cubit]

cubital /ˈkjuːbɪt(ə)l/ adj. **1** Anat. of the forearm. **2** Zool. of the corresponding part in animals. [ME f. L *cubitalis* (as CUBIT)]

cuboid /ˈkjuːbɔɪd/ adj. & n. —adj. cube-shaped; like a cube. —n. **1** Geom. a rectangular parallelepiped. **2** (in full **cuboid bone**) Anat. the outer bone of the tarsus. □□ **cuboidal** /-ˈbɔɪd(ə)l/ adj. [mod.L *cuboides* f. Gk *kuboeidēs* (as CUBE)]

cucking-stool /ˈkʌkɪŋˌstuːl/ n. hist. a chair on which disorderly women were ducked as a punishment. [ME f. obs. *cuck* defecate]

cuckold /ˈkʌkəʊld/ n. & v. —n. the husband of an adulteress. —v.tr. make a cuckold of. □□ **cuckoldry** n. [ME *cukeweld, cokewold*, f. OF *cucu* cuckoo]

cuckoo /ˈkʊkuː/ n. & adj. —n. any bird of the family Cuculidae, esp. *Cuculus canorus*, having a characteristic cry, and depositing its eggs in the nests of small birds. —predic.adj. sl. crazy, foolish. □ **cuckoo clock** a clock that strikes the hour with a sound like a cuckoo's call, usu. with the emergence on each note of a mechanical cuckoo. **cuckoo flower 1** a meadow plant, *Cardamine pratensis*, with pale lilac flowers. **2** = ragged robin. **cuckoo in the nest** an unwelcome intruder. **cuckoo-pint** a wild arum, *Arum maculatum*, with arrow-shaped leaves and scarlet berries: also called *lords and ladies* (see LORD).

cuckoo-spit froth exuded by larvae of insects of the family Cercopidae on leaves, stems, etc. [ME f. OF *cucu*, imit.]

cucumber /ˈkjuːkʌmbə(r)/ n. **1** a long green fleshy fruit, used in salads. **2** the climbing plant, *Cucumis sativus*, yielding this fruit. [ME f. OF *co(u)combre* f. L *cucumer*]

cucurbit /kjuːˈkɜːbɪt/ n. = GOURD. □□ **cucurbitaceous** /-ˈteɪʃəs/ adj. [L *cucurbita*]

cud /kʌd/ n. half-digested food returned from the first stomach of ruminants to the mouth for further chewing. [OE *cwidu, cudu* what is chewed, corresp. to OHG *kuti, quiti* glue]

cuddle /ˈkʌd(ə)l/ v. & n. —v. **1** tr. hug, embrace, fondle. **2** intr. nestle together, lie close and snug. —n. a prolonged and fond hug. □□ **cuddlesome** adj. [16th c.: perh. f. dial. *couth* snug]

cuddly /ˈkʌdlɪ/ adj. (**cuddlier, cuddliest**) tempting to cuddle; given to cuddling.

cuddy /ˈkʌdɪ/ n. (pl. **-ies**) Sc. **1** a donkey. **2** a stupid person. [perh. a pet-form of the name *Cuthbert*]

cudgel /ˈkʌdʒ(ə)l/ n. & v. —n. a short thick stick used as a weapon. —v.tr. (**cudgelled, cudgelling**; US **cudgeled, cudgeling**) beat with a cudgel. □ **cudgel one's brains** think hard about a problem. **take up the cudgels** (often foll. by *for*) make a vigorous defence. [OE *cycgel*, of unkn. orig.]

cudweed /ˈkʌdwiːd/ n. any wild composite plant of the genus *Gnaphalium*, with scales and round flower-heads, formerly given to cattle that had lost their cud.

cue[1] /kjuː/ n. & v. —n. **1 a** the last words of an actor's speech serving as a signal to another actor to enter or speak. **b** a similar signal to a singer or player etc.

2 a a stimulus to perception etc. **b** a signal for action. **c** a hint on how to behave in particular circumstances. **3** a facility for or an instance of cueing audio equipment (see sense 2 of *v.*). —*v.tr.* (**cues, cued, cueing** or **cuing**) **1** give a cue to. **2** put (a piece of audio equipment, esp. a record-player or tape recorder) in readiness to play a particular part of the recorded material. □**cue-bid** *Bridge* an artificial bid to show a particular card etc. in the bidder's hand. **cue in 1** insert a cue for. **2** give information to. **on cue** at the correct moment. **take one's cue from** follow the example or advice of. [16th c.: orig. unkn.]

cue² /kjuː/ *n. & v. Billiards* etc. —*n.* a long straight tapering rod for striking the ball. —*v.* (**cues, cued, cueing** or **cuing**) **1** *tr.* strike (a ball) with a cue. **2** *intr.* use a cue. □**cue-ball** the ball that is to be struck with the cue. □□ **cueist** *n.* [var. of QUEUE]

cuesta /ˈkwestə/ *n. Geog.* a gentle slope, esp. one ending in a steep drop. [Sp., = slope, f. L *costa*: see COAST]

cuff¹ /kʌf/ *n.* **1 a** the end part of a sleeve. **b** a separate band of linen worn round the wrist so as to appear under the sleeve. **c** the part of a glove covering the wrist. **2** *US* a trouser turn-up. **3** (in *pl.*) *colloq.* handcuffs. □**cuff-link** a device of two joined studs etc. to fasten the sides of a cuff together. **off the cuff** *colloq.* without preparation, extempore. □□ **cuffed** *adj.* (also in *comb.*). [ME: orig. unkn.]

cuff² /kʌf/ *v. & n.* —*v.tr.* strike with an open hand. —*n.* such a blow. [16th c.: perh. imit.]

Cufic var. of KUFIC.

cui bono? /kwiː ˈbɒnəʊ, ˈbəʊ-/ who stands, or stood, to gain? (with the implication that this person is responsible) [L, = to whom (is it) a benefit?]

cuirass /kwɪˈræs/ *n.* **1** *hist.* a piece of armour consisting of breastplate and back-plate fastened together. **2** a device for artificial respiration. [ME f. OF *cuirace*, ult. f. LL *coriaceus* f. *corium* leather]

cuirassier /ˌkwɪrəˈsɪə(r)/ *n. hist.* a cavalry soldier wearing a cuirass. [F (as CUIRASS)]

cuish var. of CUISSE.

cuisine /kwɪˈziːn/ *n.* a style or method of cooking, esp. of a particular country or establishment. [F f. L *coquina* f. *coquere* to cook]

cuisse /kwɪs/ *n.* (also **cuish** /kwɪʃ/) (usu. in *pl.*) *hist.* thigh armour. [ME, f. OF *cuisseaux* pl. of *cuissel* f. LL *coxale* f. *coxa* hip]

cul-de-sac /ˈkʌldəˌsæk, ˈkʊl-/ *n.* (*pl.* **culs-de-sac** *pronunc.* same) **1** a street or passage closed at one end. **2** a route or course leading nowhere; a position from which one cannot escape. **3** *Anat.* = DIVERTICULUM. [F, = sack-bottom]

-cule /kjuːl/ *suffix* forming (orig. diminutive) nouns (*molecule*). [F *-cule* or L *-culus*]

culinary /ˈkʌlɪnərɪ/ *adj.* of or for cooking or the kitchen. □□ **culinarily** *adv.* [L *culinarius* f. *culina* kitchen]

cull /kʌl/ *v. & n.* —*v.tr.* **1** select, choose, or gather from a large quantity or amount (*knowledge culled from books*). **2** pick or gather (flowers, fruit, etc.). **3** select (animals) according to quality, esp. poor surplus specimens for killing. —*n.* **1** an act of culling. **2** an animal or animals culled. □□ **culler** [ME f. OF *coillier* etc. ult. f. L *colligere* COLLECT¹]

cullet /ˈkʌlɪt/ *n.* recycled waste or broken glass used in glass-making. [var. of COLLET]

culm¹ /kʌlm/ *n.* **1** coal-dust, esp. of anthracite. **2** *Geol.* strata under coal measures, esp. in SW England. [ME, prob. rel. to COAL]

culm² /kʌlm/ *n. Bot.* the stem of a plant, esp. of grasses. □□ **culmiferous** /-ˈmɪfərəs/ *adj.* [L *culmus* stalk]

culminant /ˈkʌlmɪnənt/ *adj.* **1** at or forming the top. **2** *Astron.* on the meridian. [as CULMINATE + -ANT]

culminate /ˈkʌlmɪˌneɪt/ *v.* **1** *intr.* (usu. foll. by *in*) reach its highest or final point (*the antagonism culminated in war*). **2** *tr.* bring to its highest or

final point. **3** *intr. Astron.* be on the meridian. □□ **culmination** /-ˈneɪʃ(ə)n/ *n.* [LL *culminare culminat-* f. *culmen* summit]

culottes /kjuːˈlɒts/ *n.pl.* women's (usu. short) trousers cut to resemble a skirt. [F, = knee-breeches]

culpable /ˈkʌlpəb(ə)l/ *adj.* deserving blame. □□ **culpability** /-ˈbɪlɪtɪ/ *n.* **culpably** *adv.* [ME f. OF *coupable* f. L *culpabilis* f. *culpare* f. *culpa* blame]

culprit /ˈkʌlprɪt/ *n.* a person accused of or guilty of an offence. [17th c.: orig. in the formula *Culprit, how will you be tried?*, said by the Clerk of the Crown to a prisoner pleading Not Guilty: perh. abbr. of AF *Culpable: prest d'averrer* etc. (You are) guilty: (I am) ready to prove etc.]

cult /kʌlt/ *n.* **1** a system of religious worship esp. as expressed in ritual. **2 a** devotion or homage to a person or thing (*the cult of aestheticism*). **b** a popular fashion esp. followed by a specific section of society. **3** (*attrib.*) denoting a person or thing popularized in this way (*cult film; cult figure*). □□ **cultic** *adj.* **cultism** *n.* **cultist** *n.* [F *culte* or L *cultus* worship f. *colere cult-* inhabit, till, worship]

cultivar /ˈkʌltɪˌvɑː(r)/ *n. Bot.* a plant variety produced by cultivation. [CULTIVATE + VARIETY]

cultivate /ˈkʌltɪˌveɪt/ *v.tr.* **1 a** prepare and use (soil etc.) for crops or gardening. **b** break up (the ground) with a cultivator. **2 a** raise or produce (crops). **b** culture (bacteria etc.). **3 a** (often as **cultivated** *adj.*) apply oneself to improving or developing (the mind, manners, etc.). **b** pay attention to or nurture (a person or a person's friendship). □□ **cultivable** *adj.* **cultivatable** *adj.* **cultivation** /-ˈveɪʃ(ə)n/ *n.* [med.L *cultivare* f. *cultiva* (*terra*) arable (land) (as CULT)]

cultivator /ˈkʌltɪˌveɪtə(r)/ *n.* **1** a mechanical implement for breaking up the ground and uprooting weeds. **2** a person or thing that cultivates.

cultural /ˈkʌltʃər(ə)l/ *adj.* of or relating to the cultivation of the mind or manners, esp. through artistic or intellectual activity. □□ **culturally** *adv.*

culture /ˈkʌltʃə(r)/ *n. & v.* —*n.* **1 a** the arts and other manifestations of human intellectual achievement regarded collectively (*a city lacking in culture*). **b** a refined understanding of this; intellectual development (*a person of culture*). **2** the customs, civilization, and achievements of a particular time or people (*studied Chinese culture*). **3** improvement by mental or physical training. **4 a** the cultivation of plants; the rearing of bees, silkworms, etc. **b** the cultivation of the soil. **5** a quantity of micro-organisms and the nutrient material supporting their growth. —*v.tr.* maintain (bacteria etc.) in conditions suitable for growth. □**culture shock** the feeling of disorientation experienced by a person suddenly subjected to an unfamiliar culture or way of life. **culture vulture** *colloq.* a person eager to acquire culture. **the two cultures** the arts and science. [ME f. F *culture* or L *cultura* (as CULT): (v.) f. obs. F *culturer* or med.L *culturare*]

cultured /ˈkʌltʃəd/ *adj.* having refined taste and manners and a good education. □**cultured pearl** a pearl formed by an oyster after the insertion of a foreign body into its shell.

cultus /ˈkʌltəs/ *n.* a system of religious worship; a cult. [L: see CULT]

culverin /ˈkʌlvərɪn/ *n. hist.* **1** a long cannon. **2** a small firearm. [ME f. OF *coulevrine* f. *couleuvre* snake ult. f. L *colubra*]

culvert /ˈkʌlvət/ *n.* **1** an underground channel carrying water across a road etc. **2** a channel for an electric cable. [18th c.: orig. unkn.]

cum /kʌm/ *prep.* (usu. in *comb.*) with, combined with, also used as (*a bedroom-cum-study*). [L]

cumber /ˈkʌmbə(r)/ *v. & n.* —*v.tr. literary* hamper, hinder, inconvenience. —*n.* a hindrance, obstruction, or burden. [ME, prob. f. ENCUMBER]

cumbersome /ˈkʌmbəsəm/ *adj.* inconvenient in size, weight, or shape; unwieldy. □□ **cumbersomely** *adv.* **cumbersomeness** *n.* [ME f. CUMBER + -SOME¹]

Cumbrian /ˈkʌmbrɪən/ *adj.* & *n.* —*adj.* **1** of Cumberland. **2 a** of the ancient British kingdom of Cumbria. **b** of the modern county of Cumbria. —*n.* a native of Cumberland or of ancient or modern Cumbria. [med.L *Cumbria* f. Welsh *Cymry* Welshmen + -AN]

cumbrous /ˈkʌmbrəs/ *adj.* = CUMBERSOME. □□ **cumbrously** *adv.* **cumbrousness** *n.* [CUMBER + -OUS]

cum grano salis /kʌm ˌɡrɑːnəʊ ˈsɑːlɪs/ *adv.* with a grain of salt (see *take with a pinch of salt* (see SALT)). [L]

cumin /ˈkʌmɪn/ *n.* (also **cummin**) **1** an umbelliferous plant, *Cuminum cyminum*, bearing aromatic seeds. **2** these seeds used as flavouring, esp. ground and used in curry powder. [ME f. OF *cumin*, *comin* f. L *cuminum* f. Gk *kuminon*, prob. of Semitic orig.]

cummerbund /ˈkʌməˌbʌnd/ *n.* a waist sash. [Hind. & Pers. *kamar-band* loin-band]

cummin var. of CUMIN.

cumquat var. of KUMQUAT.

cumulate *v.* & *adj.* —*v.tr.* & *intr.* /ˈkjuːmjʊˌleɪt/ accumulate, amass; combine. —*adj.* /ˈkjuːmjʊlət/ heaped up, massed. □□ **cumulation** /-ˈleɪʃ(ə)n/ *n.* [L *cumulare* f. *cumulus* heap]

cumulative /ˈkjuːmjʊlətɪv/ *adj.* **1 a** increasing or increased in amount, force, etc., by successive additions (*cumulative evidence*). **b** formed by successive additions (*learning is a cumulative process*). **2** Stock Exch. (of shares) entitling holders to arrears of interest before any other distribution is made. □ **cumulative error** an error that increases with the size of the sample revealing it. **cumulative voting** a system in which each voter has as many votes as there are candidates and may give all to one candidate. □□ **cumulatively** *adv.* **cumulativeness** *n.*

cumulo- /ˈkjuːmjʊləʊ/ *comb. form* cumulus (cloud).

cumulus /ˈkjuːmjʊləs/ *n.* (*pl.* **cumuli** /-ˌlaɪ/) a cloud formation consisting of rounded masses heaped on each other above a horizontal base. □□ **cumulous** *adj.* [L, = heap]

cuneate /ˈkjuːnɪət/ *adj.* wedge-shaped. [L *cuneus* wedge]

cuneiform /ˈkjuːnɪˌfɔːm/ *adj.* & *n.* —*adj.* **1** wedge-shaped. **2** of, relating to, or using the wedge-shaped writing impressed usu. in clay in ancient Babylonian etc. inscriptions. —*n.* cuneiform writing. [F *cunéiforme* or mod.L *cuneiformis* f. L *cuneus* wedge]

cunjevoi /ˈkʌndʒɪˌvɔɪ/ *n. Austral.* **1** the green arum or spoon lily *Alocasia macrorrhiza*. **2** a sea squirt. [Aboriginal]

cunnilingus /ˌkʌnɪˈlɪŋɡəs/ *n.* (also **cunnilinctus** /-ˈlɪŋktəs/) oral stimulation of the female genitals. [L f. *cunnus* vulva + *lingere* lick]

cunning /ˈkʌnɪŋ/ *adj.* & *n.* —*adj.* (**cunninger**, **cunningest**) **1 a** skilled in ingenuity or deceit. **b** selfishly clever or crafty. **2** ingenious (*a cunning device*). **3** *US* attractive, quaint. —*n.* **1** craftiness; skill in deceit. **2** skill, ingenuity. □□ **cunningly** *adv.* **cunningness** *n.* [ME f. ON *kunnandi* knowing f. *kunna* know: cf. CAN¹]

cunt /kʌnt/ *n. coarse sl.* **1** the female genitals. **2** *offens.* an unpleasant or stupid person. ¶ A highly taboo word. [ME f. Gmc]

CUP *abbr.* Cambridge University Press.

cup /kʌp/ *n.* & *v.* —*n.* **1** a small bowl-shaped container, usu. with a handle for drinking from. **2 a** its contents (*a cup of tea*). **b** = CUPFUL. **3** a cup-shaped thing, esp. the calyx of a flower or the socket of a bone. **4** flavoured wine, cider, etc., usu. chilled. **5** an ornamental cup-shaped trophy as a prize for victory or prowess, esp. in a sports contest. **6** one's fate or fortune (*a bitter cup*). **7** either of the two cup-shaped parts of a brassière. **8** the chalice used or the wine taken at the Eucharist. **9** *Golf* the hole on a putting-green or the metal container in it. —*v.tr.*

(**cupped, cupping**) **1** form (esp. one's hands) into the shape of a cup. **2** take or hold as in a cup. **3** *hist.* bleed (a person) by using a glass in which a partial vacuum is formed by heating. □ **cup-cake** a small cake baked in a cup-shaped foil or paper container and often iced. **Cup Final** a final match in a competition for a cup. **cup lichen** a lichen, *Cladonia pyxidata*, with cup-shaped processes arising from the thallus. **one's cup of tea** *colloq.* what interests or suits one. **cup-tie** a match in a competition for a cup. **in one's cups** while drunk; drunk. [OE *cuppe* f. med.L *cuppa* cup, prob. differentiated from L *cupa* tub]

cupbearer /ˈkʌpˌbeərə(r)/ *n.* a person who serves wine, esp. an officer of a royal or noble household.

cupboard /ˈkʌbəd/ *n.* a recess or piece of furniture with a door and (usu.) shelves, in which things are stored. □ **cupboard love** a display of affection meant to secure some gain. [ME f. CUP + BOARD]

cupel /ˈkjuːp(ə)l/ *n.* & *v.* —*n.* a small flat porous vessel used in assaying gold or silver in the presence of lead. —*v.tr.* (**cupelled, cupelling**; *US* **cupeled, cupeling**) assay or refine in a cupel. □□ **cupellation** /-ˈleɪʃ(ə)n/ *n.* [F *coupelle* f. LL *cupella* dimin. of *cupa*: see CUP]

cupful /ˈkʌpfʊl/ *n.* (*pl.* **-fuls**) **1** the amount held by a cup, esp. *US* a half-pint or 8-ounce measure in cookery. **2** a cup full of a substance (*drank a cupful of water*). ¶ A *cupful* is a measure, and so *three cupfuls* is a quantity regarded in terms of a cup; *three cups full* denotes the actual cups, as in *three cups full of water*. Sense 2 is an intermediate use.

Cupid /ˈkjuːpɪd/ *n.* **1** (in Roman mythology) the Roman god of love represented as a naked winged boy with a bow and arrows. **2** (also **cupid**) a representation of Cupid. □ **Cupid's bow** the upper lip etc. shaped like the double-curved bow carried by Cupid. [ME f. L *Cupido* f. *cupere* desire]

cupidity /kjuːˈpɪdɪtɪ/ *n.* greed for gain; avarice. [ME f. OF *cupidité* or L *cupiditas* f. *cupidus* desirous]

cupola /ˈkjuːpələ/ *n.* **1 a** a rounded dome forming a roof or ceiling. **b** a small rounded dome adorning a roof. **2** a revolving dome protecting mounted guns on a warship or in a fort. **3** (in full **cupola-furnace**) a furnace for melting metals. □□ **cupolaed** /-ləd/ *adj.* [It. f. LL *cupula* dimin. of *cupa* cask]

cuppa /ˈkʌpə/ *n.* (also **cupper** /ˈkʌpə(r)/) *Brit. colloq.* **1** a cup of. **2** a cup of tea. [corruption]

cuprammonium /ˌkjuːprəˈməʊnɪəm/ *n.* a complex ion of divalent copper and ammonia, solutions of which dissolve cellulose. [LL *cuprum* + AMMONIUM]

cupreous /ˈkjuːprɪəs/ *adj.* of or like copper. [LL *cupreus* f. *cuprum* copper]

cupric /ˈkjuːprɪk/ *adj.* of copper, esp. divalent copper. □□ **cupriferous** /-ˈprɪfərəs/ *adj.* [LL *cuprum* copper]

cupro- /ˈkjuːprəʊ/ *comb. form* copper (*cupro-nickel*).

cupro-nickel /ˌkjuːprəʊˈnɪk(ə)l/ *n.* an alloy of copper and nickel, esp. in the proportions 3:1 as used in 'silver' coins.

cuprous /ˈkjuːprəs/ *adj.* of copper, esp. monovalent copper. [LL *cuprum* copper]

cupule /ˈkjuːpjuːl/ *n. Bot.* & *Zool.* a cup-shaped organ, receptacle, etc. [LL *cupula* CUPOLA]

cur /kɜː(r)/ *n.* **1** a worthless or snappy dog. **2** a contemptible person. [ME, prob. orig. in *cur-dog*, perh. f. ON *kurr* grumbling]

curable /ˈkjʊərəb(ə)l/ *adj.* that can be cured. □□ **curability** /-ˈbɪlɪtɪ/ *n.* [CURE]

curaçao /ˌkjʊərəˈsəʊ/ *n.* (also **curaçoa** /-ˈsəʊə/) (*pl.* **-os** or **curaçoas**) a liqueur of spirits flavoured with the peel of bitter oranges. [F *Curaçao*, name of the Caribbean island producing these oranges]

curacy /ˈkjʊərəsɪ/ *n.* (*pl.* **-ies**) a curate's office or the tenure of it.

curare /kjʊəˈrɑːrɪ/ *n.* a resinous bitter substance prepared from S. American plants of the genera *Strychnos* and *Chondodendron*, paralysing the motor nerves, used by American Indians to poison arrows and blowpipe darts, and formerly used as a muscle relaxant in surgery. [Carib]

curassow /ˈkjʊərəˌsəʊ/ n. any game bird of the family Cracidae, found in Central and S. America. [Anglicized f. CURAÇAO]

curate /ˈkjʊərət/ n. **1** a member of the clergy engaged as assistant to a parish priest. **2** archaic an ecclesiastical pastor. □ **curate-in-charge** a curate appointed to take charge of a parish in place of a priest. **curate's egg** a thing that is partly good and partly bad. [ME f. med.L curatus f. L cura CURE]

curative /ˈkjʊərətɪv/ adj. & n. —adj. tending or able to cure (esp. disease). —n. a curative medicine or agent. [F curatif -ive f. med.L curativus f. L curare CURE]

curator /kjʊəˈreɪtə(r)/ n. a keeper or custodian of a museum or other collection. □□ **curatorial** /ˌkjʊərəˈtɔːrɪəl/ adj. **curatorship** n. [ME f. AF curatour (OF -eur) or L curator (as CURATIVE)]

curb /kɜːb/ n. & v. —n. **1** a check or restraint. **2** a strap etc. fastened to the bit and passing under a horse's lower jaw, used as a check. **3** an enclosing border or edging such as the frame round the top of a well or a fender round a hearth. **4** = KERB. —v.tr. **1** restrain. **2** put a curb on (a horse). □ **curb roof** a roof of which each face has two slopes, the lower one steeper. [ME f. OF courber f. L curvare bend, CURVE]

curcuma /ˈkɜːkjuːmə/ n. **1** the spice turmeric. **2** any tuberous plant of the genus Curcuma, yielding this and other commercial substances. [med.L or mod.L f. Arab. kurkum saffron f. Skr. kuṅkuma^m]

curd /kɜːd/ n. **1** (often in pl.) a coagulated substance formed by the action of acids on milk, which may be made into cheese or eaten as food. **2** a fatty substance found between flakes of boiled salmon flesh. **3** the edible head of a cauliflower. □ **curds and whey** the result of acidulating milk. **curd soap** a white soap made of tallow and soda. □□ **curdy** adj. [ME: orig. unkn.]

curdle /ˈkɜːd(ə)l/ v.tr. & intr. make into or become curds; congeal. □ **make one's blood curdle** fill one with horror. □□ **curdler** n. [frequent. form of CURD (as verb)]

cure /kjʊə(r)/ v. & n. —v. **1** tr. (often foll. by of) restore (a person or animal) to health (was cured of pleurisy). **2** tr. eliminate (a disease, evil, etc.). **3** tr. preserve (meat, fruit, tobacco, or skins) by salting, drying, etc. **4** tr. a vulcanize (rubber). **b** harden (concrete or plastic). **5** intr. effect a cure. **6** intr. undergo a process of curing. —n. **1** restoration to health. **2** a thing that effects a cure. **3** a course of medical or healing treatment. **4 a** the office or function of a curate. **b** a parish or other sphere of spiritual ministration. **5 a** the process of curing rubber or plastic. **b** (with qualifying adj.) the degree of this. □ **cure-all** a panacea; a universal remedy. □□ **curer** n. [ME f. OF curer f. L curare take care of f. cura care]

curé /ˈkjʊəreɪ/ n. a parish priest in France etc. [F f. med.L curatus: see CURATE]

curettage /kjʊəˈretɪdʒ, -riˈtɑːdʒ/ n. the use of or an operation involving the use of a curette. [F (as CURETTE)]

curette /kjʊəˈret/ n. & v. —n. a surgeon's small scraping-instrument. —v.tr. & intr. clean or scrape with a curette. [F, f. curer cleanse (as CURE)]

curfew /ˈkɜːfjuː/ n. **1 a** a regulation restricting or forbidding the public circulation of people, esp. requiring people to remain indoors between specified hours, usu. at night. **b** the hour designated as the beginning of such a restriction. **c** a daily signal indicating this. **2** hist. **a** a medieval regulation requiring people to extinguish fires at a fixed hour in the evening. **b** the hour for this. **c** the bell announcing it. **3** the ringing of a bell at a fixed evening hour. [ME f. AF coeverfu, OF cuevrefeu f. the stem of couvrir COVER + feu fire]

Curia /ˈkjʊərɪə/ n. (also **curia**) the papal court; the government departments of the Vatican. □□ **Curial** adj. [L: orig. a division of an ancient Roman tribe, the senate house at Rome, a feudal court of justice]

curie /ˈkjʊərɪ/ n. **1** a unit of radioactivity, corresponding to 3.7 × 10¹⁰ disintegrations per second. ¶ Abbr.: **Ci**. **2** a quantity of radioactive substance having this activity. [P. Curie, Fr. scientist d. 1906]

curio /ˈkjʊərɪəʊ/ n. (pl. **-os**) a rare or unusual object or person. [19th-c. abbr. of CURIOSITY]

curiosa /ˌkjʊərɪˈəʊsə/ n.pl. **1** curiosities. **2** erotic or pornographic books. [neut. pl. of L curiosus: see CURIOUS]

curiosity /ˌkjʊərɪˈɒsɪtɪ/ n. (pl. **-ies**) **1** an eager desire to know; inquisitiveness. **2** strangeness. **3** a strange, rare, or interesting object. [ME f. OF curiouseté f. L curiositas -tatis (as CURIOUS)]

curious /ˈkjʊərɪəs/ adj. **1** eager to learn; inquisitive. **2** strange, surprising, odd. **3** euphem. (of books etc.) erotic, pornographic. □□ **curiously** adv. **curiousness** n. [ME f. OF curios f. L curiosus careful f. cura care]

curium /ˈkjʊərɪəm/ n. an artificially made transuranic radioactive metallic element, first produced by bombarding plutonium with helium ions. ¶ Symb.: **Cm**. [M. Curie d. 1934 and P. Curie d. 1906, Fr. scientists]

curl /kɜːl/ v. & n. —v. **1** tr. & intr. (often foll. by up) bend or coil into a spiral; form or cause to form curls. **2** intr. move in a spiral form (smoke curling upwards). **3 a** intr. (of the upper lip) be raised slightly on one side as an expression of contempt or disapproval. **b** tr. cause (the lip) to do this. **4** intr. play curling. —n. **1** a lock of curled hair. **2** anything spiral or curved inwards. **3 a** a curling movement or act. **b** the state of being curled. **4** a disease of plants in which the leaves are curled up. □ **curl up** lie or sit with the knees drawn up. **2** colloq. writhe with embarrassment or horror. **make a person's hair curl** colloq. shock or horrify a person. **out of curl** lacking energy. [ME; earliest form crolled, crulled f. obs. adj. crolle, crulle curly f. MDu. krul]

curler /ˈkɜːlə(r)/ n. **1** a pin or roller etc. for curling the hair. **2** a player in the game of curling.

curlew /ˈkɜːljuː/ n. any wading bird of the genus Numenius, esp. N. arquatus, possessing a usu. long slender down-curved bill. [ME f. OF courlieu, courlis orig. imit., but assim. to courliu courier f. courre run + lieu place]

curlicue /ˈkɜːlɪˌkjuː/ n. a decorative curl or twist. [CURLY + CUE² (= pigtail) or Q¹]

curling /ˈkɜːlɪŋ/ n. **1** in senses of CURL v. **2** a game played on ice, esp. in Scotland, in which large round flat stones are slid across the surface towards a mark. □ **curling-tongs** (or **-iron** or **-pins**) a heated device for twisting the hair into curls.

curly /ˈkɜːlɪ/ adj. (**curlier**, **curliest**) **1** having or arranged in curls. **2** moving in curves. □ **curly kale** see KALE. □□ **curliness** n.

curmudgeon /kəˈmʌdʒ(ə)n/ n. a bad-tempered person. □□ **curmudgeonly** adj. [16th c.: orig. unkn.]

currach /ˈkʌrə/ n. (also **curragh**) Ir. a coracle. [Ir.: cf. CORACLE]

currajong var. of KURRAJONG.

currant /ˈkʌrənt/ n. **1** a dried fruit of a small seedless variety of grape grown in the Levant and much used in cookery. **2 a** any of various shrubs of the genus Ribes producing red, white, or black berries. **b** a berry of these shrubs. □ **flowering currant** an ornamental species of currant native to N. America. [ME raysons of coraunce f. AF, = grapes of Corinth (the orig. source)]

currawong /ˈkʌrəˌwɒŋ/ n. Austral. any crowlike songbird of the genus Strepera, possessing a resonant call. [Aboriginal]

currency /ˈkʌrənsɪ/ n. (pl. **-ies**) **1 a** the money in general use in a country. **b** any other commodity used as a medium of exchange. **2** the condition of being current; prevalence (e.g. of words or ideas). **3** the time during which something is current.

current /'kʌrənt/ *adj. & n.* —*adj.* **1** belonging to the present time; happening now (*current events*; *the current week*). **2** (of money, opinion, a rumour, a word, etc.) in general circulation or use. —*n.* **1** a body of water, air, etc., moving in a definite direction, esp. through a stiller surrounding medium. **2 a** an ordered movement of electrically charged particles. **b** a quantity representing the intensity of such movement. **3** (usu. foll. by *of*) a general tendency or course (of events, opinions, etc.). □**current account** a bank account from which money may be drawn without notice. **pass current** be generally accepted as true or genuine. □□**currentness** *n.* [ME f. OF *corant* f. L *currere* run]

currently /'kʌrəntlɪ/ *adv.* at the present time; now.

curricle /'kʌrɪk(ə)l/ *n. hist.* a light open two-wheeled carriage drawn by two horses abreast. [L *curriculum*: see CURRICULUM]

curriculum /kə'rɪkjʊləm/ *n.* (*pl.* **curricula** /-lə/) **1** the subjects that are studied or prescribed for study in a school (*not part of the school curriculum*). **2** any programme of activities. □□**curricular** *adj.* [L, = course, race-chariot, f. *currere* run]

curriculum vitae /kə'rɪkjʊləm 'viːtaɪ/ *n.* a brief account of one's education, qualifications, and previous occupations. [L, = course of life]

currier /'kʌrɪə(r)/ *n.* a person who dresses and colours tanned leather. [ME f. OF *corier*, f. L *coriarius* f. *corium* leather]

currish /'kɜːrɪʃ/ *adj.* **1** like a cur; snappish. **2** ignoble. □□**currishly** *adv.* **currishness** *n.*

curry[1] /'kʌrɪ/ *n. & v.* —*n.* (*pl.* **-ies**) a dish of meat, vegetables, etc., cooked in a sauce of hot-tasting spices, usu. served with rice. —*v.tr.* (**-ies, -ied**) prepare or flavour with a sauce of hot-tasting spices (*curried eggs*). □**curry-powder** a preparation of turmeric and other spices for making curry. [Tamil]

curry[2] /'kʌrɪ/ *v.tr.* (**-ies, -ied**) **1** groom (a horse) with a curry-comb. **2** treat (tanned leather) to improve its properties. **3** thrash. □**curry-comb** a hand-held metal serrated device for grooming horses. **curry favour** ingratiate oneself. [ME f. OF *correier* ult. f. Gmc]

curse /kɜːs/ *n. & v.* —*n.* **1** a solemn utterance intended to invoke a supernatural power to inflict destruction or punishment on a person or thing. **2** the evil supposedly resulting from a curse. **3** a violent exclamation of anger; a profane oath. **4** a thing that causes evil or harm. **5** (prec. by *the*) *colloq.* menstruation. **6** a sentence of excommunication. —*v.* **1** *tr.* **a** utter a curse against. **b** (in *imper.*) may God curse. **2** *tr.* (usu. in *passive*; foll. by *with*) afflict with (*cursed with blindness*). **3** *intr.* utter expletive curses; swear. **4** *tr.* excommunicate. □□**curser** *n.* [OE *curs*, *cursian*, of unkn. orig.]

cursed /'kɜːsɪd, kɜːst/ *adj.* damnable, abominable. □□ **cursedly** *adv.* **cursedness** *n.*

cursillo /kʊə'sɪləʊ/ *n.* (*pl.* **-os**) *RC Ch.* a short informal spiritual retreat by a group of devotees esp. in Latin America. [Sp., = little course]

cursive /'kɜːsɪv/ *adj. & n.* —*adj.* (of writing) done with joined characters. —*n.* cursive writing (cf. PRINT *v.* 4, UNCIAL). □□**cursively** *adv.* [med.L (*scriptura*) *cursiva* f. L *currere curs-* run]

cursor /'kɜːsə(r)/ *n.* **1** *Math.* etc. a transparent slide engraved with a hairline and forming part of a slide-rule. **2** *Computing* a movable indicator on a VDU screen identifying a particular position in the display, esp. the position that the program will operate on with the next keystroke. [L, = runner (as CURSIVE)]

cursorial /kɜː'sɔːrɪəl/ *adj. Anat.* having limbs adapted for running. [as CURSOR + -IAL]

cursory /'kɜːsərɪ/ *adj.* hasty, hurried (*a cursory glance*). □□**cursorily** *adv.* **cursoriness** *n.* [L *cursorius* of a runner (as CURSOR)]

curst *archaic* var. of CURSED.

curt /kɜːt/ *adj.* noticeably or rudely brief. □□ **curtly** *adv.* **curtness** *n.* [L *curtus* cut short, abridged]

curtail /kɜː'teɪl/ *v.tr.* **1** cut short; reduce; terminate esp. prematurely (*curtailed his visit to America*). **2** (foll. by *of*) *archaic* deprive of. □□**curtailment** *n.* [obs. *curtal* horse with docked tail f. F *courtault* f. *court* short f. L *curtus*: assim. to *tail*]

curtain /'kɜːt(ə)n/ *n. & v.* —*n.* **1** a piece of cloth etc. hung up as a screen, usu. moveable sideways or upwards, esp. at a window or between the stage and auditorium of a theatre. **2** *Theatr.* **a** the rise or fall of the stage curtain at the beginning or end of an act or scene. **b** = *curtain-call*. **3** a partition or cover. **4** (in *pl.*) *sl.* the end. —*v.tr.* **1** furnish or cover with a curtain or curtains. **2** (foll. by *off*) shut off with a curtain or curtains. □**curtain-call** *Theatr.* an audience's summons to actor(s) to take a bow after the fall of the curtain. **curtain-fire** *Mil.* a concentration of rapid and continuous fire. **curtain lecture** a wife's private reproof to her husband, orig. behind bed-curtains. **curtain-raiser 1** *Theatr.* a piece prefaced to the main performance. **2** a preliminary event. **curtain-wall 1** *Fortification* the plain wall of a fortified place, connecting two towers etc. **2** *Archit.* a piece of plain wall not supporting a roof. [ME f. OF *cortine* f. LL *cortina* transl. Gk *aulaia* f. *aulē* court]

curtana /kɜː'teɪnə, -'tɑːnə/ *n. Brit.* an unpointed sword borne before English sovereigns at their coronation, as an emblem of mercy. [ME f. AL *curtana* (*spatha* sword) f. AF *curtain*, OF *cortain* name of Roland's similar sword f. *cort* short (as CURT)]

curtilage /'kɜːtɪlɪdʒ/ *n.* an area attached to a dwelling-house and forming one enclosure with it. [ME f. AF *curtilage*, OF *co(u)rtillage* f. *co(u)rtil* small court f. *cort* COURT]

curtsy /'kɜːtsɪ/ *n. & v.* (also **curtsey**) —*n.* (*pl.* **-ies** or **-eys**) a woman's or girl's formal greeting or salutation made by bending the knees and lowering the body. —*v.intr.* (**-ies, -ied** or **-eys, -eyed**) make a curtsy. [var. of COURTESY]

curule /'kjʊəruːl/ *adj. Rom.Hist.* designating or relating to the authority exercised by the senior Roman magistrates, chiefly the consul and praetor, who were entitled to use the *sella curulis* ('curule seat' or seat of office). [L *curulis* f. *currus* chariot (in which the chief magistrate was conveyed to the seat of office)]

curvaceous /kɜː'veɪʃəs/ *adj. colloq.* (esp. of a woman) having a shapely curved figure.

curvature /'kɜːvətʃə(r)/ *n.* **1** the act or state of curving. **2** a curved form. **3** *Geom.* **a** the deviation of a curve from a straight line, or of a curved surface from a plane. **b** the quantity expressing this. [OF f. L *curvatura* (as CURVE)]

curve /kɜːv/ *n. & v.* —*n.* **1** a line or surface having along its length a regular deviation from being straight or flat, as exemplified by the surface of a sphere or lens. **2** a curved form or thing. **3** a curved line on a graph. **4** *Baseball* a ball caused to deviate by the pitcher's spin. —*v.tr. & intr.* bend or shape so as to form a curve. □□**curved** *adj.* [orig. as *adj.* (in *curve line*) f. L *curvus* bent; (*v.*) f. L *curvare*]

curvet /kɜː'vet/ *n. & v.* —*n.* a horse's leap with the forelegs raised together and the hind legs raised with a spring before the forelegs reach the ground. —*v.intr.* (**curvetted, curvetting** or **curveted, curveting**) (of a horse or rider) make a curvet. [It. *corvetta* dimin. of *corva* CURVE]

curvi- /'kɜːvɪ/ *comb. form* curved. [L *curvus* curved]

curvifoliate /ˌkɜːvɪ'fəʊlɪət/ *adj. Bot.* with the leaves bent back.

curviform /'kɜːvɪˌfɔːm/ *adj.* having a curved shape.

curvilinear /ˌkɜːvɪ'lɪnɪə(r)/ *adj.* contained by or consisting of curved lines. □□**curvilinearly** *adv.* [CURVI- after *rectilinear*]

curvirostral /ˌkɜːvɪˈrɒstr(ə)l/ *adj.* with a curved beak.

curvy /ˈkɜːvɪ/ *adj.* (**curvier, curviest**) **1** having many curves. **2** (of a woman's figure) shapely. □□ **curviness** *n.*

cuscus[1] /ˈkʌskəs/ *n.* the aromatic fibrous root of an Indian grass, *Vetiveria zizanoides*, used for making fans etc. [Pers. *ḳaškaš*]

cuscus[2] /ˈkʌskəs/ *n.* any of several nocturnal, usu. arboreal, marsupial mammals of the genus *Phalanger*, native to New Guinea and N. Australia. [native name]

cusec /ˈkjuːsek/ *n.* a unit of flow (esp. of water) equal to one cubic foot per second. [abbr.]

cush /kʊʃ/ *n.* esp. *Billiards colloq.* a cushion. [abbr.]

cushat /ˈkʌʃət/ *n.* Sc. a woodpigeon. [OE *cūscute*, of unkn. orig.]

cush-cush /ˈkʊʃkʊʃ/ *n.* a yam, *Dioscorea trifida*, native to S. America. [native name]

cushion /ˈkʊʃ(ə)n/ *n. & v.* —*n.* **1** a bag of cloth etc. stuffed with a mass of soft material, used as a soft support for sitting or leaning on etc. **2** a means of protection against shock. **3** the elastic lining of the sides of a billiard-table, from which the ball rebounds. **4** a body of air supporting a hovercraft etc. **5** the frog of a horse's hoof. —*v.tr.* **1** provide or protect with a cushion or cushions. **2** provide with a defence; protect. **3** mitigate the adverse effects of (*cushioned the blow*). **4** quietly suppress. **5** place or bounce (the ball) against the cushion in billiards. □□ **cushiony** *adj.* [ME f. OF *co(i)ssin, cu(i)ssin* f. Gallo-Roman f. L *culcita* mattress, cushion]

Cushitic /kʊˈʃɪtɪk/ *n. & adj.* —*n.* a group of E. African languages of the Hamitic type. —*adj.* of this group. [*Cush* an ancient country in the Nile valley + -ITE[1] + -IC]

cushy /ˈkʊʃɪ/ *adj.* (**cushier, cushiest**) *colloq.* **1** (of a job etc.) easy and pleasant. **2** *US* (of a seat, surroundings, etc.) soft, comfortable. □□ **cushiness** *n.* [Anglo-Ind. f. Hind. *k̲h̲ush* pleasant]

cusp /kʌsp/ *n.* **1** an apex or peak. **2** the horn of a crescent moon etc. **3** *Astrol.* the initial point of a house. **4** *Archit.* a projecting point between small arcs in Gothic tracery. **5** *Geom.* the point at which two arcs meet from the same direction terminating with a common tangent. **6** *Bot.* a pointed end, esp. of a leaf. **7** a cone-shaped prominence on the surface of a tooth esp. a molar or premolar. **8** a pocket or fold in a valve of the heart. □□ **cuspate** /-speɪt/ *adj.* **cusped** *adj.* **cuspidal** *adj.* [L *cuspis, -idis* point, apex]

cuspidor /ˈkʌspɪˌdɔː(r)/ *n. US* a spittoon. [Port., = spitter f. *cuspir* spit f. L *conspuere*]

cuss /kʌs/ *n. & v. colloq.* —*n.* **1** a curse. **2** usu. *derog.* a person; a creature. —*v.tr. & intr.* curse. □ **cuss-word** *US* a swear-word. [var. of CURSE]

cussed /ˈkʌsɪd/ *adj. colloq.* awkward and stubborn. □□ **cussedly** *adv.* **cussedness** *n.* [var. of CURSED]

custard /ˈkʌstəd/ *n.* **1** a dish made with milk and eggs, usu. sweetened. **2** a sweet sauce made with milk and flavoured cornflour. □ **custard-apple** a W. Indian fruit, *Annona reticulata*, with a custard-like pulp. **custard-pie 1** a pie containing custard, commonly thrown in slapstick comedy. **2** (*attrib.*) denoting slapstick comedy. **custard powder** a preparation of cornflour etc. for making custard. [ME, earlier *crusta(r)de* f. AF f. OF *crouste* CRUST]

custodian /kʌˈstəʊdɪən/ *n.* a guardian or keeper, esp. of a public building etc. □□ **custodianship** *n.* [CUSTODY + -AN, after *guardian*]

custody /ˈkʌstədɪ/ *n.* **1** guardianship; protective care. **2** imprisonment. □ **take into custody** arrest. □□ **custodial** /kʌˈstəʊdɪəl/ *adj.* [L *custodia* f. *custos -odis* guardian]

custom /ˈkʌstəm/ *n.* **1 a** the usual way of behaving or acting (*a slave to custom*). **b** a particular established way of behaving (*our customs seem strange to foreigners*). **2** *Law* established usage having the force of law. **3** business patronage; regular dealings or customers (*lost a lot of custom*). **4** (in *pl.*; also treated as *sing.*) **a** a duty levied on certain imported and exported goods. **b** the official department that administers this. **c** the area at a port, frontier, etc., where customs officials deal with incoming goods, baggage, etc. □ **custom-built** (or **-made** etc.) made to a customer's order. **custom-house** the office at a port or frontier etc. at which customs duties are levied. **customs union** a group of States with an agreed common tariff, and usu. free trade with each other. [ME and OF *custume* ult. f. L *consuetudo -dinis*: see CONSUETUDE]

customary /ˈkʌstəmərɪ/ *adj. & n.* —*adj.* **1** usual; in accordance with custom. **2** *Law* in accordance with custom. —*n.* (*pl.* **-ies**) *Law* a book etc. listing the customs and established practices of a community. □□ **customarily** *adv.* **customariness** *n.* [med.L *custumarius* f. *custuma* f. AF *custume* (as CUSTOM)]

customer /ˈkʌstəmə(r)/ *n.* **1** a person who buys goods or services from a shop or business. **2** a person one has to deal with (*an awkward customer*). [ME f. AF *custumer* (as CUSTOMARY), or f. CUSTOM + -ER[1]]

customize /ˈkʌstəˌmaɪz/ *v.tr.* (also **-ise**) make to order or modify according to individual requirements.

cut /kʌt/ *v. & n.* —*v.* (**cutting**; *past* and *past part.* **cut**) **1** *tr.* (also *absol.*) penetrate or wound with a sharp-edged instrument (*cut his finger*; *the knife won't cut*). **2** *tr. & intr.* (often foll. by *into*) divide or be divided with a knife etc. (*cut the bread*; *cut cloth into metre lengths*). **3** *tr.* **a** trim or reduce the length of (hair, a hedge, etc.) by cutting. **b** detach all or the significant part of (flowers, corn, etc.) by cutting. **4** *tr.* (foll. by *loose, open*, etc.) make loose, open, etc. by cutting. **5** *tr.* (esp. as **cutting** *adj.*) cause sharp physical or mental pain to (*a cutting remark*; *a cutting wind*; *was cut to the quick*). **6** *tr.* (often foll. by *down*) **a** reduce (wages, prices, time, etc.). **b** reduce or cease (services etc.). **7** *tr.* **a** shape or fashion (a coat, gem, key, record, etc.) by cutting. **b** make (a path, tunnel, etc.) by removing material. **8** *tr.* perform, execute, make (*cut a caper*; *cut a sorry figure*). **9** *tr.* (also *absol.*) cross, intersect (*the line cuts the circle at two points*; *the two lines cut*). **10** *intr.* (foll. by *across, through*, etc.) pass or traverse, esp. in a hurry or as a shorter way (*cut across the grass*). **11** *tr.* **a** ignore or refuse to recognize (a person). **b** renounce (a connection). **12** *tr.* esp. *US* deliberately fail to attend (a class etc.). **13** *Cards* **a** divide (a pack) into two parts. **b** *intr.* select a dealer etc. by dividing the pack. **14** *Cinematog.* **a** *tr.* edit (a film or tape). **b** *intr.* (often in *imper.*) stop filming or recording. **c** *intr.* (foll. by *to*) go quickly to (another shot). **15** *tr.* switch off (an engine etc.). **16** *tr.* **a** hit (a ball) with a chopping motion. **b** *Golf* slice (the ball). **17** *tr. US* dilute, adulterate. **18** *tr.* (as **cut** *adj.*) *Brit. sl.* drunk. **19** *intr. Cricket* (of the ball) turn sharply on pitching. **20** *intr. sl.* run. **21** *tr.* castrate. —*n.* **1** an act of cutting. **2** a division or wound made by cutting. **3** a stroke with a knife, sword, whip, etc. **4 a** a reduction (in prices, wages, etc.). **b** a cessation (of a power supply etc.). **5** an excision of part of a play, film, book, etc. **6** a wounding remark or act. **7** the way or style in which a garment, the hair, etc., is cut. **8** a piece of meat etc. cut from a carcass. **9** *colloq.* commission; a share of profits. **10** *Tennis & Cricket* etc. a stroke made by cutting. **11** ignoring of or refusal to recognize a person. **12 a** an engraved block for printing. **b** = WOODCUT. **13** a railway cutting. **14** a new channel made for a river. □ **a cut above** colloq. noticeably superior to. **be cut out** (foll. by *for*, or *to* + infin.) be suited (*was not cut out to be a teacher*). **cut across 1** transcend or take no account of (normal limitations etc.) (*their concern cuts across normal rivalries*). **2** see sense 10 of *v.* **cut-and-come-again** abundance. **cut and dried 1** completely decided; prearranged; inflexible. **2** (of opinions etc.) ready-made, lacking freshness. **cut**

and run *sl.* run away. **cut and thrust 1** a lively interchange of argument etc. **2** the use of both the edge and the point of a sword. **cut back 1** reduce (expenditure etc.). **2** prune (a tree etc.). **3** *Cinematog.* repeat part of a previous scene for dramatic effect. **cut-back** *n.* an instance or the act of cutting back, esp. a reduction in expenditure. **cut both ways 1** serve both sides of an argument etc. **2** (of an action) have both good and bad effects. **cut one's coat according to one's cloth 1** adapt expenditure to resources. **2** limit ambition to what is feasible. **cut a corner** go across and not round it. **cut corners** do a task etc. perfunctorily or incompletely, esp. to save time. **cut a dash** see DASH. **cut dead** completely refuse to recognize (a person). **cut down 1 a** bring or throw down by cutting. **b** kill by means of a sword or disease. **2** see sense 6 of *v.* **3** reduce the length of (*cut down the trousers to make shorts*). **4** (often foll. by *on*) reduce one's consumption (*tried to cut down on beer*). **cut a person down to size** *colloq.* ruthlessly expose the limitations of a person's importance, ability, etc. **cut one's eye-teeth** attain worldly wisdom. **cut glass** glass with patterns and designs cut on it. **cut in 1** interrupt. **2** pull in too closely in front of another vehicle (esp. having overtaken it). **3** give a share of profits etc. to (a person). **4** connect (a source of electricity). **5** join in a card-game by taking the place of a player who cuts out. **6** interrupt a dancing couple to take over from one partner. **cut into 1** make a cut in (*they cut into the cake*). **2** interfere with and reduce (*travelling cuts into my free time*). **cut it fine** see FINE[1]. **cut it out** (usu. in *imper.*) *sl.* stop doing that (esp. quarrelling). **cut the knot** solve a problem in an irregular but efficient way. **cut-line 1** a caption to an illustration. **2** the line in squash above which a served ball must strike the wall. **cut loose 1** begin to act freely. **2** see sense 4 of *v.* **cut one's losses** (or **a loss**) abandon an unprofitable enterprise before losses become too great. **cut the mustard** *US sl.* reach the required standard. **cut no ice** *sl.* **1** have no influence or importance. **2** achieve little or nothing. **cut off 1** remove (an appendage) by cutting. **2 a** (often in *passive*) bring to an abrupt end or (esp. early) death. **b** intercept, interrupt; prevent from continuing (*cut off supplies; cut off the gas*). **c** disconnect (a person engaged in a telephone conversation) (*was suddenly cut off*). **3 a** prevent from travelling or venturing out (*was cut off by the snow*). **b** (as **cut off** *adj.*) isolated, remote (*felt cut off in the country*). **4** disinherit (*was cut off without a penny*). **cut-off** *n.* **1** the point at which something is cut off. **2** a device for stopping a flow. **3** *US* a short cut. **cut out 1** remove from the inside by cutting. **2** make by cutting from a larger whole. **3** omit; leave out. **4** *colloq.* stop doing or using (something) (*managed to cut out chocolate; let's cut out the arguing*). **5** cease or cause to cease functioning (*the engine cut out*). **6** outdo or supplant (a rival). **7** *US* detach (an animal) from the herd. **8** *Cards* be excluded from a card-game as a result of cutting the pack. **cut-out 1** a figure cut out of paper etc. **2** a device for automatic disconnection, the release of exhaust gases, etc. **cut-out box** *US* = *fuse-box* (see FUSE[1]). **cut-price** (or **-rate**) selling or sold at a reduced price. **cut short 1** interrupt; terminate prematurely (*cut short his visit*). **2** make shorter or more concise. **cut one's teeth on** acquire initial practice or experience from (something). **cut a tooth** have it appear through the gum. **cut up 1** cut into pieces. **2** destroy utterly. **3** (usu. in *passive*) distress greatly (*was very cut up about it*). **4** criticize severely. **5** *US* behave in a comical or unruly manner. **cut up rough** *Brit. sl.* show anger or resentment. **cut up well** *sl.* bequeath a large fortune. **have one's work cut out** see WORK. [ME *cutte, kitte, kette,* perh. f. OE *cyttan* (unrecorded)]

cutaneous /kjuːˈteɪnɪəs/ *adj.* of the skin. [mod.L *cutaneus* f. L *cutis* skin]

cutaway /ˈkʌtəˌweɪ/ *adj.* **1** (of a diagram etc.) with some parts left out to reveal the interior. **2** (of a coat) with the front below the waist cut away.

cutch var. of COUCH[2].

cute /kjuːt/ *adj. colloq.* **1** esp. *US* **a** attractive, quaint. **b** affectedly attractive. **2** clever, ingenious. □□ **cutely** *adv.* **cuteness** *n.* [shortening of ACUTE]

cuticle /ˈkjuːtɪk(ə)l/ *n.* **1 a** the dead skin at the base of a fingernail or toenail. **b** the epidermis or other superficial skin. **2** *Bot.* a thin surface film on plants. □□ **cuticular** /-ˈtɪkjʊlə(r)/ *adj.* [L *cuticula,* dimin. of *cutis* skin]

cutie /ˈkjuːtɪ/ *n. sl.* an attractive young woman.

cutis /ˈkjuːtɪs/ *n. Anat.* the true skin or dermis, underlying the epidermis. [L, = skin]

cutlass /ˈkʌtləs/ *n.* a short sword with a slightly curved blade, esp. of the type formerly used by sailors. [F *coutelas* ult. f. L *cultellus:* see CUTLER]

cutler /ˈkʌtlə(r)/ *n.* a person who makes or deals in knives and similar utensils. [ME f. AF *cotillere,* OF *coutelier* f. *coutel* f. L *cultellus* dimin. of *culter* COULTER]

cutlery /ˈkʌtlərɪ/ *n.* knives, forks, and spoons for use at table. [OF & F *coutel(l)erie* (as CUTLER)]

cutlet /ˈkʌtlɪt/ *n.* **1** a neck-chop of mutton or lamb. **2** a small piece of veal etc. for frying. **3** a flat cake of minced meat or nuts and breadcrumbs etc. [F *côte-lette,* OF *costelet* dimin. of *coste* rib f. L *costa*]

cutpurse /ˈkʌtpɜːs/ *n. archaic* a pickpocket; a thief.

cutter /ˈkʌtə(r)/ *n.* **1** a tailor etc. who takes measurements and cuts cloth. **2** *Naut.* **a** a small fast sailing-ship. **b** a small boat carried by a large ship. **3** *Cricket* a ball turning sharply on pitching. **4** *US* a light horse-drawn sleigh.

cutthroat /ˈkʌtθrəʊt/ *n. & adj.* —*n.* **1** a murderer. **2** (in full **cutthroat razor**) a razor having a long blade set in a handle and usu. folding like a penknife. **3** a species of trout, *Salmo clarki,* with a red mark under the jaw. —*adj.* **1** (of competition) ruthless and intense. **2** (of a card-game) three-handed.

cutting /ˈkʌtɪŋ/ *n. & adj.* —*n.* **1** a piece cut from a newspaper etc. **2** a piece cut from a plant for propagation. **3** an excavated channel through high ground for a railway or road. —*adj.* see CUT *v.* 5. □□ **cuttingly** *adv.*

cuttle /ˈkʌt(ə)l/ *n.* = CUTTLEFISH. □ **cuttle-bone** the internal shell of the cuttlefish crushed and used for polishing teeth etc. or as a supplement to the diet of a cage-bird. [OE *cudele,* ME *codel,* rel. to *cod* bag, with ref. to its ink-bag]

cuttlefish /ˈkʌt(ə)lfɪʃ/ *n.* any marine cephalopod mollusc of the genera *Sepia* and *Sepiola,* having ten arms and ejecting a black fluid when threatened or pursued.

cutty /ˈkʌtɪ/ *adj. & n. Sc. & N.Engl.* —*adj.* cut short; abnormally short. —*n.* (*pl.* **-ies**) a short tobacco pipe. □ **cutty-stool** *hist.* a stool of repentance.

cutwater /ˈkʌtˌwɔːtə(r)/ *n.* **1** the forward edge of a ship's prow. **2** a wedge-shaped projection from a pier or bridge.

cutworm /ˈkʌtwɜːm/ *n.* any of various caterpillars that eat through the stems of young plants level with the ground.

cuvée /kjuːˈveɪ/ *n.* a blend or batch of wine. [F, = vatful f. *cuve* cask f. L *cupa*]

cuvette /kjuːˈvet/ *n.* a shallow vessel for liquid. [F, dimin. of *cuve* cask f. L *cupa*]

c.v. *abbr.* curriculum vitae.

CVO *abbr.* Commander of the Royal Victorian Order.

CVS *abbr.* chorionic villus sample, a test on a pregnant woman to detect any chromosomal abnormalities in the foetus.

Cwlth. *abbr.* Commonwealth.

cwm /kuːm/ *n.* **1** (in Wales) = COOMB. **2** *Geog.* a cirque. [Welsh]

c.w.o. *abbr.* cash with order.

cwt. *abbr.* hundredweight.

-cy /sɪ/ *suffix* (see also -ACY, -ANCY, -CRACY, -ENCY,

-MANCY). 1 denoting state or condition (*bankruptcy*; *idiocy*). **2** denoting rank or status (*captaincy*). [from or after L *-cia*, *-tia*, Gk *-k(e)ia*, *-t(e)ia*]

cyan /ˈsaɪæn/ *adj. & n.* —*adj.* of a greenish-blue. —*n.* a greenish-blue colour. [Gk *kuan(e)os* dark blue]

cyanamide /saɪˈænəmaɪd/ *n. Chem.* a colourless crystalline amide of cyanogen; any salt of this, esp. the calcium one which is used as a fertilizer. ¶ Chem. formula: CH₂N₂. [CYANOGEN + AMIDE]

cyanic acid /saɪˈænɪk/ *n.* an unstable colourless pungent acid gas. ¶ Chem. formula: HCNO. [CYANOGEN]

cyanide /ˈsaɪənaɪd/ *n.* any of the highly poisonous salts or esters of hydrocyanic acid, esp. the potassium salt used in the extraction of gold and silver. [CY-ANOGEN + -IDE]

cyanobacterium /ˌsaɪæˌnəʊbækˈtɪərɪəm/ *n.* any prokaryotic organism of the division Cyanobacteria, found in many environments and capable of photosynthesizing. Also called *blue-green alga* (see BLUE¹). [CYANOGEN + BACTERIUM]

cyanocobalamin /ˌsaɪəˌnəʊkəˈbæləmɪn/ *n.* a vitamin of the B complex, found in foods of animal origin such as liver, fish, and eggs, a deficiency of which can cause pernicious anaemia. Also called *vitamin B₁₂*. [CYANOGEN + *cobalamin* f. COBALT + VITAMIN]

cyanogen /saɪˈænədʒ(ə)n/ *n. Chem.* a colourless highly poisonous gas intermediate in the preparation of many fertilizers. ¶ Chem. formula: C₂N₂. [F *cyanogène* f. Gk *kuanos* dark-blue mineral, as being a constituent of Prussian blue]

cyanosis /ˌsaɪəˈnəʊsɪs/ *n. Med.* a bluish discoloration of the skin due to the presence of oxygen-deficient blood. □□ **cyanotic** /-ˈnɒtɪk/ *adj.* [mod.L f. Gk *kuanōsis* blueness (as CYANOGEN)]

cybernation /ˌsaɪbəˈneɪʃ(ə)n/ *n.* control by machines. □□ **cybernate** /ˈsaɪ-/ *v.tr.* [f. CYBERNETICS + -ATION]

cybernetics /ˌsaɪbəˈnetɪks/ *n.pl.* (usu. treated as *sing.*) the science of communications and automatic control systems in both machines and living things. □□ **cybernetic** *adj.* **cybernetician** /-ˈtrɪʃ(ə)n/ *n.* **cyberneticist** /-sɪst/ *n.* [Gk *kubernētēs* steersman]

cycad /ˈsaɪkæd/ *n. Bot.* any of the palmlike plants of the order Cycadales (including fossil forms) inhabiting tropical and subtropical regions and often growing to a great height. [mod.L *cycas*, *cycad-* f. supposed Gk *kukas*, scribal error for *koikas*, pl. of *koix* Egyptian palm]

Cycladic /saɪˈklædɪk, sɪ-/ *adj.* of the Cyclades, a group of islands east of the Greek mainland, esp. of the Bronze Age civilization that flourished there. [*Cyclades*, L f. Gk *Kuklades* f. *kuklos* circle (of islands)]

cyclamate /ˈsaɪkləmeɪt, ˈsɪk-/ *n.* any of various salts or esters of sulphamic acid formerly used as artificial sweetening agents. [Chem. name *cyclohexylsulphamate*]

cyclamen /ˈsɪkləmən/ *n.* **1** any plant of the genus Cyclamen, originating in Europe, having pink, red, or white flowers with reflexed petals, often grown in pots. **2** the shade of colour of the red or pink cyclamen flower. [med.L f. Gk *kuklaminos*, perh. f. *kuklos* circle, with ref. to its bulbous roots]

cycle /ˈsaɪk(ə)l/ *n. & v.* —*n.* **1 a** a recurrent round or period (of events, phenomena, etc.). **b** the time needed for one such round or period. **2 a** *Physics* etc. a recurrent series of operations or states. **b** *Electr.* = HERTZ. **3** a series of songs, poems, etc., usu. on a single theme. **4** a bicycle, tricycle, or similar machine. —*v.intr.* **1** ride a bicycle etc. **2** move in cycles. □ **cycle-track** (or **-way**) a path or road for bicycles. [ME f. OF, or f. LL *cyclus* f. Gk *kuklos* circle]

cyclic /ˈsaɪklɪk/ *adj.* **1 a** recurring in cycles. **b** belonging to a chronological cycle. **2** *Chem.* with constituent atoms forming a ring. **3** of a cycle of songs etc. **4** *Bot.* (of a flower) with its parts arranged

in whorls. **5** *Math.* of a circle or cycle. [F *cyclique* or L *cyclicus* f. Gk *kuklikos* (as CYCLE)]

cyclical /ˈsaɪklɪk(ə)l, ˈsɪk-/ *adj.* = CYCLIC 1. □□ **cyclically** *adv.*

cyclist /ˈsaɪklɪst/ *n.* a rider of a bicycle.

cyclo- /ˈsaɪkləʊ/ *comb. form* circle, cycle, or cyclic (*cyclometer*; *cyclorama*). [Gk *kuklos* circle]

cycloalkane /ˌsaɪkləʊˈælkeɪn/ *n. Chem.* a saturated cyclic hydrocarbon.

cyclo-cross /ˈsaɪkləʊˌkrɒs/ *n.* cross-country racing on bicycles.

cyclograph /ˈsaɪkləˌgrɑːf/ *n.* an instrument for tracing circular arcs.

cyclohexane /ˌsaɪkləʊˈhekseɪn/ *n. Chem.* a colourless liquid cycloalkane used as a solvent and paint remover. ¶ Chem. formula: C₆H₁₂.

cycloid /ˈsaɪklɔɪd/ *n. Math.* a curve traced by a point on a circle when the circle is rolled along a straight line. □□ **cycloidal** /-ˈklɔɪd(ə)l/ *adj.* [Gk *kukloeidēs* (as CYCLE, -OID)]

cyclometer /saɪˈklɒmɪtə(r)/ *n.* **1** an instrument for measuring circular arcs. **2** an instrument for measuring the distance traversed by a bicycle etc.

cyclone /ˈsaɪkləʊn/ *n.* **1** a system of winds rotating inwards to an area of low barometric pressure; a depression. **2** a violent hurricane of limited diameter. □□ **cyclonic** /-ˈklɒnɪk/ *adj.* **cyclonically** /-ˈklɒnɪkəli/ *adv.* [prob. repr. Gk *kuklōma* wheel, coil of a snake]

cyclopaedia /ˌsaɪkləˈpiːdɪə/ *n.* (also **cyclopedia**) an encyclopaedia. □□ **cyclopaedic** *adj.* [shortening of ENCYCLOPAEDIA]

cycloparaffin /ˌsaɪkləʊˈpærəfɪn/ *n. Chem.* = CYCLO-ALKANE.

Cyclopean /ˌsaɪkləˈpiːən, -ˈkləʊpɪən/ *adj.* (also **Cyclopian**) **1** (of ancient masonry) made with massive irregular blocks. **2** of or resembling a Cyclops.

cyclopropane /ˌsaɪkləʊˈprəʊpeɪn/ *n. Chem.* a colourless gaseous cycloalkane used as a general anaesthetic. ¶ Chem. formula: C₃H₆.

Cyclops /ˈsaɪklɒps/ *n.* **1** (*pl.* **Cyclops** or **Cyclopses** or **Cyclopes** /saɪˈkləʊpiːz/) (in Greek mythology) a member of a race of one-eyed giants. **2** (**cyclops**) (*pl.* **cyclops** or **cyclopes**) *Zool.* a crustacean of the genus *Cyclops*, with a single central eye. [L f. Gk *Kuklōps* f. *kuklos* circle + *ōps* eye]

cyclorama /ˌsaɪkləʊˈrɑːmə/ *n.* a circular panorama, curved wall, or cloth at the rear of a stage, esp. one used to represent the sky. □□ **cycloramic** /-ˈræmɪk/ *adj.*

cyclostome /ˈsaɪkləˌstəʊm/ *n.* any fishlike jawless vertebrate of the subclass Cyclostomata, having a large sucking mouth, e.g. a lamprey. □□ **cyclostomate** /-ˈklɒstəmət/ *adj.* [CYCLO- + Gk *stoma* mouth]

cyclostyle /ˈsaɪkləˌstaɪl/ *n. & v.* —*n.* an apparatus for printing copies of writing from a stencil. —*v.tr.* print or reproduce with this.

cyclothymia /ˌsaɪkləʊˈθaɪmɪə/ *n. Psychol.* a disorder characterized by the occurrence of marked swings of mood from cheerfulness to misery. □□ **cyclothymic** *adj.* [CYCLO- + Gk *thumos* temper]

cyclotron /ˈsaɪkləˌtrɒn/ *n. Physics* an apparatus in which charged atomic and subatomic particles are accelerated by an alternating electric field while following an outward spiral or circular path in a magnetic field.

cyder var. of CIDER.

cygnet /ˈsɪgnɪt/ *n.* a young swan. [ME f. AF *cignet* dimin. of OF *cigne* swan f. med.L *cycnus* f. Gk *kuknos*]

cylinder /ˈsɪlɪndə(r)/ *n.* **1 a** a uniform solid or hollow body with straight sides and a circular section. **b** a thing of this shape, e.g. a container for liquefied gas. **2** a cylinder-shaped part of various machines, esp. a piston-chamber in an engine. **3** *Printing* a metal roller. □ **cylinder saw** = *crown saw*. **cylinder seal** *Antiq.* a small barrel-shaped object of stone or baked clay bearing a cuneiform inscription, esp. for use

b *but* d *dog* f *few* g *get* h *he* j *yes* k *cat* l *leg* m *man* n *no* p *pen* r *red* s *sit* t *top* v *voice*

as a seal. □□**cylindrical** /-'lɪndrɪk(ə)l/ adj.
cylindrically /-'lɪndrɪkəlɪ/ adv. [L cylindrus f. Gk
kulindros f. kulindō roll]

cyma /'saɪmə/ n. **1** Archit. an ogee moulding of a
cornice. **2** = CYME. [mod.L f. Gk kuma wave, wavy
moulding]

cymbal /'sɪmb(ə)l/ n. a musical instrument consisting of a concave brass or bronze plate, struck
with another or with a stick etc. to make a ringing
sound. □□**cymbalist** n. [ME f. L cymbalum f. Gk
kumbalon f. kumbē cup]

cymbidium /sɪm'bɪdɪəm/ n. any tropical orchid of
the genus Cymbidium, with a recess in the flower-lip.
[mod.L f. Gk kumbē cup]

cymbiform /'sɪmbɪˌfɔːm/ adj. Anat. & Bot. boat-
shaped. [L cymba f. Gk kumbē boat + -FORM]

cyme /saɪm/ n. Bot. an inflorescence in which the
primary axis bears a single terminal flower that
develops first, the system being continued by the
axes of secondary and higher orders each with a
flower (cf. RACEME). □□**cymose** adj. [F, var. of cime
summit, ult. f. Gk kuma wave]

Cymric /'kɪmrɪk/ adj. Welsh. [Welsh Cymru Wales]

cynic /'sɪnɪk/ n. & adj. —n. **1** a person who has little
faith in human sincerity and goodness. **2 (Cynic)**
one of a school of ancient Greek philosophers founded by Antisthenes, marked by ostentatious contempt for ease and pleasure. —adj. **1 (Cynic)** of
the Cynics. **2** = CYNICAL. □□**cynicism** /-ˌsɪz(ə)m/
n. [L cynicus f. Gk kunikos f. kuōn kunos dog,
nickname for a Cynic]

cynical /'sɪnɪk(ə)l/ adj. **1** of or characteristic of a
cynic; incredulous of human goodness. **2** (of behaviour etc.) disregarding normal standards. **3** sneering, mocking. □□**cynically** adv.

cynocephalus /ˌsaɪnəʊ'sefələs/ n. **1** a fabled dog-
headed man. **2** any flying lemur of the genus
Cynocephalus, native to SE Asia. [Gk kunokephalos
f. kuōn kunos dog + kephalē head]

cynosure /'saɪnəˌzjʊə(r), 'sɪn-/ n. **1** a centre of
attraction or admiration. **2** a guiding star. [F cynosure
or L cynosura f. Gk kunosoura dog's tail, Ursa Minor
f. kuōn kunos dog + oura tail]

cypher var. of CIPHER.

cy pres /siː 'preɪ/ adv. & adj. Law as near as possible
to the testator's or donor's intentions when these
cannot be precisely followed. [AF, = si près so near]

cypress /'saɪprəs/ n. **1** any coniferous tree of the
genus Cupressus or Chamaecyparis, with hard wood
and dark foliage. **2** this, or branches from it, as a
symbol of mourning. [ME f. OF cipres f. LL cypressus
f. Gk kuparissos]

Cyprian /'sɪprɪən/ n. & adj. = CYPRIOT. [L Cyprius
of Cyprus]

cyprinoid /'sɪprɪˌnɔɪd/ adj. & n. —adj. of or like a
carp. —n. a carp or related fish. [L cyprinus f. Gk
kuprinos carp]

Cypriot /'sɪprɪət/ n. & adj. (also **Cypriote** /-əʊt/)
—n. a native or national of Cyprus. —adj. of
Cyprus. [Gk Kupriōtes f. Kupros Cyprus in E. Mediter-
ranean]

cypripedium /ˌsɪprɪ'piːdɪəm/ n. any orchid
of the genus Cypripedium, esp. the lady's slipper.
[mod.L f. Gk Kupris Aphrodite + pedilon slipper]

cypsela /'sɪpsɪlə/ n. (pl. **cypselae** /-ˌliː/) Bot. a dry
single-seeded fruit formed from a double ovary of
which only one develops into a seed, characteristic

of the daisy family Compositae. [mod.L f. Gk kupselē
hollow vessel]

Cyrillic /sɪ'rɪlɪk/ adj. & n. —adj. denoting the
alphabet used by the Slavonic peoples of the Orthodox Church; now used esp. for Russian and
Bulgarian. —n. this alphabet. [St Cyril d. 869, its
reputed inventor]

cyst /sɪst/ n. **1** Med. a sac containing morbid matter,
a parasitic larva, etc. **2** Biol. **a** a hollow organ,
bladder, etc., in an animal or plant, containing
a liquid secretion. **b** a cell or cavity enclosing
reproductive bodies, an embryo, parasite, micro-
organism, etc. [LL cystis f. Gk kustis bladder]

cysteine /'sɪstɪˌiːn, -tiːn/ n. Biochem. a sulphur-
containing amino acid, essential in the human diet
and a constituent of many enzymes. [CYSTINE + -eine
(var. of -INE⁴)]

cystic /'sɪstɪk/ adj. **1** of the urinary bladder. **2** of the
gall-bladder. **3** of the nature of a cyst. □**cystic
fibrosis** Med. a hereditary disease affecting the
exocrine glands and usu. resulting in respiratory
infections. [F cystique or mod.L cysticus (as CYST)]

cystitis /sɪ'staɪtɪs/ n. an inflammation of the urinary
bladder, often caused by infection, and usu. accompanied by frequent painful urination.

cysto- /'sɪstəʊ/ comb. form the urinary bladder (cystoscope; cystotomy). [Gk kustē, kustis bladder]

cystoscope /'sɪstəˌskəʊp/ n. an instrument inserted
in the urethra for examining the urinary bladder. □□
cystoscopic /-'skɒpɪk/ adj. **cystoscopy** /sɪ'stɒskəpɪ/ n.

cystotomy /sɪ'stɒtəmɪ/ n. (pl. -ies) a surgical incision
into the urinary bladder.

-cyte /saɪt/ comb. form Biol. a mature cell (leucocyte)
(cf. -BLAST). [Gk kutos vessel]

cytidine /'saɪtɪˌdiːn/ n. a nucleoside obtained from
RNA by hydrolysis. [G Cytidin (as -CYTE)]

cyto- /'saɪtəʊ/ comb. form Biol. cells or a cell. [as
-CYTE]

cytochrome /'saɪtəʊˌkrəʊm/ n. Biochem. a compound consisting of a protein linked to a haem,
which is involved in electron transfer reactions.

cytogenetics /ˌsaɪtəʊdʒɪ'netɪks/ n. the study of inheritance in relation to the structure and function
of cells. □□**cytogenetic** adj. **cytogenetical** adj.
cytogenetically adv. **cytogeneticist** /-sɪst/ n.

cytology /saɪ'tɒlədʒɪ/ n. the study of cells. □□
cytological /ˌsaɪtə'lɒdʒɪk(ə)l/ adj. **cytologically**
/ˌsaɪtə'lɒdʒɪkəlɪ/ adv. **cytologist** n.

cytoplasm /'saɪtəʊˌplæz(ə)m/ n. the protoplasmic
content of a cell apart from its nucleus. □□
cytoplasmic /-'plæzmɪk/ adj.

cytosine /'saɪtəʊˌsiːn/ n. one of the principal component bases of the nucleotides and the nucleic acids
DNA and RNA, derived from pyrimidine.

cytotoxic /ˌsaɪtəʊ'tɒksɪk/ adj. toxic to cells.

czar etc. var. of TSAR etc.

czardas var. of CSARDAS.

Czech /tʃek/ n. & adj. —n. **1** a native or national of
Czechoslovakia, including Bohemia, Moravia, and
Slovakia (cf. SLOVAK). **2** one of the two official
languages of Czechoslovakia (cf. SLOVAK). —adj.
of or relating to Czechoslovakia or its people or
language. [Pol. spelling of Bohemian Čech]

Czechoslovak /ˌtʃekə'sləʊvæk/ n. & adj. (also
Czechoslovakian /-slə'vækɪən/) —n. a native or
national of Czechoslovakia. —adj. of or relating to
Czechoslovakia. [CZECH + SLOVAK]

D

D[1] /diː/ *n.* (also **d**) (*pl.* **Ds** or **D's**) **1** the fourth letter of the alphabet. **2** *Mus.* the second note of the diatonic scale of C major. **3** (as a Roman numeral) 500. **4** = DEE. **5** the fourth highest class or category (of academic marks etc.).

D[2] *symb. Chem.* the element deuterium.

D[3] *abbr.* (also **D.**) **1** *US* Democrat. **2** dimension (*3-D*).

d. *abbr.* **1** died. **2** departs. **3** delete. **4** daughter. **5** *Brit.* (pre-decimal) penny. **6** depth. **7** deci-. [sense 5 f. L *denarius* silver coin]

'd *v. colloq.* (usu. after pronouns) had, would (*I'd; he'd*). [abbr.]

DA *abbr.* **1** *US* District Attorney. **2** *sl.* = *duck's arse* (see DUCK¹).

D/A *abbr. Computing* digital to analogue.

da *abbr.* deca-.

dab¹ /dæb/ *v. & n.* —*v.* (**dabbed, dabbing**) **1** *tr.* press (a surface) briefly with a cloth, sponge, etc., without rubbing, esp. in cleaning or to apply a substance. **2** *tr.* press (a sponge etc.) lightly on a surface. **3** *tr.* (foll. by *on*) apply (a substance) by dabbing a surface. **4** *intr.* (usu. foll. by *at*) aim a feeble blow; tap. **5** *tr.* strike lightly; tap. —*n.* **1** a brief application of a cloth, sponge, etc., to a surface without rubbing. **2** a small amount of something applied in this way (*a dab of paint*). **3** a light blow or tap. **4** (in *pl.*) *Brit. sl.* fingerprints. □□ **dabber** *n.* [ME, imit.]

dab² /dæb/ *n.* any flat-fish of the genus *Limanda*. [15th c.: orig. unkn.]

dab³ /dæb/ *adj.* esp. *Brit. colloq.* □ **dab hand** (usu. foll. by *at*) a person especially skilled (in) (*a dab hand at cooking*). [17th c.: orig. unkn.]

dabble /'dæb(ə)l/ *v.* **1** *intr.* (usu. foll. by *in, at*) take a casual or superficial interest or part (in a subject or activity). **2** *intr.* move the feet, hands, etc. about in (usu. a small amount of) liquid. **3** *tr.* wet partly or intermittently; moisten, stain, splash. □□ **dabbler** *n.* [16th c.: f. Du. *dabbelen* or DAB¹]

dabchick /'dæbtʃɪk/ *n.* = *little grebe* (see GREBE). [16th c., in earlier forms *dap-, dop-*: perh. rel. to OE *dūfedoppa*, DEEP, DIP]

da capo /dɑː 'kɑːpəʊ/ *adv. Mus.* repeat from the beginning. [It.]

dace /deɪs/ *n.* (*pl.* same) any small freshwater fish, esp. of the genus *Leuciscus*, related to the carp. [OF *dars*: see DART]

dacha /'dætʃə/ *n.* a country house or cottage in Russia. [Russ., = gift]

dachshund /'dækshʊnd/ *n.* **1** a dog of a short-legged long-bodied breed. **2** this breed. [G, = badger-dog]

dacoit /də'kɔɪt/ *n.* (in India or Burma) a member of a band of armed robbers. [Hindi *ḍakait* f. *ḍākā* gang-robbery]

dactyl /'dæktɪl/ *n.* a metrical foot (‾ ˘ ˘) consisting of one long (or stressed) syllable followed by two short (or unstressed). [ME f. L *dactylus* f. Gk *daktulos* finger, the three bones corresponding to the three syllables]

dactylic /dæk'tɪlɪk/ *adj. & n.* —*adj.* of or using dactyls. —*n.* (usu. in *pl.*) dactylic verse. [L *dactylicus* f. Gk *daktulikos* (as DACTYL)]

dad /dæd/ *n. colloq.* father. [perh. imit. of a child's *da, da* (cf. DADDY)]

Dada /'dɑːdɑː/ *n.* an early 20th-c. international movement in art, literature, music, and film, repudiating and mocking artistic and social conventions □□ **Dadaism** /-dəˌɪz(ə)m/ *n.* **Dadaist** /-dəɪst/ *n. & adj.* **Dadaistic** /-ɪstɪk/ *adj.* [F (the title of an early 20th-c. review) f. *dada* hobby-horse]

daddy /'dædɪ/ *n.* (*pl.* **-ies**) *colloq.* **1** father. **2** (usu. foll. by *of*) the oldest or supreme example (*had a daddy of a headache*). □ **daddy-long-legs 1** a crane-fly. **2** *US* a harvestman. [DAD + -Y³]

dado /'deɪdəʊ/ *n.* (*pl.* **-os**) **1** the lower part of the wall of a room when visually distinct from the upper part. **2** the plinth of a column. **3** the cube of a pedestal between the base and the cornice. [It., = DIE²]

daemon var. of DEMON 5.

daemonic var. of DEMONIC.

daff /dæf/ *n. colloq.* = DAFFODIL. [abbr.]

daffodil /'dæfədɪl/ *n.* **1 a** a bulbous plant, *Narcissus pseudonarcissus*, with a yellow trumpet-shaped crown. **b** any of various other large-flowered plants of the genus *Narcissus*. **c** a flower of any of these plants. **2** a pale-yellow colour. [earlier *affodill*, as ASPHODEL]

daffy /'dæfɪ/ *adj.* (**daffier, daffiest**) *sl.* = DAFT. □□ **daffily** *adv.* **daffiness** *n.* [*daff* simpleton + -Y²]

daft /dɑːft/ *adj.* esp. *Brit. colloq.* **1** silly, foolish, crazy. **2** (foll. by *about*) fond of; infatuated with. [ME *daffte* = OE *gedæfte* mild, meek, f. Gmc]

dag¹ /dæg/ *n. & v. Austral. & NZ* —*n.* (usu. in *pl.*) a lock of wool clotted with dung on the hinder parts of a sheep. —*v.tr.* (**dagged, dagging**) remove dags from (a sheep). □ **rattle one's dags** *sl.* hurry up. □□ **dagger** *n.* [orig. Engl. dial.]

dag² /dæg/ *n. Austral. & NZ sl.* an eccentric or noteworthy person; a character (*he's a bit of a dag*). [orig. Engl. dial., = a dare, challenge]

dagga /'dægə/ *n. S.Afr.* **1** hemp used as a narcotic. **2** any plant of the genus *Leontis* used similarly. [Afrik. f. Hottentot *dachab*]

dagger /'dægə(r)/ *n.* **1** a short stabbing-weapon with a pointed and edged blade. **2** *Printing* = OBELUS. □ **at daggers drawn** in bitter enmity. **look daggers at** glare angrily or venomously at. [ME, perh. f. obs. *dag* pierce, infl. by OF *dague* long dagger]

dago /'deɪgəʊ/ *n.* (*pl.* **-os**) *sl. offens.* a foreigner, esp. a Spaniard, Portuguese, or Italian. [Sp. *Diego* = James]

daguerreotype /də'gerəʊˌtaɪp/ *n.* **1** a photograph taken by an early photographic process employing an iodine-sensitized silvered plate and mercury vapour. **2** this process. [L. *Daguerre*, Fr. inventor d. 1851]

dah /dɑː/ *n.* esp. *US Telegraphy* (in the Morse system) = DASH (cf. DIT). [imit.]

dahlia /'deɪlɪə/ *n.* any composite garden plant of the genus *Dahlia*, of Mexican origin, cultivated for its many-coloured single or double flowers. [A. *Dahl*, Sw. botanist d. 1789]

Dáil /dɔɪl/ *n.* (in full **Dáil Éireann** /'eɪrən/) the lower house of parliament in the Republic of Ireland. [Ir., = assembly (of Ireland)]

daily /'deɪlɪ/ *adj., adv., & n.* —*adj.* **1** done, produced, or occurring every day or every weekday. **2** constant, regular. —*adv.* **1** every day; from day to day. **2** constantly. —*n.* (*pl.* **-ies**) *colloq.* **1** a daily newspaper. **2** *Brit.* a charwoman or domestic help working daily. □ **daily bread** necessary food; a livelihood. **daily dozen** *Brit. colloq.* regular exercises, esp. on rising. [ME f. DAY + -LY¹, -LY²]

daimon /'daɪməʊn/ *n.* = DEMON 5. □□ **daimonic** /-'mɒnɪk/ *adj.* [Gk, = deity]

dainty /'deɪntɪ/ *adj. & n.* —*adj.* (**daintier, daintiest**) **1** delicately pretty. **2** delicate of build or in movement. **3** (of food) choice. **4** fastidious; having delicate taste and sensibility. —*n.* (*pl.* **-ies**) a choice morsel; a delicacy. □□ **daintily** *adv.* **daintiness** *n.* [AF *dainté*, OF *daintié*, *deintié* f. L *dignitas -tatis* f. *dignus* worthy]

æ *cat* ɑː *arm* e *bed* ɜː *her* ɪ *sit* iː *see* ɒ *hot* ɔː *saw* ʌ *run* ʊ *put* uː *too* ə *ago* aɪ *my*

daiquiri /'dækərɪ, 'daɪ-/ n. (pl. **daiquiris**) a cocktail of rum, lime-juice, etc. [*Daiquiri* in Cuba]

dairy /'deərɪ/ n. (pl. **-ies**) **1** a building or room for the storage, processing, and distribution of milk and its products. **2** a shop where milk and milk products are sold. **3** (*attrib.*) **a** of, containing, or concerning milk and its products (and sometimes eggs). **b** used for dairy products (*dairy cow*). [ME *deierie* f. *deie* maidservant f. OE *dæge* kneader of dough]

dairying /'deərɪɪŋ/ n. the business of producing, storing, and distributing milk and its products.

dairymaid /'deərɪˌmeɪd/ n. a woman employed in a dairy.

dairyman /'deərɪmən/ n. (pl. **-men**) **1** a man dealing in dairy products. **2** a man employed in a dairy.

dais /'deɪɪs/ n. a low platform, usu. at the upper end of a hall and used to support a table, lectern, etc. [ME f. OF *deis* f. L *discus* disc, dish, in med.L = table]

daisy /'deɪzɪ/ n. (pl. **-ies**) **1 a** a small composite plant, *Bellis perennis*, bearing flowers each with a yellow disc and white rays. **b** any other plant with daisy-like flowers, esp. the larger ox-eye daisy, the Michaelmas daisy, or the Shasta daisy. **2** *sl.* a first-rate specimen of anything. □**daisy-chain** a string of daisies threaded together. **daisy-cutter** *Cricket* a ball bowled so as to roll along the ground. **daisy wheel** *Computing* a disc of spokes extending radially from a central hub, each terminating in a printing character, used as a printer in word processors and typewriters. **pushing up the daisies** *sl.* dead and buried. [OE *dæges ēage* day's eye, the flower opening in the morning]

Dak. *abbr.* Dakota.

dal var. of DHAL.

Dalai lama /ˌdælaɪ 'lɑːmə/ n. the spiritual head of Tibetan Buddhism, formerly also the chief ruler of Tibet (see LAMA). [Mongolian *dalai* ocean; see LAMA]

dale /deɪl/ n. a valley, esp. in N. England. [OE *dæl* f. Gmc]

dalesman /'deɪlzmən/ n. (pl. **-men**) an inhabitant of the dales in Northern England.

dalliance /'dælɪəns/ n. a leisurely or frivolous passing of time. [DALLY + -ANCE]

dally /'dælɪ/ v.intr. (**-ies**, **-ied**) **1** delay; waste time, esp. frivolously. **2** (often foll. by *with*) play about; flirt, treat frivolously (*dallied with her affections*). □**dally away** waste or fritter (one's time, life, etc.). [ME f. OF *dalier* chat]

Dalmatian /dæl'meɪʃ(ə)n/ n. **1** a dog of a large white short-haired breed with dark spots. **2** this breed. [*Dalmatia* in Yugoslavia]

dalmatic /dæl'mætɪk/ n. a wide-sleeved long loose vestment open at the sides, worn by deacons and bishops, and by a monarch at his or her coronation. [ME f. OF *dalmatique* or LL *dalmatica* (*vestis* robe) of Dalmatia]

dal segno /dæl 'seɪnjəʊ/ adv. *Mus.* repeat from the point marked by a sign. [It., = from the sign]

daltonism /'dɔːltəˌnɪz(ə)m/ n. colour-blindness, esp. a congenital inability to distinguish between red and green. [F *daltonisme* f. J. *Dalton*, Engl. chemist d. 1844, who suffered from it]

dam[1] /dæm/ n. & v. — n. **1** a barrier constructed to hold back water and raise its level, forming a reservoir or preventing flooding. **2** a barrier constructed in a stream by a beaver. **3** anything functioning as a dam does. **4** a causeway. — v.tr. (**dammed, damming**) **1** furnish or confine with a dam. **2** (often foll. by *up*) block up; hold back; obstruct. [ME f. MLG, MDu.]

dam[2] /dæm/ n. the female parent of an animal, esp. a four-footed one. [ME: var. of DAME]

damage /'dæmɪdʒ/ n. & v. — n. **1** harm or injury impairing the value or usefulness of something, or the health or normal function of a person. **2** (in pl.) *Law* a sum of money claimed or awarded in compensation for a loss or an injury. **3** the loss of what is desirable. **4** (prec. by *the*) *sl.* cost (*what's the*

damage?). — v.tr. **1** inflict damage on. **2** (esp. as **damaging** *adj.*) detract from the reputation of (*a most damaging admission*). □□**damagingly** *adv.* [ME f. OF *damage* (n.), *damagier* (v.), f. *dam(me)* loss f. L *damnum* loss, damage]

damascene /'dæməˌsiːn, ˌdæmə'siːn/ v., n., & adj. — v.tr. decorate (metal, esp. iron or steel) by etching or inlaying esp. with gold or silver, or with a watered pattern produced in welding. — n. a design or article produced in this way. — adj. of, relating to, or produced by this process. [*Damascene* of Damascus, f. L *Damascenus* f. Gk *Damaskēnos*]

damask /'dæməsk/ n., adj., & v. — n. **1 a** a figured woven fabric (esp. silk or linen) with a pattern visible on both sides. **b** twilled table linen with woven designs shown by the reflection of light. **2** a tablecloth made of this material. **3** *hist.* steel with a watered pattern produced in welding. — adj. **1** made of or resembling damask. **2** coloured like a damask rose, velvety pink or vivid red. — v.tr. **1** weave with figured designs. **2** = DAMASCENE v. **3** ornament. □**damask rose** an old sweet-scented variety of rose, with very soft velvety petals, used to make attar. [ME, ult. f. L *Damascus*]

dame /deɪm/ n. **1 (Dame) a** (in the UK) the title given to a woman with the rank of Knight Commander or holder of the Grand Cross in the Orders of Chivalry. **b** a woman holding this title. **2** *Brit.* a comic middle-aged woman in modern pantomime, usu. played by a man. **3** *archaic* a mature woman. **4** *US sl.* a woman. □**dame-school** *hist.* a primary school kept by an elderly woman. [ME f. OF f. L *domina* mistress]

damfool /'dæmfuːl/ adj. *colloq.* foolish, stupid. [DAMN + FOOL[1]]

dammar /'dæmə(r)/ n. **1** any E. Asian tree, esp. one of the genus *Agathis* or *Shorea*, yielding a resin used in varnish-making. **2** this resin. [Malay *damar*]

dammit /'dæmɪt/ int. damn it.

damn /dæm/ v., n., adj., & adv. — v.tr. **1** (often *absol.* or as *int.* of anger or annoyance, = *may God damn*) curse (a person or thing). **2** doom to hell; cause the damnation of. **3** condemn, censure (*a review damning the performance*). **4 a** (often as **damning** *adj.*) (of a circumstance, piece of evidence, etc.) show or prove to be guilty; bring condemnation upon (*evidence against them was damning*). **b** be the ruin of. — n. **1** an uttered curse. **2** *sl.* a negligible amount (*not worth a damn*). — adj. & adv. *colloq.* = DAMNED. □**damn all** *sl.* nothing at all. **damn well** *colloq.* (as an emphatic) simply (*damn well do as I say*). **damn with faint praise** commend so unenthusiastically as to imply disapproval. **I'm** (or **I'll be**) **damned if** *colloq.* I certainly do not, will not, etc. **not give a damn** see GIVE. **well I'm** (or **I'll be**) **damned** *colloq.* exclamation of surprise, dismay, etc. □□**damningly** *adv.* [ME f. OF *damner* f. L *damnare* inflict loss on f. *damnum* loss]

damnable /'dæmnəb(ə)l/ adj. hateful, annoying. □□ **damnably** *adv.* [ME f. OF *damnable* (as DAMN)]

damnation /dæm'neɪʃ(ə)n/ n. & int. — n. condemnation to eternal punishment, esp. in hell. — int. expressing anger or annoyance. [ME f. OF *damnation* (as DAMN)]

damnatory /'dæmnətərɪ/ adj. conveying or causing censure or damnation. [L *damnatorius* (as DAMN)]

damned /dæmd/ adj. & adv. *colloq.* — adj. damnable, infernal, unwelcome. — adv. extremely (*damned hot*; *damned lovely*). □**damned well** (as an emphatic) simply (*you've damned well got to*). **do one's damnedest** do one's utmost.

damnify /'dæmnɪˌfaɪ/ v.tr. (**-ies**, **-ied**) *Law* cause injury to. □□**damnification** /-frˈkeɪʃ(ə)n/ n. [OF *damnifier* etc. f. LL *damnificare* injure (as DAMN)]

damp /dæmp/ adj., n., & v. — adj. slightly wet; moist. — n. **1** diffused moisture in the air, on a surface, or in a solid, esp. as a cause of inconvenience or danger. **2** dejection; discouragement. **3** = FIREDAMP. — v.tr.

1 make damp; moisten. **2** (often foll. by *down*) **a** take the force or vigour out of (*damp one's enthusiasm*). **b** make flaccid or spiritless. **c** make (a fire) burn less strongly by reducing the flow of air to it. **3** reduce or stop the vibration of (esp. the strings of a musical instrument). **4** quieten. □**damp** (or **damp-proof**) **course** a layer of waterproof material in the wall of a building near the ground, to prevent rising damp. **damp off** (of a plant) die from a fungus attack in damp conditions. **damp squib** an unsuccessful attempt to impress etc. □□**damply** *adv.* **dampness** *n.* [ME f. MLG, = vapour etc., OHG *dampf* steam f. WG]

dampen /'dæmpən/ *v.* **1** *v.tr. & intr.* make or become damp. **2** *tr.* make less forceful or vigorous; stifle, choke. □□**dampener** *n.*

damper /'dæmpə(r)/ *n.* **1** a person or thing that discourages, or tempers enthusiasm. **2** a device that reduces shock or noise. **3** a metal plate in a flue to control the draught, and so the rate of combustion. **4** *Mus.* a pad silencing a piano string except when removed by means of a pedal or by the note's being struck. **5** esp. *Austral. & NZ* unleavened bread or cake of flour and water baked in wood ashes. □**put a damper on** take the vigour or enjoyment out of.

damsel /'dæmz(ə)l/ *n. archaic* or *literary* a young unmarried woman. [ME f. OF *dam(e)isele* ult. f. L *domina* mistress]

damselfish /'dæmz(ə)lfɪʃ/ *n.* a small brightly-coloured fish, *Chromis chromis*, found in or near coral reefs.

damselfly /'dæmz(ə)l,flaɪ/ *n.* (*pl.* **-flies**) any of various insects of the order Odonata, like a dragonfly but with its wings folded over the body when resting.

damson /'dæmz(ə)n/ *n. & adj.* —*n.* **1** (in full **damson plum**) **a** a small dark-purple plumlike fruit. **b** the small deciduous tree, *Prunus institia*, bearing this. **2** a dark-purple colour. —*adj.* damson-coloured. □**damson cheese** a solid preserve of damsons and sugar. [ME *damacene*, *-scene*, *-sene* f. L *damascenum* (*prunum* plum) of *Damascus*: see DAMASCENE]

Dan. *abbr.* Daniel (Old Testament).

dan[1] /dæn/ *n.* **1** any of twelve degrees of advanced proficiency in judo. **2** a person who has achieved any of these. [Jap.]

dan[2] /dæn/ *n.* (in full **dan buoy**) a small buoy used as a marker in deep-sea fishing, or to mark the limits of an area cleared by minesweepers. [17th c.: orig. unkn.]

dance /dɑːns/ *v. & n.* —*v.* **1** *intr.* move about rhythmically alone or with a partner or in a set, usu. in fixed steps or sequences to music, for pleasure or as entertainment. **2** *intr.* move in a lively way; skip or jump about. **3** *tr.* **a** perform (a specified dance or form of dancing). **b** perform (a specified role) in a ballet etc. **4** *intr.* move up and down (on water, in the field of vision, etc.). **5** *tr.* move (esp. a child) up and down; dandle. —*n.* **1 a** a piece of dancing; a sequence of steps in dancing. **b** a special form of this. **2** a single round or turn of a dance. **3** a social gathering for dancing, a ball. **4** a piece of music for dancing to or in a dance rhythm. **5** a dancing or lively motion. □**dance attendance on** follow or wait on (a person) obsequiously. **dance of death** a medieval dance in which a personified Death is represented as leading all to the grave. **dance to a person's tune** accede obsequiously to a person's demands and wishes. **lead a person a dance** (or **merry dance**) *Brit.* cause a person much trouble in following a course one has instigated. □□**danceable** *adj.* [ME f. OF *dance*, *danse* (n.), *dancer*, *danser* (v.), f. Rmc, of unkn. orig.]

dancehall /'dɑːnshɔːl/ *n.* a public hall for dancing.

dancer /'dɑːnsə(r)/ *n.* **1** a person who performs a dance. **2** a person whose profession is dancing.

d. and c. *n.* dilatation (of the cervix) and curettage (of the uterus), performed after a miscarriage or for the removal of cysts, tumours, etc.

dandelion /'dændɪ,laɪən/ *n.* a composite plant, *Taraxacum officinale*, with jagged leaves and a large bright-yellow flower on a hollow stalk, followed by a globular head of seeds with downy tufts. □**dandelion clock** the downy seed-head of a dandelion. **dandelion coffee** dried and powdered dandelion roots; a drink made from this. [F *dent-de-lion* transl. med.L *dens leonis* lion's tooth]

dander /'dændə(r)/ *n. colloq.* temper, anger, indignation. □**get one's dander up** lose one's temper; become angry. [19th c.: orig. uncert.]

dandify /'dændɪ,faɪ/ *v.tr.* (**-ies**, **-ied**) cause to resemble a dandy.

dandle /'dænd(ə)l/ *v.tr.* **1** dance (a child) on one's knees or in one's arms. **2** pamper, pet. [16th c.: orig. unkn.]

dandruff /'dændrʌf/ *n.* **1** dead skin in small scales among the hair. **2** the condition of having this. [16th c.: *-ruff* perh. rel. to ME *rove* scurfiness f. ON *hrufa* or MLG, MDu. *rōve*]

dandy /'dændɪ/ *n. & adj.* —*n.* (*pl.* **-ies**) **1** a man unduly devoted to style, smartness, and fashion in dress and appearance. **2** *colloq.* an excellent thing. —*adj.* (**dandier**, **dandiest**) esp. *US colloq.* very good of its kind; splendid, first-rate. □**dandy-brush** a brush for grooming a horse. **dandy roll** (or **roller**) a device for solidifying, and impressing a watermark in, paper during manufacture. □□**dandyish** *adj.* **dandyism** *n.* [18th c.: perh. orig. = *Andrew*, in *Jack-a-dandy*]

Dane /deɪn/ *n.* **1** a native or national of Denmark. **2** *hist.* a Viking invader of England in the 9th–11th c. □**Great Dane** a dog of a very large short-haired breed. **2** this breed. [ME f. ON *Danir* (pl.), LL *Dani*]

Danegeld /'deɪngeld/ *n. hist.* **1** (in pre-Conquest England) an annual tax to raise funds for protection against Danish invaders. **2** appeasement by bribery. [OE (as DANE + ON *gjald* payment)]

Danelaw /'deɪnlɔː/ *n. hist.* the part of N. & E. England occupied or administered by Danes in the 9th–11th c. [OE *Dena lagu* Danes' law]

danger /'deɪndʒə(r)/ *n.* **1** liability or exposure to harm. **2** a thing that causes or is likely to cause harm. **3** the status of a railway signal directing a halt or caution. □**danger list** a list of those dangerously ill, esp. in a hospital. **danger money** extra payment for dangerous work. **in danger of** likely to incur or to suffer from. [earlier sense 'jurisdiction, power': ME f. OF *dangier* ult. f. L *dominus* lord]

dangerous /'deɪndʒərəs/ *adj.* involving or causing danger. □□**dangerously** *adv.* **dangerousness** *n.* [ME f. AF *dangerous*, *daungerous*, OF *dangereus* (as DANGER)]

dangle /'dæŋg(ə)l/ *v.* **1** *intr.* be loosely suspended, so as to be able to sway to and fro. **2** *tr.* hold or carry loosely suspended. **3** *tr.* hold out (a hope, temptation, etc.) enticingly. □□**dangler** *n.* [16th c. (imit.): cf. Sw. *dangla*, Da. *dangle*]

Daniell cell /'dænj(ə)l/ *n. Physics & Chem.* a primary voltaic cell with a copper anode and a zinc-amalgam cathode giving a standard electromotive force when either copper sulphate or sulphuric acid is used as the electrolyte. [John *Daniell*, Brit. chemist d. 1845, its inventor]

Danish /'deɪnɪʃ/ *adj. & n.* —*adj.* of or relating to Denmark or the Danes. —*n.* **1** the Danish language. **2** (prec. by *the*; treated as *pl.*) the Danish people. □**Danish blue** a soft salty white cheese with blue veins. **Danish pastry** a cake of sweetened yeast pastry topped with icing, fruit, nuts, etc. [ME f. AF *danes*, OF *daneis* f. med.L *Danensis* (as DANE)]

dank /dæŋk/ *adj.* disagreeably damp and cold. □□**dankly** *adv.* **dankness** *n.* [ME prob. f. Scand.: cf. Sw. *dank* marshy spot]

danse macabre /,dɑ̃s mə'kɑːbr/ *n.* = *dance of death.* [F (as DANCE, MACABRE)]

danseur /dɑ̃'sɜ:(r)/ *n.* (*fem.* **danseuse** /-'sɜ:z/) a ballet-dancer. [F, = dancer]

Dantean /'dæntɪən, dæn'ti:ən/ *adj. & n.* —*adj.* **1** of Dante. **2** in the style of or reminiscent of Dante's writings. —*n.* a student or imitator of Dante. □□ **Dantesque** /-'tesk/ *adj.* [*Dante* Alighieri, It. poet d. 1321]

danthonia /dæn'θəʊnɪə/ *n. Austral. & NZ* any tufted pasture grass of the genus *Danthonia*. [mod.L f. E. *Danthoine* 19th-c. Fr. botanist]

dap /dæp/ *v.* (**dapped, dapping**) **1** *intr.* fish by letting the bait bob on the water. **2** *tr. & intr.* dip lightly. **3** *tr. & intr.* bounce on the ground. [cf. DAB¹]

daphne /'dæfnɪ/ *n.* any flowering shrub of the genus *Daphne*, e.g. the spurge laurel or mezereon. [ME, = laurel, f. Gk *daphnē*]

daphnia /'dæfnɪə/ *n.* any freshwater branchiopod crustacean of the genus *Daphnia*, enclosed in a transparent carapace and with long antennae and prominent eyes. Also called *freshwater flea.* [mod.L f. *Daphne* name of a nymph in Gk mythol., f. DAPHNE]

dapper /'dæpə(r)/ *adj.* **1** neat and precise, esp. in dress or movement. **2** sprightly. □□ **dapperly** *adv.* **dapperness** *n.* [ME f. MLG, MDu. *dapper* strong, stout]

dapple /'dæp(ə)l/ *v. & n.* —*v.* **1** *tr.* mark with spots or rounded patches of colour or shade. **2** *intr.* become marked in this way. —*n.* **1** a dappled effect. **2** a dappled animal, esp. a horse. □ **dapple grey 1** (of an animal's coat) grey or white with darker spots. **2** a horse of this colour. [ME *dappled, dappeld,* (adj.), of unkn. orig.]

darbies /'dɑ:bɪz/ *n.pl. Brit. sl.* handcuffs. [allusive use of *Father Darby's bands,* some rigid form of agreement for debtors (16th c.)]

Darby and Joan /ˌdɑ:bɪ ənd 'dʒəʊn/ *n.* a devoted old married couple. □ **Darby and Joan club** *Brit.* a club for people over 60. [18th c.: perh. f. a poem of 1735 in the *Gentleman's Magazine*]

dare /deə(r)/ *v. & n.* —*v.tr.* (*3rd sing. present* usu. **dare** before an expressed or implied infinitive without *to*) **1** (foll. by infin. with or without *to*) venture (to); have the courage or impudence (to) (*dare he do it?; if they dare to come; how dare you?; I dare not speak; I do not dare to jump*). **2** (usu. foll. by *to* + infin.) defy or challenge (a person) (*I dare you to own up*). **3** *literary* attempt; take the risk of (*dare all things; dared their anger*). —*n.* **1** an act of daring. **2** a challenge, esp. to prove courage. □ **I dare say 1** (often foll. by *that* + clause) it is probable. **2** probably; I grant that much (*I dare say, but you are still wrong*). □□ **darer** *n.* [OE *durran* with Gmc cognates: cf. Skr. *dhṛsh,* Gk *tharseō* be bold]

daredevil /'deəˌdev(ə)l/ *n. & adj.* —*n.* a recklessly daring person. —*adj.* recklessly daring. □□ **daredevilry** *n.* **daredeviltry** *n.*

darg /dɑ:g/ *n. Sc., N.Engl., & Austral.* **1** a day's work. **2** a definite amount of work; a task. [ME f. *daywerk* or *daywark* day-work]

daring /'deərɪŋ/ *n. & adj.* —*n.* adventurous courage. —*adj.* adventurous, bold; prepared to take risks. □□ **daringly** *adv.*

dariole /'dærɪˌəʊl/ *n.* a savoury or sweet dish cooked and served in a small mould usu. shaped like a flowerpot. [ME f. OF]

Darjeeling /dɑ:'dʒi:lɪŋ/ *n.* a high-quality tea from Darjeeling in NE India.

dark /dɑ:k/ *adj. & n.* —*adj.* **1** with little or no light. **2** of a deep or sombre colour. **3** (of a person) with deep brown or black hair, complexion, or skin. **4** gloomy, depressing, dismal (*dark thoughts*). **5** evil, sinister (*dark deeds*). **6** sullen, angry (*a dark mood*). **7** remote, secret, mysterious, little-known (*the dark and distant past; keep it dark*). **8** ignorant, unenlightened. —*n.* **1** absence of light. **2** nightfall (*don't go out after dark*). **3** a lack of knowledge. **4** a dark area or colour, esp. in painting (*the skilled use of lights and darks*). □ **the Dark Ages** (or **Age**) **1** the period of European history preceding the Middle Ages, esp. the 5th-10th c. **2** any period of supposed unenlightenment. **the Dark Continent** a name for Africa, esp. when little known to Europeans. **dark glasses** spectacles with dark-tinted lenses. **dark horse** a little-known person who is unexpectedly successful or prominent. **dark star** an invisible star known to exist from reception of physical data other than light. **in the dark** lacking information. □□ **darkish** *adj.* **darkly** *adv.* **darkness** *n.* **darksome** *poet. adj.* [OE *deorc* prob. f. Gmc]

darken /'dɑ:kən/ *v.* **1** *tr.* make dark or darker. **2** *intr.* become dark or darker. □ **never darken a person's door** keep away permanently. □□ **darkener** *n.*

darkie var. of DARKY.

darkling /'dɑ:klɪŋ/ *adj. & adv. poet.* in the dark; in the night.

darkroom /'dɑ:kru:m, -rʊm/ *n.* a room for photographic work, with normal light excluded.

darky /'dɑ:kɪ/ *n.* (also **darkie**) (*pl.* **-ies**) *sl. offens.* a Black person.

darling /'dɑ:lɪŋ/ *n. & adj.* —*n.* **1** a beloved or lovable person or thing. **2** a favourite. **3** *colloq.* a pretty or endearing person or thing. —*adj.* **1** beloved, lovable. **2** favourite. **3** *colloq.* charming or pretty. [OE *dēorling* (as DEAR, -LING¹)]

darn¹ /dɑ:n/ *v. & n.* —*v.tr.* **1** mend (esp. knitted material, or a hole in it) by interweaving yarn across the hole with a needle. **2** embroider with a large running stitch. —*n.* a darned area in material. □ **darning needle 1** a long needle with a large eye, used in darning. **2** *US* a dragonfly. [16th c.: perh. f. obs. *dern* hide]

darn² /dɑ:n/ *v.tr., int., adj., & adv.* (*US* **durn** /dɜ:n/) *colloq.* = DAMN (in imprecatory senses). [corrupt. of DAMN]

darned /dɑ:nd/ *adj. & adv.* (*US* **durned** /dɜ:nd/) *colloq.* = DAMNED.

darnel /'dɑ:n(ə)l/ *n.* any of several grasses of the genus *Lolium,* growing as weeds among cereal crops. [ME: cf. Walloon *darnelle*]

darner /'dɑ:nə(r)/ *n.* a person or thing that darns, esp. a darning needle.

darning /'dɑ:nɪŋ/ *n.* **1** the action of a person who darns. **2** things to be darned.

dart /dɑ:t/ *n. & v.* —*n.* **1** a small pointed missile used as a weapon or in a game. **2** (in *pl.;* usu. treated as *sing.*) an indoor game in which light feathered darts are thrown at a circular target to score points. **3** a sudden rapid movement. **4** *Zool.* a dartlike structure, such as an insect's sting or the calcareous projections of a snail (used during copulation). **5** a tapering tuck stitched in a garment. —*v.* **1** *intr.* (often foll. by *out, in, past,* etc.) move or go suddenly or rapidly (*darted into the shop*). **2** *tr.* throw (a missile). **3** *tr.* direct suddenly (a glance etc.). [ME f. OF *darz, dars,* f. Frank.]

dartboard /'dɑ:tbɔ:d/ *n.* a circular board marked with numbered segments, used as a target in darts.

darter /'dɑ:tə(r)/ *n.* **1** any large water-bird of the genus *Anhinga,* having a narrow head and long thin neck. **2** any of various small quick-moving freshwater fish of the family Percidae, native to N. America.

Dartmoor pony /'dɑ:tmʊə, -mɔ:/ *n.* **1** a small pony of a shaggy-coated breed. **2** this breed. [*Dartmoor* in SW England]

Darwinian /dɑ:'wɪnɪən/ *adj. & n.* —*adj.* of or relating to Darwin's theory of the evolution of species by the action of natural selection. —*n.* an adherent of this theory. □□ **Darwinism** /'dɑ:-/ *n.* **Darwinist** /'dɑ:-/ *n.* [C. *Darwin,* Engl. naturalist d. 1882]

dash /dæʃ/ *v. & n.* —*v.* **1** *intr.* rush hastily or forcefully (*dashed up the stairs*). **2** *tr.* strike or fling with great force, esp. so as to shatter (*dashed it to the ground; the cup was dashed from my hand*). **3** *tr.* frustrate, daunt, dispirit (*dashed their hopes*). **4** *tr.*

colloq. (esp. **dash it** or **dash it all**) = DAMN *v.* 1. —*n.* **1** a rush or onset; a sudden advance (*made a dash for shelter*). **2** a horizontal stroke in writing or printing to mark a pause or break in sense or to represent omitted letters or words. **3** impetuous vigour or the capacity for this. **4** showy appearance or behaviour. **5** *US* a sprinting-race. **6** the longer signal of the two used in Morse code (cf. DOT¹ *n.* 3). **7** a slight admixture, esp. of a liquid. **8** = DASHBOARD. □**cut a dash** make a brilliant show. **dash down** (or **off**) write or finish hurriedly. [ME, prob. imit.]

dashboard /ˈdæʃbɔːd/ *n.* **1** the surface below the windscreen of a motor vehicle or aircraft, containing instruments and controls. **2** *hist.* a board of wood or leather in front of a carriage, to keep out mud.

dashiki /daːˈʃɪkɪ/ *n.* a loose brightly-coloured shirt worn by American Blacks. [W. Afr.]

dashing /ˈdæʃɪŋ/ *adj.* **1** spirited, lively. **2** showy. □□ **dashingly** *adv.* **dashingness** *n.*

dashpot /ˈdæʃpɒt/ *n.* a device for damping shock or vibration.

dassie /ˈdæsɪ, ˈdɑːsɪ/ *n.* *S.Afr.* **1** the Cape hyrax *Procavia capensis.* Also called *rock-rabbit* (see ROCK¹). **2** a small coastal fish *Diplodus sargus* with rows of black stripes. [Afrik. f. Du. *dasje* dimin. of *das* badger]

dastardly /ˈdæstədlɪ/ *adj.* cowardly, despicable. □□ **dastardliness** *n.* [*dastard* base coward, prob. f. *dazed* past part. + -ARD, or obs. *dasart* dullard, DOTARD]

dasyure /ˈdæsɪjʊə(r)/ *n.* any small flesh-eating marsupial of the genus *Dasyurus.* [F f. mod.L *dasyurus* f. Gk *dasus* rough + *oura* tail]

DAT *abbr.* digital audio tape.

data /ˈdeɪtə/ *n.pl.* (also treated as *sing.*, as in *that is all the data we have,* although the singular form is strictly *datum*) **1** known facts or things used as a basis for inference or reckoning. **2** quantities or characters operated on by a computer etc. □**data bank 1** a store or source of data. **2** = DATABASE. **data capture** the action or process of entering data into a computer. **data processing** a series of operations on data, esp. by a computer, to retrieve or classify etc. information. **data processor** a machine, esp. a computer, that carries out data processing. **data protection** legal control over access to data stored in computers. [pl. of DATUM]

database /ˈdeɪtəbeɪs/ *n.* a structured set of data held in a computer, esp. one that is accessible in various ways.

datable /ˈdeɪtəb(ə)l/ *adj.* (often foll. by *to*) capable of being dated (to a particular time).

date¹ /deɪt/ *n.* & *v.* —*n.* **1** a day of the month, esp. specified by a number. **2** a particular day or year, esp. when a given event occurred. **3** a statement (usu. giving the day, month, and year) in a document or inscription etc., of the time of composition or publication. **4** the period to which a work of art etc. belongs. **5** the time when an event happens or is to happen. **6** *colloq.* **a** an engagement or appointment, esp. with a person of the opposite sex. **b** *US* a person with whom one has a social engagement. —*v.* **1** *tr.* mark with a date. **2** *tr.* **a** assign a date to (an object, event, etc.). **b** (foll. by *to*) assign to a particular time, period, etc. **3** *intr.* (often foll. by *from, back to,* etc.) have its origins at a particular time. **4** *intr.* be recognizable as from a past or particular period; become evidently out of date (*a design that does not date*). **5** *tr.* indicate or expose as being out of date (*that hat really dates you*). **6** *colloq.* **a** *tr.* make an arrangement with (a person) to meet socially. **b** *intr.* meet socially by agreement (*they are now dating regularly*). □**date-line 1** the line from north to south partly along the meridian 180° from Greenwich, to the east of which the date is a day earlier than it is to the west. **2** a line at the head of a dispatch or special article in a newspaper showing the date and place of writing. **date-stamp** *n.* **1** an adjustable rubber stamp etc. used to record a date. **2** the

impression made by this. —*v.tr.* mark with a date-stamp. **out of date** (*attrib.* **out-of-date**) old-fashioned, obsolete. **to date** until now. **up to date** (*attrib.* **up-to-date**) meeting or according to the latest requirements, knowledge, or fashion; modern. [ME f. OF f. med.L *data,* fem. past part. of *dare* give: from the L formula used in dating letters, *data* (*epistola*) (letter) given or delivered (at a particular time or place)]

date² /deɪt/ *n.* **1** a dark oval single-stoned fruit. **2** (in full **date-palm**) the tall tree *Phoenix dactylifera,* native to W. Asia and N. Africa, bearing this fruit. [ME f. OF f. L *dactylus* f. Gk *daktulos* finger, from the shape of its leaf]

dateless /ˈdeɪtlɪs/ *adj.* **1** having no date. **2** of immemorial age. **3** not likely to become out of date.

dative /ˈdeɪtɪv/ *n.* & *adj. Gram.* —*n.* the case of nouns and pronouns (and words in grammatical agreement with them) indicating an indirect object or recipient. —*adj.* of or in the dative. □□ **datival** /dəˈtaɪv(ə)l/ *adj.* **datively** /dəˈtaɪvəlɪ/ *adv.* [ME f. L (*casus*) *dativus* f. *dare* dat- give]

datum /ˈdeɪtəm, ˈdɑːtəm/ *n.* (*pl.* **data:** see DATA as main entry). **1** a piece of information. **2** a thing known or granted; an assumption or premiss from which inferences may be drawn (see *sense-datum*). **3** a fixed starting-point of a scale etc. (*datum-line*). [L, = thing given, neut. past part. of *dare* give]

datura /dəˈtjʊərə/ *n.* any poisonous plant of the genus *Datura,* e.g. the thorn apple. [mod.L f. Hindi *dhatura*]

daub /dɔːb/ *v.* & *n.* —*v.tr.* **1** spread (paint, plaster, or some other thick substance) crudely or roughly on a surface. **2** coat or smear (a surface) with paint etc. **3 a** (also *absol.*) paint crudely or unskilfully. **b** lay (colours) on crudely and clumsily. —*n.* **1** paint or other substance daubed on a surface. **2** plaster, clay, etc., for coating a surface, esp. mixed with straw and applied to laths or wattles to form a wall. **3** a crude painting. [ME f. OF *dauber* f. L *dealbare* whitewash f. *albus* white]

daube /dəʊb/ *n.* a stew of braised meat (usu. beef) with wine etc. [F]

dauber /ˈdɔːbə(r)/ *n.* a person or implement that daubs, esp. in painting. □**get one's dauber down** *US sl.* become dispirited or depressed.

daughter /ˈdɔːtə(r)/ *n.* **1** a girl or woman in relation to either or both of her parents. **2** a female descendant. **3** (foll. by *of*) a female member of a family, nation, etc. **4** (foll. by *of*) a woman who is regarded as the spiritual descendant of, or as spiritually attached to, a person or thing. **5** a product or attribute personified as a daughter in relation to its source (*Fortune and its daughter Confidence*). **6** *Physics* a nuclide formed by the radioactive decay of another. **7** *Biol.* a cell etc. formed by the division etc. of another. □**daughter-in-law** (*pl.* **daughters-in-law**) the wife of one's son. □□ **daughterhood** *n.* **daughterly** *adj.* [OE *dohtor* f. Gmc]

daunt /dɔːnt/ *v.tr.* discourage, intimidate. □□ **daunting** *adj.* **dauntingly** *adv.* [ME f. AF *daunter,* OF *danter, donter* f. L *domitare* frequent. of *domare* tame]

dauntless /ˈdɔːntlɪs/ *adj.* intrepid, persevering. □□ **dauntlessly** *adv.* **dauntlessness** *n.*

dauphin /ˈdɔːfɪn, ˈdəʊfæ̃/ *n. hist.* the eldest son of the King of France. [ME f. F, ult. f. L *delphinus* DOLPHIN, as a family name]

Davenport /ˈdævənpɔːt/ *n.* **1** *Brit.* an ornamental writing-desk with drawers and a sloping surface for writing. **2** *US* a large heavily upholstered sofa. [19th c.: from the name *Davenport*]

davit /ˈdævɪt, ˈdeɪvɪt/ *n.* a small crane on board a ship, esp. one of a pair for suspending or lowering a lifeboat. [AF & OF *daviot* dimin. of *Davi* David]

Davy /ˈdeɪvɪ/ *n.* (*pl.* **-ies**) (in full **Davy lamp**) a miner's safety lamp with the flame enclosed by wire gauze to prevent an explosion of gas. [Sir H. *Davy,* Engl. chemist d. 1829, who invented it]

Davy Jones /ˌdeɪvɪ ˈdʒəʊnz/ *n. sl.* **1** (in full **Davy Jones's locker**) the bottom of the sea, esp. regarded as the grave of those drowned at sea. **2** the evil spirit of the sea. [18th c.: orig. unkn.]

daw /dɔː/ *n.* = JACKDAW. [ME: cf. OHG *tāha*]

dawdle /ˈdɔːd(ə)l/ *v. & n.* —*v.* **1** *intr.* **a** walk slowly and idly. **b** delay; waste time. **2** *tr.* (foll. by *away*) waste (time). —*n.* an act or instance of dawdling. □□ **dawdler** *n.* [perh. rel. to dial. *daddle, doddle* idle, dally]

dawn /dɔːn/ *n. & v.* —*n.* **1** the first light of day; daybreak. **2** the beginning or incipient appearance of something. —*v.intr.* **1** (of a day) begin; grow light. **2** (often foll. by *on, upon*) begin to become evident or understood (by a person). □**dawn chorus** the singing of many birds at the break of day. [orig. as verb: back-form. f. *dawning*, ME f. earlier *dawing* after Scand. (as DAY)]

dawning /ˈdɔːnɪŋ/ *n.* **1** daybreak. **2** the first beginning of something.

day /deɪ/ *n.* **1** the time between sunrise and sunset. **2 a** a period of 24 hours as a unit of time, esp. from midnight to midnight, corresponding to a complete revolution of the earth on its axis. **b** a corresponding period on other planets (*Martian day*). **3** daylight (*clear as day*). **4** the time in a day during which work is normally done (*an eight-hour day*). **5 a** (also *pl.*) a period of the past or present (*the modern day; the old days*). **b** (prec. by *the*) the present time (*the issues of the day*). **6** the lifetime of a person or thing, esp. regarded as useful or productive (*have had my day; in my day things were different*). **7** a point of time (*will do it one day*). **8 a** the date of a specific festival. **b** a day associated with a particular event or purpose (*graduation day; payday; Christmas day*). **9** a particular date; a date agreed on. **10** a day's endeavour, or the period of an endeavour, esp. as bringing success (*win the day*). □**all in a** (or the) **day's work** part of normal routine. **at the end of the day** in the final reckoning, when all is said and done. **call it a day** end a period of activity, esp. resting content that enough has been done. **day after day** without respite. **day and night** all the time. **day-boy** (or **-girl**) *Brit.* a boy or girl who goes daily from home to school, esp. a school that also has boarders. **day by day** gradually. **day care** the supervision of young children during the working day. **day centre** a place providing care for the elderly or handicapped during the day. **day-dream** *n.* a pleasant fantasy or reverie. —*v.intr.* indulge in this. **day-dreamer** a person who indulges in day-dreams. **day in, day out** routinely, constantly. **day labourer** an unskilled labourer hired by the day. **day lily** any plant of the genus *Hemerocallis*, whose flowers last only a day. **day nursery** a nursery where children are looked after during the working day. **day off** a day's holiday from work. **Day of Judgement** = *Judgement Day.* **day of reckoning** see RECKONING. **day of rest** the Sabbath. **day out** a trip or excursion for a day. **day-owl** any owl hunting by day esp. the short-eared owl. **day release** *Brit.* a system of allowing employees days off work for education. **day return** a fare or ticket at a reduced rate for a journey out and back in one day. **day-room** a room, esp. a communal room in an institution, used during the day. **day-school** a school for pupils living at home. **day-to-day** mundane, routine. **day-trip** a trip or excursion completed in one day. **day-tripper** a person who goes on a day-trip. **not one's day** a day of successive misfortunes for a person. **on one's day** at one's peak of capability. **one of these days** before very long. **one of those days** a day when things go badly. **some day** at some point in the future. **that will be the day** *colloq.* that will never happen. **this day and age** the present time or period. □□ **dayless** *adj.* [OE *dæg* f. Gmc]

Dayak var. of DYAK.

daybook /ˈdeɪbʊk/ *n.* an account-book in which a day's transactions are entered, for later transfer to a ledger.

daybreak /ˈdeɪbreɪk/ *n.* the first appearance of light in the morning.

Day-Glo /ˈdeɪɡləʊ/ *n. & adj.* —*n. propr.* a make of fluorescent paint or other colouring. —*adj.* coloured with or like this. [DAY + GLOW]

daylight /ˈdeɪlaɪt/ *n.* **1** the light of day. **2** dawn (*before daylight*). **3 a** openness, publicity. **b** open knowledge. **4** a visible gap or interval, e.g. between boats in a race. **5** (usu. in *pl.*) *sl.* one's life or consciousness (orig. the internal organs) esp. as representing vulnerability to fear, attack, etc. (*scared the daylights out of me; beat the living daylights out of them*). □**daylight robbery** *colloq.* a blatantly excessive charge. **daylight saving** the achieving of longer evening daylight, esp. in summer, by setting the time an hour ahead of the standard time. **see daylight** begin to understand what was previously obscure.

daylong /ˈdeɪlɒŋ/ *adj.* lasting for a day.

dayside /ˈdeɪsaɪd/ *n.* **1** *US* staff, esp. of a newspaper, who work during the day. **2** *Astron.* the side of a planet that faces the sun.

daytime /ˈdeɪtaɪm/ *n.* the part of the day when there is natural light.

daywork /ˈdeɪwɜːk/ *n.* work paid for according to the time taken.

daze /deɪz/ *v. & n.* —*v.tr.* stupefy, bewilder. —*n.* a state of confusion or bewilderment (*in a daze*). □□ **dazedly** /-zɪdlɪ/ *adv.* [ME *dased* past part., f. ON *dasathr* weary]

dazzle /ˈdæz(ə)l/ *v. & n.* —*v.* **1** *tr.* blind temporarily or confuse the sight of by an excess of light. **2** *tr.* impress or overpower (a person) with knowledge, ability, or any brilliant display or prospect. **3** *intr. archaic* (of eyes) be dazzled. —*n.* bright confusing light. □□ **dazzlement** *n.* **dazzler** *n.* **dazzling** *adj.* **dazzlingly** *adv.* [ME, f. DAZE + -LE⁴]

dB *abbr.* decibel(s).

DBE *abbr.* (in the UK) Dame Commander of the Order of the British Empire.

DBS *abbr.* **1** direct-broadcast satellite. **2** direct broadcasting by satellite.

DC *abbr.* **1** (also **d.c.**) direct current. **2** District of Columbia. **3** da capo. **4** District Commissioner.

DCB *abbr.* (in the UK) Dame Commander of the Order of the Bath.

DCL *abbr.* Doctor of Civil Law.

DCM *abbr.* (in the UK) Distinguished Conduct Medal.

DCMG *abbr.* (in the UK) Dame Commander of the Order of St Michael and St George.

DCVO *abbr.* (in the UK) Dame Commander of the Royal Victorian Order.

DD *abbr.* Doctor of Divinity.

D-Day /ˈdiːdeɪ/ *n.* **1** the day (6 June 1944) on which British and American forces invaded N. France. **2** the day on which an important operation is to begin or a change to take effect. [*D* for *day* + DAY]

DDT *abbr.* dichlorodiphenyltrichloroethane, a colourless chlorinated hydrocarbon used as an insecticide.

DE *abbr. US* Delaware (in official postal use).

de- /dɪ, di:/ *prefix* **1** forming verbs and their derivatives: **a** down, away (*descend; deduct*). **b** completely (*declare; denude; deride*). **2** added to verbs and their derivatives to form verbs and nouns implying removal or reversal (*decentralize; de-ice; demoralization*). [from or after L *de* (adv. & prep.) = off, from: sense 2 through OF *des-* f. L *dis-*]

deacon /ˈdiːkən/ *n. & v.* —*n.* **1** (in Episcopal churches) a minister of the third order, below bishop and priest. **2** (in Nonconformist churches) a lay officer attending to a congregation's secular affairs. **3** (in the early Church) an appointed minister of charity. —*v.tr.* appoint or ordain as a deacon. □□ **deaconate** *n.* **deaconship** *n.* [OE *diacon* f. eccl.L *diaconus* f. Gk *diakonos* servant]

deaconess /ˌdiːkəˈnes, ˈdiːkənɪs/ *n.* a woman in the early Church and in some modern Churches with functions analogous to a deacon's. [DEACON, after LL *diaconissa*]

deactivate /diːˈæktɪˌveɪt/ *v.tr.* make inactive or less reactive. □□ **deactivation** /-ˈveɪʃ(ə)n/ *n.* **deactivator** *n.*

dead /ded/ *adj., adv.,* & *n.* —*adj.* **1** no longer alive. **2** *colloq.* extremely tired or unwell. **3** benumbed; affected by loss of sensation (*my fingers are dead*). **4** (foll. by *to*) unappreciative or unconscious of; insensitive to. **5** no longer effective or in use; obsolete, extinct. **6** (of a match, of coal, etc.) no longer burning; extinguished. **7** inanimate. **8 a** lacking force or vigour; dull, lustreless, muffled. **b** (of sound) not resonant. **c** (of sparkling wine etc.) no longer effervescent. **9 a** quiet; lacking activity (*the dead season*). **b** motionless, idle. **10 a** (of a microphone, telephone, etc.) not transmitting any sound, esp. because of a fault. **b** (of a circuit, conductor, etc.) carrying or transmitting no current; not connected to a source of electricity (*a dead battery*). **11** (of the ball in a game) out of play. **12** abrupt, complete, exact, unqualified, unrelieved (*come to a dead stop; a dead faint; a dead calm; in dead silence; a dead certainty*). **13** without spiritual life. —*adv.* **1** absolutely, exactly, completely (*dead on target; dead level; dead tired*). **2** *colloq.* very, extremely (*dead good; dead easy*). —*n.* (prec. by *the*) **1** (treated as *pl.*) those who have died. **2** a time of silence or inactivity (*the dead of night*). □**dead-and-alive** *Brit.* (of a place, person, activity, etc.) dull, monotonous; lacking interest. **dead as the dodo** see DODO. **dead as a doornail** see DOORNAIL. **dead bat** *Cricket* a bat held loosely so that it imparts no motion to the ball when struck. **dead beat 1** *colloq.* exhausted. **2** *Physics* (of an instrument) without recoil. **dead-beat** *n.* **1** *colloq.* a penniless person. **2** *US sl.* a person constantly in debt. **dead centre 1** the exact centre. **2** the position of a crank etc. in line with the connecting-rod and not exerting torque. **dead cert** see CERT. **dead duck** *sl.* an unsuccessful or useless person or thing. **dead end 1** a closed end of a road, passage, etc. **2** (often (with hyphen) *attrib.*) a situation offering no prospects of progress or advancement. **dead-eye** *Naut.* a round flat three-holed block for extending shrouds. **dead from the neck up** *colloq.* stupid. **dead hand** an oppressive persisting influence, esp. posthumous control. **dead heat 1** a race in which two or more competitors finish exactly level. **2** the result of such a race. **dead-heat** *v.intr.* run a dead heat. **dead language** a language no longer commonly spoken, e.g. Latin. **dead letter** a law or practice no longer observed or recognized. **dead lift** the exertion of one's utmost strength to lift something. **dead loss 1** *colloq.* a useless person or thing. **2** a complete loss. **dead man's fingers 1** a kind of orchis, *Orchis mascula.* **2** any soft coral of the genus *Alcyonium*, with spongy lobes. **3** the finger-like divisions of a lobster's or crab's gills. **dead man's handle** (or **pedal** etc.) a controlling-device on an electric train, allowing power to be connected only as long as the operator presses on it. **dead march** a funeral march. **dead men** *colloq.* bottles after the contents have been drunk. **dead-nettle** any plant of the genus *Lamium*, having nettle-like leaves but without stinging hairs. **dead-on** exactly right. **dead reckoning** *Naut.* calculation of a ship's position from the log, compass, etc., when observations are impossible. **dead ringer** see RINGER. **dead shot** one who is extremely accurate. **dead time** *Physics* the period after the recording of a pulse etc. when the detector is unable to record another. **dead to the world** *colloq.* fast asleep; unconscious. **dead weight** (or **dead-weight**) **1 a** an inert mass. **b** a heavy weight or burden. **2** a debt not covered by assets. **3** the total weight carried on a ship. **dead wood** *colloq.* one or more useless people or things. **make a dead set at**

see SET². **wouldn't be seen dead in** (or **with** etc.) *colloq.* shall have nothing to do with; shall refuse to wear etc. □□ **deadness** *n.* [OE *dēad* f. Gmc, rel. to DIE¹]

deadbolt /ˈdedbəʊlt/ *n.* esp. *US* a bolt engaged by turning a knob or key, rather than by spring action.

deaden /ˈded(ə)n/ *v.* **1** *tr.* & *intr.* deprive of or lose vitality, force, brightness, sound, feeling, etc. **2** *tr.* (foll. by *to*) make insensitive. □□ **deadener** *n.*

deadeye /ˈdedaɪ/ *n.* **1** *Naut.* a circular wooden block with a groove round the circumference to take a lanyard, used singly or in pairs to tighten a shroud. **2** *US colloq.* an expert marksman.

deadfall /ˈdedfɔːl/ *n. US* a trap in which a raised weight is made to fall on and kill esp. large game.

deadhead /ˈdedhed/ *n.* & *v.* —*n.* **1** a faded flowerhead. **2** a passenger or member of an audience who has made use of a free ticket. **3** a useless or unenterprising person. —*v.* **1** *tr.* remove deadheads from (a plant). **2** *intr. US* (of a driver etc.) complete a journey with an empty train, bus, etc.

deadlight /ˈdedlaɪt/ *n. Naut.* **1** a shutter inside a porthole. **2** *US* a skylight that cannot be opened.

deadline /ˈdedlaɪn/ *n.* **1** a time-limit for the completion of an activity etc. **2** *hist.* a line beyond which prisoners were not allowed to go.

deadlock /ˈdedlɒk/ *n.* & *v.* —*n.* **1** a situation, esp. one involving opposing parties, in which no progress can be made. **2** a type of lock requiring a key to open or close it. —*v.tr.* & *intr.* bring or come to a standstill.

deadly /ˈdedlɪ/ *adj.* & *adv.* —*adj.* (**deadlier, deadliest**) **1 a** causing or able to cause fatal injury or serious damage. **b** poisonous (*deadly snake*). **2** intense, extreme (*deadly dullness*). **3** (of an aim etc.) extremely accurate or effective. **4** deathlike (*deadly pale; deadly faintness; deadly gloom*). **5** *colloq.* dreary, dull. **6** implacable. —*adv.* **1** like death; as if dead (*deadly faint*). **2** extremely, intensely (*deadly serious*). □**deadly nightshade** = BELLADONNA. **deadly sin** a sin regarded as leading to damnation, esp. pride, covetousness, lust, gluttony, envy, anger, and sloth. □□ **deadliness** *n.* [OE *dēadlic, dēadlīce* (as DEAD, -LY¹)]

deadpan /ˈdedpæn/ *adj.* & *adv.* with a face or manner totally lacking expression or emotion.

deadstock /ˈdedstɒk/ *n.* slaughtered farm stock, esp. diseased animals.

de-aerate /diːˈeəˌreɪt/ *v.tr.* remove air from. □□ **de-aeration** /-ˈreɪʃ(ə)n/ *n.*

deaf /def/ *adj.* **1** wholly or partly without hearing (*deaf in one ear*). **2** (foll. by *to*) refusing to listen or comply. **3** insensitive to harmony, rhythm, etc. (*tone-deaf*). □**deaf-aid** *Brit.* a hearing-aid. **deaf-and-dumb alphabet** (or **language** etc.) = sign language. ¶ *Sign language* is preferred in official use. **deaf as a post** completely deaf. **deaf mute** a deaf and dumb person. **fall on deaf ears** be ignored. **turn a deaf ear** (usu. foll. by *to*) be unresponsive. □□ **deafly** *adv.* **deafness** *n.* [OE *dēaf* f. Gmc]

deafen /ˈdef(ə)n/ *v.tr.* **1** (often as **deafening** *adj.*) overpower with sound. **2** deprive of hearing by noise, esp. temporarily. □□ **deafeningly** *adv.*

deal¹ /diːl/ *v.* & *n.* —*v.* (*past* and *past part.* **dealt** /delt/) **1** *intr.* (foll. by *with*) **a** take measures concerning (a problem, person, etc.), esp. in order to put something right. **b** do business with; associate with. **c** discuss or treat (a subject). **d** (often foll. by *by*) behave in a specified way towards a person (*dealt honourably by them*). **2** *intr.* (foll. by *in*) sell or be concerned with commercially (*deals in insurance*). **3** *tr.* (often foll. by *out, round*) distribute or apportion to several people etc. **4** *tr.* (also *absol.*) distribute (cards) to players for a game or round. **5** *tr.* cause to be received; administer (*deal a heavy blow*). **6** *tr.* assign as a share or deserts to a person (*Providence dealt them much happiness*). **7** *tr.* (foll. by *in*) *colloq.* include (a person) in an activity (*you can deal me in*). —*n.* **1** (usu. **a good** or **great deal**) *colloq.* **a** a large amount (*a good deal of trouble*). **b** to a considerable

extent (*is a great deal better*). **2** *colloq.* a business arrangement; a transaction. **3** a specified form of treatment given or received (*gave them a rough deal*; *got a fair deal*). **4 a** the distribution of cards by dealing. **b** a player's turn to do this (*it's my deal*). **c** the round of play following this. **d** a set of hands dealt to players. □**it's a deal** *colloq.* expressing assent to an agreement. [OE *dǣl*, *dǣlan*, f. Gmc]

deal[2] /diːl/ *n.* **1** fir or pine timber, esp. sawn into boards of a standard size. **2 a** a board of this timber. **b** such boards collectively. [ME f. MLG, MDu. *dele* plank f. Gmc]

dealer /'diːlə(r)/ *n.* **1** a person or business dealing in (esp. retail) goods (*contact your dealer*; *car-dealer*; *a dealer in tobacco*). **2** the player dealing at cards. **3** a jobber on the Stock Exchange. ¶ In the UK from Oct. 1986 the name has been merged with **broker** (see BROKER 2, JOBBER 1). □□ **dealership** *n.* (in sense 1).

dealings /'diːlɪŋz/ *n.pl.* contacts or transactions, esp. in business. □**have dealings with** associate with.

dealt *past* and *past part.* of DEAL[1].

dean[1] /diːn/ *n.* **1 a** the head of the chapter of a cathedral or collegiate church. **b** (usu. **rural dean**) *Brit.* a member of the clergy exercising supervision over a group of parochial clergy within a division of an archdeaconry. **2 a** a college or university official, esp. one of several fellows of a college, with disciplinary and advisory functions. **b** the head of a university faculty or department or of a medical school. **3** = DOYEN. □**Dean of Faculty** the president of the Faculty of Advocates in Scotland. [ME f. AF *deen*, OF *deien*, f. LL *decanus* f. *decem* ten; orig. = chief of a group of ten]

dean[2] var. of DENE[1].

deanery /'diːnərɪ/ *n.* (*pl.* **-ies**) **1** a dean's house or office. **2** *Brit.* the group of parishes presided over by a rural dean.

dear /dɪə(r)/ *adj.*, *n.*, *adv.*, & *int.* —*adj.* **1 a** beloved or much esteemed. **b** as a merely polite or ironic form (*my dear man*). **2** used as a formula of address, esp. at the beginning of letters (*Dear Sir*). **3** (often foll. by *to*) precious; much cherished. **4** (usu. in *superl.*) earnest, deeply felt (*my dearest wish*). **5 a** high-priced relative to its value. **b** having high prices. **c** (of money) available as a loan only at a high rate of interest. —*n.* (esp. as a form of address) dear person. —*adv.* at a high price or great cost (*buy cheap and sell dear*; *will pay dear*). —*int.* expressing surprise, dismay, pity, etc. (*dear me!*; *oh dear!*; *dear, dear!*). □**Dear John** *colloq.* a letter terminating a personal relationship. **for dear life** see LIFE. □□ **dearly** *adv.* (esp. in sense 3 of *adj.*). **dearness** *n.* [OE *dēore* f. Gmc]

dearie /'dɪərɪ/ *n.* (esp. as a form of address) usu. *joc.* or *iron.* my dear. □**dearie me!** *int.* expressing surprise, dismay, etc.

dearth /dɜːθ/ *n.* scarcity or lack, esp. of food. [ME, formed as DEAR]

deasil /'desɪl/ *adv.* *Sc.* in the direction of the sun's apparent course (considered as lucky); clockwise. [Gael. *deiseil*]

death /deθ/ *n.* **1** the final cessation of vital functions in an organism; the ending of life. **2** the event that terminates life. **3 a** the fact or process of being killed or killing (*stone to death*; *fought to the death*). **b** the fact or state of being dead (*eyes closed in death*; *their deaths caused rioting*). **4 a** the destruction or permanent cessation of something (*was the death of our hopes*). **b** *colloq.* something terrible or appalling. **5** (usu. **Death**) a personification of death, esp. as a destructive power, usu. represented by a skeleton. **6** a lack of religious faith or spiritual life. □**as sure as death** quite certain. **at death's door** close to death. **be in at the death 1** be present when an animal is killed, esp. in hunting. **2** witness the (esp. sudden) ending of an enterprise etc. **be the death of 1** cause the death of. **2** be very harmful to. **catch one's death** *colloq.* catch a serious chill etc. **death adder**

any of various venomous snakes of the genus *Acanthopis* esp. *A. antarcticus* of Australia. **death cap** a poisonous toadstool, *Amanita phalloides*. **death cell** a prison cell for a person condemned to death. **death certificate** an official statement of the cause and date and place of a person's death. **death duty** *Brit.* *hist.* a tax levied on property after the owner's death. ¶ Replaced in 1975 by *capital transfer tax* and in 1986 by *inheritance tax*. **death grant** *Brit.* a State grant towards funeral expenses. **death-knell 1** the tolling of a bell to mark a person's death. **2** an event that heralds the end or destruction of something. **death-mask** a cast taken of a dead person's face. **death penalty** punishment by being put to death. **death rate** the number of deaths per thousand of population per year. **death-rattle** a gurgling sound sometimes heard in a dying person's throat. **death-roll 1** those killed in an accident, battle, etc. **2** a list of these. **death row** *US* a prison block or section for prisoners sentenced to death. **death's head** a human skull as an emblem of mortality. **death's head moth** a large dark hawk moth, *Acherontia atropos*, with skull-like markings on the back of the thorax. **death squad** an armed paramilitary group formed to kill political enemies etc. **death tax** *US* a tax on property payable on the owner's death. **death-toll** the number of people killed in an accident, battle, etc. **death-trap** *colloq.* a dangerous or unhealthy building, vehicle, etc. **death-warrant 1** an order for the execution of a condemned person. **2** anything that causes the end of an established practice etc. **death-watch** (in full **death-watch beetle**) a small beetle (*Xestobium rufovillosum*) which makes a sound like a watch ticking, once supposed to portend death, and whose larva bores in old wood. **death-wish** *Psychol.* a desire (usu. unconscious) for the death of oneself or another. **do to death 1** kill. **2** overdo. **fate worse than death** *colloq.* a disastrous misfortune or experience. **like death warmed up** *sl.* very tired or ill. **put to death** kill or cause to be killed. **to death** to the utmost, extremely (*bored to death*; *worked to death*). □□ **deathless** *adj.* **deathlessness** *n.* **deathlike** *adj.* [OE *dēath* f. Gmc: rel. to DIE[1]]

deathbed /'deθbed/ *n.* a bed as the place where a person is dying or has died.

deathblow /'deθbləʊ/ *n.* **1** a blow or other action that causes death. **2** an event or circumstance that abruptly ends an activity, enterprise, etc.

deathly /'deθlɪ/ *adj.* & *adv.* —*adj.* (**deathlier**, **deathliest**) suggestive of death (*deathly silence*). —*adv.* in a deathly way (*deathly pale*).

deb /deb/ *n.* *colloq.* a débutante. [abbr.]

débâcle /deɪ'bɑːk(ə)l/ *n.* (*US* **debacle**) **1 a** an utter defeat or failure. **b** a sudden collapse or downfall. **2** a confused rush or rout; a stampede. **3 a** a break-up of ice in a river, with resultant flooding. **b** a sudden rush of water carrying along blocks of stone and other debris. [F f. *débâcler* unbar]

debag /diː'bæg/ *v.tr.* (**debagged**, **debagging**) *Brit.* *sl.* remove the trousers of (a person), esp. as a joke.

debar /diː'bɑː(r)/ *v.tr.* (**debarred**, **debarring**) (foll. by *from*) exclude from admission or from a right; prohibit from an action (*was debarred from entering*). □□ **debarment** *n.* [ME f. F *débarrer*, OF *desbarrer* (as DE-, BAR[1])]

debark[1] /diː'bɑːk, dɪ-/ *v.tr.* & *intr.* land from a ship. □□ **debarkation** /-'keɪʃ(ə)n/ *n.* [F *débarquer* (as DE-, BARK[3])]

debark[2] /diː'bɑːk/ *v.tr.* remove the bark from (a tree).

debase /dɪ'beɪs/ *v.tr.* **1** lower in quality, value, or character. **2** depreciate (coin) by alloying etc. □□ **debasement** *n.* **debaser** *n.* [DE- + obs. *base* for ABASE]

debatable /dɪ'beɪtəb(ə)l/ *adj.* **1** questionable; subject to dispute. **2** capable of being debated. □□ **debatably** *adv.* [OF *debatable* or AL *debatabilis* (as DEBATE)]

debate /dɪ'beɪt/ *v.* & *n.* —*v.* **1** *tr.* (also *absol.*)

discuss or dispute about (an issue, proposal, etc.) esp. formally in a legislative assembly, public meeting, etc. **2 a** *tr.* consider, ponder (a matter). **b** *intr.* consider different sides of a question. —*n.* **1** a formal discussion on a particular matter, esp. in a legislative assembly etc. **2** debating, discussion (*open to debate*). □**debating point** an inessential matter used to gain advantage in a debate. □□**debater** *n.* [ME f. OF *debatre, debat* f. Rmc (as DE-, BATTLE)]

debauch /dɪˈbɔːtʃ/ *v. & n.* —*v.tr.* **1** corrupt morally. **2** make intemperate or sensually indulgent. **3** deprave or debase (taste or judgement). **4** (as **debauched** *adj.*) dissolute. **5** seduce (a woman). —*n.* **1** a bout of sensual indulgence. **2** debauchery. □□**debaucher** *n.* [F *débauche(r)*, OF *desbaucher*, of unkn. orig.]

debauchee /ˌdɪbɔːˈtʃiː, ˌdeb-/ *n.* a person addicted to excessive sensual indulgence. [F *débauché* past part.: see DEBAUCH]

debauchery /dɪˈbɔːtʃərɪ/ *n.* excessive sensual indulgence.

debenture /dɪˈbentʃə(r)/ *n.* **1** *Brit.* an acknowledgement of indebtedness, esp. a bond of a company or corporation acknowledging a debt and providing for payment of interest at fixed intervals. **2** *US* (in full **debenture bond**) a fixed-interest bond of a company or corporation, backed by general credit rather than specified assets. □**debenture stock** *Brit.* stock comprising debentures, with only the interest secured. [ME f. L *debentur* are owing f. *debēre* owe: assim. to -URE]

debilitate /dɪˈbɪlɪˌteɪt/ *v.tr.* enfeeble, enervate. □□ **debilitatingly** *adv.* **debilitation** /-ˈteɪʃ(ə)n/ *n.* **debilitative** /-tətɪv/ *adj.* [L *debilitare* (as DEBILITY)]

debility /dɪˈbɪlɪtɪ/ *n.* feebleness, esp. of health. [ME f. OF *debilité* f. L *debilitas -tatis* f. *debilis* weak]

debit /ˈdebɪt/ *n. & v.* —*n.* **1** an entry in an account recording a sum owed. **2** the sum recorded. **3** the total of such sums. **4** the debit side of an account. —*v.tr.* (**debited, debiting**) **1** (foll. by *against, to*) enter (an amount) on the debit side of an account (*debited £500 against me*). **2** (foll. by *with*) enter (a person) on the debit side of an account (*debited me with £500*). [F *débit* f. L *debitum* DEBT]

debonair /ˌdebəˈneə(r)/ *adj.* **1** carefree, cheerful, self-assured. **2** having pleasant manners. □□ **debonairly** *adv.* [ME f. OF *debonaire = de bon aire* of good disposition]

debouch /dɪˈbaʊtʃ, -ˈbuːʃ/ *v.intr.* **1** (of troops or a stream) issue from a ravine, wood, etc., into open ground. **2** (often foll. by *into*) (of a river, road, etc.) merge into a larger body or area. □□**debouchment** *n.* [F *déboucher* (as DE-, *bouche* mouth)]

debrief /diːˈbriːf/ *v.tr. colloq.* interrogate (a person, e.g. a diplomat or pilot) about a completed mission or undertaking. □□**debriefing** *n.*

debris /ˈdebriː, ˈdeɪ-/ *n.* **1** scattered fragments, esp. of something wrecked or destroyed. **2** *Geol.* an accumulation of loose material, e.g. from rocks or plants. [F *débris* f. obs. *débriser* break down (as DE-, *briser* break)]

debt /det/ *n.* **1** something that is owed, esp. money. **2** a state of obligation to pay something owed (*in debt; out of debt; get into debt*). □**debt-collector** a person who is employed to collect debts for creditors. **debt of honour** a debt not legally recoverable, esp. a sum lost in gambling. **in a person's debt** under an obligation to a person. [ME *det(te)* f. OF *dette* (later *debte*) ult. f. L *debitum* past part. of *debēre* owe]

debtor /ˈdetə(r)/ *n.* a person who owes a debt, esp. money. [ME f. OF *det(t)or, -our* f. L *debitor* (as DEBT)]

debug /diːˈbʌg/ *v.tr.* (**debugged, debugging**) **1** *colloq.* trace and remove concealed listening devices from (a room etc.). **2** *colloq.* identify and remove defects from (a machine, computer program, etc.). **3** remove bugs from.

debunk /diːˈbʌŋk/ *v.tr. colloq.* **1** show the good reputation or aspirations of (a person, institution,

etc.) to be spurious. **2** expose the falseness of (a claim etc.). □□**debunker** *n.*

debus /diːˈbʌs/ *v.tr. & intr.* (**debussed, debussing**) esp. *Mil.* unload (personnel or stores) or alight from a motor vehicle.

début /ˈdeɪbjuː, -buː/ *n.* (*US* **debut**) **1** the first public appearance of a performer on stage etc. **2** the first appearance of a débutante in society. [F f. *débuter* lead off]

débutante /ˈdebjuːˌtɑːnt, ˈdeɪb-/ *n.* (*US* **debutante**) a (usu. wealthy) young woman making her social début. [F, fem. part. of *débuter*: see DÉBUT]

Dec. *abbr.* December.

dec. *abbr.* **1** deceased. **2** declared.

deca- /ˈdekə/ *comb. form* (also **dec-** before a vowel) **1** having ten. **2** tenfold. **3** ten, esp. of a metric unit (*decagram; decalitre*). [Gk *deka* ten]

decade /ˈdekeɪd, *disp.* dɪˈkeɪd/ *n.* **1** a period of ten years. **2** a set, series, or group of ten. □□**decadal** /ˈdekəd(ə)l/ *adj.* [ME f. F *décade* f. LL *decas -adis* f. Gk f. *deka* ten]

decadence /ˈdekəd(ə)ns/ *n.* **1** moral or cultural deterioration, esp. after a peak or culmination of achievement. **2** decadent behaviour; a state of decadence. [F *décadence* f. med.L *decadentia* f. *decadere* DECAY]

decadent /ˈdekəd(ə)nt/ *adj. & n.* —*adj.* **1 a** in a state of moral or cultural deterioration; showing or characterized by decadence. **b** of a period of decadence. **2** self-indulgent. —*n.* a decadent person. □□**decadently** *adv.* [F *décadent* (as DECADENCE)]

decaffeinate /diːˈkæfɪˌneɪt/ *v.tr.* **1** remove the caffeine from. **2** reduce the quantity of caffeine in (usu. coffee).

decagon /ˈdekəgən/ *n.* a plane figure with ten sides and angles. □□**decagonal** /dɪˈkægən(ə)l/ *adj.* [med.L *decagonum* f. Gk *dekagōnon* (as DECA-, -GON)]

decagynous /deˈkædʒɪnəs/ *adj. Bot.* having ten pistils. [mod.L *decagynus* (as DECA-, Gk *gunē* woman)]

decahedron /ˌdekəˈhiːdrən/ *n.* a solid figure with ten faces. □□**decahedral** *adj.* [DECA- + -HEDRON after POLYHEDRON]

decal /ˈdiːkæl/ *n.* = DECALCOMANIA 2. [abbr.]

decalcify /diːˈkælsɪˌfaɪ/ *v.tr.* (**-ies, -ied**) remove lime or calcareous matter from (a bone, tooth, etc.). □□ **decalcification** /-fɪˈkeɪʃ(ə)n/ *n.* **decalcifier** *n.*

decalcomania /diːˌkælkəˈmeɪnɪə/ *n. US* **1** a process of transferring designs from specially prepared paper to the surface of glass, porcelain, etc. **2** a picture or design made by this process. [F *décalcomanie* f. *décalquer* transfer]

decalitre /ˈdekəˌliːtə(r)/ *n.* a metric unit of capacity, equal to 10 litres.

Decalogue /ˈdekəˌlɒg/ *n.* the Ten Commandments. [ME f. F *décalogue* or eccl.L *decalogus* f. Gk *dekalogos* (after *hoi deka logoi* the Ten Commandments)]

decametre /ˈdekəˌmiːtə(r)/ *n.* a metric unit of length, equal to 10 metres.

decamp /dɪˈkæmp/ *v.intr.* **1** break up or leave a camp. **2** depart suddenly; abscond. □□**decampment** *n.* [F *décamper* (as DE-, CAMP[1])]

decanal /dɪˈkeɪn(ə)l, ˈdekə-/ *adj.* **1** of a dean or deanery. **2** of the south side of a choir, the side on which the dean sits (cf. CANTORIAL). [med.L *decanalis* f. LL *decanus* DEAN[1]]

decandrous /dɪˈkændrəs/ *adj. Bot.* having ten stamens. [DECA- + Gk *andr-* man (= male organ)]

decani /dɪˈkeɪnaɪ/ *adj. Mus.* to be sung by the decanal side in antiphonal singing (cf. CANTORIS). [L, genit. of *decanus* DEAN[1]]

decant /dɪˈkænt/ *v.tr.* gradually pour off (liquid, esp. wine or a solution) from one container to another, esp. without disturbing the sediment. [med.L *decanthare* (as DE-, L *canthus* f. Gk *kanthos* canthus, used of the lip of a beaker)]

decanter /dɪˈkæntə(r)/ *n.* a stoppered glass container into which wine or spirit is decanted.

decapitate /dɪˈkæpɪˌteɪt/ *v.tr.* **1** behead (esp. as a

æ cat ɑː arm e bed ɜː her ɪ sit iː see ɒ hot ɔː saw ʌ run ʊ put uː too ə ago aɪ my

form of capital punishment). **2** cut the head or end from. ▢▢ **decapitation** /-'teɪʃ(ə)n/ *n.* **decapitator** *n.* [LL *decapitare* (as DE-, *caput -itis* head)]

decapod /'dekə,pɒd/ *n.* **1** any crustacean of the chiefly marine order Decapoda, characterized by five pairs of walking legs, e.g. shrimps, crabs, and lobsters. **2** any of various molluscs of the class Cephalopoda, having ten tentacles, e.g. squids and cuttlefish. ▢▢ **decapodan** /dɪ'kæpəd(ə)n/ *adj.* [F *décapode* f. Gk *deka* ten + *pous podos* foot]

decarbonize /di:'kɑːbə,naɪz/ *v.tr.* (also **-ise**) remove carbon or carbonaceous deposits from (an internal-combustion engine etc.). ▢▢ **decarbonization** /-'zeɪʃ(ə)n/ *n.*

decastyle /'dekə,staɪl/ *n.* & *adj.* *Archit.* —*n.* a ten-columned portico. —*adj.* having ten columns. [Gk *dekastulos* f. *deka* ten + *stulos* column]

decasyllable /'dekə,sɪləb(ə)l/ *n.* a metrical line of ten syllables. ▢▢ **decasyllabic** /-sɪ'læbɪk/ *adj.* & *n.*

decathlon /dɪ'kæθlən/ *n.* an athletic contest in which each competitor takes part in ten events. ▢▢ **decathlete** /-li:t/ *n.* [DECA- + Gk *athlon* contest]

decay /dɪ'keɪ/ *v.* & *n.* —*v.* **1 a** *intr.* rot, decompose. **b** *tr.* cause to rot or decompose. **2** *intr.* & *tr.* decline or cause to decline in quality, power, wealth, energy, beauty, etc. **3** *intr.* *Physics* **a** (usu. foll. by *to*) (of a substance etc.) undergo change by radioactivity. **b** undergo a gradual decrease in magnitude of a physical quantity. —*n.* **1** a rotten or ruinous state; a process of wasting away. **2** decline in health, quality, etc. **3** *Physics* **a** change into another substance etc. by radioactivity. **b** a decrease in the magnitude of a physical quantity, esp. the intensity of radiation or amplitude of oscillation. **4** decayed tissue. ▢▢ **decayable** *adj.* [ME f. OF *decair* f. Rmc (as DE-, L *cadere* fall)]

decease /dɪ'si:s/ *n.* & *v.* formal esp. *Law* —*n.* death. —*v.intr.* die. [ME f. OF *deces* f. L *decessus* f. *decedere* (as DE-, *cedere cess-* go)]

deceased /dɪ'si:st/ *adj.* & *n.* formal —*adj.* dead. —*n.* (usu. prec. by *the*) a person who has died, esp. recently.

decedent /dɪ'si:d(ə)nt/ *n.* US *Law* a deceased person. [L *decedere* die: see DECEASE]

deceit /dɪ'si:t/ *n.* **1** the act or process of deceiving or misleading, esp. by concealing the truth. **2** a dishonest trick or stratagem. **3** willingness to deceive. [ME f. OF f. past part. of *deceveir* f. L *decipere* deceive (as DE-, *capere* take)]

deceitful /dɪ'si:tfʊl/ *adj.* **1** (of a person) using deceit, esp. habitually. **2** (of an act, practice, etc.) intended to deceive. ▢▢ **deceitfully** *adv.* **deceitfulness** *n.*

deceive /dɪ'si:v/ *v.* **1** *tr.* make (a person) believe what is false, mislead purposely. **2** *tr.* be unfaithful to, esp. sexually. **3** *intr.* use deceit. **4** *tr.* archaic disappoint (esp. hopes). ▢**be deceived** be mistaken or deluded. **deceive oneself** persist in a mistaken belief. ▢▢ **deceivable** *adj.* **deceiver** *n.* [ME f. OF *deceivre* or *deceiv-* stressed stem of *deceveir* (as DECEIT)]

decelerate /di:'selə,reɪt/ *v.* **1** *intr.* & *tr.* begin or cause to begin to reduce speed. **2** *tr.* make slower (*decelerated motion*). ▢▢ **deceleration** /-'reɪʃ(ə)n/ *n.* **decelerator** *n.* **decelerometer** /-'rɒmɪtə(r)/ *n.* [DE-, after ACCELERATE]

December /dɪ'sembə(r)/ *n.* the twelfth month of the year. [ME f. OF *decembre* f. L *December* f. *decem* ten: orig. the tenth month of the Roman year]

decency /'di:sənsɪ/ *n.* (*pl.* **-ies**) **1** correct and tasteful standards of behaviour as generally accepted. **2** conformity with current standards of behaviour or propriety. **3** avoidance of obscenity. **4** (in *pl.*) the requirements of correct behaviour. [L *decentia* f. *decēre* be fitting]

decennial /dɪ'senɪ(ə)l/ *adj.* **1** lasting ten years. **2** recurring every ten years. ▢▢ **decennially** *adv.* [L *decennis* of ten years f. *decem* ten + *annus* year]

decent /'di:s(ə)nt/ *adj.* **1 a** conforming with current standards of behaviour or propriety. **b** avoiding obscenity. **2** respectable. **3** acceptable, passable; good enough. **4** *Brit.* kind, obliging, generous (*was decent enough to apologize*). ▢▢ **decently** *adv.* [F *décent* or L *decēre* be fitting]

decentralize /di:'sentrə,laɪz/ *v.tr.* (also **-ise**) **1** transfer (powers etc.) from a central to a local authority. **2** reorganize (a centralized institution, organization, etc.) on the basis of greater local autonomy. ▢▢ **decentralist** /-lɪst/ *n.* & *adj.* **decentralization** /-'zeɪʃ(ə)n/ *n.*

deception /dɪ'sepʃ(ə)n/ *n.* **1** the act or an instance of deceiving; the process of being deceived. **2** a thing that deceives; a trick or sham. [ME f. OF or LL *deceptio* f. *decipere* (as DECEIT)]

deceptive /dɪ'septɪv/ *adj.* apt to deceive; easily mistaken for something else or as having a different quality. ▢▢ **deceptively** *adv.* **deceptiveness** *n.* [OF *deceptif -ive* or LL *deceptivus* (as DECEPTION)]

decerebrate /di:'serɪbrət/ *adj.* having had the cerebrum removed.

deci- /'desɪ/ *comb. form* one-tenth, esp. of a unit in the metric system (*decilitre*; *decimetre*). [L *decimus* tenth]

decibel /'desɪ,bel/ *n.* a unit (one-tenth of a bel) used in the comparison of two power levels relating to electrical signals or sound intensities, one of the pair usually being taken as a standard. ¶ Abbr.: **dB**.

decide /dɪ'saɪd/ *v.* **1 a** *intr.* (often foll. by *on*, *about*) come to a resolution as a result of consideration. **b** *tr.* (usu. foll. by *to* + infin., or *that* + clause) have or reach as one's resolution about something (*decided to stay*; *decided that we should leave*). **2** *tr.* **a** cause (a person) to reach a resolution (*was unsure about going but the weather decided me*). **b** resolve or settle (a question, dispute, etc.). **3** *intr.* (usu. foll. by *between*, *for*, *against*, *in favour of*, or *that* + clause) give a judgement concerning a matter. ▢▢ **decidable** *adj.* [ME f. F *décider* or f. L *decidere* (as DE-, *cædere* cut)]

decided /dɪ'saɪdɪd/ *adj.* **1** (usu. *attrib.*) definite, unquestionable (*a decided difference*). **2** (of a person, esp. as a characteristic) having clear opinions, resolute, not vacillating. ▢▢ **decidedness** *n.*

decidedly /dɪ'saɪdɪdlɪ/ *adv.* undoubtedly, undeniably.

decider /dɪ'saɪdə(r)/ *n.* **1** a game, race, etc., to decide between competitors finishing equal in a previous contest. **2** any person or thing that decides.

deciduous /dɪ'sɪdjʊəs/ *adj.* **1** (of a tree) shedding its leaves annually. **2** (of leaves, horns, teeth, etc.) shed periodically. **3** (of an ant etc.) shedding its wings after copulation. **4** fleeting, transitory. ▢▢ **deciduousness** *n.* [L *deciduus* f. *decidere* f. *cadere* fall]

decigram /'desɪ,græm/ *n.* (also **decigramme**) a metric unit of mass, equal to 0.1 gram.

decile /'desɪl, -saɪl/ *n.* *Statistics* any of the nine values of a random variable which divide a frequency distribution into ten groups, each containing one-tenth of the total population. [F *décile*, ult. f. L *decem* ten]

decilitre /'desɪ,li:tə(r)/ *n.* a metric unit of capacity, equal to 0.1 litre.

decimal /'desɪm(ə)l/ *adj.* & *n.* —*adj.* **1** (of a system of numbers, weights, measures, etc.) based on the number ten, in which the smaller units are related to the principal units as powers of ten (units, tens, hundreds, thousands, etc.). **2** of tenths or ten; reckoning or proceeding by tens. —*n.* a decimal fraction. ▢**decimal fraction** a fraction whose denominator is a power of ten, esp. when expressed positionally by units to the right of a decimal point. **decimal point** a full point or dot placed before a numerator in a decimal fraction. **decimal scale** a scale with successive places denoting units, tens, hundreds, etc. ▢▢ **decimally** *adv.* [mod.L *decimalis* f. L *decimus* tenth]

decimalize /'desɪmə‚laɪz/ v.tr. (also **-ise**) **1** express as a decimal. **2** convert to a decimal system (esp. of coinage). □□ **decimalization** /-'zeɪʃ(ə)n/ n.

decimate /'desɪ‚meɪt/ v.tr. **1** disp. destroy a large proportion of. ¶ Now the usual sense, although often deplored as an inappropriate use. **2** orig. Mil. kill or remove one in every ten of. □□ **decimation** /-'meɪʃ(ə)n/ n. **decimator** n. [L decimare take the tenth man f. decimus tenth]

decimetre /'desɪ‚miːtə(r)/ n. a metric unit of length, equal to 0.1 metre.

decipher /dɪ'saɪfə(r)/ v.tr. **1** convert (a text written in cipher) into an intelligible script or language. **2** determine the meaning of (anything obscure or unclear). □□ **decipherable** adj. **decipherment** n.

decision /dɪ'sɪʒ(ə)n/ n. **1** the act or process of deciding. **2** a conclusion or resolution reached, esp. as to future action, after consideration (have made my decision). **3** (often foll. by of) **a** the settlement of a question. **b** a formal judgement. **4** a tendency to decide firmly; resoluteness. [ME f. OF decision or L decisio (as DECIDE)]

decisive /dɪ'saɪsɪv/ adj. **1** that decides an issue; conclusive. **2** (of a person, esp. as a characteristic) able to decide quickly and effectively. □□ **decisively** adv. **decisiveness** n. [F décisif -ive f. med.L decisivus (as DECIDE)]

deck /dek/ n. & v. —n. **1 a** a platform in a ship covering all or part of the hull's area at any level and serving as a floor. **b** the accommodation on a particular deck of a ship. **2** anything compared to a ship's deck, e.g. the floor or compartment of a bus. **3** a component, usu. a flat horizontal surface, that carries a particular recording medium (such as a disc or tape) in sound-reproduction equipment. **4** US **a** a pack of cards. **b** sl. a packet of narcotics. **5** sl. the ground. **6** any floor or platform, esp. the floor of a pier or a platform for sunbathing. —v.tr. **1** (often foll. by out) decorate, adorn. **2** furnish with or cover as a deck. □ **below deck** (or **decks**) in or into the space below the main deck. **deck-chair** a folding chair of wood and canvas, of a kind used on deck on passenger ships. **deck-hand** a person employed in cleaning and odd jobs on a ship's deck. **deck quoits** a game in which rope quoits are aimed at a peg. **deck tennis** a game in which a quoit of rope, rubber, etc., is tossed to and fro over a net. **on deck 1** in the open air on a ship's main deck. **2** esp. US ready for action, work, etc. [ME, = covering f. MDu. dec roof, cloak]

-decker /'dekə(r)/ comb. form having a specified number of decks or layers (double-decker).

deckle /'dek(ə)l/ n. a device in a paper-making machine for limiting the size of the sheet. □ **deckle-edge** the rough uncut edge formed by a deckle. □□ **deckle-edged** adj. [G Deckel dimin. of Decke cover]

declaim /dɪ'kleɪm/ v. **1** intr. & tr. speak or utter rhetorically or affectedly. **2** intr. practise oratory or recitation. **3** intr. (foll. by against) protest forcefully. **4** intr. deliver an impassioned (rather than reasoned) speech. □□ **declaimer** n. [ME f. F déclamer or f. L declamare (as DE-, CLAIM)]

declamation /‚deklə'meɪʃ(ə)n/ n. **1** the act or art of declaiming. **2** a rhetorical exercise or set speech. **3** an impassioned speech; a harangue. □□ **declamatory** /dɪ'klæmətərɪ/ adj. [F déclamation or L declamatio (as DECLAIM)]

declarant /dɪ'kleərənt/ n. a person who makes a legal declaration. [F déclarant part. of déclarer (as DECLARE)]

declaration /‚deklə'reɪʃ(ə)n/ n. **1** the act or process of declaring. **2 a** a formal, emphatic, or deliberate statement or announcement. **b** a statement asserting or protecting a legal right. **3** a written public announcement of intentions, terms of an agreement, etc. **4** Cricket an act of declaring an innings closed. **5** Cards **a** the naming of trumps. **b** an announcement

of a combination held. **6** Law **a** a plaintiff's statement of claim. **b** an affirmation made instead of taking an oath. **7** (in full **declaration of the poll**) a public official announcement of the votes cast for candidates in an election. [ME f. L declaratio (as DECLARE)]

declare /dɪ'kleə(r)/ v. **1** tr. announce openly or formally (declare war; declare a dividend). **2** tr. pronounce (a person or thing) to be something (declared him to be an impostor; declared it invalid). **3** tr. (usu. foll. by that + clause) assert emphatically; state explicitly. **4** tr. acknowledge possession of (dutiable goods, income, etc.). **5** tr. (as **declared** adj.) who admits to be such (a declared atheist). **6** tr. (also absol.) Cricket close (an innings) voluntarily before all the wickets have fallen. **7** tr. Cards **a** (also absol.) name (the trump suit). **b** announce that one holds (certain combinations of cards etc.). **8** tr. (of things) make evident, prove (your actions declare your honesty). **9** intr. (foll. by for, against) take the side of one party or another. □ **declare oneself** reveal one's intentions or identity. **well, I declare** (or **I do declare**) an exclamation of incredulity, surprise, or vexation. □□ **declarable** adj. **declarative** /-'klærətɪv/ adj. **declaratively** /-'klærətɪvlɪ/ adv. **declaratory** /-'klærətərɪ/ adj. **declaredly** /-rɪdlɪ/ adv. **declarer** n. [ME f. L declarare (as DE-, clarare f. clarus clear)]

déclassé /deɪ'klæseɪ/ adj. (fem. **déclassée**) that has fallen in social status. [F]

declassify /diː'klæsɪ‚faɪ/ v.tr. (**-ies**, **-ied**) declare (information etc.) to be no longer secret. □□ **declassification** /-fɪ'keɪʃ(ə)n/ n.

declension /dɪ'klenʃ(ə)n/ n. **1** Gram. **a** the variation of the form of a noun, pronoun, or adjective, by which its grammatical case, number, and gender are identified. **b** the class in which a noun etc. is put according to the exact form of this variation. **2** deterioration, declining. □□ **declensional** adj. [OF declinaison f. decliner DECLINE after L declinatio: assim. to ASCENSION etc.]

declination /‚deklɪ'neɪʃ(ə)n/ n. **1** a downward bend or turn. **2** Astron. the angular distance of a star etc. north or south of the celestial equator. **3** Physics the angular deviation of a compass needle from true north. **4** US a formal refusal. □□ **declinational** adj. [ME f. L declinatio (as DECLINE)]

decline /dɪ'klaɪn/ v. & n. —v. **1** intr. deteriorate; lose strength or vigour; decrease. **2 a** tr. reply with formal courtesy that one will not accept (an invitation, honour, etc.). **b** tr. refuse, esp. formally and courteously (declined to make use of; declined doing anything). **c** tr. turn away from (a challenge, battle, discussion, etc.). **d** intr. give or send a refusal. **3** intr. slope downwards. **4** intr. bend down, droop. **5** tr. Gram. state the forms of (a noun, pronoun, or adjective) corresponding to cases, number, and gender. **6** intr. (of a day, life, etc.) draw to a close. **7** intr. decrease in price etc. **8** tr. bend down. —n. **1** gradual loss of vigour or excellence (on the decline). **2** decay, deterioration. **3** setting; the last part of the course (of the sun, of life, etc.). **4** a fall in price. **5** archaic tuberculosis or a similar wasting disease. □ **declining years** old age. □□ **declinable** adj. **decliner** n. [ME f. OF decliner f. L declinare (as DE-, clinare bend)]

declivity /dɪ'klɪvɪtɪ/ n. (pl. **-ies**) a downward slope, esp. a piece of sloping ground. □□ **declivitous** adj. [L declivitas f. declivis (as DE-, clivus slope)]

declutch /diː'klʌtʃ/ v.intr. disengage the clutch of a motor vehicle. □ **double-declutch** release and re-engage the clutch twice when changing gear.

Deco /'dekəʊ/ n. (also **deco**) (usu. attrib.) = art deco. [F décoratif DECORATIVE]

decoct /dɪ'kɒkt/ v.tr. extract the essence from by decoction. [ME f. L decoquere boil down]

decoction /dɪ'kɒkʃ(ə)n/ n. **1** a process of boiling down so as to extract some essence. **2** the extracted liquor resulting from this. [ME f. OF *decoction* or LL *decoctio* (as DE-, L *coquere coct-* boil)]

decode /diːˈkəʊd/ *v.tr.* convert (a coded message) into intelligible language. □□ **decodable** *adj.*

decoder /diːˈkəʊdə(r)/ *n.* **1** a person or thing that decodes. **2** an electronic device for analysing signals and feeding separate amplifier-channels.

decoke *v.* & *n. Brit. colloq.* —*v.tr.* /diːˈkəʊk/ remove carbon or carbonaceous material from (an internal-combustion engine). —*n.* /ˈdiːkəʊk/ the process of decoking.

decollate /dɪˈkɒleɪt/ *v.tr. formal* **1** behead. **2** truncate. □□ **decollation** /ˌdiːkɒˈleɪʃ(ə)n/ *n.* [L *decollare decollat-* (as DE-, *collum* neck)]

décolletage /ˌdeɪkɒlˈtɑːʒ/ *n.* a low neckline of a woman's dress etc. [F (as DE-, *collet* collar of a dress)]

décolleté /deɪˈkɒlteɪ/ *adj.* & *n.* —*adj.* (also **décolletée**) **1** (of a dress etc.) having a low neckline. **2** (of a woman) wearing a dress with a low neckline. —*n.* a low neckline. [F (as DÉCOLLETAGE)]

decolonize /diːˈkɒləˌnaɪz/ *v.tr.* (also **-ise**) (of a State) withdraw from (a colony), leaving it independent. □□ **decolonization** /-ˈzeɪʃ(ə)n/ *n.*

decolorize /diːˈkʌləˌraɪz/ *v.* (also **-ise**) **1** *tr.* remove the colour from. **2** *intr.* lose colour. □□ **decolorization** /-ˈzeɪʃ(ə)n/ *n.*

decommission /ˌdiːkəˈmɪʃ(ə)n/ *v.tr.* **1** close down (a nuclear reactor etc.). **2** take (a ship) out of service.

decompose /ˌdiːkəmˈpəʊz/ *v.* **1** *intr.* decay, rot. **2** *tr.* separate (a substance, light, etc.) into its elements or simpler constituents. **3** *intr.* disintegrate; break up. □□ **decomposition** /ˌdiːkɒmpəˈzɪʃ(ə)n/ *n.* [F *décomposer* (as DE-, COMPOSE)]

decompress /ˌdiːkəmˈpres/ *v.tr.* subject to decompression; relieve or reduce the compression on.

decompression /ˌdiːkəmˈpreʃ(ə)n/ *n.* **1** release from compression. **2** a gradual reduction of air pressure on a person who has been subjected to high pressure (esp. underwater). □**decompression chamber** an enclosed space for subjecting a person to decompression. **decompression sickness** a condition caused by the sudden lowering of air pressure and formation of bubbles in the blood: also called *caisson disease, the bends* (see BEND 14).

decompressor /ˌdiːkəmˈpresə(r)/ *n.* a device for reducing pressure in the engine of a motor vehicle.

decongestant /ˌdiːkənˈdʒest(ə)nt/ *adj.* & *n.* —*adj.* that relieves (esp. nasal) congestion. —*n.* a medicinal agent that relieves nasal congestion.

deconsecrate /diːˈkɒnsɪˌkreɪt/ *v.tr.* transfer (esp. a building) from sacred to secular use. □□ **deconsecration** /-ˈkreɪʃ(ə)n/ *n.*

deconstruct /ˌdiːkənˈstrʌkt/ *v.tr.* subject to deconstruction. □□ **deconstructive** *adj.* [back-form. f. DECONSTRUCTION]

deconstruction /ˌdiːkənˈstrʌkʃ(ə)n/ *n.* a method of critical analysis of philosophical and literary language. □□ **deconstructionism** *n.* **deconstructionist** *adj.* & *n.* [F *déconstruction* (as DE-, CONSTRUCTION)]

decontaminate /ˌdiːkənˈtæmɪˌneɪt/ *v.tr.* remove contamination from (an area, person, clothes, etc.). □□ **decontamination** /-ˈneɪʃ(ə)n/ *n.*

decontrol /ˌdiːkənˈtrəʊl/ *v.* & *n.* —*v.tr.* (**decontrolled, decontrolling**) release (a commodity etc.) from controls or restrictions, esp. those imposed by the State. —*n.* the act of decontrolling.

décor /ˈdeɪkɔː(r), ˈde-/ *n.* **1** the furnishing and decoration of a room etc. **2** the decoration and scenery of a stage. [F f. *décorer* (as DECORATE)]

decorate /ˈdekəˌreɪt/ *v.tr.* **1** provide with adornments. **2** provide (a room or building) with new paint, wallpaper, etc. **3** serve as an adornment to. **4** confer an award or distinction on. □**Decorated style** *Archit.* the second stage of English Gothic (14th c.), with increasing use of decoration and geometrical tracery. [L *decorare decorat-* f. *decus -oris* beauty]

decoration /ˌdekəˈreɪʃ(ə)n/ *n.* **1** the process or art of

decorating. **2** a thing that decorates or serves as an ornament. **3** a medal etc. conferred and worn as an honour. **4** (in *pl.*) flags etc. put up on an occasion of public celebration. □**Decoration Day** *US* Memorial Day. [F *décoration* or LL *decoratio* (as DECORATE)]

decorative /ˈdekərətɪv/ *adj.* serving to decorate. □□ **decoratively** *adv.* **decorativeness** *n.* [F *décoratif* (as DECORATE)]

decorator /ˈdekəˌreɪtə(r)/ *n.* a person who decorates, esp. one who paints or papers houses professionally.

decorous /ˈdekərəs/ *adj.* **1** respecting good taste or propriety. **2** dignified and decent. □□ **decorously** *adv.* **decorousness** *n.* [L *decorus* seemly]

decorticate /diːˈkɔːtɪˌkeɪt/ *v.tr.* **1** remove the bark, rind, or husk from. **2** remove the outside layer from (the kidney, brain, etc.). [L *decorticare decorticat-* (as DE-, *cortex -icis* bark)]

decortication /diːˌkɔːtɪˈkeɪʃ(ə)n/ *n.* **1** the removal of the outside layer from an organ (e.g. the kidney) or structure. **2** an operation removing the blood clot and scar tissue formed after bleeding in the chest cavity.

decorum /dɪˈkɔːrəm/ *n.* **1 a** seemliness, propriety. **b** behaviour required by politeness or decency. **2** a particular requirement of this kind. **3** etiquette. [L, neut. of *decorus* seemly]

découpage /ˌdeɪkuːˈpɑːʒ/ *n.* the decoration of surfaces with paper cut-outs. [F, = the action of cutting out]

decouple /diːˈkʌp(ə)l/ *v.tr.* **1** *Electr.* make the interaction between (oscillators etc.) so weak that there is little transfer of energy between them. **2** separate, disengage, dissociate.

decoy *n.* & *v.* —*n.* /ˈdiːkɔɪ, dɪˈkɔɪ/ **1 a** a person or thing used to lure an animal or person into a trap or danger. **b** a bait or enticement. **2** a pond with narrow netted arms into which wild duck may be tempted in order to catch them. —*v.tr.* /dɪˈkɔɪ, ˈdiːkɔɪ/ (often foll. by *into, out of*) allure or entice, esp. by means of a decoy. [17th c.: perh. f. Du. *de kooi* the decoy f. *de* THE + *kooi* f. L *cavea* cage]

decrease *v.* & *n.* —*v.tr.* & *intr.* /dɪˈkriːs/ make or become smaller or fewer. —*n.* /ˈdiːkriːs/ **1** the act or an instance of decreasing. **2** the amount by which a thing decreases. □□ **decreasingly** *adv.* [ME f. OF *de(s)creiss-*, pres. stem of *de(s)creistre* ult. f. L *decrescere* (as DE-, *crescere cret-* grow)]

decree /dɪˈkriː/ *n.* & *v.* —*n.* **1** an official order issued by a legal authority. **2** a judgement or decision of certain lawcourts, esp. in matrimonial cases. —*v.tr.* (**decrees, decreed, decreeing**) ordain by decree. □**decree absolute** a final order for divorce, enabling either party to remarry. **decree nisi** a provisional order for divorce, made absolute unless cause to the contrary is shown within a fixed period. [ME f. OF *decré* f. L *decretum* neut. past part. of *decernere* decide (as DE-, *cernere* sift)]

decrement /ˈdekrɪmənt/ *n.* **1** *Physics* the ratio of the amplitudes in successive cycles of a damped oscillation. **2** the amount lost by diminution or waste. **3** the act of decreasing. [L *decrementum* (as DECREASE)]

decrepit /dɪˈkrepɪt/ *adj.* **1** weakened or worn out by age and infirmity. **2** worn out by long use; dilapidated. □□ **decrepitude** *n.* [ME f. L *decrepitus* (as DE-, *crepitus* past part. of *crepare* creak)]

decrepitate /dɪˈkrepɪˌteɪt/ *v.* **1** *tr.* roast or calcine (a mineral or salt) until it stops crackling. **2** *intr.* crackle under heat. □□ **decrepitation** /-ˈteɪʃ(ə)n/ *n.* [prob. mod.L *decrepitare* f. DE- + L *crepitare* crackle]

decrescendo /ˌdiːkreˈʃendəʊ, ˌdeɪkrɪ-/ *adv., adj.,* & *n.* (*pl.* **-os**) = DIMINUENDO. [It., part. of *decrescere* DECREASE]

decrescent /dɪˈkres(ə)nt/ *adj.* (usu. of the moon) waning, decreasing. [L *decrescere*: see DECREASE]

decretal /dɪˈkriːt(ə)l/ *n.* **1** a papal decree. **2** (in *pl.*) a collection of these, forming part of canon law. [ME f. med.L *decretale* f. LL (*epistola*) *decretalis* (letter) of decree f. L *decernere*: see DECREE]

decriminalize /diːˈkrɪmɪnəˌlaɪz/ *v.tr.* (also **-ise**)

cease to treat (an action etc.) as criminal. □□
decriminalization /-'zeɪʃ(ə)n/ n.
decry /dɪ'kraɪ/ v.tr. (-ies, -ied) disparage, belittle. □□
decrier n. [after F *décrier*: cf. *cry down*]
decrypt /di:'krɪpt/ v.tr. decipher (a cryptogram),
with or without knowledge of its key. □□ **decryption**
n. [DE- + CRYPTOGRAM]
decumbent /dɪ'kʌmbənt/ adj. Bot. & Zool. (of a
plant, shoot, or bristles) lying along the ground or a
surface. [L *decumbere decumbent-* lie down]
decurve /di:'kɜːv/ v.tr. & intr. Zool. & Bot. (esp. as
decurved adj.) curve or bend down (*a decurved bill*).
□□ **decurvature** n.
decussate /di:'kʌseɪt/ adj. & v. —adj. 1 X-shaped. 2
Bot. with pairs of opposite leaves etc. each at right
angles to the pair below. —v.tr. & intr. 1 arrange or
be arranged in a decussate form. 2 intersect. □□
decussation /-'seɪʃ(ə)n/ n. [L *decussatus* past part.
of *decussare* divide in a cross shape f. *decussis* the
numeral ten or the shape X f. *decem* ten]
dedans /də'dɑ̃/ n. 1 (in real tennis) the open gallery at
the end of the service side of a court. 2 the spectators
watching a match. [F, = inside]
dedicate /'dedɪ,keɪt/ v.tr. 1 (foll. by *to*) devote (esp.
oneself) to a special task or purpose. 2 (foll. by *to*)
address (a book, piece of music, etc.) as a compliment
to a friend, patron, etc. 3 (often foll. by *to*) devote (a
building etc.) to a deity or a sacred person or purpose.
4 (as **dedicated** adj.) **a** (of a person) devoted to an
aim or vocation; having single-minded loyalty or
integrity. **b** (of equipment, esp. a computer) designed
for a specific purpose. □□ **dedicatee** /-kə'ti:/ n.
dedicative adj. **dedicator** n. **dedicatory** adj. [L
dedicare (DE-, *dicare* declare, dedicate)]
dedication /,dedɪ'keɪʃ(ə)n/ n. 1 the act or an instance
of dedicating; the process of being dedicated. 2 the
words with which a book etc. is dedicated. 3 a
dedicatory inscription. [ME f. OF *dedicacion* or L
dedicatio (as DEDICATE)]
deduce /dɪ'dju:s/ v.tr. 1 (often foll. by *from*) infer;
draw as a logical conclusion. 2 archaic trace the
course or derivation of. □□ **deducible** adj. [L *deducere*
(as DE-, *ducere duct-* lead)]
deduct /dɪ'dʌkt/ v.tr. (often foll. by *from*) subtract,
take away, withhold (an amount, portion, etc.). [L
(as DEDUCE)]
deductible /dɪ'dʌktɪb(ə)l/ adj. & n. —adj. that may
be deducted, esp. from tax to be paid or taxable
income. —n. US = EXCESS n. 6.
deduction /dɪ'dʌkʃ(ə)n/ n. 1 **a** the act of deducting.
b an amount deducted. 2 **a** the inferring of particular
instances from a general law (cf. INDUCTION). **b** a
conclusion deduced. [ME f. OF *deduction* or L *de-
ductio* (as DEDUCE)]
deductive /dɪ'dʌktɪv/ adj. of or reasoning by
deduction. □□ **deductively** adv. [med.L *deductivus*
(as DEDUCE)]
dee /di:/ n. 1 the letter D. 2 **a** a thing shaped like this.
b Physics either of two hollow semicircular electrodes
in a cyclotron. [the name of the letter]
deed /di:d/ n. & v. —n. 1 a thing done intentionally
or consciously. 2 a brave, skilful, or conspicuous act.
3 actual fact or performance (*kind in word and deed*;
in deed and not in name). 4 Law a written or printed
document often used for a legal transfer of ownership
and bearing the disposer's signature. —v.tr. US
convey or transfer by legal deed. □**deed-box** a strong
box for keeping deeds and other documents. **deed of
covenant** an agreement to pay a specified amount
regularly to a charity etc., enabling the recipient to
recover the tax paid by the donor on an equivalent
amount of income. **deed poll** a deed made and
executed by one party only, esp. to change one's
name (the paper being polled or cut even, not
indented). [OE *dēd* f. Gmc: rel. to DO[1]]
deejay /di:'dʒeɪ/ n. sl. a disc jockey. [abbr. *DJ*]
deem /di:m/ v.tr. formal regard, consider, judge
(*deem it my duty*; *was deemed sufficient*). [OE *dēman*
f. Gmc, rel. to DOOM]
de-emphasize /di:'emfə,saɪz/ v.tr. (also **-ise**) 1 remove emphasis from. 2 reduce emphasis on.
deemster /'di:mstə(r)/ n. a judge in the Isle of Man.
[DEEM + -STER]
deep /di:p/ adj., n., & adv. —adj. 1 **a** extending far
down from the top (*deep hole*; *deep water*). **b** extending
far in from the surface or edge (*deep wound*; *deep
plunge*; *deep shelf*; *deep border*). 2 (predic.) **a** extending to or lying at a specified depth (*water 6 feet
deep*; *ankle-deep in mud*). **b** in a specified number of
ranks one behind another (*soldiers drawn up six
deep*). 3 situated far down or back or in (*hands deep
in his pockets*). 4 coming or brought from far
down or in (*deep breath*; *deep sigh*). 5 low-pitched,
full-toned, not shrill (*deep voice*; *deep note*; *deep bell*).
6 intense, vivid, extreme (*deep disgrace*; *deep sleep*;
deep colour; *deep secret*). 7 heartfelt, absorbing (*deep
affection*; *deep feelings*; *deep interest*). 8 (predic.) fully
absorbed or overwhelmed (*deep in a book*; *deep
in debt*). 9 profound, penetrating, not superficial;
difficult to understand (*deep thinker*; *deep thought*;
deep insight; *deep learning*). 10 Cricket distant from
the batsman (*deep mid-off*). 11 Football distant from
the front line of one's team. 12 sl. cunning or
secretive (*a deep one*). —n. 1 (prec. by *the*) poet. the
sea. 2 a deep part of the sea. 3 an abyss, pit, or
cavity. 4 (prec. by *the*) Cricket the position of a fielder
distant from the batsman. 5 a deep state (*deep of the
night*). 6 poet. a mysterious region of thought or
feeling. —adv. deeply; far down or in (*dig deep*; *read
deep into the night*). □**deep breathing** breathing
with long breaths, esp. as a form of exercise.
deep-drawn (of metal etc.) shaped by forcing
through a die when cold. **deep-fry** (**-fries**, **-fried**)
fry (food) in an amount of fat or oil sufficient to cover
it. **deep kiss** a kiss with contact between tongues.
deep-laid (of a scheme) secret and elaborate. **deep
mourning** mourning expressed by wearing only
black clothes. **deep-mouthed** (esp. of a dog) having
a deep voice. **deep-rooted** (esp. of convictions) firmly
established. **deep sea** the deeper parts of the ocean.
deep-seated (of emotion, disease, etc.) firmly
established, profound. **Deep South** the States of the
US bordering the Gulf of Mexico. **deep space** the
regions beyond the solar system or the earth's
atmosphere. **deep therapy** curative treatment with
short-wave X-rays of high penetrating power. **go off**
(or **go in off**) **the deep end** colloq. give way to anger
or emotion. **in deep water** (or **waters**) in trouble or
difficulty. **jump** (or **be thrown**) **in at the deep end**
face a difficult problem, undertaking, etc., with little
experience of it. □□ **deeply** adv. **deepness** n. [OE
dēop (adj.), *dīope*, *dēope* (adv.), f. Gmc: rel. to DIP]
deepen /'di:pən/ v.tr. & intr. make or become deep or
deeper.
deep-freeze /di:p'fri:z/ n. & v. —n. 1 a refrigerator
in which food can be quickly frozen and kept for long
periods at a very low temperature. 2 a suspension of
activity. —v.tr. (**-froze**, **-frozen**) freeze or store
(food) in a deep-freeze.
deer /dɪə(r)/ n. (pl. same) any four-hoofed grazing
animal of the family Cervidae, the males of which
usu. have deciduous branching antlers. □**deer fly**
any bloodsucking fly of the genus *Chrysops*.
deer-forest an extensive area of wild land reserved
for the stalking of deer. **deer-hound** a large
rough-haired greyhound. **deer-lick** a spring or damp
spot impregnated with salt etc. where deer come to
lick. [OE *dēor* animal, deer]
deerskin /'dɪəskɪn/ n. & adj. —n. leather from a
deer's skin. —adj. made from a deer's skin.
deerstalker /'dɪə,stɔ:kə(r)/ n. 1 a soft cloth cap with
peaks in front and behind and ear-flaps often joined
at the top. 2 a person who stalks deer.
de-escalate /di:'eskə,leɪt/ v.tr. reduce the level or
intensity of. □□ **de-escalation** /-'leɪʃ(ə)n/ n.

æ cat ɑː arm e bed ɜː her ɪ sit iː see ɒ hot ɔː saw ʌ run ʊ put uː too ə ago aɪ my

deface /dɪˈfeɪs/ v.tr. **1** spoil the appearance of; disfigure. **2** make illegible. □□ **defaceable** adj. **defacement** n. **defacer** n. [ME f. F défacer f. OF desfacier (as DE-, FACE)]

de facto /diː ˈfæktəʊ, deɪ/ adv., adj., & n. —adv. in fact, whether by right or not. —adj. that exists or is such in fact (a de facto ruler). —n. (in full **de facto wife** or **husband**) a person living with another as if married. [L]

defalcate /ˈdiːfælˌkeɪt/ v.intr. formal misappropriate property in one's charge, esp. money. □□ **defalcator** n. [med.L defalcare lop (as DE-, L falx -cis sickle)]

defalcation /ˌdiːfælˈkeɪʃ(ə)n/ n. formal **1** Law **a** a misappropriation of money. **b** an amount misappropriated. **2** a shortcoming. **3** defection. [ME f. med.L defalcatio (as DEFALCATE)]

defame /dɪˈfeɪm/ v.tr. attack the good reputation of; speak ill of. □□ **defamation** /ˌdefəˈmeɪʃ(ə)n, ˌdiːf-/ n. **defamatory** /dɪˈfæmətərɪ/ adj. **defamer** n. [ME f. OF diffamer etc. f. L diffamare spread evil report (as DIS-, fama report)]

defat /diːˈfæt/ v.tr. (**defatted, defatting**) remove fat or fats from.

default /dɪˈfɔːlt, -ˈfɒlt/ n. & v. —n. **1** failure to fulfil an obligation, esp. to appear, pay, or act in some way. **2** lack, absence. **3** a preselected option adopted by a computer program when no alternative is specified by the user or programmer. —v. **1** intr. fail to fulfil an obligation, esp. to pay money or to appear in a lawcourt. **2** tr. declare (a party) in default and give judgement against that party. □ **go by default 1** be ignored because of absence. **2** be absent. **in default of** because of the absence of. **judgement by default** judgement given for the plaintiff on the defendant's failure to plead. **win by default** win because an opponent fails to be present. [ME f. OF defaut(e) f. defaillir fail f. Rmc (as DE-, L fallere deceive): cf. FAIL]

defaulter /dɪˈfɔːltə(r), -ˈfɒltə(r)/ n. a person who defaults, esp. Brit. a soldier guilty of a military offence.

defeasance /dɪˈfiːz(ə)ns/ n. the act or process of rendering null and void. [ME f. OF defesance f. de(s)faire undo (as DE-, faire make f. L facere)]

defeasible /dɪˈfiːzɪb(ə)l/ adj. **1** capable of annulment. **2** liable to forfeiture. □□ **defeasibility** /-ˈbɪlɪtɪ/ n. **defeasibly** adv. [AF (as DEFEASANCE)]

defeat /dɪˈfiːt/ v. & n. —v.tr. **1** overcome in a battle or other contest. **2** frustrate, baffle. **3** reject (a motion etc.) by voting. **4** Law annul. —n. the act or process of defeating or being defeated. [ME f. OF deffait, desfait past part. of desfaire f. med.L disfacere (as DIS-, L facere do)]

defeatism /dɪˈfiːtɪz(ə)m/ n. **1** an excessive readiness to accept defeat. **2** conduct conducive to this. □□ **defeatist** n. & adj. [F défaitisme f. défaite DEFEAT]

defecate /ˈdefɪˌkeɪt/ v.intr. discharge faeces from the body. □□ **defecation** /-ˈkeɪʃ(ə)n/ n. [earlier as adj., = purified, f. L defaecare (as faex faecis dregs)]

defect /dɪˈfekt/ n. & v. —n. /also ˈdiːfekt/ **1** lack of something essential or required; imperfection. **2** a shortcoming or failing. **3** a blemish. **4** the amount by which a thing falls short. —v.intr. abandon one's country or cause in favour of another. □□ **defector** n. [L defectus f. deficere desert, fail (as DE-, facere do)]

defection /dɪˈfekʃ(ə)n/ n. **1** the abandonment of one's country or cause. **2** ceasing in allegiance to a leader, party, religion, or duty. [L defectio (as DEFECT)]

defective /dɪˈfektɪv/ adj. & n. —adj. **1** having a defect or defects; incomplete, imperfect, faulty. **2** mentally subnormal. **3** (usu. foll. by in) lacking, deficient. **4** Gram. not having all the usual inflections. —n. a mentally defective person. □□ **defectively** adv. **defectiveness** n. [ME f. OF defectif -ive or LL defectivus (as DEFECT)]

defence /dɪˈfens/ n. (US **defense**) **1** the act of defending from or resisting attack. **2 a** a means of resisting attack. **b** a thing that protects. **c** the military resources of a country. **3** (in pl.) fortifications. **4 a** justification, vindication. **b** a speech or piece of writing used to this end. **5 a** the defendant's case in a lawsuit. **b** the counsel for the defendant. **6 a** the action or role of defending one's goal etc. against attack. **b** the players in a team who perform this role. □ **defence mechanism 1** the body's reaction against disease organisms. **2** a usu. unconscious mental process to avoid conscious conflict or anxiety. □□ **defenceless** adj. **defencelessly** adv. **defencelessness** n. [ME f. OF defens(e) f. LL defensum, -a, past part. of defendere: see DEFEND]

defend /dɪˈfend/ v.tr. (also absol.) **1** (often foll. by against, from) resist an attack made on; protect (a person or thing) from harm or danger. **2** support or uphold by argument; speak or write in favour of. **3** conduct the case for (a defendant in a lawsuit). □□ **defendable** adj. **defender** n. [ME f. OF defendre f. L defendere: cf. OFFEND]

defendant /dɪˈfend(ə)nt/ n. a person etc. sued or accused in a court of law. [ME f. OF, part. of defendre: see DEFEND]

defenestration /ˌdiːfenɪˈstreɪʃ(ə)n/ n. formal or joc. the action of throwing (esp. a person) out of a window. □□ **defenestrate** /diːˈfenɪˌstreɪt/ v.tr. [mod.L defenestratio (as DE-, L fenestra window)]

defense US var. of DEFENCE.

defensible /dɪˈfensɪb(ə)l/ adj. **1** justifiable; supportable by argument. **2** that can be easily defended militarily. □□ **defensibility** /-ˈbɪlɪtɪ/ n. **defensibly** adv. [ME f. LL defensibilis (as DEFEND)]

defensive /dɪˈfensɪv/ adj. **1** done or intended for defence or to defend. **2** (of a person or attitude) concerned to challenge criticism. □ **on the defensive 1** expecting criticism. **2** in an attitude or position of defence. □□ **defensively** adv. **defensiveness** n. [ME f. F défensif -ive f. med.L defensivus (as DEFEND)]

defer[1] /dɪˈfɜː(r)/ v.tr. (**deferred, deferring**) **1** put off to a later time; postpone. **2** US postpone the conscription of (a person). □ **deferred payment** payment by instalments. □□ **deferment** n. **deferrable** adj. **deferral** n. [ME, orig. the same as DIFFER]

defer[2] /dɪˈfɜː(r)/ v.intr. (**deferred, deferring**) (foll. by to) yield or make concessions in opinion or action. □□ **deferrer** n. [ME f. F déférer f. L deferre (as DE-, ferre bring)]

deference /ˈdefərəns/ n. **1** courteous regard, respect. **2** compliance with the advice or wishes of another (pay deference to). □ **in deference to** out of respect for. [F déférence (as DEFER[2])]

deferential /ˌdefəˈrenʃ(ə)l/ adj. showing deference; respectful. □□ **deferentially** adv. [DEFERENCE, after PRUDENTIAL etc.]

defiance /dɪˈfaɪəns/ n. **1** open disobedience; bold resistance. **2** a challenge to fight or maintain a cause, assertion, etc. □ **in defiance of** disregarding; in conflict with. [ME f. OF (as DEFY)]

defiant /dɪˈfaɪənt/ adj. **1** showing defiance. **2** openly disobedient. □□ **defiantly** adv.

defibrillation /ˌdiːfɪbrɪˈleɪʃ(ə)n/ n. Med. the stopping of the fibrillation of the heart. □□ **defibrillator** /ˌdiːˈfɪbrɪˌleɪtə(r)/ n.

deficiency /dɪˈfɪʃənsɪ/ n. (pl. **-ies**) **1** the state or condition of being deficient. **2** (usu. foll. by of) a lack or shortage. **3** a thing lacking. **4** the amount by which a thing, esp. revenue, falls short. □ **deficiency disease** a disease caused by the lack of some essential or important element in the diet.

deficient /dɪˈfɪʃ(ə)nt/ adj. **1** (usu. foll. by in) incomplete; not having enough of a specified quality or ingredient. **2** insufficient in quantity, force, etc. **3** (in full **mentally deficient**) incapable of adequate social or intellectual behaviour through imperfect mental development. □□ **deficiently** adv. [L deficiens part. of deficere (as DEFECT)]

deficit /ˈdefɪsɪt/ n. **1** the amount by which a thing (esp. a sum of money) is too small. **2** an excess of liabilities over assets in a given period, esp. a financial year (opp. SURPLUS). □**deficit financing** financing of (esp. State) spending by borrowing. **deficit spending** spending, esp. by the State, financed by borrowing. [F *déficit* f. L *deficit* 3rd sing. pres. of *deficere* (as DEFECT)]

defier /dɪˈfaɪə(r)/ *n.* a person who defies.

defilade /ˌdefɪˈleɪd/ *v.* & *n.* —*v.tr.* secure (a fortification) against enfilading fire. —*n.* this precaution or arrangement. [DEFILE² + -ADE]

defile¹ /dɪˈfaɪl/ *v.tr.* **1** make dirty; pollute, befoul. **2** corrupt. **3** desecrate, profane. **4** deprive (esp. a woman) of virginity. **5** make ceremonially unclean. □□ **defilement** *n.* **defiler** *n.* [ME *defoul* f. OF *defouler* trample down, outrage (as DE-, *fouler* tread, trample) altered after obs. *befile* f. OE *befȳlan* (BE-, *fūl* FOUL)]

defile² /dɪˈfaɪl/ *n.* & *v.* —*n.* /also 'diːfaɪl/ **1** a narrow way through which troops can only march in file. **2** a gorge. —*v.intr.* march in file. [F *défiler* and *défilé* past part. (as DE-, FILE²)]

define /dɪˈfaɪn/ *v.tr.* **1** give the exact meaning of (a word etc.). **2** describe or explain the scope of (*define one's position*). **3** make clear, esp. in outline (*well-defined image*). **4** mark out the boundary or limits of. **5** (of properties) make up the total character of. □□ **definable** *adj.* **definer** *n.* [ME f. OF *definer* ult. f. L *definire* (as DE-, *finire* finish, f. *finis* end)]

definite /ˈdefɪnɪt/ *adj.* **1** having exact and discernible limits. **2** clear and distinct; not vague. ¶ See the note at *definitive*. □**definite article** see ARTICLE. **definite integral** see INTEGRAL. □□**definiteness** *n.* [L *definitus* past part. of *definire* (as DEFINE)]

definitely /ˈdefɪnɪtlɪ/ *adv.* & *int.* —*adv.* **1** in a definite manner. **2** certainly; without doubt (*they were definitely there*). —*int. colloq.* yes, certainly.

definition /ˌdefɪˈnɪʃ(ə)n/ *n.* **1 a** the act or process of defining. **b** a statement of the meaning of a word or the nature of a thing. **2 a** the degree of distinctness in outline of an object or image (esp. of an image produced by a lens or shown in a photograph or on a cinema or television screen). **b** making or being distinct in outline. [ME f. OF f. L *definitio* (as DEFINE)]

definitive /dɪˈfɪnɪtɪv/ *adj.* **1** (of an answer, treaty, verdict, etc.) decisive, unconditional, final. ¶ Often confused in this sense with *definite*, which does not have connotations of authority and conclusiveness: *a definite no* is a firm refusal, whereas *a definitive no* is an authoritative judgement or decision that something is not the case. **2** (of an edition of a book etc.) most authoritative. **3** *Philately* (of a series of stamps) for permanent use, not commemorative etc. □□**definitively** *adv.* [ME f. OF *definitif -ive* f. L *definitivus* (as DEFINE)]

deflagrate /ˈdefləgreɪt, 'diː-/ *v.tr.* & *intr.* burn away with sudden flame. □□**deflagration** /-ˈreɪʃ(ə)n/ *n.* **deflagrator** *n.* [L *deflagrare* (as DE-, *flagrare* blaze)]

deflate /dɪˈfleɪt/ *v.* **1 a** *tr.* let air or gas out of (a tyre, balloon, etc.). **b** *intr.* be emptied of air or gas. **2 a** *tr.* cause to lose confidence or conceit. **b** *intr.* lose confidence. **3** *Econ.* **a** *tr.* subject (a currency or economy) to deflation. **b** *intr.* pursue a policy of deflation. **4** *tr.* reduce the importance of, depreciate. □□**deflator** *n.* [DE- + INFLATE]

deflation /dɪˈfleɪʃ(ə)n/ *n.* **1** the act or process of deflating or being deflated. **2** *Econ.* reduction in the amount of money in circulation to increase its value as a measure against inflation. **3** *Geol.* the removal of particles of rock etc. by the wind. □□**deflationary** *adj.* **deflationist** *n.*

deflect /dɪˈflekt/ *v.* **1** *tr.* & *intr.* bend or turn aside from a straight course or intended purpose. **2** (often foll. by *from*) *a tr.* cause to deviate. **b** *intr.* deviate. [L *deflectere* (as DE-, *flectere flex-* bend)]

deflection /dɪˈflekʃ(ə)n/ *n.* (also **deflexion**) **1** the act or process of deflecting or being deflected. **2** a lateral bend or turn; a deviation. **3** *Physics* the displacement of a pointer on an instrument from its zero position. [LL *deflexio* (as DEFLECT)]

deflector /dɪˈflektə(r)/ *n.* a thing that deflects, esp. a device for deflecting a flow of air etc.

defloration /ˌdiːflɔːˈreɪʃ(ə)n/ *n.* deflowering. [ME f. OF or f. LL *defloratio* (as DEFLOWER)]

deflower /dɪˈflaʊə(r)/ *v.tr.* **1** deprive (esp. a woman) of virginity. **2** ravage, spoil. **3** strip of flowers. [ME f. OF *deflourer, des-,* ult. f. LL *deflorare* (as DE-, L *flos floris* flower)]

defocus /diːˈfəʊkəs/ *v.tr.* & *intr.* (**defocused, defocusing** or **defocussed, defocussing**) put or go out of focus.

defoliate /diːˈfəʊlɪˌeɪt/ *v.tr.* remove leaves from, esp. as a military tactic. □□**defoliant** *n.* & *adj.* **defoliation** /-ˈeɪʃ(ə)n/ *n.* **defoliator** *n.* [LL *defoliare* f. *folium* leaf]

deforest /diːˈfɒrɪst/ *v.tr.* clear of forests or trees. □□ **deforestation** /-ˈsteɪʃ(ə)n/ *n.*

deform /dɪˈfɔːm/ *v.* **1** *tr.* make ugly, deface. **2** *tr.* put out of shape, misshape. **3** *intr.* undergo deformation; be deformed. □□**deformable** *adj.* [ME f. OF *deformer* etc. f. med.L *difformare* ult. f. L *deformare* (as DE-, *formare* f. *forma* shape)]

deformation /ˌdiːfɔːˈmeɪʃ(ə)n/ *n.* **1** disfigurement. **2** *Physics* **a** (often foll. by *of*) change in shape. **b** a quantity representing the amount of this change. **3** a perverted form of a word (e.g. *dang* for *damn*). □□ **deformational** *adj.* [ME f. OF *deformation* or L *deformatio* (as DEFORM)]

deformed /dɪˈfɔːmd/ *adj.* (of a person or limb) misshapen.

deformity /dɪˈfɔːmɪtɪ/ *n.* (*pl.* -**ies**) **1** the state of being deformed; ugliness, disfigurement. **2** a malformation, esp. of body or limb. **3** a moral defect; depravity. [ME f. OF *deformité* etc. f. L *deformitas -tatis* f. *deformis* (as DE-, *forma* shape)]

defraud /dɪˈfrɔːd/ *v.tr.* (often foll. by *of*) cheat by fraud. □□**defrauder** *n.* [ME f. OF *defrauder* or L *defraudare* (as DE-, FRAUD)]

defray /dɪˈfreɪ/ *v.tr.* provide money to pay (a cost or expense). □□**defrayable** *adj.* **defrayal** *n.* **defrayment** *n.* [F *défrayer* (as DE-, obs. *frai(t)* cost, f. med.L *fredum, -us* fine for breach of the peace)]

defrock /diːˈfrɒk/ *v.tr.* deprive (a person, esp. a priest) of ecclesiastical status. [F *défroquer* (as DE-, FROCK)]

defrost /diːˈfrɒst/ *v.* **1** *tr.* **a** free (the interior of a refrigerator) of excess frost, usu. by turning it off for a period. **b** remove frost or ice from (esp. the windscreen of a motor vehicle). **2** *tr.* unfreeze (frozen food). **3** *intr.* become unfrozen. □□**defroster** *n.*

deft /deft/ *adj.* neatly skilful or dextrous; adroit. □□ **deftly** *adv.* **deftness** *n.* [ME, var. of DAFT in obs. sense 'meek']

defunct /dɪˈfʌŋkt/ *adj.* **1** no longer existing. **2** no longer used or in fashion. **3** dead or extinct. □□ **defunctness** *n.* [L *defunctus* dead, past part. of *defungi* (as DE-, *fungi* perform)]

defuse /diːˈfjuːz/ *v.tr.* **1** remove the fuse from (an explosive device). **2** reduce the tension or potential danger in (a crisis, difficulty, etc.).

defy /dɪˈfaɪ/ *v.tr.* (-**ies**, -**ied**) **1** resist openly; refuse to obey. **2** (of a thing) present insuperable obstacles to (*defies solution*). **3** (foll. by *to* + infin.) challenge (a person) to do or prove something. **4** *archaic* challenge to combat. [ME f. OF *defier* f. Rmc (as DIS-, L *fidus* faithful)]

deg. *abbr.* degree.

dégagé /deɪɡɑːˈʒeɪ/ *adj.* (*fem.* **dégagée**) easy, unconstrained. [F, past part. of *dégager* set free]

degas /diːˈɡæs/ *v.tr.* (**degassed, degassing**) remove unwanted gas from.

degauss /diːˈɡaʊs/ *v.tr.* neutralize the magnetism in (a thing) by encircling it with a current-carrying conductor. □□**degausser** *n.* [DE- + GAUSS]

degenerate *adj., n.,* & *v.* —*adj.* /dɪˈdʒenərət/ **1** having lost the qualities that are normal and desirable or proper to its kind; fallen from former excellence. **2** *Biol.* having changed to a lower type.

—*n.* /dɪˈdʒenərət/ a degenerate person or animal. —*v.intr.* /dɪˈdʒenəˌreɪt/ become degenerate. □□ **degeneracy** *n.* **degenerately** *adv.* [L *degeneratus* past part. of *degenerare* (as DE-, *genus -eris* race)]

degeneration /dɪˌdʒenəˈreɪʃ(ə)n/ *n.* **1 a** the process of becoming degenerate. **b** the state of being degenerate. **2** *Med.* morbid deterioration of tissue or change in its structure. [ME f. F *dégéneration* or f. LL *degeneratio* (as DEGENERATE)]

degenerative /dɪˈdʒenərətɪv/ *adj.* **1** of or tending to degeneration. **2** (of disease) characterized by progressive often irreversible deterioration.

degrade /dɪˈɡreɪd/ *v.* **1** *tr.* reduce to a lower rank, esp. as a punishment. **2** *tr.* bring into dishonour or contempt. **3** *tr.* *Chem.* reduce to a simpler molecular structure. **4** *tr.* *Physics* reduce (energy) to a less convertible form. **5** *tr.* *Geol.* wear down (rocks etc.) by disintegration. **6** *intr.* degenerate. **7** *intr.* *Chem.* disintegrate. □□ **degradable** *adj.* **degradation** /ˌdeɡrəˈdeɪʃ(ə)n/ *n.* **degradative** /-dətɪv/ *adj.* **degrader** *n.* [ME f. OF *degrader* f. eccl.L *degradare* (as DE-, L *gradus* step)]

degrading /dɪˈɡreɪdɪŋ/ *adj.* humiliating; causing a loss of self-respect. □□ **degradingly** *adv.*

degrease /diːˈɡriːs/ *v.tr.* remove unwanted grease or fat from.

degree /dɪˈɡriː/ *n.* **1** a stage in an ascending or descending scale, series, or process. **2** a stage in intensity or amount (*to a high degree*; *in some degree*). **3** relative condition (*each is good in its degree*). **4** *Math.* a unit of measurement of angles, one-ninetieth of a right angle or the angle subtended by one-three-hundred-and-sixtieth of the circumference of a circle. ¶ Symb.: ° (as in *45°*). **5** *Physics* a unit in a scale of temperature, hardness, etc. ¶ Abbr.: **deg.** (or omitted in the Kelvin scale of temperature). **6** *Med.* an extent of burns on a scale characterized by the destruction of the skin. **7** an academic rank conferred by a college or university after examination or after completion of a course, or conferred as an honour on a distinguished person. **8** a grade of crime or criminality (*murder in the first degree*). **9** a step in direct genealogical descent. **10** social or official rank. **11** *Math.* the highest power of unknowns or variables in an equation etc. (*equation of the third degree*). **12** a masonic rank. **13** a thing placed like a step in a series; a tier or row. **14** *Mus.* the classification of a note by its position in the scale. □ **by degrees** a little at a time; gradually. **degree of freedom 1** *Physics* the independent direction in which motion can occur. **2** *Chem.* the number of independent factors required to specify a system at equilibrium. **3** *Statistics* the number of independent values or quantities which can be assigned to a statistical distribution. **degrees of comparison** see COMPARISON. **forbidden** (or **prohibited**) **degrees** a number of degrees of descent too few to allow of marriage between two related persons. **to a degree** *colloq.* considerably. □□ **degreeless** *adj.* [ME f. OF *degré* f. Rmc (as DE-, L *gradus* step)]

degressive /dɪˈɡresɪv/ *adj.* **1** (of taxation) at successively lower rates on low amounts. **2** reducing in amount. [L *degredi* (as DE-, *gradi* walk)]

de haut en bas /də ˌəʊt ɑ̃ ˈbɑː/ *adv.* in a condescending or superior manner. [F, = from above to below]

dehisce /diːˈhɪs/ *v.intr.* gape or burst open (esp. of a pod or seed-vessel or of a cut or wound). □□ **dehiscence** *n.* **dehiscent** *adj.* [L *dehiscere* (as DE-, *hiscere* incept. of *hiare* gape)]

dehorn /diːˈhɔːn/ *v.tr.* remove the horns from (an animal).

dehumanize /diːˈhjuːməˌnaɪz/ *v.tr.* (also **-ise**) **1** deprive of human characteristics. **2** make impersonal or machine-like. □□ **dehumanization** /-ˈzeɪʃ(ə)n/ *n.*

dehumidify /ˌdiːhjuːˈmɪdɪˌfaɪ/ *v.tr.* (**-ies, -ied**) reduce the degree of humidity of; remove moisture from (a gas, esp. air). □□ **dehumidification** /-fɪˈkeɪʃ(ə)n/ *n.* **dehumidifier** *n.*

dehydrate /diːˈhaɪdreɪt, ˌdiːhaɪˈdreɪt/ *v.* **1** *tr.* **a** remove water from (esp. foods for preservation and storage in bulk). **b** make dry, esp. make (the body) deficient in water. **c** render lifeless or uninteresting. **2** *intr.* lose water. □□ **dehydration** /-ˈdreɪʃ(ə)n/ *n.* **dehydrator** *n.*

dehydrogenate /ˌdiːhaɪˈdrɒdʒɪˌneɪt/ *v.tr.* *Chem.* remove a hydrogen atom or atoms from (a compound). □□ **dehydrogenation** /-ˈneɪʃ(ə)n/ *n.*

de-ice /diːˈaɪs/ *v.tr.* **1** remove ice from. **2** prevent the formation of ice on.

de-icer /diːˈaɪsə(r)/ *n.* a device or substance for de-icing, esp. a windscreen or ice on an aircraft.

deicide /ˈdiːɪˌsaɪd, ˈdeɪɪs-/ *n.* **1** the killer of a god. **2** the killing of a god. [eccl.L *deicida* f. L *deus* god + -CIDE]

deictic /ˈdaɪktɪk/ *adj.* & *n.* *Philol.* & *Gram.* —*adj.* pointing, demonstrative. —*n.* a deictic word. [Gk *deiktikos* f. *deiktos* capable of proof f. *deiknumi* show]

deify /ˈdiːɪˌfaɪ, ˈdeɪɪ-/ *v.tr.* (**-ies, -ied**) **1** make a god of. **2** regard or worship as a god. □□ **deification** /-fɪˈkeɪʃ(ə)n/ *n.* [ME f. OF *deifier* f. eccl.L *deificare* f. *deus* god]

deign /deɪn/ *v.* **1** *intr.* (foll. by *to* + infin.) think fit, condescend. **2** *tr.* (usu. with *neg.*) *archaic* condescend to give (an answer etc.). [ME f. OF *degnier*, *deigner*, *daigner* f. L *dignare*, *-ari* deem worthy f. *dignus* worthy]

Dei gratia /ˌdeɪɪ ˈɡrɑːtɪə, -ʃɪə/ *adv.* by the grace of God. [L]

deinstitutionalize /diːˌɪnstɪˈtjuːʃənəˌlaɪz/ *v.tr.* (also **-ise**) (usu. as **deinstitutionalized** *adj.*) remove from an institution or from the effects of institutional life. □□ **deinstitutionalization** /-ˈzeɪʃ(ə)n/ *n.*

deionize /diːˈaɪəˌnaɪz/ *v.tr.* (also **-ise**) remove the ions or ionic constituents from (water, air, etc.). □□ **deionization** /-ˈzeɪʃ(ə)n/ *n.* **deionizer** *n.*

deism /ˈdiːɪz(ə)m, ˈdeɪ-/ *n.* belief in the existence of a supreme being arising from reason rather than revelation (cf. THEISM). □□ **deist** *n.* **deistic** /-ˈɪstɪk/ *adj.* **deistical** /-ˈɪstɪk(ə)l/ *adj.* [L *deus* god + -ISM]

deity /ˈdiːɪtɪ, ˈdeɪɪ-/ *n.* (*pl.* **-ies**) **1** a god or goddess. **2** divine status, quality, or nature. **3** (**the Deity**) the Creator, God. [ME f. OF *deité* f. eccl.L *deitas -tatis* transl. Gk *theotēs* f. *theos* god]

déjà vu /ˌdeɪʒɑː ˈvuː/ *n.* **1** *Psychol.* an illusory feeling of having already experienced a present situation. **2** something tediously familiar. [F, = already seen]

deject /dɪˈdʒekt/ *v.tr.* (usu. as **dejected** *adj.*) make sad or dispirited; depress. □□ **dejectedly** *adv.* [ME f. L *dejicere* (DE-, *jacère* throw)]

dejection /dɪˈdʒekʃ(ə)n/ *n.* a dejected state; low spirits. [ME f. L *dejectio* (as DEJECT)]

de jure /diː ˈdʒʊərɪ, deɪ ˈjʊəreɪ/ *adj.* & *adv.* —*adj.* rightful. —*adv.* rightfully; by right. [L]

dekko /ˈdekəʊ/ *n.* (*pl.* **-os**) *Brit.* *sl.* a look or glance (*took a quick dekko*). [Hindi *dekho*, imper. of *dekhnā* look]

Del. *abbr.* Delaware.

delate /dɪˈleɪt/ *v.tr.* *archaic* **1** inform against; impeach (a person). **2** report (an offence). □□ **delation** /-ˈleɪʃ(ə)n/ *n.* **delator** *n.* [L *delat-* (as DE-, *lat-* past part. stem of *ferre* carry)]

delay /dɪˈleɪ/ *v.* & *n.* —*v.* **1** *tr.* postpone; defer. **2** *tr.* make late (*was delayed at the traffic lights*). **3** *intr.* loiter; be late (*don't delay!*). —*n.* **1** the act or an instance of delaying; the process of being delayed. **2** time lost by inaction or the inability to proceed. **3** a hindrance. □ **delayed-action** (*attrib.*) (esp. of a bomb, camera, etc.) operating some time after being primed or set. **delay line** *Electr.* a device producing a desired delay in the transmission of a signal. □□ **delayer** *n.* [ME f. OF *delayer* (v.), *delai* (n.), prob. f. *des-* DIS- + *laier* leave: see RELAY]

dele /ˈdiːlɪ/ *v.* & *n.* *Printing* —*v.tr.* (**deled, deleing**) delete or mark for deletion (a letter, word, etc., struck out of a text). —*n.* a sign marking something

to be deleted; a deletion. [L, imper. of *delēre*: see
DELETE]

delectable /dɪˈlektəb(ə)l/ *adj*. esp. *literary*. delightful, pleasant. □□ **delectability** /-ˈbɪlɪtɪ/ *n*. **delectably**
adv. [ME f. OF f. L *delectabilis* f. *delectare* DELIGHT]

delectation /ˌdiːlekˈteɪʃ(ə)n/ *n*. *literary* pleasure, enjoyment (*sang for his delectation*). [ME f. OF (as
DELECTABLE)]

delegacy /ˈdelɪgəsɪ/ *n*. (*pl*. **-ies**) **1** a system of
delegating. **2 a** an appointment as a delegate. **b** a
body of delegates; a delegation.

delegate *n*. & *v*. —*n*. /ˈdelɪgət/ **1** an elected representative sent to a conference. **2** a member of a
committee. **3** a member of a deputation. —*v.tr*.
/ˈdelɪˌgeɪt/ **1** (often foll. by *to*) **a** commit (authority,
power, etc.) to an agent or deputy. **b** entrust (a task)
to another person. **2** send or authorize (a person) as
a representative; depute. □□ **delegable** /ˈdelɪgəb(ə)l/
adj. [ME f. L *delegatus* (as DE-, *legare* depute)]

delegation /ˌdelɪˈgeɪʃ(ə)n/ *n*. **1** a body of delegates; a
deputation. **2** the act or process of delegating or
being delegated. [L *delegatio* (as DELEGATE)]

delete /dɪˈliːt/ *v.tr*. remove or obliterate (written or
printed matter), esp. by striking out. □□ **deletion**
/-ˈliːʃ(ə)n/ *n*. [L *delēre* *delet-* efface]

deleterious /ˌdelɪˈtɪərɪəs/ *adj*. harmful (to the mind
or body). □□ **deleteriously** *adv*. [med.L *deleterius* f.
Gk *dēlētērios* noxious]

delft /delft/ *n*. (also **delftware** /ˈdelftweə(r)/) glazed,
usu. blue and white, earthenware, made in Delft in
Holland.

deli /ˈdelɪ/ *n*. (*pl*. **delis**) esp. *US colloq*. a delicatessen
shop. [abbr.]

deliberate *adj*. & *v*. —*adj*. /dɪˈlɪbərət/ **1 a** intentional
(*a deliberate foul*). **b** fully considered; not impulsive
(*made a deliberate choice*). **2** slow in deciding; cautious (*a ponderous and deliberate mind*). **3** (of movement etc.) leisurely and unhurried. —*v*. /dɪˈlɪbəˌreɪt/
1 *intr*. think carefully; take counsel (*the jury deliberated for an hour*). **2** *tr*. consider, discuss carefully
(*deliberated the question*). □□ **deliberately**
/dɪˈlɪbərətlɪ/ *adv*. **deliberateness** /dɪˈlɪbərətnɪs/ *n*.
deliberator /dɪˈlɪbəˌreɪtə(r)/ *n*. [L *deliberatus* past
part. of *deliberare* (as DE-, *librare* weigh f. *libra*
balance)]

deliberation /ˌdɪlɪbəˈreɪʃ(ə)n/ *n*. **1** careful consideration. **2 a** the discussion of reasons for and
against. **b** a debate or discussion. **3 a** caution and
care. **b** (of movement) slowness or ponderousness.
[ME f. OF f. L *deliberatio -onis* (as DELIBERATE)]

deliberative /dɪˈlɪbərətɪv/ *adj*. of, or appointed for
the purpose of, deliberation or debate (*a deliberative assembly*). □□ **deliberatively** *adv*.
deliberativeness *n*. [F *délibératif -ive* or L *de-
liberativus* (as DELIBERATE)]

delicacy /ˈdelɪkəsɪ/ *n*. (*pl*. **-ies**) **1** (esp. in craftsmanship or artistic or natural beauty) fineness or
intricacy of structure or texture; gracefulness. **2**
susceptibility to injury or disease; weakness. **3**
the quality of requiring discretion or sensitivity (*a
situation of some delicacy*). **4** a choice or expensive
food. **5 a** consideration for the feelings of others. **b**
avoidance of immodesty or vulgarity. **6** (esp. in a
person, a sense, or an instrument) accuracy of
perception; sensitiveness. [ME f. DELICATE + -ACY]

delicate /ˈdelɪkət/ *adj*. **1 a** fine in texture or structure;
soft, slender, or slight. **b** of exquisite quality or
workmanship. **c** (of colour) subtle or subdued; not
bright. **d** subtle, hard to appreciate. **2** (of a person)
easily injured; susceptible to illness. **3 a** requiring
careful handling; tricky (*a delicate situation*). **b** (of
an instrument) highly sensitive. **4** deft (*a delicate
touch*). **5** (of a person) avoiding the immodest or
offensive. **6** (esp. of actions) considerate. **7** (of food)
dainty; suitable for an invalid. □**in a delicate
condition** *archaic* pregnant. □□ **delicately** *adv*.
delicateness *n*. [ME f. OF *delicat* or L *delicatus*, of
unkn. orig.]

delicatessen /ˌdelɪkəˈtes(ə)n/ *n*. **1** a shop selling
cooked meats, cheeses, and unusual or foreign prepared foods. **2** (often *attrib*.) such foods collectively
(*a delicatessen counter*). [G *Delikatessen* or Du. *delicatessen* f. F *délicatesse* f. *délicat* (as DELICATE)]

delicious /dɪˈlɪʃəs/ *adj*. **1** highly delightful and
enjoyable to the taste or sense of smell. **2** (of a joke
etc.) very witty. □□ **deliciously** *adv*. **deliciousness**
n. [ME f. OF f. LL *deliciosus* f. L *deliciae* delight]

delict /dɪˈlɪkt, ˈdiː-/ *n*. *archaic* a violation of the law;
an offence. [L *delictum* neut. past part. of *delinquere*
offend (as DE-, *linquere* leave)]

delight /dɪˈlaɪt/ *v*. & *n*. —*v*. **1** *tr*. (often foll. by *with*)
please greatly (*the gift delighted them*; *was delighted
that you won*; *delighted with the result*). **2** *intr*. (often
foll. by *in*, or *to* + infin.) take great pleasure; be
highly pleased (*delighted in her success*; *was delighted
to help*). —*n*. **1** great pleasure. **2** something giving
pleasure (*her singing is a delight*). □□ **delighted** *adj*.
delightedly *adv*. [ME f. OF *delitier*, *delit*, f. L
delectare frequent. of *delicere*: alt. after *light* etc.]

delightful /dɪˈlaɪtfʊl/ *adj*. causing great delight;
pleasant, charming. □□ **delightfully** *adv*.
delightfulness *n*.

Delilah /dɪˈlaɪlə/ *n*. a seductive and wily temptress.
[*Delilah*, betrayer of Samson (Judges 16)]

delimit /dɪˈlɪmɪt/ *v.tr*. (**delimited**, **delimiting**) **1**
determine the limits of. **2** fix the territorial boundary
of. □□ **delimitation** /-ˈteɪʃ(ə)n/ *n*. [F *délimiter* f. L
delimitare (as DE-, *limitare* f. *limes -itis* boundary)]

delimitate /dɪˈlɪmɪˌteɪt/ *v.tr*. = DELIMIT.

delineate /dɪˈlɪnɪˌeɪt/ *v.tr*. portray by drawing etc. or
in words (*delineated her character*). □□ **delineation**
/-ˈeɪʃ(ə)n/ *n*. **delineator** *n*. [L *delineare* *delineat-* (as
DE-, *lineare* f. *linea* line)]

delinquency /dɪˈlɪŋkwənsɪ/ *n*. (*pl*. **-ies**) **1 a** a crime,
usu. not of a serious kind; a misdeed. **b** minor
crime in general, esp. that of young people (*juvenile
delinquency*). **2** wickedness (*moral delinquency*; an
act of delinquency). **3** neglect of one's duty. [eccl. L
delinquentia f. L *delinquens* part. of *delinquere* (as
DELICT)]

delinquent /dɪˈlɪŋkwənt/ *n*. & *adj*. —*n*. an offender
(*juvenile delinquent*). —*adj*. **1** guilty of a minor crime
or a misdeed. **2** failing in one's duty. **3** *US* in arrears.
□□ **delinquently** *adv*.

deliquesce /ˌdelɪˈkwes/ *v.intr*. **1** become liquid, melt.
2 *Chem*. dissolve in water absorbed from the air. □□
deliquescence *n*. **deliquescent** *adj*. [L *deliquescere*
(as DE-, *liquescere* incept. of *liquēre* be liquid)]

delirious /dɪˈlɪrɪəs/ *adj*. **1** affected with delirium;
temporarily or apparently mad; raving. **2** wildly
excited, ecstatic. **3** (of behaviour) betraying delirium
or ecstasy. □□ **deliriously** *adv*.

delirium /dɪˈlɪrɪəm/ *n*. **1** an acutely disordered state
of mind involving incoherent speech, hallucinations,
and frenzied excitement, occurring in metabolic
disorders, intoxication, fever, etc. **2** great excitement,
ecstasy. □**delirium tremens** /ˈtriːmenz/ a psychosis
of chronic alcoholism involving tremors and hallucinations. [L f. *delirare* be deranged (as DE-, *lira*
ridge between furrows)]

deliver /dɪˈlɪvə(r)/ *v.tr*. **1 a** distribute (letters, parcels,
ordered goods, etc.) to the addressee or the
purchaser. **b** (often foll. by *to*) hand over (*delivered
the boy safely to his teacher*). **2** (often foll. by *from*)
save, rescue, or set free (*delivered him from his
enemies*). **3 a** give birth to (*delivered a girl*). **b** (in
passive; often foll. by *of*) give birth (*was delivered of
a child*). **c** assist at the birth of (*delivered six babies
that week*). **d** assist in giving birth (*delivered the
patient successfully*). **4 a** (often *refl*.) utter or recite
(an opinion, a speech, etc.) (*delivered himself of the
observation*; *delivered the sermon well*). **b** (of a judge)
pronounce (a judgement). **5** (often foll. by *up*, *over*)
abandon; resign; hand over (*delivered his soul up to
God*). **6** present or render (an account). **7** launch or
aim (a blow, a ball, or an attack). **8** *Law* hand over

formally (esp. a sealed deed to a grantee). **9** *colloq.* = *deliver the goods.* **10** *US* cause (voters etc.) to support a candidate. □**deliver the goods** *colloq.* carry out one's part of an agreement. □□**deliverable** *adj.* **deliverer** *n.* [ME f. OF *delivrer* f. Gallo-Roman (as DE-, LIBERATE)]

deliverance /dɪ'lɪvərəns/ *n.* **1 a** the act or an instance of rescuing; the process of being rescued. **b** a rescue. **2** a formally expressed opinion. [ME f. OF *delivrance* (as DELIVER)]

delivery /dɪ'lɪvərɪ/ *n.* (*pl.* -ies) **1 a** the delivering of letters etc. **b** a regular distribution of letters etc. (*two deliveries a day*). **c** something delivered. **2 a** the process of childbirth. **b** an act of this. **3** deliverance. **4 a** an act of throwing, esp. of a cricket ball. **b** the style of such an act (*a good delivery*). **5** the act of giving or surrendering (*delivery of the town to the enemy*). **6 a** the uttering of a speech etc. **b** the manner or style of such a delivery (*a measured delivery*). **7** *Law* **a** the formal handing over of property. **b** the transfer of a deed to a grantee or a third party. □**take delivery of** receive (something purchased). [ME f. AF *delivree* fem. past part. of *delivrer* (as DELIVER)]

dell /del/ *n.* a small usu. wooded hollow or valley. [OE f. Gmc]

Della Cruscan /delə 'krʌskən/ *adj.* & *n.* —*adj.* **1** of or relating to the Academy della Crusca in Florence, concerned with the purity of Italian. **2** of or concerning a late 18th-c. school of English poets with an artificial style. —*n.* a member of the Academy della Crusca or the late 18th-c. school of English poets. [It. (*Accademia*) *della Crusca* (Academy) of the bran (with ref. to sifting)]

delocalize /di:'ləʊkə,laɪz/ *v.tr.* (also -**ise**) **1 a** detach or remove (a thing) from its place. **b** not limit to a particular location. **2** (as **delocalized** *adj.*) *Chem.* (of electrons) shared among more than two atoms in a molecule. □□**delocalization** /-'zeɪʃ(ə)n/ *n.*

delouse /di:'laʊs/ *v.tr.* rid (a person or animal) of lice.

Delphic /'delfɪk/ *adj.* (also **Delphian** /-fɪən/) **1** (of an utterance, prophecy, etc.) obscure, ambiguous, or enigmatic. **2** of or concerning the ancient Greek oracle at Delphi.

delphinium /del'fɪnɪəm/ *n.* any ranunculaceous garden plant of the genus *Delphinium*, with tall spikes of usu. blue flowers. [mod.L f. Gk *delphinion* larkspur f. *delphin* dolphin]

delphinoid /'delfɪ,nɔɪd/ *adj.* & *n.* —*adj.* **1** of the family that includes dolphins, porpoises, grampuses, etc. **2** dolphin-like. —*n.* **1** a member of the delphinoid family of aquatic mammals. **2** a dolphin-like animal. [Gk *delphinoeidēs* f. *delphin* dolphin]

delta /'deltə/ *n.* **1** a triangular tract of deposited earth, alluvium, etc., at the mouth of a river, formed by its diverging outlets. **2 a** the fourth letter of the Greek alphabet (Δ, δ). **b** a fourth-class mark given for a piece of work or in an examination. **3** *Astron.* the fourth star in a constellation. **4** *Math.* an increment of a variable. □**delta connection** *Electr.* a triangular arrangement of three-phase windings with circuit wire from each angle. **delta rays** *Physics* rays of low penetrative power consisting of slow electrons ejected from an atom by the impact of ionizing radiation. **delta rhythm** (or **wave**) low-frequency electrical activity of the brain during sleep. **delta wing** the triangular swept-back wing of an aircraft. □□**deltaic** /del'teɪɪk/ *adj.* [ME f. Gk f. Phoen. *daleth*]

deltiology /,deltɪ'ɒlədʒɪ/ *n.* the collecting and study of postcards. □□**deltiologist** *n.* [Gk *deltion* dimin. of *deltos* writing-tablet + -LOGY]

deltoid /'deltɔɪd/ *adj.* & *n.* —*adj.* triangular; like a river delta. —*n.* (in full **deltoid muscle**) a thick triangular muscle covering the shoulder joint and used for raising the arm away from the body. [F

deltoïde or mod.L *deltoides* f. Gk *deltoeidēs* (as DELTA, -OID)]

delude /dɪ'lu:d, -'lju:d/ *v.tr.* deceive or mislead (*deluded by false optimism*). □□**deluder** *n.* [ME f. L *deludere* mock (as DE-, *ludere lus-* play)]

deluge /'delju:dʒ/ *n.* & *v.* —*n.* **1** a great flood. **2** (**the Deluge**) the biblical Flood (Gen. 6–8). **3** a great outpouring (of words, paper, etc.). **4** a heavy fall of rain. —*v.tr.* **1** flood. **2** inundate with a great number or amount (*deluged with complaints*). [ME f. OF f. L *diluvium*, rel. to *lavare* wash]

delusion /dɪ'lu:ʒ(ə)n, -'lju:ʒ(ə)n/ *n.* **1** a false belief or impression. **2** *Psychol.* this as a symptom or form of mental disorder. □**delusions of grandeur** a false idea of oneself as being important, noble, famous, etc. □□**delusional** *adj.* [ME f. LL *delusio* (as DELUDE)]

delusive /dɪ'lu:sɪv, -'lju:sɪv/ *adj.* **1** deceptive or unreal. **2** disappointing. □□**delusively** *adv.* **delusiveness** *n.*

delusory /dɪ'lu:sərɪ, dɪ'lju:-/ *adj.* = DELUSIVE. [LL *delusorius* (as DELUSION)]

delustre /di:'lʌstə(r)/ *v.tr.* (*US* **deluster**) remove the lustre from (a textile).

de luxe /də 'lʌks, 'lʊks/ *adj.* **1** luxurious or sumptuous. **2** of a superior kind. [F, = of luxury]

delve /delv/ *v.* **1** *intr.* (often foll. by *in, into*) **a** search energetically (*delved into his pocket*). **b** make a laborious search in documents etc.; research (*delved into his family history*). **2** *tr.* & *intr.* *poet.* dig. □□ **delver** *n.* [OE *delfan* f. WG]

Dem. *abbr.* *US* Democrat.

demagnetize /di:'mægnɪ,taɪz/ *v.tr.* (also -**ise**) remove the magnetic properties of. □□**demagnetization** /-'zeɪʃ(ə)n/ *n.* **demagnetizer** *n.*

demagogue /'demə,gɒg/ *n.* (*US* -**gog**) **1** a political agitator appealing to the basest instincts of a mob. **2** *hist.* a leader of the people, esp. in ancient times. □□ **demagogic** /-'gɒgɪk/ *adj.* **demagoguery** /-'gɒgərɪ/ *n.* **demagogy** /-'gɒgɪ/ *n.* [Gk *dēmagōgos* f. *dēmos* the people + *agōgos* leading]

demand /dɪ'mɑ:nd/ *n.* & *v.* —*n.* **1** an insistent and peremptory request, made as of right. **2** *Econ.* the desire of purchasers or consumers for a commodity (*no demand for solid tyres these days*). **3** an urgent claim (*care of her mother makes demands on her*). —*v.tr.* **1** (often foll. by *of, from*, or *to* + infin., or *that* + clause) ask for (something) insistently and urgently, as of right (*demanded to know*; *demanded five pounds from him*; *demanded that his wife be present*). **2** require or need (*a task demanding skill*). **3** insist on being told (*demanded her business*). **4** (as **demanding** *adj.*) making demands; requiring skill, effort, etc. (*a demanding but worthwhile job*). □**demand feeding** the practice of feeding a baby when it cries for a feed rather than at set times. **demand note 1** a written request for payment. **2** *US* a bill payable at sight. **demand pull** *Econ.* available money as a factor causing economic inflation. **in demand** sought after. **on demand** as soon as a demand is made (*a cheque payable on demand*). □□**demandable** *adj.* **demander** *n.* **demandingly** *adv.* [ME f. OF *demande* (n.), *demander* (v.) f. L *demandare* entrust (as DE-, *mandare* order: see MANDATE)]

demantoid /dɪ'mæntɔɪd/ *n.* a lustrous green garnet. [G]

demarcation /,di:mɑ:'keɪʃ(ə)n/ *n.* **1** the act of marking a boundary or limits. **2** the trade-union practice of strictly assigning specific jobs to different unions. □**demarcation dispute** an inter-union dispute about who does a particular job. □□**demarcate** /'di:-/ *v.tr.* **demarcator** /'di:-/ *n.* [Sp. *demarcación* f. *demarcar* mark the bounds of (as DE-, MARK[1])]

démarche /deɪ'mɑ:ʃ/ *n.* a political step or initiative. [F f. *démarcher* take steps (as DE-, MARCH[1])]

dematerialize /,di:mə'tɪərɪə,laɪz/ *v.tr.* & *intr.* (also -**ise**) make or become non-material or spiritual (esp.

of psychic phenomena etc.). □□ **dematerialization** /-'zeɪʃ(ə)n/ n.

deme /diːm/ n. **1 a** a political division of Attica in ancient Greece. **b** an administrative division in modern Greece. **2** Biol. a local population of closely related plants or animals. [Gk dēmos the people]

demean[1] /dɪ'miːn/ v.tr. (usu. refl.) lower the dignity of (would not demean myself to take it). [DE- + MEAN²,· after debase]

demean[2] /dɪ'miːn/ v.refl. (with adv.) behave (demeaned himself well). [ME f. OF demener f. Rmc (as DE-, L minare drive animals f. minari threaten)]

demeanour /dɪ'miːnə(r)/ n. (US **demeanor**) outward behaviour or bearing. [DEMEAN²,· prob. after obs. havour behaviour]

dement /dɪ'ment/ n. archaic a demented person. [orig. adj. f. F dément or L demens (as DEMENTED)]

demented /dɪ'mentɪd/ adj. mad; crazy. □□ **dementedly** adv. **dementedness** n. [past part. of dement verb f. OF dementer or f. LL dementare f. demens out of one's mind (as DE-, mens mentis mind)]

démenti /deɪ'mɑ̃tɪ/ n. an official denial of a rumour etc. [F f. démentir accuse of lying]

dementia /dɪ'menʃə/ n. Med. a chronic or persistent disorder of the mental processes marked by memory disorders, personality changes, impaired reasoning, etc., due to brain disease or injury. □**dementia praecox** /'priːkɒks/ schizophrenia. [L f. demens (as DEMENTED)]

demerara /ˌdeməˈreərə/ n. light-brown cane sugar coming orig. and chiefly from Demerara. [Demerara in Guyana]

demerit /diːˈmerɪt/ n. **1** a quality or action deserving blame; a fault. **2** US a mark given to an offender. □□ **demeritorious** /-'tɔːrɪəs/ adj. [ME f. OF de(s)merite or L demeritum neut. past part. of demerēri deserve]

demersal /dɪˈmɜːs(ə)l/ adj. (of a fish etc.) being or living near the sea-bottom (cf. PELAGIC). [L demersus past part. of demergere (as DE-, mergere plunge)]

demesne /dɪˈmiːn, -ˈmeɪn/ n. **1 a** a sovereign's or State's territory; a domain. **b** land attached to a mansion etc. **c** landed property; an estate. **2** (usu. foll. by of) a region or sphere. **3** Law hist. possession (of real property) as one's own. □**held in demesne** (of an estate) occupied by the owner, not by tenants. [ME f. AF, OF demeine (later AF demesne) belonging to a lord f. L dominicus (as DOMINICAL)]

demi- /'demɪ/ prefix **1** half; half-size. **2** partially or imperfectly such (demigod). [ME f. F f. med.L dimedius half, for L dimidius]

demigod /'demɪˌɡɒd/ n. (fem. **-goddess** /-ˌɡɒdɪs/) **1 a** a partly divine being. **b** the offspring of a god or goddess and a mortal. **2** colloq. a person of compelling beauty, powers, or personality.

demijohn /'demɪˌdʒɒn/ n. a bulbous narrow-necked bottle holding from 3 to 10 gallons and usu. in a wicker cover. [prob. corrupt. of F dame-jeanne Lady Jane, assim. to DEMI- + the name John]

demilitarize /diːˈmɪlɪtəˌraɪz/ v.tr. (also -ise) remove a military organization or forces from (a frontier, a zone, etc.). □□ **demilitarization** /-'zeɪʃ(ə)n/ n.

demi-mondaine /'demɪmɒnˌdeɪn, -mɔ̃ˌdeɪn/ n. a woman of a demi-monde.

demi-monde /'demɪˌmɒnd, -ˈmɔ̃d/ n. **1 a** hist. a class of women in 19th-c. France considered to be of doubtful social standing and morality. **b** a similar class of women in any society. **2** any group considered to be on the fringes of respectable society. [F, = half-world]

demineralize /diːˈmɪnərəˌlaɪz/ v.tr. (also -ise) remove salts from (sea water etc.). □□ **demineralization** /-'zeɪʃ(ə)n/ n.

demi-pension /dəmɪˈpɑ̃sjɔ̃/ n. hotel accommodation with bed, breakfast, and one main meal per day. [F (as DEMI-, PENSION²)]

demirep /'demɪˌrep/ n. archaic a woman of doubtful sexual reputation. [abbr. of demi-reputable]

demise /dɪˈmaɪz/ n. & v. —n. **1** death (left a will on

her demise; the demise of the agreement). **2** Law conveyance or transfer (of property, a title, etc.) by demising. —v.tr. Law **1** convey or grant (an estate) by will or lease. **2** transmit (a title etc.) by death. [AF use of past part. of OF de(s)mettre DISMISS, in refl. abdicate]

demisemiquaver /ˌdemɪˈsemɪˌkweɪvə(r)/ 'demɪ-/ n. Mus. a note having the time value of half a semiquaver and represented by a large dot with a three-hooked stem. Also called thirty-second note.

demist /diːˈmɪst/ v.tr. clear mist from (a windscreen etc.). □□ **demister** n.

demit /dɪˈmɪt/ v.tr. (**demitted**, **demitting**) (often absol.) resign or abdicate (an office etc.). □□ **demission** /-'mɪʃ(ə)n/ n. [F démettre f. L demittere (as DE-, mittere miss- send)]

demitasse /'demɪˌtæs, dəmɪˈtæs/ n. **1** a small coffee-cup. **2** its contents. [F, = half-cup]

demiurge /'demɪˌɜːdʒ/ n. **1** (in the philosophy of Plato) the creator of the universe. **2** (in Gnosticism etc.) a heavenly being subordinate to the Supreme Being. □□ **demiurgic** /-'ɜːdʒɪk/ adj. [eccl.L f. Gk dēmiourgos craftsman f. dēmios public f. dēmos people + -ergos working]

demo /'deməʊ/ n. (pl. **-os**) colloq. = DEMONSTRATION 2, 3. [abbr.]

demob /diːˈmɒb/ v. & n. Brit. colloq. —v.tr. (**demobbed**, **demobbing**) demobilize. —n. demobilization. [abbr.]

demobilize /diːˈməʊbɪˌlaɪz/ v.tr. (also -ise) disband (troops, ships, etc.). □□ **demobilization** /-'zeɪʃ(ə)n/ n. [F démobiliser (as DE-, MOBILIZE)]

democracy /dɪˈmɒkrəsɪ/ n. (pl. **-ies**) **1 a** a system of government by the whole population, usu. through elected representatives. **b** a State so governed. **c** any organization governed on democratic principles. **2** a classless and tolerant form of society. **3** US **a** the principles of the Democratic Party. **b** its members. [F démocratie f. LL democratia f. Gk dēmokratia f. dēmos the people + -CRACY]

democrat /'deməˌkræt/ n. **1** an advocate of democracy. **2** (**Democrat**) (in the US) a member of the Democratic Party. □□ **democratism** /dɪˈmɒkrəˌtɪz(ə)m/ n. [F démocrate (as DEMOCRACY), after aristocrate]

democratic /ˌdeməˈkrætɪk/ adj. **1** of, like, practising, advocating, or constituting democracy or a democracy. **2** favouring social equality. □**democratic centralism** an organizational system in which policy is decided centrally and is binding on all members. **Democratic Party** one of the two main US political parties, considered to support social reform and international commitment (cf. Republican Party). □□ **democratically** adv. [F démocratique f. med.L democraticus f. Gk dēmokratikos f. dēmokratia DEMOCRACY]

democratize /dɪˈmɒkrəˌtaɪz/ v.tr. (also -ise) make (a State, institution, etc.) democratic. □□ **democratization** /-'zeɪʃ(ə)n/ n.

démodé /ˌdeɪmɒˈdeɪ/ adj. out of fashion. [F, past part. of démoder (as DE-, mode fashion)]

demodulate /diːˈmɒdjʊˌleɪt/ v.tr. Physics extract a modulating signal) from its carrier. □□ **demodulation** /ˌdiːmɒdjʊˈleɪʃ(ə)n/ n. **demodulator** n.

demography /dɪˈmɒɡrəfɪ/ n. the study of the statistics of births, deaths, disease, etc., as illustrating the conditions of life in communities. □□ **demographer** n. **demographic** /ˌdeməˈɡræfɪk/ adj. **demographical** /ˌdeməˈɡræfɪk(ə)l/ **demographically** /ˌdeməˈɡræfɪkəlɪ/ adv. [Gk dēmos the people + -GRAPHY]

demoiselle /ˌdemwæˈzel/ n. **1** Zool. a small crane, Anthropoides virgo, native to Asia and N. Africa. **2 a** a damselfly. **b** a damselfish. **3** archaic a young woman. [F, = DAMSEL]

demolish /dɪˈmɒlɪʃ/ v.tr. **1 a** pull down (a building). **b** completely destroy or break. **2** overthrow (an institution). **3** refute (an argument, theory, etc.). **4** *joc.* eat up completely and quickly. □□ **demolisher** *n.* **demolition** /ˌdemə'lɪʃ(ə)n/ *n.* **demolitionist** /ˌdemə'lɪʃənɪst/ *n.* [F *démolir* f. L *demoliri* (as DE-, *moliri molit-* construct f. *moles* mass)]

demon /'diːmən/ *n.* **1 a** an evil spirit or devil, esp. one thought to possess a person. **b** the personification of evil passion. **2** a malignant supernatural being; the Devil. **3** (often *attrib.*) a forceful, fierce, or skilful performer (*a demon on the tennis court; a demon player*). **4** a cruel or destructive person. **5** (also **daemon**) **a** an inner or attendant spirit; a genius (*the demon of creativity*). **b** a supernatural being in ancient Greece. □**demon bowler** *Cricket* a very fast bowler. **a demon for work** *colloq.* a person who works strenuously. [ME f. med.L *demon* f. L *daemon* f. Gk *daimōn* deity]

demonetize /diːˈmʌnɪˌtaɪz/ *v.tr.* (also **-ise**) withdraw (a coin etc.) from use as money. □□ **demonetization** /-ˈzeɪʃ(ə)n/ *n.* [F *démonétiser* (as DE-, L *moneta* MONEY)]

demoniac /dɪˈməʊnɪˌæk/ *adj. & n.* —*adj.* **1** fiercely energetic or frenzied. **2 a** supposedly possessed by an evil spirit. **b** of or concerning such possession. **3** of or like demons. —*n.* a person possessed by an evil spirit. □□ **demoniacal** /ˌdiːmə'naɪək(ə)l/ *adj.* **demoniacally** /ˌdiːmə'naɪəkəlɪ/ *adv.* [ME f. OF *demoniaque* f. eccl.L *daemoniacus* f. *daemonium* f. Gk *daimonion* dimin. of *daimōn*: see DEMON]

demonic /dɪˈmɒnɪk/ *adj.* (also **daemonic**) **1** = DEMONIAC. **2** having or seeming to have supernatural genius or power. [LL *daemonicus* f. Gk *daimonikos* (as DEMON)]

demonism /'diːməˌnɪz(ə)m/ *n.* belief in the power of demons.

demonize /'diːməˌnaɪz/ *v.tr.* (also **-ise**) **1** make into or like a demon. **2** represent as a demon.

demonolatry /ˌdiːmə'nɒlətrɪ/ *n.* the worship of demons.

demonology /ˌdiːmə'nɒlədʒɪ/ *n.* the study of demons etc. □□ **demonologist** *n.*

demonstrable /'demɒnstrəb(ə)l, dɪˈmɒnstrəb(ə)l/ *adj.* capable of being shown or logically proved. □□ **demonstrability** /-'bɪlɪtɪ/ *n.* **demonstrably** *adv.* [ME f. L *demonstrabilis* (as DEMONSTRATE)]

demonstrate /'demənˌstreɪt/ *v.* **1** *tr.* show evidence of (feelings etc.). **2** *tr.* describe and explain (a scientific proposition, machine, etc.) by experiment, practical use, etc. **3** *tr.* **a** logically prove the truth of. **b** be proof of the existence of. **4** *intr.* take part in or organize a public demonstration. **5** *intr.* act as a demonstrator. [L *demonstrare* (as DE-, *monstrare* show)]

demonstration /ˌdemən'streɪʃ(ə)n/ *n.* **1** (foll. by *of*) **a** the outward showing of feeling etc. **b** an instance of this. **2** a public meeting, march, etc., for a political or moral purpose. **3 a** the exhibiting or explaining of specimens or experiments as a method of esp. scientific teaching. **b** an instance of this. **4** proof provided by logic, argument, etc. **5** *Mil.* a show of military force. □□ **demonstrational** *adj.* [ME f. OF *demonstration* or L *demonstratio* (as DEMONSTRATE)]

demonstrative /dɪˈmɒnstrətɪv/ *adj. & n.* —*adj.* **1** given to or marked by an open expression of feeling, esp. of affection (*a very demonstrative person*). **2** (usu. foll. by *of*) logically conclusive; giving proof (*the work is demonstrative of their skill*). **3 a** serving to point out or exhibit. **b** involving esp. scientific demonstration (*demonstrative technique*). **4** *Gram.* (of an adjective or pronoun) indicating the person or thing referred to (e.g. *this, that, those*). —*n. Gram.* a demonstrative adjective or pronoun. □□ **demonstratively** *adv.* **demonstrativeness** *n.* [ME f. OF *demonstratif -ive* f. L *demonstrativus* (as DEMONSTRATE)]

demonstrator /'demənˌstreɪtə(r)/ *n.* **1** a person who takes part in a political demonstration etc. **2** a person who demonstrates, esp. machines, equipment, etc., to prospective customers. **3** a person who teaches

by demonstration, esp. in a laboratory etc. [L (as DEMONSTRATE)]

demoralize /dɪˈmɒrəˌlaɪz/ *v.tr.* (also **-ise**) **1** destroy (a person's) morale; make hopeless. **2** *archaic* corrupt (a person's) morals. □□ **demoralization** /-ˈzeɪʃ(ə)n/ *n.* **demoralizing** *adj.* **demoralizingly** *adv.* [F *démoraliser* (as DE-, MORAL)]

demote /dɪˈməʊt, diː-/ *v.tr.* reduce to a lower rank or class. □□ **demotion** /-ˈməʊʃ(ə)n/ *n.* [DE- + PROMOTE]

demotic /dɪˈmɒtɪk/ *n. & adj.* —*n.* **1** the popular colloquial form of a language. **2** a popular simplified form of ancient Egyptian writing (cf. HIERATIC). —*adj.* **1** (esp. of language) popular, colloquial, or vulgar. **2** of or concerning the ancient Egyptian or modern Greek demotic. [Gk *dēmotikos* f. *dēmotēs* one of the people (*dēmos*)]

demotivate /ˌdiːˈməʊtɪˌveɪt/ *v.tr.* (also *absol.*) cause to lose motivation; discourage. □□ **demotivation** /-ˈveɪʃ(ə)n/ *n.*

demount /diːˈmaʊnt/ *v.tr.* **1** take (apparatus, a gun, etc.) from its mounting. **2** dismantle for later reassembly. □□ **demountable** *adj. & n.* [F *démonter*: cf. DISMOUNT]

demulcent /dɪˈmʌls(ə)nt/ *adj. & n.* —*adj.* soothing. —*n.* an agent that forms a protective film soothing irritation or inflammation in the mouth. [L *demulcēre* (as DE-, *mulcēre* soothe)]

demur /dɪˈmɜː(r)/ *v. & n.* —*v.intr.* (**demurred, demurring**) **1** (often foll. by *to, at*) raise scruples or objections. **2** *Law* put in a demurrer. —*n.* (also **demurral** /dɪˈmʌr(ə)l/) (usu. in *neg.*) **1** an objection (*agreed without demur*). **2** the act or process of objecting. □□ **demurrant** /dɪˈmʌrənt/ *n.* (in sense 2 of *v.*). [ME f. OF *demeure* (n.), *demeurer* (v.) f. Rmc (as DE-, L *morari* delay)]

demure /dɪˈmjʊə(r)/ *adj.* (**demurer, demurest**) **1** composed, quiet, and reserved; modest. **2** affectedly shy and quiet; coy. **3** decorous (*a demure high collar*). □□ **demurely** *adv.* **demureness** *n.* [ME, perh. f. AF *demuré* f. OF *demoré* past part. of *demorer* remain, stay (as DEMUR): infl. by OF *meür* f. L *maturus* ripe]

demurrable /dɪˈmʌrəb(ə)l/ *adj.* esp. *Law* open to objection.

demurrage /dɪˈmʌrɪdʒ/ *n.* **1 a** a rate or amount payable to a shipowner by a charterer for failure to load or discharge a ship within the time agreed. **b** a similar charge on railway trucks or goods. **2** such a detention or delay. [OF *demo(u)rage* f. *demorer* (as DEMUR)]

demurrer /dɪˈmʌrə(r)/ *n. Law* an objection raised or exception taken. [AF (infin. as noun), = DEMUR]

demy /dɪˈmaɪ/ *n. Printing* a size of paper, 564 × 444 mm. [ME, var. of DEMI-]

demystify /diːˈmɪstɪˌfaɪ/ *v.tr.* (**-ies, -ied**) **1** clarify (obscure beliefs or subjects etc.). **2** reduce or remove the irrationality in (a person). □□ **demystification** /-fɪˈkeɪʃ(ə)n/ *n.*

demythologize /ˌdiːmɪˈθɒləˌdʒaɪz/ *v.tr.* (also **-ise**) **1** remove mythical elements from (a legend, famous person's life, etc.). **2** reinterpret what some consider to be the mythological elements in (the Bible).

den /den/ *n.* **1** a wild animal's lair. **2** a place of crime or vice (*den of iniquity; opium den*). **3** a small private room for pursuing a hobby etc. [OE *denn* f. Gmc, rel. to DEAN[2]]

denarius /dɪˈneərɪəs/ *n.* (*pl.* **denarii** /-rɪˌaɪ/) an ancient Roman silver coin. [L, = (coin) of ten asses (as DENARY: see AS[2])]

denary /'diːnərɪ/ *adj.* of ten; decimal. □**denary scale** = *decimal scale.* [L *denarius* containing ten (*deni* by tens)]

denationalize /diːˈnæʃənəˌlaɪz/ *v.tr.* (also **-ise**) **1** transfer (a nationalized industry or institution etc.) from public to private ownership. **2 a** deprive (a nation) of its status or characteristics as a nation. **b** deprive (a person) of nationality or national characteristics. □□ **denationalization** /-ˈzeɪʃ(ə)n/ *n.* [F *dénationaliser* (as DE-, NATIONAL)]

denaturalize /diːˈnætʃərəˌlaɪz/ *v.tr.* (also **-ise**) **1** change the nature or properties of; make unnatural. **2** deprive of the rights of citizenship. **3** = DENATURE *v.* **1**. □□ **denaturalization** /-ˈzeɪʃ(ə)n/ *n.*

denature /diːˈneɪtʃə(r)/ *v.tr.* **1** change the properties of (a protein etc.) by heat, acidity, etc. **2** make (alcohol) unfit for drinking esp. by the addition of another substance. □□ **denaturant** *n.* **denaturation** /diːˌnætʃəˈreɪʃ(ə)n/ *n.* [F *dénaturer* (as DE-, NATURE)]

dendrite /ˈdendraɪt/ *n.* **1 a** a stone or mineral with natural treelike or mosslike markings. **b** such marks on stones or minerals. **2** *Chem.* a crystal with branching treelike growth. **3** *Zool.* & *Anat.* a branching process of a nerve-cell conducting signals to a cell body. [F f. Gk *dendritēs* (adj.) f. *dendron* tree]

dendritic /denˈdrɪtɪk/ *adj.* **1** of or like a dendrite. **2** treelike in shape or markings. □□ **dendritically** *adv.*

dendrochronology /ˌdendrəʊkrəˈnɒlədʒɪ/ *n.* **1** a system of dating using the characteristic patterns of annual growth rings of trees to assign dates to timber. **2** the study of these growth rings. □□ **dendrochronological** /-ˌkrɒnəˈlɒdʒɪk(ə)l/ *adj.* **dendrochronologist** *n.* [Gk *dendron* tree + CHRONOLOGY]

dendroid /ˈdendrɔɪd/ *adj.* tree-shaped. [Gk *dendrōdēs* treelike + -OID]

dendrology /denˈdrɒlədʒɪ/ *n.* the scientific study of trees. □□ **dendrological** /-drəˈlɒdʒɪk(ə)l/ *adj.* **dendrologist** *n.* [Gk *dendron* tree + -LOGY]

dene[1] /diːn/ *n.* (also **dean**) *Brit.* **1** a narrow wooded valley. **2** a vale (esp. as the ending of place-names). [OE *denu*, rel. to DEN]

dene[2] /diːn/ *n.* *Brit.* a bare sandy tract, or a low sand-hill, by the sea. [orig. unkn.: cf. DUNE]

dengue /ˈdeŋgɪ/ *n.* an infectious viral disease of the tropics causing a fever and acute pains in the joints. [W. Ind. Sp., f. Swahili *denga*, *dinga*, with assim. to Sp. *dengue* fastidiousness, with ref. to the stiffness of the patient's neck and shoulders]

deniable /dɪˈnaɪəb(ə)l/ *adj.* that may be denied.

denial /dɪˈnaɪəl/ *n.* **1** the act or an instance of denying. **2** a refusal of a request or wish. **3** a statement that a thing is not true; a rejection (*denial of the accusation*). **4** a disavowal of a person as one's leader etc. **5** = SELF-DENIAL.

denier /ˈdenjə(r)/ *n.* a unit of weight by which the fineness of silk, rayon, or nylon yarn is measured. [orig. the name of a small coin: ME f. OF f. L *denarius*]

denigrate /ˈdenɪˌgreɪt/ *v.tr.* defame or disparage the reputation of (a person); blacken. □□ **denigration** /-ˈgreɪʃ(ə)n/ *n.* **denigrator** *n.* **denigratory** /-ˈgreɪtərɪ/ *adj.* [L *denigrare* (as DE-, *nigrare* f. *niger* black)]

denim /ˈdenɪm/ *n.* **1** (often *attrib.*) a usu. blue hard-wearing cotton twill fabric used for jeans, overalls, etc. (*a denim skirt*). **2** (in *pl.*) *colloq.* jeans, overalls, etc. made of this. [for *serge de Nim* f. *Nîmes* in S. France]

denitrify /diːˈnaɪtrɪˌfaɪ/ *v.tr.* (**-ies**, **-ied**) remove the nitrates or nitrites from (soil etc.). □□ **denitrification** /-fɪˈkeɪʃ(ə)n/ *n.*

denizen /ˈdenɪz(ə)n/ *n.* **1** a foreigner admitted to certain rights in his or her adopted country. **2** a naturalized foreign word, animal, or plant. **3** (usu. foll. by *of*) *poet.* an inhabitant or occupant. □□ **denizenship** *n.* [ME f. AF *deinzein* f. OF *deinz* within f. L *de* from + *intus* within + -*ein* f. L -*aneus*: see -ANEOUS]

denominate /dɪˈnɒmɪˌneɪt/ *v.tr.* **1** give a name to. **2** call or describe (a person or thing) as. [L *denominare* (as DE-, NOMINATE)]

denomination /dɪˌnɒmɪˈneɪʃ(ə)n/ *n.* **1** a Church or religious sect. **2** a class of units within a range or sequence of numbers, weights, money, etc. (*money of small denominations*). **3 a** a name or designation, esp. a characteristic or class name. **b** a class or kind having a specific name. **4** the rank of a playing-card

within a suit, or of a suit relative to others. □ **denominational education** education according to the principles of a Church or sect. □□ **denominational** *adj.* [ME f. OF *denomination* or L *denominatio* (as DENOMINATE)]

denominative /dɪˈnɒmɪnətɪv/ *adj.* serving as or giving a name. [LL *denominativus* (as DENOMINATION)]

denominator /dɪˈnɒmɪˌneɪtə(r)/ *n.* *Math.* the number below the line in a vulgar fraction; a divisor. □ **common denominator** **1** a common multiple of the denominators of several fractions. **2** a common feature of members of a group. **least** (or **lowest**) **common denominator** the lowest common multiple as above. [F *dénominateur* or med.L *denominator* (as DE-, NOMINATE)]

de nos jours /də nəʊ ˈʒʊə(r)/ *adj.* (placed after noun) of the present time. [F, = of our days]

denote /dɪˈnəʊt/ *v.tr.* **1** be a sign of; indicate (*the arrow denotes direction*). **2** (usu. foll. by *that* + clause) mean, convey. **3** stand as a name for; signify. □□ **denotation** /diːnəˈteɪʃ(ə)n/ *n.* **denotative** /-tətɪv/ *adj.* [F *dénoter* or f. L *denotare* (as DE-, *notare* mark f. *nota* NOTE)]

denouement /deɪˈnuːmɑ̃/ *n.* (also **dénouement**) **1** the final unravelling of a plot or complicated situation. **2** the final scene in a play, novel, etc., in which the plot is resolved. [F *dénouement* f. *dénouer* unknot (as DE-, L *nodare* f. *nodus* knot)]

denounce /dɪˈnaʊns/ *v.tr.* **1** accuse publicly; condemn (*denounced him as a traitor*). **2** inform against (*denounced her to the police*). **3** give notice of the termination of (an armistice, treaty, etc.). □□ **denouncement** *n.* **denouncer** *n.* [ME f. OF *denoncier* f. L *denuntiare* (as DE-, *nuntiare* make known f. *nuntius* messenger)]

de nouveau /də nuːˈvəʊ/ *adv.* starting again; anew. [F]

de novo /diː ˈnəʊvəʊ, deɪ/ *adv.* starting again; anew. [L]

dense /dens/ *adj.* **1** closely compacted in substance; thick (*dense fog*). **2** crowded together (*the population is less dense on the outskirts*). **3** *colloq.* stupid. □□ **densely** *adv.* **denseness** *n.* [F *dense* or L *densus*]

densitometer /ˌdensɪˈtɒmɪtə(r)/ *n.* an instrument for measuring the photographic density of an image on a film or photographic print.

density /ˈdensɪtɪ/ *n.* (*pl.* **-ies**) **1** the degree of compactness of a substance. **2** *Physics* degree of consistency measured by the quantity of mass per unit volume. **3** the opacity of a photographic image. **4** a crowded state. **5** stupidity. [F *densité* or L *densitas* (as DENSE)]

dent /dent/ *n.* & *v.* —*n.* **1** a slight mark or hollow in a surface made by, or as if by, a blow with a hammer etc. **2** a noticeable effect (*lunch made a dent in our funds*). —*v.tr.* **1** mark with a dent. **2** have (esp. an adverse) effect on (*the news dented our hopes*). [ME, prob. f. INDENT[1]]

dental /ˈdent(ə)l/ *adj.* **1** of the teeth; of or relating to dentistry. **2** *Phonet.* (of a consonant) produced with the tongue-tip against the upper front teeth (as *th*) or the ridge of the teeth (as *n*, *s*, *t*). □ **dental floss** a thread of floss silk etc. used to clean between the teeth. **dental mechanic** a person who makes and repairs artificial teeth. **dental surgeon** a dentist. □□ **dentalize** *v.tr.* (also **-ise**). [LL *dentalis* f. L *dens dentis* tooth]

dentalium /denˈteɪlɪəm/ *n.* (*pl.* **dentalia** /-lɪə/) **1** any marine mollusc of the genus *Dentalium*, having a conical foot protruding from a tusklike shell. **2** this shell used as an ornament or as a form of currency. [mod.L f. LL *dentalis*: see DENTAL]

dentate /ˈdenteɪt/ *adj.* *Bot.* & *Zool.* toothed; with toothlike notches; serrated. [L *dentatus* f. *dens dentis* tooth]

denticle /ˈdentɪk(ə)l/ *n.* *Zool.* a small tooth or toothlike projection, scale, etc. □□ **denticulate**

/den'tɪkjʊlət/ *adj.* [ME f. L *denticulus* dimin. of *dens dentis* tooth]

dentifrice /'dentɪfrɪs/ *n.* a paste or powder for cleaning the teeth. [F f. L *dentifricium* f. *dens dentis* tooth + *fricare* rub]

dentil /'dentɪl/ *n.* *Archit.* each of a series of small rectangular blocks as a decoration under the moulding of a cornice in classical architecture. [obs. F *dentille* dimin. of *dent* tooth f. L *dens dentis*]

dentilingual /ˌdentɪ'lɪŋgw(ə)l/ *adj.* *Phonet.* formed by the teeth and the tongue.

dentine /'denti:n/ *n.* (*US* **dentin** /-tɪn/) a hard dense bony tissue forming the bulk of a tooth. □□ **dentinal** /'dentɪn(ə)l/ *adj.* [L *dens dentis* tooth + -INE⁴]

dentist /'dentɪst/ *n.* a person who is qualified to treat the diseases and conditions that affect the mouth, jaws, teeth, and their supporting tissues, esp. the repair and extraction of teeth and the insertion of artificial ones. □□ **dentistry** *n.* [F *dentiste* f. *dent* tooth]

dentition /den'tɪʃ(ə)n/ *n.* **1** the type, number, and arrangement of teeth in a species etc. **2** the cutting of teeth; teething. [L *dentitio* f. *dentire* to teethe]

denture /'dentʃə(r)/ *n.* a removable artificial replacement for one or more teeth carried on a removable plate or frame. [F f. *dent* tooth]

denuclearize /di:'nju:klɪəˌraɪz/ *v.tr.* (also **-ise**) remove nuclear armaments from (a country etc.). □□ **denuclearization** /-'zeɪʃ(ə)n/ *n.*

denude /dɪ'nju:d/ *v.tr.* **1** make naked or bare. **2** (foll. by *of*) **a** strip of clothing, a covering, etc. **b** deprive of a possession or attribute. **3** *Geol.* lay (rock or a formation etc.) bare by removing what lies above. □□ **denudation** /ˌdi:nju:'deɪʃ(ə)n/ *n.* **denudative** /-dətɪv/ *adj.* [L *denudare* (as DE-, *nudus* naked)]

denumerable /dɪ'nju:mərəb(ə)l/ *adj.* *Math.* countable by correspondence with the infinite set of integers. □□ **denumerability** /-'bɪlɪtɪ/ *n.* **denumerably** *adv.* [LL *denumerare* (as DE-, *numerare* NUMBER)]

denunciation /dɪˌnʌnsɪ'eɪʃ(ə)n/ *n.* **1** the act of denouncing (a person, policy, etc.); public condemnation. **2** an instance of this. □□ **denunciate** /-'nʌnsɪˌeɪt/ *v.tr.* **denunciative** /-'nʌnsɪətɪv/ *adj.* **denunciator** /-'nʌnsɪˌeɪtə(r), -'nʌnʃɪˌeɪtə(r)/ *n.* **denunciatory** /dɪ'nʌnsɪətərɪ, -'nʌnʃɪətərɪ/ *adj.* [F *dénonciation* or L *denunciatio* (as DENOUNCE)]

deny /dɪ'naɪ/ *v.tr.* (-ies, -ied) **1** declare untrue or non-existent (*denied the charge*; *denied that it is so*; *denied having lied*). **2** repudiate or disclaim (*denied his faith*; *denied his signature*). **3** (often foll. by *to*) refuse (a person or thing, or something to a person) (*this was denied to me*; *denied him the satisfaction*). **4** refuse access to (a person sought) (*denied him his son*). □**deny oneself** be abstinent. □□ **denier** *n.* [ME f. OF *denier* f. L *denegare* (as DE-, *negare* say no)]

deoch an doris /ˌdɒx ən 'dɒrɪs, ˌdɒk/ *n.* (also **doch an dorris**) *Sc.* & *Ir.* a drink taken at parting; a stirrup-cup. [Gael. *deoch an doruis* drink at the door]

deodar /'di:əˌdɑː(r)/ *n.* the Himalayan cedar *Cedrus deodara*, the tallest of the cedar family, with drooping branches bearing large barrel-shaped cones. [Hindi *dē' odār* f. Skr. *deva-dāru* divine tree]

deodorant /di:'əʊdərənt/ *n.* (often *attrib.*) a substance sprayed or rubbed on to the body or sprayed into the air to remove or conceal unpleasant smells (*a roll-on deodorant*; *has a deodorant effect*). [as DEODORIZE + -ANT]

deodorize /di:'əʊdəˌraɪz/ *v.tr.* (also **-ise**) remove or destroy the (usu. unpleasant) smell of. □□ **deodorization** /-'zeɪʃ(ə)n/ *n.* **deodorizer** *n.* [DE- + L *odor* smell]

Deo gratias /ˌdeɪəʊ 'grɑːtɪəs, -ʃɪəs/ *int.* thanks be to God. [L, = (we give) thanks to God]

deontic /di:'ɒntɪk/ *adj.* *Philos.* of or relating to duty and obligation as ethical concepts. [Gk *deont-* part. stem of *dei* it is right]

deontology /ˌdi:ɒn'tɒlədʒɪ/ *n.* *Philos.* the study of duty. □□ **deontological** /-tə'lɒdʒɪk(ə)l/ *adj.* **deontologist** *n.*

Deo volente /ˌdeɪəʊ və'lenteɪ/ *adv.* God willing; if nothing prevents it. [L]

deoxygenate /di:'ɒksɪdʒəˌneɪt/ *v.tr.* remove oxygen, esp. free oxygen, from. □□ **deoxygenation** /-'neɪʃ(ə)n/ *n.*

deoxyribonucleic acid /ˌdi:ɒksɪˌraɪbəʊnjuˈkleɪɪk/ *n.* see DNA. [DE- + OXYGEN + RIBONUCLEIC (ACID)]

dep. *abbr.* **1** departs. **2** deputy.

depart /dɪ'pɑːt/ *v.* **1** *intr.* **a** (usu. foll. by *from*) go away; leave (*the train departs from this platform*). **b** (usu. foll. by *for*) start; set out (*trains depart for Crewe every hour*). **2** *intr.* (usu. foll. by *from*) diverge; deviate (*departs from standard practice*). **3** **a** *intr.* leave by death; die. **b** *tr.* *formal* or *literary* leave by death (*departed this life*). [ME f. OF *departir* ult. f. L *dispertire* divide]

departed /dɪ'pɑːtɪd/ *adj.* & *n.* —*adj.* bygone (*departed greatness*). —*n.* (prec. by *the*) *euphem.* a particular dead person or dead people (*we are here to mourn the departed*).

department /dɪ'pɑːtmənt/ *n.* **1** a separate part of a complex whole, esp.: **a** a branch of municipal or State administration (*Housing Department*; *Department of Social Security*). **b** a branch of study and its administration at a university, school, etc. (*the physics department*). **c** a specialized section of a large store (*hardware department*). **2** *colloq.* an area of special expertise. **3** an administrative district in France and other countries. □**department store** a large shop stocking many varieties of goods in different departments. [F *département* (as DEPART)]

departmental /ˌdi:pɑːt'ment(ə)l/ *adj.* of or belonging to a department. □**departmental store** = *department store*. □□ **departmentalism** *n.* **departmentalize** *v.tr.* (also **-ise**). **departmentalization** /-'zeɪʃ(ə)n/ *n.* **departmentally** *adv.*

departure /dɪ'pɑːtʃə(r)/ *n.* **1** the act or an instance of departing. **2** (often foll. by *from*) a deviation (from the truth, a standard, etc.). **3** (often *attrib.*) the starting of a train, an aircraft, etc. (*the departure was late*; *departure lounge*). **4** a new course of action or thought (*driving a car is rather a departure for him*). **5** *Naut.* the amount of a ship's change of longitude. [OF *departeüre* (as DEPART)]

depasture /di:'pɑːstʃə(r)/ *v.* **1 a** *tr.* (of cattle) graze upon. **b** *intr.* graze. **c** *tr.* put (cattle) to graze. **2** *tr.* (of land) provide pasturage for (cattle). □□ **depasturage** /-ɪdʒ/ *n.*

dépaysé /deɪ'peɪzeɪ/ *adj.* (*fem.* **dépaysée** pronunc. same) removed from one's habitual surroundings. [F, = removed from one's own country]

depend /dɪ'pend/ *v.intr.* **1** (often foll. by *on, upon*) be controlled or determined by (*success depends on hard work*; *it depends on whether they agree*; *it depends how you tackle the problem*). **2** (foll. by *on, upon*) **a** be unable to do without (*depends on her mother*). **b** rely on (*I'm depending on you to come*). **3** (foll. by *on, upon*) be grammatically dependent on. **4** (often foll. by *from*) *archaic poet.* hang down. □**depend upon it!** you may be sure! **it** (or **it all** or **that**) **depends** expressing uncertainty or qualification in answering a question (*Will they come? It depends*). [ME f. OF *dependre* ult. f. L *dependēre* (as DE-, *pendēre* hang)]

dependable /dɪ'pendəb(ə)l/ *adj.* reliable. □□ **dependability** /-'bɪlɪtɪ/ *n.* **dependableness** *n.* **dependably** *adv.*

dependant /dɪ'pend(ə)nt/ *n.* (*US* **dependent**) **1** a person who relies on another esp. for financial support. **2** a servant. [F *dépendant* pres. part. of *dépendre* (as DEPEND)]

dependence /dɪ'pend(ə)ns/ *n.* **1** the state of being dependent, esp. on financial or other support. **2** reliance; trust; confidence (*shows great dependence on his judgement*). [F *dépendance* (as DEPEND)]

dependency /dɪ'pendənsɪ/ *n.* (*pl.* **-ies**) **1** a country or province controlled by another. **2** anything subordinate or dependent.

dependent /dɪ'pend(ə)nt/ *adj. & n.* —*adj.* **1** (usu. foll. by *on*) depending, conditional, or subordinate. **2** unable to do without (esp. a drug). **3** maintained at another's cost. **4** *Math.* (of a variable) having a value determined by that of another variable. **5** *Gram.* (of a clause, phrase, or word) subordinate to a sentence or word. —*n. US* var. of DEPENDANT. □□ **dependently** *adv.* [ME, earlier *-ant* = DEPENDANT]

depersonalization /di:ˌpɜːsənəlaɪ'zeɪʃ(ə)n/ *n.* (also **-isation**) esp. *Psychol.* the loss of one's sense of identity.

depersonalize /di:'pɜːsənəˌlaɪz/ *v.tr.* (also **-ise**) **1** make impersonal. **2** deprive of personality.

depict /dɪ'pɪkt/ *v.tr.* **1** represent in a drawing or painting etc. **2** portray in words; describe (*the play depicts him as vain and petty*). □□ **depicter** *n.* **depiction** /-'pɪkʃ(ə)n/ *n.* **depictive** *adj.* **depictor** *n.* [L *depingere depict-* (as DE-, *pingere* paint)]

depilate /'depɪˌleɪt/ *v.tr.* remove the hair from. □□ **depilation** /-'leɪʃ(ə)n/ *n.* [L *depilare* (as DE-, *pilare* f. *pilus* hair)]

depilatory /dɪ'pɪlətərɪ/ *adj. & n.* —*adj.* that removes unwanted hair. —*n.* (*pl.* **-ies**) a depilatory substance.

deplane /di:'pleɪn/ *v.* esp. *US* **1** *intr.* disembark from an aeroplane. **2** *tr.* remove from an aeroplane.

deplete /dɪ'pliːt/ *v.tr.* (esp. in *passive*) **1** reduce in numbers or quantity (*depleted forces*). **2** empty out; exhaust (*their energies were depleted*). □□ **depletion** /-'pliːʃ(ə)n/ *n.* [L *deplēre* (as DE-, *plēre plet-* fill)]

deplorable /dɪ'plɔːrəb(ə)l/ *adj.* **1** exceedingly bad (*a deplorable meal*). **2** that can be deplored. □□ **deplorably** *adv.*

deplore /dɪ'plɔː(r)/ *v.tr.* **1** grieve over; regret. **2** be scandalized by; find exceedingly bad. □□ **deploringly** *adv.* [F *déplorer* or It. *deplorare* f. L *deplorare* (as DE-, *plorare* bewail)]

deploy /dɪ'plɔɪ/ *v.* **1** *Mil.* **a** *tr.* cause (troops) to spread out from a column into a line. **b** *intr.* (of troops) spread out in this way. **2** *tr.* bring (arguments, forces, etc.) into effective action. □□ **deployment** *n.* [F *déployer* f. L *displicare* (as DIS-, *plicare* fold) & LL *deplicare* explain]

deplume /di:'pluːm/ *v.tr.* **1** strip of feathers, pluck. **2** deprive of honours etc. [ME f. F *déplumer* or f. med.L *deplumare* (as DE-, L *pluma* feather)]

depolarize /di:'pəʊləˌraɪz/ *v.tr.* (also **-ise**) *Physics* reduce or remove the polarization of. □□ **depolarization** /-'zeɪʃ(ə)n/ *n.*

depoliticize /ˌdi:pə'lɪtɪˌsaɪz/ *v.tr.* (also **-ise**) **1** make (a person, an organization, etc.) non-political. **2** remove from political activity or influence. □□ **depoliticization** /-'zeɪʃ(ə)n/ *n.*

depolymerize /di:'pɒlɪməˌraɪz/ *v.tr. & intr.* (also **-ise**) *Chem.* break down into monomers or other smaller units. □□ **depolymerization** /-'zeɪʃ(ə)n/ *n.*

deponent /dɪ'pəʊnənt/ *adj. & n.* —*adj. Gram.* (of a verb, esp. in Latin or Greek) passive or middle in form but active in meaning. —*n.* **1** *Gram.* a deponent verb. **2** *Law* **a** a person making a deposition under oath. **b** a witness giving written testimony for use in court etc. [L *deponere* (as DE-, *ponere posit-* place): adj. from the notion that the verb had laid aside the passive sense]

depopulate /di:'pɒpjʊˌleɪt/ *v.* **1** *tr.* reduce the population of. **2** *intr.* decline in population. □□ **depopulation** /-'leɪʃ(ə)n/ *n.* [L *depopulari* (as DE-, *populari* lay waste f. *populus* people)]

deport /dɪ'pɔːt/ *v.tr.* **1 a** remove (an immigrant or foreigner) forcibly to another country; banish. **b** exile (a native) to another country. **2** *refl.* conduct (oneself) or behave (in a specified manner) (*deported himself well*). □□ **deportable** *adj.* **deportation** /ˌdi:pɔː'teɪʃ(ə)n/ *n.* [OF *deporter* and (sense 1) F *déporter* (as DE-, L *portare* carry)]

deportee /ˌdi:pɔː'ti:/ *n.* a person who has been or is being deported.

deportment /dɪ'pɔːtmənt/ *n.* bearing, demeanour, or manners, esp. of a cultivated kind. [F *déportement* (as DEPORT)]

depose /dɪ'pəʊz/ *v.* **1** *tr.* remove from office, esp. dethrone. **2** *intr. Law* (usu. foll. by *to*, or *that* + clause) bear witness, esp. on oath in court. [ME f. OF *deposer* after L *deponere*: see DEPONENT, POSE¹]

deposit /dɪ'pɒzɪt/ *n. & v.* —*n.* **1 a** *Brit.* a sum of money kept in an account in a bank. **b** anything stored or entrusted for safe keeping, usu. in a bank. **2 a** a sum payable as a first instalment on an item bought on hire purchase, or as a pledge for a contract. **b** a returnable sum payable on the short-term hire of a car, boat, etc. **3 a** a natural layer of sand, rock, coal, etc. **b** a layer of precipitated matter on a surface, e.g. fur on a kettle. —*v.tr.* (**deposited, depositing**) **1 a** put or lay down in a (usu. specified) place (*deposited the book on the floor*). **b** (of water, wind, etc.) leave (matter etc.) lying in a displaced position. **2 a** store or entrust for keeping. **b** pay (a sum of money) into a bank account, esp. a deposit account. **3** pay (a sum) as a first instalment or as a pledge for a contract. □**deposit account** *Brit.* a bank account that pays interest but from which money cannot usu. be withdrawn without notice or loss of interest. **on deposit** (of money) placed in a deposit account. [L *depositum* (n.), med.L *depositare* f. L *deponere deposit-* (as DEPONENT)]

depositary /dɪ'pɒzɪtərɪ/ *n.* (*pl.* **-ies**) a person to whom something is entrusted; a trustee. [LL *depositarius* (as DEPOSIT)]

deposition /ˌdi:pə'zɪʃ(ə)n, ˌdep-/ *n.* **1** the act or an instance of deposing, esp. a monarch; dethronement. **2** *Law* **a** the process of giving sworn evidence; allegation. **b** an instance of this. **c** evidence given under oath; a testimony. **3** the act or an instance of depositing. **4 (the Deposition) a** the taking down of the body of Christ from the Cross. **b** a representation of this. [ME f. OF f. L *depositio -onis* f. *deponere*: see DEPOSIT]

depositor /dɪ'pɒzɪtə(r)/ *n.* a person who deposits money, property, etc.

depository /dɪ'pɒzɪtərɪ/ *n.* (*pl.* **-ies**) **1 a** a storehouse for furniture etc. **b** a store (of wisdom, knowledge, etc.) (*the book is a depository of wit*). **2** = DEPOSITARY. [LL *depositorium* (as DEPOSIT)]

depot /'depəʊ/ *n.* **1** a storehouse. **2** *Mil.* **a** a storehouse for equipment etc. **b** the headquarters of a regiment. **3 a** a building for the servicing, parking, etc. of esp. buses, trains, or goods vehicles. **b** *US* a railway or bus station. [F *dépôt*, OF *depost* f. L (as DEPOSIT)]

deprave /dɪ'preɪv/ *v.tr.* pervert or corrupt, esp. morally. □□ **depravation** /ˌdeprə'veɪʃ(ə)n/ *n.* [ME f. OF *depraver* or L *depravare* (as DE-, *pravare* f. *pravus* crooked)]

depravity /dɪ'prævɪtɪ/ *n.* (*pl.* **-ies**) **1 a** moral corruption; wickedness. **b** an instance of this; a wicked act. **2** *Theol.* the innate corruptness of human nature. [DE- + obs. *pravity* f. L *pravitas* (as DEPRAVE)]

deprecate /'deprɪˌkeɪt/ *v.tr.* **1** express disapproval of or a wish against; deplore (*deprecate hasty action*). ¶ Often confused with *depreciate*. **2** plead earnestly against. **3** *archaic* pray against. □□ **deprecatingly** *adv.* **deprecation** /-'keɪʃ(ə)n/ *n.* **deprecative** /'deprɪkətɪv/ *adj.* **deprecator** *n.* **deprecatory** /-'keɪtərɪ/ *adj.* [L *deprecari* (as DE-, *precari* pray)]

depreciate /dɪ'priːʃɪˌeɪt, -sɪˌeɪt/ *v.* **1** *tr. & intr.* diminish in value (*the car has depreciated*). **2** *tr.* disparage; belittle (*they are always depreciating his taste*). **3** *tr.* reduce the purchasing power of (money). □□ **depreciatingly** *adv.* **depreciatory** /dɪ'priːʃɪətərɪ/ *adj.* [LL *depretiare* (as DE-, *pretiare* f. *pretium* price)]

depreciation /dɪˌpriːʃɪ'eɪʃ(ə)n, -sɪ'eɪʃ(ə)n/ *n.* **1** the amount of wear and tear (of a property etc.) for which a reduction may be made in a valuation, an estimate, or a balance sheet. **2** *Econ.* a decrease in the value of a currency. **3** the act or an instance of depreciating; belittlement.

b *but* d *dog* f *few* g *get* h *he* j *yes* k *cat* l *leg* m *man* n *no* p *pen* r *red* s *sit* t *top* v *voice*

depredation /ˌdeprɪˈdeɪʃ(ə)n/ n. (usu. in pl.) **1** despoiling, ravaging, or plundering. **2** an instance or instances of this. [F *déprédation* f. LL *depraedatio* (as DE-, *praedatio* -*onis* f. L *praedari* plunder)]

depredator /ˈdeprɪˌdeɪtə(r)/ n. a despoiler or pillager. □□ **depredatory** /ˈdeprɪˌdeɪtərɪ, dɪˈpredɪtərɪ/ adj. [LL *depraedator* (as DEPREDATION)]

depress /dɪˈpres/ v.tr. **1** push or pull down; lower (*depressed the lever*). **2** make dispirited or dejected. **3** *Econ.* reduce the activity of (esp. trade). **4** (as **depressed** adj.) **a** dispirited or miserable. **b** *Psychol.* suffering from depression. □ **depressed area** an area suffering from economic depression. □□ **depressible** adj. **depressing** adj. **depressingly** adv. [ME f. OF *depresser* f. LL *depressare* (as DE-, *pressare* frequent. of *premere* press)]

depressant /dɪˈpres(ə)nt/ adj. & n. —adj. **1** that depresses. **2** *Med.* sedative. —n. **1** *Med.* an agent, esp. a drug, that sedates. **2** an influence that depresses.

depression /dɪˈpreʃ(ə)n/ n. **1 a** *Psychol.* a state of extreme dejection or morbidly excessive melancholy; a mood of hopelessness and feelings of inadequacy, often with physical symptoms. **b** a reduction in vitality, vigour, or spirits. **2 a** a long period of financial and industrial decline; a slump. **b** (**the Depression**) the depression of 1929-34. **3** *Meteorol.* a lowering of atmospheric pressure, esp. the centre of a region of minimum pressure or the system of winds round it. **4** a sunken place or hollow on a surface. **5 a** a lowering or sinking (often foll. by *of*: *depression of freezing-point*). **b** pressing down. **6** *Astron.* & *Geog.* the angular distance of an object below the horizon or a horizontal plane. [ME f. OF or L *depressio* (as DE-, *premere press-* press)]

depressive /dɪˈpresɪv/ adj. & n. —adj. **1** tending to depress. **2** *Psychol.* involving or characterized by depression. —n. *Psychol.* a person suffering or with a tendency to suffer from depression. [F *dépressif* -*ive* or med.L *depressivus* (as DEPRESSION)]

depressor /dɪˈpresə(r)/ n. **1** *Anat.* **a** (in full **depressor muscle**) a muscle that causes the lowering of some part of the body. **b** a nerve that lowers blood pressure. **2** *Surgery* an instrument for pressing down an organ etc. [L (as DEPRESSION)]

depressurize /diːˈpreʃəˌraɪz/ v.tr. (also **-ise**) cause an appreciable drop in the pressure of the gas inside (a container), esp. to the ambient level. □□ **depressurization** /-ˈzeɪʃ(ə)n/ n.

deprivation /ˌdeprɪˈveɪʃ(ə)n, ˌdiːprʌɪ-/ n. **1** (usu. foll. by *of*) the act or an instance of depriving; the state of being deprived (*deprivation of liberty*; *suffered many deprivations*). **2 a** deposition from esp. an ecclesiastical office. **b** an instance of this. [med.L *deprivatio* (as DEPRIVE)]

deprive /dɪˈpraɪv/ v.tr. **1** (usu. foll. by *of*) strip, dispossess; debar from enjoying (*illness deprived him of success*). **2** (as **deprived** adj.) **a** (of a child etc.) suffering from the effects of a poor or loveless home. **b** (of an area) with inadequate housing, facilities, employment, etc. **3** *archaic* depose (esp. a clergyman) from office. □□ **deprivable** adj. **deprival** n. [ME f. OF *depriver* f. med.L *deprivare* (as DE-, L *privare* deprive)]

de profundis /ˌdeɪ prəˈfʊndɪs/ adv. & n. —adv. from the depths (of sorrow etc.). —n. a cry from the depths. [opening L words of Ps. 130]

Dept. abbr. Department.

depth /depθ/ n. **1 a** deepness (*the depth is not great at the edge*). **b** the measurement from the top down, from the surface inwards, or from the front to the back (*depth of the drawer is 12 inches*). **2** difficulty; abstruseness. **3 a** sagacity; wisdom. **b** intensity of emotion etc. (*the poem has little depth*). **4** an intensity of colour, darkness, etc. **5** (in pl.) **a** deep water, a deep place; an abyss. **b** a low, depressed state. **c** the lowest or inmost part (*the depths of the country*). **6** the middle (*in the depth of winter*). □ **depth-bomb** (or **-charge**) a bomb capable of exploding under

water, esp. for dropping on a submerged submarine etc. **depth psychology** psychoanalysis to reveal hidden motives etc. **in depth** comprehensively, thoroughly, or profoundly. **in-depth** adj. thorough; done in depth. **out of one's depth 1** in water over one's head. **2** engaged in a task or on a subject too difficult for one. [ME (as DEEP, -TH²)]

depthless /ˈdepθlɪs/ adj. **1** extremely deep; fathomless. **2** shallow, superficial.

depurate /ˈdepjʊəˌreɪt/ v.tr. & intr. make or become free from impurities. □□ **depuration** /-ˈreɪʃ(ə)n/ n. **depurative** /dɪˈpjʊərətɪv/ adj. & n. **depurator** n. [med.L *depurare* (as DE-, *purus* pure)]

deputation /ˌdepjʊˈteɪʃ(ə)n/ n. a group of people appointed to represent others, usu. for a specific purpose; a delegation. [ME f. LL *deputatio* (as DEPUTE)]

depute v. & n. —v.tr. /dɪˈpjuːt/ (often foll. by *to*) **1** appoint as a deputy. **2** delegate (a task, authority, etc.) (*deputed the leadership to her*). —n. /ˈdepjuːt/ *Sc.* a deputy. [ME f. OF *député* past part. of *deputer* f. L *deputare* regard as, allot (as DE-, *putare* think)]

deputize /ˈdepjʊˌtaɪz/ v.intr. (also **-ise**) (usu. foll. by *for*) act as a deputy or understudy.

deputy /ˈdepjʊtɪ/ n. (pl. **-ies**) **1** a person appointed or delegated to act for another or others (also attrib.: *deputy manager*). **2** *Polit.* a parliamentary representative in certain countries, e.g. France. **3** a coalmine official responsible for safety. □ **by deputy** by proxy. **Chamber of Deputies** the lower legislative assembly in some parliaments. **deputy lieutenant** *Brit.* the deputy of the Lord Lieutenant of a county. □□ **deputyship** n. [ME var. of DEPUTE n.]

deracinate /diːˈræsɪˌneɪt/ v.tr. *literary* **1** tear up by the roots. **2** obliterate, expunge. □□ **deracination** /-ˈneɪʃ(ə)n/ n. [F *déraciner* (as DE-, *racine* f. LL *radicina* dimin. of *radix* root)]

derail /dɪˈreɪl, diː-/ v.tr. (usu. in passive) cause (a train etc.) to leave the rails. □□ **derailment** n. [F *dérailler* (as DE-, RAIL¹)]

derange /dɪˈreɪndʒ/ v.tr. **1** throw into confusion; disorganize; cause to act irregularly. **2** (esp. as **deranged** adj.) make insane (*deranged by the tragic events*). **3** disturb; interrupt. □□ **derangement** n. [F *déranger* (as DE-, *rang* RANK¹)]

derate /diːˈreɪt/ v. **1** tr. remove part or all of the burden of rates from. **2** intr. diminish or remove rates.

deration /diːˈræʃ(ə)n/ v.tr. free (food etc.) from rationing.

Derby /ˈdɑːbɪ/ n. (pl. **-ies**) **1 a** an annual horse-race run on the flat at Epsom. **b** a similar race elsewhere (*Kentucky Derby*). **2** any important sporting contest. **3** (**derby**) *US* a bowler hat. □ **Derby Day** the day on which the Derby is run. **local Derby** a match between two teams from the same district. [the 12th Earl of *Derby* d. 1834, founder of the horse-race]

deregister /diːˈredʒɪstə(r)/ v.tr. remove from a register. □□ **deregistration** /-ˈstreɪʃ(ə)n/ n.

de règle /də ˈreɡl/ predic.adj. customary; proper. [F, = of rule]

derelict /ˈderəlɪkt, ˈderɪ-/ adj. & n. —adj. **1** abandoned, ownerless (esp. of a ship at sea or an empty decrepit property). **2** (esp. of property) ruined; dilapidated. **3** *US* negligent (of duty etc.). —n. **1 a** social outcast; a person without a home, a job, or property. **2** abandoned property, esp. a ship. [L *derelictus* past part. of *derelinquere* (as DE-, *relinquere* leave)]

dereliction /ˌderɪˈlɪkʃ(ə)n/ n. **1** (usu. foll. by *of*) **a** neglect; failure to carry out one's obligations (*dereliction of duty*). **b** an instance of this. **2** the act or an instance of abandoning; the process of being abandoned. **3 a** the retreat of the sea exposing new land. **b** the land so exposed. [L *derelictio* (as DERELICT)]

derequisition /diːˌrekwɪˈzɪʃ(ə)n/ v.tr. return (requisitioned property) to its former owner.

derestrict /ˌdiːrɪˈstrɪkt/ v.tr. **1** remove restrictions from. **2** remove speed restrictions from (a road, area, etc.). □□ **derestriction** *n.*

deride /dɪˈraɪd/ *v.tr.* laugh scornfully at; mock. □□ **derider** *n.* **deridingly** *adv.* [L *deridēre* (as DE-, *ridēre* ris- laugh)]

de rigueur /də rɪˈgɜː(r)/ *predic.adj.* required by custom or etiquette (*evening dress is de rigueur*). [F, = of strictness]

derision /dɪˈrɪʒ(ə)n/ *n.* ridicule; mockery (*bring into derision*). □**hold** (or **have**) **in derision** *archaic* mock at. □□ **derisible** /dɪˈrɪzɪb(ə)l/ *adj.* [ME f. OF f. LL *derisio -onis* (as DERIDE)]

derisive /dɪˈraɪsɪv/ *adj.* = DERISORY. □□ **derisively** *adv.* **derisiveness** *n.*

derisory /dɪˈraɪsərɪ/ *adj.* **1** scoffing; ironical; scornful (*derisory cheers*). **2** so small or unimportant as to be ridiculous (*derisory offer*; *derisory costs*). [LL *derisorius* (as DERISION)]

derivation /ˌderɪˈveɪʃ(ə)n/ *n.* **1** the act or an instance of deriving or obtaining from a source; the process of being derived. **2 a** the formation of a word from another word or from a root. **b** a derivative. **c** the tracing of the origin of a word. **d** a statement or account of this. **3** extraction, descent. **4** *Math.* a sequence of statements showing that a formula, theorem, etc., is a consequence of previously accepted statements. □□ **derivational** *adj.* [F *dérivation* or L *derivatio* (as DERIVE)]

derivative /dəˈrɪvətɪv, dɪ-/ *adj.* & *n.* —*adj.* derived from another source; not original (*his music is derivative and uninteresting*). —*n.* **1** something derived from another source, esp.: **a** a word derived from another or from a root (e.g. *quickly* from *quick*). **b** *Chem.* a chemical compound that is derived from another. **2** *Math.* a quantity measuring the rate of change of another. □□ **derivatively** *adv.* [F *dérivatif -ive* f. L *derivativus* (as DERIVE)]

derive /dɪˈraɪv/ *v.* **1** *tr.* (usu. foll. by *from*) get, obtain, or form (*derived satisfaction from work*). **2** *intr.* (foll. by *from*) arise from, originate in, be descended or obtained from (*happiness derives from many things*). **3** *tr.* gather or deduce (*derived the information from the clues*). **4** *tr.* **a** trace the descent of (a person). **b** show the origin of (a thing). **5** *tr.* (usu. foll. by *from*) show or state the origin or formation of (a word etc.) (*derived the word from Latin*). **6** *tr.* *Math.* obtain (a function) by differentiation. □□ **derivable** *adj.* [ME f. OF *deriver* or f. L *derivare* (as DE-, *rivus* stream)]

derm (also **derma**) var. of DERMIS.

dermatitis /ˌdɜːməˈtaɪtɪs/ *n.* inflammation of the skin. [Gk *derma -atos* skin + -ITIS]

dermatoglyphics /ˌdɜːmətəʊˈglɪfɪks/ *n.* the science or study of skin markings or patterns, esp. of the fingers, hands, and feet. □□ **dermatoglyphic** *adj.* **dermatoglyphically** *adv.* [as DERMATITIS + Gk *gluphē* carving: see GLYPH]

dermatology /ˌdɜːməˈtɒlədʒɪ/ *n.* the study of the diagnosis and treatment of skin disorders. □□ **dermatological** /-tə'lɒdʒɪk(ə)l/ *adj.* **dermatologist** *n.* [as DERMATITIS + -LOGY]

dermis /ˈdɜːmɪs/ *n.* (also **derm** /dɜːm/ or **derma** /ˈdɜːmə/) **1** (in general use) the skin. **2** *Anat.* the true skin, the thick layer of living tissue below the epidermis. □□ **dermal** *adj.* **dermic** *adj.* [mod.L, after EPIDERMIS]

dernier cri /ˌdernjeɪ ˈkriː/ *n.* the very latest fashion. [F, = last cry]

derogate /ˈderəˌɡeɪt/ *v.intr.* (foll. by *from*) *formal* **1** take away a part from; detract from (a merit, a right, etc.). **2** deviate from (correct behaviour etc.). □□ **derogative** /dɪˈrɒɡətɪv/ *adj.* [L *derogare* (as DE-, *rogare* ask)]

derogation /ˌderəˈɡeɪʃ(ə)n/ *n.* **1** (foll. by *of*) a lessening or impairment of (a law, authority, position, dignity, etc.). **2** deterioration; debasement. [ME f. F *dérogation* or L *derogatio* (as DEROGATE)]

derogatory /dɪˈrɒɡətərɪ/ *adj.* (often foll. by *to*) involving disparagement or discredit; insulting, depreciatory (*made a derogatory remark*; *derogatory to my position*). □□ **derogatorily** *adv.* [LL *derogatorius* (as DEROGATE)]

derrick /ˈderɪk/ *n.* **1** a kind of crane for moving or lifting heavy weights, having a movable pivoted arm. **2** the framework over an oil well or similar excavation, holding the drilling machinery. [obs. senses *hangman*, *gallows*, f. the name of a London hangman *c.*1600]

derrière /ˌderɪˈeə(r)/ *n. colloq. euphem.* the buttocks. [F, = behind]

derring-do /ˌderɪŋˈduː/ *n. literary joc.* heroic courage or action. [ME, = *daring to do*, misinterpreted by Spenser and by Scott]

derringer /ˈderɪndʒə(r)/ *n.* a small large-bore pistol. [H. *Deringer*, Amer. inventor d. 1868]

derris /ˈderɪs/ *n.* **1** any woody tropical climbing leguminous plant of the genus *Derris*, bearing leathery pods. **2** an insecticide made from the powdered root of some kinds of derris. [mod.L f. Gk, = leather covering (with ref. to its pod)]

derry /ˈderɪ/ *n.* □**have a derry on** *Austral.* & *NZ colloq.* be prejudiced against (a person). [app. f. the song-refrain *derry down*]

derv /dɜːv/ *n. Brit.* diesel oil for road vehicles. [f. *d*iesel-*e*ngined *r*oad-*v*ehicle]

dervish /ˈdɜːvɪʃ/ *n.* a member of any of several Muslim fraternities vowed to poverty and austerity. □**whirling** (or **dancing** or **howling**) **dervish** a dervish performing a wild dance, or howling, according to which sect he belongs to. [Turk. *derviş* f. Pers. *darvēsh* poor, a mendicant]

DES *abbr.* (in the UK) Department of Education and Science.

desalinate /diːˈsælɪˌneɪt/ *v.tr.* remove salt from (esp. sea water). □□ **desalination** /-ˈneɪʃ(ə)n/ *n.*

desalt /diːˈsɔːlt/ *v.tr.* = DESALINATE.

descale /diːˈskeɪl/ *v.tr.* remove the scale from.

descant /ˈdeskænt/ *n.* & *v.* —*n.* **1** *Mus.* an independent treble melody usu. sung or played above a basic melody, esp. of a hymn tune. **2** *poet.* a melody; a song. —*v.intr.* /dɪsˈkænt/ **1** (foll. by *on*, *upon*) talk lengthily and prosily, esp. in praise of. **2** *Mus.* sing or play a descant. □**descant recorder** the most common size of recorder, with a range of two octaves. [ME f. OF *deschant* f. med.L *discantus* (as DIS-, *cantus* song, CHANT)]

descend /dɪˈsend/ *v.* **1** *tr.* & *intr.* go or come down (a hill, stairs, etc.). **2** *intr.* (of a thing) sink, fall (*rain descended heavily*). **3** *intr.* slope downwards, lie along a descending slope (*fields descended to the beach*). **4** *intr.* (usu. foll. by *on*) **a** make a sudden attack. **b** make an unexpected and usu. unwelcome visit (*hope they don't descend on us at the weekend*). **5** *intr.* (usu. foll. by *from*, *to*) of property, qualities, rights, etc.) be passed by inheritance (*the house descends from my grandmother*; *the property descended to me*). **6** *intr.* a sink in rank, quality, etc. **b** (foll. by *to*) degrade oneself morally to (an unworthy act) (*descend to violence*). **7** *intr.* *Mus.* (of sound) become lower in pitch. **8** *intr.* (usu. foll. by *to*) proceed (in discourse or writing): **a** in time (to a subsequent event etc.). **b** from the general (to the particular) (*now let's descend to details*). **9** *tr.* go along (a river etc.) to the sea etc. **10** *intr.* *Printing* (of a letter) have its tail below the line. □**be descended from** have as an ancestor. □□ **descendent** *adj.* [ME f. OF *descendre* f. L *descendere* (as DE-, *scandere* climb)]

descendant /dɪˈsend(ə)nt/ *n.* (often foll. by *of*) a person or thing descended from another (*a descendant of Charles I*). [F, part. of *descendre* (as DESCEND)]

descender /dɪˈsendə(r)/ *n. Printing* a part of a letter that extends below the line.

descendible /dɪˈsendɪb(ə)l, -dəb(ə)l/ *adj.* **1** (of a slope etc.) that may be descended. **2** *Law* capable of descending by inheritance. [OF *descendable* (as DESCEND)]

descent /dɪ'sent/ *n.* **1 a** the act of descending. **b** an instance of this. **c** a downward movement. **2 a** a way or path etc. by which one may descend. **b** a downward slope. **3 a** being one descended; lineage, family origin (*traces his descent from William the Conqueror*). **b** the transmission of qualities, property, privileges, etc., by inheritance. **4 a** a decline; a fall. **b** a lowering (of pitch, temperature, etc.). **5** a sudden violent attack. [ME f. OF *descente* f. *descendre* DESCEND]

descramble /diː'skræmb(ə)l/ *v.tr.* **1** convert or restore (a signal) to intelligible form. **2** counteract the effects of (a scrambling device). **3** recover an original signal from (a scrambled signal). □□ **descrambler** *n.*

describe /dɪ'skraɪb/ *v.tr.* **1 a** state the characteristics, appearance, etc. of, in spoken or written form (*described the landscape*). **b** (foll. by *as*) assert to be; call (*described him as a habitual liar*). **2 a** mark out or draw (esp. a geometrical figure) (*described a triangle*). **b** move in (a specified way, esp. a curve) (*described a parabola through the air*). □□ **describable** *adj.* **describer** *n.* [L *describere* (as DE-, *scribere* script-write)]

description /dɪ'skrɪpʃ(ə)n/ *n.* **1 a** the act or an instance of describing; the process of being described. **b** a spoken or written representation (of a person, object, or event). **2** a sort, kind, or class (*no food of any description*). □ **answers** (or **fits**) **the description** has the qualities specified. [ME f. OF f. L *descriptio -onis* (as DESCRIBE)]

descriptive /dɪ'skrɪptɪv/ *adj.* **1** serving or seeking to describe (*a descriptive writer*). **2** describing or classifying without expressing feelings or judging (*a purely descriptive account*). **3** *Linguistics* describing a language without comparing, endorsing, or condemning particular usage, vocabulary, etc. **4** *Gram.* (of an adjective) describing the noun, rather than its relation, position, etc., e.g. *blue* as distinct from *few*. □□ **descriptively** *adv.* **descriptiveness** *n.* [LL *descriptivus* (as DESCRIBE)]

descriptor /dɪ'skrɪptə(r)/ *n. Linguistics* a word or expression etc. used to describe or identify. [L, = describer (as DESCRIBE)]

descry /dɪ'skraɪ/ *v.tr.* (**-ies**, **-ied**) *literary* catch sight of; discern (*descried him in the crowd*; *descries no glimmer of light in her situation*). [ME (earlier senses 'proclaim, DECRY') f. OF *descrier*: prob. confused with var. of obs. *descrive* f. OF *descrivre* DESCRIBE]

desecrate /'desɪ,kreɪt/ *v.tr.* **1** violate (a sacred place or thing) with violence, profanity, etc. **2** deprive (a church, a sacred object, etc.) of sanctity; deconsecrate. □□ **desecration** /-'kreɪʃ(ə)n/ *n.* **desecrator** *n.* [DE- + CONSECRATE]

deseed /diː'siːd/ *v.tr.* remove the seeds from (a plant, vegetable, etc.).

desegregate /diː'segrɪ,geɪt/ *v.tr.* abolish racial segregation in (schools etc.) or of (people etc.). □□ **desegregation** /-'geɪʃ(ə)n/ *n.*

deselect /ˌdiːsɪ'lekt/ *v.tr. Polit.* decline to select or retain as a constituency candidate in an election. □□ **deselection** *n.*

desensitize /diː'sensɪ,taɪz/ *v.tr.* (also **-ise**) reduce or destroy the sensitiveness of (photographic materials, an allergic person, etc.). □□ **desensitization** /-'zeɪʃ(ə)n/ *n.* **desensitizer** *n.*

desert¹ /dɪ'zɜːt/ *v.* **1** *tr.* abandon, give up, leave (*deserted the sinking ship*). **2** *tr.* forsake or abandon (a cause or a person, people, etc., having claims on one) (*deserted his wife and children*). **3** *tr.* fail (*his presence of mind deserted him*). **4** *intr. Mil.* run away (esp. from military service). **5** *tr.* (as **deserted** *adj.*) empty, abandoned (*a deserted house*). □□ **deserter** *n.* (in sense 4 of *v.*). **desertion** /-'zɜːʃ(ə)n/ *n.* [F *déserter* f. LL *desertare* f. L *desertus* (as DESERT²)]

desert² /'dezət/ *n.* & *adj.* —*n.* a dry barren often sand-covered area of land, characteristically desolate, waterless, and without vegetation; an uninteresting or barren subject, period, etc. (*a cultural desert*). —*adj.* **1** uninhabited, desolate. **2** uncultivated, barren. □ **desert boot** a suede etc. boot reaching to or extending just above the ankle. **desert island** a remote (usu. tropical) island presumed to be uninhabited. **desert rat** *Brit. colloq.* a soldier of the 7th British armoured division (with the jerboa as a badge) in the N. African desert campaign of 1941-2. [ME f. OF f. L *desertus*, eccl.L *desertum* (n.), past part. of *deserere* leave, forsake]

desert³ /dɪ'zɜːt/ *n.* **1** (in *pl.*) **a** acts or qualities deserving reward or punishment. **b** such reward or punishment (*has got his deserts*). **2** the fact of being worthy of reward or punishment; deservingness. [ME f. OF f. *deservir* DESERVE]

desertification /dɪ,sɜːtɪfɪ'keɪʃ(ə)n/ *n.* the process of making or becoming a desert.

deserve /dɪ'zɜːv/ *v.tr.* (often foll. by *to* + infin.) show conduct or qualities worthy of (reward, punishment, etc.) (*deserves to be imprisoned*; *deserves a prize*). □ **deserve well** (or **ill**) **of** be worthy of good (or bad) treatment at the hands of (*deserves well of the electorate*). □□ **deservedly** /-vɪdlɪ/ *adv.* **deservedness** /-vɪdnɪs/ *n.* **deserver** *n.* [ME f. OF *deservir* f. L *deservire* (as DE-, *servire* serve)]

deserving /dɪ'zɜːvɪŋ/ *adj.* meritorious. □ **deserving of** showing conduct or qualities worthy of (praise, blame, help, etc.). □□ **deservingly** *adv.* **deservingness** *n.*

desex /diː'seks/ *v.tr.* **1** castrate or spay (an animal). **2** deprive of sexual qualities or attractions.

desexualize /diː'seksjuə,laɪz/ *v.tr.* (also **-ise**) deprive of sexual character or of the distinctive qualities of a sex.

déshabillé /ˌdezæ'biːeɪ/ *n.* (also **déshabille** /ˌdeɪzæ'biːl/, **dishabille** /ˌdɪsæ'biːl/) a state of being only partly or carelessly clothed. [F, = undressed]

desiccant /'desɪkənt/ *n. Chem.* a hygroscopic substance used as a drying agent.

desiccate /'desɪ,keɪt/ *v.tr.* remove the moisture from, dry (esp. food for preservation) (*desiccated coconut*). □□ **desiccation** /-'keɪʃ(ə)n/ *n.* **desiccative** /-kətɪv/ *adj.* [L *desiccare* (as DE-, *siccus* dry)]

desiccator /'desɪ,keɪtə(r)/ *n.* **1** an apparatus for desiccating. **2** *Chem.* an apparatus containing a drying agent to remove the moisture from specimens.

desiderate /dɪ'zɪdə,reɪt, -'sɪdə,reɪt/ *v.tr. archaic* feel to be missing; regret the absence of; wish to have. [L *desiderare* (as DE-, *siderare* as in CONSIDER)]

desiderative /dɪ'zɪdərətɪv, -'sɪdərətɪv/ *adj.* & *n.* —*adj.* **1** *Gram.* (of a verb, conjugation, etc.) formed from another verb etc. and denoting a desire to perform the action of that verb etc. **2** desiring. —*n. Gram.* a desiderative verb, conjugation, etc. [LL *desiderativus* (as DESIDERATE)]

desideratum /dɪ,zɪdə'rɑːtəm, dɪ,sɪd-/ *n.* (*pl.* **desiderata** /-tə/) something lacking but needed or desired. [L neut. past part.: see DESIDERATE]

design /dɪ'zaɪn/ *n.* & *v.* —*n.* **1 a** a preliminary plan or sketch for the making or production of a building, machine, garment, etc. **b** the art of producing these. **2** a scheme of lines or shapes forming a pattern or decoration. **3** a plan, purpose, or intention. **4 a** the general arrangement or layout of a product. **b** an established version of a product (*one of our most popular designs*). —*v.* **1** *tr.* produce a design for (a building, machine, picture, garment, etc.). **2** *tr.* intend, plan, or purpose (*the remark was designed to offend*; *a course designed for beginners*; *designed an attack*). **3** *absol.* be a designer. □ **argument from design** *Theol.* the argument that God's existence is provable by the evidence of design in the universe. **by design** on purpose. **have designs on** plan to harm or appropriate. [F *désigner* appoint or obs. F *desseing* ult. f. L *designare* DESIGNATE]

designate *v.* & *adj.* —*v.tr.* /'dezɪg,neɪt/ **1** (often foll.

by *as*) appoint to an office or function (*designated him as postmaster general*; *designated his own successor*). **2** specify or particularize (*receives guests at designated times*). **3** (often foll. by *as*) describe as; entitle, style. **4** serve as the name or distinctive mark of (*English uses French words to designate ballet steps*). —*adj.* /'dezɪgnət/ (placed after noun) appointed to an office but not yet installed (*bishop designate*). □□ **designator** /-ˌneɪtə(r)/ *n.* [L *designare*, past part. *designatus* (as DE-, *signare* f. *signum* mark)]

designation /ˌdezɪg'neɪʃ(ə)n/ *n.* **1** a name, description, or title. **2** the act or process of designating. [ME f. OF *designation* or L *designatio* (as DESIGNATE)]

designedly /dɪ'zaɪnɪdlɪ/ *adv.* by design; on purpose.

designer /dɪ'zaɪnə(r)/ *n.* **1** a person who makes artistic designs or plans for construction, e.g. for clothing, machines, theatre sets; a draughtsman. **2** (*attrib.*) (of clothing etc.) bearing the name or label of a famous designer; prestigious. □**designer drug** a synthetic analogue, not itself illegal, of an illegal drug.

designing /dɪ'zaɪnɪŋ/ *adj.* crafty, artful, or scheming. □□ **designingly** *adv.*

desirable /dɪ'zaɪərəb(ə)l/ *adj.* **1** worth having or wishing for (*it is desirable that nobody should smoke*). **2** arousing sexual desire; very attractive. □□ **desirability** /-'bɪlɪtɪ/ *n.* **desirableness** *n.* **desirably** *adv.* [ME f. OF (as DESIRE)]

desire /dɪ'zaɪə(r)/ *n.* & *v.* —*n.* **1 a** an unsatisfied longing or craving. **b** an expression of this; a request (*expressed a desire to rest*). **2** lust. **3** something desired (*achieved his heart's desire*). —*v.tr.* **1** (often foll. by *to* + infin., or *that* + clause) long for; crave. **2** request (*desires a cup of tea*). **3** *archaic* pray, entreat, or command (*desire him to wait*). [ME f. OF *desir* f. *desirer* f. L *desiderare* DESIDERATE]

desirous /dɪ'zaɪərəs/ *predic.adj.* **1** (usu. foll. by *of*) ambitious, desiring (*desirous of stardom*; *desirous of doing well*). **2** (usu. foll. by *to* + infin., or *that* + clause) wishful; hoping (*desirous to do the right thing*). [ME f. AF *desirous*, OF *desireus* f. Rmc (as DESIRE)]

desist /dɪ'zɪst/ *v.intr.* (often foll. by *from*) *literary* abstain; cease (*please desist from interrupting*; *when requested, he desisted*). [OF *desister* f. L *desistere* (as DE-, *sistere* stop, redupl. f. *stare* stand)]

desk /desk/ *n.* **1** a piece of furniture or a portable box with a flat or sloped surface for writing on, and often drawers. **2** a counter in a hotel, bank, etc., which separates the customer from the assistant. **3** a section of a newspaper office etc. dealing with a specified topic (*the sports desk*; *the features desk*). **4** *Mus.* a music stand in an orchestra regarded as a unit of two players. □**desk-bound** obliged to remain working at a desk. [ME f. med.L *desca* f. L DISCUS disc]

desktop /'desktɒp/ *n.* **1** the working surface of a desk. **2** (*attrib.*) (esp. of a microcomputer) suitable for use at an ordinary desk. □**desktop publishing** the production of printed matter with a desktop computer and printer.

desman /'desmən/ *n.* (*pl.* **desmans**) any aquatic flesh-eating shrewlike mammal of two species, one originating in Russia (*Desmana moschata*) and one in the Pyrenees (*Galemys pyrenaicus*). [F & G f. Sw. *desman-råtta* musk-rat]

desolate *adj.* & *v.* —*adj.* /'desələt/ **1** left alone; solitary. **2** (of a building or place) uninhabited, ruined, neglected, barren, dreary, empty (*a desolate moor*). **3** forlorn; wretched; miserable (*was left desolate and weeping*). —*v.tr.* /'desəˌleɪt/ **1** depopulate or devastate; lay waste to. **2** (esp. as **desolated** *adj.*) make wretched or forlorn (*desolated by grief*; *inconsolable and desolated*). □□ **desolately** /-lətlɪ/ *adv.* **desolateness** /-lətnɪs/ *n.* **desolator** /-ˌleɪtə(r)/ *n.* [ME f. L *desolatus* past part. of *desolare* (as DE-, *solare* f. *solus* alone)]

desolation /ˌdesə'leɪʃ(ə)n/ *n.* **1 a** the act of desolating.

b the process of being desolated. **2** loneliness, grief, or wretchedness, esp. caused by desertion. **3** a neglected, ruined, barren, or empty state. [ME f. LL *desolatio* (as DESOLATE)]

desorb /diː'zɔːb/ *v.* **1** *tr.* cause the release of (an adsorbed substance) from a surface. **2** *intr.* (of an adsorbed substance) become released. □□ **desorbent** *adj.* & *n.* **desorption** *n.* [DE-, after ADSORB]

despair /dɪ'speə(r)/ *n.* & *v.* —*n.* the complete loss or absence of hope. —*v.intr.* **1** (often foll. by *of*) lose or be without hope (*despaired of ever seeing her again*). **2** (foll. by *of*) lose hope about (*his life is despaired of*). □**be the despair of** be the cause of despair by badness or unapproachable excellence (*he's the despair of his parents*). □□ **despairingly** *adv.* [ME f. OF *desespeir*, *desperer* f. L *desperare* (as DE-, *sperare* hope)]

despatch var. of DISPATCH.

desperado /ˌdespə'rɑːdəʊ/ *n.* (*pl.* **-oes** or *US* **-os**) a desperate or reckless person, esp. a criminal. [after DESPERATE (obs. n.) & words in -ADO]

desperate /'despərət/ *adj.* **1** reckless from despair; violent and lawless. **2 a** extremely dangerous or serious (*a desperate situation*). **b** staking all on a small chance (*a desperate remedy*). **3** very bad (*a desperate night*; *desperate poverty*). **4** (usu. foll. by *for*) needing or desiring very much (*desperate for recognition*). □□ **desperately** *adv.* **desperateness** *n.* **desperation** /-'reɪʃ(ə)n/ *n.* [ME f. L *desperatus* past part. of *desperare* (as DE-, *sperare* hope)]

despicable /'despɪkəb(ə)l, dɪ'spɪk-/ *adj.* vile; contemptible, esp. morally. □□ **despicably** *adv.* [LL *despicabilis* f. *despicari* (as DE-, *specere* look at)]

despise /dɪ'spaɪz/ *v.tr.* look down on as inferior, worthless, or contemptible. □□ **despiser** *n.* [ME f. *despis-* pres. stem of OF *despire* f. L *despicere* (as DE-, *specere* look at)]

despite /dɪ'spaɪt/ *prep.* & *n.* —*prep.* in spite of. —*n.* *archaic* or *literary* **1** outrage, injury. **2** malice, hatred (*died of mere despite*). □**despite** (or **in despite**) **of** *archaic* in spite of. □□ **despiteful** *adj.* [ME f. OF *despit* f. L *despectus* noun f. *despicere* (as DESPISE)]

despoil /dɪ'spɔɪl/ *v.tr.* *literary* (often foll. by *of*) plunder; rob; deprive (*despoiled the roof of its lead*). □□ **despoiler** *n.* **despoilment** *n.* **despoliation** /dɪˌspəʊlɪ'eɪʃ(ə)n/ *n.* [ME f. OF *despoill(i)er* f. L *despoliare* (as DE-, *spoliare* SPOIL)]

despond /dɪ'spɒnd/ *v.* & *n.* —*v.intr.* lose heart or hope; be dejected. —*n.* *archaic* despondency. [L *despondēre* give up, abandon (as DE-, *spondēre* promise)]

despondent /dɪ'spɒnd(ə)nt/ *adj.* in low spirits, dejected. □□ **despondence** *n.* **despondency** *n.* **despondently** *adv.*

despot /'despɒt/ *n.* **1** an absolute ruler. **2** a tyrant or oppressor. □□ **despotic** /-'spɒtɪk/ *adj.* **despotically** /-'spɒtɪkəlɪ/ *adv.* [F *despote* f. med.L *despota* f. Gk *despotēs* master, lord]

despotism /'despəˌtɪz(ə)m/ *n.* **1 a** rule by a despot. **b** a country ruled by a despot. **2** absolute power or control; tyranny.

desquamate /'deskwəˌmeɪt/ *v.intr.* *Med.* (esp. of the skin) come off in scales (as in some diseases). □□ **desquamation** /-'meɪʃ(ə)n/ *n.* **desquamative** /-'skwæmətɪv/ *adj.* **desquamatory** /-'skwæmətərɪ/ *adj.* [L *desquamare* (as DE-, *squama* scale)]

des res /dez 'rez/ *n. sl.* a desirable residence. [abbr.]

dessert /dɪ'zɜːt/ *n.* **1** the sweet course of a meal, served at or near the end. **2** *Brit.* a course of fruit, nuts, etc., served after a meal. □**dessert wine** usu. sweet wine drunk with or following dessert. [F, past part. of *desservir* clear the table (as DIS-, *servir* SERVE)]

dessertspoon /dɪ'zɜːtˌspuːn/ *n.* **1** a spoon used for dessert, smaller than a tablespoon and larger than a teaspoon. **2** the amount held by this. □□ **dessertspoonful** *n.* (*pl.* **-fuls**).

destabilize /diː'steɪbɪˌlaɪz/ *v.tr.* (also **-ise**) **1** render

unstable. **2** subvert (esp. a foreign government). □□
destabilization /-'zeɪʃ(ə)n/ *n.*

destination /ˌdestɪ'neɪʃ(ə)n/ *n.* a place to which a person or thing is going. [OF *destination* or L *destinatio* (as DESTINE)]

destine /'destɪn/ *v.tr.* (often foll. by *to*, *for*, or *to* + infin.) set apart; appoint; preordain; intend (*destined him for the navy*). □**be destined to** be fated or preordained to (*was destined to become a great man*). [ME f. F *destiner* f. L *destinare* (as DE-, *stanare* (unrecorded) settle f. *stare* stand)]

destiny /'destɪnɪ/ *n.* (*pl.* **-ies**) **1 a** the predetermined course of events; fate. **b** this regarded as a power. **2** what is destined to happen to a particular person etc. (*it was their destiny to be rejected*). [ME f. OF *destinée* f. Rmc, past part. of *destinare*: see DESTINE]

destitute /'destɪtjuːt/ *adj.* **1** without food, shelter, etc.; completely impoverished. **2** (usu. foll. by *of*) lacking (*destitute of friends*). □□**destitution** /-'tjuːʃ(ə)n/ *n.* [ME f. L *destitutus* past part. of *destituere* forsake (as DE-, *statuere* place)]

destrier /'destrɪə(r)/ *n. hist.* a war-horse. [ME f. AF *destrer*, OF *destrier* ult. f. L DEXTER[1] right (as the knight's horse was led by the squire with the right hand)]

destroy /dɪ'strɔɪ/ *v.tr.* **1** pull or break down; demolish (*destroyed the bridge*). **2** end the existence of (*the accident destroyed her confidence*). **3** kill (esp. a sick or savage animal). **4** make useless; spoil utterly. **5** ruin financially, professionally, or in reputation. **6** defeat (*destroyed the enemy*). [ME f. OF *destruire* ult. f. L *destruere* (as DE-, *struere struct-* build)]

destroyer /dɪ'strɔɪə(r)/ *n.* **1** a person or thing that destroys. **2** *Naut.* a fast warship with guns and torpedoes used to protect other ships.

destruct /dɪ'strʌkt/ *v. & n. US* esp. *Astronaut.* —*v.* **1** *tr.* destroy (one's own rocket etc.) deliberately, esp. for safety reasons. **2** *intr.* be destroyed in this way. —*n.* an act of destructing. [L *destruere* (as DESTROY) or as back-form. f. DESTRUCTION]

destructible /dɪ'strʌktɪb(ə)l/ *adj.* able to be destroyed. □□**destructibility** /-'bɪlɪtɪ/ *n.* [F *destructible* or LL *destructibilis* (as DESTROY)]

destruction /dɪ'strʌkʃ(ə)n/ *n.* **1** the act or an instance of destroying; the process of being destroyed. **2** a cause of ruin; something that destroys (*greed was their destruction*). [ME f. OF f. L *destructio -onis* (as DESTROY)]

destructive /dɪ'strʌktɪv/ *adj.* **1** (often foll. by *to*, *of*) destroying or tending to destroy (*destructive of her peace of mind*; *is destructive to organisms*; *a destructive child*). **2** negative in attitude or criticism; refuting without suggesting, helping, amending, etc. (opp. CONSTRUCTIVE) (*has only destructive criticism to offer*). □□**destructively** *adv.* **destructiveness** *n.* [ME f. OF *destructif -ive* f. LL *destructivus* (as DESTROY)]

destructor /dɪ'strʌktə(r)/ *n. Brit.* a refuse-burning furnace.

desuetude /dɪ'sjuːɪˌtjuːd, 'deswɪ-/ *n.* a state of disuse (*the custom fell into desuetude*). [F *désuétude* or L *desuetudo* (as DE-, *suescere suet-* be accustomed)]

desultory /'dezəltərɪ/ *adj.* **1** going constantly from one subject to another, esp. in a half-hearted way. **2** disconnected; unmethodical; superficial. □□ **desultorily** *adv.* **desultoriness** *n.* [L *desultorius* superficial f. *desultor* vaulter f. *desult-* (as DE-, *salt-* past part. stem of *salire* leap)]

detach /dɪ'tætʃ/ *v.tr.* **1** (often foll. by *from*) unfasten or disengage and remove (*detached the buttons*; *detached himself from the group*). **2** *Mil.* send (a ship, regiment, officer, messenger, etc.) on a separate mission. **3** (as **detached** *adj.*) **a** impartial; unemotional (*a detached viewpoint*). **b** (esp. of a house) not joined to another or others; separate. □□ **detachable** *adj.* **detachedly** /dɪ'tætʃɪdlɪ/ *adv.* [F *détacher* (as DE-, ATTACH)]

detachment /dɪ'tætʃmənt/ *n.* **1 a** a state of aloofness

from or indifference to other people, one's surroundings, public opinion, etc. **b** disinterested independence of judgement. **2 a** the act or process of detaching or being detached. **b** an instance of this. **3** *Mil.* a separate group or unit of an army etc. used for a specific purpose. [F *détachement* (as DETACH)]

detail /'diːteɪl/ *n. & v.* —*n.* **1 a** a small or subordinate particular; an item. **b** such a particular, considered (ironically) to be unimportant (*the truth of the statement is just a detail*). **2 a** small items or particulars (esp. in an artistic work) regarded collectively (*has an eye for detail*). **b** the treatment of them (*the detail was insufficient and unconvincing*). **3** (often in *pl.*) a number of particulars; an aggregate of small items (*filled in the details on the form*). **4 a** a minor decoration on a building, in a picture, etc. **b** a small part of a picture etc. shown alone. **5** *Mil.* **a** the distribution of orders for the day. **b** a small detachment of soldiers etc. for special duty. —*v.tr.* **1** give particulars of (*detailed the plans*). **2** relate circumstantially (*detailed the anecdote*). **3** *Mil.* assign for special duty. **4** (as **detailed** *adj.*) **a** (of a picture, story, etc.) having many details. **b** itemized (*a detailed list*). □**go into detail** give all the items or particulars. **in detail** item by item, minutely. [F *détail*, *détailler* (as DE-, *tailler* cut, formed as TAIL[2])]

detain /dɪ'teɪn/ *v.tr.* **1** keep in confinement or under restraint. **2** keep waiting; delay. □□**detainment** *n.* [ME f. OF *detenir* ult. f. L *detinēre detent-* (as DE-, *tenēre* hold)]

detainee /ˌdiːteɪ'niː/ *n.* a person detained in custody, esp. for political reasons.

detainer /dɪ'teɪnə(r)/ *n. Law* **1** the wrongful detaining of goods taken from the owner for distraint etc. **2** the detention of a person in prison etc. [AF *detener* f. OF *detenir* (as DETAIN)]

detect /dɪ'tekt/ *v.tr.* **1 a** (often foll. by *in*) reveal the guilt of; discover (*detected him in his crime*). **b** discover (a crime). **2** discover or perceive the existence or presence of (*detected a smell of burning*; *do I detect a note of sarcasm?*). **3** *Physics* use an instrument to observe (a signal, radiation, etc.). □□ **detectable** *adj.* **detectably** *adv.* [L *detegere detect-* (as DE-, *tegere* cover)]

detection /dɪ'tekʃ(ə)n/ *n.* **1 a** the act or an instance of detecting; the process of being detected. **b** an instance of this. **2** the work of a detective. **3** *Physics* the extraction of a desired signal; a demodulation. [LL *detectio* (as DETECT)]

detective /dɪ'tektɪv/ *n. & adj.* —*n.* (often *attrib.*) a person, esp. a member of a police force, employed to investigate crime. —*adj.* serving to detect. □**private detective** a usu. freelance detective carrying out investigations for a private employer. [DETECT]

detector /dɪ'tektə(r)/ *n.* **1** a person or thing that detects. **2** *Physics* a device for the detection or demodulation of signals.

detent /dɪ'tent/ *n.* **1** a catch by the removal of which machinery is allowed to move. **2** (in a clock etc.) a catch that regulates striking. [F *détente* f. OF *destente* f. *destendre* slacken (as DE-, L *tendere*)]

détente /deɪ'tɑːt/ *n.* an easing of strained relations esp. between States. [F, = relaxation]

detention /dɪ'tenʃ(ə)n/ *n.* **1** detaining or being detained. **2 a** being kept in school after hours as a punishment. **b** an instance of this. **3** custody; confinement. □**detention centre** *Brit.* an institution for the brief detention of young offenders. [F *détention* or LL *detentio* (as DETAIN)]

deter /dɪ'tɜː(r)/ *v.tr.* (**deterred**, **deterring**) **1** (often foll. by *from*) discourage or prevent (a person) through fear or dislike of the consequences. **2** discourage, check, or prevent (a thing, process, etc.). □□ **determent** *n.* [L *deterrēre* (as DE-, *terrēre* frighten)]

detergent /dɪ'tɜːdʒ(ə)nt/ *n. & adj.* —*n.* a cleansing agent, esp. a synthetic substance (usu. other than soap) used with water as a means of removing dirt etc. —*adj.* cleansing, esp. in the manner of a detergent. [L *detergēre* (as DE-, *tergēre ters-* wipe)]

deteriorate /dɪ'tɪərɪəˌreɪt/ *v.tr.* & *intr.* make or become bad or worse (*food deteriorates in hot weather*; *his condition deteriorated after the operation*). □□ **deterioration** /-'reɪʃ(ə)n/ *n.* **deteriorative** /-'rətɪv/ *adj.* [LL *deteriorare deteriorat-* f. L *deterior* worse]

determinant /dɪ'tɜ:mɪnənt/ *adj.* & *n.* —*adj.* serving to determine or define. —*n.* **1** a determining factor, element, word, etc. **2** *Math.* a quantity obtained by the addition of products of the elements of a square matrix according to a given rule. [L *determinare* (as DETERMINE)]

determinate /dɪ'tɜ:mɪnət/ *adj.* **1** limited in time, space, or character. **2** of definite scope or nature. □□ **determinacy** *n.* **determinately** *adv.* **determinateness** *n.* [ME f. L *determinatus* past part. (as DETERMINE)]

determination /dɪˌtɜ:mɪ'neɪʃ(ə)n/ *n.* **1** firmness of purpose, resoluteness. **2** the process of deciding, determining, or calculating. **3 a** the conclusion of a dispute by the decision of an arbitrator. **b** the decision reached. **4** *Law* the cessation of an estate or interest. **5** *Law* a judicial decision or sentence. **6** *archaic* a tendency to move in a fixed direction. [ME (in sense 4) f. OF f. L *determinatio -onis* (as DETERMINE)]

determinative /dɪ'tɜ:mɪnətɪv/ *adj.* & *n.* —*adj.* serving to define, qualify, or direct. —*n.* a determinative thing or circumstance. □□ **determinatively** *adv.* [F *déterminatif -ive* (as DETERMINE)]

determine /dɪ'tɜ:mɪn/ *v.* **1** *tr.* find out or establish precisely (*have to determine the extent of the problem*). **2** *tr.* decide or settle (*determined who should go*). **3** *tr.* be a decisive factor in regard to (*demand determines supply*). **4** *intr.* & *tr.* make or cause (a person) to make a decision (*we determined to go at once*; *what determined you to do it?*). **5** *tr.* & *intr.* esp. *Law* bring or come to an end. **6** *tr. Geom.* fix or define the position of. □**be determined** be resolved (*was determined not to give up*). □□ **determinable** *adj.* [ME f. OF *determiner* f. L *determinare* (as DE-, *terminus* end)]

determined /dɪ'tɜ:mɪnd/ *adj.* showing determination; resolute, unflinching. □□ **determinedly** *adv.* **determinedness** *n.*

determiner /dɪ'tɜ:mɪnə(r)/ *n.* **1** a person or thing that determines. **2** *Gram.* any of a class of words (e.g. *a*, *the*, *every*) that determine the kind of reference a noun or noun-substitute has.

determinism /dɪ'tɜ:mɪˌnɪz(ə)m/ *n. Philos.* the doctrine that all events, including human action, are determined by causes regarded as external to the will. □□ **determinist** *n.* **deterministic** /-'nɪstɪk/ *adj.* **deterministically** /-'nɪstɪkəlɪ/ *adv.*

deterrent /dɪ'terənt/ *adj.* & *n.* —*adj.* that deters. —*n.* a deterrent thing or factor, esp. a nuclear weapon regarded as deterring an enemy from attack. □□ **deterrence** *n.*

detest /dɪ'test/ *v.tr.* hate, loathe. □□ **detester** *n.* [L *detestari* (as DE-, *testari* call to witness f. *testis* witness)]

detestable /dɪ'testəb(ə)l/ *adj.* intensely disliked; hateful. □□ **detestably** *adv.*

detestation /ˌdiːte'steɪʃ(ə)n/ *n.* **1** intense dislike, hatred. **2** a detested person or thing. [ME f. OF f. L *detestatio -onis* (as DETEST)]

dethrone /diː'θrəʊn/ *v.tr.* **1** remove from the throne, depose. **2** remove from a position of authority or influence. □□ **dethronement** *n.*

detonate /'detəˌneɪt/ *v.intr.* & *tr.* explode with a loud noise. □□ **detonative** *adj.* [L *detonare detonat-* (as DE-, *tonare* thunder)]

detonation /ˌdetə'neɪʃ(ə)n/ *n.* **1 a** the act or process of detonating. **b** a loud explosion. **2** the premature combustion of fuel in an internal-combustion engine, causing it to pink. [F *détonation* f. *détoner* (as DETONATE)]

detonator /'detəˌneɪtə(r)/ *n.* **1** a device for detonating an explosive. **2** a fog-signal that detonates, e.g. as used on railways.

detour /'diːtʊə(r)/ *n.* & *v.* —*n.* a divergence from a direct or intended route; a roundabout course. —*v.intr.* & *tr.* make or cause to make a detour. [F *détour* change of direction f. *détourner* turn away (as DE-, TURN)]

detoxicate /diː'tɒksɪˌkeɪt/ *v.tr.* = DETOXIFY. □□ **detoxication** /-'keɪʃ(ə)n/ *n.* [DE- + L *toxicum* poison, after *intoxicate*]

detoxify /diː'tɒksɪˌfaɪ/ *v.tr.* remove the poison from. □□ **detoxification** /-fɪ'keɪʃ(ə)n/ *n.* [DE- + L *toxicum* poison]

detract /dɪ'trækt/ *v.tr.* (usu. foll. by *from*) take away (a part of something); reduce, diminish (*self-interest detracted nothing from their achievement*). □□ **detraction** *n.* **detractive** *adj.* **detractor** *n.* [L *detrahere detract-* (as DE-, *trahere* draw)]

detrain /diː'treɪn/ *v.intr.* & *tr.* alight or cause to alight from a train. □□ **detrainment** *n.*

detribalize /diː'traɪbəˌlaɪz/ *v.tr.* (also **-ise**) **1** make (a person) no longer a member of a tribe. **2** destroy the tribal habits of. □□ **detribalization** /-'zeɪʃ(ə)n/ *n.*

detriment /'detrɪmənt/ *n.* **1** harm, damage. **2** something causing this. [ME f. OF *detriment* or L *detrimentum* (as DE-, *terere trit-* rub, wear)]

detrimental /ˌdetrɪ'ment(ə)l/ *adj.* harmful; causing loss. □□ **detrimentally** *adv.*

detrition /dɪ'trɪʃ(ə)n/ *n.* wearing away by friction. [med.L *detritio* (as DETRIMENT)]

detritus /dɪ'traɪtəs/ *n.* matter produced by erosion, such as gravel, sand, silt, rock-debris, etc.; debris. □□ **detrital** /dɪ'traɪt(ə)l/ *adj.* [after F *détritus* f. L *detritus* (n.) = wearing down (as DETRIMENT)]

de trop /də 'trəʊ/ *predic.adj.* not wanted, unwelcome, in the way. [F, = excessive]

detumescence /ˌdiːtjuː'mes(ə)ns/ *n.* subsidence from a swollen state. [L *detumescere* (as DE-, *tumescere* swell)]

deuce¹ /djuːs/ *n.* **1** the two on dice or playing cards. **2** (in lawn tennis) the score of 40 all, at which two consecutive points are needed to win. [OF *deus* f. L *duo* (accus. *duos*) two]

deuce² /djuːs/ *n.* misfortune, the Devil, used esp. *colloq.* as an exclamation of surprise or annoyance (*who the deuce are you?*). □**a** (or **the**) **deuce of a** a very bad or remarkable (*a deuce of a problem*; *a deuce of a fellow*). **the deuce to pay** trouble to be expected. [LG *duus*, formed as DEUCE¹,· two aces at dice being the worst throw]

deuced /'djuːsɪd, djuːst/ *adj.* & *adv. archaic* damned, confounded (*a deuced liar*). □□ **deucedly** /'djuːsɪdlɪ/ *adv.*

deus ex machina /ˌdeɪʊs eks 'mækɪnə, ˌdiːəs/ *n.* an unexpected power or event saving a seemingly hopeless situation, esp. in a play or novel. [mod.L transl. of Gk *theos ek mēkhanēs*, = god from the machinery (by which in the Greek theatre the gods were suspended above the stage)]

Deut. *abbr.* Deuteronomy (Old Testament).

deuteragonist /ˌdjuːtə'rægənɪst/ *n.* the person second in importance to the protagonist in a drama. [Gk *deuteragōnistēs* (as DEUTERO-, *agōnistēs* actor)]

deuterate /'djuːtəˌreɪt/ *v.tr.* replace the usual isotope of hydrogen in (a substance) by deuterium. □□ **deuteration** /-'reɪʃ(ə)n/ *n.*

deuterium /djuː'tɪərɪəm/ *n. Chem.* a stable isotope of hydrogen with a mass about double that of the usual isotope. [mod.L, formed as DEUTERO- + -IUM]

deutero- /'djuːtərəʊ/ *comb. form* second. [Gk *deuteros* second]

Deutero-Isaiah /ˌdjuːtərəʊaɪ'zaɪə/ *n.* the supposed later author of Isaiah 40-55.

deuteron /'djuːtəˌrɒn/ *n. Physics* the nucleus of a deuterium atom, consisting of a proton and a neutron. [DEUTERIUM + -ON]

Deutsche Mark /'dɔɪtʃə mɑːk/ *n.* (also

Deutschmark /'dɔɪtʃmɑːk/) the chief monetary unit of the Federal Republic of Germany. [G, = German mark (see MARK²)]

deutzia /'djuːtsɪə, 'dɔɪtsɪə/ n. any ornamental shrub of the genus *Deutzia*, with usu. white flowers. [J. *Deutz* 18th-c. Du. patron of botany]

devalue /diːˈvæljuː/ v.tr. (**devalues, devalued, devaluing**) **1** reduce the value of. **2** *Econ.* reduce the value of (a currency) in relation to other currencies or to gold (opp. REVALUE). □□ **devaluation** /-'eɪʃ(ə)n/ n.

Devanagari /ˌdeɪvəˈnɑːgərɪ/ n. the alphabet used for Sanskrit, Hindi, and other Indian languages. [Skr., = divine town script]

devastate /'devəˌsteɪt/ v.tr. **1** lay waste; cause great destruction to. **2** (often in *passive*) overwhelm with shock or grief; upset deeply. □□ **devastation** /-'steɪʃ(ə)n/ n. **devastator** n. [L *devastare devastat-* (as DE-, *vastare* lay waste)]

devastating /'devəˌsteɪtɪŋ/ adj. crushingly effective; overwhelming. □□ **devastatingly** adv.

develop /dɪˈveləp/ v. (**developed, developing**) **1** tr. & intr. **a** make or become bigger or fuller or more elaborate or systematic (*the new town developed rapidly*). **b** bring or come to an active or visible state or to maturity (*developed a plan of action*). **2** tr. begin to exhibit or suffer from (*developed a rattle*). **3** tr. **a** construct new buildings on (land). **b** convert (land) to a new purpose so as to use its resources more fully. **4** tr. treat (photographic film etc.) to make the latent image visible. **5** tr. *Mus.* elaborate (a theme) by modification of the melody, harmony, rhythm, etc. **6** tr. *Chess* bring (a piece) into position for effective use. □ **developing country** a poor or primitive country that is developing better economic and social conditions. □□ **developer** n. [F *développer* f. Rmc (as DIS-, orig. of second element unknown)]

developable /dɪˈveləpəb(ə)l/ adj. that can be developed. □ **developable surface** *Geom.* a surface that can be flattened into a plane without overlap or separation, e.g. a cylinder.

development /dɪˈveləpmənt/ n. **1** the act or an instance of developing; the process of being developed. **2 a** a stage of growth or advancement. **b** a thing that has developed, esp. an event or circumstance (*the latest developments*). **3** a full-grown state. **4** the process of developing a photograph. **5** a developed area of land. **6** *Mus.* the elaboration of a theme or themes, esp. in the middle section of a sonata movement. **7** *Chess* the developing of pieces from their original position. □ **development area** *Brit.* one where new industries are encouraged in order to counteract unemployment.

developmental /dɪˌveləp'ment(ə)l/ adj. **1** incidental to growth (*developmental diseases*). **2** evolutionary. □□ **developmentally** adv.

deviant /'diːvɪənt/ adj. & n. —adj. that deviates from the normal, esp. with reference to sexual practices. —n. a deviant person or thing. □□ **deviance** n. **deviancy** n. [ME (as DEVIATE)]

deviate /'diːvɪˌeɪt/ v. & n. —v.intr. (often foll. by *from*) turn aside or diverge (from a course of action, rule, truth, etc.); digress. —n. /-vɪət/ a deviant, esp. a sexual pervert. □□ **deviator** n. **deviatory** /-vɪətərɪ/ adj. [LL *deviare deviat-* (as DE-, *via* way)]

deviation /ˌdiːvɪˈeɪʃ(ə)n/ n. **1 a** deviating, digressing. **b** an instance of this. **2** *Polit.* a departure from accepted (esp. Communist) party doctrine. **3** *Statistics* the amount by which a single measurement differs from the mean. **4** *Naut.* the deflection of a ship's compass-needle caused by iron in the ship etc. □ **standard deviation** *Statistics* a quantity calculated to indicate the extent of deviation for a group as a whole. □□ **deviational** adj. **deviationism** n. **deviationist** n. [F *déviation* f. med.L *deviatio -onis* (as DEVIATE)]

device /dɪˈvaɪs/ n. **1** a thing made or adapted for a particular purpose, esp. a mechanical contrivance. **2** a plan, scheme, or trick. **3 a** an emblematic or heraldic design. **b** a drawing or design. **4** *archaic* make, look (*things of rare device*). □ **leave a person to his** or **her own devices** leave a person to do as he or she wishes. [ME f. OF *devis* ult. f. L (as DIVIDE)]

devil /'dev(ə)l/ n. & v. **1** (usu. **the Devil**) (in Christian and Jewish belief) the supreme spirit of evil; Satan. **2 a** an evil spirit; a demon; a superhuman malignant being. **b** a personified evil force or attribute. **3 a** a wicked or cruel person. **b** a mischievously energetic, clever, or self-willed person. **4** *colloq.* a person, a fellow (*lucky devil*). **5** fighting spirit, mischievousness (*the devil is in him tonight*). **6** *colloq.* something difficult or awkward (*this door is a devil to open*). **7** (**the devil** or **the Devil**) *colloq.* used as an exclamation of surprise or annoyance (*who the devil are you?*). **8** a literary hack exploited by an employer. **9** *Brit.* a junior legal counsel. **10** = Tasmanian devil. **11** applied to various instruments and machines, esp. when used for destructive work. **12** *S.Afr.* = dust devil. —v. (**devilled, devilling**; *US* **deviled, deviling**) **1** tr. cook (food) with hot seasoning. **2** intr. act as a devil for an author or barrister. **3** tr. *US* harass, worry. □ **between the devil and the deep blue sea** in a dilemma. **devil-may-care** cheerful and reckless. **a devil of** *colloq.* a considerable, difficult, or remarkable. **devil a one** not even one. **devil ray** any cartilaginous fish of the family Mobulidae, esp. the manta. **devil's advocate** a person who tests a proposition by arguing against it. **devil's bit** any of various plants whose roots look bitten off, esp. a kind of scabious (*Succisa pratensis*). **devil's coach-horse** *Brit.* a large rove-beetle, *Staphylinus olens*. **devil's darning-needle** a dragonfly or damselfly. **devil's dozen** thirteen. **devils-on-horseback** a savoury of prune or plum wrapped in slices of bacon. **devil's own** *colloq.* very difficult or unusual (*the devil's own job*). **devil take the hindmost** a motto of selfish competition. **the devil to pay** trouble to be expected. **go to the devil 1** be damned. **2** (in *imper.*) depart at once. **like the devil** with great energy. **play the devil with** cause severe damage to. **printer's devil** *hist.* an errand-boy in a printing office. **speak** (or **talk**) **of the devil** said when a person appears just after being mentioned. **the very devil** (*predic.*) *colloq.* a great difficulty or nuisance. [OE *dēofol* f. LL *diabolus* f. Gk *diabolos* accuser, slanderer f. *dia* across + *ballō* to throw]

devilfish /'dev(ə)lfɪʃ/ n. (*pl.* same or **-fishes**) **1** = devil ray. **2** any of various fish, esp. the stonefish. **3** *hist.* an octopus.

devilish /'devəlɪʃ/ adj. & adv. —adj. **1** of or like a devil; wicked. **2** mischievous. —adv. *colloq.* very, extremely. □□ **devilishly** adv. **devilishness** n.

devilment /'devəlmənt/ n. mischief, wild spirits.

devilry /'devɪlrɪ/ n. (also **deviltry**) (*pl.* **-ies**) **1 a** wickedness; reckless mischief. **b** an instance of this. **2 a** black magic. **b** the Devil and his works. [OF *diablerie* f. *diable* DEVIL: *-try* wrongly after *harlotry* etc.]

devious /'diːvɪəs/ adj. **1** (of a person etc.) not straightforward, underhand. **2** winding, circuitous. **3** erring, straying. □□ **deviously** adv. **deviousness** n. [L *devius* f. DE- + *via* way]

devise /dɪˈvaɪz/ v. & n. —v.tr. **1** plan or invent by careful thought. **2** *Law* leave (real estate) by the terms of a will (cf. BEQUEATH). —n. **1** the act or an instance of devising. **2** *Law* a devising clause in a will. □□ **devisable** adj. **devisee** /-'ziː/ n. (in sense 2 of *v.*). **deviser** n. **devisor** n. (in sense 2 of *v.*). [ME f. OF *deviser* ult. f. L *dividere divis-* DIVIDE: (n.) f. OF *devise* f. med.L *divisa* fem. past part. of *dividere*]

devitalize /diːˈvaɪtəˌlaɪz/ v.tr. (also **-ise**) take away strength and vigour from. □□ **devitalization** /-ˈzeɪʃ(ə)n/ n.

devitrify /diːˈvɪtrɪˌfaɪ/ v.tr. (**-ies, -ied**) deprive of vitreous qualities; make (glass or vitreous rock) opaque and crystalline. □□ **devitrification** /-frˈkeɪʃ(ə)n/ *n*.

devoid /dɪˈvɔɪd/ *predic.adj*. (foll. by *of*) quite lacking or free from (*a book devoid of all interest*). [ME, past part. of obs. *devoid* f. OF *devoidier* (as DE-, VOID)]

devoir /deˈvwɑː(r)/ *n. archaic* 1 duty, one's best (*do one's devoir*). 2 (in *pl*.) courteous or formal attentions; respects (*pay one's devoirs to*). [ME f. AF *dever* = OF *deveir* f. L *debēre* owe]

devolute /ˈdiːvəˌluːt, -ˌljuːt/ *v.tr.* transfer by devolution. [as DEVOLVE]

devolution /ˌdiːvəˈluːʃ(ə)n, -ˈljuːʃ(ə)n/ *n*. 1 the delegation of power, esp. by central government to local or regional administration. 2 a descent or passing on through a series of stages. b descent by natural or due succession from one to another of property or qualities. 3 the lapse of an unexercised right to an ultimate owner. 4 *Biol.* degeneration. □□ **devolutionary** *adj*. **devolutionist** *n*. [LL *devolutio* (as DEVOLVE)]

devolve /dɪˈvɒlv/ *v*. 1 (foll. by *on*, *upon*, etc.) a *tr.* pass (work or duties) to (a deputy etc.). b *intr.* (of work or duties) pass to (a deputy etc.). 2 *intr.* (foll. by *on*, *to*, *upon*) *Law* (of property etc.) descend or fall by succession to. □□ **devolvement** *n*. [ME f. L *devolvere devolut-* (as DE-, *volvere* roll)]

Devonian /dɪˈvəʊnɪən/ *adj. & n.* —*adj.* 1 of or relating to Devon in SW England. 2 *Geol.* of or relating to the fourth period of the Palaeozoic era with evidence of the first amphibians and tree forests. ¶ Cf. Appendix II. —*n.* 1 this period or system. 2 a native of Devon. [med.L *Devonia* Devonshire]

dévot /deɪˈvəʊ/ *n.* (*fem.* **dévote** /-ˈvəʊt/) a devotee. [F f. OF (as DEVOUT)]

devote /dɪˈvəʊt/ *v.tr. & refl.* 1 (foll. by *to*) apply or give over (resources etc. or oneself) to (a particular activity or purpose or person) (*devoted their time to reading*; *devoted himself to his guests*). 2 *archaic* doom to destruction. □□ **devotement** *n*. [L *devovēre devot-* (as DE-, *vovēre* vow)]

devoted /dɪˈvəʊtɪd/ *adj*. very loving or loyal (*a devoted husband*). □□ **devotedly** *adv*. **devotedness** *n*.

devotee /ˌdevəˈtiː/ *n*. 1 (usu. foll. by *of*) a zealous enthusiast or supporter. 2 a zealously pious or fanatical person.

devotion /dɪˈvəʊʃ(ə)n/ *n*. 1 (usu. foll. by *to*) enthusiastic attachment or loyalty (to a person or cause); great love. 2 a religious worship. b (in *pl*.) prayers. c devoutness, religious fervour. □□ **devotional** *adj*. [ME f. OF *devotion* or L *devotio* (as DEVOTE)]

devour /dɪˈvaʊə(r)/ *v.tr.* 1 eat hungrily or greedily. 2 (of fire etc.) engulf, destroy. 3 take in greedily with the eyes or ears (*devoured each other book*). 4 absorb the attention of (*devoured by anxiety*). □□ **devourer** *n*. **devouringly** *adv*. [ME f. OF *devorer* f. L *devorare* (as DE-, *vorare* swallow)]

devout /dɪˈvaʊt/ *adj*. 1 earnestly religious. 2 earnestly sincere (*devout hope*). □□ **devoutly** *adv*. **devoutness** *n*. [ME f. OF *devot* f. L *devotus* past part. (as DEVOTE)]

DEW *abbr*. distant early warning.

dew /djuː/ *n. & v.* —*n.* 1 atmospheric vapour condensing in small drops on cool surfaces at night. 2 beaded or glistening moisture resembling this, e.g. tears. 3 freshness, refreshing quality. —*v.tr.* wet with or as with dew. □ **dew-claw** 1 a rudimentary inner toe found on some dogs. 2 a false hoof on a deer etc. **dew-fall** 1 the time when dew begins to form. 2 evening. **dew-point** the temperature at which dew forms. **dew-pond** a shallow usu. artificial pond once supposed to have been fed by atmospheric condensation. [OE *dēaw* f. Gmc]

dewan /dɪˈwɑːn/ *n.* the prime minister or finance minister of an Indian state. [Arab. & Pers. *diwān* fiscal register]

dewar /ˈdjuːə(r)/ *n. Physics* a double-walled flask with a vacuum between the walls to reduce the transfer of heat. [Sir James *Dewar*, Brit. physicist d. 1923]

dewberry /ˈdjuːbəri/ *n.* (*pl.* **-ies**) 1 a bluish fruit like the blackberry. 2 the shrub, *Rubus caesius*, bearing this.

dewdrop /ˈdjuːdrɒp/ *n.* a drop of dew.

Dewey system /ˈdjuːɪ/ *n.* a decimal system of library classification. [M. *Dewey*, Amer. librarian d. 1931, its deviser]

dewlap /ˈdjuːlæp/ *n.* 1 a loose fold of skin hanging from the throat of cattle, dogs, etc. 2 similar loose skin round the throat of an elderly person. [ME f. DEW + LAP[1], perh. after ON (unrecorded) *döggleppr*]

dewy /ˈdjuːɪ/ *adj*. (**dewier**, **dewiest**) 1 a wet with dew. b moist as if with dew. 2 of or like dew. □ **dewy-eyed** innocently trusting; naïvely sentimental. □□ **dewily** *adv*. **dewiness** *n*. [OE *dēawig* (as DEW, -Y[1])]

dexter[1] /ˈdekstə(r)/ *adj*. esp. *Heraldry* on or of the right-hand side (the observer's left) of a shield etc. [L, = on the right]

dexter[2] /ˈdekstə(r)/ *n.* 1 an animal of a small hardy breed of Irish cattle. 2 this breed. [19th c.: perh. f. the name of a breeder]

dexterity /dekˈsterɪtɪ/ *n.* 1 skill in handling. 2 manual or mental adroitness. 3 right-handedness, using the right hand. [F *dextérité* f. L *dexteritas* (as DEXTER[1])]

dexterous /ˈdekstrəs/ *adj*. (also **dextrous**) having or showing dexterity. □□ **dexterously** *adv*. **dexterousness** *n*. [L DEXTER[1] + -OUS]

dextral /ˈdekstr(ə)l/ *adj. & n.* —*adj.* 1 (of a person) right-handed. 2 of or on the right. 3 *Zool.* (of a spiral shell) with whorls rising to the right and coiling in an anticlockwise direction. 4 *Zool.* (of a flat-fish) with the right side uppermost. —*n.* a right-handed person. □□ **dextrality** /-ˈstrælɪtɪ/ *n.* **dextrally** *adv*. [med.L *dextralis* f. L *dextra* right hand]

dextran /ˈdekstræn/ *n. Chem. & Pharm.* 1 an amorphous gum formed by the fermentation of sucrose etc. 2 a degraded form of this used as a substitute for blood-plasma. [G (as DEXTRO- + -*an* as in Chem. names)]

dextrin /ˈdekstrɪn/ *n. Chem.* a soluble gummy substance obtained from starch and used as an adhesive. [F *dextrine* f. L *dextra*: see DEXTRO-, -IN]

dextro- /ˈdekstrəʊ/ *comb. form* on or to the right (*dextrorotatory*; *dextrose*). [L *dexter*, *dextra* on or to the right]

dextrorotatory /ˌdekstrəʊrəʊˈteɪtəri/ *adj. Chem.* having the property of rotating the plane of a polarized light ray to the right (cf. LAEVOROTATORY). □□ **dextrorotation** *n*.

dextrorse /ˈdekstrɔːs/ *adj*. rising towards the right, esp. of a spiral stem. [L *dextrorsus* (as DEXTRO-)]

dextrose /ˈdekstrəʊs/ *n. Chem.* the dextrorotatory form of glucose. [formed as DEXTRO- + -OSE[2]]

dextrous var. of DEXTEROUS.

DF *abbr*. 1 Defender of the Faith. 2 direction-finder. [in sense 1 f. L *Defensor Fidei*]

DFC *abbr. Brit.* Distinguished Flying Cross.

DFM *abbr. Brit.* Distinguished Flying Medal.

DG *abbr*. 1 *Dei gratia*. 2 *Deo gratias*. 3 director-general.

dhal /dɑːl/ *n.* (also **dal**) 1 a kind of split pulse, a common foodstuff in India. 2 a dish made with this. [Hindi]

dharma /ˈdɑːmə/ *n. Ind.* 1 social custom; the right behaviour. 2 the Buddhist truth. 3 the Hindu social or moral law. [Skr., = decree, custom]

dhobi /ˈdəʊbi/ *n.* (*pl.* **dhobis**) *Ind.* etc. a washerman or washerwoman. □ **dhobi** (or **dhobi's**) **itch** a tropical skin disease; an allergic dermatitis. [Hindi *dhobī* f. *dhob* washing]

dhoti /ˈdəʊti/ *n.* (*pl.* **dhotis**) the loincloth worn by male Hindus. [Hindi *dhotī*]

dhow /daʊ/ *n.* a lateen-rigged ship used on the Arabian sea. [19th c.: orig. unkn.]

b *but* d *dog* f *few* g *get* h *he* j *yes* k *cat* l *leg* m *man* n *no* p *pen* r *red* s *sit* t *top* v *voice*

DHSS *abbr. hist.* (in the UK) Department of Health and Social Security (cf. DoH, DSS).

dhurra var. of DURRA.

DI *abbr. Brit.* Defence Intelligence.

di-¹ /daɪ/ *comb. form* **1** twice, two-, double. **2** *Chem.* containing two atoms, molecules, or groups of a specified kind (*dichromate*; *dioxide*). [Gk f. *dis* twice]

di-² /daɪ, dɪ/ *prefix* form of DIS- occurring before *l*, *m*, *n*, *r*, *s* (foll. by a consonant), *v*, usu. *g*, and sometimes *j*. [L var. of *dis-*]

di-³ /daɪ/ *prefix* form of DIA- before a vowel.

dia. *abbr.* diameter.

dia- /'daɪə/ *prefix* (also **di-** before a vowel) **1** through (*diaphanous*). **2** apart (*diacritical*). **3** across (*diameter*). [Gk f. *dia* through]

diabetes /ˌdaɪə'biːtiːz/ *n.* **1** any disorder of the metabolism with excessive thirst and the production of large amounts of urine. **2** (in full **diabetes mellitus**) the commonest form of diabetes in which sugar and starch are not properly absorbed from the blood, with thirst, emaciation, and excessive excretion of urine with glucose. □**diabetes insipidus** a rare metabolic disorder due to a pituitary deficiency, with excessive urination and thirst. [orig. = siphon: L f. Gk f. *diabainō* go through]

diabetic /ˌdaɪə'betɪk/ *adj. & n.* —*adj.* **1** of or relating to or having diabetes. **2** for use by diabetics. —*n.* a person suffering from diabetes.

diablerie /dɑr'ɑːbləri/ *n.* **1** the devil's work; sorcery. **2** wild recklessness. **3** the realm of devils; devil-lore. [F f. *diable* f. L *diabolus* DEVIL]

diabolic /ˌdaɪə'bɒlɪk/ *adj.* (also **diabolical** /-'bɒlɪk(ə)l/) **1** of the Devil. **2** devilish; inhumanly cruel or wicked. **3** fiendishly clever or cunning or annoying. □□ **diabolically** *adv.* [ME f. OF *diabolique* or LL *diabolicus* f. L *diabolus* (as DEVIL)]

diabolism /dɑr'æbə,lɪz(ə)m/ *n.* **1 a** belief in or worship of the Devil. **b** sorcery. **2** devilish conduct or character. □□ **diabolist** *n.* [Gk *diabolos* DEVIL]

diabolize /dɑr'æbə,laɪz/ *v.tr.* (also **-ise**) make into or represent as a devil.

diabolo /dɪ'æbələʊ, daɪ-/ *n.* (*pl.* **-os**) **1** a game in which a two-headed top is thrown up and caught with a string stretched between two sticks. **2** the top itself. [It., = DEVIL: formerly called *devil on two sticks*]

diachronic /ˌdaɪə'krɒnɪk/ *adj.* Linguistics etc. concerned with the historical development of a subject (esp. a language) (opp. SYNCHRONIC). □□ **diachronically** *adv.* **diachronism** /daɪ'ækrə,nɪz(ə)m/ *n.* **diachronistic** /daɪ,ækrə'nɪstɪk/ *adj.* **diachronous** /daɪ'ækrənəs/ *adj.* **diachrony** /daɪ'ækrənɪ/ *n.* [F *diachronique* (as DIA-, CHRONIC)]

diaconal /daɪ'ækən(ə)l/ *adj.* of a deacon. [eccl.L *diaconalis* f. *diaconus* DEACON]

diaconate /daɪ'ækə,neɪt, -nət/ *n.* **1 a** the office of deacon. **b** a person's time as deacon. **2** a body of deacons. [eccl.L *diaconatus* (as DIACONAL)]

diacritic /ˌdaɪə'krɪtɪk/ *n. & adj.* —*n.* a sign (e.g. an accent, diaeresis, cedilla) used to indicate different sounds or values of a letter. —*adj.* = DIACRITICAL. [Gk *diakritikos* (as DIA-, CRITIC)]

diacritical /ˌdaɪə'krɪtɪk(ə)l/ *adj. & n.* —*adj.* distinguishing, distinctive. —*n.* (in full **diacritical mark** or **sign**) = DIACRITIC.

diadelphous /ˌdaɪə'delfəs/ *adj.* Bot. with the stamens united in two bundles (cf. MONADELPHOUS, POLYADELPHOUS). [DI-¹ + Gk *adelphos* brother]

diadem /'daɪə,dem/ *n. & v.* —*n.* **1** a crown or headband worn as a sign of sovereignty. **2** a wreath of leaves or flowers worn round the head. **3** sovereignty. **4** a crowning distinction or glory. —*v.tr.* (esp. as **diademed** *adj.*) adorn with or as with a diadem. [ME f. OF *diademe* f. L *diadema* f. Gk *diadēma* (as DIA-, *deō* bind)]

diaeresis /daɪ'ɪərəsɪs/ *n.* (US **dieresis**) (*pl.* **-ses** /-,siːz/) **1** a mark (as in *naïve*) over a vowel to indicate that it is sounded separately. **2** Prosody a break

where a foot ends at the end of a word. [L f. Gk, = separation]

diagenesis /ˌdaɪə'dʒenɪsɪs/ *n.* Geol. the transformation occurring during the conversion of sedimentation to sedimentary rock.

diagnose /'daɪəg,nəʊz/ *v.tr.* make a diagnosis of (a disease, a mechanical fault, etc.) from its symptoms. □□ **diagnosable** *adj.*

diagnosis /ˌdaɪəg'nəʊsɪs/ *n.* (*pl.* **diagnoses** /-,siːz/) **1 a** the identification of a disease by means of a patient's symptoms. **b** an instance or formal statement of this. **2 a** the identification of the cause of a mechanical fault etc. **b** an instance of this. **3 a** the distinctive characterization in precise terms of a genus, species, etc. **b** an instance of this. [mod.L f. Gk (as DIA-, *gignōskō* recognize)]

diagnostic /ˌdaɪəg'nɒstɪk/ *adj. & n.* —*adj.* of or assisting diagnosis. —*n.* a symptom. □□ **diagnostically** *adv.* **diagnostician** /-nɒ'stɪʃ(ə)n/ *n.* [Gk *diagnōstikos* (as DIAGNOSIS)]

diagnostics /ˌdaɪəg'nɒstɪks/ *n.* **1** (treated as *pl.*) *Computing* programs and other mechanisms used to detect and identify faults in hardware or software. **2** (treated as *sing.*) the science or study of diagnosing disease.

diagonal /daɪ'ægən(ə)l/ *adj. & n.* —*adj.* **1** crossing a straight-sided figure from corner to corner. **2** slanting, oblique. —*n.* a straight line joining two non-adjacent corners. □□ **diagonally** *adv.* [L *diagonalis* f. Gk *diagōnios* (as DIA-, *gōnia* angle)]

diagram /'daɪə,græm/ *n. & v.* —*n.* **1** a drawing showing the general scheme or outline of an object and its parts. **2** a graphic representation of the course or results of an action or process. **3** Geom. a figure made of lines used in proving a theorem etc. —*v.tr.* (**diagrammed**, **diagramming**; US **diagramed**, **diagraming**) represent by means of a diagram. □□ **diagrammatic** /-grə'mætɪk/ *adj.* **diagrammatically** /-grə'mætɪkəlɪ/ *adv.* [L *diagramma* f. Gk (as DIA-, -GRAM)]

diagrid /'daɪəgrɪd/ *n.* Archit. a supporting structure of diagonally intersecting ribs of metal etc. [DIAGONAL + GRID]

diakinesis /ˌdaɪəkɪ'niːsɪs, -kaɪ'niːsɪs/ *n.* (*pl.* **diakineses** /-siːz/) *Biol.* a stage during the prophase of meiosis when the separation of homologous chromosomes is complete and crossing over has occurred. [mod.L f. G *Diakinese* (as DIA-, Gk *kinēsis* motion)]

dial /'daɪ(ə)l/ *n. & v.* —*n.* **1** the face of a clock or watch, marked to show the hours etc. **2** a similar flat plate marked with a scale for measuring weight, volume, pressure, consumption, etc., indicated by a pointer. **3** a movable disc on a telephone, with finger-holes and numbers for making a connection. **4 a** a plate or disc etc. on a radio or television set for selecting wavelength or channel. **b** a similar selecting device on other equipment, e.g. a washing machine. **5** Brit. sl. a person's face. —*v.* (**dialled**, **dialling**; US **dialed**, **dialing**) **1** *tr.* (also *absol.*) select (a telephone number) by means of a dial or set of buttons (*dialled 999*). **2** *tr.* measure, indicate, or regulate by means of a dial. □**dialling code** a sequence of numbers dialled to connect a telephone with the exchange of the telephone being called. **dialling tone** (US **dial tone**) a sound indicating that a caller may start to dial. □□ **dialler** *n.* [ME, = sundial, f. med.L *diale* clock-dial ult. f. L *dies* day]

dialect /'daɪə,lekt/ *n.* **1** a form of speech peculiar to a particular region. **2** a subordinate variety of a language with non-standard vocabulary, pronunciation, or grammar. □□ **dialectal** /-'lekt(ə)l/ *adj.* **dialectology** /-'tɒlədʒɪ/ *n.* **dialectologist** /-'tɒlədʒɪst/ *n.* [F *dialecte* or L *dialectus* f. Gk *dialektos* discourse f. *dialegomai* converse]

dialectic /ˌdaɪə'lektɪk/ *n. & adj.* Philos. —*n.* **1 a** the art of investigating the truth of opinions; the testing of truth by discussion. **b** logical disputation. **2 a** inquiry into metaphysical contradictions and their solutions, esp. in the thought of Kant and Hegel. **b** the existence or action of opposing social forces etc. —*adj.* **1** of or relating to logical disputation. **2** fond of or skilled in logical disputation. [ME f. OF *dialectique* or L *dialectica* f. Gk *dialektikē* (*tekhnē*) (art) of debate (as DIALECT)]

dialectical /ˌdaɪəˈlɛktɪk(ə)l/ *adj.* of dialectic or dialectics. □**dialectical materialism** the Marxist theory that political and historical events are due to a conflict of social forces caused by man's material needs. □□**dialectically** *adv.*

dialectician /ˌdaɪəlɛkˈtɪʃ(ə)n/ *n.* a person skilled in dialectic. [F *dialecticien* f. L *dialecticus*]

dialectics /ˌdaɪəˈlɛktɪks/ *n.* (treated as *sing.* or *pl.*) = DIALECTIC *n.* 1.

dialogic /ˌdaɪəˈlɒdʒɪk/ *adj.* of or in dialogue. [LL *dialogicus* f. Gk *dialogikos* (as DIALOGUE)]

dialogist /daɪˈælədʒɪst/ *n.* a speaker in or writer of dialogue. [LL *dialogista* f. Gk *dialogistēs* (as DIALOGUE)]

dialogue /ˈdaɪəˌlɒg/ *n.* (*US* **dialog**) **1 a** conversation. **b** conversation in written form; this as a form of composition. **2 a** a discussion, esp. one between representatives of two political groups. **b** a conversation, a talk (*long dialogues between the two main characters*). [ME f. OF *dialoge* f. L *dialogus* f. Gk *dialogos* f. *dialegomai* converse]

dialyse /ˈdaɪəˌlaɪz/ *v.tr.* (*US* **dialyze**) separate by means of dialysis.

dialysis /daɪˈælɪsɪs/ *n.* (*pl.* **dialyses** /-ˌsiːz/) **1** *Chem.* the separation of particles in a liquid by differences in their ability to pass through a membrane into another liquid. **2** *Med.* the clinical purification of blood by this technique. □□**dialytic** /ˌdaɪəˈlɪtɪk/ *adj.* [L f. Gk *dialusis* (as DIA-, *luō* set free)]

diamagnetic /ˌdaɪəmægˈnɛtɪk/ *adj.* & *n.* —*adj.* tending to become magnetized in a direction at right angles to the applied magnetic field. —*n.* a diamagnetic body or substance. □□**diamagnetically** *adv.* **diamagnetism** /-ˈmægnɪˌtɪz(ə)m/ *n.*

diamanté /dɪəˈmɑːteɪ/ *adj.* & *n.* —*adj.* decorated with powdered crystal or another sparkling substance. —*n.* fabric or costume jewellery so decorated. [F, past part. of *diamanter* set with diamonds f. *diamant* DIAMOND]

diamantiferous /ˌdaɪəmænˈtɪfərəs/ *adj.* diamond-yielding. [F *diamantifère* f. *diamant* DIAMOND]

diamantine /ˌdaɪəˈmæntaɪn/ *adj.* of or like diamonds. [F *diamantin* (as DIAMANTIFEROUS)]

diameter /daɪˈæmɪtə(r)/ *n.* **1 a** a straight line passing from side to side through the centre of a body or figure, esp. a circle or sphere. **b** the length of this line. **2** a transverse measurement; width, thickness. **3** a unit of linear measurement of magnifying power (*a lens magnifying 2000 diameters*). □□**diametral** *adj.* [ME f. OF *diametre* f. L *diametrus* f. Gk *diametros* (*grammē*) (line) measuring across f. *metron* measure]

diametrical /ˌdaɪəˈmɛtrɪk(ə)l/ *adj.* (also **diametric**) **1** of or along a diameter. **2** (of opposition, difference, etc.) complete, like that between opposite ends of a diameter. □□**diametrically** *adv.* [Gk *diametrikos* (as DIAMETER)]

diamond /ˈdaɪəmənd/ *n.*, *adj.*, & *v.* —*n.* **1** a precious stone of pure carbon crystallized in octahedrons etc., the hardest naturally-occurring substance. **2** a figure shaped like the cross-section of a diamond; a rhombus. **3 a** a playing-card of a suit denoted by a red rhombus. **b** (in *pl.*) this suit. **4** a glittering particle or point (of frost etc.). **5** a tool with a small diamond for glass-cutting. **6** *Baseball* **a** the space delimited by the bases. **b** the entire field. —*adj.* **1** made of or set with diamonds or a diamond. **2** rhombus-shaped. —*v.tr.* adorn with or as with diamonds. □**diamond cut diamond** wit or cunning is met by its like. **diamond jubilee** the 60th (or 75th) anniversary of an event, esp. a sovereign's accession. **diamond wedding** a 60th (or 75th) wedding anniversary. □□**diamondiferous** /-ˈdɪfərəs/ *adj.* [ME f. OF *diamant* f. med.L *diamas diamant-* var. of L *adamas* ADAMANT f. Gk]

diamondback /ˈdaɪəməndˌbæk/ *n.* **1** an edible freshwater terrapin, *Malaclemys terrapin*, native to N. America, with lozenge-shaped markings on its shell. **2** any rattlesnake of the genus *Crotalus*, native to N. America, with diamond-shaped markings.

diandrous /daɪˈændrəs/ *adj.* having two stamens. [DI-[1] + Gk *anēr andr-* man]

dianthus /daɪˈænθəs/ *n.* any flowering plant of the genus *Dianthus*, e.g. a carnation or pink. [Gk *Dios* of Zeus + *anthos* flower]

diapason /ˌdaɪəˈpeɪz(ə)n, -ˈpeɪs(ə)n/ *n. Mus.* **1** the compass of a voice or musical instrument. **2** a fixed standard of musical pitch. **3** (in full **open** or **stopped diapason**) either of two main organ-stops extending through the organ's whole compass. **4 a** a combination of notes or parts in a harmonious whole. **b** a melodious succession of notes, esp. a grand swelling burst of harmony. **5** an entire compass, range, or scope. [ME in sense 'octave' f. L *diapason* f. Gk *dia pasōn* (*khordōn*) through all (notes)]

diapause /ˈdaɪəˌpɔːz/ *n.* a period of retarded or suspended development in some insects.

diaper /ˈdaɪəpə(r)/ *n.* & *v.* —*n.* **1** *US* a baby's nappy. **2 a** a linen or cotton fabric with a small diamond pattern. **b** this pattern. **3** a similar ornamental design of diamonds etc. for panels, walls, etc. —*v.tr.* decorate with a diaper pattern. [ME f. OF *diapre* f. med.L *diasprum* f. med.Gk *diaspros* (adj.) (as DIA-, *aspros* white)]

diaphanous /daɪˈæfənəs/ *adj.* (of fabric etc.) light and delicate, and almost transparent. □□**diaphanously** *adv.* [med.L *diaphanus* f. Gk *diaphanes* (as DIA-, *phainō* show)]

diaphoresis /ˌdaɪəfəˈriːsɪs/ *n. Med.* sweating, esp. artificially induced. [LL f. Gk f. *diaphoreō* carry through]

diaphoretic /ˌdaɪəfəˈrɛtɪk/ *adj.* & *n.* —*adj.* inducing perspiration. —*n.* an agent inducing perspiration. [LL *diaphoreticus* f. Gk *diaphorētikos* (formed as DIAPHORESIS)]

diaphragm /ˈdaɪəˌfræm/ *n.* **1** a muscular partition separating the thorax from the abdomen in mammals. **2** a partition in animal and plant tissues. **3** a disc pierced by one or more holes in optical and acoustic systems etc. **4** a device for varying the effective aperture of the lens in a camera etc. **5** a thin contraceptive cap fitting over the cervix. **6** a thin sheet of material used as a partition etc. □**diaphragm pump** a pump using a flexible diaphragm in place of a piston. □□**diaphragmatic** /-frægˈmætɪk/ *adj.* [ME f. LL *diaphragma* f. Gk (as DIA-, *phragma -atos* f. *phrassō* fence in)]

diapositive /ˌdaɪəˈpɒzɪtɪv/ *n.* a positive photographic slide or transparency.

diarchy /ˈdaɪɑːkɪ/ *n.* (also **dyarchy**) (*pl.* **-ies**) **1** government by two independent authorities (esp. in India 1921-37). **2** an instance of this. □□**diarchal** /daɪˈɑːk(ə)l/ *adj.* **diarchic** /daɪˈɑːkɪk/ *adj.* [DI-[1] + Gk *-arkhia* rule, after *monarchy*]

diarist /ˈdaɪərɪst/ *n.* a person who keeps a diary. □□**diaristic** /-ˈrɪstɪk/ *adj.*

diarize /ˈdaɪəˌraɪz/ *v.* (also **-ise**) **1** *intr.* keep a diary. **2** *tr.* enter in a diary.

diarrhoea /ˌdaɪəˈrɪə/ *n.* (esp. *US* **diarrhea**) a condition of excessively frequent and loose bowel movements. □□**diarrhoeal** *adj.* **diarrhoeic** *adj.* [ME f. LL f. Gk *diarrhoia* (as DIA-, *rheō* flow)]

diary /ˈdaɪərɪ/ *n.* (*pl.* **-ies**) **1** a daily record of events or thoughts. **2** a book for this or for noting future engagements, usu. printed and with a calendar and other information. [L *diarium* f. *dies* day]

diascope /ˈdaɪəˌskəʊp/ *n.* an optical projector giving images of transparent objects.

Diaspora /daɪˈæspərə/ *n.* **1** (prec. by *the*) **a** the dispersion of the Jews among the Gentiles mainly in the 8th-6th c. BC. **b** Jews dispersed in this way. **2** (also **diaspora**) **a** any group of people similarly dispersed. **b** their dispersion. [Gk f. *diaspeirō* (as DIA-, *speirō* scatter)]

diastase /ˈdaɪəˌsteɪz/ *n.* Biochem. = AMYLASE. □□ **diastasic** /-ˈsteɪzɪk/ *adj.* **diastatic** /-ˈstætɪk/ *adj.* [F f. Gk *diastasis* separation (as DIA-, *stasis* placing)]

diastole /daɪˈæstəlɪ/ *n.* Physiol. the period between two contractions of the heart when the heart muscle relaxes and allows the chambers to fill with blood (cf. SYSTOLE). □□ **diastolic** /ˌdaɪəˈstɒlɪk/ *adj.* [LL f. Gk *diastellō* (as DIA-, *stellō* place)]

diathermancy /ˌdaɪəˈθɜːmənsɪ/ *n.* the quality of transmitting radiant heat. □□ **diathermic** *adj.* **diathermous** *adj.* [F *diathermansie* f. Gk *dia* through + *thermansis* heating: assim. to -ANCY]

diathermy /ˈdaɪəˌθɜːmɪ/ *n.* the application of high-frequency electric currents to produce heat in the deeper tissues of the body. [G *Diathermie* f. Gk *dia* through + *thermon* heat]

diathesis /daɪˈæθɪsɪs/ *n.* Med. a constitutional predisposition to a certain state, esp. a diseased one. [mod.L f. Gk f. *diatithēmi* arrange]

diatom /ˈdaɪətəm/ *n.* a microscopic unicellular alga with a siliceous cell-wall, found as plankton and forming fossil deposits. □□ **diatomaceous** /-ˈmeɪʃəs/ *adj.* [mod.L *Diatoma* (genus-name) f. Gk *diatomos* (as DIA-, *temnō* cut)]

diatomic /ˌdaɪəˈtɒmɪk/ *adj.* consisting of two atoms. [DI-¹ + ATOM]

diatomite /daɪˈætəˌmaɪt/ *n.* a deposit composed of the siliceous skeletons of diatoms.

diatonic /ˌdaɪəˈtɒnɪk/ *adj.* Mus. **1** (of a scale, interval, etc.) involving only notes proper to the prevailing key without chromatic alteration. **2** (of a melody or harmony) constructed from such a scale. [F *diatonique* or LL *diatonicus* f. Gk *diatonikos* at intervals of a tone (as DIA-, TONIC)]

diatribe /ˈdaɪəˌtraɪb/ *n.* a forceful verbal attack; a piece of bitter criticism. [F f. L *diatriba* f. Gk *diatribē* spending of time, discourse f. *diatribō* (as DIA-, *tribō* rub)]

diazepam /daɪˈæzɪˌpæm/ *n.* a tranquillizing muscle-relaxant drug with anticonvulsant properties used to relieve anxiety, tension, etc. [benzo*diaze*pine + *am*]

diazo /daɪˈeɪzəʊ/ *n.* (in full **diazotype**) a copying or colouring process using a diazo compound decomposed by light. □ **diazo compound** Chem. a chemical compound containing two usu. multiply-bonded nitrogen atoms, often highly coloured and used as dyes. [DI-¹ + AZO-]

dib /dɪb/ *v.intr.* (**dibbed, dibbing**) = DAP. [var. of DAB¹]

dibasic /daɪˈbeɪsɪk/ *adj.* Chem. having two replaceable protons. [DI-¹ + BASE¹ 6]

dibber /ˈdɪbə(r)/ *n.* = DIBBLE.

dibble /ˈdɪb(ə)l/ *n.* & *v.* —*n.* a hand-tool for making holes in the ground for seeds or young plants. —*v.* **1** *tr.* sow or plant with a dibble. **2** *tr.* prepare (soil) with a dibble. **3** *intr.* use a dibble. [ME: perh. rel. to DIB]

dibs /dɪbz/ *n.pl.* sl. money. [earlier sense 'pebbles for game', also *dib-stones*, perh. f. DIB]

dice /daɪs/ *n.* & *v.* —*n.pl.* **1** **a** small cubes with faces bearing 1-6 spots used in games of chance. **b** (treated as *sing.*) one of these cubes (see DIE²). **2** a game played with one or more such cubes. **3** food cut into small cubes for cooking. —*v.* **1** **a** *intr.* play dice. **b** *intr.* take great risks, gamble (*dicing with death*). **c** *tr.* (foll. by *away*) gamble away. **2** *tr.* cut (food) into small cubes. **3** *tr.* Austral. sl. reject; leave alone. **4** *tr.* chequer, mark with squares. □ **no dice** sl. no success or prospect of it. □□ **dicer** *n.* (in sense 1 of *v.*). [pl. of DIE²]

dicey /ˈdaɪsɪ/ *adj.* (**dicier, diciest**) sl. risky, unreliable. [DICE + -Y¹]

dichotomy /daɪˈkɒtəmɪ/ *n.* (*pl.* **-ies**) **1** **a** a division

into two, esp. a sharply defined one. **b** the result of such a division. **2** binary classification. **3** Bot. & Zool. repeated bifurcation. □□ **dichotomic** /-kəˈtɒmɪk/ *adj.* **dichotomize** *v.* **dichotomous** *adj.* [mod.L *dichotomia* f. Gk *dikhotomia* f. *dikho-* apart + -TOMY]

dichroic /daɪˈkrəʊɪk/ *adj.* (esp. of doubly refracting crystals) showing two colours. □□ **dichroism** *n.* [Gk *dikhroos* (as DI-¹, · *khrōs* colour)]

dichromatic /ˌdaɪkrəʊˈmætɪk/ *adj.* **1** two-coloured. **2** **a** (of animal species) having individuals that show different colorations. **b** having vision sensitive to only two of the three primary colours. □□ **dichromatism** /daɪˈkrəʊməˌtɪz(ə)m/ *n.* [DI-¹ + Gk *khrōmatikos* f. *khrōma -atos* colour]

dick¹ /dɪk/ *n.* **1** Brit. colloq. (in certain set phrases) fellow; person (*clever dick*). **2** coarse sl. the penis. ¶ In sense 2 usually considered a taboo word. [pet form of the name *Richard*]

dick² /dɪk/ *n. sl.* a detective. [perh. abbr.]

dick³ /dɪk/ *n.* □ **take one's dick** (often foll. by *that* + clause) *sl.* swear, affirm. [abbr. of *declaration*]

dicken /ˈdɪkən/ *int.* Austral. sl. an expression of disgust or disbelief. [usu. assoc. with DICKENS or the name *Dickens*]

dickens /ˈdɪkɪnz/ *n.* (usu. prec. by *how, what, why,* etc., *the*) colloq. (esp. in exclamations) deuce; the Devil (*what the dickens are you doing here?*). [16th c.: prob. a use of the surname *Dickens*]

Dickensian /dɪˈkenzɪən/ *adj.* & *n.* —*adj.* **1** of or relating to Charles Dickens, Engl. novelist d. 1870, or his work. **2** resembling or reminiscent of the situations, poor social conditions, or comically repulsive characters described in Dickens's work. —*n.* an admirer or student of Dickens or his work. □□ **Dickensianly** *adv.*

dicker /ˈdɪkə(r)/ *v.* & *n.* esp. US —*v.* **1 a** *intr.* bargain, haggle. **b** *tr.* barter, exchange. **2** *intr.* dither, hesitate. —*n.* a deal, a barter. □□ **dickerer** *n.* [perh. f. *dicker* set of ten (hides), as a unit of trade]

dicky¹ /ˈdɪkɪ/ *n.* (also **dickey**) (*pl.* **-ies** or **-eys**) colloq. **1** a false shirt-front. **2** (in full **dicky-bird**) a child's word for a little bird. **3** Brit. a driver's seat in a carriage. **4** Brit. an extra folding seat at the back of a vehicle. **5** (in full **dicky bow**) Brit. a bow-tie. [some senses f. *Dicky* (as DICK¹)]

dicky² /ˈdɪkɪ/ *adj.* (**dickier, dickiest**) Brit. sl. unsound, likely to collapse or fail. [19th c.: perh. f. 'as queer as Dick's hatband']

dicot /ˈdaɪkɒt/ *n.* = DICOTYLEDON. [abbr.]

dicotyledon /ˌdaɪkɒtɪˈliːd(ə)n/ *n.* any flowering plant having two cotyledons. □□ **dicotyledonous** *adj.* [mod.L *dicotyledones* (as DI-¹, COTYLEDON)]

dicrotic /daɪˈkrɒtɪk/ *adj.* (of the pulse) having a double beat. [Gk *dikrotos*]

dicta *pl.* of DICTUM.

Dictaphone /ˈdɪktəˌfəʊn/ *n. propr.* a machine for recording and playing back dictated words. [DICTATE + PHONE]

dictate /dɪkˈteɪt/ *v.* & *n.* —*v.* **1** *tr.* say or read aloud (words to be written down or recorded). **2 a** *tr.* prescribe or lay down authoritatively (terms, things to be done). **b** *intr.* lay down the law; give orders. —*n.* /ˈdɪk-/ (usu. in *pl.*) an authoritative instruction (*dictates of conscience*). [L *dictare dictat-* frequent. of *dicere dict-* say]

dictation /dɪkˈteɪʃ(ə)n/ *n.* **1 a** the saying of words to be written down or recorded. **b** an instance of this, esp. as a school exercise. **c** the material that is dictated. **2 a** authoritative prescription. **b** an instance of this. **c** a command. □ **dictation speed** a slow rate of speech suitable for dictation.

dictator /dɪkˈteɪtə(r)/ *n.* **1** a ruler with (often usurped) unrestricted authority. **2** a person with supreme authority in any sphere. **3** a domineering person. **4** a person who dictates for transcription. **5** Rom.Hist. a chief magistrate with absolute power, appointed in an emergency. [ME f. L (as DICTATE)]

dictatorial /ˌdɪktəˈtɔːrɪəl/ *adj.* **1** of or like a dictator.

aʊ h**ow** eɪ d**ay** əʊ n**o** eə h**air** ɪə n**ear** ɔɪ b**oy** ʊə p**oor** aɪə f**ire** aʊə s**our**   (*see over for consonants*)

2 imperious, overbearing. □□ **dictatorially** adv. [L dictatorius (as DICTATOR)]

dictatorship /dɪk'teɪtəʃɪp/ n. **1** a State ruled by a dictator. **2 a** the position, rule, or period of rule of a dictator. **b** rule by a dictator. **3** absolute authority in any sphere.

diction /'dɪkʃ(ə)n/ n. **1** the manner of enunciation in speaking or singing. **2** the choice of words or phrases in speech or writing. [F diction or L dictio f. dicere dict- say]

dictionary /'dɪkʃənrɪ, -nərɪ/ n. (pl. -ies) **1** a book that lists (usu. in alphabetical order) and explains the words of a language or gives equivalent words in another language. **2** a reference book on any subject, the items of which are arranged in alphabetical order (dictionary of architecture). [med.L dictionarium (manuale manual) & dictionarius (liber book) f. L dictio (as DICTION)]

dictum /'dɪktəm/ n. (pl. dicta /-tə/ or dictums) **1** a formal utterance or pronouncement. **2** a saying or maxim. **3** Law = OBITER DICTUM. [L, = neut. past part. of dicere say]

dicty /'dɪktɪ/ adj. US sl. **1** conceited, snobbish. **2** elegant, stylish. [20th c.: orig. unkn.]

did past of DO[1].

didactic /daɪ'dæktɪk, dɪ-/ adj. **1** meant to instruct. **2** (of a person) tediously pedantic. □□ **didactically** adv. **didacticism** /-tɪ,sɪz(ə)m/ n. [Gk didaktikos f. didaskō teach]

didakai var. of DIDICOI.

diddicoy var. of DIDICOI.

diddle /'dɪd(ə)l/ v. colloq. **1** tr. cheat, swindle. **2** intr. US waste time. □□ **diddler** n. [prob. back-form. f. Jeremy Diddler in Kenney's 'Raising the Wind' (1803)]

diddums /'dɪdəmz/ int. expressing commiseration esp. to a child. [= did 'em, i.e. did they (tease you etc.)?]

didgeridoo /,dɪdʒərɪ'du:/ n. (also **didjeridoo**) an Australian Aboriginal musical wind instrument of long tubular shape. [imit.]

didicoi /'dɪdɪ,kɔɪ/ n. (also **didakai**, **diddicoy**) sl. a gypsy; an itinerant tinker. [Romany]

didn't /'dɪd(ə)nt/ contr. did not.

dido /'daɪdəʊ/ n. (pl. -oes or -os) US colloq. an antic, a caper, a prank. □**cut** (or **cut up**) **didoes** play pranks. [19th c.: orig. unkn.]

didst /dɪdst/ archaic 2nd sing. past of DO[1].

didymium /dɪ'dɪmɪəm/ n. a mixture of prae-sodymium and neodymium, orig. regarded as an element. [mod.L f. Gk didumos twin (from being closely associated with lanthanum)]

die[1] /daɪ/ v. (**dies, died, dying** /'daɪɪŋ/) **1** intr. (often foll. by of) (of a person, animal, or plant) cease to live; expire, lose vital force (died of hunger). **2** intr. **a** come to an end, cease to exist, fade away (the project died within six months). **b** cease to function; break down (the engine died). **c** (of a flame) go out. **3** intr. (foll. by on) die or cease to function while in the presence or charge of (a person). **4** intr. (usu. foll. by of, from, with) be exhausted or tormented (nearly died of boredom; was dying from the heat). **5** tr. suffer (a specified death) (died a natural death). □**be dying** (foll. by for, or to + infin.) wish for longingly or intently (was dying for a drink; am dying to see you). **die away** become weaker or fainter to the point of extinction. **die-away** adj. languishing. **die back** (of a plant) decay from the tip towards the root. **die down** become less loud or strong. **die hard** die reluctantly, not without a struggle (old habits die hard). **die-hard** n. a conservative or stubborn person. **die out** become extinct, cease to exist. **never say die** keep up courage, not give in. [ME, prob. f. ON deyja f. Gmc]

die[2] /daɪ/ n. **1** sing. of DICE n. 1a. ¶ Dice is now standard in general use in this sense. **2** (pl. dies) **a** an engraved device for stamping a design on coins, medals, etc. **b** a device for stamping, cutting, or moulding material into a particular shape. **3** (pl. dice /daɪs/) Archit. the cubical part of a pedestal between the base and the cornice; a dado or plinth. □**as straight** (or **true**) **as a die 1** quite straight. **2** entirely honest or loyal. **die-cast** cast (hot metal) in a die or mould. **die-casting** the process or product of casting from metal moulds. **the die is cast** an irrevocable step has been taken. **die-sinker** an engraver of dies. **die-stamping** embossing paper etc. with a die. [ME f. OF de f. L datum neut. past part. of dare give, play]

dieldrin /dɪ'eldrɪn/ n. a crystalline insecticide produced by the oxidation of aldrin. [O. Diels, Ger. chemist d. 1954 + ALDRIN]

dielectric /,daɪɪ'lektrɪk/ adj. & n. Electr. —adj. insulating. —n. an insulating medium or substance. □**dielectric constant** permittivity. □□ **dielectrically** adv. [DI-[3] + ELECTRIC = through which electricity is transmitted (without conduction)]

diene /'daɪi:n/ n. Chem. any organic compound possessing two double bonds between carbon atoms. [DI-[1] + -ENE]

dieresis US var. of DIAERESIS.

diesel /'di:z(ə)l/ n. **1** (in full **diesel engine**) an internal-combustion engine in which the heat produced by the compression of air in the cylinder ignites the fuel. **2** a vehicle driven by a diesel engine. **3** fuel for a diesel engine. □**diesel-electric** n. a vehicle driven by the electric current produced by a diesel-engined generator. —adj. of or powered by this means. **diesel oil** a heavy petroleum fraction used as fuel in diesel engines. □□ **dieselize** v.tr. (also -ise). [R. Diesel, Ger. engineer d. 1913]

Dies irae /,di:eɪz 'ɪəraɪ/ n. a Latin hymn sung in a Mass for the dead. [L (its first words), = day of wrath]

dies non /,daɪi:z 'nɒn/ n. Law **1** a day on which no legal business can be done. **2** a day that does not count for legal purposes. [L, short for dies non juridicus non-judicial day]

diet[1] /'daɪət/ n. & v. —n. **1** the kinds of food that a person or animal habitually eats. **2** a special course of food to which a person is restricted, esp. for medical reasons or to control weight. **3** a regular occupation or series of activities to which one is restricted or which form one's main concern, usu. for a purpose (a diet of light reading and fresh air). —v. (**dieted, dieting**) **1** intr. restrict oneself to small amounts or special kinds of food, esp. to control one's weight. **2** tr. restrict (a person or animal) to a special diet. □□ **dieter** n. [ME f. OF diete (n.), dieter (v.) f. L diaeta f. Gk diaita a way of life]

diet[2] /'daɪət/ n. **1** a legislative assembly in certain countries. **2** hist. a national or international conference, esp. of a federal State or confederation. **3** Sc. Law a meeting or session of a court. [ME f. med.L dieta day's work, wages, etc.]

dietary /'daɪətrɪ/ adj. & n. —adj. of or relating to a diet. —n. (pl. -ies) a regulated or restricted diet. [ME f. med.L dietarium (as DIET[1])]

dietetic /,daɪə'tetɪk/ adj. of or relating to diet. □□ **dietetically** adv. [L dieteticus f. Gk diaitētikos (as DIET[1])]

dietetics /,daɪə'tetɪks/ n.pl. (usu. treated as sing.) the scientific study of diet and nutrition.

diethyl ether /daɪ'i:θaɪl/ n. Chem. = ETHER 1.

dietitian /,daɪə'tɪʃ(ə)n/ n. (also **dietician**) an expert in dietetics.

dif- /dɪf/ prefix assim. form of DIS- before f. [L var. of DIS-]

differ /'dɪfə(r)/ v.intr. **1** (often foll. by from) be unlike or distinguishable. **2** (often foll. by with) disagree; be at variance (with a person). [ME f. OF differer f. L differre, differ, DEFER[1], (as DIS-, ferre bear, tend)]

difference /'dɪfrəns/ n. & v. —n. **1** the state or condition of being different or unlike. **2** a point in which things differ; a distinction. **3** a degree of unlikeness. **4 a** the quantity by which amounts differ; a deficit (*will have to make up the difference*). **b** the remainder left after subtraction. **5 a** a disagreement, quarrel, or dispute. **b** the grounds of disagreement (*put aside their differences*). **6** *Heraldry* an alteration in a coat of arms distinguishing members of a family. —*v.tr.* *Heraldry* alter (a coat of arms) to distinguish members of a family. □ **make a** (or **all the** etc.) **difference** (often foll. by *to*) have a significant effect or influence (on a person, situation, etc.). **make no difference** (often foll. by *to*) have no effect (on a person, situation, etc.). **with a difference** having a new or unusual feature. [ME f. OF f. L *differentia* (as DIFFERENT)]

different /'dɪfrənt/ *adj.* **1** (often foll. by *from*, *to*, *than*) unlike, distinguishable in nature, form, or quality (from another). ¶ *Different from* is generally regarded as the most acceptable collocation; *to* is common in less formal use; *than* is established in US use and also found in British use, esp. when followed by a clause, e.g. *I am a different person than I was a year ago.* **2** distinct, separate; not the same one (as another). **3** *colloq.* unusual (*wanted to do something different*). □□ **differently** *adv.* **differentness** *n.* [ME f. OF *different* f. L *different-* (as DIFFER)]

differentia /ˌdɪfə'renʃɪə/ *n.* (*pl.* **differentiae** /-ʃɪ,iː/) a distinguishing mark, esp. between species within a genus. [L: see DIFFERENCE]

differential /ˌdɪfə'renʃ(ə)l/ *adj. & n.* —*adj.* **1 a** of, exhibiting, or depending on a difference. **b** varying according to circumstances. **2** *Math.* relating to infinitesimal differences. **3** constituting a specific difference; distinctive; relating to specific differences (*differential diagnosis*). **4** *Physics & Mech.* concerning the difference of two or more motions, pressures, etc. —*n.* **1** a difference between individuals or examples of the same kind. **2** *Brit.* a difference in wage or salary between industries or categories of employees in the same industry. **3** a difference between rates of interest etc. **4** *Math.* **a** an infinitesimal difference between successive values of a variable. **b** a function expressing this as a rate of change with respect to another variable. **5** (in full **differential gear**) a gear allowing a vehicle's driven wheels to revolve at different speeds in cornering. □ **differential calculus** *Math.* a method of calculating rates of change, maximum or minimum values, etc. (cf. INTEGRAL). **differential coefficient** *Math.* = DERIVATIVE. **differential equation** *Math.* an equation involving differentials among its quantities. □□ **differentially** *adv.* [med. & mod.L *differentialis* (as DIFFERENTIAL)]

differentiate /ˌdɪfə'renʃɪ,eɪt/ *v.* **1** *tr.* constitute a difference between or in. **2** *tr.* & (often foll. by *between*) *intr.* find differences (between); discriminate. **3** *tr.* & *intr.* make or become different in the process of growth or development (species, word-forms, etc.). **4** *tr.* *Math.* transform (a function) into its derivative. □□ **differentiation** /-'eɪʃ(ə)n/ *n.* **differentiator** *n.* [med.L *differentiare differentiat-* (as DIFFERENCE)]

difficult /'dɪfɪkəlt/ *adj.* **1 a** needing much effort or skill. **b** troublesome, perplexing. **2** (of a person): **a** not easy to please or satisfy. **b** uncooperative, troublesome. **3** characterized by hardships or problems (*a difficult period in his life*). □□ **difficultly** *adv.* **difficultness** *n.* [ME, back-form. f. DIFFICULTY]

difficulty /'dɪfɪkəltɪ/ *n.* (*pl.* **-ies**) **1** the state or condition of being difficult. **2 a** a difficult thing; a problem or hindrance. **b** (often in *pl.*) a cause of distress or hardship (*in financial difficulties; there was someone in difficulties in the water*). □ **make difficulties** be intransigent or unaccommodating. **with difficulty** not easily. [ME f. L *difficultas* (as DIS-, *facultas* FACULTY)]

diffident /'dɪfɪd(ə)nt/ *adj.* **1** shy, lacking self-confidence. **2** excessively modest and reticent. □□

diffidence *n.* **diffidently** *adv.* [L *diffidere* (as DIS-, *fidere* trust)]

diffract /dɪ'frækt/ *v.tr.* *Physics* (of the edge of an opaque body, a narrow slit, etc.) break up (a beam of light) into a series of dark or light bands or coloured spectra, or (a beam of radiation or particles) into a series of alternately high and low intensities. □□ **diffraction** *n.* **diffractive** *adj.* **diffractively** *adv.* [L *diffringere diffract-* (as DIS-, *frangere* break)]

diffractometer /ˌdɪfræk'tɒmɪtə(r)/ *n.* an instrument for measuring diffraction, esp. in crystallographic work.

diffuse *adj. & v.* —*adj.* /dɪ'fjuːs/ **1** (of light, inflammation, etc.) spread out, diffused, not concentrated. **2** (of prose, speech, etc.) not concise, long-winded, verbose. —*v.tr.* & *intr.* /dɪ'fjuːz/ disperse or be dispersed from a centre. **2** spread or be spread widely; reach a large area. **3** *Physics* (esp. of fluids) intermingle by diffusion. □□ **diffusely** /dɪ'fjuːslɪ/ *adv.* **diffuseness** /dɪ'fjuːsnɪs/ *n.* **diffusible** /dɪ'fjuːzɪb(ə)l/ *adj.* **diffusive** /dɪ'fjuːsɪv/ *adj.* [ME f. F *diffus* or L *diffusus* extensive (as DIS-, *fusus* past part. of *fundere* pour)]

diffuser /dɪ'fjuːzə(r)/ *n.* (also **diffusor**) **1** a person or thing that diffuses, esp. a device for diffusing light. **2** *Engin.* a duct for broadening an airflow and reducing its speed.

diffusion /dɪ'fjuːʒ(ə)n/ *n.* **1** the act or an instance of diffusing; the process of being diffused. **2** *Physics & Chem.* the interpenetration of substances by the natural movement of their particles. **3** *Anthropol.* the spread of elements of culture etc. to another region or people. □□ **diffusionist** *n.* [ME f. L *diffusio* (as DIFFUSE)]

dig /dɪg/ *v. & n.* —*v.* (**digging**; *past* and *past part.* **dug** /dʌg/) **1** *intr.* break up and remove or turn over soil, ground, etc., with a tool, one's hands, (of an animal) claws, etc. **2** *tr.* **a** break up and displace (the ground etc.) in this way. **b** (foll. by *up*) break up the soil of (fallow land). **3** *tr.* make (a hole, grave, tunnel, etc.) by digging. **4** *tr.* (often foll. by *up*, *out*) **a** obtain or remove by digging. **b** find or discover after searching. **5** *tr.* (also *absol.*) excavate (an archaeological site). **6** *tr. sl.* like, appreciate, or understand. **7** *tr. & intr.* (foll. by *in*, *into*) thrust or poke into or down into. **8** *intr.* make one's way by digging (*dug through the mountainside*). —*n.* **1** a piece of digging. **2** a thrust or poke (*a dig in the ribs*). **3** *colloq.* (often foll. by *at*) a pointed or critical remark. **4** an archaeological excavation. **5** (in *pl.*) *Brit. colloq.* lodgings. □ **dig one's feet** (or **heels** or **toes**) **in** be obstinate. **dig in** *colloq.* begin eating. **dig oneself in 1** prepare a defensive trench or pit. **2** establish one's position. [ME *digge*, of uncert. orig.: cf. OE *dīc* ditch]

digamma /daɪ'gæmə/ *n.* the sixth letter (*F, ϝ*) of the early Greek alphabet (prob. pronounced w), later disused. [L f. Gk (as DI-¹, GAMMA)]

digastric /daɪ'gæstrɪk/ *adj. & n.* *Anat.* —*adj.* (of a muscle) having two wide parts with a tendon between. —*n.* the muscle that opens the jaw. [mod.L *digastricus* (as DI-¹,· Gk *gastēr* belly)]

digest *v. & n.* —*v.tr.* /daɪ'dʒest, dɪ-/ **1** assimilate (food) in the stomach and bowels. **2** understand and assimilate mentally. **3** *Chem.* treat (a substance) with heat, enzymes, or a solvent in order to decompose it, extract the essence, etc. **4 a** reduce to a systematic or convenient form; classify; summarize. **b** think over; arrange in the mind. —*n.* /'daɪdʒest/ **1 a** a methodical summary esp. of a body of laws. **b** (**the Digest**) the compendium of Roman law compiled in the reign of Justinian (6th c. AD). **2** a regular or occasional synopsis of current literature or news. □□ **digester** *n.* **digestible** *adj.* **digestibility** /-'bɪlɪtɪ/ *n.* [ME f. L *digerere digest-* distribute, dissolve, digest (as DI-², *gerere* carry)]

digestion /daɪ'dʒestʃ(ə)n/ *n.* **1** the process of digesting. **2** the capacity to digest food (*has a weak digestion*). **3** digesting a substance by means of heat, enzymes, or a solvent. [ME f. OF f. L *digestio -onis* (as DIGEST)]

digestive /dɪˈdʒestɪv, daɪ-/ *adj.* & *n.* —*adj.* **1** of or relating to digestion. **2** aiding or promoting digestion. —*n.* **1** a substance that aids digestion. **2** (in full **digestive biscuit**) *Brit.* a usu. round semi-sweet wholemeal biscuit. □□ **digestively** *adv.* [ME f. OF *digestif -ive* or L *digestivus* (as DIGEST)]

digger /ˈdɪgə(r)/ *n.* **1** a person or machine that digs, esp. a mechanical excavator. **2** a miner, esp. a gold-digger. **3** *colloq.* an Australian or New Zealander, esp. a private soldier. **4** *Austral.* & *NZ colloq.* (as a form of address) mate, fellow.

diggings /ˈdɪgɪŋz/ *n.pl.* **1 a** a mine or goldfield. **b** material dug out of a mine etc. **2** *Brit. colloq.* lodgings, accommodation.

dight /daɪt/ *adj. archaic* clothed, arrayed. [past part. of *dight* (v.) f. OE *dihtan* f. L *dictare* DICTATE]

digit /ˈdɪdʒɪt/ *n.* **1** any numeral from 0 to 9, esp. when forming part of a number. **2** *Anat.* & *Zool.* a finger, thumb, or toe. [ME f. L *digitus*]

digital /ˈdɪdʒɪt(ə)l/ *adj.* **1** of or using a digit or digits. **2** (of a clock, watch, etc.) that gives a reading by means of displayed digits instead of hands. **3** (of a computer) operating on data represented as a series of usu. binary digits or in similar discrete form. **4 a** (of a recording) with sound-information represented in digits for more reliable transmission. **b** (of a recording medium) using this process. □ **digital audio tape** magnetic tape on which sound is recorded digitally. **digital to analog converter** *Computing* a device for converting digital values to analog form. □□ **digitalize** *v.tr.* (also **-ise**). **digitally** *adv.* [L *digitalis* (as DIGIT)]

digitalin /ˌdɪdʒɪˈteɪlɪn/ *n.* the pharmacologically active constituent(s) of the foxglove. [DIGITALIS + -IN]

digitalis /ˌdɪdʒɪˈteɪlɪs/ *n.* a drug prepared from the dried leaves of foxgloves and containing substances that stimulate the heart muscle. [mod.L, genus-name of foxglove after G *Fingerhut* thimble: see DIGITAL]

digitate /ˈdɪdʒɪˌteɪt/ *adj.* **1** *Zool.* having separate fingers or toes. **2** *Bot.* having deep radiating divisions. □□ **digitately** *adv.* **digitation** /-ˈteɪʃ(ə)n/ *n.* [L *digitatus* (as DIGIT)]

digitigrade /ˈdɪdʒɪtɪˌgreɪd/ *adj.* & *n. Zool.* —*adj.* (of an animal) walking on its toes and not touching the ground with its heels, e.g. dogs, cats, and rodents. —*n.* a digitigrade animal (cf. PLANTIGRADE). [F f. L *digitus* + *-gradus* -walking]

digitize /ˈdɪdʒɪˌtaɪz/ *v.tr.* (also **-ise**) convert (data etc.) into digital form, esp. for processing by a computer. □□ **digitization** /-ˈzeɪʃ(ə)n/ *n.*

dignified /ˈdɪgnɪˌfaɪd/ *adj.* having or expressing dignity; noble or stately in appearance or manner. □□ **dignifiedly** *adv.*

dignify /ˈdɪgnɪˌfaɪ/ *v.tr.* (**-ies**, **-ied**) **1** give dignity or distinction to. **2** ennoble; make worthy or illustrious. **3** give the form or appearance of dignity to (*dignified the house with the name of mansion*). [obs. F *dignifier* f. OF *dignefier* f. LL *dignificare* f. *dignus* worthy]

dignitary /ˈdɪgnɪtərɪ/ *n.* (*pl.* **-ies**) a person holding high rank or office. [DIGNITY + -ARY¹, after PROPRIETARY]

dignity /ˈdɪgnɪtɪ/ *n.* (*pl.* **-ies**) **1** a composed and serious manner or style. **2** the state of being worthy of honour or respect. **3** worthiness, excellence (*the dignity of work*). **4** a high or honourable rank or position. **5** high regard or estimation. □ **beneath one's dignity** not considered worthy enough for one to do. **stand on one's dignity** insist (esp. by one's manner) on being treated with due respect. [ME f. OF *digneté*, *dignité* f. L *dignitas -tatis* f. *dignus* worthy]

digraph /ˈdaɪgrɑːf/ *n.* a group of two letters representing one sound, as in *ph* and *ey*. □□ **digraphic** /-ˈgræfɪk/ *adj.*

digress /daɪˈgres/ *v.intr.* depart from the main subject temporarily in speech or writing. □□ **digresser** *n.* **digression** *n.* **digressive** *adj.* **digressively** *adv.* **digressiveness** *n.* [L *digredi digress-* (as DI-², *gradi* walk)]

digs see DIG *n.* 5.

dihedral /daɪˈhiːdr(ə)l/ *adj.* & *n.* —*adj.* having or contained by two plane faces. —*n.* = *dihedral angle.* □ **dihedral angle** an angle formed by two plane surfaces, esp. by an aircraft wing with the horizontal. [*dihedron* f. DI-¹ + -HEDRON]

dihydric /daɪˈhaɪdrɪk/ *adj. Chem.* containing two hydroxyl groups. [DI-¹ + HYDRIC]

dik-dik /ˈdɪkdɪk/ *n.* any dwarf antelope of the genus *Madoqua*, native to Africa. [name in E. Africa and in Afrik.]

dike¹ var. of DYKE¹.

dike² var. of DYKE².

diktat /ˈdɪktæt/ *n.* a categorical statement or decree, esp. terms imposed after a war by a victor. [G, = DICTATE]

dilapidate /dɪˈlæpɪˌdeɪt/ *v.intr.* & *tr.* fall or cause to fall into disrepair or ruin. [L *dilapidare* demolish, squander (as DI-², *lapis lapid-* stone)]

dilapidated /dɪˈlæpɪˌdeɪtɪd/ *adj.* in a state of disrepair or ruin, esp. as a result of age or neglect.

dilapidation /dɪˌlæpɪˈdeɪʃ(ə)n/ *n.* **1 a** the process of dilapidating. **b** a state of disrepair. **2** (in *pl.*) repairs required at the end of a tenancy or lease. **3** *Eccl.* a sum charged against an incumbent for wear and tear during a tenancy. [ME f. LL *dilapidatio* (as DILAPIDATE)]

dilatation /ˌdaɪləˈteɪʃ(ə)n/ *n.* **1** the widening or expansion of a hollow organ or cavity. **2** the process of dilating. □ **dilatation and curettage** an operation in which the cervix is expanded and the womb-lining scraped off with a curette.

dilate /daɪˈleɪt/ *v.* **1** *tr.* & *intr.* make or become wider or larger (esp. of an opening in the body) (*dilated pupils*). **2** *intr.* (often foll. by *on, upon*) speak or write at length. □□ **dilatable** *adj.* **dilation** *n.* [ME f. OF *dilater* f. L *dilatare* spread out (as DI-², *latus* wide)]

dilator /daɪˈleɪtə(r)/ *n.* **1** *Anat.* a muscle that dilates an organ. **2** *Surgery* an instrument for dilating a tube or cavity in the body.

dilatory /ˈdɪlətərɪ/ *adj.* given to or causing delay. □□ **dilatorily** *adv.* **dilatoriness** *n.* [LL *dilatorius* (as DI-², *dilat-* past part. stem of *differre* DEFER¹)]

dildo /ˈdɪldəʊ/ *n.* (*pl.* **-os**) an object shaped like an erect penis and used, esp. by women, for sexual stimulation. [17th c.: orig. unkn.]

dilemma /daɪˈlemə, dɪ-/ *n.* **1** a situation in which a choice has to be made between two equally undesirable alternatives. **2** a state of indecision between two alternatives. **3** *disp.* a difficult situation. **4** an argument forcing an opponent to choose either of two unfavourable alternatives. [L f. Gk (as DI-¹, *lēmma* premiss)]

dilettante /ˌdɪlɪˈtæntɪ/ *n.* & *adj.* —*n.* (*pl.* **dilettanti** /-tɪ/ or **dilettantes**) **1** a person who studies a subject or area of knowledge superficially. **2** a person who enjoys the arts. —*adj.* trifling, not thorough; amateurish. □□ **dilettantish** *adj.* **dilettantism** *n.* [It. f. pres. part. of *dilettare* delight f. L *delectare*]

diligence¹ /ˈdɪlɪdʒ(ə)ns/ *n.* **1** careful and persistent application or effort. **2** (as a characteristic) industriousness. [ME f. OF f. L *diligentia* (as DILIGENT)]

diligence² /ˈdɪlɪdʒ(ə)ns, ˌdiːliːˈʒɑ̃s/ *n. hist.* a public stagecoach, esp. in France. [F, for *carrosse de diligence* coach of speed]

diligent /ˈdɪlɪdʒ(ə)nt/ *adj.* **1** careful and steady in application to one's work or duties. **2** showing care and effort. □□ **diligently** *adv.* [ME f. OF f. L *diligens* assiduous, part. of *diligere* love, take delight in (as DI-², *legere* choose)]

dill¹ /dɪl/ *n.* **1** an umbelliferous herb, *Anethum graveolens*, with yellow flowers and aromatic seeds. **2** the leaves or seeds of this plant used for flavouring and medicinal purposes. □**dill pickle** pickled cucumber etc. flavoured with dill. **dill-water** a distillate of dill used as a carminative. [OE *dile*]

dill² /dɪl/ *n. Austral. sl.* **1** a fool or simpleton. **2** the victim of a trickster. [app. back-form. f. DILLY²]

dilly¹ /'dɪlɪ/ *n.* (*pl.* **-ies**) esp. *US sl.* a remarkable or excellent person or thing. [*dilly* (adj.) f. DELIGHTFUL or DELICIOUS]

dilly² /'dɪlɪ/ *adj. Austral. sl.* **1** odd or eccentric. **2** foolish, stupid, mad. [perh. f. DAFT, SILLY]

dillybag /'dɪlɪˌbæg/ *n. Austral.* a small bag or basket. [Aboriginal *dilly* + BAG]

dilly-dally /ˌdɪlɪ'dælɪ/ *v.intr.* (**-ies**, **-ied**) *colloq.* **1** dawdle, loiter. **2** vacillate. [redupl. of DALLY]

diluent /'dɪljʊənt/ *adj. & n. Chem. & Biochem.* —*adj.* that serves to dilute. —*n.* a diluting agent. [L *diluere diluent-* DILUTE]

dilute /daɪ'ljuːt/ *v. & adj.* —*v.tr.* **1** reduce the strength of (a fluid) by adding water or another solvent. **2** weaken or reduce the strength or forcefulness of, esp. by adding something. —*adj.* /also 'daɪ-/ **1** (esp. of a fluid) diluted, weakened. **2** (of a colour) washed out; low in saturation. **3** *Chem.* **a** (of a solution) having relatively low concentration of solute. **b** (of a substance) in solution (*dilute sulphuric acid*). □□ **diluter** *n.* **dilution** *n.* [L *diluere dilut-* (as DI-²,· *luere* wash)]

diluvial /daɪ'luːvɪəl, dɪ-, -'ljuːvɪəl/ *adj.* **1** of a flood, esp. of the Flood in Genesis. **2** *Geol.* of the Glacial Drift formation (see DRIFT *n.* 8). [LL *diluvialis* f. *diluvium* DELUGE]

diluvium /daɪ'luːvɪəm, dɪ-, -'ljuːvɪəm/ *n.* (*pl.* **diluvia** /-vɪə/) *Geol.* = DRIFT *n.* 8. [L: see DILUVIAL]

dim /dɪm/ *adj. & v.* —*adj.* (**dimmer**, **dimmest**) **1 a** only faintly luminous or visible; not bright. **b** obscure; ill-defined. **2** not clearly perceived or remembered. **3** *colloq.* stupid; slow to understand. **4** (of the eyes) not seeing clearly. —*v.* (**dimmed**, **dimming**) **1** *tr. & intr.* make or become dim or less bright. **2** *tr. US* dip (headlights). □**dim-wit** *colloq.* a stupid person. **dim-witted** *colloq.* stupid, unintelligent. **take a dim view of** *colloq.* **1** disapprove of. **2** feel gloomy about. □□ **dimly** *adv.* **dimmish** *adj.* **dimness** *n.* [OE *dim, dimm,* of unkn. orig.]

dim. *abbr.* diminuendo.

dime /daɪm/ *n. US & Can. colloq.* **1** a ten-cent coin. **2** a small amount of money. □**a dime a dozen** very cheap or commonplace. **dime novel** a cheap popular novel. **turn on a dime** *US colloq.* make a sharp turn in a vehicle. [ME (orig. = tithe) f. OF *disme* f. L *decima pars* tenth part]

dimension /daɪ'menʃ(ə)n, dɪ-/ *n. & v.* —*n.* **1 a** measurable extent of any kind, as length, breadth, depth, area, and volume. **2** (in *pl.*) size, scope, extent. **3** an aspect or facet of a situation, problem, etc. **4** *Algebra* one of a number of unknown or variable quantities contained as factors in a product (x^3, x^2y, *xyz, are all of three dimensions*). **5** *Physics* the product of mass, length, time, etc., raised to the appropriate power, in a derived physical quantity. —*v.tr.* (usu. as **dimensioned** *adj.*) mark the dimensions on (a diagram etc.). □□ **dimensional** *adj.* (also in *comb.*). **dimensionless** *adj.* [ME f. OF f. L *dimensio -onis* (as DI-²,· *metiri mensus* measure)]

dimer /'daɪmə(r)/ *n. Chem.* a compound consisting of two identical molecules linked together (cf. MONOMER). □□ **dimeric** /-'merɪk/ *adj.* [DI-¹ + *-mer* after POLYMER]

dimerous /'daɪmərəs/ *adj.* (of a plant) having two parts in a whorl etc. [mod.L *dimerus* f. Gk *dimerēs* bipartite]

dimeter /'dɪmɪtə(r)/ *n. Prosody* a line of verse consisting of two metrical feet. [LL *dimetrus* f. Gk *dimetros* (as DI-¹, METER)]

diminish /dɪ'mɪnɪʃ/ *v.* **1** *tr. & intr.* make or become smaller or less. **2** *tr.* lessen the reputation or influence of (a person). □**law of diminishing returns** *Econ.*

the fact that the increase of expenditure, investment, taxation, etc., beyond a certain point ceases to produce a proportionate yield. □□ **diminishable** *adj.* [ME, blending of earlier *minish* f. OF *menusier* (formed as MINCE) and *diminue* f. OF *diminuer* f. L *diminuere diminut-* break up small]

diminished /dɪ'mɪnɪʃt/ *adj.* **1** reduced; made smaller or less. **2** *Mus.* (of an interval, usu. a seventh or fifth) less by a semitone than the corresponding minor or perfect interval. □**diminished responsibility** *Law* the limitation of criminal responsibility on the ground of mental weakness or abnormality.

diminuendo /dɪˌmɪnjʊ'endəʊ/ *adv. & n. Mus.* —*adv.* with a gradual decrease in loudness. —*n.* (*pl.* **-os**) a passage to be played in this way. [It., part. of *diminuire* DIMINISH]

diminution /ˌdɪmɪ'njuːʃ(ə)n/ *n.* **1 a** the act or an instance of diminishing. **b** the amount by which something diminishes. **2** *Mus.* the repetition of a passage in notes shorter than those originally used. [ME f. OF f. L *diminutio -onis* (as DIMINISH)]

diminutive /dɪ'mɪnjʊtɪv/ *adj. & n.* —*adj.* **1** remarkably small; tiny. **2** *Gram.* (of a word or suffix) implying smallness, either actual or imputed in token of affection, scorn, etc. (e.g. *-let, -kins*). —*n. Gram.* a diminutive word or suffix. □□ **diminutival** /-'taɪv(ə)l/ *adj.* **diminutively** *adv.* **diminutiveness** *n.* [ME f. OF *diminutif, -ive* f. LL *diminutivus* (as DIMINISH)]

dimissory /dɪ'mɪsərɪ/ *adj.* **1** ordering or permitting to depart. **2** *Eccl.* granting permission for a candidate to be ordained outside the bishop's own see (*dimissory letters*). [ME f. LL *dimissorius* f. *dimittere dimiss-* send away (as DI-²,· *mittere* send)]

dimity /'dɪmɪtɪ/ *n.* (*pl.* **-ies**) a cotton fabric woven with stripes or checks. [ME f. It. *dimito* or med.L *dimitum* f. Gk *dimitos* (as DI-¹, *mitos* warp-thread)]

dimmer /'dɪmə(r)/ *n.* **1** a device for varying the brightness of an electric light. **2** *US* **a** (in *pl.*) small parking lights on a motor vehicle. **b** a headlight on low beam.

dimorphic /daɪ'mɔːfɪk/ *adj.* (also **dimorphous** /daɪ'mɔːfəs/) *Biol., Chem., & Mineral.* exhibiting, or occurring in, two distinct forms. □□ **dimorphism** *n.* [Gk *dimorphos* (as DI-¹, *morphē* form)]

dimple /'dɪmp(ə)l/ *n. & v.* —*n.* a small hollow or dent in the flesh, esp. in the cheeks or chin. —*v.* **1** *intr.* produce or show dimples. **2** *tr.* produce dimples in (a cheek etc.). □□ **dimply** *adj.* [ME prob. f. OE *dympel* (unrecorded) f. a Gmc root *dump-*, perh. a nasalized form rel. to DEEP]

dim sum /dɪm 'sʌm/ *n.* (also **dim sim** /'sɪm/) **1** a meal or course of savoury Cantonese-style snacks. **2** (usu. **dim sim**) *Austral.* a dish of Cantonese origin, consisting of steamed or fried meat cooked in thin dough. [Cantonese *dim-sām*, lit. 'dot of the heart']

DIN /dɪn/ *n.* any of a series of technical standards originating in W. Germany and used internationally, esp. to designate electrical connections, film speeds, and paper sizes. [G, f. *Deutsche Industrie-Norm*]

din /dɪn/ *n. & v.* —*n.* a prolonged loud and distracting noise. —*v.* (**dinned**, **dinning**) **1** *tr.* (foll. by *into*) instil (something to be learned) by constant repetition. **2** *intr.* make a din. [OE *dyne, dynn, dynian* f. Gmc]

dinar /'diːnɑː(r)/ *n.* **1** the chief monetary unit of Yugoslavia. **2** the chief monetary unit of certain countries of the Middle East and N. Africa. [Arab. & Pers. *dīnār* f. Gk *dēnarion* f. L *denarius*: see DENIER]

dine /daɪn/ *v.* **1** *intr.* eat dinner. **2** *tr.* give dinner to. □**dine out 1** dine away from home. **2** (foll. by *on*) be entertained to dinner etc. on account of (one's ability to relate an interesting event, story, etc.). **dining-car** a railway carriage equipped as a restaurant. **dining-room** a room in which meals are eaten. [ME f. OF *diner, disner*, ult. f. DIS- + LL *jejunare* f. *jejunus* fasting]

diner /'daɪnə(r)/ *n.* **1** a person who dines, esp. in a restaurant. **2** a railway dining-car. **3** *US* a small restaurant. **4** a small dining-room.

dinette /daɪˈnet/ *n.* a small room or part of a room used for eating meals.

ding[1] /dɪŋ/ *v. & n.* —*v.intr.* make a ringing sound. —*n.* a ringing sound, as of a bell. [imit.: infl. by DIN]

ding[2] /dɪŋ/ *n. Austral. sl.* a party or celebration, esp. a wild one. [perh. f. DING-DONG or WINGDING]

Ding an sich /ˌdɪŋ æn ˈzɪx/ *n. Philos.* a thing in itself. [G]

dingbat /ˈdɪŋbæt/ *n. sl.* **1** *US & Austral.* a stupid or eccentric person. **2** (in *pl.*) *Austral. & NZ* **a** madness. **b** discomfort, unease (*gives me the dingbats*). [19th c.: perh. f. *ding* to beat + BAT[1]]

ding-dong /ˈdɪŋdɒŋ/ *n., adj., & adv.* —*n.* **1** the sound of alternate chimes, as of two bells. **2** *colloq.* an intense argument or fight. **3** *colloq.* a riotous party. —*adj.* (of a contest etc.) evenly matched and intensely waged; thoroughgoing. —*adv.* with vigour and energy (*hammer away at it ding-dong*). [16th c.: imit.]

dinge /dɪndʒ/ *n. & v.* —*n.* a dent or hollow caused by a blow. —*v.tr.* make such a dent in. [17th c.: orig. unkn.]

dinghy /ˈdɪŋɪ, ˈdɪŋɡɪ/ *n.* (*pl.* **-ies**) **1** a small boat carried by a ship. **2** a small pleasure-boat. **3** a small inflatable rubber boat (esp. for emergency use). [orig. a rowing-boat used on Indian rivers, f. Hindi *ḍĩgī, ḍēṅgī*]

dingle /ˈdɪŋɡ(ə)l/ *n.* a deep wooded valley or dell. [ME: orig. unkn.]

dingo /ˈdɪŋɡəʊ/ *n.* (*pl.* **-oes**) **1** a wild or half-domesticated Australian dog, *Canis dingo*. **2** *Austral. sl.* a coward or scoundrel. [Aboriginal]

dingy /ˈdɪndʒɪ/ *adj.* (**dingier, dingiest**) dirty-looking, drab, dull-coloured. □□**dingily** *adv.* **dinginess** *n.* [perh. ult. f. OE *dynge* DUNG]

dinkum /ˈdɪŋkəm/ *adj. & n. Austral. & NZ colloq.* —*adj.* genuine, right. —*n.* work, toil. □**dinkum oil** the honest truth. [19th c.: orig. unkn.]

dinky[1] /ˈdɪŋkɪ/ *adj.* (**dinkier, dinkiest**) *colloq.* **1** *Brit. colloq.* (esp. of a thing) neat and attractive; small, dainty. **2** *US* trifling, insignificant. [Sc. *dink* neat, trim, of unkn. orig.]

dinky[2] /ˈdɪŋkɪ/ *n.* (*pl.* **-ies**) **1** a well-off young working couple with no children. **2** either partner of this. [contr. of *double income no kids* + -Y[2]]

dinner /ˈdɪnə(r)/ *n.* **1** the main meal of the day, taken either at midday or in the evening. **2** a formal evening meal, often in honour of a person or event. □**dinner-dance** a formal dinner followed by dancing. **dinner-jacket** a man's short usu. black formal jacket for evening wear. **dinner lady** a woman who supervises children's lunch in a school. **dinner service** a set of usu. matching crockery for serving a meal. [ME f. OF *diner, disner*: see DINE]

dinosaur /ˈdaɪnəˌsɔː(r)/ *n.* **1** an extinct reptile of the Mesozoic era, often of enormous size. **2** a large unwieldy system or organization, esp. one not adapting to new conditions. □□**dinosaurian** /-ˈsɔːrɪən/ *adj. & n.* [mod.L *dinosaurus* f. Gk *deinos* terrible + *sauros* lizard]

dinothere /ˈdaɪnəˌθɪə(r)/ *n.* any elephant-like animal of the extinct genus *Deinotherium*, having downward curving tusks. [mod.L *dinotherium* f. Gk *deinos* terrible + *thērion* wild beast]

dint /dɪnt/ *n. & v.* —*n.* **1** a dent. **2** *archaic* a blow or stroke. —*v.tr.* mark with dints. □**by dint of** by force or means of. [ME f. OE *dynt*, and partly f. cogn. ON *dyntr*: ult. orig. unkn.]

diocesan /daɪˈɒsɪs(ə)n/ *adj. & n.* —*adj.* of or concerning a diocese. —*n.* the bishop of a diocese. [ME f. F *diocésain* f. LL *diocesanus* (as DIOCESE)]

diocese /ˈdaɪəsɪs/ *n.* a district under the pastoral care of a bishop. [ME f. OF *diocise* f. LL *diocesis* f. L *dioecesis* f. Gk *dioikēsis* administration (as DI-[3],· *oikeō* inhabit)]

diode /ˈdaɪəʊd/ *n. Electronics* **1** a semiconductor allowing the flow of current in one direction only and having two terminals. **2** a thermionic valve having two electrodes. [DI-[1] + ELECTRODE]

dioecious /daɪˈiːʃəs/ *adj.* **1** *Bot.* having male and female organs on separate plants. **2** *Zool.* having the two sexes in separate individuals (cf. MONOECIOUS). [DI-[1] + Gk *-oikos* -housed]

diol /ˈdaɪɒl/ *n. Chem.* any alcohol containing two hydroxyl groups in each molecule. [DI-[1] + -OL[1]]

Dionysiac /ˌdaɪəˈnɪsɪˌæk/ *adj.* (also **Dionysian** /-sɪən/) **1** wildly sensual; unrestrained. **2** (in Greek mythology) of or relating to Dionysus, the Greek god of wine, or his worship. [LL *Dionysiacus* f. L *Dionysus* f. Gk *Dionusos*]

Diophantine equation /ˌdaɪəˈfæntɪn, -taɪn/ *n. Math.* an equation with integral coefficients for which integral solutions are required. [*Diophantus* of Alexandria, mathematician of uncert. date]

dioptre /daɪˈɒptə(r)/ *n.* (*US* **diopter**) *Optics* a unit of refractive power of a lens, equal to the reciprocal of its focal length in metres. [F *dioptre* f. L *dioptra* f. Gk *dioptra*: see DIOPTRIC]

dioptric /daɪˈɒptrɪk/ *adj. Optics* **1** serving as a medium for sight; assisting sight by refraction (*dioptric glass; dioptric lens*). **2** of refraction; refractive. [Gk *dioptrikos* f. *dioptra* a kind of theodolite]

dioptrics /daɪˈɒptrɪks/ *n. Optics* the part of optics dealing with refraction.

diorama /ˌdaɪəˈrɑːmə/ *n.* **1** a scenic painting in which changes in colour and direction of illumination simulate a sunrise etc. **2** a small representation of a scene with three-dimensional figures, viewed through a window etc. **3** a small-scale model or film-set. □□**dioramic** /-ˈræmɪk/ *adj.* [DI-[3] + Gk *horama -atos* f. *horaō* see]

diorite /ˈdaɪəˌraɪt/ *n.* a coarse-grained plutonic igneous rock containing quartz. □□**dioritic** /-ˈrɪtɪk/ *adj.* [F f. Gk *diorizō* distinguish]

dioxan /daɪˈɒks(ə)n/ *n.* (also **dioxane** /-eɪn/) *Chem.* a colourless toxic liquid used as a solvent. ¶ Chem. formula: $C_4H_8O_2$.

dioxide /daɪˈɒksaɪd/ *n. Chem.* an oxide containing two atoms of oxygen which are not linked together (*carbon dioxide*).

DIP /dɪp/ *n. Computing* a form of integrated circuit consisting of a small plastic or ceramic slab with two parallel rows of pins. □**DIP-switch** an arrangement of switches on a printer for selecting a printing mode. [abbr. of *dual in-line package*]

Dip. *abbr.* Diploma.

dip /dɪp/ *v. & n.* —*v.* (**dipped, dipping**) **1** *tr.* put or let down briefly into liquid etc.; immerse. **2** *intr.* **a** go below a surface or level (*the sun dipped below the horizon*). **b** (of a level of income, activity, etc.) decline slightly, esp. briefly (*profits dipped in May*). **3** *intr.* extend downwards; take or have a downward slope (*the road dips after the bend*). **4** *intr.* go under water and emerge quickly. **5** *intr.* (foll. by *into*) **a** read briefly from (a book etc.). **b** take a cursory interest in (a subject). **6** (foll. by *into*) **a** *intr.* put a hand, ladle, etc., into a container to take something out. **b** *tr.* put (a hand etc.) into a container to do this. **c** *intr.* spend from or make use of one's resources (*dipped into our savings*). **7** *tr. & intr.* lower or be lowered, esp. in salute. **8** *tr. Brit.* lower the beam of (a vehicle's headlights) to reduce dazzle. **9** *tr.* colour (a fabric) by immersing it in dye. **10** *tr.* wash (sheep) by immersion in a vermin-killing liquid. **11** *tr.* make (a candle) by immersing a wick briefly in hot tallow. **12** *tr.* baptize by immersion. **13** *tr.* (often foll. by *up, out of*) remove or scoop up (liquid, grain, etc., or something from liquid). —*n.* **1** an act of dipping or being dipped. **2** a liquid into which something is dipped. **3** a brief bathe in the sea, river, etc. **4** a brief downward slope, followed by an upward one, in a road etc. **5** a sauce or dressing into which food is dipped before eating. **6** a depression in the skyline. **7** *Astron. & Surveying* the apparent depression of the horizon from the line of observation, due to the curvature of the earth. **8** *Physics* the angle made with the horizontal at any point by the earth's magnetic field. **9** *Geol.* the angle a stratum makes with the horizon. **10** *sl.* a pickpocket. **11** a quantity dipped up. **12** a candle made by dipping. □**dip-switch** a switch for dipping a vehicle's headlight beams. [OE *dyppan* f. Gmc: rel. to DEEP]

Dip. A.D. *abbr. Brit.* Diploma in Art and Design.

Dip. Ed. *abbr.* Diploma in Education.

dipeptide /daɪˈpeptaɪd/ *n. Biochem.* a peptide formed by the combination of two amino acids.

Dip. H.E. *abbr. Brit.* Diploma of Higher Education.

diphtheria /dɪfˈθɪərɪə, *disp.* dɪp-/ *n.* an acute infectious bacterial disease with inflammation of a mucous membrane esp. of the throat, resulting in the formation of a false membrane causing difficulty in breathing and swallowing. □□**diphtherial** *adj.* **diphtheric** /-ˈθerɪk/ *adj.* **diphtheritic** /-θəˈrɪtɪk/ *adj.* **diphtheroid** /ˈdɪfθəˌrɔɪd/ *adj.* [mod.L f. F *diphthérie*, earlier *diphthérite* f. Gk *diphthera* skin, hide]

diphthong /ˈdɪfθɒŋ/ *n.* **1** a speech sound in one syllable in which the articulation begins as for one vowel and moves as for another (as in *coin*, *loud*, and *side*). **2 a** a digraph representing the sound of a diphthong or single vowel (as in *feat*). **b** a compound vowel character; a ligature (as *æ*). □□**diphthongal** /-ˈθɒŋ(ə)l/ *adj.* [F *diphtongue* f. LL *diphthongus* f. Gk *diphthoggos* (as DI-¹,· *phthoggos* voice)]

diphthongize /ˈdɪfθɒŋˌaɪz/ *v.tr.* (also **-ise**) pronounce as a diphthong. □□**diphthongization** /-ˈzeɪʃ(ə)n/ *n.*

diplo- /ˈdɪpləʊ/ *comb. form* double. [Gk *diplous* double]

diplococcus /ˌdɪpləˈkɒkəs/ *n.* (*pl.* **diplococci** /-kaɪ/) *Biol.* any coccus that occurs mainly in pairs.

diplodocus /dɪpˈlɒdəkəs, ˌdɪpləʊˈdəʊkəs/ *n.* a giant plant-eating dinosaur of the order Sauropoda, with a long neck and tail. [DIPLO- + Gk *dokos* wooden beam]

diploid /ˈdɪplɔɪd/ *adj.* & *n. Biol.* —*adj.* (of an organism or cell) having two complete sets of chromosomes per cell. —*n.* a diploid cell or organism. [G (as DIPLO-, -OID)]

diploidy /ˈdɪplɔɪdɪ/ *n. Biol.* the condition of being diploid.

diploma /dɪˈpləʊmə/ *n.* **1** a certificate of qualification awarded by a college etc. **2** a document conferring an honour or privilege. **3** a State paper; an official document; a charter. □□**diplomaed** /-məd/ *adj.* (also **diploma'd**). [L f. Gk *diplōma -atos* folded paper f. *diploō* to fold f. *diplous* double]

diplomacy /dɪpˈləʊməsɪ/ *n.* **1 a** the management of international relations. **b** expertise in this. **2** adroitness in personal relations; tact. [F *diplomatie* f. *diplomatique* DIPLOMATIC after *aristocratic*]

diplomat /ˈdɪpləˌmæt/ *n.* **1** an official representing a country abroad; a member of a diplomatic service. **2** a tactful person. [F *diplomate*, back-form. f. *diplomatique*: see DIPLOMATIC]

diplomate /ˈdɪpləˌmeɪt/ *n.* esp. *US* a person who holds a diploma, esp. in medicine.

diplomatic /ˌdɪpləˈmætɪk/ *adj.* **1 a** of or involved in diplomacy. **b** skilled in diplomacy. **2** tactful; adroit in personal relations. **3** (of an edition etc.) exactly reproducing the original. □**diplomatic bag** a container in which official mail etc. is dispatched to or from an embassy, not usu. subject to customs inspection. **diplomatic corps** the body of diplomats representing other countries at a seat of government. **diplomatic immunity** the exemption of diplomatic staff abroad from arrest, taxation, etc. **diplomatic service** *Brit.* the branch of public service concerned with the representation of a country abroad. □□ **diplomatically** *adv.* [mod.L *diplomaticus* and F *diplomatique* f. L DIPLOMA]

diplomatist /dɪˈpləʊmətɪst/ *n.* = DIPLOMAT.

diplont /ˈdɪplənt/ *n. Biol.* an animal or plant which

has a diploid number of chromosomes in its somatic cells. [DIPLO- + Gk *ont-* stem of *ōn* being]

diplotene /ˈdɪpləʊˌtiːn/ *n. Biol.* a stage during the prophase of meiosis where paired chromosomes begin to separate. [DIPLO- + Gk *tainia* band]

dipolar /daɪˈpəʊlə(r)/ *adj.* having two poles, as in a magnet.

dipole /ˈdaɪpəʊl/ *n.* **1** *Physics* two equal and oppositely charged or magnetized poles separated by a distance. **2** *Chem.* a molecule in which a concentration of positive charges is separated from a concentration of negative charges. **3** an aerial consisting of a horizontal metal rod with a connecting wire at its centre.

dipper /ˈdɪpə(r)/ *n.* **1** a diving bird, *Cinclus cinclus*. Also called *water ouzel*. **2** a ladle. **3** *colloq.* an Anabaptist or Baptist.

dippy /ˈdɪpɪ/ *adj.* (**dippier, dippiest**) *sl.* crazy, silly. [20th c.: orig. uncert.]

dipso /ˈdɪpsəʊ/ *n.* (*pl.* **-os**) *colloq.* a dipsomaniac. [abbr.]

dipsomania /ˌdɪpsəˈmeɪnɪə/ *n.* an abnormal craving for alcohol. □□**dipsomaniac** /-ˈmeɪnɪˌæk/ *n.* [Gk *dipso-* f. *dipsa* thirst + -MANIA]

dipstick /ˈdɪpstɪk/ *n.* a graduated rod for measuring the depth of a liquid, esp. in a vehicle's engine.

dipteral /ˈdɪptər(ə)l/ *adj. Archit.* having a double peristyle. [L *dipteros* f. Gk (as DI-¹, *pteron* wing)]

dipteran /ˈdɪptərən/ *n.* & *adj.* —*n.* a dipterous insect. —*adj.* = DIPTEROUS 1. [mod.L *diptera* f. Gk *diptera* neut. pl. of *dipterous* two-winged (as DI-², *pteron* wing)]

dipterous /ˈdɪptərəs/ *adj.* **1** (of an insect) of the order Diptera, having two membranous wings, e.g. the fly, gnat, or mosquito. **2** *Bot.* having two winglike appendages. [mod.L *dipterus* f. Gk *dipteros*: see DIPTERAN]

diptych /ˈdɪptɪk/ *n.* **1** a painting, esp. an altarpiece, on two hinged usu. wooden panels which may be closed like a book. **2** an ancient writing-tablet consisting of two hinged leaves with waxed inner sides. [LL *diptycha* f. Gk *diptukha* (as DI-¹, *ptukhē* fold)]

dire /ˈdaɪə(r)/ *adj.* **1 a** calamitous, dreadful (*in dire straits*). **b** ominous (*dire warnings*). **2** urgent (*in dire need*). □□**direly** *adv.* **direness** *n.* [L *dirus*]

direct /daɪˈrekt, dɪ-/ *adj., adv., & v.* —*adj.* **1** extending or moving in a straight line or by the shortest route; not crooked or circuitous. **2 a** straightforward; going straight to the point. **b** frank; not ambiguous. **3** without intermediaries or the intervention of other factors (*direct rule*; *the direct result*; *made a direct approach*). **4** (of descent) lineal, not collateral. **5** exact, complete, greatest possible (esp. where contrast is implied) (*the direct opposite*). **6** *Mus.* (of an interval or chord) not inverted. **7** *Astron.* (of planetary etc. motion) proceeding from East to West; not retrograde. —*adv.* **1** in a direct way or manner; without an intermediary or intervening factor (*dealt with them direct*). **2** frankly; without evasion. **3** by a direct route (*send it direct to London*). —*v.tr.* **1** control, guide; govern the movements of. **2** (foll. by *to* + infin., or *that* + clause) give a formal order or command to. **3** (foll. by *to*) **a** address or give indications for the delivery of (a letter etc.). **b** tell or show (a person) the way to a destination. **4** (foll. by *at*, *to*, *towards*) **a** point, aim, or cause (a blow or missile) to move in a certain direction. **b** point or address (one's attention, a remark, etc.). **5** guide as an adviser, as a principle, etc. (*I do as duty directs me*). **6 a** (also *absol.*) supervise the performing, staging, etc., of (a film, play, etc.). **b** supervise the performance of (an actor etc.). **7** (also *absol.*) guide the performance of (a group of musicians), esp. as a participant. □**direct access** the facility of retrieving data immediately from any part of a computer file. **direct action** action such as a strike or sabotage directly affecting the community and meant to reinforce demands on a government, employer, etc. **direct address** *Computing* an address (see ADDRESS *n.* 1c) which specifies the location of data to be used in an operation. **direct current** an electric current flowing in one direction only. ¶ Abbr.: **DC, d.c. direct debit** an arrangement for the regular debiting of a bank account at the request of the payee. **direct-grant school** *hist.* (in the UK) a school receiving funds from the Government and not from a local authority. **direct method** a system of teaching a foreign language using only that language and without the study of formal grammar. **direct object** *Gram.* the primary object of the action of a transitive verb. **direct proportion** a relation between quantities whose ratio is constant. **direct speech** (or **oration**) words actually spoken, not reported in the third person. **direct tax** a tax levied on the person who ultimately bears the burden of it, esp. on income. □□ **directness** *n.* [ME f. L *directus* past part. of *dirigere direct-* (as DI-², *regere* put straight)]

direction /daɪˈrekʃ(ə)n, dɪ-/ *n.* **1** the act or process of directing; supervision. **2** (usu. in *pl.*) an order or instruction, esp. each of a set guiding use of equipment etc. **3 a** the course or line along which a person or thing moves or looks, or which must be taken to reach a destination (*sailed in an easterly direction*). **b** (in *pl.*) guidance on how to reach a destination. **c** the point to or from which a person or thing moves or looks. **4** the tendency or scope of a theme, subject, or inquiry. □ **direction-finder** a device for determining the source of radio waves, esp. as an aid in navigation. □□ **directionless** *adj.* [ME f. F *direction* or L *directio* (as DIRECT)]

directional /daɪˈrekʃən(ə)l, dɪ-/ *adj.* **1** of or indicating direction. **2** *Electronics* **a** concerned with the transmission of radio or sound waves in a particular direction. **b** (of equipment) designed to receive radio or sound waves most effectively from a particular direction or directions and not others. □□ **directionality** /-ˈnælɪtɪ/ *n.* **directionally** *adv.*

directive /daɪˈrektɪv, dɪ-/ *n. & adj.* —*n.* a general instruction from one in authority. —*adj.* serving to direct. [ME f. med.L *directivus* (as DIRECT)]

directly /daɪˈrektlɪ, dɪ-/ *adv. & conj.* —*adv.* **1 a** at once; without delay. **b** presently, shortly. **2** exactly, immediately (*directly opposite; directly after lunch*). **3** in a direct manner. —*conj. colloq.* as soon as (*will tell you directly they come*).

Directoire /dɪrekˈtwɑː(r)/ *adj. Needlework & Art* in imitation of styles prevalent during the French Directory. □ **Directoire drawers** (or **knickers**) knickers which are straight, full, and knee-length. [F (as DIRECTORY)]

director /daɪˈrektə(r), dɪ-/ *n.* **1** a person who directs or controls something. **2** a member of the managing board of a commercial company. **3** a person who directs a film, play, etc., esp. professionally. **4** a person acting as spiritual adviser. **5** esp. *US* = CONDUCTOR 1. □ **director-general** the chief executive of a large (esp. public) organization. **director of public prosecutions** *Brit.* = *public prosecutor.* □□ **directorial** /-ˈtɔːrɪəl/ *adj.* **directorship** *n.* (esp. in sense 2). [AF *directour* f. LL *director* governor (as DIRECT)]

directorate /daɪˈrektərət, dɪ-/ *n.* **1** a board of directors. **2** the office of director.

directory /daɪˈrektərɪ, dɪ-/ *n.* (*pl.* **-ies**) **1** a book listing alphabetically or thematically a particular group of individuals (e.g. telephone subscribers) or organizations with various details. **2** (**Directory**) *hist.* the revolutionary executive of five persons in power in France 1795-9. **3** a book of rules, esp. for the order of private or public worship. [LL *directorium* (as DIRECT)]

directress /daɪˈrektrɪs, dɪ-/ *n.* (also **directrice**) a woman director. [DIRECTOR, F *directrice* (as DIRECTRIX)]

directrix /daɪˈrektrɪks, dɪ-/ *n.* (*pl.* **directrices** /-trɪˌsiːz/) *Geom.* a fixed line used in describing a curve or surface. [med.L f. LL *director*: see DIRECTOR, -TRIX]

direful /ˈdaɪəˌfʊl/ *adj. literary* terrible, dreadful. □□ **direfully** *adv.* [DIRE + -FUL]

dirge /dɜːdʒ/ *n.* **1** a lament for the dead, esp. forming part of a funeral service. **2** any mournful song or lament. □□ **dirgeful** *adj.* [ME f. L *dirige* (imper.) direct, the first word in the Latin antiphon (from Ps. 5:8) in the Matins part of the Office for the Dead]

dirham /ˈdɜːhæm/ *n.* the principal monetary unit of Morocco and the United Arab Emirates. [Arab. f. L DRACHMA]

dirigible /ˈdɪrɪdʒɪb(ə)l, dɪˈrɪdʒ-/ *adj. & n.* —*adj.* capable of being guided. —*n.* a dirigible balloon or airship. [L *dirigere* arrange, direct: see DIRECT]

diriment /ˈdɪrɪmənt/ *adj. Law* nullifying. □ **diriment impediment** a factor (e.g. the existence of a prior marriage) rendering a marriage null and void from the beginning. [L *dirimere* f. *dir-* = DIS- + *emere* take]

dirk /dɜːk/ *n.* a long dagger, esp. as formerly worn by Scottish Highlanders. [17th-c. *durk*, of unkn. orig.]

dirndl /ˈdɜːnd(ə)l/ *n.* **1** a woman's dress styled in imitation of Alpine peasant costume, with close-fitting bodice, tight waistband, and full skirt. **2** a full skirt of this kind. [G dial., dimin. of *Dirne* girl]

dirt /dɜːt/ *n.* **1** unclean matter that soils. **2 a** earth, soil. **b** earth, cinders, etc., used to make a surface for a road etc. (usu. *attrib.*: *dirt track; dirt road*). **3** foul or malicious words or talk. **4** excrement. **5** a dirty condition. **6** a person or thing considered worthless. □ **dirt bike** a motor cycle designed for use on unmade roads and tracks, esp. in scrambling. **dirt cheap** *colloq.* extremely cheap. **dirt-track** a course made of rolled cinders, soil, etc., for motorcycle racing or flat racing. **do a person dirt** *sl.* harm or injure a person's reputation maliciously. **eat dirt 1** suffer insults etc. without retaliating. **2** *US* make a humiliating confession. **treat like dirt** treat (a person) contemptuously; abuse. [ME f. ON *drit* excrement]

dirty /ˈdɜːtɪ/ *adj., adv., & v.* —*adj.* (**dirtier, dirtiest**) **1** soiled, unclean. **2** causing one to become dirty (*a dirty job*). **3** sordid, lewd, morally illicit or questionable (*dirty joke*). **4** unpleasant, nasty. **5** dishonest, dishonourable, unfair (*dirty play*). **6** (of weather) rough, squally. **7** (of a colour) not pure or clear, dingy. **8** *colloq.* (of a nuclear weapon) producing considerable radioactive fallout. —*adv. sl.* (with adjectives expressing magnitude) very (*a dirty great diamond*). —*v.tr. & intr.* (**-ies, -ied**) make or become dirty. □ **dirty dog** *colloq.* a scoundrel; a despicable person. **the dirty end of the stick** *colloq.* the difficult or unpleasant part of an undertaking, situation, etc. **dirty linen** (or **washing**) *colloq.* intimate secrets, esp. of a scandalous nature. **dirty look** *colloq.* a look of disapproval, anger, or disgust. **dirty money** extra money paid to those who handle dirty materials. **dirty trick 1** a dishonourable and deceitful act. **2** (in *pl.*) underhand political activity, esp. to discredit an opponent. **dirty weekend** *colloq.* a weekend spent clandestinely with a lover. **dirty word 1** an offensive or indecent word. **2** a word for something which is disapproved of (*profit is a dirty word*). **dirty work** dishonourable or illegal activity, esp. done clandestinely. **do the dirty on** *colloq.* play a mean trick on. □□ **dirtily** *adv.* **dirtiness** *n.*

dis- /dɪs/ *prefix* forming nouns, adjectives, and verbs: **1** expressing negation (*dishonest*). **2** indicating reversal or absence of an action or state (*disengage; disbelieve*). **3** indicating removal of a thing or quality (*dismember; disable*). **4** indicating separation (*distinguish; dispose*). **5** indicating completeness or intensification of the action (*disembowel; disgruntled*). **6** indicating expulsion from (*disbar*). [L *dis-*, sometimes through OF *des-*]

disability /ˌdɪsəˈbɪlɪtɪ/ n. (pl. **-ies**) **1** physical incapacity, either congenital or caused by injury, disease, etc. **2** a lack of some asset, quality, or attribute, that prevents one's doing something. **3** a legal disqualification.

disable /dɪsˈeɪb(ə)l/ v.tr. **1** render unable to function; deprive of an ability. **2** (often as **disabled** adj.) deprive of or reduce the power to walk or do other normal activities, esp. by crippling. □□ **disablement** n.

disabuse /ˌdɪsəˈbjuːz/ v.tr. **1** (foll. by of) free from a mistaken idea. **2** disillusion, undeceive.

disaccord /ˌdɪsəˈkɔːd/ n. & v. —n. disagreement, disharmony. —v.intr. (usu. foll. by with) disagree; be at odds. [ME f. F désaccorder (as ACCORD)]

disadvantage /ˌdɪsədˈvɑːntɪdʒ/ n. & v. —n. **1** an unfavourable circumstance or condition. **2** damage to one's interest or reputation. —v.tr. cause disadvantage to. □**at a disadvantage** in an unfavourable position or aspect. [ME f. OF desavantage: see ADVANTAGE]

disadvantaged /ˌdɪsədˈvɑːntɪdʒd/ adj. placed in unfavourable circumstances (esp. of a person lacking the normal social opportunities).

disadvantageous /ˌdɪsˌædvənˈteɪdʒəs/ adj. **1** involving disadvantage or discredit. **2** derogatory. □□ **disadvantageously** adv.

disaffected /ˌdɪsəˈfektɪd/ adj. **1** disloyal, esp. to one's superiors. **2** estranged; no longer friendly; discontented. □□ **disaffectedly** adv. [past part. of disaffect (v.), orig. = dislike, disorder (as DIS-, AFFECT)]

disaffection /ˌdɪsəˈfekʃ(ə)n/ n. **1** disloyalty. **2** political discontent.

disaffiliate /ˌdɪsəˈfɪlɪˌeɪt/ v. **1** tr. end the affiliation of. **2** intr. end one's affiliation. **3** tr. & intr. detach. □□ **disaffiliation** /-ˈeɪʃ(ə)n/ n.

disaffirm /ˌdɪsəˈfɜːm/ v.tr. Law **1** reverse (a previous decision). **2** repudiate (a settlement). □□ **disaffirmation** /ˌdɪsˌæfəˈmeɪʃ(ə)n/ n.

disafforest /ˌdɪsəˈfɒrɪst/ v.tr. Brit. **1** clear of forests or trees. **2** reduce from the legal status of forest to that of ordinary land. □□ **disafforestation** /-ˈsteɪʃ(ə)n/ n. [ME f. AL disafforestare (as DIS-, AFFOREST)]

disagree /ˌdɪsəˈgriː/ v.intr. (**-agrees**, **-agreed**, **-agreeing**) (often foll. by with) **1** hold a different opinion. **2** quarrel. **3** (of factors or circumstances) not correspond. **4** have an adverse effect upon (a person's health, digestion, etc.). □□ **disagreement** n. [ME f. OF desagreer (as DIS-, AGREE)]

disagreeable /ˌdɪsəˈgriːəb(ə)l/ adj. **1** unpleasant, not to one's liking. **2** quarrelsome; rude or bad-tempered. □□ **disagreeableness** n. **disagreeably** adv. [ME f. OF desagreable (as DIS-, AGREEABLE)]

disallow /ˌdɪsəˈlaʊ/ v.tr. refuse to allow or accept as valid; prohibit. □□ **disallowance** n. [ME f. OF desalouer (as DIS-, ALLOW)]

disambiguate /ˌdɪsæmˈbɪgjʊˌeɪt/ v.tr. remove ambiguity from. □□ **disambiguation** /-ˈeɪʃ(ə)n/ n.

disamenity /ˌdɪsəˈmiːnɪtɪ, -ˈmenɪtɪ/ n. (pl. **-ies**) an unpleasant feature (of a place etc.); a disadvantage.

disappear /ˌdɪsəˈpɪə(r)/ v.intr. **1** cease to be visible; pass from sight. **2** cease to exist or be in circulation or use (trams had all but disappeared). □□ **disappearance** n.

disappoint /ˌdɪsəˈpɔɪnt/ v.tr. **1** (also absol.) fail to fulfil a desire or expectation of (a person). **2** frustrate (hopes etc.); cause the failure of (a plan etc.). □**be disappointed** (foll. by with, at, in, or to + infin., or that + clause) fail to have one's expectation etc. fulfilled in some regard (was disappointed with you; disappointed at the result; am disappointed to be last). □□ **disappointedly** adv. **disappointing** adj. **disappointingly** adv. [ME f. F désappointer (as DIS-, APPOINT)]

disappointment /ˌdɪsəˈpɔɪntmənt/ n. **1** an event, thing, or person that disappoints. **2** a feeling of distress, vexation, etc., resulting from this (I cannot hide my disappointment).

disapprobation /dɪsˌæprəˈbeɪʃ(ə)n/ n. strong (esp. moral) disapproval.

disapprove /ˌdɪsəˈpruːv/ v. **1** intr. (usu. foll. by of) have or express an unfavourable opinion. **2** tr. be displeased with. □□ **disapproval** n. **disapprover** n. **disapproving** adj. **disapprovingly** adv.

disarm /dɪsˈɑːm/ v. **1** tr. **a** take weapons away from (a person, State, etc.) (often foll. by of: were disarmed of their rifles). **b** Fencing etc. deprive of a weapon. **2** tr. deprive (a ship etc.) of its means of defence. **3** intr. (of a State etc.) disband or reduce its armed forces. **4** tr. remove the fuse from (a bomb etc.). **5** tr. deprive of the power to injure. **6** tr. pacify or allay the hostility or suspicions of; mollify; placate. □□ **disarmer** n. **disarming** adj. (esp. in sense 6). **disarmingly** adv. [ME f. OF desarmer (as DIS-, ARM²)]

disarmament /dɪsˈɑːməmənt/ n. the reduction by a State of its military forces and weapons.

disarrange /ˌdɪsəˈreɪndʒ/ v.tr. bring into disorder. □□ **disarrangement** n.

disarray /ˌdɪsəˈreɪ/ n. & v. —n. (often prec. by in, into) disorder, confusion (esp. among people). —v.tr. throw into disorder.

disarticulate /ˌdɪsɑːˈtɪkjʊˌleɪt/ v.tr. & intr. separate at the joints. □□ **disarticulation** /-ˈleɪʃ(ə)n/ n.

disassemble /ˌdɪsəˈsemb(ə)l/ v.tr. take (a machine etc.) to pieces. □□ **disassembly** n.

disassociate /ˌdɪsəˈsəʊʃɪˌeɪt, -sɪˌeɪt/ v.tr. & intr. = DISSOCIATE. □□ **disassociation** /-ˈeɪʃ(ə)n/ n.

disaster /dɪˈzɑːstə(r)/ n. **1** a great or sudden misfortune. **2 a** complete failure. **b** a person or enterprise ending in failure. □□ **disastrous** adj. **disastrously** adv. [orig. 'unfavourable aspect of a star', f. F désastre or It. disastro (as DIS-, astro f. L astrum star)]

disavow /ˌdɪsəˈvaʊ/ v.tr. disclaim knowledge of, responsibility for, or belief in. □□ **disavowal** n. [ME f. OF desavouer (as DIS-, AVOW)]

disband /dɪsˈbænd/ v. **1** intr. (of an organized group etc.) cease to work or act together; disperse. **2** tr. cause (such a group) to disband. □□ **disbandment** n. [obs. F desbander (as DIS-, BAND¹ 6)]

disbar /dɪsˈbɑː(r)/ v.tr. (**disbarred**, **disbarring**) deprive (a barrister) of the right to practise; expel from the Bar. □□ **disbarment** n.

disbelieve /ˌdɪsbɪˈliːv/ v. **1** tr. be unable or unwilling to believe (a person or statement). **2** intr. have no faith. □□ **disbelief** n. **disbeliever** n. **disbelievingly** adv.

disbound /dɪsˈbaʊnd/ adj. (of a pamphlet etc.) removed from a bound volume.

disbud /dɪsˈbʌd/ v.tr. (**disbudded**, **disbudding**) remove (esp. superfluous) buds from.

disburden /dɪsˈbɜːd(ə)n/ v.tr. **1** relieve (a person, one's mind, etc.) of a burden (often foll. by of: was disburdened of all worries). **2** get rid of, discharge (a duty, anxiety, etc.).

disburse /dɪsˈbɜːs/ v. **1** tr. expend (money). **2** tr. defray (a cost). **3** intr. pay money. □□ **disbursal** n. **disbursement** n. **disburser** n. [OF desbourser (as DIS-, BOURSE)]

disc /dɪsk/ n. (also **disk** esp. US and in sense 4) **1 a** a flat thin circular object. **b** a round flat or apparently flat surface (the sun's disc). **c** a mark of this shape. **2** a layer of cartilage between vertebrae. **3** a gramophone record. **4 a** (usu. **disk**; in full **magnetic disk**) a computer storage device consisting of several flat circular magnetically coated plates formed into a rotatable disc. **b** (in full **optical disc**) a smooth non-magnetic disc with large storage capacity for data recorded and read by laser. **5** a device with a pointer or rotating disc indicating time of arrival or latest permitted time of departure, for display in a parked motor vehicle. □**disc brake** a brake employing the friction of pads against a disc. **disk drive**

---

aʊ how eɪ day əʊ no eə hair ɪə near ɔɪ boy ʊə poor aɪə fire aʊə sour (see over for consonants)

Computing a mechanism for rotating a disk and reading or writing data from or to it. **disc harrow** a harrow with cutting edges consisting of a row of concave discs set at an oblique angle. **disc jockey** the presenter of a selection of gramophone records of popular music, esp. in a broadcast. [F *disque* or L *discus*: see DISCUS]

discalced /dɪsˈkælst/ *adj.* (of a friar or a nun) barefoot or wearing only sandals. [var. of *discalceated* (after F *déchaux*) f. L *discalceatus* (as DIS-, *calceatus* f. *calceus* shoe)]

discard *v. & n.* —*v.tr.* /dɪsˈkɑːd/ **1** reject or get rid of as unwanted or superfluous. **2** (also *absol.*) *Cards* remove or put aside (a card) from one's hand. —*n.* /ˈdɪskɑːd/ a discarded item, esp. a card in a card-game. □□ **discardable** /-ˈkɑːdəb(ə)l/ *adj.* [DIS- + CARD[1]]

discarnate /dɪsˈkɑːnət/ *adj.* having no physical body; separated from the flesh. [DIS-, L *caro carnis* flesh]

discern /dɪˈsɜːn/ *v.tr.* **1** perceive clearly with the mind or the senses. **2** make out by thought or by gazing, listening, etc. □□ **discerner** *n.* **discernible** *adj.* **discernibly** *adv.* [ME f. OF *discerner* f. L (as DIS-, *cernere cret-* separate)]

discerning /dɪˈsɜːnɪŋ/ *adj.* having or showing good judgement or insight. □□ **discerningly** *adv.*

discernment /dɪˈsɜːnmənt/ *n.* good judgement or insight.

discerptible /dɪˈsɜːptɪb(ə)l/ *adj. literary* able to be plucked apart; divisible. □□ **discerptibility** /-ˈbɪlɪtɪ/ *n.* [L *discerpere discerpt-* (as DIS-, *carpere* pluck)]

discerption /dɪˈsɜːpʃ(ə)n/ *n. archaic* **1 a** a pulling apart; severance. **b** an instance of this. **2** a severed piece. [LL *discerptio* (as DISCERPTIBLE)]

discharge *v. & n.* —*v.* /dɪsˈtʃɑːdʒ/ **1** *tr.* **a** let go, release, esp. from a duty, commitment, or period of confinement. **b** relieve (a bankrupt) of residual liability. **2** *tr.* dismiss from office, employment, army commission, etc. **3** *tr.* **a** fire (a gun etc.). **b** (of a gun etc.) fire (a bullet etc.). **4** *tr.* (also *absol.*) pour out or cause to pour out (pus, liquid, etc.) (*the wound was discharging*). **b** *tr.* throw; eject (*discharged a stone at the cat*). **c** *tr.* utter (abuse etc.). **d** *intr.* (foll. by *into*) (of a river etc.) flow into (esp. the sea). **5** *tr.* **a** carry out, perform (a duty or obligation). **b** relieve oneself of (a financial commitment) (*discharged his debt*). **6** *tr. Law* cancel (an order of court). **7** *tr. Physics* release an electrical charge from. **8** *tr.* **a** relieve (a ship etc.) of its cargo. **b** unload (a cargo) from a ship. —*n.* /ˈdɪstʃɑːdʒ, dɪsˈtʃɑːdʒ/ **1** the act or an instance of discharging; the process of being discharged. **2** a dismissal, esp. from the armed services. **3 a** a release, exemption, acquittal, etc. **b** a written certificate of release etc. **4** an act of firing a gun etc. **5 a** an emission (of pus, liquid, etc.). **b** the liquid or matter so discharged. **6** (usu. foll. by *of*) **a** the payment (of a debt). **b** the performance (of a duty etc.). **7** *Physics* **a** the release of a quantity of electric charge from an object. **b** a flow of electricity through the air or other gas esp. when accompanied by the emission of light. **c** the conversion of chemical energy in a cell into electrical energy. **8** the unloading (of a ship or a cargo). □□ **dischargeable** *adj.* **discharger** *n.* (in sense 7 of *v.*). [ME f. OF *descharger* (as DIS-, CHARGE)]

disciple /dɪˈsaɪp(ə)l/ *n.* **1** a follower or pupil of a leader, teacher, philosophy, etc. (*a disciple of Zen Buddhism*). **2** any early believer in Christ, esp. one of the twelve Apostles. □□ **discipleship** *n.* **discipular** /dɪˈsɪpjʊlə(r)/ *adj.* [OE *discipul* f. L *discipulus* f. *discere* learn]

disciplinarian /ˌdɪsɪplɪˈneərɪən/ *n.* a person who upholds or practises firm discipline (*a strict disciplinarian*).

disciplinary /ˈdɪsɪplɪnərɪ, -ˈplɪnərɪ/ *adj.* of, promoting, or enforcing discipline. [med.L *disciplinarius* (as DISCIPLINE)]

discipline /ˈdɪsɪplɪn/ *n. & v.* —*n.* **1 a** control or order exercised over people or animals, esp. children,

prisoners, military personnel, church members, etc. **b** the system of rules used to maintain this control. **c** the behaviour of groups subjected to such rules (*poor discipline in the ranks*). **2 a** mental, moral, or physical training. **b** adversity as used to bring about such training (*left the course because he couldn't take the discipline*). **3** a branch of instruction or learning (*philosophy is a hard discipline*). **4** punishment. **5** *Eccl.* mortification by physical self-punishment, esp. scourging. —*v.tr.* **1** punish, chastise. **2** bring under control by training in obedience; drill. □□ **disciplinable** *adj.* **disciplinal** /ˌdɪsɪˈplaɪn(ə)l, ˈdɪsɪplɪn(ə)l/ *adj.* [ME f. OF *discipliner* or LL & med.L *disciplinare, disciplina* f. *discipulus* DISCIPLE]

disclaim /dɪsˈkleɪm/ *v.tr.* **1** deny or disown (*disclaim all responsibility*). **2** (often *absol.*) *Law* renounce a legal claim to (property etc.). [ME f. AF *desclaim-* stressed stem of *desclamer* (as DIS-, CLAIM)]

disclaimer /dɪsˈkleɪmə(r)/ *n.* a renunciation or disavowal, esp. of responsibility. [ME f. AF (= DISCLAIM as noun)]

disclose /dɪsˈkləʊz/ *v.tr.* **1** make known; reveal (*disclosed the truth*). **2** remove the cover from; expose to view. □□ **discloser** *n.* [ME f. OF *desclos-* stem of *desclore* f. Gallo-Roman (as DIS-, CLOSE[2])]

disclosure /dɪsˈkləʊʒə(r)/ *n.* **1** the act or an instance of disclosing; the process of being disclosed. **2** something disclosed; a revelation. [DISCLOSE + -URE after *closure*]

disco /ˈdɪskəʊ/ *n. & v. colloq.* —*n.* (*pl.* **-os**) = DISCOTHÈQUE. —*v.intr.* (**-oes**, **-oed**) **1** attend a discothèque. **2** dance to disco music (*discoed the night away*). □**disco music** popular dance music characterized by a heavy bass rhythm. [abbr.]

discobolus /dɪsˈkɒbələs/ *n.* (*pl.* **discoboli** /-ˌlaɪ/) **1** a discus-thrower in ancient Greece. **2** a statue of a discobolus. [L f. Gk *diskobolos* f. *diskos* DISCUS + *-bolos* -throwing f. *ballō* to throw]

discography /dɪsˈkɒɡrəfɪ/ *n.* (*pl.* **-ies**) **1** a descriptive catalogue of gramophone records, esp. of a particular performer or composer. **2** the study of gramophone records. □□ **discographer** *n.* [DISC + -GRAPHY after *biography*]

discoid /ˈdɪskɔɪd/ *adj.* disc-shaped. [Gk *diskoeidēs* (as DISCUS, -OID)]

discolour /dɪsˈkʌlə(r)/ *v.tr. & intr.* (*US* **discolor**) spoil or cause to spoil the colour of; stain; tarnish. □□ **discoloration** /-ˈreɪʃ(ə)n/ *n.* (also **discolouration**). [ME f. OF *descolorer* or med.L *discolorare* (as DIS-, COLOUR)]

discombobulate /ˌdɪskəmˈbɒbjʊˌleɪt/ *v.tr. US joc.* disturb; disconcert. [prob. based on *discompose* or *discomfit*]

discomfit /dɪsˈkʌmfɪt/ *v.tr.* (**discomfited**, **discomfiting**) **1 a** disconcert or baffle. **b** thwart. **2** *archaic* defeat in battle. □□ **discomfiture** *n.* [ME f. *disconfit* f. OF past part. of *desconfire* f. Rmc (as DIS-, L *conficere* put together: see CONFECTION)]

discomfort /dɪsˈkʌmfət/ *n. & v.* —*n.* **1 a** a lack of ease; slight pain (*tight collar caused discomfort*). **b** mental uneasiness (*his presence caused her discomfort*). **2** a lack of comfort. —*v.tr.* make uneasy. [ME f. OF *desconfort(er)* (as DIS-, COMFORT)]

discommode /ˌdɪskəˈməʊd/ *v.tr.* inconvenience (a person etc.). □□ **discommodious** *adj.* [obs. F *discommoder* var. of *incommoder* (as DIS-, INCOMMODE)]

discompose /ˌdɪskəmˈpəʊz/ *v.tr.* disturb the composure of; agitate; disturb. □□ **discomposure** /-ˈpəʊʒə(r)/ *n.*

disconcert /ˌdɪskənˈsɜːt/ *v.tr.* **1** disturb the composure of; agitate; fluster (*disconcerted by his expression*). **2** spoil or upset (plans etc.). □□ **disconcertedly** *adv.* **disconcerting** *adj.* **disconcertingly** *adv.* **disconcertion** /-ˈsɜːʃ(ə)n/ *n.* **disconcertment** *n.* [obs. F *desconcerter* (as DIS-, CONCERT)]

disconfirm /ˌdɪskənˈfɜːm/ *v.tr. formal* disprove or

tend to disprove (a hypothesis etc.). □□ **disconfirmation** /-ˌkɒnfə'meɪʃ(ə)n/ n.

disconformity /ˌdɪskən'fɔːmɪtɪ/ n. (pl. **-ies**) **1 a** lack of conformity. **b** an instance of this. **2** Geol. a difference of plane between two parallel, approximately horizontal sets of strata.

disconnect /ˌdɪskə'nekt/ v.tr. **1** (often foll. by from) break the connection of (things, ideas, etc.). **2** put (an electrical device) out of action by disconnecting the parts, esp. by pulling out the plug.

disconnected /ˌdɪskə'nektɪd/ adj. (of speech, writing, argument, etc.) incoherent and illogical. □□ **disconnectedly** adv. **disconnectedness** n.

disconnection /ˌdɪskə'nekʃ(ə)n/ n. (also **disconnexion**) the act or an instance of disconnecting; the state of being disconnected.

disconsolate /dɪs'kɒnsələt/ adj. **1** forlorn or inconsolable. **2** unhappy or disappointed. □□ **disconsolately** adv. **disconsolateness** n. **disconsolation** /-'leɪʃ(ə)n/ n. [ME f. med.L disconsolatus (as DIS-, consolatus past part. of L consolari console)]

discontent /ˌdɪskən'tent/ n., adj., & v. —n. lack of contentment; restlessness, dissatisfaction. —adj. dissatisfied (was discontent with his lot). —v.tr. (esp. as **discontented** adj.) make dissatisfied. □□ **discontentedly** adv. **discontentedness** n. **discontentment** n.

discontinue /ˌdɪskən'tɪnjuː/ v. (**-continues, -continued, -continuing**) **1** intr. & tr. cease or cause to cease to exist or be made (a discontinued line). **2** tr. give up, cease from (discontinued his visits). **3** tr. cease taking or paying (a newspaper, a subscription, etc.). □□ **discontinuance** n. **discontinuation** /-'eɪʃ(ə)n/ n. [ME f. OF discontinuer f. med.L discontinuare (as DIS-, CONTINUE)]

discontinuous /ˌdɪskən'tɪnjʊəs/ adj. lacking continuity in space or time; intermittent. □□ **discontinuity** /-ˌkɒntɪ'njuːɪtɪ/ n. **discontinuously** adv. [med.L discontinuus (as DIS-, CONTINUOUS)]

discord n. & v. —n. /'dɪskɔːd/ **1** disagreement; strife. **2** harsh clashing noise; clangour. **3** Mus. **a** a lack of harmony between notes sounding together. **b** an unpleasing or unfinished chord needing to be completed by another. **c** any interval except unison, an octave, a perfect fifth and fourth, a major and minor third and sixth, and their octaves. **d** a single note dissonant with another. —v.intr. /dɪs'kɔːd/ **1** (usu. foll. by with) **a** disagree or quarrel. **b** be different or inconsistent. **2** jar, clash, be dissonant. [ME f. OF descord (n.), descorder (v.) f. L discordare f. discors discordant (as DIS-, cor cord- heart)]

discordant /dɪs'kɔːd(ə)nt/ adj. (usu. foll. by to, from, with) **1** disagreeing; at variance. **2** (of sounds) not in harmony; dissonant. □□ **discordance** n. **discordancy** n. **discordantly** adv. [ME f. OF, part. of discorder: see DISCORD]

discothèque /'dɪskə,tek/ n. **1** a club etc. for dancing to recorded popular music. **2 a** the professional lighting and sound equipment used at a discothèque. **b** a business that provides this. **3** a party with dancing to popular music, esp. using such equipment. [F, = record-library]

discount n. & v. —n. /'dɪskaʊnt/ **1** a deduction from a bill or amount due given esp. in consideration of prompt or advance payment or to a special class of buyers. **2** a deduction from the amount of a bill of exchange etc. by a person who gives value for it before it is due. **3** the act or an instance of discounting. —v.tr. /dɪs'kaʊnt/ **1** disregard as being unreliable or unimportant (discounted his story). **2** reduce the effect of (an event etc.) by previous action. **3** detract from; lessen; deduct (esp. an amount from a bill etc.). **4** give or get the present worth of (a bill not yet due). □**at a discount 1** below the nominal or usual price (cf. PREMIUM). **2** not in demand; depreciated. **discount house 1** Brit. a firm that discounts bills. **2** US = discount store. **discount rate** US the minimum lending rate. **discount store** esp. US a shop etc. that sells goods at less than the normal retail price. □□ **discountable** /-'skaʊntəb(ə)l/ adj. **discounter** /-'skaʊntə(r)/ n. [obs. F descompte, -conte, descompter or It. (di)scontare (as DIS-, COUNT[1])]

discountenance /dɪs'kaʊntɪnəns/ v.tr. **1** (esp. in passive) disconcert (was discountenanced by his abruptness). **2** refuse to countenance; show disapproval of.

discourage /dɪs'kʌrɪdʒ/ v.tr. **1** deprive of courage, confidence, or energy. **2** (usu. foll. by from) dissuade (discouraged him from going). **3** show disapproval of (smoking is discouraged). □□ **discouragement** n. **discouragingly** adv. [ME f. OF descouragier (as DIS-, COURAGE)]

discourse n. & v. —n. /'dɪskɔːs, -'skɔːs/ **1** literary **a** conversation; talk. **b** a dissertation or treatise on an academic subject. **c** a lecture or sermon. **2** Linguistics a connected series of utterances; a text. —v. /dɪs'kɔːs/ **1** intr. talk; converse. **2** intr. (usu. foll. by of, on, upon) speak or write learnedly or at length (on a subject). **3** tr. archaic give forth (music etc.). [ME f. L discursus (as DIS-, COURSE): (v.) partly after F discourir]

discourteous /dɪs'kɜːtɪəs/ adj. impolite; rude. □□ **discourteously** adv. **discourteousness** n.

discourtesy /dɪs'kɜːtəsɪ/ n. (pl. **-ies**) **1** bad manners; rudeness. **2** an impolite act or remark.

discover /dɪs'kʌvə(r)/ v.tr. **1** (often foll. by that + clause) **a** find out or become aware of, whether by research or searching or by chance (discovered a new entrance; discovered that they had been overpaid). **b** be the first to find or find out (who discovered America?). **2** give (check) in a game of chess by removing one's own obstructing piece. **3** (in show business) find and promote as a new singer, actor, etc. **4** archaic **a** make known. **b** exhibit; manifest. **c** disclose; betray. □□ **discoverable** adj. **discoverer** n. [ME f. OF descovrir f. LL discooperire (as DIS-, COVER)]

discovery /dɪs'kʌvərɪ/ n. (pl. **-ies**) **1 a** the act or process of discovering or being discovered. **b** an instance of this (the discovery of a new planet). **2** a person or thing discovered. **3** Law the compulsory disclosure, by a party to an action, of facts or documents on which the other party wishes to rely. [DISCOVER after recover, recovery]

discredit /dɪs'kredɪt/ n. & v. —n. **1** harm to reputation (brought discredit on the enterprise). **2** a person or thing causing this (he is a discredit to his family). **3** lack of credibility; doubt (throws discredit on her story). **4** the loss of commercial credit. —v.tr. (**-credited, -crediting**) **1** harm the good reputation of. **2** cause to be disbelieved. **3** refuse to believe.

discreditable /dɪs'kredɪtəb(ə)l/ adj. bringing discredit; shameful. □□ **discreditably** adv.

discreet /dɪs'kriːt/ adj. (**discreeter, discreetest**) **1 a** circumspect in speech or action, esp. to avoid social disgrace or embarrassment. **b** tactful; trustworthy. **2** unobtrusive (a discreet touch of rouge). □□ **discreetly** adv. **discreetness** n. [ME f. OF discret -ete f. L discretus separate (as DIS-, cretus past part. of cernere sift), with LL sense f. its derivative discretio discernment]

discrepancy /dɪs'krepənsɪ/ n. (pl. **-ies**) **1** difference; failure to correspond; inconsistency. **2** an instance of this. □□ **discrepant** adj. [L discrepare be discordant (as DIS-, crepare creak)]

discrete /dɪs'kriːt/ adj. individually distinct; separate, discontinuous. □□ **discretely** adv. **discreteness** n. [ME f. L discretus: see DISCREET]

discretion /dɪs'kreʃ(ə)n/ n. **1** being discreet; discreet behaviour (treats confidences with discretion). **2** prudence; self-preservation. **3** the freedom to act and think as one wishes, usu. within legal limits (it is within his discretion to leave). **4** Law a court's freedom to decide a sentence etc. □**at discretion** as one pleases. **at the discretion of** to be settled or disposed of according to the judgement or choice of. **discretion is the better part of valour** reckless courage is often self-defeating. **use one's discretion** act according to one's own judgement. **years (or age) of discretion** the esp. legal age at which a person is able to manage his or her own affairs. □□ **discretionary** *adj.* [ME f. OF f. L *discretio -onis* (as DISCREET)]

discriminate /dɪˈskrɪmɪˌneɪt/ *v.* **1** *intr.* (often foll. by *between*) make or see a distinction; differentiate (*cannot discriminate between right and wrong*). **2** *intr.* make a distinction, esp. unjustly and on the basis of race, colour, or sex. **3** *intr.* (foll. by *against*) select for unfavourable treatment. **4** *tr.* (usu. foll. by *from*) make or see or constitute a difference in or between (*many things discriminate one person from another*). **5** *intr.* observe distinctions carefully; have good judgement. **6** *tr.* mark as distinctive; be a distinguishing feature of. □□ **discriminately** /-nətlɪ/ *adv.* **discriminative** /-nətɪv/ *adj.* **discriminator** *n.* **discriminatory** /-nətərɪ/ *adj.* [L *discriminare* f. *discrimen -minis* distinction f. *discernere* DISCERN]

discriminating /dɪˈskrɪmɪˌneɪtɪŋ/ *adj.* **1** able to discern, esp. distinctions. **2** having good taste. □□ **discriminatingly** *adv.*

discrimination /dɪˌskrɪmɪˈneɪʃ(ə)n/ *n.* **1** unfavourable treatment based on prejudice, esp. regarding race, colour, or sex. **2** good taste or judgement in artistic matters etc. **3** the power of discriminating or observing differences. **4** a distinction made with the mind or in action.

discursive /dɪˈskɜːsɪv/ *adj.* **1** rambling or digressive. **2** *Philos.* proceeding by argument or reasoning (opp. INTUITIVE). □□ **discursively** *adv.* **discursiveness** *n.* [med.L *discursivus* f. L *discurrere discurs-* (as DIS-, *currere* run)]

discus /ˈdɪskəs/ *n.* (*pl.* **discuses**) **1** a heavy thick-centred disc thrown in ancient Greek games. **2** a similar disc thrown in modern field sports. [L f. Gk *diskos*]

discuss /dɪˈskʌs/ *v.tr.* **1** hold a conversation about (*discussed their holidays*). **2** examine by argument, esp. written; debate. □□ **discussable** *adj.* **discussant** *n.* **discusser** *n.* **discussible** *adj.* [ME f. L *discutere discuss-* disperse (as DIS-, *quatere* shake)]

discussion /dɪˈskʌʃ(ə)n/ *n.* **1** a conversation, esp. on specific subjects; a debate (*had a discussion about what they should do*). **2** an examination by argument, written or spoken. [ME f. OF f. LL *discussio -onis* (as DISCUSS)]

disdain /dɪsˈdeɪn/ *n.* & *v.* —*n.* scorn; contempt. —*v.tr.* **1** regard with disdain. **2** think oneself superior to; reject (*disdained his offer*; *disdained to enter*; *disdained answering*). [ME f. OF *desdeign(ier)* ult. f. L *dedignari* (as DE-, *dignari* f. *dignus* worthy)]

disdainful /dɪsˈdeɪnfʊl/ *adj.* showing disdain or contempt. □□ **disdainfully** *adv.* **disdainfulness** *n.*

disease /dɪˈziːz/ *n.* **1** an unhealthy condition of the body (or a part of it) or the mind; illness, sickness. **2** a corresponding physical condition of plants. **3** a particular kind of disease with special symptoms or location. [ME f. OF *desaise*]

diseased /dɪˈziːzd/ *adj.* **1** affected with disease. **2** abnormal, disordered. [ME, past part. of *disease* (v.) f. OF *desaisier* (as DISEASE)]

diseconomy /ˌdɪsɪˈkɒnəmɪ/ *n.* *Econ.* the absence or reverse of economy, esp. the increase of costs in a large-scale operation.

disembark /ˌdɪsɪmˈbɑːk/ *v.tr.* & *intr.* put or go ashore or land from a ship or an aircraft. □□ **disembarkation** /-ˈkeɪʃ(ə)n/ *n.* [F *désembarquer* (as DIS-, EMBARK)]

disembarrass /ˌdɪsɪmˈbærəs/ *v.tr.* **1** (usu. foll. by *of*) relieve (of a load etc.). **2** free from embarrassment. □□ **disembarrassment** *n.*

disembody /ˌdɪsɪmˈbɒdɪ/ *v.tr.* (**-ies**, **-ied**) **1** separate or free (esp. the soul) from the body or a concrete form (*disembodied spirit*). **2** *archaic* disband (troops). □□ **disembodiment** *n.*

disembogue /ˌdɪsɪmˈbəʊg/ *v.tr.* & *intr.* (**disembogues**, **disembogued**, **disemboguing**) (of a river etc.) pour forth (waters) at the mouth. [Sp. *desembocar* (as DIS-, *en* in, *boca* mouth)]

disembowel /ˌdɪsɪmˈbaʊəl/ *v.tr.* (**-embowelled**, **-embowelling**; *US* **-emboweled**, **-emboweling**) remove the bowels or entrails of. □□ **disembowelment** *n.*

disembroil /ˌdɪsɪmˈbrɔɪl/ *v.tr.* extricate from confusion or entanglement.

disenchant /ˌdɪsɪnˈtʃɑːnt/ *v.tr.* free from enchantment; disillusion. □□ **disenchantingly** *adv.* **disenchantment** *n.* [F *désenchanter* (as DIS-, ENCHANT)]

disencumber /ˌdɪsɪnˈkʌmbə(r)/ *v.tr.* free from encumbrance.

disendow /ˌdɪsɪnˈdaʊ/ *v.tr.* strip (esp. the Church) of endowments. □□ **disendowment** *n.*

disenfranchise /ˌdɪsɪnˈfræntʃaɪz/ *v.tr.* (also **disfranchise** /dɪsˈfræntʃaɪz/) **1 a** deprive (a person) of the right to vote. **b** deprive (a place) of the right to send a representative to parliament. **2** deprive (a person) of rights as a citizen or of a franchise held. □□ **disenfranchisement** *n.*

disengage /ˌdɪsɪnˈgeɪdʒ/ *v.* & *n.* —*v.* **1** *tr.* detach, free, loosen, or separate (parts etc.) (*disengaged the clutch*). **2** *tr.* *Mil.* remove (troops) from a battle or a battle area. **3** *intr.* become detached. **4** *intr.* *Fencing* pass the point of one's sword to the other side of one's opponent's. **5** *intr.* (as **disengaged** *adj.*) **a** unoccupied; free; vacant. **b** uncommitted, esp. politically. —*n.* *Fencing* a disengaging movement.

disengagement /ˌdɪsɪnˈgeɪdʒmənt/ *n.* **1 a** the act of disengaging. **b** an instance of this. **2** freedom from ties; detachment. **3** the dissolution of an engagement to marry. **4** ease of manner or behaviour. **5** *Fencing* = DISENGAGE.

disentail /ˌdɪsɪnˈteɪl/ *v.tr.* *Law* free (property) from entail; break the entail of.

disentangle /ˌdɪsɪnˈtæŋg(ə)l/ *v.* **1** *tr.* **a** unravel, untwist. **b** free from complications; extricate (*disentangled her from the difficulty*). **2** *intr.* become disentangled. □□ **disentanglement** *n.*

disenthral /ˌdɪsɪnˈθrɔːl/ *v.tr.* (*US* **disenthrall**) (**-enthralled**, **-enthralling**) *literary* free from enthralment. □□ **disenthralment** *n.*

disentitle /ˌdɪsɪnˈtaɪt(ə)l/ *v.tr.* (usu. foll. by *to*) deprive of any rightful claim.

disentomb /ˌdɪsɪnˈtuːm/ *v.tr.* *literary* **1** remove from a tomb; disinter. **2** unearth. □□ **disentombment** /-ˈtuːmmənt/ *n.*

disequilibrium /ˌdɪsiːkwɪˈlɪbrɪəm/ *n.* a lack or loss of equilibrium; instability.

disestablish /ˌdɪsɪˈstæblɪʃ/ *v.tr.* **1** deprive (a Church) of State support. **2** depose from an official position. **3** terminate the establishment of. □□ **disestablishment** *n.*

disesteem /ˌdɪsɪˈstiːm/ *v.* & *n.* —*v.tr.* have a low opinion of; despise. —*n.* low esteem or regard.

diseuse /diːˈzɜːz/ *n.* (*masc.* **diseur** /diːˈzɜː(r)/) a female artiste entertaining with spoken monologues. [F, = talker f. *dire dis-* say]

disfavour /dɪsˈfeɪvə(r)/ *n.* & *v.* (*US* **disfavor**) —*n.* **1** disapproval or dislike. **2** the state of being disliked (*fell into disfavour*). —*v.tr.* regard or treat with disfavour.

disfigure /dɪsˈfɪgə(r)/ *v.tr.* spoil the beauty of; deform; deface. □□ **disfigurement** *n.* [ME f. OF *desfigurer* f. Rmc (as DIS-, FIGURE)]

disforest /dɪsˈfɒrɪst/ *v.tr.* *Brit.* = DISAFFOREST. □□ **disforestation** /-ˈsteɪʃ(ə)n/ *n.*

disfranchise var. of DISENFRANCHISE.

disfrock /dɪsˈfrɒk/ *v.tr.* unfrock.

disgorge /dɪsˈgɔːdʒ/ *v.tr.* **1** eject from the throat or stomach. **2** pour forth, discharge (contents, ill-gotten gains, etc.). □□ **disgorgement** *n*. [ME f. OF *desgorger* (as DIS-, GORGE)]

disgrace /dɪs'greɪs/ *n*. & *v*. —*n*. 1 the loss of reputation; shame; ignominy (*brought disgrace on his family*). 2 a dishonourable, inefficient, or shameful person, thing, state of affairs, etc. (*the bus service is a disgrace*). —*v.tr*. 1 bring shame or discredit on; be a disgrace to. 2 degrade from a position of honour; dismiss from favour. □in **disgrace** having lost respect or reputation; out of favour. [F *disgrâce*, *disgracier* f. It. *disgrazia, disgraziare* (as DIS-, GRACE)]

disgraceful /dɪs'greɪsfʊl/ *adj*. shameful; dishonourable; degrading. □□ **disgracefully** *adv*.

disgruntled /dɪs'grʌnt(ə)ld/ *adj*. discontented; moody; sulky. □□ **disgruntlement** *n*. [DIS- + *gruntle* obs. frequent. of GRUNT]

disguise /dɪs'gaɪz/ *v*. & *n*. —*v.tr*. 1 (often foll. by *as*) alter the appearance, sound, smell, etc., of so as to conceal the identity; make unrecognizable (*disguised herself as a policewoman; disguised the taste by adding sugar*). 2 misrepresent or cover up (*disguised the truth; disguised their intentions*). —*n*. 1 a a costume, false beard, make-up, etc., used to alter the appearance so as to conceal or deceive. b any action, manner, etc., used for deception. 2 a the act or practice of disguising; the concealment of reality. b an instance of this. □in **disguise** 1 wearing a concealing costume etc. 2 appearing to be the opposite (*a blessing in disguise*). □□ **disguisement** *n*. [ME f. OF *desguis(i)er* (as DIS-, GUISE)]

disgust /dɪs'gʌst/ *n*. & *v*. —*n*. (usu. foll. by *at, for*) 1 strong aversion; repugnance. 2 indignation. —*v.tr*. cause disgust in (*their behaviour disgusts me; was disgusted to find a slug*). □in **disgust** as a result of disgust (*left in disgust*). □□ **disgustedly** *adv*. [OF *degout, desgouster*, or It. *disgusto, disgustare* (as DIS-, GUSTO)]

disgustful /dɪs'gʌstfʊl/ *adj*. 1 disgusting; repulsive. 2 (of curiosity etc.) caused by disgust.

disgusting /dɪs'gʌstɪŋ/ *adj*. arousing aversion or indignation (*disgusting behaviour*). □□ **disgustingly** *adv*. **disgustingness** *n*.

dish /dɪʃ/ *n*. & *v*. —*n*. 1 a a shallow, usu. flat-bottomed container for cooking or serving food, made of glass, ceramics, metal, etc. b the food served in a dish (*all the dishes were delicious*). c a particular kind of food (*a meat dish*). 2 (in *pl*.) dirty plates, cutlery, cooking pots, etc. after a meal. 3 a a dish-shaped receptacle, object, or cavity. b = *satellite dish*. 4 *sl*. a sexually attractive person. —*v.tr*. 1 put (food) into a dish ready for serving. 2 *colloq*. a outmanœuvre. b *Brit*. destroy (one's hopes, chances, etc.). 3 make concave or dish-shaped. □dish **out** *sl*. distribute, esp. carelessly or indiscriminately. dish **up** 1 serve or prepare to serve (food). 2 *colloq*. seek to present (facts, argument, etc.) attractively. □□ **dishful** *n*. (*pl*. -fuls). **dishlike** *adj*. [OE *disc* plate, bowl (with Gmc and ON cognates) f. L *discus* DISC]

dishabille var. of DÉSHABILLÉ.

disharmony /dɪs'hɑːmənɪ/ *n*. a lack of harmony; discord. □□ **disharmonious** /-'məʊnɪəs/ *adj*. **disharmoniously** /-'məʊnɪəslɪ/ *adv*. **disharmonize** /-ˌnaɪz/ *v.tr*.

dishcloth /'dɪʃklɒθ/ *n*. a usu. open-weave cloth for washing dishes. □dishcloth **gourd** a loofah.

dishearten /dɪs'hɑːt(ə)n/ *v.tr*. cause to lose courage or confidence; make despondent. □□ **dishearteningly** *adv*. **disheartenment** *n*.

dishevelled /dɪ'ʃev(ə)ld/ *adj*. (*US* **disheveled**) (of the hair, a person, etc.) untidy; ruffled; disordered. □□ **dishevel** *v.tr*. (**dishevelled, dishevelling**; *US* **disheveled, disheveling**). **dishevelment** *n*. [ME *dischevelee* f. OF *descheveté* past part. (as DIS-, *chevel* hair f. L *capillus*)]

dishonest /dɪs'ɒnɪst/ *adj*. (of a person, act, or statement) fraudulent or insincere. □□ **dishonestly** *adv*. [ME f. OF *deshoneste* (as DIS-, HONEST)]

dishonesty /dɪs'ɒnɪstɪ/ *n*. (*pl*. -ies) 1 a a lack of

honesty. b deceitfulness, fraud. 2 a dishonest or fraudulent act. [ME f. OF *deshon(n)esté* (as DISHONEST)]

dishonour /dɪs'ɒnə(r)/ *n*. & *v*. (*US* **dishonor**) —*n*. 1 a state of shame or disgrace; discredit. 2 something that causes dishonour (*a dishonour to his profession*). —*v.tr*. 1 treat without honour or respect. 2 disgrace (*dishonoured his name*). 3 refuse to accept or pay (a cheque or a bill of exchange). 4 *archaic* violate the chastity of; rape. [ME f. OF *deshonor, deshonorer* f. med.L *dishonorare* (as DIS-, HONOUR)]

dishonourable /dɪs'ɒnərəb(ə)l/ *adj*. (*US* **dishonorable**) 1 causing disgrace; ignominious. 2 unprincipled. □□ **dishonourableness** *n*. **dishonourably** *adv*.

dishrag /'dɪʃræg/ *n*. = DISHCLOTH.

dishwasher /'dɪʃˌwɒʃə(r)/ *n*. 1 a machine for automatically washing dishes. 2 a person employed to wash dishes.

dishwater /'dɪʃˌwɔːtə(r)/ *n*. water in which dishes have been washed.

dishy /'dɪʃɪ/ *adj*. (**dishier, dishiest**) *Brit. colloq*. sexually attractive. [DISH *n*. 4 + -Y[1]]

disillusion /ˌdɪsɪ'luːʒ(ə)n, -'ljuːʒ(ə)n/ *n*. & *v*. —*n*. freedom from illusions; disenchantment. —*v.tr*. rid of illusions; disenchant. □□ **disillusionize** *v.tr*. (also **-ise**). **disillusionment** *n*.

disincentive /ˌdɪsɪn'sentɪv/ *n*. & *adj*. —*n*. 1 something that tends to discourage a particular action etc. 2 *Econ*. a source of discouragement to productivity or progress. —*adj*. tending to discourage.

disinclination /ˌdɪsɪnklɪ'neɪʃ(ə)n/ *n*. (usu. foll. by *for*, or *to* + infin.) the absence of willingness; a reluctance (*a disinclination for work; disinclination to go*).

disincline /ˌdɪsɪn'klaɪn/ *v.tr*. (usu. foll. by *to* + infin. or *for*) make unwilling or reluctant.

disincorporate /ˌdɪsɪn'kɔːpəˌreɪt/ *v.tr*. dissolve (a corporate body).

disinfect /ˌdɪsɪn'fekt/ *v.tr*. cleanse (a wound, a room, clothes, etc.) of infection, esp. with a disinfectant. □□ **disinfection** *n*. [F *désinfecter* (as DIS-, INFECT)]

disinfectant /ˌdɪsɪn'fekt(ə)nt/ *n*. & *adj*. —*n*. a usu. commercially produced chemical liquid that destroys germs etc. —*adj*. causing disinfection.

disinfest /ˌdɪsɪn'fest/ *v.tr*. rid (a person, a building, etc.) of vermin, infesting insects, etc. □□ **disinfestation** /-'steɪʃ(ə)n/ *n*.

disinflation /ˌdɪsɪn'fleɪʃ(ə)n/ *n*. *Econ*. a policy designed to counteract inflation without causing deflation. □□ **disinflationary** *adj*.

disinformation /ˌdɪsɪnfə'meɪʃ(ə)n/ *n*. false information, intended to mislead.

disingenuous /ˌdɪsɪn'dʒenjʊəs/ *adj*. having secret motives; insincere. □□ **disingenuously** *adv*. **disingenuousness** *n*.

disinherit /ˌdɪsɪn'herɪt/ *v.tr*. (**disinherited, disinheriting**) reject as one's heir; deprive of the right of inheritance. □□ **disinheritance** *n*. [ME f. DIS- + INHERIT in obs. sense 'make heir']

disintegrate /dɪs'ɪntɪˌgreɪt/ *v*. 1 *tr*. & *intr*. a separate into component parts or fragments. b lose or cause to lose cohesion. 2 *intr. colloq*. deteriorate mentally or physically. 3 *intr*. & *tr*. *Physics* undergo or cause to undergo disintegration. □□ **disintegrator** *n*.

disintegration /dɪsˌɪntɪ'greɪʃ(ə)n/ *n*. 1 the act or an instance of disintegrating. 2 *Physics* any process in which a nucleus emits a particle or particles or divides into smaller nuclei.

disinter /ˌdɪsɪn'tɜː(r)/ *v.tr*. (**disinterred, disinterring**) 1 remove (esp. a corpse) from the ground; unearth; exhume. 2 find after a protracted search (*disinterred the letter from the back of the drawer*). □□ **disinterment** *n*. [F *désenterrer* (as DIS-, INTER)]

disinterest /dɪs'ɪntrɪst/ *n*. 1 impartiality. 2 *disp*. lack of interest; unconcern.

disinterested /dɪs'ɪntrɪstɪd/ *adj*. 1 not influenced by one's own advantage; impartial. **2** *disp*. uninterested. □□ **disinterestedly** *adv*. **disinterestedness** *n*. [past part. of *disinterest* (v.) divest of interest]

disinvest /ˌdɪsɪn'vest/ *v.intr*. (foll. by *from*, or *absol*.) reduce or dispose of one's investment (in a place, company, etc.). □□ **disinvestment** *n*.

disjecta membra /dɪsˌdʒektə 'membrə/ *n.pl*. scattered remains; fragments, esp. of written work. [L, alt. of *disjecti membra poetae* (Horace) limbs of a dismembered poet]

disjoin /dɪs'dʒɔɪn/ *v.tr*. separate or disunite; part. [ME f. OF *desjoindre* f. L *disjungere* (as DIS-, *jungere*, *junct-* join)]

disjoint /dɪs'dʒɔɪnt/ *v*. & *adj*. —*v.tr*. **1** take apart at the joints. **2** (as **disjointed** *adj*.) (esp. of conversation) incoherent; desultory. **3** disturb the working or connection of; dislocate. —*adj*. (of two or more sets) having no elements in common. □□ **disjointedly** *adv*. **disjointedness** *n*. [ME f. obs. *disjoint* (adj.) f. past part. of OF *desjoindre* (as DISJOIN)]

disjunction /dɪs'dʒʌŋkʃ(ə)n/ *n*. **1** the process of disjoining; separation. **2** an instance of this. [ME f. OF *disjunction* or L *disjunctio* (as DISJOIN)]

disjunctive /dɪs'dʒʌŋktɪv/ *adj*. & *n*. —*adj*. **1** involving separation; disjoining. **2** *Gram*. (esp. of a conjunction) expressing a choice between two words etc., e.g. *or* in *asked if he was going or staying* (cf. COPULATIVE). **3** *Logic* (of a proposition) expressing alternatives. —*n*. **1** *Gram*. a disjunctive conjunction or other word. **2** *Logic* a disjunctive proposition. □□ **disjunctively** *adv*. [ME f. L *disjunctivus* (as DISJOIN)]

disk var. of DISC (esp. *US* & *Computing*).

diskette /dɪ'sket/ *n*. *Computing* = *floppy disk*.

dislike /dɪs'laɪk/ *v*. & *n*. —*v.tr*. have an aversion or objection to; not like. —*n*. **1** a feeling of repugnance or not liking. **2** an object of dislike. □□ **dislikable** *adj*. (also **dislikeable**).

dislocate /'dɪsləˌkeɪt/ *v.tr*. **1** disturb the normal connection of (esp. a joint in the body). **2** disrupt; put out of order. **3** displace. [prob. back-form. f. DISLOCATION]

dislocation /ˌdɪslə'keɪʃ(ə)n/ *n*. **1** the act or result of dislocating. **2** *Crystallog*. the displacement of part of a crystal lattice structure. [ME f. OF *dislocation* or med.L *dislocatio* f. *dislocare* (as DIS-, *locare* place)]

dislodge /dɪs'lɒdʒ/ *v.tr*. remove from an established or fixed position (*was dislodged from his directorship*). □□ **dislodgement** *n*. (also **dislodgment**). [ME f. OF *dislog(i)er* (as DIS-, LODGE)]

disloyal /dɪs'lɔɪəl/ *adj*. (often foll. by *to*) **1** not loyal; unfaithful. **2** untrue to one's allegiance; treacherous to one's government etc. □□ **disloyalist** *n*. **disloyally** *adv*. **disloyalty** *n*. [ME f. OF *desloial* (as DIS-, LOYAL)]

dismal /'dɪzm(ə)l/ *adj*. **1** causing or showing gloom; miserable. **2** dreary or sombre (*dismal brown walls*). **3** *colloq*. feeble or inept (*a dismal performance*). □ **the dismals** *colloq*. melancholy. **the dismal science** *joc*. economics. □□ **dismally** *adv*. **dismalness** *n*. [orig. noun = unlucky days: ME f. AF *dis mal* f. med.L *dies mali* two days in each month held to be unpropitious]

dismantle /dɪs'mænt(ə)l/ *v.tr*. **1** take to pieces; pull down. **2** deprive of defences or equipment. **3** (often foll. by *of*) strip of covering or protection. □□ **dismantlement** *n*. **dismantler** *n*. [OF *desmanteler* (as DIS-, MANTLE)]

dismast /dɪs'mɑːst/ *v.tr*. deprive (a ship) of masts; break down the mast or masts of.

dismay /dɪs'meɪ/ *v*. & *n*. —*v.tr*. fill with consternation or anxiety; discourage or depress; reduce to despair. —*n*. **1** consternation or anxiety. **2** depression or despair. [ME f. OF *desmaiier* (unrecorded) ult. f. a Gmc root = deprive of power (as DIS-, MAY)]

dismember /dɪs'membə(r)/ *v.tr*. **1** tear or cut the limbs from. **2** partition or divide up (an empire, country, etc.). □□ **dismemberment** *n*. [ME f. OF *desmembrer* f. Rmc (as DIS-, L *membrum* limb)]

dismiss /dɪs'mɪs/ *v*. **1 a** *tr*. send away, cause to leave one's presence, disperse; disband (an assembly or army). **b** *intr*. (of an assembly etc.) disperse; break ranks. **2** *tr*. discharge from employment, office, etc., esp. dishonourably. **3** *tr*. put out of one's thoughts; cease to feel or discuss (*dismissed him from memory*). **4** *tr*. treat (a subject) summarily (*dismissed his application*). **5** *tr*. *Law* refuse further hearing to (a case); send out of court. **6** *tr*. *Cricket* put (a batsman or a side) out (*was dismissed for 75 runs*). **7** *intr*. (in *imper*.) *Mil*. a word of command at the end of drilling. □□ **dismissal** *n*. **dismissible** *adj*. **dismission** *n*. [ME, orig. as past part. after OF *desmis* f. med.L *dismissus* (as DIS-, L *mittere miss-* send)]

dismissive /dɪs'mɪsɪv/ *adj*. tending to dismiss from consideration; disdainful. □□ **dismissively** *adv*. **dismissiveness** *n*.

dismount /dɪs'maʊnt/ *v*. **1 a** *intr*. alight from a horse, bicycle, etc. **b** *tr*. (usu. in *passive*) throw from a horse, unseat. **2** *tr*. remove (a thing) from its mounting (esp. a gun from its carriage).

disobedient /ˌdɪsə'biːdɪənt/ *adj*. disobeying; rebellious, rule-breaking. □□ **disobedience** *n*. **disobediently** *adv*. [ME f. OF *desobedient* (as DIS-, OBEDIENT)]

disobey /ˌdɪsə'beɪ/ *v.tr*. (also *absol*.) fail or refuse to obey; disregard (orders); break (rules) (*disobeyed his mother; how dare you disobey!*). □□ **disobeyer** *n*. [ME f. OF *desobeir* f. Rmc (as DIS-, OBEY)]

disoblige /ˌdɪsə'blaɪdʒ/ *v.tr*. **1** refuse to consider the convenience or wishes of. **2** (as **disobliging** *adj*.) uncooperative. [F *désobliger* f. Rmc (as DIS-, OBLIGE)]

disorder /dɪs'ɔːdə(r)/ *n*. & *v*. —*n*. **1** a lack of order; confusion. **2** a riot; a commotion. **3** *Med*. a usu. minor ailment or disease. —*v.tr*. **1** throw into confusion; disarrange. **2** *Med*. put out of good health; upset. [ME, alt. after ORDER *v*. of earlier *disordain* f. OF *desordener* (as DIS-, ORDAIN)]

disorderly /dɪs'ɔːdəlɪ/ *adj*. **1** untidy; confused. **2** irregular; unruly; riotous. **3** *Law* contrary to public order or morality. □ **disorderly house** *Law* a brothel. □□ **disorderliness** *n*.

disorganize /dɪs'ɔːɡəˌnaɪz/ *v.tr*. (also **-ise**) **1** destroy the system or order of; throw into confusion. **2** (as **disorganized** *adj*.) lacking organization or system. □□ **disorganization** /-'zeɪʃ(ə)n/ *n*. [F *désorganiser* (as DIS-, ORGANIZE)]

disorient /dɪs'ɔːrɪənt/ *v.tr*. = DISORIENTATE. [F *désorienter* (as DIS-, ORIENT *v*.)]

disorientate /dɪs'ɔːrɪənˌteɪt/ *v.tr*. **1** confuse (a person) as to his or her whereabouts or bearings. **2** confuse (a person) (*disorientated by his unexpected behaviour*). □□ **disorientation** /-'teɪʃ(ə)n/ *n*.

disown /dɪs'əʊn/ *v.tr*. **1** refuse to recognize; repudiate; disclaim. **2** renounce one's connection with or allegiance to. □□ **disowner** *n*.

disparage /dɪ'spærɪdʒ/ *v.tr*. **1** speak slightingly of; depreciate. **2** bring discredit on. □□ **disparagement** *n*. **disparagingly** *adv*. [ME f. OF *desparagier* marry unequally (as DIS-, *parage* equality of rank ult. f. L *par* equal)]

disparate /'dɪspərət/ *adj*. & *n*. —*adj*. essentially different in kind; without comparison or relation. —*n*. (in *pl*.) things so unlike that there is no basis for their comparison. □□ **disparately** *adv*. **disparateness** *n*. [L *disparatus* separated (as DIS-, *paratus* past part. of *parare* prepare), infl. in sense by L *dispar* unequal]

disparity /dɪ'spærɪtɪ/ *n*. (*pl*. **-ies**) **1** inequality; difference; incongruity. **2** an instance of this. [F *disparité* f. LL *disparitas -tatis* (as DIS-, PARITY[1])]

dispassionate /dɪ'spæʃənət/ *adj*. free from passion; calm; impartial. □□ **dispassionately** *adv*. **dispassionateness** *n*.

dispatch /dɪ'spætʃ/ *v*. & *n*. (also **despatch**) —*v.tr*. **1** send off to a destination or for a purpose (*dispatched him with the message). **2** perform (business, a task, etc.) promptly; finish off. **3** kill, execute (dispatched him with the revolver). **4** colloq. eat (food, a meal, etc.) quickly. —n. **1** the act or an instance of sending (a messenger, letter, etc.). **2** the act or an instance of killing; execution. **3 a** an official written message on State or esp. military affairs. **b** a report sent in by a newspaper's correspondent, usu. from a foreign country. **4** promptness, efficiency (done with dispatch). □dispatch-box (or -case) a container for esp. official State or military documents or dispatches. **dispatch-rider** a motor cyclist or rider on horseback carrying military dispatches. □□**dispatcher** n. [It. dispacciare or Sp. despachar expedite (as DIS-, It. impacciare and Sp. empachar hinder, of uncert. orig.)]

dispel /dɪˈspel/ v.tr. (**dispelled, dispelling**) dissipate; disperse; scatter (the dawn dispelled their fears). □□**dispeller** n. [L dispellere (as DIS-, pellere drive)]

dispensable /dɪˈspensəb(ə)l/ adj. **1** able to be done without; unnecessary. **2** (of a law etc.) able to be relaxed in special cases. □□**dispensability** /-ˈbɪlɪtɪ/ n. [med.L dispensabilis (as DISPENSE)]

dispensary /dɪˈspensərɪ/ n. (pl. -ies) **1** a place where medicines etc. are dispensed. **2** a public or charitable institution for medical advice and the dispensing of medicines. [med.L dispensarius (as DISPENSE)]

dispensation /ˌdɪspenˈseɪʃ(ə)n/ n. **1 a** the act or an instance of dispensing or distributing. **b** (foll. by with) the state of doing without (a thing). **c** something distributed. **2** (usu. foll. by from) **a** exemption from a penalty or duty; an instance of this. **b** exemption from a religious observance; an instance of this. **3 a** religious or political system obtaining in a nation etc. (the Christian dispensation). **4 a** the ordering or management of the world by Providence. **b** a specific example of such ordering (of a community, a person, etc.). □□**dispensational** adj. [ME f. OF dispensation or L dispensatio (as DISPENSE)]

dispense /dɪˈspens/ v. **1** tr. distribute; deal out. **2** tr. administer (a sacrament, justice, etc.). **3** tr. make up and give out (medicine etc.) according to a doctor's prescription. **4** tr. (usu. foll. by from) grant a dispensation to (a person) from an obligation, esp. a religious observance. **5** intr. (foll. by with) **a** do without; render needless. **b** give exemption from (a rule). □**dispensing chemist** a chemist qualified to make up and give out medicine etc. [ME f. OF despenser f. L dispensare frequent. of dispendere weigh or pay out (as DIS-, pendere pens- weigh)]

dispenser /dɪˈspensə(r)/ n. **1** a person or thing that dispenses something, e.g. medicine, good advice. **2** an automatic machine that dispenses an item or a specific amount of something (e.g. cash).

dispersant /dɪˈspɜːs(ə)nt/ n. Chem. an agent used to disperse small particles in a medium.

disperse /dɪˈspɜːs/ v. **1** intr. & tr. go, send, drive, or distribute in different directions or over a wide area. **2 a** intr. (of people at a meeting etc.) leave and go their various ways. **b** tr. cause to do this. **3** tr. send to or station at separate points. **4** tr. put in circulation; disseminate. **5** tr. Chem. distribute (small particles) uniformly in a medium. **6** tr. Physics divide (white light) into its coloured constituents. □□**dispersible** adj. **dispersal** n. **disperser** n. **dispersible** adj. **dispersive** adj. [ME f. L dispergere dispers- (as DIS-, spargere scatter)]

dispersion /dɪˈspɜːʃ(ə)n/ n. **1** the act or an instance of dispersing; the process of being dispersed. **2** Chem. a mixture of one substance dispersed in another. **3** Physics the separation of white light into colours or of any radiation according to wavelength. **4** Statistics the extent to which values of a variable differ from the mean. **5** (**the Dispersion**) the Jews dispersed among the Gentiles after the Captivity in Babylon. [ME f. LL dispersio (as DISPERSE), transl. Gk diaspora: see DIASPORA]

dispirit /dɪˈspɪrɪt/ v.tr. **1** (esp. as **dispiriting** adj.) make despondent; discourage. **2** (as **dispirited** adj.) dejected; discouraged. □□**dispiritedly** adv. **dispiritedness** n. **dispiritingly** adv.

displace /dɪsˈpleɪs/ v.tr. **1** shift from its accustomed place. **2** remove from office. **3** take the place of; oust. □**displaced person** a person who is forced to leave his or her home country because of war, persecution, etc.; a refugee.

displacement /dɪsˈpleɪsmənt/ n. **1 a** the act or an instance of displacing; the process of being displaced. **b** an instance of this. **2** Physics the amount of a fluid displaced by a solid floating or immersed in it (a ship with a displacement of 11,000 tons). **3** Psychol. **a** the substitution of one idea or impulse for another. **b** the unconscious transfer of strong unacceptable emotions from one object to another. **4** the amount by which a thing is shifted from its place.

display /dɪˈspleɪ/ v. & n. —v.tr. **1** expose to view; exhibit; show. **2** show ostentatiously. **3** allow to appear; reveal; betray (displayed his ignorance). —n. **1** the act or an instance of displaying. **2** an exhibition or show. **3** ostentation; flashiness. **4** the distinct behaviour of some birds and fish, esp. used to attract a mate. **5 a** the presentation of signals or data on a visual display unit etc. **b** the information so presented. **6** Printing the arrangement and choice of type in order to attract attention. □□**displayer** n. [ME f. OF despleier f. L displicare (as DIS-, plicare fold): cf. DEPLOY]

displease /dɪsˈpliːz/ v.tr. make indignant or angry; offend; annoy. □**be displeased** (often foll. by at, with) be indignant or dissatisfied; disapprove. □□**displeasing** adj. **displeasingly** adv. [ME f. OF desplaisir (as DIS-, L placēre please)]

displeasure /dɪsˈpleʒə(r)/ n. & v. —n. disapproval; anger; dissatisfaction. —v.tr. archaic cause displeasure to; annoy. [ME f. OF (as DISPLEASE): assim. to PLEASURE]

disport /dɪˈspɔːt/ v. & n. —v.intr. & refl. frolic; gambol; enjoy oneself (disported on the sand; disported themselves in the sea). —n. archaic **1** relaxation. **2** a pastime. [ME f. AF & OF desporter (as DIS-, porter carry f. L portare)]

disposable /dɪˈspəʊzəb(ə)l/ adj. & n. —adj. **1** intended to be used once and then thrown away (disposable nappies). **2** that can be got rid of, made over, or used. **3** (esp. of financial assets) at the owner's disposal. —n. a thing designed to be thrown away after one use. □**disposable income** income after tax etc. □□**disposability** /-ˈbɪlɪtɪ/ n.

disposal /dɪˈspəʊz(ə)l/ n. (usu. foll. by of) **1** the act or an instance of disposing of something. **2** the arrangement, disposition, or placing of something. **3** control or management (of a person, business, etc.). **4** (esp. as **waste disposal**) the disposing of rubbish. □**at one's disposal 1** available for one's use. **2** subject to one's orders or decisions.

dispose /dɪˈspəʊz/ v. **1** tr. (usu. foll. by to, or to + infin.) **a** make willing; incline (disposed him to the idea; was disposed to release them). **b** give a tendency to (the wheel was disposed to buckle). **2** tr. place suitably or in order (disposed the pictures in sequence). **3** tr. (as **disposed** adj.) have a specified mental inclination (usu. in comb.: ill-disposed). **4** intr. determine the course of events (man proposes, God disposes). □**dispose of 1 a** deal with. **b** get rid of. **c** finish. **d** kill. **2** sell. **3** prove (a claim, an argument, an opponent, etc.) to be incorrect. **4** consume (food). □□**disposer** n. [ME f. OF disposer (as DIS-, POSE¹) after L disponere disposit-]

disposition /ˌdɪspəˈzɪʃ(ə)n/ n. **1** (often foll. by to) a natural tendency; an inclination; a person's temperament (a happy disposition; a disposition to overeat). **2 a** setting in order; arranging. **b** the relative position of parts; an arrangement. **3** (usu. in pl.) **a** Mil. the stationing of troops ready for attack or defence. **b** preparations; plans. **4 a** a bestowal by deed or will. **b** control; the power of disposing. **5** ordinance, dispensation. [ME f. OF f. L *dispositio* (as DIS-, *ponere posit-* place)]

dispossess /ˌdɪspəˈzes/ *v.tr.* **1** dislodge; oust (a person). **2** (usu. foll. by *of*) deprive. □□ **dispossession** /-ˈzeʃ(ə)n/ *n.* [OF *despossesser* (as DIS-, POSSESS)]

dispraise /dɪsˈpreɪz/ *v. & n.* —*v.tr.* express disapproval or censure of. —*n.* disapproval, censure. [ME f. OF *despreisier* ult. f. LL *depretiare* DEPRECIATE]

disproof /dɪsˈpruːf/ *n.* **1** something that disproves. **2** a refutation. **b** an instance of this.

disproportion /ˌdɪsprəˈpɔːʃ(ə)n/ *n.* **1** a lack of proportion. **2** an instance of this. □□ **disproportional** *adj.* **disproportionally** *adv.*

disproportionate /ˌdɪsprəˈpɔːʃənət/ *adj.* **1** lacking proportion. **2** relatively too large or small, long or short, etc. □□ **disproportionately** *adv.* **disproportionateness** *n.*

disprove /dɪsˈpruːv/ *v.tr.* prove false; refute. □□ **disprovable** *adj.* **disproval** *n.* [ME f. OF *desprover* (as DIS-, PROVE)]

disputable /dɪˈspjuːtəb(ə)l, ˈdɪspjʊ-/ *adj.* open to question; uncertain. □□ **disputably** *adv.* [F or f. L *disputabilis* (as DISPUTE)]

disputation /ˌdɪspjuːˈteɪʃ(ə)n/ *n.* **1 a** disputing, debating. **b** an argument; a controversy. **2** a formal debate. [ME f. F *disputation* or L *disputatio* (as DISPUTE)]

disputatious /ˌdɪspjuːˈteɪʃəs/ *adj.* fond of or inclined to argument. □□ **disputatiously** *adv.* **disputatiousness** *n.*

dispute *v. & n.* —*v.* /dɪˈspjuːt/ **1** *intr.* (usu. foll. by *with*, *against*) a debate, argue (*was disputing with them about the meaning of life*). **b** quarrel. **2** *tr.* discuss, esp. heatedly (*disputed whether it was true*). **3** *tr.* question the truth or correctness or validity of (a statement, alleged fact, etc.) (*I dispute that number*). **4** *tr.* contend for; strive to win (*disputed the crown*; *disputed the field*). **5** *tr.* resist (a landing, advance, etc.). —*n.* /dɪˈspjuːt, ˈdɪspjuːt/ **1** a controversy; a debate. **2** a quarrel. **3** a disagreement between management and employees, esp. one leading to industrial action. □ **beyond** (or **past** or **without**) **dispute** certainly; indisputably. **in dispute 1** being argued about. **2** (of a workforce) involved in industrial action. □□ **disputant** /-ˈspjuːt(ə)nt/ *n.* **disputer** *n.* [ME f. OF *desputer* f. L *disputare* estimate (as DIS-, *putare* reckon)]

disqualification /dɪsˌkwɒlɪfɪˈkeɪʃ(ə)n/ *n.* **1** the act or an instance of disqualifying; the state of being disqualified. **2** something that disqualifies.

disqualify /dɪsˈkwɒlɪˌfaɪ/ *v.tr.* (-ies, -ied) **1** (often foll. by *from*) debar from a competition or pronounce ineligible as a winner because of an infringement of the rules etc. (*disqualified from the race for taking drugs*). **2** (often foll. by *for*, *from*) make or pronounce ineligible or unsuitable (*his age disqualifies him for the job*; *a criminal record disqualified him from applying*). **3** (often foll. by *from*) incapacitate legally; pronounce unqualified (*disqualified from practising as a doctor*).

disquiet /dɪsˈkwaɪət/ *v. & n.* —*v.tr.* deprive of peace; worry. —*n.* anxiety; unrest. □□ **disquieting** *adj.* **disquietingly** *adv.*

disquietude /dɪsˈkwaɪəˌtjuːd/ *n.* a state of uneasiness; anxiety.

disquisition /ˌdɪskwɪˈzɪʃ(ə)n/ *n.* a long or elaborate treatise or discourse on a subject. □□ **disquisitional** *adj.* [F f. L *disquisitio* (as DIS-, *quaerere quaesit-* seek)]

disrate /dɪsˈreɪt/ *v.tr. Naut.* reduce (a sailor) to a lower rating or rank.

disregard /ˌdɪsrɪˈɡɑːd/ *v. & n.* —*v.tr.* **1** pay no attention to; ignore. **2** treat as of no importance. —*n.* (often foll. by *of*, *for*) indifference; neglect. □□ **disregardful** *adj.* **disregardfully** *adv.*

disrelish /dɪsˈrelɪʃ/ *n. & v.* —*n.* dislike; distaste. —*v.tr.* regard with dislike or distaste.

disremember /ˌdɪsrɪˈmembə(r)/ *v.tr. & intr.* esp. *US* or *dial.* fail to remember; forget.

disrepair /ˌdɪsrɪˈpeə(r)/ *n.* poor condition due to neglect (*in disrepair*; *in a state of disrepair*).

disreputable /dɪsˈrepjʊtəb(ə)l/ *adj.* **1** of bad reputation; discreditable. **2** not respectable in appearance; dirty, untidy. □□ **disreputableness** *n.* **disreputably** *adv.*

disrepute /ˌdɪsrɪˈpjuːt/ *n.* a lack of good reputation or respectability; discredit (esp. *fall into disrepute*).

disrespect /ˌdɪsrɪˈspekt/ *n.* a lack of respect; discourtesy. □□ **disrespectful** *adj.* **disrespectfully** *adv.*

disrobe /dɪsˈrəʊb/ *v.tr. & refl.* (also *absol.*) **1** divest (oneself or another) of a robe or a garment; undress. **2** divest (oneself or another) of office, authority, etc.

disrupt /dɪsˈrʌpt/ *v.tr.* **1** interrupt the flow or continuity of (a meeting, speech, etc.); bring disorder to. **2** separate forcibly; shatter. □□ **disrupter** *n.* (also **disruptor**). **disruption** *n.* **disruptive** *adj.* **disruptively** *adv.* **disruptiveness** *n.* [L *disrumpere disrupt-* (as DIS-, *rumpere* break)]

dissatisfy /dɪˈsætɪsˌfaɪ/ *v.tr.* (-ies, -ied) make discontented; fail to satisfy (*dissatisfied with the accommodation*; *dissatisfied to find him gone*). □□ **dissatisfaction** /-ˈfækʃ(ə)n/ *n.* **dissatisfactory** /-ˈfæktəri/ *adj.* **dissatisfiedly** *adv.*

dissect /dɪˈsekt/ *v.tr.* **1** cut into pieces. **2** cut up (a plant or animal) to examine its parts, structure, etc., or (a corpse) for a post mortem. **3** analyse; criticize or examine in detail. □□ **dissection** *n.* **dissector** *n.* [L *dissecare dissect-* (as DIS-, *secare* cut)]

dissemble /dɪˈsemb(ə)l/ *v.* **1** *intr.* conceal one's motives; talk or act hypocritically. **2** *tr.* **a** disguise or conceal (a feeling, intention, act, etc.). **b** simulate (*dissembled grief in public*). □□ **dissemblance** *n.* **dissembler** *n.* **dissemblingly** *adv.* [ME, alt. after *semblance* of obs. *dissimule* f. OF *dissimuler* f. L *dissimulare* (as DIS-, SIMULATE)]

disseminate /dɪˈsemɪˌneɪt/ *v.tr.* scatter about, spread (esp. ideas) widely. □ **disseminated sclerosis** = SCLEROSIS 2. □□ **dissemination** /-ˈneɪʃ(ə)n/ *n.* **disseminator** *n.* [L *disseminare* (as DIS-, *semen -inis* seed)]

dissension /dɪˈsenʃ(ə)n/ *n.* disagreement giving rise to discord. [ME f. OF f. L *dissensio* (as DIS-, *sentire sens-* feel)]

dissent /dɪˈsent/ *v. & n.* —*v.intr.* (often foll. by *from*) **1** think differently, disagree; express disagreement. **2** differ in religious opinion, esp. from the doctrine of an established or orthodox church. —*n.* **1 a** a difference of opinion. **b** an expression of this. **2** the refusal to accept the doctrines of an established or orthodox church; nonconformity. □□ **dissenting** *adj.* **dissentingly** *adv.* [ME f. L *dissentire* (as DIS-, *sentire* feel)]

dissenter /dɪˈsentə(r)/ *n.* **1** a person who dissents. **2** (**Dissenter**) *Brit.* a member of a non-established church; a Nonconformist.

dissentient /dɪˈsenʃ(ə)nt/ *adj. & n.* —*adj.* disagreeing with a majority or official view. —*n.* a person who dissents. [L *dissentire* (as DIS-, *sentire* feel)]

dissertation /ˌdɪsəˈteɪʃ(ə)n/ *n.* a detailed discourse on a subject, esp. one submitted in partial fulfilment of the requirements of a degree or diploma. □□ **dissertational** *adj.* [L *dissertatio* f. *dissertare* discuss, frequent. of *disserere dissert-* examine (as DIS-, *serere* join)]

disservice /dɪsˈsɜːvɪs/ *n.* an ill turn; an injury, esp. done when trying to help. □□ **disserve** *v.tr. archaic.*

dissever /dɪˈsevə(r)/ *v.tr. & intr.* sever; divide into parts. □□ **disseverance** *n.* **disseverment** *n.* [ME f. AF *dis(c)everer*, OF *dessevrer* f. LL *disseparare* (as DIS-, SEPARATE)]

dissidence /ˈdɪsɪd(ə)ns/ *n.* disagreement; dissent. [F *dissidence* or L *dissidentia* (as DISSIDENT)]

dissident /ˈdɪsɪd(ə)nt/ *adj. & n.* —*adj.* disagreeing, esp. with an established government, system, etc. —*n.* a dissident person. [F or f. L *dissidēre* disagree (as DIS-, *sedēre* sit)]

dissimilar /dɪˈsɪmɪlə(r)/ *adj.* (often foll. by *to*) unlike, not similar. □□ **dissimilarity** /-ˈlærɪtɪ/ *n.* (*pl.* -ies). **dissimilarly** *adv.*

dissimilate /dɪˈsɪmɪˌleɪt/ *v.* (often foll. by *to*) *Phonet.* **1** *tr.* change (a sound or sounds in a word) to another when the word originally had the same sound repeated, as in *cinnamon*, orig. *cinnamom*. **2** *intr.* (of a sound) be changed in this way. □□ **dissimilation** /-ˈleɪʃ(ə)n/ *n.* **dissimilatory** /-lətərɪ/ *adj.* [L *dissimilis* (as DIS-, *similis* like), after *assimilate*]

dissimilitude /ˌdɪsɪˈmɪlɪˌtjuːd/ *n.* unlikeness, dissimilarity. [L *dissimilitudo* (as DISSIMILATE)]

dissimulate /dɪˈsɪmjʊˌleɪt/ *v.tr.* & *intr.* dissemble. □□ **dissimulation** /-ˈleɪʃ(ə)n/ *n.* **dissimulator** *n.* [L *dissimulare* (as DIS-, SIMULATE)]

dissipate /ˈdɪsɪˌpeɪt/ *v.* **1 a** *tr.* cause (a cloud, vapour, fear, darkness, etc.) to disappear or disperse. **b** *intr.* disperse, scatter, disappear. **2** *intr.* & *tr.* break up; bring or come to nothing. **3** *tr.* squander or fritter away (money, energy, etc.). **4** *intr.* (as **dissipated** *adj.*) given to dissipation, dissolute. □□ **dissipater** *n.* **dissipative** *adj.* **dissipator** *n.* [L *dissipare dissipat-* (as DIS-, *sipare* (unrecorded) throw)]

dissipation /ˌdɪsɪˈpeɪʃ(ə)n/ *n.* **1** intemperate, dissolute, or debauched living. **2** (usu. foll. by *of*) wasteful expenditure (*dissipation of resources*). **3** scattering, dispersion, or disintegration. **4** a frivolous amusement. [F *dissipation* or L *dissipatio* (as DISSIPATE)]

dissociate /dɪˈsəʊʃɪˌeɪt, -sɪˌeɪt/ *v.* **1** *tr.* & *intr.* (usu. foll. by *from*) disconnect or become disconnected; separate (*dissociated her from their guilt*). **2** *tr. Chem.* decompose, esp. reversibly. **3** *tr. Psychol.* cause (a person's mind) to develop more than one centre of consciousness. □**dissociated personality** *Psychol.* the pathological coexistence of two or more distinct personalities in the same person. **dissociate oneself from 1** declare oneself unconnected with. **2** decline to support or agree with (a proposal etc.). □□ **dissociative** /-ətɪv/ *adj.* [L *dissociare* (as DIS-, *socius* companion)]

dissociation /dɪˌsəʊsɪˈeɪʃ(ə)n, -ʃɪˈeɪʃ(ə)n/ *n.* **1** the act or an instance of dissociating. **2** *Psychol.* the state of suffering from dissociated personality.

dissoluble /dɪˈsɒljʊb(ə)l/ *adj.* able to be disintegrated, loosened, or disconnected; soluble. □□ **dissolubility** /-ˈbɪlɪtɪ/ *n.* **dissolubly** *adv.* [F *dissoluble* or L *dissolubilis* (as DIS-, SOLUBLE)]

dissolute /ˈdɪsəˌluːt, -ˌljuːt/ *adj.* lax in morals; licentious. □□ **dissolutely** *adv.* **dissoluteness** *n.* [ME f. L *dissolutus* past part. of *dissolvere* DISSOLVE]

dissolution /ˌdɪsəˈluːʃ(ə)n, -ˈljuːʃ(ə)n/ *n.* **1** disintegration; decomposition. **2** (usu. foll. by *of*) the undoing or relaxing of a bond, esp.: **a** a marriage. **b** a partnership. **c** an alliance. **3** the dismissal or dispersal of an assembly, esp. of a parliament at the end of its term. **4** death. **5** bringing or coming to an end; fading away; disappearance. **6** dissipation; debauchery. [ME f. OF *dissolution* or L *dissolutio* (as DISSOLVE)]

dissolve /dɪˈzɒlv/ *v.* & *n.* —*v.* **1** *tr.* & *intr.* make or become liquid, esp. by immersion or dispersion in a liquid. **2** *intr.* & *tr.* disappear or cause to disappear gradually. **3 a** *tr.* dismiss or disperse (an assembly, esp. parliament). **b** *intr.* (of an assembly) be dissolved (cf. DISSOLUTION). **4** *tr.* annul or put an end to (a partnership, marriage, etc.). **5** *intr.* (of a person) become enfeebled or emotionally overcome (*completely dissolved when he saw her*; *dissolved into tears*). **6** *intr.* (often foll. by *into*) *Cinematog.* change gradually (from one picture into another). —*n. Cinematog.* the act or process of dissolving a picture. □□ **dissolvable** *adj.* [ME f. L *dissolvere dissolut-* (as DIS-, *solvere* loosen)]

dissolvent /dɪˈzɒlv(ə)nt/ *adj.* & *n.* —*adj.* tending to

dissolve or dissipate. —*n.* a dissolvent substance. [L *dissolvere* (as DISSOLVE)]

dissonant /ˈdɪsənənt/ *adj.* **1** *Mus.* harsh-toned; unharmonious. **2** incongruous; clashing. □□ **dissonance** *n.* **dissonantly** *adv.* [ME f. OF *dissonant* or L *dissonare* (as DIS-, *sonare* sound)]

dissuade /dɪˈsweɪd/ *v.tr.* (often foll. by *from*) discourage (a person); persuade against (*dissuaded him from continuing*; *was dissuaded from his belief*). □□ **dissuader** *n.* **dissuasion** /-ˈsweɪʒ(ə)n/ *n.* **dissuasive** /-ˈsweɪsɪv/ *adj.* [L *dissuadēre* (as DIS-, *suadēre suas-* persuade)]

dissyllable var. of DISYLLABLE.

dissymmetry /dɪˈsɪmɪtrɪ/ *n.* (*pl.* -ies) **1 a** lack of symmetry. **b** an instance of this. **2** symmetry as of mirror images or the left and right hands (esp. of crystals with two corresponding forms). □□ **dissymmetrical** /-ˈmetrɪk(ə)l/ *adj.*

distaff /ˈdɪstɑːf/ *n.* **1 a** a cleft stick holding wool or flax wound for spinning by hand. **b** the corresponding part of a spinning-wheel. **2** women's work. □**distaff side** the female branch of a family. [OE *distæf* (as STAFF¹), the first element being app. rel. to LG *diesse*, MLG *dise(ne)* bunch of flax]

distal /ˈdɪst(ə)l/ *adj. Anat.* situated away from the centre of the body or point of attachment; terminal. □□ **distally** *adv.* [DISTANT + -AL]

distance /ˈdɪst(ə)ns/ *n.* & *v.* —*n.* **1** the condition of being far off; remoteness. **2 a** a space or interval between two things. **b** the length of this (*a distance of twenty miles*). **3** a distant point or place (*came from a distance*). **4** the avoidance of familiarity; aloofness; reserve (*there was a certain distance between them*). **5** a remoter field of vision (*saw him in the distance*). **6** an interval of time (*can't remember what happened at this distance*). **7 a** the full length of a race etc. **b** *Brit. Racing* a length of 240 yards from the winning-post on a racecourse. **c** *Boxing* the scheduled length of a fight. —*v.tr.* (often *refl.*) **1** place far off (*distanced herself from them*; *distanced the painful memory*). **2** leave far behind in a race or competition. □**at a distance** far off. **distance-post** *Racing* a post at the distance on a racecourse, used to disqualify runners who have not reached it by the end of the race. **distance runner** an athlete who competes in long- or middle-distance races. **go the distance 1** *Boxing* complete a fight without being knocked out. **2** complete, esp. a hard task; endure an ordeal. **keep one's distance** maintain one's reserve. **middle distance** the part of a landscape or painting between the foreground and the furthest part. **within hailing (or walking) distance** near enough to reach by hailing or walking. [ME f. OF *distance, destance* f. L *distantia* f. *distare* stand apart (as DI-², *stare* stand)]

distant /ˈdɪst(ə)nt/ *adj.* **1 a** far away in space or time. **b** (usu. *predic.*; often foll. by *from*) at a specified distance (*three miles distant from them*). **2** remote or far apart in position, time, resemblance, etc. (*a distant prospect*; *a distant relation*; *a distant likeness*). **3** not intimate; reserved; cool (*a distant bow*). **4** remote; abstracted (*a distant stare*). **5** faint, vague (*he was a distant memory to her*). □**distant early warning** *US* a radar system for the early detection of a missile attack. **distant signal** *Railways* a railway signal preceding a home signal to give warning. □□ **distantly** *adv.* [ME f. OF *distant* or L *distant-* part. stem of *distare*: see DISTANCE]

distaste /dɪsˈteɪst/ *n.* (usu. foll. by *for*) dislike; repugnance; aversion, esp. slight (*a distaste for prunes*; *a distaste for polite company*). □□ **distasteful** *adj.* **distastefully** *adv.* **distastefulness** *n.*

distemper¹ /dɪsˈtempə(r)/ *n.* & *v.* —*n.* **1** a kind of paint using glue or size instead of an oil-base, for use on walls or for scene-painting. **2** a method of mural and poster painting using this. —*v.tr.* paint (walls etc.) with distemper. [earlier as verb, f. OF *destremper* or LL *distemperare* soak, macerate: see DISTEMPER²]

distemper[2] /dɪ'stempə(r)/ n. **1** a disease of some animals, esp. dogs, causing fever, coughing, and catarrh. **2** archaic political disorder. [earlier as verb, = upset, derange: ME f. LL distemperare (as DIS-, temperare mingle correctly)]

distend /dɪ'stend/ v.tr. & intr. swell out by pressure from within (distended stomach). □□ **distensible** /-'stensɪb(ə)l/ adj. **distensibility** /-'bɪlɪtɪ/ n. **distension** /-'stenʃ(ə)n/ n. [ME f. L distendere (as DIS-, tendere tens- stretch)]

distich /'dɪstɪk/ n. Prosody a pair of verse lines; a couplet. [L distichon f. Gk distikhon (as DI-[1], stikhos line)]

distichous /'dɪstɪkəs/ adj. Bot. arranged in two opposite vertical rows. [L distichus (as DISTICH)]

distil /dɪ'stɪl/ v. (US **distill**) (**distilled**, **distilling**) **1** tr. Chem. purify (a liquid) by vaporizing it with heat, then condensing it with cold and collecting the result. **2** tr. **a** Chem. extract the essence of (a plant etc.) usu. by heating it in a solvent. **b** extract the essential meaning or implications of (an idea etc.). **3** tr. make (whisky, essence, etc.) by distilling raw materials. **4** tr. (foll. by off, out) Chem. drive (the volatile constituent) off or out by heat. **5** tr. & intr. come as or give forth in drops; exude. **6** intr. undergo distillation. □□ **distillatory** adj. [ME f. L distillare f. destillare (as DE-, stilla drop)]

distillate /'dɪstɪˌleɪt/ n. a product of distillation.

distillation /ˌdɪstɪ'leɪʃ(ə)n/ n. **1** the process of distilling or being distilled (in various senses). **2** something distilled.

distiller /dɪ'stɪlə(r)/ n. a person who distils, esp. a manufacturer of alcoholic liquor.

distillery /dɪ'stɪlərɪ/ n. (pl. **-ies**) a place where alcoholic liquor is distilled.

distinct /dɪ'stɪŋkt/ adj. **1** (often foll. by from) **a** not identical; separate; individual. **b** different in kind or quality; unlike. **2 a** clearly perceptible; plain. **b** clearly understandable; definite. **3** unmistakable, decided (had a distinct impression of being watched). □□ **distinctly** adv. **distinctness** n. [ME f. L distinctus past part. of distinguere DISTINGUISH]

distinction /dɪ'stɪŋkʃ(ə)n/ n. **1 a** the act or an instance of discriminating or distinguishing. **b** an instance of this. **c** the difference made by distinguishing. **2 a** something that differentiates, e.g. a mark, name, or title. **b** the fact of being different. **3** special consideration or honour. **4** distinguished character; excellence; eminence (a film of distinction; shows distinction in his bearing). **5** a grade in an examination denoting great excellence (passed with distinction). □ **distinction** without a **difference** a merely nominal or artificial distinction. [ME f. OF f. L distinctio -onis (as DISTINGUISH)]

distinctive /dɪ'stɪŋktɪv/ adj. distinguishing, characteristic. □□ **distinctively** adv. **distinctiveness** n.

distingué /dɪ'stæŋɡeɪ, dɪstæˈɡeɪ/ adj. (fem. **distinguée** pronunc. same) having a distinguished air, features, manner, etc. [F, past part. of distinguer: see DISTINGUISH]

distinguish /dɪ'stɪŋgwɪʃ/ v. **1** tr. (often foll. by from) **a** see or point out the difference of; draw distinctions (cannot distinguish one from the other). **b** constitute such a difference (the mole distinguishes him from his twin). **c** draw distinctions between; differentiate. **2** tr. be a mark or property of; characterize (distinguished by his greed). **3** tr. discover by listening, looking, etc. (could distinguish two voices). **4** tr. (usu. refl.; often foll. by by) make prominent or noteworthy (distinguished himself by winning first prize). **5** tr. (often foll. by into) divide; classify. **6** intr. (foll. by between) make or point out a difference between. □□ **distinguishable** adj. [F distinguer or L distinguere (as DIS-, stinguere stinct- extinguish): cf. EXTINGUISH]

distinguished /dɪ'stɪŋgwɪʃt/ adj. **1** (often foll. by for, by) of high standing; eminent; famous. **2** = DISTINGUÉ.

distort /dɪ'stɔːt/ v.tr. **1 a** put out of shape; make crooked or unshapely. **b** distort the appearance of, esp. by curved mirrors etc. **2** misrepresent (motives, facts, statements, etc.). □□ **distortedly** adv. **distortedness** n. [L distorquēre distort- (as DIS-, torquēre twist)]

distortion /dɪ'stɔːʃ(ə)n/ n. **1** the act or an instance of distorting; the process of being distorted. **2** Electronics a change in the form of a signal during transmission etc. usu. with some impairment of quality. □□ **distortional** adj. **distortionless** adj. [L distortio (as DISTORT)]

distract /dɪ'strækt/ v.tr. **1** (often foll. by from) draw away the attention of (a person, the mind, etc.). **2** bewilder, perplex. **3** (as **distracted** adj.) mad or angry (distracted by grief; distracted with worry). **4** amuse, esp. in order to take the attention from pain or worry. □□ **distractedly** adv. [ME f. L distrahere distract- (as DIS-, trahere draw)]

distraction /dɪ'strækʃ(ə)n/ n. **1 a** the act of distracting, esp. the mind. **b** something that distracts; an interruption. **2** a relaxation from work; an amusement. **3** a lack of concentration. **4** confusion; perplexity. **5** frenzy; madness. □ **to distraction** almost to a state of madness. [ME f. OF distraction or L distractio (as DISTRACT)]

distrain /dɪ'streɪn/ v.intr. Law (usu. foll. by upon) impose distraint (on a person, goods, etc.). □□ **distrainee** /-'niː/ n. **distrainer** n. **distrainment** n. **distrainor** n. [ME f. OF destreindre f. L distringere (as DIS-, stringere strict- draw tight)]

distraint /dɪ'streɪnt/ n. Law the seizure of chattels to make a person pay rent etc. or meet an obligation, or to obtain satisfaction by their sale. [DISTRAIN, after constraint]

distrait /dɪ'streɪ/ adj. (fem. **distraite** /-'streɪt/) not paying attention; absent-minded; distraught. [ME f. OF destrait past part. of destraire (as DISTRACT)]

distraught /dɪ'strɔːt/ adj. distracted with worry, fear, etc.; extremely agitated. [ME, alt. of obs. distract (adj.) (as DISTRACT), after straught obs. past part. of STRETCH]

distress /dɪ'stres/ n. & v. —n. **1** severe pain, sorrow, anguish, etc. **2** the lack of money or comforts. **3** Law = DISTRAINT. **4** breathlessness; exhaustion. —v.tr. **1** subject to distress; exhaust, afflict. **2** cause anxiety to; make unhappy; vex. □ **distress-signal** a signal from a ship in danger. **distress-warrant** Law a warrant authorizing distraint. **in distress 1** suffering or in danger. **2** (of a ship, aircraft, etc.) in danger or damaged. □□ **distressful** adj. **distressingly** adv. [ME f. OF destresse etc., AF destresser, OF -ecier f. Gallo-Roman (as DISTRAIN)]

distressed /dɪ'strest/ adj. **1** suffering from distress. **2** impoverished (distressed gentlefolk; in distressed circumstances). **3** (of furniture, leather, etc.) having simulated marks of age and wear. □ **distressed area** Brit. a region of high unemployment and poverty.

distributary /dɪ'strɪbjʊtərɪ/ n. (pl. **-ies**) a branch of a river or glacier that does not return to the main stream after leaving it (as in a delta).

distribute /dɪ'strɪbjuːt, 'dɪ-/ v.tr. **1** give shares of; deal out. **2** spread about; scatter (distributed the seeds evenly over the garden). **3** divide into parts; arrange; classify. **4** Printing separate (type that has been set up) and return the characters to their separate boxes. **5** Logic use (a term) to include every individual of the class to which it refers. □□ **distributable** adj. [ME f. L distribuere distribut- (as DIS-, tribuere assign)]

distribution /ˌdɪstrɪ'bjuːʃ(ə)n/ n. **1** the act or an instance of distributing; the process of being distributed. **2** Econ. **a** the dispersal of goods etc. among consumers, brought about by commerce. **b** the extent to which different groups, classes, or individuals share in the total production or wealth of a community. **3** Statistics the way in which a characteristic is spread over members of a class. □□ **distributional**

adj. [ME f. OF *distribution* or L *distributio* (as DISTRIBUTE)]

distributive /dɪ'strɪbjʊtɪv/ *adj. & n.* —*adj.* **1** of, concerned with, or produced by distribution. **2** *Logic & Gram.* (of a pronoun etc.) referring to each individual of a class, not to the class collectively (e.g. *each, either*). —*n. Gram.* a distributive word. □□ **distributively** *adv.* [ME f. F *distributif -ive* or LL *distributivus* (as DISTRIBUTE)]

distributor /dɪ'strɪbjʊtə(r)/ *n.* **1** a person or thing that distributes. **2** an agent who supplies goods. **3** *Electr.* a device in an internal-combustion engine for passing current to each spark-plug in turn.

district /'dɪstrɪkt/ *n. & v.* —*n.* **1 a** (often *attrib.*) a territory marked off for special administrative purposes. **b** *Brit.* a division of a county or region electing its own councillors. **2** an area which has common characteristics; a region (*the wine-growing district*). —*v.tr. US* divide into districts. □**district attorney** (in the US) the prosecuting officer of a district. **district court** (in the US) the Federal court of first instance. **district heating** a supply of heat or hot water from one source to a district or a group of buildings. **district nurse** *Brit.* a peripatetic nurse serving a rural or urban area. **district visitor** *Brit.* a person working for a member of the clergy in a section of a parish. [F f. med.L *districtus* (territory of) jurisdiction (as DISTRAIN)]

distrust /dɪs'trʌst/ *n. & v.* —*n.* a lack of trust; doubt; suspicion. —*v.tr.* have no trust or confidence in; doubt. □□ **distruster** *n.* **distrustful** *adj.* **distrustfully** *adv.*

disturb /dɪ'stɜːb/ *v.tr.* **1** break the rest, calm, or quiet of; interrupt. **2** agitate; worry (*your story disturbs me*). **3** move from a settled position, disarrange (*the papers had been disturbed*). **4** (as **disturbed** *adj.*) *Psychol.* emotionally or mentally unstable or abnormal. □□ **disturber** *n.* **disturbing** *adj.* **disturbingly** *adv.* [ME f. OF *desto(u)rber* f. L *disturbare* (as DIS-, *turbare* f. *turba* tumult)]

disturbance /dɪ'stɜːbəns/ *n.* **1** the act or an instance of disturbing; the process of being disturbed. **2** a tumult; an uproar. **3** agitation; worry. **4** an interruption. **5** *Law* interference with rights or property; molestation. [ME f. OF *desto(u)rbance* (as DISTURB)]

disulphide /daɪ'sʌlfaɪd/ *n.* (*US* **disulfide**) *Chem.* a binary chemical containing two atoms of sulphur in each molecule.

disunion /dɪs'juːnɪən/ *n.* a lack of union; separation; dissension. □□ **disunite** /-'naɪt/ *v.tr. & intr.* **disunity** *n.*

disuse *n. & v.* —*n.* /dɪs'juːs/ **1** lack of use or practice; discontinuance. **2** a disused state. —*v.tr.* /-'juːz/ cease to use. □**fall into disuse** cease to be used. [ME f. OF *desuser* (as DIS-, USE)]

disutility /ˌdɪsjuː'tɪlɪtɪ/ *n.* (*pl.* **-ies**) **1** harmfulness, injuriousness. **2** a factor tending to nullify the utility of something; a drawback.

disyllable /dɪ'sɪləb(ə)l, 'daɪ-/ *n.* (also **dissyllable** /dɪ'sɪl-/) *Prosody* a word or metrical foot of two syllables. □□ **disyllabic** /-'læbɪk/ *adj.* [F *disyllabe* f. L *disyllabus* f. Gk *disullabos* (as DI-¹, SYLLABLE)]

dit /dɪt/ *n. Telegraphy* (in the Morse system) = DOT (cf. DAH). [imit.]

ditch /dɪtʃ/ *n. & v.* —*n.* **1** a long narrow excavated channel esp. for drainage or to mark a boundary. **2** a watercourse, stream, etc. —*v.* **1** *intr.* make or repair ditches (*hedging and ditching*). **2** *tr.* provide with ditches; drain. **3** *tr. sl.* leave in the lurch; abandon. **4** *tr. colloq.* **a** bring (an aircraft) down on the sea in an emergency. **b** drive (a vehicle) into a ditch. **5** *intr. colloq.* (of an aircraft) make a forced landing on the sea. **6** *tr. sl.* defeat; frustrate. **7** *tr. US* derail (a train). □**ditch-water** stagnant water in a ditch. **dull as ditch-water** extremely dull. **last ditch** a place of final desperate defence (*fight to the

last ditch*). □□ **ditcher** *n.* [OE *dīc*, of unkn. orig.: cf. DIKE¹]

ditheism /'daɪθiːˌɪz(ə)m/ *n. Theol.* **1** a belief in two gods; dualism. **2** a belief in equal independent ruling principles of good and evil. □□ **ditheist** *n.*

dither /'dɪðə(r)/ *v. & n.* —*v.intr.* **1** hesitate; be indecisive. **2** *dial.* tremble; quiver. —*n. colloq.* **1** a state of agitation or apprehension. **2** a state of hesitation; indecisiveness. □**all of a dither** *colloq.* in a state of extreme agitation or vacillation. □□ **ditherer** *n.* **dithery** *adj.* [var. of *didder*, DODDER¹]

dithyramb /'dɪθɪˌræm, -ˌræmb/ *n.* **1** a wild choral hymn in ancient Greece, esp. to Dionysus. **b** a Bacchanalian song. **2** any passionate or inflated poem, speech, etc. □□ **dithyrambic** /-'ræmbɪk/ *adj.* [L *dithyrambus* f. Gk *dithurambos*, of unkn. orig.]

dittany /'dɪtənɪ/ *n.* (*pl.* **-ies**) any herb of the genus *Dictamnus*, formerly used medicinally. [ME f. OF *dita(i)n* f. med.L *dictamus* f. L *dictamnus* f. Gk *diktamnon* perh. f. *Diktē*, a mountain in Crete]

ditto /'dɪtəʊ/ *n. & v.* —*n.* (*pl.* **-os**) **1** (in accounts, inventories, lists, etc.) the aforesaid, the same. ¶ Often represented by ‚‚ under the word or sum to be repeated. **2** *colloq.* (replacing a word or phrase to avoid repetition) the same (*came in late last night and ditto the night before*). **3** a similar thing; a duplicate. —*v.tr.* (**-oes, -oed**) repeat (another's action or words). □**ditto marks** inverted commas etc. representing 'ditto'. **say ditto to** *colloq.* agree with; endorse. [It. dial. f. L *dictus* past part. of *dicere* say]

dittography /dɪ'tɒgrəfɪ/ *n.* (*pl.* **-ies**) **1** a copyist's mistaken repetition of a letter, word, or phrase. **2** an example of this. □□ **dittographic** /-'græfɪk/ *adj.* [Gk *dittos* double + -GRAPHY]

ditty /'dɪtɪ/ *n.* (*pl.* **-ies**) a short simple song. [ME f. OF *dité* composition f. L *dictatum* neut. past part. of *dictare* DICTATE]

ditty-bag /'dɪtɪˌbæg/ *n.* (also **ditty-box** /-ˌbɒks/) a sailor's or fisherman's receptacle for odds and ends. [19th c.: orig. unkn.]

diuresis /ˌdaɪjʊ'riːsɪs/ *n. Med.* an increased excretion of urine. [mod.L f. Gk (as DI-³, *ourēsis* urination)]

diuretic /ˌdaɪjʊ'retɪk/ *adj. & n.* —*adj.* causing increased output of urine. —*n.* a diuretic drug. [ME f. OF *diuretique* or LL *diureticus* f. Gk *diourētikos* f. *dioureō* urinate]

diurnal /daɪ'ɜːn(ə)l/ *adj.* **1** of or during the day; not nocturnal. **2** daily; of each day. **3** *Astron.* occupying one day. **4** *Zool.* (of animals) active in the daytime. **5** *Bot.* (of plants) open only during the day. □□ **diurnally** *adv.* [ME f. LL *diurnalis* f. L *diurnus* f. *dies* day]

Div. *abbr.* Division.

diva /'diːvə/ *n.* (*pl.* **divas**) a great or famous woman singer; a prima donna. [It. f. L, = goddess]

divagate /'daɪvəˌgeɪt/ *v.intr. literary* stray; digress. □□ **divagation** /-'geɪʃ(ə)n/ *n.* [L *divagari* (as DI-², *vagari* wander)]

divalent /daɪ'veɪlənt, 'daɪ-/ *adj. Chem.* **1** having a valency of two; bivalent. **2** having two valencies. □□ **divalency** *n.* [DI-¹ + *valent-* part. stem (as VALENCY)]

divan /dɪ'væn, daɪ-, 'daɪ-/ *n.* **1 a** a long, low, padded seat set against a room-wall; a backless sofa. **b** a bed consisting of a base and mattress, usu. with no board at either end. **2** an oriental State legislative body, council-chamber, or court of justice. **3** *archaic* **a** a cigar-shop. **b** a smoking-room attached to such a shop. [F *divan* or It. *divano* f. Turk. *dīvān* f. Arab. *dīwān* f. Pers. *dīvān* anthology, register, court, bench]

divaricate /daɪ'værɪˌkeɪt, dɪ-/ *v.intr.* diverge, branch; separate widely. □□ **divaricate** /-kət/ *adj.* **divarication** /-'keɪʃ(ə)n/ *n.* [L *divaricare* (as DI-², *varicus* straddling)]

dive /daɪv/ *v. & n.* —*v.* (**dived** or *US* **dove** /dəʊv/) **1** *intr.* plunge head first into water, esp. as a sport. **2** *intr.* **a** *Aeron.* (of an aircraft) plunge steeply downwards at speed. **b** *Naut.* (of a submarine) submerge. **c** (of a person) plunge downwards. **3** *intr.*

(foll. by *into*) *colloq.* **a** put one's hand into (a pocket, handbag, vessel, etc.) quickly and deeply. **b** occupy oneself suddenly and enthusiastically with (a subject, meal, etc.). **4** *tr.* (foll. by *into*) plunge (a hand etc.) into. —*n.* **1** an act of diving; a plunge. **2 a** the submerging of a submarine. **b** the steep descent of an aircraft. **3** a sudden darting movement. **4** *colloq.* a disreputable nightclub etc.; a drinking-den (*found themselves in a low dive*). **5** *Boxing sl.* a pretended knockout (*took a dive in the second round*). □ **dive-bomb** bomb (a target) while diving in an aircraft. **dive-bomber** an aircraft designed to dive-bomb. **dive in** *colloq.* help oneself (to food). **diving-bell** an open-bottomed box or bell, supplied with air, in which a person can descend into deep water. **diving-board** an elevated board used for diving from. **diving-suit** a watertight suit usu. with a helmet and an air-supply, worn for working under water. [OE *dūfan* (v.intr.) dive, sink, and *dȳfan* (v.tr.) immerse, f. Gmc: rel. to DEEP, DIP]

diver /'daɪvə(r)/ *n.* **1** a person who dives. **2 a** a person who wears a diving-suit to work under water for long periods. **b** a pearl-diver etc. **3** any of various diving birds, esp. large water-birds of the family Gaviidae.

diverge /daɪ'vɜːdʒ/ *v.* **1** *intr.* **a** proceed in a different direction or in different directions from a point (*diverging rays*; *the path diverges here*). **b** take a different course or different courses (*their interests diverged*). **2** *intr.* **a** (often foll. by *from*) depart from a set course (*diverged from the track*; *diverged from his parents' wishes*). **b** differ markedly (*they diverged as to the best course*). **3** *tr.* cause to diverge; deflect. **4** *intr. Math.* (of a series) increase indefinitely as more of its terms are added. [med.L *divergere* (as DI-², L *vergere* incline)]

divergent /daɪ'vɜːdʒ(ə)nt/ *adj.* **1** diverging. **2** *Psychol.* (of thought) tending to reach a variety of possible solutions when analysing a problem. **3** *Math.* (of a series) increasing indefinitely as more of its terms are added; not convergent. □□ **divergence** *n.* **divergency** *n.* **divergently** *adv.*

divers /'daɪvɜːz/ *adj. archaic* or *literary* more than one; sundry; several. [ME f. OF f. L *diversus* DIVERSE (as DI-², *versus* past part. of *vertere* turn)]

diverse /daɪ'vɜːs, 'daɪ-, dɪ-/ *adj.* unlike in nature or qualities; varied. □□ **diversely** *adv.* [ME (as DIVERS)]

diversify /daɪ'vɜːsɪˌfaɪ/ *v.* (-ies, -ied) **1** *tr.* make diverse; vary; modify. **2** *tr. Commerce* **a** spread (investment) over several enterprises or products, esp. to reduce the risk of loss. **b** introduce a spread of investment in (an enterprise etc.). **3** *intr.* (often foll. by *into*) esp. *Commerce* (of a firm etc.) expand the range of products handled. □□ **diversification** /-fɪ'keɪʃ(ə)n/ *n.* [ME f. OF *diversifier* f. med.L *diversificare* (as DIVERS)]

diversion /daɪ'vɜːʃ(ə)n, dɪ-/ *n.* **1 a** the act of diverting; deviation. **b** an instance of this. **2 a** the diverting of attention deliberately. **b** a stratagem for this purpose (*created a diversion to secure their escape*). **3** a recreation or pastime. **4** *Brit.* an alternative route when a road is temporarily closed to traffic. □□ **diversional** *adj.* **diversionary** *adj.* [LL *diversio* (as DIVERT)]

diversionist /daɪ'vɜːʃənɪst/ *n.* **1** a person who engages in disruptive or subversive activities. **2** *Polit.* (esp. used by communists) a conspirator against the State; a saboteur.

diversity /daɪ'vɜːsɪtɪ, dɪ-/ *n.* (pl. -ies) **1** being diverse; variety. **2** a different kind; a variety. [ME f. OF *diversité* f. L *diversitas -tatis* (as DIVERS)]

divert /daɪ'vɜːt, dɪ-/ *v.tr.* **1** (often foll. by *from, to*) **a** turn aside; deflect. **b** draw the attention of; distract. **2** (often as **diverting** *adj.*) entertain; amuse. □□ **divertingly** *adv.* [ME f. F *divertir* f. L *divertere* (as DI-², *vertere* turn)]

diverticular /ˌdaɪvɜː'tɪkjʊlə(r)/ *adj. Med.* of or relating to a diverticulum. □ **diverticular disease** a condition with abdominal pain as a result of muscle spasms in the presence of diverticula.

diverticulitis /ˌdaɪvɜːˌtɪkjʊ'laɪtɪs/ *n. Med.* inflammation of a diverticulum.

diverticulum /ˌdaɪvɜː'tɪkjʊləm/ *n.* (pl. **diverticula** /-lə/) *Anat.* a blind tube forming at weak points in a cavity or passage esp. of the alimentary tract. □□ **diverticulosis** /-'ləʊsɪs/ *n.* [med.L, var. of L *deverticulum* byway f. *devertere* (as DE-, *vertere* turn)]

divertimento /dɪˌvɜːtɪ'mentəʊ, dɪˌveə-/ *n.* (pl. **divertimenti** /-tɪ/ or **-os**) *Mus.* a light and entertaining composition, often in the form of a suite for chamber orchestra. [It., = diversion]

divertissement /ˌdiːveə'tiːsmɑ̃/ *n.* **1** a diversion; an entertainment. **2** a short ballet etc. between acts or longer pieces. [F, f. *divertiss-* stem of *divertir* DIVERT]

Dives /'daɪviːz/ *n.* a rich man. [L, in Vulgate transl. of Luke 16]

divest /daɪ'vest/ *v.tr.* **1** (usu. foll. by *of*; often *refl.*) unclothe; strip (*divested himself of his jacket*). **2** deprive, dispossess; free, rid (*cannot divest himself of the idea*). □□ **divestiture** *n.* **divestment** *n.* **divesture** *n.* [earlier *devest* f. OF *desvestir* etc. (as DIS-, L *vestire* f. *vestis* garment)]

divi var. of DIVVY.

divide /dɪ'vaɪd/ *v. & n.* —*v.* **1** *tr. & intr.* (often foll. by *in, into*) separate or be separated into parts; break up; split (*the river divides into two*; *the road divides*; *divided them into three groups*). **2** *tr. & intr.* (often foll. by *out*) distribute; deal; share (*divided it out between them*). **3** *tr.* **a** cut off; separate; part (*divide the sheep from the goats*). **b** mark out into parts (*a ruler divided into inches*). **c** specify different kinds of, classify (*people can be divided into two types*). **4** *tr.* cause to disagree; set at variance (*religion divided them*). **5** *Math.* **a** *tr.* find how many times (a number) contains another (*divide 20 by 4*). **b** *intr.* (of a number) be contained in (a number) without a remainder (*3 divides into 20*). **c** *intr.* be susceptible of division (*10 divides by 2 and 5*). **d** *tr.* find how many times (a number) is contained in another (*divide 4 into 20*). **6** *intr. Math.* do division (*can divide well*). **7** *Parl.* **a** *intr.* (of a legislative assembly etc.) part into two groups for voting (*the House divided*). **b** *tr.* so divide (a Parliament etc.) for voting. —*n.* **1** a dividing or boundary line (*the divide between rich and poor*). **2 a** watershed. □ **divided against itself** formed into factions. **divided highway** *US* a dual carriageway. **divided skirt** culottes. **the Great Divide** the boundary between life and death. [ME f. L *dividere divis-* (as DI-², *vid-* separate)]

dividend /'dɪvɪˌdend/ *n.* **1 a** a sum of money to be divided among a number of persons, esp. that paid by a company to shareholders. **b** a similar sum payable to winners in a football pool, to members of a cooperative, or to creditors of an insolvent estate. **c** an individual's share of a dividend. **2** *Math.* a number to be divided by a divisor. **3** a benefit from any action (*their long training paid dividends*). □ **dividend stripping** the evasion of tax on dividends by arrangement between the company liable to pay tax and another able to claim repayment of tax. **dividend warrant** *Brit.* the documentary authority for a shareholder to receive a dividend. **dividend yield** a dividend expressed as a percentage of a current share price. [AF *dividende* f. L *dividendum* (as DIVIDE)]

divider /dɪ'vaɪdə(r)/ *n.* **1** a screen, piece of furniture, etc., dividing a room into two parts. **2** (in *pl.*) measuring-compass, esp. with a screw for setting small intervals.

divi-divi /'dɪvɪˌdɪvɪ/ *n.* (pl. **divi-divis**) **1** a small tree, *Caesalpinia coriaria*, native to tropical Africa, bearing curved pods. **2** this pod used as a source of tannin. [Carib]

divination /ˌdɪvɪ'neɪʃ(ə)n/ *n.* **1** supposed insight into the future or the unknown gained by supernatural means. **2 a** a skilful and accurate forecast. **b** a good

æ *cat* ɑː *arm* e *bed* ɜː *her* ɪ *sit* iː *see* ɒ *hot* ɔː *saw* ʌ *run* ʊ *put* uː *too* ə *ago* aɪ *my*

guess. □□ **divinatory** adj. [ME f. OF divination or L divinatio (as DIVINE)]

divine /dɪˈvaɪn/ adj., v., & n. —adj. (**diviner**, **divinest**) **1 a** of, from, or like God or a god. **b** devoted to God; sacred (divine service). **2 a** more than humanly excellent, gifted, or beautiful. **b** colloq. excellent; delightful. —v. **1** tr. discover by guessing, intuition, inspiration, or magic. **2** tr. foresee, predict, conjecture. **3** intr. practise divination. —n. **1** a cleric, usu. an expert in theology. **2** (**the Divine**) providence or God. □**divine office** see OFFICE. **divine right of kings** the doctrine that kings derive their sovereignty and authority from God, not from their subjects. **divining-rod** = dowsing-rod (see DOWSE¹). □□ **divinely** adv. **divineness** n. **diviner** n. **divinize** /ˈdɪvɪ-/ v.tr. (also -**ise**). [ME f. OF devin -ine f. L divinus f. divus godlike]

divinity /dɪˈvɪnɪtɪ/ n. (pl. -**ies**) **1** the state or quality of being divine. **2 a** a god; a divine being. **b** (as the **Divinity**) God. **3** the study of religion; theology. [ME f. OF divinité f. L divinitas -tatis (as DIVINE)]

divisible /dɪˈvɪzɪb(ə)l/ adj. **1** capable of being divided, physically or mentally. **2** (foll. by by) Math. containing (a number) a number of times without a remainder (15 is divisible by 3 and 5). □□ **divisibility** /-ˈbɪlɪtɪ/ n. [F divisible or LL divisibilis (as DIVIDE)]

division /dɪˈvɪʒ(ə)n/ n. **1** the act or an instance of dividing; the process of being divided. **2** Math. the process of dividing one number by another (see also long division (see LONG¹), short division). **3** disagreement or discord (division of opinion). **4** Parl. the separation of members of a legislative body into two sets for counting votes for and against. **5** one of two or more parts into which a thing is divided. **6 a** major unit of administration or organization, esp.: **a** a group of army brigades or regiments. **b** Sport a grouping of teams within a league, usu. by ability. **7 a** a district defined for administrative purposes. **b** Brit. a part of a county or borough returning a Member of Parliament. **8 a** Bot. a major taxonomic grouping. **b** Zool. a subsidiary category between major levels of classification. **9** Logic a classification of kinds, parts, or senses. □**division of labour** the improvement of efficiency by giving different parts of a manufacturing process etc. to different people. **division sign** the sign (÷) indicating that one quantity is to be divided by another. □□ **divisional** adj. **divisionally** adv. **divisionary** adj. [ME f. OF divisiun f. L divisio -onis (as DIVIDE)]

divisive /dɪˈvaɪsɪv/ adj. tending to divide, esp. in opinion; causing disagreement. □□ **divisively** adv. **divisiveness** n. [LL divisivus (as DIVIDE)]

divisor /dɪˈvaɪzə(r)/ n. Math. **1** a number by which another is to be divided. **2** a number that divides another without a remainder. [ME f. F diviseur or L divisor (as DIVIDE)]

divorce /dɪˈvɔːs/ n. & v. —n. **1 a** the legal dissolution of a marriage. **b** a legal decree of this. **2** a severance or separation (a divorce between thought and feeling). —v. **1 a** tr. (usu. as **divorced** adj.) (often foll. by from) legally dissolve the marriage of (a divorced couple; he wants to get divorced from her). **b** intr. separate by divorce (they divorced last year). **c** tr. end one's marriage with (divorced him for neglect). **2** tr. (often foll. by from) detach, separate (divorced from reality). **3** tr. archaic dissolve (a union). □□ **divorcement** n. [ME f. OF divorce (n.), divorcer (v.) f. LL divortiare f. L divortium f. divortere (as DI-², vertere turn)]

divorcee /ˌdɪvɔːˈsiː/ n. (also masc. **divorcé**, fem. **divorcée** /-ˈseɪ/) a divorced person.

divot /ˈdɪvət/ n. **1** a piece of turf cut out by a golf club in making a stroke. **2** esp. Sc. a piece of turf; a sod. [16th c.: orig. unkn.]

divulge /daɪˈvʌldʒ, dɪ-/ v.tr. disclose; reveal (a secret etc.). □□ **divulgation** /-ˈgeɪʃ(ə)n/ n. **divulgement** n. **divulgence** n. [L divulgare (as DI-²,· vulgare publish f. vulgus common people)]

divvy /ˈdɪvɪ/ n. & v. (also **divi**) colloq. —n. (pl. -**ies**) **1** Brit. a dividend; a share, esp. of profits earned by a cooperative. **2** a distribution. —v.tr. (-**ies**, -**ied**) (often foll. by up) share out; divide. [abbr. of DIVIDEND]

Diwali /dɪˈwɑːlɪ/ n. a Hindu festival with illuminations, held between September and November. [Hind. dīwalī f. Skr. dīpāvalī row of lights f. dīpa lamp]

Dixie /ˈdɪksɪ/ n. the southern States of the US. [19th c.: orig. uncert.]

dixie /ˈdɪksɪ/ n. a large iron cooking pot used by campers etc. [Hind. degchī cooking pot f. Pers. degcha dimin. of deg pot]

Dixieland /ˈdɪksɪˌlænd/ n. **1** = DIXIE. **2** a kind of jazz with a strong two-beat rhythm and collective improvisation. [DIXIE]

DIY abbr. Brit. do-it-yourself.

dizzy /ˈdɪzɪ/ adj. & v. —adj. (**dizzier**, **dizziest**) **1 a** giddy, unsteady. **b** feeling confused. **2** causing giddiness (dizzy heights; dizzy speed). —v.tr. **1** make dizzy. **2** bewilder. □□ **dizzily** adv. **dizziness** n. [OE dysig f. WG]

DJ abbr. **1** Brit. dinner-jacket. **2** disc jockey.

djellaba /ˈdʒeləbə/ n. (also **djellabah**, **jellaba**) a loose hooded woollen cloak worn or as worn by Arab men. [Arab. jallaba, jallābīya]

djibba (also **djibbah**) var. of JIBBA.

djinn var. of JINNEE.

DL abbr. Deputy Lieutenant.

dl abbr. decilitre(s).

D-layer /ˈdiːˌleɪə(r)/ n. the lowest layer of the ionosphere able to reflect low-frequency radio waves. [D (arbitrary)]

D.Litt. abbr. Doctor of Letters. [L Doctor Litterarum]

DM abbr. (also **D-mark**) Deutschmark.

dm abbr. decimetre(s).

D.Mus. abbr. Doctor of Music.

DMZ abbr. US demilitarized zone.

DNA abbr. deoxyribonucleic acid, the self-replicating material present in nearly all living organisms, esp. as a constituent of chromosomes, which is the carrier of genetic information.

DNB abbr. Dictionary of National Biography.

D-notice /ˈdiːˌnəʊtɪs/ n. Brit. a government notice to news editors not to publish items on specified subjects, for reasons of security. [defence + NOTICE]

do¹ /duː, də/ v. & n. —v. (3rd sing. present **does** /dʌz/; past **did** /dɪd/; past part. **done** /dʌn/) **1** tr. perform, carry out, achieve, complete (work etc.) (did his homework; there's a lot to do; he can do anything). **2** tr. **a** produce, make (she was doing a painting; I did a translation; decided to do a casserole). **b** provide (do you do lunches?). **3** tr. bestow, grant; have a specified effect on (a walk would do you good; do me a favour). **4** intr. act, behave, proceed (do as I do; she would do well to accept the offer). **5** tr. work at, study; be occupied with (what does your father do?; he did chemistry at university; we're doing Chaucer next term). **6 a** intr. be suitable or acceptable; suffice (this dress won't do for a wedding; a sandwich will do until we get home; that will never do). **b** tr. satisfy; be suitable for (that hotel will do me nicely). **7** tr. deal with; put in order (the garden needs doing; the barber will do you next; I must do my hair before we go). **8** intr. **a** fare; get on (the patients were doing excellently; he did badly in the test). **b** perform, work (could do better). **9** tr. **a** solve; work out (we did the puzzle). **b** (prec. by can or be able to) be competent at (can you do cartwheels?; I never could do maths). **10** tr. **a** traverse (a certain distance) (we did fifty miles today). **b** travel at a specified speed (he overtook us doing about eighty). **11** tr. colloq. **a** act or behave like (did a Houdini). **b** play the part of (she was asked to do hostess). **12** intr. **a** colloq. finish (have you done annoying me?; I've done in the bathroom). **b** (as **done** adj.) be over (the day is done). **13** tr. produce or give a performance of (the school does many plays and concerts; we've never done 'Pygmalion'). **14** tr. cook, esp. to the right degree (*do it in the oven*; *the potatoes aren't done yet*). **15** *intr.* be in progress (*what's doing?*). **16** *tr. colloq.* visit; see the sights of (*we did all the art galleries*). **17** *tr. colloq.* **a** (often as **done** *adj.*) exhaust; tire out (*the climb has completely done me*). **b** beat up, defeat, kill. **c** ruin (*now you've done it*). **18** *tr.* (foll. by *into*) translate or transform (*the book was done into French*). **19** *tr. colloq.* (with qualifying adverb) provide food etc. for in a specified way (*they do one very well here*). **20** *tr. sl.* **a** rob (*they did a shop in Soho*). **b** swindle (*I was done at the market*). **21** *tr. sl.* prosecute, convict (*they were done for shoplifting*). **22** *tr. sl.* undergo (a specified term of imprisonment) (*he did two years for fraud*). **23** *tr. coarse sl.* have sexual intercourse with. **24** *tr. sl.* take (a drug). —*v.aux.* **1 a** (except with *be*, *can*, *may*, *ought*, *shall*, *will*) in questions and negative statements (*do you understand?*; *I don't smoke*). **b** (except with *can*, *may*, *ought*, *shall*, *will*) in negative commands (*don't be silly*; *do not come tomorrow*). **2** *ellipt.* or in place of verb or verb and object (*you know her better than I do*; *I wanted to go and I did so*; *tell me*, *do!*). **3** forming emphatic present and past tenses (*I do want to*; *do tell me*; *they did go but she was out*). **4** in inversion for emphasis (*rarely does it happen*; *did he but know it*). —*n.* (*pl.* **dos** or **do's**) **1** *colloq.* an elaborate event, party, or operation. **2** *Brit. sl.* a swindle or hoax. □ **be done with** see DONE. **be nothing to do with 1** be no business or concern of (*his financial situation is nothing to do with me*). **2** be unconnected with (*his depression is nothing to do with his father's death*). **be to do with** be concerned or connected with (*the argument was to do with money*). **do about** see ABOUT *prep.* 1d. **do away with** *colloq.* **1** abolish. **2** kill. **do battle** enter into combat. **do one's best** see BEST. **do one's bit** see BIT. **do by** treat or deal with in a specified way (*do as you would be done by*). **do credit to** see CREDIT. **do down** *colloq.* **1** cheat, swindle. **2** get the better of; overcome. **do for 1** be satisfactory or sufficient for. **2** *colloq.* (esp. as **done for** *adj.*) destroy, ruin, kill (*he knew he was done for*). **3** *colloq.* act as housekeeper for. **do one's head** (or **nut**) *sl.* be extremely angry or agitated. **do the honours** see HONOUR. **do in 1** *sl.* **a** kill. **b** ruin, do injury to. **2** *colloq.* exhaust, tire out. **do-it-yourself** *adj.* (of work, esp. building, painting, decorating, etc.) done or to be done by an amateur at home. —*n.* such work. **do justice to** see JUSTICE. **do nothing for** (or **to**) *colloq.* detract from the appearance or quality of (*such behaviour does nothing for our reputation*). **do or die** persist regardless of danger. **do out** *colloq.* clean or redecorate (a room). **do a person out of** *colloq.* unjustly deprive a person of; swindle out of (*he was done out of his holiday*). **do over 1** *sl.* attack; beat up. **2** *colloq.* redecorate, refurbish. **3** *US colloq.* do again. **do proud** see PROUD. **dos and don'ts** rules of behaviour. **do something for** (or **to**) *colloq.* enhance the appearance or quality of (*that carpet does something for the room*). **do one's stuff** see STUFF. **do to** (*archaic* **unto**) = *do by*. **do to death** see DEATH. **do the trick** see TRICK. **do up 1** fasten, secure. **2** *colloq.* **a** refurbish, renovate. **b** adorn, dress up. **3** *sl.* **a** ruin, get the better of. **b** beat up. **do well for oneself** prosper. **do well out of** profit by. **do with** (prec. by *could*) would be glad to have; would profit by (*I could do with a rest*; *you could do with a wash*). **do without** manage without; forgo (also *absol.*: *we shall just have to do without*). **have nothing to do with 1** have no connection or dealings with (*our problem has nothing to do with the latest news*; *after the disagreement he had nothing to do with his father*). **2** be no business or concern of (*the decision has nothing to do with him*). **have to do** (or **something to do**) **with** be connected with (*his limp has to do with a car accident*). [OE *dōn* f. Gmc: rel. to Skr *dádhāmi* put, Gk *tithemi* place, L *facere* do]

do² var. of DOH.

do. *abbr.* ditto.

DOA *abbr.* dead on arrival (at hospital etc.).

doable /ˈduːəb(ə)l/ *adj.* that can be done.

dob /dɒb/ *v.tr.* (**dobbed**, **dobbing**) (foll. by *in*) *Austral. sl.* inform against; implicate; betray. [var. of DAB¹]

dobbin /ˈdɒbɪn/ *n.* a draught-horse; a farm horse. [pet-form of the name *Robert*]

dobe /ˈdəʊbɪ/ *n. US colloq.* adobe. [abbr.]

Dobermann /ˈdəʊbəmən/ *n.* (in full **Dobermann pinscher** /ˈpɪnʃə(r)/) **1** a large dog of a German breed with a smooth coat. **2** this breed. [L. *Dobermann*, 19th-c. Ger. dog-breeder + G *Pinscher* terrier]

doc /dɒk/ *n. colloq.* doctor. [abbr.]

doch an dorris var. of DEOCH AN DORIS.

docile /ˈdəʊsaɪl/ *adj.* **1** submissive, easily managed. **2** *archaic* teachable. □□ **docilely** /ˈdəʊsaɪllɪ/ *adv.* **docility** /-ˈsɪlɪtɪ/ *n.* [ME f. L *docilis* f. *docēre* teach]

dock¹ /dɒk/ *n. & v.* —*n.* **1** an artificially enclosed body of water for the loading, unloading, and repair of ships. **2** (in *pl.*) a range of docks with wharves and offices; a dockyard. **3** *US* a ship's berth, a wharf. **4** = *dry dock*. **5** *Theatr.* = *scene-dock*. —*v.* **1** *tr. & intr.* bring or come into a dock. **2 a** *tr.* join (spacecraft) together in space. **b** *intr.* (of spacecraft) be joined. **3** *tr.* provide with a dock or docks. □ **dock-glass** a large glass for wine-tasting. **in dock** *Brit. colloq.* in hospital or (of a vehicle) laid up for repairs. [MDu. *docke*, of unkn. orig.]

dock² /dɒk/ *n.* the enclosure in a criminal court for the accused. □ **dock brief** a brief handed direct to a barrister selected by a prisoner in the dock. **in the dock** on trial. [16th c.: prob. orig. cant = Flem. *dok* cage, of unkn. orig.]

dock³ /dɒk/ *n.* any weed of the genus *Rumex*, with broad leaves. [OE *docce*]

dock⁴ /dɒk/ *v. & n.* —*v.tr.* **1 a** cut short (an animal's tail). **b** cut short the tail of (an animal). **2 a** (often foll. by *from*) deduct (a part) from wages, supplies, etc. **b** reduce (wages etc.) in this way. —*n.* **1** the solid bony part of an animal's tail. **2** the crupper of a saddle or harness. □ **dock-tailed** having a docked tail. [ME, of uncert. orig.]

dockage /ˈdɒkɪdʒ/ *n.* **1** the charge made for using docks. **2** dock accommodation. **3** the berthing of vessels in docks.

docker /ˈdɒkə(r)/ *n.* a person employed to load and unload ships.

docket /ˈdɒkɪt/ *n. & v.* —*n.* **1** *Brit.* **a** a document or label listing goods delivered or the contents of a package, or recording payment of customs dues etc. **b** a voucher; an order form. **2** *US* a list of causes for trial or persons having causes pending. **3** *US* a list of things to be done. —*v.tr.* (**docketed**, **docketing**) label with a docket. [15th c.: orig. unkn.]

dockland /ˈdɒklənd/ *n.* a district near docks. [DOCK¹]

dockyard /ˈdɒkjɑːd/ *n.* an area with docks and equipment for building and repairing ships, esp. for naval use.

doctor /ˈdɒktə(r)/ *n. & v.* —*n.* **1 a** a qualified practitioner of medicine; a physician. **b** *US* a qualified dentist or veterinary surgeon. **2** a person who holds a doctorate (*Doctor of Civil Law*). **3** *colloq.* a person who carries out repairs. **4** *archaic* a teacher or learned man. **5** *sl.* a cook on board a ship or in a camp. **6** (in full **doctor-blade**) *Printing* a blade for removing surplus ink etc. **7** an artificial fishing-fly. —*v. colloq.* **1 a** *tr.* treat medically. **b** *intr.* (esp. as **doctoring** *n.*) practise as a physician. **2** *tr.* castrate or spay. **3** *tr.* patch up (machinery etc.); mend. **4** *tr.* adulterate. **5** *tr.* tamper with, falsify. **6** *tr.* confer a degree of doctor on. □ **Doctor of the Church** any of several early Christian Fathers of the Church. **Doctor of Philosophy** a doctorate in any faculty except law, medicine, or sometimes theology. **go for the doctor** *Austral. sl.* **1** make an all-out effort. **2** bet all one has. **what the doctor ordered** *colloq.* something beneficial or desirable. □□ **doctorhood** *n.*

doctorial /-'tɔ:rɪəl/ adj. doctorly adj. doctorship n. [ME f. OF doctour f. L doctor f. docēre doct- teach]

doctoral /'dɒktər(ə)l/ adj. of or for a degree of doctor.

doctorate /'dɒktərət/ n. the highest university degree in any faculty, often honorary.

doctrinaire /ˌdɒktrɪ'neə(r)/ adj. & n. —adj. seeking to apply a theory or doctrine in all circumstances without regard to practical considerations; theoretical and impractical. —n. a doctrinaire person; a pedantic theorist. □□ **doctrinairism** n. **doctrinarian** n. [F f. doctrine DOCTRINE + -aire -ARY¹]

doctrinal /dɒk'traɪn(ə)l, 'dɒktrɪn(ə)l/ adj. of or inculcating a doctrine or doctrines. □□ **doctrinally** adv. [LL doctrinalis (as DOCTRINE)]

doctrine /'dɒktrɪn/ n. **1** what is taught; a body of instruction. **2 a** a principle of religious or political etc. belief. **b** a set of such principles; dogma. □□ **doctrinism** n. **doctrinist** n. [ME f. OF f. L doctrina teaching (as DOCTOR)]

docudrama /'dɒkjʊˌdrɑ:mə/ n. a dramatized television film based on real events. [DOCUMENTARY + DRAMA]

document /'dɒkjʊmənt/ n. & v. Law —n. a piece of written or printed matter that provides a record or evidence of events, an agreement, ownership, identification, etc. —v.tr. /'dɒkjʊˌment/ **1** prove by or provide with documents or evidence. **2** record in a document. □□ **documental** /-'ment(ə)l/ adj. [ME f. OF f. L documentum proof f. docēre teach]

documentalist /ˌdɒkjʊ'mentəlɪst/ n. a person engaged in documentation.

documentary /ˌdɒkjʊ'mentərɪ/ adj. & n. —adj. **1** consisting of documents (documentary evidence). **2** providing a factual record or report. —n. (pl. -ies) a documentary film etc. □□ **documentarily** adv.

documentation /ˌdɒkjʊmen'teɪʃ(ə)n/ n. **1** the accumulation, classification, and dissemination of information. **2** the material collected or disseminated. **3** the collection of documents relating to a process or event, esp. the written specification and instructions accompanying a computer program.

DOD abbr. US Department of Defense.

dodder¹ /'dɒdə(r)/ v.intr. tremble or totter, esp. from age. □ **dodder-grass** quaking-grass. □□ **dodderer** n. [17th c.: var. of obs. dial. dadder]

dodder² /'dɒdə(r)/ n. any climbing parasitic plant of the genus Cuscuta, with slender leafless threadlike stems. [ME f. Gmc]

doddered /'dɒdəd/ adj. (of a tree, esp. an oak) having lost its top or branches. [prob. f. obs. dod poll, lop]

doddery /'dɒdərɪ/ adj. tending to tremble or totter, esp. from age. □□ **dodderiness** n. [DODDER¹ + -Y¹]

doddle /'dɒd(ə)l/ n. Brit. colloq. an easy task. [perh. f. doddle = TODDLE]

dodeca- /'dəʊdekə/ comb. form twelve. [Gk dōdeka twelve]

dodecagon /dəʊ'dekəgən/ n. a plane figure with twelve sides.

dodecahedron /ˌdəʊdekə'hi:drən/ n. a solid figure with twelve faces. □□ **dodecahedral** adj.

dodecaphonic /ˌdəʊdekə'fɒnɪk/ adj. Mus. = twelve-note.

dodge /dɒdʒ/ v. & n. —v. **1** intr. (often foll. by about, behind, round) move quickly to one side or quickly change position, to elude a pursuer, blow, etc. (dodged behind the chair). **2** tr. **a** evade by cunning or trickery (dodged paying the fare). **b** elude (a pursuer, opponent, blow, etc.) by a sideward movement etc. **3** tr. Austral. sl. acquire dishonestly. **4** intr. (of a bell in change-ringing) move one place contrary to the normal sequence. —n. **1** a quick movement to avoid or evade something. **2** a clever trick or expedient. **3** the dodging of a bell in change-ringing. □ **dodge the column** see COLUMN. [16th c.: orig. unkn.]

dodgem /'dɒdʒəm/ n. each of a number of small electrically-driven cars in an enclosure at a funfair,

driven round and bumped into each other. [DODGE + 'EM]

dodger /'dɒdʒə(r)/ n. **1** a person who dodges, esp. an artful or elusive person. **2** a screen on a ship's bridge etc. as protection from spray etc. **3** US a small handbill. **4** US a maize-flour cake. **5** sl. a sandwich; bread; food.

dodgy /'dɒdʒɪ/ adj. (dodgier, dodgiest) **1** colloq. awkward, unreliable, tricky. **2** Brit. cunning, artful.

dodo /'dəʊdəʊ/ n. (pl. -os or -oes) **1** any large flightless bird of the extinct family Raphidae, formerly native to Mauritius. **2** an old-fashioned, stupid, or inactive person. □ **as dead as the** (or **a**) **dodo 1** completely or unmistakably dead. **2** entirely obsolete. [Port. doudo simpleton]

DoE abbr. (in the UK) Department of the Environment.

doe /dəʊ/ n. a female fallow deer, reindeer, hare, or rabbit. [OE dā]

doek /dʊk/ n. S.Afr. a cloth, esp. a head-cloth. [Afrik.]

doer /'du:ə(r)/ n. **1** a person who does something. **2** one who acts rather than merely talking or thinking. **3** (in full **hard doer**) Austral. an eccentric or amusing person.

does 3rd sing. present of DO¹.

doeskin /'dəʊskɪn/ n. **1 a** the skin of a doe fallow deer. **b** leather made from this. **2** a fine cloth resembling it.

doesn't /'dʌz(ə)nt/ contr. does not.

doest /'du:ɪst/ archaic 2nd sing. present of DO¹.

doeth /'du:ɪθ/ archaic = DOTH.

doff /dɒf/ v.tr. literary take off (one's hat, clothing). [ME, = do off]

dog /dɒg/ n. & v. —n. **1** any four-legged flesh-eating animal of the genus Canis, of many breeds domesticated and wild, kept as pets or for work or sport. **2** the male of the dog, or of the fox (also **dog-fox**) or wolf (also **dog-wolf**). **3** colloq. **a** a despicable person. **b** a person or fellow of a specified kind (a lucky dog). **c** US & Austral. sl. an informer; a traitor. **d** sl. a horse that is difficult to handle. **4** a mechanical device for gripping. **5** US sl. something poor; a failure. **6** = FIREDOG. **7** (in pl.; prec. by the) Brit. colloq. greyhound-racing. —v.tr. (**dogged**, **dogging**) **1** follow closely and persistently; pursue, track. **2** Mech. grip with a dog. □ **die like a dog** die miserably or shamefully. **dog-biscuit** a hard thick biscuit for feeding dogs. **dog-box** Austral. sl. a compartment in a railway carriage without a corridor. **dog-clutch** Mech. a device for coupling two shafts in the transmission of power, one member having teeth which engage with slots in another. **dog-collar 1** a collar for a dog. **2 a** colloq. a clerical collar. **b** a straight high collar. **dog days** the hottest period of the year (reckoned in antiquity from the heliacal rising of the dog-star). **dog-eared** (of a book etc.) with the corners worn or battered with use. **dog-eat-dog** colloq. ruthlessly competitive. **dog-end** sl. a cigarette-end. **dog-fall** a fall in which wrestlers touch the ground together. **dog in the manger** a person who prevents others from using something, although that person has no use for it. **dog-leg** (or **-legged**) bent like a dog's hind leg. **dog-leg hole** Golf a hole at which a player cannot aim directly at the green from the tee. **dog-paddle** n. an elementary swimming-stroke like that of a dog. —v.intr. swim using this stroke. **dog-rose** a wild hedge-rose, Rosa canina: also called brier-rose. **dog's breakfast** (or **dinner**) colloq. a mess. **dog's disease** Austral. sl. influenza. **dog's life** a life of misery or harassment. **dog's meat** horse's or other flesh as food for dogs; carrion. **dogs of war** poet. the havoc accompanying war. **dog's-** (or **dog-**) **tail** any grass of the genus Cynosurus, esp. C. cristatus, a common pasture grass. **dog-star** the chief star of the constellation Canis Major or Minor, esp. Sirius. **dog's tooth** (in full **dog's tooth violet**) **1** any liliaceous plant of the genus Erythronium, esp. E. dens-canis with speckled leaves, purple flowers, and a toothed perianth. **2** = *dog-tooth* 2. **dog-tired** tired out. **dog-tooth 1** a small pointed ornament or moulding esp. in Norman and Early English architecture. **2** a broken check pattern used esp. in cloth for suits. **dog trials** *Austral. & NZ* a public competitive display of the skills of sheepdogs. **dog-violet** any of various scentless wild violets, esp. *Viola riviniana.* **go to the dogs** *sl.* deteriorate, be ruined. **hair of the dog** further drink to cure the effects of drink. **like a dog's dinner** *colloq.* smartly or flashily (dressed, arranged, etc.). **not a dog's chance** no chance at all. **put on dog** *colloq.* behave pretentiously. □□ **doglike** *adj.* [OE *docga,* of unkn. orig.]

dogberry /'dɒgbərɪ/ *n.* (*pl.* **-ies**) the fruit of the dogwood.

dogcart /'dɒgkɑːt/ *n.* a two-wheeled driving-cart with cross seats back to back.

doge /dəʊdʒ/ *n. hist.* the chief magistrate of Venice or Genoa. [F f. It. f. Venetian *doze* f. L *dux ducis* leader]

dogfight /'dɒgfaɪt/ *n.* **1** a close combat between fighter aircraft. **2** uproar; a fight like that between dogs.

dogfish /'dɒgfɪʃ/ *n.* (*pl.* same or **dogfishes**) any of various small sharks esp. of the families Scyliorhinidae or Squalidae.

dogged /'dɒgɪd/ *adj.* tenacious; grimly persistent. □ **it's dogged as does it** *colloq.* persistence succeeds. □□ **doggedly** *adv.* **doggedness** *n.* [ME f. DOG + -ED¹]

dogger¹ /'dɒgə(r)/ *n.* a two-masted bluff-bowed Dutch fishing-boat. [ME f. MDu., = fishing-boat]

dogger² /'dɒgə(r)/ *n. Geol.* a large spherical concretion occurring in sedimentary rock. [dial., = kind of iron-stone, perh. f. DOG]

doggerel /'dɒgər(ə)l/ *n.* poor or trivial verse. [ME, app. f. DOG: cf. -REL]

doggie var. of DOGGY *n.*

doggish /'dɒgɪʃ/ *adj.* **1** of or like a dog. **2** currish, malicious, snappish. □□ **doggishly** *adv.* **doggishness** *n.*

doggo /'dɒgəʊ/ *adv.* □ **lie doggo** *sl.* lie motionless or hidden, making no sign. [prob. f. DOG: cf. -o]

doggone /'dɒgɒn/ *adj., adv., & int. esp. US sl.* —*adj. & adv.* damned. —*int.* expressing annoyance. [prob. f. *dog on it = God damn it*]

doggy /'dɒgɪ/ *adj. & n.* —*adj.* **1** of or like a dog. **2** devoted to dogs. —*n.* (also **doggie**) (*pl.* **-ies**) a little dog; a pet name for a dog. □ **doggy bag** a bag given to a customer in a restaurant or to a guest at a party etc. for putting leftovers in to take home. □□ **dogginess** *n.*

doghouse /'dɒghaʊs/ *n. US* a dog's kennel. □ **in the doghouse** *sl.* in disgrace or disfavour.

dogie /'dəʊgɪ/ *n. US* a motherless or neglected calf. [19th c.: orig. unkn.]

dogma /'dɒgmə/ *n.* **1 a** a principle, tenet, or system of these, esp. as laid down by the authority of a Church. **b** such principles collectively. **2** an arrogant declaration of opinion. [L f. Gk *dogma -matos* opinion f. *dokeō* seem]

dogman /'dɒgmən/ *n.* (*pl.* **-men**) *Austral.* a person giving directional signals to the operator of a crane, often while sitting on the crane's load.

dogmatic /dɒg'mætɪk/ *adj.* **1 a** (of a person) given to asserting or imposing personal opinions; arrogant. **b** intolerantly authoritative. **2 a** of or in the nature of dogma; doctrinal. **b** based on a priori principles, not on induction. □□ **dogmatically** *adv.* [LL *dogmaticus* f. Gk *dogmatikos* (as DOGMA)]

dogmatics /dɒg'mætɪks/ *n.* **1** the study of religious dogmas; dogmatic theology. **2** a system of dogma. [DOGMATIC]

dogmatism /'dɒgmə,tɪz(ə)m/ *n.* a tendency to be dogmatic. □□ **dogmatist** *n.* [F *dogmatisme* f. med.L *dogmatismus* (as DOGMA)]

dogmatize /'dɒgmə,taɪz/ *v.* (also **-ise**) **1** *intr.* make positive unsupported assertions; speak dogmatically.

2 *tr.* express (a principle etc.) as a dogma. [F *dogmatiser* or f. LL *dogmatizare* f. Gk (as DOGMA)]

do-gooder /du:'gʊdə(r)/ *n.* a well-meaning but unrealistic philanthropist or reformer. □□ **do-good** /'du:gʊd/ *adj. & n.* **do-goodery** *n.* **do-goodism** *n.*

dogsbody /'dɒgz,bɒdɪ/ *n.* (*pl.* **-ies**) **1** *colloq.* a drudge. **2** *Naut. sl.* a junior officer.

dogshore /'dɒgʃɔː(r)/ *n.* a temporary wooden support for a ship just before launching.

dogskin /'dɒgskɪn/ *n.* leather made of or imitating dog's skin, used for gloves.

dogtrot /'dɒgtrɒt/ *n.* a gentle easy trot.

dogwatch /'dɒgwɒtʃ/ *n. Naut.* either of two short watches (4–6 or 6–8 p.m.).

dogwood /'dɒgwʊd/ *n.* **1** any of various shrubs of the genus *Cornus,* esp. the wild cornel with dark red branches, greenish-white flowers, and purple berries, found in woods and hedgerows. **2** any of various similar trees. **3** the wood of the dogwood.

DoH *abbr.* (in the UK) Department of Health.

doh /dəʊ/ *n.* (also **do**) *Mus.* **1** (in tonic sol-fa) the first and eighth note of a major scale. **2** the note C in the fixed-doh system. [18th c.: f. It. *do*]

doily /'dɔɪlɪ/ *n.* (also **doyley**) (*pl.* **-ies** or **-eys**) a small ornamental mat of paper, lace, etc., on a plate for cakes etc. [orig. the name of a fabric: f. *Doiley,* the name of a draper]

doing /'du:ɪŋ/ *n.* **1 a** an action; the performance of a deed (*famous for his doings*; *it was my doing*). **b** activity, effort (*it takes a lot of doing*). **2** *colloq.* a scolding; a beating. **3** (in *pl.*) *sl.* things needed; adjuncts; things whose names are not known (*have we got all the doings?*).

doit /dɔɪt/ *n. archaic* a very small amount of money. [MLG *doyt,* MDu. *duit,* of unkn. orig.]

dojo /'dəʊdʒəʊ/ *n.* (*pl.* **-os**) **1** a room or hall in which judo and other martial arts are practised. **2** a mat on which judo etc. is practised. [Jap.]

dol. *abbr.* dollar(s).

Dolby /'dɒlbɪ/ *n. propr.* an electronic noise-reduction system used esp. in tape-recording to reduce hiss. [R. M. *Dolby,* US inventor]

dolce far niente /,dɒltʃeɪ ,fɑː nɪ'entɪ/ *n.* pleasant idleness. [It., = sweet doing nothing]

dolce vita /,dɒltʃeɪ 'viːtə/ *n.* a life of pleasure and luxury. [It., = sweet life]

doldrums /'dɒldrəmz/ *n.pl.* (usu. prec. by *the*) **1** low spirits; a feeling of boredom or depression. **2** a period of inactivity or state of stagnation. **3** an equatorial ocean region of calms, sudden storms, and light unpredictable winds. [prob. after *dull* and *tantrum*]

dole¹ /dəʊl/ *n. & v.* —*n.* **1** (usu. prec. by *the*) *Brit. colloq.* benefit claimable by the unemployed from the State. **2 a** a charitable distribution. **b** a charitable (esp. sparing, niggardly) gift of food, clothes, or money. **3** *archaic* one's lot or destiny. —*v.tr.* (usu. foll. by *out*) deal out sparingly. □ **dole-bludger** *Austral. sl.* one who allegedly prefers the dole to work. **on the dole** *Brit. colloq.* receiving State benefit for the unemployed. [OE *dāl* f. Gmc]

dole² /dəʊl/ *n. poet.* grief, woe; lamentation. [ME f. OF *do(e)l* etc. f. pop.L *dolus* f. L *dolēre* grieve]

doleful /'dəʊlfʊl/ *adj.* **1** mournful, sad. **2** dreary, dismal. □□ **dolefully** *adv.* **dolefulness** *n.* [ME f. DOLE² + -FUL]

dolerite /'dɒlə,raɪt/ *n.* a coarse basaltic rock. [F *dolérite* f. Gk *doleros* deceptive (because it is difficult to distinguish from diorite)]

dolichocephalic /,dɒlɪ,kəʊsɪ'fælɪk/ *adj.* (also **dolichocephalous** /-'sefələs/) having a long or narrow head. [Gk *dolikhos* long + -CEPHALIC, -CEPHALOUS]

dolina /də'liːnə/ *n.* (also **doline** /də'liːn/) *Geol.* an extensive depression or basin. [Russ. *dolina* valley]

doll /dɒl/ *n. & v.* —*n.* **1** a small model of a human figure, esp. a baby or a child, as a child's toy. **2 a** *colloq.* a pretty but silly young woman. **b** *sl.* a young woman, esp. an attractive one. **3** a ventriloquist's

dummy. —*v.tr.* & *intr.* (foll. by *up*) dress up smartly.
□**doll's house** **1** a miniature toy house for dolls. **2** a very small house. [pet form of the name *Dorothy*]

dollar /'dɒlə(r)/ *n.* **1** the chief monetary unit in the US, Canada, and Australia. **2** the chief monetary unit of certain countries in the Pacific, West Indies, SE Asia, Africa, and S. America. □**dollar area** the area in which currency is linked to the US dollar. **dollar diplomacy** diplomatic activity aimed at advancing a country's international influence by furthering its financial and commercial interests abroad. **dollar gap** the excess of a country's import trade with the dollar area over the corresponding export trade. **dollar mark** (or **sign**) the sign $, representing a dollar. **dollar spot** **1** a fungal disease of lawns etc. **2** a discoloured patch caused by this. [LG *daler* f. G *Taler*, short for *Joachimstaler*, a coin from the silver-mine of *Joachimstal* in Czechoslovakia]

dollhouse /'dɒlhaʊs/ *n. US* = *doll's house* (see DOLL).

dollop /'dɒləp/ *n.* & *v.* —*n.* a shapeless lump of food etc. —*v.tr.* (**dolloped**, **dolloping**) (usu. foll. by *out*) serve out in large shapeless quantities. [perh. f. Scand.]

dolly /'dɒlɪ/ *n.*, *v.*, & *adj.* —*n.* (*pl.* **-ies**) **1** a child's name for a doll. **2** a movable platform for a cine-camera. **3** *Cricket colloq.* an easy catch or hit. **4** a stick for stirring in clothes-washing. **5** = *corn dolly* (see CORN¹). **6** *colloq.* = *dolly-bird*. —*v.* (**-ies**, **-ied**) **1** *tr.* (foll. by *up*) dress up smartly. **2** *intr.* (foll. by *in*, *up*) move a cine-camera in or up to a subject, or out from it. —*adj.* (**dollier**, **dolliest**) **1** *Brit. colloq.* (esp. of a girl) attractive, stylish. **2** *Cricket colloq.* easily hit or caught. □**dolly-bird** *Brit. colloq.* an attractive and stylish young woman. **dolly mixture** any of a mixture of small variously shaped and coloured sweets.

Dolly Varden /,dɒlɪ 'vɑːd(ə)n/ *n.* **1** a woman's large hat with one side drooping and with a floral trimming. **2** a brightly spotted char, *Salvelinus malma*, of western N. America. [a character in Dickens's *Barnaby Rudge*]

dolma /'dɒlmə/ *n.* (*pl.* **dolmas** or **dolmades** /-'mɑːðez/) an E. European delicacy of spiced rice or meat etc. wrapped in vine or cabbage leaves. [Turk. f. *dolmak* fill, be filled: *dolmades* f. mod.Gk]

dolman /'dɒlmən/ *n.* **1** a long Turkish robe open in front. **2** a hussar's jacket worn with the sleeves hanging loose. **3** a woman's mantle with capelike or dolman sleeves. □**dolman sleeve** a loose sleeve cut in one piece with the body of the coat etc. [ult. f. Turk. *dolama*]

dolmen /'dɒlmən/ *n.* a megalithic tomb with a large flat stone laid on upright ones. [F, perh. f. Cornish *tolmên* hole of stone]

dolomite /'dɒləmʌɪt/ *n.* a mineral or rock of calcium magnesium carbonate. □□**dolomitic** /,dɒlə'mɪtɪk/ *adj.* [F f. D. de *Dolomieu*, Fr. geologist d. 1801]

dolorous /'dɒlərəs/ *adj. literary* or *joc.* **1** distressing, painful; doleful, dismal. **2** distressed, sad. □□ **dolorously** *adv.* [ME f. OF *doleros* f. LL *dolorosus* (as DOLOUR)]

dolour /'dɒlə(r)/ *n.* (*US* **dolor**) *literary* sorrow, distress. [ME f. OF f. L *dolor -oris* pain, grief]

dolphin /'dɒlfɪn/ *n.* **1** any of various porpoise-like sea mammals of the family Delphinidae having a slender beaklike snout. **2** (in general use) = DORADO 1. **3** a bollard, pile, or buoy for mooring. **4** a structure for protecting the pier of a bridge. **5** a curved fish in heraldry, sculpture, etc. [ME, also *delphin* f. L *delphinus* f. Gk *delphis -inos*]

dolphinarium /,dɒlfɪ'neərɪəm/ *n.* (*pl.* **dolphinariums**) an aquarium for dolphins, esp. one open to the public.

dolt /dəʊlt/ *n.* a stupid person. □□**doltish** *adj.* **doltishly** *adv.* **doltishness** *n.* [app. related to *dol*, *dold*, obs. var. of DULL]

Dom /dɒm/ *n.* **1** a title prefixed to the names of some Roman Catholic dignitaries, and Benedictine and Carthusian monks. **2** the Portuguese equivalent of Don (see DON¹). [L *dominus* master: sense 2 through Port.]

-dom /dəm/ *suffix* forming nouns denoting: **1** state or condition (*freedom*). **2** rank or status (*earldom*). **3** domain (*kingdom*). **4** a class of people (or the attitudes etc. associated with them) regarded collectively (*officialdom*). [OE *-dōm*, orig. = DOOM]

domain /də'meɪn/ *n.* **1** an area under one rule; a realm. **2** an estate or lands under one control. **3** a sphere of control or influence. **4** *Math.* the set of possible values of an independent variable. **5** *Physics* a discrete region of magnetism in ferromagnetic material. □□**domanial** /də'meɪnɪəl/ *adj.* [ME f. F *domaine*, OF *demeine* DEMESNE, assoc. with L *dominus* lord]

domaine /də'meɪn/ *n.* a vineyard. [F: see DOMAIN]

dome /dəʊm/ *n.* & *v.* —*n.* **1 a** a rounded vault as a roof, with a circular, elliptical, or polygonal base; a large cupola. **b** the revolving openable hemispherical roof of an observatory. **2 a** a natural vault or canopy (of the sky, trees, etc.). **b** the rounded summit of a hill etc. **3** *Geol.* a dome-shaped structure. **4** *sl.* the head. **5** *poet.* a stately building. —*v.tr.* (usu. as **domed** *adj.*) cover with or shape as a dome. □□ **domelike** *adj.* [F *dôme* f. It. *duomo* cathedral, dome f. L *domus* house]

Domesday /'duːmzdeɪ/ *n.* (in full **Domesday Book**) a record of the lands of England made in 1086 by order of William I. [ME var. of doomsday, as being a book of final authority]

domestic /də'mestɪk/ *adj.* & *n.* —*adj.* **1** of the home, household, or family affairs. **2 a** of one's own country, not foreign or international. **b** home-grown or home-made. **3** (of an animal) kept by or living with man. **4** fond of home life. —*n.* a household servant. □**domestic science** the study of household management. □□**domestically** *adv.* [F *domestique* f. L *domesticus* f. *domus* home]

domesticate /də'mestɪ,keɪt/ *v.tr.* **1** tame (an animal) to live with humans. **2** accustom to home life and management. **3** naturalize (a plant or animal). □□ **domesticable** /-kəb(ə)l/ *adj.* **domestication** /-'keɪʃ(ə)n/ *n.* [med.L *domesticare* (as DOMESTIC)]

domesticity /,dɒme'stɪsɪtɪ, ,dəʊ-/ *n.* **1** the state of being domestic. **2** domestic or home life.

domicile /'dɒmɪ,sʌɪl, -sɪl/ *n.* & *v.* (also **domicil** /-sɪl/) —*n.* **1** a dwelling-place; one's home. **2** *Law* **a** a place of permanent residence. **b** the fact of residing. **3** the place at which a bill of exchange is made payable. —*v.tr.* **1** (usu. as **domiciled** *adj.*) (usu. foll. by *at*, *in*) establish or settle in a place. **2** (usu. foll. by *at*) make (a bill of exchange) payable at a certain place. [ME f. OF f. L *domicilium* f. *domus* home]

domiciliary /,dɒmɪ'sɪlɪərɪ/ *adj.* of a dwelling place (esp. of a doctor's, official's, etc., visit to a person's home). [F *domiciliaire* f. med.L *domiciliarius* (as DOMICILE)]

dominance /'dɒmɪnəns/ *n.* **1** the state of being dominant. **2** control, authority.

dominant /'dɒmɪnənt/ *adj.* & *n.* —*adj.* **1** dominating, prevailing, most influential. **2** (of a high place) prominent, overlooking others. **3 a** (of an allele) expressed even when inherited from only one parent. **b** (of an inherited characteristic) appearing in an individual even when its allelic counterpart is also inherited (cf. RECESSIVE). —*n. Mus.* the fifth note of the diatonic scale of any key. □□**dominantly** *adv.* [F f. L *dominari* (as DOMINATE)]

dominate /'dɒmɪ,neɪt/ *v.* **1** *tr.* & (foll. by *over*) *intr.* have a commanding influence on; exercise control over (*fear dominated them for years*; *dominates over his friends*). **2** *intr.* (of a person, sound, feature of a scene, etc.) be the most influential or conspicuous. **3** *tr.* & (foll. by *over*) *intr.* (of a building etc.) have a commanding position over; overlook. □□**dominator** *n.* [L *dominari dominat-* f. *dominus* lord]

domination /ˌdɒmɪˈneɪʃ(ə)n/ *n.* **1** command, control. **2** the act or an instance of dominating; the process of being dominated. **3** (in *pl.*) angelic beings of the fourth order of the celestial hierarchy. [ME f. OF f. L *dominatio -onis* (as DOMINATE)]

domineer /ˌdɒmɪˈnɪə(r)/ *v.intr.* (often as **domineering** *adj.*) behave in an arrogant and overbearing way. □□ **domineeringly** *adv.* [Du. *domineren* f. F *dominer*]

dominical /dəˈmɪnɪk(ə)l/ *adj.* **1** of the Lord's day, of Sunday. **2** of the Lord (Jesus Christ). □ **dominical letter** the one of the seven letters A–G indicating the dates of Sundays in a year. [F *dominical* or L *dominicalis* f. L *dominicus* f. *dominus* lord]

Dominican /dəˈmɪnɪkən/ *adj. & n.* —*adj.* **1** of or relating to St Dominic or the order of preaching friars which he founded in 1215–16. **2** of or relating to either of the two orders of female religious founded on Dominican principles. —*n.* a Dominican friar, nun, or sister (see also *Black Friar*). [med.L *Dominicanus* f. *Dominicus* L name of *Domingo* de Guzmán (St Dominic)]

dominie /ˈdɒmɪnɪ/ *n. Sc.* a schoolmaster. [later spelling of *domine* sir, voc. of L *dominus* lord]

dominion /dəˈmɪnjən/ *n.* **1** sovereignty, control. **2** the territory of a sovereign or government; a domain. **3** *hist.* the title of each of the self-governing territories of the British Commonwealth. [ME f. OF f. med.L *dominio -onis* f. L *dominium* f. *dominus* lord]

domino /ˈdɒmɪˌnəʊ/ *n.* (*pl.* **-oes**) **1 a** any of 28 small oblong pieces marked with 0–6 pips in each half. **b** (in *pl.*, usu. treated as *sing.*) a game played with these. **2** a loose cloak with a mask for the upper part of the face, worn at masquerades. □ **domino theory** the theory that a political event etc. in one country will cause similar events in neighbouring countries, like a row of falling dominoes. [F, prob. f. L *dominus* lord, but unexplained]

don[1] /dɒn/ *n.* **1** a university teacher, esp. a senior member of a college at Oxford or Cambridge. **2** (**Don**) **a** a Spanish title prefixed to a forename. **b** a Spanish gentleman; a Spaniard. [Sp. f. L *dominus* lord]

don[2] /dɒn/ *v.tr.* (**donned, donning**) put on (clothing). [= *do on*]

dona /ˈdəʊnə/ *n.* (also **donah**) *Brit. sl.* a woman; a sweetheart. [Sp. *doña* or Port. *dona* f. L (as DONNA)]

donate /dəʊˈneɪt/ *v.tr.* give or contribute (money etc.), esp. voluntarily to a fund or institution. □□ **donator** *n.* [back-form. f. DONATION]

donation /dəʊˈneɪʃ(ə)n/ *n.* **1** the act or an instance of donating. **2** something, esp. an amount of money, donated. [ME f. OF f. L *donatio -onis* f. *donare* give f. *donum* gift]

donative /ˈdəʊnətɪv, ˈdɒn-/ *n. & adj.* —*n.* a gift or donation, esp. one given formally or officially as a largess. —*adj.* **1** given as a donation or bounty. **2** *hist.* (of a benefice) given directly, not presentative. [ME f. L *donativum* gift, largess f. *donare*: see DONATION]

done /dʌn/ *past part.* of DO[1]. —*adj.* **1** *colloq.* socially acceptable (*the done thing*; *it isn't done*). **2** (often with *in, up*) *colloq.* tired out. **3** (esp. as *int.* in reply to an offer etc.) accepted. □ **be done with** have finished with, be finished with. **done for** *colloq.* in serious trouble. **have done** have ceased or finished. **have done with** be rid of; have finished dealing with.

donee /dəʊˈniː/ *n.* the recipient of a gift. [DONOR + -EE]

dong[1] /dɒŋ/ *v. & n.* —*v.* **1** *intr.* make the deep sound of a large bell. **2** *tr. Austral. & NZ colloq.* hit, punch. —*n.* **1** the deep sound of a large bell. **2** *Austral. & NZ colloq.* a heavy blow. [imit.]

dong[2] /dɒŋ/ *n.* the chief monetary unit of Vietnam. [Vietnamese]

donga /ˈdɒŋgə/ *n. S.Afr. & Austral.* **1** a dry watercourse. **2** a ravine caused by erosion. [Zulu]

dongle /ˈdɒŋg(ə)l/ *n. Computing* a security attachment required by a computer to enable protected software to be used. [arbitrary form.]

donjon /ˈdɒndʒ(ə)n, ˈdʌn-/ *n.* the great tower or innermost keep of a castle. [archaic spelling of DUNGEON]

Don Juan /ˌdɒn ˈdʒuːən, ˌdɒn ˈwɑːn/ *n.* a seducer of women; a libertine. [name of a legendary Sp. nobleman celebrated in fiction, e.g. by Byron]

donkey /ˈdɒŋkɪ/ *n.* (*pl.* **-eys**) **1** a domestic ass. **2** *colloq.* a stupid or foolish person. □ **donkey engine** a small auxiliary engine. **donkey jacket** a thick weatherproof jacket worn by workers and as a fashion garment. **donkey's years** *colloq.* a very long time. **donkey-work** the laborious part of a job; drudgery. [earlier with pronunc. as *monkey*: perh. f. DUN[1], or the Christian name *Duncan*]

donna /ˈdɒnə/ *n.* **1** an Italian, Spanish, or Portuguese lady. **2** (**Donna**) the title of such a lady. [It. f. L *domina* mistress fem. of *dominus*: cf. DON[1]]

donnée /ˈdɒneɪ/ *n.* (also **donné**) **1** the subject or theme of a story etc. **2** a basic fact or assumption. [F, fem. or masc. past part. of *donner* give]

donnish /ˈdɒnɪʃ/ *adj.* like or resembling a college don, esp. in supposed pedantry. □□ **donnishly** *adv.* **donnishness** *n.*

donor /ˈdəʊnə(r)/ *n.* **1** a person who gives or donates something (e.g. to a charity). **2** one who provides blood for a transfusion, semen for insemination, or an organ or tissue for transplantation. **3** *Chem.* an atom or molecule that provides a pair of electrons in forming a coordinate bond. **4** *Physics* an impurity atom in a semiconductor which contributes a conducting electron to the material. □ **donor card** an official card authorizing use of organs for transplant, carried by the donor. [ME f. AF *donour*, OF *doneur* f. L *donator -oris* f. *donare* give]

don't /dəʊnt/ *contr.* do not. —*n.* a prohibition (*dos and don'ts*).

donut *US* var. of DOUGHNUT.

doodad /ˈduːdæd/ *n. US* = DOODAH. [20th c.: orig. unkn.]

doodah /ˈduːdɑː/ *n.* **1** a fancy article; a trivial ornament. **2** a gadget or 'thingummy'. □ **all of a doodah** excited, dithering. [from the refrain of the song *Camptown Races*]

doodle /ˈduːd(ə)l/ *v. & n.* —*v.intr.* scribble or draw, esp. absent-mindedly. —*n.* a scrawl or drawing made. □ **doodle-bug 1** *US* any of various insects, esp. the larva of an ant-lion. **2** *US* an unscientific device for locating minerals. **3** *colloq.* a flying bomb. □□ **doodler** *n.* [orig. = foolish person; cf. LG *dudelkopf*]

doohickey /ˈduːˌhɪkɪ/ *n.* (*pl.* **-eys**) *US colloq.* a small object, esp. mechanical. [DOODAD + HICKEY]

doom /duːm/ *n. & v.* —*n.* **1 a** a grim fate or destiny. **b** death or ruin. **2 a** a condemnation; a judgement or sentence. **b** the Last Judgement (*the crack of doom*). **3** *hist.* a statute, law, or decree. —*v.tr.* **1** (usu. foll. by *to*) condemn or destine (*a city doomed to destruction*). **2** (esp. as **doomed** *adj.*) consign to misfortune or destruction. [OE *dōm* statute, judgement f. Gmc: rel. to DO[1]]

doomsday /ˈduːmzdeɪ/ *n.* the day of the Last Judgement. □ **till doomsday** for ever (cf. DOOMESDAY). [OE *dōmes dæg*: see DOOM]

doomwatch /ˈduːmwɒtʃ/ *n.* organized vigilance or observation to avert danger, esp. from environmental pollution. □□ **doomwatcher** *n.*

door /dɔː(r)/ *n.* **1 a** a hinged, sliding, or revolving barrier for closing and opening an entrance to a building, room, cupboard, etc. **b** this as representing a house etc. (*lives two doors away*). **2 a** an entrance or exit; a doorway. **b** a means of access or approach. □ **close the door** to exclude the opportunity for. **door-case** (or **-frame**) the structure into which a door is fitted. **door-head** the upper part of a door-case. **door-keeper** = DOORMAN. **door-plate** a plate on the door of a house or room bearing the name of the occupant. **door-to-door** (of selling etc.) done at each house in turn. **lay** (or **lie**) **at the door of** impute (or be imputable) to. **leave the door open** ensure that an option remains available. **next door** in or to the next house or room. **next door to 1** in the next house to. **2** nearly, almost, near to. **open the door to** create an opportunity for. **out of doors** in or into the open air. □□ **doored** *adj.* (also in *comb.*). [OE *duru, dor* f. Gmc]

doorbell /ˈdɔːbel/ *n.* a bell in a house etc. rung by visitors outside to signal their arrival.

doorknob /ˈdɔːnɒb/ *n.* a knob for turning to release the latch of a door.

doorman /ˈdɔːmən/ *n.* (*pl.* **-men**) a person on duty at the door to a large building; a janitor or porter.

doormat /ˈdɔːmæt/ *n.* **1** a mat at an entrance for wiping mud etc. from the shoes. **2** a feebly submissive person.

doornail /ˈdɔːneɪl/ *n.* a nail with which doors were studded for strength or ornament. □ **dead as a doornail** completely or unmistakably dead.

doorpost /ˈdɔːpəʊst/ *n.* each of the uprights of a door-frame, on one of which the door is hung.

doorstep /ˈdɔːstep/ *n. & v.* —*n.* **1** a step leading up to the outer door of a house etc. **2** *sl.* a thick slice of bread. —*v.intr.* (**-stepped, -stepping**) go from door to door selling, canvassing, etc. □ **on one's** (or **the**) **doorstep** very close.

doorstop /ˈdɔːstɒp/ *n.* a device for keeping a door open or to prevent it from striking a wall etc. when opened.

doorway /ˈdɔːweɪ/ *n.* an opening filled by a door.

dooryard /ˈdɔːjɑːd/ *n. US* a yard or garden near a house-door.

dop /dɒp/ *n. S.Afr.* **1** a cheap kind of brandy. **2** a tot of liquor. [Afrik.]

dopa /ˈdəʊpə/ *n. Pharm.* a crystalline amino acid derivative used in the treatment of Parkinsonism. [G f. *Dioxyphenylalanine,* former name of the compound]

dopant /ˈdəʊpənt/ *n. Electronics* a substance used in doping a semiconductor.

dope /dəʊp/ *n. & v.* —*n.* **1** a varnish applied to the cloth surface of aeroplane parts to strengthen them, keep them airtight, etc. **2** a thick liquid used as a lubricant etc. **3** a substance added to petrol etc. to increase its effectiveness. **4 a** *sl.* a narcotic; a stupefying drug. **b** a drug etc. given to a horse or greyhound, or taken by an athlete, to affect performance. **5** *sl.* a stupid person. **6** *sl.* **a** information about a subject, esp. if not generally known. **b** misleading information. —*v.* **1** *tr.* administer dope to, drug. **2** *tr. Electronics* add an impurity to (a semiconductor) to produce a desired electrical characteristic. **3** *tr.* smear, daub; apply dope to. **4** *intr.* take addictive drugs. □ **dope out** *sl.* discover. □□ **doper** *n.* [Du. *doop* sauce f. *doopen* to dip]

dopey /ˈdəʊpɪ/ *adj.* (also **dopy**) (**dopier, dopiest**) *colloq.* **1 a** half asleep. **b** stupefied by or as if by a drug. **2** stupid, silly. □□ **dopily** *adv.* **dopiness** *n.*

doppelgänger /ˈdɒp(ə)l.genə(r)/ *n.* an apparition or double of a living person. [G, = double-goer]

Dopper /ˈdɒpə(r)/ *n. S.Afr.* a member of the Gereformeerde Kerk, a strictly orthodox Calvinistic denomination, usu. regarded as old-fashioned in ideas etc.

Doppler effect /ˈdɒplə(r)/ *n.* (also **Doppler shift**) *Physics* an increase (or decrease) in the frequency of sound, light, or other waves as the source and observer move towards (or away) from each other. [C. J. *Doppler,* Austrian physicist d. 1853]

dopy var. of DOPEY.

dorado /dəˈrɑːdəʊ/ *n.* (*pl.* **-os**) **1** a blue and silver marine fish, *Coryphaena hippurus,* showing brilliant colours when dying out of water. **2** a brightly

coloured freshwater-fish, *Salminus maxillosus,* native to S. America. [Sp. f. LL *deauratus* gilt f. *aurum* gold]

Dorian /ˈdɔːrɪən/ *n. & adj.* —*n.* (in *pl.*) a Greek-speaking people thought to have entered Greece from the north *c.*1100 BC and settled in parts of Central and S. Greece. —*adj.* of or relating to the Dorians or to Doris in Central Greece. □ **Dorian mode** *Mus.* the mode represented by the natural diatonic scale D-D. [L *Dorius* f. Gk *Dōrios* f. *Dōros,* the mythical ancestor]

Doric /ˈdɒrɪk/ *adj. & n.* —*adj.* **1** (of a dialect) broad, rustic. **2** *Archit.* of the oldest, sturdiest, and simplest of the Greek orders. —*n.* **1** rustic English or esp. Scots. **2** *Archit.* the Doric order. **3** the dialect of the Dorians in ancient Greece. [L *Doricus* f. Gk *Dōrikos* (as DORIAN)]

dorm /dɔːm/ *n. colloq.* dormitory. [abbr.]

dormant /ˈdɔːmənt/ *adj.* **1** lying inactive as in sleep; sleeping. **2 a** (of a volcano etc.) temporarily inactive. **b** (of potential faculties etc.) in abeyance. **3** (of plants) alive but not actively growing. **4** *Heraldry* (of a beast) lying with its head on its paws. □□ **dormancy** *n.* [ME f. OF, pres. part. of *dormir* f. L *dormire* sleep]

dormer /ˈdɔːmə(r)/ *n.* (in full **dormer window**) a projecting upright window in a sloping roof. [OF *dormëor* (as DORMANT)]

dormitory /ˈdɔːmɪtərɪ/ *n.* (*pl.* **-ies**) **1** a sleeping-room with several beds, esp. in a school or institution. **2** (in full **dormitory town** etc.) a small town or suburb from which people travel to work in a city etc. **3** *US* a university or college hall of residence or hostel. [ME f. L *dormitorium* f. *dormire dormit-* sleep]

Dormobile /ˈdɔːmə.biːl/ *n. propr.* a type of motor caravan with a rear compartment convertible for sleeping and eating in. [blend of DORMITORY, AUTOMOBILE]

dormouse /ˈdɔːmaʊs/ *n.* (*pl.* **dormice**) any small mouselike hibernating rodent of the family Gliridae, having a long bushy tail. [ME: orig. unkn.]

dormy /ˈdɔːmɪ/ *adj. Golf* (of a player or side) ahead by as many holes as there are holes left to play (*dormy five*). [19th c.: orig. unkn.]

doronicum /dəˈrɒnɪkəm/ *n.* = *leopard's bane* (see LEOPARD). [mod.L (Linnaeus) ult. f. Arab. *darānaj*]

dorp /dɔːp/ *n. S.Afr.* a village or small township. [Du. (as THORP)]

dorsal /ˈdɔːs(ə)l/ *adj. Anat., Zool., & Bot.* **1** of, on, or near the back (cf. VENTRAL). **2** ridge-shaped. □□ **dorsally** *adv.* [F *dorsal* or LL *dorsalis* f. L *dorsum* back]

dory[1] /ˈdɔːrɪ/ *n.* (*pl.* **-ies**) any of various marine fish having a compressed body and flat head, esp. the John Dory, used as food. [ME f. F *dorée* fem. past part. of *dorer* gild (as DORADO)]

dory[2] /ˈdɔːrɪ/ *n.* (*pl.* **-ies**) *US* a flat-bottomed fishing-boat with high sides. [Miskito *dóri* dugout]

DOS /dɒs/ *n. Computing* a program for manipulating information on a disk. [abbr. of *d*isk *o*perating *s*ystem]

dos-à-dos /ˌdəʊzəˈdəʊ/ *adj. & n.* —*adj.* (of two books) bound together with a shared central board and facing in opposite directions. —*n.* (*pl.* same) a seat, carriage, etc., in which the occupants sit back to back (cf. DO-SE-DO). [F, = back to back]

dosage /ˈdəʊsɪdʒ/ *n.* **1** the giving of medicine in doses. **2** the size of a dose.

dose /dəʊs/ *n. & v.* —*n.* **1** an amount of a medicine or drug for taking or taken at one time. **2** a quantity of something administered or allocated (e.g. work, praise, punishment, etc.). **3** the amount of ionizing radiation received by a person or thing. **4** *sl.* a venereal infection. —*v.tr.* **1** treat (a person or animal) with doses of medicine. **2** give a dose or doses to. **3** adulterate or blend (esp. wine with spirit). □ **like a dose of salts** *colloq.* very fast and efficiently. [F f. LL *dosis* f. Gk *dosis* gift f. *didōmi* give]

do-se-do /ˌdəʊzɪˈdəʊ, ˌdəʊsɪ-/ *n.* (also **do-si-do**) (*pl.*

-os) a figure in which two dancers pass round each other back to back and return to their original positions. [corrupt. of DOS-À-DOS]

dosh /dɒʃ/ n. sl. money. [20th c.: orig. unkn.]

dosimeter /dəʊˈsɪmɪtə(r)/ n. a device used to measure an absorbed dose of ionizing radiation. □□ **dosimetric** /-ˈmetrɪk/ adj. **dosimetry** n.

doss /dɒs/ v. & n. Brit. sl. —v.intr. (often foll. by down) sleep, esp. roughly or in cheap lodgings. —n. a bed, esp. in cheap lodgings. □**doss-house** a cheap lodging-house, esp. for vagrants. [prob. = doss ornamental covering for a seat-back etc. f. OF dos ult. f. L dorsum back]

dossal /ˈdɒs(ə)l/ n. a hanging cloth behind an altar or round a chancel. [med.L dossale f. LL dorsalis DORSAL]

dosser /ˈdɒsə(r)/ n. Brit. sl. 1 a person who dosses. 2 = doss-house.

dossier /ˈdɒsɪə(r), -ɪeɪ/ n. a set of documents, esp. a collection of information about a person, event, or subject. [F, so called from the label on the back, f. dos back f. L dorsum]

dost /dʌst/ archaic 2nd sing. present of DO[1].

DoT abbr. (in the UK) Department of Transport.

dot[1] /dɒt/ n. & v. —n. 1 a a small spot, speck, or mark. b such a mark written or printed as part of an i or j, as a diacritical mark, as one of a series of marks to signify omission, or as a full stop. c a decimal point. 2 Mus. a dot used to denote the lengthening of a note or rest, or to indicate staccato. 3 the shorter signal of the two used in Morse code (cf. DASH n. 6). 4 a tiny or apparently tiny object (a dot on the horizon). —v.tr. (**dotted, dotting**) 1 a mark with a dot or dots. b place a dot over (a letter). 2 Mus. mark (a note or rest) to show that the time value is increased by half. 3 (often foll. by about) scatter like dots. 4 partly cover as with dots (a sea dotted with ships). 5 sl. hit (dotted him one in the eye). □**dot the i's and cross the t's** colloq. 1 be minutely accurate, emphasize details. 2 add the final touches to a task, exercise, etc. **dot matrix printer** Computing a printer with characters formed from dots printed by configurations of the tips of small wires. **dotted line** a line of dots on a document, esp. to show a place left for a signature. **on the dot** exactly on time. **the year dot** Brit. colloq. far in the past. □□ **dotter** n. [OE dott head of a boil, perh. infl. by Du. dot knot]

dot[2] /dɒt/ n. a woman's dowry. [F f. L dos dotis]

dotage /ˈdəʊtɪdʒ/ n. feeble-minded senility (in his dotage).

dotard /ˈdəʊtəd/ n. a person who is feeble-minded, esp. from senility. [ME f. DOTE + -ARD]

dote /dəʊt/ v.intr. 1 (foll. by on, upon) be foolishly or excessively fond of. 2 be silly or feeble-minded, esp. from old age. □□ **doter** n. **dotingly** adv. [ME, corresp. to MDu. doten be silly]

doth /dʌθ/ archaic 3rd sing. present of DO[1].

dotterel /ˈdɒtər(ə)l/ n. a small migrant plover, Eudromias morinellus. [ME f. DOTE + -REL, named from the ease with which it is caught, taken to indicate stupidity]

dottle /ˈdɒt(ə)l/ n. a remnant of unburnt tobacco in a pipe. [DOT[1] + -LE[1]]

dotty /ˈdɒtɪ/ adj. (**dottier, dottiest**) colloq. 1 feeble-minded, silly. 2 eccentric. 3 absurd. 4 (foll. by about, on) infatuated with; obsessed by. □□ **dottily** adv. **dottiness** n. [earlier = unsteady: f. DOT[1] + -Y[1]]

douane /duːˈɑːn/ n. a foreign custom-house. [F f. It. do(g)ana f. Turk. duwan, Arab. dīwān: cf. DIVAN]

Douay Bible /ˈduːeɪ, ˈdaʊeɪ/ n. (also **Douay version**) an English translation of the Bible formerly used in the Roman Catholic Church, completed at Douai in France early in the seventeenth century.

double /ˈdʌb(ə)l/ adj., adv., n., & v. —adj. 1 a consisting of two usu. equal parts or things; twofold. b consisting of two identical parts. 2 twice as much or many (double the amount; double the number;

double thickness). 3 having twice the usual size, quantity, strength, etc. (double whisky). 4 designed for two people (double bed). 5 a having some part double. b (of a flower) having more than one circle of petals. c (of a domino) having the same number of pips on each half. 6 having two different roles or interpretations, esp. implying confusion or deceit (double meaning; leads a double life). 7 Mus. lower in pitch by an octave (double bassoon). —adv. 1 at or to twice the amount etc. (counts double). 2 two together (sleep double). —n. 1 a a double quantity or thing; twice as much or many. b colloq. a double measure of spirits. 2 a a counterpart of a person or thing; a person who looks exactly like another. b an understudy. c a wraith. 3 (in pl.) Sport (in lawn tennis) a game between two pairs of players. 4 Sport a pair of victories over the same team, a pair of championships at the same game, etc. 5 a system of betting in which the winnings and stake from the first bet are transferred to a second. 6 Bridge the doubling of an opponent's bid. 7 Darts a hit on the narrow ring enclosed by the two outer circles of a dartboard, scoring double. 8 a sharp turn, esp. of the tracks of a hunted animal, or the course of a river. —v. 1 tr. & intr. make or become twice as much or many; increase twofold; multiply by two. 2 tr. amount to twice as much as. 3 a tr. fold or bend (paper, cloth, etc.) over on itself. b intr. become folded. 4 a tr. (of an actor) play (two parts) in the same piece. b intr. (often foll. by for) be understudy etc. 5 intr. (usu. foll. by as) play a twofold role. 6 intr. turn sharply in flight or pursuit; take a tortuous course. 7 tr. Naut. sail round (a headland). 8 tr. Bridge make a call increasing the value of the points to be won or lost on (an opponent's bid). 9 Mus. a intr. (often foll. by on) play two or more musical instruments (the clarinettist doubles on tenor sax). b tr. add the same note in a higher or lower octave to (a note). 10 tr. clench (a fist). 11 intr. move at twice the usual speed; run. 12 Billiards a intr. rebound. b tr. cause to rebound. □**at the double** running, hurrying. **bent double** folded, stooping. **double acrostic** see ACROSTIC. **double agent** one who spies simultaneously for two rival countries etc. **double axe** an axe with two blades. **double back** take a new direction opposite to the previous one. **double-banking 1** double-parking. **2** Austral. & NZ riding two on a horse etc. **double-barrelled 1** (of a gun) having two barrels. **2** Brit. (of a surname) having two parts joined by a hyphen. **3** twofold. **double-bass 1** the largest and lowest-pitched instrument of the violin family. **2** its player. **double bill** a programme with two principal items. **double bind** a dilemma. **double-blind** adj. (of a test or experiment) in which neither the tester nor the subject has knowledge of identities etc. that might lead to bias. —n. such a test or experiment. **double bluff** an action or statement intended to appear as a bluff, but in fact genuine. **double boiler** a saucepan with a detachable upper compartment heated by boiling water in the lower one. **double bond** Chem. a pair of bonds between two atoms in a molecule. **double-book** accept two reservations simultaneously for (the same seat, room, etc.). **double-breasted** (of a coat etc.) having two fronts overlapping across the body. **double-check** verify twice or in two ways. **double chin** a chin with a fold of loose flesh below it. **double-chinned** having a double chin. **double concerto** a concerto for two solo instruments. **double cream** thick cream with a high fat-content. **double-cross** v.tr. deceive or betray (a person one is supposedly helping). —n. an act of doing this. **double-crosser** a person who double-crosses. **double dagger** Printing = double obelus. **double-dealer** a deceiver. **double-dealing** n. deceit, esp. in business. —adj. deceitful; practising deceit. **double-decker 1** esp. Brit. a bus having an upper and lower deck. **2** colloq. anything consisting of two layers. **double-declutch** see DECLUTCH. **double decomposition** *Chem.* a chemical reaction involving exchange of radicals between two reactants: also called METATHESIS. **double density** *Computing* designating a storage device, esp. a disk, having twice the basic capacity. **double dummy** *Bridge* play with two hands exposed, allowing every card to be located. **double Dutch** *Brit. colloq.* incomprehensible talk. **double-dyed** deeply affected with guilt. **double eagle 1** a figure of a two-headed eagle. **2** *US Golf* = ALBATROSS. **3** *US* a coin worth twenty dollars. **double-edged 1** having two functions or (often contradictory) applications. **2** (of a knife etc.) having two cutting-edges. **double entry** a system of bookkeeping in which each transaction is entered as a debit in one account and a credit in another. **double exposure** *Photog.* the accidental or deliberate repeated exposure of a plate, film, etc. **double-faced 1** insincere. **2** (of a fabric or material) finished on both sides so that either may be used as the right side. **double fault** (in lawn tennis) two consecutive faults in serving. **double feature** a cinema programme with two full-length films. **double figures** the numbers from 10 to 99. **double first** *Brit.* **1** first-class honours in two subjects or examinations at a university. **2** a person achieving this. **double-fronted** (of a house) with principal windows on either side of the front door. **double-ganger** = DOPPELGÄNGER. **double glazing 1** a window consisting of two layers of glass with a space between them, designed to reduce loss of heat and exclude noise. **2** the provision of this. **double Gloucester** a kind of hard cheese orig. made in Gloucestershire. **double header 1** a train pulled by two locomotives coupled together. **2** *US* two games etc. in succession between the same opponents. **3** *Austral. colloq.* a coin with a head on both sides. **double helix** a pair of parallel helices with a common axis, esp. in the structure of the DNA molecule. **double-jointed** having joints that allow unusual bending of the fingers, limbs, etc. **double-lock** lock by a double turn of the key. **double negative** *Gram.* a negative statement containing two negative elements (e.g. *didn't say nothing*). ¶ Considered ungrammatical in standard English. **double obelus** (or **obelisk**) *Printing* a sign (‡) used to introduce a reference. **double or quits** a gamble to decide whether a player's loss or debt be doubled or cancelled. **double-park** park (a vehicle) alongside one that is already parked at the roadside. **double play** *Baseball* putting out two runners. **double pneumonia** pneumonia affecting both lungs. **double-quick** very quick or quickly. **double refraction** *Optics* refraction forming two separate rays from a single incident ray. **double rhyme** a rhyme including two syllables. **double salt** *Chem.* a salt composed of two simple salts and having different crystal properties from either. **double saucepan** *Brit.* = **double boiler**. **double shuffle** *Dancing* a shuffle executed twice with one foot and then twice with the other. **double standard 1** a rule or principle applied more strictly to some people than to others (or to oneself). **2** bimetallism. **double star** two stars actually or apparently very close together. **double-stopping** *Mus.* the sounding of two strings at once on a violin etc. **double take** a delayed reaction to a situation etc. immediately after one's first reaction. **double-talk** verbal expression that is (usu. deliberately) ambiguous or misleading. **double-think** the mental capacity to accept contrary opinions or beliefs at the same time esp. as a result of political indoctrination. **double time 1** payment of an employee at twice the normal rate. **2** *Mil.* the regulation running-pace. **double-tonguing** rapid articulation in playing a wind instrument. **double top** *Darts* a score of double twenty. **double up 1 a** bend or curl up. **b** cause to do this, esp. by a blow. **2** be overcome with pain or laughter. **3** share or assign

to a room, quarters, etc., with another or others. **4** fold or become folded. **5** use winnings from a bet as stake for another. □□ **doubler** *n.* **doubly** *adv.* [ME f. OF *doble*, *duble* (n.), *dobler*, *dubler* (v.) f. L *duplus* DUPLE]

double entendre /ˌduːb(ə)l ɑːnˈtɑːndrə/ *n.* **1** a word or phrase open to two interpretations, one usu. *risqué* or indecent. **2** humour using such words or phrases. [obs. F, = double understanding]

doublet /ˈdʌblɪt/ *n.* **1** either of a pair of similar things, esp. either of two words of the same derivation but different sense (e.g. *fashion* and *faction*, *cloak* and *clock*). **2** *hist.* a man's short close-fitting jacket, with or without sleeves. **3** a historical or biblical account occurring twice in differing contexts, usu. traceable to different sources. **4** (in *pl.*) the same number on two dice thrown at once. **5** a pair of associated lines close together in a spectrum. **6** a combination of two simple lenses. [ME f. OF f. *double*: see DOUBLE]

doubloon /dʌbˈluːn, dəb-/ *n.* **1** *hist.* a Spanish gold coin. **2** (in *pl.*) *sl.* money. [F *doublon* or Sp. *doblón* (as DOUBLE)]

doublure /duːbˈljʊə(r)/ *n.* an ornamental lining, usu. leather, inside a book-cover. [F, = lining (*doubler* to line)]

doubt /daʊt/ *n. & v.* —*n.* **1** a feeling of uncertainty; an undecided state of mind (*be in no doubt about*; *have no doubt that*). **2** (often foll. by *of*, *about*) an inclination to disbelieve (*have one's doubts about*). **3** an uncertain state of things. **4** a lack of full proof or clear indication (*benefit of the doubt*). —*v.* **1** *tr.* (often foll. by *whether*, *if*, *that* + clause; also foll. (after *neg.* or *interrog.*) by *but*, *but that*) feel uncertain or undecided about (*I doubt that you are right*; *I do not doubt but that you are wrong*). **2** *tr.* hesitate to believe or trust. **3** *intr.* (often foll. by *of*) feel uncertain or undecided; have doubts (*never doubted of success*). **4** *tr.* call in question. **5** *tr. Brit. archaic* or *dial.* rather think that; suspect or fear that (*I doubt we are late*). □ **beyond doubt** certainly. **doubting Thomas** an incredulous or sceptical person (after John 20:24–29). **in doubt** uncertain; open to question. **no doubt** certainly; probably; admittedly. **without doubt** (or **a doubt**) certainly. □□ **doubtable** *adj.* **doubter** *n.* **doubtingly** *adv.* [ME *doute* f. OF *doute* (n.), *douter* (v.) f. L *dubitare* hesitate; mod. spelling after L]

doubtful /ˈdaʊtfʊl/ *adj.* **1** feeling doubt or misgivings; unsure or guarded in one's opinion. **2** causing doubt; ambiguous; uncertain in meaning etc. **3** unreliable (*a doubtful ally*). □□ **doubtfully** *adv.* **doubtfulness** *n.*

doubtless /ˈdaʊtlɪs/ *adv.* (often qualifying a sentence) **1** certainly; no doubt. **2** probably. □□ **doubtlessly** *adv.*

douce /duːs/ *adj. Sc.* sober, gentle, sedate. [ME f. OF *dous douce* f. L *dulcis* sweet]

douche /duːʃ/ *n. & v.* —*n.* **1** a jet of liquid applied to part of the body for cleansing or medicinal purposes. **2** a device for producing such a jet. —*v.* **1** *tr.* treat with a douche. **2** *intr.* use a douche. [F f. It. *doccia* pipe f. *docciare* pour by drops ult. f. L *ductus*: see DUCT]

dough /dəʊ/ *n.* **1** a thick mixture of flour etc. and liquid (usu. water), for baking into bread, pastry, etc. **2** *sl.* money. [OE *dāg* f. Gmc]

doughboy /ˈdəʊbɔɪ/ *n.* **1** a boiled dumpling. **2** *US colloq.* a United States infantryman, esp. in the war of 1914–18.

doughnut /ˈdəʊnʌt/ *n.* (*US* **donut**) **1** a small fried cake of sweetened dough, usu. in the shape of a ball or ring. **2** a ring-shaped object, esp. *Physics* a vacuum chamber for acceleration of particles in a betatron or synchrotron.

doughty /ˈdaʊtɪ/ *adj.* (**doughtier**, **doughtiest**) *archaic* or *joc.* valiant, stout-hearted. □□ **doughtily** *adv.* **doughtiness** *n.* [OE *dohtig* var. of *dyhtig* f. Gmc]

doughy /'dəʊɪ/ adj. (**doughier, doughiest**) **1** having the form or consistency of dough. **2** pale and sickly in colour. □□ **doughiness** n.

Douglas fir /'dʌgləs/ n. (also **Douglas pine** or **spruce**) any large conifer of the genus *Pseudotsuga*, of Western N. America. [D. *Douglas*, Sc. botanist d. 1834]

doum /daʊm, duːm/ n. (in full **doum-palm**) a palm-tree, *Hyphaene thebaica*, with edible fruit. [Arab. *dawm, dūm*]

dour /dʊə(r)/ adj. severe, stern, or sullenly obstinate in manner or appearance. □□ **dourly** adv. **dourness** n. [ME (orig. Sc.), prob. f. Gael. *dúr* dull, obstinate, perh. f. L *durus* hard]

douroucouli /ˌdʊərʊˈkuːlɪ/ n. (pl. **douroucoulis**) any nocturnal monkey of the genus *Aotus*, native to S. America, having large staring eyes. [Indian name]

douse /daʊs/ v.tr. (also **dowse**) **1 a** throw water over. **b** plunge into water. **2** extinguish (a light). **3** Naut. **a** lower (a sail). **b** close (a porthole). [16th c.: perh. rel. to MDu., LG *dossen* strike]

dove[1] /dʌv/ n. **1** any bird of the family Columbidae, with short legs, small head, and large breast. **2** a gentle or innocent person. **3** Polit. an advocate of peace or peaceful policies (cf. HAWK[1]). **4** (**Dove**) Relig. a representation of the Holy Spirit (John 1:32). **5** a soft grey colour. □ **dove's-foot** a cranesbill, *Geranium molle*. **dove-tree** a tree with dovelike flowers, *Davidia involucrata*, native to China. □□ **dovelike** adj. [ME f. ON *dúfa* f. Gmc]

dove[2] US past and past part. of DIVE.

dovecote /'dʌvkɒt/ n. (also **dovecot**) a shelter with nesting-holes for domesticated pigeons.

dovetail /'dʌvteɪl/ n. & v. —n. **1** a joint formed by a mortise with a tenon shaped like a dove's spread tail or a reversed wedge. **2** such a tenon. —v. **1** tr. join together by means of a dovetail. **2** tr. & intr. (often foll. by *into, with*) fit readily together; combine neatly or compactly.

dowager /'daʊədʒə(r)/ n. **1** a widow with a title or property derived from her late husband (*Queen dowager; dowager duchess*). **2** colloq. a dignified elderly woman. [ᴐF *douag(i)ere* f. *douage* (as DOWER)]

dowdy /'daʊdɪ/ aaj. & n. —adj. (**dowdier, dowdiest**) **1** (of clothes) unattractively dull; unfashionable. **2** (of a person, esp. a woman) dressed in dowdy clothes. —n. (pl. **-ies**) a dowdy woman. □□ **dowdily** adv. **dowdiness** n. [ME *dowd* slut, of unkn. orig.]

dowel /'daʊəl/ n. & v. —n. a headless peg of wood, metal, or plastic for holding together components of a structure. —v.tr. (**dowelled, dowelling**; US **doweled, doweling**) fasten with a dowel or dowels. [ME f. MLG *dovel*: cf. THOLE[1]]

dowelling /'daʊəlɪŋ/ n. (US **doweling**) round rods for cutting into dowels.

dower /'daʊə(r)/ n. & v. —n. **1** a widow's share for life of her husband's estate. **2** archaic a dowry. **3** a natural gift or talent. —v.tr. **1** archaic give a dowry to. **2** (foll. by *with*) endow with talent etc. □ **dower house** Brit. a smaller house near a big one, forming part of a widow's dower. □□ **dowerless** adj. [ME f. OF *douaire* f. med.L *dotarium* f. L *dos dotis*]

Dow-Jones index /daʊˈdʒəʊnz/ n. (also **Dow-Jones average**) a figure based on the average price of selected stocks, indicating the relative price of shares on the New York Stock Exchange. [C. H. *Dow* d. 1902 & E. D. *Jones* d. 1920, Amer. economists]

down[1] /daʊn/ adv., prep., adj., v., & n. —adv. (superl. **downmost**) **1** into or towards a lower place, esp. to the ground (*fall down; knelt down*). **2** in a lower place or position (*blinds were down*). **3** to or in a place regarded as lower, esp.: **a** southwards. **b** Brit. away from a major city or a university. **4 a** in or into a low or weaker position or condition (*hit a man when he's down; many down with colds*). **b** Brit. in a position of lagging or loss (*our team was three goals down; £5 down on the transaction*). **c** (of a computer system) out of action or unavailable for use (esp. temporarily). **5**

from an earlier to a later time (*customs handed down; down to 1600*). **6** to a finer or thinner consistency or a smaller amount or size (*grind down; water down; boil down*). **7** cheaper; lower in price or value (*bread is down; shares are down*). **8** into a more settled state (*calm down*). **9** in writing; in or into recorded or listed form (*copy it down; I got it down on tape; you are down to speak next*). **10** (of part of a larger whole) paid, dealt with (*£5 down, £20 to pay; three down, six to go*). **11** Naut. **a** with the current or wind. **b** (of a ship's helm) with the rudder to windward. **12** inclusively of the lower limit in a series (*read down to the third paragraph*). **13** (as int.) lie down, put (something) down, etc. **14** (of a crossword clue or answer) read vertically (*cannot do five down*). **15** downstairs, esp. after rising (*is not down yet*). **16** swallowed (*could not get the pill down*). **17** Amer. Football (of the ball) out of play. —prep. **1** downwards along, through, or into. **2** from top to bottom of. **3** along (*walk down the road; cut down the middle*). **4** at or in a lower part of (*situated down the river*). —adj. (superl. **downmost**) **1** directed downwards. **2** Brit. of travel away from a capital or centre (*the down train; the down platform*). —v.tr. colloq. **1** knock or bring down. **2** swallow (a drink). —n. **1** an act of putting down (esp. an opponent in wrestling, or the ball in American football). **2** a reverse of fortune (*ups and downs*). **3** colloq. a period of depression. **4** the play of the first piece in dominoes. □ **be** (or **have a**) **down on** colloq. disapprove of; show animosity towards. **be down to 1** be attributable to. **2** be the responsibility of. **3** have used up everything except (*down to their last tin of rations*). **down and out 1** penniless, destitute. **2** Boxing unable to resume the fight. **down-and-out** n. a destitute person. **down at heel 1** (of a shoe) with the heel worn down. **2** (of a person) wearing such shoes; shabby, slovenly. **down draught** a downward draught, esp. one down a chimney into a room. **down grade 1** a descending slope of a road or railway. **2** a deterioration (see also DOWNGRADE). **down in the mouth** colloq. looking unhappy. **down-market** adj. & adv. colloq. towards or relating to the cheaper or less affluent sector of the market. **down on one's luck** colloq. **1** temporarily unfortunate. **2** dispirited by misfortune. **down payment** a partial payment made at the time of purchase. **down stage** Theatr. at or to the front of the stage. **down-stroke** a stroke made or written downwards. **down time** time during which a machine, esp. a computer, is out of action or unavailable for use. **down-to-earth** practical, realistic. **down to the ground** colloq. completely. **down tools** colloq. cease work, esp. to go on strike. **down town 1** into a town from a higher or outlying part. **2** US to or in the business part of a city (see also DOWNTOWN). **down under** colloq. in the antipodes, esp. Australia. **down wind** in the direction in which the wind is blowing (see also DOWNWIND). **down with** int. expressing strong disapproval or rejection of a specified person or thing. [OE *dūn(e)* f. *adūne* ADOWN]

down[2] /daʊn/ n. **1 a** the first covering of young birds. **b** a bird's under-plumage, used in cushions etc. **c** a layer of fine soft feathers. **2** fine soft hair esp. on the face. **3** short soft hairs on some leaves, fruit, seeds, etc. **4** a fluffy substance, e.g. thistledown. [ME f. ON *dúnn*]

down[3] /daʊn/ n. **1** an area of open rolling land. **2** (in pl.; usu. prec. by *the*) **a** undulating chalk and limestone uplands esp. in S. England, with few trees and used mainly for pasture. **b** (**Downs**) a part of the sea (opposite the North Downs) off E. Kent. □□ **downy** adj. [OE *dūn* perh. f. OCelt.]

downbeat /'daʊnbiːt/ n. & adj. —n. Mus. an accented beat, usu. the first of the bar. —adj. **1** pessimistic, gloomy. **2** relaxed.

downcast /'daʊnkɑːst/ adj. & n. —adj. **1** (of eyes) looking downwards. **2** (of a person) dejected. —n. a shaft dug in a mine for extra ventilation.

downcomer /'daʊn,kʌmə(r)/ n. a pipe for downward transport of water or gas.

downer /'daʊnə(r)/ n. sl. **1** a depressant or tranquillizing drug, esp. a barbiturate. **2** a depressing person or experience; a failure. **3** = DOWNTURN.

downfall /'daʊnfɔːl/ n. **1 a** a fall from prosperity or power. **b** the cause of this. **2** a sudden heavy fall of rain etc.

downfold /'daʊnfəʊld/ n. Geol. a syncline.

downgrade /'daʊngreɪd/ v. & n. —v.tr. **1** make lower in rank or status. **2** speak disparagingly of. —n. US a downward grade. □on the downgrade US in decline.

downhearted /daʊn'hɑːtɪd/ adj. dejected; in low spirits. □□ downheartedly adv. downheartedness n.

downhill adv., adj., & n. —adv. /daʊn'hɪl/ in a descending direction, esp. towards the bottom of an incline. —adj. /'daʊnhɪl/ **1** sloping down, descending. **2** declining; deteriorating. —n. /'daʊnhɪl/ **1** Skiing a downhill race. **2** a downward slope. **3** a decline. □go downhill colloq. decline, deteriorate (in health, state of repair, moral state, etc.).

downland /'daʊnlənd/ n. = DOWN³.

download /daʊn'ləʊd/ v.tr. Computing transfer (data) from one storage device or system to another (esp. smaller remote one).

downmost /'daʊnməʊst/ adj. & adv. the furthest down.

downpipe /'daʊnpaɪp/ n. Brit. a pipe to carry rainwater from a roof to a drain or to ground level.

downplay /daʊn'pleɪ/ v.tr. play down; minimize the importance of.

downpour /'daʊnpɔː(r)/ n. a heavy fall of rain.

downright /'daʊnraɪt/ adj. & adv. —adj. **1** plain, definite, straightforward, blunt. **2** utter, complete (a downright lie; downright nonsense). —adv. thoroughly, completely, positively (downright rude). □□ downrightness n.

downscale /'daʊnskeɪl/ v. & adj. US —v.tr. reduce or restrict in size, scale, or extent. —adj. at the lower end of a scale, esp. a social scale; inferior.

downside /'daʊnsaɪd/ n. a downward movement of share prices etc.

downspout /'daʊnspaʊt/ n. US = DOWNPIPE.

Down's syndrome /daʊnz/ n. Med. a congenital disorder due to a chromosome defect, characterized by mental retardation and physical abnormalities (cf. MONGOLISM). [J. L. H. Down, Engl. physician d. 1896]

downstairs adv., adj., & n. —adv. /daʊn'steəz/ down a flight of stairs. **2** to or on a lower floor. —adj. /'daʊnsteəz/ (also **downstair**) situated downstairs. —n. /daʊn'steəz/ the lower floor.

downstate /'daʊnsteɪt/ adj., n., & adv. US —adj. of or in a part of a state remote from large cities, esp. the southern part. —n. a downstate area. —adv. in a downstate area.

downstream /'daʊnstriːm/ adv. & adj. —adv. in the direction of the flow of a stream etc. —adj. moving downstream.

downthrow /'daʊnθrəʊ/ n. Geol. a downward dislocation of strata.

downtown /'daʊntaʊn/ adj., n., & adv. US —adj. of or in the lower or more central part, or the business part, of a town or city. —n. a downtown area. —adv. in or into a downtown area.

downtrodden /'daʊn,trɒd(ə)n/ adj. oppressed; badly treated; kept under.

downturn /'daʊntɜːn/ n. a decline, esp. in economic or business activity.

downward /'daʊnwəd/ adv. & adj. —adv. (also **downwards**) towards what is lower, inferior, less important, or later. —adj. moving, extending, pointing, or leading downward. □□ downwardly adv.

downwarp /'daʊnwɔːp/ n. Geol. a broad surface depression; a syncline.

downwind /'daʊnwɪnd/ adj. & adv. in the direction in which the wind is blowing.

downy /'daʊnɪ/ adj. (**downier, downiest**) **1 a** of, like, or covered with down. **b** soft and fluffy. **2** Brit. sl. aware, knowing. □□ downily adv. downiness n.

dowry /'daʊərɪ/ n. (pl. **-ies**) **1** property or money brought by a bride to her husband. **2** a talent, a natural gift. [ME f. AF dowarie, OF douaire DOWER]

dowse¹ /daʊz/ v.intr. search for underground water or minerals by holding a Y-shaped stick or rod which dips abruptly when over the right spot. □dowsing-rod such a stick or rod. □□dowser n. [17th c.: orig. unkn.]

dowse² var. of DOUSE.

doxology /dɒk'sɒlədʒɪ/ n. (pl. **-ies**) a liturgical formula of praise to God. □□doxological /-sə'lɒdʒɪk(ə)l/ adj. [med.L doxologia f. Gk doxologia f. doxa glory + -LOGY]

doxy /'dɒksɪ/ n. (pl. **-ies**) literary **1** a lover or mistress. **2** a prostitute. [16th-c. cant: orig. unkn.]

doyen /'dɔɪən, 'dwɑːjæ/ n. (fem. **doyenne** /dɔɪ'en, dwɑːˈjen/) the senior member of a body of colleagues, esp. the senior ambassador at a court. [F (as DEAN¹)]

doyley var. of DOILY.

doz. abbr. dozen.

doze /dəʊz/ v. & n. —v.intr. sleep lightly; be half asleep. —n. a short light sleep. □doze off fall lightly asleep. □□ dozer n. [17th c.: cf. Da. døse make drowsy]

dozen /'dʌz(ə)n/ n. **1** (prec. by a or a number) (pl. **dozen**) twelve, regarded collectively (a dozen eggs; two dozen packets; ordered three dozen). **2** a set or group of twelve (packed in dozens). **3** colloq. about twelve, a fairly large indefinite number. **4** (in pl.; usu. foll. by of) colloq. very many (made dozens of mistakes). **5** (the dozens) a Black American game or ritualized exchange of verbal insults. □by the dozen in large quantities. **talk nineteen to the dozen** Brit. talk incessantly. □□ dozenth adj. & n. [ME f. OF dozeine, ult. f. L duodecim twelve]

dozer /'dəʊzə(r)/ n. colloq. = BULLDOZER. [abbr.]

dozy /'dəʊzɪ/ adj. (**dozier, doziest**) **1** drowsy; tending to doze. **2** Brit. colloq. stupid or lazy. □□ dozily adv. doziness n.

DP abbr. **1** data processing. **2** displaced person.

D.Phil. abbr. Doctor of Philosophy.

DPP abbr. (in the UK) Director of Public Prosecutions.

Dr abbr. **1** Doctor. **2** Drive. **3** debtor.

dr. abbr. **1** drachm(s). **2** drachma(s). **3** dram(s).

drab¹ /dræb/ adj. & n. —adj. (**drabber, drabbest**) **1** dull, uninteresting. **2** of a dull brownish colour. —n. **1** drab colour. **2** monotony. □□ drably adv. drabness n. [prob. f. obs. drap cloth f. OF f. LL drappus, perh. of Celt. orig.]

drab² see DRIBS AND DRABS.

drab³ /dræb/ n. **1** a slut; a slattern. **2** a prostitute. [perh. rel. to LG drabbe mire, Du. drab dregs]

drabble /'dræb(ə)l/ v.intr. & tr. become or make dirty and wet with water or mud. [ME f. LG drabbelen paddle in water or mire: cf. DRAB³]

drachm /dræm/ n. Brit. a weight or measure formerly used by apothecaries, equivalent to 60 grains or one eighth of an ounce, or (in full **fluid drachm**) 60 minims, one eighth of a fluid ounce. [ME dragme f. OF dragme or LL dragma f. L drachma f. Gk drakhmē Attic weight and coin]

drachma /'drækmə/ n. (pl. **drachmas** or **drachmae** /-miː/) **1** the chief monetary unit of Greece. **2** a silver coin of ancient Greece. [L f. Gk drakhmē]

drack /dræk/ adj. Austral. sl. **1** (esp. of a woman) unattractive. **2** dismal, dull. [20th c.: orig. unkn.]

dracone /'drækəʊn/ n. a large flexible container for liquids, towed on the surface of the sea. [L draco -onis (as DRAGON)]

Draconian /drə'kəʊnɪən, dreɪ-/ adj. (also **Draconic** /-'kɒnɪk/) very harsh or severe (esp. of laws and their application). [Drakōn, 7th-c. BC Athenian legislator]

draff /dræf, drɑːf/ n. **1** dregs, lees. **2** refuse. [ME, perh. repr. OE dræf (unrecorded)]

draft /drɑːft/ *n. & v.* —*n.* **1 a** a preliminary written version of a speech, document, etc. **b** a rough preliminary outline of a scheme. **c** a sketch of work to be carried out. **2 a** a written order for payment of money by a bank. **b** the drawing of money by means of this. **3** (foll. by *on*) a demand made on a person's confidence, friendship, etc. **4 a** a party detached from a larger group for a special duty or purpose. **b** the selection of this. **5** *US* compulsory military service. **6** a reinforcement. **7** *US* = DRAUGHT. —*v.tr.* **1** prepare a draft of (a document, scheme, etc.). **2** select for a special duty or purpose. **3** *US* conscript for military service. □□ **draftee** /-'tiː/ *n.* **drafter** *n.* [phonetic spelling of DRAUGHT]

draftsman /'drɑːftsmən/ *n.* (*pl.* **-men**) **1** a person who drafts documents. **2** = DRAUGHTSMAN 1. [phonetic spelling of DRAUGHTSMAN]

drafty *US* var. of DRAUGHTY.

drag /dræg/ *v. & n.* —*v.* (**dragged, dragging**) **1** *tr.* pull along with effort or difficulty. **2 a** *tr.* allow (one's feet, tail, etc.) to trail along the ground. **b** *intr.* trail along the ground. **c** *intr.* (of time etc.) go or pass heavily or slowly or tediously. **3 a** *intr.* (usu. foll. by *for*) use a grapnel or drag (to find a drowned person or lost object). **b** *tr.* search the bottom of (a river etc.) with grapnels, nets, or drags. **4** *tr.* (often foll. by *to*) *colloq.* take (a person to a place etc., esp. against his or her will). **5** *intr.* (foll. by *on, at*) draw on (a cigarette etc.). **6** *intr.* (often foll. by *on*) continue at tedious length. —*n.* **1 a** an obstruction to progress. **b** *Aeron.* the longitudinal retarding force exerted by air. **c** slow motion; impeded progress. **d** an iron shoe for retarding a horse-drawn vehicle downhill. **2** *colloq.* a boring or dreary person, duty, performance, etc. **3 a** a strong-smelling lure drawn before hounds as a substitute for a fox. **b** a hunt using this. **4** an apparatus for dredging or recovering drowned persons etc. from under water. **5** = drag-net. **6** *sl.* a draw on a cigarette etc. **7** *sl.* a women's clothes worn by men. **b** a party at which these are worn. **c** clothes in general. **8** an act of dragging. **9 a** *sl.* a motor car. **b** (in full **drag race**) an acceleration race between cars usu. for a quarter of a mile. **10** *US sl.* influence, pull. **11** *US sl.* a street or road (*the main drag*). **12** *hist.* a private vehicle like a stagecoach, drawn by four horses. □ **drag anchor** (of a ship) move from a moored position when the anchor fails to hold. **drag-anchor** *n.* = sea anchor. **drag one's feet** (or **heels**) be deliberately slow or reluctant to act. **drag-hound** a hound used to hunt with a drag. **drag in** introduce (a subject) irrelevantly. **drag-line** an excavator with a bucket pulled in by a wire rope. **drag-net 1** a net drawn through a river or across ground to trap fish or game. **2** a systematic hunt for criminals etc. **drag out** protract. **drag queen** *sl.* a male homosexual transvestite. **drag up** *colloq.* **1** deliberately mention (an unwelcome subject). **2** rear (a child) roughly and without proper training. [ME f. OE *dragan* or ON *draga* DRAW]

dragée /'drɑːʒeɪ/ *n.* **1** a sugar-coated almond etc. **2** a small silver ball for decorating a cake. **3** a chocolate-coated sweet. [F: see DREDGE²]

draggle /'dræg(ə)l/ *v.* **1** *tr.* make dirty or wet or limp by trailing. **2** *intr.* hang trailing. **3** *intr.* lag; straggle in the rear. □ **draggle-tailed** (of a woman) with untidily trailing skirts. [DRAG + -LE⁴]

draggy /'drægɪ/ *adj.* (**draggier, draggiest**) *colloq.* **1** tedious. **2** unpleasant.

dragoman /'drægəmən/ *n.* (*pl.* **dragomans** or **dragomen**) an interpreter or guide, esp. in countries speaking Arabic, Turkish, or Persian. [F f. It. *dragomano* f. med.Gk *dragomanos* f. Arab. *tarjumān* f. *tarjama* interpret, f. Aram. *targēm* f. Assyr. *targumānu* interpreter]

dragon /'drægən/ *n.* **1** a mythical monster like a reptile, usu. with wings and claws and able to breathe out fire. **2** a fierce person, esp. a woman. **3** (in full **flying dragon**) a lizard, *Draco volans*, with a long tail

and membranous winglike structures. Also called *flying lizard*. □ **dragon's blood** a red gum that exudes from the fruit of some palms and the dragon-tree. **dragon's teeth** *Mil. colloq.* obstacles resembling teeth pointed upwards, used esp. against tanks. **dragon-tree** a tree, *Dracaena draco*, native to the Canary Isles. [ME f. OF f. L *draco -onis* f. Gk *drakōn* serpent]

dragonet /'drægənɪt/ *n.* any marine spiny fish of the family Callionymidae, the males of which are brightly coloured. [ME f. F, dimin. of DRAGON]

dragonfish /'drægənfɪʃ/ *n.* (*pl.* same or **-fishes**) any marine deep-water fish of the family Stomiatidae, having a long slender body and a barbel on the chin with luminous tissue, serving to attract prey.

dragonfly /'drægən,flaɪ/ *n.* (*pl.* **-ies**) any of various insects of the order Odonata, having a long slender body and two pairs of large transparent wings usu. spread while resting.

dragonnade /,drægə'neɪd/ *n. & v.* —*n.* a persecution by use of troops, esp. (in *pl.*) of French Protestants under Louis XIV by quartering dragoons on them. —*v.tr.* subject to a dragonnade. [F f. *dragon*: see DRAGOON]

dragoon /drə'guːn/ *n. & v.* —*n.* **1** a cavalryman (orig. a mounted infantryman armed with a carbine). **2** a rough fierce fellow. **3** a variety of pigeon. —*v.tr.* **1** (foll. by *into*) coerce into doing something, esp. by use of strong force. **2** persecute, esp. with troops. [orig. = carbine (thought of as breathing fire) f. F *dragon* DRAGON]

dragster /'drægstə(r)/ *n.* a car built or modified to take part in drag races.

drail /dreɪl/ *n.* a fish-hook and line weighted with lead for dragging below the surface of the water. [app. var. of TRAIL]

drain /dreɪn/ *v. & n.* —*v.* **1** *tr.* draw off liquid from, esp.: **a** make (land etc.) dry by providing an outflow for moisture. **b** (of a river) carry off the superfluous water of (a district). **c** remove purulent matter from (an abscess). **2** *tr.* (foll. by *off, away*) draw off (liquid) esp. by a pipe. **3** *intr.* (foll. by *away, off, through*) flow or trickle away. **4** *intr.* (of a wet cloth, a vessel, etc.) become dry as liquid flows away (*put it there to drain*). **5** *tr.* (often foll. by *of*) exhaust or deprive (a person or thing) of strength, resources, property, etc. **6** *tr.* **a** drink (liquid) to the dregs. **b** empty (a vessel) by drinking the contents. —*n.* **1 a** a channel, conduit, or pipe carrying off liquid, esp. an artificial conduit for water or sewage. **b** a tube for drawing off the discharge from an abscess etc. **2** a constant outflow, withdrawal, or expenditure (*a great drain on my resources*). □ **down the drain** *colloq.* lost, wasted. **laugh like a drain** laugh copiously; guffaw. [OE *drē(a)hnian* f. Gmc]

drainage /'dreɪnɪdʒ/ *n.* **1** the process or means of draining (*the land has poor drainage*). **2** a system of drains, artificial or natural. **3** what is drained off, esp. sewage.

drainboard /'dreɪnbɔːd/ *n.* *US* = DRAINING-BOARD.

drainer /'dreɪnə(r)/ *n.* **1** a device for draining; anything on which things are put to drain, e.g. a draining-board. **2** a person who drains.

draining-board /'dreɪnɪŋˌbɔːd/ *n.* a sloping usu. grooved surface beside a sink, on which washed dishes etc. are left to drain.

drainpipe /'dreɪnpaɪp/ *n.* **1** a pipe for carrying off water, sewage, etc., from a building. **2** (*attrib.*) (of trousers etc.) very narrow. **3** (in *pl.*) very narrow trousers.

drake /dreɪk/ *n.* a male duck. [ME prob. f. Gmc]

Dralon /'dreɪlɒn/ *n. propr.* **1** a synthetic acrylic fibre used in textiles. **2** a fabric made from this. [after NYLON]

dram /dræm/ *n.* **1** a small drink of spirits. **2** = DRACHM. [ME f. OF *drame* or med.L *drama, dragma*: cf. DRACHM]

drama /'drɑːmə/ *n.* **1** a play for acting on stage or for broadcasting. **2** (often prec. by *the*) the art of writing and presenting plays. **3** an exciting or emotional event, set of circumstances, etc. **4** dramatic quality (*the drama of the situation*). [LL f. Gk *drama -atos* f. *draō* do]

dramatic /drə'mætɪk/ *adj.* **1** of drama or the study of drama. **2** (of an event, circumstance, etc.) sudden and exciting or unexpected. **3** vividly striking. **4** (of a gesture etc.) theatrical, overdone, absurd. □**dramatic irony** = *tragic irony*. □□**dramatically** *adv.* [LL *dramaticus* f. Gk *dramatikos* (as DRAMA)]

dramatics /drə'mætɪks/ *n.pl.* (often treated as *sing.*) **1** the production and performance of plays. **2** exaggerated or showy behaviour.

dramatis personae /ˌdræmətɪs pɜː'səʊnaɪ, -niː/ *n.pl.* (often treated as *sing.*) **1** the characters in a play. **2** a list of these. [L, = persons of the drama]

dramatist /'dræmətɪst/ *n.* a writer of dramas.

dramatize /'dræmə,taɪz/ *v.* (also **-ise**) **1 a** *tr.* adapt (a novel etc.) to form a stage play. **b** *intr.* admit of such adaptation. **2** *tr.* make a drama or dramatic scene of. **3** *tr.* (also *absol.*) express or react to in a dramatic way. □□**dramatization** /-'zeɪʃ(ə)n/ *n.*

dramaturge /'dræmə,tɜːdʒ/ *n.* **1** a specialist in theatrical production. **2** a dramatist. [F f. Gk *dramatourgos* (as DRAMA, *-ergos* worker)]

dramaturgy /'dræmə,tɜːdʒɪ/ *n.* **1** the art of theatrical production; the theory of dramatics. **2** the application of this. □□**dramaturgic** /-'tɜːdʒɪk/ *adj.* **dramaturgical** /-'tɜːdʒɪk(ə)l/ *adj.*

Drambuie /dræm'bjuːɪ, -'buːɪ/ *n. propr.* a Scotch whisky liqueur. [Gael. *dram buidheach* satisfying drink]

drank *past* of DRINK.

drape /dreɪp/ *v.* & *n.* —*v.tr.* **1** hang, cover loosely, or adorn with cloth etc. **2** arrange (clothes or hangings) carefully in folds. —*n.* **1** (often in *pl.*) a curtain or drapery. **2** a piece of drapery. **3** the way in which a garment or fabric hangs. [ME f. OF *draper* f. *drap* f. LL *drappus* cloth]

draper /'dreɪpə(r)/ *n. Brit.* a retailer of textile fabrics. [ME f. AF, OF *drapier* (as DRAPE)]

drapery /'dreɪpərɪ/ *n.* (*pl.* **-ies**) **1** clothing or hangings arranged in folds. **2** (often in *pl.*) a curtain or hanging. **3** *Brit.* cloth; textile fabrics. **4** *Brit.* the trade of a draper. **5** the arrangement of clothing in sculpture or painting. [ME f. OF *draperie* f. *drap* cloth]

drastic /'dræstɪk, 'drɑː-/ *adj.* having a strong or far-reaching effect; severe. □□**drastically** *adv.* [Gk *drastikos* f. *draō* do]

drat /dræt/ *v.* & *int. colloq.* —*v.tr.* (**dratted, dratting** (usu. as an exclam.)) curse, confound (*drat the thing!*). —*int.* expressing anger or annoyance. □□ **dratted** *adj.* [for '*od* (= God) *rot*]

draught /drɑːft/ *n.* & *v.* (*US* **draft**) —*n.* **1** a current of air in a confined space (e.g. a room or chimney). **2** pulling, traction. **3** *Naut.* the depth of water needed to float a ship. **4** the drawing of liquor from a cask etc. **5 a** a single act of drinking. **b** the amount drunk in this. **c** a dose of liquid medicine. **6** (in *pl.*; usu. treated as *sing.*) *Brit.* a game for two played with 12 pieces each on a draughtboard. **7 a** the drawing in of a fishing-net. **b** the fish taken at one drawing. **8** = DRAFT. —*v.tr.* = DRAFT. □**draught beer** beer drawn from a cask, not bottled. **draught-horse** a horse used for pulling heavy loads, esp. a cart or plough. **feel the draught** *colloq.* suffer from adverse (usu. financial) conditions. [ME *draht*, perh. f. ON *drahtr, dráttr* f. Gmc, rel. to DRAW]

draughtboard /'drɑːftbɔːd/ *n.* a chequered board, identical to a chessboard, used in draughts.

draughtsman /'drɑːftsmən/ *n.* (*pl.* **-men**) **1** a person who makes drawings, plans, or sketches. **2** /'drɑːftsmæn/ a piece in the game of draughts. **3** = DRAFTSMAN. □□**draughtsmanship** *n.* [*draught's* + MAN]

draughty /'drɑːftɪ/ *adj.* (*US* **drafty**) (**-ier, -iest**) (of

a room etc.) letting in sharp currents of air. □□**draughtily** *adv.* **draughtiness** *n.*

Dravidian /drə'vɪdɪən/ *n.* & *adj.* —*n.* **1** a member of a dark-skinned aboriginal people of S. India and Sri Lanka (including the Tamils and Kanarese). **2** any of the group of languages spoken by this people. —*adj.* of or relating to this people or group of languages. [Skr. *Dravida,* a province of S. India]

draw /drɔː/ *v.* & *n.* —*v.* (*past* **drew** /druː/; *past part.* **drawn** /drɔːn/) **1** *tr.* pull or cause to move towards or after one. **2** *tr.* pull (a thing) up, over, or across. **3** *tr.* pull (curtains etc.) open or shut. **4** *tr.* take (a person) aside, esp. to talk to. **5** *tr.* attract; bring to oneself or to something; take in (*drew a deep breath*; *I felt drawn to her; drew my attention to the matter; draw him into conversation; the match drew large crowds*). **6** *intr.* (foll. by *at, on*) suck smoke from (a cigarette, pipe, etc.). **7** *tr.* (also *absol.*) take out; remove (e.g. a tooth, a gun from a holster, etc.). **8** *tr.* obtain or take from a source (*draw a salary; draw inspiration; drew £100 from my account*). **9** *tr.* trace (a line, mark, furrow, or figure). **10 a** *tr.* produce (a picture) by tracing lines and marks. **b** *tr.* represent (a thing) by this means. **c** *absol.* make a drawing. **11** *tr.* (also *absol.*) finish (a contest or game) with neither side winning. **12** *intr.* make one's or its way, proceed, move, come (*drew near the bridge; draw to a close; the second horse drew level; drew ahead of the field; the time draws near*). **13** *tr.* infer, deduce (a conclusion). **14** *tr.* **a** elicit, evoke. **b** bring about, entail (*draw criticism; draw ruin upon oneself*). **c** induce (a person) to reveal facts, feelings, or talent (*refused to be drawn*). **d** (foll. by *to* + infin.) induce (a person) to do something. **e** *Cards* cause to be played (*drew all the trumps*). **15** *tr.* haul up (water) from a well. **16** *tr.* bring out (liquid from a vessel or blood from a wound). **17** *tr.* extract a liquid essence from. **18** *intr.* (of a chimney or pipe) promote or allow a draught. **19** *intr.* (of tea) infuse. **20 a** *tr.* obtain by lot (*drew the winner*). **b** *absol.* draw lots. **21** *intr.* (foll. by *on*) make a demand on a person, a person's skill, memory, imagination, etc. **22** *tr.* write out (a bill, cheque, or draft) (*drew a cheque on the bank*). **23** *tr.* frame (a document) in due form, compose. **24** *tr.* formulate or perceive (a comparison or distinction). **25** *tr.* (of a ship) require (a specified depth of water) to float in. **26** *tr.* disembowel (*hang, draw, and quarter; draw the fowl before cooking it*). **27** *tr. Hunting* search (cover) for game. **28** *tr.* drag (a badger or fox) from a hole. **29** *tr.* **a** protract, stretch, elongate (*long-drawn agony*). **b** make (wire) by pulling a piece of metal through successively smaller holes. **30** *tr.* **a** *Golf* drive (the ball) to the left (or, of a left-handed player, the right) esp. purposely. **b** *Bowls* cause (a bowl) to travel in a curve to the desired point. **31** *intr.* (of a sail) swell tightly in the wind. —*n.* **1** an act of drawing. **2 a** a person or thing that draws custom, attention, etc. **b** the power to attract attention. **3** the drawing of lots, esp. a raffle. **4** a drawn game. **5** a suck on a cigarette etc. **6** the act of removing a gun from its holster in order to shoot (*quick on the draw*). **7** strain, pull. **8** *US* the movable part of a drawbridge. □**draw back** withdraw from an undertaking. **draw a bead on** see BEAD. **draw bit** = *draw rein.* **draw a blank** see BLANK. **draw bridle** = *draw rein.* **draw a person's fire** attract hostility, criticism, etc., away from a more important target. **draw in 1 a** (of successive days) become shorter because of the changing seasons. **b** (of a day) approach its end. **c** (of successive evenings or nights) start earlier because of the changing seasons. **2** persuade to join, entice. **3** (of a train etc.) arrive at a station. **draw in one's horns** become less assertive or ambitious; draw back. **draw the line** at set a limit (of tolerance etc.) at. **draw lots** see LOT. **draw off** withdraw (troops). **draw on 1** approach, come near. **2** lead to, bring about. **3** allure. **4** put (gloves, boots, etc.) on. **draw out 1** prolong. **2** elicit. **3** induce to talk. **4** (of successive days) become longer because of the changing seasons. **5** (of a train etc.) leave a station etc. **6** write out in proper form. **7** lead out, detach, or array (troops). **draw rein** see REIN. **draw-sheet** a sheet that can be taken from under a patient without remaking the bed. **draw-string** a string that can be pulled to tighten the mouth of a bag, the waist of a garment, etc. **draw stumps** *Cricket* take the stumps out of the ground at the close of play. **draw one's sword against** attack. **draw up 1** compose or draft (a document etc.). **2** bring or come into regular order. **3** come to a halt. **4** make (oneself) stiffly erect. **5** (foll. by *with, to*) gain on or overtake. **draw-well** a deep well with a rope and a bucket. **quick on the draw** quick to act or react. [OE *dragan* f. Gmc]

drawback /ˈdrɔːbæk/ *n.* **1** a thing that impairs satisfaction; a disadvantage. **2** (foll. by *from*) a deduction. **3** an amount of excise or import duty paid back or remitted on goods exported. □**drawback lock** a lock with a spring bolt that can be drawn back by an inside knob.

drawbridge /ˈdrɔːbrɪdʒ/ *n.* a bridge, esp. over water, hinged at one end so that it may be raised to prevent passage or to allow ships etc. to pass.

drawee /drɔːˈiː/ *n.* the person on whom a draft or bill is drawn.

drawer /ˈdrɔː(r)/ *n.* **1** a person or thing that draws, esp. a person who draws a cheque etc. **2** /drɔː(r), ˈdrɔːə(r)/ a boxlike storage compartment without a lid, sliding in and out of a frame, table, etc. (*chest of drawers*). **3** (in *pl.*) an undergarment worn next to the body below the waist. □□**drawerful** *n.* (*pl.* **-fuls**).

drawing /ˈdrɔːɪŋ/ *n.* **1 a** the art of representing by line. **b** delineation without colour or with a single colour. **c** the art of representing with pencils, pens, crayons, etc., rather than paint. **2** a picture produced in this way. □**drawing-board** a board for spreading drawing-paper on. **drawing-paper** stout paper for drawing pictures etc. on. **drawing-pin** *Brit.* a flat-headed pin for fastening paper etc. (orig. drawing-paper) to a surface. **out of drawing** incorrectly depicted.

drawing-room /ˈdrɔːɪŋruːm, -ˌrʊm/ *n.* **1** a room for comfortable sitting or entertaining in a private house. **2** (*attrib.*) restrained; observing social proprieties (*drawing-room conversation*). **3** *US* a private compartment in a train. **4** *hist.* a levee, a formal reception esp. at court. [earlier *withdrawing-room*, because orig. used for women to withdraw to after dinner]

drawl /drɔːl/ *v.* & *n.* —*v.* **1** *intr.* speak with drawn-out vowel sounds. **2** *tr.* utter in this way. —*n.* a drawling utterance or way of speaking. □□**drawler** *n.* [16th c.: prob. orig. cant, f. LG, Du. *dralen* delay, linger]

drawn /drɔːn/ *past part.* of DRAW. —*adj.* **1** looking strained from fear, anxiety, or pain. **2** (of butter) melted. **3** (of a position in chess etc.) that will result in a draw if both players make the best moves available. □**drawn-work** (or **drawn-thread-work**) ornamental work on linen etc., done by drawing out threads, usu. with additional needlework.

dray¹ /dreɪ/ *n.* **1** a low cart without sides for heavy loads, esp. beer-barrels. **2** *Austral.* & *NZ* a two-wheeled cart. □**dray-horse** a large, powerful horse. [ME f. OE *dræge* drag-net, *dragan* DRAW]

dray² var. of DREY.

drayman /ˈdreɪmən/ *n.* (*pl.* **-men**) a brewer's driver.

dread /dred/ *v., n.,* & *adj.* —*v.tr.* **1** (foll. by *that,* or *to* + infin.) fear greatly. **2** shrink from; look forward to with great apprehension. **3** be in great fear of. —*n.* **1** great fear, apprehension, awe. **2** an object of fear or awe. —*adj.* **1** dreaded. **2** *archaic* awe-inspiring, revered. [OE *ādrǣdan, ondrǣdan*]

dreadful /ˈdredfʊl/ *adj.* **1** terrible; inspiring fear or awe. **2** *colloq.* troublesome, disagreeable; very bad. □□**dreadfully** *adv.* **dreadfulness** *n.*

dreadlocks /ˈdredlɒks/ *n.pl.* **1** a Rastafarian hairstyle in which the hair is twisted into tight braids or

ringlets hanging down on all sides. **2** hair dressed in this way.

dreadnought /ˈdrednɔːt/ *n.* **1** (usu. **Dreadnought**) *hist.* a type of battleship greatly superior in armament to all its predecessors (from the name of the first, launched in 1906). **2** *archaic* a fearless person. **3** *archaic* **a** a thick coat for stormy weather. **b** the cloth used for such coats.

dream /driːm/ *n.* & *v.* —*n.* **1 a** a series of pictures or events in the mind of a sleeping person. **b** the act or time of seeing this. **c** (in full **waking dream**) a similar experience of one awake. **2** a day-dream or fantasy. **3** an ideal, aspiration, or ambition, esp. of a nation. **4** a beautiful or ideal person or thing. **5** a state of mind without proper perception of reality (*goes about in a dream*). —*v.* (*past* and *past part.* **dreamt** /dremt, drempt/ or **dreamed**) **1** *intr.* experience a dream. **2** *tr.* imagine in or as if in a dream. **3** (usu. with *neg.*) **a** *intr.* (foll. by *of*) contemplate the possibility of, have any conception or intention of (*would not dream of upsetting them*). **b** *tr.* (often foll. by *that* + clause) think of as a possibility (*never dreamt that he would come*). **4** *tr.* (foll. by *away*) spend (time) unprofitably. **5** *intr.* be inactive or unpractical. **6** *intr.* fall into a reverie. □**dream-time** *Austral.* the alcheringa. **dream up** imagine, invent. **like a dream** *colloq.* easily, effortlessly. □□ **dreamful** *adj.* **dreamless** *adj.* **dreamlike** *adj.* [ME f. OE *drēam* joy, music]

dreamboat /ˈdriːmbəʊt/ *n. colloq.* **1** a very attractive or ideal person, esp. of the opposite sex. **2** a very desirable or ideal thing.

dreamer /ˈdriːmə(r)/ *n.* **1** a person who dreams. **2** a romantic or unpractical person.

dreamland /ˈdriːmlænd/ *n.* an ideal or imaginary land.

dreamy /ˈdriːmɪ/ *adj.* (**dreamier, dreamiest**) **1** given to day-dreaming; fanciful; unpractical. **2** dreamlike; vague; misty. **3** *colloq.* delightful; marvellous. **4** *poet.* full of dreams. □□**dreamily** *adv.* **dreaminess** *n.*

drear /drɪə(r)/ *adj. poet.* = DREARY. [abbr.]

dreary /ˈdrɪərɪ/ *adj.* (**drearier, dreariest**) dismal, dull, gloomy. □□**drearily** *adv.* **dreariness** *n.* [OE *drēorig* f. *drēor* gore: rel. to *drēosan* to drop f. Gmc]

dredge¹ /dredʒ/ *v.* & *n.* —*v.* **1** *tr.* **a** (often foll. by *up*) bring up (lost or hidden material) as if with a dredge (*don't dredge all that up again*). **b** (often foll. by *away, up, out*) bring up or clear (mud etc.) from a river, harbour, etc. with a dredge. **2** *tr.* clean (a harbour, river, etc.) with a dredge. **3** *intr.* use a dredge. —*n.* an apparatus used to scoop up oysters, specimens, etc., or to clear mud etc., from a river or sea bed. [15th-c. Sc. *dreg*, perh. rel. to MDu. *dregghe*]

dredge² /dredʒ/ *v.tr.* **1** sprinkle with flour, sugar, etc. **2** (often foll. by *over*) sprinkle (flour, sugar, etc.) on. [obs. *dredge* sweetmeat f. OF *dragie, dragee*, perh. f. L *tragemata* f. Gk *tragēmata* spices]

dredger¹ /ˈdredʒə(r)/ *n.* **1** a machine used for dredging rivers etc.; a dredge. **2** a boat containing this.

dredger² /ˈdredʒə(r)/ *n.* a container with a perforated lid used for sprinkling flour, sugar, etc.

dree /driː/ *v.tr.* (**drees, dreed, dreeing**) *Sc.* or *archaic* endure. □**dree one's weird** submit to one's destiny. [OE *drēogan* f. Gmc]

dreg /dreg/ *n.* **1** (usu. in *pl.*) **a** a sediment; grounds, lees, etc. **b** a worthless part; refuse (*the dregs of humanity*). **2** a small remnant (*not a dreg*). □**drain** (or **drink**) **to the dregs** consume leaving nothing (*drained life to the dregs*). □□**dreggy** *adj. colloq.* [ME prob. f. ON *dreggjar*]

drench /drentʃ/ *v.* & *n.* —*v.tr.* **1 a** wet thoroughly (*was drenched by the rain*). **b** saturate; soak (in liquid). **2** force (an animal) to take medicine. **3** *archaic* cause to drink. —*n.* **1** a soaking; a downpour. **2** medicine administered to an animal. **3** *archaic* a medicinal or poisonous draught. [OE *drencan, drenc* f. Gmc: rel. to DRINK]

Dresden china /'drezd(ə)n/ *n.* (also **Dresden porcelain**) **1** delicate and elaborate chinaware orig. made at Dresden in Germany, now made at nearby Meissen. **2** (*attrib.*) delicately pretty.

dress /dres/ *v. & n.* —*v.* **1 a** *tr.* clothe; array (*dressed in rags; dressed her quickly*). **b** *intr.* wear clothes of a specified kind or in a specified way (*dresses well*). **2** *intr.* **a** put on clothes. **b** put on formal or evening clothes, esp. for dinner. **3** *tr.* decorate or adorn. **4** *tr. Med.* **a** treat (a wound) with ointment etc. **b** apply a dressing to (a wound). **5** *tr.* trim, comb, brush, or smooth (the hair). **6** *tr.* a clean and prepare (poultry, a crab, etc.) for cooking or eating. **b** add a dressing to (a salad etc.). **7** *tr.* apply manure etc. to a field, garden, etc. **8** *tr.* finish the surface of (fabric, building-stone, etc.). **9** *tr.* groom (a horse). **10** *tr.* curry (leather etc.). **11** *Mil.* **a** *tr.* correct the alignment of (troops etc.). **b** *intr.* (of troops) come into alignment. **12** *tr.* make (an artificial fly) for use in fishing. —*n.* **1** a one-piece woman's garment consisting of a bodice and skirt. **2** clothing, esp. a whole outfit etc. (*fussy about his dress; wore the dress of a highlander*). **3** formal or ceremonial costume (*evening dress; morning dress*). **4** an external covering; the outward form (*birds in their winter dress*). □**dress circle** the first gallery in a theatre, in which evening dress was formerly required. **dress coat** a man's swallow-tailed evening coat. **dress down** *colloq.* reprimand or scold. **dress length** a piece of material sufficient to make a dress. **dress out** attire conspicuously. **dress parade 1** *Mil.* a military parade in full dress uniform. **2** a display of clothes worn by models. **dress rehearsal** the final rehearsal of a play etc., wearing costume. **dress-shield** (or **-preserver**) a piece of waterproof material fastened in the armpit of a dress to protect it from sweat. **dress-shirt** a man's usu. starched white shirt worn with evening dress. **dress up 1** dress (oneself or another) elaborately for a special occasion. **2** dress in fancy dress. **3** disguise (unwelcome facts) by embellishment. [ME f. OF *dresser* ult. f. L *directus* DIRECT]

dressage /'dresɑːʒ, -sɑːdʒ/ *n.* the training of a horse in obedience and deportment, esp. for competition. [F f. *dresser* to train]

dresser[1] /'dresə(r)/ *n.* **1** a kitchen sideboard with shelves above for displaying plates etc. **2** *US* a dressing-table or chest of drawers. [ME f. OF *dresseur* f. *dresser* prepare: cf. med.L *directorium*]

dresser[2] /'dresə(r)/ *n.* **1** a person who assists actors to dress, takes care of their costumes, etc. **2** *Med.* a surgeon's assistant in operations. **3** a person who dresses elegantly or in a specified way (*a snappy dresser*).

dressing /'dresɪŋ/ *n.* **1** in senses of DRESS *v.* **2 a** an accompaniment to salads, usu. a mixture of oil with other ingredients; a sauce or seasoning (*French dressing*). **b** *US* stuffing. **3 a** a bandage for a wound. **b** ointment etc. used to dress a wound. **4** size or stiffening used to finish fabrics. **5** compost etc. spread over land (*a top dressing of peat*). □**dressing-case** a case containing toiletries etc. **dressing-down** *colloq.* a scolding; a severe reprimand. **dressing-gown** a loose usu. belted robe worn over nightwear or while resting. **dressing-room 1** a room for changing the clothes etc. in a theatre, sports-ground, etc. **2** a small room attached to a bedroom, containing clothes. **dressing-station** esp. *Mil.* a place for giving emergency treatment to wounded people. **dressing-table** a table with a mirror, drawers, etc., used while applying make-up etc.

dressmaker /'dres,meɪkə(r)/ *n.* a woman who makes clothes professionally. □□**dressmaking** *n.*

dressy /'dresɪ/ *adj.* (**dressier**, **dressiest**) **1 a** fond of smart clothes. **b** overdressed. **c** (of clothes) stylish or elaborate. **2** over-elaborate (*the design is rather dressy*). □□**dressiness** *n.*

drew *past* of DRAW.

drey /dreɪ/ *n.* (also **dray**) a squirrel's nest. [17th c.: orig. unkn.]

dribble /'drɪb(ə)l/ *v. & n.* —*v.* **1** *intr.* allow saliva to flow from the mouth. **2** *intr. & tr.* flow or allow to flow in drops or a trickling stream. **3** *tr.* (also *absol.*) esp. *Football & Hockey* move (the ball) forward with slight touches of the feet, the stick, etc. —*n.* **1** the act or an instance of dribbling. **2** a small trickling stream. □□**dribbler** *n.* **dribbly** *adj.* [frequent. of obs. *drib*, var. of DRIP]

driblet /'drɪblɪt/ *n.* **1 a** a small quantity. **b** a petty sum. **2** a thin stream; a dribble. [*drib* (see DRIBBLE) + -LET]

dribs and drabs /ˌdrɪbz ənd 'dræbz/ *n.pl. colloq.* small scattered amounts (*did the work in dribs and drabs*). [as DRIBBLE + *drab* redupl.]

dried *past* and *past part.* of DRY.

drier[1] *compar.* of DRY.

drier[2] /'draɪə(r)/ *n.* (also **dryer**) **1** a machine for drying the hair, laundry, etc. **2** a substance mixed with oil-paint or ink to promote drying.

driest *superl.* of DRY.

drift /drɪft/ *n. & v.* —*n.* **1 a** slow movement or variation. **b** such movement caused by a slow current. **2** the intention, meaning, scope, etc. of what is said etc. (*didn't understand his drift*). **3** a large mass of snow, sand, etc., accumulated by the wind. **4** esp. *derog.* a state of inaction. **5 a** *Naut.* a ship's deviation from its course, due to currents. **b** *Aeron.* an aircraft's deviation due to side winds. **c** a projectile's deviation due to its rotation. **d** a controlled slide of a racing car etc. **6** *Mining* a horizontal passage following a mineral vein. **7** a large mass of esp. flowering plants (*a drift of bluebells*). **8** *Geol.* **a** material deposited by the wind, a current of water, etc. **b** (**Drift**) Pleistocene ice detritus, e.g. boulder clay. **9** the movement of cattle, esp. a gathering on an appointed day to determine ownership etc. **10** a tool for enlarging or shaping a hole in metal. **11** *S.Afr.* a ford. —*v.* **1** *intr.* be carried by or as if by a current of air or water. **2** *intr.* move or progress passively, casually, or aimlessly (*drifted into teaching*). **3 a** *tr. & intr.* pile or be piled by the wind into drifts. **b** *tr.* cover (a field, a road, etc.) with drifts. **4** *tr.* form or enlarge (a hole) with a drift. **5** *tr.* (of a current) carry. □**drift-ice** ice driven or deposited by water. **drift-net** a large net for herrings etc., allowed to drift with the tide. □□**driftage** *n.* [ME f. ON & MDu., MHG *trift* movement of cattle: rel. to DRIVE]

drifter /'drɪftə(r)/ *n.* **1** an aimless or rootless person. **2** a boat used for drift-net fishing.

driftwood /'drɪftwʊd/ *n.* wood etc. driven or deposited by water or wind.

drill[1] /drɪl/ *n. & v.* —*n.* **1** a pointed, esp. revolving, steel tool or machine used for boring cylindrical holes, sinking wells, etc. **2 a** esp. *Mil.* instruction or training in military exercises. **b** rigorous discipline or methodical instruction, esp. when learning or performing tasks. **c** routine procedure to be followed in an emergency (*fire-drill*). **d** a routine or exercise (*drills in irregular verb patterns*). **3** *colloq.* a recognized procedure (*I expect you know the drill*). **4** any of various molluscs, esp. *Urosalpinx cinera*, that bore into the shells of young oysters. —*v.* **1** *tr.* (also *absol.*) **a** (of a person or a tool) make a hole with a drill through or into (wood, metal, etc.). **b** make (a hole) with a drill. **2** *tr. & intr.* esp. *Mil.* subject to or undergo discipline by drill. **3** *tr.* impart (knowledge etc.) by a strict method. **4** *tr. sl.* shoot with a gun (*drilled him full of holes*). □□**driller** *n.* [earlier as verb, f. MDu. *drillen* bore, of unkn. orig.]

drill[2] /drɪl/ *n. & v.* —*n.* **1** a machine used for making furrows, sowing, and covering seed. **2** a small furrow for sowing seed in. **3** a ridge with such furrows on top. **4** a row of plants so sown. —*v.tr.* **1** sow (seed) with a drill. **2** plant (the ground) in drills. [perh. f. obs. *drill* rill (17th c., of unkn. orig.)]

drill³ /drɪl/ n. a W. African baboon, *Papio leuco-phaeus*, related to the mandrill. [prob. a native name: cf. MANDRILL]

drill⁴ /drɪl/ n. a coarse twilled cotton or linen fabric. [earlier *drilling* f. G *Drillich* f. L *trilix -licis* f. *tri-* three + *licium* thread]

drily /'draɪlɪ/ adv. (also **dryly**) **1** (said) in a dry manner; humorously. **2** in a dry way or condition.

drink /drɪŋk/ v. & n. —v. (past **drank** /dræŋk/; past part. **drunk** /drʌŋk/) **1 a** tr. swallow (a liquid). **b** tr. swallow the liquid contents of (a vessel). **c** intr. swallow liquid, take draughts (*drank from the stream*). **2** intr. take alcohol, esp. to excess (*I have heard that he drinks*). **3** tr. (of a plant, porous material, etc.) absorb (moisture). **4** refl. bring (oneself etc.) to a specified condition by drinking (*drank himself into a stupor*). **5** tr. (usu. foll. by *away*) spend (wages etc.) on drink (*drank away the money*). **6** tr. wish (a person's good health, luck, etc.) by drinking (*drank his health*). —n. **1 a** a liquid for drinking (*milk is a sustaining drink*). **b** a draught or specified amount of this (*had a drink of milk*). **2 a** alcoholic liquor (*got the drink in for Christmas*). **b** a portion, glass, etc. of this (*have a drink*). **c** excessive indulgence in alcohol (*drink is his vice*). **3** (as the **drink**) colloq. the sea. □**drink deep** take a large draught or draughts. **drink-driver** a person who drives a vehicle with an excess of alcohol in the blood. **drink-driving** the act or an instance of this. **drink in** listen to closely or eagerly (*drank in his every word*). **drinking-song** a song sung while drinking, usu. concerning drink. **drinking-up time** Brit. a short period legally allowed for finishing drinks bought before closing time in a public house. **drinking-water** water pure enough for drinking. **drink off** drink the whole (contents) of at once. **drink to** toast; wish success to. **drink a person under the table** remain sober longer than one's drinking companion. **drink up** drink the whole of; empty. **in drink** drunk. **strong drink** alcohol, esp. spirits. □□ **drinkable** adj. **drinker** n. [OE *drincan* (v.), *drinc(a)* (n.) f. Gmc]

drip /drɪp/ v. & n. —v. (**dripped**, **dripping**) **1** intr. & tr. fall or let fall in drops. **2** intr. (often foll. by *with*) be so wet as to shed drops (*dripped with blood*). —n. **1 a** the act or an instance of dripping (*the steady drip of rain*). **b** a drop of liquid (*a drip of paint*). **c** a sound of dripping. **2** colloq. a stupid, dull, or ineffective person. **3** (*Med.* **drip-feed**) the drip-by-drip intravenous administration of a solution of salt, sugar, etc. **4** Archit. a projection, esp. from a window-sill, keeping the rain off the walls. □**drip-dry** v. (**-dries**, **-dried**) **1** intr. (of fabric etc.) dry crease-free when hung up to drip. **2** tr. leave (a garment etc.) hanging up to dry. —adj. able to be drip-dried. **drip-mat** a small mat under a glass. **drip-moulding** (or **-stone**) Archit. a stone etc. projection that deflects rain etc. from walls. **dripping wet** very wet. [MDa. *drippe* f. Gmc (cf. DROP)]

dripping /'drɪpɪŋ/ n. **1** fat melted from roasted meat and used for cooking or as a spread. **2** (in *pl.*) water, grease, etc., dripping from anything.

drippy /'drɪpɪ/ adj. (**drippier**, **drippiest**) **1** tending to drip. **2** sl. (of a person) ineffectual; sloppily sentimental. □□ **drippily** adv. **drippiness** n.

drive /draɪv/ v. & n. —v. (past **drove** /drəʊv/; past part. **driven** /'drɪv(ə)n/) **1** tr. (usu. foll. by *away*, *back*, *in*, *out*, *to*, etc.) urge in some direction, esp. forcibly (*drove back the wolves*). **2** tr. **a** (usu. foll. by *to* + infin., or *to* + verbal noun) compel or constrain forcibly (*was driven to complain*; *drove her to stealing*). **b** (often foll. by *to*) force into a specified state (*drove him mad*; *driven to despair*). **c** (often refl.) urge to overwork (*drives himself too hard*). **3 a** tr. (also *absol.*) operate and direct the course of (a vehicle, a locomotive, etc.) (*drove a sports car*; *drives well*). **b** tr. & intr. convey or be conveyed in a vehicle (*drove them to the station*; *drove to the station in a*

bus) (cf. RIDE). **c** tr. (also *absol.*) be licensed or competent to drive (a vehicle) (*does he drive?*). **d** tr. (also *absol.*) urge and direct the course of (an animal drawing a vehicle or plough). **4** tr. (of wind, water, etc.) carry along, propel, send, or cause to go in some direction (*pure as the driven snow*). **5** tr. **a** (often foll. by *into*) force (a stake, nail, etc.) into place by blows (*drove the nail home*). **b** Mining bore (a tunnel, horizontal cavity, etc.). **6** tr. effect or conclude forcibly (*drove a hard bargain*; *drove his point home*). **7** tr. (of steam or other power) set or keep (machinery) going. **8** intr. (usu. foll. by *at*) work hard; dash, rush, or hasten. **9** tr. *Cricket & Tennis* hit (the ball) hard from a freely swung bat or racket. **10** tr. (often *absol.*) *Golf* strike (a ball) with a driver from the tee. **11** tr. chase or frighten (game, wild beasts, an enemy in warfare, etc.) from a large area to a smaller, to kill or capture; corner. **12** tr. Brit. hold a drift in (a forest etc.) (see DRIFT n. 9). —n. **1** an act of driving in a motor vehicle; a journey or excursion in such a vehicle (*went for a pleasant drive*; *lives an hour's drive from us*). **2 a** the capacity for achievement; motivation and energy (*lacks the drive needed to succeed*). **b** Psychol. an inner urge to attain a goal or satisfy a need (*unconscious emotional drives*). **3 a** a usu. landscaped street or road. **b** a usu. private road through a garden or park to a house. **4** Cricket, Golf, & Tennis a driving stroke of the bat etc. **5** an organized effort to achieve a usu. charitable purpose (*a famine-relief drive*). **6 a** the transmission of power to machinery, the wheels of a motor vehicle, etc. (*belt drive*; *front-wheel drive*). **b** the position of a steering-wheel in a motor vehicle (*left-hand drive*). **c** Computing = disk drive (see DISC). **7** Brit. an organized competition, for many players, of whist, bingo, etc. **8** an act of driving game or an enemy. **9** Austral. & NZ a line of partly cut trees on a hillside felled when the top one topples on the others. □**drive at** seek, intend, or mean (*what is he driving at?*). **drive-in** attrib.adj. (of a bank, cinema, etc.) able to be used while sitting in one's car. —n. such a bank, cinema, etc. **drive-on** (of a ship) on to which motor vehicles may be driven. **drive out** take the place of; oust; exorcize, cast out (evil spirits etc.). **driving-licence** a licence permitting a person to drive a motor vehicle. **driving rain** an excessive windblown downpour. **driving-range** Golf an area for practising drives. **driving test** an official test of a motorist's competence which must be passed to obtain a driving licence. **driving-wheel 1** the large wheel of a locomotive. **2** a wheel communicating motive power in machinery. **let drive** aim a blow or missile. □□ **drivable** adj. [OE *drīfan* f. Gmc]

drivel /'drɪv(ə)l/ n. & v. —n. silly nonsense; twaddle. —v. (**drivelled**, **drivelling**; US **driveled**, **driveling**) **1** intr. run at the mouth or nose; dribble. **2** intr. talk childishly or idiotically. **3** tr. (foll. by *away*) fritter; squander away. □□ **driveller** n. (*US* **driveler**). [OE *dreflian* (v.)]

driven past part. of DRIVE.

driver /'draɪvə(r)/ n. **1** (often in *comb.*) a person who drives a vehicle (*bus-driver*; *engine-driver*). **2** Golf a club with a flat face and wooden head, used for driving from the tee. **3** Electr. a device or part of a circuit providing power for output. **4** Mech. a wheel etc. receiving power directly and transmitting motion to other parts. □**in the driver's seat** in charge. □□ **driverless** adj.

driveway /'draɪvweɪ/ n. = DRIVE n. 3b.

drizzle /'drɪz(ə)l/ n. & v. —n. very fine rain. —v.intr. (esp. of rain) fall in very fine drops (*it's drizzling again*). □□ **drizzly** adj. [prob. f. ME *drēse*, OE *drēosan* fall]

drogue /drəʊg/ n. **1** Naut. **a** a buoy at the end of a harpoon line. **b** a sea anchor. **2** Aeron. a truncated cone of fabric used as a brake, a target for gunnery, a wind-sock, etc. [18th c.: orig. unkn.]

droit /drɔɪt/ n. *Law* a right or due. [ME f. OF f. L *directum* (n.) f. *directus* DIRECT]

droit de seigneur /ˌdrwɑː də senˈjɜː(r)/ n. *hist.* the alleged right of a feudal lord to have sexual intercourse with a vassal's bride on her wedding night. [F, = lord's right]

droll /drəʊl/ adj. & n. —adj. **1** quaintly amusing. **2** strange; odd; surprising. —n. *archaic* **1** a jester; an entertainer. **2** a quaintly amusing person. □□ **drollery** n. (pl. **-ies**). **drolly** /ˈdrəʊllɪ/ adv. **drollness** n. [F *drôle*, perh. f. MDu. *drolle* little man]

drome /drəʊm/ n. *colloq. archaic* aerodrome. [abbr.]

-drome /drəʊm/ comb. form forming nouns denoting: **1** a place for running, racing, or other forms of movement (*aerodrome*; *hippodrome*). **2** a thing that runs or proceeds in a certain way (*palindrome*; *syndrome*). [Gk *dromos* course, running]

dromedary /ˈdrɒmɪdərɪ, ˈdrʌm-/ n. (pl. **-ies**) a one-humped camel, *Camelus dromedarius*, bred for riding and racing. Also called *Arabian camel*. [ME f. OF *dromedaire* or LL *dromedarius* ult. f. Gk *dromas -ados* runner]

dromond /ˈdrɒmənd, ˈdrʌm-/ n. *hist.* a large medieval ship used for war or commerce. [ME f. OF *dromon(t)* f. LL *dromo -onis* f. late Gk *dromōn* light vessel]

drone /drəʊn/ n. & v. —n. **1** a non-working male of the honey-bee, whose sole function is to mate with fertile females. **2** an idler. **3** a deep humming sound. **4** a monotonous speech or speaker. **5 a** a pipe, esp. of a bagpipe, sounding a continuous note of fixed low pitch. **b** the note emitted by this. **6** a remote-controlled pilotless aircraft or missile. —v. **1** *intr.* make a deep humming sound. **2** *intr.* & *tr.* speak or utter monotonously. **3 a** *intr.* be idle. **b** *tr.* (often foll. by *away*) idle away (one's time etc.). [OE *drān, drǣn* prob. f. WG]

drongo /ˈdrɒŋgəʊ/ n. (pl. **-os** or **-oes**) **1** any black bird of the family Dicruridae, native to India, Africa, and Australia, having a long forked tail. **2** *Austral.* & *NZ sl. derog.* a simpleton. [Malagasy]

droob /druːb/ n. *Austral. sl.* a hopeless-looking in-effectual person. [perh. f. DROOP]

drool /druːl/ v. & n. —v.intr. **1** drivel; slobber. **2** (often foll. by *over*) show much pleasure or infatuation. —n. slobbering; drivelling. [contr. of *drivel*]

droop /druːp/ v. & n. —v. **1** *intr.* & *tr.* hang or allow to hang down; languish, decline, or sag, esp. from weariness. **2** *intr.* **a** (of the eyes) look downwards. **b** *poet.* (of the sun) sink. **3** *intr.* lose heart; be dejected; flag. —n. **1** a drooping attitude. **2** a loss of spirit or enthusiasm. □**droop-snoot** *colloq.* —adj. (of an aircraft) having an adjustable nose or leading-edge flap. —n. such an aircraft. [ME f. ON *drúpa* hang the head f. Gmc: cf. DROP]

droopy /ˈdruːpɪ/ adj. (**droopier**, **droopiest**) **1** drooping. **2** dejected, gloomy. □□**droopily** adv. **droopiness** n.

drop /drɒp/ n. & v. —n. **1 a** a small round or pear-shaped portion of liquid that hangs or falls or adheres to a surface (*drops of dew*; *tears fell in large drops*). **b** a very small amount of usu. drinkable liquid (*just a drop left in the glass*). **c** a glass etc. of alcoholic liquor (*take a drop with us*). **2 a** an abrupt fall or slope. **b** the amount of this (*a drop of fifteen feet*). **c** an act of falling or dropping (*had a nasty drop*). **d** a reduction in prices, temperature, etc. **e** a deterioration or worsening (*a drop in status*). **3** something resembling a drop, esp.: **a** a pendant or earring. **b** a crystal ornament on a chandelier etc. **c** (often in *comb.*) a sweet or lozenge (*pear-drop*; *cough drop*). **4** something that drops or is dropped, esp.: **a** *Theatr.* a painted curtain or scenery let down on to the stage. **b** a platform or trapdoor on a gallows, the opening of which causes the victim to fall. **5** *Med.* **a** the smallest separable quantity of a liquid. **b** (in *pl.*) liquid medicine to be measured in drops (*eye drops*). **6** a minute quantity (*not a drop of pity*). **7** *sl.* **a** a hiding-place for stolen or illicit goods. **b** a secret place where documents etc. may be left or passed on in espionage. **8** *sl.* a bribe. **9** *US* a box for letters etc. —v. (**dropped**, **dropping**) **1** *intr.* & *tr.* fall or let fall in drops (*tears dropped on to the book*; *dropped the soup down his shirt*). **2** *intr.* & *tr.* fall or allow to fall; relinquish; let go (*dropped the box*; *the egg dropped from my hand*). **3 a** *intr.* & *tr.* sink or cause to sink or fall to the ground from exhaustion, a blow, a wound, etc. **b** *intr.* die. **4 a** *intr.* & *tr.* cease or cause to cease; lapse or let lapse; abandon (*the connection dropped*; *dropped the friendship*; *drop everything and come at once*). **b** *tr.* *colloq.* cease to associate with. **5** *tr.* set down (a passenger etc.) (*drop me at the station*). **6** *tr.* & *intr.* utter or be uttered casually (*dropped a hint*; *the remark dropped into the conversation*). **7** *tr.* send casually (*drop me a postcard*). **8 a** *intr.* & *tr.* fall or allow to fall in direction, amount, condition, degree, pitch, etc. (*his voice dropped*; *the wind dropped*; *we dropped the price by £20*; *the road dropped south-wards*). **b** *intr.* (of a person) jump down lightly; let oneself fall. **c** *tr.* remove (clothes, esp. trousers) rapidly, allowing them to fall to the ground. **9** *tr. colloq.* lose (money, esp. in gambling). **10** *tr.* omit (a letter, esp. aitch, a syllable etc.) in speech. **11** *tr.* (as **dropped** adj.) in a lower position than usual (*dropped handlebars*; *dropped waist*). **12** *tr.* give birth to (esp. a lamb, a kitten, etc.). **13 a** *intr.* (of a card) be played in the same trick as a higher card. **b** *tr.* play or cause (a card) to be played in this way. **14** *tr. Sport* lose (a game, a point, a contest, a match, etc.). **15** *tr. Aeron.* deliver (supplies etc.) by parachute. **16** *tr. Football* **a** send (a ball) by a drop-kick. **b** score (a goal) by a drop-kick. **17** *tr. colloq.* dismiss or omit (*was dropped from the team*). □**at the drop of a hat** given the slightest excuse. **drop anchor** moor ship. **drop asleep** fall gently asleep. **drop away** decrease or depart gradually. **drop back** (or **behind** or **to the rear**) fall back; get left behind. **drop back into** return to (a habit etc.). **drop a brick** *colloq.* make an indiscreet or embarrassing remark. **drop-curtain** (or **-scene**) *Theatr.* a painted curtain or scenery (cf. sense 4 of n.). **drop a curtsy** make a curtsy. **drop dead!** *sl.* an exclamation of intense scorn. **drop down** descend a hill etc. **drop-forging** a method of forcing white-hot metal through an open-ended die by a heavy weight. **drop-hammer** a heavy weight raised mechanically and allowed to drop, as used in drop-forging and pile-driving. **drop-head** *Brit.* the adjustable fabric roof of a car. **drop in** (or **by**) *colloq.* call casually as a visitor. **drop-in centre** a meeting-place where people may call casually for advice, conversation, etc. **a drop in the ocean** (or **a bucket**) a very small amount, esp. compared with what is needed or expected. **drop into** *colloq.* **1** call casually at (a place). **2** fall into (a habit etc.). **drop it!** *sl.* stop that! **drop-kick** *Football* a kick made by dropping the ball and kicking it on the bounce. **drop-leaf** (of a table etc.) having a hinged flap. **drop off** **1** decline gradually. **2** *colloq.* fall asleep. **3** = sense 5 of v. **drop on** reprimand or punish. **drop out** *colloq.* cease to participate, esp. in a race, a course of study, or in conventional society. **drop-out** n. **1** *colloq.* a person who has dropped out. **2** the restarting of a game by a drop-kick. **drop scone** *Brit.* a small thick pancake made by dropping batter into a frying pan etc. **drop-shot** (in lawn tennis) a shot dropping abruptly over the net. **drop a stitch** let a stitch fall off the end of a knitting-needle. **drop-test** *Engin.* n. a test done by dropping under standard conditions. —v.tr. carry out a drop-test on. **drop to** *sl.* become aware of. **fit** (or **ready**) **to drop** extremely tired. **have the drop on** *colloq.* have the advantage over. **have had a drop too much** *colloq.* be slightly drunk. □□**droplet** n. [OE *dropa*, *drop(p)ian* ult. f. Gmc: cf. DRIP, DROOP]

dropper /ˈdrɒpə(r)/ n. **1** a device for administering liquid, esp. medicine, in drops. **2** *Austral.*, *NZ*, & *S.Afr.* a light vertical stave in a fence.

droppings /ˈdrɒpɪŋz/ *n.pl.* **1** the dung of animals or birds. **2** something that falls or has fallen in drops, e.g. wax from candles.

dropsy /ˈdrɒpsɪ/ *n.* (*pl.* -ies) **1** = OEDEMA. **2** *sl.* a tip or bribe. □□ **dropsical** *adj.* (in sense 1). [ME f. *idrop(e)sie* f. OF *idropesie* ult. f. L *hydropisis* f. Gk *hudrōps* dropsy (as HYDRO-)]

dropwort /ˈdrɒpwɜːt/ *n.* a plant, *Filipendula vulgaris*, with tuberous root fibres.

droshky /ˈdrɒʃkɪ/ *n.* (*pl.* -ies) a Russian low four-wheeled open carriage. [Russ. *drozhki* dimin. of *drogi* wagon f. *droga* shaft]

drosophila /drəˈsɒfɪlə/ *n.* any fruit fly of the genus *Drosophila*, used extensively in genetic research. [mod.L f. Gk *drosos* dew, moisture + *philos* loving]

dross /drɒs/ *n.* **1** rubbish, refuse. **2 a** the scum separated from metals in melting. **b** foreign matter mixed with anything; impurities. □□ **drossy** *adj.* [OE *drōs*: cf. MLG *drōsem*, OHG *truosana*]

drought /draʊt/ *n.* **1** the continuous absence of rain; dry weather. **2** the prolonged lack of something. **3** *archaic* a lack of moisture; thirst; dryness. □□ **droughty** *adj.* [OE *drūgath* f. *drȳge* DRY]

drouth /draʊθ/ *n.* Sc., Ir., US, & *poet.* var. of DROUGHT.

drove[1] *past of* DRIVE.

drove[2] /drəʊv/ *n.* **1 a** a large number (of people etc.) moving together; a crowd; a multitude; a shoal. **b** (in *pl.*) *colloq.* a great number (*people arrived in droves*). **2** a herd or flock being driven or moving together. □ **drove-road** an ancient cattle track. [OE *drāf* f. *drīfan* DRIVE]

drover /ˈdrəʊvə(r)/ *n.* a person who drives herds to market; a cattle-dealer. □□ **drove** *v.tr.* **droving** *n.*

drown /draʊn/ *v.* **1** *tr.* & *intr.* kill or be killed by submersion in liquid. **2** *tr.* submerge; flood; drench (*drowned the fields in six feet of water*). **3** *tr.* (often foll. by *in*) deaden (grief etc.) with drink (*drowned his sorrows in drink*). **4** *tr.* (often foll. by *out*) make (a sound) inaudible by means of a louder sound. □ **drowned valley** a valley partly or wholly submerged by a change in land-levels. **drown out** drive out by flood. **like a drowned rat** *colloq.* extremely wet and bedraggled. [ME (orig. north.) *drun(e)*, *droun(e)*, perh. f. OE *drūnian* (unrecorded), rel. to DRINK]

drowse /draʊz/ *v.* & *n.* —*v.* **1** *intr.* be dull and sleepy or half asleep. **2** *tr.* **a** (often foll. by *away*) pass (the time) in drowsing. **b** make drowsy. **3** *intr.* *archaic* be sluggish. —*n.* a condition of sleepiness. [back-form. f. DROWSY]

drowsy /ˈdraʊzɪ/ *adj.* (**drowsier**, **drowsiest**) **1** half asleep; dozing. **2** soporific; lulling. **3** sluggish. □□ **drowsily** *adv.* **drowsiness** *n.* [prob. rel. to OE *drūsian* be languid or slow, *drēosan* fall: cf. DREARY]

drub /drʌb/ *v.tr.* (**drubbed**, **drubbing**) **1** thump; belabour. **2** beat in a fight. **3** (usu. foll. by *into*, *out of*) beat (an idea, attitude, etc.) into or out of a person. □□ **drubbing** *n.* [ult. f. Arab. *ḍaraba* beat]

drudge /drʌdʒ/ *n.* & *v.* —*n.* a servile worker, esp. at menial tasks; a hack. —*v.intr.* (often foll. by *at*) work slavishly (at menial, hard, or dull work). □□ **drudgery** /ˈdrʌdʒərɪ/ *n.* [15th c.: perh. rel. to DRAG]

drug /drʌg/ *n.* & *v.* —*n.* **1** a medicinal substance. **2** a narcotic, hallucinogen, or stimulant, esp. one causing addiction. —*v.* (**drugged**, **drugging**) **1** *tr.* add a drug to (food or drink). **2** *tr.* **a** administer a drug to. **b** stupefy with a drug. **3** *intr.* take drugs as an addict. □ **drug addict** a person who is addicted to a narcotic drug. **drug on the market** a commodity that is plentiful but no longer in demand. **drug peddler** (*colloq.* **pusher**) a person who sells esp. addictive drugs illegally. **drug squad** a division of a police force investigating crimes involving illegal drugs. [ME *drogges*, *drouges* f. OF *drogue*, of unkn. orig.]

drugget /ˈdrʌgɪt/ *n.* **1** a coarse woven fabric used as a floor or table covering. **2** such a covering. [F *droguet*, of unkn. orig.]

druggist /ˈdrʌgɪst/ *n.* esp. *US* a pharmacist. [F *droguiste* (as DRUG)]

druggy /ˈdrʌgɪ/ *n.* & *adj.* *colloq.* —*n.* (also **druggie**) (*pl.* -ies) a drug addict. —*adj.* of or associated with narcotic drugs.

drugstore /ˈdrʌgstɔː(r)/ *n.* *US* a chemist's shop also selling light refreshments and other articles.

Druid /ˈdruːɪd/ *n.* (*fem.* **Druidess**) **1** an ancient Celtic priest, magician, or soothsayer of Gaul, Britain, or Ireland. **2** a member of a Welsh etc. Druidic order, esp. the Gorsedd. □□ **Druidism** *n.* **Druidic** /-ˈɪdɪk/ *adj.* **Druidical** /-ˈɪdɪk(ə)l/ *adj.* [F *druide* or L pl. *druidae*, *-des*, Gk *druidai* f. Gaulish *druides*]

drum[1] /drʌm/ *n.* & *v.* —*n.* **1 a** a percussion instrument or toy made of a hollow cylinder or hemisphere covered at one or both ends with stretched skin or parchment and sounded by striking (*bass drum*; *kettledrum*). **b** (often in *pl.*) a drummer or a percussion section (*the drums are playing too loud*). **c** a sound made by or resembling that of a drum. **2** something resembling a drum in shape, esp.: **a** a cylindrical container or receptacle for oil, dried fruit, etc. **b** a cylinder or barrel in machinery on which something is wound etc. **c** *Archit.* the solid part of a Corinthian or composite capital. **d** *Archit.* a stone block forming a section of a shaft. **e** *Austral.* & *NZ* swag, a bundle. **3** *Zool.* & *Anat.* the membrane of the middle ear; the eardrum. **4** *sl.* **a** a house. **b** a nightclub. **c** a brothel. **5** (in full **drum-fish**) any marine fish of the family Sciaenidae, having a swim-bladder that produces a drumming sound. **6** *hist.* an evening or afternoon tea party. **7** *Austral. sl.* a piece of reliable information, esp. a racing tip. —*v.* (**drummed**, **drumming**) **1** *intr.* & *tr.* play on a drum. **2** *tr.* & *intr.* beat, tap, or thump (knuckles, feet, etc.) continuously (on something) (*drummed on the table*; *drummed his feet*; *drumming at the window*). **3** *intr.* (of a bird or an insect) make a loud, hollow noise with quivering wings. **4** *tr.* *Austral. sl.* provide with reliable information. □ **drum brake** a brake in which shoes on a vehicle press against the drum on a wheel. **drum into** drive (a lesson) into (a person) by persistence. **drum machine** an electronic device that imitates the sound of percussion instruments. **drum major 1** the leader of a marching band. **2** *archaic* an NCO commanding the drummers of a regiment. **drum majorette** esp. *US* a member of a female baton-twirling parading group. **drum out** *Mil.* cashier (a soldier) by the beat of a drum; dismiss with ignominy. **drum up** summon, gather, or call up (*needs to drum up more support*). [obs. *drombslade*, *drombyllsclad*, f. LG *trommelslag* drum-beat f. *trommel* drum + *slag* beat]

drum[2] /drʌm/ *n.* (also **drumlin** /ˈdrʌmlɪn/) *Geol.* a long oval mound of boulder clay moulded by glacial action. □□ **drumlinoid** *n.* [Gael. & Ir. *druim* ridge: *-lin* perh. for -LING[1]]

drumfire /ˈdrʌmfaɪə(r)/ *n.* **1** *Mil.* heavy continuous rapid artillery fire, usu. heralding an infantry attack. **2** a barrage of criticism etc.

drumhead /ˈdrʌmhed/ *n.* **1** the skin or membrane of a drum. **2** an eardrum. **3** the circular top of a capstan. **4** (*attrib.*) improvised (*drumhead court martial*).

drumlin var. of DRUM[2].

drummer /ˈdrʌmə(r)/ *n.* **1** a person who plays a drum or drums. **2** esp. *US* *colloq.* a commercial traveller. **3** *sl.* a thief.

drumstick /ˈdrʌmstɪk/ *n.* **1** a stick used for beating a drum. **2** the lower joint of the leg of a cooked chicken, turkey, etc.

drunk /drʌŋk/ *adj.* & *n.* —*adj.* **1** rendered incapable by alcohol (*blind drunk*; *dead drunk*; *drunk as a lord*). **2** (often foll. by *with*) overcome or elated with joy, success, power, etc. —*n.* **1** a habitually drunk person. **2** *sl.* a drinking-bout; a period of drunkenness. [past part. of DRINK]

drunkard /'drʌŋkəd/ *n.* a person who is drunk, esp. habitually.

drunken /'drʌŋkən/ *adj.* (usu. *attrib.*) **1** = DRUNK. **2** caused by or exhibiting drunkenness (*a drunken brawl*). **3** fond of drinking; often drunk. □□ **drunkenly** *adv.* **drunkenness** *n.*

drupe /dru:p/ *n.* any fleshy or pulpy fruit enclosing a stone containing one or a few seeds, e.g. an olive, plum, or peach. □□ **drupaceous** /-'peɪʃəs/ *adj.* [L *drupa* f. Gk *druppa* olive]

drupel /'dru:p(ə)l/ *n.* (also **drupelet** /'dru:plɪt/) a small drupe usu. in an aggregate fruit, e.g. a blackberry or raspberry.

Druse /dru:z/ *n.* (often *attrib.*) a member of a political or religious sect linked with Islam and living near Mt. Lebanon (*Druse militia*). [F f. Arab. *durūz* (pl.), prob. f. their founder *al-Darazī* (11th c.)]

druse /dru:z/ *n.* **1** a crust of crystals lining a rock-cavity. **2** a cavity lined with this. [F f. G, = weathered ore]

dry /draɪ/ *adj., v., & n. —adj.* (**drier** /'draɪə(r)/; **driest** /'draɪɪst/) **1** free from moisture, not wet, esp.: **a** with any moisture having evaporated, drained, or been wiped away (*the clothes are not dry yet*). **b** (of the eyes) free from tears. **c** (of a climate etc.) with insufficient rainfall; not rainy (*a dry spell*). **d** (of a river, well, etc.) dried up; not yielding water. **e** (of a liquid) having disappeared by evaporation etc. **f** not connected with or for use without moisture (*dry shampoo*). **g** (of a shave) with an electric razor. **2** (of wine etc.) not sweet (*dry sherry*). **3 a** meagre, plain, or bare (*dry facts*). **b** uninteresting; dull (*dry as dust*). **4** (of a sense of humour, a joke, etc.) subtle, ironic, and quietly expressed; not obvious. **5** (of a country, of legislation, etc.) prohibiting the sale of alcoholic drink. **6** (of toast, bread, etc.) without butter, margarine, etc. **7** (of provisions, groceries, etc.) solid, not liquid (*dry goods*). **8** impassive, unsympathetic; hard; cold. **9** (of a cow etc.) not yielding milk. **10** *colloq.* thirsty or thirst-making (*feel dry; this is dry work*). **11** *Polit. colloq.* of or being a political 'dry'. *—v.* (**dries, dried**) **1** *tr. & intr.* make or become dry by wiping, evaporation, draining, etc. **2** *tr.* (usu. as **dried** *adj.*) preserve (food etc.) by removing the moisture (*dried egg; dried fruit; dried flowers*). **3** *intr.* (often foll. by *up*) *Theatr. colloq.* forget one's lines. **4** *tr. & intr.* (often foll. by *off*) cease or cause (a cow etc.) to cease yielding milk. *—n.* (*pl.* **dries**) **1** the process or an instance of drying. **2** *sl.* a politician, esp. a Conservative, who advocates individual responsibility, free trade, and economic stringency, and opposes high government spending. **3 a** (prec. by *the*) esp. *Austral. colloq.* the dry season. **b** *Austral.* a desert area, waterless country. **4 a** dry ginger ale. **b** dry wine, sherry, etc. □**dry battery** *Electr.* an electric battery consisting of dry cells. **dry cell** *Electr.* a cell in which the electrolyte is absorbed in a solid and cannot be spilled. **dry-clean** clean (clothes etc.) with organic solvents without using water. **dry-cleaner** a firm that specializes in dry-cleaning. **dry cough** a cough not producing phlegm. **dry-cure** cure (meat etc.) without pickling in liquid. **dry dock** an enclosure for the building or repairing of ships, from which water can be pumped out. **dry-fly** *adj.* (of fishing) with an artificial fly floating on the surface. *—v.intr.* (**-flies, -flied**) fish by such a method. **dry ice** solid carbon dioxide. **dry land** land as opposed to the sea, a river, etc. **dry measure** a measure of capacity for dry goods. **dry milk** *US* dried milk. **dry-nurse** a nurse for young children, not required to breast-feed. **dry out 1** become fully dry. **2** (of a drug addict, alcoholic, etc.) undergo treatment to cure addiction. **dry-plate** *Photog.* a photographic plate with sensitized film hard and dry for convenience of keeping, developing at leisure, etc. **dry-point 1** a needle for engraving on a bare copper plate without acid. **2** an engraving produced with this. **dry rot 1** a decayed state of

wood when not ventilated, caused by certain fungi. **2** these fungi. **dry run** *colloq.* a rehearsal. **dry-salt** = *dry-cure*. **dry-salter** a dealer in dyes, gums, drugs, oils, pickles, tinned meats, etc. **dry-shod** without wetting the shoes. **dry up 1** make utterly dry. **2** dry dishes. **3** (of moisture) disappear utterly. **4** (of a well etc.) cease to yield water. **5** *colloq.* (esp. in *imper.*) cease talking. **go dry** enact legislation for the prohibition of alcohol. □□ **dryish** *adj.* **dryness** *n.* [OE *drŷge, drygan,* rel. to MLG *dröge,* MDu. *dröghe,* f. Gmc]

dryad /'draɪæd, 'draɪəd/ *n. Mythol.* a nymph inhabiting a tree; a wood nymph. [ME f. OF *dryade* f. L f. Gk *druas -ados* f. *drus* tree]

dryer var. of DRIER[2].

dryly var. of DRILY.

drystone /'draɪstəʊn/ *adj.* (of a wall etc.) built without mortar.

DS *abbr.* **1** dal segno. **2** disseminated sclerosis.

DSC *abbr.* Distinguished Service Cross.

D.Sc. *abbr.* Doctor of Science.

DSM *abbr.* Distinguished Service Medal.

DSO *abbr.* (in the UK) Distinguished Service Order.

DSS *abbr.* (in the UK) Department of Social Security (formerly DHSS).

DT *abbr.* (also **DT's** /di:'ti:z/) delirium tremens.

DTI *abbr.* (in the UK) Department of Trade and Industry.

dual /'dju:əl/ *adj., n., & v. —adj.* **1** of two; twofold. **2** divided in two; double (*dual ownership*). **3** *Gram.* (in some languages) denoting two persons or things (additional to singular and plural). *—n.* (also **dual number**) *Gram.* a dual form of a noun, verb, etc. *—v.tr.* (**dualled, dualling**) *Brit.* convert (a road) into a dual carriageway. □**dual carriageway** *Brit.* a road with a dividing strip between the traffic in opposite directions. **dual control** (of a vehicle or an aircraft) having two sets of controls, one of which is used by the instructor. **dual in-line package** *Computing* see DIP. **dual-purpose** (of a vehicle) usable for passengers or goods. □□ **duality** /-'ælɪtɪ/ *n.* **dualize** *v.tr.* (also **-ise**). **dually** *adv.* [L *dualis* f. *duo* two]

dualism /'dju:ə,lɪz(ə)m/ *n.* **1** being twofold; duality. **2** *Philos.* the theory that in any domain of reality there are two independent underlying principles, e.g. mind and matter, form and content (cf. IDEALISM, MATERIALISM). **3** *Theol.* **a** the theory that the forces of good and evil are equally balanced in the universe. **b** the theory of the dual (human and divine) personality of Christ. □□ **dualist** *n.* **dualistic** /-'lɪstɪk/ *adj.* **dualistically** /-'lɪstɪkəlɪ/ *adv.*

dub[1] /dʌb/ *v.tr.* (**dubbed, dubbing**) **1** make (a person) a knight by touching his shoulders with a sword. **2** give (a person) a name, nickname, or title (*dubbed him a crank*). **3** *Brit.* dress (an artificial fishing-fly). **4** smear (leather) with grease. [OE f. AF *duber, aduber,* OF *adober* equip with armour, repair, of unkn. orig.]

dub[2] /dʌb/ *v.tr.* (**dubbed, dubbing**) **1** provide (a film etc.) with an alternative soundtrack, esp. in a different language. **2** add (sound effects or music) to a film or a broadcast. **3** combine (soundtracks) into one. **4** transfer or make a copy of (a soundtrack). [abbr. of DOUBLE]

dub[3] /dʌb/ *n.* esp. *US sl.* an inexperienced or unskilful person. [perh. f. DUB[1] in sense 'beat flat']

dub[4] /dʌb/ *v.intr.* (**dubbed, dubbing**) *sl.* (foll. by *in, up*) pay up; contribute money. [19th c.: orig. uncert.]

dubbin /'dʌbɪn/ *n. & v. —n.* (also **dubbing** /'dʌbɪŋ/) prepared grease for softening and waterproofing leather. *—v.tr.* (**dubbined, dubbining**) apply dubbin to (boots etc.). [see DUB[1] 4]

dubbing /'dʌbɪŋ/ *n.* an alternative soundtrack to a film etc.

dubiety /dju:'baɪətɪ/ *n.* (*pl.* **-ies**) *literary* **1** a feeling of doubt. **2** a doubtful matter. [LL *dubietas* f. *dubium* doubt]

dubious /'dju:bɪəs/ adj. **1** hesitating or doubting (*dubious about going*). **2** of questionable value or truth (*a dubious claim*). **3** unreliable; suspicious (*dubious company*). **4** of doubtful result (*a dubious undertaking*). □□ **dubiously** adv. **dubiousness** n. [L *dubiosus* f. *dubium* doubt]

dubitation /ˌdju:bɪ'teɪʃ(ə)n/ n. literary doubt, hesitation. [ME f. OF *dubitation* or L *dubitatio* f. *dubitare* DOUBT]

dubitative /'dju:bɪtətɪv/ adj. literary of, expressing, or inclined to doubt or hesitation. □□ **dubitatively** adv. [F *dubitatif* -*ive* or LL *dubitativus* (as DUBITATION)]

Dublin Bay prawn /'dʌblɪn/ n. **1** the Norway lobster. **2** (in pl.) scampi. [*Dublin* in Ireland]

Dubonnet /dju:'bɒneɪ/ n. propr. **1** a sweet French aperitif. **2** a glass of this. [name of a family of French wine-merchants]

ducal /'dju:k(ə)l/ adj. of, like, or bearing the title of a duke. [F f. *duc* DUKE]

ducat /'dʌkət/ n. **1** hist. a gold coin, formerly current in most European countries. **2 a** a coin. **b** (in pl.) money. [ME f. It. *ducato* or med.L *ducatus* DUCHY]

Duce /'du:tʃeɪ/ n. a leader, esp. (**Il Duce**) the title assumed by Mussolini (d. 1945). [It., = leader]

duchess /'dʌtʃɪs/ n. (as a title usu. **Duchess**) **1** a duke's wife or widow. **2** a woman holding the rank of duke in her own right. [ME f. OF *duchesse* f. med.L *ducissa* (as DUKE)]

duchesse /du:'ʃes, 'dʌtʃɪs/ n. **1** a soft heavy kind of satin. **2** a dressing-table with a pivoting mirror. □ **duchesse lace** a kind of Brussels pillow-lace. **duchesse potatoes** mashed potatoes mixed with egg, baked or fried, and served as small cakes. **duchesse set** a cover or a set of covers for a dressing-table. [F, = DUCHESS]

duchy /'dʌtʃɪ/ n. (pl. -**ies**) **1** the territory of a duke or duchess; a dukedom. **2** (often as **the Duchy**) the royal dukedom of Cornwall or Lancaster, each with certain estates, revenues, and jurisdiction of its own. [ME f. OF *duché(e)* f. med.L *ducatus* f. L *dux ducis* leader]

duck[1] /dʌk/ n. (pl. same or **ducks**) **1 a** any of various swimming-birds of the family Anatidae, esp. the domesticated form of the mallard or wild duck. **b** the female of this (opp. DRAKE). **c** the flesh of a duck as food. **2** Cricket (in full **duck's-egg**) the score of a batsman dismissed for nought. **3** (also **ducks**) Brit. colloq. (esp. as a form of address) dear, darling. □ **duck-hawk 1** Brit. a marsh-harrier. **2** US a peregrine. **ducks and drakes** a game of making a flat stone skim along the surface of water. **duck's arse** sl. a haircut with the hair on the back of the head shaped like a duck's tail. **duck soup** US sl. an easy task. **like a duck to water** adapting very readily. **like water off a duck's back** colloq. (of remonstrances etc.) producing no effect. **play ducks and drakes with** colloq. squander. [OE *duce, dūce*; rel. to DUCK[2]]

duck[2] /dʌk/ v. & n. —v. **1** intr. & tr. plunge, dive, or dip under water and emerge (*ducked him in the pond*). **2** intr. & tr. bend (the head or the body) quickly to avoid a blow or being seen, or as a bow or curtsy; bob (*ducked out of sight*; *ducked his head under the beam*). **3** tr. & intr. colloq. avoid or dodge; withdraw (from) (*ducked out of the engagement*; *ducked the meeting*). **4** intr. Bridge lose a trick deliberately by playing a low card. —n. **1** a quick dip or swim. **2** a quick lowering of the head etc. □ **ducking-stool** hist. a chair fastened to the end of a pole, which could be plunged into a pond, used formerly for ducking scolds etc. □□ **ducker** n. [OE *dūcan* (unrecorded) f. Gmc]

duck[3] /dʌk/ n. **1** a strong untwilled linen or cotton fabric used for small sails and the outer clothing of sailors. **2** (in pl.) trousers made of this (*white ducks*). [MDu. *doek*, of unkn. orig.]

duck[4] /dʌk/ n. colloq. an amphibious landing-craft. [DUKW, its official designation]

duckbill /'dʌkbɪl/ n. (also **duck-billed platypus**) = PLATYPUS.

duckboard /'dʌkbɔːd/ n. (usu. in pl.) a path of wooden slats placed over muddy ground or in a trench.

duckling /'dʌklɪŋ/ n. **1** a young duck. **2** its flesh as food.

duckweed /'dʌkwiːd/ n. any of various aquatic plants, esp. of the genus *Lemna*, growing on the surface of still water.

ducky /'dʌkɪ/ n. & adj. Brit. colloq. —n. (pl. -**ies**) darling, dear. —adj. sweet, pretty; splendid.

duct /dʌkt/ n. & v. —n. **1** a channel or tube for conveying fluid, cable, etc. **2 a** a tube in the body conveying secretions such as tears etc. **b** Bot. a tube formed by cells that have lost their intervening end walls, holding air, water, etc. —v.tr. convey through a duct. [L *ductus* leading, aqueduct f. *ducere duct-* lead]

ductile /'dʌktaɪl/ adj. **1** (of a metal) capable of being drawn into wire; pliable, not brittle. **2** (of a substance) easily moulded. **3** (of a person) docile, gullible. □□ **ductility** /-'tɪlɪtɪ/ n. [ME f. OF *ductile* or L *ductilis* f. *ducere duct-* lead]

ducting /'dʌktɪŋ/ n. **1** a system of ducts. **2** material in the form of a duct or ducts.

ductless /'dʌktlɪs/ adj. lacking or not using a duct or ducts. □ **ductless gland** a gland secreting directly into the bloodstream: also called *endocrine gland*.

dud /dʌd/ n. & adj. sl. —n. **1** a futile or ineffectual person or thing (*a dud at the job*). **2** a counterfeit article. **3** a shell etc. that fails to explode. **4** (in pl.) clothes. —adj. **1** useless, worthless, unsatisfactory or futile. **2** counterfeit. [ME: orig. unkn.]

dude /dju:d, du:d/ n. US sl. **1** a fastidious aesthetic person, esp. male; a dandy. **2** a holiday-maker on a ranch in the western US, esp. when unused to ranch life. **3** a fellow; a guy. □ **dude ranch** a cattle ranch converted to a holiday centre for tourists etc. □□ **dudish** adj. [19th c.: prob. f. G dial. *dude* fool]

dudgeon /'dʌdʒ(ə)n/ n. a feeling of offence; resentment. □ **in high dudgeon** very angry or angrily. [16th c.: orig. unkn.]

due /dju:/ adj., n., & adv. —adj. **1** (predic.) owing or payable as a debt or an obligation (*our thanks are due to him*; *£500 was due on the 15th*). **2** (often foll. by to) merited; appropriate; fitting (*his due reward*; *received the applause due to a hero*). **3** rightful; proper; adequate (*after due consideration*). **4** (predic.; foll. by to) to be ascribed to (a cause, an agent, etc.) (*the discovery was due to Newton*). **5** (predic.) intended to arrive at a certain time (*a train is due at 7.30*). **6** (foll. by to + infin.) under an obligation or agreement to do something (*due to speak tonight*). —n. **1** a person's right; what is owed to a person (*a fair hearing is my due*). **2** (in pl.) **a** what one owes (*pays his dues*). **b** a legally demandable toll or fee (*harbour dues*; *university dues*). —adv. (of a point of the compass) exactly, directly (*went due east*; *a due north wind*). □ **due to** disp. because of, owing to (*was late due to an accident*) (cf. sense 4 of adj.). **fall** (or **become**) **due** (of a bill etc.) be immediately payable. **in due course 1** at about the appropriate time. **2** in the natural order. [ME f. OF *deü* ult. f. L *debitus* past part. of *debēre* owe]

duel /'dju:əl/ n. & v. —n. **1** hist. a contest with deadly weapons between two people, in the presence of two seconds, to settle a point of honour. **2** any contest between two people, parties, causes, animals, etc. (*a duel of wits*). —v.intr. (**duelled**, **duelling**; US **dueled**, **dueling**) fight a duel or duels. □□ **dueller** n. (US **dueler**). **duellist** n. (US **duelist**). [It. *duello* or L *duellum* (archaic form of *bellum* war), in med.L = single combat]

duende /duˈendɪ/ n. **1** an evil spirit. **2** inspiration. [Sp.]

duenna /djuːˈenə/ n. an older woman acting as a

governess and companion in charge of girls, esp. in a Spanish family; a chaperon. [Sp. *dueña* f. L *domina* mistress]

duet /dju:'et/ *n.* **1** *Mus.* **a** a performance by two voices, instrumentalists, etc. **b** a composition for two performers. **2** a dialogue. □□ **duettist** *n.* [G *Duett* or It. *duetto* dimin. of *duo* duet f. L *duo* two]

duff[1] /dʌf/ *n.* a boiled pudding. [N.Engl. form of DOUGH]

duff[2] /dʌf/ *adj. Brit. sl.* **1** worthless, counterfeit. **2** useless, broken. [perh. = DUFF[1]]

duff[3] /dʌf/ *v.tr. sl.* **1** *Brit. Golf* mishit (a shot, a ball); bungle. **2** *Austral.* steal and alter brands on (cattle). □ **duff up** *sl.* beat; thrash. [perh. back-form. f. DUFFER]

duffer /'dʌfə(r)/ *n. sl.* **1** an inefficient, useless, or stupid person. **2** *Austral.* a person who duffs cattle. **3** *Austral.* an unproductive mine. [perh. f. Sc. *doofart* stupid person f. *douf* spiritless]

duffle /'dʌf(ə)l/ *n.* (also **duffel**) **1** a coarse woollen cloth with a thick nap. **2** *US* a sportsman's or camper's equipment. □ **duffle bag** a cylindrical canvas bag closed by a draw-string and carried over the shoulder. **duffle-coat** a hooded overcoat of duffle, usu. fastened with toggles. [*Duffel* in Belgium]

dug[1] *past* and *past part.* of DIG.

dug[2] /dʌg/ *n.* **1** the udder, breast, teat, or nipple of a female animal. **2** *derog.* the breast of a woman. [16th c.: orig. unkn.]

dugong /'du:gɒŋ/ *n.* (*pl.* same or **dugongs**) a marine mammal, *Dugong dugon*, of Asian seas and coasts. Also called *sea cow*. [ult. f. Malay *dūyong*]

dugout /'dʌgaʊt/ *n.* **1 a** a roofed shelter esp. for troops in trenches. **b** an underground air-raid or nuclear shelter. **2** a canoe made from a hollowed tree-trunk. **3** *sl.* a retired officer etc. recalled to service.

duiker /'daɪkə(r)/ *n.* **1** (also **duyker**) any African antelope of the genus *Cephalophus*, usu. having a crest of long hair between its horns. **2** *S.Afr.* the long-tailed cormorant, *Phalacrocorax africanus*. [Du. *duiker* diver: in sense 1, from plunging through bushes when pursued]

duke /dju:k/ *n.* (as a title usu. **Duke**) **1 a** a person holding the highest hereditary title of the nobility. **b** a sovereign prince ruling a duchy or small State. **2** (usu. in *pl.*) *sl.* the hand; the fist (*put up your dukes!*). **3** *Bot.* a kind of cherry, neither very sweet nor very sour. □ **royal duke** a duke who is also a royal prince. [ME f. OF *duc* f. L *dux ducis* leader]

dukedom /'dju:kdəm/ *n.* **1** a territory ruled by a duke. **2** the rank of duke.

dulcet /'dʌlsɪt/ *adj.* (esp. of sound) sweet and soothing. [ME, earlier *doucet* f. OF dimin. of *doux* f. L *dulcis* sweet]

dulcify /'dʌlsɪfaɪ/ *v.tr.* (**-ies, -ied**) *literary* **1** make gentle. **2** sweeten. □□ **dulcification** /-fɪ'keɪʃ(ə)n/ *n.* [L *dulcificare* f. *dulcis* sweet]

dulcimer /'dʌlsɪmə(r)/ *n.* a musical instrument with strings of graduated length stretched over a sounding-board or box, played by being struck with hammers. [OF *doulcemer*, said to repr. L *dulce* sweet, *melos* song]

dulcitone /'dʌlsɪtəʊn/ *n. Mus.* a keyboard instrument with steel tuning-forks which are struck by hammers. [L *dulcis* sweet + TONE]

dulia /'dju:lɪə/ *n. RC Ch.* the reverence accorded to saints and angels. [med.L f. Gk *douleia* servitude f. *doulos* slave]

dull /dʌl/ *adj. & v.* —*adj.* **1** slow to understand; stupid. **2** tedious; boring. **3** (of the weather) overcast; gloomy. **4 a** (esp. of a knife edge etc.) blunt. **b** (of colour, light, sound, or taste) not bright, vivid, or keen. **5** (of a pain etc.) usu. prolonged and indistinct; not acute (*a dull ache*). **6 a** (of a person, an animal, trade, etc.) sluggish, slow-moving, or stagnant. **b** (of a person) listless; depressed (*he's a dull fellow since the accident*). **7** (of the ears, eyes, etc.) without keen perception. —*v.tr. & intr.* make or become dull.

□ **dull the edge of** make less sensitive, interesting, effective, amusing, etc.; blunt. □□ **dullish** *adj.* **dullness** *n.* (also **dulness**). **dully** /'dʌllɪ/ *adv.* [ME f. MLG, MDu. *dul*, corresp. to OE *dol* stupid]

dullard /'dʌləd/ *n.* a stupid person.

dulse /dʌls/ *n.* an edible seaweed, *Rhodymenia palmata*, with red wedge-shaped fronds. [Ir. & Gael. *duileasg*]

duly /'dju:lɪ/ *adv.* **1** in due time or manner. **2** rightly, properly, fitly.

duma /'du:mə/ *n. hist.* a Russian council of State, esp. the elected body existing between 1905 and 1917. [Russ.: orig. an elective municipal council]

dumb /dʌm/ *adj.* **1 a** (of a person) unable to speak, usu. because of a congenital defect or deafness. **b** (of an animal) naturally unable to speak (*our dumb friends*). **2** silenced by surprise, shyness, etc. (*struck dumb by this revelation*). **3** taciturn or reticent, esp. insultingly (*dumb insolence*). **4** (of an action etc.) performed without speech. **5** (often in *comb.*) giving no sound; without voice or some other property normally belonging to things of the name (*a dumb piano*). **6** *colloq.* esp. *US* stupid; ignorant. **7** (usu. of a class, population, etc.) having no voice in government; inarticulate (*the dumb masses*). **8** (of a computer terminal etc.) able only to transmit data to or receive data from a computer; not programmable (opp. INTELLIGENT). □ **dumb animals** animals, esp. as objects of pity. **dumb-bell 1** a short bar with a weight at each end, used for exercise, muscle-building, etc. **2** *sl.* a stupid person, esp. a woman. **dumb blonde** a pretty but stupid blonde woman. **dumb cluck** *sl.* a stupid person. **dumb crambo** see CRAMBO. **dumb-iron** the curved side-piece of a motor-vehicle chassis, joining it to the front springs. **dumb piano** *Mus.* a silent or dummy keyboard. **dumb show 1** significant gestures or mime, used when words are inappropriate. **2** a part of a play in early drama, acted in mime. **dumb waiter 1** a small lift for carrying food, plates, etc., between floors. **2** a movable table, esp. with revolving shelves, used in a dining-room. □□ **dumbly** /'dʌmlɪ/ *adv.* **dumbness** /'dʌmnɪs/ *n.* [OE: orig. unkn.: sense 6 f. G *dumm*]

dumbfound /dʌm'faʊnd/ *v.tr.* (also **dumfound**) strike dumb; confound; nonplus. [DUMB, CONFOUND]

dumbhead /'dʌmhed/ *n.* esp. *US sl.* a stupid person.

dumbo /'dʌmbəʊ/ *n.* (*pl.* **-os**) *sl.* a stupid person; a fool. [DUMB + -o]

dumbstruck /'dʌmstrʌk/ *adj.* greatly shocked or surprised and so lost for words.

dumdum /'dʌmdʌm/ *n.* (in full **dumdum bullet**) a kind of soft-nosed bullet that expands on impact and inflicts laceration. [*Dum-Dum* in India, where it was first produced]

dummy /'dʌmɪ/ *n., adj., & v.* —*n.* (*pl.* **-ies**) **1** a model of a human being, esp.: **a** a ventriloquist's doll. **b** a figure used to model clothes in a shop window etc. **c** a target used for firearms practice. **2** (often *attrib.*) **a** a counterfeit object used to replace or resemble a real or normal one. **b** a prototype, esp. in publishing. **3** *colloq.* a stupid person. **4** a person taking no significant part; a figurehead. **5** *Brit.* a rubber or plastic teat for a baby to suck on. **6** an imaginary fourth player at whist, whose hand is turned up and played by a partner. **7** *Bridge* **a** the partner of the declarer, whose cards are exposed after the first lead. **b** this player's hand. **8** *Mil.* a blank round of ammunition. **9** *colloq.* a dumb person. —*adj.* sham; counterfeit. —*v.intr.* (**-ies, -ied**) *Football* make a pretended pass or swerve etc. □ **dummy run 1** a practice attack, etc.; a trial run. **2** a rehearsal. **dummy up** *US sl.* keep quiet; give no information. **sell the** (or **a**) **dummy** *Rugby Football colloq.* deceive (an opponent) by pretending to pass the ball. [DUMB + -Y[2]]

dump /dʌmp/ *n. & v.* —*n.* **1 a** a place for depositing rubbish. **b** a heap of rubbish. **2** *colloq.* an unpleasant or dreary place. **3** *Mil.* a temporary store of ammunition, provisions, etc. **4** an accumulated pile of ore, earth, etc. **5** *Computing* **a** a printout of stored data. **b** the process or result of dumping data. —*v.tr.* **1** put down firmly or clumsily (*dumped the shopping on the table*). **2** shoot or deposit (rubbish etc.). **3** *colloq.* abandon, desert. **4** *Mil.* leave (ammunition etc.) in a dump. **5** *Econ.* send (goods unsaleable at a high price in the home market) to a foreign market for sale at a low price, to keep up the price at home, and to capture a new market. **6** *Computing* **a** copy (stored data) to a different location. **b** reproduce the contents of (a store) externally. □**dump on** esp. *US* criticize or abuse; get the better of. **dump truck** a truck with a body that tilts or opens at the back for unloading. [ME perh. f. Norse; cf. Da. *dumpe*, Norw. *dumpa* fall suddenly]

dumper /'dʌmpə(r)/ *n.* **1** a person or thing that dumps. **2** *Austral.* & *NZ* a large wave that breaks and hurls the swimmer or surfer on to the beach.

dumpling /'dʌmplɪŋ/ *n.* **1 a** a small ball of usu. suet, flour, and water, boiled in stew or water, and eaten. **b** a pudding consisting of apple or other fruit enclosed in dough and baked. **2** a small fat person. [app. dimin., of *dump* small round object, but recorded much earlier]

dumps /dʌmps/ *n.pl. colloq.* depression; melancholy (*in the dumps*). [prob. f. LG or Du., fig. use of MDu. *domp* exhalation, haze, mist: rel. to DAMP]

dumpy /'dʌmpɪ/ *adj.* (**dumpier, dumpiest**) short and stout. □□ **dumpily** *adv.* **dumpiness** *n.* [*dump* (cf. DUMPLING) + -Y[1]]

dun[1] /dʌn/ *adj.* & *n.* —*adj.* **1** dull greyish-brown. **2** *poet.* dark, dusky. —*n.* **1** a dun colour. **2** a dun horse. **3** a dark fishing-fly. □**dun-bird** a pochard. **dun diver** a female or young male goosander. [OE *dun, dunn*]

dun[2] /dʌn/ *n.* & *v.* —*n.* **1** a debt-collector; an importunate creditor. **2** a demand for payment. —*v.tr.* (**dunned, dunning**) importune for payment of a debt; pester. [abbr. of obs. *dunkirk* privateer, f. *Dunkirk* in France]

dunce /dʌns/ *n.* a person slow at learning; a dullard. □**dunce's cap** a paper cone formerly put on the head of a dunce at school as a mark of disgrace. [John *Duns* Scotus, scholastic theologian d. 1308, whose followers were ridiculed by 16th-c. humanists and reformers as enemies of learning]

Dundee cake /dʌn'diː/ *n.* esp. *Brit.* a rich fruit cake usu. decorated with almonds. [*Dundee* in Scotland]

dunderhead /'dʌndəˌhed/ *n.* a stupid person. □□ **dunderheaded** *adj.* [17th c.: perh. rel. to dial. *dunner* resounding noise]

dune /djuːn/ *n.* a mound or ridge of loose sand etc. formed by the wind, esp. beside the sea or in a desert. □**dune buggy** = *beach buggy*. [F f. MDu. *dūne*: cf. DOWN[3]]

dung /dʌŋ/ *n.* & *v.* —*n.* the excrement of animals; manure. —*v.tr.* apply dung to; manure (land). □**dung-beetle** any of a family of beetles whose larvae develop in dung. **dung-fly** any of various flies feeding on dung. **dung-worm** any of various worms found in cow-dung and used as bait. [OE, rel. to OHG *tunga*, Icel. *dyngja*, of unkn. orig.]

dungaree /ˌdʌŋgəˈriː/ *n.* **1** a coarse Indian calico. **2** (in *pl.*) **a** overalls etc. made of dungaree or similar material, worn esp. by workers. **b** trousers with a bib worn by children or as a fashion garment. [Hindi *dungrī*]

dungeon /'dʌndʒ(ə)n/ *n.* & *v.* —*n.* **1** a strong underground cell for prisoners. **2** *archaic* a donjon. —*v.tr.* *archaic* (usu. foll. by *up*) imprison in a dungeon. [orig. = *donjon*: ME f. OF *donjon* ult. f. L *dominus* lord]

dunghill /'dʌŋhɪl/ *n.* a heap of dung or refuse, esp. in a farmyard.

dunk /dʌŋk/ *v.tr.* **1** dip (bread, a biscuit, etc.) into soup, coffee, etc. while eating. **2** immerse, dip (*was dunked in the river*). [Pennsylvanian G *dunke* to dip f. G *tunken*]

dunlin /'dʌnlɪn/ *n.* a long-billed sandpiper, *Calidris alpina*. [prob. f. DUN[1] + -LING[1]]

dunnage /'dʌnɪdʒ/ *n. Naut.* **1** mats, brushwood, etc. stowed under or among cargo to prevent wetting or chafing. **2** *colloq.* miscellaneous baggage. [AL *dennagium*, of unkn. orig.]

dunno /dəˈnəʊ/ *colloq.* (I) do not know. [corrupt.]

dunnock /'dʌnək/ *n. Brit.* the hedge sparrow. [app. f. DUN[1] + -OCK, from its brown and grey plumage]

dunny /'dʌnɪ/ *n.* (*pl.* -**ies**) **1** *Sc.* an underground passage or cellar, esp. in a tenement. **2** esp. *Austral.* & *NZ sl.* an earth-closet; an outdoor privy. [20th c.: orig. uncert.]

duo /'djuːəʊ/ *n.* (*pl.* -**os**) **1** a pair of actors, entertainers, singers, etc. (*a comedy duo*). **2** *Mus.* a duet. [It. f. L, = two]

duodecimal /ˌdjuːəʊˈdesɪm(ə)l/ *adj.* & *n.* —*adj.* relating to or using a system of numerical notation that has 12 as a base. —*n.* **1** the duodecimal system. **2** duodecimal notation. □□ **duodecimally** *adv.* [L *duodecimus* twelfth f. *duodecim* twelve]

duodecimo /ˌdjuːəʊˈdesɪˌməʊ/ *n.* (*pl.* -**os**) *Printing* **1** a book-size in which each leaf is one-twelfth of the size of the printing-sheet. **2** a book of this size. [L (*in*) *duodecimo* in a twelfth (as DUODECIMAL)]

duodenary /ˌdjuːəʊˈdiːnərɪ/ *adj.* proceeding by twelves or in sets of twelve. [L *duodenarius* f. *duodeni* distrib. of *duodecim* twelve]

duodenum /ˌdjuːəʊˈdiːnəm/ *n. Anat.* the first part of the small intestine immediately below the stomach. □□ **duodenal** *adj.* **duodenitis** /-'naɪtɪs/ *n.* [ME f. med.L f. *duodeni* (see DUODENARY) from its length of about 12 fingers' breadth]

duologue /'djuːəˌlɒg/ *n.* **1** a conversation between two people. **2** a play or part of a play for two actors. [irreg. f. L *duo* or Gk *duo* two, after *monologue*]

duomo /'dwəʊməʊ/ *n.* (*pl.* -**os**) an Italian cathedral. [It., = DOME]

duopoly /djuːˈɒpəlɪ/ *n.* (*pl.* -**ies**) *Econ.* the possession of trade in a commodity etc. by only two sellers. [Gk *duo* two + *pōleō* sell, after *monopoly*]

duotone /'djuːəˌtəʊn/ *n.* & *adj. Printing* —*n.* **1** a half-tone illustration in two colours from the same original with different screen angles. **2** the process of making a duotone. —*adj.* in two colours. [L *duo* two + TONE]

dupe /djuːp/ *n.* & *v.* —*n.* a victim of deception. —*v.tr.* make a fool of; cheat; gull. □□ **dupable** *adj.* **duper** *n.* **dupery** *n.* [F f. dial. F *dupe* hoopoe, from the bird's supposedly stupid appearance]

dupion /'djuːpɪən/ *n.* **1** a rough silk fabric woven from the threads of double cocoons. **2** an imitation of this with other fibres. [F *doupion* f. It. *doppione* f. *doppio* double]

duple /'djuːp(ə)l/ *adj.* of two parts. □**duple ratio** *Math.* a ratio of 2 to 1. **duple time** *Mus.* that with two beats to the bar. [L *duplus* f. *duo* two]

duplex /'djuːpleks/ *n.* & *adj.* —*n.* esp. *US* **1** a flat or maisonette on two levels. **2** a house subdivided for two families. —*adj.* **1** having two elements; twofold. **2** esp. *US* **a** (of a flat) two-storeyed. **b** (of a house) for two families. **3** *Computing* (of a circuit) allowing the transmission of signals in both directions simultaneously (opp. SIMPLEX). □**half-duplex** *Computing* (of a circuit) allowing the transmission of signals in both directions but not simultaneously. [L *duplex duplicis* f. *duo* two + *plic-* fold]

duplicate *adj., n.,* & *v.* —*adj.* /'djuːplɪkət/ **1** exactly like something already existing; copied (esp. in large numbers). **2 a** having two corresponding parts. **b** existing in two examples; paired. **c** twice as large or many; doubled. —*n.* /'djuːplɪkət/ **1 a** one of two identical things, esp. a copy of an original. **b** one of two or more specimens of a thing exactly or almost identical. **2** *Law* a second copy of a letter or document. **3** (in full **duplicate bridge** or **whist**) a form of bridge or whist in which the same hands are played successively by different players. **4** *archaic* a pawnbroker's ticket. —*v.tr.* /'dju:plɪˌkeɪt/ **1** multiply by two; double. **2 a** make or be an exact copy of. **b** make or supply copies of (*duplicated the leaflet for distribution*). **3** repeat (an action etc.), esp. unnecessarily. □**duplicate ratio** *Math.* the proportion of the squares of two numbers. **in duplicate** consisting of two exact copies. □□**duplicable** /-kəb(ə)l/ *adj.* **duplication** /-'keɪʃ(ə)n/ *n.* [L *duplicatus* past part. of *duplicare* (as DUPLEX)]

duplicator /'dju:plɪˌkeɪtə(r)/ *n.* **1** a machine for making copies of a document, leaflet, etc. **2** a person or thing that duplicates.

duplicity /dju:'plɪsɪtɪ/ *n.* **1** double-dealing; deceitfulness. **2** *archaic* doubleness. □□**duplicitous** *adj.* [ME f. OF *duplicité* or LL *duplicitas* (as DUPLEX)]

duppy /'dʌpɪ/ *n.* (*pl.* -**ies**) *W.Ind.* a malevolent spirit or ghost. [perh. of Afr. orig.]

dura var. of DURRA.

durable /'djʊərəb(ə)l/ *adj. & n.* —*adj.* **1** capable of lasting; hard-wearing. **2** (of goods) not for immediate consumption; able to be kept. —*n.* (in *pl.*) durable goods. □□**durability** /-'bɪlɪtɪ/ *n.* **durableness** *n.* **durably** *adv.* [ME f. OF f. L *durabilis* f. *durare* endure f. *durus* hard]

Duralumin /djʊə'ræljʊmɪn/ *n. propr.* a light hard alloy of aluminium with copper etc. [perh. f. *Düren* in the Rhineland or L *durus* hard + ALUMINIUM]

dura mater /ˌdjʊərə 'meɪtə(r)/ *n. Anat.* the tough outermost membrane enveloping the brain and spinal cord (see MENINX). [med.L = hard mother, transl. Arab. *al-'umm al-jāfiya* ('mother' in Arab. indicating the relationship of things)]

duramen /djʊə'reɪmen/ *n.* = HEARTWOOD. [L f. *durare* harden]

durance /'djʊərəns/ *n. archaic* imprisonment (*in durance vile*). [ME f. F f. *durer* last f. L *durare*: see DURABLE]

duration /djʊə'reɪʃ(ə)n/ *n.* **1** the length of time for which something continues. **2** a specified length of time (*after the duration of a minute*). □**for the duration 1** until the end of the war. **2** for a very long time. □□**durational** *adj.* [ME f. OF f. med.L *duratio -onis* (as DURANCE)]

durative /'djʊərətɪv/ *adj. Gram.* denoting continuing action.

durbar /'dɜ:bɑ:(r)/ *n. hist.* **1** the court of an Indian ruler. **2** a public levee of an Indian prince or an Anglo-Indian governor or viceroy. [Urdu f. Pers. *darbār* court]

durchkomponiert /'dʊəxˌkɒmpɒˌniət/ *adj. Mus.* (of a song) having different music for each verse. [G f. *durch* through + *komponiert* composed]

duress /djʊə'res, 'djʊə-/ *n.* **1** compulsion, esp. imprisonment, threats, or violence, illegally used to force a person to act against his or her will (*under duress*). **2** forcible restraint or imprisonment. [ME f. OF *duresse* f. L *duritia* f. *durus* hard]

Durex /'djʊəreks/ *n. propr.* a contraceptive sheath; a condom. [20th c.: orig. uncert.]

durian /'dʊərɪən/ *n.* **1** a large tree, *Durio zibethinus*, native to SE Asia, bearing oval spiny fruits containing a creamy pulp with a fetid smell and an agreeable taste. **2** this fruit. [Malay *durīan* f. *dūrī* thorn]

during /'djʊərɪŋ/ *prep.* **1** throughout the course or duration of (*read during the meal*). **2** at some point in the duration of (*came in during the evening*). [ME f. OF *durant* ult. f. L *durare* last, continue]

durmast /'dɜ:mɑ:st/ *n.* an oak tree, *Quercus petraea*, having sessile flowers. [*dur-* (perh. erron. for DUN[1]· + MAST[2]]

durn *US* var. of DARN[2].

durned *US* var. of DARNED.

durra /'dʌrə/ *n.* (also **dura**, **dhurra**) a kind of sorghum, *Sorghum vulgare*, native to Asia, Africa, and the US. [Arab. *dura*, *durra*]

durst /dɜ:st/ *archaic past* of DARE.

durum /'djʊərəm/ *n.* a kind of wheat, *Triticum turgidum*, having hard seeds and yielding a flour used in the manufacture of spaghetti etc. [L, neut. of *durus* hard]

durzi /'dɜ:zɪ/ *n.* (*pl.* **durzis**) an Indian tailor. [Hindi f. Pers. *darzī* f. *darz* sewing]

dusk /dʌsk/ *n., adj., & v.* —*n.* **1** the darker stage of twilight. **2** shade; gloom. —*adj. poet.* shadowy; dim; dark-coloured. —*v.tr. & intr. poet.* make or become shadowy or dim. [ME *dosk*, *dusk* f. OE *dox* dark, swarthy, *doxian* darken in colour]

dusky /'dʌskɪ/ *adj.* (**duskier**, **duskiest**) **1** shadowy; dim. **2** dark-coloured, darkish. □□**duskily** *adv.* **duskiness** *n.*

dust /dʌst/ *n. & v.* —*n.* **1 a** finely powdered earth, dirt, etc., lying on the ground or on surfaces, and blown about by the wind. **b** fine powder of any material (*pollen dust*; *gold-dust*). **c** a cloud of dust. **2** a dead person's remains (*honoured dust*). **3** confusion or turmoil (*raised quite a dust*). **4** *archaic* or *poet.* the mortal human body (*we are all dust*). **5** the ground; the earth (*kissed the dust*). —*v.* **1** *tr.* (also *absol.*) clear (furniture etc.) of dust etc. by wiping, brushing, etc. **2** *tr.* **a** sprinkle (esp. a cake) with powder, dust, sugar, etc. **b** sprinkle or strew (sugar, powder, etc.). **3** *tr.* make dusty. **4** *intr. archaic* (of a bird) take a dust-bath. □**dust and ashes** something very disappointing. **dust-bath** a bird's rolling in dust to freshen its feathers. **dust bowl** an area denuded of vegetation by drought or erosion and reduced to desert. **dust cover 1** = *dust-sheet*. **2** = *dust-jacket*. **dust devil** *S.Afr.* a whirlwind visible as a column of dust. **dust down 1** dust the clothes of (a person). **2** *colloq.* reprimand. **3** = *dust off*. **dusting-powder 1** talcum powder. **2** any dusting or drying powder. **dust-jacket** a usu. decorated paper cover used to protect a book from dirt etc. **dust off 1** remove the dust from (an object on which it has long been allowed to settle). **2** use and enjoy again after a long period of neglect. **dust-sheet** *Brit.* a cloth put over furniture to protect it from dust. **dust-shot** the smallest size of shot. **dust-storm** a storm with clouds of dust carried in the air. **dust-trap** something on, in, or under which dust gathers. **dust-up** *colloq.* a fight. **dust-wrapper** = *dust-jacket.* **in the dust 1** humiliated. **2** dead. **when the dust settles** when things quieten down. □□**dustless** *adj.* [OE *dūst*: cf. LG *dunst* vapour]

dustbin /'dʌstbɪn, 'dʌsbɪn/ *n. Brit.* a container for household refuse, esp. one kept outside.

dustcart /'dʌstkɑ:t/ *n. Brit.* a vehicle used for collecting household refuse.

duster /'dʌstə(r)/ *n.* **1 a** a cloth for dusting furniture etc. **b** a person or contrivance that dusts. **2** a woman's light, loose, full-length coat.

dustman /'dʌstmən, 'dʌsmən/ *n.* (*pl.* -**men**) *Brit.* **1** a man employed to clear household refuse. **2** the sandman.

dustpan /'dʌstpæn/ *n.* a small pan into which dust etc. is brushed from the floor.

dusty /'dʌstɪ/ *adj.* (**dustier**, **dustiest**) **1** full of, covered with, or resembling dust. **2** dry as dust; uninteresting. **3** (of a colour) dull or muted. □**dusty answer** a curt rejection of a request. **dusty miller 1** any of various plants, esp. *Artemisia stelleriana*, having white dust on the leaves and flowers. **2** an artificial fishing-fly. **not so dusty** *Brit. sl.* fairly good. □□**dustily** *adv.* **dustiness** *n.* [OE *dūstig* (as DUST)]

Dutch /dʌtʃ/ *adj. & n.* —*adj.* **1** of, relating to, or associated with the Netherlands. **2** *US sl.* German. **3** *S.Afr.* of Dutch descent. **4** *archaic* of Germany including the Netherlands. —*n.* **1 a** the language of the Netherlands. **b** *S.Afr.* usu. *derog.* Afrikaans. **2** (prec. by *the*; treated as *pl.*) **a** the people of the Netherlands. **b** *S.Afr.* Afrikaans-speakers. **3** *archaic* the language of Germany including the Netherlands.

□**beat the Dutch** *US colloq.* do something remarkable. **Dutch auction** see AUCTION. **Dutch bargain** a bargain concluded by drinking together. **Dutch barn** *Brit.* a barn roof over hay etc., set on poles and having no walls. **Dutch cap 1** a contraceptive diaphragm. **2** a woman's lace cap with triangular flaps on each side. **Dutch courage** false courage gained from alcohol. **Dutch doll** a jointed wooden doll. **Dutch door** a door divided into two parts horizontally allowing one part to be shut and the other open. **Dutch elm disease** a disease affecting elms caused by the fungus *Ceratocystis ulmi*, first found in the Netherlands. **Dutch hoe** a hoe pushed forward by the user. **Dutch interior** a painting of Dutch domestic life, esp. by P. de Hooch (d. 1683). **Dutch metal** a copper-zinc alloy imitating gold leaf. **Dutch oven 1** a metal box the open side of which is turned towards a fire. **2** a covered cooking pot for braising etc. **Dutch treat** a party, outing, etc. to which each person makes a contribution. **Dutch uncle** a person giving advice with benevolent firmness. **Dutch wife** a framework of cane etc., or a bolster, used for resting the legs in bed. **go Dutch** share expenses equally. [MDu. *dutsch* etc. Holland-ish, Netherlandish, German, OHG *diutisc* national]

dutch /dʌtʃ/ *n. Brit. sl.* a wife (esp. *old dutch*). [abbr. of *duchess* (also in this sense)]

Dutchman /ˈdʌtʃmən/ *n.* (*pl.* -**men**; *fem.* **Dutchwoman**, *pl.* -**women**) **1 a** a native or national of the Netherlands. **b** a person of Dutch descent. **2** a Dutch ship. **3** *US sl.* a German. □**Dutchman's breeches** *US* a plant, *Dicentra cucullaria*, with white flowers and finely divided leaves. **Flying Dutchman 1** a ghostly ship. **2** its captain. **I'm a Dutchman** expression of disbelief or refusal.

duteous /ˈdjuːtɪəs/ *adj. literary* (of a person or conduct) dutiful; obedient. □□**duteously** *adv.* **duteousness** *n.* [DUTY + -OUS: cf. *beauteous*]

dutiable /ˈdjuːtɪəb(ə)l/ *adj.* liable to customs or other duties.

dutiful /ˈdjuːtɪfʊl/ *adj.* doing or observant of one's duty; obedient. □□**dutifully** *adv.* **dutifulness** *n.*

duty /ˈdjuːtɪ/ *n.* (*pl.* -**ies**) **1 a** a moral or legal obligation; a responsibility (*his duty to report it*). **b** the binding force of what is right (*strong sense of duty*). **c** what is required of one (*do one's duty*). **2** payment to the public revenue, esp.: **a** that levied on the import, export, manufacture, or sale of goods (*customs duty*). **b** that levied on the transfer of property, licences, the legal recognition of documents, etc. (*death duty*; *probate duty*). **3** a job or function (*his duties as caretaker*). **4** the behaviour due to a superior; deference; respect. **5** the measure of an engine's effectiveness in units of work done per unit of fuel. **6** *Eccl.* the performance of church services. □**do duty for** serve as or pass for (something else). **duty-bound** obliged by duty. **duty-free** (of goods) on which duty is not leviable. **duty-free shop** a shop at an airport etc. at which duty-free goods can be bought. **duty-officer** the officer currently on duty. **duty-paid** (of goods) on which duty has been paid. **duty visit** a visit paid from obligation, not from pleasure. **on** (or **off**) **duty** engaged (or not engaged) in one's work. [AF *deweté*, *dueté* (as DUE)]

duumvir /djuːˈʌmvə(r), ˈdjuːəm-/ *n. Rom.Hist.* one of two coequal magistrates or officials. □□**duumvirate** /-vɪrət/ *n.* [L f. *duum virum* of the two men]

duvet /ˈduːveɪ/ *n.* a thick soft quilt with a detachable cover, used instead of an upper sheet and blankets. [F]

dux /dʌks/ *n. Sc., NZ,* & *S.Afr.* etc. the top pupil in a class or in a school. [L, = leader]

duyker var. of DUIKER 1.

DV *abbr.* Deo volente.

Dvr. *abbr.* Driver.

dwale /dweɪl/ *n.* = BELLADONNA 1. [prob. f. Scand.]

dwarf /dwɔːf/ *n.* & *v.* —*n.* (*pl.* **dwarfs** or **dwarves** /dwɔːvz/) **1 a** a person of abnormally small stature, esp. one with a normal-sized head and body but short limbs. ¶ The term *person of restricted growth* is now often preferred. **b** an animal or plant much below the ordinary size for the species. **2** a small mythological being with supernatural powers. **3** (in full **dwarf star**) a small usu. dense star. **4** (*attrib.*) **a** of a kind very small in size (*dwarf bean*). **b** puny, stunted. —*v.tr.* **1** stunt in growth. **2** cause (something similar or comparable) to seem small or insignificant (*efforts dwarfed by their rivals' achievements*). □□**dwarfish** *adj.* [OE *dweorg* f. Gmc]

dwarfism /ˈdwɔːfɪz(ə)m/ *n.* the condition of being a dwarf.

dwell /dwel/ *v.* & *n.* —*v.intr.* (*past* and *past part.* **dwelt** or **dwelled**) **1** *literary* (usu. foll. by *in, at, near, on,* etc.) live, reside (*dwelt in the forest*). **2** (of a horse) be slow in raising its feet; pause before taking a fence. —*n.* a slight, regular pause in the motion of a machine. □**dwell on** (or **upon**) **1** spend time on, linger over; write, brood, or speak at length on (a specified subject) (*always dwells on his grievances*). **2** prolong (a note, a syllable, etc.). □□**dweller** *n.* [OE *dwellan* lead astray, later 'continue in a place', f. Gmc]

dwelling /ˈdwelɪŋ/ *n.* (also **dwelling-place**) *formal* a house; a residence; an abode. □**dwelling-house** a house used as a residence, not as an office etc.

dwindle /ˈdwɪnd(ə)l/ *v.intr.* **1** become gradually smaller; shrink; waste away. **2** lose importance; decline; degenerate. [*dwine* fade away f. OE *dwīnan*, ON *dvina*]

dwt. *abbr. hist.* pennyweight.

d.w.t. *abbr.* dead-weight tonnage.

Dy *symb. Chem.* the element dysprosium.

dyad /ˈdaɪæd/ *n. Math.* an operator which is a combination of two vectors. □□**dyadic** /-ˈædɪk/ *adj.* [LL *dyas dyad-* f. Gk *duas duados* f. *duo* two]

Dyak /ˈdaɪæk/ *n.* (also **Dayak**) an aboriginal of Borneo or Sarawak. [Malay *dayak* up-country]

dyarchy var. of DIARCHY.

dybbuk /ˈdɪbʊk/ *n.* (*pl.* **dybbukim** /-kɪm/ or **dybbuks**) a malevolent spirit in Jewish folklore. [Heb. *dibbūk* f. *dābaḳ* cling]

dye /daɪ/ *n.* & *v.* —*n.* **1 a** a substance used to change the colour of hair, fabric, wood, etc. **b** a colour produced by this. **2** (in full **dyestuff**) a substance yielding a dye, esp. for colouring materials in solution. —*v.tr.* (**dyeing**) **1** impregnate with dye. **2** make (a thing) a specified colour with dye (*dyed it yellow*). □**dyed in the wool** (or **grain**) **1** out and out; unchangeable, inveterate. **2** (of a fabric) made of yarn dyed in its raw state. **dye-line** a print made by the diazo process. □□**dyeable** *adj.* [OE *deag, deagian*]

dyer /ˈdaɪə(r)/ *n.* a person who dyes cloth etc. □**dyer's broom** (or **greenweed** or **oak** etc.) names of plants yielding dyes.

dying /ˈdaɪɪŋ/ *adj.* connected with, or at the time of, death (*his dying words*). □**dying oath** an oath made at, or with the solemnity proper to, death. **to one's dying day** for the rest of one's life. [pres. part. of DIE¹]

dyke¹ /daɪk/ *n.* & *v.* (also **dike**) —*n.* **1** a long wall or embankment built to prevent flooding, esp. from the sea. **2 a** a ditch or artificial watercourse. **b** *Brit.* a natural watercourse. **3 a** a low wall, esp. of turf. **b** a causeway. **4** a barrier or obstacle; a defence. **5** *Geol.* an intrusion of igneous rock across sedimentary strata. **6** esp. *Austral. sl.* a lavatory. —*v.tr.* provide or defend with a dyke or dykes. [ME f. ON *dík* or MLG *dīk* dam, MDu. *dijc* ditch, dam: cf. DITCH]

dyke² /daɪk/ *n.* (also **dike**) *sl.* a lesbian. [20th c.: orig. unkn.]

dyn *abbr.* dyne.

dynamic /daɪˈnæmɪk/ *adj.* & *n.* —*adj.* (also **dynamical**) **1** energetic; active; potent. **2** *Physics* **a** concerning motive force (opp. STATIC). **b** concerning force in actual operation. **3** of or concerning dynamics. **4** *Mus.* relating to the volume of sound. **5** *Philos.* relating to dynamism. **6** (as **dynamical**) *Theol.* (of inspiration) endowing with divine power, not impelling mechanically. —*n.* **1** an energizing or motive force. **2** *Mus.* = DYNAMICS 3. □**dynamic equilibrium** see EQUILIBRIUM. **dynamic viscosity** see VISCOSITY. □□**dynamically** *adv.* [F *dynamique* f. Gk *dunamikos* f. *dunamis* power]

dynamics /daɪ'næmɪks/ *n.pl.* **1** (usu. treated as *sing.*) **a** *Mech.* the branch of mechanics concerned with the motion of bodies under the action of forces (cf. STATICS). **b** the branch of any science in which forces or changes are considered (*aerodynamics*; *population dynamics*). **2** the motive forces, physical or moral, affecting behaviour and change in any sphere. **3** *Mus.* the varying degree of volume of sound in musical performance. □□**dynamicist** /-sɪst/ *n.* (in sense 1).

dynamism /'daɪnə,mɪz(ə)m/ *n.* **1** energizing or dynamic action or power. **2** *Philos.* the theory that phenomena of matter or mind are due to the action of forces (rather than to motion or matter). □□ **dynamist** *n.* [Gk *dunamis* power + -ISM]

dynamite /'daɪnə,maɪt/ *n. & v.* —*n.* **1** a high explosive consisting of nitroglycerine mixed with an absorbent. **2** a potentially dangerous person, thing, or situation. **3** *sl.* a narcotic, esp. heroin. —*v.tr.* charge or shatter with dynamite. □□**dynamiter** *n.* [formed as DYNAMIS + -ITE[1]]

dynamo /'daɪnə,məʊ/ *n.* (*pl.* **-os**) **1** a machine converting mechanical into electrical energy, esp. by rotating coils of copper wire in a magnetic field. **2** *colloq.* an energetic person. [abbr. of *dynamo-electric machine* f. Gk *dunamis* power, force]

dynamometer /,daɪnə'mɒmɪtə(r)/ *n.* an instrument measuring energy expended. [F *dynamomètre* f. Gk *dunamis* power, force]

dynast /'dɪnæst, 'daɪ-/ *n.* **1** a ruler. **2** a member of a dynasty. [L f. Gk *dunastēs* f. *dunamai* be able]

dynasty /'dɪnəstɪ/ *n.* (*pl.* **-ies**) **1** a line of hereditary rulers. **2** a succession of leaders in any field. □□ **dynastic** /-'næstɪk/ *adj.* **dynastically** /-'næstɪkəlɪ/ *adv.* [F *dynastie* or LL *dynastia* f. Gk *dunasteia* lordship (as DYNAST)]

dynatron /'daɪnə,trɒn/ *n.* *Electronics* a thermionic valve, used to generate continuous oscillations. [Gk *dunamis* power + -TRON]

dyne /daɪn/ *n.* *Physics* a unit of force that, acting on a mass of one gram, increases its velocity by one centimetre per second every second along the direction that it acts. ¶ Abbr.: **dyn.** [F f. Gk *dunamis* force, power]

dys- /dɪs/ *comb. form* esp. *Med.* bad, difficult. [Gk *dus-* bad]

dysentery /'dɪsəntərɪ, -trɪ/ *n.* a disease with inflammation of the intestines, causing severe diarrhoea with blood and mucus. □□**dysenteric** /-'terɪk/ *adj.* [OF *dissenterie* or L *dysenteria* f. Gk *dusenteria* (as DYS-, *enteria* f. *entera* bowels)]

dysfunction /dɪs'fʌŋkʃ(ə)n/ *n.* an abnormality or impairment of function. □□**dysfunctional** *adj.*

dysgraphia /dɪs'græfɪə/ *n.* an inability to write coherently. □□**dysgraphic** *adj.* [DYS- + Gk *graphia* writing]

dyslexia /dɪs'leksɪə/ *n.* an abnormal difficulty in reading and spelling, caused by a condition of the brain. □□**dyslexic** *adj. & n.* **dyslectic** /-'lektɪk/ *adj. & n.* [G *Dyslexie* (as DYS-, Gk *lexis* speech)]

dysmenorrhoea /,dɪsmenə'rɪə/ *n.* painful or difficult menstruation.

dyspepsia /dɪs'pepsɪə/ *n.* indigestion. [L *dyspepsia* f. Gk *duspepsia* (as DYS-, *peptos* cooked, digested)]

dyspeptic /dɪs'peptɪk/ *adj. & n.* —*adj.* of or relating to dyspepsia or the resulting depression. —*n.* a person suffering from dyspepsia.

dysphasia /dɪs'feɪzɪə/ *n.* *Med.* lack of coordination in speech, owing to brain damage. □□**dysphasic** *adj.* [Gk *dusphatos* hard to utter (as DYS-, PHATIC)]

dysphoria /dɪs'fɔːrɪə/ *n.* a state of unease or mental discomfort. □□**dysphoric** /-'fɒrɪk/ *adj.* [Gk *dusphoria* f. *dusphoros* hard to bear (as DYS-, *pherō* bear)]

dysplasia /dɪs'pleɪzɪə/ *n.* *Med.* abnormal growth of tissues etc. □□**dysplastic** /-'plæstɪk/ *adj.* [mod.L, formed as DYS- + Gk *plasis* formation]

dyspnoea /dɪsp'niːə/ *n.* (*US* **dyspnea**) *Med.* difficult or laboured breathing. □□**dyspnoeic** *adj.* [L f. Gk *duspnoia* (as DYS-, *pneō* breathe)]

dysprosium /dɪs'prəʊzɪəm/ *n.* *Chem.* a naturally occurring soft metallic element of the lanthanide series, used as a component in certain magnetic alloys. ¶ Symb.: **Dy.** [mod.L f. Gk *dusprositos* hard to get at + -IUM]

dystocia /dɪs'təʊʃə/ *n.* *Med.* difficult or prolonged childbirth. [DYS- + Gk *tokos* childbirth]

dystrophy /'dɪstrəfɪ/ *n.* defective nutrition. □ **muscular dystrophy** a hereditary progressive weakening and wasting of the muscles. □□ **dystrophic** /dɪs'trɒfɪk/ *adj.* [mod.L *dystrophia* formed as DYS- + Gk *-trophia* nourishment]

dysuria /dɪs'jʊərɪə/ *n.* painful or difficult urination. [LL f. Gk *dusouria* (as DYS-, *ouron* urine)]

dzho /zəʊ/ *n.* (also **dzo, zho**) (*pl.* same or **-os**) a hybrid of a cow and a yak. [Tibetan *mdso*]

E

E^1 /iː/ *n.* (also **e**) (*pl.* **Es** or **E's**) **1** the fifth letter of the alphabet. **2** *Mus.* the third note of the diatonic scale of C major.

E^2 *abbr.* (also **E.**) **1** east, eastern. **2** Egyptian (*£E*). **3** Engineering (*M.I.Mech.E.* etc.). **4** see E-NUMBER.

e *symb.* **1** *Math.* the base of natural logarithms, equal to approx. 2.71828. **2** used on packaging (in conjunction with specification of weight, size, etc.) to indicate compliance with EEC regulations.

e- /ɪ, e/ *prefix* form of EX-^{1} 1 before some consonants.

ea. *abbr.* each.

each /iːtʃ/ *adj.* & *pron.* —*adj.* every one of two or more persons or things, regarded separately (*each person; five in each class*). —*pron.* each person or thing (*each of us; have two books each; cost a penny each*). □**each and every** every single. **each other** one another (used as a compound reciprocal pron.: *they hate each other; they wore each other's hats*). **each way** *Brit.* (of a bet) backing a horse etc. for both a win and a place. [OE *ǣlc* f. WG (as AYE, ALIKE)]

eager /ˈiːgə(r)/ *adj.* **1 a** full of keen desire, enthusiastic. **b** (of passions etc.) keen, impatient. **2** keen, impatient, strongly desirous (*eager to learn; eager for news*). □**eager beaver** *colloq.* a very or excessively diligent person. □□**eagerly** *adv.* **eagerness** *n.* [ME f. AF *egre*, OF *aigre* keen, ult. f. L *acer acris*]

eagle /ˈiːg(ə)l/ *n.* **1 a** any of various large birds of prey of the family Accipitridae, with keen vision and powerful flight. **b** a figure of an eagle, esp. as a symbol of the US, or formerly as a Roman or French ensign. **2** *Golf* a score of two strokes under par at any hole. **3** *US* a coin worth ten dollars. □**eagle eye** keen sight, watchfulness. **eagle-eyed** keen-sighted, watchful. **eagle owl** any large owl of the genus *Bubo*, with long ear tufts. [ME f. AF *egle*, OF *aigle* f. L *aquila*]

eaglet /ˈiːglɪt/ *n.* a young eagle.

eagre /ˈeɪgə(r), ˈiːgə(r)/ *n.* = BORE^3. [17th c.: orig. unkn.]

-ean /ˈiːən, ɪən/ *suffix* var. of -AN.

E. & O. E. *abbr.* errors and omissions excepted.

ear^1 /ɪə(r)/ *n.* **1 a** the organ of hearing and balance in man and vertebrates, esp. the external part of this. **b** an organ sensitive to sound in other animals. **2** the faculty for discriminating sounds (*an ear for music*). **3** an ear-shaped thing, esp. the handle of a jug. **4** listening, attention. □**all ears** listening attentively. **bring about one's ears** bring down upon oneself. **ear-drops 1** medicinal drops for the ear. **2** hanging earrings. **ear lobe** the lower soft pendulous external part of the ear. **ear-piercing** loud and shrill. **ear-splitting** excessively loud. **ear-trumpet** a trumpet-shaped device formerly used as a hearing-aid. **give ear to** listen to. **have a person's ear** receive a favourable hearing. **have** (or **keep**) **an ear to the ground** be alert to rumours or the trend of opinion. **in one ear and out the other** heard but disregarded or quickly forgotten. **out on one's ear** dismissed ignominiously. **up to one's ears** (often foll. by *in*) *colloq.* deeply involved or occupied. □□ **eared** *adj.* (also in *comb.*). **earless** *adj.* [OE *ēare* f. Gmc: rel. to L *auris*, Gk *ous*]

ear^2 /ɪə(r)/ *n.* the seed-bearing head of a cereal plant. [OE *ēar* f. Gmc]

earache /ˈɪəreɪk/ *n.* a (usu. prolonged) pain in the ear.

earbash /ˈɪəbæʃ/ *v.tr.* esp. *Austral. sl.* talk inordinately to; harangue. □□**earbasher** *n.* **earbashing** *n.*

eardrum /ˈɪədrʌm/ *n.* the membrane of the middle ear (= *tympanic membrane*).

earful /ˈɪəfʊl/ *n.* (*pl.* **-fuls**) *colloq.* **1** a copious or prolonged amount of talking. **2** a strong reprimand.

earl /ɜːl/ *n.* a British nobleman ranking between a marquess and a viscount (cf. COUNT^2). □**Earl Marshal** (in the UK) the officer presiding over the College of Heralds, with ceremonial duties on various royal occasions. **Earl Palatine** *hist.* an earl having royal authority within his country or domain. □□**earldom** *n.* [OE *eorl*, of unkn. orig.]

early /ˈɜːlɪ/ *adj.*, *adv.*, & *n.* —*adj.* & *adv.* (**earlier, earliest**) **1** before the due, usual, or expected time (*was early for my appointment; the train arrived early*). **2 a** not far on in the day or night, or in time (*early evening; at the earliest opportunity*). **b** prompt (*early payment appreciated; at your earliest convenience*). **3 a** not far on in a period, development, or process of evolution; being the first stage (*Early English architecture; the early Christians; early Spring*). **b** of the distant past (*early man*). **c** not far on in a sequence or serial order (*the early chapters; appears early in the list*). **4 a** of childhood, esp. the preschool years (*early learning*). **b** (of a piece of writing, music, etc.) immature, youthful (*an early work*). **5** forward in flowering, ripening, etc. (*early peaches*). —*n.* (*pl.* **-ies**) (usu. in *pl.*) an early fruit or vegetable, esp. potatoes. □**at the earliest** (often placed after a specified time) not before (*will arrive on Monday at the earliest*). **early bird** *colloq.* one who arrives, gets up, etc. early. **early closing** *Brit.* the shutting of business premises on the afternoon of one particular day of the week. **early days** early in time for something to happen etc. **early grave** an untimely or premature death. **early hours** the very early morning, usu. before dawn. **early** (or **earlier**) **on** at an early (or earlier) stage. **early warning** advance warning of an imminent (esp. nuclear) attack. □□**earliness** *n.* [orig. as *adv.*, f. OE *ǣrlīce*, *ǣrlīce* (*ǣr* ERE)]

earmark /ˈɪəmɑːk/ *n.* & *v.* —*n.* **1** an identifying mark. **2** an owner's mark on the ear of an animal. —*v.tr.* **1** set aside (money etc.) for a special purpose. **2** mark (sheep etc.) with such a mark.

earmuff /ˈɪəmʌf/ *n.* a wrap or cover for the ears, protecting them from cold, noise, etc.

earn /ɜːn/ *v.tr.* **1** (also *absol.*) **a** (of a person) obtain (income) in the form of money in return for labour or services (*earn a weekly wage; happy to be earning at last*). **b** (of capital invested) bring in as interest or profit. **2 a** deserve; be entitled to; obtain as the reward for hard work or merit (*have earned a holiday; earned our admiration; earn one's keep*). **b** incur (a reproach, reputation, etc.). □**earned income** income derived from wages etc. (opp. *unearned income*). [OE *earnian* f. WG, rel. to Gmc roots assoc. with reaping]

earner /ˈɜːnə(r)/ *n.* **1** a person or thing that earns (often in *comb.*: *wage-earner*). **2** *sl.* a lucrative job or enterprise.

earnest^1 /ˈɜːnɪst/ *adj.* & *n.* —*adj.* ardently or intensely serious; zealous; not trifling or joking. —*n.* seriousness. □**in** (or **in real**) **earnest** serious(ly), not joking(ly); with determination. □□**earnestly** *adv.* **earnestness** *n.* [OE *eornust*, *eornost* (with Gmc cognates): cf. ON *ern* vigorous]

earnest^2 /ˈɜːnɪst/ *n.* **1** money paid as an instalment, esp. to confirm a contract etc. **2** a token or foretaste (*in earnest of what is to come*). [ME *ernes*, prob. var.

---

b *but* d *dog* f *few* g *get* h *he* j *yes* k *cat* l *leg* m *man* n *no* p *pen* r *red* s *sit* t *top* v *voice*

of *erles, arles* prob. f. med.L *arrhula* (unrecorded) f. *arr(h)a* pledge]

earnings /'ɜːnɪŋz/ *n.pl.* money earned. □**earnings-related** (of benefit, a pension, etc.) calculated on the basis of past or present income.

earphone /'ɪəfəʊn/ *n.* a device applied to the ear to aid hearing or receive radio or telephone communications.

earpiece /'ɪəpiːs/ *n.* the part of a telephone etc. applied to the ear during use.

earplug /'ɪəplʌg/ *n.* a piece of wax etc. placed in the ear to protect against cold air, water, or noise.

earring /'ɪərɪŋ/ *n.* a piece of jewellery worn in or on (esp. the lobe of) the ear.

earshot /'ɪəʃɒt/ *n.* the distance over which something can be heard (esp. *within* or *out of earshot*).

earth /ɜːθ/ *n. & v.* —*n.* **1 a** (also **Earth**) one of the planets of the solar system orbiting about the sun between Venus and Mars; the planet on which we live. **b** land and sea, as distinct from sky. **2 a** dry land; the ground (*fell to earth*). **b** soil, clay, mould. **c** bodily matter (*earth to earth*). **3** *Relig.* the present abode of mankind, as distinct from heaven or hell; the world. **4** *Brit. Electr.* the connection to the earth as an arbitrary reference voltage in an electrical circuit. **5** the hole of a badger, fox, etc. **6** (prec. by *the*) *colloq.* a huge amount; everything (*cost the earth*; *want the earth*). —*v.* **1** *tr.* (foll. by *up*) cover (the roots and lower stems of plants) with heaped-up earth. **2 a** *tr.* drive (a fox) to its earth. **b** *intr.* (of a fox etc.) run to its earth. **3** *tr. Brit. Electr.* connect to the earth. □**come back** (or **down**) **to earth** return to realities. **earth-closet** a lavatory with dry earth used to cover excreta. **earth-hog** (or **-pig**) = AARDVARK. **earth mother 1** *Mythol.* a spirit or deity symbolizing the earth. **2** a sensual and maternal woman. **earth-nut** any of various plants, or its edible roundish tuber, esp.: **1** an umbelliferous woodland plant, *Conopodium majus.* **2** the peanut. **earth sciences** the sciences concerned with the earth or part of it, or its atmosphere (e.g. geology, oceanography, meteorology). **earth-shattering** having a traumatic or devastating effect. **earth-shatteringly** *colloq.* devastatingly, remarkably. **earth tremor** see TREMOR *n.* 3. **gone to earth** in hiding. **on earth** *colloq.* existing anywhere; emphatically (*the happiest man on earth*; *looked like nothing on earth*; *what on earth?*). □□**earthward** *adj. & adv.* **earthwards** *adv.* [OE *eorthe* f. Gmc]

earthbound /'ɜːθbaʊnd/ *adj.* **1** attached to the earth or earthly things. **2** moving towards the earth.

earthen /'ɜːθ(ə)n/ *adj.* **1** made of earth. **2** made of baked clay.

earthenware /'ɜːθ(ə)nˌweə(r)/ *n. & adj.* —*n.* pottery, vessels, etc., made of clay fired to a porous state which can be made impervious to liquids by the use of a glaze (cf. PORCELAIN). —*adj.* made of fired clay. [EARTHEN + WARE¹]

earthling /'ɜːθlɪŋ/ *n.* an inhabitant of the earth, esp. as regarded in fiction by outsiders.

earthly /'ɜːθlɪ/ *adj.* **1** of the earth or human life on earth; terrestrial. **2** (usu. with *neg.*) *colloq.* remotely possible or conceivable (*is no earthly use*; *there wasn't an earthly reason*). □**not an earthly** *colloq.* no chance whatever. □□**earthliness** *n.*

earthquake /'ɜːθkweɪk/ *n.* **1** a convulsion of the superficial parts of the earth due to the release of accumulated stress as a result of faults in strata or volcanic action. **2** a social etc. disturbance.

earthshine /'ɜːθʃaɪn/ *n. Astron.* **1** the unillumined portion of a crescent moon shining faintly because of sunlight reflected from the earth on to the moon. **2** illumination on the moon's surface caused by this.

earthstar /'ɜːθstɑː(r)/ *n.* any woodland fungus of the genus *Geastrum*, esp. *G. triplex*, with a spherical spore-containing fruit body surrounded by a fleshy star-shaped structure.

earthwork /'ɜːθwɜːk/ *n.* **1** an artificial bank of earth in fortification or road-building etc. **2** the process of excavating soil in civil engineering work.

earthworm /'ɜːθwɜːm/ *n.* any of various annelid worms, esp. of the genus *Lumbricus* or *Allolobophora*, living and burrowing in the ground.

earthy /'ɜːθɪ/ *adj.* (**earthier, earthiest**) **1** of or like earth or soil. **2** somewhat coarse or crude; unrefined (*earthy humour*). □□**earthily** *adv.* **earthiness** *n.*

earwax /'ɪəwæks/ *n.* a yellow waxy secretion produced by the ear, = CERUMEN.

earwig /'ɪəwɪg/ *n. & v.* —*n.* **1** any small elongate insect of the order Dermaptera, with a pair of terminal appendages in the shape of forceps. **2** *US* a small centipede. —*v.tr.* (**earwigged, earwigging**) *archaic* influence (a person) by secret communication. [OE *ēarwicga* f. *ēare* EAR¹ + *wicga* earwig, prob. rel. to *wiggle*: once thought to enter the head through the ear]

ease /iːz/ *n. & v.* —*n.* **1** absence of difficulty; facility, effortlessness (*did it with ease*). **2 a** freedom or relief from pain, anxiety, or trouble. **b** freedom from embarrassment or awkwardness. **c** freedom or relief from constraint or formality. —*v.* **1** *tr.* relieve from pain or anxiety, etc. (often foll. by *of*; *eased my mind*; *eased me of the burden*). **2** *intr.* (often foll. by *off, up*) **a** become less painful or burdensome. **b** relax; begin to take it easy. **c** slow down; moderate one's behaviour, habits, etc. **3** *tr. joc.* rob or extract money etc. from (*let me ease you of your loose change*). **4** *intr. Meteorol.* become less severe (*the wind will ease tonight*). **5 a** *tr.* relax; slacken; make a less tight fit. **b** *tr. & intr.* (foll. by *through, into*, etc.) move or be moved carefully into place (*eased it into the hole*). **6** *intr.* (often foll. by *off*) *Stock Exch.* (of shares etc.) descend in price or value. □**at ease 1** free from anxiety or constraint. **2** *Mil.* **a** in a relaxed attitude, with the feet apart. **b** the order to stand in this way. **at one's ease** free from embarrassment, awkwardness, or undue formality. **ease away** (or **down** or **off**) *Naut.* slacken (a rope, sail, etc.). □□**easer** *n.* [ME f. AF *ese*, OF *eise*, ult. f. L *adjacens* ADJACENT]

easel /'iːz(ə)l/ *n.* **1** a standing frame, usu. of wood, for supporting an artist's work, a blackboard, etc. **2** an artist's work collectively. [Du. *ezel* = G *Esel* ASS¹]

easement /'iːzmənt/ *n. Law* a right of way or a similar right over another's land. [ME f. OF *aisement*]

easily /'iːzɪlɪ/ *adv.* **1** without difficulty. **2** by far (*easily the best*). **3** very probably (*it could easily snow*).

east /iːst/ *n., adj., & adv.* —*n.* **1 a** the point of the horizon where the sun rises at the equinoxes (cardinal point 90° to the right of north). **b** the compass point corresponding to this. **c** the direction in which this lies. **2** (usu. **the East**) **a** the regions or countries lying to the east of Europe. **b** the Communist States of eastern Europe. **3** the eastern part of a country, town, etc. **4** (**East**) *Bridge* a player occupying the position designated 'east'. —*adj.* **1** towards, at, near, or facing east. **2** coming from the east (*east wind*). —*adv.* **1** towards, at, or near the east. **2** (foll. by *of*) further east than. □**East End** the part of London east of the City as far as the River Lea. **East Ender** an inhabitant of the East End. **East Indiaman** *hist.* a large ship engaged in trade with the East Indies. **East Indies** the islands etc. east of India, esp. the Malay archipelago. **east-north** (or **-south**) **-east** the direction or compass point midway between east and north-east (or south-east). **to the east** (often foll. by *of*) in an easterly direction. [OE *ēast-* f. Gmc]

eastbound /'iːstbaʊnd/ *adj.* travelling or leading eastwards.

Easter /'iːstə(r)/ *n.* **1** (also **Easter Day** or **Sunday**) the festival (held on a variable Sunday in March or April) commemorating Christ's resurrection. **2** the season in which this occurs, esp. the weekend from Good Friday to Easter Monday. □**Easter egg** an artificial usu. chocolate egg given at Easter, esp. to children. **Easter week** the week beginning on Easter

Sunday. [OE *ēastre* app. f. *Ēostre*, a goddess associated with spring, f. Gmc]

easterly /'i:stəli/ *adj.*, *adv.*, & *n.* —*adj.* & *adv.* **1** in an eastern position or direction. **2** (of a wind) blowing from the east. —*n.* (*pl.* -**ies**) a wind blowing from the east.

eastern /'i:st(ə)n/ *adj.* **1** of or in the east; inhabiting the east. **2** lying or directed towards the east. **3** (**Eastern**) of or in the Far, Middle, or Near East. □**Eastern Church** the Orthodox Church. **Eastern hemisphere** the half of the earth containing Europe, Asia, and Africa. **Eastern Time** standard time used in eastern Canada and the US or in eastern Australia. □□ **easternmost** *adj.* [OE *ēasterne* (as EAST, -ERN)]

easterner /'i:stənə(r)/ *n.* a native or inhabitant of the east.

Eastertide /'i:stə,taɪd/ *n.* the period including Easter.

easting /'i:stɪŋ/ *n. Naut.* etc. the distance travelled or the angle of longitude measured eastward from either a defined north-south grid line or a meridian.

eastward /'i:stwəd/ *adj.*, *adv.*, & *n.* —*adj.* & *adv.* (also **eastwards**) towards the east. —*n.* an eastward direction or region. □□ **eastwardly** *adj.* & *adv.*

easy /'i:zɪ/ *adj.*, *adv.*, & *int.* (**easier, easiest**) —*adj.* **1** not difficult; achieved without great effort. **2 a** free from pain, discomfort, anxiety, etc. **b** comfortably off, affluent (*easy circumstances*). **3** free from embarrassment, awkwardness, constraint, etc.; relaxed and pleasant (*an easy manner*). **4** compliant, obliging; easily persuaded (*an easy touch*). **5** *Stock Exch.* (of goods, money on loan, etc.) not much in demand. —*adv.* with ease; in an effortless or relaxed manner. —*int.* go carefully; move gently. □**easy as pie** see PIE[1]. **easy chair** a large comfortable chair, usu. an armchair. **easy come easy go** *colloq.* what is easily got is soon lost or spent. **easy does it** *colloq.* go carefully. **easy money** money got without effort (esp. of dubious legality). **easy of access** easily entered or approached. **easy on the eye** (or ear etc.) *colloq.* pleasant to look at (or listen to etc.). **easy-peasy** *sl.* very simple. **Easy Street** *colloq.* affluence. **easy terms** payment by instalments. **go easy** (foll. by *with*, *on*) be sparing or cautious. **I'm easy** *colloq.* I have no preference. **of easy virtue** (of a woman) sexually promiscuous. **stand easy!** *Brit. Mil.* permission to a squad standing at ease to relax their attitude further. **take it easy 1** proceed gently or carefully. **2** relax; avoid overwork. □□ **easiness** *n.* [ME f. AF *aisé*, OF *aisié* past part. of *aisier* EASE]

easygoing /,i:zɪ'gəʊɪŋ/ *adj.* **1** placid and tolerant; relaxed in manner; accepting things as they are. **2** (of a horse) having an easy gait.

eat /i:t/ *v.* (*past* **ate** /et, eɪt/; *past part.* **eaten** /'i:t(ə)n/) **1 a** *tr.* take into the mouth, chew, and swallow (food). **b** *intr.* consume food; take a meal. **c** *tr.* devour (*eaten by a lion*). **2** *intr.* (foll. by (*away*) *at*, *into*) **a** destroy gradually, esp. by corrosion, erosion, disease, etc. **b** begin to consume or diminish (resources etc.). **3** *tr. colloq.* trouble, vex (*what's eating you?*). □**eat dirt** see DIRT. **eat one's hat** *colloq.* admit one's surprise in being wrong (only as a proposition unlikely to be fulfilled: *said he would eat his hat*). **eat one's heart out** suffer from excessive longing or envy. **eat humble pie** see HUMBLE. **eat out** have a meal away from home, esp. in a restaurant. **eat out of a person's hand** be entirely submissive to a person. **eat salt with** see SALT. **eat up 1** (also *absol.*) eat or consume completely. **2** use or deal with rapidly or wastefully (*eats up petrol*; *eats up the miles*). **3** encroach upon or annex (*eating up the neighbouring States*). **4** absorb, preoccupy (*eaten up with pride*). **eat one's words** admit that one was wrong. [OE *etan* f. Gmc]

eatable /'i:təb(ə)l/ *adj.* & *n.* —*adj.* that is in a condition to be eaten (cf. EDIBLE). —*n.* (usu. in *pl.*) food.

eater /'i:tə(r)/ *n.* **1** a person who eats (*a big eater*). **2** *Brit.* an eating apple etc.

eatery /'i:təri/ *n. US* (*pl.* -**ies**) *colloq.* a restaurant or eating-place.

eating /'i:tɪŋ/ *adj.* **1** suitable for eating (*eating apple*). **2** used for eating (*eating-house*).

eats /i:ts/ *n.pl. colloq.* food.

eau-de-Cologne /,əʊdəkə'ləʊn/ *n.* an alcohol-based perfume of a kind made orig. at Cologne. [F, lit. 'water of Cologne']

eau-de-Nil /,əʊdə'ni:l/ *n.* a pale greenish colour. [F, lit. 'water of the Nile' (from the supposed resemblance)]

eau-de-vie /,əʊdə'vi:/ *n.* spirits, esp. brandy. [F, lit. 'water of life']

eaves /i:vz/ *n.pl.* the underside of a projecting roof. [orig. sing., f. OE *efes*: prob. rel. to OVER]

eavesdrop /'i:vzdrɒp/ *v.intr.* (-**dropped**, -**dropping**) listen secretly to a private conversation. □□ **eavesdropper** *n.* [*eavesdropper* orig. 'one who listens under walls' prob. f. ON *upsardropi* (cf. OE *yfæsdrypæ*): *eavesdrop* by back-form.]

ebb /eb/ *n.* & *v.* —*n.* **1** the movement of the tide out to sea (also *attrib.*: *ebb tide*). **2** the process of draining away of flood-water etc. —*v.intr.* (often foll. by *away*) **1** (of tidewater) flow out to sea; recede; drain away. **2** decline; run low (*his life was ebbing away*). □**at a low ebb** in a poor condition or state of decline. **ebb and flow** a continuing process of decline and upturn in circumstances. **on the ebb** in decline. [OE *ebba*, *ebbian*]

ebonite /'ebə,naɪt/ *n.* = VULCANITE. [EBONY + -ITE[1]]

ebony /'ebəni/ *n.* & *adj.* —*n.* (*pl.* -**ies**) **1** a heavy hard dark wood used for furniture. **2** any of various trees of the genus *Diospyros* producing this. —*adj.* **1** made of ebony. **2** black like ebony. [earlier *hebeny* f. (*h)eben(e)* = *ebon*, perh. after *ivory*]

ebullient /ɪ'bʌlɪənt, *disp.* ɪ'bʊlɪənt/ *adj.* **1** exuberant, high-spirited. **2** *Chem.* boiling. □□ **ebullience** *n.* **ebulliency** *n.* **ebulliently** *adv.* [L *ebullire ebullient-* bubble out (as E-, *bullire* boil)]

EC *abbr.* **1** East Central (London postal district). **2** executive committee. **3 a** European Community. **b** European Commission.

ecad /'i:kæd/ *n. Ecol.* an organism modified by its environment. [Gk *oikos* house + -AD]

écarté /eɪ'kɑ:teɪ/ *n.* **1** a card-game for two persons in which cards from a player's hand may be exchanged for others from the pack. **2** a position in classical ballet with one arm and leg extended. [F, past part. of *écarter* discard]

Ecce Homo /,ekeɪ 'hɒməʊ/ *n. Art* one of the subjects of the Passion cycle: in Renaissance painting typically a depiction of Christ wearing the crown of thorns. [L, = 'behold the man', the words of Pilate to the Jews after the crowning with thorns (John 19:5)]

eccentric /ɪk'sentrɪk, ek-/ *adj.* & *n.* —*adj.* **1** odd or capricious in behaviour or appearance; whimsical. **2 a** not placed, not having its axis etc. placed centrally. **b** (often foll. by *to*) (of a circle) not concentric (to another). **c** (of an orbit) not circular. —*n.* **1** an eccentric person. **2** *Mech.* an eccentric contrivance for changing rotatory into backward-and-forward motion, e.g. the cam used in an internal-combustion engine. □□ **eccentrically** *adv.* **eccentricity** /-'trɪsɪtɪ/ *n.* (*pl.* -**ies**). [LL *eccentricus* f. Gk *ekkentros* f. *ek* out of + *kentros* CENTRE]

Eccles. *abbr.* Ecclesiastes (Old Testament).

Eccles cake /'ek(ə)lz/ *n.* a round flat cake made of pastry filled with currants etc. [*Eccles* in N. England]

ecclesial /ɪ'kli:zj(ə)l/ *adj.* of or relating to a Church. [Gk *ekklesia* assembly, church f. *ekklētos* summoned out f. *ek* out + *kaleō* call]

ecclesiastic /ɪ,kli:zɪ'æstɪk/ *n.* & *adj.* —*n.* a priest or clergyman. —*adj.* = ECCLESIASTICAL. □□ **ecclesiasticism** /-,sɪz(ə)m/ *n.* [F *ecclésiastique* or LL *ecclesiasticus* f. Gk *ekklēsiastikos* f. *ekklēsia* assembly, church: see ECCLESIAL]

ecclesiastical /ɪ,kli:zɪ'æstɪk(ə)l/ *adj.* of the Church or the clergy. □□ **ecclesiastically** *adv.*

ecclesiology /ɪˌkliːzɪˈɒlədʒɪ/ n. **1** the study of churches, esp. church building and decoration. **2** theology as applied to the nature and structure of the Christian Church. □□ **ecclesiological** /-zɪəˈlɒdʒɪk(ə)l/ adj. **ecclesiologist** n. [Gk ekklēsia assembly, church (see ECCLESIAL) + -LOGY]

Ecclus. /ˈekləs/ abbr. Ecclesiasticus (Apocrypha).

eccrine /ˈekriːn/ adj. (of a gland, e.g. a sweat gland) secreting without loss of cell material. [Gk ek out of + krinō sift]

ecdysis /ekˈdaɪsɪs/ n. the action of casting off skin or shedding an exoskeleton etc. [mod.L f. Gk ekdusis f. ekduō put off]

ECG abbr. electrocardiogram.

echelon /ˈeʃəˌlɒn, ˈeɪʃəˌlɔ̃/ n. & v. —n. **1** a level or rank in an organization, in society, etc.; those occupying it (often in pl.: the upper echelons). **2** Mil. a formation of troops, ships, aircraft, etc., in parallel rows with the end of each row projecting further than the one in front (in echelon). —v.tr. arrange in an echelon. [F échelon f. échelle ladder f. L scala]

echeveria /ˌetʃəˈvɪərɪə/ n. any succulent plant of the genus Echeveria, native to Central and S. America. [M. Echeveri, 19th-c. Mex. botanical draughtsman]

echidna /ɪˈkɪdnə/ n. any of several egg-laying pouch-bearing mammals native to Australia and New Guinea, with a covering of spines, and having a long snout and long claws. Also called spiny anteater. [mod.L f. Gk ekhidna viper]

echinoderm /ɪˈkaɪnəˌdɜːm, ˈekɪn-/ n. any marine invertebrate of the phylum Echinodermata, usu. having a spiny skin, e.g. starfish and sea urchins. [ECHINUS + Gk derma -atos skin]

echinoid /ɪˈkaɪnɔɪd/ n. a sea urchin.

echinus /ɪˈkaɪnəs/ n. **1** any sea urchin of the genus Echinus, including the common European edible urchin, E. esculentus. **2** Archit. a rounded moulding below an abacus on a Doric or Ionic capital. [ME f. L f. Gk ekhinos hedgehog, sea urchin]

echo /ˈekəʊ/ n. & v. —n. (pl. -oes) **1 a** the repetition of a sound by the reflection of sound waves. **b** the secondary sound produced. **2** a reflected radio or radar beam. **3** a close imitation or repetition of something already done. **4** a person who slavishly repeats the words or opinions of another. **5** (often in pl.) circumstances or events reminiscent of or remotely connected with earlier ones. **6** Bridge etc. a conventional mode of play to show the number of cards held in the suit led etc. —v. (-oes, -oed) **1** intr. **a** (of a place) resound with an echo. **b** (of a sound) be repeated; resound. **2** tr. repeat (a sound) by an echo. **3** tr. **a** repeat (another's words). **b** imitate the words, opinions, or actions of (a person). □ **echo chamber** an enclosure with sound-reflecting walls. **echo location** the location of objects by reflected sound. **echo-sounder** sounding apparatus for determining the depth of the sea beneath a ship by measuring the time taken for an echo to be received. **echo-sounding** the use of an echo-sounder. **echo verse** a verse form in which a line repeats the last syllables of the previous line. □□ **echoer** n. **echoless** adj. [ME f. OF or L f. Gk ēkhō, rel. to ēkhē a sound]

echocardiogram /ˌekəʊˈkɑːdɪəˌgræm/ n. Med. a record produced by echocardiography.

echocardiography /ˌekəʊˌkɑːdɪˈɒɡrəfɪ/ n. Med. the use of ultrasound waves to investigate the action of the heart. □□ **echocardiograph** /ˌekəʊˈkɑːdɪəˌɡrɑːf/ n. **echocardiographer** n.

echoencephalogram /ˌekəʊenˈsefələʊˌgræm/ n. Med. a record produced by echoencephalography.

echoencephalography /ˌekəʊenˌsefəˈlɒɡrəfɪ/ n. Med. the use of ultrasound waves to investigate intracranial structures.

echogram /ˈekəʊˌɡræm/ n. a record made by an echo-sounder.

echograph /ˈekəʊˌɡrɑːf/ n. a device for automatically recording echograms.

echoic /eˈkəʊɪk/ adj. Phonet. (of a word) imitating the sound it represents; onomatopoeic. □□ **echoically** adv.

echoism /ˈekəʊˌɪz(ə)m/ n. = ONOMATOPOEIA.

echolalia /ˌekəʊˈleɪlɪə/ n. **1** the meaningless repetition of another person's spoken words. **2** the repetition of speech by a child learning to talk. [mod.L f. Gk ēkhō echo + lalia talk]

echovirus /ˈekəʊˌvaɪərəs/ n. (also **ECHO virus**) any of a group of enteroviruses sometimes causing mild meningitis, encephalitis, etc. [f. enteric cytopathogenic human orphan (because not originally assignable to any known disease) + VIRUS]

echt /ext/ adj. authentic, genuine, typical. [G]

éclair /eɪˈkleə(r), ɪˈkleə(r)/ n. a small elongated cake of choux pastry filled with cream and iced with chocolate or coffee icing. [F, lit. lightning, flash]

éclaircissement /ˌeɪkleəˈsiːsmã/ n. archaic an enlightening explanation of something hitherto inexplicable (e.g. conduct etc.). [F f. éclaircir clear up]

eclampsia /ɪˈklæmpsɪə/ n. a condition involving convulsions leading to coma, occurring esp. in pregnant women. □□ **eclamptic** adj. [mod.L f. F éclampsie f. Gk eklampsis sudden development f. eklampō shine forth]

éclat /eɪˈklɑː, ˈeɪklɑː/ n. **1** brilliant display; dazzling effect. **2** social distinction; conspicuous success; universal approbation (with great éclat). [F f. éclater burst out]

eclectic /ɪˈklektɪk/ adj. & n. —adj. **1** deriving ideas, tastes, style, etc., from various sources. **2** Philos. & Art selecting one's beliefs etc. from various sources; attached to no particular school of philosophy. —n. **1** an eclectic person. **2** a person who subscribes to an eclectic school of thought. □□ **eclectically** adv. **eclecticism** /-ˌsɪz(ə)m/ n. [Gk eklektikos f. eklegō pick out]

eclipse /ɪˈklɪps/ n. & v. —n. **1** the obscuring of the reflected light from one celestial body by the passage of another between it and the eye or between it and its source of illumination. **2** a deprivation of light or the period of this. **3** a rapid or sudden loss of importance or prominence, esp. in relation to another or a newly-arrived person or thing. —v.tr. **1** (of a celestial body) obscure the light from or to (another). **2** intercept (light, esp. of a lighthouse). **3** deprive of prominence or importance; outshine, surpass. □ **in eclipse 1** surpassed; in decline. **2** (of a bird) having lost its courting plumage. □□ **eclipser** n. [ME f. OF f. L f. Gk ekleipsis f. ekleipō fail to appear, be eclipsed f. leipō leave]

ecliptic /ɪˈklɪptɪk/ n. & adj. —n. the sun's apparent path among the stars during the year. —adj. of an eclipse or the ecliptic. [ME f. L f. Gk ekleiptikos (as ECLIPSE)]

eclogue /ˈeklɒɡ/ n. a short poem, esp. a pastoral dialogue. [L ecloga f. Gk eklogē selection f. eklegō pick out]

eclosion /ɪˈkləʊʒ(ə)n/ n. the emergence of an insect from a pupa-case or of a larva from an egg. [F éclosion f. éclore hatch (as EX-¹, L claudere to close)]

eco- /ˈiːkəʊ/ comb. form ecology, ecological.

ecoclimate /ˈiːkəʊˌklaɪmɪt, -mət/ n. climate considered as an ecological factor.

ecology /ɪˈkɒlədʒɪ/ n. **1** the branch of biology dealing with the relations of organisms to one another and to their physical surroundings. **2** (in full **human ecology**) the study of the interaction of people with their environment. □□ **ecological** /ˌiːkəˈlɒdʒɪk(ə)l/ adj. **ecologically** /ˌiːkəˈlɒdʒɪkəlɪ/ adv. **ecologist** n. [G Ökologie f. Gk oikos house]

Econ. abbr. Economics.

econometrics /ɪˌkɒnəˈmetrɪks/ n.pl. (usu. treated as sing.) a branch of economics concerned with the application of mathematical economics to economic data by the use of statistics. □□ **econometric** adj. **econometrical** /-məˈtrɪʃ(ə)n/ n. **econometrist** n. [ECONOMY + METRIC]

economic /ˌiːkəˈnɒmɪk, ˌek-/ adj. **1** of or relating to economics. **2** maintained for profit; on a business footing. **3** adequate to repay or recoup expenditure with some profit (*not economic to run buses on Sunday; an economic rent*). **4** practical; considered or studied with regard to human needs (*economic geography*). □□ **economically** *adv.* [ME f. OF *econ-omique* or L *oeconomicus* f. Gk *oikonomikos* (as ECONOMY)]

economical /ˌiːkəˈnɒmɪk(ə)l, ˌek-/ *adj.* sparing in the use of resources; avoiding waste. □□ **economically** *adv.*

economics /ˌiːkəˈnɒmɪks, ˌek-/ *n.pl.* (treated as *sing.*) **1 a** a science of the production and distribution of wealth. **b** the application of this to a particular subject (*the economics of publishing*). **2** the condition of a country etc. as regards material prosperity.

economist /ɪˈkɒnəmɪst/ *n.* **1** an expert in or student of economics. **2** a person who manages financial or economic matters. [Gk *oikonomos* (as ECONOMY) + -IST]

economize /ɪˈkɒnəˌmaɪz/ *v.intr.* (also **-ise**) **1** be economical; make economies; reduce expenditure. **2** (foll. by *on*) use sparingly; spend less on. □□ **economization** /-ˈzeɪʃ(ə)n/ *n.* **economizer** *n.*

economy /ɪˈkɒnəmɪ/ *n.* (*pl.* **-ies**) **1 a** the wealth and resources of a community, esp. in terms of the production and consumption of goods and services. **b** a particular kind of this (*a capitalist economy*). **c** the administration or condition of an economy. **2 a** the careful management of (esp. financial) resources; frugality. **b** (often in *pl.*) an instance of this (*made many economies*). **3** sparing or careful use (*economy of language*). **4** (also **economy class**) the cheapest class of air travel. **5** (*attrib.*) (also **economy-size** of goods) consisting of a large quantity for a pro-portionally lower cost. [F *économie* or L *oeconomia* f. Gk *oikonomia* household management f. *oikos* house + *nemō* manage]

ecosphere /ˈiːkəʊˌsfɪə(r)/ *n.* the region of space in-cluding planets where conditions are such that living things can exist.

écossaise /ˌeɪkɒˈseɪz/ *n.* **1** an energetic dance in duple time. **2** the music for this. [F, fem. of *écossais* Scottish]

ecosystem /ˈiːkəʊˌsɪstəm/ *n.* a biological community of interacting organisms and their physical environment.

ecru /ˈeɪkruː/ *n.* the colour of unbleached linen; light fawn. [F *écru* unbleached]

ecstasize /ˈekstəˌsaɪz/ *v.tr.* & *intr.* (also **-ise**) throw or go into ecstasies.

ecstasy /ˈekstəsɪ/ *n.* (*pl.* **-ies**) **1** an overwhelming feeling of joy or rapture. **2** *Psychol.* an emotional or religious frenzy or trancelike state. **3** *sl.* me-thylenedioxymethamphetamine, a powerful stim-ulant and hallucinatory drug (see MDMA). [ME f. OF *extasie* f. LL *extasis* f. Gk *ekstasis* standing outside oneself f. *ek* out + *histēmi* to place]

ecstatic /ɪkˈstætɪk/ *adj.* & *n.* —*adj.* **1** in a state of ecstasy. **2** very enthusiastic or excited (*was ecstatic about his new job*). **3** producing ecstasy; sublime (*an ecstatic embrace*). —*n.* a person subject to (usu. religious) ecstasy. □□ **ecstatically** *adv.* [F *extatique* f. Gk *ekstatikos* (as ECSTASY)]

ECT *abbr.* electroconvulsive therapy.

ecto- /ˈektəʊ/ *comb. form* outside. [Gk *ekto-* stem of *ektos* outside]

ectoblast /ˈektəʊˌblæst/ *n.* = ECTODERM. □□ **ectoblastic** /-ˈblæstɪk/ *adj.*

ectoderm /ˈektəʊˌdɜːm/ *n.* *Biol.* the outermost layer of an animal embryo in early development. □□ **ectodermal** /-ˈdɜːm(ə)l/ *adj.*

ectogenesis /ˌektəʊˈdʒenɪsɪs/ *n.* *Biol.* the production of structures outside the organism. □□ **ectogenetic** /-dʒɪˈnetɪk/ *adj.* **ectogenic** /-ˈdʒenɪk/ *adj.* **ectogenous** /ekˈtɒdʒɪnəs/ *adj.* [mod.L (as ECTO-, GENESIS)]

ectomorph /ˈektəʊˌmɔːf/ *n.* a person with a lean and delicate build of body and large skin surface in comparison with weight (cf. ENDOMORPH, MESOMORPH). □□ **ectomorphic** /-ˈmɔːfɪk/ *adj.*

ectomorphy *n.* [ECTO- + Gk *morphē* form]

-ectomy /ˈektəmɪ/ *comb. form* denoting a surgical operation in which a part of the body is removed (*appendectomy*). [Gk *ektomē* excision f. *ek* out + *temnō* cut]

ectopic /ekˈtɒpɪk/ *adj.* *Med.* in an abnormal place or position. □ **ectopic pregnancy** a pregnancy oc-curring outside the womb. [mod.L *ectopia* f. Gk *ektopos* out of place]

ectoplasm /ˈektəʊˌplæz(ə)m/ *n.* **1** the dense outer layer of the cytoplasm (cf. ENDOPLASM). **2** the sup-posed viscous substance exuding from the body of a spiritualistic medium during a trance. □□ **ectoplasmic** /-ˈplæzmɪk/ *adj.*

ectozoon /ˌektəʊˈzəʊɒn/ *n.* *Biol.* a parasite that lives on the outside of its host.

ECU *abbr.* European currency unit.

ecumenical /ˌiːkjuːˈmenɪk(ə)l, ˌek-/ *adj.* **1** of or representing the whole Christian world. **2** seeking or promoting worldwide Christian unity. □□ **ecumenically** *adv.* [LL *oecumenicus* f. Gk *oikou-menikos* of the inhabited earth f. *oikoumenē*]

ecumenicalism /ˌiːkjuːˈmenɪkəˌlɪz(ə)m, ˌek-/ *n.* (also **ecumenicism** /iːˈkjuːməˌnɪz(ə)m/) the principle or aim of the unity of Christians worldwide.

eczema /ˈeksɪmə/ *n.* inflammation of the skin, with itching and discharge from blisters. □□ **eczematous** /ekˈziːmətəs, ekˈzem-/ *adj.* [mod.L f. Gk *ekzema -atos* f. *ek* out + *zeō* boil]

ed. *abbr.* **1** edited by. **2** edition. **3** editor. **4** educated; education.

-ed[1] /əd, ɪd/ *suffix* forming adjectives: **1** from nouns, meaning 'having, wearing, affected by, etc.' (*talented*; *trousered*; *diseased*). **2** from phrases of adjective and noun (*good-humoured*; *three-cornered*). [OE *-ede*]

-ed[2] /əd, ɪd/ *suffix* forming: **1** the past tense and past participle of weak verbs (*needed*; *risked*). **2** participial adjectives (*escaped prisoner*; *a pained look*). [OE *-ed*, *-ad*, *-od*]

Edam /ˈiːdæm/ *n.* a round Dutch cheese, usu. pale yellow with a red rind. [*Edam* in Holland]

edaphic /ɪˈdæfɪk/ *adj.* **1** *Bot.* of the soil. **2** *Ecol.* produced or influenced by the soil. [G *edaphisch* f. Gk *edaphos* floor]

Edda /ˈedə/ *n.* **1** (also **Elder Edda**, **Poetic Edda**) a collection of medieval Icelandic poems on Norse legends. **2** (also **Younger Edda**, **Prose Edda**) a 13th-c. miscellaneous handbook to Icelandic poetry. [perh. a name in a Norse poem or f. ON *óthr* poetry]

eddo /ˈedəʊ/ *n.* (*pl.* **-oes**) = TARO. [Afr. word]

eddy /ˈedɪ/ *n.* & *v.* (*pl.* **-ies**) **1** a circular movement of water causing a small whirlpool. **2** a movement of wind, fog, or smoke resembling this. —*v.tr.* & *intr.* (**-ies**, **-ied**) whirl round in eddies. □ **eddy current** *Electr.* a localized current induced in a conductor by a varying magnetic field. [prob. OE *ed-* again, back, perh. of Scand. orig.]

edelweiss /ˈeɪd(ə)lˌvaɪs/ *n.* an Alpine plant, *Leon-topodium alpinum*, with woolly white bracts around the flower-heads, growing in rocky places. [G f. *edel* noble + *weiss* white]

edema *US* var. of OEDEMA.

Eden /ˈiːd(ə)n/ *n.* (also **Garden of Eden**) a place or state of great happiness; paradise (with reference to the abode of Adam and Eve in the biblical account of the Creation). [ME f. LL f. Gk *Edēn* f. Heb. *'ēden*, orig. = delight]

edentate /ɪˈdenteɪt/ *adj.* & *n.* —*adj.* having no or few teeth. —*n.* any mammal, esp. of the order Edentata, having no or few teeth, e.g. an anteater or sloth. [L *edentatus* (as E-, *dens dentis* tooth)]

edge /edʒ/ *n.* & *v.* —*n.* **1** a boundary line or margin of an area or surface. **2** a narrow surface of a thin object. **3** the meeting-line of two surfaces of a solid. **4 a** the sharpened side of the blade of a cutting instrument or weapon. **b** the sharpness of this (*the knife has lost its edge*). **5** the area close to a steep drop (*along the edge of the cliff*). **6** anything compared to an edge, esp. the crest of a ridge. **7 a** (as a personal attribute) incisiveness, excitement. **b** keenness, excitement (esp. as an element in an otherwise routine situation). —*v.* **1** *tr.* & *intr.* (often foll. by *in, into, out*, etc.) move gradually or furtively towards an objective (*edged it into the corner; they all edged towards the door*). **2** *tr.* **a** provide with an edge or border. **b** form a border to. **c** trim the edge of. **3** *tr.* sharpen (a knife, tool, etc.). **4** *tr. Cricket* strike (the ball) with the edge of the bat. □**have the edge on** (or **over**) have a slight advantage over. **on edge 1** tense and restless or irritable. **2** eager, excited. **on the edge of** almost involved in or affected by. **set a person's teeth on edge** (of a taste or sound) cause an unpleasant nervous sensation. **take the edge off** dull, weaken; make less effective or intense. □□ **edgeless** *adj.* **edger** *n.* [OE *ecg* f. Gmc]

edgeways /'edʒweɪz/ *adv.* (also **edgewise** /-waɪz/) **1** with the edge uppermost or towards the viewer. **2** edge to edge. □**get a word in edgeways** contribute to a conversation when the dominant speaker pauses briefly.

edging /'edʒɪŋ/ *n.* **1** something forming an edge or border, e.g. a fringe or lace. **2** the process of making an edge. □**edging-shears** shears for trimming the edges of a lawn.

edgy /'edʒɪ/ *adj.* (**edgier, edgiest**) **1** irritable; nervously anxious. **2** disjointed (*edgy rhythms*). □□ **edgily** *adv.* **edginess** *n.*

edh var. of ETH.

edible /'edɪb(ə)l/ *adj.* & *n.* —*adj.* fit or suitable to be eaten (cf. EATABLE). —*n.* (in *pl.*) food. □□ **edibility** /-'bɪlɪtɪ/ *n.* [LL *edibilis* f. *edere* eat]

edict /'iːdɪkt/ *n.* an order proclaimed by authority. □□ **edictal** /ɪ'dɪkt(ə)l/ *adj.* [ME f. L *edictum* f. *edicere* proclaim]

edifice /'edɪfɪs/ *n.* **1** a building, esp. a large imposing one. **2** a complex organizational or conceptual structure. [ME f. OF f. L *aedificium* f. *aedis* dwelling + *-ficium* f. *facere* make]

edify /'edɪˌfaɪ/ *v.tr.* (**-ies, -ied**) (of a circumstance, experience, etc.) instruct and improve morally or intellectually. □□ **edification** /-fɪ'keɪʃ(ə)n/ *n.* **edifying** *adj.* **edifyingly** *adv.* [ME f. OF *edifier* f. L *aedificare* (as EDIFICE)]

edit /'edɪt/ *v.* & *n.* —*v.tr.* (**edited, editing**) **1 a** assemble, prepare, or modify (written material, esp. the work of another or others) for publication. **b** prepare an edition of (an author's work). **2** be in overall charge of the content and arrangement of (a newspaper, journal, etc.). **3** take extracts from and collate (films, tape-recordings, etc.) to form a unified sequence. **4 a** prepare (data) for processing by a computer. **b** alter (a text entered in a word processor etc.). **5 a** reword to correct, or to alter the emphasis. **b** (foll. by *out*) remove (part) from a text etc. —*n.* **1 a** a piece of editing. **b** an edited item. **2** a facility for editing. [F *éditer* (as EDITION): partly a back-form. f. EDITOR]

edition /ɪ'dɪʃ(ə)n/ *n.* **1 a** one of the particular forms in which a literary work etc. is published (*paperback edition; pocket edition*). **b** a copy of a book in a particular form (*a first edition*). **2** a whole number of copies of a book, newspaper, etc., issued at one time. **3** a particular version or instance of a broadcast, esp. of a regular programme or feature. **4** a person or thing similar to or resembling another (*a miniature edition of her mother*). [F *édition* f. L *editio -onis* f. *edere edit-* put out (as E-, *dare* give)]

editio princeps /ɪˌdɪʃɪəʊ 'prɪnseps/ *n.* (*pl.* ***editiones principes*** /-ˌəʊniːz -sɪˌpiːz/) the first printed edition of a book, text, etc. [L]

editor /'edɪtə(r)/ *n.* **1** a person who edits material for publication or broadcasting. **2** a person who directs the preparation of a newspaper or periodical, or a particular section of one (*sports editor*). **3** a person who selects or commissions material for publication. **4** a person who edits film, sound track, etc. **5** a computer program for modifying data. □□ **editorship** *n.* [LL, = producer (of games), publisher (as EDIT)]

editorial /ˌedɪ'tɔːrɪəl/ *adj.* & *n.* —*adj.* **1** of or concerned with editing or editors. **2** written or approved by an editor. —*n.* a newspaper article written by or on behalf of an editor, esp. one giving an opinion on a topical issue. □□ **editorialist** *n.* **editorialize** *v.intr.* (also **-ise**). **editorially** *adv.*

-edly /ɪdlɪ/ *suffix* forming adverbs from verbs, meaning 'in a manner characterized by performance of or undergoing of the verbal action' (*allegedly; disgustedly; hurriedly*).

EDP *abbr.* electronic data processing.

EDT *abbr.* *US* Eastern Daylight Time.

educate /'edjʊˌkeɪt/ *v.tr.* (also *absol.*) **1** give intellectual, moral, and social instruction to (a pupil, esp. a child), esp. as a formal and prolonged process. **2** provide education for. **3** (often foll. by *in*, or *to* + infin.) train or instruct for a particular purpose. **4** advise; give information to. □□ **educable** /-kəb(ə)l/ *adj.* **educability** /-kə'bɪlɪtɪ/ *n.* **educatable** *adj.* **educative** /-kətɪv/ *adj.* **educator** *n.* [L *educare educat-*, rel. to *educere* EDUCE]

educated /'edjʊˌkeɪtɪd/ *adj.* **1** having had an education, esp. to a higher level than average. **2** resulting from a (good) education (*an educated accent*). **3** based on experience or study (*an educated guess*).

education /ˌedjʊ'keɪʃ(ə)n/ *n.* **1** the act or process of educating or being educated; systematic instruction. **2** a particular kind of or stage in education (*further education; a classical education*). **3 a** development of character or mental powers. **b** a stage in or aspect of this (*travel will be an education for you*). □□ **educational** *adj.* **educationalist** *n.* **educationally** *adv.* **educationist** *n.* [F *éducation* or L *educatio* (as EDUCATE)]

educe /ɪ'djuːs/ *v.tr.* **1** bring out or develop from latent or potential existence; elicit. **2** infer; elicit a principle, number, etc., from data. □□ **educible** *adj.* **eduction** /ɪ'dʌkʃ(ə)n/ *n.* **eductive** /ɪ'dʌktɪv/ *adj.* [ME f. L *educere educt-* lead out (as E-, *ducere* lead)]

Edw. *abbr.* Edward.

Edwardian /ed'wɔːdɪən/ *adj.* & *n.* —*adj.* of, characteristic of, or associated with the reign of King Edward VII (1901-10). —*n.* a person belonging to this period.

-ee /iː/ *suffix* forming nouns denoting: **1** the person affected by the verbal action (*addressee; employee; lessee*). **2** a person concerned with or described as (*absentee; bargee; refugee*). **3** an object of smaller size (*bootee*). [from or after AF past part. in *-é* f. L *-atus*]

EEC *abbr.* European Economic Community.

EEG *abbr.* electroencephalogram.

eel /iːl/ *n.* **1** any of various snakelike fish, with slender body and poorly developed fins. **2** a slippery or evasive person or thing. □**eel-grass 1** any marine plant of the genus *Zostera*, with long ribbon-like leaves. **2** any submerged freshwater plant of the genus *Vallisneria*. □□ **eel-like** *adj.* **eely** *adj.* [OE *æl* f. Gmc]

eelpout /'iːlpaʊt/ *n.* **1** any fish of the family Zoarcidae, with slender body and dorsal and anal fins meeting to fuse with the tail. Also called POUT². **2** = BURBOT. [OE *æleputa* (as EEL, POUT²)]

eelworm /'iːlwɜːm/ *n.* any of various small nematode worms infesting plant roots.

e'en¹ /iːn/ *archaic* or *poet.* var. of EVEN¹.

e'en² /iːn/ *Sc.* var. of EVEN².

-een /iːn/ *suffix Ir.* forming diminutive nouns (*colleen*). [Ir. *-ín* dimin. suffix]

e'er /eə(r)/ *poet.* var. of EVER.

-eer /ɪə(r)/ *suffix* forming: **1** nouns meaning 'person concerned with or engaged in' (*auctioneer; mountaineer; profiteer*). **2** verbs meaning 'be concerned

eerie /'ɪərɪ/ adj. (**eerier**, **eeriest**) gloomy and strange; weird, frightening (an eerie silence). □□ **eerily** adv. **eeriness** n. [orig. N.Engl. and Sc. eri, of obscure orig.: cf. OE earg cowardly]

EETPU abbr. (in the UK) Electrical, Electronic, Telecommunications, and Plumbing Union.

ef- /ɪf, ef/ prefix assim. form of EX-¹ before f.

eff /ef/ v. sl. euphem. **1** tr. & intr. (often foll. by off) = FUCK (in expletive use). **2** intr. say fuck or similar coarse slang words. □**effing and blinding** using coarse slang. [name of the letter F, as a euphemistic abbr.]

efface /ɪ'feɪs/ v. **1** tr. rub or wipe out (a mark etc.). **2** tr. (in abstract senses) obliterate; wipe out (effaced it from his memory). **3** tr. utterly surpass; eclipse (success has effaced all previous attempts). **4** refl. treat or regard oneself as unimportant (self-effacing). □□ **effacement** n. [F effacer (as EX-¹, FACE)]

effect /ɪ'fekt/ n. & v. —n. **1** the result or consequence of an action etc. **2** efficacy (had little effect). **3** an impression produced on a spectator, hearer, etc. (lights had a pretty effect; my words had no effect). **4** (in pl.) property, luggage. **5** (in pl.) the lighting, sound, etc., used to accompany a play, film, broadcast, etc. **6** Physics a physical phenomenon, usually named after its discoverer (Doppler effect). **7** the state of being operative. —v.tr. **1** bring about; accomplish. **2** cause to exist or occur. □**bring** (or **carry**) **into effect** accomplish. **for effect** to create an impression. **give effect to** make operative. **in effect** for practical purposes; in reality. **take effect** become operative. **to the effect that** the general substance or gist being. **to that effect** having that result or implication. **with effect from** coming into operation at or on (a stated time or day). [ME f. OF effect or L effectus (as EX-¹, facere make)]

effective /ɪ'fektɪv/ adj. & n. —adj. **1** having a definite or desired effect. **2** powerful in effect; impressive. **3 a** actual; existing in fact rather than officially or theoretically (took effective control in their absence). **b** actually usable; realizable; equivalent in its effect (effective money; effective demand). **4** coming into operation (effective as from 1 May). **5** (of manpower) fit for work or service. —n. a soldier available for service. □□ **effectively** adv. **effectiveness** n. [ME f. L effectivus (as EFFECT)]

effector /ɪ'fektə(r)/ adj. & n. Biol. —adj. acting in response to a stimulus. —n. an effector organ.

effectual /ɪ'fektʃʊəl, -tjʊəl/ adj. **1** capable of producing the required result or effect; answering its purpose. **2** valid. □□ **effectuality** /-'ælɪtɪ/ n. **effectually** adv. **effectualness** n. [ME f. med.L effectualis (as EFFECT)]

effectuate /ɪ'fektjʊ,eɪt/ v.tr. cause to happen; accomplish. □□ **effectuation** /-'eɪʃ(ə)n/ n. [med.L effectuare (as EFFECT)]

effeminate /ɪ'femɪnət/ adj. (of a man) feminine in appearance or manner; unmasculine. □□ **effeminacy** n. **effeminately** adv. [ME f. L effeminatus past part. of effeminare (as EX-¹, femina woman)]

effendi /e'fendɪ/ n. (pl. **effendis**) **1** a man of education or standing in Eastern Mediterranean or Arab countries. **2** a former title of respect or courtesy in Turkey. [f. Turk. efendi f. mod. Gk afentēs f. Gk authentēs lord, master: see AUTHENTIC]

efferent /'efərənt/ adj. Physiol. conducting outwards (efferent nerves; efferent vessels) (opp. AFFERENT). □□ **efference** n. [L efferre (as EX-¹, ferre carry)]

effervesce /,efə'ves/ v.intr. **1** give off bubbles of gas; bubble. **2** (of a person) be lively or energetic. □□ **effervescence** n. **effervescency** n. **effervescent** adj. [L effervescere (as EX-¹, fervēre be hot)]

effete /ɪ'fiːt/ adj. **1** feeble and incapable. **2** worn out; exhausted of its essential quality or vitality. □□ **effeteness** n. [L effetus worn out by bearing young (as EX-¹, FOETUS)]

efficacious /,efɪ'keɪʃəs/ adj. (of a thing) producing or sure to produce the desired effect. □□ **efficaciously** adv. **efficaciousness** n. **efficacy** /'efɪkəsɪ/ n. [L efficax (as EFFICIENT)]

efficiency /ɪ'fɪʃənsɪ/ n. (pl. **-ies**) **1** the state or quality of being efficient. **2** Mech. & Physics the ratio of useful work performed to the total energy expended or heat taken in. □**efficiency bar** a point on a salary scale requiring evidence of efficiency for further promotion. [L efficientia (as EFFICIENT)]

efficient /ɪ'fɪʃ(ə)nt/ adj. **1** productive with minimum waste or effort. **2** (of a person) capable; acting effectively. □**efficient cause** Philos. an agent that brings a thing into being or initiates a change. □□ **efficiently** adv. [ME f. L efficere (as EX-¹, facere make, accomplish)]

effigy /'efɪdʒɪ/ n. (pl. **-ies**) a sculpture or model of a person. □**in effigy** in the form of a (usu. crude) representation of a person. [L effigies f. effingere to fashion]

effleurage /,eflɜː'rɑːʒ/ n. & v. —n. a form of massage involving a circular inward stroking movement made with the palm of the hand, used esp. during childbirth. —v.intr. massage with a circular stroking movement. [F f. effleurer to skim]

effloresce /,eflɔː'res/ v.intr. **1** burst out into flower. **2** Chem. **a** (of a substance) turn to a fine powder on exposure to air. **b** (of salts) come to the surface and crystallize on it. **c** (of a surface) become covered with salt particles. □□ **efflorescence** n. **efflorescent** adj. [L efflorescere (as EX-¹, florēre to bloom f. flos floris flower)]

effluence /'efluəns/ n. **1** a flowing out (of light, electricity, etc.). **2** that which flows out. [F effluence or med.L effluentia f. L effluere efflux- flow out (as EX-¹, fluere flow)]

effluent /'efluənt/ adj. & n. —adj. flowing forth or out. —n. **1** sewage or industrial waste discharged into a river, the sea, etc. **2** a stream or lake flowing from a larger body of water.

effluvium /ɪ'fluːvɪəm/ n. (pl. **effluvia** /-vɪə/) an unpleasant or noxious odour or exhaled substance affecting the lungs or the sense of smell etc. [L (as EFFLUENT)]

efflux /'eflʌks/ n. = EFFLUENCE. □□ **effluxion** /e'flʌkʃ(ə)n/ n. [med.L effluxus (as EFFLUENT)]

effort /'efət/ n. **1** strenuous physical or mental exertion. **2** a vigorous or determined attempt. **3** Mech. a force exerted. **4** colloq. the result of an attempt; something accomplished (not bad for a first effort). □□ **effortful** adj. [F f. OF esforcier ult. f. L fortis strong]

effortless /'efətlɪs/ adj. **1** seemingly without effort; natural, easy. **2** requiring no effort (effortless contemplation). □□ **effortlessly** adv. **effortlessness** n.

effrontery /ɪ'frʌntərɪ/ n. (pl. **-ies**) **1** shameless insolence; impudent audacity (esp. have the effrontery to). **2** an instance of this. [F effronterie f. effronté ult. f. LL effrons -ontis shameless (as EX-¹, frons forehead)]

effulgent /ɪ'fʌldʒ(ə)nt/ adj. literary radiant; shining brilliantly. □□ **effulgence** n. **effulgently** adv. [L effulgēre shine forth (as EX-¹, fulgēre shine)]

effuse adj. & v. —adj. /ɪ'fjuːs/ Bot. (of an inflorescence etc.) spreading loosely. —v.tr. /ɪ'fjuːz/ **1** pour forth (liquid, light, etc.). **2** give out (ideas etc.). [ME f. L effusus past part. of effundere effus- pour out (as EX-¹, fundere pour)]

effusion /ɪ'fjuːʒ(ə)n/ n. **1** a copious outpouring. **2** usu. derog. an unrestrained flow of speech or writing. [ME f. OF effusion or L effusio (as EFFUSE)]

effusive /ɪ'fjuːsɪv/ adj. **1** gushing, demonstrative, exuberant (effusive praise). **2** Geol. (of igneous rock) poured out when molten and later solidified, volcanic. □□ **effusively** adv. **effusiveness** n.

EFL abbr. English as a foreign language.

eft /eft/ n. a newt. [OE efeta, of unkn. orig.]

æ cat ɑː arm e bed ɜː her ɪ sit iː see ɒ hot ɔː saw ʌ run ʊ put uː too ə ago aɪ my

Efta /'eftə/ n. (also **EFTA**) European Free Trade Association. [abbr.]

e.g. abbr. for example. [L exempli gratia]

egad /i:'gæd/ int. archaic or joc. by God. [prob. orig. a ah + GOD]

egalitarian /ɪ,gælɪ'teərɪən/ adj. & n. —adj. **1** of or relating to the principle of equal rights and opportunities for all (an egalitarian society). **2** advocating this principle. —n. a person who advocates or supports egalitarian principles. □□ **egalitarianism** n. [F égalitaire f. égal EQUAL]

egg[1] /eg/ n. **1 a** the spheroidal reproductive body produced by females of animals such as birds, reptiles, fish, etc., enclosed in a protective layer and capable of developing into a new individual. **b** the egg of the domestic hen, used for food. **2** Biol. the female reproductive cell in animals and plants. **3** colloq. a person or thing qualified in some way (a tough egg). **4** anything resembling or imitating an egg, esp. in shape or appearance. □ **as sure as eggs is** (or **are**) **eggs** colloq. without any doubt. **egg-beater 1** a device for beating eggs. **2** US sl. a helicopter. **egg-custard** = CUSTARD[1]. **egg-flip** (or **-nog**) a drink of alcoholic spirit with beaten egg, milk, etc. **eggs** (or **egg**) **and bacon** any of various yellow- and orange-shaded plants, esp. the snapdragon or toadflax. **egg-spoon** a small spoon for eating a boiled egg. **egg-timer** a device for timing the cooking of an egg. **egg-tooth** a projection of an embryo bird or reptile used for breaking out of the shell. **egg-white** the white of an egg. **have** (or **put**) **all one's eggs in one basket** colloq. risk everything on a single venture. **with egg on one's face** colloq. made to look foolish. □□ **eggless** adj. **eggy** adj. (**eggier**, **eggiest**). [ME f. ON, rel. to OE ǣg]

egg[2] /eg/ v.tr. (foll. by on) urge (egged us on to it; egged them on to do it). [ME f. ON eggja = EDGE]

eggcup /'egkʌp/ n. a cup for holding a boiled egg.

egger /'egə(r)/ n. (also **eggar**) any of various large moths of the family Lasiocampidae, esp. Lasiocampa quercus, with an egg-shaped cocoon. [prob. f. EGG[1] + -ER[1]]

egghead /'eghed/ n. colloq. an intellectual; an expert.

eggplant /'egplɑːnt/ n. = AUBERGINE.

eggshell /'egʃel/ n. & adj. —n. **1** the shell of an egg. **2** anything very fragile. —adj. **1** (of china) thin and fragile. **2** (of paint) with a slight gloss finish.

eglantine /'eglən,taɪn/ n. sweet-brier. [ME f. F églantine f. OF aiglent ult. f. L acus needle]

ego /'i:gəʊ/ n. (pl. **-os**) **1** Metaphysics a conscious thinking subject. **2** Psychol. the part of the mind that reacts to reality and has a sense of individuality. **3** self-esteem. □ **ego-ideal 1** Psychol. the part of the mind developed from the ego by an awareness of social standards. **2** (in general use) idealization of oneself. **ego-trip** colloq. activity etc. devoted entirely to one's own interests or feelings. [L, = I]

egocentric /,i:gəʊ'sentrɪk/ adj. **1** centred in the ego. **2** self-centred, egoistic. □□ **egocentrically** adv. **egocentricity** /-'trɪsɪtɪ/ n. [EGO + -CENTRIC after geocentric etc.]

egoism /'i:gəʊ,ɪz(ə)m/ n. **1** an ethical theory that treats self-interest as the foundation of morality. **2** systematic selfishness. **3** self-opinionatedness. **4** = EGOTISM. □□ **egoist** n. **egoistic** /-'ɪstɪk/ adj. **egoistical** /-'ɪstɪk(ə)l/ adj. [F égoïsme ult. f. mod.L egoismus (as EGO)]

egomania /,i:gəʊ'meɪnɪə/ n. morbid egotism. □□ **egomaniac** /-'meɪnɪ,æk/ n. **egomaniacal** /-mə'naɪək(ə)l/ adj.

egotism /'i:gə,tɪz(ə)m/ n. **1** excessive use of 'I' and 'me'. **2** the practice of talking about oneself. **3** an exaggerated opinion of oneself. **4** selfishness. □□ **egotist** n. **egotistic** /-'tɪstɪk/ adj. **egotistical** /-'tɪstɪk(ə)l/ adj. **egotistically** /-'tɪstɪkəlɪ/ adv. **egotize** v.intr. (also **-ise**). [EGO + -ISM with intrusive -t-]

egregious /ɪ'griːdʒəs/ adj. **1** outstandingly bad; shocking (egregious folly; an egregious ass). **2** archaic or joc. remarkable. □□ **egregiously** adv. **egregiousness** n. [L egregius illustrious, lit. 'standing out from the flock' f. grex gregis flock]

egress /'iːgres/ n. **1 a** going out. **b** the right of going out. **2** an exit; a way out. **3** Astron. the end of an eclipse or transit. □□ **egression** /iː'greʃ(ə)n/ n. (in senses 1, 2). [L egressus f. egredi egress- (as E-, gradi to step)]

egret /'iːgrɪt/ n. any of various herons of the genus Egretta or Bulbulcus, usu. having long white feathers in the breeding season. [ME, var. of AIGRETTE]

Egyptian /ɪ'dʒɪpʃ(ə)n/ adj. & n. —adj. **1** of or relating to Egypt in NE Africa. **2** of or for Egyptian antiquities (e.g. in a museum) (Egyptian room). —n. **1** a native of ancient or modern Egypt; a national of the Arab Republic of Egypt. **2** the Hamitic language used in ancient Egypt until the 3rd c. AD. □□ **Egyptianize** v.tr. (also **-ise**) **Egyptianization** /-'zeɪʃ(ə)n/ n.

Egyptology /,iːdʒɪp'tɒlədʒɪ/ n. the study of the language, history, and culture of ancient Egypt. □□ **Egyptologist** n.

eh /eɪ/ int. colloq. **1** expressing enquiry or surprise. **2** inviting assent. **3** asking for something to be repeated or explained. [ME ey, instinctive exclam.]

-eian /ɪən/ suffix corresp. to -ey (or -y) + -an (Bodleian; Rugbeian).

Eid /iːd/ n. a Muslim week-long festival celebrating the end of the fast of Ramadan. [Arab. 'īd feast]

eider /'aɪdə(r)/ n. **1** (in full **eider duck**) any of various large northern ducks, esp. of the genus Somateria. **2** (in full **eider-down**) small soft feathers from the breast of the eider duck. [Icel. aethr]

eiderdown /'aɪdə,daʊn/ n. a quilt stuffed with down (orig. from the eider) or some other soft material, esp. as the upper layer of bedclothes.

eidetic /aɪ'detɪk/ adj. & n. —adj. Psychol. (of a mental image) having unusual vividness and detail, as if actually visible. —n. a person able to see eidetic images. □□ **eidetically** adv. [G eidetisch f. Gk eidētikos f. eidos form]

eidolon /aɪ'dəʊlɒn/ n. (pl. **eidolons** or **eidola** /-lə/) **1** a spectre; a phantom. **2** an idealized figure. [Gk eidōlon: see IDOL]

eigen- /'aɪgən/ comb. form Math. & Physics proper, characteristic. [G eigen OWN]

eigenfrequency /'aɪgən,friːkwənsɪ/ n. (pl. **-ies**) Math. & Physics one of the natural resonant frequencies of a system.

eigenfunction /'aɪgən,fʌŋkʃ(ə)n/ n. Math. & Physics that function which under a given operation generates some multiple of itself.

eigenvalue /'aɪgən,væljuː/ n. Math. & Physics that value by which an eigenfunction of an operation is multiplied after the eigenfunction has been subjected to that operation.

eight /eɪt/ n. & adj. —n. **1** one more than seven, or two less than ten; the product of two units and four units. **2** a symbol for this (8, viii, VIII). **3** a figure resembling the form of 8. **4** a size etc. denoted by eight. **5** an eight-oared rowing-boat or its crew. **6** the time of eight o'clock (is it eight yet?). **7** a card with eight pips. —adj. that amount to eight. □ **have one over the eight** sl. get slightly drunk. [OE ehta, eahta]

eighteen /eɪ'tiːn/ n. & adj. —n. **1** one more than seventeen, or eight more than ten; the product of two units and nine units. **2** a symbol for this (18, xviii, XVIII). **3** a size etc. denoted by eighteen. **4** a set or team of eighteen individuals. **5** (18) Brit. (of films) classified as suitable for persons of 18 years and over. —adj. that amount to eighteen. □□ **eighteenth** adj. & n. [OE ehtatēne, eaht-]

eighteenmo /eɪ'tiːnməʊ/ n. = OCTODECIMO.

eightfold /'eɪtfəʊld/ adj. & adv. **1** eight times as much or as many. **2** consisting of eight parts. **3** amounting to eight.

eighth /eɪtθ/ n. & adj. —n. **1** the position in a

sequence corresponding to the number 8 in the sequence 1-8. **2** something occupying this position. **3** one of eight equal parts of a thing. —*adj.* that is the eighth. □**eighth note** esp. *US Mus.* = QUAVER. □□ **eighthly** *adv.*

eightsome /'eɪtsəm/ *n.* **1** (in full **eightsome reel**) a lively Scottish reel for eight dancers. **2** the music for this.

8vo *abbr.* octavo.

eighty /'eɪtɪ/ *n.* & *adj.* —*n.* (*pl.* **-ies**) **1** the product of eight and ten. **2** a symbol for this (80, lxxx, LXXX). **3** (in *pl.*) the numbers from 80 to 89, esp. the years of a century or of a person's life. —*adj.* that amount to eighty. □**eighty-first, -second,** etc. the ordinal numbers between eightieth and ninetieth. **eighty-one, -two,** etc. the cardinal numbers between eighty and ninety. □□ **eightieth** *adj.* & *n.* **eightyfold** *adj.* & *adv.* [OE *-eahtatig* (as EIGHT, -TY²)]

einkorn /'aɪnkɔːn/ *n.* a kind of wheat (*Triticum monococcum*). [G f. *ein* one + *Korn* seed]

einsteinium /aɪn'staɪnɪəm/ *n. Chem.* a transuranic radioactive metallic element produced artificially from plutonium. ¶ Symb.: **Es.** [A. *Einstein*, Ger.-Amer. physicist d. 1955]

eirenic var. of IRENIC.

eirenicon /aɪ'riːnɪˌkɒn/ *n.* (also **irenicon**) a proposal made as a means of achieving peace. [Gk, neut. of *eirēnikos* (adj.) f. *eirēnē* peace]

eisteddfod /aɪ'steðvɒd, -'stedfəd/ *n.* (*pl.* **eisteddfods** or **eisteddfodau** /-ˌdaɪ/) a congress of Welsh bards; a national or local festival for musical competitions etc. □□ **eisteddfodic** /-'fɒdɪk/ *adj.* [Welsh, lit. = session, f. *eistedd* sit]

either /'aɪðə(r), 'iːðə(r)/ *adj.*, *pron.*, *adv.*, & *conj.* —*adj.* & *pron.* **1** one or the other of two (*either you can go; you may have either book*). **2** each of two (*houses on either side of the road; either will do*). —*adv.* & *conj.* **1** as one possibility (*is either black or white*). **2** as one choice or alternative; which way you will (*either come in or go out*). **3** (with *neg.* or *interrog.*) **a** any more than the other (*I didn't like it either; if you do not go, I shall not either*). **b** moreover (*there is no time to lose, either*). □**either-or** *n.* an unavoidable choice between alternatives. —*adj.* involving such a choice. **either way** in either case or event. [OE *ǣgther* f. Gmc]

ejaculate *v.* & *n.* —*v.tr.* /ɪ'dʒækjʊˌleɪt/ (also *absol.*) **1** utter suddenly (words esp. of prayer or other emotion). **2** eject (fluid etc., esp. semen) from the body. —*n.* /ɪ'dʒækjʊlət/ semen that has been ejaculated from the body. □□ **ejaculation** /-'leɪʃ(ə)n/ *n.* **ejaculator** /ɪ'dʒækjʊˌleɪtə(r)/ *n.* **ejaculatory** /ɪ'dʒækjʊˌleɪtərɪ/ *adj.* [L *ejaculari* to dart (as E-, *jaculum* javelin)]

eject /ɪ'dʒekt/ *v.tr.* **1** send or drive out precipitately or by force, esp. from a building or other property; compel to leave. **2 a** cause (the pilot etc.) to be propelled from an aircraft or spacecraft in an emergency. **b** (*absol.*) (of the pilot etc.) be ejected in this way (*they both ejected at 1,000 feet*). **3** cause to be removed or drop out (e.g. a spent cartridge from a gun). **4** dispossess (a tenant etc.) by legal process. **5** dart forth; emit. □□ **ejective** *adj.* **ejectment** *n.* [L *ejicere eject-* (as E-, *jacere* throw)]

ejection /ɪ'dʒekʃ(ə)n/ *n.* the act or an instance of ejecting; the process of being ejected. □**ejection seat** = *ejector seat.*

ejector /ɪ'dʒektə(r)/ *n.* a device for ejecting. □**ejector seat** a device for the automatic ejection of the pilot etc. of an aircraft or spacecraft in an emergency.

eke /iːk/ *v.tr.* □**eke out 1** (foll. by *with, by*) supplement; make the best use of (defective means etc.). **2** contrive to make (a livelihood) or support (an existence). [OE *ēacan*, rel. to L *augēre* increase]

ekka /'ekə/ *n. Ind.* a small one-horse vehicle. [Hindi *ekkā* unit]

-el var. of -LE².

elaborate *adj.* & *v.* —*adj.* /ɪ'læbərət/ **1** carefully

or minutely worked out. **2** highly developed or complicated. —*v.tr.* /ɪ'læbəˌreɪt/ **1 a** work out or explain in detail. **b** (*absol.*) go into details (*I need not elaborate*). **2** produce by labour. **3** (of a natural agency) produce (a substance etc.) from its elements or sources. □□ **elaborately** /-rətlɪ/ *adv.* **elaborateness** /-rətnɪs/ *n.* **elaboration** /-'reɪʃ(ə)n/ *n.* **elaborative** /-rətɪv/ *adj.* **elaborator** /-ˌreɪtə(r)/ *n.* [L *elaboratus* past part. of *elaborare* (as E-, *labor* work)]

élan /eɪ'lɑ̃/ *n.* vivacity, dash. [F f. *élancer* launch]

eland /'iːlənd/ *n.* any antelope of the genus *Taurotragus*, native to Africa, having spirally twisted horns, esp. the largest of living antelopes *T. derbianus.* [Du., = elk]

elapse /ɪ'læps/ *v.intr.* (of time) pass by. [L *elabor elaps-* slip away]

elasmobranch /ɪ'læzməˌbræŋk/ *n. Zool.* any cartilaginous fish of the subclass Chondrichthyes, e.g. sharks, skates, rays. [mod.L *elasmobranchii* f. Gk *elasmos* beaten metal + *bragkhia* gills]

elasmosaurus /ɪˌlæzmə'sɔːrəs/ *n.* a large extinct marine reptile with paddle-like limbs and tough crocodile-like skin. [mod.L f. Gk *elasmos* beaten metal + *sauros* lizard]

elastic /ɪ'læstɪk, ɪ'lɑːstɪk/ *adj.* & *n.* —*adj.* **1** able to resume its normal bulk or shape spontaneously after contraction, dilatation, or distortion. **2** springy. **3** (of a person or feelings) buoyant. **4** flexible, adaptable (*elastic conscience*). **5** *Econ.* (of demand) variable according to price. **6** *Physics* (of a collision) involving no decrease of kinetic energy. —*n.* elastic cord or fabric, usu. woven with strips of rubber. □**elastic band** = *rubber band* (see RUBBER¹). □□ **elastically** *adv.* **elasticity** /ɪlæs'tɪsɪtɪ/ *n.* **elasticize** /ɪ'læstɪˌsaɪz/ *v.tr.* (also **-ise**). [mod.L *elasticus* f. Gk *elastikos* propulsive f. *elaunō* drive]

elasticated /ɪ'læstɪˌkeɪtɪd, ɪ'lɑːst-/ *adj.* (of a fabric) made elastic by weaving with rubber thread.

elastomer /ɪ'læstəmə(r)/ *n.* a natural or synthetic rubber or rubber-like plastic. □□ **elastomeric** /-'merɪk/ *adj.* [ELASTIC, after *isomer*]

elate /ɪ'leɪt/ *v.* & *adj.* —*v.tr.* **1** (esp. as **elated** *adj.*) inspirit, stimulate. **2** make proud. —*adj. archaic* in high spirits; exultant, proud. □□ **elatedly** *adv.* **elatedness** *n.* **elation** *n.* [ME f. L *efferre elat-* raise]

elater /'elətə(r)/ *n.* a click beetle. [mod.L f. Gk *elatēr* driver f. *elaunō* drive]

E-layer /'iːˌleɪə(r)/ *n.* a layer of the ionosphere able to reflect medium-frequency radio waves. [*E* (arbitrary) + LAYER]

elbow /'elbəʊ/ *n.* & *v.* —*n.* **1 a** the joint between the forearm and the upper arm. **b** the part of the sleeve of a garment covering the elbow. **2** an elbow-shaped bend or corner; a short piece of piping bent through a right angle. —*v.tr.* (foll. by *in, out, aside,* etc.) **1** thrust or jostle (a person or oneself). **2** make (one's way) by thrusting or jostling. □**at one's elbow** close at hand. **elbow-grease** *colloq.* vigorous polishing; hard work. **elbow-room** plenty of room to move or work in. **give a person the elbow** *colloq.* send a person away; dismiss or reject a person. **out at elbows 1** (of a coat) worn out. **2** (of a person) ragged, poor. [OE *elboga, elnboga,* f. Gmc (as ELL, BOW¹)]

eld /eld/ *n. archaic* or *poet.* **1** old age. **2** olden time. [OE *(i)eldu* f. Gmc: cf. OLD]

elder¹ /'eldə(r)/ *adj.* & *n.* —*attrib.adj.* (of two indicated persons, esp. when related) senior; of a greater age (*my elder brother*). —*n.* (often prec. by *the*) **1** the older or more senior of two indicated (esp. related) persons (*which is the elder?; is my elder by ten years*). **2** (in *pl.*) **a** persons of greater age or seniority (*respect your elders*). **b** persons venerable because of age. **3** a person advanced in life. **4** *hist.* a member of a senate or governing body. **5** an official in the early Christian, Presbyterian, or Mormon Churches. □**elder brother** (*pl.* **elder brethren**) *Brit.* each of thirteen senior members of Trinity

House. **elder hand** *Cards* the first player. **elder statesman** an influential experienced person, esp. a politician, of advanced age. □□**eldership** *n.* [OE *eldra*, rel. to OLD]

elder² /ˈeldə(r)/ *n.* any shrub or tree of the genus *Sambucus*, with white flowers and usu. blue-black or red berries. [OE *ellærn*]

elderberry /ˈeldəbərɪ/ *n.* (*pl.* **-ies**) the berry of the elder, esp. common elder (*Sambucus nigra*) used for making jelly, wine, etc.

elderly /ˈeldəlɪ/ *adj.* **1** somewhat old. **2** (of a person) past middle age. □□**elderliness** *n.*

eldest /ˈeldɪst/ *adj.* & *n.* first-born or oldest surviving (member of a family, son, daughter, etc.). —*n.* (often prec. by *the*) the eldest of three or more indicated (*who is the eldest?*). □**eldest hand** *Cards* the first player. [OE (as ELDER¹)]

eldorado /ˌeldəˈrɑːdəʊ/ *n.* (*pl.* **-os**) **1** any imaginary country or city abounding in gold. **2** a place of great abundance. [Sp. *el dorado* the gilded]

eldritch /ˈeldrɪtʃ/ *adj.* *Sc.* **1** weird. **2** hideous. [16th c.: perh. f. OE *elfrice* (unrecorded) 'fairy realm']

elecampane /ˌelɪkæmˈpeɪn/ *n.* **1** a sunflower-like plant, *Inula helenium*, with bitter aromatic leaves and roots, used in herbal medicine and cookery. **2** an esp. candied sweetmeat flavoured with this. [corrupt. of med.L *enula* (for L *inula* f. Gk *helenion*) *campana* (prob. = of the fields)]

elect /ɪˈlekt/ *v.* & *adj.* —*v.tr.* (usu. foll. by *to* + infin.) **1** choose (*the principles they elected to follow*). **2** choose (a person) by vote (*elected a new chairman*). **3** *Theol.* (of God) choose (persons) in preference to others for salvation. —*adj.* **1** chosen. **2** select, choice. **3** *Theol.* chosen by God. **4** (after a noun designating office) chosen but not yet in office (*president elect*). [ME f. L *electus* past part. of *eligere elect-* (as E-, *legere* pick)]

election /ɪˈlekʃn/ *n.* **1** the process of electing or being elected, esp. of members of a political body. **2** the act or an instance of electing. [ME f. OF f. L *electio -onis* (as ELECT)]

electioneer /ɪˌlekʃəˈnɪə(r)/ *v.* & *n.* —*v.intr.* take part in an election campaign. —*n.* a person who electioneers.

elective /ɪˈlektɪv/ *adj.* & *n.* —*adj.* **1 a** (of an office or its holder) filled or appointed by election. **b** (of authority) derived from election. **2** (of a body) having the power to elect. **3** having a tendency to act on or be concerned with some things rather than others (*elective affinity*). **4** (of a course of study) chosen by the student; optional. **5** (of a surgical operation etc.) optional; not urgently necessary. —*n.* *US* an elective course of study. □□**electively** *adv.* [F *électif -ive* f. LL *electivus* (as ELECT)]

elector /ɪˈlektə(r)/ *n.* **1** a person who has the right of voting to elect an MP etc. **2** (**Elector**) *hist.* a German prince entitled to take part in the election of the Emperor. **3** *US* a member of an electoral college. □□**electorship** *n.* [ME f. F *électeur* f. L *elector* (as ELECT)]

electoral /ɪˈlektər(ə)l/ *adj.* relating to or ranking as electors. □**electoral college 1** a body of persons representing the States of the US, who cast votes for the election of the President. **2** a body of electors. □□**electorally** *adv.*

electorate /ɪˈlektərət/ *n.* **1** a body of electors. **2** *Austral.* & *NZ* an area represented by one member of parliament. **3** *hist.* the office or territories of the German Elector.

Electra complex /ɪˈlektrə/ *n.* *Psychol.* a daughter's subconscious sexual attraction to her father and hostility towards her mother, corresponding to the Oedipus complex in a son. [*Electra* in Gk tragedy, who caused her mother to be murdered for having murdered Electra's father]

electret /ɪˈlektrɪt/ *n.* *Physics* a permanently polarized piece of dielectric material, analogous to a permanent magnet. [ELECTRICITY + MAGNET]

electric /ɪˈlektrɪk/ *adj.* & *n.* —*adj.* **1** of, worked by, or charged with electricity; producing or capable of generating electricity. **2** causing or charged with sudden and dramatic excitement (*the news had an electric effect*; *the atmosphere was electric*). —*n.* **1** an electric light, vehicle, etc. **2** (in *pl.*) electrical equipment. □**electric blanket** a blanket that can be heated electrically by an internal element. **electric blue** a steely or brilliant light blue. **electric chair** (in the US) an electrified chair used for capital punishment. **electric eel** an eel-like freshwater fish, *Electrophorus electricus*, native to S. America, that kills its prey by electric shock. **electric eye** *colloq.* a photoelectric cell operating a relay when the beam of light illuminating it is obscured. **electric fence** a fence charged with electricity, often consisting of one strand. **electric field** a region of electrical influence. **electric fire** an electrically operated incandescent or convector heater, usu. portable and for domestic use. **electric guitar** a guitar with a built-in electrical sound pick-up rather than a soundbox. **electric organ 1** *Biol.* the organ in some fishes giving an electric shock. **2** *Mus.* an electrically-operated organ. **electric ray** any of several rays which can give an electric shock (see RAY²). **electric shaver** (or **razor**) an electrical device for shaving, with oscillating blades behind a metal guard. **electric shock** the effect of a sudden discharge of electricity on a person or animal, usually with stimulation of the nerves and contraction of the muscles. **electric storm** a violent disturbance of the electrical condition of the atmosphere. □□**electrically** *adv.* [mod.L *electricus* f. L *electrum* f. Gk *ēlektron* amber, the rubbing of which causes electrostatic phenomena]

electrical /ɪˈlektrɪk(ə)l/ *adj.* **1** of or concerned with or of the nature of electricity. **2** operating by electricity. **3** suddenly or dramatically exciting (*the effect was electrical*).

electrician /ˌɪlekˈtrɪʃ(ə)n/ *n.* a person who installs or maintains electrical equipment, esp. professionally.

electricity /ˌɪlekˈtrɪsɪtɪ, ˌel-/ *n.* **1** a form of energy resulting from the existence of charged particles (electrons, protons, etc.), either statically as an accumulation of charge or dynamically as a current. **2** the branch of physics dealing with electricity. **3** a supply of electric current for heating, lighting, etc.

electrify /ɪˈlektrɪˌfaɪ/ *v.tr.* (**-ies**, **-ied**) **1** charge (a body) with electricity. **2** convert (machinery or the place or system employing it) to the use of electric power. **3** cause dramatic or sudden excitement in. □□**electrification** /-frˈkeɪʃ(ə)n/ *n.* **electrifier** *n.*

electro /ɪˈlektrəʊ/ *n.* & *v.* —*n.* (*pl.* **-os**) **1** = ELECTROTYPE *n.* **2** = ELECTROPLATE *n.* —*v.tr.* (**-oes**, **-oed**) *colloq.* **1** = ELECTROTYPE *v.* **2** = ELECTROPLATE *v.* [abbr.]

electro- /ɪˈlektrəʊ/ *comb. form Electr.* of, relating to, or caused by electricity (*electrocute*; *electromagnet*). [Gk *ēlektron* amber: see ELECTRIC]

electrobiology /ɪˌlektrəʊbaɪˈɒlədʒɪ/ *n.* the study of the electrical phenomena of living things.

electrocardiogram /ɪˌlektrəʊˈkɑːdɪəˌgræm/ *n.* a record of the heartbeat traced by an electrocardiograph. [G *Elektrocardiogramm* (as ELECTRO-, CARDIO-, -GRAM)]

electrocardiograph /ɪˌlektrəʊˈkɑːdɪəˌgrɑːf/ *n.* an instrument recording the electric currents generated by a person's heartbeat. □□**electrocardiographic** /-ˈgræfɪk/ *adj.* **electrocardiography** /-ˈɒgrəfɪ/ *n.*

electrochemical /ɪˌlektrəʊˈkemɪk(ə)l/ *adj.* involving electricity as applied to or occurring in chemistry. □□**electrochemist** *n.* **electrochemistry** *n.*

electroconvulsive /ɪˌlektrəʊkənˈvʌlsɪv/ *adj.* (of a therapy) employing the use of the convulsive response to the application of electric shocks.

electrocute /ɪˈlektrəˌkjuːt/ *v.tr.* **1** kill by electricity (as a form of capital punishment). **2** cause death of by electric shock. □□ **electrocution** /-'kju:ʃ(ə)n/ *n*. [ELECTRO-, after EXECUTE]

electrode /ɪ'lektrəud/ *n*. a conductor through which electricity enters or leaves an electrolyte, gas, vacuum, etc. [ELECTRIC + Gk *hodos* way]

electrodialysis /ɪ,lektrəudaɪ'ælɪsɪs/ *n*. dialysis in which electrodes are placed on either side of a semi-permeable membrane, as used in obtaining pure water from salt water.

electrodynamics /ɪ,lektrəudaɪ'næmɪks/ *n.pl*. (usu. treated as *sing*.) the branch of mechanics concerned with electric current applied to motive forces. □□ **electrodynamic** *adj*.

electroencephalogram /ɪ,lektrəuɪn'sefələ,græm/ *n*. a record of the brain's activity traced by an electroencephalograph. [G *Elektrenkephalogramm* (as ELECTRO-, ENCEPHALO-, -GRAM)]

electroencephalograph /ɪ,lektrəuɪn'sefələ,grɑ:f/ *n*. an instrument recording the electrical activity of the brain. □□ **electroencephalography** /-'lɒgrəfɪ/ *n*.

electroluminescence /ɪ,lektrəu,lu:mɪ'nes(ə)ns/ *n*. *Chem*. luminescence produced electrically, esp. by the application of a voltage. □□ **electroluminescent** *adj*.

electrolyse /ɪ'lektrə,laɪz/ *v.tr*. (US **-yze**) subject to or treat by electrolysis. □□ **electrolyser** *n*. [ELECTROLYSIS after *analyse*]

electrolysis /ɪlek'trɒlɪsɪs, ,el-/ *n*. **1** *Chem*. the decomposition of a substance by the application of an electric current. **2** *Surgery* this process applied to the destruction of tumours, hair-roots, etc. □□ **electrolytic** /ɪ,lektrəu'lɪtɪk/ *adj*. **electrolytical** /-'lɪtɪk(ə)l/ *adj*. **electrolytically** /-'lɪtɪkəlɪ/ *adv*. [ELECTRO- -LYSIS]

electrolyte /ɪ'lektrə,laɪt/ *n*. **1** a substance which conducts electricity when molten or in solution, esp. in an electric cell or battery. **2** a solution of this. [ELECTRO- + Gk *lutos* released f. *luō* loosen]

electromagnet /ɪ,lektrəu'mægnɪt/ *n*. a soft metal core made into a magnet by the passage of electric current through a coil surrounding it. □□ **electromagnetically** /-'netɪkəlɪ/ *adv*.

electromagnetic /ɪ,lektrəumæg'netɪk/ *adj*. having both an electrical and a magnetic character or properties. □ **electromagnetic radiation** a kind of radiation including visible light, radio waves, gamma rays, X-rays, etc., in which electric and magnetic fields vary simultaneously. **electromagnetic spectrum** the range of wavelengths over which electromagnetic radiation extends. **electromagnetic units** a system of units derived primarily from the magnetic properties of electric currents.

electromagnetism /ɪ,lektrəu'mægnɪ,tɪz(ə)m/ *n*. **1** the magnetic forces produced by electricity. **2** the study of this.

electromechanical /ɪ,lektrəumɪ'kænɪk(ə)l/ *adj*. relating to the application of electricity to mechanical processes, devices, etc.

electrometer /,ɪlek'trɒmɪtə(r), ,el-/ *n*. an instrument for measuring electrical potential without drawing any current from the circuit. □□ **electrometric** /-'metrɪk/ *adj*. **electrometry** *n*.

electromotive /ɪ,lektrəu'məutɪv/ *adj*. producing or tending to produce an electric current. □ **electromotive force** a force set up in an electric circuit by a difference in potential.

electron /ɪ'lektrɒn/ *n*. a stable elementary particle with a charge of negative electricity, found in all atoms and acting as the primary carrier of electricity in solids. □ **electron beam** a stream of electrons in a gas or vacuum. **electron diffraction** the diffraction of a beam of electrons by atoms or molecules, used for determining crystal structures etc. **electron gun** a device for producing a narrow stream of electrons from a heated cathode. **electron lens** a device for focusing a stream of electrons by means of electric or magnetic fields. **electron microscope** a microscope

with high magnification and resolution, employing electron beams in place of light and using electron lenses. **electron pair** an electron and a positron. **electron spin resonance** a spectroscopic method of locating electrons within the molecules of a paramagnetic substance. ¶ Abbr.: ESR. [ELECTRIC + -ON]

electronegative /ɪ,lektrəu'negətɪv/ *adj*. **1** electrically negative. **2** *Chem*. (of an element) tending to acquire electrons.

electronic /,ɪlek'trɒnɪk, ,el-/ *adj*. **1 a** produced by or involving the flow of electrons. **b** of or relating to electrons or electronics. **2** (of a device) using electronic components. **3 a** (of music) produced by electronic means and usu. recorded on tape. **b** (of a musical instrument) producing sounds by electronic means. □ **electronic flash** a flash from a gas-discharge tube, used in high-speed photography. **electronic mail** messages distributed by electronic means esp. from one computer system to one or more recipients: also called EMAIL. □□ **electronically** *adv*.

electronics /,ɪlek'trɒnɪks, ,el-/ *n.pl*. (treated as *sing*.) **1** a branch of physics and technology concerned with the behaviour and movement of electrons in a vacuum, gas, semiconductor, etc. **2** the circuits used in this.

electronvolt /ɪ'lektrɒn,vɒlt/ *n*. a unit of energy equal to the work done on an electron in accelerating it through a potential difference of one volt. ¶ Abbr.: eV.

electrophilic /ɪ,lektrəu'fɪlɪk/ *adj*. *Chem*. having an affinity for electrons. □□ **electrophile** /ɪ'lektrəu,faɪl/ *n*.

electrophoresis /ɪ,lektrəufɔː'ri:sɪs/ *n*. *Physics* & *Chem*. the movement of colloidal particles in a fluid under the influence of an electric field. □□ **electrophoretic** /-fə'retɪk/ *adj*. [ELECTRO- + Gk *phorēsis* being carried]

electrophorus /,ɪlek'trɒfərəs, el-/ *n*. a device for repeatedly generating static electricity by induction. [mod.L f. ELECTRO- + Gk *-phoros* bearing]

electroplate /ɪ'lektrə,pleɪt/ *v*. & *n*. —*v.tr*. coat (a utensil etc.) by electrolytic deposition with chromium, silver, etc. —*n*. electroplated articles. □□ **electroplater** *n*.

electroplexy /ɪ'lektrə,pleksɪ/ *n*. *Brit*. electroconvulsive therapy. [ELECTRO- + APOPLEXY]

electropositive /ɪ,lektrəu'pɒsɪtɪv/ *adj*. **1** electrically positive. **2** *Chem*. (of an element) tending to lose electrons.

electroscope /ɪ'lektrə,skəup/ *n*. an instrument for detecting and measuring electricity, esp. as an indication of the ionization of air by radioactivity. □□ **electroscopic** /-'skɒpɪk/ *adj*.

electro-shock /ɪ'lektrəu,ʃɒk/ *attrib.adj*. (of medical treatment) by means of electric shocks.

electrostatic /ɪ,lektrəu'stætɪk/ *adj*. of electricity at rest. □ **electrostatic units** a system of electric units based primarily on the forces between electric charges. [ELECTRO- + STATIC after *hydrostatic*]

electrostatics /ɪ,lektrəu'stætɪks/ *n.pl*. (treated as *sing*.) the study of electricity at rest.

electrotechnology /ɪ,lektrəutek'nɒlədʒɪ/ *n*. the science of the application of electricity in technology. □□ **electrotechnic** /-'teknɪk/ *adj*. **electrotechnical** /-'teknɪk(ə)l/ *adj*. **electrotechnics** /-'teknɪks/ *n*.

electrotherapy /ɪ,lektrəu'θerəpɪ/ *n*. the treatment of diseases by the use of electricity. □□ **electrotherapeutic** /-'pju:tɪk/ *adj*. **electrotherapeutical** /-'pju:tɪk(ə)l/ *adj*. **electrotherapist** *n*.

electrothermal /ɪ,lektrəu'θɜːm(ə)l/ *adj*. relating to heat electrically derived.

electrotype /ɪ'lektrəu,taɪp/ *v*. & *n*. —*v.tr*. copy by the electrolytic deposition of copper on a mould, esp. for printing. —*n*. a copy so formed. □□ **electrotyper** *n*.

æ *cat* ɑ: *arm* e *bed* ɜ: *her* ɪ *sit* i: *see* ɒ *hot* ɔ: *saw* ʌ *run* ʊ *put* u: *too* ə *ago* aɪ *my*

electrovalent /ɪˌlektrəʊˈveɪlənt/ adj. Chem. linking ions by a bond resulting from electrostatic attraction. □□ **electrovalence** n. **electrovalency** n. [ELECTRO- + -valent after trivalent etc.]

electrum /ɪˈlektrəm/ n. **1** an alloy of silver and gold used in ancient times. **2** native argentiferous gold ore. [ME f. L f. Gk ēlektron amber, electrum]

electuary /ɪˈlektjʊərɪ/ n. (pl. -ies) medicinal powder etc. mixed with honey or other sweet substance. [ME f. LL electuarium, prob. f. Gk ekleikton f. ekleikhō lick up]

eleemosynary /ˌeliːˈmɒsɪnərɪ, -ˈmɒzɪnərɪ/ adj. **1** of or dependent on alms. **2** charitable. **3** gratuitous. [med.L eleemosynarius f. LL eleemosyna: see ALMS]

elegant /ˈelɪgənt/ adj. **1** graceful in appearance or manner. **2** tasteful, refined. **3** (of a mode of life etc.) of refined luxury. **4** ingeniously simple and pleasing. **5** US excellent. □□ **elegance** n. **elegantly** adv. [F élégant or L elegant-, rel. to eligere: see ELECT]

elegiac /ˌelɪˈdʒaɪək/ adj. & n. —adj. **1** (of a metre) used for elegies. **2** mournful. —n. (in pl.) verses in an elegiac metre. □ **elegiac couplet** a pair of lines consisting of a dactylic hexameter and a pentameter, esp. in Greek and Latin verse. □□ **elegiacally** adv. [F élégiaque or f. LL elegiacus f. Gk elegeiakos: see ELEGY]

elegize /ˈelɪˌdʒaɪz/ v. (also -ise) **1** intr. (often foll. by upon) write an elegy. **2** intr. write in a mournful strain. **3** tr. write an elegy upon. □□ **elegist** n.

elegy /ˈelɪdʒɪ/ n. (pl. -ies) **1** a song of lament, esp. for the dead (sometimes vaguely used of other poems). **2** a poem in elegiac metre. [F élégie or L elegia f. Gk elegeia f. elegos mournful poem]

element /ˈelɪmənt/ n. **1** a component part; a contributing factor or thing. **2** Chem. & Physics any of the hundred or so substances that cannot be resolved by chemical means into simpler substances. **3 a** any of the four substances (earth, water, air, and fire) in ancient and medieval philosophy. **b** any of these as a being's natural abode or environment. **4** Electr. a resistance wire that heats up in an electric heater, cooker, etc.; an electrode. **5** (in pl.) atmospheric agencies, esp. wind and storm. **6** (in pl.) the rudiments of learning or of a branch of knowledge. **7** (in pl.) the bread and wine of the Eucharist. **8** Math. & Logic an entity that is a single member of a set. □ **in** (or **out of**) **one's element** in (or out of) one's accustomed or preferred surroundings. **reduced to its elements** analysed. [ME f. OF f. L elementum]

elemental /ˌelɪˈment(ə)l/ adj. & n. —adj. **1** of the four elements. **2** of the powers of nature (elemental worship). **3** comparable to a force of nature (elemental grandeur; elemental tumult). **4** uncompounded (elemental oxygen). **5** essential. —n. an entity or force thought to be physically manifested by occult means. □□ **elementalism** n. (in senses 1, 2). [med.L elementalis (as ELEMENT)]

elementary /ˌelɪˈmentərɪ/ adj. **1 a** dealing with or arising from the simplest facts of a subject; rudimentary, introductory. **b** simple. **2** Chem. not decomposable. □ **elementary particle** Physics any of several subatomic particles supposedly not decomposable into simpler ones. **elementary school** a school in which elementary subjects are taught to young children. □□ **elementarily** adv. **elementariness** n. [ME f. L elementarius (as ELEMENT)]

elenchus /ɪˈleŋkəs/ n. (pl. **elenchi** /-kaɪ/) Logic logical refutation. □ **Socratic elenchus** an attempted refutation of an opponent's position by short question and answer. □□ **elenctic** adj. [L f. Gk elegkhos]

elephant /ˈelɪfənt/ n. (pl. same or **elephants**) **1** the largest living land animal, of which two species survive, the larger African (Loxodonta africana) and the smaller Indian (Elephas maximus), both with a trunk and long curved ivory tusks. **2** a size of paper (711 × 584 mm). □ **elephant grass** any of various tall African grasses, esp. Pennisetum purpureum.

elephant seal = sea elephant. **elephant shrew** any small insect-eating mammal of the family Macroscelididae, native to Africa, having a long snout and long hind limbs. □□ **elephantoid** /-ˈfæntɔɪd/ adj. [ME olifaunt etc. f. OF oli-, elefant ult. f. L elephantus, elephans f. Gk elephas -antos ivory, elephant]

elephantiasis /ˌelɪfənˈtaɪəsɪs/ n. gross enlargement of the body, esp. the limbs, due to lymphatic obstruction esp. by a nematode parasite. [L f. Gk (as ELEPHANT)]

elephantine /ˌelɪˈfæntaɪn/ adj. **1** of elephants. **2 a** huge. **b** clumsy, unwieldy (elephantine movements; elephantine humour). [L elephantinus f. Gk elephantinos (as ELEPHANT)]

Eleusinian /ˌeljuːˈsɪnɪən/ adj. of or relating to Eleusis near Athens. □ **Eleusinian mysteries** Gk Hist. the annual celebrations held at ancient Eleusis in honour of Demeter. [L Eleusinius f. Gk Eleusinios]

elevate /ˈelɪˌveɪt/ v.tr. **1** bring to a higher position. **2** Eccl. hold up (the Host or the chalice) for adoration. **3** raise, lift (one's eyes etc.). **4** raise the axis of (a gun). **5** raise (a railway etc.) above ground level. **6** exalt in rank etc. **7** (usu. as **elevated** adj.) raise morally or intellectually (elevated style). **8** (as **elevated** adj.) colloq. slightly drunk. □□ **elevatory** adj. [L elevare raise (as E-, levis light)]

elevation /ˌelɪˈveɪʃ(ə)n/ n. **1 a** the process of elevating or being elevated. **b** the angle with the horizontal, esp. of a gun or of the direction of a heavenly body. **c** the height above a given level, esp. sea level. **d** a high place or position. **2 a** a drawing or diagram made by projection on a vertical plane (cf. PLAN). **b** a flat drawing of the front, side, or back of a house etc. **3** Ballet **a** the capacity of a dancer to attain height in springing movements. **b** the action of tightening the muscles and uplifting the body. □□ **elevational** adj. (in sense 2). [ME f. OF elevation or L elevatio: see ELEVATE]

elevator /ˈelɪˌveɪtə(r)/ n. **1** a hoisting machine. **2** Aeron. the movable part of a tailplane for changing the pitch of an aircraft. **3** US **a** = LIFT n. 3. **b** a place for lifting and storing quantities of grain. **4** that which elevates, esp. a muscle that raises a limb. [mod.L (as ELEVATE)]

eleven /ɪˈlev(ə)n/ n. & adj. —n. **1** one more than ten; the sum of six units and five units. **2** a symbol for this (11, xi, XI). **3** a size etc. denoted by eleven. **4** a set or team of eleven individuals. **5** the time of eleven o'clock (is it eleven yet?). —adj. that amount to eleven. □ **eleven-plus** esp. hist. (in the UK) an examination taken at the age of 11–12 to determine the type of secondary school a child should enter. [OE endleofon f. Gmc]

elevenfold /ɪˈlev(ə)nˌfəʊld/ adj. & adv. **1** eleven times as much or as many. **2** consisting of eleven parts.

elevenses /ɪˈlevənzɪz/ n. (usu. in pl.) Brit. colloq. light refreshment, usu. with tea or coffee, taken about 11 a.m.

eleventh /ɪˈlevənθ/ n. & adj. —n. **1** the position in a sequence corresponding to the number 11 in the sequence 1–11. **2** something occupying this position. **3** one of eleven equal parts of a thing. **4** Mus. **a** an interval or chord spanning an octave and a fourth in the diatonic scale. **b** a note separated from another by this interval. —adj. that is the eleventh. □ **the eleventh hour** the last possible moment.

elevon /ˈelɪˌvɒn/ n. Aeron. the movable part of the trailing edge of a delta wing. [ELEVATOR + AILERON]

elf /elf/ n. (pl. **elves** /elvz/) **1** a mythological being, esp. one that is small and mischievous. **2** a sprite or little creature. □ **elf-lock** a tangled mass of hair. □□ **elfish** adj. **elvish** adj. [OE f. Gmc]

elfin /ˈelfɪn/ adj. & n. —adj. of elves; elflike. —n. archaic a dwarf; a child. [ELF, perh. infl. by ME elvene genit. pl. of elf, and by Elphin in Arthurian romance]

elicit /ɪˈlɪsɪt, eˈlɪsɪt/ v.tr. (**elicited, eliciting**) **1** draw out, evoke (an admission, response, etc.). **2** draw forth (what is latent). □□ **elicitation** /-'teɪʃ(ə)n/ *n.* **elicitor** *n.* [L *elicere elicit-* (as E-, *lacere* entice)]

elide /ɪ'laɪd/ *v.tr.* omit (a vowel or syllable) by elision. [L *elidere elis-* crush out (as E-, *laedere* knock)]

eligible /'elɪdʒɪb(ə)l/ *adj.* **1** (often foll. by *for*) fit or entitled to be chosen (*eligible for a rebate*). **2** desirable or suitable, esp. as a partner in marriage. □□ **eligibility** /-'bɪlɪtɪ/ *n.* **eligibly** *adv.* [F *éligible* f. LL *eligibilis* (as ELECT)]

eliminate /ɪ'lɪmɪ,neɪt/ *v.tr.* **1** remove, get rid of. **2** exclude from consideration; ignore as irrelevant. **3** exclude from further participation in a competition etc. on defeat. **4** *Physiol.* discharge (waste matter). **5** *Chem.* remove (a simpler substance) from a compound. **6** *Algebra* remove (a quantity) by combining equations. □□ **eliminable** /-nəb(ə)l/ *adj.* **elimination** /-'neɪʃ(ə)n/ *n.* **eliminator** *n.* **eliminatory** /-nətərɪ/ *adj.* [L *eliminare* (as E-, *limen liminis* threshold)]

elision /ɪ'lɪʒ(ə)n/ *n.* **1** the omission of a vowel or syllable in pronouncing (as in *I'm, let's, e'en*). **2** the omission of a passage in a book etc. [LL *elisio* (as ELIDE)]

élite /eɪ'liːt, ɪ-/ *n.* **1** (prec. by *the*) the best or choice part of a larger body or group. **2** a select group or class. **3** a size of letter in typewriting (12 per inch). [F f. past part. of *élire* f. Rmc: rel. to ELECT]

élitism /eɪ'liːtɪz(ə)m, ɪ-/ *n.* **1** advocacy of or reliance on leadership or dominance by a select group. **2** a sense of belonging to an élite. □□ **élitist** *n. & adj.*

elixir /ɪ'lɪksɪə(r)/ *n.* **1** *Alchemy* **a** a preparation supposedly able to change metals into gold. **b** (in full **elixir of life**) a preparation supposedly able to prolong life indefinitely. **c** a supposed remedy for all ills. **2** *Pharm.* an aromatic solution used as a medicine or flavouring. [ME f. med.L f. Arab. *al-iksīr* f. *al* the + *iksīr* prob. f. Gk *xērion* powder for drying wounds f. *xēros* dry]

Elizabethan /ɪ,lɪzə'biːθ(ə)n/ *adj. & n.* —*adj.* of the time of Queen Elizabeth I (1558-1603) or of Queen Elizabeth II (1952-). —*n.* a person, esp. a writer, of the time of Queen Elizabeth I or II.

elk /elk/ *n.* (*pl.* same or **elks**) **1** a large deer, *Alces alces*, of N. Europe and Asia, with palmate antlers and a growth of skin hanging from the neck; a moose. **2** *US* a wapiti. □**elk-hound** a large Scandinavian hunting dog with a shaggy coat. [ME, prob. repr. OE *elh, eolh*]

ell /el/ *n. hist.* a former measure of length, about 45 inches. [OE *eln*, rel. to L *ulna*: see ULNA]

ellipse /ɪ'lɪps/ *n.* a regular oval, traced by a point moving in a plane so that the sum of its distances from two other points is constant, or resulting when a cone is cut by a plane which does not intersect the base and makes a smaller angle with the base than the side of the cone makes (cf. HYPERBOLA). [F f. L *ellipsus* f. Gk *elleipsis* f. *elleipō* come short f. *en* in + *leipō* leave]

ellipsis /ɪ'lɪpsɪs/ *n.* (also **ellipse**) (*pl.* **ellipses** /-siːz/) **1** the omission from a sentence of words needed to complete the construction or sense. **2** the omission of a sentence at the end of a paragraph. **3** a set of three dots etc. indicating an omission.

ellipsoid /ɪ'lɪpsɔɪd/ *n.* a solid of which all the plane sections normal to one axis are circles and all the other plane sections are ellipses. □□ **ellipsoidal** /,elɪp'sɔɪd(ə)l/ *adj.*

elliptic /ɪ'lɪptɪk/ *adj.* (also **elliptical**) of, relating to, or having the form of an ellipse or ellipsis. □□ **elliptically** *adv.* **ellipticity** /,elɪp'tɪsɪtɪ/ *n.* [Gk *elleiptikos* defective f. *elleipō* (as ELLIPSE)]

elm /elm/ *n.* **1** any tree of the genus *Ulmus*, esp. *U. procera* with rough serrated leaves. **2** (in full **elmwood**) the wood of the elm. □□ **elmy** *adj.* [OE, rel. to L *ulmus*]

elocution /,elə'kjuːʃ(ə)n/ *n.* **1** the art of clear and expressive speech, esp. of distinct pronunciation and articulation. **2** a particular style of speaking. □□

elocutionary *adj.* **elocutionist** *n.* [L *elocutio* f. *eloqui elocut-* speak out (as E-, *loqui* speak)]

elongate /'iːlɒŋ,geɪt/ *v. & adj.* —*v.* **1** lengthen, prolong. **2** *intr. Bot.* be of slender or tapering form. —*adj. Bot. & Zool.* long in proportion to width. [LL *elongare* (as E-, L *longus* long)]

elongation /,iːlɒŋ'geɪʃ(ə)n/ *n.* **1** the act or an instance of lengthening; the process of being lengthened. **2** a part of a line etc. formed by lengthening. **3** *Mech.* the amount of extension under stress. **4** *Astron.* the angular separation of a planet from the sun or of a satellite from a planet. [ME f. LL *elongatio* (as ELONGATE)]

elope /ɪ'ləʊp/ *v.intr.* **1** run away to marry secretly, esp. without parental consent. **2** run away with a lover. □□ **elopement** *n.* **eloper** *n.* [AF *aloper* perh. f. a ME form *alope*, rel. to LEAP]

eloquence /'eləkwəns/ *n.* **1** fluent and effective use of language. **2** rhetoric. [ME f. OF f. L *eloquentia* f. *eloqui* speak out (as E-, *loqui* speak)]

eloquent /'eləkwənt/ *adj.* **1** possessing or showing eloquence. **2** (often foll. by *of*) clearly expressive or indicative. □□ **eloquently** *adv.* [ME f. OF f. L *eloqui* (as ELOQUENCE)]

Elsan /'elsæn/ *n. Brit. propr.* a type of transportable chemical lavatory. [app. f. *E. L.* Jackson (its manufacturer) + SANITATION]

else /els/ *adv.* **1** (prec. by indef. or interrog. pron.) besides; in addition (*someone else; nowhere else; who else*). **2** instead; other, different (*what else could I say?; he did not love her, but someone else*). **3** otherwise; if not (*run, (or) else you will be late*). [OE *elles*, rel. to L *alius*, Gk *allos*]

elsewhere /'elsweə(r), els'weə(r)/ *adv.* in or to some other place. [OE *elles hwǣr* (as ELSE, WHERE)]

eluant var. of ELUENT.

eluate /'eljuː,eɪt/ *n. Chem.* a solution or gas stream obtained by elution. [formed as ELUENT]

elucidate /ɪ'luːsɪ,deɪt, ɪ'ljuː,s-/ *v.tr.* throw light on; explain. □□ **elucidation** /-'deɪʃ(ə)n/ *n.* **elucidative** *adj.* **elucidator** *n.* **elucidatory** *adj.* [LL *elucidare* (as E-, LUCID)]

elude /ɪ'luːd, ɪ'ljuːd/ *v.tr.* **1** escape adroitly from (a danger, difficulty, pursuer, etc.); dodge. **2** avoid compliance with (a law, request, etc.) or fulfilment of (an obligation). **3** (of a fact, solution, etc.) escape from or baffle (a person's memory or understanding). □□ **elusion** /-ʒ(ə)n/ *n.* **elusory** *adj.* [L *eludere elus-* (as E-, *ludere* play)]

eluent /'eljuːənt/ *n.* (also **eluant**) *Chem.* a fluid used for elution. [L *eluere* wash out (as E-, *luere lut-* wash)]

elusive /ɪ'luːsɪv, ɪ'ljuːsɪv/ *adj.* **1** difficult to find or catch; tending to elude. **2** difficult to remember or recall. **3** (of an answer etc.) avoiding the point raised; seeking to elude. □□ **elusively** *adv.* **elusiveness** *n.*

elute /ɪ'ljuːt/ *v.tr. Chem.* remove (an adsorbed substance) by washing. □□ **elution** *n.* [G *eluieren* (as ELUENT)]

elutriate /ɪ'luːtrɪ,eɪt/ *v.tr. Chem.* separate (lighter and heavier particles in a mixture) by suspension in an upward flow of liquid or gas. □□ **elutriation** /-'eɪʃ(ə)n/ *n.* [L *elutriare elutriat-* (as E-, *lutriare* wash)]

elver /'elvə(r)/ *n.* a young eel. [var. of *eel-fare* (see FARE) = a brood of young eels]

elves *pl.* of ELF.

elvish see ELF.

Elysium /ɪ'lɪzɪəm/ *n.* **1** (also **Elysian Fields**) (in Greek mythology) the abode of the blessed after death. **2** a place or state of ideal happiness. □□ **Elysian** *adj.* [L f. Gk *Elusion (pedion* plain)]

elytron /'elɪ,trɒn/ *n.* (*pl.* **elytra** /-trə/) the outer hard usu. brightly coloured wing-case of a coleopterous insect. [Gk *elutron* sheath]

em /em/ *n. Printing* **1** a unit for measuring the amount of printed matter in a line, usually equal to the nominal width of capital M. **2** a unit of measurement equal to 12 points. □**em rule** (or **dash**)

b *but* d *dog* f *few* g *get* h *he* j *yes* k *cat* l *leg* m *man* n *no* p *pen* r *red* s *sit* t *top* v *voice*

a long dash used in punctuation. [name of the letter M]

em- /ɪm, em/ *prefix* assim. form of EN-[1], EN-[2] before *b*, *p*.

'em /əm/ *pron. colloq.* them (*let 'em all come*). [orig. a form of ME *hem*, dative and accus. 3rd pers. pl. pron.: now regarded as an abbr. of THEM]

emaciate /ɪˈmeɪsɪˌeɪt, ɪˈmeɪʃɪˌeɪt/ *v.tr.* (esp. as **emaciated** *adj.*) make abnormally thin or feeble. □□ **emaciation** /-ˈeɪʃ(ə)n/ *n.* [L *emaciare emaciat-* (as E-, *macies* leanness)]

email /ˈiːmeɪl/ *n.* (also **e-mail**) = *electronic mail*.

emanate /ˈeməˌneɪt/ *v.* **1** *intr.* (usu. foll. by *from*) (of an idea, rumour, etc.) issue, originate (from a source). **2** *intr.* (usu. foll. by *from*) (of gas, light, etc.) proceed, issue. **3** *tr.* emit; send forth. [L *emanare* flow out]

emanation /ˌeməˈneɪʃ(ə)n/ *n.* **1** the act or process of emanating. **2** something that emanates from a source (esp. of virtues, qualities, etc.). **3** *Chem.* a radioactive gas formed by radioactive decay. □□ **emanative** *adj.* [LL *emanatio* (as EMANATE)]

emancipate /ɪˈmænsɪˌpeɪt/ *v.tr.* **1** free from restraint, esp. legal, social, or political. **2** (usu. as **emancipated** *adj.*) cause to be less inhibited by moral or social convention. **3** free from slavery. □□ **emancipation** /-ˈpeɪʃ(ə)n/ *n.* **emancipator** *n.* **emancipatory** *adj.* [L *emancipare* transfer property (as E-, *manus* hand + *capere* take)]

emasculate *v. & adj.* —*v.tr.* /ɪˈmæskjʊˌleɪt/ **1** deprive of force or vigour; make feeble or ineffective. **2** castrate. —*adj.* /ɪˈmæskjʊlət/ **1** deprived of force or vigour. **2** castrated. **3** effeminate. □□ **emasculation** /-ˈleɪʃ(ə)n/ *n.* **emasculator** *n.* **emasculatory** /-lətərɪ/ *adj.* [L *emasculatus* past part. of *emasculare* (as E-, *masculus* dimin. of *mas* male)]

embalm /ɪmˈbɑːm/ *v.tr.* **1** preserve (a corpse) from decay orig. with spices, now by means of arterial injection. **2** preserve from oblivion. **3** endue with balmy fragrance. □□ **embalmer** *n.* **embalmment** *n.* [ME f. OF *embaumer* (as EN-[1], BALM)]

embank /ɪmˈbæŋk/ *v.tr.* shut in or confine (a river etc.) with an artificial bank.

embankment /ɪmˈbæŋkmənt/ *n.* an earth or stone bank for keeping back water, or for carrying a road or railway.

embargo /emˈbɑːgəʊ, ɪm-/ *n. & v.* —*n.* (*pl.* **-oes**) **1** an order of a State forbidding foreign ships to enter, or any ships to leave, its ports. **2** an official suspension of commerce or other activity (*be under an embargo*). **3** an impediment. —*v.tr.* (**-oes**, **-oed**) **1** place (ships, trade, etc.) under embargo. **2** seize (a ship, goods) for State service. [Sp. f. *embargar* arrest f. Rmc (as IN-[2], BAR[1])]

embark /ɪmˈbɑːk/ *v.* **1** *tr. & intr.* (often foll. by *for*) put or go on board a ship or aircraft (to a destination). **2** *intr.* (foll. by *on, upon*) engage in an activity or undertaking. □□ **embarkation** /ˌembɑːˈkeɪʃ(ə)n/ *n.* (in sense 1). [F *embarquer* (as IN-[2], BARK[3])]

embarras de choix /ˌɑ̃bæˌrɑː də ˈʃwɑː/ *n.* (also *embarras de richesse(s)* /riˈʃes/) more choices than one needs or can deal with. [F, = embarrassment of choice, riches]

embarrass /ɪmˈbærəs/ *v.tr.* **1** cause (a person) to feel awkward or self-conscious or ashamed. **2** (as **embarrassed** *adj.*) encumbered with debts. **3** encumber, impede. **4** complicate (a question etc.). **5** perplex. □□ **embarrassedly** *adv.* **embarrassingly** *adv.* **embarrassment** *n.* [F *embarrasser* (orig. = hamper) f. Sp. *embarazar* f. It. *imbarrare* bar in (as IN-[2], BAR[1])]

embassy /ˈembəsɪ/ *n.* (*pl.* **-ies**) **1 a** the residence or offices of an ambassador. **b** the ambassador and staff attached to an embassy. **2** a deputation or mission to a foreign country. [earlier *ambassy* f. OF *ambassée* etc. f. med.L *ambasciata* f. Rmc (as AMBASSADOR)]

embattle /ɪmˈbæt(ə)l/ *v.tr.* **1 a** set (an army etc.) in battle array. **b** fortify against attack. **2** provide (a building or wall) with battlements. **3** (as **embattled**

adj.) **a** prepared or arrayed for battle. **b** involved in a conflict or difficult undertaking. **c** *Heraldry* like battlements in form. [ME f. OF *embataillier* (as EN-[1], BATTLE): see BATTLEMENT]

embay /ɪmˈbeɪ/ *v.tr.* **1** enclose in or as in a bay; shut in. **2** form (a coast) into bays. □□ **embayment** *n.*

embed /ɪmˈbed/ *v.tr.* (also **imbed**) (**-bedded**, **-bedding**) **1** (esp. as **embedded** *adj.*) fix firmly in a surrounding mass (*embedded in concrete*). **2** (of a mass) surround so as to fix firmly. **3** place in or as in a bed. □□ **embedment** *n.*

embellish /ɪmˈbelɪʃ/ *v.tr.* **1** beautify, adorn. **2** add interest to (a narrative) with fictitious additions. □□ **embellisher** *n.* **embellishment** *n.* [ME f. OF *embellir* (as EN-[1], *bel* handsome f. L *bellus*)]

ember[1] /ˈembə(r)/ *n.* **1** (usu. in *pl.*) a small piece of glowing coal or wood in a dying fire. **2** an almost extinct residue of a past activity, feeling, etc. [OE *æmyrge* f. Gmc]

ember[2] /ˈembə(r)/ *n.* (in full **ember-goose**) = *great northern diver.* [Norw. *emmer*]

ember days /ˈembə(r)/ *n.pl.* any of the days traditionally reserved for fasting and prayer in the Christian Church, now associated with ordinations. [OE *ymbren* (n.), perh. f. *ymbryne* period f. *ymb* about + *ryne* course]

embezzle /ɪmˈbez(ə)l/ *v.tr.* (also *absol.*) divert (money etc.) fraudulently to one's own use. □□ **embezzlement** *n.* **embezzler** *n.* [AF *embesiler* (as EN-[1], OF *besillier* maltreat, ravage, of unkn. orig.)]

embitter /ɪmˈbɪtə(r)/ *v.tr.* **1** arouse bitter feelings in (a person). **2** make more bitter or painful. **3** render (a person or feelings) hostile. □□ **embitterment** *n.*

emblazon /ɪmˈbleɪz(ə)n/ *v.tr.* **1 a** portray conspicuously, as on a heraldic shield. **b** adorn (a shield) with heraldic devices. **2** adorn brightly and conspicuously. **3** celebrate, extol. □□ **emblazonment** *n.*

emblem /ˈembləm/ *n.* **1** a symbol or representation typifying or identifying an institution, quality, etc. **2** (foll. by *of*) (of a person) the type (*the very emblem of courage*). **3** a heraldic device or symbolic object as a distinctive badge. □□ **emblematic** /-ˈmætɪk/ *adj.* **emblematical** /-ˈmætɪk(ə)l/ *adj.* **emblematically** /-ˈmætɪkəlɪ/ *adv.* [ME f. L *emblema* f. Gk *emblēma* -*matos* insertion f. *emballō* throw in (as EN-[1], *ballō* throw)]

emblematize /ɪmˈblemaˌtaɪz/ *v.tr.* (also **-ise**) **1** serve as an emblem of. **2** represent by an emblem.

emblements /ˈemblɪmənts/ *n.pl. Law* crops normally harvested annually, regarded as personal property. [ME f. OF *emblaement* f. *emblaier* (as EN-[1], *blé* corn)]

embody /ɪmˈbɒdɪ/ *v.tr.* (**-ies**, **-ied**) **1** give a concrete or discernible form to (an idea, concept, etc.). **2** (of a thing or person) be an expression of (an idea etc.). **3** express tangibly (*courage embodied in heroic actions*). **4** form into a body. **5** include, comprise. **6** provide (a spirit) with bodily form. □□ **embodiment** *n.*

embolden /ɪmˈbəʊld(ə)n/ *v.tr.* (often foll. by *to* + infin.) make bold; encourage.

embolism /ˈembəˌlɪz(ə)m/ *n.* an obstruction of any artery by a clot of blood, air-bubble, etc. [ME, = 'intercalation' f. LL *embolismus* f. Gk *embolismos* f. *emballō* (as EMBLEM)]

embolus /ˈembələs/ *n.* (*pl.* **emboli** /-ˌlaɪ/) an object causing an embolism. [L, = piston, f. Gk *embolos* peg, stopper]

embonpoint /ˌɑ̃bɔ̃ˈpwæ̃/ *n.* plumpness (of a person). [F *en bon point* in good condition]

embosom /ɪmˈbʊz(ə)m/ *v.tr. literary* **1** embrace. **2** enclose, surround.

emboss /ɪmˈbɒs/ *v.tr.* **1** carve or mould in relief. **2** form figures etc. so that they stand out on (a surface). **3** make protuberant. □□ **embosser** *n.* **embossment** *n.* [ME, f. OF (as EN-[1], BOSS[2])]

embouchure /ˈɒmbʊˌʃʊə(r)/ *n.* **1** *Mus.* **a** the mode of applying the mouth to the mouthpiece of a brass or wind instrument. **b** the mouthpiece of some instruments. **2** the mouth of a river. **3** the opening of a valley. [F f. *s'emboucher* discharge itself by the mouth (as EN-[1], *bouche* mouth)]

embowel /ɪm'baʊəl/ *v.tr.* (**embowelled, embowelling**; *US* **emboweled, emboweling**) *archaic* = DISEMBOWEL. [OF *emboweler* f. *esboueler* (as EX-[1], BOWEL)]

embower /ɪm'baʊə(r)/ *v.tr. literary* enclose as in a bower.

embrace /ɪm'breɪs/ *v. & n. —v.tr.* **1 a** hold (a person) closely in the arms, esp. as a sign of affection. **b** (*absol.*, of two people) hold each other closely. **2** clasp, enclose. **3** accept eagerly (an offer, opportunity, etc.). **4** adopt (a course of action, doctrine, cause, etc.). **5** include, comprise. **6** take in with the eye or mind. *—n.* an act of embracing; holding in the arms. □□**embraceable** *adj.* **embracement** *n.* **embracer** *n.* [ME f. OF *embracer*, ult. f. L *in-* IN-[1] + *bracchium* arm]

embranchment /ɪm'brɑ:ntʃmənt/ *n.* a branching-out (of the arm of a river etc.). [F *embranchement* BRANCH (as EN-[1], BRANCH)]

embrasure /ɪm'breɪʒə(r)/ *n.* **1** the bevelling of a wall at the sides of a door or window; splaying. **2** a small opening in a parapet of a fortified building, splayed on the inside. □□**embrasured** *adj.* [F f. *embraser* splay, of unkn. orig.]

embrittle /ɪm'brɪt(ə)l/ *v.tr.* make brittle. □□ **embrittlement** *n.*

embrocation /ˌembrəʊ'keɪʃ(ə)n/ *n.* a liquid used for rubbing on the body to relieve muscular pain etc. [F *embrocation* or med.L *embrocatio* ult. f. Gk *embrokhē* lotion]

embroider /ɪm'brɔɪdə(r)/ *v.tr.* **1** (also *absol.*) **a** decorate (cloth etc.) with needlework. **b** create (a design) in this way. **2** add interest to (a narrative) with fictitious additions. □□**embroiderer** *n.* [ME f. AF *enbrouder* (as EN-[1], OF *brouder, broisder* f. Gmc)]

embroidery /ɪm'brɔɪdərɪ/ *n.* (*pl.* -**ies**) **1** the art of embroidering. **2** embroidered work; a piece of this. **3** unnecessary or extravagant ornament. [ME f. AF *enbrouderie* (as EMBROIDER)]

embroil /ɪm'brɔɪl/ *v.tr.* **1** (often foll. by *with*) involve (a person) in conflict or difficulties. **2** bring (affairs) into a state of confusion. □□**embroilment** *n.* [F *embrouiller* (as EN-[1], BROIL[2])]

embryo /'embrɪəʊ/ *n.* (*pl.* -**os**) **1 a** an unborn or unhatched offspring. **b** a human offspring in the first eight weeks from conception. **2** a rudimentary plant contained in a seed. **3** a thing in a rudimentary stage. **4** (*attrib.*) undeveloped, immature. □**in embryo** undeveloped. □□**embryoid** *adj.* **embryonal** /'embrɪən(ə)l/ *adj.* **embryonic** /ˌembrɪ'ɒnɪk/ *adj.* **embryonically** /-'ɒnɪkəlɪ/ *adv.* [LL *embryo -onis* f. Gk *embruon* foetus (as EN-[2], *bruō* swell, grow)]

embryo- /'embrɪəʊ/ *comb. form* embryo.

embryogenesis /ˌembrɪəʊ'dʒenɪsɪs/ *n.* the formation of an embryo.

embryology /ˌembrɪ'ɒlədʒɪ/ *n.* the study of embryos. □□ **embryologic** /-brɪə'lɒdʒɪk/ *adj.* **embryological** /-brɪə'lɒdʒɪk(ə)l/ *adj.* **embryologically** /-brɪə'lɒdʒɪkəlɪ/ *adv.* **embryologist** *n.*

embus /ɪm'bʌs/ *v.* (**embused, embusing** or **embussed, embussing**) *Mil.* **1** *tr.* put (men or equipment) into a motor vehicle. **2** *intr.* board a motor vehicle.

emcee /em'si:/ *n. & v. colloq. —n.* a master of ceremonies or compère. *—v.tr. & intr.* (**emcees, emceed**) compère. [the letters *MC*]

-eme /i:m/ *suffix Linguistics* forming nouns denoting units of structure etc. (*grapheme; morpheme*). [F *-ème* unit f. Gk *-ēma*]

emend /ɪ'mend/ *v.tr.* edit (a text etc.) to remove errors and corruptions. □□**emendation** /ˌi:men'deɪʃ(ə)n/ *n.* **emendator** /'i:men,deɪtə(r)/ *n.* **emendatory** *adj.* [ME f. L *emendare* (as E-, *menda* fault)]

emerald /'emər(ə)ld/ *n.* **1** a bright-green precious stone, a variety of beryl. **2** (also **emerald green**) the colour of this. □**Emerald Isle** *literary* Ireland. □□ **emeraldine** /-ˌdaɪn, -dɪn/ *adj.* [ME f. OF *emeraude, esm-,* ult. f. Gk *smaragdos*]

emerge /ɪ'mɜ:dʒ/ *v.intr.* (often foll. by *from*) **1** come up or out into view, esp. when formerly concealed. **2** come up out of a liquid. **3** (of facts, circumstances, etc.) come to light, become known, esp. as a result of inquiry etc. **4** become recognized or prominent (*emerged as a leading contender*). **5** (of a question, difficulty, etc.) become apparent. **6** survive (an ordeal etc.) with a specified result (*emerged unscathed*). □□ **emergence** *n.* [L *emergere emers-* (as E-, *mergere* dip)]

emergency /ɪ'mɜ:dʒənsɪ/ *n.* (*pl.* -**ies**) **1** a sudden state of danger, conflict, etc., requiring immediate action. **2 a** a medical condition requiring immediate treatment. **b** a patient with such a condition. **3** (*attrib.*) characterized by or for use in an emergency. **4** *Austral. Sport* a reserve player. □**state of emergency** a condition of danger or disaster affecting a country, esp. with normal constitutional procedures suspended. [med.L *emergentia* (as EMERGE)]

emergent /ɪ'mɜ:dʒ(ə)nt/ *adj.* **1** becoming apparent; emerging. **2** (of a nation) newly formed or made independent.

emeritus /ɪ'merɪtəs/ *adj.* **1** retired and retaining one's title as an honour (*emeritus professor*; *professor emeritus*). **2** honourably discharged from service. [L, past part. of *emereri* (as E-, *merēri* earn)]

emersion /ɪ'mɜ:ʃ(ə)n/ *n.* **1** the act or an instance of emerging. **2** *Astron.* the reappearance of a celestial body after its eclipse or occultation. [LL *emersio* (as EMERGE)]

emery /'emərɪ/ *n.* **1** a coarse rock of corundum and magnetite or haematite used for polishing metal or other hard materials. **2** (*attrib.*) covered with emery. □**emery-board** a strip of thin wood or board coated with emery or another abrasive, used as a nail-file. **emery-paper** cloth or paper covered with emery, used for polishing or cleaning metals etc. [F *émeri(l)* f. It. *smeriglio* ult. f. Gk *smuris, smēris* polishing powder]

emetic /ɪ'metɪk/ *adj. & n. —adj.* that causes vomiting. *—n.* an emetic medicine. [Gk *emetikos* f. *emeō* vomit]

EMF *abbr.* electromotive force.

-emia *US* var. of -AEMIA.

emigrant /'emɪgrənt/ *n. & adj. —n.* a person who emigrates. *—adj.* emigrating.

emigrate /'emɪˌgreɪt/ *v.* **1** *intr.* leave one's own country to settle in another. **2** *tr.* assist (a person) to emigrate. □□**emigration** /-'greɪʃ(ə)n/ *n.* **emigratory** *adj.* [L *emigrare emigrat-* (as E-, *migrare* depart)]

émigré /'emɪˌgreɪ/ *n.* an emigrant, esp. a political exile. [F, past part. of *émigrer* EMIGRATE]

eminence /'emɪnəns/ *n.* **1** distinction; recognized superiority. **2** a piece of rising ground. **3** (**Eminence**) a title used in addressing or referring to a cardinal (*Your Eminence*; *His Eminence*). **4** an important person. [L *eminentia* (as EMINENT)]

éminence grise /ˌeɪmɪˌnɑːs 'griːz/ *n.* **1** a person who exercises power or influence without holding office. **2** a confidential agent. [F, = grey cardinal (see EMINENCE): orig. applied to Cardinal Richelieu's private secretary, Père Joseph d. 1638]

eminent /'emɪnənt/ *adj.* **1** distinguished, notable. **2** (of qualities) remarkable in degree. □**eminent domain** sovereign control over all property in a State, with the right of expropriation. □□ **eminently** *adv.* [ME f. L *eminēre eminent-* jut]

emir /e'mɪə(r)/ *n.* **1** a title of various Muslim rulers. **2** *archaic* a male descendant of Muhammad. [F *émir* f. Arab. *'amīr*: cf. AMIR]

emirate /'emɪərət/ *n.* the rank, domain, or reign of an emir.

emissary /'emɪsərɪ/ *n.* (*pl.* -**ies**) a person sent on a special mission (usu. diplomatic, formerly usu. odious or underhand). [L *emissarius* scout, spy (as EMIT)]

emission /ɪ'mɪʃ(ə)n/ *n.* **1** (often foll. by *of*) the process or an act of emitting. **2** a thing emitted. [L *emissio* (as EMIT)]

emissive /ɪ'mɪsɪv/ *adj.* having the power to radiate light, heat, etc. ▫▫ **emissivity** /ˌiːmɪ'sɪvɪtɪ/ *n.*

emit /ɪ'mɪt/ *v.tr.* (**emitted, emitting**) **1 a** send out (heat, light, vapour, etc.). **b** discharge from the body. **2** utter (a cry etc.). [L *emittere emiss-* (as E-, *mittere* send)]

emitter /ɪ'mɪtə(r)/ *n.* that which emits, esp. a region in a transistor producing carriers of current.

Emmental /'emən,taːl/ *n.* (also **Emmenthal**) a kind of hard Swiss cheese with many holes in it, similar to Gruyère. [G *Emmentaler* f. *Emmental* in Switzerland]

emmer /'emə(r)/ *n.* a kind of wheat, *Triticum dicoccum*, grown mainly for fodder. [G dial.]

emmet /'emɪt/ *n. archaic* or *dial.* an ant. [OE *ǣmete*: see ANT]

Emmy /'emɪ/ *n.* (*pl.* **-ies**) (in the US) a statuette awarded annually to an outstanding television programme or performer. [perh. f. *Immy = image orthicon tube*]

emollient /ɪ'mɒlɪənt/ *adj.* & *n.* —*adj.* that softens or soothes the skin. —*n.* an emollient agent. ▫▫ **emollience** *n.* [L *emollire* (as E-, *mollis* soft)]

emolument /ɪ'mɒljʊmənt/ *n.* a salary, fee, or profit from employment or office. [ME f. OF *emolument* or L *emolumentum*, orig. prob. 'payment for corn-grinding', f. *emolere* (as E-, *molere* grind)]

emote /ɪ'məʊt/ *v.intr. colloq.* show excessive emotion. ▫▫ **emoter** *n.* [back-form. f. EMOTION]

emotion /ɪ'məʊʃ(ə)n/ *n.* a strong mental or instinctive feeling such as love or fear. [earlier = agitation, disturbance of the mind, f. F *émotion* f. *émouvoir* excite]

emotional /ɪ'məʊʃən(ə)l/ *adj.* **1** of or relating to the emotions. **2** (of a person) liable to excessive emotion. **3** expressing or based on emotion (*an emotional appeal*). **4** likely to excite emotion (*an emotional issue*). ▫▫ **emotionalism** *n.* **emotionalist** *n.* **emotionality** /-'nælɪtɪ/ *n.* **emotionalize** *v.tr.* (also **-ise**). **emotionally** *adv.*

emotive /ɪ'məʊtɪv/ *adj.* **1** of or characterized by emotion. **2** tending to excite emotion. **3** arousing feeling; not purely descriptive. ▫▫ **emotively** *adv.* **emotiveness** *n.* **emotivity** /ˌiːməʊ'tɪvɪtɪ/ *n.* [L *emovēre emot-* (as E-, *movēre* move)]

empanel /ɪm'pæn(ə)l/ *v.tr.* (also **impanel**) (**-panelled, -panelling;** *US* **-paneled, -paneling**) enrol or enter on a panel (those eligible for jury service). ▫▫ **empanelment** *n.* [AF *empaneller* (as EN-¹, PANEL)]

empathize /'empə,θaɪz/ *v. Psychol.* **1** *intr.* (usu. foll. by *with*) exercise empathy. **2** *tr.* treat with empathy.

empathy /'empəθɪ/ *n. Psychol.* the power of identifying oneself mentally with (and so fully comprehending) a person or object of contemplation. ▫▫ **empathetic** /-'θetɪk/ *adj.* **empathetically** /-'θetɪkəlɪ/ *adv.* **empathic** /em'pæθɪk/ *adj.* **empathically** /em'pæθ-/ *adv.* **empathist** *n.* [transl. G *Einfühlung* f. *ein* in + *Fühlung* feeling, after Gk *empatheia*: see SYMPATHY]

empennage /em'penɪdʒ/ *n. Aeron.* an arrangement of stabilizing surfaces at the tail of an aircraft. [F f. *empenner* to feather (an arrow)]

emperor /'empərə(r)/ *n.* **1** the sovereign of an empire. **2** a sovereign of higher rank than a king. ▫ **emperor moth** a large moth, *Saturnia pavonia*, of the silk-moth family, with eye-spots on all four wings. **emperor penguin** the largest known penguin, *Aptenodytes forsteri*, of the Antarctic. ▫▫ **emperorship** *n.* [ME f. OF *emperere, empereor* f. L *imperator -oris* f. *imperare* command]

emphasis /'emfəsɪs/ *n.* (*pl.* **emphases** /-ˌsiːz/) **1** special importance or prominence attached to a thing, fact, idea, etc. (*emphasis on economy*). **2** stress

laid on a word or words to indicate special meaning or importance. **3** vigour or intensity of expression, feeling, action, etc. **4** prominence, sharpness of contour. [L f. Gk f. *emphainō* exhibit (as EN-², *phainō* show)]

emphasize /'emfə,saɪz/ *v.tr.* (also **-ise**) **1** bring (a thing, fact, etc.) into special prominence. **2** lay stress on (a word in speaking).

emphatic /ɪm'fætɪk/ *adj.* **1** (of language, tone, or gesture) forcibly expressive. **2** of words: **a** bearing the stress. **b** used to give emphasis. **3** expressing oneself with emphasis. **4** (of an action or process) forcible, significant. ▫▫ **emphatically** *adv.* [LL *emphaticus* f. Gk *emphatikos* (as EMPHASIS)]

emphysema /ˌemfɪ'siːmə/ *n.* **1** enlargement of the air sacs of the lungs causing breathlessness. **2** a swelling caused by the presence of air in the connective tissues of the body. [LL f. Gk *emphusēma* f. *emphusaō* puff up]

empire /'empaɪə(r)/ *n.* **1** an extensive group of States or countries under a single supreme authority, esp. an emperor. **2 a** supreme dominion. **b** (often foll. by *over*) *archaic* absolute control. **3** a large commercial organization etc. owned or directed by one person or group. **4** (**the Empire**) *hist.* **a** the British Empire. **b** the Holy Roman Empire. **5** a type or period of government in which the sovereign is called emperor. **6** (**Empire**) (*attrib.*) **a** denoting a style of furniture or dress fashionable during the first (1804–14) or second (1852–70) French Empire. **b** *Brit.* denoting produce from the Commonwealth. ▫ **empire-builder** a person who deliberately acquires extra territory, authority, etc. esp. unnecessarily. **Empire Day** *hist.* the former name of Commonwealth Day, orig. 24 May. [ME f. OF f. L *imperium* rel. to *imperare*: see EMPEROR]

empiric /ɪm'pɪrɪk/ *adj.* & *n.* —*adj.* = EMPIRICAL. —*n. archaic* **1** a person relying solely on experiment. **2** a quack doctor. ▫▫ **empiricism** *n.* **empiricist** *n.* [L *empiricus* f. Gk *empeirikos* f. *empeiria* experience f. *empeiros* skilled]

empirical /ɪm'pɪrɪk(ə)l/ *adj.* **1** based or acting on observation or experiment, not on theory. **2** *Philos.* regarding sense-data as valid information. **3** deriving knowledge from experience alone. ▫ **empirical formula** *Chem.* a formula showing the constituents of a compound but not their configuration. ▫▫ **empirically** *adv.*

emplacement /ɪm'pleɪsmənt/ *n.* **1** the act or an instance of putting in position. **2** a platform or defended position where a gun is placed for firing. **3** situation, position. [F (as EN-¹, PLACE)]

emplane /ɪm'pleɪn/ *v.intr.* & *tr.* (also **enplane** /ɪn-/) go or put on board an aeroplane.

employ /ɪm'plɔɪ/ *v.* & *n.* —*v.tr.* **1** use the services of (a person) in return for payment; keep (a person) in one's service. **2** (often foll. by *for, in, on*) use (a thing, time, energy, etc.) esp. to good effect. **3** (often foll. by *in*) keep (a person) occupied. —*n.* the state of being employed, esp. for wages. ▫ **in the employ of** employed by. ▫▫ **employable** *adj.* **employability** /-'bɪlɪtɪ/ *n.* **employer** *n.* [ME f. OF *employer* ult. f. L *implicari* be involved f. *implicare* enfold: see IMPLICATE]

employee /ˌemplɔɪ'iː, -'plɔɪ/ *n.* (*US* **employe**) a person employed for wages or salary, esp. at non-executive level.

employment /ɪm'plɔɪmənt/ *n.* **1** the act of employing or the state of being employed. **2** a person's regular trade or profession. ▫ **employment agency** a business that finds employers or employees for those seeking them. **employment office** (formerly **employment exchange**) *Brit.* any of a number of government offices concerned with advising and finding work for the unemployed.

empolder var. of IMPOLDER.

emporium /em'pɔːrɪəm/ *n.* (*pl.* **emporia** /-rɪə/ or **-ums**) **1** a large retail store selling a wide variety of goods. **2** a centre of commerce, a market. [L f. Gk *emporion* f. *emporos* merchant]

empower /ɪm'paʊə(r)/ *v.tr.* (foll. by *to* + infin.) **1** authorize, license. **2** give power to; make able. □□ **empowerment** *n.*

empress /'emprɪs/ *n.* **1** the wife or widow of an emperor. **2** a woman emperor. [ME f. OF *emperesse* fem. of *emperere* EMPEROR]

empty /'emptɪ/ *adj.*, *v.*, & *n.* —*adj.* (**emptier**, **emptiest**) **1** containing nothing. **2** (of a house etc.) unoccupied or unfurnished. **3** (of a transport vehicle etc.) without a load, passengers, etc. **4 a** meaningless, hollow, insincere (*empty threats*; *an empty gesture*). **b** without substance or purpose (*an empty existence*). **5** *colloq.* hungry. **6** (foll. by *of*) devoid, lacking. —*v.* (**-ies**, **-ied**) **1** *tr.* **a** make empty; remove the contents of. **b** (foll. by *of*) deprive of certain contents (*emptied the room of its chairs*). **2** *tr.* (often foll. by *into*) transfer (the contents of a container). **3** *intr.* become empty. **4** *intr.* (usu. foll. by *into*) (of a river) discharge itself (into the sea etc.). —*n.* (*pl.* **-ies**) *colloq.* a container (esp. a bottle) left empty of its contents. □**empty-handed 1** bringing or taking nothing. **2** having achieved or obtained nothing. **empty-headed** foolish; lacking common sense. **empty-nester** *US* either of a couple whose children have grown up and left home. **on an empty stomach** see STOMACH. □□ **emptily** *adv.* **emptiness** *n.* [OE *ǣmtig*, *ǣmetig* f. *ǣmetta* leisure]

empurple /ɪm'pɜːp(ə)l/ *v.tr.* **1** make purple or red. **2** make angry.

empyema /ˌempaɪ'iːmə, ˌempɪ-/ *n.* a collection of pus in a cavity, esp. in the pleura. [LL f. Gk *empuēma* f. *empueō* suppurate (as EN-², *puon* pus)]

empyrean /ˌempaɪ'riːən, empɪ-/ *n.* & *adj.* —*n.* **1** the highest heaven, as the sphere of fire in ancient cosmology or as the abode of God in early Christianity. **2** the visible heavens. —*adj.* of the empyrean. □□ **empyreal** /ˌempaɪ'riːəl, empɪ-, em'pɪr-/ *adj.* [med.L *empyreus* f. Gk *empurios* (as EN-², *pur* fire)]

EMS *abbr.* European Monetary System.

emu /'iːmjuː/ *n.* a large flightless bird, *Dromaius novaehollandiae*, native to Australia, and capable of running at high speed. [earlier *emia*, *eme* f. Port. *ema*]

e.m.u. *abbr.* electromagnetic unit(s).

emulate /'emjʊˌleɪt/ *v.tr.* **1** try to equal or excel. **2** imitate zealously. **3** rival. □□ **emulation** /-'leɪʃ(ə)n/ *n.* **emulative** /-lətɪv/ *adj.* **emulator** *n.* [L *aemulari* (as EMULOUS)]

emulous /'emjʊləs/ *adj.* **1** (usu. foll. by *of*) seeking to emulate. **2** actuated by a spirit of rivalry. □□ **emulously** *adv.* [ME f. L *aemulus* rival]

emulsifier /ɪ'mʌlsɪˌfaɪə(r)/ *n.* **1** any substance that stabilizes an emulsion, esp. a food additive used to stabilize processed foods. **2** an apparatus used for producing an emulsion.

emulsify /ɪ'mʌlsɪˌfaɪ/ *v.tr.* (**-ies**, **-ied**) convert into an emulsion. □□ **emulsifiable** *adj.* **emulsification** /-fɪ'keɪʃ(ə)n/ *n.*

emulsion /ɪ'mʌlʃ(ə)n/ *n.* **1** a fine dispersion of one liquid in another, esp. as paint, medicine, etc. **2** a mixture of a silver compound suspended in gelatin etc. for coating plates or films. □**emulsion paint** a water-thinned paint containing a non-volatile substance, e.g. synthetic resin, as its binding medium. □□ **emulsionize** *v.tr.* (also **-ise**). **emulsive** *adj.* [F *émulsion* or mod.L *emulsio* f. *emulgēre* (as E-, *mulgēre* *muls-* to milk)]

en /en/ *n.* *Printing* a unit of measurement equal to half an em. □**en rule** (or **dash**) a short dash used in punctuation. [name of the letter *N*]

en-¹ /en, ɪn/ *prefix* (also **em-** before *b*, *p*) forming verbs, = IN-¹: **1** from nouns, meaning 'put into or on' (*engulf*; *entrust*; *embed*). **2** from nouns or adjectives, meaning 'bring into the condition of' (*enslave*); often with the suffix *-en* (*enlighten*). **3** from verbs: **a** in

the sense 'in, into, on' (*enfold*). **b** as an intensive (*entangle*). [from or after F *en-* f. L *in-*]

en-² /en, ɪn/ *prefix* (also **em-** before *b*, *p*) in, inside (*energy*; *enthusiasm*). [Gk]

-en¹ /ən/ *suffix* forming verbs: **1** from adjectives, usu. meaning 'make or become so or more so' (*deepen*; *fasten*; *moisten*). **2** from nouns (*happen*; *strengthen*). [OE *-nian* f. Gmc]

-en² /ən/ *suffix* (also **-n**) forming adjectives from nouns, meaning: **1** made or consisting of (often with extended and figurative senses) (*wooden*). **2** resembling; of the nature of (*golden*; *silvern*). [OE f. Gmc]

-en³ /ən/ *suffix* (also **-n**) forming past participles of strong verbs: **1** as a regular inflection (*spoken*; *sworn*). **2** with restricted sense (*drunken*). [OE f. Gmc]

-en⁴ /ən/ *suffix* forming the plural of a few nouns (*children*; *brethren*; *oxen*). [ME reduction of OE *-an*]

-en⁵ /ən/ *suffix* forming diminutives of nouns (*chicken*; *maiden*). [OE f. Gmc]

-en⁶ /ən/ *suffix* **1** forming feminine nouns (*vixen*). **2** forming abstract nouns (*burden*). [OE f. Gmc]

enable /ɪ'neɪb(ə)l/ *v.tr.* **1** (foll. by *to* + infin.) give (a person etc.) the means or authority to do something. **2** make possible. **3** esp. *Computing* make (a device) operational; switch on. □**enabling act 1** a statute empowering a person or body to take certain action. **2** *US* a statute legalizing something otherwise unlawful. □□ **enabler** *n.*

enact /ɪ'nækt/ *v.tr.* **1 a** (often foll. by *that* + clause) ordain, decree. **b** make (a bill etc.) law. **2** play (a part or scene on stage or in life). □□ **enactable** *adj.* **enaction** *n.* **enactive** *adj.* **enactor** *n.* **enactory** *adj.*

enactment /ɪ'næktmənt/ *n.* **1** a law enacted. **2** the process of enacting.

enamel /ɪ'næm(ə)l/ *n.* & *v.* —*n.* **1** a glasslike opaque or semi-transparent coating on metallic or other hard surfaces for ornament or as a preservative lining. **2 a** a smooth hard coating. **b** a cosmetic simulating this. **3** the hard glossy natural coating over the crown of a tooth. **4** painting done in enamel. **5** *poet.* a smooth bright surface colouring, verdure, etc. —*v.tr.* (**enamelled**, **enamelling**; *US* **enameled**, **enameling**) **1** inlay or encrust (a metal etc.) with enamel. **2** portray (figures etc.) with enamel. **3** *archaic* adorn with varied colours. □**enamel paint** a paint that dries to give a smooth hard coat. □□ **enameller** *n.* **enamelling** *n.* [ME f. AF *enameler*, *enamailler* (as EN-¹, OF *esmail* f. Gmc)]

enamelware /ɪ'næm(ə)l,weə(r)/ *n.* enamelled kitchenware.

enamour /ɪ'næmə(r)/ *v.tr.* (*US* **enamor**) (usu. in *passive*; foll. by *of*) **1** inspire with love or liking. **2** charm, delight. [ME f. OF *enamourer* f. *amourer* (as EN-¹, AMOUR)]

enanthema /ˌenæn'θiːmə/ *n.* *Med.* an eruption occurring on a mucus-secreting surface such as the inside of the mouth. [mod.L f. Gk *enanthēma* eruption (as EN-¹, EXANTHEMA)]

enantiomer /en'æntɪəmə(r)/ *n.* *Chem.* a molecule with a mirror image. □□ **enantiomeric** /-'merɪk/ *adj.* [Gk *enantios* opposite + -MER]

enantiomorph /en'æntɪəˌmɔːf/ *n.* a mirror image; a form (esp. of a crystal structure etc.) related to another as an object is to its mirror image. □□ **enantiomorphic** /-'mɔːfɪk/ *adj.* **enantiomorphism** /-'mɔːfɪz(ə)m/ *n.* **enantiomorphous** /-'mɔːfəs/ *adj.* [G f. Gk *enantios* opposite + *morphē* form]

enarthrosis /ˌenɑː'θrəʊsɪs/ *n.* (*pl.* **enarthroses** /-siːz/) *Anat.* a ball-and-socket joint. [Gk f. *enarthros* jointed (as EN-², *arthron* joint)]

en bloc /ɑ̃ 'blɒk/ *adv.* in a block; all at the same time; wholesale. [F]

en brosse /ɑ̃ 'brɒs/ *adj.* (of hair) cut short and bristly. [F]

encaenia /en'siːnɪə/ *n.* **1** (at Oxford University) an annual celebration in memory of founders and benefactors. **2** a dedication festival. [L f. Gk *egkainia* (as EN-², *kainos* new)]

encage /ɪnˈkeɪdʒ/ *v.tr.* confine in or as in a cage.

encamp /ɪnˈkæmp/ *v.tr. & intr.* **1** settle in a military camp. **2** lodge in the open in tents.

encampment /ɪnˈkæmpmənt/ *n.* **1** a place where troops etc. are encamped. **2** the process of setting up a camp.

encapsulate /ɪnˈkæpsjʊˌleɪt/ *v.tr.* **1** enclose in or as in a capsule. **2** summarize; express the essential features of. **3** isolate. □□ **encapsulation** /-ˈleɪʃ(ə)n/ *n.* [EN-¹ + L *capsula* CAPSULE]

encase /ɪnˈkeɪs/ *v.tr.* (also **incase**) **1** put into a case. **2** surround as with a case. □□ **encasement** *n.*

encash /ɪnˈkæʃ/ *v.tr. Brit.* **1** convert (bills etc.) into cash. **2** receive in the form of cash; realize. □□ **encashable** *adj.* **encashment** *n.*

encaustic /ɪnˈkɔːstɪk/ *adj. & n.* —*adj.* **1** (in painting, ceramics, etc.) using pigments mixed with hot wax, which are burned in as an inlay. **2** (of bricks and tiles) inlaid with differently coloured clays burnt in. —*n.* **1** the art of encaustic painting. **2** a painting done with this technique. [L *encausticus* f. Gk *egkaustikos* (as EN-², CAUSTIC)]

-ence /əns/ *suffix* forming nouns expressing: **1** a quality or state or an instance of one (*patience*; *an impertinence*). **2** an action (*reference*; *reminiscence*). [from or after F *-ence* f. L *-entia*, *-antia* (cf. *-ANCE*) f. pres. part. stem *-ent-*, *-ant-*]

enceinte /ɑ̃ˈsæt/ *n. & adj.* —*n.* an enclosure, esp. in fortification. —*adj. archaic* pregnant. [F, ult. f. L *cingere cinct-* gird: see CINCTURE]

encephalic /ˌenkɪˈfælɪk, ˌens-/ *adj.* of or relating to the brain. [Gk *egkephalos* brain (as EN-², *kephalē* head)]

encephalin var. of ENKEPHALIN.

encephalitis /enˌkefəˈlaɪtɪs, enˌsef-/ *n.* inflammation of the brain. □ **encephalitis lethargica** /lɪˈθɑːdʒɪkə/ an infectious encephalitis caused by a virus, with headache and drowsiness leading to coma; sleepy sickness. □□ **encephalitic** /-ˈlɪtɪk/ *adj.*

encephalo- /enˈkefələʊ, enˈsef-/ *comb. form* brain. [Gk *egkephalos* brain]

encephalogram /enˈkefələˌgræm, enˈsef-/ *n.* an X-ray photograph of the brain.

encephalograph /enˈkefələʊˌgrɑːf, enˈsef-/ *n.* an instrument for recording the electrical activity of the brain.

encephalon /enˈkefəˌlɒn, enˈsef-/ *n. Anat.* the brain.

encephalopathy /enˌkefəˈlɒpəθɪ, enˌsef-/ *n.* disease of the brain.

enchain /ɪnˈtʃeɪn/ *v.tr.* **1** chain up, fetter. **2** hold fast (the attention, emotions, etc.). □□ **enchainment** *n.* [ME f. F *enchaîner* ult. f. L *catena* chain]

enchant /ɪnˈtʃɑːnt/ *v.tr.* **1** charm, delight. **2** bewitch. □□ **enchantedly** *adv.* **enchanting** *adj.* **enchantingly** *adv.* **enchantment** *n.* [ME f. F *enchanter* f. L *incantare* (as IN-², *canere cant-* sing)]

enchanter /ɪnˈtʃɑːntə(r)/ *n.* (*fem.* **enchantress**) a person who enchants, esp. by supposed use of magic. □ **enchanter's nightshade** a small plant, *Circaea lutetiana*, with white flowers.

enchase /ɪnˈtʃeɪs/ *v.tr.* **1** (foll. by *in*) place (a jewel) in a setting. **2** (foll. by *with*) set (gold etc.) with gems. **3** inlay with gold etc. **4** adorn with figures in relief. **5** engrave. [ME f. F *enchâsser* (as EN-¹, CHASE³)]

enchilada /ˌentʃɪˈlɑːdə/ *n.* a tortilla with chilli sauce and usu. a filling, esp. meat. [Amer. Sp., fem. past part. of *enchilar* season with chilli]

enchiridion /ˌenkaɪəˈrɪdɪən/ *n.* (*pl.* **enchiridions** or **enchiridia** /-dɪə/) *formal* a handbook. [LL f. Gk *egkheiridion* (as EN-², *kheir* hand, *-idion* dimin. suffix)]

encipher /ɪnˈsaɪfə(r)/ *v.tr.* **1** write (a message etc.) in cipher. **2** convert into coded form using a cipher. □□ **encipherment** *n.*

encircle /ɪnˈsɜːk(ə)l/ *v.tr.* **1** (usu. foll. by *with*)

surround, encompass. **2** form a circle round. □□ **encirclement** *n.*

encl. *abbr.* **1** enclosed. **2** enclosure.

en clair /ɑ̃ ˈkleə(r)/ *adj. & adv.* (of a telegram, official message, etc.) in ordinary language (not in code or cipher). [F, lit. 'in clear']

enclasp /ɪnˈklɑːsp/ *v.tr.* hold in a clasp or embrace.

enclave /ˈenkleɪv/ *n.* **1** a portion of territory of one State surrounded by territory of another or others, as viewed by the surrounding territory (cf. EXCLAVE). **2** a group of people who are culturally, intellectually, or socially distinct from those surrounding them. [F f. *enclaver* ult. f. L *clavis* key]

enclitic /enˈklɪtɪk/ *adj. & n. Gram.* —*adj.* (of a word) pronounced with so little emphasis that it forms part of the preceding word. —*n.* such a word, e.g. *not* in *cannot*. □□ **enclitically** *adv.* [LL *encliticus* f. Gk *egklitikos* (as EN-², *klinō* lean)]

enclose /ɪnˈkləʊz/ *v.tr.* (also **inclose**) **1** (often foll. by *with*, *in*) **a** surround with a wall, fence, etc. **b** shut in on all sides. **2** fence in (common land) so as to make it private property. **3** put in a receptacle (esp. in an envelope together with a letter). **4** (usu. as **enclosed** *adj.*) seclude (a religious community) from the outside world. **5** esp. *Math.* bound on all sides; contain. [ME f. OF *enclos* past part. of *enclore* ult. f. L *includere* (as INCLUDE)]

enclosure /ɪnˈkləʊʒə(r)/ *n.* (also **inclosure**) **1** the act of enclosing, esp. of common land. **2** *Brit.* an enclosed space or area, esp. for a special class of persons at a sporting event. **3** a thing enclosed with a letter. **4** an enclosing fence etc. [AF & OF (as ENCLOSE)]

encode /ɪnˈkəʊd/ *v.tr.* put (a message etc.) into code or cipher. □□ **encoder** *n.*

encomiast /enˈkəʊmɪˌæst/ *n.* **1** the composer of an encomium. **2** a flatterer. □□ **encomiastic** /-ˈæstɪk/ *adj.* [Gk *egkōmiastēs* (as ENCOMIUM)]

encomium /enˈkəʊmɪəm/ *n.* (*pl.* **encomiums** or **encomia** /-mɪə/) a formal or high-flown expression of praise. [L f. Gk *egkōmion* (as EN-², *kōmos* revelry)]

encompass /ɪnˈkʌmpəs/ *v.tr.* **1** surround or form a circle about, esp. to protect or attack. **2** contain. □□ **encompassment** *n.*

encore /ˈɒŋkɔː(r)/ *n., v., & int.* —*n.* **1** a call by an audience or spectators for the repetition of an item, or for a further item. **2** such an item. —*v.tr.* **1** call for the repetition of (an item). **2** call back (a performer) for this. —*int.* /also -ˈkɔː(r)/ again, once more. [F, = once again]

encounter /ɪnˈkaʊntə(r)/ *v. & n.* —*v.tr.* **1** meet by chance or unexpectedly. **2** meet as an adversary. —*n.* **1** a meeting by chance. **2** a meeting in conflict. **3** participation in an encounter group. □ **encounter group** a group of persons seeking psychological benefit through close contact with one another. [ME f. OF *encontrer*, *encontre* ult. f. L *contra* against]

encourage /ɪnˈkʌrɪdʒ/ *v.tr.* **1** give courage, confidence, or hope to. **2** (foll. by *to* + infin.) urge, advise. **3** stimulate by help, reward, etc. **4** promote or assist (an enterprise, opinion, etc.). □□ **encouragement** *n.* **encourager** *n.* **encouraging** *adj.* **encouragingly** *adv.* [ME f. F *encourager* (as EN¹, COURAGE)]

encroach /ɪnˈkrəʊtʃ/ *v.intr.* **1** (foll. by *on*, *upon*) intrude, esp. on another's territory or rights. **2** advance gradually beyond due limits. □□ **encroacher** *n.* **encroachment** *n.* [ME f. OF *encrochier* (as EN-¹, *crochier* f. *croc* hook: see CROOK)]

encrust /ɪnˈkrʌst/ *v.* (also **incrust**) **1** *tr.* cover with a crust. **2** *tr.* overlay with an ornamental crust of precious material. **3** *intr.* form a crust. □□ **encrustment** *n.* [F *incruster* f. L *incrustare* (as IN-², *crustare* f. *crusta* CRUST)]

encrustation var. of INCRUSTATION.

encrypt /ɪnˈkrɪpt/ *v.tr.* **1** convert (data) into code, esp. to prevent unauthorized access. **2** conceal by

w *we* z *zoo* ʃ *she* ʒ *decision* θ *thin* ð *this* ŋ *ring* x *loch* tʃ *chip* dʒ *jar* (*see over for vowels*)

this means. □□ **encryption** *n.* [EN-¹ + Gk *kruptos* hidden]

encumber /ɪnˈkʌmbə(r)/ *v.tr.* **1** be a burden to. **2** hamper, impede. **3** burden (a person or estate) with debts, esp. mortgages. **4** fill or block (a place) esp. with lumber. □□ **encumberment** *n.* [ME f. OF *encombrer* block up f. Rmc]

encumbrance /ɪnˈkʌmbrəns/ *n.* **1** a burden. **2** an impediment. **3** a mortgage or other charge on property. **4** an annoyance. □ **without encumbrance** having no children. [ME f. OF *encombrance* (as ENCUMBER)]

-ency /ənsɪ/ *suffix* forming nouns denoting a quality (*efficiency*; *fluency*) or state (*presidency*) but not action (cf. -ENCE). [L *-entia* (cf. -ANCY)]

encyclical /enˈsɪklɪk(ə)l/ *n. & adj.* —*n.* a papal letter sent to all bishops of the Roman Catholic Church. —*adj.* (of a letter) for wide circulation. [LL *encyclicus* f. Gk *egkuklios* (as EN-², *kuklos* circle)]

encyclopaedia /enˌsaɪkləˈpiːdɪə, ɪn-/ *n.* (also **encyclopedia**) a book, often in several volumes, giving information on many subjects, or on many aspects of one subject, usu. arranged alphabetically. [mod.L f. spurious Gk *egkuklopaideia* for *egkuklios paideia* all-round education: cf. ENCYCLICAL]

encyclopaedic /enˌsaɪkləˈpiːdɪk, ɪn-/ *adj.* (also **encyclopedic**) (of knowledge or information) comprehensive.

encyclopaedism /enˌsaɪkləˈpiːdɪz(ə)m, ɪn-/ *n.* (also **encyclopedism**) encyclopaedic learning.

encyclopaedist /enˌsaɪkləˈpiːdɪst, ɪn-/ *n.* (also **encyclopedist**) a person who writes, edits, or contributes to an encyclopaedia.

encyst /ɪnˈsɪst/ *v.tr. & intr. Biol.* enclose or become enclosed in a cyst. □□ **encystation** /-ˈteɪʃ(ə)n/ *n.* **encystment** *n.*

end /end/ *n. & v.* —*n.* **1 a** the extreme limit; the point beyond which a thing does not continue. **b** an extremity of a line, or of the greatest dimension of an object. **c** the furthest point (*to the ends of the earth*). **2** the surface bounding a thing at either extremity; an extreme part (*a strip of wood with a nail in one end*). **3 a** conclusion, finish (*no end to his misery*). **b** the latter or final part. **c** death, destruction, downfall (*met an untimely end*). **d** result, outcome. **e** an ultimate state or condition. **4 a** a thing one seeks to attain; a purpose (*will do anything to achieve his ends*; *to what end?*). **b** the object for which a thing exists. **5** a remnant; a piece left over (*cigarette-end*). **6** (prec. by *the*) *colloq.* the limit of endurability. **7** the half of a sports pitch or court occupied by one team or player. **8** the part or share with which a person is concerned (*no problem at my end*). **9** *Bowls* a unit of play in which play is from one side of the green towards the other. **10** *US Football* a player at the extremity of a line or team. —*v.* **1** *tr. & intr.* bring or come to an end. **2** *tr.* put an end to; destroy. **3** *intr.* (foll. by *in*) have as its result (*will end in tears*). **4** *intr.* (foll. by *by*) do or achieve eventually (*ended by marrying an heiress*). □ **all ends up** completely. **at an end** exhausted or completed. **at the end of one's tether** see TETHER. **come to a bad** (or **sticky**) **end** meet with ruin or disgrace. **come to an end 1** be completed or finished. **2** become exhausted. **end-around** *n. US Football* an offensive play in which an end carries the ball round the opposite end. —*adj. Computing* involving the transfer of a digit from one end of a register to the other. **end-game** the final stage of a game (esp. chess), when few pieces remain. **end it all** (or **end it**) *colloq.* commit suicide. **end of the road** the point at which a hope or endeavour has to be abandoned. **end of the world** the cessation of mortal life. **end on** with the end facing one, or with the end adjoining the end of the next object. **end-play** *Bridge* a method of play in the last few tricks to force an opponent to make a disadvantageous lead. **end-point** the final stage of a process, esp. the point at which an effect is observed

in titration, dilution, etc. **end-product** the final product of manufacture, radioactive decay, etc. **end result** final outcome. **end run** *US* **1** *Football* an attempt by the ball-carrier to run round his or her own end. **2** an evasive tactic esp. in war or politics. **end standard** a standard of length in the form of a metal bar or block with the end faces the standard distance apart. **end-stopped** (of verse) having a pause at the end of each line. **end to end** with the end of each of a series adjoining the end of the next. **end up** reach a specified state, action, or place eventually (*ended up a drunkard*; *ended up making a fortune*). **end-user** the person, customer, etc., who is the ultimate user of a product. **in the end** finally; after all. **keep one's end up** do one's part despite difficulties. **make an end of** put a stop to. **make ends** (or **both ends**) **meet** live within one's income. **no end** *colloq.* to a great extent, very much. **no end of** *colloq.* much or many of. **on end 1** upright (*hair stood on end*). **2** continuously (*for three weeks on end*). **put an end to 1** stop (an activity etc.). **2** abolish, destroy. □□ **ender** *n.* [OE *ende*, *endian*, f. Gmc]

-end /end, ənd/ *suffix* forming nouns in the sense 'person or thing to be treated in a specified way' (*dividend*; *reverend*). [L gerundive ending *-endus*]

endanger /ɪnˈdeɪndʒə(r)/ *v.tr.* place in danger. □ **endangered species** a species in danger of extinction. □□ **endangerment** *n.*

endear /ɪnˈdɪə(r)/ *v.tr.* (usu. foll. by *to*) make dear to or beloved by.

endearing /ɪnˈdɪərɪŋ/ *adj.* inspiring affection. □□ **endearingly** *adv.*

endearment /ɪnˈdɪəmənt/ *n.* **1** an expression of affection. **2** liking, affection.

endeavour /ɪnˈdevə(r)/ *v. & n.* (*US* **endeavor**) —*v.* **1** *tr.* (foll. by *to* + infin.) try earnestly. **2** *intr.* (foll. by *after*) *archaic* strive. —*n.* (often foll. by *at*, or *to* + infin.) an earnest attempt. [ME f. *put oneself in* DEVOIR]

endemic /enˈdemɪk/ *adj. & n.* —*adj.* regularly or only found among a particular people or in a certain region. —*n.* an endemic disease or plant. □□ **endemically** *adv.* **endemicity** /ˌendɪˈmɪsɪtɪ/ *n.* **endemism** /ˈendɪˌmɪz(ə)m/ *n.* [F *endémique* or mod.L *endemicus* f. Gk *endēmos* native (as EN-², *dēmos* the people)]

endermic /enˈdɜːmɪk/ *adj.* acting on or through the skin. □□ **endermically** *adv.* [EN-² + Gk *derma* skin]

ending /ˈendɪŋ/ *n.* **1** an end or final part, esp. of a story. **2** an inflected final part of a word. [OE (as END, -ING¹)]

endive /ˈendaɪv, -dɪv/ *n.* **1** a curly-leaved plant, *Cichorium endivia*, used in salads. **2** *US* a chicory crown. [ME f. OF f. LL *endivia* ult. f. Gk *entubon*]

endless /ˈendlɪs/ *adj.* **1** infinite; without end; eternal. **2** continual, incessant (*tired of their endless complaints*). **3** *colloq.* innumerable. **4** (of a belt, chain, etc.) having the ends joined for continuous action over wheels etc. □ **endless screw** a short length of screw revolving to turn a cog-wheel. □□ **endlessly** *adv.* **endlessness** *n.* [OE *endelēas* (as END, -LESS)]

endmost /ˈendməʊst/ *adj.* nearest the end.

endnote /ˈendnəʊt/ *n.* a note printed at the end of a book or section of a book.

endo- /ˈendəʊ/ *comb. form* internal. [Gk *endon* within]

endocarditis /ˌendəʊkɑːˈdaɪtɪs/ *n.* inflammation of the endocardium. □□ **endocarditic** /-ˈdɪtɪk/ *adj.*

endocardium /ˌendəʊˈkɑːdɪəm/ *n.* the lining membrane of the heart. [ENDO- + Gk *kardia* heart]

endocarp /ˈendəʊˌkɑːp/ *n.* the innermost layer of the pericarp. □□ **endocarpic** /-ˈkɑːpɪk/ *adj.* [ENDO- + PERICARP]

endocrine /ˈendəʊˌkraɪn, -ˌkrɪn/ *adj.* (of a gland) secreting directly into the blood; ductless. [ENDO- + Gk *krinō* sift]

endocrinology /ˌendəʊkrɪˈnɒlədʒɪ/ *n.* the study of the structure and physiology of endocrine glands.

□□ **endocrinological** /-nə'lɒdʒɪk(ə)l/ *adj.* **endocrinologist** *n.*

endoderm /'endəʊ,dɜːm/ *n. Biol.* the innermost layer of an animal embryo in early development. □□ **endodermal** /-'dɜːm(ə)l/ *adj.* **endodermic** /-'dɜːmɪk/ *adj.* [ENDO- + Gk *derma* skin]

endogamy /en'dɒɡəmɪ/ *n.* **1** *Anthropol.* marrying within the same tribe. **2** *Bot.* pollination from the same plant. □□ **endogamous** *adj.* [ENDO- + Gk *gamos* marriage]

endogenous /en'dɒdʒɪnəs/ *adj.* growing or originating from within. □□ **endogenesis** /,endə'dʒenɪsɪs/ *n.* **endogeny** /en'dɒdʒɪnɪ/ *n.*

endolymph /'endəʊlɪmf/ *n.* the fluid in the membranous labyrinth of the ear.

endometrium /,endəʊ'miːtrɪəm/ *n. Anat.* the membrane lining the womb. □□ **endometritis** /,endəʊmɪ'traɪtɪs/ *n.* [ENDO- + Gk *mētra* womb]

endomorph /'endəʊ,mɔːf/ *n.* **1** a person with a soft round build of body and a high proportion of fat tissue (cf. ECTOMORPH, MESOMORPH). **2** *Mineral.* a mineral enclosed within another. □□ **endomorphic** /-'mɔːfɪk/ *adj.* **endomorphy** *n.* [ENDO- + Gk *morphē* form]

endoparasite /,endəʊ'pærə,saɪt/ *n.* a parasite that lives on the inside of its host. Also called ENTOPARASITE.

endoplasm /'endəʊ,plæz(ə)m/ *n.* the inner fluid layer of the cytoplasm.

endoplasmic reticulum /,endəʊ'plæzmɪk/ *n. Biol.* a system of membranes within the cytoplasm of a eukaryotic cell forming a link between the cell and nuclear membranes and usu. having ribosomes attached to its surface.

endorphin /en'dɔːfɪn/ *n. Biochem.* any of a group of peptide neurotransmitters occurring naturally in the brain and having pain-relieving properties. [F *endorphine* f. *endogène* endogenous + MORPHINE]

endorse /ɪn'dɔːs/ *v.tr.* (also **indorse**) **1 a** confirm (a statement or opinion). **b** declare one's approval of. **2** sign or write on the back of (a document), esp. the back of (a bill, cheque, etc.) as the payee or to specify another as payee. **3** write (an explanation or comment) on the back of a document. **4** *Brit.* enter details of a conviction for a motoring offence on (a driving licence). □□ **endorsable** *adj.* **endorsee** /,endɔː'siː/ *n.* **endorser** *n.* [med.L *indorsare* (as IN-², L *dorsum* back)]

endorsement /ɪn'dɔːsmənt/ *n.* **1** the act or an instance of endorsing. **2** something with which a document etc. is endorsed, esp. a signature. **3** a record in a driving licence of a conviction for a motoring offence.

endoscope /'endəʊ,skəʊp/ *n. Surgery* an instrument for viewing the internal parts of the body. □□ **endoscopic** /-'skɒpɪk/ *adj.* **endoscopically** /-'skɒpɪkəlɪ/ *adv.* **endoscopist** /en'dɒskəpɪst/ *n.* **endoscopy** /en'dɒskəpɪ/ *n.*

endoskeleton /'endəʊ,skelɪt(ə)n/ *n.* an internal skeleton, as found in vertebrates.

endosperm /'endəʊ,spɜːm/ *n.* albumen enclosed with the germ in seeds.

endospore /'endəʊ,spɔː(r)/ *n.* **1** a spore formed by certain bacteria. **2** the inner coat of a spore.

endothelium /,endəʊ'θiːlɪəm/ *n. Anat.* a layer of cells lining the blood-vessels, heart, and lymphatic vessels. [ENDO- + Gk *thēlē* teat]

endothermic /,endəʊ'θɜːmɪk/ *adj.* occurring or formed with the absorption of heat.

endow /ɪn'daʊ/ *v.tr.* **1** bequeath or give a permanent income to (a person, institution, etc.). **2** (esp. as **endowed** *adj.*) (usu. foll. by *with*) provide (a person) with talent, ability, etc. □□ **endower** *n.* [ME f. AF *endouer* (as EN-¹, OF *douer* f. L *dotare* f. *dos dotis* DOWER)]

endowment /ɪn'daʊmənt/ *n.* **1** the act or an instance of endowing. **2** assets, esp. property or income with which a person or body is endowed. **3** (usu. in *pl.*) skill, talent, etc., with which a person is endowed. **4** (*attrib.*) denoting forms of life insurance involving payment by the insurer of a fixed sum on a specified date, or on the death of the insured person if earlier. □ **endowment mortgage** a mortgage linked to endowment insurance of the mortgagor's life, the capital being paid from the sum insured.

endpaper /'end,peɪpə(r)/ *n.* a usu. blank leaf of paper at the beginning and end of a book, fixed to the inside of the cover.

endue /ɪn'djuː/ *v.tr.* (also **indue**) (foll. by *with*) invest or provide (a person) with qualities, powers, etc. [earlier = induct, put on clothes: ME f. OF *enduire* f. L *inducere* lead in, assoc. in sense with L *induere* put on (clothes)]

endurance /ɪn'djʊərəns/ *n.* **1** the power or habit of enduring (*beyond endurance*). **2** the ability to withstand prolonged strain (*endurance test*). **3** the act of enduring. [OF f. *endurer*: see ENDURE]

endure /ɪn'djʊə(r)/ *v.* **1** *tr.* **a** undergo (a difficulty, hardship, etc.). **b** tolerate (a person) (*cannot endure him*). **b** (esp. with *neg.*; foll. by *to* + infin.) bear. **2** *intr.* remain in existence; last. **4** *tr.* submit to. □□ **endurable** *adj.* **endurability** /-'bɪlɪtɪ/ *n.* **enduringly** *adv.* [ME f. OF *endurer* f. L *indurare* harden (as IN-², *durus* hard)]

enduro /ɪn'djʊərəʊ/ *n.* (*pl.* **-os**) a long-distance race for motor vehicles, designed to test endurance.

endways /'endweɪz/ *adv.* **1** with its end uppermost or foremost or turned towards the viewer. **2** end to end.

endwise /'endwaɪz/ *adv.* = ENDWAYS.

ENE *abbr.* east-north-east.

-ene /iːn/ *suffix* **1** forming names of inhabitants of places (*Nazarene*). **2** *Chem.* forming names of unsaturated hydrocarbons containing a double bond (*benzene*; *ethylene*). [from or after Gk *-ēnos*]

enema /'enɪmə/ *n.* (*pl.* **enemas** or **enemata** /ɪ'nemətə/) **1** the injection of liquid or gas into the rectum, esp. to expel its contents. **2** a fluid or syringe used for this. [LL f. Gk *enema* f. *eniēmi* inject (as EN-², *hiēmi* send)]

enemy /'enəmɪ/ *n.* (*pl.* **-ies**) **1** a person or group actively opposing or hostile to another, or to a cause etc. **2 a** a hostile nation or army, esp. in war. **b** a member of this. **c** a hostile ship or aircraft. **3** (usu. foll. by *of, to*) an adversary or opponent. **4** a thing that harms or injures. **5** (*attrib.*) of or belonging to an enemy (*destroyed by enemy action*). [ME f. OF *enemi* f. L *inimicus* (as IN-¹, *amicus* friend)]

energetic /,enə'dʒetɪk/ *adj.* **1** strenuously active. **2** forcible, vigorous. **3** powerfully operative. □□ **energetically** *adv.* [Gk *energētikos* f. *energeō* (as EN-², *ergon* work)]

energetics /,enə'dʒetɪks/ *n.pl.* the science of energy.

energize /'enə,dʒaɪz/ *v.tr.* (also **-ise**) **1** infuse energy into (a person or work). **2** provide energy for the operation of (a device). □□ **energizer** *n.*

energumen /,enɜː'gjuːmen/ *n.* an enthusiast or fanatic. [LL *energumenus* f. Gk *energoumenos* passive part. of *energeō*: see ENERGETIC]

energy /'enədʒɪ/ *n.* (*pl.* **-ies**) **1** force, vigour; capacity for activity. **2** (in *pl.*) individual powers in use (*devote your energies to this*). **3** *Physics* the capacity of matter or radiation to do work. **4** the means of doing work by utilizing matter or radiation. [F *énergie* or LL *energia* f. Gk *energeia* f. *ergon* work]

enervate *v. & adj.* —*v.tr.* /'enə,veɪt/ deprive of vigour or vitality. —*adj.* /ɪ'nɜːvət/ enervated. □□ **enervation** /,enə'veɪʃ(ə)n/ *n.* [L *enervatus* past part. of *enervare* (as E-, *nervus* sinew)]

en famille /,ɑ̃ fæ'miːj/ *adv.* **1** in or with one's family. **2** at home. [F, = in family]

enfant gâté /,ɑ̃fɑ̃ ɡæ'teɪ/ *n.* a person given undue flattery or indulgence. [F, = spoilt child]

enfant terrible /,ɑ̃fɑ̃ te'riːbl/ *n.* a person who causes embarrassment by indiscreet or unruly behaviour. [F, = terrible child]

enfeeble /ɪnˈfiːb(ə)l/ v.tr. make feeble. □□ **enfeeblement** n. [ME f. OF enfeblir (as EN-[1], FEEBLE)]

en fête /ã ˈfeɪt/ adv. & predic.adj. holding or ready for a holiday or celebration. [F, = in festival]

enfetter /ɪnˈfetə(r)/ v.tr. literary 1 bind in or as in fetters. 2 (foll. by to) enslave.

enfilade /ˌenfɪˈleɪd/ n. & v. —n. gunfire directed along a line from end to end. —v.tr. direct an enfilade at (troops, a road, etc.). [F f. enfiler (as EN-[1], fil thread)]

enfold /ɪnˈfəʊld/ v.tr. (also **infold**) 1 (usu. foll. by in, with) wrap up; envelop. 2 clasp, embrace.

enforce /ɪnˈfɔːs/ v.tr. 1 compel observance of (a law etc.). 2 (foll. by on, upon) impose (an action, conduct, one's will). 3 persist in (a demand or argument). □□ **enforceable** adj. **enforceability** /-səˈbɪlɪtɪ/ n. **enforcedly** /-sɪdlɪ/ adv. **enforcer** n. [ME f. OF enforcir, -ier ult. f. L fortis strong]

enforcement /ɪnˈfɔːsmənt/ n. the act or an instance of enforcing. □ **enforcement notice** Brit. an official notification to remedy a breach of planning legislation. [ME f. OF, as ENFORCE + -MENT]

enfranchise /ɪnˈfræntʃaɪz/ v.tr. 1 give (a person) the right to vote. 2 give (a town) municipal rights, esp. that of representation in parliament. 3 hist. free (a slave, villein, etc.). □□ **enfranchisement** /-ɪzmənt/ n. [OF enfranchir (as EN-[1], franc franche FRANK)]

ENG abbr. electronic news gathering.

engage /ɪnˈɡeɪdʒ/ v. 1 tr. employ or hire (a person). 2 tr. a (usu. in passive) employ busily; occupy (are you engaged tomorrow?). b hold fast (a person's attention). 3 tr. (usu. in passive) bind by a promise, esp. of marriage. 4 tr. (usu. foll. by to + infin.) bind by a contract. 5 tr. arrange beforehand to occupy (a room, seat, etc.). 6 (usu. foll. by with) Mech. a tr. interlock (parts of a gear etc.); cause (a part) to interlock. b intr. (of a part, gear, etc.) interlock. 7 a intr. (usu. foll. by with) (of troops etc.) come into battle. b tr. bring (troops) into battle. c tr. come into battle with (an enemy etc.). 8 intr. take part (engage in politics). 9 intr. (foll. by that + clause or to + infin.) pledge oneself. 10 tr. (usu. as **engaged** adj.) Archit. attach (a column) to a wall. 11 tr. (of fencers etc.) interlock (weapons). □□ **engager** n. [F engager, rel. to GAGE[1]]

engagé /ã ˈɡæʒeɪ/ adj. (of a writer etc.) morally committed. [F, past part. of engager: see ENGAGE]

engaged /ɪnˈɡeɪdʒd/ adj. 1 under a promise to marry. 2 a occupied, busy. b reserved, booked. 3 Brit. (of a telephone line) unavailable because already in use. □ **engaged signal** (or **tone**) Brit. a sound indicating that a telephone line is engaged.

engagement /ɪnˈɡeɪdʒmənt/ n. 1 the act or state of engaging or being engaged. 2 an appointment with another person. 3 a betrothal. 4 an encounter between hostile forces. 5 a moral commitment. □ **engagement ring** a finger-ring given by a man to a woman when they promise to marry. [F f. engager: see ENGAGE]

engaging /ɪnˈɡeɪdʒɪŋ/ adj. attractive, charming. □□ **engagingly** adv. **engagingness** n.

engender /ɪnˈdʒendə(r)/ v.tr. 1 give rise to; bring about (a feeling etc.). 2 archaic beget. [ME f. OF engendrer f. L ingenerare (as IN-[2], generare GENERATE)]

engine /ˈendʒɪn/ n. 1 a mechanical contrivance consisting of several parts working together, esp. as a source of power. 2 a a railway locomotive. b = fire-engine. c = steam engine. 3 archaic a machine or instrument, esp. a contrivance used in warfare. □ **engine-driver** the driver of an engine, esp. a railway locomotive. **engine-room** a room containing engines (esp. in a ship). □□ **engined** adj. (also in comb.). **engineless** adj. [OF engin f. L ingenium talent, device: cf. INGENIOUS]

engineer /ˌendʒɪˈnɪə(r)/ n. & v. —n. 1 a person qualified in a branch of engineering, esp. as a professional. 2 = civil engineer. 3 a person who

makes or is in charge of engines. 4 US an engine-driver. 5 a person who designs and constructs military works; a soldier trained for this purpose. 6 (foll. by of) a skilful or artful contriver. —v. 1 tr. arrange, contrive, or bring about, esp. artfully. 2 intr. act as an engineer. 3 tr. construct or manage as an engineer. □□ **engineership** n. [ME f. OF engineor f. med.L ingeniator -oris f. ingeniare (as ENGINE)]

engineering /ˌendʒɪˈnɪərɪŋ/ n. the application of science to the design, building, and use of machines, constructions, etc. □ **engineering science** engineering as a field of study.

enginery /ˈendʒɪnrɪ/ n. engines and machinery generally.

engird /ɪnˈɡɜːd/ v.tr. surround with or as with a girdle.

engirdle /ɪnˈɡɜːd(ə)l/ v.tr. engird.

English /ˈɪŋɡlɪʃ/ adj. & n. —adj. of or relating to England or its people or language. —n. 1 the language of England, now used in many varieties in the British Isles, the United States, and most Commonwealth or ex-Commonwealth countries, and often internationally. 2 (prec. by the; treated as pl.) the people of England. 3 US Billiards = SIDE n. 10. □ **English bond** Building a bond of brickwork arranged in alternate courses of stretchers and headers. **English horn** = COR ANGLAIS. **the Queen's** (or **King's**) **English** the English language as correctly written or spoken in Britain. □□ **Englishness** n. [OE englisc, ænglisc (as ANGLE, -ISH[1])]

Englishman /ˈɪŋɡlɪʃmən/ n. (pl. -men) a man who is English by birth or descent.

Englishwoman /ˈɪŋɡlɪʃˌwʊmən/ n. (pl. -women) a woman who is English by birth or descent.

engorge /ɪnˈɡɔːdʒ/ v.tr. 1 (in passive) a be crammed. b Med. be congested with blood. 2 devour greedily. □□ **engorgement** n. [F engorger (as EN-[1], GORGE)]

engraft /ɪnˈɡrɑːft/ v.tr. (also **ingraft**) 1 Bot. (usu. foll. by into, upon) insert (a scion of one tree into another). 2 (usu. foll. by in) implant (principles etc.) in a person's mind. 3 (usu. foll. by into) incorporate permanently. □□ **engraftment** n.

engrail /ɪnˈɡreɪl/ v.tr. (usu. as **engrailed** adj.) esp. Heraldry indent the edge of; give a serrated appearance to. [ME f. OF engresler (as EN-[1], gresle hail)]

engrain /ɪnˈɡreɪn/ v.tr. 1 implant (a habit, belief, or attitude) ineradicably in a person (see also INGRAINED). 2 cause (dye etc.) to sink deeply into a thing. [ME f. OF engrainer dye in grain (en graine): see GRAIN]

engrained /ɪnˈɡreɪnd/ adj. inveterate (see also INGRAINED).

engram /ˈenɡræm/ n. a memory-trace, a supposed permanent change in the brain accounting for the existence of memory. □□ **engrammatic** /-ɡrəˈmætɪk/ adj. [G Engramm f. Gk en in + gramma letter of the alphabet]

engrave /ɪnˈɡreɪv/ v.tr. 1 (often foll. by on) inscribe, cut, or carve (a text or design) on a hard surface. 2 (often foll. by with) inscribe or ornament (a surface) in this way. 3 cut (a design) as lines on a metal plate for printing. 4 (often foll. by on) impress deeply on a person's memory etc. □□ **engraver** n. [EN-[1] + GRAVE[3]]

engraving /ɪnˈɡreɪvɪŋ/ n. a print made from an engraved plate.

engross /ɪnˈɡrəʊs/ v.tr. 1 absorb the attention of; occupy fully (engrossed in studying). 2 make a fair copy of a legal document. 3 reproduce (a document etc.) in larger letters or larger format. 4 archaic monopolize (a conversation etc.). □□ **engrossing** adj. (in sense 1). **engrossment** n. [ME f. AF engrosser: senses 2 and 3 f. en in + grosse large writing: senses 1 and 4 f. en gros wholesale]

engulf /ɪnˈɡʌlf/ v.tr. (also **ingulf**) 1 flow over and swamp; overwhelm. 2 swallow or plunge into a gulf. □□ **engulfment** n.

enhance /ɪnˈhɑːns/ v.tr. heighten or intensify (qualities, powers, value, etc.); improve (something already of good quality). □□ **enhancement** n. **enhancer** n. [ME f. AF enhauncer, prob. alt. f. OF enhaucier ult. f. L altus high]

enharmonic /ˌenhɑːˈmɒnɪk/ adj. Mus. of or having intervals smaller than a semitone (esp. such intervals as that between G sharp and A flat, these notes being made the same in a scale of equal temperament). □□ **enharmonically** adv. [LL enharmonicus f. Gk enarmonikos (as EN-², harmonia HARMONY)]

enigma /ɪˈnɪgmə/ n. 1 a puzzling thing or person. 2 a riddle or paradox. □□ **enigmatic** /ˌenɪgˈmætɪk/ adj. **enigmatical** /ˌenɪgˈmætɪk(ə)l/ adj. **enigmatically** /ˌenɪgˈmætɪkəlɪ/ adv. **enigmatize** v.tr. (also -ise). [L aenigma f. Gk ainigma -matos f. ainissomai speak allusively f. ainos fable]

enjambment /enˈdʒæmmənt/ n. (also **enjambement**) Prosody the continuation of a sentence without a pause beyond the end of a line, couplet, or stanza. [F enjambement f. enjamber (as EN-¹, jambe leg)]

enjoin /ɪnˈdʒɔɪn/ v.tr. 1 a (foll. by to + infin.) command or order (a person). b (foll. by that + clause) issue instructions. 2 (often foll. by on) impose or prescribe (an action or conduct). 3 (usu. foll. by from) Law prohibit (a person) by order. □□ **enjoinment** n. [ME f. OF enjoindre f. L injungere (as IN-², jungere join)]

enjoy /ɪnˈdʒɔɪ/ v.tr. 1 take delight or pleasure in. 2 have the use or benefit of. 3 experience (enjoy poor health). □ **enjoy oneself** experience pleasure. □□ **enjoyer** n. **enjoyment** n. [ME f. OF enjoier give joy to or enjoïr enjoy, ult. f. L gaudēre rejoice]

enjoyable /ɪnˈdʒɔɪəb(ə)l/ adj. pleasant; giving enjoyment. □□ **enjoyability** /-ˈbɪlɪtɪ/ n. **enjoyableness** n. **enjoyably** adv.

enkephalin /enˈkefəlɪn/ n. (also **encephalin** /en'sef-/) Biochem. either of two morphine-like peptides occurring naturally in the brain and thought to control levels of pain. [Gk egkephalos brain]

enkindle /ɪnˈkɪnd(ə)l/ v.tr. literary 1 a cause (flames) to flare up. b stimulate (feeling, passion, etc.). 2 inflame with passion.

enlace /ɪnˈleɪs/ v.tr. 1 encircle tightly. 2 entwine. 3 enfold. □□ **enlacement** n. [ME f. OF enlacier ult. f. L laqueus noose]

enlarge /ɪnˈlɑːdʒ/ v. 1 tr. & intr. make or become larger or wider. 2 a tr. describe in greater detail. b intr. (usu. foll. by upon) expatiate. 3 tr. Photog. produce an enlargement of (a negative). [ME f. OF enlarger (as EN-¹, LARGE)]

enlargement /ɪnˈlɑːdʒmənt/ n. 1 the act or an instance of enlarging; the state of being enlarged. 2 Photog. a print that is larger than the negative from which it is produced.

enlarger /ɪnˈlɑːdʒə(r)/ n. Photog. an apparatus for enlarging or reducing negatives or positives.

enlighten /ɪnˈlaɪt(ə)n/ v.tr. 1 (often foll. by on) instruct or inform (about a subject). 2 (esp. as **enlightened** adj.) free from prejudice or superstition. 3 rhet. or poet. a shed light on (an object). b give spiritual insight to (a person). □□ **enlightener** n.

enlightenment /ɪnˈlaɪtənmənt/ n. 1 the act or an instance of enlightening; the state of being enlightened. 2 (**the Enlightenment**) the 18th-c. philosophy emphasizing reason and individualism rather than tradition.

enlist /ɪnˈlɪst/ v. 1 intr. & tr. enrol in the armed services. 2 tr. secure as a means of help or support. □ **enlisted man** US a soldier or sailor below the rank of officer. □□ **enlister** n. **enlistment** n.

enliven /ɪnˈlaɪv(ə)n/ v.tr. 1 give life or spirit to. 2 make cheerful, brighten (a picture or scene). □□ **enlivener** n. **enlivenment** n.

en masse /ɑ̃ ˈmæs/ adv. 1 all together. 2 in a mass. [F]

enmesh /ɪnˈmeʃ/ v.tr. entangle in or as in a net. □□ **enmeshment** n.

enmity /ˈenmɪtɪ/ n. (pl. **-ies**) 1 the state of being an enemy. 2 a feeling of hostility. [ME f. OF enemitié f. Rmc (as ENEMY)]

ennead /ˈenɪˌæd/ n. a group of nine. [Gk enneas enneados f. ennea nine]

ennoble /ɪˈnəʊb(ə)l/ v.tr. 1 make (a person) a noble. 2 make noble; elevate. □□ **ennoblement** n. [F ennoblir (as EN-¹, NOBLE)]

ennui /ɒˈnwiː/ n. mental weariness from lack of occupation or interest; boredom. [F f. L in odio: cf. ODIUM]

enology US var. of OENOLOGY.

enormity /ɪˈnɔːmɪtɪ/ n. (pl. **-ies**) 1 extreme wickedness. 2 an act of extreme wickedness. 3 a serious error. 4 disp. great size; enormousness. [ME f. F énormité f. L enormitas -tatis f. enormis (as ENORMOUS)]

enormous /ɪˈnɔːməs/ adj. very large; huge (enormous animals; an enormous difference). □□ **enormously** adv. **enormousness** n. [L enormis (as E-, norma pattern, standard)]

enosis /ˈenəʊsɪs/ n. the political union of Cyprus and Greece, as an ideal or proposal. [mod. Gk enōsis f. ena one]

enough /ɪˈnʌf/ adj., n., adv., & int. —adj. as much or as many as required (we have enough apples; we do not have enough sugar; earned enough money to buy a house). —n. an amount or quantity that is enough (we have enough of everything now; enough is as good as a feast). —adv. 1 to the required degree, adequately (are you warm enough?). 2 fairly (she sings well enough). 3 very, quite (you know well enough what I mean; oddly enough). —int. that is enough (in various senses, esp. to put an end to an action, thing said, etc.). □ **have had enough of** want no more of; be satiated with or tired of. [OE genog f. Gmc]

en passant /ˌɑ̃ pæˈsɑ̃/ adv. 1 by the way. 2 Chess used with reference to the permitted capture of an opponent's pawn that has just advanced two squares in its first move with a pawn that could have taken it if it had advanced only one square. [F, = in passing]

en pension /ˌɑ̃ pɑ̃ˈsjɔ̃/ adv. as a boarder or resident. [F: see PENSION²]

enplane var. of EMPLANE.

enprint /ˈenprɪnt/ n. a standard-sized photographic print. [enlarged print]

enquire /ɪnˈkwaɪə(r), ɪŋ-/ v. 1 intr. (often foll. by of) seek information; ask a question (of a person). 2 intr. = INQUIRE. 3 intr. (foll. by after, for) ask about a person, a person's health, etc. 4 intr. (foll. by for) ask about the availability of. 5 tr. ask for information as to (enquired my name; enquired whether we were coming). □□ **enquirer** n. [ME enquere f. OF enquerre ult. f. L inquirere (as IN-², quaerere quaesit- seek)]

enquiry /ɪnˈkwaɪərɪ, ɪŋ-/ n. (pl. **-ies**) 1 the act or an instance of asking or seeking information. 2 = INQUIRY.

enrage /ɪnˈreɪdʒ/ v.tr. (often foll. by at, by, with) make furious. □□ **enragement** n. [F enrager (as EN-¹, RAGE)]

en rapport /ˌɑ̃ ræˈpɔː(r)/ adv. (usu. foll. by with) in harmony or rapport. [F: see RAPPORT]

enrapture /ɪnˈræptʃə(r)/ v.tr. give intense delight to.

enrich /ɪnˈrɪtʃ/ v.tr. 1 make rich or richer. 2 make richer in quality, flavour, nutritive value, etc. 3 add to the contents of (a collection, museum, or book). 4 increase the content of an isotope in (material) esp. enrich uranium with isotope U-235. □□ **enrichment** n. [ME f. OF enrichir (as EN-¹, RICH)]

enrobe /ɪnˈrəʊb/ v.intr. put on a robe, vestment, etc.

enrol /ɪnˈrəʊl/ v. (US **enroll**) (**enrolled**, **enrolling**) 1 intr. enter one's name on a list, esp. as a commitment to membership. 2 tr. a write the name of (a person) on a list. b (usu. foll. by in) incorporate (a person) as a member of a society etc. **3** *tr. hist.* enter (a deed etc.) among the rolls of a court of justice. **4** *tr.* record. □□ **enrollee** /-'li:/ *n.* **enroller** *n.* [ME f. OF *enroller* (as EN-[1], *rolle* ROLL)]

enrolment /ɪn'rəʊlmənt/ *n.* (*US* **enrollment**) **1** the act or an instance of enrolling; the state of being enrolled. **2** *US* the number of persons enrolled, esp. at a school or college.

en route /ɑ̃ 'ru:t/ *adv.* (usu. foll. by *to, for*) on the way. [F]

ensconce /ɪn'skɒns/ *v.tr.* (usu. *refl.* or in *passive*) establish or settle comfortably, safely, or secretly.

ensemble /ɒn'sɒmb(ə)l/ *n.* **1 a** a thing viewed as the sum of its parts. **b** the general effect of this. **2** a set of clothes worn together; an outfit. **3** a group of actors, dancers, musicians, etc., performing together, esp. subsidiary dancers in ballet etc. **4** *Mus.* **a** a concerted passage for an ensemble. **b** the manner in which this is performed (*good ensemble*). **5** *Math.* a group of systems with the same constitution but possibly in different states. [F, ult. f. L *insimul* (as IN-[2], *simul* at the same time)]

enshrine /ɪn'ʃraɪn/ *v.tr.* **1** enclose in or as in a shrine. **2** serve as a shrine for. **3** preserve or cherish. □□ **enshrinement** *n.*

enshroud /ɪn'ʃraʊd/ *v.tr. literary* **1** cover with or as with a shroud. **2** cover completely; hide from view.

ensign /'ensaɪn, -s(ə)n/ *n.* **1 a** a banner or flag, esp. the military or naval flag of a nation. **b** *Brit.* a flag with the union in the corner. **2** a standard-bearer. **3 a** *hist.* the lowest commissioned infantry officer. **b** *US* the lowest commissioned officer in the navy. □ **blue ensign** the ensign of government departments and formerly of the naval reserve etc. **red ensign** the ensign of the merchant service. **white ensign** the ensign of the Royal Navy and the Royal Yacht Squadron. □□ **ensigncy** *n.* [ME f. OF *enseigne* f. L *insignia*: see INSIGNIA]

ensilage /'ensɪlɪdʒ/ *n. & v.* —*n.* = SILAGE. —*v.tr.* treat (fodder) by ensilage. [F (as ENSILE)]

ensile /ɪn'saɪl/ *v.tr.* **1** put (fodder) into a silo. **2** preserve (fodder) in a silo. [F *ensiler* f. Sp. *ensilar* (as EN-[1], SILO)]

enslave /ɪn'sleɪv/ *v.tr.* make (a person) a slave. □□ **enslavement** *n.* **enslaver** *n.*

ensnare /ɪn'sneə(r)/ *v.tr.* catch in or as in a snare; entrap. □□ **ensnarement** *n.*

ensue /ɪn'sju:/ *v.intr.* **1** happen afterwards. **2** (often foll. by *from, on*) occur as a result. [ME f. OF *ensuivre* ult. f. L *sequi* follow]

en suite /ɑ̃ 'swi:t/ *adv.* forming a single unit (*bedroom with bathroom en suite*). [F, = in sequence]

ensure /ɪn'ʃʊə(r)/ *v.tr.* **1** (often foll. by *that* + clause) make certain. **2** (usu. foll. by *to, for*) secure (a thing for a person etc.). **3** (usu. foll. by *against*) make safe. □□ **ensurer** *n.* [ME f. AF *enseürer* f. OF *aseürer* ASSURE]

enswathe /ɪn'sweɪð/ *v.tr.* bind or wrap in or as in a bandage. □□ **enswathement** *n.*

ENT *abbr.* ear, nose, and throat.

-ent /ənt, ent/ *suffix* **1** forming adjectives denoting attribution of an action (*consequent*) or state (*existent*). **2** forming nouns denoting an agent (*coefficient; president*). [from or after F *-ent* or L *-ent-* pres. part. stem of verbs (cf. -ANT)]

entablature /ɪn'tæblətʃə(r)/ *n. Archit.* the upper part of a classical building supported by columns or a colonnade, comprising architrave, frieze, and cornice. [It. *intavolatura* f. *intavolare* board up (as IN-[2], *tavola* table)]

entablement /ɪn'teɪb(ə)lmənt/ *n.* a platform supporting a statue, above the dado and base. [F, f. *entabler* (as IN-[2], TABLE)]

entail /ɪn'teɪl, en-/ *v. & n.* —*v.tr.* **1** necessitate or involve unavoidably (*the work entails much effort*). **2** *Law* bequeath (property etc.) so that it remains within a family. **3** (usu. foll. by *on*) bestow (a thing) inalienably. —*n. Law* **1** an entailed estate. **2** the

succession to such an estate. □□ **entailment** *n.* [ME, f. EN-[1] + AF *taile* TAIL[2]]

entangle /ɪn'tæŋg(ə)l/ *v.tr.* **1** cause to get caught in a snare or among obstacles. **2** cause to become tangled. **3** involve in difficulties or illicit activities. **4** make (a thing) tangled or intricate; complicate.

entanglement /ɪn'tæŋg(ə)lmənt/ *n.* **1** the act or condition of entangling or being entangled. **2 a** a thing that entangles. **b** *Mil.* an extensive barrier erected to obstruct an enemy's movements (esp. one made of stakes and interlaced barbed wire). **3** a compromising (esp. amorous) relationship.

entasis /'entəsɪs/ *n. Archit.* a slight convex curve in a column shaft to correct the visual illusion that straight sides give of curving inwards. [mod.L f. Gk f. *enteinō* to stretch]

entellus /ɪn'teləs/ *n.* = HANUMAN. [name of a Trojan in Virgil's *Aeneid*]

entente /ɒn'tɒnt/ *n.* **1** = ENTENTE CORDIALE. **2** a group of States in such a relation. [F, = understanding (as INTENT)]

entente cordiale /ɑ̃, tɑ̃t kɔːdɪ'ɑːl/ *n.* a friendly understanding between States, esp. (often **Entente Cordiale**) that reached in 1904 between Britain and France. [F, = cordial understanding: see ENTENTE]

enter /'entə(r)/ *v.* **1 a** *intr.* (often foll. by *into*) go or come in. **b** *tr.* go or come into. **c** *intr.* come on stage (as a direction: *enter Macbeth*). **2** *tr.* penetrate; go through (*a bullet entered his chest*). **3** *tr.* (often foll. by *up*) write (a name, details, etc.) in a list, book, etc. **4 a** *intr.* register or announce oneself as a competitor (*entered for the long jump*). **b** *tr.* become a competitor in (an event). **c** *tr.* record the name of (a person etc.) as a competitor (*entered two horses for the Derby*). **5** *tr.* **a** become a member of (a society etc.). **b** enrol as a member or prospective member of a society, school, etc.; admit or obtain admission for. **6** *tr.* make known; present for consideration (*entered a protest*). **7** *tr.* put into an official record. **8** *intr.* (foll. by *into*) **a** engage in (conversation, relations, an undertaking, etc.). **b** subscribe to; bind oneself by (an agreement etc.). **c** form part of (one's calculations, plans, etc.). **d** sympathize with (feelings etc.). **9** *intr.* (foll. by *on, upon*) **a** begin, undertake; begin to deal with (a subject). **b** assume the functions of (an office). **c** assume possession of (property). **10** *intr.* (foll. by *up*) complete a series of entries in (account-books etc.). □□ **enterer** *n.* [ME f. OF *entrer* f. L *intrare*]

enteric /en'terɪk/ *adj. & n.* —*adj.* of the intestines. —*n.* (in full **enteric fever**) typhoid. □□ **enteritis** /,entə'raɪtɪs/ *n.* [Gk *enterikos* (as ENTERO-)]

entero- /'entərəʊ/ *comb. form* intestine. [Gk *enteron* intestine]

enterostomy /,entə'rɒstəmɪ/ *n.* (*pl.* **-ies**) *Surgery* a surgical operation in which the small intestine is brought through the abdominal wall and opened, in order to bypass the stomach or the colon.

enterotomy /,entə'rɒtəmɪ/ *n.* (*pl.* **-ies**) *Surgery* the surgical cutting open of the intestine.

enterovirus /,entərəʊ'vaɪərəs/ *n.* a virus infecting the intestines and sometimes spreading to other parts of the body, esp. the central nervous system.

enterprise /'entə,praɪz/ *n.* **1** an undertaking, esp. a bold or difficult one. **2** (as a personal attribute) readiness to engage in such undertakings (*has no enterprise*). **3** a business firm. □ **enterprise zone** *Brit.* a depressed (usu. urban) area where State incentives such as tax concessions are designed to encourage investment. □□ **enterpriser** *n.* [ME f. OF *entreprise* fem. past part. of *entreprendre* var. of *emprendre* ult. f. L *prendere, prehendere* take]

enterprising /'entə,praɪzɪŋ/ *adj.* **1** ready to engage in enterprises. **2** resourceful, imaginative, energetic. □□ **enterprisingly** *adv.*

entertain /,entə'teɪn/ *v.tr.* **1** amuse; occupy agreeably. **2 a** receive or treat as a guest. **b** (*absol.*) receive guests (*they entertain a great deal*). **3** give attention or consideration to (an idea, feeling, or proposal). [ME f. F *entretenir* ult. f. L *tenēre* hold]

entertainer /ˌentəˈteɪnə(r)/ *n.* a person who entertains, esp. professionally on stage etc.

entertaining /ˌentəˈteɪnɪŋ/ *adj.* amusing, diverting.

entertainment /ˌentəˈteɪnmənt/ *n.* **1** the act or an instance of entertaining; the process of being entertained. **2** a public performance or show. **3** diversions or amusements for guests etc. **4** amusement (*much to my entertainment*). **5** hospitality.

enthalpy /ˈenθəlpɪ, enˈθælpɪ/ *n. Physics* the total thermodynamic heat content of a system. [Gk *enthalpō* warm in (as EN-¹, *thalpō* to heat)]

enthral /ɪnˈθrɔːl/ *v.tr.* (*US* **enthrall, inthrall**) (**-thralled, -thralling**) **1** captivate, please greatly. **2** enslave. □□ **enthralment** *n.* (*US* **enthrallment**). [EN-¹ + THRALL]

enthrone /ɪnˈθrəʊn/ *v.tr.* **1** install (a king, bishop, etc.) on a throne, esp. ceremonially. **2** exalt. □□ **enthronement** *n.*

enthuse /ɪnˈθjuːz, -ˈθuːz/ *v.intr.* & *tr. colloq.* be or make enthusiastic. [back-form. f. ENTHUSIASM]

enthusiasm /ɪnˈθjuːzɪˌæz(ə)m, -ˈθuːzɪˌæz(ə)m/ *n.* **1** (often foll. by *for, about*) **a** strong interest or admiration. **b** great eagerness. **2** an object of enthusiasm. **3** *archaic* extravagant religious emotion. [F *enthousiasme* or LL *enthusiasmus* f. Gk *enthousiasmos* f. *entheos* possessed by a god, inspired (as EN-², *theos* god)]

enthusiast /ɪnˈθjuːzɪˌæst, -ˈθuːzɪˌæst/ *n.* **1** (often foll. by *for*) a person who is full of enthusiasm. **2** a visionary; a self-deluded person. [F *enthousiaste* or eccl.L *enthusiastes* f. Gk (as ENTHUSIASM)]

enthusiastic /ɪnˌθjuːzɪˈæstɪk, -ˌθuːzɪˈæstɪk/ *adj.* having or showing enthusiasm. □□ **enthusiastically** *adv.* [Gk *enthousiastikos* (as ENTHUSIASM)]

enthymeme /ˈenθɪˌmiːm/ *n. Logic* a syllogism in which one premiss is not explicitly stated. [L *enthymema* f. Gk *enthumēma* f. *enthumeomai* consider (as EN-², *thumos* mind)]

entice /ɪnˈtaɪs/ *v.tr.* (often foll. by *from, into*, or *to* + infin.) persuade by the offer of pleasure or reward. □□ **enticement** *n.* **enticer** *n.* **enticingly** *adv.* [ME f. OF *enticier* prob. f. Rmc]

entire /ɪnˈtaɪə(r)/ *adj.* & *n.* —*adj.* **1** whole, complete. **2** not broken or decayed. **3** unqualified, absolute (*an entire success*). **4** in one piece; continuous. **5** not castrated. **6** *Bot.* without indentation. **7** pure, unmixed. —*n.* an uncastrated animal. [ME f. AF *enter*, OF *entier* f. L *integer* (as IN-², *tangere* touch)]

entirely /ɪnˈtaɪəlɪ/ *adv.* **1** wholly, completely (*the stock is entirely exhausted*). **2** solely, exclusively (*did it entirely for my benefit*).

entirety /ɪnˈtaɪərətɪ/ *n.* (*pl.* **-ies**) **1** completeness. **2** (usu. foll. by *of*) the sum total. □**in its entirety** in its complete form; completely. [ME f. OF *entiereté* f. L *integritas -tatis* f. *integer* (as ENTIRE)]

entitle /ɪnˈtaɪt(ə)l/ *v.tr.* **1 a** (usu. foll. by *to*) give (a person etc.) a just claim. **b** (foll. by *to* + infin.) give (a person etc.) a right. **2 a** give (a book etc.) the title of. **b** *archaic* give (a person) the title of (*entitled him sultan*). □□ **entitlement** *n.* [ME f. AF *entitler*, OF *entiteler* f. LL *intitulare* (as IN-², TITLE)]

entity /ˈentɪtɪ/ *n.* (*pl.* **-ies**) **1** a thing with distinct existence, as opposed to a quality or relation. **2** a thing's existence regarded distinctly. □□ **entitative** /-tətɪv/ *adj.* [F *entité* or med.L *entitas* f. LL *ens* being]

ento- /ˈentəʊ/ *comb. form* within.

entomb /ɪnˈtuːm/ *v.tr.* **1** place in or as in a tomb. **2** serve as a tomb for. □□ **entombment** *n.* [OF *entomber* (as EN-¹, TOMB)]

entomo- /ˈentəməʊ/ *comb. form* insect. [Gk *entomos* cut up (in neut. = INSECT) f. EN-² + *temnō* cut]

entomology /ˌentəˈmɒlədʒɪ/ *n.* the study of the forms and behaviour of insects. □□ **entomological** /-məˈlɒdʒɪk(ə)l/ *adj.* **entomologist** *n.* [F *entomologie* or mod.L *entomologia* (as ENTOMO-, -LOGY)]

entomophagous /ˌentəˈmɒfəgəs/ *adj. Zool.* insect-eating.

entomophilous /ˌentəˈmɒfɪləs/ *adj. Biol.* pollinated by insects.

entoparasite /ˌentəʊˈpærəˌsaɪt/ *n. Biol.* = ENDOPARASITE.

entophyte /ˈentəʊˌfaɪt/ *n. Bot.* a plant growing inside a plant or animal.

entourage /ˌɒntʊəˈrɑːʒ/ *n.* **1** people attending an important person. **2** surroundings. [F f. *entourer* surround]

entr'acte /ˈɒntrækt/ *n.* **1** an interval between two acts of a play. **2** a piece of music or a dance performed during this. [F f. *entre* between + *acte* act]

entrails /ˈentreɪlz/ *n.pl.* **1** the bowels and intestines of a person or animal. **2** the innermost parts (*entrails of the earth*). [ME f. OF *entrailles* f. med.L *intralia* alt. f. L *interaneus* internal f. *inter* among]

entrain¹ /ɪnˈtreɪn/ *v.intr.* & *tr.* go or put on board a train. □□ **entrainment** *n.*

entrain² /ɪnˈtreɪn/ *v.tr.* **1** (of a fluid) carry (particles etc.) along in its flow. **2** drag along. □□ **entrainment** *n.* [F *entrainer* (as EN-¹, *traîner* drag, formed as TRAIN)]

entrain³ /ɑ̃ˈtræ/ *n.* enthusiasm, animation. [F]

entrammel /ɪnˈtræm(ə)l/ *v.tr.* (**entrammelled, entrammelling**; *US* **entrammeled, entrammeling**) entangle, hamper.

entrance¹ /ˈentrəns/ *n.* **1** the act or an instance of going or coming in. **2** a door, passage, etc., by which one enters. **3** right of admission. **4** the coming of an actor on stage. **5** *Mus.* = ENTRY 8. **6** (foll. by *into, upon*) entering into office etc. **7** (in full **entrance fee**) a fee paid for admission to a society, club, exhibition, etc. [OF (as ENTER, -ANCE)]

entrance² /ɪnˈtrɑːns/ *v.tr.* **1** enchant, delight. **2** put into a trance. **3** (often foll. by *with*) overwhelm with strong feeling. □□ **entrancement** *n.* **entrancing** *adj.* **entrancingly** *adv.*

entrant /ˈentrənt/ *n.* a person who enters (esp. an examination, profession, etc.). [F, part. of *entrer*: see ENTER]

entrap /ɪnˈtræp/ *v.tr.* (**entrapped, entrapping**) **1** catch in or as in a trap. **2** (often foll. by *into* + verbal noun) beguile or trick (a person). □□ **entrapper** *n.* [OF *entraper* (as EN-¹, TRAP¹)]

entrapment /ɪnˈtræpmənt/ *n.* **1** the act or an instance of entrapping; the process of being entrapped. **2** *Law* inducement to commit a crime, esp. by the authorities to secure a prosecution.

entreat /ɪnˈtriːt/ *v.tr.* **1 a** (foll. by *to* + infin. or *that* + clause) ask (a person) earnestly. **b** ask earnestly for (a thing). **2** *archaic* treat; act towards (a person). □□ **entreatingly** *adv.* [ME f. OF *entraiter* (as EN-¹, *traiter* TREAT)]

entreaty /ɪnˈtriːtɪ/ *n.* (*pl.* **-ies**) an earnest request; a supplication. [ENTREAT, after TREATY]

entrechat /ˌɒntrəˈʃɑː/ *n.* a leap in ballet, with one or more crossings of the legs while in the air. [F f. It. (*capriola*) *intrecciata* complicated (caper)]

entrecôte /ˈɒntrəˌkəʊt/ *n.* a boned steak cut off the sirloin. [F f. *entre* between + *côte* rib]

entrée /ˈɒntreɪ, ˈɑ̃treɪ/ *n.* **1** *Cookery* **a** *Brit.* a dish served between the fish and meat courses. **b** esp. *US* the main dish of a meal. **2** the right or privilege of admission, esp. at Court. [F, = ENTRY]

entremets /ˌɒntrəˈmeɪ/ *n.* **1** a sweet dish. **2** any light dish served between two courses. [F f. *entre* between + *mets* dish]

entrench /ɪnˈtrentʃ/ *v.* (also **intrench**) **1** *tr.* establish firmly (in a defensible position, in office, etc.). **2** *tr.* surround (a post, army, town, etc.) with a trench as a fortification. **3** *tr.* apply extra safeguards to (rights etc. guaranteed by legislation). **4** *intr.* entrench oneself. **5** *intr.* (foll. by *upon*) encroach, trespass. □**entrench oneself** adopt a well-defended position. □□ **entrenchment** *n.*

entre nous /ˌɒntrə 'nuː/ *adv.* **1** between you and me. **2** in private. [F, = between ourselves]

entrepôt /'ɒntrəˌpəʊ/ *n.* **1** a warehouse for temporary storage of goods in transit. **2** a commercial centre for import and export, and for collection and distribution. [F f. *entreposer* store f. *entre-* INTER- + *poser* place]

entrepreneur /ˌɒntrəprə'nɜː(r)/ *n.* **1** a person who undertakes an enterprise or business, with the chance of profit or loss. **2** a contractor acting as an intermediary. **3** the person in effective control of a commercial undertaking. □□ **entrepreneurial** /-'nɜːrɪəl, -'njʊərɪəl/ *adj.* **entrepreneurialism** /-'nɜːrɪəˌlɪz(ə)m, -'njʊərɪəˌlɪz(ə)m/ *n.* (also **entrepreneurism**). **entrepreneurially** /-'nɜːrɪəlɪ, -'njʊərɪəlɪ/ *adv.* **entrepreneurship** *n.* [F f. *entreprendre* undertake: see ENTERPRISE]

entresol /'ɒntrəˌsɒl/ *n.* a low storey between the first and the ground floor; a mezzanine floor. [F f. *entre* between + *sol* ground]

entrism var. of ENTRYISM.

entropy /'entrəpɪ/ *n.* **1** *Physics* a measure of the unavailability of a system's thermal energy for conversion into mechanical work. **2** *Physics* a measure of the disorganization or degradation of the universe. **3** a measure of the rate of transfer of information in a message etc. □□ **entropic** /-'trɒpɪk/ *adj.* **entropically** /-'trɒpɪkəlɪ/ *adv.* [G *Entropie* (as EN-², Gk *tropē* transformation)]

entrust /ɪn'trʌst/ *v.tr.* (also **intrust**) **1** (foll. by *to*) give responsibility for (a person or a thing) to a person in whom one has confidence. **2** (foll. by *with*) assign responsibility for a thing to (a person). □□ **entrustment** *n.*

entry /'entrɪ/ *n.* (*pl.* **-ies**) **1 a** the act or an instance of going or coming in. **b** the coming of an actor on stage. **c** ceremonial entrance. **2** liberty to go or come in. **3 a** a place of entrance; a door, gate, etc. **b** a lobby. **4** *Brit.* a passage between buildings. **5** the mouth of a river. **6 a** an item entered in a diary, list, account-book, etc. **b** the recording of this. **7 a** a person or thing competing in a race, contest, etc. **b** a list of competitors. **8** the start or resumption of music for a particular instrument in an ensemble. **9** *Law* the act of taking possession. **10** *Bridge* **a** the transfer of the lead to one's partner's hand. **b** a card providing this. □ **entry form** an application form for a competition. **entry permit** an authorization to enter a particular country etc. [ME f. OF *entree* ult. f. L *intrare* ENTER]

entryism /'entrɪˌɪz(ə)m/ *n.* (also **entrism**) infiltration into a political organization to change or subvert its policies or objectives. □□ **entrist** *n.* **entryist** *n.*

Entryphone /'entrɪˌfəʊn/ *n. propr.* an intercom device at an entrance to a building by which callers may identify themselves to gain admission.

entwine /ɪn'twaɪn/ *v.tr.* (also **intwine**) **1** (foll. by *with*, *about*, *round*) twine together (a thing with or round another). **2** interweave. □□ **entwinement** *n.*

enucleate /ɪ'njuːklɪˌeɪt/ *v.tr. Surgery* extract (a tumour etc.). □□ **enucleation** /-'eɪʃ(ə)n/ *n.* [L *enucleare* (as E-, NUCLEUS)]

E-number /'iːˌnʌmbə(r)/ *n.* the letter E followed by a code number, designating food additives according to EEC directives.

enumerate /ɪ'njuːməˌreɪt/ *v.tr.* **1** specify (items); mention one by one. **2** count; establish the number of. □□ **enumerable** *adj.* **enumeration** /-'reɪʃ(ə)n/ *n.* **enumerative** /-rətɪv/ *adj.* [L *enumerare* (as E-, NUMBER)]

enumerator /ɪ'njuːməˌreɪtə(r)/ *n.* **1** a person who enumerates. **2** a person employed in census-taking.

enunciate /ɪ'nʌnsɪˌeɪt/ *v.tr.* **1** pronounce (words) clearly. **2** express (a proposition or theory) in definite terms. **3** proclaim. □□ **enunciation** /-'eɪʃ(ə)n/ *n.*

enunciative /-sɪətɪv/ *adj.* **enunciator** *n.* [L *enuntiare* (as E-, *nuntiare* announce f. *nuntius* messenger)]

enure /ɪ'njʊə(r)/ *v.intr. Law* take effect. [var. of INURE]

enuresis /ˌenjʊə'riːsɪs/ *n. Med.* involuntary urination. □□ **enuretic** /-'retɪk/ *adj.* & *n.* [mod.L f. Gk *enoureō* urinate in (as EN-², *ouron* urine)]

envelop /ɪn'veləp/ *v.tr.* (**enveloped**, **enveloping**) **1** (often foll. by *in*) **a** wrap up or cover completely. **b** make obscure; conceal (*was enveloped in mystery*). **2** *Mil.* completely surround (an enemy). □□ **envelopment** *n.* [ME f. OF *envoluper* (as EN-¹: cf. DEVELOP)]

envelope /'envəˌləʊp, 'ɒn-/ *n.* **1** a folded paper container, usu. with a sealable flap, for a letter etc. **2** a wrapper or covering. **3** the structure within a balloon or airship containing the gas. **4** the outer metal or glass housing of a vacuum tube, electric light, etc. **5** *Electr.* a curve joining the successive peaks of a modulated wave. **6** *Bot.* any enveloping structure esp. the calyx or corolla (or both). **7** *Math.* a line or curve tangent to each line or curve of a given family. [F *enveloppe* (as ENVELOP)]

envenom /ɪn'venəm/ *v.tr.* **1** put poison on or into; make poisonous. **2** infuse venom or bitterness into (feelings, words, or actions). [ME f. OF *envenimer* (as EN-¹, *venim* VENOM)]

enviable /'envɪəb(ə)l/ *adj.* (of a person or thing) exciting or likely to excite envy. □□ **enviably** *adv.*

envious /'envɪəs/ *adj.* (often foll. by *of*) feeling or showing envy. □□ **enviously** *adv.* [ME f. AF *envious*, OF *envieus* f. *envie* ENVY]

environ /ɪn'vaɪərən/ *v.tr.* encircle, surround (esp. hostilely or protectively). [ME f. OF *environer* f. *environ* surroundings f. *en* in + *viron* circuit f. *virer* turn, VEER¹]

environment /ɪn'vaɪərənmənt/ *n.* **1** physical surroundings and conditions, esp. as affecting people's lives. **2** conditions or circumstances of living. **3** *Ecol.* external conditions affecting the growth of plants and animals. **4** a structure designed to be experienced from inside as a work of art. □□ **environmental** /-'ment(ə)l/ *adj.* **environmentally** /-'mentəlɪ/ *adv.*

environmentalist /ɪnˌvaɪərən'mentəlɪst/ *n.* **1** a person who is concerned with or advocates the protection of the environment. **2** a person who considers that environment has the primary influence on the development of a person or group. □□ **environmentalism** *n.*

environs /ɪn'vaɪərənz, 'envɪrənz/ *n.pl.* a surrounding district, esp. round an urban area.

envisage /ɪn'vɪzɪdʒ/ *v.tr.* **1** have a mental picture of (a thing or conditions not yet existing). **2** contemplate or conceive, esp. as possible or desirable. **3** *archaic* **a** face (danger, facts, etc.). **b** look in the face of. □□ **envisagement** *n.* [F *envisager* (as EN-¹, VISAGE)]

envision /ɪn'vɪʒ(ə)n/ *v.tr.* envisage, visualize.

envoy¹ /'envɔɪ/ *n.* **1** a messenger or representative, esp. on a diplomatic mission. **2** (in full **envoy extraordinary**) a minister plenipotentiary, ranking below ambassador and above chargé d'affaires. □□ **envoyship** *n.* [F *envoyé*, past part. of *envoyer* send f. *en voie* on the way f. L *via*]

envoy² /'envɔɪ/ *n.* (also **envoi**) **1** a short stanza concluding a ballade etc. **2** *archaic* an author's concluding words. [ME f. OF *envoi* f. *envoyer* (as ENVOY¹)]

envy /'envɪ/ *n.* & *v.* —*n.* (*pl.* **-ies**) **1** a feeling of discontented or resentful longing aroused by another's better fortune etc. **2** the object or ground of this feeling (*their house is the envy of the neighbourhood*). —*v.tr.* (**-ies**, **-ied**) feel envy of (a person, circumstances, etc.) (*I envy you your position*). □□ **envier** *n.* [ME f. OF *envie* f. L *invidia* f. *invidēre* envy (as IN-¹, *vidēre* see)]

enweave var. of INWEAVE.

enwrap /ɪn'ræp/ *v.tr.* (also **inwrap**) (**-wrapped, -wrapping**) (often foll. by *in*) *literary* wrap or enfold.

enwreathe /ɪn'riːð/ *v.tr.* (also **inwreathe**) *literary* surround with or as with a wreath.

Enzed /en'zed/ *n. Austral.* & *NZ colloq.* a popular written form of: **1** New Zealand. **2** a New Zealander. □□ **Enzedder** *n.* [pronunc. of *NZ*]

enzootic /ˌenzəʊ'ɒtɪk/ *adj.* & *n.* —*adj.* regularly affecting animals in a particular district or at a particular season (cf. ENDEMIC, EPIZOOTIC). —*n.* an enzootic disease. [Gk *en* in + *zōion* animal]

enzyme /'enzaɪm/ *n. Biochem.* a protein acting as a catalyst in a specific biochemical reaction. □□ **enzymatic** /-'mætɪk/ *adj.* **enzymic** /-'zaɪmɪk/ *adj.* **enzymology** /-'mɒlədʒɪ/ *n.* [G *Enzym* f. med. Gk *enzumos* leavened f. Gk *en* in + *zumē* leaven]

EOC *abbr.* Equal Opportunities Commission.

Eocene /'iːəʊˌsiːn/ *adj.* & *n. Geol.* —*adj.* of or relating to the second epoch of the Tertiary period with evidence of an abundance of mammals including horses, bats, and whales. ¶ Cf. Appendix II. —*n.* this epoch or system. [Gk *ēōs* dawn + *kainos* new]

eolian *US* var. of AEOLIAN.

eolith /'iːəlɪθ/ *n. Archaeol.* any of various flint objects found in Tertiary strata and thought to be early artefacts. [Gk *ēōs* dawn + *lithos* stone]

eolithic /ˌiːə'lɪθɪk/ *adj. Archaeol.* of the period preceding the palaeolithic age, thought to include the earliest use of flint tools. [F *éolithique* (as EOLITH)]

eon var. of AEON.

eosin /'iːəsɪn/ *n.* a red fluorescent dyestuff used esp. as a stain in optical microscopy. [Gk *ēōs* dawn + -IN]

eosinophil /ˌiːə'sɪnəfɪl/ *n.* a white blood cell readily stained by eosin.

-eous /ɪəs/ *suffix* forming adjectives meaning 'of the nature of' (*erroneous; gaseous*).

EP *abbr.* **1** electroplate. **2** extended-play (gramophone record).

Ep. *abbr.* Epistle.

ep- /ep, ɪp, iːp/ *prefix* form of EPI- before a vowel or *h*.

e.p. *abbr. Chess* en passant.

EPA *abbr.* (in the US) Environmental Protection Agency.

epact /'iːpækt/ *n.* the number of days by which the solar year exceeds the lunar year. [F *épacte* f. LL *epactae* f. Gk *epaktai* (*hēmerai*) intercalated (days) f. *epagō* intercalate (as EPI-, *agō* bring)]

eparch /'epɑːk/ *n.* the chief bishop of an eparchy. [Gk *eparkhos* (as EPI-, *arkhos* ruler)]

eparchy /'epɑːkɪ/ *n.* (*pl.* **-ies**) a province of the Orthodox Church. [Gk *eparkhia* (as EPARCH)]

epaulette /'epələt, 'epɔːˌlet, 'epəʊˌlet, ˌepə'let/ *n.* (*US* **epaulet**) an ornamental shoulder-piece on a coat, dress, etc., esp. on a uniform. [F *épaulette* dimin. of *épaule* shoulder f. L *spatula*: see SPATULA]

épée /'eɪpeɪ/ *n.* a sharp-pointed duelling-sword, used (with the end blunted) in fencing. □□ **épéeist** *n.* [F, = sword, f. OF *espee*: see SPAY]

epeirogenesis /eˌpaɪərəʊ'dʒenɪsɪs/ *n.* (also **epeirogeny** /-'rɒdʒənɪ/) *Geol.* the regional uplift of extensive areas of the earth's crust. □□ **epeirogenic** /-'dʒenɪk/ *adj.* [Gk *ēpeiros* mainland + -GENESIS, -GENY]

epenthesis /e'penθɪsɪs, ɪ-/ *n.* (*pl.* **epentheses** /-siːz/) the insertion of a letter or sound within a word, e.g. *b* in *thimble*. □□ **epenthetic** /ˌepen'θetɪk/ *adj.* [LL f. Gk f. *epentithēmi* insert (as EPI- + EN-² + *tithēmi* place)]

epergne /ɪ'pɜːn/ *n.* an ornament (esp. in branched form) for the centre of a dinner-table, holding flowers or fruit. [18th c.: perh. a corrupt. of F *épargne* saving, economy]

epexegesis /eˌpeksɪ'dʒiːsɪs/ *n.* (*pl.* **epexegeses** /-siːz/) **1** the addition of words to clarify meaning (e.g. *to do* in *difficult to do*). **2** the words added. □□ **epexegetic** /-'dʒetɪk/ *adj.* **epexegetical** /-'dʒetɪk(ə)l/ *adj.* **epexegetically** /-'dʒetɪkəlɪ/ *adv.* [Gk *epexēgēsis* (as EPI-, EXEGESIS)]

Eph. *abbr.* Ephesians (New Testament).

ephebe /'efiːb/ *n. Gk Hist.* a young man of 18-20 undergoing military training. □□ **ephebic** /e'fiːbɪk/ *adj.* [L *ephebus* f. Gk *ephēbos* (as EPI-, *hēbē* early manhood)]

ephedra /ɪ'fedrə/ *n.* any evergreen shrub of the genus *Ephedra*, with trailing stems and scalelike leaves. [mod.L f. Gk *ephedra* sitting upon]

ephedrine /'efedrɪn/ *n.* an alkaloid drug found in some ephedras, causing constriction of the blood-vessels and widening of the bronchial passages, used to relieve asthma, etc. [EPHEDRA + -INE⁴]

ephemera¹ /ɪ'femərə, ɪ'fiːm-/ *n.* (*pl.* **ephemeras** or **ephemerae** /-ˌriː/) **1 a** an insect living only a day or a few days. **b** any insect of the order Ephemeroptera, e.g. the mayfly. **2** = EPHEMERON. [mod.L f. Gk *ephēmeros* lasting only a day (as EPI-, *hēmera* day)]

ephemera² *pl.* of EPHEMERON 1.

ephemeral /ɪ'femər(ə)l, ɪ'fiːm-/ *adj.* **1** lasting or of use for only a short time; transitory. **2** lasting only a day. **3** (of an insect, flower, etc.) lasting a day or a few days. □□ **ephemerality** /-'rælɪtɪ/ *n.* **ephemerally** *adv.* **ephemeralness** *n.* [Gk *ephēmeros*: see EPHEMERA]

ephemeris /ɪ'femərɪs, ɪ'fiːm-/ *n.* (*pl.* **ephemerides** /ˌefɪ'merɪˌdiːz/) *Astron.* an astronomical almanac or table of the predicted positions of celestial bodies. [L f. Gk *ephēmeris* diary (as EPHEMERAL)]

ephemerist /ɪ'femərɪst/ *n.* a collector of ephemera.

ephemeron /ɪ'femərən, ɪ'fiːm-/ *n.* **1** (*pl.* **ephemera** /-rə/) (usu. in *pl.*) **a** a thing (esp. a printed item) of short-lived interest or usefulness. **b** a short-lived thing. **2** (*pl.* **ephemerons**) = EPHEMERA¹ 1. [as EPHEMERA¹]

ephod /'iːfɒd, 'efɒd/ *n.* a Jewish priestly vestment. [ME f. Heb. '*ēpôd*]

ephor /'efɔː(r)/ *n. Gk Hist.* any of five senior magistrates in ancient Sparta. □□ **ephorate** *n.* [Gk *ephoros* overseer (as EPI-, *horaō* see)]

epi- /'epɪ-/ *prefix* (usu. **ep-** before a vowel or *h*) **1** upon (*epicycle*). **2** above (*epicotyl*). **3** in addition (*epiphenomenon*). [Gk *epi* (prep.)]

epiblast /'epɪˌblæst/ *n. Biol.* the outermost layer of a gastrula etc.; the ectoderm. [EPI- + -BLAST]

epic /'epɪk/ *n.* & *adj.* —*n.* **1** a long poem narrating the adventures or deeds of one or more heroic or legendary figures, e.g. the *Iliad*, *Paradise Lost*. **2** an imaginative work of any form, embodying a nation's conception of its past history. **3** a book or film based on an epic narrative or heroic in type or scale. **4** a subject fit for recital in an epic. —*adj.* **1** of or like an epic. **2** grand, heroic. □□ **epical** *adj.* **epically** *adv.* [L *epicus* f. Gk *epikos* f. *epos* word, song]

epicarp /'epɪˌkɑːp/ *n. Bot.* the outermost layer of the pericarp. [EPI- + Gk *karpos* fruit]

epicedium /ˌepɪ'siːdɪəm/ *n.* (*pl.* **epicedia** /-dɪə/) a funeral ode. □□ **epicedian** *adj.* [L f. Gk *epikēdeion* (as EPI-, *kēdos* care)]

epicene /'epɪˌsiːn/ *adj.* & *n.* —*adj.* **1** *Gram.* denoting either sex without change of gender. **2** of, for, or used by both sexes. **3** having characteristics of both sexes. **4** having no characteristics of either sex. **5** effete, effeminate. —*n.* an epicene person. [ME f. LL *epicoenus* f. Gk *epikoinos* (as EPI-, *koinos* common)]

epicentre /'epɪˌsentə(r)/ *n.* (*US* **epicenter**) **1** *Geol.* the point at which an earthquake reaches the earth's surface. **2** the central point of a difficulty. □□ **epicentral** /-'sentr(ə)l/ *adj.* [Gk *epikentros* (adj.) (as EPI-, CENTRE)]

epicontinental /ˌepɪˌkɒntɪ'nent(ə)l/ *adj.* (of the sea) over the continental shelf.

epicotyl /ˌepɪ'kɒtɪl/ *n. Bot.* the region of an embryo or seedling stem above the cotyledon(s).

epicure /'epɪˌkjʊə(r)/ *n.* a person with refined tastes, esp. in food and drink. □□ **epicurism** *n.* [med.L *epicurus* one preferring sensual enjoyment: see EPICUREAN]

Epicurean /ˌepɪkjʊə'riːən/ *n.* & *adj.* —*n.* **1** a disciple or student of the Greek philosopher Epicurus (d. 270 BC), who taught that the highest good is personal happiness. **2** (**epicurean**) a person devoted to (esp. sensual) enjoyment. —*adj.* **1** of or concerning Epicurus or his ideas. **2** (**epicurean**) characteristic of an epicurean. □□ **Epicureanism** *n.* [F *épicurien* or L *epicureus* f. Gk *epikoureios* f. *Epikouros* Epicurus]

epicycle /'epɪ,saɪk(ə)l/ *n. Geom.* a small circle moving round the circumference of a larger one. □□ **epicyclic** /-'saɪklɪk, -'sɪklɪk/ *adj.* [ME f. OF or LL *epicyclus* f. Gk *epikuklos* (as EPI-, *kuklos* circle)]

epicycloid /,epɪ'saɪklɔɪd/ *n. Math.* a curve traced by a point on the circumference of a circle rolling on the exterior of another circle. □□ **epicycloidal** /-'klɔɪd(ə)l/ *adj.*

epideictic /,epɪ'daɪktɪk/ *adj.* meant for effect or display, esp. in speaking. [Gk *epideiktikos* (as EPI-, *deiknumi* show)]

epidemic /,epɪ'demɪk/ *n. & adj.* —*n.* **1** a widespread occurrence of a disease in a community at a particular time. **2** such a disease. **3** (foll. by *of*) a wide prevalence of something usu. undesirable. —*adj.* in the nature of an epidemic (cf. ENDEMIC). □□ **epidemically** *adv.* [F *épidémique* f. *épidémie* f. LL *epidemia* f. Gk *epidēmia* prevalence of disease f. *epidēmios* (adj.) (as EPI-, *dēmos* the people)]

epidemiology /,epɪdiːmɪ'ɒlədʒɪ/ *n.* the study of the incidence and distribution of diseases, and of their control and prevention. □□ **epidemiological** /-mɪə'lɒdʒɪk(ə)l/ *adj.* **epidemiologist** *n.*

epidermis /,epɪ'dɜːmɪs/ *n.* **1** the outer cellular layer of the skin. **2** Bot. the outer layer of cells of leaves, stems, roots, etc. □□ **epidermal** *adj.* **epidermic** *adj.* **epidermoid** *adj.* [LL f. Gk (as EPI-, DERMIS)]

epidiascope /,epɪ'daɪə,skəʊp/ *n.* an optical projector capable of giving images of both opaque and transparent objects. [EPI- + DIA- + -SCOPE]

epididymis /,epɪ'dɪdɪmɪs/ *n.* (*pl.* **epididymides** /-'dɪmɪ,diːz/) *Anat.* a convoluted duct behind the testis, along which sperm passes to the vas deferens. [Gk *epididumis* (as EPI-, *didumoi* testicles)]

epidural /,epɪ'djʊər(ə)l/ *adj. & n.* —*adj.* **1** *Anat.* on or around the dura mater. **2** (of an anaesthetic) introduced into the space around the dura mater of the spinal cord. —*n.* an epidural anaesthetic, used esp. in childbirth to produce loss of sensation below the waist. [EPI- + DURA (MATER)]

epifauna /'epɪ,fɔːnə/ *n.* animals living on the seabed, either attached to animals, plants, etc., or free-living. [Da. (as EPI-, FAUNA)]

epigastrium /,epɪ'gæstrɪəm/ *n.* (*pl.* **epigastria** /-rɪə/) *Anat.* the part of the abdomen immediately over the stomach. □□ **epigastric** *adj.* [LL f. Gk *epigastrion* (neut. adj.) (as EPI-, *gastēr* belly)]

epigeal /,epɪ'dʒiːəl/ *adj. Bot.* **1** having one or more cotyledons above the ground. **2** growing above the ground. [Gk *epigeios* (as EPI-, *gē* earth)]

epigene /'epɪ,dʒiːn/ *adj. Geol.* produced on the surface of the earth. [F *épigène* f. Gk *epigenēs* (as EPI-, *genēs* born)]

epiglottis /,epɪ'glɒtɪs/ *n. Anat.* a flap of cartilage at the root of the tongue, which is depressed during swallowing to cover the windpipe. □□ **epiglottal** *adj.* **epiglottic** *adj.* [Gk *epiglōttis* (as EPI-, *glōtta* tongue)]

epigone /'epɪ,gəʊn/ *n.* (*pl.* **epigones** or **epigoni** /e'pɪgə,naɪ/) one of a later (and less distinguished) generation. [pl. f. F *épigones* f. L *epigoni* f. Gk *epigonoi* those born afterwards (as EPI-, root of *gignomai* be born)]

epigram /'epɪ,græm/ *n.* **1** a short poem with a witty ending. **2** a pointed saying. **3** a pointed mode of expression. □□ **epigrammatic** /-grə'mætɪk/ *adj.* **epigrammatically** /-grə'mætɪkəlɪ/ *adv.* **epigrammatist** /-'græmətɪst/ *n.* **epigrammatize** /-'græmə,taɪz/ *v.tr. & intr.* (also -ise). [F *épigramme* or L *epigramma* f. Gk *epigramma -atos* (as EPI-, -GRAM)]

epigraph /'epɪ,grɑːf/ *n.* an inscription on a statue or coin, at the head of a chapter, etc. [Gk *epigraphē* f. *epigraphō* (as EPI-, *graphō* write)]

epigraphy /e'pɪgrəfɪ/ *n.* the study of (esp. ancient) inscriptions. □□ **epigraphic** /-'græfɪk/ *adj.* **epigraphical** /-'græfɪk(ə)l/ *adj.* **epigraphically** /-'græfɪkəlɪ/ *adv.* **epigraphist** *n.*

epilate /'epɪ,leɪt/ *v.tr.* remove hair from. □□ **epilation** /-'leɪʃ(ə)n/ *n.* [F *épiler* (cf. DEPILATE)]

epilepsy /'epɪ,lepsɪ/ *n.* a nervous disorder with convulsions and often loss of consciousness. [F *épilepsie* or LL *epilepsia* f. Gk *epilēpsia* f. *epilambanō* attack (as EPI-, *lambanō* take)]

epileptic /,epɪ'leptɪk/ *adj. & n.* —*adj.* of or relating to epilepsy. —*n.* a person with epilepsy. [F *épileptique* f. LL *epilepticus* f. Gk *epilēptikos* (as EPILEPSY)]

epilimnion /,epɪ'lɪmnɪən/ *n.* (*pl.* **epilimnia** /-nɪə/) the upper layer of water in a stratified lake. [EPI- + Gk *limnion* dimin. of *limnē* lake]

epilogist /ɪ'pɪlədʒɪst/ *n.* the writer or speaker of an epilogue.

epilogue /'epɪ,lɒg/ *n.* **1 a** the concluding part of a literary work. **b** an appendix. **2 a** speech or short poem addressed to the audience by an actor at the end of a play. **3** *Brit.* a short piece at the end of a day's broadcasting (cf. PROLOGUE). [ME f. F *épilogue* f. L *epilogus* f. Gk *epilogos* (as EPI-, *logos* speech)]

epimer /'epɪmə(r)/ *n. Chem.* either of two isomers with different configurations of atoms about one of several asymmetric carbon atoms present. □□ **epimeric** /-'merɪk/ *adj.* **epimerism** /e'pɪm-/ *n.* [G (as EPI-, -MER)]

epimerize /e'pɪmə,raɪz/ *v.tr.* (also -ise) *Chem.* convert (one epimer) into the other.

epinasty /'epɪ,næstɪ/ *n. Bot.* a tendency in plant-organs to grow more rapidly on the upper side. [EPI- + Gk *nastos* pressed]

epinephrine /,epɪ'nefrɪn/ *n. Biochem.* = ADRENALIN. [Gk *epi* upon + *nephros* kidney]

epiphany /e'pɪfənɪ, ɪ'pɪf-/ *n.* (*pl.* **-ies**) **1** (**Epiphany**) **a** the manifestation of Christ to the Magi according to the biblical account. **b** the festival commemorating this on 6 January. **2** any manifestation of a god or demigod. □□ **epiphanic** /,epɪ'fænɪk/ *adj.* [ME f. Gk *epiphaneia* manifestation f. *epiphainō* reveal (as EPI-, *phainō* show): sense 1 through OF *epiphanie* and eccl.L *epiphania*]

epiphenomenon /,epɪfɪ'nɒmɪnən/ *n.* (*pl.* **epiphenomena** /-nə/) **1** a secondary symptom, which may occur simultaneously with a disease etc. but is not regarded as its cause or result. **2** *Psychol.* consciousness regarded as a by-product of brain activity. □□ **epiphenomenal** *adj.*

epiphysis /e'pɪfɪsɪs/ *n.* (*pl.* **epiphyses** /-,siːz/) *Anat.* **1** the end part of a long bone, initially growing separately from the shaft. **2** = *pineal body*. [mod.L f. Gk *epiphusis* (as EPI-, *phusis* growth)]

epiphyte /'epɪ,faɪt/ *n.* a plant growing but not parasitic on another, e.g. a moss. □□ **epiphytal** /-'faɪt(ə)l/ *adj.* **epiphytic** /,epɪ'fɪtɪk/ *adj.* [EPI- + Gk *phuton* plant]

episcopacy /ɪ'pɪskəpəsɪ/ *n.* (*pl.* **-ies**) **1** government of a Church by bishops. **2** (prec. by *the*) the bishops.

episcopal /ɪ'pɪskəp(ə)l/ *adj.* **1** of a bishop or bishops. **2** (of a Church) constituted on the principle of government by bishops. □ **Episcopal Church** the Anglican Church in Scotland and the US, with elected bishops. □□ **episcopalism** *n.* **episcopally** *adv.* [ME f. F *épiscopal* or eccl.L *episcopalis* f. *episcopus* BISHOP]

episcopalian /ɪ,pɪskə'peɪlɪən/ *adj. & n.* —*adj.* **1** of or advocating government of a Church by bishops. **2** of or belonging to an episcopal Church or (**Episcopalian**) the Episcopal Church. —*n.* **1** an adherent of episcopacy. **2** (**Episcopalian**) a member of the Episcopal Church. □□ **episcopalianism** *n.*

episcopate /ɪ'pɪskəpət/ *n.* **1** the office or tenure of a bishop. **2** (prec. by *the*) the bishops collectively. [eccl.L *episcopatus* f. *episcopus* BISHOP]

episcope /'epɪˌskəʊp/ *n.* an optical projector giving images of opaque objects.

episematic /ˌepɪsɪ'mætɪk/ *adj. Zool.* (of coloration, markings, etc.) serving to help recognition by animals of the same species. [EPI- + Gk *sēma sēmatos* sign]

episiotomy /eˌpɪsɪ'ɒtəmɪ, eˌpiːz-/ *n.* (*pl.* **-ies**) a surgical cut made at the opening of the vagina during childbirth, to aid delivery. [Gk *epision* pubic region]

episode /'epɪˌsəʊd/ *n.* **1** one event or a group of events as part of a sequence. **2** each of the parts of a serial story or broadcast. **3** an incident or set of incidents in a narrative. **4** an incident that is distinct but contributes to a whole (*a romantic episode in her life*). **5** *Mus.* a passage containing distinct material or introducing a new subject. **6** the part between two choric songs in Greek tragedy. [Gk *epeisodion* (as EPI- + *eisodos* entry f. *eis* into + *hodos* way)]

episodic /ˌepɪ'sɒdɪk/ *adj.* (also **episodical** /-'sɒdɪk(ə)l/) **1** in the nature of an episode. **2** sporadic; occurring at irregular intervals. □□ **episodically** *adv.*

epistaxis /ˌepɪ'stæksɪs/ *n. Med.* a nosebleed. [mod.L f. Gk (as EPI-, *stazō* drip)]

epistemic /ˌepɪ'stiːmɪk, -'stemɪk/ *adj. Philos.* relating to knowledge or to the degree of its validation. □□ **epistemically** *adv.* [Gk *epistēmē* knowledge]

epistemology /ɪˌpɪstɪ'mɒlədʒɪ/ *n.* the theory of knowledge, esp. with regard to its methods and validation. □□ **epistemological** /-mə'lɒdʒ ɪk(ə)l/ *adj.* **epistemologically** /-mə'lɒdzɪkəlɪ/ *adv.* **epistemologist** *n.*

epistle /ɪ'pɪs(ə)l/ *n.* **1** *formal* or *joc.* a letter, esp. a long one on a serious subject. **2** (**Epistle**) **a** any of the letters of the apostles in the New Testament. **b** an extract from an Epistle read in a church service. **3** a poem or other literary work in the form of a letter or series of letters. [ME f. OF f. L *epistola* f. Gk *epistolē* f. *epistellō* send news (as EPI-, *stellō* send)]

epistolary /ɪ'pɪstələrɪ/ *adj.* **1** in the style or form of a letter or letters. **2** of, carried by, or suited to letters. [F *épistolaire* or L *epistolaris* (as EPISTLE)]

epistrophe /ɪ'pɪstrəfɪ/ *n.* the repetition of a word at the end of successive clauses. [Gk (as EPI-, *strophē* turning)]

epistyle /'epɪˌstaɪl/ *n. Archit.* = ARCHITRAVE. [F *épistyle* or L *epistylium* f. Gk *epistulion* (as EPI-, *stulos* pillar)]

epitaph /'epɪˌtɑːf/ *n.* words written in memory of a person who has died, esp. as a tomb inscription. [ME f. OF *epitaphe* f. L *epitaphium* f. Gk *epitaphion* funeral oration (as EPI-, *taphos* tomb)]

epitaxy /'epɪˌtæksɪ/ *n. Crystallog.* the growth of a thin layer on a single-crystal substrate that determines the lattice-structure of the layer. □□ **epitaxial** /-'tæksɪəl/ *adj.* [F *épitaxie* (as EPI-, Gk *taxis* arrangement)]

epithalamium /ˌepɪθə'leɪmɪəm/ *n.* (*pl.* **epithalamiums** or **epithalamia** /-mɪə/) a song or poem celebrating a marriage. □□ **epithalamial** *adj.* **epithalamic** /-'læmɪk/ *adj.* [L f. Gk *epithalamion* (as EPI-, *thalamos* bridal chamber)]

epithelium /ˌepɪ'θiːlɪəm/ *n.* (*pl.* **epitheliums** or **epithelia** /-lɪə/) the tissue forming the outer layer of the body surface and lining many hollow structures. □□ **epithelial** *adj.* [mod.L f. EPI- + Gk *thēlē* teat]

epithet /'epɪˌθet/ *n.* **1** an adjective or other descriptive word expressing a quality or attribute, esp. used with or as a name. **2** such a word as a term of abuse. □□ **epithetic** /-'θetɪk/ *adj.* **epithetical** /-'θetɪk(ə)l/ *adj.* **epithetically** /-'θetɪkəlɪ/ *adv.* [F *épithète* or L *epitheton* f. Gk *epitheton* f. *epitithēmi* add (as EPI-, *tithēmi* place)]

epitome /ɪ'pɪtəmɪ/ *n.* **1** a person or thing embodying a quality, class, etc. **2** a thing representing another in miniature. **3** a summary of a written work; an abstract. □□ **epitomist** *n.* [L f. Gk *epitomē* f. *epitemnō* abridge (as EPI-, *temnō* cut)]

epitomize /ɪ'pɪtəˌmaɪz/ *v.tr.* (also **-ise**) **1** be a perfect example of (a quality etc.); typify. **2** make an epitome of (a work). □□ **epitomization** /-'zeɪʃ(ə)n/ *n.*

epizoon /ˌepɪ'zəʊɒn/ *n.* (*pl.* **epizoa** /-'zəʊə/) an animal living on another animal. [mod.L (as EPI-, Gk *zōion* animal)]

epizootic /ˌepɪzəʊ'ɒtɪk/ *adj. & n.* —*adj.* (of a disease) temporarily prevalent among animals (cf. ENZOOTIC). —*n.* an outbreak of such a disease. [F *épizootique* f. *épizootie* (as EPIZOON)]

EPNS *abbr.* electroplated nickel silver.

epoch /'iːpɒk/ *n.* **1** a period of history or of a person's life marked by notable events. **2** the beginning of an era. **3** *Geol.* a division of a period, corresponding to a set of strata. □ **epoch-making** remarkable, historic; of major importance. □□ **epochal** /'epək(ə)l/ *adj.* [mod.L *epocha* f. Gk *epokhē* stoppage]

epode /'epəʊd/ *n.* **1** a form of lyric poem written in couplets each of a long line followed by a shorter one. **2** the third section of an ancient Greek choral ode or of one division of it. [F *épode* or L *epodos* f. Gk *epōidos* (as EPI-, ODE)]

eponym /'epənɪm/ *n.* **1** a person (real or imaginary) after whom a discovery, invention, place, institution, etc., is named or thought to be named. **2** the name given. □□ **eponymous** /ɪ'pɒnɪməs/ *adj.* [Gk *epōnumos* (as EPI-, *-ōnumos* f. *onoma* name)]

EPOS /'iːpɒs/ *abbr.* electronic point-of-sale (of retail outlets recording information electronically).

epoxide /ɪ'pɒksaɪd/ *n. Chem.* a compound containing an oxygen atom bonded in a triangular arrangement to two carbon atoms. [EPI- + OXIDE]

epoxy /ɪ'pɒksɪ/ *adj. Chem.* relating to or derived from an epoxide. □ **epoxy resin** a synthetic thermosetting resin containing epoxy groups. [EPI- + OXY-²]

epsilon /'epsɪˌlɒn/ *n.* the fifth letter of the Greek alphabet (E, ϵ). [ME f. Gk, = bare E f. *psilos* bare]

Epsom salts /'epsəm/ *n.* a preparation of magnesium sulphate used as a purgative etc. [*Epsom* in Surrey, where it was first found occurring naturally]

epyllion /e'pɪlɪən/ *n.* (*pl.* **epyllia** /-lɪə/) a miniature epic poem. [Gk *epullion* dimin. of *epos* word, song]

equable /'ekwəb(ə)l/ *adj.* **1** even; not varying. **2** uniform and moderate (*an equable climate*). **3** (of a person) not easily disturbed or angered. □□ **equability** /-'bɪlɪtɪ/ *n.* **equably** *adv.* [L *aequabilis* (as EQUATE)]

equal /'iːkw(ə)l/ *adj., n., & v.* —*adj.* **1** (often foll. by *to, with*) the same in quantity, quality, size, degree, rank, level, etc. **2** evenly balanced (*an equal contest*). **3** having the same rights or status (*human beings are essentially equal*). **4** uniform in application or effect (*equal opportunities*). —*n.* a person or thing equal to another, esp. in rank, status, or characteristic quality (*their treatment of the subject has no equal; is the equal of any man*). —*v.tr.* (**equalled**, **equalling**; *US* **equaled**, **equaling**) **1** be equal to in number, quality, etc. **2** achieve something that is equal to (an achievement) or to the achievement of (a person). □ **be equal to** have the ability or resources for. **equal opportunity** (often in *pl.*) the opportunity or right to be employed, paid, etc., without discrimination on grounds of sex, race, etc. **equal (or equals) sign** the symbol =. [ME f. L *aequalis* f. *aequus* even]

equalitarian /iːˌkwɒlɪ'teərɪən/ *n.* = EGALITARIAN. □□ **equalitarianism** *n.* [EQUALITY, after *humanitarian* etc.]

equality /ɪ'kwɒlɪtɪ/ *n.* the state of being equal. [ME f. OF *equalité* f. L *aequalitas -tatis* (as EQUAL)]

equalize /'iːkwəˌlaɪz/ *v.* (also **-ise**) **1** *tr. & intr.* make or become equal. **2** *intr.* reach one's opponent's score in a game, after being behind. □□ **equalization** /-'zeɪʃ(ə)n/ *n.*

equalizer /'iːkwəˌlaɪzə(r)/ *n.* **1** an equalizing score or goal etc. in a game. **2** *sl.* a weapon, esp. a gun. **3**

Electr. a connection in a system which compensates for any undesirable frequency or phase response with the system.

equally /'i:kwəlɪ/ *adv.* **1** in an equal manner (*treated them all equally*). **2** to an equal degree (*is equally important*). ¶ In sense 2 construction with *as* (*equally as important*) is often found, but is *disp.*

equanimity /ˌekwə'nɪmɪtɪ, ˌi:k-/ *n.* mental composure, evenness of temper, esp. in misfortune. □□ **equanimous** /ɪ'kwænɪməs/ *adj.* [L *aequanimitas* f. *aequanimis* f. *aequus* even + *animus* mind]

equate /ɪ'kweɪt/ *v.* **1** *tr.* (usu. foll. by *to, with*) regard as equal or equivalent. **2** *intr.* (foll. by *with*) **a** be equal or equivalent to. **b** agree or correspond. □□ **equatable** *adj.* [ME f. L *aequare aequat-* f. *aequus* equal]

equation /ɪ'kweɪʒ(ə)n/ *n.* **1** the process of equating or making equal; the state of being equal. **2** *Math.* a statement that two mathematical expressions are equal (indicated by the sign $=$). **3** *Chem.* a formula indicating a chemical reaction by means of symbols for the elements taking part. □ **equation of the first order, second order**, etc. an equation involving only the first derivative, second derivative, etc. □□ **equational** *adj.* [ME f. OF *equation* or L *aequatio* (as EQUATE)]

equator /ɪ'kweɪtə(r)/ *n.* **1** an imaginary line round the earth or other body, equidistant from the poles. **2** *Astron.* = *celestial equator*. [ME f. OF *equateur* or med.L *aequator* (as EQUATION)]

equatorial /ˌekwə'tɔ:rɪəl, ˌi:k-/ *adj.* of or near the equator. □ **equatorial telescope** a telescope attached to an axis perpendicular to the plane of the equator. □□ **equatorially** *adv.*

equerry /'ekwərɪ, ɪ'kwerɪ/ *n.* (*pl.* **-ies**) **1** an officer of the British royal household attending members of the royal family. **2** *hist.* an officer of a prince's or noble's household having charge over the horses. [earlier *esquiry* f. OF *esquierie* company of squires, prince's stables, f. OF *esquier* ESQUIRE: perh. assoc. with L *equus* horse]

equestrian /ɪ'kwestrɪən/ *adj. & n.* —*adj.* **1** of or relating to horses and horse-riding. **2** on horseback. —*n.* (*fem.* **equestrienne** /-trɪ'en/) a rider or performer on horseback. □□ **equestrianism** *n.* [L *equestris* f. *eques* horseman, knight, f. *equus* horse]

equi- /'i:kwɪ/ *comb. form* equal. [L *aequi-* f. *aequus* equal]

equiangular /ˌi:kwɪ'æŋgjʊlə(r)/ *adj.* having equal angles.

equidistant /ˌi:kwɪ'dɪst(ə)nt/ *adj.* at equal distances. □□ **equidistantly** *adv.*

equilateral /ˌi:kwɪ'lætər(ə)l/ *adj.* having all its sides equal in length.

equilibrate /ɪ'kwɪlɪˌbreɪt, ˌi:kwɪ'laɪbreɪt/ *v.* **1** *tr.* cause (two things) to balance. **2** *intr.* be in equilibrium; balance. □□ **equilibration** /-'breɪʃ(ə)n/ *n.* **equilibrator** /ɪ'kwɪlɪˌbreɪtə(r)/ *n.* [LL *aequilibrare aequilibrat-* (as EQUI-, *libra* balance)]

equilibrist /ɪ'kwɪlɪbrɪst/ *n.* an acrobat, esp. on a high rope.

equilibrium /ˌi:kwɪ'lɪbrɪəm/ *n.* (*pl.* **equilibria** /-rɪə/ or **equilibriums**) **1** a state of physical balance. **2** a state of mental or emotional equanimity. **3** a state in which the energy in a system is evenly distributed and forces, influences, etc., balance each other. [L (as EQUI-, *libra* balance)]

equine /'i:kwaɪn, 'ek-/ *adj.* of or like a horse. [L *equinus* f. *equus* horse]

equinoctial /ˌi:kwɪ'nɒkʃ(ə)l, ˌek-/ *adj. & n.* —*adj.* **1** happening at or near the time of an equinox (*equinoctial gales*). **2** of or relating to equal day and night. **3** at or near the (terrestrial) equator. —*n.* (in full **equinoctial line**) = *celestial equator.* □ **equinoctial point** the point at which the ecliptic cuts the celestial equator (twice each year at an equinox). **equinoctial year** see YEAR. [ME f. OF *equinoctial* or L *aequinoctialis* (as EQUINOX)]

equinox /'i:kwɪˌnɒks, 'ek-/ *n.* **1** the time or date (twice each year) at which the sun crosses the celestial equator, when day and night are of equal length. **2** = *equinoctial point.* □ **autumn** (or **autumnal**) **equinox** about 22 Sept. **spring** (or **vernal**) **equinox** about 20 March. [ME f. OF *equinoxe* or med.L *equinoxium* for L *aequinoctium* (as EQUI-, *nox noctis* night)]

equip /ɪ'kwɪp/ *v.tr.* (**equipped, equipping**) supply with what is needed. □□ **equipper** *n.* [F *équiper*, prob. f. ON *skipa* to man (a ship) f. *skip* SHIP]

equipage /'ekwɪpɪdʒ/ *n.* **1 a** requisites for an undertaking. **b** an outfit for a special purpose. **2** a carriage and horses with attendants. [F *équipage* (as EQUIP)]

equipment /ɪ'kwɪpmənt/ *n.* **1** the necessary articles, clothing, etc., for a purpose. **2** the process of equipping or being equipped. [F *équipement* (as EQUIP)]

equipoise /'ekwɪˌpɔɪz, 'i:-/ *n. & v.* —*n.* **1** equilibrium; a balanced state. **2** a counterbalancing thing. —*v.tr.* counterbalance.

equipollent /ˌi:kwɪ'pɒlənt/ *adj. & n.* —*adj.* **1** equal in power, force, etc. **2** practically equivalent. —*n.* an equipollent thing. □□ **equipollence** *n.* **equipollency** *n.* [ME f. OF *equipolent* f. L *aequipollens -entis* of equal value (as EQUI-, *pollēre* be strong)]

equipotential /ˌi:kwɪpə'tenʃ(ə)l/ *adj. & n. Physics* —*adj.* (of a surface or line) having the potential of a force the same or constant at all its points. —*n.* an equipotential line or surface.

equiprobable /ˌi:kwɪ'prɒbəb(ə)l/ *adj. Logic* equally probable. □□ **equiprobability** /-'bɪlɪtɪ/ *n.*

equitable /'ekwɪtəb(ə)l/ *adj.* **1** fair, just. **2** *Law* valid in equity as distinct from law. □□ **equitableness** *n.* **equitably** *adv.* [F *équitable* (as EQUITY)]

equitation /ˌekwɪ'teɪʃ(ə)n/ *n.* the art and practice of horsemanship and horse-riding. [F *équitation* or L *equitatio* f. *equitare* ride a horse f. *eques equitis* horseman f. *equus* horse]

equity /'ekwɪtɪ/ *n.* (*pl.* **-ies**) **1** fairness. **2** the application of the principles of justice to correct or supplement the law. **3 a** the value of the shares issued by a company. **b** (in *pl.*) stocks and shares not bearing fixed interest. **4** the net value of a mortgaged property after the deduction of charges. **5** (**Equity**) *Brit.* the actors' trade union. [ME f. OF *equité* f. L *aequitas -tatis* f. *aequus* fair]

equivalent /ɪ'kwɪvələnt/ *adj. & n.* —*adj.* **1** (often foll. by *to*) equal in value, amount, importance, etc. **2** corresponding. **3** (of words) having the same meaning. **4** having the same result. **5** *Chem.* (of a substance) equal in combining or displacing capacity. —*n.* **1** an equivalent thing, amount, word, etc. **2** (in full **equivalent weight**) *Chem.* the weight of a substance that can combine with or displace one gram of hydrogen or eight grams of oxygen. □□ **equivalence** *n.* **equivalency** *n.* **equivalently** *adv.* [ME f. OF f. LL *aequivalēre* (as EQUI-, *valēre* be worth)]

equivocal /ɪ'kwɪvək(ə)l/ *adj.* **1** of double or doubtful meaning; ambiguous. **2** of uncertain nature. **3** (of a person, character, etc.) questionable, suspect. □□ **equivocality** /-'kælɪtɪ/ *n.* **equivocally** *adv.* **equivocalness** *n.* [LL *aequivocus* (as EQUI-, *vocare* call)]

equivocate /ɪ'kwɪvəˌkeɪt/ *v.intr.* use ambiguity to conceal the truth. □□ **equivocation** /-'keɪʃ(ə)n/ *n.* **equivocator** *n.* **equivocatory** *adj.* [ME f. LL *aequivocare* (as EQUIVOCAL)]

equivoque /'ekwɪˌvəʊk, 'i:-/ *n.* (also **equivoke**) a pun or ambiguity. [ME in the sense 'equivocal' f. OF *equivoque* or LL *aequivocus* EQUIVOCAL]

ER *abbr.* **1** Queen Elizabeth. **2** King Edward. [L *Elizabetha Regina, Edwardus Rex*]

Er *symb. Chem.* the element erbium.

er /ɜ:(r)/ *int.* expressing hesitation or a pause in speech. [imit.]

b *but* d *dog* f *few* g *get* h *he* j *yes* k *cat* l *leg* m *man* n *no* p *pen* r *red* s *sit* t *top* v *voice*

-er[1] /ə(r)/ *suffix* forming nouns from nouns, adjectives, and many verbs, denoting: **1** a person, animal, or thing that performs a specified action or activity (*cobbler*; *lover*; *executioner*; *poker*; *computer*; *eye-opener*). **2** a person or thing that has a specified attribute or form (*foreigner*; *four-wheeler*; *second-rater*). **3** a person concerned with a specified thing or subject (*hatter*; *geographer*). **4** a person belonging to a specified place or group (*villager*; *New Zealander*; *sixth-former*). [orig. 'one who has to do with': OE *-ere* f. Gmc]

-er[2] /ə(r)/ *suffix* forming the comparative of adjectives (*wider*; *hotter*) and adverbs (*faster*). [OE *-ra* (adj.), *-or* (adv.) f. Gmc]

-er[3] /ə(r)/ *suffix* used in slang formations usu. distorting the root word (*rugger*; *soccer*). [prob. an extension of -ER[1]]

-er[4] /ə(r)/ *suffix* forming iterative and frequentative verbs (*blunder*; *glimmer*; *twitter*). [OE *-erian, -rian* f. Gmc]

-er[5] /ə(r)/ *suffix* **1** forming nouns and adjectives through OF or AF, corresponding to: **a** L *-aris* (*sampler*) (cf. -AR[1]). **b** L *-arius, -arium* (*butler*; *carpenter*; *danger*). **c** (through OF *-eüre*) L *-atura* or (through OF *-eör*) L *-atorium* (see COUNTER[1], FRITTER[2]). **2** = -OR.

-er[6] /ə(r)/ *suffix* esp. *Law* forming nouns denoting verbal action or a document effecting this (*cesser*; *disclaimer*; *misnomer*). ¶ The same ending occurs in *dinner* and *supper*. [AF infin. ending of verbs]

era /ˈɪərə/ *n.* **1** a system of chronology reckoning from a noteworthy event (*the Christian era*). **2** a large distinct period of time, esp. regarded historically (*the pre-Roman era*). **3** a date at which an era begins. **4** *Geol.* a major division of time. [LL *aera* number expressed in figures (pl. of *aes aeris* money, treated as fem. sing.)]

eradicate /ɪˈrædɪˌkeɪt/ *v.tr.* root out; destroy completely; get rid of. □□ **eradicable** *adj.* **eradication** /-ˈkeɪʃ(ə)n/ *n.* **eradicator** *n.* [ME f. L *eradicare* tear up by the roots (as E-, *radix -icis* root)]

erase /ɪˈreɪz/ *v.tr.* **1** rub out; obliterate. **2** remove all traces of (*erased it from my memory*). **3** remove recorded material from (a magnetic tape or medium). □□ **erasable** *adj.* **erasure** *n.* [L *eradere eras-* (as E-, *radere* scrape)]

eraser /ɪˈreɪzə(r)/ *n.* a thing that erases, esp. a piece of rubber or plastic used for removing pencil and ink marks.

erbium /ˈɜːbɪəm/ *n.* *Chem.* a soft silvery metallic element of the lanthanide series, occurring naturally in apatite and xenotine. ¶ Symb.: **Er**. [mod.L f. *Ytterby* in Sweden]

ere /eə(r)/ *prep. & conj. poet.* or *archaic* before (of time) (*ere noon*; *ere they come*). [OE *ǣr* f. Gmc]

erect /ɪˈrekt/ *adj. & v.* —*adj.* **1** upright, vertical. **2** (of the penis, clitoris, or nipples) enlarged and rigid, esp. in sexual excitement. **3** (of hair) bristling, standing up from the skin. —*v.tr.* **1** raise; set upright. **2** build. **3** establish (*erect a theory*). □□ **erectable** *adj.* **erectly** *adv.* **erectness** *n.* **erector** *n.* [ME f. L *erigere erect-* set up (as E-, *regere* direct)]

erectile /ɪˈrektaɪl/ *adj.* that can be erected or become erect. □ **erectile tissue** *Physiol.* animal tissue that is capable of becoming rigid, esp. with sexual excitement. [F *érectile* (as ERECT)]

erection /ɪˈrekʃ(ə)n/ *n.* **1** the act or an instance of erecting; the state of being erected. **2** a building or structure. **3** *Physiol.* an enlarged and erect state of erectile tissue, esp. of the penis. [F *érection* or L *erectio* (as ERECTILE)]

E-region var. of E-LAYER.

eremite /ˈerɪˌmaɪt/ *n.* a hermit or recluse (esp. Christian). □□ **eremitic** /-ˈmɪtɪk/ *adj.* **eremitical** /-ˈmɪtɪk(ə)l/ *adj.* **eremitism** *n.* [ME f. OF, var. of *hermite, ermite* HERMIT]

erethism /ˈerɪˌθɪz(ə)m/ *n.* **1** an excessive sensitivity to stimulation of any part of the body, esp. the sexual organs. **2** a state of abnormal mental excitement or irritation. [F *éréthisme* f. Gk *erethismos* f. *erethizō* irritate]

erg[1] /ɜːg/ *n.* *Physics* a unit of work or energy, equal to the work done by a force of one dyne when its point of application moves one centimetre in the direction of action of the force. [Gk *ergon* work]

erg[2] /ɜːg/ *n.* (pl. **ergs** or **areg** /ˈɑːreg/) an area of shifting sand-dunes in the Sahara. [F f. Arab. *'irj*]

ergo /ˈɜːgəʊ/ *adv.* therefore. [L]

ergocalciferol /ˌɜːgəʊkælˈsɪfəˌrɒl/ *n.* = CALCIFEROL. [ERGOT + CALCIFEROL]

ergonomics /ˌɜːgəˈnɒmɪks/ *n.* the study of the efficiency of persons in their working environment. □□ **ergonomic** *adj.* □□ **ergonomist** /ɜːˈgɒnəmɪst/ *n.* [Gk *ergon* work: cf. ECONOMICS]

ergosterol /ɜːˈgɒstəˌrɒl/ *n.* *Biochem.* a plant sterol that is converted to vitamin D$_2$ when irradiated with ultraviolet light. [ERGOT, after CHOLESTEROL]

ergot /ˈɜːgət/ *n.* **1** a disease of rye and other cereals caused by the fungus *Claviceps purpurea*. **2 a** this fungus. **b** the dried spore-containing structures of this, used as a medicine to aid childbirth. [F f. OF *argot* cock's spur, from the appearance produced]

ergotism /ˈɜːgəˌtɪz(ə)m/ *n.* poisoning produced by eating food affected by ergot.

erica /ˈerɪkə/ *n.* any shrub or heath of the genus *Erica*, with small leathery leaves and bell-like flowers. □□ **ericaceous** /-ˈkeɪʃəs/ *adj.* [L f. Gk *ereikē* heath]

erigeron /ɪˈrɪgəˌrɒn/ *n.* any hardy composite herb of the genus *Erigeron*, with daisy-like flowers. [Gk *ērigerōn* f. *ēri* early + *gerōn* old man, because some species bear grey down]

Erin /ˈerɪn, ˈɪərɪn/ *n. archaic* or *poet.* Ireland. [Ir.]

Erinys /eˈrɪnɪs/ *n.* (pl. **Erinyes** /eˈrɪnɪˌiːz/) *Mythol.* a Fury. [Gk]

eristic /eˈrɪstɪk/ *adj. & n.* —*adj.* **1** of or characterized by disputation. **2** (of an argument or arguer) aiming at winning rather than at reaching the truth. —*n.* **1** the practice of disputation. **2** an exponent of disputation. □□ **eristically** *adv.* [Gk *eristikos* f. *erizō* wrangle f. *eris* strife]

erk /ɜːk/ *n. Brit. sl.* **1** a naval rating. **2** an aircraftman. **3** a disliked person. [20th c.: orig. unkn.]

erl-king /ˈɜːlkɪŋ/ *n.* (in Germanic mythology) a bearded giant or goblin who lures little children to the land of death. [G *Erlkönig* alder-king, a mistransl. of Da. *ellerkonge* king of the elves]

ermine /ˈɜːmɪn/ *n.* (pl. same or **ermines**) **1** the stoat, esp. when in its white winter fur. **2** its white fur, used as trimming for the robes of judges, peers, etc. **3** *Heraldry* a white fur marked with black spots. □□ **ermined** *adj.* [ME f. OF *(h)ermine* prob. f. med.L *(mus) Armenius* Armenian (mouse)]

ern *US* var. of ERNE.

-ern /ən/ *suffix* forming adjectives (*northern*). [OE *-erne* f. Gmc]

erne /ɜːn/ *n.* (*US* **ern**) *poet.* a sea eagle. [OE *earn* f. Gmc]

Ernie /ˈɜːnɪ/ *n.* (in the UK) a device for drawing prize-winning numbers of Premium Bonds. [initial letters of *electronic random number indicator equipment*]

erode /ɪˈrəʊd/ *v.* **1** *tr. & intr.* wear away, destroy or be destroyed gradually. **2** *tr. Med.* (of ulcers etc.) destroy (tissue) little by little. □□ **erodible** *adj.* [F *éroder* or L *erodere eros-* (as E-, *rodere ros-* gnaw)]

erogenous /ɪˈrɒdʒɪnəs/ *adj.* **1** (esp. of a part of the body) sensitive to sexual stimulation. **2** giving rise to sexual desire or excitement. [as EROTIC + -GENOUS]

erosion /ɪˈrəʊʒ(ə)n/ *n.* **1** *Geol.* the wearing away of the earth's surface by the action of water, wind, etc. **2** the act or an instance of eroding; the process of being eroded. □□ **erosional** *adj.* **erosive** *adj.* [F *érosion* f. L *erosio* (as ERODE)]

erotic /ɪˈrɒtɪk/ *adj.* of or causing sexual love, esp. tending to arouse sexual desire or excitement. □□

erotically *adv.* [F *érotique* f. Gk *erōtikos* f. *erōs erōtos* sexual love]

erotica /ɪ'rɒtɪkə/ *n.pl.* erotic literature or art.

eroticism /ɪ'rɒtɪ,sɪz(ə)m/ *n.* **1** erotic nature or character. **2** the use of or response to erotic images or stimulation.

erotism /'erə,tɪz(ə)m/ *n.* sexual desire or excitement; eroticism.

eroto- /ɪ,rɒtəʊ, ɪ,rəʊt-/ *comb. form* erotic, eroticism. [Gk *erōs erōtos* sexual love]

erotogenic /ɪ,rɒtə'dʒenɪk/ *adj.* (also **erotogenous** /,erə'tɒdʒɪnəs/) = EROGENOUS.

erotology /,erə'tɒlədʒɪ/ *n.* the study of sexual love.

erotomania /ɪ,rəʊtə'meɪnɪə/ *n.* **1** excessive or morbid erotic desire. **2** a preoccupation with sexual passion. □□ **erotomaniac** /-nɪæk/ *n.*

err /ɜː(r)/ *v.intr.* **1** be mistaken or incorrect. **2** do wrong; sin. □ **err on the right side** act so that the least harmful of possible errors is the most likely to occur. **err on the side of** act with a specified bias (*errs on the side of generosity*). [ME f. OF *errer* f. L *errare* stray: rel. to Goth. *airzei* error, *airzjan* lead astray]

errand /'erənd/ *n.* **1** a short journey, esp. on another's behalf, to take a message, collect goods, etc. **2** the object of such a journey. □ **errand of mercy** a journey to relieve suffering etc. [OE *ǣrende* f. Gmc]

errant /'erənt/ *adj.* **1** erring; deviating from an accepted standard. **2** *literary* or *archaic* travelling in search of adventure (*knight errant*). □□ **errancy** *n.* (in sense 1). **errantry** *n.* (in sense 2). [ME: sense 1 formed as ERR: sense 2 f. OF *errer* ult. f. LL *itinerare* f. *iter* journey]

erratic /ɪ'rætɪk/ *adj.* **1** inconsistently variable in conduct, opinions, etc. **2** uncertain in movement. □ **erratic block** *Geol.* a large rock carried from a distance by glacial action. □□ **erratically** *adv.* [ME f. OF *erratique* f. L *erraticus* (as ERR)]

erratum /ɪ'rɑːtəm/ *n.* (*pl.* **errata** /-tə/) an error in printing or writing, esp. (in *pl.*) a list of corrected errors attached to a book etc. [L, neut. past part. (as ERR)]

erroneous /ɪ'rəʊnɪəs/ *adj.* incorrect; arising from error. □□ **erroneously** *adv.* **erroneousness** *n.* [ME f. OF *erroneus* or L *erroneus* f. *erro -onis* vagabond (as ERR)]

error /'erə(r)/ *n.* **1** a mistake. **2** the condition of being wrong in conduct or judgement (*led into error*). **3** a wrong opinion or judgement. **4** the amount by which something is incorrect or inaccurate in a calculation or measurement. □□ **errorless** *adj.* [ME f. OF *errour* f. L *error -oris* (as ERR)]

ersatz /'ɜːzæts, 'eə-/ *adj. & n.* —*adj.* substitute, imitation (esp. of inferior quality). —*n.* an ersatz thing. [G, = replacement]

Erse /ɜːs/ *adj. & n.* —*adj.* Irish or Highland Gaelic. —*n.* the Gaelic language. [early Sc. form of IRISH]

erst /ɜːst/ *adv. archaic* formerly; of old. [OE *ǣrest* superl. of *ǣr:* see ERE]

erstwhile /'ɜːstwaɪl/ *adj. & adv.* —*adj.* former, previous. —*adv. archaic* = ERST.

erubescent /,eru:'bes(ə)nt/ *adj.* reddening, blushing. [L *erubescere* (as E-, *rubescere* f. *rubēre* be red)]

eructation /,iːrʌk'teɪʃ(ə)n/ *n.* the act or an instance of belching. [L *eructatio* f. *eructare* (as E-, *ructare* belch)]

erudite /'eru:,daɪt/ *adj.* **1** (of a person) learned. **2** (of writing etc.) showing great learning. □□ **eruditely** *adv.* **erudition** /-'dɪʃ(ə)n/ *n.* [ME f. L *eruditus* past part. of *erudire* instruct, train (as E-, *rudis* untrained)]

erupt /ɪ'rʌpt/ *v.intr.* **1** break out suddenly or dramatically. **2** (of a volcano) become active and eject lava etc. **3 a** (of a rash, boil, etc.) appear on the skin. **b** (of the skin) produce a rash etc. **4** (of the teeth) break through the gums in normal development. □□ **eruption** *n.* **eruptive** *adj.* [L *erumpere erupt-* (as E-, *rumpere* break)]

-ery /ərɪ/ *suffix* forming nouns denoting: **1** a class or kind (*greenery; machinery; citizenry*). **2** employment; state or condition (*archery; dentistry; slavery; bravery*). **3** a place of work or cultivation or breeding (*brewery; orangery; rookery*). **4** behaviour (*mimicry*). **5** often *derog.* all that has to do with (*knavery; popery; tomfoolery*). [ME, from or after F *-erie, -ere* ult. f. L *-ario-, -ator*]

erysipelas /,erɪ'sɪpɪləs/ *n. Med.* a streptococcal infection producing inflammation and a deep red colour on the skin, esp. of the face and scalp. [ME f. L f. Gk *erusipelas*, perh. rel. to *eruthros* red + a root *pel-* skin]

erythema /,erɪ'θiːmə/ *n.* a superficial reddening of the skin, usu. in patches. □□ **erythemal** *adj.* **erythematic** /e,rɪθɪ'mætɪk/ *adj.* [mod.L f. Gk *eruthēma* f. *eruthainō* be red f. *eruthros* red]

erythro- /ɪ'rɪθrəʊ/ *comb. form* red. [Gk *eruthros* red]

erythroblast /ɪ'rɪθrəʊ,blæst/ *n.* an immature erythrocyte. [G]

erythrocyte /ɪ'rɪθrəʊ,saɪt/ *n.* a red blood cell, which contains the pigment haemoglobin and transports oxygen and carbon dioxide to and from the tissues. □□ **erythrocytic** /-'sɪtɪk/ *adj.*

erythroid /'erɪ,θrɔɪd/ *adj.* of or relating to erythrocytes.

Es *symb. Chem.* the element einsteinium.

-es[1] /ɪz/ *suffix* forming plurals of nouns ending in sibilant sounds (such words in *-e* dropping the *e*) (*kisses; cases; boxes; churches*). [var. of -s[1]]

-es[2] /ɪz, z/ *suffix* forming the 3rd person sing. present of verbs ending in sibilant sounds (such words in *-e* dropping the *e*) and ending in *-o* (but not *-oo*) (*goes; places; pushes*). [var. of -s[2]]

ESA *abbr.* European Space Agency.

escadrille /,eskə'drɪl/ *n.* a French squadron of aeroplanes. [F]

escalade /,eskə'leɪd/ *n.* the scaling of fortified walls with ladders, as a military attack. [F f. Sp. *escalada, -ado* f. med.L *scalare* f. *scala* ladder]

escalate /'eskə,leɪt/ *v.* **1** *intr. & tr.* increase or develop (usu. rapidly) by stages. **2** *tr.* cause (an action, activity, or process) to become more intense. □□ **escalation** /-'leɪʃ(ə)n/ *n.* [back-form. f. ESCALATOR]

escalator /'eskə,leɪtə(r)/ *n.* a moving staircase consisting of a circulating belt forming steps. [f. the stem of *escalade* 'climb a wall by ladder' + -ATOR]

escallonia /,eskə'ləʊnɪə/ *n.* any evergreen shrub of the genus *Escallonia*, bearing rose-red flowers. [*Escallon*, 18th-c. Sp. traveller]

escallop /ɪ'skæləp/ *n.* **1** = SCALLOP 1, 2. **2** = ESCALOPE. **3** (in *pl.*) = SCALLOP 3. **4** *Heraldry* a scallop shell as a device. [formed as ESCALOPE]

escalope /'eskə,lɒp/ *n.* a thin slice of meat without any bone, esp. from a leg of veal. [F (in OF = shell): see SCALLOP]

escapade /'eskə,peɪd, ,eskə'peɪd/ *n.* a piece of daring or reckless behaviour. [F f. Prov. or Sp. *escapada* (as ESCAPE)]

escape /ɪ'skeɪp/ *v. & n.* —*v.* **1** *intr.* (often foll. by *from*) get free of the restriction or control of a place, person, etc. **2** *intr.* (of a gas, liquid, etc.) leak from a container or pipe etc. **3** *intr.* succeed in avoiding danger, punishment, etc.; get off safely. **4** *tr.* get completely free of (a person, grasp, etc.). **5** *tr.* avoid or elude (a commitment, danger, etc.). **6** *tr.* elude the notice or memory of (*nothing escapes you; the name escaped me*). **7** *tr.* (of words etc.) issue unawares from (a person, a person's lips). —*n.* **1** the act or an instance of escaping; avoidance of danger, injury, etc. **2** the state of having escaped (*was a narrow escape*). **3** a means of escaping (often *attrib.: escape hatch*). **4** a leakage of gas etc. **5** a temporary relief from reality or worry. **6** a garden plant running wild. □ **escape clause** *Law* a clause specifying the conditions under which a contracting party is free from an obligation. **escape road** a road for a vehicle to turn into if unable to negotiate a bend, descent, etc., safely (esp. on a racetrack). **escape velocity**

the minimum velocity needed to escape from the gravitational field of a body. **escape wheel** a toothed wheel in the escapement of a watch or clock. □□ **escapable** *adj.* **escaper** *n.* [ME f. AF, ONF *escaper* ult. f. med.L (as EX-[1], *cappa* cloak)]

escapee /ɪskeɪˈpiː/ *n.* a person, esp. a prisoner, who has escaped.

escapement /ɪˈskeɪpmənt/ *n.* **1** the part of a clock or watch that connects and regulates the motive power. **2** the part of the mechanism in a piano that enables the hammer to fall back immediately it has struck the string. **3** *archaic* a means of escape. [F *échappement* f. *échapper* ESCAPE]

escapism /ɪˈskeɪpɪz(ə)m/ *n.* the tendency to seek distraction and relief from reality, esp. in the arts or through fantasy. □□ **escapist** *n. & adj.*

escapology /ˌeskəˈpɒlədʒɪ/ *n.* the methods and techniques of escaping from confinement, esp. as a form of entertainment. □□ **escapologist** *n.*

escargot /eˈskɑːgəʊ/ *n.* an edible snail. [F]

escarpment /ɪˈskɑːpmənt/ *n.* (also **escarp**) *Geol.* a long steep slope at the edge of a plateau etc. [F *escarpement* f. *escarpe* SCARP]

-esce /es/ *suffix* forming verbs, usu. initiating action (*effervesce*; *fluoresce*). [from or after L *-escere*]

-escent /ˈes(ə)nt/ *suffix* forming adjectives denoting the beginning of a state or action (*effervescent*; *fluorescent*). □□ **-escence** *suffix* forming nouns. [from or after F *-escent* or L *-escent-*, pres. part. stem of verbs in *-escere*]

eschatology /ˌeskəˈtɒlədʒɪ/ *n.* the part of theology concerned with death and final destiny. □□ **eschatological** /-təˈlɒdʒɪk(ə)l/ *adj.* **eschatologist** *n.* [Gk *eskhatos* last + -LOGY]

escheat /ɪsˈtʃiːt/ *n. & v. hist.* —*n.* **1** the reversion of property to the State, or (in feudal law) to a lord, on the owner's dying without legal heirs. **2** property affected by this. —*v.* **1** *tr.* hand over (property) as an escheat. **2** *tr.* confiscate. **3** *intr.* revert by escheat. [ME f. OF *eschete*, ult. f. L *excidere* (as EX-[1], *cadere* fall)]

eschew /ɪsˈtʃuː/ *v.tr. literary* avoid; abstain from. □□ **eschewal** *n.* [ME f. OF *eschiver*, ult. f. Gmc: rel. to SHY[1]]

eschscholtzia /ɪsˈkɒlʃə, eˈʃɒltsɪə/ *n.* any yellow-flowering plant of the genus *Eschscholtzia*, esp. the Californian poppy (see POPPY). [J. F. von *Eschscholtz*, Ger. botanist d. 1831]

escort *n. & v.* —*n.* /ˈeskɔːt/ **1** one or more persons, vehicles, ships, etc., accompanying a person, vehicle, etc., esp. for protection or security or as a mark of rank or status. **2** a person accompanying a person of the opposite sex socially. —*v.tr.* /ɪˈskɔːt/ act as an escort to. [F *escorte*, *escorter* f. It. *scorta* fem. past part. of *scorgere* conduct]

escritoire /ˌeskrɪˈtwɑː(r)/ *n.* a writing-desk with drawers etc. [F f. L *scriptorium* writing-room: see SCRIPTORIUM]

escrow /eˈskrəʊ/ *n. & v. Law* —*n.* **1** money, property, or a written bond, kept in the custody of a third party until a specified condition has been fulfilled. **2** the status of this (*in escrow*). —*v.tr.* place in escrow. [AF *escrowe*, OF *escroe* scrap, scroll, f. med.L *scroda* f. Gmc]

escudo /eˈskjuːdəʊ/ *n.* (*pl.* -os) the principal monetary unit of Portugal and Chile. [Sp. & Port. f. L *scutum* shield]

esculent /ˈeskjʊlənt/ *adj. & n.* —*adj.* fit to eat; edible. —*n.* an edible substance. [L *esculentus* f. *esca* food]

escutcheon /ɪˈskʌtʃ(ə)n/ *n.* **1** a shield or emblem bearing a coat of arms. **2** the middle part of a ship's stern where the name is placed. **3** the protective plate around a keyhole or door-handle. □□ **escutcheoned** *adj.* [AF & ONF *escuchon* ult. f. L *scutum* shield]

Esd. *abbr.* Esdras (Apocrypha).

ESE *abbr.* east-south-east.

-ese /iːz/ *suffix* forming adjectives and nouns denoting: **1** an inhabitant or language of a country or city (*Japanese*; *Milanese*; *Viennese*). ¶ Plural forms are the same. **2** often *derog.* character or style, esp. of language (*officialese*). [OF *-eis* ult. f. L *-ensis*]

esker /ˈeskə(r)/ *n.* (also **eskar**) *Geol.* a long ridge of post-glacial gravel in river valleys. [Ir. *eiscir*]

Eskimo /ˈeskɪˌməʊ/ *n. & adj.* —*n.* (*pl.* same or **-os**) **1** a member of a people inhabiting N. Canada, Alaska, Greenland, and E. Siberia. **2** the language of this people. —*adj.* of or relating to the Eskimos or their language. ¶ The term *Inuit* is preferred by the people themselves. [Da. f. F *Esquimaux* (pl.) f. Algonquian]

Esky /ˈeskɪ/ *n.* (*pl.* **-ies**) *Austral. propr.* a portable insulated container for keeping food or drink cool. [prob. f. ESKIMO, with ref. to their cold climate]

ESN *abbr.* educationally subnormal.

esophagus US var. of OESOPHAGUS.

esoteric /ˌiːsəʊˈterɪk, ˌe-/ *adj.* **1** intelligible only to those with special knowledge. **2** (of a belief etc.) intended only for the initiated. □□ **esoterical** *adj.* **esoterically** *adv.* **esotericism** /-ˌsɪz(ə)m/ *n.* **esotericist** /-sɪst/ *n.* [Gk *esōterikos* f. *esōterō* compar. of *esō* within]

ESP *abbr.* extrasensory perception.

espadrille /ˌespəˈdrɪl/ *n.* a light canvas shoe with a plaited fibre sole. [F f. Prov. *espardillo* f. *espart* ESPARTO]

espalier /ɪˈspælɪə(r)/ *n.* **1** a lattice-work along which the branches of a tree or shrub are trained to grow flat against a wall etc. **2** a tree or shrub trained in this way. [F f. It. *spalliera* f. *spalla* shoulder]

esparto /eˈspɑːtəʊ/ *n.* (*pl.* -os) (in full **esparto grass**) a coarse grass, *Stipa tenacissima*, native to Spain and N. Africa, with tough narrow leaves, used to make ropes, wickerwork, and good-quality paper. [Sp. f. L *spartum* f. Gk *sparton* rope]

especial /ɪˈspeʃ(ə)l/ *adj.* **1** notable, exceptional. **2** attributed or belonging chiefly to one person or thing (*your especial charm*). [ME f. OF f. L *specialis* special]

especially /ɪˈspeʃəlɪ, -ʃlɪ/ *adv.* chiefly; much more than in other cases.

Esperanto /ˌespəˈræntəʊ/ *n.* an artificial universal language devised in 1887, based on roots common to the chief European languages. □□ **Esperantist** *n.* [the pen-name (f. L *sperare* hope) of its inventor, L. L. Zamenhof, Polish physician d. 1917]

espial /ɪˈspaɪəl/ *n.* **1** the act or an instance of catching sight of or of being seen. **2** *archaic* spying. [ME f. OF *espiaille* f. *espier*: see ESPY]

espionage /ˈespɪəˌnɑːʒ/ *n.* the practice of spying or of using spies, esp. by governments. [F *espionnage* f. *espionner* f. *espion* SPY]

esplanade /ˌespləˈneɪd/ *n.* **1** a long open level area for walking on, esp. beside the sea. **2** a level space separating a fortress from a town. [F f. Sp. *esplanada* f. *esplanar* make level f. L *explanare* (as EX-[1], *planus* level)]

espousal /ɪˈspaʊz(ə)l/ *n.* **1** (foll. by *of*) the espousing of a cause etc. **2** *archaic* a marriage or betrothal. [ME f. OF *espousailles* f. L *sponsalia* neut. pl. of *sponsalis* (as ESPOUSE)]

espouse /ɪˈspaʊz/ *v.tr.* **1** adopt or support (a cause, doctrine, etc.) **2** *archaic* **a** (usu. of a man) marry. **b** (usu. foll. by *to*) give (a woman) in marriage. □□ **espouser** *n.* [ME f. OF *espouser* f. L *sponsare* f. *sponsus* past part. of *spondēre* betroth]

espresso /eˈspresəʊ/ *n.* (also **expresso** /ekˈspresəʊ/) (*pl.* -os) **1** strong concentrated black coffee made under steam pressure. **2** a machine for making this. [It., = pressed out]

esprit /eˈspriː, ˈesprɪ/ *n.* sprightliness, wit. □ **esprit de corps** /də ˈkɔː(r)/ a feeling of devotion to and pride in the group one belongs to. **esprit de l'escalier** /də leˈskælɪeɪ/ an apt retort or clever remark that comes to mind after the chance to make it is gone. [F f. L *spiritus* SPIRIT (+ *corps* body, *escalier* stairs)]

espy /ɪˈspaɪ/ *v.tr.* (**-ies**, **-ied**) *literary* catch sight of; perceive. [ME f. OF *espier*: see SPY]

Esq. *abbr.* Esquire.

-esque /esk/ *suffix* forming adjectives meaning 'in the style of' or 'resembling' (*romanesque*; *Schumannesque*; *statuesque*). [F f. It. *-esco* f. med.L *-iscus*]

Esquimau /'eskɪˌməʊ/ *n.* (*pl.* **-aux** /-əʊz/) = ESKIMO. [F]

esquire /ɪ'skwaɪə(r)/ *n.* **1** (usu. as abbr. **Esq.**) *Brit.* a title appended to a man's surname when no other form of address is used, esp. as a form of address for letters. **2** *archaic* = SQUIRE. [ME f. OF *esquier* f. L *scutarius* shield-bearer f. *scutum* shield]

ESR *abbr.* *Physics* electron spin resonance.

-ess[1] /ɪs/ *suffix* forming nouns denoting females (*actress*; *lioness*; *mayoress*). [from or after F *-esse* f. LL *-issa* f. Gk *-issa*]

-ess[2] /es/ *suffix* forming abstract nouns from adjectives (*duress*). [ME f. F *-esse* f. L *-itia*; cf. -ICE]

essay *n.* & *v.* —*n.* /'eseɪ/ **1** a composition, usu. short and in prose, on any subject. **2** (often foll. by *at, in*) *formal* an attempt. —*v.tr.* /e'seɪ/ *formal* attempt, try. □□ **essayist** *n.* [ME f. ASSAY, assim. to F *essayer* ult. f. LL *exagium* weighing f. *exigere* weigh: see EXACT]

essence /'es(ə)ns/ *n.* **1** the indispensable quality or element identifying a thing or determining its character; fundamental nature or inherent characteristics. **2 a** an extract obtained by distillation etc., esp. a volatile oil. **b** a perfume or scent, esp. made from a plant or animal substance. **3** the constituent of a plant that determines its chemical properties. **4** an abstract entity; the reality underlying a phenomenon or all phenomena. □ **in essence** fundamentally. **of the essence** indispensable, vital. [ME f. OF f. L *essentia* f. *esse* be]

Essene /'esiːn, e'siːn/ *n.* a member of an ancient Jewish ascetic sect living communally. [L pl. *Esseni* f. Gk pl. *Essēnoi*]

essential /ɪ'senʃ(ə)l/ *adj.* & *n.* —*adj.* **1** absolutely necessary; indispensable. **2** fundamental, basic. **3** of or constituting the essence of a person or thing. **4** (of a disease) with no known external stimulus or cause; idiopathic. —*n.* (esp. in *pl.*) a basic or indispensable element or thing. □ **essential element** any of various elements required by living organisms for normal growth. **essential oil** a volatile oil derived from a plant etc. with its characteristic odour. □□ **essentiality** /-ʃɪ'ælɪtɪ/ *n.* **essentially** *adv.* **essentialness** *n.* [ME f. LL *essentialis* (as ESSENCE)]

EST *abbr.* **1** *US* Eastern Standard Time. **2** electroshock treatment.

-est[1] /ɪst/ *suffix* forming the superlative of adjectives (*widest*; *nicest*; *happiest*) and adverbs (*soonest*). [OE *-ost-, -ust-, -ast-*]

-est[2] /ɪst/ *suffix* (also **-st**) *archaic* forming the 2nd person sing. of verbs (*canst*; *findest*; *gavest*). [OE *-est, -ast, -st*]

establish /ɪ'stæblɪʃ/ *v.tr.* **1** set up or consolidate (a business, system, etc.) on a permanent basis. **2** (foll. by *in*) settle (a person or oneself) in some capacity. **3** (esp. as **established** *adj.*) achieve permanent acceptance for (a custom, belief, practice, institution, etc.). **4** validate; place beyond dispute (a fact etc.). □ **Established Church** the Church recognized by the State as the national Church. □□ **establisher** *n.* [ME f. OF *establir* (stem *establiss-*) f. L *stabilire* f. *stabilis* STABLE[1]]

establishment /ɪ'stæblɪʃmənt/ *n.* **1** the act or an instance of establishing; the process of being established. **2 a** a business organization or public institution. **b** a place of business. **c** a residence. **3 a** the staff or equipment of an organization. **b** a household. **4** any organized body permanently maintained for a purpose. **5** a Church system organized by law. **6** (**the Establishment**) **a** the group in a society exercising authority or influence, and seen as resisting change. **b** any influential or controlling group (*the literary Establishment*).

establishmentarian /ɪˌstæblɪʃmən'teərɪən/ *adj.* & *n.* —*adj.* adhering to or advocating the principle of

an established Church. —*n.* a person adhering to or advocating this. □□ **establishmentarianism** *n.*

estaminet /e'stæmɪˌneɪ/ *n.* a small French café etc. selling alcoholic drinks. [F f. Walloon *staminé* byre f. *stamo* a pole for tethering a cow, prob. f. G *Stamm* stem]

estate /ɪ'steɪt/ *n.* **1** a property consisting of an extensive area of land usu. with a large house. **2** *Brit.* a modern residential or industrial area with integrated design or purpose. **3** all of a person's assets and liabilities, esp. at death. **4** a property where rubber, tea, grapes, etc., are cultivated. **5** (in **full estate of the realm**) an order or class forming (or regarded as) a part of the body politic. **6** *archaic* or *literary* a state or position in life (*the estate of holy matrimony*; *poor man's estate*). **7** *colloq.* = estate car. □ **estate agent** *Brit.* **1** a person whose business is the sale or lease of buildings and land on behalf of others. **2** the steward of an estate. **estate car** *Brit.* a car with the passenger area extended and combined with space for luggage, usu. with an extra door at the rear. **estate duty** *Brit. hist.* death duty levied on property. ¶ Replaced in 1975 by *capital transfer tax* and in 1986 by *inheritance tax.* **the Three Estates** Lords Spiritual (the heads of the Church), Lords Temporal (the peerage), and the Commons. [ME f. OF *estat* (as STATUS)]

esteem /ɪ'stiːm/ *v.* & *n.* —*v.tr.* **1** (usu. in *passive*) have a high regard for; greatly respect; think favourably of. **2** *formal* consider, deem (*esteemed it an honour*). —*n.* high regard; respect; favour (*held them in esteem*). [ME f. OF *estimer* f. L *aestimare* fix the price of]

ester /'estə(r)/ *n.* *Chem.* any of a class of organic compounds produced by replacing the hydrogen of an acid by an alkyl, aryl, etc. radical, many of which occur naturally as oils and fats. □□ **esterify** /e'sterɪˌfaɪ/ *v.tr.* (**-ies, -ied**). [G, prob. f. *Essig* vinegar + *Äther* ether]

Esth. *abbr.* Esther (Old Testament & Apocrypha).

esthete *US* var. of AESTHETE.

esthetic *US* var. of AESTHETIC.

estimable /'estɪməb(ə)l/ *adj.* worthy of esteem. □□ **estimably** *adv.* [F f. L *aestimabilis* (as ESTEEM)]

estimate *n.* & *v.* —*n.* /'estɪmət/ **1** an approximate judgement, esp. of cost, value, size, etc. **2** a price specified as that likely to be charged for work to be undertaken. —*v.tr.* (also *absol.*) /'estɪˌmeɪt/ **1** form an estimate or opinion of. **2** (foll. by *that* + clause) make a rough calculation. **3** (often foll. by *at*) form an estimate; adjudge. **4** fix (a price etc.) by estimate. □□ **estimative** /-mətɪv/ *adj.* **estimator** /-ˌmeɪtə(r)/ *n.* [L *aestimare aestimat-* fix the price of]

estimation /ˌestɪ'meɪʃ(ə)n/ *n.* **1** the process or result of estimating. **2** judgement or opinion of worth (*in my estimation*). **3** *archaic* esteem (*hold in estimation*). [ME f. OF *estimation* or L *aestimatio* (as ESTIMATE)]

estival *US* var. of AESTIVAL.

estivate *US* var. of AESTIVATE.

Estonian /ɪ'stəʊnɪən/ *n.* & *adj* —*n.* **1 a** a native of Estonia, a Baltic republic of the USSR. **b** a person of Estonian descent. **2** the Finno-Ugric language of Estonia. —*adj.* of or relating to Estonia or its people or language.

estop /ɪ'stɒp/ *v.tr.* (**estopped, estopping**) (foll. by *from*) *Law* bar or preclude, esp. by estoppel. □□ **estoppage** *n.* [ME f. AF, OF *estoper* f. LL *stuppare* stop up f. L *stuppa* tow: cf. STOP, STUFF]

estoppel /ɪ'stɒp(ə)l/ *n. Law* the principle which precludes a person from asserting something contrary to what is implied by a previous action or statement of that person or by a previous pertinent judicial determination. [OF *estouppail* bung f. *estoper* (as ESTOP)]

estovers /ɪ'stəʊvəz/ *n.pl. hist.* necessaries allowed by law to a tenant (esp. fuel, or wood for repairs). [AF *estover*, OF *estoveir* be necessary, f. L *est opus*]

estrange /ɪ'streɪndʒ/ *v.tr.* (usu. in *passive*; often foll.

by *from*) cause (a person or group) to turn away in feeling or affection; alienate. □□ **estrangement** *n.* [ME f. AF *estraunger*, OF *estranger* f. L *extraneare* treat as a stranger f. *extraneus* stranger]

estreat /ɪ'striːt/ *n.* & *v. Law* —*n.* **1** a copy of a court record of a fine etc. for use in prosecution. **2** the enforcement of a fine or forfeiture of a recognizance. —*v.tr.* enforce the forfeit of (a fine etc., esp. surety for bail). [ME f. AF *estrete*, OF *estraite* f. *estraire* f. L *extrahere* EXTRACT]

estrogen *US* var. of OESTROGEN.

estrus etc. *US* var. of OESTRUS etc.

estuary /'estjʊərɪ/ *n.* (*pl.* -ies) a wide tidal mouth of a river. □□ **estuarine** /-ˌraɪn/ *adj.* [L *aestuarium* tidal channel f. *aestus* tide]

e.s.u. *abbr.* electrostatic unit(s).

esurient /ɪ'sjʊərɪənt/ *adj. archaic* or *joc.* **1** hungry. **2** impecunious and greedy. □□ **esuriently** *adv.* [L *esurire* (v.) hunger f. *edere* es- eat]

ET *abbr.* extraterrestrial.

-et[1] /ɪt/ *suffix* forming nouns (orig. diminutives) (*baronet*; *bullet*; *sonnet*). [OF -*et* -*ete*]

-et[2] /ɪt/ *suffix* (also -**ete** /iːt/) forming nouns usu. denoting persons (*comet*; *poet*; *athlete*). [Gk -*ētēs*]

ETA[1] *abbr.* estimated time of arrival.

ETA[2] /'etə/ *n.* a Basque separatist movement. [Basque abbr., f. *Euzkadi ta Azkatasuna* Basque homeland and liberty]

eta /'iːtə/ *n.* the seventh letter of the Greek alphabet (*H*, η). [Gk]

et al. /et 'æl/ *abbr.* and others. [L *et alii, et alia,* etc.]

etalon /'etəˌlɒn/ *n. Physics* a device consisting of two reflecting plates, for producing interfering light-beams. [F *étalon* standard]

etc. *abbr.* = ET CETERA.

et cetera /et 'setərə, 'setrə/ *adv.* & *n.* (also **etcetera**) —*adv.* **1** and the rest; and similar things or people. **b** or similar things or people. **2** and so on. —*n.* (in *pl.*) the usual sundries or extras. [ME f. L]

etch /etʃ/ *v.* & *n.* —*v.* **1** a *tr.* reproduce (a picture etc.) by engraving a design on a metal plate with acid (esp. to print copies). **b** *tr.* engrave (a plate) in this way. **2** *intr.* practise this craft. **3** *tr.* (foll. by *on, upon*) impress deeply (esp. on the mind). —*n.* the action or process of etching. □□ **etcher** *n.* [Du. *etsen* f. G *ätzen* etch f. OHG *azzen* cause to eat or to be eaten f. Gmc]

etchant /'etʃ(ə)nt/ *n.* a corrosive used in etching.

etching /'etʃɪŋ/ *n.* **1** a print made from an etched plate. **2** the art of producing these plates.

-ete *suffix* var. of -ET[2].

eternal /ɪ'tɜːn(ə)l/ *adj.* **1** existing always; without an end or (usu.) beginning in time. **2** essentially unchanging (*eternal truths*). **3** *colloq.* constant; seeming not to cease (*your eternal nagging*). □ **the Eternal** God. **Eternal City** Rome. **eternal triangle** a complex of emotional relationships involving two people of one sex and one of the other sex. □□ **eternality** /-'nælɪtɪ/ *n.* **eternalize** *v.tr.* (also -**ise**). **eternally** *adv.* **eternalness** *n.* **eternize** *v.tr.* (also -**ise**). [ME f. OF f. LL *aeternalis* f. *aeternus* f. *aevum* age]

eternity /ɪ'tɜːnɪtɪ/ *n.* (*pl.* -ies) **1** infinite or unending (esp. future) time. **2** *Theol.* endless life after death. **3** the state of being eternal. **4** *colloq.* (often prec. by *an*) a very long time. **5** (in *pl.*) eternal truths. □ **eternity ring** a finger-ring set with gems all round, usu. given as a token of lasting affection. [ME f. OF *eternité* f. L *aeternitas -tatis* f. *aeternus:* see ETERNAL]

Etesian /ɪ'tiːʒ(ə)n/ *adj.* □ **Etesian winds** NW winds blowing each summer in the E. Mediterranean. [L *etesius* f. Gk *etēsios* annual f. *etos* year]

eth /eθ/ *n.* (also **edh** /eð/) the name of an Old English and Icelandic letter, = th. [Icel.]

-eth[1] var. of -TH[1].

-eth[2] /ɪθ/ *suffix* (also -**th**) *archaic* forming the 3rd person sing. present of verbs (*doeth*; *saith*). [OE -*eth*, -*ath*, -*th*]

ethanal /'eθəˌnæl/ *n.* = ACETALDEHYDE. [ETHANE + ALDEHYDE]

ethane /'eθeɪn, 'iːθ-/ *n. Chem.* a gaseous hydrocarbon of the alkane series, occurring in natural gas. ¶ Chem. formula: C_2H_6. [ETHER + -ANE[2]]

ethanediol /'eθeɪnˌdaɪɒl, 'iːθ-/ *n. Chem.* = *ethylene glycol.* [ETHANE + DIOL]

ethanol /'eθəˌnɒl/ *n. Chem.* = ALCOHOL 1. [ETHANE + ALCOHOL]

ethene /'eθiːn, 'iːθ-/ *n. Chem.* = ETHYLENE. [ETHER + -ENE]

ether /'iːθə(r)/ *n.* **1** *Chem.* **a** a colourless volatile organic liquid used as an anaesthetic or solvent. Also called DIETHYL ETHER, ETHOXYETHANE. ¶ Chem. formula: $C_2H_5OC_2H_5$. **b** any of a class of organic compounds with a similar structure to this, having an oxygen joined to two alkyl etc. groups. **2** a clear sky; the upper regions of air beyond the clouds. **3** *hist.* **a** a medium formerly assumed to permeate space and fill the interstices between particles of matter. **b** a medium through which electromagnetic waves were formerly thought to be transmitted. □□ **etheric** /iː'θerɪk/ *adj.* [ME f. OF *ether* or L *aether* f. Gk *aithēr* f. root of *aithō* burn, shine]

ethereal /ɪ'θɪərɪəl/ *adj.* (also **etherial**) **1** light, airy. **2** highly delicate, esp. in appearance. **3** heavenly, celestial. **4** *Chem.* of or relating to ether. □□ **ethereality** /-'ælɪtɪ/ *n.* **ethereally** *adv.* [L *aethereus, -ius* f. Gk *aitherios* (as ETHER)]

etherial var. of ETHEREAL.

etherize /'iːθəˌraɪz/ *v.tr.* (also -**ise**) *hist.* treat or anaesthetize with ether. □□ **etherization** /-'zeɪʃ(ə)n/ *n.*

ethic /'eθɪk/ *n.* & *adj.* —*n.* a set of moral principles (*the Quaker ethic*). —*adj.* = ETHICAL. [ME f. OF *éthique* or L *ethicus* f. Gk *ēthikos* (as ETHOS)]

ethical /'eθɪk(ə)l/ *adj.* **1** relating to morals, esp. as concerning human conduct. **2** morally correct; honourable. **3** (of a medicine or drug) not advertised to the general public, and usu. available only on a doctor's prescription. □□ **ethicality** /-'kælɪtɪ/ *n.* **ethically** *adv.*

ethics /'eθɪks/ *n.pl.* (also treated as *sing.*) **1** the science of morals in human conduct. **2 a** moral principles; rules of conduct. **b** a set of these (*medical ethics*). □□ **ethicist** /-sɪst/ *n.*

Ethiopian /ˌiːθɪ'əʊpɪən/ *n.* & *adj.* —*n.* **1 a** a native or national of Ethiopia in NE Africa. **b** a person of Ethiopian descent. **2** *archaic* a Black person. —*adj.* of or relating to Ethiopia. [*Ethiopia* f. L *Aethiops* f. Gk *Aithiops* f. *aithō* burn + *ōps* face]

Ethiopic /ˌiːθɪ'ɒpɪk, -'əʊpɪk/ *n.* & *adj.* —*n.* the Christian liturgical language of Ethiopia. —*adj.* of or in this language. [L *aethiopicus* f. Gk *aithiopikos:* see ETHIOPIAN]

ethmoid /'eθmɔɪd/ *adj.* sievelike. □ **ethmoid bone** a square bone at the root of the nose, with many perforations through which the olfactory nerves pass to the nose. □□ **ethmoidal** /-'mɔɪd(ə)l/ *adj.* [Gk *ēthmoeidēs* f. *ēthmos* sieve]

ethnic /'eθnɪk/ *adj.* & *n.* —*adj.* **1 a** (of a social group) having a common national or cultural tradition. **b** (of clothes etc.) resembling those of a non-European exotic people. **2** denoting origin by birth or descent rather than nationality (*ethnic Turks*). **3** relating to race or culture (*ethnic group*; *ethnic origins*). **4** *archaic* pagan, heathen. —*n.* **1** *US* a member of an (esp. minority) ethnic group. **2** (in *pl.*, usu. treated as *sing.*) = ETHNOLOGY. □ **ethnic minority** a (usu. identifiable) group differentiated from the main population of a community by racial origin or cultural background. □□ **ethnically** *adv.* **ethnicity** /-'nɪsɪtɪ/ *n.* [ME f. eccl.L *ethnicus* f. Gk *ethnikos* heathen f. *ethnos* nation]

ethnical /'eθnɪk(ə)l/ *adj.* relating to ethnology.

ethno- /'eθnəʊ/ *comb. form* ethnic, ethnological. [Gk *ethnos* nation]

ethnoarchaeology /ˌeθnəʊˌɑːkɪ'ɒlədʒɪ/ *n.* the study

ethnocentric of a society's institutions based on examination of its material attributes. □□ **ethnoarchaeological** /-kɪəˈlɒdʒɪk(ə)l/ *adj.* **ethnoarchaeologist** *n.*

ethnocentric /ˌeθnəʊˈsentrɪk/ *adj.* evaluating other races and cultures by criteria specific to one's own. □□ **ethnocentrically** *adv.* **ethnocentricity** /-ˈtrɪsɪtɪ/ *n.* **ethnocentrism** *n.*

ethnography /eθˈnɒɡrəfɪ/ *n.* the scientific description of races and cultures of mankind. □□ **ethnographer** *n.* **ethnographic** /-nəˈɡræfɪk/ *adj.* **ethnographical** /-nəˈɡræfɪk(ə)l/ *adj.*

ethnology /eθˈnɒlədʒɪ/ *n.* the comparative scientific study of human peoples. □□ **ethnologic** /-nəˈlɒdʒɪk/ *adj.* **ethnological** /-nəˈlɒdʒɪk(ə)l/ *adj.* **ethnologist** *n.*

ethnomusicology /ˌeθnəʊˌmjuːzɪˈkɒlədʒɪ/ *n.* the study of the music of one or more (esp. non-European) cultures. □□ **ethnomusicologist** *n.*

ethogram /ˈiːθəˌɡræm/ *n.* Zool. a list of the kinds of behaviour or activity observed in an animal. [Gk *ētho-* (see ETHOS) + -GRAM]

ethology /iːˈθɒlədʒɪ/ *n.* **1** the science of animal behaviour. **2** the science of character-formation in human behaviour. □□ **ethological** /ˌiːθəˈlɒdʒɪk(ə)l/ *adj.* **ethologist** *n.* [L *ethologia* f. Gk *ēthologia* (as ETHOS)]

ethos /ˈiːθɒs/ *n.* the characteristic spirit or attitudes of a community, people, or system, or of a literary work etc. [mod.L f. Gk *ēthos* nature, disposition]

ethoxyethane /iːˌθɒksɪˈiːθeɪn/ *n.* Chem. = ETHER 1a. [ETHER + OXY-² + ETHANE]

ethyl /ˈiːθaɪl, ˈeθɪl/ *n.* (attrib.) Chem. the univalent radical derived from ethane by removal of a hydrogen atom (*ethyl alcohol*). [G (as ETHER, -YL)]

ethylene /ˈeθɪˌliːn/ *n.* Chem. a gaseous hydrocarbon of the alkene series, occurring in natural gas and used in the manufacture of polythene. Also called ETHENE. ¶ Chem. formula: C_2H_4. □ **ethylene glycol** Chem. a colourless viscous hygroscopic liquid used as an antifreeze and in the manufacture of polyesters. ¶ Chem. formula: $C_2H_6O_2$.: also called ETHANEDIOL. □□ **ethylenic** /-ˈliːnɪk/ *adj.*

-etic /ˈetɪk/ *suffix* forming adjectives and nouns (*ascetic*; *emetic*; *genetic*; *synthetic*). [Gk *-ētikos* or *-ētikos*: cf. -IC]

etiolate /ˈiːtɪəʊˌleɪt/ *v.tr.* **1** make (a plant) pale by excluding light. **2** give a sickly hue to (a person). □□ **etiolation** /-ˈleɪʃ(ə)n/ *n.* [F *étioler* f. Norman F *étieuler* make into haulm f. *éteule* ult. f. L *stipula* straw]

etiology US var. of AETIOLOGY.

etiquette /ˈetɪˌket, -ˈket/ *n.* **1** the conventional rules of social behaviour. **2 a** the customary behaviour of members of a profession towards each other. **b** the unwritten code governing this (*medical etiquette*). [F *étiquette* label, etiquette]

Eton collar /ˈiːt(ə)n/ *n.* a broad stiff collar worn outside the coat-collar, esp. of an Eton jacket.

Etonian /iːˈtəʊnɪən/ *n.* a past or present member of Eton College in S. England.

Eton jacket /ˈiːt(ə)n/ *n.* a short jacket reaching only to the waist, as formerly worn by pupils of Eton College.

étrier /ˈeɪtrɪˌeɪ/ *n.* Mountaineering a short rope ladder with a few rungs of wood or metal. [F, = stirrup]

Etruscan /ɪˈtrʌskən/ *adj. & n.* —*adj.* of ancient Etruria in Italy, esp. its pre-Roman civilization and physical remains. —*n.* **1** a native of Etruria. **2** the language of Etruria. □□ **Etruscology** /-ˈkɒlədʒɪ/ *n.* [L *Etruscus*]

et seq. *abbr.* (also **et seqq.**) and the following (pages etc.). [L *et sequentia*]

-ette /et/ *suffix* forming nouns meaning: **1** small (*kitchenette*; *cigarette*). **2** imitation or substitute (*leatherette*; *flannelette*). **3** female (*usherette*; *suffragette*). [from or after OF *-ette*, fem. of -ET¹]

étude /ˈeɪtjuːd, -ˈtjuːd/ *n.* a short musical composition or exercise, usu. for one instrument, designed to improve the technique of the player. [F, = study]

étui /eˈtwiː/ *n.* a small case for needles etc. [F *étui* f. OF *estui* prison]

-etum /ˈiːtəm/ *suffix* forming nouns denoting a collection of trees or other plants (*arboretum*; *pinetum*). [L]

etymologize /ˌetɪˈmɒləˌdʒaɪz/ *v.* (also **-ise**) **1** *tr.* give or trace the etymology of. **2** *intr.* study etymology. [med.L *etymologizare* f. L *etymologia* (as ETYMOLOGY)]

etymology /ˌetɪˈmɒlədʒɪ/ *n.* (pl. **-ies**) **1 a** the historically verifiable sources of the formation of a word and the development of its meaning. **b** an account of these. **2** the branch of linguistic science concerned with etymologies. □□ **etymological** /-məˈlɒdʒɪk(ə)l/ *adj.* **etymologically** /-məˈlɒdʒɪkəlɪ/ *adv.* **etymologist** *n.* [OF *ethimologie* f. L *etymologia* f. Gk *etumologia* (as ETYMON, -LOGY)]

etymon /ˈetɪmən/ *n.* (pl. **etyma** /-mə/) the word that gives rise to a derivative or a borrowed or later form. [L f. Gk *etumon* (neut. of *etumos* true), the literal sense or original form of a word]

Eu *symb.* Chem. the element europium.

eu- /juː/ *comb. form* well, easily. [Gk]

eucalyptus /ˌjuːkəˈlɪptəs/ *n.* (also **eucalypt**) (pl. **eucalyptuses** or **eucalypti** /-taɪ/ or **eucalypts**) **1** any tree of the genus *Eucalyptus*, native to Australasia, cultivated for its timber and for the oil from its leaves. **2** (in full **eucalyptus oil**) this oil used as an antiseptic etc. [mod.L f. EU- + Gk *kaluptos* covered f. *kaluptō* to cover, the unopened flower being protected by a cap]

eucaryote var. of EUKARYOTE.

eucharis /ˈjuːkərɪs/ *n.* any bulbous plant of the genus *Eucharis*, native to S. America, with white umbellate flowers. [Gk *eukharis* pleasing (as EU-, *kharis* grace)]

Eucharist /ˈjuːkərɪst/ *n.* **1** the Christian sacrament commemorating the Last Supper, in which bread and wine are consecrated and consumed. **2** the consecrated elements, esp. the bread (*receive the Eucharist*). □□ **Eucharistic** /-ˈrɪstɪk/ *adj.* **Eucharistical** /-ˈrɪstɪk(ə)l/ *adj.* [ME f. OF *eucariste*, ult. f. eccl.Gk *eukharistia* thanksgiving f. Gk *eukharistos* grateful (as EU-, *kharizomai* offer willingly)]

euchre /ˈjuːkə(r)/ *n. & v.* —*n.* an American card-game for two, three, or four players. —*v.tr.* **1** (in euchre) gain the advantage over (another player) when that player fails to take three tricks. **2** deceive, outwit. **3** Austral. exhaust, ruin. [19th c.: orig. unkn.]

Euclidean /juːˈklɪdɪən/ *adj.* of or relating to Euclid, 3rd-c. BC Alexandrian geometrician, esp. the system of geometry based on his principles. □ **Euclidean space** space for which Euclidean geometry is valid. [L *Euclideus* f. Gk *Eukleideios*]

eudemonic /ˌjuːdɪˈmɒnɪk/ *adj.* (also **eudaemonic**) conducive to happiness. [Gk *eudaimonikos* (as EUDEMONISM)]

eudemonism /juːˈdiːməˌnɪz(ə)m/ *n.* (also **eudaemonism**) a system of ethics that bases moral obligation on the likelihood of actions producing happiness. □□ **eudemonist** *n.* **eudemonistic** /-ˈnɪstɪk/ *adj.* [Gk *eudaimonismos* system of happiness f. *eudaimōn* happy (as EU-, *daimōn* guardian spirit)]

eudiometer /ˌjuːdɪˈɒmɪtə(r)/ *n.* Chem. a graduated glass tube in which gases may be chemically combined by an electric spark, used to measure changes in volume of gases during chemical reactions. □□ **eudiometric** /-dɪəˈmetrɪk/ *adj.* **eudiometrical** /-dɪəˈmetrɪk(ə)l/ *adj.* **eudiometry** *n.* [Gk *eudios* clear (weather): orig. used to measure the amount of oxygen, thought to be greater in clear air]

eugenics /juːˈdʒenɪks/ *n.pl.* (also treated as *sing.*) the science of improving the (esp. human) population by controlled breeding for desirable inherited characteristics. □□ **eugenic** *adj.* **eugenically** *adv.* **eugenicist** /juːˈdʒenɪsɪst/ *n.* **eugenist** /ˈjuːdʒɪnɪst/ *n.*

æ cat ɑ: arm e bed ɜ: her ɪ sit iː see ɒ hot ɔ: saw ʌ run ʊ put uː too ə ago aɪ my

eukaryote /ˈjuːkærɪˌɒt/ n. (also **eucaryote**) Biol. an organism consisting of a cell or cells in which the genetic material is contained within a distinct nucleus (cf. PROKARYOTE). □□ **eukaryotic** /-ˈɒtɪk/ adj. [EU- + KARYO- + -ote as in ZYGOTE]

eulogium /juːˈləʊdʒɪəm/ n. (pl. **eulogia** /-dʒɪə/ or **-ums**) = EULOGY. [med.L: see EULOGY]

eulogize /ˈjuːləˌdʒaɪz/ v.tr. (also **-ise**) praise in speech or writing. □□ **eulogist** n. **eulogistic** /-ˈdʒɪstɪk/ adj. **eulogistically** /-ˈdʒɪstɪkəlɪ/ adv.

eulogy /ˈjuːlədʒɪ/ n. (pl. **-ies**) **1 a** speech or writing in praise of a person. **b** an expression of praise. **2** US a funeral oration in praise of a person. [med.L eulogium f. (app. by confusion with L elogium epitaph) LL eulogia praise f. Gk]

eunuch /ˈjuːnək/ n. **1** a castrated man, esp. one formerly employed at an oriental harem or court. **2** a person lacking effectiveness (political eunuch). [ME f. L eunuchus f. Gk eunoukhos lit. bedchamber attendant f. eunē bed + second element rel. to ekhō hold]

euonymus /juːˈɒnɪməs/ n. any tree of the genus Euonymus, e.g. the spindle tree. [L f. Gk euōnumos of lucky name (as EU-, onoma name)]

eupeptic /juːˈpɛptɪk/ adj. of or having good digestion. [Gk eupeptos (as EU-, peptō digest)]

euphemism /ˈjuːfɪˌmɪz(ə)m/ n. **1** a mild or vague expression substituted for one thought to be too harsh or direct (e.g. pass over for die). **2** the use of such expressions. □□ **euphemist** n. **euphemistic** /-ˈmɪstɪk/ adj. **euphemistically** /-ˈmɪstɪkəlɪ/ adv. **euphemize** v.tr. & intr. (also **-ise**). [Gk euphēmismos f. euphēmos (as EU-, phēmē speaking)]

euphonious /juːˈfəʊnɪəs/ adj. **1** sounding pleasant, harmonious. **2** concerning euphony. □□ **euphoniously** adv.

euphonium /juːˈfəʊnɪəm/ n. a brass wind instrument of the tuba family. [mod.L f. Gk euphōnos (as EUPHONY)]

euphony /ˈjuːfənɪ/ n. (pl. **-ies**) **1 a** pleasantness of sound, esp. of a word or phrase; harmony. **b** a pleasant sound. **2** the tendency to make a phonetic change for ease of pronunciation. □□ **euphonic** /-ˈfɒnɪk/ adj. **euphonize** v.tr. (also **-ise**). [F euphonie f. LL euphonia f. Gk euphōnia (as EU-), phōnē sound)]

euphorbia /juːˈfɔːbɪə/ n. any plant of the genus Euphorbia, including spurges. [ME f. L euphorbea f. Euphorbus, 1st-c. Gk physician]

euphoria /juːˈfɔːrɪə/ n. a feeling of well-being, esp. one based on over-confidence or over-optimism. □□ **euphoric** /-ˈfɒrɪk/ adj. **euphorically** /-ˈfɒrɪkəlɪ/ adv. [Gk f. euphoros well-bearing (as EU-, pherō bear)]

euphoriant /juːˈfɔːrɪənt/ adj. & n. —adj. inducing euphoria. —n. a euphoriant drug.

euphuism /ˈjuːfjuːˌɪz(ə)m/ n. an affected or high-flown style of writing or speaking. □□ **euphuist** n. **euphuistic** /-ˈɪstɪk/ adj. **euphuistically** /-ˈɪstɪkəlɪ/ adv. [Gk euphuēs well endowed by nature: orig. of writing imitating Lyly's Euphues (1578–80)]

Eurasian /jʊəˈreɪʒ(ə)n/ adj. & n. —adj. **1** of mixed European and Asian (esp. Indian) parentage. **2** of Europe and Asia. —n. a Eurasian person.

Euratom /jʊəˈrætəm/ n. European Atomic Energy Community. [abbr.]

eureka /jʊəˈriːkə/ int. & n. —int. I have found it! (announcing a discovery etc.). —n. the exultant cry of 'eureka'. [Gk heurēka 1st pers. sing. perfect of heuriskō find: attributed to Archimedes]

eurhythmic /jʊəˈrɪðmɪk/ adj. of or in harmonious proportion (esp. of architecture). [eurhythmy harmony of proportions f. L eur(h)ythmia f. Gk eurhuthmia (as EU-, rhuthmos proportion, rhythm)]

eurhythmics /jʊəˈrɪðmɪks/ n.pl. (also treated as sing.) (US **eurythmics**) harmony of bodily movement, esp. as developed with music and dance into a system of education.

Euro- /ˈjʊərəʊ/ comb. form Europe, European. [abbr.]

euro /ˈjʊərəʊ/ n. (pl. **-os**) Austral. a large reddish kangaroo. [Aboriginal]

Eurocommunism /ˌjʊərəʊˈkɒmjʊˌnɪz(ə)m/ n. a form of Communism in Western European countries that is independent of the Soviet Communist Party. □□ **Eurocommunist** adj. & n.

Eurocrat /ˈjʊərəʊˌkræt/ n. usu. derog. a bureaucrat in the administration of the European Economic Community.

Eurodollar /ˈjʊərəʊˌdɒlə(r)/ n. a dollar held in a bank in Europe.

European /ˌjʊərəˈpɪən/ adj. & n. —adj. **1** of or in Europe. **2 a** descended from natives of Europe. **b** originating in or characteristic of Europe. **3 a** happening in or extending over Europe. **b** concerning Europe as a whole rather than its individual countries. **4** of or relating to the European Economic Community. —n. **1 a** a native or inhabitant of Europe. **b** a person descended from natives of Europe. **c** a White person. **2** a person concerned with European matters. □**European Economic Community** (or **European Community**) an economic and political association of certain European countries as a unit with internal free trade and common external tariffs. **European plan** US a system of charging for a hotel room only without meals. □□ **Europeanism** n. **Europeanize** v.tr. & intr. (also **-ise**). **Europeanization** /-ˈzeɪʃ(ə)n/ n. [F européen f. L europaeus f. L Europa f. Gk Europē Europe]

europium /jʊˈrəʊpɪəm/ n. Chem. a soft silvery metallic element of the lanthanide series, occurring naturally in small quantities. ¶ Symb.: **Eu**. [mod.L f. Europe]

Eurovision /ˈjʊərəʊˌvɪʒ(ə)n/ n. a network of European television production administered by the European Broadcasting Union.

eurythmics US var. of EURHYTHMICS.

Eustachian tube /juːˈsteɪʃ(ə)n/ n. Anat. a tube leading from the pharynx to the cavity of the middle ear and equalizing the pressure on each side of the eardrum. [L Eustachius = B. Eustachio, It. anatomist d. 1574]

eustasy /ˈjuːstəsɪ/ n. a change in sea level throughout the world caused by tectonic movements, melting of glaciers, etc. □□ **eustatic** /-ˈstætɪk/ adj. [back-form. f. G eustatisch (adj.) (as EU-, STATIC)]

eutectic /juːˈtɛktɪk/ adj. & n. Chem. —adj. (of a mixture, alloy, etc.) having the lowest freezing-point of any possible proportions of its constituents. —n. a eutectic mixture. □**eutectic point** (or **temperature**) the minimum freezing-point for a eutectic mixture. [Gk eutēktos (as EU-, tēkō melt)]

euthanasia /ˌjuːθəˈneɪzɪə/ n. **1** the bringing about of a gentle and easy death in the case of incurable and painful disease. **2** such a death. [Gk (as EU-, thanatos death)]

eutrophic /juːˈtrɒfɪk, -ˈtrəʊfɪk/ adj. (of a lake etc.) rich in nutrients and therefore supporting a dense plant population, which kills animal life by depriving it of oxygen. □□ **eutrophicate** v.tr. **eutrophication** /-ˈkeɪʃ(ə)n/ n. **eutrophy** /ˈjuːtrəfɪ/ n. [eutrophy f. Gk eutrophia (as EU-, trephō nourish)]

eV abbr. electronvolt.

EVA abbr. Astronaut. extravehicular activity.

evacuate /ɪˈvækjʊˌeɪt/ v.tr. **1 a** remove (people) from a place of danger to stay elsewhere for the duration of the danger. **b** empty (a place) in this way. **2** make empty (a vessel of air etc.). **3** (of troops) withdraw from (a place). **4 a** empty (the bowels or other bodily organ). **b** discharge (faeces etc.). □□ **evacuant** n. & adj. **evacuation** /-ˈeɪʃ(ə)n/ n. **evacuative** /-kjʊətɪv/ adj. & n. **evacuator** n. [L evacuare (as E-, vacuus empty)]

evacuee /ɪˌvækjuːˈiː/ n. a person evacuated from a place of danger.

evade /ɪˈveɪd/ v.tr. **1 a** escape from, avoid, esp. by guile or trickery. **b** avoid doing (one's duty etc.). **c**

avoid answering (a question) or yielding to (an argument). **2 a** fail to pay (tax due). **b** defeat the intention of (a law etc.), esp. while complying with its letter. **3** (of a thing) elude or baffle (a person). □□ **evadable** *adj.* **evader** *n.* [F *évader* f. L *evadere* (as E-, *vadere* vas- go)]

evaginate /ɪˈvædʒɪˌneɪt/ *v.tr.* *Med.* & *Physiol.* turn (a tubular organ) inside out. □□ **evagination** /-ˈneɪʃ(ə)n/ *n.* [L *evaginare* (as E-, *vaginare* as VAGINA)]

evaluate /ɪˈvæljuˌeɪt/ *v.tr.* **1** assess, appraise. **2 a** find or state the number or amount of. **b** find a numerical expression for. □□ **evaluation** /-ˈeɪʃ(ə)n/ *n.* **evaluative** /-ətɪv/ *adj.* **evaluator** *n.* [back-form. f. *evaluation* f. F *évaluation* f. *évaluer* (as E-, VALUE)]

evanesce /ˌiːvəˈnes, ˌe-/ *v.intr.* **1** fade from sight; disappear. **2** become effaced. [L *evanescere* (as E-, *vanus* empty)]

evanescent /ˌiːvəˈnes(ə)nt, ˌe-/ *adj.* (of an impression or appearance etc.) quickly fading. □□ **evanescence** *n.* **evanescently** *adv.*

evangel /ɪˈvændʒ(ə)l/ *n.* **1** *archaic* **a** the gospel. **b** any of the four Gospels. **2** a basic doctrine or set of principles. **3** *US* = EVANGELIST. [ME f. OF *evangile* f. eccl.L *evangelium* f. Gk *euaggelion* good news (as EU-, ANGEL)]

evangelic /ˌiːvænˈdʒelɪk/ *adj.* = EVANGELICAL.

evangelical /ˌiːvænˈdʒelɪk(ə)l/ *adj.* & *n.* —*adj.* **1** of or according to the teaching of the gospel or the Christian religion. **2** of the Protestant school maintaining that the doctrine of salvation by faith in the Atonement is the essence of the gospel. —*n.* a member of the evangelical school. □□ **evangelicalism** *n.* **evangelically** *adv.* [eccl.L *evangelicus* f. eccl.Gk *euaggelikos* (as EVANGEL)]

evangelism /ɪˈvændʒəˌlɪz(ə)m/ *n.* **1** the preaching or promulgation of the gospel. **2** evangelicalism.

evangelist /ɪˈvændʒəlɪst/ *n.* **1** any of the writers of the four Gospels (Matthew, Mark, Luke, John). **2** a preacher of the gospel. **3** a lay person doing missionary work.

evangelistic /ɪˌvændʒəˈlɪstɪk/ *adj.* **1** = EVANGELICAL. **2** of preachers of the gospel. **3** of the four evangelists.

evangelize /ɪˈvændʒəˌlaɪz/ *v.tr.* (also **-ise**) **1** (also *absol.*) preach the gospel to. **2** convert (a person) to Christianity. □□ **evangelization** /-ˈzeɪʃ(ə)n/ *n.* **evangelizer** *n.* [ME f. eccl.L *evangelizare* f. Gk *euaggelizomai* (as EVANGEL)]

evaporate /ɪˈvæpəˌreɪt/ *v.* **1** *intr.* turn from solid or liquid into vapour. **2** *intr.* & *tr.* lose or cause to lose moisture as vapour. **3** *intr.* & *tr.* disappear or cause to disappear (*our courage evaporated*). □ **evaporated milk** milk concentrated by partial evaporation. □□ **evaporable** *adj.* **evaporation** /-ˈreɪʃ(ə)n/ *n.* **evaporative** /-rətɪv/ *adj.* **evaporator** *n.* [L *evaporare* (as E-, *vaporare* as VAPOUR)]

evasion /ɪˈveɪʒ(ə)n/ *n.* **1** the act or a means of evading. **2 a** a subterfuge or prevaricating excuse. **b** an evasive answer. [ME f. OF f. L *evasio -onis* (as EVADE)]

evasive /ɪˈveɪsɪv/ *adj.* **1** seeking to evade something. **2** not direct in one's answers etc. **3** enabling or effecting evasion (*evasive action*). **4** (of a person) tending to evasion; habitually practising evasion. □□ **evasively** *adv.* **evasiveness** *n.*

eve /iːv/ *n.* **1** the evening or day before a church festival or any date or event (*Christmas Eve*; *the eve of the funeral*). **2** the time just before anything (*the eve of the election*). **3** *archaic* evening. [ME, = EVEN²]

evection /ɪˈvekʃ(ə)n/ *n.* *Astron.* a perturbation of the moon's motion caused by the sun's attraction. [L *evectio* (as E-, *vehere vect-* carry)]

even¹ /ˈiːv(ə)n/ *adj.*, *adv.*, & *v.* —*adj.* (**evener**, **evenest**) **1** level; flat and smooth. **2 a** uniform in quality; constant. **b** equal in number or amount or value etc. **c** equally balanced. **3** (usu. foll. by *with*) in the same plane or line. **4** (of a person's temper etc.) equable, calm. **5 a** (of a number such as 4, 6) divisible by two without a remainder. **b** bearing such a

number (*no parking on even dates*). **c** not involving fractions; exact (*in even dozens*). —*adv.* **1** used to invite comparison of the stated assertion, negation, etc., with an implied one that is less strong or remarkable (*never even opened* [let alone read] *the letter*; *does he even suspect* [not to say realize] *the danger?*; *ran even faster* [not just as fast as before]; *even if my watch is right we shall be late* [later if it is slow]). **2** used to introduce an extreme case (*even you must realize it*; *it might even cost £100*). —*v.* **1** *tr.* & *intr.* (often foll. by *up*) make or become even. **2** *tr.* (often foll. by *to*) *archaic* treat as equal or comparable. □ **even as** at the very moment that. **even break** *colloq.* an equal chance. **even chance** an equal chance of success or failure. **even money 1** betting odds offering the gambler the chance of winning the amount he or she staked. **2** equally likely to happen or not (*it's even money he'll fail to arrive*). **even now 1** now as well as before. **2** at this very moment. **even so 1** notwithstanding that; nevertheless. **2** quite so. **3** in that case as well as in others. **get** (or **be**) **even with** have one's revenge on. **of even date** *Law* & *Commerce* of the same date. **on an even keel 1** (of a ship or aircraft) not listing. **2** (of a plan or person) untroubled. □□ **evenly** *adv.* **evenness** *n.* [OE *efen*, *efne*]

even² /ˈiːv(ə)n/ *n.* *poet.* evening. [OE *æfen*]

even-handed /ˌiːv(ə)nˈhændɪd/ *adj.* impartial, fair. □□ **even-handedly** *adv.* **even-handedness** *n.*

evening /ˈiːvnɪŋ/ *n.* & *int.* —*n.* **1** the end part of the day, esp. from about 6 p.m. to bedtime (*this evening*; *during the evening*; *evening meal*). **2** this time spent in a particular way (*had a lively evening*). **3** a time compared with this, esp. the last part of a person's life. —*int.* = *good evening* (see GOOD *adj.* 14). □ **evening dress** formal dress for evening wear. **evening primrose** any plant of the genus *Oenothera* with pale yellow flowers that open in the evening. **evening star** a planet, esp. Venus, conspicuous in the west after sunset. [OE *æfnung*, rel. to EVEN²]

evens /ˈiːv(ə)nz/ *n.pl.* *Brit.* = *even money*.

evensong /ˈiːv(ə)nˌsɒŋ/ *n.* a service of evening prayer in the Church of England. [EVEN² + SONG]

event /ɪˈvent/ *n.* **1** a thing that happens or takes place, esp. one of importance. **2 a** the fact of a thing's occurring. **b** a result or outcome. **3** an item in a sports programme, or the programme as a whole. **4** *Physics* a single occurrence of a process, e.g. the ionization of one atom. **5** something on the result of which money is staked. □ **at all events** (or **in any event**) whatever happens. **event horizon** *Astron.* the gravitational boundary enclosing a black hole, from which no light escapes. **in the event** as it turns (or turned) out. **in the event of** if (a specified thing) happens. **in the event that** *disp.* if it happens that. [L *eventus* f. *evenire event-* happen (as E-, *venire* come)]

eventful /ɪˈventfʊl/ *adj.* marked by noteworthy events. □□ **eventfully** *adv.* **eventfulness** *n.*

eventide /ˈiːv(ə)nˌtaɪd/ *n.* *archaic* or *poet.* = EVENING. □ **eventide home** a home for the elderly, orig. one run by the Salvation Army. [OE *æfentīd* (as EVEN², TIDE)]

eventing /ɪˈventɪŋ/ *n.* *Brit.* participation in equestrian competitions, esp. dressage and showjumping. [EVENT 3 as in *three-day event*]

eventless /ɪˈventlɪs/ *adj.* without noteworthy or remarkable events. □□ **eventlessly** *adv.*

eventual /ɪˈventjʊəl/ *adj.* occurring or existing in due course or at last; ultimate. □□ **eventually** *adv.* [as EVENT, after *actual*]

eventuality /ɪˌventjʊˈælɪtɪ/ *n.* (*pl.* **-ies**) a possible event or outcome.

eventuate /ɪˈventjʊˌeɪt/ *v.intr.* *formal* **1** turn out in a specified way as the result. **2** (often foll. by *in*) result. □□ **eventuation** /-ˈeɪʃ(ə)n/ *n.* [as EVENT, after *actuate*]

ever /ˈevə(r)/ *adv.* **1** at all times; always (*ever hopeful*; *ever after*). **2** at any time (*have you ever been to*

b *but* d *dog* f *few* g *get* h *he* j *yes* k *cat* l *leg* m *man* n *no* p *pen* r *red* s *sit* t *top* v *voice*

Paris?; *nothing ever happens*; *as good as ever*). **3** as an emphatic word: **a** in any way; at all (*how ever did you do it?*; *when will they ever learn?*). **b** (prec. by *as*) in any manner possible (*be as quick as ever you can*). **4** (in *comb.*) constantly (*ever-present*; *ever-recurring*). **5** (foll. by *so, such*) *Brit. colloq.* very; very much (*is ever so easy*; *was ever such a nice man*; *thanks ever so*). **6** (foll. by *compar.*) constantly, increasingly (*grew ever larger*). □**did you ever?** *colloq.* did you ever hear or see the like? **ever since** throughout the period since. **for ever 1** for all future time. **2** *colloq.* for a long time (cf. FOREVER). [OE *ǣfre*]

evergreen /'evəˌgriːn/ *adj. & n.* —*adj.* **1** always green or fresh. **2** (of a plant) retaining green leaves throughout the year. —*n.* an evergreen plant (cf. DECIDUOUS).

everlasting /ˌevəˈlɑːstɪŋ/ *adj. & n.* —*adj.* **1** lasting for ever. **2** lasting for a long time, esp. so as to become unwelcome. **3** (of flowers) keeping their shape and colour when dried. —*n.* **1** eternity. **2** = IMMORTELLE. □□**everlastingly** *adv.* **everlastingness** *n.*

evermore /ˌevəˈmɔː(r)/ *adv.* for ever; always.

evert /ɪˈvɜːt/ *v.tr. Physiol.* turn (an organ etc.) outwards or inside out. □□**eversion** *n.* [L *evertere* (as E-, *vertere vers-* turn)]

every /'evrɪ/ *adj.* **1** each single (*heard every word*; *watched her every movement*). **2** each at a specified interval in a series (*take every third one*; *comes every four days*). **3** all possible; the utmost degree of (*there is every prospect of success*). □**every bit as** *colloq.* (in comparisons) quite as (*every bit as good*). **every now and again** (or **now and then**) from time to time. **every one** each one (see also EVERYONE). **every other** each second in a series (*every other day*). **every so often** at intervals; occasionally. **every time** *colloq.* **1** without exception. **2** without hesitation. **every which way** *US colloq.* **1** in all directions. **2** in a disorderly manner. [OE *ǣfre ǣlc* ever each]

everybody /'evrɪˌbɒdɪ/ *pron.* every person.

everyday /'evrɪˌdeɪ, -ˈdeɪ/ *adj.* **1** occurring every day. **2** suitable for or used on ordinary days. **3** commonplace, usual.

Everyman /'evrɪˌmæn/ *n.* the ordinary or typical human being; the 'man in the street'. [the principal character in a 15th-c. morality play]

everyone /'evrɪˌwʌn/ *pron.* every person; everybody.

everything /'evrɪθɪŋ/ *pron.* **1** all things; all the things of a group or class. **2** *colloq.* a great deal (*gave me everything*). **3** an essential consideration (*speed is everything*). □**have everything** *colloq.* possess all the desired attributes etc.

everywhere /'evrɪˌweə(r)/ *adv.* **1** in every place. **2** *colloq.* in many places.

evict /ɪˈvɪkt/ *v.tr.* expel (a tenant) from a property by legal process. □□**eviction** *n.* **evictor** *n.* [L *evincere evict-* (as E-, *vincere* conquer)]

evidence /'evɪd(ə)ns/ *n. & v.* —*n.* **1** (often foll. by *for, of*) the available facts, circumstances, etc. supporting or otherwise a belief, proposition, etc., or indicating whether or not a thing is true or valid. **2** *Law* **a** information given personally or drawn from a document etc. and tending to prove a fact or proposition. **b** statements or proofs admissible as testimony in a lawcourt. **3** clearness, obviousness. —*v.tr.* be evidence of; attest. □**call in evidence** *Law* summon (a person) as a witness. **in evidence** noticeable, conspicuous. **Queen's** (or **King's** or **State's**) **evidence** *Law* evidence for the prosecution given by a participant in or accomplice to the crime at issue. [ME f. OF f. L *evidentia* (as EVIDENT)]

evident /'evɪd(ə)nt/ *adj.* **1** plain or obvious (visually or intellectually); manifest. **2** seeming, apparent (*his evident anxiety*). [ME f. OF *evident* or L *evidēre evident-* (as E-, *vidēre* see)]

evidential /ˌevɪˈdenʃ(ə)l/ *adj.* of or providing evidence. □□**evidentially** *adv.*

evidentiary /ˌevɪˈdenʃərɪ/ *adj.* = EVIDENTIAL.

evidently /'evɪdəntlɪ/ *adv.* **1** as shown by evidence. **2** seemingly; as it appears (*was evidently unwilling to go*).

evil /'iːv(ə)l, -ɪl/ *adj. & n.* —*adj.* **1** morally bad; wicked. **2** harmful or tending to harm, esp. intentionally or characteristically. **3** disagreeable or unpleasant (*has an evil temper*). **4** unlucky; causing misfortune (*evil days*). —*n.* **1** an evil thing; an instance of something evil. **2** evil quality; wickedness, harm. □**evil eye** a gaze or stare superstitiously believed to be able to cause material harm. **speak evil of** slander. □□ **evilly** *adv.* **evilness** *n.* [OE *yfel* f. Gmc]

evince /ɪˈvɪns/ *v.tr.* **1** indicate or make evident. **2** show that one has (a quality). □□**evincible** *adj.* **evincive** *adj.* [L *evincere*: see EVICT]

eviscerate /ɪˈvɪsəˌreɪt/ *v.tr. formal* **1** disembowel. **2** empty or deprive of essential contents. □□ **evisceration** /-ˈreɪʃ(ə)n/ *n.* [L *eviscerare eviscerat-* (as E-, VISCERA)]

evocative /ɪˈvɒkətɪv/ *adj.* tending to evoke (esp. feelings or memories). □□**evocatively** *adv.* **evocativeness** *n.*

evoke /ɪˈvəʊk/ *v.tr.* **1** inspire or draw forth (memories, feelings, a response, etc.). **2** summon (a supposed spirit from the dead). □□**evocation** /ˌevəˈkeɪʃ(ə)n/ *n.* **evoker** *n.* [L *evocare* (as E-, *vocare* call)]

evolute /'iːvəˌljuːt, 'ev-, -ˌluːt/ *n.* (in full **evolute curve**) *Math.* a curve which is the locus of the centres of curvature of another curve that is its involute. [L *evolutus* past part. (as EVOLVE)]

evolution /ˌiːvəˈluːʃ(ə)n, -ˈljuːʃ(ə)n/ *n.* **1** gradual development, esp. from a simple to a more complex form. **2** a process by which species develop from earlier forms, as an explanation of their origins. **3** the appearance or presentation of events etc. in due succession (*the evolution of the plot*). **4** a change in the disposition of troops or ships. **5** the giving off or evolving of gas, heat, etc. **6** an opening out. **7** the unfolding of a curve. **8** *Math.* the extraction of a root from any given power (cf. INVOLUTION). □□ **evolutional** *adj.* **evolutionally** *adv.* **evolutionary** *adj.* **evolutionarily** *adv.* [L *evolutio* unrolling (as EVOLVE)]

evolutionist /ˌiːvəˈluːʃənɪst, -ˈljuːʃənɪst/ *n.* a person who believes in evolution as explaining the origin of species. □□**evolutionism** *n.* **evolutionistic** /-ˈnɪstɪk/ *adj.*

evolve /ɪˈvɒlv/ *v.* **1** *intr. & tr.* develop gradually by a natural process. **2** *tr.* work out or devise (a theory, plan, etc.). **3** *intr. & tr.* unfold; open out. **4** *tr.* give off (gas, heat, etc.). □□**evolvable** *adj.* **evolvement** *n.* [L *evolvere evolut-* (as E-, *volvere* roll)]

evzone /'evzəʊn/ *n.* a member of a select Greek infantry regiment. [mod. Gk *euzōnos* f. Gk, = dressed for exercise (as EU-, *zōnē* belt)]

ewe /juː/ *n.* a female sheep. □**ewe lamb** one's most cherished possession (2 Sam. 12). [OE *ēowu* f. Gmc]

ewer /'juːə(r)/ *n.* a large pitcher or water-jug with a wide mouth. [ME f. ONF *eviere*, OF *aiguiere*, ult. f. L *aquarius* of water f. *aqua* water]

ex¹ /eks/ *prep.* **1** (of goods) sold from (*ex-works*). **2** (of stocks or shares) without, excluding. [L, = out of]

ex² /eks/ *n. colloq.* a former husband or wife. [absol. use of EX-¹]

ex-¹ /eks/ *prefix* (also **e-** before some consonants, **ef-** before *f*) **1** forming verbs meaning: **a** out, forth (*exclude*; *exit*). **b** upward (*extol*). **c** thoroughly (*excruciate*). **d** bring into a state (*exasperate*). **e** remove or free from (*expatriate*; *exonerate*). **2** forming nouns from titles of office, status, etc., meaning 'formerly' (*ex-convict*; *ex-president*; *ex-wife*). [L f. *ex* out of]

ex-² /eks/ *prefix* out (*exodus*). [Gk f. *ex* out of]

exa- /'eksə/ *comb. form* denoting a factor of 10^{18}. [perh. f. HEXA-]

exacerbate /ekˈsæsəˌbeɪt, ɪg-/ *v.tr.* **1** make (pain,

anger, etc.) worse. **2** irritate (a person). □□
exacerbation /-'beɪʃ(ə)n/ *n.* [L *exacerbare* (as EX-[1], *acerbus* bitter)]

exact /ɪg'zækt/ *adj. & v.* —*adj.* **1** accurate; correct in all details (*an exact description*). **2 a** precise. **b** (of a person) tending to precision. —*v.tr.* (often foll. by *from, of*) **1** demand and enforce payment of (money, fees, etc.) from a person. **2 a** demand; insist on. **b** (of circumstances) require urgently. □**exact science** a science admitting of absolute or quantitative precision. □□**exactable** *adj.* **exactitude** *n.* **exactness** *n.* **exactor** *n.* [L *exigere exact-* (as EX-[1], *agere* drive)]

exacting /ɪg'zæktɪŋ/ *adj.* **1** making great demands. **2** calling for much effort. □□**exactingly** *adv.* **exactingness** *n.*

exaction /ɪg'zækʃ(ə)n/ *n.* **1** the act or an instance of exacting; the process of being exacted. **2 a** an illegal or exorbitant demand; an extortion. **b** a sum or thing exacted. [ME f. L *exactio* (as EXACT)]

exactly /ɪg'zæktlɪ/ *adv.* **1** accurately, precisely; in an exact manner (*worked it out exactly*). **2** in exact terms (*exactly when did it happen?*). **3** (said in reply) quite so; I quite agree. □**not exactly** *colloq.* **1** by no means. **2** not precisely.

exaggerate /ɪg'zædʒə,reɪt/ *v.tr.* **1** (also *absol.*) give an impression of (a thing), esp. in speech or writing, that makes it seem larger or greater etc. than it really is. **2** enlarge or alter beyond normal or due proportions (*spoke with exaggerated politeness*). □□**exaggeratedly** *adv.* **exaggeratingly** *adv.* **exaggeration** /-'reɪʃ(ə)n/ *n.* **exaggerative** /-rətɪv/ *adj.* **exaggerator** *n.* [L *exaggerare* (as EX-[1], *aggerare* heap up f. *agger* heap)]

exalt /ɪg'zɔːlt/ *v.tr.* **1** raise in rank or power etc. **2** praise highly. **3** (usu. as **exalted** *adj.*) make lofty or noble (*exalted aims; an exalted style*). □□**exaltedly** *adv.* **exaltedness** *n.* **exalter** *n.* [ME f. L *exaltare* (as EX-[1], *altus* high)]

exaltation /,egzɔːl'teɪʃ(ə)n/ *n.* **1** the act or an instance of exalting; the state of being exalted. **2** elation; rapturous emotion. [ME f. OF *exaltation* or LL *exaltatio* (as EXALT)]

exam /ɪg'zæm/ *n.* = EXAMINATION 3.

examination /ɪg,zæmɪ'neɪʃ(ə)n/ *n.* **1** the act or an instance of examining; the state of being examined. **2** a detailed inspection. **3** the testing of the proficiency or knowledge of students or other candidates for a qualification by oral or written questions. **4** an instance of examining or being examined medically. **5** *Law* the formal questioning of the accused or of a witness in court. □**examination paper 1** the printed questions in an examination. **2** a candidate's set of answers. □□**examinational** *adj.* [ME f. OF f. L *examinatio -onis* (as EXAMINE)]

examine /ɪg'zæmɪn/ *v.* **1** *tr.* inquire into the nature or condition etc. of. **2** *tr.* look closely or analytically at. **3** *tr.* test the proficiency of, esp. by examination (see EXAMINATION 3). **4** *tr.* check the health of (a patient) by inspection or experiment. **5** *tr. Law* formally question (the accused or a witness) in court. **6** *intr.* (foll. by *into*) inquire. □□**examinable** *adj.* **examinee** /-'niː/ *n.* **examiner** *n.* [ME f. OF *examiner* f. L *examinare* weigh, test f. *examen* tongue of a balance, ult. f. *exigere* examine, weigh: see EXACT]

example /ɪg'zɑːmp(ə)l/ *n. & v.* —*n.* **1** a thing characteristic of its kind or illustrating a general rule. **2** a person, thing, or piece of conduct, regarded in terms of its fitness to be imitated (*must set him an example; you are a bad example*). **3** a circumstance or treatment seen as a warning to others; a person so treated (*shall make an example of you*). **4** a problem or exercise designed to illustrate a rule. —*v.tr.* (usu. in *passive*) serve as an example of. □**for example** by way of illustration. [ME f. OF f. L *exemplum* (as EXEMPT)]

exanthema /,eksæn'θiːmə/ *n. Med.* a skin rash accompanying any eruptive disease or fever. [LL f. Gk

exanthēma eruption f. *exantheō* (as EX-[2], *anthos* blossom)]

exarch /'eksɑːk/ *n.* in the Orthodox Church, a bishop lower in rank than a patriarch and having jurisdiction wider than the metropolitan of a diocese. □□**exarchate** *n.* [eccl.L f. Gk *exarkhos* (as EX-[2], *arkhos* ruler)]

exasperate /ɪg'zɑːspə,reɪt/ *v.tr.* **1** (often as **exasperated** *adj.* or **exasperating** *adj.*) irritate intensely. **2** make (a pain, ill feeling, etc.) worse. □□**exasperatedly** *adv.* **exasperatingly** *adv.* **exasperation** /-'reɪʃ(ə)n/ *n.* [L *exasperare exasperat-* (as EX-[1], *asper* rough)]

ex cathedra /,eks kə'θiːdrə/ *adj. & adv.* with full authority (esp. of a papal pronouncement, implying infallibility as doctrinally defined). [L, = from the (teacher's) chair]

excavate /'ekskə,veɪt/ *v.tr.* **1 a** make (a hole or channel) by digging. **b** dig out material from (the ground). **2** reveal or extract by digging. **3** (also *absol.*) *Archaeol.* dig systematically into the ground to explore (a site). □□**excavation** /-'veɪʃ(ə)n/ *n.* **excavator** *n.* [L *excavare* (as EX-[1], *cavus* hollow)]

exceed /ɪk'siːd/ *v.tr.* **1** (often foll. by *by* an amount) be more or greater than (in number, extent, etc.). **2** go beyond or do more than is warranted by (a set limit, esp. of one's instructions or rights). **3** surpass, excel (a person or achievement). [ME f. OF *exceder* f. L *excedere* (as EX-[1], *cedere cess-* go)]

exceeding /ɪk'siːdɪŋ/ *adj. & adv.* —*adj.* **1** surpassing in amount or degree. **2** pre-eminent. —*adv. archaic* = EXCEEDINGLY 2.

exceedingly /ɪk'siːdɪŋlɪ/ *adv.* **1** very; to a great extent. **2** surpassingly, pre-eminently.

excel /ɪk'sel/ *v.* (**excelled, excelling**) (often foll. by *in, at*) **1** *tr.* be superior to. **2** *intr.* be pre-eminent or the most outstanding (*excels at games*). □**excel oneself** surpass one's previous performance. [ME f. L *excellere* (as EX-[1], *celsus* lofty)]

excellence /'eksələns/ *n.* **1** the state of excelling; surpassing merit or quality. **2** the activity etc. in which a person excels. [ME f. OF *excellence* or L *excellentia* (as EXCEL)]

Excellency /'eksələnsɪ/ *n.* (*pl.* **-ies**) (usu. prec. by *Your, His, Her, Their*) a title used in addressing or referring to certain high officials, e.g. ambassadors and governors, and (in some countries) senior Church dignitaries. [ME f. L *excellentia* (as EXCEL)]

excellent /'eksələnt/ *adj.* extremely good; pre-eminent. □□**excellently** *adv.* [ME f. OF (as EXCEL)]

excelsior /ɪk'selsɪˌɔː(r)/ *int. & n.* —*int.* higher, outstanding (esp. as a motto or trade mark). —*n.* soft wood shavings used for stuffing, packing, etc. [L, compar. of *excelsus* lofty]

excentric var. of ECCENTRIC (in technical senses).

except /ɪk'sept/ *v., prep., & conj.* —*v.tr.* (often as **excepted** *adj.* placed after object) exclude from a general statement, condition, etc. (*excepted him from the amnesty; present company excepted*). —*prep.* (often foll. by *for*) not including; other than (*all failed except him; all here except for John; is all right except that it is too long*). —*conj. archaic* unless (*except he be born again*). [ME f. L *excipere except-* (as EX-[1], *capere* take)]

excepting /ɪk'septɪŋ/ *prep. & conj.* —*prep.* = EXCEPT *prep.* —*conj. archaic* = EXCEPT *conj.*

exception /ɪk'sepʃ(ə)n/ *n.* **1** the act or an instance of excepting; the state of being excepted (*made an exception in my case*). **2** a thing that has been or will be excepted. **3** an instance that does not follow a rule. □**take exception** (often foll. by *to*) object; be resentful (about). **with the exception of** except; not including. [ME f. OF f. L *exceptio -onis* (as EXCEPT)]

exceptionable /ɪk'sepʃənəb(ə)l/ *adj.* open to objection. □□**exceptionably** *adv.*

exceptional /ɪkˈsepʃən(ə)l/ *adj.* **1** forming an exception. **2** unusual; not typical (*exceptional circumstances*). **3** unusually good; outstanding. □□ **exceptionality** /-ˈnælɪtɪ/ *n.* **exceptionally** *adv.*

excerpt *n.* & *v.* —*n.* /ˈeksɜːpt/ a short extract from a book, film, piece of music, etc. —*v.tr.* /ɪkˈsɜːpt/ (also *absol.*) **1** take an excerpt or excerpts from (a book etc.). **2** take (an extract) from a book etc. □□ **excerptible** /-ˈsɜːptɪb(ə)l/ *adj.* **excerption** /-ˈsɜːpʃ(ə)n/ *n.* [L *excerpere excerpt-* (as EX-[1], *carpere* pluck)]

excess /ɪkˈses, ˈekses/ *n.* & *adj.* —*n.* **1** the state or an instance of exceeding. **2** the amount by which one quantity or number exceeds another. **3** exceeding of a proper or permitted limit. **4 a** the overstepping of the accepted limits of moderation, esp. intemperance in eating or drinking. **b** (in *pl.*) outrageous or immoderate behaviour. **5** an extreme or improper degree or extent (*an excess of cruelty*). **6** part of an insurance claim to be paid by the insured, esp. by prior agreement. —*attrib.adj.* /usu. ˈekses/ **1** that exceeds a limited or prescribed amount (*excess weight*). **2** required as extra payment (*excess postage*). □ **excess baggage** (or **luggage**) that exceeding a weight allowance and liable to an extra charge. **in** (or **to**) **excess** exceeding the proper amount or degree. **in excess of** more than; exceeding. [ME f. OF *exces* f. L *excessus* (as EXCEED)]

excessive /ɪkˈsesɪv/ *adj.* **1** too much or too great. **2** more than what is normal or necessary. □□ **excessively** *adv.* **excessiveness** *n.*

exchange /ɪksˈtʃeɪndʒ/ *n.* & *v.* —*n.* **1** the act or an instance of giving one thing and receiving another in its place. **2 a** the giving of money for its equivalent in the money of the same or another country. **b** the fee or percentage charged for this. **3** the central telephone office of a district, where connections are effected. **4** a place where merchants, bankers, etc. gather to transact business. **5 a** an office where certain information is given or a service provided, usu. involving two parties. **b** an employment office. **6** a system of settling debts between persons (esp. in different countries) without the use of money, by bills of exchange (see BILL[1]). **7 a** a short conversation, esp. a disagreement or quarrel. **b** a sequence of letters between correspondents. **8** *Chess* the capture of an important piece (esp. a rook) by one player at the loss of a minor piece to the opposing player. **9** (*attrib.*) forming part of an exchange, e.g. of personnel between institutions (*an exchange student*). —*v.* **1** *tr.* (often foll. by *for*) give or receive (one thing) in place of another. **2** *tr.* give and receive as equivalents (e.g. things or people, blows, information, etc.); give one and receive another of. **3** *intr.* (often foll. by *with*) make an exchange. □ **exchange rate** the value of one currency in terms of another. **in exchange** (often foll. by *for*) as a thing exchanged (for). □□ **exchangeable** *adj.* **exchangeability** /-ˈbɪlɪtɪ/ *n.* **exchanger** *n.* [ME f. OF *eschangier* f. Rmc (as EX-[1], CHANGE)]

exchequer /ɪksˈtʃekə(r)/ *n.* **1** *Brit.* the former government department in charge of national revenue. ¶ Its functions now belong to the Treasury, although the name formally survives, esp. in the title *Chancellor of the Exchequer*. **2** a royal or national treasury. **3** the money of a private individual or group. [ME f. AF *escheker*, OF *eschequier* f. med.L *scaccarium* chessboard (its orig. sense, with ref. to keeping accounts on a chequered cloth)]

excise[1] /ˈeksaɪz/ *n.* & *v.* —*n.* **1 a** a duty or tax levied on goods and commodities produced or sold within the country of origin. **b** a tax levied on certain licences. **2** *Brit.* a former government office collecting excise. ¶ Now the *Board of Customs and Excise*. —*v.tr.* **1** charge excise on (goods). **2** force (a person) to pay excise. [MDu. *excijs, accijs*, perh. f. Rmc: rel. to CENSUS]

excise[2] /ɪkˈsaɪz, ek-/ *v.tr.* **1** remove (a passage of a

book etc.). **2** cut out (an organ etc.) by surgery. □□ **excision** /ɪkˈsɪʒ(ə)n/ *n.* [L *excidere excis-* (as EX-[1], *caedere* cut)]

exciseman /ˈeksaɪzˌmæn/ *n.* (*pl.* **-men**) *Brit. hist.* an officer responsible for collecting excise duty.

excitable /ɪkˈsaɪtəb(ə)l/ *adj.* **1** (esp. of a person) easily excited. **2** (of an organism, tissue, etc.) responding to a stimulus, or susceptible to stimulation. □□ **excitability** /-ˈbɪlɪtɪ/ *n.* **excitably** *adv.*

excitation /ˌeksɪˈteɪʃ(ə)n/ *n.* **1 a** the act or an instance of exciting. **b** the state of being excited; excitement. **2** the action of an organism, tissue, etc., resulting from stimulation. **3** *Electr.* **a** the process of applying current to the winding of an electromagnet to produce a magnetic field. **b** the process of applying a signal voltage to the control electrode of an electron tube or the base of a transistor. **4** *Physics* the process in which an atom etc. acquires a higher energy state.

excite /ɪkˈsaɪt/ *v.tr.* **1 a** rouse the feelings or emotions of (a person). **b** bring into play; rouse up (feelings, faculties, etc.). **c** arouse sexually. **2** provoke; bring about (an action or active condition). **3** promote the activity of (an organism, tissue, etc.) by stimulus. **4** *Electr.* **a** cause (a current) to flow in the winding of an electromagnet. **b** supply a signal. **5** *Physics* **a** cause the emission of (a spectrum). **b** cause (a substance) to emit radiation. **c** put (an atom etc.) into a state of higher energy. □□ **excitant** /ˈeksɪt(ə)nt, ɪkˈsaɪt(ə)nt/ *adj.* & *n.* **excitative** /-tətɪv/ *adj.* **excitatory** /-tətərɪ/ *adj.* **excitedly** *adv.* **excitedness** *n.* **excitement** *n.* **exciter** *n.* (esp. in senses 4, 5). [ME f. OF *exciter* or L *excitare* frequent. of *exciēre* (as EX-[1], *ciēre* set in motion)]

exciting /ɪkˈsaɪtɪŋ/ *adj.* arousing great interest or enthusiasm. □□ **excitingly** *adv.* **excitingness** *n.*

exciton /ˈeksaɪtɒn, ˈeksɪˌtɒn/ *n.* *Physics* a combination of an electron with a hole in a crystalline solid. [EXCITATION + -ON]

exclaim /ɪkˈskleɪm/ *v.* **1** *intr.* cry out suddenly, esp. in anger, surprise, pain, etc. **2** *tr.* (foll. by *that*) utter by exclaiming. [F *exclamer* or L *exclamare* (as EX-[1]: cf. CLAIM)]

exclamation /ˌekskləˈmeɪʃ(ə)n/ *n.* **1** the act or an instance of exclaiming. **2** words exclaimed; a strong sudden cry. □ **exclamation mark** (*US* **point**) a punctuation mark (!) indicating an exclamation. [ME f. OF *exclamation* or L *exclamatio* (as EXCLAIM)]

exclamatory /ɪkˈsklæmətərɪ/ *adj.* of or serving as an exclamation.

exclave /ˈekskleɪv/ *n.* a portion of territory of one State completely surrounded by territory of another or others, as viewed by the home territory (cf. ENCLAVE). [EX-[1] + ENCLAVE]

exclosure /ekˈskləʊʒə(r)/ *n.* *Forestry* etc. an area from which unwanted animals are excluded. [EX-[1] + ENCLOSURE]

exclude /ɪkˈskluːd/ *v.tr.* **1** shut or keep out (a person or thing) from a place, group, privilege, etc. **2** expel and shut out. **3** remove from consideration (*no theory can be excluded*). **4** prevent the occurrence of; make impossible (*excluded all doubt*). □ **excluded middle** *Logic* the principle that of two contradictory propositions one must be true. □□ **excludable** *adj.* **excluder** *n.* [ME f. L *excludere exclus-* (as EX-[1], *claudere* shut)]

exclusion /ɪkˈskluːʒ(ə)n/ *n.* the act or an instance of excluding; the state of being excluded. □ **exclusion order** *Brit.* an official order preventing a person (esp. a suspected terrorist) from entering the UK. **exclusion principle** *Physics* see PAULI EXCLUSION PRINCIPLE. **to the exclusion of** so as to exclude. □□ **exclusionary** *adj.* [L *exclusio* (as EXCLUDE)]

exclusionist /ɪkˈskluːʒənɪst/ *adj.* & *n.* —*adj.* favouring exclusion, esp. from rights or privileges. —*n.* a person favouring exclusion.

exclusive /ɪkˈskluːsɪv/ *adj.* & *n.* —*adj.* **1** excluding other things. **2** (*predic.*; foll. by *of*) not including; except for. **3** tending to exclude others, esp. socially;

select. **4** catering for few or select customers; high-class. **5 a** (of a commodity) not obtainable elsewhere. **b** (of a newspaper article) not published elsewhere. **6** (*predic.*; foll. by *to*) restricted or limited to; existing or available only in. **7** (of terms etc.) excluding all but what is specified. **8** employed or followed or held to the exclusion of all else (*my exclusive occupation*; *exclusive rights*). —*n.* an article or story published by only one newspaper or periodical. □**Exclusive Brethren** a more exclusive section of the Plymouth Brethren. □□**exclusively** *adv.* **exclusiveness** *n.* **exclusivity** /-'sɪvɪtɪ/ *n.* [med.L *exclusivus* (as EXCLUDE)]

excogitate /eks'kɒdʒɪ,teɪt/ *v.tr.* think out; contrive. □□**excogitation** /-'teɪʃ(ə)n/ *n.* [L *excogitare excogitat-* (as EX-¹, *cogitare* COGITATE)]

excommunicate *v.*, *adj.*, & *n. Eccl.* —*v.tr.* /,ekskə'mju:nɪ,keɪt/ officially exclude (a person) from participation in the sacraments, or from formal communion with the Church. —*adj.* /,ekskə'mju:nɪkət/ excommunicated. —*n.* /,ekskə'mju:nɪkət/ an excommunicated person. □□**excommunication** /-'keɪʃ(ə)n/ *n.* **excommunicative** /-kətɪv/ *adj.* **excommunicator** *n.* **excommunicatory** /-'keɪtərɪ/ *adj.* [L *excommunicare -atus* (as EX-¹, *communis* COMMON)]

ex-con /eks'kɒn/ *n. colloq.* an ex-convict; a former inmate of a prison. [abbr.]

excoriate /eks'kɔ:rɪ,eɪt/ *v.tr.* **1 a** remove part of the skin of (a person etc.) by abrasion. **b** strip or peel off (skin). **2** censure severely. □□**excoriation** /-'eɪʃ(ə)n/ *n.* [L *excoriare excoriat-* (as EX-¹, *corium* hide)]

excrement /'ekskrɪmənt/ *n.* (in *sing.* or *pl.*) faeces. □□**excremental** /-'ment(ə)l/ *adj.* [F *excrément* or L *excrementum* (as EXCRETE)]

excrescence /ɪk'skres(ə)ns/ *n.* **1** an abnormal or morbid outgrowth on the body or a plant. **2** an ugly addition. □□**excrescent** *adj.* **excrescential** /,ekskrɪ'senʃ(ə)l/ *adj.* [L *excrescentia* (as EX-¹, *crescere* grow)]

excreta /ek'skri:tə, ɪk-/ *n.pl.* waste discharged from the body, esp. faeces and urine. [L neut. pl.: see EXCRETE]

excrete /ɪk'skri:t/ *v.tr.* (of an animal or plant) separate and expel waste matter as a result of metabolism. □□**excreter** *n.* **excretion** *n.* **excretive** *adj.* **excretory** *adj.* [L *excernere excret-* (as EX-¹, *cernere* sift)]

excruciate /ɪk'skru:ʃɪ,eɪt/ *v.tr.* (esp. as **excruciating** *adj.*) torment acutely (a person's senses); torture mentally. □□**excruciatingly** *adv.* **excruciation** /-'eɪʃ(ə)n/ *n.* [L *excruciare excruciat-* (as EX-¹, *cruciare* torment f. *crux crucis* cross)]

exculpate /'ekskʌl,peɪt/ *v.tr. formal* **1** free from blame. **2** (foll. by *from*) clear (a person) of a charge. □□**exculpation** /-'peɪʃ(ə)n/ *n.* **exculpatory** /-'kʌlpətərɪ/ *adj.* [med.L *exculpare exculpat-* (as EX-¹, *culpa* blame)]

excursion /ɪk'skɜ:ʃ(ə)n/ *n.* **1** a short journey or ramble for pleasure, with return to the starting-point. **2** a digression. **3** *Astron.* a deviation from a regular path. **4** *archaic* a sortie (see ALARUM). □□**excursional** *adj.* **excursionary** *adj.* **excursionist** *n.* [L *excursio* f. *excurrere excurs-* (as EX-¹, *currere* run)]

excursive /ɪk'skɜ:sɪv/ *adj.* digressive; diverse. □□**excursively** *adv.* **excursiveness** *n.*

excursus /ek'skɜ:səs, ɪk-/ *n.* **1** a detailed discussion of a special point in a book, usu. in an appendix. **2** a digression in a narrative. [L, verbal noun formed as EXCURSION]

excuse *v.* & *n.* —*v.tr.* /ɪk'skju:z/ **1** attempt to lessen the blame attaching to (a person, act, or fault). **2** (of a fact or circumstance) serve in mitigation of (a person or act). **3** obtain exemption for (a person or oneself). **4** (foll. by *from*) release (a person) from a duty etc. (*excused from supervision duties*). **5** overlook or forgive (a fault or offence). **6** (foll. by *for*) forgive (a person) for a fault. **7** not insist upon (what is due). **8** *refl.* apologize for leaving. —*n.* /ɪk'skju:s, ek-/ **1 a**

reason put forward to mitigate or justify an offence, fault, etc. **2** an apology (*made my excuses*). **3** (foll. by *for*) a poor or inadequate example of. □**be excused** be allowed to leave a room etc., e.g. to go to the lavatory. **excuse me** a polite apology for lack of ceremony, for an interruption etc., or for disagreeing. **excuse-me** a dance in which dancers may interrupt other pairs to change partners. □□**excusable** /-'kju:zəb(ə)l/ *adj.* **excusably** /-'kju:zəblɪ/ *adv.* **excusatory** /-'kju:zətərɪ/ *adj.* [ME f. OF *escuser* f. L *excusare* (as EX-¹, *causa* CAUSE, accusation)]

ex-directory /,eksdaɪ'rektərɪ/ *adj. Brit.* not listed in a telephone directory, at the wish of the subscriber.

ex div. *abbr.* ex dividend.

ex dividend /eks 'dɪvɪ,dend/ *adj.* & *adv.* (of stocks or shares) not including the next dividend.

exeat /'eksɪ,æt/ *n. Brit.* permission granted to a student by a college for temporary absence or permission granted to a priest by a bishop to move to another diocese. [L, 3rd sing. pres. subjunctive of *exire* go out (as EX-¹, *ire* go)]

exec /ɪk'zek/ *n.* an executive. [abbr.]

execrable /'eksɪkrəb(ə)l/ *adj.* abominable, detestable. □□**execrably** *adv.* [ME f. OF f. L *execrabilis* (as EXECRATE)]

execrate /'eksɪ,kreɪt/ *v.* **1** *tr.* express or feel abhorrence for. **2** *tr.* curse (a person or thing). **3** *intr.* utter curses. □□**execration** /-'kreɪʃ(ə)n/ *n.* **execrative** *adj.* **execratory** *adj.* [L *exsecrare* (as EX-¹, *sacrare* devote f. *sacer* sacred, accursed)]

executant /ɪg'zekjʊt(ə)nt/ *n. formal* **1** a performer, esp. of music. **2** one who carries something into effect. [F *exécutant* pres. part. (as EXECUTE)]

execute /'eksɪ,kju:t/ *v.tr.* **1 a** carry out a sentence of death on (a condemned person). **b** kill as a political act. **2** carry into effect, perform (a plan, duty, command, operation, etc.). **3 a** carry out a design for (a product of art or skill). **b** perform (a musical composition, dance, etc.). **4** make (a legal instrument) valid by signing, sealing, etc. **5** put into effect (a judicial sentence, the terms of a will, etc.). □□**executable** *adj.* [ME f. OF *executer* f. med.L *executare* f. L *exsequi exsecut-* (as EX-¹, *sequi* follow)]

execution /,eksɪ'kju:ʃ(ə)n/ *n.* **1** the carrying out of a sentence of death. **2** the act or an instance of carrying out or performing something. **3** technique or style of performance in the arts, esp. music. **4 a** seizure of the property or person of a debtor in default of payment. **b** a judicial writ enforcing a judgement. □□**executionary** *adj.* [ME f. OF f. L *executio -onis* (as EXECUTE)]

executioner /,eksɪ'kju:ʃənə(r)/ *n.* an official who carries out a sentence of death.

executive /ɪg'zekjʊtɪv/ *n.* & *adj.* —*n.* **1** a person or body with managerial or administrative responsibility in a business organization etc.; a senior businessman. **2** a branch of a government or organization concerned with executing laws, agreements, etc., or with other administration or management. —*adj.* **1** concerned with executing laws, agreements, etc., or with other administration or management. **2** relating to or having the function of executing. □**executive session** *US* a usu. private meeting of a legislative body for executive business. □□**executively** *adv.* [med.L *executivus* (as EXECUTE)]

executor /ɪg'zekjʊtə(r)/ *n.* (*fem.* **executrix** /-trɪks/) a person appointed by a testator to carry out the terms of his or her will. □**literary executor** a person entrusted with a writer's papers, unpublished works, etc. □□**executorial** /-'tɔ:rɪəl/ *adj.* **executorship** *n.* **executory** *adj.* [ME f. AF *executor*, *-our* f. L *executor -oris* (as EXECUTE)]

exegesis /,eksɪ'dʒi:sɪs/ *n.* (*pl.* **exegeses** /-si:z/) critical explanation of a text, esp. of Scripture. □□**exegete** /'eksɪ,dʒi:t/ *n.* **exegetic** /-'dʒetɪk/ *adj.* **exegetical** /-'dʒetɪk(ə)l/ *adj.* **exegetist** /-'dʒi:tɪst/ *n.* [Gk *exēgēsis* f. *exēgeomai* interpret (as EX-², *hēgeomai* lead)]

exemplar /ɪg'zemplə(r), -plɑ:(r)/ *n.* **1** a model or

pattern. **2** a typical instance of a class of things. **3** a parallel instance. [ME f. OF *exemplaire* f. LL *exemplarium* (as EXAMPLE)]

exemplary /ɪgˈzempləri/ *adj.* **1** fit to be imitated; outstandingly good. **2 a** serving as a warning. **b** *Law* (of damages) exceeding the amount needed for simple compensation. **3** illustrative, representative. □□ **exemplarily** *adv.* **exemplariness** *n.* [LL *exemplaris* (as EXAMPLE)]

exemplify /ɪgˈzemplɪˌfaɪ/ *v.tr.* (**-ies, -ied**) **1** illustrate by example. **2** be an example of. **3** *Law* make an attested copy of (a document) under an official seal. □□ **exemplification** /-fɪˈkeɪʃ(ə)n/ *n.* [ME f. med.L *exemplificare* (as EXAMPLE)]

exemplum /ɪgˈzempləm/ *n.* (*pl.* **exempla** /-plə/) an example or model, esp. a moralizing or illustrative story. [L: see EXAMPLE]

exempt /ɪgˈzempt/ *adj.*, *n.*, & *v.* —*adj.* **1** free from an obligation or liability etc. imposed on others. **2** (foll. by *from*) not liable to. —*n.* **1** a person who is exempt, esp. from payment of tax. **2** *Brit.* = EXON. —*v.tr.* (foll. by *from*) free from an obligation, esp. one imposed on others. □□ **exemption** *n.* [ME f. L *exemptus* past part. of *eximere* exempt- (as EX-¹, *emere* take)]

exequies /ˈeksɪkwɪz/ *n.pl. formal* funeral rites. [ME f. OF f. L *exsequiae* (as EX-¹, *sequi* follow)]

exercise /ˈeksəˌsaɪz/ *n.* & *v.* —*n.* **1** activity requiring physical effort, done esp. as training or to sustain or improve health. **2** mental or spiritual activity, esp. as practice to develop a skill. **3** (often in *pl.*) a particular task or set of tasks devised as exercise, practice in a technique, etc. **4 a** the use or application of a mental faculty, right, etc. **b** practice of an ability, quality, etc. **5** (often in *pl.*) military drill or manœuvres. **6** (foll. by *in*) a process directed at or concerned with something specified (*was an exercise in public relations*). —*v.* **1** *tr.* use or apply (a faculty, right, influence, restraint, etc.). **2** *tr.* perform (a function). **3 a** *intr.* take (esp. physical) exercise; do exercises. **b** *tr.* provide (an animal) with exercise. **c** *tr.* train (a person). **4** *tr.* **a** tax the powers of. **b** perplex, worry. □**exercise book 1** a book containing exercises. **2** a book for writing school work, notes, etc., in. □□ **exercisable** *adj.* **exerciser** *n.* [ME f. OF *exercice* f. L *exercitium* f. *exercere* exercit- keep at work (as EX-¹, *arcēre* restrain)]

exergue /egˈzɜːg, ˈek-/ *n.* **1** a small space usu. on the reverse of a coin or medal, below the principal device. **2** an inscription on this space. [F f. med.L *exergum* f. Gk ex- (as EX-²) + *ergon* work]

exert /ɪgˈzɜːt/ *v.tr.* **1** exercise, bring to bear (a quality, force, influence, etc.). **2** *refl.* (often foll. by *for*, or *to* + *infin.*) use one's efforts or endeavours; strive. □□ **exertion** *n.* [L *exserere* exsert- put forth (as EX-¹, *serere* bind)]

exeunt /ˈeksɪˌʌnt/ *v.intr.* (as a stage direction) (actors) leave the stage. □*exeunt omnes* all leave the stage. [L, = they go out: 3rd pl. pres. of *exire* go out: see EXIT]

exfiltrate /ˈeksfɪlˌtreɪt/ *v.tr.* (also *absol.*) withdraw (troops, spies, etc.) surreptitiously, esp. from danger. □□ **exfiltration** /-ˈtreɪʃ(ə)n/ *n.*

exfoliate /eksˈfəʊlɪˌeɪt/ *v.intr.* **1** (of bone, the skin, a mineral, etc.) come off in scales or layers. **2** (of a tree) throw off layers of bark. □□ **exfoliation** /-ˈeɪʃ(ə)n/ *n.* **exfoliative** /-lɪətɪv/ *adj.* [LL *exfoliare exfoliat-* (as EX-¹, *folium* leaf)]

ex gratia /eks ˈgreɪʃə/ *adv.* & *adj.* —*adv.* as a favour rather than from an (esp. legal) obligation. —*adj.* granted on this basis. [L, = from favour]

exhalation /ˌekshəˈleɪʃ(ə)n/ *n.* **1 a** an expiration of air. **b** a puff of breath. **2** a mist, vapour. **3** an emanation or effluvium. [ME f. L *exhalatio* (as EXHALE)]

exhale /eksˈheɪl, ɪgz-/ *v.* **1** *tr.* breathe out (esp. air or smoke) from the lungs. **2** *tr.* & *intr.* give off or be

given off in vapour. □□ **exhalable** *adj.* [ME f. OF *exhaler* f. L *exhalare* (as EX-¹, *halare* breathe)]

exhaust /ɪgˈzɔːst/ *v.* & *n.* —*v.tr.* **1** consume or use up the whole of. **2** (often as **exhausted** *adj.* or **exhausting** *adj.*) use up the strength or resources of; tire out. **3** study or expound on (a subject) completely. **4** (often foll. by *of*) empty (a vessel etc.) of its contents. —*n.* **1 a** waste gases etc. expelled from an engine after combustion. **b** (also **exhaust-pipe**) the pipe or system by which these are expelled. **c** the process of expulsion of these gases. **2 a** the production of an outward current of air by the creation of a partial vacuum. **b** an apparatus for this. □□ **exhauster** *n.* **exhaustible** *adj.* **exhaustibility** /-ˈbɪlɪtɪ/ *n.* **exhaustibly** *adv.* [L *exhaurire exhaust-* (as EX-¹, *haurire* draw (water), drain)]

exhaustion /ɪgˈzɔːstʃ(ə)n/ *n.* **1** the act or an instance of exhausting; the state of being exhausted. **2** a total loss of strength. **3** the process of establishing a conclusion by eliminating alternatives. [LL *exhaustio* (as EXHAUST)]

exhaustive /ɪgˈzɔːstɪv/ *adj.* **1** thorough, comprehensive. **2** tending to exhaust a subject. □□ **exhaustively** *adv.* **exhaustiveness** *n.*

exhibit /ɪgˈzɪbɪt/ *v.* & *n.* —*v.tr.* (**exhibited, exhibiting**) **1** show or reveal publicly (for amusement, in competition, etc.). **2 a** show, display. **b** manifest (a quality). **3** submit for consideration. —*n.* **1** a thing or collection of things forming part or all of an exhibition. **2** a document or other item or object produced in a lawcourt as evidence. □□ **exhibitory** *adj.* [L *exhibēre exhibit-* (as EX-¹, *habēre* hold)]

exhibition /ˌeksɪˈbɪʃ(ə)n/ *n.* **1** a display (esp. public) of works of art, industrial products, etc. **2** the act or an instance of exhibiting; the state of being exhibited. **3** *Brit.* a scholarship, esp. from the funds of a school, college, etc. □**make an exhibition of oneself** behave so as to appear ridiculous or foolish. [ME f. OF f. LL *exhibitio -onis* (as EXHIBIT)]

exhibitioner /ˌeksɪˈbɪʃənə(r)/ *n. Brit.* a student who has been awarded an exhibition.

exhibitionism /ˌeksɪˈbɪʃəˌnɪz(ə)m/ *n.* **1** a tendency towards display or extravagant behaviour. **2** *Psychol.* a mental condition characterized by the compulsion to display one's genitals indecently in public. □□ **exhibitionist** *n.* **exhibitionistic** /-ˈnɪstɪk/ *adj.* **exhibitionistically** /-ˈnɪstɪkəlɪ/ *adv.*

exhibitor /ɪgˈzɪbɪtə(r)/ *n.* a person who provides an item or items for an exhibition.

exhilarate /ɪgˈzɪləˌreɪt/ *v.tr.* (often as **exhilarating** *adj.* or **exhilarated** *adj.*) affect with great liveliness or joy; raise the spirits of. □□ **exhilarant** *adj.* & *n.* **exhilaratingly** *adv.* **exhilaration** /-ˈreɪʃ(ə)n/ *n.* **exhilarative** /-rətɪv/ *adj.* [L *exhilarare* (as EX-¹, *hilaris* cheerful)]

exhort /ɪgˈzɔːt/ *v.tr.* (often foll. by *to* + infin.) urge or advise strongly or earnestly. □□ **exhortative** /-tətɪv/ *adj.* **exhortatory** /-tətərɪ/ *adj.* **exhorter** *n.* [ME f. OF *exhorter* or L *exhortari* (as EX-¹, *hortari* exhort)]

exhortation /ˌegzɔːˈteɪʃ(ə)n, ˌeks-/ *n.* **1** the act or an instance of exhorting; the state of being exhorted. **2** a formal or liturgical address. [ME f. OF *exhortation* or L *exhortatio* (as EXHORT)]

exhume /eksˈhjuːm, ɪgˈzjuːm/ *v.tr.* dig out, unearth (esp. a buried corpse). □□ **exhumation** /-ˈmeɪʃ(ə)n/ *n.* [F *exhumer* f. med.L *exhumare* (as EX-¹, *humus* ground)]

ex hypothesi /ˌeks haɪˈpɒθəsɪ/ *adv.* according to the hypothesis proposed. [mod.L]

exigency /ˈeksɪdʒənsɪ, ɪgˈzɪdʒ-/ *n.* (*pl.* **-ies**) (also **exigence** /ˈeksɪdʒ(ə)ns/) **1** an urgent need or demand. **2** an emergency. [F *exigence* & LL *exigentia* (as EXIGENT)]

exigent /ˈeksɪdʒ(ə)nt/ *adj.* **1** requiring much; exacting. **2** urgent, pressing. [ME f. L *exigere* EXACT]

exiguous /egˈzɪgjʊəs, ɪg-/ *adj.* scanty, small. □□

exiguity /-'gju:ɪtɪ/ *n.* **exiguously** *adv.*
exiguousness *n.* [L *exiguus* scanty f. *exigere* weigh
exactly: see EXACT]

exile /'eksaɪl, 'egz-/ *n. & v.* —*n.* **1** expulsion, or the
state of being expelled, from one's native land or
(**internal exile**) native town etc. **2** long absence
abroad, esp. enforced. **3** a person expelled or long
absent from his or her native country. **4** (**the Exile**)
the captivity of the Jews in Babylon in the 6th c. BC.
—*v.tr.* (foll. by *from*) officially expel (a person) from
his or her native country or town etc. □□**exilic**
/-'sɪlɪk, -'zɪlɪk/ *adj.* (esp. in sense 4 of *n.*). [ME f. OF
exil, exiler f. L *exilium* banishment]

exist /ɪg'zɪst/ *v.intr.* **1** have a place as part of objective
reality. **2 a** have being under specified conditions. **b**
(foll. by *as*) exist in the form of. **3** (of circumstances
etc.) occur; be found. **4** live with no pleasure under
adverse conditions (*felt he was merely existing*). **5**
continue in being; maintain life (*can hardly exist on
this salary*). **6** be alive, live. [prob. back-form. f.
EXISTENCE; cf. LL *existere*]

existence /ɪg'zɪst(ə)ns/ *n.* **1** the fact or condition of
being or existing. **2** the manner of one's existing or
living, esp. under adverse conditions (*a wretched
existence*). **3** an existing thing. **4** all that exists. [ME
f. OF *existence* or LL *existentia* f. L *exsistere* (as EX-[1],
stare stand)]

existent /ɪg'zɪst(ə)nt/ *adj.* existing, actual, current.

existential /ˌegzɪ'stenʃ(ə)l/ *adj.* **1** of or relating to
existence. **2** *Logic* (of a proposition etc.) affirming or
implying the existence of a thing. **3** *Philos.* concerned
with existence, esp. with human existence as viewed
by existentialism. □□**existentially** *adv.* [LL *ex-
istentialis* (as EXISTENCE)]

existentialism /ˌegzɪ'stenʃə‚lɪz(ə)m/ *n.* a philosophical theory emphasizing the existence of
the individual person as a free and responsible
agent determining his or her own development.
□□**existentialist** *n.* [G *Existentialismus* (as
EXISTENTIAL)]

exit /'eksɪt, 'egzɪt/ *n. & v.* —*n.* **1** a passage or door by
which to leave a room, building, etc. **2 a** the act of
going out. **b** the right to go out. **3** a place where
vehicles can leave a motorway or major road. **4** the
departure of an actor from the stage. **5** death.
—*v.intr.* (**exited, exiting**) **1** go out of a room, building, etc. **2** (as a stage direction) (an actor) leaves the
stage (*exit Macbeth*). **3** die. □**exit permit** (or **visa**
etc.) authorization to leave a particular country. [L,
3rd sing. pres. of *exire* go out (as EX-[1], *ire* go): cf. L
exitus going out]

ex-libris /eks'li:brɪs/ *n.* (*pl.* same) a usu. decorated
bookplate or label bearing the owner's name, pasted
into the front of a book. [L *ex libris* among the books
of]

ex nihilo /eks 'naɪhɪ‚ləʊ/ *adv.* out of nothing (*creation
ex nihilo*). [L]

exo- /'eksəʊ/ *comb. form* external. [Gk *exō* outside]

exobiology /ˌeksəʊbaɪ'ɒlədʒɪ/ *n.* the study of life
outside the earth. □□**exobiologist** *n.*

Exocet /'eksə‚set/ *n. propr.* a short-range guided
missile used esp. in sea warfare. [F *exocet* flying fish]

exocrine /'eksəʊ‚kraɪn/ *adj.* (of a gland) secreting
through a duct (cf. ENDOCRINE). [EXO- + Gk *krinō* sift]

Exod. *abbr.* Exodus (Old Testament).

exoderm /'eksəʊ‚dɜːm/ *n. Biol.* = ECTODERM.

exodus /'eksədəs/ *n.* **1** a mass departure of people
(esp. emigrants). **2** (**Exodus**) *Bibl.* **a** the departure
of the Israelites from Egypt. **b** the book of the Old
Testament relating this. [eccl.L f. Gk *exodos* (as EX-[2],
hodos way)]

ex officio /ˌeks ə'fɪʃɪəʊ/ *adv. & adj.* by virtue of one's
office or status. [L]

exogamy /ek'sɒgəmɪ/ *n.* **1** *Anthropol.* marriage of a
man outside his own tribe. **2** *Biol.* the fusion of
reproductive cells from distantly related or unrelated
individuals. □□**exogamous** *adj.*

exogenous /ek'sɒdʒɪnəs/ *adj. Biol.* growing or originating from outside. □□**exogenously** *adv.*

exon /'eksɒn/ *n. Brit.* each of the four officers acting
as commanders of the Yeomen of the Guard. [repr.
F pronunc. of EXEMPT]

exonerate /ɪg'zɒnə‚reɪt/ *v.tr.* (often foll. by *from*) **1**
free or declare free from blame etc. **2** release from a
duty etc. □□**exoneration** /-'reɪʃ(ə)n/ *n.* **exonerative**
/-rətɪv/ *adj.* [L *exonerare exonerat-* (as EX-[1], *onus,
oneris* burden)]

exophthalmos /ˌeksɒf'θælməs/ *n.* (also
exophthalmus, exophthalmia /-mɪə/) *Med.* abnormal protrusion of the eyeball. □□**exophthalmic**
adj. [mod.L f. Gk *exophthalmos* having prominent
eyes (as EX-[2], *ophthalmos* eye)]

exoplasm /'eksəʊ‚plæz(ə)m/ *n. Biol.* = ECTOPLASM.

exor. *abbr.* executor.

exorbitant /ɪg'zɔːbɪt(ə)nt/ *adj.* (of a price, demand,
etc.) grossly excessive. □□**exorbitance** *n.*
exorbitantly *adv.* [LL *exorbitare* (as EX-[1], *orbita*
ORBIT)]

exorcize /'eksɔː‚saɪz/ *v.tr.* (also **-ise**) **1** expel (a
supposed evil spirit) by invocation or by use of a
holy name. **2** (often foll. by *of*) free (a person or
place) of a supposed evil spirit. □□**exorcism** *n.*
exorcist *n.* **exorcization** /-'zeɪʃ(ə)n/ *n.* [F *exorciser*
or eccl.L *exorcizare* f. Gk *exorkizō* (as EX-[2], *horkos*
oath)]

exordium /ek'sɔːdɪəm/ *n.* (*pl.* **exordiums** or **exordia**
/-dɪə/) the beginning or introductory part, esp. of a
discourse or treatise. □□**exordial** *adj.* **exordially**
adv. [L f. *exordiri* (as EX-[1], *ordiri* begin)]

exoskeleton /ˌeksəʊ'skelɪt(ə)n/ *n.* a rigid external
covering for the body in certain animals, esp.
arthropods, providing support and protection.
□□**exoskeletal** *adj.*

exosphere /'eksəʊ‚sfɪə(r)/ *n.* the layer of atmosphere
furthest from the earth.

exothermic /ˌeksəʊ'θɜːmɪk/ *adj.* (also **exothermal**
/-m(ə)l/) esp. *Chem.* occurring or formed with the
evolution of heat. □□**exothermally** *adv.*
exothermically *adv.*

exotic /ɪg'zɒtɪk/ *adj. & n.* —*adj.* **1** introduced from
or originating in a foreign (esp. tropical) country
(*exotic fruits*). **2** attractively or remarkably strange
or unusual; bizarre. **3** (of a fuel, metal, etc.) of a kind
newly brought into use. —*n.* an exotic person or
thing. □**exotic dancer** a striptease dancer. □□
exotically *adv.* **exoticism** /-tɪ‚sɪz(ə)m/ *n.* [L *exoticus*
f. Gk *exōtikos* f. *exō* outside]

exotica /ɪg'zɒtɪkə/ *n.pl.* remarkably strange or rare
objects. [L, neut. pl. of *exoticus*: see EXOTIC]

expand /ɪk'spænd/ *v.* **1** *tr. & intr.* increase in size or
bulk or importance. **2** *intr.* (often foll. by *on*) give a
fuller description or account. **3** *intr.* become more
genial or effusive; discard one's reserve. **4** *tr.* set or
write out in full (something condensed or abbreviated). **5** *tr. & intr.* spread out flat. □**expanded
metal** sheet metal slit and stretched into a mesh,
used to reinforce concrete and other brittle materials.
□□**expandable** *adj.* **expander** *n.* **expansible** *adj.*
expansibility /-'bɪlɪtɪ/ *n.* [ME f. L *expandere expans-*
spread out (as EX-[1], *pandere* spread)]

expanse /ɪk'spæns/ *n.* **1** a wide continuous area or
extent of land, space, etc. **2** an amount of expansion.
[mod.L *expansum* neut. past part. (as EXPAND)]

expansile /ɪk'spænsaɪl/ *adj.* **1** of expansion. **2**
capable of expansion.

expansion /ɪk'spænʃ(ə)n/ *n.* **1** the act or an instance
of expanding; the state of being expanded. **2** enlargement of the scale or scope of (esp. commercial)
operations. **3** increase in the amount of a State's
territory or area of control. **4** an increase in the
volume of fuel etc. on combustion in the cylinder of
an engine. □□**expansionary** *adj.* **expansionism** *n.*
expansionist *n.* **expansionistic** /-'nɪstɪk/ *adj.* (all
in senses 2, 3). [LL *expansio* (as EXPAND)]

expansive /ɪk'spænsɪv/ *adj.* **1** able or tending to

æ cat ɑː arm e bed ɜː her ɪ sit iː see ɒ hot ɔː saw ʌ run ʊ put uː too ə ago aɪ my

expand. **2** extensive, wide-ranging. **3** (of a person, feelings, or speech) effusive, open. □□ **expansively** *adv.* **expansiveness** *n.* **expansivity** /-'sɪvɪtɪ/ *n.*

ex parte /eks 'pɑːtɪ/ *adj. & adv. Law* in the interests of one side only or of an interested outside party. [L]

expat /eks'pæt/ *n. & adj. colloq.* = EXPATRIATE. [abbr.]

expatiate /ɪk'speɪʃɪˌeɪt/ *v.intr.* (usu. foll. by *on, upon*) speak or write at length or in detail. □□ **expatiation** /-'eɪʃ(ə)n/ *n.* **expatiatory** /-ʃɪətərɪ/ *adj.* [L *exspatiari* digress (as EX-¹, *spatium* SPACE)]

expatriate *adj., n., & v.* —*adj.* /eks'pætrɪət, -'peɪtrɪət/ **1** living abroad, esp. for a long period. **2** expelled from one's country; exiled. —*n.* /eks'pætrɪət, -'peɪtrɪət/ an expatriate person. —*v.tr.* /eks'pætrɪ,eɪt, -'peɪtrɪ,eɪt/ **1** expel or remove (a person) from his or her native country. **2** *refl.* withdraw (oneself) from one's citizenship or allegiance. □□ **expatriation** /-'eɪʃ(ə)n/ *n.* [med.L *expatriare* (as EX-¹, *patria* native country)]

expect /ɪk'spekt/ *v.tr.* **1** (often foll. by *to* + infin., or *that* + clause) **a** regard as likely; assume as a future event or occurrence. **b** (often foll. by *of*) look for as appropriate or one's due (from a person) (*I expect cooperation; expect you to be here*; *expected better of you*). **2** *colloq.* (often foll. by *that* + clause) think, suppose (*I expect we'll be on time*). **3** be shortly to have (a baby) (*is expecting twins*). □ **be expecting** *colloq.* be pregnant. □□ **expectable** *adj.* [L *exspectare* (as EX-¹, *spectare* look, frequent. of *specere* see)]

expectancy /ɪk'spektənsɪ/ *n.* (*pl.* **-ies**) **1** a state of expectation. **2** a prospect, esp. of future possession. **3** (foll. by *of*) a prospective chance. [L *exspectantia, exp-* (as EXPECT)]

expectant /ɪk'spekt(ə)nt/ *adj. & n.* —*adj.* **1** (often foll. by *of*) expecting. **2** having the expectation of possession, status, etc. **3** expecting a baby (said of the mother or father). —*n.* **1** one who expects. **2** a candidate for office etc. □□ **expectantly** *adv.*

expectation /,ekspek'teɪʃ(ə)n/ *n.* **1** the act or an instance of expecting or looking forward. **2** something expected or hoped for. **3** (foll. by *of*) the probability of an event. **4** (in *pl.*) one's prospects of inheritance. [L *exspectatio* (as EXPECT)]

expectorant /ek'spektərənt/ *adj. & n.* —*adj.* causing the coughing out of phlegm etc. —*n.* an expectorant medicine.

expectorate /ek'spektə,reɪt/ *v.tr.* (also *absol.*) cough or spit out (phlegm etc.) from the chest or lungs. □□ **expectoration** /-'reɪʃ(ə)n/ *n.* **expectorator** *n.* [L *expectorare expectorat-* (as EX-¹, *pectus -oris* breast)]

expedient /ɪk'spiːdɪənt/ *adj. & n.* —*adj.* **1** advantageous; advisable on practical rather than moral grounds. **2** suitable, appropriate. —*n.* a means of attaining an end; a resource. □□ **expedience** *n.* **expediency** *n.* **expediently** *adv.* [ME f. L *expedire*: see EXPEDITE]

expedite /'ekspɪ,daɪt/ *v.tr.* **1** assist the progress of; hasten (an action, process, etc.). **2** accomplish (business) quickly. □□ **expediter** *n.* [L *expedire expedit-* extricate, put in order (as EX-¹, *pes pedis* foot)]

expedition /,ekspɪ'dɪʃ(ə)n/ *n.* **1** a journey or voyage for a particular purpose, esp. exploration, scientific research, or war. **2** the personnel or ships etc. undertaking this. **3** promptness, speed. □□ **expeditionist** *n.* [ME f. OF f. L *expeditio -onis* (as EXPEDITE)]

expeditionary /,ekspɪ'dɪʃənərɪ/ *adj.* of or used in an expedition, esp. military.

expeditious /,ekspɪ'dɪʃəs/ *adj.* **1** acting or done with speed and efficiency. **2** suited for speedy performance. □□ **expeditiously** *adv.* **expeditiousness** *n.* [EXPEDITION + -OUS]

expel /ɪk'spel/ *v.tr.* (**expelled, expelling**) (often foll. by *from*) **1** deprive (a person) of the membership of or involvement in (a school, society, etc.). **2** force out or eject (a thing from its container etc.). **3** order or force to leave a building etc. □□ **expellable** *adj.*

expellee /-'liː/ *n.* **expellent** *adj.* **expeller** *n.* [ME f. L *expellere expuls-* (as EX-¹, *pellere* drive)]

expend /ɪk'spend/ *v.tr.* spend or use up (money, time, etc.). [ME f. L *expendere expens-* (as EX-¹, *pendere* weigh)]

expendable /ɪk'spendəb(ə)l/ *adj.* **1** that may be sacrificed or dispensed with, esp. to achieve a purpose. **2 a** not regarded as worth preserving or saving. **b** unimportant, insignificant. **3** not normally reused. □□ **expendability** /-'bɪlɪtɪ/ *n.* **expendably** *adv.*

expenditure /ɪk'spendɪtʃə(r)/ *n.* **1** the process or an instance of spending or using up. **2** a thing (esp. a sum of money) expended. [EXPEND, after obs. *expenditor* officer in charge of expenditure, f. med.L f. *expenditus* irreg. past part. of L *expendere*]

expense /ɪk'spens/ *n.* **1** cost incurred; payment of money. **2** (usu. in *pl.*) **a** costs incurred in doing a particular job etc. (*will pay your expenses*). **b** an amount paid to reimburse this (*offered me £40 per day expenses*). **3** a thing that is a cause of much expense (*the house is a real expense to run*). □ **at the expense of** so as to cause loss or damage or discredit to. **expense account** a list of an employee's expenses payable by the employer. [ME f. AF, alt. of OF *espense* f. LL *expensa* (money) spent, past part. of L *expendere* EXPEND]

expensive /ɪk'spensɪv/ *adj.* **1** costing much. **2** making a high charge. **3** causing much expense (*has expensive tastes*). □□ **expensively** *adv.* **expensiveness** *n.*

experience /ɪk'spɪərɪəns/ *n. & v.* —*n.* **1** actual observation of or practical acquaintance with facts or events. **2** knowledge or skill resulting from this. **3 a** an event regarded as affecting one (*an unpleasant experience*). **b** the fact or process of being so affected (*learnt by experience*). —*v.tr.* **1** have experience of; undergo. **2** feel or be affected by (an emotion etc.). □□ **experienceable** *adj.* [ME f. OF f. L *experientia* f. *experiri expert-* try]

experienced /ɪk'spɪərɪənst/ *adj.* **1** having had much experience. **2** skilled from experience (*an experienced driver*).

experiential /ɪk,spɪərɪ'enʃ(ə)l/ *adj.* involving or based on experience. □ **experiential philosophy** a philosophy that treats all knowledge as based on experience. □□ **experientialism** *n.* **experientialist** *n.* **experientially** *adv.*

experiment /ɪk'sperɪmənt, -,ment/ *n. & v.* —*n.* **1** a procedure adopted on the chance of its succeeding, for testing a hypothesis etc., or to demonstrate a known fact. **2** (foll. by *of*) a test or trial of. —*v.intr.* (often foll. by *on, with*) make an experiment. □□ **experimentation** /-men'teɪʃ(ə)n/ *n.* **experimenter** *n.* [ME f. OF *experiment* or L *experimentum* (as EXPERIENCE)]

experimental /ɪk,sperɪ'ment(ə)l/ *adj.* **1** based on or making use of experiment (*experimental psychology*). **2 a** used in experiments. **b** serving or resulting from (esp. incomplete) experiment; tentative, provisional. **3** based on experience, not on authority or conjecture. □□ **experimentalism** *n.* **experimentalist** *n.* **experimentalize** *v.intr.* (also **-ise**). **experimentally** *adv.* [ME f. med.L *experimentalis* (as EXPERIMENT)]

expert /'eksp3ːt/ *adj. & n.* —*adj.* **1** (often foll. by *at, in*) having special knowledge or skill in a subject. **2** involving or resulting from this (*expert evidence; an expert piece of work*). —*n.* (often foll. by *at, in*) a person having special knowledge or skill. □□ **expertly** *adv.* **expertness** *n.* [ME f. OF f. L *expertus* past part. of *experiri*: see EXPERIENCE]

expertise /,eksp3ː'tiːz/ *n.* expert skill, knowledge, or judgement. [F (as EXPERT)]

expertize /'eksp3ː,taɪz/ *v.* (also **-ise**) **1** *intr.* give an expert opinion. **2** *tr.* give an expert opinion concerning.

expiate /'ekspɪ,eɪt/ v.tr. **1** pay the penalty for (wrongdoing). **2** make amends for. □□ **expiable** /'ekspɪəb(ə)l/ adj. **expiatory** /-pɪətərɪ, -pɪ,eɪtərɪ/ adj. **expiation** /-'eɪʃ(ə)n/ n. **expiator** n. [L expiare expiat- (as EX-¹, pius devout)]

expiration /,ekspɪ'reɪʃ(ə)n/ n. **1** breathing out. **2** expiry. [L expiratio (as EXPIRE)]

expire /ɪk'spaɪə(r)/ v. **1** intr. (of a period of time, validity, etc.) come to an end. **2** intr. (of a document, authorization, etc.) cease to be valid; become void. **3** intr. (of a person) die. **4** tr. (usu. foll. by from; also absol.) exhale (air etc.) from the lungs. □□ **expiratory** adj. (in sense 4). [ME f. OF expirer f. L exspirare (as EX-¹, spirare breathe)]

expiry /ɪk'spaɪərɪ/ n. **1** the end of the validity or duration of something. **2** death.

explain /ɪk'spleɪn/ v.tr. **1** make clear or intelligible with detailed information etc. (also absol.: let me explain). **2** (foll. by that + clause) say by way of explanation. **3** account for (one's conduct etc.). □**explain away** minimize the significance of (a difficulty or mistake) by explanation. **explain oneself 1** make one's meaning clear. **2** give an account of one's motives or conduct. □□ **explainable** adj. **explainer** n. [L explanare (as EX-¹, planus flat, assim. to PLAIN¹)]

explanation /,eksplə'neɪʃ(ə)n/ n. **1** the act or an instance of explaining. **2** a statement or circumstance that explains something. **3** a declaration made with a view to mutual understanding or reconciliation. [ME f. L explanatio (as EXPLAIN)]

explanatory /ɪk'splænətərɪ/ adj. serving or intended to serve to explain. □□ **explanatorily** adv. [LL explanatorius (as EXPLAIN)]

explant /eks'plɑ:nt/ v. & n. Biol. —v.tr. transfer (living cells, tissues, or organs) from animals or plants to a nutrient medium. —n. a piece of explanted tissue etc. □□ **explantation** /-'teɪʃ(ə)n/ n. [mod.L explantare (as EX-¹, plantare PLANT)]

expletive /ɪk'spli:tɪv/ n. & adj. —n. **1** an oath, swear-word, or other expression, used in an exclamation. **2** a word used to fill out a sentence etc., esp. in verse. —adj. serving to fill out (esp. a sentence, line of verse, etc.). [LL expletivus (as EX-¹, plēre plet- fill)]

explicable /ɪk'splɪkəb(ə)l, 'ek-/ adj. that can be explained.

explicate /'eksplɪ,keɪt/ v.tr. **1** develop the meaning or implication of (an idea, principle, etc.). **2** make clear, explain (esp. a literary text). □□ **explication** /-'keɪʃ(ə)n/ n. **explicative** /ek'splɪkətɪv, 'eksplɪ,keɪtɪv/ adj. **explicator** n. **explicatory** /ek'splɪkətərɪ, 'eksplɪ,keɪtərɪ/ adj. [L explicare explicat- unfold (as EX-¹, plicare plicat- or plicit- fold)]

explicit /ɪk'splɪsɪt/ adj. **1** expressly stated, leaving nothing merely implied; stated in detail. **2** (of knowledge, a notion, etc.) definite, clear. **3** (of a person, book, etc.) expressing views unreservedly; outspoken. □□ **explicitly** adv. **explicitness** n. [F explicite or L explicitus (as EXPLICATE)]

explode /ɪk'spləʊd/ v. **1 a** intr. (of gas, gunpowder, a bomb, a boiler, etc.) expand suddenly with a loud noise owing to a release of internal energy. **b** tr. cause (a bomb etc.) to explode. **2** intr. give vent suddenly to emotion, esp. anger. **3** intr. (of a population etc.) increase suddenly or rapidly. **4** tr. show (a theory etc.) to be false or baseless. **5** tr. (as **exploded** adj.) (of a drawing etc.) showing the components of a mechanism as if separated by an explosion but in the normal relative positions. □□ **exploder** n. [earliest in sense 4: L explodere hiss off the stage (as EX-¹, plodere plos- = plaudere clap)]

exploit n. & v. —n. /'eksplɔɪt/ a bold or daring feat. —v.tr. /ɪk'splɔɪt/ **1** make use of (a resource etc.); derive benefit from. **2** usu. derog. utilize or take advantage of (esp. a person) for one's own ends. □□ **exploitable** /ɪk'splɔɪtəb(ə)l/ adj. **exploitation** /,eksplɔɪ'teɪʃ(ə)n/ n. **exploitative** /ɪk'splɔɪtətɪv/ adj.

exploiter n. **exploitive** /ɪk'splɔɪtɪv/ adj. [ME f. OF esploit, exploiter ult. f. L explicare: see EXPLICATE]

exploration /,eksplə'reɪʃ(ə)n/ n. **1** an act or instance of exploring. **2** the process of exploring. □□ **explorational** adj.

exploratory /ɪk'splɒrətərɪ/ adj. **1** (of discussion etc.) preliminary, serving to establish procedure etc. **2** of or concerning exploration or investigation (exploratory surgery).

explore /ɪk'splɔː(r)/ v.tr. **1** travel extensively through (a country etc.) in order to learn or discover about it. **2** inquire into; investigate thoroughly. **3** Surgery examine (a part of the body) in detail. □□ **explorative** /ɪk'splɒrətɪv/ adj. [F explorer f. L explorare]

explorer /ɪk'splɔːrə(r)/ n. a traveller into undiscovered or uninvestigated territory, esp. to get scientific information.

explosion /ɪk'spləʊʒ(ə)n/ n. **1** the act or an instance of exploding. **2** a loud noise caused by something exploding. **3 a** a sudden outburst of noise. **b** a sudden outbreak of feeling, esp. anger. **4** a rapid or sudden increase, esp. of population. [L explosio scornful rejection (as EXPLODE)]

explosive /ɪk'spləʊsɪv/ adj. & n. —adj. **1** able or tending or likely to explode. **2** likely to cause a violent outburst etc.; (of a situation etc.) dangerously tense. —n. an explosive substance. □□ **explosively** adv. **explosiveness** n.

Expo /'ekspəʊ/ n. (also **expo**) (pl. -os) a large international exhibition. [abbr. of EXPOSITION 4]

exponent /ɪk'spəʊnənt/ n. & adj. —n. **1** a person who favours or promotes an idea etc. **2** a representative or practitioner of an activity, profession, etc. **3** a person who explains or interprets something. **4** an executant (of music etc.). **5** a type or representative. **6** Math. a raised symbol or expression beside a numeral indicating how many times it is to be multiplied by itself (e.g. $2^3 = 2 \times 2 \times 2$). —adj. that sets forth or interprets. [L exponere (as EX-¹, ponere posit- put)]

exponential /,ekspə'nenʃ(ə)l/ adj. **1** Math. of or indicated by a mathematical exponent. **2** (of an increase etc.) more and more rapid. □**exponential function** Math. a function which increases as a quantity raised to a power determined by the variable on which the function depends. **exponential growth** Biol. a form of population growth in which the rate of growth is related to the number of individuals present. [F exponentiel (as EXPONENT)]

export v. & n. —v.tr. /ek'spɔːt, 'ek-/ send out (goods or services) esp. for sale in another country. —n. /'ekspɔːt/ **1** the process of exporting. **2 a** an exported article or service. **b** (in pl.) an amount exported (exports exceeded £50m.). **3** (attrib.) suitable for export, esp. of better quality. □**export reject** an article sold in its country of manufacture, as being below the standard for export. □□ **exportable** adj. **exportability** /-'bɪlɪtɪ/ n. **exportation** /-'teɪʃ(ə)n/ n. **exporter** /-'spɔːtə(r)/ n. [L exportare (as EX-¹, portare carry)]

expose /ɪk'spəʊz/ v.tr. **1** leave uncovered or unprotected, esp. from the weather. **2** (foll. by to) cause to be liable to or in danger of (was exposed to great danger). **3** (as **exposed** adj.) **a** (foll. by to) open to; unprotected from (exposed to the east). **b** vulnerable, risky. **4** Photog. subject (a film) to light, esp. by operation of a camera. **5** reveal the identity or fact of (esp. a person or thing disapproved of or guilty of crime etc.). **6** disclose; make public. **7** exhibit, display. **8** put up for sale. □**expose oneself** display one's body, esp. the genitals, publicly and indecently. □□ **exposer** n. [ME f. OF exposer after L exponere: see EXPONENT, POSE¹]

exposé /ek'spəʊzeɪ/ n. **1** an orderly statement of facts. **2** the act or an instance of revealing something discreditable. [F, past part. of exposer (as EXPOSE)]

exposition /,ekspə'zɪʃ(ə)n/ n. **1** an explanatory statement or account. **2** an explanation or commentary. **3** Mus. the part of a movement, esp. in sonata form, in which the principal themes are first presented. **4** a large public exhibition. **5** *archaic* exposure. □□ **expositional** *adj.* **expositive** /-'spɒzɪtɪv/ *adj.* [ME f. OF *exposition*, or L *expositio* (as EXPONENT)]

expositor /ɪk'spɒzɪtə(r)/ *n.* an expounder or interpreter. □□ **expository** *adj.*

ex post facto /ˌeks pəʊst 'fæktəʊ/ *adj.* & *adv.* with retrospective action or force. [L *ex postfacto* in the light of subsequent events]

expostulate /ɪk'spɒstjʊˌleɪt/ *v.intr.* (often foll. by *with* a person) make a protest; remonstrate earnestly. □□ **expostulation** /-'leɪʃ(ə)n/ *n.* **expostulatory** /-lətərɪ/ *adj.* [L *expostulare expostulat-* (as EX-[1], *postulare* demand)]

exposure /ɪk'spəʊʒə(r)/ *n.* (foll. by *to*) **1** the act or condition of exposing or being exposed (to air, cold, danger, etc.). **2** the condition of being exposed to the elements, esp. in severe conditions (*died from exposure*). **3** the revelation of an identity or fact, esp. when concealed or likely to find disapproval. **4** *Photog.* **a** the action of exposing a film etc. to the light. **b** the duration of this action. **c** the area of film etc. affected by it. **5** an aspect or outlook (*has a fine southern exposure*). □**exposure meter** *Photog.* a device for measuring the strength of the light to determine the correct duration of exposure. [EXPOSE after *enclosure* etc.]

expound /ɪk'spaʊnd/ *v.tr.* **1** set out in detail (a doctrine etc.). **2** explain or interpret (esp. Scripture). □□ **expounder** *n.* [ME f. OF *espondre* (as EXPONENT)]

express[1] /ɪk'spres/ *v.tr.* **1** represent or make known (thought, feelings, etc.) in words or by gestures, conduct, etc. **2** *refl.* say what one thinks or means. **3** esp. *Math.* represent by symbols. **4** squeeze out (liquid or air). □□ **expresser** *n.* **expressible** *adj.* [ME f. OF *expresser* f. Rmc (as EX-[1], PRESS[1])]

express[2] /ɪk'spres/ *adj., adv., n.,* & *v.* —*adj.* **1** operating at high speed. **2** /also 'ekspres/ **a** definitely stated, not merely implied. **b** *archaic* (of a likeness) exact. **3 a** done, made, or sent for a special purpose. **b** (of messages or goods) delivered by a special messenger or service. —*adv.* **1** at high speed. **2** by express messenger or train. —*n.* **1 a** an express train or messenger. **b** an express rifle. **2** *US* a company undertaking the transport of parcels etc. —*v.tr.* send by express messenger or service. □**express rifle** a rifle that discharges a bullet at high speed. **express train** a fast train, stopping at few intermediate stations. □□ **expressly** *adv.* (in sense 2 of *adj.*). [ME f. OF *expres* f. L *expressus* distinctly shown, past part. of *exprimere* (as EX-[1], *premere* press)]

expression /ɪk'spreʃ(ə)n/ *n.* **1** the act or an instance of expressing. **2** a word or phrase expressed. **3** *Math.* a collection of symbols expressing a quantity. **4** a person's facial appearance or intonation of voice, esp. as indicating feeling. **5** depiction of feeling, movement, etc., in art. **6** conveying of feeling in the performance of a piece of music. □**expression-mark** *Mus.* a sign or word indicating the required manner of performance. □□ **expressional** *adj.* **expressionless** *adj.* **expressionlessly** *adv.* **expressionlessness** *n.* [ME f. OF *expression* or L *expressio* f. *exprimere*: see EXPRESS[1]]

expressionism /ɪk'spreʃəˌnɪz(ə)m/ *n.* a style of painting, music, drama, etc., in which an artist or writer seeks to express emotional experience rather than impressions of the external world. □□ **expressionist** *n.* & *adj.* **expressionistic** /-'nɪstɪk/ *adj.* **expressionistically** /-'nɪstɪkəlɪ/ *adv.*

expressive /ɪk'spresɪv/ *adj.* **1** full of expression (*an expressive look*). **2** (foll. by *of*) serving to express (*words expressive of contempt*). □□ **expressively** *adv.* **expressiveness** *n.* **expressivity** /-'sɪvɪtɪ/ *n.* [ME f. F *expressif -ive* or med.L *expressivus* (as EXPRESSION)]

expresso var. of ESPRESSO.

expressway /ɪk'spresweɪ/ *n. US* an urban motorway.

expropriate /eks'prəʊprɪˌeɪt/ *v.tr.* **1** (esp. of the State) take away (property) from its owner. **2** (foll. by *from*) dispossess. □□ **expropriation** /-'eɪʃ(ə)n/ *n.* **expropriator** *n.* [med.L *expropriare expropriat-* (as EX-[1], *proprium* property: see PROPER)]

expulsion /ɪk'spʌlʃ(ə)n/ *n.* the act or an instance of expelling; the process of being expelled. □□ **expulsive** /-sɪv/ *adj.* [ME f. L *expulsio* (as EXPEL)]

expunge /ɪk'spʌndʒ/ *v.tr.* (foll. by *from*) erase, remove (esp. a passage from a book or a name from a list). □□ **expunction** /ɪk'spʌŋkʃ(ə)n/ *n.* **expunger** *n.* [L *expungere expunct-* (as EX-[1], *pungere* prick)]

expurgate /'ekspəˌgeɪt/ *v.tr.* **1** remove matter thought to be objectionable from (a book etc.). **2** remove (such matter). □□ **expurgation** /-'geɪʃ(ə)n/ *n.* **expurgator** *n.* **expurgatorial** /ˌekspɜːgə'tɔːrɪəl/ *adj.* **expurgatory** /ek'spɜːgətərɪ/ *adj.* [L *expurgare expurgat-* (as EX-[1], *purgare* cleanse)]

exquisite /'ekskwɪzɪt, ek'skwɪzɪt/ *adj.* & *n.* —*adj.* **1** extremely beautiful or delicate. **2** acute; keenly felt (*exquisite pleasure*). **3** keen; highly sensitive or discriminating (*exquisite taste*). —*n.* a person of refined (esp. affected) tastes. □□ **exquisitely** *adv.* **exquisiteness** *n.* [ME f. L *exquirere exquisit-* (as EX-[1], *quaerere* seek)]

exsanguinate /ek'sæŋgwɪˌneɪt/ *Med. v.tr.* drain of blood. □□ **exsanguination** /-'neɪʃ(ə)n/ *n.* [L *exsanguinatus* (as EX-[1], *sanguis -inis* blood)]

exsert /ɪk'sɜːt/ *v.tr. Biol.* put forth. [L *exserere*: see EXERT]

ex-service /eks'sɜːvɪs/ *adj.* **1** having formerly been a member of the armed forces. **2** relating to former servicemen and -women.

ex-serviceman /eks'sɜːvɪsmən/ *n.* (*pl.* **-men**) a former member of the armed forces.

ex-servicewoman /eks'sɜːvɪsˌwʊmən/ *n.* (*pl.* **-women**) a former woman member of the armed forces.

ex silentio /ˌeks sɪ'lenʃɪəʊ/ *adv.* by the absence of contrary evidence. [L, = from silence]

ext. *abbr.* **1** exterior. **2** external.

extant /ek'stænt, ɪk'st-, 'ekst(ə)nt/ *adj.* (esp. of a document etc.) still existing, surviving. [L *exstare exstant-* (as EX-[1], *stare* stand)]

extemporaneous /ɪkˌstempə'reɪnɪəs/ *adj.* spoken or done without preparation. □□ **extemporaneously** *adv.* **extemporaneousness** *n.*

extemporary /ɪk'stempərərɪ/ *adj.* = EXTEMPORANEOUS. □□ **extemporarily** *adv.* **extemporariness** *n.*

extempore /ɪk'stempərɪ/ *adj.* & *adv.* **1** without preparation. **2** offhand. [L *ex tempore* on the spur of the moment, lit. out of the time f. *tempus* time]

extemporize /ɪk'stempəˌraɪz/ *v.tr.* (also **-ise**) (also *absol.*) compose or produce (music, a speech, etc.) without preparation; improvise. □□ **extemporization** /-'zeɪʃ(ə)n/ *n.*

extend /ɪk'stend/ *v.* **1** *tr.* & *intr.* lengthen or make larger in space or time. **2** *tr.* stretch or lay out at full length. **3** *intr.* & *tr.* (foll. by *to, over*) reach or be or make continuous over a certain area. **4** *intr.* (foll. by *to*) have a certain scope (*the permit does not extend to camping*). **5** *tr.* offer or accord (an invitation, hospitality, kindness, etc.). **6** *tr.* (usu. *refl.* or in *passive*) tax the powers of (an athlete, horse, etc.) to the utmost. □**extended family** a family including relatives living near. **extended-play** (of a gramophone record) playing for longer than most singles, usu. at 45 r.p.m. □□ **extendable** *adj.* **extendability** /-də'bɪlɪtɪ/ *n.* **extendible** *adj.* **extendibility** /-dɪ'bɪlɪtɪ/ *n.* **extensible** /-sɪb(ə)l/ *adj.* **extensibility** /-sɪ'bɪlɪtɪ/ *n.* [ME f. L *extendere extens-* or *extent-* stretch out (as EX-[1], *tendere* stretch)]

extender /ɪk'stendə(r)/ *n.* **1** a person or thing that extends. **2** a substance added to paint, ink, glue, etc., to dilute its colour or increase its bulk.

extensile /ɪk'stensaɪl/ *adj.* capable of being stretched out or protruded.

extension /ɪk'stenʃ(ə)n/ n. **1** the act or an instance of extending; the process of being extended. **2** prolongation; enlargement. **3** a part enlarging or added on to a main structure or building. **4** an additional part of anything. **5 a** a subsidiary telephone on the same line as the main one. **b** its number. **6 a** an additional period of time, esp. extending allowance for a project etc. **b** permission for the sale of alcoholic drinks until later than usual, granted to licensed premises on special occasions. **7** extramural instruction by a university or college (*extension course*). **8** extent, range. **9** *Logic* a group of things denoted by a term. □□ **extensional** adj. [ME f. LL *extensio* (as EXTEND)]

extensive /ɪk'stensɪv/ adj. **1** covering a large area in space or time. **2** having a wide scope; far-reaching, comprehensive (*an extensive knowledge of music*). **3** *Agriculture* involving cultivation from a large area, with a minimum of special resources (cf. INTENSIVE). □□ **extensively** adv. **extensiveness** n. [F *extensif* -*ive* or LL *extensivus* (as EXTENSION)]

extensometer /ˌeksten'sɒmɪtə(r)/ n. **1** an instrument for measuring deformation of metal under stress. **2** an instrument using such deformation to record elastic strains in other materials. [L *extensus* (as EXTEND) + -METER]

extensor /ɪk'stensə(r)/ n. (in full **extensor muscle**) *Anat.* a muscle that extends or straightens out part of the body (cf. FLEXOR). [mod.L (as EXTEND)]

extent /ɪk'stent/ n. **1** the space over which a thing extends. **2** the width or limits of application; scope (*to a great extent; to the full extent of their power*). [ME f. AF *extente* f. med.L *extenta* past part. of L *extendere*: see EXTEND]

extenuate /ɪk'stenjʊˌeɪt/ v.tr. (often as **extenuating** adj.) lessen the seeming seriousness of (guilt or an offence) by reference to some mitigating factor. □□ **extenuatingly** adv. **extenuation** /-'eɪʃ(ə)n/ n. **extenuatory** /-jʊətərɪ/ adj. [L *extenuare extenuat-* (as EX-[1], *tenuis* thin)]

exterior /ɪk'stɪərɪə(r)/ adj. & n. —adj. **1 a** of or on the outer side (opp. INTERIOR). **b** (foll. by *to*) situated on the outside of (a building etc.). **c** coming from outside. **2** *Cinematog.* outdoor. —n. **1** the outward aspect or surface of a building etc. **2** the outward or apparent behaviour or demeanour of a person. **3** *Cinematog.* an outdoor scene. □ **exterior angle** the angle between the side of a rectilinear figure and the adjacent side extended outward. □□ **exteriority** /-'ɒrɪtɪ/ n. **exteriorize** v.tr. (also **-ise**). **exteriorly** adv. [L, compar. of *exterus* outside]

exterminate /ɪk'stɜːmɪˌneɪt/ v.tr. **1** destroy utterly (esp. something living). **2** get rid of; eliminate (a pest, disease, etc.). □□ **extermination** /-'neɪʃ(ə)n/ n. **exterminator** n. **exterminatory** /-nətərɪ/ adj. [L *exterminare exterminat-* (as EX-[1], *terminus* boundary)]

external /ɪk'stɜːn(ə)l/ adj. & n. —adj. **1 a** of or situated on the outside or visible part (opp. INTERNAL). **b** coming or derived from the outside or an outside source. **2** relating to a country's foreign affairs. **3** outside the conscious subject (*the external world*). **4** (of medicine etc.) for use on the outside of the body. **5** for or concerning students taking the examinations of a university without attending it. —n. (in *pl.*) **1** the outward features or aspect. **2** external circumstances. **3** inessentials. □ **external evidence** evidence derived from a source independent of the thing discussed. □□ **externality** /ˌekstɜː'nælɪtɪ/ n. (*pl.* **-ies**). **externally** adv. [med.L f. L *externus* f. *exterus* outside]

externalize /ɪk'stɜːnəˌlaɪz/ v.tr. (also **-ise**) give or attribute external existence to. □□ **externalization** /-'zeɪʃ(ə)n/ n.

exteroceptive /ˌekstərəʊ'septɪv/ adj. *Biol.* relating to stimuli produced outside an organism. [irreg. f. L *externus* exterior + RECEPTIVE]

exterritorial /ˌeksterɪ'tɔːrɪəl/ adj. = EXTRATERRITORIAL. □□ **exterritoriality** /-'ælɪtɪ/ n.

extinct /ɪk'stɪŋkt/ adj. **1** (of a family, class, or species) that has died out. **2 a** (of fire etc.) no longer burning. **b** (of a volcano) that no longer erupts. **3** (of life, hope, etc.) terminated, quenched. **4** (of an office etc.) obsolete. **5** (of a title of nobility) having no qualified claimant. [ME f. L *exstinguere exstinct-* (as EX-[1], *stinguere* quench)]

extinction /ɪk'stɪŋkʃ(ə)n/ n. **1** the act of making extinct; the state of being or process of becoming extinct. **2** the act of extinguishing; the state of being extinguished. **3** total destruction or annihilation. **4** the wiping out of a debt. **5** *Physics* a reduction in the intensity of radiation by absorption, scattering, etc. □□ **extinctive** adj. [L *extinctio* (as EXTINCT)]

extinguish /ɪk'stɪŋgwɪʃ/ v.tr. **1** cause (a flame, light, etc.) to die out; put out. **2** make extinct; annihilate, destroy (*a programme to extinguish disease*). **3** put an end to; terminate; obscure utterly (a feeling, quality, etc.). **4 a** abolish; wipe out (a debt). **b** *Law* render void. **5** *colloq.* reduce to silence (*the argument extinguished the opposition*). □□ **extinguishable** adj. **extinguishment** n. [irreg. f. L *extinguere* (as EXTINCT): cf. *distinguish*]

extinguisher /ɪk'stɪŋgwɪʃə(r)/ n. a person or thing that extinguishes, esp. = *fire extinguisher*.

extirpate /'ekstəˌpeɪt/ v.tr. root out; destroy completely. □□ **extirpation** /-'peɪʃ(ə)n/ n. **extirpator** n. [L *exstirpare exstirpat-* (as EX-[1], *stirps* stem)]

extol /ɪk'stəʊl, ɪk'stɒl/ v.tr. (**extolled**, **extolling**) praise enthusiastically. □□ **extoller** n. **extolment** n. [L *extollere* (as EX-[1], *tollere* raise)]

extort /ɪk'stɔːt/ v.tr. obtain by force, threats, persistent demands, etc. □□ **extorter** n. **extortive** adj. [L *extorquēre extort-* (as EX-[1], *torquēre* twist)]

extortion /ɪk'stɔːʃ(ə)n/ n. **1** the act or an instance of extorting, esp. money. **2** illegal exaction. □□ **extortioner** n. **extortionist** n. [ME f. LL *extortio* (as EXTORT)]

extortionate /ɪk'stɔːʃənət/ adj. **1** (of a price etc.) exorbitant. **2** using or given to extortion (*extortionate methods*). □□ **extortionately** adv.

extra /'ekstrə/ adj., adv., & n. —adj. additional; more than is usual or necessary or expected. —adv. **1** more than usually. **2** additionally (*was charged extra*). —n. **1** an extra thing. **2** a thing for which an extra charge is made. **3** a person engaged temporarily to fill out a scene in a film or play, esp. as one of a crowd. **4** a special issue of a newspaper etc. **5** *Cricket* a run scored other than from a hit with the bat. □ **extra cover** *Cricket* **1** a fielding position on a line between cover-point and mid-off, but beyond these. **2** a fielder at this position. **extra size** outsize. **extra time** *Sport* a further period of play at the end of a match when the scores are equal. [prob. a shortening of EXTRAORDINARY]

extra- /'ekstrə/ comb. form **1** outside, beyond (*extragalactic*). **2** beyond the scope of (*extracurricular*). [med.L f. L *extra* outside]

extracellular /ˌekstrə'seljʊlə(r)/ adj. situated or taking place outside a cell or cells.

extract v. & n. —v.tr. /ɪk'strækt/ **1** remove or take out, esp. by effort or force (anything firmly rooted). **2** obtain (money, an admission, etc.) with difficulty or against a person's will. **3** obtain (a natural resource) from the earth. **4** select or reproduce for quotation or performance (a passage of writing, music, etc.). **5** obtain (juice etc.) by suction, pressure, distillation, etc. **6** derive (pleasure etc.). **7** *Math.* find (the root of a number). **8** *archaic* deduce (a principle etc.). —n. /'ekstrækt/ **1** a short passage taken from a book, piece of music, etc.; an excerpt. **2** a preparation containing the active principle of a substance in concentrated form (*malt extract*). □□ **extractable** adj. **extractability** /-'bɪlɪtɪ/ n. [L *extrahere extract-* (as EX-[1], *trahere* draw)]

extraction /ɪk'strækʃ(ə)n/ n. **1** the act or an instance of extracting; the process of being extracted. **2** the removal of a tooth. **3** origin, lineage, descent (*of Indian extraction*). [ME f. F f. LL *extractio -onis* (as EXTRACT)]

extractive /ık'stræktıv/ *adj.* of or involving extraction, esp. extensive extracting of natural resources without provision for their renewal.

extractor /ık'stræktə(r)/ *n.* **1** a person or machine that extracts. **2** (*attrib.*) (of a device) that extracts bad air etc. or ventilates a room (*extractor fan*; *extractor hood*).

extracurricular /ˌekstrəkə'rıkjʊlə(r)/ *adj.* (of a subject of study) not included in the normal curriculum.

extraditable /'ekstrəˌdaıtəb(ə)l/ *adj.* **1** liable to extradition. **2** (of a crime) warranting extradition.

extradite /'ekstrəˌdaıt/ *v.tr.* hand over (a person accused or convicted of a crime) to the foreign State etc. in which the crime was committed.

extradition /ˌekstrə'dıʃ(ə)n/ *n.* **1** the extraditing of a person accused or convicted of a crime. **2** *Psychol.* the localizing of a sensation at a distance from the centre of sensation.

extrados /ek'streıdɒs/ *n. Archit.* the upper or outer curve of an arch (opp. INTRADOS). [EXTRA- + *dos* back f. L *dorsum*]

extragalactic /ˌekstrəgə'læktık/ *adj.* occurring or existing outside the Galaxy.

extrajudicial /ˌekstrədʒu:'dıʃ(ə)l/ *adj.* **1** not legally authorized. **2** (of a confession) not made in court. □□ **extrajudicially** *adv.*

extramarital /ˌekstrə'mærıt(ə)l/ *adj.* (esp. of sexual relations) occurring outside marriage. □□ **extramaritally** *adv.*

extramundane /ˌekstrə'mʌndeın/ *adj.* outside or beyond the physical world.

extramural /ˌekstrə'mjʊər(ə)l/ *adj.* & *n.* —*adj.* **1** taught or conducted off the premises of a university, college, or school. **2** additional to normal teaching or studies, esp. for non-resident students. **3** outside the walls or boundaries of a town or city. —*n.* an extramural lesson, course, etc. □□ **extramurally** *adv.* [L *extra muros* outside the walls]

extraneous /ık'streınıəs/ *adj.* **1** of external origin. **2** (often foll. by *to*) **a** separate from the object to which it is attached etc. **b** external to; irrelevant or unrelated to. □□ **extraneously** *adv.* **extraneousness** *n.* [L *extraneus*]

extraordinary /ık'strɔ:dınərı, ˌekstrə'ɔ:dınərı/ *adj.* **1** unusual or remarkable; out of the usual course. **2** unusually great (*an extraordinary talent*). **3 a** (of an official etc.) additional; specially employed (*envoy extraordinary*). **b** (of a meeting) specially convened. □□ **extraordinarily** *adv.* **extraordinariness** *n.* [L *extraordinarius* f. *extra ordinem* outside the usual order]

extrapolate /ık'stræpəˌleıt/ *v.tr.* (also *absol.*) **1** *Math.* & *Philos.* **a** calculate approximately from known values, data, etc. (others which lie outside the range of those known). **b** calculate on the basis of (known facts) to estimate unknown facts, esp. extend (a curve) on a graph. **2** infer more widely from a limited range of known facts. □□ **extrapolation** /-'leıʃ(ə)n/ *n.* **extrapolative** /-lətıv/ *adj.* **extrapolator** *n.* [EXTRA- + INTERPOLATE]

extrasensory /ˌekstrə'sensərı/ *adj.* regarded as derived by means other than the known senses, e.g. by telepathy, clairvoyance, etc. □ **extrasensory perception** a person's supposed faculty of perceiving by such means.

extraterrestrial /ˌekstrətı'restrıəl/ *adj.* & *n.* —*adj.* **1** outside the earth or its atmosphere. **2** (in science fiction) from outer space. —*n.* (in science fiction) a being from outer space.

extraterritorial /ˌekstrəˌterı'tɔ:rıəl/ *adj.* **1** situated or (of laws etc.) valid outside a country's territory. **2** (of an ambassador etc.) free from the jurisdiction of the territory of residence. □□ **extraterritoriality** /-'ælıtı/ *n.* [L *extra territorium* outside the territory]

extravagance /ık'strævəgəns/ *n.* **1** excessive spending or use of resources; being extravagant. **2** an instance or item of this. □□ **extravagancy** *n.* (*pl.* **-ies**). [F (as EXTRAVAGANT)]

extravagant /ık'strævəgənt/ *adj.* **1** spending (esp. money) excessively; immoderate or wasteful in use of resources. **2** exorbitant; costing much. **3** exceeding normal restraint or sense; unreasonable, absurd (*extravagant claims*). □□ **extravagantly** *adv.* [ME f. med.L *extravagari* (as EXTRA-, *vagari* wander)]

extravaganza /ık,strævə'gænzə/ *n.* **1** a fanciful literary, musical, or dramatic composition. **2** a spectacular theatrical or television production, esp. of light entertainment. [It. *estravaganza* extravagance]

extravasate /ık'strævə,seıt/ *v.* **1** *tr.* force out (a fluid, esp. blood) from its proper vessel. **2** *intr.* (of blood, lava, etc.) flow out. □□ **extravasation** /-'seıʃ(ə)n/ *n.* [L *extra* outside + *vas* vessel]

extravehicular /ˌekstrəvi:'hıkjʊlə(r)/ *adj.* outside a vehicle, esp. a spacecraft.

extrema *pl.* of EXTREMUM.

extreme /ık'stri:m/ *adj.* & *n.* —*adj.* **1** reaching a high or the highest degree; exceedingly great or intense (*extreme old age*; *in extreme danger*). **2 a** severe, stringent; lacking restraint or moderation (*take extreme measures*; *an extreme reaction*). **b** (of a person, opinion, etc.) going to great lengths; advocating immoderate measures. **3** outermost; furthest from the centre; situated at either end (*the extreme edge*). **4** *Polit.* on the far left or right of a party. **5** utmost; last. —*n.* **1** (often in *pl.*) one or other of two things as remote as or as different as possible. **2** a thing at either end of anything. **3** the highest degree of anything. **4** *Math.* the first or the last term of a ratio or series. **5** *Logic* the subject or predicate in a proposition; the major or the minor term in a syllogism. □ **extreme unction** the last rites in the Roman Catholic and Orthodox Churches. **go to extremes** take an extreme course of action. **go to the other extreme** take a diametrically opposite course of action. **in the extreme** to an extreme degree. □□ **extremely** *adv.* **extremeness** *n.* [ME f. OF f. L *extremus* superl. of *exterus* outward]

extremist /ık'stri:mıst/ *n.* (also *attrib.*) a person who holds extreme or fanatical political or religious views and esp. resorts to or advocates extreme action. □□ **extremism** *n.*

extremity /ık'stremıtı/ *n.* (*pl.* **-ies**) **1** the extreme point; the very end. **2** (in *pl.*) the hands and feet. **3** a condition of extreme adversity or difficulty. [ME f. OF *extremité* or L *extremitas* (as EXTREME)]

extremum /ek'stri:məm/ *n.* (*pl.* **extremums** or **extrema** /-mə/) *Math.* the maximum or minimum value of a function. □□ **extremal** *adj.* [L, neut. of *extremus* EXTREME]

extricate /'ekstrı,keıt/ *v.tr.* (often foll. by *from*) free or disentangle from a constraint or difficulty. □□ **extricable** *adj.* **extrication** /-'keıʃ(ə)n/ *n.* [L *extricat-* (as EX-¹, *tricae* perplexities)]

extrinsic /ek'strınsık/ *adj.* **1** not inherent or intrinsic; not essential (opp. INTRINSIC). **2** (often foll. by *to*) extraneous; lying outside; not belonging (to). **3** originating or operating from without. □□ **extrinsically** *adv.* [LL *extrinsicus* outward f. L *extrinsecus* (adv.) f. *exter* outside + *secus* beside]

extrovert /'ekstrə,vɜ:t/ *n.* & *adj.* —*n.* **1** *Psychol.* a person predominantly concerned with external things or objective considerations. **2** an outgoing or sociable person. —*adj.* typical or characteristic of an extrovert. □□ **extroversion** /-'vɜ:ʃ(ə)n/ *n.* **extroverted** *adj.* [*extro-* = EXTRA- (after *intro-*) + L *vertere* turn]

extrude /ık'stru:d/ *v.tr.* **1** (foll. by *from*) thrust or force out. **2** shape metal, plastics, etc. by forcing them through a die. □□ **extrusion** /-ʒ(ə)n/ *n.* **extrusile** /-saıl/ *adj.* **extrusive** /-sıv/ *adj.* [L *extrudere extrus-* (as EX-¹, *trudere* thrust)]

au how eı day əʊ no eə hair ıə near ɔı boy ʊə poor aıə fire aʊə sour (*see over for consonants*)

exuberant /ɪɡˈzjuːbərənt/ adj. **1** lively, high-spirited. **2** (of a plant etc.) prolific; growing copiously. **3** (of feelings etc.) abounding, lavish, effusive. □□ **exuberance** n. **exuberantly** adv. [F exubérant f. L exuberare (as EX-¹, uberare be fruitful f. uber fertile)]

exuberate /ɪɡˈzjuːbəˌreɪt/ v.intr. be exuberant.

exude /ɪɡˈzjuːd/ v. **1** tr. & intr. (of a liquid, moisture, etc.) escape or cause to escape gradually; ooze out; give off. **2** tr. emit (a smell). **3** tr. display (an emotion etc.) freely or abundantly (exuded displeasure). □□ **exudate** /ˈeɡzjʊˌdeɪt/ n. **exudation** /-ˈdeɪʃ(ə)n/ n. **exudative** /ɪɡˈzjuːdətɪv/ adj. [L exsudare (as EX-¹, sudare sweat)]

exult /ɪɡˈzʌlt/ v.intr. (often foll. by at, in, over, or to + infin.) **1** be greatly joyful. **2** (often foll. by over) have a feeling of triumph (over a person). □□ **exultancy** n. **exultation** /-ˈteɪʃ(ə)n/ n. **exultant** adj. **exultantly** adv. **exultingly** adv. [L exsultare (as EX-¹, saltare frequent. of salire salt- leap)]

exurb /ˈeksɜːb/ n. a district outside a city or town, esp. a prosperous area beyond the suburbs. □□ **exurban** /ekˈsɜːbən/ adj. **exurbanite** /ekˈsɜːbəˌnaɪt/ n. [L ex out of + urbs city, or back-form. f. exurban (as EX-¹ + URBAN, after suburban)]

exurbia /ekˈsɜːbɪə/ n. the exurbs collectively; the region beyond the suburbs. [EX-¹, after suburbia]

exuviae /ɪɡˈzjuːvɪˌiː/ n.pl. (also treated as sing.) an animal's cast skin or covering. □□ **exuvial** adj. [L, = animal's skins, spoils of the enemy, f. exuere divest oneself of]

exuviate /ɪɡˈzjuːvɪˌeɪt/ v.tr. shed (a skin etc.). □□ **exuviation** /-ˈeɪʃ(ə)n/ n.

ex voto /eks ˈvəʊtəʊ/ n. (pl. -os) an offering made in pursuance of a vow. [L, = out of a vow]

-ey /ɪ/ suffix var. of -Y².

eyas /ˈaɪəs/ n. a young hawk, esp. one taken from the nest for training in falconry. [orig. nyas f. F niais ult. f. L nidus nest: for loss of n- cf. ADDER]

eye /aɪ/ n. & v. —n. **1 a** the organ of sight in man and other animals. **b** the light-detecting organ in some invertebrates. **2** the eye characterized by the colour of the iris (has blue eyes). **3** the region round the eye (eyes red from weeping). **4** a glass or plastic ball serving as an artificial eye (his eye fell out). **5** (in sing. or pl.) sight; the faculty of sight (demonstrate to the eye; need perfect eyes to be a pilot). **6** a particular visual faculty or talent; visual appreciation (a straight eye; cast an expert eye over). **7** (in sing. or pl.) a look, gaze, or glance, esp. as indicating the disposition of the viewer (a friendly eye). **8** mental awareness; consciousness. **9** a person or animal etc. that sees on behalf of another. **10 a** = electric eye. **b** = private eye. **11** a thing like an eye, esp.: **a** a spot on a peacock's tail (cf. EYELET n. 3). **b** the leaf bud of a potato. **12** the centre of something circular, e.g. a flower or target. **13** the relatively calm region at the centre of a storm or hurricane. **14** an aperture in an implement, esp. a needle, for the insertion of something, e.g. thread. **15** a ring or loop for a bolt or hook etc. to pass through. —v.tr. (**eyes, eyed, eyeing** or **eying**) watch or observe closely, esp. admiringly or with curiosity or suspicion. □**all eyes 1** watching intently. **2** general attention (all eyes were on us). **before one's** (or **one's very**) **eyes** right in front of one. **do a person in the eye** colloq. defraud or thwart a person. **eye-bolt** a bolt or bar with an eye at the end for a hook etc. **eye-catching** colloq. striking, attractive. **eye contact** looking directly into another person's eyes. **an eye for an eye** retaliation in kind (Exodus 21:24). **eye language** the process of communication by the expression of the eyes. **eye-level** the level seen by the eyes looking horizontally (eye-level grill). **eye-liner** a cosmetic applied as a line round the eye. **eye mask 1** a covering of soft material saturated with a lotion for refreshing the eyes. **2** a covering for the eyes. **eye-opener** colloq. **1** an enlightening experience; an unexpected revelation. **2** US an alcoholic drink taken on waking up. **eye-rhyme** a correspondence of words in spelling but not in pronunciation (e.g. love and move). **eyes front** (or **left** or **right**) Mil. a command to turn the head in the direction stated. **eye-shade** a device to protect the eyes, esp. from strong light. **eye-shadow** a coloured cosmetic applied to the skin round the eyes. **eye-spot 1 a** a light-sensitive area on the bodies of some invertebrate animals, e.g. flatworms, starfish, etc.; an ocellus. **b** Bot. an area of light-sensitive pigment found in some algae etc. **2** any of several fungus diseases of plants characterized by yellowish oval spots on the leaves and stems. **eye-stalk** Zool. a movable stalk carrying the eye, esp. in crabs, shrimps, etc. **eye strain** fatigue of the (internal or external) muscles of the eye. **eye-tooth** a canine tooth just under or next to the eye, esp. in the upper jaw. **eye-worm** a nematode worm, Loa loa, parasitic on man and other primates in Central and West Africa. **get** (or **keep**) **one's eye in** Sport accustom oneself (or keep oneself accustomed) to the conditions of play so as to judge speed, distance, etc. **have an eye for** be capable of perceiving or appreciating. **have one's eye on** wish or plan to procure. **have eyes for** be interested in; wish to acquire. **have an eye to** have as one's objective; prudently consider. **hit a person in the eye** (or **between the eyes**) colloq. be very obvious or impressive. **keep an eye on 1** pay attention to. **2** look after; take care of. **keep an eye open** (or **out**) (often foll. by for) watch carefully. **keep one's eyes open** (or **peeled** or **skinned**) watch out; be on the alert. **lower one's eyes** look modestly or sheepishly down or away. **make eyes** (or **sheep's eyes**) (foll. by at) look amorously or flirtatiously at. **my** (or **all my**) **eye** sl. nonsense. **one in the eye** (foll. by for) a disappointment or setback. **open a person's eyes** be enlightening or revealing to a person. **raise one's eyes** look upwards. **see eye to eye** (often foll. by with) be in full agreement. **set eyes on** catch sight of. **take one's eyes off** (usu. in neg.) stop watching; stop paying attention to. **under the eye of** under the supervision or observation of. **up to the** (or **one's**) **eyes in 1** deeply engaged or involved in; inundated with (up to the eyes in work). **2** to the utmost limit (mortgaged up to the eyes). **with one's eyes open** deliberately; with full awareness. **with one's eyes shut** (or **closed**) **1** easily; with little effort. **2** without awareness; unobservant (goes around with his eyes shut). **with an eye to** with a view to; prudently considering. **with a friendly** (or **jealous** etc.) **eye** with a feeling of friendship, jealousy, etc. **with one eye on** directing one's attention partly to. **with one eye shut** colloq. easily; with little effort (could do this with one eye shut). □□ **eyed** adj. (also in comb.). **eyeless** adj. [OE ēage f. Gmc]

eyeball /ˈaɪbɔːl/ n. & v. —n. the ball of the eye within the lids and socket. —v. US sl. **1** tr. look or stare at. **2** intr. look or stare. □**eyeball to eyeball** colloq. confronting closely. **to** (or **up to**) **the eyeballs** colloq. completely (permeated, soaked, etc.).

eyebath /ˈaɪbɑːθ/ n. (also **eyecup** /ˈaɪkʌp/) a small glass or vessel for applying lotion etc. to the eye.

eyeblack /ˈaɪblæk/ n. = MASCARA.

eyebright /ˈaɪbraɪt/ n. any plant of the genus Euphrasia, formerly used as a remedy for weak eyes.

eyebrow /ˈaɪbraʊ/ n. the line of hair growing on the ridge above the eye-socket. □**raise one's eyebrows** show surprise, disbelief, or mild disapproval.

eyeful /ˈaɪfʊl/ n. (pl. **-fuls**) colloq. **1** a long steady look. **2** a visually striking person or thing. **3** anything thrown or blown into the eye.

eyeglass /ˈaɪɡlɑːs/ n. **1 a** a lens for correcting or assisting defective sight. **b** (in pl.) a pair of these held in the hand or kept in position on the nose by means of a frame or a spring. **2** a small glass vessel for applying lotion etc. to the eye.

eyehole /'aɪhəʊl/ n. a hole to look through.

eyelash /'aɪlæʃ/ n. each of the hairs growing on the edges of the eyelids. □**by an eyelash** by a very small margin.

eyelet /'aɪlɪt/ n. & v. —n. **1** a small hole in paper, leather, cloth, etc., for string or rope etc. to pass through. **2** a metal ring reinforcement for this. **3** a small eye, esp. the ocellus on a butterfly's wing (cf. EYE n. 11a). **4** a form of decoration in embroidery. **5** a small hole for observation, shooting through, etc. —v.tr. (**eyeleted**, **eyeleting**) provide with eyelets. [ME f. OF *oillet* dimin. of *oil* eye f. L *oculus*]

eyelid /'aɪlɪd/ n. the upper or lower fold of skin closing to cover the eye.

eyepiece /'aɪpiːs/ n. the lens or lenses to which the eye is applied at the end of a microscope, telescope, etc.

eyeshot /'aɪʃɒt/ n. seeing-distance (*out of eyeshot*).

eyesight /'aɪsaɪt/ n. the faculty or power of seeing.

eyesore /'aɪsɔː(r)/ n. a visually offensive or ugly thing, esp. a building.

Eyetie /'aɪtaɪ/ n. & adj. sl. offens. Italian. [joc. pronunc. of *Italian*]

eyewash /'aɪwɒʃ/ n. **1** lotion for the eye. **2** sl. nonsense, bunkum; pretentious or insincere talk.

eyewitness /'aɪˌwɪtnɪs/ n. a person who has personally seen a thing done or happen and can give evidence of it.

eyot var. of AIT.

eyra /'eərə/ n. Zool. a red form of jaguarundi. [Tupi (e)irara]

eyrie /'aɪrɪ, 'ɪərɪ, 'ɜːrɪ/ n. (also **aerie**) **1** a nest of a bird of prey, esp. an eagle, built high up. **2** a house etc. perched high up. [med.L *aeria*, *aerea*, etc., prob. f. OF *aire* lair ult. f. L *agrum* piece of ground]

Ezek. abbr. Ezekiel (Old Testament).

F

F *abbr. Electr.* faraday.

F^1 /ef/ *n.* (also **f**) (*pl.* **Fs** or **F's**) **1** the sixth letter of the alphabet. **2** *Mus.* the fourth note of the diatonic scale of C major.

F^2 *abbr.* (also **F.**) **1** Fahrenheit. **2** farad(s). **3** female. **4** fine (pencil-lead). **5** *Biol.* filial generation (as F$_1$ for the first filial generation, F$_2$ for the second, etc.).

F^3 *symb. Chem.* the element fluorine.

f *abbr.* (also **f.**) **1** female. **2** feminine. **3** following page etc. **4** *Mus.* forte. **5** folio. **6** focal length (cf. F-NUMBER). **7** femto-. **8** filly. **9** foreign. **10** frequency.

FA *abbr.* **1** (in the UK) Football Association. **2** = FANNY ADAMS 1.

fa var. of FAH.

FAA *abbr.* Fleet Air Arm.

fab /fæb/ *adj. colloq.* fabulous, marvellous. [abbr.]

Fabian /'feɪbɪən/ *n. & adj.* —*n.* a member or supporter of the Fabian Society, an organization of socialists aiming at a gradual rather than revolutionary achievement of socialism. —*adj.* **1** relating to or characteristic of the Fabians. **2** employing a cautiously persistent and dilatory strategy to wear out an enemy (*Fabian tactics*). □□ **Fabianism** *n.* **Fabianist** *n.* [L *Fabianus* f. the name of Q. *Fabius* Maximus Cunctator (= delayer), Roman general of the 3rd c. BC, noted for cautious strategies]

fable /'feɪb(ə)l/ *n. & v.* —*n.* **1 a** a story, esp. a supernatural one, not based on fact. **b** a tale, esp. with animals as characters, conveying a moral. **2** (*collect.*) myths and legendary tales (*in fable*). **3 a** a false statement; a lie. **b** a thing only supposed to exist. —*v.* **1** *intr.* tell fictitious tales. **2** *tr.* describe fictitiously. **3** *tr.* (as **fabled** *adj.*) celebrated in fable; famous, legendary. □□ **fabler** /'feɪblə(r)/ *n.* [ME f. OF *fabler* f. L *fabulari* f. *fabula* discourse f. *fari* speak]

fabliau /'fæblɪəʊ/ *n.* (*pl.* **fabliaux** /-əʊz/) a metrical tale in early French poetry, often coarsely humorous. [F f. OF dialect *fabliaux*, *-ax* pl. of *fablel* dimin. (as FABLE)]

fabric /'fæbrɪk/ *n.* **1 a** a woven material; a textile. **b** other material resembling woven cloth. **2** a structure or framework, esp. the walls, floor, and roof of a building. **3** (in abstract senses) the essential structure or essence of a thing (*the fabric of society*). [ME f. F *fabrique* f. L *fabrica* f. *faber* metal-worker etc.]

fabricate /'fæbrɪˌkeɪt/ *v.tr.* **1** construct or manufacture, esp. from prepared components. **2** invent or concoct (a story, evidence, etc.). **3** forge (a document). □□ **fabrication** /-'keɪʃ(ə)n/ *n.* **fabricator** *n.* [L *fabricare fabricat-* (as FABRIC)]

fabulist /'fæbjʊlɪst/ *n.* **1** a composer of fables. **2** a liar. [F *fabuliste* f. L *fabula*: see FABLE]

fabulous /'fæbjʊləs/ *adj.* **1** incredible, exaggerated, absurd (*fabulous wealth*). **2** *colloq.* marvellous (*looking fabulous*). **3 a** celebrated in fable. **b** legendary, mythical. □□ **fabulosity** /-'lɒsɪtɪ/ *n.* **fabulously** *adv.* **fabulousness** *n.* [F *fabuleux* or L *fabulosus* (as FABLE)]

façade /fə'sɑːd/ *n.* **1** the face of a building, esp. its principal front. **2** an outward appearance or front, esp. a deceptive one. [F (as FACE)]

face /feɪs/ *n. & v.* —*n.* **1** the front of the head from the forehead to the chin. **2** the expression of the facial features (*had a happy face*). **3** composure, coolness, effrontery. **4** the surface of a thing, esp. as regarded or approached, esp.: **a** the visible part of a celestial body. **b** a side of a mountain etc. (*the north face*). **c** the (usu. vertical) surface of a coal-seam. **d** *Geom.* each surface of a solid. **e** the façade of a building. **f** the plate of a clock or watch bearing the digits, hands, etc. **5 a** the functional or working side of a tool etc. **b** the distinctive side of a playing card. **c** the obverse of a coin. **6** = TYPEFACE. **7** the outward appearance or aspect (*the unacceptable face of capitalism*). **8** a person, esp. conveying some quality or association (*a face from the past; some young faces for a change*). —*v.* **1** *tr. & intr.* look or be positioned towards or in a certain direction (*face towards the window; facing the window; the room faces north*). **2** *tr.* be opposite (*facing page 20*). **3** *tr.* **a** (often foll. by *out*) meet resolutely or defiantly; confront (*face one's critics*). **b** not shrink from (*face the facts*). **4** *tr.* present itself to; confront (*the problem that faces us; faces us with a problem*). **5** *tr.* **a** cover the surface of a thing with a coating, extra layer, etc. **b** put a facing on (a garment). **6** *intr. & tr.* turn or cause to turn in a certain direction. □ **face-ache 1** neuralgia. **2** *sl.* a mournful-looking person. **face-card** = *court-card*. **face-cloth 1** a cloth for washing one's face. **2** a smooth-surfaced woollen cloth. **face-cream** a cosmetic cream applied to the face to improve the complexion. **face down** (or **downwards**) with the face or surface turned towards the ground, floor, etc. **face facts** (or **the facts**) recognize the truth. **face-flannel** = *face-cloth* 1. **face-lift 1** (also **face-lifting**) cosmetic surgery to remove wrinkles etc. by tightening the skin of the face. **2** a procedure to improve the appearance of a thing. **face the music** *colloq.* put up with or stand up to unpleasant consequences, esp. criticism. **face-pack** a preparation beneficial to the complexion, spread over the face and removed when dry. **face-powder** a cosmetic powder for reducing the shine on the face. **face-saving** preserving one's reputation, credibility, etc. **face to face** (often foll. by *with*) facing; confronting each other. **face up** (or **upwards**) with the face or surface turned upwards to view. **face up to** accept bravely; confront; stand up to. **face value 1** the nominal value as printed or stamped on money. **2** the superficial appearance or implication of a thing. **face-worker** a miner who works at the coalface. **have the face** be shameless enough. **in one's** (or **the**) **face 1** straight against one; as one approaches. **2** confronting. **in face** (or **the face**) **of 1** despite. **2** confronted by. **let's face it** *colloq.* we must be honest or realistic about it. **on the face of it** as it would appear. **put a bold** (or **brave**) **face on it** accept difficulty etc. cheerfully or with courage. **put one's face on** *colloq.* apply make-up to one's face. **put a good face on** make (a matter) look well. **put a new face on** alter the aspect of. **save face** preserve esteem; avoid humiliation. **save a person's face** enable a person to save face; forbear from humiliating a person. **set one's face against** oppose or resist with determination. **to a person's face** openly in a person's presence. □□ **faced** *adj.* (also in *comb.*). **facing** *adj.* (also in *comb.*). [ME f. OF ult. f. L *facies*]

faceless /'feɪslɪs/ *adj.* **1** without identity; purposely not identifiable. **2** lacking character. **3** without a face. □□ **facelessly** *adv.* **facelessness** *n.*

facer /'feɪsə(r)/ *n. colloq.* **1** a sudden difficulty or obstacle. **2** a blow in the face.

facet /'fæsɪt/ *n.* **1** a particular aspect of a thing. **2** one side of a many-sided body, esp. of a cut gem. **3** one segment of a compound eye. □□ **faceted** *adj.* (also in *comb.*). [F *facette* dimin. (as FACE, -ETTE)]

facetiae /fə'siːʃɪˌiː/ *n.pl.* **1** pleasantries, witticisms. **2** (in bookselling) pornography. [L, pl. of *facetia* jest f. *facetus* witty]

facetious /fə'si:ʃəs/ adj. 1 characterized by flippant or inopportune humour. 2 (of a person) intending to be amusing, esp. inopportunely. □□ **facetiously** adv. **facetiousness** n. [F facétieux f. facétie f. L facetia jest]

facia var. of FASCIA.

facial /'feɪʃ(ə)l/ adj. & n. —adj. of or for the face. —n. a beauty treatment for the face. □□ **facially** adv. [med.L facialis (as FACE)]

-facient /'feɪʃ(ə)nt/ comb. form forming adjectives and nouns indicating an action or state produced (abortifacient). [from or after L -faciens -entis part. of facere make]

facies /'feɪʃiːz/ n. (pl. same) 1 Med. the appearance or facial expression of an individual. 2 Geol. the character of rock etc. expressed by its composition, fossil content, etc. [L, = FACE]

facile /'fæsaɪl/ adj. usu. derog. 1 easily achieved but of little value. 2 (of speech, writing, etc.) fluent, ready, glib. □□ **facilely** adv. **facileness** n. [F facile or L facilis f. facere do]

facilitate /fə'sɪlɪˌteɪt/ v.tr. make easy or less difficult or more easily achieved. □□ **facilitation** /-'teɪʃ(ə)n/ n. **facilitative** /-tətɪv/ adj. **facilitator** n. [F faciliter f. It. facilitare f. facile easy f. L facilis]

facility /fə'sɪlɪtɪ/ n. (pl. -ies) 1 ease; absence of difficulty. 2 fluency, dexterity, aptitude (facility of expression). 3 (esp. in pl.) an opportunity, the equipment, or the resources for doing something. 4 US a plant, installation, or establishment. [F facilité or L facilitas (as FACILE)]

facing /'feɪsɪŋ/ n. 1 a a layer of material covering part of a garment etc. for contrast or strength. b (in pl.) the cuffs, collar, etc., of a military jacket. 2 an outer layer covering the surface of a wall etc.

facsimile /fæk'sɪmɪlɪ/ n. & v. —n. 1 an exact copy, esp. of writing, printing, a picture, etc. (often attrib.: facsimile edition). 2 a production of an exact copy of a document etc. by electronic scanning and transmission of the resulting data (see also FAX). b a copy produced in this way. —v.tr. (**facsimiled**, **facsimileing**) make a facsimile of. □**in facsimile** as an exact copy. [mod.L f. L fac imper. of facere make + simile neut. of similis like]

fact /fækt/ n. 1 a thing that is known to have occurred, to exist, or to be true. 2 a datum of experience (often foll. by an explanatory clause or phrase: the fact that fire burns; the fact of my having seen them). 3 (usu. in pl.) an item of verified information; a piece of evidence. 4 truth, reality. 5 a thing assumed as the basis for argument or inference. □**before** (or **after**) **the fact** before (or after) the committing of a crime. **a fact of life** something that must be accepted. **facts and figures** precise details. **fact-sheet** a paper setting out relevant information. **the facts of life** information about sexual functions and practices. **in** (or **in point of**) **fact 1** in reality; as a matter of fact. **2** (in summarizing) in short. [L factum f. facere do]

factice /'fæktɪs/ n. Chem. a rubber-like substance obtained by vulcanizing unsaturated vegetable oils. [G Faktis f. L facticius FACTITIOUS]

faction[1] /'fækʃ(ə)n/ n. 1 a small organized dissentient group within a larger one, esp. in politics. 2 a state of dissension within an organization. [F f. L factio -onis f. facere fact- do, make]

faction[2] /'fækʃ(ə)n/ n. a book, film, etc., using real events as a basis for a fictional narrative or dramatization. [blend of FACT and FICTION]

-faction /'fækʃ(ə)n/ comb. form forming nouns of action from verbs in -fy (petrifaction; satisfaction). [from or after L -factio -factionis f. -facere do, make]

factional /'fækʃən(ə)l/ adj. 1 of or characterized by faction. 2 belonging to a faction. □□ **factionalism** n. **factionalize** v.tr. & intr. (also -ise). **factionally** adv. [FACTION[1]]

factious /'fækʃəs/ adj. of, characterized by, or inclined to faction. □□ **factiously** adv. **factiousness** n.

factitious /fæk'tɪʃəs/ adj. 1 specially contrived, not genuine (factitious value). 2 artificial, not natural (factitious joy). □□ **factitiously** adv. **factitiousness** n. [L facticius f. facere fact- do, make]

factitive /'fæktɪtɪv/ adj. Gram. (of a verb) having a sense of regarding or designating, and taking a complement as well as an object (e.g. appointed me captain). [mod.L factitivus, irreg. f. L factitare frequent. of facere fact- do, make]

factoid /'fæktɔɪd/ n. & adj. —n. an assumption or speculation that is reported and repeated so often that it becomes accepted as fact; a simulated or imagined fact. —adj. being or having the character of a factoid; containing factoids.

factor /'fæktə(r)/ n. & v. —n. 1 a circumstance, fact, or influence contributing to a result. 2 Math. a whole number etc. that when multiplied with another produces a given number or expression. 3 Biol. a gene etc. determining hereditary character. 4 (foll. by identifying number) Med. any of several substances in the blood contributing to coagulation (factor eight). 5 a a business agent; a merchant buying and selling on commission. b Sc. a land-agent or steward. c an agent or a deputy. 6 a company that buys a manufacturer's invoices and takes responsibility for collecting the payments due on them. —v.tr. 1 Math. resolve into factors or components. 2 tr. sell (one's receivable debts) to a factor. □**factor analysis** Statistics a process by which the relative importance of variables in the study of a sample is assessed by mathematical techniques. □□ **factorable** adj. [F facteur or L factor f. facere fact- do, make]

factorage /'fæktərɪdʒ/ n. commission or charges payable to a factor.

factorial /fæk'tɔːrɪəl/ n. & adj. Math. —n. 1 the product of a number and all the whole numbers below it (factorial four = 4 × 3 × 2 × 1). ¶ Symb.: ! (as in 4!). 2 the product of a series of factors in an arithmetical progression. —adj. of a factor or factorial. □□ **factorially** adv.

factorize /'fæktəˌraɪz/ v. (also -ise) Math. 1 tr. resolve into factors. 2 intr. be capable of resolution into factors. □□ **factorization** /-'zeɪʃ(ə)n/ n.

factory /'fæktərɪ/ n. (pl. -ies) 1 a building or buildings containing plant or equipment for manufacturing machinery or goods. 2 hist. a merchant company's foreign trading station. □**factory farm** a farm employing factory farming. **factory farming** a system of rearing livestock using industrial or intensive methods. **factory floor** workers in industry as distinct from management. **factory ship** Brit. a fishing ship with facilities for immediate processing of the catch. [Port. feitoria and LL factorium]

factotum /fæk'təʊtəm/ n. (pl. **factotums**) an employee who does all kinds of work. [med.L f. L fac imper. of facere do, make + totum neut. of totus whole]

factual /'fæktjʊəl/ adj. 1 based on or concerned with fact or facts. 2 actual, true. □□ **factuality** /-'ælɪtɪ/ n. **factually** adv. **factualness** n. [FACT, after actual]

factum /'fæktəm/ n. (pl. **factums** or **facta** /-tə/) Law 1 an act or deed. 2 a statement of the facts. [F f. L: see FACT]

facture /'fæktʃə(r)/ n. the quality of execution esp. of the surface of a painting. [ME f. OF f. L factura f. facere fact- do, make]

facula /'fækjʊlə/ n. (pl. **faculae** /-ˌliː/) Astron. a bright spot or streak on the sun. □□ **facular** adj. **faculous** adj. [L, dimin. of fax facis torch]

facultative /'fækəltətɪv/ adj. 1 Law enabling an act to take place. 2 that may occur. 3 Biol. not restricted to a particular function, mode of life, etc. 4 of a faculty. □□ **facultatively** adv. [F facultatif -ive (as FACULTY)]

faculty /'fækəltɪ/ n. (pl. -ies) 1 an aptitude or ability for a particular activity. 2 an inherent mental or physical power. **3 a** a group of university departments concerned with a major division of knowledge (*faculty of modern languages*). **b** *US* the staff of a university or college. **c** a branch of art or science; those qualified to teach it. **4** the members of a particular profession, esp. medicine. **5** authorization, esp. by a Church authority. □**Faculty of Advocates** *Law* the society constituting the Scottish Bar. [ME f. OF *faculté* f. L *facultas -tatis* f. *facilis* easy]

FAD *abbr.* flavin adenine dinucleotide.

fad /fæd/ *n.* **1** a craze. **2** a peculiar notion or idiosyncrasy. □□**faddish** *adj.* **faddishly** *adv.* **faddishness** *n.* **faddism** *n.* **faddist** *n.* [19th c. (orig. dial.): prob. f. *fidfad* f. FIDDLE-FADDLE]

faddy /ˈfædɪ/ *adj.* (**faddier, faddiest**) having arbitrary likes and dislikes, esp. about food. □□**faddily** *adv.* **faddiness** *n.*

fade /feɪd/ *v. & n.* —*v.* **1** *intr. & tr.* lose or cause to lose colour. **2** *intr.* lose freshness or strength; (of flowers etc.) droop, wither. **3** *intr.* **a** (of colour, light, etc.) disappear gradually; grow pale or dim. **b** (of sound) grow faint. **4** *intr.* (of a feeling etc.) diminish. **5** *intr.* (foll. by *away, out*) (of a person etc.) disappear or depart gradually. **6** *tr.* (foll. by *in, out*) *Cinematog. & Broadcasting* **a** cause (a picture) to come gradually in or out of view on a screen, or to merge into another shot. **b** make (the sound) more or less audible. **7** *intr.* (of a radio signal) vary irregularly in intensity. **8** *intr.* (of a brake) temporarily lose effectiveness. **9** *Golf* **a** *intr.* (of a ball) deviate from a straight course, esp. in a deliberate slice. **b** *tr.* cause (a ball) to fade. —*n.* the action or an instance of fading. □**do a fade** *sl.* depart. **fade away** *colloq.* languish, grow thin. **fade-in** *Cinematog. & Broadcasting* the action or an instance of fading in a picture or sound. **fade-out 1** *colloq.* disappearance, death. **2** *Cinematog. & Broadcasting* the action or an instance of fading out a picture or sound. □□**fadeless** *adj.* **fader** *n.* (in sense 6 of *v.*). [ME f. OF *fader* f. *fade* dull, insipid prob. ult. f. L *fatuus* silly + *vapidus* VAPID]

fadge /fædʒ/ *n. Austral. & NZ* **1** a limp package of wool. **2** a loosely packed wool bale. [16th-c. Engl. dial.: orig. uncert.]

faeces /ˈfiːsiːz/ *n.pl.* (*US* **feces**) waste matter discharged from the bowels. □□**faecal** /ˈfiːk(ə)l/ *adj.* [L, pl. of *faex* dregs]

faerie /ˈfeɪərɪ/ *n.* (also **faery**) *archaic* **1** Fairyland; the fairies esp. as represented by Spenser (*the Faerie Queene*). **2** (*attrib.*) visionary, fancied. [var. of FAIRY]

Faeroese /ˌfeərəʊˈiːz/ *adj. & n.* (also **Faroese**) —*adj.* of or relating to the Faeroes, an island group in the N. Atlantic between Norway and Iceland. —*n.* (*pl.* same) **1** a native of the Faeroes; a person of Faeroese descent. **2** the Norse language of this people.

faff /fæf/ *v. & n. Brit. colloq.* —*v.intr.* (often foll. by *about, around*) fuss, dither. —*n.* a fuss. [imit.]

fag[1] /fæg/ *n. & v.* —*n.* **1** esp. *Brit. colloq.* a piece of drudgery; a wearisome or unwelcome task. **2** *sl.* a cigarette. **3** *Brit.* (at public schools) a junior pupil who runs errands for a senior. —*v.* (**fagged, fagging**) **1 a** *tr.* (often foll. by *out*) tire out; exhaust. **b** *intr.* toil. **2** *intr. Brit.* (in public schools) act as a fag. **3** *tr. Naut.* (often foll. by *out*) fray (the end of a rope etc.). □**fag-end** *sl.* **1** *Brit.* a cigarette-end. **2** an inferior or useless remnant. [orig. unkn.: cf. FLAG[1]]

fag[2] /fæg/ *n. US sl.* often *offens.* a male homosexual. [abbr. of FAGGOT]

faggot /ˈfægət/ *n. & v.* (*US* **fagot**) —*n.* **1** (usu. in *pl.*) a ball or roll of seasoned chopped liver etc., baked or fried. **2** a bundle of sticks or twigs bound together as fuel. **3** a bundle of iron rods for heat treatment. **4** a bunch of herbs. **5** *sl. derog.* **a** an unpleasant woman. **b** *US* often *offens.* a male homosexual. —*v.tr.* (**faggoted, faggoting**) **1** bind in or make into faggots. **2** join by faggoting (see FAGGOTING). □□**faggoty** *adj.* [ME f. OF *fagot*, of uncert. orig.]

faggoting /ˈfægətɪŋ/ *n.* **1** embroidery in which

threads are fastened together like a faggot. **2** the joining of materials in a similar manner.

fagot *US* var. of FAGGOT.

fah /fɑː/ *n.* (also **fa**) *Mus.* **1** (in tonic sol-fa) the fourth note of a major scale. **2** the note F in the fixed-doh system. [ME *fa* f. L *famuli*: see GAMUT]

Fahr. *abbr.* Fahrenheit.

Fahrenheit /ˈfærənˌhaɪt/ *adj.* of or measured on a scale of temperature on which water freezes at 32° and boils at 212° under standard conditions. [G. *Fahrenheit*, Ger. physicist d. 1736]

faience /ˈfaɪɑ̃s/ *n.* decorated and glazed earthenware and porcelain, e.g. delft or majolica. [F *faïence* f. *Faenza* in Italy]

fail /feɪl/ *v. & n.* —*v.* **1** *intr.* not succeed (*failed in persuading; failed to qualify; tried but failed*). **2 a** *tr. & intr.* be unsuccessful in (an examination, test, interview, etc.); be rejected as a candidate. **b** *tr.* (of a commodity etc.) not pass (a test of quality). **c** *tr.* reject (a candidate etc.); adjudge unsuccessful. **3** *intr.* be unable to; neglect to; choose not to (*I fail to see the reason; he failed to appear*). **4** *tr.* disappoint; let down; not serve when needed. **5** *intr.* (of supplies, crops, etc.) be or become lacking or insufficient. **6** *intr.* become weaker; cease functioning; break down (*her health is failing; the engine has failed*). **7** *intr.* **a** (of an enterprise) collapse; come to nothing. **b** become bankrupt. —*n.* a failure in an examination or test. □**fail-safe** reverting to a safe condition in the event of a breakdown etc. **without fail** for certain, whatever happens. [ME f. OF *faillir* (v.), *fail(l)e* (n.) ult. f. L *fallere* deceive]

failed /feɪld/ *adj.* **1** unsuccessful; not good enough (*a failed actor*). **2** weak, deficient; broken down (*a failed crop; a failed battery*).

failing /ˈfeɪlɪŋ/ *n. & prep.* —*n.* a fault or shortcoming; a weakness, esp. in character. —*prep.* in default of; if not.

failure /ˈfeɪljə(r)/ *n.* **1** lack of success; failing. **2** an unsuccessful person, thing, or attempt. **3** non-performance, non-occurrence. **4** breaking down or ceasing to function (*heart failure; engine failure*). **5** running short of supply etc. **6** bankruptcy, collapse. [earlier *failer* f. AF, = OF *faillir* FAIL]

fain /feɪn/ *adj. & adv. archaic* —*predic.adj.* (foll. by *to* + infin.) **1** willing under the circumstances to. **2** left with no alternative but to. —*adv.* gladly (esp. *would fain*). [OE *fægen* f. Gmc]

fainéant /ˈfeɪneɪˌɑ̃/ *n. & adj.* —*n.* an idle or ineffective person. —*adj.* idle, inactive. [F f. *fait* does + *néant* nothing]

faint /feɪnt/ *adj., v., & n.* —*adj.* **1** indistinct, pale, dim; not clearly perceived. **2** (of a person) weak or giddy; inclined to faint. **3** slight, remote, inadequate (*a faint chance*). **4** feeble, half-hearted (*faint praise*). **5** timid (*a faint heart*). **6** (also **feint**) (of ruled paper) with inconspicuous lines to guide writing. —*v.intr.* **1** lose consciousness. **2** become faint. —*n.* a sudden loss of consciousness; fainting. □**faint-hearted** cowardly, timid. **faint-heartedly** in a faint-hearted manner. **faint-heartedness** cowardliness, timidity. **not have the faintest** *colloq.* have no idea. □□ **faintness** *n.* [ME f. OF, past part. of *faindre* FEIGN]

faintly /ˈfeɪntlɪ/ *adv.* **1** very slightly (*faintly amused*). **2** indistinctly, feebly.

fair[1] /feə(r)/ *adj., adv., n., & v.* —*adj.* **1** just, unbiased, equitable; in accordance with the rules. **2** blond; light or pale in colour or complexion. **3 a** of (only) moderate quality or amount; average. **b** considerable, satisfactory (*a fair chance of success*). **4** (of weather) fine and dry; (of the wind) favourable. **5** clean, clear, unblemished (*fair copy*). **6** beautiful, attractive. **7** *archaic* kind, gentle. **8 a** specious (*fair speeches*). **b** complimentary (*fair words*). **9** *Austral. & NZ* complete, unquestionable. —*adv.* **1** in a fair manner (*play fair*). **2** exactly, completely (*was hit fair on the jaw*). —*n.* **1** a fair thing. **2** *archaic* a beautiful woman. —*v.* **1** *tr.* make (the surface of a ship, aircraft, etc.) smooth and streamlined. **2** *intr.* *dial.* (of the weather) become fair. □**fair and square** *adv.* & *adj.* **1** exactly. **2** straightforward, honest, above-board. **fair crack of the whip** see CRACK. **a fair deal** equitable treatment. **fair dos** /duːz/ *colloq.* fair shares. **fair enough** *colloq.* that is reasonable or acceptable. **fair game** a thing or person one may legitimately pursue, exploit, etc. **fair-minded** just, impartial. **fair-mindedly** justly, impartially. **fair-mindedness** a sense of justice; impartiality. **fair name** a good reputation. **fair play** reasonable treatment or behaviour. **fair rent** the amount of rent which a tenant may reasonably be expected to pay according to established guidelines. **the fair sex** women. **fair's fair** *colloq.* all involved should act fairly. **fair-spoken** courteous. **a fair treat** *colloq.* a very enjoyable or attractive thing or person. **fair-weather friend** a friend or ally who is unreliable in times of difficulty. **for fair** *US sl.* completely. **in a fair way** to likely to. □□**fairish** *adj.* **fairness** *n.* [OE *fæger* f. Gmc]

fair[2] /feə(r)/ *n.* **1** a gathering of stalls, amusements, etc., for public (usu. outdoor) entertainment. **2** a periodical gathering for the sale of goods, often with entertainments. **3** an exhibition, esp. to promote particular products. [ME f. OF *feire* f. LL *feria* sing. f. L *feriae* holiday]

fairground /ˈfeəgraʊnd/ *n.* an outdoor area where a fair is held.

fairing[1] /ˈfeərɪŋ/ *n.* **1** a streamlining structure added to a ship, aircraft, vehicle, etc. **2** the process of streamlining. [FAIR[1] v. 1 + -ING[1]]

fairing[2] /ˈfeərɪŋ/ *n.* *Brit.* *archaic* a present bought at a fair.

Fair Isle /ˈfeəraɪl/ *n.* (also *attrib.*) a piece of knitwear knitted in a characteristic particoloured design. [*Fair Isle* in the Shetlands, where the design was first devised]

fairlead /ˈfeəliːd/ *n.* *Naut.* a device to guide rope etc., e.g. to prevent cutting or chafing.

fairly /ˈfeəlɪ/ *adv.* **1** in a fair manner; justly. **2** moderately, acceptably (*fairly good*). **3** to a noticeable degree (*fairly narrow*). **4** utterly, completely (*fairly beside himself*). **5** actually (*fairly jumped for joy*). □**fairly and squarely** = *fair and square* (see FAIR[1]).

fairwater /ˈfeəˌwɔːtə(r)/ *n.* a structure on a ship etc. assisting its passage through water.

fairway /ˈfeəweɪ/ *n.* **1** a navigable channel; a regular course or track of a ship. **2** the part of a golf-course between a tee and its green, kept free of rough grass.

fairy /ˈfeərɪ/ *n.* & *adj.* —*n.* (*pl.* -ies) **1** a small imaginary being with magical powers. **2** *sl.* *derog.* a male homosexual. —*adj.* of fairies, fairy-like, delicate, small. □**fairy cake** a small individual iced sponge cake. **fairy cycle** a small bicycle for a child. **fairy godmother** a benefactress. **fairy lights** small coloured lights esp. for outdoor decoration. **fairy ring** a ring of darker grass caused by fungi. **fairy story** (or **tale**) **1** a tale about fairies. **2** an incredible story; a fabrication. □□**fairy-like** *adj.* [ME f. OF *faerie* f. *fae* FAY]

fairyland /ˈfeərɪlænd/ *n.* **1** the imaginary home of fairies. **2** an enchanted region.

fait accompli /ˌfeɪt əˈkɒmpliː, əˈkɔ̃pliː/ *n.* a thing that has been done and is past arguing against or altering. [F]

faith /feɪθ/ *n.* **1** complete trust or confidence. **2** firm belief, esp. without logical proof. **3 a** a system of religious belief (*the Christian faith*). **b** belief in religious doctrines. **c** spiritual apprehension of divine truth apart from proof. **d** things believed or to be believed. **4** duty or commitment to fulfil a trust, promise, etc. (*keep faith*). **5** (*attrib.*) concerned with a supposed ability to cure by faith rather than treatment (*faith-healing*). □**bad faith** intent to deceive. **good faith** honesty or sincerity of intention. [ME f. AF *fed* f. OF *feid* f. L *fides*]

faithful /ˈfeɪθfʊl/ *adj.* **1** showing faith. **2** (often foll.

by *to*) loyal, trustworthy, constant. **3** accurate; true to fact (*a faithful account*). **4** (**the Faithful**) the believers in a religion, esp. Muslims and Christians. □□**faithfulness** *n.*

faithfully /ˈfeɪθfʊlɪ/ *adv.* in a faithful manner. □**yours faithfully** a formula for ending a business or formal letter.

faithless /ˈfeɪθlɪs/ *adj.* **1** false, unreliable, disloyal. **2** without religious faith. □□**faithlessly** *adv.* **faithlessness** *n.*

fake[1] /feɪk/ *n.*, *adj.*, & *v.* —*n.* **1** a thing or person that is not genuine. **2** a trick. —*adj.* counterfeit; not genuine. —*v.tr.* **1** make (a false thing) appear genuine; forge, counterfeit. **2** make a pretence of having (a feeling, illness, etc.). □□**faker** *n.* **fakery** *n.* [obs. *feak, feague* thrash f. G *fegen* sweep, thrash]

fake[2] /feɪk/ *n.* & *v.* *Naut.* —*n.* one round of a coil of rope. —*v.tr.* coil (rope). [ME: cf. Scottish *faik* fold]

fakir /ˈfeɪkɪə(r), fəˈkɪə(r)/ *n.* (also **faquir**) a Muslim or (rarely) Hindu religious mendicant or ascetic. [Arab. *faḳīr* needy man]

falafel var. of FELAFEL.

Falange /fæˈlændʒ/ *n.* the Fascist movement in Spain, founded in 1933. □□**Falangism** *n.* **Falangist** *n.* [Sp., = PHALANX]

falcate /ˈfælkeɪt/ *adj.* *Anat.* curved like a sickle. [L *falcatus* f. *falx falcis* sickle]

falchion /ˈfɔːltʃ(ə)n/ *n.* *hist.* a broad curved sword with a convex edge. [ME *fauchoun* f. OF *fauchon* ult. f. L *falx falcis* sickle]

falciform /ˈfælsɪfɔːm/ *adj.* *Anat.* curved like a sickle. [L *falx falcis* sickle]

falcon /ˈfɔːlkən, ˈfɒlkən/ *n.* **1** any diurnal bird of prey of the family Falconidae, having long pointed wings, and sometimes trained to hunt small game for sport. **2** (in falconry) a female falcon (cf. TERCEL). [ME f. OF *faucon* f. LL *falco -onis*, perh. f. L *falx* scythe or f. Gmc]

falconer /ˈfɔːlkənə(r), ˈfɒl-/ *n.* **1** a keeper and trainer of hawks. **2** a person who hunts with hawks. [ME f. AF *fauconer*, OF *fauconier* (as FALCON)]

falconet /ˈfɔːlkənɪt, ˈfɒl-/ *n.* **1** *hist.* a light cannon. **2** *Zool.* a small falcon. [sense 1 f. It. *falconetto* dimin. of *falcone* FALCON: sense 2 f. FALCON + -ET[1]]

falconry /ˈfɔːlkənrɪ, ˈfɒl-/ *n.* the breeding and training of hawks; the sport of hawking. [F *fauconnerie* (as FALCON)]

falderal /ˈfældəˌræl/ *n.* (also **folderol** /ˈfɒldəˌrɒl/) **1** a gewgaw or trifle. **2** a nonsensical refrain in a song. [perh. f. *falbala* trimming on a dress]

faldstool /ˈfɔːldstuːl/ *n.* **1** a bishop's backless folding chair. **2** *Brit.* a small movable desk for kneeling at prayer. [OE *fældestōl* f. med.L *faldistolium* f. WG (as FOLD[1], STOOL)]

fall /fɔːl/ *v.* & *n.* —*v.intr.* (*past* **fell** /fel/; *past part.* **fallen** /ˈfɔːlən/) **1 a** go or come down freely; descend rapidly from a higher to a lower level (*fell from the top floor; rain was falling*). **b** drop or be dropped (*supplies fell by parachute; the curtain fell*). **2 a** (often foll. by *over*) cease to stand; come suddenly to the ground from loss of balance etc. **b** collapse forwards or downwards esp. of one's own volition (*fell into my arms; fell over the chair*). **3** become detached and descend or disappear. **4** take a downward direction: **a** (of hair, clothing, etc.) hang down. **b** (of ground etc.) slope. **c** (foll. by *into*) (of a river etc.) discharge into. **5 a** find a lower level; sink lower. **b** subside, abate. **6** (of a barometer, thermometer, etc.) show a lower reading. **7** occur; become apparent or present (*darkness fell*). **8** decline, diminish (*demand is falling; standards have fallen*). **9 a** (of the face) show dismay or disappointment. **b** (of the eyes or a glance) look downwards. **10 a** lose power or status (*the government will fall*). **b** lose esteem, moral integrity, etc. **11** commit sin; yield to temptation. **12** take or have a particular direction or place (*his eye fell on me; the accent falls on the first syllable*). **13 a** find a place; be naturally divisible (*the subject falls into three parts*).

b (foll. by *under, within*) be classed among. **14** occur at a specified time (*Easter falls early this year*). **15** come by chance or duty (*it fell to me to answer*). **16 a** pass into a specified condition (*fall into decay; fell ill*). **b** become (*fall asleep*). **17 a** (of a position etc.) be overthrown or captured; succumb to attack. **b** be defeated; fail. **18** die (*fall in battle*). **19** (foll. by *on, upon*) **a** attack. **b** meet with. **c** embrace or embark on avidly. **20** (foll. by *to* + verbal noun) begin (*fell to wondering*). **21** (foll. by *to*) lapse, revert (*revenues fall to the Crown*). —*n.* **1** the act or an instance of falling; a sudden rapid descent. **2** that which falls or has fallen, e.g. snow, rocks, etc. **3** the recorded amount of rainfall etc. **4** a decline or diminution. **5** overthrow, downfall (*the fall of Rome*). **6 a** succumbing to temptation. **b** (**the Fall**) the sin of Adam and its consequences, as described in Genesis. **7** (of material, land, light, etc.) a downward direction; a slope. **8** (also **Fall**) *US* autumn. **9** (esp. in *pl.*) a waterfall, cataract, or cascade. **10** *Mus.* a cadence. **11 a** a wrestling-bout; a throw in wrestling which keeps the opponent on the ground for a specified time. **b** a controlled act of falling, esp. as a stunt or in judo etc. **12 a** the birth of young of certain animals. **b** the number of young born. **13** a rope of a hoisting-tackle. □**fall about** *colloq.* be helpless, esp. with laughter. **fall apart** (or **to pieces**) **1** break into pieces. **2** (of a situation etc.) disintegrate; be reduced to chaos. **3** lose one's capacity to cope. **fall away 1** (of a surface) incline abruptly. **2** become few or thin; gradually vanish. **3** desert, revolt; abandon one's principles. **fall back** retreat. **fall-back** (*attrib.*) emergency, esp. (of wages) the minimum paid when no work is available. **fall back on** have recourse to in difficulty. **fall behind 1** be outstripped by one's competitors etc.; lag. **2** be in arrears. **fall down** (often foll. by *on*) *colloq.* fail; perform poorly; fail to deliver (payment etc.). **fall for** *colloq.* **1** be captivated or deceived by. **2** admire; yield to the charms or merits of. **fall foul of** come into conflict with; quarrel with. **fall guy** *sl.* **1** an easy victim. **2** a scapegoat. **fall in 1** take one's place in military formation. **b** (as *int.*) the order to do this. **2** collapse inwards. **falling star** a meteor. **fall in love** see LOVE. **fall into line 1** take one's place in the ranks. **2** conform or collaborate with others. **fall into place** begin to make sense or cohere. **fall in with 1** meet by chance. **2** agree with; accede to; humour. **3** coincide with. **fall off 1** (of demand etc.) decrease, deteriorate. **2** withdraw. **fall-off** *n.* a decrease, deterioration, withdrawal, etc. **fall out 1** quarrel. **2** (of the hair, teeth, etc.) become detached. **3** *Mil.* come out of formation. **4** result; come to pass; occur. **fall out of** gradually discontinue (a habit etc.). **fall over oneself** *colloq.* **1** be eager or competitive. **2** be awkward, stumble through haste, confusion, etc. **fall-pipe** a downpipe. **fall short 1** be or become deficient or inadequate. **2** (of a missile etc.) not reach its target. **fall short of** fail to reach or obtain. **fall through** fail; come to nothing; miscarry. **fall to** begin an activity, e.g. eating or working. [OE *fallan, feallan* f. Gmc]

fallacy /ˈfæləsɪ/ *n.* (*pl.* -ies) **1** a mistaken belief, esp. based on unsound argument. **2** faulty reasoning; misleading or unsound argument. **3** *Logic* a flaw that vitiates an argument. □□**fallacious** /fəˈleɪʃəs/ *adj.* **fallaciously** /fəˈleɪʃəslɪ/ *adv.* **fallaciousness** /fəˈleɪʃəsnɪs/ *n.* [L *fallacia* f. *fallax -acis* deceiving f. *fallere* deceive]

fallen *past part.* of FALL *v.* —*adj.* **1** (*attrib.*) having lost one's honour or reputation. **2** killed in war. □□ **fallenness** *n.*

fallfish /ˈfɔːlfɪʃ/ *n.* *US* a N. American freshwater fish like the chub.

fallible /ˈfælɪb(ə)l/ *adj.* **1** capable of making mistakes. **2** liable to be erroneous. □□**fallibility** /-ˈbɪlɪtɪ/ *n.* **fallibly** *adv.* [med.L *fallibilis* f. L *fallere* deceive]

Fallopian tube /fəˈləʊpɪən/ *n.* *Anat.* either of two tubes in female mammals along which ova travel from the ovaries to the uterus. [*Fallopius*, Latinized name of G. *Fallopio*, It. anatomist d. 1562]

fallout /ˈfɔːlaʊt/ *n.* **1** radioactive debris caused by a nuclear explosion or accident. **2** the adverse side-effects of a situation etc.

fallow[1] /ˈfæləʊ/ *adj., n.,* & *v.* —*adj.* **1 a** (of land) ploughed and harrowed but left unsown for a year. **b** uncultivated. **2** (of an idea etc.) potentially useful but not yet in use. **3** inactive. **4** (of a sow) not pregnant. —*n.* fallow or uncultivated land. —*v.tr.* break up (land) for sowing or to destroy weeds. □□ **fallowness** *n.* [ME f. OE *fealh* (n.), *fealgian* (v.)]

fallow[2] /ˈfæləʊ/ *adj.* of a pale brownish or reddish yellow. □**fallow deer** any small deer of the genus *Dama*, having a white-spotted reddish-brown coat in the summer. [OE *falu, fealu* f. Gmc]

false /fɔːls/ *adj.* & *adv.* —*adj.* **1** not according with fact; wrong, incorrect (*a false idea*). **2 a** spurious, sham, artificial (*false gods; false teeth; false modesty*). **b** acting as such; appearing to be such, esp. deceptively (*a false lining*). **3** illusory; not actually so (*a false economy*). **4** improperly so called (*false acacia*). **5** deceptive. **6** (foll. by *to*) deceitful, treacherous, or unfaithful. **7** illegal (*false imprisonment*). —*adv.* in a false manner (esp. *play false*). □**false acacia** see ACACIA. **false alarm** an alarm given needlessly. **false bedding** *Geol.* = CROSS-BEDDING. **false colours** deceitful pretence. **false dawn** a transient light in the east before dawn. **false gharial** see GHARIAL. **false pretences** misrepresentations made with intent to deceive (esp. *under false pretences*). **false rib** = *floating rib*. **false start 1** an invalid or disallowed start in a race. **2** an unsuccessful attempt to begin something. **false step** a slip; a mistake. **false topaz** = CITRINE. □□**falsely** *adv.* **falseness** *n.* **falsity** *n.* (*pl.* -ies). [OE *fals* and OF *fals, faus* f. L *falsus* past part. of *fallere* deceive]

falsehood /ˈfɔːlshʊd, ˈfɔːls-/ *n.* **1** the state of being false, esp. untrue. **2** a false or untrue thing. **3 a** the act of lying. **b** a lie or lies.

falsetto /fɔːlˈsetəʊ, fɔːl-/ *n.* (*pl.* -os) **1** a method of voice production used by male singers, esp. tenors, to sing notes higher than their normal range. **2** a singer using this method. [It., dimin. of *falso* FALSE]

falsework /ˈfɔːlswɜːk/ *n.* a temporary framework or support used during building to form arches etc.

falsies /ˈfɔːlsɪz, ˈfɔːls-/ *n.pl. colloq.* padded material to increase the apparent size of the breasts.

falsify /ˈfɔːlsɪˌfaɪ, ˈfɔːls-/ *v.tr.* (-ies, -ied) **1** fraudulently alter or make false (a document, evidence, etc.). **2** misrepresent. **3** make wrong; pervert. **4** show to be false. **5** disappoint (a hope, fear, etc.). □□**falsifiable** *adj.* **falsifiability** /-ˌfaɪəˈbɪlɪtɪ/ *n.* **falsification** /-frˈkeɪʃ(ə)n/ *n.* [ME f. F *falsifier* or med.L *falsificare* f. L *falsificus* making false f. *falsus* false]

falter /ˈfɔːltə(r), ˈfɔːl-/ *v.* **1** *intr.* stumble, stagger; go unsteadily. **2** *intr.* waver; lose courage. **3** *tr.* & *intr.* stammer; speak hesitatingly. □□**falterer** *n.* **falteringly** *adv.* [ME: orig. uncert.]

fame /feɪm/ *n.* **1** renown; the state of being famous. **2** reputation. **3** *archaic* public report; rumour. □**house of ill fame** *archaic* a brothel. **ill fame** disrepute. [ME f. OF f. L *fama*]

famed /feɪmd/ *adj.* **1** (foll. by *for*) famous; much spoken of (*famed for its good food*). **2** *archaic* currently reported.

familial /fəˈmɪlɪəl/ *adj.* of, occurring in, or characteristic of a family or its members. [F f. L *familia* FAMILY]

familiar /fəˈmɪlɪə(r)/ *adj.* & *n.* —*adj.* **1 a** (often foll. by *to*) well known; no longer novel. **b** common, usual; often encountered or experienced. **2** (foll. by *with*) knowing a thing well or in detail (*am familiar with all the problems*). **3** (often foll. by *with*) **a** well acquainted (with a person); in close friendship; intimate. **b** sexually intimate. **4** excessively informal; impertinent. **5** unceremonious, informal. —*n.* **1 a**

close friend or associate. **2** *RC Ch.* a person rendering certain services in a pope's or bishop's household. **3** (in full **familiar spirit**) a demon supposedly attending and obeying a witch etc. □□**familiarly** *adv.* [ME f. OF *familier* f. L *familiaris* (as FAMILY)]

familiarity /fə‚mɪlɪ'ærɪtɪ/ *n.* (*pl.* -**ies**) **1** the state of being well known (*the familiarity of the scene*). **2** (foll. by *with*) close acquaintance. **3** a close relationship. **4 a** sexual intimacy. **b** (in *pl.*) acts of physical intimacy. **5** familiar or informal behaviour, esp. excessively so. [ME f. OF *familiarité* f. L *familiaritas -tatis* (as FAMILIAR)]

familiarize /fə'mɪlɪə‚raɪz/ *v.tr.* (also -**ise**) **1** (foll. by *with*) make (a person) conversant or well acquainted. **2** make (a thing) well known. □□**familiarization** /-'zeɪʃ(ə)n/ *n.* [F *familiariser* f. *familiaire* (as FAMILIAR)]

famille /fæ'miːj/ *n.* a Chinese enamelled porcelain with a predominant colour: (*famille jaune* /ʒəʊn/) yellow, (*famille noire* /nwɑ:(r)/) black, (*famille rose* /rɒz/) red, (*famille verte* /veət/) green. [F, = family]

family /'fæmɪlɪ, 'fæmlɪ/ *n.* (*pl.* -**ies**) **1** a set of parents and children, or of relations, living together or not. **2 a** the members of a household, esp. parents and their children. **b** a person's children. **c** (*attrib.*) serving the needs of families (*family butcher*). **3 a** all the descendants of a common ancestor. **b** a race or group of peoples from a common stock. **4** all the languages ultimately derived from a particular early language, regarded as a group. **5** a brotherhood of persons or nations united by political or religious ties. **6** a group of objects distinguished by common features. **7** *Math.* a group of curves etc. obtained by varying one quantity. **8** *Biol.* a group of related genera of organisms within an order in taxonomic classification. □**family allowance** *Brit.* a former name for *child benefit*. **family credit** (or **income supplement**) (in the UK) a regular payment by the State to a family with an income below a certain level. **Family Division** (in the UK) a division of the High Court dealing with adoption, divorce, etc. **family man** a man having a wife and children, esp. one fond of family life. **family name** a surname. **family planning** birth control. **family tree** a chart showing relationships and lines of descent. **in the family way** *colloq.* pregnant. [ME f. L *familia* household f. *famulus* servant]

famine /'fæmɪn/ *n.* **1 a** extreme scarcity of food. **b** a shortage of something specified (*water famine*). **2** *archaic* hunger, starvation. [ME f. OF f. *faim* f. L *fames* hunger]

famish /'fæmɪʃ/ *v.tr. & intr.* (usu. in *passive*) **1** reduce or be reduced to extreme hunger. **2** *colloq.* feel very hungry. [ME f. obs. *fame* f. OF *afamer* ult. f. L *fames* hunger]

famous /'feɪməs/ *adj.* **1** (often foll. by *for*) celebrated; well known. **2** *colloq.* excellent. □□**famousness** *n.* [ME f. AF, OF *fameus* f. L *famosus* f. *fama* fame]

famously /'feɪməslɪ/ *adv.* **1** *colloq.* excellently (*got on famously*). **2** notably.

famulus /'fæmjʊləs/ *n.* (*pl.* **famuli** /-‚laɪ/) *hist.* an attendant on a magician or scholar. [L, = servant]

fan[1] /fæn/ *n. & v.* — *n.* **1** an apparatus, usu. with rotating blades, giving a current of air for ventilation etc. **2** a device, usu. folding and forming a semicircle when spread out, for agitating the air to cool oneself. **3** anything spread out like a fan, e.g. a bird's tail or kind of ornamental vaulting (*fan tracery*). **4** a device for winnowing grain. **5** a fan-shaped deposit of alluvium esp. where a stream begins to descend a gentler slope. **6** a small sail for keeping the head of a windmill towards the wind. — *v.* (**fanned, fanning**) **1** *tr.* **a** blow a current of air on, with or as with a fan. **b** agitate (the air) with a fan. **2** *tr.* (of a breeze) blow gently on; cool. **3** *tr.* **a** winnow (grain). **b** winnow away (chaff). **4** *tr.* sweep away by or as by the wind from a fan. **5** *intr. & tr.* (usu. foll. by *out*) spread out in the shape of a fan. □**fan belt** a belt that drives a

fan to cool the radiator in a motor vehicle. **fan dance** a dance in which the dancer is (apparently) nude and partly concealed by fans. **fan heater** an electric heater in which a fan drives air over an element. **fan-jet** = TURBOFAN. **fan palm** a palm-tree with fan-shaped leaves. □□**fanlike** *adj.* **fanner** *n.* [OE *fann* in sense 4 of *n.*) f. L *vannus* winnowing-fan]

fan[2] /fæn/ *n.* a devotee of a particular activity, performer, etc. (*film fan; football fan*). □**fan club** an organized group of devotees. **fan mail** letters from fans. □□**fandom** *n.* [abbr. of FANATIC]

fanatic /fə'nætɪk/ *n. & adj.* — *n.* a person filled with excessive and often misguided enthusiasm for something. — *adj.* excessively enthusiastic. □□ **fanatical** *adj.* **fanatically** *adv.* **fanaticism** /-tɪ‚sɪz(ə)m/ *n.* **fanaticize** /-tɪ‚saɪz/ *v.intr. & tr.* (also -**ise**). [F *fanatique* or L *fanaticus* f. *fanum* temple (orig. in religious sense)]

fancier /'fænsɪə(r)/ *n.* a connoisseur or follower of some activity or thing (*dog-fancier*).

fanciful /'fænsɪ‚fʊl/ *adj.* **1** existing only in the imagination or fancy. **2** indulging in fancies; whimsical, capricious. **3** fantastically designed, ornamented, etc.; odd-looking. □□**fancifully** *adv.* **fancifulness** *n.*

fancy /'fænsɪ/ *n., adj., & v.* — *n.* (*pl.* -**ies**) **1** an individual taste or inclination (*take a fancy to*). **2** a caprice or whim. **3** a thing favoured, e.g. a horse to win a race. **4** an arbitrary supposition. **5 a** the faculty of using imagination or of inventing imagery. **b** a mental image. **6** delusion; unfounded belief. **7** (prec. by *the*) those who have a certain hobby; fanciers, esp. patrons of boxing. — *adj.* (usu. *attrib.*) (**fancier, fanciest**) **1** ornamental; not plain. **2** capricious, whimsical, extravagant (*at a fancy price*). **3** based on imagination, not fact. **4** *US* (of foods etc.) above average quality. **5** (of flowers etc.) particoloured. **6** (of an animal) bred for particular points of beauty etc. — *v.tr.* (-**ies, -ied**) **1** (foll. by *that* + clause) be inclined to suppose; rather think. **2** *Brit. colloq.* feel a desire for (*do you fancy a drink?*). **3** *Brit. colloq.* find sexually attractive. **4** *colloq.* have an unduly high opinion of (oneself, one's ability, etc.). **5** (in *imper.*) an exclamation of surprise (*fancy their doing that!*). **6** picture to oneself; conceive, imagine. □**catch** (or **take**) **the fancy of** please; appeal to. **fancy dress** fanciful costume, esp. for masquerading as a different person or as an animal etc. at a party. **fancy-free** without (esp. emotional) commitments. **fancy goods** ornamental novelties etc. **fancy man** *sl. derog.* **1** a woman's lover. **2** a pimp. **fancy woman** *sl. derog.* a mistress. **fancy-work** ornamental sewing etc. □□**fanciable** *adj.* (in sense 3 of *v.*). **fancily** *adv.* **fanciness** *n.* [contr. of FANTASY]

fandangle /fæn'dæŋg(ə)l/ *n.* **1** a fantastic ornament. **2** nonsense, tomfoolery. [perh. f. FANDANGO after *newfangle*]

fandango /fæn'dæŋgəʊ/ *n.* (*pl.* -**oes** or -**os**) **1 a** a lively Spanish dance for two. **b** the music for this. **2** nonsense, tomfoolery. [Sp.: orig. unkn.]

fane /feɪn/ *n. poet.* = TEMPLE[1]. [ME f. L *fanum*]

fanfare /'fænfeə(r)/ *n.* **1** a short showy or ceremonious sounding of trumpets, bugles, etc. **2** an elaborate welcome. [F, imit.]

fanfaronade /‚fænfærə'neɪd/ *n.* **1** arrogant talk; brag. **2** a fanfare. [F *fanfaronnade* f. *fanfaron* braggart (as FANFARE)]

fang /fæŋ/ *n.* **1** a canine tooth, esp. of a dog or wolf. **2** the tooth of a venomous snake, by which poison is injected. **3** the root of a tooth or its prong. **4** *Brit. colloq.* a person's tooth. □□**fanged** *adj.* (also in *comb.*). **fangless** *adj.* [OE f. ON *fang* f. a Gmc root = to catch]

fanlight /'fænlaɪt/ *n.* a small, orig. semicircular window over a door or another window.

fanny /'fænɪ/ *n.* (*pl.* -**ies**) **1** *Brit. coarse sl.* the female genitals. **2** *US sl.* the buttocks. ¶ Usually considered a taboo word in *Brit.* use. [20th c.: orig. unkn.]

Fanny Adams /ˌfænɪ 'ædəmz/ n. Brit. sl. **1** (also **sweet Fanny Adams**) nothing at all. ¶ Sometimes understood as a euphemism for fuck all. **2** Naut. **a** tinned meat. **b** stew. [name of a murder victim c.1870]

fantail /'fænteɪl/ n. **1** a pigeon with a broad-shaped tail. **2** any flycatcher of the genus Rhipidura, with a fan-shaped tail. **3** a fan-shaped tail or end. **4** the fan of a windmill. **5** the projecting part of a boat's stern. □□ **fantailed** adj.

fan-tan /'fæntæn/ n. **1** a Chinese gambling game in which players try to guess the remainder after the banker has divided a number of hidden objects into four groups. **2** a card-game in which players build on sequences of sevens. [Chin., = repeated divisions]

fantasia /fæn'teɪzɪə, ˌfæntə'zɪə/ n. a musical or other composition free in form and often in improvisatory style, or which is based on several familiar tunes. [It., = FANTASY]

fantasize /'fæntəˌsaɪz/ v. (also **phantasize, -ise**) **1** intr. have a fantasy or fanciful vision. **2** tr. imagine; create a fantasy about. □□ **fantasist** n.

fantast /'fæntæst/ n. (also **phantast**) a visionary; a dreamer. [med.L f. Gk phantastēs boaster f. phantazomai make a show f. phainō show]

fantastic /fæn'tæstɪk/ adj. (also **fantastical**) **1** colloq. excellent, extraordinary. **2** extravagantly fanciful; capricious, eccentric. **3** grotesque or quaint in design etc. □□ **fantasticality** /-'kælɪtɪ/ n. **fantastically** adv. [ME f. OF fantastique f. med.L fantasticus f. LL phantasticus f. Gk phantastikos (as FANTAST)]

fantasticate /fæn'tæstɪˌkeɪt/ v.tr. make fantastic. □□ **fantastication** /-'keɪʃ(ə)n/ n.

fantasy /'fæntəsɪ, -zɪ/ n. & v. (also **phantasy**) —n. (pl. **-ies**) **1** the faculty of inventing images, esp. extravagant or visionary ones. **2** a fanciful mental image; a day-dream. **3** a whimsical speculation. **4** a fantastic invention or composition; a fantasia. —v.tr. (**-ies, -ied**) imagine in a visionary manner. [ME f. OF fantasie f. L phantasia appearance f. Gk (as FANTAST)]

Fanti /'fæntɪ/ n. (also **Fante** /'fæntɪ/) (pl. same or **Fantis**) **1** a member of a Black tribe native to Ghana. **2** the language of this tribe. [native name]

FAO abbr. Food and Agriculture Organization (of the United Nations).

far /fɑː(r)/ adv. & adj. (**further, furthest** or **farther, farthest**) —adv. **1** at or to or by a great distance (far away; far off; far out). **2** a long way (off) in space or time (are you travelling far?; we talked far into the night). **3** to a great extent or degree; by much (far better; far the best; far too early). —adj. **1** situated at or extending over a great distance in space or time; remote (a far cry; a far country). **2** more distant (the far end of the hall). □ **as far as 1** to the distance of (a place). **2** to the extent that (travel as far as you like). **by far** by a great amount. **far and away** by a very large amount. **far and near** everywhere. **far and wide** over a large area. **far-away 1** remote; long-past. **2** (of a look) dreamy. **3** (of a voice) sounding as if from a distance. **far be it from me** (foll. by to + infin.) I am reluctant to (esp. express criticism etc.). **far cry** a long way. **the Far East** China, Japan, and other countries of E. Asia. **Far Eastern** of or in the Far East. **far-fetched** (of an explanation etc.) strained, unconvincing. **far-flung** extending far; widely distributed. **far from** very different from being; tending to the opposite of (the problem is far from being solved). **far gone 1** advanced in time. **2** colloq. in an advanced state of illness, drunkenness, etc. **far-off** remote. **far-out 1** distant. **2** avant-garde, unconventional, excellent. **far-reaching 1** widely applicable. **2** having important consequences or implications. **far-seeing** shrewd in judgement; prescient. **go far 1** achieve much. **2** contribute greatly. **3** be adequate. **go too far** go beyond the limits of what is reasonable, polite, etc. **how far** to what extent. **so far 1** to such an extent or distance; to this point. **2** until now. **so** (or **in so**) **far as** (or

that) to the extent that. **so far so good** progress has been satisfactory up to now. □□ **farness** n. [OE feorr]

farad /'færəd/ n. Electr. the SI unit of capacitance, such that one coulomb of charge causes a potential difference of one volt. ¶ Abbr.: **F**. [shortening of FARADAY]

faradaic /ˌfærə'deɪɪk/ adj. (also **faradic** /fə'rædɪk/) Electr. inductive, induced. [see FARADAY]

faraday /'færəˌdeɪ/ n. (also **Faraday's constant**) Electr. the quantity of electric charge carried by one mole of electrons. ¶ Abbr.: **F**. □ **Faraday cage** Electr. an earthed metal screen used for excluding electrostatic influences. **Faraday effect** Physics the rotation of the plane of polarization of electromagnetic waves in certain substances in a magnetic field. [M. Faraday, Engl. physicist d. 1867]

farandole /ˌfærən'dɒl/ n. **1** a lively Provençal dance. **2** the music for this. [F f. mod. Prov. farandoulo]

farce /fɑːs/ n. **1 a** a coarsely comic dramatic work based on ludicrously improbable events. **b** this branch of drama. **2** absurdly futile proceedings; pretence, mockery. [F, orig. = stuffing, f. OF farsir f. L farcire to stuff, used metaph. of interludes etc.]

farceur /fɑː'sɜː(r)/ n. **1** a joker or wag. **2** an actor or writer of farces. [F f. farcer act farces]

farcical /'fɑːsɪk(ə)l/ adj. **1** extremely ludicrous or futile. **2** of or like farce. □□ **farcicality** /-'kælɪtɪ/ n. **farcically** adv.

farcy /'fɑːsɪ/ n. glanders with inflammation of the lymph vessels. □ **farcy bud** (or **button**) a small lymphatic tumour as a result of farcy. [ME f. earlier & OF farcin f. LL farciminum f. farcire to stuff]

farded /'fɑːdɪd/ adj. archaic (of a face etc.) painted with cosmetics. [past part. of obs. fard f. OF farder]

fare /feə(r)/ n. & v. —n. **1 a** the price a passenger has to pay to be conveyed by bus, train, etc. **b** a passenger paying to travel in a public vehicle. **2** a range of food provided by a restaurant etc. —v.intr. literary **1** progress; get on (how did you fare?). **2** happen; turn out. **3** journey, go, travel. □ **fare-stage** Brit. **1** a section of a bus etc. route for which a fixed fare is charged. **2** a stop marking this. [OE fær, faru journeying, faran (v.), f. Gmc]

farewell /feə'wel/ int. & n. —int. goodbye, adieu. —n. **1** leave-taking, departure (also attrib.: a farewell kiss). **2** parting good wishes. [ME f. imper. of FARE + WELL[1]]

farina /fə'raɪnə, -'riːnə/ n. **1** the flour or meal of cereal, nuts, or starchy roots. **2** a powdery substance. **3** Brit. starch. □□ **farinaceous** /ˌfærɪ'neɪʃəs/ adj. [L f. far corn]

farl /fɑːl/ n. Sc. a thin cake, orig. quadrant-shaped, of oatmeal or flour. [obs. fardel quarter (as FOURTH, DEAL[1])]

farm /fɑːm/ n. & v. —n. **1** an area of land and its buildings used under one management for growing crops, rearing animals, etc. **2** a place or establishment for breeding a particular type of animal, growing fruit, etc. (trout-farm; mink-farm). **3** = FARMHOUSE. **4** a place for the storage of oil or oil products. **5** = sewage farm. —v. **1 a** tr. use (land) for growing crops, rearing animals, etc. **b** intr. be a farmer; work on a farm. **2** tr. breed (fish etc.) commercially. **3** tr. (often foll. by out) **a** delegate or subcontract (work) to others. **b** contract (the collection of taxes) to another for a fee. **c** arrange for (a person, esp. a child) to be looked after by another, with payment. **4** tr. let the labour of (a person) for hire. **5** tr. contract to maintain and care for (a person, esp. a child) for a fixed sum. □ **farm-hand** a worker on a farm. □□ **farmable** adj. **farming** n. [ME f. OF ferme f. med.L firma fixed payment f. L firmus FIRM[1]: orig. applied only to leased land]

farmer /'fɑːmə(r)/ n. **1** a person who cultivates a farm. **2** a person to whom the collection of taxes is contracted for a fee. **3** a person who looks after children for payment. [ME f. AF fermer, OF fermier f. med.L firmarius, firmator f. firma FIRM[2]]

farmhouse /'fɑːmhaʊs/ n. a dwelling-place (esp. the main one) attached to a farm.

farmstead /'fɑːmsted/ n. a farm and its buildings regarded as a unit.

farmyard /'fɑːmjɑːd/ n. a yard or enclosure attached to a farmhouse.

faro /'feərəʊ/ n. a gambling card-game in which bets are placed on the order of appearance of the cards. [F *pharaon* PHARAOH (said to have been the name of the king of hearts)]

Faroese var. of FAEROESE.

farouche /fəˈruːʃ/ adj. sullen, shy. [F f. OF *faroche, forache* f. med.L *forasticus* f. L *foras* out of doors]

farrago /fəˈrɑːgəʊ/ n. (pl. **-os** or US **-oes**) a medley or hotchpotch. □□ **farraginous** /-ˈrædʒɪnəs/ adj. [L *farrago farraginis* mixed fodder f. *far* corn]

farrier /'færɪə(r)/ n. Brit. **1** a smith who shoes horses. **2** a horse-doctor. □□ **farriery** n. [OF *ferrier* f. L *ferrarius* f. *ferrum* iron, horseshoe]

farrow /'færəʊ/ n. & v. —n. **1** a litter of pigs. **2** the birth of a litter. —v.tr. (also *absol.*) (of a sow) produce (pigs). [OE *fearh, færh* pig f. WG]

farruca /fəˈruːkə/ n. a type of flamenco dance. [Sp.]

Farsi /'fɑːsiː/ n. the modern Persian language. [Pers.: cf. PARSEE]

far-sighted /fɑːˈsaɪtɪd, 'fɑː-/ adj. **1** having foresight, prudent. **2** esp. US = LONG-SIGHTED. □□ **far-sightedly** adv. **far-sightedness** n.

fart /fɑːt/ v. & n. coarse sl. —v.intr. **1** emit wind from the anus. **2** (foll. by *about, around*) behave foolishly; waste time. —n. **1** an emission of wind from the anus. **2** an unpleasant person. ¶ Usually considered a taboo word. [OE (recorded in *feorting* verbal noun) f. Gmc]

farther var. of FURTHER (esp. with ref. to physical distance).

farthest var. of FURTHEST (esp. with ref. to physical distance).

farthing /'fɑːðɪŋ/ n. **1** (in the UK) a coin and monetary unit formerly worth a quarter of an old penny. ¶ Withdrawn in 1961. **2** the least possible amount (*it doesn't matter a farthing*). [OE *feorthing* f. *feortha* fourth]

farthingale /'fɑːðɪŋˌgeɪl/ n. hist. a hooped petticoat or a stiff curved roll to extend a woman's skirt. [earlier *vardingale, verd-* f. F *verdugale* f. Sp. *verdugado* f. *verdugo* rod]

fartlek /'fɑːtlek/ n. Athletics a method of training for middle- and long-distance running, mixing fast with slow work. [Sw. f. *fart* speed + *lek* play]

fasces /'fæsiːz/ n.pl. Rom.Hist. **1** a bundle of rods with a projecting axe-blade, carried by a lictor as a symbol of a magistrate's power. **2** hist. (in Fascist Italy) emblems of authority. [L, pl. of *fascis* bundle]

fascia /'feɪʃə/ n. (also **facia**) **1** Brit. **a** the instrument panel of a motor vehicle. **b** any similar panel or plate for operating machinery. **2** the upper part of a shop-front with the proprietor's name etc. **3** Archit. **a** a long flat surface between mouldings on the architrave in classical architecture. **b** a flat surface, usu. of wood, covering the ends of rafters. **4** a stripe or band. **5** /'fæʃə/ Anat. a thin sheath of fibrous tissue. □□ **fascial** adj. [L, = band, door-frame, etc.]

fasciate /'fæʃɪˌeɪt/ adj. (also **fasciated**) **1** Bot. (of contiguous parts) compressed or growing into one. **2** striped or banded. □□ **fasciation** /-ˈeɪʃ(ə)n/ n. [L *fasciatus* past part. of *fasciare* swathe (as FASCIA)]

fascicle /'fæsɪk(ə)l/ n. **1** (also **fascicule** /-ˌkjuːl/) a separately published instalment of a book, usu. not complete in itself. **2** a bunch or bundle. **3** (also **fasciculus** /fæˈsɪkjʊləs/) Anat. a bundle of fibres. □□ **fascicled** adj. **fascicular** /-ˈsɪkjʊlə(r)/ adj. **fasciculate** /-ˈsɪkjʊlət/ adj. **fasciculation** /-ˈeɪʃ(ə)n/ n. [L *fasciculus* bundle, dimin. of *fascis*: see FASCES]

fascinate /'fæsɪˌneɪt/ v.tr. **1** capture the interest of; attract irresistibly. **2** (esp. of a snake) paralyse (a victim) with fear. □□ **fascinated** adj. **fascinating** adj. **fascinatingly** adv. **fascination** /-ˈneɪʃ(ə)n/ n. **fascinator** n. [L *fascinare* f. *fascinum* spell]

fascine /fæˈsiːn/ n. a long faggot used for engineering purposes and (esp. in war) for lining trenches, filling ditches, etc. [F f. L *fascina* f. *fascis* bundle: see FASCES]

Fascism /'fæʃɪz(ə)m/ n. **1** the totalitarian principles and organization of the extreme right-wing nationalist movement in Italy (1922–43). **2** (also **fascism**) **a** any similar nationalist and authoritarian movement. **b** disp. any system of extreme right-wing or authoritarian views. □□ **Fascist** n. & adj. (also **fascist**). **Fascistic** /-ˈʃɪstɪk/ adj. (also **fascistic**). [It. *fascismo* f. *fascio* political group f. L *fascis* bundle: see FASCES]

fashion /'fæʃ(ə)n/ n. & v. —n. **1** the current popular custom or style, esp. in dress or social conduct. **2** a manner or style of doing something (*in a peculiar fashion*). **3** (in *comb.*) in a specified manner (*walk crab-fashion*). **4** fashionable society (*a woman of fashion*). —v.tr. (often foll. by *into*) make into a particular or the required form. □**after** (or **in**) **a fashion** as well as is practicable, though not satisfactorily. **in** (or **out of**) **fashion** fashionable (or not fashionable) at the time in question. □□ **fashioner** n. [ME f. AF *fasun*, OF *façon*, f. L *factio -onis* f. *facere fact-* do, make]

fashionable /'fæʃnəb(ə)l/ adj. **1** following, suited to, or influenced by the current fashion. **2** characteristic of or favoured by those who are leaders of social fashion. □□ **fashionableness** n. **fashionably** adv.

fast¹ /fɑːst/ adj. & adv. —adj. **1** rapid, quick-moving. **2** capable of high speed (*a fast car*). **3** enabling or causing or intended for high speed (*a fast road; fast lane*). **4** (of a clock etc.) showing a time ahead of the correct time. **5** (of a pitch or ground etc. in a sport) likely to make the ball bounce or run quickly. **6 a** (of a photographic film) needing only a short exposure. **b** (of a lens) having a large aperture. **7 a** firmly fixed or attached. **b** secure; firmly established (*a fast friendship*). **8** (of a colour) not fading in light or when washed. **9** (of a person) immoral, dissipated. —adv. **1** quickly; in quick succession. **2** firmly, fixedly, tightly, securely (*stand fast; eyes fast shut*). **3** soundly, completely (*fast asleep*). □**fast breeder** (or **fast breeder reactor**) a reactor using fast neutrons to produce the same fissile material as it uses. **fast buck** see BUCK². **fast food** food that can be prepared and served quickly and easily, esp. in a snack bar or restaurant. **fast neutron** a neutron with high kinetic energy, esp. not slowed by a moderator etc. **fast reactor** a nuclear reactor using mainly fast neutrons. **fast-talk** US colloq. persuade by rapid or deceitful talk. **fast-wind** wind (magnetic tape) rapidly backwards or forwards. **fast worker** colloq. a person who achieves quick results, esp. in love affairs. **pull a fast one** colloq. try to deceive or gain an unfair advantage. [OE *fæst* f. Gmc]

fast² /fɑːst/ v. & n. —v.intr. abstain from all or some kinds of food or drink, esp. as a religious observance. —n. an act or period of fasting. □□ **faster** n. [ON *fasta* f. Gmc (as FAST¹)]

fastback /'fɑːstbæk/ n. **1** a motor car with the rear sloping continuously down to the bumper. **2** such a rear.

fasten /'fɑːs(ə)n/ v. **1** tr. make or become fixed or secure. **2** tr. (foll. by *in, up*) lock securely; shut in. **3** tr. **a** (foll. by *on, upon*) direct (a look, thoughts, etc.) fixedly or intently. **b** focus or direct the attention fixedly upon (*fastened him with her eyes*). **4** tr. (foll. by *on, upon*) fix (a designation or imputation etc.). **5** intr. (foll. by *on, upon*) **a** take hold of. **b** single out. □□ **fastener** n. [OE *fæstnian* f. Gmc]

fastening /'fɑːsnɪŋ/ n. a device that fastens something; a fastener.

fastidious /fæˈstɪdɪəs/ adj. **1** very careful in matters of choice or taste; fussy. **2** easily disgusted;

squeamish. ◻◻ **fastidiously** *adv.* **fastidiousness** *n.* [ME f. L *fastidiosus* f. *fastidium* loathing]

fastigiate /fæˈstɪdʒət/ *adj. Bot.* **1** having a conical or tapering outline. **2** having parallel upright branches. [L *fastigium* gable-top]

fastness /ˈfɑːstnɪs/ *n.* **1** a stronghold or fortress. **2** the state of being secure. [OE *fæstnes* (as FAST¹)]

fat /fæt/ *n., adj., & v.* — *n.* **1** a natural oily or greasy substance occurring esp. in animal bodies. **2** the part of anything containing this. **3** excessive presence of fat in a person or animal; corpulence. **4** *Chem.* any of a group of natural esters of glycerol and various fatty acids existing as solids at room temperature. — *adj.* (**fatter**, **fattest**) **1** (of a person or animal) having excessive fat; corpulent. **2** (of an animal) made plump for slaughter; fatted. **3** containing much fat. **4** greasy, oily, unctuous. **5** (of land or resources) fertile, rich; yielding abundantly. **6 a** thick, substantial in content (*a fat book*). **b** substantial as an asset or opportunity (*a fat cheque*; *was given a fat part in the play*). **7 a** (of coal) bituminous. **b** (of clay etc.) sticky. **8** *colloq. iron.* very little; not much (*a fat chance*; *a fat lot*). — *v.tr. & intr.* (**fatted**, **fatting**) make or become fat. ◻**fat cat** *sl.* **1** *US* a wealthy person, esp. as a benefactor. **2** *Austral.* a highly paid executive or official. **fat-head** *colloq.* a stupid person. **fat-headed** stupid. **fat-headedness** stupidity. **fat hen** the white goosefoot, *Chenopodium album.* **the fat is in the fire** trouble is imminent. **kill the fatted calf** celebrate, esp. at a prodigal's return (Luke 15). **live off** (or **on**) **the fat of the land** have the best of everything. ◻◻ **fatless** *adj.* **fatly** *adv.* **fatness** *n.* **fattish** *adj.* [OE *fæt* (adj.), *fǣttian* (v.) f. Gmc]

fatal /ˈfeɪt(ə)l/ *adj.* **1** causing or ending in death (*a fatal accident*). **2** (often foll. by *to*) destructive; ruinous; ending in disaster (*was fatal to their chances*; *made a fatal mistake*). **3** fateful, decisive. ◻◻ **fatally** *adv.* **fatalness** *n.* [ME f. OF *fatal* or L *fatalis* (as FATE)]

fatalism /ˈfeɪtə,lɪz(ə)m/ *n.* **1** the belief that all events are predetermined and therefore inevitable. **2** a submissive attitude to events as being inevitable. ◻◻ **fatalist** *n.* **fatalistic** /-ˈlɪstɪk/ *adj.* **fatalistically** /-ˈlɪstɪkəlɪ/ *adv.*

fatality /fəˈtælətɪ/ *n.* (*pl.* **-ies**) **1 a** an occurrence of death by accident or in war etc. **b** a person killed in this way. **2** a fatal influence. **3** a predestined liability to disaster. **4** subjection to or the supremacy of fate. [F *fatalité* or LL *fatalitas* f. L *fatalis* FATAL]

fate /feɪt/ *n. & v.* — *n.* **1** a power regarded as predetermining events unalterably. **2 a** the future regarded as determined by such a power. **b** an individual's appointed lot. **c** the ultimate condition or end of a person or thing (*that sealed our fate*). **3** death, destruction. **4** (usu. **Fate**) a goddess of destiny, esp. one of three Greek or Scandinavian goddesses. — *v.tr.* **1** (usu. in *passive*) preordain (*was fated to win*). **2** (as **fated** *adj.*) doomed to destruction. ◻**fate worse than death** see DEATH. [ME f. It. *fato* & L *fatum* that which is spoken, f. *fari* speak]

fateful /ˈfeɪtfʊl/ *adj.* **1** important, decisive; having far-reaching consequences. **2** controlled as if by fate. **3** causing or likely to cause disaster. **4** prophetic. ◻◻ **fatefully** *adv.* **fatefulness** *n.*

father /ˈfɑːðə(r)/ *n. & v.* — *n.* **1 a** a man in relation to a child or children born from his fertilization of an ovum. **b** (in full **adoptive father**) a man who has continuous care of a child, esp. by adoption. **2** any male animal in relation to its offspring. **3** (usu. in *pl.*) a progenitor or forefather. **4** an originator, designer, or early leader. **5** a person who deserves special respect (*the father of his country*). **6** (**Fathers** or **Fathers of the Church**) early Christian theologians whose writings are regarded as especially authoritative. **7** (also **Father**) **a** (often as a title or form of address) a priest, esp. of a religious order. **b** a religious leader. **8** (**the Father**) (in Christian belief) the first person of the Trinity. **9** (**Father**) a venerable person, esp. as a title in personifications (*Father Time*). **10** the oldest member or doyen (*Father of the House*). **11** (usu. in *pl.*) the leading men or elders in a city or State (*city fathers*). — *v.tr.* **1** beget; be the father of. **2** behave as a father towards. **3** originate (a scheme etc.). **4** appear as or admit that one is the father or originator of. **5** (foll. by *on*) assign the paternity of (a child, book) to a person. ◻**father-figure** an older man who is respected like a father; a trusted leader. **father-in-law** (*pl.* **fathers-in-law**) the father of one's husband or wife. **father of chapel** see CHAPEL. **Father's Day** a day (usu. the third Sunday in June) established for a special tribute to fathers. **Father Time** see TIME. ◻◻ **fatherhood** *n.* **fatherless** *adj.* **fatherlessness** *n.* **fatherlike** *adj. & adv.* **fathership** *n.* [OE *fæder* with many Gmc cognates: rel. to L *pater*, Gk *patēr*]

fatherland /ˈfɑːðə,lænd/ *n.* one's native country.

fatherly /ˈfɑːðəlɪ/ *adj.* **1** like or characteristic of a father in affection, care, etc. (*fatherly concern*). **2** of or proper to a father. ◻◻ **fatherliness** *n.*

fathom /ˈfæð(ə)m/ *n. & v.* — *n.* (*pl.* often **fathom** when prec. by a number) **1** a measure of six feet, esp. used in taking depth soundings. **2** *Brit.* a quantity of wood six feet square in cross-section. — *v.tr.* **1** grasp or comprehend (a problem or difficulty). **2** measure the depth of (water) with a sounding-line. ◻◻ **fathomable** *adj.* **fathomless** *adj.* [OE *fæthm* outstretched arms f. Gmc]

Fathometer /fəˈðɒmɪtə(r)/ *n.* a type of echo-sounder.

fatigue /fəˈtiːg/ *n. & v.* — *n.* **1** extreme tiredness after exertion. **2** weakness in materials, esp. metal, caused by repeated variations of stress. **3** a reduction in the efficiency of a muscle, organ, etc., after prolonged activity. **4** an activity that causes fatigue. **5 a** a non-military duty in the army, often as a punishment. **b** (in full **fatigue-party**) a group of soldiers ordered to do fatigues. — *v.tr.* (**fatigues**, **fatigued**, **fatiguing**) cause fatigue in; tire, exhaust. ◻◻ **fatiguable** *adj.* (also **fatigable**). **fatiguability** /-gəˈbɪlɪtɪ/ *n.* (also **fatigability**). **fatigueless** *adj.* [F *fatigue*, *fatiguer* f. L *fatigare* tire out]

Fatiha /ˈfɑːtɪ,hɑː/ *n.* (also **Fatihah**) the short first sura of the Koran, used by Muslims as a prayer. [Arab. *fātiḥa* opening f. *fataḥa* to open]

Fatimid /ˈfætɪmɪd/ *n.* (also **Fatimite** /-,maɪt/) **1** a descendant of Fatima, the daughter of Muhammad. **2** a member of a dynasty ruling in N. Africa in the 10th-12th c.

fatling /ˈfætlɪŋ/ *n.* a young fatted animal.

fatso /ˈfætsəʊ/ *n.* (*pl.* **-oes**) *sl. joc.* or *offens.* a fat person. [prob. f. FAT or the designation *Fats*]

fatstock /ˈfætstɒk/ *n.* livestock fattened for slaughter.

fatten /ˈfæt(ə)n/ *v.* **1** *tr. & intr.* (esp. with ref. to meat-producing animals) make or become fat. **2** *tr.* enrich (soil).

fatty /ˈfætɪ/ *adj. & n.* — *adj.* (**fattier**, **fattiest**) **1** like fat; oily, greasy. **2** consisting of or containing fat; adipose. **3** marked by abnormal deposition of fat, esp. in fatty degeneration. — *n.* (*pl.* **-ies**) *colloq.* a fat person (esp. as a nickname). ◻**fatty acid** *Chem.* any of a class of organic compounds consisting of a hydrocarbon chain and a terminal carboxyl group, esp. those occurring as constituents of lipids. **fatty oil** = *fixed oil.* ◻◻ **fattily** *adv.* **fattiness** *n.*

fatuous /ˈfætjʊəs/ *adj.* vacantly silly; purposeless, idiotic. ◻◻ **fatuity** /fəˈtjuːɪtɪ/ *n.* (*pl.* **-ies**). **fatuously** *adv.* **fatuousness** *n.* [L *fatuus* foolish]

fatwa /ˈfætwɑː/ *n.* (in Islamic countries) an authoritative ruling on a religious matter. [Arab. *fatwa*]

faubourg /ˈfəʊbʊəg/ *n.* a suburb, esp. of Paris. [F: cf. med.L *falsus burgus* not the city proper]

fauces /ˈfɔːsiːz/ *n.pl. Anat.* a cavity at the back of the mouth. ◻◻ **faucial** /ˈfɔːʃ(ə)l/ *adj.* [L, = throat]

faucet /ˈfɔːsɪt/ *n.* esp. *US* a tap. ¶ In Brit. use only in special applications. [ME f. OF *fausset* vent-peg f. Prov. *falset* f. *falsar* to bore]

fault /fɒlt, fɔːlt/ n. & v. —n. **1** a defect or imperfection of character or of structure, appearance, etc. **2** a break or other defect in an electric circuit. **3** a transgression, offence, or thing wrongly done. **4 a** *Tennis* etc. a service of the ball not in accordance with the rules. **b** (in showjumping) a penalty for an error. **5** responsibility for wrongdoing, error, etc. (*it will be your own fault*). **6** a defect regarded as the cause of something wrong (*the fault lies in the teaching methods*). **7** *Geol.* an extended break in the continuity of strata or a vein. —v. **1** tr. find fault with; blame. **2** tr. declare to be faulty. **3** tr. *Geol.* break the continuity of (strata or a vein). **4** intr. commit a fault. **5** intr. *Geol.* show a fault. □ **at fault** guilty; to blame. **fault-finder** a person given to continually finding fault. **fault-finding** continual criticism. **find fault** (often foll. by *with*) make an adverse criticism; complain. **to a fault** (usu. of a commendable quality etc.) excessively (*generous to a fault*). [ME *faut(e)* f. OF ult. f. L *fallere* FAIL]

faultless /ˈfɒltlɪs, ˈfɔːlt-/ adj. without fault; free from defect or error. □□ **faultlessly** adv. **faultlessness** n.

faulty /ˈfɒltɪ, ˈfɔːltɪ/ (**faultier, faultiest**) adj. having faults; imperfect, defective. □□ **faultily** adv. **faultiness** n.

faun /fɔːn/ n. a Latin rural deity with a human face and torso and a goat's horns, legs, and tail. [ME f. OF *faune* or L *Faunus*, a Latin god identified with Gk Pan]

fauna /ˈfɔːnə/ n. (pl. **faunae** /-niː/ or **faunas**) **1** the animal life of a region or geological period (cf. FLORA). **2** a treatise on or list of this. □□ **faunal** adj. **faunist** n. **faunistic** /-ˈnɪstɪk/ adj. [mod.L f. the name of a rural goddess, sister of Faunus: see FAUN]

faute de mieux /ˌfəʊt də ˈmjɜː/ adv. for want of a better alternative. [F]

fauteuil /fəʊˈtɜːɪ/ n. a kind of wooden seat in the form of an armchair with open sides and upholstered arms. [F f. OF *faudestuel, faldestoel* FALDSTOOL]

fauve /fəʊv/ n. a person who practises or favours fauvism.

fauvism /ˈfəʊvɪz(ə)m/ n. a style of painting with vivid use of colour. □□ **fauvist** n. [F *fauve* wild beast, applied to painters of the school of Matisse]

faux pas /fəʊ ˈpɑː/ n. (pl. same /ˈpɑːz/) **1** a tactless mistake; a blunder. **2** a social indiscretion. [F, = false step]

fave /feɪv/ n. & adj. sl. = FAVOURITE (esp. in show business). [abbr.]

favela /fəˈvelə/ n. a Brazilian shack, slum, or shanty town. [Port.]

favour /ˈfeɪvə(r)/ n. & v. (US **favor**) —n. **1** an act of kindness beyond what is due or usual (*did it as a favour*). **2** esteem, liking, approval, goodwill; friendly regard (*gained their favour; look with favour on*). **3** partiality; too lenient or generous treatment. **4** aid, support (*under favour of night*). **5** a thing given or worn as a mark of favour or support, e.g. a badge or a knot of ribbons. **6** *archaic* leave, pardon (*by your favour*). **7** *Commerce archaic* a letter (*your favour of yesterday*). —v.tr. **1** regard or treat with favour or partiality. **2** give support or approval to; promote, prefer. **3 a** be to the advantage of (a person). **b** facilitate (a process etc.). **4** tend to confirm (an idea or theory). **5** (foll. by *with*) oblige (*favour me with a reply*). **6** (as **favoured** adj.) having special advantages. **7** colloq. resemble in features. □ **in favour 1** meeting with approval. **2** (foll. by *of*) **a** in support of. **b** to the advantage of. **out of favour** lacking approval. □□ **favourer** n. [ME f. OF f. L *favor -oris* f. *favēre* show kindness to]

favourable /ˈfeɪvərəb(ə)l/ adj. (US **favorable**) **1 a** well-disposed; propitious. **b** commendatory, approving. **2** giving consent (*a favourable answer*). **3** promising, auspicious, satisfactory (*a favourable*

aspect). **4** (often foll. by *to*) helpful, suitable. □□ **favourableness** n. **favourably** adv. [ME f. OF *favorable* f. L *favorabilis* (as FAVOUR)]

favourite /ˈfeɪvərɪt/ adj. & n. (US **favorite**) —adj. preferred to all others (*my favourite book*). —n. **1** a specially favoured person. **2** *Sport* a competitor thought most likely to win. □ **favourite son** *US* a person preferred as the presidential candidate by delegates from the candidate's home State. [obs. F *favorit* f. It. *favorito* past part. of *favorire* favour]

favouritism /ˈfeɪvərɪˌtɪz(ə)m/ n. (US **favoritism**) the unfair favouring of one person or group at the expense of another.

fawn[1] /fɔːn/ n., adj., & v. —n. **1** a young deer in its first year. **2** a light yellowish brown. —adj. fawn-coloured. —v.tr. (also *absol.*) (of a deer) bring forth (young). □ **in fawn** (of a deer) pregnant. [ME f. OF *faon* etc. ult. f. L *fetus* offspring: cf. FOETUS]

fawn[2] /fɔːn/ v.intr. **1** (often foll. by *on, upon*) (of a person) behave servilely, cringe. **2** (of an animal, esp. a dog) show extreme affection. □□ **fawner** n. **fawning** adj. **fawningly** adv. [OE *fagnian, fægnian* (as FAIN)]

fax /fæks/ n. & v. —n. **1** facsimile transmission (see FACSIMILE n. 2). **2** a copy produced by this. —v.tr. transmit (a document) in this way. [abbr. of FACSIMILE]

fay /feɪ/ n. *literary* a fairy. [ME f. OF *fae, faie* f. L *fata* (pl.) the Fates]

faze /feɪz/ v.tr. (often as **fazed** adj.) colloq. disconcert, perturb, disorientate. [var. of *feeze* drive off, f. OE *fēsian*, of unkn. orig.]

FBA abbr. Fellow of the British Academy.

FBI abbr. (in the US) Federal Bureau of Investigation.

FC abbr. Football Club.

FCC abbr. (in the US) Federal Communications Commission.

FCO abbr. (in the UK) Foreign and Commonwealth Office.

fcp. abbr. foolscap.

FD abbr. Defender of the Faith. [L *Fidei Defensor*]

FDA abbr. **1** (in the US) Food and Drugs Administration. **2** (in the UK) First Division (Civil Servants) Association (cf. AFDCS).

Fe symb. *Chem.* the element iron.

fealty /ˈfiːəltɪ/ n. (pl. **-ies**) **1** hist. **a** a feudal tenant's or vassal's fidelity to a lord. **b** an acknowledgement of this. **2** allegiance. [ME f. OF *feaulté* f. L *fidelitas -tatis* f. *fidelis* faithful f. *fides* faith]

fear /fɪə(r)/ n. & v. —n. **1 a** an unpleasant emotion caused by exposure to danger, expectation of pain, etc. **b** a state of alarm (*be in fear*). **2** a cause of fear (*all fears removed*). **3** (often foll. by *of*) dread or fearful respect (towards) (*had a fear of heights*). **4** anxiety for the safety of (*in fear of their lives*). **5** danger; likelihood (of something unwelcome) (*there is little fear of failure*). —v. **1 a** tr. feel fear about or towards (a person or thing). **b** intr. feel fear. **2** intr. (foll. by *for*) feel anxiety or apprehension about (*feared for my life*). **3** tr. apprehend; have uneasy expectation of (*fear the worst*). **4** tr. (usu. foll. by *that* + clause) apprehend with fear or regret (*I fear that you are wrong*). **5** tr. **a** (foll. by *to* + infin.) hesitate. **b** (foll. by verbal noun) shrink from; be apprehensive about (*he feared meeting his ex-wife*). **6** tr. show reverence towards. □ **for fear of** (or **that**) to avoid the risk of (or that). **never fear** there is no danger of that. **no fear** colloq. expressing strong denial or refusal. **without fear or favour** impartially. [OE f. Gmc]

fearful /ˈfɪəfʊl/ adj. **1** (usu. foll. by *of*, or *that* + clause) afraid. **2** terrible, awful. **3** colloq. extremely unwelcome or unpleasant (*a fearful row*). □□ **fearfully** adv. **fearfulness** n.

fearless /ˈfɪəlɪs/ adj. **1** courageous, brave. **2** (foll. by *of*) without fear. □□ **fearlessly** adv. **fearlessness** n.

fearsome /ˈfɪəsəm/ adj. appalling or frightening,

esp. in appearance. □□**fearsomely** *adv.*
fearsomeness *n.*

feasibility /ˌfiːzɪˈbɪlɪtɪ/ *n.* the state or degree of being feasible. □**feasibility study** a study of the practicability of a proposed project.

feasible /ˈfiːzɪb(ə)l/ *adj.* **1** practicable, possible; easily or conveniently done. **2** *disp.* likely, probable (*it is feasible that it will rain*). □□**feasibly** *adv.* [ME f. OF *faisable*, *-ible* f. *fais-* stem of *faire* f. L *facere* do, make]

feast /fiːst/ *n. & v.* —*n.* **1** a large or sumptuous meal. **2** a gratification to the senses or mind. **3 a** an annual religious celebration. **b** a day dedicated to a particular saint. **4** an annual village festival. —*v.* **1** *intr.* partake of a feast; eat and drink sumptuously. **2** *tr.* **a** regale. **b** pass (time) in feasting. □**feast-day** a day on which a feast (esp. in sense 3) is held. **feast one's eyes on** take pleasure in beholding. **feast of reason** intellectual talk. □□**feaster** *n.* [ME f. OF *feste*, *fester* f. L *festus* joyous]

feat /fiːt/ *n.* a noteworthy act or achievement. [ME f. OF *fait*, *fet* (as FACT)]

feather /ˈfeðə(r)/ *n. & v.* —*n.* **1** any of the appendages growing from a bird's skin, with a horny hollow stem and fine strands. **2** one or more of these as decoration etc. **3** (*collect.*) **a** plumage. **b** game-birds. —*v.* **1** *tr.* cover or line with feathers. **2** *tr. Rowing* turn (an oar) so that it passes through the air edgeways. **3** *tr. Aeron. & Naut.* **a** cause (the propeller blades) to rotate in such a way as to lessen the air or water resistance. **b** vary the angle of incidence of (helicopter blades). **4** *intr.* float, move, or wave like feathers. □**feather bed** a bed with a mattress stuffed with feathers. **feather-bed** *v.tr.* (**-bedded, -bedding**) provide with (esp. financial) advantages. **feather-bedding** the employment of excess staff. **feather-brain** (or **-head**) a silly or absent-minded person. **feather-brained** (or **-headed**) silly, absent-minded. **feather-edge** the fine edge of a wedge-shaped board. **a feather in one's cap** an achievement to one's credit. **feather one's nest** enrich oneself. **feather-stitch** ornamental zigzag sewing. **in fine** (or **high**) **feather** *colloq.* in good spirits. □□**feathered** *adj.* (also in *comb.*). **featherless** *adj.* **feathery** *adj.* **featheriness** *n.* [OE *fether*, *gefithrian*, f. Gmc]

feathering /ˈfeðərɪŋ/ *n.* **1** bird's plumage. **2** the feathers of an arrow. **3** a feather-like structure in an animal's coat. **4** *Archit.* cusps in tracery.

featherweight /ˈfeðəˌweɪt/ *n.* **1 a** a weight in certain sports intermediate between bantamweight and lightweight, in the amateur boxing scale 54-7kg but differing for professionals, wrestlers, and weight-lifters. **b** a sportsman of this weight. **2** a very light person or thing. **3** (usu. *attrib.*) a trifling or unimportant thing.

feature /ˈfiːtʃə(r)/ *n. & v.* —*n.* **1** a distinctive or characteristic part of a thing. **2** (usu. in *pl.*) a distinctive part of the face, esp. with regard to shape and visual effect. **3** a distinctive or regular article in a newspaper or magazine. **4 a** (in full **feature film**) a full-length film intended as the main item in a cinema programme. **b** (in full **feature programme**) a broadcast devoted to a particular topic. —*v.* **1** *tr.* make a special display or attraction of; give special prominence to. **2** *tr. & intr.* have as or be an important actor, participant, or topic in a film, broadcast, etc. **3** *intr.* be a feature. □□**featured** *adj.* (also in *comb.*). **featureless** *adj.* [ME f. OF *feture, faiture* form f. L *factura* formation: see FACTURE]

Feb. *abbr.* February.

febrifuge /ˈfebrɪˌfjuːdʒ/ *n.* a medicine or treatment that reduces fever; a cooling drink. □□**febrifugal** /fɪˈbrɪfjʊg(ə)l, ˌfebrɪˈfjuːg(ə)l/ *adj.* [F *fébrifuge* f. L *febris* fever + -FUGE]

febrile /ˈfiːbraɪl/ *adj.* of or relating to fever; feverish. □□**febrility** /fɪˈbrɪlɪtɪ/ *n.* [F *fébrile* or med.L *febrilis* f. L *febris* fever]

February /ˈfebrʊərɪ/ *n.* (*pl.* **-ies**) the second month

of the year. [ME f. OF *fevrier* ult. f. L *februarius* f. *februa* a purification feast held in this month]

feces *US* var. of FAECES.

feckless /ˈfeklɪs/ *adj.* **1** feeble, ineffective. **2** unthinking, irresponsible (*feckless gaiety*). □□**fecklessly** *adv.* **fecklessness** *n.* [Sc. *feck* f. *effeck* var. of EFFECT]

feculent /ˈfekjʊlənt/ *adj.* **1** murky; filthy. **2** containing sediments or dregs. □□**feculence** *n.* [F *féculent* or L *faeculentus* (as FAECES)]

fecund /ˈfiːkənd, ˈfek-/ *adj.* **1** prolific, fertile. **2** fertilizing. □□**fecundability** /fɪˌkʌndəˈbɪlɪtɪ/ *n.* **fecundity** /fɪˈkʌndɪtɪ/ *n.* [ME f. F *fécond* or L *fecundus*]

fecundate /ˈfiːkənˌdeɪt, ˈfek-/ *v.tr.* **1** make fruitful. **2** = FERTILIZE. □□**fecundation** /-ˈdeɪʃ(ə)n/ *n.* [L *fecundare* f. *fecundus* fruitful]

Fed /fed/ *n. US sl.* a federal official, esp. a member of the FBI. [abbr. of FEDERAL]

fed *past* and *past part.* of FEED. □**fed up** (or **fed to death**) (often foll. by *with*) discontented or bored, esp. from a surfeit of something (*am fed up with the rain*). **fed-upness** the state of being fed up.

fedayeen /ˌfedəˈjiːn/ *n.pl.* Arab guerrillas operating esp. against Israel. [colloq. Arab. *fidāʾiyīn* pl. f. Arab. *fidāʾī* adventurer]

federal /ˈfedər(ə)l/ *adj.* **1** of a system of government in which several States form a unity but remain independent in internal affairs. **2** relating to or affecting such a federation (*federal laws*). **3** relating to or favouring centralized government. **4** (**Federal**) *US* of the Northern States in the Civil War. **5** comprising an association of largely independent units. □**federal reserve** (in the US) a national system of reserve cash available to banks. □□**federalism** *n.* **federalist** *n.* **federalize** *v.tr.* (also **-ise**). **federalization** /-ˈzeɪʃ(ə)n/ *n.* **federally** *adv.* [L *foedus -eris* league, covenant]

federate *v. & adj.* —*v.tr. & intr.* /ˈfedəˌreɪt/ organize or be organized on a federal basis. —*adj.* /ˈfedərət/ having a federal organization. □□**federative** /ˈfedərətɪv/ *adj.* [LL *foederare foederat-* (as FEDERAL)]

federation /ˌfedəˈreɪʃ(ə)n/ *n.* **1** a federal group of States. **2** a federated society or group. **3** the act or an instance of federating. □□**federationist** *n.* [F *fédération* f. LL *foederatio* (as FEDERAL)]

fedora /frˈdɔːrə/ *n.* a low soft felt hat with a crown creased lengthways. [*Fédora*, drama by V. Sardou (1882)]

fee /fiː/ *n. & v.* —*n.* **1** a payment made to a professional person or to a professional or public body in exchange for advice or services. **2** money paid as part of a special transaction, for a privilege, admission to a society, etc. (*enrolment fee*). **3** (in *pl.*) money regularly paid (esp. to a school) for continuing services. **4** *Law* an inherited estate, unlimited (**fee simple**) or limited (**fee tail**) as to the category of heir. **5** *hist.* a fief; a feudal benefice. —*v.tr.* (**fee'd** or **feed**) **1** pay a fee to. **2** engage for a fee. [ME f. AF, = OF *feu, fieu*, etc. f. med.L *feodum, feudum*, perh. f. Frank.: cf. FEUD[2], FIEF]

feeble /ˈfiːb(ə)l/ *adj.* **1** weak, infirm. **2** lacking energy, force, or effectiveness. **3** dim, indistinct. **4** deficient in character or intelligence. □□**feebleness** *n.* **feeblish** *adj.* **feebly** *adv.* [ME f. AF & OF *feble, fieble, fleible* f. L *flebilis* lamentable f. *flēre* weep]

feeble-minded /ˌfiːb(ə)lˈmaɪndɪd/ *adj.* **1** unintelligent. **2** mentally deficient. □□**feeble-mindedly** *adv.* **feeble-mindedness** *n.*

feed /fiːd/ *v. & n.* —*v.* (*past* and *past part.* **fed** /fed/) **1** *tr.* **a** supply with food. **b** put food into the mouth of. **2** *tr.* **a** give as food, esp. to animals. **b** graze (cattle). **3** *tr.* serve as food for. **4** *intr.* (usu. foll. by *on*) (esp. of animals, or *colloq.* of people) take food; eat. **5** *tr.* nourish; make grow. **6 a** *tr.* maintain supply of raw material, fuel, etc., to (a fire, machine, etc.). **b** *tr.* (foll. by *into*) supply (material) to a machine etc. **c** *intr.* (often foll. by *into*) (of a river etc.) flow into another body of water. **d** *tr.* insert further coins into (a meter) to continue its function, validity, etc. **7** *intr.* (foll. by *on*) **a** be nourished by. **b** derive benefit from. **8** *tr.* use (land) as pasture. **9** *tr. Theatr. sl.* supply (an actor etc.) with cues. **10** *tr. Sport* send passes to (a player) in a ball-game. **11** *tr.* gratify (vanity etc.). **12** *tr.* provide (advice, information, etc.) to. —*n.* **1** an amount of food, esp. for animals or infants. **2** the act or an instance of feeding; the giving of food. **3** *colloq.* a meal. **4** pasturage; green crops. **5 a** a supply of raw material to a machine etc. **b** the provision of this or a device for it. **6** the charge of a gun. **7** *Theatr. sl.* an actor who supplies another with cues. □**feed back** produce feedback. **feed the fishes 1** meet one's death by drowning. **2** be seasick. **feeding-bottle** a bottle with a teat for feeding infants. **feed up 1** fatten. **2** satiate (cf. *fed up* (see FED)). □□**feedable** *adj.* [OE *fēdan* f. Gmc]

feedback /ˈfiːdbæk/ *n.* **1** information about the result of an experiment etc.; response. **2** *Electronics* **a** the return of a fraction of the output signal from one stage of a circuit, amplifier, etc., to the input of the same or a preceding stage. **b** a signal so returned. **3** *Biol.* etc. the modification or control of a process or system by its results or effects, esp. by the difference between the desired and the actual result.

feeder /ˈfiːdə(r)/ *n.* **1** a person or thing that feeds. **2** a person who feeds in a specified manner. **3** a child's feeding-bottle. **4** *Brit.* a bib for an infant. **5** a tributary stream. **6** a branch road, railway line, etc., linking outlying districts with a main communication system. **7** *Electr.* a main carrying electricity to a distribution point. **8** a hopper or feeding apparatus in a machine.

feel /fiːl/ *v.* & *n.* —*v.* (*past* and *past part.* **felt** /felt/) **1** *tr.* **a** examine or search by touch. **b** (*absol.*) have the sensation of touch (*was unable to feel*). **2** *tr.* perceive or ascertain by touch; have a sensation of (*could feel the warmth; felt that it was cold*). **3** *tr.* **a** undergo, experience (*shall feel my anger*). **b** exhibit or be conscious of (an emotion, sensation, conviction, etc.). **4 a** *intr.* have a specified feeling or reaction (*felt strongly about it*). **b** *tr.* be emotionally affected by (*felt the rebuke deeply*). **5** *tr.* (foll. by *that* + clause) have a vague or unreasoned impression (*I feel that I am right*). **6** *tr.* consider, think (*I feel it useful to go*). **7** *intr.* seem; give an impression of being; be perceived as (*the air feels chilly*). **8** *intr.* be consciously; consider oneself (*I feel happy; do not feel well*). **9** *intr.* **a** (foll. by *with*) have sympathy with. **b** (foll. by *for*) have pity or compassion for. **10** *tr.* (often foll. by *up*) *sl.* fondle the genitals of. —*n.* **1** the act or an instance of feeling; testing by touch. **2** the sensation characterizing a material, situation, etc. **3** the sense of touch. □**feel free** (often foll. by *to* + infin.) not be reluctant or hesitant (*do feel free to criticize*). **feel like** have a wish for; be inclined towards. **feel one's oats** see OAT. **feel oneself** be fit or confident etc. **feel out** investigate cautiously. **feel strange** see STRANGE. **feel up to** be ready to face or deal with. **feel one's way** proceed carefully; act cautiously. **get the feel of** become accustomed to using. **make one's influence** (or **presence** etc.) **felt** assert one's influence; make others aware of one's presence etc. [OE *fēlan* f. WG]

feeler /ˈfiːlə(r)/ *n.* **1** an organ in certain animals for testing things by touch or for searching for food. **2** a tentative proposal or suggestion, esp. to elicit a response (*put out feelers*). **3** a person or thing that feels. □**feeler gauge** a gauge equipped with blades for measuring narrow gaps etc.

feeling /ˈfiːlɪŋ/ *n.* & *adj.* —*n.* **1 a** the capacity to feel; a sense of touch (*lost all feeling in his arm*). **b** a physical sensation. **2 a** (often foll. by *of*) a particular emotional reaction (*a feeling of despair*). **b** (in *pl.*) emotional susceptibilities or sympathies (*hurt my feelings; had strong feelings about it*). **3** a particular sensitivity (*had a feeling for literature*). **4 a** an opinion or notion, esp. a vague or irrational one (*my

feelings on the subject; had a feeling she would be there*). **b** vague awareness (*had a feeling of safety*). **c** sentiment (*the general feeling was against it*). **5** readiness to feel sympathy or compassion. **6 a** the general emotional response produced by a work of art, piece of music, etc. **b** emotional commitment or sensibility in artistic execution (*played with feeling*). —*adj.* **1** sensitive, sympathetic. **2** showing emotion or sensitivity. □□**feelingless** *adj.* **feelingly** *adv.*

feet *pl.* of FOOT.

feign /feɪn/ *v.* **1** *tr.* simulate; pretend to be affected by (*feign madness*). **2** *tr. archaic* invent (an excuse etc.). **3** *intr.* indulge in pretence. [ME f. *feign-* stem of OF *feindre* f. L *fingere* mould, contrive]

feijoa /feɪˈdʒəʊə, faɪ-/ *n.* **1** any evergreen shrub or tree of the genus *Feijoa*, bearing edible guava-like fruit. **2** this fruit. [mod.L f. J. da Silva *Feijo*, 19th-c. Sp. naturalist]

feint¹ /feɪnt/ *n.* & *v.* —*n.* **1** a sham attack or blow etc. to divert attention or fool an opponent or enemy. **2** pretence. —*v.intr.* make a feint. [F *feinte*, fem. past part. of *feindre* FEIGN]

feint² /feɪnt/ *adj.* esp. *Printing* = FAINT *adj.* 6 (*feint lines*). [ME f. OF (as FEINT¹):· see FAINT]

feisty /ˈfaɪstɪ/ *adj.* (**feistier, feistiest**) *US sl.* **1** aggressive, exuberant. **2** touchy. □□**feistiness** *n.* [*feist* (= fist) small dog]

felafel /feˈlɑːf(ə)l/ *n.* (also **falafel**) (in Near Eastern countries) a spicy dish of fried rissoles made from mashed chick peas or beans. [Arab. *falāfil*]

feldspar /ˈfeldspɑː(r)/ *n.* (also **felspar** /ˈfelspɑː(r)/) *Mineral.* any of a group of aluminium silicates of potassium, sodium, or calcium, which are the most abundant minerals in the earth's crust. □□ **feldspathic** /-ˈspæθɪk/ *adj.* **feldspathoid** /ˈfeldspə,θɔɪd/ *n.* [G *Feldspat, -spath* f. *Feld* FIELD + *Spat, Spath* SPAR³:· *felspar* by false assoc. with G *Fels* rock]

felicitate /fəˈlɪsɪ,teɪt/ *v.tr.* (usu. foll. by *on*) congratulate. □□**felicitation** /-ˈteɪʃ(ə)n/ *n.* (usu. in *pl.*). [LL *felicitare* make happy f. L *felix -icis* happy]

felicitous /fəˈlɪsɪtəs/ *adj.* (of an expression, quotation, civilities, or a person making them) strikingly apt; pleasantly ingenious. □□**felicitously** *adv.* **felicitousness** *n.*

felicity /fəˈlɪsɪtɪ/ *n.* (*pl.* **-ies**) **1** intense happiness; being happy. **2** a cause of happiness. **3 a** a capacity for apt expression; appropriateness. **b** an appropriate or well-chosen phrase. **4** a fortunate state. [ME f. OF *felicité* f. L *felicitas -tatis* f. *felix -icis* happy]

feline /ˈfiːlaɪn/ *adj.* & *n.* —*adj.* **1** of or relating to the cat family. **2** catlike, esp. in beauty or slyness. —*n.* an animal of the cat family Felidae. □□**felinity** /frˈlɪnɪtɪ/ *n.* [L *felinus* f. *feles* cat]

fell¹ *past* of FALL *v.*

fell² /fel/ *v.* & *n.* —*v.tr.* **1** cut down (esp. a tree). **2** strike or knock down (a person or animal). **3** stitch down (the edge of a seam) to lie flat. —*n.* an amount of timber cut. □□ **feller** *n.* [OE *fellan* f. Gmc, rel. to FALL]

fell³ /fel/ *n. N.Engl.* **1** a hill. **2** a stretch of hills or moorland. [ME f. ON *fjall, fell* hill]

fell⁴ /fel/ *adj. poet.* or *rhet.* **1** fierce, ruthless. **2** terrible, destructive. □**at** (or **in**) **one fell swoop** in a single (orig. deadly) action. [ME f. OF *fel* f. Rmc FELON¹]

fell⁵ /fel/ *n.* an animal's hide or skin with its hair. [OE *fel, fell* f. Gmc]

fellah /ˈfelə/ *n.* (*pl.* **fellahin** /-əˈhiːn/) an Egyptian peasant. [Arab. *fallāḥ* husbandman f. *falaḥa* till the soil]

fellatio /fɪˈleɪʃɪəʊ, feˈlɑːtɪəʊ/ *n.* oral stimulation of the penis. □□ **fellate** /fɪˈleɪt/ *v.tr.* **fellator** /fɪˈleɪtə(r)/ *n.* [mod.L f. L *fellare* suck]

feller /ˈfelə(r)/ *n.* = FELLOW 1, 2. [repr. an affected or sl. pronunc.]

felloe /ˈfeləʊ/ *n.* (also **felly** /ˈfelɪ/) (*pl.* **-oes** or **-ies**) the outer circle (or a section of it) of a wheel, to which the spokes are fixed. [OE *felg*, of unkn. orig.]

fellow /'feləʊ/ n. **1** colloq. a man or boy (*poor fellow!*; *my dear fellow*). **2** derog. a person regarded with contempt. **3** (usu. in *pl.*) a person associated with another; a comrade (*were separated from their fellows*). **4** a counterpart or match; the other of a pair. **5** an equal; one of the same class. **6** a contemporary. **7 a** an incorporated senior member of a college. **b** an elected graduate receiving a stipend for a period of research. **c** a member of the governing body in some universities. **8** a member of a learned society. **9** (*attrib.*) belonging to the same class or activity (*fellow soldier*; *fellow-countryman*). □**fellow-feeling** sympathy from common experience. **fellow-traveller 1** a person who travels with another. **2** a sympathizer with, or a secret member of, the Communist Party. [OE *fēolaga* f. ON *félagi* f. *fé* cattle, property, money: see LAY¹]

fellowship /'feləʊʃɪp/ n. **1** companionship, friendliness. **2** participation, sharing; community of interest. **3** a body of associates; a company. **4** a brotherhood or fraternity. **5** a guild or corporation. **6** the status or emoluments of a fellow of a college or society.

felly var. of FELLOE.

felon¹ /'felən/ n. & adj. —n. a person who has committed a felony. —adj. archaic cruel, wicked. □□**felonry** n. [ME f. OF f. med.L *felo -onis*, of unkn. orig.]

felon² /'felən/ n. an inflammatory sore on the finger near the nail. [ME, perh. as FELON¹: cf. med.L *felo, fello* in the same sense]

felonious /fɪ'ləʊnɪəs/ adj. **1** criminal. **2** Law **a** of or involving felony. **b** who has committed felony. □□ **feloniously** adv.

felony /'felənɪ/ n. (pl. -**ies**) a crime regarded by the law as grave, and usu. involving violence. [ME f. OF *felonie* (as FELON¹)]

felspar var. of FELDSPAR.

felt¹ /felt/ n. & v. —n. **1** a kind of cloth made by rolling and pressing wool etc., or by weaving and shrinking it. **2** a similar material made from other fibres. —v. **1** tr. make into felt; mat together. **2** tr. cover with felt. **3** intr. become matted. □**felt-tipped** (or **felt-tip**) **pen** a pen with a writing-point made of felt or fibre. □□ **felty** adj. [OE f. WG]

felt² past and past part. of FEEL.

felucca /fɪ'lʌkə/ n. a small Mediterranean coasting vessel with oars or lateen sails or both. [It. *felucca* f. obs. Sp. *faluca* f. Arab. *fulk*, perh. f. Gk *epholkion* sloop]

felwort /'felwɜːt/ n. a purple-flowered gentian, *Gentianella amarella*. [OE *feldwyrt* (as FIELD, WORT)]

female /'fiːmeɪl/ adj. & n. —adj. **1** of the sex that can bear offspring or produce eggs. **2** (of plants or their parts) fruit-bearing; having a pistil and no stamens. **3** of or consisting of women or female animals or female plants. **4** (of a screw, socket, etc.) manufactured hollow to receive a corresponding inserted part. —n. a female person, animal, or plant. □**female impersonator** a male performer impersonating a woman. □□ **femaleness** n. [ME f. OF *femelle* (n.) f. L *femella* dimin. of *femina* a woman, assim. to *male*]

feme /fiːm/ n. Law a woman or wife. □**feme covert** a married woman. **feme sole** a woman without a husband (esp. if divorced). [ME f. AF & OF f. L *femina* woman]

feminal /'femɪn(ə)l/ adj. archaic womanly. □□ **feminality** /-'nælɪtɪ/ n. [med.L *feminalis* f. L *femina* woman]

femineity /ˌfemɪ'niːɪtɪ/ n. archaic womanliness; womanishness. [L *femineus* womanish f. *femina* woman]

feminine /'femɪnɪn/ adj. & n. —adj. **1** of or characteristic of women. **2** having qualities associated with women. **3** womanly, effeminate. **4** Gram. of or denoting the gender proper to women's names. —n.

Gram. a feminine gender or word. □□**femininely** adv. **feminineness** n. **femininity** /-'nɪnɪtɪ/ n. [ME f. OF *feminin -ine* or L *femininus* f. *femina* woman]

feminism /'femɪˌnɪz(ə)m/ n. **1** the advocacy of women's rights on the ground of the equality of the sexes. **2** Med. the development of female characteristics in a male person. □□ **feminist** n. (in sense 1). [L *femina* woman (in sense 1 after F *féminisme*)]

feminity /fe'mɪnɪtɪ/ n. = FEMININITY (see FEMININE). [ME f. OF *feminité* f. med.L *feminitas -tatis* f. L *femina* woman]

feminize /'femɪˌnaɪz/ v.tr. & intr. (also -**ise**) make or become feminine or female. □□ **feminization** /-'zeɪʃ(ə)n/ n.

femme fatale /ˌfæm fæ'taːl/ n. (pl. **femmes fatales** pronunc. same) a seductively attractive woman. [F]

femto- /'femtəʊ/ comb. form denoting a factor of 10^{-15} (*femtometre*). [Da. or Norw. *femten* fifteen]

femur /'fiːmə(r)/ n. (pl. **femurs** or **femora** /'femərə/) **1** Anat. the thigh-bone, the thick bone between the hip and the knee. **2** the corresponding part of an insect. □□ **femoral** /'femər(ə)l/ adj. [L *femur femoris* thigh]

fen /fen/ n. **1** a low marshy or flooded area of land. **2** (**the Fens**) flat low-lying areas in and around Cambridgeshire. □**fen-berry** (pl. -**berries**) a cranberry. **fen-fire** will-o'-the-wisp. □□ **fenny** adj. [OE *fenn* f. Gmc]

fence /fens/ n. & v. —n. **1** a barrier or railing or other upright structure enclosing an area of ground, esp. to prevent or control access. **2** a large upright obstacle in steeplechasing or showjumping. **3** sl. a receiver of stolen goods. **4** a guard or guide in machinery. —v. **1** tr. surround with or as with a fence. **2** tr. **a** (foll. by *in*, *off*) enclose or separate with or as with a fence. **b** (foll. by *up*) seal with or as with a fence. **3** tr. (foll. by *from*, *against*) screen, shield, protect. **4** tr. (foll. by *out*) exclude with or as with a fence; keep out. **5** tr. (also *absol.*) sl. deal in (stolen goods). **6** intr. practise the sport of fencing; use a sword. **7** intr. (foll. by *with*) evade answering (a person or question). **8** intr. (of a horse etc.) leap fences. □**sit on the fence** remain neutral or undecided in a dispute etc. □□ **fenceless** adj. **fencer** n. [ME f. DEFENCE]

fencible /'fensɪb(ə)l/ n. hist. a soldier liable only for home service. [ME f. DEFENSIBLE]

fencing /'fensɪŋ/ n. **1** a set or extent of fences. **2** material for making fences. **3** the art or sport of swordplay.

fend /fend/ v. **1** intr. (foll. by *for*) look after (esp. oneself). **2** tr. (usu. foll. by *off*) keep away; ward off (an attack etc.). [ME f. DEFEND]

fender /'fendə(r)/ n. **1** a low frame bordering a fireplace to keep in falling coals etc. **2** Naut. a piece of old cable, matting, etc., hung over a vessel's side to protect it against impact. **3 a** a thing used to keep something off, prevent a collision, etc. **b** US a bumper or mudguard of a motor vehicle.

fenestella /ˌfenɪ'stelə/ n. Archit. a niche in a wall south of an altar, holding the piscina and often the credence. [L, dimin. of *fenestra* window]

fenestra /fɪ'nestrə/ n. (pl. **fenestrae** /-triː/) **1** Anat. a small hole or opening in a bone etc., esp. one of two (**fenestra ovalis**, **fenestra rotunda**) in the inner ear. **2** a perforation in a surgical instrument. **3** a hole made by surgical fenestration. [L, = window]

fenestrate /fɪ'nestreɪt/ adj. Bot. & Zool. having small window-like perforations or transparent areas. [L *fenestratus* past part. of *fenestrare* f. *fenestra* window]

fenestrated /fɪ'nestreɪtɪd/ adj. **1** Archit. having windows. **2** perforated. **3** = FENESTRATE. **4** Surgery having fenestrae.

fenestration /ˌfenɪ'streɪʃ(ə)n/ n. **1** Archit. the arrangement of windows in a building. **2** Bot. & Zool. being fenestrate. **3** a surgical operation in which a new opening is formed, esp. in the bony labyrinth of

æ cat ɑː arm e bed ɜː her ɪ sit iː see ɒ hot ɔː saw ʌ run ʊ put uː too ə ago aɪ my

the inner ear, as a form of treatment in some cases of deafness.

Fenian /'fi:nɪən/ n. & adj. —n. hist. a member of a 19th-c. league among the Irish in the US & Ireland for promoting revolution and overthrowing British government in Ireland. —adj. of or relating to the Fenians. □□ **Fenianism** n. [OIr. féne name of an ancient Irish people, confused with fíann guard of legendary kings]

fennec /'fenɪk/ n. a small fox, Vulpes zerda, native to N. Africa, having large pointed ears. [Arab. fanak]

fennel /'fen(ə)l/ n. **1** a yellow-flowered fragrant umbelliferous plant, Foeniculum vulgare, with leaves or leaf-stalks used in salads, soups, etc. **2** the seeds of this used as flavouring. [OE finugl etc. & OF fenoil f. L feniculum f. fenum hay]

fenugreek /'fenju:ˌgri:k/ n. **1** a leguminous plant, Trigonella foenum-graecum, having aromatic seeds. **2** these seeds used as flavouring, esp. ground and used in curry powder. [OE fenogrecum, superseded in ME f. OF fenugrec f. L faenugraecum (fenum graecum Greek hay), used by the Romans as fodder]

feoffment /'fefmənt/ n. hist. a mode of conveying a freehold estate by a formal transfer of possession. □□ **feoffee** /fe'fi:/ n. **feoffor** n. [ME f. AF feoffement, rel. to FEE]

feral /'fɪər(ə)l, 'fer(ə)l/ adj. **1** (of an animal or plant) wild, untamed, uncultivated. **2 a** (of an animal) in a wild state after escape from captivity. **b** born in the wild of such an animal. **3** brutal. [L ferus wild]

fer de lance /ˌfeə də 'lɑ:ns/ n. a large highly venomous snake, Bothrops atrox, native to Central and S. America. [F, = iron (head) of a lance]

feretory /'feritəri/ n. (pl. -ies) **1** a shrine for a saint's relics. **2** a chapel containing such a shrine. [ME f. OF fiertre f. L feretrum f. Gk pheretron f. pherō bear]

ferial /'fɪərɪəl, 'fer-/ adj. Eccl. **1** (of a day) ordinary; not appointed for a festival or fast. **2** (of a service etc.) for use on a ferial day. [ME f. OF ferial or med.L ferialis f. L feriae: see FAIR²]

fermata /fə'mɑ:tə/ n. (pl. **fermatas**) Mus. **1** an unspecified prolongation of a note or rest. **2** a sign indicating this. [It.]

ferment n. & v. —n. /'f3:ment/ **1** agitation, excitement, tumult. **2 a** fermenting, fermentation. **b** a fermenting-agent or leaven. —v. /fə'ment/ **1** intr. & tr. undergo or subject to fermentation. **2** intr. & tr. effervesce or cause to effervesce. **3** tr. excite; stir up; foment. □□ **fermentable** /-'mentəb(ə)l/ adj. **fermenter** /-'mentə(r)/ n. [ME f. OF ferment or L fermentum f. L fervēre boil]

fermentation /ˌf3:men'teɪʃ(ə)n/ n. **1** the breakdown of a substance by micro-organisms, such as yeasts and bacteria, usu. in the absence of oxygen, esp. of sugar to ethyl alcohol in making beers, wines, and spirits. **2** agitation, excitement. □□ **fermentative** /-'mentətɪv/ adj. [ME f. LL fermentatio (as FERMENT)]

fermi /'f3:mi/ n. (pl. **fermis**) a unit of length equal to 10^{-15} metre, formerly used in nuclear physics. [E. Fermi, Ital.-Amer. physicist d. 1954]

fermion /'f3:mɪˌɒn/ n. Physics any of several elementary particles with half-integral spin, e.g. nucleons (cf. BOSON). [as FERMI + -ON]

fermium /'f3:mɪəm/ n. Chem. a transuranic radioactive metallic element produced artificially. ¶ Symb.: **Fm**. [as FERMI + -IUM]

fern /f3:n/ n. (pl. same or **ferns**) any flowerless plant of the order Filicales, reproducing by spores and usu. having feathery fronds. □□ **fernery** n. (pl. -ies). **fernless** adj. **ferny** adj. [OE fearn f. WG]

ferocious /fə'rəʊʃəs/ adj. fierce, savage; wildly cruel. □□ **ferociously** adv. **ferociousness** n. [L ferox -ocis]

ferocity /fə'rɒsɪti/ n. (pl. -ies) a ferocious nature or act. [F férocité or L ferocitas (as FEROCIOUS)]

-ferous /fərəs/ comb. form (usu. **-iferous**) forming adjectives with the sense 'bearing', 'having' (auriferous; odoriferous). □□ **-ferously** suffix

-ferousness suffix [from or after F -fère or L -fer producing f. ferre bear]

ferrate /'fereɪt/ n. Chem. a salt of (the hypothetical) ferric acid. [L ferrum iron]

ferrel var. of FERRULE.

ferret /'ferɪt/ n. & v. —n. **1** a small half-domesticated polecat, Mustela putorius furo, used in catching rabbits, rats, etc. **2** a person who searches assiduously. —v. **1** intr. hunt with ferrets. **2** intr. rummage; search about. **3** tr. (often foll. by about, away, out, etc.) **a** clear out (holes or an area of ground) with ferrets. **b** take or drive away (rabbits etc.) with ferrets. **4** tr. (foll. by out) search out (secrets, criminals, etc.). □□ **ferreter** n. **ferrety** adj. [ME f. OF fu(i)ret alt. f. fu(i)ron f. LL furo -onis f. L fur thief]

ferri- /'feri/ comb. form Chem. containing iron, esp. in ferric compounds. [L ferrum iron]

ferriage /'feriɪdʒ/ n. **1** conveyance by ferry. **2** a charge for using a ferry.

ferric /'ferik/ adj. **1** of iron. **2** Chem. containing iron in a trivalent form (cf. FERROUS).

ferrimagnetism /ˌferi'mægnɪˌtɪz(ə)m/ n. Physics a form of ferromagnetism with non-parallel alignment of neighbouring atoms or ions. □□ **ferrimagnetic** /-mæg'netɪk/ adj. [F ferrimagnétisme (as FERRI-, MAGNETISM)]

Ferris wheel /'feris/ n. a fairground ride consisting of a tall revolving vertical wheel with passenger cars suspended on its outer edge. [G. W. G. Ferris, Amer. engineer d. 1896]

ferrite /'ferait/ n. Chem. **1** a salt of (the hypothetical) ferrous acid $H_2Fe_2O_4$, often with magnetic properties. **2** an allotrope of pure iron occurring in low-carbon steel. □□ **ferritic** /fe'ritik/ adj. [L ferrum iron]

ferro- /'ferəʊ/ comb. form Chem. **1** iron, esp. in ferrous compounds. **2** (of alloys) containing iron (ferrocyanide; ferromanganese). [L ferrum iron]

ferroconcrete /ˌferəʊ'kɒŋkri:t/ n. & adj. —n. concrete reinforced with steel. —adj. made of reinforced concrete.

ferroelectric /ˌferəʊi'lektrik/ adj. & n. Physics —adj. exhibiting permanent electric polarization which varies in strength with the applied electric field. —n. a ferroelectric substance. □□ **ferroelectricity** /-'trisiti/ n. [ELECTRIC after ferromagnetic]

ferromagnetism /ˌferəʊ'mægnɪˌtiz(ə)m/ n. Physics a phenomenon in which there is a high susceptibility to magnetization, the strength of which varies with the applied magnetizing field, and which may persist after removal of the applied field. □□ **ferromagnetic** /-mæg'netik/ adj.

ferrous /'ferəs/ adj. **1** containing iron (ferrous and non-ferrous metals). **2** Chem. containing iron in a divalent form (cf. FERRIC). [L ferrum iron]

ferruginous /fə'ru:dʒɪnəs/ adj. **1** of or containing iron-rust, or iron as a chemical constituent. **2** rust-coloured; reddish-brown. [L ferrugo -ginis rust f. ferrum iron]

ferrule /'feru:l/ n. (also **ferrel** /'fer(ə)l/) **1** a ring or cap strengthening the end of a stick or tube. **2** a band strengthening or forming a joint. [earlier verrel etc. f. OF virelle, virol(e), f. L viriola dimin. of viriae bracelet: assim. to L ferrum iron]

ferry /'feri/ n. & v. —n. (pl. -ies) **1** a boat or aircraft etc. for conveying passengers and goods, esp. across water and as a regular service. **2** the service itself or the place where it operates. —v. (-ies, -ied) **1** tr. & intr. convey or go in a boat etc. across water. **2** intr. (of a boat etc.) pass to and fro across water. **3** tr. transport from one place to another, esp. as a regular service. □□ **ferryman** n. (pl. -men). [ME f. ON ferja f. Gmc]

fertile /'f3:taɪl/ adj. **1 a** (of soil) producing abundant vegetation or crops. **b** fruitful. **2 a** (of a seed, egg, etc.) capable of becoming a new individual. **b** (of animals and plants) able to conceive young or produce fruit. **3** (of the mind) inventive. **4** (of nuclear material) able to become fissile by the capture of neutrons. □**Fertile Crescent** the fertile region extending in a crescent shape from the E. Mediterranean to the Persian Gulf. □□**fertility** /-'tɪlɪtɪ/ *n.* [ME f. F f. L *fertilis*]

fertilization /ˌfɜːtɪlaɪ'zeɪʃ(ə)n/ *n.* (also **-isation**) **1** *Biol.* the fusion of male and female gametes during sexual reproduction to form a zygote. **2 a** the act or an instance of fertilizing. **b** the process of being fertilized.

fertilize /'fɜːtɪˌlaɪz/ *v.tr.* (also **-ise**) **1** make (soil etc.) fertile or productive. **2** cause (an egg, female animal, or plant) to develop a new individual by introducing male reproductive material. □□**fertilizable** *adj.* **fertilizer** *n.*

ferula /'ferʊlə/ *n.* **1** any plant of the genus *Ferula*, esp. the giant fennel (*F. communis*), having a tall sticklike stem and thick roots. **2** = FERULE. [ME f. L, = giant fennel, rod]

ferule /'feruːl/ *n. & v.* —*n.* a flat ruler with a widened end formerly used for beating children. —*v.tr.* beat with a ferule. [ME (as FERULA)]

fervent /'fɜːv(ə)nt/ *adj.* **1** ardent, impassioned, intense (*fervent admirer; fervent hatred*). **2** hot, glowing. □□**fervency** *n.* **fervently** *adv.* [ME f. OF f. L *fervēre* boil]

fervid /'fɜːvɪd/ *adj.* **1** ardent, intense. **2** *poet.* hot, glowing. □□**fervidly** *adv.* [L *fervidus* (as FERVENT)]

fervour /'fɜːvə(r)/ *n.* (*US* **fervor**) **1** vehemence, passion, zeal. **2** a glowing condition; intense heat. [ME f. OF f. L *fervor -oris* (as FERVENT)]

fescue /'feskjuː/ *n.* any grass of the genus *Festuca*, valuable for pasture and fodder. [ME *festu(e)* f. OF *festu* ult. f. L *festuca* stalk, straw]

fess /fes/ *n.* (also **fesse**) *Heraldry* a horizontal stripe across the middle of a shield. □**fess point** a point at the centre of a shield. **in fess** arranged horizontally. [ME f. OF f. L *fascia* band]

festal /'fest(ə)l/ *adj.* **1** joyous, merry. **2** engaging in holiday activities. **3** of a feast. □□**festally** *adv.* [OF f. LL *festalis* (as FEAST)]

fester /'festə(r)/ *v.* **1** *tr. & intr.* make or become septic. **2** *intr.* cause continuing annoyance. **3** *intr.* rot, stagnate. [ME f. obs. *fester* (n.) or OF *festrir* f. OF *festre* f. L *fistula*: see FISTULA]

festival /'festɪv(ə)l/ *n. & adj.* —*n.* **1** a day or period of celebration, religious or secular. **2** a concentrated series of concerts, plays, etc., held regularly in a town etc. (*Bath Festival*). —*attrib.adj.* of or concerning a festival. [earlier as adj.: ME f. OF f. med.L *festivalis* (as FESTIVE)]

festive /'festɪv/ *adj.* **1** of or characteristic of a festival. **2** joyous. **3** fond of feasting, jovial. □□**festively** *adv.* **festiveness** *n.* [L *festivus* f. *festum* (as FEAST)]

festivity /fe'stɪvɪtɪ/ *n.* (*pl.* **-ies**) **1** gaiety, rejoicing. **2 a** a festive celebration. **b** (in *pl.*) festive proceedings. [ME f. OF *festivité* or L *festivitas* (as FESTIVE)]

festoon /fe'stuːn/ *n. & v.* —*n.* **1** a chain of flowers, leaves, ribbons, etc., hung in a curve as a decoration. **2** a carved or moulded ornament representing this. —*v.tr.* (often foll. by *with*) adorn with or form into festoons; decorate elaborately. □□**festoonery** *n.* [F *feston* f. It. *festone* f. *festa* FEAST]

Festschrift /'festʃrɪft/ *n.* (also **festschrift**) (*pl.* **-schriften** or **-schrifts**) a collection of writings published in honour of a scholar. [G f. *Fest* celebration + *Schrift* writing]

feta /'fetə/ *n.* (also **fetta**) a soft white ewe's-milk or goat's-milk cheese made esp. in Greece. [mod.Gk *pheta*]

fetch[1] /fetʃ/ *v. & n.* —*v.tr.* **1** go for and bring back (a person or thing) (*fetch a doctor*). **2** be sold for; realize (a price) (*fetched £10*). **3** cause (blood, tears, etc.) to flow. **4** draw (breath), heave (a sigh). **5** *colloq.* give a blow, slap, etc. (usu. with recipient stated: *fetched him a slap on the face*). **6** excite the emotions of, delight or irritate. —*n.* **1** an act of fetching. **2 a** dodge or trick. **3** *Naut.* **a** the distance travelled by

wind or waves across open water. **b** the distance a vessel must sail to reach open water. □**fetch and carry** run backwards and forwards with things, be a mere servant. **fetch up** *colloq.* **1** arrive, come to rest. **2** vomit. □□**fetcher** *n.* [OE *fecc(e)an* var. of *fetian*, prob. rel. to a Gmc root = grasp]

fetch[2] /fetʃ/ *n.* a person's wraith or double. [18th c.: orig. unkn.]

fetching /'fetʃɪŋ/ *adj.* attractive. □□**fetchingly** *adv.*

fête /feɪt/ *n. & v.* —*n.* **1** an outdoor function with the sale of goods, amusements, etc., esp. to raise funds for charity. **2** a great entertainment; a festival. **3** a saint's day. —*v.tr.* honour or entertain lavishly. [F *fête* (as FEAST)]

fête champêtre /feɪt ʃɑ̃'peɪtr/ *n.* an outdoor entertainment; a rural festival. [F (as FÊTE, *champêtre* rural)]

fetid /'fetɪd, 'fiːtɪd/ *adj.* (also **foetid**) stinking. □□**fetidly** *adv.* **fetidness** *n.* [L *fetidus* f. *fetēre* stink]

fetish /'fetɪʃ/ *n.* **1** *Psychol.* a thing abnormally stimulating or attracting sexual desire. **2 a** an inanimate object worshipped by primitive peoples for its supposed inherent magical powers or as being inhabited by a spirit. **b** a thing evoking irrational devotion or respect. □□**fetishism** *n.* **fetishist** *n.* **fetishistic** /-'ʃɪstɪk/ *adj.* [F *fétiche* f. Port. *feitiço* charm: orig. adj. = made by art, f. L *factitius* FACTITIOUS]

fetlock /'fetlɒk/ *n.* part of the back of a horse's leg above the hoof where a tuft of hair grows. [ME *fetlak* etc. rel. to G *Fessel* fetlock f. Gmc]

fetor /'fiːtə(r)/ *n.* a stench. [L (as FETID)]

fetta var. of FETA.

fetter /'fetə(r)/ *n. & v.* —*n.* **1 a** a shackle for holding a prisoner by the ankles. **b** any shackle or bond. **2** (in *pl.*) captivity. **3** a restraint or check. —*v.tr.* **1** put into fetters. **2** restrict, restrain, impede. [OE *feter* f. Gmc]

fetterlock /'fetəˌlɒk/ *n.* **1** a D-shaped fetter for tethering a horse by the leg. **2** a heraldic representation of this.

fettle /'fet(ə)l/ *n. & v.* —*n.* condition or trim (*in fine fettle*). —*v.tr.* trim or clean (the rough edge of a metal casting, pottery before firing, etc.). [earlier as verb, f. dial. *fettle* (n.) = girdle, f. OE *fetel* f. Gmc]

fettler /'fetlə(r)/ *n.* **1** *Brit. & Austral.* a railway maintenance worker. **2** a person who fettles.

fetus *US* var. of FOETUS.

feu /fjuː/ *n. & v. Sc.* —*n.* **1** a perpetual lease at a fixed rent. **2** a piece of land so held. —*v.tr.* (**feus, feued, feuing**) grant (land) on feu. [OF: see FEE]

feud[1] /fjuːd/ *n. & v.* —*n.* **1** prolonged mutual hostility, esp. between two families, tribes, etc., with murderous assaults in revenge for a previous injury (*a family feud; be at feud with*). **2** a prolonged or bitter quarrel or dispute. —*v.intr.* conduct a feud. [ME *fede* f. OF *feide, fede* f. MDu., MLG *vēde* f. Gmc, rel. to FOE]

feud[2] /fjuːd/ *n.* a piece of land held under the feudal system or in fee; a fief. [med.L *feudum*: see FEE]

feudal /'fjuːd(ə)l/ *adj.* **1** of, according to, or resembling the feudal system. **2** of a feud or fief. **3** outdated (*had a feudal attitude*). □**feudal system** the social system in medieval Europe whereby a vassal held land from a superior in exchange for allegiance and service. □□**feudalism** *n.* **feudalist** *n.* **feudalistic** /-'lɪstɪk/ *adj.* **feudalize** *v.tr.* (also **-ise**). **feudalization** /-'zeɪʃ(ə)n/ *n.* **feudally** *adv.* [med.L *feudalis, feodalis* f. *feudum, feodum* FEE, perh. f. Gmc]

feudality /fjuː'dælɪtɪ/ *n.* (*pl.* **-ies**) **1** the feudal system or its principles. **2** a feudal holding, a fief. [F *féodalité* f. *féodal* (as FEUDAL)]

feudatory /'fjuːdətərɪ/ *adj. & n.* —*adj.* (often foll. by *to*) feudally subject, under overlordship. —*n.* (*pl.* **-ies**) a feudal vassal. [med.L *feudatorius* f. *feudare* enfeoff (as FEUD[2])]

feu de joie /ˌfɜː də 'ʒwɑː/ *n.* (*pl.* **feux** *pronunc.* same) a salute by firing rifles etc. on a ceremonial occasion. [F, = fire of joy]

feudist /'fju:dɪst/ n. US a person who is conducting a feud.

feuilleton /,fɜ:jə'tõ/ n. **1** a part of a newspaper etc. devoted to fiction, criticism, light literature, etc. **2** an item printed in this. [F, = leaflet]

fever /'fi:və(r)/ n. & v. —n. **1 a** an abnormally high body temperature, often with delirium etc. **b** a disease characterized by this (scarlet fever; typhoid fever). **2** nervous excitement; agitation. —v.tr. (esp. as **fevered** adj.) affect with fever or excitement. □**fever pitch** a state of extreme excitement. [OE fēfor & AF fevre, OF fievre f. L febris]

feverfew /'fi:və,fju:/ n. an aromatic bushy plant, Tenacetum parthenium, with feathery leaves and white daisy-like flowers, formerly used to reduce fever. [OE feferfuga f. L febrifuga (as FEBRIFUGE)]

feverish /'fi:vərɪʃ/ adj. **1** having the symptoms of a fever. **2** excited, fitful, restless. **3** (of a place) infested by fever; feverous. □□**feverishly** adv. **feverishness** n.

feverous /'fi:vərəs/ adj. **1** infested with or apt to cause fever. **2** archaic feverish.

few /fju:/ adj. & n. —adj. not many (few doctors smoke; visitors are few). —n. (as pl.) **1** (prec. by a) some but not many (a few words should be added; a few of his friends were there). **2** a small number, not many (many are called but few are chosen). **3** (prec. by the) **a** the minority. **b** the elect. **4** (the Few) colloq. the RAF pilots who took part in the Battle of Britain. □**every few** once in every small group of (every few days). **few and far between** scarce. **a good few** colloq. a fairly large number. **have a few** colloq. take several alcoholic drinks. **no fewer than** as many as (a specified number). **not a few** a considerable number. **some few** some but not at all many. □□**fewness** n. [OE fēawe, fēawa f. Gmc]

fey /feɪ/ adj. **1 a** strange, other-worldly; elfin; whimsical. **b** clairvoyant. **2** Sc. **a** fated to die soon. **b** overexcited or elated, as formerly associated with the state of mind of a person about to die. □□**feyly** adv. **feyness** n. [OE fǣge f. Gmc]

fez /fez/ n. (pl. **fezzes**) a flat-topped conical red cap with a tassel, worn by men in some Muslim countries. □□**fezzed** adj. [Turk., perh. f. Fez (now Fès) in Morocco]

ff abbr. Mus. fortissimo.

ff. abbr. **1** following pages etc. **2** folios.

fiacre /fɪ'ɑ:kr/ n. hist. a small four-wheeled cab. [the Hôtel de St Fiacre, Paris]

fiancé /fɪ'ɒnseɪ, fɪ'ãseɪ/ n. (fem. **fiancée** pronunc. same) a person to whom another is engaged to be married. [F, past part. of fiancer betroth f. OF fiance a promise, ult. f. L fidere to trust]

fianchetto /,fjæn'tʃetəʊ/ n. & v. Chess —n. (pl. **-oes**) the development of a bishop to a long diagonal of the board. —v.tr. (**-oes, -oed**) develop (a bishop) in this way. [It., dimin. of fianco FLANK]

fiasco /fɪ'æskəʊ/ n. (pl. **-os**) a ludicrous or humiliating failure or breakdown (orig. in a dramatic or musical performance); an ignominious result. [It., = bottle (with unexplained allusion): see FLASK]

fiat /'faɪæt, 'faɪət/ n. **1** an authorization. **2** a decree or order. □**fiat money** US inconvertible paper money made legal tender by a Government decree. [L, = let it be done]

fib /fɪb/ n. & v. —n. a trivial or venial lie. —v.intr. (**fibbed, fibbing**) tell a fib. □□**fibber** n. **fibster** n. [perh. f. obs. fible-fable nonsense, redupl. of FABLE]

fiber US var. of FIBRE.

Fibonacci series /,fɪbə'nɑ:tʃɪ/ n. Math. a series of numbers in which each number (**Fibonacci number**) is the sum of the two preceding numbers, esp. 1, 1, 2, 3, 5, 8, etc. [L. Fibonacci, It. mathematician fl. 1200]

fibre /'faɪbə(r)/ n. (US **fiber**) **1** Biol. any of the threads or filaments forming animal or vegetable tissue and textile substances. **2** a piece of glass in the form of a thread. **3 a** a substance formed of fibres. **b** a substance that can be spun, woven, or felted. **4** the structure, grain, or character of something (lacks moral fibre). **5** dietary material that is resistant to the action of digestive enzymes; roughage. □**fibre optics** optics employing thin glass fibres, usu. for the transmission of light, esp. modulated to carry signals. □□**fibred** adj. (also in comb.). **fibreless** adj. **fibriform** /'faɪbrɪ,fɔ:m/ adj. [ME f. F f. L fibra]

fibreboard /'faɪbə,bɔ:d/ n. (US **fiberboard**) a building material made of wood or other plant fibres compressed into boards.

fibreglass /'faɪbə,glɑ:s/ n. (US **fiberglass**) **1** a textile fabric made from woven glass fibres. **2** a plastic reinforced by glass fibres.

fibril /'faɪbrɪl/ n. **1** a small fibre. **2** a subdivision of a fibre. □□**fibrillar** adj. **fibrillary** adj. [mod.L fibrilla dimin. of L fibra fibre]

fibrillate /'fɪbrɪ,leɪt, 'faɪ-/ v. **1** intr. **a** (of a fibre) split up into fibrils. **b** (of a muscle, esp. in the heart) undergo a quivering movement in fibrils. **2** tr. break (a fibre) into fibrils. □□**fibrillation** /-'leɪʃ(ə)n/ n.

fibrin /'faɪbrɪn/ n. an insoluble protein formed during blood-clotting from fibrinogen. □□**fibrinoid** adj. [FIBRE + -IN]

fibrinogen /faɪ'brɪnədʒ(ə)n/ n. a soluble blood-plasma protein which produces fibrin when acted upon by the enzyme thrombin.

fibro /'faɪbrəʊ/ n. (pl. **-os**) Austral. **1** fibro-cement. **2** a house constructed mainly of this. [abbr.]

fibro- /'faɪbrəʊ/ comb. form fibre.

fibro-cement /,faɪbrəʊsɪ'ment/ n. a mixture of any of various fibrous materials, such as glass fibre, cellulose fibre, etc. and cement, used in sheets for building etc.

fibroid /'faɪbrɔɪd/ adj. & n. —adj. **1** of or characterized by fibrous tissue. **2** resembling or containing fibres. —n. a benign tumour of muscular and fibrous tissues, one or more of which may develop in the wall of the womb.

fibroin /'faɪbrəʊɪn/ n. a protein which is the chief constituent of silk. [FIBRO- + -IN]

fibroma /faɪ'brəʊmə/ n. (pl. **fibromas** or **fibromata** /-mətə/) a fibrous tumour. [mod.L f. L fibra fibre + -OMA]

fibrosis /faɪ'brəʊsɪs/ n. Med. a thickening and scarring of connective tissue, usu. as a result of injury. □□**fibrotic** /-'brɒtɪk/ adj. [mod.L f. L fibra fibre + -OSIS]

fibrositis /,faɪbrə'saɪtɪs/ n. an inflammation of fibrous connective tissue, usu. rheumatic and painful. □□**fibrositic** /-'sɪtɪk/ adj. [mod.L f. L fibrosus fibrous + -ITIS]

fibrous /'faɪbrəs/ adj. consisting of or like fibres. □□ **fibrously** adv. **fibrousness** n.

fibula /'fɪbjʊlə/ n. (pl. **fibulae** /-,li:/ or **fibulas**) **1** Anat. the smaller and outer of the two bones between the knee and the ankle in terrestrial vertebrates. **2** Antiq. a brooch or clasp. □□**fibular** adj. [L, perh. rel. to figere fix]

-fic /fɪk/ suffix (usu. as **-ific**) forming adjectives meaning 'producing', 'making' (prolific; pacific). □□ **-fically** suffix forming adverbs. [from or after F -fique or L -ficus f. facere do, make]

-fication /fɪ'keɪʃ(ə)n/ suffix (usu. as **-ification**) forming nouns of action from verbs in -fy (acidification; purification; simplification). [from or after F -fication or L -ficatio -onis f. -ficare: see -FY]

fiche /fi:ʃ/ n. (pl. same or **fiches**) a microfiche. [F, = slip of paper]

fichu /'fi:ʃu:, 'fɪ:ʃu:/ n. a woman's small triangular shawl of lace etc. for the shoulders and neck. [F]

fickle /'fɪk(ə)l/ adj. inconstant, changeable, esp. in loyalty. □□**fickleness** n. **fickly** adv. [OE ficol; cf. befician deceive, fǣcne deceitful]

fictile /'fɪktaɪl/ adj. **1** made of earth or clay by a potter. **2** of pottery. [L fictilis f. fingere fict- fashion]

fiction /'fɪkʃ(ə)n/ n. **1** an invented idea or statement or narrative; an imaginary thing. **2** literature, esp. novels, describing imaginary events and people. **3** a conventionally accepted falsehood (*legal fiction*; *polite fiction*). **4** the act or process of inventing imaginary things. □□ **fictional** adj. **fictionality** /-'nælɪtɪ/ n. **fictionalize** v.tr. (also -**ise**). **fictionalization** /-'zeɪʃ(ə)n/ n. **fictionally** adv. **fictionist** n. [ME f. OF f. L *fictio -onis* (as FICTILE)]

fictitious /fɪk'tɪʃəs/ adj. **1** imaginary, unreal. **2** counterfeit; not genuine. **3** (of a name or character) assumed. **4** of or in novels. **5** regarded as what it is called by a legal or conventional fiction. □□ **fictitiously** adv. **fictitiousness** n. [L *ficticius* (as FICTILE)]

fictive /'fɪktɪv/ adj. **1** creating or created by imagination. **2** not genuine. □□ **fictively** adv. **fictiveness** n. [F *fictif -ive* or med.L *fictivus* (as FICTILE)]

fid /fɪd/ n. **1** a small thick piece or wedge or heap of anything. **2** *Naut.* **a** a square wooden or iron bar to support the topmast. **b** a conical wooden pin used in splicing. [17th c.: orig. unkn.]

Fid. Def. abbr. *Brit.* Defender of the Faith. [L *Fidei Defensor*]

fiddle /'fɪd(ə)l/ n. & v. —n. **1** colloq. or derog. a stringed instrument played with a bow, esp. a violin. **2** colloq. an instance of cheating or fraud. **3** *Naut.* a contrivance for stopping things from rolling or sliding off a table in bad weather. —v. **1** intr. **a** (often foll. by with, at) play restlessly. **b** (often foll. by about) move aimlessly. **c** act idly or frivolously. **d** (usu. foll. by with) make minor adjustments; tinker (esp. in an attempt to make improvements). **2** tr. sl. **a** cheat, swindle. **b** falsify. **c** get by cheating. **3** **a** intr. play the fiddle. **b** tr. play (a tune etc.) on the fiddle. □ **as fit as a fiddle** in very good health. **face as long as a fiddle** a dismal face. **fiddle-back** a fiddle-shaped back of a chair or front of a chasuble. **fiddle-head** a scroll-like carving at a ship's bows. **fiddle pattern** the pattern of spoons and forks with fiddle-shaped handles. **play second** (or **first**) **fiddle** take a subordinate (or leading) role. [OE *fithele* f. Gmc f. a Rmc root rel. to VIOL]

fiddle-de-dee /ˌfɪdəldɪ'diː/ int. & n. nonsense.

fiddle-faddle /'fɪd(ə)lˌfæd(ə)l/ n., v., int., & adj. —n. trivial matters. —v.intr. fuss, trifle. —int. nonsense! —adj. (of a person or thing) petty, fussy. [redupl. of FIDDLE]

fiddler /'fɪdlə(r)/ n. **1** a fiddle-player. **2** sl. a swindler, a cheat. **3** any small N. American crab of the genus *Uca*, the male having one of its claws held in a position like a violinist's arm. [OE *fithelere* (as FIDDLE)]

fiddlestick /'fɪd(ə)lstɪk/ n. **1** (usu. in pl.; as int.) nonsense! **2** colloq. a bow for a fiddle.

fiddling /'fɪdlɪŋ/ adj. **1 a** petty, trivial. **b** contemptible, futile. **2** colloq. = FIDDLY. **3** that fiddles.

fiddly /'fɪdlɪ/ adj. (**fiddlier**, **fiddliest**) colloq. intricate, awkward, or tiresome to do or use.

fideism /'faɪdɪˌɪz(ə)m, 'fiːdeɪ-/ n. the doctrine that all or some knowledge depends on faith or revelation. □□ **fideist** n. **fideistic** /-'ɪstɪk/ adj. [L *fides* faith + -ISM]

fidelity /fɪ'delɪtɪ/ n. **1** (often foll. by to) faithfulness, loyalty. **2** strict conformity to truth or fact. **3** exact correspondence to the original. **4** precision in reproduction of sound (*high fidelity*). □ **fidelity insurance** insurance taken out by an employer against losses incurred through an employee's dishonesty etc. [F *fidélité* or L *fidelitas* (as FEALTY)]

fidget /'fɪdʒɪt/ v. & n. —v. (**fidgeted**, **fidgeting**) **1** intr. move or act restlessly or nervously, usu. while maintaining basically the same posture. **2** intr. be uneasy, worry. **3** tr. make (a person) uneasy or uncomfortable. —n. **1** a person who fidgets. **2** (usu. in pl.) **a** a bodily uneasiness seeking relief in spasmodic movements; such movements. **b** a restless mood. □□

fidgety adj. **fidgetiness** n. [obs. or dial. *fidge* to twitch]

Fido /'faɪdəʊ/ n. a device enabling aircraft to land by dispersing fog by means of petrol-burners on the ground. [initials of *Fog Intensive Dispersal Operation*]

fiducial /fɪ'djuːʃ(ə)l/ adj. *Surveying*, *Astron.*, etc. (of a line, point, etc.) assumed as a fixed basis of comparison. [LL *fiducialis* f. *fiducia* trust f. *fidere* to trust]

fiduciary /fɪ'djuːʃərɪ/ adj. & n. —adj. **1 a** of a trust, trustee, or trusteeship. **b** held or given in trust. **2** (of a paper currency) depending for its value on public confidence or securities. —n. (pl. -**ies**) a trustee. [L *fiduciarius* (as FIDUCIAL)]

fidus Achates /ˌfaɪdəs ə'keɪtiːz/ n. a faithful friend; a devoted follower. [L, = faithful Achates (a companion of Aeneas in Virgil's *Aeneid*)]

fie /faɪ/ int. expressing disgust, shame, or a pretence of outraged propriety. [ME f. OF f. L *fi* exclam. of disgust at a stench]

fief /fiːf/ n. **1** a piece of land held under the feudal system or in fee. **2** a person's sphere of operation or control. [F (as FEE)]

fiefdom /'fiːfdəm/ n. a fief.

field /fiːld/ n. & v. —n. **1** an area of open land, esp. one used for pasture or crops, often bounded by hedges, fences, etc. **2** an area rich in some natural product (*gas field*; *diamond field*). **3** a piece of land for a specified purpose, esp. an area marked out for games (*football field*). **4 a** the participants in a contest or sport. **b** all the competitors in a race or all except those specified. **5** *Cricket* **a** the side fielding. **b** a fielder. **6** an expanse of ice, snow, sea, sky, etc. **7 a** the ground on which a battle is fought; a battlefield (*left his rival in possession of the field*). **b** the scene of a campaign. **c** (attrib.) (of artillery etc.) light and mobile for use on campaign. **d** a battle. **8** an area of operation or activity; a subject of study (*each supreme in his own field*). **9 a** the region in which a force is effective (*gravitational field*; *magnetic field*). **b** the force exerted in such an area. **10** a range of perception (*field of view*; *wide field of vision*; *filled the field of the telescope*). **11** *Math.* a system subject to two operations analogous to those for the multiplication and addition of real numbers. **12** (attrib.) **a** (of an animal or plant) found in the countryside, wild (*field mouse*). **b** carried out or working in the natural environment, not in a laboratory etc. (*field test*). **13 a** the background of a picture, coin, flag, etc. **b** *Heraldry* the surface of an escutcheon or of one of its divisions. **14** *Computing* a part of a record, representing an item of data. —v. **1** *Cricket*, *Baseball*, etc. **a** intr. act as a fieldsman. **b** tr. stop (and return) (the ball). **2** tr. select (a team or individual) to play in a game. **3** tr. deal with (a succession of questions etc.). □ **field-book** a book used in the field by a surveyor for technical notes. **field-cornet** *S.Afr. hist.* a minor magistrate. **field-day 1** wide scope for action or success; a time occupied with exciting events (*when crowds form, pickpockets have a field-day*). **2** *Mil.* an exercise, esp. in manœuvring; a review. **3** a day spent in exploration, scientific investigation, etc., in the natural environment. **field events** athletic sports other than races (e.g. shot-putting, jumping, discus-throwing). **field-glasses** binoculars for outdoor use. **field goal** *US Football & Basketball* a goal scored when the ball is in normal play. **field hockey** *US* = HOCKEY[1]. **field hospital** a temporary hospital near a battlefield. **Field Marshal** *Brit.* an army officer of the highest rank. **field mouse** a small rodent, *Apodemus sylvaticus*, with beady eyes, prominent ears, and a long tail. **field mushroom** the edible fungus *Agaricus campestris*. **field mustard** charlock. **field officer** an army officer of field rank. **field of honour** the place where a duel or battle is fought. **field rank** any rank in the army above captain and below general. **field sports** outdoor sports, esp. hunting, shooting, and fishing. **field**

telegraph a movable telegraph for use on campaign. **hold the field** not be superseded. **in the field 1** campaigning. **2** working etc. away from one's laboratory, headquarters, etc. **keep the field** continue a campaign. **play the field** *colloq.* avoid exclusive attachment to one person or activity etc. **take the field 1** begin a campaign. **2** (of a sports team) go on to a pitch to begin a game. [OE *feld* f. WG]

fielder /ˈfiːldə(r)/ *n.* = FIELDSMAN.

fieldfare /ˈfiːldfeə(r)/ *n.* a thrush, *Turdus pilaris*, having grey plumage with a speckled breast. [ME *feldefare*, perh. as FIELD + FARE]

fieldsman /ˈfiːldzmən/ *n.* (*pl.* **-men**) *Cricket, Baseball*, etc. a member (other than the bowler or pitcher) of the side that is fielding.

fieldstone /ˈfiːldstəʊn/ *n.* stone used in its natural form.

fieldwork /ˈfiːldwɜːk/ *n.* **1** the practical work of a surveyor, collector of scientific data, sociologist, etc. , conducted in the natural environment rather than a laboratory, office, etc. **2** a temporary fortification. □□ **fieldworker** *n.*

fiend /fiːnd/ *n.* **1 a** an evil spirit, a demon. **b** (prec. by *the*) the Devil. **2 a** a very wicked or cruel person. **b** a person causing mischief or annoyance. **3** (with a qualifying word) *sl.* a devotee or addict (*a fitness fiend*). **4** something difficult or unpleasant. □□ **fiendish** *adj.* **fiendishly** *adv.* **fiendishness** *n.* **fiendlike** *adj.* [OE *fēond* f. Gmc]

fierce /fɪəs/ *adj.* (**fiercer, fiercest**) **1** vehemently aggressive or frightening in temper or action, violent. **2** eager, intense, ardent. **3** unpleasantly strong or intense; uncontrolled (*fierce heat*). **4** (of a mechanism) not smooth or easy in action. □□ **fiercely** *adv.* **fierceness** *n.* [ME f. AF *fers*, OF *fiers fier* proud f. L *ferus* savage]

fieri facias /ˌfaɪəraɪ ˈfeɪʃɪˌæs/ *n. Law* a writ to a sheriff for executing a judgement. [L, = cause to be made or done]

fiery /ˈfaɪərɪ/ *adj.* (**fierier, fieriest**) **1 a** consisting of or flaming with fire. **b** (of an arrow etc.) fire-bearing. **2** like fire in appearance, bright red. **3 a** hot as fire. **b** acting like fire; producing a burning sensation. **4 a** flashing, ardent (*fiery eyes*). **b** eager, pugnacious, spirited, irritable (*fiery temper*). **c** (of a horse) mettlesome. **5** (of gas, a mine, etc.) inflammable; liable to explosions. **6** *Cricket* (of a pitch) making the ball rise dangerously. □ **fiery cross** a wooden cross charred or set on fire as a symbol. □□ **fierily** *adv.* **fieriness** *n.*

fiesta /fɪˈestə/ *n.* **1** a holiday or festivity. **2** a religious festival in Spanish-speaking countries. [Sp., = feast]

FIFA /ˈfiːfə/ *abbr.* International Football Federation. [F *Fédération Internationale de Football Association*]

fi. fa. *abbr.* fieri facias.

fife /faɪf/ *n. & v.* —*n.* **1** a kind of small shrill flute used with the drum in military music. **2** its player. —*v.* **1** *intr.* play the fife. **2** *tr.* play (an air etc.) on the fife. □□ **fifer** *n.* [G *Pfeife* PIPE, or F *fifre* f. Swiss G *Pfifre* piper]

fife-rail /ˈfaɪfreɪl/ *n. Naut.* a rail round the mainmast with belaying-pins. [18th c.: orig. unkn.]

fifteen /fɪfˈtiːn, ˈfɪf-/ *n. & adj.* —*n.* **1** one more than fourteen, or five more than ten; the product of three units and five units. **2** a symbol for this (15, xv, XV). **3** a size etc. denoted by fifteen. **4** a team of fifteen players, esp. in Rugby football. **5** (**the Fifteen**) *hist.* the Jacobite rebellion of 1715. **6** (15) *Brit.* (of films) classified as suitable for persons of 15 years and over. —*adj.* that amount to fifteen. □□ **fifteenth** *adj. & n.* [OE *fīftēne* (as FIVE, -TEEN)]

fifth /fɪfθ/ *n. & adj.* —*n.* **1** the position in a sequence corresponding to that of the number 5 in the sequence 1-5. **2** something occupying this position. **3** the fifth person etc. in a race or competition. **4** any of five equal parts of a thing. **5** *Mus.* **a** an interval or chord spanning five consecutive notes in the diatonic scale

(e.g. C to G). **b** a note separated from another by this interval. **6** *US colloq.* **a** a fifth of a gallon of liquor. **b** a bottle containing this. —*adj.* that is the fifth. □ **fifth column** a group working for an enemy within a country at war etc. (from General Mola's reference to such support in besieged Madrid in 1936). **fifth-columnist** a member of a fifth column; a traitor or spy. **Fifth Monarchy** the last of the five great kingdoms predicted in Daniel 2:44. **Fifth-monarchy-man** *hist.* a 17th-c. zealot expecting the immediate second coming of Christ and repudiating all other government. **fifth part** = sense 3 of *n.* **fifth wheel 1** an extra wheel of a coach. **2** a superfluous person or thing. **3** a horizontal turntable over the front axle of a carriage as an extra support to prevent its tipping. **take the fifth** (in the US) exercise the right guaranteed by the Fifth Amendment to the Constitution of refusing to answer questions in order to avoid incriminating oneself. □□ **fifthly** *adv.* [earlier and dial. *fift* f. OE *fīfta* f. Gmc, assim. to FOURTH]

fifty /ˈfɪftɪ/ *n. & adj.* —*n.* (*pl.* **-ies**) **1** the product of five and ten. **2** a symbol for this (50, l, L). **3** (in *pl.*) the numbers from 50 to 59, esp. the years of a century or of a person's life. **4** a set of fifty persons or things. **5** a large indefinite number (*have fifty things to tell you*). —*adj.* that amount to fifty. □ **fifty-fifty** equal, with equal shares or chances (*on a fifty-fifty basis*). —*adv.* equally, half and half (*go fifty-fifty*). **fifty-first, -second**, etc. the ordinal numbers between fiftieth and sixtieth. **fifty-one, -two**, etc. the cardinal numbers between fifty and sixty. □□ **fiftieth** *adj. & n.* **fiftyfold** *adj. & adv.* [OE *fīftig* (as FIVE, -TY²)]

fig¹ /fɪg/ *n.* **1 a** a soft pear-shaped fruit with many seeds, eaten fresh or dried. **b** (in full **fig-tree**) any deciduous tree of the genus *Ficus*, esp. *F. carica*, having broad leaves and bearing figs. **2** a valueless thing (*don't care a fig for*). □ **fig-leaf 1** a leaf of a fig-tree. **2** a device for concealing something, esp. the genitals (Gen. 3:7). [ME f. OF *figue* f. Prov. *fig(u)a* ult. f. L *ficus*]

fig² /fɪg/ *n. & v.* —*n.* **1** dress or equipment (*in full fig*). **2** condition or form (*in good fig*). —*v.tr.* (**figged, figging**) **1** (foll. by *out*) dress up (a person). **2** (foll. by *out*, *up*) make (a horse) lively. [var. of obs. *feague* (v.) f. G *fegen*: see FAKE¹]

fig. *abbr.* figure.

fight /faɪt/ *v. & n.* —*v.* (*past* and *past part.* **fought** /fɔːt/) **1** *intr.* (often foll. by *against, with*) contend or struggle in war, battle, single combat, etc. **2** *tr.* contend with (an opponent) in this way. **3** *tr.* take part or engage in (a battle, war, duel, etc.). **4** *tr.* contend about (an issue, an election); maintain (a lawsuit, cause, etc.) against an opponent. **5** *intr.* campaign or strive determinedly to achieve something. **6** *tr.* strive to overcome (disease, fire, fear, etc.). **7** *tr.* make (one's way) by fighting. **8** *tr.* cause (cocks or dogs) to fight. **9** *tr.* handle (troops, a ship, etc.) in battle. —*n.* **1 a** a combat, esp. unpremeditated, between two or more persons, animals, or parties. **b** a boxing-match. **c** a battle. **2** a conflict or struggle; a vigorous effort in the face of difficulty. **3** power or inclination to fight (*has no fight left; showed fight*). □ **fight back 1** counter-attack. **2** suppress (one's feelings, tears, etc.). **fight down** suppress (one's feelings, tears, etc.). **fight for 1** fight on behalf of. **2** fight to secure (a thing). **fighting chair** *US* a fixed chair on a boat for use when catching large fish. **fighting chance** an opportunity of succeeding by great effort. **fighting fish** (in full **Siamese fighting fish**) a freshwater fish, *Betta splendens*, native to Thailand, the males of which sometimes kill each other during fights for territory. **fighting fit** fit enough to fight; at the peak of fitness. **fighting fund** money raised to support a campaign. **fighting-top** *Naut.* a circular gun-platform high on a warship's mast. **fighting words** *colloq.* words indicating a willingness to fight. **fight off** repel with effort. **fight out** (usu. **fight it out**) settle (a dispute etc.) by fighting. **fight shy of** avoid; be unwilling to approach (a person, task, etc.). **make a fight of it** (or **put up a fight**) offer resistance. [OE *feohtan, feoht(e),* f. WG]

fighter /'faɪtə(r)/ *n.* **1** a person or animal that fights. **2** a fast military aircraft designed for attacking other aircraft. □**fighter-bomber** an aircraft serving as both fighter and bomber.

figment /'fɪgmənt/ *n.* a thing invented or existing only in the imagination. [ME f. L *figmentum,* rel. to *fingere* fashion]

figura /fɪ'gjʊərə/ *n.* **1** a person or thing representing or symbolizing a fact etc. **2** *Theol.* a type of a person etc. [mod.L f. L, = FIGURE]

figural /'fɪgjʊr(ə)l/ *adj.* **1** figurative. **2** relating to figures or shapes. **3** *Mus.* florid in style. [OF *figural* or LL *figuralis* f. *figura* FIGURE]

figurant /'fɪgjʊərənt/ *n.* (*fem.* **figurante** *pronunc.* same) a ballet-dancer appearing only in a group. [F, pres. part. of *figurer* FIGURE]

figurante /ˌfɪgjʊ'rænti/ *n.* (*pl.* **figuranti** /-ti:/) = FIGURANT. [It., pres. part. of *figurare* FIGURE]

figuration /ˌfɪgjʊ'reɪʃ(ə)n/ *n.* **1 a** the act of formation. **b** a mode of formation; a form. **c** a shape or outline. **2 a** ornamentation by designs. **b** *Mus.* ornamental patterns of scales, arpeggios, etc., often derived from an earlier motif. **3** allegorical representation. [ME f. F or f. L *figuratio* (as FIGURE)]

figurative /'fɪgjʊrətɪv, 'fɪgər-/ *adj.* **1 a** metaphorical, not literal. **b** metaphorically so called. **2** characterized by or addicted to figures of speech. **3** of pictorial or sculptural representation. **4** emblematic, serving as a type. □□**figuratively** *adv.* **figurativeness** *n.* [ME f. LL *figurativus* (as FIGURE)]

figure /'fɪgə(r)/ *n. & v.* —*n.* **1 a** the external form or shape of a thing. **b** bodily shape (*has a well-developed figure*). **2 a** a person as seen in outline but not identified (*saw a figure leaning against the door*). **b** a person as contemplated mentally (*a public figure*). **3** appearance as giving a certain impression (*cut a poor figure*). **4 a** a representation of the human form in drawing, sculpture, etc. **b** an image or likeness. **c** an emblem or type. **5** *Geom.* a two-dimensional space enclosed by a line or lines, or a three-dimensional space enclosed by a surface or surfaces; any of the classes of these, e.g. the triangle, the sphere. **6 a** a numerical symbol, esp. any of the ten in Arabic notation. **b** a number so expressed. **c** an amount of money, a value (*cannot put a figure on it*). **d** (in *pl.*) arithmetical calculations. **7** a diagram or illustrative drawing. **8** a decorative pattern. **9 a** a division of a set dance, an evolution. **b** (in skating) a prescribed pattern of movements from a stationary position. **10** *Mus.* a short succession of notes producing a single impression, a brief melodic or rhythmic formula out of which longer passages are developed. **11** (in full **figure of speech**) a recognized form of rhetorical expression giving variety, force, etc., esp. metaphor or hyperbole. **12** *Gram.* a permitted deviation from the usual rules of construction, e.g. ellipsis. **13** *Logic* the form of a syllogism, classified according to the position of the middle term. **14** a horoscope. —*v.* **1** *intr.* appear or be mentioned, esp. prominently. **2** *tr.* represent in a diagram or picture. **3** *tr.* imagine; picture mentally. **4** *tr.* **a** embellish with a pattern (*figured satin*). **b** *Mus.* embellish with figures. **5** *tr.* mark with numbers (*figured bass*) or prices. **6 a** *tr.* calculate. **b** *intr.* do arithmetic. **7** *tr.* be a symbol of, represent typically. **8** esp. *US* **a** *tr.* understand, ascertain, consider. **b** *intr. colloq.* be likely or understandable (*that figures*). □**figured bass** *Mus.* = CONTINUO. **figure of fun** a ridiculous person. **figure on** *US* count on, expect. **figure out 1** work out by arithmetic or logic. **2** estimate. **3** understand. **figure-skater** a person who practises figure-skating. **figure-skating** skating in prescribed patterns from a stationary position. □□**figureless** *adj.* [ME f. OF

figure (n.), **figurer** (v.) f. L *figura, figurare,* rel. to *fingere* fashion]

figurehead /'fɪgə,hed/ *n.* **1** a nominal leader or head without real power. **2** a carving, usu. a bust or a full-length figure, at a ship's prow.

figurine /ˌfɪgjʊ'ri:n, 'fɪg-/ *n.* a statuette. [F f. It. *figurina* dimin. of *figura* FIGURE]

figwort /'fɪgwɜ:t/ *n.* any aromatic green-flowered plant of the genus *Scrophularia,* once believed to be useful against scrofula.

filagree var. of FILIGREE.

filament /'fɪləmənt/ *n.* **1** a slender threadlike body or fibre (esp. in animal or vegetable structures). **2** a conducting wire or thread with a high melting-point in an electric bulb or thermionic valve, heated or made incandescent by an electric current. **3** *Bot.* the part of the stamen that supports the anther. **4** *archaic* (of air, light, etc.) a notional train of particles following each other. □□**filamentary** /-'mentərɪ/ *adj.* **filamented** *adj.* **filamentous** /-'mentəs/ *adj.* [F *filament* or mod.L *filamentum* f. LL *filare* spin f. L *filum* thread]

filaria /fɪ'leərɪə/ *n.* (*pl.* **filariae** /-rɪ,i:/) any threadlike parasitic nematode worm of the family Filariidae introduced into the blood by certain biting flies and mosquitoes. □□**filarial** *adj.* [mod.L f. L *filum* thread]

filariasis /ˌfɪlə'raɪəsɪs, fɪˌleərɪ'eɪsɪs/ *n.* a disease common in the tropics, caused by the presence of filarial worms in the lymph vessels.

filature /'fɪlətʃə(r)/ *n.* an establishment for or the action of reeling silk from cocoons. [F f. It. *filatura* f. *filare* spin]

filbert /'fɪlbət/ *n.* **1** the cultivated hazel, *Corylus maxima,* bearing edible ovoid nuts. **2** this nut. [ME *philliberd* etc. f. AF *philbert,* dial. F *noix de filbert,* a nut ripe about St Philibert's day (20 Aug.)]

filch /fɪltʃ/ *v.tr.* pilfer, steal. □□**filcher** *n.* [16th-c. thieves' sl.: orig. unkn.]

file[1] /faɪl/ *n. & v.* —*n.* **1** a folder, box, etc., for holding loose papers, esp. arranged for reference. **2** a set of papers kept in this. **3** *Computing* a collection of (usu. related) data stored under one name. **4** a series of issues of a newspaper etc. in order. **5** a stiff pointed wire on which documents etc. are impaled for keeping. —*v.tr.* **1** place (papers) in a file or among (esp. public) records. **2** submit (a petition for divorce, an application for a patent, etc.) to the appropriate authority. **3** (of a reporter) send (a story, information, etc.) to a newspaper. □**filing cabinet** a case with drawers for storing documents. □□**filer** *n.* [F *fil* f. L *filum* thread]

file[2] /faɪl/ *n. & v.* —*n.* **1** a line of persons or things one behind another. **2** (foll. by *of*) *Mil.* a small detachment of men (now usu. two). **3** *Chess* a line of squares from player to player (cf. RANK[1]). —*v.intr.* walk in a file. □**file off** (or **away**) *Mil.* go off by files. [F *file* f. LL *filare* spin or L *filum* thread]

file[3] /faɪl/ *n. & v.* —*n.* a tool with a roughened surface or surfaces, usu. of steel, for smoothing or shaping wood, fingernails, etc. —*v.tr.* **1** smooth or shape with a file. **2** elaborate or improve (a thing, esp. a literary work). □**file away** remove (roughness etc.) with a file. **file-fish** any fish of the family Ostracionidae, with sharp dorsal fins and usu. bright coloration. □□**filer** *n.* [OE *fíl* f. WG]

filet /'fɪlɪt/ *n.* **1** a kind of net or lace with a square mesh. **2** a fillet of meat. □**filet mignon** /'mi:njɔ̃/ a small tender piece of beef from the end of the undercut. [F, = thread]

filial /'fɪlɪəl/ *adj.* **1** of or due from a son or daughter. **2** *Biol.* bearing the relation of offspring (cf. F[2] 5). □□**filially** *adv.* [ME f. OF *filial* or LL *filialis* f. *filius* son, *filia* daughter]

filiation /ˌfɪlɪ'eɪʃ(ə)n/ *n.* **1** being the child of one or two specified parents. **2** (often foll. by *from*) descent or transmission. **3** the formation of offshoots. **4** a branch of a society or language. **5** a genealogical relation or arrangement. [F f. LL *filiatio -onis* f. L *filius* son]

filibeg /'fɪlɪˌbeg/ *n.* (also **philabeg** /'fɪlə-/) *Sc.* a kilt. [Gael. *feileadh-beag* little fold]

filibuster /'fɪlɪˌbʌstə(r)/ *n.* & *v.* —*n.* **1 a** the obstruction of progress in a legislative assembly, esp. by prolonged speaking. **b** esp. *US* a person who engages in a filibuster. **2** esp. *hist.* a person engaging in unauthorized warfare against a foreign State. —*v.* **1** *intr.* act as a filibuster. **2** *tr.* act in this way against (a motion etc.). □□ **filibusterer** *n.* [ult. f. Du. *vrijbuiter* FREEBOOTER, infl. by F *flibustier*, Sp. *filibustero*]

filigree /'fɪlɪˌgriː/ *n.* (also **filagree** /'fɪləˌgriː/) **1** ornamental work of gold or silver or copper as fine wire formed into delicate tracery; fine metal openwork. **2** anything delicate resembling this. □□ **filigreed** *adj.* [earlier *filigreen*, *filigrane* f. F *filigrane* f. It. *filigrana* f. L *filum* thread + *granum* seed]

filing /'faɪlɪŋ/ *n.* (usu. in *pl.*) a particle rubbed off by a file.

Filipino /ˌfɪlɪ'piːnəʊ/ *n.* & *adj.* —*n.* (*pl.* **-os**; *fem.* **Filipina** /-nə/) a native or national of the Philippines, a group of islands in the SW Pacific. —*adj.* of or relating to the Philippines or the Filipinos. [Sp., = Philippine]

fill /fɪl/ *v.* & *n.* —*v.* **1** *tr.* & *intr.* (often foll. by *with*) make or become full. **2** *tr.* occupy completely; spread over or through; pervade. **3** *tr.* block up (a cavity or hole in a tooth) with cement, amalgam, gold, etc.; drill and put a filling into (a decayed tooth). **4** *tr.* appoint a person to hold (a vacant post). **5** *tr.* hold (a position); discharge the duties of (an office). **6** *tr.* carry out or supply (an order, commission, etc.). **7** *tr.* occupy (vacant time). **8** *intr.* (of a sail) be distended by wind. **9** *tr.* (usu. as **filling** *adj.*) (esp. of food) satisfy, satiate. **10** *tr. Poker* etc. complete (a holding) by drawing the necessary cards. **11** *tr.* stock abundantly. —*n.* **1** (prec. by possessive) as much as one wants or can bear (*eat your fill*). **2** enough to fill something (*a fill of tobacco*). **3** earth etc. used to fill a cavity. □ **fill the bill** be suitable or adequate. **fill in 1** add information to complete (a form, document, blank cheque, etc.). **2 a** complete (a drawing etc.) within an outline. **b** fill (an outline) in this way. **3** fill (a hole etc.) completely. **4** (often foll. by *for*) act as a substitute. **5** occupy oneself during (time between other activities). **6** *colloq.* inform (a person) more fully. **7** *sl.* thrash, beat. **fill out 1** enlarge to the required size. **2** become enlarged or plump. **3** *US* fill in (a document etc.). **fill up 1** make or become completely full. **2** fill in (a document etc.). **3** fill the petrol tank of (a car etc.). **4** provide what is needed to occupy vacant parts or places or deal with deficiencies in. **5** do away with (a pond etc.) by filling. **fill-up** *n.* a thing that fills something up. [OE *fyllan* f. Gmc, rel. to FULL¹]

fille de joie /ˌfiːj də 'zwɑː/ *n.* a prostitute. [F, lit. 'daughter of joy']

filler /'fɪlə(r)/ *n.* **1** material or an object used to fill a cavity or increase bulk. **2** an item filling space in a newspaper etc. **3** a person or thing that fills. □ **filler cap** a cap closing the filling-pipe leading to the petrol tank of a motor vehicle.

fillet /'fɪlɪt/ *n.* & *v.* —*n.* **1 a** a fleshy boneless piece of meat from near the loins or the ribs. **b** (in full **fillet steak**) the undercut of a sirloin. **c** a boned longitudinal section of a fish. **2 a** a headband, ribbon, string, or narrow band, for binding the hair or worn round the head. **b** a band or bandage. **3 a** a thin narrow strip of anything. **b** a raised rim or ridge on any surface. **4** *Archit.* **a** a narrow flat band separating two mouldings. **b** a small band between the flutes of a column. **5** *Carpentry* an added triangular piece of wood to round off an interior angle. **6 a** a plain line impressed on the cover of a book. **b** a roller used to impress this. **7** *Heraldry* a horizontal division of a shield, a quarter of the depth of a chief. —*v.tr.*

(**filleted, filleting**) **1 a** remove bones from (fish or meat). **b** divide (fish or meat) into fillets. **2** bind or provide with a fillet or fillets. **3** encircle with an ornamental band. □□ **filleter** *n.* [ME f. OF *filet* f. Rmc dimin. of L *filum* thread]

filling /'fɪlɪŋ/ *n.* **1** any material that fills or is used to fill, esp.: **a** a piece of material used to fill a cavity in a tooth. **b** the edible substance between the bread in a sandwich or between the pastry in a pie. **2** *US* weft. □ **filling-station** an establishment selling petrol etc. to motorists.

fillip /'fɪlɪp/ *n.* & *v.* —*n.* **1** a stimulus or incentive. **2 a** a sudden release of a finger or thumb when it has been bent and checked by a thumb or finger. **b** a slight smart stroke given in this way. —*v.* (**filliped, filliping**) **1** *tr.* stimulate (*fillip one's memory*). **2** *tr.* strike slightly and smartly. **3** *tr.* propel (a coin, marble, etc.) with a fillip. **4** *intr.* make a fillip. [imit.]

fillis /'fɪlɪs/ *n. Hort.* loosely-twisted string used as a tying material. [F *filasse* tow]

fillister /'fɪlɪstə(r)/ *n.* a rabbet or rabbet plane for window-sashes etc. [19th c.: perh. f. F *feuilleret*]

filly /'fɪlɪ/ *n.* (*pl.* **-ies**) **1** a young female horse, usu. before it is four years old. **2** *colloq.* a girl or young woman. [ME, prob. f. ON *fylja* f. Gmc (as FOAL)]

film /fɪlm/ *n.* & *v.* —*n.* **1** a thin coating or covering layer. **2** *Photog.* a strip or sheet of plastic or other flexible base coated with light-sensitive emulsion for exposure in a camera, either as individual visual representations or as a sequence which form the illusion of movement when shown in rapid succession. **3 a** a representation of a story, episode, etc., on a film, with the illusion of movement. **b** a story represented in this way. **c** (in *pl.*) the cinema industry. **4** a slight veil or haze etc. **5** a dimness or morbid growth affecting the eyes. **6** a fine thread or filament. —*v.* **1 a** *tr.* make a photographic film of (a scene, person, etc.). **b** *tr.* (also *absol.*) make a cinema or television film of (a book etc.). **c** *intr.* be (well or ill) suited for reproduction on film. **2** *tr.* & *intr.* cover or become covered with or as with a film. □ **film-goer** a person who frequents the cinema. **film star** a celebrated actor or actress in films. **film-strip** a series of transparencies in a strip for projection. [OE *filmen* membrane f. WG, rel. to FELL⁵]

filmic /'fɪlmɪk/ *adj.* of or relating to films or cinematography.

filmography /fɪl'mɒgrəfɪ/ *n.* (*pl.* **-ies**) a list of films by one director etc. or on one subject. [FILM + -GRAPHY after *bibliography*]

filmset /'fɪlmset/ *v.tr.* (**-setting**; *past* and *past part.* **-set**) *Printing* set (material for printing) by filmsetting. □□ **filmsetter** *n.*

filmsetting /'fɪlmˌsetɪŋ/ *n. Printing* typesetting using characters on photographic film.

filmy /'fɪlmɪ/ *adj.* (**filmier, filmiest**) **1** thin and translucent. **2** covered with or as with a film. □□ **filmily** *adv.* **filminess** *n.*

Filofax /'faɪləʊˌfæks/ *n. propr.* a portable loose-leaf filing system for personal or office use. [FILE¹ + *facts* pl. of FACT]

filoselle /'fɪləˌsel/ *n.* floss silk. [F]

fils /fiːs/ *n.* (added to a surname to distinguish a son from a father) the son, junior (cf. PÈRE). [F, = son]

filter /'fɪltə(r)/ *n.* & *v.* —*n.* **1** a porous device for removing impurities or solid particles from a liquid or gas passed through it. **2** = *filter tip*. **3** a screen or attachment for absorbing or modifying light, X-rays, etc. **4** a device for suppressing electrical or sound waves of frequencies not required. **5** *Brit.* **a** an arrangement for filtering traffic. **b** a traffic-light signalling this. —*v.intr.* & *tr.* **1** pass or cause to pass through a filter. **2** (foll. by *through, into*, etc.) make way gradually. **3** (foll. by *out*) leak or cause to leak. **4** *Brit.* allow (traffic) or (of traffic) be allowed to pass to the left or right at a junction while traffic going straight ahead is halted (esp. at traffic lights). □ **filter-bed** a tank or pond containing a layer of

sand etc. for filtering large quantities of liquid.
filter-paper porous paper for filtering. **filter tip 1** a filter attached to a cigarette for removing impurities from the inhaled smoke. **2** a cigarette with this. **filter-tipped** having a filter tip. [F *filtre* f. med.L *filtrum* felt used as a filter, f. WG]

filterable /ˈfɪltərəb(ə)l/ *adj.* (also **filtrable** /ˈfɪltrəb(ə)l/) **1** *Med.* (of a virus) able to pass through a filter that retains bacteria. **2** that can be filtered.

filth /fɪlθ/ *n.* **1** repugnant or extreme dirt. **2** vileness, corruption, obscenity. **3** foul or obscene language. **4** (prec. by *the*) *sl.* the police. [OE *fÿlth* (as FOUL, -TH²)]

filthy /ˈfɪlθɪ/ *adj.* & *adv.* —*adj.* (**filthier, filthiest**) **1** extremely or disgustingly dirty. **2** obscene. **3** *colloq.* (of weather) very unpleasant. **4** vile. —*adv.* **1** filthily (*filthy dirty*). **2** *colloq.* extremely (*filthy rich*). □**filthy lucre 1** dishonourable gain (Tit. 1:11). **2** *joc.* money. □□**filthily** *adv.* **filthiness** *n.*

filtrable var. of FILTERABLE.

filtrate /ˈfɪltreɪt/ *v.* & *n.* —*v.tr.* filter. —*n.* filtered liquid. □□**filtration** /-ˈtreɪʃ(ə)n/ *n.* [mod.L *filtrare* (as FILTER)]

fimbriate /ˈfɪmbrɪˌeɪt/ *adj.* (also **fimbriated**) **1** *Bot.* & *Zool.* fringed or bordered with hairs etc. **2** *Heraldry* having a narrow border. [L *fimbriatus* f. *fimbriae* fringe]

fin /fɪn/ *n.* & *v.* —*n.* **1** an organ on various parts of the body of many aquatic vertebrates and some invertebrates, including fish and cetaceans, for propelling, steering, and balancing (*dorsal fin*; *anal fin*). **2** a small projecting surface or attachment on an aircraft, rocket, or motor car for ensuring aerodynamic stability. **3** an underwater swimmer's flipper. **4** a sharp lateral projection on the share or coulter of a plough. **5** a finlike projection on any device, for improving heat transfer etc. —*v.* (**finned, finning**) **1** *tr.* provide with fins. **2** *intr.* swim under water. □**fin-back** (or **fin whale**) a rorqual, *Balaenoptera physalus*. □□**finless** *adj.* **finned** *adj.* (also in *comb.*). [OE *fin(n)*]

finable see FINE².

finagle /fɪˈneɪg(ə)l/ *v.intr.* & *tr. colloq.* act or obtain dishonestly. □□**finagler** *n.* [dial. *fainaigue* cheat]

final /ˈfaɪn(ə)l/ *adj.* & *n.* —*adj.* **1** situated at the end, coming last. **2** conclusive, decisive, unalterable, putting an end to doubt. **3** concerned with the purpose or end aimed at. —*n.* **1** the last or deciding heat or game in sports or in a competition (*Cup Final*). **2** the edition of a newspaper published latest in the day. **3** (usu. in *pl.*) the series of examinations at the end of a degree course. **4** *Mus.* the principal note in any mode. □**final cause** *Philos.* the end towards which a thing naturally develops or at which an action aims. **final clause** *Gram.* a clause expressing purpose, introduced by *in order that, lest*, etc. **final drive** the last part of the transmission system in a motor vehicle. **final solution** the Nazi policy (1941-5) of exterminating European Jews. □□**finally** *adv.* [ME f. OF or f. L *finalis* f. *finis* end]

finale /fɪˈnɑːlɪ, -leɪ/ *n.* **1 a** the last movement of an instrumental composition. **b** a piece of music closing an act in an opera. **2** the close of a drama etc. **3** a conclusion. [It. (as FINAL)]

finalism /ˈfaɪnəˌlɪz(ə)m/ *n.* the doctrine that natural processes (e.g. evolution) are directed towards some goal. □□**finalistic** /-ˈlɪstɪk/ *adj.*

finalist /ˈfaɪnəlɪst/ *n.* a competitor in the final of a competition etc.

finality /faɪˈnælɪtɪ/ *n.* (*pl.* **-ies**) **1** the quality or fact of being final. **2** the belief that something is final. **3** a final act, state, or utterance. **4** the principle of final cause viewed as operative in the universe. [F *finalité* f. LL *finalitas -tatis* (as FINAL)]

finalize /ˈfaɪnəˌlaɪz/ *v.tr.* (also **-ise**) **1** put into final form. **2** complete; bring to an end. **3** approve the final form or details of. □□**finalization** /-ˈzeɪʃ(ə)n/ *n.*

finance /ˈfaɪnæns, fɪˈnæns, faɪˈnæns/ *n.* & *v.* —*n.* **1** the management of (esp. public) money. **2** monetary support for an enterprise. **3** (in *pl.*) the money resources of a State, company, or person. —*v.tr.* provide capital for (a person or enterprise). □**finance company** (or **house**) a company concerned mainly with providing money for hire-purchase transactions. [ME f. OF f. *finer* settle a debt f. *fin* end: see FINE²]

financial /faɪˈnænʃ(ə)l, fɪ-/ *adj.* **1** of finance. **2** *Austral.* & *NZ sl.* possessing money. □**financial year** a year as reckoned for taxing or accounting (e.g. the British tax year, reckoned from 6 April). □□ **financially** *adv.*

financier *n.* & *v.* —*n.* /faɪˈnænsɪə(r), ˌfɪ-/ a person engaged in large-scale finance. —*v.intr.* /ˌfaɪnænˈsɪə(r), fɪ-/ usu. *derog.* conduct financial operations. [F (as FINANCE)]

finch /fɪntʃ/ *n.* any small seed-eating passerine bird of the family Fringillidae (esp. one of the genus *Fringilla*), including crossbills, canaries, and chaffinches. [OE *finc* f. WG]

find /faɪnd/ *v.* & *n.* —*v.tr.* (*past* and *past part.* **found** /faʊnd/) **1 a** discover by chance or effort (*found a key*). **b** become aware of. **c** (*absol.*) discover game, esp. a fox. **2 a** get possession of by chance (*found a treasure*). **b** obtain, receive (*idea found acceptance*). **c** succeed in obtaining (*cannot find the money*; *can't find time to read*). **d** summon up (*found courage to protest*). **e** *sl.* steal. **3 a** seek out and provide (*will find you a book*). **b** supply, furnish (*each finds his own equipment*). **4** ascertain by study or calculation or inquiry (*could not find the answer*). **5 a** perceive or experience (*find no sense in it*; *find difficulty in breathing*). **b** (often in *passive*) recognize or discover to be present (*the word is not found in Shakespeare*). **c** regard or discover from experience (*finds England too cold*; *you'll find it pays*; *find it impossible to reply*). **6** *Law* (of a jury, judge, etc.) decide and declare (*found him guilty*; *found that he had done it*; *found it murder*). **7** reach by a natural or normal process (*water finds its own level*). **8 a** (of a letter) reach (a person). **b** (of an address) be adequate to enable a letter etc. to reach (a person). **9** *archaic* reach the conscience of. —*n.* **1 a** a discovery of treasure, minerals, etc. **b** *Hunting* the finding of a fox. **2 a** thing or person discovered, esp. when of value. □**all found** (of an employee's wages) with board and lodging provided free. **find against** *Law* decide against (a person), judge to be guilty. **find fault** see FAULT. **find favour** prove acceptable. **find one's feet 1** become able to walk. **2** develop one's independent ability. **find for** *Law* decide in favour of (a person), judge to be innocent. **find it in one's heart** (esp. with *neg.*; foll. by *to* + infin.) prevail upon oneself, be willing. **find oneself 1** discover that one is (*woke to find myself in hospital*; *found herself agreeing*). **2** discover one's vocation. **3** provide for one's own needs. **find out 1** discover or detect (a wrongdoer etc.). **2** (often foll. by *about*) get information (*find out about holidays abroad*). **3** discover (*find out where we are*). **4** (often foll. by *about*) discover the truth, a fact, etc. (*he never found out*). **5** devise. **6** solve. **find-spot** *Archaeol.* the place where an object is found. **find one's way 1** (often foll. by *to*) manage to reach a place. **2** (often foll. by *into*) be brought or get. □□**findable** *adj.* [OE *findan* f. Gmc]

finder /ˈfaɪndə(r)/ *n.* **1** a person who finds. **2** a small telescope attached to a large one to locate an object for observation. **3** the viewfinder of a camera. □**finders keepers** *colloq.* whoever finds a thing is entitled to keep it.

fin de siècle /ˌfæ̃ də ˈsjekl/ *adj.* **1** characteristic of the end of the nineteenth century. **2** decadent. [F, = end of century]

finding /ˈfaɪndɪŋ/ *n.* **1** (often in *pl.*) a conclusion reached by an inquiry. **2** (in *pl.*) *US* small parts or tools used by workmen.

fine¹ /faɪn/ *adj.*, *n.*, *adv.*, & *v.* —*adj.* **1** of high quality. **2 a** excellent; of notable merit (*a fine painting*). **b**

good, satisfactory (*that will be fine*). **c** fortunate (*has been a fine thing for him*). **d** well conceived or expressed (*a fine saying*). **3 a** pure, refined. **b** (of gold or silver) containing a specified proportion of pure metal. **4** of handsome appearance or size; imposing, dignified (*fine buildings*; *a person of fine presence*). **5** in good health (*I'm fine, thank you*). **6** (of weather etc.) bright and clear with sunshine; free from rain. **7 a** thin; sharp. **b** in small particles. **c** worked in slender thread. **d** (esp. of print) small. **e** (of a pen) narrow-pointed. **8** *Cricket* behind the wicket and near the line of flight of the ball. **9** tritely complimentary; euphemistic (*say fine things about a person*; *call things by fine names*). **10** ornate, showy, smart. **11** fastidious, dainty, pretending refinement; (of speech or writing) affectedly ornate. **12 a** capable of delicate perception or discrimination. **b** perceptible only with difficulty (*a fine distinction*). **13 a** delicate, subtle, exquisitely fashioned. **b** (of feelings) refined, elevated. **14** (of wine or other goods) of a high standard; conforming to a specified grade. —*n.* **1** fine weather (*in rain or fine*). **2** (in *pl.*) very small particles in mining, milling, etc. —*adv.* **1** finely. **2** *colloq.* very well (*suits me fine*). —*v.* **1** (often foll. by *down*) **a** *tr.* make (beer or wine) clear. **b** *intr.* (of liquid) become clear. **2** *tr. & intr.* (often foll. by *away, down, off*) make or become finer, thinner, or less coarse; dwindle or taper, or cause to do so. □**cut** (or **run**) **it fine** allow very little margin of time etc. **fine arts** those appealing to the mind or to the sense of beauty, as poetry, music, and esp. painting, sculpture, and architecture. **fine chemicals** see CHEMICAL. **fine-draw** sew together (two pieces of cloth, edges of a tear, parts of a garment) so that the join is imperceptible. **fine-drawn 1** extremely thin. **2** subtle. **fine print** detailed printed information, esp. in legal documents, instructions, etc. **fine-spun 1** delicate. **2** (of a theory etc.) too subtle, unpractical. **fine-tooth comb** a comb with narrow close-set teeth. **fine-tune** make small adjustments to (a mechanism etc.) in order to obtain the best possible results. **fine up** *Austral. colloq.* (of the weather) become fine. **go over with a fine-tooth comb** check or search thoroughly. **not to put too fine a point on it** (as a parenthetic remark) to speak bluntly. □□ **finely** *adv.* **fineness** *n.* [ME f. OF *fin* ult. f. L *finire* finish]

fine² /faɪn/ *n. & v.* —*n.* **1** a sum of money exacted as a penalty. **2** *hist.* a sum of money paid by an incoming tenant in return for the rent's being small. —*v.tr.* punish by a fine (*fined him £5*). □**in fine** to sum up; in short. □□ **finable** /ˈfaɪnəb(ə)l/ *adj.* [ME f. OF *fin* f. med.L *finis* sum paid on settling a lawsuit f. L *finis* end]

fine³ /fiːn/ *n.* = FINE CHAMPAGNE. [abbr.]

fine champagne /ˌfiːn ʃɑ̃ˈpɑːnj/ *n.* old liqueur brandy. [F, = fine (brandy from) Champagne (vineyards in Charente)]

finery¹ /ˈfaɪnərɪ/ *n.* showy dress or decoration. [FINE¹ + -ERY, after BRAVERY]

finery² /ˈfaɪnərɪ/ *n.* (*pl.* -ies) *hist.* a hearth where pig iron was converted into wrought iron. [F *finerie* f. *finer* refine, FINE¹]

fines herbes /fiːnz ˈeəb/ *n.pl.* mixed herbs used in cooking, esp. chopped as omelette-flavouring. [F, = fine herbs]

finesse /fɪˈnes/ *n. & v.* —*n.* **1** refinement. **2** subtle or delicate manipulation. **3** artfulness, esp. in handling a difficulty tactfully. **4** *Cards* an attempt to win a trick with a card that is not the highest held. —*v.* **1** *intr. & tr.* use or achieve by finesse. **2** *Cards* **a** *intr.* make a finesse. **b** *tr.* play (a card) by way of finesse. **3** *tr.* evade or trick by finesse. [F, rel. to FINE¹]

finger /ˈfɪŋgə(r)/ *n. & v.* —*n.* **1** any of the terminal projections of the hand (including or excluding the thumb). **2** the part of a glove etc. intended to cover a finger. **3 a** a finger-like object (*fish finger*). **b** a long narrow structure. **4** *colloq.* a measure of liquor in a glass, based on the breadth of a finger. **5** *sl.* **a** an

informer. **b** a pickpocket. **c** a policeman. —*v.tr.* **1** touch, feel, or turn about with the fingers. **2** *Mus.* **a** play (a passage) with fingers used in a particular way. **b** mark (music) with signs showing which fingers are to be used. **c** play upon (an instrument) with the fingers. **3** *US sl.* indicate (a victim, or a criminal to the police). □**all fingers and thumbs** clumsy. **finger alphabet** a form of sign language using the fingers. **finger-board** a flat strip at the top end of a stringed instrument, against which the strings are pressed to determine tones. **finger-bowl** (or **-glass**) a small bowl for rinsing the fingers during a meal. **finger language** language expressed by means of the finger alphabet. **finger-mark** a mark left on a surface by a finger. **finger-paint** *n.* paint that can be applied with the fingers. —*v.intr.* apply paint with the fingers. **finger-plate** a plate fixed to a door above the handle to prevent finger-marks. **finger-post** a signpost at a road junction. **one's fingers itch** (often foll. by *to* + infin.) one is longing or impatient. **finger-stall** a cover to protect a finger, esp. when injured. **get** (or **pull**) **one's finger out** *sl.* cease prevaricating and start to act. **have a finger in the pie** be (esp. officiously) concerned in the matter. **lay a finger on** touch however slightly. **put one's finger on** locate or identify exactly. **put the finger on** *sl.* **1** inform against. **2** identify (an intended victim). **twist** (or **wind**) **round one's finger** (or **little finger**) persuade (a person) without difficulty, dominate (a person) completely. **work one's fingers to the bone** see BONE. □□ **fingered** *adj.* (also in *comb.*). **fingerless** *adj.* [OE f. Gmc]

fingering¹ /ˈfɪŋgərɪŋ/ *n.* **1** a manner or technique of using the fingers, esp. to play an instrument. **2** an indication of this in a musical score.

fingering² /ˈfɪŋgərɪŋ/ *n.* fine wool for knitting. [earlier *fingram*, perh. f. F *fin grain*, as GROGRAM f. *gros grain*]

fingerling /ˈfɪŋgəlɪŋ/ *n.* a parr.

fingernail /ˈfɪŋgəneɪl/ *n.* the nail at the tip of each finger.

fingerprint /ˈfɪŋgəprɪnt/ *n. & v.* —*n.* **1** an impression made on a surface by the fingertips, esp. as used for identifying individuals. **2** a distinctive characteristic. —*v.tr.* record the fingerprints of (a person).

fingertip /ˈfɪŋgətɪp/ *n.* the tip of a finger. □**have at one's fingertips** be thoroughly familiar with (a subject etc.).

finial /ˈfɪnɪəl/ *n. Archit.* **1** an ornament finishing off the apex of a roof, pediment, gable, tower-corner, canopy, etc. **2** the topmost part of a pinnacle. [ME f. OF *fin* f. L *finis* end]

finical /ˈfɪnɪk(ə)l/ *adj.* = FINICKY. □□ **finicality** /-ˈkælɪtɪ/ *n.* **finically** *adv.* **finicalness** *n.* [16th c.: prob. orig. university sl. f. FINE¹ + -ICAL]

finicking /ˈfɪnɪkɪŋ/ *adj.* = FINICKY. [FINICAL + -ING²]

finicky /ˈfɪnɪkɪ/ *adj.* **1** over-particular, fastidious. **2** needing much attention to detail; fiddly. □□ **finickiness** *n.*

finis /ˈfɪnɪs, ˈfiːnɪs, ˈfaɪnɪs/ *n.* **1** (at the end of a book) the end. **2** the end of anything, esp. of life. [L]

finish /ˈfɪnɪʃ/ *v. & n.* —*v.* **1** *tr.* **a** (often foll. by *off*) bring to an end; come to the end of; complete. **b** (usu. foll. by *off*) *colloq.* kill; overcome completely. **c** (often foll. by *off, up*) consume or get through the whole or the remainder of (food or drink) (*finish up your dinner*). **2** *intr.* **a** come to an end, cease. **b** reach the end, esp. of a race. **c** = *finish up*. **3** *tr.* **a** complete the manufacture of (cloth, woodwork, etc.) by surface treatment. **b** put the final touches to; make perfect or highly accomplished (*finished manners*). **c** prepare (a girl) for entry into fashionable society. —*n.* **1 a** the end, the last stage. **b** the point at which a race etc. ends. **c** the death of a fox in a hunt (*be in at the finish*). **2** a method, material, or texture used in surface treatment of wood, cloth, etc. (*mahogany finish*). **3** what serves to give completeness. **4** an accomplished or completed state. □**fight to a finish**

fight till one party is completely beaten.
finishing-school a private college where girls are prepared for entry into fashionable society. **finish off** provide with an ending. **finish up** (often foll. by *in*, *by*) end in something, end by doing something (*he finished up last in the race*; *the plan finished up in the waste-paper basket*; *finished up by apologizing*). **finish with** have no more to do with, complete one's use of or association with. [ME f. OF *fenir* f. L *finire* f. *finis* end]

finisher /'fɪnɪʃə(r)/ *n.* **1** a person who finishes something. **2** a worker or machine doing the last operation in manufacture. **3** *colloq.* a discomfiting thing, a crushing blow, etc.

finite /'faɪnaɪt/ *adj.* **1** limited, bounded; not infinite. **2** *Gram.* (of a part of a verb) having a specific number and person. **3** not infinitely small. □□ **finitely** *adv.* **finiteness** *n.* **finitude** /'fɪnɪˌtjuːd/ *n.* [L *finitus* past part. of *finire* FINISH]

finitism /'faɪnaɪˌtɪz(ə)m/ *n.* belief in the finiteness of the world, God, etc. □□ **finitist** *n.*

fink /fɪŋk/ *n. & v. US sl.* —*n.* **1** an unpleasant person. **2** an informer. **3** a strikebreaker; a blackleg. —*v.intr.* (foll. by *on*) inform on. [20th c.: orig. unkn.]

Finn /fɪn/ *n.* a native or national of Finland; a person of Finnish descent. [OE *Finnas* pl.]

finnan /'fɪnən/ *n.* (in full **finnan haddock**) a haddock cured with the smoke of green wood, turf, or peat. [*Findhorn* or *Findon* in Scotland]

finnesko /'fɪnəˌskəʊ/ *n.* (*pl.* same) a boot of tanned reindeer-skin with the hair on the outside. [Norw. *finnsko* (as FINN, *sko* SHOE)]

Finnic /'fɪnɪk/ *adj.* **1** of the group of peoples related to the Finns. **2** of the group of languages related to Finnish.

Finnish /'fɪnɪʃ/ *adj. & n.* —*adj.* of the Finns or their language. —*n.* the language of the Finns.

Finno-Ugric /ˌfɪnəʊˈuːgrɪk, -ˈjuːgrɪk/ *adj. & n.* (also **Finno-Ugrian** /-ˈuːgrɪən/) —*adj.* belonging to the group of Ural-Altaic languages including Finnish, Estonian, Lapp, and Magyar. —*n.* this group.

finny /'fɪnɪ/ *adj.* **1** having fins; like a fin. **2** *poet.* of or teeming with fish.

fino /'fiːnəʊ/ *n.* (*pl.* **-os**) a light-coloured dry sherry. [Sp., = fine]

fiord /fjɔːd/ *n.* (also **fjord**) a long narrow inlet of sea between high cliffs, as in Norway. [Norw. f. ON *fjörthr* f. Gmc: cf. FIRTH, FORD]

fioritura /fɪˌɔːrɪˈtʊərə/ *n.* (*pl.* **fioriture** *pronunc.* same) *Mus.* the usu. improvised decoration of a melody. [It., = flowering f. *fiorire* to flower]

fipple /'fɪp(ə)l/ *n.* a plug at the mouth-end of a wind instrument. □ **fipple flute** a flute played by blowing endwise, e.g. a recorder. [17th c.: orig. unkn.]

fir /fɜː(r)/ *n.* **1** (in full **fir-tree**) any evergreen coniferous tree, esp. of the genus *Abies*, with needles borne singly on the stems (cf. PINE¹). **2** the wood of the fir. □ **fir-cone** the fruit of the fir. □□ **firry** *adj.* [ME, prob. f. ON *fyri-* f. Gmc]

fire /'faɪə(r)/ *n. & v.* —*n.* **1 a** the state or process of combustion, in which substances combine chemically with oxygen from the air and usu. give out bright light and heat. **b** the active principle operative in this. **c** flame or incandescence. **2** a conflagration, a destructive burning (*forest fire*). **3 a** burning fuel in a grate, furnace, etc. **b** = *electric fire*. **c** = *gas fire*. **4** firing of guns. **5 a** fervour, spirit, vivacity. **b** poetic inspiration, lively imagination. **c** vehement emotion. **6** burning heat, fever. **7** luminosity, glow (*St Elmo's fire*). —*v.* **1 a** *tr.* discharge (a gun etc.). **b** *tr.* propel (a missile) from a gun etc. **c** *intr.* (often foll. by *at*, *into*, *on*) fire a gun or missile. **d** *tr.* produce (a broadside, salute, etc.) by discharge of guns. **e** *intr.* (of a gun etc.) be discharged. **2** *tr.* cause (explosive) to explode. **3** *tr.* deliver or utter in rapid succession (*fired insults at us*). **4** *tr. sl.* dismiss (an employee) from a job. **5** *tr.* **a** set fire to with the intention of destroying. **b** kindle (explosives). **6** *intr.* catch fire. **7** *intr.* (of an

internal-combustion engine, or a cylinder in one) undergo ignition of its fuel. **8** *tr.* supply (a furnace, engine, boiler, or power station) with fuel. **9** *tr.* **a** stimulate (the imagination). **b** fill (a person) with enthusiasm. **10** *tr.* **a** bake or dry (pottery, bricks, etc.). **b** cure (tea or tobacco) by artificial heat. **11** *intr.* become heated or excited. **12** *tr.* cause to glow or redden. □ **catch fire** begin to burn. **fire-alarm** a device for giving warning of fire. **fire and brimstone** the supposed torments of hell. **fire away** *colloq.* begin; go ahead. **fire-ball** **1** a large meteor. **2** a ball of flame, esp. from a nuclear explosion. **3** an energetic person. **4** ball lightning. **5** *Mil. hist.* a ball filled with combustibles. **fire-balloon** a balloon made buoyant by the heat of a fire burning at its mouth. **fire-blight** a disease of plants, esp. hops and fruit trees, causing a scorched appearance. **fire-bomb** an incendiary bomb. **fire-break** an obstacle to the spread of fire in a forest etc., esp. an open space. **fire-brick** a fireproof brick used in a grate. **fire brigade** esp. *Brit.* an organized body of firemen trained and employed to extinguish fires. **fire-bug** *colloq.* a pyromaniac. **fire company** **1** = *fire brigade*. **2** a fire-insurance company. **fire-control** a system of regulating the fire of a ship's or a fort's guns. **fire department** *US* = *fire brigade*. **fire door** a fire-resistant door to prevent the spread of fire. **fire-drake** (in Germanic mythology) a fiery dragon. **fire-drill** **1** a rehearsal of the procedures to be used in case of fire. **2** a primitive device for kindling fire with a stick and wood. **fire-eater** **1** a conjuror who appears to swallow fire. **2** a person fond of quarrelling or fighting. **fire-engine** a vehicle carrying equipment for fighting large fires. **fire-escape** an emergency staircase or apparatus for escape from a building on fire. **fire extinguisher** an apparatus with a jet for discharging liquid chemicals, water, or foam to extinguish a fire. **fire-fighter** a person whose task is to extinguish fires. **fire-guard** **1** a protective screen or grid placed in front of a fireplace. **2** *US* a fire-watcher. **3** *US* fire-break. **fire-hose** a hose-pipe used in extinguishing fires. **fire-irons** tongs, poker, and shovel, for tending a domestic fire. **fire-lighter** *Brit.* a piece of inflammable material to help start a fire in a grate. **fire-office** a fire-insurance company. **fire-opal** girasol. **fire-plug** a hydrant for a fire-hose. **fire-power** **1** the destructive capacity of guns etc. **2** financial, intellectual, or emotional strength. **fire-practice** a fire-drill. **fire-raiser** *Brit.* an arsonist. **fire-raising** *Brit.* arson. **fire-screen** **1** a screen to keep off the direct heat of a fire. **2** a fire-guard. **3** an ornamental screen for a fireplace. **fire-ship** *hist.* a ship loaded with combustibles and sent adrift to ignite an enemy's ships etc. **fire station** the headquarters of a fire brigade. **fire-step** = *firing-step*. **fire-stone** stone that resists fire, used for furnaces etc. **fire-storm** a high wind or storm following a fire caused by bombs. **fire-tongs** tongs for picking up pieces of coal etc. in tending a fire. **fire-trap** a building without proper provision for escape in case of fire. **fire up** show sudden anger. **fire-walking** the (often ceremonial) practice of walking barefoot over white-hot stones, wood-ashes, etc. **fire warden** *US* a person employed to prevent or extinguish fires. **fire-watcher** a person keeping watch for fires, esp. those caused by bombs. **fire-water** *colloq.* strong alcoholic liquor. **go on fire** *Sc. & Ir.* catch fire. **go through fire and water** face all perils. **on fire** **1** burning. **2** excited. **set fire to** (or **set on fire**) ignite, kindle, cause to burn. **set the world** (or **Thames**) **on fire** do something remarkable or sensational. **take fire** catch fire. **under fire** **1** being shot at. **2** being rigorously criticized or questioned. □□ **fireless** *adj.* **firer** *n.* [OE *fȳr*, *fȳrian*, f. WG]

firearm /'faɪərˌɑːm/ *n.* (usu. in *pl.*) a gun, esp. a pistol or rifle.

fireback /'faɪəˌbæk/ *n.* **1 a** the back wall of a fireplace.

b an iron sheet for this. **2** a SE Asian pheasant of the genus *Lophura*.

firebox /'faɪəˌbɒks/ *n.* the fuel-chamber of a steam engine or boiler.

firebrand /'faɪəˌbrænd/ *n.* **1** a piece of burning wood. **2** a cause of trouble, esp. a person causing unrest.

fireclay /'faɪəˌkleɪ/ *n.* clay capable of withstanding high temperatures, often used to make fire-bricks.

firecracker /'faɪəˌkrækə(r)/ *n.* *US* an explosive firework.

firecrest /'faɪəˌkrest/ *n.* a warbler, *Regulus ignicapillus*, with red and orange crown feathers which may be erected.

firedamp /'faɪəˌdæmp/ *n.* a miners' name for methane, which is explosive when mixed in certain proportions with air.

firedog /'faɪəˌdɒg/ *n.* a metal support for burning wood or for a grate or fire-irons.

firefly /'faɪəˌflaɪ/ *n.* (*pl.* **-flies**) any soft-bodied beetle of the family Lampyridae, emitting phosphorescent light, including glow-worms.

firehouse /'faɪəˌhaʊs/ *n.* *US* a fire station.

firelight /'faɪəˌlaɪt/ *n.* light from a fire in a fireplace. [OE *fyr-leoht* (as FIRE, LIGHT¹)]

firelock /'faɪəˌlɒk/ *n.* *hist.* a musket in which the priming was ignited by sparks.

fireman /'faɪəmən/ *n.* (*pl.* **-men**) **1** a member of a fire brigade; a person employed to extinguish fires. **2** a person who tends a furnace or the fire of a steam engine or steamship.

fireplace /'faɪəˌpleɪs/ *n. Archit.* **1** a place for a domestic fire, esp. a grate or hearth at the base of a chimney. **2** a structure surrounding this. **3** the area in front of this.

fireproof /'faɪəˌpruːf/ *adj. & v.* —*adj.* able to resist fire or great heat. —*v.tr.* make fireproof.

fireside /'faɪəˌsaɪd/ *n.* **1** the area round a fireplace. **2** a person's home or home-life. □**fireside chat** an informal talk.

firewood /'faɪəˌwʊd/ *n.* wood for use as fuel.

firework /'faɪəˌwɜːk/ *n.* **1** a device containing combustible chemicals that cause explosions or spectacular effects. **2** (in *pl.*) **a** an outburst of passion, esp. anger. **b** a display of wit or brilliance.

firing /'faɪərɪŋ/ *n.* **1** the discharging of guns. **2** material for a fire, fuel. **3** the heating process which hardens clay into pottery etc. □**firing-line 1** the front line in a battle. **2** the leading part in an activity etc. **firing-party** a group detailed to fire the salute at a military funeral. **firing-squad 1** a group detailed to shoot a condemned person. **2** a firing-party. **firing-step** a step on which soldiers in a trench stand to fire.

firkin /'fɜːkɪn/ *n.* **1** a small cask for liquids, butter, fish, etc. **2** *Brit.* (as a measure) half a kilderkin (8 or 9 gallons). [ME *ferdekyn*, prob. f. MDu. *vierdekijn* (unrecorded) dimin. of *vierde* fourth]

firm¹ /fɜːm/ *adj., adv., & v.* —*adj.* **1 a** of solid or compact structure. **b** fixed, stable. **c** steady; not shaking. **2 a** resolute, determined. **b** not easily shaken (*firm belief*). **c** steadfast, constant (*a firm friend*). **3 a** (of an offer etc.) not liable to cancellation after acceptance. **b** (of a decree, law, etc.) established, immutable. **4** *Commerce* (of prices or goods) maintaining their level or value. —*adv.* firmly (*stand firm; hold firm to*). —*v.* **1** *tr.* & *intr.* make or become firm, secure, compact, or solid. **2** *tr.* fix (plants) firmly in the soil. □□**firmly** *adv.* **firmness** *n.* [ME f. OF *ferme* f. L *firmus*]

firm² /fɜːm/ *n.* **1 a** a business concern. **b** the partners in such a concern. **2** a group of persons working together, esp. of hospital doctors and assistants. [earlier = signature, style: Sp. & It. *firma* f. med.L, f. L *firmare* confirm f. *firmus* FIRM¹]

firmament /'fɜːməmənt/ *n. literary* the sky regarded as a vault or arch. □□**firmamental** /-'ment(ə)l/ *adj.* [ME f. OF f. L *firmamentum* f. *firmare* (as FIRM²)]

firman /fɜː'mɑːn, 'fɜːmən/ *n.* **1** an oriental sovereign's edict. **2** a grant or permit. [Pers. *fermān*, Skr. *pramāṇam* right measure]

firmware /'fɜːmweə(r)/ *n. Computing* a permanent kind of software programmed into a read-only memory.

firry see FIR.

first /fɜːst/ *adj., n., & adv.* —*adj.* **1 a** earliest in time or order. **b** coming next after a specified or implied time (*shall take the first train; the first cuckoo*). **2** foremost in position, rank, or importance (*First Lord of the Treasury; first mate*). **3** *Mus.* performing the highest or chief of two or more parts for the same instrument or voice. **4** most willing or likely (*should be the first to admit the difficulty*). **5** basic or evident (*first principles*). —*n.* **1** (prec. by *the*) the person or thing first mentioned or occurring. **2** the first occurrence of something notable. **3 a** a place in the first class in an examination. **b** a person having this. **4** the first day of a month. **5** first gear. **6 a** first place in a race. **b** the winner of this. **7** (in *pl.*) goods of the best quality. —*adv.* **1** before any other person or thing (*first of all; first and foremost; first come first served*). **2** before someone or something else (*must get this done first*). **3** for the first time (*when did you first see her?*). **4** in preference; rather (*will see him damned first*). **5** first-class (*I usually travel first*). □**at first** at the beginning. **at first hand** directly from the original source. **first aid** help given to an injured person until proper medical treatment is available. **first and last** taking one thing with another, on the whole. **first blood** see BLOOD. **first-born** *adj.* eldest. —*n.* the eldest child of a person. **First Cause** the Creator of the universe. **first class 1** a set of persons or things grouped together as the best. **2** the best accommodation in a train, ship, etc. **3** the class of mail given priority in handling. **4 a** the highest division in an examination list. **b** a place in this. **first-class** *adj.* **1** belonging to or travelling by the first class. **2** of the best quality; very good. —*adv.* by the first class (*travels first-class*). **first cousin** see COUSIN. **first-day cover** an envelope with stamps postmarked on their first day of issue. **first-degree** *Med.* denoting burns that affect only the surface of the skin, causing reddening. **first finger** the finger next to the thumb. **first floor** see FLOOR. **first-foot** *Sc. n.* the first person to cross a threshold in the New Year. —*v.intr.* be a first-foot. **first-fruit** (usu. in *pl.*) **1** the first agricultural produce of a season, esp. as offered to God. **2** the first results of work etc. **3** *hist.* a payment to a superior by the new holder of an office. **first gear** see GEAR. **first intention** see INTENTION. **First Lady** (in the US) the wife of the President. **first lesson** the first of several passages from the Bible read at a service in the Church of England. **first lieutenant** *US* an army or air force officer next below captain. **first light** the time when light first appears in the morning. **first mate** (on a merchant ship) the officer second in command to the master. **first name** a personal or Christian name. **first night** the first public performance of a play etc. **first-nighter** a habitual attender of first nights. **first off** *US colloq.* at first, first of all. **first offender** a criminal against whom no previous conviction is recorded. **first officer** the mate on a merchant ship. **first or last** sooner or later. **first past the post 1** winning a race etc. by being the first to reach the finishing line. **2** (of an electoral system) selecting a candidate or party by simple majority (see also *proportional representation, single transferable vote*). **first person** see PERSON. **first post** see POST³. **first-rate** *adj.* of the highest class, excellent. —*adv. colloq.* **1** very well (*feeling first-rate*). **2** excellently. **first reading** the occasion when a Bill is presented to a legislature to permit its introduction. **first refusal** see REFUSAL. **first school** *Brit.* a school for children from 5 to 9 years old. **first sergeant** *US* the highest-ranking non-commissioned officer in a company. **first-strike** denoting a first aggressive attack with nuclear weapons. **first thing** *colloq.* before anything else; very early in the morning (*shall do it first thing*). **the first thing** even the most elementary fact or principle (*does not know the first thing about it*). **first things first** the most important things before any others (*we must do first things first*). **first up** *Austral.* first of all; at the first attempt. **from the first** from the beginning. **from first to last** throughout. **get to first base** *US* achieve the first step towards an objective. **in the first place** as the first consideration. **of the first water** see WATER. [OE *fyrst* f. Gmc]

firsthand /fɜːstˈhænd, *attrib.* ˈfɜːst-/ *adj.* & *adv.* from the original source; direct.

firstling /ˈfɜːstlɪŋ/ *n.* (usu. in *pl.*) **1** the first result of anything, first-fruits. **2** the first offspring; the first born in a season.

firstly /ˈfɜːstlɪ/ *adv.* (in enumerating topics, arguments, etc.) in the first place, first (cf. FIRST *adv.*).

firth /fɜːθ/ *n.* (also **frith** /frɪθ/) **1** a narrow inlet of the sea. **2** an estuary. [ME (orig. Sc.) f. ON *fjörthr* FIORD]

fisc /fɪsk/ *n.* *Rom.Hist.* the public treasury; the emperor's privy purse. [F *fisc* or L *fiscus* rush-basket, purse, treasury]

fiscal /ˈfɪsk(ə)l/ *adj.* & *n.* —*adj.* of public revenue. —*n.* **1** a legal official in some countries. **2** *Sc.* = *procurator fiscal.* □**fiscal year** = *financial year.* □□ **fiscally** *adv.* [F *fiscal* or L *fiscalis* (as FISC)]

fiscality /fɪˈskælɪtɪ/ *n.* (*pl.* -**ies**) **1** (in *pl.*) fiscal matters. **2** excessive regard for these.

fish¹ /fɪʃ/ *n.* & *v.* —*n.* (*pl.* same or **fishes**) **1** a vertebrate cold-blooded animal with gills and fins living wholly in water. **2** any animal living wholly in water, e.g. cuttlefish, shellfish, jellyfish. **3** the flesh of fish as food. **4** *colloq.* a person remarkable in some way (usu. unfavourable) (*an odd fish*). **5** (**the Fish** or **Fishes**) the zodiacal sign or constellation Pisces. **6** *Naut. sl.* a torpedo; a submarine. —*v.* **1** *intr.* try to catch fish, esp. with a line or net. **2** *tr.* fish for (a certain kind of fish) or in (a certain stretch of water). **3** *intr.* (foll. by *for*) **a** a search for in water or a concealed place. **b** seek by indirect means (*fishing for compliments*). **4** *tr.* (foll. by *up, out,* etc.) retrieve with careful or awkward searching. □**drink like a fish** drink excessively. **fish-bowl** a usu. round glass bowl for keeping pet fish in. **fish cake** a cake of shredded fish and mashed potato, usu. eaten fried. **fish eagle 1** any large eagle of the genus *Haliaeetus,* with long broad wings, strong legs, and a strong tail. **2** any of several other eagles catching and feeding on fish. **fish-eye lens** a very wide-angle lens with a curved front. **fish farm** a place where fish are bred for food. **fish finger** *Brit.* a small oblong piece of fish in batter or breadcrumbs. **fish-glue** isinglass. **fish-hawk** an osprey, *Pandion haliaeetus.* **fish-hook** a barbed hook for catching fish. **fish-kettle** an oval pan for boiling fish. **fish-knife** a knife for eating or serving fish. **fish-meal** ground dried fish used as fertilizer or animal feed. **fish out of water** a person in an unsuitable or unwelcome environment or situation. **fish-pond** (or **-pool**) a pond or pool in which fish are kept. **fish-slice** a flat utensil for lifting fish and fried foods during and after cooking. **other fish to fry** other matters to attend to. [OE *fisc, fiscian* f. Gmc]

fish² /fɪʃ/ *n.* & *v.* —*n.* **1** a flat plate of iron, wood, etc., to strengthen a beam or joint. **2** *Naut.* a piece of wood, convex and concave, used to strengthen a mast etc. —*v.tr.* **1** mend or strengthen (a spar etc.) with a fish. **2** join (rails) with a fish-plate. □**fish-bolt** a bolt used to fasten fish-plates and rails together. **fish-plate a** a flat piece of iron etc. connecting railway rails. **b** a flat piece of metal with ends like a fish's tail, used to position masonry. □□ **fishlike** *adj.* [orig. as verb: f. F *ficher* fix ult. f. L *figere*]

fish³ /fɪʃ/ *n.* a piece of ivory etc. used as a counter in games. [F *fiche* (*ficher;* see FISH²)]

fisher /ˈfɪʃə(r)/ *n.* **1** an animal that catches fish, esp. a pekan. **2** *archaic* a fisherman. [OE *fiscere* f. Gmc (as FISH¹)]

fisherman /ˈfɪʃəmən/ *n.* (*pl.* -**men**) **1** a person who catches fish as a livelihood or for sport. **2** a fishing-boat.

fishery /ˈfɪʃərɪ/ *n.* (*pl.* -**ies**) **1** a place where fish are caught or reared. **2** the occupation or industry of catching or rearing fish.

fishing /ˈfɪʃɪŋ/ *n.* the activity of catching fish, esp. for food or as a sport. □**fishing-line** a long thread of silk etc. with a baited hook, sinker, float, etc., used for catching fish. **fishing-rod** a long tapering usu. jointed rod to which a fishing-line is attached.

fishmonger /ˈfɪʃˌmʌŋgə(r)/ *n.* esp. *Brit.* a dealer in fish.

fishnet /ˈfɪʃnet/ *n.* (often *attrib.*) an open-meshed fabric (*fishnet stockings*).

fishpot /ˈfɪʃpɒt/ *n.* a wicker trap for eels, lobsters, etc.

fishtail /ˈfɪʃteɪl/ *n.* & *v.* —*n.* a device etc. shaped like a fish's tail. —*v.intr.* move the tail of a vehicle from side to side. □**fishtail burner** a kind of burner producing a broadening jet of flame.

fishwife /ˈfɪʃwaɪf/ *n.* (*pl.* -**wives**) **1** a coarse-mannered or noisy woman. **2** a woman who sells fish.

fishy /ˈfɪʃɪ/ *adj.* (**fishier, fishiest**) **1 a** smelling or tasting like fish. **b** like that of a fish. **c** (of an eye) dull, vacant-looking. **d** consisting of fish (*a fishy repast*). **e** *joc.* or *poet.* abounding in fish. **2** *sl.* of dubious character, questionable, suspect. □□ **fishily** *adv.* **fishiness** *n.*

fisk /fɪsk/ *n.* *Sc.* the State treasury, the exchequer. [var. of FISC]

fissile /ˈfɪsaɪl/ *adj.* **1** capable of undergoing nuclear fission. **2** cleavable; tending to split. □□ **fissility** /-ˈsɪlɪtɪ/ *n.* [L *fissilis* (as FISSURE)]

fission /ˈfɪʃ(ə)n/ *n.* & *v.* —*n.* **1** *Physics* the spontaneous or impact-induced splitting of a heavy atomic nucleus, accompanied by a release of energy. **2** *Biol.* the division of a cell etc. into new cells etc. as a mode of reproduction. —*v.intr.* & *tr.* undergo or cause to undergo fission. □**fission bomb** an atomic bomb. □□ **fissionable** *adj.* [L *fissio* (as FISSURE)]

fissiparous /fɪˈsɪpərəs/ *adj.* **1** *Biol.* reproducing by fission. **2** tending to split. □□ **fissiparity** /-ˈpærɪtɪ/ *n.* **fissiparously** *adv.* **fissiparousness** *n.* [L *fissus* past part. (as FISSURE) after *viviparous*]

fissure /ˈfɪʃə(r)/ *n.* & *v.* —*n.* **1** an opening, usu. long and narrow, made esp. by cracking, splitting, or separation of parts. **2** *Bot.* & *Anat.* a narrow opening in an organ etc., esp. a depression between convolutions of the brain. **3** a cleavage. —*v.tr.* & *intr.* split or crack. [ME f. OF *fissure* or L *fissura* f. *findere fiss-* cleave]

fist /fɪst/ *n.* & *v.* —*n.* **1** a tightly closed hand. **2** *sl.* handwriting (*writes a good fist; I know his fist*). **3** *sl.* a hand (*give us your fist*). —*v.tr.* **1** strike with the fist. **2** *Naut.* handle (a sail, an oar, etc.). □**make a good** (or **poor** etc.) **fist** (foll. by *at, of*) *colloq.* make a good (or poor etc.) attempt at. □□ **fisted** *adj.* (also in *comb.*). **fistful** *n.* (*pl.* -**fuls**) [OE *fÿst* f. WG]

fistic /ˈfɪstɪk/ *adj.* (also **fistical**) *joc.* pugilistic.

fisticuffs /ˈfɪstɪˌkʌfs/ *n.pl.* fighting with the fists. [prob. obs. *fisty* adj. = FISTIC, + CUFF²]

fistula /ˈfɪstjʊlə/ *n.* (*pl.* **fistulas** or **fistulae** /-ˌliː/) **1** an abnormal or surgically made passage between a hollow organ and the body surface or between two hollow organs. **2** a natural pipe or spout in whales, insects, etc. □□ **fistular** *adj.* **fistulous** *adj.* [L, = pipe, flute]

fit¹ /fɪt/ *adj.*, *v.*, *n.*, & *adv.* —*adj.* (**fitter, fittest**) **1 a** (usu. foll. by *for*, or *to* + infin.) well adapted or suited. **b** (foll. by *to* + infin.) qualified, competent, worthy. **c** (foll. by *for*, or *to* + infin.) in a suitable condition, ready. **d** (foll. by *for*) good enough (*a dinner fit for a king*). **e** (foll. by *to* + infin.) sufficiently exhausted, troubled, or angry (*fit to drop*). **2** in good health or athletic condition. **3** proper, becoming, right (*it is fit that*). —*v.* (**fitted, fitting**) **1 a** *tr.* (also *absol.*) be of the right shape and size for (*the dress fits her; the key doesn't fit the lock; these shoes don't fit*). **b** *tr.* make, fix, or insert (a thing) so that it is of the right size or shape (*fitted shelves in the alcoves*). **c** *intr.* (often foll. by *in, into*) (of a component) be correctly positioned (*that bit fits here*). **d** *tr.* find room for (*can't fit another person on the bench*). **2** *tr.* (foll. by *for*, or *to* + infin.) **a** make suitable; adapt. **b** make competent (*fitted him to be a priest*). **3** *tr.* (usu. foll. by *with*) supply, furnish (*fitted the boat with a new rudder*). **4** *tr.* fix in place (*fit a lock on the door*). **5** *tr.* = *fit on*. **6** *tr.* be in harmony with, befit, become (*it fits the occasion; the punishment fits the crime*). —*n.* the way in which a garment, component, etc., fits (*a bad fit; a tight fit*). —*adv.* (foll. by *to* + infin.) *colloq.* in a suitable manner, appropriately (*was laughing fit to bust*). □**fit the bill** = *fill the bill*. **fit in 1** (often foll. by *with*) be (esp. socially) compatible or accommodating (*doesn't fit in with the rest of the group; tried to fit in with their plans*). **2** find space or time for (an object, engagement, etc.) (*the dentist fitted me in at the last minute*). **fit on** try on (a garment). **fit out** (or **up**) (often foll. by *with*) equip. **fit-up** *Theatr. sl.* **1** a temporary stage etc. **2** a travelling company. **see** (or **think**) **fit** (often foll. by *to* + infin.) decide or choose (a specified course of action). □□**fitly** *adv.* **fitness** *n.* [ME: orig. unkn.]

fit[2] /fɪt/ *n.* **1 a** a sudden seizure of epilepsy, hysteria, apoplexy, fainting, or paralysis, with unconsciousness or convulsions. **2** a sudden brief attack of an illness or of symptoms (*fit of coughing*). **3** a sudden short bout or burst (*fit of energy; fit of giggles*). **4** *colloq.* an attack of strong feeling (*fit of rage*). **5** a capricious impulse; a mood (*when the fit was on him*). □**by** (or **in**) **fits and starts** spasmodically. **give a person a fit** *colloq.* surprise or outrage him or her. **have a fit** *colloq.* be greatly surprised or outraged. **in fits** laughing uncontrollably. [ME, = position of danger, perh. = OE *fitt* conflict (?)]

fit[3] /fɪt/ *n.* (also **fytte**) *archaic* a section of a poem. [OE *fitt*]

fitch /fɪtʃ/ *n.* **1** a polecat. **2 a** the hair of a polecat. **b** a brush made from this or similar hair. [MDu. *fisse* etc.: cf. FITCHEW]

fitchew /'fɪtʃuː/ *n.* a polecat. [14th c. f. OF *ficheau, fissel* dimin. of MDu. *fisse*]

fitful /'fɪtfʊl/ *adj.* active or occurring spasmodically or intermittently. □□**fitfully** *adv.* **fitfulness** *n.*

fitment /'fɪtmənt/ *n.* (usu. in *pl.*) a fixed item of furniture.

fitted /'fɪtɪd/ *adj.* **1** made or shaped to fill a space or cover something closely or exactly (*a fitted carpet*). **2** provided with appropriate equipment, fittings, etc. (*a fitted kitchen*). **3** built-in; filling an alcove etc. (*fitted cupboards*).

fitter /'fɪtə(r)/ *n.* **1** a person who supervises the cutting, fitting, altering, etc. of garments. **2** a mechanic who fits together and adjusts machinery.

fitting /'fɪtɪŋ/ *n. & adj.* —*n.* **1** the process or an instance of having a garment etc. fitted (*needed several fittings*). **2 a** (in *pl.*) the fixtures and fitments of a building. **b** a piece of apparatus or furniture. —*adj.* proper, becoming, right. □**fitting-shop** a place where machine parts are put together. □□**fittingly** *adv.* **fittingness** *n.*

FitzGerald contraction /fɪts'dʒer(ə)ld/ *n.* (also **FitzGerald effect**) (in full **FitzGerald-Lorentz**) *Physics* the shortening of a moving body in the direction of its motion esp. at speeds close to that of light. [G. F. *FitzGerald*, Ir. physicist d. 1901 and H. A. *Lorentz*, Du. physicist d. 1928]

five /faɪv/ *n. & adj.* —*n.* **1** one more than four or one half of ten; the sum of three units and two units. **2** a symbol for this (5, v, V). **3** a size etc. denoted by five. **4** a set or team of five individuals. **5** the time of five

o'clock (*is it five yet?*). **6** a card with five pips. **7** *Cricket* a hit scoring five runs. —*adj.* that amount to five. □**bunch of fives** *Brit. sl.* a hand or fist. **five-corner** (or **-corners**) *Austral.* **1** a shrub of the genus *Styphelia.* **2** the pentagonal fruit of this. **five-eighth** *Austral. & NZ Rugby Football* either of two players between the scrum-half and the centre three-quarter. **five-finger exercise 1** an exercise on the piano involving all the fingers. **2** an easy task. **five hundred** a form of euchre in which 500 points make a game. **five o'clock shadow** beard-growth visible on a man's face in the latter part of the day. **five-star** of the highest class. **five-year plan 1** (in the USSR) a government plan for economic development over five years, inaugurated in 1928. **2** a similar plan in another country. [OE *fīf* f. Gmc]

fivefold /'faɪvfəʊld/ *adj. & adv.* **1** five times as much or as many. **2** consisting of five parts. **3** amounting to five.

fiver /'faɪvə(r)/ *n. colloq.* **1** *Brit.* a five-pound note. **2** *US* a five-dollar bill.

fives /faɪvz/ *n.* a game in which a ball is hit with a gloved hand or a bat against the walls of a court with three walls (**Eton fives**) or four walls (**Rugby fives**). [*pl.* of FIVE used as *sing.*: significance unkn.]

fivestones /'faɪvstəʊnz/ *n. Brit.* jacks played with five pieces of metal etc. and usu. without a ball.

fix /fɪks/ *v. & n.* —*v.* **1** *tr.* make firm or stable; fasten, secure (*fixed a picture to the wall*). **2** *tr.* decide, settle, specify (a price, date, etc.). **3** *tr.* mend, repair. **4** *tr.* implant (an idea or memory) in the mind (*couldn't get the rules fixed in his head*). **5** *tr.* **a** (foll. by *on, upon*) direct steadily, set (one's eyes, gaze, attention, or affection). **b** attract and hold (a person's attention, eyes, etc.). **c** (foll. by *with*) single out with one's eyes etc. **6** *tr.* place definitely or permanently, establish, station. **7** *tr.* determine the exact nature, position, etc., of; refer (a thing or person) to a definite place or time; identify, locate. **8 a** *tr.* make (eyes, features, etc.) rigid. **b** *intr.* (of eyes, features, etc.) become rigid. **9** *tr. US colloq.* prepare (food or drink) (*fixed me a drink*). **10 a** *tr.* deprive of fluidity or volatility; congeal. **b** *intr.* lose fluidity or volatility, become congealed. **11** *tr. colloq.* punish, kill, silence, deal with (a person). **12** *tr. colloq.* **a** secure the support of (a person) fraudulently, esp. by bribery. **b** arrange the result of (a race, match, etc.) fraudulently (*the competition was fixed*). **13** *sl.* **a** inject (a person, esp. oneself) with a narcotic. **b** *intr.* take an injection of a narcotic. **14** *tr.* make (a colour, photographic image, or microscope-specimen) fast or permanent. **15** *tr.* (of a plant or micro-organism) assimilate (nitrogen or carbon dioxide) by forming a nongaseous compound. **16** *tr.* castrate or spay (an animal). **17** *tr.* arrest changes or development in (a language or literature). **18** *tr.* determine the incidence of (liability etc.). **19** *intr. archaic* take up one's position. —*n.* **1** *colloq.* a position hard to escape from; a dilemma or predicament. **2 a** the act of finding one's position by bearings or astronomical observations. **b** a position found in this way. **3** *sl.* a dose of a narcotic drug to which one is addicted. **4** *US sl.* bribery. □**be fixed** (usu. foll. by *for*) be disposed or affected (regarding) (*how is he fixed for money?; how are you fixed for Friday?*). **fixed capital** machinery etc. that remains in the owner's use. **fixed-doh** *Mus.* applied to a system of sight-singing in which C is called 'doh', D is called 'ray', etc., irrespective of the key in which they occur (cf. *movable-doh*). **fixed focus** a camera focus at a distance from a lens that is not adjustable. **fixed idea** = IDÉE FIXE. **fixed income** income deriving from a pension, investment at fixed interest, etc. **fixed odds** predetermined odds in racing etc. (opp. *starting price*). **fixed oil** an oil of animal or plant origin used in varnishes, lubricants, illuminants, soaps, etc. **fixed point** *Physics* a well-defined reproducible temperature. **fixed star** *Astron.* a star so far from the earth as to appear motionless. **fix on** (or **upon**) choose, decide on. **fix up 1** arrange, organize, prepare. **2** accommodate. **3** (often foll. by *with*) provide (a person) (*fixed me up with a job*). □□ **fixable** *adj.* **fixedly** /ˈfɪksɪdlɪ/ *adv.* **fixedness** /ˈfɪksɪdnɪs/ *n.* [ME, partly f. obs. *fix* fixed f. OF *fix* or L *fixus* past part. of *figere* fix, fasten, partly f. med.L *fixare* f. *fixus*]

fixate /fɪkˈseɪt/ *v.tr.* **1** direct one's gaze on. **2** *Psychol.* **a** (usu. in *passive*; often foll. by *on, upon*) cause (a person) to acquire an abnormal attachment to persons or things (*was fixated on his son*). **b** arrest (part of the libido) at an immature stage, causing such attachment. [L *fixus* (see FIX) + -ATE³]

fixation /fɪkˈseɪʃ(ə)n/ *n.* **1** the act or an instance of being fixated. **2** an obsession, concentration on a single idea. **3** fixing or being fixed. **4** the process of rendering solid; coagulation. **5** the process of assimilating a gas to form a solid compound. [ME f. med.L *fixatio* f. *fixare*: see FIX]

fixative /ˈfɪksətɪv/ *adj. & n.* —*adj.* tending to fix or secure. —*n.* a substance used to fix colours, hair, microscope-specimens, etc.

fixer /ˈfɪksə(r)/ *n.* **1** a person or thing that fixes. **2** *Photog.* a substance used for fixing a photographic image etc. **3** *colloq.* a person who makes arrangements, esp. of an illicit kind.

fixings /ˈfɪksɪŋz/ *n.pl.* US **1** apparatus or equipment. **2** the trimmings for a dish. **3** the trimmings of a dress etc.

fixity /ˈfɪksɪtɪ/ *n.* **1** a fixed state. **2** stability; permanence. [obs. *fix* fixed: see FIX]

fixture /ˈfɪkstʃə(r)/ *n.* **1 a** something fixed or fastened in position. **b** (usu. *predic.*) *colloq.* a person or thing confined to or established in one place (*he seems to be a fixture*). **2 a** a sporting event, esp. a match, race, etc. **b** the date agreed for this. **3** (in *pl.*) *Law* articles attached to a house or land and regarded as legally part of it. [alt. of obs. *fixure* f. LL *fixura* f. L *figere* fix-fix]

fizgig /ˈfɪzɡɪɡ/ *n. & adj. archaic* —*n.* **1** a silly or flirtatious young woman. **2** a kind of small firework; a cracker. **3** *Austral. sl.* a police informer. —*adj.* flighty. [prob. f. FIZZ + obs. *gig* flighty girl]

fizz /fɪz/ *v. & n.* —*v.intr.* **1** make a hissing or spluttering sound. **2** (of a drink) make bubbles; effervesce. —*n.* **1** effervescence. **2** *colloq.* an effervescent drink, esp. champagne. [imit.]

fizzle /ˈfɪz(ə)l/ *v. & n.* —*v.intr.* make a feeble hissing or spluttering sound. —*n.* such a sound. □ **fizzle out** end feebly (*the party fizzled out at 10 o'clock*). [formed as FIZZ + -LE⁴]

fizzy /ˈfɪzɪ/ *adj.* (**fizzier, fizziest**) effervescent. □□ **fizzily** *adv.* **fizziness** *n.*

FJI *abbr.* Fellow of the Institute of Journalists.

fjord var. of FIORD.

FL *abbr.* US Florida (in official postal use).

fl. *abbr.* **1** floor. **2** floruit. **3** fluid.

Fla. *abbr.* Florida.

flab /flæb/ *n. colloq.* fat; flabbiness. [imit., or back-form. f. FLABBY]

flabbergast /ˈflæbəˌɡɑːst/ *v.tr.* (esp. as **flabbergasted** *adj.*) *colloq.* overwhelm with astonishment; dumbfound. [18th c.: perh. f. FLABBY + AGHAST]

flabby /ˈflæbɪ/ *adj.* (**flabbier, flabbiest**) **1** (of flesh etc.) hanging down; limp; flaccid. **2** (of language or character) feeble. □□ **flabbily** *adv.* **flabbiness** *n.* [alt. of earlier *flappy* f. FLAP]

flaccid /ˈflæksɪd, ˈflæsɪd/ *adj.* **1 a** (of flesh etc.) hanging loose or wrinkled; limp, flabby. **b** (of plant tissue) soft; less rigid. **2** relaxed, drooping. **3** lacking vigour; feeble. □□ **flaccidity** /-ˈsɪdɪtɪ/ *n.* **flaccidly** *adv.* [F *flaccide* or L *flaccidus* f. *flaccus* flabby]

flack¹ /flæk/ *n.* US *sl.* a publicity agent. [20th c.: orig. unkn.]

flack² var. of FLAK.

flag¹ /flæɡ/ *n. & v.* —*n.* **1 a** a piece of cloth, usu.

oblong or square, attachable by one edge to a pole or rope and used as a country's emblem or as a standard, signal, etc. **b** a small toy, device, etc., resembling a flag. **2** *Brit.* an oblong strip of metal etc. that can be raised or lowered to indicate whether a taxi is for hire or occupied. **3** *Naut.* a flag carried by a flagship as an emblem of an admiral's rank afloat. —*v.* (**flagged, flagging**) **1** *intr.* **a** grow tired; lose vigour; lag (*his energy flagged after the first lap*). **b** hang down; droop; become limp. **2** *tr.* **a** place a flag on or over. **b** mark out with or as if with a flag or flags. **3** *tr.* (often foll. by *that*) **a** inform (a person) by flag-signals. **b** communicate (information) by flagging. □ **black flag 1** a pirate's ensign. **2** *hist.* a flag hoisted outside a prison to announce an execution. **flag-boat** a boat serving as a mark in sailing-matches. **flag-captain** the captain of a flagship. **flag-day** *Brit.* a day on which money is raised for a charity by the sale of small paper flags etc. in the street. **Flag Day** US 14 June, the anniversary of the adoption of the Stars and Stripes in 1777. **flag down** signal to (a vehicle or driver) to stop. **flag-lieutenant** *Naut.* an admiral's ADC. **flag-list** *Naut.* a roll of flag-officers. **flag of convenience** a foreign flag under which a ship is registered, usu. to avoid financial charges etc. **flag-officer** *Naut.* an admiral, vice admiral, or rear admiral, or the commodore of a yacht-club. **flag of truce** a white flag indicating a desire for a truce. **flag-pole** = FLAGSTAFF. **flag-rank** *Naut.* the rank attained by flag-officers. **flag-station** a station at which trains stop only if signalled. **flag-wagging** *sl.* **1** signalling with hand-held flags. **2** = *flag-waving.* **flag-waver** a populist agitator; a chauvinist. **flag-waving** populist agitation, chauvinism. **keep the flag flying** continue the fight. **put the flag out** celebrate victory, success, etc. **show the flag 1** make an official visit to a foreign port etc. **2** ensure that notice is taken of one's country, oneself, etc.; make a patriotic display. □□ **flagger** *n.* [16th c.: perh. f. obs. *flag* drooping]

flag² /flæɡ/ *n. & v.* —*n.* (also **flagstone**) **1** a flat usu. rectangular stone slab used for paving. **2** (in *pl.*) a pavement made of these. —*v.tr.* (**flagged, flagging**) pave with flags. [ME, = sod: cf. Icel. *flag* spot from which a sod has been cut out, ON *flaga* slab of stone, and FLAKE¹]

flag³ /flæɡ/ *n.* **1** any plant with a bladed leaf (esp. several of the genus *Iris*) growing on moist ground. **2** the long slender leaf of such a plant. [ME: cf. MDu. *flag*, Da. *flæg*]

flag⁴ /flæɡ/ *n.* (in full **flag-feather**) a quill-feather of a bird's wing. [perh. rel. to obs. *fag* loose flap: cf. FLAG¹ *v.*]

flagellant /ˈflædʒələnt, fləˈdʒelənt/ *n. & adj.* —*n.* **1** a person who scourges himself or herself or others as a religious discipline. **2** a person who engages in flogging as a sexual stimulus. —*adj.* of or concerning flagellation. [L *flagellare* to whip f. FLAGELLUM]

flagellate¹ /ˈflædʒəˌleɪt/ *v.tr.* scourge, flog (cf. FLAGELLANT). □□ **flagellation** /-ˈleɪʃ(ə)n/ *n.* **flagellator** *n.* **flagellatory** /-lətərɪ/ *adj.*

flagellate² /ˈflædʒɪlɪt/ *adj. & n.* —*adj.* having flagella (see FLAGELLUM). —*n.* a protozoan having one or more flagella.

flagellum /fləˈdʒeləm/ *n.* (*pl.* **flagella** /-lə/) **1** *Biol.* a long lashlike appendage found principally on microscopic organisms. **2** *Bot.* a runner; a creeping shoot. □□ **flagellar** *adj.* **flagelliform** *adj.* [L, = whip, dimin. of *flagrum* scourge]

flageolet¹ /ˌflædʒəˈlet, ˈflædʒ-/ *n.* **1** a small flute blown at the end, like a recorder but with two thumb-holes. **2** an organ stop having a similar sound. [F, dimin. of OF *flag(e)ol* f. Prov. *flajol*, of unkn. orig.]

flageolet² /ˌflædʒəʊˈleɪ, -ˈlet/ *n.* a kind of French kidney bean. [F]

flagitious /fləˈdʒɪʃəs/ *adj.* deeply criminal; utterly villainous. □□ **flagitiously** *adv.* **flagitiousness** *n.* [ME f. L *flagitiosus* f. *flagitium* shameful crime]

flagman /'flægmən/ n. (pl. **-men**) a person who signals with or as with a flag, e.g. at races.

flagon /'flægən/ n. **1** a large bottle in which wine, cider, etc., are sold, usu. holding 1.13 litres. **2 a** a large vessel usu. with a handle, spout, and lid, to hold wine etc. **b** a similar vessel used for the Eucharist. [ME *flakon* f. OF *flacon* ult. f. LL *flasco -onis* FLASK]

flagrant /'fleɪgrənt/ adj. (of an offence or an offender) glaring; notorious; scandalous. □□ **flagrancy** /-grənsɪ/ n. **flagrantly** adv. [F *flagrant* or L *flagrant-* part. stem of *flagrare* blaze]

flagship /'flægʃɪp/ n. **1** a ship having an admiral on board. **2** something that is held to be the best or most important of its kind; a leader.

flagstaff /'flægstɑːf/ n. a pole on which a flag may be hoisted.

flagstone /'flægstəʊn/ n. = FLAG².

flail /fleɪl/ n. & v. —n. a threshing-tool consisting of a wooden staff with a short heavy stick swinging from it. —v. **1** tr. beat or strike with or as if with a flail. **2** intr. wave or swing wildly or erratically (*went into the fight with arms flailing*). [OE prob. f. L FLAGELLUM]

flair /fleə(r)/ n. **1** an instinct for selecting or performing what is excellent, useful, etc.; a talent (*has a flair for knowing what the public wants*; *has a flair for languages*). **2** talent or ability, esp. artistic or stylistic. [F *flairer* to smell ult. f. L *fragrare*: see FRAGRANT]

flak /flæk/ n. (also **flack**) **1** anti-aircraft fire. **2** adverse criticism; abuse. □ **flak jacket** a protective jacket of heavy camouflage fabric reinforced with metal, worn by soldiers etc. [abbr. of G *Flieger-abwehrkanone*, lit. aviator-defence-gun]

flake¹ /fleɪk/ n. & v. —n. **1 a** a small thin light piece of snow. **b** a similar piece of another material. **2 a** thin broad piece of material peeled or split off. **3** *Archaeol.* a piece of hard stone chipped off and used as a tool. **4** a natural division of the flesh of some fish. **5** the dogfish or other shark as food. —v.tr. & intr. (often foll. by *away*, *off*) **1** take off or come away in flakes. **2** sprinkle with or fall in snowlike flakes. □ **flake out** colloq. fall asleep or drop from exhaustion; faint. [ME: orig. unkn.: cf. ON *flakna* flake off]

flake² /fleɪk/ n. **1** a stage for drying fish etc. **2** a rack for storing oatcakes etc. [ME, perh. f. ON *flaki*, *fleki* wicker shield]

flaky /'fleɪkɪ/ adj. (**flakier**, **flakiest**) **1** of or like flakes; separating easily into flakes. **2** esp. *US sl.* crazy, eccentric. □ **flaky pastry** pastry consisting of thin light layers. □□ **flakily** adv. **flakiness** n.

flambé /'flɒmbeɪ/ adj. (of food) covered with alcohol and set alight briefly. [F, past part. of *flamber* singe (as FLAMBEAU)]

flambeau /'flæmbəʊ/ n. (pl. **flambeaus** or **flambeaux** /-əʊz/) **1** a flaming torch, esp. composed of several thick waxed wicks. **2** a branched candlestick. [F f. *flambe* f. L *flammula* dimin. of *flamma* flame]

flamboyant /flæm'bɔɪənt/ adj. **1** ostentatious; showy. **2** floridly decorated. **3** gorgeously coloured. **4** *Archit.* (of decoration) marked by wavy flamelike lines. □□ **flamboyance** n. **flamboyancy** n. **flamboyantly** adv. [F (in Archit. sense), pres. part. of *flamboyer* f. *flambe*: see FLAMBEAU]

flame /fleɪm/ n. & v. —n. **1 a** ignited gas (*the fire burnt with a steady flame*). **b** one portion of this (*the flame flickered and died*). **c** (usu. in *pl.*) visible combustion (*burst into flames*). **2 a** a bright light; brilliant colouring. **b** a brilliant orange-red colour. **3 a** strong passion, esp. love (*fan the flame*). **b** colloq. a boyfriend or girlfriend. —v. **1** intr. & tr. (often foll. by *away*, *forth*, *out*, *up*) emit or cause to emit flames. **2** intr. (often foll. by *out*, *up*) **a** (of passion) break out. **b** (of a person) become angry. **3** intr. shine or glow like flame (*leaves flamed in the autumn sun*). **4** intr.

poet. move like flame. **5** tr. send (a signal) by means of flame. **6** tr. subject to the action of flame. □ **flame gun** a device for throwing flames to destroy weeds etc. **flame out** (of a jet engine) lose power through the extinction of the flame in the combustion chamber. **flame-proof** (esp. of a fabric) treated so as to be non-flammable. **flame-thrower** (or **-projector**) a weapon for throwing a spray of flame. **flame-tree** any of various trees with brilliant red flowers esp. flame-of-the-forest, *Delonix regia*. **go up in flames** be consumed by fire. □□ **flameless** adj. **flamelike** adj. **flamy** adj. [ME f. OF *flame*, *flam(m)er* f. L *flamma*]

flamen /'fleɪmən/ n. *Rom.Hist.* a priest serving a particular deity. [ME f. L]

flamenco /flə'meŋkəʊ/ n. (pl. **-os**) **1** a style of music played (esp. on the guitar) and sung by Spanish gypsies. **2** a dance performed to this music. [Sp., = Flemish]

flaming /'fleɪmɪŋ/ adj. **1** emitting flames. **2** very hot (*flaming June*). **3** colloq. **a** passionate; intense (*a flaming row*). **b** expressing annoyance, or as an intensifier (*that flaming dog*). **4** bright-coloured (*flaming red hair*).

flamingo /flə'mɪŋgəʊ/ n. (pl. **-os** or **-oes**) any tall long-necked web-footed wading bird of the family Phoenicopteridae, with crooked bill and pink, scarlet, and black plumage. [Port. *flamengo* f. Prov. *flamenc* f. *flama* flame + -*enc* = -ING³]

flammable /'flæməb(ə)l/ adj. inflammable. ¶ Often used because *inflammable* can be mistaken for a negative (the true negative being *non-flammable*). □□ **flammability** /-'bɪlɪtɪ/ n. [L *flammare* f. *flamma* flame]

flan /flæn/ n. **1 a** a pastry case with a savoury or sweet filling. **b** a sponge base with a sweet topping. **2** a disc of metal from which a coin etc. is made. [F (orig. = round cake) f. OF *flaon* f. med.L *flado -onis* f. Frank.]

flanch /flɑːntʃ/ v.tr. & intr. (also **flaunch** /flɔːntʃ/) (esp. with ref. to a chimney) slope inwards or cause to slope inwards towards the top. □□ **flanching** n. [perh. f. OF *flanchir* f. *flanche*, *flanc* FLANK]

flânerie /flæn'riː/ n. idling, idleness. [F f. *flâner* lounge]

flâneur /flæ'nɜːr/ n. an idler; a lounger. [F (as FLÂNERIE)]

flange /flændʒ/ n. & v. *Engin.* —n. a projecting flat rim, collar, or rib, used for strengthening or attachment. —v.tr. provide with a flange. □□ **flangeless** n. [17th c.: perh. f. *flange* widen out f. OF *flangir* (as FLANCH)]

flank /flæŋk/ n. & v. —n. **1 a** the side of the body between the ribs and the hip. **b** the side of an animal carved as meat (*flank of beef*). **2** the side of a mountain, building, etc. **3** the right or left side of an army or other body of persons. —v.tr. **1** (often in passive) be situated at both sides of (*a road flanked by mountains*). **2** *Mil.* **a** guard or strengthen on the flank. **b** menace the flank of. **c** rake with sweeping gunfire; enfilade. □ **flank forward** *Rugby Football* a wing forward. **in flank** at the side. [ME f. OF *flanc* f. Frank.]

flanker /'flæŋkə(r)/ n. **1** *Mil.* a fortification guarding or menacing the flank. **2** anything that flanks another thing. **3** (in Rugby and American Football) a flank forward. **4** *sl.* a trick; a swindle (*pulled a flanker*).

flannel /'flæn(ə)l/ n. & v. —n. **1 a** a kind of woven woollen fabric, usu. without a nap. **b** (in *pl.*) flannel garments, esp. trousers. **2** *Brit.* a small usu. towelling cloth, used for washing oneself. **3** *Brit. sl.* nonsense; flattery. —v. (**flannelled**, **flannelling**; *US* **flanneled**, **flanneling**) **1** *Brit. sl.* **a** tr. flatter. **b** intr. use flattery. **2** tr. wash or clean with a flannel. □ **flannel-mouth** *US sl.* a flatterer; a braggart. □□ **flannelly** adj. [perh. f. Welsh *gwlanen* f. *gwlân* wool]

flannelboard /'flæn(ə)l,bɔːd/ n. a piece of flannel as

a base for paper or cloth cut-outs, used as a toy or a teaching aid.

flannelette /ˌflænə'let/ *n.* a napped cotton fabric imitating flannel. [FLANNEL]

flannelgraph /'flæn(ə)lˌgrɑːf/ *n.* = FLANNELBOARD.

flannelled /'flæn(ə)ld/ *adj.* (*US* also **flanneled**) wearing flannel trousers. [FLANNEL]

flap /flæp/ *v. & n.* —*v.* (**flapped, flapping**) **1 a** *tr.* move (wings, the arms, etc.) up and down when flying, or as if flying. **b** *intr.* (of wings, the arms, etc.) move up and down; beat. **2** *intr. colloq.* be agitated or panicky. **3** *intr.* (esp. of curtains, loose cloth, etc.) swing or sway about; flutter. **4** *tr.* (usu. foll. by *away, off*) strike (flies etc.) with something broad; drive. **5** *intr. colloq.* (of ears) listen intently. —*n.* **1** a piece of cloth, wood, paper, etc. hinged or attached by one side only and often used to cover a gap, e.g. a pocket-cover, the folded part of an envelope, a table-leaf. **2** one up-and-down motion of a wing, an arm, etc. **3** *colloq.* a state of agitation; panic (*don't get into a flap*). **4** a hinged or sliding section of a wing used to control lift; an aileron. **5** a light blow with something broad. **6** an open mushroom-top. □□ **flappy** *adj.* [ME, prob. imit.]

flapdoodle /flæp'duːd(ə)l, 'flæp-/ *n. colloq.* nonsense. [19th c.: orig. unkn.]

flapjack /'flæpdʒæk/ *n.* **1** a cake made from oats and golden syrup etc. **2** esp. *US* a pancake. [FLAP + JACK¹]

flapper /'flæpə(r)/ *n.* **1** a person or thing that flaps. **2** an instrument that is flapped to kill flies, scare birds, etc. **3** a person who panics easily or is easily agitated. **4** *sl.* (in the 1920s) a young unconventional or lively woman. **5** a young mallard or partridge.

flare /fleə(r)/ *v. & n.* —*v.* **1** *intr. & tr.* widen or cause to widen gradually towards the top or bottom (*flared trousers*). **2** *intr. & tr.* burn or cause to burn suddenly with a bright unsteady flame. **3** *intr.* burst into anger; burst forth. —*n.* **1 a** a dazzling irregular flame or light, esp. in the open air. **b** a sudden outburst of flame. **2 a** a signal light used at sea. **b** a bright light used as a signal. **c** a flame dropped from an aircraft to illuminate a target etc. **3** *Astron.* a sudden burst of radiation from a star. **4 a** a gradual widening, esp. of a skirt or trousers. **b** (in *pl.*) wide-bottomed trousers. **5** an outward bulge in a ship's sides. **6** *Photog.* unnecessary illumination on a lens caused by internal reflection etc. □**flare-path** an area illuminated to enable an aircraft to land or take off. **flare up 1** burst into a sudden blaze. **2** become suddenly angry or active. **flare-up** *n.* an outburst of flame, anger, activity, etc. [16th c.: orig. unkn.]

flash /flæʃ/ *v., n., & adj.* —*v.* **1** *intr. & tr.* emit or reflect or cause to emit or reflect light briefly, suddenly, or intermittently; gleam or cause to gleam. **2** *intr.* break suddenly into flame; give out flame or sparks. **3** *tr.* send or reflect like a sudden flame or blaze (*his eyes flashed fire*). **4** *intr.* **a** burst suddenly into view or perception (*the explanation flashed upon me*). **b** move swiftly (*the train flashed through the station*). **5** *tr.* **a** send (news etc.) by radio, telegraph, etc. (*flashed a message to her*). **b** signal to (a person) by shining lights or headlights briefly. **6** *tr. colloq.* show ostentatiously (*flashed her engagement ring*). **7** *intr.* (of water) rush along; rise and flow. **8** *intr. sl.* indecently expose oneself. —*n.* **1** a sudden bright light o.ᵣ flame, e.g. of lightning. **2** a very brief time; an instant (*all over in a flash*). **3 a** a brief, sudden burst of feeling (*a flash of hope*). **b** a sudden display (of wit, understanding, etc.). **4** = NEWSFLASH. **5** *Photog.* = FLASHLIGHT 1. **6 a** a rush of water, esp. down a weir to take a boat over shallows. **b** a contrivance for producing this. **7** *Brit. Mil.* a coloured patch of cloth on a uniform etc. as a distinguishing emblem. **8** vulgar display, ostentation. **9** a bright patch of colour. **10** *Cinematog.* the momentary exposure of a scene. **11** excess plastic or metal oozing from a mould during moulding. —*adj. colloq.* **1**

gaudy; showy; vulgar (*a flash car*). **2** counterfeit (*flash notes*). **3** connected with thieves, the underworld, etc. □**flash-board** a board used for sending more water from a mill-dam into a mill-race. **flash bulb** *Photog.* a bulb for a flashlight. **flash burn** a burn caused by sudden intense heat, esp. from a nuclear explosion. **flash card** a card containing a small amount of information, held up for pupils to see, as an aid to learning. **flash-cube** *Photog.* a set of four flash bulbs arranged as a cube and operated in turn. **flash-flood** a sudden local flood due to heavy rain etc. **flash-gun** *Photog.* a device used to operate a camera flashlight. **flashing-point** = FLASHPOINT. **flash in the pan** a promising start followed by failure (from the priming of old guns). **flash-lamp** a portable flashing electric lamp. **flash out** (or **up**) show sudden passion. **flash over** *Electr.* make an electric circuit by sparking across a gap. **flash-over** *n.* an instance of this. [ME orig. with ref. to the rushing of water: cf. SPLASH]

flashback /'flæʃbæk/ *n. Cinematog.* a scene set in a time earlier than the main action.

flasher /'flæʃə(r)/ *n.* **1** *Brit. sl.* a man who indecently exposes himself. **2 a** an automatic device for switching lights rapidly on and off. **b** a sign or signal using this. **3** a person or thing that flashes.

flashing /'flæʃɪŋ/ *n.* a usu. metallic strip used to prevent water penetration at the junction of a roof with a wall etc. [dial. *flash* seal with lead sheets or obs. *flash* flashing]

flashlight /'flæʃlaɪt/ *n.* **1 a** a light giving an intense flash, used for photographing by night, indoors, etc. **b** a picture so taken. **2** *US* an electric torch. **3** a flashing light used for signals and in lighthouses.

flashpoint /'flæʃpɔɪnt/ *n.* **1** the temperature at which vapour from oil etc. will ignite in air. **2** the point at which anger, indignation, etc. becomes uncontrollable.

flashy /'flæʃɪ/ *adj.* (**flashier, flashiest**) showy; gaudy; cheaply attractive. □□**flashily** *adv.* **flashiness** *n.*

flask /flɑːsk/ *n.* **1** a narrow-necked bulbous bottle for wine etc. or as used in chemistry. **2** = *hip-flask* (see HIP¹). **3** = *vacuum flask.* **4** *hist.* = *powder-flask.* [F *flasque* & (prob.) It. *fiasco* f. med.L *flasca, flasco*: cf. FLAGON]

flat¹ /flæt/ *adj., adv., n., & v.* —*adj.* (**flatter, flattest**) **1 a** horizontally level (*a flat roof*). **b** even; smooth; unbroken; without projection or indentation (*a flat stomach*). **c** with a level surface and little depth; shallow (*a flat cap; a flat heel*). **2** unqualified; plain; downright (*a flat refusal; a flat denial*). **3 a** dull; lifeless; monotonous (*spoke in a flat tone*). **b** without energy; dejected. **4** (of a fizzy drink) having lost its effervescence. **5** (of an accumulator, a battery, etc.) having exhausted its charge. **6** *Mus.* **a** below true or normal pitch (*the violins are flat*). **b** (of a key) having a flat or flats in the signature. **c** (as **B**, **E**, etc. **flat**) a semitone lower than B, E, etc. **7** *Photog.* lacking contrast. **8 a** (of paint etc.) not glossy; matt. **b** (of a tint) uniform. **9** (of a tyre) punctured; deflated. **10** (of a market, prices, etc.) inactive; sluggish. **11** of or relating to flat-racing. —*adv.* **1** lying at full length; spread out, esp. on another surface (*lay flat on the floor; the ladder was flat against the wall*). **2** *colloq.* **a** completely; absolutely (*turned it down flat; flat broke*). **b** exactly (*in five minutes flat*). **3** *Mus.* below the true or normal pitch (*always sings flat*). —*n.* **1** the flat part of anything; something flat (*the flat of the hand*). **2** level ground, esp. a plain or swamp. **3** *Mus.* **a** a note lowered a semitone below natural pitch. **b** the sign (♭) indicating this. **4** (as **the flat**) *Brit.* a flat racing. **b** the flat racing season. **5** *Theatr.* a flat section of scenery mounted on a frame. **6** esp. *US colloq.* a flat tyre. **7** *sl.* a foolish person. —*v.tr.* (**flatted, flatting**) **1** make flat, flatten (esp. in technical use). **2** *US Mus.* make (a note) flat. □**fall flat** fail to live up to expectations; not win applause.

flat arch *Archit.* an arch with a flat lower or inner curve. **flat** (or **flat-bottomed**) **boat** a boat with a flat bottom for transport in shallow water. **flat-fish** any marine fish of various families having an asymmetric appearance with both eyes on one side of a flattened body, including sole, turbot, plaice, etc. **flat foot** a foot with a less than normal arch. **flat-four** (of an engine) having four cylinders all horizontal, two on each side of the crankshaft. **flat-head 1** any marine fish of the family Platycephalidae, having a flattened body with both eyes on the top side. **2** *sl.* a foolish person. **flat-iron** *hist.* an iron heated externally and used for pressing clothes etc. **flat out 1** at top speed. **2** using all one's strength, energy, or resources. **flat race** a horse race over level ground, as opposed to a steeplechase or hurdles. **flat-racing** the racing of horses in flat races. **flat rate** a rate that is the same in all cases, not proportional. **flat spin 1** *Aeron.* a nearly horizontal spin. **2** *colloq.* a state of agitation or panic. **flat-top 1** *US Aeron. sl.* an aircraft-carrier. **2** *sl.* a man's short flat haircut. **that's flat** *colloq.* let there be no doubt about it. □□ **flatly** *adv.* **flatness** *n.* **flattish** *adj.* [ME f. ON *flatr* f. Gmc]

flat² /flæt/ *n.* & *v.* —*n.* a set of rooms, usu. on one floor, used as a residence. —*v.intr.* (**flatted**, **flatting**) (often foll. by *with*) *Austral.* share a flat with. □□ **flatlet** *n.* [alt. f. obs. *flet* floor, dwelling f. Gmc (as FLAT¹)]

flatcar /'flætkɑ:(r)/ *n.* a railway wagon without raised sides or ends.

flatfoot /'flætfʊt/ *n.* (*pl.* **-foots** or **-feet**) *sl.* a policeman.

flat-footed /'flæt,fʊtɪd/ *adj.* **1** having flat feet. **2** *colloq.* downright, positive. **3** *colloq.* unprepared; off guard (*was caught flat-footed*). □□ **flat-footedly** *adv.* **flat-footedness** *n.*

flatmate /'flætmeɪt/ *n.* *Brit.* a person in relation to one or more others living in the same flat.

flatten /'flæt(ə)n/ *v.* **1** *tr.* & *intr.* make or become flat. **2** *tr. colloq.* **a** humiliate. **b** knock down. □ **flatten out** bring an aircraft parallel to the ground. □□ **flattener** *n.*

flatter /'flætə(r)/ *v.tr.* **1** compliment unduly; over-praise, esp. for gain or advantage. **2** (usu. *refl.*; usu. foll. by *that* + clause) please, congratulate, or delude (oneself etc.) (*I flatter myself that I can sing*). **3 a** (of a colour, a style, etc.) make (a person) appear to the best advantage (*that blouse flatters you*). **b** (esp. of a portrait, a painter, etc.) represent too favourably. **4** gratify the vanity of; make (a person) feel honoured. **5** inspire (a person) with hope, esp. unduly (*was flattered into thinking himself invulnerable*). **6** please or gratify (the ear, the eye, etc.). □ **flattering unction** a salve that one administers to one's own conscience or self-esteem (Shakesp. esp. *Hamlet* III. iv. 136). □□ **flatterer** *n.* **flattering** *adj.* **flatteringly** *adv.* [ME, perh. rel. to OF *flater* to smooth]

flattery /'flætərɪ/ *n.* (*pl.* **-ies**) **1** exaggerated or insincere praise. **2** the act or an instance of flattering.

flattie /'flætɪ/ *n.* (also **flatty**) (*pl.* **-ies**) *colloq.* **1** a flat-heeled shoe. **2** a flat-bottomed boat. **3** a policeman.

flatulent /'flætjʊlənt/ *adj.* **1 a** causing formation of gas in the alimentary canal. **b** caused by or suffering from this. **2** (of speech etc.) inflated, pretentious. □□ **flatulence** *n.* **flatulency** *n.* **flatulently** *adv.* [F f. mod.L *flatulentus* (as FLATUS)]

flatus /'fleɪtəs/ *n.* wind in or from the stomach or bowels. [L, = blowing f. *flare* blow]

flatware /'flætweə(r)/ *n.* **1** plates, saucers, etc. (opp. HOLLOWWARE). **2** *US* domestic cutlery.

flatworm /'flætwɜ:m/ *n.* any worm of the phylum Platyhelminthes, having a flattened body and no body-cavity or blood vessels, including turbellaria, flukes, etc.

flaunch var. of FLANCH.

flaunt /flɔ:nt/ *v.* & *n.* —*v.tr.* & *intr.* **1** (often *refl.*) display ostentatiously (oneself or one's finery); show off; parade (*liked to flaunt his gold cuff-links; flaunted themselves before the crowd*). ¶ Often confused with *flout.* **2** wave or cause to wave proudly (*flaunted the banner*). —*n.* an act or instance of flaunting. □□ **flaunter** *n.* **flaunty** *adj.* [16th c.: orig. unkn.]

flautist /'flɔ:tɪst/ *n.* a flute-player. [It. *flautista* f. *flauto* FLUTE]

flavescent /flə'ves(ə)nt/ *adj.* turning yellow; yellowish. [L *flavescere* f. *flavus* yellow]

flavin /'fleɪvɪn/ *n.* (also **flavine** /-vi:n/) **1** the chemical compound forming the nucleus of various natural yellow pigments. **2** a yellow dye obtained from dyer's oak. □ **flavin adenine dinucleotide** a coenzyme derived from riboflavin, important in various biochemical reactions. ¶ Abbr.: **FAD**. [L *flavus* yellow + -IN]

flavine /'fleɪvi:n/ *n.* *Pharm.* an antiseptic derived from acridine. [as FLAVIN + -INE⁴]

flavone /'fleɪvəʊn/ *n.* *Biochem.* any of a group of naturally occurring white or yellow pigments found in plants. [as FLAVINE + -ONE]

flavoprotein /,fleɪvəʊ'prəʊti:n/ *n.* *Biochem.* any of a group of conjugated proteins containing flavin that are involved in oxidation reactions in cells. [FLAVINE + PROTEIN]

flavorous /'fleɪvərəs/ *adj.* having a pleasant or pungent flavour.

flavour /'fleɪvə(r)/ *n.* & *v.* (*US* **flavor**) —*n.* **1** a distinctive mingled sensation of smell and taste (*has a cheesy flavour*). **2** an indefinable characteristic quality (*music with a romantic flavour*). **3** (usu. foll. by *of*) a slight admixture of a usu. undesirable quality (*the flavour of failure hangs over the enterprise*). **4** esp. *US* = FLAVOURING. —*v.tr.* give flavour to; season. □ **flavour of the month** (or **week**) a temporary trend or fashion. □□ **flavourful** *adj.* **flavourless** *adj.* **flavoursome** *adj.* [ME f. OF *flaor* perh. f. L *flatus* blowing & *foetor* stench: assim. to *savour*]

flavouring /'fleɪvərɪŋ/ *n.* a substance used to flavour food or drink.

flaw¹ /flɔ:/ *n.* & *v.* —*n.* **1** an imperfection; a blemish (*has a character without a flaw*). **2** a crack or similar fault (*the cup has a flaw*). **3** *Law* an invalidating defect in a legal matter. —*v.tr.* & *intr.* crack; damage; spoil. □□ **flawless** *adj.* **flawlessly** *adv.* **flawlessness** *n.* [ME perh. f. ON *flaga* slab f. Gmc: cf. FLAKE¹, FLAG²]

flaw² /flɔ:/ *n.* a squall of wind; a short storm. [prob. f. MDu. *vlāghe*, MLG *vlāge*, perh. = stroke]

flax /flæks/ *n.* **1 a** a blue-flowered plant, *Linum usitatissimum*, cultivated for its textile fibre and its seeds (see LINSEED). **b** a plant resembling this. **2 a** dressed or undressed flax fibres. **b** *archaic* linen, cloth of flax. □ **flax-lily** (*pl.* **-ies**) *NZ* any plant of the genus *Phormium*, yielding valuable fibre. **flax-seed** linseed. [OE *flæx* f. WG]

flaxen /'flæks(ə)n/ *adj.* **1** of flax. **2** (of hair) coloured like dressed flax; pale yellow.

flay /fleɪ/ *v.tr.* **1** strip the skin or hide off, esp. by beating. **2** criticize severely (*the play was flayed by the critics*). **3** peel off (skin, bark, peel, etc.). **4** strip (a person) of wealth by extortion or exaction. □□ **flayer** *n.* [OE *flēan* f. Gmc]

F-layer /'ef,leɪə(r)/ *n.* the highest and most strongly ionized region of the ionosphere. [*F* (arbitrary) + LAYER]

flea /fli:/ *n.* **1** a small wingless jumping insect of the order Siphonaptera, feeding on human and other blood. **2 a** (in full **flea beetle**) a small jumping beetle infesting hops, cabbages, etc. **b** (in full **water flea**) daphnia. □ **flea-bite 1** the bite of a flea. **2** a trivial injury or inconvenience. **flea-bitten 1** bitten by or infested with fleas. **2** shabby. **flea-bug** *US* = FLEA 2a. **flea-circus** a show of performing fleas. **flea-collar** an insecticidal collar for pets. **a flea in one's ear** a sharp reproof. **flea market** a street market selling second-hand goods etc. **flea-pit** a dingy dirty place, esp. a run-down cinema. **flea-wort** any of several plants supposed to drive away fleas. [OE *flēa*, *flēah* f. Gmc]

fleabag /'fliːbæg/ *n. sl.* a shabby or unattractive person or thing.

fleabane /'fliːbeɪn/ *n.* any of various composite plants of the genus *Inula* or *Pulicaria*, supposed to drive away fleas.

flèche /fleɪʃ, fleʃ/ *n.* a slender spire, often perforated with windows, esp. at the intersection of the nave and the transept of a church. [F, orig. = arrow]

fleck /flek/ *n. & v.* —*n.* **1** a small patch of colour or light (*eyes with green flecks*). **2** a small particle or speck, esp. of dust. **3** a spot on the skin; a freckle. —*v.tr.* mark with flecks; dapple; variegate. [perh. f. ON *flekkr* (n.), *flekka* (v.), or MLG, MDu. *vlecke*, OHG *flec*, *fleccho*]

flection *US* var. of FLEXION.

fled *past* and *past part.* of FLEE.

fledge /fledʒ/ *v.* **1** *intr.* (of a bird) grow feathers. **2** *tr.* provide (an arrow) with feathers. **3** *tr.* bring up (a young bird) until it can fly. **4** *tr.* (as **fledged** *adj.*) **a** able to fly. **b** independent; mature. **5** *tr.* deck or provide with feathers or down. [obs. *fledge* (adj.) 'fit to fly', f. OE *flycge* (recorded in *unfligge*) f. a Gmc root rel. to FLY[1]]

fledgling /'fledʒlɪŋ/ *n.* (also **fledgeling**) **1** a young bird. **2** an inexperienced person. [FLEDGE + -LING[1]]

flee /fliː/ *v.* (*past* and *past part.* **fled** /fled/) **1** *intr.* (often foll. by *from*, *before*) **a** run away. **b** seek safety by fleeing. **2** *tr.* run away from; leave abruptly; shun (*fled the room*; *fled his attentions*). **3** *intr.* vanish; cease; pass away. □□ **fleer** /'fliːə(r)/ *n.* [OE *flēon* f. Gmc]

fleece /fliːs/ *n. & v.* —*n.* **1 a** the woolly covering of a sheep or a similar animal. **b** the amount of wool sheared from a sheep at one time. **2** something resembling a fleece, esp.: **a** a woolly or rough head of hair. **b** a soft warm fabric with a pile, used for lining coats etc. **c** a white cloud, a blanket of snow, etc. **3** *Heraldry* a representation of a fleece suspended from a ring. —*v.tr.* **1** (often foll. by *of*) strip (a person) of money, valuables, etc.; swindle. **2** remove the fleece from (a sheep etc.); shear. **3** cover as if with a fleece (*a sky fleeced with clouds*). □ **fleece-picker** *Austral. & NZ* = FLEECY. **Golden Fleece** see GOLDEN. □□ **fleeceable** *adj.* **fleeced** *adj.* (also in *comb.*). [OE *flēos*, *flēs* f. WG]

fleecy /'fliːsɪ/ *adj. & n.* —*adj.* (**fleecier**, **fleeciest**) **1** of or like a fleece. **2** covered with a fleece. —*n.* (also **fleecie**) (*pl.* **-ies**) *Austral. & NZ* a person whose job is to pick up fleeces in a shearing shed. □□ **fleecily** *adv.* **fleeciness** *n.*

fleer /'flɪə(r)/ *v. & n.* —*v.intr.* laugh impudently or mockingly; sneer; jeer. —*n.* a mocking look or speech. [ME, prob. f. Scand.: cf. Norw. & Sw. dial. *flira* to grin]

fleet[1] /fliːt/ *n.* **1 a** a number of warships under one commander-in-chief. **b** (prec. by *the*) all the warships and merchant-ships of a nation. **2** a number of ships, aircraft, buses, lorries, taxis, etc. operating together or owned by one proprietor. □ **Fleet Admiral** see ADMIRAL. **Fleet Air Arm** *hist.* the aviation service of the Royal Navy. [OE *flēot* ship, shipping f. *flēotan* float, FLEET[5]]

fleet[2] /fliːt/ *adj. poet. literary* swift; nimble. □□ **fleetly** *adv.* **fleetness** *n.* [prob. f. ON *fljótr* f. Gmc: cf. FLEET[5]]

fleet[3] /fliːt/ *n. dial.* **1** a creek; an inlet. **2** (**the Fleet**) **a** an underground stream running into the Thames east of Fleet St. **b** *hist.* a prison that stood near it. □ **Fleet Street 1** the London press. **2** British journalism or journalists. [OE *flēot* creek: cf. FLEET[5]]

fleet[4] /fliːt/ *adj. & adv. dial.* —*adj.* (of water) shallow. —*adv.* at or to a small depth (*plough fleet*). [orig. uncert.: perh. f. OE *flēat* (unrecorded), rel. to FLEET[5]]

fleet[5] /fliːt/ *v.intr. archaic* **1** glide away; vanish; be transitory. **2** (usu. foll. by *away*) (of time) pass

rapidly; slip away. **3** move swiftly; fly. [OE *flēotan* float, swim f. Gmc]

fleeting /'fliːtɪŋ/ *adj.* transitory; brief. □□ **fleetingly** *adv.* [FLEET[5] + -ING[2]]

Fleming /'flemɪŋ/ *n.* **1** a native of medieval Flanders in the Low Countries. **2** a member of a Flemish-speaking people inhabiting N. and W. Belgium (see also WALLOON). [OE f. ON *Flæmingi* & MDu. *Vlāming* f. root of *Vlaanderen* Flanders]

Flemish /'flemɪʃ/ *adj. & n.* —*adj.* of or relating to Flanders. —*n.* the language of the Flemings. □ **Flemish bond** *Building* a bond in which each course consists of alternate headers and stretchers. [MDu. *Vlāmisch* (as FLEMING)]

flense /flenz/ *v.tr.* (also **flench** /flentʃ/, **flinch** /flɪntʃ/) **1** cut up (a whale or seal). **2** flay (a seal). [Da. *flense*: cf. Norw. *flinsa*, *flunsa* flay]

flesh /fleʃ/ *n. & v.* —*n.* **1 a** the soft, esp. muscular, substance between the skin and bones of an animal or a human. **b** plumpness; fat (*has put on flesh*). **c** *archaic* meat, esp. excluding poultry, game, and offal. **2** the body as opposed to the mind or the soul, esp. considered as sinful. **3** the pulpy substance of a fruit or a plant. **4 a** the visible surface of the human body with ref. to its colour or appearance. **b** (also **flesh-colour**) a yellowish pink colour. **5** animal or human life. —*v.tr.* **1** embody in flesh. **2** incite (a hound etc.) by the taste of blood. **3** initiate, esp. by aggressive or violent means, esp.: **a** use (a sword etc.) for the first time on flesh. **b** use (wit, the pen, etc.) for the first time. **c** inflame (a person) by the foretaste of success. □ **all flesh** all human and animal creation. **flesh and blood** —*n.* **1** the body or its substance. **2** humankind. **3** human nature, esp. as being fallible. —*adj.* actually living, not imaginary or supernatural. **flesh-fly** (*pl.* **-flies**) any fly of the family Sarcophagidae that deposits eggs or larvae in dead flesh. **flesh out** make or become substantial. **flesh side** the side of a hide that adjoined the flesh. **flesh tints** flesh-colours as rendered by a painter. **flesh-wound** a wound not reaching a bone or a vital organ. **in the flesh** in bodily form, in person. **lose** (or **put on**) **flesh** grow thinner or fatter. **make a person's flesh creep** frighten or horrify a person, esp. with tales of the supernatural etc. **one flesh** (of two people) intimately united, esp. by virtue of marriage (Gen. 2:24). **one's own flesh and blood** near relatives; descendants. **sins of the flesh** unchastity. **the way of all flesh** experience common to all mankind. □□ **fleshless** *adj.* [OE *flǣsc* f. Gmc]

flesher /'fleʃə(r)/ *n. Sc.* a butcher.

fleshings /'fleʃɪŋz/ *n.pl.* an actor's flesh-coloured tights.

fleshly /'fleʃlɪ/ *adj.* (**fleshlier**, **fleshliest**) **1** (of desire etc.) bodily; lascivious; sensual. **2** mortal, not divine. **3** worldly. □□ **fleshliness** *n.* [OE *flǣsclic* (as FLESH)]

fleshpots /'fleʃpɒts/ *n.pl.* luxurious living (Exod. 16: 3).

fleshy /'fleʃɪ/ *adj.* (**fleshier**, **fleshiest**) **1** plump, fat. **2** of flesh, without bone. **3** (of plant or fruit tissue) pulpy. **4** like flesh. □□ **fleshiness** *n.*

fletcher /'fletʃə(r)/ *n. archaic* a maker or seller of arrows. [ME f. OF *flech(i)er* f. *fleche* arrow]

fleur-de-lis /ˌflɜːdə'liː/ *n.* (also **fleur-de-lys**) (*pl.* **fleurs-** *pronunc.* same) **1** the iris flower. **2** *Heraldry* **a** a lily composed of three petals bound together near their bases. **b** the former royal arms of France. [ME f. OF *flour de lys* flower of lily]

fleuret /fluə'ret/ *n.* an ornament like a small flower. [F *fleurette* f. *fleur* flower]

fleuron /flɜː'rɔ̃/ *n.* a flower-shaped ornament on a building, a coin, a book, etc. [ME f. OF *floron* f. *flour* FLOWER]

fleury /'fluərɪ/ *adj.* (also **flory** /'flɔːrɪ/) *Heraldry* decorated with fleurs-de-lis. [ME f. OF *flo(u)ré* (as FLEURON)]

flew *past* of FLY[1].

flews /fluːz/ *n.pl.* the hanging lips of a bloodhound etc. [16th c.: orig. unkn.]

flex[1] /fleks/ *v.* **1** *tr.* & *intr.* bend (a joint, limb, etc.) or be bent. **2** *tr.* & *intr.* move (a muscle) or (of a muscle) be moved to bend a joint. **3** *tr. Geol.* bend (strata). **4** *tr. Archaeol.* place (a corpse) with the legs drawn up under the chin. [L *flectere flex-* bend]

flex[2] /fleks/ *n. Brit.* a flexible insulated cable used for carrying electric current to an appliance. [abbr. of FLEXIBLE]

flexible /ˈfleksɪb(ə)l/ *adj.* **1** able to bend without breaking; pliable; pliant. **2** easily led; manageable; docile. **3** adaptable; versatile; variable (*works flexible hours*). □□ **flexibility** /-ˈbɪlɪtɪ/ *n.* **flexibly** *adv.* [ME f. OF *flexible* or L *flexibilis* (as FLEX[1])]

flexile /ˈfleksaɪl/ *adj. archaic* **1** supple; mobile. **2** tractable; manageable. **3** versatile. □□ **flexility** /-ˈsɪlɪtɪ/ *n.* [L *flexilis* (as FLEX[1])]

flexion /ˈflekʃ(ə)n/ *n.* (*US* **flection**) **1 a** the act of bending or the condition of being bent, esp. of a limb or joint. **b** a bent part; a curve. **2** *Gram.* inflection. **3** *Math.* = FLEXURE. □□ **flexional** *adj.* (in sense 2). **flexionless** *adj.* (in sense 2). [L *flexio* (as FLEX[1])]

flexitime /ˈfleksɪˌtaɪm/ *n. Brit.* **1** a system of working a set number of hours with the starting and finishing times chosen within agreed limits by the employee. **2** the hours worked in this way. [FLEXIBLE + TIME]

flexography /flekˈsɒɡrəfɪ/ *n. Printing* a rotary letterpress technique using rubber or plastic plates and synthetic inks or dyes for printing on fabrics, plastics, etc., as well as on paper. □□ **flexographic** /-səˈɡræfɪk/ *adj.* [L *flexus* a bending f. *flectere* bend + -GRAPHY]

flexor /ˈfleksə(r)/ *n.* (in full **flexor muscle**) a muscle that bends part of the body (cf. EXTENSOR). [mod.L (as FLEX[1])]

flexuous /ˈfleksjʊəs/ *adj.* full of bends; winding. □□ **flexuosity** /-ˈɒsɪtɪ/ *n.* **flexuously** *adv.* [L *flexuosus* f. *flexus* bending formed as FLEX[1]]

flexure /ˈflekʃə(r)/ *n.* **1 a** the act of bending or the condition of being bent. **b** a bend, curve, or turn. **2** *Math.* the curving of a line, surface, or solid, esp. from a straight line, plane, etc. **3** *Geol.* the bending of strata under pressure. □□ **flexural** *adj.* [L *flexura* (as FLEX[1])]

flibbertigibbet /ˌflɪbətɪˈdʒɪbɪt, ˈflɪb-/ *n.* a gossiping, frivolous, or restless person. [imit. of chatter]

flick /flɪk/ *n.* & *v.* —*n.* **1 a** a light, sharp, quickly retracted blow with a whip etc. **b** the sudden release of a bent finger or thumb, esp. to propel a small object. **2** a sudden movement or jerk. **3** a quick turn of the wrist in playing games, esp. in throwing or striking a ball. **4** a slight, sharp sound. **5** *Brit. colloq.* **a** a cinema film. **b** (in *pl.*; prec. by *the*) the cinema. —*v.* **1** *tr.* (often foll. by *away*, *off*) strike or move with a flick (*flicked the ash off his cigar; flicked away the dust*). **2** *tr.* give a flick with (a whip, towel, etc.). **3** *intr.* make a flicking movement or sound. □ **flick-knife** a weapon with a blade that springs out from the handle when a button is pressed. **flick through 1** turn over (cards, pages, etc.). **2 a** turn over the pages etc. of, by a rapid movement of the fingers. **b** look cursorily through (a book etc.). [ME, imit.]

flicker[1] /ˈflɪkə(r)/ *v.* & *n.* —*v.intr.* **1** (of light) shine unsteadily or fitfully. **2** (of a flame) burn unsteadily, alternately flaring and dying down. **3 a** (of a flag, a reptile's tongue, an eyelid, etc.) move or wave to and fro; quiver; vibrate. **b** (of the wind) blow lightly and unsteadily. **4** (of hope etc.) increase and decrease unsteadily and intermittently. —*n.* a flickering movement or light. □ **flicker out** die away after a final flicker. [OE *flicorian, flycerian*]

flicker[2] /ˈflɪkə(r)/ *n.* any woodpecker of the genus *Colaptes*, native to N. America. [imit. of its note]

flier var. of FLYER.

flight[1] /flaɪt/ *n.* & *v.* —*n.* **1 a** the act or manner of flying through the air (*studied swallows' flight*). **b** the swift movement or passage of a projectile etc.

through the air (*the flight of an arrow*). **2 a** a journey made through the air or in space. **b** a timetabled journey made by an airline. **c** an RAF unit of about six aircraft. **3 a** a flock or large body of birds, insects, etc., esp. when migrating. **b** a migration. **4** (usu. foll. by *of*) a series, esp. of stairs between floors, or of hurdles across a race track (*lives up six flights*). **5** an extravagant soaring, a mental or verbal excursion or sally (of wit etc.) (*a flight of fancy; a flight of ambition*). **6** the trajectory and pace of a ball in games. **7** the distance that a bird, aircraft, or missile can fly. **8** (usu. foll. by *of*) a volley (*a flight of arrows*). **9** the tail of a dart. **10** the pursuit of game by a hawk. **11** swift passage (of time). —*v.tr.* **1** vary the trajectory and pace of (a cricket-ball etc.). **2** provide (an arrow) with feathers. **3** shoot (wildfowl etc.) in flight. □ **flight bag** a small, zipped, shoulder bag carried by air travellers. **flight control** an internal or external system directing the movement of aircraft. **flight-deck 1** the deck of an aircraft-carrier used for take-off and landing. **2** the accommodation for the pilot, navigator, etc. in an aircraft. **flight-feather** a bird's wing or tail feather. **flight lieutenant** an RAF officer next in rank below squadron leader. **flight officer** a rank in the WRAF, corresponding to flight lieutenant. **flight path** the planned course of an aircraft or spacecraft. **flight-recorder** a device in an aircraft to record technical details during a flight, that may be used in the event of an accident to discover its cause. **flight sergeant** *Mil.* an RAF rank next above sergeant. **flight-test** test (an aircraft, rocket, etc.) during flight. **in the first (**or **top) flight** taking a leading place. **take (**or **wing) one's flight** fly. [OE *flyht* f. WG: rel to FLY[1]]

flight[2] /flaɪt/ *n.* **1 a** the act or manner of fleeing. **b** a hasty retreat. **2** *Econ.* the selling of currency, investments, etc. in anticipation of a fall in value (*flight from sterling*). □ **put to flight** cause to flee. **take (**or **take to) flight** flee. [OE f. Gmc: rel. to FLEE]

flightless /ˈflaɪtlɪs/ *adj.* (of a bird etc.) naturally unable to fly.

flighty /ˈflaɪtɪ/ *adj.* (**flightier, flightiest**) **1** (usu. of a girl) frivolous, fickle, changeable. **2** crazy. □□ **flightily** *adv.* **flightiness** *n.* [FLIGHT[1] + -Y[1]]

flimflam /ˈflɪmflæm/ *n.* & *v.* —*n.* **1** a trifle; nonsense; idle talk. **2** humbug; deception. —*v.tr.* (**flimflammed, flimflamming**) cheat; deceive. □□ **flimflammer** *n.* **flimflammery** *n.* (*pl.* -**ies**). [imit. redupl.]

flimsy /ˈflɪmzɪ/ *adj.* & *n.* —*adj.* (**flimsier, flimsiest**) **1** lightly or carelessly assembled; insubstantial, easily damaged (*a flimsy structure*). **2** (of an excuse etc.) unconvincing (*a flimsy pretext*). **3** paltry; trivial; superficial (*a flimsy play*). **4** (of clothing) thin (*a flimsy blouse*). —*n.* (*pl.* -**ies**) **1 a** very thin paper. **b** a document, esp. a copy, made on this. **2** a flimsy thing, esp. women's underwear. □□ **flimsily** *adv.* **flimsiness** *n.* [17th c.: prob. f. FLIMFLAM: cf. TIPSY]

flinch[1] /flɪntʃ/ *v.* & *n.* —*v.intr.* **1** draw back in pain or expectation of a blow etc.; wince. **2** (often foll. by *from*) give way; shrink, turn aside (*flinched from his duty*). —*n.* an act or instance of flinching. □□ **flincher** *n.* **flinchingly** *adv.* [OF *flenchir, flainchir* f. WG]

flinch[2] var. of FLENSE.

flinders /ˈflɪndəz/ *n.pl.* fragments; splinters. [ME, prob. f. Scand.]

fling /flɪŋ/ *v.* & *n.* —*v.* (*past* and *past part.* **flung** /flʌŋ/) **1** *tr.* throw or hurl (an object) forcefully. **2** *refl.* **a** (usu. foll. by *into*) rush headlong (into a person's arms, a train, etc.). **b** (usu. foll. by *into*) embark wholeheartedly (on an enterprise). **c** (usu. foll. by *on*) throw (oneself) on a person's mercy etc. **3** *tr.* utter (words) forcefully. **4** *tr.* (usu. foll. by *out*) suddenly spread (the arms). **5** *tr.* (foll. by *on, off*) put on or take off (clothes) carelessly or rapidly. **6** *intr.* go angrily or violently; rush (*flung out of the room*). **7** *tr.* put or send suddenly or violently (*was flung into jail*). **8** *tr.* (foll. by *away*) discard or put aside

w *we* z *zoo* ʃ *she* ʒ *decision* θ *thin* ð *this* ŋ *ring* x *loch* tʃ *chip* dʒ *jar* (*see over for vowels*)

thoughtlessly or rashly (*flung away their reputation*). **9** *intr.* (usu. foll. by *out*) (of a horse etc.) kick and plunge. **10** *tr. archaic* send, emit (sound, light, smell). —*n.* **1** an act or instance of flinging; a throw; a plunge. **2** a spell of indulgence or wild behaviour (*he's had his fling*). **3** an impetuous, whirling Scottish dance, esp. the Highland fling. □**have a fling at 1** make an attempt at. **2** jeer at. □□**flinger** *n.* [ME, perh. f. ON]

flint /flɪnt/ *n.* **1 a** a hard grey stone of nearly pure silica occurring naturally as nodules or bands in chalk. **b** a piece of this esp. as flaked or ground to form a primitive tool or weapon. **2** a piece of hard alloy of rare-earth metals used to give an igniting spark in a cigarette-lighter etc. **3** a piece of flint used with steel to produce fire, esp. in a flintlock gun. **4** anything hard and unyielding. □**flint corn** a variety of maize having hard translucent grains. **flint glass** a pure lustrous kind of glass orig. made with flint. □□**flinty** *adj.* (**flintier, flintiest**). **flintily** *adv.* **flintiness** *n.* [OE]

flintlock /ˈflɪntlɒk/ *n. hist.* **1** an old type of gun fired by a spark from a flint. **2** the lock producing such a spark.

flip[1] /flɪp/ *v., n., & adj.* —*v.* (**flipped, flipping**) **1** *tr.* **a** flick or toss (a coin, pellet, etc.) with a quick movement so that it spins in the air. **b** remove (a small object) from a surface with a flick of the fingers. **2** *tr.* **a** strike or flick (a person's ear, cheek, etc.) lightly or smartly. **b** move (a fan, whip, etc.) with a sudden jerk. **3** *tr.* turn (a small object) over. **4** *intr.* **a** make a fillip or flicking noise with the fingers. **b** (foll. by *at*) strike smartly at. **5** *intr.* move about with sudden jerks. **6** *intr. sl.* become suddenly excited or enthusiastic. —*n.* **1** a smart light blow; a flick. **2** *colloq.* **a** a short pleasure flight in an aircraft. **b** a quick tour etc. **3** an act of flipping over (*gave the stone a flip*). —*adj. colloq.* glib; flippant. □**flip chart** a large pad erected on a stand and bound so that one page can be turned over at the top to reveal the next. **flip one's lid** *sl.* **1** lose self-control. **2** go mad. **flip side** *colloq.* the less important side of a gramophone record. **flip through** = *flick through*. [prob. f. FILLIP]

flip[2] /flɪp/ *n.* **1** a drink of heated beer and spirit. **2** = *egg-flip*. [perh. f. FLIP[1] in the sense *whip up*]

flip-flop /ˈflɪpflɒp/ *n. & v.* —*n.* **1 a** usu. rubber sandal with a thong between the big and second toe. **2** esp. *US* a backward somersault. **3** an electronic switching circuit changed from one stable state to another, or through an unstable state back to its stable state, by a triggering pulse. —*v.intr.* (**-flopped, -flopping**) move with a sound or motion suggested by 'flip-flop'. [imit.]

flippant /ˈflɪpənt/ *adj.* lacking in seriousness; treating serious things lightly; disrespectful. □□ **flippancy** *n.* **flippantly** *adv.* [FLIP[1] + -ANT]

flipper /ˈflɪpə(r)/ *n.* **1** a broadened limb of a turtle, penguin, etc., used in swimming. **2** a flat rubber etc. attachment worn on the foot for underwater swimming. **3** *sl.* a hand.

flipping /ˈflɪpɪŋ/ *adj. & adv. Brit. sl.* expressing annoyance, or as an intensifier (*where's the flipping towel?*; *he flipping beat me*). [FLIP[1] + -ING[2]]

flirt /flɜːt/ *v. & n.* —*v.* **1** *intr.* (usu. foll. by *with*) behave in a frivolously amorous or sexually enticing manner. **2** *intr.* (usu. foll. by *with*) **a** superficially interest oneself (with an idea etc.). **b** trifle (with danger etc.) (*flirted with disgrace*). **3** *tr.* wave or move (a fan, a bird's tail, etc.) briskly. **4** *intr. & tr.* move or cause to move with a jerk. —*n.* **1** a person who indulges in flirting. **2** a quick movement; a sudden jerk. □□ **flirtation** /-ˈteɪʃ(ə)n/ *n.* **flirtatious** /-ˈteɪʃəs/ *adj.* **flirtatiously** /-ˈteɪʃəslɪ/ *adv.* **flirtatiousness** /-ˈteɪʃəsnɪs/ *n.* **flirty** *adj.* (**flirtier, flirtiest**). [imit.]

flit /flɪt/ *v. & n.* —*v.intr.* (**flitted, flitting**) **1** move lightly, softly, or rapidly (*flitted from one room to another*). **2** fly lightly; make short flights (*flitted from branch to branch*). **3** *Brit. colloq.* leave one's house etc. secretly to escape creditors or obligations. **4** esp. *Sc. & N.Engl.* change one's home; move. —*n.* **1** an act of flitting. **2** (also **moonlight flit**) a secret change of abode in order to escape creditors etc. □□ **flitter** *n.* [ME f. ON *flytja*: rel. to FLEET[5]]

flitch /flɪtʃ/ *n.* **1** a side of bacon. **2** a slab of timber from a tree-trunk, usu. from the outside. **3** (in full **flitch-plate**) a strengthening plate in a beam etc. □**flitch-beam** a compound beam, esp. of an iron plate between two slabs of wood. [OE *flicce* f. Gmc]

flitter /ˈflɪtə(r)/ *v.intr.* flit about; flutter. □**flitter-mouse** = BAT[2]. [FLIT + -ER[4]]

flivver /ˈflɪvə(r)/ *n. US sl.* **1** a cheap car or aircraft. **2** a failure. [20th c.: orig. uncert.]

flixweed /ˈflɪkswiːd/ *n.* a cruciferous plant, *Descurainia sophia*, formerly thought to cure dysentery. [earlier *fluxweed*]

float /fləʊt/ *v. & n.* —*v.* **1** *intr. & tr.* **a** rest or move or cause (a buoyant object) to rest or move on the surface of a liquid without sinking. **b** get afloat or set (a stranded ship) afloat. **2** *intr.* move with a liquid or current of air; drift (*the clouds floated high up*). **3** *intr. colloq.* **a** move in a leisurely or casual way (*floated about humming quietly*). **b** (often foll. by *before*) hover before the eye or mind (*the prospect of lunch floated before them*). **4** *intr.* (often foll. by *in*) move or be suspended freely in a liquid or a gas. **5** *tr.* **a** bring (a company, scheme, etc.) into being; launch. **b** offer (stock, shares, etc.) on the stock market. **6** *Commerce* **a** *intr.* (of currency) be allowed to have a fluctuating exchange rate. **b** *tr.* cause (currency) to float. **c** *intr.* (of an acceptance) be in circulation. **7** *tr.* (of water etc.) support; bear along (a buoyant object). **8** *intr. & tr.* circulate or cause (a rumour or idea) to circulate. **9** *tr.* waft (a buoyant object) through the air. **10** *tr. archaic* cover with liquid; inundate. —*n.* **1** a thing that floats, esp.: **a** a raft. **b** a cork or quill on a fishing-line as an indicator of a fish biting. **c** a cork supporting the edge of a fishing-net. **d** the hollow or inflated part or organ supporting a fish etc. in the water; an air bladder. **e** a hollow structure fixed underneath an aircraft enabling it to float on water. **f** a floating device on the surface of water, petrol, etc., controlling the flow. **2** a small vehicle or cart, esp. one powered by electricity (*milk float*). **3** a platform mounted on a lorry and carrying a display in a procession etc. **4** **a** a sum of money used at the beginning of a period of selling in a shop, a fête, etc. to provide change. **b** a small sum of money for minor expenditure; petty cash. **5** *Theatr.* (in *sing.* or *pl.*) footlights. **6** a tool used for smoothing plaster. □**float-board** one of the boards of a water-wheel or paddle-wheel. **float glass** a kind of glass made by drawing the molten glass continuously on to a surface of molten metal for hardening. **float process** the process used to make float glass. **float-stone** a light, porous stone that floats. □□ **floatable** *adj.* **floatability** /-ˈbɪlɪtɪ/ *n.* [OE *flot, flotian* float, OE *flota* ship, ON *flota, floti* rel. to FLEET[5]: in ME infl. by OF *floter*]

floatage /ˈfləʊtɪdʒ/ *n.* **1** the act or state of floating. **2** *Brit.* **a** a floating objects or masses; flotsam. **b** the right of appropriating flotsam. **3 a** a ships etc. afloat on a river. **b** the part of a ship above the water-line. **4** buoyancy; floating power.

floatation var. of FLOTATION.

floater /ˈfləʊtə(r)/ *n.* **1** a person or thing that floats. **2** a floating voter. **3** *sl.* a mistake; a gaffe. **4** a person who frequently changes occupation. **5** *Stock Exch.* a government stock certificate etc. recognized as a security.

floating /ˈfləʊtɪŋ/ *adj.* not settled in a definite place; fluctuating; variable (*the floating population*). □ **floating anchor** a sea anchor. **floating bridge 1** a bridge on pontoons etc. **2** a ferry working on chains. **floating debt** a debt repayable on demand, or at a stated time. **floating dock** a floating structure usable as a dry dock. **floating kidney 1** an abnormal condition in which the kidneys are unusually movable. **2** such a kidney. **floating light 1** a lightship. **2** a lifebuoy with a lantern. **floating point** *Computing* a decimal etc. point that does not occupy a fixed position in the numbers processed. **floating rib** any of the lower ribs, which are not attached to the breastbone. **floating voter** a voter without allegiance to any political party. □□ **floatingly** *adv.*

floaty /ˈfləʊtɪ/ *adj.* (esp. of a woman's garment or a fabric) light and airy. [FLOAT]

floc /flɒk/ *n.* a flocculent mass of fine particles. [abbr. of FLOCCULUS]

flocculate /ˈflɒkjʊˌleɪt/ *v.tr.* & *intr.* form into flocculent masses. □□ **flocculation** /-ˈleɪʃ(ə)n/ *n.*

floccule /ˈflɒkjuːl/ *n.* a small portion of matter resembling a tuft of wool.

flocculent /ˈflɒkjʊlənt/ *adj.* **1** like tufts of wool. **2** consisting of or showing tufts, downy. **3** *Chem.* (of precipitates) loosely massed. □□ **flocculence** *n.* [L *floccus* FLOCK²]

flocculus /ˈflɒkjʊləs/ *n.* (*pl.* **flocculi** /-ˌlaɪ/) **1** a floccule. **2** *Anat.* a small ovoid lobe in the undersurface of the cerebellum. **3** *Astron.* a small cloudy wisp on the sun's surface. [mod.L, dimin. of FLOCCUS]

floccus /ˈflɒkəs/ *n.* (*pl.* **flocci** /ˈflɒksaɪ/) a tuft of woolly hairs or filaments. [L, = FLOCK²]

flock¹ /flɒk/ *n.* & *v.* —*n.* **1 a** a number of animals of one kind, esp. birds, feeding or travelling together. **b** a number of domestic animals, esp. sheep, goats, or geese, kept together. **2** a large crowd of people. **3 a a** Christian congregation or body of believers, esp. in relation to one minister. **b** a family of children, a number of pupils, etc. —*v.intr.* **1** congregate; mass. **2** (usu. foll. by *to, in, out, together*) go together in a crowd; troop (*thousands flocked to Wembley*). [OE *flocc*]

flock² /flɒk/ *n.* **1** a lock or tuft of wool, cotton, etc. **2 a** (also in *pl.*; often *attrib.*) material for quilting and stuffing made of wool-refuse or torn-up cloth (*a flock pillow*). **b** powdered wool or cloth. □ **flock-paper** (or **-wallpaper**) wallpaper sized and sprinkled with powdered wool to make a raised pattern. □□ **flocky** *adj.* [ME f. OF *floc* f. L *floccus*]

floe /fləʊ/ *n.* a sheet of floating ice. [prob. f. Norw. *flo* f. ON *fló* layer]

flog /flɒg/ *v.* (**flogged**, **flogging**) **1** *tr.* **a** beat with a whip, stick, etc. (as a punishment or to urge on). **b** make work through violent effort (*flogged the engine*). **2** *tr. Brit. sl.* sell. **3** *tr.* (usu. foll. by *into, out of*) drive (a quality, knowledge, etc.) into or out of a person, esp. by physical punishment. **4** *intr.* & *refl. sl.* proceed by violent or painful effort. □ **flog a dead horse** waste energy on something unalterable. **flog to death** *colloq.* talk about or promote at tedious length. □□ **flogger** *n.* [17th-c. cant: prob. imit. or f. L *flagellare* to whip]

flong /flɒŋ/ *n. Printing* prepared paper for making stereotype moulds. [F *flan* FLAN]

flood /flʌd/ *n.* & *v.* —*n.* **1 a** an overflowing or influx of water beyond its normal confines, esp. over land; an inundation. **b** the water that overflows. **2 a** an outpouring of water; a torrent (*a flood of rain*). **b** something resembling a torrent (*a flood of tears*; *a flood of relief*). **3** the inflow of the tide (also in *comb.*: *flood-tide*). **4** *colloq.* a floodlight. **5** (**the Flood**) the flood described in Genesis. **6** *poet.* a river; a stream; a sea. —*v.* **1** *tr.* **a** cover with or overflow in a flood (*rain flooded the cellar*). **b** overflow as if with a flood (*the market was flooded with foreign goods*). **2** *tr.* irrigate (*flooded the paddy fields*). **3** *tr.* deluge (a burning house, a mine, etc.) with water. **4** *intr.* (often foll. by *in, through*) arrive in great quantities (*complaints flooded in*; *fear flooded through them*). **5** *intr.* become inundated (*the bathroom flooded*). **6** *tr.* overfill (a carburettor) with petrol. **7** *intr.* experience a uterine haemorrhage. **8** *tr.* (of rain etc.) fill (a river) to overflowing. □ **flood and field** sea and land. **flood**

out drive out (of one's home etc.) with a flood. **flood-tide** the periodical exceptional rise of the tide because of lunar or solar attraction. [OE *flōd* f. Gmc]

floodgate /ˈflʌdgeɪt/ *n.* **1** a gate opened or closed to admit or exclude water, esp. the lower gate of a lock. **2** (usu. in *pl.*) a last restraint holding back tears, rain, anger, etc.

floodlight /ˈflʌdlaɪt/ *n.* & *v.* —*n.* **1** a large powerful light (usu. one of several) to illuminate a building, sportsground, stage, etc. **2** the illumination so provided. —*v.tr.* illuminate with floodlight.

floor /flɔː(r)/ *n.* & *v.* —*n.* **1 a** the lower surface of a room. **b** the boards etc. of which it is made. **2 a** the bottom of the sea, a cave, a cavity, etc. **b** any level area. **3** all the rooms etc. on the same level of a building; a storey (*lives on the ground floor*; *walked up to the sixth floor*). **4 a** (in a legislative assembly) the part of the house in which members sit and from which they speak. **b** the right to speak next in debate (*gave him the floor*). **5** *Stock Exch.* the large central hall where trading takes place. **6** the minimum of prices, wages, etc. **7** *colloq.* the ground. —*v.tr.* **1** furnish with a floor; pave. **2** bring to the ground; knock (a person) down. **3** *colloq.* confound, baffle (*was floored by the puzzle*). **4** *colloq.* get the better of; overcome. **5** serve as the floor of (*leopard skins floored the hall*). □ **first** (*US* **second**) **floor** the floor above the ground floor. **floor-lamp** *US* a standard lamp. **floor-leader** *US* the leader of a party in a legislative assembly. **floor manager 1** the stage manager of a television production. **2** a shopwalker. **floor plan** a diagram of the rooms etc. on one storey of a building. **floor-polish** a manufactured substance used for polishing floors. **floor show** an entertainment presented on the floor (as opposed to the stage) of a nightclub etc. **floor-walker** *US* a shopwalker. **from the floor** (of a speech etc.) given by a member of the audience, not by those on the platform etc. **take the floor 1** begin to dance on a dance-floor etc. **2** speak in a debate. □□ **floorless** *adj.* [OE *flōr* f. Gmc]

floorboard /ˈflɔːbɔːd/ *n.* a long wooden board used for flooring.

floorcloth /ˈflɔːklɒθ/ *n.* a cloth for washing the floor.

flooring /ˈflɔːrɪŋ/ *n.* the boards etc. of which a floor is made.

floozie /ˈfluːzɪ/ *n.* (also **floozy**) (*pl.* **-ies**) *colloq.* a girl or a woman, esp. a disreputable one. [20th c.: cf. FLOSSY and dial. *floosy* fluffy]

flop /flɒp/ *v., n.,* & *adv.* —*v.intr.* (**flopped, flopping**) **1** sway about heavily or loosely (*hair flopped over his face*). **2** move in an ungainly way (*flopped along the beach in flippers*). **3** (often foll. by *down, on, into*) sit, kneel, lie, or fall awkwardly or suddenly (*flopped down on to the bench*). **4** *sl.* (esp. of a play, film, book, etc.) fail; collapse (*flopped on Broadway*). **5** *sl.* sleep. **6** make a dull sound as of a soft body landing, or of a flat thing slapping water. —*n.* **1 a** a flopping movement. **b** the sound made by it. **2** *sl.* a failure. **3** *sl.* a bed. —*adv.* with a flop. □ **flop-house** *sl.* esp. *US* a doss-house. [var. of FLAP]

floppy /ˈflɒpɪ/ *adj.* & *n.* —*adj.* (**floppier, floppiest**) tending to flop; not firm or rigid. —*n.* (*pl.* **-ies**) (in full **floppy disk**) *Computing* a flexible removable magnetic disc for the storage of data. □□ **floppily** *adv.* **floppiness** *n.*

flor. *abbr.* floruit.

flora /ˈflɔːrə/ *n.* (*pl.* **floras** or **florae** /-riː/) **1** the plants of a particular region, geological period, or environment. **2** a treatise on or list of these. [mod.L f. the name of the goddess of flowers f. L *flos floris* flower]

floral /ˈflɔːr(ə)l, ˈflɒ-/ *adj.* **1** of flowers. **2** decorated with or depicting flowers. **3** of flora or floras. □□ **florally** *adv.* [L *floralis* or *flos floris* flower]

floreat /ˈflɒrɪˌæt/ *v.intr.* may (he, she, or it) flourish. [L, 3rd sing. pres. subj. of *florēre* flourish]

Florentine /ˈflɒrənˌtaɪn/ *adj.* & *n.* —*adj.* **1** of or relating to Florence in Italy. **2** (**florentine** /-,ti:n/) (of a dish) served on a bed of spinach. —*n.* a native or citizen of Florence. [F *Florentin -ine* or L *Florentinus* f. *Florentia* Florence]

florescence /flɔːˈres(ə)ns, flɒ-/ *n.* the process, state, or time of flowering. [mod.L *florescentia* f. L *florescere* f. *florēre* bloom]

floret /ˈflɒrɪt, ˈflɔː-/ *n. Bot.* **1** each of the small flowers making up a composite flower-head. **2** each of the flowering stems making up a head of cauliflower, broccoli, etc. **3** a small flower. [L *flos floris* flower]

floriate /ˈflɔːrɪˌeɪt/ *v.tr.* decorate with flower-designs etc.

floribunda /ˌflɒrɪˈbʌndə, ˌflɔː-/ *n.* a plant, esp. a rose, bearing dense clusters of flowers. [mod.L f. *floribundus* freely flowering f. L *flos floris* flower, infl. by L *abundus* copious]

floriculture /ˈflɒrɪˌkʌltʃə(r), ˈflɔː-/ *n.* the cultivation of flowers. □□ **floricultural** /-ˈkʌltʃər(ə)l/ *adj.* **floriculturist** /-ˈkʌltʃərɪst/ *n.* [L *flos floris* flower + CULTURE, after *horticulture*]

florid /ˈflɒrɪd/ *adj.* **1** ruddy; flushed; high-coloured (*a florid complexion*). **2** (of a book, a picture, music, architecture, etc.) elaborately ornate; ostentatious; showy. **3** adorned with or as with flowers; flowery. □□ **floridity** /-ˈrɪdɪti/ *n.* **floridly** *adv.* **floridness** *n.* [F *floride* or L *floridus* f. *flos floris* flower]

floriferous /flɔːˈrɪfərəs, flɒ-/ *adj.* (of a seed or plant) producing many flowers. [L *florifer* f. *flos floris* flower]

florilegium /ˌflɒrɪˈliːdʒɪəm/ *n.* (*pl.* **florilegia** /-ˈliːdʒɪə/ or **florilegiums**) an anthology. [mod.L f. L *flos floris* flower + *legere* gather, transl. of Gk *anthologion* ANTHOLOGY]

florin /ˈflɒrɪn/ *n. hist.* **1 a** a British silver or alloy two-shilling coin of the 19th-20th c. (now worth 10 pence at face value). **b** an English gold coin of the 14th c., worth 6s. 8d. (33 pence). **2** a foreign coin of gold or silver, esp. a Dutch guilder. [ME f. OF f. It. *fiorino* dimin. of *fiore* flower f. L *flos floris*, the orig. coin having a figure of a lily on it]

florist /ˈflɒrɪst/ *n.* a person who deals in or grows flowers. □□ **floristry** *n.* [L *flos floris* flower + -IST]

floristic /flɒˈrɪstɪk/ *adj.* relating to the study of the distribution of plants. □□ **floristically** *adv.* **floristics** *n.*

floruit /ˈflɒrʊɪt, ˈflɔː-/ *v. & n.* —*v.intr.* (he or she) was alive and working; flourished (used of a person, esp. a painter, a writer, etc., whose exact dates are unknown). —*n.* the period or date at which a person lived or worked. [L, = he or she flourished]

flory var. of FLEURY.

floscular /ˈflɒskjʊlə(r)/ *adj.* (also **flosculous** /-kjʊləs/) having florets or composite flowers. [L *flosculus* dimin. of *flos* flower]

floss /flɒs/ *n. & v.* —*n.* **1** the rough silk enveloping a silkworm's cocoon. **2** untwisted silk thread used in embroidery. **3** = *dental floss.* —*v.tr.* (also *absol.*) clean (the teeth) with dental floss. □ **floss silk** a rough silk used in cheap goods. [F (*soie*) *floche* floss(-silk) f. OF *flosche* down, nap of velvet]

flossy /ˈflɒsi/ *adj.* (**flossier**, **flossiest**) **1** of or like floss. **2** *colloq.* fancy, showy.

flotation /fləʊˈteɪʃ(ə)n/ *n.* (also **floatation**) **1** the process of launching or financing a commercial enterprise. **2** the separation of the components of crushed ore etc. by their different capacities to float. **3** the capacity to float. □ **centre of flotation** the centre of gravity in a floating body. [alt. of *floatation* f. FLOAT, after *rotation* etc.]

flotilla /fləˈtɪlə/ *n.* **1** a small fleet. **2** a fleet of boats or small ships. [Sp., dimin. of *flota* fleet, OF *flote* multitude]

flotsam /ˈflɒtsəm/ *n.* wreckage found floating. □ **flotsam and jetsam 1** odds and ends; rubbish. **2** vagrants etc. [AF *floteson* f. *floter* FLOAT]

flounce¹ /flaʊns/ *v. & n.* —*v.intr.* (often foll. by *away, about, off, out*) go or move with an agitated,

violent, or impatient motion (*flounced out in a huff*). —*n.* a flouncing movement. [16th c.: orig. unkn.: perh. imit., as *bounce, pounce*]

flounce² /flaʊns/ *n. & v.* —*n.* a wide ornamental strip of material gathered and sewn to a skirt, dress, etc.; a frill. —*v.tr.* trim with a flounce or flounces. [alt. of earlier *frounce* fold, pleat, f. OF *fronce* f. *froncir* wrinkle]

flounder¹ /ˈflaʊndə(r)/ *v. & n.* —*v.intr.* **1** struggle in mud, or as if in mud, or when wading. **2** perform a task badly or without knowledge; be out of one's depth. —*n.* an act of floundering. □□ **flounderer** *n.* [imit.: perh. assoc. with *founder, blunder*]

flounder² /ˈflaʊndə(r)/ *n.* **1** an edible flat-fish, *Pleuronectes flesus,* native to European shores. **2** any of various flat-fish native to N. American shores. [ME f. AF *floundre,* OF *flondre,* prob. of Scand. orig.]

flour /ˈflaʊə(r)/ *n. & v.* —*n.* **1** a meal or powder obtained by grinding and usu. sifting cereals, esp. wheat. **2** any fine powder. —*v.tr.* **1** sprinkle with flour. **2** *US* grind into flour. □□ **floury** *adj.* (**flourier**, **flouriest**). **flouriness** *n.* [ME, different. spelling of FLOWER in the sense 'finest part']

flourish /ˈflʌrɪʃ/ *v. & n.* —*v.* **1** *intr.* **a** grow vigorously; thrive. **b** prosper; be successful. **c** be in one's prime. **d** be in good health. **2** *intr.* (usu. foll. by *in, at, about*) spend one's life; be active (at a specified time) (*flourished in the Middle Ages*) (cf. FLORUIT). **3** *tr.* show ostentatiously (*flourished his cheque-book*). **4** *tr.* wave (a weapon, one's limbs, etc.) vigorously. —*n.* **1** an ostentatious gesture with a weapon, a hand, etc. (*removed his hat with a flourish*). **2** an ornamental curving decoration of handwriting. **3** a florid verbal expression; a rhetorical embellishment. **4** *Mus.* **a** a fanfare played by brass instruments. **b** an ornate musical passage. **c** an extemporized addition played esp. at the beginning or end of a composition. **5** *archaic* an instance of prosperity; a flourishing. □□ **flourisher** *n.* **flourishy** *adj.* [ME f. OF *florir* ult. f. L *florēre* f. *flos floris* flower]

flout /flaʊt/ *v. & n.* —*v.* **1** *tr.* express contempt for (the law, rules, etc.) by word or action; mock; insult (*flouted convention by shaving her head*). ¶ Often confused with *flaunt.* **2** *intr.* (often foll. by *at*) mock or scoff at. —*n.* a flouting speech or act. [perh. f. Du. *fluiten* whistle, hiss: cf. FLUTE]

flow /fləʊ/ *v. & n.* —*v.intr.* **1** glide along as a stream (*the Thames flows under London Bridge*). **2 a** (of a liquid, esp. water) gush out; spring. **b** (of blood, liquid, etc.) be spilt. **3** (of blood, money, electric current, etc.) circulate. **4** (of people or things) come or go in large numbers or smoothly (*traffic flowed down the hill*). **5** (of talk, literary style, etc.) proceed easily and smoothly. **6** (of a garment, hair, etc.) hang easily or gracefully; undulate. **7** (often foll. by *from*) result from; be caused by (*his failure flows from his diffidence*). **8** (esp. of the tide) be in flood; run full. **9** (of wine) be poured out copiously. **10** (of a rock or metal) undergo a permanent change of shape under stress. **11** (foll. by *with*) *archaic* be richly supplied with (*land flowing with milk and honey*). —*n.* **1 a** a flowing movement in a stream. **b** the manner in which a thing flows (*a sluggish flow*). **c** a flowing liquid (*couldn't stop the flow*). **d** a copious outpouring; a stream (*a continuous flow of complaints*). **2** the rise of a tide or a river (*ebb and flow*). **3** the gradual deformation of a rock or metal under stress. **4** *Sc.* a bog or morass. □ **flow chart** (or **diagram** or **sheet**) **1** a diagram of the movement or action of things or persons engaged in a complex activity. **2** a graphical representation of a computer program in relation to its sequence of functions (as distinct from the data it processes). **flow of spirits** habitual cheerfulness. **flow-on** *Austral.* a wage or salary adjustment made as a consequence of one already made in a similar or related occupation. [OE *flōwan* f. Gmc, rel. to FLOOD]

flower /ˈflaʊə(r)/ *n. & v.* —*n.* **1** the part of a plant from which the fruit or seed is developed. **2** the reproductive organ in a plant containing one or more pistils or stamens or both, and usu. a corolla and calyx. **3** a blossom, esp. on a stem and used in bunches for decoration. **4** a plant cultivated or noted for its flowers. **5** (in *pl.*) ornamental phrases (*flowers of speech*). —*v.* **1** *intr.* (of a plant) produce flowers; bloom or blossom. **2** *intr.* reach a peak. **3** *tr.* cause or allow (a plant) to flower. **4** *tr.* decorate with worked flowers or a floral design. □**flower-bed** a garden bed in which flowers are grown. **flower-girl** a woman who sells flowers, esp. in the street. **flower-head** = HEAD *n.* 4d. **the flower of** the best or best part of. **flower people** hippies carrying or wearing flowers as symbols of peace and love. **flower power** the ideas of the flower people regarded as an instrument in changing the world. **flowers of sulphur** *Chem.* a fine powder produced when sulphur evaporates and condenses. **in flower** with the flowers out. □□ **flowered** *adj.* (also in *comb.*). **flowerless** *adj.* **flowerlike** *adj.* [ME f. AF *flur*, OF *flour*, *flor*, f. L *flos floris*]

flowerer /ˈflaʊərə(r)/ *n.* a plant that flowers at a specified time (*a late flowerer*).

floweret /ˈflaʊərɪt/ *n.* a small flower.

flowering /ˈflaʊərɪŋ/ *adj.* (of a plant) capable of producing flowers.

flowerpot /ˈflaʊəˌpɒt/ *n.* a pot in which a plant may be grown.

flowery /ˈflaʊərɪ/ *adj.* **1** decorated with flowers or floral designs. **2** (of literary style, manner of speech, etc.) high-flown; ornate. **3** full of flowers (*a flowery meadow*). □□ **floweriness** *n.*

flowing /ˈfləʊɪŋ/ *adj.* **1** (of literary style etc.) fluent; easy. **2** (of a line, a curve, or a contour) smoothly continuous, not abrupt. **3** (of hair, a garment, a sail, etc.) unconfined. □□ **flowingly** *adv.*

flown *past part.* of FLY[1].

flowstone /ˈfləʊstəʊn/ *n.* rock deposited in a thin sheet by a flow of water.

FLQ *abbr.* Front de Libération du Québec.

Flt. Lt. *abbr.* Flight Lieutenant.

Flt. Off. *abbr.* Flight Officer.

Flt. Sgt. *abbr.* Flight Sergeant.

flu /fluː/ *n. colloq.* influenza. [abbr.]

flub /flʌb/ *v. & n. US colloq.* —*v.tr.* & *intr.* (**flubbed**, **flubbing**) botch; bungle. —*n.* something badly or clumsily done. [20th c.: orig. unkn.]

fluctuate /ˈflʌktjʊˌeɪt/ *v.intr.* vary irregularly; be unstable, vacillate; rise and fall, move to and fro. □□ **fluctuation** /-ˈeɪʃ(ə)n/ *n.* [L *fluctuare* f. *fluctus* flow, wave f. *fluere fluct-* flow]

flue /fluː/ *n.* **1** a smoke-duct in a chimney. **2** a channel for conveying heat, esp. a hot-air passage in a wall; a tube for heating water in some kinds of boiler. □**flue-cure** cure (tobacco) by artificial heat from flues. **flue-pipe** an organ pipe into which the air enters directly, not striking a reed. [16th c.: orig. unkn.]

fluence /ˈfluːəns/ *n. colloq.* influence. □**put the fluence on** apply hypnotic etc. power to (a person). [shortening of INFLUENCE]

fluency /ˈfluːənsɪ/ *n.* **1** a smooth, easy flow, esp. in speech or writing. **2** a ready command of words or of a specified foreign language.

fluent /ˈfluːənt/ *adj.* **1 a** (of speech or literary style) flowing naturally and readily. **b** having command of a foreign language (*is fluent in German*). **c** able to speak quickly and easily. **2** flowing easily or gracefully (*the fluent line of her arabesque*). **3** *archaic* liable to change; unsettled. □□ **fluently** *adv.* [L *fluere* flow]

fluff /flʌf/ *n. & v.* —*n.* **1** soft, light, feathery material coming off blankets etc. **2** soft fur or feathers. **3** *sl.* a mistake in delivering theatrical lines, in playing music, etc. **b** a mistake in playing a game. —*v.* **1** *tr.* & *intr.* (often foll. by *up*) shake into or become a soft mass. **2** *tr.* & *intr. colloq.* make a mistake in (a theatrical part, a game, playing music, a speech,

etc.); blunder (*fluffed his opening line*). **3** *tr.* make into fluff. **4** *tr.* put a soft surface on (the flesh side of leather). □**bit of fluff** *sl. offens.* a woman regarded as an object of sexual desire. [prob. dial. alt. of *flue* fluff]

fluffy /ˈflʌfɪ/ *adj.* (**fluffier, fluffiest**) **1** of or like fluff. **2** covered in fluff; downy. □□ **fluffily** *adv.* **fluffiness** *n.*

flugelhorn /ˈfluːg(ə)lˌhɔːn/ *n.* a valved brass wind instrument like a cornet but with a broader tone. [G *Flügelhorn* f. *Flügel* wing + *Horn* horn]

fluid /ˈfluːɪd/ *n. & adj.* —*n.* **1** a substance, esp. a gas or liquid, lacking definite shape and capable of flowing and yielding to the slightest pressure. **2** a fluid part or secretion. —*adj.* **1** able to flow and alter shape freely. **2** constantly changing or fluctuating (*the situation is fluid*). **3** (of a clutch, coupling, etc.) in which liquid is used to transmit power. □**fluid drachm** see DRACHM. **fluid ounce** see OUNCE[1]. □□ **fluidity** /-ˈɪdɪˌfaɪ/ *v.tr.* (**-ies, -ied**). **fluidity** /-ˈɪdɪtɪ/ *n.* **fluidly** *adv.* **fluidness** *n.* [F *fluide* or L *fluidus* f. *fluere* flow]

fluidics /fluːˈɪdɪks/ *n.pl.* (usu. treated as *sing.*) the study and technique of using small interacting flows and fluid jets for functions usu. performed by electronic devices. □□ **fluidic** *adj.*

fluidize /ˈfluːɪˌdaɪz/ *v.tr.* (also **-ise**) cause (a finely divided solid) to acquire the characteristics of a fluid by the upward passage of a gas etc. □□ **fluidization** /-ˈzeɪʃ(ə)n/ *n.*

fluidounce /ˈfluːɪdˌaʊns/ *n. US* a fluid ounce (see OUNCE[1]).

fluidram /ˈfluːɪˌdræm/ *n. US* a fluid drachm (see DRACHM).

fluke[1] /fluːk/ *n. & v.* —*n.* **1** a lucky accident (*won by a fluke*). **2** a chance breeze. —*v.tr.* achieve by a fluke (*fluked that shot*). [19th c.: perh. f. dial. *fluke* guess]

fluke[2] /fluːk/ *n.* **1** any parasitic flatworm of the class Digenea or Monogenea, including liver flukes and blood flukes. **2** a flat-fish, esp. a flounder. [OE *flōc*]

fluke[3] /fluːk/ *n.* **1** *Naut.* a broad triangular plate on the arm of an anchor. **2** the barbed head of a lance, harpoon, etc. **3** *Zool.* either of the lobes of a whale's tail. [16th c.: perh. f. FLUKE[2]]

fluky /ˈfluːkɪ/ *adj.* (**flukier, flukiest**) of the nature of a fluke; obtained more by chance than skill. □□ **flukily** *adv.* **flukiness** *n.*

flume /fluːm/ *n. & v.* —*n.* **1** an artificial channel conveying water etc. for industrial use. **2** a ravine with a stream. —*v.* **1** *intr.* build flumes. **2** *tr.* convey down a flume. [ME f. OF *flum*, *flun* f. L *flumen* river f. *fluere* flow]

flummery /ˈflʌmərɪ/ *n.* (*pl.* **-ies**) **1** empty compliments; trifles; nonsense. **2** a sweet dish made with beaten eggs, sugar, etc. [Welsh *llymru*, of unkn. orig.]

flummox /ˈflʌməks/ *v.tr. colloq.* bewilder, confound, disconcert. [19th c.: prob. dial., imit.]

flump /flʌmp/ *v. & n.* —*v.* (often foll. by *down*) **1** *intr.* fall or move heavily. **2** *tr.* set or throw down with a heavy thud. —*n.* the action or sound of flumping. [imit.]

flung *past* and *past part.* of FLING.

flunk /flʌŋk/ *v. & n. US colloq.* —*v.* **1** *tr.* **a** fail (an examination etc.). **b** fail (an examination candidate). **2** *intr.* (often foll. by *out*) fail utterly; give up. —*n.* an instance of flunking. □**flunk out** be dismissed from school etc. after failing an examination. [cf. FUNK[1] and obs. *flink* be a coward]

flunkey /ˈflʌŋkɪ/ *n.* (also **flunky**) (*pl.* **-eys** or **-ies**) usu. *derog.* **1** a liveried servant; a footman. **2** a toady; a snob. **3** *US* a cook, waiter, etc. □□ **flunkeyism** *n.* [18th c. (orig. Sc.): perh. f. FLANK with the sense 'sidesman, flanker']

fluoresce /flʊəˈrɛs/ *v.intr.* be or become fluorescent.

fluorescence /flʊəˈrɛs(ə)ns/ *n.* **1** the visible or invisible radiation produced from certain substances as a result of incident radiation of a shorter wavelength as X-rays, ultraviolet light, etc. **2** the property of absorbing light of short (invisible) wavelength and emitting light of longer (visible) wavelength. [FLUORSPAR (which fluoresces) after *opalescence*]

fluorescent /fluə'res(ə)nt/ *adj.* (of a substance) having or showing fluorescence. □**fluorescent lamp** (or **bulb**) a lamp or bulb radiating largely by fluorescence, esp. a tubular lamp in which phosphor on the inside surface of the tube is made to fluoresce by ultraviolet radiation from mercury vapour. **fluorescent screen** a screen coated with fluorescent material to show images from X-rays etc.

fluoridate /'fluəri,deit/ *v.tr.* add traces of fluoride to (drinking-water etc.).

fluoridation /,fluəri'deiʃ(ə)n/ *n.* (also **fluoridization** /-dai'zeiʃ(ə)n/) the addition of traces of fluoride to drinking-water in order to prevent or reduce tooth-decay.

fluoride /'fluəraid/ *n.* any binary compound of fluorine.

fluorinate /'fluəri,neit/ *v.tr.* 1 = FLUORIDATE. 2 introduce fluorine into (a compound) (*fluorinated hydrocarbons*). □□ **fluorination** /-'neiʃ(ə)n/ *n.*

fluorine /'fluəri:n/ *n.* a poisonous pale-yellow gaseous element of the halogen group occurring naturally in fluorite and cryolite, and the most reactive of all elements. ¶ Symb.: F. [F (as FLUORSPAR)]

fluorite /'fluərait/ *n.* a mineral form of calcium fluoride. [It. (as FLUORSPAR)]

fluoro- /'fluərəʊ/ *comb. form* 1 fluorine (*fluorocarbon*). 2 fluorescence (*fluoroscope*). [FLUORINE, FLUORESCENCE]

fluorocarbon /,fluərəʊ'ka:bən/ *n.* a compound formed by replacing one or more of the hydrogen atoms in a hydrocarbon with fluorine atoms.

fluoroscope /'fluərə,skəʊp/ *n.* an instrument with a fluorescent screen on which X-ray images may be viewed without taking and developing X-ray photographs.

fluorosis /fluə'rəʊsis/ *n.* poisoning by fluorine or its compounds. [F *fluorose* (as FLUORO- 1)]

fluorspar /'fluəspa:(r)/ *n.* = FLUORITE. [*fluor* a flow, any of the minerals used as fluxes, fluorspar, f. L *fluor* f. *fluere* flow + SPAR³]

flurry /'flʌri/ *n. & v.* —*n.* (*pl.* -**ies**) 1 a gust or squall (of snow, rain, etc.). 2 a sudden burst of activity. 3 a commotion; excitement; nervous agitation (*a flurry of speculation; the flurry of the city*). —*v.tr.* (-**ies**, -**ied**) confuse by haste or noise; agitate. [imit.: cf. obs. *flurr* ruffle, *hurry*]

flush¹ /flʌʃ/ *v. & n.* —*v.* 1 *intr.* **a** blush, redden (*he flushed with embarrassment*). **b** glow with a warm colour (*sky flushed pink*). 2 *tr.* (usu. as **flushed** *adj.*) cause to glow or blush (often foll. by *with*: *flushed with pride*). 3 *tr.* **a** cleanse (a drain, lavatory, etc.) by a rushing flow of water. **b** (often foll. by *away, down*) dispose of (an object) in this way (*flushed away the cigarette*). 4 *intr.* rush out, spurt. 5 *tr.* flood (*the river flushed the meadow*). 6 *intr.* (of a plant) throw out fresh shoots. —*n.* 1 **a** a blush. **b** a glow of light or colour. 2 **a** a rush of water. **b** the cleansing of a drain, lavatory, etc. by flushing. 3 **a** a rush of emotion. **b** the elation produced by a victory etc. (*the flush of triumph*). 4 sudden abundance. 5 freshness; vigour (*in the first flush of womanhood*). 6 **a** (also **hot flush**) a sudden feeling of heat during the menopause. **b** a feverish temperature. **c** facial redness, esp. caused by fever, alcohol, etc. 7 a fresh growth of grass etc. □□ **flusher** *n.* [ME, perh. ≡ FLUSH⁴ infl. by *flash* and *blush*]

flush² /flʌʃ/ *adj. & v.* —*adj.* 1 (often foll. by *with*) in the same plane; level; even (*the sink is flush with the cooker; fitted it flush with the wall*). 2 (usu. *predic.*) *colloq.* **a** having plenty of money. **b** (of money) abundant, plentiful. 3 full to overflowing; in flood. —*v.tr.* 1 make (surfaces) level. 2 fill in (a joint) level with a surface. □□ **flushness** *n.* [prob. f. FLUSH¹]

flush³ /flʌʃ/ *n.* a hand of cards all of one suit, esp. in poker. □**royal flush** a straight poker flush headed

by an ace. **straight flush** a flush that is a numerical sequence. [OF *flus, flux* f. L *fluxus* FLUX]

flush⁴ /flʌʃ/ *v.* 1 *tr.* cause (esp. a game bird) to fly up. 2 *intr.* (of a bird) fly up and away. □**flush out** 1 reveal. 2 drive out. [ME, imit.: cf. *fly, rush*]

fluster /'flʌstə(r)/ *v. & n.* —*v.* 1 *tr. & intr.* make or become nervous or confused; flurry (*was flustered by the noise; he flusters easily*). 2 *tr.* confuse with drink; half-intoxicate. 3 *intr.* bustle. —*n.* a confused or agitated state. [ME: orig. unkn.: cf. Icel. *flaustr(a)* hurry, bustle]

flute /flu:t/ *n. & v.* —*n.* 1 **a** a high-pitched woodwind instrument of metal or wood, having holes along it stopped by the fingers or keys, and held across the body. **b** an organ stop having a similar sound. **c** any of various wind instruments resembling a flute. **d** a flute-player. 2 **a** *Archit.* an ornamental vertical groove in a column. **b** a trumpet-shaped frill on a dress etc. **c** any similar cylindrical groove. 3 **a** tall narrow wineglass. —*v.* 1 *intr.* play the flute. 2 *intr.* speak, sing, or whistle in a fluting way. 3 *tr.* make flutes or grooves in. 4 *tr.* play (a tune etc.) on a flute. □□ **flutelike** *adj.* **fluting** *n.* **flutist** *n.* US (cf. FLAUTIST). **fluty** *adj.* (in sense 1a of *n.*). [ME f. OF *fleute, flaute, flahute,* prob. f. Prov. *flaüt*]

flutter /'flʌtə(r)/ *v. & n.* —*v.* 1 **a** *intr.* flap the wings in flying or trying to fly (*butterflies fluttered in the sunshine*). **b** *tr.* flap (the wings). 2 *intr.* fall with a quivering motion (*leaves fluttered to the ground*). 3 *intr. & tr.* move or cause to move irregularly or tremblingly (*the wind fluttered the flag*). 4 *intr.* go about restlessly; flit; hover. 5 *tr.* agitate, confuse. 6 *intr.* (of a pulse or heartbeat) beat feebly or irregularly. 7 *intr.* tremble with excitement or agitation. —*n.* 1 **a** the act of fluttering. **b** an instance of this. 2 tremulous excitement; a sensation (*was in a flutter; caused a flutter with his behaviour*). 3 *Brit. sl.* a small bet, esp. on a horse. 4 an abnormally rapid but regular heartbeat. 5 *Aeron.* an undesired oscillation in a part of an aircraft etc. under stress. 6 *Mus.* a rapid movement of the tongue (as when rolling one's rs) in playing a wind instrument. 7 *Electronics* a rapid variation of pitch, esp. of recorded sound (cf. wow²). 8 a vibration. □**flutter the dovecots** cause alarm among normally imperturbable people. □□ **flutterer** *n.* **fluttery** *adj.* [OE *floterian, flotorian,* frequent. form rel. to FLEET⁵]

fluvial /'flu:viəl/ *adj.* of or found in a river or rivers. [ME f. L *fluvialis* f. *fluvius* river f. *fluere* flow]

fluviatile /'flu:viə,tail/ *adj.* of, found in, or produced by a river or rivers. [F f. L *fluviatilis* f. *fluviatus* moistened f. *fluvius*]

fluvio- /'flu:viəʊ/ *comb. form* river (*fluviometer*). [L *fluvius* river f. *fluere* flow]

fluvioglacial /,flu:viəʊ'gleisiəl, -ʃ(ə)l/ *adj.* of or caused by streams from glacial ice, or the combined action of rivers and glaciers.

fluviometer /,flu:vi'ɒmit(ə)r/ *n.* an instrument for measuring the rise and fall of rivers.

flux /flʌks/ *n. & v.* —*n.* 1 a process of flowing or flowing out. 2 an issue or discharge. 3 continuous change (*in a state of flux*). 4 *Metallurgy* a substance mixed with a metal etc. to promote fusion. 5 *Physics* **a** the rate of flow of any fluid across a given area. **b** the amount of fluid crossing an area in a given time. 6 *Physics* the amount of radiation or particles incident on an area in a given time. 7 *Electr.* the total electric or magnetic field passing through a surface. 8 *Med.* an abnormal discharge of blood or excrement from the body. —*v.* 1 *tr. & intr.* make or become fluid. 2 *tr.* a fuse. **b** treat with a fusing flux. [ME f. OF *flux* or L *fluxus* f. *fluere flux-* flow]

fluxion /'flʌkʃ(ə)n/ *n. Math.* the rate at which a variable quantity changes; a derivative. [F *fluxion* or L *fluxio* (as FLUX)]

fly¹ /flai/ *v. & n.* —*v.* (**flies**; *past* **flew** /flu:/; *past part.* **flown** /fləʊn/) 1 *intr.* move through the air under control, esp. with wings. 2 (of an aircraft or its

æ **cat** ɑ: **arm** e **bed** ɜ: **her** ɪ **sit** i: **see** ɒ **hot** ɔ: **saw** ʌ **run** ʊ **put** u: **too** ə **ago** ai **my** occupants): **a** *intr.* travel through the air or through space. **b** *tr.* traverse (a region or distance) (*flew the Channel*). **3** *tr.* **a** control the flight of (esp. an aircraft). **b** transport in an aircraft. **4 a** *tr.* cause to fly or remain aloft. **b** *intr.* (of a flag, hair, etc.) wave or flutter. **5** *intr.* pass or rise quickly through the air or over an obstacle. **6** *intr.* go or move quickly; pass swiftly (*time flies*). **7** *intr.* **a** flee. **b** *colloq.* depart hastily. **8** *intr.* be driven or scattered; be forced off suddenly (*sent me flying*; *the door flew open*). **9** *intr.* (foll. by *at, upon*) **a** hasten or spring violently. **b** attack or criticize fiercely. **10** *tr.* flee from; escape in haste. —*n.* (*pl.* -ies) **1** (usu. in *pl.*) **a** a flap on a garment, esp. trousers, to contain or cover a fastening. **b** this fastening. **2** a flap at the entrance of a tent. **3** (in *pl.*) the space over the proscenium in a theatre. **4** the act or an instance of flying. **5** (*pl.* usu. **flys**) *Brit. hist.* a one-horse hackney carriage. **6** a speed-regulating device in clockwork and machinery. □**fly-away** (of hair etc.) tending to fly out or up; streaming. **fly-by** (*pl.* -**bys**) a flight past a position, esp. the approach of a spacecraft to a planet for observation. **fly-by-night** *adj.* unreliable. —*n.* an unreliable person. **fly-half** *Rugby Football* a stand-off half. **fly high 1** pursue a high ambition. **2** excel, prosper. **fly in the face of** openly disregard or disobey; conflict roundly with (probability, the evidence, etc.). **fly into a rage** (or **temper** etc.) become suddenly or violently angry. **fly a kite 1** try something out; test public opinion. **2** raise money by an accommodation bill. **fly off the handle** *colloq.* lose one's temper suddenly and unexpectedly. **fly-past** a ceremonial flight of aircraft past a person or a place. **fly-pitcher** *sl.* a street-trader. **fly-pitching** *sl.* street-trading. □□**flyable** *adj.* [OE *flēogan* f. Gmc]

fly² /flaɪ/ *n.* (*pl.* **flies**) **1** any insect of the order Diptera with two usu. transparent wings. **2** any other winged insect, e.g. a firefly or mayfly. **3** a disease of plants or animals caused by flies. **4** a natural or artificial fly used as bait in fishing. □**fly agaric** a poisonous fungus *Amanita Muscaria*, forming bright-red mushrooms with white flecks. **fly-blow** flies' eggs contaminating food, esp. meat. **fly-blown** *adj.* tainted, esp. by flies. **fly-fish** *v.intr.* fish with a fly. **fly in the ointment** a minor irritation that spoils enjoyment. **fly on the wall** an unnoticed observer. **fly-paper** sticky treated paper for catching flies. **fly-post** display (posters etc.) rapidly in unauthorized places. **fly-tip** illegally dump (waste). **fly-tipper** a person who engages in fly-tipping. **fly-trap** any of various plants that catch flies, esp. the Venus fly-trap. **like flies** in large numbers (usu. of people dying in an epidemic etc.). **no flies on** *colloq.* nothing to diminish (a person's) astuteness. [OE *flȳge, flēoge* f. WG]

fly³ /flaɪ/ *adj. Brit. sl.* knowing, clever, alert. □□ **flyness** *n.* [19th c.: orig. unkn.]

flycatcher /'flaɪ,kætʃə(r)/ *n.* any bird of the families Tyrannidae and Muscicapidae, catching insects esp. in short flights from a perch.

flyer /'flaɪə(r)/ *n.* (also **flier**) *colloq.* **1** an airman or airwoman. **2** a thing that flies in a specified way (*a poor flyer*). **3** a fast-moving animal or vehicle. **4** an ambitious or outstanding person. **5** *US* a small handbill. **6** *US* a speculative investment. **7** a flying jump.

flying /'flaɪɪŋ/ *adj. & n.* —*adj.* **1** fluttering or waving in the air; hanging loose. **2** hasty, brief (*a flying visit*). **3** designed for rapid movement. **4** (of an animal) able to make very long leaps by using winglike membranes etc. —*n.* flight, esp. in an aircraft. □**flying boat** a seaplane with a boatlike fuselage. **flying bomb** a pilotless aircraft with an explosive warhead. **flying buttress** a buttress slanting from a separate column, usu. forming an arch with the wall it supports. **flying doctor** a doctor (esp. in a large sparsely populated area) who visits distant patients by aircraft. **flying fish** any tropical

fish of the family Exocoetidae, with winglike pectoral fins for gliding through the air. **flying fox** any of various fruit-eating bats esp. of the genus *Pteropus*, with a fox-like head. **flying lemur** either of two mammals of the genus *Cyanocephalus* of S. Asia, with a lemur-like appearance and having a membrane between the fore and hind limbs for gliding from tree to tree. **flying lizard** any lizard of the genus *Draco*, having membranes on elongated ribs for gliding. **flying officer** the RAF rank next below flight lieutenant. **flying phalanger** any of various phalangers having a membrane between the fore and hind limbs for gliding. **flying picket** an industrial picket that can be moved rapidly from one site to another, esp. to reinforce local pickets. **flying saucer** any unidentified, esp. circular, flying object, popularly supposed to have come from space. **flying squad** a police detachment or other body organized for rapid movement. **flying squirrel** any of various squirrels, esp. of the genus *Pteromys*, with skin joining the fore and hind limbs for gliding from tree to tree. **flying start 1** a start (of a race etc.) in which the starting-point is passed at full speed. **2** a vigorous start giving an initial advantage. **flying wing** an aircraft with little or no fuselage and no tailplane. **with flying colours** with distinction.

flyleaf /'flaɪliːf/ *n.* (*pl.* -**leaves**) a blank leaf at the beginning or end of a book.

flyover /'flaɪ,əʊvə(r)/ *n.* **1** *Brit.* a bridge carrying one road or railway over another. **2** *US* = *fly-past* (see FLY¹).

flysheet /'flaɪʃiːt/ *n.* **1** a tract or circular of two or four pages. **2** a canvas cover pitched outside and over a tent to give extra protection against bad weather.

flyweight /'flaɪweɪt/ *n.* **1** a weight in certain sports intermediate between light flyweight and bantamweight, in the amateur boxing scale 48–51 kg but differing for professionals, wrestlers, and weightlifters. **2** a sportsman of this weight. □**light flyweight 1** a weight in amateur boxing up to 48 kg. **2** an amateur boxer of this weight.

flywheel /'flaɪwiːl/ *n.* a heavy wheel on a revolving shaft used to regulate machinery or accumulate power.

FM *abbr.* **1** Field Marshal. **2** frequency modulation.

Fm *symb. Chem.* the element fermium.

fm. *abbr.* (also **fm**) fathom(s).

f-number /'ef,nʌmbə(r)/ *n. Photog.* the ratio of the focal length to the effective diameter of a lens (e.g. *f*5, indicating that the focal length is five times the diameter). [*f* (denoting focal length) + NUMBER]

FO *abbr.* **1** Flying Officer. **2** *hist.* (in the UK) Foreign Office.

fo. *abbr.* folio.

foal /fəʊl/ *n. & v.* —*n.* the young of a horse or related animal. —*v.tr.* (of a mare etc.) give birth to (a foal). □**in** (or **with**) **foal** (of a mare etc.) pregnant. [OE *fola* f. Gmc: cf. FILLY]

foam /fəʊm/ *n. & v.* —*n.* **1** a mass of small bubbles formed on or in liquid by agitation, fermentation, etc. **2** a froth of saliva or sweat. **3** a substance resembling these, e.g. rubber or plastic in a cellular mass. —*v.intr.* **1** emit foam; froth. **2** run with foam. **3** (of a vessel) be filled and overflow with foam. □**foam at the mouth** be very angry. □□**foamless** *adj.* **foamy** *adj.* (**foamier, foamiest**). [OE *fām* f. WG]

fob¹ /fɒb/ *n. & v.* —*n.* **1** (in full **fob-chain**) a chain attached to a watch for carrying in a waistcoat or waistband pocket. **2** a small pocket for carrying a watch. **3** a tab on a key-ring. —*v.tr.* (**fobbed, fobbing**) put in one's fob; pocket. [orig. cant, prob. f. G]

fob² /fɒb/ *v.tr.* (**fobbed, fobbing**) □**fob off 1** (often foll. by *with* a thing) deceive into accepting something inferior. **2** (often foll. by *on to* a person) palm or pass off (an inferior thing). [16th c.: cf. obs. *fop* to dupe, G *foppen* to banter]

f.o.b. *abbr.* free on board.

focal /ˈfəʊk(ə)l/ *adj.* of, at, or in terms of a focus. □**focal distance** (or **length**) the distance between the centre of a mirror or lens and its focus. **focal plane** the plane through the focus perpendicular to the axis of a mirror or lens. **focal point** = FOCUS *n.* 1. [mod.L *focalis* (as FOCUS)]

focalize /ˈfəʊkəˌlaɪz/ *v.tr.* (also **-ise**) = FOCUS *v.* □□ **focalization** /-ˈzeɪʃ(ə)n/ *n.*

fo'c's'le var. of FORECASTLE.

focus /ˈfəʊkəs/ *n. & v.* —*n.* (*pl.* **focuses** or **foci** /ˈfəʊsaɪ/) **1** *Physics* **a** the point at which rays or waves meet after reflection or refraction. **b** the point from which diverging rays or waves appear to proceed. Also called *focal point.* **2 a** *Optics* the point at which an object must be situated for an image of it given by a lens or mirror to be well defined (*bring into focus*). **b** the adjustment of the eye or a lens necessary to produce a clear image (*the binoculars were not in focus*). **c** a state of clear definition (*the photograph was out of focus*). **3** the centre of interest or activity (*focus of attention*). **4** *Geom.* one of the points from which the distances to any point of a given curve are connected by a linear relation. **5** *Med.* the principal site of an infection or other disease. **6** *Geol.* the place of origin of an earthquake. —*v.* (**focused, focusing** or **focussed, focussing**) **1** *tr.* bring into focus. **2** *tr.* adjust the focus of (a lens, the eye, etc.). **3** *tr. & intr.* (often foll. by *on*) concentrate or be concentrated on. **4** *intr. & tr.* converge or make converge to a focus. □□ **focuser** *n.* [L, = hearth]

fodder /ˈfɒdə(r)/ *n. & v.* —*n.* dried hay or straw etc. for cattle, horses, etc. —*v.tr.* give fodder to. [OE *fōdor* f. Gmc, rel. to FOOD]

foe /fəʊ/ *n.* esp. *poet.* or *formal* an enemy or opponent. [OE *fāh* hostile, rel. to FEUD[1]]

foehn var. of FÖHN.

foetid var. of FETID.

foetus /ˈfiːtəs/ *n.* (*US* **fetus**) an unborn or unhatched offspring of a mammal esp. a human one more than eight weeks after conception. □□ **foetal** *adj.* **foeticide** /-tɪˌsaɪd/ *n.* [ME f. L *fetus* offspring]

fog[1] /fɒg/ *n. & v.* —*n.* **1 a** a thick cloud of water droplets or smoke suspended in the atmosphere at or near the earth's surface restricting or obscuring visibility. **b** obscurity in the atmosphere caused by this. **2** *Photog.* cloudiness on a developed negative etc. obscuring the image. **3** an uncertain or confused position or state. —*v.* (**fogged, fogging**) **1** *tr.* **a** envelop or cover with fog or condensed vapour. **b** bewilder or confuse as if with a fog. **2** *intr.* become covered with fog or condensed vapour. **3** *tr. Photog.* make (a negative etc.) obscure or cloudy. □**fog-bank** a mass of fog at sea. **fog-bound** unable to proceed because of fog. **fog-bow** a manifestation like a rainbow, produced by light on fog. **fog-lamp** a lamp used to improve visibility in fog. **fog-signal** a detonator placed on a railway line in fog to warn train drivers. **in a fog** puzzled; at a loss. [perh. back-form. f. FOGGY]

fog[2] /fɒg/ *n. & v.* esp. *Brit.* —*n.* **1** a second growth of grass after cutting; aftermath. **2** long grass left standing in winter. —*v.tr.* (**fogged, fogging**) **1** leave (land) under fog. **2** feed (cattle) on fog. [ME: orig. unkn.]

fogey var. of FOGY.

foggy /ˈfɒgɪ/ *adj.* (**foggier, foggiest**) **1** (of the atmosphere) thick or obscure with fog. **2** of or like fog. **3** vague, confused, unclear. □**not have the foggiest** *colloq.* have no idea at all. □□ **foggily** *adv.* **fogginess** *n.*

foghorn /ˈfɒghɔːn/ *n.* **1** a deep-sounding instrument for warning ships in fog. **2** *colloq.* a loud penetrating voice.

fogy /ˈfəʊgɪ/ *n.* (also **fogey**) (*pl.* **-ies** or **-eys**) a dull

old-fashioned person (esp. *old fogy*). □□ **fogydom** *n.* **fogyish** *adj.* [18th c.: rel. to sl. *fogram*, of unkn. orig.]

föhn /fɜːn/ *n.* (also **foehn**) **1** a hot southerly wind on the northern slopes of the Alps. **2** a warm dry wind on the lee side of mountains. [G, ult. f. L *Favonius* mild west wind]

foible /ˈfɔɪb(ə)l/ *n.* **1** a minor weakness or idiosyncrasy. **2** *Fencing* the part of a sword-blade from the middle to the point. [F, obs. form of *faible* (as FEEBLE)]

foie gras /fwɑː ˈgrɑː/ *n. colloq.* = *pâté de foie gras.*

foil[1] /fɔɪl/ *v. & n.* —*v.tr.* **1** frustrate, baffle, defeat. **2** *Hunting* **a** run over or cross (ground or a scent) to confuse the hounds. **b** (*absol.*) (of an animal) spoil the scent in this way. —*n.* **1** *Hunting* the track of a hunted animal. **2** *archaic* a repulse or defeat. [ME, = trample down, perh. f. OF *fouler* to full cloth, trample, ult. f. L *fullo* FULLER[1]]

foil[2] /fɔɪl/ *n.* **1 a** metal hammered or rolled into a thin sheet (*tin foil*). **b** a sheet of this, or of tin amalgam, attached to mirror glass as a reflector. **c** a leaf of foil placed under a precious stone etc. to brighten or colour it. **2 a** person or thing that enhances the qualities of another by contrast. **3** *Archit.* a leaf-shaped curve formed by the cusping of an arch or circle. [ME f. OF f. L *folium* leaf, and f. OF *foille* f. L *folia* (pl.)]

foil[3] /fɔɪl/ *n.* a light blunt-edged sword with a button on its point used in fencing. □□ **foilist** *n.* [16th c.: orig. unkn.]

foil[4] /fɔɪl/ *n.* = HYDROFOIL. [abbr.]

foist /fɔɪst/ *v.tr.* (foll. by *off*) *on*, (*off*) *upon*) **1** present (a thing) falsely as genuine or superior. **2** falsely fix the ownership of. **3** (foll. by *in*, *into*) introduce surreptitiously or unwarrantably. [orig. of palming a false die, f. Du. dial. *vuisten* take in the hand f. *vuist* FIST]

fol. *abbr.* folio.

folacin /ˈfəʊləsɪn/ *n.* = FOLIC ACID. [*folic acid* + -IN]

fold[1] /fəʊld/ *v. & n.* —*v.* **1** *tr.* **a** bend or close (a flexible thing) over upon itself. **b** (foll. by *back, over, down*) bend a part of (a flexible thing) in the manner specified (*fold down the flap*). **2** *intr.* become or be able to be folded. **3** *tr.* (foll. by *away, up*) make compact by folding. **4** *intr.* (often foll. by *up*) *colloq.* **a** collapse, disintegrate. **b** (of an enterprise) fail; go bankrupt. **5** *tr. poet.* embrace (esp. *fold in the arms* or *to the breast*). **6** *tr.* (foll. by *about, round*) clasp (the arms); wrap, envelop. **7** *tr.* (foll. by *in*) mix (an ingredient with others) using a gentle cutting and turning motion. —*n.* **1** the act or an instance of folding. **2** a line made by or for folding. **3** a folded part. **4** a hollow among hills. **5** *Geol.* a curvature of strata. □**fold one's arms** place one's arms across the chest, side by side or entwined. **fold one's hands** clasp them. **folding door** a door with jointed sections, folding on itself when opened. **folding money** esp. *US colloq.* banknotes. **fold-out** an oversize page in a book etc. to be unfolded by the reader. □□ **foldable** *adj.* [OE *falden, fealden* f. Gmc]

fold[2] /fəʊld/ *n. & v.* —*n.* **1** = SHEEPFOLD. **2** a body of believers or members of a Church. —*v.tr.* enclose (sheep) in a fold. [OE *fald*]

-fold /fəʊld/ *suffix* forming adjectives and adverbs from cardinal numbers, meaning: **1** in an amount multiplied by (*repaid tenfold*). **2** consisting of so many parts (*threefold blessing*). [OE *-fald, -feald*, rel. to FOLD[1]: orig. sense 'folded in so many layers']

foldaway /ˈfəʊldəˌweɪ/ *adj.* adapted or designed to be folded away.

folder /ˈfəʊldə(r)/ *n.* **1** a folding cover or holder for loose papers. **2** a folded leaflet.

folderol var. of FALDERAL.

foliaceous /ˌfəʊlɪˈeɪʃəs/ *adj.* **1** of or like leaves. **2** having organs like leaves. **3** laminated. [L *foliaceus* leafy f. *folium* leaf]

foliage /ˈfəʊlɪɪdʒ/ *n.* **1** leaves, leafage. **2** a design in art resembling leaves. □**foliage leaf** a leaf excluding petals and other modified leaves. [ME f. F *feuillage* f. *feuille* leaf f. OF *foille*: see FOIL²]

foliar /ˈfəʊlɪə(r)/ *adj.* of or relating to leaves. □**foliar feed** feed supplied to leaves of plants. [mod.L *foliaris* f. L *folium* leaf]

foliate *adj.* & *v.* —*adj.* /ˈfəʊlɪət/ 1 leaflike. 2 having leaves. 3 (in *comb.*) having a specified number of leaflets (*trifoliate*). —*v.* /ˈfəʊlɪˌeɪt/ 1 *intr.* split into laminae. 2 *tr.* decorate (an arch or door-head) with foils. 3 *tr.* number leaves (not pages) of (a volume) consecutively. □□**foliation** /-ˈeɪʃ(ə)n/ *n.* [L *foliatus* leaved f. *folium* leaf]

foliole /ˈfəʊlɪˌəʊl/ *n.* a division of a compound leaf; a leaflet. [F f. LL *foliolum* dimin. of L *folium* leaf]

folic acid /ˈfəʊlɪk/ *n.* a vitamin of the B complex, found in leafy green vegetables, liver, and kidney, a deficiency of which causes pernicious anaemia. Also called FOLACIN or PTEROYLGLUTAMIC ACID. [L *folium* leaf (because found esp. in green leaves) + -IC]

folio /ˈfəʊlɪəʊ/ *n.* & *adj.* —*n.* (*pl.* -os) 1 a leaf of paper etc., esp. one numbered only on the front. 2 a leaf-number of a book. 3 a sheet of paper folded once making two leaves of a book. 4 a book made of such sheets. —*adj.* (of a book) made of folios, of the largest size. □**in folio** made of folios. [L, ablat. of *folium* leaf, = *on leaf* (as specified)]

folk /fəʊk/ *n.* (*pl.* **folk** or **folks**) 1 (treated as *pl.*) people in general or of a specified class (*few folk about*; *townsfolk*). 2 (in *pl.*) (usu. **folks**) one's parents or relatives. 3 (treated as *sing.*) a people. 4 (treated as *sing.*) *colloq.* traditional music. 5 (*attrib.*) of popular origin; traditional (*folk art*). □**folk-dance 1** a dance of popular origin. 2 the music for such a dance. **folk etymology** a popular modifying of the form of a word or phrase to make it seem to be derived from a more familiar word (e.g. *forlorn hope*). **folk memory** recollection of the past persisting among a people. **folk-singer** a singer of folk-songs. **folk-song** a song of popular or traditional origin or style. **folk-tale** a popular or traditional story. **folk-ways** the traditional behaviour of a people. [OE *folc* f. Gmc]

folkish /ˈfəʊkɪʃ/ *adj.* of the common people; traditional, unsophisticated.

folklore /ˈfəʊklɔː(r)/ *n.* the traditional beliefs and stories of a people; the study of these. □□**folkloric** *adj.* **folklorist** *n.* **folkloristic** /-ˈrɪstɪk/ *adj.*

folksy /ˈfəʊksɪ/ *adj.* (**folksier, folksiest**) 1 friendly, sociable, informal. 2 a having the characteristics of folk art, culture, etc. b ostensibly or artificially folkish. □□**folksiness** *n.*

folkweave /ˈfəʊkwiːv/ *n.* a rough loosely woven fabric.

folky /ˈfəʊkɪ/ *adj.* (**folkier, folkiest**) 1 = FOLKSY 2. 2 = FOLKISH. □□**folkiness** *n.*

follicle /ˈfɒlɪk(ə)l/ *n.* 1 a small sac or vesicle. 2 a small sac-shaped secretory gland or cavity. 3 *Bot.* a single-carpelled dry fruit opening on one side only to release its seeds. □□**follicular** /fɒˈlɪkjʊlə(r)/ *adj.* **folliculate** /fɒˈlɪkjʊlət/ *adj.* **folliculated** /fɒˈlɪkjʊˌleɪtɪd/ *adj.* [L *folliculus* dimin. of *follis* bellows]

follow /ˈfɒləʊ/ *v.* 1 *tr.* or (foll. by *after*) *intr.* go or come after (a person or thing proceeding ahead). 2 *tr.* go along (a route, path, etc.). 3 *tr.* & *intr.* come after in order or time (*Nero followed Claudius*; *dessert followed*; *my reasons are as follows*). 4 *tr.* take as a guide or leader. 5 *tr.* conform to (*follow your example*). 6 *tr.* practise (a trade or profession). 7 *tr.* undertake (a course of study etc.). 8 *tr.* understand the meaning or tendency of (a speaker or argument). 9 *tr.* maintain awareness of the current state or progress of (events etc. in a particular sphere). 10 *tr.* (foll. by *with*) provide with a sequel or successor. 11 *intr.* happen after something else; ensue. 12 *intr.* a be necessarily true as a result of something else. b (foll. by *from*) be a result of. 13 *tr.* strive after; aim at; pursue (*followed fame and fortune*).

□**follow-my-leader** a game in which players must do as the leader does. **follow one's nose** trust to instinct. **follow on 1** continue. 2 (of a cricket team) have to bat again immediately after the first innings. **follow-on** *n.* an instance of this. **follow out** carry out; adhere precisely to (instructions etc.). **follow suit 1** *Cards* play a card of the suit led. 2 conform to another person's actions. **follow through 1** continue (an action etc.) to its conclusion. 2 *Sport* continue the movement of a stroke after the ball has been struck. **follow-through** *n.* the action of following through. **follow up** (foll. by *with*) 1 pursue, develop, supplement. 2 make further investigation of. **follow-up** *n.* a subsequent or continued action, measure, experience, etc. [OE *folgian* f. Gmc]

follower /ˈfɒləʊə(r)/ *n.* 1 an adherent or devotee. 2 a person or thing that follows.

following /ˈfɒləʊɪŋ/ *prep.*, *n.*, & *adj.* —*prep.* coming after in time; as a sequel to. —*n.* a body of adherents or devotees. —*adj.* that follows or comes after.

folly /ˈfɒlɪ/ *n.* (*pl.* -ies) 1 foolishness; lack of good sense. 2 a foolish act, behaviour, idea, etc. 3 an ornamental building, usu. a tower or mock Gothic ruin. 4 (in *pl.*) *Theatr.* a a revue with glamorous female performers, esp. scantily-clad. b the performers. [ME f. OF *folie* f. *fol* mad, FOOL¹]

foment /fəˈment, fəʊ-/ *v.tr.* 1 instigate or stir up (trouble, sedition, etc.). 2 a bathe with warm or medicated liquid. b apply warmth to. □□**fomenter** *n.* [ME f. F *fomenter* f. LL *fomentare* f. L *fomentum* poultice, lotion f. *fovēre* heat, cherish]

fomentation /ˌfəʊmenˈteɪʃ(ə)n/ *n.* 1 the act or an instance of fomenting. 2 materials prepared for application to a wound etc. [ME f. OF or LL *fomentatio* (as FOMENT)]

fond /fɒnd/ *adj.* 1 (foll. by *of*) having affection or a liking for. 2 affectionate, loving, doting. 3 (of beliefs etc.) foolishly optimistic or credulous; naïve. □□**fondly** *adv.* **fondness** *n.* [ME f. obs. *fon* fool, be foolish]

fondant /ˈfɒnd(ə)nt/ *n.* a soft sweet of flavoured sugar. [F, pres. part. of *fondre* melt f. L *fundere* pour]

fondle /ˈfɒnd(ə)l/ *v.tr.* touch or stroke lovingly; caress. □□**fondler** *n.* [back-form. f. *fondling* fondled person (as FOND, -LING¹)]

fondue /ˈfɒndjuː, -duː/ *n.* a dish of flavoured melted cheese. [F, fem. past part. of *fondre* melt f. L *fundere* pour]

font¹ /fɒnt/ *n.* 1 a receptacle in a church for baptismal water. 2 the reservoir for oil in a lamp. □□**fontal** *adj.* (in sense 1). [OE *font, fant* f. OIr. *fant, font* f. L *fons fontis* fountain, baptismal water]

font² var. of FOUNT².

fontanel *US* var. of FONTANELLE.

fontanelle /ˌfɒntəˈnel/ *n.* (*US* **fontanel**) a membranous space in an infant's skull at the angles of the parietal bones. [F *fontanelle* f. mod.L *fontanella* f. OF *fontenelle* dimin. of *fontaine* fountain]

food /fuːd/ *n.* 1 a nutritious substance, esp. solid in form, that can be taken into an animal or a plant to maintain life and growth. 2 ideas as a resource for or stimulus to mental work (*food for thought*). □**food additive** a substance added to food to enhance its colour, flavour, or presentation, or for any other non-nutritional purpose. **food-chain** *Ecol.* a series of organisms each dependent on the next for food. **food poisoning** illness due to bacteria or other toxins in food. **food processor** a machine for chopping and mixing food materials. **food value** the relative nourishing power of a food. [OE *fōda* f. Gmc: cf. FEED]

foodie /ˈfuːdɪ/ *n.* (also **foody**) (*pl.* -ies) *colloq.* a person who is particular about food; a gourmet.

foodstuff /ˈfuːdstʌf/ *n.* any substance suitable as food.

fool¹ /fuːl/ *n.*, *v.*, & *adj.* —*n.* 1 a person who acts unwisely or imprudently; a stupid person. 2 *hist.* a jester; a clown. 3 a dupe. —*v.* 1 *tr.* deceive so as to cause to appear foolish. **2** *tr.* (foll. by *into* + verbal noun, or *out of*) trick; cause to do something foolish. **3** *tr.* play tricks on; dupe. **4** *intr.* act in a joking, frivolous, or teasing way. **5** *intr.* (foll. by *about*, *around*) behave in a playful or silly way. —*adj. US colloq.* foolish, silly. □**act** (or **play**) **the fool** behave in a silly way. **fool's errand** a fruitless venture. **fool's gold** iron pyrites. **fool's paradise** happiness founded on an illusion. **fool's parsley** a species of hemlock resembling parsley. **make a fool of** make (a person or oneself) look foolish; trick or deceive. **no** (or **nobody's**) **fool** a shrewd or prudent person. [ME f. OF *fol* f. L *follis* bellows, empty-headed person]

fool² /fuːl/ *n.* a dessert of usu. stewed fruit crushed and mixed with cream, custard, etc. [16th c.: perh. f. FOOL¹]

foolery /ˈfuːlərɪ/ *n.* (*pl.* **-ies**) **1** foolish behaviour. **2** a foolish act.

foolhardy /ˈfuːlˌhɑːdɪ/ *adj.* (**foolhardier**, **foolhardiest**) rashly or foolishly bold; reckless. □□**foolhardily** *adv.* **foolhardiness** *n.* [ME f. OF *folhardi* f. *fol* foolish + *hardi* bold]

foolish /ˈfuːlɪʃ/ *adj.* (of a person, action, etc.) lacking good sense or judgement; unwise. □□**foolishly** *adv.* **foolishness** *n.*

foolproof /ˈfuːlpruːf/ *adj.* (of a procedure, mechanism, etc.) so straightforward or simple as to be incapable of misuse or mistake.

foolscap /ˈfuːlskæp/ *n. Brit.* a size of paper, about 330 × 200 (or 400) mm. [named from the former watermark representing a fool's cap]

foot /fʊt/ *n. & v.* —*n.* (*pl.* **feet** /fiːt/) **1 a** the lower extremity of the leg below the ankle. **b** the part of a sock etc. covering the foot. **2 a** the lower or lowest part of anything, e.g. a mountain, a page, stairs, etc. **b** the lower end of a table. **c** the end of a bed where the user's feet normally rest. **3** the base, often projecting, of anything extending vertically. **4** a step, pace, or tread; a manner of walking (*fleet of foot*). **5** (*pl.* **feet** or **foot**) a unit of linear measure equal to 12 inches (30.48 cm). **6** *Prosody* **a** a group of syllables (one usu. stressed) constituting a metrical unit. **b** a similar unit of speech etc. **7** *Brit. hist.* infantry (*a regiment of foot*). **8** *Zool.* the locomotive or adhesive organ of invertebrates. **9** *Bot.* the part by which a petal is attached. **10** a device on a sewing-machine for holding the material steady as it is sewn. **11** (*pl.* **foots**) **a** dregs; oil refuse. **b** coarse sugar. —*v.tr.* **1** (usu. as **foot it**) **a** traverse (esp. a long distance) by foot. **b** dance. **2** pay (a bill, esp. one considered large). □**at a person's feet** as a person's disciple or subject. **feet of clay** a fundamental weakness in a person otherwise revered. **foot-and-mouth disease** a contagious viral disease of cattle etc. **foot-fault** (in lawn tennis) incorrect placement of the feet while serving. **foot-pound** the amount of energy required to raise 1 lb. a distance of 1 foot. **foot-pound-second system** a system of measurement with these as basic units. **foot-rot** a bacterial disease of the feet in sheep and cattle. **foot-rule** a ruler 1 foot long. **foot-soldier** a soldier who fights on foot. **get one's feet wet** begin to participate. **have one's** (or **both**) **feet on the ground** be practical. **have a foot in the door** have a prospect of success. **have one foot in the grave** be near death or very old. **my foot!** *int.* expressing strong contradiction. **not put a foot wrong** make no mistakes. **off one's feet** so as to be unable to stand, or in a state compared with this (*was rushed off my feet*). **on foot** walking, not riding etc. **put one's best foot forward** make every effort; proceed with determination. **put one's feet up** *colloq.* take a rest. **put one's foot down** *colloq.* **1** be firmly insistent or repressive. **2** accelerate a motor vehicle. **put one's foot in it** *colloq.* commit a blunder or indiscretion. **set foot on** (or **in**) enter; go into. **set on foot** put (an action, process, etc.) in motion. **under one's feet** in the way. **under foot** on the

ground. □□**footed** *adj.* (also in *comb.*). **footless** *adj.* [OE *fōt* f. Gmc]

footage /ˈfʊtɪdʒ/ *n.* **1** length or distance in feet. **2** an amount of film made for showing, broadcasting, etc.

football /ˈfʊtbɔːl/ *n. & v.* —*n.* **1** any of several outdoor games between two teams played with a ball on a pitch with goals at each end, esp. = *Association Football*. **2** a large inflated ball of a kind used in these. **3** a topical issue or problem that is the subject of continued argument or controversy. —*v.intr.* play football. □**football pool** (or **pools**) a form of gambling on the results of football matches, the winners receiving sums accumulated from entry money. □□**footballer** *n.*

footboard /ˈfʊtbɔːd/ *n.* **1** a board to support the feet or a foot. **2** an upright board at the foot of a bed.

footbrake /ˈfʊtbreɪk/ *n.* a brake operated by the foot in a motor vehicle.

footbridge /ˈfʊtbrɪdʒ/ *n.* a bridge for use by pedestrians.

footer¹ /ˈfʊtə(r)/ *n.* (in *comb.*) a person or thing of so many feet in length or height (*six-footer*).

footer² /ˈfʊtə(r)/ *n. Brit. colloq.* = FOOTBALL 1.

footfall /ˈfʊtfɔːl/ *n.* the sound of a footstep.

foothill /ˈfʊthɪl/ *n.* (often in *pl.*) any of the low hills around the base of a mountain.

foothold /ˈfʊthəʊld/ *n.* **1** a place, esp. in climbing, where a foot can be supported securely. **2** a secure initial position or advantage.

footing /ˈfʊtɪŋ/ *n.* **1** a foothold; a secure position (*lost his footing*). **2** the basis on which an enterprise is established or operates; the position or status of a person in relation to others (*on an equal footing*). **3** the foundations of a wall, usu. with a course of brickwork wider than the base of the wall.

footle /ˈfuːt(ə)l/ *v.intr.* (usu. foll. by *about*) *colloq.* behave foolishly or trivially. [19th c.: perh. f. dial. *footer* idle]

footlights /ˈfʊtlaɪts/ *n.pl.* a row of lights along the front of a stage at the level of the actors' feet.

footling /ˈfuːtlɪŋ/ *adj. colloq.* trivial, silly.

footloose /ˈfʊtluːs/ *adj.* free to go where or act as one pleases.

footman /ˈfʊtmən/ *n.* (*pl.* **-men**) **1** a liveried servant attending at the door, at table, or on a carriage. **2** *hist.* an infantryman.

footmark /ˈfʊtmɑːk/ *n.* a footprint.

footnote /ˈfʊtnəʊt/ *n. & v.* —*n.* a note printed at the foot of a page. —*v.tr.* supply with a footnote or footnotes.

footpad /ˈfʊtpæd/ *n. hist.* an unmounted highwayman.

footpath /ˈfʊtpɑːθ/ *n.* a path for pedestrians; a pavement.

footplate /ˈfʊtpleɪt/ *n. esp. Brit.* the platform in the cab of a locomotive for the crew.

footprint /ˈfʊtprɪnt/ *n.* **1** the impression left by a foot or shoe. **2** *Computing* the area of desk space etc. occupied by a microcomputer or other piece of hardware.

footrest /ˈfʊtrest/ *n.* a support for the feet or a foot.

footsie /ˈfʊtsɪ/ *n. colloq.* amorous play with the feet. [joc. dimin. of FOOT]

footslog /ˈfʊtslɒg/ *v. & n.* —*v.intr.* (**-slogged**, **-slogging**) walk or march, esp. laboriously for a long distance. —*n.* a laborious walk or march. □□ **footslogger** *n.*

footsore /ˈfʊtsɔː(r)/ *adj.* having sore feet, esp. from walking.

footstalk /ˈfʊtstɔːk/ *n.* **1** *Bot.* a stalk of a leaf or peduncle of a flower. **2** *Zool.* an attachment of a barnacle etc.

footstep /ˈfʊtstep/ *n.* **1** a step taken in walking. **2** the sound of this. □**follow** (or **tread**) **in a person's footsteps** do as another person did before.

footstool /ˈfʊtstuːl/ *n.* a stool for resting the feet on when sitting.

footway /ˈfʊtweɪ/ *n.* a path or way for pedestrians.

footwear /'fʊtweə(r)/ n. shoes, socks, etc.

footwork /'fʊtwɜːk/ n. the use of the feet, esp. skilfully, in sports, dancing, etc.

fop /fɒp/ n. an affectedly elegant or fashionable man; a dandy. □□**foppery** n. **foppish** adj. **foppishly** adv. **foppishness** n. [17th c.: perh. f. earlier fop fool]

for /fə(r), fɔː(r)/ prep. & conj. —prep. **1** in the interest or to the benefit of; intended to go to (these flowers are for you; wish to see it for myself; did it all for my country; silly for you to go). **2** in defence, support, or favour of (fight for one's rights). **3** suitable or appropriate to (a dance for beginners; not for me to say). **4** in respect of or with reference to; regarding; so far as concerns (usual for ties to be worn; don't care for him at all; ready for bed; MP for Lincoln). **5** representing or in place of (here for my uncle). **6** in exchange against (swopped it for a bigger one). **7** **a** as the price of (give me £5 for it). **b** at the price of (bought it for £5). **c** to the amount of (a bill for £100; all out for 45). **8** as the penalty of (fined them heavily for it). **9** in requital of (that's for upsetting my sister). **10** as a reward for (here's £5 for your trouble). **11** **a** with a view to; in the hope or quest of; in order to get (go for a walk; run for a doctor; did it for the money). **b** on account of (could not speak for laughing). **12** corresponding to (word for word). **13** to reach; in the direction of; towards (left for Rome; ran for the end of the road). **14** conducive or conducively to; in order to achieve (take the pills for a sound night's sleep). **15** so as to start promptly at (the meeting is at seven-thirty for eight). **16** through or over (a distance or period); during (walked for miles; sang for two hours). **17** in the character of; as being (for the last time; know it for a lie; I for one refuse). **18** because of; on account of (could not see for tears). **19** in spite of; notwithstanding (for all we know; for all your fine words). **20** considering or making due allowance in respect of (good for a beginner). **21** in order to be (gone for a soldier). —conj. because, since, seeing that. □**be for it** Brit. colloq. be in imminent danger of punishment or other trouble. **for ever** see EVER; (cf. FOREVER). **o** (or **oh**) **for** I wish I had. [OE, prob. a reduction of Gmc fora (unrecorded) BEFORE (of place and time)]

for- /fɔː, fə/ prefix forming verbs and their derivatives meaning: **1** away, off, apart (forget; forgive). **2** prohibition (forbid). **3** abstention or neglect (forgo; forsake). **4** excess or intensity (forlorn). [OE for-, fær-]

f.o.r. abbr. free on rail.

forage /'fɒrɪdʒ/ n. & v. —n. **1** food for horses and cattle. **2** the act or an instance of searching for food. —v. **1** intr. go searching; rummage (esp. for food). **2** tr. collect food from; ravage. **3** tr. **a** get by foraging. **b** supply with food. □**forage cap** an infantry undress cap. □□**forager** n. [ME f. OF fourrage, fourrager, rel. to FODDER]

foramen /fɒ'reɪmen/ n. (pl. **foramina** /-'ræmɪnə/) Anat. an opening, hole, or passage, esp. in a bone. □□**foraminate** /-'ræmɪnət/ adj. [L foramen -minis f. forare bore a hole]

foraminifer /,fɒrə'mɪnɪfə(r)/ n. (also **foraminiferan** /-'nɪfərən/) any protozoan of the order Foraminifera, having a perforated shell through which amoeba-like pseudopodia emerge. □□ **foraminiferous** /-'nɪfərəs/ adj.

foraminiferan var. of FORAMINIFER.

forasmuch as /,fɒrəz'mʌtʃ/ conj. archaic because, since. [= for as much]

foray /'fɒreɪ/ n. & v. —n. a sudden attack; a raid or incursion. —v.intr. make or go on a foray. [ME, prob. earlier as verb: back-form. f. forayer f. OF forrier forager, rel. to FODDER]

forbade (also **forbad**) past of FORBID.

forbear[1] /fɔː'beə(r)/ v.intr. & tr. (past **forbore** /-'bɔː(r)/; past part. **forborne** /-'bɔːn/) (often foll. by from, or to + infin.) literary abstain or desist (from) (could not forbear (from) speaking out; forbore to mention it). [OE forberan (as FOR-, BEAR[1])]

forbear[2] var. of FOREBEAR.

forbearance /fɔː'beərəns/ n. patient self-control; tolerance.

forbid /fə'bɪd/ v.tr. (**forbidding**; past **forbade** /-'bæd, -'beɪd/ or **forbad** /-'bæd/; past part. **forbidden** /-'bɪd(ə)n/) **1** (foll. by to + infin.) order not (I forbid you to go). **2** refuse to allow (a thing, or a person to have a thing) (I forbid it; was forbidden any wine). **3** refuse a person entry to (the gardens are forbidden to children). □**forbidden degrees** see DEGREE. **forbidden fruit** something desired or enjoyed all the more because not allowed. **God forbid!** may it not happen! [OE forbēodan (as FOR-, BID)]

forbidding /fə'bɪdɪŋ/ adj. uninviting, repellent, stern. □□**forbiddingly** adv.

forbore past of FORBEAR[1].

forborne past part. of FORBEAR[1].

forbye /fɔː'baɪ/ prep. & adv. archaic or Sc. —prep. besides. —adv. in addition.

force[1] /fɔːs/ n. & v. —n. **1** power; exerted strength or impetus; intense effort. **2** coercion or compulsion, esp. with the use or threat of violence. **3 a** military strength. **b** (in pl.) troops; fighting resources. **c** an organized body of people, esp. soldiers, police, or workers. **4** binding power; validity. **5** effect; precise significance (the force of their words). **6 a** mental or moral strength; influence, efficacy (force of habit). **b** vividness of effect (described with much force). **7** Physics **a** an influence tending to cause the motion of a body. **b** the intensity of this equal to the mass of the body and its acceleration. **8** a person or thing regarded as exerting influence (is a force for good). —v. **1** tr. constrain (a person) by force or against his or her will. **2** tr. make a way through or into by force; break open by force. **3** tr. (usu. with prep. or adv.) drive or propel violently or against resistance (forced it into the hole; the wind forced them back). **4** tr. (foll. by on, upon) impose or press (on a person) (forced their views on us). **5** tr. **a** cause or produce by effort (forced a smile). **b** attain by strength or effort (forced an entry; must force a decision). **6** tr. strain or increase to the utmost; overstrain. **7** tr. artificially hasten the development or maturity of (a plant). **8** tr. seek or demand quick results from; accelerate the process of (force the pace). **9** intr. Cards make a play that compels another particular play. □**by force of** by means of. **force the bidding** (at an auction) make bids to raise the price rapidly. **forced labour** compulsory labour, esp. under harsh conditions. **forced landing** the unavoidable landing of an aircraft in an emergency. **forced march** a long and vigorous march esp. by troops. **force-feed** force (esp. a prisoner) to take food. **force field** (in science fiction) an invisible barrier of force. **force a person's hand** make a person act prematurely or unwillingly. **force the issue** render an immediate decision necessary. **force-land** land an aircraft in an emergency. **force-pump** a pump that forces water under pressure. **in force 1** valid, effective. **2** in great strength or numbers. **join forces** combine efforts. □□**forceable** adj. **forceably** adv. **forcer** n. [ME f. OF force, forcer ult. f. L fortis strong]

force[2] /fɔːs/ n. N.Engl. a waterfall. [ON fors]

forceful /'fɔːsfʊl/ adj. **1** vigorous, powerful. **2** (of speech) compelling, impressive. □□**forcefully** adv. **forcefulness** n.

force majeure /,fɔːs mæ'ʒɜː(r)/ n. **1** irresistible compulsion or coercion. **2** an unforeseeable course of events excusing a person from the fulfilment of a contract. [F, = superior strength]

forcemeat /'fɔːsmiːt/ n. meat etc. chopped and seasoned for use as a stuffing or a garnish. [obs. force, farce stuff f. OF farsir: see FARCE]

forceps /'fɔːseps/ n. (pl. same) **1** surgical pincers, used for grasping and holding. **2** Bot. & Zool. an organ or structure resembling forceps. □□**forcipate** /-sɪpət/ adj. [L forceps forcipis]

forcible /'fɔːsɪb(ə)l/ adj. done by or involving force;

forceful. □□ **forcibleness** *n.* **forcibly** *adv.* [ME f. AF & OF (as FORCE¹)]

ford /fɔːd/ *n. & v.* —*n.* a shallow place where a river or stream may be crossed by wading or in a vehicle. —*v.tr.* cross (water) at a ford. □□ **fordable** *adj.* **fordless** *adj.* [OE f. WG]

fore /fɔː(r)/ *adj., n., int., & prep.* situated in front. —*n.* the front part, esp. of a ship; the bow. —*int. Golf* a warning to a person in the path of a ball. —*prep. archaic* (in oaths) in the presence of (*fore God*). □ **come to the fore** take a leading part. **fore and aft** at bow and stern; all over the ship. **fore-and-aft** *adj.* (of a sail or rigging) set lengthwise, not on the yards. **to the fore** in front; conspicuous. [OE f. Gmc.: (adj. & n.) ME f. compounds with FORE-]

fore- /fɔː(r)/ *prefix* forming: **1** verbs meaning: **a** in front (*foreshorten*). **b** beforehand; in advance (*foreordain; forewarn*). **2** nouns meaning: **a** situated in front of (*forecourt*). **b** the front part of (*forehead*). **c** of or near the bow of a ship (*forecastle*). **d** preceding (*forerunner*).

forearm¹ /ˈfɔːrɑːm/ *n.* **1** the part of the arm from the elbow to the wrist or the fingertips. **2** the corresponding part in a foreleg or wing.

forearm² /fɔːrˈɑːm/ *v.tr.* prepare or arm beforehand.

forebear /ˈfɔːbeə(r)/ *n.* (also **forbear**) (usu. in *pl.*) an ancestor. [FORE + obs. *bear, beer* (as BE, -ER¹)]

forebode /fɔːˈbəʊd/ *v.tr.* **1** betoken; be an advance warning of (an evil or unwelcome event). **2** have a presentiment of (usu. evil).

foreboding /fɔːˈbəʊdɪŋ/ *n.* an expectation of trouble or evil; a presage or omen. □□ **forebodingly** *adv.*

forecast /ˈfɔːkɑːst/ *v. & n.* —*v.tr.* (*past* and *past part.* **-cast** or **-casted**) predict; estimate or calculate beforehand. —*n.* a calculation or estimate of something future, esp. coming weather. □□ **forecaster** *n.*

forecastle /ˈfəʊks(ə)l/ *n.* (also **fo'c's'le**) *Naut.* **1** the forward part of a ship where the crew has quarters. **2** *hist.* a short raised deck at the bow.

foreclose /fɔːˈkləʊz/ *v.tr.* **1** (also *absol.*; foll. by *on*) stop (a mortgage) from being redeemable or (a mortgager) from redeeming, esp. as a result of defaults in payment. **2** exclude, prevent. **3** shut out; bar. □□ **foreclosure** *n.* [ME f. OF *forclos* past part. of *forclore* f. *for-* out f. L *foras* + CLOSE²]

forecourt /ˈfɔːkɔːt/ *n.* **1** an enclosed space in front of a building. **2** the part of a filling-station where petrol is supplied. **3** (in lawn tennis) the part of a tennis-court between the service line and the net.

foredoom /fɔːˈduːm/ *v.tr.* (often foll. by *to*) doom or condemn beforehand.

fore-edge /ˈfɔːredʒ/ *n.* (also **foredge**) the front or outer edge (esp. of the pages of a book).

forefather /ˈfɔːfɑːðə(r)/ *n.* (usu. in *pl.*) **1** an ancestor. **2** a member of a past generation of a family or people.

forefinger /ˈfɔːfɪŋɡə(r)/ *n.* the finger next to the thumb.

forefoot /ˈfɔːfʊt/ *n.* (*pl.* **-feet**) **1** either of the front feet of a four-footed animal. **2** *Naut.* the foremost section of a ship's keel.

forefront /ˈfɔːfrʌnt/ *n.* **1** the foremost part. **2** the leading position.

foregather var. of FORGATHER.

forego¹ /fɔːˈɡəʊ/ *v.tr. & intr.* (**-goes**; *past* **-went** /-ˈwent/; *past part.* **-gone** /-ˈɡɒn/) precede in place or time. □□ **foregoer** *n.* [OE *foregān*]

forego² var. of FORGO.

foregoing /fɔːˈɡəʊɪŋ, ˈfɔː-/ *adj.* preceding; previously mentioned.

foregone /fɔːˈɡɒn/ *past part.* of FOREGO¹. —*attrib.adj.* /ˈfɔːɡɒn/ previous, preceding, completed. □ **foregone conclusion** an easily foreseen or predictable result.

foreground /ˈfɔːɡraʊnd/ *n.* **1** the part of a view, esp. in a picture, that is nearest the observer. **2** the most conspicuous position. [Du. *voorgrond* (as FORE-, GROUND¹)]

forehand /ˈfɔːhænd/ *n.* **1** *Tennis* etc. **a** a stroke played with the palm of the hand facing the opponent. **b** (*attrib.*) (also **forehanded**) of or made with a forehand. **2** the part of a horse in front of the seated rider.

forehead /ˈfɔːrɪd, ˈfɔːhed/ *n.* the part of the face above the eyebrows. [OE *forhēafod* (as FORE-, HEAD)]

forehock /ˈfɔːhɒk/ *n.* a foreleg cut of pork or bacon.

foreign /ˈfɒrɪn, ˈfɒrən/ *adj.* **1** of or from or situated in or characteristic of a country or a language other than one's own. **2** dealing with other countries (*foreign service*). **3** of another district, society, etc. **4** (often foll. by *to*) unfamiliar, strange, uncharacteristic (*his behaviour is foreign to me*). **5** coming from outside (*a foreign body lodged in my eye*). □ **foreign aid** money, food, etc. given or lent by one country to another. **foreign exchange 1** the currency of other countries. **2** dealings in these. **foreign legion** a body of foreign volunteers in an army (esp. the French army). **foreign minister** (or **secretary**) a government minister in charge of his or her country's relations with other countries. **foreign office** a government department dealing with other countries. □□ **foreignness** *n.* [ME f. OF *forein, forain* ult. f. L *foras, -is* outside: for *-g-* cf. *sovereign*]

foreigner /ˈfɒrɪnə(r), ˈfɒrənə(r)/ *n.* **1** a person born in or coming from a foreign country or place. **2** *dial.* a non-native of a place. **3 a** a foreign ship. **b** an imported animal or article.

forejudge /fɔːˈdʒʌdʒ/ *v.tr.* judge or determine before knowing the evidence.

foreknow /fɔːˈnəʊ/ *v.tr.* (*past* **-knew** /-ˈnjuː/; *past part.* **-known** /-ˈnəʊn/) know beforehand; have prescience of. □□ **foreknowledge** /fɔːˈnɒlɪdʒ/ *n.*

forelady /ˈfɔːˌleɪdɪ/ *n.* (*pl.* **-ies**) *US* = FOREWOMAN.

foreland /ˈfɔːlænd/ *n.* **1** a cape or promontory. **2** a piece of land in front of something.

foreleg /ˈfɔːleɡ/ *n.* each of the front legs of a quadruped.

forelimb /ˈfɔːlɪm/ *n.* any of the front limbs of an animal.

forelock /ˈfɔːlɒk/ *n.* a lock of hair growing just above the forehead. □ **take time by the forelock** seize an opportunity.

foreman /ˈfɔːmən/ *n.* (*pl.* **-men**) **1** a worker with supervisory responsibilities. **2** the member of a jury who presides over its deliberations and speaks on its behalf.

foremast /ˈfɔːmɑːst, -məst/ *n.* the forward (lower) mast of a ship.

foremost /ˈfɔːməʊst/ *adj. & adv.* —*adj.* **1** the chief or most notable. **2** the most advanced in position; the front. —*adv.* before anything else in position; in the first place (*first and foremost*). [earlier *formost, formest*, superl. of OE *forma* first, assim. to FORE, MOST]

forename /ˈfɔːneɪm/ *n.* a first or Christian name.

forenoon /ˈfɔːnuːn/ *n. Naut.* or *Law* or *archaic* the part of the day before noon.

forensic /fəˈrensɪk/ *adj.* of or used in connection with courts of law (*forensic science*). □ **forensic medicine** the application of medical knowledge to legal problems. □□ **forensically** *adv.* [L *forensis* f. FORUM]

foreordain /ˌfɔːrɔːˈdeɪn/ *v.tr.* predestinate; ordain beforehand. □□ **foreordination** /-dɪˈneɪʃ(ə)n/ *n.*

forepaw /ˈfɔːpɔː/ *n.* either of the front paws of a quadruped.

forepeak /ˈfɔːpiːk/ *n. Naut.* the end of the forehold in the angle of the bows.

foreplay /ˈfɔːpleɪ/ *n.* stimulation preceding sexual intercourse.

forerun /fɔːˈrʌn/ *v.tr.* (**-running**; *past* **-ran** /-ˈræn/; *past part.* **-run**) **1** go before. **2** indicate the coming of; foreshadow.

forerunner /ˈfɔːˌrʌnə(r)/ *n.* **1** a predecessor. **2** an advance messenger.

foresail /ˈfɔːseɪl, -s(ə)l/ *n. Naut.* the principal sail on a foremast (the lowest square sail, or the fore-and-aft bent on the mast, or the triangular before the mast).

foresee /fɔː'siː/ v.tr. (past **-saw** /-'sɔː/; past part. **-seen** /-'siːn/) (often foll. by that + clause) see or be aware of beforehand. □□ **foreseeable** adj. **foreseeability** /-'bɪlɪtɪ/ n. **foreseer** /-'siːə(r)/ n. [OE foreseōn (as FORE- + SEE¹)]

foreshadow /fɔː'ʃædəʊ/ v.tr. be a warning or indication of (a future event).

foresheets /'fɔːʃiːts/ n.pl. Naut. the inner part of the bows of a boat with gratings for the bowman to stand on.

foreshore /'fɔːʃɔː(r)/ n. the part of the shore between high- and low-water marks, or between the water and cultivated or developed land.

foreshorten /fɔː'ʃɔːt(ə)n/ v.tr. show or portray (an object) with the apparent shortening due to visual perspective.

foreshow /fɔː'ʃəʊ/ v.tr. (past part. **-shown** /-ʃəʊn/) **1** foretell. **2** foreshadow, portend, prefigure.

foresight /'fɔːsaɪt/ n. **1** regard or provision for the future. **2** the process of foreseeing. **3** the front sight of a gun. **4** Surveying a sight taken forwards. □□ **foresighted** /-'saɪtɪd/ adj. **foresightedly** /-'saɪtɪdlɪ/ adv. **foresightedness** /-'saɪtɪdnɪs/ n. [ME, prob. after ON forsjá, forsjó (as FORE-, SIGHT)]

foreskin /'fɔːskɪn/ n. the fold of skin covering the end of the penis. Also called PREPUCE.

forest /'fɒrɪst/ n. & v. —n. **1 a** (often attrib.) a large area covered chiefly with trees and undergrowth. **b** the trees growing in it. **c** a large number or dense mass of vertical objects (a forest of masts). **2** a district formerly a forest but now cultivated (Sherwood Forest). **3** hist. an area usu. owned by the sovereign and kept for hunting. —v.tr. **1** plant with trees. **2** convert into a forest. □**forest-tree** a large tree suitable for a forest. [ME f. OF f. LL forestis silva wood outside the walls of a park f. L foris outside]

forestall /fɔː'stɔːl/ v.tr. **1** act in advance of in order to prevent. **2** anticipate (the action of another, or an event). **3** anticipate the action of. **4** deal with beforehand. **5** hist. buy up (goods) in order to profit by an enhanced price. □□**forestaller** n. **forestalment** n. [ME in sense 5: cf. AL forestallare f. OE foresteall an ambush (as FORE-, STALL)]

forestay /'fɔːsteɪ/ n. Naut. a stay from the head of the foremast to the ship's deck to support the foremast.

forester /'fɒrɪstə(r)/ n. **1** a person in charge of a forest or skilled in forestry. **2** a person or animal living in a forest. **3** (**Forester**) a member of the Ancient Order of Foresters (a friendly society). [ME f. OF forestier (as FOREST)]

forestry /'fɒrɪstrɪ/ n. **1** the science or management of forests. **2** wooded country; forests.

foretaste n. & v. —n. /'fɔːteɪst/ partial enjoyment or suffering in advance; anticipation. —v.tr. /fɔː'teɪst/ taste beforehand; anticipate the experience of.

foretell /fɔː'tel/ v.tr. (past and past part. **-told** /-'təʊld/) **1** tell of (an event etc.) before it takes place; predict, prophesy. **2** presage; be a precursor of. □□**foreteller** n.

forethought /'fɔːθɔːt/ n. **1** care or provision for the future. **2** previous thinking or devising. **3** deliberate intention.

foretoken n. & v. —n. /'fɔːtəʊkən/ a sign of something to come. —v.tr. /fɔː'təʊkən/ portend; indicate beforehand. [OE foretācn (as FORE-, TOKEN)]

foretold past and past part. of FORETELL.

foretop /'fɔːtɒp/ n. Naut. a platform at the top of a foremast (see TOP¹ n. 9). □**foretop-gallant mast** the mast above the fore-topmast. **foretop-gallant-sail** the sail above the fore-topsail.

fore-topmast /fɔː'tɒpmɑːst/ n. Naut. the mast above the foremast.

fore-topsail /fɔː'tɒpseɪl, -s(ə)l/ n. Naut. the sail above the foresail.

forever /fə'revə(r)/ adv. continually, persistently (is forever complaining) (cf. for ever).

forevermore /fəˌrevə'mɔː(r)/ adv. esp. US an emphatic form of FOREVER or for ever (see EVER).

forewarn /fɔː'wɔːn/ v.tr. warn beforehand. □□ **forewarner** n.

forewent past of FOREGO¹, FOREGO².

forewoman /'fɔːˌwʊmən/ n. (pl. **-women**) **1** a female worker with supervisory responsibilities. **2** a woman who presides over a jury's deliberations and speaks on its behalf.

foreword /'fɔːwɜːd/ n. introductory remarks at the beginning of a book, often by a person other than the author. [FORE- + WORD after G Vorwort]

foreyard /'fɔːjɑːd/ n. Naut. the lowest yard on a foremast.

forfeit /'fɔːfɪt/ n., adj., & v. —n. **1** a penalty for a breach of contract or neglect; a fine. **2 a** a trivial fine for a breach of rules in clubs etc. or in games. **b** (in pl.) a game in which forfeits are exacted. **3** something surrendered as a penalty. **4** the process of forfeiting. **5** Law property or a right or privilege lost as a legal penalty. —adj. lost or surrendered as a penalty. —v.tr. (**forfeited, forfeiting**) lose the right to, be deprived of, or have to pay as a penalty. □□ **forfeitable** adj. **forfeiter** n. **forfeiture** n. [ME (= crime) f. OF forfet, forfait past part. of forfaire transgress (f. L foris outside) + faire f. L facere do]

forfend /fɔː'fend/ v.tr. **1** US protect by precautions. **2** archaic avert; keep off.

forgather /fɔː'gæðə(r)/ v.intr. (also **foregather**) assemble; meet together; associate. [16th-c. Sc. f. Du. vergaderen, assim. to FOR-, GATHER]

forgave past of FORGIVE.

forge¹ /fɔːdʒ/ v. & n. —v.tr. **1 a** make (money etc.) in fraudulent imitation. **b** write (a document or signature) in order to pass it off as written by another. **2** fabricate, invent. **3** shape (esp. metal) by heating in a fire and hammering. —n. **1 a** a blacksmith's workshop; a smithy. **2 a** a furnace or hearth for melting or refining metal. **b** a workshop containing this. □□ **forgeable** adj. **forger** n. [ME f. OF forge (n.), forger (v.) f. L fabricare FABRICATE]

forge² /fɔːdʒ/ v.intr. move forward gradually or steadily. □**forge ahead 1** take the lead in a race. **2** move forward or make progress rapidly. [18th c.: perh. an aberrant pronunc. of FORCE¹]

forgery /'fɔːdʒərɪ/ n. (pl. **-ies**) **1** the act or an instance of forging, counterfeiting, or falsifying a document etc. **2** a forged or spurious thing, esp. a document or signature.

forget /fə'get/ v. (**forgetting**; past **forgot** /-'gɒt/; past part. **forgotten** /-'gɒt(ə)n/ or esp. US **forgot**) **1** tr. & (often foll. by about) intr. lose the remembrance of; not remember (a person or thing). **2** tr. (foll. by clause or to + infin.) not remember; neglect (forgot to come; forgot how to do it). **3** tr. inadvertently omit to bring or mention or attend to. **4** tr. (also absol.) put out of mind; cease to think of (forgive and forget). □**forget-me-not** any plant of the genus Myosotis, esp. M. alpestris with small yellow-eyed bright blue flowers. **forget oneself 1** neglect one's own interests. **2** act unbecomingly or unworthily. □□ **forgettable** adj. **forgetter** n. [OE forgietan f. WG (as FOR-, GET)]

forgetful /fə'getfʊl/ adj. **1** apt to forget, absent-minded. **2** (often foll. by of) forgetting, neglectful. □□ **forgetfully** adv. **forgetfulness** n.

forgive /fə'gɪv/ v.tr. (also absol. or with double object) (past **forgave**; past part. **forgiven**) **1** cease to feel angry or resentful towards; pardon (an offender or offence) (forgive us our mistakes). **2** remit or let off (a debt or debtor). □□ **forgivable** adj. **forgivably** adv. **forgiver** n. [OE forgiefan (as FOR-, GIVE)]

forgiveness /fə'gɪvnɪs/ n. the act of forgiving; the state of being forgiven. [OE forgiefenes (as FORGIVE)]

forgiving /fɔː'gɪvɪŋ/ adj. inclined readily to forgive. □□ **forgivingly** adv.

forgo /fɔːˈgəʊ/ *v.tr.* (also **forego**) (**-goes**; *past* **-went** /-ˈwent/; *past part.* **-gone** /-ˈgɒn/) **1** abstain from; go without; relinquish. **2** omit or decline to take or use (a pleasure, advantage, etc.). [OE *forgān* (as FOR-, GO¹)]

forgot *past* of FORGET.

forgotten *past part.* of FORGET.

forint /ˈfɒrɪnt/ *n.* the chief monetary unit of Hungary. [Magyar f. It. *fiorino*: see FLORIN]

fork /fɔːk/ *n. & v.* —*n.* **1** an instrument with two or more prongs used in eating or cooking. **2** a similar much larger instrument used for digging, lifting, etc. **3** any pronged device or component (*tuning-fork*). **4** a forked support for a bicycle wheel. **5 a** a divergence of anything, e.g. a stick or road, or *US* a river, into two parts. **b** the place where this occurs. **c** either of the two parts (*take the left fork*). **6** a flash of forked lightning. **7** *Chess* a simultaneous attack on two pieces by one. —*v.* **1** *intr.* form a fork or branch by separating into two parts. **2** *intr.* take one or other road etc. at a fork (*fork left for Banbury*). **3** *tr.* dig or lift etc. with a fork. **4** *tr. Chess* attack (two pieces) simultaneously with one. □**fork-lift truck** a vehicle with a horizontal fork in front for lifting and carrying loads. **fork lunch** (or **supper** etc.) a light meal eaten with a fork at a buffet etc. **fork out** (or **up**) *sl.* hand over or pay, usu. reluctantly. [OE *forca*, *force* f. L *furca*]

forked /fɔːkt/ *adj.* **1** having a fork or forklike end or branches. **2** divergent, cleft. **3** (in *comb.*) having so many prongs (*three-forked*). □**forked lightning** a lightning-flash in the form of a zigzag or branching line.

forlorn /fɔːˈlɔːn/ *adj.* **1** sad and abandoned or lonely. **2** in a pitiful state; of wretched appearance. **3** desperate, hopeless, forsaken. □**forlorn hope 1** a faint remaining hope or chance. **2** a desperate enterprise. □□**forlornly** *adv.* **forlornness** *n.* [*past part.* of obs. *forlese* f. OE *forlēosan* (as FOR-, LOSE): *forlorn hope* f. Du. *verloren hoop* lost troop, orig. of a storming-party etc.]

form /fɔːm/ *n. & v.* —*n.* **1 a** a shape; an arrangement of parts. **b** the outward aspect (esp. apart from colour) or shape of a body. **2** a person or animal as visible or tangible (*the familiar form of the postman*). **3** the mode in which a thing exists or manifests itself (*took the form of a book*). **4** a species, kind, or variety. **5 a** a printed document with blank spaces for information to be inserted. **b** a regularly drawn document. **6** esp. *Brit.* a class in a school. **7** a customary method; what is usually done (*common form*). **8** a set order of words; a formula. **9** behaviour according to a rule or custom. **10** (prec. by *the*) correct procedure (*knows the form*). **11 a** (of an athlete, horse, etc.) condition of health and training (*is in top form*). **b** *Racing* details of previous performances. **12** general state or disposition (*was in great form*). **13** *sl.* a criminal record. **14** formality or mere ceremony. **15** *Gram.* **a** one of the ways in which a word may be spelt or pronounced or inflected. **b** the external characteristics of words apart from meaning. **16** arrangement and style in literary or musical composition. **17** *Philos.* the essential nature of a species or thing. **18** a long bench without a back. **19** esp. *US Printing* = FORME. **20** a hare's lair. **21** = FORMWORK. —*v.* **1** *tr.* make or fashion into a certain shape or form. **2** *intr.* take a certain shape; be formed. **3** *tr.* be the material of; make up or constitute (*together form a unit*; *forms part of the structure*). **4** *tr.* train or instruct. **5** *tr.* develop or establish as a concept, institution, or practice (*form an idea*; *formed an alliance*; *form a habit*). **6** *tr.* (foll. by *into*) embody, organize. **7** *tr.* articulate (a word). **8** *tr. & intr.* (often foll. by *up*) esp. *Mil.* bring or be brought into a certain arrangement or formation. **9** *tr.* construct (a new word) by derivation, inflection, etc. □**bad form** an offence against current social conventions. **form class** *Linguistics* a class of linguistic forms with

grammatical or syntactical features in common. **form criticism** textual analysis of the Bible etc. by tracing the history of its content by forms (e.g. proverbs, myths). **form letter** a standardized letter to deal with frequently occurring matters. **good form** what complies with current social conventions. **in form** fit for racing etc. **off form** not playing or performing well. **on form** playing or performing well. **out of form** not fit for racing etc. [ME f. OF *forme* f. L *forma* mould, form]

-form /fɔːm/ *comb. form* (usu. as **-iform**) forming adjectives meaning: **1** having the form of (*cruciform*; *cuneiform*). **2** having such a number of (*uniform*; *multiform*). [from or after F *-forme* f. L *-formis* f. *forma* FORM]

formal /ˈfɔːm(ə)l/ *adj. & n.* —*adj.* **1** used or done or held in accordance with rules, convention, or ceremony (*formal dress*; *a formal occasion*). **2** ceremonial; required by convention (*a formal call*). **3** precise or symmetrical (*a formal garden*). **4** prim or stiff in manner. **5** perfunctory, having the form without the spirit. **6** valid or correctly so called because of its form; explicit and definite (*a formal agreement*). **7** in accordance with recognized forms or rules. **8** of or concerned with (outward) form or appearance, esp. as distinct from content or matter. **9** *Logic* concerned with the form and not the matter of reasoning. **10** *Philos.* of the essence of a thing; essential not material. —*n.* *US* **1** evening dress. **2** an occasion on which evening dress is worn. □□ **formally** *adv.* **formalness** *n.* [ME f. L *formalis* (as FORM)]

formaldehyde /fɔːˈmældɪˌhaɪd/ *n.* a colourless pungent gas used as a disinfectant and preservative and in the manufacture of synthetic resins. ¶ Chem. formula: CH_2O. Also called METHANAL. [FORMIC (ACID) + ALDEHYDE]

formalin /ˈfɔːməlɪn/ *n.* a colourless solution of formaldehyde in water used as a preservative for biological specimens etc.

formalism /ˈfɔːməˌlɪz(ə)m/ *n.* **1 a** excessive adherence to prescribed forms. **b** the use of forms without regard to inner significance. **2** *derog.* an artist's concentration on form at the expense of content. **3** the treatment of mathematics as a manipulation of meaningless symbols. **4** *Theatr.* a symbolic and stylized manner of production. **5** *Physics & Math.* the mathematical description of a physical situation etc. □□ **formalist** *n.* **formalistic** /-ˈlɪstɪk/ *adj.*

formality /fɔːˈmælɪtɪ/ *n.* (*pl.* **-ies**) **1 a** a formal or ceremonial act, requirement of etiquette, regulation, or custom (often with an implied lack of real significance). **b** a thing done simply to comply with a rule. **2** the rigid observance of rules or convention. **3** ceremony; elaborate procedure. **4** being formal; precision of manners. **5** stiffness of design. [F *formalité* or med.L *formalitas* (as FORMAL)]

formalize /ˈfɔːməˌlaɪz/ *v.tr.* (also **-ise**) **1** give definite shape or legal formality to. **2** make ceremonious, precise, or rigid; imbue with formalism. □□ **formalization** /-ˈzeɪʃ(ə)n/ *n.*

formant /ˈfɔːmənt/ *n.* **1** the characteristic pitch-constituent of a vowel. **2** a morpheme occurring only in combination in a word or word-stem. [G f. L *formare* *formant-* to form]

format /ˈfɔːmæt/ *n. & v.* —*n.* **1** the shape and size of a book, periodical, etc. **2** the style or manner of an arrangement or procedure. **3** *Computing* a defined structure for holding data etc. in a record for processing or storage. —*v.tr.* (**formatted**, **formatting**) **1** arrange or put into a format. **2** *Computing* prepare (a storage medium) to receive data. [F f. G f. L *formatus* (*liber*) shaped (book), past part. of *formare* FORM]

formate see FORMIC ACID.

formation /fɔːˈmeɪʃ(ə)n/ *n.* **1** the act or an instance of forming; the process of being formed. **2** a thing formed. **3** a structure or arrangement of parts. **4** a particular arrangement, e.g. of troops, aircraft in flight, etc. **5** *Geol.* an assemblage of rocks or series of strata having some common characteristic. □□ **formational** *adj.* [ME f. OF *formation* or L *formatio* (as FORM)]

formative /ˈfɔːmətɪv/ *adj. & n.* —*adj.* **1** serving to form or fashion; of formation. **2** *Gram.* (of a flexional or derivative suffix or prefix) used in forming words. —*n. Gram.* a formative element. □□ **formatively** *adv.* [ME f. OF *formatif -ive* or med.L *formativus* (as FORM)]

forme /fɔːm/ *n.* (*US* form: see FORM *n.* 19) *Printing* **1** a body of type secured in a chase for printing at one impression. **2** a quantity of film arranged for making a plate etc. [var. of FORM]

former[1] /ˈfɔːmə(r)/ *attrib.adj.* **1** of or occurring in the past or an earlier period (*in former times*). **2** having been previously (*her former husband*). **3** (prec. by *the*; often *absol.*) the first or first mentioned of two (opp. LATTER). [ME f. *forme* first, after FOREMOST]

former[2] /ˈfɔːmə(r)/ *n.* **1** a person or thing that forms. **2** *Electr.* a frame or core for winding a coil on. **3** *Aeron.* a transverse strengthening member in a wing or fuselage. **4** (in *comb.*) a pupil of a specified form in a school (*fourth-former*).

formerly /ˈfɔːməlɪ/ *adv.* in the past; in former times.

Formica /fɔːˈmaɪkə/ *n. propr.* a hard durable plastic laminate used for working surfaces, cupboard doors, etc. [20th c.: orig. uncert.]

formic acid /ˈfɔːmɪk/ *n.* a colourless irritant volatile acid (HCOOH) contained in the fluid emitted by some ants. Also called METHANOIC ACID. □□ **formate** /-meɪt/ *n.* [L *formica* ant]

formication /ˌfɔːmɪˈkeɪʃ(ə)n/ *n.* a sensation as of ants crawling over the skin. [L *formicatio* f. *formica* ant]

formidable /ˈfɔːmɪdəb(ə)l, *disp.* fɔːˈmɪd-/ *adj.* **1** inspiring fear or dread. **2** inspiring respect or awe. **3** likely to be hard to overcome, resist, or deal with. □□ **formidableness** *n.* **formidably** *adv.* [F *formidable* or L *formidabilis* f. *formidare* fear]

formless /ˈfɔːmlɪs/ *adj.* shapeless; without determinate or regular form. □□ **formlessly** *adv.* **formlessness** *n.*

formula /ˈfɔːmjʊlə/ *n.* (*pl.* **formulas** or (esp. in senses 1, 2) **formulae** /-ˌliː/) **1** *Chem.* a set of chemical symbols showing the constituents of a substance and their relative proportions. **2** *Math.* a mathematical rule expressed in symbols. **3 a** a fixed form of words, esp. one used on social or ceremonial occasions. **b** a rule unintelligently or slavishly followed; an established or conventional usage. **c** a form of words embodying or enabling agreement, resolution of a dispute, etc. **4 a** a list of ingredients; a recipe. **b** *US* an infant's food made up from a recipe. **5** a classification of racing car, esp. by the engine capacity. □□ **formulaic** /-ˈleɪɪk/ *adj.* **formularize** *v.tr.* (also -ise). **formulize** *v.tr.* (also -ise). [L, dimin. of *forma* FORM]

formulary /ˈfɔːmjʊlərɪ/ *n. & adj.* —*n.* (*pl.* -ies) **1** a collection of formulas or set forms, esp. for religious use. **2** *Pharm.* a compendium of formulae used in the preparation of medicinal drugs. —*adj.* **1** using formulae. **2** in or of formulae. [(n.) F *formulaire* or f. med.L *formularius* (*liber* book) f. L (as FORMULA): (adj.) f. FORMULA]

formulate /ˈfɔːmjʊˌleɪt/ *v.tr.* **1** express in a formula. **2** express clearly and precisely. □□ **formulation** /-ˈleɪʃ(ə)n/ *n.*

formulism /ˈfɔːmjʊˌlɪz(ə)m/ *n.* adherence to or dependence on conventional formulas. □□ **formulist** *n.* **formulistic** /-ˈlɪstɪk/ *adj.*

formwork /ˈfɔːmwɜːk/ *n.* = SHUTTERING 1.

fornicate /ˈfɔːnɪˌkeɪt/ *v.intr.* archaic or joc. (of people not married or not married to each other) have sexual intercourse voluntarily. □□ **fornication** /-ˈkeɪʃ(ə)n/ *n.* **fornicator** *n.* [eccl.L *fornicari* f. L *fornix -icis* brothel]

forrader /ˈfɒrədə(r)/ *colloq. compar.* of FORWARD.

forsake /fəˈseɪk, fɔː-/ *v.tr.* (*past* **forsook** /-ˈsʊk/; *past part.* **forsaken** /-ˈseɪkən/) **1** give up; break off from; renounce. **2** withdraw one's help, friendship, or companionship from; desert, abandon. □□ **forsakenness** *n.* **forsaker** *n.* [OE *forsacan* deny, renounce, refuse, f. WG; cf. OE *sacan* quarrel]

forsooth /fəˈsuːθ, fɔː-/ *adv. archaic or joc.* truly; in truth; no doubt. [OE *forsōth* (as FOR, SOOTH)]

forswear /fɔːˈsweə(r)/ *v.tr.* (*past* **forswore** /-ˈswɔː(r)/; *past part.* **forsworn** /-ˈswɔːn/) **1** abjure; renounce on oath. **2** (as **forsworn** *adj.*) perjured. □ **forswear oneself** swear falsely; perjure oneself. [OE *forswerian* (as FOR-, SWEAR)]

forsythia /fɔːˈsaɪθɪə/ *n.* any ornamental shrub of the genus *Forsythia* bearing bright-yellow flowers in early spring. [mod.L f. W. *Forsyth*, Engl. botanist d. 1804]

fort /fɔːt/ *n.* **1** a fortified building or position. **2** *hist.* a trading-station, orig. fortified. [F *fort* or It. *forte* f. L *fortis* strong]

forte[1] /ˈfɔːteɪ/ *n.* **1** a person's strong point; a thing in which a person excels. **2** *Fencing* the part of a sword-blade from the hilt to the middle (cf. FOIBLE 2). [F *fort* strong f. L *fortis*]

forte[2] /ˈfɔːtɪ/ *adj., adv., & n. Mus.* —*adj.* performed loudly. —*adv.* loudly. —*n.* a passage to be performed loudly. □ **forte piano** *adj. & adv.* loud and then immediately soft. [It., = strong, loud]

fortepiano /ˌfɔːtɪpɪˈænəʊ/ *n.* (*pl.* -os) *Mus.* = PIANOFORTE esp. with ref. to an instrument of the 18th to early 19th c. [FORTE[2] + PIANO[2]]

forth /fɔːθ/ *adv. archaic* except in set phrases and after certain verbs, esp. *bring, come, go,* and *set* **1** forward; into view. **2** onwards in time (*from this time forth; henceforth*). **3** forwards. **4** out from a starting-point (*set forth*). □ **and so forth** and so on; and the like. [OE f. Gmc]

forthcoming /fɔːθˈkʌmɪŋ, *attrib.* ˈfɔːθ-/ *adj.* **1 a** about or likely to appear or become available. **b** approaching. **2** produced when wanted (*no reply was forthcoming*). **3** (of a person) informative, responsive. □□ **forthcomingness** *n.*

forthright *adj. & adv.* —*adj.* /ˈfɔːθraɪt/ **1** direct and outspoken; straightforward. **2** decisive, unhesitating. —*adv.* /fɔːθˈraɪt/ in a direct manner; bluntly. □□ **forthrightly** *adv.* **forthrightness** *n.* [OE *forthriht* (as FORTH, RIGHT)]

forthwith /fɔːθˈwɪθ, -ˈwɪð/ *adv.* immediately; without delay. [earlier *forthwithal* (as FORTH, WITH, ALL)]

fortification /ˌfɔːtɪfɪˈkeɪʃ(ə)n/ *n.* **1** the act or an instance of fortifying; the process of being fortified. **2** *Mil.* **a** the art or science of fortifying. **b** (usu. in *pl.*) defensive works fortifying a position. [ME f. F f. LL *fortificatio -onis* act of strengthening (as FORTIFY)]

fortify /ˈfɔːtɪˌfaɪ/ *v.tr.* (-ies, -ied) **1** provide or equip with defensive works so as to strengthen against attack. **2** strengthen or invigorate mentally or morally; encourage. **3** strengthen the structure of. **4** strengthen (wine) with alcohol. **5** increase the nutritive value of (food, esp. with vitamins). □□ **fortifiable** *adj.* **fortifier** *n.* [ME f. OF *fortifier* f. LL *fortificare* f. L *fortis* strong]

fortissimo /fɔːˈtɪsɪˌməʊ/ *adj., adv., & n. Mus.* —*adj.* performed very loudly. —*adv.* very loudly. —*n.* (*pl.* -os or **fortissimi** /-ˌmiː/) a passage to be performed very loudly. [It., superl. of FORTE[2]]

fortitude /ˈfɔːtɪˌtjuːd/ *n.* courage in pain or adversity. [ME f. F f. L *fortitudo -dinis* f. *fortis* strong]

fortnight /ˈfɔːtnaɪt/ *n.* **1** a period of two weeks. **2** (prec. by a specified day) two weeks after (that day) (*Tuesday fortnight*). [OE *fēowertīene niht* fourteen nights]

fortnightly /ˈfɔːtˌnaɪtlɪ/ *adj., adv., & n.* —*adj.* done, produced, or occurring once a fortnight. —*adv.* every fortnight. —*n.* (*pl.* -ies) a magazine etc. issued every fortnight.

Fortran /ˈfɔːtræn/ *n.* (also **FORTRAN**) *Computing*

a high-level programming language used esp. for scientific calculations. [*formula* translation]

fortress /ˈfɔːtrɪs/ n. a military stronghold, esp. a strongly fortified town fit for a large garrison. [ME f. OF *forteresse*, ult. f. L *fortis* strong]

fortuitous /fɔːˈtjuːɪtəs/ adj. due to or characterized by chance; accidental, casual. ▫▫ **fortuitously** adv. **fortuitousness** n. [L *fortuitus* f. *forte* by chance]

fortuity /fɔːˈtjuːɪtɪ/ n. (pl. **-ies**) **1** a chance occurrence. **2** accident or chance; fortuitousness.

fortunate /ˈfɔːtjʊnət, -tʃənət/ adj. **1** favoured by fortune; lucky, prosperous. **2** auspicious, favourable. [ME f. L *fortunatus* (as FORTUNE)]

fortunately /ˈfɔːtjʊnətlɪ, -tʃənətlɪ/ adv. **1** luckily, successfully. **2** (qualifying a whole sentence) it is fortunate that.

fortune /ˈfɔːtjuːn, -tʃuːn/ n. **1 a** chance or luck as a force in human affairs. **b** a person's destiny. **2** (**Fortune**) this force personified, often as a deity. **3** (in *sing.* or *pl.*) luck (esp. favourable) that befalls a person or enterprise. **4** good luck. **5** prosperity; a prosperous condition. **6** (also *colloq.* **small fortune**) great wealth; a huge sum of money. ▫ **fortune-hunter** *colloq.* a person seeking wealth by marriage. **fortune-teller** a person who claims to predict future events in a person's life. **fortune-telling** the practice of this. **make a** (or **one's**) **fortune** acquire wealth or prosperity. **tell a person's fortune** make predictions about a person's future. [ME f. OF f. L *fortuna* luck, chance]

forty /ˈfɔːtɪ/ n. & adj. —n. (pl. **-ies**) **1** the product of four and ten. **2** a symbol for this (40, xl, XL). **3** (in *pl.*) the numbers from 40 to 49, esp. the years of a century or of a person's life. **4** (**the Forties**) *Brit.* the sea area between the NE coast of Scotland and the SW coast of Norway (so called from its depth of forty fathoms or more). —adj. that amount to forty. ▫ **forty-first, -second,** etc. the ordinal numbers between fortieth and fiftieth. **forty-five** a gramophone record played at 45 r.p.m. **the Forty-five** the Jacobite rebellion of 1745. **forty-niner** *US* a seeker for gold etc., esp. in the Californian gold-rush of 1849. **forty-one, -two,** etc. the cardinal numbers between forty and fifty. **forty winks** *colloq.* a short sleep. ▫▫ **fortieth** adj. & n. **fortyfold** adj. & adv. [OE *fēowertig* (as FOUR, -TY²)]

forum /ˈfɔːrəm/ n. **1** a place of or meeting for public discussion. **2** a periodical etc. giving an opportunity for discussion. **3** a court or tribunal. **4** *hist.* a public square or market-place in an ancient Roman city used for judicial and other business. [L, in sense 4]

forward /ˈfɔːwəd/ adj., n., adv., & v. —adj. **1** lying in one's line of motion. **2 a** onward or towards the front. **b** *Naut.* belonging to the fore part of a ship. **3** precocious; bold in manner; presumptuous. **4** *Commerce* relating to future produce, delivery, etc. (*forward contract*). **5 a** advanced; progressing towards or approaching maturity or completion. **b** (of a plant etc.) well advanced or early. —n. an attacking player positioned near the front of a team in football, hockey, etc. —adv. **1** to the front; into prominence (*come forward; move forward*). **2** in advance; ahead (*sent them forward*). **3** onward so as to make progress (*not getting any further forward*). **4** towards the future; continuously onwards (*from this time forward*). **5** (also **forwards**) **a** towards the front in the direction one is facing. **b** in the normal direction of motion or of traversal. **c** with continuous forward motion (*backwards and forwards; rushing forward*). **6** *Naut.* & *Aeron.* in, near, or towards the bow or nose. —v.tr. **1 a** send (a letter etc.) on to a further destination. **b** dispatch (goods etc.) (*forwarding agent*). **2** help to advance; promote. ▫ **forward-looking** progressive; favouring change. ▫▫ **forwarder** n. **forwardly** adv. **forwardness** n. (esp. in sense 3 of adj.). [OE *forweard*, var. of *forthweard* (as FORTH, -WARD)]

forwards var. of FORWARD adv. 5.

forwent past of FORGO.

fossa /ˈfɒsə/ n. (pl. **fossae** /-siː/) *Anat.* a shallow depression or cavity. [L, = ditch, fem. past part. of *fodere* dig]

fosse /fɒs/ n. **1** a long narrow trench or excavation, esp. in a fortification. **2** *Anat.* = FOSSA. [ME f. OF f. L *fossa*: see FOSSA]

fossick /ˈfɒsɪk/ v.intr. *Austral.* & *NZ colloq.* **1** (foll. by *about, around*) rummage, search. **2** search for gold etc. in abandoned workings. ▫▫ **fossicker** n. [19th c.: cf. dial. *fossick* bustle about]

fossil /ˈfɒs(ə)l/ n. & adj. —n. **1** the remains or impression of a (usu. prehistoric) plant or animal hardened in rock (often *attrib.: fossil bones; fossil shells*). **2** *colloq.* an antiquated or unchanging person or thing. **3** a word that has become obsolete except in set phrases or forms, e.g. *hue* in *hue and cry*. —adj. **1** of or like a fossil. **2** antiquated; out of date. ▫ **fossil fuel** a natural fuel such as coal or gas formed in the geological past from the remains of living organisms. **fossil ivory** see IVORY. ▫▫ **fossiliferous** /ˌfɒsɪˈlɪfərəs/ adj. **fossilize** v.tr. & intr. (also -ise). **fossilization** /-ˈzeɪʃ(ə)n/ n. [F *fossile* f. L *fossilis* f. *fodere foss-* dig]

fossorial /fɒˈsɔːrɪəl/ adj. **1** (of animals) burrowing. **2** (of limbs etc.) used in burrowing. [med.L *fossorius* f. *fossor* digger (as FOSSIL)]

foster /ˈfɒstə(r)/ v. & adj. —v.tr. **1 a** promote the growth or development of. **b** encourage or harbour (a feeling). **2** (of circumstances) be favourable to. **3 a** bring up (a child that is not one's own by birth). **b** *Brit.* (of a local authority etc.) assign a (child) to be fostered. **4** cherish; have affectionate regard for (an idea, scheme, etc.). —adj. **1** having a family connection by fostering and not by birth (*foster-brother; foster-child; foster-parent*). **2** involving or concerned with fostering a child (*foster care; foster home*). ▫▫ **fosterage** n. (esp. in sense 3 of v.). **fosterer** n. [OE *fōstrian, fōster*, rel. to FOOD]

fosterling /ˈfɒstəlɪŋ/ n. a foster-child; a nursling or protégé. [OE *fōsterling* (as FOSTER)]

fouetté /fweˈteɪ/ n. *Ballet* a quick whipping movement of the raised leg. [F, past part. of *fouetter* whip]

fought past and past part. of FIGHT.

foul /faʊl/ adj., n., adv., & v. —adj. **1** offensive to the senses; loathsome, stinking. **2** dirty, soiled, filthy. **3** *colloq.* revolting, disgusting. **4 a** containing or charged with noxious matter (*foul air*). **b** clogged, choked. **5** morally polluted; disgustingly abusive or offensive (*foul language; foul deeds*). **6** unfair; against the rules of a game etc. (*by fair means or foul*). **7** (of the weather) wet, rough, stormy. **8** (of a rope etc.) entangled. **9** (of a ship's bottom) overgrown with weeds, barnacles, etc. —n. **1** *Sport* an unfair or invalid stroke or piece of play. **2** a collision or entanglement, esp. in riding, rowing, or running. **3** a foul thing. —adv. unfairly; contrary to the rules. —v. **1** tr. & intr. make or become foul or dirty. **2** tr. (of an animal) make dirty with excrement. **3 a** tr. *Sport* commit a foul against (a player). **b** intr. commit a foul. **4 a** tr. (often foll. by *up*) cause (an anchor, cable, etc.) to become entangled or muddled. **b** intr. become entangled. **5** tr. jam or block (a crossing, railway line, or traffic). **6** tr. (usu. foll. by *up*) *colloq.* spoil or bungle. **7** tr. run foul of; collide with. **8** tr. pollute with guilt; dishonour. ▫ **foul brood** a fatal disease of larval bees caused by bacteria. **foul mouth** a person who uses foul language. **foul play 1** unfair play in games. **2** treacherous or violent activity, esp. murder. **foul-up** a muddled or bungled situation. ▫▫ **foully** adv. **foulness** n. [OE *fūl* f. Gmc]

foulard /fuːˈlɑːd/ n. **1** a thin soft material of silk or silk and cotton. **2** an article made of this. [F]

foumart /ˈfuːmɑːt/ n. a polecat. [ME *fulmert* etc. (as FOUL, *mart* MARTEN)]

found[1] past and past part. of FIND.

found[2] /faʊnd/ v. **1** tr. **a** establish (esp. with an endowment). **b** originate or initiate (an institution).

2 *tr.* be the original builder or begin the building of (a town etc.). **3** *tr.* lay the base of (a building etc.). **4** (foll. by *on*, *upon*) **a** *tr.* construct or base (a story, theory, rule, etc.) according to a specified principle or ground. **b** *intr.* have a basis in. □**founding father** a person associated with a founding, esp. an American statesman at the time of the Revolution. [ME f. OF *fonder* f. L *fundare* f. *fundus* bottom]

found³ /faʊnd/ *v.tr.* **1 a** melt and mould (metal). **b** fuse (materials for glass). **2** make by founding. □□ **founder** *n.* [ME f. OF *fondre* f. L *fundere fus-* pour]

foundation /faʊnˈdeɪʃ(ə)n/ *n.* **1 a** the solid ground or base, natural or artificial, on which a building rests. **b** (usu. in *pl.*) the lowest load-bearing part of a building, usu. below ground level. **2** a body or ground on which other parts are overlaid. **3** a basis or underlying principle; groundwork (*the report has no foundation*). **4 a** the act or an instance of establishing or constituting (esp. an endowed institution) on a permanent basis. **b** such an institution, e.g. a monastery, college, or hospital. **5** (in full **foundation garment**) a woman's supporting undergarment, e.g. a corset. □**foundation cream** a cream used as a base for applying cosmetics. **foundation-stone 1** a stone laid with ceremony to celebrate the founding of a building. **2** the main ground or basis of something. □□**foundational** *adj.* [ME f. OF *fondation* f. L *fundatio -onis* (as FOUND²)]

founder¹ /ˈfaʊndə(r)/ *n.* a person who founds an institution. □□ **foundership** *n.*

founder² /ˈfaʊndə(r)/ *v.* & *n.* —*v.* **1 a** *intr.* (of a ship) fill with water and sink. **b** *tr.* cause (a ship) to founder. **2** *intr.* (of a plan etc.) fail. **3** *intr.* (of earth, a building, etc.) fall down or in, give way. **4 a** *intr.* (of a horse or its rider) fall to the ground, fall from lameness, stick fast in mud etc. **b** *tr.* cause (a horse) to break down, esp. with founder. —*n.* **1** inflammation of a horse's foot from overwork. **2** rheumatism of the chest-muscles in horses. [ME f. OF *fondrer*, *esfondrer* submerge, collapse, ult. f. L *fundus* bottom]

foundling /ˈfaʊndlɪŋ/ *n.* an abandoned infant of unknown parentage. [ME, perh. f. obs. *funding* (as FIND, -ING³),· assim. to -LING¹]

foundry /ˈfaʊndrɪ/ *n.* (*pl.* **-ies**) a workshop for or a business of casting metal.

fount¹ /faʊnt/ *n. poet.* a spring or fountain; a source. [back-form. f. FOUNTAIN after MOUNT²]

fount² /faʊnt, fɒnt/ *n.* (also **font** /fɒnt/) *Printing* a set of type of one face or size. [F *fonte* f. *fondre* FOUND³]

fountain /ˈfaʊntɪn/ *n.* **1 a** a jet or jets of water made to spout for ornamental purposes or for drinking. **b** a structure provided for this. **2** a structure for the constant public supply of drinking-water. **3** a natural spring of water. **4** a source (in physical or abstract senses). **5** = *soda-fountain*. **6** a reservoir for oil, ink, etc. □**fountain-head** an original source. **fountain-pen** a pen with a reservoir or cartridge holding ink. □□**fountained** *adj.* (also in *comb.*). [ME f. OF *fontaine* f. LL *fontana* fem. of L *fontanus* (adj.) f. *fons fontis* a spring]

four /fɔː(r)/ *n.* & *adj.* —*n.* **1** one more than three, or six less than ten; the product of two units and two units. **2** a symbol for this (4, iv, IV, rarely iiii, IIII). **3** a size etc. denoted by four. **4** a four-oared rowing-boat or its crew. **5** the time of four o'clock (*is it four yet?*). **6** a card with four pips. **7** a hit at cricket scoring four runs. —*adj.* that amount to four. □**four-eyes** *sl.* a person wearing glasses. **four-flush** *US Cards* a poker hand of little value, having four cards of the same suit and one of another. **four-flusher** *US* a bluffer or humbug. **four hundred** *US* the social élite of a community. **four-in-hand 1** a vehicle with four horses driven by one person. **2** *US* a necktie worn with a knot and two hanging ends superposed. **four-leaf** (or **-leaved**) **clover** a clover leaf with four leaflets thought to bring good luck. **four-letter word**

any of several short words referring to sexual or excretory functions, regarded as coarse or offensive. **four o'clock** = *marvel of Peru*. **four-part** *Mus.* arranged for four voices to sing or instruments to play. **four-poster** a bed with a post at each corner supporting a canopy. **four-square** *adj.* **1** solidly based. **2** steady, resolute; forthright. **3** square-shaped. —*adv.* steadily, resolutely. **four-stroke** (of an internal-combustion engine) having a cycle of four strokes (intake, compression, combustion, and exhaust). **four-wheel drive** drive acting on all four wheels of a vehicle. **on all fours** on hands and knees. [OE *fēower* f. Gmc]

fourchette /fʊəˈʃet/ *n. Anat.* a thin fold of skin at the back of the vulva. [F, dimin. of *fourche* (as FORK)]

fourfold /ˈfɔːfəʊld/ *adj.* & *adv.* **1** four times as much or as many. **2** consisting of four parts. **3** amounting to four.

Fourier analysis /ˈfʊərɪˌeɪ/ *n. Math.* the resolution of periodic data into harmonic functions using a Fourier series. [J. B. J. *Fourier*, Fr. mathematician d. 1830]

Fourier series /ˈfʊərɪˌeɪ/ *n. Math.* an expansion of a periodic function as a series of trigonometric functions.

fourpence /ˈfɔːpəns/ *n. Brit.* the sum of four pence, esp. before decimalization.

fourpenny /ˈfɔːpənɪ/ *adj. Brit.* costing four pence, esp. before decimalization. □**fourpenny one** *colloq.* a hit or blow.

fourscore /fɔːˈskɔː(r)/ *n. archaic* eighty.

foursome /ˈfɔːsəm/ *n.* **1** a group of four persons. **2** a golf match between two pairs with partners playing the same ball.

fourteen /fɔːˈtiːn/ *n.* & *adj.* —*n.* **1** one more than thirteen, or four more than ten; the product of two units and seven units. **2** a symbol for this (14, xiv, XIV). **3** a size etc. denoted by fourteen. —*adj.* that amount to fourteen. □□ **fourteenth** *adj.* & *n.* [OE *fēowertīene* (as FOUR, -TEEN)]

fourth /fɔːθ/ *n.* & *adj.* —*n.* **1** the position in a sequence corresponding to that of the number 4 in the sequence 1–4. **2** something occupying this position. **3** the fourth person etc. in a race or competition. **4** each of four equal parts of a thing; a quarter. **5** the fourth (and often highest) in a sequence of gears. **6** *Mus.* **a** an interval or chord spanning four consecutive notes in the diatonic scale (e.g. C to F). **b** a note separated from another by this interval. —*adj.* that is the fourth. □**fourth dimension 1** a postulated dimension additional to those determining area and volume. **2** time regarded as equivalent to linear dimensions. **fourth estate** *joc.* the press; journalism. □□ **fourthly** *adv.* [OE *fēortha*, *fēowertha* f. Gmc]

4to *abbr.* quarto.

fovea /ˈfəʊvɪə/ *n.* (*pl.* **foveae** /-vɪ,iː/) *Anat.* a small depression or pit, esp. the pit in the retina of the eye for focusing images. □□ **foveal** *adj.* **foveate** /-vɪ,eɪt/ *adj.* [L]

fowl /faʊl/ *n.* & *v.* (*pl.* same or **fowls**) —*n.* **1** any domestic cock or hen of various gallinaceous birds, kept for eggs and flesh. **2** the flesh of birds, esp. a domestic cock or hen, as food. **3** *archaic* (except in *comb.* or *collect.*) a bird (*guineafowl*; *wildfowl*). —*v.intr.* catch or hunt wildfowl. □**fowl cholera** see CHOLERA. **fowl pest** an infectious virus disease of fowls. **fowl-run 1** a place where fowls may run. **2** a breeding establishment for fowls. □□ **fowler** *n.* **fowling** *n.* [OE *fugol* f. Gmc]

fox /fɒks/ *n.* & *v.* —*n.* **1 a** any of various wild flesh-eating mammals of the dog family, esp. of the genus *Vulpes*, with a sharp snout, bushy tail, and red or grey fur. **b** the fur of a fox. **2** a cunning or sly person. **3** *US sl.* an attractive young woman. —*v.* **1 a** *intr.* act craftily. **b** *tr.* deceive, baffle, trick. **2** *tr.* (usu. as **foxed** *adj.*) discolour (the leaves of a book, engraving, etc.) with brownish marks. □**fox-terrier**

1 a terrier of a short-haired breed originally used for unearthing foxes. **2** this breed. □□ **foxing** *n*. (in sense 2 of *v*.). **foxlike** *adj*. [OE f. WG]

foxglove /'fɒksglʌv/ *n*. any tall plant of the genus *Digitalis*, with erect spikes of purple or white flowers like glove-fingers.

foxhole /'fɒkshəʊl/ *n*. **1** *Mil*. a hole in the ground used as a shelter against enemy fire or as a firing-point. **2** a place of refuge or concealment.

foxhound /'fɒkshaʊnd/ *n*. a kind of hound bred and trained to hunt foxes.

fox-hunt /'fɒkshʌnt/ *n*. & *v*. —*n*. **1** the hunting of foxes with hounds. **2** a particular group of people engaged in this. —*v.intr*. engage in a fox-hunt. □□ **fox-hunter** *n*. **fox-hunting** *n*. & *adj*.

foxtail /'fɒksteɪl/ *n*. any of several grasses of the genus *Alopecurus*, with brushlike spikes.

foxtrot /'fɒkstrɒt/ *n*. & *v*. —*n*. **1** a ballroom dance with slow and quick steps. **2** the music for this. —*v.intr*. (**foxtrotted, foxtrotting**) perform this dance.

foxy /'fɒksɪ/ *adj*. (**foxier, foxiest**) **1** of or like a fox. **2** sly or cunning. **3** reddish-brown. **4** (of paper) damaged, esp. by mildew. **5** *US sl*. (of a woman) sexually attractive. □□ **foxily** *adv*. **foxiness** *n*.

foyer /'fɔɪeɪ/ *n*. the entrance hall or other large area in a hotel, theatre, etc. [F, = hearth, home, ult. f. L *focus* fire]

FP *abbr*. freezing-point.

fp *abbr*. forte piano.

FPA *abbr*. (in the UK) Family Planning Association.

FPS *abbr*. Fellow of the Pharmaceutical Society of Great Britain.

fps *abbr*. (also **f.p.s.**) **1** feet per second. **2** foot-pound-second.

Fr *symb*. *Chem*. the element francium.

Fr. *abbr*. (also **Fr**) **1** Father. **2** French.

fr. *abbr*. franc(s).

Fra /frɑː/ *n*. a prefixed title given to an Italian monk or friar. [It., abbr. of *frate* brother]

frabjous /'fræbdʒəs/ *adj*. delightful, joyous. □□ **frabjously** *adv*. [devised by Lewis Carroll, app. to suggest *fair* and *joyous*]

fracas /'frækɑː/ *n*. (*pl*. same /-kɑːz/) a noisy disturbance or quarrel. [F f. *fracasser* f. It. *fracassare* make an uproar]

fraction /'frækʃ(ə)n/ *n*. **1** a numerical quantity that is not a whole number (e.g. ½, 0.5). **2** a small, esp. very small, part, piece, or amount. **3** a portion of a mixture separated by distillation etc. **4** *Polit*. any organized dissentient group, esp. a group of communists in a non-communist organization. **5** the division of the Eucharistic bread. □□ **fractionary** *adj*. **fractionize** *v.tr*. (also **-ise**). [ME f. OF f. LL *fractio -onis* f. L *frangere* fract- break]

fractional /'frækʃən(ə)l/ *adj*. **1** of or relating to or being a fraction. **2** very slight; incomplete. **3** *Chem*. relating to the separation of parts of a mixture by making use of their different physical properties (*fractional crystallization*; *fractional distillation*). □□ **fractionalize** *v.tr*. (also **-ise**). **fractionally** *adv*. (esp. in sense 2).

fractionate /'frækʃə,neɪt/ *v.tr*. **1** break up into parts. **2** separate (a mixture) by fractional distillation etc. □□ **fractionation** /-'neɪʃ(ə)n/ *n*.

fractious /'frækʃəs/ *adj*. **1** irritable, peevish. **2** unruly. □□ **fractiously** *adv*. **fractiousness** *n*. [FRACTION in obs. sense 'brawling', prob. after *factious* etc.]

fracto- /'fræktəʊ/ *comb. form* *Meteorol*. (of a cloud form) broken or fragmentary (*fracto-cumulus*; *fracto-nimbus*). [L *fractus* broken: see FRACTION]

fracture /'fræktʃə(r)/ *n*. & *v*. —*n*. **1 a** breakage or breaking, esp. of a bone or cartilage. **b** the result of breaking; a crack or split. **2** the surface appearance of a freshly broken rock or mineral. **3** *Linguistics* **a** the substitution of a diphthong for a simple vowel owing to an influence esp. of a following consonant. **b** a diphthong substituted in this way. —*v.intr*. & *tr*.

1 *Med*. undergo or cause to undergo a fracture. **2** break or cause to break. [ME f. F *fracture* or f. L *fractura* (as FRACTION)]

fraenulum /'friːnjuːləm/ *n*. (also **frenulum**) (*pl*. **-la** /-lə/) *Anat*. a small fraenum. [mod.L, dimin. of FRAENUM]

fraenum /'friːnəm/ *n*. (also **frenum**) (*pl*. **-na** /-nə/) *Anat*. a fold of mucous membrane or skin esp. under the tongue, checking the motion of an organ. [L, = bridle]

fragile /'frædʒaɪl, -dʒɪl/ *adj*. **1** easily broken; weak. **2** of delicate frame or constitution; not strong. □□ **fragilely** *adv*. **fragility** /frə'dʒɪlɪtɪ/ *n*. [F *fragile* or L *fragilis* f. *frangere* break]

fragment *n*. & *v*. —*n*. /'frægmənt/ **1** a part broken off; a detached piece. **2** an isolated or incomplete part. **3** the remains of an otherwise lost or destroyed whole, esp. the extant remains or unfinished portion of a book or work of art. —*v.tr*. & *intr*. /fræg'ment/ break or separate into fragments. □□ **fragmental** /-'ment(ə)l/ *adj*. **fragmentize** /'frægmən,taɪz/ *v.tr*. (also **-ise**). [ME f. F *fragment* or L *fragmentum* (as FRAGILE)]

fragmentary /'frægməntərɪ/ *adj*. **1** consisting of fragments. **2** disconnected. **3** *Geol*. composed of fragments of previously existing rocks. □□ **fragmentarily** *adv*.

fragmentation /,frægmən'teɪʃ(ə)n/ *n*. the process or an instance of breaking into fragments. □ **fragmentation bomb** a bomb designed to break up into small rapidly-moving fragments when exploded.

fragrance /'freɪgrəns/ *n*. **1** sweetness of smell. **2** a sweet scent. [F *fragrance* or L *fragrantia* (as FRAGRANT)]

fragrancy /'freɪgrənsɪ/ *n*. (*pl*. **-ies**) = FRAGRANCE.

fragrant /'freɪgrənt/ *adj*. sweet-smelling. □□ **fragrantly** *adv*. [ME f. F *fragrant* or L *fragrare* smell sweet]

frail /freɪl/ *adj*. & *n*. —*adj*. **1** fragile, delicate. **2** in weak health. **3** morally weak; unable to resist temptation. **4** transient, insubstantial. —*n*. *US sl*. a woman. □□ **frailly** *adv*. **frailness** *n*. [ME f. OF *fraile*, *frele* f. L *fragilis* FRAGILE]

frailty /'freɪltɪ/ *n*. (*pl*. **-ies**) **1** the condition of being frail. **2** liability to err or yield to temptation. **3** a fault, weakness, or foible. [ME f. OF *frailté* f. L *fragilitas -tatis* (as FRAGILE)]

Fraktur /'fræktʊə(r)/ *n*. a German style of black-letter type. [G]

framboesia /fræm'biːzɪə/ *n*. (*US* **frambesia**) *Med*. = YAWS. [mod.L f. F *framboise* raspberry f. L *fraga ambrosia* ambrosial strawberry]

frame /freɪm/ *n*. & *v*. —*n*. **1** a case or border enclosing a picture, window, door, etc. **2** the basic rigid supporting structure of anything, e.g. of a building, motor vehicle, or aircraft. **3** (in *pl*.) the structure of spectacles holding the lenses. **4** a human or animal body, esp. with reference to its size or structure (*his frame shook with laughter*). **5** a framed work or structure (*the frame of heaven*). **6 a** an established order, plan, or system (*the frame of society*). **b** construction, constitution, build. **7** a temporary state (esp. in **frame of mind**). **8** a single complete image or picture on a cinema film or transmitted in a series of lines by television. **9 a** a triangular structure for positioning the balls in snooker etc. **b** the balls positioned in this way. **c** a round of play in snooker etc. **10** *Hort*. a boxlike structure of glass etc. for protecting plants. **11** a removable box of slats for the building of a honeycomb in a beehive. **12** *US sl*. = frame-up. —*v.tr*. **1 a** set in or provide with a frame. **b** serve as a frame for. **2** construct by a combination of parts or in accordance with a design or plan. **3** formulate or devise the essentials of (a complex thing, idea, theory, etc.). **4** (foll. by *to*, *into*) adapt or fit. **5** *sl*. concoct a false charge or evidence against; devise a plot with regard to. **6** articulate (words). □**frame-house** a house constructed of a wooden skeleton covered with boards etc. **frame of reference 1** a set of standards or principles governing behaviour, thought, etc. **2** *Geom.* a system of geometrical axes for defining position. **frame-saw** a saw stretched in a frame to make it rigid. **frame-up** *colloq.* a conspiracy, esp. to make an innocent person appear guilty. □□**framable** *adj.* **frameless** *adj.* **framer** *n.* [OE *framian* be of service f. *fram* forward: see FROM]

framework /'freɪmwɜːk/ *n.* **1** an essential supporting structure. **2** a basic system.

framing /'freɪmɪŋ/ *n.* a framework; a system of frames.

franc /fræŋk/ *n.* the chief monetary unit of France, Belgium, Switzerland, Luxemburg, and several other countries. [ME f. OF f. *Francorum Rex* king of the Franks, the legend on the earliest gold coins so called (14th c.): see FRANK]

franchise /'fræntʃaɪz/ *n.* & *v.* —*n.* **1 a** the right to vote at State (esp. parliamentary) elections. **b** the principle of qualification for this. **2** full membership of a corporation or State; citizenship. **3** authorization granted to an individual or group by a company to sell its goods or services in a particular way. **4** *hist.* legal immunity or exemption from a burden or jurisdiction. **5** a right or privilege granted to a person or corporation. —*v.tr.* grant a franchise to. □□ **franchisee** /-'ziː/ *n.* **franchiser** *n.* (also **franchisor**). [ME f. OF f. *franc, franche* free: see FRANK]

Franciscan /fræn'sɪskən/ *n.* & *adj.* —*n.* a monk, nun, or sister of an order founded in 1209 by St Francis of Assisi (see also *Grey Friar*). —*adj.* of St Francis or his order. [F *franciscain* f. mod.L *Franciscanus* f. *Franciscus* Francis]

francium /'fræŋkɪəm/ *n. Chem.* a radioactive metallic element occurring naturally in uranium and thorium ores. ¶ Symb.: **Fr**. [mod.L f. *France* (the discoverer's country)]

Franco- /'fræŋkəʊ/ *comb. form* **1** French; French and (*Franco-German*). **2** regarding France or the French (*Francophile*). [med.L *Francus* FRANK]

francolin /'fræŋkəʊlɪn/ *n.* any medium-sized partridge of the genus *Francolinus*. [F f. It. *francolino*]

Francophile /'fræŋkə,faɪl/ *n.* a person who is fond of France or the French.

francophone /'fræŋkə,fəʊn/ *n.* & *adj.* —*n.* a French-speaking person. —*adj.* French-speaking. [FRANCO- + Gk *phōnē* voice]

frangible /'frændʒɪb(ə)l/ *adj.* breakable, fragile. [OF *frangible* or med.L *frangibilis* f. L *frangere* to break]

frangipane /'frændʒɪ,peɪn/ *n.* **1 a** an almond-flavoured cream or paste. **b** a flan filled with this. **2** = FRANGIPANI. [F prob. f. Marquis *Frangipani*, 16th-c. It. inventor of the perfume]

frangipani /,frændʒɪ'pɑːnɪ/ *n.* (*pl.* **frangipanis**) **1** any tree or shrub of the genus *Plumeria*, native to tropical America, esp. *P. rubra* with clusters of fragrant white, pink, or yellow flowers. **2** the perfume from this plant. [var. of FRANGIPANE]

franglais /'frãgleɪ/ *n.* a corrupt version of French using many words and idioms borrowed from English. [F f. *français* French + *anglais* English]

Frank /fræŋk/ *n.* **1** a member of the Germanic nation or coalition that conquered Gaul in the 6th c. **2** (in the Levant) a person of Western nationality. □□ **Frankish** *adj.* [OE *Franca*, OHG *Franko*, perh. f. the name of a weapon: cf. OE *franca* javelin]

frank /fræŋk/ *adj., v.,* & *n.* —*adj.* **1** candid, outspoken (*a frank opinion*). **2** undisguised, avowed (*frank admiration*). **3** ingenuous, open (*a frank face*). **4** *Med.* unmistakable. —*v.tr.* **1** stamp (a letter) with an official mark (esp. other than a normal postage stamp) to record the payment of postage. **2** *hist.* superscribe (a letter etc.) with a signature ensuring conveyance without charge; send without charge. **3** *archaic* facilitate the coming and going of (a person).

—*n.* **1** a franking signature or mark. **2** a franked cover. □□ **frankable** *adj.* **franker** *n.* **frankness** *n.* [ME f. OF *franc* f. med.L *francus* free, f. FRANK (since only Franks had full freedom in Frankish Gaul)]

Frankenstein /'fræŋkən,staɪn/ *n.* (in full **Frankenstein's monster**) a thing that becomes terrifying to its maker; a monster. [Baron *Frankenstein*, a character in and the title of a novel (1818) by Mary Shelley]

frankfurter /'fræŋk,fɜːtə(r)/ *n.* a seasoned smoked sausage made of beef and pork. [G *Frankfurter Wurst* Frankfurt sausage]

frankincense /'fræŋkɪn,sens/ *n.* an aromatic gum resin obtained from trees of the genus *Boswellia*, used for burning as incense. [ME f. OF *franc encens* pure incense]

franklin /'fræŋklɪn/ *n. hist.* a landowner of free but not noble birth in the 14th and 15th c. in England. [ME *francoleyn* etc. f. AL *francalanus* f. *francalis* held without dues f. *francus* free: see FRANK]

frankly /'fræŋklɪ/ *adv.* **1** in a frank manner. **2** (qualifying a whole sentence) to be frank.

frantic /'fræntɪk/ *adj.* **1** wildly excited; frenzied. **2** characterized by great hurry or anxiety; desperate, violent. **3** *colloq.* extreme; very great. □□ **frantically** *adv.* **franticly** *adv.* **franticness** *n.* [ME *frentik, frantik* f. OF *frenetique* f. L *phreneticus*: see PHRENETIC]

frap /fræp/ *v.tr.* (**frapped, frapping**) *Naut.* bind tightly. [F *frapper* bind, strike]

frappé /'fræpeɪ/ *adj.* & *n.* —*adj.* (esp. of wine) iced, cooled. —*n.* **1** an iced drink. **2** a soft water-ice. [F, past part. of *frapper* strike, ice (drinks)]

frass /fræs/ *n.* **1** a fine powdery refuse left by insects boring. **2** the excrement of insect larvae. [G f. *fressen* devour (as FRET¹)]

fraternal /frə'tɜːn(ə)l/ *adj.* **1** of a brother or brothers. **2** suitable to a brother; brotherly. **3** (of twins) developed from separate ova and not necessarily closely similar. **4** *US* of or concerning a fraternity (see FRATERNITY 3). □□ **fraternalism** *n.* **fraternally** *adv.* [med.L *fraternalis* f. L *fraternus* f. *frater* brother]

fraternity /frə'tɜːnɪtɪ/ *n.* (*pl.* **-ies**) **1** a religious brotherhood. **2** a group or company with common interests, or of the same professional class. **3** *US* a male students' society in a university or college. **4** being fraternal; brotherliness. [ME f. OF *fraternité* f. L *fraternitas -tatis* (as FRATERNAL)]

fraternize /'frætə,naɪz/ *v.intr.* (also **-ise**) (often foll. by *with*) **1** associate; make friends; behave as intimates. **2** (of troops) enter into friendly relations with enemy troops or the inhabitants of an occupied country. □□ **fraternization** /-'zeɪʃ(ə)n/ *n.* [F *fraterniser* & med.L *fraternizare* f. L *fraternus*: see FRATERNAL]

fratricide /'frætrɪ,saɪd/ *n.* **1** the killing of one's brother or sister. **2** a person who does this. □□ **fratricidal** /-'saɪd(ə)l/ *adj.* [F *fratricide* or LL *fratricidium*, L *fratricida*, f. *frater fratris* brother]

Frau /frau/ *n.* (*pl.* **Frauen** /'frauən/) (often as a title) a married or widowed German woman. [G]

fraud /frɔːd/ *n.* **1** criminal deception; the use of false representations to gain an unjust advantage. **2** a dishonest artifice or trick. **3** a person or thing not fulfilling what is claimed or expected of it. [ME f. OF *fraude* f. L *fraus fraudis*]

fraudulent /'frɔːdjʊlənt/ *adj.* **1** characterized or achieved by fraud. **2** guilty of fraud; intending to deceive. □□ **fraudulence** *n.* **fraudulently** *adv.* [ME f. OF *fraudulent* or L *fraudulentus* (as FRAUD)]

fraught /frɔːt/ *adj.* **1** (foll. by *with*) filled or attended with (*fraught with danger*). **2** *colloq.* causing or affected by great anxiety or distress. [ME, past part. of obs. *fraught* (v.) load with cargo f. MDu. *vrachten* f. *vracht* FREIGHT]

Fräulein /'frɔɪlaɪn/ *n.* (often as a title or form of address) an unmarried (esp. young) German woman. [G, dimin. of FRAU]

Fraunhofer lines /ˈfraʊnˌhəʊfə(r)/ *n.pl.* the dark lines visible in solar and stellar spectra. [J. von *Fraunhofer*, Bavarian physicist d. 1826]

fraxinella /ˌfræksɪˈnelə/ *n.* an aromatic plant *Dictamnus albus*, having foliage that emits an ethereal inflammable oil. Also called DITTANY, *gas plant*, *burning bush*. [mod.L, dimin. of L *fraxinus* ash-tree]

fray[1] /freɪ/ *v.* **1** *tr.* & *intr.* wear through or become worn, esp. (of woven material) unweave at the edges. **2** *intr.* (of nerves, temper, etc.) become strained; deteriorate. [F *frayer* f. L *fricare* rub]

fray[2] /freɪ/ *n.* **1** conflict, fighting (*eager for the fray*). **2** a noisy quarrel or brawl. [ME f. *fray* to quarrel f. *affray* (v.) (as AFFRAY)]

frazil /ˈfreɪzɪl/ *n.* US ice crystals that form in a stream or on its bed. [Can.F *frasil* snow floating in the water; cf. F *fraisil* cinders]

frazzle /ˈfræz(ə)l/ *n.* & *v.* *colloq.* —*n.* a worn or exhausted state (*burnt to a frazzle*). —*v.tr.* (usu. as **frazzled** *adj.*) wear out; exhaust. [orig. uncert.]

freak /friːk/ *n.* & *v.* —*n.* **1** (also **freak of nature**) a monstrosity; an abnormally developed individual or thing. **2** (often *attrib.*) an abnormal, irregular, or bizarre occurrence (*a freak storm*). **3** *colloq.* **a** an unconventional person. **b** a person with a specified enthusiasm or interest (*health freak*). **c** a person who undergoes hallucinations; a drug addict (use sense 2 of *v.*). **4 a** a caprice or vagary. **b** capriciousness. —*v.* (often foll. by *out*) *colloq.* **1** *intr.* & *tr.* become or make very angry. **2** *intr.* & *tr.* undergo or cause to undergo hallucinations or a strong emotional experience, esp. from use of narcotics. **3** *intr.* adopt a wildly unconventional lifestyle. □**freak-out** *colloq.* an act of freaking out; a hallucinatory or strong emotional experience. [16th c.: prob. f. dial.]

freakish /ˈfriːkɪʃ/ *adj.* **1** of or like a freak. **2** bizarre, unconventional. □□ **freakishly** *adv.* **freakishness** *n.*

freaky /ˈfriːkɪ/ *adj.* (**freakier**, **freakiest**) = FREAKISH. □□ **freakily** *adv.* **freakiness** *n.*

freckle /ˈfrek(ə)l/ *n.* & *v.* —*n.* (often in *pl.*) a light brown spot on the skin, usu. caused by exposure to the sun. —*v.* **1** *tr.* (usu. as **freckled** *adj.*) spot with freckles. **2** *intr.* be spotted with freckles. □□ **freckly** *adj.* [ME *fracel* etc. f. dial. *freken* f. ON *freknur* (pl.)]

free /friː/ *adj.*, *adv.*, & *v.* —*adj.* (**freer** /ˈfriːə(r)/; **freest** /ˈfriːɪst/) **1** not in bondage to or under the control of another; having personal rights and social and political liberty. **2** (of a State, or its citizens or institutions) subject neither to foreign domination nor to despotic government; having national and civil liberty (*a free press; a free society*). **3 a** unrestricted, unimpeded; not restrained or fixed. **b** at liberty; not confined or imprisoned. **c** released from ties or duties; unimpeded. **d** unrestrained as to action; independent (*set free*). **4** (foll. by *of*, *from*) **a** not subject to; exempt from (*free of tax*). **b** not containing or subject to a specified (usu. undesirable) thing (*free of preservatives; free from disease*). **5** (foll. by *to* + infin.) able or permitted to take a specified action (*you are free to choose*). **6** unconstrained (*free gestures*). **7 a** available without charge; costing nothing. **b** not subject to tax, duty, trade-restraint, or fees. **8 a** clear of engagements or obligations (*are you free tomorrow?*). **b** not occupied or in use (*the bathroom is free now*). **c** clear of obstructions. **9** spontaneous, unforced (*free compliments*). **10** open to all comers. **11** lavish, profuse; using or used without restraint (*very free with their money*). **12** frank, unreserved. **13** (of a literary style) not observing the strict laws of form. **14** (of a translation) conveying the broad sense; not literal. **15** forward, familiar, impudent. **16** (of talk, stories, etc.) slightly indecent. **17** *Physics* a not modified by an external force. **b** not bound in an atom or molecule. **18** *Chem.* not combined (*free oxygen*). **19** (of power or energy) disengaged or available. —*adv.* **1** in a free manner. **2** without cost

or payment. **3** *Naut.* not close-hauled. —*v.tr.* **1** make free; set at liberty. **2** (foll. by *of*, *from*) relieve from (something undesirable). **3** disengage, disentangle. □**free agent** a person with freedom of action. **free and easy** informal, unceremonious. **free association** *Psychol.* a method of investigating a person's unconscious by eliciting from him or her spontaneous associations with ideas proposed by the examiner. **free-born** inheriting a citizen's rights and liberty. **Free Church** a Church dissenting or seceding from an established Church. **free enterprise** a system in which private business operates in competition and largely free of State control. **free fall** movement under the force of gravity only, esp.: **1** the part of a parachute descent before the parachute opens. **2** the movement of a spacecraft in space without thrust from the engines. **free fight** a general fight in which all present join. **free-for-all** a free fight, unrestricted discussion, etc. **free-form** (*attrib.*) of an irregular shape or structure. **free hand** freedom to act at one's own discretion (see also FREE-HAND). **free-handed** generous. **free-handedly** generously. **free-handedness** generosity. **free house** *Brit.* an inn or public house not controlled by a brewery and therefore not restricted to selling particular brands of beer or liquor. **free kick** *Football* a set kick allowed to be taken by one side without interference from the other. **free labour** the labour of workmen not in a trade union. **free-living 1** indulgence in pleasures, esp. that of eating. **2** *Biol.* living freely and independently; not attached to a substrate. **free love** sexual relations according to choice and unrestricted by marriage. **free market** a market in which prices are determined by unrestricted competition. **free on board** (or **rail**) without charge for delivery to a ship or railway wagon. **free pass** an authorization of free admission, travel, etc. **free port 1** a port area where goods in transit are exempt from customs duty. **2** a port open to all traders. **free radical** *Chem.* an unchanged atom or group of atoms with one or more unpaired electrons. **free-range** esp. *Brit.* (of hens etc.) kept in natural conditions with freedom of movement. **free rein** see REIN. **free school 1** a school for which no fees are charged. **2** a school run on the basis of freedom from restriction for the pupils. **free speech** the right to express opinions freely. **free-spoken** speaking candidly; not concealing one's opinions. **free-standing** not supported by another structure. **free trade** international trade left to its natural course without restriction on imports or exports. **free verse** = VERS LIBRE. **free vote** a Parliamentary vote not subject to party discipline. **free wheel** the driving wheel of a bicycle, able to revolve with the pedals at rest. **free-wheel** *v.intr.* **1** ride a bicycle with the pedals at rest, esp. downhill. **2** move or act without constraint or effort. **free will 1** the power of acting without the constraint of necessity or fate. **2** the ability to act at one's own discretion (*I did it of my own free will*). **free world** esp. *US* the non-Communist countries. □□ **freely** *adv.* **freeness** *n.* [OE *frēo*, *frēon* f. Gmc]

-free /friː/ *comb. form* free of or from (*duty-free; fancy-free*).

freebase /ˈfriːbeɪs/ *n.* & *v. sl.* —*n.* cocaine that has been purified by heating with ether, and is taken by inhaling the fumes or smoking the residue. —*v.tr.* purify (cocaine) for smoking or inhaling.

freebie /ˈfriːbɪ/ *n.* esp. *US colloq.* a thing provided free of charge. [arbitrary f. FREE]

freeboard /ˈfriːbɔːd/ *n.* the part of a ship's side between the water-line and the deck.

freebooter /ˈfriːˌbuːtə(r)/ *n.* a pirate or lawless adventurer. □□ **freeboot** *v.intr.* [Du. *vrijbuiter* (as FREE, BOOTY): cf. FILIBUSTER]

freedman /ˈfriːdmən/ *n.* (*pl.* **-men**) an emancipated slave.

freedom /ˈfriːdəm/ *n.* **1** the condition of being free or unrestricted. **2** personal or civic liberty; absence of slave status. **3** the power of self-determination; independence of fate or necessity. **4** the state of being free to act (often foll. by *to* + infin.: *we have the freedom to leave*). **5** frankness, outspokenness; undue familiarity. **6** (foll. by *from*) the condition of being exempt from or not subject to (a defect, burden, etc.). **7** (foll. by *of*) **a** full or honorary participation in (membership, privileges, etc.). **b** unrestricted use of (facilities etc.). **8** a privilege possessed by a city or corporation. **9** facility or ease in action. **10** boldness of conception. □**the four freedoms** freedom of speech and religion, and freedom from fear and want. **freedom fighter** a person who takes part in violent resistance to an established political system etc. [OE *frēodōm* (as FREE, -DOM)]

freehand /'friːhænd/ *adj. & adv.* —*adj.* (of a drawing or plan etc.) done by hand without special instruments or guides. —*adv.* in a freehand manner.

freehold /'friːhəʊld/ *n. & adj.* —*n.* **1** tenure of land or property in fee simple or fee tail or for life. **2** land or property or an office held by such tenure. —*adj.* held by or having the status of freehold. □□ **freeholder** *n.*

freelance /'friːlɑːns/ *n., v., & adj.* —*n.* **1 a** (also **freelancer**) a person, usu. self-employed, offering services on a temporary basis, esp. to several businesses etc. for particular assignments. **b** (*attrib.*) (a *freelance editor*). **2** (usu. **free lance**) *hist.* a medieval mercenary. —*v.intr.* act as a freelance. —*adv.* as a freelance. [19th c.: orig. in sense 2 of *n.*]

freeloader /'friːˌləʊdə(r)/ *n. US sl.* a person who eats or drinks at others' expense; a sponger. □□ **freeload** /-'ləʊd/ *v.intr.*

freeman /'friːmən/ *n.* (*pl.* -men) **1** a person who has the freedom of a city, company, etc. **2** a person who is not a slave or serf.

freemartin /'friːˌmɑːtɪn/ *n.* a hermaphrodite or imperfect female calf of oppositely sexed twins. [17th c.: orig. unkn.]

Freemason /'friːˌmeɪs(ə)n/ *n.* a member of an international fraternity for mutual help and fellowship (the *Free and Accepted Masons*), with elaborate secret rituals.

Freemasonry /'friːˌmeɪsənrɪ/ *n.* **1** the system and institutions of the Freemasons. **2** (**freemasonry**) instinctive sympathy or understanding.

freepost /'friːpəʊst/ *n.* a system of sending business post in envelopes prepaid by the recipient.

freer *compar.* of FREE.

freesia /'friːzjə, -ʒə/ *n.* any bulbous plant of the genus *Freesia*, native to Africa, having fragrant coloured flowers. [mod.L f. F. H. T. *Freese*, Ger. physician d. 1876]

freest *superl.* of FREE.

freestone /'friːstəʊn/ *n.* **1** any fine-grained stone which can be cut easily, esp. sandstone or limestone. **2** a stone-fruit, esp. a peach, in which the stone is loose when the fruit is ripe (cf. CLINGSTONE).

freestyle /'friːstaɪl/ *adj.* (of a race or contest) in which all styles are allowed, esp.: **1** *Swimming* in which any stroke may be used. **2** *Wrestling* with few restrictions on the holds permitted.

freethinker /friː'θɪŋkə(r)/ *n.* a person who rejects dogma or authority, esp. in religious belief. □□ **freethinking** *n. & adj.*

freeway /'friːweɪ/ *n. US* **1** an express highway, esp. with controlled access. **2** a toll-free highway.

freeze /friːz/ *v. & n.* —*v.* (*past* **froze** /frəʊz/; *past part.* **frozen** /'frəʊz(ə)n/) **1** *tr. & intr.* **a** turn or be turned into ice or another solid by cold. **b** (often foll. by *over*, *up*) make or become rigid or solid as a result of the cold. **2** *intr.* be or feel very cold. **3** *tr. & intr.* cover or become covered with ice. **4** *intr.* (foll. by *to*, *together*) adhere or be fastened by frost (*the curtains froze to the window*). **5** *tr.* preserve (food) by refrigeration below freezing-point. **6** *tr. & intr.* **a** make or become motionless or powerless through fear,

surprise, etc. **b** react or cause to react with sudden aloofness or detachment. **7** *tr.* stiffen or harden, injure or kill, by chilling (*frozen to death*). **8** *tr.* make (credits, assets, etc.) temporarily or permanently unrealizable. **9** *tr.* fix or stabilize (prices, wages, etc.) at a certain level. **10** *tr.* arrest (an action) at a certain stage of development. **11** *tr.* arrest (a movement in a film) by repeating a frame or stopping the film at a frame. —*n.* **1** a state of frost; a period or the coming of frost or very cold weather. **2** the fixing or stabilization of prices, wages, etc. **3** a film-shot in which movement is arrested by the repetition of a frame. □**freeze-dry** (**-dries, -dried**) freeze and dry by the sublimation of ice in a high vacuum. **freeze-frame** = sense 3 of *n.* **freeze on to** *colloq.* take or keep tight hold of. **freeze out** *US colloq.* exclude from business, society, etc. by competition or boycott etc. **freeze up** obstruct or be obstructed by the formation of ice. **freeze-up** *n.* a period or conditions of extreme cold. **freezing-mixture** salt and snow or some other mixture used to freeze liquids. **freezing-point** the temperature at which a liquid, esp. water, freezes. **freezing works** *Austral. & NZ* a place where animals are slaughtered and carcasses frozen for export. **frozen mitt** *colloq.* a cool reception. □□ **freezable** *adj.* **frozenly** *adv.* [OE *frēosan* f. Gmc]

freezer /'friːzə(r)/ *n.* a refrigerated cabinet or room for preserving food at very low temperatures; = DEEP-FREEZE *n.*

freight /freɪt/ *n. & v.* —*n.* **1** the transport of goods in containers or by water or air or *US* by land. **2** goods transported; cargo. **3** a charge for transportation of goods. **4** the hire of a ship or aircraft for transporting goods. **5** a load or burden. —*v.tr.* **1** transport (goods) as freight. **2** load with freight. **3** hire or let out (a ship) for the carriage of goods and passengers. □**freight ton** see TON¹. [MDu., MLG *vrecht* var. of *vracht*: cf. FRAUGHT]

freightage /'freɪtɪdʒ/ *n.* **1 a** the transportation of freight. **b** the cost of this. **2** freight transported.

freighter /'freɪtə(r)/ *n.* **1** a ship or aircraft designed to carry freight. **2** *US* a wagon for freight. **3** a person who loads or charters and loads a ship. **4** a person who consigns goods for carriage inland. **5** a person whose business is to receive and forward freight.

freightliner /'freɪtˌlaɪnə(r)/ *n.* a train carrying goods in containers.

French /frentʃ/ *adj. & n.* —*adj.* **1** of or relating to France or its people or language. **2** having the characteristics attributed to the French people. —*n.* **1** the language of France, also used in Belgium, Switzerland, Canada, and elsewhere. **2** (**the French**) (*pl.*) the people of France. **3** *colloq.* bad language (*excuse my French*). **4** *colloq.* dry vermouth (*gin and French*). □**French bean** *Brit.* a beanplant, *Phaseolus vulgaris*, having many varieties cultivated for their pods and seeds. **2 a** the pod used as food. **b** the seed used as food: also called HARICOT, *kidney bean*. **French bread** white bread in a long crisp loaf. **French Canadian** *n.* a Canadian whose principal language is French. —*adj.* of or relating to French-speaking Canadians. **French chalk** a kind of steatite used for marking cloth and removing grease and as a dry lubricant. **French cricket** an informal type of cricket without stumps and played with a soft ball. **French cuff** a cuff of double thickness. **French curve** a template used for drawing curved lines. **French door** = *French window*. **French dressing** a salad dressing of vinegar and oil, usu. seasoned. **French fried potatoes** (*US* **French fries**) potato chips. **French horn** a coiled brass wind instrument with a wide bell. **French kiss** a kiss with one partner's tongue inserted in the other's mouth. **French knickers** wide-legged knickers. **French leave** absence without permission. **French letter** *Brit. colloq.* a condom. **French mustard** *Brit.* a mild mustard mixed with

w *we*   z *zoo*   ʃ *she*   ʒ *decision*   θ *thin*   ð *this*   ŋ *ring*   x *loch*   tʃ *chip*   dʒ *jar*   (*see over for vowels*)

vinegar. **French polish** shellac polish for wood. **French-polish** *v.tr.* polish with this. **French roof** a mansard. **French seam** a seam with the raw edges enclosed. **French toast** 1 *Brit.* bread buttered on one side and toasted on the other. 2 bread dipped in egg and milk and fried. **French vermouth** dry vermouth. **French window** a glazed door in an outside wall, serving as a window and door. □□ **Frenchness** *n.* [OE *frencisc* f. Gmc]

Frenchify /ˈfrentʃɪˌfaɪ/ *v.tr.* (-**ies**, -**ied**) (usu. as **Frenchified** *adj.*) make French in form, character, or manners.

Frenchman /ˈfrentʃmən/ *n.* (*pl.* -**men**) a man who is French by birth or descent.

Frenchwoman /ˈfrentʃˌwʊmən/ *n.* (*pl.* -**women**) a woman who is French by birth or descent.

frenetic /frəˈnetɪk/ *adj.* 1 frantic, frenzied. 2 fanatic. □□ **frenetically** *adv.* [ME f. OF *frenetique* f. L *phreneticus* f. Gk *phrenitikos* f. *phrenitis* delirium f. *phrēn phrenos* mind]

frenulum var. of FRAENULUM.

frenum var. of FRAENUM.

frenzy /ˈfrenzɪ/ *n.* & *v.* —*n.* (*pl.* -**ies**) 1 mental derangement; wild excitement or agitation. 2 delirious fury. —*v.tr.* (-**ies**, -**ied**) (usu. as **frenzied** *adj.*) drive to frenzy; infuriate. □□ **frenziedly** *adv.* [ME f. OF *frenesie* f. med.L *phrenesia* f. L *phrenesis* f. Gk *phrēn* mind]

Freon /ˈfriːɒn/ *n. propr.* any of a group of halogenated hydrocarbons containing fluorine, chlorine, and sometimes bromine, used in aerosols, refrigerants, etc. (see also CFC).

frequency /ˈfriːkwənsɪ/ *n.* (*pl.* -**ies**) 1 commonness of occurrence. 2 **a** the state of being frequent; frequent occurrence. **b** the process of being repeated at short intervals. 3 *Physics* the rate of recurrence of a vibration, oscillation, cycle, etc.; the number of repetitions in a given time, esp. per second. ¶ Abbr.: *f.* 4 *Statistics* the ratio of the number of actual to possible occurrences of an event. □ **frequency band** *Electronics* = BAND[1] 3a. **frequency distribution** *Statistics* a measurement of the frequency of occurrence of the values of a variable. **frequency modulation** *Electronics* a modulation in which the frequency of the carrier wave is varied. ¶ Abbr.: FM. **frequency response** *Electronics* the dependence on signal-frequency of the output–input ratio of an amplifier etc. [L *frequentia* (as FREQUENT)]

frequent *adj.* & *v.* —*adj.* /ˈfriːkwənt/ 1 occurring often or in close succession. 2 habitual, constant (*a frequent caller*). 3 found near together; numerous, abundant. 4 (of the pulse) rapid. —*v.tr.* /frɪˈkwent/ attend or go to habitually. □□ **frequentation** /ˌfriːkwenˈteɪʃ(ə)n/ *n.* **frequenter** /frɪˈkwentə(r)/ *n.* **frequently** /ˈfriːkwəntlɪ/ *adv.* [F *fréquent* or L *frequens -entis* crowded]

frequentative /frɪˈkwentətɪv/ *adj.* & *n. Gram.* —*adj.* expressing frequent repetition or intensity of action. —*n.* a verb or verbal form or conjugation expressing this (e.g. *chatter, twinkle*). [F *fréquentatif -ive* or L *frequentativus* (as FREQUENT)]

fresco /ˈfreskəʊ/ *n.* (*pl.* -**os** or -**oes**) 1 a painting done in water-colour on a wall or ceiling while the plaster is still wet. 2 this method of painting (esp. *in fresco*). □ **fresco secco** = SECCO. □□ **frescoed** *adj.* [It., = cool, fresh]

fresh /freʃ/ *adj.*, *adv.*, & *n.* —*adj.* 1 newly made or obtained (*fresh sandwiches*). 2 **a** other, different; not previously known or used (*start a fresh page; we need fresh ideas*). **b** additional (*fresh supplies*). 3 (foll. by *from*) lately arrived from (a specified place or situation). 4 not stale or musty or faded (*fresh flowers; fresh memories*). 5 (of food) not preserved by salting, tinning, freezing, etc. 6 not salty (*fresh water*). 7 **a** pure, untainted, refreshing, invigorating (*fresh air*). **b** bright and pure in colour (*a fresh complexion*). 8 (of the wind) brisk; of fair strength. 9 alert, vigorous, fit (*never felt fresher*). 10 *colloq.* **a**

cheeky, presumptuous. **b** amorously impudent. 11 young and inexperienced. —*adv.* newly, recently (esp. in *comb.*: *fresh-baked; fresh-cut*). —*n.* the fresh part of the day, year, etc. (*in the fresh of the morning*). □□ **freshly** *adv.* **freshness** *n.* [ME f. OF *freis fresche* ult. f. Gmc]

freshen /ˈfreʃ(ə)n/ *v.* 1 *tr.* & *intr.* make or become fresh or fresher. 2 *intr.* & *tr.* (foll. by *up*) **a** wash, change one's clothes, etc. **b** revive, refresh, renew.

fresher /ˈfreʃə(r)/ *n. Brit. colloq.* = FRESHMAN.

freshet /ˈfreʃɪt/ *n.* 1 a rush of fresh water flowing into the sea. 2 the flood of a river from heavy rain or melted snow. [prob. f. OF *freschete* f. *frais* FRESH]

freshman /ˈfreʃmən/ *n.* (*pl.* -**men**) a first-year student at university or *US* at high school.

freshwater /ˈfreʃˌwɔːtə(r)/ *adj.* 1 of or found in fresh water; not of the sea. 2 *US* (of a school or college) rustic or provincial. □ **freshwater flea** = DAPHNIA.

fret[1] /fret/ *v.* & *n.* —*v.* (**fretted, fretting**) 1 *intr.* **a** be greatly and visibly worried or distressed. **b** be irritated or resentful. 2 *tr.* **a** cause anxiety or distress to. **b** irritate, annoy. 3 *tr.* wear or consume by gnawing or rubbing. 4 *tr.* form (a channel or passage) by wearing away. 5 *intr.* (of running water) flow or rise in little waves. —*n.* irritation, vexation, querulousness (esp. *in a fret*). [OE *fretan* f. Gmc, rel. to EAT]

fret[2] /fret/ *n.* & *v.* —*n.* 1 an ornamental pattern made of continuous combinations of straight lines joined usu. at right angles. 2 *Heraldry* a device of narrow bands and a diamond interlaced. —*v.tr.* (**fretted, fretting**) 1 embellish or decorate with a fret. 2 adorn (esp. a ceiling) with carved or embossed work. [ME f. OF *frete* trellis-work and *freter* (v.)]

fret[3] /fret/ *n.* each of a sequence of bars or ridges on the finger-board of some stringed musical instruments (esp. the guitar) fixing the positions of the fingers to produce the desired notes. □□ **fretless** *adj.* [15th c.: orig. unkn.]

fretful /ˈfretfʊl/ *adj.* visibly anxious, distressed, or irritated. □□ **fretfully** *adv.* **fretfulness** *n.*

fretsaw /ˈfretsɔː/ *n.* a saw consisting of a narrow blade stretched on a frame, for cutting thin wood in patterns.

fretwork /ˈfretwɜːk/ *n.* ornamental work in wood, done with a fretsaw.

Freudian /ˈfrɔɪdɪən/ *adj.* & *n. Psychol.* —*adj.* of or relating to the Austrian psychologist Sigmund Freud (d. 1939) or his methods of psychoanalysis, esp. with reference to the importance of sexuality in human behaviour. —*n.* a follower of Freud or his methods. □ **Freudian slip** an unintentional error regarded as revealing subconscious feelings. □□ **Freudianism** *n.*

Fri. *abbr.* Friday.

friable /ˈfraɪəb(ə)l/ *adj.* easily crumbled. □□ **friability** /-ˈbɪlɪtɪ/ *n.* **friableness** *n.* [F *friable* or L *friabilis* f. *friare* crumble]

friar /ˈfraɪə(r)/ *n.* a member of any of certain religious orders of men, esp. the four mendicant orders Augustinians, Carmelites, Dominicans, and Franciscans. □ **friar's** (or **friars'**) **balsam** a tincture of benzoin etc. used esp. as an inhalant. □□ **friarly** *adj.* [ME & OF *frere* f. L *frater fratris* brother]

friary /ˈfraɪərɪ/ *n.* (*pl.* -**ies**) a convent of friars.

fricandeau /ˈfrɪkənˌdəʊ/ *n.* & *v.* —*n.* (*pl.* **fricandeaus** /-ˌdəʊz/) 1 a cushion-shaped piece of meat, esp. veal, cut from the leg. 2 a dish made from this, usu. fried or stewed and served with a sauce. —*v.tr.* (**fricandeaus, fricandeaued, fricandeauing**) make into fricandeaux. [F]

fricassee /ˈfrɪkəˌsiː, -ˈsiː/ *n.* & *v.* —*n.* a dish of stewed or fried pieces of meat served in a thick white sauce. —*v.tr.* (**fricassees, fricasseed**) make a fricassee of. [F, fem. past part. of *fricasser* (v.)]

fricative /ˈfrɪkətɪv/ *adj.* & *n. Phonet.* —*adj.* made by the friction of breath in a narrow opening. —*n.* a consonant made in this way, e.g. *f* and *th*. [mod.L *fricativus* f. L *fricare* rub]

gash[2] /gæʃ/ *adj. Brit. sl.* spare, extra. [20th-c. Naut. sl.: orig. unkn.]

gasholder /'gæs,həʊldə(r)/ *n.* a large receptacle for storing gas; a gasometer.

gasify /'gæsɪ,faɪ/ *v.tr. & intr.* (-ies, -ied) convert or be converted into gas. □□ **gasification** /-fɪ'keɪʃ(ə)n/ *n.*

gasket /'gæskɪt/ *n.* **1** a sheet or ring of rubber etc., shaped to seal the junction of metal surfaces. **2** a small cord securing a furled sail to a yard. □ **blow a gasket** *sl.* lose one's temper. [perh. f. F *garcette* thin rope (orig. little girl)]

gaskin /'gæskɪn/ *n.* the hinder part of a horse's thigh. [perh. erron. f. GALLIGASKINS]

gaslight /'gæslaɪt/ *n.* **1** a jet of burning gas, usu. heating a mantle, to provide light. **2** light emanating from this.

gasman /'gæsmən/ *n.* (*pl.* -men) a man who instals or services gas appliances, or reads gas meters.

gasolene var. of GASOLINE.

gasoline /'gæsə,liːn/ *n.* (also **gasolene**) **1** a volatile inflammable liquid distilled from petroleum and used for heating and lighting. **2** *US* petrol. [GAS + -OL[2] + -INE[4], -ENE]

gasometer /gæ'sɒmɪtə(r)/ *n.* a large tank in which gas is stored for distribution by pipes to users. [F *gazomètre* f. *gaz* gas + -*mètre* -METER]

gasp /gɑːsp/ *v. & n.* —*v.* **1** *intr.* catch one's breath with an open mouth as in exhaustion or astonishment. **2** *intr.* (foll. by *for*) strain to obtain by gasping (*gasped for air*). **3** *tr.* (often foll. by *out*) utter with gasps. —*n.* a convulsive catching of breath. □ **at one's last gasp 1** at the point of death. **2** exhausted. [ME f. ON *geispa*: cf. *geip* idle talk]

gasper /'gɑːspə(r)/ *n.* **1** a person who gasps. **2** *Brit. sl.* a cigarette.

gasser /'gæsə(r)/ *n.* **1** *colloq.* an idle talker. **2** *sl.* a very attractive or impressive person or thing.

gassy /'gæsɪ/ *adj.* (**gassier, gassiest**) **1 a** of or like gas. **b** full of gas. **2** *colloq.* (of talk etc.) pointless, verbose. □□ **gassiness** *n.*

gasteropod var. of GASTROPOD.

gasthaus /'gæsthaʊs/ *n.* a small inn or hotel in German-speaking countries. [G f. *Gast* GUEST + *Haus* HOUSE]

gastrectomy /gæ'strektəmɪ/ *n.* (*pl.* -ies) a surgical operation in which the whole or part of the stomach is removed. [GASTRO- + -ECTOMY]

gastric /'gæstrɪk/ *adj.* of the stomach. □ **gastric flu** a popular name for an intestinal disorder of unknown cause. **gastric juice** a thin clear virtually colourless acid fluid secreted by the stomach glands and active in promoting digestion. [mod.L *gastricus* f. Gk *gastēr gast(e)ros* stomach]

gastritis /gæ'straɪtɪs/ *n.* inflammation of the lining of the stomach.

gastro- /'gæstrəʊ/ *comb. form* (also **gastr-** before a vowel) stomach. [Gk *gastēr gast(e)ros* stomach]

gastro-enteric /,gæstrəʊen'terɪk/ *adj.* of or relating to the stomach and intestines.

gastro-enteritis /,gæstrəʊ,entə'raɪtɪs/ *n. Med.* inflammation of the stomach and intestines.

gastronome /'gæstrə,nəʊm/ *n.* a gourmet. [F f. *gastronomie* GASTRONOMY]

gastronomy /gæ'strɒnəmɪ/ *n.* the practice, study, or art of eating and drinking well. □□ **gastronomic** /,gæstrə'nɒmɪk/ *adj.* **gastronomical** /,gæstrə'nɒmɪk(ə)l/ *adj.* **gastronomically** /,gæstrə'nɒmɪkəlɪ/ *adv.* [F *gastronomie* f. Gk *gastronomia* (as GASTRO-, -*nomia* f. *nomos* law)]

gastropod /'gæstrə,pɒd/ *n.* (also **gasteropod**) any mollusc of the class Gastropoda that moves along by means of a large muscular foot, e.g. a snail, slug, etc. □□ **gastropodous** /gæ'strɒpədəs/ *adj.* [F *gastéropode* f. mod.L *gasteropoda* (as GASTRO-, Gk *pous podos* foot)]

gastroscope /'gæstrə,skəʊp/ *n.* an optical instrument used for inspecting the interior of the stomach.

gastrula /'gæstrʊlə/ *n.* (*pl.* **gastrulae** /-,liː/) *Zool.* an embryonic stage developing from the blastula. [mod.L f. Gk *gastēr gast(e)ros* belly]

gasworks /'gæswɜːks/ *n.* a place where gas is manufactured and processed.

gat[1] /gæt/ *n. sl.* a revolver or other firearm. [abbr. of GATLING]

gat[2] /gæt/ *archaic past of* GET *v.*

gate[1] /geɪt/ *n. & v.* —*n.* **1** a barrier, usu. hinged, used to close an opening made for entrance and exit through a wall, fence, etc. **2** such an opening, esp. in the wall of a city, enclosure, or large building. **3** a means of entrance or exit. **4** a numbered place of access to aircraft at an airport. **5** a mountain pass. **6** an arrangement of slots into which the gear lever of a motor vehicle moves to engage the required gear. **7** a device for holding the frame of a cine film momentarily in position behind the lens of a camera or projector. **8 a** an electrical signal that causes or controls the passage of other signals. **b** an electrical circuit with an output which depends on the combination of several inputs. **9** a device regulating the passage of water in a lock etc. **10 a** the number of people entering by payment at the gates of a sports ground etc. **b** (in full **gate-money**) the proceeds taken for admission. **11** *sl.* the mouth. **12** *US sl.* dismissal. **13** = *starting-gate.* —*v.tr.* **1** *Brit.* confine to college or school entirely or after certain hours. **2** (as **gated** *adj.*) (of a road) having a gate or gates to control the movement of traffic or animals. [OE *gæt, geat,* pl. *gatu,* f. Gmc]

gate[2] /geɪt/ *n.* (prec. or prefixed by a name) *Brit.* a street (*Westgate*). [ME f. ON *gata,* f. Gmc]

gateau /'gætəʊ/ *n.* (*pl.* **gateaus** or **gateaux**) any of various rich cakes, usu. containing cream or fruit. [F *gâteau* cake]

gatecrasher /'geɪt,kræʃə(r)/ *n.* an uninvited guest at a party etc. □□ **gatecrash** *v.tr. & intr.*

gatefold /'geɪtfəʊld/ *n.* a page in a book or magazine etc. that folds out to be larger than the page-format.

gatehouse /'geɪthaʊs/ *n.* **1** a house standing by a gateway, esp. to a large house or park. **2** *hist.* a room over a city gate, often used as a prison.

gatekeeper /'geɪt,kiːpə(r)/ *n.* **1** an attendant at a gate, controlling entrance and exit. **2** any of several large brown species of butterfly, esp. *Maniola tithonus*, frequenting hedgerows and woodland.

gateleg /'geɪtleg/ *n.* (in full **gateleg table**) a table with folding flaps supported by legs swung open like a gate. □□ **gatelegged** *adj.*

gateman /'geɪtmən/ *n.* (*pl.* -men) = GATEKEEPER 1.

gatepost /'geɪtpəʊst/ *n.* a post on which a gate is hung or against which it shuts. □ **between you and me and the gatepost** in strict confidence.

gateway /'geɪtweɪ/ *n.* **1** an entrance with or opening for a gate. **2** a frame or structure built over a gate.

gather /'gæðə(r)/ *v. & n.* —*v.* **1** *tr. & intr.* bring or come together; assemble, accumulate. **2** *tr.* (usu. foll. by *up*) **a** bring together from scattered places or sources. **b** take up together from the ground, a surface, etc. **c** draw into a smaller compass. **3** *tr.* acquire by gradually collecting; amass. **4** *tr.* **a** pick a quantity of (flowers etc.). **b** collect (grain etc.) as a harvest. **5** *tr.* (often foll. by *that* + clause) infer or understand. **6** *tr.* be subjected to or affected by the accumulation or increase of (*unread books gathering dust; gather speed; gather strength*). **7** *tr.* (often foll. by *up*) summon up (one's thoughts, energy, etc.) for a purpose. **8** *tr.* gain or recover (one's breath). **9** *tr.* **a** draw (material, or one's brow) together in folds or wrinkles. **b** pucker or draw together (part of a dress) by running a thread through. **10** *intr.* come to a head; develop a purulent swelling. —*n.* (in *pl.*) a part of a garment that is gathered or drawn in. □ **gather way** (of a ship) begin to move. □□ **gatherer** *n.* [OE *gaderian* f. WG]

gathering /'gæðərɪŋ/ *n.* **1** an assembly or meeting. **2**

friction /'frɪkʃ(ə)n/ n. **1** the action of one object rubbing against another. **2** the resistance an object encounters in moving over another. **3** a clash of wills, temperaments, or opinions; mutual animosity arising from disagreement. **4** (in comb.) of devices that transmit motion by frictional contact (friction-clutch; friction-disc). □**friction-ball** a ball used in bearings to lessen friction. □□**frictional** adj. **frictionless** adj. [F f. L frictio -onis f. fricare frict-rub]

Friday /'fraɪdeɪ, -dɪ/ n. & adv. —n. the sixth day of the week, following Thursday. —adv. colloq. **1** on Friday. **2** (Fridays) on Fridays; each Friday. □**girl** (or **man**) **Friday** a helper or follower (after Man Friday in Defoe's Robinson Crusoe). [OE frígedæg f. Gmc (named after Frigg the wife of Odin)]

fridge /frɪdʒ/ n. Brit. colloq. = REFRIGERATOR. □**fridge-freezer** an upright unit comprising a refrigerator and a freezer, each self-contained. [abbr.]

friend /frend/ n. & v. —n. **1** a person with whom one enjoys mutual affection and regard (usu. exclusive of sexual or family bonds). **2** a sympathizer, helper, or patron (no friend to virtue; a friend of order). **3** a person who is not an enemy or who is on the same side (friend or foe?). **4 a** a person already mentioned or under discussion (my friend at the next table then left the room). **b** a person known by sight. **c** used as a polite or ironic form of address. **5** (usu. in pl.) a regular contributor of money or other assistance to an institution. **6** (**Friend**) a member of the Society of Friends, a Quaker. **7** (in pl.) one's near relatives, those responsible for one. **8** a helpful thing or quality. —v.tr. archaic or poet. befriend, help. □**be** (or **keep**) **friends with** be friendly with. **friend at court** a friend whose influence may be made use of. **my honourable friend** Brit. used in the House of Commons to refer to another member of one's own party. **my learned friend** used by a lawyer in court to refer to another lawyer. **my noble friend** Brit. used in the House of Lords to refer to another member of one's own party. □□**friended** adj. **friendless** adj. [OE frēond f. Gmc]

friendly /'frendlɪ/ adj., n., & adv. —adj. (**friendlier**, **friendliest**) **1** acting as or like a friend, well-disposed, kindly. **2 a** (often foll. by with) on amicable terms. **b** not hostile. **3** characteristic of friends, showing or prompted by kindness. **4** favourably disposed, ready to approve or help. **5 a** (of a thing) serviceable, convenient, opportune. **b** = user-friendly. —n. (pl. **-ies**) = friendly match. —adv. in a friendly manner. □**friendly action** Law an action brought merely to get a point decided. **friendly match** a match played for enjoyment and not in competition for a cup etc. **Friendly Society** Brit. = benefit society. □□**friendlily** adv. **friendliness** n.

friendship /'frendʃɪp/ n. **1** being friends, the relationship between friends. **2** a friendly disposition felt or shown. [OE frēondscipe (as FRIEND, -SHIP)]

frier var. of FRYER.

Friesian /'friːʒ(ə)n, -zɪən/ n. & adj. Brit. —n. **1** a large animal of a usu. black and white breed of dairy cattle orig. from Friesland. **2** this breed. —adj. of or concerning Friesians. [var. of FRISIAN]

frieze[1] /friːz/ n. **1** the part of an entablature between the architrave and the cornice. **2** a horizontal band of sculpture filling this. **3** a band of decoration elsewhere, esp. along a wall near the ceiling. [F frise f. med.L frisium, frigium f. L Phrygium (opus) (work) of Phrygia]

frieze[2] /friːz/ n. coarse woollen cloth with a nap, usu. on one side only. [ME f. F frise, prob. rel. to FRISIAN]

frig[1] /frɪg/ v. & n. coarse sl. —v. (**frigged**, **frigging**) **1** tr. & intr. **a** have sexual intercourse (with). **b** masturbate. **2** tr. (usu. as an exclamation) = FUCK v. **3**. **3** intr. (foll. by about, around) mess about; fool around. **4** intr. (foll. by off) go away. —n. an act of frigging. ¶ Usually considered a taboo word. [perh. imit.: orig. senses 'move about, rub']

frig[2] /frɪdʒ/ n. Brit. colloq. = REFRIGERATOR. [abbr.]

frigate /'frɪgɪt/ n. **1 a** Brit. a naval escort-vessel between a corvette and a destroyer in size. **b** US a similar ship between a destroyer and a cruiser in size. **2** hist. a warship next in size to ships of the line. □**frigate-bird** any marine bird of the family Fregatidae, found in tropical seas, with a wide wingspan and deeply forked tail: also called hurricane-bird. [F frégate f. It. fregata, of unkn. orig.]

fright /fraɪt/ n. & v. —n. **1 a** sudden or extreme fear. **b** an instance of this (gave me a fright). **2** a person or thing looking grotesque or ridiculous. —v.tr. poet. frighten. □**take fright** become frightened. [OE fryhto, metathetic form of fyrhto, f. Gmc]

frighten /'fraɪt(ə)n/ v.tr. **1** fill with fright; terrify (was frightened at the bang; is frightened of dogs). **2** (foll. by away, off, out of, into) drive or force by fright (frightened it out of the room; frightened them into submission; frightened me into agreeing). □□ **frightening** adj. **frighteningly** adv.

frightener /'fraɪtənə(r)/ n. a person or thing that frightens. □**put the frighteners on** sl. intimidate.

frightful /'fraɪtfʊl/ adj. **1 a** dreadful, shocking, revolting. **b** ugly, hideous. **2** colloq. extremely bad (a frightful idea). **3** colloq. very great, extreme. □□ **frightfully** adv.

frightfulness /'fraɪtfʊlnɪs/ n. **1** being frightful. **2** (transl. G Schrecklichkeit) the terrorizing of a civilian population as a military resource.

frigid /'frɪdʒɪd/ adj. **1 a** lacking friendliness or enthusiasm; apathetic, formal, forced. **b** dull, flat, insipid. **c** chilling, depressing. **2** (of a woman) sexually unresponsive. **3** (esp. of climate or air) cold. □**frigid zones** the parts of the earth north of the Arctic Circle and south of the Antarctic Circle. □□ **frigidity** /-'dʒɪdɪtɪ/ n. **frigidly** adv. **frigidness** n. [L frigidus f. frigēre be cold f. frigus (n.) cold]

frijoles /fri:'həʊleɪs/ n.pl. beans. [Sp., pl. of frijol f. L phaseolus]

frill /frɪl/ n. & v. —n. **1 a** a strip of material with one side gathered or pleated and the other left loose with a fluted appearance, used as an ornamental edging. **b** a similar paper ornament on a ham-knuckle, chop, etc. **c** a natural fringe of feathers, hair, etc., on an animal (esp. a bird) or a plant. **2** (in pl.) **a** unnecessary embellishments or accomplishments. **b** airs, affectation (put on frills). —v.tr. **1** decorate with a frill. **2** form into a frill. □**frill** (or **frilled**) **lizard** a large N. Australian lizard, Chlamydosaurus kingii, with an erectile membrane round the neck. □□**frilled** adj. **frillery** n. [16th c.: orig. unkn.]

frilling /'frɪlɪŋ/ n. **1** a set of frills. **2** material for frills.

frilly /'frɪlɪ/ adj. & n. —adj. (**frillier**, **frilliest**) **1** having a frill or frills. **2** resembling a frill. —n. (pl. **-ies**) (in pl.) colloq. frilled underwear. □□**frilliness** n.

fringe /frɪndʒ/ n. & v. —n. **1 a** an ornamental bordering of threads left loose or formed into tassels or twists. **b** such a bordering made separately. **c** any border or edging. **2 a** a portion of the front hair hanging over the forehead. **b** a natural border of hair etc. in an animal or plant. **3** an outer edge or margin; the outer limit of an area, population, etc. (often attrib.: fringe theatre). **4** a thing, part, or area of secondary or minor importance. **5 a** a band of contrasting brightness or darkness produced by diffraction or interference of light. **b** a strip of false colour in an optical image. **6** US a fringe benefit. —v.tr. **1** adorn or encircle with a fringe. **2** serve as a fringe to. □**fringe benefit** an employee's benefit supplementing a money wage or salary. **fringe medicine** systems of treatment of disease etc. not regarded as orthodox by the medical profession. **fringing reef** a coral reef that fringes the shore. □□ **fringeless** adj. **fringy** adj. [ME & OF frenge ult. f. LL fimbria (earlier only in pl.) fibres, fringe]

fringing /'frɪndʒɪŋ/ n. material for a fringe or fringes.

frippery /ˈfrɪpərɪ/ n. & adj. —n. (pl. **-ies**) **1** showy, tawdry, or unnecessary finery or ornament, esp. in dress. **2** empty display in speech, literary style, etc. **3 a** knick-knacks, trifles. **b** a knick-knack or trifle. —adj. **1** frivolous. **2** contemptible. [F friperie f. OF freperie f. frepe rag]

frippet /ˈfrɪpɪt/ n. sl. a frivolous or showy young woman. [20th c.: orig. unkn.]

Frisbee /ˈfrɪzbɪ/ n. propr. a concave plastic disc for skimming through the air as an outdoor game. [perh. f. Frisbie bakery (Bridgeport, Conn.), whose pie-tins could be used similarly]

Frisian /ˈfrɪzɪən/ adj. & n. —adj. of Friesland (an area comprising the NW Netherlands and adjacent islands). —n. **1** a native or inhabitant of Friesland. **2** the language of Friesland. [L Frisii pl. f. OFris. Frīsa, Frēsa]

frisk /frɪsk/ v. & n. —v. **1** intr. leap or skip playfully. **2** tr. sl. feel over or search (a person) for a weapon etc. (usu. rapidly). —n. **1** a playful leap or skip. **2** sl. the frisking of a person. □□ **frisker** n. [obs. frisk (adj.) f. OF frisque lively, of unkn. orig.]

frisket /ˈfrɪskɪt/ n. Printing a thin iron frame keeping the sheet in position during printing on a hand-press. [F frisquette f. Prov. frisqueto f. Sp. frasqueta]

frisky /ˈfrɪskɪ/ adj. (**friskier**, **friskiest**) lively, playful. □□ **friskily** adv. **friskiness** n.

frisson /ˈfriːsɒn, -sɔ̃/ n. an emotional thrill. [F, = shiver]

frit /frɪt/ n. & v. —n. **1** a calcined mixture of sand and fluxes as material for glass-making. **2** a vitreous composition from which soft porcelain, enamel, etc., are made. —v.tr. (**fritted**, **fritting**) make into frit, partially fuse, calcine. [It. fritta fem. past part. of friggere FRY[1]]

frit-fly /ˈfrɪtflaɪ/ n. (pl. **-flies**) a small fly, Oscinella frit, of which the larvae are destructive to cereals. [19th c.: orig. unkn.]

frith var. of FIRTH.

fritillary /frɪˈtɪlərɪ, ˈfrɪ-/ n. (pl. **-ies**) **1** any liliaceous plant of the genus Fritillaria, esp. snake's head, having pendent bell-like flowers. **2** any of various butterflies, esp. of the genus Argynnis, having red-brown wings chequered with black. [mod.L fritillaria f. L fritillus dice-box]

fritter[1] /ˈfrɪtə(r)/ v.tr. **1** (usu. foll. by away) waste (money, time, energy, etc.) triflingly, indiscriminately, or on divided aims. **2** archaic subdivide. [obs. n. fritter(s) fragments = obs. fitters (n.pl.), perh. rel. to MHG vetze rag]

fritter[2] /ˈfrɪtə(r)/ n. a piece of fruit, meat, etc., coated in batter and deep-fried (apple fritter). [ME f. OF friture ult. f. L frigere frict- FRY[1]]

fritto misto /ˌfrɪtəʊ ˈmɪstəʊ/ n. a mixed grill. [It., = mixed fry]

fritz /frɪts/ n. □ **on the fritz** US sl. out of order, unsatisfactory. [20th c.: orig. unkn.]

frivol /ˈfrɪv(ə)l/ v. (**frivolled**, **frivolling**; US **frivoled**, **frivoling**) **1** intr. be a trifler; trifle. **2** tr. (foll. by away) spend (money or time) foolishly. [back-form. f. FRIVOLOUS]

frivolous /ˈfrɪvələs/ adj. **1** paltry, trifling, trumpery. **2** lacking seriousness; given to trifling; silly. □□ **frivolity** /-ˈvɒlɪtɪ/ n. (pl. **-ies**). **frivolously** adv. **frivolousness** n. [L frivolus silly, trifling]

frizz /frɪz/ v. & n. —v.tr. **1** form (hair) into a mass of small curls. **2** dress (wash-leather etc.) with pumice or a scraping-knife. —n. **1 a** frizzed hair. **b** a row of curls. **2** a frizzed state. [F friser, perh. f. the stem of frire FRY[1]]

frizzle[1] /ˈfrɪz(ə)l/ v.intr. & tr. **1** fry, toast, or grill, with a sputtering noise. **2** (often foll. by up) burn or shrivel. [frizz (in the same sense) f. FRY[1], with imit. ending + -LE[4]]

frizzle[2] /ˈfrɪz(ə)l/ v. & n. —v. **1** tr. form (hair) into tight curls. **2** intr. (often foll. by up) (of hair etc.) curl tightly. —n. frizzled hair. [16th c.: orig. unkn. (earlier than FRIZZ)]

frizzly /ˈfrɪzlɪ/ adj. in tight curls.

frizzy /ˈfrɪzɪ/ adj. (**frizzier**, **frizziest**) in a mass of small curls. □□ **frizziness** n.

Frl. abbr. Fräulein.

fro /frəʊ/ adv. back (now only in to and fro: see TO). [ME f. ON frá FROM]

frock /frɒk/ n. & v. —n. **1** a woman's or girl's dress. **2 a** a monk's or priest's long gown with loose sleeves. **b** priestly office. **3** a smock. **4 a** a frock-coat. **b** a military coat of similar shape. **5** a sailor's woollen jersey. —v.tr. invest with priestly office (cf. UNFROCK). □ **frock-coat** a man's long-skirted coat not cut away in front. [ME f. OF froc f. Frank.]

froe /frəʊ/ n. (also **frow**) US a cleaving tool with a handle at right angles to the blade. [abbr. of frower f. FROWARD 'turned away']

Froebel system /ˈfrəʊb(ə)l, ˈfrɜːb(ə)l/ n. a system of education of children by means of kindergartens. □□ **Froebelian** /-ˈbiːlɪən/ adj. **Froebelism** n. [F. W. A. Fröbel, Ger. teacher d. 1852]

frog[1] /frɒg/ n. **1** any of various small amphibians of the order Anura, having a tailless smooth-skinned body with legs developed for jumping. **2** (**Frog**) Brit. sl. offens. a Frenchman. **3** a hollow in the top face of a brick for holding the mortar. **4** the nut of a violin-bow etc. □ **frog-fish** = angler-fish. **frog in the** (or **one's**) **throat** colloq. hoarseness. **frog-spawn** the spawn of a frog. [OE frogga f. Gmc]

frog[2] /frɒg/ n. an elastic horny substance in the sole of a horse's foot. [17th c.: orig. uncert. (perh. a use of FROG[1])]

frog[3] /frɒg/ n. **1** an ornamental coat-fastening of a spindle-shaped button and loop. **2** an attachment to a waist-belt to support a sword, bayonet, etc. □□ **frogged** adj. **frogging** n. [18th c.: orig. unkn.]

frog[4] /frɒg/ n. a grooved piece of iron at a place in a railway where tracks cross. [19th c.: orig. unkn.]

froggy /ˈfrɒgɪ/ adj. & n. —adj. **1** of or like a frog or frogs. **2 a** cold as a frog. **b** abounding in frogs. **3** Brit. sl. offens. French. —n. (**Froggy**) (pl. **-ies**) sl. derog. a Frenchman.

froghopper /ˈfrɒg,hɒpə(r)/ n. any jumping insect of the family Cercopidae, sucking sap and as larvae producing a protective mass of froth (see cuckoo-spit).

frogman /ˈfrɒgmən/ n. (pl. **-men**) a person equipped with a rubber suit, flippers, and an oxygen supply for underwater swimming.

frogmarch /ˈfrɒgmɑːtʃ/ v. & n. esp. Brit. —v.tr. **1** hustle (a person) forward holding and pinning the arms from behind. **2** carry (a person) in a frogmarch. —n. the carrying of a person face downwards by four others each holding a limb.

frogmouth /ˈfrɒgmaʊθ/ n. any of various birds of Australia and SE Asia, esp. of the family Podargidae, having large wide mouths.

frolic /ˈfrɒlɪk/ v., n., & adj. —v.intr. (**frolicked**, **frolicking**) play about cheerfully, gambol. —n. **1** cheerful play. **2** a prank. **3** a merry party. **4** an outburst of gaiety. **5** merriment. —adj. archaic **1** full of pranks, sportive. **2** joyous, mirthful. □□ **frolicker** n. [Du. vrolijk (adj.) f. vro glad + -lijk -LY[1]]

frolicsome /ˈfrɒlɪksəm/ adj. merry, playful. □□ **frolicsomely** adv. **frolicsomeness** n.

from /frəm, frɒm/ prep. expressing separation or origin, followed by: **1** a person, place, time, etc., that is the starting-point of motion or action, or of extent in place or time (rain comes from the clouds; repeated from mouth to mouth; dinner is served from 8; from start to finish). **2** a place, object, etc. whose distance or remoteness is reckoned or stated (ten miles from Rome; I am far from admitting it; absent from home; apart from its moral aspect). **3 a** a source (dig gravel from a pit; a man from Italy; draw a conclusion from premisses; quotations from Shaw). **b** a giver or sender (presents from Father Christmas; have not heard from her). **4 a** a thing or person avoided, escaped, lost, etc. (released him from prison; cannot refrain from laughing; dissuaded from folly). **b** a person or thing deprived (*took his gun from him*). **5** a reason, cause, or motive (*died from fatigue; suffering from mumps; did it from jealousy; from his looks you might not believe it*). **6** a thing distinguished or unlike (*know black from white*). **7** a lower limit (*saw from 10 to 20 boats; tickets from £5*). **8** a state changed for another (*from being the victim he became the attacker; raised the penalty from a fine to imprisonment*). **9** an adverb or preposition of time or place (*from long ago; from abroad; from under the bed*). **10** the position of a person who observes or considers (*saw it from the roof; from his point of view*). **11** a model (*painted it from nature*). □**from a child** since childhood. **from day to day** (or **hour to hour** etc.) daily (or hourly etc.); as the days (or hours etc.) pass. **from home** out, away. **from now on** henceforward. **from time to time** occasionally. **from year to year** each year; as the years pass. [OE *fram, from* f. Gmc]

frond /frɒnd/ n. **1** Bot. **a** a large usu. divided foliage leaf in various flowerless plants, esp. ferns and palms. **b** the leaflike thallus of some algae. **2** Zool. a leaflike expansion. □□ **frondage** n. **frondose** adj. [L *frons frondis* leaf]

frondeur /frɒn'dɜ:(r)/ n. a political rebel. [F, = slinger, applied to a party (the Fronde) rebelling during the minority of Louis XIV of France]

front /frʌnt/ n., adj., & v. —n. **1** the side or part normally nearer or towards the spectator or the direction of motion (*the front of the car; the front of the chair; the front of the mouth*). **2** any face of a building, esp. that of the main entrance. **3** Mil. **a** the foremost line or part of an army etc. **b** line of battle. **c** the part of the ground towards a real or imaginary enemy. **d** a scene of actual fighting (*go to the front*). **e** the direction in which a formed line faces (*change front*). **4 a** a sector of activity regarded as resembling a military front. **b** an organized political group. **5 a** demeanour, bearing (*show a bold front*). **b** outward appearance. **6** a forward or conspicuous position (*come to the front*). **7 a** a bluff. **b** a pretext. **8** a person etc. serving to cover subversive or illegal activities. **9** (prec. by *the*) the promenade of a seaside resort. **10** Meteorol. the forward edge of an advancing mass of cold or warm air. **11** (prec. by *the*) the auditorium of a theatre. **12 a** a face. **b** poet. or rhet. a forehead. **13 a** the breast of a man's shirt. **b** a false shirt-front. **14** impudence. —attrib.adj. **1** of the front. **2** situated in front. **3** Phonet. formed at the front of the mouth. —v. **1** intr. (foll. by *on, to, towards, upon*) have the front facing or directed. **2** intr. (foll. by *for*) sl. act as a front or cover for. **3** tr. furnish with a front (*fronted with stone*). **4** tr. lead (a band). **5** tr. a stand opposite to, front towards. **b** have its front on the side of (a street etc.). **6** tr. archaic confront, meet, oppose. □**front bench** Brit. the foremost seats in Parliament, occupied by leading members of the government and opposition. **front-bencher** Brit. such a member. **front door 1** the chief entrance of a house. **2** a chief means of approach or access to a place, situation, etc. **front line** Mil. = sense 3 of n. **front-line States** countries in Southern Africa bordering on and opposed to South Africa. **front man** a person acting as a front or cover. **front matter** Printing the title-page, preface, etc. preceding the text proper. **front office** a main office, esp. police headquarters. **front page** the first page of a newspaper, esp. as containing important or remarkable news. **front passage** colloq. the vagina. **front runner 1** the contestant most likely to succeed. **2** an athlete or horse running best when in the lead. **in front 1** in an advanced position. **2** facing the spectator. **in front of 1** ahead of, in advance of. **2** in the presence of, confronting. **on the front burner** see BURNER. □□ **frontless** adj. **frontward** adj. & adv. **frontwards** adv. [ME f. OF *front* (n.), *fronter* (v.) f. L *frons frontis*]

frontage /'frʌntɪdʒ/ n. **1** the front of a building. **2 a** land abutting on a street or on water. **b** the land between the front of a building and the road. **3** extent of front (*a shop with little frontage*). **4 a** the way a thing faces. **b** outlook. □**frontage road** US a service road. □□ **frontager** n.

frontal[1] /'frʌnt(ə)l/ adj. **1 a** of, at, or on the front (*a frontal attack*). **b** of the front as seen by an onlooker (*a frontal view*). **2** of the forehead or front part of the skull (*frontal bone*). □□ **frontally** adv. [mod.L *frontalis* (as FRONT)]

frontal[2] /'frʌnt(ə)l/ n. **1** a covering for the front of an altar. **2** the façade of a building. [ME f. OF *frontel* f. L *frontale* (as FRONT)]

frontier /'frʌntɪə(r), -'tɪə(r)/ n. **1 a** the border between two countries. **b** the district on each side of this. **2** the limits of attainment or knowledge in a subject. **3** US the borders between settled and unsettled country. □□ **frontierless** adj. [ME f. AF *frounter*, OF *frontiere* ult. f. L *frons frontis* FRONT]

frontiersman /'frʌntɪəzmən, -'tɪəzmən/ n. (pl. -**men**) a person living in the region of a frontier, esp. between settled and unsettled country.

frontispiece /'frʌntɪs,pi:s/ n. **1** an illustration facing the title-page of a book or of one of its divisions. **2** Archit. **a** the principal face of a building. **b** a decorated entrance. **c** a pediment over a door etc. [F *frontispice* or LL *frontispicium* façade f. L *frons frontis* FRONT + -spicium f. specere look: assim. to PIECE]

frontlet /'frʌntlɪt/ n. **1** a piece of cloth hanging over the upper part of an altar frontal. **2** a band worn on the forehead. **3** a phylactery. **4** an animal's forehead. [OF *frontlet* (as FRONTAL[2])]

fronton /'frʌnt(ə)n/ n. a pediment. [F f. It. *frontone* f. *fronte* forehead]

frore /frɔ:(r)/ adj. poet. frozen, frosty. [archaic past part. of FREEZE]

frost /frɒst/ n. & v. —n. **1 a** (also **white frost**) a white frozen dew coating esp. the ground at night (*windows covered with frost*). **b** a consistent temperature below freezing-point causing frost to form. **2** a chilling dispiriting atmosphere. **3** sl. a failure. —v. **1** intr. (usu. foll. by *over, up*) become covered with frost. **2** tr. **a** cover with or as if with frost, powder, etc. **b** injure (a plant etc.) with frost. **3** tr. give a roughened or finely granulated surface to (glass, metal) (*frosted glass*). **4** tr. US cover or decorate (a cake etc.) with icing. □**black frost** a frost without white dew. **degrees of frost** Brit. degrees below freezing-point (*ten degrees of frost tonight*). **frost-work** tracery made by frost on glass etc. □□ **frostless** adj. [OE f. Gmc]

frostbite /'frɒstbaɪt/ n. injury to body tissues, esp. the nose, fingers, or toes, due to freezing and often resulting in gangrene.

frosting /'frɒstɪŋ/ n. **1** US icing. **2** a rough surface on glass etc.

frosty /'frɒstɪ/ adj. (**frostier, frostiest**) **1** cold with frost. **2** covered with or as with hoar-frost. **3** unfriendly in manner, lacking in warmth of feeling. □□ **frostily** adv. **frostiness** n.

froth /frɒθ/ n. & v. —n. **1 a** a collection of small bubbles in liquid, caused by shaking, fermenting, etc.; foam. **b** impure matter on liquid, scum. **2 a** idle talk or ideas. **b** anything unsubstantial or of little worth. —v. **1** intr. emit or gather froth (*frothing at the mouth*). **2** tr. cause (beer etc.) to foam. □**froth-blower** Brit. joc. a beer-drinker (esp. as a designation of a member of a charitable organization). □□ **frothily** adv. **frothiness** n. **frothy** adj. (**frothier, frothiest**). [ME f. ON *frotha, frauth* f. Gmc]

frottage /frɒ'tɑ:ʒ/ n. **1** Psychol. an abnormal desire for contact between the clothed bodies of oneself and another. **2** Art the technique or process of taking a rubbing from an uneven surface to form the basis of a work of art. [F, = rubbing f. *frotter* rub f. OF *froter*]

frou-frou /'fru:fru:/ n. a rustling, esp. of a dress. [F, imit.]

frow[1] /frau/ n. **1** a Dutchwoman. **2** a housewife. [ME f. Du. *vrouw* woman]

frow[2] var. of FROE.

froward /'frəʊəd/ *adj. archaic* perverse; difficult to deal with. □□**frowardly** *adv.* **frowardness** *n.* [ME f. FRO + -WARD]

frown /fraʊn/ *v. & n.* —*v.* **1** *intr.* wrinkle one's brows, esp. in displeasure or deep thought. **2** *intr.* (foll. by *at, on, upon*) express disapproval. **3** *intr.* (of a thing) present a gloomy aspect. **4** *tr.* compel with a frown (*frowned them into silence*). **5** *tr.* express (defiance etc.) with a frown. —*n.* **1** an action of frowning; a vertically furrowed or wrinkled state of the brow. **2** a look expressing severity, disapproval, or deep thought. □□**frowner** *n.* **frowningly** *adv.* [ME f. OF *frongnier, froignier* f. *froigne* surly look f. Celt.]

frowst /fraʊst/ *n. & v. Brit. colloq.* —*n.* fusty warmth in a room. —*v.intr.* stay in or enjoy frowst. □□ **frowster** *n.* [back-form. f. FROWSTY]

frowsty /'fraʊstɪ/ *adj. Brit.* (**frowstier, frowstiest**) fusty, stuffy. □□**frowstiness** *n.* [var. of FROWZY]

frowzy /'fraʊzɪ/ *adj.* (also **frowsy**) (**-ier, -iest**) **1** fusty, musty, ill-smelling, close. **2** slatternly, unkempt, dingy. □□**frowziness** *n.* [17th c.: orig. unkn.: cf. earlier *frowy*]

froze *past* of FREEZE.

frozen *past part.* of FREEZE.

FRS *abbr.* (in the UK) Fellow of the Royal Society.

FRSE *abbr.* Fellow of the Royal Society of Edinburgh.

fructiferous /frʌk'tɪfərəs/ *adj.* bearing fruit. [L *fructifer* f. *fructus* FRUIT]

fructification /ˌfrʌktɪfɪ'keɪʃ(ə)n/ *n. Bot.* **1** the process of fructifying. **2** any spore-bearing structure esp. in ferns, fungi, and mosses. [LL *fructificatio* (as FRUCTIFY)]

fructify /'frʌktɪˌfaɪ/ *v.* (**-ies, -ied**) **1** *intr.* bear fruit. **2** *tr.* make fruitful; impregnate. [ME f. OF *fructifier* f. L *fructificare* f. *fructus* FRUIT]

fructose /'frʌktəʊz, -əʊs, 'frʊk-/ *n. Chem.* a simple sugar found in honey and fruits. Also called LAE-VULOSE, *fruit sugar.* [L *fructus* FRUIT + -OSE 2]

fructuous /'frʌktjʊəs/ *adj.* full of or producing fruit. [ME f. OF *fructuous* or L *fructuosus* (as FRUIT)]

frugal /'fruːg(ə)l/ *adj.* **1** (often foll. by *of*) sparing or economical, esp. as regards food. **2** sparingly used or supplied, meagre, costing little. □□**frugality** /-'gælɪtɪ/ *n.* **frugally** *adv.* **frugalness** *n.* [L *frugalis* f. *frugi* economical]

frugivorous /fruː'dʒɪvərəs/ *adj.* feeding on fruit. [L *frux frugis* fruit + -VOROUS]

fruit /fruːt/ *n. & v.* —*n.* **1 a** the usu. sweet and fleshy edible product of a plant or tree, containing seed. **b** (in *sing.*) these in quantity (*eats fruit*). **2** the seed of a plant or tree with its covering, e.g. an acorn, pea pod, cherry, etc. **3** (usu. in *pl.*) vegetables, grains, etc. used for food (*fruits of the earth*). **4** (usu. in *pl.*) the result of action etc., esp. as financial reward (*fruits of his labours*). **5** *sl.* esp. *US* a male homosexual. **6** *Bibl.* an offspring (*the fruit of the womb; the fruit of his loins*). —*v.intr. & tr.* bear or cause to bear fruit. □**fruit bar** a piece of dried and pressed fruit. **fruit-bat** any large bat of the suborder Megachiroptera, feeding on fruit. **fruit- (or fruiting-) body** (*pl.* **-ies**) the spore-bearing part of a fungus. **fruit cake 1** a cake containing dried fruit. **2** *sl.* an eccentric or mad person. **fruit cocktail** a finely-chopped usu. tinned fruit salad. **fruit fly** (*pl.* **flies**) any of various flies, esp. of the genus *Drosophila*, having larvae that feed on fruit. **fruit machine** *Brit.* a coin-operated gaming machine giving random combinations of symbols often representing fruit. **fruit salad 1** various fruits cut up and served in syrup, juice, etc. **2** *sl.* a display of medals etc. **fruit sugar** fructose. **fruit-tree** a tree grown for its fruit. **fruit-wood** the wood of a fruit-tree, esp. when used in furniture. □□**fruitage** *n.* **fruited** *adj.* (also in *comb.*). [ME f. OF f. L *fructus* fruit, enjoyment f. *frui* enjoy]

fruitarian /fruː'teərɪən/ *n.* a person who eats only fruit. [FRUIT, after *vegetarian*]

fruiter /'fruːtə(r)/ *n.* **1** a tree producing fruit, esp. with reference to its quality (*a poor fruiter*). **2** *Brit.* a fruit grower. **3** a ship carrying fruit. [ME f. OF *fruitier* (as FRUIT, -ER[5]): later f. FRUIT + -ER[1]]

fruiterer /'fruːtərə(r)/ *n.* esp. *Brit.* a dealer in fruit.

fruitful /'fruːtfʊl/ *adj.* **1** producing much fruit; fertile; causing fertility. **2** producing good results, successful; beneficial, remunerative. **3** producing offspring, esp. prolifically. □□**fruitfully** *adv.* **fruitfulness** *n.*

fruition /fruː'ɪʃ(ə)n/ *n.* **1 a** the bearing of fruit. **b** the production of results. **2** the realization of aims or hopes. **3** enjoyment. [ME f. OF f. LL *fruitio -onis* f. *frui* enjoy, erron. assoc. with FRUIT]

fruitless /'fruːtlɪs/ *adj.* **1** not bearing fruit. **2** useless, unsuccessful, unprofitable. □□**fruitlessly** *adv.* **fruitlessness** *n.*

fruitlet /'fruːtlɪt/ *n.* = DRUPEL.

fruity /'fruːtɪ/ *adj.* (**fruitier, fruitiest**) **1 a** of fruit. **b** tasting or smelling like fruit, esp. (of wine) tasting of the grape. **2** (of a voice etc.) of full rich quality. **3** *colloq.* full of rough humour or (usu. scandalous) interest; suggestive. □□**fruitily** *adv.* **fruitiness** *n.*

frumenty /'fruːməntɪ/ *n.* (also **furmety** /'fɜːmɪtɪ/) hulled wheat boiled in milk and seasoned with cinnamon, sugar, etc. [ME f. OF *frumentee* f. *frument* f. L *frumentum* corn]

frump /frʌmp/ *n.* a dowdy unattractive old-fashioned woman. □□**frumpish** *adj.* **frumpishly** *adv.* [16th c.: perh. f. dial. *frumple* (v.) wrinkle f. MDu. *verrompelen* (as FOR-, RUMPLE)]

frumpy /'frʌmpɪ/ *adj.* (**frumpier, frumpiest**) dowdy, unattractive, and old-fashioned. □□**frumpily** *adv.* **frumpiness** *n.*

frustrate *v. & adj.* —*v.tr.* /frʌ'streɪt, 'frʌs-/ **1** make (efforts) ineffective. **2** prevent (a person) from achieving a purpose. **3** (as **frustrated** *adj.*) **a** discontented because unable to achieve one's desire. **b** sexually unfulfilled. **4** disappoint (a hope). —*adj.* /'frʌstreɪt/ *archaic* frustrated. □□**frustratedly** *adv.* **frustrater** *n.* **frustrating** *adj.* **frustratingly** *adv.* **frustration** *n.* [ME f. L *frustrari frustrat-* f. *frustra* in vain]

frustule /'frʌstjuːl/ *n. Bot.* the siliceous cell wall of a diatom. [F f. L *frustulum* (as FRUSTUM)]

frustum /'frʌstəm/ *n.* (*pl.* **frusta** /-tə/ or **frustums**) *Geom.* **1** the remainder of a cone or pyramid whose upper part has been cut off by a plane parallel to its base. **2** the part of a cone or pyramid intercepted between two planes. [L = piece cut off]

frutescent /fruː'tes(ə)nt/ *adj. Bot.* of the nature of a shrub. [irreg. f. L *frutex* bush]

frutex /'fruːteks/ *n.* (*pl.* **frutices** /-tɪˌsiːz/) *Bot.* a woody-stemmed plant smaller than a tree; a shrub. [L *frutex fruticis*]

fruticose /'fruːtɪˌkəʊz, -ˌkəʊs/ *adj. Bot.* resembling a shrub. [L *fruticosus* (as FRUTEX)]

fry[1] /fraɪ/ *v. & n.* —*v.* (**fries, fried**) **1** *tr. & intr.* cook or be cooked in hot fat. **2** *tr. & intr. sl.* electrocute or be electrocuted. **3** *tr.* (as **fried** *adj.*) *sl.* drunk. —*n.* (*pl.* **fries**) **1** various internal parts of animals usu. eaten fried (*lamb's fry*). **2** a dish of fried food, esp. meat. **3** *US* a social gathering to eat fried food. □**frying- (US fry-) pan** a shallow pan used in frying. **fry up** heat or reheat (food) in a frying-pan. **fry-up** *n. Brit. colloq.* a dish of miscellaneous fried food. **out of the frying-pan into the fire** from a bad situation to a worse one. [ME f. OF *frire* f. L *frigere*]

fry[2] /fraɪ/ *n.pl.* **1** young or newly hatched fishes. **2** the young of other creatures produced in large numbers, e.g. bees or frogs. □**small fry** people of little importance; children. [ME f. ON *frjó*]

fryer /'fraɪə(r)/ *n.* (also **frier**) **1** a person who fries. **2** a vessel for frying esp. fish. **3** *US* a chicken suitable for frying.

FSA *abbr.* Fellow of the Society of Antiquaries.

FSH *abbr.* follicle-stimulating hormone.

Ft. abbr. Fort.

ft. abbr. foot, feet.

FTC abbr. US Federal Trade Commission.

fubsy /'fʌbzɪ/ adj. (**fubsier, fubsiest**) Brit. fat or squat. [obs. fubs small fat person + -Y¹]

fuchsia /'fju:ʃə/ n. any shrub of the genus Fuchsia, with drooping red or purple or white flowers. [mod.L f. L. Fuchs, Ger. botanist d. 1566]

fuchsine /'fu:ksi:n, -ɪn/ n. a deep red aniline dye used in the pharmaceutical and textile-processing industries, rosaniline. [FUCHSIA (from its resemblance to the colour of the flower)]

fuck /fʌk/ v., int., & n. coarse sl. —v. 1 tr. & intr. have sexual intercourse (with). 2 intr. (foll. by about, around) mess about; fool around. 3 tr. (usu. as an exclam.) curse, confound (fuck the thing!). 4 intr. (as **fucking** adj., adv.) used as an intensive to express annoyance etc. —int. expressing anger or annoyance. —n. 1 a an act of sexual intercourse. b a partner in sexual intercourse. 2 the slightest amount (don't give a fuck). □**fuck all** nothing. **fuck off** go away. **fuck up** make a mess of. **fuck-up** n. a mess or muddle. ¶ A highly taboo word. □□**fucker** n. (often as a term of abuse). [16th c.: orig. unkn.]

fucus /'fju:kəs/ n. (pl. **fuci** /'fju:saɪ/) any seaweed of the genus Fucus, with flat leathery fronds. □□**fucoid** adj. [L, = rock-lichen, f. Gk phukos, of Semitic orig.]

fuddle /'fʌd(ə)l/ v. & n. —v. 1 tr. confuse or stupefy, esp. with alcoholic liquor. 2 intr. tipple, booze. —n. 1 confusion. 2 intoxication. 3 a spell of drinking (on the fuddle). [16th c.: orig. unkn.]

fuddy-duddy /'fʌdɪˌdʌdɪ/ adj. & n. sl. —adj. old-fashioned or quaintly fussy. —n. (pl. **-ies**) a fuddy-duddy person. [20th c.: orig. unkn.]

fudge /fʌdʒ/ n., v., & int. —n. 1 a soft toffee-like sweet made with milk, sugar, butter, etc. 2 nonsense. 3 a piece of dishonesty or faking. 4 a piece of late news inserted in a newspaper page. —v. 1 tr. put together in a makeshift or dishonest way; fake. 2 tr. deal with incompetently. 3 intr. practise such methods. —int. expressing disbelief or annoyance. [perh. f. obs. fadge (v.) fit]

fuehrer var. of FÜHRER.

fuel /'fju:əl/ n. & v. —n. 1 material, esp. coal, wood, oil, etc., burnt or used as a source of heat or power. 2 food as a source of energy. 3 material used as a source of nuclear energy. 4 anything that sustains or inflames emotion or passion. —v. (**fuelled, fuelling**; US **fueled, fueling**) 1 tr. supply with fuel. 2 tr. sustain or inflame (an argument, feeling, etc.) (drink fuelled his anger). 3 intr. take in or get fuel. □**fuel cell** a cell producing an electric current direct from a chemical reaction. **fuel element** an element of nuclear fuel etc. for use in a reactor. **fuel injection** the direct introduction of fuel under pressure into the combustion units of an internal-combustion engine. **fuel oil** oil used as fuel in an engine or furnace. [ME f. AF fuaille, fewaile, OF fouaille, ult. f. L focus hearth]

fug /fʌg/ n. & v. colloq. —n. stuffiness or fustiness of the air in a room. —v.intr. (**fugged, fugging**) stay in or enjoy a fug. □□**fuggy** adj. [19th c.: orig. unkn.]

fugacious /fju:'geɪʃəs/ adj. literary fleeting, evanescent, hard to capture or keep. □□**fugaciously** adv. **fugaciousness** n. **fugacity** /-'gæsɪtɪ/ n. [L fugax fugacis f. fugere flee]

fugal /'fju:g(ə)l/ adj. of the nature of a fugue. □□ **fugally** adv.

-fuge /fju:dʒ/ comb. form forming adjectives and nouns denoting expelling or dispelling (febrifuge; vermifuge). [from or after mod.L -fugus f. L fugare put to flight]

fugitive /'fju:dʒɪtɪv/ adj. & n. —adj. 1 fleeing; that runs or has run away. 2 transient, fleeting; of short duration. 3 (of literature) of passing interest, ephemeral. 4 flitting, shifting. —n. 1 (often foll. by from) a person who flees, esp. from justice, an enemy, danger, or a master. 2 an exile or refugee. □□

fugitively adv. [ME f. OF fugitif -ive f. L fugitivus f. fugere fugit- flee]

fugle /'fju:g(ə)l/ v.intr. act as a fugleman. [back-form. f. FUGLEMAN]

fugleman /'fju:g(ə)lmən/ n. (pl. **-men**) 1 hist. a soldier placed in front of a regiment etc. while drilling to show the motions and time. 2 a leader, organizer, or spokesman. [G Flügelmann f. Flügel wing + Mann man]

fugue /fju:g/ n. & v. —n. 1 Mus. a contrapuntal composition in which a short melody or phrase (the subject) is introduced by one part and successively taken up by others and developed by interweaving the parts. 2 Psychol. loss of awareness of one's identity, often coupled with flight from one's usual environment. —v.intr. (**fugues, fugued, fuguing**) Mus. compose or perform a fugue. □□**fuguist** n. [F or It. f. L fuga flight]

fugued /fju:gd/ adj. in the form of a fugue.

führer /'fjʊərə(r)/ n. (also **fuehrer**) a leader, esp. a tyrannical one. [G, = leader: part of the title assumed in 1934 by Hitler (see HITLER)]

-ful /fʊl/ comb. form forming: 1 adjectives from nouns, meaning: a full of (beautiful). b having the qualities of (masterful). 2 adjectives from adjectives or Latin stems with little change of sense (direful; grateful). 3 adjectives from verbs, meaning 'apt to', 'able to', 'accustomed to' (forgetful; mournful; useful). 4 nouns (pl. **-fuls**) meaning 'the amount needed to fill' (handful; spoonful).

fulcrum /'fʊlkrəm, 'fʌl-/ n. (pl. **fulcra** /-rə/ or **fulcrums**) 1 the point against which a lever is placed to get a purchase or on which it turns or is supported. 2 the means by which influence etc. is brought to bear. [L, = post of a couch, f. fulcire to prop]

fulfil /fʊl'fɪl/ v.tr. (US **fulfill**) (**fulfilled, fulfilling**) 1 bring to consummation, carry out (a prophecy or promise). 2 satisfy (a desire or prayer). 3 a execute, obey (a command or law). b perform, carry out (a task). 4 comply with (conditions). 5 answer (a purpose). 6 bring to an end, finish, complete (a period or piece of work). □**fulfil oneself** develop one's gifts and character to the full. □□**fulfillable** adj. **fulfiller** n. **fulfilment** n. (US **fulfillment**). [OE fullfyllan (as FULL¹, FILL)]

fulgent /'fʌldʒ(ə)nt/ adj. poet. or rhet. shining, brilliant. [ME f. L fulgēre shine]

fulguration /ˌfʌlgjʊ'reɪʃ(ə)n/ n. Surgery the destruction of tissue by means of high-voltage electric sparks. [L fulguratio sheet lightning f. fulgur lightning]

fulgurite /'fʌlgjʊˌraɪt/ n. Geol. a rocky substance of sand fused or vitrified by lightning. [L fulgur lightning]

fuliginous /fju:'lɪdʒɪnəs/ adj. sooty, dusky. [LL fuliginosus f. fuligo -ginis soot]

full¹ /fʊl/ adj., adv., n., & v. —adj. 1 (often foll. by of) holding all its limits will allow (the bucket is full; full of water). 2 having eaten to one's limits or satisfaction. 3 abundant, copious, satisfying, sufficient (a full programme of events; led a full life; turned it to full account; give full details; the book is very full on this point). 4 (foll. by of) having or holding an abundance of, showing marked signs of (full of vitality; full of interest; full of mistakes). 5 (foll. by of) a engrossed in thinking about (full of himself; full of his work). b unable to refrain from talking about (full of the news). 6 a complete, perfect, reaching the specified or usual or utmost limit (full membership; full daylight; waited a full hour; it was full summer; in full bloom). b Bookbinding used for the entire cover (full leather). 7 a (of tone or colour) deep and clear, mellow. b (of light) intense. c (of motion etc.) vigorous (a full pulse; at full gallop). 8 plump, rounded, protuberant (a full figure). 9 (of clothes) made of much material arranged in folds or gathers. 10 (of the heart etc.) overcharged with emotion. 11 sl. drunk. 12 (foll. by of) archaic having had plenty of (*full of years and honours*). —*adv.* **1** very (*you know full well*). **2** quite, fully (*full six miles*; *full ripe*). **3** exactly (*hit him full on the nose*). **4** more than sufficiently (*full early*). —*n.* **1** height, acme (*season is past the full*). **2** the state or time of full moon. **3** the whole (*cannot tell you the full of it*). —*v.intr.* & *tr.* be or become or make (esp. clothes) full. □**at full length 1** lying stretched out. **2** without abridgement. **come full circle** see CIRCLE. **full age** adult status (esp. with ref. to legal rights and duties). **full and by** *Naut.* close-hauled but with sails filling. **full back** a defensive player, or a position near the goal, in football, hockey, etc. **full blood** pure descent. **full-blooded 1** vigorous, hearty, sensual. **2** not hybrid. **full-bloodedly** forcefully, wholeheartedly. **full-bloodedness** being full-blooded. **full-blown** fully developed, complete, (of flowers) quite open. **full board** provision of accommodation and all meals at a hotel etc. **full-bodied** rich in quality, tone, etc. **full-bottomed** (of a wig) long at the back. **full brother** a brother born of the same parents. **full-cream** of or made from unskimmed milk. **full dress** formal clothes worn on great occasions. **full-dress** *adj.* (of a debate etc.) of major importance. **full employment 1** the condition in which there is no idle capital or labour of any kind that is in demand. **2** the condition in which virtually all who are able and willing to work are employed. **full face** with all the face visible to the spectator. **full-fashioned** = *fully-fashioned*. **full-fledged** mature. **full-frontal 1** (of nudity or a nude figure) with full exposure at the front. **2** unrestrained, explicit; with nothing concealed. **full-grown** having reached maturity. **full hand** *Poker* a hand with three of a kind and a pair. **full-hearted** full of feeling; confident, zealous. **full-heartedly** in a full-hearted manner. **full-heartedness** fullness of feeling, ardour, zeal. **full house 1** a maximum or large attendance at a theatre, in Parliament, etc. **2** = *full hand*. **full-length 1** not shortened or abbreviated. **2** (of a mirror, portrait, etc.) showing the whole height of the human figure. **full lock** see LOCK¹. **full marks** the maximum award in an examination, in assessment of a person, etc. **full measure** not less than the professed amount. **full moon 1** the moon with its whole disc illuminated. **2** the time when this occurs. **full-mouthed 1** (of cattle or sheep) having a full set of teeth. **2** (of a dog) baying loudly. **3** (of oratory etc.) sonorous, vigorous. **full out 1** *Printing* flush with the margin. **2** at full power. **3** complete. **full page** an entire page of a newspaper etc. **full pitch** = *full toss*. **full point** = *full stop* 1. **full professor** a professor of the highest grade in a university etc. **full-scale** not reduced in size, complete. **full score** *Mus.* a score giving the parts for all performers on separate staves. **full service** a church service performed by a choir without solos, or performed with music wherever possible. **full sister** a sister born of the same parents. **full speed** (or **steam**) **ahead!** an order to proceed at maximum speed or to pursue a course of action energetically. **full stop 1** a punctuation mark (.) used at the end of a sentence or an abbreviation. **2** a complete cessation. **full term** the completion of a normal pregnancy. **full tilt** see TILT. **full time 1** the total normal duration of work etc. **2** the end of a football etc. match. **full-time** *adj.* occupying or using the whole of the available working time. **full-timer** a person who does a full-time job. **full toss** *Cricket n.* a ball pitched right up to the batsman. —*adv.* without the ball's having touched the ground. **full up** *colloq.* completely full. **in full 1** without abridgement. **2** to or for the full amount (*paid in full*). **in full swing** at the height of activity. **in full view** entirely visible. **on a full stomach** see STOMACH. **to the full** to the utmost extent. [OE f. Gmc]

full² /fʊl/ *v.tr.* cleanse and thicken (cloth). [ME, back-form. f. FULLER¹: cf. OF *fouler* (FOIL¹)]

fuller¹ /'fʊlə(r)/ *n.* a person who fulls cloth. □**fuller's earth** a type of clay used in fulling cloth and as an adsorbent. [OE *fullere* f. L *fullo*]

fuller² /'fʊlə(r)/ *n.* & *v.* —*n.* **1 a** grooved or rounded tool on which iron is shaped. **2** a groove made by this esp. in a horseshoe. —*v.tr.* stamp with a fuller. [19th c.: orig. unkn.]

fullness /'fʊlnɪs/ *n.* (also **fulness**) **1** being full. **2** (of sound, colour, etc.) richness, volume, body. **3** all that is contained (in the world etc.). □**the fullness of the heart** emotion, genuine feelings. **the fullness of time** the appropriate or destined time.

fully /'fʊlɪ/ *adv.* **1** completely, entirely (*am fully aware*). **2** no less or fewer than (*fully 60*). □**fully-fashioned** (of women's clothing) shaped to fit the body. **fully-fledged** mature. [OE *fullīce* (as FULL¹, -LY²)]

-fully /'fʊlɪ/ *comb. form* forming adverbs corresp. to adjectives in *-ful.*

fulmar /'fʊlmə(r)/ *n.* any medium-sized sea bird of the genus *Fulmarus*, with stout body, robust bill, and rounded tail. [orig. Hebridean dial.: perh. f. ON *fúll* FOUL (with ref. to its smell) + *már* gull (cf. MEW²)]

fulminant /'fʌlmɪnənt, 'fʊl-/ *adj.* **1** fulminating. **2** *Med.* (of a disease or symptom) developing suddenly. [F *fulminant* or L *fulminant-* (as FULMINATE)]

fulminate /'fʌlmɪˌneɪt, 'fʊl-/ *v.* & *n.* —*v.intr.* **1** (often foll. by *against*) express censure loudly and forcefully. **2** explode violently; flash like lightning (*fulminating mercury*). **3** *Med.* (of a disease or symptom) develop suddenly. —*n.* *Chem.* a salt or ester of fulminic acid. □□**fulmination** /-'neɪʃ(ə)n/ *n.* **fulminatory** *adj.* [L *fulminare fulminat-* f. *fulmen -minis* lightning]

fulminic acid /fʌl'mɪnɪk, fʊl-/ *n.* *Chem.* an isomer of cyanic acid that is stable only in solution. ¶ Chem. formula: HONC. [L *fulmen*: see FULMINATE]

fulness var. of FULLNESS.

fulsome /'fʊlsəm/ *adj.* **1** disgusting by excess of flattery, servility, or expressions of affection; excessive, cloying. **2** *disp.* copious. ¶ In *fulsome praise*, *fulsome* means 'excessive', not 'generous'. □□ **fulsomely** *adv.* **fulsomeness** *n.* [ME f. FULL¹ + -SOME¹]

fulvous /'fʌlvəs/ *adj.* reddish-yellow, tawny. □□ **fulvescent** /-'ves(ə)nt/ *adj.* [L *fulvus*]

fumarole /'fju:məˌrəʊl/ *n.* an opening in or near a volcano, through which hot vapours emerge. □□ **fumarolic** /-'rɒlɪk/ *adj.* [F *fumarolle*]

fumble /'fʌmb(ə)l/ *v.* & *n.* —*v.* **1** *intr.* (often foll. by *at, with, for, after*) use the hands awkwardly, grope about. **2** *tr.* **a** handle or deal with clumsily or nervously. **b** *Sport* fail to stop (a ball) cleanly. —*n.* an act of fumbling. □□ **fumbler** *n.* **fumblingly** *adv.* [LG *fummeln, fommeln*, Du. *fommelen*]

fume /fju:m/ *n.* & *v.* —*n.* **1** (usu. in *pl.*) exuded gas or smoke or vapour, esp. when harmful or unpleasant. **2** a fit of anger (*in a fume*). —*v.* **1 a** *intr.* emit fumes. **b** *tr.* give off as fumes. **2** *intr.* (often foll. by *at*) be affected by (esp. suppressed) anger (*was fuming at their inefficiency*). **3** *tr.* **a** fumigate. **b** subject to fumes esp. those of ammonia (to darken tints in oak, photographic film, etc.). **4** *tr.* perfume with incense. □**fume cupboard** (or **chamber** etc.) a ventilated structure in a laboratory, for storing or experimenting with noxious chemicals. □□ **fumeless** *adj.* **fumingly** *adv.* **fumy** *adj.* (in sense 1 of *n.*). [ME f. OF *fum* f. L *fumus* smoke & OF *fume* f. *fumer* f. L *fumare* to smoke]

fumigate /'fju:mɪˌgeɪt/ *v.tr.* **1** disinfect or purify with fumes. **2** apply fumes to. □□ **fumigant** *n.* **fumigation** /-'geɪʃ(ə)n/ *n.* **fumigator** *n.* [L *fumigare fumigat-* f. *fumus* smoke]

fumitory /'fju:mɪtərɪ/ *n.* any plant of the genus *Fumaria*, esp. *F. officinalis*, formerly used against scurvy. [ME f. OF *fumeterre* f. med.L *fumus terrae* earth-smoke]

fun /fʌn/ *n.* & *adj.* —*n.* **1** amusement, esp. lively or playful. **2** a source of this. **3** (in full **fun and games**) exciting or amusing goings-on. —*adj. disp. colloq.* amusing, entertaining, enjoyable (*a fun thing to do*). □**for fun** (or **for the fun of it**) not for a serious purpose. **fun run** *colloq.* an uncompetitive run, esp. for sponsored runners in support of a charity. **have fun** enjoy oneself. **in fun** as a joke, not seriously. **is great** (or **good**) **fun** is very amusing. **like fun 1** vigorously, quickly. **2** much. **3** *iron.* not at all. **what fun!** how amusing! [obs. *fun* (v.) var. of *fon* befool: cf. FOND]

funambulist /fju:'næmbjʊlɪst/ *n.* a rope-walker. [F *funambule* or L *funambulus* f. *funis* rope + *ambulare* walk]

function /'fʌŋkʃ(ə)n/ *n. & v.* —*n.* **1 a** an activity proper to a person or institution. **b** a mode of action or activity by which a thing fulfils its purpose. **c** an official or professional duty; an employment, profession, or calling. **2 a** a public ceremony or occasion. **b** a social gathering, esp. a large, formal, or important one. **3** *Math.* a variable quantity regarded in relation to another or others in terms of which it may be expressed or on which its value depends (*x is a function of y and z*). **4** a part of a program that corresponds to a single value. —*v.intr.* fulfil a function, operate; be in working order. □□ **functionless** *adj.* [F *fonction* f. L *functio -onis* f. *fungi funct-* perform]

functional /'fʌŋkʃən(ə)l/ *adj.* **1** of or serving a function. **2** (esp. of buildings) designed or intended to be practical rather than attractive; utilitarian. **3** *Physiol.* **a** (esp. of disease) of or affecting only the functions of an organ etc., not structural or organic. **b** (of mental disorder) having no discernible organic cause. **c** (of an organ) having a function, not functionless or rudimentary. **4** *Math.* of a function. □**functional group** *Chem.* a group of atoms that determine the reactions of a compound containing the group. □□**functionality** /-'nælɪtɪ/ *n.* **functionally** *adv.*

functionalism /'fʌŋkʃənə,lɪz(ə)m/ *n.* belief in or stress on the practical application of a thing. □□ **functionalist** *n.*

functionary /'fʌŋkʃənərɪ/ *n.* (*pl.* **-ies**) a person who has to perform official functions or duties; an official.

fund /fʌnd/ *n. & v.* —*n.* **1** a permanent stock of something ready to be drawn upon (*a fund of knowledge*; *a fund of tenderness*). **2** a stock of money, esp. one set apart for a purpose. **3** (in *pl.*) money resources. **4** (in *pl.*; prec. by *the*) *Brit.* the stock of the National Debt (as a mode of investment). —*v.tr.* **1** provide with money. **2** convert (a floating debt) into a more or less permanent debt at fixed interest. **3** put into a fund. □**fund-raiser** a person who seeks financial support for a cause, enterprise, etc. **fund-raising** the seeking of financial support. **in funds** *colloq.* having money to spend. [L *fundus* bottom, piece of land]

fundament /'fʌndəmənt/ *n. joc.* the buttocks. [ME f. OF *fondement* f. L *fundamentum* (as FOUND²)]

fundamental /,fʌndə'ment(ə)l/ *adj. & n.* —*adj.* of, affecting, or serving as a base or foundation, essential, primary, original (*a fundamental change*; *the fundamental rules*; *the fundamental form*). —*n.* **1** (usu. in *pl.*) a fundamental rule, principle, or article. **2** *Mus.* a fundamental note or tone. □**fundamental note** *Mus.* the lowest note of a chord in its original (uninverted) form. **fundamental particle** an elementary particle. **fundamental tone** *Mus.* the tone produced by vibration of the whole of a sonorous body (opp. HARMONIC). □□**fundamentality** /-'tælɪtɪ/ *n.* **fundamentally** *adv.* [ME f. F *fondamental* or LL *fundamentalis* (as FUNDAMENT)]

fundamentalism /,fʌndə'mentə,lɪz(ə)m/ *n.* **1** strict maintenance of traditional Protestant beliefs such as the inerrancy of Scripture and literal acceptance of the creeds as fundamentals of Christianity. **2** strict

maintenance of ancient or fundamental doctrines of any religion, esp. Islam. □□ **fundamentalist** *n.*

fundus /'fʌndəs/ *n.* (*pl.* **fundi** /-daɪ/) *Anat.* the base of a hollow organ; the part furthest from the opening. [L, = bottom]

funeral /'fju:nər(ə)l/ *n. & adj.* —*n.* **1 a** the burial or cremation of a dead person with its ceremonies. **b** a burial or cremation procession. **c** *US* a burial or cremation service. **2** *sl.* one's (usu. unpleasant) concern (*that's your funeral*). —*attrib.adj.* of or used etc. at a funeral (*funeral oration*). □**funeral director** an undertaker. **funeral parlour** (*US* **home**) an establishment where the dead are prepared for burial or cremation. **funeral pile** (or **pyre**) a pile of wood etc. on which a corpse is burnt. **funeral urn** an urn holding the ashes of a cremated body. [ME f. OF *funeraille* f. med.L *funeralia* neut. pl. of LL *funeralis* f. L *funus -eris* funeral: (adj.) OF f. L *funeralis*]

funerary /'fju:nərərɪ/ *adj.* of or used at a funeral or funerals. [LL *funerarius* (as FUNERAL)]

funereal /fju:'nɪərɪəl/ *adj.* **1** of or appropriate to a funeral. **2** gloomy, dismal, dark. □□**funereally** *adv.* [L *funereus* (as FUNERAL)]

funfair /'fʌnfeə(r)/ *n. Brit.* a fair, or part of one, consisting of amusements and sideshows.

fungi *pl.* of FUNGUS.

fungible /'fʌndʒɪb(ə)l/ *adj. Law* (of goods etc. contracted for, when an individual specimen is not meant) that can serve for, or be replaced by, another answering to the same definition. □□**fungibility** /-'bɪlɪtɪ/ *n.* [med.L *fungibilis* f. *fungi* (*vice*) serve (in place of)]

fungicide /'fʌndʒɪ,saɪd/ *n.* a fungus-destroying substance. □□**fungicidal** /-'saɪd(ə)l/ *adj.*

fungistatic /,fʌndʒɪ'stætɪk/ *adj.* inhibiting the growth of fungi. □□**fungistatically** *adv.*

fungoid /'fʌŋɡɔɪd/ *adj. & n.* —*adj.* **1** resembling a fungus in texture or in rapid growth. **2** *Brit.* of a fungus or fungi. —*n.* a fungoid plant.

fungous /'fʌŋɡəs/ *adj.* **1** having the nature of a fungus. **2** springing up like a mushroom; transitory. [ME f. L *fungosus* (as FUNGUS)]

fungus /'fʌŋɡəs/ *n.* (*pl.* **fungi** /-ɡaɪ, -dʒaɪ/ or **funguses**) **1** any of a group of unicellular, multicellular, or multinucleate non-photosynthetic organisms feeding on organic matter, which include moulds, yeast, mushrooms, and toadstools. **2** anything similar usu. growing suddenly and rapidly. **3** *Med.* a spongy morbid growth. **4** *sl.* a beard. □□**fungal** *adj.* **fungiform** /'fʌndʒɪ,fɔ:m/ *adj.* **fungivorous** /-'dʒɪvərəs/ *adj.* [L, perh. f. Gk *sp(h)oggos* SPONGE]

funicular /fju:'nɪkjʊlə(r)/ *adj. & n.* —*adj.* **1** (of a railway, esp. on a mountainside) operating by cable with ascending and descending cars counterbalanced. **2** of a rope or its tension. —*n.* a funicular railway. [L *funiculus* f. *funis* rope]

funk¹ /fʌŋk/ *n. & v. sl.* —*n.* **1** fear, panic. **2** a coward. —*v. Brit.* **1** *intr.* flinch, shrink, show cowardice. **2** *tr.* try to evade (an undertaking), shirk. **3** *tr.* be afraid of. [18th-c. Oxford sl.: perh. f. sl. FUNK² = tobacco-smoke]

funk² /fʌŋk/ *n. sl.* **1** funky music. **2** *US* a strong smell. [*funk* blow smoke on, perh. f. F dial. *funkier* f. L (as FUMIGATE)]

funkia /'fʌŋkɪə/ *n.* = HOSTA. [mod.L f. H. C. *Funck*, Prussian botanist d. 1839]

funky¹ /'fʌŋkɪ/ *adj.* (**funkier**, **funkiest**) *sl.* **1** (esp. of jazz or rock music) earthy, bluesy, with a heavy rhythmical beat. **2** fashionable. **3** *US* having a strong smell. □□**funkily** *adv.* **funkiness** *n.*

funky² /'fʌŋkɪ/ *adj.* (**funkier**, **funkiest**) *sl.* **1** terrified. **2** cowardly.

funnel /'fʌn(ə)l/ *n. & v.* —*n.* **1** a narrow tube or pipe widening at the top, for pouring liquid, powder, etc., into a small opening. **2** a metal chimney on a steam engine or ship. **3** something resembling a funnel in shape or use. —*v.tr. & intr.* (**funnelled**, **funnelling**; *US* **funneled**, **funneling**) guide or move through or as through a funnel. □□ **funnel-like** adj. [ME f. Prov. fonilh f. LL fundibulum f. L infundibulum f. infundere (as IN-², fundere pour)]

funniosity /ˌfʌnɪˈɒsɪtɪ/ n. (pl. -ies) joc. 1 comicality. 2 a comical thing. [FUNNY + -OSITY]

funny /ˈfʌnɪ/ adj. & n. —adj. (**funnier, funniest**) 1 amusing, comical. 2 strange, perplexing, hard to account for. 3 colloq. slightly unwell, eccentric, etc. —n. (pl. -ies) (usu. in pl.) colloq. 1 a comic strip in a newspaper. 2 a joke. □**funny-bone** the part of the elbow over which the ulnar nerve passes. **funny business** 1 sl. misbehaviour or deception. 2 comic behaviour, comedy. **funny-face** joc. colloq. an affectionate form of address. **funny farm** sl. a mental hospital. **funny-ha-ha** colloq. = sense 1 of adj. **funny man** a clown or comedian, esp. a professional. **funny money** colloq. inflated currency. **funny paper** a newspaper etc. containing humorous matter. **funny-peculiar** colloq. = senses 2, 3 of adj. □□ **funnily** adv. **funniness** n. [FUN + -Y¹]

fur /fɜ:(r)/ n. & v. —n. 1 a the short fine soft hair of certain animals, distinguished from the longer hair. b the skin of such an animal with the fur on it; a pelt. 2 a the coat of certain animals as material for making, trimming, or lining clothes. b a trimming or lining made of the dressed coat of such animals, or of material imitating this. c a garment made of or trimmed or lined with fur. 3 (collect.) furred animals. 4 a a coating formed on the tongue in sickness. b Brit. a coating formed on the inside surface of a pipe, kettle, etc., by hard water. c a crust adhering to a surface, e.g. a deposit from wine. 5 Heraldry a representation of tufts on a plain ground. —v. (**furred, furring**) 1 tr. (esp. as **furred** adj.) a line or trim (a garment) with fur. b provide (an animal) with fur. c clothe (a person) with fur. d coat (a tongue, the inside of a kettle) with fur. 2 intr. (often foll. by up) (of a kettle etc.) become coated with fur. 3 tr. level (floor-timbers) by inserting strips of wood. □**fur and feather** game animals and birds. **fur-seal** a sea lion with a valuable undercoat. **make the fur fly** colloq. cause a disturbance, stir up trouble. □□ **furless** adj. [ME (earlier as v.) f. OF forrer f. forre, fuerre sheath f. Gmc]

fur. abbr. furlong(s).

furbelow /ˈfɜ:bɪˌləʊ/ n. & v. —n. 1 a gathered strip or pleated border of a skirt or petticoat. 2 (in pl.) derog. showy ornaments. —v.tr. adorn with a furbelow or furbelows. [18th-c. var. of falbala flounce, trimming]

furbish /ˈfɜ:bɪʃ/ v.tr. (often foll. by up) 1 remove rust from, polish, burnish. 2 give a new look to, renovate, revive (something antiquated). □□ **furbisher** n. [ME f. OF forbir f. Gmc]

furcate /ˈfɜ:keɪt/ adj. & v. —adj. /also ˈfɜ:kət/ forked, branched. —v.intr. form a fork, divide. □□ **furcation** /fɜ:ˈkeɪʃ(ə)n/ n. [L furca fork: (adj.) f. LL furcatus]

furfuraceous /ˌfɜ:fəˈreɪʃəs/ adj. 1 Med. (of skin) resembling bran or dandruff; scaly. 2 Bot. covered with branlike scales. [furfur scurf f. L furfur bran]

furious /ˈfjʊərɪəs/ adj. 1 extremely angry. 2 full of fury. 3 raging, violent, intense. □**fast and furious** adv. 1 rapidly. 2 eagerly, uproariously. —adj. (of mirth etc.) eager, uproarious. □□ **furiously** adv. **furiousness** n. [ME f. OF furieus f. L furiosus (as FURY)]

furl /fɜ:l/ v. 1 tr. roll up and secure (a sail, umbrella, flag, etc.). 2 intr. become furled. 3 tr. a close (a fan). b fold up (wings). c draw away (a curtain). d relinquish (hopes). □□ **furlable** adj. [F ferler f. OF fer(m) FIRM¹ + lier bind f. L ligare]

furlong /ˈfɜ:lɒŋ/ n. an eighth of a mile, 220 yards. [OE furlang f. furh FURROW + lang LONG¹: orig. = length of a furrow in a common field]

furlough /ˈfɜ:ləʊ/ n. & v. —n. leave of absence, esp. granted to a member of the services or to a missionary. —v. US 1 tr. grant furlough to. 2 intr. spend furlough. [Du. verlof after G Verlaub (as FOR-, LEAVE²)]

furmety var. of FRUMENTY.

furnace /ˈfɜ:nɪs/ n. 1 an enclosed structure for intense heating by fire, esp. of metals or water. 2 a very hot place. [ME f. OF fornais f. L fornax -acis f. fornus oven]

furnish /ˈfɜ:nɪʃ/ v.tr. 1 provide (a house, room, etc.) with all necessary contents, esp. movable furniture. 2 (foll. by with) cause to have possession or use of. 3 provide, afford, yield. [OF furnir ult. f. WG]

furnished /ˈfɜ:nɪʃt/ adj. (of a house, flat, etc.) let with furniture.

furnisher /ˈfɜ:nɪʃə(r)/ n. 1 a person who sells furniture. 2 a person who furnishes.

furnishings /ˈfɜ:nɪʃɪŋz/ n.pl. the furniture and fitments in a house, room, etc.

furniture /ˈfɜ:nɪtʃə(r)/ n. 1 the movable equipment of a house, room, etc., e.g. tables, chairs, and beds. 2 Naut. a ship's equipment, esp. tackle etc. 3 accessories, e.g. the handles and lock of a door. 4 Printing pieces of wood or metal placed round or between type to make blank spaces and fasten the matter in the chase. □**furniture beetle** a beetle, Anobium punctatum, the larvae of which bore into wood (see WOODWORM). **furniture van** a large van used to move furniture from one house to another. **part of the furniture** colloq. a person or thing taken for granted. [F fourniture f. fournir (as FURNISH)]

furore /fjʊəˈrɔ:rɪ/ n. (US furor /ˈfjʊərɔ:(r)/) 1 an uproar; an outbreak of fury. 2 a wave of enthusiastic admiration, a craze. [It. f. L furor -oris f. furere be mad]

furphy /ˈfɜ:fɪ/ n. (pl. -ies) Austral. sl. 1 a false report or rumour. 2 an absurd story. [water and sanitary Furphy carts of the war of 1914-18, made at a foundry set up by the Furphy family]

furrier /ˈfʌrɪə(r)/ n. a dealer in or dresser of furs. [ME furrour f. OF forreor f. forrer trim with fur, assim. to -IER]

furriery /ˈfʌrɪərɪ/ n. the work of a furrier.

furrow /ˈfʌrəʊ/ n. & v. —n. 1 a narrow trench made in the ground by a plough. 2 a rut, groove, or deep wrinkle. 3 a ship's track. —v.tr. 1 plough. 2 a make furrows, grooves, etc. in. b mark with wrinkles. □**furrow-slice** the slice of earth turned up by the mould-board of a plough. □□ **furrowless** adj. **furrowy** adj. [OE furh f. Gmc]

furry /ˈfɜ:rɪ/ adj. (**furrier, furriest**) 1 of or like fur. 2 covered with or wearing fur. □□ **furriness** n.

further /ˈfɜ:ðə(r)/ adv., adj., & v. —adv. (also **farther** /ˈfɑ:ðə(r)/ esp. with ref. to physical distance) 1 to or at a more advanced point in space or time (unsafe to proceed further). 2 at a greater distance (nothing was further from his thoughts). 3 to a greater extent, more (will enquire further). 4 in addition; furthermore (I may add further). —adj. (also **farther** /ˈfɑ:ðə(r)/) 1 more distant or advanced (on the further side). 2 more, additional, going beyond what exists or has been dealt with (threats of further punishment). —v.tr. promote, favour, help on (a scheme, undertaking, movement, or cause). □**further education** Brit. education for persons above school age but usu. below degree level. **further to** formal following on from (esp. an earlier letter etc.). **till further notice** (or **orders**) to continue until explicitly changed. □□ **furtherer** n. **furthermost** adj. [OE furthor (adv.), furthra (adj.), fyrthrian (v.), formed as FORTH, -ER³]

furtherance /ˈfɜ:ðərəns/ n. furthering or being furthered; the advancement of a scheme etc.

furthermore /ˌfɜ:ðəˈmɔ:(r)/ adv. in addition, besides (esp. introducing a fresh consideration in an argument).

furthest /ˈfɜ:ðɪst/ adj. & adv. (also **farthest** /ˈfɑ:ðɪst/ esp. with ref. to physical distance) —adj. most distant. —adv. to or at the greatest distance. □**at the**

furthest (or **at furthest**) at the greatest distance; at the latest; at most. [ME, superl. f. FURTHER]

furtive /ˈfɜːtɪv/ adj. **1** done by stealth, clandestine, meant to escape notice. **2** sly, stealthy. **3** stolen, taken secretly. **4** thievish, pilfering. □□ **furtively** adv. **furtiveness** n. [F furtif -ive or L furtivus f. furtum theft]

furuncle /ˈfjʊərʌnk(ə)l/ n. Med. = BOIL². □□ **furuncular** /-ˈrʌŋkjʊlə(r)/ adj. **furunculous** /-ˈrʌŋkjʊləs/ adj. [L furunculus f. fur thief]

furunculosis /fjʊˌrʌŋkjʊˈləʊsɪs/ n. **1** a diseased condition in which boils appear. **2** a bacterial disease of salmon and trout. [mod.L (as FURUNCLE)]

fury /ˈfjʊərɪ/ n. (pl. **-ies**) **1 a** wild and passionate anger, rage. **b** a fit of rage (in a blind fury). **c** impetuosity in battle etc. **2** violence of a storm, disease, etc. **3** (**Fury**) (usu. in pl.) (in Greek mythology) each of three goddesses sent from Tartarus to avenge crime, esp. against kinship. **4** an avenging spirit. **5** an angry or malignant woman, a virago. □ **like fury** colloq. with great force or effect. [ME f. OF furie f. L furia f. furere be mad]

furze /fɜːz/ n. Brit. = GORSE. □□ **furzy** /ˈfɜːzɪ/ adj. [OE fyrs, of unkn. orig.]

fuscous /ˈfʌskəs/ adj. sombre, dark-coloured. [L fuscus dusky]

fuse¹ /fjuːz/ v. & n. —v. **1** tr. & intr. melt with intense heat; liquefy. **2** tr. & intr. blend or amalgamate into one whole by or as by melting. **3** tr. provide (a circuit, plug, etc.) with a fuse. **4 a** intr. (of an appliance) cease to function when a fuse blows. **b** tr. cause (an appliance) to do this. —n. a device or component for protecting an electric circuit, containing a strip of wire of easily melted metal and placed in the circuit so as to break it by melting when an excessive current passes through. □ **fuse-box** a box housing the fuses for circuits in a building. [L fundere fuspour, melt]

fuse² /fjuːz/ n. & v. (also **fuze**) —n. **1** a device for igniting a bomb or explosive charge, consisting of a tube or cord etc. filled or saturated with combustible matter. **2** a component in a shell, mine, etc., designed to detonate an explosive charge on impact, after an interval, or when subjected to a magnetic or vibratory stimulation. —v.tr. fit a fuse to. □□ **fuseless** adj. [It. fuso f. L fusus spindle]

fusee /fjuːˈziː/ n. (US **fuzee**) **1** a conical pulley or wheel esp. in a watch or clock. **2** a large-headed match for lighting a cigar or pipe in a wind. **3** US a railway signal-flare. [F fusée spindle ult. f. L fusus]

fuselage /ˈfjuːzəˌlɑːʒ, -lɪdʒ/ n. the body of an aeroplane. [F f. fuseler cut into a spindle f. fuseau spindle f. OF fusel ult. f. L fusus]

fusel oil /ˈfjuːz(ə)l/ n. a mixture of several alcohols, chiefly amyl alcohol, produced usu. in small amounts during alcoholic fermentation. [G Fusel bad brandy etc.: cf. fuseln to bungle]

fusible /ˈfjuːzɪb(ə)l/ adj. that can be easily fused or melted. □□ **fusibility** /-ˈbɪlɪtɪ/ n.

fusiform /ˈfjuːzɪˌfɔːm/ adj. Bot. & Zool. shaped like a spindle or cigar, tapering at both ends. [L fusus spindle + -FORM]

fusil /ˈfjuːzɪl/ n. hist. a light musket. [F ult. f. L focus hearth, fire]

fusilier /ˌfjuːzɪˈlɪə(r), -zəˈlɪə(r)/ n. (US **fusileer**) **1** a member of any of several British regiments formerly armed with fusils. **2** hist. a soldier armed with a fusil. [F (as FUSIL)]

fusillade /ˌfjuːzɪˈleɪd/ n. & v. —n. **1 a** a continuous discharge of firearms. **b** a wholesale execution by this means. **2** a sustained outburst of criticism etc. —v.tr. **1** assault (a place) by a fusillade. **2** shoot down (persons) with a fusillade. [F f. fusiller shoot]

fusion /ˈfjuːʒ(ə)n/ n. **1** the act or an instance of fusing or melting. **2** a fused mass. **3** the blending of different things into one. **4** a coalition. **5** Physics = nuclear fusion. □ **fusion bomb** a bomb involving nuclear

fusion, esp. a hydrogen bomb. □□ **fusional** adj. [F fusion or L fusio (as FUSE¹)]

fuss /fʌs/ n. & v. —n. **1** excited commotion, bustle, ostentatious or nervous activity. **2 a** excessive concern about a trivial thing. **b** abundance of petty detail. **3** a sustained protest or dispute. **4** a person who fusses. —v. **1** intr. **a** make a fuss. **b** busy oneself restlessly with trivial things. **c** (often foll. by about, up and down) move fussily. **2** tr. agitate, worry. □ **make a fuss** complain vigorously. **make a fuss of** (or **over**) treat (a person or animal) with great or excessive attention. □□ **fusser** n. [18th c.: perh. Anglo-Ir.]

fusspot /ˈfʌspɒt/ n. colloq. a person given to fussing.

fussy /ˈfʌsɪ/ adj. (**fussier, fussiest**) **1** inclined to fuss. **2** full of unnecessary detail or decoration. **3** fastidious. □□ **fussily** adv. **fussiness** n.

fustanella /ˌfʌstəˈnelə/ n. a man's stiff white kilt worn in Albania and Greece. [It. dimin. of mod. Gk phoustani prob. f. It. fustagno FUSTIAN]

fustian /ˈfʌstɪən/ n. & adj. —n. **1** thick twilled cotton cloth with a short nap, usu. dyed in dark colours. **2** turgid speech or writing, bombast. —adj. **1** made of fustian. **2** bombastic. **3** worthless. [ME f. OF fustaigne f. med.L fustaneus (adj.) relating to cloth from Fostat a suburb of Cairo]

fustic /ˈfʌstɪk/ n. a yellow dye obtained from either of two kinds of wood, esp. old fustic. □ **old fustic 1** a tropical tree, Chlorophora tinctoria, native to America. **2** the wood of this tree. **young fustic 1** a sumac, Cotinus coggyria, native to Europe (also called Venetian sumac). **2** the wood of this tree. [F f. Sp. fustoc f. Arab. fustuḳ f. Gk pistakē pistachio]

fusty /ˈfʌstɪ/ adj. (**fustier, fustiest**) **1** stale-smelling, musty, mouldy. **2** stuffy, close. **3** antiquated, old-fashioned. □□ **fustily** adv. **fustiness** n. [ME f. OF fusté smelling of the cask f. fust cask, tree-trunk, f. L fustis cudgel]

futhorc /ˈfuːθɔːk/ n. the Scandinavian runic alphabet. [its first six letters f, u, th, ö, r, k]

futile /ˈfjuːtaɪl/ adj. **1** useless, ineffectual, vain. **2** frivolous, trifling. □□ **futilely** adv. **futility** /-ˈtɪlɪtɪ/ n. [L futilis leaky, futile, rel. to fundere pour]

futon /ˈfuːtɒn/ n. a Japanese quilted mattress rolled out on the floor for use as a bed. [Jap.]

futtock /ˈfʌtək/ n. each of the middle timbers of a ship's frame, between the floor and the top timbers. [ME votekes etc. pl. f. MLG f. fōt FOOT + -ken -KIN]

future /ˈfjuːtʃə(r)/ adj. & n. —adj. **1 a** going or expected to happen or be or become (his future career). **b** that will be something specified (my future wife). **c** that will be after death (a future life). **2 a** of time to come (future years). **b** Gram. (of a tense or participle) describing an event yet to happen. —n. **1** time to come (past, present, and future). **2** what will happen in the future (the future is uncertain). **3** the future condition of a person, country, etc. **4** a prospect of success etc. (there's no future in it). **5** Gram. the future tense. **6** (in pl.) Stock Exch. **a** goods and stocks sold for future delivery. **b** contracts for these. □ **for the future** = in future. **future perfect** Gram. a tense giving the sense will have done. **future shock** inability to cope with rapid progress. in future from now onwards. □□ **futureless** adj. [ME f. OF futur -ure f. L futurus future part. of esse be f. stem fu- be]

futurism /ˈfjuːtʃəˌrɪz(ə)m/ n. a movement in art, literature, music, etc., with violent departure from traditional forms so as to express movement and growth. [FUTURE + -ISM, after It. futurismo, F futurisme]

futurist /ˈfjuːtʃərɪst/ n. (often attrib.) **1** an adherent of futurism. **2** a believer in human progress. **3** a student of the future. **4** Theol. one who believes that biblical prophecies, esp. those of the Apocalypse, are still to be fulfilled.

futuristic /ˌfjuːtʃəˈrɪstɪk/ adj. **1** suitable for the future; ultra-modern. **2** of futurism. **3** relating to the future. □□ **futuristically** *adv.*

futurity /fjuːˈtjʊərɪtɪ/ *n.* (*pl.* **-ies**) **1** future time. **2** (in *sing.* or *pl.*) future events. **3** future condition; existence after death. □ **futurity stakes** *US* stakes raced for long after entries or nominations are made.

futurology /ˌfjuːtʃəˈrɒlədʒɪ/ *n.* systematic forecasting of the future esp. from present trends in society. □□ **futurologist** *n.*

fuze var. of FUSE[2].

fuzee *US* var. of FUSEE.

fuzz /fʌz/ *n.* **1** fluff. **2** fluffy or frizzled hair. **3** *sl.* **a** the police. **b** a policeman. □ **fuzz-ball** a puff-ball fungus. [17th c.: prob. f. LG or Du.: sense 3 perh. a different word]

fuzzy /ˈfʌzɪ/ *adj.* (**fuzzier**, **fuzziest**) **1 a** like fuzz. **b** frayed, fluffy. **c** frizzy. **2** blurred, indistinct.

□ **fuzzy-wuzzy** (*pl.* **-ies**) *offens.* **1** *colloq. hist.* a Sudanese soldier. **2** *sl.* a Coloured native of any country. □□ **fuzzily** *adv.* **fuzziness** *n.*

fwd *abbr.* forward.

f.w.d. *abbr.* **1** four-wheel drive. **2** front-wheel drive.

f.y. *abbr. US* fiscal year.

-fy /faɪ/ *suffix* forming: **1** verbs from nouns, meaning: **a** make, produce (*pacify*; *satisfy*). **b** make into (*deify*; *petrify*). **2** verbs from adjectives, meaning 'bring or come into such a state' (*Frenchify*; *solidify*). **3** verbs in causative sense (*horrify*; *stupefy*). [from or after F *-fier* f. L *-ficare*, *-facere* f. *facere* do, make]

fylfot /ˈfɪlfɒt/ *n.* a swastika. [perh. f. *fill-foot*, pattern to fill the foot of a painted window]

fyrd /fɜːd/ *n. hist.* **1** the English militia before 1066. **2** the duty to serve in this. [OE f. Gmc (as FARE)]

fytte var. of FIT[3].

G

G¹ /dʒi:/ n. (also **g**) (pl. **Gs** or **G's**) **1** the seventh letter of the alphabet. **2** *Mus.* the fifth note in the diatonic scale of C major.

G² abbr. (also **G.**) **1** gauss. **2** giga-. **3** gravitational constant. **4** *US sl.* = GRAND n. 2.

g abbr. (also **g.**) **1** gelding. **2** gram(s). **3 a** gravity. **b** acceleration due to gravity.

GA abbr. *US* Georgia (in official postal use).

Ga symb. *Chem.* the element gallium.

Ga. abbr. Georgia (US).

gab /gæb/ n. *colloq.* talk, chatter, twaddle. □**gift of the gab** the facility of speaking eloquently or profusely. □□ **gabber** n. [17th-c. var. of GOB¹]

gabardine /ˈgæbə.di:n, -ˈdi:n/ n. (also **gaberdine**) **1** a smooth durable twill-woven cloth esp. of worsted or cotton. **2** a garment made of this, esp. a raincoat. [var. of GABERDINE]

gabble /ˈgæb(ə)l/ v. & n. —v. **1** *intr.* **a** talk volubly or inarticulately. **b** read aloud too fast. **2** *tr.* utter too fast, esp. in reading aloud. —n. fast unintelligible talk. □□ **gabbler** n. [MDu. *gabbelen* (imit.)]

gabbro /ˈgæbrəʊ/ n. (pl. **-os**) a dark granular plutonic rock of crystalline texture. □□ **gabbroic** /-ˈbrəʊɪk/ adj. **gabbroid** adv. [It. f. *Gabbro* in Tuscany]

gabby /ˈgæbɪ/ adj. (**gabbier, gabbiest**) *colloq.* talkative. [GAB + -Y¹]

gaberdine /ˈgæbə.di:n, -ˈdi:n/ n. **1** var. of GABARDINE. **2** *hist.* a loose long upper garment worn esp. by Jews and almsmen. [OF *gauvardine* perh. f. MHG *wallevart* pilgrimage]

gabion /ˈgeɪbɪən/ n. a cylindrical wicker or metal basket for filling with earth or stones, used in engineering or (formerly) in fortification. □□ **gabionage** n. [F f. It. *gabbione* f. *gabbia* CAGE]

gable /ˈgeɪb(ə)l/ n. **1 a** the triangular upper part of a wall at the end of a ridged roof. **b** (in full **gable-end**) a gable-topped wall. **2** a gable-shaped canopy over a window or door. □□ **gabled** adj. (also in *comb.*). [ME *gable* f. ON *gafl*]

gad¹ /gæd/ v. & n. —v.intr. (**gadded, gadding**) (foll. by *about, abroad, around*) go about idly or in search of pleasure. —n. idle wandering or adventure (esp. in **on the gad**). [back-form. f. obs. *gadling* companion f. OE *gædeling* f. *gæd* fellowship]

gad² /gæd/ int. (also **by gad**) an expression of surprise or emphatic assertion. [= *God*]

gadabout /ˈgædə.baʊt/ n. a person who gads about; an idle pleasure-seeker.

Gadarene /ˈgædə.ri:n/ adj. involving or engaged in headlong or suicidal rush or flight. [LL *Gadarenus* f. Gk *Gadarēnos* of Gadara in anc. Palestine, with ref. to Matthew 8:28–32]

gadfly /ˈgædflaɪ/ n. (pl. **-flies**) **1** a cattle-biting fly, esp. a warble fly, horsefly, or bot-fly. **2** an irritating or harassing person. [obs. *gad* goad, spike f. ON *gaddr*, rel. to YARD¹]

gadget /ˈgædʒɪt/ n. any small and usu. ingenious mechanical device or tool. □□ **gadgeteer** /-ˈtɪə(r)/ n. **gadgetry** n. **gadgety** adj. [19th-c. Naut.: orig. unkn.]

gadoid /ˈgeɪdɔɪd/ n. & adj. —n. any marine fish of the cod family Gadidae, including haddock and whiting. —adj. belonging to or resembling the Gadidae. [mod.L *gadus* f. Gk *gados* cod + -OID]

gadolinite /ˈgædəlɪ.naɪt/ n. a dark crystalline mineral consisting of ferrous silicate of beryllium. [J. *Gadolin*, Finnish mineralogist d. 1852]

gadolinium /ˌgædəˈlɪnɪəm/ n. *Chem.* a soft silvery metallic element of the lanthanoid series, occurring naturally in gadolinite. ¶ Symb.: **Gd**. [mod.L f. GADOLINITE]

gadroon /gəˈdru:n/ n. a decoration on silverware etc., consisting of convex curves in a series forming an ornamental edge like inverted fluting. [F *godron*: cf. *goder* pucker]

gadwall /ˈgædwɔ:l/ n. a brownish-grey freshwater duck, *Anas strepera*. [17th c.: orig. unkn.]

gadzooks /gædˈzu:ks/ int. *archaic* an expression of asseveration etc. [GAD² + *zooks* of unkn. orig.]

Gael /geɪl/ n. **1** a Scottish Celt. **2** a Gaelic-speaking Celt. □□ **Gaeldom** n. [Gael. *Gaidheal*]

Gaelic /ˈgeɪlɪk, ˈgæ-/ n. & adj. —n. any of the Celtic languages spoken in Ireland, Scotland, and the Isle of Man. —adj. of or relating to the Celts or the Celtic languages.

Gaeltacht /ˈgeɪltəxt/ n. any of the regions in Ireland where the vernacular language is Irish. [Ir.]

gaff¹ /gæf/ n. & v. —n. **1 a** a stick with an iron hook for landing large fish. **b** a barbed fishing-spear. **2** a spar to which the head of a fore-and-aft sail is bent. —v.tr. seize (a fish) with a gaff. [ME f. Prov. *gaf* hook]

gaff² /gæf/ n. *Brit. sl.* □**blow the gaff** let out a plot or secret. [19th c., = nonsense: orig. unkn.]

gaffe /gæf/ n. a blunder; an indiscreet act or remark. [F]

gaffer /ˈgæfə(r)/ n. **1** an old fellow; an elderly rustic. **2** *Brit. colloq.* a foreman or boss. **3** *colloq.* the chief electrician in a film or television production unit. [prob. contr. of GODFATHER]

gag /gæg/ n. & v. —n. **1** a piece of cloth etc. thrust into or held over the mouth to prevent speaking or crying out, or to hold it open in surgery. **2** a joke or comic scene in a play, film, etc., or as part of a comedian's act. **3** an actor's interpolation in a dramatic dialogue. **4** a thing or circumstance restricting free speech. **5 a** a joke or hoax. **b** a humorous action or situation. **6** an imposture or deception. **7** *Parl.* a closure or guillotine. —v. (**gagged, gagging**) **1** *tr.* apply a gag to. **2** *tr.* silence; deprive of free speech. **3** *tr.* apply a gag-bit to (a horse). **4 a** *intr.* choke or retch. **b** *tr.* cause to do this. **5** *intr. Theatr.* make gags. □**gag-bit** a specially powerful bit for horse-breaking. **gag man** a deviser or performer of theatrical gags. [ME, orig. as verb: orig. uncert.]

gaga /ˈgɑːgɑː/ adj. *sl.* **1** senile. **2** fatuous; slightly crazy. [F, = senile]

gage¹ /geɪdʒ/ n. & v. —n. **1** a pledge; a thing deposited as security. **2 a** a challenge to fight. **b** a symbol of this, esp. a glove thrown down. —v.tr. *archaic* stake, pledge; offer as a guarantee. [ME f. OF *gage* (n.), F *gager* (v.) ult. f. Gmc, rel. to WED]

gage² *US* var. of GAUGE.

gage³ /geɪdʒ/ n. = GREENGAGE. [abbr.]

gaggle /ˈgæg(ə)l/ n. & v. —n. **1** a flock of geese. **2** *colloq.* a disorderly group of people. —v.intr. (of geese) cackle. [ME, imit.: cf. *gabble*, *cackle*]

gagster /ˈgægstə(r)/ n. = gag man.

gaiety /ˈgeɪətɪ/ n. (*US* **gayety**) **1** the state of being light-hearted or merry; mirth. **2** merrymaking, amusement. **3** a bright appearance. □**gaiety of nations** the cheerfulness or pleasure of numerous people. [F *gaieté* (as GAY)]

gaillardia /geɪˈlɑːdɪə/ n. any composite plant of the genus *Gaillardia*, with showy flowers. [mod.L f. *Gaillard* de Marentoneau, 18th-c. Fr. botanist]

gaily /ˈgeɪlɪ/ adv. **1** in a gay or light-hearted manner. **2** with a bright or colourful appearance.

gain /geɪn/ v. & n. —v. **1** *tr.* obtain or secure (usu. something desired or favourable) (*gain an* *advantage*; *gain recognition*). **2** *tr.* acquire (a sum) as profits or as a result of changed conditions; earn. **3** *tr.* obtain as an increment or addition (*gain momentum*; *gain weight*). **4** *tr.* **a** win (a victory). **b** reclaim (land from the sea). **5** *intr.* (foll. by *in*) make a specified advance or improvement (*gained in stature*). **6** *intr.* & *tr.* (of a clock etc.) become fast, or be fast by (a specified amount of time). **7** *intr.* (often foll. by *on*, *upon*) come closer to a person or thing pursued. **8** *tr.* **a** bring over to one's interest or views. **b** (foll. by *over*) win by persuasion etc. **9** *tr.* reach or arrive at (a desired place). —*n.* **1** something gained, achieved, etc. **2** an increase of possessions etc.; a profit, advance, or improvement. **3** the acquisition of wealth. **4** (in *pl.*) sums of money acquired by trade etc., emoluments, winnings. **5** an increase in amount. **6** *Electronics* **a** the factor by which power etc. is increased. **b** the logarithm of this. □**gain ground** see GROUND[1]. **gain time** improve one's chances by causing or accepting delay. □□ **gainable** *adj.* **gainer** *n.* **gainings** *n.pl.* [OF *gaigner*, *gaaignier* to till, acquire, ult. f. Gmc]

gainful /'geɪnfʊl/ *adj.* **1** (of employment) paid. **2** lucrative, remunerative. □□ **gainfully** *adv.* **gainfulness** *n.*

gainsay /geɪn'seɪ/ *v.tr.* (*past* and *past part.* **gainsaid** /-'sed/) *archaic* or *literary* deny, contradict. □□ **gainsayer** *n.* [ME f. obs. *gain-* against f. ON *gegn* straight f. Gmc + SAY]

'gainst /genst/ *prep. poet.* = AGAINST. [abbr.]

gait /geɪt/ *n.* **1** a manner of walking; one's bearing or carriage as one walks. **2** the manner of forward motion of a runner, horse, vehicle, etc. □**go one's** (or **one's own**) **gait** pursue one's own course. [var. of GATE[2]]

gaiter /'geɪtə(r)/ *n.* a covering of cloth, leather, etc. for the leg below the knee, for the ankle, for part of a machine, etc. □□ **gaitered** *adj.* [F *guêtre*, prob. rel. to WRIST]

Gal. *abbr.* Galatians (New Testament).

gal[1] /gæl/ *n. sl.* a girl. [repr. var. pronunc.]

gal[2] /gæl/ *n. Physics* a unit of acceleration for a gravitational field, equal to one centimetre per second per second. [*Galileo*: see GALILEAN[1]]

gal. *abbr.* gallon(s).

gala /'gɑːlə/ *n.* **1** a festive occasion. **2** *Brit.* a festive gathering for sports, esp. swimming. [F or It. f. Sp. f. OF *gale* rejoicing f. Gmc]

galactagogue /gə'læktəgɒg/ *adj.* & *n.* —*adj.* inducing a flow of milk. —*n.* a galactagogue substance. [Gk *gala galaktos* milk, + *agōgos* leading]

galactic /gə'læktɪk/ *adj.* of or relating to a galaxy or galaxies, esp. the Galaxy. [Gk *galaktias*, var. of *galaxias*: see GALAXY]

galago /gə'leɪgəʊ/ *n.* (*pl.* **-os**) any small tree-climbing primate of the genus *Galago*, found in southern Africa, with large eyes and ears and a long tail. Also called *bush-baby*. [mod.L]

galah /gə'lɑː/ *n. Austral.* **1** a small rose-breasted grey-backed cockatoo, *Cacatua roseicapilla*. **2** *sl.* a fool or simpleton. [Aboriginal]

Galahad /'gæləhæd/ *n.* a person characterized by nobility, integrity, courtesy, etc. [name of a knight of the Round Table in Arthurian legend]

galantine /'gælənˌtiːn/ *n.* white meat or fish boned, cooked, pressed, and served cold in aspic etc. [ME f. OF, alt. f. *galatine* jellied meat f. med.L *galatina*]

galaxy /'gæləksɪ/ *n.* (*pl.* **-ies**) **1** any of many independent systems of stars, gas, dust, etc., held together by gravitational attraction. **2** (**the Galaxy**) the galaxy of which the solar system is a part. **3** (**the Galaxy**) the irregular luminous band of stars indistinguishable to the naked eye encircling the heavens, the Milky Way. **4** (foll. by *of*) a brilliant company or gathering. [ME f. OF *galaxie* f. med.L *galaxia*, LL *galaxias* f. Gk f. *gala galaktos* milk]

galbanum /'gælbənəm/ *n.* a bitter aromatic gum resin produced from kinds of ferula. [ME f. L f. Gk *khalbanē*, prob. of Semitic orig.]

gale[1] /geɪl/ *n.* **1** a very strong wind, esp. (on the Beaufort scale) one of 32-54 m.p.h. **2** *Naut.* a storm. **3** an outburst, esp. of laughter. [16th c.: orig. unkn.]

gale[2] /geɪl/ *n.* (in full **sweet-gale**) bog myrtle. [OE *gagel(le)*, MDu. *gaghel*]

galea /'geɪlɪə/ *n.* (*pl.* **galeae** /-lɪˌiː/ or **-as**) *Bot.* & *Zool.* a structure like a helmet in shape, form, or function. □□ **galeate** /-ɪət/ *adj.* **galeated** /-ˌeɪtɪd/ *adj.* [L, = helmet]

galena /gə'liːnə/ *n.* a bluish, grey or black mineral ore of lead sulphide. ¶ Chem. formula: PbS. [L, = lead ore (in a partly purified state)]

galenic /gə'lenɪk/ *adj.* & *n.* (also **galenical** /-'lenɪk(ə)l/) —*adj.* **1** of or relating to Galen, a Greek physician of the 2nd c. AD, or his methods. **2** made of natural as opposed to synthetic components. —*n.* a drug or medicament produced directly from animal or vegetable tissues.

galenical var. of GALENIC.

Galilean[1] /ˌgælɪ'liːən/ *adj.* of or relating to Galileo, Italian astronomer d. 1642, or his methods.

Galilean[2] /ˌgælɪ'liːən/ *adj.* & *n.* —*adj.* **1** of Galilee in Palestine. **2** Christian. —*n.* **1** a native of Galilee. **2** a Christian. **3** (prec. by *the*) *derog.* Christ.

galingale /'gælɪŋˌgeɪl/ *n.* **1** an aromatic rhizome of an E. Asian plant of the genus *Alpinia*, formerly used in cookery and medicine. **2** (in full **English galingale**) a sedge (*Cyperus longus*) having a root with similar properties. [OE *gallengar* OF *galingal* f. Arab. *ḳalanjān* f. Chin. *ge-liang-jiang* mild ginger from Ge in Canton]

galiot var. of GALLIOT.

galipot /'gælɪˌpɒt/ *n.* a hardened deposit of resin formed on the stem of the cluster pine. [F: orig. unkn.]

gall[1] /gɔːl/ *n.* **1** *sl.* impudence. **2** asperity, rancour. **3** bitterness; anything bitter (*gall and wormwood*). **4** the bile of animals. **5** the gall-bladder and its contents. □**gall-bladder** the vessel storing bile after its secretion by the liver and before release into the intestine. [ON, corresp. to OE *gealla*, f. Gmc]

gall[2] /gɔːl/ *n.* & *v.* —*n.* **1** a sore on the skin made by chafing. **2** **a** mental soreness or vexation. **b** a cause of this. **3** a place rubbed bare. —*v.tr.* **1** rub sore; injure by rubbing. **2** vex, annoy, humiliate. □□ **gallingly** *adv.* [ME f. LG or Du. *galle*, corresp. to OE *gealla* sore on a horse]

gall[3] /gɔːl/ *n.* **1** a growth produced by insects or fungus etc. on plants and trees, esp. on oak. **2** (*attrib.*) of insects producing galls (*gall-fly*). [ME f. OF *galle* f. L *galla*]

gall. *abbr.* gallon(s).

gallant *adj.*, *n.*, & *v.* —*adj.* /'gælənt/ **1** brave, chivalrous. **2** **a** (of a ship, horse, etc.) grand, fine, stately. **b** *archaic* finely dressed. **3** /'gælənt, gə'lænt/ **a** markedly attentive to women. **b** concerned with sexual love; amatory. —*n.* /'gælənt, gə'lænt/ **1** a ladies' man; a lover or paramour. **2** *archaic* a man of fashion; a fine gentleman. —*v.* /gə'lænt/ **1** *tr.* flirt with. **2** *tr.* escort; act as a cavalier to (a lady). **3** *intr.* **a** play the gallant. **b** (foll. by *with*) flirt. □□ **gallantly** /'gæləntlɪ/ *adv.* [ME f. OF *galant* part. of *galer* make merry]

gallantry /'gæləntrɪ/ *n.* (*pl.* **-ies**) **1** bravery; dashing courage. **2** courtliness; devotion to women. **3** a polite act or speech. **4** the conduct of a gallant; sexual intrigue; immorality. [F *galanterie* (as GALLANT)]

galleon /'gælɪən/ *n. hist.* **1** a ship of war (usu. Spanish). **2** a large Spanish ship used in American trade. **3** a vessel shorter and higher than a galley. [MDu. *galjoen* f. F *galion* f. *galie* galley, or f. Sp. *galeón*]

gallery /'gælərɪ/ *n.* (*pl.* **-ies**) **1** a room or building for showing works of art. **2** a balcony, esp. a platform projecting from the inner wall of a church, hall, etc., providing extra room for spectators etc. or reserved for musicians etc. (*minstrels' gallery*). **3 a** the highest balcony in a theatre. **b** its occupants. **4 a** a covered space for walking in, partly open at the side; a portico or colonnade. **b** a long narrow passage in the thickness of a wall or supported on corbels, open towards the interior of the building. **5** a long narrow room, passage, or corridor. **6** *Mil.* & *Mining* a horizontal underground passage. **7** a group of spectators at a golf-match etc. □**play to the gallery** seek to win approval by appealing to popular taste. □□ **galleried** *adj.* [F *galerie* f. It. *galleria* f. med.L *galeria*]

galleryite /'gælərɪˌaɪt/ *n.* a person occupying a seat in a gallery; a playgoer.

galley /'gælɪ/ *n.* (*pl.* -eys) **1** *hist.* **a** a low flat single-decked vessel using sails and oars, and usu. rowed by slaves or criminals. **b** an ancient Greek or Roman warship with one or more banks of oars. **c** a large open rowing-boat, e.g. that used by the captain of a man-of-war. **2** a ship's or aircraft's kitchen. **3** *Printing* **a** an oblong tray for set type. **b** the corresponding part of a composing-machine. **c** (in full **galley proof**) a proof in the form of long single-column strips from type in a galley, not in sheets or pages. □**galley-slave 1** *hist.* a person condemned to row in a galley. **2** a drudge. [ME f. OF *galie* f. med.L *galea*, med.Gk *galaia*]

galliard /'gælɪˌɑːd/ *n. hist.* **1** a lively dance usu. in triple time for two persons. **2** the music for this. [ME f. OF *gaillard* valiant]

Gallic /'gælɪk/ *adj.* **1** French or typically French. **2** of the Gauls; Gaulish. □□ **Gallicize** /-ˌsaɪz/ *v.tr.* & *intr.* (also -**ise**). [L *Gallicus* f. *Gallus* a Gaul]

gallic acid /'gælɪk/ *n. Chem.* an acid extracted from gallnuts etc., formerly used in making ink. [F *gallique* f. *galle* GALL³]

gallice /'gælɪˌsiː/ *adv.* in French. [L, = in Gaulish]

Gallicism /'gælɪˌsɪz(ə)m/ *n.* a French idiom, esp. one adopted in another language. [F *gallicisme* (as GALLIC)]

galligaskins /ˌgælɪ'gæskɪnz/ *n.pl. hist.* or *joc.* breeches, trousers. [orig. wide hose of the 16th–17th c., f. obs. F *garguesque* for *greguesque* f. It. *grechesca* fem. of *grechesco* Greek]

gallimaufry /ˌgælɪ'mɔːfrɪ/ *n.* (*pl.* -**ies**) a heterogeneous mixture; a jumble or medley. [F *galimafrée*, of unkn. orig.]

gallinaceous /ˌgælɪ'neɪʃəs/ *adj.* of or relating to the order Galliformes, which includes domestic poultry, pheasants, partridges, etc. [L *gallinaceus* f. *gallina* hen f. *gallus* cock]

gallinule /'gælɪˌnjuːl/ *n.* **1** a moorhen. **2** any of various similar birds of the genus *Porphyrula* or *Porphyrio*. [mod.L *gallinula*, dimin. of L *gallina* hen f. *gallus* cock]

galliot /'gælɪət/ *n.* (also **galiot**) **1** a Dutch cargo-boat or fishing-vessel. **2** a small (usu. Mediterranean) galley. [ME f. OF *galiote* f. It. *galeotta* f. med.L *galea* galley]

gallipot /'gælɪˌpɒt/ *n.* a small pot of earthenware, metal, etc., used for ointments etc. [prob. GALLEY + POT¹, because brought in galleys from the Mediterranean]

gallium /'gælɪəm/ *n. Chem.* a soft bluish-white metallic element occurring naturally in zinc blende, bauxite, and kaolin. ¶ Symb.: **Ga**. [mod.L f. L *Gallia* France (so named patriotically by its discoverer Lecoq de Boisbaudran d. 1912)]

gallivant /'gælɪˌvænt/ *v.intr. colloq.* **1** gad about. **2** flirt. [orig. uncert.]

galliwasp /'gælɪˌwɒsp/ *n.* a W. Indian lizard, *Diploglossus monotropis*. [18th c.: orig. unkn.]

gallnut /'gɔːlnʌt/ *n.* = GALL³.

Gallo- /'gæləʊ/ *comb. form* **1** French; French and. **2** Gaul (*Gallo-Roman*). [L *Gallus* a Gaul]

gallon /'gælən/ *n.* **1 a** (in full **imperial gallon**) *Brit.* a measure of capacity equal to eight pints and equivalent to 4546 cc, used for liquids and corn etc. **b**

US a measure of capacity equivalent to 3785 cc, used for liquids. **2** (usu. in *pl.*) *colloq.* a large amount. □□ **gallonage** *n.* [ME f. ONF *galon*, OF *jalon*, f. base of med.L *galleta*, *galletum*, perh. of Celtic orig.]

galloon /gə'luːn/ *n.* a narrow close-woven braid of gold, silver, silk, cotton, nylon, etc., for binding dresses etc. [F *galon* f. *galonner* trim with braid, of unkn. orig.]

gallop /'gæləp/ *n.* & *v.* —*n.* **1** the fastest pace of a horse or other quadruped, with all the feet off the ground together in each stride. **2** a ride at this pace. **3** a track or ground for this. —*v.* (**galloped**, **galloping**) **1 a** *intr.* (of a horse etc. or its rider) go at the pace of a gallop. **b** *tr.* make (a horse etc.) gallop. **2** *intr.* (foll. by *through*, *over*) read, recite, or talk at great speed. **3** *intr.* move or progress rapidly (*galloping inflation*). □**at a gallop** at the pace of a gallop. □□ **galloper** *n.* [OF *galop*, *galoper*: see WALLOP]

galloway /'gæləˌweɪ/ *n.* **1** an animal of a breed of hornless black beef cattle from Galloway in SW Scotland. **2** this breed.

gallows /'gæləʊz/ *n.pl.* (usu. treated as *sing.*) **1** a structure, usu. of two uprights and a crosspiece, for the hanging of criminals. **2** (prec. by *the*) execution by hanging. □**gallows humour** grim and ironical humour. [ME f. ON *gálgi*]

gallstone /'gɔːlstəʊn/ *n.* a small hard mass forming in the gall-bladder.

Gallup poll /'gæləp/ *n.* an assessment of public opinion by questioning a representative sample, esp. as the basis for forecasting the results of voting. [G. H. *Gallup*, Amer. statistician d. 1984]

galluses /'gæləsɪz/ *n.pl. dial.* & *US* trouser-braces. [pl. of *gallus* var. of GALLOWS]

galoot /gə'luːt/ *n. colloq.* a person, esp. a strange or clumsy one. [19th-c. Naut. sl.: orig. unkn.]

galop /'gæləp/ *n.* & *v.* **1** a lively dance in duple time. **2** the music for this. —*v.intr.* (**galoped**, **galoping**) perform this dance. [F: see GALLOP]

galore /gə'lɔː(r)/ *adv.* in abundance (placed after noun: *flowers galore*). [Ir. *go leór* to sufficiency]

galosh /gə'lɒʃ/ *n.* (also **golosh**) (usu. in *pl.*) a waterproof overshoe, usu. of rubber. [ME f. OF *galoche* f. LL *gallicula* small Gallic shoe]

galumph /gə'lʌmf/ *v.intr. colloq.* **1** move noisily or clumsily. **2** go prancing in triumph. [coined by Lewis Carroll (in sense 2), perh. f. GALLOP + TRIUMPH]

galvanic /gæl'vænɪk/ *adj.* **1 a** sudden and remarkable (*had a galvanic effect*). **b** stimulating; full of energy. **2** of or producing an electric current by chemical action. □□ **galvanically** *adv.*

galvanism /'gælvəˌnɪz(ə)m/ *n. hist.* **1** electricity produced by chemical action. **2** the use of electricity for medical purposes. □□ **galvanist** *n.* [F *galvanisme* f. L. *Galvani*, It. physiologist d. 1798]

galvanize /'gælvəˌnaɪz/ *v.tr.* (also -**ise**) **1** (often foll. by *into*) rouse forcefully, esp. by shock or excitement (*was galvanized into action*). **2** stimulate by or as if by electricity. **3** coat (iron) with zinc (usu. without the use of electricity) as a protection against rust. □□ **galvanization** /-'zeɪʃ(ə)n/ *n.* **galvanizer** *n.* [F *galvaniser*: see GALVANISM]

galvanometer /ˌgælvə'nɒmɪtə(r)/ *n.* an instrument for detecting and measuring small electric currents. □□ **galvanometric** /-nə'metrɪk/ *adj.*

gambade /gæm'bɑːd/ *n.* (also **gambado** /-'bɑːdəʊ/) (*pl.* **gambades**; -**os** or -**oes**) **1** a horse's leap or bound. **2** a fantastic movement. **3** an escapade. [F *gambade* & Sp. *gambado* f. It. & Sp. *gamba* leg]

gambier /'gæmbɪə(r)/ *n.* an astringent extract of an Eastern plant used in tanning etc. [Malay *gambir* name of the plant]

gambit /'gæmbɪt/ *n.* **1** a chess opening in which a player sacrifices a piece or pawn to secure an advantage. **2** an opening move in a discussion etc. **3** a trick or device. [earlier *gambett* f. It. *gambetto* tripping up f. *gamba* leg]

gamble /'gæmb(ə)l/ v. & n. —v. **1** intr. play games of chance for money, esp. for high stakes. **2** tr. **a** bet (a sum of money) in gambling. **b** (often foll. by *away*) lose (assets) by gambling. **3** intr. take great risks in the hope of substantial gain. **4** intr. (foll. by *on*) act in the hope or expectation of (*gambled on fine weather*). —n. **1** a risky undertaking or attempt. **2** a spell of gambling. ▫▫ **gambler** n. [obs. *gamel* to sport, *gamene* GAME¹]

gamboge /gæm'bəʊʒ, -'buːʒ/ n. a gum resin produced by various E. Asian trees and used as a yellow pigment and as a purgative. [mod.L *gambaugium* f. *Cambodia* in SE Asia]

gambol /'gæmb(ə)l/ v. & n. —v.intr. (**gambolled**, **gambolling**; US **gamboled**, **gamboling**) skip or frolic playfully. —n. a playful frolic. [GAMBADE]

gambrel /'gæmbr(ə)l/ n. (in full **gambrel roof**) **1** Brit. a roof like a hipped roof but with gable-like ends. **2** US = curb roof. [ONF *gamberel* f. *gambier* forked stick f. *gambe* leg (from the resemblance to the shape of a horse's hind leg)]

game¹ /geɪm/ n., adj., & v. —n. **1** a form or spell of play or sport, esp. a competitive one played according to rules and decided by skill, strength, or luck. **2** a single portion of play forming a scoring unit in some contests, e.g. bridge or tennis. **3** (in pl.) **a** athletics or sports as organized in a school etc. **b** a meeting for athletic etc. contests (*Olympic Games*). **4** a winning score in a game; the state of the score in a game (*the game is two all*). **5** the equipment for a game. **6** one's level of achievement in a game, as specified (*played a good game*). **7 a** a piece of fun; a jest (*was only playing a game with you*). **b** (in pl.) dodges, tricks (*none of your games!*). **8** a scheme or undertaking etc. regarded as a game (*so that's your game*). **9** a policy or line of action. **10** (collect.) **a** wild animals or birds hunted for sport or food. **b** the flesh of these. **11** a hunted animal; a quarry or object of pursuit or attack. **12** a kept flock of swans. —adj. **1** spirited; eager and willing. **2** (foll. by *for*, or *to* + infin.) having the spirit or energy; eagerly prepared. —v. intr. play at games of chance for money; gamble. ▫**the game is up** the scheme is revealed or foiled. **game plan** esp. US **1** a winning strategy worked out in advance for a particular match. **2** a plan of campaign, esp. in politics. **game point** Tennis etc. a point which, if won, would win the game. **game** (or **games**) **theory** the mathematical analysis of conflict in war, economics, games of skill, etc. **game-warden** an official locally supervising game and hunting. **gaming-house** a place frequented for gambling; a casino. **gaming-table** a table used for gambling. **make game** (or **a game**) **of** mock, taunt. **off** (or **on**) **one's game** playing badly (or well). **on the game** Brit. sl. involved in prostitution or thieving. **play the game** behave fairly or according to the rules. ▫▫ **gamely** adv. **gameness** n. **gamester** n. [OE *gamen*]

game² /geɪm/ adj. (of a leg, arm, etc.) lame, crippled. [18th-c. dial.: orig. unkn.]

gamebook /'geɪmbʊk/ n. a book for recording game killed by a sportsman.

gamecock /'geɪmkɒk/ n. (also **gamefowl** /-faʊl/) a cock bred and trained for cock-fighting.

gamekeeper /'geɪm,kiːpə(r)/ n. a person employed to breed and protect game.

gamelan /'gæmə,læn/ n. **1** a type of orchestra found in SE Asia (esp. Indonesia), with string and woodwind instruments, and a wide range of percussion instruments. **2** a kind of xylophone used in this. [Jav.]

gamesman /'geɪmzmən/ n. (pl. **-men**) an exponent of gamesmanship.

gamesmanship /'geɪmzmənʃɪp/ n. the art or practice of winning games or other contests by gaining a psychological advantage over an opponent.

gamesome /'geɪmsəm/ adj. merry, sportive. ▫▫ **gamesomely** adv. **gamesomeness** n.

gametangium /,gæmɪ'tændʒɪəm/ n. (pl.

gametangia /-dʒɪə/) Bot. an organ in which gametes are formed. [as GAMETE + *aggeion* vessel]

gamete /'gæmiːt, gə'miːt/ n. Biol. a mature germ cell able to unite with another in sexual reproduction. ▫▫ **gametic** /gə'metɪk/ adj. [mod.L *gameta* f. Gk *gametē* wife f. *gamos* marriage]

gameto- /gə'miːtəʊ/ comb. form Biol. gamete.

gametocyte /gə'miːtəʊ,saɪt/ n. Biol. any cell that is in the process of developing into one or more gametes.

gametogenesis /gə,miːtəʊ'dʒenɪsɪs/ n. Biol. the process by which cells undergo meiosis to form gametes.

gametophyte /gə'miːtəʊ,faɪt/ n. the gamete-producing form of a plant that has alternation of generations between this and the asexual form. ▫▫ **gametophytic** /-'fɪtɪk/ adj.

gamin /'gæmɪn/ n. **1** a street urchin. **2** an impudent child. [F]

gamine /gæ'miːn/ n. **1** a girl gamin. **2** a girl with mischievous or boyish charm. [F]

gamma /'gæmə/ n. **1** the third letter of the Greek alphabet (Γ, γ). **2** a third-class mark given for a piece of work or in an examination. **3** Astron. the third brightest star in a constellation. **4** the third member of a series. ▫**gamma radiation** (or **rays**) electromagnetic radiation of very short wavelength emitted by some radioactive substances. [ME f. Gk]

gammer /'gæmə(r)/ n. archaic an old woman, esp. as a rustic name. [prob. contr. of GODMOTHER: cf. GAFFER]

gammon¹ /'gæmən/ n. & v. —n. **1** the bottom piece of a flitch of bacon including a hind leg. **2** the ham of a pig cured like bacon. —v.tr. cure (bacon). [ONF *gambon* f. *gambe* leg: cf. JAMB]

gammon² /'gæmən/ n. & v. —n. a kind of victory scoring two games at backgammon. —v.tr. defeat in this way. [app. = ME *gamen* GAME¹]

gammon³ /'gæmən/ n. & v. colloq. —n. humbug, deception. —v. **1** intr. **a** talk speciously. **b** pretend. **2** tr. hoax, deceive. [18th c.: orig. uncert.]

gammy /'gæmɪ/ adj. (**gammier**, **gammiest**) Brit. sl. (esp. of a leg) lame; permanently injured. [dial. form of GAME²]

gamp /gæmp/ n. Brit. colloq. an umbrella, esp. a large unwieldy one. [Mrs *Gamp* in Dickens's *Martin Chuzzlewit*]

gamut /'gæmət/ n. **1** the whole series or range or scope of anything (*the whole gamut of crime*). **2** Mus. **a** the whole series of notes used in medieval or modern music. **b** a major diatonic scale. **c** a people's or a period's recognized scale. **d** a voice's or instrument's compass. **3** Mus. the lowest note in the medieval sequence of hexachords, = modern G on the lowest line of the bass staff. [med.L *gamma ut* f. GAMMA taken as the name for a note one tone lower than A of the classical scale + *ut* the first of six arbitrary names of notes forming the hexachord, being syllables (*ut, re, mi, fa, so, la*) of the Latin hymn beginning *Ut queant laxis*]

gamy /'geɪmɪ/ adj. (**gamier**, **gamiest**) **1** having the flavour or scent of game kept till it is high. **2** US scandalous, sensational. **3** = GAME¹ adj. ▫▫ **gamily** adv. **gaminess** n.

gander /'gændə(r)/ n. & v. —n. **1** a male goose. **2** sl. a look, a glance (*take a gander*). —v.intr. look or glance. [OE *gandra*, rel. to GANNET]

gang¹ /gæŋ/ n. & v. —n. **1 a** a band of persons acting or going about together, esp. for criminal purposes. **b** colloq. such a band pursuing a purpose causing disapproval. **2** a set of workers, slaves, or prisoners. **3** a set of tools arranged to work simultaneously. —v.tr. arrange (tools etc.) to work in coordination. ▫**gang-bang** sl. an occasion on which several men successively have sexual intercourse with one woman. **gang up** colloq. **1** (often foll. by *with*) act in concert. **2** (foll. by *on*) combine against. [orig. = going, journey, f. ON *gangr*, *ganga* GOING, corresp. to OE *gang*]

gang² /gæŋ/ *v.intr. Sc.* go. □**gang agley** (of a plan etc.) go wrong. [OE *gangan*: cf. GANG¹]

gangboard /'gæŋbɔːd/ *n.* = GANGPLANK.

ganger /'gæŋə(r)/ *n. Brit.* the foreman of a gang of workers, esp. navvies.

gangle /'gæŋg(ə)l/ *v.intr.* move ungracefully. [back-form. f. GANGLING]

gangling /'gæŋglɪŋ/ *adj.* (of a person) loosely built; lanky. [frequent. of GANG²]

ganglion /'gæŋglɪən/ *n.* (*pl.* **ganglia** /-lɪə/ or **ganglions**) **1 a** an enlargement or knot on a nerve etc. containing an assemblage of nerve-cells. **b** a mass of grey matter in the central nervous system forming a nerve-nucleus. **2** *Med.* a cyst, esp. on a tendon sheath. **3** a centre of activity or interest. □□ **gangliar** *adj.* **gangliform** *adj.* **ganglionated** *adj.* **ganglionic** /-'ɒnɪk/ *adj.* [Gk *gagglion*]

gangly /'gæŋglɪ/ *adj.* (**ganglier, gangliest**) = GANGLING.

gangplank /'gæŋplæŋk/ *n.* a movable plank usu. with cleats nailed on it for boarding or disembarking from a ship etc.

gangrene /'gæŋgriːn/ *n. & v.* —*n.* **1** *Med.* death and decomposition of a part of the body tissue, usu. resulting from obstructed circulation. **2** moral corruption. —*v.tr. & intr.* affect or become affected with gangrene. □□ **gangrenous** /'gæŋgrɪnəs/ *adj.* [F *gangrène* f. L *gangraena* f. Gk *gaggraina*]

gangster /'gæŋstə(r)/ *n.* a member of a gang of violent criminals. □□ **gangsterism** *n.*

gangue /gæŋ/ *n.* valueless earth etc. in which ore is found. [F f. G *Gang* lode = GANG¹]

gangway /'gæŋweɪ/ *n. & int.* —*n.* **1** *Brit.* a passage, esp. between rows of seats. **2 a** an opening in the bulwarks by which a ship is entered or left. **b** a bridge laid from ship to shore. **c** a passage on a ship, esp. a platform connecting the quarterdeck and forecastle. **3** a temporary bridge on a building site etc. —*int.* make way!

ganister /'gænɪstə(r)/ *n.* a close-grained hard siliceous stone found in the coal measures of northern England, and used for furnace-linings. [19th c.: orig. unkn.]

ganja /'gænd͡ʒə/ *n.* marijuana. [Hindi *gānjhā*]

gannet /'gænɪt/ *n.* **1** any sea bird of the genus *Sula*, esp. *Sula bassana*, catching fish by plunge-diving. **2** *sl.* a greedy person. □□ **gannetry** *n.* (*pl.* **-ies**). [OE *ganot* f. Gmc, rel. to GANDER]

ganoid /'gænɔɪd/ *adj. & n.* —*adj.* **1** (of fish scales) enamelled; smooth and bright. **2** having ganoid scales. —*n.* a fish having ganoid scales. [F *ganoïde* f. Gk *ganos* brightness]

gantlet *US* var. of GAUNTLET².

gantry /'gæntrɪ/ *n.* (*pl.* **-ies**) **1** an overhead structure with a platform supporting a travelling crane, or railway or road signals. **2** a structure supporting a space rocket prior to launching. **3** (also **gauntry** /'gɔːntrɪ/) a wooden stand for barrels. [prob. f. *gawn*, dial. form of GALLON + TREE]

gaol *Brit.* var. of JAIL.

gaoler *Brit.* var. of JAILER.

gap /gæp/ *n.* **1** an unfilled space or interval; a blank; a break in continuity. **2** a breach in a hedge, fence, or wall. **3** a wide (usu. undesirable) divergence in views, sympathies, development, etc. (*generation gap*). **4** a gorge or pass. □**fill** (or **close** etc.) **a gap** make up a deficiency. **gap-toothed** having gaps between the teeth. □□ **gapped** *adj.* **gappy** *adj.* [ME f. ON, = chasm, rel. to GAPE]

gape /geɪp/ *v. & n.* —*v.intr.* **1 a** open one's mouth wide, esp. in amazement or wonder. **b** be or become wide open. **2** (foll. by *at*) gaze curiously or wondrously. **3** split; part asunder. **4** yawn. —*n.* **1** an open-mouthed stare. **2** a yawn. **3** (in *pl.*; prec. by *the*) **a** a disease of birds with gaping as a symptom, caused by infestation with gapeworm. **b** *joc.* a fit of yawning. **4 a** an expanse of open mouth or beak. **b** the part of

a beak that opens. **5** a rent or opening. □□ **gapingly** *adv.* [ME f. ON *gapa*]

gaper /'geɪpə(r)/ *n.* **1** any bivalve mollusc of the genus *Mya*, with the shell open at one or both ends. **2** the comber fish, which gapes when dead. **3** a person who gapes.

gapeworm /'geɪpwɜːm/ *n.* a nematode worm, *Syngamus tracheae*, that infests the trachea and bronchi of birds and causes the gapes.

gar /gɑː(r)/ *n.* = GARFISH 2.

garage /'gærɑːʒ, -rɪdʒ/ *n. & v.* —*n.* **1** a building or shed for the storage of a motor vehicle or vehicles. **2** an establishment selling petrol etc., or repairing and selling motor vehicles. —*v.tr.* put or keep (a motor vehicle) in a garage. □**garage sale** *US* a sale of miscellaneous household goods, usu. for charity, held in the garage of a private house. [F f. *garer* shelter]

garb /gɑːb/ *n. & v.* —*n.* **1** clothing, esp. of a distinctive kind. **2** the way a person is dressed. —*v.tr.* **1** (usu. in *passive* or *refl.*) put (esp. distinctive) clothes on (a person). **2** attire. [obs. F *garbe* f. It. *garbo* f. Gmc, rel. to GEAR]

garbage /'gɑːbɪdʒ/ *n.* **1 a** refuse, filth. **b** domestic waste. **2** foul or rubbishy literature etc. □**garbage can** *US* a dustbin. [AF: orig. unkn.]

garble /'gɑːb(ə)l/ *v.tr.* **1** unintentionally distort or confuse (facts, messages, etc.). **2 a** mutilate in order to misrepresent. **b** make (usu. unfair or malicious) selections from (facts, statements, etc.). □□ **garbler** *n.* [It. *garbellare* f. Arab. *garbala* sift, perh. f. LL *cribellare* to sieve f. L *cribrum* sieve]

garboard /'gɑːbəd/ *n.* (in full **garboard strake**) the first range of planks or plates laid on a ship's bottom next to the keel. [Du. *gaarboord*, perh. f. *garen* GATHER + *boord* BOARD]

garçon /'gɑːsɔ̃/ *n.* a waiter in a French restaurant, hotel, etc. [F, lit. 'boy']

Garda /'gɑːdə/ *n.* **1** the State police force of the Irish Republic. **2** (also **garda**) (*pl.* **-dai** /-diː/) a member of this. [Ir. *Garda Síochána* Civic Guard]

garden /'gɑːd(ə)n/ *n. & v.* —*n.* **1** esp. *Brit.* a piece of ground, usu. partly grassed and adjoining a private house, used for growing flowers, fruit, or vegetables, and as a place of recreation. **2** (esp. in *pl.*) ornamental grounds laid out for public enjoyment (*botanical gardens*). **3** a similar place with the service of refreshments (*tea garden*). **4** (*attrib.*) **a** (of plants) cultivated, not wild. **b** for use in a garden (*garden seat*). **5** (usu. in *pl.* prec. by a name) *Brit.* a street, square, etc. (*Onslow Gardens*). **6** an especially fertile region. **7** *US* a large public hall. **8** (**the Garden**) the philosophy or school of Epicurus. —*v.intr.* cultivate or work in a garden. □**garden centre** an establishment where plants and garden equipment etc. are sold. **garden city** an industrial or other town laid out systematically with spacious surroundings, parks, etc. **garden cress** a cruciferous plant, *Lepidium sativum*, used in salads. **garden party** a social event held on a lawn or in a garden. **garden suburb** *Brit.* a suburb laid out spaciously with open spaces, parks, etc. **garden warbler** a European woodland songbird, *Sylvia borin*. □□ **gardenesque** /-'nesk/ *adj.* [ME f. ONF *gardin* (OF *jardin*) ult. f. Gmc: cf. YARD²]

gardener /'gɑːdnə(r)/ *n.* a person who gardens or is employed to tend a garden. □**gardener-bird** a bowerbird making a 'garden' of moss etc. in front of a bower. [ME ult. f. OF *jardinier* (as GARDEN)]

gardenia /gɑː'diːnɪə/ *n.* any tree or shrub of the genus *Gardenia*, with large white or yellow flowers and usu. a fragrant scent. [mod.L f. Dr A. *Garden*, Sc. naturalist d. 1791]

garfish /'gɑːfɪʃ/ *n.* (*pl.* same) **1** any mainly marine fish of the family *Belonidae*, esp. *Belone belone*, having long beaklike jaws with sharp teeth. Also called NEEDLEFISH. **2** *US* any similar freshwater fish of the genus *Lepisosteus*, with ganoid scales. Also called GAR or GARPIKE. **3** *NZ & Austral.* either of two marine fish of the genus *Hemiramphus.* Also called HALFBEAK. [app. f. OE *gār* spear + *fisc* FISH¹]

garganey /ˈgɑːnɪ/ *n.* (*pl.* **-eys**) a small duck, *Anas querquedula*, the drake of which has a white stripe from the eye to the neck. [It., dial. var. of *garganello*]

gargantuan /gɑːˈgæntjʊən/ *adj.* enormous, gigantic. [the name of a giant in Rabelais' book *Gargantua* (1534)]

garget /ˈgɑːgɪt/ *n.* **1** inflammation of a cow's or ewe's udder. **2** *US* pokeweed. [perh. f. obs. *garget* throat f. OF *gargate, -guete*]

gargle /ˈgɑːg(ə)l/ *v. & n.* —*v.* **1** *tr.* (also *absol.*) wash (one's mouth and throat), esp. for medicinal purposes, with a liquid kept in motion by breathing through it. **2** *intr.* make a sound as when doing this. —*n.* **1** a liquid used for gargling. **2** *sl.* an alcoholic drink. [F *gargouiller* f. *gargouille*: see GARGOYLE]

gargoyle /ˈgɑːgɔɪl/ *n.* a grotesque carved human or animal face or figure projecting from the gutter of (esp. a Gothic) building usu. as a spout to carry water clear of a wall. [OF *gargouille* throat, gargoyle]

gargoylism /ˈgɑːgɔɪˌlɪz(ə)m/ *n. Med.* = HURLER'S SYNDROME.

garibaldi /ˌgærɪˈbɔːldɪ/ *n.* (*pl.* **garibaldis**) **1** a kind of woman's or child's loose blouse, orig. of bright red material imitating the shirts worn by Garibaldi and his followers. **2** *Brit.* a biscuit containing a layer of currants. **3** *US* a small red Californian fish, *Hypsypops rubicundus.* [G. *Garibaldi,* It. patriot d. 1882]

garish /ˈgeərɪʃ/ *adj.* **1** obtrusively bright; showy. **2** gaudy; over-decorated. □□ **garishly** *adv.* **garishness** *n.* [16th-c. *gaurish* app. f. obs. *gaure* stare]

garland /ˈgɑːlənd/ *n. & v.* —*n.* **1** a wreath of flowers, leaves, etc., worn on the head or hung as a decoration. **2** a prize or distinction. **3** a literary anthology or miscellany. —*v.tr.* **1** adorn with garlands. **2** crown with a garland. [ME f. OF *garlande,* of unkn. orig.]

garlic /ˈgɑːlɪk/ *n.* **1** any of various alliaceous plants, esp. *Allium sativum.* **2** the strong-smelling pungent-tasting bulb of this plant, used as a flavouring in cookery. □□ **garlicky** *adj.* [OE *gārlēac* f. *gār* spear + *lēac* LEEK]

garment /ˈgɑːmənt/ *n. & v.* —*n.* **1 a** an article of dress. **b** (in *pl.*) clothes. **2** the outward and visible covering of anything. —*v.tr.* (usu. in *passive*) *rhet.* attire. [ME f. OF *garnement* (as GARNISH)]

garner /ˈgɑːnə(r)/ *v. & n.* —*v.tr.* **1** collect. **2** store, deposit. —*n. literary* a storehouse or granary. [ME (orig. as noun) f. OF *gernier* f. L *granarium* GRANARY]

garnet /ˈgɑːnɪt/ *n.* a vitreous silicate mineral, esp. a transparent deep-red kind used as a gem. [ME f. OF *grenat* f. med.L *granatum* POMEGRANATE, from its resemblance to the pulp of the fruit]

garnish /ˈgɑːnɪʃ/ *v. & n.* —*v.tr.* **1** decorate or embellish (esp. food). **2** *Law* **a** serve notice on (a person) for the purpose of legally seizing money belonging to a debtor or defendant. **b** summon (a person) as a party to litigation started between others. —*n.* (also **garnishing**) a decoration or embellishment, esp. to food. □□ **garnishment** *n.* (in sense 2). [ME f. OF *garnir* f. Gmc]

garnishee /ˌgɑːnɪˈʃiː/ *n. & v. Law* —*n.* a person garnished. —*v.tr.* (**garnishees, garnisheed**) **1** garnish (a person). **2** attach (money etc.) by way of garnishment.

garniture /ˈgɑːnɪtʃə(r)/ *n.* **1** decoration or trimmings, esp. of food. **2** accessories, appurtenances. [F (as GARNISH)]

garotte var. of GARROTTE.

garpike /ˈgɑːpaɪk/ *n.* a gar or garfish (see GARFISH 2). [OE *gār* spear + PIKE¹]

garret /ˈgærɪt/ *n.* **1** a top-floor or attic room, esp. a dismal one. **2** an attic. [ME f. OF *garite* watch-tower f. Gmc]

garrison /ˈgærɪs(ə)n/ *n. & v.* —*n.* **1** the troops stationed in a fortress, town, etc., to defend it. **2** the building occupied by them. —*v.tr.* **1** provide (a place)

with or occupy as a garrison. **2** place on garrison duty. □ **garrison town** a town having a permanent garrison. [ME f. OF *garison* f. *garir* defend, furnish f. Gmc]

garrotte /gəˈrɒt/ *v. & n.* (also **garotte**; *US* **garrote**) —*v.tr.* **1** execute or kill by strangulation, esp. with an iron or wire collar etc. **2** throttle in order to rob. —*n.* **1 a** a Spanish method of execution by garrotting. **b** the apparatus used for this. **2** highway robbery in which the victim is throttled. [F *garrotter* or Sp. *garrotear* f. *garrote* a cudgel, of unkn. orig.]

garrulous /ˈgærʊləs/ *adj.* **1** talkative, esp. on trivial matters. **2** loquacious, wordy. □□ **garrulity** /gəˈruːlɪtɪ/ *n.* **garrulously** *adv.* **garrulousness** *n.* [L *garrulus* f. *garrire* chatter]

garter /ˈgɑːtə(r)/ *n. & v.* —*n.* **1** a band worn to keep a sock or stocking up. **2** (**the Garter**) *Brit.* **a** the highest order of English knighthood. **b** the badge of this. **c** membership of this. **3** *US* a suspender for a sock or stocking. —*v.tr.* fasten (a stocking) or encircle (a leg) with a garter. □ **garter-belt** *US* a suspender belt. **Garter King of Arms** see *King of Arms.* **garter-snake** any water-snake of the genus *Thamnophis,* native to N. America, having lengthwise stripes. **garter stitch** a plain knitting stitch or pattern, forming ridges in alternate rows. [ME f. OF *gartier* f. *garet* bend of the knee]

garth /gɑːθ/ *n. Brit.* **1** an open space within cloisters. **2** *archaic* **a** a close or yard. **b** a garden or paddock. [ME f. ON *garthr* = OE *geard* YARD²]

gas /gæs/ *n. & v.* —*n.* (*pl.* **gases**) **1** any airlike substance which moves freely to fill any space available, irrespective of its quantity. **2 a** such a substance (esp. found naturally or extracted from coal) used as a domestic or industrial fuel (also *attrib.*: *gas cooker*; *gas fire*). **b** an explosive mixture of firedamp with air. **3** nitrous oxide or another gas used as an anaesthetic (esp. in dentistry). **4** a gas or vapour used as a poisonous agent to disable an enemy in warfare. **5** *US colloq.* petrol, gasoline. **6** *sl.* pointless idle talk; boasting. **7** *sl.* an enjoyable, attractive, or amusing thing or person. —*v.* (**gases, gassed, gassing**) **1** *tr.* expose to gas, esp. to kill or make unconscious. **2** *intr.* give off gas. **3** *tr.* (usu. foll. by *up*) *US colloq.* fill (the tank of a motor vehicle) with petrol. **4** *intr. colloq.* talk idly or boastfully. □ **gas chamber** an airtight chamber that can be filled with poisonous gas to kill people or animals. **gas chromatography** chromatography employing gas as the eluent. **gas-cooled** (of a nuclear reactor etc.) cooled by a current of gas. **gas fire** a domestic fire using gas as its fuel. **gas-fired** using gas as the fuel. **gas gangrene** a rapidly spreading gangrene of injured tissue infected by a soil bacterium and accompanied by the evolution of gas. **gas mask** a respirator used as a defence against poison gas. **gas meter** an apparatus recording the amount of gas consumed. **gas oil** a type of fuel oil distilled from petroleum and heavier than paraffin oil. **gas plant** *Bot.* fraxinella. **gas-proof** impervious to gas. **gas ring** a hollow ring perforated with gas jets, used esp. for cooking. **gas station** *US* a filling-station. **gas-tight** proof against the leakage of gas. **gas turbine** a turbine driven by a flow of gas or by gas from combustion. [invented by J. B. van Helmont, Belgian chemist d. 1644, after Gk *khaos* chaos]

gasbag /ˈgæsbæg/ *n.* **1** a container of gas, esp. for holding the gas for a balloon or airship. **2** *sl.* an idle talker.

Gascon /ˈgæskən/ *n.* **1** a native of Gascony. **2** (**gascon**) a braggart. [F f. L *Vasco -onis*]

gaseous /ˈgæsɪəs/ *adj.* of or like gas. □□ **gaseousness** *n.*

gash¹ /gæʃ/ *n. & v.* —*n.* **1** a long and deep slash, cut, or wound. **2 a** a cleft such as might be made by a slashing cut. **b** the act of making such a cut. —*v.tr.* make a gash in; cut. [var. of ME *garse* f. OF *garcer* scarify, perh. ult. f. Gk *kharassō*]

a purulent swelling. **3** a group of leaves taken together in bookbinding.

Gatling /'gætlɪŋ/ *n.* (in full **Gatling gun**) a machine-gun with clustered barrels. [R. J. *Gatling*, Amer. inventor d. 1903]

GATT /gæt/ *abbr.* (also **Gatt**) General Agreement on Tariffs and Trade.

gauche /gəʊʃ/ *adj.* **1** lacking ease or grace; socially awkward. **2** tactless. □□ **gauchely** *adv.* **gaucheness** *n.* [F, = left-handed, awkward]

gaucherie /'gəʊʃəri:/ *n.* **1** gauche manners. **2** a gauche action. [F]

gaucho /'gaʊtʃəʊ/ *n.* (*pl.* **-os**) a cowboy from the S. American pampas. [Sp. f. Quechua]

gaud /gɔːd/ *n.* **1** a gaudy thing; a showy ornament. **2** (in *pl.*) showy ceremonies. [perh. through AF f. OF *gaudir* rejoice f. L *gaudēre*]

gaudy[1] /'gɔːdɪ/ *adj.* (**gaudier, gaudiest**) tastelessly or extravagantly bright or showy. □□ **gaudily** *adv.* **gaudiness** *n.* [prob. f. GAUD + -Y[1]]

gaudy[2] /'gɔːdɪ/ *n.* (*pl.* **-ies**) *Brit.* an annual feast or entertainment, esp. a college dinner for old members etc. [L *gaudium* joy or *gaude* imper. of *gaudēre* rejoice]

gauge /geɪdʒ/ *n. & v.* (*US* **gage**: see also sense 7) —*n.* **1** a standard measure to which certain things must conform, esp.: **a** the measure of the capacity or contents of a barrel. **b** the fineness of a textile. **c** the diameter of a bullet. **d** the thickness of sheet metal. **2** any of various instruments for measuring or determining this, or for measuring length, thickness, or other dimensions or properties. **3** the distance between a pair of rails or the wheels on one axle. **4** the capacity, extent, or scope of something. **5** a means of estimating; a criterion or test. **6** a graduated instrument measuring the force or quantity of rain-fall, stream, tide, wind, etc. **7** (usu. **gage**) *Naut.* a relative position with respect to the wind. —*v.tr.* **1** measure exactly (esp. objects of standard size). **2** determine the capacity or content of. **3** estimate or form a judgement of (a person, temperament, situation, etc.). **4** make uniform; bring to a standard size or shape. □ **gauge pressure** the amount by which a pressure exceeds that of the atmosphere. **take the gauge of** estimate. □□ **gaugeable** *adj.* **gauger** *n.* [ME f. ONF *gauge, gauger*, of unkn. orig.]

Gaul /gɔːl/ *n.* a native or inhabitant of ancient Gaul. [*Gaul* the country f. F *Gaule* f. Gmc]

gauleiter /'gaʊˌlaɪtə(r)/ *n.* **1** an official governing a district under Nazi rule. **2** a local or petty tyrant. [G f. *Gau* administrative district + *Leiter* leader]

Gaulish /'gɔːlɪʃ/ *adj. & n.* —*adj.* of or relating to the ancient Gauls. —*n.* their language.

Gaullism /'gəʊlɪz(ə)m/ *n.* **1** the principles and policies of Charles de Gaulle, French military and political leader (d. 1970), characterized by their conservatism, nationalism, and advocacy of centralized government. **2** adherence to these. □□ **Gaullist** *n.* [F *Gaullisme*]

gault /gɔːlt/ *n. Geol.* **1** a series of clay and marl beds between the upper and lower greensand in S. England. **2** clay obtained from these beds. [16th c.: orig. unkn.]

gaunt /gɔːnt/ *adj.* **1** lean, haggard. **2** grim or desolate in appearance. □□ **gauntly** *adv.* **gauntness** *n.* [ME: orig. unkn.]

gauntlet[1] /'gɔːntlɪt/ *n.* **1** a stout glove with a long loose wrist. **2** *hist.* an armoured glove. **3** the part of a glove covering the wrist. **4** a challenge (esp. in **throw down the gauntlet**). [ME f. OF *gantelet* dimin. of *gant* glove f. Gmc]

gauntlet[2] /'gɔːntlɪt/ *n.* (*US* **gantlet** /'gænt-/) □ **run the gauntlet 1** be subjected to harsh criticism. **2** pass between two rows of people and receive blows from them, as a punishment or ordeal. [earlier *gantlope* f. Sw. *gatlopp* f. *gata* lane, *lopp* course, assim. to GAUNTLET[1]]

gauntry var. of GANTRY 3.

gaur /'gaʊə(r)/ *n.* a wild species of Indian cattle, *Bos gaurus*. [Hind.]

gauss /gaʊs/ *n.* (*pl.* same or **gausses**) a unit of magnetic induction, equal to one ten-thousandth of a tesla. ¶ Abbr.: **G**. [K. *Gauss*, Ger. mathematician d. 1855]

Gaussian distribution /'gaʊsɪən/ *n. Statistics* = *normal distribution*. [as GAUSS]

gauze /gɔːz/ *n.* **1** a thin transparent fabric of silk, cotton, etc. **2** a fine mesh of wire etc. **3** a slight haze. [F *gaze* f. *Gaza* in Palestine]

gauzy /'gɔːzɪ/ *adj.* (**gauzier, gauziest**) **1** like gauze; thin and translucent. **2** flimsy, delicate. □□ **gauzily** *adv.* **gauziness** *n.*

gave past of GIVE.

gavel /'gæv(ə)l/ *n. & v.* —*n.* a small hammer used by an auctioneer, or for calling a meeting to order. —*v.* (**gavelled, gavelling**; *US* **gaveled, gaveling**) **1** *intr.* use a gavel. **2** *tr.* (often foll. by *down*) end (a meeting) or dismiss (a speaker) by use of a gavel. [19th c.: orig. unkn.]

gavial var. of GHARIAL.

gavotte /gə'vɒt/ *n.* **1** an old French dance in common time beginning on the third beat of the bar. **2** the music for this, or a piece of music in the rhythm of this as a movement in a suite. [F f. Prov. *gavoto* f. *Gavot* native of a region in the Alps]

gawk /gɔːk/ *v. & n.* —*v.intr. colloq.* stare stupidly. —*n.* an awkward or bashful person. □□ **gawkish** *adj.* [rel. to obs. *gaw* gaze f. ON *gá* heed]

gawky /'gɔːkɪ/ *adj.* (**gawkier, gawkiest**) awkward or ungainly. □□ **gawkily** *adv.* **gawkiness** *n.*

gawp /gɔːp/ *v.intr. Brit. colloq.* stare stupidly or obtrusively. □□ **gawper** *n.* [earlier *gaup, galp* f. ME *galpen* yawn, rel. to YELP]

gay /geɪ/ *adj. & n.* —*adj.* **1** light-hearted and carefree; mirthful. **2** characterized by cheerfulness or pleasure (*a gay life*). **3** brightly coloured; showy, brilliant (*a gay scarf*). **4** *colloq.* **a** homosexual. **b** intended for or used by homosexuals (*a gay bar*). ¶ Generally informal in use, but favoured by homosexuals with ref. to themselves. **5** *colloq.* dissolute, immoral. —*n. colloq.* a homosexual, esp. male. □ **Gay Liberation** the advocacy of homosexuals' freedom from social discrimination. □□ **gayness** *n.* [ME f. OF *gai*, of unkn. orig.]

gayal /gə'jæl/ *n.* a wild species of Indian cattle, *Bos fontalis*. [Hindi]

gayety *US* var. of GAIETY.

gazania /gə'zeɪnɪə/ *n.* any herbaceous plant of the genus *Gazania*, with showy yellow or orange daisy-shaped flowers. [18th c.: f. Theodore of *Gaza*, Greek scholar d. 1478]

gaze /geɪz/ *v. & n.* —*v.intr.* (foll. by *at, into, on, upon*, etc.) look fixedly. —*n.* a fixed or intent look. □□ **gazer** *n.* [ME: orig. unkn.; cf. obs. *gaw* GAWK]

gazebo /gə'zi:bəʊ/ *n.* (*pl.* **-os** or **-oes**) a small building or structure such as a summer-house or turret, designed to give a wide view. [perh. joc. f. GAZE, in imitation of L futures in *-ēbo*: cf. LAVABO]

gazelle /gə'zel/ *n.* any of various small graceful soft-eyed antelopes of Asia or Africa, esp. of the genus *Gazella*. [F prob. f. Sp. *gacela* f. Arab. *gazāl*]

gazette /gə'zet/ *n. & v.* —*n.* **1** a newspaper, esp. the official one of an organization or institution (*University Gazette*). **2** *hist.* a news-sheet; a periodical publication giving current events. **3** *Brit.* an official journal with a list of government appointments, bankruptcies, and other public notices (*London Gazette*). —*v.tr. Brit.* announce or publish in an official gazette. [F f. It. *gazzetta* f. *gazeta*, a Venetian small coin]

gazetteer /ˌgæzɪ'tɪə(r)/ *n.* a geographical index or dictionary. [earlier = journalist, for whom such an index was provided: f. F *gazettier* f. It. *gazzettiere* (as GAZETTE)]

gazpacho /gæ'spætʃəʊ/ *n.* (*pl.* **-os**) a Spanish soup made with oil, garlic, onions, etc., and served cold. [Sp.]

gazump /gə'zʌmp/ v.tr. (also absol.) Brit. colloq. **1** (of a seller) raise the price of a property after having accepted an offer by (an intending buyer). **2** swindle. □□ **gazumper** n. [20th c.: orig. uncert.]

gazunder /gə'zʌndə(r)/ v.tr. (also absol.) Brit. colloq. (of a buyer) lower the amount of an offer made to (the seller for a property), esp. just before exchange of contracts. [GAZUMP + UNDER]

GB abbr. Great Britain.

GBE abbr. (in the UK) Knight (or Dame) Grand Cross (of the Order) of the British Empire.

GBH abbr. grievous bodily harm.

GC abbr. (in the UK) George Cross.

GCB abbr. (in the UK) Knight (or Dame) Grand Cross (of the Order) of the Bath.

GCE abbr. (in the UK) General Certificate of Education.

GCHQ abbr. (in the UK) Government Communications Headquarters.

GCMG abbr. (in the UK) Knight (or Dame) Grand Cross (of the Order) of St Michael & St George.

GCSE abbr. (in the UK) General Certificate of Secondary Education.

GCVO abbr. (in the UK) Knight (or Dame) Grand Cross of the Royal Victorian Order.

Gd symb. Chem. the element gadolinium.

Gdn. abbr. Garden.

Gdns. abbr. Gardens.

GDP abbr. gross domestic product.

GDR abbr. German Democratic Republic.

Ge symb. Chem. the element germanium.

gear /gɪə(r)/ n. & v. —n. **1** (often in pl.) **a** a set of toothed wheels that work together to transmit and control motion from an engine, esp. to the road wheels of a vehicle. **b** a mechanism for doing this. **2** a particular function or state of adjustment of engaged gears (low gear; second gear). **3** a mechanism of wheels, levers, etc., usu. for a special purpose (winding-gear). **4** a particular apparatus or mechanism, as specified (landing-gear). **5** equipment or tackle for a special purpose. **6** colloq. clothing, esp. when modern or fashionable. **7** goods; household utensils. **8** rigging. **9** a harness for a draught animal. —v. **1** tr. (foll. by to) adjust or adapt to suit a special purpose or need. **2** tr. (often foll. by up) equip with gears. **3** tr. (foll. by up) make ready or prepared. **4** tr. put (machinery) in gear. **5** intr. **a** be in gear. **b** (foll. by with) work smoothly with. □ **be geared** (or **all geared**) **up** (often foll. by for, or to + infin.) colloq. be ready or enthusiastic. **first** (or **bottom**) **gear** the lowest gear in a series. **gear down** (or **up**) provide with a low (or high) gear. **gear lever** (or **shift**) a lever used to engage or change gear, esp. in a motor vehicle. **high** (or **low**) **gear** a gear such that the driven end of a transmission revolves faster (or slower) than the driving end. **in gear** with a gear engaged. **out of gear** **1** with no gear engaged. **2** out of order. **top gear** the highest gear in a series. [ME f. ON gervi f. Gmc]

gearbox /'gɪəbɒks/ n. **1** the casing that encloses a set of gears. **2** a set of gears with its casing, esp. in a motor vehicle.

gearing /'gɪərɪŋ/ n. **1** a set or arrangement of gears in a machine. **2** Brit. Commerce **a** the allocation of part of a dividend to preferred recipients. **b** the amount of this part.

gearwheel /'gɪəwiːl/ n. **1** a toothed wheel in a set of gears. **2** (in a bicycle) the cog-wheel driven directly by the chain.

gecko /'gekəʊ/ n. (pl. -os or -oes) any of various house lizards found in warm climates, with adhesive feet for climbing vertical surfaces. [Malay chichak etc., imit. of its cry]

gee[1] /dʒiː/ int. (also **gee whiz** /wɪz/) US colloq. a mild expression of surprise, discovery, etc. [perh. abbr. of JESUS]

gee[2] /dʒiː/ int. (often foll. by up) a command to a horse etc., esp. to go faster. [17th c.: orig. unkn.]

gee[3] /dʒiː/ n. US sl. (usu. in pl.) a thousand dollars. [the letter G, as initial of GRAND]

gee-gee /'dʒiːdʒiː/ n. Brit. colloq. a horse. [orig. a child's word, f. GEE[2]]

geek /giːk/ n. Austral. sl. a look. [E dial.]

geese pl. of GOOSE.

gee-string var. of G-STRING 2.

geezer /'giːzə(r)/ n. sl. a person, esp. an old man. [dial. pronunc. of guiser mummer]

Gehenna /gɪ'henə/ n. **1** (in the New Testament) hell. **2** a place of burning, torment, or misery. [eccl.L f. Gk f. Heb. gê' hinnōm hell, orig. the valley of Hinnom near Jerusalem, where children were sacrificed]

Geiger counter /'gaɪgə(r)/ n. a device for measuring radioactivity by detecting and counting ionizing particles. [H. Geiger, Ger. physicist d. 1945]

geisha /'geɪʃə/ n. (pl. same or **geishas**) **1** a Japanese hostess trained in entertaining men with dance and song. **2** a Japanese prostitute. [Jap.]

Geissler tube /'gaɪslə/ n. a sealed tube of glass or quartz with a central constriction, filled with vapour for the production of a luminous electrical discharge. [H. Geissler, Ger. mechanic d. 1879]

gel /dʒel/ n. & v. —n. a semi-solid colloidal suspension or jelly, of a solid dispersed in a liquid. —v.intr. (**gelled, gelling**) form a gel. □□ **gelation** /-'leɪʃ(ə)n/ n. [abbr. of GELATIN]

gelatin /'dʒelatɪn/ n. (also **gelatine** /-ˌtiːn/) a virtually colourless tasteless transparent water-soluble protein derived from collagen and used in food preparation, photography, etc. □ **gelatin paper** a paper coated with sensitized gelatin for photography. □□ **gelatinize** /dʒɪ'lætɪˌnaɪz/ v.tr. & intr. (also **-ise**). **gelatinization** /dʒɪˌlætɪnaɪ'zeɪʃ(ə)n/ n. [F gélatine f. It. gelatina f. gelata JELLY]

gelatinous /dʒɪ'lætɪnəs/ adj. **1** of or like gelatin. **2** of a jelly-like consistency. □□ **gelatinously** adv.

gelation /dʒɪ'leɪʃ(ə)n/ n. solidification by freezing. [L gelatio f. gelare freeze]

geld /geld/ v.tr. **1** deprive (usu. a male animal) of the ability to reproduce. **2** castrate or spay; excise the testicles or ovaries of. [ME f. ON gelda f. geldr barren f. Gmc]

gelding /'geldɪŋ/ n. a gelded animal, esp. a male horse. [ME f. ON geldingr: see GELD]

gelid /'dʒelɪd/ adj. **1** icy, ice-cold. **2** chilly, cool. [L gelidus f. gelu frost]

gelignite /'dʒelɪgˌnaɪt/ n. an explosive made from nitroglycerine, cellulose nitrate, sodium nitrate, and wood pulp. [GELATIN + L ignis fire + -ITE[1]]

gelly /'dʒelɪ/ n. Brit. sl. gelignite. [abbr.]

gem /dʒem/ n. & v. —n. **1** a precious stone, esp. when cut and polished or engraved. **2** an object or person of great beauty or worth. —v.tr. (**gemmed, gemming**) adorn with or as with gems. □□ **gemlike** adj. **gemmy** adj. [ME f. OF gemme f. L gemma bud, jewel]

Gemara /gɪ'mɑːrə/ n. a rabbinical commentary on the Mishnah, forming the second part of the Talmud. [Aram. gᵉmārâ completion]

geminal /'dʒemɪn(ə)l/ adj. Chem. (of molecules) having two functional groups attached to the same atom. □□ **geminally** adv. [as GEMINATE + -AL]

geminate adj. & v. —adj. /'dʒemɪnət/ combined in pairs. —v.tr. /'dʒemɪˌneɪt/ **1** double, repeat. **2** arrange in pairs. □□ **gemination** /-'neɪʃ(ə)n/ n. [L geminatus past part. of geminare f. geminus twin]

Gemini /'dʒemɪˌnaɪ, -ˌniː/ n. **1** a constellation, traditionally regarded as contained in the figures of twins. **2 a** the third sign of the zodiac (the Twins). **b** a person born when the sun is in this sign. □□ **Geminean** /ˌdʒemɪ'niːən/ n. & adj. [ME f. L, = twins]

gemma /'dʒemə/ n. (pl. **gemmae** /-miː/) a small cellular body in cryptogams that separates from the mother-plant and starts a new one; an asexual spore. [L: see GEM]

gemmation /dʒeˈmeɪʃ(ə)n/ *n.* reproduction by gemmae. [F f. *gemmer* to bud, *gemme* bud]

gemmiferous /dʒeˈmɪfərəs/ *adj.* 1 producing precious stones. 2 bearing buds. [L *gemmifer* (as GEMMA, -FEROUS)]

gemmiparous /dʒeˈmɪpərəs/ *adj.* of or propagating by gemmation. [mod.L *gemmiparus* f. L *gemma* bud + *parere* bring forth]

gemmology /dʒeˈmɒlədʒɪ/ *n.* the study of gems. □□ **gemmologist** *n.* [L *gemma* gem + -LOGY] \

gemmule /ˈdʒemjuːl/ *n.* an encysted embryonic cell-cluster in sponges. [F *gemmule* or L *gemmula* little bud (as GEM)]

gemstone /ˈdʒemstəʊn/ *n.* a precious stone used as a gem.

gemütlich /gəˈmuːtlɪx/ *adj.* 1 pleasant and comfortable. 2 genial, agreeable. [G]

Gen. *abbr.* 1 General. 2 Genesis (Old Testament).

gen /dʒen/ *n. & v. Brit. sl.* —*n.* information. —*v.tr. & intr.* (**genned, genning**) (foll. by *up*) provide with or obtain information. [perh. f. first syll. of *general information*]

-gen /dʒ(ə)n/ *comb. form* 1 *Chem.* that which produces (*hydrogen*; *antigen*). 2 *Bot.* growth (*endogen*; *exogen*; *acrogen*). [F -*gène* f. Gk -*genēs* -born, of a specified kind f. *gen*- root of *gignomai* be born, become]

gendarme /ˈʒɒndɑːm/ *n.* 1 a soldier, mounted or on foot, employed in police duties esp. in France. 2 a rock-tower on a mountain, occupying and blocking an arête. [F f. *gens d'armes* men of arms]

gendarmerie /ʒɒnˈdɑːmərɪ/ *n.* 1 a force of gendarmes. 2 the headquarters of such a force.

gender /ˈdʒendə(r)/ *n.* 1 a the grammatical classification of nouns and related words, roughly corresponding to the two sexes and sexlessness. b each of the classes of nouns (see MASCULINE, FEMININE, NEUTER, COMMON *adj.* 6). 2 (of nouns and related words) the property of belonging to such a class. 3 *colloq.* a person's sex. [ME f. OF *gendre* ult. f. L GENUS]

gene /dʒiːn/ *n.* a unit of heredity composed of DNA or RNA and forming part of a chromosome etc., that determines a particular characteristic of an individual. [G *Gen*: see -GEN]

genealogical /ˌdʒiːnɪəˈlɒdʒɪk(ə)l/ *adj.* 1 of or concerning genealogy. 2 tracing family descent. □**genealogical tree** a chart like an inverted branching tree showing the descent of a family or of an animal species. □□ **genealogically** *adv.* [F *généalogique* f. Gk *genealogikos* (as GENEALOGY)]

genealogy /ˌdʒiːnɪˈælədʒɪ/ *n.* (*pl.* -**ies**) 1 a a line of descent traced continuously from an ancestor. b an account or exposition of this. 2 the study and investigation of lines of descent. 3 a plant's or animal's line of development from earlier forms. □□ **genealogist** *n.* **genealogize** *v.tr. & intr.* (also -**ise**). [ME f. OF *genealogie* f. LL *genealogia* f. Gk *genealogia* f. *genea* race]

genera *pl.* of GENUS.

general /ˈdʒenər(ə)l/ *adj. & n.* —*adj.* 1 a completely or almost universal. b including or affecting all or nearly all parts or cases of things. 2 prevalent, widespread, usual. 3 not partial, particular, local, or sectional. 4 not limited in application; relating to whole classes or all cases. 5 including points common to the individuals of a class and neglecting the differences (*a general term*). 6 not restricted or specialized (*general knowledge*). 7 a roughly corresponding or adequate. b sufficient for practical purposes. 8 not detailed (*a general resemblance*; *a general idea*). 9 vague, indefinite (*spoke only in general terms*). 10 chief or principal; having overall authority (*general manager*; *Secretary-General*). —*n.* 1 a an army officer ranking next below Field Marshal or above lieutenant-general. b *US* = lieutenant-general, major-general. 2 a commander of an army. 3 a tactician or strategist of specified merit (*a great general*). 4 the head of a religious order, e.g.

of the Jesuits or Dominicans or the Salvation Army. 5 (prec. by *the*) *archaic* the public. □**as a general rule** in most cases. **General American** a form of US speech not markedly dialectal or regional. **General Certificate of Education** 1 an examination set esp. for secondary-school pupils at advanced level in England and Wales. 2 the certificate gained by passing it. **General Certificate of Secondary Education** an examination replacing and combining the GCE ordinary level and CSE examinations. **general delivery** *US* the delivery of letters to callers at a post office. **general election** the election of representatives to a legislature (esp. in the UK to the House of Commons) from constituencies throughout the country. **general headquarters** the headquarters of a military commander. **general meeting** a meeting open to all the members of a society etc. **general of the army** (or **air force**) *US* the officer of the highest rank in the army or air force. **general practice** the work of a general practitioner. **general practitioner** a doctor working in the community and treating cases of all kinds in the first instance, as distinct from a consultant or specialist. **general staff** the staff assisting a military commander in planning and administration. **general strike** a strike of workers in all or most trades. **General Synod** the highest governing body in the Church of England. **in general** 1 as a normal rule; usually. 2 for the most part. □□ **generalness** *n.* [ME f. OF f. L *generalis* (as GENUS)]

generalissimo /ˌdʒenərəˈlɪsɪˌməʊ/ *n.* (*pl.* -**os**) the commander of a combined military force consisting of army, navy, and air-force units. [It., superl. of *generale* GENERAL]

generalist /ˈdʒenərəlɪst/ *n.* a person competent in several different fields or activities (opp. SPECIALIST).

generality /ˌdʒenəˈrælɪtɪ/ *n.* (*pl.* -**ies**) 1 a statement or principle etc. having general validity or force. 2 applicability to a whole class of instances. 3 vagueness; lack of detail. 4 the state of being general. 5 (foll. by *of*) the main body or majority. [F *généralité* f. LL *generalitas -tatis* (as GENERAL)]

generalization /ˌdʒenərəlaɪˈzeɪʃ(ə)n/ *n.* (also -**isation**) 1 a general notion or proposition obtained by inference from (esp. limited or inadequate) particular cases. 2 the act or an instance of generalizing. [F *généralisation* (as GENERALIZE)]

generalize /ˈdʒenərəˌlaɪz/ *v.* (also -**ise**) 1 *intr.* a speak in general or indefinite terms. b form general principles or notions. 2 *tr.* reduce to a general statement, principle, or notion. 3 *tr.* a give a general character to. b call by a general name. 4 *tr.* infer (a law or conclusion) by induction. 5 *tr. Math. & Philos.* express in a general form; extend the application of. 6 *tr.* (in painting) render only the typical characteristics of. 7 *tr.* bring into general use. □□ **generalizable** *adj.* **generalizability** /-zəˈbɪlɪtɪ/ *n.* **generalizer** *n.* [F *généraliser* (as GENERAL)]

generally /ˈdʒenərəlɪ/ *adv.* 1 usually; in most cases. 2 in a general sense; without regard to particulars or exceptions (*generally speaking*). 3 for the most part; extensively (*not generally known*). 4 in most respects (*they were generally well-behaved*).

generalship /ˈdʒenər(ə)lʃɪp/ *n.* 1 the art or practice of exercising military command. 2 military skill; strategy. 3 skilful management; tact, diplomacy.

generate /ˈdʒenəˌreɪt/ *v.tr.* 1 bring into existence; produce, evolve. 2 produce (electricity). 3 *Math.* (of a point or line or surface conceived as moving) make (a line or surface or solid). 4 *Math. & Linguistics* produce (a set or sequence of items) by the formulation and application of precise criteria. □□ **generable** /-rəb(ə)l/ *adj.* [L *generare* beget (as GENUS)]

generation /ˌdʒenəˈreɪʃ(ə)n/ *n.* 1 all the people born at a particular time, regarded collectively (*my generation*; *the rising generation*). 2 a single step in descent or pedigree (*have known them for three*

æ cat ɑː arm e bed ɜː her ɪ sit iː see ɒ hot ɔː saw ʌ run ʊ put uː too ə ago aɪ my

generations). **3** a stage in (esp. technological) development (*fourth-generation computers*). **4** the average time in which children are ready to take the place of their parents (usu. reckoned at about 30 years). **5** production by natural or artificial process, esp. the production of electricity or heat. **6 a** procreation; the propagation of species. **b** the act of begetting or being begotten. □**generation gap** differences of outlook or opinion between those of different generations. □□**generational** *adj.* [ME f. OF f. L *generatio -onis* (as GENERATE)]

generative /ˈdʒenərətɪv/ *adj.* **1** of or concerning procreation. **2** able to produce, productive. □**generative grammar** a set of rules whereby permissible sentences may be generated from the elements of a language. [ME f. OF *generatif* or LL *generativus* (as GENERATE)]

generator /ˈdʒenəˌreɪtə(r)/ *n.* **1** a machine for converting mechanical into electrical energy; a dynamo. **2** an apparatus for producing gas, steam, etc. **3** a person who generates an idea etc.; an originator.

generic /dʒɪˈnerɪk/ *adj.* **1** characteristic of or relating to a class; general, not specific or special. **2** *Biol.* characteristic of or belonging to a genus. **3** (of goods, esp. a drug) having no brand name; not protected by a registered trade mark. □□**generically** *adv.* [F *générique* f. L GENUS]

generous /ˈdʒenərəs/ *adj.* **1** giving or given freely. **2** magnanimous, noble-minded, unprejudiced. **3 a** ample, abundant, copious (*a generous portion*). **b** (of wine) rich and full. □□**generosity** /-ˈrɒsɪtɪ/ *n.* **generously** *adv.* **generousness** *n.* [OF *genereus* f. L *generosus* noble, magnanimous (as GENUS)]

genesis /ˈdʒenɪsɪs/ *n.* **1** the origin, or mode of formation or generation, of a thing. **2** (**Genesis**) the first book of the Old Testament, with an account of the creation of the world. [L f. Gk f. *gen-* be produced, root of *gignomai* become]

genet /ˈdʒenɪt/ *n.* (also **genette** /dʒɪˈnet/) **1** any catlike mammal of the genus *Genetta*, native to Africa and S. Europe, with spotted fur and a long ringed bushy tail. **2** the fur of the genet. [ME f. OF *genete* f. Arab. *jarnaiṭ*]

genetic /dʒɪˈnetɪk/ *adj.* **1** of genetics or genes; inherited. **2** of, in, or concerning origin; causal. □**genetic code** *Biochem.* the means by which genetic information is stored as sequences of nucleotide bases in the chromosomal DNA. **genetic engineering** the deliberate modification of the characters of an organism by the manipulation of DNA and the transformation of certain genes. **genetic fingerprinting** (or **profiling**) the analysis of characteristic patterns in DNA as a means of identifying individuals. □□**genetically** *adv.* [GENESIS after *antithetic*]

genetics /dʒɪˈnetɪks/ *n.pl.* (treated as *sing.*) the study of heredity and the variation of inherited characteristics. □□**geneticist** /-tɪsɪst/ *n.*

genette var. of GENET.

geneva /dʒɪˈniːvə/ *n.* Hollands gin. [Du. *genever* f. OF *genevre* f. L *juniperus*, with assim. to the place name *Geneva*]

Geneva bands /dʒɪˈniːvə/ *n.pl.* two white cloth strips attached to the collar of some Protestants' clerical dress. [*Geneva* in Switzerland, where orig. worn by Calvinists]

Geneva Convention /dʒɪˈniːvə/ *n.* an international agreement first made at Geneva in 1864 and later revised, governing the status and treatment of captured and wounded military personnel in wartime.

genial[1] /ˈdʒiːnɪəl/ *adj.* **1** jovial, sociable, kindly, cheerful. **2** (of the climate) mild and warm; conducive to growth. **3** cheering, enlivening. □□**geniality** /-ˈælɪtɪ/ *n.* **genially** *adv.* [L *genialis* (as GENIUS)]

genial[2] /dʒɪˈniːəl/ *adj.* *Anat.* of or relating to the chin. [Gk *geneion* chin f. *genus* jaw]

genic /ˈdʒiːnɪk/ *adj.* of or relating to genes.

-genic /ˈdʒenɪk/ *comb. form* forming adjectives meaning: **1** producing (*carcinogenic*; *pathogenic*). **2** well suited to (*photogenic*; *radiogenic*). **3** produced by (*iatrogenic*). □□**-genically** *suffix* forming adverbs. [-GEN + -IC]

genie /ˈdʒiːnɪ/ *n.* (*pl.* usu. **genii** /ˈdʒiːnɪˌaɪ/) a jinnee, goblin, or familiar spirit of Arabian folklore. [F *génie* f. L GENIUS: cf. JINNEE]

genii *pl.* of GENIE, GENIUS.

genista /dʒɪˈnɪstə/ *n.* any almost leafless shrub of the genus *Genista*, with a profusion of yellow pea-shaped flowers, e.g. dyer's broom. [L]

genital /ˈdʒenɪt(ə)l/ *adj.* & *n.* of or relating to animal reproduction. —*n.* (in *pl.*) the external reproductive organs. [OF *génital* or L *genitalis* f. *gignere genit-* beget]

genitalia /dʒenɪˈteɪlɪə/ *n.pl.* the genitals. [L, neut. pl. of *genitalis*: see GENITAL]

genitive /ˈdʒenɪtɪv/ *n.* & *adj.* *Gram.* —*n.* the case of nouns and pronouns (and words in grammatical agreement with them) corresponding to *of*, *from*, and other prepositions and indicating possession or close association. —*adj.* of or in the genitive. □□**genitival** /-ˈtaɪv(ə)l/ *adj.* **genitivally** /-ˈtaɪvəlɪ/ *adv.* [ME f. OF *genetif*, *-ive* or L *genitivus* f. *gignere genit-* beget]

genito- /ˈdʒenɪtəʊ/ *comb. form* genital.

genito-urinary /ˌdʒenɪtəʊˈjʊərɪnərɪ/ *adj.* of the genital and urinary organs.

genius /ˈdʒiːnɪəs/ *n.* (*pl.* **geniuses** or **genii** /-nɪˌaɪ/) **1** (*pl.* **geniuses**) **a** an exceptional intellectual or creative power or other natural ability or tendency. **b** a person having this. **2** the tutelary spirit of a person, place, institution, etc. **3** a person or spirit regarded as powerfully influencing a person for good or evil. **4** the prevalent feeling or associations etc. of a nation, age, etc. [L (in sense 2) f. the root of *gignere* beget]

genizah /dʒeˈniːzə/ *n.* a room attached to a synagogue and housing damaged, discarded, or heretical books etc., and sacred relics. [Heb. *gĕnīzāh*, lit. hiding-place f. *gānaz* hide, set aside]

Genoa cake /ˈdʒenəʊə/ *n.* a rich fruit cake with almonds on top. [*Genoa* in Italy]

Genoa jib /ˈdʒenəʊə/ *n.* a large jib or foresail used esp. on yachts.

genocide /ˈdʒenəˌsaɪd/ *n.* the deliberate extermination of a people or nation. □□**genocidal** /-ˈsaɪd(ə)l/ *adj.* [Gk *genos* race + -CIDE]

genome /ˈdʒiːnəʊm/ *n.* **1** the haploid set of chromosomes of an organism. **2** the genetic material of an organism. [GENE + CHROMOSOME]

genotype /ˈdʒiːnəˌtaɪp/ *n.* *Biol.* the genetic constitution of an individual. □□**genotypic** /-ˈtɪpɪk/ *adj.* [G *Genotypus* (as GENE, TYPE)]

-genous /ˈdʒenəs/ *comb. form* forming adjectives meaning 'produced' (*endogenous*).

genre /ˈʒɑːr/ *n.* **1** a kind or style, esp. of art or literature (e.g. novel, drama, satire). **2** (in full **genre painting**) the painting of scenes from ordinary life. [F, = a kind (as GENDER)]

gens /dʒenz/ *n.* (*pl.* **gentes** /-tiːz/) **1** *Rom.Hist.* a group of families sharing a name and claiming a common origin. **2** *Anthropol.* a number of people sharing descent through the male line. [L, f. the root of *gignere* beget]

gent /dʒent/ *n. colloq.* (often *joc.*) **1** a gentleman. **2** (in *pl.*) in shop titles) men (*gents' outfitters*). **3** (the **Gents**) *Brit. colloq.* a men's public lavatory. [abbr. of GENTLEMAN]

genteel /dʒenˈtiːl/ *adj.* **1** affectedly or ostentatiously refined or stylish. **2** often *iron.* of or appropriate to the upper classes. □□**genteelly** *adv.* **genteelness** *n.* [earlier *gentile*, readoption of F *gentil* GENTLE]

genteelism /dʒenˈtiːlɪz(ə)m/ *n.* a word used because it is thought to be less vulgar than the commoner word (e.g. *perspire* for *sweat*).

gentes *pl.* of GENS.

gentian /ˈdʒenʃ(ə)n, -ʃɪən/ *n.* **1** any plant of the genus *Gentiana* or *Gentianella*, found esp. in mountainous regions, and having usu. vivid blue flowers. **2** (in full **gentian bitter**) a liquor extracted from the root of the gentian. □**gentian violet** a violet dye used as an antiseptic, esp. in the treatment of burns. [OE f. L *gentiana* f. *Gentius* king of Illyria]

gentile /'dʒentaɪl/ *adj. & n. —adj.* **1** (**Gentile**) not Jewish; heathen. **2** of or relating to a nation or tribe. **3** *Gram.* (of a word) indicating nationality. *—n.* **1** (**Gentile**) a person who is not Jewish. **2** *Gram.* a word indicating nationality. [ME f. L *gentilis* f. *gens gentis* family: see GENS]

gentility /dʒen'tɪlɪtɪ/ *n.* **1** social superiority. **2** good manners; habits associated with the nobility. **3** people of noble birth. [ME f. OF *gentilité* (as GENTLE)]

gentle /'dʒent(ə)l/ *adj., v., & n. —adj.* (**gentler**, **gentlest**) **1** not rough; mild or kind, esp. in temperament. **2** moderate; not severe or drastic (*a gentle rebuke*; *a gentle breeze*). **3** (of birth, pursuits, etc.) honourable, of or fit for people of good social position. **4** quiet; requiring patience (*gentle art*). **5** *archaic* generous, courteous. *—v.tr.* **1** make gentle or docile. **2** handle (a horse etc.) firmly but gently. *—n.* a maggot, the larva of the meat-fly or bluebottle used as fishing-bait. □□**gentleness** *n.* **gently** *adv.* [ME f. OF *gentil* f. L *gentilis*: see GENTILE]

gentlefolk /'dʒent(ə)l,fəʊk/ *n.pl. literary* people of good family.

gentleman /'dʒent(ə)lmən/ *n.* (*pl.* **-men**) **1** a man (in polite or formal use). **2** a chivalrous or well-bred man. **3** a man of good social position or of wealth and leisure (*country gentleman*). **4** a man of gentle birth attached to a royal household (*gentleman in waiting*). **5** (in *pl.* as a form of address) a male audience or the male part of an audience. □**gentleman-at-arms** one of a sovereign's bodyguard. **gentleman farmer** a country gentleman who farms. **gentleman's** (or **-men's**) **agreement** one which is binding in honour but not legally enforceable. [GENTLE + MAN after OF *gentilz hom*]

gentlemanly /'dʒent(ə)lmənlɪ/ *adj.* like a gentleman in looks or behaviour; befitting a gentleman. □□ **gentlemanliness** *n.*

gentlewoman /'dʒent(ə)l,wʊmən/ *n.* (*pl.* **-women**) *archaic* a woman of good birth or breeding.

gentoo /'dʒentuː/ *n.* a penguin, *Pygoscelis papua*, esp. abundant in the Falkland Islands. [perh. f. Anglo-Ind. *Gentoo* = Hindu, f. Port. *gentio* GENTILE]

gentrification /,dʒentrɪfɪ'keɪʃ(ə)n/ *n.* the social advancement of an inner urban area by the arrival of affluent middle-class residents. □□**gentrify** /-,faɪ/ *v.tr.* (**-ies, -ied**).

gentry /'dʒentrɪ/ *n.pl.* **1** the people next below the nobility in position and birth. **2** *derog.* people (*these gentry*). [prob. f. obs. *gentrice* f. OF *genterise* var. of *gentelise* nobility f. *gentil* GENTLE]

genuflect /'dʒenjʊ,flekt/ *v.intr.* bend the knee, esp. in worship or as a sign of respect. □□**genuflection** /-'flekʃ(ə)n/ *n.* (also **genuflexion**). **genuflector** *n.* [eccl.L *genuflectere genuflex-* f. L *genu* the knee + *flectere* bend]

genuine /'dʒenjʊɪn/ *adj.* **1** really coming from its stated, advertised, or reputed source. **2** properly so called; not sham. **3** pure-bred. □□**genuinely** *adv.* **genuineness** *n.* [L *genuinus* f. *genu* knee, with ref. to a father's acknowledging a new-born child by placing it on his knee: later associated with GENUS]

genus /'dʒiːnəs, 'dʒenəs/ *n.* (*pl.* **genera** /'dʒenərə/) **1** *Biol.* a taxonomic grouping of organisms having common characteristics distinct from those of other genera, usu. containing several or many species and being one of a series constituting a taxonomic family. **2** a kind or class having common characteristics. **3** *Logic* kinds of things including subordinate kinds of species. [L *genus -eris* birth, race, stock]

-geny /dʒənɪ/ *comb. form* forming nouns meaning 'mode of production or development of' (*anthropogeny*; *ontogeny*; *pathogeny*). [F *-génie* (as -GEN, -Y³)]

Geo. *abbr.* George.

geo- /'dʒiːəʊ/ *comb. form* earth. [Gk *geō-* f. *gē* earth]

geobotany /,dʒiːəʊ'bɒtənɪ/ *n.* the study of the geographical distribution of plants. □□**geobotanist** *n.*

geocentric /,dʒiːəʊ'sentrɪk/ *adj.* **1** considered as viewed from the centre of the earth. **2** having or representing the earth as the centre; not heliocentric. □**geocentric latitude** the latitude at which a planet would appear if viewed from the centre of the earth. □□ **geocentrically** *adv.*

geochemistry /,dʒiːəʊ'kemɪstrɪ/ *n.* the chemistry of the earth and its rocks, minerals, etc. □□ **geochemical** *adj.* **geochemist** *n.*

geochronology /,dʒiːəʊkrə'nɒlədʒɪ/ *n.* **1** the study and measurement of geological time by means of geological events. **2** the ordering of geological events. □□ **geochronological** /-,krɒnə'lɒdʒɪk(ə)l/ *adj.* **geochronologist** *n.*

geode /'dʒiːəʊd/ *n.* **1** a small cavity lined with crystals or other mineral matter. **2** a rock containing such a cavity. □□ **geodic** /dʒiː'ɒdɪk/ *adj.* [L *geodes* f. Gk *geōdēs* earthy f. *gē* earth]

geodesic /,dʒiːəʊ'diːzɪk/ *adj.* (also **geodetic** /-'detɪk/) **1** of or relating to geodesy. **2** of, involving, or consisting of a geodesic line. □**geodesic dome** a dome constructed of short struts along geodesic lines. **geodesic line** the shortest possible line between two points on a curved surface.

geodesy /dʒiː'ɒdɪsɪ/ *n.* the branch of mathematics dealing with the figures and areas of the earth or large portions of it. □□**geodesist** *n.* [mod.L f. Gk *geōdaisia* (as GEO-, *daiō* divide)]

geodetic var. of GEODESIC.

geographic var. of GEOGRAPHICAL.

geographical /,dʒiːə'græfɪk(ə)l/ *adj.* (also **geographic** /-'græfɪk/) of or relating to geography. □**geographical latitude** the angle made with the plane of the equator by a perpendicular to the earth's surface at any point. **geographical mile** a distance equal to one minute of longitude or latitude at the equator (about 1850 metres). □□ **geographically** *adv.* [*geographic* f. F *géographique* or LL *geographicus* f. Gk *geōgraphikos* (as GEO-, -GRAPHIC)]

geography /dʒɪ'ɒgrəfɪ/ *n.* **1** the study of the earth's physical features, resources, and climate, and the physical aspects of its population. **2** the main physical features of an area. **3** the layout or arrangement of rooms in a building. □□ **geographer** *n.* [F *géographie* or L *geographia* f. Gk *geōgraphia* (as GEO-, -GRAPHY)]

geoid /'dʒiːɔɪd/ *n.* **1** the shape of the earth. **2** a shape formed by the mean sea level and its imagined extension under land areas. **3** an oblate spheroid. [Gk *geōeidēs* (as GEO-, -OID)]

geology /dʒɪ'ɒlədʒɪ/ *n.* **1** the science of the earth, including the composition, structure, and origin of its rocks. **2** this science applied to any other planet or celestial body. **3** the geological features of a district. □□ **geologic** /,dʒiːə'lɒdʒɪk/ *adj.* **geological** /,dʒiːə'lɒdʒɪk(ə)l/ *adj.* **geologically** /,dʒiːə'lɒdʒɪkəlɪ/ *adv.* **geologist** *n.* **geologize** *v.tr. & intr.* (also **-ise**). [mod.L *geologia* (as GEO-, -LOGY)]

geomagnetism /,dʒiːəʊ'mægnɪ,tɪz(ə)m/ *n.* the study of the magnetic properties of the earth. □□ **geomagnetic** /-mæg'netɪk/ *adj.* **geomagnetically** /-mæg'netɪkəlɪ/ *adv.*

geomancy /'dʒiːəʊ,mænsɪ/ *n.* divination from the configuration of a handful of earth or random dots. □□**geomantic** /-'mæntɪk/ *adj.*

geometer /dʒɪ'ɒmɪtə(r)/ *n.* **1** a person skilled in geometry. **2** any moth, esp. of the family *Geometridae*, having twiglike larvae which move in a looping fashion, seeming to measure the ground. [ME f. LL *geometra* f. L *geometres* f. Gk *geōmetrēs* (as GEO-, *metrēs* measurer)]

geometric /,dʒɪə'metrɪk/ *adj.* (also **geometrical**) **1** of, according to, or like geometry. **2** (of a design, architectural feature, etc.) characterized by or decorated with regular lines and shapes. □**geometric**

mean the central number in a geometric progression, also calculable as the nth root of a product of n numbers (as 9 from 3 and 27). **geometric progression** a progression of numbers with a constant ratio between each number and the one before (as 1, 3, 9, 27, 81). **geometric tracery** tracery with openings of geometric form. □□ **geometrically** *adv.* [F *géometrique* f. L *geometricus* f. Gk *geōmetrikos* (as GEOMETER)]

geometry /dʒɪ'ɒmɪtrɪ/ *n.* **1** the branch of mathematics concerned with the properties and relations of points, lines, surfaces, and solids. **2** the relative arrangement of objects or parts. □□ **geometrician** /ˌdʒiːəmɪ'trɪʃ(ə)n/ *n.* [ME f. OF *geometrie* f. L *geometria* f. Gk (as GEO-, -METRY)]

geomorphology /ˌdʒiːəmɔː'fɒlədʒɪ/ *n.* the study of the physical features of the surface of the earth and their relation to its geological structures. □□ **geomorphological** /-fə'lɒdʒɪk(ə)l/ *adj.* **geomorphologist** *n.*

geophagy /dʒɪ'ɒfədʒɪ/ *n.* the practice of eating earth. [GEO- + Gk *phagō* eat]

geophysics /ˌdʒiːəʊ'fɪzɪks/ *n.* the physics of the earth. □□ **geophysical** *adj.* **geophysicist** /-sɪst/ *n.*

geopolitics /ˌdʒiːəʊ'pɒlɪtɪks/ *n.* **1** the politics of a country as determined by its geographical features. **2** the study of this. □□ **geopolitical** /-pə'lɪtɪk(ə)l/ *adj.* **geopolitically** /-pə'lɪtɪkəlɪ/ *adv.* **geopolitician** /-'tɪʃ(ə)n/ *n.*

Geordie /'dʒɔːdɪ/ *n. Brit. colloq.* a native of Tyneside. [GEORGE + -IE]

George /dʒɔːdʒ/ *n. Brit. sl.* the automatic pilot of an aircraft. [the name *George*]

George Cross /dʒɔːdʒ/ *n.* (also **George Medal**) (in the UK) decorations for bravery awarded esp. to civilians, instituted in 1940 by King George VI.

georgette /dʒɔː'dʒet/ *n.* a thin silk or crêpe dress-material. [*Georgette* de la Plante, Fr. dressmaker]

Georgian[1] /'dʒɔːdʒ(ə)n/ *adj.* **1** of or characteristic of the time of Kings George I–IV (1714–1830). **2** of or characteristic of the time of Kings George V and VI (1910–52), esp. of the literature of 1910–20.

Georgian[2] /'dʒɔːdʒ(ə)n/ *adj. & n.* —*adj.* of or relating to Georgia in the Caucasus (USSR). —*n.* **1** a native of Georgia; a person of Georgian descent. **2** the language of Georgia.

Georgian[3] /'dʒɔːdʒ(ə)n/ *adj. & n.* —*adj.* of or relating to Georgia in the US. —*n.* a native of Georgia.

geosphere /'dʒiːə,sfɪə(r)/ *n.* **1** the solid surface of the earth. **2** any of the almost spherical concentric regions of the earth and its atmosphere.

geostationary /ˌdʒiːəʊ'steɪʃənərɪ/ *adj. Electronics* (of an artificial satellite of the earth) moving in such an orbit as to remain above the same point on the earth's surface (see also GEOSYNCHRONOUS).

geostrophic /ˌdʒiːəʊ'strɒfɪk/ *adj. Meteorol.* depending upon the rotation of the earth. [GEO- + Gk *strophē* a turning f. *strephō* to turn]

geosynchronous /ˌdʒiːəʊ'sɪŋkrənəs/ *adj.* (of an artificial satellite of the earth) moving in an orbit equal to the earth's period of rotation (see also GEOSTATIONARY).

geothermal /ˌdʒiːəʊ'θɜːm(ə)l/ *adj.* relating to, originating from, or produced by the internal heat of the earth.

geotropism /dʒɪ'ɒtrə,pɪz(ə)m/ *n.* plant growth in relation to gravity. □**negative geotropism** the tendency of stems etc. to grow away from the centre of the earth. **positive geotropism** the tendency of roots to grow towards the centre of the earth. □□ **geotropic** /ˌdʒiːəʊ'trɒpɪk/ *adj.* [GEO- + Gk *tropikos* f. *tropē* a turning f. *trepō* to turn]

Ger. *abbr.* German.

geranium /dʒə'reɪnɪəm/ *n.* **1** any herb or shrub of the genus *Geranium* bearing fruit shaped like the bill of a crane, e.g. cranesbill. **2** (in general use) a cultivated pelargonium. **3** the colour of the scarlet geranium. [L f. Gk *geranion* f. *geranos* crane]

gerbera /'dʒɜːbərə/ *n.* any composite plant of the genus *Gerbera* of Africa or Asia, esp. the Transvaal daisy. [T. *Gerber*, Ger. naturalist d. 1743]

gerbil /'dʒɜːbɪl/ *n.* (also **jerbil**) a mouselike desert rodent of the subfamily Gerbillinae, with long hind legs. [F *gerbille* f. mod.L *gerbillus* dimin. of *gerbo* JERBOA]

gerenuk /'dʒerə,nʊk/ *n.* an antelope, *Litocranius walleri*, native to E. Africa, with a very long neck and small head. [Somali]

gerfalcon var. of GYRFALCON.

geriatric /ˌdʒerɪ'ætrɪk/ *adj. & n.* —*adj.* **1** of or relating to old people. **2** *colloq.* old, outdated. —*n.* **1** an old person, esp. one receiving special care. **2** *colloq.* a person or thing considered as relatively old or outdated. [Gk *gēras* old age + *iatros* doctor]

geriatrics /ˌdʒerɪ'ætrɪks/ *n.pl.* (usu. treated as *sing.*) a branch of medicine or social science dealing with the health and care of old people. □□ **geriatrician** /-ə'trɪʃ(ə)n/ *n.*

germ /dʒɜːm/ *n.* **1** a micro-organism, esp. one which causes disease. **2 a** a portion of an organism capable of developing into a new one; the rudiment of an animal or plant. **b** an embryo of a seed (*wheat germ*). **3** an original idea etc. from which something may develop; an elementary principle. □**germ-cell 1** a cell containing half the number of chromosomes of a somatic cell and able to unite with one from the opposite sex to form a new individual; a gamete. **2** any embryonic cell with the potential of developing into a gamete. **germ warfare** the systematic spreading of micro-organisms to cause disease in an enemy population. **in germ** not yet developed. □□ **germy** *adj.* [F *germe* f. L *germen germinis* sprout]

German /'dʒɜːmən/ *n. & adj.* —*n.* **1** a native or national of Germany; a person of German descent. **2** the language of Germany, also used in Austria and Switzerland. —*adj.* of or relating to Germany or its people or language. □**German measles** a contagious disease, rubella, with symptoms like mild measles. **German shepherd** (or **shepherd dog**) an Alsatian. **German silver** a white alloy of nickel, zinc, and copper. **High German** a literary and cultured form of German. **Low German** German dialects other than High German. [L *Germanus* with ref. to related peoples of Central and N. Europe, a name perh. given by Celts to their neighbours: cf. OIr. *gair* neighbour]

german /'dʒɜːmən/ *adj.* (placed after *brother, sister,* or *cousin*) **1** having both parents the same (*brother german*). **2** having both grandparents the same on one side (*cousin german*). **3** *archaic* germane. [ME f. OF *germain* f. L *germanus* genuine, of the same parents]

germander /dʒɜː'mændə(r)/ *n.* any plant of the genus *Teucrium*. □**germander speedwell** a creeping plant, *Veronica chamaedrys*, with germander-like leaves and blue flowers. [ME f. med.L *germandra* ult. f. Gk *khamaidrus* f. *khamai* on the ground + *drus* oak]

germane /dʒɜː'meɪn/ *adj.* (usu. foll. by *to*) relevant (to a subject under consideration). □□ **germanely** *adv.* **germaneness** *n.* [var. of GERMAN]

Germanic /dʒɜː'mænɪk/ *adj. & n.* —*adj.* **1** having German characteristics. **2** *hist.* of the Germans. **3** of the Scandinavians, Anglo-Saxons, or Germans. **4** of the languages or language group called Germanic. —*n.* **1** the branch of Indo-European languages including English, German, Dutch, and the Scandinavian languages. **2** the (unrecorded) early language from which other Germanic languages developed. □**East Germanic** an extinct group including Gothic. **North Germanic** the Scandinavian languages. **West Germanic** a group including High and Low German, English, Frisian, and Dutch. [L *Germanicus* (as GERMAN)]

germanic /dʒɜː'mænɪk/ *adj. Chem.* of or containing germanium, esp. in its quadrivalent state.

Germanist /'dʒɜːmənɪst/ *n.* an expert in or student of

the language, literature, and civilization of Germany, or Germanic languages.

germanium /dʒɜːˈmeɪnɪəm/ n. Chem. a lustrous brittle semi-metallic element occurring naturally in sulphide ores and used in semiconductors. ¶ Symb.: Ge. [mod.L f. Germanus GERMAN]

Germanize /ˈdʒɜːməˌnaɪz/ v.tr. & intr. (also -ise) make or become German; adopt or cause to adopt German customs etc. □□ **Germanization** /-ˈzeɪʃ(ə)n/ n. **Germanizer** n.

Germano- /dʒɜːˈmænəʊ/ comb. form German; German and.

germanous /dʒɜːˈmeɪnəs/ adj. Chem. containing germanium in the bivalent state.

germicide /ˈdʒɜːmɪˌsaɪd/ n. a substance destroying germs, esp. those causing disease. □□ **germicidal** /-ˈsaɪd(ə)l/ adj.

germinal /ˈdʒɜːmɪn(ə)l/ adj. 1 relating to or of the nature of a germ or germs (see GERM 1). 2 in the earliest stage of development. 3 productive of new ideas. □□ **germinally** adv. [L germen germin- sprout: see GERM]

germinate /ˈdʒɜːmɪˌneɪt/ v. 1 a intr. sprout, bud, or put forth shoots. b tr. cause to sprout or shoot. 2 a tr. cause (ideas etc.) to originate or develop. b intr. come into existence. □□ **germination** /-ˈneɪʃ(ə)n/ n. **germinative** /-nətɪv/ adj. **germinator** n. [L germinare germinat- (as GERM)]

germon /ˈdʒɜːmən/ n. = ALBACORE 1. [F]

gerontology /ˌdʒerɒnˈtɒlədʒɪ/ n. the scientific study of old age, the process of ageing, and the special problems of old people. □□ **gerontological** /-təˈlɒdʒɪk(ə)l/ adj. **gerontologist** n. [Gk gerōn -ontos old man + -LOGY]

-gerous /dʒərəs/ comb. form forming adjectives meaning 'bearing' (lanigerous).

gerrymander /ˌdʒerɪˈmændə(r)/ v. & n. (also **jerrymander**) —v.tr. 1 manipulate the boundaries of (a constituency etc.) so as to give undue influence to some party or class. 2 manipulate (a situation etc.) to gain advantage. —n. this practice. □□ **gerrymanderer** n. [the name of Governor Gerry of Massachusetts + (SALA)MANDER, from the shape of a district on a political map drawn when he was in office (1812)]

gerund /ˈdʒerənd/ n. Gram. a form of a verb functioning as a noun, orig. in Latin ending in -ndum (declinable), in English ending in -ing and used distinctly as a part of a verb (e.g. do you mind my asking you?). [LL gerundium f. gerundum var. of gerendum, the gerund of L gerere do]

gerundive /dʒeˈrʌndɪv/ n. Gram. a form of a Latin verb, ending in -ndus (declinable) and functioning as an adjective meaning 'that should or must be done' etc. [LL gerundivus (modus mood) f. gerundium: see GERUND]

gesso /ˈdʒesəʊ/ n. (pl. -oes) plaster of Paris or gypsum as used in painting or sculpture. [It. f. L gypsum: see GYPSUM]

gestalt /ɡəˈstɑːlt/ n. Psychol. an organized whole that is perceived as more than the sum of its parts. □ **gestalt psychology** a system maintaining that perceptions, reactions, etc., are gestalts. □□ **gestaltism** n. **gestaltist** n. [G, = form, shape]

Gestapo /ɡeˈstɑːpəʊ/ n. 1 the German secret police under Nazi rule. 2 derog. an organization compared to this. [G, f. Geheime Staatspolizei]

gestate /dʒeˈsteɪt/ v.tr. 1 carry (a foetus) in gestation. 2 develop (an idea etc.).

gestation /dʒeˈsteɪʃ(ə)n/ n. 1 a the process of carrying or being carried in the womb between conception and birth. b this period. 2 the private development of a plan, idea, etc. [L gestatio f. gestare frequent. of gerere carry]

gesticulate /dʒeˈstɪkjʊˌleɪt/ v. 1 intr. use gestures instead of or in addition to speech. 2 tr. express with gestures. □□ **gesticulation** /-ˈleɪʃ(ə)n/ n. **gesticulative** /-lətɪv/ adj. **gesticulator** n.

gesticulatory /-lətərɪ/ adj. [L gesticulari f. gesticulus dimin. of gestus GESTURE]

gesture /ˈdʒestʃə(r)/ n. & v. —n. 1 a significant movement of a limb or the body. 2 the use of such movements esp. to convey feeling or as a rhetorical device. 3 an action to evoke a response or convey intention, usu. friendly. —v.tr. & intr. gesticulate. □□ **gestural** adj. **gesturer** n. [ME f. med.L gestura f. L gerere gest- wield]

gesundheit /ɡəˈzʊnthaɪt/ int. expressing a wish of good health, esp. before drinking or to a person who has sneezed. [G, = health]

get /ɡet/ v. & n. —v. (getting; past **got** /ɡɒt/; past part. **got** or US (and in comb.) **gotten** /ˈɡɒt(ə)n/) 1 tr. come into the possession of; receive or earn (get a job; got £200 a week; got first prize). 2 tr. fetch, obtain, procure, purchase (get my book for me; got a new car). 3 tr. go to reach or catch (a bus, train, etc.). 4 tr. prepare (a meal etc.). 5 intr. & tr. reach or cause to reach a certain state or condition; become or cause to become (get rich; get one's feet wet; get to be famous; got them ready; got him into trouble; cannot get the key into the lock). 6 tr. obtain as a result of calculation. 7 tr. contract (a disease etc.). 8 tr. establish or be in communication with via telephone or radio; receive (a radio signal). 9 tr. experience or suffer; have inflicted on one; receive as one's lot or penalty (got four years in prison). 10 a tr. succeed in bringing, placing, etc. (get it round the corner; get it on to the agenda; flattery will get you nowhere). b intr. & tr. succeed or cause to succeed in coming or going (will get you there somehow; got absolutely nowhere). 11 tr. (prec. by have) a possess (have not got a penny). b (foll. by to + infin.) be bound or obliged (have got to see you). 12 tr. (foll. by to + infin.) induce; prevail upon (got them to help me). 13 tr. colloq. understand (a person or an argument) (have you got that?; I get your point; do you get me?). 14 tr. colloq. inflict punishment or retribution on, esp. in retaliation (I'll get you for that). 15 tr. colloq. a annoy. b move; affect emotionally. c attract, obsess. d amuse. 16 tr. (foll. by to + infin.) develop an inclination as specified (am getting to like it). 17 intr. (foll. by verbal noun) begin (get going). 18 tr. (esp. in past or perfect) catch in an argument; corner, puzzle. 19 tr. establish (an idea etc.) in one's mind. 20 intr. sl. be off; go away. 21 tr. archaic beget. 22 tr. archaic learn; acquire (knowledge) by study. —n. 1 a an act of begetting (of animals). b an offspring (of animals). 2 sl. a fool or idiot. □ **get about** (or **around**) 1 travel extensively or fast; go from place to place. 2 manage to walk, move about, etc. (esp. after illness). 3 (of news) be circulated, esp. orally. **get across** 1 manage to communicate (an idea etc.). 2 (of an idea etc.) be communicated successfully. 3 colloq. annoy, irritate. **get along** (or **on**) 1 (foll. by together, with) live harmoniously, accord. 2 be off! nonsense! **get at** 1 reach; get hold of. 2 colloq. imply (what are you getting at?). **get away** 1 escape. 2 (as imper.) colloq. expressing disbelief or scepticism. 3 (foll. by with) escape blame or punishment for. **get back at** colloq. retaliate against. **get by** colloq. 1 just manage, even with difficulty. 2 be acceptable. **get down** 1 alight, descend (from a vehicle, ladder, etc.). 2 record in writing. **get a person down** depress or deject him or her. **get down to** begin working on or discussing. **get even** (often foll. by with) 1 achieve revenge; act in retaliation. 2 equalize the score. **get his** (or **hers** etc.) sl. be killed. **get hold of** 1 grasp (physically). 2 grasp (intellectually); understand. 3 make contact with (a person). 4 acquire. **get in** 1 enter. 2 be elected. **get into** become interested or involved in. **get it** sl. be punished or in trouble. **get it into one's head** (foll. by that + clause) firmly believe or maintain; realize. **get off** 1 colloq. be acquitted; escape with little or no punishment. 2 start. 3 alight; alight from (a bus etc.). 4 go, or cause to go, to sleep. 5 (foll. by with, together) Brit. colloq. form an amorous or sexual relationship, esp. abruptly or quickly. **get a person off** *colloq.* cause a person to be acquitted. **get on 1** make progress; manage. **2** enter (a bus etc.). **3** = *get along* 1. **get on to** *colloq.* **1** make contact with. **2** understand; become aware of. **get out 1** leave or escape. **2** manage to go outdoors. **3** alight from a vehicle. **4** transpire; become known. **5** succeed in uttering, publishing, etc. **6** solve or finish (a puzzle etc.). **7** *Cricket* be dismissed. **get-out** *n.* a means of avoiding something. **get a person out 1** help a person to leave or escape. **2** *Cricket* dismiss (a batsman). **get out of 1** avoid or escape (a duty etc.). **2** abandon (a habit) gradually. **get a thing out of** manage to obtain it from (a person) esp. with difficulty. **get outside** (or **outside of**) *sl.* eat or drink. **get over 1** recover from (an illness, upset, etc.). **2** overcome (a difficulty). **3** manage to communicate (an idea etc.). **get a thing over** (or **over with**) complete (a tedious task) promptly. **get one's own back** *colloq.* have one's revenge. **get-rich-quick** *adj.* designed to make a lot of money fast. **get rid of** see RID. **get round** (*US* **around**) **1** successfully coax or cajole (a person) esp. to secure a favour. **2** evade (a law etc.). **get round to** deal with (a task etc.) in due course. **get somewhere** make progress; be initially successful. **get there** *colloq.* **1** succeed. **2** understand what is meant. **get through 1** pass or assist in passing (an examination, an ordeal, etc.). **2** finish or use up (esp. resources). **3** make contact by telephone. **4** (foll. by *to*) succeed in making (a person) listen or understand. **get a thing through** cause it to overcome obstacles, difficulties, etc. **get to 1** reach. **2** = *get down to*. **get together** gather, assemble. **get-together** *n.* *colloq.* a social gathering. **get up 1** rise or cause to rise from sitting etc., or from bed after sleeping or an illness. **2** ascend or mount, e.g. on horseback. **3** (of fire, wind, or the sea) begin to be strong or agitated. **4** prepare or organize. **5** enhance or refine one's knowledge of (a subject). **6** work up (a feeling, e.g. anger). **7** produce or stimulate (*get up steam*; *get up speed*). **8** (often *refl.*) dress or arrange elaborately; make presentable; arrange the appearance of. **9** (foll. by *to*) *colloq.* indulge or be involved in (*always getting up to mischief*). **get-up** *n.* *colloq.* a style or arrangement of dress etc., esp. an elaborate one. **get-up-and-go** *colloq.* energy, vim, enthusiasm. **get the wind up** see WIND[1]. **get with child** *archaic* make pregnant. **have got it bad** (or **badly**) *sl.* be obsessed or affected emotionally. □□ **gettable** *adj.* [ME f. ON *geta* obtain, beget, guess, corresp. to OE *gietan* (recorded only in compounds), f. Gmc]

get-at-able /get'ætəb(ə)l/ *adj. colloq.* accessible.

getaway /'getə,weɪ/ *n.* an escape, esp. after committing a crime.

getter /'getə(r)/ *n. & v.* —*n.* **1** in senses of GET *v.* **2** *Physics* a substance used to remove residual gas from an evacuated vessel. —*v.tr. Physics* remove (gas) or evacuate (a vessel) with a getter.

geum /'dʒiːəm/ *n.* any rosaceous plant of the genus *Geum* including herb bennet, with rosettes of leaves and yellow, red, or white flowers. [mod.L, var. of L *gaeum*]

GeV *abbr.* gigaelectronvolt (equivalent to 10[9] electronvolts).

gewgaw /'gjuː,gɔː/ *n.* a gaudy plaything or ornament; a bauble. [ME: orig. unkn.]

geyser /'gaɪzə(r), 'giː-/ *n.* **1** an intermittently gushing hot spring that throws up a tall column of water. **2** /'giːzə(r)/ *Brit.* an apparatus for heating water rapidly for domestic use. [Icel. *Geysir*, the name of a particular spring in Iceland, rel. to *geysa* to gush]

GG *abbr.* Governor-General.

Ghanaian /gɑː'neɪən/ *adj. & n.* —*adj.* of or relating to Ghana in W. Africa. —*n.* a native or national of Ghana; a person of Ghanaian descent.

gharial /'geərɪəl, 'gærɪəl/ *n.* (also **gavial** /'geɪvɪəl/) a large Indian crocodile, *Gavialis gangeticus*, having a long narrow snout widening at the nostrils. □ **false gharial** a similar crocodile, *Tomistoma schlegelii*, of Indonesia and Malaya. [Hind.]

ghastly /'gɑːstlɪ/ *adj. & adv.* —*adj.* (**ghastlier**, **ghastliest**) **1** horrible, frightful. **2** *colloq.* objectionable, unpleasant. **3** deathlike, pallid. —*adv.* in a ghastly or sickly way (*ghastly pale*). □□ **ghastlily** *adv.* **ghastliness** *n.* [ME *gastlich* f. obs. *gast* terrify: *gh* after *ghost*]

ghat /gɔːt/ *n.* (also **ghaut**) in India: **1** steps leading down to a river. **2** a landing-place. **3** a defile or mountain pass. [Hindi *ghāṭ*]

Ghazi /'gɑːzɪ/ *n.* (*pl.* **Ghazis**) a Muslim fighter against non-Muslims. [Arab. *al-ġāzī* part. of *ġazā* raid]

ghee /giː/ *n.* (also **ghi**) Indian clarified butter esp. from the milk of a buffalo or cow. [Hindi *ghī* f. Skr. *ghritá-* sprinkled]

gherao /ge'raʊ/ *n.* (*pl.* **-os**) (in India and Pakistan) coercion of employers, by which their workers prevent them from leaving the premises until certain demands are met. [Hind. *gherna* besiege]

gherkin /'gɜːkɪn/ *n.* **1** a small variety of cucumber, or a young green cucumber, used for pickling. **2 a** a trailing plant, *Cucumis sativus*, with cucumber-like fruits used for pickling. **b** this fruit. [Du. *gurkkijn* (unrecorded), dimin. of *gurk*, f. Slavonic, ult. f. med. Gk *aggourion*]

ghetto /'getəʊ/ *n. & v.* —*n.* (*pl.* **-os**) **1** a part of a city, esp. a slum area, occupied by a minority group or groups. **2** *hist.* the Jewish quarter in a city. **3** a segregated group or area. —*v.tr.* (**-oes**, **-oed**) put or keep (people) in a ghetto. □ **ghetto-blaster** *sl.* a large portable radio, esp. used to play loud pop music. [perh. f. It. *getto* foundry (applied to the site of the first ghetto in Venice in 1516)]

ghi var. of GHEE.

ghillie var. of GILLIE.

ghost /gəʊst/ *n. & v.* —*n.* **1** the supposed apparition of a dead person or animal; a disembodied spirit. **2** a shadow or mere semblance (*not a ghost of a chance*). **3** an emaciated or pale person. **4** a secondary or duplicated image produced by defective television reception or by a telescope. **5** *archaic* a spirit or soul. —*v.* **1** *intr.* (often foll. by *for*) act as ghost-writer. **2** *tr.* act as ghost-writer of (a work). □ **ghost town** a deserted town with few or no remaining inhabitants. **ghost-write** *v.tr. & intr.* act as ghost-writer (of). **ghost-writer** a person who writes on behalf of the credited author of a work. □□ **ghostlike** *adj.* [OE *gāst* f. WG: *gh-* occurs first in Caxton, prob. infl. by Flem. *gheest*]

ghosting /'gəʊstɪŋ/ *n.* the appearance of a 'ghost' (see GHOST *n.* 4) or secondary image in a television picture.

ghostly /'gəʊstlɪ/ *adj.* (**ghostlier**, **ghostliest**) like a ghost; spectral. □□ **ghostliness** *n.* [OE *gāstlic* (as GHOST)]

ghoul /guːl/ *n.* **1** a person morbidly interested in death etc. **2** an evil spirit or phantom. **3** a spirit in Muslim folklore preying on corpses. □□ **ghoulish** *adj.* **ghoulishly** *adv.* **ghoulishness** *n.* [Arab. *ġūl* protean desert demon]

GHQ *abbr.* General Headquarters.

ghyll *Brit.* var. of GILL[3].

GI /dʒiː'aɪ/ *n. & adj.* —*n.* a private soldier in the US Army. —*adj.* of or for US servicemen. [abbr. of *government* (or *general*) *issue*]

giant /'dʒaɪənt/ *n. & adj.* —*n.* **1** an imaginary or mythical being of human form but superhuman size. **2** (in Greek mythology) one of such beings who fought against the gods. **3** an abnormally tall or large person, animal, or plant. **4** a person of exceptional ability, integrity, courage, etc. **5** a large star. —*attrib.adj.* **1** of extraordinary size or force, gigantic; monstrous. **2** *colloq.* extra large (*giant packet*). **3** (of a plant or animal) of a very large kind. □ **giant-killer** a person who defeats a seemingly much more powerful opponent. □□ **giantism** *n.* **giant-like**

adj. [ME *geant* (later infl. by L) f. OF, ult. f. L *gigas gigant-* f. Gk]

giaour /'dʒaʊə(r)/ *n. derog.* or *literary* a non-Muslim, esp. a Christian (orig. a Turkish name). [Pers. *gaur*, *gōr*]

Gib. /dʒɪb/ *n. colloq.* Gibraltar. [abbr.]

gib /dʒɪb, gɪb/ *n.* a wood or metal bolt, wedge, or pin for holding a machine part etc. in place. [18th c.: orig. unkn.]

gibber[1] /'dʒɪbə(r)/ *v.* & *n.* —*v.intr.* speak fast and inarticulately; chatter incoherently. —*n.* such speech or sound. [imit.]

gibber[2] /'gɪbə(r)/ *n. Austral.* a boulder or large stone. [Aboriginal]

gibberellin /,dʒɪbə'relɪn/ *n.* one of a group of plant hormones that stimulate the growth of leaves and shoots. [*Gibberella* a genus of fungi, dimin. of genus-name *Gibbera* f. L *gibber* hump]

gibberish /'dʒɪbərɪʃ/ *n.* unintelligible or meaningless speech; nonsense. [perh. f. GIBBER[1] (but attested earlier) + -ISH[1] as used in *Spanish*, *Swedish*, etc.]

gibbet /'dʒɪbɪt/ *n.* & *v.* —*n. hist.* **1 a** a gallows. **b** an upright post with an arm on which the bodies of executed criminals were hung up. **2** (prec. by *the*) death by hanging. —*v.tr.* (**gibbeted**, **gibbeting**) **1** put to death by hanging. **2 a** expose on a gibbet. **b** hang up as on a gibbet. **3** hold up to contempt. [ME f. OF *gibet* gallows dimin. of *gibe* club, prob. f. Gmc]

gibbon /'gɪbən/ *n.* any small ape of the genus *Hylobates*, native to SE Asia, having a slender body and long arms. [F f. a native name]

gibbous /'gɪbəs/ *adj.* **1** convex or protuberant. **2** (of a moon or planet) having the bright part greater than a semicircle and less than a circle. **3** humped or humpbacked. □□ **gibbosity** /-'bɒsɪtɪ/ *n.* **gibbously** *adv.* **gibbousness** *n.* [ME f. LL *gibbosus* f. *gibbus* hump]

gibe /dʒaɪb/ *v.* & *n.* (also **jibe**) —*v.intr.* (often foll. by *at*) jeer, mock. —*n.* an instance of gibing; a taunt. □□ **giber** *n.* [perh. f. OF *giber* handle roughly]

giblets /'dʒɪblɪts/ *n.pl.* the liver, gizzard, neck, etc., of a bird, usu. removed and kept separate when the bird is prepared for cooking. [OF *gibelet* game stew, perh. f. *gibier* game]

giddy /'gɪdɪ/ *adj.* & *v.* —*adj.* (**giddier**, **giddiest**) **1** having a sensation of whirling and a tendency to fall, stagger, or spin round. **2 a** overexcited as a result of success, pleasurable emotion, etc.; mentally intoxicated. **b** excitable, frivolous. **3** tending to make one giddy. —*v.tr.* & *intr.* (**-ies**, **-ied**) make or become giddy. □□ **giddily** *adv.* **giddiness** *n.* [OE *gidig* insane, lit. 'possessed by a god']

gie /gi:/ *v.tr.* & *intr. Sc.* = GIVE.

gift /gɪft/ *n.* & *v.* —*n.* **1** a thing given; a present. **2** a natural ability or talent. **3** the power to give (*in his gift*). **4** the act or an instance of giving. **5** *colloq.* an easy task. —*v.tr.* **1** endow with gifts. **2 a** (foll. by *with*) give to as a gift. **b** bestow as a gift. □ **gift of tongues** see TONGUE. **gift token** (or **voucher**) a voucher used as a gift and exchangeable for goods. **gift-wrap** (**-wrapped**, **-wrapping**) wrap attractively as a gift. **look a gift-horse in the mouth** (usu. *neg.*) find fault with what has been given. [ME f. ON *gipt* f. Gmc, rel. to GIVE]

gifted /'gɪftɪd/ *adj.* exceptionally talented or intelligent. □□ **giftedly** *adv.* **giftedness** *n.*

gig[1] /gɪg/ *n.* **1** a light two-wheeled one-horse carriage. **2** a light ship's boat for rowing or sailing. **3** a rowing-boat esp. for racing. [ME in var. senses: prob. imit.]

gig[2] /gɪg/ *n.* & *v. colloq.* —*n.* an engagement of an entertainer, esp. of musicians to play jazz or dance music, usu. for a single appearance. —*v.intr.* (**gigged, gigging**) perform a gig. [20th c.: orig. unkn.]

gig[3] /gɪg/ *n.* a kind of fishing-spear. [short for *fizgig, fishgig*: cf. Sp. *fisga* harpoon]

giga- /'gaɪgə, 'gɪgə/ *comb. form* denoting a factor of 10⁹. [Gk *gigas* giant]

gigametre /'gɪgə,mi:tə(r)/ *n.* a metric unit equal to 10^9 metres.

gigantic /dʒaɪ'gæntɪk/ *adj.* **1** very large; enormous. **2** like or suited to a giant. □□ **gigantesque** /-'tesk/ *adj.* **gigantically** *adv.* [L *gigas gigantis* GIANT]

gigantism /'dʒaɪgən,tɪz(ə)m/ *n.* abnormal largeness, esp. *Med.* excessive growth due to hormonal imbalance, or to polyploidy in plants.

giggle /'gɪg(ə)l/ *v.* & *n.* —*v.intr.* laugh in half-suppressed spasms, esp. in an affected or silly manner. —*n.* **1** such a laugh. **2** *colloq.* an amusing person or thing; a joke. □□ **giggler** *n.* **giggly** *adj.* (**gigglier, giggliest**). **giggliness** *n.* [imit.: cf. Du. *gichelen*, G *gickeln*]

gigolo /'ʒɪgə,ləʊ, 'dʒɪg-/ *n.* (*pl.* **-os**) **1** a young man paid by an older woman to be her escort or lover. **2** a professional male dancing-partner or escort. [F, formed as masc. of *gigole* dance-hall woman]

gigot /'dʒɪgət/ *n.* a leg of mutton or lamb. □ **gigot sleeve** a leg-of-mutton sleeve. [F, dimin. of dial. *gigue* leg]

gigue /ʒi:g/ *n.* **1** = JIG 1. **2** *Mus.* a lively dance usu. in a dotted rhythm with two sections each repeated. [F: see JIG[1]]

gild[1] /gɪld/ *v.tr.* (*past part.* **gilded** or as adj. in sense 1 **gilt**) **1** cover thinly with gold. **2** tinge with a golden colour or light. **3** give a specious or false brilliance to. □ **gilded cage** luxurious but restrictive surroundings. **gilded youth** young people of wealth, fashion, and flair. **gild the lily** try to improve what is already beautiful or excellent. □□ **gilder** *n.* [OE *gyldan* f. Gmc]

gild[2] var. of GUILD.

gilding /'gɪldɪŋ/ *n.* **1** the act or art of applying gilt. **2** material used in applying gilt.

gilet /dʒɪ'leɪ/ *n.* a light often padded waistcoat, usu. worn for warmth by women. [F, = waistcoat]

gilgai /'gɪlgaɪ/ *n. Austral.* a saucer-like natural reservoir for rainwater. [Aboriginal]

gill[1] /gɪl/ *n.* & *v.* —*n.* (usu. in *pl.*) **1** the respiratory organ in fishes and other aquatic animals. **2** the vertical radial plates on the underside of mushrooms and other fungi. **3** the flesh below a person's jaws and ears (*green about the gills*). **4** the wattles or dewlap of fowls. —*v.tr.* **1** gut (a fish). **2** cut off the gills of (a mushroom). **3** catch in a gill-net. □ **gill-cover** a bony case protecting a fish's gills; an operculum. **gill-net** a net for entangling fishes by the gills. □□ **gilled** *adj.* (also in *comb.*). [ME f. ON *gil* (unrecorded) f. Gmc]

gill[2] /dʒɪl/ *n.* **1** a unit of liquid measure, equal to a quarter of a pint. **2** *Brit. dial.* half a pint. [ME f. OF *gille*, med.L *gillo* f. LL *gello, gillo* water-pot]

gill[3] /gɪl/ *n.* (also **ghyll**) *Brit.* **1** a deep usu. wooded ravine. **2** a narrow mountain torrent. [ME f. ON *gil* glen]

gill[4] /dʒɪl/ *n.* (also Gill, jill, Jill) **1** *derog.* a young woman. **2** *colloq.* or *dial.* a female ferret. [ME, abbr. of *Gillian* f. OF *Juliane* f. L *Juliana* (*Julius*)]

gillie /'gɪlɪ/ *n.* (also **ghillie**) *Sc.* **1** a man or boy attending a person hunting or fishing. **2** *hist.* a Highland chief's attendant. [Gael. *gille* lad, servant]

gillion /'dʒɪlɪən/ *n.* **1** a thousand million. **2** a large number. ¶ Mainly used to avoid the ambiguity of *billion*. [GIGA- + MILLION]

gillyflower /'dʒɪlɪ,flaʊə(r)/ *n.* **1** (in full **clove gillyflower**) a clove-scented pink (see CLOVE[1] 2). **2** any of various similarly scented flowers such as the wallflower or white stock. [ME *gilofre, gerofle* f. OF *gilofre, girofle*, f. med.L f. Gk *karuophullon* clove-tree f. *karuon* nut + *phullon* leaf, assim. to FLOWER]

gilt[1] /gɪlt/ *adj.* & *n.* —*adj.* **1** covered thinly with gold. **2** gold-coloured. —*n.* **1** gold or a goldlike substance applied in a thin layer to a surface. **2** (often in *pl.*) a gilt-edged security. □ **gilt-edged 1** (of securities, stocks, etc.) having a high degree of reliability as an investment. **2** having a gilded edge. [past part. of GILD[1]]

gilt² /gɪlt/ n. a young unbred sow. [ME f. ON *gyltr*]

gimbals /'dʒɪmb(ə)lz/ n.pl. a contrivance, usu. of rings and pivots, for keeping instruments such as a compass and chronometer horizontal at sea, in the air, etc. [var. of earlier *gimmal* f. OF *gemel* double finger-ring f. L *gemellus* dimin. of *geminus* twin]

gimcrack /'dʒɪmkræk/ adj. & n. —adj. showy but flimsy and worthless. —n. a cheap showy ornament; a knick-knack. ▫▫ **gimcrackery** n. **gimcracky** adj. [ME *gibecrake* a kind of ornament, of unkn. orig.]

gimlet /'gɪmlɪt/ n. 1 a small tool with a screw-tip for boring holes. 2 a cocktail usu. of gin and lime-juice. ▫**gimlet eye** an eye with a piercing glance. [ME f. OF *guimbelet*, dimin. of *guimble*]

gimmick /'gɪmɪk/ n. colloq. a trick or device, esp. to attract attention, publicity, or trade. ▫▫ **gimmickry** n. **gimmicky** adj. [20th-c. US: orig. unkn.]

gimp¹ /gɪmp/ n. (also **guimp**, **gymp**) 1 a twist of silk etc. with cord or wire running through it, used esp. as trimming. 2 fishing-line of silk etc. bound with wire. 3 a coarser thread outlining the design of lace. [Du.: orig. unkn.]

gimp² /gɪmp/ n. sl. a lame person or leg.

gin¹ /dʒɪn/ n. an alcoholic spirit distilled from grain or malt and flavoured with juniper berries. ▫**gin rummy** a form of the card-game rummy. [abbr. of GENEVA]

gin² /dʒɪn/ n. & v. —n. 1 a snare or trap. 2 a machine for separating cotton from its seeds. 3 a kind of crane and windlass. —v.tr. (**ginned**, **ginning**) 1 treat (cotton) in a gin. 2 trap. ▫▫ **ginner** n. [ME f. OF *engin* ENGINE]

gin³ /dʒɪn/ n. Austral. an Aboriginal woman. [Aboriginal]

ginger /'dʒɪndʒə(r)/ n., adj., & v. —n. 1 a a hot spicy root usu. powdered for use in cooking, or preserved in syrup, or candied. b the plant, *Zingiber officinale*, of SE Asia, having this root. 2 a light reddish-yellow colour. 3 spirit, mettle. 4 stimulation. —adj. of a ginger colour. —v.tr. 1 flavour with ginger. 2 (foll. by *up*) rouse or enliven. ▫**black ginger** unscraped ginger. **ginger ale** an effervescent non-alcoholic clear drink flavoured with ginger extract. **ginger beer** an effervescent mildly alcoholic cloudy drink, made by fermenting a mixture of ginger and syrup. **ginger group** Brit. a group within a party or movement that presses for stronger or more radical policy or action. **ginger-nut** a ginger-flavoured biscuit. **ginger-pop** colloq. = *ginger ale*. **ginger-snap** a thin brittle biscuit flavoured with ginger. **ginger wine** a drink of fermented sugar, water, and bruised ginger. ▫▫ **gingery** adj. [ME f. OE *gingiber* & OF *gingi(m)bre*, both f. med.L *gingiber* ult. f. Skr. *śṛṅgaveram* f. *śṛṅgam* horn + *-vera* body, with ref. to the antler-shape of the root]

gingerbread /'dʒɪndʒə,bred/ n. 1 a cake made with treacle or syrup and flavoured with ginger. 2 (often *attrib.*) a gaudy or tawdry decoration or ornament.

gingerly /'dʒɪndʒəlɪ/ adv. & adj. —adv. in a careful or cautious manner. —adj. showing great care or caution. ▫▫ **gingerliness** n. [perh. f. OF *gensor* delicate, compar. of *gent* graceful f. L *genitus* (well-)born]

gingham /'gɪŋəm/ n. a plain-woven cotton cloth esp. striped or checked. [Du. *gingang* f. Malay *ginggang* (orig. adj. = striped)]

gingili /'dʒɪndʒɪlɪ/ n. 1 sesame. 2 sesame oil. [Hindi *jinjalī* f. Arab. *juljulān*]

gingiva /'dʒɪndʒɪvə/ n. (pl. **gingivae** /-,viː/) the gum. ▫▫ **gingival** /-'dʒaɪv(ə)l/ adj. [L]

gingivitis /,dʒɪndʒɪ'vaɪtɪs/ n. inflammation of the gums.

gingko var. of GINKGO.

ginglymus /'dʒɪŋglɪməs/ n. (pl. **ginglymi** /-,maɪ/) Anat. a hingelike joint in the body with motion in one plane only, e.g. the elbow or knee. [mod.L f. Gk *gigglumos* hinge]

gink /gɪŋk/ n. sl. often derog. a fellow; a man. [20th-c. US: orig. unkn.]

ginkgo /'gɪŋkgəʊ/ n. (also **gingko** /'gɪŋkəʊ/) (pl. -os or -oes) an orig. Chinese and Japanese tree, *Ginkgo biloba*, with fan-shaped leaves and yellow flowers. Also called *maidenhair tree*. [Jap. *ginkyo* f. Chin. *yinxing* silver apricot]

ginormous /dʒaɪ'nɔːməs/ adj. Brit. sl. very large; enormous. [GIANT + ENORMOUS]

ginseng /'dʒɪnseŋ/ n. 1 any of several medicinal plants of the genus *Panax*, found in E. Asia and N. America. 2 the root of this. [Chin. *renshen* perh. = man-image, with allusion to its forked root]

gippy tummy /'dʒɪpɪ/ n. (also **gyppy tummy**) colloq. diarrhoea affecting visitors to hot countries. [abbr. of EGYPTIAN]

gipsy var. of GYPSY.

giraffe /dʒɪ'rɑːf, -'ræf/ n. (pl. same or **giraffes**) a ruminant mammal, *Giraffa camelopardalis* of Africa, the tallest living animal, with a long neck and forelegs and a skin of dark patches separated by lighter lines. [F *girafe*, It. *giraffa*, ult. f. Arab. *zarāfa*]

girandole /'dʒɪrən,dəʊl/ n. 1 a revolving cluster of fireworks. 2 a branched candle-bracket or candlestick. 3 an earring or pendant with a large central stone surrounded by small ones. [F f. It. *girandola* f. *girare* GYRATE]

girasol /'dʒɪrə,sɒl/ n. (also **girasole** /-,səʊl/) a kind of opal reflecting a reddish glow; a fire-opal. [orig. = sunflower, f. F *girasol* or It. *girasole* f. *girare* (as GIRANDOLE) + *sole* sun]

gird¹ /gɜːd/ v.tr. (past and past part. **girded** or **girt**) literary 1 encircle, attach, or secure with a belt or band. 2 secure (clothes) on the body with a girdle or belt. 3 enclose or encircle. 4 a (foll. by *with*) equip with a sword in a belt. b fasten (a sword) with a belt. 5 (foll. by *round*) place (cord etc.) round. ▫**gird** (or **gird up**) **one's loins** prepare for action. [OE *gyrdan* f. Gmc (as GIRTH)]

gird² /gɜːd/ v. & n. —v.intr. (foll. by *at*) jeer or gibe. —n. a gibe or taunt. [ME, = strike etc.: orig. unkn.]

girder /'gɜːdə(r)/ n. a large iron or steel beam or compound structure for bearing loads, esp. in bridge-building. [GIRD¹ + -ER¹]

girdle¹ /'gɜːd(ə)l/ n. & v. —n. 1 a belt or cord worn round the waist. 2 a woman's corset extending from waist to thigh. 3 a thing that surrounds like a girdle. 4 the bony support for a limb (*pelvic girdle*). 5 the part of a cut gem dividing the crown from the base and embraced by the setting. 6 a ring round a tree made by the removal of bark. —v.tr. 1 surround with a girdle. 2 remove a ring of bark from (a tree), esp. to make it more fruitful. [OE *gyrdel*: see GIRD¹]

girdle² /'gɜːd(ə)l/ n. Sc. & N.Engl. a circular iron plate placed over a fire or otherwise heated for baking, toasting, etc. [var. of GRIDDLE]

girl /gɜːl/ n. 1 a female child or youth. 2 colloq. a young (esp. unmarried) woman. 3 colloq. a girlfriend or sweetheart. 4 a female servant. ▫**girl Friday** see FRIDAY. ▫▫ **girlhood** n. [ME *gurle*, *girle*, *gerle*, perh. rel. to LG *göre* child]

girlfriend /'gɜːlfrend/ n. 1 a regular female companion or lover. 2 a female friend.

girlie /'gɜːlɪ/ adj. colloq. (of a magazine etc.) depicting nude or partially nude young women in erotic poses.

girlish /'gɜːlɪʃ/ adj. of or like a girl. ▫▫ **girlishly** adv. **girlishness** n.

giro /'dʒaɪrəʊ/ n. & v. —n. (pl. -os) 1 a system of credit transfer between banks, post offices, etc. 2 a cheque or payment by giro. —v.tr. (-oes, -oed) pay by giro. [G f. It., = circulation (of money)]

girt¹ past part. of GIRD¹.

girt² var. of GIRTH.

girth /gɜːθ/ n. & v. (also **girt** /gɜːt/) —n. 1 the distance around a thing. 2 a band round the body of a horse to secure the saddle etc. —v. 1 tr. a secure (a saddle etc.) with a girth. b put a girth on (a horse).

2 *tr.* surround, encircle. **3** *intr.* measure (an amount) in girth. [ME f. ON *gjǫrth*, Goth. *gairda* f. Gmc]

gismo /ˈgɪzməʊ/ *n.* (also **gizmo**) (*pl.* -os) *sl.* a gadget. [20th c.: orig. unkn.]

gist /dʒɪst/ *n.* **1** the substance or essence of a matter. **2** *Law* the real ground of an action etc. [OF, 3rd sing. pres. of *gesir* lie f. L *jacēre*]

git /gɪt/ *n. Brit. sl.* a silly or contemptible person. [var. of GET *n.*]

gîte /ʒiːt/ *n.* a furnished holiday house in France, usu. small and in a rural district. [orig. = lodging: F f. OF *giste*, rel. to *gésir* lie]

gittern /ˈgɪt(ə)n/ *n.* a medieval stringed instrument, a forerunner of the guitar. [ME f. OF *guiterne*: cf. CITTERN, GUITAR]

give /gɪv/ *v. & n.* —*v.* (*past* **gave** /geɪv/; *past part.* **given** /ˈgɪv(ə)n/) **1** *tr.* (also *absol.*; often foll. by *to*) transfer the possession of freely; hand over as a present (*gave them her old curtains*; *gives to cancer research*). **2** *tr.* **a** transfer the ownership of with or without actual delivery; bequeath (*gave him £200 in her will*). **b** transfer, esp. temporarily or for safe keeping; hand over; provide with (*gave him the dog to hold*; *gave them a drink*). **c** administer (medicine). **d** deliver (a message) (*give her my best wishes*). **3** *tr.* (usu. foll. by *for*) make over in exchange or payment; pay; sell (*gave him £30 for the bicycle*). **4** *tr.* **a** confer; grant (a benefit, an honour, etc.). **b** accord; bestow (one's affections, confidence, etc.). **c** award; administer (one's approval, blame, etc.); tell, offer (esp. something unpleasant) (*gave him a talking-to*; *gave him my blessing*; *gave him the sack*). **d** pledge, assign as a guarantee (*gave his word*). **5** *tr.* **a** effect or perform (an action etc.) (*gave him a kiss*; *gave a jump*). **b** utter (*gave a shriek*). **6** *tr.* allot; assign; grant (*was given the contract*). **7** *tr.* (in *passive*; foll. by *to*) be inclined to or fond of (*is given to speculation*). **8** *tr.* yield as a product or result (*the lamp gives a bad light*; *the field gives fodder for twenty cows*). **9** *intr.* **a** yield to pressure; become relaxed; lose firmness (*this elastic doesn't give properly*). **b** collapse (*the roof gave under the pressure*). **10** *intr.* (usu. foll. by *of*) grant; bestow (*gave freely of his time*). **11** *tr.* **a** commit, consign, or entrust (*gave him into custody*; *give her into your care*). **b** sanction the marriage of (a daughter etc.). **12** *tr.* devote; dedicate (*gave his life to table tennis*; *shall give it my attention*). **13** *tr.* (usu. *absol.*) *colloq.* tell what one knows (*What happened? Come on, give!*). **14** *tr.* present; show; hold out (*gives no sign of life*; *gave her his arm*; *give him your ear*). **15** *tr. Theatr.* read, recite, perform, act, etc. (*gave them Hamlet's soliloquy*). **16** *tr.* impart; be a source of (*gave him my sore throat*; *gave its name to the battle*; *gave me much pain*; *gives him a right to complain*). **17** *tr.* allow (esp. a fixed amount of time) (*can give you five minutes*). **18** *tr.* (usu. foll. by *for*) value (something) (*gives nothing for their opinions*). **19** *tr.* concede; yield (*I give you the victory*). **20** *tr.* deliver (a judgement etc.) authoritatively (*gave his verdict*). **21** *tr. Cricket* (of an umpire) declare (a batsman) out or not out. **22** *tr.* toast (a person, cause, etc.) (*I give you our President*). **23** *tr.* provide (a party, meal, etc.) as host (*gave a banquet*). —*n.* **1** capacity to yield or bend under pressure; elasticity (*there is no give in a stone floor*). **2** ability to adapt or comply (*no give in his attitudes*). □**give and take** *v.tr.* exchange (words, blows, or concessions). —*n.* an exchange of words etc.; a compromise. **give as good as one gets** retort adequately in words or blows. **give away 1** transfer as a gift. **2** hand over (a bride) ceremonially to a bridegroom. **3** betray or expose to ridicule or detection. **4** *Austral.* abandon, desist from, give up, lose faith or interest in. **give-away** *n. colloq.* **1** an inadvertent betrayal or revelation. **2** an act of giving away. **3** a free gift; a low price. **give back** return (something) to its previous owner or in exchange. **give a person the best** see BEST. **give birth (to)** see BIRTH. **give chase** pursue a person,

animal, etc.; hunt. **give down** (often *absol.*) (of a cow) let (milk) flow. **give forth** emit; publish; report. **give the game** (or **show**) **away** reveal a secret or intention. **give a hand** see HAND. **give a person** (or **the devil**) **his** or **her due** acknowledge, esp. grudgingly, a person's rights, abilities, etc. **give in 1** cease fighting or arguing; yield. **2** hand in (a document etc.) to an official etc. **give in marriage** sanction the marriage of (one's daughter etc.). **give it to a person** *colloq.* scold or punish. **give me** I prefer or admire (*give me the Greek islands*). **give off** emit (vapour etc.). **give oneself** (of a woman) yield sexually. **give oneself airs** act pretentiously or snobbishly. **give oneself up to 1** abandon oneself to an emotion, esp. despair. **2** addict oneself to. **give on to** (or **into**) (of a window, corridor, etc.) overlook or lead into. **give or take** *colloq.* add or subtract (a specified amount or number) in estimating. **give out 1** announce; emit; distribute. **2** cease or break down from exhaustion etc. **3** run short. **give over 1** *colloq.* cease from doing; abandon (a habit etc.); desist (*give over sniffing*). **2** hand over. **3** devote. **give rise to** cause, induce, suggest. **give tongue 1** speak one's thoughts. **2** (of hounds) bark, esp. on finding a scent. **give a person to understand** inform authoritatively. **give up 1** resign; surrender. **2** part with. **3** deliver (a wanted person etc.). **4** pronounce incurable or insoluble; renounce hope of. **5** renounce or cease (an activity). **give up the ghost** *archaic* or *colloq.* die. **give way** see WAY. **give a person what for** *colloq.* punish or scold severely. **give one's word** (or **word of honour** etc.) promise solemnly. **not give a damn** (or **monkey's** or **toss** etc.) *colloq.* not care at all. **what gives?** *colloq.* what is the news?; what's happening? **would give the world** (or **one's ears, eyes,** etc.) **for** covet or wish for desperately. □□**giveable** *adj.* **giver** *n.* [OE *g(i)efan* f. Gmc]

given /ˈgɪv(ə)n/ *adj. & n.* —*adj.* **1** as previously stated or assumed; granted; specified (*given that he is a liar, we cannot trust him*; *a given number of people*). **2** *Law* (of a document) signed and dated (*given this day the 30th June*). —*n.* a known fact or situation. □**given name** *US* a name given at, or as if at, baptism; a Christian name. [past part. of GIVE]

gizmo var. of GISMO.

gizzard /ˈgɪzəd/ *n.* **1** the second part of a bird's stomach, for grinding food usu. with grit. **2** a muscular stomach of some fish, insects, molluscs, and other invertebrates. □**stick in one's gizzard** *colloq.* be distasteful. [ME *giser* f. OF *giser, gesier* etc., ult. f. L *gigeria* cooked entrails of fowl]

glabella /gləˈbelə/ *n.* (*pl.* **glabellae** /-liː/) the smooth part of the forehead above the nose and between the eyebrows. □□**glabellar** *adj.* [mod.L f. L *glabellus* (adj.) dimin. of *glaber* smooth]

glabrous /ˈgleɪbrəs/ *adj.* free from hair or down; smooth skinned. [L *glaber* smooth: hairless]

glacé /ˈglaseɪ/ *adj.* **1** (of fruit, esp. cherries) preserved in sugar, usu. resulting in a glossy surface. **2** (of cloth, leather, etc.) smooth; polished. □**glacé icing** icing made with icing sugar and water. [F, past part. of *glacer* to ice, gloss f. *glace* ice: see GLACIER]

glacial /ˈgleɪʃ(ə)l, -sɪəl/ *adj.* **1** of ice; icy. **2** *Geol.* characterized or produced by the presence or agency of ice. **3** *Chem.* forming icelike crystals upon freezing (*glacial acetic acid*). □**glacial epoch** (or **period**) a period when ice-sheets were exceptionally extensive. □□**glacially** *adv.* [F *glacial* or L *glacialis* icy f. *glacies* ice]

glaciated /ˈgleɪsɪˌeɪtɪd, ˈglæs-/ *adj.* **1** marked or polished by the action of ice. **2** covered or having been covered by glaciers or ice sheets. □□**glaciation** /-ˈeɪʃ(ə)n/ *n.* [past part. of *glaciate* f. L *glaciare* freeze f. *glacies* ice]

glacier /ˈglæsɪə(r)/ *n.* a mass of land ice formed by the accumulation of snow on high ground. [F f. *glace* ice ult. f. L *glacies*]

æ **cat** ɑː **arm** e **bed** ɜː **her** ɪ **sit** iː **see** ɒ **hot** ɔː **saw** ʌ **run** ʊ **put** uː **too** ə **ago** aɪ **my**

glaciology /ˌgleɪsɪˈɒlədʒɪ/ n. the science of the internal dynamics and effects of glaciers. □□ **glaciological** /-əˈlɒdʒɪk(ə)l/ adj. **glaciologist** n. [L glacies ice + -LOGY]

glacis /ˈglæsɪs, -siː/ n. (pl. same /-sɪz, -siːz/) a bank sloping down from a fort, on which attackers are exposed to the defenders' missiles etc. [F f. OF glacier to slip f. glace ice: see GLACIER]

glad[1] /glæd/ adj. & v. —adj. (**gladder, gladdest**) 1 (predic.; usu. foll. by of, about, or to + infin.) pleased; willing (shall be glad to come; would be glad of a chance to talk about it). 2 a marked by, filled with, or expressing, joy (a glad expression). b (of news, events, etc.) giving joy (glad tidings). 3 (of objects) bright; beautiful. —v.tr. (**gladded, gladding**) archaic make glad. □**the glad eye** colloq. an amorous glance. **glad hand** the hand of welcome. **glad-hand** v.tr. greet cordially; welcome. **glad rags** colloq. best clothes; evening dress. □□ **gladly** adv. **gladness** n. **gladsome** adj. poet. [OE glæd f. Gmc]

glad[2] /glæd/ n. (also Austral. **gladdie** /ˈglædɪ/) colloq. a gladiolus. [abbr.]

gladden /ˈglæd(ə)n/ v.tr. & intr. make or become glad. □□**gladdener** n.

gladdie Austral. var. of GLAD[2].

glade /gleɪd/ n. an open space in a wood or forest. [16th c.: orig. unkn.]

gladiator /ˈglædɪeɪtə(r)/ n. 1 hist. a man trained to fight with a sword or other weapons at ancient Roman shows. 2 a person defending or opposing a cause; a controversialist. □□ **gladiatorial** /-əˈtɔːrɪəl/ adj. [L f. gladius sword]

gladiolus /ˌglædɪˈəʊləs/ n. (pl. **gladioli** /-laɪ/ or **gladioluses**) any iridaceous plant of the genus Gladiolus with sword-shaped leaves and usu. brightly coloured flower-spikes. [L, dimin. of gladius sword]

Gladstone bag /ˈglædst(ə)n/ n. a bag like a briefcase having two equal compartments joined by a hinge. [W. E. Gladstone, Engl. statesman d. 1898]

Glagolitic /ˌglægəˈlɪtɪk/ adj. of or relating to the alphabet ascribed to St Cyril and formerly used in writing some Slavonic languages. [mod.L glagoliticus f. Serbo-Croatian glagolica Glagolitic alphabet f. OSlav. glagol word]

glair /gleə(r)/ n. (also **glaire**) 1 white of egg. 2 an adhesive preparation made from this, used in bookbinding etc. □□ **glaireous** adj. **glairy** adj. [ME f. OF glaire, ult. f. L clara fem. of clarus clear]

glaire var. of GLAIR.

glaive /gleɪv/ n. archaic poet. 1 a broadsword. 2 any sword. [ME f. OF, app. f. L gladius sword]

Glam. abbr. Glamorgan.

glam /glæm/ adj., n., & v. colloq. —adj. glamorous. —n. glamour. —v.tr. (**glammed, glamming**) glamorize. [abbr.]

glamorize /ˈglæməˌraɪz/ v.tr. (also **glamourize, -ise**) make glamorous or attractive. □□ **glamorization** /-ˈzeɪʃ(ə)n/ n.

glamour /ˈglæmə(r)/ n. & v. (US **glamor**) —n. 1 physical attractiveness, esp. when achieved by make-up etc. 2 alluring or exciting beauty or charm (the glamour of New York). —v.tr. 1 poet. affect with glamour; bewitch; enchant. 2 colloq. make glamorous. □**cast a glamour over** enchant. **glamour girl** (or **boy**) an attractive young woman (or man), esp. a model etc. □□ **glamorous** adj. **glamorously** adv. [18th c.: var. of GRAMMAR, with ref. to the occult practices associated with learning in the Middle Ages]

glance[1] /glɑːns/ v. & n. —v. 1 intr. (often foll. by down, up, etc.) cast a momentary look (glanced up at the sky). 2 intr. (often foll. by off) (esp. of a weapon) glide or bounce (off an object). 3 intr. (usu. foll. by over, off, from) (of talk or a talker) pass quickly over a subject or subjects (glanced over the question of payment). 4 intr. (of a bright beam or light) flash, dart, or gleam; reflect (the sun glanced off the knife).

5 tr. (esp. of a weapon) strike (an object) obliquely. 6 tr. Cricket deflect (the ball) with an oblique stroke. —n. 1 (usu. foll. by at, into, over, etc.) a brief look (took a glance at the paper; threw a glance over her shoulder). 2 a a flash or gleam (a glance of sunlight). b a sudden movement producing this. 3 a swift oblique movement or impact. 4 Cricket a stroke with the bat's face turned slantwise to deflect the ball. □**at a glance** immediately upon looking. **glance at** 1 give a brief look at. 2 make a passing and usu. sarcastic allusion to. **glance one's eye** (foll. by at, over, etc.) look at briefly (esp. a document). **glance over** (or **through**) read cursorily. □□ **glancingly** adv. [ME glence etc., prob. a nasalized form of obs. glace in the same sense, f. OF glacier to slip: see GLACIS]

glance[2] /glɑːns/ n. any lustrous sulphide ore (copper glance; lead glance). [G Glanz lustre]

gland[1] /glænd/ n. 1 a an organ in an animal body secreting substances for use in the body or for ejection. b a structure resembling this, such as a lymph gland. 2 Bot. a secreting cell or group of cells on the surface of a plant-structure. [F glande f. OF glandre f. L glandulae throat-glands]

gland[2] /glænd/ n. a sleeve used to produce a seal round a moving shaft. [19th c.: perh. var. of glam, glan a vice, rel. to CLAMP[1]]

glanders /ˈglændəz/ n.pl. (also treated as sing.) 1 a contagious disease of horses, caused by a bacterium and characterized by swellings below the jaw and mucous discharge from the nostrils. 2 this disease in humans or other animals. □□ **glandered** adj. **glanderous** adj. [OF glandre: see GLAND[1]]

glandular /ˈglændjʊlə(r)/ adj. of or relating to a gland or glands. □**glandular fever** an infectious viral disease characterized by swelling of the lymph glands and prolonged lassitude, infectious mononucleosis (see MONONUCLEOSIS). [F glandulaire (as GLAND[1])]

glans /glænz/ n. (pl. **glandes** /ˈglændiːz/) the rounded part forming the end of the penis or clitoris. [L, = acorn]

glare[1] /gleə(r)/ v. & n. —v. 1 intr. (usu. foll. by at, upon) look fiercely or fixedly. 2 intr. shine dazzlingly or disagreeably. 3 tr. express (hate, defiance, etc.) by a look. 4 intr. be over-conspicuous or obtrusive. —n. 1 a strong fierce light, esp. sunshine. b oppressive public attention (the glare of fame). 2 a fierce or fixed look (a glare of defiance). 3 tawdry brilliance. □□ **glary** adj. [ME, prob. ult. rel. to GLASS: cf. MDu. and MLG glaren gleam, glare]

glare[2] /gleə(r)/ adj. US (esp. of ice) smooth and glassy. [perh. f. glare frost (16th c., of uncert. orig.)]

glaring /ˈgleərɪŋ/ adj. 1 obvious, conspicuous (a glaring error). 2 shining oppressively. 3 staring fiercely. □□ **glaringly** adv. **glaringness** n.

glasnost /ˈglæznɒst, ˈglɑːs-/ n. (in the Soviet Union) the policy or practice of more open consultative government and wider dissemination of information. [Russ. glasnost', lit. = publicity, openness]

glass /glɑːs/ n., v., & adj. —n. 1 a (often attrib.) a hard, brittle, usu. transparent, translucent, or shiny substance, made by fusing sand with soda and lime and sometimes other ingredients (a glass jug) (cf. crown glass, flint glass, plate glass). b a substance of similar properties or composition. 2 (often collect.) an object or objects made from, or partly from, glass, esp.: a a drinking vessel. b a mirror; a looking-glass. c an hour- or sand-glass. d a window. e a greenhouse (rows of lettuce under glass). f glass ornaments. g a barometer. h a glass disc covering a watch-face. i a magnifying lens. j a monocle. 3 (in pl.) a spectacles. b field-glasses; opera-glasses. 4 the amount of liquid contained in a glass; a drink (he likes a glass). —v.tr. 1 (usu. as **glassed** adj.) fit with glass; glaze. 2 poet. reflect as in a mirror. 3 Mil. look at or for with field-glasses. —adj. of or made from glass. □**glass-blower** a person who blows semi-molten glass to make glassware. **glass-blowing** this occupation. **glass case** an exhibition display case made mostly from glass. **glass-cloth 1** a linen cloth for drying glasses. **2** a cloth covered with powdered glass or abrasive, like glass-paper. **glass cloth** a woven fabric of fine-spun glass. **glass-cutter 1** a worker who cuts glass. **2** a tool used for cutting glass. **glass eye** a false eye made from glass. **glass fibre 1** a filament or filaments of glass made into fabric. **2** such filaments embedded in plastic as reinforcement. **glass-gall** = SANDIVER. **glass-making** the manufacture of glass. **glass-paper** paper covered with glass-dust or abrasive and used for smoothing and polishing. **glass snake** any snakelike lizard of the genus *Ophisaurus*, with a very brittle tail. **glass wool** glass in the form of fine fibres used for packing and insulation. **has had a glass too much** is rather drunk. □□**glassful** *n.* (*pl.* **-fuls**). **glassless** *adj.* **glasslike** *adj.* [OE *glæs* f. Gmc: cf. GLAZE]

glasshouse /ˈglɑːshaʊs/ *n.* **1** a greenhouse. **2** *Brit. sl.* a military prison. **3** a building where glass is made.

glassie var. of GLASSY *n.*

glassine /ˈglɑːsiːn/ *n.* a glossy transparent paper. [GLASS]

glassware /ˈglɑːsweə(r)/ *n.* articles made from glass, esp. drinking glasses, tableware, etc.

glasswort /ˈglɑːswɜːt/ *n.* any plant of the genus *Salicornia* or *Salsola* formerly burnt for use in glass-making.

glassy /ˈglɑːsɪ/ *adj. & n.* —*adj.* (**glassier, glassiest**) **1** of or resembling glass, esp. in smoothness. **2** (of the eye, the expression, etc.) abstracted; dull; fixed (*fixed her with a glassy stare*). —*n.* (also **glassie**) *Austral.* a glass marble. □**the** (or **just the**) **glassy** *Austral.* the most excellent person or thing. □□ **glassily** *adv.* **glassiness** *n.*

Glaswegian /glæzˈwiːdʒ(ə)n, glɑː-/ *adj. & n.* —*adj.* of or relating to Glasgow in Scotland. —*n.* a native of Glasgow. [*Glasgow* after *Norwegian* etc.]

Glauber's salt /ˈglaʊbə(r)z, ˈglɔː-/ *n.* (also **Glauber's salts**) a crystalline hydrated form of sodium sulphate used esp. as a laxative. [J. R. *Glauber*, Ger. chemist d. 1668]

glaucoma /glɔːˈkəʊmə/ *n.* an eye-condition with increased pressure within the eyeball, causing gradual loss of sight. □□**glaucomatous** *adj.* [L f. Gk *glaukōma -atos*, ult. f. *glaukos*: see GLAUCOUS]

glaucous /ˈglɔːkəs/ *adj.* **1** of a dull greyish green or blue. **2** covered with a powdery bloom as of grapes. [L *glaucus* f. Gk *glaukos*]

glaze /gleɪz/ *v. & n.* —*v.* **1** *tr.* **a** fit (a window, picture, etc.) with glass. **b** provide (a building) with glass windows. **2** *tr.* **a** cover (pottery etc.) with a glaze. **b** fix (paint) on pottery with a glaze. **3** *tr.* cover (pastry, meat, etc.) with a glaze. **4** *intr.* (often foll. by *over*) (of the eyes) become fixed or glassy (*his eyes glazed over*). **5** *tr.* cover (cloth, paper, leather, a painted surface, etc.) with a glaze. **6** *tr.* give a glassy surface to, e.g. by rubbing. —*n.* **1** a vitreous substance, usu. a special glass, used to glaze pottery. **2** a smooth shiny coating of milk, sugar, gelatine, etc., on food. **3** a thin topcoat of transparent paint used to modify the tone of the underlying colour. **4** a smooth surface formed by glazing. **5** *US* a thin coating of ice. □**glazed frost** a glassy coating of ice caused by frozen rain or a sudden thaw succeeded by a frost. **glaze in** enclose (a building, a window frame, etc.) with glass. □□ **glazer** *n.* **glazy** *adj.* [ME f. an oblique form of GLASS]

glazier /ˈgleɪzɪə(r)/ *n.* a person whose trade is glazing windows etc. □□**glaziery** *n.*

glazing /ˈgleɪzɪŋ/ *n.* **1** the act or an instance of glazing. **2** windows (see also *double glazing*). **3** material used to produce a glaze.

GLC *abbr. hist.* (in the UK) Greater London Council.

gleam /gliːm/ *n. & v.* —*n.* **1** a faint or brief light (*a gleam of sunlight*). **2** a faint, sudden, intermittent, or temporary show (*not a gleam of hope*). —*v.intr.* **1** emit gleams. **2** shine with a faint or intermittent brightness. **3** (of a quality) be indicated (*fear gleamed in his eyes*). □□**gleamingly** *adv.* **gleamy** *adj.* [OE *glǣm*: cf. GLIMMER]

glean /gliːn/ *v.* **1** *tr.* collect or scrape together (news, facts, gossip, etc.) in small quantities. **2 a** *tr.* (also *absol.*) gather (ears of corn etc.) after the harvest. **b** *tr.* strip (a field etc.) after a harvest. □□ **gleaner** *n.* [ME f. OF *glener* f. LL *glennare*, prob. of Celt. orig.]

gleanings /ˈgliːnɪŋz/ *n.pl.* things gleaned, esp. facts.

glebe /gliːb/ *n.* **1** a piece of land serving as part of a clergyman's benefice and providing income. **2** *poet.* earth; land; a field. [ME f. L *gl(a)eba* clod, soil]

glee /gliː/ *n.* **1** mirth; delight (*watched the enemy's defeat with glee*). **2** a song for three or more, esp. adult male, voices, singing different parts simultaneously, usu. unaccompanied. □**glee club** a society for singing part-songs. □□ **gleesome** *adj.* [OE *glīo, glēo* minstrelsy, jest f. Gmc]

gleeful /ˈgliːfʊl/ *adj.* joyful. □□**gleefully** *adv.* **gleefulness** *n.*

Gleichschaltung /ˈglaɪxˌʃæltʊŋ/ *n.* the standardization of political, economic, and social institutions in authoritarian States. [G]

glen /glen/ *n.* a narrow valley. [Gael. & Ir. *gleann*]

glengarry /glenˈgærɪ/ *n.* (*pl.* **-ies**) a brimless Scottish hat with a cleft down the centre and usu. two ribbons hanging at the back. [*Glengarry* in Scotland]

glenoid cavity /ˈgliːnɔɪd/ *n.* a shallow depression on a bone, esp. the scapula and temporal bone, receiving the projection of another bone to form a joint. [F *glénoïde* f. Gk *glēnoeidēs* f. *glēnē* socket]

gley /gleɪ/ *n.* a tacky waterlogged soil grey to blue in colour. [Ukrainian, = sticky blue clay, rel. to CLAY]

glia /ˈglaɪə/ *n.* = NEUROGLIA. □□**glial** *adj.* [Gk, = glue]

glib /glɪb/ *adj.* (**glibber, glibbest**) **1** (of a speaker, speech, etc.) fluent and voluble but insincere and shallow. **2** *archaic* smooth; unimpeded. □□**glibly** *adv.* **glibness** *n.* [rel. to obs. *glibbery* slippery f. Gmc: perh. imit.]

glide /glaɪd/ *v. & n.* —*v.* **1** *intr.* (of a stream, bird, snake, ship, train, skater, etc.) move with a smooth continuous motion. **2** *intr.* (of an aircraft, esp. a glider) fly without engine-power. **3** *intr.* of time etc.: **a** pass gently and imperceptibly. **b** (often foll. by *into*) pass and change gradually and imperceptibly (*night glided into day*). **4** *intr.* move quietly or stealthily. **5** *tr.* cause to glide (*breezes glided the ship on its course*). **6** *tr.* cross in a glider. —*n.* **1 a** the act of gliding. **b** an instance of this. **2** *Phonet.* a gradually changing sound made in passing from one position of the speech-organs to another. **3** a gliding dance or dance-step. **4** a flight in a glider. **5** *Cricket* = GLANCE *n.* 4. □**glide clip** *Austral.* a paper fastener made of bent wire. **glide path** an aircraft's line of descent to land, esp. as indicated by ground radar. □□ **glidingly** *adv.* [OE *glīdan* f. WG]

glider /ˈglaɪdə(r)/ *n.* **1 a** an aircraft that flies without an engine. **b** a glider pilot. **2** a person or thing that glides.

glim /glɪm/ *n.* **1** a faint light. **2** *archaic sl.* a candle; a lantern. [17th c.: perh. abbr. of GLIMMER or GLIMPSE]

glimmer /ˈglɪmə(r)/ *v. & n.* —*v.intr.* shine faintly or intermittently. —*n.* **1** a feeble or wavering light. **2** (usu. foll. by *of*) a faint gleam (of hope, understanding, etc.). **3** a glimpse. □□ **glimmeringly** *adv.* [ME prob. f. Scand. f. WG: see GLEAM]

glimmering /ˈglɪmərɪŋ/ *n.* **1** = GLIMMER *n.* **2** an act of glimmering.

glimpse /glɪmps/ *n. & v.* —*n.* (often foll. by *of*) **1** a momentary or partial view (*caught a glimpse of her*). **2** a faint and transient appearance (*glimpses of the truth*). —*v.* **1** *tr.* see faintly or partly (*glimpsed his face in the crowd*). **2** *intr.* (often foll. by *at*) cast a passing glance. **3** *intr.* **a** shine faintly or intermittently. **b** *poet.* appear faintly; dawn. [ME *glimse* corresp. to MHG *glimsen* f. WG (as GLIMMER)]

glint /glɪnt/ v. & n. —v.intr. & tr. flash or cause to flash; glitter; sparkle; reflect (*eyes glinted with amusement*; *the sword glinted fire*). —n. a brief flash of light; a sparkle. [alt. of ME *glent*, prob. of Scand. orig.]

glissade /glɪˈsɑːd, -ˈseɪd/ n. & v. —n. 1 an act of sliding down a steep slope of snow or ice, usu. on the feet with the support of an ice-axe etc. 2 a gliding step in ballet. —v.intr. perform a glissade. [F f. *glisser* slip, slide]

glissando /glɪˈsændəʊ/ n. (*pl.* **glissandi** /-dɪ/ *or* **-os**) *Mus.* a continuous slide of adjacent notes upwards or downwards. [It. f. F *glissant* sliding (as GLISSADE)]

glissé /gliːˈseɪ/ n. (also *pas glissé* /pɑː/) *Ballet* a sliding step in which the flat of the foot is often used. [F, past part. of *glisser*: see GLISSADE]

glisten /ˈglɪs(ə)n/ v. & n. —v.intr. shine, esp. like a wet object, snow, etc.; glitter. —n. a glitter; a sparkle. [OE *glisnian* f. *glisian* shine]

glister /ˈglɪstə(r)/ v. & n. archaic —v.intr. sparkle; glitter. —n. a sparkle; a gleam. [ME f. MLG *glistern*, MDu *glisteren*, rel. to GLISTEN]

glitch /glɪtʃ/ n. colloq. a sudden irregularity or malfunction (of equipment etc.). [20th c.: orig. unkn.]

glitter /ˈglɪtə(r)/ v. & n. —v.intr. 1 shine, esp. with a bright reflected light; sparkle. 2 (usu. foll. by *with*) a be showy or splendid (*glittered with diamonds*). b be ostentatious or flashily brilliant (*glittering rhetoric*). —n. 1 a gleam; a sparkle. 2 showiness; splendour. 3 tiny pieces of sparkling material as on Christmas-tree decorations. □□ **glitteringly** adv. **glittery** adj. [ME f. ON *glitra* f. Gmc]

glitterati /ˌglɪtəˈrɑːtɪ/ n.pl. sl. the fashionable set of literary or show-business people. [GLITTER + LITERATI]

glitz /glɪts/ n. sl. extravagant but superficial display; show-business glamour. [back-form. f. GLITZY]

glitzy /ˈglɪtsɪ/ adj. (**glitzier, glitziest**) sl. extravagant, ostentatious; tawdry, gaudy. □□ **glitzily** adv. **glitziness** n. [GLITTER, after RITZY: cf. G *glitzerig* glittering]

gloaming /ˈgləʊmɪŋ/ n. poet. twilight; dusk. [OE *glōmung* f. *glōm* twilight, rel. to GLOW]

gloat /gləʊt/ v. & n. —v.intr. (often foll. by *on*, *upon*, *over*) consider or contemplate with lust, greed, malice, triumph, etc. (*gloated over his collection*). —n. 1 the act of gloating. 2 a look or expression of triumphant satisfaction. □□ **gloater** n. **gloatingly** adv. [16th c.: orig. unkn., but perh. rel. to ON *glotta* grin, MHG *glotzen* stare]

glob /glɒb/ n. a mass or lump of semi-liquid substance, e.g. mud. [20th c.: perh. f. BLOB and GOB[1]]

global /ˈgləʊb(ə)l/ adj. 1 worldwide (*global conflict*). 2 relating to or embracing a group of items etc.; total. □**global warming** the increase in temperature of the earth's atmosphere caused by the greenhouse effect. □□ **globally** adv. [F (as GLOBE)]

globe /gləʊb/ n. & v. —n. 1 a (prec. by *the*) the planet earth. b a planet, star, or sun. c any spherical body; a ball. 2 a spherical representation of the earth or of the constellations with a map on the surface. 3 a golden sphere as an emblem of sovereignty; an orb. 4 any spherical glass vessel, esp. a fish bowl, a lamp, etc. 5 the eyeball. —v.tr. & intr. make (usu. in *passive*) or become globular. □**globe artichoke** the partly edible head of the artichoke plant. **globe-fish** any tropical fish of the family Tetraodontidae, able to inflate itself into a spherical form: also called PUFFER-FISH. **globe-flower** any ranunculaceous plant of the genus *Trollius* with globular usu. yellow flowers. **globe lightning** = *ball lightning* (see BALL[1]). **globe-trotter** a person who travels widely. **globe-trotting** such travel. □□ **globelike** adj. **globoid** adj. & n. **globose** adj. [F *globe* or L *globus*]

globigerina /gləʊˌbɪdʒəˈraɪnə, -ˈriːnə/ n. any planktonic protozoan of the genus *Globigerina*, living near the surface of the sea. [mod.L f. L *globus* globe + -*ger* carrying + -INA]

globular /ˈglɒbjʊlə(r)/ adj. 1 globe-shaped, spherical. 2 composed of globules. □□ **globularity** /-ˈlærɪtɪ/ n. **globularly** adv.

globule /ˈglɒbjuːl/ n. 1 a small globe or round particle; a drop. 2 a pill. □□ **globulous** adj. [F *globule* or L *globulus* (as GLOBE)]

globulin /ˈglɒbjʊlɪn/ n. any of a group of proteins found in plant and animal tissues and esp. responsible for the transport of molecules etc.

glockenspiel /ˈglɒkənˌspiːl, -ˌʃpiːl/ n. a musical instrument consisting of a series of bells or metal bars or tubes suspended or mounted in a frame and struck by hammers. [G, = bell-play]

glom /glɒm/ v. US sl. (**glommed, glomming**) 1 tr. steal; grab. 2 intr. (usu. foll. by *on to*) steal; grab. [var. of Sc. *glaum* (18th c., of unkn. orig.)]

glomerate /ˈglɒmərət/ adj. Bot. & Anat. compactly clustered. [L *glomeratus* past part. of *glomerare* f. *glomus -eris* ball]

glomerule /ˈglɒməˌruːl/ n. a clustered flower-head.

glomerulus /gləˈmɛrələs/ n. (*pl.* **glomeruli** /-ˌlaɪ/) a cluster of small organisms, tissues, or blood vessels, esp. of the capillaries of the kidney. □□ **glomerular** adj. [mod.L, dimin. of L *glomus -eris* ball]

gloom /gluːm/ n. & v. —n. 1 darkness; obscurity. 2 melancholy; despondency. 3 poet. a dark place. —v. 1 intr. be gloomy or melancholy; frown. 2 intr. (of the sky etc.) be dull or threatening; lour. 3 intr. appear darkly or obscurely. 4 tr. cover with gloom; make dark or dismal. [ME *gloum(b)e*, of unkn. orig.: cf. GLUM]

gloomy /ˈgluːmɪ/ adj. (**gloomier, gloomiest**) 1 dark; unlighted. 2 depressed; sullen. 3 dismal; depressing. □□ **gloomily** adv. **gloominess** n.

glop /glɒp/ n. US sl. a liquid or sticky mess, esp. inedible food. [imit.: cf. obs. *glop* swallow greedily]

Gloria /ˈglɔːrɪə/ n. 1 any of various doxologies beginning with *Gloria*, esp. the hymn beginning with *Gloria in excelsis Deo* (Glory be to God in the highest). 2 an aureole. [L, = glory]

glorify /ˈglɔːrɪˌfaɪ/ v.tr. (**-ies, -ied**) 1 exalt to heavenly glory; make glorious. 2 transform into something more splendid. 3 extol; praise. 4 (as **glorified** adj.) seeming or pretending to be more splendid than in reality (*just a glorified office boy*). □□ **glorification** /-fɪˈkeɪʃ(ə)n/ n. **glorifier** n. [ME f. OF *glorifier* f. eccl.L *glorificare* f. LL *glorificus* f. L *gloria* glory]

gloriole /ˈglɔːrɪˌəʊl/ n. an aureole; a halo. [F f. L *gloriola* dimin. of *gloria* glory]

glorious /ˈglɔːrɪəs/ adj. 1 possessing glory; illustrious. 2 conferring glory; honourable. 3 colloq. splendid; magnificent; delightful (*a glorious day*; *glorious fun*). 4 iron. intense; unmitigated (*a glorious muddle*). 5 colloq. happily intoxicated. □□ **gloriously** adv. **gloriousness** n. [ME f. AF *glorious*, OF *glorios*, -*eus* f. L *gloriosus* (as GLORY)]

glory /ˈglɔːrɪ/ n. & v. —n. (*pl.* **-ies**) 1 high renown or fame; honour. 2 adoring praise and thanksgiving (*Glory to the Lord*). 3 resplendent majesty or magnificence; great beauty (*the glory of Versailles*; *the glory of the rose*). 4 a thing that brings renown or praise; a distinction. 5 the bliss and splendour of heaven. 6 colloq. a state of exaltation, prosperity, happiness, etc. (*is in his glory playing with his trains*). 7 an aureole, a halo. 8 an anthelion. —v.intr. (often foll. by *in*, or *to* + infin.) pride oneself; exult (*glory in their skill*). □**glory be! 1** a devout ejaculation. 2 colloq. an exclamation of surprise or delight. **glory-box** Austral. & NZ a box for women's clothes etc., stored in preparation for marriage. **glory-hole** 1 colloq. an untidy room, drawer, or receptacle. 2 US an open quarry. **glory-of-the-snow** = CHIONODOXA. **go to glory** sl. die; be destroyed. [ME f. AF & OF *glorie* f. L *gloria*]

Glos. /glɒs/ abbr. Gloucestershire.

gloss[1] /glɒs/ n. & v. —n. 1 a surface shine or lustre. b an instance of this; a smooth finish. 2 a deceptively attractive appearance. b an instance of this. 3 (in full **gloss paint**) paint formulated to give a hard glossy finish (cf. MATT). —*v.tr.* make glossy. □**gloss over 1** seek to conceal beneath a false appearance. **2** conceal or evade by mentioning briefly or misleadingly. □□ **glosser** *n.* [16th c.: orig. unkn.]

gloss[2] /glɒs/ *n. & v.* —*n.* **1 a** an explanatory word or phrase inserted between the lines or in the margin of a text. **b** a comment, explanation, interpretation, or paraphrase. **2** a misrepresentation of another's words. **3 a** a glossary. **b** an interlinear translation or annotation. —*v.* **1** *tr.* **a** add a gloss or glosses to (a text, word, etc.). **b** read a different sense into; explain away. **2** *intr.* (often foll. by *on*) make (esp. unfavourable) comments. **3** *intr.* write or introduce glosses. □□ **glosser** *n.* [alt. of GLOZE after med.L *glossa*]

glossal /'glɒs(ə)l/ *adj. Anat.* of the tongue; lingual. [Gk *glōssa* tongue]

glossary /'glɒsərɪ/ *n.* (*pl.* **-ies**) **1** (also **gloss**) an alphabetical list of terms or words found in or relating to a specific subject or text, esp. dialect, with explanations; a brief dictionary. **2** a collection of glosses. □□ **glossarial** /glɒ'seərɪəl/ *adj.* **glossarist** *n.* [L *glossarium* f. *glossa* GLOSS[2]]

glossator /glɒ'seɪtə(r)/ *n.* **1** a writer of glosses. **2** *hist.* a commentator on, or interpreter of, medieval law-texts. [ME f. med.L f. *glossare* f. *glossa* GLOSS[2]]

glosseme /'glɒsi:m/ *n.* any meaningful feature of a language that cannot be analysed into smaller meaningful units. [Gk *glōssēma* f. *glōssa* GLOSS[2]]

glossitis /glɒ'saɪtɪs/ *n.* inflammation of the tongue. [Gk *glōssa* tongue]

glossographer /glɒ'sɒgrəfə(r)/ *n.* a writer of glosses or commentaries. [GLOSS[2] + -GRAPHER]

glossolalia /ˌglɒsə'leɪlɪə/ *n.* = *gift of tongues* (see TONGUE). [mod.L f. Gk *glōssa* tongue + *-lalia* speaking]

glosso-laryngeal /ˌglɒsəʊlæ'rɪndʒɪəl/ *adj.* of the tongue and larynx. [Gk *glōssa* tongue + LARYNGEAL]

glossy /'glɒsɪ/ *adj. & n.* —*adj.* (**glossier, glossiest**) **1** having a shine; smooth. **2** (of paper etc.) smooth and shiny. **3** (of a magazine etc.) printed on such paper. —*n.* (*pl.* **-ies**) *colloq.* **1** a glossy magazine. **2** a photograph with a glossy surface. □□ **glossily** *adv.* **glossiness** *n.*

glottal /'glɒt(ə)l/ *adj.* of or produced by the glottis. □**glottal stop** a sound produced by the sudden opening or shutting of the glottis.

glottis /'glɒtɪs/ *n.* the space at the upper end of the windpipe and between the vocal cords, affecting voice modulation through expansion or contraction. □□ **glottic** *adj.* [mod.L f. Gk *glōttis* f. *glōtta* var. of *glōssa* tongue]

Gloucester /'glɒstə(r)/ *n.* (usu. **double Gloucester**, orig. a richer kind) a kind of hard cheese orig. made in Gloucestershire in S. England.

glove /glʌv/ *n. & v.* —*n.* **1** a covering for the hand, of wool, leather, cotton, etc., worn esp. for protection against cold or dirt, and usu. having separate fingers. **2** a padded protective glove, esp.: **a** a boxing glove. **b** a wicket-keeper's glove. —*v.tr.* cover or provide with a glove or gloves. □**fit like a glove** fit exactly. **glove box 1** a box for gloves. **2** a closed chamber with sealed-in gloves for handling radioactive material etc. **3** = *glove compartment*. **glove compartment** a recess for small articles in the dashboard of a motor vehicle. **glove puppet** a small cloth puppet fitted on the hand and worked by the fingers. **throw down** (or **take up**) **the glove** issue (or accept) a challenge. **with the gloves off** mercilessly; unfairly; with no compunction. □□ **gloveless** *adj.* **glover** *n.* [OE *glōf*, corresp. to ON *glófi*, perh. f. Gmc]

glow /gləʊ/ *v. & n.* —*v.intr.* **1 a** throw out light and heat without flame; be incandescent. **b** shine like something heated in this way. **2** (of the cheeks) redden, esp. from cold or exercise. **3** (often foll. by *with*) **a** (of the body) be heated, esp. from exertion; sweat. **b** express or experience strong emotion

(*glowed with pride*; *glowing with indignation*). **4** showing a warm colour (*the painting glows with warmth*). **5** (as **glowing** *adj.*) expressing pride or satisfaction (*a glowing report*). —*n.* **1** a glowing state. **2** a bright warm colour, esp. the red of cheeks. **3** ardour; passion. **4** a feeling induced by good health, exercise, etc.; well-being. □**glow discharge** a luminous sparkless electrical discharge from a pointed conductor in a gas at low pressure. **glow-worm** any beetle of the genus *Lampyris* whose wingless female emits light from the end of the abdomen. **in a glow** *colloq.* hot or flushed; sweating. □□ **glowingly** *adv.* [OE *glōwan* f. Gmc]

glower /'glaʊə(r)/ *v. & n.* —*v.intr.* (often foll. by *at*) stare or scowl, esp. angrily. —*n.* a glowering look. □□ **gloweringly** *adv.* [orig. uncert.: perh. Sc. var. of ME *glore* f. LG or Scand., or f. obs. (ME) *glow* stare + -ER[4]]

gloxinia /glɒk'sɪnɪə/ *n.* any tropical plant of the genus *Gloxinia*, native to S. America, with large bell flowers of various colours. [mod.L f. B. P. *Gloxin*, 18th-c. Ger. botanist]

gloze /gləʊz/ *v.* **1** *tr.* (also **gloze over**) explain away; extenuate; palliate. **2** *intr. archaic* **a** (usu. foll. by *on, upon*) comment. **b** talk speciously; fawn. [ME f. OF *gloser* f. *glose* f. med.L *glosa, gloza* f. L *glossa* tongue, GLOSS[2]]

glucagon /'glu:kəgən/ *n.* a polypeptide hormone formed in the pancreas, which aids the breakdown of glycogen. [Gk *glukus* sweet + *agōn* leading]

glucose /'glu:kəʊs, -kəʊz/ *n.* **1** a simple sugar containing six carbon atoms, found mainly in its dextrorotatory form (see DEXTROSE), which is an important energy source in living organisms and obtainable from some carbohydrates by hydrolysis. ¶Chem. formula: $C_6H_{12}O_6$. **2** a syrup containing glucose sugars from the incomplete hydrolysis of starch. [F f. Gk *gleukos* sweet wine, rel. to *glukus* sweet]

glucoside /'glu:kəˌsaɪd/ *n.* a compound giving glucose and other products upon hydrolysis. □□ **glucosidic** /-'sɪdɪk/ *adj.*

glue /glu:/ *n. & v.* —*n.* an adhesive substance used for sticking objects or materials together. —*v.tr.* (**glues, glued, gluing** or **glueing**) **1** fasten or join with glue. **2** keep or put very close (*an eye glued to the keyhole*). □**glue-pot 1** a pot with an outer vessel holding water to heat glue. **2** *colloq.* an area of sticky mud etc. **glue-sniffer** a person who inhales the fumes from adhesives as a drug. □□ **gluelike** *adj.* **gluer** *n.* **gluey** /'glu:ɪ/ *adj.* (**gluier, gluiest**). **glueyness** *n.* [ME f. OF *glu* (n.), *gluer* (v.), f. LL *glus glutis* f. L *gluten*]

glum /glʌm/ *adj.* (**glummer, glummest**) looking or feeling dejected; sullen; displeased. □□ **glumly** *adv.* **glumness** *n.* [rel. to dial. *glum* (v.) frown, var. of *gloume* GLOOM *v.*]

glume /glu:m/ *n.* **1** a membranous bract surrounding the spikelet of grasses or the florets of sedges. **2** the husk of grain. □□ **glumaceous** /-'meɪʃəs/ *adj.* **glumose** *adj.* [L *gluma* husk]

gluon /'glu:ɒn/ *n. Physics* any of a group of elementary particles that are thought to bind quarks together. [GLUE + -ON]

glut /glʌt/ *v. & n.* —*v.tr.* (**glutted, glutting**) **1** feed (a person, one's stomach, etc.) or indulge (an appetite, a desire, etc.) to the full; satiate; cloy. **2** fill to excess; choke up. **3** *Econ.* overstock (a market) with goods. —*n.* **1** *Econ.* supply exceeding demand; a surfeit (*a glut in the market*). **2** full indulgence; one's fill. [ME prob. f. OF *gloutir* swallow f. L *gluttire*: cf. GLUTTON]

glutamate /'glu:təˌmeɪt/ *n.* any salt or ester of glutamic acid, esp. a sodium salt used to enhance the flavour of food.

glutamic acid /glu:'tæmɪk/ *n.* a naturally occurring amino acid, a constituent of many proteins. [GLUTEN + AMINE + -IC]

gluten /'glu:t(ə)n/ *n.* **1** a mixture of proteins present

æ *cat* ɑ: *arm* e *bed* ɜ: *her* ɪ *sit* i: *see* ɒ *hot* ɔ: *saw* ʌ *run* ʊ *put* u: *too* ə *ago* aɪ *my*

in cereal grains. **2** *archaic* a sticky substance. [F f. L *gluten glutinis* glue]

gluteus /'gluːtɪəs/ *n.* (*pl.* **glutei** /-tɪ,aɪ/) any of the three muscles in each buttock. □□ **gluteal** *adj.* [mod.L f. Gk *gloutos* buttock]

glutinous /'gluːtɪnəs/ *adj.* sticky; like glue. □□ **glutinously** *adv.* **glutinousness** *n.* [F *glutineux* or L *glutinosus* (as GLUTEN)]

glutton /'glʌt(ə)n/ *n.* **1** an excessively greedy eater. **2** (often foll. by *for*) *colloq.* a person insatiably eager (*a glutton for work*). **3** a voracious animal *Gulo gulo*, of the weasel family. Also called WOLVERINE. □ **a glutton for punishment** a person eager to take on hard or unpleasant tasks. □□ **gluttonize** *v.intr.* (also **-ise**). **gluttonous** *adj.* **gluttonously** *adv.* [ME f. OF *gluton, gloton* f. L *glutto -onis* f. *gluttire* swallow, *gluttus* greedy]

gluttony /'glʌtənɪ/ *n.* habitual greed or excess in eating. [OF *glutonie* (as GLUTTON)]

glyceride /'glɪsə,raɪd/ *n.* any fatty-acid ester of glycerol.

glycerine /'glɪsə,riːn/ *n.* (*US* **glycerin** /-rɪn/) = GLYCEROL. [F *glycerin* f. Gk *glukeros* sweet]

glycerol /'glɪsə,rɒl/ *n.* a colourless sweet viscous liquid formed as a by-product in the manufacture of soap, used as an emollient and laxative, in explosives, etc. ¶ Chem. formula: $C_3H_8O_3$. Also called GLYCERINE. [GLYCERINE + -OL¹]

glycine /'glaɪsiːn/ *n.* the simplest naturally occurring amino acid, a general constituent of proteins. [G *Glycin* f. Gk *glukus* sweet]

glyco- /'glaɪkəʊ/ *comb. form* sugar. [Gk *glukus* sweet]

glycogen /'glaɪkədʒ(ə)n/ *n.* a polysaccharide serving as a store of carbohydrates, esp. in animal tissues, and yielding glucose on hydrolysis. □□ **glycogenic** /-'dʒenɪk/ *adj.*

glycogenesis /,glaɪkəʊ'dʒenɪsɪs/ *n. Biochem.* the formation of glycogen from sugar.

glycol /'glaɪkɒl/ *n.* a diol, esp. ethylene glycol. □□ **glycolic** /-'kɒlɪk/ *adj.* **glycollic** /-'kɒlɪk/ *adj.* [GLYCERINE + -OL¹,· orig. as being intermediate between glycerine and alcohol]

glycolysis /glaɪ'kɒlɪsɪs/ *n. Biochem.* the breakdown of glucose by enzymes in most living organisms to release energy and pyruvic acid.

glycoprotein /,glaɪkəʊ'prəʊtiːn/ *n.* any of a group of compounds consisting of a protein combined with a carbohydrate.

glycoside /'glaɪkə,saɪd/ *n.* any compound giving sugar and other products on hydrolysis. □□ **glycosidic** /-'sɪdɪk/ *adj.* [GLYCO-, after GLUCOSIDE]

glycosuria /,glaɪkə'sjʊərɪə/ *n.* a condition characterized by an excess of sugar in the urine, associated with diabetes, kidney disease, etc. □□ **glycosuric** *adj.* [F *glycose* glucose + -URIA]

glyph /glɪf/ *n.* **1** a sculptured character or symbol. **2** a vertical groove, esp. that on a Greek frieze. □□ **glyphic** *adj.* [F *glyphe* f. Gk *gluphē* carving f. *gluphō* carve]

glyptal /'glɪptæl/ *n.* an alkyd resin, esp. one formed from glycerine and phthalic acid or anhydride. [perh. f. *glycerol* + *phthalic*]

glyptic /'glɪptɪk/ *adj.* of or concerning carving, esp. on precious stones. [F *glyptique* or Gk *gluptikos* f. *gluptēs* carver f. *gluphō* carve]

glyptodont /'glɪptə,dɒnt/ *n.* any extinct armadillo-like edentate animal of the genus *Glyptodon* native to S. America, having fluted teeth and a body covered in a hard thick bony shell. [mod.L f. Gk *gluptos* carved + *odous odontos* tooth]

glyptography /glɪp'tɒgrəfɪ/ *n.* the art or scientific study of gem-engraving. [Gk *gluptos* carved + -GRAPHY]

GM *abbr.* **1** (in the UK) George Medal. **2** (in the US) General Motors. **3** general manager.

gm *abbr.* gram(s).

G-man /'dʒiːmæn/ *n.* (*pl.* **G-men**) **1** *US colloq.* a federal criminal-investigation officer. **2** *Ir.* a political detective. [Government + MAN]

GMT *abbr.* Greenwich mean time.

GMWU *abbr.* (in the UK) General & Municipal Workers' Union.

gnamma /'næmə/ *n.* (also **namma**) *Austral.* a natural hole in a rock, containing water; a waterhole. [Aboriginal]

gnarled /nɑːld/ *adj.* (also **gnarly** /'nɑːlɪ/) (of a tree, hands, etc.) knobbly, twisted, rugged. [var. of *knarled*, rel. to KNURL]

gnash /næʃ/ *v. & n.* —*v.* **1** *tr.* grind (the teeth). **2** *intr.* (of the teeth) strike together; grind. —*n.* an act of grinding the teeth. [var. of obs. *gnacche* or *gnast*, rel. to ON *gnastan* a gnashing (imit.)]

gnat /næt/ *n.* **1** any small two-winged biting fly of the genus *Culex*, esp. *C. pipiens*. **2** an insignificant annoyance. **3** a tiny thing. [OE *gnætt*]

gnathic /'næθɪk/ *adj.* of or relating to the jaws. [Gk *gnathos* jaw]

gnaw /nɔː/ *v.* (*past part.* **gnawed** or **gnawn**) **1 a** *tr.* (usu. foll. by *away, off, in two,* etc.) bite persistently; wear away by biting. **b** *intr.* (often foll. by *at, into*) bite, nibble. **2 a** *intr.* (often foll. by *at, into*) (of a destructive agent, pain, fear, etc.) corrode; waste away; consume; torture. **b** *tr.* corrode, consume, torture, etc. with pain, fear, etc. (*was gnawed by doubt*). **3** *tr.* (as **gnawing** *adj.*) persistent; worrying. □□ **gnawingly** *adv.* [OE *gnagen*, ult. imit.]

gneiss /naɪs/ *n.* a usu. coarse-grained metamorphic rock foliated by mineral layers, principally of feldspar, quartz, and ferromagnesian minerals. □□ **gneissic** *adj.* **gneissoid** *adj.* **gneissose** *adj.* [G]

gnocchi /'nɒkɪ, 'njɒkɪ/ *n.pl.* an Italian dish of small dumplings usu. made from potato, semolina flour, etc., or from spinach and cheese. [It., pl. of *gnocco* f. *nocchio* knot in wood]

gnome¹ /nəʊm/ *n.* **1 a** a dwarfish legendary creature supposed to guard the earth's treasures underground; a goblin. **b** a figure of a gnome, esp. as a garden ornament. **2** (esp. in *pl.*) *colloq.* a person with sinister influence; esp. financial (*gnomes of Zurich*). □□ **gnomish** *adj.* [F f. mod.L *gnomus* (word invented by Paracelsus)]

gnome² /'nəʊmɪ, nəʊm/ *n.* a maxim; an aphorism. [Gk *gnōmē* opinion f. *gignōskō* know]

gnomic /'nəʊmɪk/ *adj.* **1** of, consisting of, or using gnomes or aphorisms; sententious (see GNOME²). **2** *Gram.* (of a tense) used without the implication of time to express a general truth, e.g. *men were deceivers ever.* □□ **gnomically** *adv.* [Gk *gnōmikos* (as GNOME²)]

gnomon /'nəʊmɒn/ *n.* **1** the rod or pin etc. on a sundial that shows the time by the position of its shadow. **2** *Geom.* the part of a parallelogram left when a similar parallelogram has been taken from its corner. **3** *Astron.* a column etc. used in observing the sun's meridian altitude. □□ **gnomonic** /-'mɒnɪk/ *adj.* [F or L *gnomon* f. Gk *gnōmōn* indicator etc. f. *gignōskō* know]

gnosis /'nəʊsɪs/ *n.* knowledge of spiritual mysteries. [Gk *gnōsis* knowledge (as GNOMON)]

gnostic /'nɒstɪk/ *adj. & n.* —*adj.* **1** relating to knowledge, esp. esoteric mystical knowledge. **2** (**Gnostic**) concerning the Gnostics; occult; mystic. —*n.* (**Gnostic**) (usu. in *pl.*) a Christian heretic of the 1st–3rd c. claiming gnosis. □□ **Gnosticism** /-,sɪz(ə)m/ *n.* **gnosticize** /-,saɪz/ *v.tr. & intr.* [eccl.L *gnosticus* f. Gk *gnōstikos* (as GNOSIS)]

GNP *abbr.* gross national product.

Gnr. *abbr. Brit.* Gunner.

gns. *abbr. Brit. hist.* guineas.

gnu /nuː, njuː/ *n.* any antelope of the genus *Connochaetes*, native to S. Africa, with a large erect head and brown stripes on the neck and shoulders. Also called WILDEBEEST. [Bushman *nqu*, prob. through Du. *gnoe*]

go¹ /gəʊ/ *v., n., & adj.* —*v.* (*3rd sing. present* **goes**

/gəʊz/; *past* **went** /went/; *past part.* **gone** /gɒn/) **1** *intr.* **a** start moving or be moving from one place or point in time to another; travel, proceed. **b** (foll. by *to* + infin., or *and* + verb) proceed in order to (*went to find him*; *go and buy some bread*). **c** (foll. by *and* + verb) *colloq.* expressing annoyance (*you went and told him*; *they've gone and broken it*; *she went and won*). **2** *intr.* (foll. by verbal noun) make a special trip for; participate in; proceed to do (*went skiing*; *then went shopping*; *often goes running*). **3** *intr.* lie or extend in a certain direction (*the road goes to London*). **4** *intr.* leave; depart (*they had to go*). **5** *intr.* move, act, work, etc. (*the clock doesn't go*; *his brain is going all the time*). **6** *intr.* **a** make a specified movement (*go like this with your foot*). **b** make a sound (often of a specified kind) (*the gun went bang*; *the door bell went*). **c** *colloq.* say (*so he goes to me 'Why didn't you like it?'*). **d** (of an animal) make (its characteristic cry) (*the cow went 'moo'*). **7** *intr.* be in a specified state (*go hungry*; *went in fear of his life*). **8** *intr.* **a** pass into a specified condition (*gone bad*; *went mad*; *went to sleep*). **b** *colloq.* die. **c** proceed or escape in a specified condition (*the poet went unrecognized*; *the crime went unnoticed*). **9** *intr.* (of time or distance) pass, elapse; be traversed (*ten days to go before Easter*; *the last mile went quickly*). **10** *intr.* **a** (of a document, verse, song, etc.) have a specified content or wording; run (*the tune goes like this*). **b** be current or accepted (*so the story goes*). **c** be suitable; fit; match (*the shoes don't go with the hat*). **d** be regularly kept or put (*the forks go here*). **e** find room; fit (*this won't go into the cupboard*). **11** *intr.* **a** turn out, proceed; take a course or view (*things went well*; *Liverpool went Labour*). **b** be successful (*make the party go*; *went like a bomb*). **c** progress (*we've still a long way to go*). **12** *intr.* **a** be sold (*went for £1*; *went cheap*). **b** (of money) be spent (*£200 went on a new jacket*). **13** *intr.* **a** be relinquished, dismissed, or abolished (*the car will have to go*). **b** fail, decline; give way, collapse (*his sight is going*; *the bulb has gone*). **14** *intr.* be acceptable or permitted; be accepted without question (*anything goes*; *what I say goes*). **15** *intr.* (often foll. by *by, with, on, upon*) be guided by; judge or act on or in harmony with (*have nothing to go on*; *a good rule to go by*). **16** *intr.* attend or visit or travel to regularly (*goes to church*; *goes to school*; *this train goes to Bristol*). **17** *intr.* (foll. by pres. part.) *colloq.* proceed (often foolishly) to do (*went running to the police*; *don't go making him angry*). **18** *intr.* act or proceed to a certain point (*will go so far and no further*; *went as high as £100*). **19** *intr.* (of a number) be capable of being contained in another (*6 into 12 goes twice*; *6 into 5 won't go*). **20** *tr.* *Cards* bid; declare (*go nap*; *has gone two spades*). **21** *intr.* (usu. foll. by *to*) be allotted or awarded; pass (*first prize went to the girl*; *the job went to his rival*). **22** *intr.* (foll. by *to, towards*) amount to; contribute to (*12 inches go to make a foot*; *this will go towards your holiday*). **23** *intr.* (in *imper.*) begin motion (a starter's order in a race) (*ready, steady, go!*). **24** *intr.* (usu. foll. by *to*) refer or appeal (*go to him for help*). **25** *intr.* (often foll. by *on*) take up a specified profession (*went on the stage*; *gone soldiering*; *went to sea*). **26** *intr.* (usu. foll. by *by, under*) be known or called (*goes by the name of Droopy*). **27** *tr.* *colloq.* proceed to (*go jump in the lake*). **28** *intr.* (foll. by *for*) apply to; have relevance for (*that goes for me too*). —*n.* (*pl.* **goes**) **1** the act or an instance of going. **2** mettle; spirit; dash; animation (*she has a lot of go in her*). **3** vigorous activity (*it's all go*). **4** *colloq.* a success (*made a go of it*). **5** *colloq.* a turn; an attempt (*I'll have a go*; *it's my go*; *all in one go*). **6** *colloq.* a state of affairs (*a rum go*). **7** *colloq.* an attack of illness (*a bad go of flu*). **8** *colloq.* a quantity of liquor, food, etc. served at one time. —*adj.* *colloq.* **1** functioning properly (*all systems are go*). **2** fashionable; progressive. □**all the go** *colloq.* in fashion. **as** (or **so**) **far as it goes** an expression of caution against taking a statement too positively (*the*

work is good as far as it goes). **as** (**a person or thing**) **goes** as the average is (*a good actor as actors go*). **from the word go** *colloq.* from the very beginning. **give it a go** *colloq.* make an effort to succeed. **go about 1** busy oneself with; set to work at. **2** be socially active. **3** (foll. by pres. part.) make a habit of doing (*goes about telling lies*). **4** *Naut.* change to an opposite tack. **go ahead** proceed without hesitation. **go-ahead** *n.* permission to proceed. —*adj.* enterprising. **go along with** agree to; take the same view as. **go around** **1** (foll. by *with*) be regularly in the company of. **2** = *go about* 3. **go-as-you-please** untrammelled; free. **go at** take in hand energetically; attack. **go away** depart, esp. from home for a holiday etc. **go back on** fail to keep (one's word, promise, etc.). **go bail** see BAIL[1]. **go begging** see BEG. **go-between** an intermediary; a negotiator. **go by 1** pass. **2** be dependent on; be guided by. **go-by** *colloq.* a snub; a slight (*gave it the go-by*). **go by default** see DEFAULT. **go-cart 1** a handcart; a pushchair. **2** = *go-kart*. **3** *archaic* a baby-walker. **go-devil** *US* an instrument used to clean the inside of pipes etc. **go down 1 a** (of an amount) become less (*the coffee has gone down a lot*). **b** subside (*the flood went down*). **c** decrease in price; lose value. **2 a** (of a ship) sink. **b** (of the sun) set. **3** (usu. foll. by *to*) be continued to a specified point. **4** deteriorate; fail; (of a computer network etc.) cease to function. **5** be recorded in writing. **6** be swallowed. **7** (often foll. by *with*) find acceptance. **8** *Brit. colloq.* leave university. **9** *colloq.* be sent to prison (*went down for ten years*). **10** (often foll. by *before*) fall (before a conqueror). **go down with** *Brit.* begin to suffer from (a disease). **go Dutch** see DUTCH. **go far** be very successful. **go for 1** go to fetch. **2** be accounted as or achieve (*went for nothing*). **3** prefer; choose (*that's the one I go for*). **4** *colloq.* strive to attain (*go for it!*). **5** *colloq.* attack (*the dog went for him*). **go-getter** *colloq.* an aggressively enterprising person, esp. a businessman. **go-go** *colloq.* **1** (of a dancer, music, etc.) in modern style, lively and rhythmic. **2** unrestrained; energetic. **3** (of investment) speculative. **go great guns** see GUN. **go halves** (or **shares**) (often foll. by *with*) share equally. **go in 1** enter a room, house, etc. **2** (usu. foll. by *for*) enter as a competitor. **3** *Cricket* take or begin an innings. **4** (of the sun etc.) become obscured by cloud. **go in for** take as one's object, style, pursuit, principle, etc. **going!, gone!** an auctioneer's announcement that bidding is closing or closed. **go into 1** enter (a profession, Parliament, etc.). **2** take part in; be a part of. **3** investigate. **4** allow oneself to pass into (hysterics etc.). **5** dress oneself in (mourning etc.). **6** frequent (society). **go it** *colloq.* **1** act vigorously, furiously, etc. **2** indulge in dissipation. **go it alone** see ALONE. **go it strong** *colloq.* go to great lengths; exaggerate. **go-kart** a miniature racing car with a skeleton body. **go a long way 1** (often foll. by *towards*) have a great effect. **2** (of food, money, etc.) last a long time, buy much. **3** = *go far*. **go off 1** explode. **2** leave the stage. **3** gradually cease to be felt. **4** (esp. of foodstuffs) deteriorate; decompose. **5** go to sleep; become unconscious. **6** begin. **7** die. **8** be got rid of by sale etc. **9** *Brit. colloq.* begin to dislike (*I've gone off him*). **go-off** *colloq.* a start (*at the first go-off*). **go off at** *Austral. & NZ sl.* reprimand, scold. **go off well** (or **badly** etc.) (of an enterprise etc.) be received or accomplished well (or badly etc.). **go on 1** (often foll. by pres. part.) continue, persevere (*decided to go on with it*; *went on trying*; *unable to go on*). **2** *colloq.* **a** talk at great length. **b** (foll. by *at*) admonish (*went on and on at him*). **3** (foll. by *to* + infin.) proceed (*went on to become a star*). **4** happen. **5** conduct oneself (*shameful, the way they went on*). **6** *Theatr.* appear on stage. **7** *Cricket* begin bowling. **8** (of a garment) be large enough for its wearer. **9** take one's turn to do something. **10** (also **go upon**) *colloq.* use as evidence (*police don't have anything to go on*).

11 *colloq.* (esp. in *neg.*) **a** concern oneself about. **b** care for (*don't go much on red hair*). **12** become chargeable to (the parish etc.). **go on!** *colloq.* an expression of encouragement or disbelief. **go out 1** leave a room, house, etc. **2** be broadcast. **3** be extinguished. **4** (often foll. by *with*) be courting. **5** (of a government) leave office. **6** cease to be fashionable. **7** (usu. foll. by *to*) depart, esp. to a colony etc. **8** *colloq.* lose consciousness. **9** (of workers) strike. **10** (usu. foll. by *to*) (of the heart etc.) expand with sympathy etc. towards (*my heart goes out to them*). **11** *Golf* play the first nine holes in a round. **12** *Cards* be the first to dispose of one's hand. **13** (of a tide) turn to low tide. **go over 1** inspect the details of; rehearse; retouch. **2** (often foll. by *to*) change one's allegiance or religion. **3** (of a play etc.) be successful (*went over well in Dundee*). **go round 1** spin, revolve. **2** be long enough to encompass. **3** (of food etc.) suffice for everybody. **4** (usu. foll. by *to*) visit informally. **5** = *go around*. **go slow** work slowly, as a form of industrial action. **go-slow** *Brit.* such industrial action. **go through 1** be dealt with or completed. **2** discuss in detail; scrutinize in sequence. **3** perform (a ceremony, a recitation, etc.). **4** undergo. **5** *colloq.* use up; spend (money etc.). **6** make holes in. **7** (of a book) be successively published (in so many editions). **8** *Austral. sl.* abscond. **go through with** not leave unfinished; complete. **go to!** *archaic* an exclamation of disbelief, impatience, admonition, etc. **go to the bar** become a barrister. **go to blazes** (or **hell** or **Jericho** etc.) *sl.* an exclamation of dismissal, contempt, etc. **go to the country** see COUNTRY. **go together 1** match; fit. **2** be courting. **go to it!** *colloq.* begin work! **go-to-meeting** (of a hat, clothes, etc.) suitable for going to church in. **go to show** (or **prove**) serve to demonstrate (or prove). **go under** sink; fail; succumb. **go up 1** increase in price. **2** *Brit. colloq.* enter university. **3** be consumed (in flames etc.); explode. **go well** (or **ill** etc.) (often foll. by *with*) turn out well, (or ill etc.). **go with 1** be harmonious with; match. **2** agree to; take the same view as. **3 a** be a pair with. **b** be courting. **4** follow the drift of. **go without** manage without; forgo (also *absol.: we shall just have to go without*). **go with the tide** (or **times**) do as others do; follow the drift. **have a go at 1** attack, criticize. **2** attempt, try. **on the go** *colloq.* **1** in constant motion. **2** constantly working. **to go** *US* (of refreshments etc.) to be eaten or drunk off the premises. **who goes there?** a sentry's challenge. [OE *gān* f. Gmc: *went* orig. past of WEND]

go² /gəʊ/ *n.* a Japanese board game of territorial possession and capture. [Jap.]

goad /gəʊd/ *n. & v.* —*n.* **1** a spiked stick used for urging cattle forward. **2** anything that torments, incites, or stimulates. —*v.tr.* **1** urge on with a goad. **2** (usu. foll. by *on, into*) irritate; stimulate (*goaded him into retaliating; goaded me on to win*). [OE *gād*, rel. to Lombard *gaida* arrowhead f. Gmc]

goal /gəʊl/ *n.* **1** the object of a person's ambition or effort; a destination; an aim (*fame is his goal; London was our goal*). **2 a** *Football* a pair of posts with a crossbar between which the ball has to be sent to score. **b** a cage or basket used similarly in other games. **c** a point won (*scored 3 goals*). **3** a point marking the end of a race. □**goal average** *Football* the ratio of the numbers of goals scored for and against a team in a series of matches. **goal difference** *Football* the difference of goals scored for and against. **goal-kick 1** *Assoc. Football* a kick by the defending side after attackers send the ball over the goal-line without scoring. **2** *Rugby Football* an attempt to kick a goal. **goal-line** *Football* a line between each pair of goalposts, extended to form the end-boundary of a field of play (cf. *touch-line*). **goal-minder** (or **-tender**) *US* a goalkeeper at ice hockey. **goal-mouth** *Football* the space between or near the goalposts. **in goal** in the position of

goalkeeper. □□**goalless** *adj.* [16th c.: orig. unkn.: perh. identical with ME *gol* boundary]

goalball /ˈgəʊlbɔːl/ *n.* a team ball game for blind and visually handicapped players.

goalie /ˈgəʊlɪ/ *n. colloq.* = GOALKEEPER.

goalkeeper /ˈgəʊlˌkiːpə(r)/ *n.* a player stationed to protect the goal in various sports.

goalpost /ˈgəʊlpəʊst/ *n.* either of the two upright posts of a goal. □**move the goalposts** alter the basis or scope of a procedure during its course, so as to fit adverse circumstances encountered.

goanna /gəʊˈænə/ *n. Austral.* a monitor lizard. [corrupt. of IGUANA]

goat /gəʊt/ *n.* **1 a** a hardy lively frisky short-haired domesticated mammal, *Capra aegagrus*, having horns and (in the male) a beard, and kept for its milk and meat. **b** either of two similar mammals, the mountain goat and the Spanish goat. **2** any other mammal of the genus *Capra*, including the ibex. **3** a lecherous man. **4** *colloq.* a foolish person. **5** (**the Goat**) the zodiacal sign or constellation Capricorn. **6** *US* a scapegoat. □**get a person's goat** *colloq.* irritate a person. **goat-antelope** any antelope-like member of the goat family, including the chamois and goral. **goat-god** Pan. **goat moth** any of various large moths of the family Cossidae. **goat's-beard 1** a meadow plant, *Tragopogon pratensis*. **2** a herbaceous plant, *Aruncus dioicus*, with long plumes of white flowers. □□**goatish** *adj.* **goaty** *adj.* [OE *gāt* she-goat f. Gmc]

goatee /gəʊˈtiː/ *n.* a small pointed beard like that of a goat.

goatherd /ˈgəʊthɜːd/ *n.* a person who tends goats.

goatskin /ˈgəʊtskɪn/ *n.* **1** the skin of a goat. **2** a garment or bottle made out of goatskin.

goatsucker /ˈgəʊtˌsʌkə(r)/ *n.* = NIGHTJAR.

gob¹ /gɒb/ *n.* esp. *Brit. sl.* the mouth. □**gob-stopper** a very large hard sweet. [perh. f. Gael. & Ir., = beak, mouth]

gob² /gɒb/ *n. & v. Brit. sl.* —*n.* a clot of slimy matter. —*v.intr.* (**gobbed, gobbing**) spit. [ME f. OF *go(u)be* mouthful]

gob³ /gɒb/ *n. sl.* a US sailor. [20th c.: cf. GOBBY]

gobbet /ˈgɒbɪt/ *n.* **1** a piece or lump of raw meat, flesh, food, etc. **2** an extract from a text, esp. one set for translation or comment in an examination. [ME f. OF *gobet* (as GOB²)]

gobble¹ /ˈgɒb(ə)l/ *v.tr. & intr.* eat hurriedly and noisily. □□**gobbler** *n.* [prob. dial. f. GOB²]

gobble² /ˈgɒb(ə)l/ *v.intr.* **1** (of a turkeycock) make a characteristic swallowing sound in the throat. **2** make such a sound when speaking, esp. when excited, angry, etc. [imit.: perh. based on GOBBLE¹]

gobbledegook /ˈgɒb(ə)ldɪˌguːk, -ˌgʊk/ *n.* (also **gobbledygook**) *colloq.* pompous or unintelligible jargon. [prob. imit. of a turkeycock]

gobbler /ˈgɒblə(r)/ *n. colloq.* a turkeycock.

gobby /ˈgɒbɪ/ *n.* (*pl.* **-ies**) *sl.* **1** a coastguard. **2** an American sailor. [perh. f. GOB² + -Y¹]

Gobelin /ˈgəʊbəlɪn, gɔˈblæ̃/ *n.* (in full **Gobelin tapestry**) **1** a tapestry made at the Gobelins factory. **2** a tapestry imitating this. [name of a State factory in Paris, called *Gobelins* after its orig. owners]

gobemouche /ˈgɒbmuːʃ/ *n.* (*pl.* **gobemouches** pronunc. same) a gullible listener. [F *gobe-mouches,* = fly-catcher f. *gober* swallow + *mouches* flies]

goblet /ˈgɒblɪt/ *n.* **1** a drinking-vessel with a foot and a stem, usu. of glass. **2** *archaic* a metal or glass bowl-shaped drinking-cup without handles, sometimes with a foot and a cover. **3** *poet.* a drinking-cup. [ME f. OF *gobelet* dimin. of *gobel* cup, of unkn. orig.]

goblin /ˈgɒblɪn/ *n.* a mischievous ugly dwarflike creature of folklore. [ME prob. f. AF *gobelin,* med.L *gobelinus,* prob. f. name dimin. of *Gobel,* rel. to G *Kobold:* cf. COBALT]

goby /ˈgəʊbɪ/ *n.* (*pl.* **-ies**) any small marine fish of the family Gabiidae, having ventral fins joined to form a sucker or disc. [L *gobius*, *cobius* f. Gk *kōbios* GUDGEON[1]]

GOC *abbr.* General Officer Commanding.

god /gɒd/ *n.* **1 a** (in many religions) a superhuman being or spirit worshipped as having power over nature, human fortunes, etc.; a deity. **b** an image, idol, animal, or other object worshipped as divine or symbolizing a god. **2 (God)** (in Christian and other monotheistic religions) the creator and ruler of the universe; the supreme being. **3 a** an adored, admired, or influential person. **b** something worshipped like a god (*makes a god of success*). **4** *Theatr.* (in *pl.*) **a** the gallery. **b** the people sitting in it. **5 (God!)** an exclamation of surprise, anger, etc. ▫**by God!** an exclamation of surprise etc. **for God's sake!** see SAKE[1]. **God-awful** *sl.* extremely unpleasant, nasty, etc. **God bless** an expression of good wishes on parting. **God bless me** (or **my soul**) see BLESS. **God damn** (you, him, etc.) may (you etc.) be damned. **god-damn** (or **-dam** or **-damned**) *sl.* accursed, damnable. **god-daughter** a female godchild. **God the Father, Son, and Holy Ghost** (in the Christian tradition) the Persons of the Trinity. **God-fearing** earnestly religious. **God forbid** (foll. by *that* + clause, or *absol.*) may it not happen! **God-forsaken** devoid of all merit; dismal; dreary. **God grant** (foll. by *that* + clause) may it happen. **God help (you, him,** etc.) an expression of concern for or sympathy with a person. **God knows 1** it is beyond all knowledge (*God knows what will become of him*). **2** I call God to witness that (*God knows we tried hard enough*). **God's Acre** a churchyard. **God's book** the Bible. **God's gift** often *iron.* a godsend. **God's own country** an earthly paradise, esp. the United States. **God squad** *sl.* **1** a religious organization, esp. an evangelical Christian group. **2** its members. **God's truth** the absolute truth. **God willing** if Providence allows. **good God!** an exclamation of surprise, anger, etc. **in God's name** an appeal for help. **my** (or **oh**) **God!** an exclamation of surprise, anger, etc. **play God** assume importance or superiority. **thank God!** an exclamation of pleasure or relief. **with God** dead and in Heaven. ▫▫ **godhood** *n.* **godship** *n.* **godward** *adj.* & *adv.* **godwards** *adv.* [OE f. Gmc]

godchild /ˈgɒdtʃaɪld/ *n.* a person in relation to a godparent.

goddess /ˈgɒdɪs/ *n.* **1** a female deity. **2** a woman who is adored, esp. for her beauty.

godet /ˈgəʊdeɪ/ *n.* a triangular piece of material inserted in a dress, glove, etc. [F]

godetia /gəˈdiːʃə/ *n.* any plant of the genus *Godetia*, having showy rose-purple or reddish flowers. [mod.L f. C. H. *Godet*, Swiss botanist d. 1879]

godfather /ˈgɒdˌfɑːðə(r)/ *n.* **1** a male godparent. **2** esp. *US* a person directing an illegal organization, esp. the Mafia. ▫**my godfathers!** *euphem.* my God!

godhead /ˈgɒdhed/ *n.* (also **Godhead**) **1 a** the state of being God or a god. **b** divine nature. **2** a deity. **3 (the Godhead)** God.

godless /ˈgɒdlɪs/ *adj.* **1** impious; wicked. **2** without a god. **3** not recognizing God. ▫▫ **godlessness** *n.*

godlike /ˈgɒdlaɪk/ *adj.* **1** resembling God or a god in some quality, esp. in physical beauty. **2** befitting or appropriate to a god.

godly /ˈgɒdlɪ/ *adj.* religious, pious, devout. ▫▫ **godliness** *n.*

godmother /ˈgɒdˌmʌðə(r)/ *n.* a female godparent.

godown /gəʊˈdaʊn/ *n.* a warehouse in parts of E. Asia, esp. in India. [Port. *gudão* f. Malay *godong* perh. f. Telugu *gidaṅgi* place where goods lie f. *kidu* lie]

godparent /ˈgɒdˌpeərənt/ *n.* a person who presents a child at baptism and responds on the child's behalf.

godsend /ˈgɒdsend/ *n.* an unexpected but welcome event or acquisition.

godson /ˈgɒdsʌn/ *n.* a male godchild.

Godspeed /gɒdˈspiːd/ *int.* an expression of good wishes to a person starting a journey.

godwit /ˈgɒdwɪt/ *n.* any wading bird of the genus *Limosa*, with long legs and a long straight or slightly upcurved bill. [16th c.: of unkn. orig.]

Godwottery /gɒdˈwɒtərɪ/ *n. joc.* affected, archaic, or excessively elaborate speech or writing, esp. regarding gardens. [*God wot* (in a poem on gardens, by T. E. Brown 1876)]

goer /ˈgəʊə(r)/ *n.* **1** a person or thing that goes (*a slow goer*). **2** (often in *comb.*) a person who attends, esp. regularly (*a churchgoer*). **3** *colloq.* **a** a lively or persevering person. **b** a sexually promiscuous person. **4** *Austral. colloq.* a project likely to be accepted or to succeed.

goes *3rd sing. present* of GO[1].

goest /ˈgəʊɪst/ *archaic 2nd sing. present* of GO[1].

goeth /ˈgəʊɪθ/ *archaic 3rd sing. present* of GO[1].

Goethean /ˈgɜːtɪən/ *adj.* & *n.* (also **Goethian**) —*adj.* of, relating to, or characteristic of the German writer J. W. von Goethe (d. 1832). —*n.* an admirer or follower of Goethe.

gofer /ˈgəʊfə(r)/ *n.* esp. *US sl.* a person who runs errands, esp. on a film set or in an office; a dogsbody. [*go for* (see GO[1])]

goffer /ˈgəʊfə(r), ˈgɒf-/ *v.* & *n.* —*v.tr.* **1** make wavy, flute, or crimp (a lace edge, a trimming, etc.) with heated irons. **2** (as **goffered** *adj.*) (of the edges of a book) embossed. —*n.* **1** an iron used for goffering. **2** ornamental plaiting used for frills etc. [F *gaufrer* stamp with a patterned tool f. *gaufre* honeycomb, rel. to WAFER, WAFFLE[2]]

goggle /ˈgɒg(ə)l/ *v.*, *adj.*, & *n.* —*v.* **1** *intr.* **a** (often foll. by *at*) look with wide-open eyes. **b** (of the eyes) be rolled about; protrude. **2** *tr.* turn (the eyes) sideways or from side to side. —*adj.* (usu. *attrib.*) (of the eyes) protuberant or rolling. —*n.* **1** (in *pl.*) **a** spectacles for protecting the eyes from glare, dust, water, etc. **b** *colloq.* spectacles. **2** (in *pl.*) a sheep disease, the staggers. **3** a goggling expression. ▫ **goggle-box** *Brit. colloq.* a television set. **goggle-dive** an underwater dive in goggles. **goggle-eyed** having staring or protuberant eyes. [ME, prob. from a base *gog* (unrecorded) expressive of oscillating movement]

goglet /ˈgɒglɪt/ *n. Ind.* a long-necked usu. porous earthenware vessel used for keeping water cool. [Port. *gorgoleta*]

Goidel /ˈgɔɪd(ə)l/ *n.* a Celt who speaks Irish Gaelic, Scottish Gaelic, or Manx. ▫▫ **Goidelic** /-ˈdelɪk/ *n.* [OIr. *Góidel*]

going /ˈgəʊɪŋ/ *n.* & *adj.* —*n.* **1 a** the act or process of going. **b** an instance of this; a departure. **2 a** the condition of the ground for walking, riding, etc. **b** progress affected by this (*found the going hard*). —*adj.* **1** in or into action (*set the clock going*). **2** existing, available; to be had (*there's cold beef going*; *one of the best fellows going*). **3** current, prevalent (*the going rate*). ▫**get going** start steadily talking, working, etc. (*can't stop him when he gets going*). **going away** a departure, esp. on a honeymoon. **going concern** a thriving business. **going for one** *colloq.* acting in one's favour (*he has got a lot going for him*). **going on fifteen** etc. esp. *US* approaching one's fifteenth etc. birthday. **going on for** approaching (a time, an age, etc.) (*must be going on for 6 years*). **going-over 1** *colloq.* an inspection or overhaul. **2** *sl.* a thrashing. **3** *US colloq.* a scolding. **goings-on** /ˌgəʊɪŋzˈɒn/ behaviour, esp. morally suspect. **going to** intending or intended to; about to; likely to (*it's going to sink!*). **heavy going** slow or difficult to progress with (*found Proust heavy going*). **to be going on with** to start with; for the time being. **while the going is good** while conditions are favourable. [GO[1]: in some senses f. earlier *a-going*: see A[2]]

goitre /ˈgɔɪtə(r)/ *n.* (*US* **goiter**) *Med.* a swelling of the neck resulting from enlargement of the thyroid gland. ▫▫ **goitred** *adj.* **goitrous** *adj.* [F, back-form. f. *goitreux* or f. Prov. *goitron*, ult. f. L *guttur* throat]

Golconda /gɒl'kɒndə/ *n.* a mine or source of wealth, advantages, etc. [city near Hyderabad, India]

gold /gəʊld/ *n.* & *adj.* —*n.* **1** a yellow malleable ductile high density metallic element resistant to chemical reaction, occurring naturally in quartz veins and gravel, and precious as a monetary medium, in jewellery, etc. ¶ Symb.: **Au.** **2** the colour of gold. **3 a** coins or articles made of gold. **b** money in large sums, wealth. **4** something precious, beautiful, or brilliant (*all that glitters is not gold*). **5** = *gold medal.* **6** gold used for coating a surface or as a pigment, gilding. **7** the bull's-eye of an archery target (usu. gilt). —*adj.* **1** made wholly or chiefly of gold. **2** coloured like gold. □**age of gold** = *golden age.* **gold amalgam** an easily-moulded combination of gold with mercury. **gold-beater** a person who beats gold out into gold leaf. **gold-beater's skin** a membrane used to separate leaves of gold during beating, or as a covering for slight wounds. **gold bloc** a bloc of countries having a gold standard. **gold brick** *sl.* **1** a thing with only a surface appearance of value, a sham or fraud. **2** *US* a lazy person. **gold-digger 1** *sl.* a woman who wheedles money out of men. **2** a person who digs for gold. **gold-dust 1** gold in fine particles as often found naturally. **2** a plant, *Alyssum saxatile*, with many small yellow flowers. **gold-field** a district in which gold is found as a mineral. **gold foil** gold beaten into a thin sheet. **gold leaf** gold beaten into a very thin sheet. **gold medal** a medal of gold, usu. awarded as first prize. **gold-mine 1** a place where gold is mined. **2** *colloq.* a source of wealth. **gold of pleasure** an annual yellow-flowered plant, *Camelina sativa.* **gold plate 1** vessels made of gold. **2** material plated with gold. **gold-plate** *v.tr.* plate with gold. **gold reserve** a reserve of gold coins or bullion held by a central bank etc. **gold-rush** a rush to a newly-discovered gold-field. **gold standard** a system by which the value of a currency is defined in terms of gold, for which the currency may be exchanged. **Gold Stick 1** (in the UK) a gilt rod carried on State occasions by the colonel of the Life Guards or the captain of the gentlemen-at-arms. **2** the officer carrying this rod. **gold thread 1** a thread of silk etc. with gold wire wound round it. **2** a bitter plant, *Coptis tinfolia.* [OE f. Gmc]

goldcrest /'gəʊldkrest/ *n.* a small bird, *Regulus regulus*, with a golden crest.

golden /'gəʊld(ə)n/ *adj.* **1 a** made or consisting of gold (*golden sovereign*). **b** yielding gold. **2** coloured or shining like gold (*golden hair*). **3** precious; valuable; excellent; important (*a golden memory*; *a golden opportunity*). □**golden age** a supposed past age when people were happy and innocent. **2** the period of a nation's greatest prosperity, literary merit, etc. **golden-ager** *US* an old person. **golden balls** a pawnbroker's sign. **golden boy** (or **girl**) *colloq.* a popular or successful person. **golden calf** wealth as an object of worship (Exod. 32). **golden chain** the laburnum. **golden delicious** a variety of dessert apple. **golden disc** an award given to a performer after the sale of 500,000 copies of a record. **golden eagle** a large eagle, *Aquila chrysaetos*, with yellow-tipped head-feathers. **golden-eye** any marine duck of the genus *Bucephala.* **Golden Fleece** (in Greek mythology) a fleece of gold sought and won by Jason. **golden goose** a continuing source of wealth or profit. **golden hamster** a usu. tawny hamster, *Mesocricetus auratus*, kept as a pet or laboratory animal. **golden handshake** *colloq.* a payment given on redundancy or early retirement. **golden hello** *colloq.* a payment made by an employer to a keenly sought recruit. **Golden Horde** the Tartar horde that overran E. Europe in the 13th c. (from the richness of the leader's tent). **Golden Horn** the harbour of Istanbul. **golden jubilee 1** the fiftieth anniversary of a sovereign's accession. **2** any other fiftieth anniversary. **golden mean 1** the principle

of moderation, as opposed to excess. **2** = *golden section.* **golden number** the number of a year in the Metonic lunar cycle, used to fix the date of Easter. **golden oldie** *colloq.* an old hit record or film etc. that is still well known and popular. **golden opinions** high regard. **golden oriole** a European oriole, *Oriolus oriolus*, of which the male has yellow and black plumage and the female has mainly green plumage. **golden perch** *Austral.* = CALLOP. **golden retriever** a retriever with a thick golden-coloured coat. **golden rod** any plant of the genus *Solidago* with a rodlike stem and a spike of small bright-yellow flowers. **golden rule** a basic principle of action, esp. 'do as you would be done by'. **golden section** the division of a line so that the whole is to the greater part as that part is to the smaller part. **Golden State** *US* California. **golden syrup** *Brit.* a pale treacle. **golden wedding** the fiftieth anniversary of a wedding. □□**goldenly** *adv.* **goldenness** *n.*

goldfinch /'gəʊldfɪntʃ/ *n.* any of various bright-coloured songbirds of the genus *Carduelis*, esp. the Eurasian *C. carduelis*, with a yellow band across each wing. [OE *goldfinc* (as GOLD, FINCH)]

goldfish /'gəʊldfɪʃ/ *n.* a small reddish-golden Chinese carp kept for ornament, *Carassius auratus.* □**goldfish bowl 1** a globular glass container for goldfish. **2** a situation lacking privacy.

goldilocks /'gəʊldɪˌlɒks/ *n.* **1** a person with golden hair. **2 a** a kind of buttercup, *Ranunculus auricomus.* **b** a composite plant, *Aster linosyris*, like the golden rod. [*goldy* f. GOLD + LOCK²]

goldsmith /'gəʊldsmɪθ/ *n.* a worker in gold, a manufacturer of gold articles. [OE (as GOLD, SMITH)]

golem /'gəʊləm/ *n.* **1** a clay figure supposedly brought to life in Jewish legend. **2** an automaton; a robot. [Yiddish *goylem* f. Heb. *gōlem* shapeless mass]

golf /gɒlf/ *n.* & *v.* —*n.* a game played on a course set in open country, in which a small hard ball is driven with clubs into a series of 18 or 9 holes with the fewest possible strokes. —*v.intr.* play golf. □**golf-bag** a bag used for carrying clubs and balls. **golf ball 1** a ball used in golf. **2** *colloq.* a small ball used in some electric typewriters to carry the type. **golf cart 1** a trolley used for carrying clubs in golf. **2** a motorized cart for golfers and equipment. **golf club 1** a club used in golf. **2** an association for playing golf. **3** the premises used by a golf club. **golf-course** (or **-links**) the course on which golf is played. [15th-c. Sc.: orig. unkn.]

golfer /'gɒlfə(r)/ *n.* **1** a golf-player. **2** a cardigan.

Golgi body /'gɒldʒɪ/ *n.* (also **Golgi apparatus**) *Biol.* an organelle of vesicles and folded membranes within the cytoplasm of most eukaryotic cells, involved esp. in the secretion of substances. [C. *Golgi*, It. cytologist d. 1926]

Goliath beetle /gə'laɪəθ/ *n.* any large beetle of the genus *Goliathus*, esp. *G. giganteus* native to Africa. [LL f. Heb. *golyat* giant slain by David (1 Sam. 17)]

golliwog /'gɒlɪ,wɒg/ *n.* a black-faced brightly dressed soft doll with fuzzy hair. [19th c.: perh. f. GOLLY¹ + POLLIWOG]

gollop /'gɒləp/ *v.* & *n.* *colloq.* —*v.tr.* (**golloped**, **golloping**) swallow hastily or greedily. —*n.* a hasty gulp. [perh. f. GULP, infl. by GOBBLE¹]

golly¹ /'gɒlɪ/ *int.* expressing surprise. [euphem. for GOD]

golly² /'gɒlɪ/ *n.* (*pl.* **-ies**) *colloq.* = GOLLIWOG. [abbr.]

golosh *Brit.* var. of GALOSH.

GOM *abbr.* Grand Old Man (name orig. applied to W. E. Gladstone).

gombeen /gɒm'biːn/ *n.* *Ir.* usury. □**gombeen-man** a moneylender. [Ir. *gaimbín* perh. f. the same OCelt. source as med.L *cambire* CHANGE]

-gon /gən/ *comb. form* forming nouns denoting plane figures with a specified number of angles (*hexagon*; *polygon*; *n-gon*). [Gk *-gōnos* -angled]

gonad /'gəʊnæd/ *n.* an animal organ producing gametes, e.g. the testis or ovary. □□**gonadal** /gəʊ'neɪd(ə)l/

adj. [mod.L *gonas gonad-* f. Gk *gonē, gonos* generation, seed]

gonadotrophic hormone /ˌgəʊnədəʊˈtrəʊfɪk/ *n.* (also **gonadotropic** /-ˈtrɒpɪk, -ˈtrəʊpɪk/) *Biochem.* any of various hormones stimulating the activity of the gonads.

gonadotrophin /ˌgəʊnədəʊˈtrəʊfɪn/ *n.* = GONADO- TROPHIC HORMONE.

gondola /ˈgɒndələ/ *n.* **1** a light flat-bottomed boat used on Venetian canals, with a central cabin and a high point at each end, worked by one oar at the stern. **2** a car suspended from an airship or balloon. **3** an island of shelves used to display goods in a supermarket. **4** (also **gondola car**) *US* a flat-bottomed open railway goods wagon. **5** a car attached to a ski-lift. [Venetian It., of obscure orig.]

gondolier /ˌgɒndəˈlɪə(r)/ *n.* the oarsman on a gondola. [F f. It. *gondoliere* (as GONDOLA)]

gone /gɒn/ *adj.* **1** (of time) past (*not until gone nine*). **2 a** lost; hopeless. **b** dead. **3** *colloq.* pregnant for a specified time (*already three months gone*). **4** *sl.* completely enthralled or entranced, esp. by rhythmic music, drugs, etc. □**be gone** depart; leave temporarily (cf. BEGONE). **gone away!** a huntsman's cry, indicating that a fox has been started. **gone goose** (or **gosling**) *colloq.* a person or thing beyond hope. **gone on** *sl.* infatuated with. [past part. of GO¹]

goner /ˈgɒnə(r)/ *n. sl.* a person or thing that is doomed, ended, irrevocably lost, etc.; a dead person.

gonfalon /ˈgɒnfələn/ *n.* **1** a banner, often with streamers, hung from a crossbar. **2** *hist.* such a banner as the standard of some Italian republics. □□ **gonfalonier** /ˌgɒnfələˈnɪə(r)/ *n.* [It. *gonfalone* f. Gmc (cf. VANE)]

gong /gɒŋ/ *n. & v.* —*n.* **1** a metal disc with a turned rim, giving a resonant note when struck. **2** a saucer-shaped bell. **3** *Brit. sl.* a medal; a decoration. —*v.tr.* **1** summon with a gong. **2** (of traffic police) sound a gong etc. to direct (a motorist) to stop. [Malay *gong, gung* of imit. orig.]

goniometer /ˌgəʊnɪˈɒmɪtə(r)/ *n.* an instrument for measuring angles. □□ **goniometry** *n.* **goniometric** /-əˈmetrɪk/ *adj.* **goniometrical** /-əˈmetrɪk(ə)l/ *adj.* [F *goniomètre* f. Gk *gōnia* angle]

gonococcus /ˌgɒnəˈkɒkəs/ *n.* (*pl.* **gonococci** /-kaɪ/) a bacterium causing gonorrhoea. □□ **gonococcal** *adj.* [Gk *gonos* generation, semen + COCCUS]

gonorrhoea /ˌgɒnəˈrɪə/ *n.* (*US* **gonorrhea**) a venereal disease with inflammatory discharge from the urethra or vagina. □□ **gonorrhoeal** *adj.* [LL f. Gk *gonorrhoia* f. *gonos* semen + *rhoia* flux]

goo /guː/ *n.* **1** a sticky or slimy substance. **2** sickly sentiment. [20th c.: perh. f. *burgoo* (Naut. sl.) = porridge]

good /gʊd/ *adj., n., & adv.* —*adj.* (**better, best**) **1** having the right or desired qualities; satisfactory, adequate. **2 a** (of a person) efficient, competent (*good at French; a good driver*). **b** (of a thing) reliable, efficient (*good brakes*). **c** (of health etc.) strong (*good eyesight*). **3 a** kind, benevolent (*good of you to come*). **b** morally excellent; virtuous (*a good deed*). **c** charitable (*good works*). **d** well-behaved (*a good child*). **4** enjoyable, agreeable (*a good party; good news*). **5** thorough, considerable (*gave it a good wash*). **6 a** not less than (*waited a good hour*). **b** considerable in number, quality, etc. (*a good many people*). **7** healthy, beneficial (*milk is good for you*). **8 a** valid, sound (*a good reason*). **b** financially sound (*his credit is good*). **9** in exclamations of surprise (*good heavens!*). **10** right, proper, expedient (*thought it good to have a try*). **11** fresh, eatable, untainted (*is the meat still good?*). **12** (sometimes patronizing) commendable, worthy (*good old George; your good lady wife; good men and true; my good man*). **13** well shaped, attractive (*has good legs; good looks*). **14** in courteous greetings and farewells (*good afternoon*). —*n.* **1** (only in *sing.*) that which is good; what is beneficial or morally right (*only good can come of it;*

did it for your own good; what good will it do?). **2** (only in *sing.*) a desirable end or object; a thing worth attaining (*sacrificing the present for a future good*). **3** (in *pl.*) **a** movable property or merchandise. **b** *Brit.* things to be transported, as distinct from passengers. **c** (prec. by *the*) *colloq.* what one has undertaken to supply (esp. *deliver the goods*). **d** (prec. by *the*) *sl.* the real thing; the genuine article. **4** (as *pl.*; prec. by *the*) virtuous people. —*adv. US colloq.* well (*doing pretty good*). □**as good as** practically (*he as good as told me*). **be so good as** (or **be good enough) to** (often in a request) be kind and do (a favour) (*be so good as to open the window*). **be (a certain amount) to the good** have as net profit or advantage. **do good** show kindness, act philanthropically. **do a person good** be beneficial to. **for good (and all)** finally, permanently. **good and** *colloq.* used as an intensifier before an adj. or adv. (*raining good and hard; was good and angry*). **the good book** the Bible. **good breeding** correct or courteous manners. **good faith** see FAITH. **good for 1** beneficial to; having a good effect on. **2** able to perform; inclined for (*good for a ten-mile walk*). **3** able to be trusted to pay (*is good for £100*). **good form** see FORM. **good-for-nothing** (or **-nought**) *adj.* worthless. —*n.* a worthless person. **good for you!** (or **him!, her!,** etc.) exclamation of approval towards a person. **Good Friday** the Friday before Easter Sunday commemorating the Crucifixion of Christ. **good-hearted** kindly, well-meaning. **good humour** a genial mood. **a good job** a fortunate state of affairs (*it's a good job you came early*). **good-looker** a handsome or attractive person. **good-looking** handsome; attractive. **good luck 1** good fortune, happy chance. **2** exclamation of well-wishing. **good money 1** genuine money; money that might usefully have been spent elsewhere. **2** *colloq.* high wages. **good nature** a friendly disposition. **good oil** *Austral. sl.* reliable information. **good on you!** (or **him!** etc.) = *good for you!* **goods and chattels** see CHATTEL. **good-time** recklessly pursuing pleasure. **good-timer** a person who recklessly pursues pleasure. **good times** a period of prosperity. **good will** the intention and hope that good will result (see also GOODWILL). **a good word** (often in phr. **put in a good word for**) words in recommendation or defence of a person. **good works** charitable acts. **have a good mind** see MIND. **have the goods on a person** *sl.* have advantageous information about a person. **have a good time** enjoy oneself. **in a person's good books** see BOOK. **in good faith** with honest or sincere intentions. **in good time 1** with no risk of being late. **2** (also **all in good time**) in due course but without haste. **make good 1** make up for, compensate for, pay (an expense). **2** fulfil (a promise); effect (a purpose or an intended action). **3** demonstrate the truth of (a statement); substantiate (a charge). **4** gain and hold (a position). **5** replace or restore (a thing lost or damaged). **6** (*absol.*) accomplish what one intended. **no good 1** mischief (*is up to no good*). **2** useless; to no advantage (*it is no good arguing*). **no-good** —*adj.* useless. —*n.* a useless thing or person. **take in good part** not be offended by. **to the good** having as profit or benefit. □□ **goodish** *adj.* [OE *gōd* f. Gmc]

goodbye /gʊdˈbaɪ/ *int. & n.* (*US* **goodby**) —*int.* expressing good wishes on parting, ending a telephone conversation, etc., or said with reference to a thing got rid of or irrevocably lost. —*n.* (*pl.* **goodbyes** or *US* **goodbys**) the saying of 'goodbye'; a parting; a farewell. [contr. of *God be with you!* with *good* substituted after *good night* etc.]

good-humoured /gʊdˈhjuːməd/ *adj.* genial, cheerful, amiable. □□ **good-humouredly** *adv.*

goodie var. of GOODY¹ *n.*

goodly /ˈgʊdlɪ/ *adj.* (**goodlier, goodliest**) **1** comely, handsome. **2** of imposing size etc. □□ **goodliness** *n.* [OE *gōdlic* (as GOOD, -LY¹)]

goodman /'gʊdmən/ n. (pl. **-men**) Sc. archaic the head of a household.

good-natured /gʊd'neɪtʃəd/ adj. kind, patient; easygoing. □□ **good-naturedly** adv.

goodness /'gʊdnɪs/ n. & int. —n. **1** virtue; excellence, esp. moral. **2** kindness, generosity (had the goodness to wait). **3** what is good or beneficial in a thing (vegetables with all the goodness boiled out). —int. (as a substitution for 'God') expressing surprise, anger, etc. (goodness me!; goodness knows; for goodness' sake!). [OE gōdnes (as GOOD, -NESS)]

goodo /'gʊdəʊ/ adj. Austral. & NZ = GOOD adj. 10.

good-tempered /gʊd'tempəd/ adj. having a good temper; not easily annoyed. □□ **good-temperedly** adv.

goodwife /'gʊdwaɪf/ n. (pl. **-wives**) Sc. archaic the mistress of a household.

goodwill /gʊd'wɪl/ n. **1** kindly feeling. **2** the established reputation of a business etc. as enhancing its value. **3** cheerful consent or acquiescence; readiness, zeal.

goody[1] /'gʊdɪ/ n. & int. —n. (also **goodie**) (pl. **-ies**) **1** colloq. a good or favoured person, esp. a hero in a story, film, etc. **2** (usu. in pl.) something good or attractive, esp. to eat. **3** = GOODY-GOODY n. —int. expressing childish delight.

goody[2] /'gʊdɪ/ n. (pl. **goodies**) archaic (often as a title prefixed to a surname) an elderly woman of humble station (Goody Blake). [for GOODWIFE: cf. HUSSY]

goody-goody /'gʊdɪ,gʊdɪ/ n. & adj. colloq. —n. a smug or obtrusively virtuous person. —adj. obtrusively or smugly virtuous.

gooey /'gu:ɪ/ adj. (**gooier**, **gooiest**) sl. **1** viscous, sticky. **2** sickly, sentimental. □□ **gooeyness** n. (also **gooiness**). [GOO + -Y[2]]

goof /gu:f/ n. & v. sl. —n. **1** a foolish or stupid person. **2** a mistake. —v. **1** tr. bungle, mess up. **2** intr. blunder, make a mistake. **3** intr. (often foll. by off) idle. **4** tr. (as **goofed** adj.) stupefied with drugs. [var. of dial. goff f. F goffe f. It. goffo f. med.L gufus coarse]

goofy /'gu:fɪ/ adj. (**goofier**, **goofiest**) **1** stupid, silly, daft. **2** having protruding or crooked front teeth. □□ **goofily** adv. **goofiness** n.

goog /gʊg/ n. Austral. sl. an egg. □ **full as a goog** very drunk. [20th c.: orig. unkn.]

googly /'gu:glɪ/ n. (pl. **-ies**) Cricket an off-break ball bowled with apparent leg-break action. [20th c.: orig. unkn.]

googol /'gu:gɒl/ n. ten raised to the hundredth power (10[100]). ¶ Not in formal use. [arbitrary formation]

gook /gu:k, gʊk/ n. US sl. offens. a foreigner, esp. a coloured person from E. Asia. [20th c.: orig. unkn.]

goolie /'gu:lɪ/ n. (also **gooly**) (pl. **-ies**) **1** (usu. in pl.) sl. a testicle. **2** Austral. sl. a stone or pebble. [app. of Ind. orig.; cf. Hind. golī bullet, ball, pill]

goon /gu:n/ n. sl. **1** a stupid or playful person. **2** esp. US a person hired by racketeers etc. to terrorize political or industrial opponents. [perh. f. dial. gooney booby: infl. by the subhuman cartoon character 'Alice the Goon']

goop /gu:p/ n. sl. a stupid or fatuous person. [20th c.: cf. GOOF]

goopy /'gu:pɪ/ adj. sl. (**goopier**, **goopiest**) stupid, fatuous. □□ **goopiness** n.

goosander /gu:'sændə(r)/ n. a large diving duck, Mergus merganser, with a narrow serrated bill. [prob. f. GOOSE + -ander in bergander sheldrake]

goose /gu:s/ n. & v. —n. (pl. **geese** /gi:s/) **1 a** any of various large water-birds of the family Anatidae, with short legs, webbed feet, and a broad bill. **b** the female of this (opp. GANDER). **c** the flesh of a goose as food. **2** colloq. a simpleton. **3** (pl. **gooses**) a tailor's smoothing-iron, having a handle like a goose's neck. —v.tr. sl. poke (a person) in the bottom. □ **goose bumps** US = goose-flesh. **goose-egg** US a zero score in a game. **goose-flesh** (or **-pimples** or **-skin**) a bristling state of the skin produced by cold or fright.

goose-step a military marching step in which the knees are kept stiff. [OE gōs f. Gmc]

gooseberry /'gʊzbərɪ/ n. (pl. **-ies**) **1** a round edible yellowish-green berry with a thin usu. translucent skin enclosing seeds in a juicy flesh. **2** the thorny shrub, Ribes grossularia, bearing this fruit. □ **play gooseberry** Brit. colloq. be an unwanted extra (usu. third) person. [perh. f. GOOSE + BERRY]

goosefoot /'gu:sfʊt/ n. (pl. **-foots**) any plant of the genus Chenopodium, having leaves shaped like the foot of a goose.

goosegog /'gʊzgɒg/ n. Brit. colloq. a gooseberry. [joc. corrupt.]

goosegrass /'gu:sgrɑ:s/ n. cleavers.

GOP abbr. US Grand Old Party (the Republican Party).

gopher[1] /'gəʊfə(r)/ n. **1** (in full **pocket gopher**) any burrowing rodent of the family Geomyidae, native to N. America, having external cheek pouches and sharp front teeth. **2** a N. American ground squirrel. **3** a tortoise, Gopherus polyphemus, native to the southern US, that excavates tunnels as shelter from the sun. □ **gopher snake** a cribo. [18th c.: orig. uncert.]

gopher[2] /'gəʊfə(r)/ n. **1** Bibl. a tree from the wood of which Noah's ark was made. **2** (in full **gopher-wood**) a tree, Cladrastis lutea, yielding yellowish timber. [Heb. gōper]

goral /'gɔ:r(ə)l/ n. a goat-antelope, Nemorhaedus goral, native to mountainous regions of N. India, having short horns curving to the rear. [native name]

gorblimey /gɔ:'blaɪmɪ/ int. & n. Brit. colloq. —int. an expression of surprise, indignation, etc. —n. (pl. **-eys**) a soft service cap. [corrupt. of God blind me]

gorcock /'gɔ:kɒk/ n. Sc. & N.Engl. the male of the red grouse. [gor- (of unkn. orig.) + COCK[1]]

Gordian knot /'gɔ:dɪən/ n. **1** an intricate knot. **2** a difficult problem or task. □ **cut the Gordian knot** solve a problem by force or by evasion. [Gordius, king of Phrygia, who tied an intricate knot that remained tied until cut by Alexander the Great]

Gordon setter /'gɔ:d(ə)n/ n. **1** a setter of a black and tan breed, used as a gun dog. **2** this breed. [4th Duke of Gordon, d. 1827, promoter of the breed]

gore[1] /gɔ:(r)/ n. blood shed and clotted. [OE gor dung, dirt]

gore[2] /gɔ:(r)/ v.tr. pierce with a horn, tusk, etc. [ME: orig. unkn.]

gore[3] /gɔ:(r)/ n. & v. —n. **1** a wedge-shaped piece in a garment. **2** a triangular or tapering piece in an umbrella etc. —v.tr. shape with a gore. [OE gāra triangular piece of land, rel. to OE gār spear, a spearhead being triangular]

gorge /gɔ:dʒ/ n. & v. —n. **1** a narrow opening between hills or a rocky ravine, often with a stream running through it. **2** an act of gorging; a feast. **3** the contents of the stomach; what has been swallowed. **4** the neck of a bastion or other outwork; the rear entrance to a work. **5** US a mass of ice etc. blocking a narrow passage. —v. **1** intr. feed greedily. **2** tr. **a** (often refl.) satiate, glut. **b** swallow, devour greedily. □ **cast the gorge at** reject with loathing. **one's gorge rises at** one is sickened by. □□ **gorger** n. [ME f. OF gorge throat ult. f. L gurges whirlpool]

gorgeous /'gɔ:dʒəs/ adj. **1** richly coloured, sumptuous, magnificent. **2** colloq. very pleasant, splendid (gorgeous weather). **3** colloq. strikingly beautiful. □□ **gorgeously** adv. **gorgeousness** n. [earlier gorgayse, -yas f. OF gorgias fine, elegant, of unkn. orig.]

gorget /'gɔ:gɪt/ n. **1** hist. **a** a piece of armour for the throat. **b** a woman's wimple. **2** a patch of colour on the throat of a bird, insect, etc. [OF gorgete (as GORGE)]

Gorgio /'gɔ:dʒɪəʊ/ n. (pl. **-os**) the Gypsy name for a non-Gypsy. [Romany]

gorgon /'gɔ:gən/ n. **1** (in Greek mythology) each of three snake-haired sisters (esp. Medusa) with the power to turn anyone who looked at them to stone.

2 a frightening or repulsive person, esp. a woman. □□ **gorgonian** /gɔːˈgəʊnɪən/ *adj.* [L *Gorgo -onis* f. Gk *Gorgō* f. *gorgos* terrible]

gorgonian /gɔːˈgəʊnɪən/ *n. & adj.* —*n.* a usu. brightly coloured horny coral of the order Gorgonacea, having a treelike skeleton bearing polyps, e.g. a sea fan. —*adj.* of or relating to the Gorgonacea. [mod.L (as GORGON), with ref. to its petrifaction]

gorgonize /ˈgɔːgəˌnaɪz/ *v.tr.* (also -**ise**) **1** stare at like a gorgon. **2** paralyse with terror etc.

Gorgonzola /ˌgɔːgənˈzəʊlə/ *n.* a type of rich cheese with bluish-green veins. [*Gorgonzola* in Italy]

gorilla /gəˈrɪlə/ *n.* the largest anthropoid ape, *Gorilla gorilla*, native to Central Africa, having a large head, short neck, and prominent mouth. [adopted as the specific name in 1847 f. Gk *Gorillai* an African tribe noted for hairiness]

gormandize /ˈgɔːmənˌdaɪz/ *v. & n.* (also -**ise**) —*v.* **1** *intr. & tr.* eat or devour voraciously. **2** *intr.* indulge in good eating. —*n.* = GOURMANDISE. □□ **gormandizer** *n.* [as GOURMANDISE]

gormless /ˈgɔːmlɪs/ *adj.* esp. *Brit. colloq.* foolish, lacking sense. □□ **gormlessly** *adv.* **gormlessness** *n.* [orig. *gaumless* f. dial. *gaum* understanding]

gorse /gɔːs/ *n.* any spiny yellow-flowered shrub of the genus *Ulex*, esp. growing on European wastelands. Also called FURZE. □□ **gorsy** *adj.* [OE *gors(t)* rel. to OHG *gersta*, L *hordeum*, barley]

Gorsedd /ˈgɔːseð/ *n.* a meeting of Welsh etc. bards and druids (esp. as a daily preliminary to the eisteddfod). [Welsh, lit. 'throne']

gory /ˈgɔːrɪ/ *adj.* (**gorier, goriest**) **1** involving bloodshed; bloodthirsty (*a gory film*). **2** covered in gore. □□ **gorily** *adv.* **goriness** *n.*

gosh /gɒʃ/ *int.* expressing surprise. [euphem. for GOD]

goshawk /ˈgɒshɔːk/ *n.* a large short-winged hawk, *Accipiter gentilis*. [OE *gōs-hafoc* (as GOOSE, HAWK[1])]

gosling /ˈgɒzlɪŋ/ *n.* a young goose. [ME, orig. *gesling* f. ON *gæslingr*]

gospel /ˈgɒsp(ə)l/ *n.* **1** the teaching or revelation of Christ. **2** (**Gospel**) **a** the record of Christ's life and teaching in the first four books of the New Testament. **b** each of these books. **c** a portion from one of them read at a service. **3** a thing regarded as absolutely true (*take my word as gospel*). **4** a principle one acts on or advocates. **5** (in full **gospel music**) Black American evangelical religious singing. □ **Gospel side** the north side of the altar, at which the Gospel is read. **gospel truth** something as true as the Gospel. [OE *gōdspel* (as GOOD, *spel* news, SPELL[1]), rendering eccl.L *bona annuntiatio, bonus nuntius* = *evangelium* EVANGEL: assoc. with GOD]

gospeller /ˈgɒspələ(r)/ *n.* the reader of the Gospel in a Communion service. □ **hot gospeller** a zealous puritan; a rabid propagandist.

gossamer /ˈgɒsəmə(r)/ *n. & adj.* —*n.* **1** a filmy substance of small spiders' webs. **2** delicate filmy material. **3** a thread of gossamer. —*adj.* light and flimsy as gossamer. □□ **gossamered** *adj.* **gossamery** *adj.* [ME *gos(e)somer(e)*, app. f. GOOSE + SUMMER[1] (*goose summer* = St Martin's summer, i.e. early November when geese are eaten, gossamer being common then)]

gossip /ˈgɒsɪp/ *n. & v.* —*n.* **1** a easy or unconstrained talk or writing esp. about persons or social incidents. **b** idle talk; groundless rumour. **2** an informal chat, esp. about persons or social incidents. **3** a person who indulges in gossip. —*v.intr.* (**gossiped, gossiping**) talk or write gossip. □ **gossip column** a section of a newspaper devoted to gossip about well-known people. **gossip columnist** a regular writer of gossip columns. **gossip-monger** a perpetrator of gossip. □□ **gossiper** *n.* **gossipy** *adj.* [earlier sense 'godparent': f. OE *godsibb* person related to one in GOD: see SIB]

gossoon /gɒˈsuːn/ *n. Ir.* a lad. [earlier *garsoon* f. F *garçon* boy]

got *past* and *past part.* of GET.

Goth /gɒθ/ *n.* **1** a member of a Germanic tribe that invaded the Roman Empire in the 3rd-5th c. **2** an uncivilized or ignorant person. [LL *Gothi* (pl.) f. Gk *Go(t)thoi* f. Goth.]

Gothic /ˈgɒθɪk/ *adj. & n.* —*adj.* **1** of the Goths or their language. **2** in the style of architecture prevalent in W. Europe in the 12th-16th c., characterized by pointed arches. **3** (of a novel etc.) in a style popular in the 18th-19th c., with supernatural or horrifying events. **4** barbarous, uncouth. **5** *Printing* (of type) old-fashioned German, black letter, or sanserif. —*n.* **1** the Gothic language. **2** Gothic architecture. **3** *Printing* Gothic type. □□ **Gothically** *adv.* **Gothicism** /-ˌsɪz(ə)m/ *n.* **Gothicize** /-ˌsaɪz/ *v.tr. & intr.* (also -**ise**). [F *gothique* or LL *gothicus* f. *Gothi*: see GOTH]

gotta /ˈgɒtə/ *colloq.* have got a; have got to (*I gotta pain; we gotta go*). [corrupt.]

gotten *US past part.* of GET.

Götterdämmerung /ˌgɜːtəˈdeməˌrʊŋ/ *n.* **1** the twilight (i.e. downfall) of the gods. **2** the complete downfall of a regime etc. [G, esp. as the title of an opera by Wagner]

gouache /guˈɑːʃ, gwɑːʃ/ *n.* **1** a method of painting in opaque pigments ground in water and thickened with a gluelike substance. **2** these pigments. **3** a picture painted in this way. [F f. It. *guazzo*]

Gouda /ˈgaʊdə/ *n.* a flat round usu. Dutch cheese with a yellow rind. [*Gouda* in Holland, where orig. made]

gouge /gaʊdʒ/ *n. & v.* —*n.* **1 a** a chisel with a concave blade, used in carpentry, sculpture, and surgery. **b** an indentation or groove made with or as with this. **2** *US colloq.* a swindle. —*v.* **1** *tr.* cut with or as with a gouge. **2** *tr.* **a** (foll. by *out*) force out (esp. an eye with the thumb) with or as with a gouge. **b** force out the eye of (a person). **3** *tr. US colloq.* swindle; extort money from. **4** *intr. Austral.* dig for opal. □□ **gouger** *n.* [F f. LL *gubia*, perh. of Celt. orig.]

goulash /ˈguːlæʃ/ *n.* **1** a highly-seasoned Hungarian dish of meat and vegetables, usu. flavoured with paprika. **2** (in contract bridge) a re-deal, several cards at a time, of the four hands (unshuffled, but with each hand arranged in suits and order of value) when no player has bid. [Magyar *gulyás-hús* f. *gulyás* herdsman + *hús* meat]

gourami /ˈgʊərəmɪ, -ˈrɑːmɪ/ *n.* **1 a** a large freshwater fish, *Osphronemus goramy*, native to SE Asia, used as food. **b** any small fish of the family Osphronemidae, usu. kept in aquariums. **2** any small brightly coloured freshwater fish of the family Belontiidae, usu. kept in aquariums. Also called LABYRINTH FISH. [Malay *gurāmi*]

gourd /gʊəd/ *n.* **1 a** any of various fleshy usu. large fruits with a hard skin, often used as containers, ornaments, etc. **b** any of various climbing or trailing plants of the family Cucurbitaceae bearing this fruit. Also called CUCURBIT. **2** the hollow hard skin of the gourd-fruit, dried and used as a drinking-vessel, water container, etc. □□ **gourdful** *n.* (*pl.* -**fuls**). [ME f. AF *gurde*, OF *gourde* ult. f. L *cucurbita*]

gourmand /ˈgʊəmænd/ *n. & adj.* —*n.* **1** a glutton. **2** *disp.* a gourmet. —*adj.* gluttonous; fond of eating, esp. to excess. □□ **gourmandism** *n.* [ME f. OF, of unkn. orig.]

gourmandise /ˌgʊəmɑˈdiːz/ *n.* the habits of a gourmand; gluttony. [F (as GOURMAND)]

gourmet /ˈgʊəmeɪ/ *n.* a connoisseur of good or delicate food. [F, = wine-taster: sense infl. by GOURMAND]

gout /gaʊt/ *n.* **1** a disease with inflammation of the smaller joints, esp. the toe, as a result of excess uric acid salts in the blood. **2** *archaic* **a** a drop, esp. of blood. **b** a splash or spot. □□ **gouty** *adj.* **goutily** *adv.* **goutiness** *n.* [ME f. OF *goute* f. L *gutta* drop, with ref. to the medieval theory of the flowing down of humours]

Gov. *abbr.* **1** Government. **2** Governor.

gov. *abbr.* governor.

govern /'gʌv(ə)n/ *v.* **1 a** *tr.* rule or control (a State, subject, etc.) with authority; conduct the policy and affairs of (an organization etc.). **b** *intr.* be in government. **2 a** *tr.* influence or determine (a person or a course of action). **b** *intr.* be the predominating influence. **3** *tr.* be a standard or principle for; constitute a law for; serve to decide (a case). **4** *tr.* check or control (esp. passions). **5** *tr. Gram.* (esp. of a verb or preposition) have (a noun or pronoun or its case) depending on it. **6** *tr.* be in military command of (a fort, town). ▫**governing body** the managers of an institution. ▫▫**governable** *adj.* **governability** /-nə'bɪlɪtɪ/ *n.* **governableness** *n.* [ME f. OF *governer* f. L *gubernare* steer, rule f. Gk *kubernaō*]

governance /'gʌvənəns/ *n.* **1** the act or manner of governing. **2** the office or function of governing. **3** sway, control. [ME f. OF (as GOVERN)]

governess /'gʌvənɪs/ *n.* a woman employed to teach children in a private household. [earlier *governeress* f. OF *governeresse* (as GOVERNOR)]

governessy /'gʌvənɪsɪ/ *adj.* characteristic of a governess; prim.

government /'gʌvənmənt/ *n.* **1** the act or manner of governing. **2** the system by which a State or community is governed. **3 a** a body of persons governing a State. **b** (usu. **Government**) a particular ministry in office. **4** the State as an agent. **5** *Gram.* the relation between a governed and a governing word. ▫**Government House** the official residence of a governor. **government issue** *US* (of equipment) provided by the government. **government paper** (or **securities**) bonds etc. issued by the government. **government surplus** unused equipment sold by the government. ▫▫**governmental** /-'ment(ə)l/ *adj.* **governmentally** /-'mentəlɪ/ *adv.* [ME f. OF *governement* (as GOVERN)]

governor /'gʌvənə(r)/ *n.* **1** a person who governs; a ruler. **2 a** an official governing a province, town, etc. **b** a representative of the Crown in a colony. **3** the executive head of each State of the US. **4** an officer commanding a fortress or garrison. **5** the head or a member of a governing body of an institution. **6** the official in charge of a prison. **7 a** *sl.* one's employer. **b** *sl.* one's father. **c** *colloq.* (as a form of address) sir. **8** *Mech.* an automatic regulator controlling the speed of an engine etc. ▫**Governor-General** the representative of the Crown in a Commonwealth country that regards the Queen as Head of State. ▫▫ **governorate** /-rət/ *n.* **governorship** *n.* [ME f. AF *gouvernour*, OF *governëo(u)r* f. L *gubernator -oris* (as GOVERN)]

Govt. *abbr.* Government.

gowan /'gaʊən/ *n. Sc.* **1** a daisy. **2** any white or yellow field-flower. [prob. var. of dial. *gollan* ranunculus etc., and rel. to *gold* in *marigold*]

gowk /gaʊk/ *n. dial.* **1** a cuckoo. **2** an awkward or halfwitted person; a fool. [ME f. ON *gaukr* f. Gmc]

gown /gaʊn/ *n. & v.* —*n.* **1** a loose flowing garment, esp. a long dress worn by a woman. **2** the official robe of an alderman, judge, cleric, member of a university, etc. **3** a surgeon's overall. **4** the members of a university as distinct from the permanent residents of the university town (cf. TOWN). —*v.tr.* (usu. as **gowned** *adj.*) attire in a gown. [ME f. OF *goune, gon(n)e* f. LL *gunna* fur garment: cf. med. Gk *gouna* fur]

goy /gɔɪ/ *n.* (*pl.* **goyim** /'gɔɪɪm/ or **goys**) *sl. derog.* a Jewish name for a non-Jew. ▫▫**goyish** *adj.* (also **goyisch**). [Heb. *gōy* people, nation]

GP *abbr.* **1** general practitioner. **2** Grand Prix.

Gp. Capt. *abbr.* (in the RAF) Group Captain.

GPI *abbr.* general paralysis of the insane.

GPO *abbr.* **1** General Post Office. **2** *US* Government Printing Office.

GR *abbr.* King George. [L *Georgius Rex*]

gr *abbr.* (also **gr.**) **1** gram(s). **2** grains. **3** gross. **4** grey.

Graafian follicle /'grɑːfɪən/ *n.* a follicle in the mammalian ovary in which an ovum develops prior to ovulation. [R. de *Graaf*, Du. anatomist d. 1673]

grab /græb/ *v. & n.* —*v.* (**grabbed, grabbing**) **1** *tr.* **a** seize suddenly. **b** capture, arrest. **2** *tr.* take greedily or unfairly. **3** *tr. sl.* attract the attention of, impress. **4** *intr.* (foll. by *at*) make a sudden snatch at. **5** *intr.* (of the brakes of a motor vehicle) act harshly or jerkily. —*n.* **1** a sudden clutch or attempt to seize. **2** a mechanical device for clutching. **3** the practice of grabbing; rapacious proceedings esp. in politics and commerce. **4** a children's card-game in which certain cards may be snatched from the table. ▫**grab-bag** *US* a lucky dip. **grab handle** (or **rail** etc.) a handle or rail etc. to steady passengers in a moving vehicle. **up for grabs** *sl.* easily obtainable; inviting capture. ▫▫**grabber** *n.* [MLG, MDu. *grabben*: cf. GRIP, GRIPE, GROPE]

grabble /'græb(ə)l/ *v.intr.* **1** grope about, feel for something. **2** (often foll. by *for*) sprawl on all fours, scramble (for something). [Du. & LG *grabbeln* scramble for a thing (as GRAB)]

grabby /'græbɪ/ *adj. colloq.* tending to grab; greedy, grasping.

graben /'grɑːbən/ *n.* (*pl.* same or **grabens**) *Geol.* a depression of the earth's surface between faults. [G, orig. = ditch]

grace /greɪs/ *n. & v.* —*n.* **1** attractiveness, esp. in elegance of proportion or manner or movement; gracefulness. **2** courteous good will (*had the grace to apologize*). **3** an attractive feature; an accomplishment (*social graces*). **4 a** (in Christian belief) the unmerited favour of God; a divine saving and strengthening influence. **b** the state of receiving this. **c** a divinely given talent. **5** goodwill, favour (*fall from grace*). **6** delay granted as a favour (*a year's grace*). **7** a short thanksgiving before or after a meal. **8** (**Grace**) (in Greek mythology) each of three beautiful sister goddesses, bestowers of beauty and charm. **9** (**Grace**) (prec. by *His, Her, Your*) forms of description or address for a duke, duchess, or archbishop. —*v.tr.* (often foll. by *with*) add grace to, enhance; confer honour or dignity on (*graced us with his presence*). ▫**days of grace** the time allowed by law for payment of a sum due. **grace and favour house** etc. *Brit.* a house etc. occupied by permission of a sovereign etc. **grace-note** *Mus.* an extra note as an embellishment not essential to the harmony or melody. **in a person's good** (or **bad**) **graces** regarded by a person with favour (or disfavour). **with good** (or **bad**) **grace** as if willingly (or reluctantly). [ME f. OF f. L *gratia* f. *gratus* pleasing: cf. GRATEFUL]

graceful /'greɪsfʊl/ *adj.* having or showing grace or elegance. ▫▫**gracefully** *adv.* **gracefulness** *n.*

graceless /'greɪslɪs/ *adj.* lacking grace or elegance or charm. ▫▫**gracelessly** *adv.* **gracelessness** *n.*

gracile /'græsaɪl, -sɪl/ *adj.* slender; gracefully slender. [L *gracilis* slender]

gracility /grə'sɪlɪtɪ/ *n.* **1** slenderness. **2** (of literary style) unornamented simplicity.

gracious /'greɪʃəs/ *adj. & int.* —*adj.* **1** kind; indulgent and beneficent to inferiors. **2** (of God) merciful, benign. **3** *poet.* kindly, courteous. **4** a polite epithet used of royal persons or their acts (*the gracious speech from the throne*). —*int.* expressing surprise. ▫**gracious living** an elegant way of life. ▫▫ **graciosity** /ˌgreɪsɪ'ɒsɪtɪ/ *n.* **graciously** *adv.* **graciousness** *n.* [ME f. OF f. L *gratiosus* (as GRACE)]

grackle /'græk(ə)l/ *n.* **1** any of various orioles, esp. of the genus *Quiscalus*, native to America, the males of which are shiny black with a blue-green sheen. Also called BLACKBIRD. **2** any of various minas, esp. of the genus *Gracula*, native to Asia. [mod.L *Gracula* f. L *graculus* jackdaw]

---

grad /græd/ *n. colloq.* = GRADUATE *n.* 1. [abbr.]

gradate /grə'deɪt/ *v.* **1** *v.intr. & tr.* pass or cause to pass by gradations from one shade to another. **2** *tr.* arrange in steps or grades of size etc. [back-form. f. GRADATION]

gradation /grə'deɪʃ(ə)n/ *n.* (usu. in *pl.*) **1** a stage of transition or advance. **2 a** a certain degree in rank, intensity, merit, divergence, etc. **b** such a degree; an arrangement in such degrees. **3** (of paint etc.) the gradual passing from one shade, tone, etc., to another. **4** *Philol.* ablaut. □□ **gradational** *adj.* **gradationally** *adv.* [L *gradatio* f. *gradus* step]

grade /greɪd/ *n. & v.* —*n.* **1 a** a certain degree in rank, merit, proficiency, quality, etc. **b** a class of persons or things of the same grade. **2 a** a mark indicating the quality of a student's work. **b** an examination, esp. in music. **3** *US* a class in school, concerned with a particular year's work and usu. numbered from the first upwards. **4 a** a gradient or slope. **b** the rate of ascent or descent. **5 a** a variety of cattle produced by crossing native stock with a superior breed. **b** a group of animals at a similar level of development. **6** *Philol.* a relative position in a series of forms involving ablaut. —*v.* **1** *tr.* arrange in or allocate to grades; class, sort. **2** *intr.* (foll. by *up, down, off, into,* etc.) pass gradually between grades, or into a grade. **3** *tr.* give a grade to (a student). **4** *tr.* blend so as to affect the grade of colour with tints passing into each other. **5** *tr.* reduce (a road etc.) to easy gradients. **6** *tr.* (often foll. by *up*) cross (livestock) with a better breed. □ **at grade** *US* on the same level. **grade crossing** *US* = *level crossing.* **grade school** *US* elementary school. **make the grade** *colloq.* succeed; reach the desired standard. [F *grade* or L *gradus* step]

grader /'greɪdə(r)/ *n.* **1** a person or thing that grades. **2** a wheeled machine for levelling the ground, esp. in road-making. **3** (in *comb.*) *US* a pupil of a specified grade in a school.

gradient /'greɪdɪənt/ *n.* **1 a** a stretch of road, railway, etc., that slopes from the horizontal. **b** the amount of such a slope. **2** the rate of rise or fall of temperature, pressure, etc., in passing from one region to another. [prob. formed on GRADE after *salient*]

gradine /'greɪdɪn/ *n.* (also **gradin** /-dɪn/) **1** each of a series of low steps or a tier of seats. **2** a ledge at the back of an altar. [It. *gradino* dimin. of *grado* GRADE]

gradual /'grædjʊəl/ *adj. & n.* —*adj.* **1** taking place or progressing slowly or by degrees. **2** not rapid or steep or abrupt. —*n. Eccl.* **1** a response sung or recited between the Epistle and Gospel in the Mass. **2** a book of music for the sung Mass service. □□ **gradually** *adv.* **gradualness** *n.* [med.L *gradualis, -ale* f. L *gradus* step, the noun referring to the altar-steps on which the response is sung]

gradualism /'grædjʊə,lɪz(ə)m/ *n.* a policy of gradual reform rather than sudden change or revolution. □□ **gradualist** *n.* **gradualistic** /-'lɪstɪk/ *adj.*

graduand /'grædjʊ,ænd/ *n. Brit.* a person about to receive an academic degree. [med.L *graduandus* gerundive of *graduare* GRADUATE]

graduate *n. & v.* —*n.* /'grædjʊət/ **1** a person who has been awarded an academic degree (also *attrib.*: *graduate student*). **2** *US* a person who has completed a school course. —*v.* /'grædjʊ,eɪt/ **1 a** *intr.* take an academic degree. **b** *tr. US* admit to an academic degree or a certificate of completion of School Studies. **2** *intr.* **a** (foll. by *from*) be a graduate of a specified university. **b** (foll. by *in*) be a graduate in a specified subject. **3** *tr. US* send out as a graduate from a university etc. **4** *intr.* **a** (foll. by *to*) move up to (a higher grade of activity etc.). **b** (foll. by *as, in*) gain specified qualifications. **5** *tr.* mark out in degrees or parts. **6** *tr.* arrange in gradations; apportion (e.g. tax) according to a scale. **7** *intr.* (foll. by *into, away*) pass by degrees. □ **graduated pension** (in the UK) a system of pension contributions by employees in proportion to their wages or salary. **graduate**

school a department of a university for advanced work by graduates. □□ **graduator** *n.* [med.L *graduari* take a degree f. L *gradus* step]

graduation /,grædjʊ'eɪʃ(ə)n/ *n.* **1** the act or an instance of graduating or being graduated. **2** a ceremony at which degrees are conferred. **3** each or all of the marks on a vessel or instrument indicating degrees of quantity etc.

Graecism /'griːkɪz(ə)m, -sɪz(ə)m/ *n.* (also **Grecism**) **1** a Greek idiom, esp. as imitated in another language. **2 a** the Greek spirit, style, mode of expression, etc. **b** the imitation of these. [F *grécisme* or med.L *Graecismus* f. *Graecus* GREEK]

Graecize /'griːkaɪz/ *v.tr.* (also **Grecize, -ise**) give a Greek character or form to. [L *Graecizare* (as GRAECISM)]

Graeco- /'griːkəʊ/ *comb. form* (also **Greco-**) Greek; Greek and. [L *Graecus* GREEK]

Graeco-Roman /,griːkəʊ'rəʊmən/ *adj.* **1** of or relating to the Greeks and Romans. **2** *Wrestling* denoting a style attacking only the upper part of the body.

graffito /grə'fiːtəʊ/ *n.* (*pl.* **graffiti** /-tiː/) **1** (usu. in *pl.*) a piece of writing or drawing scribbled, scratched, or sprayed on a surface. ¶ Not a mass noun in this sense, and so a plural construction is needed, e.g. *graffiti are* (not *is*) *an art form.* **2** *Art* a form of decoration made by scratches on wet plaster, showing a different-coloured under-surface. [It. f. *graffio* scratch]

graft¹ /grɑːft/ *n. & v.* —*n.* **1** *Bot.* **a** a shoot or scion inserted into a slit of stock, from which it receives sap. **b** the place where a graft is inserted. **2** *Surgery* a piece of living tissue, organ, etc., transplanted surgically. **3** *sl.* hard work. —*v.* **1** *tr.* **a** (often foll. by *into, on, together,* etc.) insert (a scion) as a graft. **b** insert a graft on (a stock). **2** *intr.* insert a graft. **3** *tr. Surgery* transplant (living tissue). **4** *tr.* (foll. by *in, on*) insert or fix (a thing) permanently to another. **5** *intr. sl.* work hard. □ **grafting-clay** (or **-wax**) a substance for covering the united parts of a graft and stock. □□ **grafter** *n.* [ME (earlier *graff*) f. OF *grafe, grefe* f. L *graphium* f. Gk *graphion* stylus f. *graphō* write]

graft² /grɑːft/ *n. & v. colloq.* —*n.* **1** practices, esp. bribery, used to secure illicit gains in politics or business. **2** such gains. —*v.intr.* seek or make such gains. □□ **grafter** *n.* [19th c.: orig. unkn.]

Grail /greɪl/ *n.* (in full **Holy Grail**) **1** (in medieval legend) the cup or platter used by Christ at the Last Supper, and in which Joseph of Arimathea received Christ's blood at the Cross, esp. as the object of quests by medieval knights. **2** any object of a quest. [ME f. OF *graal* etc. f. med.L *gradalis* dish, of unkn. orig.]

grain /greɪn/ *n. & v.* —*n.* **1** a fruit or seed of a cereal. **2 a** (*collect.*) wheat or any allied grass used as food, corn. **b** (*collect.*) their fruit. **c** any particular species of corn. **3 a** a small hard particle of salt, sand, etc. **b** a discrete particle or crystal, usu. small, in a rock or metal. **c** a piece of solid propellant for use in a rocket engine. **4** the smallest unit of weight in the troy system (equivalent to 1/480 of an ounce), and in the avoirdupois system (equivalent to 1/437.5 of an ounce). **5** the smallest possible quantity (*not a grain of truth in it*). **6 a** roughness of surface. **b** *Photog.* a granular appearance on a photograph or negative. **7** the texture of skin, wood, stone, etc.; the arrangement and size of constituent particles. **8 a** a pattern of lines of fibre in wood or paper. **b** lamination or planes of cleavage in stone, coal, etc. **9** nature, temper, tendency. **10 a** *hist.* kermes or cochineal, or dye made from either of these. **b** *poet.* dye; colour. —*v.* **1** *tr.* paint in imitation of the grain of wood or marble. **2** *tr.* give a granular surface to. **3** *tr.* dye in grain. **4** *tr. & intr.* form into grains. **5** *tr.* remove hair from (hides). □ **against the grain** contrary to one's natural inclination or feeling. **grain-leather**

leather dressed with grain-side out. **grain-side** the side of a hide on which the hair was. **grains of Paradise** capsules of a W. African plant (*Aframomum melegueta*), used as a spice and a drug. **in grain** thorough, genuine, by nature, downright, indelible. □□**grained** *adj.* (also in *comb.*). **grainer** *n.* **grainless** *adj.* [ME f. OF f. L *granum*]

grainy /ˈgreɪnɪ/ *adj.* (**grainier**, **grainiest**) 1 granular. 2 resembling the grain of wood. 3 *Photog.* having a granular appearance. □□**graininess** *n.*

grallatorial /ˌgræləˈtɔːrɪəl/ *adj. Zool.* of or relating to long-legged wading birds, e.g. storks, flamingos, etc. [mod.L *grallatorius* f. L *grallator* stilt-walker f. *grallae* stilts]

gram[1] /græm/ *n.* (also **gramme**) a metric unit of mass equal to one-thousandth of a kilogram. □**gram-atom** *Chem.* the quantity of a chemical element equal to its relative atomic mass in grams (see MOLE[4]). **gram-equivalent** *Chem.* the quantity of a substance equal to its equivalent weight in grams. **gram-molecule** *Chem.* the quantity of a substance equal to its relative molecular mass in grams. [F *gramme* f. Gk *gramma* small weight]

gram[2] /græm/ *n.* any of various pulses used as food. [Port. *grão* f. L *granum* grain]

-gram /græm/ *comb. form* forming nouns denoting a thing written or recorded (often in a certain way) (*anagram*; *epigram*; *monogram*; *telegram*). □□ **-grammatic** /grəˈmætɪk/ *comb. form* forming adjectives. [from or after Gk *gramma* *-atos* thing written, letter of the alphabet, f. *graphō* write]

graminaceous /ˌgræmɪˈneɪʃəs/ *adj.* of or like grass; grassy. [L *gramen -inis* grass]

gramineous /grəˈmɪnɪəs/ *adj.* = GRAMINACEOUS. [L *gramineus* f. *gramen -inis* grass]

graminivorous /ˌgræmɪˈnɪvərəs/ *adj.* feeding on grass, cereals, etc. [L *gramen -inis* grass + -VOROUS]

grammalogue /ˈgræməˌlɒg/ *n.* 1 a word represented by a single shorthand sign. 2 a logogram. [irreg. f. Gk *gramma* letter of the alphabet + *logos* word]

grammar /ˈgræmə(r)/ *n.* 1 a the study or rules of a language's inflections or other means of showing the relation between words, including its phonetic system. b a body of form and usages in a specified language (*Latin grammar*). 2 a person's manner or quality of observance or application of the rules of grammar (*bad grammar*). 3 a book on grammar. 4 the elements or rudiments of an art or science. 5 *Brit. colloq.* = grammar school. □**grammar school** 1 *Brit.* esp. *hist.* a selective State secondary school with a mainly academic curriculum. 2 *Brit. hist.* a school founded in or before the 16th c. for teaching Latin, later becoming a secondary school teaching academic subjects. 3 *US* a school intermediate between primary and high school. □□**grammarless** *adj.* [ME f. AF *gramere*, OF *gramaire* f. L *grammatica* f. Gk *grammatikē* (*tekhnē*) (art) of letters f. *gramma* *-atos* letter of the alphabet]

grammarian /grəˈmeərɪən/ *n.* an expert in grammar or linguistics; a philologist. [ME f. OF *gramarien*]

grammatical /grəˈmætɪk(ə)l/ *adj.* 1 a of or relating to grammar. b determined by grammar, esp. by form or inflection (*grammatical gender*). 2 conforming to the rules of grammar, or to the formal principles of an art, science, etc. □□**grammatically** *adv.* **grammaticalness** *n.* [F *grammatical* or LL *grammaticalis* f. L *grammaticus* f. Gk *grammatikos* (as GRAMMAR)]

gramme var. of GRAM[1].

gramophone /ˈgræməˌfəʊn/ *n.* an instrument reproducing recorded sound by a stylus resting on a rotating grooved disc. ¶ Now more usually called *record-player*. □□**gramophonic** /-ˈfɒnɪk/ *adj.* [formed by inversion of PHONOGRAM]

grampus /ˈgræmpəs/ *n.* (*pl.* **grampuses**) 1 a dolphin, *Grampus griseus*, with a blunt snout and long pointed black flippers. 2 a person breathing heavily and loudly. [earlier *graundepose*, *grapeys* f. OF *grapois* etc. f. med.L *craspiscis* f. L *crassus piscis* fat fish]

Gram's method /græmz/ *n. Biol.* a method of differentiating bacteria by staining with a dye, then attempting to remove the dye with a solvent, for purposes of identification. □**Gram-positive** (or **negative**) (of bacteria) that do (or do not) retain the dye. [H. C. J. *Gram*, Da. physician d. 1938]

gran /græn/ *n. colloq.* grandmother (cf. GRANNY). [abbr.]

granadilla /ˌgrænəˈdɪlə/ *n.* (also **grenadilla** /ˌgren-/) a passion-fruit. [Sp., dimin. of *granada* pomegranate]

granary /ˈgrænərɪ/ *n.* (*pl.* **-ies**) 1 a storehouse for threshed grain. 2 a region producing, and esp. exporting, much corn. [L *granarium* f. *granum* grain]

grand /grænd/ *adj. & n.* —*adj.* 1 a splendid, magnificent, imposing, dignified. b solemn or lofty in conception, execution, or expression; noble. 2 main; of chief importance (*grand staircase*; *grand entrance*). 3 (**Grand**) of the highest rank, esp. in official titles (*Grand Cross*; *grand vizier*; *Grand Inquisitor*). 4 *colloq.* excellent, enjoyable (*had a grand time*; *in grand condition*). 5 belonging to high society; wealthy (*the grand folk at the big house*). 6 (in *comb.*) in names of family relationships, denoting the second degree of ascent or descent (*granddaughter*). 7 (**Grand**) (in French phrases or imitations) great (*grand army*; *Grand Monarch*; *Grand Hotel*). 8 *Law* serious, important (*grand larceny*) (cf. COMMON, PETTY). —*n.* 1 = grand piano. 2 (*pl.* same) (usu. in *pl.*) esp. *US sl.* a thousand dollars or pounds. □**grand aunt** a great-aunt (see GREAT *adj.* 11). **grand duchy** a State ruled by a grand duke or duchess. **grand duke** (or **duchess**) 1 a prince (or princess) or noble person ruling over a territory. 2 (**Grand Duke**) *hist.* the son or grandson of a Russian tsar. **grand jury** esp. *US Law* a jury selected to examine the validity of an accusation prior to trial. **grand master** 1 a chess-player of the highest class. 2 the head of a military order of knighthood, of Freemasons, etc. **Grand National** a steeplechase held annually at Aintree, Liverpool. **grand nephew** (or **niece**) a great-nephew or -niece (see GREAT *adj.* 11). **grand opera** opera on a serious theme, or in which the entire libretto (including dialogue) is sung. **grand piano** a large full-toned piano standing on three legs, with the body, strings, and soundboard arranged horizontally and in line with the keys. **grand slam** 1 *Sport* the winning of all of a group of championships. 2 *Bridge* the winning of 13 tricks. **grand total** the final amount after everything is added up; the sum of other totals. **grand tour** *hist.* a cultural tour of Europe, esp. in the 18th c. for educational purposes. □□**grandly** *adv.* **grandness** *n.* [ME f. AF *graunt*, OF *grant* f. L *grandis* full-grown]

grandad /ˈgrændæd/ *n.* (also **grand-dad**) *colloq.* 1 grandfather. 2 an elderly man.

grandam /ˈgrændæm/ *n.* 1 (also **grandame**) *archaic* grandmother. 2 an old woman. 3 an ancestress. [ME f. AF *graund dame* (as GRAND, DAME)]

grandchild /ˈgræntʃaɪld, ˈgrænd-/ *n.* (*pl.* **-children**) a child of one's son or daughter.

granddaughter /ˈgrænˌdɔːtə(r)/ *n.* a female grandchild.

grande dame /grɑ̃d ˈdɑːm/ *n.* a dignified lady of high rank. [F]

grandee /grænˈdiː/ *n.* 1 a Spanish or Portuguese nobleman of the highest rank. 2 a person of high rank or eminence. [Sp. & Port. *grande*, assim. to -EE]

grandeur /ˈgrændjə(r), -ndʒə(r)/ *n.* 1 majesty, splendour; dignity of appearance or bearing. 2 high rank, eminence. 3 nobility of character. [F f. *grand* great, GRAND]

grandfather /ˈgrænˌfɑːðə(r), ˈgrænd-/ *n.* a male grandparent. □**grandfather clock** a clock in a tall wooden case, driven by weights. □□**grandfatherly** *adj.*

Grand Guignol /ˌgrɑ̃ giːˈnjɒl/ *n.* a dramatic entertainment of a sensational or horrific nature. [the name (= Great Punch) of a theatre in Paris]

grandiflora /ˌgrændɪˈflɔːrə/ *adj.* bearing large flowers. [mod.L (often used in specific names of large-flowered plants) f. L *grandis* great + FLORA]

grandiloquent /ˌgrænˈdɪləkwənt/ *adj.* **1** pompous or inflated in language. **2** given to boastful talk. □□ **grandiloquence** *n.* **grandiloquently** *adv.* [L *grandiloquus* (as GRAND, *-loquus* -speaking f. *loqui* speak), after *eloquent* etc.]

grandiose /ˈgrændɪˌəʊs/ *adj.* **1** producing or meant to produce an imposing effect. **2** planned on an ambitious or magnificent scale. □□ **grandiosely** *adv.* **grandiosity** /-ˈɒsɪtɪ/ *n.* [F f. It. *grandioso* (as GRAND, -OSE¹)]

grandma /ˈgrænmɑː, ˈgrænd-/ *n. colloq.* grandmother.

grand mal /grɑ̃ ˈmæl/ *n.* a serious form of epilepsy with loss of consciousness (cf. PETIT MAL). [F, = great sickness]

grandmama /ˈgrænməˌmɑː, ˈgrænd-/ *n. archaic colloq.* = GRANDMA.

grandmother /ˈgrænˌmʌðə(r), ˈgrænd-/ *n.* a female grandparent. □ **grandmother clock** a clock like a grandfather clock but in a smaller case. **teach one's grandmother to suck eggs** presume to advise a more experienced person. □□ **grandmotherly** *adj.*

grandpa /ˈgrænpɑː, ˈgrænd-/ *n. colloq.* grandfather.

grandpapa /ˈgrænpəˌpɑː, ˈgrænd-/ *n. archaic colloq.* = GRANDPA.

grandparent /ˈgrænˌpeərənt, ˈgrænd-/ *n.* a parent of one's father or mother.

Grand Prix /grɑ̃ ˈpriː/ *n.* any of several important international motor or motor-cycle racing events. [F, = great or chief prize]

grand siècle /grɑ̃ sɪˈeklə/ *n.* the classical or golden age, esp. the 17th c. in France. [F, = great century or age]

grandsire /ˈgrænˌsaɪə(r)/ *n. archaic* **1** grandfather, old man, ancestor. **2** *Bell-ringing* a method of change-ringing.

grandson /ˈgrænsʌn, ˈgrænd-/ *n.* a male grandchild.

grandstand /ˈgrænstænd, ˈgrænd-/ *n.* the main stand, usu. roofed, for spectators at a racecourse etc. □ **grandstand finish** a close and exciting finish to a race etc.

grange /greɪndʒ/ *n.* **1** a country house with farm-buildings. **2** *archaic* a barn. [ME f. AF *graunge*, OF *grange* f. med.L *granica* (*villa*) ult. f. L *granum* GRAIN]

graniferous /grəˈnɪfərəs/ *adj.* producing grain or a grainlike seed. □□ **graniform** /ˈgrænɪˌfɔːm/ *adj.* [L *granum* GRAIN]

granite /ˈgrænɪt/ *n.* **1** a granular crystalline igneous rock of quartz, mica, feldspar, etc., used for building. **2** a determined or resolute quality, attitude, etc. □□ **granitic** /grəˈnɪtɪk/ *adj.* **granitoid** *adj.* & *n.* [It. *granito*, lit. grained f. *grano* f. L *granum* GRAIN]

graniteware /ˈgrænɪtˌweə(r)/ *n.* **1** a speckled form of earthenware imitating the appearance of granite. **2** a kind of enamelled ironware.

granivorous /grəˈnɪvərəs/ *adj.* feeding on grain. □□ **granivore** /ˈgrænɪˌvɔː(r)/ *n.* [L *granum* GRAIN]

granny /ˈgrænɪ/ *n.* (also **grannie**) (*pl. -ies*) *colloq.* grandmother. □ **granny bond** *Brit. colloq.* a form of National Savings certificate orig. available only to pensioners. **granny flat** (or **annexe**) *Brit.* part of a house made into self-contained accommodation for an elderly relative. **granny knot** a reef-knot crossed the wrong way and therefore insecure. [obs. *grannam* for GRANDAM + -Y²]

Granny Smith /ˌgrænɪ ˈsmɪθ/ *n.* an Australian green variety of apple. [Maria Ann ('Granny') Smith d. 1870]

grant /grɑːnt/ *v.* & *n.* —*v.tr.* **1 a** consent to fulfil (a request, wish, etc.) (*granted all he asked*). **b** allow (a person) to have (a thing) (*granted me my freedom*). **c** (as **granted**) *colloq.* apology accepted; pardon given.

2 give (rights, property, etc.) formally; transfer legally. **3** (often foll. by *that* + clause) admit as true; concede, esp. as a basis for argument. —*n.* **1** the process of granting or a thing granted. **2** a sum of money given by the State for any of various purposes, esp. to finance education. **3** *Law* **a** a legal conveyance by written instrument. **b** formal conferment. □ **grant-in-aid** (*pl.* **grants-in-aid**) a grant by central government to local government or an institution. **take for granted 1** assume something to be true or valid. **2** cease to appreciate through familiarity. □□ **grantable** *adj.* **grantee** /-ˈtiː/ *n.* (esp. in sense 2 of *v.*). **granter** *n.* **grantor** /-ˈtɔː(r)/ *n.* (esp. in sense 2 of *v.*). [ME f. OF *gr(e)anter* var. of *creanter* ult. f. part. of L *credere* entrust]

Granth /grʌnt/ *n.* (also **Grunth**) the sacred scriptures of the Sikhs. [Hindi, = book, code f. Skr. *grantha* tying, literary composition]

gran turismo /ˌgræn tuːˈrɪzməʊ/ *n.* (*pl. -os*) a touring-car. [It., = great touring]

granular /ˈgrænjʊlə(r)/ *adj.* **1** of or like grains or granules. **2** having a granulated surface or structure. □□ **granularity** /-ˈlærɪtɪ/ *n.* **granularly** *adv.* [LL *granulum* GRANULE]

granulate /ˈgrænjʊˌleɪt/ *v.* **1** *tr.* & *intr.* form into grains (*granulated sugar*). **2** *tr.* roughen the surface of. **3** *intr.* (of a wound etc.) form small prominences as the beginning of healing; heal, join. □□ **granulation** /-ˈleɪʃ(ə)n/ *n.* **granulator** *n.*

granule /ˈgrænjuːl/ *n.* a small grain. [LL *granulum*, dimin. of L *granum* grain]

granulocyte /ˈgrænjʊləˌsaɪt/ *n. Physiol.* any of various white blood cells having granules in their cytoplasm. □□ **granulocytic** /-ˈsɪtɪk/ *adj.*

granulometric /ˌgrænjʊləˈmetrɪk/ *adj.* relating to the distribution of grain sizes in sand etc. [F *granulométrique* (as GRANULE, METRIC)]

grape /greɪp/ *n.* **1** a berry (usu. green, purple, or black) growing in clusters on a vine, used as fruit and in making wine. **2** (prec. by *the*) *colloq.* wine. **3** = GRAPESHOT. **4** (in *pl.*) a diseased growth like a bunch of grapes on the pastern of a horse etc., or on a pleura in cattle. □ **grape hyacinth** any liliaceous plant of the genus *Muscari*, with clusters of usu. blue flowers. **grape-sugar** dextrose. □□ **grapey** *adj.* (also **grapy**). [ME f. OF *grape* bunch of grapes prob. f. *graper* gather (grapes) f. *grap(p)e* hook, ult. f. Gmc]

grapefruit /ˈgreɪpfruːt/ *n.* (*pl.* same) **1** a large round yellow citrus fruit with an acid juicy pulp. **2** the tree, *Citrus paradisi*, bearing this fruit.

grapeshot /ˈgreɪpʃɒt/ *n. hist.* small balls used as charge in a cannon and scattering when fired.

grapevine /ˈgreɪpvaɪn/ *n.* **1** any of various vines of the genus *Vitis*, esp. *Vitis vinifera*. **2** *colloq.* the means of transmission of unofficial information or rumour (*heard it through the grapevine*).

graph¹ /grɑːf, græf/ *n.* & *v.* —*n.* **1** a diagram showing the relation between variable quantities, usu. of two variables, each measured along one of a pair of axes at right angles. **2** *Math.* a collection of points whose coordinates satisfy a given relation. —*v.tr.* plot or trace on a graph. □ **graph paper** paper printed with a network of lines as a basis for drawing graphs. [abbr. of *graphic formula*]

graph² /grɑːf, græf/ *n. Linguistics* a visual symbol, esp. a letter or letters, representing a unit of sound or other feature of speech. [Gk *graphē* writing]

-graph /grɑːf/ *comb. form* forming nouns and verbs meaning: **1** a thing written or drawn etc. in a specified way (*autograph; photograph*). **2** an instrument that records (*heliograph; seismograph; telegraph*).

grapheme /ˈgræfiːm/ *n. Linguistics* **1** a class of letters etc. representing a unit of sound. **2** a feature of a written expression that cannot be analysed into smaller meaningful units. □□ **graphematic** /-ˈmætɪk/ *adj.* **graphemic** /grəˈfiːmɪk/ *adj.* **graphemically** /grəˈfiːmɪkəlɪ/ *adv.* [GRAPH² + -EME]

-grapher /grəfə(r)/ *comb. form* forming nouns denoting a person concerned with a subject (*geographer*; *radiographer*). [from or after Gk *-graphos* writer + -ER¹]

graphic /'græfɪk/ *adj. & n.* —*adj.* 1 of or relating to the visual or descriptive arts, esp. writing and drawing. 2 vividly descriptive. 3 (of minerals) showing marks like writing on the surface or in a fracture. 4 = GRAPHICAL. —*n.* a product of the graphic arts (cf. GRAPHICS). □**graphic arts** the visual and technical arts involving design, writing, drawing, printing, etc. **graphic equalizer** a device for the separate control of the strength and quality of selected frequency bands. □□ **graphically** *adv.* **graphicness** *n.* [L *graphicus* f. Gk *graphikos* f. *graphē* writing]

-graphic /'græfɪk/ *comb. form* (also **-graphical**) forming adjectives corresponding to nouns in *-graphy* (see -GRAPHY). □□-**graphically** *comb. form* forming adverbs. [from or after Gk *-graphikos* (as GRAPHIC)]

graphicacy /'græfɪkəsɪ/ *n.* the ability to read a map, graph, etc., or to present information by means of diagrams. [GRAPHIC, after *literacy*, *numeracy*]

graphical /'græfɪk(ə)l/ *adj.* 1 of or in the form of graphs (see GRAPH¹). 2 graphic. □□ **graphically** *adv.*

graphics /'græfɪks/ *n.pl.* (usu. treated as *sing.*) 1 the products of the graphic arts, esp. commercial design or illustration. 2 the use of diagrams in calculation and design. 3 (in full **computer graphics**) *Computing* a mode of processing and output in which a significant part of the information is in pictorial form.

graphite /'græfaɪt/ *n.* a crystalline allotropic form of carbon used as a solid lubricant, in pencils, and as a moderator in nuclear reactors etc. Also called PLUMBAGO, *black lead*. □□ **graphitic** /-'fɪtɪk/ *adj.* **graphitize** /-fɪ,taɪz/ *v.tr. & intr.* (also **-ise**). [G *Graphit* f. Gk *graphō* write]

graphology /grə'fɒlədʒɪ/ *n.* 1 the study of handwriting esp. as a supposed guide to character. 2 a system of graphic formulae; notation for graphs (see GRAPH¹). 3 *Linguistics* the study of systems of writing. □□ **graphological** /-fə'lɒdʒɪk(ə)l/ *adj.* **graphologist** *n.* [Gk *graphē* writing]

-graphy /grəfɪ/ *comb. form* forming nouns denoting: 1 a descriptive science (*bibliography*; *geography*). 2 a technique of producing images (*photography*; *radiography*). 3 a style or method of writing, drawing, etc. (*calligraphy*). [from or after F or G *-graphie* f. L *-graphia* f. Gk *-graphia* writing]

grapnel /'græpn(ə)l/ *n.* 1 a device with iron claws, attached to a rope and used for dragging or grasping. 2 a small anchor with several flukes. [ME f. AF f. OF *grapon* f. Gmc: cf. GRAPE]

grappa /'græpə/ *n.* a brandy distilled from the fermented residue of grapes after they have been pressed in wine-making. [It.]

grapple /'græp(ə)l/ *v. & n.* —*v.* 1 *intr.* (often foll. by *with*) fight at close quarters or in close combat. 2 *intr.* (foll. by *with*) try to manage or overcome a difficult problem etc. 3 *tr.* **a** grip with the hands; come to close quarters with. **b** seize with or as with a grapnel; grasp. —*n.* 1 **a** a hold or grip in or as in wrestling. **b** a contest at close quarters. 2 a clutching-instrument; a grapnel. □**grappling-iron** (or **-hook**) = GRAPNEL. □□ **grappler** *n.* [OF *grapil* (n.) f. Prov., dimin. of *grapa* hook (as GRAPNEL)]

graptolite /'græptə,laɪt/ *n.* an extinct marine invertebrate animal found as a fossil in lower Palaeozoic rocks. [Gk *graptos* marked with letters + -LITE]

grasp /grɑːsp/ *v. & n.* —*v.* 1 *tr.* **a** clutch at; seize greedily. **b** hold firmly; grip. 2 *intr.* (foll. by *at*) try to seize; accept avidly. 3 *tr.* understand or realize (a fact or meaning). —*n.* 1 a firm hold; a grip. 2 (foll. by *of*) **a** mastery or control (*a grasp of the situation*). **b** a mental hold or understanding (*a grasp of the*

facts). 3 mental agility (*a quick grasp*). □**grasp at a straw** see STRAW. **grasp the nettle** tackle a difficulty boldly. **within one's grasp** capable of being grasped or comprehended by one. □□ **graspable** *adj.* **grasper** *n.* [ME *graspe*, *grapse* perh. f. OE *grǣpsan* (unrecorded) f. Gmc, rel. to GROPE: cf. LG *grapsen*]

grasping /'grɑːspɪŋ/ *adj.* avaricious, greedy. □□ **graspingly** *adv.* **graspingness** *n.*

grass /grɑːs/ *n. & v.* —*n.* 1 **a** vegetation belonging to a group of small plants with green blades that are eaten by cattle, horses, sheep, etc. **b** any species of this. **c** any plant of the family Gramineae, which includes cereals, reeds, and bamboos. 2 pasture land. 3 grass-covered ground, a lawn (*keep off the grass*). 4 grazing (*out to grass*; *be at grass*). 5 *sl.* marijuana. 6 *Brit. sl.* an informer, esp. a police informer. 7 the earth's surface above a mine; the pit-head. 8 *sl.* asparagus. —*v.* 1 *tr.* cover with turf. 2 *tr. US* provide with pasture. 3 *Brit. sl.* **a** *tr.* betray, esp. to the police. **b** *intr.* inform the police. 4 *tr.* knock down; fell (an opponent). 5 *tr.* **a** bring (a fish) to the bank. **b** bring down (a bird) by a shot. □**at grass** out of work, on holiday, etc. **grass bird** *Austral.* any of various warblers, esp. of the genus *Megalurus*, living among reeds. **grass-box** a receptacle for cut grass on a lawnmower. **grass-cloth** a linen-like cloth woven from ramie etc. **grass court** a grass-covered lawn-tennis court. **grass of Parnassus** a herbaceous plant, *Parnassia palustris*. **grass parakeet** *Austral.* a parakeet, esp. of the genus *Neophema*, frequenting grassland. **grass roots** 1 a fundamental level or source. 2 ordinary people, esp. as voters; the rank and file of an organization, esp. a political party. **grass skirt** a skirt made of long grass and leaves fastened to a waistband. **grass snake** 1 *Brit.* the common ringed snake, *Natrix natrix*. 2 *US* the common greensnake, *Opheodrys vernalis*. **grass tree** = BLACKBOY. **grass widow** (or **widower**) a person whose husband (or wife) is away for a prolonged period. **grass-wrack** eel-grass. **not let the grass grow under one's feet** be quick to act or to seize an opportunity. □□ **grassless** *adj.* **grasslike** *adj.* [OE *grǣs* f. Gmc, rel. to GREEN, GROW]

grasshopper /'grɑːs,hɒpə(r)/ *n.* a jumping and chirping plant-eating insect of the order Saltatoria.

grassland /'grɑːslænd/ *n.* a large open area covered with grass, esp. one used for grazing.

grassy /'grɑːsɪ/ *adj.* (**grassier**, **grassiest**) 1 covered with or abounding in grass. 2 resembling grass. 3 of grass. □□ **grassiness** *n.*

grate¹ /greɪt/ *v.* 1 *tr.* reduce to small particles by rubbing on a serrated surface. 2 *intr.* (often foll. by *against*, *on*) rub with a harsh scraping sound. 3 *tr.* utter in a harsh tone. 4 *intr.* (often foll. by *on*) **a** sound harshly or discordantly. **b** have an irritating effect. 5 *tr.* grind (one's teeth). 6 *intr.* (of a hinge etc.) creak. [ME f. OF *grater* ult. f. WG]

grate² /greɪt/ *n.* 1 the recess of a fireplace or furnace. 2 a metal frame confining fuel in a grate. [ME, = grating f. OF ult. f. L *cratis* hurdle]

grateful /'greɪtfʊl/ *adj.* 1 thankful; feeling or showing gratitude (*am grateful to you for helping*). 2 pleasant, acceptable. □□ **gratefully** *adv.* **gratefulness** *n.* [obs. *grate* (adj.) f. L *gratus* + -FUL]

grater /'greɪtə(r)/ *n.* a device for reducing cheese or other food to small particles.

graticule /'grætɪ,kjuːl/ *n.* 1 fine lines or fibres incorporated in a telescope or other optical instrument as a measuring scale or as an aid in locating objects. 2 *Surveying* a network of lines on paper representing meridians and parallels. [F f. med.L *graticula* for *craticula* gridiron f. L *cratis* hurdle]

gratify /'grætɪ,faɪ/ *v.tr.* (**-fies**, **-fied**) 1 **a** please, delight. **b** please by compliance; assent to the wish of. 2 indulge in or yield to (a feeling or desire). □□ **gratification** /-fɪ'keɪʃ(ə)n/ *n.* **gratifier** *n.* **gratifying** *adj.* **gratifyingly** *adv.* [F *gratifier* or L *gratificari* do a favour to, make a present of, f. *gratus* pleasing]

---

aʊ *how* eɪ *day* əʊ *no* eə *hair* ɪə *near* ɔɪ *boy* ʊə *poor* aɪə *fire* aʊə *sour*   (*see over for consonants*)

grating[1] /'greɪtɪŋ/ *adj.* **1** sounding harsh or discordant (*a grating laugh*). **2** having an irritating effect. □□ **gratingly** *adv.*

grating[2] /'greɪtɪŋ/ *n.* **1** a framework of parallel or crossed metal bars. **2** *Optics* a set of parallel wires, lines ruled on glass, etc., for producing spectra by diffraction.

gratis /'grɑːtɪs, 'greɪ-/ *adv. & adj.* free; without charge. [L, contracted ablat. pl. of *gratia* favour]

gratitude /'grætɪˌtjuːd/ *n.* being thankful; readiness to show appreciation for and to return kindness. [F *gratitude* or med.L *gratitudo* f. *gratus* thankful]

gratuitous /grə'tjuːɪtəs/ *adj.* **1** given or done free of charge. **2** uncalled for; unwarranted; lacking good reason (*a gratuitous insult*). □□ **gratuitously** *adv.* **gratuitousness** *n.* [L *gratuitus* spontaneous: cf. *fortuitous*]

gratuity /grə'tjuːɪtɪ/ *n.* (*pl.* -ies) money given in recognition of services; a tip. [OF *gratuité* or med.L *gratuitas* gift f. L *gratus* grateful]

gratulatory /'grætjʊlətərɪ/ *adj.* expressing congratulation. [LL *gratulatorius* f. L *gratus* grateful]

graunch /grɔːntʃ/ *v.intr. & tr.* make or cause to make a crunching or grinding sound. [imit.]

gravamen /grə'veɪmen/ *n.* (*pl.* **gravamens** or **gravamina** /-mɪnə/) **1** the essence or most serious part of an argument. **2** a grievance. [LL, = inconvenience, f. L *gravare* to load f. *gravis* heavy]

grave[1] /greɪv/ *n.* **1 a** a trench dug in the ground to receive a coffin on burial. **b** a mound or memorial stone placed over this. **2** (prec. by *the*) death, esp. as indicating mortal finality. **3** something compared to or regarded as a grave. □ **turn in one's grave** (of a dead person) be thought of in certain circumstances as likely to have been shocked or angry when alive. □□ **graveless** *adj.* **graveward** *adv. & adj.* [OE *græf* f. WG]

grave[2] /greɪv/ *adj. & n.* —*adj.* **1 a** serious, weighty, important (*a grave matter*). **b** dignified, solemn, sombre (*a grave look*). **2** extremely serious or threatening (*grave danger*). **3** /grɑːv/ (of sound) low-pitched, not acute. —*n.* /grɑːv/ = *grave accent*. □ **grave accent** /grɑːv/ a mark (`) placed over a vowel in some languages to denote pronunciation, length, etc., orig. indicating low or falling pitch. □□ **gravely** *adv.* **graveness** *n.* [F *grave* or L *gravis* heavy, serious]

grave[3] /greɪv/ *v.tr.* (*past part.* **graven** or **graved**) **1** (foll. by *in*, *on*) fix indelibly (on one's memory). **2** *archaic* engrave, carve. □ **graven image** an idol. [OE *grafan* dig, engrave f. Gmc: cf. GROOVE]

grave[4] /greɪv/ *v.tr.* clean (a ship's bottom) by burning off accretions and by tarring. □ **graving dock** = *dry dock*. [perh. F dial. *grave* = OF *greve* shore]

gravedigger /'greɪvˌdɪgə(r)/ *n.* **1** a person who digs graves. **2** (in full **gravedigger beetle**) a sexton beetle.

gravel /'græv(ə)l/ *n. & v.* —*n.* **1 a** a mixture of coarse sand and small water-worn or pounded stones, used for paths and roads and as an aggregate. **b** *Geol.* a stratum of this. **2** *Med.* aggregations of crystals formed in the urinary tract. —*v.tr.* (**gravelled**, **gravelling**; *US* **graveled**, **graveling**) **1** lay or strew with gravel. **2** perplex, puzzle, nonplus (from an obs. sense 'run (a ship) aground'). □ **gravel-blind** *literary* almost completely blind ('more than sand-blind', in Shakesp. *Merchant of Venice* II. ii. 33). [ME f. OF *gravel(e)* dimin. of *grave* (as GRAVE[4])]

gravelly /'grævəlɪ/ *adj.* **1** of or like gravel. **2** having or containing gravel. **3** (of a voice) deep and rough-sounding.

graven *past part.* of GRAVE[3].

graver /'greɪvə(r)/ *n.* **1** an engraving tool; a burin. **2** *archaic* an engraver; a carver.

Graves /grɑːv/ *n.* a light usu. white wine from Graves in France.

Graves' disease /greɪvz/ *n.* exophthalmic goitre with characteristic swelling of the neck and protrusion of the eyes, resulting from an overactive thyroid gland. [R. J. *Graves*, Ir. physician d. 1853]

gravestone /'greɪvstəʊn/ *n.* a stone (usu. inscribed) marking a grave.

graveyard /'greɪvjɑːd/ *n.* a burial-ground, esp. by a church.

gravid /'grævɪd/ *adj. literary* or *Zool.* pregnant. [L *gravidus* f. *gravis* heavy]

gravimeter /grə'vɪmɪtə(r)/ *n.* an instrument for measuring the difference in the force of gravity from one place to another. [F *gravimètre* f. L *gravis* heavy]

gravimetric /ˌgrævɪ'metrɪk/ *adj.* **1** of or relating to the measurement of weight. **2** denoting chemical analysis based on weight.

gravimetry /grə'vɪmɪtrɪ/ *n.* the measurement of weight.

gravitas /'grævɪˌtæs, -ˌtɑːs/ *n.* solemn demeanour; seriousness. [L f. *gravis* serious]

gravitate /'grævɪteɪt/ *v.* **1** *intr.* (foll. by *to*, *towards*) move or be attracted to some source of influence. **2** *tr. & intr.* **a** move or tend by force of gravity towards. **b** sink by or as if by gravity. [mod.L *gravitare* as GRAVITAS]

gravitation /ˌgrævɪ'teɪʃ(ə)n/ *n. Physics* **1** a force of attraction between any particle of matter in the universe and any other. **2** the effect of this, esp. the falling of bodies to the earth. [mod.L *gravitatio* (as GRAVITY)]

gravitational /ˌgrævɪ'teɪʃən(ə)l/ *adj.* of or relating to gravitation. □ **gravitational constant** the constant in Newton's law of gravitation relating gravity to the masses and separation of particles. ¶ Symb.: **G**. **gravitational field** the region of space surrounding a body in which another body experiences a force of attraction. □□ **gravitationally** *adv.*

gravity /'grævɪtɪ/ *n.* **1 a** the force that attracts a body to the centre of the earth or other celestial body. **b** the degree of intensity of this measured by acceleration. **c** gravitational force. **2** the property of having weight. **3 a** importance, seriousness; the quality of being grave. **b** solemnity, sobriety; serious demeanour. □ **gravity feed** the supply of material by its fall under gravity. [F *gravité* or L *gravitas* f. *gravis* heavy]

gravure /grə'vjʊə(r)/ *n.* = PHOTOGRAVURE. [abbr.]

gravy /'greɪvɪ/ *n.* (*pl.* -ies) **1 a** the juices exuding from meat during and after cooking. **b** a dressing or sauce for food, made from these or from other materials, e.g. stock. **2** *sl.* unearned or unexpected money. □ **gravy-boat** a boat-shaped vessel for serving gravy. **gravy train** *sl.* a source of easy financial benefit. [ME, perh. from a misreading as *gravé* of OF *grané*, prob. f. *grain* spice: see GRAIN]

gray[1] /greɪ/ *n. Physics* the SI unit of the absorbed dose of ionizing radiation, corresponding to one joule per kilogram. ¶ Abbr.: **Gy**. [L. H. *Gray*, Engl. radiobiologist d. 1965]

gray[2] *US* var. of GREY.

grayling /'greɪlɪŋ/ *n.* **1** any silver-grey freshwater fish of the genus *Thymallus*, with a long high dorsal fin. **2** a butterfly, *Hipparchia semele*, having wings with grey undersides and bright eye-spots on the upper side. [*gray* var. of GREY + -LING[2]]

graywacke *US* var. of GREYWACKE.

graze[1] /greɪz/ *v.* **1** *intr.* (of cattle, sheep, etc.) eat growing grass. **2** *tr.* **a** feed (cattle etc.) on growing grass. **b** feed on (grass). **3** *intr.* pasture cattle. □□ **grazer** *n.* [OE *grasian* f. *græs* GRASS]

graze[2] /greɪz/ *v. & n.* —*v.* **1** *tr.* rub or scrape (a part of the body, esp. the skin) so as to break the surface without causing bleeding. **2 a** *tr.* touch lightly in passing. **b** *intr.* (foll. by *against*, *along*, etc.) move with a light passing contact. —*n.* an act or instance of grazing. [perh. a specific use of GRAZE[1], as if 'take off the grass close to the ground' (of a shot etc.)]

grazier /'greɪzɪə(r)/ *n.* **1** a person who feeds cattle for market. **2** *Austral.* a large-scale sheep-farmer or cattle-farmer. □□ **graziery** *n.* [GRASS + -IER]

grazing /'greɪzɪŋ/ *n.* grassland suitable for pasturage.

grease /griːs/ *n. & v.* —*n.* **1** oily or fatty matter esp. as a lubricant. **2** the melted fat of a dead animal. **3** oily matter in unprocessed wool. —*v.tr.* /griːs, griːz/ smear or lubricate with grease. □ **grease-gun** a device for pumping grease under pressure to a particular point. **grease the palm** of *colloq.* bribe. **like greased lightning** *colloq.* very fast. □□ **greaseless** *adj.* [ME f. AF *grece, gresse,* OF *graisse* ult. f. L *crassus* (adj.) fat]

greasepaint /'griːspeɪnt/ *n.* a waxy composition used as make-up for actors.

greaseproof /'griːspruːf/ *adj.* impervious to the penetration of grease.

greaser /'griːsə(r)/ *n.* **1** a person or thing that greases. **2** *sl.* a member of a gang of youths with long hair and riding motor cycles. **3** *US sl. offens.* a Mexican or Spanish-American. **4** *sl.* a gentle landing of an aircraft.

greasy /'griːsɪ, -zɪ/ *adj.* (**greasier, greasiest**) **1 a** of or like grease. **b** smeared or covered with grease. **c** containing or having too much grease. **2 a** slippery. **b** (of a person or manner) unpleasantly unctuous, smarmy. **c** objectionable. □□ **greasily** *adv.* **greasiness** *n.*

great /greɪt/ *adj. & n.* —*adj.* **1 a** of a size, amount, extent, or intensity considerably above the normal or average; big (*made a great hole; take great care; lived to a great age*). **b** also with implied surprise, admiration, contempt, etc., esp. in exclamations (*you great idiot!; great stuff!; look at that great wasp*). **c** reinforcing other words denoting size, quantity, etc. (*a great big hole; a great many*). **2** important, pre-eminent; worthy or most worthy of consideration (*the great thing is not to get caught*). **3** grand, imposing (*a great occasion; the great hall*). **4 a** (esp. of a public or historic figure) distinguished; prominent. **b** (**the Great**) as a title denoting the most important of the name (*Alfred the Great*). **5 a** (of a person) remarkable in ability, character, achievement, etc. (*great men; a great thinker*). **b** (of a thing) outstanding of its kind (*the Great Fire*). **6** (foll. by *at, on*) competent, skilled, well-informed. **7** fully deserving the name of; doing a thing habitually or extensively (*a great reader; a great believer in tolerance; not a great one for travelling*). **8** (also **greater**) the larger of the name, species, etc. (*great auk; greater celandine*). **9** (**Greater**) (of a city etc.) including adjacent urban areas (*Greater Manchester*). **10** *colloq.* **a** very enjoyable or satisfactory; attractive, fine (*had a great time; it would be great if we won*). **b** (as an exclam.) fine, very good. **11** (in *comb.*) (in names of family relationships) denoting one degree further removed upwards or downwards (*great-uncle; great-great-grandmother*). —*n.* **1** a great or outstanding person or thing. **2** (in *pl.*) (**Greats**) *colloq.* (at Oxford University) an honours course or final examinations in classics and philosophy. □ **great and small** all classes or types. **the Great Bear** see BEAR². **Great Britain** England, Wales, and Scotland. **great circle** see CIRCLE. **Great Dane** see DANE. **great deal** see DEAL¹. **great-hearted** magnanimous; having a noble or generous mind. **great-heartedness** magnanimity. **the great majority** by far the most. **great northern diver** a diving sea bird, *Gavia immer,* of the northern hemisphere. **great organ** the chief manual in a large organ, with its related pipes and mechanism. **Great Russian** *n.* a member or the language of the principal ethnic group in the USSR; Russian. —*adj.* of or relating to this people or language. **great tit** a Eurasian songbird, *Parus major,* with black and white head markings. **great toe** the big toe. **Great War** the world war of 1914–18. **to a great extent** largely. □□ **greatness** *n.* [OE *grēat* f. WG]

greatcoat /'greɪtkəʊt/ *n.* a long heavy overcoat.

greatly /'greɪtlɪ/ *adv.* by a considerable amount; much (*greatly admired; greatly superior*).

greave /griːv/ *n.* (usu. in *pl.*) armour for the shin. [ME f. OF *greve* shin, greave, of unkn. orig.]

grebe /griːb/ *n.* any diving bird of the family Podicipedidae, with a long neck, lobed toes, and almost no tail. □ **little grebe** a small water bird of the grebe family, *Tachybaptus ruficollis.* [F *grèbe,* of unkn. orig.]

Grecian /'griːʃ(ə)n/ *adj.* (of architecture or facial outline) following Greek models or ideals. □ **Grecian nose** a straight nose that continues the line of the forehead without a dip. [OF *grecien* or med.L *graecianus* (unrecorded) f. L *Graia* Greece]

Grecism var. of GRAECISM.

Grecize var. of GRAECIZE.

Greco- var. of GRAECO-.

greed /griːd/ *n.* an excessive desire, esp. for food or wealth. [back-form. f. GREEDY]

greedy /'griːdɪ/ *adj.* (**greedier, greediest**) **1** having or showing an excessive appetite for food or drink. **2** wanting wealth or pleasure to excess. **3** (foll. by *for,* or *to* + infin.) very keen or eager; needing intensely (*greedy for affection; greedy to learn*). □□ **greedily** *adv.* **greediness** *n.* [OE *grǣdig* f. Gmc]

Greek /griːk/ *n. & adj.* —*n.* **1 a** a native or national of modern Greece; a person of Greek descent. **b** a native or citizen of any of the ancient States of Greece; a member of the Greek people. **2** the Indo-European language of Greece. —*adj.* of Greece or its people or language; Hellenic. □ **Greek** (or **Greek Orthodox**) **Church** the national Church of Greece (see also *Orthodox Church*). **Greek cross** a cross with four equal arms. **Greek fire** *hist.* a combustible composition for igniting enemy ships etc. **Greek to me** *colloq.* incomprehensible to me. □□ **Greekness** *n.* [OE *Grēcas* (pl.) f. Gmc f. L *Graecus* Greek f. Gk *Graikoi,* the prehistoric name of the Hellenes (in Aristotle)]

green /griːn/ *adj., n., & v.* —*adj.* **1** of the colour between blue and yellow in the spectrum; coloured like grass, emeralds, etc. **2 a** covered with leaves or grass. **b** mild and without snow (*a green Christmas*). **3** (of fruit etc. or wood) unripe or unseasoned. **4** not dried, smoked, or tanned. **5** inexperienced, naïve, gullible. **6 a** (of the complexion) pale, sickly-hued. **b** jealous, envious. **7** young, flourishing. **8** not withered or worn out (*a green old age*). **9** vegetable (*green food; green salad*). **10** (also **Green**) concerned with or supporting protection of the environment as a political principle. **11** *archaic* fresh; not healed (*a green wound*). —*n.* **1** a green colour or pigment. **2** green clothes or material (*dressed in green*). **3 a** a piece of public or common grassy land (*village green*). **b** a grassy area used for a special purpose (*putting-green; bowling-green*). **c** *Golf* a putting-green. **d** *Golf* a fairway. **4** (in *pl.*) green vegetables. **5** vigour, youth, virility (*in the green*). **6** a green light. **7** a green ball, piece, etc., in a game or sport. **8** (also **Green**) a member or supporter of an environmentalist group or party. **9** (in *pl.*) *sl.* sexual intercourse. **10** *sl.* low-grade marijuana. **11** *sl.* money. **12** green foliage or growing plants. —*v.* **1** *tr. & intr.* make or become green. **2** *tr. sl.* hoax; take in. □ **green belt** an area of open land round a city, designated for preservation. **Green Beret** *colloq.* a British or American commando. **green card** an international insurance document for motorists. **green cheese 1** cheese coloured green with sage. **2** whey cheese. **3** unripened cheese. **Green Cloth** (in full **Board of Green Cloth**) (in the UK) the Lord Steward's department of the Royal Household. **green crop** a crop used as fodder in a green state rather than as hay etc. **green drake** the common mayfly. **green earth** a hydrous silicate of potassium, iron, and other metals. **green-eyed** jealous. **the green-eyed monster** jealousy. **green fat** part of a turtle, highly regarded by gourmets. **green-fee** *Golf* a charge for playing one round on a course. **green fingers** skill in growing plants. **green goose** a goose killed under four months old and eaten without stuffing. **green in a person's eye** a sign of gullibility (*do you see any green in my eye?*). **green leek** any of several green-faced Australian parakeets. **green light 1** a signal to proceed on a road, railway, etc. **2** *colloq.* permission to go ahead with a project. **green linnet** = GREENFINCH. **green manure** growing plants ploughed into the soil as fertilizer. **green meat** grass and green vegetables as food. **Green Paper** (in the UK) a preliminary report of Government proposals, for discussion. **green plover** a lapwing. **green pound** the exchange rate for the pound for payments for agricultural produce in the EEC. **green revolution** greatly increased crop production in underdeveloped countries. **green-room** a room in a theatre for actors and actresses who are off stage. **green-stick fracture** a bone-fracture, esp. in children, in which one side of the bone is broken and one only bent. **green tea** tea made from steam-dried, not fermented, leaves. **green thumb** = *green fingers*. **green turtle** a green-shelled sea turtle, *Chelonia mydas*, highly regarded as food. **green vitriol** ferrous sulphate crystals. □□ **greenish** *adj.* **greenly** *adv.* **greenness** *n.* [OE *grēne* (adj. & n.), *grēnian* (v.), f. Gmc, rel. to GROW]

greenback /ˈgriːnbæk/ *n.* *US* **1** a US legal-tender note. **2** any of various green-backed animals.

greenbottle /ˈgriːnbɒt(ə)l/ *n.* any fly of the genus *Lucilia*, esp. *L. sericata* which lays eggs in the flesh of sheep.

greenery /ˈgriːnərɪ/ *n.* green foliage or growing plants.

greenfeed /ˈgriːnfiːd/ *n.* *Austral. & NZ* forage grown to be fed fresh to livestock.

greenfield /ˈgriːnfiːld/ *n.* (*attrib.*) (of a site, in terms of its potential development) having no previous building development on it.

greenfinch /ˈgriːnfɪntʃ/ *n.* a finch, *Carduelis chloris*, with green and yellow plumage.

greenfly /ˈgriːnflaɪ/ *n.* (*pl.* **-flies**) *Brit.* **1** a green aphid. **2** these collectively.

greengage /ˈgriːngeɪdʒ/ *n.* a roundish green fine-flavoured variety of plum. [Sir W. *Gage* d. 1727]

greengrocer /ˈgriːnˌgrəʊsə(r)/ *n.* *Brit.* a retailer of fruit and vegetables.

greengrocery /ˈgriːnˌgrəʊsərɪ/ *n.* (*pl.* **-ies**) *Brit.* **1** the business of a greengrocer. **2** goods sold by a greengrocer.

greenhead /ˈgriːnhed/ *n.* **1** any biting fly of the genus *Chrysops*. **2** an Australian ant, *Chalcoponera metallica*, with a painful sting.

greenheart /ˈgriːnhɑːt/ *n.* **1** any of several tropical American trees, esp. *Ocotea rodiaei*. **2** the hard greenish wood of one of these.

greenhorn /ˈgriːnhɔːn/ *n.* an inexperienced or foolish person; a new recruit.

greenhouse /ˈgriːnhaʊs/ *n.* a light structure with the sides and roof mainly of glass, for rearing delicate plants or hastening the growth of plants. □ **greenhouse effect** the trapping of the sun's warmth in the lower atmosphere of the earth caused by an increase in carbon dioxide, which is more transparent to solar radiation than to the reflected radiation from the earth. **greenhouse gas** any of various gases, esp. carbon dioxide, that contribute to the greenhouse effect.

greening /ˈgriːnɪŋ/ *n.* a variety of apple that is green when ripe. [prob. f. MDu. *groeninc* (as GREEN)]

greenkeeper /ˈgriːnˌkiːpə(r)/ *n.* the keeper of a golf-course.

greenlet /ˈgriːnlɪt/ *n.* = VIREO.

greensand /ˈgriːnsænd/ *n.* **1** a greenish kind of sandstone, often imperfectly cemented. **2** a stratum largely formed of this sandstone.

greenshank /ˈgriːnʃæŋk/ *n.* a large sandpiper, *Tringa nebularia*.

greensick /ˈgriːnsɪk/ *adj.* affected with chlorosis. □□ **greensickness** *n.*

greenstone /ˈgriːnstəʊn/ *n.* **1** a greenish igneous rock containing feldspar and hornblende. **2** a variety of jade found in New Zealand, used for tools, ornaments, etc.

greenstuff /ˈgriːnstʌf/ *n.* vegetation; green vegetables.

greensward /ˈgriːnswɔːd/ *n.* **1** grassy turf. **2** an expanse of this.

greenweed /ˈgriːnwiːd/ *n.* (dyer's greenweed) a bushy plant, *Genista tinctoria*, with deep yellow flowers.

Greenwich Mean Time /ˈgrenɪtʃ, ˈgrɪnɪdʒ/ *n.* (also **Greenwich Time**) the local time on the meridian of Greenwich, used as an international basis of time-reckoning. [*Greenwich* in London, former site of the Royal Observatory]

greenwood /ˈgriːnwʊd/ *n.* a wood in summer, esp. as the scene of outlaw life.

greeny /ˈgriːnɪ/ *adj.* greenish (*greeny-yellow*).

greenyard /ˈgriːnjɑːd/ *n.* *Brit.* an enclosure for stray animals, a pound.

greet[1] /griːt/ *v.tr.* **1** address politely or welcomingly on meeting or arrival. **2** receive or acknowledge in a specified way (*was greeted with derision*). **3** (of a sight, sound, etc.) become apparent to or noticed by. □□ **greeter** *n.* [OE *grētan* handle, attack, salute f. WG]

greet[2] /griːt/ *v.intr.* *Sc.* weep. [OE *grētan*, *grēotan*, of uncert. orig.]

greeting /ˈgriːtɪŋ/ *n.* **1** the act or an instance of welcoming or addressing politely. **2** words, gestures, etc., used to greet a person. **3** (often in *pl.*) an expression of goodwill. □ **greetings card** a decorative card sent to convey greetings.

gregarious /grɪˈgeərɪəs/ *adj.* **1** fond of company. **2** living in flocks or communities. **3** growing in clusters. □□ **gregariously** *adv.* **gregariousness** *n.* [L *gregarius* f. *grex gregis* flock]

Gregorian calendar /grɪˈgɔːrɪən/ *n.* the calendar introduced in 1582 by Pope Gregory XIII, as a correction of the Julian calendar. [med.L *Gregorianus* f. LL *Gregorius* f. Gk *Grēgorios* Gregory]

Gregorian chant /grɪˈgɔːrɪən/ *n.* plainsong ritual music, named after Pope Gregory I.

Gregorian telescope /grɪˈgɔːrɪən/ *n.* a reflecting telescope in which light reflected from a secondary mirror passes through a hole in a primary mirror. [J. *Gregory*, Sc. mathematician d. 1675, who devised it]

gregory-powder /ˈgregərɪ/ *n.* *hist.* a compound powder of rhubarb, magnesia, and ginger, used as a laxative. [J. *Gregory*, Sc. physician d. 1822]

gremlin /ˈgremlɪn/ *n.* *colloq.* **1** an imaginary mischievous sprite regarded as responsible for mechanical faults, esp. in aircraft. **2** any similar cause of trouble. [20th c.: orig. unkn., but prob. after *goblin*]

grenade /grɪˈneɪd/ *n.* **1** a small bomb thrown by hand (**hand-grenade**) or shot from a rifle. **2** a glass receptacle containing chemicals which disperse on impact, for testing drains, extinguishing fires, etc. [F f. OF *grenate* and Sp. *granada* POMEGRANATE]

grenadier /ˌgrenəˈdɪə(r)/ *n.* **1 a** *Brit.* (**Grenadiers** or **Grenadier Guards**) the first regiment of royal household infantry. **b** *hist.* a soldier armed with grenades. **2** any deep-sea fish of the family Macrouridae, with a long tapering body and pointed tail, and secreting luminous bacteria when disturbed. [F (as GRENADE)]

grenadilla var. of GRANADILLA.

grenadine[1] /ˈgrenəˌdiːn/ *n.* a French cordial syrup of pomegranates etc. [F f. *grenade*: see GRENADE]

grenadine[2] /ˈgrenəˌdiːn/ *n.* a dress-fabric of loosely woven silk or silk and wool. [F, earlier *grenade* grained silk f. *grenu* grained]

Gresham's law /ˈgreʃəmz/ *n.* the tendency for money of lower intrinsic value to circulate more freely than money of higher intrinsic and equal nominal value. [Sir T. *Gresham*, Engl. financier d. 1579]

gressorial /gre'sɔːrɪəl/ *adj. Zool.* **1** walking. **2** adapted for walking. [mod.L *gressorius* f. L *gradi gress-* walk]

grew *past* of GROW.

grey /greɪ/ *adj., n.,* & *v.* (*US* **gray**) —*adj.* **1** of a colour intermediate between black and white, as of ashes or lead. **2 a** (of the weather etc.) dull, dismal; heavily overcast. **b** bleak, depressing; (of a person) depressed. **3 a** (of hair) turning white with age etc. **b** (of a person) having grey hair. **4** anonymous, nondescript, unidentifiable. —*n.* **1 a** a grey colour or pigment. **b** grey clothes or material (*dressed in grey*). **2** a cold sunless light. **3** a grey or white horse. —*v.tr.* & *intr.* make or become grey. □**grey area 1** a situation or topic sharing features of more than one category and not clearly attributable to any one category. **2** *S.Afr.* an area where Black and Coloured people live (usu. illicitly) alongside White. **3** *Brit.* an area in economic decline. **grey eminence** = ÉMINENCE GRISE. **Grey Friar** a Franciscan friar. **grey goose** = GREYLAG. **grey-hen** the female of the black grouse (cf. BLACKCOCK). **grey matter 1** the darker tissues of the brain and spinal cord consisting of nerve-cell bodies and branching dendrites. **2** *colloq.* intelligence. **grey squirrel** an American squirrel, *Sciurus carolinensis*, brought to Europe in the 19th c. □□**greyish** *adj.* **greyly** *adv.* **greyness** *n.* [OE *græg* f. Gmc]

greybeard /'greɪbɪəd/ *n. archaic* **1** an old man. **2** a large stoneware jug for spirits. **3** *Brit.* clematis in seed.

greyhound /'greɪhaʊnd/ *n.* **1** a dog of a tall slender breed having keen sight and capable of high speed, used in racing and coursing. **2** this breed. [OE *grīghund* f. *grīeg* bitch (unrecorded: cf. ON *grey*) + *hund* dog, rel. to HOUND]

greylag /'greɪlæg/ *n.* (in full **greylag goose**) a wild goose, *Anser anser*, native to Europe. [GREY + LAG[1] (because of its late migration)]

greywacke /'greɪ,wækə, -wæk/ *n.* (*US* **graywacke**) *Geol.* a dark and coarse-grained sandstone, usu. with an admixture of clay. [Anglicized f. G *Grauwacke* f. *grau* grey: see WACKE]

grid /grɪd/ *n.* **1** a framework of spaced parallel bars; a grating. **2** a system of numbered squares printed on a map and forming the basis of map references. **3** a network of lines, electric-power connections, gas-supply lines, etc. **4** a pattern of lines marking the starting-places on a motor-racing track. **5** the wire network between the filament and the anode of a thermionic valve etc. **6** an arrangement of town streets in a rectangular pattern. □**grid bias** *Electr.* a fixed voltage applied between the cathode and the control grid of a thermionic valve which determines its operating conditions. □□**gridded** *adj.* [back-form. f. GRIDIRON]

griddle /'grɪd(ə)l/ *n.* & *v.* —*n.* **1** = GIRDLE[2]. **2** a miner's wire-bottomed sieve. —*v.tr.* **1** cook with a griddle; grill. **2** sieve with a griddle. [ME f. OF *gredil, gridil* gridiron ult. f. L *craticula* dimin. of *cratis* hurdle; cf. GRATE[2], GRILL[1]]

gridiron /'grɪd,aɪən/ *n.* **1** a cooking utensil of metal bars for broiling or grilling. **2** a frame of parallel beams for supporting a ship in dock. **3** *US* a football field (with parallel lines marking out the area of play). **4** *Theatr.* a plank structure over a stage supporting the mechanism for drop-scenes etc. **5** = GRID 6. [ME *gredire*, var. of *gredil* GRIDDLE, later assoc. with IRON]

grief /griːf/ *n.* **1** deep or intense sorrow or mourning. **2** the cause of this. □**come to grief** meet with disaster; fail. **good** (or **great**) **grief!** an exclamation of surprise, alarm, etc. [ME f. AF *gref*, OF *grief* f. *grever* GRIEVE[1]]

grievance /'griːv(ə)ns/ *n.* a real or fancied cause for complaint. [ME, = injury, f. OF *grevance* (as GRIEF)]

grieve[1] /griːv/ *v.* **1** *tr.* cause grief or great distress to. **2** *intr.* suffer grief, esp. at another's death. □□**griever** *n.* [ME f. OF *grever* ult. f. L *gravare* f. *gravis* heavy]

grieve[2] /griːv/ *n. Sc.* a farm-bailiff; an overseer. [OE *grǣfa*: cf. REEVE[1]]

grievous /'griːvəs/ *adj.* **1** (of pain etc.) severe. **2** causing grief or suffering. **3** injurious. **4** flagrant, heinous. □**grievous bodily harm** *Law* serious injury inflicted intentionally on a person. □□**grievously** *adv.* **grievousness** *n.* [ME f. OF *grevos* (as GRIEVE[1])]

griffin /'grɪfɪn/ *n.* (also **gryphon** /-f(ə)n/) a fabulous creature with an eagle's head and wings and a lion's body. [ME f. OF *grifoun* ult. f. LL *gryphus* f. L *gryps* f. Gk *grups*]

griffon /'grɪf(ə)n/ *n.* **1 a** a dog of a small terrier-like breed with coarse or smooth hair. **b** this breed. **2** (in full **griffon vulture**) a large vulture, *Gyps fulvus*. **3** = GRIFFIN. [F (in sense 1) or var. of GRIFFIN]

grig /grɪg/ *n.* **1** a small eel. **2** a grasshopper or cricket. □**merry** (or **lively**) **as a grig** full of fun; extravagantly lively. [ME, orig. = dwarf: orig. unkn.]

grill[1] /grɪl/ *n.* & *v.* —*n.* **1 a** a device on a cooker for radiating heat downwards. **b** = GRIDIRON[1]. **2** a dish of food cooked on a grill. **3** (in full **grill room**) a restaurant serving grilled food. —*v.* **1** *tr.* & *intr.* cook or be cooked under a grill or on a gridiron. **2** *tr.* & *intr.* subject or be subjected to extreme heat, esp. from the sun. **3** *tr.* subject to severe questioning or interrogation. □□**griller** *n.* **grilling** *n.* (in sense 3 of *v.*). [F *gril* (n.), *griller* (v.), f. OF forms of GRILLE]

grill[2] var. of GRILLE.

grillage /'grɪlɪdʒ/ *n.* a heavy framework of cross-timbering or metal beams forming a foundation for building on difficult ground. [F (as GRILLE)]

grille /grɪl/ *n.* (also **grill**) **1** a grating or latticed screen, used as a partition or to allow discreet vision. **2** a metal grid protecting the radiator of a motor vehicle. [F f. OF *graïlle* f. med.L *graticula, craticula*: see GRIDDLE]

grilse /grɪls/ *n.* a young salmon that has returned to fresh water from the sea for the first time. [ME: orig. unkn.]

grim /grɪm/ *adj.* (**grimmer, grimmest**) **1** of a stern or forbidding appearance. **2** harsh, merciless, severe. **3** ghastly, joyless, sinister (*has a grim truth in it*). **4** unpleasant, unattractive. □**like grim death** with great determination. □□**grimly** *adv.* **grimness** *n.* [OE f. Gmc]

grimace /'grɪməs, grɪ'meɪs/ *n.* & *v.* —*n.* a distortion of the face made in disgust etc. or to amuse. —*v.intr.* make a grimace. □□**grimacer** *n.* [F f. Sp. *grimazo* f. *grima* fright]

grimalkin /grɪ'mælkɪn, -'mɔːlkɪn/ *n. archaic* (esp. in fiction) **1** an old she-cat. **2** a spiteful old woman. [GREY + *Malkin* dimin. of the name *Matilda*]

grime /graɪm/ *n.* & *v.* —*n.* soot or dirt ingrained in a surface, esp. of buildings or the skin. —*v.tr.* blacken with grime; befoul. [orig. as verb: f. MLG & MDu.]

grimy /'graɪmɪ/ *adj.* (**grimier, grimiest**) covered with grime; dirty. □□**grimily** *adv.* **griminess** *n.*

grin /grɪn/ *v.* & *n.* —*v.* (**grinned, grinning**) **1** *intr.* **a** smile broadly, showing the teeth. **b** make a forced, unrestrained, or stupid smile. **2** *tr.* express by grinning (*grinned his satisfaction*). —*n.* the act or action of grinning. □**grin and bear it** take pain or misfortune stoically. □□**grinner** *n.* **grinningly** *adv.* [OE *grennian* f. Gmc]

grind /graɪnd/ *v.* & *n.* —*v.* (*past* and *past part.* **ground** /graʊnd/) **1 a** *tr.* reduce to small particles or powder by crushing esp. by passing through a mill. **b** *intr.* (of a mill, machine, etc.) move with a crushing action. **2 a** *tr.* reduce, sharpen, or smooth by friction. **b** *tr.* & *intr.* rub or rub together gratingly (*grind one's teeth*). **3** *tr.* (often foll. by *down*) oppress; harass with exactions (*grinding poverty*). **4** *intr.* **a** (often foll. by *away*) work or study hard. **b** (foll. by *out*) produce with effort (*grinding out verses*). **c**

(foll. by *on*) (of a sound) continue gratingly or monotonously. **5** *tr.* turn the handle of e.g. a coffee-mill, barrel-organ, etc. **6** *intr. sl.* (of a dancer) rotate the hips. **7** *intr. coarse sl.* have sexual intercourse. —*n.* **1** the act or an instance of grinding. **2** *colloq.* hard dull work; a laborious task (*the daily grind*). **3** the size of ground particles. **4** *sl.* a dancer's rotary movement of the hips. **5** *coarse sl.* an act of sexual intercourse. □**grind to a halt** stop laboriously. **ground glass 1** glass made non-transparent by grinding etc. **2** glass ground to a powder. □□ **grindingly** *adv.* [OE *grindan*, of unkn. orig.]

grinder /ˈgraɪndə(r)/ *n.* **1** a person or thing that grinds, esp. a machine (often in *comb.*: *coffee-grinder*; *organ-grinder*). **2** a molar tooth.

grindstone /ˈgraɪndstəʊn/ *n.* **1** a thick revolving disc used for grinding, sharpening, and polishing. **2** a kind of stone used for this. □**keep one's nose to the grindstone** work hard and continuously.

gringo /ˈgrɪŋgəʊ/ *n.* (*pl.* -os) *colloq.* a foreigner, esp. a British or N. American person, in a Spanish-speaking country. [Sp., = gibberish]

grip /grɪp/ *v. & n.* —*v.* (**gripped, gripping**) **1 a** *tr.* grasp tightly; take a firm hold of. **b** *intr.* take a firm hold, esp. by friction. **2** *tr.* (of a feeling or emotion) deeply affect (a person) (*was gripped by fear*). **3** *tr.* compel the attention or interest of (*a gripping story*). —*n.* **1 a** a firm hold; a tight grasp or clasp. **b** a manner of grasping or holding. **2** the power of holding attention. **3 a** mental or intellectual understanding or mastery. **b** effective control of a situation or one's behaviour etc. (*lose one's grip*). **4 a** a part of a machine that grips or holds something. **b** a part or attachment by which a tool, implement, weapon, etc., is held in the hand. **5** = HAIRGRIP. **6** a travelling bag. **7** an assistant in a theatre, film studio, etc. **8** *Austral. sl.* a job or occupation. □**come** (or **get**) **to grips with** approach purposefully; begin to deal with. **in the grip of** dominated or affected by (esp. an adverse circumstance or unpleasant sensation). □□ **gripper** *n.* **grippingly** *adv.* [OE *gripe, gripa* handful (as GRIPE)]

gripe /graɪp/ *v. & n.* —*v.* **1** *intr. colloq.* complain, esp. peevishly. **2** *tr.* affect with gastric or intestinal pain. **3** *tr. archaic* clutch, grip. **4** *Naut.* **a** *tr.* secure with gripes. **b** *intr.* turn to face the wind in spite of the helm. —*n.* **1** (usu. in *pl.*) gastric or intestinal pain; colic. **2** *colloq.* **a** a complaint. **b** the act of griping. **3** a grip or clutch. **4** (in *pl.*) *Naut.* lashings securing a boat in its place. □**Gripe Water** *propr.* a carminative solution to relieve colic and stomach ailments in infants. □□ **griper** *n.* **gripingly** *adv.* [OE *grīpan* f. Gmc: cf. GROPE]

grippe /grɪp/ *n. archaic* or *colloq.* influenza. [F f. *gripper* seize]

grisaille /grɪˈzeɪl, -ˈzaɪl/ *n.* **1** a method of painting in grey monochrome, often to imitate sculpture. **2** a painting or stained-glass window of this kind. [F f. *gris* grey]

griseofulvin /ˌgrɪzɪəʊˈfʊlvɪn/ *n.* an antibiotic used against fungal infections of the hair and skin. [mod.L *griseofulvum* f. med.L *griseus* grey + L *fulvus* reddish-yellow]

grisette /griˈzet/ *n.* a young working-class French-woman. [F, orig. a grey dress-material, f. *gris* grey]

grisly /ˈgrɪzlɪ/ *adj.* (**grislier, grisliest**) causing horror, disgust, or fear. □□ **grisliness** *n.* [OE *grislic* terrifying]

grison /ˈgrɪz(ə)n/ *n.* any weasel-like mammal of the genus *Galictis*, with dark fur and a white stripe across the forehead. [F, app. f. *grison* grey]

grist /grɪst/ *n.* **1** corn to grind. **2** malt crushed for brewing. □**grist to the** (or **a person's**) **mill** a source of profit or advantage. [OE f. Gmc, rel. to GRIND]

gristle /ˈgrɪs(ə)l/ *n.* tough flexible tissue in vertebrates; cartilage. □□ **gristly** /-slɪ/ *adj.* [OE *gristle*]

grit /grɪt/ *n. & v.* —*n.* **1** particles of stone or sand, esp. as causing discomfort, clogging machinery, etc.

2 coarse sandstone. **3** *colloq.* pluck, endurance; strength of character. —*v.* (**gritted, gritting**) **1** *tr.* spread grit on (icy roads etc.). **2** *tr.* clench (the teeth). **3** *intr.* make or move with a grating sound. □□ **gritter** *n.* **gritty** *adj.* (**grittier, grittiest**). **grittily** *adv.* **grittiness** *n.* [OE *grēot* f. Gmc: cf. GRITS, GROATS]

grits /grɪts/ *n.pl.* **1** coarsely ground grain, esp. oatmeal. **2** oats that have been husked but not ground. [OE *grytt(e)*: cf. GRIT, GROATS]

grizzle /ˈgrɪz(ə)l/ *v.intr. Brit. colloq.* **1** (esp. of a child) cry fretfully. **2** complain whiningly. □□ **grizzler** *n.* **grizzly** *adj.* [19th c.: orig. unkn.]

grizzled /ˈgrɪz(ə)ld/ *adj.* having, or streaked with, grey hair. [*grizzle* grey f. OF *grisel* f. *gris* grey]

grizzly /ˈgrɪzlɪ/ *adj. & n.* —*adj.* (**grizzlier, grizzliest**) grey, greyish, grey-haired. —*n.* (*pl.* -ies) (in full **grizzly bear**) a large variety of brown bear, found in N. America and N. Russia.

groan /grəʊn/ *v. & n.* —*v.* **1 a** *intr.* make a deep sound expressing pain, grief, or disapproval. **b** *tr.* utter with groans. **2** *intr.* complain inarticulately. **3** *intr.* (usu. foll. by *under, beneath, with*) be loaded or oppressed. —*n.* the sound made in groaning. □**groan inwardly** be distressed. □□ **groaner** *n.* **groaningly** *adv.* [OE *grānian* f. Gmc, rel. to GRIN]

groat /grəʊt/ *n. hist.* **1** a silver coin worth four old pence. **2** *archaic* a small sum (*don't care a groat*). [ME f. MDu. *groot*, orig. = great, i.e. thick (penny): cf. GROSCHEN]

groats /grəʊts/ *n.pl.* hulled or crushed grain, esp. oats. [OE *grotan* (pl.): cf. *grot* fragment, *grēot* GRIT, *grytt* bran]

grocer /ˈgrəʊsə(r)/ *n.* a dealer in food and household provisions. [ME & AF *grosser*, orig. one who sells in the gross, f. OF *grossier* f. med.L *grossarius* (as GROSS)]

grocery /ˈgrəʊsərɪ/ *n.* (*pl.* -ies) **1** a grocer's trade or shop. **2** (in *pl.*) provisions, esp. food, sold by a grocer.

grockle /ˈgrɒk(ə)l/ *n. dial. & sl.* a visitor or holiday-maker, esp. from the North or Midlands to SW England. [20th c.: orig. uncert.]

grog /grɒg/ *n.* **1** a drink of spirit (orig. rum) and water. **2** *Austral. & NZ colloq.* alcoholic liquor, esp. beer. [said to be from 'Old *Grog*', the reputed nickname (f. his GROGRAM cloak) of Admiral Vernon, who in 1740 first had diluted instead of neat rum served out to sailors]

groggy /ˈgrɒgɪ/ *adj.* (**groggier, groggiest**) incapable or unsteady from being dazed or semi-conscious. □□ **groggily** *adv.* **grogginess** *n.*

grogram /ˈgrɒgrəm/ *n.* a coarse fabric of silk, mohair, and wool, or a mixture of these, often stiffened with gum. [F *gros grain* coarse grain (as GROSS, GRAIN)]

groin[1] /grɔɪn/ *n. & v.* —*n.* **1** the depression between the belly and the thigh. **2** *Archit.* **a** an edge formed by intersecting vaults. **b** an arch supporting a vault. —*v.tr. Archit.* build with groins. [ME *grynde*, perh. f. OE *grynde* depression]

groin[2] *US* var. of GROYNE.

grommet /ˈgrɒmɪt/ *n.* (also **grummet** /ˈgrʌmɪt/) **1** a metal, plastic, or rubber eyelet placed in a hole to protect or insulate a rope or cable etc. passed through it. **2** a tube passed through the eardrum in surgery to make a communication with the middle ear. [obs. F *grommette* f. *gourmer* to curb, of unkn. orig.]

gromwell /ˈgrɒmw(ə)l/ *n.* any of various plants of the genus *Lithospermum*, with hard seeds formerly used in medicine. [ME f. OF *gromil*, prob. f. med.L *gruinum milium* (unrecorded) crane's millet]

groom /gruːm/ *n. & v.* —*n.* **1** a person employed to take care of horses. **2** = BRIDEGROOM. **3** *Brit. Mil.* any of certain officers of the Royal Household. —*v.tr.* **1** a curry or tend (a horse). **b** give a neat appearance to (a person etc.). **2** (of an ape or monkey etc.) clean and comb the fur (of its fellow) with the fingers. **3** prepare or train (a person) for a particular purpose or activity (*was groomed for the top job*). [ME, orig. = boy: orig. unkn.]

groove /gruːv/ *n. & v.* —*n.* **1 a** a channel or hollow, esp. one made to guide motion or receive a corresponding ridge. **b** a spiral track cut in a gramophone record. **2** an established routine or habit, esp. a monotonous one. —*v.* **1** *tr.* make a groove or grooves in. **2** *intr. sl.* **a** enjoy oneself. **b** (often foll. by *with*) make progress; get on well. ¶ Often with ref. to popular music or jazz; now largely disused in general contexts. □**in the groove** *sl.* **1** doing or performing well. **2** fashionable. [ME, = mine-shaft, f. obs. Du. *groeve* furrow f. Gmc]

groovy /ˈgruːvɪ/ *adj.* (**groovier, grooviest**) **1** *sl.* fashionable and exciting; enjoyable, excellent. **2** of or like a groove. □□**groovily** *adv.* **grooviness** *n.*

grope /grəʊp/ *v. & n.* —*v.* **1** *intr.* (usu. foll. by *for*) feel about or search blindly or uncertainly with the hands. **2** *intr.* (foll. by *for*, *after*) search mentally (*was groping for the answer*). **3** *tr.* feel (one's way) towards something. **4** *tr. sl.* fondle clumsily for sexual pleasure. —*n.* the process or an instance of groping. □□**groper** *n.* **gropingly** *adv.* [OE *grāpian* f. Gmc]

groper /ˈgrəʊpə(r)/ *n.* esp. *Austral. & NZ* = GROUPER. [var. of GROUPER]

grosbeak /ˈgrəʊsbiːk/ *n.* any of various finches of the families Cardinalidae and Fringillidae, having stout conical bills and usu. brightly coloured plumage. [F *grosbec* (as GROSS)]

groschen /ˈgrɒʃ(ə)n/ *n.* **1** an Austrian coin and monetary unit, one hundredth of a schilling. **2** *colloq.* a German 10-pfennig piece. **3** *hist.* a small German silver coin. [G f. MHG *gros, grosse* f. med.L (*denarius*) *grossus* thick (penny): cf. GROAT]

grosgrain /ˈgrəʊgreɪn/ *n.* a corded fabric of silk etc. [F, = coarse grain (as GROSS, GRAIN)]

gros point /grəʊ ˈpwæ̃/ *n.* cross-stitch embroidery on canvas. [F (as GROSS, POINT)]

gross /grəʊs/ *adj., v., & n.* —*adj.* **1** overfed, bloated; repulsively fat. **2** (of a person, manners, or morals) noticeably coarse, unrefined, or indecent. **3** flagrant; conspicuously wrong (*gross negligence*). **4** total; without deductions; not net (*gross tonnage; gross income*). **5 a** luxuriant, rank. **b** thick, solid, dense. **6** (of the senses etc.) dull; lacking sensitivity. —*v.tr.* produce or earn as gross profit or income. —*n.* (*pl.* same) an amount equal to twelve dozen. □**by the gross** in large quantities; wholesale. **gross domestic product** the total value of goods produced and services provided in a country in one year. **gross national product** the gross domestic product plus the total of net income from abroad. **gross out** *US sl.* disgust, esp. by repulsive or obscene behaviour. **gross up** increase (a net amount) to its value before deductions. □□**grossly** *adv.* **grossness** *n.* [ME f. OF *gros grosse* large f. LL *grossus*: (n.) f. F *grosse douzaine* large dozen]

grot /grɒt/ *n. & adj. Brit. sl.* —*n.* rubbish, junk. —*adj.* dirty. [back-form. f. GROTTY]

grotesque /grəʊˈtesk/ *adj. & n.* —*adj.* **1** comically or repulsively distorted; monstrous, unnatural. **2** incongruous, ludicrous, absurd. —*n.* **1** a decorative form interweaving human and animal features. **2** a comically distorted figure or design. **3** *Printing* a family of sanserif typefaces. □□**grotesquely** *adv.* **grotesqueness** *n.* **grotesquerie** /-ˈteskərɪ/ *n.* [earlier *crotesque* f. F *crotesque* f. It. *grottesca* grotto-like (painting etc.) fem. of *grottesco* (as GROTTO, -ESQUE)]

grotto /ˈgrɒtəʊ/ *n.* (*pl.* **-oes** or **-os**) **1** a small picturesque cave. **2** an artificial ornamental cave, e.g. in a park or large garden. □□**grottoed** *adj.* [It. *grotta* ult. f. L *crypta* f. Gk *kruptē* CRYPT]

grotty /ˈgrɒtɪ/ *adj.* (**grottier, grottiest**) *Brit. sl.* unpleasant, dirty, shabby, unattractive. □□ **grottiness** *n.* [shortening of GROTESQUE + -Y¹]

grouch /graʊtʃ/ *v. & n. colloq.* —*v.intr.* grumble.

—*n.* **1** a discontented person. **2** a fit of grumbling or the sulks. **3** a cause of discontent. [var. of *grutch*: see GRUDGE]

grouchy /ˈgraʊtʃɪ/ *adj.* (**grouchier, grouchiest**) *colloq.* discontented, grumpy. □□**grouchily** *adv.* **grouchiness** *n.*

ground¹ /graʊnd/ *n. & v.* —*n.* **1 a** the surface of the earth, esp. as contrasted with the air around it. **b** a part of this specified in some way (*low ground*). **2** the substance of the earth's surface; soil, earth (*stony ground; dug deep into the ground*). **3 a** a position, area, or distance on the earth's surface. **b** the extent of activity etc. achieved or of a subject dealt with (*the book covers a lot of ground*). **4** (often in *pl.*) a foundation, motive, or reason (*there is ground for concern; there are grounds for believing; excused on the grounds of ill-health*). **5** an area of a special kind or designated for special use (often in *comb.*: *cricket-ground; fishing-grounds*). **6** (in *pl.*) an area of usu. enclosed land attached to a house etc. **7** an area or basis for consideration, agreement, etc. (*common ground; on firm ground*). **8 a** (in painting) the prepared surface giving the predominant colour or tone. **b** (in embroidery, ceramics, etc.) the undecorated surface. **9** (in full **ground bass**) *Mus.* a short theme in the bass constantly repeated with the upper parts of the music varied. **10** (in *pl.*) solid particles, esp. of coffee, forming a residue. **11** *Electr.* = EARTH. **12** the bottom of the sea (*the ship touched ground*). **13** *Brit.* the floor of a room etc. **14** a piece of wood fixed to a wall as a base for boards, plaster, or joinery. **15** (*attrib.*) **a** (of animals) living on or in the ground; (of fish) living at the bottom of water; (of plants) dwarfish or trailing. **b** relating to or concerned with the ground (*ground staff*). —*v.* **1** *tr.* refuse authority for (a pilot or an aircraft) to fly. **2 a** *tr.* run (a ship) aground; strand. **b** *intr.* (of a ship) run aground. **3** *tr.* (foll. by *in*) instruct thoroughly (in a subject). **4** *tr.* (often as **grounded** *adj.*) (foll. by *on*) base (a principle, conclusion, etc.) on. **5** *tr. Electr.* = EARTH *v.* **6** *intr.* alight on the ground. **7** *tr.* place or lay (esp. weapons) on the ground. □**break new** (or **fresh**) **ground** treat a subject previously not dealt with. **cut the ground from under a person's feet** anticipate and pre-empt a person's arguments, plans, etc. **down to the ground** *Brit. colloq.* thoroughly; in every respect. **fall to the ground** (of a plan etc.) fail. **gain** (or **make**) **ground 1** advance steadily; make progress. **2** (foll. by *on*) catch (a person) up. **get in on the ground floor** become part of an enterprise in its early stages. **get off the ground** *colloq.* make a successful start. **give** (or **lose**) **ground 1** retreat, decline. **2** lose the advantage or one's position in an argument, contest, etc. **go to ground 1** (of a fox etc.) enter its earth or burrow etc. **2** (of a person) become inaccessible for a prolonged period. **ground-bait** bait thrown to the bottom of a fishing-ground. **ground control** the personnel directing the landing etc. of aircraft or spacecraft. **ground cover** plants covering the surface of the earth, esp. low-growing spreading plants that inhibit the growth of weeds. **ground elder** a garden weed, *Aegopodium podagraria*, spreading by means of underground stems. **ground floor** the floor of a building at ground level. **ground frost** frost on the surface of the ground or in the top layer of soil. **ground level 1** the level of the ground; the ground floor. **2** *Physics* the lowest energy state of an atom etc. **ground-plan 1** the plan of a building at ground level. **2** the general outline of a scheme. **ground-rent** rent for land leased for building. **ground rule** a basic principle. **ground speed** an aircraft's speed relative to the ground. **ground-squirrel 1** a squirrel-like rodent, e.g. a chipmunk, gopher, etc. **2** any squirrel of the genus *Spermophilus* living in burrows. **ground staff** the non-flying personnel of an airport or airbase. **ground state** *Physics* = *ground level* 2. **ground stroke** *Tennis* a stroke played near the ground after the ball has bounced. **ground swell 1** a heavy sea caused by a distant or past storm or an earthquake. **2** an increasingly forceful presence (esp. of public opinion). **ground zero** the point on the ground under an exploding (usu. nuclear) bomb. **hold one's ground** not retreat or give way. **on the ground** at the point of production or operation; in practical conditions. **on one's own ground** on one's own territory or subject; on one's own terms. **thin on the ground** not numerous. **work** (or **run** etc.) **oneself into the ground** colloq. work etc. to the point of exhaustion. □□ **grounder** n. [OE *grund* f. Gmc]

ground² past and past part. of GRIND.

groundage /'graʊndɪdʒ/ n. Brit. duty levied on a ship entering a port or lying on a shore.

groundhog /'graʊndhɒg/ n. **1** = AARDVARK. **2** US a marmot; a woodchuck.

grounding /'graʊndɪŋ/ n. basic training or instruction in a subject.

groundless /'graʊndlɪs/ adj. without motive or foundation. □□ **groundlessly** adv. **groundlessness** n. [OE *grundlēas* (as GROUND¹, -LESS)]

groundling /'graʊndlɪŋ/ n. **1 a** a creeping or dwarf plant. **b** an animal that lives near the ground, at the bottom of a lake, etc., esp. a ground-fish. **2** a person on the ground as opposed to one in an aircraft. **3** a spectator or reader of inferior taste (with ref. to Shakesp. *Hamlet* III. ii. 11).

groundnut /'graʊndnʌt/ n. **1** Brit. = PEANUT. **2 a** a N. American wild bean. **b** its edible tuber.

groundsel /'graʊns(ə)l/ n. any composite plant of the genus *Senecio*, esp. *S. vulgaris*, used as a food for cage-birds. [OE *grundeswylige, gundæswelgiæ* (perh. = pus-absorber f. *gund* pus, with ref. to use for poultices)]

groundsheet /'graʊndʃiːt/ n. a waterproof sheet for spreading on the ground, esp. in a tent.

groundsman /'graʊndzmən/ n. (pl. **-men**) a person who maintains a sports ground.

groundwater /'graʊnd,wɔːtə(r)/ n. water found in soil or in pores, crevices, etc., in rock.

groundwork /'graʊndwɜːk/ n. **1** preliminary or basic work. **2** a foundation or basis.

group /gruːp/ n. & v. —n. **1** a number of persons or things located close together, or considered or classed together. **2** (attrib.) concerning or done by a group (a group photograph; group sex). **3** a number of people working together or sharing beliefs, e.g. part of a political party. **4** a number of commercial companies under common ownership. **5** an ensemble playing popular music. **6** a division of an air force or air-fleet. **7** Math. a set of elements, together with an associative binary operation, which contains an inverse for each element and an identity element. **8** Chem. **a** a set of ions or radicals giving a characteristic qualitative reaction. **b** a set of elements having similar properties. **c** a combination of atoms having a recognizable identity in a number of compounds. —v. **1** tr. & intr. form or be formed into a group. **2** tr. (often foll. by with) place in a group or groups. **3** tr. form (colours, figures, etc.) into a well-arranged and harmonious whole. **4** tr. classify. □ **group captain** an RAF officer next below air commodore. **group dynamics** Psychol. the field of social psychology concerned with the nature, development, and interactions of human groups. **group practice** a medical practice in which several doctors are associated. **group therapy** therapy in which patients with a similar condition are brought together to assist one another psychologically. **group velocity** the speed of travel of the energy of a wave or wave-group. □□ **groupage** n. [F *groupe* f. It. *gruppo* f. Gmc, rel. to CROP]

grouper /'gruːpə(r)/ n. any marine fish of the family Serranidae, with heavy body, big head, and wide mouth. [Port. *garupa*, prob. f. native name in S. America]

groupie /'gruːpɪ/ n. sl. an ardent follower of touring pop groups, esp. a young woman seeking sexual relations with them.

grouping /'gruːpɪŋ/ n. a process or system of allocation to groups.

grouse¹ /graʊs/ n. (pl. same) **1** any of various game-birds of the family Tetraonidae, with a plump body and feathered legs. **2** the flesh of a grouse used as food. [16th c.: orig. uncert.]

grouse² /graʊs/ v. & n. colloq. —v.intr. grumble or complain pettily. —n. a complaint. □□ **grouser** n. [19th c.: orig. unkn.]

grout¹ /graʊt/ n. & v. —n. a thin fluid mortar for filling gaps in tiling etc. —v.tr. provide or fill with grout. □□ **grouter** n. [perh. f. GROUT²,· but cf. F dial. *grouter* grout a wall]

grout² /graʊt/ n. sediment, dregs. [OE *grūt*, rel. to GRITS, GROATS]

grouter /'graʊtə(r)/ n. Austral. sl. an unfair advantage. [20th c.: orig. uncert.]

grove /grəʊv/ n. a small wood or group of trees. □□ **grovy** adj. [OE *grāf*, rel. to *græfa* brushwood]

grovel /'grɒv(ə)l/ v.intr. (**grovelled, grovelling**; US **groveled, groveling**) **1** behave obsequiously in seeking favour or forgiveness. **2** lie prone in abject humility. □□ **groveller** n. **grovelling** adj. **grovellingly** adv. [back-form. f. obs. *grovelling* (adv.) f. *gruf* face down f. *on grufe* f. ON *á grúfu*, later taken as pres. part.]

grow /grəʊ/ v. (past **grew** /gruː/; past part. **grown** /grəʊn/) **1** intr. increase in size, height, quantity, degree, or in any way regarded as measurable (e.g. authority or reputation) (often foll. by in: grew in stature). **2** intr. **a** develop or exist as a living plant or natural product. **b** develop in a specific way or direction (began to grow sideways). **c** germinate; sprout; spring up. **3** intr. be produced; come naturally into existence; arise. **4** intr. (as **grown** adj.) fully matured; adult. **5** intr. become gradually (grow rich; grow less). **b** (foll. by to + infin.) come by degrees (grew to like it). **6** intr. (foll. by into) **a** become, having grown or developed (the acorn has grown into a tall oak; will grow into a fine athlete). **b** become large enough for or suited to (will grow into the coat; grew into her new job). **7** intr. (foll. by on) become gradually more favoured by. **8** tr. **a** produce (plants, fruit, wood, etc.) by cultivation. **b** bring forth. **c** cause (a beard etc.) to develop. **9** tr. (in passive; foll. by over, up) be covered with a growth. □ **growing bag** a bag containing peat-based potting compost in which plants may be grown. **growing pains 1** early difficulties in the development of an enterprise etc. **2** neuralgic pain in children's legs due to fatigue etc. **grown-up** adj. adult. —n. an adult person. **grow out of 1** become too large to wear (a garment). **2** become too mature to retain (a childish habit etc.). **3** be the result or development of. **grow together** coalesce. **grow up 1 a** advance to maturity. **b** (esp. in imper.) begin to behave sensibly. **2** (of a custom) arise, become common. □□ **growable** adj. [OE *grōwan* f. Gmc, rel. to GRASS, GREEN]

grower /'grəʊə(r)/ n. **1** (often in comb.) a person growing produce (fruit-grower). **2** a plant that grows in a specified way (a fast grower).

growl /graʊl/ v. & n. —v. **1** intr. **a** (often foll. by at) (esp. of a dog) make a low guttural sound, usu. of anger. **b** murmur angrily. **2** intr. rumble. **3** tr. (often foll. by out) utter with a growl. —n. **1** a growling sound, esp. made by a dog. **2** an angry murmur; complaint. **3** a rumble. □□ **growlingly** adv. [prob. imit.]

growler /'graʊlə(r)/ n. **1** a person or thing that growls, esp. sl. a dog. **2** a small iceberg.

grown past part. of GROW.

growth /grəʊθ/ n. **1** the act or process of growing. **2** an increase in size or value. **3** something that has grown or is growing. **4** Med. a morbid formation. **5**

the cultivation of produce. **6** a crop or yield of grapes. □**full growth** the size ultimately attained; maturity. **growth hormone** *Biol.* a substance which stimulates the growth of a plant or animal. **growth industry** an industry that is developing rapidly. **growth stock** etc. stock etc. that tends to increase in capital value rather than yield high income.

groyne /grɔɪn/ *n.* (*US* **groin**) a timber framework or low broad wall built out from a shore to check erosion of a beach. [dial. *groin* snout f. OF *groign* f. LL *grunium* pig's snout]

grub /grʌb/ *n.* & *v.* —*n.* **1** the larva of an insect, esp. of a beetle. **2** *colloq.* food. —*v.* (**grubbed, grubbing**) **1** *tr.* & *intr.* dig superficially. **2** *tr.* **a** clear (the ground) of roots and stumps. **b** clear away (roots etc.). **3** *tr.* (foll. by *up, out*) **a** fetch by digging (*grubbing up weeds*). **b** extract (information etc.) by searching in books etc. **4** *intr.* search, rummage. **5** *intr.* (foll. by *on, along, away*) toil, plod. □**grub-screw** a small headless screw, esp. used to attach a handle etc. to a spindle. □□ **grubber** *n.* (also in *comb.*). [ME, (v.) perh. corresp. to OE *grybban* (unrecorded) f. Gmc]

grubby /'grʌbɪ/ *adj.* (**grubbier, grubbiest**) **1** dirty, grimy, slovenly. **2** of or infested with grubs. □□ **grubbily** *adv.* **grubbiness** *n.*

grubstake /'grʌbsteɪk/ *n.* & *v.* *US colloq.* —*n.* material or provisions supplied to an enterprise in return for a share in the resulting profits (orig. in prospecting for ore). —*v.tr.* provide with a grubstake. □□ **grubstaker** *n.*

Grub Street /grʌb striːt/ *n.* (often *attrib.*) the world or class of literary hacks and impoverished authors. [name of a street (later Milton St.) in Moorgate, London, inhabited by these in the 17th c.]

grudge /grʌdʒ/ *n.* & *v.* —*n.* a persistent feeling of ill will or resentment, esp. one due to an insult or injury (*bears a grudge against me*). —*v.tr.* **1** be resentfully unwilling to give, grant, or allow (a thing). **2** (foll. by verbal noun or *to* + infin.) be reluctant to do (a thing) (*grudged paying so much*). □□ **grudger** *n.* [ME *grutch* f. OF *grouchier* murmur, of unkn. orig.]

grudging /'grʌdʒɪŋ/ *adj.* reluctant; not willing. □□ **grudgingly** *adv.* **grudgingness** *n.*

gruel /'gruːəl/ *n.* a liquid food of oatmeal etc. boiled in milk or water chiefly for invalids. [ME f. OF, ult. f. Gmc, rel. to GROUT¹]

gruelling /'gruːəlɪŋ/ *adj.* & *n.* (*US* **grueling**) —*adj.* extremely demanding, severe, or tiring. —*n.* a harsh or exhausting experience; punishment. □□ **gruellingly** *adv.* [GRUEL as verb, = exhaust, punish]

gruesome /'gruːsəm/ *adj.* horrible, grisly, disgusting. □□ **gruesomely** *adv.* **gruesomeness** *n.* [Sc. *grue* to shudder f. Scand. + -SOME¹]

gruff /grʌf/ *adj.* **1 a** (of a voice) low and harsh. **b** (of a person) having a gruff voice. **2** surly, laconic, rough-mannered. □□ **gruffly** *adv.* **gruffness** *n.* [Du., MLG *grof* coarse f. WG (rel. to ROUGH)]

grumble /'grʌmb(ə)l/ *v.* & *n.* —*v.* **1** *intr.* **a** (often foll. by *at, about, over*) complain peevishly. **b** be discontented. **2** *intr.* **a** utter a dull inarticulate sound; murmur, growl faintly. **b** rumble. **3** *tr.* (often foll. by *out*) utter complainingly. **4** *intr.* (as **grumbling** *adj.*) *colloq.* giving intermittent discomfort without causing illness (*a grumbling appendix*). —*n.* **1 a** complaint. **2 a** a dull inarticulate sound; a murmur. **b** a rumble. □□ **grumbler** *n.* **grumbling** *adj.* **grumblingly** *adv.* **grumbly** *adj.* [obs. *grumme*: cf. MDu. *grommen*, MLG *grommelen*, f. Gmc]

grummet var. of GROMMET.

grump /grʌmp/ *n.* *colloq.* **1** a grumpy person. **2** (in *pl.*) a fit of sulks. □□ **grumpish** *adj.* **grumpishly** *adv.* [imit.]

grumpy /'grʌmpɪ/ *adj.* (**grumpier, grumpiest**) morosely irritable; surly. □□ **grumpily** *adv.* **grumpiness** *n.*

Grundy /'grʌndɪ/ *n.* (*pl.* **-ies**) (in full **Mrs Grundy**) a person embodying conventional propriety and prudery. □□ **Grundyism** *n.* [a person repeatedly

mentioned in T. Morton's comedy *Speed the Plough* (1798)]

grunion /'grʌnjən/ *n.* a slender Californian marine fish, *Leuresthes tenuis*, that comes ashore to spawn. [prob. f. Sp. *gruñón* grunter]

grunt /grʌnt/ *n.* & *v.* —*n.* **1** a low guttural sound made by a pig. **2** a sound resembling this. **3** any fish of the genus *Haemulon* that grunts when caught. —*v.* **1** *intr.* (of a pig) make a grunt or grunts. **2** *intr.* (of a person) make a low inarticulate sound resembling this, esp. to express discontent, dissent, fatigue, etc. **3** *tr.* utter with a grunt. [OE *grunnettan*, prob. orig. imit.]

grunter /'grʌntə(r)/ *n.* **1** a person or animal that grunts, esp. a pig. **2** a grunting fish, esp. = GRUNT *n.* 3.

Grunth var. of GRANTH.

Gruyère /'gruːjeə(r)/ *n.* a firm pale cheese made from cow's milk. [*Gruyère*, a district in Switzerland where it was first made]

gryphon var. of GRIFFIN.

grysbok /'grɪsbɒk/ *n.* any small antelope of the genus *Raphicerus*, native to S. Africa. [S.Afr. Du. f. Du. *grijs* grey + *bok* BUCK¹]

gs. *abbr. Brit. hist.* guineas.

G-string /'dʒiːstrɪŋ/ *n.* **1** *Mus.* a string sounding the note G. **2** (also **gee-string**) a narrow strip of cloth etc. covering only the genitals and attached to a string round the waist, as worn esp. by striptease artistes.

G-suit /'dʒiːsuːt, -sjuːt/ *n.* a garment with inflatable pressurized pouches, worn by pilots and astronauts to enable them to withstand high acceleration. [*g* = gravity + SUIT]

GT /dʒiː'tiː/ *n.* a high-performance saloon car. [abbr. f. It. *gran turismo* great touring]

Gt. *abbr.* Great.

guacamole /ˌgwɑːkə'məʊlɪ/ *n.* a dish of mashed avocado pears mixed with chopped onion, tomatoes, chilli peppers, and seasoning. [Amer. Sp. f. Nahuatl *ahuacamolli* f. *ahuacatl* avocado + *molli* sauce]

guacharo /'gwɑːtʃəˌrəʊ/ *n.* (*pl.* **-os**) a nocturnal bird, *Steatornis caripensis*, native to S. America and feeding on fruit. Also called *oil-bird*. [S.Amer. Sp.]

guaiac var. of GUAIACUM 2.

guaiacum /'gwaɪəkəm/ *n.* **1** any tree of the genus *Guaiacum*, native to tropical America. **2** (also **guaiac** /'gwaɪæk/) **a** the hard dense oily timber of some of these, esp. *G. officinale*. Also called LIGNUM VITAE. **b** the resin from this used medicinally. [mod.L f. Sp. *guayaco* of Haitian orig.]

guan /gwɑːn/ *n.* any of various game-birds of the family Cracidae, of tropical America. [prob. f. a native name]

guanaco /gwə'nɑːkəʊ/ *n.* (*pl.* **-os**) a llama-like camelid, *Lama guanicoe*, with a coat of soft pale-brown hair used for wool. [Quechua *huanaco*]

guanine /'gwɑːniːn/ *n.* *Biochem.* a purine derivative found in all living organisms as a component base of DNA and RNA. [GUANO + -INE⁴]

guano /'gwɑːnəʊ/ *n.* & *v.* (*pl.* **-os**) —*n.* **1** the excrement of sea-fowl, found esp. in the islands off Peru and used as manure. **2** an artificial manure, esp. that made from fish. —*v.tr.* (**-oes, -oed**) fertilize with guano. [Sp. f. Quechua *huanu* dung]

Guarani /ˌgwɑːrə'niː/ *n.* **1 a** a member of a S. American Indian people. **b** the language of this people. **2** (**guarani**) the monetary unit of Paraguay. [Sp.]

guarantee /ˌgærən'tiː/ *n.* & *v.* —*n.* **1 a** a formal promise or assurance, esp. that an obligation will be fulfilled or that something is of a specified quality and durability. **b** a document giving such an undertaking. **2** = GUARANTY. **3** a person making a guaranty or giving a security. —*v.tr.* (**guarantees, guaranteed**) **1 a** give or serve as a guarantee for; answer for the due fulfilment of (a contract etc.) or the genuineness of (an article). **b** assure the permanence etc. of. **c** provide with a guarantee. **2** (foll. by *that* + clause, or *to* + infin.) give a promise or assurance. **3 a** (foll. by *to*) secure the possession of (a thing) for a person. **b** make (a person) secure against a risk or in possession of a thing. □**guarantee fund** a sum pledged as a contingent indemnity for loss. [earlier *garante*, perh. f. Sp. *garante* = F *garant* WARRANT: later infl. by F *garantie* guaranty]

guarantor /ˌgærənˈtɔː(r), ˈgærəntə(r)/ *n.* a person who gives a guarantee or guaranty.

guaranty /ˈgærəntɪ/ *n.* (*pl.* **-ies**) **1** a written or other undertaking to answer for the payment of a debt or for the performance of an obligation by another person liable in the first instance. **2** a thing serving as security for a guaranty. [AF *guarantie*, var. of *warantie* WARRANTY]

guard /gɑːd/ *v. & n.* —*v.* **1** *tr.* (often foll. by *from*, *against*) watch over and defend or protect from harm. **2** *tr.* keep watch by (a door etc.) so as to control entry or exit. **3** *tr.* supervise (prisoners etc.) and prevent from escaping. **4** *tr.* provide (machinery) with a protective device. **5** *tr.* keep (thoughts or speech) in check. **6** *tr.* provide with safeguards. **7** *intr.* (foll. by *against*) take precautions. **8** *tr.* (in various games) protect (a piece, card, etc.) with set moves. —*n.* **1** a state of vigilance or watchfulness. **2** a person who protects or keeps watch. **3** a body of soldiers etc. serving to protect a place or person; an escort. **4** *US* a prison warder. **5** a part of an army detached for some purpose (*advance guard*). **6** (in *pl.*) (usu. **Guards**) any of various bodies of troops nominally employed to guard a monarch. **7** a thing that protects or defends. **8** (often in *comb.*) a device fitted to a machine, vehicle, weapon, etc., to prevent injury or accident to the user (*fire-guard*). **9** *Brit.* an official who rides with and is in general charge of a train. **10** in some sports: **a** a protective or defensive player. **b** a defensive posture or motion. □**be on** (or **keep** or **stand**) **guard** (of a sentry etc.) keep watch. **guard cell** *Bot.* either of a pair of cells surrounding the stomata in plants. **guard-rail** a rail, e.g. a handrail, fitted as a support or to prevent an accident. **guard ring** *Electronics* a ring-shaped electrode used to limit the extent of an electric field, esp. in a capacitor. **guard's van** *Brit.* a coach or compartment occupied by a guard. **lower one's guard** reduce vigilance against attack. **off** (or **off one's**) **guard** unprepared for some surprise or difficulty. **on** (or **on one's**) **guard** prepared for all contingencies; vigilant. **raise one's guard** become vigilant against attack. □□**guarder** *n.* **guardless** *adj.* [ME f. OF *garde*, *garder* ult. f. WG, rel. to WARD *n.*]

guardant /ˈgɑːd(ə)nt/ *adj. Heraldry* depicted with the body sideways and the face towards the viewer.

guarded /ˈgɑːdɪd/ *adj.* (of a remark etc.) cautious, avoiding commitment. □□**guardedly** *adv.* **guardedness** *n.*

guardhouse /ˈgɑːdhaʊs/ *n.* a building used to accommodate a military guard or to detain prisoners.

guardian /ˈgɑːdɪən/ *n.* **1** a defender, protector, or keeper. **2** a person having legal custody of another person and his or her property when that person is incapable of managing his or her own affairs. **3** the superior of a Franciscan convent. □**guardian angel** a spirit conceived as watching over a person or place. □□**guardianship** *n.* [ME f. AF *gardein*, OF *garden* f. Frank., rel. to WARD, WARDEN]

guardroom /ˈgɑːdruːm, -rʊm/ *n.* a room with the same purpose as a guardhouse.

guardsman /ˈgɑːdzmən/ *n.* (*pl.* **-men**) **1** a soldier belonging to a body of guards. **2** (in the UK) a soldier of a regiment of Guards.

guava /ˈgwɑːvə/ *n.* **1** a small tropical American tree, *Psidium guajava*, bearing an edible pale yellow fruit with pink juicy flesh. **2** this fruit. [Sp. *guayaba* prob. f. a S.Amer. name]

guayule /gwaɪˈjuːlɪ/ *n.* **1** a silver-leaved shrub, *Parthenium argentatum*, native to Mexico. **2** a rubber

substitute made from the sap of this plant. [Amer. Sp. f. Nahuatl *cuauhuli*]

gubbins /ˈgʌbɪnz/ *n. Brit.* **1** a set of equipment or paraphernalia. **2** a gadget. **3** something of little value. **4** *colloq.* a foolish person (often with ref. to oneself). [orig. = fragments, f. obs. *gobbon*: perh. rel. to GOBBET]

gubernatorial /ˌgjuːbənəˈtɔːrɪəl/ *adj.* esp. *US* of or relating to a governor. [L *gubernator* governor]

gudgeon[1] /ˈgʌdʒ(ə)n/ *n.* **1** a small European freshwater fish, *Gobio gobio*, often used as bait. **2** a credulous or easily fooled person. [ME f. OF *goujon* f. L *gobio -onis* GOBY]

gudgeon[2] /ˈgʌdʒ(ə)n/ *n.* **1** any of various kinds of pivot working a wheel, bell, etc. **2** the tubular part of a hinge into which the pin fits to effect the joint. **3** a socket at the stern of a boat, into which a rudder is fitted. **4** a pin holding two blocks of stone etc. together. □**gudgeon-pin** (in an internal-combustion engine) a pin holding a piston-rod and a connecting-rod together. [ME f. OF *goujon* dimin. of *gouge* GOUGE]

guelder rose /ˈgeldə(r)/ *n.* a deciduous shrub, *Viburnum opulus*, with round bunches of creamy-white flowers. Also called *snowball tree*. [Du. *geldersch* f. *Gelderland* a province in the Netherlands]

guenon /gəˈnɒn/ *n.* any African monkey of the genus *Cercopithecus*, having a characteristic long tail, e.g. the vervet. [F: orig. unkn.]

guerdon /ˈgɜːd(ə)n/ *n. & v. poet.* —*n.* a reward or recompense. —*v.tr.* give a reward to. [ME f. OF *guerdon* f. med.L *widerdonum* f. WG *widarlōn* (as WITH, LOAN[1]), assim. to L *donum* gift]

Guernsey /ˈgɜːnzɪ/ *n.* (*pl.* **-eys**) **1 a** an animal of a breed of dairy cattle from Guernsey in the Channel Islands. **b** this breed. **2** (**guernsey**) **a** a thick (usu. blue) woollen sweater of a distinctive pattern. **b** *Austral.* a football shirt. □**get a guernsey** *Austral. colloq.* **1** be selected for a football team. **2** gain recognition. **guernsey lily** a kind of nerine orig. from S. Africa, with large pink lily-like flowers.

guerrilla /gəˈrɪlə/ *n.* (also **guerilla**) a member of a small independently acting (usu. political) group taking part in irregular fighting, esp. against larger regular forces. □**guerrilla war** (or **warfare**) fighting by or with guerrillas. [Sp. *guerrilla*, dimin. of *guerra* war]

guess /ges/ *v. & n.* —*v.* **1** *tr.* (often *absol.*) estimate without calculation or measurement, or on the basis of inadequate data. **2** *tr.* (often foll. by *that* etc. + clause, or *to* + infin.) form a hypothesis or opinion about; conjecture; think likely (*cannot guess how you did it*; *guess them to be Italian*). **3** *tr.* conjecture or estimate correctly by guessing (*you have to guess the weight*). **4** *intr.* (foll. by *at*) make a conjecture about. —*n.* an estimate or conjecture reached by guessing. □**anybody's** (or **anyone's**) **guess** something very vague or difficult to determine. **I guess** *colloq.* I think it likely; I suppose. **keep a person guessing** *colloq.* withhold information. □□**guessable** *adj.* **guesser** *n.* [ME *gesse*, of uncert. orig.: cf. OSw. *gissa*, MLG, MDu. *gissen*: f. the root of GET *v.*]

guess-rope var. of GUEST-ROPE.

guesswork /ˈgeswɜːk/ *n.* the process of or results got by guessing.

guest /gest/ *n. & v.* —*n.* **1** a person invited to visit another's house or have a meal etc. at the expense of the inviter. **2** a person lodging at a hotel, boarding-house, etc. **3 a** an outside performer invited to take part with a regular body of performers. **b** a person who takes part by invitation in a radio or television programme (often *attrib.*: *guest artist*). **4** (*attrib.*) **a** serving or set aside for guests (*guest-room*; *guest-night*). **b** acting as a guest (*guest speaker*). **5** an organism living in close association with another. —*v.intr.* be a guest on a radio or television show or in a theatrical performance etc. □**be my guest** *colloq.* make what use you wish of the available facilities. **guest-house** a private house offering paid accommodation. **guest of honour** the most important guest at an occasion. □□ **guestship** n. [ME f. ON gestr f. Gmc]

guestimate /'gestɪmət/ n. (also **guesstimate**) colloq. an estimate based on a mixture of guesswork and calculation. [GUESS + ESTIMATE]

guest-rope /'gestrəʊp, 'gesrəʊp/ n. (also **guess-rope**) 1 a second rope fastened to a boat in tow to steady it. 2 a rope slung outside a ship to give a hold for boats coming alongside. [17th c.: orig. uncert.]

guff /gʌf/ n. sl. empty talk; nonsense. [19th c., orig. = 'puff': imit.]

guffaw /gʌ'fɔː/ n. & v. —n. a coarse or boisterous laugh. —v. 1 intr. utter a guffaw. 2 tr. say with a guffaw. [orig. Sc.: imit.]

guidance /'gaɪd(ə)ns/ n. 1 advice or information aimed at resolving a problem, difficulty, etc. 2 the process of guiding or being guided.

guide /gaɪd/ n. & v. —n. 1 a person who leads or shows the way, or directs the movements of a person or group. 2 a person who conducts travellers on tours etc. 3 a professional mountain-climber in charge of a group. 4 an adviser. 5 a directing principle or standard (one's feelings are a bad guide). 6 a book with essential information on a subject, esp. = GUIDEBOOK. 7 a thing marking a position or guiding the eye. 8 a soldier, vehicle, or ship whose position determines the movements of others. 9 Mech. a a bar, rod, etc., directing the motion of something. b a gauge etc. controlling a tool. 10 (**Guide**) Brit. a member of a girls' organization similar to the Scouts. —v.tr. 1 a act as guide to; lead or direct. b arrange the course of (events). 2 be the principle, motive, or ground of (an action, judgement, etc.). 3 direct the affairs of (a State etc.). □ **guided missile** a missile directed to its target by remote control or by equipment within itself. **guide-dog** a dog trained to guide a blind person. **guide-rope** a rope guiding the movement of a crane, airship, etc. **Queen's** (or **King's**) **Guide** a Guide (sense 10) who has reached the highest rank of proficiency. □□ **guidable** adj. **guider** n. [ME f. OF guide (n.), guider (v.), earlier guier ult. f. Gmc, rel. to WIT²]

guidebook /'gaɪdbʊk/ n. a book of information about a place for visitors, tourists, etc.

guideline /'gaɪdlaɪn/ n. a principle or criterion guiding or directing action.

guidepost /'gaɪdpəʊst/ n. = SIGNPOST.

Guider /'gaɪdə(r)/ n. an adult leader of Guides (see GUIDE n. 10).

guideway /'gaɪdweɪ/ n. a groove or track that guides movement.

guidon /'gaɪd(ə)n/ n. a pennant narrowing to a point or fork at the free end, esp. one used as the standard of a regiment of dragoons. [F f. It. guidone f. guida GUIDE]

guild /gɪld/ n. (also **gild**) 1 an association of people for mutual aid or the pursuit of a common goal. 2 a medieval association of craftsmen or merchants. [ME prob. f. MLG, MDu. gilde f. Gmc: rel. to OE gild payment, sacrifice]

guilder /'gɪldə(r)/ n. 1 the chief monetary unit of the Netherlands. 2 hist. a gold coin of the Netherlands and Germany. [ME, alt. of Du. gulden: see GULDEN]

guildhall /gɪld'hɔːl, 'gɪld-/ n. 1 the meeting-place of a guild or corporation; a town hall. 2 (**the Guildhall**) the hall of the Corporation of the City of London, used for ceremonial occasions.

guildsman /'gɪldzmən/ n. (pl. -**men**; fem. **guildswoman**, pl. -**women**) a member of a guild.

guile /gaɪl/ n. treachery, deceit; cunning or sly behaviour. □□ **guileful** adj. **guilefully** adv. **guilefulness** n. **guileless** adj. **guilelessly** adv. **guilelessness** n. [ME f. OF, prob. f. Gmc]

guillemot /'gɪlɪmɒt/ n. any fast-flying sea bird of the genus Uria or Cepphus, nesting on cliffs or islands. [F f. Guillaume William]

guilloche /gɪ'lɒʃ/ n. an architectural or metalwork ornament imitating braided ribbons. [F guillochis (or guilloche the tool used)]

guillotine /'gɪlə,tiːn/ n. & v. —n. 1 a machine with a heavy knife-blade sliding vertically in grooves, used for beheading. 2 a device for cutting paper, metal, etc. 3 a surgical instrument for excising the uvula etc. 4 Parl. a method of preventing delay in the discussion of a legislative bill by fixing times at which various parts of it must be voted on. —v.tr. 1 use a guillotine on. 2 Parl. end discussion of (a bill) by applying a guillotine. □□ **guillotiner** n. [F f. J.-I. Guillotin, Fr. physician d. 1814, who recommended its use for executions in 1789]

guilt /gɪlt/ n. 1 the fact of having committed a specified or implied offence. 2 a culpability. b the feeling of this. □ **guilt complex** Psychol. a mental obsession with the idea of having done wrong. [OE gylt, of unkn. orig.]

guiltless /'gɪltlɪs/ adj. 1 (often foll. by of an offence) innocent. 2 (foll. by of) not having knowledge or possession of. □□ **guiltlessly** adv. **guiltlessness** n. [OE gyltlēas (as GUILT, -LESS)]

guilty /'gɪltɪ/ adj. (**guiltier, guiltiest**) 1 culpable of or responsible for a wrong. 2 conscious of or affected by guilt (a guilty conscience; a guilty look). 3 concerning guilt (a guilty secret). 4 a (often foll. by of) having committed a (specified) offence. b Law adjudged to have committed a specified offence, esp. by a verdict in a trial. □□ **guiltily** adv. **guiltiness** n. [OE gyltig (as GUILT, -Y¹)]

guimp var. of GIMP¹.

guinea /'gɪnɪ/ n. 1 Brit. hist. the sum of 21 old shillings (£1.05), used esp. in determining professional fees. 2 hist. a former British gold coin worth 21 shillings, first coined for the African trade. □ **guinea-fowl** any African fowl of the family Numididae, esp. Numida meleagris, with slate-coloured white-spotted plumage. **guinea-pig** 1 a domesticated S. American cavy, Cavia porcellus, kept as a pet or for research in biology etc. 2 a person or thing used as a subject for experiment. [Guinea in W. Africa]

guipure /'gi:pjʊə(r)/ n. a heavy lace of linen pieces joined by embroidery. [F f. guiper cover with silk etc. f. Gmc]

guise /gaɪz/ n. 1 an assumed appearance; a pretence (in the guise of; under the guise of). 2 external appearance. 3 archaic style of attire, garb. [ME f. OF ult. f. Gmc]

guitar /gɪ'tɑː(r)/ n. a usu. six-stringed musical instrument with a fretted finger-board, played by plucking with the fingers or a plectrum. □□ **guitarist** n. [Sp. guitarra (partly through F guitare) f. Gk kithara: see CITTERN, GITTERN]

guiver /'gaɪvə(r)/ n. (also **gyver**) Austral. & NZ sl. 1 plausible talk. 2 affectation of speech or manner. [19th c.: orig. unkn.]

Gujarati /ˌgu:dʒə'rɑ:tɪ/ n. & adj. —n. (pl. **Gujaratis**) 1 the language of Gujarat in W. India. 2 a native of Gujarat. —adj. of or relating to Gujarat or its language. [Hind.: see -I²]

gulch /gʌltʃ/ n. US a ravine, esp. one in which a torrent flows. [perh. dial. gulch to swallow]

gulden /'gʊld(ə)n/ n. = GUILDER. [Du. & G, = GOLDEN]

gules /gju:lz/ n. & adj. (usu. placed after noun) Heraldry red. [ME f. OF goules red-dyed fur neck ornaments f. gole throat]

gulf /gʌlf/ n. & v. —n. 1 a stretch of sea consisting of a deep inlet with a narrow mouth. 2 (**the Gulf**) the Persian Gulf. 3 a deep hollow; a chasm or abyss. 4 a wide difference of feelings, opinion, etc. —v.tr. engulf; swallow up. □ **Gulf Stream** an oceanic warm current flowing from the Gulf of Mexico to Newfoundland where it is deflected into the Atlantic Ocean. [ME f. OF golfe f. It. golfo ult. f. Gk kolpos bosom, gulf]

gulfweed /'gʌlfwiːd/ n. = SARGASSO.

gull¹ /gʌl/ n. any of various long-winged web-footed

sea birds of the family Laridae, usu. having white plumage with a mantle varying from pearly-grey to black, and a bright bill. □□ **gullery** n. (pl. -ies). [ME ult. f. OCelt.]

gull² /gʌl/ v.tr. (usu. in passive; foll. by into) dupe, fool. [perh. f. obs. gull yellow f. ON gulr]

Gullah /ˈgʌlə/ n. **1** a member of a Negro people living on the coast of S. Carolina or the nearby sea islands. **2** the Creole language spoken by them. [perh. a shortening of Angola, or f. a tribal name Golas]

gullet /ˈgʌlɪt/ n. **1** the food-passage extending from the mouth to the stomach; the oesophagus. **2** the throat. [ME f. OF dimin. of go(u)le throat f. L gula]

gullible /ˈgʌlɪb(ə)l/ adj. easily persuaded or deceived, credulous. □□ **gullibility** /-ˈbɪlɪtɪ/ n. **gullibly** adv. [GULL² + -IBLE]

gully /ˈgʌlɪ/ n. & v. —n. (pl. -ies) **1** a water-worn ravine. **2** a deep artificial channel; a gutter or drain. **3** Austral. & NZ a river valley. **4** Cricket **a** the fielding position between point and slips. **b** a fielder in this position. —v.tr. (-ies, -ied) **1** form (channels) by water action. **2** make gullies in. □ **gully-hole** an opening in a street to a drain or sewer. [F goulet bottle-neck (as GULLET)]

gulp /gʌlp/ v. & n. —v. **1** tr. (often foll. by down) swallow hastily, greedily, or with effort. **2** intr. swallow gaspingly or with difficulty; choke. **3** tr. (foll. by down, back) stifle, suppress (esp. tears). —n. **1** an act of gulping (drained it at one gulp). **2** an effort to swallow. **3** a large mouthful of a drink. □□ **gulper** n. **gulpingly** adv. **gulpy** adj. [ME prob. f. MDu. gulpen (imit.)]

gum¹ /gʌm/ n. & v. —n. **1 a** a viscous secretion of some trees and shrubs that hardens on drying but is soluble in water (cf. RESIN). **b** an adhesive substance made from this. **2** US chewing gum. **3** = GUMDROP. **4** = gum arabic. **5** = gum-tree. **6** a secretion collecting in the corner of the eye. **7** US = GUMBOOT. —v. (**gummed, gumming**) **1** tr. smear or cover with gum. **2** tr. (usu. foll. by down, together, etc.) fasten with gum. **3** intr. exude gum. □ **gum arabic** a gum exuded by some kinds of acacia and used as glue and in incense. **gum benjamin** benzoin. **gum dragon** tragacanth. **gum juniper** sandarac. **gum resin** a vegetable secretion of resin mixed with gum, e.g. gamboge. **gum-tree** a tree exuding gum, esp. a eucalyptus. **gum up 1** (of a mechanism etc.) become clogged or obstructed with stickiness. **2** colloq. interfere with the smooth running of (gum up the works). **up a gum-tree** colloq. in great difficulties. [ME f. OF gomme ult. f. L gummi, cummi f. Gk kommi f. Egypt. kemai]

gum² /gʌm/ n. (usu. in pl.) the firm flesh around the roots of the teeth. □ **gum-shield** a pad protecting a boxer's teeth and gums. [OE gōma rel. to OHG guomo, ON gómr roof or floor of the mouth]

gum³ /gʌm/ n. colloq. (in oaths) God (by gum!). [corrupt. of God]

gumbo /ˈgʌmbəʊ/ n. (pl. -os) US **1** okra. **2** a soup thickened with okra pods. **3** (Gumbo) a patois of Blacks and Creoles spoken esp. in Louisiana. [of Afr. orig.]

gumboil /ˈgʌmbɔɪl/ n. a small abscess on the gums.

gumboot /ˈgʌmbuːt/ n. a rubber boot; a wellington.

gumdrop /ˈgʌmdrɒp/ n. a soft coloured sweet made with gelatin or gum arabic.

gumma /ˈgʌmə/ n. (pl. **gummas** or **gummata** /-mətə/) Med. a small soft swelling occurring in the connective tissue of the liver, brain, testes, and heart, and characteristic of the late stages of syphilis. □□ **gummatous** adj. [mod.L f. L gummi GUM¹]

gummy¹ /ˈgʌmɪ/ adj. (**gummier, gummiest**) **1** viscous, sticky. **2** abounding in or exuding gum. □□ **gumminess** n. [ME f. GUM¹ + -Y¹]

gummy² /ˈgʌmɪ/ adj. & n. —adj. (**gummier, gummiest**) toothless. —n. (pl. -ies) **1** Austral. a small shark, Mustelus antarcticus, having rounded teeth with which it crushes hard-shelled prey. **2**

Austral. & NZ a toothless sheep. □□ **gummily** adv. [GUM² + -Y¹]

gumption /ˈgʌmpʃ(ə)n/ n. colloq. **1** resourcefulness, initiative; enterprising spirit. **2** common sense. [18th-c. Sc.: orig. unkn.]

gumshoe /ˈgʌmʃuː/ n. US **1** a galosh. **2** sl. a detective.

gun /gʌn/ n. & v. —n. **1** any kind of weapon consisting of a metal tube and often held in the hand with a grip at one end, from which bullets or other missiles are propelled with great force, esp. by a contained explosion. **2** any device imitative of this, e.g. a starting pistol. **3** a device for discharging insecticide, grease, electrons, etc., in the required direction (often in comb.: grease-gun). **4** a member of a shooting-party. **5** US a gunman. **6** the firing of a gun. **7** (in pl.) Naut. sl. a gunnery officer. —v. (**gunned, gunning**) **1** tr. **a** (usu. foll. by down) shoot (a person) with a gun. **b** shoot at with a gun. **2** tr. colloq. accelerate (an engine or vehicle). **3** intr. go shooting. **4** intr. (foll. by for) seek out determinedly to attack or rebuke. □ **go great guns** colloq. proceed forcefully or vigorously or successfully. **gun-carriage** a wheeled support for a gun. **gun-cotton** an explosive used for blasting, made by steeping cotton in nitric and sulphuric acids. **gun crew** a team manning a gun. **gun dog** a dog trained to follow sportsmen using guns. **gun-shy** (esp. of a sporting dog) alarmed at the report of a gun. **gun-site** a (usu. fortified) emplacement for a gun. **jump the gun** colloq. start before a signal is given, or before an agreed time. **stick to one's guns** colloq. maintain one's position under attack. □□ **gunless** adj. **gunned** adj. [ME gunne, gonne, perh. f. the Scand. name Gunnhildr]

gunboat /ˈgʌnbəʊt/ n. a small vessel of shallow draught and with relatively heavy guns. □ **gunboat diplomacy** political negotiation supported by the use or threat of military force.

gunfight /ˈgʌnfaɪt/ n. US a fight with firearms. □□ **gunfighter** n.

gunfire /ˈgʌnˌfaɪə(r)/ n. **1** the firing of a gun or guns, esp. repeatedly. **2** the noise from this.

gunge /gʌndʒ/ n. & v. Brit. colloq. —n. sticky or viscous matter, esp. when messy or indeterminate. —v.tr. (usu. foll. by up) clog or obstruct with gunge. □□ **gungy** adj. [20th c.: orig. uncert.: cf. GOO, GUNK]

gung-ho /gʌŋˈhəʊ/ adj. enthusiastic, eager. [Chin. gonghe work together, slogan adopted by US Marines in 1942]

gunk /gʌŋk/ n. sl. viscous or liquid material. [20th c.: orig. the name of a detergent (propr.)]

gunlock /ˈgʌnlɒk/ n. a mechanism by which the charge of a gun is exploded.

gunman /ˈgʌnmən/ n. (pl. -men) a man armed with a gun, esp. in committing a crime.

gun-metal /ˈgʌnˌmet(ə)l/ n. **1** a dull bluish-grey colour. **2** an alloy of copper and tin or zinc (formerly used for guns).

gunnel¹ /ˈgʌn(ə)l/ n. any small eel-shaped marine fish of the family Pholidae, esp. Pholis gunnellus. Also called BUTTERFISH. [17th c.: orig. unkn.]

gunnel² var. of GUNWALE.

gunner /ˈgʌnə(r)/ n. **1** an artillery soldier (esp. as an official term for a private). **2** Naut. a warrant-officer in charge of a battery, magazine, etc. **3** a member of an aircraft crew who operates a gun. **4** a person who hunts game with a gun.

gunnera /ˈgʌnərə/ n. any plant of the genus Gunnera from S. America and New Zealand, having large leaves and often grown for ornament. [J. E. Gunnerus, Norw. botanist d. 1773]

gunnery /ˈgʌnərɪ/ n. **1** the construction and management of large guns. **2** the firing of guns.

gunny /ˈgʌnɪ/ n. (pl. -ies) **1** coarse sacking, usu. of jute fibre. **2** a sack made of this. [Hindi & Marathi gōnī f. Skr. gōṇi sack]

gunplay /ˈgʌnpleɪ/ n. the use of guns.

gunpoint /ˈgʌnpɔɪnt/ n. the point of a gun. □ **at**

gunpoint threatened with a gun or an ultimatum etc.

gunpowder /'gʌn,paʊdə(r)/ n. **1** an explosive made of saltpetre, sulphur, and charcoal. **2** a fine green tea of granular appearance.

gunpower /'gʌn,paʊə(r)/ n. the strength or quantity of available guns.

gunroom /'gʌnruːm, -rʊm/ n. Brit. **1** a room in a house for storing sporting-guns. **2** quarters for junior officers (orig. for gunners) in a warship.

gunrunner /'gʌn,rʌnə(r)/ n. a person engaged in the illegal sale or importing of firearms. □□ **gunrunning** n.

gunship /'gʌnʃɪp/ n. a heavily-armed helicopter or other aircraft.

gunshot /'gʌnʃɒt/ n. **1** a shot fired from a gun. **2** the range of a gun (within gunshot).

gunslinger /'gʌn,slɪŋə(r)/ n. esp. US sl. a gunman. □□ **gunslinging** n.

gunsmith /'gʌnsmɪθ/ n. a person who makes, sells, and repairs small firearms.

gunstock /'gʌnstɒk/ n. the wooden mounting of the barrel of a gun.

Gunter's chain /'gʌntəz/ n. Surveying **1** a measuring chain of 66 ft. **2** this length as a unit. [E. Gunter, Engl. mathematician d. 1626]

gunwale /'gʌn(ə)l/ n. (also **gunnel**) the upper edge of the side of a boat or ship. [GUN + WALE (because formerly used to support guns)]

gunyah /'gʌnjɑː/ n. Austral. an Aboriginal bush hut. [Aboriginal]

guppy /'gʌpɪ/ n. (pl. -ies) a freshwater fish, Poecilia reticulata, of the W. Indies and S. America, frequently kept in aquariums, and giving birth to live young. [R. J. L. Guppy, 19th-c. Trinidad clergyman who sent the first specimen to the British Museum]

gurdwara /ɡɜːd'wɑːrə/ n. a Sikh temple. [Punjabi gurduārā f. Skr. guru teacher + dvāra door]

gurgle /'ɡɜːɡ(ə)l/ v. & n. —v. **1** intr. make a bubbling sound as of water from a bottle. **2** tr. utter with such a sound. —n. a gurgling sound. □□ **gurgler** n. [imit., or f. Du. gorgelen, G gurgeln, or med.L gurgulare f. L gurgulio gullet]

Gurkha /'ɡɜːkə/ n. **1** a member of the dominant Hindu race in Nepal. **2** a Nepalese soldier serving in the British army. [native name, f. Skr. gāus cow + raksh protect]

gurnard /'ɡɜːnəd/ n. (also **gurnet** /'ɡɜːnɪt/) any marine fish of the family Triglidae, having a large spiny head with mailed sides, and three finger-like pectoral rays used for walking on the sea bed etc. [ME f. OF gornart f. grondir to grunt f. L grunnire]

guru /'ɡʊruː, 'ɡuːruː/ n. **1** a Hindu spiritual teacher or head of a religious sect. **2 a** an influential teacher. **b** a revered mentor. [Hindi gurū teacher f. Skr. gurús grave, dignified]

gush /ɡʌʃ/ v. & n. —v. **1** tr. & intr. emit or flow in a sudden and copious stream. **2** intr. speak or behave with effusiveness or sentimental affectation. —n. **1** a sudden or copious stream. **2** an effusive or sentimental manner. □□ **gushing** adj. **gushingly** adv. [ME gosshe, gusche, prob. imit.]

gusher /'ɡʌʃə(r)/ n. **1** an oil well from which oil flows without being pumped. **2** an effusive person.

gushy /'ɡʌʃɪ/ adj. (gushier, gushiest) excessively effusive or sentimental. □□ **gushily** adv. **gushiness** n.

gusset /'ɡʌsɪt/ n. **1** a piece let into a garment etc. to strengthen or enlarge a part. **2** a bracket strengthening an angle of a structure. □□ **gusseted** adj. [ME f. OF gousset flexible piece filling up a joint in armour f. gousse pod, shell]

gust /ɡʌst/ n. & v. —n. **1** a sudden strong rush of wind. **2** a burst of rain, fire, smoke, or sound. **3** a passionate or emotional outburst. —v.intr. blow in gusts. [ON gustr, rel. to gjósa to gush]

gustation /ɡʌ'steɪʃ(ə)n/ n. the act or capacity of tasting. □□ **gustative** /'ɡʌstətɪv/ adj. **gustatory**

/'ɡʌstətərɪ/ adj. [F gustation or L gustatio f. gustare f. gustus taste]

gusto /'ɡʌstəʊ/ n. (pl. -oes) **1** zest; enjoyment or vigour in doing something. **2** (foll. by for) archaic relish or liking. **3** archaic a style of artistic execution. [It. f. L gustus taste]

gusty /'ɡʌstɪ/ adj. (gustier, gustiest) **1** characterized by or blowing in strong winds. **2** characterized by gusto. □□ **gustily** adv. **gustiness** n.

gut /ɡʌt/ n. & v. —n. **1** the lower alimentary canal or a part of this; the intestine. **2** (in pl.) the bowel or entrails, esp. of animals. **3** (in pl.) colloq. personal courage and determination; vigorous application and perseverance. **4** (in pl.) colloq. the belly as the source of appetite. **5** (in pl.) **a** the contents of anything, esp. representing substantiality. **b** the essence of a thing, e.g. of an issue or problem. **6 a** material for violin or racket strings or surgical use made from the intestines of animals. **b** material for fishing-lines made from the silk-glands of silkworms. **7 a** a narrow water-passage; a sound, straits. **b** a defile or narrow passage. **8** (attrib.) **a** instinctive (a gut reaction). **b** fundamental (a gut issue). —v.tr. (**gutted**, **gutting**) **1** remove or destroy (esp. by fire) the internal fittings of (a house etc.). **2** take out the guts of (a fish). **3** extract the essence of (a book etc.). □ **gut-rot** colloq. **1** = rot-gut. **2** a stomach upset. **hate a person's guts** colloq. dislike a person intensely. **sweat** (or **work**) **one's guts out** colloq. work extremely hard. [OE guttas (pl.), prob. rel. to ġēotan pour]

gutless /'ɡʌtlɪs/ adj. colloq. lacking courage or determination; feeble. □□ **gutlessly** adv. **gutlessness** n.

gutsy /'ɡʌtsɪ/ adj. (gutsier, gutsiest) colloq. **1** courageous. **2** greedy. □□ **gutsily** adv. **gutsiness** n.

gutta-percha /,ɡʌtə'pɜːtʃə/ n. a tough plastic substance obtained from the latex of various Malaysian trees. [Malay getah gum + percha name of a tree]

guttate /'ɡʌteɪt/ adj. Biol. having droplike markings. [L guttatus speckled f. gutta drop]

gutter /'ɡʌtə(r)/ n. & v. —n. **1** a shallow trough below the eaves of a house, or a channel at the side of a street, to carry off rainwater. **2** (prec. by the) a poor or degraded background or environment. **3** an open conduit along which liquid flows out. **4** a groove. **5** a track made by the flow of water. —v. **1** intr. flow in streams. **2** tr. furrow, channel. □ **gutter press** sensational journalism concerned esp. with the private lives of public figures. [ME f. AF gotere, OF gotiere ult. f. L gutta drop]

guttering /'ɡʌtərɪŋ/ n. **1 a** the gutters of a building etc. **b** a section or length of a gutter. **2** material for gutters.

guttersnipe /'ɡʌtə,snaɪp/ n. a street urchin.

guttural /'ɡʌtər(ə)l/ adj. & n. —adj. **1** throaty, harsh-sounding. **2 a** Phonet. (of a consonant) produced in the throat or by the back of the tongue and palate. **b** (of a sound) coming from the throat. **c** of the throat. —n. Phonet. a guttural consonant (e.g. k, g). □□ **gutturally** adv. [F guttural or med.L gutturalis f. L guttur throat]

guv /ɡʌv/ n. Brit. sl. = GOVERNOR 7. [abbr.]

guy¹ /ɡaɪ/ n. & v. —n. **1** colloq. a man; a fellow. **2** (usu. in pl.) US a person of either sex. **3** Brit. an effigy of Guy Fawkes in ragged clothing, burnt on a bonfire on 5 Nov. **4** Brit. a grotesquely dressed person. —v.tr. **1** ridicule. **2** exhibit in effigy. [Guy Fawkes, conspirator in the Gunpowder Plot to blow up Parliament in 1605]

guy² /ɡaɪ/ n. & v. —n. a rope or chain to secure a tent or steady a crane-load etc. —v.tr. secure with a guy or guys. [prob. of LG orig.: cf. LG & Du. gei brail etc.]

guzzle /'ɡʌz(ə)l/ v.tr. & intr. eat, drink, or consume excessively or greedily. □□ **guzzler** n. [perh. f. OF gosiller chatter, vomit f. gosier throat]

Gy abbr. = GRAY¹.

gybe /dʒaɪb/ v. & n. (US **jibe**) —v. **1** intr. (of a fore-and-aft sail or boom) swing across in wearing or running before the wind. **2** *tr.* cause (a sail) to do this. **3** *intr.* (of a ship or its crew) change course so that this happens. —*n.* a change of course causing gybing. [obs. Du. *gijben*]

gym /dʒɪm/ *n. colloq.* **1** a gymnasium. **2** gymnastics. [abbr.]

gymkhana /dʒɪmˈkɑːnə/ *n.* **1** a meeting for competition or display in sport, esp. horse-riding. **2** a public place with facilities for athletics. [Hind. *gendkhāna* ball-house, racket-court, assim. to GYMNASIUM]

gymnasium /dʒɪmˈneɪzɪəm/ *n.* (*pl.* **gymnasiums** or **gymnasia** /-zɪə/) **1** a room or building equipped for gymnastics. **2** a school in Germany or Scandinavia that prepares pupils for university entrance. □□ **gymnasial** *adj.* [L f. Gk *gumnasion* f. *gumnazō* exercise f. *gumnos* naked]

gymnast /ˈdʒɪmnæst/ *n.* an expert in gymnastics. [F *gymnaste* or Gk *gumnastēs* athlete-trainer f. *gumnazō*: see GYMNASIUM]

gymnastic /dʒɪmˈnæstɪk/ *adj.* of or involving gymnastics. □□ **gymnastically** *adv.* [L *gymnasticus* f. Gk *gumnastikos* (as GYMNASIUM)]

gymnastics /dʒɪmˈnæstɪks/ *n.pl.* (also treated as *sing.*) **1** exercises developing or displaying physical agility and coordination, usu. in competition. **2** other forms of physical or mental agility.

gymno- /ˈdʒɪmnəʊ/ *comb. form Biol.* bare, naked. [Gk *gumnos* naked]

gymnosophist /dʒɪmˈnɒsəfɪst/ *n.* a member of an ancient Hindu sect wearing little clothing and devoted to contemplation. □□ **gymnosophy** *n.* [ME f. F *gymnosophiste* f. L *gymnosophistae* (pl.) f. Gk *gumnosophistai*: see GYMNO-, SOPHIST]

gymnosperm /ˈdʒɪmnəʊˌspɜːm/ *n.* any of various plants having seeds unprotected by an ovary, including conifers, cycads, and ginkgos (opp. ANGIOSPERM). □□ **gymnospermous** /-ˈspɜːməs/ *adj.*

gymp var. of GIMP[1].

gymslip /ˈdʒɪmslɪp/ *n.* a sleeveless tunic, usu. belted, worn by schoolgirls.

gynaeceum var. of GYNOECIUM.

gynaeco- /ˈgaɪnɪkəʊ/ *comb. form* (US **gyneco-**) woman; female. [Gk *gunē gunaikos* woman]

gynaecology /ˌgaɪnɪˈkɒlədʒɪ/ *n.* (US **gynecology**) the science of the physiological functions and diseases of women and girls, esp. those affecting the reproductive system. □□ **gynaecological** /-kəˈlɒdʒɪk(ə)l/ *adj.* **gynaecologically** /-kəˈlɒdʒɪkəlɪ/ *adv.* **gynaecologist** *n.* **gynecologic** /-kəˈlɒdʒɪk/ *adj.* US.

gynaecomastia /ˌgaɪnɪkəʊˈmæstɪə/ *n.* (US **gynecomastia**) *Med.* enlargement of a man's breasts, usu. due to hormone imbalance or hormone therapy.

gynandromorph /gaɪˈnændrəˌmɔːf/ *n. Biol.* an individual, esp. an insect, having male and female characteristics. □□ **gynandromorphic** /-ˈmɔːfɪk/ *adj.* **gynandromorphism** /-ˈmɔːfɪz(ə)m/ *n.* [formed as GYNANDROUS + Gk *morphē* form]

gynandrous /gaɪˈnændrəs/ *adj. Bot.* with stamens and pistil united in one column as in orchids. [Gk *gunandros* of doubtful sex, f. *gunē* woman + *anēr andros* man]

gyneco- *comb. form* US var. of GYNAECO-.

gynoecium /gaɪˈniːsɪəm/ *n.* (also **gynaecium**) (*pl.* **-cia** /-sɪə/) *Bot.* the carpels of a flower taken collectively. [mod.L f. Gk *gunaikeion* women's apartments (as GYNAECO-, Gk *oikos* house)]

-gynous /ˈgɪnəs, ˈdʒɪnəs/ *comb. form Bot.* forming adjectives meaning 'having specified female organs or pistils' (*monogynous*). [Gk *-gunos* f. *gunē* woman]

gyp[1] /dʒɪp/ *n. Brit. colloq.* **1** pain or severe discomfort. **2** a scolding (*gave them gyp*). [19th c.: perh. f. *gee-up* (see GEE[2])]

gyp[2] /dʒɪp/ *n. Brit.* a college servant at Cambridge and Durham. [perh. f. obs. *gippo* scullion, orig. a man's short tunic, f. obs. F *jupeau*]

gyp[3] /dʒɪp/ *v. & n. sl.* —*v.tr.* (**gypped**, **gypping**) cheat, swindle. —*n.* an act of cheating; a swindle. [19th c.: perh. f. GYP[2]]

gyppy tummy var. of GIPPY TUMMY.

gypsophila /dʒɪpˈsɒfɪlə/ *n.* any plant of the genus *Gypsophila*, with a profusion of small usu. white composite flowers. [mod.L f. Gk *gupsos* chalk + *philos* loving]

gypsum /ˈdʒɪpsəm/ *n.* a hydrated form of calcium sulphate occurring naturally and used to make plaster of Paris and in the building industry. □□ **gypseous** *adj.* **gypsiferous** /-ˈsɪfərəs/ *adj.* [L f. Gk *gupsos*]

Gypsy /ˈdʒɪpsɪ/ *n.* (also **Gipsy**) (*pl.* **-ies**) **1** a member of a nomadic people of Europe and N. America, of Hindu origin with dark skin and hair, and speaking a language related to Hindi. **2** (**gypsy**) a person resembling or living like a Gypsy. □**gypsy moth** a kind of tussock moth, *Lymantria dispar*, of which the larvae are very destructive to foliage. □□ **Gypsydom** *n.* **Gypsyfied** *adj.* **Gypsyhood** *n.* **Gypsyish** *adj.* [earlier *gipcyan*, *gipsen* f. EGYPTIAN, from the supposed origin of Gypsies when they appeared in England in the early 16th c.]

gyrate *v. & adj.* —*v.intr.* /ˌdʒaɪəˈreɪt/ go in a circle or spiral; revolve, whirl. —*adj.* /ˈdʒaɪrət/ *Bot.* arranged in rings or convolutions. □□ **gyration** /-ˈreɪʃ(ə)n/ *n.* **gyrator** /ˌdʒaɪəˈreɪtə(r)/ *n.* **gyratory** /-rətərɪ, -ˈreɪtərɪ/ *adj.* [L *gyrare gyrat-* revolve f. *gyrus* ring f. Gk *guros*]

gyre /dʒaɪə(r)/ *v. & n.* esp. *poet.* —*v.intr.* whirl or gyrate. —*n.* a gyration. [L *gyrus* ring f. Gk *guros*]

gyrfalcon /ˈdʒɜːˌfɔːlkən/ *n.* (also **gerfalcon**) a large falcon, *Falco rusticolus*, of the northern hemisphere. [ME f. OF *gerfaucon* f. Frank. *gērfalco* f. ON *geirfálki*: see FALCON]

gyro /ˈdʒaɪərəʊ/ *n.* (*pl.* **-os**) *colloq.* **1** = GYROSCOPE. **2** = GYROCOMPASS. [abbr.]

gyro- /ˈdʒaɪərəʊ/ *comb. form* rotation. [Gk *guros* ring]

gyrocompass /ˈdʒaɪərəʊˌkʌmpəs/ *n.* a non-magnetic compass giving true north and bearings from it by means of a gyroscope.

gyrograph /ˈdʒaɪərəʊˌgrɑːf/ *n.* an instrument for recording revolutions.

gyromagnetic /ˌdʒaɪərəʊmægˈnetɪk/ *adj.* **1** *Physics* of the magnetic and mechanical properties of a rotating charged particle. **2** (of a compass) combining a gyroscope and a normal magnetic compass.

gyropilot /ˈdʒaɪərəʊˌpaɪlət/ *n.* a gyrocompass used for automatic steering.

gyroplane /ˈdʒaɪərəʊˌpleɪn/ *n.* a form of aircraft deriving its lift mainly from freely rotating overhead vanes.

gyroscope /ˈdʒaɪərəˌskəʊp/ *n.* a rotating wheel whose axis is free to turn but maintains a fixed direction unless perturbed, esp. used for stabilization or with the compass in an aircraft, ship, etc. □□ **gyroscopic** /-ˈskɒpɪk/ *adj.* **gyroscopically** /-ˈskɒpɪkəlɪ/ *adv.* [F (as GYRO-, SCOPE[2])]

gyrostabilizer /ˈdʒaɪərəʊˌsteɪbɪˌlaɪzə(r)/ *n.* a gyroscopic device for maintaining the equilibrium of a ship, aircraft, platform, etc.

gyrus /ˈdʒaɪərəs/ *n.* (*pl.* **gyri** /-rɪ/) a fold or convolution, esp. of the brain. [L f. Gk *guros* ring]

gyttja /ˈjɪtʃə/ *n. Geol.* a lake deposit of a usu. black organic sediment. [Sw., = mud, ooze]

gyver var. of GUIVER.

H

H¹ /eɪtʃ/ n. (also **h**) (pl. **Hs** or **H's**) **1** the eighth letter of the alphabet (see AITCH). **2** anything having the form of an H (esp. in *comb.*: *H-girder*).

H² abbr. (also **H.**) **1** hardness. **2** (of a pencil-lead) hard. **3** henry, henrys. **4** (water) hydrant. **5** sl. heroin.

H³ symb. Chem. the element hydrogen.

h. abbr. **1** hecto-. **2** height. **3** horse. **4** hot. **5** hour(s). **6** husband. **7** Planck's constant.

Ha symb. Chem. the element hahnium.

ha¹ /hɑː/ int. & v. (also **hah**) —int. expressing surprise, suspicion, triumph, etc. (cf. HA HA). —v. intr. (in **hum and ha**: see HUM¹) [ME]

ha² abbr. hectare(s).

haar /hɑː(r)/ n. a cold sea-fog on the east coast of England or Scotland. [perh. f. ON *hárr* hoar, hoary]

Hab. abbr. Habakkuk (Old Testament).

habanera /ˌhæbəˈneərə/ n. **1** a Cuban dance in slow duple time. **2** the music for this. [Sp., fem. of *habanero* of Havana in Cuba]

habeas corpus /ˌheɪbɪəs ˈkɔːpəs/ n. a writ requiring a person to be brought before a judge or into court, esp. to investigate the lawfulness of his or her detention. [L, = you must have the body]

haberdasher /ˈhæbəˌdæʃə(r)/ n. **1** Brit. a dealer in dress accessories and sewing-goods. **2** US a dealer in men's clothing. □□ **haberdashery** n. (pl. **-ies**). [ME prob. ult. f. AF *hapertas* perh. the name of a fabric]

habergeon /ˈhæbədʒ(ə)n/ n. hist. a sleeveless coat of mail. [ME f. OF *haubergeon* (as HAUBERK)]

habiliment /həˈbɪlɪmənt/ n. (usu. in pl.) **1** clothes suited to a particular purpose. **2** joc. ordinary clothes. [ME f. OF *habillement* f. *habiller* fit out f. *habile* ABLE]

habilitate /həˈbɪlɪˌteɪt/ v.intr. qualify for office (esp. as a teacher in a German university). □□ **habilitation** /-ˈteɪʃ(ə)n/ n. [med.L *habilitare* (as ABILITY)]

habit /ˈhæbɪt/ n. & v. —n. **1** a settled or regular tendency or practice (often foll. by *of* + verbal noun: *has a habit of ignoring me*). **2** a practice that is hard to give up. **3** a mental constitution or attitude. **4** Psychol. an automatic reaction to a specific situation. **5** colloq. an addictive practice, esp. of taking drugs. **6** **a** the dress of a particular class, esp. of a religious order. **b** (in full **riding-habit**) a woman's riding-dress. **c** archaic dress, attire. **7** a bodily constitution. **8** Biol. & Crystallog. a mode of growth. —v.tr. (usu. as **habited** adj.) clothe. □ **habit-forming** causing addiction. **make a habit of** do regularly. [ME f. OF *abit* f. L *habitus* f. *habēre* habit- have, be constituted]

habitable /ˈhæbɪtəb(ə)l/ adj. that can be inhabited. □□ **habitability** /-ˈbɪlɪtɪ/ n. **habitableness** n. **habitably** adv. [ME f. OF f. L *habitabilis* (as HABITANT)]

habitant n. **1** /ˈhæbɪt(ə)nt/ an inhabitant. **2** /ˌæbiːˈtɑ̃/ **a** an early French settler in Canada or Louisiana. **b** a descendant of these settlers. [F f. OF *habiter* f. L *habitare* inhabit (as HABIT)]

habitat /ˈhæbɪˌtæt/ n. **1** the natural home of an organism. **2** a habitation. [L, = it dwells: see HABITANT]

habitation /ˌhæbɪˈteɪʃ(ə)n/ n. **1** the process of inhabiting (*fit for human habitation*). **2** a house or home. [ME f. OF f. L *habitatio -onis* (as HABITANT)]

habitual /həˈbɪtjʊəl/ adj. **1** done constantly or as a habit. **2** regular, usual. **3** given to a (specified) habit (*a habitual smoker*). □□ **habitually** adv. **habitualness** n. [med.L *habitualis* (as HABIT)]

habituate /həˈbɪtjʊˌeɪt/ v.tr. (often foll. by *to*) accustom; make used to something. □□ **habituation** /-ˈeɪʃ(ə)n/ n. [LL *habituare* (as HABIT)]

habitude /ˈhæbɪˌtjuːd/ n. **1** a mental or bodily disposition. **2** a custom or tendency. [ME f. OF f. L *habitudo -dinis* f. *habēre* habit- have]

habitué /həˈbɪtjʊˌeɪ/ n. a habitual visitor or resident. [F, past part. of *habituer* (as HABITUATE)]

háček /ˈhætʃek/ n. a diacritic mark (ˇ) placed over letters to modify the sound in some Slavonic and Baltic languages. [Czech, dimin. of *hák* hook]

hachures /hæˈʃjʊə(r)/ n.pl. parallel lines used in hill-shading on maps, their closeness indicating the steepness of gradient. [F f. *hacher* HATCH³]

hacienda /ˌhæsɪˈendə/ n. in Spanish-speaking countries: **1** an estate or plantation with a dwelling-house. **2** a factory. [Sp. f. L *facienda* things to be done]

hack¹ /hæk/ v. & n. —v. **1** tr. cut or chop roughly; mangle. **2** tr. kick the shin of (an opponent at football). **3** intr. (often foll. by *at*) deliver cutting blows. **4** tr. cut (one's way) through thick foliage etc. **5** tr. colloq. gain unauthorized access to (data in a computer). **6** tr. sl. **a** manage, cope with. **b** tolerate. —n. **1** a kick with the toe of a boot. **2** a gash or wound, esp. from a kick. **3** **a** a mattock. **b** a miner's pick. □ **hacking cough** a short dry frequent cough. [OE *haccian* cut in pieces f. WG]

hack² /hæk/ n., adj., & v. —n. **1** **a** a horse for ordinary riding. **b** a horse let out for hire. **c** = JADE² 1. **2** a dull, uninspired writer. **3** a person hired to do dull routine work. **4** US a taxi. —attrib.adj. **1** used as a hack. **2** typical of a hack; commonplace (*hack work*). —v. **1** **a** intr. ride on horseback on a road at an ordinary pace. **b** tr. ride (a horse) in this way. **2** tr. make common or trite. [abbr. of HACKNEY]

hack³ /hæk/ n. **1** a board on which a hawk's meat is laid. **2** a rack holding fodder for cattle. □ **at hack** (of a young hawk) not yet allowed to prey for itself. [var. of HATCH¹]

hackberry /ˈhækbərɪ/ n. (pl. **-ies**) US **1** any tree of the genus *Celtis*, native to N. America, bearing purple edible berries. **2** the berry of this tree. [var. of *hagberry*, of Norse orig.]

hacker /ˈhækə(r)/ n. **1** a person or thing that hacks or cuts roughly. **2** colloq. a person who uses computers for a hobby, esp. to gain unauthorized access to data.

hackle /ˈhæk(ə)l/ n. & v. —n. **1** a long feather or series of feathers on the neck or saddle of a domestic cock and other birds. **2** Fishing an artificial fly dressed with a hackle. **3** a feather in a Highland soldier's bonnet. **4** (in pl.) the erectile hairs along the back of a dog, which rise when it is angry or alarmed. **5** a steel comb for dressing flax. —v.tr. dress or comb with a hackle. □ **make one's hackles rise** cause one to be angry or indignant. [ME *hechele*, *hakele*, prob. f. OE f. WG]

hackney /ˈhæknɪ/ n. (pl. **-eys**) **1** a horse of average size and quality for ordinary riding. **2** (attrib.) designating any of various vehicles kept for hire. ¶ No longer used except in *hackney carriage*, still in official use as a term for 'taxi'. [ME, perh. f. *Hackney* (formerly *Hakenei*) in London, where horses were pastured]

hackneyed /ˈhæknɪd/ adj. (of a phrase etc.) made commonplace or trite by overuse.

hacksaw /ˈhæksɔː/ n. a saw with a narrow blade set in a frame, for cutting metal.

had past and past part. of HAVE.

---

w *we*   z *zoo*   ʃ *she*   ʒ *decision*   θ *thin*   ð *this*   ŋ *ring*   x *loch*   tʃ *chip*   dʒ *jar*   (*see over for vowels*)

haddock /'hædək/ n. (pl. same) a marine fish, *Melanogrammus aeglefinus*, of the N. Atlantic, allied to cod, but smaller. [ME, prob. f. AF *hadoc*, OF (*h*)*adot*, of unkn. orig.]

hade /heɪd/ n. & v. *Geol.* —n. an incline from the vertical. —v.intr. incline from the vertical. [17th c., perh. dial. form of *head*]

Hades /'heɪdiːz/ n. (in Greek mythology) the underworld, the abode of the spirits of the dead. [Gk *haidēs*, orig. a name of Pluto]

Hadith /'hædɪθ/ n. *Relig.* a body of traditions relating to Muhammad. [Arab. *ḥadīt* tradition]

hadj var. of HAJJ.

hadji var. of HAJJI.

hadn't /'hæd(ə)nt/ contr. had not.

hadron /'hædrɒn/ n. *Physics* any strongly interacting elementary particle. □□ **hadronic** /-'drɒnɪk/ adj. [Gk *hadros* bulky]

hadst /hædst/ archaic 2nd sing. past of HAVE.

haecceity /hek'siːɪtɪ/ n. *Philos.* **1** the quality of a thing that makes it unique or describable as 'this (one)'. **2** individuality. [med.L *haecceitas* f. *haec* fem. of *hic* this]

haem /hiːm/ n. (also **heme**) a non-protein compound containing iron, and responsible for the red colour of haemoglobin. [Gk *haima* blood or f. HAEMOGLOBIN]

haemal /'hiːm(ə)l/ adj. (US **hemal**) *Anat.* **1** of or concerning the blood. **2 a** situated on the same side of the body as the heart and great blood-vessels. **b** ventral. [Gk *haima* blood]

haematic /hiː'mætɪk/ adj. (US **hematic**) *Med.* of or containing blood. [Gk *haimatikos* (as HAEMATIN)]

haematin /'hiːmətɪn/ n. (US **hematin** /'hiːm-, 'hem-/) *Anat.* a bluish-black derivative of haemoglobin, formed by removal of the protein part and oxidation of the iron atom. [Gk *haima -matos* blood]

haematite /'hiːmətaɪt/ n. (US **hematite** /'hiːm-, 'hem-/) a ferric oxide ore. [L *haematites* f. Gk *haimatitēs* (*lithos*) bloodlike (stone) (as HAEMATIN)]

haemato- /'hiːmətəʊ/ comb. form (US **hemato-**) blood. [Gk *haima haimat-* blood]

haematocele /'hiːmətəʊˌsiːl/ n. (US **hematocele** /'hiː-, 'he-/) *Med.* a swelling caused by blood collecting in a body cavity.

haematocrit /'hiːmətəʊkrɪt/ n. (US **hematocrit** /'hiː-, 'he-/) *Physiol.* **1** the ratio of the volume of red blood cells to the total volume of blood. **2** an instrument for measuring this. [HAEMATO- + Gk *kritēs* judge]

haematology /ˌhiːmə'tɒlədʒɪ/ n. (US **hematology** /'hiː-, 'he-/) the study of the physiology of the blood. □□ **haematologic** /-tə'lɒdʒɪk/ adj. **haematological** /-tə'lɒdʒɪk(ə)l/ adj. **haematologist** n.

haematoma /ˌhiːmə'təʊmə/ n. (US **hematoma** /ˌhiː-, ˌhe-/) *Med.* a solid swelling of clotted blood within the tissues.

haematuria /ˌhiːmə'tjʊərɪə/ n. (US **hematuria** /ˌhiː-, ˌhe-/) *Med.* the presence of blood in urine.

-haemia var. of -AEMIA.

haemo- /'hiːməʊ/ comb. form (US **hemo-**) = HAEMATO-. [abbr.]

haemocyanin /ˌhiːmə'saɪənɪn/ n. (US **hemocyanin** /ˌhiː-, ˌhe-/) an oxygen-carrying substance containing copper, present in the blood plasma of arthropods and molluscs. [HAEMO- + *cyanin* blue pigment (as CYAN)]

haemodyalysis /ˌhiːməʊdaɪˈælɪsɪs/ n. = DIALYSIS 2.

haemoglobin /ˌhiːmə'gləʊbɪn/ n. (US **hemoglobin** /ˌhiː-, ˌhe-/) a red oxygen-carrying substance containing iron, present in the red blood-cells of vertebrates. [shortened f. *haematoglobin*, compound of HAEMATIN + GLOBULIN]

haemolysis /hiː'mɒlɪsɪs/ n. (US **hemolysis** /hiː-, he-/) the loss of haemoglobin from red blood-cells. □□ **haemolytic** /-mə'lɪtɪk/ adj.

haemophilia /ˌhiːmə'fɪlɪə/ n. (US **hemophilia** /ˌhiː-, ˌhe-/) *Med.* a usu. hereditary disorder with a tendency to bleed severely from even a slight injury, through the failure of the blood to clot normally. □□ **haemophilic** adj. [mod.L (as HAEMO-, -PHILIA)]

haemophiliac /ˌhiːmə'fɪlɪˌæk/ n. (US **hemophiliac** /ˌhiː-, ˌhe-/) a person suffering from haemophilia.

haemorrhage /'hemərɪdʒ/ n. & v. (US **hemorrhage**) —n. **1** an escape of blood from a ruptured blood-vessel, esp. when profuse. **2** an extensive damaging loss suffered by a State, organization, etc., esp. of people or assets. —v.intr. undergo a haemorrhage. □□ **haemorrhagic** /ˌhemə'rædʒɪk/ adj. [earlier *haemorrhagy* f. F *hémorr*(*h*)*agie* f. L *haemorrhagia* f. Gk *haimorrhagia* f. *haima* blood + stem of *rhēgnumi* burst]

haemorrhoid /'hemərɔɪd/ n. (US **hemorrhoid**) (usu. in pl.) swollen veins at or near the anus; piles. □□ **haemorrhoidal** /-'rɔɪd(ə)l/ adj. [ME *emeroudis* (Bibl. *emerods*) f. OF *emeroyde* f. L f. Gk *haimorrhoides* (*phlebes*) bleeding (veins) f. *haima* blood, *-rhoos* -flowing]

haemostasis /ˌhiːməʊ'steɪsɪs/ n. (US **hemostasis**) the stopping of the flow of blood. □□ **haemostatic** /ˌhiːmə'stætɪk, ˌhe-/ adj.

haere mai /'haɪrə ˌmaɪ/ int. *NZ* welcome. [Maori, lit. 'come hither']

hafiz /'hɑːfɪz/ n. a Muslim who knows the Koran by heart. [Pers. f. Arab. *ḥāfiz* guardian]

hafnium /'hæfnɪəm/ n. *Chem.* a silvery lustrous metallic element occurring naturally with zirconium, used in tungsten alloys for filaments and electrodes. ¶ Symb.: **Hf**. [mod.L f. *Hafnia* Copenhagen]

haft /hɑːft/ n. & v. —n. the handle of a dagger or knife etc. —v.tr. provide with a haft. [OE *hæft* f. Gmc]

Hag. abbr. Haggai (Old Testament).

hag[1] /hæg/ n. **1** an ugly old woman. **2** a witch. **3** = HAGFISH. □□ **haggish** adj. [ME *hegge, hagge*, perh. f. OE *hægtesse*, OHG *hagazissa*, of unkn. orig.]

hag[2] /hæg/ n. *Sc.* & *N.Engl.* **1** a soft place on a moor. **2** a firm place in a bog. [ON *högg* gap, orig. 'cutting blow', rel. to HEW]

hagfish /'hægfɪʃ/ n. any jawless fish of the family Myxinidae, with a rasp-like tongue used for feeding on dead or dying fish. [HAG[1]]

Haggadah /hə'gɑːdə/ n. **1** a legend etc. used to illustrate a point of the Law in the Talmud; the legendary element of the Talmud. **2** a book recited at the Passover Seder service. □□ **Haggadic** /-'gædɪk, -'gɑːdɪk/ adj. [Heb., = tale, f. *higgīd* tell]

haggard /'hægəd/ adj. & n. —adj. **1** looking exhausted and distraught, esp. from fatigue, worry, privation, etc. **2** (of a hawk) caught and trained as an adult. —n. a haggard hawk. □□ **haggardly** adv. **haggardness** n. [F *hagard*, of uncert. orig.: later infl. by HAG[1]]

haggis /'hægɪs/ n. a Scottish dish consisting of a sheep's or calf's offal mixed with suet, oatmeal, etc., and boiled in a bag made from the animal's stomach or in an artificial bag. [ME: orig. unkn.]

haggle /'hæg(ə)l/ v. & n. —v.intr. (often foll. by *about, over*) dispute or bargain persistently. —n. a dispute or wrangle. □□ **haggler** n. [earlier sense 'hack' f. ON *höggva* HEW]

hagio- /'hægɪəʊ/ comb. form of saints or holiness. [Gk *hagios* holy]

Hagiographa /ˌhægɪ'ɒgrəfə/ n. the twelve books comprising the last of the three major divisions of the Hebrew Scriptures, additional to the Law and the Prophets.

hagiographer /ˌhægɪ'ɒgrəfə(r)/ n. **1** a writer of the lives of saints. **2** a writer of any of the Hagiographa.

hagiography /ˌhægɪ'ɒgrəfɪ/ n. the writing of the lives of saints. □□ **hagiographic** /-ə'græfɪk/ adj. **hagiographical** /-ə'græfɪk(ə)l/ adj.

hagiolatry /ˌhægɪ'ɒlətrɪ/ n. the worship of saints.

hagiology /ˌhægɪ'ɒlədʒɪ/ n. literature dealing with the lives and legends of saints. □□ **hagiological** /-gɪə'lɒdʒɪk(ə)l/ adj. **hagiologist** n.

hagridden /ˈhægˌrɪd(ə)n/ *adj*. afflicted by nightmares or anxieties.

hah var. of HA.

ha ha /hɑːˈhɑː/ *int*. repr. laughter. [OE: cf. HA]

ha-ha /ˈhɑːhɑː/ *n*. a ditch with a wall on its inner side below ground level, forming a boundary to a park or garden without interrupting the view. [F, perh. from the cry of surprise on encountering it]

hahnium /ˈhɑːnɪəm/ *n*. *Chem*. an artificially produced radioactive element. ¶ Symb.: **Ha**. [O. *Hahn*, Ger. chemist d. 1968 + -IUM]

haik /haɪk, heɪk/ *n*. (also **haick**) an outer covering for head and body worn by Arabs. [Moroccan Arab. *ḥāʼik*]

haiku /ˈhaɪkuː/ *n*. (*pl*. same) **1** a Japanese three-part poem of usu. 17 syllables. **2** an English imitation of this. [Jap.]

hail[1] /heɪl/ *n*. & *v*. —*n*. **1** pellets of frozen rain falling in showers from cumulonimbus clouds. **2** (foll. by *of*) a barrage or onslaught (of missiles, curses, questions, etc.). —*v*. **1** *intr*. (prec. by *it* as subject) hail falls (*it is hailing*; *if it hails*). **2 a** *tr*. pour down (blows, words, etc.). **b** *intr*. come down forcefully. [OE *hagol*, *hægl*, *hagalian* f. Gmc]

hail[2] /heɪl/ *v*., *int*., & *n*. —*v*. **1** *tr*. greet enthusiastically. **2** *tr*. signal to or attract the attention of (*hailed a taxi*). **3** *tr*. acclaim (*hailed him king*). **4** *intr*. (foll. by *from*) have one's home or origins in (a place) (*hails from Mauritius*). —*int*. expressing greeting. —*n*. **1** a greeting or act of hailing. **2** distance as affecting the possibility of hailing (*was within hail*). □**hail-fellow-well-met** intimate, esp. too intimate. **Hail Mary** the Ave Maria (see AVE). □□ **hailer** *n*. [ellipt. use of obs. *hail* (adj.) f. ON *heill* sound, WHOLE]

hailstone /ˈheɪlstəʊn/ *n*. a pellet of hail.

hailstorm /ˈheɪlstɔːm/ *n*. a period of heavy hail.

hair /heə(r)/ *n*. **1 a** any of the fine threadlike strands growing from the skin of mammals, esp. from the human head. **b** these collectively (*his hair is falling out*). **2 a** an artificially produced hairlike strand, e.g. in a brush. **b** a mass of such hairs. **3** anything resembling a hair. **4** an elongated cell growing from the epidermis of a plant. **5** a very small quantity or extent (also *attrib.*: *a hair crack*). □**get in a person's hair** *colloq*. encumber or annoy a person. **hair-drier** (or **-dryer**) an electrical device for drying the hair by blowing warm air over it. **hair-grass** any of various grasses, esp. of the genus *Deschampsia*, *Corynephous*, *Aira*, etc., with slender stems. **hair of the dog** see DOG. **hair-raising** extremely alarming; terrifying. **hair's breadth** a very small amount or margin. **hair shirt** a shirt of haircloth, worn formerly by penitents and ascetics. **hair-shirt** *adj*. (*attrib.*) austere, harsh, self-sacrificing. **hair-slide** *Brit*. a (usu. ornamental) clip for keeping the hair in position. **hair-splitter** a quibbler. **hair-splitting** *adj*. & *n*. making overfine distinctions; quibbling. **hair-trigger** a trigger of a firearm set for release at the slightest pressure. **keep one's hair on** *Brit*. *colloq*. remain calm; not get angry. **let one's hair down** *colloq*. abandon restraint; behave freely or wildly. **make one's hair stand on end** alarm or horrify one. **not turn a hair** remain apparently unmoved or unaffected. □□ **haired** *adj*. (also in *comb.*). **hairless** *adj*. **hairlike** *adj*. [OE *hǣr* f. Gmc]

hairbreadth /ˈheəbredθ/ *n*. = *hair's breadth*; (esp. *attrib.*: *a hairbreadth escape*).

hairbrush /ˈheəbrʌʃ/ *n*. a brush for arranging or smoothing the hair.

haircloth /ˈheəklɒθ/ *n*. stiff cloth woven from hair, used e.g. in upholstery.

haircut /ˈheəkʌt/ *n*. **1** a cutting of the hair. **2** the style in which the hair is cut.

hairdo /ˈheəduː/ *n*. (*pl*. **-dos**) *colloq*. the style of or an act of styling a woman's hair.

hairdresser /ˈheəˌdresə(r)/ *n*. **1** a person who cuts and styles hair, esp. professionally. **2** the business

or establishment of a hairdresser. □□ **hairdressing** *n*.

hairgrip /ˈheəgrɪp/ *n*. *Brit*. a flat hairpin with the ends close together.

hairline /ˈheəlaɪn/ *n*. **1** the edge of a person's hair, esp. on the forehead. **2** a very thin line or crack etc.

hairnet /ˈheənet/ *n*. a piece of fine mesh-work for confining the hair.

hairpiece /ˈheəpiːs/ *n*. a quantity or switch of detached hair used to augment a person's natural hair.

hairpin /ˈheəpɪn/ *n*. a U-shaped pin for fastening the hair. □**hairpin bend** a sharp U-shaped bend in a road.

hairspray /ˈheəspreɪ/ *n*. a solution sprayed on to the hair to keep it in place.

hairspring /ˈheəsprɪŋ/ *n*. a fine spring regulating the balance-wheel in a watch.

hairstreak /ˈheəstriːk/ *n*. a butterfly of the genus *Strymonidia* etc. with fine streaks or rows of spots on its wings.

hairstyle /ˈheəstaɪl/ *n*. a particular way of arranging or dressing the hair. □□ **hairstyling** *n*. **hairstylist** *n*.

hairy /ˈheərɪ/ *adj*. (**hairier**, **hairiest**) **1** made of or covered with hair. **2** having the feel of hair. **3** *sl*. alarmingly unpleasant or difficult. **b** crude, clumsy. □□ **hairily** *adv*. **hairiness** *n*.

hajj /hædʒ/ *n*. (also **hadj**) the Islamic pilgrimage to Mecca. [Arab. *ḥājj* pilgrimage]

hajji /ˈhædʒɪ/ *n*. (also **hadji**) (*pl*. **-is**) a Muslim who has been to Mecca as a pilgrim: also (**Hajji**) used as a title. [Pers. *hājī* (partly through Turk. *hacı*) f. Arab. *ḥājj*: see HAJJ]

haka /ˈhɑːkə/ *n*. *NZ* **1** a Maori ceremonial war-dance accompanied by chanting. **2** an imitation of this by members of a sports team before a match. [Maori]

hake /heɪk/ *n*. any marine fish of the genus *Merluccius*, esp. *M. merluccius* with an elongate body and large head. [ME perh. ult. f. dial. *hake* hook + FISH[1]]

hakenkreuz /ˈhɑːkənˌkrɔɪts/ *n*. a swastika, esp. as a Nazi symbol. [G f. *Haken* hook + *Kreuz* CROSS]

hakim[1] /hʌˈkiːm/ *n*. (in India and Muslim countries) a physician. [Arab. *ḥakīm* wise man, physician]

hakim[2] /ˈhɑːkɪm/ *n*. (in India and Muslim countries) a judge, ruler, or governor. [Arab. *ḥākim* governor]

Halacha /həˈlɑːxə/ *n*. (also **Halakah**) Jewish law and jurisprudence, based on the Talmud. □□ **Halachic** *adj*. [Aram. *hᵃlāḵāh* law]

halal /hɑːˈlɑːl/ *v*. & *n*. (also **hallal**) —*v.tr*. (**halalled**, **halalling**) kill (an animal) as prescribed by Muslim law. —*n*. (often *attrib.*) meat prepared in this way; lawful food. [Arab. *ḥalāl* lawful]

halation /hæˈleɪʃ(ə)n/ *n*. *Photog*. the spreading of light beyond its proper extent in a developed image, caused by internal reflection in the support of the emulsion. [irreg. f. HALO + -ATION]

halberd /ˈhælbəd/ *n*. (also **halbert**) *hist*. a combined spear and battleaxe. [ME f. F *hallebarde* f. It *alabarda* f. MHG *helmbarde* f. *helm* handle + *barde* hatchet]

halberdier /ˌhælbəˈdɪə(r)/ *n*. *hist*. a man armed with a halberd. [F *hallebardier* (as HALBERD)]

halcyon /ˈhælsɪən/ *adj*. & *n*. —*adj*. **1** calm, peaceful (*halcyon days*). **2** (of a period) happy, prosperous. —*n*. **1** any kingfisher of the genus *Halcyon*, native to Europe, Africa, and Australasia, with brightly-coloured plumage. **2** *Mythol*. a bird thought in antiquity to breed in a nest floating at sea at the winter solstice, charming the wind and waves into calm. [ME f. L (*h*)*alcyon* f. Gk (*h*)*alkuōn* kingfisher]

hale[1] /heɪl/ *adj*. (esp. of an old person) strong and healthy (esp. in **hale and hearty**). □□ **haleness** *n*. [OE *hāl* WHOLE]

hale[2] /heɪl/ *v.tr*. drag or draw forcibly. [ME f. OF *haler* f. ON *hala*]

half /hɑːf/ *n*., *adj*., & *adv*. —*n*. (*pl*. **halves** /hɑːvz/) **1** either of two equal or corresponding parts or groups into which a thing is or might be divided. **2** *colloq*. =

half-back. **3** *colloq.* half a pint, esp. of beer etc. **4** either of two equal periods of play in sports. **5** *colloq.* a half-price fare or ticket, esp. for a child. **6** *Golf* a score that is the same as one's opponent's. —*adj.* **1** of an amount or quantity equal to a half, or loosely to a part thought of as roughly a half (*take half the men; spent half the time reading; half a pint; a half-pint; half-price*). **2** forming a half (*a half share*). —*adv.* **1** (often in *comb.*) to the extent of half; partly (*only half cooked; half-frozen; half-laughing*). **2** to a certain extent; somewhat (esp. in idiomatic phrases: *half dead; am half inclined to agree*). **3** (in reckoning time) by the amount of half (an hour etc.) (*half past two*). □**at half cock** see COCK¹. **by half** (prec. by *too* + adj.) excessively (*too clever by half*). **by halves** imperfectly or incompletely (*never does things by halves*). **half-and-half** being half one thing and half another. **half-back** (in some sports) a player between the forwards and full backs. **half-baked 1** incompletely considered or planned. **2** (of enthusiasm etc.) only partly committed. **3** foolish. **half the battle** see BATTLE. **half-beak** any fish of the family Hemirhamphidae with the lower jaw projecting beyond the upper. **half-binding** a type of bookbinding in which the spine and corners are bound in one material (usu. leather) and the sides in another. **half-blood 1** a person having one parent in common with another. **2** this relationship. **3** = *half-breed*. **half-blooded** born from parents of different races. **half-blue** *Brit.* **1** a person who has represented a university, esp. Oxford or Cambridge, in a sport but who has not received a full blue. **2** this distinction (see BLUE¹ *n.* 3). **half board** provision of bed, breakfast, and one main meal at a hotel etc. **half-boot** a boot reaching up to the calf. **half-breed** often *offens.* a person of mixed race. **half-brother** a brother with only one parent in common. **half-caste** often *offens. n.* a person whose parents are of different races, esp. the offspring of a European father and an Indian mother. —*adj.* of or relating to such a person. **half a chance** *colloq.* the slightest opportunity (esp. *given half a chance*). **half-crown** (or **half a crown**) (in the UK) a former coin and monetary unit worth 2s. 6d. (12½p). **half-cut** *Brit. sl.* fairly drunk. **half-deck** the quarters of cadets and apprentices on a merchant vessel. **half-dozen** (or **half a dozen**) *colloq.* six, or about six. **half-duplex** see DUPLEX. **half an eye** the slightest degree of perceptiveness. **half-hardy** (of a plant) able to grow in the open air at all times except in severe frost. **half hitch** a noose or knot formed by passing the end of a rope round its standing part and then through the loop. **half holiday** a day of which half (usu. the afternoon) is taken as a holiday. **half-hour 1** (also **half an hour**) a period of 30 minutes. **2** a point of time 30 minutes after any hour o'clock. **half-hourly** at intervals of 30 minutes. **half-hunter** a watch with a hinged cover in which a small opening allows identification of the approximate position of the hands. **half-inch** *n.* a unit of length half as large as an inch. —*v.tr. rhyming sl.* steal (= *pinch*). **half-integral** equal to half an odd integer. **half-landing** a landing part of the way up a flight of stairs, whose length is twice the width of the flight plus the width of the well. **half-lap** the joining of rails, shafts, etc., by halving the thickness of each at one end and fitting them together. **half-length** a canvas depicting a half-length portrait. **half-life** *Physics & Biochem.* etc. the time taken for the radioactivity or some other property of a substance to fall to half its original value. **half-light** a dim imperfect light. **half-mast** the position of a flag halfway down the mast, as a mark of respect for a person who has died. **half measures** an unsatisfactory compromise or inadequate policy. **half a mind** see MIND. **half moon 1** the moon when only half its illuminated surface is visible from earth. **2** the time when this occurs. **3** a semicircular object. **half nelson** *Wrestling* see NELSON. **half-note** esp.

US Mus. = MINIM 1. **the half of it** *colloq.* the rest or more important part of something (usu. after *neg.: you don't know the half of it*). **half pay** reduced income, esp. on retirement. **half-pie** *NZ sl.* imperfect, mediocre. **half-plate 1** a photographic plate 16.5 by 10.8 cm. **2** a photograph reproduced from this. **half-seas-over** *Brit. sl.* partly drunk. **half-sister** a sister with only one parent in common. **half-sole** the sole of a boot or shoe from the shank to the toe. **half-sovereign** a former British gold coin and monetary unit worth ten shillings (50p). **half-step** *Mus.* a semitone. **half-term** *Brit.* a period about halfway through a school term, when a short holiday is usually taken. **half-timbered** *Archit.* having walls with a timber frame and a brick or plaster filling. **half-time 1** the time at which half of a game or contest is completed. **2** a short interval occurring at this time. **half the time** see TIME. **half-title 1** the title or short title of a book, printed on the recto of the leaf preceding the title-page. **2** the title of a section of a book printed on the recto of the leaf preceding it. **half-tone 1** a reproduction printed from a block (produced by photographic means) in which the various tones of grey are produced from small and large black dots. **2** *US Mus.* a semitone. **half-track 1** a propulsion system for land vehicles with wheels at the front and an endless driven belt at the back. **2** a vehicle equipped with this. **half-truth** a statement that (esp. deliberately) conveys only part of the truth. **half-volley** (*pl.* **-eys**) (in ball games) the playing of a ball as soon as it bounces off the ground. **half-yearly** at intervals of six months. **not half 1** not nearly (*not half long enough*). **2** *colloq.* not at all (*not half bad*). **3** *Brit. sl.* to an extreme degree (*he didn't half get angry*). [OE *half, healf* f. Gmc, orig. = 'side']

half-hearted /hɑːfˈhɑːtɪd/ *adj.* lacking enthusiasm; feeble. □□ **half-heartedly** *adv.* **half-heartedness** *n.*

halfpenny /ˈheɪpnɪ/ *n.* (also **ha'penny** /ˈheɪpnɪ/) (*pl.* **-pennies** or **-pence** /ˈheɪpəns/) (in the UK) a former bronze coin worth half a penny. ¶ Withdrawn in 1984. (cf. FARTHING).

halfpennyworth /ˈheɪpəθ/ *n.* (also **ha'p'orth**) **1** as much as could be bought for a halfpenny. **2** *colloq.* a negligible amount (esp. after *neg.: doesn't make a halfpennyworth of difference*).

halfway /hɑːfˈweɪ, ˈhɑːfweɪ/ *adv.* & *adj.* —*adv.* at a point equidistant between two others (*we were halfway to Rome*). **2** *US* to some extent; more or less (*is halfway decent*). —*adj.* situated halfway (*reached a halfway point*). □ **halfway house 1** a compromise. **2** the halfway point in a progression. **3** a centre for rehabilitating ex-prisoners, mental patients, or others unused to normal life. **4** an inn midway between two towns. **halfway line** a line midway between the ends of a pitch, esp. in football.

halfwit /ˈhɑːfwɪt/ *n.* **1** *colloq.* an extremely foolish or stupid person. **2** a person who is mentally deficient. □□ **halfwitted** /-ˈwɪtɪd/ *adj.* **halfwittedly** /-ˈwɪtɪdlɪ/ *adv.* **halfwittedness** /-ˈwɪtɪdnɪs/ *n.*

halibut /ˈhælɪbət/ *n.* (also **holibut** /ˈhɒl-/) (*pl.* same) a large marine flat-fish, *Hippoglossus vulgaris*, used as food. [ME f. *haly* HOLY + BUTT³ flat-fish, perh. because eaten on holy days]

halide /ˈhælaɪd, ˈheɪl-/ *n. Chem.* **1** a binary compound of a halogen with another group or element. **2** any organic compound containing a halogen.

halieutic /ˌhælɪˈjuːtɪk/ *adj. formal* of or concerning fishing. [L *halieuticus* f. Gk *halieutikos* f. *halieutēs* fisherman]

haliotis /ˌhælɪˈəʊtɪs/ *n.* any edible gastropod mollusc of the genus *Haliotis* with an ear-shaped shell lined with mother-of-pearl. [Gk *hals hali-* sea + *ous ōt-* ear]

halite /ˈhælaɪt/ *n.* rock-salt. [mod.L *halites* f. Gk *hals* salt]

halitosis /ˌhælɪˈtəʊsɪs/ *n.* = *bad breath*. [mod.L f. L *halitus* breath]

hall /hɔːl/ *n.* **1 a** a space or passage into which the front entrance of a house etc. opens. **b** *US* a corridor or passage in a building. **2 a** a large room or building for meetings, meals, concerts, etc. **b** (in *pl.*) music-halls. **3** a large country house, esp. with a landed estate. **4** (in full **hall of residence**) a university residence for students. **5 a** (in a college etc.) a common dining-room. **b** dinner in this. **6** the building of a guild (*Fishmongers' Hall*). **7 a** a large public room in a palace etc. **b** the principal living-room of a medieval house. □**Hall of Fame** *US* a building with memorials of celebrated people. **hall porter** *Brit.* a porter who carries baggage etc. in a hotel. **hall-stand** a stand in the hall of a house, with a mirror, pegs, etc. [OE = *hall* f. Gmc, rel. to HELL]

hallal var. of HALAL.

hallelujah var. of ALLELUIA.

halliard var. of HALYARD.

hallmark /ˈhɔːlmɑːk/ *n. & v.* —*n.* **1** a mark used at Goldsmiths' Hall (and by the UK assay offices) for marking the standard of gold, silver, and platinum. **2** any distinctive feature esp. of excellence. —*v.tr.* **1** stamp with a hallmark. **2** designate as excellent.

hallo var. of HELLO.

halloo /həˈluː/ *int., n., & v.* —*int.* **1** inciting dogs to the chase. **2** calling attention. **3** expressing surprise. —*n.* the cry 'halloo'. —*v.* (**halloos, hallooed**) **1** *intr.* cry 'halloo'. esp. to dogs. **2** *intr.* shout to attract attention. **3** *tr.* urge on (dogs etc.) with shouts. [perh. f. *hallow* pursue with shouts f. OF *halloer* (imit.)]

hallow /ˈhæləʊ/ *v. & n.* —*v.tr.* **1** make holy, consecrate. **2** honour as holy. —*n. archaic* a saint or holy person. □**All Hallows** All Saints' Day, 1 Nov. [OE *hālgian, hālga* f. Gmc]

Hallowe'en /ˌhæləʊˈiːn/ *n.* the eve of All Saints' Day, 31 Oct. [HALLOW + EVEN²]

Hallstatt /ˈhɑːlʃtɑːt/ *adj.* of or relating to the early Iron Age in Europe as attested by archaeological finds at Hallstatt in Upper Austria.

halluces *pl.* of HALLUX.

hallucinate /həˈluːsɪˌneɪt/ *v.* **1** *tr.* produce illusions in the mind of (a person). **2** *intr.* experience hallucinations. □□**hallucinant** *adj. & n.* **hallucinator** *n.* [L (*h*)*allucinari* wander in mind f. Gk *alussō* be uneasy]

hallucination /həˌluːsɪˈneɪʃ(ə)n/ *n.* the apparent or alleged perception of an object not actually present. □□**hallucinatory** /həˈluːsɪnətərɪ/ *adj.* [L *hallucinatio* (as HALLUCINATE)]

hallucinogen /həˈluːsɪnədʒ(ə)n/ *n.* a drug causing hallucinations. □□**hallucinogenic** /-ˈdʒenɪk/ *adj.*

hallux /ˈhælʌks/ *n.* (*pl.* **halluces** /-juːˌsiːz/) **1** the big toe. **2** the innermost digit of the hind foot of vertebrates. [mod.L f. L *allex*]

hallway /ˈhɔːlweɪ/ *n.* an entrance-hall or corridor.

halm var. of HAULM.

halma /ˈhælmə/ *n.* a game played by two or four persons on a board of 256 squares, with men advancing from one corner to the opposite corner by being moved over other men into vacant squares. [Gk, = leap]

halo /ˈheɪləʊ/ *n. & v.* —*n.* (*pl.* **-oes**) **1** a disc or circle of light shown surrounding the head of a sacred person. **2** the glory associated with an idealized person etc. **3** a circle of white or coloured light round a luminous body, esp. the sun or moon. **4** a circle or ring. —*v.tr.* (**-oes, -oed**) surround with a halo. [med.L f. L f. Gk *halōs* threshing-floor, disc of the sun or moon]

halogen /ˈhæləˌdʒ(ə)n/ *n. Chem.* any of the group of non-metallic elements: fluorine, chlorine, bromine, iodine, and astatine, which form halides (e.g. sodium chloride) by simple union with a metal. □□**halogenic** /-ˈdʒenɪk/ *adj.* [Gk *hals halos* salt]

halogenation /ˌhæləʤɪˈneɪʃ(ə)n/ *n.* the introduction of a halogen atom into a molecule.

halon /ˈheɪlɒn/ *n. Chem.* any of various gaseous compounds of carbon, bromine, and other halogens, used to extinguish fires. [as HALOGEN + -ON]

halt¹ /hɒlt, hɔːlt/ *n. & v.* —*n.* **1** a stop (usu. temporary); an interruption of progress (*come to a halt*). **2** a temporary stoppage on a march or journey. **3** *Brit.* a minor stopping-place on a local railway line, usu. without permanent buildings. —*v.intr. & tr.* stop; come or bring to a halt. □**call a halt** (**to**) decide to stop. [orig. in phr. *make halt* f. G *Halt machen* f. *halten* hold, stop]

halt² /hɒlt, hɔːlt/ *v. & adj.* —*v.intr.* **1** (esp. as **halting** *adj.*) lack smooth progress. **2** hesitate (*halt between two opinions*). **3** walk hesitatingly. **4** *archaic* be lame. —*adj. archaic* lame or crippled. □□**haltingly** *adv.* [OE *halt, healt, healtian* f. Gmc]

halter /ˈhɒltə(r), ˈhɔːl-/ *n. & v.* —*n.* **1** a rope or strap with a noose or headstall for horses or cattle. **2 a** a strap round the back of a woman's neck holding her dress-top and leaving her shoulders and back bare. **b** a dress-top held by this. **3 a** a rope with a noose for hanging a person. **b** death by hanging. —*v.tr.* **1** put a halter on (a horse etc.). **2** hang (a person) with a halter. □**halter-break** accustom (a horse) to a halter. [OE *hælftre*: cf. HELVE]

halteres /hælˈtɪəriːz/ *n.pl.* the balancing-organs of dipterous insects. [Gk, = weights used to aid leaping f. *hallomai* to leap]

halva /ˈhælvɑː/ *n.* (also **halvah**) a sweet confection of sesame flour and honey. [Yiddish f. Turk. *helva* f. Arab. *ḥalwā*]

halve /hɑːv/ *v.tr.* **1** divide into two halves or parts. **2** reduce by half. **3** share equally (with another person etc.). **4** *Golf* use the same number of strokes as one's opponent in (a hole or match). **5** fit (crossing timbers) together by cutting out half the thickness of each. [ME *halfen* f. HALF]

halves *pl.* of HALF.

halyard /ˈhæljəd/ *n.* (also **halliard, haulyard** /ˈhɔːljəd/) *Naut.* a rope or tackle for raising or lowering a sail or yard etc. [ME *halier* f. HALE² + -IER, assoc. with YARD¹]

ham /hæm/ *n. & v.* —*n.* **1 a** the upper part of a pig's leg salted and dried or smoked for food. **b** the meat from this. **2** the back of the thigh; the thigh and buttock. **3** *sl.* (often *attrib.*) an inexpert or unsubtle actor or piece of acting. **4** (in full **radio ham**) *colloq.* the operator of an amateur radio station. —*v.intr. & tr.* (**hammed, hamming**) *sl.* overact; act or treat emotionally or sentimentally. [OE *ham, hom* f. a Gmc root meaning 'be crooked']

hamadryad /ˌhæməˈdraɪæd/ *n.* **1** (in Greek and Roman mythology) a nymph who lives in a tree and dies when it dies. **2** the king cobra, *Naja bungarus.* [ME f. L *hamadryas* f. Gk *hamadruas* f. *hama* with + *drus* tree]

hamadryas /ˌhæməˈdraɪəs/ *n.* a large Arabian baboon, *Papio hamadryas*, with a silvery-grey cape of hair over the shoulders, held sacred in ancient Egypt.

hamamelis /ˌhæməˈmiːlɪs/ *n.* any shrub of the genus *Hamamelis*, e.g. wych-hazel. [mod.L f. Gk *hamamēlis* medlar]

hamba /ˈhæmbə/ *int. S.Afr.* be off; go away. [Nguni *-hambe* go]

hamburger /ˈhæmˌbɜːgə(r)/ *n.* a cake of minced beef usu. fried or grilled and eaten in a soft bread roll. [G, = of Hamburg in Germany]

hames /heɪmz/ *n.pl.* two curved pieces of iron or wood forming the collar or part of the collar of a draught-horse, to which the traces are attached. [ME f. MDu. *hame*]

ham-fisted /hæmˈfɪstɪd/ *adj. colloq.* clumsy, heavy-handed, bungling. □□**ham-fistedly** *adv.* **ham-fistedness** *n.*

ham-handed /hæmˈhændɪd/ *adj. colloq.* = HAM-FISTED. □□**ham-handedly** *adv.* **ham-handedness** *n.*

Hamitic /həˈmɪtɪk/ *n. & adj.* —*n.* a group of African

languages including ancient Egyptian and Berber. —*adj.* **1** of or relating to this group of languages. **2** of or relating to the Hamites, a group of peoples in Egypt and N. Africa, by tradition descended from Noah's son Ham (Gen. 10:6 ff.).

hamlet /ˈhæmlɪt/ *n.* a small village, esp. one without a church. [ME f. AF *hamelet(t)e*, OF *hamelet* dimin. of *hamel* dimin. of *ham* f. MLG *hamm*]

hammer /ˈhæmə(r)/ *n. & v.* —*n.* **1 a** a tool with a heavy metal head at right angles to the handle, used for breaking, driving nails, etc. **b** a machine with a metal block serving the same purpose. **c** a similar contrivance, as for exploding the charge in a gun, striking the strings of a piano, etc. **2** an auctioneer's mallet, indicating by a rap that an article is sold. **3 a** a metal ball of about 7 kg, attached to a wire for throwing in an athletic contest. **b** the sport of throwing the hammer. **4** a bone of the middle ear; the malleus. —*v.* **1 a** *tr. & intr.* hit or beat with or as with a hammer. **b** *intr.* strike loudly; knock violently (esp. on a door). **2** *tr.* **a** drive in (nails) with a hammer. **b** fasten or secure by hammering (*hammered the lid down*). **3** *tr.* (often foll. by *in*) inculcate (ideas, knowledge, etc.) forcefully or repeatedly. **4** *tr. colloq.* utterly defeat; inflict heavy damage on. **5** *intr.* (foll. by *at*, *away at*) work hard or persistently at. **6** *tr. Stock Exch.* declare (a person or a firm) a defaulter. □**come under the hammer** be sold at an auction. **hammer and sickle** the symbols of the industrial worker and the peasant used as the emblem of the USSR and of international communism. **hammer and tongs** *colloq.* with great vigour and commotion. **hammer out 1** make flat or smooth by hammering. **2** work out the details of (a plan, agreement, etc.) laboriously. **3** play (a tune, esp. on the piano) loudly or clumsily. **hammer-toe** a deformity in which the toe is bent permanently downwards. □□ **hammering** *n.* (esp. in sense 4 of *v.*). **hammerless** *adj.* [OE *hamor, hamer*]

hammerbeam /ˈhæmə,biːm/ *n.* a wooden beam (often carved) projecting from a wall to support the principal rafter or the end of an arch.

hammerhead /ˈhæmə,hed/ *n.* **1** any shark of the family Sphyrinidae, with a flattened head and eyes in lateral extensions of it. **2** a long-legged African marsh-bird, *Scopus umbretta*, with a thick bill and an occipital crest.

hammerlock /ˈhæmə,lɒk/ *n. Wrestling* a hold in which the arm is twisted and bent behind the back.

hammock /ˈhæmək/ *n.* a bed of canvas or rope network, suspended by cords at the ends, used esp. on board ship. [earlier *hamaca* f. Sp., of Carib orig.]

hammy /ˈhæmɪ/ *adj.* (**hammier**, **hammiest**) **1** of or like ham. **2** *colloq.* (of an actor or acting) over-theatrical.

hamper[1] /ˈhæmpə(r)/ *n.* **1** a large basket usu. with a hinged lid and containing food (*picnic hamper*). **2** *Brit.* a selection of food, drink, etc., for an occasion. [ME f. obs. *hanaper*, AF f. OF *hanapier* case for a goblet f. *hanap* goblet]

hamper[2] /ˈhæmpə(r)/ *v. & n.* —*v.tr.* **1** prevent the free movement or activity of; impede, hinder. —*n. Naut.* necessary but cumbersome equipment on a ship. [ME: orig. unkn.]

hamsin var. of KHAMSIN.

hamster /ˈhæmstə(r)/ *n.* any of various rodents of the subfamily Cricetinae, esp. *Cricetus cricetus*, having a short tail and large cheek pouches for storing food, kept as a pet or laboratory animal. [G f. OHG *hamustro* corn-weevil]

hamstring /ˈhæmstrɪŋ/ *n. & v. Anat.* —*n.* **1** each of five tendons at the back of the knee in humans. **2** the great tendon at the back of the hock in quadrupeds. —*v.tr.* (*past* and *past part.* **hamstrung** or **hamstringed**) **1** cripple by cutting the hamstrings of (a person or animal). **2** prevent the activity or efficiency of (a person or enterprise).

hamulus /ˈhæmjʊləs/ *n.* (*pl.* **hamuli** /-ˌlaɪ/) *Anat.,*

Zool., & Bot. a hooklike process. [L, dimin. of *hamus* hook]

hand /hænd/ *n. & v.* —*n.* **1 a** the end part of the human arm beyond the wrist, including the fingers and thumb. **b** in other primates, the end part of a forelimb, also used as a foot. **2 a** (often in *pl.*) control, management, custody, disposal (*is in good hands*). **b** agency or influence (*suffered at their hands*). **c** a share in an action; active support. **3** a thing compared with a hand or its functions, esp. the pointer of a clock or watch. **4** the right or left side or direction relative to a person or thing. **5 a** a skill, esp. in something practical (*a hand for making pastry*). **b** a person skilful in some respect. **6** a person who does or makes something, esp. distinctively (*a picture by the same hand*). **7** an individual's writing or the style of this; a signature (*a legible hand; in one's own hand; witness the hand of . . .*). **8** a person etc. as the source of information etc. (*at first hand*). **9** a pledge of marriage. **10** a person as a source of manual labour esp. in a factory, on a farm, or on board ship. **11 a** the playing-cards dealt to a player. **b** the player holding these. **c** a round of play. **12** *colloq.* applause (*got a big hand*). **13** the unit of measure of a horse's height, equal to 4 inches (10.16 cm). **14** a forehock of pork. **15** a bunch of bananas. **16** (*attrib.*) **a** operated or held in the hand (*hand-drill; hand-luggage*). **b** done by hand and not by machine (*hand-knitted*). —*v.tr.* **1** (foll. by *in*, *to*, *over*, etc.) deliver; transfer by hand or otherwise. **2** convey verbally (*handed me a lot of abuse*). **3** *colloq.* give away too readily (*handed them the advantage*). □**all hands 1** the entire crew of a ship. **2** the entire workforce. **at hand 1** close by. **2** about to happen. **by hand 1** by a person and not a machine. **2** delivered privately and not by the public post. **from hand to mouth** satisfying only one's immediate needs (also *attrib.*: *a hand-to-mouth existence*). **get** (or **have** or **keep**) **one's hand in** become (or be or remain) practised in something. **give** (or **lend**) **a hand** assist in an action or enterprise. **hand and foot** completely; satisfying all demands (*waited on them hand and foot*). **hand cream** an emollient for the hands. **hand down 1** pass the ownership or use of to another. **2 a** transmit (a decision) from a higher court etc. **b** *US* express (an opinion or verdict). **hand-grenade** see GRENADE. **hand in glove** in collusion or association. **hand in hand** in close association. **hand it to** *colloq.* acknowledge the merit of (a person). **hand-me-down** an article of clothing etc. passed on from another person. **hand off** *Rugby Football* push off (a tackling opponent) with the hand. **hand on** pass (a thing) to the next in a series or succession. **hand out 1** serve, distribute. **2** award, allocate (*the judges handed out stiff sentences*). **hand-out 1** something given free to a needy person. **2** a statement given to the press etc. **hand over** deliver; surrender possession of. **hand-over** *n.* the act or an instance of handing over. **hand-over-fist** *colloq.* with rapid progress. **hand-pick** choose carefully or personally. **hand-picked** carefully or personally chosen. **hand round** distribute. **hands down** (esp. of winning) with no difficulty. **hands off** **1** a warning not to touch or interfere with something. **2** *Computing* etc. not requiring manual use of controls. **hands on** *Computing* of or requiring personal operation at a keyboard. **hands up!** an instruction to raise one's hands in surrender or to signify assent or participation. **hand-to-hand** (of fighting) at close quarters. **have** (or **take**) **a hand in** share or take part in. **have one's hands full** be fully occupied. **have one's hands tied** *colloq.* be unable to act. **hold one's hand** = *stay one's hand* (see HAND). **in hand 1** receiving attention. **2** in reserve; at one's disposal. **3** under one's control. **lay** (or **put**) **one's hands on** see LAY[1]. **off one's hands** no longer one's responsibility. **on every hand** (or **all hands**) to or from all directions. **on hand** available. **on one's hands** resting on one as a responsibility. **on the one** (or **the other**) **hand** from one (or another) point of view. **out of hand 1** out of control. **2** peremptorily (*refused out of hand*). **put** (or **set**) **one's hand to** start work on; engage in. **stay one's hand** *archaic* or *literary* refrain from action. **to hand 1** within easy reach. **2** (of a letter) received. **turn one's hand to** undertake (as a new activity). □□ **handed** *adj.* **handless** *adj.* [OE *hand*, *hond*]

handbag /ˈhændbæg/ *n.* & *v.* —*n.* a small bag for a purse etc., carried esp. by a woman. —*v.tr.* (of a woman politician) treat (a person, idea, etc.) ruthlessly or insensitively.

handball *n.* **1** /ˈhændbɔːl/ a game with a ball thrown by hand among players or against a wall. **2** /hændˈbɔːl/ *Football* intentional touching of the ball with the hand or arm by a player other than the goalkeeper in the goal area, constituting a foul.

handbell /ˈhændbel/ *n.* a small bell, usu. tuned to a particular note and rung by hand, esp. one of a set giving a range of notes.

handbill /ˈhændbɪl/ *n.* a printed notice distributed by hand.

handbook /ˈhændbʊk/ *n.* a short manual or guidebook.

handbrake /ˈhændbreɪk/ *n.* a brake operated by hand.

h. & c. *abbr.* hot and cold (water).

handcart /ˈhændkɑːt/ *n.* a small cart pushed or drawn by hand.

handclap /ˈhændklæp/ *n.* a clapping of the hands.

handcraft /ˈhændkrɑːft/ *n.* & *v.* —*n.* = HANDICRAFT. —*v.tr.* make by handicraft.

handcuff /ˈhændkʌf/ *n.* & *v.* —*n.* (in *pl.*) a pair of lockable linked metal rings for securing a prisoner's wrists. —*v.tr.* put handcuffs on.

-handed /ˈhændɪd/ *adj.* (in *comb.*) **1** for or involving a specified number of hands (in various senses) (*two-handed*). **2** using chiefly the hand specified (*left-handed*). □□ **-handedly** *adv.* **-handedness** *n.* (both in sense 2).

handful /ˈhændfʊl/ *n.* (*pl.* **-fuls**) **1** a quantity that fills the hand. **2** a small number or amount. **3** *colloq.* a troublesome person or task.

handglass /ˈhændɡlɑːs/ *n.* **1** a magnifying glass held in the hand. **2** a small mirror with a handle.

handgrip /ˈhændɡrɪp/ *n.* **1** a grasp with the hand. **2** a handle designed for easy holding.

handgun /ˈhændɡʌn/ *n.* a small firearm held in and fired with one hand.

handhold /ˈhændhəʊld/ *n.* something for the hands to grip on (in climbing, sailing, etc.).

handicap /ˈhændɪˌkæp/ *n.* & *v.* —*n.* **1 a** a disadvantage imposed on a superior competitor in order to make the chances more equal. **b** a race or contest in which this is imposed. **2** the number of strokes by which a golfer normally exceeds par for the course. **3** a thing that makes progress or success difficult. **4** a physical or mental disability. —*v.tr.* (**handicapped**, **handicapping**) **1** impose a handicap on. **2** place (a person) at a disadvantage. □□ **handicapper** *n.* [prob. from the phrase *hand i'* (= in) *cap* describing a kind of sporting lottery]

handicapped /ˈhændɪˌkæpt/ *adj.* suffering from a physical or mental disability.

handicraft /ˈhændɪˌkrɑːft/ *n.* work that requires both manual and artistic skill. [ME, alt. of earlier HANDCRAFT after HANDIWORK]

handiwork /ˈhændɪˌwɜːk/ *n.* work done or a thing made by hand, or by a particular person. [OE *handgeweorc*]

handkerchief /ˈhæŋkətʃɪf, -ˌtʃiːf/ *n.* (*pl.* **handkerchiefs** or **-chieves** /-ˌtʃiːvz/) a square of cotton, linen, silk, etc., usu. carried in the pocket for wiping one's nose, etc.

handle /ˈhænd(ə)l/ *n.* & *v.* —*n.* **1** the part by which a thing is held, carried, or controlled. **2** a fact that may be taken advantage of (*gave a handle to his critics*). **3** *colloq.* a personal title. **4** the feel of goods, esp. textiles, when handled. —*v.tr.* **1** touch, feel, operate, or move with the hands. **2** manage or deal with; treat in a particular or correct way (*knows how to handle people*; *unable to handle the situation*). **3** deal in (goods). **4** discuss or write about (a subject). □**get a handle on** *colloq.* understand the basis of or reason for a situation, circumstance, etc. □□ **handleable** *adj.* **handleability** /-ˈlɪtɪ/ *n.* **handled** *adj.* (also in *comb.*). [OE *handle, handlian* (as HAND)]

handlebar /ˈhænd(ə)l,bɑː/ *n.* (often in *pl.*) the steering bar of a bicycle etc., with a handgrip at each end. □**handlebar moustache** a thick moustache with curved ends.

handler /ˈhændlə(r)/ *n.* **1** a person who handles or deals in certain commodities. **2** a person who trains and looks after an animal (esp. a police dog).

handlist /ˈhændlɪst/ *n.* a short list of essential reading, reference books, etc.

handmade /hændˈmeɪd/ *adj.* made by hand and not by machine, esp. as designating superior quality.

handmaid /ˈhændmeɪd/ *n.* (also **handmaiden** /-ˌmeɪd(ə)n/) *archaic* a female servant or helper.

handrail /ˈhændreɪl/ *n.* a narrow rail for holding as a support on stairs etc.

handsaw /ˈhændsɔː/ *n.* a saw worked by one hand.

handsel /ˈhæns(ə)l/ *n.* & *v.* (also **hansel**) —*n.* **1** a gift at the beginning of the new year, or on coming into new circumstances. **2** = EARNEST[2] **1**. **3** a foretaste. —*v.tr.* (**handselled, handselling**; *US* **handseled, handseling**) **1** give a handsel to. **2** inaugurate. **3** be the first to try. [ME, corresp. to OE *handselen* giving into a person's hands, ON *handsal* giving of the hand (esp. in promise), formed as HAND + OE *sellan* SELL]

handset /ˈhændset/ *n.* a telephone mouthpiece and earpiece forming one unit.

handshake /ˈhændʃeɪk/ *n.* the shaking of a person's hand with one's own as a greeting etc.

handsome /ˈhænsəm/ *adj.* (**handsomer, handsomest**) **1** (of a person) good-looking. **2** (of a building etc.) imposing, attractive. **3 a** generous, liberal (*a handsome present*; *handsome treatment*). **b** (of a price, fortune, etc., as assets gained) considerable. □□ **handsomeness** *n.* [ME, = easily handled, f. HAND + -SOME[1]]

handsomely /ˈhænsəmlɪ/ *adv.* **1** generously, liberally. **2** finely, beautifully. **3** *Naut.* carefully.

handspike /ˈhændspaɪk/ *n.* a wooden rod shod with iron, used on board ship and by artillery soldiers.

handspring /ˈhændsprɪŋ/ *n.* a somersault in which one lands first on the hands and then on the feet.

handstand /ˈhændstænd/ *n.* balancing on one's hands with the feet in the air or against a wall.

handwork /ˈhændwɜːk/ *n.* work done with the hands, esp. as opposed to machinery. □□ **handworked** *adj.*

handwriting /ˈhændˌraɪtɪŋ/ *n.* **1** writing with a pen, pencil, etc. **2** a person's particular style of writing. □□ **handwritten** /-ˌrɪt(ə)n/ *adj.*

handy /ˈhændɪ/ *adj.* (**handier, handiest**) **1** convenient to handle or use; useful. **2** ready to hand; placed or occurring conveniently. **3** clever with the hands. □□ **handily** *adv.* **handiness** *n.*

handyman /ˈhændɪˌmæn/ *n.* (*pl.* **-men**) a person able or employed to do occasional domestic repairs and minor renovations.

hang /hæŋ/ *v.* & *n.* —*v.* (*past* and *past part.* **hung** /hʌŋ/ except in sense 7) **1** *tr.* **a** secure or cause to be supported from above, esp. with the lower part free. **b** (foll. by *up*, *on*, *on to*, etc.) attach loosely by suspending from the top. **2** *tr.* set up (a door, gate, etc.) on its hinges so that it moves freely. **3** *tr.* place (a picture) on a wall or in an exhibition. **4** *tr.* attach (wallpaper) in vertical strips to a wall. **5** *tr.* (foll. by *on*) *colloq.* attach the blame for (a thing) to (a person) (*you can't hang that on me*). **6** *tr.* (foll. by *with*) decorate by hanging pictures or decorations etc. (*a hall hung with tapestries*). **7** *tr.* & *intr.* (*past* and *past* *part.* **hanged**) **a** suspend or be suspended by the neck with a noosed rope until dead, esp. as a form of capital punishment. **b** as a mild oath (*hang the expense; let everything go hang*). **8** *tr.* let droop (*hang one's head*). **9** *tr.* suspend (meat or game) from a hook and leave it until dry or tender or high. **10** *intr.* be or remain hung (in various senses). **11** *intr.* remain static in the air. **12** *intr.* (often foll. by *over*) be present or imminent, esp. oppressively or threateningly (*a hush hung over the room*). **13** *intr.* (foll. by *on*) **a** be contingent or dependent on (*everything hangs on the discussions*). **b** listen closely to (*hangs on their every word*). —*n.* **1** the way a thing hangs or falls. **2** a downward droop or bend. □**get the hang of** *colloq.* understand the technique or meaning of. **hang about** (or **around**) **1** loiter or dally; not move away. **2** (foll. by *with*) associate with (a person etc.). **hang back 1** show reluctance to act or move. **2** remain behind. **hang fire** be slow in taking action or in progressing. **hang heavily** (or **heavy**) (of time) pass slowly. **hang in** *US colloq.* **1** persist, persevere. **2** linger. **hang on** *colloq.* **1** continue or persevere, esp. with difficulty. **2** (often foll. by *to*) continue to hold or grasp. **3** (foll. by *to*) retain; fail to give back. **4 a** wait for a short time. **b** (in telephoning) continue to listen during a pause in the conversation. **hang out 1** hang from a window, clothes-line, etc. **2** protrude or cause to protrude downwards. **3** *sl.* reside or be often present. **4** (foll. by *of*) lean out of (a window etc.). **hang-out** *n. sl.* a place one lives in or frequently visits. **hang together 1** make sense. **2** remain associated. **hang up 1** hang from a hook, peg, etc. **2** (often foll. by *on*) end a telephone conversation, esp. abruptly (*then he hung up on me*). **3** cause delay or difficulty to. **4** (usu. in *passive*, foll. by *on*) *sl.* be a psychological or emotional obsession or problem to (*is really hung up on her father*). **hang-up** *n. sl.* an emotional problem or inhibition. **hung-over** *colloq.* suffering from a hangover. **hung parliament** a parliament in which no party has a clear majority. **let it all hang out** *sl.* be uninhibited or relaxed. **not care** (or **give**) **a hang** *colloq.* not care at all. [ON *hanga* (tr.) = OE *hōn*, & f. OE *hangian* (intr.), f. Gmc]

hangar /ˈhæŋə(r)/ *n.* a building with extensive floor area, for housing aircraft etc. □□ **hangarage** *n.* [F, of unkn. orig.]

hangdog /ˈhæŋdɒg/ *adj.* having a dejected or guilty appearance; shamefaced.

hanger[1] /ˈhæŋə(r)/ *n.* **1** a person or thing that hangs. **2** (in full **coat-hanger**) a shaped piece of wood or plastic etc. from which clothes may be hung. □ **hanger-on** (*pl.* **hangers-on**) a follower or dependant, esp. an unwelcome one.

hanger[2] /ˈhæŋə(r)/ *n. Brit.* a wood on the side of a steep hill. [OE *hangra* f. *hangian* HANG]

hang-glider /ˈhæŋˌglaɪdə(r)/ *n.* a frame with a fabric aerofoil stretched over it, from which the operator is suspended and controls flight by body movement. □□ **hang-glide** *v.intr.* **hang-gliding** *n.*

hanging /ˈhæŋɪŋ/ *n. & adj.* —*n.* **1 a** the practice or an act of executing by hanging a person. **b** (attrib.) meriting or causing this (*a hanging offence*). **2** (usu. in *pl.*) draperies hung on a wall etc. —*adj.* that hangs or is hung; suspended. □ **hanging gardens** gardens laid out on a steep slope. **hanging valley** a valley, usu. tributary, above the level of the valleys or plains it joins.

hangman /ˈhæŋmən/ *n.* (*pl.* **-men**) **1** an executioner who hangs condemned persons. **2** a word-game for two players, in which the tally of failed guesses is kept by drawing a representation of a gallows.

hangnail /ˈhæŋneɪl/ *n.* = AGNAIL. [alt. of AGNAIL, infl. by HANG and taking *nail* as = NAIL[1] 2]

hangover /ˈhæŋˌəʊvə(r)/ *n.* **1** a severe headache or other after-effects caused by drinking an excess of alcohol. **2** a survival from the past.

hank /hæŋk/ *n.* **1** a coil or skein of wool or thread

etc. **2** any of several measures of length of cloth or yarn, e.g. 840 yds. for cotton yarn and 560 yds. for worsted. **3** *Naut.* a ring of rope, iron, etc., for securing the staysails to the stays. [ME f. ON *hǫnk*: cf. Sw. *hank* string, Da. *hank* handle]

hanker /ˈhæŋkə(r)/ *v.intr.* (foll. by *for, after*, or *to* + infin.) long for; crave. □□ **hankerer** *n.* **hankering** *n.* [obs. *hank*, prob. rel. to HANG]

hanky /ˈhæŋkɪ/ *n.* (also **hankie**) (*pl.* **-ies**) *colloq.* a handkerchief. [abbr.]

hanky-panky /ˌhæŋkɪˈpæŋkɪ/ *n. sl.* **1** naughtiness, esp. sexual misbehaviour. **2** dishonest dealing; trickery. [orig. unkn.]

Hanoverian /ˌhænəˈvɪərɪən/ *adj.* of or relating to the British sovereigns from George I to Victoria (1714-1901). [*Hanover* in Germany, whose Elector became George I in 1714]

Hansa /ˈhænsə/ *n.* (also **Hanse**) **1 a** a medieval guild of merchants. **b** the entrance fee to a guild. **2** (also **Hanseatic League**) a medieval political and commercial league of Germanic towns. □□ **Hanseatic** /-sɪˈætɪk/ *adj.* [MHG *hanse*, OHG, Goth. *hansa* company]

Hansard /ˈhænsɑːd/ *n.* the official verbatim record of debates in the British Parliament. [T. C. *Hansard*, Engl. printer d. 1833, who first printed it]

hansel var. of HANDSEL.

Hansen's disease /ˈhæns(ə)nz/ *n.* leprosy. [G. H. A. *Hansen*, Norw. physician d. 1912]

hansom /ˈhænsəm/ *n.* (in full **hansom cab**) *hist.* a two-wheeled horse-drawn cab accommodating two inside, with the driver seated behind. [J. A. *Hansom*, Engl. architect d. 1822, who designed it]

Hants /hænts/ *abbr.* Hampshire. [OE *Hantescire*]

Hanukkah /ˈhɑːnəkə, -xə/ *n.* (also **Chanukkah**) the Jewish festival of lights, commemorating the purification of the Temple in 165 BC. [Heb. *ḥānukkāh* consecration]

hanuman /ˌhænʊˈmɑːn/ *n.* **1** an Indian langur venerated by Hindus. **2** (**Hanuman**) (in Hindu mythology) the monkey-god, a loyal helper of Rama. [Hindi]

hap /hæp/ *n. & v. archaic* —*n.* **1** chance, luck. **2** a chance occurrence. —*v.intr.* (**happed, happing**) **1** come about by chance. **2** (foll. by *to* + infin.) happen to. [ME f. ON *happ*]

hapax legomenon /ˌhæpæks lɪˈgɒmɪˌnɒn/ *n.* (*pl.* **hapax legomena** /-mɪnə/) a word of which only one instance of use is recorded. [Gk, = a thing said once]

ha'penny var. of HALFPENNY.

haphazard /hæpˈhæzəd/ *adj. & adv.* —*adj.* done etc. by chance; random. —*adv.* at random. □□ **haphazardly** *adv.* **haphazardness** *n.* [HAP + HAZARD]

hapless /ˈhæplɪs/ *adj.* unlucky. □□ **haplessly** *adv.* **haplessness** *n.* [HAP + -LESS]

haplography /hæpˈlɒgrəfɪ/ *n.* the accidental omission of letters when these are repeated in a word (e.g. *philogy* for *philology*). [Gk *haplous* single + -GRAPHY]

haploid /ˈhæplɔɪd/ *adj. & n.* —*adj. Biol.* (of an organism or cell) with a single set of chromosomes. —*n.* a haploid organism or cell. [G f. Gk *haplous* single + *eidos* form]

haplology /hæpˈlɒlədʒɪ/ *n.* the omission of a sound when this is repeated within a word (e.g. *February* pronounced /ˈfebrɪ/). [Gk *haplous* + -LOGY]

ha'p'orth *Brit.* var. of HALFPENNYWORTH.

happen /ˈhæpən/ *v. & adv.* —*v.intr.* **1** occur (by chance or otherwise). **2** (foll. by *to* + infin.) have the (good or bad) fortune to (*I happened to meet her*). **3** (foll. by *to*) be the (esp. unwelcome) fate or experience of (*what happened to you?; I hope nothing happens to them*). **4** (foll. by *on*) encounter or discover by chance. —*adv. N.Engl. dial.* perhaps, maybe (*happen it'll rain*). □**as it happens** in fact; in reality (*as it happens, it turned out well*). [ME f. HAP + -EN[1]]

happening /'hæpənɪŋ, -pnɪŋ/ n. **1** an event or occurrence. **2** an improvised or spontaneous theatrical etc. performance.

happenstance /'hæpənst(ə)ns/ n. US a thing that happens by chance. [HAPPEN + CIRCUMSTANCE]

happi /'hæpɪ/ n. (pl. **happis**) (also **happi-coat**) a loose informal Japanese coat. [Jap.]

happy /'hæpɪ/ adj. (**happier**, **happiest**) **1** feeling or showing pleasure or contentment. **2 a** fortunate; characterized by happiness. **b** (of words, behaviour, etc.) apt, pleasing. **3** colloq. slightly drunk. **4** (in comb.) colloq. inclined to use excessively or at random (trigger-happy). □**happy as a sandboy** see SANDBOY. **happy event** colloq. the birth of a child. **happy families** a card-game the object of which is to acquire four members of the same 'family'. **happy-go-lucky** cheerfully casual. **happy hour** esp. US a period of the day when drinks are sold at reduced prices in bars, hotels, etc. **happy hunting-ground** a place where success or enjoyment is obtained. **happy medium** a compromise; the avoidance of extremes. □□**happily** adv. **happiness** n. [ME f. HAP + -Y¹]

haptic /'hæptɪk/ adj. relating to the sense of touch. [Gk haptikos able to touch f. haptō fasten]

hara-kiri /ˌhærəˈkɪrɪ/ n. ritual suicide by disembowelment with a sword, formerly practised by Samurai to avoid dishonour. [colloq. Jap. f. hara belly + kiri cutting]

harangue /həˈræŋ/ n. & v. —n. a lengthy and earnest speech. —v.tr. lecture or make a harangue to. □□ **haranguer** n. [ME f. F f. OF arenge f. med.L harenga, perh. f. Gmc]

harass /'hærəs, disp. həˈræs/ v.tr. **1** trouble and annoy continually or repeatedly. **2** make repeated attacks on (an enemy or opponent). □□**harasser** n. **harassingly** adv. **harassment** n. [F harasser f. OF harer set a dog on]

harbinger /'hɑːbɪndʒə(r)/ n. **1** a person or thing that announces or signals the approach of another. **2** a forerunner. [earlier = 'one who provides lodging': ME herbergere f. OF f. herberge lodging f. Gmc]

harbour /'hɑːbə(r)/ n. & v. (US **harbor**) —n. **1** a place of shelter for ships. **2** a shelter; a place of refuge or protection. —v. **1** tr. give shelter to (esp. a criminal or wanted person). **2** tr. keep in one's mind, esp. resentfully (harbour a grudge). **3** intr. come to anchor in a harbour. □**harbour-master** an official in charge of a harbour. □□**harbourless** adj. [OE herebeorg perh. f. ON, rel. to HARBINGER]

harbourage /'hɑːbərɪdʒ/ n. (US **harborage**) a shelter or place of shelter, esp. for ships.

hard /hɑːd/ adj., adv., & n. —adj. **1** (of a substance, material, etc.) firm and solid; unyielding to pressure; not easily cut. **2 a** difficult to understand or explain (a hard problem). **b** difficult to accomplish (a hard decision). **c** (foll. by to + infin.) not easy to (hard to believe; hard to please). **3** difficult to bear; entailing suffering (a hard life). **4** (of a person) unfeeling; severely critical. **5** (of a season or the weather) severe, harsh (a hard winter; a hard frost). **6** harsh or unpleasant to the senses (a hard voice; hard colours). **7 a** strenuous, enthusiastic, intense (a hard worker; a hard fight). **b** severe, uncompromising (a hard blow; a hard bargain; hard words). **c** Polit. extreme; most radical (the hard right). **8 a** (of liquor) strongly alcoholic. **b** (of drugs) potent and addictive. **c** (of radiation) highly penetrating. **d** (of pornography) highly suggestive and explicit. **9** (of water) containing mineral salts that make lathering difficult. **10** established; not disputable; reliable (hard facts; hard data). **11** Stock Exch. (of currency, prices, etc.) high; not likely to fall in value. **12** Phonet. (of a consonant) guttural (as c in cat, g in go). —adv. **1** strenuously, intensely, copiously; with one's full effort (try hard; look hard at; is raining hard; hard-working). **2** with difficulty or effort (hard-earned). **3** so as to be hard or firm (hard-baked; the jelly set hard). —n. Brit. **1** a

sloping roadway across a foreshore. **2** sl. = hard labour (got two years hard). □**be hard on 1** be difficult for. **2** be severe in one's treatment or criticism of. **3** be unpleasant to (the senses). **be hard put to it** (usu. foll. by to + infin.) find it difficult. **go hard with** turn out to (a person's) disadvantage. **hard and fast** (of a rule or a distinction made) definite, unalterable, strict. **hard at it** colloq. busily working or occupied. **hard-boiled 1** (of an egg) boiled until the white and the yolk are solid. **2** (of a person) tough, shrewd. **hard by** near; close by. **a hard case 1** colloq. **a** an intractable person. **b** Austral. & NZ an amusing or eccentric person. **2** a case of hardship. **hard cash** negotiable coins and banknotes. **hard coal** anthracite. **hard copy** printed material produced by computer, usu. on paper, suitable for ordinary reading. **hard core 1** an irreducible nucleus. **2** colloq. **a** the most active or committed members of a society etc. **b** a conservative or reactionary minority. **3** Brit. solid material, esp. rubble, forming the foundation of a road etc. **hard-core** adj. blatant, uncompromising, esp.: **1** (of pornography) explicit, obscene. **2** (of drug addiction) relating to 'hard' drugs, esp. heroin. **hard disk** Computing a large-capacity rigid usu. magnetic storage disk. **hard-done-by** harshly or unfairly treated. **hard error** Computing a permanent error. **hard feelings** feelings of resentment. **hard hat** colloq. **1** protective headgear worn on building-sites etc. **2** a reactionary person. **hard hit** badly affected. **hard-hitting** aggressively critical. **hard labour** heavy manual work as a punishment, esp. in a prison. **hard landing 1** a clumsy or rough landing of an aircraft. **2** an uncontrolled landing in which a spacecraft is destroyed. **hard line** unyielding adherence to a firm policy. **hard-liner** a person who adheres rigidly to a policy. **hard lines** Brit. colloq. = hard luck. **hard luck** worse fortune than one deserves. **hard-nosed** colloq. realistic, uncompromising. **hard nut** sl. a tough, aggressive person. **a hard nut to crack** colloq. **1** a difficult problem. **2** a person or thing not easily understood or influenced. **hard of hearing** somewhat deaf. **hard on** (or **upon**) close to in pursuit etc. **hard-on** n. coarse sl. an erection of the penis. **hard pad** a form of distemper in dogs etc. **hard palate** the front part of the palate. **hard-paste** denoting a Chinese or 'true' porcelain made of fusible and infusible materials (usu. clay and stone) and fired at a high temperature. **hard-pressed 1** closely pursued. **2** burdened with urgent business. **hard rock** colloq. rock music with a heavy beat. **hard roe** see ROE¹. **hard sauce** a sauce of butter and sugar, often with brandy etc. added. **hard sell** aggressive salesmanship or advertising. **hard shoulder** Brit. a hardened strip alongside a motorway for stopping on in an emergency. **hard stuff** sl. strong alcoholic drink, esp. whisky. **hard tack** ship's biscuit. **hard up 1** short of money. **2** (foll. by for) at a loss for; lacking. **hard-wearing** able to stand much wear. **hard wheat** wheat with a hard grain rich in gluten. **hard-wired** involving or achieved by permanently connected circuits designed to perform a specific function. **hard-working** diligent. **put the hard word on** Austral. & NZ sl. ask a favour (esp. sexual or financial) of. □□**hardish** adj. **hardness** n. [OE hard, heard f. Gmc]

hardback /'hɑːdbæk/ adj. & n. —adj. (of a book) bound in stiff covers. —n. a hardback book.

hardball /'hɑːdbɔːl/ n. & v. US —n. **1** = BASEBALL. **2** sl. uncompromising methods or dealings, esp. in politics (play hardball). —v.tr. sl. pressure or coerce politically.

hardbitten /'hɑːdˌbɪt(ə)n/ adj. colloq. tough and cynical.

hardboard /'hɑːdbɔːd/ n. stiff board made of compressed and treated wood pulp.

harden /'hɑːd(ə)n/ v. **1** tr. & intr. make or become

hard or harder. **2** *intr.* & *tr.* become, or make (one's attitude etc.), uncompromising or less sympathetic. **3** *intr.* (of prices etc.) cease to fall or fluctuate. □**harden off** inure (a plant) to cold by gradual increase of its exposure. □□ **hardener** *n.*

hardening /'hɑːdənɪŋ/ *n.* **1** the process or an instance of becoming hard. **2** (in full **hardening of the arteries**) *Med.* = ARTERIOSCLEROSIS.

hard-headed /hɑːd'hedɪd/ *adj.* practical, realistic; not sentimental. □□ **hard-headedly** *adv.* **hard-headedness** *n.*

hard-hearted /hɑːd'hɑːtɪd/ *adj.* unfeeling, unsympathetic. □□ **hard-heartedly** *adv.* **hard-heartedness** *n.*

hardihood /'hɑːdɪˌhʊd/ *n.* boldness, daring.

hardly /'hɑːdlɪ/ *adv.* **1** scarcely; only just (*we hardly knew them*). **2** only with difficulty (*could hardly speak*). **3** harshly.

hardpan /'hɑːdpæn/ *n.* *Geol.* a hardened layer of clay occurring in or below the soil profile.

hardshell /'hɑːdʃel/ *adj.* **1** having a hard shell. **2** esp. *US* rigid, orthodox, uncompromising.

hardship /'hɑːdʃɪp/ *n.* **1** severe suffering or privation. **2** the circumstance causing this.

hardtop /'hɑːdtɒp/ *n.* a motor car with a rigid (usu. detachable) roof.

hardware /'hɑːdweə(r)/ *n.* **1** tools and household articles of metal etc. **2** heavy machinery or armaments. **3** the mechanical and electronic components of a computer etc. (cf. SOFTWARE).

hardwood /'hɑːdwʊd/ *n.* the wood from a deciduous broad-leaved tree as distinguished from that of conifers.

hardy /'hɑːdɪ/ *adj.* (**hardier, hardiest**) **1** robust; capable of enduring difficult conditions. **2** (of a plant) able to grow in the open air all the year. □**hardy annual 1** an annual plant that may be sown in the open. **2** *joc.* a subject that comes up at regular intervals. □□ **hardily** *adv.* **hardiness** *n.* [ME f. OF *hardi* past part. of *hardir* become bold, f. Gmc, rel. to HARD]

hare /heə(r)/ *n.* & *v.* —*n.* **1** any of various mammals of the family Leporidae, esp. *Lepus europaeus*, like a large rabbit, with tawny fur, long ears, short tail, and hind legs longer than forelegs, inhabiting fields, hills, etc. **2** (in full **electric hare**) a dummy hare propelled by electricity, used in greyhound racing. —*v.intr.* run with great speed. □**hare and hounds** a paperchase. **hare-brained** rash, wild. **hare's-foot** (in full **hare's-foot clover**) a clover, *Trifolium arvense*, with soft hair around the flowers. **run with the hare and hunt with the hounds** try to remain on good terms with both sides. **start a hare** raise a topic of conversation. [OE *hara* f. Gmc]

harebell /'heəbel/ *n.* **1** a plant, *Campanula rotundifolia*, with slender stems and pale-blue bell-shaped flowers. **2** = BLUEBELL 2.

Hare Krishna /ˌhɑːrɪ 'krɪʃnə/ *n.* **1** a sect devoted to the worship of the Hindu deity Krishna (an incarnation of Vishnu). **2** (*pl.* **Hare Krishnas**) a member of this sect. [the title of a mantra based on the name *Krishna*, f. Skr. *O Hari!* an epithet of Krishna]

harelip /'heəlɪp/ *n.* a congenital fissure of the upper lip. □□ **harelipped** *adj.*

harem /'hɑːriːm, hɑːˈriːm/ *n.* **1 a** the women of a Muslim household, living in a separate part of the house. **b** their quarters. **2** a group of female animals sharing a mate. [Arab. *ḥarām, ḥarīm*, orig. = prohibited, prohibited place, f. *ḥarama* prohibit]

harewood /'heəwʊd/ *n.* stained sycamore-wood used for making furniture. [G dial. *Ehre* f. L *acer* maple + WOOD]

haricot /'hærɪˌkəʊ/ *n.* **1** (in full **haricot bean**) a variety of French bean with small white seeds. **2** the dried seed of this used as a vegetable. [F]

Harijan /'hærɪdʒ(ə)n/ *n.* a member of the class of

untouchables in India. [Skr., = a person dedicated to Vishnu, f. *Hari* Vishnu, *jana* person]

hark /hɑːk/ *v.intr.* (usu. in *imper.*) *archaic* listen attentively. □**hark back** revert to a topic discussed earlier. [ME *herkien* f. OE *heorcian* (unrecorded): cf. HEARKEN: *hark back* was orig. a hunting call to retrace steps]

harken var. of HEARKEN.

harl /hɑːl/ *n.* (also **harle, herl** /hɜːl/) fibre of flax or hemp. [MLG *herle, harle* fibre of flax or hemp]

harlequin /'hɑːlɪkwɪn/ *n.* & *adj.* —*n.* **1** (**Harlequin**) **a** a mute character in pantomime, usu. masked and dressed in a diamond-patterned costume. **b** *hist.* a stock comic character in Italian *commedia dell'arte*. **2** (in full **harlequin duck**) an Icelandic duck, *Histrionicus histrionicus*, with variegated plumage. —*adj.* in varied colours; variegated. [F f. earlier *Herlequin* leader of a legendary troup of demon horsemen]

harlequinade /ˌhɑːlɪkwɪ'neɪd/ *n.* **1** the part of a pantomime featuring Harlequin. **2** a piece of buffoonery. [F *arlequinade* (as HARLEQUIN)]

harlot /'hɑːlət/ *n.* *archaic* a prostitute. □□ **harlotry** *n.* [ME f. OF *harlot, herlot* lad, knave, vagabond]

harm /hɑːm/ *n.* & *v.* —*n.* hurt, damage. —*v.tr.* cause harm to. □**out of harm's way** in safety. [OE *hearm, hearmian* f. Gmc]

harmattan /hɑːˈmæt(ə)n/ *n.* a parching dusty land-wind of the W. African coast occurring from December to February. [Fanti or Twi *haramata*]

harmful /'hɑːmfʊl/ *adj.* causing or likely to cause harm. □□ **harmfully** *adv.* **harmfulness** *n.*

harmless /'hɑːmlɪs/ *adj.* **1** not able or likely to cause harm. **2** inoffensive. □□ **harmlessly** *adv.* **harmlessness** *n.*

harmonic /hɑːˈmɒnɪk/ *adj.* & *n.* —*adj.* **1** of or characterized by harmony; harmonious. **2** *Mus.* **a** of or relating to harmony. **b** (of a tone) produced by vibration of a string etc. in an exact fraction of its length. **3** *Math.* of or relating to quantities whose reciprocals are in arithmetical progression (*harmonic progression*). —*n.* **1** *Mus.* an overtone accompanying at a fixed interval (and forming a note with) a fundamental. **2** *Physics* a component frequency of wave motion. □**harmonic motion** (in full **simple harmonic motion**) oscillatory motion under a retarding force proportional to the amount of displacement from an equilibrium position. **harmonic progression** (or **series**) *Math.* a series of quantities whose reciprocals are in arithmetical progression. □□ **harmonically** *adv.* [L *harmonicus* f. Gk *harmonikos* (as HARMONY)]

harmonica /hɑːˈmɒnɪkə/ *n.* a small rectangular wind instrument with a row of metal reeds along its length, held against the lips and moved from side to side to produce different notes by blowing or sucking. [L, fem. sing. or neut. pl. of *harmonicus*: see HARMONIC]

harmonious /hɑːˈməʊnɪəs/ *adj.* **1** sweet-sounding, tuneful. **2** forming a pleasing or consistent whole; concordant. **3** free from disagreement or dissent. □□ **harmoniously** *adv.* **harmoniousness** *n.*

harmonist /'hɑːmənɪst/ *n.* a person skilled in musical harmony, a harmonizer. □□ **harmonistic** /-'nɪstɪk/ *adj.*

harmonium /hɑːˈməʊnɪəm/ *n.* a keyboard instrument in which the notes are produced by air driven through metal reeds by bellows operated by the feet. [F f. L (as HARMONY)]

harmonize /'hɑːməˌnaɪz/ *v.* (also **-ise**) **1** *tr.* add notes to (a melody) to produce harmony. **2** *tr.* & *intr.* (often foll. by *with*) bring into or be in harmony. **3** *intr.* make or form a pleasing or consistent whole. □□ **harmonization** /-ˈzeɪʃ(ə)n/ *n.* [f. F *harmoniser* (as HARMONY)]

harmony /'hɑːmənɪ/ *n.* (*pl.* **-ies**) **1 a** a combination of simultaneously sounded musical notes to produce chords and chord progressions, esp. as having a pleasing effect. **b** the study of this. **2 a** an apt or aesthetic arrangement of parts. **b** the pleasing effect of this. **3** agreement, concord. **4** a collation of parallel narratives, esp. of the Gospels. □**in harmony 1** (of singing etc.) producing chords; not discordant. **2** (often foll. by *with*) in agreement. **harmony of the spheres** see SPHERE. [ME f. OF *harmonie* f. L *harmonia* f. Gk *harmonia* joining, concord, f. *harmos* joint]

harness /ˈhɑːnɪs/ *n. & v.* —*n.* **1** the equipment of straps and fittings by which a horse is fastened to a cart etc. and controlled. **2** a similar arrangement for fastening a thing to a person's body, for restraining a young child, etc. —*v.tr.* **1 a** put a harness on (esp. a horse). **b** (foll. by *to*) attach by a harness. **2** make use of (natural resources) esp. to produce energy. □**in harness** in the routine of daily work. □□ **harnesser** *n.* [ME f. OF *harneis* military equipment f. ON *hernest* (unrecorded) f. *herr* army + *nest* provisions]

harp /hɑːp/ *n. & v.* —*n.* **1** a large upright roughly triangular musical instrument consisting of a frame housing a graduated series of vertical strings, played by plucking with the fingers. —*v.intr.* **1** (foll. by *on*, *on about*) talk repeatedly and tediously about. **2** play on a harp. □**harp-seal** a Greenland seal, *Phoca groenlandica*, with a harp-shaped dark mark on its back. □□ **harper** *n.* **harpist** *n.* [OE *hearpe* f. Gmc]

harpoon /hɑːˈpuːn/ *n. & v.* —*n.* a barbed spearlike missile with a rope attached, for catching whales etc. —*v.tr.* spear with a harpoon. □**harpoon-gun** a gun for firing a harpoon. □□ **harpooner** *n.* [F *harpon* f. *harpe* clamp f. L *harpa* f. Gk *harpē* sickle]

harpsichord /ˈhɑːpsɪˌkɔːd/ *n.* a keyboard instrument with horizontal strings which are plucked mechanically. □□ **harpsichordist** *n.* [obs. F *harpechorde* f. LL *harpa* harp, + *chorda* string, the *-s-* being unexplained]

harpy /ˈhɑːpɪ/ *n.* (*pl.* **-ies**) **1** (in Greek and Roman mythology) a monster with a woman's head and body and bird's wings and claws. **2** a grasping unscrupulous person. □**harpy eagle** a S. American crested bird of prey, *Harpia harpyja*, one of the largest of eagles. [F *harpie* or L *harpyia* f. Gk *harpuiai* snatchers (cf. *harpazō* snatch)]

harquebus /ˈhɑːkwɪbəs/ *n.* (also **arquebus** /ˈɑːk-/) *hist.* an early type of portable gun supported on a tripod or on a forked rest. [F (*h*)*arquebuse* ult. f. MLG *hakebusse* or MHG *hakenbühse*, f. *haken* hook + *busse* gun]

harridan /ˈhærɪd(ə)n/ *n.* a bad-tempered old woman. [17th-c. cant, perhaps f. F *haridelle* old horse]

harrier[1] /ˈhærɪə(r)/ *n.* a person who harries or lays waste.

harrier[2] /ˈhærɪə(r)/ *n.* **1 a** a hound used for hunting hares. **b** (in *pl.*) a pack of these with huntsmen. **2 a** group of cross-country runners. [HARE + -IER, assim. to HARRIER[1]]

harrier[3] /ˈhærɪə(r)/ *n.* any bird of prey of the genus *Circus*, with long wings for swooping over the ground. [*harrower* f. *harrow* harry, rob, assim. to HARRIER[1]]

Harris tweed /ˈhærɪs/ *n.* a kind of tweed woven by hand in Harris in the Outer Hebrides.

harrow /ˈhærəʊ/ *n. & v.* —*n.* a heavy frame with iron teeth dragged over ploughed land to break up clods, remove weeds, cover seed, etc. —*v.tr.* **1** draw a harrow over (land). **2** (usu. as **harrowing** *adj.*) distress greatly. □□ **harrower** *n.* **harrowingly** *adv.* [ME f. ON *hervi*]

harrumph /həˈrʌmf/ *v.intr.* US clear the throat or make a similar sound, esp. ostentatiously. [imit.]

harry /ˈhærɪ/ *v.tr.* (**-ies, -ied**) **1** ravage or despoil. **2** harass, worry. [OE *herian, hergian* f. Gmc, rel. to OE *here* army]

harsh /hɑːʃ/ *adj.* **1** unpleasantly rough or sharp, esp. to the senses. **2** severe, cruel. □□ **harshen** *v.tr. &*

intr. **harshly** *adv.* **harshness** *n.* [MLG *harsch* rough, lit. 'hairy', f. *haer* HAIR]

harslet var. of HASLET.

hart /hɑːt/ *n.* the male of the deer (esp. the red deer) usu. over five years old. □**hart's tongue** a fern, *Phyllitis scolopendrium*, with narrow undivided fronds. [OE *heor(o)t* f. Gmc]

hartal /ˈhɑːt(ə)l/ *n.* the closing of shops and offices in India as a mark of protest or sorrow. [Hind. *hartāl*, *haṭṭāl* f. Skr. *haṭṭa* shop + *tālaka* lock]

hartebeest /ˈhɑːtɪˌbiːst/ *n.* any large African antelope of the genus *Alcelaphus*, with ringed horns bent back at the tips. [Afrik. f. Du. *hert* HART + *beest* BEAST]

hartshorn /ˈhɑːtʃhɔːn/ *n. archaic* **1** an ammoniac substance got from the horns of a hart. **2** (in full **spirit of hartshorn**) an aqueous solution of ammonia. [as HART, HORN[1]]

harum-scarum /ˌheərəmˈskeərəm/ *adj. & n. colloq.* —*adj.* wild and reckless. —*n.* such a person. [rhyming form. on HARE, SCARE]

haruspex /həˈruːspeks/ *n.* (*pl.* **haruspices** -spɪˌsiːz/) a Roman religious official who interpreted omens from the inspection of animals' entrails. □□ **haruspicy** /-spɪsɪ/ *n.* [L]

harvest /ˈhɑːvɪst/ *n. & v.* —*n.* **1 a** the process of gathering in crops etc. **b** the season when this takes place. **2** the season's yield or crop. **3** the product or result of any action. —*v.tr.* **1** gather as a harvest, reap. **2** experience (consequences). □**harvest festival** a thanksgiving festival in church for the harvest. **harvest home** the close of harvesting or the festival to mark this. **harvest mite** any arachnid larvae of the genus *Trombicula*, a chigger. **harvest moon** the full moon nearest to the autumn equinox (22 or 23 Sept.). **harvest mouse** a small rodent, *Micromys minutus*, that nests in the stalks of growing grain. □□ **harvestable** *adj.* [OE *hærfest* f. Gmc]

harvester /ˈhɑːvɪstə(r)/ *n.* **1** a reaper. **2** a reaping-machine, esp. with sheaf-binding.

harvestman /ˈhɑːvɪstmən/ *n.* (*pl.* **-men**) any of various arachnids of the family Opilionidae, with very long thin legs, found in humus and on tree trunks.

has *3rd sing. present* of HAVE.

has-been /ˈhæzbiːn/ *n. colloq.* a person or thing that has lost a former importance or usefulness.

hash[1] /hæʃ/ *n. & v.* —*n.* **1** a dish of cooked meat cut into small pieces and recooked. **2 a** a mixture; a jumble. **b** a mess. **3** re-used or recycled material. —*v.tr.* (often foll. by *up*) **1** make (meat etc.) into a hash. **2** recycle (old material). □**make a hash of** *colloq.* make a mess of; bungle. **settle a person's hash** *colloq.* deal with and subdue a person. [F *hacher* f. *hache* HATCHET]

hash[2] /hæʃ/ *n. colloq.* hashish. [abbr.]

hashish /ˈhæʃiːʃ/ *n.* a resinous product of the top leaves and tender parts of hemp, smoked or chewed for its narcotic effects. [f. Arab. *ḥašīš* dry herb; powdered hemp leaves]

Hasid /ˈhæsɪd/ (*pl.* **Hasidim**) a member of any of several mystical Jewish sects esp. one founded in the 18th c. □□ **Hasidic** /-ˈsɪdɪk/ *adj.* [Heb. *ḥasīd* pious]

haslet /ˈhæzlɪt/ *n.* (also **harslet** /ˈhɑː-/) pieces of (esp. pig's) offal cooked together and usu. compressed into a meat loaf. [ME f. OF *hastelet* dimin. of *haste* roast meat, spit, f. OLG, OHG *harst* roast]

hasn't /ˈhæz(ə)nt/ *contr.* has not.

hasp /hɑːsp/ *n. & v.* —*n.* a hinged metal clasp that fits over a staple and can be secured by a padlock. —*v.tr.* fasten with a hasp. [OE *hæpse, hæsp*]

hassle /ˈhæs(ə)l/ *n. & v. colloq.* —*n.* **1** a prolonged trouble or inconvenience. **2** an argument or involved struggle. —*v.* **1** *tr.* harass, annoy; cause trouble to. **2** *intr.* argue, quarrel. [20th c.: orig. dial.]

hassock /ˈhæsək/ *n.* **1** a thick firm cushion for kneeling on, esp. in church. **2** a tuft of matted grass etc. [OE *hassuc*]

hast /hæst/ *archaic 2nd sing. present* of HAVE.

hastate /'hæsteɪt/ *adj. Bot.* triangular like the head of a spear. [L *hastatus* f. *hasta* spear]

haste /heɪst/ *n. & v.* —*n.* **1** urgency of movement or action. **2** excessive hurry. —*v.intr. archaic* = HASTEN. □**in haste** quickly, hurriedly. **make haste** hurry; be quick. [ME f. OF *haste, haster* f. WG]

hasten /'heɪs(ə)n/ *v.* **1** *intr.* (often foll. by *to* + infin.) make haste; hurry. **2** *tr.* cause to occur or be ready or be done sooner.

hasty /'heɪstɪ/ *adj.* (**hastier, hastiest**) **1** hurried; acting too quickly or hurriedly. **2** said, made, or done too quickly or too soon; rash, unconsidered. **3** quick-tempered. □□**hastily** *adv.* **hastiness** *n.* [ME f. OF *hasti, hastif* (as HASTE, -IVE)]

hat /hæt/ *n. & v.* —*n.* **1** a covering for the head, often with a brim and worn out of doors. **2** *colloq.* a person's occupation or capacity, esp. one of several (*wearing his managerial hat*). —*v.tr.* (**hatted, hatting**) cover or provide with a hat. □**hat trick 1** *Cricket* the taking of three wickets by the same bowler with three successive balls. **2** the scoring of three goals, points, etc. in other sports. **keep it under one's hat** *colloq.* keep it secret. **out of a hat** by random selection. **pass the hat round** collect contributions of money. **take off one's hat to** *colloq.* acknowledge admiration for. **throw one's hat in the ring** take up a challenge. □□**hatful** *n.* (*pl.* -**fuls**). **hatless** *adj.* [OE *hætt* f. Gmc]

hatband /'hætbænd/ *n.* a band of ribbon etc. round a hat above the brim.

hatbox /'hætbɒks/ *n.* a box to hold a hat, esp. for travelling.

hatch[1] /hætʃ/ *n.* **1** an opening between two rooms, e.g. between a kitchen and a dining-room for serving food. **2** an opening or door in an aircraft, spacecraft, etc. **3** *Naut.* **a** = HATCHWAY. **b** a trapdoor or cover for this (often in *pl.*: *batten the hatches*). **4** a floodgate. □**down the hatch** *sl.* (as a drinking toast) drink up, cheers! **under hatches 1** below deck. **2 a** down out of sight. **b** brought low; dead. [OE *hæcc* f. Gmc]

hatch[2] /hætʃ/ *v. & n.* —*v.* **1** *intr.* **a** (often foll. by *out*) (of a young bird or fish etc.) emerge from the egg. **b** (of an egg) produce a young animal. **2** *tr.* incubate (an egg). **3** *tr.* (also foll. by *up*) devise (a plot etc.). —*n.* **1** the act or an instance of hatching. **2** a brood hatched. [ME *hacche*, of unkn. orig.]

hatch[3] /hætʃ/ *v.tr.* mark (a surface, e.g. a map or drawing) with close parallel lines. [ME f. F *hacher* f. *hache* HATCHET]

hatchback /'hætʃbæk/ *n.* a car with a sloping back hinged at the top to form a door.

hatchery /'hætʃərɪ/ *n.* (*pl.* -**ies**) a place for hatching eggs, esp. of fish or poultry.

hatchet /'hætʃɪt/ *n.* a light short-handled axe. □**hatchet-faced** *colloq.* sharp-featured or grim-looking. **hatchet job** *colloq.* a fierce verbal attack on a person, esp. in print. **hatchet man** *colloq.* **1** a hired killer. **2** a person employed to carry out a hatchet job. [ME f. OF *hachette* dimin. of *hache* axe f. med.L *hapia* f. Gmc]

hatching /'hætʃɪŋ/ *n. Art & Archit.* close parallel lines forming shading esp. on a map or an architectural drawing.

hatchling /'hætʃlɪŋ/ *n.* a bird or fish that has just hatched.

hatchment /'hætʃmənt/ *n.* a large usu. diamond-shaped tablet with a deceased person's armorial bearings, affixed to that person's house, tomb, etc. [contr. of ACHIEVEMENT]

hatchway /'hætʃweɪ/ *n.* an opening in a ship's deck for lowering cargo into the hold.

hate /heɪt/ *v. & n.* —*v.tr.* **1** dislike intensely; feel hatred towards. **2** *colloq.* **a** dislike. **b** (foll. by verbal noun or *to* + infin.) be reluctant (to do something) (*I hate to disturb you*). —*n.* **1** hatred. **2** *colloq.* a hated person or thing. □□**hatable** *adj.* (also **hateable**). **hater** *n.* [OE *hatian* f. Gmc]

hateful /'heɪtfʊl/ *adj.* arousing hatred. □□**hatefully** *adv.* **hatefulness** *n.*

hath /hæθ/ *archaic* 3rd *sing. present* of HAVE.

hatha yoga /'hæθə/ *n.* a system of physical exercises and breathing control used in yoga. [Skr. *haṭha* force: see YOGA]

hatpin /'hætpɪn/ *n.* a long pin, often decorative, for securing a hat to the head.

hatred /'heɪtrɪd/ *n.* intense dislike or ill will. [ME f. HATE + -*red* f. OE *rǣden* condition]

hatstand /'hætstænd/ *n.* a stand with hooks on which to hang hats.

hatter /'hætə(r)/ *n.* **1** a maker or seller of hats. **2** *Austral. & NZ* a person (esp. a miner or bushman) who lives alone.

hauberk /'hɔːbɜːk/ *n. hist.* a coat of mail. [ME f. OF *hau(s)berc* f. Frank., = neck protection, f. *hals* neck + *berg-* f. *beorg* protection]

haughty /'hɔːtɪ/ *adj.* (**haughtier, haughtiest**) arrogantly self-admiring and disdainful. □□**haughtily** *adv.* **haughtiness** *n.* [extension of *haught* (adj.), earlier *haut* f. OF *haut* f. L *altus* high]

haul /hɔːl/ *v. & n.* —*v.* **1** *tr.* pull or drag forcibly. **2** *tr.* transport by lorry, cart, etc. **3** *intr.* turn a ship's course. **4** *tr. colloq.* (usu. foll. by *up*) bring for reprimand or trial. —*n.* **1** the act or an instance of hauling. **2** an amount gained or acquired. **3** a distance to be traversed (*a short haul*). □**haul over the coals** see COAL. [var. of HALE[2]]

haulage /'hɔːlɪdʒ/ *n.* **1** the commercial transport of goods. **2** a charge for this.

hauler /'hɔːlə(r)/ *n.* **1** a person or thing that hauls. **2** a miner who takes coal from the workface to the bottom of the shaft. **3** a person or firm engaged in the transport of goods.

haulier /'hɔːlɪə(r)/ *n. Brit.* = HAULER.

haulm /hɔːm, hɑːm/ *n.* (also **halm**) **1** a stalk or stem. **2** the stalks or stems collectively of peas, beans, potatoes, etc., without the pods etc. [OE *h(e)alm* f. Gmc]

haulyard var. of HALYARD.

haunch /hɔːntʃ/ *n.* **1** the fleshy part of the buttock with the thigh, esp. in animals. **2** the leg and loin of a deer etc. as food. **3** the side of an arch between the crown and the pier. [ME f. OF *hanche*, of Gmc orig.: cf. LG *hanke* hind leg of a horse]

haunt /hɔːnt/ *v. & n.* —*v.* **1** *tr.* (of a ghost) visit (a place) regularly, usu. reputedly giving signs of its presence. **2** *tr.* (of a person or animal) frequent or be persistently in (a place). **3** *tr.* (of a memory etc.) be persistently in the mind of. **4** *intr.* (foll. by *with, in*) stay habitually. —*n.* **1** (often in *pl.*) a place frequented by a person. **2** a place frequented by animals, esp. for food and drink. □□**haunter** *n.* [ME f. OF *hanter* f. Gmc]

haunting /'hɔːntɪŋ/ *adj.* (of a memory, melody, etc.) poignant, wistful, evocative. □□**hauntingly** *adv.*

Hausa /'haʊzə/ *n. & adj.* —*n.* (*pl.* same or **Hausas**) **1 a** a people of W. Africa and the Sudan. **b** a member of this people. **2** the Hamitic language of this people, widely used in W. Africa. —*adj.* of or relating to this people or language. [native name]

hausfrau /'haʊsfraʊ/ *n.* a German housewife. [G f. *Haus* house + *Frau* woman]

hautboy *archaic* var. of OBOE.

haute couture /ˌəʊt kuːˈtjʊə(r)/ *n.* high fashion; the leading fashion houses or their products. [F, lit. = high dressmaking]

haute cuisine /ˌəʊt kwɪˈziːn/ *n.* cookery of a high standard, esp. of the French traditional school. [F, lit. = high cookery]

haute école /ˌəʊt eɪˈkɒl/ *n.* the art or practice of advanced classical dressage. [F, = high school]

hauteur /əʊˈtɜː(r)/ *n.* haughtiness of manner. [F f. *haut* high]

haut monde /əʊ ˈmɔːnd/ *n.* fashionable society. [F, lit. = high world]

Havana /həˈvænə/ *n.* a cigar made at Havana or elsewhere in Cuba.

have /hæv, həv/ *v.* & *n.* —*v.* (*3rd sing. present* **has** /hæz, həz/; *past* and *past part.* **had** /hæd/) —*v.tr.* **1** hold in possession as one's property or at one's disposal; be provided with (*has a car; had no time to read; has nothing to wear*). **2** hold in a certain relationship (*has a sister; had no equals*). **3** contain as a part or quality (*house has two floors; has green eyes*). **4 a** undergo, experience, enjoy, suffer (*had a good time; had a shock; has a headache*). **b** be subjected to a specified state (*had my car stolen; the book has a page missing*). **c** cause, instruct, or invite (a person or thing) to be in a particular state or take a particular action (*had him dismissed; had us worried; had my hair cut; had a copy made; had them to stay*). **5 a** engage in (an activity) (*had an argument; had sex*). **b** hold (a meeting, party, etc.). **6** eat or drink (*had a beer*). **7** (usu. in *neg.*) accept or tolerate; permit to (*I won't have it; will not have you say such things*). **8 a** let (a feeling etc.) be present (*have no doubt; has a lot of sympathy for me; have nothing against them*). **b** show or feel (mercy, pity, etc.) towards another person (*have pity on him; have mercy!*). **c** (foll. by *to* + infin.) show by action that one is influenced by (a feeling, quality, etc.) (*have the goodness to leave now*). **9 a** give birth to (offspring). **b** conceive mentally (an idea etc.). **10** receive, obtain (*had a letter from him; not a ticket to be had*). **11** be burdened with or committed to (*has a job to do; have my garden to attend to*). **12 a** have obtained (a qualification) (*has six O levels*). **b** know (a language) (*has no Latin*). **13** *sl.* **a** get the better of (*I had him there*). **b** (usu. in *passive*) *Brit.* cheat, deceive (*you were had*). **14** *coarse sl.* have sexual intercourse with. —*v.aux.* (with *past part.* or *ellipt.*, to form the perfect, pluperfect, and future perfect tenses, and the conditional mood) (*have worked; had seen; will have been; had I known, I would have gone; have you met her? yes, I have*). —*n.* **1** (usu. in *pl.*) *colloq.* a person who has wealth or resources. **2** *sl.* a swindle. □**had best** see BEST. **had better** would find it prudent to. **had rather** see RATHER. **have a care** see CARE. **have done, have done with** see DONE. **have an eye for, have eyes for, have an eye to** see EYE. **have a good mind to** see MIND. **have got to** *colloq.* = *have to*. **have had it** *colloq.* **1** have missed one's chance. **2** have passed one's prime. **3** have been killed, defeated, etc. **have it 1** (foll. by *that* + clause) express the view that. **2** win a decision in a vote etc. **3** *colloq.* have found the answer etc. **have it away** (or **off**) *Brit. coarse sl.* have sexual intercourse. **have it both ways** see BOTH. **have it in for** *colloq.* be hostile or ill-disposed towards. **have it out** (often foll. by *with*) *colloq.* attempt to settle a dispute by discussion or argument. **have it one's own way** see WAY. **have-not** (usu. in *pl.*) *colloq.* a person lacking wealth or resources. **have nothing to do with** see DO¹. **have on 1** be wearing (clothes). **2** be committed to (an engagement). **3** *colloq.* tease, play a trick on. **have out** get (a tooth etc.) extracted (*had her tonsils out*). **have something** (or **nothing**) **on a person 1** know something (or nothing) discreditable or incriminating about a person. **2** have an (or no) advantage or superiority over a person. **have to** be obliged to, must. **have to do with** see DO¹. **have up** *Brit. colloq.* bring (a person) before a court of justice, interviewer, etc. [OE *habban* f. Gmc, prob. rel. to HEAVE]

haven /ˈheɪv(ə)n/ *n.* **1** a harbour or port. **2** a place of refuge. [OE *hæfen* f. ON *höfn*]

haven't /ˈhæv(ə)nt/ *contr.* have not.

haver /ˈheɪvə(r)/ *v.* & *n.* —*v.intr. Brit.* **1** talk foolishly; babble. **2** vacillate, hesitate. —*n.* (usu. in *pl.*) *Sc.* foolish talk; nonsense. [18th c.: orig. unkn.]

haversack /ˈhævəsæk/ *n.* a stout bag for provisions etc., carried on the back or over the shoulder. [F *havresac* f. G *Habersack* f. *Haber* oats + *Sack* SACK¹]

haversine /ˈhævəˌsaɪn/ *n.* (also **haversin**) *Math.* half of a versed sine. [contr.]

havildar /ˈhævɪlˌdɑː(r)/ *n.* an Indian NCO corresponding to an army sergeant. [Hind. *havildār* f. Pers. *hawāldār* trust-holder]

havoc /ˈhævək/ *n.* & *v.* —*n.* widespread destruction; great confusion or disorder. —*v.tr.* (**havocked, havocking**) devastate. □**play havoc with** *colloq.* cause great confusion or difficulty to. [ME f. AF *havok* f. OF *havo(t)*, of unkn. orig.]

haw¹ /hɔː/ *n.* the hawthorn or its fruit. [OE *haga* f. Gmc, rel. to HEDGE]

haw² /hɔː/ *n.* the nictitating membrane of a horse, dog, etc., esp. when inflamed. [16th c.: orig. unkn.]

haw³ /hɔː/ *int.* & *v.* —*int.* expressing hesitation. —*v.intr.* (in **hum and haw**: see HUM¹) [imit.: cf. HA]

Hawaiian /həˈwaɪən/ *n.* & *adj.* —*n.* **1 a** a native of Hawaii, an island or island-group in the N. Pacific. **b** a person of Hawaiian descent. **2** the Malayo-Polynesian language of Hawaii. —*adj.* of or relating to Hawaii or its people or language.

hawfinch /ˈhɔːfɪntʃ/ *n.* any large stout finch of the genus *Coccothraustes*, with a thick beak for cracking seeds. [HAW¹ + FINCH]

hawk¹ /hɔːk/ *n.* & *v.* —*n.* **1** any of various diurnal birds of prey of the family Accipitridae, having a characteristic curved beak, rounded short wings, and a long tail. **2** *Polit.* a person who advocates an aggressive or warlike policy, esp. in foreign affairs. **3** a rapacious person. —*v.* **1** *intr.* hunt game with a hawk. **2** *intr.* (often foll. by *at*) & *tr.* attack, as a hawk does. **3** *intr.* (of a bird) hunt on the wing for food. □**hawk-eyed** keen-sighted. **hawk moth** any darting and hovering moth of the family Sphingidae, having narrow forewings and a stout body. **hawk-nosed** having an aquiline nose. □□**hawkish** *adj.* **hawkishness** *n.* **hawklike** *adj.* [OE *h(e)afoc, hæbuc* f. Gmc]

hawk² /hɔːk/ *v.tr.* **1** carry about or offer around (goods) for sale. **2** (often foll. by *about*) relate (news, gossip, etc.) freely. [back-form. f. HAWKER¹]

hawk³ /hɔːk/ *v.* **1** *intr.* clear the throat noisily. **2** *tr.* (foll. by *up*) bring (phlegm etc.) up from the throat. [prob. imit.]

hawk⁴ /hɔːk/ *n.* a plasterer's square board with a handle underneath for carrying plaster or mortar. [17th c.: orig. unkn.]

hawker¹ /ˈhɔːkə(r)/ *n.* a person who travels about selling goods. [16th c.: prob. f. LG or Du.; cf. HUCKSTER]

hawker² /ˈhɔːkə(r)/ *n.* a falconer. [OE *hafocere*]

hawksbill /ˈhɔːksbɪl/ *n.* (in full **hawksbill turtle**) a small turtle, *Eretmochelys imbricata*, yielding tortoiseshell.

hawkweed /ˈhɔːkwiːd/ *n.* any composite plant of the genus *Hieracium*, with yellow flowers.

hawse /hɔːz/ *n.* **1** the part of a ship's bows in which hawse-holes or hawse-pipes are placed. **2** the space between the head of an anchored vessel and the anchors. **3** the arrangement of cables when a ship is moored with port and starboard forward anchors. □**hawse-hole** a hole in the side of a ship through which a cable or anchor-rope passes. **hawse-pipe** a metal pipe lining a hawse-hole. [ME *halse*, prob. f. ON *háls* neck, ship's bow]

hawser /ˈhɔːzə(r)/ *n. Naut.* a thick rope or cable for mooring or towing a ship. [ME f. AF *haucer, hauceour* f. OF *haucier* hoist ult. f. L *altus* high]

hawthorn /ˈhɔːθɔːn/ *n.* any thorny shrub or tree of the genus *Crataegus*, esp. *C. monogyna*, with white, red, or pink blossom and small dark-red fruit or haws. [OE *hagathorn* (as HAW¹, THORN)]

hay¹ /heɪ/ *n.* & *v.* —*n.* grass mown and dried for fodder. —*v.* **1** *intr.* make hay. **2** *tr.* put (land) under grass for hay. **3** *tr.* make into hay. □**hay fever** an allergy with catarrhal and other asthmatic symptoms, caused by pollen or dust. **make hay of** throw into confusion. **make hay (while the sun shines)**

seize opportunities for profit or enjoyment. [OE *hēg*, *hīeg, hīg* f. Gmc]

hay² /heɪ/ *n.* (also **hey**) **1** a country dance with interweaving steps. **2** a figure in this. [obs. F *haie*]

haybox /'heɪbɒks/ *n.* a box stuffed with hay, in which heated food is left to continue cooking.

haycock /'heɪkɒk/ *n.* a conical heap of hay in a field.

hayfield /'heɪfiːld/ *n.* a field where hay is being or is to be made.

haymaker /'heɪˌmeɪkə(r)/ *n.* **1** a person who tosses and spreads hay to dry after mowing. **2** an apparatus for shaking and drying hay. **3** *sl.* a forceful blow or punch. □□ **haymaking** *n.*

haymow /'heɪməʊ/ *n.* hay stored in a stack or barn.

hayrick /'heɪrɪk/ *n.* = HAYSTACK.

hayseed /'heɪsiːd/ *n.* **1** grass seed obtained from hay. **2** *US colloq.* a rustic or yokel.

haystack /'heɪstæk/ *n.* a packed pile of hay with a pointed or ridged top.

haywire /'heɪˌwaɪə(r)/ *adj. colloq.* **1** badly disorganized, out of control. **2** (of a person) badly disturbed; erratic. [HAY¹ + WIRE, from the use of hay-baling wire in makeshift repairs]

hazard /'hæzəd/ *n. & v.* —*n.* **1** a danger or risk. **2** a source of this. **3** chance. **4** a dice game with a complicated arrangement of chances. **5** *Golf* an obstruction in playing a shot, e.g. a bunker, water, etc. **6** each of the winning openings in a real-tennis court. —*v.tr.* **1** venture on (*hazard a guess*). **2** run the risk of. **3** expose to hazard. [ME f. OF *hasard* f. Sp. *azar* f. Arab. *az-zahr* chance, luck]

hazardous /'hæzədəs/ *adj.* **1** risky, dangerous. **2** dependent on chance. □□ **hazardously** *adv.* **hazardousness** *n.* [F *hasardeux* (as HAZARD)]

haze¹ /heɪz/ *n.* **1** obscuration of the atmosphere near the earth by fine particles of water, smoke, or dust. **2** mental obscurity or confusion. [prob. back-form. f. HAZY]

haze² /heɪz/ *v.tr.* **1** *Naut.* harass with overwork. **2** *US* bully; seek to disconcert. [orig. uncert.: cf. obs. F *haser* tease, insult]

hazel /'heɪz(ə)l/ *n.* **1** any shrub or small tree of the genus *Corylus*, esp. *C. avellana* bearing round brown edible nuts. **2 a** wood from the hazel. **b** a stick made of this. **3** a reddish-brown or greenish-brown colour (esp. of the eyes). □ **hazel-grouse** a woodland grouse, *Tetrastes bonasia*. [OE *hæsel* f. Gmc]

hazelnut /'heɪz(ə)l,nʌt/ *n.* the fruit of the hazel.

hazy /'heɪzɪ/ *adj.* (**hazier, haziest**) **1** misty. **2** vague, indistinct. **3** confused, uncertain. □□ **hazily** *adv.* **haziness** *n.* [17th c. in Naut. use: orig. unkn.]

HB *abbr.* hard black (pencil-lead).

Hb *symb.* haemoglobin.

HBM *abbr.* Her or His Britannic Majesty (or Majesty's).

H-bomb /'eɪtʃbɒm/ *n.* = *hydrogen bomb*. [H³ + BOMB]

HC *abbr.* **1** Holy Communion. **2** (in the UK) House of Commons.

h.c. *abbr. honoris causa.*

HCF *abbr.* **1** highest common factor. **2** *Brit.* Honorary Chaplain to the Forces.

HE *abbr.* **1** His or Her Excellency. **2** His Eminence. **3** high explosive.

He *symb. Chem.* the element helium.

he /hiː, hɪ/ *pron. & n.* —*pron.* (*obj.* **him** /hɪm/; *poss.* **his** /hɪz/; *pl.* **they** /ðeɪ/) **1** the man or boy or male animal previously named or in question. **2** a person etc. of unspecified sex, esp. referring to one already named or identified (*if anyone comes he will have to wait*). —*n.* **1** a male; a man. **2** (in *comb.*) male (*he-goat*). **3** a children's chasing game, with the chaser designated 'he'. □ **he-man** (*pl.* **-men**) a masterful or virile man. [OE f. Gmc]

head /hed/ *n., adj., & v.* —*n.* **1** the upper part of the human body, or the foremost or upper part of an animal's body, containing the brain, mouth, and sense-organs. **2 a** the head regarded as the seat of intellect or repository of comprehended information.

b intelligence; imagination (*use your head*). **c** mental aptitude or tolerance (usu. foll. by *for: a good head for business; no head for heights*). **3** *colloq.* a headache, esp. resulting from a blow or from intoxication. **4** a thing like a head in form or position, esp.: **a** the operative part of a tool. **b** the flattened top of a nail. **c** the ornamented top of a pillar. **d** a mass of leaves or flowers at the top of a stem. **e** the flat end of a drum. **f** the foam on top of a glass of beer etc. **g** the upper horizontal part of a window frame, door frame, etc. **5** life when regarded as vulnerable (*it cost him his head*). **6 a** a person in charge; a director or leader (esp. the principal teacher at a school or college). **b** a position of leadership or command. **7** the front or forward part of something, e.g. a queue. **8** the upper end of something, e.g. a table or bed. **9** the top or highest part of something, e.g. a page, stairs, etc. **10** a person or individual regarded as a numerical unit (*£10 per head*). **11** (*pl.* same) **a** an individual animal as a unit. **b** (as *pl.*) a number of cattle or game as specified (*20 head*). **12 a** the side of a coin bearing the image of a head. **b** (usu. in *pl.*) this side as a choice when tossing a coin. **13 a** the source of a river or stream etc. **b** the end of a lake at which a river enters it. **14** the height or length of a head as a measure. **15** the component of a machine that is in contact with or very close to what is being processed or worked on, esp.: **a** the component on a tape recorder that touches the moving tape in play and converts the signals. **b** the part of a record-player that holds the playing cartridge and stylus. **c** = PRINTHEAD. **16 a** a confined body of water or steam in an engine etc. **b** the pressure exerted by this. **17** a promontory (esp. in place-names) (*Beachy Head*). **18** *Naut.* **a** the bows of a ship. **b** (often in *pl.*) a ship's latrine. **19** a main topic or category for consideration or discussion. **20** *Journalism* = HEADLINE *n.* **21** a culmination, climax, or crisis. **22** the fully developed top of a boil etc. **23** *sl.* a habitual taker of drugs; a drug addict. —*attrib.adj.* chief or principal (*head gardener; head office*). —*v.* **1** *tr.* be at the head or front of. **2** *tr.* be in charge of (*headed a small team*). **3** *tr.* **a** provide with a head or heading. **b** (of an inscription, title, etc.) be at the top of, serve as a heading for. **4 a** *intr.* face or move in a specified direction or towards a specified result (often foll. by *for: is heading for trouble*). **b** *tr.* direct in a specified direction. **5** *tr. Football* strike (the ball) with the head. **6 a** *tr.* (often foll. by *down*) cut the head off (a plant etc.). **b** *intr.* (of a plant etc.) form a head. □ **above** (or **over**) **one's head** beyond one's ability to understand. **come to a head** reach a crisis. **enter** (or **come into**) **one's head** *colloq.* occur to one. **from head to toe** (or **foot**) all over a person's body. **get one's head down** *sl.* **1** go to bed. **2** concentrate on the task in hand. **give a person his** or **her head** allow a person to act freely. **go out of one's head** go mad. **go to one's head 1** (of liquor) make one dizzy or slightly drunk. **2** (of success) make one conceited. **head and shoulders** *colloq.* by a considerable amount. **head back 1** get ahead of so as to intercept and turn back. **2** return home etc. **head-banger** *sl.* **1** a young person shaking violently to the rhythm of pop music. **2** a crazy or eccentric person. **head-butt** *n.* a forceful thrust with the top of the head into the chin or body of another person. —*v.tr.* attack (another person) with a head-butt. **head-dress** an ornamental covering or band for the head. **head first 1** with the head foremost. **2** precipitately. **head in the sand** refusal to acknowledge an obvious danger or difficulty. **head off 1** get ahead of so as to intercept and turn aside. **2** forestall. **head of hair** the hair on a person's head, esp. as a distinctive feature. **head-on 1** with the front foremost (*a head-on crash*). **2** in direct confrontation. **head over heels 1** turning over completely in forward motion as in a somersault etc. **2** topsy-turvy. **3** utterly, completely (*head over heels in love*).

head-shrinker *sl.* a psychiatrist. **head start** an advantage granted or gained at an early stage. **heads will roll** *colloq.* people will be disgraced or dismissed. **head-up** (of instrument readings in an aircraft, vehicle, etc.) shown so as to be visible without lowering the eyes. **head-voice** the high register of the voice in speaking or singing. **head wind** a wind blowing from directly in front. **hold up one's head** be confident or unashamed. **in one's head** 1 in one's thoughts or imagination. 2 by mental process without use of physical aids. **keep one's head** remain calm. **keep one's head above water** *colloq.* 1 keep out of debt. 2 avoid succumbing to difficulties. **keep one's head down** *colloq.* remain inconspicuous in difficult or dangerous times. **lose one's head** lose self-control; panic. **make head or tail of** (usu. with *neg.* or *interrog.*) understand at all. **off one's head** *sl.* crazy. **off the top of one's head** *colloq.* impromptu; without careful thought or investigation. **on one's** (or **one's own**) **head** as one's sole responsibility. **out of one's head** 1 *sl.* crazy. 2 from one's imagination or memory. **over one's head** 1 beyond one's ability to understand. 2 without one's knowledge or involvement, esp. when one has a right to this. 3 with disregard for one's own (stronger) claim (*was promoted over their heads*). **put heads together** consult together. **put into a person's head** suggest to a person. **take** (or **get**) **it into one's head** (foll. by *that* + clause or *to* + infin.) form a definite idea or plan. **turn a person's head** make a person conceited. **with one's head in the clouds** see CLOUD. □□ **headed** *adj.* (also in *comb.*). **headless** *adj.* **headward** *adj.* & *adv.* [OE *hēafod* f. Gmc]

-head /hed/ *suffix* = -HOOD (*godhead*; *maidenhead*). [ME *-hed*, *-hede* = -HOOD]

headache /'hedeɪk/ *n.* 1 a continuous pain in the head. 2 *colloq.* a a worrying problem. b a troublesome person. □□ **headachy** *adj.*

headband /'hedbænd/ *n.* a band worn round the head as decoration or to keep the hair off the face.

headboard /'hedbɔːd/ *n.* an upright panel placed behind the head of a bed.

headcount /'hedkaʊnt/ *n.* 1 a counting of individual people. 2 a total number of people, esp. the number of people employed in a particular organization.

header /'hedə(r)/ *n.* 1 *Football* a shot or pass made with the head. 2 *colloq.* a headlong fall or dive. 3 a brick or stone laid at right angles to the face of a wall. 4 (in full **header-tank**) a tank of water etc. maintaining pressure in a plumbing system.

headgear /'hedgɪə(r)/ *n.* a hat or head-dress.

head-hunting /'hed,hʌntɪŋ/ *n.* 1 the practice among some peoples of collecting the heads of dead enemies as trophies. 2 the practice of filling a (usu. senior) business position by approaching a suitable person employed elsewhere. □□ **head-hunt** *v.tr.* (also *absol.*). **head-hunter** *n.*

heading /'hedɪŋ/ *n.* 1 a a title at the head of a page or section of a book etc. b a division or section of a subject of discourse etc. 2 a a horizontal passage made in preparation for building a tunnel. b *Mining* = DRIFT *n.* 6. 3 material for making cask-heads. 4 the extension of the top of a curtain above the tape that carries the hooks or the pocket for a wire.

headlamp /'hedlæmp/ *n.* = HEADLIGHT.

headland *n.* 1 /'hedlənd/ a promontory. 2 /'hedlænd/ a strip left unploughed at the end of a field, for machinery to pass along.

headlight /'hedlaɪt/ *n.* 1 a strong light at the front of a motor vehicle or railway engine. 2 the beam from this.

headline /'hedlaɪn/ *n.* & *v.* —*n.* 1 a heading at the top of an article or page, esp. in a newspaper. 2 (in *pl.*) the most important items of news in a newspaper or broadcast news bulletin. —*v.tr.* give a headline to. □**hit** (or **make**) **the headlines** *colloq.* be given prominent attention as news.

headliner /'hed,laɪnə(r)/ *n.* *US* a star performer.

headlock /'hedlɒk/ *n.* *Wrestling* a hold with an arm round the opponent's head.

headlong /'hedlɒŋ/ *adv.* & *adj.* 1 with head foremost. 2 in a rush. [ME *headling* (as HEAD, -LING²),· assim. to -LONG]

headman /'hedmən/ *n.* (*pl.* **-men**) the chief man of a tribe etc.

headmaster /hed'mɑːstə(r)/ *n.* (*fem.* **headmistress** /-'mɪstrɪs/) the principal teacher in charge of a school.

headmost /'hedməʊst/ *adj.* (esp. of a ship) foremost.

headphone /'hedfəʊn/ *n.* (usu. in *pl.*) a pair of earphones joined by a band placed over the head, for listening to audio equipment etc.

headpiece /'hedpiːs/ *n.* 1 an ornamental engraving at the head of a chapter etc. 2 a helmet. 3 *archaic* intellect.

headquarters /hed'kwɑːtəz/ *n.* (as *sing.* or *pl.*) 1 the administrative centre of an organization. 2 the premises occupied by a military commander and the commander's staff.

headrest /'hedrest/ *n.* a support for the head, esp. on a seat or chair.

headroom /'hedruːm, -rʊm/ *n.* 1 the space or clearance between the top of a vehicle and the underside of a bridge etc. which it passes under. 2 the space above a driver's or passenger's head in a vehicle.

headscarf /'hedskɑːf/ *n.* a scarf worn round the head and tied under the chin, instead of a hat.

headset /'hedset/ *n.* a set of headphones, often with a microphone attached, used esp. in telephony and radio communication.

headship /'hedʃɪp/ *n.* the position of chief or leader, esp. of a headmaster or headmistress.

headsman /'hedzmən/ *n.* (*pl.* **-men**) 1 *hist.* an executioner who beheads. 2 a person in command of a whaling boat.

headspring /'hedsprɪŋ/ *n.* 1 the main source of a stream. 2 a principal source of ideas etc.

headsquare /'hedskweə(r)/ *n.* a rectangular scarf for wearing on the head.

headstall /'hedstɔːl/ *n.* the part of a halter or bridle that fits round a horse's head.

headstock /'hedstɒk/ *n.* a set of bearings in a machine, supporting a revolving part.

headstone /'hedstəʊn/ *n.* a (usu. inscribed) stone set up at the head of a grave.

headstrong /'hedstrɒŋ/ *adj.* self-willed and obstinate. □□ **headstrongly** *adv.* **headstrongness** *n.*

headwater /'hed,wɔːtə(r)/ *n.* (in *sing.* or *pl.*) streams flowing from the sources of a river.

headway /'hedweɪ/ *n.* 1 progress. 2 the rate of progress of a ship. 3 = HEADROOM 1.

headword /'hedwɜːd/ *n.* a word forming a heading, e.g. of an entry in a dictionary or encyclopaedia.

headwork /'hedwɜːk/ *n.* mental work or effort.

heady /'hedɪ/ *adj.* (**headier**, **headiest**) 1 (of liquor) potent, intoxicating. 2 (of success etc.) likely to cause conceit. 3 (of a person, thing, or action) impetuous, violent. □□ **headily** *adv.* **headiness** *n.*

heal /hiːl/ *v.* 1 *intr.* (often foll. by *up*) (of a wound or injury) become sound or healthy again. 2 *tr.* cause (a wound, disease, or person) to heal or be healed. 3 *tr.* put right (differences etc.). 4 *tr.* alleviate (sorrow etc.). □**heal-all** 1 a universal remedy, a panacea. 2 a popular name of various medicinal plants. □□ **healable** *adj.* **healer** *n.* [OE *hǣlan* f. Gmc, rel. to WHOLE]

heald /hiːld/ *n.* = HEDDLE. [app. f. OE *hefel*, *hefeld*, f. Gmc]

health /helθ/ *n.* 1 the state of being well in body or mind. 2 a person's mental or physical condition (*has poor health*). 3 soundness, esp. financial or moral (*the health of the nation*). 4 a toast drunk in someone's honour. □**health centre** the headquarters of a group of local medical services. **health certificate** a certificate stating a person's fitness for work etc. **health farm** a residential establishment where people seek improved health by a regime of dieting, exercise, etc. **health food** natural food thought to have health-giving qualities. **health service** a public service providing medical care. **health visitor** *Brit.* a trained nurse who visits those in need of medical attention in their homes. [OE *hælth* f. Gmc]

healthful /'helθfʊl/ *adj.* conducive to good health; beneficial. □□ **healthfully** *adv.* **healthfulness** *n.*

healthy /'helθɪ/ *adj.* (**healthier**, **healthiest**) **1** having, showing, or promoting good health. **2** beneficial, helpful (*a healthy respect for experience*). □□ **healthily** *adv.* **healthiness** *n.*

heap /hiːp/ *n. & v.* —*n.* **1** a collection of things lying haphazardly one on another. **2** (esp. in *pl.*) *colloq.* a large number or amount (*there's heaps of time*; *is heaps better*). **3** *sl.* an old or dilapidated thing, esp. a motor vehicle or building. —*v.* **1** *tr. & intr.* (foll. by *up, together,* etc.) collect or be collected in a heap. **2** *tr.* (foll. by *with*) load copiously or to excess. **3** *tr.* (foll. by *on, upon*) accord or offer copiously to (*heaped insults on them*). **4** *tr.* (as **heaped** *adj.*) (of a spoonful etc.) with the contents piled above the brim. □ **heap coals of fire on a person's head** cause a person remorse by returning good for evil. [OE *hēap, hēapian* f. Gmc]

hear /hɪə(r)/ *v.* (*past* and *past part.* **heard** /hɜːd/) **1** *tr.* (also *absol.*) perceive (sound etc.) with the ear. **2** *tr.* listen to (*heard them on the radio*). **3** *tr.* listen judicially to and judge (a case, plaintiff, etc.). **4** *intr.* (foll. by *about, of,* or *that* + clause) be told or informed. **5** *intr.* (foll. by *from*) be contacted by, esp. by letter or telephone. **6** *tr.* be ready to obey (an order). **7** *tr.* grant (a prayer). □ **have heard of** be aware of; know of the existence of. **hear! hear!** *int.* expressing agreement (esp. with something said in a speech). **hear a person out** listen to all that a person says. **hear say** (or **tell**) (usu. foll. by *of,* or *that* + clause) be informed. **will not hear of** will not allow or agree to. □□ **hearable** *adj.* **hearer** *n.* [OE *hīeran* f. Gmc]

hearing /'hɪərɪŋ/ *n.* **1** the faculty of perceiving sounds. **2** the range within which sounds may be heard; earshot (*within hearing*; *in my hearing*). **3** an opportunity to state one's case (*give them a fair hearing*). **4** the listening to evidence and pleadings in a law court. □ **hearing-aid** a small device to amplify sound, worn by a partially deaf person.

hearken /'hɑːkən/ *v.intr.* (also **harken**) *archaic* or *literary* (often foll. by *to*) listen. [OE *heorcnian* (as HARK)]

hearsay /'hɪəseɪ/ *n.* rumour, gossip. □ **hearsay evidence** *Law* evidence given by a witness based on information received from others rather than personal knowledge.

hearse /hɜːs/ *n.* a vehicle for conveying the coffin at a funeral. [ME f. OF *herse* harrow f. med.L *herpica* ult. f. L *hirpex -icis* large rake]

heart /hɑːt/ *n.* **1** a hollow muscular organ maintaining the circulation of blood by rhythmic contraction and dilation. **2** the region of the heart; the breast. **3 a** the heart regarded as the centre of thought, feeling, and emotion (esp. love). **b** a person's capacity for feeling emotion (*has no heart*). **4 a** courage or enthusiasm (*take heart*; *lose heart*). **b** one's mood or feeling (*change of heart*). **5 a** the central or innermost part of something. **b** the vital part or essence (*the heart of the matter*). **6** the close compact head of a cabbage, lettuce, etc. **7 a** a heart-shaped thing. **b** a conventional representation of a heart with two equal curves meeting at a point at the bottom and a cusp at the top. **8 a** a playing-card of a suit denoted by a red figure of a heart. **b** (in *pl.*) this suit. **c** (in *pl.*) a card-game in which players avoid taking tricks containing a card of this suit. **9** condition of land as regards fertility (*in good heart*).

□ **after one's own heart** such as one likes or desires. **at heart 1** in one's inmost feelings. **2** basically, essentially. **break a person's heart** overwhelm a person with sorrow. **by heart** in or from memory. **close to** (or **near**) **one's heart 1** dear to one. **2** affecting one deeply. **from the heart** (or **the bottom of one's heart**) sincerely, profoundly. **give** (or **lose**) **one's heart** (often foll. by *to*) fall in love (with). **have a heart** be merciful. **have the heart** (usu. with *neg.*; foll. by *to* + infin.) be insensitive or hard-hearted enough (*didn't have the heart to ask him*). **have** (or **put**) **one's heart in** be keenly involved in or committed to (an enterprise etc.). **have one's heart in one's mouth** be greatly alarmed or apprehensive. **have one's heart in the right place** be sincere or well-intentioned. **heart attack** a sudden occurrence of coronary thrombosis usu. resulting in the death of part of a heart muscle. **heart failure** a gradual failure of the heart to function properly, resulting in breathlessness, oedema, etc. **heart-lung machine** a machine that temporarily takes over the functions of the heart and lungs, esp. in surgery. **heart of gold** a generous nature. **heart of oak** a courageous nature. **heart of stone** a stern or cruel nature. **heart-rending** very distressing. **heart-rendingly** in a heart-rending way. **heart's-blood** lifeblood, life. **heart-searching** thorough examination of one's own feelings and motives. **heart to heart** candidly, intimately. **heart-to-heart** *adj.* (of a conversation etc.) candid, intimate. —*n.* a candid or personal conversation. **heart-warming** emotionally rewarding or uplifting. **in heart** in good spirits. **in one's heart of hearts** in one's inmost feelings. **out of heart** in low spirits. **take to heart** be much affected or distressed by. **to one's heart's content** see CONTENT[1]. **wear one's heart on one's sleeve** make one's feelings apparent. **with all one's heart** sincerely; with all goodwill. **with one's whole heart** with enthusiasm; without doubts or reservations. □□ **-hearted** *adj.* [OE *heorte* f. Gmc]

heartache /'hɑːteɪk/ *n.* mental anguish or grief.

heartbeat /'hɑːtbiːt/ *n.* a pulsation of the heart.

heartbreak /'hɑːtbreɪk/ *n.* overwhelming distress. □□ **heartbreaker** *n.* **heartbreaking** *adj.* **heartbroken** *adj.*

heartburn /'hɑːtbɜːn/ *n.* a burning sensation in the chest resulting from indigestion; pyrosis.

hearten /'hɑːt(ə)n/ *v.tr. & intr.* make or become more cheerful. □□ **hearteningly** *adv.*

heartfelt /'hɑːtfelt/ *adj.* sincere; deeply felt.

hearth /hɑːθ/ *n.* **1 a** the floor of a fireplace. **b** the area in front of a fireplace. **2** this symbolizing the home. **3** the bottom of a blast-furnace where molten metal collects. [OE *heorth* f. WG]

hearthrug /'hɑːθrʌg/ *n.* a rug laid before a fireplace.

hearthstone /'hɑːθstəʊn/ *n.* **1** a flat stone forming a hearth. **2** a soft stone used to whiten hearths, doorsteps, etc.

heartily /'hɑːtɪlɪ/ *adv.* **1** in a hearty manner; with goodwill, appetite, or courage. **2** very; to a great degree (esp. with ref. to personal feelings) (*am heartily sick of it*; *disliked him heartily*).

heartland /'hɑːtlənd/ *n.* the central or most important part of an area.

heartless /'hɑːtlɪs/ *adj.* unfeeling, pitiless. □□ **heartlessly** *adv.* **heartlessness** *n.*

heartsease /'hɑːtsiːz/ *n.* (also **heart's-ease**) a pansy.

heartsick /'hɑːtsɪk/ *adj.* very despondent. □□ **heartsickness** *n.*

heartsore /'hɑːtsɔː(r)/ *adj.* grieving, heartsick.

heartstrings /'hɑːtstrɪŋz/ *n.pl.* one's deepest feelings or emotions.

heartthrob /'hɑːtθrɒb/ *n.* **1** beating of the heart. **2** *colloq.* a person for whom one has (esp. immature) romantic feelings.

heartwood /'hɑːtwʊd/ *n.* the dense inner part of a tree-trunk yielding the hardest timber.

hearty /'hɑːtɪ/ adj. & n. —adj. (**heartier, heartiest**) **1** strong, vigorous. **2** spirited. **3** (of a meal or appetite) large. **4** warm, friendly. —n. **1** a hearty person, esp. one ostentatiously so. **2** (usu. in pl.) (as a form of address) fellows, esp. fellow sailors. □□ **heartiness** n.

heat /hiːt/ n. & v. —n. **1 a** the condition of being hot. **b** the sensation or perception of this. **c** high temperature of the body. **2** Physics **a** a form of energy arising from the random motion of the molecules of bodies, which may be transferred by conduction, convection, or radiation. **b** the amount of this needed to cause a specific process, or evolved in a process (heat of formation; heat of solution). **3** hot weather (succumbed to the heat). **4 a** warmth of feeling. **b** anger or excitement (the heat of the argument). **5** (foll. by of) the most intense part or period of an activity (in the heat of the battle). **6** a (usu. preliminary or trial) round in a race or contest. **7** the receptive period of the sexual cycle, esp. in female mammals. **8** redness of the skin with a sensation of heat (prickly heat). **9** pungency of flavour. **10** sl. intensive pursuit, e.g. by the police. —v. **1** tr. & intr. make or become hot or warm. **2** tr. inflame; excite or intensify. □ **heat barrier** the limitation of the speed of an aircraft etc. by heat resulting from air friction. **heat capacity** thermal capacity. **heat death** Physics a state of uniform distribution of energy to which the universe is thought to be tending. **heat engine** a device for producing motive power from heat. **heat-exchanger** a device for the transfer of heat from one medium to another. **heat pump** a device for the transfer of heat from a colder area to a hotter area by using mechanical energy. **heat-resistant** = HEATPROOF. **heat-seeking** (of a missile etc.) able to detect infrared radiation to guide it to its target. **heat shield** a device for protection from excessive heat, esp. fitted to a spacecraft. **heat sink** a device or substance for absorbing excessive or unwanted heat. **heat-treat** subject to heat treatment. **heat treatment** the use of heat to modify the properties of a metal etc. **heat wave** a period of very hot weather. **in the heat of the moment** during or resulting from intense activity, without pause for thought. **on heat** (of mammals, esp. females) sexually receptive. **turn the heat on** colloq. concentrate an attack or criticism on (a person). [OE *hætu* f. Gmc]

heated /'hiːtɪd/ adj. **1** (of a person, discussions, etc.) angry; inflamed with passion or excitement. **2** made hot. □□ **heatedly** adv.

heater /'hiːtə(r)/ n. **1** a device for supplying heat to its environment. **2** a container with an element etc. for heating the contents (water-heater). **3** sl. a gun.

heath /hiːθ/ n. **1** an area of flattish uncultivated land with low shrubs. **2** a plant growing on a heath, esp. of the genus *Erica* or *Calluna* (e.g. heather). □□ **heathless** adj. **heathlike** adj. **heathy** adj. [OE *hæth* f. Gmc]

heathen /'hiːð(ə)n/ n. & adj. —n. **1** a person who does not belong to a widely-held religion (esp. who is not Christian, Jew, or Muslim) as regarded by those that do. **2** an unenlightened person; a person regarded as lacking culture or moral principles. **3** (**the heathen**) heathen people collectively. **4** Bibl. a Gentile. —adj. **1** of or relating to heathens. **2** having no religion. □□ **heathendom** n. **heathenism** n. [OE *hæthen* f. Gmc]

heather /'heðə(r)/ n. **1** an evergreen shrub, *Calluna vulgaris*, with purple bell-shaped flowers. **2** any of various shrubs of the genus *Erica* or *Daboecia*, growing esp. on moors and heaths. □ **heather mixture** **1** a fabric of mixed hues supposed to resemble heather. **2** the colour of this. □□ **heathery** adj. [ME, Sc., & N.Engl. *hathir* etc., of unkn. orig.: assim. to *heath*]

Heath Robinson /hiːθ 'rɒbɪns(ə)n/ adj. absurdly

ingenious and impracticable in design or construction. [W. *Heath Robinson*, Engl. cartoonist d. 1944 who drew such contrivances]

heating /'hiːtɪŋ/ n. **1** the imparting or generation of heat. **2** equipment or devices used to provide heat, esp. to a building.

heatproof /'hiːtpruːf/ adj. & v. —adj. able to resist great heat. —v.tr. make heatproof.

heatstroke /'hiːtstrəʊk/ n. a feverish condition caused by excessive exposure to high temperature.

heatwave /'hiːtweɪv/ n. a prolonged period of abnormally hot weather.

heave /hiːv/ v. & n. —v. (past and past part. **heaved** or esp. Naut. **hove** /həʊv/) **1** tr. lift or haul (a heavy thing) with great effort. **2** tr. utter with effort or resignation (heaved a sigh). **3** tr. colloq. throw. **4** intr. rise and fall rhythmically or spasmodically. **5** tr. Naut. haul by rope. **6** intr. retch. —n. **1** an instance of heaving. **2** Geol. a sideways displacement in a fault. **3** (in pl.) a disease of horses, with laboured breathing. □ **heave-ho** a sailors' cry, esp. on raising the anchor. **heave in sight** Naut. or colloq. come into view. **heave to** esp. Naut. bring or be brought to a standstill. □□ **heaver** n. [OE *hebban* f. Gmc, rel. to L *capere* take]

heaven /'hev(ə)n/ n. **1** a place regarded in some religions as the abode of God and the angels, and of the good after death, often characterized as above the sky. **2** a place or state of supreme bliss. **3** colloq. something delightful. **4** (usu. **Heaven**) God, Providence (often, in sing. or pl. as an exclam. or mild oath: by Heaven). **5** (**the heavens**) esp. poet. the sky as the abode of the sun, moon, and stars and regarded from earth. □ **heaven-sent** providential; wonderfully opportune. **in seventh heaven** in a state of ecstasy. **move heaven and earth** (foll. by to + infin.) make extraordinary efforts. □□ **heavenward** adj. & adv. **heavenwards** adv. [OE *heofon*]

heavenly /'hevənlɪ/ adj. **1** of heaven; divine. **2** of the heavens or sky. **3** colloq. very pleasing; wonderful. □ **heavenly bodies** the sun, stars, planets, etc. □□ **heavenliness** n. [OE *heofonlic* (as HEAVEN)]

Heaviside layer /'hevɪˌsaɪd/ n. (in full **Heaviside-Kennelly layer** /ˌhevɪˌsaɪd'kenəlɪ/) = E-LAYER. [O. *Heaviside*, Engl. physicist d. 1925, and A. E. *Kennelly*, US physicist d. 1939]

heavy /'hevɪ/ adj., n., & adv. —adj. (**heavier, heaviest**) **1** of great or exceptionally high weight; difficult to lift. **2 a** of great density. **b** Physics having a greater than the usual mass (esp. of isotopes and compounds containing them). **3** abundant, considerable (a heavy crop). **4** severe, intense, extensive, excessive (heavy fighting; a heavy sleep). **5** doing something to excess (a heavy drinker). **6 a** striking or falling with force (heavy blows; heavy rain). **b** (of the sea) having large powerful waves. **7** (of machinery, artillery, etc.) very large of its kind; large in calibre etc. **8** causing a strong impact (a heavy fall). **9** needing much physical effort (heavy work). **10** (foll. by with) laden. **11** carrying heavy weapons (the heavy brigade). **12** (of a person, writing, music, etc.) serious or sombre in tone or attitude; dull, tedious. **13 a** (of food) hard to digest. **b** (of a literary work etc.) hard to read or understand. **14 a** (of temperament) dignified, stern. **b** intellectually slow. **15** (of bread etc.) too dense from not having risen. **16** (of ground) difficult to traverse or work. **17** oppressive; hard to endure (a heavy fate; heavy demands). **18 a** coarse, ungraceful (heavy features). **b** unwieldy. —n. (pl. **-ies**) **1** colloq. a large violent person; a thug. **2** a villainous or tragic role or actor in a play etc. (usu. in pl.). **3** colloq. a serious newspaper. **4** anything large or heavy of its kind, e.g. a vehicle. —adv. heavily (esp. in comb.: heavy-laden). □ **heavier-than-air** (of an aircraft) weighing more than the air it displaces. **heavy chemicals** see CHEMICAL. **heavy-duty** adj. intended to withstand hard use. **heavy-footed** awkward, ponderous. **heavy going** slow or difficult progress. **heavy-hearted** sad, doleful. **heavy hydrogen** = DEUTERIUM. **heavy industry** industry producing metal, machinery, etc. **heavy metal 1** heavy guns. **2** metal of high density. **3** *colloq.* (often *attrib.*) a type of highly-amplified rock music with a strong beat. **heavy petting** erotic fondling between two people, stopping short of intercourse. **heavy sleeper** a person who sleeps deeply. **heavy water** a substance composed entirely or mainly of deuterium oxide. **make heavy weather of** see WEATHER. □□ **heavily** *adv.* **heaviness** *n.* **heavyish** *adj.* [OE *hefig* f. Gmc, rel. to HEAVE]

heavy-handed /ˌhevɪˈhændɪd/ *adj.* **1** clumsy. **2** overbearing, oppressive. □□ **heavy-handedly** *adv.* **heavy-handedness** *n.*

heavyweight /ˈhevɪˌweɪt/ *n.* **1 a** a weight in certain sports, in the amateur boxing scale over 81 kg but differing for professional boxers, wrestlers, and weightlifters. **b** a sportsman of this weight. **2** a person, animal, or thing of above average weight. **3** *colloq.* a person of influence or importance. □ **light heavyweight 1** the weight in some sports between middleweight and heavyweight, in the amateur boxing scale 75-81 kg: also called CRUISERWEIGHT. **2** a sportsman of this weight.

Heb. *abbr.* **1** Hebrew. **2** Hebrews (New Testament).

hebdomadal /hebˈdɒməd(ə)l/ *adj. formal* weekly, esp. meeting weekly. [LL *hebdomadalis* f. Gk *hebdomas, -ados* f. *hepta* seven]

hebe /ˈhiːbɪ/ *n.* any flowering shrub of the genus *Hebe*, with usu. overlapping scale-like leaves. [mod.L after the Gk goddess *Hēbē*]

hebetude /ˈhebɪˌtjuːd/ *n. literary* dullness. [LL *hebetudo* f. *hebes, -etis* blunt]

Hebraic /hiːˈbreɪɪk/ *adj.* of Hebrew or the Hebrews. □□ **Hebraically** *adv.* [LL f. Gk *Hebraikos* (as HEBREW)]

Hebraism /ˈhiːbreɪˌɪz(ə)m/ *n.* **1** a Hebrew idiom or expression, esp. in the Greek of the Bible. **2** an attribute of the Hebrews. **3** the Hebrew system of thought or religion. □□ **Hebraistic** /-ˈɪstɪk/ *adj.* **Hebraize** *v.tr.* & *intr.* (also **-ise**). [F *hébraïsme* or mod.L *Hebraismus* f. late Gk *Hebraïsmos* (as HEBREW)]

Hebraist /ˈhiːbreɪɪst/ *n.* an expert in Hebrew.

Hebrew /ˈhiːbruː/ *n.* & *adj.* —*n.* **1** a member of a Semitic people orig. centred in ancient Palestine. **2 a** the language of this people. **b** a modern form of this used esp. in Israel. —*adj.* **1** of or in Hebrew. **2** of the Hebrews or the Jews. [ME f. OF *Ebreu* f. med.L *Ebreus* f. L *hebraeus* f. Gk *Hebraios* f. Aram. *'ibray* f. Heb. *'ibrī* one from the other side (of the river)]

Hebridean /ˌhebrɪˈdiːən/ *adj.* & *n.* —*adj.* of or relating to the Hebrides, an island group off the W. coast of Scotland. —*n.* a native of the Hebrides.

hecatomb /ˈhekəˌtuːm/ *n.* **1** (in ancient Greece or Rome) a great public sacrifice, orig. of 100 oxen. **2** any extensive sacrifice. [L *hecatombe* f. Gk *hekatombē* f. *hekaton* hundred + *bous* ox]

heck /hek/ *int. colloq.* a mild exclamation of surprise or dismay. [alt. f. HELL]

heckelphone /ˈhekəlˌfəʊn/ *n. Mus.* a bass oboe. [G *Heckelphon* f. W. *Heckel*, 20th-c. Ger. instrument-maker]

heckle /ˈhek(ə)l/ *v.tr.* **1** interrupt and harass (a public speaker). **2** dress (flax or hemp). □□ **heckler** *n.* [ME, northern and eastern form of HACKLE[1]]

hectare /ˈhekteə(r), -tɑː(r)/ *n.* a metric unit of square measure, equal to 100 ares (2.471 acres or 10,000 square metres). □□ **hectarage** /ˈhektərɪdʒ/ *n.* [F (as HECTO-, ARE[2])]

hectic /ˈhektɪk/ *adj.* & *n.* —*adj.* **1** busy and confused; excited. **2** having a hectic fever; morbidly flushed. —*n.* **1** a hectic fever or flush. **2** a patient suffering from this. □ **hectic fever** (or **flush**) *hist.* a fever which accompanies consumption and similar diseases, with

flushed cheeks and hot dry skin. □□ **hectically** *adv.* [ME *etik* f. OF *etique* f. LL *hecticus* f. Gk *hektikos* habitual f. *hexis* habit, assim. to F *hectique* or LL]

hecto- /ˈhektəʊ/ *comb. form* a hundred, esp. of a unit in the metric system. ¶ Abbr.: **ha.** [F, irreg. f. Gk *hekaton* hundred]

hectogram /ˈhektəˌgræm/ *n.* (also **hectogramme**) a metric unit of mass, equal to one hundred grams.

hectograph /ˈhektəˌgrɑːf/ *n.* an apparatus for copying documents by the use of a gelatin plate which receives an impression of the master copy.

hectolitre /ˈhektəˌliːtə(r)/ *n.* (*US* **hectoliter**) a metric unit of capacity, equal to one hundred litres.

hectometre /ˈhektəˌmiːtə(r)/ *n.* (*US* **hectometer**) a metric unit of length, equal to one hundred metres.

hector /ˈhektə(r)/ *v.* & *n.* —*v.tr.* bully, intimidate. —*n.* a bully. □□ **hectoringly** *adv.* [*Hector*, L f. Gk *Hektōr*, Trojan hero and son of Priam in Homer's *Iliad*, f. its earlier use to mean 'swaggering fellow']

he'd /hiːd, hɪd/ *contr.* **1** he had. **2** he would.

heddle /ˈhed(ə)l/ *n.* one of the sets of small cords or wires between which the warp is passed in a loom before going through the reed. [app. f. OE *hefeld*]

hedge /hedʒ/ *n.* & *v.* —*n.* **1** a fence or boundary formed by closely growing bushes or shrubs. **2** a protection against possible loss or diminution. —*v.* **1** *tr.* surround or bound with a hedge. **2** *tr.* (foll. by *in*) enclose. **3 a** *tr.* reduce one's risk of loss on (a bet or speculation) by compensating transactions on the other side. **b** *intr.* avoid a definite decision or commitment. **4** *intr.* make or trim hedges. □ **hedge-hop** fly at a very low altitude. **hedge sparrow** a common grey and brown bird, *Prunella modularis*; the dunnock. □□ **hedger** *n.* [OE *hegg* f. Gmc]

hedgehog /ˈhedʒhɒg/ *n.* **1** any small nocturnal insect-eating mammal of the genus *Erinaceus*, esp. *E. europaeus*, having a piglike snout and a coat of spines, and rolling itself up into a ball for defence. **2** a porcupine or other animal similarly covered with spines. □□ **hedgehoggy** *adj.* [ME f. HEDGE (from its habitat) + HOG (from its snout)]

hedgerow /ˈhedʒrəʊ/ *n.* a row of bushes etc. forming a hedge.

hedonic /hiːˈdɒnɪk, he-/ *adj.* **1** of or characterized by pleasure. **2** *Psychol.* of pleasant or unpleasant sensations. [Gk *hēdonikos* f. *hēdonē* pleasure]

hedonism /ˈhiːdəˌnɪz(ə)m, ˈhe-/ *n.* **1** belief in pleasure as the highest good and mankind's proper aim. **2** behaviour based on this. □□ **hedonist** *n.* **hedonistic** /-ˈnɪstɪk/ *adj.* [Gk *hēdonē* pleasure]

-hedron /ˈhiːdrən, ˈhedrən/ *comb. form* (*pl.* **-hedra**) forming nouns denoting geometrical solids with various numbers or shapes of faces (*dodecahedron*; *rhombohedron*). □□ **-hedral** *comb. form* forming adjectives. [Gk *hedra* seat]

heebie-jeebies /ˌhiːbɪˈjiːbɪz/ *n.pl.* (prec. by *the*) *sl.* a state of nervous depression or anxiety. [20th c.: orig. unkn.]

heed /hiːd/ *v.* & *n.* —*v.tr.* attend to; take notice of. —*n.* careful attention. □□ **heedful** *adj.* **heedfully** *adv.* **heedfulness** *n.* **heedless** *adj.* **heedlessly** *adv.* **heedlessness** *n.* [OE *hēdan* f. WG]

hee-haw /ˈhiːhɔː/ *n.* & *v.* —*n.* the bray of a donkey. —*v.intr.* (of or like a donkey) emit a braying sound. [imit.]

heel[1] /hiːl/ *n.* & *v.* —*n.* **1** the back part of the foot below the ankle. **2** the corresponding part in vertebrate animals. **3 a** the part of a sock etc. covering the heel. **b** the part of a shoe or boot supporting the heel. **4** a thing like a heel in form or position, e.g. the part of the palm next to the wrist, the end of a violin bow at which it is held, or the part of a golf club near where the head joins the shaft. **5** the crust end of a loaf of bread. **6** *colloq.* a person regarded with contempt or disapproval. **7** (as *int.*) a command to a dog to walk close to its owner's heel. —*v.* **1** *tr.* fit or renew a heel on (a shoe or boot). **2**

intr. touch the ground with the heel as in dancing. **3** *intr.* (foll. by *out*) *Rugby Football* pass the ball with the heel. **4** *tr. Golf* strike (the ball) with the heel of the club. □**at heel 1** (of a dog) close behind. **2** (of a person etc.) under control. **at** (or **on**) **the heels of** following closely after (a person or event). **cool** (or **kick**) **one's heels** be kept waiting. **down at heel 1** (of a shoe) with the heel worn down. **2** (of a person) shabby. **take to one's heels** run away. **to heel 1** (of a dog) close behind. **2** (of a person etc.) under control. **turn on one's heel** turn sharply round. **well-heeled** *colloq.* wealthy. □□**heelless** *adj.* [OE *hēla, hǣla* f. Gmc]

heel[2] /hiːl/ *v. & n.* —*v.* **1** *intr.* (of a ship etc.) lean over owing to the pressure of wind or an uneven load (cf. LIST[2]). **2** *tr.* cause (a ship etc.) to do this. —*n.* the act or amount of heeling. [prob. f. obs. *heeld, hield* incline, f. OE *hieldan,* OS *-heldian* f. Gmc]

heel[3] var. of HELE.

heelball /ˈhiːlbɔːl/ *n.* **1** a mixture of hard wax and lampblack used by shoemakers for polishing. **2** this or a similar mixture used in brass-rubbing.

heeltap /ˈhiːltæp/ *n.* **1** a layer of leather in a shoe heel. **2** liquor left at the bottom of a glass after drinking.

heft /heft/ *v. & n.* —*v.tr.* lift (something heavy), esp. to judge its weight. —*n. dial.* or *US* weight, heaviness. [prob. f. HEAVE after *cleft, weft*]

hefty /ˈhefti/ *adj.* (**heftier, heftiest**) **1** (of a person) big and strong. **2** (of a thing) large, heavy, powerful. □□**heftily** *adv.* **heftiness** *n.*

Hegelian /herˈgiːliən/ *adj. & n.* —*adj.* of or relating to the German philosopher G. W. F. Hegel (d. 1831) or his philosophy of objective idealism. —*n.* an adherent of Hegel or his philosophy. □□ **Hegelianism** *n.*

hegemonic /ˌhedʒɪˈmɒnɪk, ˌhegɪ-/ *adj.* ruling, supreme. [Gk *hēgemonikos* (as HEGEMONY)]

hegemony /hɪˈdʒeməni, -ˈgemənɪ/ *n.* leadership esp. by one State of a confederacy. [Gk *hēgemonia* f. *hēgemōn* leader f. *hēgeomai* lead]

hegira /ˈhedʒɪrə/ *n.* (also **hejira, hijra** /ˈhɪdʒrə/) **1** (**Hegira**) **a** Muhammad's departure from Mecca to Medina in AD 622. **b** the Muslim era reckoned from this date. **2** a general exodus or departure. [med.L *hegira* f. Arab. *hijra* departure from one's country f. *hajara* separate]

heifer /ˈhefə(r)/ *n.* **1 a** a young cow, esp. one that has not had more than one calf. **b** a female calf. **2** *sl. derog.* a woman. [OE *heahfore*]

heigh /heɪ/ *int.* expressing encouragement or enquiry. □**heigh-ho** expressing boredom, resignation, etc. [imit.]

height /haɪt/ *n.* **1** the measurement from base to top or (of a standing person) from head to foot. **2** the elevation above ground or a recognized level (usu. sea level). **3** any considerable elevation (*situated at a height*). **4 a** a high place or area. **b** rising ground. **5** the top of something. **6** *Printing* the distance from the foot to the face of type. **7 a** the most intense part or period of anything (*the battle was at its height*). **b** an extreme instance or example (*the height of fashion*). □**height of land** *US* a watershed. [OE *hēhthu* f. Gmc]

heighten /ˈhaɪt(ə)n/ *v.tr. & intr.* make or become higher or more intense.

heinous /ˈheɪnəs, ˈhiːnəs/ *adj.* (of a crime or criminal) utterly odious or wicked. □□**heinously** *adv.* **heinousness** *n.* [ME f. OF *haïneus* ult. f. *haïr* to hate f. Frank.]

heir /eə(r)/ *n.* **1** a person entitled to property or rank as the legal successor of its former owner (often foll. by *to*: *heir to the throne*). **2** a person deriving or morally entitled to some thing, quality, etc., from a predecessor. □**heir apparent** an heir whose claim cannot be set aside by the birth of another heir. **heir-at-law** (*pl.* **heirs-at-law**) an heir by right of blood, esp. to the real property of an intestate. **heir presumptive** an heir whose claim may be set aside

in this way. □□**heirdom** *n.* **heirless** *adj.* **heirship** *n.* [ME f. OF *eir* f. LL *herem* f. L *heres -edis*]

heiress /ˈeərɪs/ *n.* a female heir, esp. to wealth or high title.

heirloom /ˈeəluːm/ *n.* **1** a piece of personal property that has been in a family for several generations. **2** a piece of property received as part of an inheritance. [HEIR + LOOM[1] in the sense 'tool']

Heisenberg uncertainty principle see *uncertainty principle.*

heist /haɪst/ *n. & v. US sl.* —*n.* a robbery. —*v.tr.* rob. [repr. a local pronunc. of HOIST]

hei-tiki /heɪˈtɪkɪ/ *n. NZ* a greenstone neck-ornament worn by Maoris. [Maori f. *hei* hang, TIKI]

hejira var. of HEGIRA.

HeLa /ˈhiːlə/ *adj.* of a strain of human epithelial cells maintained in tissue culture. [*Henrietta Lacks,* whose cervical carcinoma provided the original cells]

held *past* and *past part.* of HOLD.

Heldentenor /ˈheldənteˌnɔː(r)/ *n.* **1** a powerful tenor voice suitable for heroic roles in opera. **2** a singer with this voice. [G f. *Held* a hero]

hele /hiːl/ *v.tr.* (also **heel**) (foll. by *in*) set (a plant) in the ground and cover its roots. [OE *helian* f. Gmc]

helenium /heˈliːnɪəm/ *n.* any composite plant of the genus *Helenium,* with daisy-like flowers having prominent central discs. [mod.L f. Gk *helenion,* possibly commemorating Helen of Troy]

heli- /ˈhelɪ/ *comb. form* helicopter (*heliport*).

heliacal /hɪˈlaɪək(ə)l/ *adj. Astron.* relating to or near the sun. □**heliacal rising** (or **setting**) the first rising (or setting) of a star after (or before) a period of invisibility due to conjunction with the sun. [LL *heliacus* f. Gk *hēliakos* f. *hēlios* sun]

helianthemum /ˌhiːlɪˈænθəməm/ *n.* any evergreen shrub of the genus *Helianthemum,* with saucer-shaped flowers. Also called *rock rose.* [mod.L f. Gk *hēlios* sun + *anthemon* flower]

helianthus /ˌhiːlɪˈænθəs/ *n.* any plant of the genus *Helianthus,* including the sunflower and Jerusalem artichoke. [mod.L f. Gk *hēlios* sun + *anthos* flower]

helical /ˈhelɪk(ə)l/ *adj.* having the form of a helix. □□**helically** *adv.* **helicoid** *adj. & n.*

helices *pl.* of HELIX.

helichrysum /ˌhelɪˈkraɪz(ə)m/ *n.* any composite plant of the genus *Helichrysum,* with flowers retaining their appearance when dried. [L f. Gk *helikhrusos* f. *helix* spiral + *khrusos* gold]

helicon /ˈhelɪkən/ *n.* a large spiral bass tuba played encircling the player's head and resting on the shoulder. [L f. Gk *Helikōn* mountain sacred to the Muses; later assoc. with HELIX]

helicopter /ˈhelɪˌkɒptə(r)/ *n. & v.* —*n.* a type of aircraft without wings, obtaining lift and propulsion from horizontally revolving overhead blades or rotors, and capable of moving vertically and horizontally. —*v.tr. & intr.* transport or fly by helicopter. [F *hélicoptère* f. Gk *helix* (see HELIX) + *pteron* wing]

helio- /ˈhiːlɪəʊ/ *comb. form* the sun. [Gk *hēlios* sun]

heliocentric /ˌhiːlɪəˈsentrɪk/ *adj.* **1** regarding the sun as centre. **2** considered as viewed from the sun's centre. □□ **heliocentrically** *adv.*

heliogram /ˈhiːlɪəˌgræm/ *n.* a message sent by heliograph.

heliograph /ˈhiːlɪəˌgrɑːf/ *n. & v.* —*n.* **1 a** a signalling apparatus reflecting sunlight in flashes from a movable mirror. **b** a message sent by means of this; a heliogram. **2** an apparatus for photographing the sun. **3** an engraving obtained chemically by exposure to light. —*v.tr.* send (a message) by heliograph. □□ **heliography** /-ˈɒgrəfɪ/ *n.*

heliogravure /ˌhiːlɪəʊgrəˈvjʊə(r)/ *n.* = PHOTO-GRAVURE.

heliolithic /ˌhiːlɪəˈlɪθɪk/ *adj.* (of a civilization) characterized by sun-worship and megaliths.

heliometer /ˌhiːlɪˈɒmɪtə(r)/ *n.* an instrument used

for finding the angular distance between two stars (orig. used for measuring the diameter of the sun).

heliostat /'hi:lɪəˌstæt/ n. an apparatus with a mirror driven by clockwork to reflect sunlight in a fixed direction. □□ **heliostatic** /-'stætɪk/ adj.

heliotherapy /ˌhi:lɪəʊ'θerəpɪ/ n. the use of sunlight in treating disease.

heliotrope /'hi:lɪəˌtrəʊp, 'hel-/ n. **1 a** any plant of the genus *Heliotropium*, with fragrant purple flowers. **b** the scent of these. **2** a light purple colour. **3** bloodstone. [L *heliotropium* f. Gk *hēliotropion* plant turning its flowers to the sun, f. *hēlios* sun + *-tropos* f. *trepō* turn]

heliotropism /ˌhi:lɪ'ɒtrəˌpɪz(ə)m/ n. the directional growth of a plant in response to sunlight (cf. PHOTOTROPISM). □□ **heliotropic** /ˌhi:lɪə'trɒpɪk/ adj.

heliotype /'hi:lɪəˌtaɪp/ n. a picture obtained from a sensitized gelatin film exposed to light.

heliport /'helɪˌpɔːt/ n. a place where helicopters take off and land. [HELI-, after *airport*]

helium /'hi:lɪəm/ n. *Chem.* a colourless light inert gaseous element occurring in deposits of natural gas, used in airships and as a refrigerant. ¶ Symb.: **He**. [Gk *hēlios* sun (having been first identified in the sun's atmosphere)]

helix /'hi:lɪks/ n. (pl. **helices** /'hi:lɪˌsiːz, 'hel-/) **1** a spiral curve (like a corkscrew) or a coiled curve (like a watch spring). **2** *Geom.* a curve that cuts a line on a solid cone or cylinder, at a constant angle with the axis. **3** *Archit.* a spiral ornament. **4** *Anat.* the rim of the external ear. [L *helix -icis* f. Gk *helix -ikos*]

hell /hel/ n. **1** a place regarded in some religions as the abode of the dead, or of condemned sinners and devils. **2** a place or state of misery or wickedness. **3** *colloq.* used as an exclamation of surprise or annoyance (*who the hell are you?; a hell of a mess*). **4** *US colloq.* fun; high spirits. □ **beat** (or **knock** etc.) **the hell out of** *colloq.* beat etc. without restraint. **come hell or high water** no matter what the difficulties. **for the hell of it** *colloq.* for fun; on impulse. **get** (or **catch**) **hell** *colloq.* be severely scolded or punished. **give a person hell** *colloq.* scold or punish or make things difficult for a person. **hell-bent** (foll. by *on*) recklessly determined. **hell-cat** a spiteful violent woman. **hell-fire** the fire or fires regarded as existing in hell. **hell for leather** at full speed. **hell-hole** an oppressive or unbearable place. **hell-hound** a fiend. **hell's angel** a member of a gang of male motor-cycle enthusiasts notorious for outrageous and violent behaviour. **like hell** *colloq.* **1** not at all. **2** recklessly, exceedingly. **not a hope in hell** *colloq.* no chance at all. **play hell** (or **merry hell**) **with** *colloq.* be upsetting or disruptive to. **what the hell** *colloq.* it is of no importance. □□ **hell-like** adj. **hellward** adv. & adj. [OE *hel, hell* f. Gmc]

he'll /hi:l, hɪl/ contr. he will; he shall.

Helladic /he'lædɪk/ adj. of or belonging to the Bronze Age culture of mainland Greece. [Gk *Helladikos* f. *Hellas -ados* Greece]

hellebore /'helɪˌbɔː(r)/ n. **1** any evergreen plant of the genus *Helleborus*, having large white, green, or purplish flowers, e.g. the Christmas rose. **2** a liliaceous plant, *Veratrum album.* **3** *hist.* any of various plants supposed to cure madness. [ME f. OF *ellebre, elebore* or med.L *eleborus* f. L *elleborus* f. Gk *(h)elleboros*]

helleborine /'helɪbəˌriːn/ n. any orchid of the genus *Epipactis* or *Cephalanthera*. [F or L *helleborine* or L f. Gk *helleborinē* plant like hellebore (as HELLEBORE)]

Hellene /'heliːn/ n. **1** a native of modern Greece. **2** an ancient Greek. □□ **Hellenic** /he'lenɪk, -'liːnɪk/ adj. [Gk *Hellēn* a Greek]

Hellenism /'helɪˌnɪz(ə)m/ n. **1** Greek character or culture (esp. of ancient Greece). **2** the study or imitation of Greek culture. □□ **Hellenize** v.tr. & intr. (also **-ise**). **Hellenization** /-naɪ'zeɪʃ(ə)n/ n. [Gk

hellēnismos f. *hellēnizō* speak Greek, make Greek (as HELLENE)]

Hellenist /'helɪnɪst/ n. an expert on or admirer of Greek language or culture. [Gk *Hellēnistēs* (as HELLENISM)]

Hellenistic /ˌhelɪ'nɪstɪk/ adj. of or relating to Greek history, language, and culture from the death of Alexander the Great to the time of Augustus (4th-1st c. BC).

hellgrammite /'helgrəˌmaɪt/ n. *US* an aquatic larva of an American fly, *Corydalus cornutus*, often used as fishing bait. [19th c.: orig. unkn.]

hellion /'helɪən/ n. *US colloq.* a mischievous or troublesome person, esp. a child. [perh. f. dial. *hallion* a worthless fellow, assim. to HELL]

hellish /'helɪʃ/ adj. & adv. —adj. **1** of or like hell. **2** *colloq.* extremely difficult or unpleasant. —adv. *Brit. colloq.* (as an intensifier) extremely (*hellish expensive*). □□ **hellishly** adv. **hellishness** n.

hello /hə'ləʊ/ int., n., & v. (also **hallo, hullo**) —int. **1 a** an expression of informal greeting, or of surprise. **b** used to begin a telephone conversation. **2** a cry used to call attention. —n. (pl. **-os**) a cry of 'hello'. —v.intr. (**-oes, -oed**) cry 'hello'. [var. of earlier HOLLO]

helm¹ /helm/ n. & v. —n. **1** a tiller or wheel by which a ship's rudder is controlled. **2** the amount by which this is turned (*more helm needed*). —v.tr. steer or guide as if with a helm. □ **at the helm** in control; at the head (of an organization etc.). [OE *helma*, prob. related to HELVE]

helm² /helm/ n. *archaic* helmet. □□ **helmed** adj. [OE f. Gmc]

helmet /'helmɪt/ n. **1** any of various protective head-coverings worn by soldiers, policemen, firemen, divers, motor cyclists, etc. **2** *Bot.* the arched upper part of the corolla in some flowers. **3** the shell of a gastropod mollusc of the genus *Cassis*, used in jewellery. □□ **helmeted** adj. [ME f. OF, dimin. of *helme* f. WG (as HELM²)]

helminth /'helmɪnθ/ n. any of various parasitic worms including flukes, tapeworms, and nematodes. □□ **helminthic** /-'mɪnθɪk/ adj. **helminthoid** /-'mɪnθɔɪd/ adj. **helminthology** /-mɪn'θɒlədʒɪ/ n. [Gk *helmins -inthos* intestinal worm]

helminthiasis /ˌhelmɪn'θaɪəsɪs/ n. a disease characterized by the presence of any of several parasitic worms in the body.

helmsman /'helmzmən/ n. (pl. **-men**) a steersman.

helot /'helət/ n. a serf (esp. **Helot**), of a class in ancient Sparta. □□ **helotism** n. **helotry** n. [L *helotes* pl. f. Gk *heilōtes, -ōtai*, erron. taken as = inhabitants of *Helos*, a Laconian town]

help /help/ v. & n. —v.tr. **1** provide (a person etc.) with the means towards what is needed or sought (*helped me with my work; helped me* (to) *pay my debts*). **2** (foll. by *up, down*, etc.) assist or give support to (a person) in moving etc. as specified (*helped her into the chair; helped him on with his coat*). **3** (often *absol.*) be of use or service to (a person) (*does that help?*). **4** contribute to alleviating (a pain or difficulty). **5** prevent or remedy (*it can't be helped*). **6** (usu. with *neg.*) **a** *tr.* refrain from (*can't help it; could not help laughing*). **b** *refl.* refrain from acting (*couldn't help himself*). **7** *tr.* (often foll. by *to*) serve (a person with food) (*shall I help you to greens?*). —n. **1** the act of helping or being helped (*we need your help; came to our help*). **2** a person or thing that helps. **3** a domestic servant or employee, or several collectively. **4** a remedy or escape (*there is no help for it*). □ **helping hand** assistance. **help oneself** (often foll. by *to*) **1** serve oneself (with food). **2** take without seeking help or permission. **help a person out** give a person help, esp. in difficulty. **so help me** (or **help me God**) (as an invocation or oath) I am speaking the truth. □□ **helper** n. [OE *helpan* f. Gmc]

helpful /'helpfʊl/ n. (of a person or thing) giving help; useful. □□ **helpfully** adv. **helpfulness** n.

helping /'hɛlpɪŋ/ n. a portion of food esp. at a meal.

helpless /'hɛlplɪs/ adj. **1** lacking help or protection; defenceless. **2** unable to act without help. □□ **helplessly** adv. **helplessness** n.

helpline /'hɛlplaɪn/ n. a telephone service providing help with problems.

helpmate /'hɛlpmeɪt/ n. a helpful companion or partner (usu. a husband or wife).

helter-skelter /ˌhɛltə'skɛltə(r)/ adv., adj., & n. —adv. & adj. in disorderly haste. —n. Brit. a tall spiral slide round a tower, at a fairground or funfair. [imit., orig. in a rhyming jingle, perh. f. ME skelte hasten]

helve /hɛlv/ n. the handle of a weapon or a tool. [OE helfe f. WG]

Helvetian /hɛl'viːʃ(ə)n/ adj. & n. —adj. Swiss. —n. a native of Switzerland. [L Helvetia Switzerland]

hem¹ /hɛm/ n. & v. —n. the border of a piece of cloth, esp. a cut edge turned under and sewn down. —v.tr. (**hemmed**, **hemming**) turn down and sew in the edge of (a piece of cloth etc.). □ **hem in** confine; restrict the movement of. [OE, perh. rel. to dial. ham enclosure]

hem² /hɛm, həm/ int., n., & v. —int. calling attention or expressing hesitation by a slight cough or clearing of the throat. —n. an utterance of this. —v.intr. (**hemmed**, **hemming**) say hem; hesitate in speech. □ **hem and haw** = hum and haw (see HUM¹). [imit.]

hemal etc. US var. of HAEMAL etc.

hemato- etc. US var. of HAEMATO- etc.

heme var. of HAEM.

hemerocallis /ˌhɛmərəʊ'kælɪs/ n. = day lily. [L hemerocalles f. Gk hēmerokalles a kind of lily f. hēmera day + kallos beauty]

hemi- /'hɛmɪ/ comb. form half. [Gk hēmi- = L semi-: see SEMI-]

-hemia comb. form US var. of -AEMIA.

hemianopsia /ˌhɛmɪə'nɒpsɪə/ n. (also **hemianopia** /ˌhɛmɪə'nəʊpɪə/) blindness over half the field of vision.

hemicellulose /ˌhɛmɪ'sɛljʊˌləʊz/ n. any of various polysaccharides forming the matrix of plant cell walls in which cellulose is embedded. [G (as HEMI-, CELLULOSE)]

hemicycle /'hɛmɪˌsaɪk(ə)l/ n. a semicircular figure.

hemidemisemiquaver /'hɛmɪˌdɛmɪˌsɛmɪˌkweɪvə(r)/ n. Mus. a note having the time value of half a demisemiquaver and represented by a large dot with a four-hooked stem. Also called sixty-fourth note.

hemihedral /ˌhɛmɪ'hiːdr(ə)l/ adj. Crystallog. having half the number of planes required for symmetry of the holohedral form.

hemiplegia /ˌhɛmɪ'pliːdʒɪə/ n. Med. paralysis of one side of the body. □□ **hemiplegic** n. & adj. [mod.L f. Gk hēmiplēgia paralysis (as HEMI-, plēgē stroke)]

hemipterous /hɛ'mɪptərəs/ adj. of the insect order Hemiptera including aphids, bugs, and cicadas, with piercing or sucking mouthparts. [HEMI- + Gk pteron wing]

hemisphere /'hɛmɪˌsfɪə(r)/ n. **1** half of a sphere. **2** a half of the earth, esp. as divided by the equator (into northern and southern hemisphere) or by a line passing through the poles (into eastern and western hemisphere). □□ **hemispheric** /-'sfɛrɪk/ adj. **hemispherical** /-'sfɛrɪk(ə)l/ adj. [OF emisphere & L hemisphaerium f. Gk hēmisphaira (as HEMI, SPHERE)]

hemistich /'hɛmɪstɪk/ n. half of a line of verse. [LL hemistichium f. Gk hēmistikhion (as HEMI, stikhion f. stikhos line)]

hemline /'hɛmlaɪn/ n. the line or level of the lower edge of a skirt, dress, or coat.

hemlock /'hɛmlɒk/ n. **1 a** a poisonous umbelliferous plant, Conium maculatum, with fernlike leaves and small white flowers. **b** a poisonous potion obtained from this. **2** (in full **hemlock fir** or **spruce**) **a** any coniferous tree of the genus Tsuga, having foliage

that smells like hemlock when crushed. **b** the timber or pitch of these trees. [OE hymlic(e)]

hemo- comb. form US var. of HAEMO-.

hemp /hɛmp/ n. **1** (in full **Indian hemp**) a herbaceous plant, Cannabis sativa, native to Asia. **2** its fibre extracted from the stem and used to make rope and stout fabrics. **3** any of several narcotic drugs made from the hemp plant (cf. CANNABIS, MARIJUANA). **4** any of several other plants yielding fibre, including Manila hemp and sunn hemp. □ **hemp agrimony** a composite plant, Eupatorium cannabinum, with pale-purple flowers and hairy leaves. **hemp-nettle** any of various nettle-like plants of the genus Galeopsis. [OE henep, hænep f. Gmc, rel. to Gk kannabis]

hempen /'hɛmpən/ adj. made from hemp.

hemstitch /'hɛmstɪtʃ/ n. & v. —n. a decorative stitch used in sewing hems. —v.tr. hem with this stitch.

hen /hɛn/ n. **1 a** a female bird, esp. of a domestic fowl. **b** (in pl.) domestic fowls of either sex. **2** a female lobster or crab or salmon. □ **hen and chickens** any of several plants esp. the houseleek. **hen-coop** a coop for keeping fowls in. **hen-harrier** a common harrier, Circus cyaneus. **hen-house** a small shed for fowls to roost in. **hen-party** colloq. derog. a social gathering of women. **hen-roost** a place where fowls roost at night. **hen-run** an enclosure for fowls. [OE henn f. WG]

henbane /'hɛnbeɪn/ n. **1** a poisonous herbaceous plant, Hyoscyamus niger, with sticky hairy leaves and an unpleasant smell. **2** a narcotic drug obtained from this.

hence /hɛns/ adv. **1** from this time (two years hence). **2** for this reason; as a result of inference (hence we seem to be wrong). **3** archaic from here; from this place. [ME hens, hennes, henne f. OE heonan f. the root of HE]

henceforth /hɛns'fɔːθ/ adv. (also **henceforward** /-'fɔːwəd/) from this time onwards.

henchman /'hɛntʃmən/ n. (pl. -men) **1** a trusted supporter or attendant. **2** hist. a squire; a page of honour. **3** the principal attendant of a Highland chief. [ME henxman, hengestman f. OE hengst male horse]

hendeca- /hɛn'dɛkə/ comb. form eleven. [Gk hendeka eleven]

hendecagon /hɛn'dɛkəˌgɒn/ n. a plane figure with eleven sides and angles.

hendiadys /hɛn'daɪədɪs/ n. the expression of an idea by two words connected with 'and', instead of one modifying the other, e.g. nice and warm for nicely warm. [med.L f. Gk hen dia duoin one thing by two]

henequen /'hɛnɪˌkɛn/ n. **1** a Mexican agave, Agave fourcroydes. **2** the sisal-like fibre obtained from this. [Sp. jeniquen]

henge /hɛndʒ/ n. a prehistoric monument consisting of a circle of massive stone or wood uprights. [back-form. f. Stonehenge, such a monument in S. England]

henna /'hɛnə/ n. **1** a tropical shrub, Lawsonia inermis, having small pink, red, or white flowers. **2** the reddish dye from its shoots and leaves esp. used to colour hair. [Arab. ḥinnā]

hennaed /'hɛnəd/ adj. treated with henna.

henotheism /'hɛnəˌθiːɪz(ə)m/ n. belief in or adoption of a particular god in a polytheistic system as the god of a tribe, class, etc. [Gk heis henos one + theos god]

henpeck /'hɛnpɛk/ v.tr. (of a woman) constantly harass (a man, esp. her husband).

henry /'hɛnrɪ/ n. (pl. -ies or henrys) Electr. the SI unit of inductance which gives an electromotive force of one volt in a closed circuit with a uniform rate of change of current of one ampere per second. ¶ Abbr.: **H**. [J. Henry, Amer. physicist d. 1878]

heortology /ˌhiːɔː'tɒlədʒɪ/ n. the study of Church festivals. [G Heortologie, F héortologie f. Gk heortē feast]

w we   z zoo   ʃ she   ʒ decision   θ thin   ð this   ŋ ring   x loch   tʃ chip   dʒ jar   (see over for vowels)

hep[1] var. of HIP[3].

hep[2] var. of HIP[2].

heparin /'hepərɪn/ *n. Biochem.* a substance produced in liver cells etc. which inhibits blood coagulation, and is used as an anticoagulant in the treatment of thrombosis. □□ **heparinize** *v.tr.* (also **-ise**). [L f. Gk *hēpar* liver]

hepatic /hɪ'pætɪk/ *adj.* 1 of or relating to the liver. 2 dark brownish-red; liver-coloured. [ME f. L *hepaticus* f. Gk *hēpatikos* f. *hēpar -atos* liver]

hepatica /hɪ'pætɪkə/ *n.* any plant of the genus *Hepatica*, with reddish-brown lobed leaves resembling the liver. [med.L fem. of *hepaticus*: see HEPATIC]

hepatitis /ˌhepə'taɪtɪs/ *n.* inflammation of the liver. [mod.L: see HEPATIC]

Hepplewhite /'hepəlˌwaɪt/ *n.* a light and graceful style of furniture. [G. *Hepplewhite*, Engl. cabinet-maker d. 1786]

hepta- /'heptə/ *comb. form* seven. [Gk *hepta* seven]

heptad /'heptæd/ *n.* a group of seven. [Gk *heptas -ados* set of seven (*hepta*)]

heptagon /'heptəgən/ *n.* a plane figure with seven sides and angles. □□ **heptagonal** /-'tægən(ə)l/ *adj.* [F *heptagone* or med.L *heptagonum* f. Gk (as HEPTA-, -GON)]

heptahedron /ˌheptə'hi:drən/ *n.* a solid figure with seven faces. □□ **heptahedral** *adj.* [HEPTA- + -HEDRON after POLYHEDRON]

heptameter /hep'tæmɪtə(r)/ *n.* a line or verse of seven metrical feet. [L *heptametrum* f. Gk (as HEPTA-, -METER)]

heptane /'heptem/ *n. Chem.* a liquid hydrocarbon of the alkane series, obtained from petroleum. ¶ Chem. formula: C_7H_{16}. [HEPTA- + -ANE]

heptarchy /'heptəkɪ/ *n.* (*pl.* **-ies**) 1 **a** government by seven rulers. **b** an instance of this. 2 *hist.* the supposed seven kingdoms of the Angles and the Saxons in Britain in the 7th-8th c. □□ **heptarchic** /-'ta:kɪk/ *adj.* **heptarchical** /-'ta:kɪk(ə)l/ *adj.* [HEPTA- after *tetrarchy*]

Heptateuch /'heptəˌtju:k/ *n.* the first seven books of the Old Testament. [L f. Gk f. *hepta* seven + *teukhos* book, volume]

heptavalent /ˌheptə'veɪlənt/ *adj. Chem.* having a valency of seven; septivalent.

her /hɜ:(r), hə(r)/ *pron. & poss.pron.* —*pron.* 1 *objective case* of SHE (*I like her*). 2 *colloq.* she (*it's her all right; am older than her*). 3 *archaic* herself (*she fell and hurt her*). —*poss.pron.* (*attrib.*) 1 of or belonging to her or herself (*her house; her own business*). 2 (**Her**) (in titles) that she is (*Her Majesty*). [OE *hi(e)re* dat. & gen. of *hio*, *hēo* fem. of HE]

herald /'her(ə)ld/ *n. & v.* —*n.* 1 an official messenger bringing news. 2 a forerunner (*spring is the herald of summer*). 3 **a** *hist.* an officer responsible for State ceremonial and etiquette. **b** *Brit.* an official of the Heralds' College. —*v.tr.* proclaim the approach of; usher in (*the storm heralded trouble*). □ **Heralds' College** *Brit. colloq.* = *College of Arms.* [ME f. OF *herau(l)t, heraud* f. Gmc]

heraldic /he'rældɪk/ *adj.* of or concerning heraldry. □□ **heraldically** *adv.* [HERALD]

heraldist /'herəldɪst/ *n.* an expert in heraldry. [HERALD]

heraldry /'herəldrɪ/ *n.* 1 the science or art of a herald, esp. in dealing with armorial bearings. 2 heraldic pomp. 3 armorial bearings.

herb /hɜ:b/ *n.* 1 any non-woody seed-bearing plant which dies down to the ground after flowering. 2 any plant with leaves, seeds, or flowers used for flavouring, food, medicine, scent, etc. □ **herb bennet** a common yellow-flowered plant, *Geum urbanum*. **herb Christopher** a white-flowered baneberry, *Actaea spicata*. **herb Gerard** a white-flowered plant, *Aegopodium podagraria*. **herb Paris** a plant, *Paris quadrifolia*, with a single flower and four leaves in a cross shape on an unbranched stem. **herb Robert** a common cranesbill, *Geranium robertianum*, with

red-stemmed leaves and pink flowers. **herb tea** an infusion of herbs. **herb tobacco** a mixture of herbs smoked as a substitute for tobacco. □□ **herbiferous** /-'bɪfərəs/ *adj.* **herblike** *adj.* [ME f. OF *erbe* f. L *herba* grass, green crops, herb; *herb bennet* prob. f. med.L *herba benedicta* blessed herb (thought of as expelling the Devil)]

herbaceous /hɜ:'beɪʃəs/ *adj.* of or like herbs (see HERB 1). □ **herbaceous border** a garden border containing esp. perennial flowering plants. **herbaceous perennial** a plant whose growth dies down annually but whose roots etc. survive. [L *herbaceus* grassy (as HERB)]

herbage /'hɜ:bɪdʒ/ *n.* 1 herbs collectively. 2 the succulent part of herbs, esp. as pasture. 3 *Law* the right of pasture on another person's land. [ME f. OF *erbage* f. med.L *herbaticum, herbagium* right of pasture, f. L *herba* herb]

herbal /'hɜ:b(ə)l/ *adj. & n.* —*adj.* of herbs in medicinal and culinary use. —*n.* a book with descriptions and accounts of the properties of these. [med.L *herbalis* (as HERB)]

herbalist /'hɜ:bəlɪst/ *n.* 1 a dealer in medicinal herbs. 2 a person skilled in herbs, esp. an early botanical writer.

herbarium /hɜ:'beərɪəm/ *n.* (*pl.* **herbaria** /-rɪə/) 1 a systematically arranged collection of dried plants. 2 a book, room, or building for these. [LL (as HERB)]

herbicide /'hɜ:bɪˌsaɪd/ *n.* a substance toxic to plants and used to destroy unwanted vegetation.

herbivore /'hɜ:bɪˌvɔ:(r)/ *n.* an animal that feeds on plants. □□ **herbivorous** /-'bɪvərəs/ *adj.* [L *herba* herb + -VORE (see -VOROUS)]

herby /'hɜ:bɪ/ *adj.* (**herbier, herbiest**) 1 abounding in herbs. 2 of the nature of a culinary or medicinal herb.

Herculean /ˌhɜ:kjʊ'li:ən, -'kju:lɪən/ *adj.* having or requiring great strength or effort. [L *Herculeus* (as HERCULES)]

Hercules /'hɜ:kjʊˌli:z/ *n.* a man of exceptional strength or size. □ **Hercules beetle** *Zool.* a large S. American beetle, *Dynastes hercules*, with two horns extending from the head. [ME f. L f. Gk *Hēraklēs* a hero noted for his great strength]

Hercynian /hɜ:'sɪnɪən/ *adj. Geol.* of a mountain-forming time in the E. hemisphere in the late Palaeozoic era. [L *Hercynia silva* forested mountains of central Germany]

herd /hɜ:d/ *n. & v.* —*n.* 1 a large number of animals, esp. cattle, feeding or travelling or kept together. 2 (prec. by *the*) *derog.* a large number of people; a mob (*prefers not to follow the herd*). 3 (esp. in *comb.*) a keeper of herds; a herdsman (*cowherd*). —*v.* 1 *intr.* & *tr.* go or cause to go in a herd (*herded together for warmth; herded the cattle into the field*). 2 *tr.* tend (sheep, cattle, etc.) (*he herds the goats*). □ **herd-book** a book recording the pedigrees of cattle or pigs. **the herd instinct** the tendency of associating or conforming with one's own kind for support etc. **ride herd on** *US* keep watch on. □□ **herder** *n.* [OE *heord*, (in sense 3) *hirdi*, f. Gmc]

herdsman /'hɜ:dzmən/ *n.* (*pl.* **-men**) the owner or keeper of herds (of domesticated animals).

Herdwick /'hɜ:dwɪk/ *n.* 1 an animal of a hardy breed of mountain sheep from N. England. 2 this breed. [obs. *herdwick* pasture-ground (as HERD, WICK[2]), perh. because this breed originated in Furness Abbey pastures]

here /hɪə(r)/ *adv., n., & int.* —*adv.* 1 in or at or to this place or position (*put it here; has lived here for many years; comes here every day*). 2 indicating a person's presence or a thing offered (*here is your coat; my son here will show you*). 3 at this point in the argument, situation, etc. (*here I have a question*). —*n.* this place (*get out of here; lives near here; fill it up to here*). —*int.* 1 calling attention: short for *come here, look here*, etc. (*here, where are you going with that?*). 2 indicating one's presence in a roll-call: short for *I am here*. □**here and now** at this very moment; immediately. **here and there** in various places. **here goes!** *colloq*. an expression indicating the start of a bold act. **here's to** I drink to the health of. **here we are** *colloq*. said on arrival at one's destination. **here we go again** *colloq*. the same, usu. undesirable, events are recurring. **here you are** said on handing something to somebody. **neither here nor there** of no importance or relevance. [OE *hēr* f. Gmc: cf. HE]

hereabouts /ˌhɪərəˈbaʊts/ *adv.* (also **hereabout**) near this place.

hereafter /hɪərˈɑːftə(r)/ *adv. & n.* —*adv.* **1** from now on; in the future. **2** in the world to come (after death). —*n.* **1** the future. **2** life after death.

hereat /hɪərˈæt/ *adv. archaic* as a result of this.

hereby /hɪəˈbaɪ/ *adv.* by this means; as a result of this.

hereditable /hɪˈredɪtəb(ə)l/ *adj.* that can be inherited. [obs. F *héréditable* or med.L *hereditabilis* f. eccl.L *hereditare* f. L *heres -edis* heir]

hereditament /ˌherɪˈdɪtəmənt, hɪˈredɪ-/ *n. Law* **1** any property that can be inherited. **2** inheritance. [med.L *hereditamentum* (as HEREDITABLE)]

hereditary /hɪˈredɪtərɪ/ *adj.* **1** (of disease, instinct, etc.) able to be passed down from one generation to another. **2 a** descending by inheritance. **b** holding a position by inheritance. **3** the same as or resembling what one's parents had (*a hereditary hatred*). **4** of or relating to inheritance. □□ **hereditarily** *adv.* **hereditariness** *n.* [L *hereditarius* (as HEREDITY)]

heredity /hɪˈredɪtɪ/ *n.* **1 a** the passing on of physical or mental characteristics genetically from one generation to another. **b** these characteristics. **2** the genetic constitution of an individual. [F *hérédité* or L *hereditas* heirship (as HEIR)]

Hereford /ˈherɪfəd/ *n.* **1** an animal of a breed of red and white beef cattle. **2** this breed. [*Hereford* in England, where it originated]

herein /hɪəˈrɪn/ *adv. formal* in this matter, book, etc.

hereinafter /ˌhɪərɪnˈɑːftə(r)/ *adv.* esp. *Law formal* in a later part of this document etc.

hereinbefore /ˌhɪərɪnbɪˈfɔː(r)/ *adv.* esp. *Law formal* in a preceding part of this document etc.

hereof /hɪərˈɒv/ *adv. formal* of this.

heresiarch /heˈriːzɪˌɑːk/ *n.* the leader or founder of a heresy. [eccl.L *haeresiarcha* f. Gk *hairesiarkhēs* (as HERESY + *arkhēs* ruler)]

heresy /ˈherəsɪ/ *n.* (*pl.* -**ies**) **1 a** belief or practice contrary to the orthodox doctrine of the Christian Church. **b** an instance of this. **2 a** opinion contrary to what is normally accepted or maintained (*it's heresy to suggest that instant coffee is as good as the real thing*). **b** an instance of this. □□ **heresiology** /ˌherɪsɪˈɒlədʒɪ/ *n.* [ME f. OF (*h*)*eresie* f. eccl.L *haeresis*, in L = school of thought, f. Gk *hairesis* choice, sect f. *haireomai* choose]

heretic /ˈherətɪk/ *n.* **1** the holder of an unorthodox opinion. **2** *hist.* a person believing in or practising religious heresy. □□ **heretical** /hɪˈretɪk(ə)l/ *adj.* **heretically** /hɪˈretɪkəlɪ/ *adv.* [ME f. OF *heretique* f. eccl.L *haereticus* f. Gk *hairetikos* able to choose (as HERESY)]

hereto /hɪəˈtuː/ *adv. formal* to this matter.

heretofore /ˌhɪətʊˈfɔː(r)/ *adv. formal* before this time.

hereunder /hɪərˈʌndə(r)/ *adv. formal* below (in a book, legal document, etc.).

hereunto /ˌhɪərʌnˈtuː/ *adv. archaic* to this.

hereupon /ˌhɪərəˈpɒn/ *adv.* after this; in consequence of this.

herewith /hɪəˈwɪð, -ˈwɪθ/ *adv.* with this (esp. of an enclosure in a letter etc.).

heriot /ˈherɪət/ *n. Brit. hist.* a tribute paid to a lord on the death of a tenant, consisting of a live animal, a chattel, or, orig., the return of borrowed equipment. [OE *heregeatwa* f. *here* army + *geatwa* trappings]

heritable /ˈherɪtəb(ə)l/ *adj.* **1** *Law* **a** (of property)

capable of being inherited by heirs-at-law (cf. MOVABLE). **b** capable of inheriting. **2** *Biol.* (of a characteristic) transmissible from parent to offspring. □□ **heritability** /-ˈbɪlɪtɪ/ *n.* **heritably** *adv.* [ME f. OF f. *heriter* f. eccl.L *hereditare*: see HEREDITABLE]

heritage /ˈherɪtɪdʒ/ *n.* **1** anything that is or may be inherited. **2** inherited circumstances, benefits, etc. (*a heritage of confusion*). **3** a nation's historic buildings, monuments, countryside, etc., esp. when regarded as worthy of preservation. **4** *Bibl.* **a** the ancient Israelites. **b** the Church. [ME f. OF (as HERITABLE)]

heritor /ˈherɪtə(r)/ *n.* (esp. in Scottish Law) a person who inherits. [ME f. AF *heriter*, OF *heritier* (as HEREDITARY), assim. to words in -OR[1]]

herl var. of HARL.

herm /hɜːm/ *n. Gk Antiq.* a squared stone pillar with a head (esp. of Hermes) on top, used as a boundary-marker etc. (cf. TERMINUS 6). [L *Herma* f. Gk *Hermēs* messenger of the gods]

hermaphrodite /hɜːˈmæfrəˌdaɪt/ *n. & adj.* —*n.* **1 a** *Zool.* an animal having both male and female sexual organs. **b** *Bot.* a plant having stamens and pistils in the same flower. **2** a human being in which both male and female sex organs are present, or in which the sex organs contain both ovarian and testicular tissue. **3** a person or thing combining opposite qualities or characteristics. —*adj.* **1** combining both sexes. **2** combining opposite qualities or characteristics. □**hermaphrodite brig** *hist.* a two-masted sailing ship rigged on the foremast as a brig and on the mainmast as a schooner. □□ **hermaphroditic** /-ˈdɪtɪk/ *adj.* **hermaphroditical** /-ˈdɪtɪk(ə)l/ *adj.* **hermaphroditism** *n.* [L *hermaphroditus* f. Gk *hermaphroditos*, orig. the name of a son of Hermes and Aphrodite in Greek mythology, who became joined in one body with the nymph Salmacis]

hermeneutic /ˌhɜːmɪˈnjuːtɪk/ *adj.* concerning interpretation, esp. of Scripture or literary texts. □□ **hermeneutical** *adj.* **hermeneutically** *adv.* [Gk *hermēneutikos* f. *hermēneuō* interpret]

hermeneutics /ˌhɜːmɪˈnjuːtɪks/ *n.pl.* (also treated as *sing.*) *Bibl.* interpretation, esp. of Scripture or literary texts.

hermetic /hɜːˈmetɪk/ *adj.* (also **hermetical**) **1** with an airtight closure. **2** protected from outside agencies. **3 a** of alchemy or other occult sciences (*hermetic art*). **b** esoteric. □**hermetic seal** an airtight seal (orig. as used by alchemists). □□ **hermetically** *adv.* **hermetism** /ˈhɜːmɪˌtɪz(ə)m/ *n.* [mod.L *hermeticus* irreg. f. *Hermes Trismegistus* thrice-greatest Hermes (as the founder of alchemy)]

hermit /ˈhɜːmɪt/ *n.* **1** an early Christian recluse. **2** any person living in solitude. □**hermit-crab** any crab of the family Paguridae that lives in a cast-off mollusc shell for protection. **hermit thrush** a migratory N. American thrush, *Catharus guttatus*. □□ **hermitic** /-ˈmɪtɪk/ *adj.* [ME f. OF (*h*)*ermite* or f. LL *eremita* f. Gk *erēmitēs* f. *erēmia* desert f. *erēmos* solitary]

hermitage /ˈhɜːmɪtɪdʒ/ *n.* **1** a hermit's dwelling. **2** a monastery. **3** a solitary dwelling. [ME f. OF (*h*)*ermitage* (as HERMIT)]

hernia /ˈhɜːnɪə/ *n.* (*pl.* **hernias** or **herniae** /-nɪˌiː/) the displacement and protrusion of part of an organ through the wall of the cavity containing it, esp. of the abdomen. □□ **hernial** *adj.* **herniary** *adj.* **herniated** *adj.* [L]

hero /ˈhɪərəʊ/ *n.* (*pl.* -**oes**) **1 a** a man noted or admired for nobility, courage, outstanding achievements, etc. (*Newton, a hero of science*). **b** a great warrior. **2** the chief male character in a poem, play, story, etc. **3** *Gk Antiq.* a man of superhuman qualities, favoured by the gods; a demigod. □**hero's welcome** a rapturous welcome, like that given to a successful warrior. **hero-worship** *n.* **1** idealization of an admired man. **2** *Gk Antiq.* worship of the ancient heroes. —*v.tr.* (-**worshipped**, -**worshipping**; *US* -**worshiped**,

-worshiping) worship as a hero; idolize. **hero-worshipper** a person engaging in hero-worship. [ME f. L *heros* f. Gk *hērōs*]

heroic /hɪˈrəʊɪk/ *adj.* & *n.* —*adj.* **1 a** (of an act or a quality) of or fit for a hero. **b** (of a person) like a hero. **2 a** (of language) grand, high-flown, dramatic. **b** (of a work of art) heroic in scale or subject. **3** (of poetry) dealing with the ancient heroes. —*n.* (in *pl.*) **1 a** high-flown language or sentiments. **b** unduly bold behaviour. **2** = *heroic verse*. □**the heroic age** the period in Greek history before the return from Troy. **heroic couplet** two lines of rhyming iambic pentameters. **heroic verse** a type of verse used for heroic poetry, esp. the hexameter, the iambic pentameter, or the alexandrine. □□**heroically** *adv.* [F *héroïque* or L *heroicus* f. Gk *hērōikos* (as HERO)]

heroi-comic /ˌhɪrəʊɪˈkɒmɪk/ *adj.* (also **heroi-comical**) combining the heroic with the comic. [F *héroï-comique* (as HERO, COMIC)]

heroin /ˈherəʊɪn/ *n.* a highly addictive white crystalline analgesic drug derived from morphine, often used as a narcotic. [G (as HERO, from its effects on the user's self-esteem)]

heroine /ˈherəʊɪn/ *n.* **1** a woman noted or admired for nobility, courage, outstanding achievements, etc. **2** the chief female character in a poem, play, story, etc. **3** *Gk Antiq.* a demigoddess. [F *héroïne* or L *heroina* f. Gk *hērōinē*, fem. of *hērōs* HERO]

heroism /ˈherəʊˌɪz(ə)m/ *n.* heroic conduct or qualities. [F *héroïsme* f. *héros* HERO]

heroize /ˈherəʊˌaɪz/ *v.* (also **-ise**) **1** *tr.* **a** make a hero of. **b** make heroic. **2** *intr.* play the hero.

heron /ˈherən/ *n.* any of various large wading birds of the family Ardeidae, esp. *Ardea cinerea*, with long legs and a long S-shaped neck. □□**heronry** *n.* (*pl.* **-ies**). [ME f. OF *hairon* f. Gmc]

herpes /ˈhɜːpiːz/ *n.* a virus disease with outbreaks of blisters on the skin etc. □**herpes simplex** a viral infection which may produce blisters or conjunctivitis. **herpes zoster** /ˈzɒstə(r)/ = SHINGLES. □□**herpetic** /-ˈpetɪk/ *adj.* [ME f. L f. Gk *herpēs -ētos* shingles f. *herpō* creep: *zoster* f. Gk *zōstēr* belt, girdle]

herpetology /ˌhɜːpɪˈtɒlədʒɪ/ *n.* the study of reptiles. □□**herpetological** /-tə'lɒdʒɪk(ə)l/ *adj.* **herpetologist** *n.* [Gk *herpeton* reptile f. *herpō* creep]

Herr /heə(r)/ *n.* (*pl.* **Herren** /ˈherən/) **1** the title of a German man; Mr. **2** a German man. [G f. OHG *hērro* compar. of *hēr* exalted]

Herrenvolk /ˈherənˌfɒlk, -ˌfəʊk/ *n.* **1** the German nation characterized by the Nazis as born to mastery. **2** a group regarding itself as naturally superior. [G, = master-race (as HERR, FOLK)]

herring /ˈherɪŋ/ *n.* a N. Atlantic fish, *Clupea harengus*, coming near the coast in large shoals to spawn. □**herring-gull** a large gull, *Larus argentatus*, with dark wing-tips. [OE *hæring, hēring* f. WG]

herring-bone /ˈherɪŋˌbəʊn/ *n.* & *v.* —*n.* **1** a stitch with a zigzag pattern, resembling the pattern of a herring's bones. **2** this pattern, or cloth woven in it. **3** any zigzag pattern, e.g. in building. **4** *Skiing* a method of ascending a slope with the skis pointing outwards. —*v.* **1** *tr.* **a** work with a herring-bone stitch. **b** mark with a herring-bone pattern. **2** *intr. Skiing* ascend a slope using the herring-bone technique.

Herrnhuter /ˈheənˌhuːtə(r), ˈherən-/ *n.* a member of a Christian Moravian sect (see MORAVIAN). [G f. *Herrnhut* (= the Lord's keeping), name of their first German settlement]

hers /hɜːz/ *poss.pron.* the one or ones belonging to or associated with her (*it is hers; hers are over there*). □**of hers** of or belonging to her (*a friend of hers*).

herself /həˈself/ *pron.* **1 a** *emphat. form* of SHE or HER (*she herself will do it*). **b** *refl. form* of HER (*she has hurt herself*). **2** in her normal state of body or mind (*does not feel quite herself today*). □**be herself** act in her normal unconstrained manner. **by herself** see *by oneself*. [OE *hire self* (as HER, SELF)]

Herts. /hɑːts/ *abbr.* Hertfordshire.

hertz /hɜːts/ *n.* (*pl.* same) the SI unit of frequency, equal to one cycle per second. ¶ Abbr.: **Hz**. [H. R. *Hertz*, Ger. physicist d. 1894]

Hertzian wave /ˈhɜːtsɪən/ *n.* an electromagnetic wave of a length suitable for use in radio.

he's /hiːz, hɪz/ *contr.* **1** he is. **2** he has.

hesitant /ˈhezɪt(ə)nt/ *adj.* hesitating; irresolute. □□**hesitance** *n.* **hesitancy** *n.* **hesitantly** *adv.*

hesitate /ˈhezɪˌteɪt/ *v.intr.* **1** (often foll. by *about, over*) show or feel indecision or uncertainty; pause in doubt (*hesitated over her choice*). **2** (often foll. by *to* + infin.) be deterred by scruples; be reluctant (*I hesitate to inform against him*). □□**hesitater** *n.* **hesitatingly** *adv.* **hesitation** /-ˈteɪʃ(ə)n/ *n.* **hesitative** *adj.* [L *haesitare* frequent. of *haerēre haes-* stick fast]

Hesperian /heˈspɪərɪən/ *adj. poet.* **1** western. **2** (in Greek mythology) of or concerning the Hesperides (nymphs who guarded the garden of golden apples at the western extremity of the earth). [L *Hesperius* f. Gk *Hesperios* (as HESPERUS)]

hesperidium /ˌhespəˈrɪdɪəm/ *n.* (*pl.* **hesperidia** /-dɪə/) a fruit with sectioned pulp inside a separable rind, e.g. an orange or grapefruit. [Gk *Hesperides* daughters of Hesperus, nymphs in Greek mythology who guarded a tree of golden apples]

Hesperus /ˈhespərəs/ *n.* the evening star, Venus. [ME f. L f. Gk *hesperos* (adj. & n.) western, evening (star)]

hessian /ˈhesɪən/ *n.* & *adj.* —*n.* **1** a strong coarse sacking made of hemp or jute. **2** (**Hessian**) a native of Hesse in Germany. —*adj.* (**Hessian**) of or concerning Hesse. □**Hessian boot** a tasselled high boot first worn by Hessian troops. **Hessian fly** a midge, *Mayetiola destructor*, whose larva destroys growing wheat (thought to have been brought to America by Hessian troops). [*Hesse* in Germany]

hest /hest/ *n. archaic* behest. [OE *hæs* (see HIGHT), assim. to ME nouns in *-t*]

hetaera /hɪˈtɪərə/ *n.* (also **hetaira** /-ˈtaɪrə/) (*pl.* **-as, hetaerae** /-ˈtɪəriː/, or **hetairai** /-ˈtaɪraɪ/) a courtesan or mistress, esp. in ancient Greece. [Gk *hetaira*, fem. of *hetairos* companion]

hetaerism /hɪˈtɪərɪzəm/ *n.* (also **hetairism** /-ˈtaɪrɪzəm/) **1** a recognized system of concubinage. **2** communal marriage in a tribe. [Gk *hetairismos* prostitution (as HETAERA)]

hetero /ˈhetərəʊ/ *n.* (*pl.* **-os**) *colloq.* a heterosexual. [abbr.]

hetero- /ˈhetərəʊ/ *comb. form* other, different (often opp. HOMO-). [Gk *heteros* other]

heterochromatic /ˌhetərəʊkrəˈmætɪk/ *adj.* of several colours.

heteroclite /ˈhetərəʊˌklaɪt/ *adj.* & *n.* —*adj.* **1** abnormal. **2** *Gram.* (esp. of a noun) irregularly declined. —*n.* **1** an abnormal thing or person. **2** *Gram.* an irregularly declined word, esp. a noun. [LL *heteroclitus* f. Gk (as HETERO-, *klitos* f. *klinō* bend, inflect)]

heterocyclic /ˌhetərəʊˈsaɪklɪk, -ˈsɪklɪk/ *adj. Chem.* (of a compound) with a bonded ring of atoms of more than one kind.

heterodox /ˈhetərəʊˌdɒks/ *adj.* (of a person, opinion, etc.) not orthodox. □□**heterodoxy** *n.* [LL *heterodoxus* f. Gk (as HETERO-, *doxos* f. *doxa* opinion)]

heterodyne /ˈhetərəʊˌdaɪn/ *adj.* & *v. Radio* —*adj.* relating to the production of a lower frequency from the combination of two almost equal high frequencies. —*v.intr.* produce a lower frequency in this way.

heterogamous /ˌhetəˈrɒɡəməs/ *adj.* **1** *Bot.* irregular as regards stamens and pistils. **2** *Biol.* characterized by heterogamy or heterogony.

heterogamy /ˌhetəˈrɒɡəmɪ/ *n.* **1** the alternation of generations, esp. of a sexual and parthenogenic generation. **2** sexual reproduction by fusion of unlike gametes. **3** *Bot.* a state in which the flowers of a plant are of two types.

heterogeneous /ˌhetərəʊ'dʒiːnɪəs/ *adj.* **1** diverse in character. **2** varied in content. **3** *Math.* incommensurable through being of different kinds or degrees. □□ **heterogeneity** /-dʒɪ'niːɪtɪ/ *n.* **heterogeneously** *adv.* **heterogeneousness** *n.* [med.L *heterogeneus* f. Gk *heterogenēs* (as HETERO-, *genos* kind)]

heterogenesis /ˌhetərəʊ'dʒenɪsɪs/ *n.* **1** the birth of a living being otherwise than from parents of the same kind. **2** spontaneous generation from inorganic matter. □□ **heterogenetic** /-dʒɪ'netɪk/ *adj.*

heterogony /ˌhetə'rɒgənɪ/ *n.* the alternation of generations, esp. of a sexual and hermaphroditic generation. □□ **heterogonous** *adj.*

heterograft /'hetərəʊˌgrɑːft/ *n.* living tissue grafted from one individual to another of a different species.

heterologous /ˌhetə'rɒləgəs/ *adj.* not homologous. □□ **heterology** *n.*

heteromerous /ˌhetə'rɒmərəs/ *adj.* not isomerous.

heteromorphic /ˌhetərəʊ'mɔːfɪk/ *adj.* (also **heteromorphous** /-'mɔːfəs/) *Biol.* **1** of dissimilar forms. **2** (of insects) existing in different forms at different stages in their life cycle.

heteromorphism /ˌhetərəʊ'mɔːfɪz(ə)m/ *n.* existing in various forms.

heteronomous /ˌhetə'rɒnəməs/ *adj.* **1** subject to an external law (cf. AUTONOMOUS). **2** *Biol.* subject to different laws (of growth etc.).

heteronomy /ˌhetə'rɒnəmɪ/ *n.* **1** the presence of a different law. **2** subjection to an external law.

heteropathic /ˌhetərəʊ'pæθɪk/ *adj.* **1** allopathic. **2** differing in effect.

heterophyllous /ˌhetərəʊ'fɪləs/ *adj.* bearing leaves of different forms on the same plant. □□ **heterophylly** *n.* [HETERO- + Gk *phullon* leaf]

heteropolar /ˌhetərəʊ'pəʊlə(r)/ *adj.* having dissimilar poles, esp. *Electr.* with an armature passing north and south magnetic poles alternately.

heteropteran /ˌhetə'rɒptərən/ *n.* any insect of the suborder Heteroptera, including bugs, with non-uniform fore-wings having a thickened base and membranous tip (cf. HOMOPTERAN). □□ **heteropterous** *adj.* [HETERO- + Gk *pteron* wing]

heterosexual /ˌhetərəʊ'seksjʊəl/ *adj.* & *n.* —*adj.* **1** feeling or involving sexual attraction to persons of the opposite sex. **2** concerning heterosexual relations or people. **3** relating to the opposite sex. —*n.* a heterosexual person. □□ **heterosexuality** /-'ælɪtɪ/ *n.* **heterosexually** *adv.*

heterosis /ˌhetə'rəʊsɪs/ *n.* the tendency of a cross-bred individual to show qualities superior to those of both parents. [Gk f. *heteros* different]

heterotaxy /'hetərəʊˌtæksɪ/ *n.* the abnormal disposition of organs or parts. [HETERO- + Gk *taxis* arrangement]

heterotransplant /ˌhetərəʊ'trænsplɑːnt/ *n.* = HETEROGRAFT.

heterotrophic /ˌhetərəʊ'trɒfɪk/ *adj.* *Biol.* deriving its nourishment and carbon requirements from organic substances; not autotrophic. [HETERO- + Gk *trophos* feeder]

heterozygote /ˌhetərəʊ'zaɪgəʊt/ *n.* *Biol.* **1** a zygote resulting from the fusion of unlike gametes. **2** an individual with dominant and recessive alleles determining a particular characteristic. □□ **heterozygous** *adj.*

hetman /'hetmən/ *n.* (*pl.* **-men**) a Polish or Cossack military commander. [Pol., prob. f. G *Hauptmann* captain]

het up /het ʌp/ *adj.* *colloq.* excited, overwrought. [*het* dial. past part. of HEAT]

heuchera /'hjuːkərə, 'hɔɪk-/ *n.* any N. American herbaceous plant of the genus *Heuchera*, with dark-green round or heart-shaped leaves and tiny flowers. [mod.L f. J. H. von *Heucher*, Ger. botanist d. 1747]

heuristic /hjʊə'rɪstɪk/ *adj.* & *n.* —*adj.* **1** allowing or

assisting to discover. **2** *Computing* proceeding to a solution by trial and error. —*n.* **1** the science of heuristic procedure. **2** a heuristic process or method. **3** (in *pl.*, usu. treated as *sing.*) *Computing* the study and use of heuristic techniques in data processing. □ **heuristic method** a system of education under which pupils are trained to find out things for themselves. □□ **heuristically** *adv.* [irreg. f. Gk *heuriskō* find]

hevea /'hiːvɪə/ *n.* any S. American tree of the genus *Hevea*, yielding a milky sap used for making rubber. [mod.L f. native name *hevé*]

HEW *abbr.* US Department of Health, Education, and Welfare.

hew /hjuː/ *v.* (*past part.* **hewn** /hjuːn/ or **hewed**) **1** *tr.* **a** (often foll. by *down*, *away*, *off*) chop or cut (a thing) with an axe, a sword, etc. **b** cut (a block of wood etc.) into shape. **2** *intr.* (often foll. by *at*, *among*, etc.) strike cutting blows. **3** *intr.* US (usu. foll. by *to*) conform. □ **hew one's way** make a way for oneself by hewing. [OE *hēawan* f. Gmc]

hewer /'hjuː.ə(r)/ *n.* **1** a person who hews. **2** a person who cuts coal from a seam. □ **hewers of wood and drawers of water** menial drudges; labourers (Josh. 9:21).

hex /heks/ *v.* & *n.* US —*v.* **1** *intr.* practise witchcraft. **2** *tr.* bewitch. —*n.* **1** a magic spell. **2** a witch. [Pennsylvanian G *hexe* (v.), *Hex* (n.), f. G *hexen*, *Hexe*]

hexa- /'heksə/ *comb. form* six. [Gk *hex* six]

hexachord /'heksəˌkɔːd/ *n.* a diatonic series of six notes with a semitone between the third and fourth, used at three different pitches in medieval music. [HEXA- + CHORD[1]]

hexad /'heksæd/ *n.* a group of six. [Gk *hexas -ados* f. *hex* six]

hexadecimal /ˌheksə'desɪm(ə)l/ *adj.* & *n.* esp. *Computing.* —*adj.* relating to or using a system of numerical notation that has 16 rather than 10 as a base. —*n.* the hexadecimal system; hexadecimal notation. □□ **hexadecimally** *adv.*

hexagon /'heksəgən/ *n.* a plane figure with six sides and angles. □□ **hexagonal** /-'sægən(ə)l/ *adj.* [LL *hexagonum* f. Gk (as HEXA-, -GON)]

hexagram /'heksəˌgræm/ *n.* **1** a figure formed by two intersecting equilateral triangles. **2** a figure of six lines. [HEXA- + Gk *gramma* line]

hexahedron /ˌheksə'hiːdrən/ *n.* a solid figure with six faces. □□ **hexahedral** *adj.* [Gk (as HEXA-, -HEDRON)]

hexameter /hek'sæmɪtə(r)/ *n.* a line or verse of six metrical feet. □ **dactylic hexameter** a hexameter having five dactyls and a spondee or trochee, any of the first four feet, and sometimes the fifth, being replaceable by a spondee. □□ **hexametric** /-sə'metrɪk/ *adj.* **hexametrist** *n.* [ME f. L f. Gk *hexametros* (as HEXA-, *metron* measure)]

hexane /'hekseɪn/ *n.* *Chem.* a liquid hydrocarbon of the alkane series. ¶ *Chem.* formula: C_6H_{14}. [HEXA- + -ANE]

hexapla /'heksəplə/ *n.* a sixfold text, esp. of the Old Testament, in parallel columns. [Gk neut. pl. of *hexaploos* (as HEXA-, *ploos* -fold), orig. of Origen's OT text]

hexapod /'heksəˌpɒd/ *n.* & *adj.* —*n.* any arthropod with six legs; an insect. —*adj.* having six legs. [Gk *hexapous, hexapod-* (as HEXA-, *pous pod-* foot)]

hexastyle /'heksəˌstaɪl/ *n.* & *adj.* —*n.* a six-columned portico. —*adj.* having six columns. [Gk *hexastulos* (as HEXA-, *stulos* column)]

Hexateuch /'heksəˌtjuːk/ *n.* the first six books of the Old Testament. [Gk *hex* six + *teukhos* book]

hexavalent /ˌheksə'veɪlənt/ *adj.* having a valency of six; sexivalent.

hexose /'heksəʊz/ *n.* *Biochem.* a monosaccharide with six carbon atoms in each molecule, e.g. glucose or fructose. [HEXA- + -OSE[2]]

hey[1] /heɪ/ *int.* calling attention or expressing joy, surprise, inquiry, enthusiasm, etc. □ **hey presto!** a phrase of command, or indicating a successful trick, used by a conjuror etc. [ME: cf. OF *hay*, Du., G *hei*]

hey[2] var. of HAY[2].

heyday /'heɪdeɪ/ *n.* the flush or full bloom of youth, vigour, prosperity, etc. [archaic *heyday* expression of joy, surprise, etc.: cf. LG *heidi, heida*, excl. denoting gaiety]

HF *abbr.* high frequency.

Hf *symb. Chem.* the element hafnium.

hf. *abbr.* half.

HG *abbr.* 1 Her or His Grace. 2 Home Guard.

Hg *symb. Chem.* the element mercury.

hg *abbr.* hectogram(s).

HGV *abbr. Brit.* heavy goods vehicle.

HH *abbr.* 1 Her or His Highness. 2 His Holiness. 3 double-hard (pencil-lead).

hh. *abbr.* hands (see HAND *n.* 13).

hhd. *abbr.* hogshead(s).

H-hour /'eɪtʃ‚aʊə(r)/ *n.* the hour at which an operation is scheduled to begin. [*H* for *hour* + HOUR]

HI *abbr. US* 1 Hawaii (also in official postal use). 2 the Hawaiian Islands.

hi /haɪ/ *int.* calling attention or as a greeting. [parallel form to HEY[1]]

hiatus /haɪ'eɪtəs/ *n. (pl.* **hiatuses**) 1 a break or gap, esp. in a series, account, or chain of proof. 2 *Prosody & Gram.* a break between two vowels coming together but not in the same syllable, as in *though oft the ear.* □□ **hiatal** *adj.* [L, = gaping f. *hiare* gape]

hibernate /'haɪbəneɪt/ *v.intr.* 1 (of some animals) spend the winter in a dormant state. 2 remain inactive. □□ **hibernation** /-'neɪʃ(ə)n/ *n.* **hibernator** *n.* [L *hibernare* f. *hibernus* wintry]

Hibernian /haɪ'bɜːnɪən/ *adj. & n. archaic poet.* —*adj.* of or concerning Ireland. —*n.* a native of Ireland. [L *Hibernia, Iverna* f. Gk *Iernē* f. OCelt.]

Hibernicism /haɪ'bɜːnɪ‚sɪz(ə)m/ *n.* an Irish idiom or expression; = BULL[3] 1. [as HIBERNIAN after *Anglicism* etc.]

Hiberno- /haɪ'bɜːnəʊ/ *comb. form* Irish (*Hiberno-British*). [med.L *hibernus* Irish (as HIBERNIAN)]

hibiscus /hɪ'bɪskəs/ *n.* any tree or shrub of the genus *Hibiscus*, cultivated for its large bright-coloured flowers. Also called *rose-mallow*. [L f. Gk *hibiskos* marsh mallow]

hic /hɪk/ *int.* expressing the sound of a hiccup, esp. a drunken hiccup. [imit.]

hiccup /'hɪkʌp/ *n. & v.* (also **hiccough**) —*n.* 1 a an involuntary spasm of the diaphragm and respiratory organs, with sudden closure of the glottis and characteristic coughlike sound. b (in *pl.*) an attack of such spasms. 2 a temporary or minor stoppage or difficulty. —*v.* 1 *intr.* make a hiccup or series of hiccups. 2 *tr.* utter with a hiccup. □□ **hiccupy** *adj.* [imit.]

hic jacet /hɪk 'dʒeɪset, hiːk 'jæket/ *n.* an epitaph. [L, = here lies]

hick /hɪk/ *n. esp. US colloq.* a country dweller; a provincial. [pet-form of the name *Richard*: cf. DICK[1]]

hickey /'hɪkɪ/ *n. (pl.* **-eys**) *US colloq.* a gadget (cf. DOOHICKEY). [20th c.: orig. unkn.]

hickory /'hɪkərɪ/ *n. (pl.* **-ies**) 1 any N. American tree of the genus *Carya*, yielding tough heavy wood and bearing nutlike edible fruits (see PECAN). 2 a the wood of these trees. b a stick made of this. [native Virginian *pohickery*]

hid *past* of HIDE[1].

hidalgo /hɪ'dælgəʊ/ *n. (pl.* **-os**) a Spanish gentleman. [Sp. f. *hijo dalgo* son of something]

hidden *past part.* of HIDE[1]. □□ **hiddenness** *n.*

hide[1] /haɪd/ *v. & n.* —*v.* (*past* hid; *past part.* hidden /'hɪd(ə)n/ or *archaic* hid) 1 *tr.* put or keep out of sight (*hid it under the cushion; hid her in the cupboard*). 2 *intr.* conceal oneself. 3 *tr.* (usu. foll. by *from*) keep (a fact) secret (*hid his real motive from her*). 4 *tr.* conceal (a thing) from sight intentionally or not (*trees hid the house*). —*n. Brit.* a camouflaged shelter used for observing wildlife or hunting

animals. □ **hidden reserves** extra profits, resources, etc. kept concealed in reserve. **hide-and-seek** 1 a children's game in which one or more players seek a child or children hiding. 2 a process of attempting to find an evasive person or thing. **hide one's head** keep out of sight, esp. from shame. **hide one's light under a bushel** conceal one's merits (Matthew 5:15). **hide out** (or **up**) remain in concealment. **hide-out** *colloq.* a hiding-place. **hidey-** (or **hidy-**) **hole** *colloq.* a hiding-place. □□ **hider** *n.* [OE *hȳdan* f. WG]

hide[2] /haɪd/ *n. & v.* —*n.* 1 the skin of an animal, esp. when tanned or dressed. 2 *colloq.* the human skin (*saved his own hide; I'll tan your hide*). —*v.tr. colloq.* flog. □□ **hided** *adj.* (also in *comb.*). [OE *hȳd* f. Gmc]

hide[3] /haɪd/ *n.* a former measure of land large enough to support a family and its dependants, usu. between 60 and 120 acres. [OE *hī(gi)d* f. *hīw-, hīg-* household]

hideaway /'haɪdə‚weɪ/ *n.* a hiding-place or place of retreat.

hidebound /'haɪdbaʊnd/ *adj.* 1 a narrow-minded; bigoted. b (of the law, rules, etc.) constricted by tradition. 2 (of cattle) with the skin clinging close as a result of bad feeding. [HIDE[2] + BOUND[4]]

hideosity /‚hɪdɪ'ɒsɪtɪ/ *n. (pl.* **-ies**) 1 a hideous object. 2 hideousness.

hideous /'hɪdɪəs/ *adj.* 1 frightful, repulsive, or revolting, to the senses or the mind (*a hideous monster; a hideous pattern*). 2 *colloq.* unpleasant. □□ **hideously** *adv.* **hideousness** *n.* [ME *hidous* f. AF *hidous*, OF *hidos, -eus*, f. OF *hide, hisde* fear, of unkn. orig.]

hiding[1] /'haɪdɪŋ/ *n. colloq.* a thrashing. □**on a hiding to nothing** in a position from which there can be no successful outcome. [HIDE[2] + -ING[1]]

hiding[2] /'haɪdɪŋ/ *n.* 1 the act or an instance of hiding. 2 the state of remaining hidden (*go into hiding*). □ **hiding-place** a place of concealment. [ME, f. HIDE[1] + -ING[1]]

hidrosis /hɪ'drəʊsɪs, haɪ-/ *n. Med.* perspiration. □□ **hidrotic** /-'drɒtɪk/ *adj.* [mod.L f. Gk f. *hidrōs* sweat]

hie /haɪ/ *v.intr. & refl.* (**hies, hied, hieing** or **hying**) *archaic or poet.* go quickly (*hie to your chamber; hied him to the chase*). [OE *hīgian* strive, pant, of unkn. orig.]

hierarch /'haɪə‚rɑːk/ *n.* 1 a chief priest. 2 an archbishop. □□ **hierarchal** /-'rɑːk(ə)l/ *adj.* [med.L f. Gk *hierarkhēs* f. *hieros* sacred + -*arkhēs* ruler]

hierarchy /'haɪə‚rɑːkɪ/ *n. (pl.* **-ies**) 1 a a system in which grades or classes of status or authority are ranked one above the other (*ranks third in the hierarchy*). b the hierarchical system (of government, management, etc.). 2 a priestly government. b a priesthood organized in grades. 3 a each of the three divisions of angels. b the angels. □□ **hierarchic** /-'rɑːkɪk/ *adj.* **hierarchical** /-'rɑːkɪk(ə)l/ *adj.* **hierarchism** *n.* **hierarchize** *v.tr.* (also **-ise**). [ME f. OF *ierarchie* f. med.L (*h*)*ierarchia* f. Gk *hierarkhia* (as HIERARCH)]

hieratic /‚haɪə'rætɪk/ *adj.* 1 of or concerning priests. 2 of the ancient Egyptian writing of abridged hieroglyphics as used by priests (opp. DEMOTIC). 3 of or concerning Egyptian or Greek traditional styles of art. 4 priestly. □□ **hieratically** *adv.* [L f. Gk *hieratikos* f. *hieraomai* be a priest f. *hiereus* priest]

hiero- /'haɪərəʊ/ *comb. form* sacred, holy. [Gk *hieros* sacred + -o-]

hierocracy /‚haɪə'rɒkrəsɪ/ *n. (pl.* **-ies**) 1 priestly rule. 2 a body of ruling priests. [HIERO- + -CRACY]

hieroglyph /'haɪərəglɪf/ *n.* 1 a a picture of an object representing a word, syllable, or sound, as used in ancient Egyptian and other writing. b a writing consisting of characters of this kind. 2 a secret or enigmatic symbol. 3 (in *pl.*) *joc.* writing difficult to read. [back-form. f. HIEROGLYPHIC]

hieroglyphic /‚haɪərə'glɪfɪk/ *adj. & n.* —*adj.* 1 of or written in hieroglyphs. 2 symbolical. —*n.* (in *pl.*) hieroglyphs; hieroglyphic writing. □□ **hieroglyphical** *adj.* **hieroglyphically** *adv.* [F *hiéroglyphique* or LL *hieroglyphicus* f. Gk *hiero-glyphikos* (as HIERO-, *gluphikos* f. *gluphē* carving)]

hierogram /'haɪərəʊˌgræm/ *n.* a sacred inscription or symbol.

hierograph /'haɪərəʊˌgrɑːf/ *n.* = HIEROGRAM.

hierolatry /ˌhaɪə'rɒlətrɪ/ *n.* the worship of saints or sacred things.

hierology /ˌhaɪə'rɒlədʒɪ/ *n.* sacred literature or lore.

hierophant /'haɪərəˌfænt/ *n.* **1** *Gk Antiq.* an initiating or presiding priest; an official interpreter of sacred mysteries. **2** an interpreter of sacred mysteries or any esoteric principle. □□ **hierophantic** /-'fæntɪk/ *adj.* [LL *hierophantes* f. Gk *hierophantēs* (as HIERO-, *phantēs* f. *phainō* show)]

hi-fi /'haɪfaɪ/ *adj. & n. colloq.* —*adj.* = *high fidelity.* —*n.* (*pl.* **hi-fis**) a set of equipment for high-fidelity sound reproduction. [abbr.]

higgle /'hɪg(ə)l/ *v.intr.* dispute about terms; haggle. [var. of HAGGLE]

higgledy-piggledy /ˌhɪgəldɪ'pɪgəldɪ/ *adv., adj., & n.* —*adv. & adj.* in confusion or disorder. —*n.* a state of disordered confusion. [rhyming jingle, prob. with ref. to the irregular herding together of pigs]

high /haɪ/ *adj., n., & adv.* —*adj.* **1 a** of great vertical extent (*a high building*). **b** (*predic.*; often in *comb.*) of a specified height (*one inch high; water was waist-high*). **2 a** far above ground or sea level etc. (*a high altitude*). **b** inland, esp. when raised (*High Asia*). **3** extending above the normal or average level (*high boots; jersey with a high neck*). **4** of exalted, esp. spiritual, quality (*high minds; high principles; high art*). **5** of exalted rank (*in high society; is high in the Government*). **6 a** great; intense; extreme; powerful (*high praise; high temperature*). **b** greater than normal (*high prices*). **c** extreme in religious or political opinion (*high Tory*). **7** (of physical action, esp. athletics) performed at, to, or from a considerable height (*high diving; high flying*). **8** *colloq.* (often foll. by *on*) intoxicated by alcohol or esp. drugs. **9** (of a sound or note) of high frequency; shrill; at the top end of the scale. **10** (of a period, an age, a time, etc.) at its peak (*high noon; high summer; High Renaissance*). **11 a** (of meat) beginning to go bad; off. **b** (of game) well-hung and slightly decomposed. **12** *Geog.* (of latitude) near the North or South Pole. **13** *Phonet.* (of a vowel) close (see CLOSE[1] *adj.* 14). —*n.* **1** a high, or the highest, level or figure. **2** an area of high barometric pressure; an anticyclone. **3** *sl.* a euphoric drug-induced state. **4** top gear in a motor vehicle. **5** *US colloq.* high school. **6** (**the High**) *Brit. colloq.* a High Street, esp. that in Oxford. —*adv.* **1** far up; aloft (*flew the flag high*). **2** in or to a high degree. **3** at a high price. **4** (of a sound) at or to a high pitch (*sang high*). □ **ace** (or **King** or **Queen** etc.) **high** (in card games) having the ace etc. as the highest-ranking card. **from on high** from heaven or a high place. **High Admiral** etc. a chief officer. **high altar** the chief altar of a church. **high and dry** **1** out of the current of events; stranded. **2** (of a ship) out of the water. **high and low** **1** everywhere (*searched high and low*). **2** (people) of all conditions. **high and mighty** **1** *colloq.* arrogant. **2** *archaic* of exalted rank. **high-born** of noble birth. **high camp** sophisticated camp (cf. CAMP[2]). **high card** a card that outranks others, esp. the ace or a court-card. **high chair** an infant's chair with long legs and a tray, for use at meals. **High Church** *n.* a section of the Church of England emphasizing ritual, priestly authority, and sacraments. —*adj.* of or relating to this section. **High Churchman** (*pl.* -**men**) an advocate of High Church principles. **high-class** of high quality. **high colour** a flushed complexion. **high command** an army commander-in-chief and associated staff. **High Commission** an embassy from one Commonwealth country to another. **High Commissioner** the head of such an embassy. **High Court** (also in England **High Court of Justice**) a supreme court of justice for civil cases. **high day** a

festal day. **High Dutch** see DUTCH. **high enema** an enema delivered into the colon. **higher animal** (or **plant**) an animal or plant evolved to a high degree. **higher court** *Law* a court that can overrule the decision of another. **the higher criticism** see CRITICISM. **higher education** education at university etc., esp. to degree level. **higher mathematics** advanced mathematics as taught at university etc. **higher-up** *colloq.* a person of higher rank. **highest common factor** *Math.* the highest number that can be divided exactly into each of two or more numbers. **high explosive** an extremely explosive substance used in shells, bombs, etc. **high fashion** = HAUTE COUTURE. **high fidelity** the reproduction of sound with little distortion, giving a result very similar to the original. **high finance** financial transactions involving large sums. **high-flown** (of language etc.) extravagant, bombastic. **high-flyer** (or -**flier**) **1** an ambitious person. **2** a person or thing with great potential for achievement. **high-flying** reaching a great height; ambitious. **high frequency** a frequency, esp. in radio, of 3 to 30 megahertz. **high gear** see GEAR. **High German** see GERMAN. **high-grade** of high quality. **high hat** **1** a tall hat; a top hat. **2** foot-operated cymbals. **3** a snobbish or overbearing person. **high-hat** —*adj.* supercilious; snobbish. —*v.* (-**hatted**, -**hatting**) *US* **1** *tr.* treat superciliously. **2** *intr.* assume a superior attitude. **high holiday** the Jewish New Year or the Day of Atonement. **high jinks** boisterous joking or merrymaking. **high-jump** **1** an athletic event consisting of jumping as high as possible over a bar of adjustable height. **2** *colloq.* a drastic punishment (*he's for the high-jump*). **high-key** *Photog.* consisting of light tones only. **high kick** a dancer's kick high in the air. **high-level** **1** (of negotiations etc.) conducted by high-ranking people. **2** *Computing* (of a programming language) that is not machine-dependent and is usu. at a level of abstraction close to natural language. **high life** (or **living**) a luxurious existence ascribed to the upper classes. **high-lows** *archaic* boots reaching over the ankles. **high mass** see MASS[2]. **high-octane** (of petrol etc.) having good antiknock properties. **high old** *colloq.* most enjoyable (*had a high old time*). **high opinion** of a favourable opinion of. **high-pitched** **1** (of a sound) high. **2** (of a roof) steep. **3** (of style etc.) lofty. **high places** the upper ranks of an organization etc. **high point** the maximum or best state reached. **high polymer** a polymer having a high molecular weight. **high-powered** **1** having great power or energy. **2** important or influential. **high pressure** **1** a high degree of activity or exertion. **2** a condition of the atmosphere with the pressure above average. **high priest** **1** a chief priest, esp. Jewish. **2** the head of any cult. **high profile** exposure to attention or publicity. **high-profile** *adj.* (usu. *attrib.*) having a high profile. **high-ranking** of high rank, senior. **high relief** see RELIEF. **high-rise** **1** (of a building) having many storeys. **2** such a building. **high-risk** (usu. *attrib.*) involving or exposed to danger (*high-risk sports*). **high road** **1** a main road. **2** (usu. foll. by *to*) a direct route (*on the high road to success*). **high roller** *US sl.* a person who gambles large sums or spends freely. **high school** **1** *Brit.* a grammar school. **2** *US & Sc.* a secondary school. **high sea** (or **seas**) open seas not within any country's jurisdiction. **high season** the period of the greatest number of visitors at a resort etc. **High Sheriff** see SHERIFF. **high sign** *US colloq.* a surreptitious gesture indicating that all is well or that the coast is clear. **high-sounding** pretentious, bombastic. **high-speed** **1** operating at great speed. **2** (of steel) suitable for cutting-tools even when red-hot. **high-spirited** vivacious; cheerful. **high-spiritedness** = *high spirits.* **high spirits** vivacity; energy; cheerfulness. **high spot** *sl.* an important place or feature. **high-stepper** **1** a horse that lifts its feet high when walking or trotting. **2** a stately person. **High Steward** see STEWARD *n*. **6. high street** *Brit*. a main road, esp. the principal shopping street of a town. **high-strung** = *highly-strung*. **high table** a table on a platform at a public dinner or for the fellows of a college. **high tea** *Brit*. a main evening meal usu. consisting of a cooked dish, bread and butter, tea, etc. **high tech** *n*. = *high technology*. —*adj*. **1** (of interior design etc.) imitating styles more usual in industry etc., esp. using steel, glass, or plastic in a functional way. **2** employing, requiring, or involved in high technology. **high technology** advanced technological development, esp. in electronics. **high-tensile** (of metal) having great tensile strength. **high tension** = *high voltage*. **high tide** the time or level of the tide at its flow. **high time** a time that is late or overdue (*it is high time they arrived*). **high-toned** stylish; dignified; superior. **high treason** see TREASON. **high-up** *colloq*. a person of high rank. **high voltage** electrical potential causing some danger of injury or damage. **high water 1** the tide at its fullest. **2** the time of this. **high-water mark 1** the level reached at high water. **2** the maximum recorded value or highest point of excellence. **high, wide, and handsome** *colloq*. in a carefree or stylish manner. **high wire** a high tightrope. **high words** angry talk. **high yellow** *US* a person of mixed race with a palish skin. **in high feather** see FEATHER. **the Most High** God. **on high** in or to heaven or a high place. **on one's high horse** *colloq*. behaving superciliously or arrogantly. **play high 1** play for high stakes. **2** play a card of high value. **run high 1** (of the sea) have a strong current with high tide. **2** (of feelings) be strong. [OE *hēah* f. Gmc]

highball /ˈhaɪbɔːl/ *n*. *US* **1** a drink of spirits and soda etc., served with ice in a tall glass. **2** a railway signal to proceed.

highbinder /ˈhaɪˌbaɪndə(r)/ *n*. *US* a ruffian; a swindler; an assassin.

highboy /ˈhaɪbɔɪ/ *n*. *US* a tall chest of drawers on legs.

highbrow /ˈhaɪbraʊ/ *adj*. & *n*. *colloq*. —*adj*. intellectual; cultural. —*n*. an intellectual or cultured person.

highfalutin /ˌhaɪfəˈluːtɪn/ *adj*. & *n*. (also **highfaluting** /-tɪŋ/) *colloq*. —*adj*. absurdly pompous or pretentious. —*n*. highfalutin speech or writing. [HIGH + *-falutin*, of unkn. orig.]

high-handed /haɪˈhændɪd/ *adj*. disregarding others' feelings; overbearing. □□ **high-handedly** *adv*. **high-handedness** *n*.

highland /ˈhaɪlənd/ *n*. & *adj*. —*n*. (usu. in *pl*.) **1** an area of high land. **2** (**the Highlands**) the mountainous part of Scotland. —*adj*. of or in a highland or the Highlands. □ **Highland cattle 1** cattle of a shaggy-haired breed with long curved widely-spaced horns. **2** this breed. **Highland dress** the kilt etc. **Highland fling** see FLING *n*. 3. □□ **highlander** *n*. (also **Highlander**). **Highlandman** *n*. (*pl*. **-men**). [OE *hēahlond* promontory (as HIGH, LAND)]

highlight /ˈhaɪlaɪt/ *n*. & *v*. —*n*. **1** (in a painting etc.) a light area, or one seeming to reflect light. **2** a moment or detail of vivid interest; an outstanding feature. **3** (usu. in *pl*.) a bright tint in the hair produced by bleaching. —*v.tr*. **1 a** bring into prominence; draw attention to. **b** mark with a highlighter. **2** create highlights in (the hair).

highlighter /ˈhaɪˌlaɪtə(r)/ *n*. a marker pen which overlays colour on a printed word etc., leaving it legible and emphasized.

highly /ˈhaɪlɪ/ *adv*. **1** in a high degree (*highly amusing*; *highly probable*; *commend it highly*). **2** honourably; favourably (*think highly of him*). □ **highly-strung** very sensitive or nervous. [OE *hēalīce* (as HIGH)]

high-minded /haɪˈmaɪndɪd/ *adj*. **1** having high

moral principles. **2** *archaic* proud. □□ **high-mindedly** *adv*. **high-mindedness** *n*.

high-muck-a-muck /ˈhaɪˌmʌkəˌmʌk/ *n*. *US* a person of great self-importance. [perh. f. Chinook *hiu* plenty + *muckamuck* food]

highness /ˈhaɪnɪs/ *n*. **1** the state of being high (*highness of taxation*) (cf. HEIGHT). **2** (**Highness**) a title used in addressing and referring to a prince or princess (*Her Highness*; *Your Royal Highness*). [OE *hēanes* (as HIGH)]

hight /haɪt/ *adj*. *archaic*, *poet*., or *joc*. called; named. [past part. (from 14th c.) of OE *hātan* command, call]

hightail /ˈhaɪteɪl/ *v.intr*. *US colloq*. move at high speed.

highway /ˈhaɪweɪ/ *n*. **1 a** a public road. **b** a main route (by land or water). **2** a direct course of action (*on the highway to success*). □ **Highway Code** *Brit*. the official booklet of guidance for road-users. **King's** (or **Queen's**) **highway** a public road, regarded as being under the sovereign's protection.

highwayman /ˈhaɪweɪmən/ *n*. (*pl*. **-men**) *hist*. a robber of passengers, travellers, etc., usu. mounted. [HIGHWAY]

HIH *abbr*. Her or His Imperial Highness.

hijack /ˈhaɪdʒæk/ *v*. & *n*. —*v.tr*. **1** seize control of (a loaded lorry, an aircraft in flight, etc.), esp. to force it to a different destination. **2** seize (goods) in transit. **3** take over (an organization etc.) by force or subterfuge in order to redirect it. —*n*. an instance of hijacking. □□ **hijacker** *n*. [20th c.: orig. unkn.]

hijra var. of HEGIRA.

hike /haɪk/ *n*. & *v*. —*n*. **1** a long country walk, esp. with rucksacks etc. **2** esp. *US* an increase (of prices etc.). —*v*. **1** *intr*. walk, esp. across country, for a long distance, esp. with boots, rucksack, etc. **2** (usu. foll. by *up*) **a** *tr*. hitch up (clothing etc.); hoist; shove. **b** *intr*. work upwards out of place, become hitched up. **3** *tr*. esp. *US* increase (prices etc.). □□ **hiker** *n*. [19th-c. dial.: orig. unkn.]

hila *pl*. of HILUM.

hilarious /hɪˈleərɪəs/ *adj*. **1** exceedingly funny. **2** boisterously merry. □□ **hilariously** *adv*. **hilariousness** *n*. **hilarity** /-ˈlærɪtɪ/ *n*. [L *hilaris* f. Gk *hilaros* cheerful]

Hilary term /ˈhɪlərɪ/ *n*. *Brit*. the university term beginning in January, esp. at Oxford. [*Hilarius* bishop of Poitiers d. 367, with a festival on 13 Jan.]

hill /hɪl/ *n*. & *v*. —*n*. **1 a** a naturally raised area of land, not as high as a mountain. **b** (as **the hills**) *Anglo-Ind*. = *hill-station*. **2** (often in *comb*.) a heap; a mound (*anthill*; *dunghill*). **3** a sloping piece of road. —*v.tr*. **1** form into a hill. **2** (usu. foll. by *up*) bank up (plants) with soil. □ **hill and dale** (of a gramophone record) with groove-undulations in a vertical plane. **hill-billy** (*pl*. **-ies**) *US* **1** *colloq*., often *derog*. a person from a remote rural area in a southern State (cf. HICK). **2** folk music of or like that of the southern US. **hill climb** a race for vehicles up a steep hill. **hill-fort** a fort built on a hill. **hill-station** *Anglo-Ind*. a government settlement, esp. for holidays etc. during the hot season, in the low mountains of N. India. **old as the hills** very ancient. **over the hill** *colloq*. **1** past the prime of life; declining. **2** past the crisis. **up hill and down dale** see UP. [OE *hyll*]

hillock /ˈhɪlək/ *n*. a small hill or mound. □□ **hillocky** *adj*.

hillside /ˈhɪlsaɪd/ *n*. the sloping side of a hill.

hilltop /ˈhɪltɒp/ *n*. the summit of a hill.

hillwalking /ˈhɪlˌwɔːkɪŋ/ *n*. the pastime of walking in hilly country. □□ **hillwalker** *n*.

hilly /ˈhɪlɪ/ *adj*. (**hillier**, **hilliest**) having many hills. □□ **hilliness** *n*.

hilt /hɪlt/ *n*. & *v*. —*n*. **1** the handle of a sword, dagger, etc. **2** the handle of a tool. —*v.tr*. provide with a hilt. □ **up to the hilt** completely. [OE *hilt(e)* f. Gmc]

hilum /ˈhaɪləm/ *n*. (*pl*. **hila** /-lə/) **1** *Bot*. the point of attachment of a seed to its seed-vessel. **2** *Anat*. a

b *but* d *dog* f *few* g *get* h *he* j *yes* k *cat* l *leg* m *man* n *no* p *pen* r *red* s *sit* t *top* v *voice*

notch or indentation where a vessel enters an organ. [L, = little thing, trifle]

HIM abbr. Her or His Imperial Majesty.

him /hɪm/ pron. **1** objective case of HE (I saw him). **2** colloq. he (it's him again; is taller than him). **3** archaic himself (fell and hurt him). [OE, masc. and neut. dative sing. of HE, IT¹]

Himalayan /ˌhɪmə'leɪən/ adj. of or relating to the Himalaya mountains in Nepal. [Himalaya Skr. f. hima snow + ālaya abode]

himation /hɪ'mætɪən/ n. hist. the outer garment worn by the ancient Greeks over the left shoulder and under the right. [Gk]

himself /hɪm'self/ pron. **1** emphat. form of HE or HIM (he himself will do it). **b** refl. form of HIM (he has hurt himself). **2** in his normal state of body or mind (does not feel quite himself today). **3** esp. Ir. a third party of some importance; the master of the house. □**be himself** act in his normal unconstrained manner. **by himself** see by oneself. [OE (as HIM, SELF)]

Hinayana /ˌhiːnə'jɑːnə/ n. = THERAVADA. [Skr. f. hīna lesser + yāna vehicle]

hind¹ /haɪnd/ adj. (esp. of parts of the body) situated at the back, posterior (hind leg) (opp. FORE). □**on one's hind legs** see LEG. [ME, perh. shortened f. OE bihindan BEHIND]

hind² /haɪnd/ n. a female deer (usu. a red deer or sika), esp. in and after the third year. [OE f. Gmc]

hind³ /haɪnd/ n. hist. **1** esp. Sc. a skilled farm-worker, usu. married and with a tied cottage, and formerly having charge of two horses. **2** a steward on a farm. **3** a rustic, a boor. [ME hine f. OE hīne (pl.) app. f. hī(g)na genit. pl. of hīgan, hīwan 'members of a family' (cf. HIDE³): for -d cf. SOUND¹)]

hinder¹ /'hɪndə(r)/ v.tr. (also absol.) impede; delay; prevent (you will hinder him; hindered me from working). [OE hindrian f. Gmc]

hinder² /'haɪndə(r)/ adj. rear, hind (the hinder part). [ME, perh. f. OE hinderweard backward: cf. HIND¹]

Hindi /'hɪndɪ/ n. & adj. —n. **1** a group of spoken dialects of N. India. **2** a literary form of Hindustani with a Sanskrit-based vocabulary and the Devanagari script, an official language of India. —adj. of or concerning Hindi. [Urdu hindī f. Hind India]

hindmost /'haɪndməʊst/ adj. furthest behind; most remote.

Hindoo archaic var. of HINDU.

hindquarters /haɪnd'kwɔːtəz/ n.pl. the hind legs and adjoining parts of a quadruped.

hindrance /'hɪndrəns/ n. **1** the act or an instance of hindering; the state of being hindered. **2** a thing that hinders; an obstacle.

hindsight /'haɪndsaɪt/ n. **1** wisdom after the event (realized with hindsight that they were wrong) (opp. FORESIGHT). **2** the backsight of a gun.

Hindu /'hɪnduː, -'duː/ n. & adj. —n. **1** a follower of Hinduism. **2** archaic an Indian. —adj. **1** of or concerning Hindus or Hinduism. **2** archaic Indian. [Urdu f. Pers. f. Hind India]

Hinduism /'hɪnduːˌɪz(ə)m/ n. the main religious and social system of India, including belief in reincarnation, the worship of several gods, and a caste system as the basis of society. □□ **Hinduize** v.tr. (also -ise).

Hindustani /ˌhɪndʊ'stɑːnɪ/ n. & adj. —n. **1** a language based on Western Hindi, with elements of Arabic, Persian, etc., used as a lingua franca in much of India. **2** archaic Urdu. —adj. of or relating to Hindustan or its people, or Hindustani. [Urdu f. Pers. hindūstānī (as HINDU, stān country)]

hinge /hɪndʒ/ n. & v. —n. **1 a** a movable, usu. metal, joint or mechanism such as that by which a door is hung on a side post. **b** Biol. a natural joint performing a similar function, e.g. that of a bivalve shell. **2** a central point or principle on which everything depends. —v. **1** intr. (foll. by on) **a** depend (on a principle, an event, etc.) (all hinges on his acceptance).

b (of a door etc.) hang and turn (on a post etc.). **2** tr. attach with or as if with a hinge. □**stamp-hinge** a small piece of gummed transparent paper used for fixing postage stamps in an album etc. □□ **hinged** adj. **hingeless** adj. **hingewise** adv. [ME heng etc., rel. to HANG]

hinny¹ /'hɪnɪ/ n. (pl. **-ies**) the offspring of a female donkey and a male horse. [L hinnus f. Gk hinnos]

hinny² /'hɪnɪ/ n. (also **hinnie**) (pl. **-ies**) Sc. & N.Engl. (esp. as a form of address) darling, sweetheart. □**singing hinny** a currant cake baked on a griddle. [var. of HONEY]

hint /hɪnt/ n. & v. —n. **1** a slight or indirect indication or suggestion (took the hint and left). **2** a small piece of practical information (handy hints on cooking). **3** a very small trace; a suggestion (a hint of perfume). —v.tr. (often foll. by that + clause) suggest slightly (hinted the contrary; hinted that they were wrong). □**hint at** give a hint of; refer indirectly to. [app. f. obs. hent grasp, lay hold of, f. OE hentan, f. Gmc, rel. to HUNT]

hinterland /'hɪntəˌlænd/ n. **1** the often deserted or uncharted areas beyond a coastal district or a river's banks. **2** an area served by a port or other centre. **3** a remote or fringe area. [G f. hinter behind + Land LAND]

hip¹ /hɪp/ n. **1** a projection of the pelvis and upper thigh-bone on each side of the body in human beings and quadrupeds. **2** (often in pl.) the circumference of the body at the buttocks. **3** Archit. the sharp edge of a roof from ridge to eaves where two sides meet. □**hip-bath** a portable bath in which a person sits. **hip-bone** a bone forming the hip, esp. the ilium. **hip-flask** a flask for spirits etc., carried in a hip-pocket. **hip-joint** the articulation of the head of the thigh-bone with the ilium. **hip-length** (of a garment) reaching down to the hips. **hip-pocket** a trouser-pocket just behind the hip. **hip-** (or **hipped-**) **roof** a roof with the sides and the ends inclined. **on the hip** archaic at a disadvantage. □□ **hipless** adj. **hipped** adj. (also in comb.). [OE hype f. Gmc, rel. to HOP¹]

hip² /hɪp/ n. (also **hep** /hep/) the fruit of a rose, esp. a wild kind. [OE hēope, hīope f. WG]

hip³ /hɪp/ adj. (also **hep** /hep/) (**hipper**, **hippest** or **hepper**, **heppest**) sl. **1** following the latest fashion in esp. jazz music, clothes, etc.; stylish. **2** (often foll. by to) understanding, aware. □**hip-cat** a hip person; a devotee of jazz or swing. □□ **hipness** n. [20th c.: orig. unkn.]

hip⁴ /hɪp/ int. introducing a united cheer (hip, hip, hooray). [19th c.: orig. unkn.]

hippeastrum /ˌhɪpɪ'æstrəm/ n. any S. American bulbous plant of the genus Hippeastrum with showy white or red flowers. [mod.L f. Gk hippeus horseman (the leaves appearing to ride on one another) + astron star (from the flower-shape)]

hipped /hɪpt/ adj. (usu. foll. by on) esp. US sl. obsessed, infatuated. [past part. of hip (v.) = make hip (HIP³)]

hippie /'hɪpɪ/ n. (also **hippy**) (pl. **-ies**) colloq. **1** (esp. in the 1960s) a person of unconventional appearance, typically with long hair, jeans, beads, etc., often associated with hallucinogenic drugs and a rejection of conventional values. **2** = HIPSTER². [HIP³]

hippo /'hɪpəʊ/ n. (pl. **-os**) colloq. a hippopotamus. [abbr.]

hippocampus /ˌhɪpə'kæmpəs/ n. (pl. **hippocampi** /-pɪ/) **1** any marine fish of the genus Hippocampus, swimming vertically and with a head suggestive of a horse; a sea horse. **2** Anat. the elongated ridges on the floor of each lateral ventricle of the brain, thought to be the centre of emotion and the autonomic nervous system. [L f. Gk hippokampos f. hippos horse + kampos sea monster]

hippocras /'hɪpəˌkræs/ n. hist. wine flavoured with spices. [ME f. OF ipocras Hippocrates (see HIPPOCRATIC OATH), prob. because strained through a filter called 'Hippocrates' sleeve']

w we z zoo ʃ she ʒ decision θ thin ð this ŋ ring x loch tʃ chip dʒ jar (see over for vowels)

Hippocratic oath /ˌhɪpə'krætɪk/ n. an oath formerly taken by doctors affirming their obligations and proper conduct. [med.L *Hippocraticus* f. *Hippocrates*, Gk physician of the 5th c. BC]

Hippocrene /'hɪpə,kriːn/ n. *poet.* poetic or literary inspiration. [name of a fountain on Mount Helicon sacred to the Muses: L f. Gk f. *hippos* horse + *krēnē* fountain, as having been produced by a stroke of Pegasus' hoof]

hippodrome /'hɪpə,drəʊm/ n. **1** a music- or dance-hall. **2** (in classical antiquity) a course for chariot races etc. **3** a circus. [F *hippodrome* or L *hippodromus* f. Gk *hippodromos* f. *hippos* horse + *dromos* race, course]

hippogriff /'hɪpəɡrɪf/ n. (also **hippogryph**) a mythical griffin-like creature with the body of a horse. [F *hippogriffe* f. It. *ippogrifo* f. Gk *hippos* horse + It. *grifo* GRIFFIN]

hippopotamus /ˌhɪpə'pɒtəməs/ n. (pl. **hippopotamuses** or **hippopotami** /-ˌmaɪ/) **1** a large thick-skinned four-legged mammal, *Hippopotamus amphibius*, native to Africa, inhabiting rivers, lakes, etc. **2** (in full **pigmy hippopotamus**) a smaller related mammal, *Choeropsis liberiensis*, native to Africa, inhabiting forests and swamps. [ME f. L f. Gk *hippopotamos* f. *hippos* horse + *potamos* river]

hippy[1] var. of HIPPIE.

hippy[2] /'hɪpɪ/ adj. having large hips.

hipster[1] /'hɪpstə(r)/ adj. & n. *Brit.* —adj. (of a garment) hanging from the hips rather than the waist. —n. (in pl.) trousers hanging from the hips.

hipster[2] /'hɪpstə(r)/ n. *sl.* a person who is hip; a hip-cat. □□ **hipsterism** n.

hiragana /ˌhɪərə'ɡɑːnə/ n. the cursive form of Japanese syllabic writing or kana (cf. KATAKANA). [Jap., = plain kana]

hircine /'hɜːsaɪn/ adj. goatlike. [L *hircinus* f. *hircus* he-goat]

hire /'haɪə(r)/ v. & n. —v.tr. **1** (often foll. by *from*) procure the temporary use of (a thing) for an agreed payment (*hired a van from them*). **2** esp. *US* employ (a person) for wages or a fee. **3** *US* borrow (money). —n. **1** hiring or being hired. **2** payment for this. □**for** (or **on**) **hire** ready to be hired. **hire-car** a car available for hire. **hired girl** (or **man**) *US* a domestic servant, esp. on a farm. **hire out** grant the temporary use of (a thing) for an agreed payment. **hire purchase** *Brit.* a system by which a person may purchase a thing by regular payments while having the use of it. □□ **hireable** adj. (*US* **hirable**). **hirer** n. [OE *hȳrian*, *hȳr* f. WG]

hireling /'haɪəlɪŋ/ n. usu. *derog.* a person who works for hire. [OE *hȳrling* (as HIRE, -LING[1])]

hirsute /'hɜːsjuːt/ adj. **1** hairy, shaggy. **2** untrimmed. □□ **hirsuteness** n. [L *hirsutus*]

hirsutism /'hɜːsjuː,tɪz(ə)m/ n. the excessive growth of hair on the face and body.

his /hɪz/ poss.pron. **1** (*attrib.*) of or belonging to him or himself (*his house; his own business*). **2** (**His**) (*attrib.*) (in titles) that he is (*His Majesty*). **3** the one or ones belonging to or associated with him (*it is his; his are over there*). □**his and hers** *joc.* (of matching items) for husband and wife, or men and women. **of his** of or belonging to him (*a friend of his*). [OE, genit. of HE, IT[1]]

Hispanic /hɪ'spænɪk/ adj. & n. **1** of or relating to Spain or to Spain and Portugal. **2** of Spain and other Spanish-speaking countries. —n. a Spanish-speaking person, esp. one of Latin-American descent, living in the US. □□ **Hispanicize** /-ˌsaɪz/ v.tr. (also **-ise**). [L *Hispanicus* f. *Hispania* Spain]

Hispanist /'hɪspənɪst/ n. (also **Hispanicist** /hɪ'spænɪsɪst/) an expert in or student of the language, literature, and civilization of Spain.

Hispano- /hɪ'spænəʊ/ comb. form Spanish. [L *Hispanus* Spanish]

hispid /'hɪspɪd/ adj. *Bot.* & *Zool.* **1** rough with bristles; bristly. **2** shaggy. [L *hispidus*]

hiss /hɪs/ v. & n. —v. **1** intr. (of a person, snake, goose, etc.) make a sharp sibilant sound, esp. as a sign of disapproval or derision (*audience booed and hissed; the water hissed on the hotplate*). **2** tr. express disapproval of (a person etc.) by hisses. **3** tr. whisper (a threat etc.) urgently or angrily ('*Where's the door?*' *he hissed*). —n. **1** a sharp sibilant sound as of the letter *s*. **2** *Electronics* unwanted interference at audio frequencies. □**hiss away** (or **down**) drive off etc. by hisses. **hiss off** hiss (actors etc.) so that they leave the stage. [ME: imit.]

hist /hɪst/ int. *archaic* used to call attention, enjoin silence, incite a dog, etc. [16th c.: natural excl.]

histamine /'hɪstəmɪn, 'hɪstə,miːn/ n. *Biochem.* an organic compound occurring in injured body tissues etc., and also associated with allergic reactions. □□ **histaminic** /-'mɪnɪk/ adj. [HISTO- + AMINE]

histidine /'hɪstɪ,diːn/ n. *Biochem.* an amino acid from which histamine is derived. [Gk *histos* web, tissue]

histo- /'hɪstəʊ/ comb. form (also **hist-** before a vowel) *Biol.* tissue. [Gk *histos* web]

histochemistry /ˌhɪstəʊ'kemɪstrɪ/ n. the study of the identification and distribution of the chemical constituents of tissues by means of stains, indicators, and microscopy. □□ **histochemical** adj.

histogenesis /ˌhɪstəʊ'dʒenɪsɪs/ n. the formation of tissues. □□ **histogenetic** /-dʒɪ'netɪk/ adj.

histogeny /hɪ'stɒdʒɪnɪ/ n. = HISTOGENESIS. □□ **histogenic** /ˌhɪstə'dʒenɪk/ adj.

histogram /'hɪstə,ɡræm/ n. *Statistics* a chart consisting of rectangles (usu. drawn vertically from a base line) whose areas and positions are proportional to the value or range of a number of variables. [Gk *histos* mast + -GRAM]

histology /hɪ'stɒlədʒɪ/ n. the study of the structure of tissues. □□ **histological** /ˌhɪstə'lɒdʒɪk(ə)l/ adj. **histologist** /hɪ'stɒlədʒɪst/ n.

histolysis /hɪ'stɒlɪsɪs/ n. the breaking down of tissues. □□ **histolytic** /-tə'lɪtɪk/ adj.

histone /'hɪstəʊn/ n. *Biochem.* any of a group of proteins found in chromatin. [G *Histon* perh. f. Gk *histamai* arrest, or as HISTO-]

histopathology /ˌhɪstəʊpə'θɒlədʒɪ/ n. **1** changes in tissues caused by disease. **2** the study of these.

historian /hɪ'stɔːrɪən/ n. **1** a writer of history, esp. a critical analyst, rather than a compiler. **2** a person learned in or studying history (*English historian; ancient historian*). [F *historien* f. L (as HISTORY)]

historiated /hɪ'stɔːrɪ,eɪtɪd/ adj. = STORIATED. [med.L *historiare* (as HISTORY)]

historic /hɪ'stɒrɪk/ adj. **1** famous or important in history or potentially so (*a historic moment*). **2** *Gram.* (of a tense) normally used in the narration of past events (esp. Latin & Greek imperfect and pluperfect; cf. PRIMARY). **3** *archaic* or *disp.* = HISTORICAL. □**historic infinitive** the infinitive when used instead of the indicative. **historic present** the present tense used instead of the past in vivid narration. [L *historicus* f. Gk *historikos* (as HISTORY)]

historical /hɪ'stɒrɪk(ə)l/ adj. **1** of or concerning history (*historical evidence*). **2** belonging to history, not to prehistory or legend. **3** (of the study of a subject) based on an analysis of its development over a period. **4** belonging to the past, not the present. **5** (of a novel, a film, etc.) dealing or professing to deal with historical events. **6** in connection with history, from the historian's point of view (*of purely historical interest*). □□ **historically** adv.

historicism /hɪ'stɒrɪ,sɪz(ə)m/ n. **1 a** the theory that social and cultural phenomena are determined by history. **b** the belief that historical events are governed by laws. **2** the tendency to regard historical development as the most basic aspect of human existence. **3** an excessive regard for past styles etc. □□ **historicist** n. [HISTORIC after G *Historismus*]

historicity /ˌhɪstə'rɪsɪtɪ/ n. the historical genuineness of an event etc.

historiographer /hɪ,stɔːrɪ'ɒɡrəfə(r)/ n. **1** an expert in or student of historiography. **2** a writer of history, esp. an official historian. [ME f. F *historiographe* or f. LL *historiographus* f. Gk *historiographos* (as HISTORY, -GRAPHER)]

historiography /hɪˌstɔːrɪˈɒgrəfɪ/ *n.* **1** the writing of history. **2** the study of history-writing. □□ **historiographic** /-ˈgræfɪk/ *adj.* **historiographical** /-ˈgræfɪk(ə)l/ *adj.* [med.L *historiographia* f. Gk *historiographia* (as HISTORY, -GRAPHY)]

history /ˈhɪstərɪ/ *n.* (*pl.* **-ies**) **1** a continuous, usu. chronological, record of important or public events. **2 a** the study of past events, esp. human affairs. **b** the total accumulation of past events, esp. relating to human affairs or to the accumulation of developments connected with a particular nation, person, thing, etc. (*our island history*; *the history of astronomy*). **3** an eventful past (*this house has a history*). **4 a** a systematic or critical account of or research into a past event or events etc. **b** a similar record or account of natural phenomena. **5** a historical play. □ **make history 1** influence the course of history. **2** do something memorable. [ME f. L *historia* f. Gk *historia* finding out, narrative, history f. *histōr* learned, wise man, rel. to WIT²]

histrionic /ˌhɪstrɪˈɒnɪk/ *adj.* & *n.* —*adj.* **1** of or concerning actors or acting. **2** (of behaviour) theatrical, dramatic. —*n.* **1** (in *pl.*) **a** insincere and dramatic behaviour designed to impress. **b** theatricals; theatrical art. **2** *archaic* an actor. □□ **histrionically** *adv.* [LL *histrionicus* f. L *histrio -onis* actor]

hit /hɪt/ *v.* & *n.* —*v.* (**hitting**; *past* and *past part.* **hit**) **1** *tr.* **a** strike with a blow or a missile. **b** (of a moving body) strike (*the plane hit the ground*). **c** reach (a target, a person, etc.) with a directed missile (*hit the window with the ball*). **2** *tr.* cause to suffer or affect adversely; wound (*the loss hit him hard*). **3** *intr.* (often foll. by *at*, *against*, *upon*) direct a blow. **4** *tr.* (often foll. by *against*, *on*) knock (a part of the body) (*hit his head on the door-frame*). **5** *tr.* light upon; get at (a thing aimed at) (*he's hit the truth at last; tried to hit the right tone in his apology*) (see *hit on*). **6** *tr.* *colloq.* **a** encounter (*hit a snag*). **b** arrive at (*hit an all-time low; hit the town*). **c** indulge in, esp. liquor etc. (*hit the bottle*). **7** *tr.* esp. *US sl.* rob or kill. **8** *tr.* occur forcefully to (*the seriousness of the situation only hit him later*). **9** *tr.* *Sport* **a** propel (a ball etc.) with a bat etc. to score runs or points. **b** score (runs etc.) in this way. **c** (usu. foll. by *for*) strike (a ball or a bowler) for so many runs (*hit him for six*). **10** *tr.* represent exactly. —*n.* **1 a** a blow; a stroke. **b** a collision. **2** a shot etc. that hits its target. **3** *colloq.* a popular success in entertainment. **4** a stroke of sarcasm, wit, etc. **5** a stroke of good luck. **6** esp. *US sl.* **a** a murder or other violent crime. **b** a drug injection etc. **7** a successful attempt. □ **hit and run** cause (accidental or wilful) damage and escape or leave the scene before being discovered. **hit-and-run** *attrib.adj.* relating to or (of a person) committing an act of this kind. **hit back** retaliate. **hit below the belt 1** esp. *Boxing* give a foul blow. **2** treat or behave unfairly. **hit for six** *Brit.* defeat in argument. **hit the hay** (or **sack**) *colloq.* go to bed. **hit the headlines** see HEADLINE. **hit home** make a salutary impression. **hit it off** (often foll. by *with*, *together*) agree or be congenial. **hit list** *sl.* a list of prospective victims. **hit man** (*pl.* **hit men**) *sl.* a hired assassin. **hit the nail on the head** state the truth exactly. **hit on** (or **upon**) find (what is sought), esp. by chance. **hit-or-miss** aimed at or done carelessly. **hit out** deal vigorous physical or verbal blows (*hit out at her enemies*). **hit-out** *n.* *Austral. sl.* a brisk gallop. **hit parade** *colloq.* a list of the current best-selling records of popular music. **hit the road** (*US* **trail**) *sl.* depart. **hit the roof** see ROOF. **hit up** *Cricket* score (runs) energetically. **hit wicket** *Cricket* be out by striking the wicket with the bat etc. **make a hit** (usu. foll. by *with*) be successful or popular. □□ **hitter**

n. [ME f. OE *hittan* f. ON *hitta* meet with, of unkn. orig.]

hitch /hɪtʃ/ *v.* & *n.* —*v.* **1 a** *tr.* fasten with a loop, hook, etc.; tether (*hitched the horse to the cart*). **b** *intr.* (often foll. by *in*, *on to*, etc.) become fastened in this way (*the rod hitched in to the bracket*). **2** *tr.* move (a thing) with a jerk; shift slightly (*hitched the pillow to a comfortable position*). **3** *colloq.* **a** *intr.* = HITCHHIKE. **b** *tr.* obtain (a lift) by hitchhiking. —*n.* **1** an impediment; a temporary obstacle. **2** an abrupt pull or push; a jerk. **3** a noose or knot of various kinds. **4** *colloq.* a free ride in a vehicle. **5** *US sl.* a period of service. □ **get hitched** *colloq.* marry. **half hitch** a knot formed by passing the end of a rope round its standing part and then through the bight. **hitch up** lift (esp. clothing) with a jerk. **hitch one's wagon to a star** make use of powers higher than one's own. □□ **hitcher** *n.* [ME: orig. uncert.]

hitchhike /ˈhɪtʃhaɪk/ *v.* & *n.* —*v.intr.* travel by seeking free lifts in passing vehicles. —*n.* a journey made by hitchhiking. □□ **hitchhiker** *n.*

hi-tech /ˈhaɪtek/ *n.* = *high tech.* [abbr.]

hither /ˈhɪðə(r)/ *adv.* & *adj.* *formal* —*adv.* to or towards this place. —*adj.* *archaic* situated on this side; the nearer (of two). □ **hither and thither** (or **yon**) in various directions; to and fro. [OE *hider*: cf. THITHER]

hitherto /ˌhɪðəˈtuː/ *adv.* until this time, up to now.

hitherward /ˈhɪðəwəd/ *adv.* *archaic* in this direction.

Hitler /ˈhɪtlə(r)/ *n.* a person who embodies the authoritarian characteristics of Adolf Hitler, Ger. dictator d. 1945. □□ **Hitlerite** /-ˌraɪt/ *n.* & *adj.*

Hitlerism /ˈhɪtləˌrɪz(ə)n/ *n.* the political principles or policy of the Nazi Party in Germany. [HITLER]

Hittite /ˈhɪtaɪt/ *n.* & *adj.* —*n.* **1** a member of an ancient people of Asia Minor and Syria. **2** the language of the Hittites. —*adj.* of or relating to the Hittites or their language. [Heb. *Ḥittīm*]

HIV *abbr.* human immunodeficiency virus, either of two retroviruses causing Aids.

hive /haɪv/ *n.* & *v.* —*n.* **1 a** a beehive. **b** the bees in a hive. **2** a busy swarming place. **3** a swarming multitude. **4** a thing shaped like a hive in being domed. —*v.* **1** *tr.* a place (bees) in a hive. **b** house (people etc.) snugly. **2** *intr.* **a** enter a hive. **b** live together like bees. □ **hive off 1** separate from a larger group. **2 a** form into or assign (work) to a subsidiary department or company. **b** denationalize or privatize (an industry etc.). **hive up** hoard. [OE *hȳf* f. Gmc]

hives /haɪvz/ *n.pl.* **1** a skin-eruption, esp. nettle-rash. **2** inflammation of the larynx etc. [16th c. (orig. Sc.): orig. unkn.]

hiya /ˈhaɪjə/ *int. colloq.* a word used in greeting. [corrupt. of *how are you?*]

HK *abbr.* Hong Kong.

HL *abbr.* (in the UK) House of Lords.

hl *abbr.* hectolitre(s).

HM *abbr.* **1** Her (or His) Majesty('s). **2 a** headmaster. **b** headmistress.

hm *abbr.* hectometre(s).

h'm /hm/ *int.* & *n.* (also **hmm**) = HEM², HUM².

HMG *abbr.* Her or His Majesty's Government.

HMI *abbr.* Her or His Majesty's Inspector (of Schools).

HMS *abbr.* Her or His Majesty's Ship.

HMSO *abbr.* Her or His Majesty's Stationery Office.

HMV *abbr.* (in the UK) His Master's Voice.

HNC *abbr.* (in the UK) Higher National Certificate.

HND *abbr.* (in the UK) Higher National Diploma.

Ho *symb. Chem.* the element holmium.

ho /həʊ/ *int.* **1 a** an expression of surprise, admiration, triumph, or (often repeated as **ho! ho!** etc.) derision. **b** (in *comb.*) (*heigh-ho; what ho*). **2** a call for attention. **3** (in *comb.*) *Naut.* an addition to the name of a destination etc. (*westward ho*). [ME, imit.: cf. ON *hó*]

ho. *abbr.* house.

hoar /hɔː(r)/ *adj.* & *n.* *literary* —*adj.* **1** grey-haired

with age. 2 greyish-white. **3** (of a thing) grey with age. —*n.* **1** = *hoar-frost.* **2** hoariness. □**hoar-frost** frozen water vapour deposited in clear still weather on vegetation etc. [OE *hār* f. Gmc]

hoard /hɔːd/ *n. & v.* —*n.* **1** a stock or store (esp. of money) laid by. **2** an amassed store of facts etc. **3** *Archaeol.* an ancient store of treasure etc. —*v.* **1** *tr.* (often *absol.*; often foll. by *up*) amass (money etc.) and put away; store. **2** *intr.* accumulate more than one's current requirements of food etc. in a time of scarcity. **3** *tr.* store in the mind. □□ **hoarder** *n.* [OE *hord* f. Gmc]

hoarding /ˈhɔːdɪŋ/ *n.* **1** *Brit.* a large, usu. wooden, structure used to carry advertisements etc. **2** a board fence erected round a building site etc., often used for displaying posters etc. [obs. *hoard* f. AF *h(o)urdis* f. OF *hourd, hort,* rel. to HURDLE]

hoarhound var. of HOREHOUND.

hoarse /hɔːs/ *adj.* **1** (of the voice) rough and deep; husky; croaking. **2** having such a voice. □□ **hoarsely** *adv.* **hoarsen** *v.tr. & intr.* **hoarseness** *n.* [ME f. ON *hārs* (unrecorded) f. Gmc]

hoarstone /ˈhɔːstəʊn/ *n. Brit.* an ancient boundary stone.

hoary /ˈhɔːrɪ/ *adj.* (**hoarier, hoariest**) **1 a** (of hair) grey or white with age. **b** having such hair; aged. **2** old and trite (*a hoary joke*). **3** *Bot. & Zool.* covered with short white hairs. □□ **hoarily** *adv.* **hoariness** *n.*

hoatzin /hwætˈsiːn/ *n.* a tropical American bird, *Opisthocomus hoatzin,* whose young climb by means of hooked claws on their wings. [native name, imit.]

hoax /həʊks/ *n. & v.* —*n.* a humorous or malicious deception; a practical joke. —*v.tr.* deceive (a person) with a hoax. □□ **hoaxer** *n.* [18th c.: prob. contr. f. HOCUS]

hob[1] /hɒb/ *n.* **1 a** a flat heating surface for a pan on a cooker. **b** a flat metal shelf at the side of a fireplace, having its surface level with the top of the grate, used esp. for heating a pan etc. **2** a tool used for cutting gear-teeth etc. **3** a peg or pin used as a mark in quoits etc. **4** = HOBNAIL. [perh. var. of HUB, orig. = lump]

hob[2] /hɒb/ *n.* **1** a male ferret. **2** a hobgoblin. □**play** (or **raise**) **hob** *US* cause mischief. [ME, familiar form of *Rob,* short for *Robin* or *Robert*]

hobbit /ˈhɒbɪt/ *n.* a member of an imaginary race of half-sized people in stories by Tolkien. □□ **hobbitry** *n.* [invented by J. R. R. Tolkien, Engl. writer d. 1973, and said by him to mean 'hole-dweller']

hobble /ˈhɒb(ə)l/ *v. & n.* —*v.* **1** *intr.* **a** walk lamely; limp. **b** proceed haltingly in action or speech (*hobbled lamely to his conclusion*). **2** *tr.* **a** tie together the legs of (a horse etc.) to prevent it from straying. **b** tie (a horse's etc. legs). **3** *tr.* cause (a person etc.) to limp. —*n.* **1** an uneven or infirm gait. **2** a rope, clog, etc. used for hobbling a horse etc. □**hobble skirt** a skirt so narrow at the hem as to impede walking. □□ **hobbler** *n.* [ME, prob. f. LG: cf. HOPPLE and Du. *hobbelen* rock from side to side]

hobbledehoy /ˈhɒbəldɪˌhɔɪ/ *n. colloq.* **1** a clumsy or awkward youth. **2** a hooligan. [16th c.: orig. unkn.]

hobby[1] /ˈhɒbɪ/ *n.* (*pl.* **-ies**) **1** a favourite leisure-time activity or occupation. **2** *archaic* a small horse. **3** *hist.* an early type of velocipede. □□ **hobbyist** *n.* [ME *hobyn, hoby,* f. pet-forms of *Robin*: cf. DOBBIN]

hobby[2] /ˈhɒbɪ/ *n.* (*pl.* **-ies**) any of several small long-winged falcons, esp. *Falco subbuteo,* catching prey on the wing. [ME f. OF *hobé, hobet* dimin. of *hobe* small bird of prey]

hobby-horse /ˈhɒbɪˌhɔːs/ *n.* **1** a child's toy consisting of a stick with a horse's head. **2** a preoccupation; a favourite topic of conversation. **3** a model of a horse, esp. of wicker, used in morris dancing etc. **4** a rocking horse. **5** a horse on a merry-go-round.

hobday /ˈhɒbdeɪ/ *v.tr.* operate on (a horse) to improve its breathing. [F. T. *Hobday,* veterinary surgeon d. 1939]

hobgoblin /ˈhɒbˌgɒblɪn/ *n.* a mischievous imp; a bogy; a bugbear. [HOB[2] + GOBLIN]

hobnail /ˈhɒbneɪl/ *n.* a heavy-headed nail used for boot-soles. □**hobnail** (or **hobnailed**) **liver** a liver having many small knobbly projections due to cirrhosis. □□ **hobnailed** *adj.* [HOB[1] + NAIL]

hobnob /ˈhɒbnɒb/ *v.intr.* (**hobnobbed, hobnobbing**) **1** (usu. foll. by *with*) mix socially or informally. **2** drink together. [*hob or nob* = give or take, of alternate drinking; earlier *hab nab,* = have or not have]

hobo /ˈhəʊbəʊ/ *n.* (*pl.* **-oes** or **-os**) *US* a wandering worker; a tramp. [19th c.: orig. unkn.]

Hobson's choice /ˈhɒbs(ə)nz/ *n.* a choice of taking the thing offered or nothing. [T. *Hobson,* Cambridge carrier d. 1631, who let out horses on the basis that customers must take the one nearest the door]

hock[1] /hɒk/ *n.* **1** the joint of a quadruped's hind leg between the knee and the fetlock. **2** a knuckle of pork; the lower joint of a ham. [obs. *hockshin* f. OE *hōhsinu:* see HOUGH]

hock[2] /hɒk/ *n. Brit.* a German white wine from the Rhineland (properly that of Hochheim on the river Main). [abbr. of obs. *hockamore* f. G *Hochheimer*]

hock[3] /hɒk/ *v. & n.* esp. *US colloq.* —*v.tr.* pawn; pledge. —*n.* a pawnbroker's pledge. □**in hock 1** in pawn. **2** in debt. **3** in prison. [Du. *hok* hutch, prison, debt]

hockey[1] /ˈhɒkɪ/ *n.* **1** a game played between two teams on a field with curved sticks and a small hard ball. **2** *US* = *ice hockey.* □□ **hockeyist** *n.* (in sense 2). [16th c.: orig. unkn.]

hockey[2] var. of OCHE.

Hocktide /ˈhɒktaɪd/ *n. hist.* a festival formerly kept on the second Monday and Tuesday after Easter, orig. for money-raising. [ME: orig. unkn.]

hocus /ˈhəʊkəs/ *v.tr.* (**hocussed, hocussing;** *US* **hocused, hocusing**) **1** take in; hoax. **2** stupefy (a person) with drugs. **3** drug (liquor). [obs. noun *hocus* = HOCUS-POCUS]

hocus-pocus /ˌhəʊkəsˈpəʊkəs/ *n. & v.* —*n.* **1** deception; trickery. **2** a typical verbal formula used in conjuring. —*v.* (**-pocussed, -pocussing;** *US* **-pocused, -pocusing**) **1** *intr.* (often foll. by *with*) play tricks. **2** *tr.* play tricks on, deceive. [17th-c. sham L]

hod /hɒd/ *n.* **1** a V-shaped open trough on a pole used for carrying bricks, mortar, etc. **2** a portable receptacle for coal. [prob. = dial. *hot* f. OF *hotte* pannier, f. Gmc]

hodden /ˈhɒd(ə)n/ *n. Sc.* a coarse woollen cloth. □**hodden grey** grey hodden; typical rustic clothing. [16th c.: orig. unkn.]

Hodge /hɒdʒ/ *n. Brit.* a typical English agricultural labourer. [pet-form of the name *Roger*]

hodgepodge /ˈhɒdʒpɒdʒ/ *n.* = HOTCHPOTCH 1, 3. [ME, assim. to HODGE]

Hodgkin's disease /ˈhɒdʒkɪnz/ *n.* a malignant disease of lymphatic tissues usu. characterized by enlargement of the lymph nodes. [T. *Hodgkin,* Engl. physician d. 1866]

hodiernal /ˌhɒdɪˈɜːnəl, ˌhəʊ-/ *adj. formal* of the present day. [L *hodiernus* f. *hodie* today]

hodman /ˈhɒdmæn/ *n.* (*pl.* **-men**) **1** a labourer who carries a hod. **2** a literary hack. **3** a person who works mechanically.

hodograph /ˈhɒdəˌɡrɑːf/ *n.* a curve in which the radius vector represents the velocity of a moving particle. [Gk *hodos* way + -GRAPH]

hodometer /həˈdɒmɪtə(r)/ var. of ODOMETER.

hoe /həʊ/ *n. & v.* —*n.* a long-handled tool with a thin metal blade, used for weeding etc. —*v.* (**hoes, hoed, hoeing**) **1** *tr.* weed (crops); loosen (earth); dig up or cut down with a hoe. **2** *intr.* use a hoe. □**hoe-cake** *US* a coarse cake of maize flour orig. baked on the blade of a hoe. **hoe in** *Austral. & NZ sl.* eat eagerly. **hoe into** *Austral. & NZ sl.* attack (food, a person, a task). □□ **hoer** *n.* [ME *howe* f. OF *houe* f. Gmc]

hoedown /ˈhəʊdaʊn/ n. US a lively dance or dance-party.

hog /hɒg/ n. & v. —n. 1 a a domesticated pig, esp. a castrated male reared for slaughter. b any of several other pigs of the family Suidae, e.g. a wart-hog. 2 colloq. a greedy person. 3 (also **hogg**) Brit. dial. a young sheep before the first shearing. —v. (**hogged, hogging**) 1 tr. colloq. take greedily; hoard selfishly. 2 tr. & intr. raise (the back), or rise in an arch in the centre. □**go the whole hog** colloq. do something completely or thoroughly. **hog-tie** US 1 secure by fastening the hands and feet or all four feet together. 2 restrain, impede. □□ **hogger** n. **hoggery** n. **hoggish** adj. **hoggishly** adv. **hoggishness** n. **hoglike** adj. [OE hogg, hocg, perh. of Celt. orig.]

hogan /ˈhəʊgən/ n. an American Indian hut of logs etc. [Navajo]

hogback /ˈhɒgbæk/ n. (also **hog's back**) a steep-sided ridge of a hill.

hogg var. of HOG n. 3.

hogget /ˈhɒgɪt/ n. Brit. a yearling sheep. [HOG]

hoggin /ˈhɒgɪn/ n. 1 a mixture of sand and gravel. 2 sifted gravel. [19th c.: orig. unkn.]

hogmanay /ˈhɒgmə nei, -ˈnei/ n. Sc. 1 New Year's Eve. 2 a celebration on this day. 3 a gift of cake etc. demanded by children at hogmanay. [17th c.: perh. f. Norman F hoguinané f. OF aguillanneuf (also = new year's gift)]

hog's back var. of HOGBACK.

hogshead /ˈhɒgzhed/ n. 1 a large cask. 2 a liquid or dry measure, usu. about 50 imperial gallons. [ME f. HOG, HEAD: reason for the name unkn.]

hogwash /ˈhɒgwɒʃ/ n. 1 colloq. nonsense, rubbish. 2 kitchen swill etc. for pigs.

hogweed /ˈhɒgwiːd/ n. any of various coarse weeds of the genus Heracleum, esp. H. sphondylium.

ho-ho /həʊˈhəʊ/ int. expressing surprise, triumph, or derision. [redupl. of HO]

ho-hum /ˈhəʊhʌm/ int. expressing boredom. [imit. of yawn]

hoick[1] /hɔɪk/ v. & n. colloq. —v.tr. (often foll. by out) lift or pull, esp. with a jerk. —n. a jerky pull; a jerk. [perh. var. of HIKE]

hoick[2] /hɔɪk/ v.intr. sl. spit. [perh. var. of HAWK[3]]

hoicks var. of YOICKS.

hoi polloi /ˌhɔɪ pəˈlɔɪ/ n. (often prec. by the: see note below) 1 the masses; the common people. 2 the majority. ¶ Use with the is strictly unnecessary, since hoi = 'the', but this construction is very common. [Gk, = the many]

hoist /hɔɪst/ v. & n. —v.tr. 1 raise or haul up. 2 raise by means of ropes and pulleys etc. —n. 1 an act of hoisting, a lift. 2 an apparatus for hoisting. 3 a the part of a flag nearest the staff. b a group of flags raised as a signal. □**hoist the flag** stake one's claim to discovered territory by displaying a flag. **hoist one's flag** signify that one takes command. **hoist with one's own petard** see PETARD. □□ **hoister** n. [16th c.: alt. of hoise f. (15th-c.) hysse, prob. of LG orig.: cf. LG hissen]

hoity-toity /ˌhɔɪtɪˈtɔɪtɪ/ adj., int., & n. —adj. 1 haughty; petulant; snobbish. 2 archaic frolicsome. —int. expressing surprised protest at presumption etc. —n. archaic riotous or giddy conduct. [obs. hoit indulge in riotous mirth, of unkn. orig.]

hokey /ˈhəʊkɪ/ adj. (also **hoky**) (**hokier, hokiest**) US sl. sentimental, melodramatic, artificial. □□ **hokeyness** n. (also **hokiness**). **hokily** adv. [HOKUM + -Y[2]]

hokey-cokey /ˌhəʊkɪˈkəʊkɪ/ n. a communal dance performed in a circle with synchronized shaking of the limbs in turn. [perh. f. HOCUS-POCUS]

hokey-pokey /ˌhəʊkɪˈpəʊkɪ/ n. colloq. 1 = HOCUS-POCUS. 2 ice-cream formerly sold esp. by Italian street vendors. [HOCUS-POCUS: sense 2 of unkn. orig.]

hokku /ˈhɒkʊ/ n. (pl. same) = HAIKU. [Jap.]

hokum /ˈhəʊkəm/ n. esp. US sl. 1 sentimental, popular, sensational, or unreal situations, dialogue,

etc., in a film or play etc. 2 bunkum; rubbish. [20th c.: orig. unkn.]

hoky var. of HOKEY.

Holarctic /həˈlɑːktɪk/ adj. of or relating to the geographical distribution of animals in the whole northern or arctic region. [HOLO- + ARCTIC]

hold[1] /həʊld/ v. & n. —v. (past and past part. **held** /held/) 1 tr. a keep fast; grasp (esp. in the hands or arms). b (also refl.) keep or sustain (a thing, oneself, one's head, etc.) in a particular position (hold it to the light; held himself erect). c grasp so as to control (hold the reins). 2 tr. (of a vessel etc.) contain or be capable of containing (the jug holds two pints; the hall holds 900). 3 tr. possess, gain, or have, esp.: a be the owner or tenant of (land, property, stocks, etc.) (holds the farm from the trust). b gain or have gained (a degree, record, etc.) (holds the long-jump record). c have the position of (a job or office). d have (a specified card) in one's hand. e keep possession of (a place, a person's thoughts, etc.) esp. against attack (held the fort against the enemy; held his place in her estimation). 4 intr. remain unbroken; not give way (the roof held under the storm). 5 tr. observe; celebrate; conduct (a meeting, festival, conversation, etc.). 6 tr. a keep (a person etc.) in a specified condition, place, etc. (held him prisoner; held him at arm's length). b detain, esp. in custody (hold him until I arrive). 7 tr. a engross (a person or a person's attention) (the book held him for hours). b dominate (held the stage). 8 tr. (foll. by to) make (a person etc.) adhere to (terms, a promise, etc.). 9 intr. (of weather) continue fine. 10 tr. (often foll. by to + infin., or that + clause) think; believe (held it to be self-evident; held that the earth was flat). 11 tr. regard with a specified feeling (held him in contempt). 12 tr. a cease; restrain (hold your fire). b US colloq. withhold; not use (a burger please, and hold the onions!). 13 tr. keep or reserve (will you hold our seats please?). 14 tr. be able to drink (liquor) without effect (can't hold his drink). 15 tr. (usu. foll. by that + clause) (of a judge, a court, etc.) lay down; decide. 16 intr. keep going (held on his way). 17 tr. Mus. sustain (a note). 18 intr. archaic restrain oneself. —n. 1 a grasp (catch hold of him; keep a hold on him). 2 (often in comb.) a thing to hold by (seized the handhold). 3 (foll. by on, over) influence over (has a strange hold over them). 4 a manner of holding in wrestling etc. 5 archaic a fortress. □**hold (a thing) against (a person)** resent or regard it as discreditable to (a person). **hold aloof** avoid communication with people etc. **hold back** 1 impede the progress of; restrain. 2 keep (a thing) to or for oneself. 3 (often foll. by from) hesitate; refrain. **hold-back** n. a hindrance. **hold one's breath** see BREATH. **hold by** (or to) adhere to (a choice, purpose, etc.). **hold cheap** not value highly; despise. **hold the clock on** time (a sporting event etc.). **hold court** preside over one's admirers etc., like a sovereign. **hold dear** regard with affection. **hold down** 1 repress. 2 colloq. be competent enough to keep (one's job etc.). **hold everything!** (or **it!**) cease action or movement. **hold the fort** 1 act as a temporary substitute. 2 cope in an emergency. **hold forth** 1 offer (an inducement etc.). 2 usu. derog. speak at length or tediously. **hold good** (or **true**) be valid; apply. **hold one's ground** see GROUND[1]. **hold one's hand** see HAND. **hold a person's hand** give a person guidance or moral support. **hold hands** grasp one another by the hand as a sign of affection or for support or guidance. **hold hard!** stop!; wait! **hold harmless** Law indemnify. **hold one's head high** behave proudly and confidently. **hold one's horses** colloq. stop; slow down. **hold in** keep in check, confine. **hold it good** think it advisable. **hold the line** 1 not yield. 2 maintain a telephone connection. **hold one's nose** compress the nostrils to avoid a bad smell. **hold off** 1 delay; not begin. 2 keep one's distance. **hold on** 1 keep one's grasp on something. 2 wait a moment. 3 (when telephoning) not ring off.

hold out 1 stretch forth (a hand etc.). **2** offer (an inducement etc.). **3** maintain resistance. **4** persist or last. **hold out for** continue to demand. **hold out on** *colloq.* refuse something to (a person). **hold over** postpone. **hold-over** *n. US* a relic. **hold something over** threaten (a person) constantly with something. **hold one's own** see OWN. **hold to bail** *Law* bind by bail. **hold to a draw** manage to achieve a draw against (an opponent thought likely to win). **hold together 1** cohere. **2** cause to cohere. **hold one's tongue** *colloq.* be silent. **hold to ransom 1** keep (a person) prisoner until a ransom is paid. **2** demand concessions from by threats of damaging action. **hold up 1 a** support; sustain. **b** maintain (the head etc.) erect. **2** exhibit; display. **3** arrest the progress of; obstruct. **4** stop and rob by violence or threats. **hold-up** *n.* **1** a stoppage or delay by traffic, fog, etc. **2** a robbery, esp. by the use of threats or violence. **hold water** (of reasoning) be sound; bear examination. **hold with** (usu. with *neg.*) *colloq.* approve of (*don't hold with motor bikes*). **left holding the baby** left with unwelcome responsibility. **take hold** (of a custom or habit) become established. **there is no holding him** (or **her** etc.) he (or she etc.) is restive, high-spirited, determined, etc. **with no holds barred** with no restrictions, all methods being permitted. □□ **holdable** *adj.* [OE *h(e)aldan*, *heald*]

hold² /hǝʊld/ *n.* a cavity in the lower part of a ship or aircraft in which the cargo is stowed. [obs. *holl* f. OE *hol* (orig. adj. = hollow), rel. to HOLE, assim. to HOLD¹]

holdall /ˈhǝʊldɔːl/ *n.* a portable case for miscellaneous articles.

holder /ˈhǝʊldǝ(r)/ *n.* **1** (often in *comb.*) a device or implement for holding something (*cigarette-holder*). **2 a** the possessor of a title etc. **b** the occupant of an office etc. **3** = SMALLHOLDER.

holdfast /ˈhǝʊldfɑːst/ *n.* **1** a firm grasp. **2** a staple or clamp securing an object to a wall etc. **3** the attachment-organ of an alga etc.

holding /ˈhǝʊldɪŋ/ *n.* **1 a** land held by lease (cf. SMALLHOLDING). **b** the tenure of land. **2** stocks, property, etc. held. □ **holding company** a company created to hold the shares of other companies, which it then controls. **holding operation** a manœuvre designed to maintain the *status quo*.

hole /hǝʊl/ *n. & v.* —*n.* **1 a** an empty space in a solid body. **b** an aperture in or through something. **2** an animal's burrow. **3** a cavity or receptacle for a ball in various sports or games. **4** *colloq.* a small, mean, or dingy abode. **5** *colloq.* an awkward situation. **6** *Golf* **a** a point scored by a player who gets the ball from tee to hole with the fewest strokes. **b** the terrain or distance from tee to hole. **7** a position from which an electron is absent, esp. acting as a mobile positive particle in a semiconductor. —*v.tr.* **1** make a hole or holes in. **2** pierce the side of (a ship). **3** put into a hole. **4** (also *absol.*; often foll. by *out*) send (a golf ball) into a hole. □ **hole-and-corner** secret; underhand. **hole in the heart** a congenital defect in the heart septum. **hole in one** *Golf* a shot that enters the hole from the tee. **hole in the wall** a small dingy place (esp. of business). **hole-proof** (of materials etc.) treated so as to be resistant to wear. **hole up** *US colloq.* hide oneself. **in holes** worn so much that holes have formed. **make a hole in** use a large amount of. **a round** (or **square**) **peg in a square** (or **round**) **hole** see PEG. □□ **holey** *adj.* [OE *hol*, *holian* (as HOLD²)]

holibut var. of HALIBUT.

holiday /ˈhɒlɪˌdeɪ, -dɪ/ *n. & v.* —*n.* **1** esp. *Brit.* (often in *pl.*) an extended period of recreation, esp. away from home or in travelling; a break from work (cf. VACATION). **2** a day of festivity or recreation when no work is done, esp. a religious festival etc. **3** (*attrib.*) (of clothes etc.) festive. —*v.intr.* esp. *Brit.* spend a holiday. □ **holiday camp** *Brit.* a camp for holiday-makers with accommodation, entertainment, and facilities on site. **holiday centre** a place with many tourist attractions. **holiday-maker** esp. *Brit.* a person on holiday. **on holiday** (or **one's holidays**) in the course of one's holiday. **take a** (or **make**) **holiday** have a break from work. [OE *hāligdæg* (HOLY, DAY)]

holily /ˈhǝʊlɪlɪ/ *adv.* in a holy manner. [OE *hāliglīce* (as HOLY)]

holiness /ˈhǝʊlɪnɪs/ *n.* **1** sanctity; the state of being holy. **2** (**Holiness**) a title used when referring to or addressing the Pope. [OE *hālignes* (as HOLY)]

holism /ˈhɒlɪz(ǝ)m, ˈhǝʊ-/ *n.* (also **wholism**) **1** *Philos.* the theory that certain wholes are to be regarded as greater than the sum of their parts (cf. REDUCTIONISM). **2** *Med.* the treating of the whole person including mental and social factors rather than just the symptoms of a disease. □□ **holistic** /-ˈlɪstɪk/ *adj.* **holistically** /-ˈlɪstɪkǝlɪ/ *adv.* [as HOLO- + -ISM]

holla /ˈhɒlǝ/ *int., n., & v.* —*int.* calling attention. —*n.* a cry of 'holla'. —*v.* (**hollas, hollaed** or **holla'd, hollaing**) **1** *intr.* shout. **2** *tr.* call to (hounds). [F *holà* (as HO, *là* there)]

holland /ˈhɒlǝnd/ *n.* a smooth, hard-wearing, linen fabric. □ **brown holland** unbleached holland. [*Holland* = Netherlands: Du., earlier *Holtlant* f. *holt* wood + *-lant* land, describing the Dordrecht district]

hollandaise sauce /ˌhɒlǝnˈdeɪz, ˈhɒl-/ *n.* a creamy sauce of melted butter, egg-yolks, vinegar, etc., served esp. with fish. [F, fem. of *hollandais* Dutch f. *Hollande* Holland]

Hollander /ˈhɒlǝndǝ(r)/ *n.* **1** a native of Holland (the Netherlands). **2** a Dutch ship.

Hollands /ˈhɒlǝndz/ *n.* gin made in Holland. [Du. *hollandsch genever* Dutch gin]

holler /ˈhɒlǝ(r)/ *v. & n. US colloq.* —*v.* **1** *intr.* make a loud cry or noise. **2** *tr.* express with a loud cry or shout. —*n.* a loud cry, noise, or shout. [var. of HOLLO]

hollo /ˈhɒlǝʊ/ *int., n., & v.* —*int.* = HOLLA. —*n.* (*pl.* **-os**) = HOLLA. —*v.* (**-oes, -oed**) (also **hollow** *pronunc.* same) = HOLLA. [rel. to HOLLA]

hollow /ˈhɒlǝʊ/ *adj., n., v., & adv.* —*adj.* **1 a** having a hole or cavity inside; not solid throughout. **b** having a depression; sunken (*hollow cheeks*). **2** (of a sound) echoing, as though made in or on a hollow container. **3** empty; hungry. **4** without significance; meaningless (*a hollow triumph*). **5** insincere; cynical; false (*a hollow laugh; hollow promises*). —*n.* **1** a hollow place; a hole. **2** a valley; a basin. —*v.tr.* (often foll. by *out*) make hollow; excavate. —*adv. colloq.* completely (*beaten hollow*). □ **hollow-eyed** with eyes deep sunk. **hollow-hearted** insincere. **hollow square** *Mil. hist.* a body of infantry drawn up in a square with a space in the middle. **in the hollow of one's hand** entirely subservient to one. □□ **hollowly** *adv.* **hollowness** *n.* [ME *holg, holu, hol(e)we* f. OE *holh* cave, rel. to HOLE]

hollowware /ˈhɒlǝʊˌweǝ(r)/ *n.* hollow articles of metal, china, etc., such as pots, kettles, jugs, etc. (opp. FLATWARE).

holly /ˈhɒlɪ/ *n.* (*pl.* **-ies**) **1** an evergreen shrub, *Ilex aquifolium*, with prickly usu. dark-green leaves, small white flowers, and red berries. **2** its branches and foliage used as decorations at Christmas. □ **holly oak** a holm-oak. [OE *hole(g)n*]

hollyhock /ˈhɒlɪˌhɒk/ *n.* a tall plant, *Alcea rosea*, with large showy flowers of various colours. [ME (orig. = marsh mallow) f. HOLY + obs. *hock* mallow, OE *hoc*, of unkn. orig.]

Hollywood /ˈhɒlɪˌwʊd/ *n.* the American cinema industry or its products, with its principal centre at Hollywood in California.

holm¹ /hǝʊm/ *n.* (also **holme**) *Brit.* **1** an islet, esp. in a river or near a mainland. **2** a piece of flat ground by a river, which is submerged in time of flood. [ON *holmr*]

holm² /hǝʊm/ *n.* (in full **holm-oak**) an evergreen

oak, *Quercus ilex*, with holly-like young leaves. [ME alt. of obs. *holin* (as HOLLY)]

holmium /'həʊlmɪəm/ *n. Chem.* a soft silvery metallic element of the lanthanide series occurring naturally in apatite. ¶ Symb.: **Ho**. [mod.L f. *Holmia* Stockholm]

holo- /'hɒləʊ/ *comb. form* whole (*Holocene*; *holocaust*). [Gk *holos* whole]

holocaust /'hɒlə,kɔːst/ *n.* **1** a case of large-scale destruction, esp. by fire or nuclear war. **2** (**the Holocaust**) the mass murder of the Jews by the Nazis 1939–45. **3** a sacrifice wholly consumed by fire. [ME f. OF *holocauste* f. LL *holocaustum* f. Gk *holokauston* (as HOLO-, *kaustos* burnt f. *kaiō* burn)]

Holocene /'hɒlə,siːn/ *adj. & n. Geol.* —*adj.* of or relating to the most recent epoch of the Quaternary period with evidence of human development and intervention, and the extinction of large mammals. ¶ Cf. Appendix II. —*n.* this period or system. Also called RECENT. [HOLO- + Gk *kainos* new]

holoenzyme /,hɒləʊ'enzaɪm/ *n. Biochem.* a complex enzyme consisting of several components.

hologram /'hɒlə,græm/ *n. Physics* **1** a three-dimensional image formed by the interference of light beams from a coherent light source. **2** a photograph of the interference pattern, which when suitably illuminated produces a three-dimensional image.

holograph /'hɒlə,grɑːf/ *adj. & n.* —*adj.* wholly written by hand by the person named as the author. —*n.* a holograph document. [F *holographe* or LL *holographus* f. Gk *holographos* (as HOLO-, -GRAPH)]

holography /həˈlɒgrəfɪ/ *n. Physics* the study or production of holograms. □□ **holographic** /-lə-'græfɪk/ *adj.* **holographically** /-lə'græfɪkəlɪ/ *adv.*

holohedral /,hɒlə'hiːdr(ə)l/ *adj. Crystallog.* having the full number of planes required by the symmetry of a crystal system.

holophyte /'hɒlə,faɪt/ *n.* an organism that synthesizes complex organic compounds by photosynthesis. □□ **holophytic** /-'fɪtɪk/ *adj.*

holothurian /,hɒlə'θjʊərɪən/ *n. & adj.* —*n.* any echinoderm of the class Holothurioidea, with a wormlike body, e.g. a sea cucumber. —*adj.* of or relating to this class. [mod.L *Holothuria* (n.pl.) f. Gk *holothourion*, a zoophyte]

holotype /'hɒlə,taɪp/ *n.* the specimen used for naming and describing a species.

hols /hɒlz/ *n.pl. Brit. colloq.* holidays. [abbr.]

Holstein /'hɒlstiːn/ *n. & adj. US* = FRIESIAN. [*Holstein* in NW Germany]

holster /'həʊlstə(r)/ *n.* a leather case for a pistol or revolver, worn on a belt or under an arm or fixed to a saddle. [17th c., synonymous with Du. *holster*: orig. unkn.]

holt¹ /həʊlt/ *n.* **1** an animal's (esp. an otter's) lair. **2** *colloq.* or *dial.* grip, hold. [var. of HOLD¹]

holt² /həʊlt/ *n. archaic* or *dial.* **1** a wood or copse. **2** a wooded hill. [OE f. Gmc]

holus-bolus /,həʊləs'bəʊləs/ *adv.* all in a lump, altogether. [app. sham L]

holy /'həʊlɪ/ *adj.* (**holier**, **holiest**) **1** morally and spiritually excellent or perfect, and to be revered. **2** belonging to, devoted to, or empowered by, God. **3** consecrated, sacred. **4** used in trivial exclamations (*holy cow!*; *holy mackerel!*; *holy Moses!*; *holy smoke!*). □ **holier-than-thou** *colloq.* self-righteous. **Holy City 1** a city held sacred by the adherents of a religion, esp. Jerusalem. **2** Heaven. **Holy Communion** see COMMUNION. **Holy Cross Day** the festival of the Exaltation of the Cross, 14 Sept. **holy day** a religious festival. **Holy Family** the young Jesus with his mother and St Joseph (often with St John the Baptist, St Anne, etc.) as grouped in pictures etc. **Holy Father** the Pope. **Holy Ghost** = *Holy Spirit*. **Holy Grail** see GRAIL. **holy Joe** *orig. Naut. sl.* **1** a clergyman. **2** a pious person. **Holy Land 1** W. Palestine, esp. Judaea. **2** a region similarly revered

in non-Christian religions. **Holy Name** *RC Ch.* the name of Jesus as an object of formal devotion. **Holy Office** the Inquisition. **holy of holies 1** the inner chamber of the sanctuary in the Jewish temple, separated by a veil from the outer chamber. **2** an innermost shrine. **3** a thing regarded as most sacred. **holy orders** see ORDER. **holy place 1** (in *pl.*) places to which religious pilgrimage is made. **2** the outer chamber of the sanctuary in the Jewish temple. **Holy Roman Empire** see ROMAN. **Holy Rood Day 1** the festival of the Invention of the Cross, 3 May. **2** = *Holy Cross Day*. **Holy Sacrament** see SACRAMENT. **Holy Saturday** Saturday in Holy Week. **Holy Scripture** the Bible. **Holy See** the papacy or the papal court. **Holy Spirit** the Third Person of the Trinity, God as spiritually acting. **holy terror** see TERROR. **Holy Thursday 1** *Anglican Ch.* Ascension Day. **2** *RC Ch.* Maundy Thursday. **Holy Trinity** see TRINITY. **holy war** a war waged in support of a religious cause. **holy water** water dedicated to holy uses, or blessed by a priest. **Holy Week** the week before Easter. **Holy Writ** holy writings collectively, esp. the Bible. **Holy Year** *RC Ch.* a period of remission from the penal consequences of sin, granted under certain conditions for a year usu. at intervals of 25 years. [OE *hālig* f. Gmc, rel. to WHOLE]

holystone /'həʊlɪ,stəʊn/ *n. & v. Naut.* —*n.* a piece of soft sandstone used for scouring decks. —*v.tr.* scour with this. [19th c.: prob. f. HOLY + STONE: the stones were called *bibles* etc., perh. because used while kneeling]

hom /həʊm/ *n.* (also **homa** /'həʊmə/) **1** the soma plant. **2** the juice of this plant as a sacred drink of the Parsees. [Pers. *hōm*, *hūm*, Avestan *haoma*]

homage /'hɒmɪdʒ/ *n.* **1** acknowledgement of superiority, dutiful reverence (*pay homage to*; *do homage to*). **2** *hist.* formal public acknowledgement of feudal allegiance. [ME f. OF (*h*)*omage* f. med.L *hominaticum* f. L *homo -minis* man]

hombre /'ɒmbreɪ/ *n. US* a man. [Sp.]

Homburg /'hɒmbɜːg/ *n.* a man's felt hat with a narrow curled brim and a lengthwise dent in the crown. [*Homburg* in W. Germany, where first worn]

home /həʊm/ *n., adj., adv., & v.* —*n.* **1 a** the place where one lives; the fixed residence of a family or household. **b** a dwelling-house. **2** the members of a family collectively; one's family background (*comes from a good home*). **3** the native land of a person or of a person's ancestors. **4** an institution for persons needing care, rest, or refuge (*nursing home*). **5** the place where a thing originates or is native or most common. **6 a** the finishing-point in a race. **b** (in games) the place where one is free from attack; the goal. **c** *Lacrosse* a player in an attacking position near the opponents' goal. **7** *Sport* a home match or win. —*attrib.adj.* **1 a** of or connected with one's home. **b** carried on, done, or made, at home. **c** proceeding from home. **2 a** carried on or produced in one's own country (*home industries*; *the home market*). **b** dealing with the domestic affairs of a country. **3** *Sport* played on one's own ground etc. (*home match*; *home win*). **4** in the neighbourhood of home. —*adv.* **1 a** to one's home or country (*go home*). **b** arrived at home (*is he home yet?*). **c** *US* at home (*stay home*). **2 a** to the point aimed at (*the thrust went home*). **b** as far as possible (*drove the nail home*; *pressed his advantage home*). —*v.* **1** *intr.* (esp. of a trained pigeon) return home (cf. HOMING 1). **2** *intr.* (often foll. by *on, in on*) (of a vessel, missile, etc.) be guided towards a destination or target by a landmark, radio beam, etc. **3** *tr.* send or guide homewards. **4** *tr.* provide with a home. □ **at home 1** in one's own house or native land. **2** at ease as if in one's own home (*make yourself at home*). **3** (usu. foll. by *in, on, with*) familiar or well informed. **4** available to callers. **at-home** *n.* a social reception in a person's

564

home. **come home to** become fully realized by. **come home to roost** see ROOST¹. **home and dry** having achieved one's purpose. **home away from home** = *home from home*. **home-bird** a person who likes to stay at home. **home-brew** beer or other alcoholic drink brewed at home. **home-brewed** (of beer etc.) brewed at home. **home-coming** arrival at home. **Home Counties** the counties closest to London. **home economics** the study of household management. **home farm** *Brit.* a farm (one of several on an estate) set aside to provide produce for the owner. **home-felt** felt intimately. **home from home** a place other than one's home where one feels at home; a place providing homelike amenities. **home-grown** grown or produced at home. **Home Guard** *hist.* **1** the British citizen army organized in 1940 to defend the UK against invasion, and disbanded in 1957. **2** a member of this. **home help** *Brit.* a woman employed to help in a person's home, esp. one provided by a local authority. **home, James!** *joc.* drive home quickly! **home-made** made at home. **home-making** creation of a (pleasant) home. **home movie** a film made at home or of one's own activities. **Home Office 1** the British government department dealing with law and order, immigration, etc., in England and Wales. **2** the building used for this. **home of lost causes** Oxford University. **home-owner** a person who owns his or her own home. **home perm** a permanent wave made with domestic equipment. **home plate** *Baseball* a plate beside which the batter stands. **home port** the port from which a ship originates. **home rule** the government of a country or region by its own citizens. **home run** *Baseball* a hit that allows the batter to make a complete circuit of the bases. **Home Secretary** (in the UK) the Secretary of State in charge of the Home Office. **home signal** a signal indicating whether a train may proceed into a station or to the next section of the line. **home straight** (*US* **stretch**) the concluding stretch of a racecourse. **home town** the town of one's birth or early life or present fixed residence. **home trade** trade carried on within a country. **home truth** basic but unwelcome information concerning oneself. **home unit** *Austral.* a private residence, usu. occupied by the owner, as one of several in a building. **near home** affecting one closely. □□ **homelike** *adj.* [OE *hām* f. Gmc]

homebody /ˈhəʊmˌbɒdɪ/ *n.* (*pl.* -**ies**) a person who likes to stay at home.

homeland /ˈhəʊmlænd/ *n.* **1** one's native land. **2** an area in S. Africa reserved for a particular African people (the official name for a Bantustan).

homeless /ˈhəʊmlɪs/ *adj.* lacking a home. □□ **homelessness** *n.*

homely /ˈhəʊmlɪ/ *adj.* (**homelier, homeliest**) **1 a** simple, plain. **b** unpretentious. **c** primitive. **2** *US* (of people or their features) not attractive in appearance, ugly. **3** comfortable in the manner of a home, cosy. **4** skilled at housekeeping. □□ **homeliness** *n.*

homeopath etc. *US* var. of HOMOEOPATH etc.

homeostasis *US* var. of HOMOEOSTASIS.

homer /ˈhəʊmə(r)/ *n.* **1** a homing pigeon. **2** *Baseball* a home run.

Homeric /həʊˈmerɪk, hɒˈm-/ *adj.* **1** of, or in the style of, Homer or the epic poems ascribed to him. **2** of Bronze Age Greece as described in these poems. **3** epic, large-scale, titanic (*Homeric conflict*). [L *Homericus* f. Gk *Homērikos* f. *Homēros* Homer, traditional author of the *Iliad* and the *Odyssey*]

homesick /ˈhəʊmsɪk/ *adj.* depressed by longing for one's home during absence from it. □□ **homesickness** *n.*

homespun /ˈhəʊmspʌn/ *adj.* & *n.* —*adj.* **1 a** (of cloth) made of yarn spun at home. **b** (of yarn) spun at home. **2** plain, simple, unsophisticated, homely. —*n.* **1** homespun cloth. **2** anything plain or homely.

homestead /ˈhəʊmsted, -stɪd/ *n.* **1** a house, esp. a farmhouse, and outbuildings. **2** *Austral.* & *NZ* the

owner's residence on a sheep or cattle station. **3** *US* an area of land (usu. 160 acres) granted to a settler as a home. □□ **homesteader** *n.* [OE *hāmstede* (as HOME, STEAD)]

homestyle /ˈhəʊmstaɪl/ *adj. US* (esp. of food) of a kind made or done at home, homely.

homeward /ˈhəʊmwəd/ *adv.* & *adj.* —*adv.* (also **homewards** /-wədz/) towards home. —*adj.* going or leading towards home. □ **homeward-bound** (esp. of a ship) preparing to go, or on the way, home. [OE *hāmweard(es)* (as HOME, -WARD)]

homework /ˈhəʊmwɜːk/ *n.* **1** work to be done at home, esp. by a school pupil. **2** preparatory work or study.

homey /ˈhəʊmɪ/ *adj.* (also **homy**) (**homier, homiest**) suggesting home; cosy. □□ **homeyness** *n.* (also **hominess**).

homicide /ˈhɒmɪˌsaɪd/ *n.* **1** the killing of a human being by another. **2** a person who kills a human being. □□ **homicidal** /-ˈsaɪd(ə)l/ *adj.* [ME f. OF f. L *homicidium* (sense 1), *homicida* (sense 2) (HOMO man)]

homiletic /ˌhɒmɪˈletɪk/ *adj.* & *n.* —*adj.* of homilies. —*n.* (usu. in *pl.*) the art of preaching. [LL *homileticus* f. Gk *homilētikos* f. *homileō* hold converse, consort (as HOMILY)]

homiliary /hɒˈmɪlɪərɪ/ *n.* (*pl.* -**ies**) a book of homilies. [med.L *homeliarius*]

homily /ˈhɒmɪlɪ/ *n.* (*pl.* -**ies**) **1** a sermon. **2** a tedious moralizing discourse. □□ **homilist** *n.* [ME f. OF *omelie* f. eccl.L *homilia* f. Gk *homilia* f. *homilos* crowd]

homing /ˈhəʊmɪŋ/ *attrib.adj.* **1** (of a pigeon) trained to fly home, bred for long-distance racing. **2** (of a device) for guiding to a target etc. **3** that goes home. □ **homing instinct** the instinct of certain animals to return to the territory from which they have been moved.

hominid /ˈhɒmɪnɪd/ *n.* & *adj.* —*n.* any member of the primate family Hominidae, including humans and their fossil ancestors. —*adj.* of or relating to this family. [mod.L *Hominidae* f. L *homo hominis* man]

hominoid /ˈhɒmɪˌnɔɪd/ *adj.* & *n.* —*adj.* **1** like a human. **2** hominid or pongid. —*n.* an animal resembling a human.

hominy /ˈhɒmɪnɪ/ *n.* esp. *US* coarsely ground maize kernels esp. boiled with water or milk. [Algonquian]

Homo /ˈhəʊməʊ, ˈhɒməʊ/ *n.* any primate of the genus *Homo*, including modern humans and various extinct species. [L, = man]

homo /ˈhəʊməʊ/ *n.* (*pl.* -**os**) *colloq.* a homosexual. [abbr.]

homo- /ˈhəʊməʊ, ˈhɒməʊ/ *comb. form* same (often opp. HETERO-). [Gk *homos* same]

homocentric /ˌhəʊməʊˈsentrɪk, ˌhɒməʊ-/ *adj.* having the same centre.

homoeopath /ˈhəʊmɪəʊˌpæθ, ˈhɒmɪ-/ *n.* (*US* **homeopath**) a person who practises homoeopathy. [G *Homöopath* (as HOMOEOPATHY)]

homoeopathy /ˌhəʊmɪˈɒpəθɪ, ˌhɒmɪ-/ *n.* (*US* **homeopathy**) the treatment of disease by minute doses of drugs that in a healthy person would produce symptoms of the disease (cf. ALLOPATHY). □□ **homoeopathic** /-ˈpæθɪk/ *adj.* **homoeopathist** *n.* [G *Homöopathie* f. Gk *homoios* like + *patheia* -PATHY]

homoeostasis /ˌhəʊmɪəʊˈsteɪsɪs, ˌhɒm-/ *n.* (*US* **homeostasis**) (*pl.* -**stases** /-siːz/) the tendency towards a relatively stable equilibrium between interdependent elements, esp. as maintained by physiological processes. □□ **homoeostatic** /-ˈstætɪk/ *adj.* [mod.L f. Gk *homoios* like + -STASIS]

homoeotherm /ˈhɒmɪəʊˌθɜːm/ *n.* (also **homoiotherm**) an organism that maintains its body temperature at a constant level, usu. above that of the environment, by its metabolic activity; a warm-blooded organism (cf. POIKILOTHERM). □□ **homoeothermal** /-ˈθɜːm(ə)l/ *adj.* **homoeothermic**

/-'θɜːmɪk/ *adj*. **homoeothermy** *n*. [mod.L f. Gk *homoios* like + *thermē* heat]

homoerotic /ˌhəʊməʊɪ'rɒtɪk, ˌhɒməʊ-/ *adj*. homosexual.

homogametic /ˌhəʊməʊgə'miːtɪk, ˌhɒməʊ-/ *adj. Biol*. (of a sex or individuals of a sex) producing gametes that carry the same sex chromosome.

homogamy /hə'mɒgəmɪ/ *n. Bot*. **1** a state in which the flowers of a plant are hermaphrodite or of the same sex. **2** the simultaneous ripening of the stamens and pistils of a flower. □□ **homogamous** *adj*. [Gk *homogamos* (as HOMO-, *gamos* marriage)]

homogenate /hə'mɒdʒɪˌneɪt/ *n*. a suspension produced by homogenizing.

homogeneous /ˌhəʊməʊ'dʒiːnɪəs, ˌhɒməʊ-/ *adj*. **1** of the same kind. **2** consisting of parts all of the same kind; uniform. **3** *Math*. containing terms all of the same degree. □□ **homogeneity** /-dʒɪ'niːɪtɪ/ *n*. **homogeneously** *adv*. **homogeneousness** *n*. [med.L *homogeneus* f. Gk *homogenēs* (as HOMO-, *genēs* f. *genos* kind)]

homogenetic /ˌhəʊməʊdʒɪ'netɪk, ˌhɒməʊ-/ *adj. Biol*. having a common descent or origin.

homogenize /hə'mɒdʒɪˌnaɪz/ *v*. (also **-ise**) **1** *tr*. & *intr*. make or become homogeneous. **2** *tr*. treat (milk) so that the fat droplets are emulsified and the cream does not separate. □□ **homogenization** /-'zeɪʃ(ə)n/ *n*. **homogenizer** *n*.

homogeny /hə'mɒdʒɪnɪ/ *n. Biol*. similarity due to common descent. □□ **homogenous** *adj*.

homograft /'hɒməˌgrɑːft/ *n*. a graft of living tissue from one to another of the same species but different genotype.

homograph /'hɒməˌgrɑːf/ *n*. a word spelt like another but of different meaning or origin (e.g. POLE¹, POLE²).

homoiotherm var. of HOMOEOTHERM.

homoiousian /ˌhɒmɔɪ'uːsɪən, -'aʊsɪən/ *n. hist*. a person who held that God the Father and God the Son are of like but not identical substance (cf. HOMOOUSIAN). [eccl.L f. Gk *homoiousios* f. *homoios* like + *ousia* essence]

homolog US var. of HOMOLOGUE.

homologate /hə'mɒləˌgeɪt/ *v.tr*. **1** acknowledge, admit. **2** confirm, accept. **3** approve (a car, boat, engine, etc.) for use in a particular class of racing. □□ **homologation** /-'geɪʃ(ə)n/ *n*. [med.L *homologare* agree f. Gk *homologeō* (as HOMO-, *logos* word)]

homologize /hə'mɒləˌdʒaɪz/ *v*. (also **-ise**) **1** *intr*. be homologous; correspond. **2** *tr*. make homologous.

homologous /hə'mɒləgəs/ *adj*. **1 a** having the same relation, relative position, etc. **b** corresponding. **2** *Biol*. (of organs etc.) similar in position and structure but not necessarily in function. **3** *Biol*. (of chromosomes) pairing at meiosis and having the same structural features and pattern of genes. **4** *Chem*. (of a series of chemical compounds) having the same functional group but differing in composition by a fixed group of atoms. [med.L *homologus* f. Gk (as HOMO-, *logos* ratio, proportion)]

homologue /'hɒməˌlɒg/ *n*. (US **homolog**) a homologous thing. [F f. Gk *homologon* (neut. adj.) (as HOMOLOGOUS)]

homology /hə'mɒlədʒɪ/ *n*. a homologous state or relation; correspondence. □□ **homological** /ˌhɒmə'lɒdʒɪk(ə)l/ *adj*.

homomorphic /ˌhəʊməʊ'mɔːfɪk, ˌhɒməʊ-/ *adj*. (also **homomorphous**) of the same or similar form. □□ **homomorphically** *adv*. **homomorphism** *n*. **homomorphy** *n*.

homonym /'hɒmənɪm/ *n*. **1** a word of the same spelling or sound as another but of different meaning; a homograph or homophone. **2** a namesake. □□ **homonymic** /-'nɪmɪk/ *adj*. **homonymous** /hə'mɒnɪməs/ *adj*. [L *homonymum* f. Gk *homōnumon* (neut. adj.) (as HOMO-, *onoma* name)]

homoousian /ˌhɒməʊ'uːsɪən, ˌhəʊm-, -'aʊsɪən/ *n*. (also **homousian** /hɒ'muː-, hɒ'maʊ-/) *hist*. a person who

held that God the Father and God the Son are of the same substance (cf. HOMOIOUSIAN). [eccl.L *homoousianus* f. LL *homousius* f. Gk *homoousios* (as HOMO-, *ousia* essence)]

homophobia /ˌhəʊmə'fəʊbɪə/ *n*. a hatred or fear of homosexuals. □□ **homophobe** /'həʊm-/ *n*. **homophobic** /-'fəʊbɪk/ *adj*.

homophone /'hɒməˌfəʊn/ *n*. **1** a word having the same sound as another but of different meaning or origin (e.g. *pair, pear*). **2** a symbol denoting the same sound as another.

homophonic /ˌhɒməʊ'fɒnɪk/ *adj. Mus*. in unison; characterized by movement of all parts to the same melody. □□ **homophonically** *adv*.

homophonous /hə'mɒfənəs/ *adj*. **1** (of music) homophonic. **2** (of a word or symbol) that is a homophone. □□ **homophony** *n*.

homopolar /ˌhəʊməʊ'pəʊlə(r), ˌhɒməʊ-/ *adj*. **1** electrically symmetrical. **2** *Electr*. (of a generator) producing direct current without the use of commutators. **3** *Chem*. (of a covalent bond) in which one atom supplies both electrons.

homopteran /hə'mɒptərən/ *n*. any insect of the suborder Homoptera, including aphids and cicadas, with wings of uniform texture (cf. HETEROPTERAN). □□ **homopterous** *adj*. [HOMO- + Gk *pteron* wing]

Homo sapiens /ˌhəʊməʊ 'sæpɪenz/ *n*. modern humans regarded as a species. [L, = wise man]

homosexual /ˌhəʊməʊ'seksjʊəl, ˌhɒm-/ *adj*. & *n*. —*adj*. **1** feeling or involving sexual attraction only to persons of the same sex. **2** concerning homosexual relations or people. **3** relating to the same sex. —*n*. a homosexual person. □□ **homosexuality** /-'ælɪtɪ/ *n*. **homosexually** *adv*.

homousian var. of HOMOOUSIAN.

homozygote /ˌhəʊməʊ'zaɪgəʊt, ˌhɒməʊ-/ *n. Biol*. **1** an individual with identical alleles determining a particular characteristic. **2** an individual that is homozygous and so breeds true. □□ **homozygous** *adj*.

homunculus /hə'mʌŋkjʊləs/ *n*. (also **homuncule** /-kjuːl/) (*pl*. **homunculi** /-ˌlaɪ/ or **homuncules**) a little man, a manikin. [L *homunculus* f. *homo -minis* man]

homy var. of HOMEY.

Hon. *abbr*. **1** Honorary. **2** Honourable.

hon /hʌn/ *n. colloq*. = HONEY 5. [abbr.]

honcho /'hɒntʃəʊ/ *n*. & *v. US sl*. —*n*. (*pl*. **-os**) **1** a leader or manager, the person in charge. **2** an admirable man. —*v.tr*. (**-oes**, **-oed**) be in charge of, oversee. [Jap. *han'chō* group leader]

hone /həʊn/ *n*. & *v*. —*n*. **1** a whetstone, esp. for razors. **2** any of various stones used as material for this. —*v.tr*. sharpen on or as on a hone. [OE *hān* stone f. Gmc]

honest /'ɒnɪst/ *adj*. & *adv*. —*adj*. **1** fair and just in character or behaviour, not cheating or stealing. **2** free of deceit and untruthfulness, sincere. **3** fairly earned (*an honest living*). **4** (of an act or feeling) showing fairness. **5** (with patronizing effect) blameless but undistinguished (cf. WORTHY). **6** (of a thing) unadulterated, unsophisticated. —*adv. colloq*. genuinely, really. □ **earn** (or **turn**) **an honest penny** earn money fairly. **honest broker** a mediator in international, industrial, etc., disputes (orig. of Bismarck). **honest Injun** *colloq*. genuinely, really. **honest-to-God** (or **-goodness**) *colloq. adj*. genuine, real. —*adv*. genuinely, really. **make an honest woman of** *colloq*. marry (esp. a pregnant woman). [ME f. OF (*h*)*oneste* f. L *honestus* f. *honos* HONOUR]

honestly /'ɒnɪstlɪ/ *adv*. **1** in an honest way. **2** really (*I don't honestly know; honestly, the cheek of it!*).

honesty /'ɒnɪstɪ/ *n*. **1** being honest. **2** truthfulness. **3** a plant of the genus *Lunaria* with purple or white flowers, so called from its flat round semi-transparent seed-pods. [ME f. OF (*h*)*onesté* f. L *honestas -tatis* (as HONEST)]

honey /'hʌnɪ/ *n*. (*pl*. **-eys**) **1** a sweet sticky yellowish fluid made by bees and other insects from nectar collected from flowers. **2** the colour of this. **3 a** sweetness. **b** a sweet thing. **4** a person or thing excellent of its kind. **5** esp. *US* (usu. as a form of address) darling, sweetheart. □**honey-badger** a ratel. **honey-bee** any of various bees of the genus *Apis*, esp. the common hive-bee (*A. mellifera*). **honey-bun** (or **-bunch**) (esp. as a form of address) darling. **honey-buzzard** any bird of prey of the genus *Pernis* feeding on the larvae of bees and wasps. **honey-eater** any Australasian bird of the family Meliphagidae with a long tongue that can take nectar from flowers. **honey-fungus** a parasitic fungus, *Armillaria mellea*, with honey-coloured edible toadstools. **honey-guide 1** any small bird of the family Indicatoridae which feeds on beeswax and insects. **2** a marking on the corolla of a flower thought to guide bees to nectar. **honey-parrot** a lorikeet. **honey-pot 1** a pot for honey. **2** a posture with the hands clasped under the hams. **3** something very attractive or tempting. **honey sac** an enlarged part of a bee's gullet where honey is formed. **honey-sweet** sweet as honey. [OE *hunig* f. Gmc]

honeycomb /ˈhʌnɪˌkəʊm/ *n. & v.* —*n.* **1** a structure of hexagonal cells of wax, made by bees to store honey and eggs. **2 a** a pattern arranged hexagonally. **b** fabric made with a pattern of raised hexagons etc. **3** tripe from the second stomach of a ruminant. **4** a cavernous flaw in metalwork, esp. in guns. —*v.tr.* **1** fill with cavities or tunnels, undermine. **2** mark with a honeycomb pattern. [OE *hunigcamb* (as HONEY, COMB)]

honeydew /ˈhʌnɪˌdjuː/ *n.* **1** a sweet sticky substance found on leaves and stems, excreted by aphids. **2** a variety of melon with smooth pale skin and sweet green flesh. **3** an ideally sweet substance. **4** tobacco sweetened with molasses.

honeyed /ˈhʌnɪd/ *adj.* (also **honied**) **1** of or containing honey. **2** sweet.

honeymoon /ˈhʌnɪˌmuːn/ *n. & v.* —*n.* **1** a holiday spent together by a newly married couple. **2** an initial period of enthusiasm or goodwill. —*v.intr.* (usu. foll. by *in, at*) spend a honeymoon. □□ **honeymooner** *n.* [HONEY + MOON, orig. with ref. to waning affection, not to a period of a month]

honeysuckle /ˈhʌnɪˌsʌk(ə)l/ *n.* any climbing shrub of the genus *Lonicera* with fragrant yellow and pink flowers. [ME *hunisuccle, -soukel*, extension of *hunisuce, -souke*, f. OE *hunigsūce, -sūge* (as HONEY, SUCK)]

honied var. of HONEYED.

honk /hɒŋk/ *n. & v.* —*n.* **1** the cry of a wild goose. **2** the harsh sound of a car horn. —*v.* **1** *intr.* emit or give a honk. **2** *tr.* cause to do this. [imit.]

honky /ˈhɒŋkɪ/ *n.* (*pl.* **-ies**) *US Black sl. offens.* **1** a White person. **2** White people collectively. [20th c.: orig. unkn.]

honky-tonk /ˈhɒŋkɪˌtɒŋk/ *n. colloq.* **1** ragtime piano music. **2** a cheap or disreputable nightclub, dance-hall, etc. [20th c.: orig. unkn.]

honnête homme /ˌɒnɛt ˈɒm/ *n.* an honest and decent man. [F]

honor *US* var. of HONOUR.

honorable *US* var. of HONOURABLE.

honorand /ˈɒnəˌrænd/ *n.* a person to be honoured, esp. with an honorary degree. [L *honorandus* (as HONOUR)]

honorarium /ˌɒnəˈreərɪəm/ *n.* (*pl.* **honorariums** or **honoraria** /-rɪə/) a fee, esp. a voluntary payment for professional services rendered without the normal fee. [L, neut. of *honorarius*: see HONORARY]

honorary /ˈɒnərərɪ/ *adj.* **1 a** conferred as an honour, without the usual requirements, functions, etc. (*honorary degree*). **b** holding such a title or position (*honorary colonel*). **2** (of an office or its holder) unpaid (*honorary secretaryship; honorary treasurer*). **3** (of an obligation) depending on honour, not legally enforceable. [L *honorarius* (as HONOUR)]

honorific /ˌɒnəˈrɪfɪk/ *adj. & n.* —*adj.* **1** conferring honour. **2** (esp. of Oriental forms of speech) implying respect. —*n.* an honorific form of words. □□ **honorifically** *adv.* [L *honorificus* (as HONOUR)]

honoris causa /ɒˌnɔːrɪs ˈkaʊzə/ *adv.* (esp. of a degree awarded without examination) as a mark of esteem. [L, = for the sake of honour]

honour /ˈɒnə(r)/ *n. & v.* (*US* **honor**) —*n.* **1** high respect; glory; credit, reputation, good name. **2** adherence to what is right or to a conventional standard of conduct. **3** nobleness of mind, magnanimity (*honour among thieves*). **4** a thing conferred as a distinction, esp. an official award for bravery or achievement. **5** (foll. by *of* + verbal noun, or *to* + infin.) privilege, special right (*had the honour of being invited*). **6 a** exalted position. **b** (**Honour**) (prec. by *your, his*, etc.) a title of a circuit judge, *US* a mayor, and *Ir.* or in rustic speech any person of rank. **7** (foll. by *to*) a person or thing that brings honour (*she is an honour to her profession*). **8 a** (of a woman) chastity. **b** the reputation for this. **9** (in *pl.*) **a** special distinction for proficiency in an examination. **b** a course of degree studies more specialized than for an ordinary pass. **10 a** *Bridge* the ace, king, queen, jack, and ten, esp. of trumps, or the four aces at no trumps. **b** *Whist* the ace, king, queen, and jack, esp. of trumps. **11** *Golf* the right of driving off first as having won the last hole (*it is my honour*). —*v.tr.* **1** respect highly. **2** confer honour on. **3** accept or pay (a bill or cheque) when due. **4** acknowledge. □**do the honours** perform the duties of a host to guests etc. **honour bright** *colloq.* = *on my honour*. **honour point** *Heraldry* the point halfway between the top of a shield and the fesse point. **honours are even** there is equality in the contest. **honours list** a list of persons awarded honours. **honours of war** privileges granted to a capitulating force, e.g. that of marching out with colours flying. **honour system** a system of examinations etc. without supervision, relying on the honour of those concerned. **honour-trick** = *quick trick*. **in honour bound** = *on one's honour*. **in honour of** as a celebration of. **on one's honour** (usu. foll. by *to* + infin.) under a moral obligation. **on** (or **upon**) **my honour** an expression of sincerity. [ME f. OF (*h*)*onor* (n.), *onorer* (v.) f. L *honor, honorare*]

honourable /ˈɒnərəb(ə)l/ *adj.* (*US* **honorable**) **1 a** worthy of honour. **b** bringing honour to its possessor. **c** showing honour, not base. **d** consistent with honour. **e** *colloq.* (of the intentions of a man courting a woman) directed towards marriage. **2** (**Honourable**) a title indicating eminence or distinction, given to certain high officials, the children of certain ranks of the nobility, and MPs. □**honourable mention** an award of merit to a candidate in an examination, a work of art, etc., not awarded a prize. □□ **honourableness** *n.* **honourably** *adv.* [ME f. OF *honorable* f. L *honorabilis* (as HONOUR)]

Hon. Sec. *abbr.* Honorary Secretary.

hooch /huːtʃ/ *n.* (also **hootch**) *US colloq.* alcoholic liquor, esp. inferior or illicit whisky. [abbr. of Alaskan *hoochinoo*, name of a liquor-making tribe]

hood[1] /hʊd/ *n. & v.* —*n.* **1 a** a covering for the head and neck, whether part of a cloak etc. or separate. **b** a separate hoodlike garment worn over a university gown or a surplice to indicate the wearer's degree. **2** *Brit.* a folding waterproof top of a motor car, pram, etc. **3** *US* the bonnet of a motor vehicle. **4** a canopy to protect users of machinery or to remove fumes etc. **5** the hoodlike part of a cobra, seal, etc. **6** a leather covering for a hawk's head. —*v.tr.* cover with a hood. □**hood-mould** (or **-moulding**) *Archit.* a dripstone. □□ **hoodless** *adj.* **hoodlike** *adj.* [OE *hōd* f. WG, rel. to HAT]

hood[2] /hʊd/ *n. US sl.* a gangster or gunman. [abbr. of HOODLUM]

-hood /hʊd/ *suffix* forming nouns: **1** of condition or state (*childhood; falsehood*). **2** indicating a collection or group (*sisterhood*; *neighbourhood*). [OE -*hād*, orig. an independent noun, = person, condition, quality]

hooded /ˈhʊdɪd/ *adj.* having a hood; covered with a hood. □**hooded crow** a piebald grey and black crow, *Corvus cornix*.

hoodie /ˈhʊdɪ/ *n.* = *hooded crow*.

hoodlum /ˈhuːdləm/ *n.* **1** a street hooligan, a young thug. **2** a gangster. [19th c.: orig. unkn.]

hoodoo /ˈhuːduː/ *n. & v. esp. US* —*n.* **1 a** bad luck. **b** a thing or person that brings or causes this. **2** voodoo. **3** a fantastic rock pinnacle or column of rock formed by erosion etc. —*v.tr.* (**hoodoos, hoodooed**) **1** make unlucky. **2** bewitch. [alt. of VOODOO]

hoodwink /ˈhʊdwɪŋk/ *v.tr.* deceive, delude. [orig. 'blindfold', f. HOOD¹ n. + WINK]

hooey /ˈhuːɪ/ *n. & int. sl.* nonsense, humbug. [20th c.: orig. unkn.]

hoof /huːf/ *n. & v.* —*n.* (*pl.* **hoofs** or **hooves** /-vz/) the horny part of the foot of a horse, antelope, and other ungulates. —*v.* **1** *tr.* strike with a hoof. **2** *tr. sl.* kick or shove. □**hoof it** *sl.* **1** go on foot. **2** dance. **on the hoof** (of cattle) not yet slaughtered. □□ **hoofed** *adj.* (also in *comb.*). [OE *hōf* f. Gmc]

hoofer /ˈhuːfə(r)/ *n. sl.* a professional dancer.

hoo-ha /ˈhuːhɑː/ *n. sl.* a commotion, a row; uproar, trouble. [20th c.: orig. unkn.]

hook /hʊk/ *n. & v.* —*n.* **1 a** a piece of metal or other material bent back at an angle or with a round bend, for catching hold or for hanging things on. **b** (in full **fish-hook**) a bent piece of wire, usu. barbed and baited, for catching fish. **2** a curved cutting instrument (*reaping-hook*). **3 a** a sharp bend, e.g. in a river. **b** a projecting point of land (*Hook of Holland*). **c** a sand-spit with a curved end. **4 a** *Cricket & Golf* a hooking stroke (see sense 5 of *v.*). **b** *Boxing* a short swinging blow with the elbow bent and rigid. **5 a** trap, a snare. **6 a** a curved stroke in handwriting, esp. as made in learning to write. **b** *Mus.* an added stroke transverse to the stem in the symbol for a quaver etc. **7** (in *pl.*) *sl.* fingers. —*v.* **1** *tr.* **a** grasp with a hook. **b** secure with a hook or hooks. **2** (often foll. by *on, up*) **a** *tr.* attach with or as with a hook. **b** *intr.* be or become attached with a hook. **3** *tr.* catch with or as with a hook (*he hooked a fish; she hooked a husband*). **4** *tr. sl.* steal. **5** *tr.* a *Cricket* play (the ball) round from the off to the on side with an upward stroke. **b** (also *absol.*) *Golf* strike (the ball) so that it deviates towards the striker. **6** *tr. Rugby Football* secure (the ball) and pass it backward with the foot in the scrum. **7** *tr. Boxing* strike (one's opponent) with the elbow bent and rigid. □**be hooked on** *sl.* be addicted to or captivated by. **by hook or by crook** by one means or another, by fair means or foul. **hook and eye** a small metal hook and loop as a fastener on a garment. **hook it** *sl.* make off, run away. **hook, line, and sinker** entirely. **hook-nose** an aquiline nose. **hook-nosed** having an aquiline nose. **hook-up** a connection, esp. an interconnection of broadcasting equipment for special transmissions. **off the hook 1** *colloq.* no longer in difficulty or trouble. **2** (of a telephone receiver) not on its rest, and so preventing incoming calls. **off the hooks** *sl.* dead. **on one's own hook** *sl.* on one's own account. **sling** (or **take**) **one's hook** *sl.* = *hook it.* □□ **hookless** *adj.* **hooklet** *n.* **hooklike** *adj.* [OE *hōc*: sense 3 of *n.* prob. influenced by Du. *hoek* corner]

hookah /ˈhʊkə/ *n.* an oriental tobacco-pipe with a long tube passing through water for cooling the smoke as it is drawn through. [Urdu f. Arab. *ḥuḳḳah* casket]

hooked /hʊkt/ *adj.* **1** hook-shaped (*hooked nose*). **2** furnished with a hook or hooks. **3** in senses of HOOK *v.* **4** (of a rug or mat) made by pulling woollen yarn through canvas with a hook.

hooker¹ /ˈhʊkə(r)/ *n.* **1** *Rugby Football* the player in the middle of the front row of the scrum who tries to hook the ball. **2** *sl.* a prostitute. **3** a person or thing that hooks.

hooker² /ˈhʊkə(r)/ *n.* **1** a small Dutch or Irish fishing-vessel. **2** *derog.* any ship. [Du. *hoeker* f. *hoek* HOOK]

Hooke's law /hʊks/ *n.* the law that the strain in a solid is proportional to the applied stress within the elastic limit of that solid. [R. *Hooke*, Engl. scientist d. 1703]

hookey /ˈhʊkɪ/ *n.* (also **hooky**) *US* □**blind hookey** a gambling guessing-game at cards. **play hookey** *sl.* play truant. [19th c.: orig. unkn.]

hookworm /ˈhʊkwɜːm/ *n.* **1** any of various nematode worms, with hooklike mouthparts for attachment and feeding, infesting humans and animals. **2** a disease caused by one of these, often resulting in severe anaemia.

hooligan /ˈhuːlɪgən/ *n.* a young ruffian, esp. a member of a gang. □□ **hooliganism** *n.* [19th c.: orig. unkn.]

hoop¹ /huːp/ *n. & v.* —*n.* **1** a circular band of metal, wood, etc., esp. for binding the staves of casks etc. or for forming part of a framework. **2 a** a ring bowled along by a child. **b** a large ring usu. with paper stretched over it for circus performers to jump through. **3** an arch of iron etc. through which the balls are hit in croquet. **4** *hist.* **a** a circle of flexible material for expanding a woman's petticoat or skirt. **b** (in full **hoop petticoat**) a petticoat expanded with this. **5 a** a band in contrasting colour on a jockey's blouse, sleeves, or cap. **b** *Austral. colloq.* a jockey. —*v.tr.* **1** bind with a hoop or hoops. **2** encircle with or as with a hoop. □**be put** (or **go**) **through the hoop** (or **hoops**) undergo an ordeal. **hoop-iron** iron in long thin strips for binding casks etc. **hoop-la 1** *Brit.* a game in which rings are thrown in an attempt to encircle one of various prizes. **2** *sl.* commotion. **3** *sl.* pretentious nonsense. [OE *hōp* f. WG]

hoop² var. of WHOOP.

hoopoe /ˈhuːpuː/ *n.* a salmon-pink bird, *Upupa epops*, with black and white wings and tail, a large erectile crest, and a long decurved bill. [alt. of ME *hoop* f. OF *huppe* f. L *upupa*, imit. of its cry]

hooray /hʊˈreɪ/ *int.* **1** = HURRAH. **2** *Austral. & NZ* goodbye. □**Hooray Henry** /ˈhuːreɪ/ *Brit. sl.* a rich ineffectual young man, esp. one who is fashionable, extroverted, and conventional. [var. of HURRAH]

hoosegow /ˈhuːsgaʊ/ *n. US sl.* a prison. [Amer. Sp. *juzgao*, Sp. *juzgado* tribunal f. L *judicatum* neut. past part. of *judicare* JUDGE]

hoot /huːt/ *n. & v.* —*n.* **1** an owl's cry. **2** the sound made by a motor horn or a steam whistle. **3** a shout expressing scorn or disapproval; an inarticulate shout. **4** *colloq.* **a** laughter. **b** a cause of this. **5** (also **two hoots**) *sl.* anything at all (*don't care a hoot; don't give a hoot; doesn't matter two hoots*). —*v.* **1** *intr.* **a** (of an owl) utter its cry. **b** (of a motor horn or steam whistle) make a hoot. **c** (often foll. by *at*) make loud sounds, esp. of scorn or disapproval or *colloq.* merriment (*hooted with laughter*). **2** *tr.* **a** assail with scornful shouts. **b** (often foll. by *out, away*) drive away by hooting. **3** *tr.* sound (a motor horn or steam whistle). [ME *hūten* (v.), perh. imit.]

hootch var. of HOOCH.

hootenanny /ˈhuːtənænɪ/ *n.* (*pl.* -**ies**) *US colloq.* an informal gathering with folk music. [orig. dial., = 'gadget']

hooter /ˈhuːtə(r)/ *n.* **1** *Brit.* a siren or steam whistle, esp. as a signal for work to begin or cease. **2** *Brit.* the horn of a motor vehicle. **3** *sl.* a nose. **4** a person or animal that hoots.

hoots /huːts/ *int. Sc. & N.Engl.* expressing dissatisfaction or impatience. [natural exclam.: cf. Sw. *hut* begone, Welsh *hwt* away, Ir. *ut* out, all in similar sense]

Hoover /ˈhuːvə(r)/ *n. & v.* —*n. propr.* a vacuum cleaner (properly one made by the Hoover company). —*v.* (**hoover**) **1** *tr.* (also *absol.*) clean (a carpet etc.) with a vacuum cleaner. **2** (foll. by *up*) **a** *tr.* suck up with or as with a vacuum cleaner (*hoovered up the* *crumbs).* **b** *absol.* clean a room etc. with a vacuum cleaner *(decided to hoover up before they arrived).* [W. H. *Hoover,* Amer. manufacturer d. 1932]

hooves *pl.* of HOOF.

hop¹ /hɒp/ *v. & n.* —*v.* (**hopped, hopping**) **1** *intr.* (of a bird, frog, etc.) spring with two or all feet at once. **2** *intr.* (of a person) jump on one foot. **3** *tr.* cross (a ditch etc.) by hopping. **4** *intr. colloq.* **a** make a quick trip. **b** make a quick change of position or location. **5** *tr. colloq.* **a** jump into (a vehicle). **b** obtain (a ride) in this way. **6** *tr.* (usu. as **hopping** *n.*) (esp. of aircraft) pass quickly from one (place of a specified type) to another *(cloud-hopping; hedge-hopping).* —*n.* **1** a hopping movement. **2** *colloq.* an informal dance. **3** a short flight in an aircraft; the distance travelled by air without landing; a stage of a flight or journey. □**hop in** (or **out**) *colloq.* get into (or out of) a car etc. **hop it** *Brit. sl.* go away. **hopping mad** *colloq.* very angry. **hop, skip** (or **step**), **and jump** = *triple jump.* **hop the twig** (or **stick**) *sl.* **1** depart suddenly. **2** die. **on the hop** *colloq.* **1** unprepared *(caught on the hop).* **2** bustling about. [OE *hoppian*]

hop² /hɒp/ *n. & v.* —*n.* **1** a climbing plant, *Humulus lupulus,* cultivated for the cones borne by the female. **2** (in *pl.*) **a** the ripe cones of this, used to give a bitter flavour to beer. **b** *Austral. & NZ colloq.* beer. **3** *US sl.* opium or any other narcotic. —*v.* (**hopped, hopping**) **1** *tr.* flavour with hops. **2** *intr.* produce or pick hops. **3** *tr. US sl.* (foll. by *up*) stimulate with a drug. (esp. as **hopped up**). □**hop-bind** (or **-bine**) the climbing stem of the hop. **hop-sack** (or **-sacking**) **1 a** a coarse material made from hemp etc. **b** sacking for hops made from this. **2** a coarse clothing fabric of a loose plain weave. [ME *hoppe* f. MLG, MDu. *hoppe*]

hope /həʊp/ *n. & v.* —*n.* **1** (in *sing.* or *pl.*; often foll. by *of, that*) expectation and desire combined, e.g. for a certain thing to occur *(hope of getting the job).* **2 a** a person, thing, or circumstance that gives cause for hope. **b** ground of hope, promise. **3** what is hoped for. **4** *archaic* a feeling of trust. —*v.* **1** *intr.* (often foll. by *for*) feel hope. **2** *tr.* expect and desire. **3** *tr.* feel fairly confident. □**hope against hope** cling to a mere possibility. **hope chest** *US* = *bottom drawer.* **not a** (or **some**) **hope!** *colloq.* no chance at all. □□ **hoper** *n.* [OE *hopa*]

hopeful /ˈhəʊpfʊl/ *adj. & n.* —*adj.* **1** feeling hope. **2** causing or inspiring hope. **3** likely to succeed, promising. —*n.* (in full **young hopeful**) **1** a person likely to succeed. **2** *iron.* a person likely to be disappointed. □□ **hopefulness** *n.*

hopefully /ˈhəʊpfʊlɪ/ *adv.* **1** in a hopeful manner. **2** *disp.* (qualifying a whole sentence) it is to be hoped *(hopefully, the car will be ready by then).*

hopeless /ˈhəʊplɪs/ *adj.* **1** feeling no hope. **2** admitting no hope *(a hopeless case).* **3** inadequate, incompetent *(am hopeless at tennis).* □□ **hopelessly** *adv.* **hopelessness** *n.*

hophead /ˈhɒphed/ *n. sl.* **1** *US* a drug addict. **2** *Austral. & NZ* a drunkard.

hoplite /ˈhɒplaɪt/ *n.* a heavily-armed foot-soldier of ancient Greece. [Gk *hoplitēs* f. *hoplon* weapon]

hopper¹ /ˈhɒpə(r)/ *n.* **1** a person who hops. **2** a hopping arthropod, esp. a flea or cheese-maggot or young locust. **3 a** a container tapering downward (orig. having a hopping motion) through which grain passes into a mill. **b** a similar contrivance in various machines. **4 a** a barge carrying away mud etc. from a dredging-machine and discharging it. **b** a railway truck able to discharge coal etc. through its floor.

hopper² /ˈhɒpə(r)/ *n.* a hop-picker.

hopple /ˈhɒp(ə)l/ *v. & n.* —*v.tr.* fasten together the legs of (a horse etc.) to prevent it from straying etc. —*n.* an apparatus for this. [prob. LG: cf. HOBBLE and early Flem. *hoppelen* = MDu. *hobelen* jump, dance]

hopscotch /ˈhɒpskɒtʃ/ *n.* a children's game of hopping over squares or oblongs marked on the ground to retrieve a flat stone etc. [HOP¹ + SCOTCH¹]

horary /ˈhɔːrərɪ/ *adj. archaic* **1** of the hours. **2** occurring every hour, hourly. [med.L *horarius* f. L *hora* HOUR]

horde /hɔːd/ *n.* **1 a** usu. *derog.* a large group, a gang. **b** a moving swarm or pack (of insects, wolves, etc.). **2** a troop of Tartar or other nomads. [Pol. *horda* f. Turki *ordī, ordū* camp: cf. URDU]

horehound /ˈhɔːhaʊnd/ *n.* (also **hoarhound**) **1 a** a herbaceous plant, *Marrubium vulgare,* with a white cottony covering on its stem and leaves. **b** its bitter aromatic juice used against coughs etc. **2** a herbaceous plant, *Ballota nigra,* with an unpleasant aroma. [OE *hāre hūne* f. *hār* HOAR + *hūne* a plant]

horizon /həˈraɪz(ə)n/ *n.* **1 a** the line at which the earth and sky appear to meet. **b** (in full **apparent** or **sensible** or **visible horizon**) the line at which the earth and sky would appear to meet but for irregularities and obstructions; a circle where the earth's surface touches a cone whose vertex is at the observer's eye. **c** (in full **celestial** or **rational** or **true horizon**) a great circle of the celestial sphere, the plane of which passes through the centre of the earth and is parallel to that of the apparent horizon of a place. **2** limit of mental perception, experience, interest, etc. **3** a geological stratum or set of strata, or layer of soil, with particular characteristics. **4** *Archaeol.* the level at which a particular set of remains is found. □**on the horizon** (of an event) just imminent or becoming apparent. [ME f. OF *orizon(te)* f. LL *horizon -ontis* f. Gk *horizōn (kuklos)* limiting (circle)]

horizontal /ˌhɒrɪˈzɒnt(ə)l/ *adj. & n.* —*adj.* **1 a** parallel to the plane of the horizon, at right angles to the vertical *(horizontal plane).* **b** (of machinery etc.) having its parts working in a horizontal direction. **2 a** combining firms engaged in the same stage of production *(horizontal integration).* **b** involving social groups of equal status etc. **3** of or at the horizon. —*n.* a horizontal line, plane, etc. □□ **horizontality** /-ˈtælɪtɪ/ *n.* **horizontally** *adv.* **horizontalness** *n.* [F *horizontal* or mod.L *horizontalis* (as HORIZON)]

hormone /ˈhɔːməʊn/ *n.* **1** *Biochem.* a regulatory substance produced in an organism and transported in tissue fluids such as blood or sap to stimulate cells or tissues into action. **2** a synthetic substance with a similar effect. □□ **hormonal** /-ˈməʊn(ə)l/ *adj.* [Gk *hormōn* part. of *hormaō* impel]

horn /hɔːn/ *n. & v.* —*n.* **1 a** a hard permanent outgrowth, often curved and pointed, on the head of cattle, rhinoceroses, giraffes, and other esp. hoofed mammals, found singly, in pairs, or one in front of another. **b** the structure of a horn, consisting of a core of bone encased in keratinized skin. **2** each of two deciduous branched appendages on the head of (esp. male) deer. **3** a hornlike projection on the head of other animals, e.g. a snail's tentacle, the crest of a horned owl, etc. **4** the substance of which horns are composed. **5** anything resembling or compared to a horn in shape. **6** *Mus.* **a** = *French horn.* **b** a wind instrument played by lip vibration, orig. made of horn, now usu. of brass. **c** a horn player. **7** an instrument sounding a warning or other signal *(car horn; foghorn).* **8** a receptacle or instrument made of horn, e.g. a drinking-vessel or powder-flask etc. **9** a horn-shaped projection. **10** the extremity of the moon or other crescent. **11 a** an arm or branch of a river, bay, etc. **b** (**the Horn**) Cape Horn. **12** a pyramidal peak formed by glacial action. **13** *coarse sl.* an erect penis. **14** the hornlike emblem of a cuckold. —*v.tr.* **1** (esp. as **horned** *adj.*) provide with horns. **2** gore with the horns. □**horn in** *sl.* **1** (usu. foll. by *on*) intrude. **2** interfere. **horn of plenty** a cornucopia. **horn-rimmed** (esp. of spectacles) having rims made of horn or a substance resembling it. **on the horns of a dilemma** faced with a decision involving equally unfavourable alternatives. □□ **hornist** *n.* (in sense 6 of *n.*). **hornless** *adj.* **hornlike** *adj.* [OE f. Gmc, rel. to L *cornu*]

hornbeam /'hɔːnbiːm/ n. any tree of the genus *Carpinus*, with a smooth bark and a hard tough wood.

hornbill /'hɔːnbɪl/ n. any bird of the family Bucerotidae, with a hornlike excrescence on its large red or yellow curved bill.

hornblende /'hɔːnblend/ n. a dark-brown, black, or green mineral occurring in many igneous and metamorphic rocks, and composed of calcium, magnesium, and iron silicates. [G (as HORN, BLENDE)]

hornbook /'hɔːnbʊk/ n. hist. a leaf of paper containing the alphabet, the Lord's Prayer, etc., mounted on a wooden tablet with a handle, and protected by a thin plate of horn.

horned /hɔːnd/ adj. having a horn. □**horned owl** an owl, *Bubo virginianus*, with hornlike feathers over the ears. **horned toad 1** an American lizard, *Phrynosoma cornutum*, covered with spiny scales. **2** any SE Asian toad of the family Pelobatidae, with horn-shaped extensions over the eyes.

hornet /'hɔːnɪt/ n. a large wasp, *Vespa crabro*, with a brown and yellow striped body, and capable of inflicting a serious sting. □**stir up a hornets' nest** provoke or cause trouble or opposition. [prob. f. MLG, MDu. *horn(e)te*, corresp. to OE *hyrnet*, perh. rel. to HORN]

hornpipe /'hɔːnpaɪp/ n. **1** a lively dance, usu. by one person (esp. associated with sailors). **2** the music for this. [name of an obs. wind instrument partly of horn: ME, f. HORN + PIPE]

hornstone /'hɔːnstəʊn/ n. a brittle siliceous rock.

hornswoggle /'hɔːn,swɒg(ə)l/ v.tr. sl. cheat, hoax. [19th c.: orig. unkn.]

hornwort /'hɔːnwɜːt/ n. any aquatic rootless plant of the genus *Ceratophyllum*, with forked leaves.

horny /'hɔːnɪ/ adj. (**hornier, horniest**) **1** of or like horn. **2** hard like horn, callous (*horny-handed*). **3** sl. sexually excited. □□ **horniness** n.

horologe /'hɒrə,lɒdʒ/ n. archaic a timepiece. [ME f. OF *orloge* f. L *horologium* f. Gk *hōrologion* f. *hōra* time + *-logos* -telling]

horology /hə'rɒlədʒɪ/ n. the art of measuring time or making clocks, watches, etc.; the study of this. □□ **horologer** n. **horologic** /,hɒrə'lɒdʒɪk/ adj. **horological** /,hɒrə'lɒdʒɪk(ə)l/ adj. **horologist** n. [Gk *hōra* time + -LOGY]

horoscope /'hɒrə,skəʊp/ n. Astrol. **1** a forecast of a person's future based on a diagram showing the relative positions of the stars and planets at that person's birth. **2** such a diagram (*cast a horoscope*). **3** observation of the sky and planets at a particular moment, esp. at a person's birth. □□ **horoscopic** /-'skɒpɪk/ adj. **horoscopical** /-'skɒpɪk(ə)l/ adj. **horoscopy** /hə'rɒskəpɪ/ n. [F f. L *horoscopus* f. Gk *hōroskopos* f. *hōra* time + *skopos* observer]

horrendous /hə'rendəs/ adj. horrifying. □□ **horrendously** adv. **horrendousness** n. [L *horrendus* gerundive of *horrēre*: see HORRID]

horrent /'hɒrənt/ adj. poet. **1** bristling. **2** shuddering. [L *horrēre*: see HORRID]

horrible /'hɒrɪb(ə)l/ adj. **1** causing or likely to cause horror; hideous, shocking. **2** colloq. unpleasant, excessive (*horrible weather*; *horrible noise*). □□ **horribleness** n. **horribly** adv. [ME f. OF (*h*)*orrible* f. L *horribilis* f. *horrēre*: see HORRID]

horrid /'hɒrɪd/ adj. **1** horrible, revolting. **2** colloq. unpleasant, disagreeable (*horrid weather*; *horrid children*). **3** poet. rough, bristling. □□ **horridly** adv. **horridness** n. [L *horridus* f. *horrēre* bristle, shudder]

horrific /hə'rɪfɪk/ adj. horrifying. □□ **horrifically** adv. [F *horrifique* or L *horrificus* f. *horrēre*: see HORRID]

horrify /'hɒrɪ,faɪ/ v.tr. (**-ies, -ied**) arouse horror in; shock, scandalize. □□ **horrification** /-fɪ'keɪʃ(ə)n/ n. **horrifiedly** /-,faɪdlɪ/ adv. **horrifying** adj. **horrifyingly** adv. [L *horrificare* (as HORRIFIC)]

horripilation /,hɒrɪpɪ'leɪʃ(ə)n/ n. literary = *gooseflesh*. [LL *horripilatio* f. L *horrēre* to bristle + *pilus* hair]

horror /'hɒrə(r)/ n. & adj. —n. **1** a painful feeling of loathing and fear. **2 a** (often foll. by *of*) intense dislike. **b** (often foll. by *at*) colloq. intense dismay. **3 a** a person or thing causing horror. **b** colloq. a bad or mischievous person etc. **4** (in pl.; prec. by *the*) a fit of horror, depression, or nervousness, esp. as in delirium tremens. **5** a terrified and revolted shuddering. **6** (in pl.) an exclamation of dismay. —attrib. adj. (of literature, films, etc.) designed to attract by arousing pleasurable feelings of horror. □**Chamber of Horrors** a place full of horrors (orig. a room of criminals etc. in Madame Tussaud's waxworks). **horror-struck** (or **-stricken**) horrified, shocked. [ME f. OF (*h*)*orrour* f. L *horror -oris* (as HORRID)]

hors concours /,ɒr kɔ̃'kʊə(r)/ adj. **1** unrivalled, unequalled. **2** (of an exhibit or exhibitor) not competing for a prize. [F, lit. 'outside competition']

hors de combat /,ɒr də 'kɔ̃ba:/ adj. out of the fight, disabled. [F]

hors-d'œuvre /ɔː'dɜːvr, -'dɜːv/ n. an appetizer served at the beginning of a meal or (occasionally) during a meal. [F, lit. 'outside the work']

horse /hɔːs/ n. & v. —n. **1 a** a solid-hoofed plant-eating quadruped, *Equus caballus*, with flowing mane and tail, used for riding and to carry and pull loads. **b** an adult male horse; a stallion or gelding. **c** any other four-legged mammal of the genus *Equus*, including asses and zebras. **d** (collect.; as sing.) cavalry. **e** a representation of a horse. **2** a vaulting-block. **3** a supporting frame esp. with legs (*clothes-horse*). **4** sl. heroin. **5** colloq. a unit of horsepower. **6** Naut. any of various ropes and bars. **7** Mining an obstruction in a vein. —v. **1** intr. (foll. by *around*) fool about. **2** tr. provide (a person or vehicle) with a horse or horses. **3** intr. mount or go on horseback. □**from the horse's mouth** (of information etc.) from the person directly concerned or another authoritative source. **horse-and-buggy** US old-fashioned, bygone. **horse-block** a small platform of stone or wood for mounting a horse. **horse-brass** see BRASS. **horse-breaker** one who breaks in horses. **horse chestnut 1** any large ornamental tree of the genus *Aesculus*, with upright conical clusters of white or pink or red flowers. **2** the dark brown fruit of this (like an edible chestnut, but with a coarse bitter taste). **horse-cloth** a cloth used to cover a horse, or as part of its trappings. **horse-coper** a horse-dealer. **horse-doctor** a veterinary surgeon attending horses. **horse-drawn** (of a vehicle) pulled by a horse or horses. **Horse Guards 1** (in the UK) the cavalry brigade of the household troops. **2** the headquarters of such cavalry, esp. a building in Whitehall. **horse latitudes** a belt of calms in each hemisphere between the trade winds and the westerlies. **horse-mackerel** any large fish of the mackerel type, e.g. the scad or the tunny. **horse-mushroom** a large edible mushroom, *Agaricus arvensis*. **horse opera** US sl. a western film. **horse-pistol** a pistol for use by a horseman. **horse-pond** a pond for watering and washing horses, proverbial as a place for ducking obnoxious persons. **horse-race** a race between horses with riders. **horse-racing** the sport of conducting horse-races. **horse sense** colloq. plain common sense. **horses for courses** the matching of tasks and talents. **horse's neck** sl. a drink of flavoured ginger ale usu. with spirits. **horse-soldier** a soldier mounted on a horse. **horse-trading 1** US dealing in horses. **2** shrewd bargaining. **to horse!** (as a command) mount your horses. □□ **horseless** adj. **horselike** adj. [OE *hors* f. Gmc]

horseback /'hɔːsbæk/ n. the back of a horse, esp. as sat on in riding. □**on horseback** mounted on a horse.

horsebean /'hɔːsbiːn/ n. a broad bean used as fodder.

horsebox /'hɔːsbɒks/ n. Brit. a closed vehicle for transporting a horse or horses.

horseflesh /'hɔːsfleʃ/ n. **1** the flesh of a horse, esp. as food. **2** horses collectively.

horsefly /'hɔːsflaɪ/ n. (pl. **-flies**) any of various biting dipterous insects of the family Tabanidae troublesome esp. to horses.

horsehair /'hɔːsheə(r)/ n. hair from the mane or tail of a horse, used for padding etc.

horseleech /'hɔːsliːtʃ/ n. **1** a large kind of leech feeding by swallowing not sucking. **2** an insatiable person (cf. Prov. 30:15).

horseless /'hɔːslɪs/ adj. without a horse. □**horseless carriage** archaic a motor car.

horseman /'hɔːsmən/ n. (pl. **-men**) **1** a rider on horseback. **2** a skilled rider.

horsemanship /'hɔːsmənʃɪp/ n. the art of riding on horseback; skill in doing this.

horseplay /'hɔːspleɪ/ n. boisterous play.

horsepower /'hɔːs,paʊə(r)/ n. (pl. same) **1** an imperial unit of power equal to 550 foot-pounds per second (about 750 watts). ¶ Abbr.: **hp**. **2** the power of an engine etc. measured in terms of this.

horseradish /'hɔːs,rædɪʃ/ n. **1** a cruciferous plant, Armoracia rusticana, with large lobed leaves. **2** the pungent root of this scraped or grated as a condiment, often made into a sauce.

horseshoe /'hɔːʃʃuː, 'hɔːsʃuː/ n. **1** an iron shoe for a horse shaped like the outline of the hard part of the hoof. **2** a thing of this shape; an object shaped like C or U (e.g. a magnet, a table, a Spanish or Islamic arch). □**horseshoe crab** a large marine arthropod, Xiphosura polyphemus, with a horseshoe-shaped shell and a long tail-spine: also called king-crab.

horsetail /'hɔːsteɪl/ n. **1** the tail of a horse (formerly used in Turkey as a standard, or as an ensign denoting the rank of a pasha). **2** any cryptogamous plant of the genus Equisetum, like a horse's tail, with a hollow jointed stem and scale-like leaves. **3** = pony-tail.

horsewhip /'hɔːswɪp/ n. & v. —n. a whip for driving horses. —v.tr. (**-whipped**, **-whipping**) beat with a horsewhip.

horsewoman /'hɔːs,wʊmən/ n. (pl. **-women**) **1** a woman who rides on horseback. **2** a skilled woman rider.

horst /hɔːst/ n. Geol. a raised elongated block of land bounded by faults on both sides. [G, = heap]

horsy /'hɔːsɪ/ adj. (also **horsey**) (**horsier**, **horsiest**) **1** of or like a horse. **2** concerned with or devoted to horses or horse-racing. **3** affectedly using the dress and language of a groom or jockey. □□ **horsily** adv. **horsiness** n.

hortative /'hɔːtətɪv/ adj. (also **hortatory** /'hɔːtətərɪ/) tending or serving to exhort. □□ **hortation** /hɔːˈteɪʃ(ə)n/ n. [L hortativus f. hortari exhort]

hortensia /hɔːˈtensɪə/ n. a kind of hydrangea, Hydrangea macrophylla, with large rounded infertile flower heads. [mod.L f. Hortense Lepaute, 18th-c. Frenchwoman]

horticulture /'hɔːtɪ,kʌltʃə(r)/ n. the art of garden cultivation. □□ **horticultural** /-ˈkʌltʃər(ə)l/ adj. **horticulturist** /-ˈkʌltʃərɪst/ n. [L hortus garden, after AGRICULTURE]

hortus siccus /ˌhɔːtəs 'sɪkəs/ n. **1** an arranged collection of dried plants. **2** a collection of uninteresting facts etc. [L, = dry garden]

Hos. abbr. Hosea (Old Testament).

hosanna /həʊˈzænə/ n. & int. a shout of adoration (Matt. 21:9, 15, etc.). [ME f. LL f. Gk hōsanna f. Heb. hôša'nā for hôšî'a-nnā save now!]

hose /həʊz/ n. & v. —n. **1** (also **hose-pipe**) a flexible tube conveying water for watering plants etc., putting out fires, etc. **2 a** (collect.; as pl.) stockings and socks (esp. in trade use). **b** hist. breeches (doublet and hose). —v.tr. **1** (often foll. by down) water or spray or drench with a hose. **2** provide with hose. □**half-hose** socks. [OE f. Gmc]

hosier /'həʊzɪə(r), 'həʊʒə(r)/ n. a dealer in hosiery.

hosiery /'həʊzɪərɪ, 'həʊʒərɪ/ n. **1** stockings and socks. **2** Brit. knitted or woven underwear.

hospice /'hɒspɪs/ n. **1** Brit. a home for people who are ill (esp. terminally) or destitute. **2** a lodging for travellers, esp. one kept by a religious order. [F f. L hospitium (as HOST²)]

hospitable /'hɒspɪtəb(ə)l, hɒˈspɪt-/ adj. giving or disposed to give welcome and entertainment to strangers or guests. □□ **hospitably** adv. [F f. hospiter f. med.L hospitare entertain (as HOST²)]

hospital /'hɒspɪt(ə)l/ n. **1** an institution providing medical and surgical treatment and nursing care for ill or injured people. **2** hist. **a** a hospice. **b** an establishment of the Knights Hospitallers. **3** Law a charitable institution (also in proper names, e.g. Christ's Hospital). □**hospital corners** a way of tucking in sheets, used by nurses. **hospital fever** a kind of typhus formerly prevalent in crowded hospitals. **hospital ship** a ship to receive sick and wounded seamen, or to take sick and wounded soldiers home. **hospital train** a train taking wounded soldiers from a battlefield. [ME f. OF f. med.L hospitale neut. of L hospitalis (adj.) (as HOST²)]

hospitaler US var. of HOSPITALLER.

hospitalism /'hɒspɪtə,lɪz(ə)m/ n. the adverse effects of a prolonged stay in hospital.

hospitality /,hɒspɪˈtælɪtɪ/ n. the friendly and generous reception and entertainment of guests or strangers. [ME f. OF hospitalité f. L hospitalitas -tatis (as HOSPITAL)]

hospitalize /'hɒspɪtə,laɪz/ v.tr. (also **-ise**) send or admit (a patient) to hospital. □□ **hospitalization** /-ˈzeɪʃ(ə)n/ n.

hospitaller /'hɒspɪtələ(r)/ n. (US **hospitaler**) **1** a member of a charitable religious order. **2** a chaplain (in some London hospitals). [ME f. OF hospitalier f. med.L hospitalarius (as HOSPITAL)]

host¹ /həʊst/ n. **1** (usu. foll. by of) a large number of people or things. **2** archaic an army. **3** (in full **heavenly host**) Bibl. **a** the sun, moon, and stars. **b** the angels. □**host** (or **hosts**) **of heaven** = sense 3 of n. **is a host in himself** can do as much as several ordinary people. **Lord** (or **Lord God**) **of hosts** God as Lord over earthly or heavenly armies. [ME f. OF f. L hostis stranger, enemy, in med.L 'army']

host² /həʊst/ n. & v. —n. **1** a person who receives or entertains another as a guest. **2** the landlord of an inn (mine host). **3** Biol. an animal or plant having a parasite or commensal. **4** an animal or person that has received a transplanted organ etc. **5** the compère of a show, esp. of a television or radio programme. —v.tr. act as host to (a person) or at (an event). [ME f. OF oste f. L hospes -pitis host, guest]

host³ /həʊst/ n. the bread consecrated in the Eucharist. [ME f. OF (h)oiste f. L hostia victim]

hosta /'hɒstə/ n. any perennial garden plant of the genus Hosta (formerly Funkia) with green or variegated ornamental leaves and loose clusters of tubular mauve or white flowers. [mod.L, f. N. T. Host, Austrian physician d. 1834]

hostage /'hɒstɪdʒ/ n. **1** a person seized or held as security for the fulfilment of a condition. **2** a pledge or security. □**a hostage to fortune** an acquisition, commitment, etc., regarded as endangered by unforeseen circumstances. □□ **hostageship** n. [ME f. OF (h)ostage ult. f. LL obsidatus hostageship f. L obses obsidis hostage]

hostel /'hɒst(ə)l/ n. **1** Brit. a house of residence or lodging for students, nurses, etc. **2** = youth hostel. **3** archaic an inn. [ME f. OF (h)ostel f. med.L (as HOSPITAL)]

hostelling /'hɒstəlɪŋ/ n. (US **hosteling**) the practice of staying in youth hostels, esp. while travelling. □□ **hosteller** n.

hostelry /'hɒstəlrɪ/ n. (pl. **-ies**) archaic or literary an inn. [ME f. OF (h)ostelerie f. (h)ostelier innkeeper (as HOSTEL)]

hostess /'həʊstɪs/ n. **1** a woman who receives or entertains a guest. **2** a woman employed to welcome and entertain customers at a nightclub etc. **3** a stewardess on an aircraft, train, etc. (*air hostess*). [ME f. OF (*h*)*ostesse* (as HOST²)]

hostile /'hɒstaɪl/ adj. **1** of an enemy. **2** (often foll. by *to*) unfriendly, opposed. □**hostile witness** *Law* a witness who appears hostile to the party calling him or her and therefore untrustworthy. □□**hostilely** adv. [F *hostile* or L *hostilis* (as HOST¹)]

hostility /hɒ'stɪlɪtɪ/ n. (*pl.* **-ies**) **1** being hostile, enmity. **2** a state of warfare. **3** (in *pl.*) acts of warfare. **4** opposition (in thought etc.). [F *hostilité* or LL *hostilitas* (as HOSTILE)]

hostler /'ɒslə(r)/ n. **1** = OSTLER. **2** *US* a person in charge of vehicles or machines, esp. railway engines, when they are not in use. [ME f. *hosteler* (as OSTLER)]

hot /hɒt/ adj., v., & adv. —adj. (**hotter, hottest**) **1 a** having a relatively or noticeably high temperature. **b** (of food or drink) prepared by heating and served without cooling. **2** producing the sensation of heat (*hot fever*; *hot flush*). **3** (of pepper, spices, etc.) pungent. **4** (of a person) feeling heat. **5 a** ardent, passionate, excited. **b** (often foll. by *for*, *on*) eager, keen (*in hot pursuit*). **c** angry or upset. **d** lustful. **e** exciting. **6 a** (of news etc.) fresh, recent. **b** *Brit. colloq.* (of Treasury bills) newly issued. **7** *Hunting* (of the scent) fresh and strong, indicating that the quarry has passed recently. **8 a** (of a player) very skilful. **b** (of a competitor in a race or other sporting event) strongly fancied to win (*a hot favourite*). **c** (of a hit, return, etc., in ball games) difficult for an opponent to deal with. **9** (of music, esp. jazz) strongly rhythmical and emotional. **10** *sl.* **a** (of goods) stolen, esp. easily identifiable and hence difficult to dispose of. **b** (of a person) wanted by the police. **11** *sl.* radioactive. **12** *colloq.* (of information) unusually reliable (*hot tip*). —v. (**hotted, hotting**) (usu. foll. by *up*) *Brit. colloq.* **1** *tr.* & *intr.* make or become hot. **2** *tr.* & *intr.* make or become active, lively, exciting, or dangerous. —adv. **1** angrily, severely (*give it him hot*). **2** eagerly. □**go hot and cold** feel alternately hot and cold owing to fear etc. **have the hots for** *sl.* be sexually attracted to. **hot air** *sl.* empty, boastful, or excited talk. **hot-air balloon** a balloon (see BALLOON *n.* 2) consisting of a bag in which air is heated by burners located below it, causing it to rise. **hot blast** a blast of heated air forced into a furnace. **hot-blooded** ardent, passionate. **hot cathode** a cathode heated to emit electrons. **hot cross bun** see BUN. **hot dog** *n. colloq.* a hot sausage sandwiched in a soft roll. —*int.* *US sl.* expressing approval. **hot flush** see FLUSH¹. **hot gospeller** see GOSPELLER. **hot line** a direct exclusive line of communication, esp. for emergencies. **hot metal** *Printing* using type made from molten metal. **hot money** capital transferred at frequent intervals. **hot potato** *colloq.* a controversial or awkward matter or situation. **hot-press** *n.* a press of glazed boards and hot metal plates for smoothing paper or cloth or making plywood. —*v.tr.* press (paper etc.) in this. **hot rod** a motor vehicle modified to have extra power and speed. **hot seat** *sl.* **1** a position of difficult responsibility. **2** the electric chair. **hot-short** (of metal) brittle in its hot state (cf. COLD-SHORT). **hot spot 1** a small region that is relatively hot. **2** a lively or dangerous place. **hot spring** a spring of naturally hot water. **hot stuff** *colloq.* **1** a formidably capable person. **2** an important person or thing. **3** a sexually attractive person. **4** a spirited, strong-willed, or passionate person. **5** a book, film, etc. with a strongly erotic content. **hot-tempered** impulsively angry. **hot under the collar** angry, resentful, or embarrassed. **hot war** an open war, with active hostilities. **hot water** *colloq.* difficulty, trouble, or disgrace (*be in hot water*; *get into hot water*). **hot-water bottle** (*US* **bag**) a container, usu. made of rubber, filled with hot water, esp. to warm a bed.

hot well 1 = *hot spring.* **2** a reservoir in a condensing steam engine. **hot-wire** operated by the expansion of heated wire. **like hot cakes** see CAKE. **make it** (or **things**) **hot for a person** persecute a person. **not so hot** *colloq.* only mediocre. □□**hotly** adv. **hotness** *n.* **hottish** adj. [OE *hāt* f. Gmc: cf. HEAT]

hotbed /'hɒtbed/ n. **1** a bed of earth heated by fermenting manure. **2** (foll. by *of*) an environment promoting the growth of something, esp. something unwelcome (*hotbed of vice*).

hotchpotch /'hɒtʃpɒtʃ/ n. (also esp. in sense 3) **hotchpot** /-pɒt/) **1** a confused mixture, a jumble. **2** a dish of many mixed ingredients, esp. a mutton broth or stew with vegetables. **3** *Law* the reunion and blending of properties for the purpose of securing equal division (esp. of the property of an intestate parent). [ME f. AF & OF *hochepot* f. OF *hocher* shake + POT¹:· -*potch* by assim.]

hotel /həʊ'tel/ n. **1** an establishment providing accommodation and meals for payment. **2** *Austral.* & *NZ* a public house. [F *hôtel*, later form of HOSTEL]

hotelier /həʊ'telɪə(r)/ n. a hotel-keeper. [F *hôtelier* f. OF *hostelier*: see HOSTELRY]

hotfoot /'hɒtfʊt/ adv., v., & adj. —adv. in eager haste. —*v.tr.* hurry eagerly (esp. *hotfoot it*). —adj. acting quickly.

hothead /'hɒthed/ n. an impetuous person.

hotheaded /hɒt'hedɪd/ adj. impetuous, excitable. □□**hotheadedly** adv. **hotheadedness** *n.*

hothouse /'hɒthaʊs/ n. **1** a heated building, usu. largely of glass, for rearing plants out of season or in a climate colder than is natural for them. **2** an environment that encourages the rapid growth or development of something.

hotplate /'hɒtpleɪt/ n. a heated metal plate etc. (or a set of these) for cooking food or keeping it hot.

hotpot /'hɒtpɒt/ n. a casserole of meat and vegetables, usu. with a layer of potato on top.

hotshot /'hɒtʃɒt/ n. & adj. esp. *US colloq.* —*n.* an important or exceptionally able person. —adj. (*attrib.*) important, able, expert, suddenly prominent.

hotspur /'hɒtspɜ:(r)/ n. a rash person. [sobriquet of Sir H. Percy, d. 1403]

Hottentot /'hɒtən‚tɒt/ n. & adj. —*n.* **1** a member of a stocky Negroid people of SW Africa. **2** their language. —adj. of this people. [Afrik., perh. = stammerer, with ref. to their mode of pronunc.]

hottie /'hɒtɪ/ n. (also **hotty**) (*pl.* **-ies**) *colloq.* a hot-water bottle.

Houdini /hu:'di:nɪ/ n. **1** an ingenious escape. **2** a person skilled at escaping. [H. *Houdini*, professional name of E. Weiss, American escapologist d. 1926]

hough /hɒk/ n. & v. *Brit.* —*n.* **1** = HOCK¹. **2** a cut of beef etc. from this and the leg above it. —*v.tr.* hamstring. □□**hougher** *n.* [ME *ho*(*u*)*gh* = OE *hōh* (heel) in *hōhsinu* hamstring]

hoummos var. of HUMMUS.

hound /haʊnd/ n. & v. —*n.* **1 a** a dog used for hunting, esp. one able to track by scent. **b** (**the hounds**) *Brit.* a pack of foxhounds. **2** *colloq.* a despicable man. **3** a runner who follows a trail in hare and hounds. **4** a person keen in pursuit of something (usu. in *comb.*: *news-hound*). —*v.tr.* **1** harass or pursue relentlessly. **2** chase or pursue with a hound. **3** (foll. by *at*) set (a dog or person) on (a quarry). **4** urge on or nag (a person). □**hound's tongue** *Bot.* a tall plant, *Cynoglossum officinale*, with tongue-shaped leaves. **hound's-tooth** a check pattern with notched corners suggestive of a canine tooth. **ride to hounds** go fox-hunting on horseback. □□**hounder** *n.* **houndish** adj. [OE *hund* f. Gmc]

hour /aʊə(r)/ n. **1** a twenty-fourth part of a day and night, 60 minutes. **2** a time of day, a point in time (*a late hour*; *what is the hour?*). **3** (in *pl.* with preceding numerals in form 18.00, 20.30, etc.) this number of hours and minutes past midnight on the 24-hour clock (*will assemble at 20.00 hours*). **4 a** a period set aside for some purpose (*lunch hour*; *keep regular* *hours*). **b** (in *pl.*) a fixed period of time for work, use of a building, etc. (*office hours*; *opening hours*). **5** a short indefinite period of time (*an idle hour*). **6** the present time (*question of the hour*). **7** a time for action etc. (*the hour has come*). **8** the distance traversed in one hour by a means of transport stated or implied (*we are an hour from London*). **9** *RC Ch.* **a** prayers to be said at one of seven fixed times of day (*book of hours*). **b** any of these times. **10** (prec. by *the*) each time o'clock of a whole number of hours (*buses leave on the hour; on the half hour; at quarter past the hour*). **11** *Astron.* 15° of longitude or right ascension. □**after hours** after closing-time. **hour-hand** the hand on a clock or watch which shows the hour. **hour-long** *adj.* lasting for one hour. —*adv.* for one hour. **till all hours** till very late. [ME *ure* etc. f. AF *ure*, OF *ore*, *eure* f. L *hora* f. Gk *hōra* season, hour]

hourglass /ˈauəˌglɑːs/ *n.* a reversible device with two connected glass bulbs containing sand that takes an hour to pass from the upper to the lower bulb.

houri /ˈhuəri/ *n.* a beautiful young woman, esp. in the Muslim Paradise. [F f. Pers. *ḥūrī* f. Arab. *ḥūr* pl. of *ḥawrā* gazelle-like (in the eyes)]

hourly /ˈauəli/ *adj. & adv.* —*adj.* **1** done or occurring every hour. **2** frequent, continual. **3** reckoned hour by hour (*hourly wage*). —*adv.* **1** every hour. **2** frequently, continually.

house *n. & v.* —*n.* /haus/ (*pl.* /ˈhauzɪz/) **1 a** a building for human habitation. **b** (*attrib.*) (of an animal) kept in, frequenting, or infesting houses (*house-cat*; *housefly*). **2** a building for a special purpose (*opera-house*; *summer-house*). **3** a building for keeping animals or goods (*hen-house*). **4 a** a religious community. **b** the buildings occupied by it. **5 a** a body of pupils living in the same building at a boarding-school. **b** such a building. **c** a division of a day-school for games, competitions, etc. **6 a** a college of a university. **b** (**the House**) Christ Church, Oxford. **7** a family, esp. a royal family; a dynasty (*House of York*). **8 a** a firm or institution. **b** its place of business. **c** (**the House**) *Brit. colloq.* the Stock Exchange. **9 a** a legislative or deliberative assembly. **b** the building where it meets. **c** (**the House**) (in the UK) the House of Commons or Lords; (in the US) the House of Representatives. **10 a** an audience in a theatre, cinema, etc. **b** a performance in a theatre or cinema (*second house starts at 9 o'clock*). **c** a theatre. **11** *Astrol.* a twelfth part of the heavens. **12** (*attrib.*) living in a hospital as a member of staff (*house officer*; *house physician*; *house surgeon*). **13 a** a place of public refreshment, a restaurant or inn (*coffee-house*; *public house*). **b** (*attrib.*) (of wine) selected by the management of a restaurant, hotel, etc. to be offered at a special price. **14** *US* a brothel. **15** *Sc.* a dwelling that is one of several in a building. **16** *Brit. sl.* = HOUSEY-HOUSEY. **17** an animal's den, shell, etc. **18** (**the House**) *Brit. hist. euphem.* the workhouse. —*v.tr.* /hauz/ **1** provide (a person, a population, etc.) with a house or houses or other accommodation. **2** store (goods etc.). **3** enclose or encase (a part or fitting). **4** fix in a socket, mortise, etc. □**as safe as houses** thoroughly or completely safe. **house-agent** *Brit.* an agent for the sale and letting of houses. **house and home** (as an emphatic) home. **house arrest** detention in one's own house etc., not in prison. **house-broken** = *house-trained*. **house church 1** a charismatic church independent of traditional denominations. **2** a group meeting in a house as part of the activities of a church. **house-dog** a dog kept to guard a house. **house-father** a man in charge of a house, esp. of a home for children. **house-flag** a flag indicating to what firm a ship belongs. **house guest** a guest staying for some days in a private house. **house-hunting** seeking a house to live in. **house-husband** a husband who carries out the household duties traditionally carried out by a housewife. **house lights** the lights in the

auditorium of a theatre. **house magazine** a magazine published by a firm and dealing mainly with its own activities. **house-martin** a black and white swallow-like bird, *Delichon urbica*, which builds a mud nest on house walls etc. **house-mother** a woman in charge of a house, esp. of a home for children. **house of cards 1** an insecure scheme etc. **2** a structure built (usu. by a child) out of playing cards. **House of Commons** (in the UK) the elected chamber of Parliament. **house of God** a church, a place of worship. **house of ill fame** *archaic* a brothel. **House of Keys** (in the Isle of Man) the elected chamber of Tynwald. **House of Lords 1** (in the UK) the chamber of Parliament composed of peers and bishops. **2** a committee of specially qualified members of this appointed as the ultimate judicial appeal court. **House of Representatives** the lower house of the US Congress and other legislatures. **house-parent** a house-mother or house-father. **house party** a group of guests staying at a country house etc. **house-plant** a plant grown indoors. **house-proud** attentive to, or unduly preoccupied with, the care and appearance of the home. **Houses of Parliament 1** the Houses of Lords and Commons regarded together. **2** the buildings where they meet. **house sparrow** a common brown and grey sparrow, *Passer domesticus*, which nests in the eaves and roofs of houses. **house style** a particular printer's or publisher's etc. preferred way of presentation. **house-to-house** performed at or carried to each house in turn. **house-trained** *Brit.* **1** (of animals) trained to be clean in the house. **2** *colloq.* well-mannered. **house-warming** a party celebrating a move to a new home. **keep house** provide for or manage a household. **keep** (or **make**) **a House** secure the presence of enough members for a quorum in the House of Commons. **keep open house** provide general hospitality. **keep to the house** (or **keep the house**) stay indoors. **like a house on fire 1** vigorously, fast. **2** successfully, excellently. **on the house** at the management's expense, free. **play house** play at being a family in its home. **put** (or **set**) **one's house in order** make necessary reforms. **set up house** begin to live in a separate dwelling. □□ **houseful** *n.* (*pl.* **-fuls**). **houseless** *adj.* [OE *hūs*, *hūsian*, f. Gmc]

houseboat /ˈhausbəut/ *n.* a boat fitted up for living in.

housebound /ˈhausbaund/ *adj.* unable to leave one's house through illness etc.

houseboy /ˈhausbɔɪ/ *n.* a boy or man as a servant in a house.

housebreaker /ˈhausˌbreɪkə(r)/ *n.* **1** a person guilty of housebreaking. **2** *Brit.* a person who is employed to demolish houses.

housebreaking /ˈhausˌbreɪkɪŋ/ *n.* the act of breaking into a building, esp. in daytime, to commit a crime. ¶ In 1968 replaced as a statutory crime in English law by *burglary*.

housecarl /ˈhauskɑːl/ *n.* (also **housecarle**) *hist.* a member of the bodyguard of a Danish or English king or noble. [OE *húscarl* f. ON *húskarl* f. *hús* HOUSE + *karl* man: cf. CARL]

housecoat /ˈhauskəut/ *n.* a woman's garment for informal wear in the house, usu. a long dresslike coat.

housecraft /ˈhauskrɑːft/ *n. Brit.* skill in household management.

housefly /ˈhausflaɪ/ *n.* any fly of the family Muscidae, esp. *Musca domestica*, breeding in decaying organic matter and often entering houses.

household /ˈhaushəuld/ *n.* **1** the occupants of a house regarded as a unit. **2** a house and its affairs. **3** (prec. by *the*) (in the UK) the royal household. □**household gods 1** gods presiding over a household, esp. the lares and penates. **2** the essentials of home life. **household troops** (in the UK) troops nominally employed to guard the sovereign. **household word**

(or **name**) **1** a familiar name or saying. **2** a familiar person or thing.

householder /ˈhaʊsˌhəʊldə(r)/ *n*. **1** a person who owns or rents a house. **2** the head of a household.

housekeep /ˈhaʊskiːp/ *v.intr.* (*past* and *past part.* **-kept**) *colloq.* keep house.

housekeeper /ˈhaʊsˌkiːpə(r)/ *n*. **1** a person, esp. a woman, employed to manage a household. **2** a person in charge of a house, office, etc.

housekeeping /ˈhaʊsˌkiːpɪŋ/ *n*. **1** the management of household affairs. **2** money allowed for this. **3** operations of maintenance, record-keeping, etc., in an organization.

houseleek /ˈhaʊsliːk/ *n*. a plant, *Sempervivum tectorum*, with pink flowers, growing on walls and roofs.

housemaid /ˈhaʊsmeɪd/ *n*. a female servant in a house, esp. in charge of reception rooms and bedrooms. □**housemaid's knee** inflammation of the kneecap, often due to excessive kneeling.

houseman /ˈhaʊsmən/ *n*. (*pl.* **-men**) **1** *Brit.* a resident doctor at a hospital etc. **2** = HOUSEBOY.

housemaster /ˈhaʊsˌmɑːstə(r)/ *n*. (*fem.* **housemistress** /ˈhaʊsˌmɪstrɪs/) the teacher in charge of a house at a boarding-school.

houseroom /ˈhaʊsruːm, -rʊm/ *n*. space or accommodation in one's house. □**not give houseroom to** not have in any circumstances.

housetop /ˈhaʊstɒp/ *n*. the roof of a house. □**proclaim** (or **shout** etc.) **from the housetops** announce publicly.

housewife /ˈhaʊswaɪf/ *n*. (*pl.* **-wives**) **1** a woman (usu. married) managing a household. **2** /ˈhʌzɪf/ a case for needles, thread, etc. □□ **housewifely** *adj.* **housewifeliness** *n*. [ME *hus(e)wif* f. HOUSE + WIFE]

housewifery /ˈhaʊsˌwɪfrɪ/ *n*. **1** housekeeping. **2** skill in this, housecraft.

housework /ˈhaʊswɜːk/ *n*. regular work done in housekeeping, e.g. cleaning and cooking.

housey-housey /ˌhaʊsɪˈhaʊsɪ, ˌhaʊzɪˈhaʊzɪ/ *n*. (also **housie-housie**) *Brit. sl.* a gambling form of lotto.

housing[1] /ˈhaʊzɪŋ/ *n*. **1 a** dwelling-houses collectively. **b** the provision of these. **2** shelter, lodging. **3** a rigid casing, esp. for moving or sensitive parts of a machine. **4** the hole or niche cut in one piece of wood to receive some part of another in order to join them. □**housing estate** a residential area planned as a unit.

housing[2] /ˈhaʊzɪŋ/ *n*. a cloth covering put on a horse for protection or ornament. [ME = covering, f. obs. *house* f. OF *houce* f. med.L *hultia* f. Gmc]

hove *past* of HEAVE.

hovel /ˈhɒv(ə)l/ *n*. **1** a small miserable dwelling. **2** a conical building enclosing a kiln. **3** an open shed or outhouse. [ME: orig. unkn.]

hover /ˈhɒvə(r)/ *v.* & *n*. —*v.intr.* **1** (of a bird, helicopter, etc.) remain in one place in the air. **2** (often foll. by *about*, *round*) wait close at hand, linger. **3** remain undecided. —*n*. **1** hovering. **2** a state of suspense. □**hover-fly** (*pl.* **-flies**) any fly of the family Syrphidae which hovers with rapidly beating wings. □□ **hoverer** *n*. [ME f. obs. *hove* hover, linger]

hovercraft /ˈhɒvəˌkrɑːft/ *n*. (*pl.* same) a vehicle or craft that travels over land or water on a cushion of air provided by a downward blast.

hoverport /ˈhɒvəˌpɔːt/ *n*. a terminal for hovercraft.

hovertrain /ˈhɒvəˌtreɪn/ *n*. a train that travels on a cushion of air like a hovercraft.

how[1] /haʊ/ *adv., conj.,* & *n*. —*interrog. adv.* **1** by what means, in what way (*how do you do it?; tell me how you do it; how could you behave so disgracefully?; but how to bridge the gap?*). **2** in what condition, esp. of health (*how is the patient?; how do things stand?*). **3 a** to what extent (*how far is it?; how would you like to take my place?; how we laughed!*). **b** to what extent good or well, what . . . like (*how was the film?; how did they play?*). —*rel. adv.* in whatever way, as (*do it how you can*). —*conj. colloq.* that (*told us how he'd been in India*). —*n*. the way a thing is done (*the how*

and why of it). □**and how!** *sl.* very much so (chiefly used ironically or intensively). **here's how!** I drink to your good health. **how about** I would you like (*how about a game of chess?*). **2** what is to be done about. **3** what is the news about. **how are you? 1** what is your state of health? **2** = *how do you do?* **how come?** see COME. **how do?** an informal greeting on being introduced to a stranger. **how do you do?** a formal greeting. **how-do-you-do** (or **how-d'ye-do**) *n*. (*pl.* **-dos**) an awkward situation. **how many** what number. **how much 1** what amount (*how much do I owe you?; did not know how much to take*). **2** what price (*how much is it?*). **3** (as *interrog.*) *joc.* what? ('*She is a hedonist.*' '*A how much?*'). **how now?** *archaic* what is the meaning of this? **how so?** how can you show that that is so? **how's that? 1** what is your opinion or explanation of that? **2** *Cricket* (said to an umpire) is the batsman out or not? [OE *hū* f. WG]

how[2] /haʊ/ *int*. a greeting used by N. American Indians. [perh. f. Sioux *háo*, Omaha *hau*]

howbeit /haʊˈbiːɪt/ *adv. archaic* nevertheless.

howdah /ˈhaʊdə/ *n*. a seat for two or more, usu. with a canopy, for riding on the back of an elephant or camel. [Urdu *hawda* f. Arab. *hawdaj* litter]

howdy /ˈhaʊdɪ/ *int. US* = *how do you do?* [corrupt.]

however /haʊˈevə(r)/ *adv*. **1 a** in whatever way (*do it however you want*). **b** to whatever extent, no matter how (*must go however inconvenient*). **2** nevertheless. **3** *colloq.* (as an emphatic) in what way, by what means (*however did that happen?*).

howitzer /ˈhaʊɪtsə(r)/ *n*. a short gun for high-angle firing of shells at low velocities. [Du. *houwitser* f. G *Haubitze* f. Czech *houfnice* catapult]

howl /haʊl/ *n.* & *v*. —*n*. **1** a long loud doleful cry uttered by a dog, wolf, etc. **2** a prolonged wailing noise, e.g. as made by a strong wind. **3** a loud cry of pain or rage. **4** a yell of derision or merriment. **5** *Electronics* a howling noise in a loudspeaker due to electrical or acoustic feedback. —*v*. **1** *intr.* make a howl. **2** *intr.* weep loudly. **3** *tr.* utter (words) with a howl. □**howl down** prevent (a speaker) from being heard by howls of derision. [ME *houle* (v.), prob. imit.: cf. OWL]

howler /ˈhaʊlə(r)/ *n*. **1** *colloq.* a glaring mistake. **2** a S. American monkey of the genus *Alouatta*. **3** a person or animal that howls.

howling /ˈhaʊlɪŋ/ *adj*. **1** that howls. **2** *sl.* extreme (*a howling shame*). **3** *archaic* dreary (*howling wilderness*). □**howling dervish** see DERVISH.

howsoever /ˌhaʊsəʊˈevə(r)/ *adv*. (also *poet.* **howsoe'er** /-ˈeə(r)/) **1** in whatsoever way. **2** to whatsoever extent.

hoy[1] /hɔɪ/ *int.* & *n*. —*int.* used to call attention, drive animals, or *Naut.* hail or call aloft. —*n. Austral.* a game of chance resembling bingo, using playing cards. [ME: natural cry]

hoy[2] /hɔɪ/ *n. hist.* a small vessel, usu. rigged as a sloop, carrying passengers and goods esp. for short distances. [MDu. *hoei, hoede*, of unkn. orig.]

hoy[3] /hɔɪ/ *v.tr. Austral. sl.* throw. [Brit. dial.: orig. unkn.]

hoya /ˈhɔɪə/ *n*. any climbing shrub of the genus *Hoya*, with pink, white, or yellow waxy flowers. [mod.L f. T. *Hoy*, Engl. gardener d. 1821]

hoyden /ˈhɔɪd(ə)n/ *n*. a boisterous girl. □□ **hoydenish** *adj*. [orig. = rude fellow, prob. f. MDu. *heiden* (= HEATHEN)]

Hoyle /hɔɪl/ *n*. □**according to Hoyle** *adv*. correctly, exactly. —*adj*. correct, exact. [E. *Hoyle*, Engl. writer on card-games d. 1769]

h.p. *abbr*. **1** horsepower. **2** hire purchase. **3** high pressure.

HQ *abbr*. headquarters.

HR *abbr. US* House of Representatives.

hr. *abbr*. hour.

HRH *abbr*. Her or His Royal Highness.

hrs. *abbr*. hours.

HSH abbr. Her or His Serene Highness.

HT abbr. high tension.

hub /hʌb/ n. **1** the central part of a wheel, rotating on or with the axle, and from which the spokes radiate. **2** a central point of interest, activity, etc. □**hub-cap** a cover for the hub of a vehicle's wheel. [16th c.: perh. = HOB¹]

hubble-bubble /'hʌb(ə)l,bʌb(ə)l/ n. **1** a rudimentary form of hookah. **2** a bubbling sound. **3** confused talk. [redupl. of BUBBLE]

hubbub /'hʌbʌb/ n. **1** a confused din, esp. from a crowd of people. **2** a disturbance or riot. [perh. of Ir. orig.: cf. Gael. *ubub* int. of contempt, Ir. *abú*, used in battle-cries]

hubby /'hʌbɪ/ n. (pl. **-ies**) colloq. a husband. [abbr.]

hubris /'hju:brɪs/ n. **1** arrogant pride or presumption. **2** (in Greek tragedy) excessive pride towards or defiance of the gods, leading to nemesis. □□ **hubristic** /-'brɪstɪk/ adj. [Gk]

huckaback /'hʌkə,bæk/ n. a stout linen or cotton fabric with a rough surface, used for towelling. [17th c.: orig. unkn.]

huckleberry /'hʌkəlbərɪ/ n. (pl. **-ies**) **1** any low-growing N. American shrub of the genus *Gaylussacia*. **2** the blue or black soft fruit of this plant. [prob. alt. of *hurtleberry*, WHORTLEBERRY]

huckster /'hʌkstə(r)/ n. & v. —n. **1** a mercenary person. **2** US a publicity agent, esp. for broadcast material. **3** a pedlar or hawker. —v. **1** intr. bargain, haggle. **2** tr. carry on a petty traffic in. **3** tr. adulterate. [ME prob. f. LG: cf. dial. *huck* to bargain, HAWKER¹]

huddle /'hʌd(ə)l/ v. & n. —v. **1** tr. & intr. (often foll. by *up*) crowd together; nestle closely. **2** intr. & refl. (often foll. by *up*) coil one's body into a small space. **3** tr. Brit. heap together in a muddle. —n. **1** a confused or crowded mass of people or things. **2** colloq. a close or secret conference (esp. in **go into a huddle**). **3** confusion, bustle. [16th c.: perh. f. LG and ult. rel. to HIDE³]

hue /hju:/ n. **1 a** a colour or tint. **b** a variety or shade of colour caused by the admixture of another. **2** the attribute of a colour by virtue of which it is discernible as red, green, etc. □□ **-hued** adj. **hueless** adj. [OE *hīew, hēw* form, beauty f. Gmc: cf. ON *hȳ* down on plants]

hue and cry /hju:/ n. **1** a loud clamour or outcry. **2** hist. **a** a loud cry raised for the pursuit of a wrongdoer. **b** a proclamation for the capture of a criminal. [AF *hu e cri* f. OF *hu* outcry (f. *huer* shout) + *e* and + *cri* cry]

huff /hʌf/ v. & n. —v. **1** intr. give out loud puffs of air, steam, etc. **2** intr. bluster loudly or threateningly (*huffing and puffing*). **3** intr. & tr. take or cause to take offence. **4** tr. Draughts remove (an opponent's man that could have made a capture) from the board as a forfeit (orig. after blowing on the piece). —n. a fit of petty annoyance. □**in a huff** annoyed and offended. □□ **huffish** adj. [imit. of the sound of blowing]

huffy /'hʌfɪ/ adj. (**huffier, huffiest**) **1** apt to take offence. **2** offended. □□ **huffily** adv. **huffiness** n.

hug /hʌg/ v. & n. —v.tr. (**hugged, hugging**) **1** squeeze tightly in one's arms, esp. with affection. **2** (of a bear) squeeze (a person) between its forelegs. **3** keep close to (the shore, kerb, etc.). **4** cherish or cling to (prejudices etc.). **5** refl. congratulate or be pleased with (oneself). —n. **1** a strong clasp with the arms. **2** a squeezing grip in wrestling. □□ **huggable** adj. [16th c.: prob. f. Scand.: cf. ON *hugga* console]

huge /hju:dʒ/ adj. **1** extremely large; enormous. **2** (of immaterial things) very great (*a huge success*). □□ **hugeness** n. [ME *huge* f. OF *ahuge, ahoge*, of unkn. orig.]

hugely /'hju:dʒlɪ/ adv. **1** enormously (*hugely successful*). **2** very much (*enjoyed it hugely*).

hugger-mugger /'hʌgə,mʌgə(r)/ adj., adv., n., & v. —adj. & adv. **1** in secret. **2** confused; in confusion. —n. **1** secrecy. **2** confusion. —v.intr. proceed in a secret or muddled fashion. [prob. rel. to ME *hoder huddle, mokere* conceal: cf. 15th-c. *hoder moder*, 16th-c. *hucker mucker* in the same sense]

Huguenot /'hju:gə,nəʊ, -,nɒt/ n. hist. a French Protestant. [F, assim. of *eiguenot* (f. Du. *eedgenot* f. Swiss G *Eidgenoss* confederate) to the name of a Geneva burgomaster *Hugues*]

huh /hə/ int. expressing disgust, surprise, etc. [imit.]

hula /'hu:lə/ n. (also **hula-hula**) a Polynesian dance performed by women, with flowing movements of the arms. □**hula hoop** a large hoop for spinning round the body with hula-like movements. **hula skirt** a long grass skirt. [Hawaiian]

hulk /hʌlk/ n. **1 a** the body of a dismantled ship, used as a store vessel etc. **b** (in pl.) hist. this used as a prison. **2** an unwieldy vessel. **3** colloq. a large clumsy-looking person or thing. [OE *hulc* & MLG, MDu. *hulk*: cf. Gk *holkas* cargo ship]

hulking /'hʌlkɪŋ/ adj. colloq. bulky; large and clumsy.

hull¹ /hʌl/ n. & v. —n. the body or frame of a ship, airship, flying boat, etc. —v.tr. pierce the hull of (a ship) with gunshot etc. [ME, perh. rel. to HOLD²]

hull² /hʌl/ n. & v. —n. **1** the outer covering of a fruit, esp. the pod of peas and beans, the husk of grain, or the green calyx of a strawberry. **2** a covering. —v.tr. remove the hulls from (fruit etc.). [OE *hulu* ult. f. *helan* cover: cf. HELE]

hullabaloo /,hʌləbə'lu:/ n. (pl. **hullabaloos**) an uproar or clamour. [18th c.: redupl. of *hallo, hullo*, etc.]

hullo var. of HELLO.

hum¹ /hʌm/ v. & n. —v. (**hummed, humming**) **1** intr. make a low steady continuous sound like that of a bee. **2** tr. (also absol.) sing (a wordless tune) with closed lips. **3** intr. utter a slight inarticulate sound. **4** intr. colloq. be in an active state (*really made things hum*). **5** intr. Brit. colloq. smell unpleasantly. —n. **1** a humming sound. **2** an unwanted low-frequency noise caused by variation of electric current, usu. the alternating frequency of the mains, in an amplifier etc. **3** Brit. colloq. a bad smell. □**hum and haw** (or **ha**) hesitate, esp. in speaking. □□ **hummable** adj. **hummer** n. [ME, imit.]

hum² /həm/ int. expressing hesitation or dissent. [imit.]

human /'hju:mən/ adj. & n. —adj. **1** of or belonging to the genus *Homo*. **2** consisting of human beings (*the human race*). **3** of or characteristic of mankind as opposed to God or animals or machines, esp. susceptible to the weaknesses of mankind (*is only human*). **4** showing (esp. the better) qualities of man (*proved to be very human*). —n. a human being. □**human being** any man or woman or child of the species *Homo sapiens*. **human chain** a line of people formed for passing things along, e.g. buckets of water to the site of a fire. **human engineering 1** the management of industrial labour, esp. as regards man-machine relationships. **2** the study of this. **human equation** a bias or prejudice. **human interest** (in a newspaper story etc.) reference to personal experience and emotions etc. **human nature** the general characteristics and feelings of mankind. **human relations** relations with or between people or individuals. **human rights** rights held to be justifiably belonging to any person. □□ **humanness** n. [ME *humain(e)* f. OF f. L *humanus* f. *homo* human being]

humane /hju:'meɪn/ adj. **1** benevolent, compassionate. **2** inflicting the minimum of pain. **3** (of a branch of learning) tending to civilize or confer refinement. □**humane killer** an instrument for the painless slaughter of animals. □□ **humanely** adv. **humaneness** n. [var. of HUMAN, differentiated in sense in the 18th c.]

humanism /'hju:mə,nɪz(ə)m/ n. **1** an outlook or system of thought concerned with human rather than divine or supernatural matters. **2** a belief or outlook emphasizing common human needs and

seeking solely rational ways of solving human problems, and concerned with mankind as responsible
and progressive intellectual beings. **3** (often
Humanism) literary culture, esp. that of the Renaissance humanists.

humanist /ˈhjuːmənɪst/ *n.* **1** an adherent of humanism. **2** a humanitarian. **3** a student (esp. in the
14th-16th c.) of Roman and Greek literature and
antiquities. □□ **humanistic** /-ˈnɪstɪk/ *adj.*
humanistically /-ˈnɪstɪkəlɪ/ *adv.* [F *humaniste* f. It.
umanista (as HUMAN)]

humanitarian /hjuːˌmænɪˈteərɪən/ *n. & adj.* —*n.* **1**
a person who seeks to promote human welfare. **2** a
person who advocates or practises humane action; a
philanthropist. —*adj.* relating to or holding the
views of humanitarians. □□ **humanitarianism** *n.*

humanity /hjuːˈmænɪtɪ/ *n.* (*pl.* -**ies**) **1 a** the human
race. **b** human beings collectively. **c** the fact or
condition of being human. **2** humaneness, bene-
volence. **3** (in *pl.*) human attributes. **4** (in *pl.*) learning
or literature concerned with human culture, esp. the
study of Latin and Greek literature and philosophy.
[ME f. OF *humanité* f. L *humanitas -tatis* (as HUMAN)]

humanize /ˈhjuːmənaɪz/ *v.tr.* (also -**ise**) **1** make
human; give a human character to. **2** make humane.
□□ **humanization** /-ˈzeɪʃ(ə)n/ *n.* [F *humaniser* (as
HUMAN)]

humankind /ˈhjuːmənˌkaɪnd/ *n.* human beings
collectively.

humanly /ˈhjuːmənlɪ/ *adv.* **1** by human means (*I
will do it if it is humanly possible*). **2** in a human
manner. **3** from a human point of view. **4** with
human feelings.

humble /ˈhʌmb(ə)l/ *adj. & v.* —*adj.* **1 a** having or
showing a low estimate of one's own importance. **b**
offered with or affected by such an estimate (*if you
want my humble opinion*). **2** of low social or political
rank (*humble origins*). **3** (of a thing) of modest
pretensions, dimensions, etc. —*v.tr.* **1** make humble;
bring low; abase. **2** lower the rank or status of.
□ **eat humble pie** make a humble apology; accept
humiliation. □□ **humbleness** *n.* **humbly** *adv.* [ME
umble, humble f. OF *umble* f. L *humilis* lowly f.
humus ground: *humble pie* f. UMBLES]

humble-bee /ˈhʌmb(ə)lˌbiː/ *n.* = BUMBLE-BEE. [ME
prob.f. MLG *hummelbē*, MDu. *hommel*, OHG *humbal*]

humbug /ˈhʌmbʌɡ/ *n. & v.* —*n.* **1** deceptive or false
talk or behaviour. **2** an impostor. **3** *Brit.* a hard
boiled sweet usu. flavoured with peppermint. —*v.*
(**humbugged, humbugging**) **1** *intr.* be or behave
like an impostor. **2** *tr.* deceive, hoax. □□
humbuggery *n.* [18th c.: orig. unkn.]

humdinger /ˈhʌmˌdɪŋə(r)/ *n. sl.* an excellent or
remarkable person or thing. [20th c.: orig. unkn.]

humdrum /ˈhʌmdrʌm/ *adj. & n.* —*adj.* **1** commonplace, dull. **2** monotonous. —*n.* **1** commonplaceness, dullness. **2** a monotonous routine etc.
[16th c.: prob.f. HUM¹ by redupl.]

humectant /hjuːˈmekt(ə)nt/ *adj. & n.* —*adj.* retaining or preserving moisture. —*n.* a substance,
esp. a food additive, used to reduce loss of moisture.
[L (*h*)*umectant-* part. stem of (*h*)*umectare* moisten f.
umēre be moist]

humeral /ˈhjuːmər(ə)l/ *adj.* **1** of the humerus or
shoulder. **2** worn on the shoulder. [F *huméral* & LL
humeralis (as HUMERUS)]

humerus /ˈhjuːmərəs/ *n.* (*pl.* **humeri** /-ˌraɪ/) **1** the
bone of the upper arm in man. **2** the corresponding
bone in other vertebrates. [L, = shoulder]

humic /ˈhjuːmɪk/ *adj.* of or consisting of humus.

humid /ˈhjuːmɪd/ *adj.* (of the air or climate) warm
and damp. □□ **humidly** *adv.* [F *humide* or L *humidus*
f. *umēre* be moist]

humidifier /hjuːˈmɪdɪˌfaɪə(r)/ *n.* a device for keeping
the atmosphere moist in a room etc.

humidify /hjuːˈmɪdɪˌfaɪ/ *v.tr.* (-**ies, -ied**) make (air
etc.) humid or damp. □□ **humidification** /-fɪ
ˈkeɪʃ(ə)n/ *n.*

humidity /hjuːˈmɪdɪtɪ/ *n.* (*pl.* -**ies**) **1** a humid state.
2 moisture. **3** the degree of moisture esp. in the
atmosphere. □ **relative humidity** the proportion of
moisture to the value for saturation at the same
temperature. [ME f. OF *humidité* or L *humiditas* (as
HUMID)]

humidor /ˈhjuːmɪˌdɔː(r)/ *n.* a room or container
for keeping cigars or tobacco moist. [HUMID after
cuspidor]

humify /ˈhjuːmɪˌfaɪ/ *v.tr. & intr.* (-**ies, -ied**) make or
be made into humus. □□ **humification** /-fɪˈkeɪʃ(ə)n/
n.

humiliate /hjuːˈmɪlɪˌeɪt/ *v.tr.* make humble; injure
the dignity or self-respect of. □□ **humiliating** *adj.*
humiliatingly *adv.* **humiliation** /-ˈeɪʃ(ə)n/ *n.*
humiliator *n.* [LL *humiliare* (as HUMBLE)]

humility /hjuːˈmɪlɪtɪ/ *n.* **1** humbleness, meekness. **2**
a humble condition. [ME f. OF *humilité* f. L *humilitas
-tatis* (as HUMBLE)]

hummingbird /ˈhʌmɪŋˌbɜːd/ *n.* any small nectar-
feeding tropical bird of the family Trochilidae that
makes a humming sound by the vibration of its
wings when it hovers.

humming-top /ˈhʌmɪŋˌtɒp/ *n.* a child's top which
hums as it spins.

hummock /ˈhʌmək/ *n.* **1** a hillock or knoll. **2** *US* a
piece of rising ground, esp. in a marsh. **3** a hump or
ridge in an ice-field. □□ **hummocky** *adj.* [16th c.:
orig. unkn.]

hummus /ˈhʊməs/ *n.* (also **hoummos**) a thick sauce
or spread made from ground chick-peas and sesame
oil flavoured with lemon and garlic. [Turk. *humus*
mashed chick-peas]

humor *US* var. of HUMOUR.

humoral /ˈhjuːmər(ə)l/ *adj.* **1** *hist.* of the four bodily
humours. **2** *Med.* relating to body fluids, esp. as
distinct from cells. [F *humoral* or med.L *humoralis*
(as HUMOUR)]

humoresque /ˌhjuːməˈresk/ *n.* a short lively piece
of music. [G *Humoreske* f. *Humor* HUMOUR]

humorist /ˈhjuːmərɪst/ *n.* **1** a facetious person. **2** a
humorous talker, actor, or writer. □□ **humoristic**
/-ˈrɪstɪk/ *adj.*

humorous /ˈhjuːmərəs/ *adj.* **1** showing humour or a
sense of humour. **2** facetious, comic. □□ **humorously**
adv. **humorousness** *n.*

humour /ˈhjuːmə(r)/ *n. & v.* (*US* **humor**) —*n.* **1**
a the condition of being amusing or comic (less
intellectual and more sympathetic than wit). **b** the
expression of humour in literature, speech, etc. **2** (in
full **sense of humour**) the ability to perceive or
express humour or take a joke. **3** a mood or state of
mind (*bad humour*). **4** an inclination or whim (*in the
humour for fighting*). **5** (in full **cardinal humour**)
hist. each of the four chief fluids of the body (blood,
phlegm, choler, melancholy), thought to determine
a person's physical and mental qualities. —*v.tr.* **1**
gratify or indulge (a person or taste etc.). **2** adapt
oneself to; make concessions to. □ **out of humour**
displeased. □□ **-humoured** *adj.* **humourless** *adj.*
humourlessly *adv.* **humourlessness** *n.* [ME f.
AF *umour, humour*, OF *umor, humor* f. L *humor*
moisture (as HUMID)]

humous /ˈhjuːməs/ *adj.* like or consisting of humus.

hump /hʌmp/ *n. & v.* —*n.* **1** a rounded protuberance
on the back of a camel etc., or as an abnormality on
a person's back. **2** a rounded raised mass of earth
etc. **3** a mound over which railway vehicles are
pushed so as to run by gravity to the required place
in a marshalling yard. **4** a critical point in an
undertaking, ordeal, etc. **5** (prec. by *the*) *Brit. sl.* a fit
of depression or vexation (*it gives me the hump*).
—*v.tr.* **1 a** (often foll. by *about*) *colloq.* lift or carry
(heavy objects etc.) with difficulty. **b** esp. *Austral.*
hoist up, shoulder (one's pack etc.). **2** make hump-
shaped. **3** annoy, depress. **4** *coarse sl.* have sexual
intercourse with. ¶ In sense 4 usually considered a
taboo word. □ **hump bridge** = *humpback bridge.*

live on one's hump *colloq*. be self-sufficient. **over the hump** over the worst; well begun. □□ **humped** *adj*. **humpless** *adj*. [17th c.: perh. rel. to LG *humpel* hump, LG *humpe*, Du. *homp* lump, hunk (of bread)]

humpback /ˈhʌmpbæk/ *n*. **1 a** a deformed back with a hump. **b** a person having this. **2** a baleen whale, *Megaptera novaeangliae*, with a dorsal fin forming a hump. □ **humpback bridge** *Brit*. a small bridge with a steep ascent and descent. □□ **humpbacked** *adj*.

humph /həmf/ *int*. & *n*. an inarticulate sound expressing doubt or dissatisfaction. [imit.]

humpty-dumpty /ˌhʌmptɪˈdʌmptɪ/ *n*. (*pl*. **-ies**) **1** a short dumpy person. **2** a person or thing that once overthrown cannot be restored. [the nursery rhyme *Humpty-Dumpty*, perh. ult. f. HUMPY¹, DUMPY]

humpy¹ /ˈhʌmpɪ/ *adj*. (**humpier, humpiest**) **1** having a hump or humps. **2** humplike.

humpy² /ˈhʌmpɪ/ *n*. (*pl*. **-ies**) *Austral*. a primitive hut. [Aboriginal *oompi*, infl. by HUMP]

humus /ˈhjuːməs/ *n*. the organic constituent of soil, usu. formed by the decomposition of plants and leaves by soil bacteria. □□ **humusify** *v.tr*. & *intr*. (**-ies, -ied**). [L, = soil]

Hun /hʌn/ *n*. **1** a member of a warlike Asiatic nomadic people who invaded and ravaged Europe in the 4th–5th c. **2** *offens*. a German (esp. in military contexts). **3** an uncivilized devastator; a vandal. □□ **Hunnish** *adj*. [OE *Hūne* pl. f. LL *Hunni* f. Gk *Hounnoi* f. Turki *Hun-yü*]

hunch /hʌntʃ/ *v*. & *n*. —*v*. **1** *tr*. bend or arch into a hump. **2** *tr*. thrust out or up to form a hump. **3** *intr*. (usu. foll. by *up*) *US* sit with the body hunched. —*n*. **1** an intuitive feeling or conjecture. **2** a hint. **3** a hump. **4** a thick piece. [16th c.: orig. unkn.]

hunchback /ˈhʌntʃbæk/ *n*. = HUMPBACK. □□ **hunchbacked** *adj*.

hundred /ˈhʌndrəd/ *n*. & *adj*. —*n*. (*pl*. **hundreds** or (in sense 1) **hundred**) (in *sing*., prec. by *a* or *one*) **1** the product of ten and ten. **2** a symbol for this (100, c, C). **3** a set of a hundred things. **4** (in *sing*. or *pl*.) *colloq*. a large number. **5** (in *pl*.) the years of a specified century (*the seventeen hundreds*). **6** *Brit. hist*. a subdivision of a county or shire, having its own court. —*adj*. **1** that amount to a hundred. **2** used to express whole hours in the 24-hour system (*thirteen hundred hours*). □ **a** (or **one**) **hundred per cent** *adv*. entirely, completely. —*adj*. **1** entire, complete. **2** (usu. with *neg*.) fully recovered. **hundreds and thousands** tiny coloured sweets used chiefly for decorating cakes etc. □□ **hundredfold** *adj*. & *adv*. **hundredth** *adj*. & *n*. [OE f. Gmc]

hundredweight /ˈhʌndrədˌweɪt/ *n*. (*pl*. same or **-weights**) **1** (in full **long hundredweight**) *Brit*. a unit of weight equal to 112 lb. avoirdupois (about 50.8 kg). **2** (in full **metric hundredweight**) a unit of weight equal to 50 kg. **3** (in full **short hundredweight**) *US* a unit of weight equal to 100 lb. (about 45.4 kg).

hung *past* and *past part*. of HANG.

Hungarian /hʌŋˈgeərɪən/ *n*. & *adj*. —*n*. **1 a** a native or national of Hungary in E. Europe. **b** a person of Hungarian descent. **2** the Finno-Ugric language of Hungary. —*adj*. of or relating to Hungary or its people or language. [med.L *Hungaria* f. *Hungari* Magyar nation]

hunger /ˈhʌŋgə(r)/ *n*. & *v*. —*n*. **1** a feeling of pain or discomfort, or (in extremes) an exhausted condition, caused by lack of food. **2** (often foll. by *for, after*) a strong desire. —*v.intr*. **1** (often foll. by *for, after*) have a craving or strong desire. **2** feel hunger. □ **hunger march** a march undertaken by a body of unemployed etc. to call attention to their condition. **hunger marcher** a person who goes on a hunger march. **hunger strike** the refusal of food as a form of protest, esp. by prisoners. **hunger striker** a

person who takes part in a hunger strike. [OE *hungor, hyngran* f. Gmc]

hungry /ˈhʌŋgrɪ/ *adj*. (**hungrier, hungriest**) **1** feeling or showing hunger; needing food. **2** inducing hunger (*a hungry air*). **3 a** eager, greedy, craving. **b** *Austral*. mean, stingy. **4** (of soil) poor, barren. □□ **hungrily** *adv*. **hungriness** *n*. [OE *hungrig* (as HUNGER)]

hunk /hʌŋk/ *n*. **1 a** a large piece cut off (*a hunk of bread*). **b** a thick or clumsy piece. **2** *colloq*. **a** a very large person. **b** esp. *US* a sexually attractive man. □□ **hunky** *adj*. (**hunkier, hunkiest**). [19th c.: prob. f. Flem. *hunke*]

hunkers /ˈhʌŋkəz/ *n.pl*. the haunches. [orig. Sc., f. *hunker* crouch, squat]

hunky-dory /ˌhʌŋkɪˈdɔːrɪ/ *adj*. esp. *US colloq*. excellent. [19th c.: orig. unkn.]

hunt /hʌnt/ *v*. & *n*. **1** *tr*. (also *absol*.) **a** pursue and kill (wild animals, esp. foxes, or game), esp. on horseback and with hounds, for sport or food. **b** (of an animal) chase (its prey). **2** *intr*. (foll. by *after, for*) seek, search (*hunting for a pen*). **3** *intr*. **a** oscillate. **b** (of an engine etc.) run alternately too fast and too slow. **4** *tr*. (foll. by *away* etc.) drive off by pursuit. **5** *tr*. scour (a district) in pursuit of game. **6** *tr*. (as **hunted** *adj*.) (of a look etc.) expressing alarm or terror as of one being hunted. **7** *tr*. (foll. by *down, up*) move the place of (a bell) in ringing the changes. —*n*. **1** the practice of hunting or an instance of this. **2 a** an association of people engaged in hunting with hounds. **b** an area where hunting takes place. **3** an oscillating motion. □ **hunt down** pursue and capture. **hunt out** find by searching; track down. [OE *huntian*, weak grade of *hentan* seize]

huntaway /ˈhʌntəˌweɪ/ *n*. *Austral*. & *NZ* a dog trained to drive sheep forward.

hunter /ˈhʌntə(r)/ *n*. **1 a** (*fem*. **huntress**) a person or animal that hunts. **b** a horse used in hunting. **2** a person who seeks something. **3** a watch with a hinged cover protecting the glass. □ **hunter's moon** the next full moon after the harvest moon.

hunting /ˈhʌntɪŋ/ *n*. the practice of pursuing and killing wild animals, esp. for sport. □ **hunting-crop** see CROP *n*. 3. **hunting-ground 1** a place suitable for hunting. **2** a source of information or object of exploitation likely to be fruitful. **hunting horn** a straight horn used in hunting. **hunting-pink** see PINK¹. [OE *huntung* (as HUNT)]

Huntington's chorea /ˈhʌntɪŋt(ə)nz/ *n*. *Med*. see CHOREA. [G. *Huntington*, Amer. neurologist, d. 1916]

huntsman /ˈhʌntsmən/ *n*. (*pl*. **-men**) **1** a hunter. **2** a hunt official in charge of hounds.

hurdle /ˈhɜːd(ə)l/ *n*. & *v*. —*n*. **1** *Athletics* **a** each of a series of light frames to be cleared by athletes in a race. **b** (in *pl*.) a hurdle-race. **2** an obstacle or difficulty. **3** a portable rectangular frame strengthened with withes or wooden bars, used as a temporary fence etc. **4** *hist*. a frame on which traitors were dragged to execution. —*v*. **1** *Athletics* **a** *intr*. run in a hurdle-race. **b** *tr*. clear (a hurdle). **2** *tr*. fence off etc. with hurdles. **3** *tr*. overcome (a difficulty). [OE *hyrdel* f. Gmc]

hurdler /ˈhɜːdlə(r)/ *n*. **1** *Athletics* a person who runs in hurdle-races. **2** a person who makes hurdles.

hurdy-gurdy /ˈhɜːdɪˌgɜːdɪ/ *n*. (*pl*. **-ies**) **1** a musical instrument with a droning sound, played by turning a handle, esp. one with a rosined wheel turned by the right hand to sound the drone-strings, and keys played by the left hand. **2** *colloq*. a barrel-organ. [prob. imit.]

hurl /hɜːl/ *v*. & *n*. —*v*. **1** *tr*. throw with great force. **2** *tr*. utter (abuse etc.) vehemently. **3** *intr*. play hurling. —*n*. **1** a forceful throw. **2** the act of hurling. [ME, prob. imit., but corresp. in form and partly in sense with LG *hurreln*]

Hurler's syndrome /ˈhɜːləz/ *n*. *Med*. a defect in metabolism resulting in mental retardation, a protruding abdomen, and deformities of the bones, including an abnormally large head. Also called GARGOYLISM. [G. *Hurler*, Ger. paediatrician]

hurling /ˈhɜːlɪŋ/ *n.* (also **hurley** /ˈhɜːlɪ/) **1** an Irish game somewhat resembling hockey, played with broad sticks. **2** a stick used in this.

hurly-burly /ˈhɜːlɪˌbɜːlɪ/ *n.* boisterous activity; commotion. [redupl. f. HURL]

hurrah /hʊˈrɑː/ *int.*, *n.*, & *v.* (also **hurray** /hʊˈreɪ/) —*int.* & *n.* an exclamation of joy or approval. —*v.intr.* cry or shout 'hurrah' or 'hurray'. [alt. of earlier *huzza*, perh. orig. a sailor's cry when hauling]

hurricane /ˈhʌrɪkən, -ˌkeɪn/ *n.* **1** a storm with a violent wind, esp. a W. Indian cyclone. **2** *Meteorol.* a wind of 65 knots (75 m.p.h.) or more, force 12 on the Beaufort scale. **3** a violent commotion. □ **hurricane-bird** a frigate-bird. **hurricane-deck** a light upper deck on a ship etc. **hurricane-lamp** an oil-lamp designed to resist a high wind. [Sp. *huracan* & Port. *furacão* of Carib orig.]

hurry /ˈhʌrɪ/ *n.* & *v.* —*n.* (*pl.* -ies) **1 a** great haste. **b** (with *neg.* or *interrog.*) a need for haste (*there is no hurry*; *what's the hurry?*). **2** (often foll. by *for*, or *to* + infin.) eagerness to get a thing done quickly. —*v.* (-ies, -ied) **1** move or act with great or undue haste. **2** *tr.* (often foll. by *away*, *along*) cause to move or proceed in this way. **3** *tr.* (as **hurried** *adj.*) hasty; done rapidly owing to lack of time. □ **hurry along** (or **up**) make or cause to make haste. **in a hurry 1** hurrying, rushed; in a rushed manner. **2** *colloq.* easily or readily (*you will not beat that in a hurry*; *shall not ask again in a hurry*). □□ **hurriedly** *adv.* **hurriedness** *n.* [16th c.: imit.]

hurry-scurry /ˌhʌrɪˈskʌrɪ/ *n.*, *adj.*, & *adv.* —*n.* disorderly haste. —*adj.* & *adv.* in confusion. [jingling redupl. of HURRY]

hurst /hɜːst/ *n.* **1** a hillock. **2** a sandbank in the sea or a river. **3** a wood or wooded eminence. [OE *hyrst*, rel. to OS, OHG *hurst*, *horst*]

hurt /hɜːt/ *v.* & *n.* —*v.* (*past* and *past part.* **hurt**) **1** *tr.* (also *absol.*) cause pain or injury to. **2** *tr.* cause mental pain or distress to (a person, feelings, etc.). **3** *intr.* suffer pain or harm (*my arm hurts*). —*n.* **1** bodily or material injury. **2** harm, wrong. □□ **hurtless** *adj.* [ME f. OF *hurter*, *hurt* ult. perh. f. Gmc]

hurtful /ˈhɜːtfʊl/ *adj.* causing (esp. mental) hurt. □□ **hurtfully** *adv.* **hurtfulness** *n.*

hurtle /ˈhɜːt(ə)l/ *v.* **1** *intr.* & *tr.* move or hurl rapidly or with a clattering sound. **2** *intr.* come with a crash. [HURT in obs. sense 'strike forcibly']

husband /ˈhʌzbənd/ *n.* & *v.* —*n.* a married man esp. in relation to his wife. —*v.tr.* manage thriftily; use (resources) economically. □□ **husbander** *n.* **husbandhood** *n.* **husbandless** *adj.* **husbandlike** *adj.* **husbandly** *adj.* **husbandship** *n.* [OE *hūsbonda* house-dweller f. ON *húsbóndi* (as HOUSE, *bóndi* one who has a household)]

husbandry /ˈhʌzbəndrɪ/ *n.* **1** farming. **2 a** management of resources. **b** careful management.

hush /hʌʃ/ *v.*, *int.*, & *n.* —*v.tr.* & *intr.* make or become silent or quiet. —*int.* calling for silence. —*n.* an expectant stillness or silence. □ **hush money** money paid to prevent the disclosure of a discreditable matter. **hush puppy** *US* quickly fried maize bread. **hush up** suppress public mention of (an affair). [back-form. f. obs. *husht* int., = quiet!, taken as a past part.]

hushaby /ˈhʌʃəˌbaɪ/ *int.* (also **hushabye**) used to lull a child.

hush-hush /ˌhʌʃˈhʌʃ/ *adj.* *colloq.* (esp. of an official plan or enterprise etc.) highly secret or confidential.

husk /hʌsk/ *n.* & *v.* —*n.* **1** the dry outer covering of some fruits or seeds, esp. of a nut or *US* maize. **2** the worthless outside part of a thing. —*v.tr.* remove a husk or husks from. [ME, prob. f. LG *hūske* sheath, dimin. f. *hūs* HOUSE]

husky¹ /ˈhʌskɪ/ *adj.* (**huskier**, **huskiest**) **1** (of a person or voice) dry in the throat; hoarse. **2** of or full of husks. **3** dry as a husk. **4** tough, strong, hefty. □□ **huskily** *adv.* **huskiness** *n.*

husky² /ˈhʌskɪ/ *n.* (*pl.* **-ies**) **1** a dog of a powerful breed used in the Arctic for pulling sledges. **2** this breed. [perh. contr. f. ESKIMO]

huss /hʌs/ *n.* dogfish as food. [ME *husk*, of unkn. orig.]

hussar /hʊˈzɑː(r)/ *n.* **1** a soldier of a light cavalry regiment. **2** a Hungarian light horseman of the 15th c. [Magyar *huszár* f. OSerb. *husar* f. It. *corsaro* CORSAIR]

Hussite /ˈhʌsaɪt/ *n.* *hist.* a member or follower of the movement begun by John *Huss*, Bohemian religious and nationalist reformer d. 1415. □□ **Hussitism** *n.*

hussy /ˈhʌsɪ/ *n.* (*pl.* **-ies**) *derog.* an impudent or immoral girl or woman. [phonetic reduction of HOUSEWIFE (the orig. sense)]

hustings /ˈhʌstɪŋz/ *n.* **1** parliamentary election proceedings. **2** *Brit.* *hist.* a platform from which (before 1872) candidates for Parliament were nominated and addressed electors. [late OE *husting* f. ON *hústhing* house of assembly]

hustle /ˈhʌs(ə)l/ *v.* & *n.* —*v.* **1** *tr.* push roughly; jostle. **2** *tr.* **a** (foll. by *into*, *out of*, etc.) force, coerce, or deal with hurriedly or unceremoniously (*hustled them out of the room*). **b** (foll. by *into*) coerce hurriedly (*was hustled into agreeing*). **3** *intr.* push one's way; hurry, bustle. **4** *tr.* *sl.* **a** obtain by forceful action. **b** swindle. **5** *intr.* *sl.* engage in prostitution. —*n.* **1** an act or instance of hustling. **2** *colloq.* a fraud or swindle. [MDu. *husselen* shake, toss, frequent. of *hutsen*, orig. imit.]

hustler /ˈhʌslə(r)/ *n.* *sl.* **1** an active, enterprising, or unscrupulous individual. **2** a prostitute.

hut /hʌt/ *n.* & *v.* —*n.* **1** a small simple or crude house or shelter. **2** *Mil.* a temporary wooden etc. house for troops. —*v.* (**hutted**, **hutting**) **1** *tr.* provide with huts. **2** *tr.* *Mil.* place (troops etc.) in huts. **3** *intr.* lodge in a hut. □□ **hutlike** *adj.* [F *hutte* f. MHG *hütte*]

hutch /hʌtʃ/ *n.* **1** a box or cage, usu. with a wire mesh front, for keeping small pet animals. **2** *derog.* a small house. [ME, = coffer, f. OF *huche* f. med.L *hutica*, of unkn. orig.]

hutment /ˈhʌtmənt/ *n.* *Mil.* an encampment of huts.

HWM *abbr.* high-water mark.

hwyl /ˈhuːɪl/ *n.* an emotional quality inspiring impassioned eloquence. [Welsh]

Hy. *abbr.* Henry.

hyacinth /ˈhaɪəsɪnθ/ *n.* **1** any bulbous plant of the genus *Hyacinthus* with racemes of usu. purplish-blue, pink, or white bell-shaped fragrant flowers. **2** = *grape hyacinth*. **3** the purplish-blue colour of the hyacinth flower. **4** an orange variety of zircon used as a precious stone. **5** *poet.* hair or locks like the hyacinth flower (as a Homeric epithet of doubtful sense). □ **wild** (or **wood**) **hyacinth** = BLUEBELL 1. □□ **hyacinthine** /-ˈsɪnθiːn/ *adj.* [F *hyacinthe* f. L *hyacinthus* f. Gk *huakinthos*, flower and gem, also the name of a youth loved by Apollo]

Hyades /ˈhaɪəˌdiːz/ *n.pl.* a group of stars in Taurus near the Pleiades, whose heliacal rising was once thought to foretell rain. [ME f. Gk *Huades* (by popular etym. f. *huō* rain, but perh. f. *hus* pig)]

hyaena var. of HYENA.

hyalin /ˈhaɪəlɪn/ *n.* a clear glassy substance produced as a result of the degeneration of certain body tissues. [Gk *hualos* glass + -IN]

hyaline /ˈhaɪəlɪn, -ˌlaɪn, -ˌliːn/ *adj.* & *n.* —*adj.* glasslike, vitreous, transparent. —*n.* *literary* a smooth sea, clear sky, etc. □ **hyaline cartilage** *n.* a common type of cartilage. [L *hyalinus* f. Gk *hualinos* f. *hualos* glass]

hyalite /ˈhaɪəˌlaɪt/ *n.* a colourless variety of opal. [Gk *hualos* glass]

hyaloid /ˈhaɪəˌlɔɪd/ *adj.* *Anat.* glassy. □ **hyaloid membrane** a thin transparent membrane enveloping the vitreous humour of the eye. [F *hyaloïde* f. LL *hyaloides* f. Gk *hualoeidēs* (as HYALITE)]

w *we* z zoo ʃ *she* ʒ deci*s*ion θ *th*in ð *th*is ŋ ri*ng* x lo*ch* tʃ *ch*ip dʒ *j*ar (*see over for vowels*)

hybrid /'haɪbrɪd/ *n. & adj.* —*n.* **1** *Biol.* the offspring of two plants or animals of different species or varieties. **2** often *offens.* a person of mixed racial or cultural origin. **3** a thing composed of incongruous elements, e.g. a word with parts taken from different languages. —*adj.* **1** bred as a hybrid from different species or varieties. **2** *Biol.* heterogeneous. □**hybrid vigour** heterosis. □□ **hybridism** *n.* **hybridity** /-'brɪdɪtɪ/ *n.* [L *hybrida*, (h)*ibrida* offspring of a tame sow and wild boar, child of a freeman and slave, etc.]

hybridize /'haɪbrɪˌdaɪz/ *v.* (also **-ise**) **1** *tr.* subject (a species etc.) to cross-breeding. **2** *intr.* **a** produce hybrids. **b** (of an animal or plant) interbreed. □□ **hybridizable** *adj.* **hybridization** /-'zeɪʃ(ə)n/ *n.*

hydatid /'haɪdətɪd/ *n. Med.* **1** a cyst containing watery fluid (esp. one formed by, and containing, a tapeworm larva). **2** a tapeworm larva. □□ **hydatidiform** /-'tɪdɪˌfɔːm/ *adj.* [mod.L *hydatis* f. Gk *hudatis -idos* watery vesicle f. *hudōr hudatos* water]

hydra /'haɪdrə/ *n.* **1** a freshwater polyp of the genus *Hydra* with tubular body and tentacles around the mouth. **2** any water-snake. **3** something which is hard to destroy. [ME f. L f. Gk *hudra* water-snake, esp. a fabulous one with many heads that grew again when cut off]

hydrangea /haɪ'dreɪndʒə/ *n.* any shrub of the genus *Hydrangea* with large white, pink, or blue flowers. [mod.L f. Gk *hudōr* water + *aggos* vessel (from the cup-shape of its seed-capsule)]

hydrant /'haɪdrənt/ *n.* a pipe (esp. in a street) with a nozzle to which a hose can be attached for drawing water from the main. [irreg. f. HYDRO- + -ANT]

hydrate /'haɪdreɪt/ *n. & v.* —*n. Chem.* a compound of water combined with another compound or with an element. —*v.tr.* **1** combine chemically with water. **b** (as **hydrated** *adj.*) chemically bonded to water. **2** cause to absorb water. □□ **hydratable** *adj.* **hydration** /-'dreɪʃ(ə)n/ *n.* **hydrator** *n.* [F f. Gk *hudōr* water]

hydraulic /haɪ'drɔːlɪk, -'drɒlɪk/ *adj.* **1** (of water, oil, etc.) conveyed through pipes or channels usu. by pressure. **2** (of a mechanism etc.) operated by liquid moving in this manner (*hydraulic brakes*; *hydraulic lift*). **3** of or concerned with hydraulics (*hydraulic engineer*). **4** hardening under water (*hydraulic cement*). □**hydraulic press** a device in which the force applied to a fluid creates a pressure which when transmitted to a larger volume of fluid gives rise to a greater force. **hydraulic ram** an automatic pump in which the kinetic energy of a descending column of water raises some of the water above its original level. □□ **hydraulically** *adv.* **hydraulicity** /-'lɪsɪtɪ/ *n.* [L *hydraulicus* f. Gk *hudraulikos* f. *hudōr* water + *aulos* pipe]

hydraulics /haɪ'drɔːlɪks, -'drɒlɪks/ *n.pl.* (usu. treated as *sing.*) the science of the conveyance of liquids through pipes etc. esp. as motive power.

hydrazine /'haɪdrəˌziːn/ *n. Chem.* a colourless alkaline liquid which is a powerful reducing agent and is used as a rocket propellant. ¶ Chem. formula: N₂H₄. [HYDROGEN + AZO- + -INE⁴]

hydride /'haɪdraɪd/ *n. Chem.* a binary compound of hydrogen with an element, esp. with a metal.

hydriodic acid /ˌhaɪdrɪ'ɒdɪk, -aɪ'ɒdɪk/ *n. Chem.* a solution of the colourless gas hydrogen iodide in water. ¶ Chem. formula: HI. [HYDROGEN + IODINE]

hydro /'haɪdrəʊ/ *n.* (*pl.* **-os**) *colloq.* **1** a hotel or clinic etc. orig. providing hydropathic treatment. **2** a hydroelectric power plant. [abbr.]

hydro- /'haɪdrəʊ/ *comb. form* (also **hydr-** before a vowel) **1** having to do with water (*hydroelectric*). **2** *Med.* affected with an accumulation of serous fluid (*hydrocele*). **3** *Chem.* combined with hydrogen (*hydrochloric*). [Gk *hudro-* f. *hudōr* water]

hydrobromic acid /ˌhaɪdrəʊ'brəʊmɪk/ *n. Chem.* a solution of the colourless gas hydrogen bromide in water. ¶ Chem. formula: HBr.

hydrocarbon /ˌhaɪdrəʊ'kɑːbən/ *n. Chem.* a compound of hydrogen and carbon.

hydrocele /'haɪdrəˌsiːl/ *n. Med.* the accumulation of serous fluid in a body sac.

hydrocephalus /ˌhaɪdrə'sefələs/ *n. Med.* an abnormal amount of fluid within the brain, esp. in young children, which makes the head enlarge and can cause mental deficiency. □□ **hydrocephalic** /-sɪ'fælɪk/ *adj.*

hydrochloric acid /ˌhaɪdrə'klɒrɪk, -'klɒrɪk/ *n. Chem.* a solution of the colourless gas hydrogen chloride in water. ¶ Chem. formula: HCl.

hydrochloride /ˌhaɪdrə'klɒraɪd/ *n. Chem.* a compound of an organic base with hydrochloric acid.

hydrocortisone /ˌhaɪdrə'kɔːtɪˌzəʊn/ *n. Biochem.* a steroid hormone produced by the adrenal cortex, used medicinally to treat inflammation and rheumatism.

hydrocyanic acid /ˌhaɪdrəsaɪ'ænɪk/ *n. Chem.* a highly poisonous volatile liquid with a characteristic odour of bitter almonds. ¶ Chem. formula: HCN. Also called *prussic acid.*

hydrodynamics /ˌhaɪdrəʊdaɪ'næmɪks/ *n.* the science of forces acting on or exerted by fluids (esp. liquids). □□ **hydrodynamic** *adj.* **hydrodynamical** *adj.* **hydrodynamicist** /-sɪst/ *n.* [mod.L *hydro-dynamicus* (as HYDRO-, DYNAMIC)]

hydroelectric /ˌhaɪdrəʊɪ'lektrɪk/ *adj.* **1** generating electricity by utilization of water-power. **2** (of electricity) generated in this way. □□ **hydroelectricity** /-'trɪsɪtɪ/ *n.*

hydrofluoric acid /ˌhaɪdrəʊ'flʊərɪk/ *n. Chem.* a solution of the colourless liquid hydrogen fluoride in water. ¶ Chem. formula: HF.

hydrofoil /'haɪdrəˌfɔɪl/ *n.* **1** a boat equipped with a device consisting of planes for lifting its hull out of the water to increase its speed. **2** this device. [HYDRO-, after AEROFOIL]

hydrogen /'haɪdrədʒ(ə)n/ *n. Chem.* a colourless gaseous element, without taste or odour, the lightest of the elements and occurring in water and all organic compounds. ¶ Symb.: H. □**hydrogen bomb** an immensely powerful bomb utilizing the explosive fusion of hydrogen nuclei: also called H-BOMB. **hydrogen bond** a weak electrostatic interaction between an electronegative atom and a hydrogen atom bonded to a different electronegative atom. **hydrogen peroxide** a colourless viscous unstable liquid with strong oxidizing properties. ¶ Chem. formula: H₂O₂. **hydrogen sulphide** a colourless poisonous gas with a disagreeable smell, formed by rotting animal matter. ¶ Chem. formula: H₂S. □□ **hydrogenous** /-'drɒdʒɪnəs/ *adj.* [F *hydrogène* (as HYDRO-, -GEN)]

hydrogenase /haɪ'drɒdʒɪˌneɪz, -ˌneɪs/ *n. Biochem.* any enzyme which catalyses the oxidation of hydrogen and the reduction of protons.

hydrogenate /haɪ'drɒdʒɪˌneɪt, 'haɪdrədʒəˌneɪt/ *v.tr.* charge with or cause to combine with hydrogen. □□ **hydrogenation** /-'neɪʃ(ə)n/ *n.*

hydrography /haɪ'drɒgrəfɪ/ *n.* the science of surveying and charting seas, lakes, rivers, etc. □□ **hydrographer** *n.* **hydrographic** /ˌhaɪdrə'græfɪk/ *adj.* **hydrographical** /ˌhaɪdrə'græfɪk(ə)l/ *adj.* **hydrographically** /ˌhaɪdrə'græfɪkəlɪ/ *adv.*

hydroid /'haɪdrɔɪd/ *adj. & n. Zool.* any usu. polypoid hydrozoan of the order Hydroida, including hydra.

hydrolase /'haɪdrəʊˌleɪz, -ˌleɪs/ *n. Biochem.* any enzyme which catalyses the hydrolysis of a substrate.

hydrology /haɪ'drɒlədʒɪ/ *n.* the science of the properties of the earth's water, esp. of its movement in relation to land. □□ **hydrologic** /ˌhaɪdrə'lɒdʒɪk/ *adj.* **hydrological** /ˌhaɪdrə'lɒdʒɪk(ə)l/ *adj.* **hydrologically** /ˌhaɪdrə'lɒdʒɪkəlɪ/ *adv.* **hydrologist** *n.*

hydrolyse /'haɪdrəˌlaɪz/ *v.tr. & intr.* (*US* **hydrolyze**) subject to or undergo the chemical action of water.

hydrolysis /haɪ'drɒlɪsɪs/ *n.* the chemical reaction of

a substance with water, usu. resulting in decomposition. □□ **hydrolytic** /ˌhaɪdrə'lɪtɪk/ *adj.*

hydromagnetic /ˌhaɪdrəmæg'netɪk/ *adj.* involving hydrodynamics and magnetism; magnetohydrodynamic.

hydromania /ˌhaɪdrə'meɪnɪə/ *n.* a craving for water.

hydromechanics /ˌhaɪdrəʊmɪ'kænɪks/ *n.* the mechanics of liquids; hydrodynamics.

hydrometer /haɪ'drɒmɪtə(r)/ *n.* an instrument for measuring the density of liquids. □□ **hydrometric** /ˌhaɪdrə'metrɪk/ *adj.* **hydrometry** *n.*

hydronium ion /haɪ'drəʊnɪəm/ *n. Chem.* = HYDROXONIUM ION. [contr.]

hydropathy /haɪ'drɒpəθɪ/ *n.* the (medically unorthodox) treatment of disease by external and internal application of water. □□ **hydropathic** /ˌhaɪdrə'pæθɪk/ *adj.* **hydropathist** *n.* [HYDRO-, after HOMOEOPATHY etc.]

hydrophil /'haɪdrəfɪl/ *adj.* (also **hydrophile** /-ˌfaɪl/) = HYDROPHILIC. [as HYDROPHILIC]

hydrophilic /ˌhaɪdrə'fɪlɪk/ *adj.* **1** having an affinity for water. **2** wettable by water. [HYDRO- + Gk *philos* loving]

hydrophobia /ˌhaɪdrə'fəʊbɪə/ *n.* **1** a morbid aversion to water, esp. as a symptom of rabies in man. **2** rabies, esp. in man. [LL f. Gk *hudrophobia* (as HYDRO-, -PHOBIA)]

hydrophobic /ˌhaɪdrə'fəʊbɪk/ *adj.* **1** of or suffering from hydrophobia. **2 a** lacking an affinity for water. **b** not readily wettable.

hydrophone /'haɪdrəˌfəʊn/ *n.* an instrument for the detection of sound-waves in water.

hydrophyte /'haɪdrəˌfaɪt/ *n.* an aquatic plant, or a plant which needs much moisture.

hydroplane /'haɪdrəˌpleɪn/ *n. & v.* —*n.* **1** a light fast motor boat designed to skim over the surface of water. **2** a finlike attachment which enables a submarine to rise and fall in water. —*v.intr.* **1** (of a boat) skim over the surface of water with its hull lifted. **2** = AQUAPLANE *v.* 2.

hydroponics /ˌhaɪdrə'pɒnɪks/ *n.* the process of growing plants in sand, gravel, or liquid, without soil and with added nutrients. □□ **hydroponic** *adj.* **hydroponically** *adv.* [HYDRO- + Gk *ponos* labour]

hydroquinone /ˌhaɪdrə'kwɪnəʊn/ *n.* a substance formed by the reduction of quinone, used as a photographic developer.

hydrosphere /'haɪdrəˌsfɪə(r)/ *n.* the waters of the earth's surface.

hydrostatic /ˌhaɪdrə'stætɪk/ *adj.* of the equilibrium of liquids and the pressure exerted by liquid at rest. □ **hydrostatic press** = *hydraulic press.* □□ **hydrostatical** *adj.* **hydrostatically** *adv.* [prob. f. Gk *hudrostatēs* hydrostatic balance (as HYDRO-, STATIC)]

hydrostatics /ˌhaɪdrə'stætɪks/ *n.pl.* (usu. treated as *sing.*) the branch of mechanics concerned with the hydrostatic properties of liquids.

hydrotherapy /ˌhaɪdrə'θerəpɪ/ *n.* the use of water in the treatment of disorders, usu. exercises in swimming pools for arthritic or partially paralysed patients. □□ **hydrotherapist** *n.* **hydrotherapic** *adj.*

hydrothermal /ˌhaɪdrə'θɜːm(ə)l/ *adj.* of the action of heated water on the earth's crust. □□ **hydrothermally** *adv.*

hydrothorax /ˌhaɪdrə'θɔːræks/ *n.* the condition of having fluid in the pleural cavity.

hydrotropism /haɪ'drɒtrəˌpɪz(ə)m/ *adj.* a tendency of plant roots etc. to turn to or from moisture.

hydrous /'haɪdrəs/ *adj. Chem. & Mineral.* containing water. [Gk *hudōr hudro-* water]

hydroxide /haɪ'drɒksaɪd/ *n. Chem.* a metallic compound containing oxygen and hydrogen either in the form of the hydroxide ion (OH-) or the hydroxyl group (-OH).

hydroxonium ion /ˌhaɪdrɒk'səʊnɪəm/ *n. Chem.* the hydrated hydrogen ion, H_3O^+. [HYDRO- + OXY-² + -onium]

hydroxy- /haɪ'drɒksɪ/ *comb. form Chem.* having a hydroxide ion (or ions) or a hydroxyl group (or groups) (*hydroxybenzoic acid*). [HYDROGEN + OXYGEN]

hydroxyl /haɪ'drɒksɪl/ *n. Chem.* the univalent group containing hydrogen and oxygen, as -OH. [HYDROGEN + OXYGEN + -YL]

hydrozoan /ˌhaɪdrə'zəʊən/ *n. & adj.* —*n.* any aquatic coelenterate of the class *Hydrozoa* of mainly marine polyp or medusoid forms, including hydra and Portuguese man-of-war. [mod.L *Hydrozoa* (as HYDRA, Gk *zōion* animal)]

hyena /haɪ'iːnə/ *n.* (also **hyaena**) any flesh-eating mammal of the order Hyaenidae, with hind limbs shorter than forelimbs. □ **laughing hyena** *n.* a hyena, *Crocuta crocuta*, whose howl is compared to a fiendish laugh. [ME f. OF *hyene* & L *hyaena* f. Gk *huaina* fem. of *hus* pig]

hygiene /'haɪdʒiːn/ *n.* **1 a** a study, or set of principles, of maintaining health. **b** conditions or practices conducive to maintaining health. **2** sanitary science. [F *hygiène* f. mod.L *hygieina* f. Gk *hugieinē* (*tekhnē*) (art) of health f. *hugiēs* healthy]

hygienic /haɪ'dʒiːnɪk/ *adj.* conducive to hygiene; clean and sanitary. □□ **hygienically** *adv.*

hygienics /haɪ'dʒiːnɪks/ *n.pl.* (usu. treated as *sing.*) = HYGIENE 1a.

hygienist /'haɪdʒiːnɪst/ *n.* a specialist in the promotion and practice of cleanliness for the preservation of health.

hygro- /'haɪgrəʊ/ *comb. form* moisture. [Gk *hugro-* f. *hugros* wet, moist]

hygrology /haɪ'grɒlədʒɪ/ *n.* the study of the humidity of the atmosphere etc.

hygrometer /haɪ'grɒmɪtə(r)/ *n.* an instrument for measuring the humidity of the air or a gas. □□ **hygrometric** /ˌhaɪgrə'metrɪk/ *adj.* **hygrometry** *n.*

hygrophilous /haɪ'grɒfɪləs/ *adj.* (of a plant) growing in a moist environment.

hygrophyte /'haɪgrəˌfaɪt/ *n.* = HYDROPHYTE.

hygroscope /'haɪgrəˌskəʊp/ *n.* an instrument which indicates but does not measure the humidity of the air.

hygroscopic /ˌhaɪgrə'skɒpɪk/ *adj.* **1** of the hygroscope. **2** (of a substance) tending to absorb moisture from the air. □□ **hygroscopically** *adv.*

hying *pres. part.* of HIE.

hylic /'haɪlɪk/ *adj.* of matter; material. [LL *hylicus* f. Gk *hulikos* f. *hulē* matter]

hylo- /'haɪləʊ/ *comb. form* matter. [Gk *hulo-* f. *hulē* matter]

hylomorphism /ˌhaɪlə'mɔːfɪz(ə)m/ *n.* the theory that physical objects are composed of matter and form. [HYLO- + Gk *morphē* form]

hylozoism /ˌhaɪlə'zəʊɪz(ə)m/ *n.* the doctrine that all matter has life. [HYLO- + Gk *zōē* life]

hymen /'haɪmen/ *n. Anat.* a membrane which partially closes the opening of the vagina and is usu. broken at the first occurrence of sexual intercourse. □□ **hymenal** *adj.* [LL f. Gk *humēn* membrane]

hymeneal /ˌhaɪmɪ'niːəl/ *adj. literary* of or concerning marriage. [*Hymen* (L f. Gk *Humēn*) Greek and Roman god of marriage]

hymenium /haɪ'miːnɪəm/ *n.* (*pl.* **hymenia** /-nɪə/) the spore-bearing surface of certain fungi. [mod.L f. Gk *humenion* dimin. of *humēn* membrane]

hymenopteran /ˌhaɪmə'nɒptərən/ *n.* any insect of the order *Hymenoptera* having four transparent wings, including bees, wasps, and ants. □□ **hymenopterous** *adj.* [mod.L *hymenoptera* f. Gk *humenopteros* membrane-winged (as HYMENIUM, *pteron* wing)]

hymn /hɪm/ *n. & v.* —*n.* **1** a song of praise, esp. to God in Christian worship, usu. a metrical composition sung in a religious service. **2** a song of praise in honour of a god or other exalted being or thing. —*v.* **1** *tr.* praise or celebrate in hymns. **2** *intr.* sing hymns. □ **hymn-book** a book of hymns. □□ **hymnic**

/'hɪmnɪk/ adj. [ME ymne etc. f. OF ymne f. L hymnus f. Gk humnos]

hymnal /'hɪmn(ə)l/ n. & adj. —n. a hymn-book. —adj. of hymns. [ME f. med.L hymnale (as HYMN)]

hymnary /'hɪmnərɪ/ n. (pl. -ies) a hymn-book.

hymnody /'hɪmnədɪ/ n. (pl. -ies) 1 a the singing of hymns. b the composition of hymns. 2 hymns collectively. □□ **hymnodist** n. [med.L hymnodia f. Gk humnōidia f. humnos hymn: cf. PSALMODY]

hymnographer /hɪm'nɒgrəfə(r)/ n. a writer of hymns. □□ **hymnography** n. [Gk humnographos f. humnos hymn]

hymnology /hɪm'nɒlədʒɪ/ n. (pl. -ies) 1 the composition or study of hymns. 2 hymns collectively. □□ **hymnologist** n.

hyoid /'haɪɔɪd/ n. & adj. Anat. —n. (in full **hyoid bone**) a U-shaped bone in the neck which supports the tongue. —adj. of or relating to this. [F hyoïde f. mod.L hyoïdes f. Gk huoeidēs shaped like the letter upsilon (hu)]

hyoscine /'haɪə,siːn/ n. a poisonous alkaloid found in plants of the nightshade family, esp. of the genus Scopolia, and used as an antiemetic in motion sickness and a preoperative medication for examination of the eye. Also called SCOPOLAMINE.

hyoscyamine /,haɪə'saɪə,miːn/ n. a poisonous alkaloid obtained from henbane, having similar properties to hyoscine. [mod.L hyoscyamus f. Gk huoskuamos henbane f. hus huos pig + kuamos bean]

hypaesthesia /,haɪpɪs'θiːzɪə/ n. (US **hypesthesia**) a diminished capacity for sensation, esp. of the skin. □□ **hypaesthetic** /-'θetɪk/ adj. [mod.L (as HYPO-, Gk -aisthēsia f. aisthanomai perceive)]

hypaethral /haɪ'iːθr(ə)l/ adj. (also **hypethral**) 1 open to the sky; roofless. 2 open-air. [L hypaethrus f. Gk hupaithros (as HYPO-, aithēr air)]

hypallage /haɪ'pælədʒɪ/ n. Rhet. the transposition of the natural relations of two elements in a proposition (e.g. Melissa shook her doubtful curls). [LL f. Gk hupallagē (as HYPO-, allassō exchange)]

hype[1] /haɪp/ n. & v. sl. —n. 1 extravagant or intensive publicity promotion. 2 cheating; a trick. —v.tr. 1 promote (a product) with extravagant publicity. 2 cheat, trick. [20th c.: orig. unkn.]

hype[2] /haɪp/ n. sl. 1 a drug addict. 2 a hypodermic needle or injection. □ **hyped up** stimulated by or as if by a hypodermic injection. [abbr. of HYPODERMIC]

hyper- /'haɪpə(r)/ prefix meaning: 1 over, beyond, above (hyperphysical). 2 exceeding (hypersonic). 3 excessively; above normal (hyperbole; hypersensitive). [Gk huper over, beyond]

hyperactive /,haɪpə'ræktɪv/ adj. (of a person, esp. a child) abnormally active. □□ **hyperactivity** /-'tɪvɪtɪ/ n.

hyperaemia /,haɪpə'riːmɪə/ n. (US **hyperemia**) an excessive quantity of blood in the vessels supplying an organ or other part of the body. □□ **hyperaemic** adj. [mod.L (as HYPER-, -AEMIA)]

hyperaesthesia /,haɪpəriːs'θiːzɪə/ n. (US **hyperesthesia**) an excessive physical sensibility, esp. of the skin. □□ **hyperaesthetic** /-'θetɪk/ adj. [mod.L (as HYPER-, Gk -aisthēsia f. aisthanomai perceive)]

hyperbaric /,haɪpə'bærɪk/ adj. (of a gas) at a pressure greater than normal. [HYPER- + Gk barus heavy]

hyperbaton /haɪ'pɜːbə,tɒn/ n. Rhet. the inversion of the normal order of words, esp. for the sake of emphasis (e.g. this I must see). [L f. Gk huperbaton (as HYPER-, bainō go)]

hyperbola /haɪ'pɜːbələ/ n. (pl. **hyperbolas** or **hyperbolae** /-ˌliː/) Geom. the plane curve of two equal branches, produced when a cone is cut by a plane that makes a larger angle with the base than the side of the cone (cf. ELLIPSE). [mod.L f. Gk huperbolē excess (as HYPER-, ballō to throw)]

hyperbole /haɪ'pɜːbəlɪ/ n. Rhet. an exaggerated statement not meant to be taken literally. □□

hyperbolical /-'bɒlɪk(ə)l/ adj. **hyperbolically** /-'bɒlɪkəlɪ/ adv. **hyperbolism** n. [L (as HYPERBOLA)]

hyperbolic /,haɪpə'bɒlɪk/ adj. Geom. of or relating to a hyperbola. □ **hyperbolic function** a function related to a rectangular hyperbola, e.g. a hyperbolic cosine.

hyperboloid /haɪ'pɜːbə,lɔɪd/ n. Geom. a solid or surface having plane sections that are hyperbolas, ellipses, or circles. □□ **hyperboloidal** adj.

hyperborean /,haɪpəbɔː'riːən, -'bɔːrɪən/ n. & adj. —n. 1 an inhabitant of the extreme north of the earth. 2 (**Hyperborean**) (in Greek mythology) a member of a race worshipping Apollo and living in a land of sunshine and plenty beyond the north wind. —adj. of the extreme north of the earth. [LL hyperboreanus f. L hyperboreus f. Gk huperboreos (as HYPER-, Boreas god of the north wind)]

hyperconscious /,haɪpə'kɒnʃəs/ adj. (foll. by of) acutely or excessively aware.

hypercritical /,haɪpə'krɪtɪk(ə)l/ adj. excessively critical, esp. of small faults. □□ **hypercritically** adv.

hyperemia US var. of HYPERAEMIA.

hyperesthesia US var. of HYPERAESTHESIA.

hyperfocal distance /,haɪpə'fəʊk(ə)l/ n. the distance on which a camera lens can be focused to bring the maximum range of object-distances into focus.

hypergamy /haɪ'pɜːgəmɪ/ n. marriage to a person of equal or superior caste or class. [HYPER- + Gk gamos marriage]

hyperglycaemia /,haɪpəglaɪ'siːmɪə/ n. (US **hyperglycemia**) an excess of glucose in the bloodstream, often associated with diabetes mellitus. □□ **hyperglycaemic** adj. [HYPER- + GLYCO- + -AEMIA]

hypergolic /,haɪpə'gɒlɪk/ adj. (of a rocket propellant) igniting spontaneously on contact with an oxidant etc. [G Hypergol (perh. as HYPO-, ERG[1], -OL)]

hypericum /haɪ'perɪkəm/ n. any shrub of the genus Hypericum with five-petalled yellow flowers. Also called ST JOHN'S WORT. [L f. Gk hupereikon (as HYPER-, ereikē heath)]

hypermarket /'haɪpə,mɑːkɪt/ n. Brit. a very large self-service store with a wide range of goods and extensive car-parking facilities, usu. outside a town. [transl. F hypermarché (as HYPER-, MARKET)]

hypermetropia /,haɪpəmɪ'trəʊpɪə/ n. the condition of having long sight. □□ **hypermetropic** /-'trɒpɪk/ adj. [mod.L f. HYPER- + Gk metron measure, ōps eye]

hyperon /'haɪpə,rɒn/ n. Physics an unstable elementary particle which is classified as a baryon apart from the neutron or proton. [HYPER- + -ON]

hyperopia /,haɪpə'rəʊpɪə/ n. = HYPERMETROPIA. □□ **hyperopic** /-'rɒpɪk/ adj. [mod.L f. HYPER- + Gk ōps eye]

hyperphysical /,haɪpə'fɪzɪk(ə)l/ adj. supernatural. □□ **hyperphysically** adv.

hyperplasia /,haɪpə'pleɪzɪə/ n. the enlargement of an organ or tissue from the increased production of cells. [HYPER- + Gk plasis formation]

hypersensitive /,haɪpə'sensɪtɪv/ adj. abnormally or excessively sensitive. □□ **hypersensitiveness** n. **hypersensitivity** /-'tɪvɪtɪ/ n.

hypersonic /,haɪpə'sɒnɪk/ adj. 1 relating to speeds of more than five times the speed of sound (Mach 5). 2 relating to sound-frequencies above about a thousand million hertz. □□ **hypersonically** adv. [HYPER-, after SUPERSONIC, ULTRASONIC]

hypersthene /'haɪpə,sθiːn/ n. a rock-forming mineral, magnesium iron silicate, of greenish colour. [F hyperstène (as HYPER-, Gk sthenos strength, from its being harder than hornblende)]

hypertension /,haɪpə'tenʃ(ə)n/ n. 1 abnormally high blood pressure. 2 a state of great emotional tension. □□ **hypertensive** /-sɪv/ adj.

hyperthermia /,haɪpə'θɜːmɪə/ n. Med. the condition of having a body-temperature greatly above normal. □□ **hyperthermic** adj. [HYPER- + Gk thermē heat]

hyperthyroidism /,haɪpə'θaɪrɔɪ,dɪz(ə)m/ n. Med. overactivity of the thyroid gland, resulting in rapid

heartbeat and an increased rate of metabolism. □□
hyperthyroid n. & adj. **hyperthyroidic** adj.
hypertonic /ˌhaɪpəˈtɒnɪk/ adj. **1** (of muscles) having high tension. **2** (of a solution) having a greater osmotic pressure than another solution. □□
hypertonia /-ˈtəʊnɪə/ n. (in sense 1). **hypertonicity** /-təˈnɪsɪtɪ/ n.
hypertrophy /haɪˈpɜːtrəfɪ/ n. the enlargement of an organ or tissue from the increase in size of its cells. □□
hypertrophic /ˌhaɪpəˈtrɒfɪk/ adj. **hypertrophied** adj. [mod.L hypertrophia (as HYPER-, Gk -trophia nourishment)]
hyperventilation /ˌhaɪpəˌventɪˈleɪʃ(ə)n/ n. breathing at an abnormally rapid rate, resulting in an increased loss of carbon dioxide.
hypethral var. of HYPAETHRAL.
hypha /ˈhaɪfə/ n. (pl. **hyphae** /-fiː/) a filament in the mycelium of a fungus. □□ **hyphal** adj. [mod.L f. Gk huphē web]
hyphen /ˈhaɪf(ə)n/ n. & v. —n. the sign (-) used to join words semantically or syntactically (as in fruit-tree, pick-me-up, rock-forming), to indicate the division of a word at the end of a line, or to indicate a missing or implied element (as in man- and womankind). —v.tr. **1** write a (compound word) with a hyphen. **2** join (words) with a hyphen. [LL f. Gk huphen together f. hupo under + hen one]
hyphenate /ˈhaɪfəˌneɪt/ v.tr. = HYPHEN v. □□
hyphenation /-ˈneɪʃ(ə)n/ n.
hypno- /ˈhɪpnəʊ/ comb. form sleep, hypnosis. [Gk hupnos sleep]
hypnogenesis /ˌhɪpnəʊˈdʒenəsɪs/ n. the induction of a hypnotic state.
hypnology /hɪpˈnɒlədʒɪ/ n. the science of the phenomena of sleep. □□ **hypnologist** n.
hypnopaedia /ˌhɪpnəʊˈpiːdɪə/ n. learning by hearing while asleep.
hypnosis /hɪpˈnəʊsɪs/ n. **1** a state like sleep in which the subject acts only on external suggestion. **2** artificially produced sleep. [mod.L f. Gk hupnos sleep + -OSIS]
hypnotherapy /ˌhɪpnəʊˈθerəpɪ/ n. the treatment of disease by hypnosis.
hypnotic /hɪpˈnɒtɪk/ adj. & n. —adj. **1** of or producing hypnotism. **2** (of a drug) soporific. —n. **1** a thing, esp. a drug, that produces sleep. **2** a person under or open to the influence of hypnotism. □□
hypnotically adv. [F hypnotique f. LL hypnoticus f. Gk hupnōtikos f. hupnoō put to sleep]
hypnotism /ˈhɪpnəˌtɪz(ə)m/ n. the study or practice of hypnosis. □□ **hypnotist** n.
hypnotize /ˈhɪpnəˌtaɪz/ v.tr. (also **-ise**) **1** produce hypnosis in. **2** fascinate; capture the mind of (a person). □□ **hypnotizable** adj. **hypnotizer** n.
hypo[1] /ˈhaɪpəʊ/ n. Photog. the chemical sodium thiosulphate (incorrectly called hyposulphite) used as a photographic fixer. [abbr.]
hypo[2] /ˈhaɪpəʊ/ n. (pl. **-os**) colloq. = HYPODERMIC n. [abbr.]
hypo- /ˈhaɪpəʊ/ prefix (usu. **hyp-** before a vowel or h) **1** under (hypodermic). **2** below normal (hypoxia). **3** slightly (hypomania). **4** Chem. containing an element combined in low valence (hypochlorous). [Gk f. hupo under]
hypoblast /ˈhaɪpəˌblæst/ n. Biol. = ENDODERM. [mod.L hypoblastus (as HYPO-, -BLAST)]
hypocaust /ˈhaɪpəˌkɔːst/ n. a hollow space under the floor in ancient Roman houses, into which hot air was sent for heating a room or bath. [L hypocaustum f. Gk hupokauston place heated from below (as HYPO-, kaiō, kau- burn)]
hypochondria /ˌhaɪpəˈkɒndrɪə/ n. **1** abnormal anxiety about one's health. **2** morbid depression without real cause. [LL f. Gk hupokhondria soft parts of the body below the ribs, where melancholy was thought to arise (as HYPO-, khondros sternal cartilage)]
hypochondriac /ˌhaɪpəˈkɒndrɪˌæk/ n. & adj. —n. a

person suffering from hypochondria. —adj. (also **hypochondriacal** /-ˈdraɪək(ə)l/) of or affected by hypochondria. [F hypocondriaque f. Gk hupokhondriakos (as HYPOCHONDRIA)]
hypocoristic /ˌhaɪpəkɔːˈrɪstɪk/ adj. Gram. of the nature of a pet name. [Gk hupokoristikos f. hupokorizomai call by pet names]
hypocotyl /ˌhaɪpəˈkɒtɪl/ n. Bot. the part of the stem of an embryo plant beneath the stalks of the seed leaves or cotyledons and directly above the root.
hypocrisy /hɪˈpɒkrɪsɪ/ n. (pl. **-ies**) **1** the assumption or postulation of moral standards to which one's own behaviour does not conform; dissimulation, pretence. **2** an instance of this. [ME f. OF ypocrisie f. eccl.L hypocrisis f. Gk hupokrisis acting of a part, pretence (as HYPO-, krinō decide, judge)]
hypocrite /ˈhɪpəkrɪt/ n. a person given to hypocrisy. □□ **hypocritical** /-ˈkrɪtɪk(ə)l/ adj. **hypocritically** /-ˈkrɪtɪkəlɪ/ adv. [ME f. OF ypocrite f. eccl.L f. Gk hupokritēs actor (as HYPOCRISY)]
hypocycloid /ˌhaɪpəˈsaɪklɔɪd/ n. Math. the curve traced by a point on the circumference of a circle rolling on the interior of another circle. □□
hypocycloidal /-ˈklɔɪd(ə)l/ adj.
hypodermic /ˌhaɪpəˈdɜːmɪk/ adj. & n. —adj. Med. **1** of or relating to the area beneath the skin. **2 a** (of a drug etc. or its application) injected beneath the skin. **b** (of a needle, syringe, etc.) used to do this. —n. a hypodermic injection or syringe. □□
hypodermically adv. [HYPO- + Gk derma skin]
hypogastrium /ˌhaɪpəˈɡæstrɪəm/ n. (pl. **hypogastria** /-strɪə/) the part of the central abdomen which is situated below the region of the stomach. □□ **hypogastric** adj. [mod.L f. Gk hupogastrion (as HYPO-, gastēr belly)]
hypogean /ˌhaɪpəˈdʒiːən/ adj. (also **hypogeal** /-ˈdʒiːəl/) **1** (existing or growing) underground. **2** (of seed germination) with the seed leaves remaining below the ground. [LL hypogeus f. Gk hupogeios (as HYPO-, gē earth)]
hypogene /ˈhaɪpəˌdʒiːn/ adj. Geol. produced under the surface of the earth. [HYPO- + Gk gen- produce]
hypogeum /ˌhaɪpəˈdʒiːəm/ n. (pl. **hypogea** /-ˈdʒiːə/) an underground chamber. [L f. Gk hupogeion neut. of hupogeios: see HYPOGEAL]
hypoglycaemia /ˌhaɪpəʊɡlaɪˈsiːmɪə/ n. (US **hypoglycemia**) a deficiency of glucose in the bloodstream. □□ **hypoglycaemic** adj. [HYPO- + GLYCO- + -AEMIA]
hypoid /ˈhaɪpɔɪd/ n. a gear with the pinion offset from the centre-line of the wheel, to connect nonintersecting shafts. [perh. f. HYPERBOLOID]
hypolimnion /ˌhaɪpəˈlɪmnɪən/ n. (pl. **hypolimnia** /-nɪə/) the lower layer of water in stratified lakes. [HYPO- + Gk limnion dimin. of limnē lake]
hypomania /ˌhaɪpəˈmeɪnɪə/ n. a minor form of mania. □□ **hypomanic** /-ˈmænɪk/ adj. [mod.L f. G Hypomanie (as HYPO-, MANIA)]
hyponasty /ˈhaɪpəˌnæstɪ/ n. Bot. the tendency in plant-organs for growth to be more rapid on the under-side. □□ **hyponastic** /-ˈnæstɪk/ adj. [HYPO- + Gk nastos pressed]
hypophysis /haɪˈpɒfɪsɪs/ n. (pl. **hypophyses** /-ˌsiːz/) Anat. = pituitary gland. □□ **hypophyseal** /ˌhaɪpəˈfɪzɪəl/ adj. (also **-physial**). [mod.L f. Gk hupophusis offshoot (as HYPO-, phusis growth)]
hypostasis /haɪˈpɒstəsɪs/ n. (pl. **hypostases** /-ˌsiːz/) **1** Med. an accumulation of fluid or blood in the lower parts of the body or organs under the influence of gravity, in cases of poor circulation. **2** Metaphysics an underlying substance, as opposed to attributes or to that which is unsubstantial. **3** Theol. **a** the person of Christ, combining human and divine natures. **b** each of the three persons of the Trinity. □□
hypostasize v.tr. (also **-ise**) (in senses 1, 2). [eccl.L f. Gk hupostasis (as HYPO-, STASIS standing, state)]
hypostatic /ˌhaɪpəˈstætɪk/ adj. (also **hypostatical**) Theol. relating to the three persons of the Trinity.

□**hypostatic union** the divine and human natures in Christ.

hypostyle /'haɪpə,staɪl/ *adj. Archit.* having a roof supported by pillars. [Gk *hupostulos* (as HYPO-, STYLE)]

hypotaxis /,haɪpə'tæksɪs/ *n. Gram.* the subordination of one clause to another. □□**hypotactic** /-'tæktɪk/ *adj.* [Gk *hupotaxis* (as HYPO-, *taxis* arrangement)]

hypotension /,haɪpə'tenʃ(ə)n/ *n.* abnormally low blood pressure. □□**hypotensive** *adj.*

hypotenuse /haɪ'pɒtə,njuːz/ *n.* the side opposite the right angle of a right-angled triangle. [L *hypotenusa* f. Gk *hupoteinousa* (*grammē*) subtending (line) fem. part. of *hupoteinō* (as HYPO-, *teinō* stretch)]

hypothalamus /,haɪpə'θæləməs/ *n.* (*pl.* **-mi** /-,maɪ/) *Anat.* the region of the brain which controls body-temperature, thirst, hunger, etc. □□**hypothalamic** *adj.* [mod.L formed as HYPO-, THALAMUS]

hypothec /'haɪpɒθɪk/ *n.* (in Roman and Scottish law) a right established by law over property belonging to a debtor. □□**hypothecary** /haɪ'pɒθɪkəri/ *adj.* [F *hypothèque* f. LL *hypotheca* f. Gk *hupothēkē* deposit (as HYPO-, *tithēmi* place)]

hypothecate /haɪ'pɒθɪ,keɪt/ *v.tr.* pledge, mortgage. □□**hypothecation** /-'keɪʃ(ə)n/ *n.* [med.L *hypothecare* (as HYPOTHEC)]

hypothermia /,haɪpəʊ'θɜːmɪə/ *n. Med.* the condition of having an abnormally low body-temperature. [HYPO- + Gk *thermē* heat]

hypothesis /haɪ'pɒθɪsɪs/ *n.* (*pl.* **hypotheses** /-,siːz/) **1** a proposition made as a basis for reasoning, without the assumption of its truth. **2** a supposition made as a starting-point for further investigation from known facts (cf. THEORY). **3** a groundless assumption. [LL f. Gk *hupothesis* foundation (as HYPO-, THESIS)]

hypothesize /haɪ'pɒθɪ,saɪz/ *v.* (also **-ise**) **1** *intr.* frame a hypothesis. **2** *tr.* assume a hypothesis. □□**hypothesist** /-sɪst/ *n.* **hypothesizer** *n.*

hypothetical /,haɪpə'θetɪk(ə)l/ *adj.* **1** of or based on or serving as a hypothesis. **2** supposed but not necessarily real or true. □□**hypothetically** *adv.*

hypothyroidism /,haɪpəʊ'θaɪrɔɪ,dɪz(ə)m/ *n. Med.* subnormal activity of the thyroid gland, resulting in cretinism in children, and mental and physical slowing in adults. □□**hypothyroid** *n.* & *adj.* **hypothyroidic** /-'rɔɪdɪk/ *adj.*

hypoventilation /,haɪpəʊ,ventɪ'leɪʃ(ə)n/ *n.* breathing at an abnormally slow rate, resulting in an increased amount of carbon dioxide in the blood.

hypoxaemia /,haɪpɒk'siːmɪə/ *n.* (*US* **hypoxemia**) *Med.* an abnormally low concentration of oxygen in the blood. [mod.L (as HYPO-, OXYGEN, -AEMIA)]

hypoxia /haɪ'pɒksɪə/ *n. Med.* a deficiency of oxygen reaching the tissues. □□**hypoxic** *adj.* [HYPO- + OX- + -IA[1]]

hypso- /'hɪpsəʊ/ *comb. form* height. [Gk *hupsos* height]

hypsography /hɪp'sɒgrəfɪ/ *n.* a description or mapping of the contours of the earth's surface. □□**hypsographic** /-'græfɪk/ *adj.* **hypsographical** /-'græfɪk(ə)l/ *adj.*

hypsometer /hɪp'sɒmɪtə(r)/ *n.* **1** a device for calibrating thermometers at the boiling point of water. **2** this instrument when used to estimate height above sea level. □□**hypsometric** /-sə'metrɪk/ *adj.*

hyrax /'haɪræks/ *n.* any small mammal of the order *Hyracoidea*, including rock-rabbit and dassie. [mod.L f. Gk *hurax* shrew-mouse]

hyson /'haɪs(ə)n/ *n.* a kind of green China tea. [Chin. *xichun*, lit. 'bright spring']

hyssop /'hɪsəp/ *n.* **1** any small bushy aromatic herb of the genus *Hyssopus*, esp. *H. officinalis*, formerly used medicinally. **2** *Bibl.* **a** a plant whose twigs were used for sprinkling in Jewish rites. **b** a bunch of this used in purification. [OE (*h*)*ysope* (reinforced in ME by OF *ysope*) f. L *hyssopus* f. Gk *hyssōpos*, of Semitic orig.]

hysterectomy /,hɪstə'rektəmɪ/ *n.* (*pl.* **-ies**) the surgical removal of the womb. □□**hysterectomize** *v.tr.* (also **-ise**). [Gk *hustera* womb + -ECTOMY]

hysteresis /,hɪstə'riːsɪs/ *n. Physics* the lagging behind of an effect when its cause varies in amount etc., esp. of magnetic induction behind the magnetizing force. [Gk *husterēsis* f. *hustereō* be behind f. *husteros* coming after]

hysteria /hɪ'stɪərɪə/ *n.* **1** a wild uncontrollable emotion or excitement. **2** a functional disturbance of the nervous system, of psychoneurotic origin. [mod.L (as HYSTERIC)]

hysteric /hɪ'sterɪk/ *n.* & *adj.* —*n.* **1** (in *pl.*) **a** a fit of hysteria. **b** *colloq.* overwhelming mirth or laughter (*we were in hysterics*). **2** a hysterical person. —*adj.* = HYSTERICAL. [L f. Gk *husterikos* of the womb (*hustera*), hysteria being thought to occur more frequently in women than in men and to be associated with the womb]

hysterical /hɪ'sterɪk(ə)l/ *adj.* **1** of or affected with hysteria. **2** morbidly or uncontrolledly emotional. **3** *colloq.* extremely funny or amusing. □□**hysterically** *adv.*

hysteron proteron /,hɪstərɒn 'prɒtə,rɒn/ *n. Rhet.* a figure of speech in which that should come last is put first; an inversion of the natural order (e.g. *I die! I faint! I fail!*). [LL f. Gk *husteron proteron* the latter (put in place of) the former]

Hz *abbr.* hertz.

I

I¹ /aɪ/ *n.* (also **i**) (*pl.* **Is** or **I's**) **1** the ninth letter of the alphabet. **2** (as a Roman numeral) 1. □**I-beam** a girder of I-shaped section.

I² /aɪ/ *pron.* & *n.* —*pron.* (*obj.* **me**; *poss.* **my, mine**; *pl.* **we**) used by a speaker or writer to refer to himself or herself. —*n.* (**the I**) *Metaphysics* the ego; the subject or object of self-consciousness. [OE f. Gmc]

I³ *symb. Chem.* the element iodine.

I⁴ *abbr.* (also **I.**) **1** Island(s). **2** Isle(s).

-i¹ /ɪ, aɪ/ *suffix* forming the plural of nouns from Latin in *-us* or from Italian in *-e* or *-o* (*foci*; *dilettanti*; *timpani*). ¶ Plural in *-s* or *-es* is often also possible.

-i² /ɪ/ *suffix* forming adjectives from names of countries or regions in the Near or Middle East (*Israeli*; *Pakistani*). [adj. suffix in Semitic and Indo-Iranian languages]

-i- a connecting vowel esp. forming words in *-ana*, *-ferous*, *-fic*, *-form*, *-fy*, *-gerous*, *-vorous* (cf. -o-). [from or after F f. L]

IA *abbr. US* Iowa (in official postal use).

Ia. *abbr.* Iowa.

-ia¹ /ɪə/ *suffix* **1** forming abstract nouns (*mania*; *utopia*), often in *Med.* (*anaemia*; *pneumonia*). **2** *Bot.* forming names of classes and genera (*dahlia*; *fuchsia*). **3** forming names of countries (*Australia*; *India*). [from or after L & Gk]

-ia² /ɪə/ *suffix* forming plural nouns or the plural of nouns: **1** from Greek in *-ion* or Latin in *-ium* (*paraphernalia*; *regalia*; *amnia*; *labia*). **2** *Zool.* the names of groups (*Mammalia*).

IAA *abbr.* indoleacetic acid.

IAEA *abbr.* International Atomic Energy Agency.

-ial /ɪəl/ *suffix* forming adjectives (*celestial*; *dictatorial*; *trivial*). [from or after F *-iel* or L *-ialis*: cf. -AL]

iamb /'aɪæmb/ *n.* an iambus. [Anglicized f. IAMBUS]

iambic /aɪ'æmbɪk/ *adj.* & *n. Prosody* —*adj.* of or using iambuses. —*n.* (usu. in *pl.*) iambic verse. [F *iambique* f. LL *iambicus* f. Gk *iambikos* (as IAMBUS)]

iambus /aɪ'æmbəs/ *n.* (*pl.* **iambuses** or **-bi** /-baɪ/) *Prosody* a foot consisting of one short (or unstressed) followed by one long (or stressed) syllable. [L f. Gk *iambos* iambus, lampoon, f. *iaptō* assail in words, from its use by Gk satirists]

-ian /ɪən/ *suffix* var. of -AN. [from or after F *-ien* or L *-ianus*]

-iasis /'aɪəsɪs/ *suffix* the usual form of -ASIS.

IATA /aɪ'ɑːtə, iː-/ *abbr.* International Air Transport Association.

iatrogenic /aɪˌætrə'dʒenɪk/ *adj.* (of a disease etc.) caused by medical examination or treatment. [Gk *iatros* physician + -GENIC]

ib. *var.* of IBID.

IBA *abbr.* (in the UK) Independent Broadcasting Authority.

Iberian /aɪ'bɪərɪən/ *adj.* & *n.* —*adj.* of ancient Iberia, the peninsula now comprising Spain and Portugal; of Spain and Portugal. —*n.* **1** a native of ancient Iberia. **2** any of the languages of ancient Iberia. [L *Iberia* f. Gk *Ibēres* Spaniards]

Ibero- /ɪ'beərəʊ/ *comb. form* Iberian; Iberian and (*Ibero-American*).

ibex /'aɪbeks/ *n.* (*pl.* **ibexes**) a wild goat, *Capra ibex*, esp. of mountainous areas of Europe, N. Africa, and Asia, with a chin beard and thick curved ridged horns. [L]

ibid. *abbr.* (also **ib.**) in the same book or passage etc. [L *ibidem* in the same place]

-ibility /ɪ'bɪlɪtɪ/ *suffix* forming nouns from, or corresponding to, adjectives in *-ible* (*possibility*; *credibility*). [F *-ibilité* or L *-ibilitas*]

ibis /'aɪbɪs/ *n.* (*pl.* **ibises**) any wading bird of the family Threskiornithidae with a curved bill, long neck, and long legs, and nesting in colonies. □**sacred ibis** an ibis, *Threskiornis aethiopicus*, native to Africa and Madagascar, venerated by the ancient Egyptians. [ME f. L f. Gk]

-ible /'ɪb(ə)l/ *suffix* forming adjectives meaning 'that may or may be' (see -ABLE) (*terrible*; *forcible*; *possible*). [F *-ible* or L *-ibilis*]

-ibly /'ɪblɪ/ *suffix* forming adverbs corresponding to adjectives in *-ible*.

IBM *abbr.* International Business Machines.

Ibo /'iːbəʊ/ *n.* (also **Igbo**) (*pl.* same or **-os**) **1** a member of a Black people of SE Nigeria. **2** the language of this people. [native name]

IBRD *abbr.* International Bank for Reconstruction and Development (also known as the *World Bank*).

IC *abbr.* integrated circuit.

i/c *abbr.* **1** in charge. **2** in command. **3** internal combustion.

-ic /ɪk/ *suffix* **1** forming adjectives (*Arabic*; *classic*; *public*) and nouns (*critic*; *epic*; *mechanic*; *music*). **2** *Chem.* in higher valence or degree of oxidation (*ferric*; *sulphuric*) (see also -OUS). **3** denoting a particular form or instance of a noun in *-ics* (*aesthetic*; *tactic*). [from or after F *-ique* or L *-icus* or Gk *-ikos*: cf. -ATIC, -ETIC, -FIC, -OTIC]

-ical /'ɪk(ə)l/ *suffix* **1** forming adjectives corresponding to nouns or adjectives, usu. in *-ic* (*classical*; *comical*; *farcical*; *musical*). **2** forming adjectives corresponding to nouns in *-y* (*pathological*).

-ically /'ɪkəlɪ/ *suffix* forming adverbs corresponding to adjectives in *-ic* or *-ical* (*comically*; *musically*; *tragically*).

ICAO *abbr.* International Civil Aviation Organization.

ICBM *abbr.* intercontinental ballistic missile.

ICE *abbr.* **1** (in the UK) Institution of Civil Engineers. **2** internal-combustion engine.

ice /aɪs/ *n.* & *v.* —*n.* **1 a** frozen water, a brittle transparent crystalline solid. **b** a sheet of this on the surface of water (*fell through the ice*). **2** *Brit.* a portion of ice-cream or water-ice (*would you like an ice?*). **3** *sl.* diamonds. —*v.* **1** *tr.* mix with or cool in ice (*iced drinks*). **2** *tr.* & *intr.* (often foll. by *over, up*) **a** cover or become covered with ice. **b** freeze. **3** *tr.* cover (a cake etc.) with icing. □**ice age** a glacial period, esp. in the Pleistocene epoch. **ice-axe** a tool used by mountain-climbers for cutting footholds. **ice-bag** an ice-filled rubber bag for medical use. **ice-blue** a very pale blue. **ice-boat 1** a boat mounted on runners for travelling on ice. **2** a boat used for breaking ice on a river etc. **ice-bound** confined by ice. **ice-breaker 1** = *ice-boat* 2. **2** something that serves to relieve inhibitions, start a conversation, etc. **ice bucket** a bucket-like container with chunks of ice, used to keep a bottle of wine chilled. **ice-cap** a permanent covering of ice e.g. in polar regions. **ice-cold** as cold as ice. **ice-cream** a sweet creamy frozen food, usu. flavoured. **ice-cube** a small block of ice made in a refrigerator. **ice-fall** a steep part of a glacier like a frozen waterfall. **ice-field** an expanse of ice, esp. in polar regions. **ice-fish** a capelin. **ice floe** = FLOE. **ice hockey** a form of hockey played on ice with a puck. **ice house** a building often partly or wholly underground for storing ice. **ice** (or **iced**) **lolly** *Brit.* a piece of flavoured ice, often with chocolate or ice-cream, on a stick. **ice-pack 1** = *pack ice.* **2** a quantity of ice applied to the body for medical etc. purposes. **ice-pick** a needle-like implement with a handle for splitting up small pieces of ice. **ice-plant** a plant, *Mesembryanthemum crystallinum,* with leaves covered with crystals or vesicles looking like ice specks. **ice-rink** = RINK *n.* 1. **ice-skate** *n.* a skate consisting of a boot with a blade beneath, for skating on ice. —*v.intr.* skate on ice. **ice-skater** a person who skates on ice. **ice station** a meteorological research centre in polar regions. **on ice 1** (of an entertainment, sport, etc.) performed by skaters. **2** *colloq.* held in reserve; awaiting further attention. **on thin ice** in a risky situation. [OE *īs* f. Gmc]

-ice /ɪs/ *suffix* forming (esp. abstract) nouns (*avarice*; *justice*; *service*) (cf. -ISE[2]).

iceberg /ˈaɪsbɜːɡ/ *n.* **1** a large floating mass of ice detached from a glacier or ice-sheet and carried out to sea. **2** an unemotional or cold-blooded person. □**iceberg lettuce** any of various crisp lettuces with a freely blanching head. **the tip of the iceberg** a small perceptible part of something (esp. a difficulty) the greater part of which is hidden. [prob. f. Du. *ijsberg* f. *ijs* ice + *berg* hill]

iceblink /ˈaɪsblɪŋk/ *n.* a luminous appearance on the horizon, caused by a reflection from ice.

iceblock /ˈaɪsblɒk/ *n. Austral. & NZ* = *ice lolly.*

icebox /ˈaɪsbɒks/ *n. US* a refrigerator.

Icelander /ˈaɪsləndə(r)/ *n.* **1** a native or national of Iceland, an island in the N. Atlantic. **2** a person of Icelandic descent.

Icelandic /aɪsˈlændɪk/ *adj. & n.* —*adj.* of or relating to Iceland. —*n.* the language of Iceland.

Iceland lichen /ˈaɪslənd/ *n.* (also **Iceland moss**) a mountain and moorland lichen, *Cetraria islandica,* with edible branching fronds.

Iceland poppy /ˈaɪslənd/ *n.* an Arctic poppy, *Papaver nudicaule,* with red or yellow flowers.

Iceland spar /ˈaɪslənd/ *n.* a transparent variety of calcite with the optical property of strong double refraction.

iceman /ˈaɪsmən/ *n.* (*pl.* -**men**) esp. *US* **1** a man skilled in crossing ice. **2** a man who sells or delivers ice.

I.Chem.E. *abbr.* (in the UK) Institution of Chemical Engineers.

I Ching /iː ˈtʃɪŋ/ *n.* an ancient Chinese manual of divination based on symbolic trigrams and hexagrams. [Chin. *yijing* book of changes]

ichneumon /ɪkˈnjuːmən/ *n.* **1** (in full **ichneumon wasp**) any small hymenopterous insect of the family Ichneumonidae, depositing eggs in or on the larva of another insect as food for its own larva. **2** a mongoose of N. Africa, *Herpestes ichneumon,* noted for destroying crocodile eggs. [L f. Gk *ikhneumōn* spider-hunting wasp f. *ikhneuō* trace f. *ikhnos* footstep]

ichnography /ɪkˈnɒɡrəfɪ/ *n.* (*pl.* -**ies**) **1** the ground-plan of a building, map of a region, etc. **2** a drawing of this. [F *ichnographie* or L *ichnographia* f. Gk *ikhnographia* f. *ikhnos* track: see -GRAPHY]

ichor /ˈaɪkɔː(r)/ *n.* **1** (in Greek mythology) fluid flowing like blood in the veins of the gods. **2** *poet.* bloodlike fluid. **3** *hist.* a watery fetid discharge from a wound etc. □□ **ichorous** /ˈaɪkərəs/ *adj.* [Gk *ikhōr*]

ichthyo- /ˈɪkθɪəʊ/ *comb. form* fish. [Gk *ikhthus* fish]

ichthyoid /ˈɪkθɪɔɪd/ *adj. & n.* —*adj.* fishlike. —*n.* any fishlike vertebrate.

ichthyolite /ˈɪkθɪəlaɪt/ *n.* a fossil fish.

ichthyology /ˌɪkθɪˈɒlədʒɪ/ *n.* the study of fishes. □□ **ichthyological** /-əˈlɒdʒɪk(ə)l/ *adj.* **ichthyologist** *n.*

ichthyophagous /ˌɪkθɪˈɒfəɡəs/ *adj.* fish-eating. □□ **ichthyophagy** /-fədʒɪ/ *n.*

ichthyosaurus /ˌɪkθɪəˈsɔːrəs/ *n.* (also **ichthyosaur** /ˈɪkθɪəˌsɔːr/) any extinct marine reptile of the order Ichthyosauria, with long head, tapering body, four flippers, and usu. a large tail. [ICHTHYO- + Gk *sauros* lizard]

ichthyosis /ˌɪkθɪˈəʊsɪs/ *n.* a skin disease which

causes the epidermis to become dry and horny like fish scales. □□ **ichthyotic** /-ˈɒtɪk/ *adj.* [Gk *ikhthus* fish + -OSIS]

ICI *abbr.* Imperial Chemical Industries.

-ician /ˈɪʃ(ə)n/ *suffix* forming nouns denoting persons skilled in or concerned with subjects having nouns (usu.) in -*ic* or -*ics* (*magician*; *politician*). [from or after F -*icien* (as -IC, -IAN)]

icicle /ˈaɪsɪk(ə)l/ *n.* a hanging tapering piece of ice, formed by the freezing of dripping water. [ME f. ICE + *ickle* (now dial.) icicle]

icing /ˈaɪsɪŋ/ *n.* **1** a coating of sugar etc. on a cake or biscuit. **2** the formation of ice on a ship or aircraft. □**icing on the cake** an attractive though inessential addition or enhancement. **icing sugar** *Brit.* finely powdered sugar for making icing for cakes etc.

-icist /ɪsɪst/ *suffix* = -ICIAN (*classicist*). [-IC + -IST]

-icity /ˈɪsɪtɪ/ *suffix* forming abstract nouns esp. from adjectives in -*ic* (*authenticity*; *publicity*). [-IC + -ITY]

-ick /ɪk/ *suffix archaic* var. of -IC.

icky /ˈɪkɪ/ *adj.* (also **ikky**) *colloq.* **1** sweet, sticky, sickly. **2** (as a general term of disapproval) nasty, repulsive. [20th c.: orig. unkn.]

-icle /ˈɪk(ə)l/ *suffix* forming (orig. diminutive) nouns (*article*; *particle*). [formed as -CULE]

icon /ˈaɪkɒn/ *n.* (also **ikon**) **1** a devotional painting or carving, usu. on wood, of Christ or another holy figure, esp. in the Eastern Church. **2** an image or statue. **3** *Computing* a symbol or graphic representation on a VDU screen of a program, option, or window, esp. one of several for selection. **4** *Linguistics* a sign which has a characteristic in common with the thing it signifies. [L f. Gk *eikōn* image]

iconic /aɪˈkɒnɪk/ *adj.* **1** of or having the nature of an image or portrait. **2** (of a statue) following a conventional type. **3** *Linguistics* that is an icon. □□ **iconicity** /-kəˈnɪsɪtɪ/ *n.* (esp. in sense 3). [L *iconicus* f. Gk *eikonikos* (as ICON)]

icono- /aɪˈkɒnəʊ/ *comb. form* an image or likeness. [Gk *eikōn*]

iconoclasm /aɪˈkɒnəˌklæz(ə)m/ *n.* **1** the breaking of images. **2** the assailing of cherished beliefs. [ICONOCLAST after *enthusiasm* etc.]

iconoclast /aɪˈkɒnəˌklæst/ *n.* **1** a person who attacks cherished beliefs. **2** a person who destroys images used in religious worship, esp. *hist.* during the 8th–9th c. in the Churches of the East, or as a Puritan of the 16th–17th c. □□ **iconoclastic** /-ˈklæstɪk/ *adj.* **iconoclastically** /-ˈklæstɪkəlɪ/ *adv.* [med.L *iconoclastes* f. eccl.Gk *eikonoklastēs* (as ICONO-, *klaō* break)]

iconography /ˌaɪkəˈnɒɡrəfɪ/ *n.* (*pl.* -**ies**) **1** the illustration of a subject by drawings or figures. **2 a** the study of portraits, esp. of an individual. **b** the study of artistic images or symbols. **3** a treatise on pictures or statuary. **4** a book whose essence is pictures. □□ **iconographer** *n.* **iconographic** /-nəˈɡræfɪk/ *adj.* **iconographical** /-nəˈɡræfɪk(ə)l/ *adj.* **iconographically** /-nəˈɡræfɪkəlɪ/ *adv.* [Gk *eikonographia* sketch (as ICONO- + -GRAPHY)]

iconolatry /ˌaɪkəˈnɒlətrɪ/ *n.* the worship of images. □□ **iconolater** *n.* [eccl.Gk *eikonolatreia* (as ICONO-, -LATRY)]

iconology /ˌaɪkəˈnɒlədʒɪ/ *n.* **1** an artistic theory developed from iconography (see ICONOGRAPHY 2b). **2** symbolism.

iconostasis /ˌaɪkəˈnɒstəsɪs, aɪˌkɒnəˈstæsɪs/ *n.* (*pl.* **iconostases** /-ˌsiːz/) (in the Eastern Church) a screen bearing icons and separating the sanctuary from the nave. [mod.Gk *eikonostasis* (as ICONO-, STASIS)]

icosahedron /ˌaɪkəsəˈhedrən, -ˈhiːdrən/ *n.* a solid figure with twenty faces. □□ **icosahedral** *adj.* [LL *icosahedrum* f. Gk *eikosaedron* f. *eikosi* twenty + -HEDRON]

-ics /ɪks/ *suffix* (treated as *sing.* or *pl.*) forming nouns denoting arts or sciences or branches of study or action (*athletics*; *politics*) (cf. -IC 3). [from or after F pl. -*iques* or L pl. -*ica* or Gk pl. -*ika*]

icterus /'ɪktərəs/ n. Med. = JAUNDICE. □□ **icteric** /ɪk'terɪk/ adj. [L f. Gk *ikteros*]

ictus /'ɪktəs/ n. (pl. same or **ictuses**) **1** Prosody rhythmical or metrical stress. **2** Med. a stroke or seizure; a fit. [L, = blow f. *icere* strike]

icy /'aɪsɪ/ adj. (**icier, iciest**) **1** very cold. **2** covered with or abounding in ice. **3** (of a tone or manner) unfriendly, hostile (*an icy stare*). □□ **icily** adv. **iciness** n.

ID abbr. **1** esp. US identification, identity (*ID card*). **2** US Idaho (in official postal use).

id /ɪd/ n. Psychol. the inherited instinctive impulses of the individual as part of the unconscious. [L, = that, transl. G *es*]

id. abbr. = IDEM.

i.d. abbr. inner diameter.

I'd /aɪd/ contr. **1** I had. **2** I should; I would.

-id[1] /ɪd/ suffix forming adjectives (*arid; rapid*). [F *-ide* f. L *-idus*]

-id[2] /ɪd/ suffix forming nouns: **1** general (*pyramid*). **2** Biol. of structural constituents (*plastid*). **3** Bot. of a plant belonging to a family with a name in *-aceae* (*orchid*). [from or after F *-ide* f. L *-is* *-idis* f. Gk *-is* *-ida* or *-idos*]

-id[3] /ɪd/ suffix forming nouns denoting: **1** Zool. an animal belonging to a family with a name in *-idae* or a class with a name in *-ida* (*canid; arachnid*). **2** a member of a person's family (*Seleucid* from Seleucus). **3** Astron. **a** a meteor in a group radiating from a specified constellation (*Leonid* from Leo). **b** a star of a class like one in a specified constellation (*cepheid*). [from or after L *-ides*, pl. *-idae* or *-ida*]

-id[4] /ɪd/ suffix esp. US var. of -IDE.

IDA abbr. International Development Association.

ide /aɪd/ n. a freshwater fish, *Leuciscus idus*, used as food. Also called ORFE. [mod.L *idus* f. Sw. *id*]

-ide /aɪd/ suffix (also esp. US **-id**) Chem. forming nouns denoting: **1** binary compounds of an element (the suffix *-ide* being added to the abbreviated name of the more electronegative element etc.) (*sodium chloride; lead sulphide; calcium carbide*). **2** various other compounds (*amide; anhydride; peptide; saccharide*). **3** elements of a series in the periodic table (*actinide; lanthanide*). [orig. in OXIDE]

idea /aɪ'dɪə/ n. **1** a conception or plan formed by mental effort (*have you any ideas?; had the idea of writing a book*). **2 a** a mental impression or notion; a concept. **b** a vague belief or fancy (*had an idea you were married; had no idea where you were*). **3** an intention, purpose, or essential feature (*the idea is to make money*). **4** an archetype or pattern as distinguished from its realization in individual cases. **5** Philos. **a** (in Platonism) an eternally existing pattern of which individual things in any class are imperfect copies. **b** a concept of pure reason which transcends experience. □**get** (or **have**) **ideas** colloq. be ambitious, rebellious, etc. **have no idea** colloq. **1** not know at all. **2** be completely incompetent. **not one's idea of** colloq. not what one regards as (*not my idea of a pleasant evening*). **put ideas into a person's head** suggest ambitions etc. he or she would not otherwise have had. **that's an idea** colloq. that proposal etc. is worth considering. **the very idea!** colloq. an exclamation of disapproval or disagreement. □□ **idea'd** adj. **ideaed** adj. **idealess** adj. [Gk *idea* form, pattern f. stem *id-* see]

ideal /aɪ'diːəl/ adj. & n. —adj. **1 a** answering to one's highest conception. **b** perfect or supremely excellent. **2 a** existing only in idea. **b** visionary. **3** embodying an idea. **4** relating to or consisting of ideas; dependent on the mind. —n. **1** a perfect type, or a conception of this. **2** an actual thing as a standard for imitation. □**ideal gas** a hypothetical gas consisting of molecules occupying negligible space and without attraction for each other, thereby obeying simple laws. □□ **ideally** adv. [ME f. F *idéal* f. LL *idealis* (as IDEA)]

idealism /aɪ'dɪə,lɪz(ə)m/ n. **1** the practice of forming or following after ideals, esp. unrealistically (cf. REALISM). **2** the representation of things in ideal or idealized form. **3** imaginative treatment. **4** Philos. any of various systems of thought in which the objects of knowledge are held to be in some way dependent on the activity of mind (cf. REALISM). □□ **idealist** n. **idealistic** /-'lɪstɪk/ adj. **idealistically** /-'lɪstɪkəlɪ/ adv. [F *idéalisme* or G *Idealismus* (as IDEAL)]

ideality /,aɪdɪ'ælɪtɪ/ n. (pl. **-ies**) **1** the quality of being ideal. **2** an ideal thing.

idealize /aɪ'dɪə,laɪz/ v.tr. (also **-ise**) **1** regard or represent (a thing or person) in ideal form or character. **2** exalt in thought to ideal perfection or excellence. □□ **idealization** /-'zeɪʃ(ə)n/ n. **idealizer** n.

ideate /'aɪdɪ,eɪt/ v. Psychol. **1** tr. imagine, conceive. **2** intr. form ideas. □□ **ideation** /-'eɪʃ(ə)n/ n. **ideational** /-'eɪʃən(ə)l/ adj. **ideationally** /-'eɪʃənəlɪ/ adv. [med.L *ideare* form an idea (as IDEA)]

idée fixe /,iːdeɪ 'fiːks/ n. (pl. **idées fixes** pronunc. same) an idea that dominates the mind; an obsession. [F, lit. 'fixed idea']

idée reçue /iː,deɪ rə'sjuː/ n. (pl. **idées reçues** pronunc. same) a generally accepted notion or opinion. [F]

idem /'ɪdem/ adv. & n. —adv. in the same author. —n. the same word or author. [ME f. L]

identical /aɪ'dentɪk(ə)l/ adj. **1** (often foll. by *with*) (of different things) agreeing in every detail. **2** (of one thing viewed at different times) one and the same. **3** (of twins) developed from a single fertilized ovum, therefore of the same sex and usu. very similar in appearance. **4** Logic & Math. expressing an identity. □□ **identically** adv. **identicalness** n. [med.L *identicus* (as IDENTITY)]

identification /aɪ,dentɪfɪ'keɪʃ(ə)n/ n. **1** the act or an instance of identifying. **2** a means of identifying a person. **3** (*attrib.*) serving to identify (esp. the bearer) (*identification card*). □**identification parade** an assembly of persons from whom a suspect is to be identified.

identifier /aɪ'dentɪ,faɪə(r)/ n. **1** a person or thing that identifies. **2** Computing a sequence of characters used to identify or refer to a set of data.

identify /aɪ'dentɪ,faɪ/ v. (**-ies, -ied**) **1** tr. establish the identity of; recognize. **2** tr. establish or select by consideration or analysis of the circumstances (*identify the best method of solving the problem*). **3** tr. (foll. by *with*) associate (a person or oneself) inseparably or very closely (with a party, policy, etc.). **4** tr. (often foll. by *with*) treat (a thing) as identical. **5** intr. (foll. by *with*) **a** regard oneself as sharing characteristics of (another person). **b** associate oneself. □□ **identifiable** adj. [med.L *identificare* (as IDENTITY)]

Identikit /aɪ'dentɪkɪt/ n. (often *attrib.*) propr. a reconstructed picture of a person (esp. one sought by the police) assembled from transparent strips showing typical facial features according to witnesses' descriptions. [IDENTITY + KIT[1]]

identity /aɪ'dentɪtɪ/ n. (pl. **-ies**) **1 a** the quality or condition of being a specified person or thing. **b** individuality, personality (*felt he had lost his identity*). **2** identification or the result of it (*a case of mistaken identity; identity card*). **3** the state of being the same in substance, nature, qualities, etc.; absolute sameness (*no identity of interests between them*). **4** Algebra **a** the equality of two expressions for all values of the quantities expressed by letters. **b** an equation expressing this, e.g. $(x + 1)^2 = x^2 + 2x + 1$. **5** Math. **a** (in full **identity element**) an element in a set, left unchanged by any operation to it. **b** a transformation that leaves an object unchanged. □**identity crisis** a phase in which an individual feels a need to establish an identity in relation to society. **identity parade** = *identification parade*. [LL *identitas* f. L *idem* same]

ideogram /'ɪdɪə,græm/ n. a character symbolizing the idea of a thing without indicating the sequence of sounds in its name (e.g. a numeral, and many Chinese characters). [Gk *idea* form + -GRAM]

ideograph /'ɪdɪə,grɑ:f/ *n.* = IDEOGRAM. □□ **ideographic** /-'græfɪk/ *adj.* **ideography** /,ɪdɪ'ɒgrəfɪ/ *n.* [Gk *idea* form + -GRAPH]

ideologue /'aɪdɪə,lɒg/ *n.* **1** a theorist; a visionary. **2** an adherent of an ideology. [F *idéologue* f. Gk *idea* (see IDEA) + -LOGUE]

ideology /,aɪdɪ'ɒlədʒɪ/ *n.* (*pl.* -ies) **1** the system of ideas at the basis of an economic or political theory (*Marxist ideology*). **2** the manner of thinking characteristic of a class or individual (*bourgeois ideology*). **3** visionary speculation. **4** *archaic* the science of ideas. □□ **ideological** /-ə'lɒdʒɪk(ə)l/ *adj.* **ideologically** /-ə'lɒdʒɪkəlɪ/ *adv.* **ideologist** *n.* [F *idéologie* (as IDEOLOGUE)]

ides /aɪdz/ *n.pl.* the eighth day after the nones in the ancient Roman calendar (the 15th day of March, May, July, October, the 13th of other months). [ME f. OF f. L *idus* (pl.), perh. f. Etruscan]

idiocy /'ɪdɪəsɪ/ *n.* (*pl.* -ies) **1** utter foolishness; idiotic behaviour or an idiotic action. **2** extreme mental imbecility. [ME f. IDIOT, prob. after *lunacy*]

idiolect /'ɪdɪə,lekt/ *n.* the form of language used by an individual person. [Gk *idios* own + *-lect* in DIALECT]

idiom /'ɪdɪəm/ *n.* **1** a group of words established by usage and having a meaning not deducible from those of the individual words (as in *over the moon, see the light*). **2** a form of expression peculiar to a language, person, or group of people. **3 a** the language of a people or country. **b** the specific character of this. **4** a characteristic mode of expression in music, art, etc. [F *idiome* or LL *idioma* f. Gk *idiōma -matos* private property f. *idios* own, private]

idiomatic /,ɪdɪə'mætɪk/ *adj.* **1** relating to or conforming to idiom. **2** characteristic of a particular language. □□ **idiomatically** *adv.* [Gk *idiōmatikos* peculiar (as IDIOM)]

idiopathy /,ɪdɪ'ɒpəθɪ/ *n. Med.* any disease or condition of unknown cause or that arises spontaneously. □□ **idiopathic** /,ɪdɪə'pæθɪk/ *adj.* [mod.L *idiopathia* f. Gk *idiopatheia* f. *idios* own + -PATHY]

idiosyncrasy /,ɪdɪəʊ'sɪŋkrəsɪ/ *n.* (*pl.* -ies) **1** a mental constitution, view or feeling, or mode of behaviour, peculiar to a person. **2** anything highly individualized or eccentric. **3** a mode of expression peculiar to an author. **4** *Med.* a physical constitution peculiar to a person. □□ **idiosyncratic** /-'krætɪk/ *adj.* **idiosyncratically** /-'krætɪkəlɪ/ *adv.* [Gk *idiosugkrasia* f. *idios* own + *sun* together + *krasis* mixture]

idiot /'ɪdɪət/ *n.* **1** *colloq.* a stupid person; an utter fool. **2** a person deficient in mind and permanently incapable of rational conduct. □ **idiot board** (or **card**) *colloq.* a board displaying a television script to a speaker as an aid to memory. □□ **idiotic** /-'ɒtɪk/ *adj.* **idiotically** /-'ɒtɪkəlɪ/ *adv.* [ME f. OF f. L *idiota* ignorant person f. Gk *idiōtēs* private person, layman, ignorant person f. *idios* own, private]

idle /'aɪd(ə)l/ *adj.* & *v.* —*adj.* (**idler, idlest**) **1** lazy, indolent. **2** not in use; not working; unemployed. **3** (of time etc.) unoccupied. **4** having no special basis or purpose (*idle rumour; idle curiosity*). **5** useless. **6** (of an action, thought, or word) ineffective, worthless, vain. —*v.* **1 a** *intr.* (of an engine) run slowly without doing any work. **b** *tr.* cause (an engine) to idle. **2** *intr.* be idle. **3** *tr.* (foll. by *away*) pass (time etc.) in idleness. □ **idle wheel** an intermediate wheel between two geared wheels, esp. to allow them to rotate in the same direction. □□ **idleness** *n.* **idly** *adv.* [OE *īdel* empty, useless]

idler /'aɪdlə(r)/ *n.* **1** a habitually lazy person. **2** = *idle wheel.*

Ido /'i:dəʊ/ *n.* an artificial universal language based on Esperanto. [Ido, = offspring]

idol /'aɪd(ə)l/ *n.* **1** an image of a deity etc. used as an object of worship. **2** *Bibl.* a false god. **3** a person or thing that is the object of excessive or supreme adulation (*cinema idol*). **4** *archaic* a phantom. [ME f. OF *idole* f. L *idolum* f. Gk *eidōlon* phantom f. *eidos* form]

idolater /aɪ'dɒlətə(r)/ *n.* (*fem.* **idolatress** /-trɪs/) **1** a worshipper of idols. **2** (often foll. by *of*) a devoted admirer. □□ **idolatrous** *adj.* [ME *idolatrer* f. OF or f. *idolatry* or f. OF *idolâtre*, ult. f. Gk *eidōlolatrēs* (as IDOL, -LATER)]

idolatry /aɪ'dɒlətrɪ/ *n.* **1** the worship of idols. **2** great adulation. [OF *idolatrie* (as IDOLATER)]

idolize /'aɪdə,laɪz/ *v.* (also -ise) **1** *tr.* venerate or love extremely or excessively. **2** *tr.* make an idol of. **3** *intr.* practise idolatry. □□ **idolization** /-'zeɪʃ(ə)n/ *n.* **idolizer** *n.*

idyll /'ɪdɪl/ *n.* (also **idyl**) **1** a short description in verse or prose of a picturesque scene or incident, esp. in rustic life. **2** an episode suitable for such treatment, usu. a love-story. □□ **idyllist** *n.* **idyllize** *v.tr.* (also -ise). [L *idyllium* f. Gk *eidullion*, dimin. of *eidos* form]

idyllic /ɪ'dɪlɪk/ *adj.* **1** blissfully peaceful and happy. **2** of or like an idyll. □□ **idyllically** *adv.*

i.e. *abbr.* that is to say. [L *id est*]

-ie /ɪ/ *suffix* **1** var. of -Y² (*dearie; nightie*). **2** *archaic* var. of -Y¹, -Y³ (*litanie; prettie*). [earlier form of -Y]

IEE *abbr.* (in the UK) Institution of Electrical Engineers.

-ier /ɪə(r)/ *suffix* forming personal nouns denoting an occupation or interest: **1** with stress on the preceding element (*grazier*). **2** with stress on the suffix (*cashier; brigadier*). [sense 1 ME of various orig.; sense 2 F *-ier* f. L *-arius*]

IF *abbr.* intermediate frequency.

if /ɪf/ *conj.* & *n.* —*conj.* **1** introducing a conditional clause: **a** on the condition or supposition that; in the event that (*if he comes I will tell him; if you are tired we will rest*). **b** (with past tense) implying that the condition is not fulfilled (*if I were you; if I knew I would say*). **2** even though (*I'll finish it, if it takes me all day*). **3** whenever (*if I am not sure I ask*). **4** whether (*see if you can find it*). **5 a** expressing wish or surprise (*if I could just try!; if it isn't my old hat!*). **b** expressing a request (*if you wouldn't mind opening the door?*). **6** with implied reservation, = and perhaps not (*very rarely if at all*). **7** (with reduction of the protasis to its significant word) if there is or it is etc. (*took little if any*). **8** despite being (*a useful if cumbersome device*). —*n.* a condition or supposition (*too many ifs about it*). □ **if only 1** even if for no other reason than (*I'll come if only to see her*). **2** (often *ellipt.*) an expression of regret (*if only I had thought of it; if only I could swim!*). **if so** if that is the case. [OE *gif*]

IFC *abbr.* International Finance Corporation.

iff /ɪf/ *conj. Logic & Math.* = if and only if. [arbitrary extension of *if*]

iffy /'ɪfɪ/ *adj.* (**iffier, iffiest**) *colloq.* uncertain, doubtful.

Igbo var. of IBO.

igloo /'ɪglu:/ *n.* an Eskimo dome-shaped dwelling, esp. one built of snow. [Eskimo, = house]

igneous /'ɪgnɪəs/ *adj.* **1** of fire; fiery. **2** *Geol.* (esp. of rocks) produced by volcanic or magmatic action. [L *igneus* f. *ignis* fire]

ignis fatuus /,ɪgnɪs 'fætjʊəs/ *n.* (*pl.* **ignes fatui** /,ɪgniːz 'fætjʊɪ/) a will-o'-the-wisp. [mod.L, = foolish fire, because of its erratic movement]

ignite /ɪg'naɪt/ *v.* **1** *tr.* set fire to; cause to burn. **2** *intr.* catch fire. **3** *tr. Chem.* heat to the point of combustion or chemical change. **4** *tr.* provoke or excite (feelings etc.). □□ **ignitable** *adj.* **ignitability** /-tə'bɪlɪtɪ/ *n.* **ignitible** *adj.* **ignitibility** /-tɪ'bɪlɪtɪ/ *n.* [L *ignire ignit-* f. *ignis* fire]

igniter /ɪg'naɪtə(r)/ *n.* **1** a device for igniting a fuel mixture in an engine. **2** a device for causing an electric arc.

ignition /ɪgˈnɪʃ(ə)n/ n. **1** a mechanism for, or the action of, starting the combustion of mixture in the cylinder of an internal-combustion engine. **2** the act or an instance of igniting or being ignited. □**ignition key** a key to operate the ignition of a motor vehicle. [F *ignition* or med.L *ignitio* (as IGNITE)]

ignitron /ɪgˈnaɪtrən/ n. *Electr.* a mercury-arc rectifier able to carry large currents. [IGNITE + -TRON]

ignoble /ɪgˈnəʊb(ə)l/ adj. (**ignobler**, **ignoblest**) **1** dishonourable, mean, base. **2** of low birth, position, or reputation. □□**ignobility** /-nəˈbɪlɪtɪ/ n. **ignobly** adv. [F *ignoble* or L *ignobilis* (as IN-¹, *nobilis* noble)]

ignominious /ˌɪgnəˈmɪnɪəs/ adj. **1** causing or deserving ignominy. **2** humiliating. □□ **ignominiously** adv. **ignominiousness** n. [ME f. F *ignominieux* or L *ignominiosus*]

ignominy /ˈɪgnəmɪnɪ/ n. **1** dishonour, infamy. **2** *archaic* infamous conduct. [F *ignominie* or L *ignominia* (as IN-¹, *nomen* name)]

ignoramus /ˌɪgnəˈreɪməs/ n. (pl. **ignoramuses**) an ignorant person. [L, = we do not know: in legal use (formerly of a grand jury rejecting a bill) we take no notice of it; mod. sense perh. from a character in Ruggle's *Ignoramus* (1615) exposing lawyers' ignorance]

ignorance /ˈɪgnərəns/ n. (often foll. by *of*) lack of knowledge (about a thing). [ME f. OF f. L *ignorantia* (as IGNORANT)]

ignorant /ˈɪgnərənt/ adj. **1 a** lacking knowledge. **b** (foll. by *of*, *in*) uninformed (about a fact or subject). **2** *colloq.* ill-mannered, uncouth. □□ **ignorantly** adv. [ME f. OF f. L *ignorare ignorant-* (as IGNORE)]

ignore /ɪgˈnɔː(r)/ v.tr. **1** refuse to take notice of or accept. **2** intentionally disregard. □□**ignorer** n. [F *ignorer* or L *ignorare* not know, ignore (as IN-¹, *gno-* know)]

iguana /ɪgˈwɑːnə/ n. any of various large lizards of the family Iguanidae native to America, the W. Indies, and the Pacific islands, having a dorsal crest and throat appendages. [Sp. f. Carib *iwana*]

iguanodon /ɪˈgwɑːnəˌdɒn/ n. a large extinct planteating dinosaur of the genus *Iguanodon*, with forelimbs smaller than hind limbs. [IGUANA (from its resemblance to this), after *mastodon* etc.]

i.h.p. abbr. indicated horsepower.

IHS abbr. Jesus. [ME f. LL, repr. Gk *IHΣ* = *Iēs(ous)* Jesus: often taken as an abbr. of various Latin words]

ikebana /ˌɪkɪˈbɑːnə/ n. the art of Japanese flower arrangement, with formal display according to strict rules. [Jap., = living flowers]

ikky var. of ICKY.

ikon var. of ICON.

IL abbr. US Illinois (in official postal use).

il- /ɪl/ prefix assim. form of IN-¹, IN-² before *l*.

-il /ɪl/ suffix (also **-ile** /aɪl/) forming adjectives or nouns denoting relation (*civil*; *utensil*) or capability (*agile*; *sessile*). [OF f. L -*ilis*]

ilang-ilang var. of YLANG-YLANG.

ILEA /ˈɪlɪə/ abbr. Inner London Education Authority.

ilea pl. of ILEUM.

ileostomy /ˌɪlɪˈɒstəmɪ/ n. (pl. **-ies**) a surgical operation in which the ileum is brought through the abdominal wall to create an artificial opening for the evacuation of the intestinal contents. [ILEUM + Gk *stoma* mouth]

ileum /ˈɪlɪəm/ n. (pl. **ilea** /ɪlɪə/) *Anat.* the third and last portion of the small intestine. □□ **ileac** adj. [var. of ILIUM]

ileus /ˈɪlɪəs/ n. *Med.* any painful obstruction of the intestine, esp. of the ileum. [L f. Gk *(e)ileos* colic]

ilex /ˈaɪleks/ n. **1** any tree or shrub of the genus *Ilex*, esp. the common holly. **2** the holm-oak. [ME f. L]

ilia pl. of ILIUM.

iliac /ˈɪlɪˌæk/ adj. of the lower body or ilium (*iliac artery*). [LL *iliacus* (as ILIUM)]

ilium /ˈɪlɪəm/ n. (pl. **ilia** /ˈɪlɪə/) **1** the bone forming the upper part of each half of the human pelvis. **2** the corresponding bone in animals. [ME f. L]

ilk /ɪlk/ n. **1** *colloq. disp.* a family, class, or set (*not of the same ilk as you*). ¶ Usu. *derog.* and therefore best avoided. **2** (in **of that ilk**) *Sc.* of the same (name) (*Guthrie of that ilk* = of Guthrie). [OE *ilca* same]

Ill. abbr. Illinois.

ill /ɪl/ adj., adv., & n. —adj. **1** (usu. *predic.*; often foll. by *with*) out of health; sick (*is ill*; *was taken ill with pneumonia*; *mentally ill people*). **2** (of health) unsound, disordered. **3** wretched, unfavourable (*ill fortune*; *ill luck*). **4** harmful (*ill effects*). **5** hostile, unkind (*ill feeling*). **6** *archaic* morally bad. **7** faulty, unskilful (*ill taste*; *ill management*). **8** (of manners or conduct) improper. —adv. **1** badly, wrongly (*ill-matched*). **2 a** imperfectly (*ill-provided*). **b** scarcely (*can ill afford to do it*). **3** unfavourably (*it would have gone ill with them*). —n. **1** injury, harm. **2** evil; the opposite of good. □**do an ill turn to** harm (a person or a person's interests). **ill-advised 1** acting foolishly or imprudently. **2** (of a plan etc.) not well formed or considered. **ill-advisedly** /-ədˈvaɪzɪdlɪ/ in a foolish or badly considered manner. **ill-affected** (foll. by *towards*) not well disposed. **ill-assorted** not well matched. **ill at ease** embarrassed, uneasy. **ill-behaved** see BEHAVE. **ill blood** bad feeling; animosity. **ill-bred** badly brought up; rude. **ill breeding** bad manners. **ill-considered** = *ill-advised*. **ill-defined** not clearly defined. **ill-disposed 1** (often foll. by *towards*) unfavourably disposed. **2** disposed to evil; malevolent. **ill-equipped** (often foll. by *to* + infin.) not adequately equipped or qualified. **ill fame** see FAME. **ill-fated** destined to or bringing bad fortune. **ill-favoured** (*US* -favored) unattractive, displeasing, objectionable. **ill feeling** bad feeling; animosity. **ill-founded** (of an idea etc.) not well founded; baseless. **ill-gotten** gained by wicked or unlawful means. **ill humour** moroseness, irritability. **ill-humoured** bad-tempered. **ill-judged** unwise; badly considered. **ill-mannered** having bad manners; rude. **ill nature** churlishness, unkindness. **ill-natured** churlish, unkind. **ill-naturedly** churlishly. **ill-omened** attended by bad omens. **ill-starred** unlucky; destined to failure. **ill success** partial or complete failure. **ill temper** moroseness. **ill-tempered** morose, irritable. **ill-timed** done or occurring at an inappropriate time. **ill-treat** (or **-use**) treat badly; abuse. **ill-treatment** (or **ill use**) abuse; bad treatment. **ill will** bad feeling; animosity. **an ill wind** an unfavourable or untoward circumstance (with ref. to the proverb *it's an ill wind that blows nobody good*). **speak ill of** say something unfavourable about. [ME f. ON *illr*, of unkn. orig.]

I'll /aɪl/ contr. I shall; I will.

illation /ɪˈleɪʃ(ə)n/ n. **1** a deduction or conclusion. **2** a thing deduced. [L *illatio* f. *illatus* past part. of *inferre* INFER]

illative /ɪˈleɪtɪv, ˈɪlətɪv/ adj. **1 a** (of a word) stating or introducing an inference. **b** inferential. **2** *Gram.* (of a case) denoting motion into. □□ **illatively** adv. [L *illativus* (as ILLATION)]

illegal /ɪˈliːg(ə)l/ adj. **1** not legal. **2** contrary to law. □□ **illegality** /-ˈgælɪtɪ/ n. (pl. **-ies**). **illegally** adv. [F *illégal* or med.L *illegalis* (as IN-¹, LEGAL)]

illegible /ɪˈledʒɪb(ə)l/ adj. not legible. □□ **illegibility** /-ˈbɪlɪtɪ/ n. **illegibly** adv. [F

illegitimate adj., n., & v. —adj. /ˌɪlɪˈdʒɪtɪmət/ **1** (of a child) born of parents not married to each other. **2** not authorized by law; unlawful. **3** improper. **4** wrongly inferred. **5** physiologically abnormal. —n. /ˌɪlɪˈdʒɪtɪmət/ a person whose position is illegitimate, esp. by birth. —v.tr. /ˌɪlɪˈdʒɪtɪˌmeɪt/ declare or pronounce illegitimate. □□ **illegitimacy** n. **illegitimately** adv. [LL *illegitimus*, after LEGITIMATE]

illiberal /ɪˈlɪbər(ə)l/ adj. **1** intolerant, narrow-minded. **2** without liberal culture. **3** not generous; stingy. **4** vulgar, sordid. □□ **illiberality** /-ˈrælɪtɪ/ n. (pl. **-ies**). **illiberally** adv. [F *illibéral* f. L *illiberalis* mean, sordid (as IN-¹, LIBERAL)]

illicit /ɪˈlɪsɪt/ *adj.* unlawful, forbidden (*illicit dealings*). □□ **illicitly** *adv.* **illicitness** *n.*

illimitable /ɪˈlɪmɪtəb(ə)l/ *adj.* limitless. □□ **illimitability** /-ˈbɪlɪtɪ/ *n.* **illimitableness** *n.* **illimitably** *adv.* [LL *illimitatus* f. L *limitatus* (as IN-¹, L *limitatus* past part. of *limitare* LIMIT)]

illiquid /ɪˈlɪkwɪd/ *adj.* (of assets) not easily converted into cash. □□ **illiquidity** /-ˈkwɪdɪtɪ/ *n.*

illiterate /ɪˈlɪtərət/ *adj. & n.* —*adj.* **1** unable to read. **2** uneducated. —*n.* an illiterate person. □□ **illiteracy** *n.* **illiterately** *adv.* **illiterateness** *n.* [L *illitteratus* (as IN-¹, *litteratus* LITERATE)]

illness /ˈɪlnɪs/ *n.* **1** a disease, ailment, or malady. **2** the state of being ill.

illogical /ɪˈlɒdʒɪk(ə)l/ *adj.* devoid of or contrary to logic. □□ **illogicality** /-ˈkælɪtɪ/ *n.* (*pl.* **-ies**). **illogically** *adv.*

illude /ɪˈluːd, ɪˈljuːd/ *v.tr. literary* trick or deceive. [ME, = mock, f. L *illudere* (as ILLUSION)]

illume /ɪˈluːm, ɪˈljuːm/ *v.tr. poet.* light up; make bright. [shortening of ILLUMINE]

illuminant /ɪˈluːmɪnənt, ɪˈljuː-/ *n. & adj.* —*n.* a means of illumination. —*adj.* serving to illuminate. □□ **illuminance** *n.* [L *illuminant-* part. stem of *illuminare* ILLUMINATE]

illuminate /ɪˈluːmɪˌneɪt, ɪˈljuː-/ *v.tr.* **1** light up; make bright. **2** decorate (buildings etc.) with lights as a sign of festivity. **3** decorate (an initial letter, a manuscript, etc.) with gold, silver, or brilliant colours. **4** help to explain (a subject etc.). **5** enlighten spiritually or intellectually. **6** shed lustre on. □□ **illuminating** *adj.* **illuminatingly** *adv.* **illumination** /-ˈneɪʃ(ə)n/ *n.* **illuminative** /-ˌneɪtɪv, -nətɪv/ *adj.* **illuminator** *n.* [L *illuminare* (as IN-², *lumen luminis* light)]

illuminati /ɪˌluːmɪˈnɑːtɪ, ɪˌljuː-/ *n.pl.* **1** persons claiming to possess special knowledge or enlightenment. **2** (**Illuminati**) *hist.* any of various intellectual movements or societies of illuminati. □□ **illuminism** /ɪˈluːmɪˌnɪz(ə)m, ɪˈljuː-/ *n.* **illuminist** /ɪˈluːmɪnɪst, ɪˈljuː-/ *n.* [pl. of L *illuminatus* or It. *illuminato* past part. (as ILLUMINATE)]

illumine /ɪˈljuːmɪn, ɪˈluː-/ *v.tr. literary* **1** light up; make bright. **2** enlighten spiritually. [ME f. OF *illuminer* f. L (as ILLUMINATE)]

illusion /ɪˈluːʒ(ə)n, ɪˈljuː-/ *n.* **1** deception, delusion. **2** a misapprehension of the true state of affairs. **3 a** the faulty perception of an external object. **b** an instance of this. **4** a figment of the imagination. **5** = *optical illusion*. □ **be under the illusion** (foll. by *that* + clause) believe mistakenly. □□ **illusional** *adj.* [ME f. F f. L *illusio -onis* f. *illudere* mock (as IN-², *ludere lus-* play)]

illusionist /ɪˈluːʒənɪst, ɪˈljuː-/ *n.* a person who produces illusions; a conjuror. □□ **illusionism** *n.* **illusionistic** /-ˈnɪstɪk/ *adj.*

illusive /ɪˈluːsɪv, ɪˈljuː-/ *adj.* = ILLUSORY. [med.L *illusivus* (as ILLUSION)]

illusory /ɪˈluːsərɪ, ɪˈljuː-/ *adj.* **1** deceptive (esp. as regards value or content). **2** having the character of an illusion. □□ **illusorily** *adv.* **illusoriness** *n.* [eccl.L *illusorius* (as ILLUSION)]

illustrate /ˈɪləˌstreɪt/ *v.tr.* **1 a** provide (a book, newspaper, etc.) with pictures. **b** elucidate (a description etc.) by drawings or pictures. **2** serve as an example of. **3** explain or make clear, esp. by examples. [L *illustrare* (as IN-², *lustrare* light up)]

illustration /ˌɪləˈstreɪʃ(ə)n/ *n.* **1** a drawing or picture illustrating a book, magazine article, etc. **2** an example serving to elucidate. **3** the act or an instance of illustrating. □□ **illustrational** *adj.* [ME f. OF f. L *illustratio -onis* (as ILLUSTRATE)]

illustrative /ˈɪləstrətɪv/ *adj.* (often foll. by *of*) serving as an explanation or example. □□ **illustratively** *adv.*

illustrator /ˈɪləˌstreɪtə(r)/ *n.* a person who makes illustrations, esp. for magazines, books, advertising copy, etc.

illustrious /ɪˈlʌstrɪəs/ *adj.* distinguished, renowned. □□ **illustriously** *adv.* **illustriousness** *n.* [L *illustris* (as ILLUSTRATE)]

Illyrian /ɪˈlɪrɪən/ *adj. & n.* —*adj.* **1** of or relating to Illyria on the Balkan coast of the Adriatic (corresponding to parts of modern Albania and Yugoslavia). **2** of the language-group represented by modern Albanian. —*n.* **1** a native of Illyria; a person of Illyrian descent. **2 a** the language of Illyria. **b** the language-group represented by modern Albanian.

illywhacker /ˈɪlɪˌwækə(r)/ *n. Austral. sl.* a professional trickster. [20th c.: orig. unkn.]

ilmenite /ˈɪlmənaɪt/ *n.* a black ore of titanium. [*Ilmen* mountains in the Urals]

ILO *abbr.* International Labour Organization.

ILR *abbr.* Independent Local Radio.

-ily /ɪlɪ/ *suffix* forming adverbs corresponding to adjectives in *-y* (see -Y¹, -LY²).

im- /ɪm/ *prefix* assim. form of IN-¹, IN-² before *b, m, p.*

I'm /aɪm/ *contr.* I am.

image /ˈɪmɪdʒ/ *n. & v.* —*n.* **1 a** a representation of the external form of an object, e.g. a statue (esp. of a saint etc. as an object of veneration). **2** the character or reputation of a person or thing as generally perceived. **3** an optical appearance or counterpart produced by light or other radiation from an object reflected in a mirror, refracted through a lens, etc. **4** semblance, likeness (*God created man in His own image*). **5** a person or thing that closely resembles another (*is the image of his father*). **6** a typical example. **7** a simile or metaphor. **8 a** a mental representation. **b** an idea or conception. **9** *Math.* a set formed by mapping from another set. —*v.tr.* **1** make an image of; portray. **2** reflect, mirror. **3** describe or imagine vividly. **4** typify. □□ **imageable** *adj.* **imageless** *adj.* [ME f. OF f. L *imago -ginis*, rel. to IMITATE]

imagery /ˈɪmɪdʒərɪ/ *n.* **1** figurative illustration, esp. as used by an author for particular effects. **2** images collectively. **3** statuary, carving. **4** mental images collectively. [ME f. OF *imagerie* (as IMAGE)]

imaginable /ɪˈmædʒɪnəb(ə)l/ *adj.* that can be imagined (*the greatest difficulty imaginable*). □□ **imaginably** *adv.* [ME f. LL *imaginabilis* (as IMAGINE)]

imaginal /ɪˈmædʒɪn(ə)l/ *adj.* **1** of an image or images. **2** *Zool.* of an imago. [L *imago imagin-*: see IMAGE]

imaginary /ɪˈmædʒɪnərɪ/ *adj.* **1** existing only in the imagination. **2** *Math.* being the square root of a negative quantity, and plotted graphically in a direction usu. perpendicular to the axis of real quantities (see REAL¹). □□ **imaginarily** *adv.* [ME f. L *imaginarius* (as IMAGE)]

imagination /ɪˌmædʒɪˈneɪʃ(ə)n/ *n.* **1** a mental faculty forming images or concepts of external objects not present to the senses. **2** the ability of the mind to be creative or resourceful. **3** the process of imagining. [ME f. OF f. L *imaginatio -onis* (as IMAGINE)]

imaginative /ɪˈmædʒɪnətɪv/ *adj.* **1** having or showing in a high degree the faculty of imagination. **2** given to using the imagination. □□ **imaginatively** *adv.* **imaginativeness** *n.* [ME f. OF *imaginatif -ive* f. med.L *imaginativus* (as IMAGINE)]

imagine /ɪˈmædʒɪn/ *v.tr.* **1 a** form a mental image or concept of. **b** picture to oneself (something nonexistent or not present to the senses). **2** (often foll. by *to* + infin.) think or conceive (*imagined them to be soldiers*). **3** guess (*cannot imagine what they are doing*). **4** (often foll. by *that* + clause) suppose; be of the opinion (*I imagine you will need help*). **5** (in *imper.*) as an exclamation of surprise (*just imagine!*). □□ **imaginer** *n.* [ME f. OF *imaginer* f. L *imaginari* (as IMAGE)]

imagines *pl.* of IMAGO.

imaginings /ɪˈmædʒɪnɪŋz/ *n.pl.* fancies, fantasies.

imagism /ˈɪmɪˌdʒɪz(ə)m/ *n.* a movement in early 20th-c. poetry which sought clarity of expression through the use of precise images. □□ **imagist** *n.* **imagistic** /-'dʒɪstɪk/ *adj.*

imago /ɪ'meɪgəʊ/ *n.* (*pl.* **-os** or **imagines** /ɪ'mædʒɪˌniːz/) **1** the final and fully developed stage of an insect after all metamorphoses, e.g. a butterfly or beetle. **2** *Psychol.* an idealized mental picture of oneself or others, esp. a parent. [mod.L sense of *imago* IMAGE]

imam /ɪ'mɑːm/ *n.* **1** a leader of prayers in a mosque. **2** a title of various Muslim leaders, esp. of one succeeding Muhammad as leader of Islam. □□ **imamate** /-meɪt/ *n.* [Arab. *'imām* leader f. *'amma* precede]

imbalance /ɪm'bæləns/ *n.* **1** lack of balance. **2** disproportion.

imbecile /'ɪmbɪˌsiːl/ *n. & adj.* —*n.* **1** a person of abnormally weak intellect, esp. an adult with a mental age of about five. **2** *colloq.* a stupid person. —*adj.* mentally weak; stupid, idiotic. □□ **imbecilely** *adv.* **imbecilic** /-'sɪlɪk/ *adj.* **imbecility** /-'sɪlɪtɪ/ *n.* (*pl.* **-ies**). [F *imbécil(l)e* f. L *imbecillus* (as IN-¹, *baculum* stick) orig. in sense 'without supporting staff']

imbed var. of EMBED.

imbibe /ɪm'baɪb/ *v.tr.* **1** (also *absol.*) drink (esp. alcoholic liquor). **2 a** absorb or assimilate (ideas etc.). **b** absorb (moisture etc.). **3** inhale (air etc.). □□ **imbiber** *n.* **imbibition** /ˌɪmbɪ'bɪʃ(ə)n/ *n.* [ME f. L *imbibere* (as IN-², *bibere* drink)]

imbricate *v. & adj.* —*v.tr. & intr.* /'ɪmbrɪˌkeɪt/ arrange (leaves, the scales of a fish, etc.), or be arranged, so as to overlap like roof-tiles. —*adj.* /'ɪmbrɪkət/ having scales etc. arranged in this way. □□ **imbrication** /-'keɪʃ(ə)n/ *n.* [L *imbricare imbricat*-cover with rain-tiles f. *imbrex -icis* rain-tile f. *imber* shower]

imbroglio /ɪm'brəʊlɪəʊ/ *n.* (*pl.* **-os**) **1** a confused or complicated situation. **2** a confused heap. [It. *imbrogliare* confuse (as EMBROIL)]

imbrue /ɪm'bruː/ *v.tr.* (foll. by *in*, *with*) *literary* stain (one's hand, sword, etc.). [OF *embruer* bedabble (as IN-², *breu* ult. f. Gmc, rel. to BROTH)]

imbue /ɪm'bjuː/ *v.tr.* (**imbues**, **imbued**, **imbuing**) (often foll. by *with*) **1** inspire or permeate (with feelings, opinions, or qualities). **2** saturate. **3** dye. [orig. as past part., f. F *imbu* or L *imbutus* f. *imbuere* moisten]

I.Mech.E. *abbr.* (in the UK) Institution of Mechanical Engineers.

IMF *abbr.* International Monetary Fund.

imide /'ɪmaɪd/ *n. Chem.* an organic compound containing the group (−CO.NH.CO.−) formed by replacing two of the hydrogen atoms in ammonia by carbonyl groups. [orig. F: arbitrary alt. of AMIDE]

imine /'ɪmiːn/ *n. Chem.* a compound containing the group (−NH−) formed by replacing two of the hydrogen atoms in ammonia by other groups. [G *Imin* arbitrary alt. of *Amin* AMINE]

I.Min.E. *abbr.* (in the UK) Institution of Mining Engineers.

imitate /'ɪmɪˌteɪt/ *v.tr.* **1** follow the example of; copy the action(s) of. **2** mimic. **3** make a copy of; reproduce. **4** be (consciously or not) like. □□ **imitable** *adj.* **imitator** *n.* [L *imitari imitat*-, rel. to *imago* IMAGE]

imitation /ˌɪmɪ'teɪʃ(ə)n/ *n.* **1** the act or an instance of imitating or being imitated. **2** a copy. **3** counterfeit (often *attrib.*: *imitation leather*). **4** *Mus.* the repetition of a phrase etc., usu. at a different pitch, in another part or voice. [F *imitation* or L *imitatio* (as IMITATE)]

imitative /'ɪmɪtətɪv/ *adj.* **1** (often foll. by *of*) imitating; following a model or example. **2** counterfeit. **3** of a word: **a** that reproduces a natural sound (e.g. *fizz*). **b** whose sound is thought to correspond to the appearance etc. of the object or action described (e.g. *blob*). □ **imitative arts** painting and sculpture. □□ **imitatively** *adv.* **imitativeness** *n.* [LL *imitatiuus* (as IMITATE)]

immaculate /ɪ'mækjʊlət/ *adj.* **1** pure, spotless; perfectly clean. **2** perfectly or extremely well executed (*an immaculate performance*). **3** free from fault; innocent. **4** *Biol.* not spotted. □ **Immaculate Conception** *RC Ch.* the doctrine that God preserved the Virgin Mary from the taint of original sin from the moment she was conceived. □□ **immaculacy** *n.* **immaculately** *adv.* **immaculateness** *n.* [ME f. L *immaculatus* (as IN-¹, *maculatus* f. *macula* spot)]

immanent /'ɪmənənt/ *adj.* **1** (often foll. by *in*) indwelling, inherent. **2** (of the supreme being) permanently pervading the universe (opp. TRANSCENDENT). □□ **immanence** *n.* **immanency** *n.* **immanentism** *n.* **immanentist** *n.* [LL *immanēre* (as IN-², *manēre* remain)]

immaterial /ˌɪmə'tɪərɪəl/ *adj.* **1** of no essential consequence; unimportant. **2** not material; incorporeal. □□ **immateriality** /-'ælɪtɪ/ *n.* **immaterialize** *v.tr.* (also -**ise**). **immaterially** *adv.* [ME f. LL *immaterialis* (as IN-¹, MATERIAL)]

immaterialism /ˌɪmə'tɪərɪəˌlɪz(ə)m/ *n.* the doctrine that matter has no objective existence. □□ **immaterialist** *n.*

immature /ˌɪmə'tjʊə(r)/ *adj.* **1** not mature or fully developed. **2** lacking emotional or intellectual development. **3** unripe. □□ **immaturely** *adv.* **immaturity** *n.* [L *immaturus* (as IN-¹, MATURE)]

immeasurable /ɪ'meʒərəb(ə)l/ *adj.* not measurable; immense. □□ **immeasurability** /-'bɪlɪtɪ/ *n.* **immeasurableness** *n.* **immeasurably** *adv.*

immediate /ɪ'miːdɪət/ *adj.* **1** occurring or done at once or without delay (*an immediate reply*). **2** nearest, next; not separated by others (*the immediate vicinity*; *the immediate future*; *my immediate neighbour*). **3** most pressing or urgent (*our immediate concern was to get him to hospital*). **4** (of a relation or action) having direct effect; without an intervening medium or agency (*the immediate cause of death*). **5** (of knowledge) intuitive, gained without reasoning. □□ **immediacy** *n.* **immediateness** *n.* [ME f. F *immédiat* or LL *immediatus* (as IN-¹, MEDIATE)]

immediately /ɪ'miːdɪətlɪ/ *adj. & conj.* —*adv.* **1** without pause or delay. **2** without intermediary. —*conj.* as soon as.

immedicable /ɪ'medɪkəb(ə)l/ *adj.* that cannot be healed or cured. □□ **immedicably** *adv.* [L *immedicabilis* (as IN-¹, MEDICABLE)]

immemorial /ˌɪmɪ'mɔːrɪəl/ *adj.* **1** ancient beyond memory or record. **2** very old. □□ **immemorially** *adv.* [med.L *immemorialis* (as IN-¹, MEMORIAL)]

immense /ɪ'mens/ *adj.* **1** immeasurably large or great; huge. **2** very great; considerable (*made an immense difference*). **3** *colloq.* very good. □□ **immenseness** *n.* **immensity** *n.* [ME f. F f. L *immensus* immeasurable (as IN-¹, *mensus* past part. of *metiri* measure)]

immensely /ɪ'menslɪ/ *adv.* **1** very much (*enjoyed myself immensely*). **2** to an immense degree.

immerse /ɪ'mɜːs/ *v.tr.* **1 a** (often foll. by *in*) dip, plunge. **b** cause (a person) to be completely under water. **2** (often *refl.* or in *passive*; often foll. by *in*) absorb or involve deeply. **3** (often foll. by *in*) bury, embed. [L *immergere* (as IN-², *mergere mers*- dip)]

immersion /ɪ'mɜːʃ(ə)n/ *n.* **1** the act or an instance of immersing; the process of being immersed. **2** baptism by immersing the whole person in water. **3** mental absorption. **4** *Astron.* the disappearance of a celestial body behind another or in its shadow. □ **immersion heater** an electric heater designed for direct immersion in a liquid to be heated, esp. as a fixture in a hot-water tank. [ME f. LL *immersio* (as IMMERSE)]

immigrant /'ɪmɪgrənt/ *n. & adj.* —*n.* a person who immigrates. —*adj.* **1** immigrating. **2** of or concerning immigrants.

immigrate /'ɪmɪˌgreɪt/ *v.* **1** *intr.* come as a permanent resident to a country other than one's native land. **2** *tr.* bring in (a person) as an immigrant. □□ **immigration**

/-'greɪʃ(ə)n/ n. **immigratory** adj. [L immigrare (as IN-², MIGRATE)]

imminent /'ɪmɪnənt/ adj. **1** (of an event, esp. danger) impending; about to happen. **2** archaic overhanging. □□ **imminence** n. **imminently** adv. [L imminēre imminent- overhang, project]

immiscible /ɪ'mɪsɪb(ə)l/ adj. (often foll. by with) that cannot be mixed. □□ **immiscibility** /-'bɪlɪtɪ/ n. **immiscibly** adv. [LL immiscibilis (as IN-¹, MISCIBLE)]

immitigable /ɪ'mɪtɪgəb(ə)l/ adj. that cannot be mitigated. □□ **immitigably** adv. [LL immitigabilis (as IN-¹, MITIGATE)]

immittance /ɪ'mɪt(ə)ns/ n. Electr. admittance or impedance (when not distinguished). [impedance + admittance]

immixture /ɪ'mɪkstʃə(r)/ n. **1** the process of mixing up. **2** (often foll. by in) being involved.

immobile /ɪ'məʊbaɪl/ adj. **1** not moving. **2** not able to move or be moved. □□ **immobility** /-'bɪlɪtɪ/ n. [ME f. OF f. L immobilis (as IN-¹, MOBILE)]

immobilize /ɪ'məʊbɪˌlaɪz/ v.tr. (also **-ise**) **1** make or keep immobile. **2** make (a vehicle or troops) incapable of being moved. **3** keep (a limb or patient) restricted in movement for healing purposes. **4** restrict the free movement of. **5** withdraw (coins) from circulation to support banknotes. □□ **immobilization** /-'zeɪʃ(ə)n/ n. **immobilizer** n. [F immobiliser (as IMMOBILE)]

immoderate /ɪ'mɒdərət/ adj. excessive; lacking moderation. □□ **immoderately** adv. **immoderateness** n. **immoderation** /-'reɪʃ(ə)n/ n. [ME f. L immoderatus (as IN-¹, MODERATE)]

immodest /ɪ'mɒdɪst/ adj. **1** lacking modesty; forward, impudent. **2** lacking due decency. □□ **immodestly** adv. **immodesty** n. [F immodeste or L immodestus (as IN-¹, MODEST)]

immolate /'ɪməˌleɪt/ v.tr. **1** kill or offer as a sacrifice. **2** literary sacrifice (a valued thing). □□ **immolation** /-'leɪʃ(ə)n/ n. **immolator** n. [L immolare sprinkle with sacrificial meal (as IN-², mola MEAL²)]

immoral /ɪ'mɒr(ə)l/ adj. **1** not conforming to accepted standards of morality (cf. AMORAL). **2** morally wrong (esp. in sexual matters). **3** depraved, dissolute. □□ **immorality** /ˌɪmə'rælɪtɪ/ n. (pl. **-ies**). **immorally** adv.

immortal /ɪ'mɔːt(ə)l/ adj. & n. —adj. **1 a** living for ever; not mortal. **b** divine. **2** unfading, incorruptible. **3** likely or worthy to be famous for all time. —n. **1 a** an immortal being. **b** (in pl.) the gods of antiquity. **2 a** person (esp. an author) of enduring fame. **3** (Immortal) a member of the French Academy. □□ **immortality** /ˌɪmɔː'tælɪtɪ/ n. **immortalize** v.tr. (also **-ise**). **immortalization** /-'zeɪʃ(ə)n/ n. **immortally** adv. [ME f. L immortalis (as IN-¹, MORTAL)]

immortelle /ˌɪmɔː'tel/ n. a composite flower of papery texture retaining its shape and colour after being dried, esp. a helichrysum. [F, fem. of immortel IMMORTAL]

immovable /ɪ'muːvəb(ə)l/ adj. & n. (also **immoveable**) —adj. **1** that cannot be moved. **2** steadfast, unyielding. **3** emotionless. **4** not subject to change (immovable law). **5** motionless. **6** Law (of property) consisting of land, houses, etc. —n. (in pl.) Law immovable property. □**immovable feast** a religious feast-day that occurs on the same date each year. □□ **immovability** /-'bɪlɪtɪ/ n. **immovableness** n. **immovably** adv.

immune /ɪ'mjuːn/ adj. **1 a** (often foll. by against, from, to) protected against an infection owing to the presence of specific antibodies, or through inoculation or inherited or acquired resistance. **b** relating to immunity (immune mechanism). **2** (foll. by from, to) free or exempt from or not subject to (some undesirable factor or circumstance). □**immune response** the reaction of the body to the introduction into it of an antigen. [ME f. L immunis exempt from public service or charge (as IN-¹, munis ready for service): sense 1 f. F immun]

immunity /ɪ'mjuːnɪtɪ/ n. (pl. **-ies**) **1** Med. the ability of an organism to resist infection, by means of the presence of circulating antibodies and white blood cells. **2** freedom or exemption from an obligation, penalty, or unfavourable circumstance. [ME f. L immunitas (as IMMUNE): sense 1 f. F immunité]

immunize /'ɪmjuːˌnaɪz/ v.tr. (also **-ise**) make immune, esp. to infection, usu. by inoculation. □□ **immunization** /-'zeɪʃ(ə)n/ n. **immunizer** n.

immuno- /'ɪmjuːnəʊ/ comb. form immunity to infection.

immunoassay /ˌɪmjuːnəʊ'æseɪ/ n. Biochem. the determination of the presence or quantity of a substance, esp. a protein, through its properties as an antigen or antibody.

immunochemistry /ˌɪmjuːnəʊ'kemɪstrɪ/ n. the chemistry of immune systems, esp. in mammalian tissues.

immunodeficiency /ˌɪmjuːˌnəʊdɪ'fɪʃənsɪ/ n. a reduction in a person's normal immune defences.

immunogenic /ˌɪmjuːnəʊ'dʒenɪk/ adj. Biochem. of, relating to, or possessing the ability to elicit an immune response.

immunoglobulin /ˌɪmjuːnəʊ'glɒbjʊlɪn/ n. Biochem. any of a group of structurally related proteins which function as antibodies.

immunology /ˌɪmjuː'nɒlədʒɪ/ n. the scientific study of immunity. □□ **immunologic** /-nə'lɒdʒɪk/ adj. **immunological** /-nə'lɒdʒɪk(ə)l/ adj. **immunologically** /-nə'lɒdʒɪkəlɪ/ adv. **immunologist** n.

immunosuppressed /ˌɪmjuːnəʊsə'prest/ adj. (of an individual) rendered partially or completely unable to react immunologically.

immunosuppression /ˌɪmjuːnəʊsə'preʃ(ə)n/ n. Biochem. the partial or complete suppression of the immune response of an individual, esp. to maintain the survival of an organ after a transplant operation. □□ **immunosuppressant** n.

immunosuppressive /ˌɪmjuːnəʊsə'presɪv/ adj. & n. —adj. partially or completely suppressing the immune response of an individual. —n. an immunosuppressive drug.

immunotherapy /ˌɪmjuːnəʊ'θerəpɪ/ n. Med. the prevention or treatment of disease with substances that stimulate the immune response.

immure /ɪ'mjʊə(r)/ v.tr. **1** enclose within walls; imprison. **2** refl. shut oneself away. □□ **immurement** n. [F emmurer or med.L immurare (as IN-², murus wall)]

immutable /ɪ'mjuːtəb(ə)l/ adj. **1** unchangeable. **2** not subject to variation in different cases. □□ **immutability** /-'bɪlɪtɪ/ n. **immutably** adv. [ME f. L immutabilis (as IN-¹, MUTABLE)]

imp /ɪmp/ n. & v. —n. **1** a mischievous child. **2** a small mischievous devil or sprite. —v.tr. **1** add feathers to (the wing of a falcon) to restore or improve its flight. **2** archaic enlarge; add by grafting. [OE impa, impe young shoot, scion, impian graft: ult. f. Gk emphutos implanted, past part. of emphuō]

impact n. & v. —n. /'ɪmpækt/ **1** (often foll. by on, against) the action of one body coming forcibly into contact with another. **2** an effect or influence, esp. when strong. —v.tr. /ɪm'pækt/ **1** (often foll. by in, into) press or fix firmly. **2** (as **impacted** adj.) **a** (of a tooth) wedged between another tooth and the jaw. **b** (of a fractured bone) with the parts crushed together. **c** (of faeces) lodged in the intestine. □□ **impaction** /ɪm'pækʃ(ə)n/ n. [L impact- part. stem of impingere IMPINGE]

impair /ɪm'peə(r)/ v.tr. damage or weaken. □□ **impairment** n. [ME empeire f. OF empeirier (as IN-², LL pejorare f. L pejor worse)]

impala /ɪm'pɑːlə, -'pælə/ n. (pl. same) a small antelope, Aepyceros melampus, of S. and E. Africa, capable of long high jumps. [Zulu]

impale /ɪm'peɪl/ v.tr. **1** (foll. by on, upon, with) transfix or pierce with a sharp instrument. **2** Heraldry combine (two coats of arms) by placing them side by side on one shield separated by a vertical line down the middle. □□ **impalement** *n*. [F *empaler* or med.L *impalare* (as IN-², *palus* stake)]

impalpable /ɪmˈpælpəb(ə)l/ *adj*. **1** not easily grasped by the mind; intangible. **2** imperceptible to the touch. **3** (of powder) very fine; not containing grains that can be felt. □□ **impalpability** /-ˈbɪlɪtɪ/ *n*. **impalpably** *adv*. [F *impalpable* or LL *impalpabilis* (as IN-¹, PALPABLE)]

impanel var. of EMPANEL.

impark /ɪmˈpɑːk/ *v.tr*. **1** enclose (animals) in a park. **2** enclose (land) for a park. [ME f. AF *enparker*, OF *emparquer* (as IN-², *parc* PARK)]

impart /ɪmˈpɑːt/ *v.tr*. (often foll. by *to*) **1** communicate (news etc.). **2** give a share of (a thing). □□ **impartable** *adj*. **impartation** /ˌɪmpɑːˈteɪʃ(ə)n/ *n*. **impartment** *n*. [ME f. OF *impartir* f. L *impartire* (as IN-², *pars* part)]

impartial /ɪmˈpɑːʃ(ə)l/ *adj*. treating all sides in a dispute etc. equally; unprejudiced, fair. □□ **impartiality** /-ʃɪˈælɪtɪ/ *n*. **impartially** *adv*.

impassable /ɪmˈpɑːsəb(ə)l/ *adj*. that cannot be traversed. □□ **impassability** /-ˈbɪlɪtɪ/ *n*. **impassableness** *n*. **impassably** *adv*.

impasse /ˈæmpɑːs, ˈɪm-/ *n*. a position from which progress is impossible; deadlock. [F (as IN-¹, *passer* PASS¹)]

impassible /ɪmˈpæsɪb(ə)l/ *adj*. **1** impassive. **2** incapable of feeling or emotion. **3** incapable of suffering injury. **4** *Theol*. not subject to suffering. □□ **impassibility** /-ˈbɪlɪtɪ/ *n*. **impassibleness** *n*. **impassibly** *adv*. [ME f. OF f. eccl.L *impassibilis* (as IN-¹, PASSIBLE)]

impassion /ɪmˈpæʃ(ə)n/ *v.tr*. fill with passion; arouse emotionally. [It. *impassionare* (as IN-², PASSION)]

impassioned /ɪmˈpæʃ(ə)nd/ *adj*. deeply felt; ardent (*an impassioned plea*).

impassive /ɪmˈpæsɪv/ *adj*. **1 a** deficient in or incapable of feeling emotion. **b** undisturbed by passion; serene. **2** without sensation. **3** not subject to suffering. □□ **impassively** *adv*. **impassiveness** *n*. **impassivity** /-ˈsɪvɪtɪ/ *n*.

impasto /ɪmˈpæstəʊ/ *n. Art* **1** the process of laying on paint thickly. **2** this technique of painting. [It. *impastare* (as IN-², *pastare* paste)]

impatiens /ɪmˈpeɪʃɪˌenz/ *n*. any plant of the genus *Impatiens*, including busy Lizzie and touch-me-not. [mod.L f. IMPATIENT]

impatient /ɪmˈpeɪʃ(ə)nt/ *adj*. **1 a** (often foll. by *at*, *with*) lacking patience or tolerance. **b** (of an action) showing a lack of patience. **2** (often foll. by *for*, or *to* + infin.) restlessly eager. **3** (foll. by *of*) intolerant. □□ **impatience** *n*. **impatiently** *adv*. [ME f. OF f. L *impatiens* (as IN-¹, PATIENT)]

impeach /ɪmˈpiːtʃ/ *v.tr*. **1** *Brit*. charge with a crime against the State, esp. treason. **2** *US* charge (the holder of a public office) with misconduct. **3** call in question, disparage (a person's integrity etc.). □□ **impeachable** *adj*. **impeachment** *n*. [ME f. OF *empecher* impede f. LL *impedicare* entangle (as IN-², *pedica* fetter f. *pes pedis* foot)]

impeccable /ɪmˈpekəb(ə)l/ *adj*. **1** (of behaviour, performance, etc.) faultless, exemplary. **2** not liable to sin. □□ **impeccability** /-ˈbɪlɪtɪ/ *n*. **impeccably** *adv*. [L *impeccabilis* (as IN-¹, *peccare* sin)]

impecunious /ˌɪmpɪˈkjuːnɪəs/ *adj*. having little or no money. □□ **impecuniosity** /-ˈɒsɪtɪ/ *n*. **impecuniousness** *n*. [IN-¹ + obs. *pecunious* having money f. L *pecuniosus* f. *pecunia* money f. *pecu* cattle]

impedance /ɪmˈpiːd(ə)ns/ *n*. **1** *Electr*. the total effective resistance of an electric circuit etc. to alternating current, arising from ohmic resistance and reactance. **2** an analogous mechanical property. [IMPEDE + -ANCE]

impede /ɪmˈpiːd/ *v.tr*. retard by obstructing; hinder. [L *impedire* shackle the feet of (as IN-², *pes* foot)]

impediment /ɪmˈpedɪmənt/ *n*. **1** a hindrance or obstruction. **2** a defect in speech, e.g. a lisp or stammer. □□ **impedimental** /-ˈment(ə)l/ *adj*. [ME f. L *impedimentum* (as IMPEDE)]

impedimenta /ɪmˌpedɪˈmentə/ *n.pl*. **1** encumbrances. **2** travelling equipment, esp. of an army. [L, pl. of *impedimentum*: see IMPEDIMENT]

impel /ɪmˈpel/ *v.tr*. (**impelled**, **impelling**) **1** drive, force, or urge into action. **2** drive forward; propel. □□ **impellent** *adj*. & *n*. **impeller** *n*. [ME f. L *impellere* (as IN-², *pellere puls-* drive)]

impend /ɪmˈpend/ *v.intr*. **1** be about to happen. **2** (often foll. by *over*) **a** (of a danger) be threatening. **b** hang; be suspended. □□ **impending** *adj*. [L *impendēre* (as IN-², *pendēre* hang)]

impenetrable /ɪmˈpenɪtrəb(ə)l/ *adj*. **1** that cannot be penetrated. **2** inscrutable, unfathomable. **3** inaccessible to ideas, influences, etc. **4** *Physics* (of matter) having the property such that a body is incapable of occupying the same place as another body at the same time. □□ **impenetrability** /-ˈbɪlɪtɪ/ *n*. **impenetrableness** *n*. **impenetrably** *adv*. [ME f. F *impénétrable* f. L *impenetrabilis* (as IN-¹, PENETRATE)]

impenitent /ɪmˈpenɪt(ə)nt/ *adj*. not repentant or penitent. □□ **impenitence** *n*. **impenitency** *n*. **impenitently** *adv*. [eccl.L *impaenitens* (as IN-¹, PENITENT)]

imperative /ɪmˈperətɪv/ *adj*. & *n*. —*adj*. **1** urgent. **2** obligatory. **3** commanding, peremptory. **4** *Gram*. (of a mood) expressing a command (e.g. *come here!*). —*n*. **1** *Gram*. the imperative mood. **2** a command. □□ **imperatival** /ɪmˌperəˈtaɪv(ə)l/ *adj*. **imperatively** *adv*. **imperativeness** *n*. [LL *imperativus* f. *imperare* command (as IN-², *parare* make ready)]

imperator /ˌɪmpəˈrɑːtɔː(r)/ *n. Rom.Hist*. commander (a title conferred under the Republic on a victorious general and under the Empire on the emperor). □□ **imperatorial** /ˌɪmperəˈtɔːrɪəl/ *adj*. [L (as IMPERATIVE)]

imperceptible /ˌɪmpəˈseptɪb(ə)l/ *adj*. **1** that cannot be perceived. **2** very slight, gradual, or subtle. □□ **imperceptibility** /-ˈbɪlɪtɪ/ *n*. **imperceptibly** *adv*. [F *imperceptible* or med.L *imperceptibilis* (as IN-¹, PERCEPTIBLE)]

impercipient /ˌɪmpəˈsɪpɪənt/ *adj*. lacking in perception. □□ **impercipience** *n*.

imperfect /ɪmˈpɜːfɪkt/ *adj*. & *n*. —*adj*. **1** not fully formed or done; faulty, incomplete. **2** *Gram*. (of a tense) denoting a (usu. past) action in progress but not completed at the time in question (e.g. *they were singing*). **3** *Mus*. (of a cadence) ending on the dominant chord. —*n*. the imperfect tense. □ **imperfect rhyme** *Prosody* a rhyme that only partly satisfies the usual criteria (e.g. *love* and *move*). □□ **imperfectly** *adv*. [ME *imparfit* etc. f. OF *imparfait* f. L *imperfectus* (as IN-¹, PERFECT)]

imperfection /ˌɪmpəˈfekʃ(ə)n/ *n*. **1** incompleteness. **2 a** faultiness. **b** a fault or blemish. [ME f. OF *imperfection* or LL *imperfectio* (as IMPERFECT)]

imperfective /ˌɪmpəˈfektɪv/ *adj*. & *n. Gram*. —*adj*. (of a verb aspect etc.) expressing an action without reference to its completion (opp. PERFECTIVE). —*n*. an imperfective aspect or form of a verb.

imperforate /ɪmˈpɜːfərət/ *adj*. **1** not perforated. **2** *Anat*. lacking the normal opening. **3** (of a postage stamp) lacking perforations.

imperial /ɪmˈpɪərɪəl/ *adj*. & *n*. —*adj*. **1** of or characteristic of an empire or comparable sovereign State. **2 a** of or characteristic of an emperor. **b** supreme in authority. **c** majestic, august. **d** magnificent. **3** (of non-metric weights and measures) used or formerly used by statute in the UK (*imperial gallon*). —*n*. a former size of paper, 762 × 559 mm (30 × 22 inches). □□ **imperially** *adv*. [ME f. OF f. L *imperialis* f. *imperium* command, authority]

imperialism /ɪmˈpɪərɪəˌlɪz(ə)m/ *n*. **1** an imperial rule or system. **2** usu. *derog*. a policy of acquiring dependent territories or extending a country's influence through trade, diplomacy, etc. □□ **imperialistic** /-ˈlɪstɪk/ *adj*. **imperialistically** /-ˈlɪstɪkəlɪ/ *adv*. **imperialize** *v.tr*. (also **-ise**).

imperialist /ɪmˈpɪərɪəlɪst/ *n. & adj. —n.* usu. *derog.* an advocate or agent of imperial rule or of imperialism. *—adj.* of or relating to imperialism or imperialists.

imperil /ɪmˈperɪl/ *v.tr.* (**imperilled, imperilling**; *US* **imperiled, imperiling**) bring or put into danger.

imperious /ɪmˈpɪərɪəs/ *adj.* **1** overbearing, domineering. **2** urgent, imperative. □□ **imperiously** *adv.* **imperiousness** *n.* [L *imperiosus* f. *imperium* command, authority]

imperishable /ɪmˈperɪʃəb(ə)l/ *adj.* that cannot perish. □□ **imperishability** /-ˈbɪlɪtɪ/ *n.* **imperishableness** *n.* **imperishably** *adv.*

imperium /ɪmˈpɪərɪəm, -ˈperɪəm/ *n.* absolute power or authority. [L, = command, authority]

impermanent /ɪmˈpɜːmənənt/ *adj.* not permanent; transient. □□ **impermanence** *n.* **impermanency** *n.* **impermanently** *adv.*

impermeable /ɪmˈpɜːmɪəb(ə)l/ *adj.* **1** that cannot be penetrated. **2** *Physics* that does not permit the passage of fluids. □□ **impermeability** /-ˈbɪlɪtɪ/ *n.* [F *imperméable* or LL *impermeabilis* (as IN-[1], PERMEABLE)]

impermissible /ˌɪmpəˈmɪsɪb(ə)l/ *adj.* not allowable. □□ **impermissibility** /-ˈbɪlɪtɪ/ *n.*

impersonal /ɪmˈpɜːsən(ə)l/ *adj.* **1** having no personality. **2** having no personal feeling or reference. **3** *Gram.* **a** (of a verb) used only with a formal subject (usu. *it*) and expressing an action not attributable to a definite subject (e.g. *it is snowing*). **b** (of a pronoun) = INDEFINITE. □□ **impersonality** /-ˈnælɪtɪ/ *n.* **impersonally** *adv.* [LL *impersonalis* (as IN-[1], PERSONAL)]

impersonate /ɪmˈpɜːsəˌneɪt/ *v.tr.* **1** pretend to be (another person) for the purpose of entertainment or fraud. **2** act (a character). □□ **impersonation** /-ˈneɪʃ(ə)n/ *n.* **impersonator** *n.* [IN-[2] + L *persona* PERSON]

impertinent /ɪmˈpɜːtɪnənt/ *adj.* **1** rude or insolent; lacking proper respect. **2** out of place; absurd. **3** esp. *Law* irrelevant, intrusive. □□ **impertinence** *n.* **impertinently** *adv.* [ME f. OF or LL *impertinens* (as IN-[1], PERTINENT)]

imperturbable /ˌɪmpəˈtɜːbəb(ə)l/ *adj.* not excitable; calm. □□ **imperturbability** /-ˈbɪlɪtɪ/ *n.* **imperturbableness** *n.* **imperturbably** *adv.* [ME f. LL *imperturbabilis* (as IN-[1], PERTURB)]

impervious /ɪmˈpɜːvɪəs/ *adj.* (usu. foll. by *to*) **1** not responsive to an argument etc. **2** not affording passage to a fluid. □□ **imperviously** *adv.* **imperviousness** *n.* [L *impervius* (as IN-[1], PERVIOUS)]

impetigo /ˌɪmpɪˈtaɪɡəʊ/ *n.* a contagious bacterial skin infection forming pustules and yellow crusty sores. □□ **impetiginous** /ˌɪmpɪˈtɪdʒɪnəs/ *adj.* [ME f. L *impetigo -ginis* f. *impetere* assail]

impetuous /ɪmˈpetjʊəs/ *adj.* **1** acting or done rashly or with sudden energy. **2** moving forcefully or rapidly. □□ **impetuosity** /-ˈɒsɪtɪ/ *n.* **impetuously** *adv.* **impetuousness** *n.* [ME f. OF *impetueux* f. LL *impetuosus* (as IMPETUS)]

impetus /ˈɪmpɪtəs/ *n.* **1** the force or energy with which a body moves. **2** a driving force or impulse. [L, = assault, force, f. *impetere* assail (as IN-[2], *petere* seek)]

impi /ˈɪmpɪ/ *n.* (*pl.* **impis**) *S.Afr.* **1** a band of armed men. **2** *hist.* an African tribal army or regiment. [Zulu, = regiment, armed band]

impiety /ɪmˈpaɪətɪ/ *n.* (*pl.* **-ies**) **1** a lack of piety or reverence. **2** an act etc. showing this. [ME f. OF *impieté* or L *impietas* (as IN-[1], PIETY)]

impinge /ɪmˈpɪndʒ/ *v.tr.* (usu. foll. by *on, upon*) **1** make an impact; have an effect. **2** encroach. □□ **impingement** *n.* **impinger** *n.* [L *impingere* drive (a thing) at (as IN-[2], *pangere* fix, drive)]

impious /ˈɪmpɪəs/ *adj.* **1** not pious. **2** wicked, profane. □□ **impiously** *adv.* **impiousness** *n.* [L *impius* (as IN-[1], PIOUS)]

impish /ˈɪmpɪʃ/ *adj.* of or like an imp; mischievous. □□ **impishly** *adv.* **impishness** *n.*

implacable /ɪmˈplækəb(ə)l/ *adj.* that cannot be appeased; inexorable. □□ **implacability** /-ˈbɪlɪtɪ/ *n.* **implacably** *adv.* [ME f. F *implacable* or L *implacabilis* (as IN-[1], PLACABLE)]

implant *v. & n. —v.tr.* /ɪmˈplɑːnt/ **1** (often foll. by *in*) insert or fix. **2** (often foll. by *in*) instil (a principle, idea, etc.) in a person's mind. **3** plant. **4** *Med.* **a** insert (tissue etc.) in a living body. **b** (in *passive*) (of a fertilized ovum) become attached to the wall of the womb. *—n.* /ˈɪmplɑːnt/ *n.* **1** a thing implanted. **2** a thing implanted in the body, e.g. a piece of tissue or a capsule containing material for radium therapy. □□ **implantation** /-ˈteɪʃ(ə)n/ *n.* [F *implanter* or LL *implantare* engraft (as IN-[2], PLANT)]

implausible /ɪmˈplɔːzɪb(ə)l/ *adj.* not plausible. □□ **implausibility** /-ˈbɪlɪtɪ/ *n.* **implausibly** *adv.*

implead /ɪmˈpliːd/ *v.tr. Law* **1** prosecute or take proceedings against (a person). **2** involve (a person etc.) in a suit. [ME f. AF *empleder*, OF *empleidier* (as EN-[1], PLEAD)]

implement *n. & v. —n.* /ˈɪmplɪmənt/ **1** a tool, instrument, or utensil. **2** (in *pl.*) equipment; articles of furniture, dress, etc. **3** *Law* performance of an obligation. *—v.tr.* /ˈɪmplɪˌment/ **1 a** put (a decision, plan, etc.) into effect. **b** fulfil (an undertaking). **2** complete (a contract etc.). **3** fill up; supplement. □□ **implementation** /ˌɪmplɪmenˈteɪʃ(ə)n/ *n.* [ME f. med.L *implementa* (pl.) f. *implēre* employ (as IN-[2], L *plēre plet-* fill)]

implicate *v. & n. —v.tr.* /ˈɪmplɪˌkeɪt/ **1** (often foll. by *in*) show (a person) to be concerned or involved (in a charge, crime, etc.). **2** (in *passive*; often foll. by *in*) be affected or involved. **3** lead to as a consequence or inference. *—n.* /ˈɪmplɪkət/ a thing implied. □□ **implicative** /ɪmˈplɪkətɪv/ *adj.* **implicatively** /ɪmˈplɪkətɪvlɪ/ *adv.* [L *implicatus* past part. of *implicare* (as IN-[2], *plicare, plicat-* or *plicit-* fold)]

implication /ˌɪmplɪˈkeɪʃ(ə)n/ *n.* **1** what is involved in or implied by something else. **2** the act of implicating or implying. □ **by implication** by what is implied or suggested rather than by formal expression. [ME f. L *implicatio* (as IMPLICATE)]

implicit /ɪmˈplɪsɪt/ *adj.* **1** implied though not plainly expressed. **2** (often foll. by *in*) virtually contained. **3** absolute, unquestioning, unreserved (*implicit obedience*). **4** *Math.* (of a function) not expressed directly in terms of independent variables. □□ **implicitly** *adv.* **implicitness** *n.* [F *implicite* or L *implicitus* (as IMPLICATE)]

implode /ɪmˈpləʊd/ *v.intr. & tr.* burst or cause to burst inwards. □□ **implosion** /ɪmˈpləʊʒ(ə)n/ *n.* **implosive** /-sɪv, -zɪv/ *adj.* [IN-[2] + L *-plodere*, after EXPLODE]

implore /ɪmˈplɔː(r)/ *v.tr.* **1** (often foll. by *to* + infin.) entreat (a person). **2** beg earnestly for. □□ **imploringly** *adv.* [F *implorer* or L *implorare* invoke with tears (as IN-[2], *plorare* weep)]

imply /ɪmˈplaɪ/ *v.tr.* (**-ies, -ied**) **1** (often foll. by *that* + clause) strongly suggest the truth or existence of (a thing not expressly asserted). **2** insinuate, hint (*what are you implying?*). **3** signify. □□ **implied** *adj.* **impliedly** *adv.* [ME f. OF *emplier* f. L *implicare* (as IMPLICATE)]

impolder /ɪmˈpəʊldə(r)/ *v.tr.* (also **empolder**) *Brit.* **1** make a polder of. **2** reclaim from the sea. [Du. *inpolderen* (as IN-[2], POLDER)]

impolite /ˌɪmpəˈlaɪt/ *adj.* (**impolitest**) ill-mannered, uncivil, rude. □□ **impolitely** *adv.* **impoliteness** *n.* [L *impolitus* (as IN-[1], POLITE)]

impolitic /ɪmˈpɒlɪtɪk/ *adj.* **1** inexpedient, unwise. **2** not politic. □□ **impoliticly** *adv.*

imponderable /ɪmˈpɒndərəb(ə)l/ *adj. & n. —adj.* **1** that cannot be estimated or assessed in any definite way. **2** very light. **3** *Physics* having no weight. *—n.* (usu. in *pl.*) something difficult or impossible to assess. □□ **imponderability** /-'bɪlɪtɪ/ n. **imponderably** adv.

import v. & n. —v.tr. /ɪm'pɔːt, 'ɪm-/ **1** bring in (esp. foreign goods or services) to a country. **2** (often foll. by that + clause) **a** imply, indicate, signify. **b** express, make known. —n. /'ɪmpɔːt/ **1** the process of importing. **2 a** an imported article or service. **b** (in pl.) an amount imported (imports exceeded £50m.). **3** what is implied; meaning. **4** importance. □□ **importable** /ɪm'pɔːtəb(ə)l/ adj. **importation** /ˌɪmpɔː'teɪʃ(ə)n/ n. **importer** /ɪm'pɔːtə(r)/ n. (all in sense 1 of v.). [ME f. L importare bring in, in med.L = imply, be of consequence (as IN-², portare carry)]

importance /ɪm'pɔːt(ə)ns/ n. **1** the state of being important. **2** weight, significance. **3** personal consequence; dignity. [F f. med.L importantia (as IMPORT)]

important /ɪm'pɔːt(ə)nt/ adj. **1** (often foll. by to) of great effect or consequence; momentous. **2** (of a person) having high rank or status, or great authority. **3** pretentious, pompous. **4** (absol. in parenthetic construction) what is a more important point or matter (they are willing and, more important, able). ¶ Use of importantly here is disp. □□ **importantly** adv. (see note above). [F f. med.L (as IMPORT)]

importunate /ɪm'pɔːtjʊnət/ adj. **1** making persistent or pressing requests. **2** (of affairs) urgent. □□ **importunately** adv. **importunity** /ˌɪmpɔː'tjuːnɪtɪ/ n. [L importunus inconvenient (as IN-¹, portunus f. portus harbour)]

importune /ɪm'pɔːtjuːn, -'tjuːn/ v.tr. **1** solicit (a person) pressingly. **2** solicit for an immoral purpose. [F importuner or med.L importunari (as IMPORTUNATE)]

impose /ɪm'pəʊz/ v. **1** tr. (often foll. by on, upon) require (a tax, duty, charge, or obligation) to be paid or undertaken (by a person etc.). **2** tr. enforce compliance with. **3** intr. & refl. (foll. by on, upon, or absol.) demand the attention or commitment of (a person); take advantage of (I do not want to impose on you any longer; I did not want to impose). **4** tr. (often foll. by on, upon) palm (a thing) off on (a person). **5** tr. Printing lay (pages of type) in the proper order ready for printing. **6** intr. (foll. by on, upon) exert influence by an impressive character or appearance. **7** intr. (often foll. by on, upon) practise deception. **8** tr. archaic (foll. by upon) place (a thing). [ME f. F imposer f. L imponere imposit- inflict, deceive (as IN-², ponere put)]

imposing /ɪm'pəʊzɪŋ/ adj. impressive, formidable, esp. in appearance. □□ **imposingly** adv. **imposingness** n.

imposition /ˌɪmpə'zɪʃ(ə)n/ n. **1** the act or an instance of imposing; the process of being imposed. **2** an unfair or resented demand or burden. **3** a tax or duty. **4** Brit. work set as a punishment at school. [ME f. OF imposition or L impositio f. imponere: see IMPOSE]

impossibility /ɪmˌpɒsɪ'bɪlɪtɪ/ n. (pl. -ies) **1** the fact or condition of being impossible. **2** an impossible thing or circumstance. [F impossibilité or L impossibilitas (as IMPOSSIBLE)]

impossible /ɪm'pɒsɪb(ə)l/ adj. **1** not possible; that cannot occur, exist, or be done (such a thing is impossible; it is impossible to alter them). **2** (loosely) not easy; not convenient; not easily believable. **3** colloq. (of a person or thing) outrageous, intolerable. □□ **impossibly** adv. [ME f. OF impossible or L impossibilis (as IN-¹, POSSIBLE)]

impost¹ /'ɪmpəʊst/ n. **1** a tax, duty, or tribute. **2** a weight carried by a horse in a handicap race. [F f. med.L impost- part. stem of L imponere: see IMPOSE]

impost² /'ɪmpəʊst/ n. the upper course of a pillar, carrying an arch. [F imposte or It. imposta fem. past part. of imporre f. L imponere: see IMPOSE]

impostor /ɪm'pɒstə(r)/ n. (also **imposter**) **1** a person who assumes a false character or pretends to be someone else. **2** a swindler. □□ **impostorous** adj.

impostrous adj. [F imposteur f. LL impostor (as IMPOST¹)]

imposture /ɪm'pɒstʃə(r)/ n. the act or an instance of fraudulent deception. [F f. LL impostura (as IMPOST¹)]

impotent /'ɪmpət(ə)nt/ adj. **1 a** powerless; lacking all strength. **b** helpless, decrepit. **2** (esp. of a male) unable, esp. for a prolonged period, to achieve a sexual erection or orgasm. □□ **impotence** n. **impotency** n. **impotently** adv. [ME f. OF f. L impotens (as IN-¹, POTENT¹)]

impound /ɪm'paʊnd/ v.tr. **1** confiscate. **2** take possession of. **3** shut up (animals) in a pound. **4** shut up (a person or thing) as in a pound. **5** (of a dam etc.) collect or confine (water). □□ **impoundable** adj. **impounder** n. **impoundment** n.

impoverish /ɪm'pɒvərɪʃ/ v.tr. **1** make poor. **2** exhaust the strength or natural fertility of. □□ **impoverishment** n. [ME f. OF empoverir (as EN-¹, povre POOR)]

impracticable /ɪm'præktɪkəb(ə)l/ adj. **1** impossible in practice. **2** (of a road etc.) impassable. **3** (of a person or thing) unmanageable. □□ **impracticability** /-'bɪlɪtɪ/ n. **impracticableness** n. **impracticably** adv.

impractical /ɪm'præktɪk(ə)l/ adj. **1** not practical. **2** esp. US not practicable. □□ **impracticality** /-'kælɪtɪ/ n. **impractically** adv.

imprecate /'ɪmprɪˌkeɪt/ v.tr. (often foll. by upon) invoke, call down (evil). □□ **imprecatory** adj. [L imprecari (as IN-², precari pray)]

imprecation /ˌɪmprɪ'keɪʃ(ə)n/ n. **1** a spoken curse; a malediction. **2** imprecating.

imprecise /ˌɪmprɪ'saɪs/ adj. not precise. □□ **imprecisely** adv. **impreciseness** n. **imprecision** /-'sɪʒ(ə)n/ n.

impregnable¹ /ɪm'pregnəb(ə)l/ adj. **1** (of a fortified position) that cannot be taken by force. **2** resistant to attack or criticism. □□ **impregnability** /-'bɪlɪtɪ/ n. **impregnably** adv. [ME f. OF imprenable (as IN-¹, prendre take)]

impregnable² /ɪm'pregnəb(ə)l/ adj. that can be impregnated.

impregnate v. & adj. —v.tr. /'ɪmpregˌneɪt/ **1** (often foll. by with) fill or saturate. **2** (often foll. by with) imbue (with feelings, moral qualities, etc.). **3 a** make (a female) pregnant. **b** Biol. fertilize (a female reproductive cell or ovum). —adj. /ɪm'pregnət/ **1** pregnant. **2** (often foll. by with) permeated. □□ **impregnation** /ˌɪmpreg'neɪʃ(ə)n/ n. [LL impregnare impregnat- (as IN-², pregnare be pregnant)]

impresario /ˌɪmprɪ'sɑːrɪəʊ/ n. (pl. -os) an organizer of public entertainments, esp. the manager of an operatic, theatrical, or concert company. [It. f. impresa undertaking]

imprescriptible /ˌɪmprɪ'skrɪptɪb(ə)l/ adj. Law (of rights) that cannot be taken away by prescription or lapse of time. [med.L imprescriptibilis (as IN-¹, PRESCRIBE)]

impress¹ v. & n. —v.tr. /ɪm'pres/ **1** (often foll. by with) **a** affect or influence deeply. **b** evoke a favourable opinion or reaction from (a person) (was most impressed with your efforts). **2** (often foll. by on) emphasize (an idea etc.) (must impress on you the need to be prompt). **3** (often foll. by on) **a** imprint or stamp. **b** apply (a mark etc.) with pressure. **4** make a mark or design on (a thing) with a stamp, seal, etc. **5** Electr. apply (voltage etc.) from outside. —n. /'ɪmpres/ **1** the act or an instance of impressing. **2** a mark made by a seal, stamp, etc. **3** a characteristic mark or quality. **4** = IMPRESSION 1. □□ **impressible** /ɪm'presɪb(ə)l/ adj. [ME f. OF empresser (as EN-¹, PRESS¹)]

impress² /ɪm'pres/ v.tr. hist. **1** force (men) to serve in the army or navy. **2** seize (goods etc.) for public service. □□ **impressment** n. [IN-² + PRESS²]

impression /ɪm'preʃ(ə)n/ n. **1** an effect produced (esp. on the mind or feelings). **2** a notion or belief (esp. a vague or mistaken one) (my impression is they *are afraid*). **3** an imitation of a person or sound, esp. done to entertain. **4 a** the impressing of a mark. **b** a mark impressed. **5** an unaltered reprint from standing type or plates (esp. as distinct from *edition*). **6 a** the number of copies of a book, newspaper, etc., issued at one time. **b** the printing of these. **7** a print taken from a wood engraving. **8** *Dentistry* a negative copy of the teeth or mouth made by pressing them into a soft substance. □□ **impressional** *adj.* [ME f. OF f. L *impressio -onis* f. *imprimere impress-* (as IN-², PRESS¹)]

impressionable /ɪmˈpreʃənəb(ə)l/ *adj.* easily influenced; susceptible to impressions. □□ **impressionability** /-ˈbɪlɪtɪ/ *n.* **impressionably** *adv.* [F *impressionnable* f. *impressionner* (as IMPRESSION)]

impressionism /ɪmˈpreʃə,nɪz(ə)m/ *n.* **1** a style or movement in art concerned with expression of feeling by visual impression, esp. from the effect of light on objects. **2** a style of music or writing that seeks to describe a feeling or experience rather than achieve accurate depiction or systematic structure. □□ **impressionist** *n.* [F *impressionnisme* (after *Impression: Soleil levant*, title of a painting by Monet, 1872)]

impressionistic /ɪm,preʃəˈnɪstɪk/ *adj.* **1** in the style of impressionism. **2** subjective, unsystematic. □□ **impressionistically** *adv.*

impressive /ɪmˈpresɪv/ *adj.* **1** impressing the mind or senses, esp. so as to cause approval or admiration. **2** (of language, a scene, etc.) tending to excite deep feeling. □□ **impressively** *adv.* **impressiveness** *n.*

imprest /ˈɪmprest/ *n.* money advanced to a person for use in State business. [orig. *in prest* f. OF *prest* loan, advance pay: see PRESS²]

imprimatur /,ɪmprɪˈmeɪtə(r), -ˈmɑːtə(r), -tʊə(r)/ *n.* **1** RC Ch. an official licence to print (an ecclesiastical or religious book etc.). **2** official approval. [L, = let it be printed]

imprimatura /ɪm,priːməˈtʊərə/ *n.* (in painting) a coloured transparent glaze as a primer. [It. *imprimitura* f. *imprimere* IMPRESS¹]

imprint *v. & n. —v.tr.* /ɪmˈprɪnt/ **1** (often foll. by *on*) impress or establish firmly, esp. on the mind. **2 a** (often foll. by *on*) make a stamp or impression of (a figure etc.) on a thing. **b** make an impression on (a thing) with a stamp etc. *—n.* /ˈɪmprɪnt/ **1** an impression or stamp. **2** the printer's or publisher's name and other details printed in a book. [ME f. OF *empreinter empreint* f. L *imprimere*: see IMPRESSION]

imprinting /ɪmˈprɪntɪŋ/ *n.* **1** in senses of IMPRINT *v.* **2** *Zool.* the development in a young animal of a pattern of recognition and trust for its own species.

imprison /ɪmˈprɪz(ə)n/ *v.tr.* **1** put into prison. **2** confine; shut up. □□ **imprisonment** *n.* [ME f. OF *emprisoner* (as EN-¹, PRISON)]

improbable /ɪmˈprɒbəb(ə)l/ *adj.* **1** not likely to be true or to happen. **2** difficult to believe. □□ **improbability** /-ˈbɪlɪtɪ/ *n.* **improbably** *adv.* [F *improbable* or L *improbabilis* (as IN-¹, PROBABLE)]

improbity /ɪmˈprəʊbɪtɪ/ *n.* (*pl.* -ies) **1** wickedness; lack of moral integrity. **2** dishonesty. **3** a wicked or dishonest act. [L *improbitas* (as IN-¹, PROBITY)]

impromptu /ɪmˈprɒmptjuː/ *adj., adv., & n. —adj. & adv.* extempore, unrehearsed. *—n.* **1** an extempore performance or speech. **2** a short piece of usu. solo instrumental music, often songlike. [F f. L *in promptu* in readiness: see PROMPT]

improper /ɪmˈprɒpə(r)/ *adj.* **1** unseemly; indecent. **b** not in accordance with accepted rules of behaviour. **2** inaccurate, wrong. **3** not properly so called. □ **improper fraction** a fraction in which the numerator is greater than or equal to the denominator. □□ **improperly** *adv.* [F *impropre* or L *improprius* (as IN-¹, PROPER)]

impropriate /ɪmˈprəʊprɪ,eɪt/ *v.tr. Brit.* **1** annex (an ecclesiastical benefice) to a corporation or person as property. **2** place (tithes or ecclesiastical property)

in lay hands. □□ **impropriation** /-ˈeɪʃ(ə)n/ *n.* [AL *impropriare* (as IN-², *proprius* own)]

impropriator /ɪmˈprəʊprɪ,eɪtə(r)/ *n. Brit.* a person to whom a benefice is impropriated.

impropriety /,ɪmprəˈpraɪətɪ/ *n.* (*pl.* -ies) **1** lack of propriety; indecency. **2** an instance of improper conduct etc. **3** incorrectness. **4** unfitness. [F *impropriété* or L *improprietas* (as IN-¹, *proprius* proper)]

improvable /ɪmˈpruːvəb(ə)l/ *adj.* **1** that can be improved. **2** suitable for cultivation. □□ **improvability** /-ˈbɪlɪtɪ/ *n.*

improve /ɪmˈpruːv/ *v.* **1 a** *tr. & intr.* make or become better. **b** *intr.* (foll. by *on*) produce something better than. **2** *absol.* (as **improving** *adj.*) giving moral benefit (*improving literature*). [orig. *emprowe, improwe* f. AF *emprower* f. OF *emprou* f. *prou* profit, infl. by PROVE]

improvement /ɪmˈpruːvmənt/ *n.* **1** the act or an instance of improving or being improved. **2** something that improves, esp. an addition or alteration that adds to value. **3** something that has been improved. [ME f. AF *emprowement* (as IMPROVE)]

improver /ɪmˈpruːvə(r)/ *n.* **1** a person who improves. **2** *Brit.* a person who works for low wages while acquiring skill and experience in a trade.

improvident /ɪmˈprɒvɪd(ə)nt/ *adj.* **1** lacking foresight or care for the future. **2** not frugal; thriftless. **3** heedless, incautious. □□ **improvidence** *n.* **improvidently** *adv.*

improvise /ˈɪmprə,vaɪz/ *v.tr.* (also *absol.*) **1** compose or perform (music, verse, etc.) extempore. **2** provide or construct (a thing) extempore. □□ **improvisation** /-ˈzeɪʃ(ə)n/ *n.* **improvisational** /-ˈzeɪʃən(ə)l/ *adj.* **improvisatorial** /-zəˈtɔːrɪəl/ *adj.* **improvisatory** /-ˈzeɪtərɪ/ *adj.* **improviser** *n.* [F *improviser* or It. *improvvisare* f. *improvviso* extempore, f. L *improvisus* past part. (as IN-¹, PROVIDE)]

imprudent /ɪmˈpruːd(ə)nt/ *adj.* rash, indiscreet. □□ **imprudence** *n.* **imprudently** *adv.* [ME f. L *imprudens* (as IN-¹, PRUDENT)]

impudent /ˈɪmpjʊd(ə)nt/ *adj.* **1** insolently disrespectful; impertinent. **2** shamelessly presumptuous. **3** unblushing. □□ **impudence** *n.* **impudently** *adv.* [ME f. L *impudens* (as IN-¹, *pudēre* be ashamed)]

impudicity /,ɪmpjʊˈdɪsɪtɪ/ *n.* shamelessness, immodesty. [F *impudicité* f. L *impudicus* (as IMPUDENT)]

impugn /ɪmˈpjuːn/ *v.tr.* challenge or call in question (a statement, action, etc.). □□ **impugnable** *adj.* **impugnment** *n.* [ME f. L *impugnare* assail (as IN-², *pugnare* fight)]

impuissant /ɪmˈpjuːɪs(ə)nt/ *adj.* impotent, weak. □□ **impuissance** *n.* [F (as IN-¹, PUISSANT)]

impulse /ˈɪmpʌls/ *n.* **1** the act or an instance of impelling; a push. **2** an impetus. **3** *Physics* **a** an indefinitely large force acting for a very short time but producing a finite change of momentum (e.g. the blow of a hammer). **b** the change of momentum produced by this or any force. **4** a wave of excitation in a nerve. **5** mental incitement. **6** a sudden desire or tendency to act without reflection (*did it on impulse*). □ **impulse buying** the unpremeditated buying of goods as a result of a whim or impulse. [L *impulsus* (as IMPEL)]

impulsion /ɪmˈpʌlʃ(ə)n/ *n.* **1** the act or an instance of impelling. **2** a mental impulse. **3** impetus. [ME f. OF f. L *impulsio -onis* (as IMPEL)]

impulsive /ɪmˈpʌlsɪv/ *adj.* **1** (of a person or conduct etc.) apt to be affected or determined by sudden impulse. **2** tending to impel. **3** *Physics* acting as an impulse. □□ **impulsively** *adv.* **impulsiveness** *n.* [ME f. F *impulsif -ive* or LL *impulsivus* (as IMPULSION)]

impunity /ɪmˈpjuːnɪtɪ/ *n.* exemption from punishment or from the injurious consequences of an action. □ **with impunity** without having to suffer the normal injurious consequences (of an action). [L *impunitas* f. *impunis* (as IN-¹, *poena* penalty)]

impure /ɪmˈpjʊə(r)/ *adj.* **1** mixed with foreign matter; adulterated. **2** dirty. **3** unchaste. **4** (of a colour)

mixed with another colour. □□**impurely** *adv.*
impureness *n.* [ME f. L *impurus* (as IN-[1], *purus*
pure)]
impurity /ɪmˈpjʊərɪtɪ/ *n.* (*pl.* **-ies**) **1** the quality or
condition of being impure. **2** an impure thing or
constituent. [F *impurité* or L *impuritas* (as IMPURE)]
impute /ɪmˈpjuːt/ *v.tr.* (foll. by *to*) **1** regard (esp.
something undesirable) as being done or caused or
possessed by. **2** *Theol.* ascribe (righteousness, guilt,
etc.) to (a person) by virtue of a similar quality in
another. □□**imputable** *adj.* **imputation** /-ˈteɪʃ(ə)n/
n. **imputative** /-tətɪv/ *adj.* [ME f. OF *imputer* f. L
imputare enter in the account (as IN-[2], *putare* reckon)]
I.Mun.E. *abbr.* (in the UK) Institution of Municipal
Engineers.
IN *abbr. US* Indiana (in official postal use).
In *symb. Chem.* the element indium.
in /ɪn/ *prep., adv., & adj.* —*prep.* **1** expressing
inclusion or position within limits of space, time,
circumstance, etc. (*in England; in bed; in the rain*). **2**
during the time of (*in the night; in 1989*). **3** within the
time of (*will be back in two hours*). **4 a** with respect
to (*blind in one eye; good in parts*). **b** as a kind of (*the
latest thing in luxury*). **5** as a proportionate part of
(*one in three failed; a gradient of one in six*). **6** with
the form or arrangement of (*packed in tens; falling
in folds*). **7** as a member of (*in the army*). **8** concerned
with (*is in politics*). **9** as or regarding the content of
(*there is something in what you say*). **10** within the
ability of (*does he have it in him?*). **11** having the
condition of; affected by (*in bad health; in danger*).
12 having as a purpose (*in search of; in reply to*). **13**
by means of or using as material (*drawn in pencil;
modelled in bronze*). **14 a** using as the language of
expression (*written in French*). **b** (of music) having
as its key (*symphony in C*). **15** (of a word) having as a
beginning or ending (*words in un-*). **16** wearing as
dress (*in blue; in a suit*). **17** with the identity of
(*found a friend in Mary*). **18** (of an animal) pregnant
with (*in calf*). **19** into (with a verb of motion or
change: *put it in the box; cut it in two*). **20** introducing
an indirect object after a verb (*believe in; engage in;
share in*). **21** forming adverbial phrases (*in any case;
in reality; in short*). —*adv.* expressing position within
limits, or motion to such a position: **1** into a room,
house, etc. (*come in*). **2** at home, in one's office, etc.
(*is not in*). **3** so as to be enclosed or confined (*locked
in*). **4** in a publication (*is the advertisement in?*). **5** in
or to the inward side (*rub it in*). **6 a** in fashion,
season, or office (*long skirts are in; strawberries are
not yet in*). **b** elected (*the Democrat got in*). **7** exerting
favourable action or influence (*their luck was in*). **8**
Cricket (of a player or side) batting. **9** (of transport)
at the platform etc. (*the train is in*). **10** (of a season,
harvest, order, etc.) having arrived or been received.
11 *Brit.* (of a fire) continuing to burn. **12** denoting
effective action (*join in*). **13** (of the tide) at the highest
point. **14** (in *comb.*) *colloq.* denoting prolonged or
concerted action, esp. by large numbers (*sit-in; teach-
in*). —*adj.* **1** internal; living in; inside (*in-patient*). **2**
fashionable, esoteric (*the in thing to do*). **3** confined
to or shared by a group of people (*in-joke*). □**in all**
see ALL. **in at** present at; contributing to (*in at the
kill*). **in between** see BETWEEN *adv.* **in-between** *adj.*
attrib.adj. colloq. intermediate (*at an in-between
stage*). **in for 1** about to undergo (esp. something
unpleasant). **2** competing in or for. **3** involved in;
committed to. **in on** sharing in; privy to (a secret
etc.). **ins and outs** (often foll. by *of*) all the details
(of a procedure etc.). **in so far as** see FAR. **in that**
because; in so far as. **in with** on good terms with.
[OE *in, inn,* orig. as adv. with verbs of motion]
in. *abbr.* inch(es).
in-[1] /ɪn/ *prefix* (also **il-, im-, ir-**) added to: **1** adjectives,
meaning 'not' (*inedible; insane*). **2** nouns, meaning
'without, lacking' (*inaction*). [L]
in-[2] /ɪn/ *prefix* (also **il-** before *l*, **im-** before *b, m, p,* **ir-**

before *r*) in, on, into, towards, within (*induce; influx;
insight; intrude*). [IN, or from or after L *in* in IN *prep.*]
-in /ɪn/ *suffix Chem.* forming names of: **1** neutral
substances (*gelatin*). **2** antibiotics (*penicillin*). [-INE[4]]
-ina /ˈiːnə/ *suffix* denoting: **1** feminine names and titles
(*Georgina; tsarina*). **2** names of musical instruments
(*concertina*). **3** names of zoological classification
categories (*globigerina*). [It. or Sp. or L]
inability /ˌɪnəˈbɪlɪtɪ/ *n.* **1** the state of being unable. **2**
a lack of power or means.
in absentia /ˌɪn æbˈsentɪə/ *adv.* in (his, her, or their)
absence. [L]
inaccessible /ˌɪnækˈsesɪb(ə)l/ *adj.* **1** not accessible;
that cannot be reached. **2** (of a person) not open
to advances or influence; unapproachable. □□
inaccessibility /-ˈbɪlɪtɪ/ *n.* **inaccessibleness** *n.*
inaccessibly *adv.* [ME f. F *inaccessible* or LL *in-
accessibilis* (as IN-[1], ACCESSIBLE)]
inaccurate /ɪnˈækjʊrət/ *adj.* not accurate. □□
inaccuracy *n.* (*pl.* **-ies**). **inaccurately** *adv.*
inaction /ɪnˈækʃ(ə)n/ *n.* **1** lack of action. **2** sluggishness, inertness.
inactivate /ɪnˈæktɪˌveɪt/ *v.tr.* make inactive or
inoperative. □□**inactivation** /-ˈveɪʃ(ə)n/ *n.*
inactive /ɪnˈæktɪv/ *adj.* **1** not active or inclined
to act. **2** passive. **3** indolent. □□**inactively** *adv.*
inactivity /-ˈtɪvɪtɪ/ *n.*
inadequate /ɪnˈædɪkwət/ *adj.* (often foll. by *to*) **1** not
adequate; insufficient. **2** (of a person) incompetent;
unable to deal with a situation. □□**inadequacy** *n.*
(*pl.* **-ies**). **inadequately** *adv.*
inadmissible /ˌɪnədˈmɪsɪb(ə)l/ *adj.* that cannot be
admitted or allowed. □□**inadmissibility** /-ˈbɪlɪtɪ/ *n.*
inadmissibly *adv.*
inadvertent /ˌɪnədˈvɜːt(ə)nt/ *adj.* **1** (of an action)
unintentional. **2 a** not properly attentive. **b** negligent. □□**inadvertence** *n.* **inadvertency** *n.*
inadvertently *adv.* [IN-[1] + obs. *advertent* attentive
(as ADVERT[2])]
inadvisable /ˌɪnədˈvaɪzəb(ə)l/ *adj.* not advisable. □□
inadvisability /-ˈbɪlɪtɪ/ *n.* [ADVISABLE]
inalienable /ɪnˈeɪlɪənəb(ə)l/ *adj.* that cannot be
transferred to another; not alienable. □□
inalienability /-ˈbɪlɪtɪ/ *n.* **inalienably** *adv.*
inalterable /ɪnˈɒltərəb(ə)l/ *adj.* not alterable; that
cannot be changed. □□**inalterability** /-ˈbɪlɪtɪ/ *n.*
inalterably *adv.* [med.L *inalterabilis* (as IN-[1], *alter-
abilis* alterable)]
inamorato /ɪnˌæməˈrɑːtəʊ/ *n.* (*pl.* **-os**; *fem.*
inamorata /-tə/) a lover. [It., past part. of *inamorare*
enamour (as IN-[2], *amore* f. L *amor* love)]
inane /ɪˈneɪn/ *adj.* **1** silly, senseless. **2** empty, void.
□□**inanely** *adv.* **inaneness** *n.* **inanity** /-ˈænɪtɪ/ *n.*
(*pl.* **-ies**). [L *inanis* empty, vain]
inanimate /ɪnˈænɪmət/ *adj.* **1** destitute of life. **2**
not endowed with animal life. **3** spiritless, dull.
□**inanimate nature** everything other than the animal world. □□**inanimately** *adv.* **inanimation**
/-ˈmeɪʃ(ə)n/ *n.* [LL *inanimatus* (as IN-[1], ANIMATE)]
inanition /ˌɪnəˈnɪʃ(ə)n/ *n.* emptiness, esp. exhaustion
from lack of nourishment. [ME f. LL *inanitio* f. L
inanire make empty (as INANE)]
inappellable /ˌɪnəˈpeləb(ə)l/ *adj.* that cannot be
appealed against. [obs.F *inappelable* (as IN-[1], *appeler*
APPEAL)]
inapplicable /ɪnˈæplɪkəb(ə)l, ˌɪnəˈplɪk-/ *adj.* (often
foll. by *to*) not applicable; unsuitable. □□
inapplicability /-ˈbɪlɪtɪ/ *n.* **inapplicably** *adv.*
inapposite /ɪnˈæpəzɪt/ *adj.* not apposite; out of place.
□□**inappositely** *adv.* **inappositeness** *n.*
inappreciable /ˌɪnəˈpriːʃəb(ə)l/ *adj.* **1** imperceptible;
not worth reckoning. **2** that cannot be appreciated.
□□**inappreciably** *adv.*
inappreciation /ˌɪnəˌpriːʃɪˈeɪʃ(ə)n/ *n.* failure to
appreciate. □□**inappreciative** /-ˈpriːʃətɪv/ *adj.*
inappropriate /ˌɪnəˈprəʊprɪət/ *adj.* not appropriate.
□□**inappropriately** *adv.* **inappropriateness** *n.*

inapt /ɪnˈæpt/ adj. **1** not apt or suitable. **2** unskilful. □□ **inaptitude** n. **inaptly** adv. **inaptness** n.

inarch /ɪnˈɑːtʃ/ v.tr. graft (a plant) by connecting a growing branch without separation from the parent stock. [IN-² + ARCH¹ v.]

inarguable /ɪnˈɑːgjʊəb(ə)l/ adj. that cannot be argued about or disputed. □□ **inarguably** adv.

inarticulate /ˌɪnɑːˈtɪkjʊlət/ adj. **1** unable to speak distinctly or express oneself clearly. **2** (of speech) not articulate; indistinctly pronounced. **3** dumb. **4** esp. Anat. not jointed. □□ **inarticulately** adv. **inarticulateness** n. [LL inarticulatus (as IN-¹, ARTICULATE)]

inartistic /ˌɪnɑːˈtɪstɪk/ adj. **1** not following the principles of art. **2** lacking skill or talent in art; not appreciating art. □□ **inartistically** adv.

inasmuch /ˌɪnəzˈmʌtʃ/ adv. (foll. by as) **1** since, because. **2** to the extent that. [ME, orig. in as much]

inattentive /ˌɪnəˈtentɪv/ adj. **1** not paying due attention; heedless. **2** neglecting to show courtesy. □□ **inattention** n. **inattentively** adv. **inattentiveness** n.

inaudible /ɪnˈɔːdɪb(ə)l/ adj. that cannot be heard. □□ **inaudibility** /-ˈbɪlɪtɪ/ n. **inaudibly** adv.

inaugural /ɪˈnɔːgjʊr(ə)l/ adj. & n. —adj. **1** of inauguration. **2** (of a lecture etc.) given by a person being inaugurated. —n. an inaugural speech etc. [F f. inaugurer (as INAUGURATE)]

inaugurate /ɪˈnɔːgjʊˌreɪt/ v.tr. **1** admit (a person) formally to office. **2** initiate the public use of (a building etc.). **3** begin, introduce. **4** enter with ceremony upon (an undertaking etc.). □□ **inauguration** /-ˈreɪʃ(ə)n/ n. **inaugurator** n. **inauguratory** adj. [L inaugurare (as IN-², augurare take omens: see AUGUR)]

inauspicious /ˌɪnɔːˈspɪʃəs/ adj. **1** ill-omened, unpropitious. **2** unlucky. □□ **inauspiciously** adv. **inauspiciousness** n.

inboard /ˈɪnbɔːd/ adv. & adj. —adv. within the sides of or towards the centre of a ship, aircraft, or vehicle. —adj. situated inboard.

inborn /ˈɪnbɔːn/ adj. existing from birth; implanted by nature.

inbreathe /ɪnˈbriːð/ v.tr. **1** breathe in or absorb. **2** inspire (a person).

inbred /ɪnˈbred, ˈɪn-/ adj. **1** inborn. **2** produced by inbreeding.

inbreeding /ɪnˈbriːdɪŋ/ n. breeding from closely related animals or persons. □□ **inbreed** v.tr. & intr. (past and past part. **inbred**).

inbuilt /ˈɪnbɪlt/ adj. incorporated as part of a structure.

Inc. abbr. US Incorporated.

Inca /ˈɪŋkə/ n. a member of an American Indian people in Peru before the Spanish conquest. □□ **Incaic** /ɪŋˈkeɪɪk/ adj. **Incan** adj. [Quechua, = lord, royal person]

incalculable /ɪnˈkælkjʊləb(ə)l/ adj. **1** too great for calculation. **2** that cannot be reckoned beforehand. **3** (of a person, character, etc.) uncertain. □□ **incalculability** /-ˈbɪlɪtɪ/ n. **incalculably** adv.

in camera see CAMERA.

incandesce /ˌɪnkænˈdes/ v.intr. & tr. glow or cause to glow with heat. [back-form. f. INCANDESCENT]

incandescent /ˌɪnkænˈdes(ə)nt/ adj. **1** glowing with heat. **2** shining brightly. **3** (of an electric or other light) produced by a glowing white-hot filament. □□ **incandescence** n. **incandescently** adv. [F f. L incandescere (as IN-², candescere inceptive of candēre be white)]

incantation /ˌɪnkænˈteɪʃ(ə)n/ n. **1 a** a magical formula. **b** the use of this. **2** a spell or charm. □□ **incantational** adj. **incantatory** adj. [ME f. OF f. LL incantatio -onis f. incantare chant, bewitch (as IN-², cantare sing)]

incapable /ɪnˈkeɪpəb(ə)l/ adj. **1** (often foll. by of) **a** not capable. **b** lacking the required quality or characteristic (favourable or adverse) (incapable of hurting anyone). **2** not capable of rational conduct or of managing one's own affairs (drunk and incapable). □□ **incapability** /-ˈbɪlɪtɪ/ n. **incapably** adv. [F incapable or LL incapabilis (as IN-¹, capabilis CAPABLE)]

incapacitate /ˌɪnkəˈpæsɪˌteɪt/ v.tr. **1** render incapable or unfit. **2** disqualify. □□ **incapacitant** n. **incapacitation** /-ˈteɪʃ(ə)n/ n.

incapacity /ˌɪnkəˈpæsɪtɪ/ n. (pl. **-ies**) **1** inability; lack of the necessary power or resources. **2** legal disqualification. **3** an instance of incapacity. [F incapacité or LL incapacitas (as IN-¹, CAPACITY)]

incarcerate /ɪnˈkɑːsəˌreɪt/ v.tr. imprison or confine. □□ **incarceration** /-ˈreɪʃ(ə)n/ n. **incarcerator** n. [med.L incarcerare (as IN-², L carcer prison)]

incarnadine /ɪnˈkɑːnəˌdaɪn/ adj. & v. poet. —adj. flesh-coloured or crimson. —v.tr. dye this colour. [F incarnadin -ine f. It. incarnadino (for -tino) f. incarnato INCARNATE adj.]

incarnate adj. & v. —adj. /ɪnˈkɑːnət/ **1** (of a person, spirit, quality, etc.) embodied in flesh, esp. in human form (is the devil incarnate). **2** represented in a recognizable or typical form (folly incarnate). —v.tr. /ˈɪnkɑːˌneɪt, -ˈkɑːneɪt/ **1** embody in flesh. **2** put (an idea etc.) into concrete form; realize. **3** (of a person etc.) be the living embodiment of (a quality). [ME f. eccl.L incarnare incarnat- make flesh (as IN-², L caro carnis flesh)]

incarnation /ˌɪnkɑːˈneɪʃ(ə)n/ n. **1 a** embodiment in (esp. human) flesh. **b** (the Incarnation) Theol. the embodiment of God the Son in human flesh as Jesus Christ. **2** (often foll. by of) a living type (of a quality etc.). **3** Med. the process of forming new flesh. [ME f. OF f. eccl.L incarnatio -onis (as INCARNATE)]

incase var. of ENCASE.

incautious /ɪnˈkɔːʃəs/ adj. heedless, rash. □□ **incaution** n. **incautiously** adv. **incautiousness** n.

incendiary /ɪnˈsendɪərɪ/ adj. & n. —adj. **1** (of a substance or device, esp. a bomb) designed to cause fires. **2 a** of or relating to the malicious setting on fire of property. **b** guilty of this. **3** tending to stir up strife; inflammatory. —n. (pl. **-ies**) **1** an incendiary bomb or device. **2** an incendiary person. □□ **incendiarism** n. [ME f. L incendiarius f. incendium conflagration f. incendere incens- set fire to]

incense¹ /ˈɪnsens/ n. & v. —n. **1** a gum or spice producing a sweet smell when burned. **2** the smoke of this, esp. in religious ceremonial. —v.tr. **1** treat or perfume (a person or thing) with incense. **2** burn incense to (a deity etc.). **3** suffuse with fragrance. □□ **incensation** /-ˈseɪʃ(ə)n/ n. [ME f. OF encens, encenser f. eccl.L incensum a thing burnt, incense: see INCENDIARY]

incense² /ɪnˈsens/ v.tr. (often foll. by at, with, against) enrage; make angry. [ME f. OF incenser (as INCENDIARY)]

incensory /ˈɪnsensərɪ/ n. (pl. **-ies**) = CENSER. [med.L incensorium (as INCENSE¹)]

incentive /ɪnˈsentɪv/ n. & adj. —n. **1** (often foll. by to) a motive or incitement, esp. to action. **2** a payment or concession to stimulate greater output by workers. —adj. serving to motivate or incite. [ME f. L incentivus setting the tune f. incinere incent- sing to (as IN-², canere sing)]

incept /ɪnˈsept/ v. **1** tr. Biol. (of an organism) take in (food etc.). **2** intr. Brit. hist. take a master's or doctor's degree at a university. □□ **inceptor** n. (in sense 2). [L incipere incept- begin (as IN-², capere take)]

inception /ɪnˈsepʃ(ə)n/ n. a beginning. [ME f. OF inception or L inceptio (as INCEPT)]

inceptive /ɪnˈseptɪv/ adj. & n. —adj. **1 a** beginning. **b** initial. **2** Gram. (of a verb) that denotes the beginning of an action. —n. an inceptive verb. [LL inceptivus (as INCEPT)]

incertitude /ɪnˈsɜːtɪˌtjuːd/ n. uncertainty, doubt. [F incertitude or LL incertitudo (as IN-¹, CERTITUDE)]

incessant /ɪnˈses(ə)nt/ adj. unceasing, continual, repeated. □□ **incessancy** n. **incessantly** adv.

incessantness n. [F incessant or LL incessans (as IN-[1], cessans pres. part. of L cessare CEASE)]

incest /'ɪnsest/ n. sexual intercourse between persons regarded as too closely related to marry each other. [ME f. L incestus (as IN-[1], castus CHASTE)]

incestuous /ɪn'sestjʊəs/ adj. 1 involving or guilty of incest. 2 (of human relations generally) excessively restricted or resistant to wider influence. □□ **incestuously** adv. **incestuousness** n. [LL incestuosus (as INCEST)]

inch[1] /ɪntʃ/ n. & v. — n. 1 a unit of linear measure equal to one-twelfth of a foot (2.54 cm). 2 a (as a unit of rainfall) a quantity that would cover a horizontal surface to a depth of 1 inch. b (of atmospheric or other pressure) an amount that balances the weight of a column of mercury 1 inch high. 3 (as a unit of map-scale) so many inches representing 1 mile on the ground (a 4-inch map). 4 a small amount (usu. with neg.: would not yield an inch). — v.tr. & intr. move gradually in a specified way (inched forward). □ **every inch 1** entirely (looked every inch a queen). 2 the whole distance or area (combed every inch of the garden). **give a person an inch and he or she will take a mile** (or orig. **an ell**) a person once conceded to will demand much. **inch by inch** gradually; bit by bit. **within an inch of** almost to the point of. [OE ynce f. L uncia twelfth part: cf. OUNCE[1]]

inch[2] /ɪntʃ/ n. esp. Sc. a small island (esp. in place-names). [ME f. Gael. innis]

inchoate /ɪn'kəʊeɪt, 'ɪn-/ adj. & v. — adj. 1 just begun. 2 undeveloped, rudimentary, unformed. — v.tr. begin; originate. □□ **inchoately** adv. **inchoateness** n. **inchoation** /-'eɪʃ(ə)n/ n. **inchoative** /-'kəʊətɪv/ adj. [L inchoatus past part. of inchoare (as IN-[2], choare begin)]

inchworm /'ɪntʃwɜːm/ n. = measuring-worm (see MEASURE).

incidence /'ɪnsɪd(ə)ns/ n. 1 (often foll. by of) the fact, manner, or rate, of occurrence or action. 2 the range, scope, or extent of influence of a thing. 3 Physics the falling of a line, or of a thing moving in a line, upon a surface. 4 the act or an instance of coming into contact with a thing. □ **angle of incidence** the angle which an incident line, ray, etc., makes with the perpendicular to the surface at the point of incidence. [ME f. OF incidence or med.L incidentia (as INCIDENT)]

incident /'ɪnsɪd(ə)nt/ n. & adj. — n. 1 a an event or occurrence. b a minor or detached event attracting general attention or noteworthy in some way. 2 a hostile clash, esp. of troops of countries at war (a frontier incident). 3 a distinct piece of action in a play or a poem. 4 Law a privilege, burden, etc., attaching to an obligation or right. — adj. 1 a (often foll. by to) apt or liable to happen; naturally attaching or dependent. b (foll. by to) Law attaching to. 2 (often foll. by on, upon) (of light etc.) falling or striking. [ME f. F incident or L incidere (as IN-[2], cadere fall)]

incidental /ˌɪnsɪ'dent(ə)l/ adj. 1 (often foll. by to) a having a minor role in relation to a more important thing, event, etc. b not essential. 2 (foll. by to) liable to happen. 3 (foll. by on, upon) following as a subordinate event. □ **incidental music** music used as a background to the action of a film, broadcast, etc.

incidentally /ˌɪnsɪ'dentəlɪ/ adv. 1 by the way; as an unconnected remark. 2 in an incidental way.

incinerate /ɪn'sɪnəˌreɪt/ v.tr. 1 consume (a body etc.) by fire. 2 reduce to ashes. □□ **incineration** /-'reɪʃ(ə)n/ n. [med.L incinerare (as IN-[2], cinis -eris ashes)]

incinerator /ɪn'sɪnəˌreɪtə(r)/ n. a furnace or apparatus for burning esp. refuse to ashes.

incipient /ɪn'sɪpɪənt/ adj. 1 beginning. 2 in an initial stage. □□ **incipience** n. **incipiency** n. **incipiently** adv. [L incipere incipient- (as INCEPT)]

incise /ɪn'saɪz/ v.tr. 1 make a cut in. 2 engrave. [F inciser f. L incidere incis- (as IN-[2], caedere cut)]

incision /ɪn'sɪʒ(ə)n/ n. 1 a cut; a division produced by cutting; a notch. 2 the act of cutting into a thing. [ME f. OF incision or LL incisio (as INCISE)]

incisive /ɪn'saɪsɪv/ adj. 1 mentally sharp; acute. 2 clear and effective. 3 cutting, penetrating. □□ **incisively** adv. **incisiveness** n. [med.L incisivus (as INCISE)]

incisor /ɪn'saɪzə(r)/ n. a cutting-tooth, esp. at the front of the mouth. [med.L, = cutter (as INCISE)]

incite /ɪn'saɪt/ v.tr. (often foll. by to) urge or stir up. □□ **incitation** /-'teɪʃ(ə)n/ n. **incitement** n. **inciter** n. [ME f. F inciter f. L incitare (as IN-[2], citare rouse)]

incivility /ˌɪnsɪ'vɪlɪtɪ/ n. (pl. -ies) 1 rudeness, discourtesy. 2 a rude or discourteous act. [F incivilité or LL incivilitas (as IN-[1], CIVILITY)]

inclement /ɪn'klemənt/ adj. (of the weather or climate) severe, esp. cold or stormy. □□ **inclemency** n. (pl. -ies). **inclemently** adv. [F inclément or L inclemens (as IN-[1], CLEMENT)]

inclination /ˌɪnklɪ'neɪʃ(ə)n/ n. 1 (often foll. by to) a disposition or propensity. 2 (often foll. by for) a liking or affection. 3 a leaning, slope, or slant. 4 the difference of direction of two lines or planes, esp. as measured by the angle between them. 5 the dip of a magnetic needle. [ME f. OF inclination or L inclinatio (as INCLINE)]

incline v. & n. — v. /ɪn'klaɪn/ 1 tr. (usu. in passive; often foll. by to, for, or to + infin.) a make (a person, feelings, etc.) willing or favourably disposed (am inclined to think so; does not incline me to agree). b give a specified tendency to (a thing) (the door is inclined to bang). 2 intr. a be disposed (I incline to think so). b (often foll. by to, towards) tend. 3 intr. & tr. lean or turn away from a given direction, esp. the vertical. 4 tr. bend (the head, body, or oneself) forward or downward. — n. /'ɪnklaɪn/ 1 a slope. 2 an inclined plane. □ **inclined plane** a sloping plane (esp. as a means of reducing the force needed to raise a load). **incline one's ear** (often foll. by to) listen favourably. □□ **incliner** n. [ME encline f. OF encliner f. L inclinare (as IN-[2], clinare bend)]

inclinometer /ˌɪnklɪ'nɒmɪtə(r)/ n. 1 an instrument for measuring the angle between the direction of the earth's magnetic field and the horizontal. 2 an instrument for measuring the inclination of an aircraft or ship to the horizontal. 3 an instrument for measuring a slope. [L inclinare INCLINE v. + -METER]

inclose var. of ENCLOSE.

inclosure var. of ENCLOSURE.

include /ɪn'kluːd/ v.tr. 1 comprise or reckon in as part of a whole. 2 (as **including** prep.) if we include (six members, including the chairman). 3 treat or regard as so comprised. 4 (as **included** adj.) shut in; enclosed. □ **include out** colloq. or joc. specifically exclude. □□ **includable** adj. **includible** adj. **inclusion** /-ʒ(ə)n/ n. [ME f. L includere inclus- (as IN-[2], claudere shut)]

inclusive /ɪn'kluːsɪv/ adj. 1 (often foll. by of) including, comprising. 2 with the inclusion of the extreme limits stated (pages 7 to 26 inclusive). 3 including all the normal services etc. (a hotel offering inclusive terms). □□ **inclusively** adv. **inclusiveness** n. [med.L inclusivus (as INCLUDE)]

incog /ɪn'kɒg/ adj., adv., & n. colloq. = INCOGNITO. [abbr.]

incognito /ˌɪnkɒg'niːtəʊ/ adj., adv., & n. — adj. & adv. with one's name or identity kept secret (was travelling incognito). — n. (pl. -os) 1 a person who is incognito. 2 the pretended identity or anonymous character of such a person. [It., = unknown, f. L incognitus (as IN-[1], cognitus past part. of cognoscere know)]

incognizant /ɪn'kɒgnɪz(ə)nt/ adj. (foll. by of) unaware; not knowing. □□ **incognizance** n.

incoherent /ˌɪnkəʊ'hɪərənt/ adj. 1 (of a person) unable to speak intelligibly. 2 (of speech etc.) lacking logic or consistency. 3 Physics (of waves) having no definite or stable phase relationship. □□ **incoherence** n. **incoherency** n. (pl. **-ies**). **incoherently** adv.

incombustible /ˌɪnkəm'bʌstɪb(ə)l/ adj. that cannot be burnt or consumed by fire. □□ **incombustibility** /-'bɪlɪtɪ/ n. [ME f. med.L incombustibilis (as IN-¹, COMBUSTIBLE)]

income /'ɪnkʌm, 'ɪŋkəm/ n. the money or other assets received, esp. periodically or in a year, from one's business, lands, work, investments, etc. □**income group** a section of the population determined by income. **income tax** a tax levied on income. [ME (orig. = arrival), prob. f. ON innkoma: in later use f. come in]

incomer /'ɪn,kʌmə(r)/ n. 1 a person who comes in. 2 a person who arrives to settle in a place; an immigrant. 3 an intruder. 4 a successor.

-incomer /'ɪnkʌmə(r), 'ɪŋkʌmə(r)/ comb. form earning a specified kind or level of income (middle-incomer).

incoming /'ɪn,kʌmɪŋ/ adj. & n. —adj. 1 coming in (the incoming tide; incoming telephone calls). 2 succeeding another person or persons (the incoming tenant). 3 immigrant. 4 (of profit) accruing. —n. 1 (usu. in pl.) revenue, income. 2 the act of arriving or entering.

incommensurable /ˌɪnkə'menʃərəb(ə)l, -sjərəb(ə)l/ adj. (often foll. by with) 1 not comparable in respect of magnitude. 2 incapable of being measured (in comparison with). 3 Math. (of a magnitude or magnitudes) having no common factor, integral or fractional. 4 Math. irrational. □□ **incommensurability** /-'bɪlɪtɪ/ n. **incommensurably** adv. [LL incommensurabilis (as IN-¹, COMMENSURABLE)]

incommensurate /ˌɪnkə'menʃərət, -sjərət/ adj. 1 (often foll. by with, to) out of proportion; inadequate. 2 = INCOMMENSURABLE. □□ **incommensurately** adv. **incommensurateness** n.

incommode /ˌɪnkə'məʊd/ v.tr. 1 hinder, inconvenience. 2 trouble, annoy. [F incommoder or L incommodare (as IN-¹, commodus convenient)]

incommodious /ˌɪnkə'məʊdɪəs/ adj. not affording good accommodation; uncomfortable. □□ **incommodiously** adv. **incommodiousness** n.

incommunicable /ˌɪnkə'mjuːnɪkəb(ə)l/ adj. 1 that cannot be communicated or shared. 2 that cannot be uttered or told. 3 that does not communicate; uncommunicative. □□ **incommunicability** /-'bɪlɪtɪ/ n. **incommunicableness** n. **incommunicably** adv. [LL incommunicabilis (as IN-¹, COMMUNICABLE)]

incommunicado /ˌɪnkə,mjuːnɪ'kɑːdəʊ/ adj. 1 without or deprived of the means of communication with others. 2 (of a prisoner) in solitary confinement. [Sp. incomunicado past part. of incomunicar deprive of communication]

incommunicative /ˌɪnkə'mjuːnɪkətɪv/ adj. not communicative; taciturn. □□ **incommunicatively** adv. **incommunicativeness** n.

incommutable /ˌɪnkə'mjuːtəb(ə)l/ adj. 1 not changeable. 2 not commutable. □□ **incommutably** adv. [ME f. L incommutabilis (as IN-¹, COMMUTABLE)]

incomparable /ɪn'kɒmpərəb(ə)l/ adj. 1 without an equal; matchless. 2 (often foll. by with, to) not to be compared. □□ **incomparability** /-'bɪlɪtɪ/ n. **incomparableness** n. **incomparably** adv. [ME f. OF f. L incomparabilis (as IN-¹, COMPARABLE)]

incompatible /ˌɪnkəm'pætɪb(ə)l/ adj. 1 opposed in character; discordant. 2 (often foll. by with) inconsistent. 3 (of persons) unable to live, work, etc., together in harmony. 4 (of drugs) not suitable for taking at the same time. 5 (of equipment, machinery, etc.) not capable of being used in combination. □□ **incompatibility** /-'bɪlɪtɪ/ n. **incompatibleness** n. **incompatibly** adv. [med.L incompatibilis (as IN-¹, COMPATIBLE)]

incompetent /ɪn'kɒmpɪt(ə)nt/ adj. & n. —adj. 1 (often foll. by to + infin.) not qualified or able to perform a particular task or function (an incompetent builder). 2 showing a lack of skill (an incompetent performance). 3 Med. (esp. of a valve or sphincter) not able to perform its function. —n. an incompetent person. □□ **incompetence** n. **incompetency** n. **incompetently** adv. [F incompétent or LL incompetens (as IN-¹, COMPETENT)]

incomplete /ˌɪnkəm'pliːt/ adj. not complete. □□ **incompletely** adv. **incompleteness** n. [ME f. LL incompletus (as IN-¹, COMPLETE)]

incomprehensible /ɪn,kɒmprɪ'hensɪb(ə)l/ adj. (often foll. by to) that cannot be understood. □□ **incomprehensibility** /-'bɪlɪtɪ/ n. **incomprehensibleness** n. **incomprehensibly** adv. [ME f. L incomprehensibilis (as IN-¹, COMPREHENSIBLE)]

incomprehension /ɪn,kɒmprɪ'henʃ(ə)n/ n. failure to understand.

incompressible /ˌɪnkəm'presɪb(ə)l/ adj. that cannot be compressed. □□ **incompressibility** /-'bɪlɪtɪ/ n.

inconceivable /ˌɪnkən'siːvəb(ə)l/ adj. 1 that cannot be imagined. 2 colloq. very remarkable. □□ **inconceivability** /-'bɪlɪtɪ/ n. **inconceivableness** n. **inconceivably** adv.

inconclusive /ˌɪnkən'kluːsɪv/ adj. (of an argument, evidence, or action) not decisive or convincing. □□ **inconclusively** adv. **inconclusiveness** n.

incondensable /ˌɪnkən'densəb(ə)l/ adj. that cannot be condensed, esp. that cannot be reduced to a liquid or solid condition.

incongruous /ɪn'kɒŋgrʊəs/ adj. 1 out of place; absurd. 2 (often foll. by with) disagreeing; out of keeping. □□ **incongruity** /-'gruːɪtɪ/ n. (pl. **-ies**). **incongruously** adv. **incongruousness** n. [L incongruus (as IN-¹, CONGRUOUS)]

inconsecutive /ˌɪnkən'sekjʊtɪv/ adj. lacking sequence; inconsequent. □□ **inconsecutively** adv. **inconsecutiveness** n.

inconsequent /ɪn'kɒnsɪkwənt/ adj. 1 not following naturally; irrelevant. 2 lacking logical sequence. 3 disconnected. □□ **inconsequence** n. **inconsequently** adv. [L inconsequens (as IN-¹, CONSEQUENT)]

inconsequential /ɪn,kɒnsɪ'kwenʃ(ə)l, ˌɪnkɒn-/ adj. 1 unimportant. 2 = INCONSEQUENT. □□ **inconsequentiality** /-ʃɪ'ælɪtɪ/ n. (pl. **-ies**). **inconsequentially** adv. **inconsequentialness** n.

inconsiderable /ˌɪnkən'sɪdərəb(ə)l/ adj. 1 of small size, value, etc. 2 not worth considering. □□ **inconsiderableness** n. **inconsiderably** adv. [obs. F inconsidérable or LL inconsiderabilis (as IN-¹, CONSIDERABLE)]

inconsiderate /ˌɪnkən'sɪdərət/ adj. 1 (of a person or action) thoughtless, rash. 2 lacking in regard for the feelings of others. □□ **inconsiderately** adv. **inconsiderateness** n. **inconsideration** /-'reɪʃ(ə)n/ n. [L inconsideratus (as IN-¹, CONSIDERATE)]

inconsistent /ˌɪnkən'sɪst(ə)nt/ adj. 1 acting at variance with one's own principles or former conduct. 2 (often foll. by with) not in keeping; discordant, incompatible. 3 (of a single thing) incompatible or discordant; having self-contradictory parts. □□ **inconsistency** n. (pl. **-ies**). **inconsistently** adv.

inconsolable /ˌɪnkən'səʊləb(ə)l/ adj. (of a person, grief, etc.) that cannot be consoled or comforted. □□ **inconsolability** /-'bɪlɪtɪ/ n. **inconsolableness** n. **inconsolably** adv. [F inconsolable or L inconsolabilis (as IN-¹, consolabilis f. consolari CONSOLE¹)]

inconsonant /ɪn'kɒnsənənt/ adj. (often foll. by with, to) not harmonious; not compatible. □□ **inconsonance** n. **inconsonantly** adv.

inconspicuous /ˌɪnkən'spɪkjʊəs/ adj. 1 not conspicuous; not easily noticed. 2 Bot. (of flowers) small, pale, or green. □□ **inconspicuously** adv. **inconspicuousness** n. [L inconspicuus (as IN-¹, CONSPICUOUS)]

inconstant /ɪn'kɒnst(ə)nt/ adj. 1 (of a person) fickle, changeable. 2 frequently changing; variable, irregular. □□ **inconstancy** *n.* (*pl.* **-ies**). **inconstantly** *adv.* [ME f. OF f. L *inconstans -antis* (as IN-¹, CONSTANT)]

incontestable /ˌɪnkən'testəb(ə)l/ *adj.* that cannot be disputed. □□ **incontestability** /-'bɪlɪtɪ/ *n.* **incontestably** *adv.* [F *incontestable* or med.L *incontestabilis* (as IN-¹, *contestabilis* f. L *contestari* CONTEST)]

incontinent /ɪn'kɒntɪnənt/ *adj.* **1** unable to control movements of the bowels or bladder or both. **2** lacking self-restraint (esp. in regard to sexual desire). **3** (foll. by *of*) unable to control. □□ **incontinence** *n.* **incontinently** *adv.* [ME f. OF or L *incontinens* (as IN-¹, CONTINENT²)]

incontrovertible /ˌɪnkɒntrə'vɜːtɪb(ə)l/ *adj.* indisputable, indubitable. □□ **incontrovertibility** /-'bɪlɪtɪ/ *n.* **incontrovertibly** *adv.*

inconvenience /ˌɪnkən'viːnɪəns/ *n.* & *v.* —*n.* **1** lack of suitability to personal requirements or ease. **2** a cause or instance of this. —*v.tr.* cause inconvenience to. [ME f. OF f. LL *inconvenientia* (as INCONVENIENT)]

inconvenient /ˌɪnkən'viːnɪənt/ *adj.* **1** unfavourable to ease or comfort; not convenient. **2** awkward, troublesome. □□ **inconveniently** *adv.* [ME f. OF f. L *inconveniens -entis* (as IN-¹, CONVENIENT)]

inconvertible /ˌɪnkən'vɜːtɪb(ə)l/ *adj.* **1** not convertible. **2** (esp. of currency) not convertible into another form on demand. □□ **inconvertibility** /-'bɪlɪtɪ/ *n.* **inconvertibly** *adv.* [F *inconvertible* or LL *inconvertibilis* (as IN-¹, CONVERTIBLE)]

incoordination /ˌɪnkəʊˌɔːdɪ'neɪʃ(ə)n/ *n.* lack of co-ordination, esp. of muscular action.

incorporate *v.* & *adj.* —*v.* /ɪn'kɔːpəˌreɪt/ **1** *tr.* (often foll. by *in*, *with*) unite; form into one body or whole. **2** *intr.* become incorporated. **3** *tr.* combine (ingredients) into one substance. **4** *tr.* admit as a member of a company etc. **5** *tr.* **a** constitute as a legal corporation. **b** (as **incorporated** *adj.*) forming a legal corporation. —*adj.* /ɪn'kɔːpərət/ **1** (of a company etc.) formed into a legal corporation. **2** embodied. □□ **incorporation** /-'reɪʃ(ə)n/ *n.* **incorporator** *n.* [ME f. LL *incorporare* (as IN-², *corpus -oris* body)]

incorporeal /ˌɪnkɔː'pɔːrɪəl/ *adj.* **1** not composed of matter. **2** of immaterial beings. **3** *Law* having no physical existence. □□ **incorporeality** /-'ælɪtɪ/ *n.* **incorporeally** *adv.* **incorporeity** /-pə'riːɪtɪ/ *n.* [L *incorporeus* (as INCORPORATE)]

incorrect /ˌɪnkə'rekt/ *adj.* **1** not in accordance with fact; wrong. **2** (of style etc.) improper, faulty. □□ **incorrectly** *adv.* **incorrectness** *n.* [ME f. OF or L *incorrectus* (as IN-¹, CORRECT)]

incorrigible /ɪn'kɒrɪdʒɪb(ə)l/ *adj.* **1** (of a person or habit) incurably bad or depraved. **2** not readily improved. □□ **incorrigibility** /-'bɪlɪtɪ/ *n.* **incorrigibleness** *n.* **incorrigibly** *adv.* [ME f. OF *incorrigible* or L *incorrigibilis* (as IN-¹, CORRIGIBLE)]

incorruptible /ˌɪnkə'rʌptɪb(ə)l/ *adj.* **1** that cannot be corrupted, esp. by bribery. **2** that cannot decay; everlasting. □□ **incorruptibility** /-'bɪlɪtɪ/ *n.* **incorruptibly** *adv.* [ME f. OF *incorruptible* or eccl.L *incorruptibilis* (as IN-¹, CORRUPT)]

increase *v.* & *n.* —*v.* /ɪn'kriːs/ **1** *tr.* & *intr.* make or become greater in size, amount, etc., or more numerous. **2** *intr.* advance (in quality, attainment, etc.). **3** *tr.* intensify (a quality). —*n.* /'ɪnkriːs/ **1** the act or process of becoming greater or more numerous; growth, enlargement. **2** (of people, animals, or plants) growth in numbers; multiplication. **3** the amount or extent of an increase. □ **on the increase** increasing, esp. in frequency. □□ **increasable** *adj.* **increaser** *n.* **increasingly** *adv.* [ME f. OF *encreiss-* stem of *encreistre* f. L *increscere* (as IN-², *crescere* grow)]

incredible /ɪn'kredɪb(ə)l/ *adj.* **1** that cannot be believed. **2** *colloq.* hard to believe; amazing. □□ **incredibility** /-'bɪlɪtɪ/ *n.* **incredibleness** *n.*

incredibly *adv.* [ME f. L *incredibilis* (as IN-¹, CREDIBLE)]

incredulous /ɪn'kredjʊləs/ *adj.* (often foll. by *of*) unwilling to believe. □□ **incredulity** /ˌɪnkrɪ'djuːlɪtɪ/ *n.* **incredulously** *adv.* **incredulousness** *n.* [L *incredulus* (as IN-¹, CREDULOUS)]

increment /'ɪnkrɪmənt/ *n.* **1 a** an increase or addition, esp. one of a series on a fixed scale. **b** the amount of this. **2** *Math.* a small amount by which a variable quantity increases. □□ **incremental** /-'ment(ə)l/ *adj.* [ME f. L *incrementum* f. *increscere* INCREASE]

incriminate /ɪn'krɪmɪˌneɪt/ *v.tr.* **1** tend to prove the guilt of (*incriminating evidence*). **2** involve in an accusation. **3** charge with a crime. □□ **incrimination** /-'neɪʃ(ə)n/ *n.* **incriminatory** *adj.* [LL *incriminare* (as IN-², L *crimen* offence)]

incrust var. of ENCRUST.

incrustation /ˌɪnkrʌ'steɪʃ(ə)n/ *n.* **1** the process of encrusting or state of being encrusted. **2** a crust or hard coating, esp. of fine material. **3** a concretion or deposit on a surface. **4** a facing of marble etc. on a building. [F *incrustation* or LL *incrustatio* (as ENCRUST)]

incubate /'ɪŋkjʊˌbeɪt/ *v.* **1** *tr.* sit on or artificially heat (eggs) in order to bring forth young birds etc. **2** *tr.* cause the development of (bacteria etc.) by creating suitable conditions. **3** *intr.* sit on eggs; brood. [L *incubare* (as IN-², *cubare* *cubit-* or *cubat-* lie)]

incubation /ˌɪŋkjʊ'beɪʃ(ə)n/ *n.* **1 a** the act of incubating. **b** brooding. **2** *Med.* **a** a phase through which the germs causing a disease pass before the development of the first symptoms. **b** the period of this. □□ **incubational** *adj.* **incubative** /'ɪŋkjʊˌbeɪtɪv/ *adj.* **incubatory** /'ɪŋkjʊˌbeɪtərɪ/ *adj.* [L *incubatio* (as INCUBATE)]

incubator /'ɪŋkjʊˌbeɪtə(r)/ *n.* **1** an apparatus used to provide a suitable temperature and environment for a premature baby or one of low birth-weight. **2** an apparatus used to hatch eggs or grow micro-organisms.

incubus /'ɪŋkjʊbəs/ *n.* (*pl.* **incubuses** or **incubi** /-ˌbaɪ/) **1** an evil spirit supposed to descend on sleeping persons. **2** a nightmare. **3** a person or thing that oppresses like a nightmare. [ME f. LL, = L *incubo* nightmare (as INCUBATE)]

incudes *pl.* of INCUS.

inculcate /'ɪnkʌlˌkeɪt/ *v.tr.* (often foll. by *upon*, *in*) urge or impress (a fact, habit, or idea) persistently. □□ **inculcation** /-'keɪʃ(ə)n/ *n.* **inculcator** *n.* [L *inculcare* (as IN-², *calcare* tread f. *calx calcis* heel)]

inculpate /'ɪnkʌlˌpeɪt/ *v.tr.* **1** involve in a charge. **2** accuse, blame. □□ **inculpation** /-'peɪʃ(ə)n/ *n.* **inculpative** /ɪn'kʌlpətɪv/ *adj.* **inculpatory** /ɪn'kʌlpətərɪ/ *adj.* [LL *inculpare* (as IN-², *culpare* blame f. *culpa* fault)]

incumbency /ɪn'kʌmbənsɪ/ *n.* (*pl.* **-ies**) the office, tenure, or sphere of an incumbent.

incumbent /ɪn'kʌmbənt/ *adj.* & *n.* —*adj.* **1** (foll. by *on*, *upon*) resting as a duty (*it is incumbent on you to warn them*). **2** (often foll. by *on*) lying, pressing. —*n.* the holder of an office or post, esp. an ecclesiastical benefice. [ME f. AL *incumbens* pres. part. of L *incumbere* lie upon (as IN-², *cubare* lie)]

incunable /ɪn'kjuːnəb(ə)l/ *n.* = INCUNABULUM 1. [F, formed as INCUNABULUM]

incunabulum /ˌɪnkjuː'næbjʊləm/ *n.* (*pl.* **incunabula** /-lə/) **1** a book printed at an early date, esp. before 1501. **2** (in *pl.*) the early stages of the development of a thing. [L *incunabula* swaddling-clothes, cradle (as IN-², *cunae* cradle)]

incur /ɪn'kɜː(r)/ *v.tr.* (**incurred**, **incurring**) suffer, experience, or become subject to (something unpleasant) as a result of one's own behaviour etc. (*incurred huge debts*). □□ **incurrable** *adj.* [ME f. L *incurrere incurs-* (as IN-², *currere* run)]

incurable /ɪn'kjʊərəb(ə)l/ *adj.* & *n.* —*adj.* that cannot be cured. —*n.* a person who cannot be

aʊ how eɪ day əʊ no eə hair ɪə near ɔɪ boy ʊə poor aɪə fire aʊə sour (*see over for consonants*)

cured. □□ **incurability** /-'brlrtɪ/ *n*. **incurableness** *n*.
incurably *adv*. [ME f. OF *incurable* or LL *incurabilis*
(as IN-¹, CURABLE)]
incurious /ɪn'kjʊərɪəs/ *adj*. **1** lacking curiosity. **2**
heedless, careless. □□ **incuriosity** /-'ɒsɪtɪ/ *n*.
incuriously *adv*. **incuriousness** *n*. [L *incuriosus*
(as IN-¹, CURIOUS)]
incursion /ɪn'kɜ:ʃ(ə)n/ *n*. an invasion or attack, esp.
when sudden or brief. □□ **incursive** /-sɪv/ *adj*. [ME
f. L *incursio* (as INCUR)]
incurve /ɪn'kɜ:v/ *v.tr*. **1** bend into a curve. **2** (as
incurved *adj*.) curved inwards. □□ **incurvation**
/-'veɪʃ(ə)n/ *n*. [L *incurvare* (as IN-², CURVE)]
incus /'ɪŋkəs/ *n*. (*pl*. **incudes** /-'kju:di:z/) the small
anvil-shaped bone in the middle ear, in contact with
the malleus and stapes. [L, = anvil]
incuse /ɪŋ'kju:z/ *n*., *v*., & *adj*. —*n*. an impression
hammered or stamped on a coin. —*v.tr*. **1** mark (a
coin) with a figure by stamping. **2** impress (a figure)
on a coin by stamping. —*adj*. hammered or stamped
on a coin. [L *incusus* past part. of *incudere* (as IN-²,
cudere forge)]
Ind. *abbr*. **1** Independent. **2 a** India. **b** Indian. **3**
Indiana.
indaba /ɪn'dɑ:bə/ *n*. *S.Afr*. **1** a conference between
or with members of S. African native tribes. **2** *colloq*.
one's problem or concern. [Zulu, = business]
indebted /ɪn'detɪd/ *adj*. (usu. foll. by *to*) **1** owing
gratitude or obligation. **2** owing money. □□
indebtedness *n*. [ME f. OF *endetté* past part. of
endetter involve in debt (as EN-¹, *detter* f. *dette* DEBT)]
indecent /ɪn'di:s(ə)nt/ *adj*. **1** offending against recognized standards of decency. **2** unbecoming; highly
unsuitable (*with indecent haste*). □ **indecent assault**
a sexual attack not involving rape. **indecent exposure** the intentional act of publicly and indecently
exposing one's body, esp. the genitals. □□ **indecency**
n. (*pl*. **-ies**). **indecently** *adv*. [F *indécent* or L *indecens*
(as IN-¹, DECENT)]
indecipherable /,ɪndɪ'saɪfərəb(ə)l/ *adj*. that cannot
be deciphered.
indecision /,ɪndɪ'sɪʒ(ə)n/ *n*. lack of decision; hesitation. [F *indécision* (as IN-¹, DECISION)]
indecisive /,ɪndɪ'saɪsɪv/ *adj*. **1** not decisive. **2**
undecided, hesitating. □□ **indecisively** *adv*.
indecisiveness *n*.
indeclinable /,ɪndɪ'klaɪnəb(ə)l/ *adj*. *Gram*. **1** that
cannot be declined. **2** having no inflections. [ME f. F
indéclinable f. L *indeclinabilis* (as IN-¹, DECLINE)]
indecorous /ɪn'dekərəs/ *adj*. **1** improper. **2** in bad
taste. □□ **indecorously** *adv*. **indecorousness** *n*. [L
indecorus (as IN-¹, *decorus* seemly)]
indecorum /,ɪndɪ'kɔ:rəm/ *n*. **1** lack of decorum.
2 improper behaviour. [L, neut. of *indecorus*: see
INDECOROUS]
indeed /ɪn'di:d/ *adv*. & *int*. —*adv*. **1** in truth; really
(*they are, indeed, a remarkable family*). **2** expressing
emphasis or intensification (*I shall be very glad
indeed*; *indeed it is*). **3** admittedly (*there are indeed
exceptions*). **4** in point of fact (*if indeed such a thing
is possible*). **5** expressing an approving or ironic echo
(*who is this Mr Smith?—who is he indeed?*). —*int*.
expressing irony, contempt, incredulity, etc.
indefatigable /,ɪndɪ'fætɪgəb(ə)l/ *adj*. (of a person,
quality, etc.) that cannot be tired out; unwearying,
unremitting. □□ **indefatigability** /-'brlrtɪ/ *n*.
indefatigably *adv*. [obs. F *indéfatigable* or L *in-
defatigabilis* (as IN-¹, *defatigare* wear out)]
indefeasible /,ɪndɪ'fi:zɪb(ə)l/ *adj*. *literary* (esp. of a
claim, rights, etc.) that cannot be lost. □□
indefeasibility /-'brlrtɪ/ *n*. **indefeasibly** *adv*.
indefectible /,ɪndɪ'fektɪb(ə)l/ *adj*. **1** unfailing; not
liable to defect or decay. **2** faultless. [IN-¹ + *defectible*
f. LL *defectibilis* (as DEFECT)]
indefensible /,ɪndɪ'fensɪb(ə)l/ *adj*. that cannot be
defended or justified. □□ **indefensibility** /-'brlrtɪ/ *n*.
indefensibly *adv*.

indefinable /,ɪndɪ'faɪnəb(ə)l/ *adj*. that cannot be
defined or exactly described. □□ **indefinably** *adv*.
indefinite /ɪn'defɪnɪt/ *adj*. **1** vague, undefined. **2**
unlimited. **3** *Gram*. not determining the person,
thing, time, etc., referred to. □ **indefinite article**
see ARTICLE. **indefinite integral** see INTEGRAL.
indefinite pronoun *Gram*. a pronoun indicating
a person, amount, etc., without being definite or
particular, e.g. *any*, *some*, *anyone*. □□ **indefiniteness**
n. [L *indefinitus* (as IN-¹, DEFINITE)]
indefinitely /ɪn'defɪnɪtlɪ/ *adv*. **1** for an unlimited
time (*was postponed indefinitely*). **2** in an indefinite
manner.
indehiscent /,ɪndɪ'hɪs(ə)nt/ *adj*. *Bot*. (of fruit) not
splitting open when ripe. □□ **indehiscence** *n*.
indelible /ɪn'delɪb(ə)l/ *adj*. **1** that cannot be rubbed
out or (in abstract senses) removed. **2** (of ink etc.)
that makes indelible marks. □□ **indelibility** /-'brlrtɪ/
n. **indelibly** *adv*. [F *indélébile* or L *indelebilis* (as
IN-¹, *delebilis* f. *delēre* efface)]
indelicate /ɪn'delɪkət/ *adj*. **1** coarse, unrefined. **2**
tactless. **3** tending to indecency. □□ **indelicacy** *n*.
(*pl*. **-ies**). **indelicately** *adv*.
indemnify /ɪn'demnɪfaɪ/ *v.tr*. (**-ies**, **-ied**) **1** (often
foll. by *from*, *against*) protect or secure (a person) in
respect of harm, a loss, etc. **2** (often foll. by *for*)
secure (a person) against legal responsibility for
actions. **3** (often foll. by *for*) compensate (a person)
for a loss, expenses, etc. □□ **indemnification**
/-fɪ'keɪʃ(ə)n/ *n*. **indemnifier** *n*. [L *indemnis* unhurt
(as IN-¹, *damnum* loss, damage)]
indemnity /ɪn'demnɪtɪ/ *n*. (*pl*. **-ies**) **1 a** compensation
for loss incurred. **b** a sum paid for this, esp. a sum
exacted by a victor in war etc. as one condition of
peace. **2** security against loss. **3** legal exemption
from penalties etc. incurred. [ME f. F *indemnité* or
LL *indemnitas -tatis* (as INDEMNIFY)]
indemonstrable /ɪn'demənstrəb(ə)l/, ,ɪndɪ'mɒn-/
adj. that cannot be proved (esp. of primary or
axiomatic truths).
indene /'ɪndi:n/ *n*. *Chem*. a colourless flammable
liquid hydrocarbon obtained from coal tar and used
in making synthetic resins. [INDOLE + -ENE]
indent¹ *v*. & *n*. —*v*. /ɪn'dent/ **1** *tr*. start (a line of
print or writing) further from the margin than other
lines, e.g. to mark a new paragraph. **2** *tr*. **a** divide (a
document drawn up in duplicate) into its two copies
with a zigzag line dividing them and ensuring identification. **b** draw up (usu. a legal document) in exact
duplicate. **3** *Brit*. **a** *intr*. (often foll. by *on*, *upon* a
person, *for* a thing) make a requisition (orig. a
written order with a duplicate). **b** *tr*. order (goods)
by requisition. **4** *tr*. make toothlike notches in. **5** *tr*.
form deep recesses in (a coastline etc.). —*n*. /'ɪndent/
1 *Brit*. **a** an order (esp. from abroad) for goods. **b** an
official requisition for stores. **2** an indented line. **3**
indentation. **4** an indenture. □□ **indenter** *n*.
indentor *n*. [ME f. AF *endenter* f. AL *indentare* (as
IN-², L *dens dentis* tooth)]
indent² /ɪn'dent/ *v.tr*. **1** make a dent in. **2** impress (a
mark etc.). [ME f. IN-² + DENT]
indentation /,ɪnden'teɪʃ(ə)n/ *n*. **1** the act or an
instance of indenting; the process of being indented.
2 a cut or notch. **3** a zigzag. **4** a deep recess in a
coastline etc.
indention /ɪn'denʃ(ə)n/ *n*. **1** the indenting of a line
in printing or writing. **2** = INDENTATION.
indenture /ɪn'dentʃə(r)/ *n*. & *v*. —*n*. **1** an indented
document (see INDENT¹ *v*. 2). **2** a sealed agreement or
contract (usu. in *pl*.). **3** a formal list, certificate, etc.
—*v.tr*. *hist*. bind (a person) by indentures, esp. as an
apprentice. □□ **indentureship** *n*. [ME (orig. Sc.) f.
AF *endenture* (as INDENT¹)]
independence /,ɪndɪ'pend(ə)ns/ *n*. **1** (often foll.
by *of*, *from*) the state of being independent. **2**
independent income. □ **Independence Day** a day
celebrating the anniversary of national independence, esp. 4 July in the US.

independency /ˌɪndɪˈpendənsɪ/ n. (pl. **-ies**) **1** an independent State. **2** = INDEPENDENCE.

independent /ˌɪndɪˈpend(ə)nt/ adj. & n. —adj. **1 a** (often foll. by of) not depending on authority or control. **b** self-governing. **2 a** not depending on another person for one's opinion or livelihood. **b** (of income or resources) making it unnecessary to earn one's living. **3** unwilling to be under an obligation to others. **4** Polit. not belonging to or supported by a party. **5** not depending on something else for its validity, efficiency, value, etc. (independent proof). **6** (of broadcasting, a school, etc.) not supported by public funds. **7** (**Independent**) hist. Congregational. —n. **1** a person who is politically independent. **2** (**Independent**) hist. a Congregationalist. □□ **independently** adv.

in-depth see DEPTH.

indescribable /ˌɪndɪˈskraɪbəb(ə)l/ adj. **1** too unusual or extreme to be described. **2** vague, indefinite. □□ **indescribability** /-ˈbɪlɪtɪ/ n. **indescribably** adv.

indestructible /ˌɪndɪˈstrʌktɪb(ə)l/ adj. that cannot be destroyed. □□ **indestructibility** /-ˈbɪlɪtɪ/ n. **indestructibly** adv.

indeterminable /ˌɪndɪˈtɜːmɪnəb(ə)l/ adj. **1** that cannot be ascertained. **2** (of a dispute etc.) that cannot be settled. □□ **indeterminably** adv. [ME f. LL indeterminabilis (as IN-¹, L determinare DETERMINE)]

indeterminate /ˌɪndɪˈtɜːmɪnət/ adj. **1** not fixed in extent, character, etc. **2** left doubtful; vague. **3** Math. (of a quantity) not limited to a fixed value by the value of another quantity. **4** (of a judicial sentence) such that the convicted person's conduct determines the date of release. □ **indeterminate vowel** the obscure vowel /ə/ heard in 'a moment ago'; a schwa. □□ **indeterminacy** n. **indeterminately** adv. **indeterminateness** n. [ME f. LL indeterminatus (as IN-¹, DETERMINATE)]

indetermination /ˌɪndɪˌtɜːmɪˈneɪʃ(ə)n/ n. **1** lack of determination. **2** the state of being indeterminate.

indeterminism /ˌɪndɪˈtɜːmɪˌnɪz(ə)m/ n. the belief that human action is not wholly determined by motives. □□ **indeterminist** n. **indeterministic** /-ˈnɪstɪk/ adj.

index /ˈɪndeks/ n. & v. —n. (pl. **indexes** or esp. in technical use **indices** /ˈɪndɪˌsiːz/) **1** an alphabetical list of names, subjects, etc., with references, usu. at the end of a book. **2** = card index. **3** (in full **index number**) a number showing the variation of prices or wages as compared with a chosen base period (retail price index; Dow-Jones index). **4** Math. **a** the exponent of a number. **b** the power to which it is raised. **5 a** a pointer, esp. on an instrument, showing a quantity, a position on a scale, etc. **b** an indicator of a trend, direction, tendency, etc. **c** (usu. foll. by of) a sign, token, or indication of something. **6** Physics a number expressing a physical property etc. in terms of a standard (refractive index). **7** Computing a set of items each of which specifies one of the records of a file and contains information about its address. **8** (**Index**) RC Ch. hist. a list of books forbidden to Roman Catholics to read. **9** Printing a symbol shaped like a pointing hand, used to draw attention to a note etc. —v.tr. **1** provide (a book etc.) with an index. **2** enter in an index. **3** relate (wages etc.) to the value of a price index. □ **index finger** the forefinger. **index-linked** related to the value of a retail price index. □□ **indexation** /-ˈseɪʃ(ə)n/ n. **indexer** n. **indexible** /ˈɪndeks-, ɪnˈdeks-/ adj. **indexical** /ɪnˈdeks-/ adj. **indexless** adj. [ME f. L index indicis forefinger, informer, sign: sense 8 f. L Index librorum prohibitorum list of prohibited books]

India ink /ˈɪndɪə/ n. US = Indian ink. [India in Asia: see INDIAN]

Indiaman /ˈɪndɪəmən/ n. (pl. **-men**) Naut. hist. a ship engaged in trade with India or the East Indies.

Indian /ˈɪndɪən/ n. & adj. —n. **1 a** a native or national of India. **b** a person of Indian descent. **2** (in full **American Indian**) a member of the aboriginal

peoples of America or their descendants. **3** any of the languages of the aboriginal peoples of America. —adj. **1** of or relating to India, or to the subcontinent comprising India, Pakistan, and Bangladesh. **2** of or relating to the aboriginal peoples of America. □ **Indian clubs** a pair of bottle-shaped clubs swung to exercise the arms in gymnastics. **Indian corn** maize. **Indian elephant** the elephant, Elephas maximus, of India, which is smaller than the African elephant. **Indian file** = single file. **Indian hemp** see HEMP 1. **Indian ink** Brit. **1** a black pigment made orig. in China and Japan. **2** a dark ink made from this, used esp. in drawing and technical graphics. **Indian Ocean** the ocean between Africa to the west, and Australia to the east. **Indian rope-trick** the supposed Indian feat of climbing an upright unsupported length of rope. **Indian summer 1** a period of unusually dry warm weather sometimes occurring in late autumn. **2** a late period of life characterized by comparative calm. [ME f. India ult. f. Gk Indos the River Indus f. Pers. Hind: cf. HINDU]

India paper /ˈɪndɪə/ n. **1** a soft absorbent kind of paper orig. imported from China, used for proofs of engravings. **2** a very thin tough opaque printing-paper.

Indiarubber /ˌɪndɪəˈrʌbə(r)/ n. = RUBBER¹ 2.

Indic /ˈɪndɪk/ adj. & n. —adj. of the group of Indo-European languages comprising Sanskrit and its modern descendants. —n. this language-group. [L Indicus f. Gk Indikos INDIAN]

indicate /ˈɪndɪˌkeɪt/ v.tr. (often foll. by that + clause) **1** point out; make known; show. **2** be a sign or symptom of; express the presence of. **3** (often in passive) suggest; call for; require or show to be necessary (stronger measures are indicated). **4** admit to or state briefly (indicated his disapproval). **5** (of a gauge etc.) give as a reading. [L indicare (as IN-², dicare make known)]

indication /ˌɪndɪˈkeɪʃ(ə)n/ n. **1** the act or an instance of indicating. **2** something indicated or suggested. **3** a reading given by a gauge or instrument. [F f. L indicatio (as INDICATE)]

indicative /ɪnˈdɪkətɪv/ adj. & n. —adj. **1** (foll. by of) suggestive; serving as an indication. **2** Gram. (of a mood) denoting simple statement of a fact. —n. Gram. **1** the indicative mood. **2** a verb in this mood. □□ **indicatively** adv. [ME f. F indicatif -ive f. LL indicativus (as INDICATE)]

indicator /ˈɪndɪˌkeɪtə(r)/ n. **1** a person or thing that indicates. **2** a device indicating the condition of a machine etc. **3** a recording instrument attached to an apparatus etc. **4** a board in a railway station etc. giving current information. **5** a device (esp. a flashing light) on a vehicle to show that it is about to change direction. **6** a substance which changes colour at a given stage in a chemical reaction. **7** Physics & Med. a radioactive tracer.

indicatory /ˈɪndɪkətərɪ, ɪnˈdɪk-/ adj. = INDICATIVE adj. 1.

indices pl. of INDEX.

indicia /ɪnˈdɪʃɪə/ n.pl. **1** distinguishing or identificatory marks. **2** signs, indications. [pl. of L indicium (as INDEX)]

indicial /ɪnˈdɪʃ(ə)l/ adj. **1** of the nature or form of an index. **2** of the nature of indicia; indicative.

indict /ɪnˈdaɪt/ v.tr. accuse (a person) formally by legal process. □□ **indictee** /-ˈtiː/ n. **indicter** n. [ME f. AF enditer indict f. OF enditier declare f. Rmc indictare (unrecorded: as IN-², DICTATE)]

indictable /ɪnˈdaɪtəb(ə)l/ adj. **1** (of an offence) rendering the person who commits it liable to be charged with a crime. **2** (of a person) so liable.

indictment /ɪnˈdaɪtmənt/ n. **1** the act of indicting. **2 a** a formal accusation. **b** a legal process in which this is made. **c** a document containing a charge. **3** something that serves to condemn or censure. [ME f. AF enditement (as INDICT)]

w we   z zoo   ʃ she   ʒ decision   θ thin   ð this   ŋ ring   x loch   tʃ chip   dʒ jar   (see over for vowels)

indie /ˈɪndɪ/ n. colloq. an independent record or film company.

Indies /ˈɪndɪz/ n.pl. (prec. by the) archaic India and adjacent regions (see also East Indies, West Indies). [pl. of obs. Indy India]

indifference /ɪnˈdɪfrəns/ n. 1 lack of interest or attention. 2 unimportance (a matter of indifference). 3 neutrality. [L indifferentia (as INDIFFERENT)]

indifferent /ɪnˈdɪfrənt/ adj. 1 neither good nor bad; average, mediocre. 2 a not especially good. b fairly bad. 3 (often prec. by very) decidedly inferior. 4 (foll. by to) having no partiality for or against; having no interest in or sympathy for. 5 chemically, magnetically, etc., neutral. □□ indifferently adv. [ME f. OF indifferent or L indifferens (as IN-¹, DIFFERENT)]

indifferentism /ɪnˈdɪfrənˌtɪz(ə)m/ n. an attitude of indifference, esp. in religious matters. □□ indifferentist n.

indigenize /ɪnˈdɪdʒɪˌnaɪz/ v.tr. (also -ise) 1 make indigenous; subject to native influence. 2 subject to increased use of indigenous people in government etc. □□ indigenization /-ˈzeɪʃ(ə)n/ n.

indigenous /ɪnˈdɪdʒɪnəs/ adj. 1 a (esp. of flora or fauna) originating naturally in a region. b (of people) born in a region. 2 (foll. by to) belonging naturally to a place. □□ indigenously adv. indigenousness n. [L indigena f. indi- = IN-² + gen- be born]

indigent /ˈɪndɪdʒ(ə)nt/ adj. needy, poor. □□ indigence n. [ME f. OF f. LL indigēre f. indi- = IN-² + egēre need]

indigested /ˌɪndaɪˈdʒestɪd/ adj. 1 shapeless. 2 ill-considered. 3 not digested.

indigestible /ˌɪndɪˈdʒestɪb(ə)l/ adj. 1 difficult or impossible to digest. 2 too complex or awkward to read or comprehend easily. □□ indigestibility /-ˈbɪlɪtɪ/ n. indigestibly adv. [F indigestible or LL indigestibilis (as IN-¹, DIGEST)]

indigestion /ˌɪndɪˈdʒestʃ(ə)n/ n. 1 difficulty in digesting food. 2 pain or discomfort caused by this. □□ indigestive adj. [ME f. OF indigestion or LL indigestio (as IN-¹, DIGESTION)]

indignant /ɪnˈdɪɡnənt/ adj. feeling or showing scornful anger or a sense of injured innocence. □□ indignantly adv. [L indignari indignant- regard as unworthy (as IN-¹, dignus worthy)]

indignation /ˌɪndɪɡˈneɪʃ(ə)n/ n. scornful anger at supposed unjust or unfair conduct or treatment. [ME f. OF indignation or L indignatio (as INDIGNANT)]

indignity /ɪnˈdɪɡnɪtɪ/ n. (pl. -ies) 1 unworthy treatment. 2 a slight or insult. 3 the humiliating quality of something (the indignity of my position). [F indignité or L indignitas (as INDIGNANT)]

indigo /ˈɪndɪˌɡəʊ/ n. (pl. -os) 1 a a natural blue dye obtained from the indigo plant. b a synthetic form of this dye. 2 any plant of the genus Indigofera. 3 (in full indigo blue) a colour between blue and violet in the spectrum. □□ indigotic /-ˈɡɒtɪk/ adj. [16th-c. indico (f. Sp.), indigo (f. Port.) f. L indicum f. Gk indikon INDIAN (dye)]

indirect /ˌɪndaɪˈrekt/ adj. 1 not going straight to the point. 2 (of a route etc.) not straight. 3 not directly sought or aimed at (an indirect result). 4 (of lighting) from a concealed source and diffusely reflected. □ indirect object Gram. a person or thing affected by a verbal action but not primarily acted on (e.g. him in give him the book). indirect question Gram. a question in reported speech (e.g. they asked who I was). indirect speech (or oration) = reported speech (see REPORT). indirect tax a tax levied on goods and services and not on income or profits. □□ indirectly adv. indirectness n. [ME f. OF indirect or med.L indirectus (as IN-¹, DIRECT)]

indiscernible /ˌɪndɪˈsɜːnɪb(ə)l/ adj. that cannot be discerned or distinguished from another. □□ indiscernibility /-ˈbɪlɪtɪ/ n. indiscernibly adv.

indiscipline /ɪnˈdɪsɪplɪn/ n. lack of discipline.

indiscreet /ˌɪndɪˈskriːt/ adj. 1 not discreet; revealing secrets. 2 injudicious, unwary. □□ indiscreetly adv. [ME f. LL indiscretus (as IN-¹, DISCREET)]

indiscrete /ˌɪndɪˈskriːt/ adj. not divided into distinct parts. [L indiscretus (as IN-¹, DISCRETE)]

indiscretion /ˌɪndɪˈskreʃ(ə)n/ n. 1 lack of discretion; indiscreet conduct. 2 an indiscreet action, remark, etc. [ME f. OF indiscretion or LL indiscretio (as IN-¹, DISCRETION)]

indiscriminate /ˌɪndɪˈskrɪmɪnət/ adj. 1 making no distinctions. 2 confused, promiscuous. □□ indiscriminately adv. indiscriminateness n. indiscrimination /-ˈneɪʃ(ə)n/ n. indiscriminative adj. [IN-¹ + discriminate (adj.) f. L discriminatus past part. (as DISCRIMINATE)]

indispensable /ˌɪndɪˈspensəb(ə)l/ adj. 1 (often foll. by to, for) that cannot be dispensed with; necessary. 2 (of a law, duty, etc.) that is not to be set aside. □□ indispensability /-ˈbɪlɪtɪ/ n. indispensableness n. indispensably adv. [med.L indispensabilis (as IN-¹, DISPENSABLE)]

indispose /ˌɪndɪˈspəʊz/ v.tr. 1 (often foll. by for, or to + infin.) make unfit or unable. 2 (often foll. by towards, from, or to + infin.) make averse.

indisposed /ˌɪndɪˈspəʊzd/ adj. 1 slightly unwell. 2 averse or unwilling.

indisposition /ˌɪndɪspəˈzɪʃ(ə)n/ n. 1 ill health, a slight or temporary ailment. 2 disinclination. 3 aversion. [F indisposition or IN-¹ + DISPOSITION]

indisputable /ˌɪndɪˈspjuːtəb(ə)l/ adj. 1 that cannot be disputed. 2 unquestionable. □□ indisputability /-ˈbɪlɪtɪ/ n. indisputableness n. indisputably adv. [LL indisputabilis (as IN-¹, DISPUTABLE)]

indissolubilist /ˌɪndɪˈsɒljʊbɪlɪst/ n. & adj. —n. a person who believes that the Church should not remarry divorcees. —adj. of or holding this belief.

indissoluble /ˌɪndɪˈsɒljʊb(ə)l/ adj. 1 that cannot be dissolved or decomposed. 2 lasting, stable (an indissoluble bond). □□ indissolubility /-ˈbɪlɪtɪ/ n. indissolubly adv. [L indissolubilis (as IN-¹, DISSOLUBLE)]

indistinct /ˌɪndɪˈstɪŋkt/ adj. 1 not distinct. 2 confused, obscure. □□ indistinctly adv. indistinctness n. [ME f. L indistinctus (as IN-¹, DISTINCT)]

indistinctive /ˌɪndɪˈstɪŋktɪv/ adj. not having distinctive features. □□ indistinctively adv. indistinctiveness n.

indistinguishable /ˌɪndɪˈstɪŋɡwɪʃəb(ə)l/ adj. (often foll. by from) not distinguishable. □□ indistinguishableness n. indistinguishably adv.

indite /ɪnˈdaɪt/ v.tr. formal or joc. 1 put (a speech etc.) into words. 2 write (a letter etc.). [ME f. OF enditier: see INDICT]

indium /ˈɪndɪəm/ n. Chem. a soft silvery-white metallic element occurring naturally in zinc blende etc., used for electroplating and in semiconductors. ¶ Symb.: In. [L indicum indigo with ref. to its characteristic spectral lines]

indivertible /ˌɪndɪˈvɜːtɪb(ə)l/ adj. that cannot be turned aside. □□ indivertibly adv.

individual /ˌɪndɪˈvɪdjʊəl/ adj. & n. —adj. 1 single. 2 particular, special; not general. 3 having a distinct character. 4 characteristic of a particular person. 5 designed for use by one person. —n. 1 a single member of a class. 2 a single human being as distinct from a family or group. 3 colloq. a person (a most unpleasant individual). [ME, = indivisible, f. med.L individualis (as IN-¹, dividuus f. dividere DIVIDE)]

individualism /ˌɪndɪˈvɪdjʊəˌlɪz(ə)m/ n. 1 the habit or principle of being independent and self-reliant. 2 a social theory favouring the free action of individuals. 3 self-centred feeling or conduct; egoism. □□ individualist n. individualistic adj. individualistically /-ˈlɪstɪkəlɪ/ adv.

individuality /ˌɪndɪvɪdjʊˈælɪtɪ/ n. (pl. -ies) 1 individual character, esp. when strongly marked. 2 (in pl.) individual tastes etc. 3 separate existence.

individualize /ˌɪndɪˈvɪdjʊəˌlaɪz/ v.tr. (also -ise) 1

give an individual character to. **2** specify. ▫▫
individualization /-'zeɪʃ(ə)n/ *n.*

individually /ˌɪndɪ'vɪdjʊəlɪ/ *adv.* **1** personally; in an individual capacity. **2** in a distinctive manner. **3** one by one; not collectively.

individuate /ˌɪndɪ'vɪdjʊˌeɪt/ *v.tr.* individualize; form into an individual. ▫▫ **individuation** /-'eɪʃ(ə)n/ *n.* [med.L *individuare* (as INDIVIDUAL)]

indivisible /ˌɪndɪ'vɪzɪb(ə)l/ *adj.* **1** not divisible. **2** not distributable among a number. ▫▫ **indivisibility** /-'bɪlɪtɪ/ *n.* **indivisibly** *adv.* [ME f. LL *indivisibilis* (as IN-¹, DIVISIBLE)]

Indo- /'ɪndəʊ/ *comb. form* Indian; Indian and. [L *Indus* f. Gk *Indos*]

Indo-Aryan /ˌɪndəʊ'eərɪən/ *n. & adj.* —*n.* **1** a member of any of the Aryan peoples of India. **2** the Indic group of languages. —*adj.* of or relating to the Indo-Aryans or Indo-Aryan.

Indo-Chinese /ˌɪndəʊtʃaɪ'niːz/ *adj. & n.* —*adj.* of or relating to Indo-China in SE Asia. —*n.* a native of Indo-China; a person of Indo-Chinese descent.

indocile /ɪn'dəʊsaɪl/ *adj.* not docile. ▫▫ **indocility** /-də'sɪlɪtɪ/ *n.* [F *indocile* or L *indocilis* (as IN-¹, DOCILE)]

indoctrinate /ɪn'dɒktrɪˌneɪt/ *v.tr.* **1** teach (a person or group) systematically or for a long period to accept (esp. partisan or tendentious) ideas uncritically. **2** teach, instruct. ▫▫ **indoctrination** /-'neɪʃ(ə)n/ *n.* **indoctrinator** *n.* [IN-² + DOCTRINE + -ATE³]

Indo-European /ˌɪndəʊjʊərə'pɪən/ *adj. & n.* —*adj.* **1** of or relating to the family of languages spoken over the greater part of Europe and Asia as far as N. India. **2** of or relating to the hypothetical parent language of this family. —*n.* **1** the Indo-European family of languages. **2** the hypothetical parent language of all languages belonging to this family. **3** (usu. in *pl.*) a speaker of an Indo-European language.

Indo-Iranian /ˌɪndəʊɪ'reɪnɪən/ *adj. & n.* —*adj.* of or relating to the subfamily of Indo-European languages spoken chiefly in N. India and Iran. —*n.* this subfamily.

indole /'ɪndəʊl/ *n. Chem.* an organic compound with a characteristic odour formed on the reduction of indigo. [INDIGO + L *oleum* oil]

indoleacetic acid /ˌɪndəʊlə'siːtɪk/ *n. Biochem.* any of the several isomeric acetic acid derivatives of indole, esp. one found as a natural growth hormone in plants. ¶ Abbr.: **IAA.** [INDOLE + ACETIC]

indolent /'ɪndələnt/ *adj.* **1** lazy; wishing to avoid activity or exertion. **2** *Med.* causing no pain (*an indolent tumour*). ▫▫ **indolence** *n.* **indolently** *adv.* [LL *indolens* (as IN-¹, *dolēre* suffer pain)]

Indology /ɪn'dɒlədʒɪ/ *n.* the study of Indian history, literature, etc. ▫▫ **Indologist** *n.*

indomitable /ɪn'dɒmɪtəb(ə)l/ *adj.* **1** that cannot be subdued; unyielding. **2** stubbornly persistent. ▫▫ **indomitability** /-'bɪlɪtɪ/ *n.* **indomitableness** *n.* **indomitably** *adv.* [LL *indomitabilis* (as IN-¹, L *domitare* tame)]

Indonesian /ˌɪndə'niːzjən, -ʒ(ə)n, -ʃ(ə)n/ *n. & adj.* —*n.* **1 a** a native or national of Indonesia in SE Asia. **b** a person of Indonesian descent. **2** a member of the chief pre-Malay population of the E. Indies. **3** a language of the group spoken in the E. Indies, esp. the official language of the Indonesian Republic (see also BAHASA INDONESIA). —*adj.* of or relating to Indonesia or its people or language. [*Indonesia* f. INDIES after *Polynesia*]

indoor /'ɪndɔː(r)/ *adj.* situated, carried on, or used within a building or under cover (*indoor aerial*; *indoor games*). [earlier *within-door*: cf. INDOORS]

indoors /ɪn'dɔːz/ *adv.* into or within a building. [earlier *within doors*]

indorse var. of ENDORSE.

indraught /'ɪndrɑːft/ *n.* (*US* **indraft**) **1** the drawing in of something. **2** an inward flow or current.

indrawn /'ɪndrɔːn/ *adj.* **1** (of breath etc.) drawn in. **2** aloof.

indri /'ɪndrɪ/ *n.* (*pl.* **indris**) a large lemur, *Indri indri*,

of Madagascar. [Malagasy *indry* behold, mistaken for its name]

indubitable /ɪn'djuːbɪtəb(ə)l/ *adj.* that cannot be doubted. ▫▫ **indubitably** *adv.* [F *indubitable* or L *indubitabilis* (as IN-¹, *dubitare* to doubt)]

induce /ɪn'djuːs/ *v.tr.* **1** (often foll. by *to* + infin.) prevail on; persuade. **2** bring about; give rise to. **3** *Med.* bring on (labour) artificially, esp. by use of drugs. **4** *Electr.* produce (a current) by induction. **5** *Physics* cause (radioactivity) by bombardment. **6** infer; derive as a deduction. ▫▫ **inducer** *n.* **inducible** *adj.* [ME f. L *inducere* induct- (as IN-², *ducere* lead)]

inducement /ɪn'djuːsmənt/ *n.* **1** (often foll. by *to*) an attraction that leads one on. **2** a thing that induces.

induct /ɪn'dʌkt/ *v.tr.* (often foll. by *to, into*) **1** introduce formally into possession of a benefice. **2** install into a room, office, etc. **3** introduce, initiate. **4** *US* enlist (a person) for military service. ▫▫ **inductee** /ˌɪndʌk'tiː/ *n.* [ME (as INDUCE)]

inductance /ɪn'dʌkt(ə)ns/ *n. Electr.* the property of an electric circuit that causes an electromotive force to be generated by a change in the current flowing.

induction /ɪn'dʌkʃ(ə)n/ *n.* **1** the act or an instance of inducting or inducing. **2** *Med.* the process of bringing on (esp. labour) by artificial means. **3** *Logic* **a** the inference of a general law from particular instances (cf. DEDUCTION). **b** *Math.* a means of proving a theorem by showing that if it is true of any particular case it is true of the next case in a series, and then showing that it is indeed true in one particular case. **c** (foll. by *of*) the production of (facts) to prove a general statement. **4** (often *attrib.*) a formal introduction to a new job, position, etc. (*attended an induction course*). **5** *Electr.* **a** the production of an electric or magnetic state by the proximity (without contact) of an electrified or magnetized body. **b** the production of an electric current in a conductor by a change of magnetic field. **6** the drawing of a fuel mixture into the cylinders of an internal-combustion engine. **7** *US* enlistment for military service. ▫ **induction-coil** a coil for generating intermittent high voltage from a direct current. **induction heating** heating by an induced electric current. [ME f. OF *induction* or L *inductio* (as INDUCE)]

inductive /ɪn'dʌktɪv/ *adj.* **1** (of reasoning etc.) of or based on induction. **2** of electric or magnetic induction. ▫▫ **inductively** *adv.* **inductiveness** *n.* [LL *inductivus* (as INDUCE)]

inductor /ɪn'dʌktə(r)/ *n.* **1** *Electr.* a component (in a circuit) which possesses inductance. **2** a person who inducts a member of the clergy. [L (as INDUCE)]

indue var. of ENDUE.

indulge /ɪn'dʌldʒ/ *v.* **1** *intr.* (often foll. by *in*) take pleasure freely. **2** *tr.* yield freely to (a desire etc.). **3** *tr.* gratify the wishes of; favour (*indulged them with money*). **4** *intr. colloq.* take alcoholic liquor. ▫▫ **indulger** *n.* [L *indulgēre indult-* give free rein to]

indulgence /ɪn'dʌldʒ(ə)ns/ *n.* **1 a** the act of indulging. **b** the state of being indulgent. **2** something indulged in. **3** *RC Ch.* the remission of temporal punishment in purgatory, still due for sins after absolution. **4** a privilege granted. ▫ **Declaration of Indulgence** the proclamation of religious liberties, esp. under Charles II in 1672 and James II in 1687. [ME f. OF f. L *indulgentia* (as INDULGENT)]

indulgent /ɪn'dʌldʒ(ə)nt/ *adj.* **1** ready or too ready to overlook faults etc. **2** indulging or tending to indulge. ▫▫ **indulgently** *adv.* [F *indulgent* or L *indulgere indulgent-* (as INDULGE)]

indumentum /ˌɪndjʊ'mentəm/ *n.* (*pl.* **indumenta** /-tə/) *Bot.* the covering of hairs on part of a plant, esp. when dense. [L, = garment]

induna /ɪn'duːnə/ *n.* **1** *S.Afr.* a tribal councillor or headman. **2 a** an African foreman. **b** a person in authority. [Nguni *inDuna* captain, councillor]

indurate /'ɪndjʊəˌreɪt/ *v.* **1** *tr. & intr.* make or become hard. **2** *tr.* make callous or unfeeling. **3** *intr.* become inveterate. □□ **induration** /-'reɪʃ(ə)n/ *n*. **indurative** *adj*. [L *indurare* (as IN-², *durus* hard)]

indusium /ɪn'dju:zɪəm/ *n*. (*pl*. **indusia** /-zɪə/) **1 a** membranous shield covering the fruit-cluster of a fern. **2** a collection of hairs enclosing the stigma of some flowers. **3** the case of a larva. □□ **indusial** *adj*. [L, = tunic, f. *induere* put on (a garment)]

industrial /ɪn'dʌstrɪəl/ *adj*. & *n*. —*adj*. **1** of or relating to industry or industries. **2** designed or suitable for industrial use (*industrial alcohol*). **3** characterized by highly developed industries (*the industrial nations*). —*n*. (in *pl*.) shares in industrial companies. □**industrial action** *Brit*. any action, esp. a strike or work to rule, taken by employees as a protest. **industrial archaeology** the study of machines, factories, bridges, etc., formerly used in industry. **industrial estate** *Brit*. an area of land developed for the siting of industrial enterprises. **industrial relations** the relations between management and workers in industries. **the Industrial Revolution** the rapid development of a nation's industry (esp. in Britain in the late 18th and early 19th c.). □□ **industrially** *adv*. [INDUSTRY + -AL: in 19th c. partly f. F *industriel*]

industrialism /ɪn'dʌstrɪə,lɪz(ə)m/ *n*. a social or economic system in which manufacturing industries are prevalent.

industrialist /ɪn'dʌstrɪəlɪst/ *n*. a person engaged in the management of industry.

industrialize /ɪn'dʌstrɪə,laɪz/ *v*. (also **-ise**) **1** *tr*. introduce industries to (a country or region etc.). **2** *intr*. become industrialized. □□ **industrialization** /-'zeɪʃ(ə)n/ *n*.

industrious /ɪn'dʌstrɪəs/ *adj*. diligent, hard-working. □□ **industriously** *adv*. **industriousness** *n*. [F *industrieux* or LL *industriosus* (as INDUSTRY)]

industry /'ɪndəstrɪ/ *n*. (*pl*. **-ies**) **1 a** a branch of trade or manufacture. **b** trade and manufacture collectively (*incentives to industry*). **2** concerted or copious activity (*the building was a hive of industry*). **3 a** diligence. **b** *colloq*. the diligent study of a particular topic (*the Shakespeare industry*). **4** habitual employment in useful work. [ME, = skill, f. F *industrie* or L *industria* diligence]

indwell /ɪn'dwel/ *v*. (*past* and *past part*. **indwelt**) *literary* **1** *intr*. (often foll. by *in*) be permanently present as a spirit, principle, etc. **2** *tr*. inhabit spiritually. □□ **indweller** *n*.

-ine¹ /aɪn, ɪn/ *suffix* forming adjectives, meaning 'belonging to, of the nature of' (*Alpine*; *asinine*). [from or after F *-in -ine*, or f. L *-inus*]

-ine² /aɪn/ *suffix* forming adjectives esp. from names of minerals, plants, etc. (*crystalline*). [L *-inus* from or after Gk *-inos*]

-ine³ /ɪn, i:n/ *suffix* forming feminine nouns (*heroine*; *margravine*). [F f. L *-ina* f. Gk *-inē*, or f. G *-in*]

-ine⁴ *suffix* **1** /ɪn/ forming (esp. abstract) nouns (*discipline*; *medicine*). **2** /i:n, ɪn/ *Chem*. forming nouns denoting derived substances, esp. alkaloids, halogens, amines, and amino acids. [F f. L *-ina* (fem.) = -INE¹]

inebriate *v*., *adj*., & *n*. —*v.tr*. /ɪ'ni:brɪ,eɪt/ **1** make drunk; intoxicate. **2** excite. —*adj*. /ɪ'ni:brɪət/ drunken. —*n*. /ɪ'ni:brɪət/ a drunken person, esp. a habitual drunkard. □□ **inebriation** /-'eɪʃ(ə)n/ *n*. **inebriety** /-'braɪətɪ/ *n*. [ME f. L *inebriatus* past part. of *inebriare* (as IN-², *ebrius* drunk)]

inedible /ɪn'edɪb(ə)l/ *adj*. not edible, esp. not suitable for eating (cf. UNEATABLE). □□ **inedibility** /-'bɪlɪtɪ/ *n*.

inedited /ɪn'edɪtɪd/ *adj*. **1** not published. **2** published without editorial alterations or additions.

ineducable /ɪn'edjʊkəb(ə)l/ *adj*. incapable of being educated, esp. through mental retardation. □□ **ineducability** /-'bɪlɪtɪ/ *n*.

ineffable /ɪn'efəb(ə)l/ *adj*. **1** unutterable; too great for description in words. **2** that must not be uttered. □□ **ineffability** /-'bɪlɪtɪ/ *n*. **ineffably** *adv*. [ME f. OF *ineffable* or L *ineffabilis* (as IN-¹, *effari* speak out, utter)]

ineffaceable /,ɪnɪ'feɪsəb(ə)l/ *adj*. that cannot be effaced. □□ **ineffaceability** /-'bɪlɪtɪ/ *n*. **ineffaceably** *adv*.

ineffective /,ɪnɪ'fektɪv/ *adj*. **1** not producing any effect or the desired effect. **2** (of a person) inefficient; not achieving results. **3** lacking artistic effect. □□ **ineffectively** *adv*. **ineffectiveness** *n*.

ineffectual /,ɪnɪ'fektjʊəl, -ʃʊəl/ *adj*. **1 a** without effect. **b** not producing the desired or expected effect. **2** (of a person) lacking the ability to achieve results (*an ineffectual leader*). □□ **ineffectuality** /-tjʊ'ælɪtɪ/ *n*. **ineffectually** *adv*. **ineffectualness** *n*. [ME f. med.L *ineffectualis* (as IN-¹, EFFECTUAL)]

inefficacious /,ɪnefɪ'keɪʃəs/ *adj*. (of a remedy etc.) not producing the desired effect. □□ **inefficaciously** *adv*. **inefficaciousness** *n*. **inefficacy** /ɪn'efɪkəsɪ/ *n*.

inefficient /,ɪnɪ'fɪʃ(ə)nt/ *adj*. **1** not efficient. **2** (of a person) not fully capable; not well qualified. □□ **inefficiency** *n*. **inefficiently** *adv*.

inelastic /,ɪnɪ'læstɪk/ *adj*. **1** not elastic. **2** unadaptable, inflexible, unyielding. □□ **inelastically** *adv*. **inelasticity** /-'tɪsɪtɪ/ *n*.

inelegant /ɪn'elɪgənt/ *adj*. **1** ungraceful. **2 a** unrefined. **b** (of a style) unpolished. □□ **inelegance** *n*. **inelegantly** *adv*. [F *inélégant* f. L *inelegans* (as IN-¹, ELEGANT)]

ineligible /ɪn'elɪdʒɪb(ə)l/ *adj*. **1** not eligible. **2** undesirable. □□ **ineligibility** /-'bɪlɪtɪ/ *n*. **ineligibly** *adv*.

ineluctable /,ɪnɪ'lʌktəb(ə)l/ *adj*. **1** against which it is useless to struggle. **2** that cannot be escaped from. □□ **ineluctability** /-'bɪlɪtɪ/ *n*. **ineluctably** *adv*. [L *ineluctabilis* (as IN-¹, *eluctari* struggle out)]

inept /ɪ'nept/ *adj*. **1** unskilful. **2** absurd, silly. **3** out of place. □□ **ineptitude** *n*. **ineptly** *adv*. **ineptness** *n*. [L *ineptus* (as IN-¹, APT)]

inequable /ɪn'ekwəb(ə)l/ *adj*. **1** not fairly distributed. **2** not uniform. [L *inaequabilis* uneven (as IN-¹, EQUABLE)]

inequality /,ɪnɪ'kwɒlɪtɪ/ *n*. (*pl*. **-ies**) **1 a** a lack of equality in any respect. **b** an instance of this. **2** the state of being variable. **3** (of a surface) irregularity. **4** *Math*. a formula affirming that two expressions are not equal. [ME f. OF *inequalité* or L *inaequalitas* (as IN-¹, EQUALITY)]

inequitable /ɪn'ekwɪtəb(ə)l/ *adj*. unfair, unjust. □□ **inequitably** *adv*.

inequity /ɪn'ekwɪtɪ/ *n*. (*pl*. **-ies**) unfairness, bias.

ineradicable /,ɪnɪ'rædɪkəb(ə)l/ *adj*. that cannot be rooted out. □□ **ineradicably** *adv*.

inerrant /ɪn'erənt/ *adj*. not liable to err. □□ **inerrancy** *n*. [L *inerrans* (as IN-¹, ERR)]

inert /ɪ'nɜːt/ *adj*. **1** without inherent power of action, motion, or resistance. **2** without active chemical or other properties. **3** sluggish, slow. □**inert gas** = *noble gas*. □□ **inertly** *adv*. **inertness** *n*. [L *iners inert-* (as IN-¹, *ars* ART¹)]

inertia /ɪ'nɜːʃə, -ʃɪə/ *n*. **1** *Physics* a property of matter by which it continues in its existing state of rest or uniform motion in a straight line, unless that state is changed by an external force. **2** inertness, sloth. □**inertia reel** a reel device which allows a vehicle seat belt to unwind freely but which locks under force of impact or rapid deceleration. **inertia selling** the sending of unsolicited goods in the hope of making a sale. □□ **inertial** *adj*. **inertialess** *adj*. [L (as INERT)]

inescapable /,ɪnɪ'skeɪpəb(ə)l/ *adj*. that cannot be escaped or avoided. □□ **inescapability** /-'bɪlɪtɪ/ *n*. **inescapably** *adv*.

-iness /ɪnɪs/ *suffix* forming nouns corresponding to adjectives in *-y* (see -Y¹, -LY²).

inessential /,ɪnɪ'senʃ(ə)l/ *adj*. & *n*. —*adj*. **1** not necessary. **2** dispensable. —*n*. an inessential thing.

inestimable /ɪn'estɪməb(ə)l/ *adj*. too great, intense,

precious, etc., to be estimated. □□ **inestimably** *adv.* [ME f. OF f. L *inaestimabilis* (as IN-¹, ESTIMABLE)]

inevitable /ɪnˈevɪtəb(ə)l/ *adj.* **1 a** unavoidable; sure to happen. **b** that is bound to occur or appear. **2** *colloq.* that is tiresomely familiar. **3** (of character-drawing, the development of a plot, etc.) so true to nature etc. as to preclude alternative treatment or solution; convincing. □□ **inevitability** /-ˈbɪlɪtɪ/ *n.* **inevitableness** *n.* **inevitably** *adv.* [L *inevitabilis* (as IN-¹, *evitare* avoid)]

inexact /ˌɪnɪgˈzækt/ *adj.* not exact. □□ **inexactitude** *n.* **inexactly** *adv.* **inexactness** *n.*

inexcusable /ˌɪnɪkˈskjuːzəb(ə)l/ *adj.* (of a person, action, etc.) that cannot be excused or justified. □□ **inexcusably** *adv.* [ME f. L *inexcusabilis* (as IN-¹, EXCUSE)]

inexhaustible /ˌɪnɪgˈzɔːstɪb(ə)l/ *adj.* that cannot be exhausted or used up. □□ **inexhaustibility** /-ˈbɪlɪtɪ/ *n.* **inexhaustibly** *adv.*

inexorable /ɪnˈeksərəb(ə)l/ *adj.* **1** relentless. **2** (of a person or attribute) that cannot be persuaded by request or entreaty. □□ **inexorability** /-ˈbɪlɪtɪ/ *n.* **inexorably** *adv.* [F *inexorable* or L *inexorabilis* (as IN-¹, *exorare* entreat)]

inexpedient /ˌɪnɪkˈspiːdɪənt/ *adj.* not expedient. □□ **inexpediency** *n.*

inexpensive /ˌɪnɪkˈspensɪv/ *adj.* **1** not expensive, cheap. **2** offering good value for the price. □□ **inexpensively** *adv.* **inexpensiveness** *n.*

inexperience /ˌɪnɪkˈspɪərɪəns/ *n.* lack of experience, or of the resulting knowledge or skill. □□ **inexperienced** *adj.* [F *inexpérience* f. LL *inexperientia* (as IN-¹, EXPERIENCE)]

inexpert /ɪnˈekspɜːt/ *adj.* unskilful; lacking expertise. □□ **inexpertly** *adv.* **inexpertness** *n.* [OF f. L *inexpertus* (as IN-¹, EXPERT)]

inexpiable /ɪnˈekspɪəb(ə)l/ *adj.* (of an act or feeling) that cannot be expiated or appeased. □□ **inexpiably** *adv.* [L *inexpiabilis* (as IN-¹, EXPIATE)]

inexplicable /ˌɪnɪkˈsplɪkəb(ə)l, ɪnˈeks-/ *adj.* that cannot be explained or accounted for. □□ **inexplicability** /-ˈbɪlɪtɪ/ *n.* **inexplicably** *adv.* [F *inexplicable* or L *inexplicabilis* that cannot be un-folded (as IN-¹, EXPLICABLE)]

inexplicit /ˌɪnɪkˈsplɪsɪt/ *adj.* not definitely or clearly expressed. □□ **inexplicitly** *adv.* **inexpliciteness** *n.*

inexpressible /ˌɪnɪkˈspresɪb(ə)l/ *adj.* that cannot be expressed in words. □□ **inexpressibly** *adv.*

inexpressive /ˌɪnɪkˈspresɪv/ *adj.* not expressive. □□ **inexpressively** *adv.* **inexpressiveness** *n.*

inexpungible /ˌɪnɪkˈspʌndʒɪb(ə)l/ *adj.* that cannot be expunged or obliterated.

in extenso /ˌɪn ekˈstensəʊ/ *adv.* in full; at length. [L]

inextinguishable /ˌɪnɪkˈstɪŋgwɪʃəb(ə)l/ *adj.* **1** not quenchable; indestructible. **2** (of laughter etc.) irrepressible.

in extremis /ˌɪn ekˈstriːmɪs/ *adj.* **1** at the point of death. **2** in great difficulties. [L]

inextricable /ɪnˈekstrɪkəb(ə)l, ˌɪnɪkˈstrɪk-/ *adj.* **1** (of a circumstance) that cannot be escaped from. **2** (of a knot, problem, etc.) that cannot be unravelled or solved. **3** intricately confused. □□ **inextricability** /-ˈbɪlɪtɪ/ *n.* **inextricably** *adv.* [ME f. L *inextricabilis* (as IN-¹, EXTRICATE)]

infallible /ɪnˈfælɪb(ə)l/ *adj.* **1** incapable of error. **2** (of a method, test, proof, etc.) unfailing; sure to succeed. **3** *RC Ch.* (of the Pope) unable to err in pronouncing dogma as doctrinally defined. □□ **infallibility** /-ˈbɪlɪtɪ/ *n.* **infallibly** *adv.* [ME f. F *infaillible* or LL *infallibilis* (as IN-¹, FALLIBLE)]

infamous /ˈɪnfəməs/ *adj.* **1** notoriously bad; having a bad reputation. **2** abominable. **3** (in ancient law) deprived of all or some rights of a citizen on account of serious crime. □□ **infamously** *adv.* **infamy** /ˈɪnfəmɪ/ *n.* (*pl.* **-ies**). [ME f. med.L *infamosus* f. L *infamis* (as IN-¹, FAME)]

infancy /ˈɪnfənsɪ/ *n.* (*pl.* **-ies**) **1** early childhood; babyhood. **2** an early state in the development of an idea, undertaking, etc. **3** *Law* the state of being a minor. [L *infantia* (as INFANT)]

infant /ˈɪnf(ə)nt/ *n.* **1 a** a child during the earliest period of its life. **b** *Brit.* a schoolchild below the age of seven years. **2** (esp. *attrib.*) a thing in an early stage of its development. **3** *Law* a minor; a person under 18. □ **infant mortality** death before the age of one. [ME f. OF *enfant* f. L *infans* unable to speak (as IN-¹, *fans fantis* pres. part. of *fari* speak)]

infanta /ɪnˈfæntə/ *n. hist.* a daughter of the ruling monarch of Spain or Portugal (usu. the eldest daughter who is not heir to the throne). [Sp. & Port., fem. of INFANTE]

infante /ɪnˈfæntɪ/ *n. hist.* the second son of the ruling monarch of Spain or Portugal. [Sp. & Port. f. L (as INFANT)]

infanticide /ɪnˈfæntɪsaɪd/ *n.* **1** the killing of an infant soon after birth. **2** the practice of killing newborn infants. **3** a person who kills an infant. □□ **infanticidal** /-ˈsaɪd(ə)l/ *adj.* [F f. LL *infanticidium*, *-cida* (as INFANT)]

infantile /ˈɪnfəntaɪl/ *adj.* **1 a** like or characteristic of a child. **b** childish, immature (*infantile humour*). **2** in its infancy. □ **infantile paralysis** poliomyelitis. □□ **infantility** /-ˈtɪlɪtɪ/ *n.* (*pl.* **-ies**). [F *infantile* or L *infantilis* (as INFANT)]

infantilism /ɪnˈfæntɪˌlɪz(ə)m/ *n.* **1** childish behaviour. **2** *Psychol.* the persistence of infantile characteristics or behaviour in adult life.

infantry /ˈɪnfəntrɪ/ *n.* (*pl.* **-ies**) a body of soldiers who march and fight on foot; foot-soldiers collectively. [F *infanterie* f. It. *infanteria* f. *infante* youth, infantryman (as INFANT)]

infantryman /ˈɪnfəntrɪmən/ *n.* (*pl.* **-men**) a soldier of an infantry regiment.

infarct /ˈɪnfaːkt/ *n. Med.* a small localized area of dead tissue caused by an inadequate blood supply. □□ **infarction** /ɪnˈfaːkʃ(ə)n/ *n.* [mod.L *infarctus* (as IN-², L *farcire farct-* stuff)]

infatuate /ɪnˈfætjʊˌeɪt/ *v.tr.* **1** inspire with intense usu. transitory fondness or admiration. **2** affect with extreme folly. □□ **infatuation** /-ˈeɪʃ(ə)n/ *n.* [L *infatuare* (as IN-², *fatuus* foolish)]

infatuated /ɪnˈfætjʊˌeɪtɪd/ *adj.* (often foll. by *with*) affected by an intense fondness or admiration.

infauna /ˈɪnˌfɔːnə/ *n.* any animals which live just below the surface of the seabed. [Da. *ifauna* (as IN-², FAUNA)]

infeasible /ɪnˈfiːzɪb(ə)l/ *adj.* not feasible; that cannot easily be done. □□ **infeasibility** /-ˈbɪlɪtɪ/ *n.*

infect /ɪnˈfekt/ *v.tr.* **1** contaminate (air, water, etc.) with harmful organisms or noxious matter. **2** affect (a person) with disease etc. **3** instil bad feeling or opinion into (a person). □□ **infector** *n.* [ME f. L *inficere infect-* taint (as IN-², *facere* make)]

infection /ɪnˈfekʃ(ə)n/ *n.* **1 a** the process of infecting or state of being infected. **b** an instance of this; an infectious disease. **2** communication of disease, esp. by the agency of air or water etc. **3 a** moral contamination. **b** the diffusive influence of example, sympathy, etc. [ME f. OF *infection* or LL *infectio* (as INFECT)]

infectious /ɪnˈfekʃəs/ *adj.* **1** infecting with disease. **2** (of a disease) liable to be transmitted by air, water, etc. **3** (of emotions etc.) apt to spread; quickly affecting others. □□ **infectiously** *adv.* **infectiousness** *n.*

infective /ɪnˈfektɪv/ *adj.* **1** capable of infecting with disease. **2** infectious. □□ **infectiveness** *n.* [L *infectivus* (as INFECT)]

infelicitous /ˌɪnfɪˈlɪsɪtəs/ *adj.* not felicitous; unfortunate. □□ **infelicitously** *adv.*

infelicity /ˌɪnfɪˈlɪsɪtɪ/ *n.* (*pl.* **-ies**) **1 a** inaptness of expression etc. **b** an instance of this. **2 a** unhappiness. **b** a misfortune. [ME f. L *infelicitas* (as IN-¹, FELICITY)]

infer /ɪnˈfɜː(r)/ *v.tr.* (**inferred**, **inferring**) (often foll. by *that* + clause) **1** deduce or conclude from facts and reasoning. **2** *disp*. imply, suggest. □□ **inferable** *adj*. (also **inferrable**). [L *inferre* (as IN-[2], *ferre* bring)]

inference /'ɪnfərəns/ *n*. **1** the act or an instance of inferring. **2** *Logic* **a** the forming of a conclusion from premisses. **b** a thing inferred. □□ **inferential** /-'renʃ(ə)l/ *adj*. **inferentially** /-'renʃəlɪ/ *adv*. [med.L *inferentia* (as INFER)]

inferior /ɪn'fɪərɪə(r)/ *adj*. & *n*. —*adj*. **1** (often foll. by *to*) **a** lower; in a lower position. **b** of lower rank, quality, etc. **2** poor in quality. **3** (of a planet) having an orbit within the earth's. **4** *Bot*. situated below an ovary or calyx. **5** (of figures or letters) written or printed below the line. —*n*. **1** a person inferior to another, esp. in rank. **2** an inferior letter or figure. □□ **inferiorly** *adv*. [ME f. L, compar. of *inferus* that is below]

inferiority /ɪn,fɪərɪ'ɒrɪtɪ/ *n*. the state of being inferior. □ **inferiority complex** an unrealistic feeling of general inadequacy caused by actual or supposed inferiority in one sphere, sometimes marked by aggressive behaviour in compensation.

infernal /ɪn'fɜːn(ə)l/ *adj*. **1 a** of hell or the underworld. **b** hellish, fiendish. **2** *colloq*. detestable, tiresome. □□ **infernally** *adv*. [ME f. OF f. LL *infernalis* f. L *infernus* situated below]

inferno /ɪn'fɜːnəʊ/ *n*. (*pl*. **-os**) **1** a raging fire. **2** a scene of horror or distress. **3** hell, esp. with ref. to Dante's *Divine Comedy*. [It. f. LL *infernus* (as INFERNAL)]

infertile /ɪn'fɜːtaɪl/ *adj*. not fertile. □□ **infertility** /-'tɪlɪtɪ/ *n*. [F *infertile* or LL *infertilis* (as IN-[1], FERTILE)]

infest /ɪn'fest/ *v.tr*. (of harmful persons or things, esp. vermin or disease) overrun (a place) in large numbers. □□ **infestation** /-'steɪʃ(ə)n/ *n*. [ME f. F *infester* or L *infestare* assail f. *infestus* hostile]

infidel /'ɪnfɪd(ə)l/ *n*. & *adj*. —*n*. **1** a person who does not believe in religion or in a particular religion; an unbeliever. **2** *hist*. an adherent of a religion other than Christianity, esp. a Muslim. —*adj*. **1** that is an infidel. **2** of unbelievers. [ME f. F *infidèle* or L *infidelis* (as IN-[1], *fidelis* faithful)]

infidelity /,ɪnfɪ'delɪtɪ/ *n*. (*pl*. **-ies**) **1 a** disloyalty or unfaithfulness, esp. to a husband or wife. **b** an instance of this. **2** disbelief in Christianity or another religion. [ME f. F *infidélité* or L *infidelitas* (as INFIDEL)]

infield /'ɪnfiːld/ *n*. **1** *Cricket* **a** the part of the ground near the wicket. **b** the fielders stationed there. **2** *Baseball* **a** the area between the four bases. **b** the four fielders stationed on its boundaries. **3** farm land around or near a homestead. **4 a** arable land. **b** land regularly manured and cropped. □□ **infielder** *n*. (in sense 2).

infighting /'ɪn,faɪtɪŋ/ *n*. **1** hidden conflict or competitiveness within an organization. **2** boxing at closer quarters than arm's length. □□ **infighter** *n*.

infill /'ɪnfɪl/ *n*. & *v*. —*n*. **1** material used to fill a hole, gap, etc. **2** the placing of buildings to occupy the space between existing ones. —*v.tr*. fill in (a cavity etc.).

infilling /'ɪn,fɪlɪŋ/ *n*. = INFILL *n*.

infiltrate /'ɪnfɪl,treɪt/ *v*. **1** *tr*. **a** gain entrance or access to surreptitiously and by degrees (as spies etc.). **b** cause to do this. **2** *tr*. permeate by filtration. **3** *tr*. (often foll. by *into*, *through*) introduce (fluid) by filtration. □□ **infiltration** /-'treɪʃ(ə)n/ *n*. **infiltrator** *n*. [IN-[2] + FILTRATE]

infinite /'ɪnfɪnɪt/ *adj*. & *n*. —*adj*. **1** boundless, endless. **2** very great. **3** (usu. with *pl*.) innumerable; very many (*infinite resources*). **4** *Math*. **a** greater than any assignable quantity or countable number. **b** (of a series) that may be continued indefinitely. **5** *Gram*. (of a verb part) not limited by person or number, e.g. infinitive, gerund, and participle. —*n*. **1** (**the Infinite**) God. **2** (**the infinite**) infinite space. □□ **infinitely** *adv*. **infiniteness** *n*. [ME f. L *infinitus* (as IN-[1], FINITE)]

infinitesimal /,ɪnfɪnɪ'tesɪm(ə)l/ *adj*. & *n*. —*adj*.

infinitely or very small. —*n*. an infinitesimal amount. □ **infinitesimal calculus** the differential and integral calculuses regarded as one subject. □□ **infinitesimally** *adv*. [mod.L *infinitesimus* f. INFINITE: cf. CENTESIMAL]

infinitive /ɪn'fɪnɪtɪv/ *n*. & *adj*. —*n*. a form of a verb expressing the verbal notion without reference to a particular subject, tense, etc. (e.g. *see* in *we came to see*, *let him see*). —*adj*. having this form. □□ **infinitival** /-'taɪv(ə)l/ *adj*. **infinitivally** /-'taɪvəlɪ/ *adv*. [L *infinitivus* (as IN-[1], *finitivus* definite f. *finire* *finit-* define)]

infinitude /ɪn'fɪnɪ,tjuːd/ *n*. **1** the state of being infinite; boundlessness. **2** (often foll. by *of*) a boundless number or extent. [L *infinitus*: see INFINITE, -TUDE]

infinity /ɪn'fɪnɪtɪ/ *n*. (*pl*. **-ies**) **1** the state of being infinite. **2** an infinite number or extent. **3** infinite distance. **4** *Math*. infinite quantity. ¶ Symb.: ∞. [ME f. OF *infinité* or L *infinitas* (as INFINITE)]

infirm /ɪn'fɜːm/ *adj*. **1** physically weak, esp. through age. **2** (of a person, mind, judgement, etc.) weak, irresolute. □□ **infirmity** *n*. (*pl*. **-ies**). **infirmly** *adv*. [ME f. L *infirmus* (as IN-[1], FIRM[1])]

infirmary /ɪn'fɜːmərɪ/ *n*. (*pl*. **-ies**) **1** a hospital. **2** a place for those who are ill in a monastery, school, etc. [med.L *infirmaria* (as INFIRM)]

infix *v*. & *n*. —*v.tr*. /ɪn'fɪks/ **1** (often foll. by *in*) **a** fix (a thing in another). **b** impress (a fact etc. in the mind). **2** *Gram*. insert (a formative element) into the body of a word. —*n*. /'ɪnfɪks/ *Gram*. a formative element inserted in a word. □□ **infixation** /-'seɪʃ(ə)n/ *n*. [L *infigere infix-* (as IN-[2], FIX): (n.) after *prefix*, *suffix*]

in flagrante delicto /ɪn flə,græntɪ dɪ'lɪktəʊ/ *adj*. in the very act of committing an offence. [L, = in blazing crime]

inflame /ɪn'fleɪm/ *v*. **1** *tr*. & *intr*. (often foll. by *with*, *by*) provoke or become provoked to strong feeling, esp. anger. **2** *Med*. **a** *intr*. become hot, reddened, and sore. **b** *tr*. cause inflammation or fever in (a body etc.); make hot. **3** *tr*. aggravate. **4** *intr*. & *tr*. catch or set on fire. **5** *tr*. light up with or as if with flames. □□ **inflamer** *n*. [ME f. OF *enflammer* f. L *inflammare* (as IN-[2], *flamma* flame)]

inflammable /ɪn'flæməb(ə)l/ *adj*. & *n*. —*adj*. **1** easily set on fire; flammable. **2** easily excited. —*n*. (usu. in *pl*.) an inflammable substance. □□ **inflammability** /-'bɪlɪtɪ/ *n*. **inflammableness** *n*. **inflammably** *adv*. [INFLAME after F *inflammable*]

inflammation /,ɪnflə'meɪʃ(ə)n/ *n*. **1** the act or an instance of inflaming. **2** *Med*. a localized physical condition with heat, swelling, redness, and usu. pain, esp. as a reaction to injury or infection. [L *inflammatio* (as INFLAME)]

inflammatory /ɪn'flæmətərɪ/ *adj*. **1** (esp. of speeches, leaflets, etc.) tending to cause anger etc. **2** of or tending to inflammation of the body.

inflatable /ɪn'fleɪtəb(ə)l/ *adj*. & *n*. —*adj*. that can be inflated. —*n*. an inflatable plastic or rubber object.

inflate /ɪn'fleɪt/ *v.tr*. **1** distend (a balloon etc.) with air. **2** (usu. foll. by *with*; usu. in *passive*) puff up (a person with pride etc.). **3 a** (often *absol*.) bring about inflation (of the currency). **b** raise (prices) artificially. **4** (as **inflated** *adj*.) (esp. of language, sentiments, etc.) bombastic. □□ **inflatedly** *adv*. **inflatedness** *n*. **inflater** *n*. **inflator** *n*. [L *inflare inflat-* (as IN-[2], *flare* blow)]

inflation /ɪn'fleɪʃ(ə)n/ *n*. **1 a** the act or condition of inflating or being inflated. **b** an instance of this. **2** *Econ*. **a** a general increase in prices and fall in the purchasing value of money. **b** an increase in available currency regarded as causing this. □□ **inflationary** *adj*. **inflationism** *n*. **inflationist** *n*. & *adj*. [ME f. L *inflatio* (as INFLATE)]

inflect /ɪn'flekt/ *v*. **1** *tr*. change the pitch of (the voice, a musical note, etc.). **2** *Gram*. **a** *tr*. change the form of (a word) to express tense, gender, number, mood, etc. **b** *intr.* (of a word, language, etc.) undergo such change. **3** *tr.* bend inwards; curve. □□ **inflective** *adj.* [ME f. L *inflectere inflex-* (as IN-[2], *flectere* bend)]

inflection /ɪnˈflekʃ(ə)n/ *n.* (also **inflexion**) **1 a** the act or condition of inflecting or being inflected. **b** an instance of this. **2** *Gram.* **a** the process or practice of inflecting words. **b** an inflected form of a word. **c** a suffix etc. used to inflect, e.g. *-ed*. **3** a modulation of the voice. **4** *Geom.* a change of curvature from convex to concave at a particular point on a curve. □□ **inflectional** *adj.* **inflectionally** *adv.* **inflectionless** *adj.* [F *inflection* or L *inflexio* (as INFLECT)]

inflexible /ɪnˈfleksɪb(ə)l/ *adj.* **1** unbendable. **2** stiff; immovable; obstinate (*old and inflexible in his attitudes*). **3** unchangeable; inexorable. □□ **inflexibility** /-ˈbɪlɪtɪ/ *n.* **inflexibly** *adv.* [L *inflexibilis* (as IN-[1], FLEXIBLE)]

inflict /ɪnˈflɪkt/ *v.tr.* (usu. foll. by *on, upon*) **1** administer, deal (a stroke, wound, defeat, etc.). **2** (also *refl.*) often *joc.* impose (suffering, a penalty, oneself, one's company, etc.) on (*shall not inflict myself on you any longer*). □□ **inflictable** *adj.* **inflicter** *n.* **inflictor** *n.* [L *infligere inflict-* (as IN-[2], *fligere* strike)]

infliction /ɪnˈflɪkʃ(ə)n/ *n.* **1** the act or an instance of inflicting. **2** something inflicted, esp. a troublesome or boring experience. [LL *inflictio* (as INFLICT)]

inflight /ˈɪnflaɪt/ *attrib.adj.* occurring or provided during an aircraft flight.

inflorescence /ˌɪnfləˈres(ə)ns/ *n.* **1** *Bot.* **a** the complete flower-head of a plant including stems, stalks, bracts, and flowers. **b** the arrangement of this. **2** the process of flowering. [mod.L *inflorescentia* f. LL *inflorescere* (as IN-[2], FLORESCENCE)]

inflow /ˈɪnfləʊ/ *n.* **1** a flowing in. **2** something that flows in. □□ **inflowing** *n.* & *adj.*

influence /ˈɪnfluəns/ *n.* & *v.* —*n.* **1 a** (usu. foll. by *on, upon*) the effect a person or thing has on another. **b** (usu. foll. by *over, with*) moral ascendancy or power. **c** a thing or person exercising such power (*is a good influence on them*). **2** *Astrol.* an ethereal fluid supposedly flowing from the stars and affecting character and destiny. **3** *Electr. archaic* = INDUCTION. —*v.tr.* exert influence on; have an effect on. □ **under the influence** *colloq.* affected by alcoholic drink. □□ **influenceable** *adj.* **influencer** *n.* [ME f. OF *influence* or med.L *influentia* inflow f. L *influere* flow in (as IN-[2], *fluere* flow)]

influent /ˈɪnfluənt/ *adj.* & *n.* —*adj.* flowing in. —*n.* a tributary stream. [ME f. L (as INFLUENCE)]

influential /ˌɪnfluˈenʃ(ə)l/ *adj.* having a great influence or power (*influential in the financial world*). □□ **influentially** *adv.* [med.L *influentia* INFLUENCE]

influenza /ˌɪnfluˈenzə/ *n.* a highly contagious virus infection causing fever, severe aching, and catarrh, often occurring in epidemics. □□ **influenzal** *adj.* [It. f. med.L *influentia* INFLUENCE]

influx /ˈɪnflʌks/ *n.* **1** a continual stream of people or things (*an influx of complaints*). **2** (usu. foll. by *into*) a flowing in, esp. of a stream etc. [F *influx* or LL *influxus* (as IN-[2], FLUX)]

info /ˈɪnfəʊ/ *n. colloq.* information. [abbr.]

infold var. of ENFOLD.

inform /ɪnˈfɔːm/ *v.* **1** *tr.* (usu. foll. by *of, about, on,* or *that, how* + clause) tell (*informed them of their rights*; *informed us that the train was late*). **2** *intr.* (usu. foll. by *against, on*) make an accusation. **3** *tr.* (usu. foll. by *with*) *literary* inspire or imbue (a person, heart, or thing) with a feeling, principle, quality, etc. **4** *tr.* impart its quality to; permeate. □□ **informant** *n.* [ME f. OF *enfo(u)rmer* f. L *informare* give shape to, fashion, describe (as IN-[2], *forma* form)]

informal /ɪnˈfɔːm(ə)l/ *adj.* **1** without ceremony or formality (*just an informal chat*). **2** (of language, clothing, etc.) everyday; normal. □ **informal vote** *NZ & Austral.* an invalid vote or voting paper. □□ **informality** /-ˈmælɪtɪ/ *n.* (*pl.* **-ies**). **informally** *adv.*

informatics /ˌɪnfəˈmætɪks/ *n.pl.* (usu. treated as

sing.) the science of processing data for storage and retrieval; information science. [transl. Russ. *informatika* (as INFORMATION, -ICS)]

information /ˌɪnfəˈmeɪʃ(ə)n/ *n.* **1 a** something told; knowledge. **b** (usu. foll. by *on, about*) items of knowledge; news (*the latest information on the crisis*). **2** *Law* (usu. foll. by *against*) a charge or complaint lodged before a court or magistrate. **3 a** the act of informing or telling. **b** an instance of this. □ **information retrieval** the tracing of information stored in books, computers, etc. **information science** the study of the processes for storing and retrieving information. **information theory** *Math.* the quantitative study of the transmission of information by signals etc. □□ **informational** *adj.* **informationally** *adv.* [ME f. OF f. L *informatio -onis* (as INFORM)]

informative /ɪnˈfɔːmətɪv/ *adj.* (also **informatory** /ɪnˈfɔːmətərɪ/) giving information; instructive. □□ **informatively** *adv.* **informativeness** *n.* [med.L *informativus* (as INFORM)]

informed /ɪnˈfɔːmd/ *adj.* **1** knowing the facts; instructed (*his answers show that he is badly informed*). **2** educated; intelligent. □□ **informedly** /also ɪnˈfɔːmɪdlɪ/ *adv.* **informedness** /also ɪnˈfɔːmɪdnɪs/ *n.*

informer /ɪnˈfɔːmə(r)/ *n.* **1** a person who informs against another. **2** a person who informs or advises.

infra /ˈɪnfrə/ *adv.* below, further on (in a book or writing). [L, = below]

infra- /ˈɪnfrə/ *comb. form* **1** below (opp. SUPRA-). **2** *Anat.* below or under a part of the body. [from or after L *infra* below, beneath]

infraction /ɪnˈfrækʃ(ə)n/ *n.* esp. *Law* a violation or infringement. □□ **infract** *v.tr.* **infractor** *n.* [L *infractio* (as INFRINGE)]

infra dig /ˌɪnfrə ˈdɪg/ *predic.adj. colloq.* beneath one's dignity; unbecoming. [abbr. of L *infra dignitatem*]

infrangible /ɪnˈfrændʒɪb(ə)l/ *adj.* **1** unbreakable. **2** inviolable. □□ **infrangibility** /-ˈbɪlɪtɪ/ *n.* **infrangibleness** *n.* **infrangibly** *adv.* [obs.F *infrangible* or med.L *infrangibilis* (as IN-[1], FRANGIBLE)]

infrared /ˌɪnfrəˈred/ *adj.* **1** having a wavelength just greater than the red end of the visible light spectrum but less than that of radio waves. **2** of or using such radiation.

infrasonic /ˌɪnfrəˈsɒnɪk/ *adj.* of or relating to sound waves with a frequency below the lower limit of human audibility. □□ **infrasonically** *adv.*

infrasound /ˈɪnfrəsaʊnd/ *n.* sound waves with frequencies below the lower limit of human audibility.

infrastructure /ˈɪnfrəˌstrʌktʃə(r)/ *n.* **1 a** the basic structural foundations of a society or enterprise; a substructure or foundation. **b** roads, bridges, sewers, etc., regarded as a country's economic foundation. **2** permanent installations as a basis for military etc. operations. [F (as INFRA-, STRUCTURE)]

infrequent /ɪnˈfriːkwənt/ *adj.* not frequent. □□ **infrequency** *n.* **infrequently** *adv.* [L *infrequens* (as IN-[1], FREQUENT)]

infringe /ɪnˈfrɪndʒ/ *v.* **1** *tr.* **a** act contrary to; violate (a law, an oath, etc.). **b** act in defiance of (another's rights etc.). **2** *intr.* (usu. foll. by *on, upon*) encroach; trespass. □□ **infringement** *n.* **infringer** *n.* [L *infringere infract-* (as IN-[2], *frangere* break)]

infula /ˈɪnfjʊlə/ *n.* (*pl.* **infulae** /-ˌliː/) *Eccl.* either of the two ribbons on a bishop's mitre. [L, = woollen fillet worn by priest etc.]

infundibular /ˌɪnfʌnˈdɪbjʊlə(r)/ *adj.* funnel-shaped. [L *infundibulum* funnel f. *infundere* pour in (as IN-[2], *fundere* pour)]

infuriate *v.* & *adj.* —*v.tr.* /ɪnˈfjʊərɪˌeɪt/ fill with fury; enrage. —*adj.* /ɪnˈfjʊərɪət/ *literary* excited to fury; frantic. □□ **infuriating** /ɪnˈfjʊərɪˌeɪtɪŋ/ *adj.* **infuriatingly** /ɪnˈfjʊərɪˌeɪtɪŋlɪ/ *adv.* **infuriation** /-ˈeɪʃ(ə)n/ *n.* [med.L *infuriare infuriat-* (as IN-[2], L *furia* FURY)]

infuse /ɪnˈfjuːz/ *v.* **1** *tr.* (usu. foll. by *with*) imbue; pervade (*anger infused with resentment*). **2** *tr.* steep (herbs, tea, etc.) in liquid to extract the content. **3** *tr.* (usu. foll. by *into*) instil (grace, spirit, life, etc.). **4** *intr.* undergo infusion (*let it infuse for five minutes*). **5** *tr.* (usu. foll. by *into*) pour (a thing). □□ **infusable** *adj.* **infuser** *n.* **infusive** /-sɪv/ *adj.* [ME f. L *infundere infus-* (as IN-², *fundere* pour)]

infusible /ɪnˈfjuːzɪb(ə)l/ *adj.* not able to be fused or melted. □□ **infusibility** /-ˈbɪlɪtɪ/ *n.*

infusion /ɪnˈfjuːʒ(ə)n/ *n.* **1** a liquid obtained by infusing. **2** an infused element; an admixture. **3** *Med.* a slow injection of a substance into a vein or tissue. **4 a** the act of infusing. **b** an instance of this. [ME f. F *infusion* or L *infusio* (as INFUSE)]

infusorial earth /ˌɪnfjuːˈzɔːrɪəl, -ˈsɔːrɪəl/ *n.* = KIESELGUHR. [mod.L *infusoria*, formerly a class of protozoa found in decaying animal or vegetable matter (as INFUSE)]

-ing[1] /ɪŋ/ *suffix* forming gerunds and nouns from verbs (or occas. from nouns), denoting: **1 a** the verbal action or its result (*asking*; *carving*; *fighting*; *learning*). **b** the verbal action as described or classified in some way (*tough going*). **2** material used for or associated with a process etc. (*piping*; *washing*). **3** an occupation or event (*banking*; *wedding*). **4** a set or arrangement of (*colouring*; *feathering*). [OE *-ung*, *-ing* f. Gmc]

-ing[2] /ɪŋ/ *suffix* **1** forming the present participle of verbs (*asking*; *fighting*), often as adjectives (*charming*; *strapping*). **2** forming adjectives from nouns (*hulking*) and verbs (*balding*). [ME alt. of OE *-ende*, later *-inde*]

-ing[3] /ɪŋ/ *suffix* forming nouns meaning 'one belonging to' or 'one having the quality of', surviving esp. in names of coins and fractional parts (*farthing*; *gelding*; *riding*). [OE f. Gmc]

ingather /ɪnˈgæðə(r)/ *v.tr.* gather in; assemble.

ingathering /ɪnˈgæðərɪŋ/ *n.* the act or an instance of gathering in, esp. of a harvest.

ingeminate /ɪnˈdʒɛmɪneɪt/ *v.tr.* *literary* repeat; reiterate. □ **ingeminate peace** constantly urge peace. [L *ingeminare ingeminat-* (as IN-², GEMINATE)]

ingenious /ɪnˈdʒiːnɪəs/ *adj.* **1** clever at inventing, constructing, organizing, etc.; skilful; resourceful. **2** (of a machine, theory, etc.) cleverly contrived. □□ **ingeniously** *adv.* **ingeniousness** *n.* [ME, = talented, f. F *ingénieux* or L *ingeniosus* f. *ingenium* cleverness: cf. ENGINE]

ingénue /ˌæʒeɪˈnjuː/ *n.* **1** an innocent or unsophisticated young woman. **2** *Theatr.* **a** such a part in a play. **b** the actress who plays this part. [F, fem. of *ingénu* INGENUOUS]

ingenuity /ˌɪndʒɪˈnjuːɪtɪ/ *n.* skill in devising or contriving; ingeniousness. [L *ingenuitas* ingenuousness (as INGENUOUS): Engl. meaning by confusion of INGENIOUS with INGENUOUS]

ingenuous /ɪnˈdʒɛnjʊəs/ *adj.* **1** innocent; artless. **2** open; frank. □□ **ingenuously** *adv.* **ingenuousness** *n.* [L *ingenuus* free-born, frank (as IN-², root of *gignere* beget)]

ingest /ɪnˈdʒɛst/ *v.tr.* **1** take in (food etc.); eat. **2** absorb (facts, knowledge, etc.). □□ **ingestion** /ɪnˈdʒɛstʃ(ə)n/ *n.* **ingestive** *adj.* [L *ingerere ingest-* (as IN-², *gerere* carry)]

inglenook /ˈɪŋg(ə)lnʊk/ *n.* a space within the opening on either side of a large fireplace. [dial. (orig. Sc.) *ingle* fire burning on a hearth, perh. f. Gael. *aingeal* fire, light, + NOOK]

inglorious /ɪnˈglɔːrɪəs/ *adj.* **1** shameful; ignominious. **2** not famous. □□ **ingloriously** *adv.* **ingloriousness** *n.*

-ingly /ˈɪŋlɪ/ *suffix* forming adverbs esp. denoting manner of action or nature or condition (*dotingly*; *charmingly*; *slantingly*).

ingoing /ˈɪnˌgəʊɪŋ/ *adj.* **1** going in; entering. **2** penetrating; thorough.

ingot /ˈɪŋgɒt, -gət/ *n.* a usu. oblong piece of cast metal, esp. of gold, silver, or steel. [ME: perh. f. IN¹ + *goten* past part. of OE *geotan* cast]

ingraft var. of ENGRAFT.

ingrain /ˈɪngreɪn/ *adj.* **1** inherent; ingrained. **2** (of textiles) dyed in the fibre, before being woven. □ **ingrain carpet** a reversible carpet, with different colours interwoven.

ingrained /ɪnˈgreɪnd, *attrib.* ˈɪn-/ *adj.* **1** deeply rooted; inveterate. **2** thorough. **3** (of dirt etc.) deeply embedded. □□ **ingrainedly** /-ˈgreɪnɪdlɪ/ *adv.* [var. of *engrained*: see ENGRAIN]

ingrate /ˈɪngreɪt, -ˈgreɪt/ *n.* & *adj.* *formal* or *literary* —*n.* an ungrateful person. —*adj.* ungrateful. [ME f. L *ingratus* (as IN-¹, *gratus* grateful)]

ingratiate /ɪnˈgreɪʃɪeɪt/ *v.refl.* (usu. foll. by *with*) bring oneself into favour. □□ **ingratiating** *adj.* **ingratiatingly** *adv.* **ingratiation** /-ˈeɪʃ(ə)n/ *n.* [L *in gratiam* into favour]

ingratitude /ɪnˈgrætɪˌtjuːd/ *n.* a lack of due gratitude. [ME f. OF *ingratitude* or LL *ingratitudo* (as INGRATE)]

ingravescent /ˌɪngrəˈvɛs(ə)nt/ *adj.* *Med.* (of a disease etc.) growing worse. □□ **ingravescence** *n.* [L *ingravescere* (as IN-², *gravescere* grow heavy f. *gravis* heavy)]

ingredient /ɪnˈgriːdɪənt/ *n.* a component part or element in a recipe, mixture, or combination. [ME f. L *ingredi ingress-* enter (as IN-², *gradi* step)]

ingress /ˈɪngrɛs/ *n.* **1** the act or right of going in or entering. **2** *Astron.* the start of an eclipse or transit. □□ **ingression** /ɪnˈgrɛʃ(ə)n/ *n.* [ME f. L *ingressus* (as INGREDIENT)]

in-group /ˈɪngruːp/ *n.* a small exclusive group of people with a common interest.

ingrowing /ˈɪnˌgrəʊɪŋ/ *adj.* growing inwards, esp. (of a toenail) growing into the flesh. □□ **ingrown** *adj.* **ingrowth** *n.*

inguinal /ˈɪŋgwɪn(ə)l/ *adj.* of the groin. □□ **inguinally** *adv.* [L *inguinalis* f. *inguen -inis* groin]

ingulf var. of ENGULF.

ingurgitate /ɪnˈgɜːdʒɪteɪt/ *v.tr.* **1** swallow greedily. **2** engulf. □□ **ingurgitation** /-ˈteɪʃ(ə)n/ *n.* [L *ingurgitare ingurgitat-* (as IN-², *gurges gurgitis* whirlpool)]

inhabit /ɪnˈhæbɪt/ *v.tr.* (**inhabited**, **inhabiting**) (of a person or animal) dwell in; occupy (a region, town, house, etc.). □□ **inhabitability** /-əˈbɪlɪtɪ/ *n.* **inhabitable** *adj.* **inhabitant** *n.* **inhabitation** /-ˈteɪʃ(ə)n/ *n.* [ME *inhabite*, *enhabite* f. OF *enhabiter* or L *inhabitare* (as IN-², *habitare* dwell): see HABIT]

inhabitancy /ɪnˈhæbɪtənsɪ/ *n.* (also **inhabitance** /-t(ə)ns/) residence as an inhabitant, esp. during a specified period so as to acquire rights etc.

inhalant /ɪnˈheɪlənt/ *n.* a medicinal preparation for inhaling.

inhale /ɪnˈheɪl/ *v.tr.* (often *absol.*) breathe in (air, gas, tobacco-smoke, etc.). □□ **inhalation** /-həˈleɪʃ(ə)n/ *n.* [L *inhalare* breathe in (as IN-², *halare* breathe)]

inhaler /ɪnˈheɪlə(r)/ *n.* a portable device used for relieving esp. asthma by inhaling.

inharmonic /ˌɪnhɑːˈmɒnɪk/ *adj.* esp. *Mus.* not harmonic.

inharmonious /ˌɪnhɑːˈməʊnɪəs/ *adj.* esp. *Mus.* not harmonious. □□ **inharmoniously** *adv.*

inhere /ɪnˈhɪə(r)/ *v.intr.* (often foll. by *in*) **1** exist essentially or permanently in (*goodness inheres in that child*). **2** (of rights etc.) be vested in (a person etc.). [L *inhaerēre inhaes-* (as IN-², *haerēre* to stick)]

inherent /ɪnˈhɪərənt, ɪnˈhɛrənt/ *adj.* (often foll. by *in*) **1** existing in something, esp. as a permanent or characteristic attribute. **2** vested in (a person etc.) as a right or privilege. □□ **inherence** *n.* **inherently** *adv.* [L *inhaerēre inhaerent-* (as INHERE)]

inherit /ɪnˈhɛrɪt/ *v.* (**inherited**, **inheriting**) **1** *tr.* receive (property, rank, title, etc.) by legal descent or succession. **2** *tr.* derive (a quality or characteristic) genetically from one's ancestors. **3** *absol.* succeed as an heir (*a younger son rarely inherits*). □□ **inheritor** *n.* (*fem.* **inheritress** or **inheritrix**). [ME f. OF *enheriter* f. LL *inhereditare* (as IN-², L *heres heredis* heir)]

inheritable /ɪnˈhɛrɪtəb(ə)l/ *adj.* **1** capable of being inherited. **2** capable of inheriting. □□ **inheritability** /-ˈbɪlɪtɪ/ *n.* [ME f. AF (as INHERIT)]

inheritance /ɪnˈherɪt(ə)ns/ *n.* **1** something that is inherited. **2 a** the act of inheriting. **b** an instance of this. □**inheritance tax** a tax levied on property etc. acquired by gift or inheritance. ¶ Introduced in the UK in 1986 to replace *Capital Transfer Tax*. [ME f. AF *inheritaunce* f. OF *enheriter*: see INHERIT]

inhesion /ɪnˈhiːʒ(ə)n/ *n. formal* the act or fact of inhering. [LL *inhaesio* (as INHERE)]

inhibit /ɪnˈhɪbɪt/ *v.tr.* (**inhibited, inhibiting**) **1** hinder, restrain, or prevent (an action or progress). **2** (as **inhibited** *adj.*) subject to inhibition. **3 a** (usu. foll. by *from* + verbal noun) forbid or prohibit (a person etc.). **b** (esp. in ecclesiastical law) forbid (an ecclesiastic) to exercise clerical functions. □□ **inhibitive** *adj.* **inhibitor** *n.* **inhibitory** *adj.* [L *inhibēre* (as IN-², *habēre* hold)]

inhibition /ˌɪnhɪˈbɪʃ(ə)n/ *n.* **1** *Psychol.* a restraint on the direct expression of an instinct. **2** *colloq.* an emotional resistance to a thought, an action, etc. (*has inhibitions about singing in public*). **3** *Law* an order forbidding alteration to property rights. **4 a** the act of inhibiting. **b** the process of being inhibited. [ME f. OF *inhibition* or L *inhibitio* (as INHIBIT)]

inhomogeneous /ɪnˌhɒməˈdʒiːnɪəs, ɪnˌhəʊm-/ *adj.* not homogeneous. □□ **inhomogeneity** /-dʒɪˈniːɪtɪ/ *n.*

inhospitable /ˌɪnhɒˈspɪtəb(ə)l, ɪnˈhɒspɪ-/ *adj.* **1** not hospitable. **2** (of a region, coast, etc.) not affording shelter etc. □□ **inhospitableness** *n.* **inhospitably** *adv.* [obs. F (as IN-¹, HOSPITABLE)]

inhospitality /ɪnˌhɒspɪˈtælɪtɪ/ *n.* the act or process of being inhospitable. [L *inhospitalitas* (as IN-¹, HOSPITALITY)]

in-house /ˈɪnhaʊs, -ˈhaʊs/ *adj. & adv.* —*adj.* done or existing within an institution, company, etc. (*an in-house project*). —*adv.* internally, without outside assistance.

inhuman /ɪnˈhjuːmən/ *adj.* **1** (of a person, conduct, etc.) brutal; unfeeling; barbarous. **2** not of a human type. □□ **inhumanly** *adv.* [L *inhumanus* (as IN-¹, HUMAN)]

inhumane /ˌɪnhjuːˈmeɪn/ *adj.* not humane. □□ **inhumanely** *adv.* [L *inhumanus* (see INHUMAN) & f. IN-¹ + HUMANE, orig. = INHUMAN)]

inhumanity /ˌɪnhjuːˈmænɪtɪ/ *n.* (*pl.* **-ies**) **1** brutality; barbarousness; callousness. **2** an inhumane act.

inhume /ɪnˈhjuːm/ *v.tr. literary* bury. □□ **inhumation** /-ˈmeɪʃ(ə)n/ *n.* [L *inhumare* (as IN-², *humus* ground)]

inimical /ɪˈnɪmɪk(ə)l/ *adj.* (usu. foll. by *to*) **1** hostile. **2** harmful. □□ **inimically** *adv.* [LL *inimicalis* f. L *inimicus* (as IN-¹, *amicus* friend)]

inimitable /ɪˈnɪmɪtəb(ə)l/ *adj.* impossible to imitate. □□ **inimitability** /-ˈbɪlɪtɪ/ *n.* **inimitableness** *n.* **inimitably** *adv.* [F *inimitable* or L *inimitabilis* (as IN-¹, *imitabilis* imitable)]

iniquity /ɪˈnɪkwɪtɪ/ *n.* (*pl.* **-ies**) **1** wickedness; unrighteousness. **2** a gross injustice. □□ **iniquitous** *adj.* **iniquitously** *adv.* **iniquitousness** *n.* [ME f. OF *iniquité* f. L *iniquitas -tatis* f. *iniquus* (as IN-¹, *aequus* just)]

initial /ɪˈnɪʃ(ə)l/ *adj., n., & v.* —*adj.* of, existing, or occurring at the beginning (*initial stage; initial expenses*). —*n.* **1** = *initial letter*. **2** (usu. in *pl.*) the first letter or letters of the words of a (esp. a person's) name or names. —*v.tr.* (**initialled, initialling;** *US* **initialed, initialing**) mark or sign with one's initials. □**initial letter** (or **consonant**) a letter or consonant at the beginning of a word. **initial teaching alphabet** a 44-letter phonetic alphabet used to help those beginning to read and write English. □□ **initially** *adv.* [L *initialis* f. *initium* beginning f. *inire init-* go in]

initialism /ɪˈnɪʃəˌlɪz(ə)m/ *n.* a group of initial letters used as an abbreviation for a name or expression, each letter being pronounced separately (e.g. *BBC*) (cf. ACRONYM).

initialize /ɪˈnɪʃəˌlaɪz/ *v.tr.* (also **-ise**) (often foll. by *to*) *Computing* set to the value or put in the condition appropriate to the start of an operation. □□ **initialization** /-ˈzeɪʃ(ə)n/ *n.*

initiate *v., n., & adj.* —*v.tr.* /ɪˈnɪʃɪˌeɪt/ **1** begin; set going; originate. **2 a** (usu. foll. by *into*) admit (a person) into a society, an office, a secret, etc., esp. with a ritual. **b** (usu. foll. by *in, into*) instruct (a person) in science, art, etc. —*n.* /ɪˈnɪʃɪət/ a person who has been newly initiated. —*adj.* /ɪˈnɪʃɪət/ (of a person) newly initiated (*an initiate member*). □□ **initiation** /-ˈeɪʃ(ə)n/ *n.* **initiator** *n.* **initiatory** /ɪˈnɪʃjətərɪ, ɪˈnɪʃətərɪ/ *adj.* [L *initiare* f. *initium*: see INITIAL]

initiative /ɪˈnɪʃətɪv, ɪˈnɪʃɪətɪv/ *n. & adj.* —*n.* **1** the ability to initiate things; enterprise (*I'm afraid he lacks all initiative*). **2** a first step; origination (*a peace initiative*). **3** the power or right to begin something. **4** *Polit.* (esp. in Switzerland and some US States) the right of citizens outside the legislature to originate legislation. —*adj.* beginning; originating. □**have the initiative** esp. *Mil.* be able to control the enemy's movements. **on one's own initiative** without being prompted by others. **take the initiative** (usu. foll. by *in* + verbal noun) be the first to take action. [F (as INITIATE)]

inject /ɪnˈdʒekt/ *v.tr.* **1** *Med.* **a** (usu. foll. by *into*) drive or force (a solution, medicine, etc.) by or as if by a syringe. **b** (usu. foll. by *with*) fill (a cavity etc.) by injecting. **c** administer medicine etc. to (a person) by injection. **2** place or insert (an object, a quality, etc.) into something (*may I inject a note of realism?*). □□ **injectable** *adj. & n.* **injector** *n.* [L *injicere* (as IN-², *jacere* throw)]

injection /ɪnˈdʒekʃ(ə)n/ *n.* **1 a** the act of injecting. **b** an instance of this. **2** a liquid or solution (to be) injected (*prepare a morphine injection*). □**injection moulding** the shaping of rubber or plastic articles by injecting heated material into a mould. [F *injection* or L *injectio* (as INJECT)]

injudicious /ˌɪndʒuːˈdɪʃəs/ *adj.* unwise; ill-judged. □□ **injudiciously** *adv.* **injudiciousness** *n.*

Injun /ˈɪndʒ(ə)n/ *n. colloq. US* or *dial.* an American Indian. [corrupt.]

injunction /ɪnˈdʒʌŋkʃ(ə)n/ *n.* **1** an authoritative warning or order. **2** *Law* a judicial order restraining a person from an act or compelling redress to an injured party. □□ **injunctive** *adj.* [LL *injunctio* f. L *injungere* ENJOIN]

injure /ˈɪndʒə(r)/ *v.tr.* **1** do physical harm or damage to; hurt (*was injured in a road accident*). **2** harm or impair (*illness might injure her chances*). **3** do wrong to. □□ **injurer** *n.* [back-form. f. INJURY]

injured /ˈɪndʒəd/ *adj.* **1** harmed or hurt (*the injured passengers*). **2** offended; wronged (*in an injured tone*).

injurious /ɪnˈdʒʊərɪəs/ *adj.* **1** hurtful. **2** (of language) insulting; libellous. **3** wrongful. □□ **injuriously** *adv.* **injuriousness** *n.* [ME f. F *injurieux* or L *injuriosus* (as INJURY)]

injury /ˈɪndʒərɪ/ *n.* (*pl.* **-ies**) **1 a** physical harm or damage. **b** an instance of this (*suffered head injuries*). **2** esp. *Law* a wrongful action or treatment. **b** an instance of this. **3** damage to one's good name etc. □**injury time** *Brit. Football* extra playing-time allowed by a referee to compensate for time lost in dealing with injuries. [ME f. AF *injurie* f. L *injuria* a wrong (as IN-¹, *jus juris* right)]

injustice /ɪnˈdʒʌstɪs/ *n.* **1** a lack of fairness or justice. **2** an unjust act. □**do a person an injustice** judge a person unfairly. [ME f. OF f. L *injustitia* (as IN-¹, JUSTICE)]

ink /ɪŋk/ *n. & v.* —*n.* **1 a** a coloured fluid used for writing with a pen, marking with a rubber stamp, etc. **b** a thick paste used in printing, duplicating, in ball-point pens, etc. **2** *Zool.* a black liquid ejected by a cuttlefish, octopus, etc. to confuse a predator. —*v.tr.* **1** (usu. foll. by *in, over*, etc.) mark with ink. **2** cover (type etc.) with ink before printing. **3** apply ink to. **4** (as **inked** *adj.*) *Austral. sl.* drunk. □**ink-blot test** = RORSCHACH TEST. **ink-cap** any fungus of the genus *Coprinus*. **ink-horn** *hist.* a small portable horn container for ink. **ink out** obliterate with ink. **ink-pad** an ink-soaked pad, usu. in a box, used for inking a rubber stamp etc. **ink-well** a pot for ink usu. housed in a hole in a desk. □□ **inker** *n.* [ME *enke, inke* f. OF *enque* f. LL *encau(s)tum* f. Gk *egkauston* purple ink used by Roman emperors for signature (as EN-², CAUSTIC)]

inkling /'ɪŋklɪŋ/ *n.* (often foll. by *of*) a slight knowledge or suspicion; a hint. [ME *inkle* utter in an undertone, of unkn. orig.]

inkstand /'ɪŋkstænd/ *n.* a stand for one or more ink bottles, often incorporating a pen tray etc.

inky /'ɪŋkɪ/ *adj.* (**inkier, inkiest**) of, as black as, or stained with ink. □□ **inkiness** *n.*

inlaid *past* and *past part.* of INLAY.

inland /'ɪnlənd, 'ɪnlænd/ *adj., n., & adv.* —*adj.* **1** situated in the interior of a country. **2** esp. *Brit.* carried on within the limits of a country; domestic (*inland trade*). —*n.* the parts of a country remote from the sea or frontiers; the interior. —*adv.* /ɪn'lænd/ in or towards the interior of a country. □**inland duty** a tax payable on inland trade. **inland revenue** *Brit.* revenue consisting of taxes and inland duties. **Inland Revenue** (in the UK) the government department responsible for assessing and collecting such taxes. □□ **inlander** *n.* **inlandish** *adj.*

in-law /'ɪnlɔː/ *n.* (often in *pl.*) a relative by marriage.

inlay *v. & n.* —*v.tr.* /ɪn'leɪ/ (*past* and *past part.* **inlaid** /ɪn'leɪd/) **1 a** (usu. foll. by *in*) embed (a thing in another) so that the surfaces are even. **b** (usu. foll. by *with*) ornament (a thing with inlaid work). **2** (as **inlaid** *adj.*) (of a piece of furniture etc.) ornamented by inlaying. **3** insert (a page, an illustration, etc.) in a space cut in a larger thicker page. —*n.* /'ɪnleɪ/ **1** inlaid work. **2** material inlaid. **3** a filling shaped to fit a tooth-cavity. □□ **inlayer** *n.* [IN-² + LAY¹]

inlet /'ɪnlet, -lɪt/ *n.* **1** a small arm of the sea, a lake, or a river. **2** a piece inserted, esp. in dressmaking etc. **3** a way of entry. [ME f. IN + LET¹ *v.*]

inlier /'ɪn,laɪə(r)/ *n. Geol.* a structure or area of older rocks completely surrounded by newer rocks. [IN, after *outlier*]

in-line /'ɪnlaɪn/ *adj.* **1** having parts arranged in a line. **2** constituting an integral part of a continuous sequence of operations or machines.

in loco parentis /ɪn ,ləʊkəʊ pə'rentɪs/ *adv.* in the place or position of a parent (used of a teacher etc. responsible for children). [L]

inly /'ɪnlɪ/ *adv. poet.* **1** inwardly; in the heart. **2** intimately; thoroughly. [OE *innlīce* (as IN, -LY²)]

inlying /'ɪn,laɪɪŋ/ *adj.* situated within, or near a centre.

inmate /'ɪnmeɪt/ *n.* (usu. foll. by *of*) **1** an occupant of a hospital, prison, institution, etc. **2** an occupant of a house etc., esp. one of several. [prob. orig. INN + MATE¹, assoc. with IN]

in medias res /ɪn ,miːdɪæs 'reɪz/ *adv.* **1** into the midst of things. **2** into the middle of a story, without preamble. [L]

in memoriam /ɪn mɪ'mɔːrɪ,æm/ *prep. & n.* —*prep.* in memory of (a dead person). —*n.* a written article or notice etc. in memory of a dead person; an obituary. [L]

inmost /'ɪnməʊst, -məst/ *adj.* **1** most inward. **2** most intimate; deepest. [OE *innemest* (as IN, -MOST)]

inn /ɪn/ *n.* **1** a public house providing alcoholic liquor for consumption on the premises, and sometimes accommodation etc. **2** *hist.* a house providing ac-commodation, esp. for travellers. □**Inn of Court** *Brit. Law* **1** each of the four legal societies having the exclusive right of admitting people to the English bar. **2** any of the sets of buildings in London belonging to these societies. **3** a similar society in Ireland. **Inns of Chancery** *Brit. hist.* buildings in London formerly used as hostels for law students. [OE *inn* (as IN)]

innards /'ɪnədz/ *n.pl. colloq.* **1** entrails. **2** works (of an engine etc.). [dial. etc. pronunc. of *inwards*: see INWARD n.]

innate /ɪ'neɪt, 'ɪ-/ *adj.* **1** inborn; natural. **2** *Philos.* originating in the mind. □□ **innately** *adv.* **innateness** *n.* [ME f. L *innatus* (as IN-², *natus* past part. of *nasci* be born)]

inner /'ɪnə(r)/ *adj. & n.* —*adj.* (usu. *attrib.*) **1** further in; inside; interior (*the inner compartment*). **2** (of thoughts, feelings, etc.) deeper; more secret. —*n. Archery* **1** a division of the target next to the bull's-eye. **2** a shot that strikes this. □**inner bar** *Brit. Law* Queen's or King's Counsel collectively. **inner city** the central most densely populated area of a city (also (with hyphen) *attrib.*: *inner-city housing*). **inner-directed** *Psychol.* governed by standards formed in childhood. **inner man** (or **woman**) **1** the soul or mind. **2** *joc.* the stomach. **inner planet** an inferior planet (see INFERIOR *adj.* 3). **inner space 1** the region between the earth and outer space, or below the surface of the sea. **2** the part of the mind not normally accessible to consciousness. **inner-spring** *US* = *interior-sprung*. **Inner Temple** one of the two Inns of Court on the site of the Temple in London (cf. *Middle Temple*). **inner tube** a separate inflatable tube inside the cover of a pneumatic tyre. □□ **innerly** *adv.* **innermost** *adj.* **innerness** *n.* [OE *innera* (adj.), compar. of IN]

innervate /'ɪnə,veɪt, ɪ'nɜː-/ *v.tr.* supply (an organ etc.) with nerves. □□ **innervation** /-'veɪʃ(ə)n/ *n.* [IN-² + L *nervus* nerve + -ATE³]

inning /'ɪnɪŋ/ *n. US* an innings at baseball etc. [*in* (v.) go in (f. IN)]

innings /'ɪnɪŋz/ *n.* (*pl.* same or *colloq.* **inningses**) **1** esp. *Cricket* **a** the part of a game during which a side is in or batting. **b** the play of or score achieved by a player during a turn at batting. **2** a period during which a government, party, cause, etc. is in office or effective. **3 a** a period during which a person can achieve something. **b** *colloq.* a person's life span (*had a good innings and died at 94*).

innkeeper /'ɪn,kiːpə(r)/ *n.* a person who keeps an inn.

innocent /'ɪnəs(ə)nt/ *adj. & n.* —*adj.* **1** free from moral wrong; sinless. **2** (usu. foll. by *of*) not guilty (of a crime etc.). **3 a** simple; guileless; naïve. **b** pretending to be guileless. **4** harmless. **5** (foll. by *of*) *colloq.* without, lacking (*appeared, innocent of shoes*). —*n.* **1** an innocent person, esp. a young child. **2** (in *pl.*) the young children killed by Herod after the birth of Jesus (Matt. 2:16). □**Innocents'** (or **Holy Innocents'**) **Day** the day, 28 Dec., commemorating the massacre of the innocents. □□ **innocence** *n.* **innocency** *n.* **innocently** *adv.* [ME f. OF *innocent* or L *innocens innocent-* (as IN-¹, *nocēre* hurt)]

innocuous /ɪ'nɒkjʊəs/ *adj.* **1** not injurious; harmless. **2** inoffensive. □□ **innocuity** /,ɪnə'kjuːɪtɪ/ *n.* **innocuously** *adv.* **innocuousness** *n.* [L *innocuus* (as IN-¹, *nocuus* formed as INNOCENT)]

innominate /ɪ'nɒmɪnət/ *adj.* unnamed. □**innominate bone** *n. Anat.* the bone formed from the fusion of the ilium, ischium, and pubis; the hip-bone. [LL *innominatus* (as IN-¹, NOMINATE)]

innovate /'ɪnə,veɪt/ *v.intr.* **1** bring in new methods, ideas, etc. **2** (often foll. by *in*) make changes. □□ **innovation** /-'veɪʃ(ə)n/ *n.* **innovational** /-'veɪʃ(ə)nl/ *adj.* **innovator** *n.* **innovative** *adj.* **innovatory** /-,veɪtərɪ/ *adj.* [L *innovare* make new, alter (as IN-², *novus* new)]

innoxious /ɪ'nɒkʃəs/ *adj.* harmless. □□ **innoxiously** *adv.* **innoxiousness** *n.* [L *innoxius* (as IN-¹, NOXIOUS)]

innuendo /,ɪnjʊ'endəʊ/ *n. & v.* —*n.* (*pl.* **-oes** or **-os**) **1** an allusive or oblique remark or hint, usu. dispar-aging. **2** a remark with a double meaning, usu. suggestive. —*v.intr.* (**-oes, -oed**) make innuendoes. [L, = by nodding at, by pointing to: ablat. gerund of *innuere* nod at (as IN-², *nuere* nod)]

Innuit var. of INUIT.

innumerable /ɪ'njuːmərəb(ə)l/ *adj.* too many to

be counted. □□ **innumerability** /-'bɪlɪtɪ/ n. **innumerably** adv. [ME f. L innumerabilis (as IN-[1], NUMERABLE)]

innumerate /ɪ'njuːmərət/ adj. having no knowledge of or feeling for mathematical operations; not numerate. □□ **innumeracy** /-əsɪ/ n. [IN-[1], NUMERATE]

innutrition /ˌɪnjuː'trɪʃ(ə)n/ n. lack of nutrition. □□ **innutritious** adj.

inobservance /ˌɪnəb'zɜːv(ə)ns/ n. **1** inattention. **2** (usu. foll. by of) non-observance (of a law etc.). [F inobservance or L inobservantia (as IN-[1], OBSERVANCE)]

inoculate /ɪ'nɒkjʊˌleɪt/ v.tr. **1 a** treat (a person or animal) with a small quantity of the agent of a disease, in the form of vaccine or serum, usu. by injection, to promote immunity against the disease. **b** implant (a disease) by means of vaccine. **2** instil (a person) with ideas or opinions. □□ **inoculable** adj. **inoculation** /-'leɪʃ(ə)n/ n. **inoculative** /-lətɪv/ adj. **inoculator** n. [orig. in sense 'insert (a bud) into a plant': L inoculare inoculat- engraft (as IN-[2], oculus eye, bud)]

inoculum /ɪ'nɒkjʊləm/ n. (pl. **inocula** /-lə/) any substance used for inoculation. [mod.L (as INOCULATE)]

inodorous /ɪn'əʊdərəs/ adj. having no smell; odourless.

in-off /'ɪnɒf/ n. Billiards the act of pocketing a ball by bouncing it off another ball.

inoffensive /ˌɪnə'fensɪv/ adj. not objectionable; harmless. □□ **inoffensively** adv. **inoffensiveness** n.

inoperable /ɪn'ɒpərəb(ə)l/ adj. **1** Surgery that cannot suitably be operated on (inoperable cancer). **2** that cannot be operated; inoperative. □□ **inoperability** /-'bɪlɪtɪ/ n. **inoperably** adv. [F inopérable (as IN-[1], OPERABLE)]

inoperative /ɪn'ɒpərətɪv/ adj. not working or taking effect.

inopportune /ɪn'ɒpəˌtjuːn/ adj. not appropriate, esp. as regards time; unseasonable. □□ **inopportunely** adv. **inopportuneness** n. [L inopportunus (as IN-[1], OPPORTUNE)]

inordinate /ɪn'ɔːdɪnət/ adj. **1** immoderate; excessive. **2** intemperate. **3** disorderly. □□ **inordinately** adv. [ME f. L inordinatus (as IN-[1], ordinatus past part. of ordinare ORDAIN)]

inorganic /ˌɪnɔː'gænɪk/ adj. **1** Chem. (of a compound) not organic, usu. of mineral origin (opp. ORGANIC). **2** without organized physical structure. **3** not arising by natural growth; extraneous. **4** Philol. not explainable by normal etymology. □ **inorganic chemistry** the chemistry of inorganic compounds. □□ **inorganically** adv.

inosculate /ɪn'ɒskjʊˌleɪt/ v.intr. & tr. **1** join by running together. **2** join closely. □□ **inosculation** /-'leɪʃ(ə)n/ n. [IN-[2] + L osculare provide with a mouth f. osculum dimin. of os mouth]

in-patient /'ɪnˌpeɪʃ(ə)nt/ n. a patient who lives in hospital while under treatment.

in propria persona /ɪn ˌprəʊprɪə pɜː'səʊnə/ adv. in his or her own person. [L]

input /'ɪnpʊt/ n. & v. —n. **1** what is put in or taken in, or operated on by any process or system. **2** Electronics **a** a place where, or a device through which, energy, information, etc., enters a system (a tape recorder with inputs for microphone and radio). **b** energy supplied to a device or system; an electrical signal. **3** the information fed into a computer. **4** the action or process of putting in or feeding in. **5** a contribution of information etc. —v.tr. (**inputting**; past and past part. **input** or **inputted**) (often foll. by into) **1** put in. **2** Computing supply (data, programs, etc., to a computer, program, etc.). □ **input-** (or **input/**) **output** Computing etc. of, relating to, or for input and output. □□ **inputter** n.

inquest /'ɪnkwest, 'ɪŋ-/ n. **1** Law **a** an inquiry by a coroner's court into the cause of a death. **b** a judicial inquiry to ascertain the facts relating to an incident etc. **c** a coroner's jury. **2** colloq. a discussion analysing

the outcome of a game, an election, etc. [ME f. OF enqueste (as ENQUIRE)]

inquietude /ɪn'kwaɪɪˌtjuːd, ɪŋ-/ n. uneasiness of mind or body. [ME f. OF inquietude or LL inquietudo f. L inquietus (as IN-[1], quietus quiet)]

inquiline /'ɪnkwɪˌlaɪn, 'ɪŋk-/ n. an animal living in the home of another; a commensal. □□ **inquilinous** /-'laɪnəs/ adj. [L inquilinus sojourner (as IN-[2], colere dwell)]

inquire /ɪn'kwaɪə(r), ɪŋ-/ v. **1** intr. seek information formally; make a formal investigation. **2** intr. & tr. = ENQUIRE. □□ **inquirer** n. [var. of ENQUIRE]

inquiry /ɪn'kwaɪərɪ, ɪŋ-/ n. (pl. **-ies**) **1** an investigation, esp. an official one. **2** = ENQUIRY. □ **inquiry agent** Brit. a private detective.

inquisition /ˌɪnkwɪ'zɪʃ(ə)n, ˌɪŋ-/ n. **1** usu. derog. an intensive search or investigation. **2** a judicial or official inquiry. **3** (**the Inquisition**) RC Ch. hist. an ecclesiastical tribunal for the suppression of heresy, esp. in Spain, operating through torture and execution. □□ **inquisitional** adj. [ME f. OF f. L inquisitio -onis examination (as INQUIRE)]

inquisitive /ɪn'kwɪzɪtɪv, ɪŋ-/ adj. **1** unduly curious; prying. **2** seeking knowledge; inquiring. □□ **inquisitively** adv. **inquisitiveness** n. [ME f. OF inquisitif -ive f. LL inquisitivus (as INQUISITION)]

inquisitor /ɪn'kwɪzɪtə(r), ɪŋ-/ n. **1** an official investigator. **2** hist. an officer of the Inquisition. □ **Grand Inquisitor** the director of the court of Inquisition in some countries. **Inquisitor General** the head of the Spanish Inquisition. [F inquisiteur f. L inquisitor -oris (as INQUIRE)]

inquisitorial /ɪnˌkwɪzɪ'tɔːrɪəl, ɪŋ-/ adj. **1** of or like an inquisitor. **2** offensively prying. **3** Law (of a trial etc.) in which the judge has a prosecuting role (opp. ACCUSATORIAL). □□ **inquisitorially** adv. [med.L inquisitorius (as INQUISITOR)]

inquorate /ɪn'kwɔːreɪt, ɪŋ-/ adj. not constituting a quorum.

in re /ɪn 'riː, 'reɪ/ prep. = RE[1]. [L, = in the matter of]

INRI abbr. Jesus of Nazareth, King of the Jews. [L Iesus Nazarenus Rex Iudaeorum]

inroad /'ɪnrəʊd/ n. **1** (often in pl.; usu. foll. by on, into) an encroachment; a using up of resources etc. (makes inroads on my time). **2** a hostile attack; a raid. [IN + ROAD[1] in sense 'riding']

inrush /'ɪnrʌʃ/ n. a rushing in; an influx. □□ **inrushing** adj. & n.

ins. abbr. **1** inches. **2** insurance.

insalubrious /ˌɪnsə'luːbrɪəs, -'ljuːbrɪəs/ adj. (of a climate or place) unhealthy. □□ **insalubrity** n. [L insalubris (as IN-[1], SALUBRIOUS)]

insane /ɪn'seɪn/ adj. **1** not of sound mind; mad. **2** colloq. extremely foolish; irrational. □□ **insanely** adv. **insaneness** n. **insanity** /-'sænɪtɪ/ n. (pl. **-ies**). [L insanus (as IN-[1], sanus healthy)]

insanitary /ɪn'sænɪtərɪ/ adj. not sanitary; dirty or germ-carrying.

insatiable /ɪn'seɪʃəb(ə)l/ adj. **1** unable to be satisfied. **2** (usu. foll. by of) extremely greedy. □□ **insatiability** /-'bɪlɪtɪ/ n. **insatiably** adv. [ME f. OF insaciable or L insatiabilis (as IN-[1], SATIATE)]

insatiate /ɪn'seɪʃɪət/ adj. never satisfied. [L insatiatus (as IN-[1], SATIATE)]

inscape /'ɪnskeɪp/ n. literary the unique inner quality or essence of an object etc. as shown in a work of art, esp. a poem. [perh. f. IN-[2] + -SCAPE]

inscribe /ɪn'skraɪb/ v.tr. **1 a** (usu. foll. by in, on) write or carve (words etc.) on stone, metal, paper, a book, etc. **b** (usu. foll. by with) mark (a sheet, tablet, etc.) with characters. **2** (usu. foll. by to) write an informal dedication (to a person) in or on (a book etc.). **3** enter the name of (a person) on a list or in a book. **4** Geom. draw (a figure) within another so that some or all points of it lie on the boundary of the other (cf. CIRCUMSCRIBE). **5** (esp. as **inscribed** adj.) Brit. issue (stock etc.) in the form of shares with registered holders. □□ **inscribable** adj. **inscriber** n. [L inscribere inscript- (as IN-[2], scribere write)]

inscription /ɪn'skrɪpʃ(ə)n/ n. 1 words inscribed, esp. on a monument, coin, stone, or in a book etc. 2 **a** the act of inscribing, esp. the informal dedication of a book etc. **b** an instance of this. □□ **inscriptional** adj. **inscriptive** adj. [ME f. L inscriptio (as INSCRIBE)]

inscrutable /ɪn'skruːtəb(ə)l/ adj. wholly mysterious, impenetrable. □□ **inscrutability** /-'bɪlɪtɪ/ n. **inscrutableness** n. **inscrutably** adv. [ME f. eccl.L inscrutabilis (as IN-[1], scrutari search: see SCRUTINY)]

insect /'ɪnsekt/ n. 1 **a** any arthropod of the class Insecta, having a head, thorax, abdomen, two antennae, three pairs of thoracic legs, and usu. one or two pairs of thoracic wings. **b** (loosely) any other small segmented invertebrate animal. 2 an insignificant or contemptible person or creature. □□ **insectile** /-'sektaɪl/ adj. [L insectum (animal) notched (animal) f. insecare insect- (as IN-[2], secare cut)]

insectarium /ˌɪnsek'teərɪəm/ n. (also **insectary** /ɪn'sektərɪ/) (pl. **insectariums** or **insectaries**) a place for keeping insects.

insecticide /ɪn'sektɪˌsaɪd/ n. a substance used for killing insects. □□ **insecticidal** /-'saɪd(ə)l/ adj.

insectivore /ɪn'sektɪˌvɔː(r)/ n. 1 any mammal of the order Insectivora feeding on insects etc., e.g. a hedgehog or mole. 2 any plant which captures and absorbs insects. □□ **insectivorous** /-'tɪvərəs/ adj. [F f. mod.L insectivorus (as INSECT, -VORE: see -VOROUS)]

insecure /ˌɪnsɪ'kjʊə(r)/ adj. 1 (of a person or state of mind) uncertain; lacking confidence. 2 **a** unsafe; not firm or fixed. **b** (of ice, ground, etc.) liable to give way. □□ **insecurely** adv. **insecurity** /-'kjʊərɪtɪ/ n.

inselberg /'ɪns(ə)l,bɜːg, 'ɪnz-/ n. an isolated hill or mountain rising abruptly from its surroundings. [G, = island mountain]

inseminate /ɪn'semɪˌneɪt/ v.tr. 1 introduce semen into (a female) by natural or artificial means. 2 sow (seed etc.). □□ **insemination** /-'neɪʃ(ə)n/ n. **inseminator** n. [L inseminare (as IN-[2], SEMEN)]

insensate /ɪn'senseɪt/ adj. 1 without physical sensation; unconscious. 2 without sensibility; unfeeling. 3 stupid. □□ **insensately** adv. [eccl.L insensatus (as IN-[1], sensatus f. sensus SENSE)]

insensibility /ɪnˌsensɪ'bɪlɪtɪ/ n. 1 unconsciousness. 2 a lack of mental feeling or emotion; hardness. 3 (often foll. by to) indifference. [F insensibilité or LL insensibilitas (as INSENSIBLE)]

insensible /ɪn'sensɪb(ə)l/ adj. 1 **a** without one's mental faculties; unconscious. **b** (of the extremities etc.) numb; without feeling. 2 (usu. foll. by of, to) unaware; indifferent (insensible of her needs). 3 without emotion; callous. 4 too small or gradual to be perceived; inappreciable. □□ **insensibly** adv. [ME f. OF insensible or L insensibilis (as IN-[1], SENSIBLE)]

insensitive /ɪn'sensɪtɪv/ adj. (often foll. by to) 1 unfeeling; boorish; crass. 2 not sensitive to physical stimuli. □□ **insensitively** adv. **insensitiveness** n. **insensitivity** /-'tɪvɪtɪ/ n.

insentient /ɪn'senʃ(ə)nt/ adj. not sentient; inanimate. □□ **insentience** n.

inseparable /ɪn'sepərəb(ə)l/ adj. & n. —adj. 1 (esp. of friends) unable or unwilling to be separated. 2 Gram. (of a prefix, or a verb in respect of it) unable to be used as a separate word, e.g.: dis-, mis-, un-. —n. (usu. in pl.) an inseparable person or thing, esp. a friend. □□ **inseparability** /-'bɪlɪtɪ/ n. **inseparably** adv. [ME f. L inseparabilis (as IN-[1], SEPARABLE)]

insert v. & n. —v.tr. /ɪn'sɜːt/ 1 (usu. foll. by in, into, between, etc.) place, fit, or thrust (a thing) into another. 2 (usu. foll. by in, into) introduce (a letter, word, article, advertisement, etc.) into a newspaper etc. 3 (as **inserted** adj.) Anat. etc. (of a muscle etc.) attached (at a specific point). —n. /'ɪnsɜːt/ something inserted, e.g. a loose page in a magazine, a piece of cloth in a garment, a shot in a cinema film. □□ **insertable** adj. **inserter** n. [L inserere (as IN-[2], serere sert- join)]

insertion /ɪn'sɜːʃ(ə)n/ n. 1 the act or an instance of inserting. 2 an amendment etc. inserted in writing or printing. 3 each appearance of an advertisement in a newspaper etc. 4 an ornamental section of needlework inserted into plain material (lace insertions). 5 the manner or place of attachment of a muscle, an organ, etc. 6 the placing of a spacecraft in an orbit. [LL insertio (as INSERT)]

in-service /'ɪn,sɜːvɪs/ adj. (of training) intended for those actively engaged in the profession or activity concerned.

inset n. & v. —n. /'ɪnset/ 1 **a** an extra page or pages inserted in a folded sheet or in a book; an insert. **b** a small map, photograph, etc., inserted within the border of a larger one. 2 a piece let into a dress etc. —v.tr. /ɪn'set/ (**insetting**; past and past part. **inset** or **insetted**) 1 put in as an inset. 2 decorate with an inset. □□ **insetter** n.

inshallah /ɪn'ʃælə/ int. if Allah wills it. [Arab. in šā' Allah]

inshore /ɪn'ʃɔː(r), 'ɪn-/ adv. & adj. at sea but close to the shore. □**inshore of** nearer to shore than.

inside n., adj., adv., & prep. —n. /ɪn'saɪd/ 1 **a** the inner side or surface of a thing. **b** the inner part; the interior. 2 **a** (of a path) the side next to the wall or away from the road. **b** (of a double-decker bus) the lower section. 3 (usu. in pl.) colloq. the stomach and bowels (something wrong with my insides). 4 colloq. a position affording inside information (knows someone on the inside). —adj. /'ɪnsaɪd/ 1 situated on or in, or derived from, the inside. 2 Football & Hockey nearer to the centre of the field (inside forward; inside left; inside right). —adv. /ɪn'saɪd/ 1 on, in, or to the inside. 2 sl. in prison. —prep. /ɪn'saɪd/ 1 on the inner side of; within (inside the house). 2 in less than (inside an hour). □**inside country** Austral. settled areas near the coast. **inside information** information not accessible to outsiders. **inside job** colloq. a crime committed by a person living or working on the premises burgled etc. **inside of** colloq. 1 in less than (a week etc.). 2 Brit. the middle part of. **inside out** with the inner surface turned outwards. **inside track** 1 the track which is shorter, because of the curve. 2 a position of advantage. **know a thing inside out** know a thing thoroughly. **turn inside out** 1 turn the inner surface outwards. 2 colloq. cause confusion or a mess in. [IN + SIDE]

insider /ɪn'saɪdə(r)/ n. 1 a person who is within a society, organization, etc. (cf. OUTSIDER). 2 a person privy to a secret, esp. when using it to gain advantage. □**insider dealing** Stock Exch. the illegal practice of trading to one's own advantage through having access to confidential information.

insidious /ɪn'sɪdɪəs/ adj. 1 proceeding or progressing inconspicuously but harmfully (an insidious disease). 2 treacherous; crafty. □□ **insidiously** adv. **insidiousness** n. [L insidiosus cunning f. insidiae ambush (as IN-[2], sedēre sit)]

insight /'ɪnsaɪt/ n. (usu. foll. by into) 1 the capacity of understanding hidden truths etc., esp. of character or situations. 2 an instance of this. □□ **insightful** adj. **insightfully** adv. [ME, = 'discernment', prob. of Scand. & LG orig. (as IN-[2], SIGHT)]

insignia /ɪn'sɪgnɪə/ n. (treated as sing. or pl.; usu. foll. by of) 1 badges (wore his insignia of office). 2 distinguishing marks. [L, pl. of insigne neut. of insignis distinguished (as IN-[2], signis f. signum SIGN)]

insignificant /ˌɪnsɪg'nɪfɪkənt/ adj. 1 unimportant; trifling. 2 (of a person) undistinguished. 3 meaningless. □□ **insignificance** n. **insignificancy** n. **insignificantly** adv.

insincere /ˌɪnsɪn'sɪə(r)/ adj. not sincere; not candid. □□ **insincerely** adv. **insincerity** /-'serɪtɪ/ n. (pl. -ies). [L insincerus (as IN-[1], SINCERE)]

insinuate /ɪn'sɪnjʊˌeɪt/ v.tr. 1 (often foll. by that + clause) convey indirectly or obliquely; hint (insinuated that she was lying). 2 (often refl.; usu. foll. by into) **a** introduce (oneself, a person, etc.) into favour, office, etc., by subtle manipulation. **b** introduce (a

---

b but d dog f few g get h he j yes k cat l leg m man n no p pen r red s sit t top v voice

thing, oneself, etc.) subtly or deviously into a place (*insinuated himself into the Royal Box*). □□ **insinuation** /-'eɪʃ(ə)n/ *n.* **insinuative** *adj.* **insinuator** *n.* **insinuatory** /-jʊətərɪ/ *adj.* [L *insinuare insinuat-* (as IN-², *sinuare* to curve)]

insipid /ɪn'sɪpɪd/ *adj.* **1** lacking vigour or interest; dull. **2** lacking flavour; tasteless. □□ **insipidity** /-'pɪdɪtɪ/ *n.* **insipidly** *adv.* **insipidness** *n.* [F *insipide* or LL *insipidus* (as IN-¹, *sapidus* SAPID)]

insist /ɪn'sɪst/ *v.tr.* (usu. foll. by *that* + clause; also *absol.*) maintain or demand positively and assertively (*insisted that he was innocent; give me the bag! I insist!*). □ **insist on** demand or maintain (*I insist on being present; insists on his suitability*). □□ **insister** *n.* **insistingly** *adv.* [L *insistere* stand on, persist (as IN-², *sistere* stand)]

insistent /ɪn'sɪst(ə)nt/ *adj.* **1** (often foll. by *on*) insisting; demanding positively or continually (*is insistent on taking me with him*). **2** obtruding itself on the attention (*the insistent rattle of the window frame*). □□ **insistence** *n.* **insistency** *n.* **insistently** *adv.*

in situ /ɪn 'sɪtjuː/ *adv.* **1** in its place. **2** in its original place. [L]

insobriety /ˌɪnsə'braɪɪtɪ/ *n.* intemperance, esp. in drinking.

insofar /ˌɪnsəʊ'fɑː(r)/ *adv.* = *in so far* (see FAR).

insolation /ˌɪnsəʊ'leɪʃ(ə)n/ *n.* exposure to the sun's rays, esp. for bleaching. [L *insolatio* f. *insolare* (as IN-², *solare* f. *sol* sun)]

insole /'ɪnsəʊl/ *n.* **1** a removable sole worn in a boot or shoe for warmth etc. **2** the fixed inner sole of a boot or shoe.

insolent /'ɪnsələnt/ *adj.* offensively contemptuous or arrogant; insulting. □□ **insolence** *n.* **insolently** *adv.* [ME, = 'arrogant', f. L *insolens* (as IN-¹, *solens* pres. part. of *solēre* be accustomed)]

insoluble /ɪn'sɒljʊb(ə)l/ *adj.* **1** incapable of being solved. **2** incapable of being dissolved. □□ **insolubility** /-'bɪlɪtɪ/ **insolubilize** /-bɪˌlaɪz/ *v.tr.* (also **-ise**). **insolubleness** *n.* **insolubly** *adv.* [ME f. OF *insoluble* or L *insolubilis* (as IN-¹, SOLUBLE)]

insolvable /ɪn'sɒlvəb(ə)l/ *adj.* = INSOLUBLE.

insolvent /ɪn'sɒlv(ə)nt/ *adj. & n.* —*adj.* **1** unable to pay one's debts. **2** relating to insolvency (*insolvent laws*). —*n.* a debtor. □□ **insolvency** *n.*

insomnia /ɪn'sɒmnɪə/ *n.* habitual sleeplessness; inability to sleep. □□ **insomniac** /-ɪˌæk/ *n. & adj.* [L f. *insomnis* sleepless (as IN-¹, *somnus* sleep)]

insomuch /ˌɪnsəʊ'mʌtʃ/ *adv.* **1** (foll. by *that* + clause) to such an extent. **2** (foll. by *as*) inasmuch. [ME, orig. *in so much*]

insouciant /ɪn'suːsɪənt, ӕ'sʊsjã/ *adj.* carefree; unconcerned. □□ **insouciance** *n.* **insouciantly** *adv.* [F (as IN-¹, *souciant* pres. part. of *soucier* care)]

inspan /ɪn'spæn/ *v.* (**inspanned, inspanning**) *S.Afr.* **1** *tr.* (also *absol.*) **a** yoke (oxen etc.) in a team to a vehicle. **b** harness an animal or animals to (a wagon). **2** *tr.* harness (people or resources) into service. [Du. *inspannen* stretch (as IN-², SPAN²)]

inspect /ɪn'spekt/ *v.tr.* **1** look closely at or into. **2** examine (a document etc.) officially. □□ **inspection** *n.* [L *inspicere inspect-* (as IN-², *specere* look at), or its frequent. *inspectare*]

inspector /ɪn'spektə(r)/ *n.* **1** a person who inspects. **2** an official employed to supervise a service, a machine, etc., and make reports. **3** *Brit.* a police officer below a superintendent and above a sergeant in rank. □ **inspector general** a chief inspector. **inspector of taxes** (in the UK) an official of the Inland Revenue responsible for collecting taxes. □□ **inspectorate** /-rət/ *n.* **inspectorial** /-'tɔːrɪəl/ *adj.* **inspectorship** *n.* [L (as INSPECT)]

inspiration /ˌɪnspɪ'reɪʃ(ə)n/ *n.* **1 a** a supposed creative force or influence on poets, artists, musicians, etc., stimulating the production of works of art. **b** a person, principle, faith, etc. stimulating artistic or moral fervour and creativity. **c** a similar divine influence supposed to have led to the writing of Scripture etc. **2** a sudden brilliant, creative, or timely idea. **3** a drawing in of breath; inhalation. □□ **inspirational** *adj.* **inspirationism** *n.* **inspirationist** *n.* [ME f. OF f. LL *inspiratio -onis* (as INSPIRE)]

inspirator /'ɪnspɪˌreɪtə(r)/ *n.* an apparatus for drawing in air or vapour. [LL (as INSPIRE)]

inspire /ɪn'spaɪə(r)/ *v.tr.* **1** stimulate or arouse (a person) to esp. creative activity, esp. by supposed divine or supernatural agency (*your faith inspired him; inspired by God*). **2 a** (usu. foll. by *with*) animate (a person) with a feeling. **b** (usu. foll. by *into*) instil (a feeling) into a person etc. **c** (usu. foll. by *in*) create (a feeling) in a person. **3** prompt; give rise to (*the poem was inspired by the autumn*). **4** (as **inspired** *adj.*) **a** (of a work of art etc.) as if prompted by or emanating from a supernatural source; characterized by inspiration (*an inspired speech*). **b** (of a guess) intuitive but accurate. **5** (also *absol.*) breathe in (air etc.); inhale. □□ **inspiratory** /ɪn'spɪrətərɪ/ *adj.* **inspiredly** /-rɪdlɪ/ *adv.* **inspirer** *n.* **inspiring** *adj.* **inspiringly** *adv.* [ME f. OF *inspirer* f. L *inspirare* breathe in (as IN-², *spirare* breathe)]

inspirit /ɪn'spɪrɪt/ *v.tr.* (**inspirited, inspiriting**) **1** put life into; animate. **2** (usu. foll. by *to*, or *to* + infin.) encourage (a person). □□ **inspiriting** *adj.* **inspiritingly** *adv.*

inspissate /ɪn'spɪseɪt/ *v.tr.* *literary* thicken; condense. □□ **inspissation** /-'seɪʃ(ə)n/ *n.* [LL *inspissare inspissat-* (as IN-², L *spissus* thick)]

inspissator /'ɪnspɪˌseɪtə(r)/ *n.* an apparatus for thickening serum etc. by heat.

inst. *abbr.* **1** = INSTANT *adj.* 4 (*the 6th inst.*). **2** institute. **3** institution.

instability /ˌɪnstə'bɪlɪtɪ/ *n.* (*pl.* -ies) **1** a lack of stability. **2** *Psychol.* unpredictability in behaviour etc. **3** an instance of instability. [ME f. F *instabilité* f. L *instabilitas -tatis* f. *instabilis* (as IN-¹, STABLE¹)]

install /ɪn'stɔːl/ *v.tr.* (also **instal**) (**installed, installing**) **1** place (equipment, machinery, etc.) in position ready for use. **2** place (a person) in an office or rank with ceremony (*installed in the office of chancellor*). **3** establish (oneself, a person, etc.) in a place, condition, etc. (*installed herself at the head of the table*). □□ **installant** *adj. & n.* **installer** *n.* [med.L *installare* (as IN-², *stallare* f. *stallum* STALL¹)]

installation /ˌɪnstə'leɪʃ(ə)n/ *n.* **1 a** the act or an instance of installing. **b** the process or an instance of being installed. **2 a** piece of apparatus, a machine, etc. installed. [med.L *installatio* (as INSTALL)]

instalment /ɪn'stɔːlmənt/ *n.* (*US* **installment**) **1** a sum of money due as one of several usu. equal payments for something, spread over an agreed period of time. **2** any of several parts, esp. of a television or radio serial or a magazine story, published or shown in sequence at intervals. □ **instalment plan** payment by instalments, esp. hire purchase. [alt. f. obs. *estallment* f. AF *estalement* f. *estaler* fix: prob. assoc. with INSTALLATION]

instance /'ɪnst(ə)ns/ *n. & v.* —*n.* **1** an example or illustration of (*just another instance of his lack of determination*). **2** a particular case (*that's not true in this instance*). **3** *Law* a legal suit. —*v.tr.* cite (a fact, case, etc.) as an instance. □ **at the instance of** at the request or suggestion of. **court of first instance** *Law* a court of primary jurisdiction. **for instance** as an example. **in the first** (or **second** etc.) **instance** in the first (or second etc.) place; at the first (or second etc.) stage of a proceeding. [ME f. OF f. L *instantia* (as INSTANT)]

instancy /'ɪnstənsɪ/ *n.* **1** urgency. **2** pressing nature. [L *instantia*: see INSTANCE]

instant /'ɪnst(ə)nt/ *adj. & n.* —*adj.* **1** occurring immediately (*gives an instant result*). **2 a** (of food etc.) ready for immediate use, with little or no preparation. **b** prepared hastily and with little effort (*I have no instant solution*). **3** urgent; pressing. **4** *Commerce* of the current month (*the 6th instant*). **5**

archaic of the present moment. —*n.* **1** a precise moment of time, esp. the present (*come here this instant*; *went that instant*; *told you the instant I heard*). **2** a short space of time (*was there in an instant*; *not an instant too soon*). □**instant replay** the immediate repetition of part of a filmed sports event, often in slow motion. [ME f. F f. L *instare instant-* be present, press upon (as IN-², *stare* stand)]

instantaneous /ˌɪnstənˈteɪnɪəs/ *adj.* **1** occurring or done in an instant or instantly. **2** *Physics* existing at a particular instant. □□**instantaneity** /-təˈniːɪtɪ/ *n.* **instantaneously** *adv.* **instantaneousness** *n.* [med.L *instantaneus* f. L *instans* (as INSTANT) after eccl.L *momentaneus*]

instanter /ɪnˈstæntə(r)/ *adv.* archaic or *joc.* immediately; at once. [L f. *instans* (as INSTANT)]

instantiate /ɪnˈstænʃɪˌeɪt/ *v.tr.* represent by an instance. □□**instantiation** /-ˈeɪʃ(ə)n/ *n.* [L *instantia*: see INSTANCE]

instantly /ˈɪnstəntlɪ/ *adv.* **1** immediately; at once. **2** archaic urgently; pressingly.

instar /ˈɪnstɑː(r)/ *n.* a stage in the life of an insect etc. between two periods of moulting. [L, = form]

instate /ɪnˈsteɪt/ *v.tr.* (often foll. by *in*) install; establish. [IN-² + STATE]

in statu pupillari /ɪn ˌstætjuː ˌpjuːpɪˈlɑːrɪ/ *adj.* **1** under guardianship, esp. as a pupil. **2** in a junior position at university; not having a master's degree. [L]

instauration /ˌɪnstɔːˈreɪʃ(ə)n/ *n.* formal **1** restoration; renewal. **2** an act of instauration. □□ **instaurator** /ˈɪnstɔːˌreɪtə(r)/ *n.* [L *instauratio* f. *instaurare* (as IN-²: cf. RESTORE)]

instead /ɪnˈsted/ *adv.* **1** (foll. by *of*) as a substitute or alternative to; in place of (*instead of this one*; *stayed instead of going*). **2** as an alternative (*took me instead*) (cf. STEAD). [ME, f. IN + STEAD]

instep /ˈɪnstep/ *n.* **1** the inner arch of the foot between the toes and the ankle. **2** the part of a shoe etc. fitting over or under this. **3** a thing shaped like an instep. [16th c.: ult. formed as IN-² + STEP, but immed. orig. uncert.]

instigate /ˈɪnstɪˌgeɪt/ *v.tr.* **1** bring about by incitement or persuasion; provoke (*who instigated the inquiry?*). **2** (usu. foll. by *to*) urge on, incite (a person etc.) to esp. an evil act. □□**instigation** /-ˈgeɪʃ(ə)n/ *n.* **instigative** /-gətɪv/ *adj.* **instigator** *n.* [L *instigare instigat-*]

instil /ɪnˈstɪl/ *v.tr.* (US **instill**) (**instilled**, **instilling**) (often foll. by *into*) **1** introduce (a feeling, idea, etc.) into a person's mind etc. gradually. **2** put (a liquid) into something in drops. □□**instillation** /-ˈleɪʃ(ə)n/ *n.* **instiller** *n.* **instilment** *n.* [L *instillare* (as IN-², *stillare* drop): cf. DISTIL]

instinct *n.* & *adj.* —*n.* /ˈɪnstɪŋkt/ **1 a** an innate, usu. fixed, pattern of behaviour in most animals in response to certain stimuli. **b** a similar propensity in human beings to act without conscious intention; innate impulsion. **2** (usu. foll. by *for*) unconscious skill; intuition. —*predic.adj.* /ɪnˈstɪŋkt/ (foll. by *with*) imbued, filled (*with life, beauty, force,* etc.). □□ **instinctual** /-ˈstɪŋktjʊəl/ *adj.* **instinctually** /-ˈstɪŋktjʊəlɪ/ *adv.* [ME, = 'impulse', f. L *instinctus* f. *instinguere* incite (as IN-², *stinguere stinct-* prick)]

instinctive /ɪnˈstɪŋktɪv/ *adj.* **1** relating to or prompted by instinct. **2** apparently unconscious or automatic (*an instinctive reaction*). □□**instinctively** *adv.*

institute /ˈɪnstɪˌtjuːt/ *n.* & *v.* —*n.* **1 a** a society or organization for the promotion of science, education, etc. **b** a building used by an institute. **2** *Law* (usu. in *pl.*) a digest of the elements of a legal subject (*Institutes of Justinian*). **3** a principle of instruction. **4** *US* a brief course of instruction for teachers etc. —*v.tr.* **1** establish; found. **2 a** initiate (an inquiry etc.). **b** begin (proceedings) in a court. **3** (usu. foll. by *to, into*) appoint (a person) as a cleric in a church etc. [ME f. L *institutum* design, precept, neut. past part. of *instituere* establish, arrange, teach (as IN-², *statuere* set up)]

institution /ˌɪnstɪˈtjuːʃ(ə)n/ *n.* **1** the act or an instance of instituting. **2 a** a society or organization founded esp. for charitable, religious, educational, or social purposes. **b** a building used by an institution. **3** an established law, practice, or custom. **4** *colloq.* (of a person, a custom, etc.) a familiar object. **5** the establishment of a cleric etc. in a church. [ME f. OF f. L *institutio -onis* (as INSTITUTE)]

institutional /ˌɪnstɪˈtjuːʃən(ə)l/ *adj.* **1** of or like an institution. **2** typical of institutions, esp. in being regimented or unimaginative (*the food was dreadfully institutional*). **3** (of religion) expressed or organized through institutions (churches etc.). **4** *US* (of advertising) intended to create prestige rather than immediate sales. □□**institutionalism** *n.* **institutionally** *adv.*

institutionalize /ˌɪnstɪˈtjuːʃənəˌlaɪz/ *v.tr.* (also **-ise**) **1** (as **institutionalized** *adj.*) (of a prisoner, a long-term patient, etc.) made apathetic and dependent after a long period in an institution. **2** place or keep (a person) in an institution. **3** convert into an institution; make institutional. □□**institutionalization** /-ˈzeɪʃ(ə)n/ *n.*

Inst.P. *abbr.* (in the UK) Institute of Physics.

instruct /ɪnˈstrʌkt/ *v.tr.* **1** (often foll. by *in*) teach (a person) a subject etc. (*instructed her in French*). **2** (usu. foll. by *to* + infin.) direct; command (*instructed him to fill in the hole*). **3** (often foll. by *of*, or *that* etc. + clause) inform (a person) of a fact etc. **4** *Brit.* **a** (of a client or solicitor) give information to (a solicitor or counsel). **b** authorize (a solicitor or counsel) to act for one. [ME f. L *instruere instruct-* build, teach (as IN-², *struere* pile up)]

instruction /ɪnˈstrʌkʃ(ə)n/ *n.* **1** (often in *pl.*) a direction; an order (*gave him his instructions*). **2** teaching; education (*took a course of instruction*). **3** *Law* (in *pl.*) directions to a solicitor or counsel. **4** *Computing* a direction in a computer program defining and effecting an operation. □□**instructional** *adj.* [ME f. OF f. LL *instructio -onis* (as INSTRUCT)]

instructive /ɪnˈstrʌktɪv/ *adj.* tending to instruct; conveying a lesson; enlightening (*found the experience instructive*). □□**instructively** *adv.* **instructiveness** *n.*

instructor /ɪnˈstrʌktə(r)/ *n.* (*fem.* **instructress** /-ˈstrʌktrɪs/) **1** a person who instructs; a teacher, demonstrator, etc. **2** *US* a university teacher ranking below professor. □□**instructorship** *n.*

instrument /ˈɪnstrəmənt/ *n.* & *v.* —*n.* **1** a tool or implement, esp. for delicate or scientific work. **2** (in full **musical instrument**) a device for producing musical sounds by vibration, wind, percussion, etc. **3 a** a thing used in performing an action (*the meeting was an instrument in his success*). **b** a person made use of (*is merely their instrument*). **4** a measuring-device, esp. in an aeroplane, serving to determine its position in darkness etc. **5** a formal, esp. legal, document. —*v.tr.* **1** arrange (music) for instruments. **2** equip with instruments (for measuring, recording, controlling, etc.). □**instrument board** (or **panel**) a surface, esp. in a car or aeroplane, containing the dials etc. of measuring-devices. [ME f. OF *instrument* or L *instrumentum* (as INSTRUCT)]

instrumental /ˌɪnstrəˈment(ə)l/ *adj.* & *n.* —*adj.* **1** (usu. foll. by *to, in,* or *in* + verbal noun) serving as an instrument or means (*was instrumental in finding the money*). **2** (of music) performed on instruments, without singing (cf. VOCAL). **3** of, or arising from, an instrument (*instrumental error*). **4** *Gram.* of or in the instrumental. —*n.* **1** a piece of music performed by instruments, not by the voice. **2** *Gram.* the case of nouns and pronouns (and words in grammatical agreement with them) indicating a means or instrument. □□**instrumentalist** /-ˈmentəlɪst/ *n.* **instrumentality** /-ˈtælɪtɪ/ *n.* **instrumentally** *adv.* [ME f. F f. med.L *instrumentalis* (as INSTRUMENT)]

instrumentation /ˌɪnstrəmənˈteɪʃ(ə)n/ *n.* **1 a** the arrangement or composition of music for a particular group of musical instruments. **b** the instruments used in any one piece of music. **2 a** the design, provision, or use of instruments in industry, science, etc. **b** such instruments collectively. [F f. *instrumenter* (as INSTRUMENT)]

insubordinate /ˌɪnsəˈbɔːdɪnət/ *adj.* disobedient; rebellious. □□ **insubordinately** *adv.* **insubordination** /-ˈneɪʃ(ə)n/ *n.*

insubstantial /ˌɪnsəbˈstænʃ(ə)l, -ˈstɑːnʃ(ə)l/ *adj.* **1** lacking solidity or substance. **2** not real. □□ **insubstantiality** /-ʃɪˈælɪtɪ/ *n.* **insubstantially** *adv.* [LL *insubstantialis* (as IN-¹, SUBSTANTIAL)]

insufferable /ɪnˈsʌfərəb(ə)l/ *adj.* **1** intolerable. **2** unbearably arrogant or conceited etc. □□ **insufferableness** *n.* **insufferably** *adv.*

insufficiency /ˌɪnsəˈfɪʃənsɪ/ *n.* **1** the condition of being insufficient. **2** *Med.* the inability of an organ to perform its normal function (*renal insufficiency*). [ME f. LL *insufficientia* (as INSUFFICIENT)]

insufficient /ˌɪnsəˈfɪʃ(ə)nt/ *adj.* not sufficient; inadequate. □□ **insufficiently** *adv.* [ME f. OF f. LL *insufficiens* (as IN-¹, SUFFICIENT)]

insufflate /ˈɪnsəˌfleɪt/ *v.tr.* **1** *Med.* **a** blow or breathe (air, gas, powder, etc.) into a cavity of the body etc. **b** treat (the nose etc.) in this way. **2** *Theol.* blow or breathe on (a person) to symbolize spiritual influence. □□ **insufflation** /-ˈfleɪʃ(ə)n/ *n.* [LL *insufflare insufflat-* (as IN-², *sufflare* blow upon)]

insufflator /ˈɪnsəˌfleɪtə(r)/ *n.* **1** a device for blowing powder on to a surface in order to make fingerprints visible. **2** an instrument for insufflating.

insular /ˈɪnsjʊlə(r)/ *adj.* **1 a** of or like an island. **b** separated or remote, like an island. **2** ignorant of or indifferent to cultures, peoples, etc., outside one's own experience; narrow-minded. **3** of a British variant of Latin handwriting current in the Middle Ages. **4** (of climate) equable. □□ **insularism** *n.* **insularity** /-ˈlærɪtɪ/ *n.* **insularly** *adv.* [LL *insularis* (as INSULATE)]

insulate /ˈɪnsjʊˌleɪt/ *v.tr.* **1** prevent the passage of electricity, heat, or sound from (a thing, room, etc.) by interposing non-conductors. **2** detach (a person or thing) from its surroundings; isolate. **3** *archaic* make (land) into an island. □ **insulating tape** an adhesive tape used to cover exposed electrical wires etc. □□ **insulation** /-ˈleɪʃ(ə)n/ *n.* [L *insula* island + -ATE³]

insulator /ˈɪnsjʊˌleɪtə(r)/ *n.* **1** a thing or substance used for insulation against electricity, heat, or sound. **2** an insulating device to support telegraph wires etc. **3** a device preventing contact between electrical conductors.

insulin /ˈɪnsjʊlɪn/ *n.* *Biochem.* a hormone produced in the pancreas by the islets of Langerhans, regulating the amount of glucose in the blood and the lack of which causes diabetes. [L *insula* island + -IN]

insult *v.* & *n.* —*v.tr.* /ɪnˈsʌlt/ **1** speak to or treat with scornful abuse or indignity. **2** offend the self-respect or modesty of. —*n.* /ˈɪnsʌlt/ **1** an insulting remark or action. **2** *colloq.* something so worthless or contemptible as to be offensive. **3** *Med.* **a** an agent causing damage to the body. **b** such damage. □□ **insulter** *n.* **insulting** *adj.* **insultingly** *adv.* [F *insulte* or L *insultare* (as IN-², *saltare* frequent. of *salire* salt- leap)]

insuperable /ɪnˈsuːpərəb(ə)l, ɪnˈsjuː-/ *adj.* **1** (of a barrier) impossible to surmount. **2** (of a difficulty etc.) impossible to overcome. □□ **insuperability** /-ˈbɪlɪtɪ/ *n.* **insuperably** *adv.* [ME f. OF *insuperable* or L *insuperabilis* (as IN-¹, SUPERABLE)]

insupportable /ˌɪnsəˈpɔːtəb(ə)l/ *adj.* **1** unable to be endured. **2** unjustifiable. □□ **insupportableness** *n.* **insupportably** *adv.* [F (as IN-¹, SUPPORT)]

insurance /ɪnˈʃʊərəns/ *n.* **1** the act or an instance of insuring. **2 a** a sum paid for this; a premium. **b** a sum paid out as compensation for theft, damage, loss, etc. **3** = *insurance policy*. **4** a measure taken to provide for a possible contingency (*take an umbrella*

as insurance). □ **insurance agent** *Brit.* a person employed to collect premiums door to door. **insurance company** *Brit.* a company engaged in the business of insurance. **insurance policy** *Brit.* **1** a contract of insurance. **2** a document detailing such a policy and constituting a contract. **insurance stamp** *Brit. hist.* a stamp certifying the payment of a sum, usu. paid weekly, for National Insurance. [earlier *ensurance* f. OF *enseürance* (as ENSURE)]

insure /ɪnˈʃʊə(r)/ *v.tr.* **1** (often foll. by *against*; also *absol.*) secure the payment of a sum of money in the event of loss or damage to (property, life, a person, etc.) by regular payments or premiums (*insured the house for £100,000; we have insured against flood damage*) (cf. ASSURANCE). **2** (of the owner of a property, an insurance company, etc.) secure the payment of (a sum of money) in this way. **3** (usu. foll. by *against*) provide for (a possible contingency) (*insured themselves against the rain by taking umbrellas*). **4** *US* = ENSURE. □□ **insurable** *adj.* **insurability** /-ˈbɪlɪtɪ/ *n.* [ME, var. of ENSURE]

insured /ɪnˈʃʊəd/ *adj.* & *n.* —*adj.* covered by insurance. —*n.* (usu. prec. by *the*) a person etc. covered by insurance.

insurer /ɪnˈʃʊərə(r)/ *n.* **1** a person or company offering insurance policies for premiums; an underwriter. **2** a person who takes out insurance.

insurgent /ɪnˈsɜːdʒ(ə)nt/ *adj.* & *n.* —*adj.* **1** rising in active revolt. **2** (of the sea etc.) rushing in. —*n.* a rebel; a revolutionary. □□ **insurgence** *n.* **insurgency** *n.* (*pl.* **-ies**). [F f. L *insurgere insurrect-* (as IN-², *surgere* rise)]

insurmountable /ˌɪnsəˈmaʊntəb(ə)l/ *adj.* unable to be surmounted or overcome. □□ **insurmountably** *adv.*

insurrection /ˌɪnsəˈrekʃ(ə)n/ *n.* a rising in open resistance to established authority; a rebellion. □□ **insurrectional** *adj.* **insurrectionary** *adj.* **insurrectionist** *n.* [ME f. OF f. LL *insurrectio -onis* (as INSURGENT)]

insusceptible /ˌɪnsəˈseptɪb(ə)l/ *adj.* (usu. foll. by *of*, *to*) not susceptible (of treatment, to an influence, etc.). □□ **insusceptibility** /-ˈbɪlɪtɪ/ *n.*

inswinger /ˈɪnˌswɪŋə(r)/ *n.* **1** *Cricket* a ball bowled with a swing towards the batsman. **2** *Football* a pass or kick that sends the ball curving towards the goal.

int. *abbr.* **1** interior. **2** internal. **3** international.

intact /ɪnˈtækt/ *adj.* **1** entire; unimpaired. **2** untouched. □□ **intactness** *n.* [ME f. L *intactus* (as IN-¹, *tactus* past part. of *tangere* touch)]

intagliated /ɪnˈtælɪˌeɪtɪd/ *adj.* decorated with surface carving. [It. *intagliato* past part. of *intagliare* cut into]

intaglio /ɪnˈtælɪəʊ, -ˈtɑːlɪəʊ/ *n.* & *v.* —*n.* (*pl.* **-os**) **1** a gem with an incised design (cf. CAMEO). **2** an engraved design. **3** a carving, esp. incised, in hard material. **4** a process of printing from an engraved design. —*v.tr.* (**-oes**, **-oed**) **1** engrave (material) with a sunk pattern or design. **2** engrave (such a design). [It. (as INTAGLIATED)]

intake /ˈɪnteɪk/ *n.* **1 a** the action of taking in. **b** an instance of this. **2** a number or the amount taken in or received. **3** a place where water is taken into a channel or pipe from a river, or fuel or air enters an engine etc. **4** an airway into a mine. **5** *N.Engl.* land reclaimed from a moor etc.

intangible /ɪnˈtændʒɪb(ə)l/ *adj.* & *n.* —*adj.* **1** unable to be touched; not solid. **2** unable to be grasped mentally. —*n.* something that cannot be precisely measured or assessed. □□ **intangibility** /-ˈbɪlɪtɪ/ *n.* **intangibly** *adv.* [F *intangible* or med.L *intangibilis* (as IN-¹, TANGIBLE)]

intarsia /ɪnˈtɑːsɪə/ *n.* the craft of using wood inlays, esp. as practised in 15th-c. Italy. [It. *intarsio*]

integer /ˈɪntɪdʒə(r)/ *n.* **1** a whole number. **2** a thing complete in itself. [L (adj.) = untouched, whole: see ENTIRE]

integral /ˈɪntɪɡr(ə)l/ *adj.* & *n.* —*adj.* /ˈɪntɪɡr(ə)l, disp.

ɪn'tɛgr(ə)l/ **1 a** of a whole or necessary to the completeness of a whole. **b** forming a whole (*integral design*). **c** whole, complete. **2** *Math.* **a** of or denoted by an integer. **b** involving only integers, esp. as coefficients of a function. —*n.* *Math.* **1** a quantity of which a given function is the derivative, either containing an indeterminate additive constant (**indefinite integral**), or calculated as the difference between its values at specified limits (**definite integral**). **2** a function satisfying a given differential equation. □**integral calculus** mathematics concerned with finding integrals, their properties and application, etc. (cf. *differential calculus*). □□ **integrality** /-'grælɪtɪ/ *n.* **integrally** *adv.* [LL *integralis* (as INTEGER)]

integrand /'ɪntɪˌgrænd/ *n.* *Math.* a function that is to be integrated. [L *integrandus* gerundive of *integrare*: see INTEGRATE]

integrant /'ɪntɪgrənt/ *adj.* (of parts) making up a whole; component. [F *intégrant* f. *intégrer* (as INTEGRATE)]

integrate *v. & adj.* —*v.* /'ɪntɪˌgreɪt/ **1** *tr.* **a** combine (parts) into a whole. **b** complete (an imperfect thing) by the addition of parts. **2** *tr. & intr.* bring or come into equal participation in or membership of society, a school, etc. **3** *tr.* desegregate, esp. racially (a school etc.). **4** *tr.* *Math.* **a** find the integral of. **b** (as **integrated** *adj.*) indicating the mean value or total sum of (temperature, an area, etc.). —*adj.* /'ɪntɪgrət/ **1** made up of parts. **2** whole; complete. □**integrated circuit** *Electronics* a small chip etc. of material replacing several separate components in a conventional electrical circuit. □□**integrable** /'ɪntɪgrəb(ə)l/ *adj.* **integrability** /ˌɪntɪgrə'bɪlɪtɪ/ *n.* **integrative** /'ɪntɪgrətɪv/ *adj.* [L *integrare integrat*-make whole (as INTEGER)]

integration /ˌɪntɪ'greɪʃ(ə)n/ *n.* **1** the act or an instance of integrating. **2** the intermixing of persons previously segregated. **3** *Psychol.* the combination of the diverse elements of perception etc. in a personality. □□**integrationist** *n.* [L *integratio* (as INTEGRATE)]

integrator /'ɪntɪˌgreɪtə(r)/ *n.* **1** an instrument for indicating or registering the total amount or mean value of some physical quality, as area, temperature, etc. **2** a person or thing that integrates.

integrity /ɪn'tɛgrɪtɪ/ *n.* **1** moral uprightness; honesty. **2** wholeness; soundness. [ME f. F *intégrité* or L *integritas* (as INTEGER)]

integument /ɪn'tɛgjʊmənt/ *n.* a natural outer covering, as a skin, husk, rind, etc. □□**integumental** /-'ment(ə)l/ *adj.* **integumentary** /-'mentərɪ/ *adj.* [L *integumentum* f. *integere* (as IN-², *tegere* cover)]

intellect /'ɪntɪˌlɛkt/ *n.* **1 a** the faculty of reasoning, knowing, and thinking, as distinct from feeling. **b** the understanding or mental powers (of a particular person etc.) (*his intellect is not great*). **2 a** a clever or knowledgeable person. **b** the intelligentsia regarded collectively (*the combined intellect of four universities*). [ME f. OF *intellect* or L *intellectus* understanding (as INTELLIGENT)]

intellection /ˌɪntɪ'lɛkʃ(ə)n/ *n.* the action or process of understanding (opp. IMAGINATION). □□**intellective** *adj.* [ME f. med.L *intellectio* (as INTELLIGENT)]

intellectual /ˌɪntɪ'lɛktjʊəl/ *adj. & n.* —*adj.* **1** of or appealing to the intellect. **2** possessing a high level of understanding or intelligence; cultured. **3** requiring, or given to the exercise of, the intellect. —*n.* a person possessing a highly developed intellect. □□**intellectuality** /-'ælɪtɪ/ *n.* **intellectualize** /-'lɛktjʊəˌlaɪz/ *v.tr. & intr.* (also -ise). **intellectually** *adv.* [ME f. L *intellectualis* (as INTELLECT)]

intellectualism /ˌɪntɪ'lɛktjʊəˌlɪz(ə)m/ *n.* **1** the exercise, esp. when excessive, of the intellect at the expense of the emotions. **2** *Philos.* the theory that knowledge is wholly or mainly derived from pure reason. □□**intellectualist** *n.*

intelligence /ɪn'tɛlɪdʒ(ə)ns/ *n.* **1 a** the intellect;

the understanding. **b** (of a person or an animal) quickness of understanding; wisdom. **2 a** the collection of information, esp. of military or political value. **b** people employed in this. **c** *archaic* information; news. **3** an intelligent or rational being. □**intelligence department** a usu. government department engaged in collecting esp. secret information. **intelligence quotient** a number denoting the ratio of a person's intelligence to the normal or average. **intelligence test** a test designed to measure intelligence rather than acquired knowledge. □□**intelligential** /-'dʒɛnʃ(ə)l/ *adj.* [ME f. OF f. L *intelligentia* (as INTELLIGENT)]

intelligent /ɪn'tɛlɪdʒ(ə)nt/ *adj.* **1** having or showing intelligence, esp. of a high level. **2** quick of mind; clever. **3 a** (of a device or machine) able to vary its behaviour in response to varying situations and requirements and past experience. **b** (esp. of a computer terminal) having its own data-processing capability; incorporating a microprocessor (opp. DUMB). □□**intelligently** *adv.* [L *intelligere intellect*-understand (as INTER-, *legere* gather, pick out, read)]

intelligentsia /ˌɪntɛlɪ'dʒɛntsɪə/ *n.* **1** the class of intellectuals regarded as possessing culture and political initiative. **2** people doing intellectual work; intellectuals. [Russ. f. Pol. *inteligencja* f. L *intelligentia* (as INTELLIGENT)]

intelligible /ɪn'tɛlɪdʒɪb(ə)l/ *adj.* **1** (often foll. by *to*) able to be understood; comprehensible. **2** *Philos.* able to be understood only by the intellect, not by the senses. □□**intelligibility** /-'bɪlɪtɪ/ *n.* **intelligibly** *adv.* [L *intelligibilis* (as INTELLIGENT)]

Intelpost /'ɪntɛlˌpəʊst/ *n.* the international electronic transmission of messages and graphics by fax, telex, etc. [*International Electronic Post*]

Intelsat /'ɪntɛlˌsæt/ *n.* an international organization of countries operating a system of commercial communication satellites. [*International Telecommunications Satellite Consortium*]

intemperate /ɪn'tɛmpərət/ *adj.* **1** (of a person, conduct, or speech) immoderate; unbridled; violent (*used intemperate language*). **2 a** given to excessive indulgence in alcohol. **b** excessively indulgent in one's appetites. □□**intemperance** *n.* **intemperately** *adv.* **intemperateness** *n.* [ME f. L *intemperatus* (as IN-¹, TEMPERATE)]

intend /ɪn'tɛnd/ *v.tr.* **1** have as one's purpose; propose (*we intend to go; we intend going; we intend that it shall be done*). **2** (usu. foll. by *for, as*) design or destine (a person or a thing) (*I intend him to go; I intend it as a warning*). **3** mean (*what does he intend by that?*). **4** (in *passive*; foll. by *for*) **a** be meant for a person to have or use etc. (*they are intended for the children*). **b** be meant to represent (*the picture is intended for you*). **5** (as **intending** *adj.*) who intends to be (*an intending visitor*). [ME *entende, intende* f. OF *entendre, intendre* f. L *intendere intent-* or *intens*-strain, direct, purpose (as IN-², *tendere* stretch, tend)]

intendant /ɪn'tɛnd(ə)nt/ *n.* **1** (esp. as a title of foreign officials) a superintendent or manager of a department of public business etc. **2** the administrator of an opera house or theatre. □□**intendancy** *n.* [F f. L *intendere* (as INTEND)]

intended /ɪn'tɛndɪd/ *adj. & n.* —*adj.* **1** done on purpose; intentional. **2** designed, meant. —*n. colloq.* the person one intends to marry; one's fiancé or fiancée (*is this your intended?*). □□**intendedly** *adv.*

intense /ɪn'tɛns/ *adj.* (**intenser, intensest**) **1** (of a quality etc.) existing in a high degree; violent; forceful (*intense cold*). **2** (of a person) feeling, or apt to feel, strong emotion (*very intense about her music*). **3** (of a feeling or action etc.) extreme (*intense joy; intense thought*). □□**intensely** *adv.* **intenseness** *n.* [ME f. OF *intens* or L *intensus* (as INTEND)]

intensifier /ɪn'tɛnsɪˌfaɪə(r)/ *n.* **1** a person or thing that intensifies. **2** *Gram.* = INTENSIVE *n.*

intensify /ɪn'tɛnsɪˌfaɪ/ *v.* (**-ies, -ied**) **1** *tr. & intr.* make or become intense or more intense. **2** *tr.*

Photog. increase the opacity of (a negative). □□
intensification /-fɪ'keɪʃ(ə)n/ *n.*
intension /ɪn'tenʃ(ə)n/ *n.* **1** *Logic* the internal content of a concept. **2** *formal* the intensity, or high degree, of a quality. **3** *formal* the strenuous exertion of the mind or will. □□**intensional** *adj.* **intensionally** *adv.* [L *intensio* (as INTEND)]
intensity /ɪn'tensɪtɪ/ *n.* (*pl.* **-ies**) **1** the quality or an instance of being intense. **2** esp. *Physics* the measurable amount of some quality, e.g. force, brightness, a magnetic field, etc.
intensive /ɪn'tensɪv/ *adj. & n.* —*adj.* **1** thorough, vigorous; directed to a single point, area, or subject (*intensive study*; *intensive bombardment*). **2** of or relating to intensity as opp. to extent; producing intensity. **3** serving to increase production in relation to costs (*intensive farming methods*). **4** (usu. in *comb.*) *Econ.* making much use of (*a labour-intensive industry*). **5** *Gram.* (of an adjective, adverb, etc.) expressing intensity; giving force, as *really* in *my feet are really cold.* —*n. Gram.* an intensive adjective, adverb, etc. □**intensive care** medical treatment with constant monitoring etc. of a dangerously ill patient (also (with hyphen) *attrib.*: *intensive-care unit*). □□**intensively** *adv.* **intensiveness** *n.* [F *intensif -ive* or med.L *intensivus* (as INTEND)]
intent /ɪn'tent/ *n. & adj.* —*n.* (usu. without article) intention; a purpose (*with intent to defraud*; *my intent to reach the top*; *with evil intent*). —*adj.* **1** (usu. foll. by *on*) **a** resolved; bent; determined (*was intent on succeeding*). **b** attentively occupied (*intent on his books*). **2** (esp. of a look) earnest; eager; meaningful. □**to all intents and purposes** practically; virtually. □□**intently** *adv.* **intentness** *n.* [ME *entent* f. OF f. L *intentus* (as INTEND)]
intention /ɪn'tenʃ(ə)n/ *n.* **1** (often foll. by *to* + infin., or *of* + verbal noun) a thing intended; an aim or purpose (*it was not his intention to interfere*; *have no intention of staying*). **2** the act of intending (*done without intention*). **3** *colloq.* (usu. in *pl.*) a person's, esp. a man's, designs in respect to marriage (*are his intentions strictly honourable?*). **4** *Logic* a conception. □**first intention** *Med.* the healing of a wound by natural contact of the parts. **first intentions** *Logic* one's primary conceptions of things (e.g. a tree, an oak). **intention tremor** *Med.* a trembling of a part of a body when commencing a movement. **second intention** *Med.* the healing of a wound by granulation. **second intentions** *Logic* one's secondary conceptions (e.g. difference, identity, species). **special** (or **particular**) **intention** *RC Ch.* a special aim or purpose for which a mass is celebrated, prayers are said, etc. □□**intentioned** *adj.* (usu. in *comb.*). [ME *entencion* f. OF f. L *intentio* stretching, purpose (as INTEND)]
intentional /ɪn'tenʃ(ə)n(ə)l/ *adj.* done on purpose. □□ **intentionality** /-'nælɪtɪ/ *n.* **intentionally** *adv.* [F *intentionnel* or med.L *intentionalis* (as INTENTION)]
inter /ɪn'tɜ:(r)/ *v.tr.* (**interred, interring**) deposit (a corpse etc.) in the earth, a tomb, etc.; bury. [ME f. OF *enterrer* f. Rmc (as IN-², L *terra* earth)]
inter. *abbr.* intermediate.
inter- /'ɪntə(r)/ *comb. form* **1** between, among (*intercontinental*). **2** mutually, reciprocally (*interbreed*). [OF *entre-* or L *inter* between, among]
interact /ɪntər'ækt/ *v.intr.* act reciprocally; act on each other. □□**interactant** *adj. & n.*
interaction /ɪntər'ækʃ(ə)n/ *n.* **1** reciprocal action or influence. **2** *Physics* the action of atomic and subatomic particles on each other.
interactive /ɪntər'æktɪv/ *adj.* **1** reciprocally active; acting upon or influencing each other. **2** (of a computer or other electronic device) allowing a two-way flow of information between it and a user, responding to the user's input. □□**interactively** *adv.* [INTERACT, after *active*]
inter alia /ɪntər 'eɪlɪə, 'ælɪə/ *adv.* among other things. [L]

inter-allied /ɪntər'ælaɪd/ *adj.* relating to two or more allies (in war etc.).
interarticular /ɪntərɑː'tɪkjʊlə(r)/ *adj.* between the contiguous surfaces of a joint.
interatomic /ɪntərə'tɒmɪk/ *adj.* between atoms.
interbank /'ɪntəbæŋk/ *adj.* agreed, arranged, or operating between banks (*interbank loan*).
interbed /ɪntə'bed/ *v.tr.* (**-bedded, -bedding**) embed (one thing) among others.
interblend /ɪntə'blend/ *v.* **1** *tr.* (usu. foll. by *with*) mingle (things) together. **2** *intr.* blend with each other.
interbreed /ɪntə'briːd/ *v.* (*past* and *past part.* **-bred** /-'bred/) **1** *intr. & tr.* breed or cause to breed with members of a different race or species to produce a hybrid. **2** *tr.* breed within one family etc. in order to produce desired characteristics (cf. CROSS-BREED).
intercalary /ɪn'tɜːkələrɪ, -'kælərɪ/ *adj.* **1 a** (of a day or a month) inserted in the calendar to harmonize it with the solar year, e.g. 29 Feb. in leap years. **b** (of a year) having such an addition. **2** interpolated; intervening. [L *intercalari(u)s* (as INTERCALATE)]
intercalate /ɪn'tɜːkəleɪt/ *v.tr.* **1** (also *absol.*) insert (an intercalary day etc.). **2** interpose (anything out of the ordinary course). **3** (as **intercalated** *adj.*) (of strata etc.) interposed. □□**intercalation** /-'leɪʃ(ə)n/ *n.* [L *intercalare intercalat-* (as INTER-, *calare* proclaim)]
intercede /ɪntə'siːd/ *v.intr.* (usu. foll. by *with*) interpose or intervene on behalf of another; plead (*they interceded with the king for his life*). □□**interceder** *n.* [F *intercéder* or L *intercedere intercess-* intervene (as INTER-, *cedere* go)]
intercellular /ɪntə'seljʊlə(r)/ *adj. Biol.* located or occurring between cells.
intercensal /ɪntə'sens(ə)l/ *adj.* between two censuses.
intercept *v. & n.* —*v.tr.* /ɪntə'sept/ **1** seize, catch, or stop (a person, message, vehicle, ball, etc.) going from one place to another. **2** (usu. foll. by *from*) cut off (light etc.). **3** check or stop (motion etc.). **4** *Math.* mark off (a space) between two points etc. —*n.* /'ɪntəsept/ *Math.* the part of a line between two points of intersection with usu. the coordinate axes or other lines. □□ **interception** /-'sepʃ(ə)n/ *n.* **interceptive** /-'septɪv/ *adj.* [L *intercipere intercept-* (as INTER-, *capere* take)]
interceptor /ɪntə'septə(r)/ *n.* **1** an aircraft used to intercept enemy raiders. **2** a person or thing that intercepts.
intercession /ɪntə'seʃ(ə)n/ *n.* **1** the act of interceding, esp. by prayer. **2** an instance of this. **3** a prayer. □□ **intercessional** *adj.* **intercessor** *n.* **intercessorial** /-se'sɔːrɪəl/ *adj.* **intercessory** *adj.* [F *intercession* or L *intercessio* (as INTERCEDE)]
interchange *v. & n.* —*v.tr.* /ɪntə'tʃeɪndʒ/ **1** (of two people) exchange (things) with each other. **2** put each of (two things) in the other's place; alternate. —*n.* /'ɪntə,tʃeɪndʒ/ **1** (often foll. by *of*) a reciprocal exchange between two people etc. **2** alternation (*the interchange of woods and fields*). **3** a road junction designed so that traffic streams do not intersect. □□ **interchangeable** *adj.* **interchangeability** /-'bɪlɪtɪ/ *n.* **interchangeableness** *n.* **interchangeably** *adv.* [ME f. OF *entrechangier* (as INTER-, CHANGE)]
inter-city /ɪntə'sɪtɪ/ *adj.* existing or travelling between cities.
inter-class /ɪntə'klɑːs/ *adj.* existing or conducted between different social classes.
intercollegiate /ɪntəkə'liːdʒət/ *adj.* existing or conducted between colleges or universities.
intercolonial /ɪntəkə'ləʊnɪəl/ *adj.* existing or conducted between colonies.
intercom /'ɪntə,kɒm/ *n. colloq.* a system of intercommunication by radio or telephone between or within offices, aircraft, etc. [abbr.]
intercommunicate /ɪntəkə'mjuːnɪkeɪt/ *v.intr.* **1** communicate reciprocally. **2** (of rooms etc.) have free passage into each other; have a connecting door. □□ **intercommunication** /-'keɪʃ(ə)n/ *n.* **intercommunicative** /-kətɪv/ *adj.*

intercommunion /ˌɪntəkəˈmjuːnɪən/ n. **1** mutual communion. **2** a mutual action or relationship, esp. between Christian denominations.

intercommunity /ˌɪntəkəˈmjuːnɪtɪ/ n. **1** the quality of being common to various groups etc. **2** having things in common.

interconnect /ˌɪntəkəˈnekt/ v.tr. & intr. connect with each other. □□ **interconnection** /-ˈnekʃ(ə)n/ n.

intercontinental /ˌɪntəˌkɒntɪˈnent(ə)l/ adj. connecting or travelling between continents. □□ **intercontinentally** adv.

interconvert /ˌɪntəkənˈvɜːt/ v.tr. & intr. convert into each other. □□ **interconversion** n. **interconvertible** adj.

intercooling /ˈɪntəˌkuːlɪŋ/ n. the cooling of gas between successive compressions, esp. in a car or truck engine. □□ **intercool** v.tr. **intercooler** n.

intercorrelate /ˌɪntəˈkɒrəˌleɪt/ v.tr. & intr. correlate with one another. □□ **intercorrelation** /-ˈleɪʃ(ə)n/ n.

intercostal /ˌɪntəˈkɒst(ə)l/ adj. between the ribs (of the body or a ship). □□ **intercostally** adv.

intercounty /ˌɪntəˈkaʊntɪ/ adj. existing or conducted between counties.

intercourse /ˈɪntəkɔːs/ n. **1** communication or dealings between individuals, nations, etc. **2** = sexual intercourse. **3** communion between human beings and God. [ME f. OF entrecours exchange, commerce, f. L intercursus (as INTER-, currere curs- run)]

intercrop /ˌɪntəˈkrɒp/ v.tr. (also absol.) (-cropped, -cropping) raise (a crop) among plants of a different kind, usu. in the space between rows. □□ **intercropping** n.

intercross /ˌɪntəˈkrɒs/ v. **1** tr. & intr. lay or lie across each other. **2 a** intr. (of animals) breed with each other. **b** tr. cause to do this.

intercrural /ˌɪntəˈkrʊər(ə)l/ adj. between the legs.

intercurrent /ˌɪntəˈkʌrənt/ adj. **1** (of a time or event) intervening. **2** Med. **a** (of a disease) occurring during the progress of another. **b** recurring at intervals. □□ **intercurrence** n. [L intercurrere intercurrent- (as INTERCOURSE)]

intercut /ˌɪntəˈkʌt/ v.tr. (-cutting; past and past part. -cut) Cinematog. alternate (shots) with contrasting shots by cutting.

interdenominational /ˌɪntədɪˌnɒmɪˈneɪʃən(ə)l/ adj. concerning more than one (religious) denomination. □□ **interdenominationally** adv.

interdepartmental /ˌɪntəˌdiːpɑːˈtment(ə)l/ adj. concerning more than one department. □□ **interdepartmentally** adv.

interdepend /ˌɪntədɪˈpend/ v.intr. depend on each other. □□ **interdependence** n. **interdependency** n. **interdependent** adj.

interdict n. & v. —n. /ˈɪntədɪkt/ **1** an authoritative prohibition. **2** RC Ch. a sentence debarring a person, or esp. a place, from ecclesiastical functions and privileges. **3** Sc. Law an injunction. —v.tr. /ˌɪntəˈdɪkt/ **1** prohibit (an action). **2** forbid the use of. **3** (usu. foll. by from + verbal noun) restrain (a person). **4** (usu. foll. by to) forbid (a thing) to a person. □□ **interdiction** /-ˈdɪkʃ(ə)n/ n. **interdictory** /-ˈdɪktərɪ/ adj. [ME f. OF entredit f. L interdictum past part. of interdicere interpose, forbid by decree (as INTER-, dicere say)]

interdigital /ˌɪntəˈdɪdʒɪt(ə)l/ adj. between the fingers or toes. □□ **interdigitally** adv.

interdigitate /ˌɪntəˈdɪdʒɪˌteɪt/ v.intr. interlock like clasped fingers. [INTER- + L digitus finger + -ATE³]

interdisciplinary /ˌɪntəˌdɪsɪˈplɪnərɪ/ adj. of or between more than one branch of learning.

interest /ˈɪntrəst, -trɪst/ n. & v. —n. **1 a** concern; curiosity (have no interest in fishing). **b** a quality exciting curiosity or holding the attention (this magazine lacks interest). **2** a subject, hobby, etc., in which one is concerned (his interests are gardening and sport). **3** advantage or profit, esp. when financial (it is in your interest to go; look after your own interests). **4** money paid for the use of money lent, or for not requiring the repayment of a debt. **5** (usu. foll. by in) **a** a financial stake (in an undertaking etc.). **b** a legal concern, title, or right (in property). **6 a** a party or group having a common interest (the brewing interest). **b** a principle in which a party or group is concerned. **7** the selfish pursuit of one's own welfare, self-interest. —v.tr. **1** excite the curiosity or attention of (your story interests me greatly). **2** (usu. foll. by in) cause (a person) to take a personal interest or share (can I interest you in a holiday abroad?). **3** (as **interested** adj.) having a private interest; not impartial or disinterested (an interested party). □ **at interest** (of money borrowed) on the condition that interest is payable. **declare an** (or **one's**) **interest** make known one's financial etc. interests in an undertaking before it is discussed. **in the interest** (or **interests**) **of** as something that is advantageous to. **lose interest** become bored or boring. **with interest** with increased force etc. (returned the blow with interest). □□ **interestedly** adv. **interestedness** n. [ME, earlier interesse f. AF f. med.L, alt. app. after OF interest, both f. L interest, 3rd sing. pres. of interesse matter, make a difference (as INTER-, esse be)]

interesting /ˈɪntrəstɪŋ, -trɪstɪŋ/ adj. causing curiosity; holding the attention. □ **in an interesting condition** archaic pregnant. □□ **interestingly** adv. **interestingness** n.

interface /ˈɪntəˌfeɪs/ n. & v. —n. **1** esp. Physics a surface forming a common boundary between two regions. **2** a point where interaction occurs between two systems, processes, subjects, etc. (the interface between psychology and education). **3** esp. Computing an apparatus for connecting two pieces of equipment so that they can be operated jointly. —v.tr. & intr. (often foll. by with) connect with (another piece of equipment etc.) by an interface.

interfacial /ˌɪntəˈfeɪʃ(ə)l/ adj. **1** included between two faces of a crystal or other solid. **2** of or forming an interface. □□ **interfacially** adv. (esp. in sense 2).

interfacing /ˈɪntəˌfeɪsɪŋ/ n. a stiffish material, esp. buckram, between two layers of fabric in collars etc.

interfemoral /ˌɪntəˈfemər(ə)l/ adj. between the thighs.

interfere /ˌɪntəˈfɪə(r)/ v.intr. **1** (usu. foll. by with) **a** (of a person) meddle; obstruct a process etc. **b** (of a thing) be a hindrance; get in the way. **2** (usu. foll. by in) take part or intervene, esp. without invitation or necessity. **3** (foll. by with) euphem. molest or assault sexually. **4** Physics (of light or other waves) combine so as to cause interference. **5** (of a horse) knock one leg against another. □□ **interferer** n. **interfering** adj. **interferingly** adv. [OF s'entreferir strike each other (as INTER-, ferir f. L ferire strike)]

interference /ˌɪntəˈfɪərəns/ n. **1** (usu. foll. by with) **a** the act of interfering. **b** an instance of this. **2** the fading or disturbance of received radio signals by the interference of waves from different sources, or esp. by atmospherics or unwanted signals. **3** Physics the combination of two or more wave motions to form a resultant wave in which the displacement is reinforced or cancelled. □□ **interferential** /-fəˈrenʃ(ə)l/ adj.

interferometer /ˌɪntəfəˈrɒmɪt(ə)r/ n. an instrument for measuring wavelengths etc. by means of interference phenomena. □□ **interferometric** /-ˌferəˈmetrɪk/ adj. **interferometrically** /-ˌferəˈmetrɪkəlɪ/ adv. **interferometry** n.

interferon /ˌɪntəˈfɪəˌrɒn/ n. Biochem. any of various proteins that can inhibit the development of a virus in a cell etc. [INTERFERE + -ON]

interfibrillar /ˌɪntəˈfɪbrɪlə(r)/ adj. between fibrils.

interfile /ˌɪntəˈfaɪl/ v.tr. **1** file (two sequences) together. **2** file (one or more items) into an existing sequence.

interflow /ˈɪntəˌfləʊ/ v. & n. —v.intr. flow into each other. —n. the process or result of this.

interfluent /ˌɪntəˈfluːənt/ adj. flowing into each

other. [L *interfluere interfluent-* (as INTER-, *fluere* flow)]

interfuse /ˌɪntəˈfjuːz/ v. **1** tr. **a** (usu. foll. by *with*) mix (a thing) with; intersperse. **b** blend (things) together. **2** *intr.* (of two things) blend with each other. □□ **interfusion** /-ˈfjuːʒ(ə)n/ n. [L *interfundere interfus-* (as INTER-, *fundere* pour)]

intergalactic /ˌɪntəgəˈlæktɪk/ adj. of or situated between two or more galaxies. □□ **intergalactically** adv.

interglacial /ˌɪntəˈɡleɪʃ(ə)l, -sɪəl/ adj. between glacial periods.

intergovernmental /ˌɪntəˌɡʌvənˈment(ə)l/ adj. concerning or conducted between two or more governments. □□ **intergovernmentally** adv.

intergradation /ˌɪntəgrəˈdeɪʃ(ə)n/ n. the process of merging together by gradual change of the constituents.

intergrade /ˈɪntəˌɡreɪd/ v. & n. —v.intr. pass into another form by intervening grades. —n. such a grade.

intergrowth /ˈɪntəˌɡrəʊθ/ n. the growing of things into each other.

interim /ˈɪntərɪm/ n., adj., & adv. —n. the intervening time (*in the interim he had died*). —adj. intervening; provisional, temporary. —adv. *archaic* meanwhile. □**interim dividend** a dividend declared on the basis of less than a full year's results. [L, as INTER- + adv. suffix *-im*]

interior /ɪnˈtɪərɪə(r)/ adj. & n. —adj. **1** inner (opp. EXTERIOR). **2** remote from the coast or frontier; inland. **3** internal; domestic (opp. FOREIGN). **4** (usu. foll. by *to*) situated further in or within. **5** existing in the mind or soul; inward. **6** drawn, photographed, etc. within a building. **7** coming from inside. —n. **1** the interior part; the inside. **2** the interior part of a country or region. **3 a** the home affairs of a country. **b** a department dealing with these (*Minister of the Interior*). **4** a representation of the inside of a building or a room (*Dutch interior*). **5** the inner nature; the soul. □**interior angle** the angle between adjacent sides of a rectilinear figure. **interior decoration** (or **design**) the decoration or design of the interior of a building, a room, etc. **interior monologue** a form of writing expressing a character's inner thoughts. **interior-sprung** (of a mattress etc.) with internal springs. □□ **interiorize** v.tr. (also **-ise**). **interiorly** adv. [L, compar. f. *inter* among]

interject /ˌɪntəˈdʒekt/ v.tr. **1** utter (words) abruptly or parenthetically. **2** interrupt with. □□ **interjectory** adj. [L *interjicere* (as INTER-, *jacere* throw)]

interjection /ˌɪntəˈdʒekʃ(ə)n/ n. an exclamation, esp. as a part of speech (e.g. *ah!*, *dear me!*). □□ **interjectional** adj. [ME f. OF f. L *interjectio -onis* (as INTERJECT)]

interknit /ˌɪntəˈnɪt/ v.tr. & intr. (**-knitting**; *past* and *past part.* **-knitted** or **-knit**) knit together; intertwine.

interlace /ˌɪntəˈleɪs/ v. **1** tr. bind intricately together; interweave. **2** tr. mingle, intersperse. **3** intr. cross each other intricately. □□ **interlacement** n. [ME f. OF *entrelacier* (as INTER-, LACE v.)]

interlanguage /ˈɪntəˌlæŋɡwɪdʒ/ n. a language or use of language having features of two others, often a pidgin or dialect form.

interlap /ˌɪntəˈlæp/ v.intr. (**-lapped**, **-lapping**) overlap.

interlard /ˌɪntəˈlɑːd/ v.tr. (usu. foll. by *with*) mix (writing or speech) with unusual words or phrases. [F *entrelarder* (as INTER-, LARD v.)]

interleaf /ˈɪntəˌliːf/ n. (pl. **-leaves**) an extra (usu. blank) leaf between the leaves of a book.

interleave /ˌɪntəˈliːv/ v.tr. insert (usu. blank) leaves between the leaves of (a book etc.).

interleukin /ˌɪntəˈluːkɪn/ n. *Biochem.* any of several glycoproteins produced by leucocytes for regulating immune responses. [INTER- + LEUCOCYTE]

interlibrary /ˈɪntəˌlaɪbrərɪ/ adj. between libraries (esp. *interlibrary loan*).

interline[1] /ˌɪntəˈlaɪn/ v.tr. **1** insert words between the lines of (a document etc.). **2** insert (words) in this way. □□ **interlineation** /-ˌlɪnɪˈeɪʃ(ə)n/ n. [ME f. med.L *interlineare* (as INTER-, LINE[1])]

interline[2] /ˌɪntəˈlaɪn/ v.tr. put an extra lining between the ordinary lining and the fabric of (a garment).

interlinear /ˌɪntəˈlɪnɪə(r)/ adj. written or printed between the lines of a text. [ME f. med.L *interlinearis* (as INTER-, LINEAR)]

interlining /ˈɪntəˌlaɪnɪŋ/ n. material used to interline a garment.

interlink /ˌɪntəˈlɪŋk/ v.tr. & intr. link or be linked together.

interlobular /ˌɪntəˈlɒbjʊlə(r)/ adj. situated between lobes.

interlock /ˌɪntəˈlɒk/ v., adj., & n. —v. **1** intr. engage with each other by overlapping or by the fitting together of projections and recesses. **2** tr. (usu. in *passive*) lock or clasp within each other. —adj. (of a fabric) knitted with closely interlocking stitches. —n. a device or mechanism for connecting or coordinating the function of different components. □□ **interlocker** n.

interlocutor /ˌɪntəˈlɒkjʊtə(r)/ n. (*fem.* **interlocutrix** /-trɪks/) a person who takes part in a dialogue or conversation. □□ **interlocution** /-ləˈkjuːʃ(ə)n/ n. [mod.L f. L *interloqui interlocut-* interrupt in speaking (as INTER-, *loqui* speak)]

interlocutory /ˌɪntəˈlɒkjʊtərɪ/ adj. **1** of dialogue or conversation. **2** *Law* (of a decree etc.) given provisionally in a legal action. [med.L *interlocutorius* (as INTERLOCUTOR)]

interloper /ˈɪntəˌləʊpə(r)/ n. **1** an intruder. **2** a person who interferes in others' affairs, esp. for profit. □□ **interlope** v.intr. [INTER- + *loper* as in *landloper* vagabond f. MDu. *landlooper*]

interlude /ˈɪntəˌluːd, -ˌljuːd/ n. **1 a** a pause between the acts of a play. **b** something performed or done during this pause. **2 a** an intervening time, space, or event that contrasts with what goes before or after. **b** a temporary amusement or entertaining episode. **3** a piece of music played between other pieces, the verses of a hymn, etc. [ME, = a light dramatic item between the acts of a morality play, f. med.L *interludium* (as INTER-, *ludus* play)]

intermarriage /ˌɪntəˈmærɪdʒ/ n. **1** marriage between people of different races, castes, families, etc. **2** (loosely) marriage between near relations.

intermarry /ˌɪntəˈmærɪ/ v.intr. (**-ies**, **-ied**) (foll. by *with*) (of races, castes, families, etc.) become connected by marriage.

intermediary /ˌɪntəˈmiːdɪərɪ/ n. & adj. —n. (pl. **-ies**) an intermediate person or thing, esp. a mediator. —adj. acting as mediator; intermediate. [F *intermédiaire* f. It. *intermediario* f. L *intermedius* (as INTERMEDIATE)]

intermediate /ˌɪntəˈmiːdɪət/ adj., n., & v. —adj. coming between two things in time, place, order, character, etc. —n. **1** an intermediate thing. **2** a chemical compound formed by one reaction and then used in another, esp. during synthesis. —v.intr. /-dɪˌeɪt/ (foll. by *between*) act as intermediary; mediate. □**intermediate frequency** the frequency to which a radio signal is converted during heterodyne reception. □□ **intermediacy** /-sɪ/ n. **intermediately** adv. **intermediateness** n. **intermediation** /-ˈeɪʃ(ə)n/ n. **intermediator** /-ˌeɪtə(r)/ n. [med.L *intermediatus* (as INTER-, *medius* middle)]

interment /ɪnˈtɜːmənt/ n. the burial of a corpse, esp. with ceremony.

intermesh /ˌɪntəˈmeʃ/ v.tr. & intr. make or become meshed together.

intermezzo /ˌɪntəˈmetsəʊ/ n. (pl. **intermezzi** /-tsɪ/

aʊ how eɪ day əʊ no eə hair ɪə near ɔɪ boy ʊə poor aɪə fire aʊə sour (*see over for consonants*)

or -os) **1 a** a short connecting instrumental movement in an opera or other musical work. **b** a similar piece performed independently. **c** a short piece for a solo instrument. **2** a short light dramatic or other performance inserted between the acts of a play. [It. f. L *intermedium* interval (as INTERMEDIATE)]

interminable /ɪn'tɜːmɪnəb(ə)l/ *adj.* **1** endless. **2** tediously long or habitual. **3** with no prospect of an end. □□ **interminableness** *n.* **interminably** *adv.* [ME f. OF *interminable* or LL *interminabilis* (as IN-[1], TERMINATE)]

intermingle /ˌɪntə'mɪŋg(ə)l/ *v.tr.* & *intr.* (often foll. by *with*) mix together; mingle.

intermission /ˌɪntə'mɪʃ(ə)n/ *n.* **1** a pause or cessation. **2** an interval between parts of a play, film, concert, etc. **3** a period of inactivity. [F *intermission* or L *intermissio* (as INTERMIT)]

intermit /ˌɪntə'mɪt/ *v.* (**intermitted, intermitting**) **1** *intr.* esp. *Med.* stop or cease activity briefly (e.g. of a fever, or a pulse). **2** *tr.* suspend; discontinue for a time. [L *intermittere intermiss-* (as INTER-, *mittere* let go)]

intermittent /ˌɪntə'mɪt(ə)nt/ *adj.* occurring at intervals; not continuous or steady. □□ **intermittence** /-t(ə)ns/ *n.* **intermittency** /-tənsɪ/ *n.* **intermittently** *adv.* [L *intermittere intermittent-* (as INTERMIT)]

intermix /ˌɪntə'mɪks/ *v.tr.* & *intr.* mix together. □□ **intermixable** *adj.* **intermixture** *n.* [back-form. f. *intermixed, intermixt* f. L *intermixtus* past part. of *intermiscēre* mix together (as INTER-, *miscēre* mix)]

intermolecular /ˌɪntəmə'lekjʊlə(r)/ *adj.* between molecules.

intern *n.* & *v.* —*n.* /'ɪntɜːn/ (also **interne**) *US* a recent graduate or advanced student living in a hospital and acting as an assistant physician or surgeon. —*v.* **1** *tr.* /ɪn'tɜːn/ confine; oblige (a prisoner, alien, etc.) to reside within prescribed limits. **2** *intr.* /'ɪntɜːn/ *US* serve as an intern. □□ **internment** *n.* **internship** *n.* [F *interne* f. L *internus* internal]

internal /ɪn'tɜːn(ə)l/ *adj.* & *n.* —*adj.* **1** of or situated in the inside or invisible part. **2** relating or applied to the inside of the body (*internal injuries*). **3** of a nation's domestic affairs. **4** (of a student) attending a university etc. as well as taking its examinations. **5** used or applying within an organization. **6 a** of the inner nature of a thing; intrinsic. **b** of the mind or soul. —*n.* (in *pl.*) intrinsic qualities. □ **internal-combustion engine** an engine with its motive power generated by the explosion of gases or vapour with air in a cylinder. **internal energy** the energy in a system arising from the relative positions and interactions of its parts. **internal evidence** evidence derived from the contents of the thing discussed. **internal exile** see EXILE *n.* 1. **internal rhyme** a rhyme involving a word in the middle of a line and another at the end of the line or in the middle of the next. □□ **internality** /-'nælɪtɪ/ *n.* **internalize** *v.tr.* (also **-ise**). /-'zeɪʃ(ə)n/ *n.* **internally** *adv.* [mod.L *internalis* (as INTERN)]

internat. *abbr.* international.

international /ˌɪntə'næʃən(ə)l/ *adj.* & *n.* —*adj.* **1** existing, involving, or carried on between two or more nations. **2** agreed on or used by all or many nations (*international date-line; international driving licence*). —*n.* **1 a** a contest, esp. in sport, between teams representing different countries. **b** a member of such a team. **2 a** (**International**) any of four associations founded (1864-1936) to promote socialist or communist action. **b** a member of any of these. □ **international law** a body of rules established by custom or treaty and agreed as binding by nations in their relations with one another. **international system of units** a system of physical units based on the metre, kilogram, second, ampere, kelvin, candela, and mole, with prefixes to indicate multiplication or division by a power of ten.

international unit a standard quantity of a vitamin etc. □□ **internationality** /-'nælɪtɪ/ *n.* **internationally** *adv.*

Internationale /ˌɪntəˌnæʃjə'nɑːl/ *n.* **1** (prec. by *the*) an (orig. French) revolutionary song adopted by socialists. **2** = INTERNATIONAL *n.* 2a. [F, fem. of *international* (adj.) f. INTERNATIONAL]

internationalism /ˌɪntə'næʃənəˌlɪz(ə)m/ *n.* **1** the advocacy of a community of interests among nations. **2** (**Internationalism**) the principles of any of the Internationals. □□ **internationalist** *n.*

internationalize /ˌɪntə'næʃənəˌlaɪz/ *v.tr.* (also **-ise**) **1** make international. **2** bring under the protection or control of two or more nations. □□ **internationalization** /-'zeɪʃ(ə)n/ *n.*

interne *US* var. of INTERN *n.*

internecine /ˌɪntə'niːsaɪn/ *adj.* mutually destructive. [orig. = deadly, f. L *internecinus* f. *internecio* massacre f. *internecare* slaughter (as INTER-, *necare* kill)]

internee /ˌɪntɜː'niː/ *n.* a person interned.

internist /ɪn'tɜːnɪst/ *n. Med.* **1** a specialist in internal diseases. **2** *US* a general practitioner.

internode /'ɪntəˌnəʊd/ *n.* **1** *Bot.* a part of a stem between two of the knobs from which leaves arise. **2** *Anat.* a slender part between two joints, esp. the bone of a finger or toe.

internuclear /ˌɪntə'njuːklɪə(r)/ *adj.* between nuclei.

internuncial /ˌɪntə'nʌnʃ(ə)l/ *adj.* (of nerves) communicating between different parts of the system. [*internuncio* ambassador f. It. *internunzio*]

interoceanic /ˌɪntərˌəʊsɪ'ænɪk/ *adj.* between or connecting two oceans.

interoceptive /ˌɪntərəʊ'septɪv/ *adj. Biol.* relating to stimuli produced within an organism, esp. in the viscera. [irreg. f. L *internus* interior + RECEPTIVE]

interosculate /ˌɪntər'ɒskjʊˌleɪt/ *v.intr.* = IN-OSCULATE.

interosseous /ˌɪntər'ɒsɪəs/ *adj.* between bones.

interparietal /ˌɪntəpə'raɪət(ə)l/ *adj.* between the right and left parietal bones of the skull. □□ **interparietally** *adv.*

interpellate /ɪn'tɜːpeˌleɪt/ *v.tr.* (in European parliaments) interrupt the order of the day by demanding an explanation from (the Minister concerned). □□ **interpellation** /-'leɪʃ(ə)n/ *n.* **interpellator** *n.* [L *interpellare interpellat-* (as INTER-, *pellere* drive)]

interpenetrate /ˌɪntə'peniˌtreɪt/ *v.* **1** *intr.* (of two things) penetrate each other. **2** *tr.* pervade; penetrate thoroughly. □□ **interpenetration** /-'treɪʃ(ə)n/ *n.* **interpenetrative** /-trətɪv/ *adj.*

interpersonal /ˌɪntə'pɜːsən(ə)l/ *adj.* (of relations) occurring between persons, esp. reciprocally. □□ **interpersonally** *adv.*

interplait /ˌɪntə'plæt/ *v.tr.* & *intr.* plait together.

interplanetary /ˌɪntə'plænɪtərɪ/ *adj.* **1** between planets. **2** relating to travel between planets.

interplay /'ɪntəˌpleɪ/ *n.* **1** reciprocal action. **2** the operation of two things on each other.

interplead /ˌɪntə'pliːd/ *v.* **1** *intr.* litigate with each other to settle a point concerning a third party. **2** *tr.* cause to do this. □□ **interpleader** *n.* [ME f. AF *enterpleder* (as INTER-, PLEAD)]

Interpol /'ɪntəˌpɒl/ *n.* International Criminal Police Organization. [abbr.]

interpolate /ɪn'tɜːpəˌleɪt/ *v.tr.* **1 a** insert (words) in a book etc., esp. to give false impressions as to its date etc. **b** make such insertions in (a book etc.). **2** interject (a remark) in a conversation. **3** estimate (values) from known ones in the same range. □□ **interpolation** /-'leɪʃ(ə)n/ *n.* **interpolative** /-lətɪv/ *adj.* **interpolator** *n.* [L *interpolare* furnish up (as INTER-, *polire* POLISH[1])]

interpose /ˌɪntə'pəʊz/ *v.* **1** *tr.* (often foll. by *between*) place or insert (a thing) between others. **2** *tr.* say (words) as an interruption. **3** *tr.* exercise or advance (a veto or objection) so as to interfere. **4** *intr.* (foll. by

b *but* d *dog* f *few* g *get* h *he* j *yes* k *cat* l *leg* m *man* n *no* p *pen* r *red* s *sit* t *top* v *voice*

between) intervene (between parties). [F *interposer* f. L *interponere* put (as INTER-, POSE[1])]

interposition /ˌɪntəpəˈzɪʃ(ə)n/ *n.* **1** the act of interposing. **2** a thing interposed. **3** an interference. [ME f. OF *interposition* or L *interpositio* (as INTER-, POSITION)]

interpret /ɪnˈtɜːprɪt/ *v.* (**interpreted, interpreting**) **1** *tr.* explain the meaning of (foreign or abstruse words, a dream, etc.). **2** *tr.* make out or bring out the meaning of (creative work). **3** *intr.* act as an interpreter, esp. of foreign languages. **4** *tr.* explain or understand (behaviour etc.) in a specified manner (*interpreted his gesture as mocking*). □□ **interpretable** *adj.* **interpretability** /-təˈbɪlɪtɪ/ *n.* **interpretation** /-ˈteɪʃ(ə)n/ *n.* **interpretational** /-ˈteɪʃən(ə)l/ *adj.* **interpretative** /-ˈtətɪv/ *adj.* **interpretive** *adj.* **interpretively** *adv.* [ME f. OF *interpreter* or L *interpretari* explain, translate f. *interpres -pretis* explainer]

interpreter /ɪnˈtɜːprɪtə(r)/ *n.* a person who interprets, esp. one who translates speech orally. [ME f. AF *interpretour*, OF *interpreteur* f. LL *interpretator -oris* (as INTERPRET)]

interprovincial /ˌɪntəprəˈvɪnʃ(ə)l/ *adj.* situated or carried on between provinces.

interracial /ˌɪntəˈreɪʃ(ə)l/ *adj.* existing between or affecting different races. □□ **interracially** *adv.*

interregnum /ˌɪntəˈregnəm/ *n.* (*pl.* **interregnums** or **interregna** /-nə/) **1** an interval when the normal government is suspended, esp. between successive reigns or regimes. **2** an interval or pause. [L (as INTER-, *regnum* reign)]

interrelate /ˌɪntərɪˈleɪt/ *v.tr.* relate (two or more things) to each other. □□ **interrelation** *n.* **interrelationship** *n.*

interrogate /ɪnˈterəˌgeɪt/ *v.tr.* ask questions of (a person) esp. closely, thoroughly, or formally. □□ **interrogator** *n.* [ME f. L *interrogare interrogat-* ask (as INTER-, *rogare* ask)]

interrogation /ɪnˌterəˈgeɪʃ(ə)n/ *n.* **1** the act or an instance of interrogating; the process of being interrogated. **2** a question or enquiry. □ **interrogation point** (or **mark** etc.) = *question mark*. □□ **interrogational** *adj.* [ME f. F *interrogation* or L *interrogatio* (as INTERROGATE)]

interrogative /ˌɪntəˈrɒgətɪv/ *adj. & n.* —*adj.* **1 a** of or like a question; used in questions. **b** *Gram.* (of an adjective or pronoun) asking a question (e.g. *who?, which?*). **2** having the form or force of a question. **3** suggesting enquiry (*an interrogative tone*). —*n.* an interrogative word (e.g. *what?, why?*). □□ **interrogatively** *adv.* [LL *interrogativus* (as INTERROGATE)]

interrogatory /ˌɪntəˈrɒgətərɪ/ *adj. & n.* —*adj.* questioning; of or suggesting enquiry (*an interrogatory eyebrow*). —*n.* (*pl.* **-ies**) a formal set of questions, esp. *Law* one formally put to an accused person etc. [LL *interrogatorius* (as INTERROGATE)]

interrupt /ˌɪntəˈrʌpt/ *v.tr.* **1** act so as to break the continuous progress of (an action, speech, a person speaking, etc.). **2** obstruct (a person's view etc.). **3** break the continuity of. □□ **interruptible** *adj.* **interruption** /-ˈrʌpʃ(ə)n/ *n.* **interruptive** *adj.* **interruptory** *adj.* [ME f. L *interrumpere interrupt-* (as INTER-, *rumpere* break)]

interrupter /ˌɪntəˈrʌptə(r)/ *n.* (also **interruptor**) **1** a person or thing that interrupts. **2** a device for interrupting, esp. an electric circuit.

intersect /ˌɪntəˈsekt/ *v.* **1** *tr.* divide (a thing) by passing or lying across it. **2** *intr.* (of lines, roads, etc.) cross or cut each other. [L *intersecare intersect-* (as INTER-, *secare* cut)]

intersection /ˌɪntəˈsekʃ(ə)n/ *n.* **1** the act of intersecting. **2** a place where two roads intersect. **3** a point or line common to lines or planes that intersect. □□ **intersectional** *adj.* [L *intersectio* (as INTERSECT)]

interseptal /ˌɪntəˈsept(ə)l/ *adj.* between septa or partitions.

intersex /ˈɪntəˌseks/ *n.* **1** the abnormal condition of being intermediate between male and female. **2** an individual in this condition.

intersexual /ˌɪntəˈseksjʊəl/ *adj.* **1** existing between the sexes. **2** of intersex. □□ **intersexuality** /-ˈælɪtɪ/ *n.* **intersexually** *adv.*

interspace /ˈɪntəˌspeɪs/ *n. & v.* —*n.* an interval of space or time. —*v.tr.* put interspaces between.

interspecific /ˌɪntəspəˈsɪfɪk/ *adj.* formed from different species.

intersperse /ˌɪntəˈspɜːs/ *v.tr.* **1** (often foll. by *between, among*) scatter; place here and there. **2** (foll. by *with*) diversify (a thing or things with others so scattered). □□ **interspersion** *n.* [L *interspergere interspers-* (as INTER-, *spargere* scatter)]

interspinal /ˌɪntəˈspaɪn(ə)l/ *adj.* (also **interspinous** /-nəs/) between spines or spinous processes.

interstate /ˈɪntəˌsteɪt/ *adj. & n.* US —*adj.* existing or carried on between States, esp. of the US. —*n.* a motorway, esp. crossing a State boundary.

interstellar /ˌɪntəˈstelə(r)/ *adj.* occurring or situated between stars.

interstice /ɪnˈtɜːstɪs/ *n.* **1** an intervening space. **2** a chink or crevice. [L *interstitium* (as INTER-, *sistere stit-* stand)]

interstitial /ˌɪntəˈstɪʃ(ə)l/ *adj.* of, forming, or occupying interstices. □□ **interstitially** *adv.*

intertextuality /ˌɪntəˌtekstjʊˈælɪtɪ/ *n.* the relationship between esp. literary texts.

intertidal /ˌɪntəˈtaɪd(ə)l/ *adj.* of or relating to the area which is covered at high tide and uncovered at low tide.

intertribal /ˌɪntəˈtraɪb(ə)l/ *adj.* existing or occurring between different tribes.

intertrigo /ˌɪntəˈtraɪgəʊ/ *n.* (*pl.* **-os**) *Med.* inflammation from the rubbing of one area of skin on another. [L f. *interterere intertrit-* (as INTER-, *terere* rub)]

intertwine /ˌɪntəˈtwaɪn/ *v.* **1** *tr.* (often foll. by *with*) entwine (together). **2** *intr.* become entwined. □□ **intertwinement** *n.*

intertwist /ˌɪntəˈtwɪst/ *v.tr.* twist together.

interval /ˈɪntəv(ə)l/ *n.* **1** an intervening time or space. **2** *Brit.* a pause or break, esp. between the parts of a theatrical or musical performance. **3** the difference in pitch between two sounds. **4** the distance between persons or things in respect of qualities. □ **at intervals** here and there; now and then. □□ **intervallic** /-ˈvælɪk/ *adj.* [ME ult. f. L *intervallum* space between ramparts, interval (as INTER-, *vallum* rampart)]

intervene /ˌɪntəˈviːn/ *v.intr.* (often foll. by *between, in*) **1** occur in time between events. **2** interfere; come between so as to prevent or modify the result or course of events. **3** be situated between things. **4** come in as an extraneous factor or thing. **5** *Law* interpose in a lawsuit as a third party. □□ **intervener** *n.* **intervenient** *adj.* **intervenor** *n.* [L *intervenire* (as INTER-, *venire* come)]

intervention /ˌɪntəˈvenʃ(ə)n/ *n.* **1** the act or an instance of intervening. **2** interference, esp. by a State in another's affairs. **3** mediation. [ME f. F *intervention* or L *interventio* (as INTERVENE)]

interventionist /ˌɪntəˈvenʃənɪst/ *n.* a person who favours intervention.

intervertebral /ˌɪntəˈvɜːtɪbr(ə)l/ *adj.* between vertebrae.

interview /ˈɪntəˌvjuː/ *n. & v.* —*n.* **1** an oral examination of an applicant for employment, a college place, etc. **2** a conversation between a reporter etc. and a person of public interest, used as a basis of a broadcast or publication. **3** a meeting of persons face to face, esp. for consultation. —*v.tr.* **1** hold an interview with. **2** question to discover the opinions or experience of (a person). □□ **interviewee** /-vjuːˈiː/ *n.* **interviewer** *n.* [F *entrevue* f. *s'entrevoir* see each other (as INTER-, *voir* f. L *vidēre* see: see VIEW)]

interwar /ˌɪntəˈwɔː(r)/ adj. existing in the period between two wars, esp. the two world wars.

interweave /ˌɪntəˈwiːv/ v.tr. (past **-wove** /-ˈwəʊv/; past part. **-woven** /-ˈwəʊv(ə)n/) **1** (often foll. by with) weave together. **2** blend intimately.

interwind /ˌɪntəˈwaɪnd/ v.tr. & intr. (past and past part. **-wound** /-ˈwaʊnd/) wind together.

interwork /ˌɪntəˈwɜːk/ v. **1** intr. work together or interactively. **2** tr. interweave.

intestate /ɪnˈtesteɪt/ adj. & n. —adj. (of a person) not having made a will before death. —n. a person who has died intestate. □□ **intestacy** /-təsɪ/ n. [ME f. L intestatus (as IN-¹, testari testat- make a will f. testis witness)]

intestine /ɪnˈtestɪn/ n. (in sing. or pl.) the lower part of the alimentary canal from the end of the stomach to the anus. □ **large intestine** the caecum, colon, and rectum collectively. **small intestine** the duodenum, jejunum, and ileum collectively. □□ **intestinal** /also ˌɪnteˈstaɪn(ə)l/ adj. [L intestinum f. intestinus internal]

inthrall US var. of ENTHRAL.

intimacy /ˈɪntɪməsɪ/ n. (pl. **-ies**) **1** the state of being intimate. **2** an intimate act, esp. sexual intercourse. **3** an intimate remark; an endearment.

intimate¹ /ˈɪntɪmət/ adj. & n. —adj. **1** closely acquainted; familiar, close (an intimate friend; an intimate relationship). **2** private and personal (intimate thoughts). **3** (usu. foll. by with) having sexual relations. **4** (of knowledge) detailed, thorough. **5** (of a relationship between things) close. **6** (of mixing etc.) thorough. **7** essential, intrinsic. **8** (of a place etc.) friendly; promoting close personal relationships. —n. a very close friend. □□ **intimately** adv. [L intimus inmost]

intimate² /ˈɪntɪˌmeɪt/ v.tr. **1** (often foll. by that + clause) state or make known. **2** imply, hint. □□ **intimater** n. **intimation** /-ˈmeɪʃ(ə)n/ n. [LL intimare announce f. L intimus inmost]

intimidate /ɪnˈtɪmɪˌdeɪt/ v.tr. frighten or overawe, esp. to subdue or influence. □□ **intimidation** /-ˈdeɪʃ(ə)n/ n. **intimidator** n. [med.L intimidare (as IN-², timidare f. timidus TIMID]

intinction /ɪnˈtɪŋkʃ(ə)n/ n. Eccl. the dipping of the Eucharistic bread in the wine so that the communicant receives both together. [LL intinctio f. L intingere intinct- (as IN-², TINGE)]

intitule /ɪnˈtɪtjuːl/ v.tr. Brit. entitle (an Act of Parliament etc.). [OF intituler f. LL intitulare (as IN-², titulare f. titulus title)]

into /ˈɪntʊ, ˈɪntə/ prep. **1** expressing motion or direction to a point on or within (walked into a tree; ran into the house). **2** expressing direction of attention or concern (will look into it). **3** expressing a change of state (turned into a dragon; separated into groups; forced into cooperation). **4** colloq. interested in; knowledgeable about (is really into art). [OE intō (as IN, TO)]

intolerable /ɪnˈtɒlərəb(ə)l/ adj. that cannot be endured. □□ **intolerableness** n. **intolerably** adv. [ME f. OF intolerable or L intolerabilis (as IN-¹, TOLERABLE)]

intolerant /ɪnˈtɒlərənt/ adj. not tolerant, esp. of views, beliefs, or behaviour differing from one's own. □□ **intolerance** n. **intolerantly** adv. [L intolerans (as IN-¹, TOLERANT)]

intonate /ˈɪntəˌneɪt/ v.tr. intone. [med.L intonare: see INTONE]

intonation /ˌɪntəˈneɪʃ(ə)n/ n. **1** modulation of the voice; accent. **2** the act of intoning. **3** accuracy of pitch in playing or singing (has good intonation). **4** the opening phrase of a plainsong melody. □□ **intonational** adj. [med.L intonatio (as INTONE]

intone /ɪnˈtəʊn/ v.tr. **1** recite (prayers etc.) with prolonged sounds, esp. in a monotone. **2** utter with a particular tone. □□ **intoner** n. [med.L intonare (as IN-², L tonus TONE]

in toto /ɪn ˈtəʊtəʊ/ adv. completely. [L]

intoxicant /ɪnˈtɒksɪkənt/ adj. & n. —adj. intoxicating. —n. an intoxicating substance.

intoxicate /ɪnˈtɒksɪˌkeɪt/ v.tr. **1** make drunk. **2** excite or elate beyond self-control. □□ **intoxicatingly** adv. **intoxication** /-ˈkeɪʃ(ə)n/ n. [med.L intoxicare (as IN-², toxicare poison f. L toxicum): see TOXIC]

intra- /ˈɪntrə/ prefix forming adjectives usu. from adjectives, meaning 'on the inside, within' (intramural). [L intra inside]

intracellular /ˌɪntrəˈseljʊlə(r)/ adj. Biol. located or occurring within a cell or cells.

intracranial /ˌɪntrəˈkreɪnɪəl/ adj. within the skull. □□ **intracranially** adv.

intractable /ɪnˈtræktəb(ə)l/ adj. **1** hard to control or deal with. **2** difficult, stubborn. □□ **intractability** /-ˈbɪlɪtɪ/ n. **intractableness** n. **intractably** adv. [L intractabilis (as IN-¹, TRACTABLE)]

intrados /ɪnˈtreɪdɒs/ n. the lower or inner curve of an arch. [F (as INTRA-, dos back f. L dorsum)]

intramolecular /ˌɪntrəməˈlekjʊlə(r)/ adj. within a molecule.

intramural /ˌɪntrəˈmjʊər(ə)l/ adj. **1** situated or done within walls. **2** forming part of normal university or college studies. □□ **intramurally** adv.

intramuscular /ˌɪntrəˈmʌskjʊlə(r)/ adj. in or into a muscle or muscles.

intransigent /ɪnˈtrænsɪdʒ(ə)nt, -zɪdʒ(ə)nt/ adj. & n. —adj. uncompromising, stubborn. —n. an intransigent person. □□ **intransigence** /-dʒ(ə)ns/ n. **intransigency** /-dʒənsɪ/ n. **intransigently** adv. [F intransigeant f. Sp. los intransigentes extreme republicans in Cortes, ult. formed as IN-¹ + L transigere transigent- come to an understanding (as TRANS-, agere act)]

intransitive /ɪnˈtrænsɪtɪv, ɪnˈtrɑːn-, -zɪtɪv/ adj. (of a verb or sense of a verb) that does not take or require a direct object (whether expressed or implied), e.g. look in look at the sky (opp. TRANSITIVE). □□ **intransitively** adv. **intransitivity** /-ˈtɪvɪtɪ/ n. [LL intransitivus (as IN-¹, TRANSITIVE)]

intra-uterine /ˌɪntrəˈjuːtəˌraɪn, -rɪn/ adj. within the womb.

intravenous /ˌɪntrəˈviːnəs/ adj. in or into a vein or veins. □□ **intravenously** adv. [INTRA- + L vena vein]

in-tray /ˈɪntreɪ/ n. a tray for incoming documents, letters, etc.

intrepid /ɪnˈtrepɪd/ adj. fearless; very brave. □□ **intrepidity** /-trɪˈpɪdɪtɪ/ n. **intrepidly** adv. [F intrépide or L intrepidus (as IN-¹, trepidus alarmed)]

intricate /ˈɪntrɪkət/ adj. very complicated; perplexingly detailed. □□ **intricacy** /-kəsɪ/ n. (pl. **-ies**). **intricately** adv. [ME f. L intricare intricat- (as IN-², tricare f. tricae tricks)]

intrigant /ˈɪntrɪgənt/ n. (fem. **intrigante**) an intriguer. [F intriguant f. intriguer: see INTRIGUE]

intrigue v. & n. —v. /ɪnˈtriːg/ (**intrigues**, **intrigued**, **intriguing**) **1** intr. (foll. by with) **a** carry on an underhand plot. **b** use secret influence. **2** tr. arouse the curiosity of; fascinate. —n. /ɪnˈtriːg, ˈɪn-/ **1** an underhand plot or plotting. **2** archaic a secret love affair. □□ **intriguer** /ɪnˈtriːgə(r)/ n. **intriguing** adj. (esp. in sense 2 of v.) **intriguingly** /ɪnˈtriːgɪ-/ adv. [F intrigue (n.), intriguer (v.) f. It. intrigo, intrigare f. L (as INTRICATE)]

intrinsic /ɪnˈtrɪnzɪk/ adj. inherent, essential; belonging naturally (intrinsic value). □□ **intrinsically** adv. [ME, = interior, f. F intrinsèque f. LL intrinsecus f. L intrinsecus (adv.) inwardly]

intro /ˈɪntrəʊ/ n. (pl. **-os**) colloq. an introduction. [abbr.]

intro- /ˈɪntrəʊ/ comb. form into (introgression). [L intro to the inside]

introduce /ˌɪntrəˈdjuːs/ v.tr. **1** (foll. by to) make (a person or oneself) known by name to another, esp. formally. **2** announce or present to an audience. **3** bring (a custom, idea, etc.) into use. **4** bring (a piece of legislation) before a legislative assembly. **5** (foll. by to) draw the attention or extend the understanding of (a person) to a subject. **6** insert; place in. **7** bring in; usher in; bring forward. **8** begin; occur just before the start of. □□ **introducer** n. **introducible** adj. [ME f. L introducere introduct- (as INTRO-, ducere lead)]

introduction /ˌɪntrəˈdʌkʃ(ə)n/ n. **1** the act or an instance of introducing; the process of being introduced. **2** a formal presentation of one person to another. **3** an explanatory section at the beginning of a book etc. **4** a preliminary section in a piece of music, often thematically different from the main section. **5** an introductory treatise on a subject. **6** a thing introduced. [ME f. OF introduction or L introductio (as INTRODUCE)]

introductory /ˌɪntrəˈdʌktərɪ/ adj. serving as an introduction; preliminary. [LL introductorius (as INTRODUCTION)]

introit /ˈɪntrɔɪt/ n. a psalm or antiphon sung or said while the priest approaches the altar for the Eucharist. [ME f. OF f. L introitus f. introire introit-enter (as INTRO-, ire go)]

introjection /ˌɪntrəˈdʒekʃ(ə)n/ n. the unconscious incorporation of external ideas into one's mind. [INTRO- after projection]

intromit /ˌɪntrəˈmɪt/ v.tr. (**intromitted**, **intromitting**) **1** archaic (foll. by into) let in, admit. **2** insert. □□ **intromission** /-ˈmɪʃ(ə)n/ n. **intromittent** adj. [L intromittere intromiss- introduce (as INTRO-, mittere send)]

introspection /ˌɪntrəˈspekʃ(ə)n/ n. the examination or observation of one's own mental and emotional processes etc. □□ **introspective** adj. **introspectively** adv. **introspectiveness** n. [L introspicere introspect- look inwards (as INTRO-, specere look)]

introvert n., adj., & v. —n. /ˈɪntrəˌvɜːt/ **1** Psychol. a person predominantly concerned with his or her own thoughts and feelings rather than with external things. **2** a shy inwardly thoughtful person. —adj. /ˈɪntrəˌvɜːt/ (also **introverted** /-tɪd/) typical or characteristic of an introvert. —v.tr. /ˌɪntrəˈvɜːt/ **1** Psychol. direct (one's thoughts or mind) inwards. **2** Zool. withdraw (an organ etc.) within its own tube or base, like the finger of a glove. □□ **introversion** /-ˈvɜːʃ(ə)n/ n. **introversive** /-ˈvɜːsɪv/ adj. **introverted** adj. **introvertive** /-ˈvɜːtɪv/ adj. [INTRO- + vert as in INVERT]

intrude /ɪnˈtruːd/ v. (foll. by on, upon, into) **1** intr. come uninvited or unwanted; force oneself abruptly on others. **2** tr. thrust or force (something unwelcome) on a person. □□ **intrudingly** adv. [L intrudere intrus- (as IN-², trudere thrust)]

intruder /ɪnˈtruːdə(r)/ n. a person who intrudes, esp. into a building with criminal intent.

intrusion /ɪnˈtruːʒ(ə)n/ n. **1** the act or an instance of intruding. **2** an unwanted interruption etc. **3** Geol. an influx of molten rock between or through strata etc. but not reaching the surface. **4** the occupation of a vacant estate etc. to which one has no claim. **5** Phonet. the addition of a sound between words or syllables to facilitate pronunciation, e.g. the r in saw a film (/ˈsɔːrəfɪlm/). [ME f. OF intrusion or med.L intrusio (as INTRUDE)]

intrusive /ɪnˈtruːsɪv/ adj. **1** that intrudes or tends to intrude. **2** characterized by intrusion. □□ **intrusively** adv. **intrusiveness** n.

intrust var. of ENTRUST.

intubate /ˈɪntjuˌbeɪt/ v.tr. Med. insert a tube into the trachea for ventilation, usu. during anaesthesia. □□ **intubation** /-ˈbeɪʃ(ə)n/ n. [IN-² + L tuba tube]

intuit /ɪnˈtjuːɪt/ v. **1** tr. know by intuition. **2** intr. receive knowledge by direct perception. □□ **intuitable** adj. [L intueri intuit- consider (as IN-², tueri look)]

intuition /ˌɪntjuːˈɪʃ(ə)n/ n. **1** immediate apprehension by the mind without reasoning. **2** immediate apprehension by a sense. **3** immediate insight. □□ **intuitional** adj. [LL intuitio (as INTUIT)]

intuitionism /ˌɪntjuːˈɪʃəˌnɪz(ə)m/ n. (also

intuitionalism) Philos. the belief that primary truths and principles (esp. of ethics and metaphysics) are known directly by intuition. □□ **intuitionist** n.

intuitive /ɪnˈtjuːɪtɪv/ adj. **1** of, characterized by, or possessing intuition. **2** perceived by intuition. □□ **intuitively** adv. **intuitiveness** n. [med.L intuitivus (as INTUIT)]

intuitivism /ɪnˈtjuːɪtɪˌvɪz(ə)m/ n. the doctrine that ethical principles can be established by intuition. □□ **intuitivist** n.

intumesce /ˌɪntjuːˈmes/ v.intr. swell up. □□ **intumescence** n. **intumescent** adj. [L intumescere (as IN-², tumescere incept. of tumēre swell)]

intussusception /ˌɪntəsəˈsepʃ(ə)n/ n. **1** Med. the inversion of one portion of the intestine within another. **2** Bot. the deposition of new cellulose particles in a cell wall, to increase the surface area of the cell. [F intussusception or mod.L intussusceptio f. L intus within + susceptio f. suscipere take up]

intwine var. of ENTWINE.

Inuit /ˈɪnjuːɪt, ˈɪnuɪt/ n. (also **Innuit**) (pl. same or **Inuits**) a N. American Eskimo. [Eskimo inuit people]

inundate /ˈɪnənˌdeɪt/ v.tr. (often foll. by with) **1** flood. **2** overwhelm (inundated with enquiries). □□ **inundation** /-ˈdeɪʃ(ə)n/ n. [L inundare flow (as IN-², unda wave)]

inure /ɪˈnjʊə(r)/ v. **1** tr. (often in passive; foll. by to) accustom (a person) to something esp. unpleasant. **2** intr. Law come into operation; take effect. □□ **inurement** n. [ME f. AF eneurer f. phr. en eure (both unrecorded) in use or practice, f. en in + OF e(u)vre work f. L opera]

in utero /ɪn ˈjuːtəˌrəʊ/ adv. in the womb; before birth. [L]

in vacuo /ɪn ˈvækjʊəʊ/ adv. in a vacuum. [L]

invade /ɪnˈveɪd/ v.tr. (often absol.) **1** enter (a country etc.) under arms to control or subdue it. **2** swarm into. **3** (of a disease) attack (a body etc.). **4** encroach upon (a person's rights, esp. privacy). □□ **invader** n. [L invadere invas- (as IN-², vadere go)]

invaginate /ɪnˈvædʒɪˌneɪt/ v.tr. **1** put in a sheath. **2** turn (a tube) inside out. □□ **invagination** /-ˈneɪʃ(ə)n/ n. [IN-² + L vagina sheath]

invalid¹ n. & v. —n. /ˈɪnvəˌliːd, -lɪd/ **1** a person enfeebled or disabled by illness or injury. **2** (attrib.) **a** of or for invalids (invalid car; invalid diet). **b** being an invalid (caring for her invalid mother). —v. /ˈɪnvəˌliːd/ (**invalided**, **invaliding**) **1** tr. (often foll. by out etc.) remove from active service (one who has become an invalid). **2** tr. (usu. in passive) disable (a person) by illness. **3** intr. become an invalid. □□ **invalidism** n. [L invalidus weak, infirm (as IN-¹, VALID)]

invalid² /ɪnˈvælɪd/ adj. not valid, esp. having no legal force. □□ **invalidly** adv. [L invalidus (as INVALID¹)]

invalidate /ɪnˈvælɪˌdeɪt/ v.tr. **1** make (esp. an argument etc.) invalid. **2** remove the validity or force of (a treaty, contract, etc.). □□ **invalidation** /-ˈdeɪʃ(ə)n/ n. [med.L invalidare invalidat- (as IN-¹, validus VALID)]

invalidity /ˌɪnvəˈlɪdɪtɪ/ n. **1** lack of validity. **2** bodily infirmity. [F invalidité or med.L invaliditas (as INVALID¹)]

invaluable /ɪnˈvæljʊəb(ə)l/ adj. above valuation; inestimable. □□ **invaluableness** n. **invaluably** adv.

Invar /ˈɪnvɑː(r)/ n. propr. an iron-nickel alloy with a negligible coefficient of expansion, used in the manufacture of clocks and scientific instruments. [abbr. of INVARIABLE]

invariable /ɪnˈveərɪəb(ə)l/ adj. **1** unchangeable. **2** always the same. **3** Math. constant, fixed. □□ **invariability** /-ˈbɪlɪtɪ/ n. **invariableness** n. **invariably** adv. [F invariable or LL invariabilis (as IN-¹, VARIABLE)]

invariant /ɪnˈveərɪənt/ adj. & n. —adj. invariable. —n. Math. a function which remains unchanged when a specified transformation is applied. □□ **invariance** n.

invasion /ɪnˈveɪʒ(ə)n/ n. **1** the act of invading or process of being invaded. **2** an entry of a hostile army into a country. □□ **invasive** /-sɪv/ adj. [F invasion or LL invasio (as INVADE)]

invective /ɪnˈvektɪv/ n. **1 a** strongly attacking words. **b** the use of these. **2** abusive rhetoric. [ME f. OF f. LL invectivus attacking (as INVEIGH)]

inveigh /ɪnˈveɪ/ v.intr. (foll. by against) speak or write with strong hostility. [L invehi go into, assail (as IN-², vehi passive of vehere vect- carry)]

inveigle /ɪnˈveɪg(ə)l, -ˈviːg(ə)l/ v.tr. (foll. by into, or to + infin.) entice; persuade by guile. □□ **inveiglement** n. [earlier enve(u)gle f. AF envegler, OF aveugler to blind f. aveugle blind prob. f. Rmc ab oculis (unrecorded) without eyes]

invent /ɪnˈvent/ v.tr. **1** create by thought, devise; originate (a new method, an instrument, etc.). **2** concoct (a false story etc.). □□ **inventable** adj. [ME, = discover, f. L invenire invent- find, contrive (as IN-², venire vent- come)]

invention /ɪnˈvenʃ(ə)n/ n. **1** the process of inventing. **2** a thing invented; a contrivance, esp. one for which a patent is granted. **3** a fictitious story. **4** inventiveness. **5** Mus. a short piece for keyboard, developing a simple idea. [ME f. L inventio (as INVENT)]

inventive /ɪnˈventɪv/ adj. **1** able or inclined to invent; original in devising. **2** showing ingenuity of devising. □□ **inventively** adv. **inventiveness** n. [ME f. F inventif -ive or med.L inventivus (as INVENT)]

inventor /ɪnˈventə(r)/ n. (fem. **inventress** /-trɪs/) a person who invents, esp. as an occupation.

inventory /ˈɪnvəntərɪ/ n. & v. —n. (pl. -ies) **1** a complete list of goods in stock, house contents, etc. **2** the goods listed in this. **3** US the total of a firm's commercial assets. —v.tr. (-ies, -ied) **1** make an inventory of. **2** enter (goods) in an inventory. [ME f. med.L inventorium f. LL inventarium (as INVENT)]

inverse /ˈɪnvɜːs, -ˈvɜːs/ adj. & n. —adj. inverted in position, order, or relation. —n. **1** the state of being inverted. **2** (often foll. by of) a thing that is the opposite or reverse of another. **3** Math. an element which, when combined with a given element in an operation, produces the identity element for that operation. □ **inverse proportion** (or **ratio**) a relation between two quantities such that one increases in proportion as the other decreases. **inverse square law** a law by which the intensity of an effect, such as gravitational force, illumination, etc., changes in inverse proportion to the square of the distance from the source. □□ **inversely** adv. [L inversus past part. of invertere: see INVERT]

inversion /ɪnˈvɜːʃ(ə)n/ n. **1** the act of turning upside down or inside out. **2** the reversal of a normal order, position, or relation. **3** the reversal of the order of words, for rhetorical effect. **4** the reversal of the normal variation of air temperature with altitude. **5** the process or result of inverting. **6** the reversal of direction of rotation of a plane of polarized light. **7** homosexuality. □□ **inversive** /-sɪv/ adj. [L inversio (as INVERT)]

invert v. & n. —v.tr. /ɪnˈvɜːt/ **1** turn upside down. **2** reverse the position, order, or relation of. **3** Mus. change the relative position of the notes of (a chord or interval) by placing the lowest note higher, usu. by an octave. **4** subject to inversion. —n. /ˈɪnvɜːt/ **1** a homosexual. **2** an inverted arch, as at the bottom of a sewer. □ **inverted comma** = quotation mark. **inverted snob** a person who likes or takes pride in what a snob might be expected to disapprove of. **invert sugar** a mixture of dextrose and laevulose. □□ **inverter** /ɪnˈvɜːtə(r)/ n. **invertible** /ɪnˈvɜːtɪb(ə)l/ adj. **invertibility** /-ˈbɪlɪtɪ/ n. [L invertere invers- (as IN-², vertere turn)]

invertebrate /ɪnˈvɜːtɪbrət, -ˌbreɪt/ adj. & n. —adj. **1** (of an animal) not having a backbone. **2** lacking firmness of character. —n. an invertebrate animal. [mod.L invertebrata (pl.) (as IN-¹, VERTEBRA)]

invest /ɪnˈvest/ v. **1** tr. (often foll. by in) apply or use (money), esp. for profit. **2** intr. (foll. by in) **a** put money for profit (into stocks etc.). **b** colloq. buy (invested in a new car). **3** tr. **a** (foll. by with) provide, endue, or attribute (a person with qualities, insignia, or rank). **b** (foll. by in) attribute or entrust (qualities or feelings to a person). **4** tr. cover as a garment. **5** tr. lay siege to. □□ **investable** adj. **investible** adj. **investor** n. [ME f. F investir or L investire investit- (as IN-², vestire clothe f. vestis clothing): sense 1 f. It. investire]

investigate /ɪnˈvestɪˌgeɪt/ v. **1** tr. **a** inquire into; examine; study carefully. **b** make an official inquiry into. **2** intr. make a systematic inquiry or search. □□ **investigator** n. **investigatory** /-gətərɪ/ adj. [L investigare investigat- (as IN-², vestigare track)]

investigation /ɪnˌvestɪˈgeɪʃ(ə)n/ n. **1** the process or an instance of investigating. **2** a formal examination or study.

investigative /ɪnˈvestɪgətɪv/ adj. seeking or serving to investigate, esp. (of journalism) inquiring intensively into controversial issues.

investiture /ɪnˈvestɪˌtjʊə(r)/ n. **1** the formal investing of a person with honours or rank, esp. a ceremony at which a sovereign confers honours. **2** (often foll. by with) the act of enduing (with attributes). [ME f. med.L investitura (as INVEST)]

investment /ɪnˈvestmənt/ n. **1** the act or process of investing. **2** money invested. **3** property etc. in which money is invested. **4** the act of besieging; a blockade. □ **investment trust** a trust that buys and sells shares in selected companies to make a profit for its members.

inveterate /ɪnˈvetərət/ adj. **1** (of a person) confirmed in an (esp. undesirable) habit etc. (an inveterate gambler). **2 a** (of a habit etc.) long-established. **b** (of an activity, esp. an undesirable one) habitual. □□ **inveteracy** /-rəsɪ/ n. **inveterately** adv. [ME f. L inveterare inveterat- make old (as IN-², vetus veteris old)]

invidious /ɪnˈvɪdɪəs/ adj. (of an action, conduct, attitude, etc.) likely to excite resentment or indignation against the person responsible, esp. by real or seeming injustice (an invidious position; an invidious task). □□ **invidiously** adv. **invidiousness** n. [L invidiosus f. invidia ENVY]

invigilate /ɪnˈvɪdʒɪˌleɪt/ v.intr. Brit. supervise candidates at an examination. □□ **invigilation** /-ˈleɪʃ(ə)n/ n. **invigilator** n. [orig. = keep watch, f. L invigilare invigilat- (as IN-², vigilare watch f. vigil watchful)]

invigorate /ɪnˈvɪgəˌreɪt/ v.tr. give vigour or strength to. □□ **invigorating** adj. **invigoratingly** adv. **invigoration** /-ˈreɪʃ(ə)n/ n. **invigorative** /-rətɪv/ adj. **invigorator** n. [IN-² + med.L vigorare vigorat- make strong]

invincible /ɪnˈvɪnsɪb(ə)l/ adj. unconquerable; that cannot be defeated. □□ **invincibility** /-ˈbɪlɪtɪ/ n. **invincibleness** n. **invincibly** adv. [ME f. OF f. L invincibilis (as IN-¹, VINCIBLE)]

inviolable /ɪnˈvaɪələb(ə)l/ adj. not to be violated or profaned. □□ **inviolability** /-ˈbɪlɪtɪ/ n. **inviolably** adv. [F inviolable or L inviolabilis (as IN-¹, VIOLATE)]

inviolate /ɪnˈvaɪələt/ adj. not violated or profaned. □□ **inviolacy** /-ləsɪ/ n. **inviolately** adv. **inviolateness** n. [ME f. L inviolatus (as IN-¹, violare, violat- treat violently)]

invisible /ɪnˈvɪzɪb(ə)l/ adj. **1** not visible to the eye, either characteristically or because hidden. **2** too small to be seen or noticed. **3** artfully concealed (invisible mending). □ **invisible exports** (or **imports** etc.) items, esp. services, involving payment between countries but not constituting tangible commodities. □□ **invisibility** /-ˈbɪlɪtɪ/ n. **invisibleness** n. **invisibly** adv. [ME f. OF invisible or L invisibilis (as IN-¹, VISIBLE)]

invitation /ˌɪnvɪˈteɪʃ(ə)n/ n. the process of inviting or fact of being invited, esp. to a social occasion.

b but d dog f few g get h he j yes k cat l leg m man n no p pen r red s sit t top v voice

invite /ɪnˈvaɪt/ v. & n. —v. **1** tr. (often foll. by to, or to + infin.) ask (a person) courteously to come, or to do something (were invited to lunch; invited them to reply). **2** tr. make a formal courteous request for (invited comments). **3** tr. tend to call forth un-intentionally (something unwanted). **4 a** tr. attract. **b** intr. be attractive. —n. /ˈɪnvaɪt/ colloq. an invitation. □□ **invitee** /-ˈtiː/ n. **inviter** n. [F inviter or L invitare]

inviting /ɪnˈvaɪtɪŋ/ adj. **1** attractive. **2** enticing, tempting. □□ **invitingly** adv. **invitingness** n.

in vitro /ɪn ˈviːtrəʊ/ adv. Biol. (of processes or re-actions) taking place in a test-tube or other la-boratory environment (opp. IN VIVO). [L, = in glass]

in vivo /ɪn ˈviːvəʊ/ adv. Biol. (of processes) taking place in a living organism. [L, = in a living thing]

invocation /ˌɪnvəˈkeɪʃ(ə)n/ n. **1** the act or an instance of invoking, esp. in prayer. **2** an appeal to a su-pernatural being or beings, e.g. the Muses, for psychological or spiritual inspiration. **3** Eccl. the words 'In the name of the Father' etc. used as the preface to a sermon etc. □□ **invocatory** /ɪnˈvɒkətərɪ/ adj. [ME f. OF f. L invocatio -onis (as INVOKE)]

invoice /ˈɪnvɔɪs/ n. & v. —n. a list of goods shipped or sent, or services rendered, with prices and charges; a bill. —v.tr. **1** make an invoice of (goods and services). **2** send an invoice to (a person). [earlier invoyes pl. of invoy = ENVOY²]

invoke /ɪnˈvəʊk/ v.tr. **1** call on (a deity etc.) in prayer or as a witness. **2** appeal to (the law, a person's authority, etc.). **3** summon (a spirit) by charms. **4** ask earnestly for (vengeance, help, etc.). □□ **invocable** adj. **invoker** n. [F invoquer f. L invocare (as IN-², vocare call)]

involucre /ˈɪnvəˌluːkə(r), -ˌljuːkə(r)/ n. **1** a covering or envelope. **2** Anat. a membranous envelope. **3** Bot. a whorl of bracts surrounding an inflorescence. □□ **involucral** /-ˈluːkr(ə)l, -ˈljuːkr(ə)l/ adj. [F involucre or L involucrum (as INVOLVE)]

involuntary /ɪnˈvɒləntərɪ/ adj. **1** done without the exercise of the will; unintentional. **2** (of a limb, muscle, or movement) not under the control of the will. □□ **involuntarily** adv. **involuntariness** n. [LL involuntarius (as IN-¹, VOLUNTARY)]

involute /ˈɪnvəˌluːt, -ˌljuːt/ adj. & n. —adj. **1** involved, intricate. **2** curled spirally. **3** Bot. rolled inwards at the edges. —n. Geom. the locus of a point fixed on a straight line that rolls without sliding on a curve and is in the plane of that curve (cf. EVOLUTE). [L involutus past part. of involvere: see INVOLVE]

involuted /ˈɪnvəˌluːtɪd, -ˌljuːtɪd/ adj. **1** complicated, abstruse. **2** = INVOLUTE adj. 2.

involution /ˌɪnvəˈluːʃ(ə)n, -ˈljuːʃ(ə)n/ n. **1** the process of involving. **2** an entanglement. **3** intricacy. **4** curling inwards. **5** a part that curls upwards. **6** Math. the raising of a quantity to any power. **7** Physiol. the reduction in size of an organ in old age, or when its purpose has been fulfilled (esp. the uterus after childbirth). □□ **involutional** adj. [L involutio (as INVOLVE)]

involve /ɪnˈvɒlv/ v.tr. **1** (often foll. by in) cause (a person or thing) to participate, or share the experience or effect (in a situation, activity, etc.). **2** imply, entail, make necessary. **3** (foll. by in) implicate (a person in a charge, crime, etc.). **4** include or affect in its operations. **5** (as **involved** adj.) **a** (often foll. by in) concerned or interested. **b** complicated in thought or form. [ME f. L involvere involut- (as IN-², volvere roll)]

involvement /ɪnˈvɒlvmənt/ n. **1** (often foll. by in, with) the act or an instance of involving; the process of being involved. **2** financial embarrassment. **3** a complicated affair or concern.

invulnerable /ɪnˈvʌlnərəb(ə)l/ adj. that cannot be wounded or hurt, physically or mentally. □□ **invulnerability** /-ˈbɪlɪtɪ/ n. **invulnerably** adv. [L invulnerabilis (as IN-¹, VULNERABLE)]

inward /ˈɪnwəd/ adj. & adv. —adj. **1** directed toward

the inside; going in. **2** situated within. **3** mental, spiritual. —adv. (also **inwards**) **1** (of motion or position) towards the inside. **2** in the mind or soul. [OE innanweard (as IN, -WARD)]

inwardly /ˈɪnwədlɪ/ adv. **1** on the inside. **2** in the mind or soul. **3** (of speaking) not aloud; inaudibly. [OE inweardlíce (as INWARD)]

inwardness /ˈɪnwədnɪs/ n. **1** inner nature; essence. **2** the condition of being inward. **3** spirituality.

inwards var. of INWARD adv.

inweave /ɪnˈwiːv/ v.tr. (also **enweave**) (past **-wove** /-ˈwəʊv/; past part. **-woven** /-ˈwəʊv(ə)n/) **1** weave (two or more things) together. **2** intermingle.

inwrap var. of ENWRAP.

inwreathe var. of ENWREATHE.

inwrought /ɪnˈrɔːt, attrib. ˈɪnrɔːt/ adj. **1 a** (often foll. by with) (of a fabric) decorated (with a pattern). **b** (often foll. by in, on) (of a pattern) wrought (in or on a fabric). **2** closely blended.

inyala /ɪnˈjɑːlə/ n. (also **nyala** /ˈnjɑːlə/) (pl. same) a large antelope, Tragelaphus angasi, native to S. Africa, with curved horns having a single complete turn. [Zulu]

IOC abbr. International Olympic Committee.

iodic /aɪˈɒdɪk/ adj. Chem. containing iodine in chem-ical combination (iodic acid). □□ **iodate** /ˈaɪəˌdeɪt/ n.

iodide /ˈaɪəˌdaɪd/ n. Chem. any compound of iodine with another element or group.

iodinate /aɪˈɒdɪˌneɪt, ˈaɪə-/ v.tr. treat or combine with iodine. □□ **iodination** /-ˈneɪʃ(ə)n/ n.

iodine /ˈaɪəˌdiːn, -ɪn/ n. **1** Chem. a non-metallic element of the halogen group, forming black crystals and a violet vapour, used in medicine and pho-tography, and important as an essential element for living organisms. ¶ Symb.: **I**. **2** a solution of this in alcohol used as a mild antiseptic. [F iode f. Gk iōdēs violet-like f. ion violet + -INE⁴]

iodism /ˈaɪəˌdɪz(ə)m/ n. Med. a condition caused by an overdose of iodides.

iodize /ˈaɪəˌdaɪz/ v.tr. (also **-ise**) treat or impregnate with iodine. □□ **iodization** /-ˈzeɪʃ(ə)n/ n.

iodo- /aɪˈəʊdəʊ/ comb. form (usu. **iod-** before a vowel) Chem. iodine.

iodoform /aɪˈəʊdəˌfɔːm, -ˈɒdəˌfɔːm/ n. a pale yellow volatile sweet-smelling solid compound of iodine with antiseptic properties. ¶ Chem. formula: CHI_3. [IODINE after chloroform]

IOM abbr. Isle of Man.

ion /ˈaɪən/ n. an atom or group of atoms that has lost one or more electrons (= CATION), or gained one or more electrons (= ANION). □**ion exchange** the ex-change of ions of the same charge between a usu. aqueous solution and a solid, used in water-softening etc. **ion exchanger** a substance or equipment for this process. [Gk, neut. pres. part. of eimi go]

-ion suffix (usu. as **-sion, -tion, -xion**; see -ATION, -ITION, -UTION) forming nouns denoting: **1** verbal action (excision). **2** an instance of this (a suggestion). **3** a resulting state or product (vexation; concoction). [from or after F -ion or L -io -ionis]

Ionian /aɪˈəʊnɪən/ n. & adj. —n. a native or in-habitant of ancient Ionia in W. Asia Minor. —adj. of or relating to Ionia or the Ionians. □**Ionian mode** Mus. the mode represented by the natural diatonic scale C–C. [L Ionius f. Gk Iōnios]

Ionic /aɪˈɒnɪk/ adj. & n. —adj. **1** of the order of Greek architecture characterized by a column with scroll-shapes on either side of the capital. **2** of the ancient Greek dialect used in Ionia. —n. the Ionic dialect. [L Ionicus f. Gk Iōnikos]

ionic /aɪˈɒnɪk/ adj. of, relating to, or using ions. □□ **ionically** adv.

ionization /ˌaɪənaɪˈzeɪʃ(ə)n/ n. (also **-isation**) the process of producing ions as a result of solvation, heat, radiation, etc. □**ionization chamber** an in-strument for detecting ionizing radiation.

ionize /ˈaɪəˌnaɪz/ v.tr. & intr. (also **-ise**) convert or be converted into an ion or ions. □**ionizing radiation**

a radiation of sufficient energy to cause ionization in the medium through which it passes. □□ **ionizable** *adj.*

ionizer /ˈaɪəˌnaɪzə(r)/ *n.* any thing which produces ionization, esp. a device used to improve the quality of the air in a room etc.

ionosphere /aɪˈɒnəˌsfɪə(r)/ *n.* an ionized region of the atmosphere above the stratosphere, extending to about 1,000 km above the earth's surface and able to reflect radio waves for long-distance transmission round the earth (cf. TROPOSPHERE). □□ **ionospheric** /-ˈsferɪk/ *adj.*

-ior[1] /ɪə(r)/ *suffix* forming adjectives of comparison (*senior*; *ulterior*). [L]

-ior[2] var. of -IOUR.

iota /aɪˈəʊtə/ *n.* **1** the ninth letter of the Greek alphabet (*I*, ɩ). **2** (usu. with *neg.*) the smallest possible amount. [Gk *iōta*]

IOU /ˌaɪəʊˈjuː/ *n.* a signed document acknowledging a debt. [= I owe you]

-iour /ɪə(r)/ *suffix* (also **-ior**) forming nouns (*saviour*; *warrior*). [-ɪ- (as a stem element) + -OUR[2], -OR[1]]

-ious /-ɪəs, -əs/ *suffix* forming adjectives meaning 'characterized by, full of', often corresponding to nouns in *-ion* (*cautious*; *curious*; *spacious*). [from or after F *-ieux* f. L *-iosus*]

IOW *abbr.* Isle of Wight.

IPA *abbr.* International Phonetic Alphabet (or Association).

IPCS *abbr.* (in the UK) Institution of Professional Civil Servants.

ipecac /ˈɪpɪˌkæk/ *n. colloq.* ipecacuanha. [abbr.]

ipecacuanha /ˌɪpɪˌkækjʊˈɑːnə/ *n.* the root of a S. American shrub, *Cephaelis ipecacuanha*, used as an emetic and purgative. [Port. f. Tupi-Guarani *ipekaaguéne* emetic creeper]

ipomoea /ˌɪpəˈmiːə/ *n.* any twining plant of the genus *Ipomoea*, having trumpet-shaped flowers, e.g. the sweet potato and morning glory. [mod.L f. Gk *ips ipos* worm + *homoios* like]

i.p.s. *abbr.* inches per second.

ipse dixit /ˌɪpsɪ ˈdɪksɪt/ *n.* a dogmatic statement resting merely on the speaker's authority. [L, he himself said it (orig. of Pythagoras)]

ipsilateral /ˌɪpsɪˈlætər(ə)l/ *adj.* belonging to or occurring on the same side of the body. [irreg. f. L *ipse* self + LATERAL]

ipsissima verba /ɪpˌsɪsɪmə ˈvɜːbə/ *n.pl.* the precise words. [L]

ipso facto /ˌɪpsəʊ ˈfæktəʊ/ *adv.* **1** by that very fact or act. **2** thereby. [L]

IQ *abbr.* intelligence quotient.

-ique *archaic* var. of -IC.

IR *abbr.* infrared.

Ir *symb. Chem.* the element iridium.

ir- /ɪ(r)/ *prefix* assim. form of IN-[1], IN-[2] before *r*.

IRA *abbr.* Irish Republican Army.

irade /ɪˈrɑːdɪ/ *n. hist.* a written decree of the Sultan of Turkey. [Turk. f. Arab. *ʾirāda* will]

Iranian /ɪˈreɪnɪən/ *adj. & n.* —*adj.* **1** of or relating to Iran (formerly Persia) in the Middle East. **2** of the Indo-European group of languages including Persian, Pashto, Avestan, and Kurdish. —*n.* **1** a native or national of Iran. **2** a person of Iranian descent.

Iraqi /ɪˈrɑːkɪ/ *adj. & n.* —*adj.* of or relating to Iraq in the Middle East. —*n.* (*pl.* **Iraqis**) **1 a** a native or national of Iraq. **b** a person of Iraqi descent. **2** the form of Arabic spoken in Iraq.

irascible /ɪˈræsɪb(ə)l/ *adj.* irritable; hot-tempered. □□ **irascibility** /-ˈbɪlɪtɪ/ *n.* **irascibly** *adv.* [ME f. F f. LL *irascibilis* f. L *irasci* grow angry f. *ira* anger]

irate /aɪˈreɪt/ *adj.* angry, enraged. □□ **irately** *adv.* **irateness** *n.* [L *iratus* f. *ira* anger]

IRBM *abbr.* intermediate-range ballistic missile.

ire /aɪə(r)/ *n. literary* anger. □□ **ireful** *adj.* [ME f. OF f. L *ira*]

irenic /aɪˈriːnɪk/ *adj.* (also **irenical, eirenic**) *literary*

aiming or aimed at peace. [Gk *eirēnikos*: see EIRENICON]

irenicon var. of EIRENICON.

iridaceous /ˌɪrɪˈdeɪʃəs/ *adj. Bot.* of or relating to the family Iridaceae of plants growing from bulbs, corms, or rhizomes, e.g. iris, crocus, and gladiolus. [mod.L *iridaceus* (as IRIS)]

iridescent /ˌɪrɪˈdes(ə)nt/ *adj.* **1** showing rainbow-like luminous or gleaming colours. **2** changing colour with position. □□ **iridescence** *n.* **iridescently** *adv.* [L IRIS + -ESCENT]

iridium /ɪˈrɪdɪəm/ *n. Chem.* a hard white metallic element of the transition series used esp. in alloys. ¶ Symb.: **Ir.** [mod.L f. L IRIS + -IUM]

iris /ˈaɪərɪs/ *n.* **1** the flat circular coloured membrane behind the cornea of the eye, with a circular opening (pupil) in the centre. **2** any herbaceous plant of the genus *Iris*, usu. with tuberous roots, sword-shaped leaves, and showy flowers. **3** (in full **iris diaphragm**) an adjustable diaphragm of thin overlapping plates for regulating the size of a central hole esp. for the admission of light to a lens. [ME f. L *iris iridis* f. Gk *iris iridos* rainbow, iris]

Irish /ˈaɪərɪʃ/ *adj. & n.* —*adj.* of or relating to Ireland; of or like its people. —*n.* **1** the Celtic language of Ireland. **2** (prec. by *the*; treated as *pl.*) the people of Ireland. □**Irish bull** = BULL[3]. **Irish coffee** coffee mixed with a dash of whisky and served with cream on top. **Irish moss** dried carrageen. **Irish Sea** the sea between England and Wales and Ireland. **Irish stew** a stew of mutton, potato, and onion. **Irish terrier** a rough-haired light reddish-brown breed of terrier. [ME f. OE *Iras* the Irish]

Irishman /ˈaɪərɪʃmən/ *n.* (*pl.* **-men**) a man who is Irish by birth or descent.

Irishwoman /ˈaɪərɪʃˌwʊmən/ *n.* (*pl.* **-women**) a woman who is Irish by birth or descent.

iritis /ˌaɪəˈraɪtɪs/ *n.* inflammation of the iris.

irk /ɜːk/ *v.tr.* (usu. *impers.*; often foll. by *that* + clause) irritate, bore, annoy. [ME: orig. unkn.]

irksome /ˈɜːksəm/ *adj.* tedious, annoying, tiresome. □□ **irksomely** *adv.* **irksomeness** *n.* [ME, = tired etc., f. IRK + -SOME[1]]

IRO *abbr.* **1** (in the UK) Inland Revenue Office. **2** International Refugee Organization.

iroko /ɪˈrəʊkəʊ/ *n.* (*pl.* **-os**) **1** either of two African trees, *Chlorophora excelsa* or *C. regia*. **2** the light-coloured hardwood from these trees. [Ibo]

iron /ˈaɪən/ *n., adj., & v.* —*n.* **1** *Chem.* a silver-white ductile metallic element occurring naturally as haematite, magnetite, etc., much used for tools and implements, and an essential element in all living organisms. ¶ Symb.: **Fe. 2** this as a type of unyieldingness or a symbol of firmness (*man of iron*; *will of iron*). **3** a tool or implement made of iron (*branding iron*; *curling iron*). **4** a household, now usu. electrical, implement with a flat base which is heated to smooth clothes etc. **5** a golf club with an iron or steel sloping face used for lofting the ball. **6** (usu. in *pl.*) a fetter (*clapped in irons*). **7** (usu. in *pl.*) a stirrup. **8** (often in *pl.*) an iron support for a malformed leg. **9** a preparation of iron as a tonic or dietary supplement (*iron tablets*). —*adj.* **1** made of iron. **2** very robust. **3** unyielding, merciless (*iron determination*). —*v.tr.* **1** smooth (clothes etc.) with an iron. **2** furnish or cover with iron. **3** shackle with irons. □**in irons** handcuffed, chained, etc. **Iron Age** *Archaeol.* the period following the Bronze Age when iron replaced bronze in the making of implements and weapons. **iron-bark** any of various eucalyptus trees with a thick solid bark and hard dense timber. **iron-bound 1** bound with iron. **2** rigorous; hard and fast. **3** (of a coast) rock-bound. **Iron Cross** the highest German military decoration for bravery. **Iron Curtain** a notional barrier to the passage of people and information between the Soviet bloc and the West. **iron hand** firmness or inflexibility (cf. *velvet glove*). **iron in the fire** an undertaking, opportunity, or commitment (usu. in *pl.*: *too many irons in the fire*). **ironing-board** a flat surface usu. on legs and of adjustable height on which clothes etc. are ironed. **iron lung** a rigid case fitted over a patient's body, used for administering prolonged artificial respiration by means of mechanical pumps. **iron maiden** *hist.* an instrument of torture consisting of a coffin-shaped box lined with iron spikes. **iron-mould** (*US* **-mold**) a spot caused by iron-rust or an ink-stain, esp. on fabric. **iron-on** able to be fixed to the surface of a fabric etc. by ironing. **iron out** remove or smooth over (difficulties etc.). **iron pyrites** see PYRITES. **iron ration** a small emergency supply of food. □□ **ironer** *n.* **ironing** *n.* (in sense 1 of *v.*). **ironless** *adj.* **iron-like** *adj.* [OE *īren*, *īsern* f. Gmc, prob. f. Celt.]

ironclad *adj.* & *n.* —*adj.* /ˌaɪən'klæd/ **1** clad or protected with iron. **2** impregnable; rigorous. —*n.* /'aɪən,klæd/ *hist.* an early name for a 19th-c. warship built of iron or protected by iron plates.

ironic /aɪ'rɒnɪk/ *adj.* (also **ironical**) **1** using or displaying irony. **2** in the nature of irony. □□ **ironically** *adv.* [F *ironique* or LL *ironicus* f. Gk *eirōnikos* dissembling (as IRONY¹)]

ironist /'aɪrənɪst/ *n.* a person who uses irony. □□ **ironize** *v.intr.* (also **-ise**). [Gk *eirōn* dissembler + -IST]

ironmaster /'aɪən,mɑːstə(r)/ *n.* a manufacturer of iron.

ironmonger /'aɪən,mʌŋgə(r)/ *n.* *Brit.* a dealer in hardware etc. □□ **ironmongery** *n.* (*pl.* **-ies**).

Ironsides /'aɪən,saɪdz/ *n.* a man of great bravery, esp. (as *pl.*) Cromwell's troopers in the English Civil War.

ironstone /'aɪən,stəʊn/ *n.* **1** any rock containing a substantial proportion of an iron compound. **2** a kind of hard white opaque stoneware.

ironware /'aɪən,weə(r)/ *n.* articles made of iron, esp. domestic implements.

ironwork /'aɪən,wɜːk/ *n.* **1** things made of iron. **2** work in iron.

ironworks /'aɪən,wɜːks/ *n.* (as *sing.* or *pl.*) a place where iron is smelted or iron goods are made.

irony¹ /'aɪrənɪ/ *n.* (*pl.* **-ies**) **1** an expression of meaning, often humorous or sarcastic, by the use of language of a different or opposite tendency. **2** an ill-timed or perverse arrival of an event or circumstance that is in itself desirable. **3** the use of language with one meaning for a privileged audience and another for those addressed or concerned. [L *ironia* f. Gk *eirōneia* simulated ignorance f. *eirōn* dissembler]

irony² /'aɪənɪ/ *adj.* of or like iron.

Iroquoian /ˌɪrə'kwɔɪən/ *n.* & *adj.* —*n.* **1** a language family of eastern N. America, including Cherokee and Mohawk. **2** a member of the Iroquois Indians. —*adj.* of or relating to the Iroquois or the Iroquoian language family or one of its members.

Iroquois /'ɪrə,kwɔɪ/ *n.* & *adj.* —*n.* (*pl.* same) **1 a** an American Indian confederacy of five peoples formerly inhabiting New York State. **b** a member of any of these peoples. **2** any of the languages of these peoples. —*adj.* of or relating to the Iroquois or their languages. [F f. Algonquin]

irradiant /ɪ'reɪdɪənt/ *adj.* *literary* shining brightly. □□ **irradiance** *n.*

irradiate /ɪ'reɪdɪ,eɪt/ *v.tr.* **1** subject to (any form of) radiation. **2** shine upon; light up. **3** throw light on (a subject). □□ **irradiative** /-dɪətɪv/ *adj.* [L *irradiare irradiat-* (as IN-², *radiare* f. *radius* RAY¹)]

irradiation /ɪ,reɪdɪ'eɪʃ(ə)n/ *n.* **1** the process of irradiating. **2** shining, illumination. **3** the apparent extension of the edges of an illuminated object seen against a dark background. [F *irradiation* or LL *irradiatio* (as IRRADIATE)]

irrational /ɪ'ræʃ(ə)n(ə)l/ *adj.* **1** illogical; unreasonable. **2** not endowed with reason. **3** *Math.* (of a root etc.) not rational; not commensurate with the natural numbers (e.g. a non-terminating decimal). □□ **irrationality** /-'nælɪtɪ/ *n.* **irrationalize** *v.tr.* (also **-ise**). **irrationally** *adv.* [L *irrationalis* (as IN-¹, RATIONAL)]

irreclaimable /ˌɪrɪ'kleɪməb(ə)l/ *adj.* that cannot be reclaimed or reformed. □□ **irreclaimably** *adv.*

irreconcilable /ɪ'rekən,saɪləb(ə)l/ *adj.* & *n.* —*adj.* **1** implacably hostile. **2** (of ideas etc.) incompatible. —*n.* **1** an uncompromising opponent of a political measure etc. **2** (usu. in *pl.*) any of two or more items, ideas, etc., that cannot be made to agree. □□ **irreconcilability** /-'bɪlɪtɪ/ *n.* **irreconcilableness** *n.* **irreconcilably** *adv.*

irrecoverable /ˌɪrɪ'kʌvərəb(ə)l/ *adj.* that cannot be recovered or remedied. □□ **irrecoverably** *adv.*

irrecusable /ˌɪrɪ'kjuːzəb(ə)l/ *adj.* that must be accepted. [F *irrécusable* or LL *irrecusabilis* (as IN-¹, *recusare* refuse)]

irredeemable /ˌɪrɪ'diːməb(ə)l/ *adj.* **1** that cannot be redeemed. **2** hopeless, absolute. **3 a** (of a government annuity) not terminable by repayment. **b** (of paper currency) for which the issuing authority does not undertake ever to pay coin. □□ **irredeemability** /-'bɪlɪtɪ/ *n.* **irredeemably** *adv.*

irredentist /ˌɪrɪ'dentɪst/ *n.* a person, esp. in 19th-c. Italy, advocating the restoration to his or her country of any territory formerly belonging to it. □□ **irredentism** *n.* [It. *irredentista* f. (*Italia*) *irredenta* unredeemed (Italy)]

irreducible /ˌɪrɪ'djuːsɪb(ə)l/ *adj.* **1** that cannot be reduced or simplified. **2** (often foll. by *to*) that cannot be brought to a desired condition. □□ **irreducibility** /-'bɪlɪtɪ/ *n.* **irreducibly** *adv.*

irrefragable /ɪ'refrəgəb(ə)l/ *adj.* **1** (of a statement, argument, or person) unanswerable, indisputable. **2** (of rules etc.) inviolable. □□ **irrefragably** *adv.* [LL *irrefragabilis* (as IN-¹, *refragari* oppose)]

irrefrangible /ˌɪrɪ'frændʒɪb(ə)l/ *adj.* **1** inviolable. **2** *Optics* incapable of being refracted.

irrefutable /ɪ'refjʊtəb(ə)l/, /ˌɪrɪ'fjuː-/ *adj.* that cannot be refuted. □□ **irrefutability** /-'bɪlɪtɪ/ *n.* **irrefutably** *adv.* [LL *irrefutabilis* (as IN-¹, REFUTE)]

irregular /ɪ'regjʊlə(r)/ *adj.* & *n.* —*adj.* **1** not regular; unsymmetrical, uneven; varying in form. **2** (of a surface) uneven. **3** contrary to a rule, moral principle, or custom; abnormal. **4** uneven in duration, order, etc. **5** (of troops) not belonging to the regular army. **6** *Gram.* (of a verb, noun, etc.) not inflected according to the usual rules. **7** disorderly. **8** (of a flower) having unequal petals etc. —*n.* (in *pl.*) irregular troops. □□ **irregularity** /-'lærɪtɪ/ *n.* (*pl.* **-ies**). **irregularly** *adv.* [ME f. OF *irreguler* f. LL *irregularis* (as IN-¹, REGULAR)]

irrelative /ɪ'relətɪv/ *adj.* **1** (often foll. by *to*) unconnected, unrelated. **2** having no relations; absolute. **3** irrelevant. □□ **irrelatively** *adv.*

irrelevant /ɪ'relɪv(ə)nt/ *adj.* (often foll. by *to*) not relevant; not applicable (to a matter in hand). □□ **irrelevance** *n.* **irrelevancy** *n.* **irrelevantly** *adv.*

irreligion /ˌɪrɪ'lɪdʒ(ə)n/ *n.* disregard of or hostility to religion. □□ **irreligionist** *n.* [F *irréligion* or L *irreligio* (as IN-¹, RELIGION)]

irreligious /ˌɪrɪ'lɪdʒəs/ *adj.* **1** indifferent or hostile to religion. **2** lacking a religion. □□ **irreligiously** *adv.* **irreligiousness** *n.*

irremediable /ˌɪrɪ'miːdɪəb(ə)l/ *adj.* that cannot be remedied. □□ **irremediably** *adv.* [L *irremediabilis* (as IN-¹, REMEDY)]

irremissible /ˌɪrɪ'mɪsɪb(ə)l/ *adj.* **1** unpardonable. **2** unalterably obligatory. □□ **irremissibly** *adv.* [ME f. OF *irremissible* or eccl.L *irremissibilis* (as IN-¹, REMISSIBLE)]

irremovable /ˌɪrɪ'muːvəb(ə)l/ *adj.* that cannot be removed, esp. from office. □□ **irremovability** /-'bɪlɪtɪ/ *n.* **irremovably** *adv.*

irreparable /ɪ'repərəb(ə)l/ *adj.* (of an injury, loss, etc.) that cannot be rectified or made good. □□ **irreparability** /-'bɪlɪtɪ/ *n.* **irreparableness** *n.*

irreparably *adv.* [ME f. OF f. L *irreparabilis* (as IN-¹, REPARABLE)]

irreplaceable /ˌɪrɪˈpleɪsəb(ə)l/ *adj.* **1** that cannot be replaced. **2** of which the loss cannot be made good. □□ **irreplaceably** *adv.*

irrepressible /ˌɪrɪˈpresɪb(ə)l/ *adj.* that cannot be repressed or restrained. □□ **irrepressibility** /-ˈbɪlɪtɪ/ *n.* **irrepressibleness** *n.* **irrepressibly** *adv.*

irreproachable /ˌɪrɪˈprəʊtʃəb(ə)l/ *adj.* faultless, blameless. □□ **irreproachability** /-ˈbɪlɪtɪ/ *n.* **irreproachableness** *n.* **irreproachably** *adv.* [F *irréprochable* (as IN-¹, REPROACH)]

irresistible /ˌɪrɪˈzɪstɪb(ə)l/ *adj.* **1** too strong or convincing to be resisted. **2** delightful; alluring. □□ **irresistibility** /-ˈbɪlɪtɪ/ *n.* **irresistibleness** *n.* **irresistibly** *adv.* [med.L *irresistibilis* (as IN-¹, RESIST)]

irresolute /ɪˈrezəˌluːt, -ˌljuːt/ *adj.* **1** hesitant, undecided. **2** lacking in resoluteness. □□ **irresolutely** *adv.* **irresoluteness** *n.* **irresolution** /-ˈluːʃ(ə)n, -ˈljuːʃ(ə)n/ *n.*

irresolvable /ˌɪrɪˈzɒlvəb(ə)l/ *adj.* **1** that cannot be resolved into its components. **2** (of a problem) that cannot be solved.

irrespective /ˌɪrɪˈspektɪv/ *adj.* (foll. by *of*) not taking into account; regardless of. □□ **irrespectively** *adv.*

irresponsible /ˌɪrɪˈspɒnsɪb(ə)l/ *adj.* **1** acting or done without due sense of responsibility. **2** not responsible for one's conduct. □□ **irresponsibility** /-ˈbɪlɪtɪ/ *n.* **irresponsibly** *adv.*

irresponsive /ˌɪrɪˈspɒnsɪv/ *adj.* (often foll. by *to*) not responsive. □□ **irresponsively** *adv.* **irresponsiveness** *n.*

irretrievable /ˌɪrɪˈtriːvəb(ə)l/ *adj.* that cannot be retrieved or restored. □□ **irretrievability** /-ˈbɪlɪtɪ/ *n.* **irretrievably** *adv.*

irreverent /ɪˈrevərənt/ *adj.* lacking reverence. □□ **irreverence** *n.* **irreverential** /-ˈrenʃ(ə)l/ *adj.* **irreverently** *adv.* [L *irreverens* (as IN-¹, REVERENT)]

irreversible /ˌɪrɪˈvɜːsɪb(ə)l/ *adj.* not reversible or alterable. □□ **irreversibility** /-ˈbɪlɪtɪ/ *n.* **irreversibly** *adv.*

irrevocable /ɪˈrevəkəb(ə)l/ *adj.* **1** unalterable. **2** gone beyond recall. □□ **irrevocability** /-ˈbɪlɪtɪ/ *n.* **irrevocably** *adv.* [ME f. L *irrevocabilis* (as IN-¹, REVOKE)]

irrigate /ˈɪrɪˌɡeɪt/ *v.tr.* **1 a** water (land) by means of channels. **b** (of a stream etc.) supply (land) with water. **2** *Med.* supply (a wound etc.) with a constant flow of liquid. **3** refresh as with moisture. □□ **irrigable** *adj.* **irrigation** /-ˈɡeɪʃ(ə)n/ *n.* **irrigative** *adj.* **irrigator** *n.* [L *irrigare* (as IN-², *rigare* moisten)]

irritable /ˈɪrɪtəb(ə)l/ *adj.* **1** easily annoyed or angered. **2** (of an organ etc.) very sensitive to contact. **3** *Biol.* responding actively to physical stimulus. □□ **irritability** /-ˈbɪlɪtɪ/ *n.* **irritably** *adv.* [L *irritabilis* (as IRRITATE)]

irritant /ˈɪrɪt(ə)nt/ *adj.* & *n.* —*adj.* causing irritation. —*n.* an irritant substance. □□ **irritancy** *n.*

irritate /ˈɪrɪˌteɪt/ *v.tr.* **1** excite to anger; annoy. **2** stimulate discomfort or pain in (a part of the body). **3** *Biol.* stimulate (an organ) to action. □□ **irritatedly** *adv.* **irritating** *adj.* **irritatingly** *adv.* **irritation** /-ˈteɪʃ(ə)n/ *n.* **irritative** /-tətɪv/ *adj.* **irritator** *n.* [L *irritare irritat-*]

irrupt /ɪˈrʌpt/ *v.intr.* (foll. by *into*) enter forcibly or violently. □□ **irruption** /ɪˈrʌpʃ(ə)n/ *n.* [L *irrumpere irrupt-* (as IN-², *rumpere* break)]

Is. *abbr.* **1 a** Island(s). **b** Isle(s). **2** (also **Isa.**) Isaiah (Old Testament).

is *3rd sing. present* of BE.

isagogic /ˌaɪsəˈɡɒdʒɪk/ *adj.* introductory. [L *isagogicus* f. Gk *eisagōgikos* f. *eisagōgē* introduction f. *eis* into + *agōgē* leading f. *agō* lead]

isagogics /ˌaɪsəˈɡɒdʒɪks/ *n.* an introductory study, esp. of the literary and external history of the Bible.

isatin /ˈaɪsətɪn/ *n. Chem.* a red crystalline derivative of indole used in the manufacture of dyes. [L *isatis* woad f. Gk]

ISBN *abbr.* international standard book number.

ischaemia /ɪˈskiːmɪə/ *n.* (*US* **ischemia**) *Med.* a reduction of the blood supply to part of the body. □□ **ischaemic** *adj.* [mod.L f. Gk *iskhaimos* f. *iskhō* keep back]

ischium /ˈɪskɪəm/ *n.* (*pl.* **ischia** /-kɪə/) the curved bone forming the base of each half of the pelvis. □□ **ischial** *adj.* [L f. Gk *iskhion* hip-joint: cf. SCIATIC]

-ise¹ *suffix* var. of -IZE. ¶ See the note at *-ize*.

-ise² /aɪz, iːz/ *suffix* forming nouns of quality, state, or function (*exercise*; *expertise*; *franchise*; *merchandise*). [from or after F or OF *-ise* f. L *-itia* etc.]

-ise³ *suffix* var. of -ISH².

isentropic /ˌaɪsenˈtrɒpɪk/ *adj.* having equal entropy. [ISO- + ENTROPY]

-ish¹ /ɪʃ/ *suffix* forming adjectives: **1** from nouns, meaning: **a** having the qualities or characteristics of (*boyish*). **b** of the nationality of (*Danish*). **2** from adjectives, meaning 'somewhat' (*thickish*). **3** *colloq.* denoting an approximate age or time of day (*fortyish*; *six-thirtyish*). [OE *-isc*]

-ish² /ɪʃ/ *suffix* (also **-ise** /aɪz/) forming verbs (*vanish*; *advertise*). [from or after F *-iss-* (in extended stems of verbs in *-ir*) f. L *-isc-* incept. suffix]

isinglass /ˈaɪzɪŋˌɡlɑːs/ *n.* **1** a kind of gelatin obtained from fish, esp. sturgeon, and used in making jellies, glue, etc. **2** mica. [corrupt. of obs. Du. *huisenblas* sturgeon's bladder, assim. to GLASS]

Islam /ˈɪzlɑːm, -læm, -ˈlɑːm/ *n.* **1** the religion of the Muslims, a monotheistic faith regarded as revealed through Muhammad as the Prophet of Allah. **2** the Muslim world. □□ **Islamic** /ɪzˈlæmɪk/ *adj.* **Islamism** *n.* **Islamist** *n.* **Islamize** *v.tr.* (also **-ise**). **Islamization** /-aɪˈzeɪʃ(ə)n/ *n.* [Arab. *islām* submission (to God) f. *aslama* resign oneself]

island /ˈaɪlənd/ *n.* **1** a piece of land surrounded by water. **2** anything compared to an island, esp. in being surrounded in some way. **3** = *traffic island*. **4 a** a detached or isolated thing. **b** *Physiol.* a detached portion of tissue or group of cells (cf. ISLET). **5** *Naut.* a ship's superstructure, bridge, etc. [OE *īgland* f. *īg* island + LAND: first syll. infl. by ISLE]

islander /ˈaɪləndə(r)/ *n.* a native or inhabitant of an island.

isle /aɪl/ *n. poet.* (and in place-names) an island or peninsula, esp. a small one. [ME *ile* f. OF *ile* f. L *insula*: later ME & OF *isle* after L]

islet /ˈaɪlɪt/ *n.* **1** a small island. **2** *Anat.* a portion of tissue structurally distinct from surrounding tissue. **3** an isolated place. □ **islets of Langerhans** *Physiol.* groups of pancreatic cells secreting insulin and glucagon. [OF, dimin. of *isle* ISLE]

ism /ˈɪz(ə)m/ *n. colloq.* usu. *derog.* any distinctive but unspecified doctrine or practice of a kind with a name in *-ism*.

-ism /ˈɪz(ə)m/ *suffix* forming nouns, esp. denoting: **1** an action or its result (*baptism*; *organism*). **2** a system, principle, or ideological movement (*Conservatism*; *jingoism*; *feminism*). **3** a state or quality (*heroism*; *barbarism*). **4** a basis of prejudice or discrimination (*racism*; *sexism*). **5** a peculiarity in language (*Americanism*). **6** a pathological condition (*alcoholism*; *Parkinsonism*). [from or after F *-isme* f. L *-ismus* f. Gk *-ismos* or *-isma* f. *-izō* -IZE]

Ismaili /ˌɪzˈmaɪlɪ/ *n.* (*pl.* **Ismailis**) a member of a Muslim Shiite sect that arose in the 8th c. [*Ismail* a son of the patriarch Ibrāhīm (= Abraham)]

isn't /ˈɪz(ə)nt/ *contr.* is not.

ISO *abbr.* **1** (in the UK) Imperial Service Order. **2** International Organization for Standardization.

iso- /ˈaɪsəʊ/ *comb. form* **1** equal (*isometric*). **2** *Chem.* isomeric, esp. of a hydrocarbon with a branched chain of carbon atoms (*isobutane*). [Gk *isos* equal]

isobar /ˈaɪsəʊˌbɑː(r)/ *n.* **1** a line on a map connecting positions having the same atmospheric pressure at a given time or on average over a given period. **2** a curve for a physical system at constant pressure. **3** one of two or more isotopes of different elements, with the same atomic weight. ▫▫ **isobaric** /-'bærɪk/ *adj.* [Gk *isobarēs* of equal weight (as ISO-, *baros* weight)]

isocheim /'aɪsəʊ,kaɪm/ *n.* a line on a map connecting places having the same average temperature in winter. [ISO- + Gk *kheima* winter weather]

isochromatic /,aɪsəʊkrəʊ'mætɪk/ *adj.* of the same colour.

isochronous /aɪ'sɒkrənəs/ *adj.* **1** occurring at the same time. **2** occupying equal time. ▫▫ **isochronously** *adv.* [ISO- + Gk *khronos* time]

isoclinal /,aɪsəʊ'klaɪn(ə)l/ *adj.* (also **isoclinic** /-'klɪnɪk/) **1** *Geol.* (of a fold) in which the two limbs are parallel. **2** corresponding to equal values of magnetic dip. [ISO- + CLINE]

isoclinic var. of ISOCLINAL.

isodynamic /,aɪsəʊdaɪ'næmɪk/ *adj.* corresponding to equal values of (magnetic) force.

isoenzyme /'aɪsəʊ,enzaɪm/ *n. Biochem.* one of two or more enzymes with identical function but different structure.

isogeotherm /,aɪsəʊ'dʒiːəʊ,θɜːm/ *n.* a line or surface connecting points in the interior of the earth having the same temperature. ▫▫ **isogeothermal** /-'θɜːm(ə)l/ *adj.*

isogloss /'aɪsəʊ,ɡlɒs/ *n.* a line on a map marking an area having a distinct linguistic feature.

isogonic /,aɪsəʊ'ɡɒnɪk/ *adj.* corresponding to equal values of magnetic declination.

isohel /'aɪsəʊ,hel/ *n.* a line on a map connecting places having the same duration of sunshine. [ISO- + Gk *hēlios* sun]

isohyet /,aɪsəʊ'haɪɪt/ *n.* a line on a map connecting places having the same amount of rainfall in a given period. [ISO- + Gk *huetos* rain]

isolate /'aɪsə,leɪt/ *v.tr.* **1 a** place apart or alone, cut off from society. **b** place (a patient thought to be contagious or infectious) in quarantine. **2 a** identify and separate for attention (*isolated the problem*). **b** *Chem.* separate (a substance) from a mixture. **3** insulate (electrical apparatus). ▫▫ **isolable** /'aɪsələb(ə)l/ *adj.* **isolatable** *adj.* **isolator** *n.* [orig. in past part., f. F *isolé* f. It. *isolato* f. LL *insulatus* f. L *insula* island]

isolated /'aɪsə,leɪtɪd/ *adj.* **1** lonely; cut off from society or contact; remote (*feeling isolated*; *an isolated farmhouse*). **2** untypical, unique (*an isolated example*).

isolating /'aɪsə,leɪtɪŋ/ *adj.* (of a language) having each element as an independent word without inflections.

isolation /,aɪsə'leɪʃ(ə)n/ *n.* the act or an instance of isolating; the state of being isolated or separated. ▫**in isolation** considered singly and not relatively. **isolation hospital** (or **ward** etc.) a hospital, ward, etc., for patients with contagious or infectious diseases.

isolationism /,aɪsə'leɪʃə,nɪz(ə)m/ *n.* the policy of holding aloof from the affairs of other countries or groups esp. in politics. ▫▫ **isolationist** *n.*

isoleucine /,aɪsəʊ'luːsiːn/ *n. Biochem.* an amino acid that is a constituent of proteins and an essential nutrient. [G *Isoleucin* (see ISO-, LEUCINE)]

isomer /'aɪsəmə(r)/ *n.* **1** *Chem.* one of two or more compounds with the same molecular formula but a different arrangement of atoms and different properties. **2** *Physics* one of two or more atomic nuclei that have the same atomic number and the same mass number but different energy states. ▫▫ **isomeric** /-'merɪk/ *adj.* **isomerism** /aɪ'sɒmə,rɪz(ə)m/ *n.* **isomerize** /aɪ'sɒmə,raɪz/ *v.* (also **-ise**). [G f. Gk *isomerēs* sharing equally (as ISO-, *meros* share)]

isomerous /aɪ'sɒmərəs/ *adj. Bot.* (of a flower) having the same number of petals in each whorl. [Gk *isomerēs*: see ISOMER]

isometric /,aɪsəʊ'metrɪk/ *adj.* **1** of equal measure. **2** *Physiol.* (of muscle action) developing tension while the muscle is prevented from contracting. **3** (of a drawing etc.) with the plane of projection at equal angles to the three principal axes of the object shown. **4** *Math.* (of a transformation) without change of shape or size. ▫▫ **isometrically** *adv.* **isometry** /aɪ'sɒmɪtrɪ/ *n.* (in sense 4). [Gk *isometria* equality of measure (as ISO-, -METRY)]

isometrics /,aɪsəʊ'metrɪks/ *n.pl.* a system of physical exercises in which muscles are caused to act against each other or against a fixed object.

isomorph /'aɪsəʊ,mɔːf/ *n.* an isomorphic substance or organism. [ISO- + Gk *morphē* form]

isomorphic /,aɪsəʊ'mɔːfɪk/ *adj.* (also **isomorphous** /-fəs/) **1** exactly corresponding in form and relations. **2** *Crystallog.* having the same form. ▫▫ **isomorphism** *n.*

-ison /'ɪs(ə)n/ *suffix* forming nouns, = -ATION (*comparison*; *garrison*; *jettison*; *venison*). [OF *-aison* etc. f. L *-atio* etc.: see -ATION]

isophote /'aɪsəʊ,fəʊt/ *n.* a line (imaginary or in a diagram) of equal brightness or illumination. [ISO- + Gk *phōs phōtos* light]

isopleth /'aɪsəʊ,pleθ/ *n.* a line on a map connecting places having equal incidence of a meteorological feature. [ISO- + Gk *plēthos* fullness]

isopod /'aɪsəʊ,pɒd/ *n.* any crustacean of the order *Isopoda*, including woodlice and slaters, often parasitic and having a flattened body with seven pairs of legs. [F *isopode* f. mod.L *Isopoda* (as ISO-, Gk *pous podos* foot)]

isosceles /aɪ'sɒsɪ,liːz/ *adj.* (of a triangle) having two sides equal. [LL f. Gk *isoskelēs* (as ISO-, *skelos* leg)]

isoseismal /,aɪsəʊ'saɪzm(ə)l/ *adj.* & *n.* (also **isoseismic** /-mɪk/) —*adj.* having equal strength of earthquake shock. —*n.* a line on a map connecting places having an equal strength of earthquake shock.

isostasy /aɪ'sɒstəsɪ/ *n. Geol.* the general state of equilibrium of the earth's crust, with the rise and fall of land relative to sea. ▫▫ **isostatic** /,aɪsəʊ'stætɪk/ *adj.* [ISO- + Gk *stasis* station]

isothere /'aɪsəʊ,θɪə(r)/ *n.* a line on a map connecting places having the same average temperature in summer. [ISO- + Gk *theros* summer]

isotherm /'aɪsəʊ,θɜːm/ *n.* **1** a line on a map connecting places having the same temperature at a given time or on average over a given period. **2** a curve for changes in a physical system at a constant temperature. ▫▫ **isothermal** /-'θɜːm(ə)l/ *adj.* **isothermally** /-'θɜːməlɪ/ *adv.* [F *isotherme* (as ISO-, Gk *thermē* heat)]

isotonic /,aɪsəʊ'tɒnɪk/ *adj.* **1** having the same osmotic pressure. **2** *Physiol.* (of muscle action) taking place with normal contraction. ▫▫ **isotonically** *adv.* **isotonicity** /-tə'nɪsɪtɪ/ *n.* [Gk *isotonos* (as ISO-, TONE)]

isotope /'aɪsə,təʊp/ *n. Chem.* one of two or more forms of an element differing from each other in relative atomic mass, and in nuclear but not chemical properties. ▫▫ **isotopic** /-'tɒpɪk/ *adj.* **isotopically** /-'tɒpɪkəlɪ/ *adv.* **isotopy** /aɪ'sɒtəpɪ/ *n.* [ISO- + Gk *topos* place (i.e. in the periodic table of elements)]

isotropic /,aɪsəʊ'trɒpɪk/ *adj.* having the same physical properties in all directions (opp. ANISOTROPIC). ▫▫ **isotropically** *adv.* **isotropy** /aɪ'sɒtrəpɪ/ *n.* [ISO- + Gk *tropos* turn]

I-spy /aɪ'spaɪ/ *n.* a game in which players try to identify something observed by one of them, with its initial letter as a clue.

Israeli /ɪz'reɪlɪ/ *adj.* & *n.* —*adj.* of or relating to the modern State of Israel in the Middle East. —*n.* **1** a native or national of Israel. **2** a person of Israeli descent. [*Israel*, a later name of Jacob, ult. f. Heb. *yisrā'ēl* he that strives with God (Gen. 32:28) + -ɪ²]

Israelite /'ɪzrɪə,laɪt, -rə,laɪt/ *n. hist.* a native of ancient Israel; a Jew.

ISSN *abbr.* international standard serial number.

issuant /'ɪʃuːənt, 'ɪsjuː-/ *adj. Heraldry* (esp. of a beast with only the upper part shown) rising from the bottom or top of a bearing.

issue /'ɪʃuː, 'ɪsjuː/ n. & v. —n. **1 a** a giving out or circulation of shares, notes, stamps, etc. **b** a quantity of coins, supplies, copies of a newspaper or book etc., circulated or put on sale at one time. **c** an item or amount given out or distributed. **d** each of a regular series of a magazine etc. (*the May issue*). **2 a** an outgoing, an outflow. **b** a way out, an outlet esp. the place of the emergence of a stream etc. **3** a point in question; an important subject of debate or litigation. **4** a result; an outcome; a decision. **5** *Law* children, progeny (*without male issue*). **6** *archaic* a discharge of blood etc. —v. (**issues, issued, issuing**) **1** *intr.* (often foll. by *out, forth*) *literary* go or come out. **2** *tr.* **a** send forth; publish; put into circulation. **b** supply, esp. officially or authoritatively (foll. by *to, with*: *issued passports to them; issued them with passports; issued orders to the staff*). **3** *intr.* **a** (often foll. by *from*) be derived or result. **b** (foll. by *in*) end, result. **4** *intr.* (foll. by *from*) emerge from a condition. □**at issue 1** under discussion; in dispute. **2** at variance. **issue of fact** (or **law**) a dispute at law when the significance of a fact or facts is denied or when the application of the law is contested. **join** (or **take**) **issue** identify an issue for argument (foll. by *with, on*). **make an issue of** make a fuss about; turn into a subject of contention. □□**issuable** *adj.* **issuance** *n.* **issueless** *adj.* **issuer** *n.* [ME f. OF ult. f. L *exitus* past part. of *exire* EXIT]

-ist /ɪst/ *suffix* forming personal nouns (and in some senses related adjectives) denoting: **1** an adherent of a system etc. in *-ism*: see -ISM 2 (*Marxist; fatalist*). **2 a** a member of a profession (*pathologist*). **b** a person concerned with something (*tobacconist*). **3** a person who uses a thing (*violinist; balloonist; motorist*). **4** a person who does something expressed by a verb in *-ize* (*plagiarist*). **5** a person who subscribes to a prejudice or practises discrimination (*racist; sexist*). [OF *-iste*, L *-ista* f. Gk *-istēs*]

isthmian /'ɪsmɪən, 'ɪsθ-/ *adj.* of or relating to an isthmus, esp. (**Isthmian**) to the Isthmus of Corinth in southern Greece.

isthmus /'ɪsməs, 'ɪsθ-/ n. **1** a narrow piece of land connecting two larger bodies of land. **2** *Anat.* a narrow part connecting two larger parts. [L f. Gk *isthmos*]

istle /'ɪstlɪ/ n. a fibre used for cord, nets, etc., obtained from agave. [Mex. *ixtli*]

IT *abbr.* information technology.

It. *abbr.* Italian.

it[1] /ɪt/ *pron.* (*poss.* **its**; *pl.* **they**) **1** the thing (or occas. the animal or child) previously named or in question (*took a stone and threw it*). **2** the person in question (*Who is it? It is I; is it a boy or a girl?*). **3** as the subject of an impersonal verb (*it is raining; it is winter; it is Tuesday; it is two miles to Bath*). **4** as a substitute for a deferred subject or object (*it is intolerable, this delay; it is silly to talk like that; I take it that you agree*). **5** as a substitute for a vague object (*brazen it out; run for it!*). **6** as the antecedent to a relative word (*it was an owl I heard*). **7** exactly what is needed (*absolutely it*). **8** the extreme limit of achievement. **9** *colloq.* sexual intercourse; sex appeal. **10** (in children's games) a player who has to perform a required feat, esp. to catch the others. □**that's it** *colloq.* that is: **1** what is required. **2** the difficulty. **3** the end, enough. **this is it** *colloq.* **1** the expected event is at hand. **2** this is the difficulty. [OE *hit* neut. of HE]

it[2] /ɪt/ n. *colloq.* Italian vermouth (*gin and it*). [abbr.]

i.t.a. *abbr.* (also **ITA**) initial teaching alphabet.

ital. *abbr.* italic (type).

Italian /ɪ'tæljən/ n. & *adj.* —n. **1 a** a native or national of Italy. **b** a person of Italian descent. **2** the Romance language used in Italy and parts of Switzerland. —*adj.* of or relating to Italy or its people or language. □**Italian vermouth** a sweet kind of vermouth. [ME f. It. *Italiano* f. *Italia* Italy]

Italianate /ɪ'tæljəˌneɪt/ *adj.* of Italian style or appearance. [It. *Italianato*]

italic /ɪ'tælɪk/ *adj.* & n. —*adj.* **1 a** *Printing* of the sloping kind of letters now used esp. for emphasis or distinction and in foreign words. **b** (of handwriting) compact and pointed like early Italian handwriting. **2** (**Italic**) of ancient Italy. —n. **1** a letter in italic type. **2** this type. [L *italicus* f. Gk *italikos* Italian (because introduced by Aldo Manuzio of Venice)]

italicize /ɪ'tælɪˌsaɪz/ *v.tr.* (also **-ise**) print in italics. □□**italicization** /-ˈzeɪʃ(ə)n/ n.

Italiot /ɪ'tælɪət/ n. & *adj.* —n. an inhabitant of the Greek colonies in ancient Italy. —*adj.* of or relating to the Italiots. [Gk *Italiōtēs* f. *Italia* Italy]

Italo- /'ɪtələʊ/ *comb. form* Italian; Italian and.

itch /ɪtʃ/ n. & v. —n. **1** an irritation in the skin. **2** an impatient desire; a hankering. **3** (prec. by *the*) (in general use) scabies. —*v.intr.* **1** feel an irritation in the skin, causing a desire to scratch it. **2** (usu. foll. by *to* + infin.) (of a person) feel a desire to do something (*am itching to tell you the news*). □**itching palm** avarice. **itch-mite** a parasitic arthropod, *Sarcoptes scabiei*, which burrows under the skin causing scabies. [OE *gycce, gyccan* f. WG]

itchy /'ɪtʃɪ/ *adj.* (**itchier, itchiest**) having or causing an itch. □**have itchy feet** *colloq.* **1** be restless. **2** have a strong urge to travel. □□**itchiness** n.

it'd /'ɪtəd/ *contr. colloq.* **1** it had. **2** it would.

-ite[1] /aɪt/ *suffix* forming nouns meaning 'a person or thing connected with': **1** in names of persons: **a** as natives of a country (*Israelite*). **b** often *derog.* as followers of a movement etc. (*pre-Raphaelite; Trotskyite*). **2** in names of things: **a** fossil organisms (*ammonite*). **b** minerals (*graphite*). **c** constituent parts of a body or organ (*somite*). **d** explosives (*dynamite*). **e** commercial products (*ebonite; vulcanite*). **f** salts of acids having names in *-ous* (*nitrite; sulphite*). [from or after F *-ite* f. L *-ita* f. Gk *- itēs*]

-ite[2] /aɪt, ɪt/ *suffix* **1** forming adjectives (*erudite; favourite*). **2** forming nouns (*appetite*). **3** forming verbs (*expedite; unite*). [from or after L *-itus* past part. of verbs in *-ēre, -ere*, and *-ire*]

item /'aɪtəm/ n. & *adv.* —n. **1 a** any of a number of enumerated or listed things. **b** an entry in an account. **2** an article, esp. one for sale (*household items*). **3** a separate or distinct piece of news, information, etc. —*adv.* *archaic* (introducing the mention of each item) likewise, also. [orig. as *adv.*; L, = in like manner, also]

itemize /'aɪtəˌmaɪz/ *v.tr.* (also **-ise**) state or list item by item. □□**itemization** /-ˈzeɪʃ(ə)n/ n. **itemizer** n.

iterate /'ɪtəˌreɪt/ *v.tr.* repeat; state repeatedly. □□**iteration** /-ˈreɪʃ(ə)n/ n. [L *iterare iterat-* f. *iterum* again]

iterative /'ɪtərətɪv/ *adj. Gram.* = FREQUENTATIVE. □□**iteratively** *adv.*

ithyphallic /ˌɪθɪˈfælɪk/ *adj. Gk Hist.* **1 a** of the phallus carried in Bacchic festivals. **b** (of a statue etc.) having an erect penis. **2** lewd, licentious. **3** (of a poem or metre) used for Bacchic hymns. [LL *ithyphallicus* f. Gk *ithuphallikos* f. *ithus* straight, *phallos* PHALLUS]

-itic /'ɪtɪk/ *suffix* forming adjectives and nouns corresponding to nouns in *-ite, -itis*, etc. (*Semitic; arthritic; syphilitic*). [from or after F *-itique* f. L *-iticus* f. Gk *-itikos*: see -IC]

itinerant /aɪ'tɪnərənt, ɪ-/ *adj.* & n. —*adj.* travelling from place to place. —n. an itinerant person; a tramp. □**itinerant judge** (or **minister** etc.) a judge, minister, etc. travelling within a circuit. □□**itineracy** n. **itinerancy** n. [LL *itinerari* travel f. L *iter itiner-* journey]

itinerary /aɪ'tɪnərərɪ, ɪ-/ n. & *adj.* —n. (*pl.* **-ies**) **1** a detailed route. **2** a record of travel. **3** a guidebook. —*adj.* of roads or travelling. [LL *itinerarius* (adj.), *-um* (n.) f. L *iter*: see ITINERANT]

itinerate /aɪ'tɪnəˌreɪt, ɪ-/ *v.intr.* travel from place to place or (of a minister etc.) within a circuit. □□

itineration /-'reɪʃ(ə)n/ n. [LL itinerari: see ITINERANT]

-ition /'ɪʃ(ə)n/ suffix forming nouns, = -ATION (admonition; perdition; position). [from or after F -ition or L -itio -itionis]

-itious[1] /'ɪʃəs/ suffix forming adjectives corresponding to nouns in -ition (ambitious; suppositious). [L -itio etc. + -OUS]

-itious[2] /'ɪʃəs/ suffix forming adjectives meaning 'related to, having the nature of' (adventitious; supposititious). [L -icius + -OUS, commonly written with t in med.L manuscripts]

-itis /'aɪtɪs/ suffix forming nouns, esp.: **1** names of inflammatory diseases (appendicitis; bronchitis). **2** colloq. in extended uses with ref. to conditions compared to diseases (electionitis). [Gk -itis, forming fem. of adjectives in -itēs (with nosos 'disease' implied)]

-itive /'ɪtɪv/ suffix forming adjectives, = -ATIVE (positive; transitive). [from or after F -itif -itive or L -itivus f. participial stems in -it-: see -IVE]

it'll /'ɪt(ə)l/ contr. colloq. it will; it shall.

ITN abbr. (in the UK) Independent Television News.

ITO abbr. International Trade Organization.

-itor /'ɪtə(r)/ suffix forming agent nouns, usu. from Latin words (sometimes via French) (creditor). See also -OR[1].

-itory /'ɪtərɪ/ suffix forming adjectives meaning 'relating to or involving (a verbal action)' (inhibitory). See also -ORY[2]. [L -itorius]

-itous /'ɪtəs/ suffix forming adjectives corresponding to nouns in -ity (calamitous; felicitous). [from or after F -iteux f. L -itosus]

its /ɪts/ poss.pron. of it; of itself (can see its advantages).

it's /ɪts/ contr. **1** it is. **2** it has.

itself /ɪt'self/ pron. emphatic and refl. form of IT[1]. □ **by itself** apart from its surroundings, automatically, spontaneously. **in itself** viewed in its essential qualities (not in itself a bad thing). [OE f. IT[1] + SELF, but often treated as ITS + SELF (cf. its own self)]

itsy-bitsy /ˌɪtsɪ'bɪtsɪ/ adj. (also **itty-bitty** /ˌɪtɪ'bɪtɪ/) colloq. usu. derog. tiny, insubstantial, slight. [redupl. of LITTLE, infl. by BIT[1]]

ITU abbr. International Telecommunication Union.

ITV abbr. (in the UK) Independent Television.

-ity /'ɪtɪ/ suffix forming nouns denoting: **1** quality or condition (authority; humility; purity). **2** an instance or degree of this (a monstrosity; humidity). [from or after F -ité f. L -itas -itatis]

IU abbr. international unit.

IUD abbr. **1** intra-uterine (contraceptive) device. **2** intra-uterine death (of the foetus before birth).

-ium /ɪəm/ suffix forming nouns denoting esp.: **1** (also **-um**) names of metallic elements (uranium; tantalum). **2** a region of the body (pericardium;

hypogastrium). **3** a biological structure (mycelium; prothallium). [from or after L -ium f. Gk -ion]

IUPAC /'ju:pæk/ abbr. International Union of Pure and Applied Chemistry.

IV abbr. intravenous.

I've /aɪv/ contr. I have.

-ive /ɪv/ suffix forming adjectives meaning 'tending to, having the nature of', and corresponding nouns (suggestive; corrosive; palliative; coercive; talkative). □□ **-ively** suffix forming adverbs. **-iveness** suffix forming nouns. [from or after F -if -ive f. L -ivus]

IVF abbr. in vitro fertilization.

ivied /'aɪvɪd/ adj. overgrown with ivy.

ivory /'aɪvərɪ/ n. (pl. **-ies**) **1** a hard creamy-white substance composing the main part of the tusks of an elephant, hippopotamus, walrus, and narwhal. **2** the colour of this. **3** (usu. in pl.) **a** an article made of ivory. **b** sl. anything made of or resembling ivory, esp. a piano key or a tooth. □ **fossil ivory** ivory from the tusks of a mammoth. **ivory black** black pigment from calcined ivory or bone. **ivory-nut** the seed of a corozo palm, Phytelephas macrocarpa, used as a source of vegetable ivory for carving: also called corozo-nut. **ivory tower** a state of seclusion or separation from the ordinary world and the harsh realities of life. **vegetable ivory** a hard white material obtained from the endosperm of the ivory-nut. □□ **ivoried** adj. [ME f. OF yvoire ult. f. L ebur eboris]

ivy /'aɪvɪ/ n. (pl. **-ies**) **1** a climbing evergreen shrub, Hedera helix, with usu. dark-green shining five-angled leaves. **2** any of various other climbing plants including ground ivy and poison ivy. □ **Ivy League** a group of universities in the eastern US. [OE ifig]

IWW abbr. Industrial Workers of the World.

ixia /'ɪksɪə/ n. any iridaceous plant of the genus Ixia of S. Africa, with large showy flowers. [L f. Gk, a kind of thistle]

izard /'ɪzɑːd/ n. a chamois. [F isard, of unkn. orig.]

-ize /aɪz/ suffix (also **-ise**) forming verbs, meaning: **1** make or become such (Americanize; pulverize; realize). **2** treat in such a way (monopolize; pasteurize). **3 a** follow a special practice (economize). **b** have a specified feeling (sympathize). **4** affect with, provide with, or subject to (oxidize; hospitalize). ¶ The form -ize has been in use in English since the 16th c.; it is widely used in American English, but is not an Americanism. The alternative spelling -ise (reflecting a French influence) is in common use, esp. in British English, and is obligatory in certain cases: (a) where it forms part of a larger word-element, such as -mise (= sending) in compromise, and -prise (= taking) in surprise; and (b) in verbs corresponding to a noun with -s- in the stem, such as advertise and televise. □□ **-ization** /-'zeɪʃ(ə)n/ suffix forming nouns. **-izer** suffix forming agent nouns. [from or after F -iser f. LL -izare f. Gk -izō]

J

J¹ /dʒeɪ/ n. (also **j**) (pl. **Js** or **J's**) **1** the tenth letter of the alphabet. **2** (as a Roman numeral) = *i* in a final position (*ij*; *vj*).

J² abbr. (also **J.**) **1** joule(s). **2** Judge. **3** Justice.

jab /dʒæb/ v. & n. —v.tr. (**jabbed, jabbing**) **1 a** poke roughly. **b** stab. **2** (foll. by *into*) thrust (a thing) hard or abruptly. —n. **1** an abrupt blow with one's fist or a pointed implement. **2** *colloq.* a hypodermic injection, esp. a vaccination. [orig. Sc. var. of JOB²]

jabber /'dʒæbə(r)/ v. & n. —v. **1** *intr.* chatter volubly and incoherently. **2** *tr.* utter (words) fast and indistinctly. —n. meaningless jabbering; a gabble. [imit.]

jabberwocky /'dʒæbə,wɒkɪ/ n. (pl. **-ies**) a piece of nonsensical writing or speech, esp. for comic effect. [title of a poem in Lewis Carroll's *Through the Looking-Glass* (1871)]

jabiru /'dʒæbɪ,ruː/ n. **1** a large stork, *Jabiru mycteria*, of Central and S. America. **2** a black-necked stork, *Xenorhyncus asiaticus*, of Asia and Australia. [Tupi-Guarani *jabirú*]

jaborandi /,dʒæbə'rændɪ/ n. (pl. **jaborandis**) **1** any shrub of the genus *Pilocarpus*, of S. America. **2** the dried leaflets of this, having diuretic and diaphoretic properties. [Tupi-Guarani *jaburandi*]

jabot /'ʒæbəʊ/ n. an ornamental frill or ruffle of lace etc. on the front of a shirt or blouse. [F, orig. = crop of a bird]

jacana /dʒæ'kɑːnə, -sənə/ n. any of various small tropical wading birds of the family Jacanidae, with elongated toes and hind-claws which enable them to walk on floating leaves etc. [Port. *jaçanã* f. Tupi-Guarani *jasaná*]

jacaranda /,dʒækə'rændə/ n. **1** any tropical American tree of the genus *Jacaranda*, with trumpet-shaped blue flowers. **2** any tropical American tree of the genus *Dalbergia*, with hard scented wood. [Tupi-Guarani *jacarandá*]

jacinth /'dʒæsɪnθ, 'dʒeɪ-/ n. a reddish-orange variety of zircon used as a gem. [ME *iacynt* etc. f. OF *iacinte* or med.L *jacint(h)us* f. L *hyacinthus* HYACINTH]

jack¹ /dʒæk/ n. & v. —n. **1** a device for lifting heavy objects, esp. the axle of a vehicle off the ground while changing a wheel etc. **2** a court-card with a picture of a man, esp. a soldier, page, or knave, etc. **3** a ship's flag, esp. one flown from the bow and showing nationality. **4** a device using a single plug to connect an electrical circuit. **5** a small white ball in bowls, at which the players aim. **6 a** = JACKSTONE. **b** (in *pl.*) a game of jackstones. **7** (**Jack**) the familiar form of *John* esp. typifying the common man or the male of a species (*I'm all right, Jack*). **8** the figure of a man striking the bell on a clock. **9** *sl.* a detective; a policeman. **10** *US sl.* money. **11** = LUMBERJACK. **12** = STEEPLEJACK. **13** a device for turning a spit. **14** any of various marine perchlike fish of the family Carangidae, including the amberjack. **15** a device for plucking the string of a harpsichord etc., one being operated by each key. —v.tr. (usu. foll. by *up*) **1** raise with or as with a jack (in sense 1). **2** *colloq.* raise e.g. prices. □ **every man jack** each and every person. **Jack Frost** frost personified. **jack in** (or **up**) *sl.* abandon (an attempt etc.). **jack-in-the-box** a toy figure that springs out of a box when it is opened. **jack-in-office** a self-important minor official. **jack of all trades** a person who can do many different kinds of work. **jack-o'-lantern** **1** a will-o'-the-wisp. **2** a lantern made esp. from a pumpkin with holes for facial features. **jack plane** a medium-sized plane for use in rough joinery. **jack plug** a plug for use with a jack (see sense 4 of *n.*). **Jack tar** a sailor. **on one's jack** (or **Jack Jones**) *sl.* alone; on one's own. [ME *Iakke*, a pet-name for *John*, erron. assoc. with F *Jacques* James]

jack² /dʒæk/ n. **1** = BLACKJACK³. **2** *hist.* a sleeveless padded tunic worn by foot-soldiers. [ME f. OF *jaque*, of uncert. orig.]

jackal /'dʒæk(ə)l/ n. **1** any of various wild doglike mammals of the genus *Canis*, esp. *C. aureus*, found in Africa and S. Asia, usu. hunting or scavenging for food in packs. **2** *colloq.* **a** a person who does preliminary drudgery for another. **b** a person who assists another's immoral behaviour. [Turk. *çakal* f. Pers. *šagāl*]

jackanapes /'dʒækə,neɪps/ n. *archaic* **1** a pert or insolent fellow. **2** a mischievous child. **3** a tame monkey. [earliest as *Jack Napes* (1450): supposed to refer to the Duke of Suffolk, whose badge was an ape's clog and chain]

jackaroo /,dʒækə'ruː/ n. (also **jackeroo**) *Austral. colloq.* a novice on a sheep-station or cattle-station. [JACK¹ + KANGAROO]

jackass /'dʒækæs/ n. **1** a male ass. **2** a stupid person.

jackboot /'dʒækbuːt/ n. **1** a large boot reaching above the knee. **2** this as a symbol of fascism or military oppression. □□ **jackbooted** adj.

jackdaw /'dʒækdɔː/ n. a small grey-headed crow, *Corvus monedula*, often frequenting rooftops and nesting in tall buildings, and noted for its inquisitiveness (cf. DAW).

jackeroo var. of JACKAROO.

jacket /'dʒækɪt/ n. & v. —n. **1 a** a sleeved short outer garment. **b** a thing worn esp. round the torso for protection or support (*life-jacket*). **2** a casing or covering, e.g. as insulation round a boiler. **3** = *dust-jacket*. **4** the skin of a potato, esp. when baked whole. **5** an animal's coat. —v.tr. (**jacketed, jacketing**) cover with a jacket. □ **jacket potato** a baked potato served with the skin on. [ME f. OF *ja(c)quet* dimin. of *jaque* JACK²]

jackfish /'dʒækfɪʃ/ n. (pl. same) = PIKE¹.

jackfruit /'dʒækfruːt/ n. **1** an East Indian tree, *Artocarpus heterophyllus*, bearing fruit resembling breadfruit. **2** this fruit. [Port. *jaca* f. Malayalam *chakka* + FRUIT]

jackhammer /'dʒæk,hæmə(r)/ n. *US* a pneumatic hammer or drill.

jackknife /'dʒæknaɪf/ n. & v. —n. (pl. **-knives**) **1** a large clasp-knife. **2** a dive in which the body is first bent at the waist and then straightened. —v.intr. (**-knifed, -knifing**) (of an articulated vehicle) fold against itself in an accidental skidding movement.

jackpot /'dʒækpɒt/ n. a large prize or amount of winnings, esp. accumulated in a game or lottery etc. □ **hit the jackpot** *colloq.* **1** win a large prize. **2** have remarkable luck or success. [JACK¹ n. 2 + POT¹: orig. in a form of poker with two jacks as minimum to open the pool]

jackrabbit /'dʒæk,ræbɪt/ n. *US* any of various large prairie hares of the genus *Lepus* with very long ears and hind legs.

Jack Russell /dʒæk 'rʌs(ə)l/ n. **1** a terrier of a breed with short legs. **2** this breed.

jacksnipe /'dʒæksnaɪp/ n. a small snipe, *Lymnocryptes minimus*.

jackstaff /'dʒækstɑːf/ n. *Naut.* **1** a staff at the bow of a ship for a jack. **2** a staff carrying the flag that is to show above the masthead.

jackstone /'dʒækstəʊn/ n. **1** a small piece of metal etc. used with others in tossing-games. Also called

---

b *but* d *dog* f *few* g *get* h *he* j *yes* k *cat* l *leg* m *man* n *no* p *pen* r *red* s *sit* t *top* v *voice*

JACK[1]. **2** (in *pl.*) **a** a game with a ball and jackstones. **b** the game of jacks.

jackstraw /ˈdʒækstrɔː/ *n.* a spillikin.

Jacobean /ˌdʒækəˈbiːən/ *adj.* & *n.* —*adj.* **1** of or relating to the reign of James I of England. **2** (of furniture) in the style prevalent then, esp. of the colour of dark oak. —*n.* a Jacobean person. [mod.L *Jacobaeus* f. eccl.L *Jacobus* James f. Gk *Iakōbos* Jacob]

Jacobin /ˈdʒækəbɪn/ *n.* **1 a** *hist.* a member of a radical democratic club established in Paris in 1789 in the old convent of the Jacobins (see sense 2). **b** any extreme radical. **2** *archaic* a Dominican friar. **3** (**jacobin**) a pigeon with reversed feathers on the back of its neck like a cowl. □□ **Jacobinic** /-ˈbɪnɪk/ *adj.* **Jacobinical** /-ˈbɪnɪk(ə)l/ *adj.* **Jacobinism** *n.* [orig. in sense 2 by assoc. with the Rue St Jacques in Paris: ME f. F f. med.L *Jacobinus* f. eccl.L *Jacobus*]

Jacobite /ˈdʒækəˌbaɪt/ *n.* *hist.* a supporter of James II of England after his removal from the throne in 1688, or of the Stuarts. □□ **Jacobitical** /-ˈbɪtɪk(ə)l/ *adj.* **Jacobitism** *n.* [L *Jacobus* James: see JACOBEAN]

Jacob's ladder /ˈdʒeɪkəbz/ *n.* **1** a plant, *Polemonium caeruleum*, with corymbs of blue or white flowers, and leaves suggesting a ladder. **2** a rope-ladder with wooden rungs. [f. Jacob's dream of a ladder reaching to heaven, as described in Gen. 28:12]

Jacob's staff /ˈdʒeɪkəbz/ *n.* **1** a surveyor's iron-shod rod used instead of a tripod. **2** an instrument for measuring distances and heights. [f. the staffs used by Jacob, as described in Gen. 30:37–43]

jaconet /ˈdʒækənɪt/ *n.* a cotton cloth like cambric, esp. a dyed waterproof kind for poulticing etc. [Urdu *jagannāthi* f. *Jagannath* (now Puri) in India, its place of origin: see JUGGERNAUT]

Jacquard /ˈdʒækɑːd/ *n.* **1** an apparatus with perforated cards, fitted to a loom to facilitate the weaving of figured fabrics. **2** (in full **Jacquard loom**) a loom fitted with this. **3** a fabric or article made with this, with an intricate variegated pattern. [J. M. *Jacquard*, Fr. inventor d. 1834]

jactitation /ˌdʒæktɪˈteɪʃ(ə)n/ *n.* **1** *Med.* **a** the restless tossing of the body in illness. **b** the twitching of a limb or muscle. **2** *archaic* the offence of falsely claiming to be a person's wife or husband. [med.L *jactitatio* false declaration f. L *jactitare* boast, frequent. of *jactare* throw: sense 1 f. earlier *jactation*]

Jacuzzi /dʒəˈkuːzɪ/ *n.* (*pl.* **Jacuzzis**) *propr.* a large bath with underwater jets of water to massage the body. [name of the inventor and manufacturers]

jade[1] /dʒeɪd/ *n.* **1** a hard usu. green stone composed of silicates of calcium and magnesium, or of sodium and aluminium, used for ornaments and implements. **2** the green colour of jade. [F: *le jade* for *l'ejade* f. Sp. *piedra de ijada* stone of the flank, i.e. stone for colic (which it was believed to cure)]

jade[2] /dʒeɪd/ *n.* **1** an inferior or worn-out horse. **2** *derog.* a disreputable woman. [ME: orig. unkn.]

jaded /ˈdʒeɪdɪd/ *adj.* tired or worn out; surfeited. □□ **jadedly** *adv.* **jadedness** *n.*

jadeite /ˈdʒeɪdaɪt/ *n.* a green, blue, or white sodium aluminium silicate form of jade.

j'adoube /ʒɑːˈduːb/ *int.* *Chess* a declaration by a player intending to adjust the placing of a piece without making a move with it. [F, = I adjust]

jaeger /ˈjeɪɡə(r)/ *n.* (also **yager**) *US* = SKUA. [G *Jäger* hunter f. *jagen* to hunt]

Jaffa /ˈdʒæfə/ *n.* a large oval thick-skinned variety of orange. [*Jaffa* in Israel, near where it was first grown]

jag[1] /dʒæɡ/ *n.* & *v.* —*n.* a sharp projection of rock etc. —*v.tr.* (**jagged, jagging**) **1** cut or tear unevenly. **2** make indentations in. □□ **jagger** *n.* [ME, prob. imit.]

jag[2] /dʒæɡ/ *n.* *sl.* **1** a drinking bout; a spree. **2** a period of indulgence in an activity, emotion, etc. [orig. 16th c., = load for one horse: orig. unkn.]

jagged /ˈdʒæɡɪd/ *adj.* **1** with an unevenly cut or torn edge. **2** deeply indented; with sharp points. □□ **jaggedly** *adv.* **jaggedness** *n.*

jaggy /ˈdʒæɡɪ/ *adj.* (**jaggier, jaggiest**) **1** = JAGGED. **2** (also **jaggie**) *Sc.* prickly.

jaguar /ˈdʒæɡjʊə(r)/ *n.* a large flesh-eating spotted feline, *Panthera onca*, of Central and S. America. [Tupi-Guarani *jaguara*]

jaguarundi /ˌdʒæɡwəˈrʌndɪ/ *n.* (*pl.* **jaguarundis**) a long-tailed slender feline, *Felis yaguarondi*, of Central and S. America. [Tupi-Guarani]

jai alai /ˈhaɪ əˌlaɪ/ *n.* a game like pelota played with large curved wicker baskets. [Sp. f. Basque *jai* festival + *alai* merry]

jail /dʒeɪl/ *n.* & *v.* (also **gaol**) —*n.* **1** a place to which persons are committed by a court for detention. **2** confinement in a jail. —*v.tr.* put in jail. [ME *gayole* f. OF *jaiole, jeole* & ONF *gaole* f. Rmc dimin. of L *cavea* CAGE]

jailbird /ˈdʒeɪlbɜːd/ *n.* (also **gaolbird**) a prisoner or habitual criminal.

jailbreak /ˈdʒeɪlbreɪk/ *n.* (also **gaolbreak**) an escape from jail.

jailer /ˈdʒeɪlə(r)/ *n.* (also **gaoler**) a person in charge of a jail or of the prisoners in it.

Jain /dʒaɪn/ *n.* & *adj.* —*n.* an adherent of a non-Brahminical Indian religion. —*adj.* of or relating to this religion. □□ **Jainism** *n.* **Jainist** *n.* [Hindi f. Skr. *jainas* saint, victor f. *jīna* victorious]

jake /dʒeɪk/ *adj.* *Austral.* & *NZ sl.* all right; satisfactory. [20th c.: orig. uncert.]

jalap /ˈdʒæləp/ *n.* a purgative drug obtained esp. from the tuberous roots of a Mexican climbing plant, *Exogonium purga*. [F f. Sp. *jalapa* f. *Jalapa, Xalapa*, city in Mexico, f. Aztec *Xalapan* sand by the water]

jalopy /dʒəˈlɒpɪ/ *n.* (*pl.* **-ies**) *colloq.* a dilapidated old motor vehicle. [20th c.: orig. unkn.]

jalousie /ˈʒæluˌziː/ *n.* a blind or shutter made of a row of angled slats to keep out rain etc. and control the influx of light. [F (as JEALOUSY)]

Jam. *abbr.* **1** Jamaica. **2** James (New Testament).

jam[1] /dʒæm/ *n.* & *v.* —*v.tr.* & *intr.* (**jammed, jamming**) **1 a** *tr.* (usu. foll. by *into*) squeeze or wedge into a space. **b** *intr.* become wedged. **2 a** *tr.* cause (machinery or a component) to become wedged or immovable so that it cannot work. **b** *intr.* become jammed in this way. **3** *tr.* push or cram together in a compact mass. **4** *intr.* (foll. by *in, on to*) push or crowd (*they jammed on to the bus*). **5** *tr.* **a** block (a passage, road, etc.) by crowding or obstructing. **b** (foll. by *in*) obstruct the exit of (*we were jammed in*). **6** *tr.* (usu. foll. by *on*) apply (brakes etc.) forcefully or abruptly. **7** *tr.* make (a radio transmission) unintelligible by causing interference. **8** *colloq.* (in jazz etc.) extemporize with other musicians. —*n.* **1** a squeeze or crush. **2** a crowded mass (*traffic jam*). **3** *colloq.* an awkward situation or predicament. **4** a stoppage (of a machine etc.) due to jamming. **5** (in full **jam session**) *colloq.* improvised playing by a group of jazz musicians. □**jam-packed** *colloq.* full to capacity. □□**jammer** *n.* [imit.]

jam[2] /dʒæm/ *n.* & *v.* —*n.* **1** a conserve of fruit and sugar boiled to a thick consistency. **2** *Brit. colloq.* something easy or pleasant (*money for jam*). —*v.tr.* (**jammed, jamming**) **1** spread jam on. **2** make (fruit etc.) into jam. □**jam tomorrow** a pleasant thing often promised but usu. never forthcoming. [perh. = JAM[1]]

jamb /dʒæm/ *n.* *Archit.* a side post or surface of a doorway, window, or fireplace. [ME f. OF *jambe* ult. f. LL *gamba* hoof]

jambalaya /ˌdʒæmbəˈlaɪə/ *n.* a dish of rice with shrimps, chicken, etc. [Louisiana F f. mod. Prov. *jambalaia*]

jamboree /ˌdʒæmbəˈriː/ *n.* **1** a celebration or merrymaking. **2** a large rally of Scouts. [19th c.: orig. unkn.]

jamjar /ˈdʒæmdʒɑː(r)/ *n.* a glass jar for containing jam.

jammy /'dʒæmɪ/ adj. (**jammier, jammiest**) **1** covered with jam. **2** Brit. colloq. **a** lucky. **b** profitable.

Jan. abbr. January.

jane /dʒeɪn/ n. sl. a woman (a plain jane). [the name Jane]

jangle /'dʒæŋg(ə)l/ v. & n. —v. **1** intr. & tr. make, or cause (a bell etc.) to make, a harsh metallic sound. **2** tr. irritate (the nerves etc.) by discordant sound or speech etc. —n. a harsh metallic sound. [ME f. OF jangler, of uncert. orig.]

Janglish /'dʒæŋglɪʃ/ n. = JAPLISH. [Japanese + English]

janissary var. of JANIZARY.

janitor /'dʒænɪtə(r)/ n. **1** a doorkeeper. **2** a caretaker of a building. □□ **janitorial** /-'tɔːrɪəl/ adj. [L f. janua door]

janizary /'dʒænɪzərɪ/ n. (also **janissary** /-sərɪ/) (pl. **-ies**) **1** hist. a member of the Turkish infantry forming the Sultan's guard in the 14th-19th c. **2** a devoted follower or supporter. [ult. f. Turk. yeniçeri f. yeni new + çeri troops]

jankers /'dʒæŋkəz/ n. Mil. sl. punishment for defaulters. [20th c.: orig. unkn.]

January /'dʒænjʊərɪ/ n. (pl. **-ies**) the first month of the year. [ME f. AF Jenever f. L Januarius (mensis) (month) of Janus the guardian god of doors and beginnings]

Jap /dʒæp/ n. & adj. colloq. often offens. = JAPANESE. [abbr.]

japan /dʒə'pæn/ n. & v. —n. **1** a hard usu. black varnish, esp. of a kind brought orig. from Japan. **2** work in a Japanese style. —v.tr. (**japanned, japanning**) **1** varnish with japan. **2** make black and glossy as with japan. [Japan in E. Asia]

Japanese /,dʒæpə'niːz/ n. & adj. —n. (pl. same) **1 a** a native or national of Japan. **b** a person of Japanese descent. **2** the language of Japan. —adj. of or relating to Japan, its people, or its language. □ **Japanese cedar** = CRYPTOMERIA. **Japanese print** a colour print from woodblocks. **Japanese quince** = JAPONICA.

jape /dʒeɪp/ n. & v. —n. a practical joke. —v.intr. play a joke. □□ **japery** n. [ME: orig. uncert.]

Japlish /'dʒæplɪʃ/ n. a blend of Japanese and English, used in Japan. [Japanese + English]

japonica /dʒə'pɒnɪkə/ n. any flowering shrub of the genus Chaenomeles, esp. C. speciosa, with round white, green, or yellow edible fruits and bright red flowers. Also called Japanese quince. [mod.L, fem. of japonicus Japanese]

jar¹ /dʒɑː(r)/ n. **1 a** a container of glass, earthenware, plastic, etc., usu. cylindrical. **b** the contents of this. **2** Brit. colloq. a glass of beer. □□ **jarful** n. (pl. **-fuls**). [F jarre f. Arab. jarra]

jar² /dʒɑː(r)/ v. & n. —v. (**jarred, jarring**) **1** intr. (often foll. by on) (of sound, words, manner, etc.) sound discordant or grating (on the nerves etc.). **2 a** tr. (foll. by against, on) strike or cause to strike with vibration or a grating sound. **b** intr. (of a body affected) vibrate gratingly. **3** tr. send a shock through (a part of the body) (the fall jarred his neck). **4** intr. (often foll. by with) (of an opinion, fact, etc.) be at variance; be in conflict or in dispute. —n. **1** a jarring sound or sensation. **2** a physical shock or jolt. **3** lack of harmony; disagreement. [16th c.: prob. imit.]

jar³ /dʒɑː(r)/ n. □ **on the jar** ajar. [late form of obs. char turn: see AJAR¹, CHAR²]

jardinière /,ʒɑːdɪ'njeə(r)/ n. **1** an ornamental pot or stand for the display of growing plants. **2** a dish of mixed vegetables. [F]

jargon¹ /'dʒɑːgən/ n. **1** words or expressions used by a particular group or profession (medical jargon). **2** barbarous or debased language. **3** gibberish. □□ **jargonic** /-'gɒnɪk/ adj. **jargonistic** /-'nɪstɪk/ adj. **jargonize** v.tr. & intr. (also **-ise**). [ME f. OF: orig. unkn.]

jargon² /'dʒɑːgən/ n. (also **jargoon** /dʒɑː'guːn/) a translucent, colourless, or smoky variety of zircon. [F f. It. giargone, prob. ult. formed as ZIRCON]

jargonelle /,dʒɑːgə'nel/ n. an early-ripening variety of pear. [F, dimin. of JARGON²]

jarl /jɑːl/ n. hist. a Norse or Danish chief. [ON, orig. = man of noble birth, rel. to EARL]

jarrah /'dʒærə/ n. **1** the Australian mahogany gumtree, Eucalyptus marginata. **2** the durable timber of this. [Aboriginal djarryl]

Jas. abbr. James (also in New Testament).

jasmine /'dʒæsmɪn, 'dʒæz-/ n. (also **jasmin**, **jessamin** /'dʒesəmɪn/, **jessamine** /'dʒesəmɪn/) any of various ornamental shrubs of the genus Jasminum usu. with white or yellow flowers. □ **jasmine tea** a tea perfumed with dried jasmine blossom. [F jasmin, jessemin f. Arab. yās(a)mīn f. Pers. yāsamīn]

jaspé /'dʒæspeɪ/ adj. like jasper; randomly coloured (esp. of cotton fabric). [F, past part. of jasper marble f. jaspe JASPER]

jasper /'dʒæspə(r)/ n. an opaque variety of quartz, usu. red, yellow, or brown in colour. [ME f. OF jasp(r)e f. L iaspis f. Gk, of oriental orig.]

Jat /dʒɑːt/ n. a member of an Indo-Aryan people widely distributed in NW India. [Hindi jāt]

jato /'dʒeɪtəʊ/ n. (pl. **-os**) Aeron. **1** jet-assisted take-off. **2** an auxiliary power unit providing extra thrust at take-off. [abbr.]

jaundice /'dʒɔːndɪs/ n. & v. —n. **1** Med. a condition with yellowing of the skin or whites of the eyes, often caused by obstruction of the bile duct or by liver disease. **2** disordered (esp. mental) vision. **3** envy. —v.tr. **1** affect with jaundice. **2** (esp. as **jaundiced** adj.) affect (a person) with envy, resentment, or jealousy. [ME iaunes f. OF jaunice yellowness f. jaune yellow]

jaunt /dʒɔːnt/ n. & v. —n. a short excursion for enjoyment. —v.intr. take a jaunt. □ **jaunting car** a light two-wheeled horse-drawn vehicle formerly used in Ireland. [16th c.: orig. unkn.]

jaunty /'dʒɔːntɪ/ adj. (**jauntier, jauntiest**) **1** cheerful and self-confident. **2** sprightly. □□ **jauntily** adv. **jauntiness** n. [earlier jentee f. F gentil GENTLE]

Java Man /'dʒɑːvə/ n. a prehistoric type of man whose remains were found in Java. [Java in Indonesia]

Javan /'dʒɑːv(ə)n/ n. & adj. = JAVANESE.

Javanese /,dʒɑːvə'niːz/ n. & adj. —n. (pl. same) **1 a** a native of Java in Indonesia. **b** a person of Javanese descent. **2** the language of Java. —adj. of or relating to Java, its people, or its language.

Java sparrow /'dʒɑːvə/ n. a finch, Padda oryzivora.

javelin /'dʒævəlɪn, -vlɪn/ n. **1** a light spear thrown in a competitive sport or as a weapon. **2** the athletic event or sport of throwing the javelin. [F javeline, javelot f. Gallo-Roman gabalottus]

jaw /dʒɔː/ n. & v. —n. **1 a** each of the upper and lower bony structures in vertebrates forming the framework of the mouth and containing the teeth. **b** the parts of certain invertebrates used for the ingestion of food. **2 a** (in pl.) the mouth with its bones and teeth. **b** the narrow mouth of a valley, channel, etc. **c** the gripping parts of a tool or machine. **d** gripping-power (jaws of death). **3** colloq. **a** talkativeness; tedious talk (hold your jaw). **b** a sermonizing talk; a lecture. —v. colloq. **1** intr. speak esp. at tedious length. **2** tr. **a** persuade by talking. **b** admonish or lecture. □ **jaw-breaker** colloq. a word that is very long or hard to pronounce. [ME f. OF joe cheek, jaw, of uncert. orig.]

jawbone /'dʒɔːbəʊn/ n. **1** each of the two bones forming the lower jaw in most mammals. **2** these two combined into one in other mammals.

jay /dʒeɪ/ n. **1 a** a noisy chattering European bird, Garrulus glandarius, with vivid pinkish-brown, blue, black, and white plumage. **b** any other bird of the subfamily Garrulinae. **2** a person who chatters impertinently. [ME f. OF f. LL gaius, gaia, perh. f. L praenomen Gaius: cf. jackdaw, robin]

jaywalk /ˈdʒeɪwɔːk/ v.intr. cross or walk in the street or road without regard for traffic. □□**jaywalker** n.

jazz /dʒæz/ n. & v. —n. **1** music of US Negro origin characterized by improvisation, syncopation, and usu. a regular or forceful rhythm. **2** sl. pretentious talk or behaviour, nonsensical stuff (all that jazz). —v.intr. play or dance to jazz. □**jazz up** brighten or enliven. □□**jazzer** n. [20th c.: orig. uncert.]

jazzman /ˈdʒæzmæn/ n. (pl. -men) a jazz-player.

jazzy /ˈdʒæzɪ/ adj. (**jazzier**, **jazziest**) **1** of or like jazz. **2** vivid, unrestrained, showy. □□**jazzily** adv. **jazziness** n.

JCB /ˌdʒeɪsiːˈbiː/ n. propr. a type of mechanical excavator with a shovel at the front and a digging arm at the rear. [J. C. Bamford, the makers]

JCL abbr. Computing job-control language.

JCR abbr. Brit. Junior Common (or Combination) Room.

jealous /ˈdʒeləs/ adj. **1** (often foll. by of) fiercely protective (of rights etc.). **2** afraid, suspicious, or resentful of rivalry in love or affection. **3** (often foll. by of) envious or resentful (of a person or a person's advantages etc.). **4** (of God) intolerant of disloyalty. **5** (of inquiry, supervision, etc.) vigilant. □□**jealously** adv. [ME f. OF gelos f. med.L zelosus ZEALOUS]

jealousy /ˈdʒeləsɪ/ n. (pl. -ies) **1** a jealous state or feeling. **2** an instance of this. [ME f. OF gelosie (as JEALOUS)]

jean /dʒiːn/ n. twilled cotton cloth. [ME, attrib. use of Jene f. OF Janne f. med.L Janua Genoa]

jeans /dʒiːnz/ n.pl. trousers made of jean or (more usually) denim, for informal wear.

Jeep /dʒiːp/ n. propr. a small sturdy esp. military motor vehicle with four-wheel drive. [orig. US, f. GP = general purposes, infl. by 'Eugene the Jeep', an animal in a comic strip]

jeepers /ˈdʒiːpəz/ int. US sl. expressing surprise etc. [corrupt. of Jesus]

jeer /dʒɪə(r)/ v. & n. —v. **1** intr. (usu. foll. by at) scoff derisively. **2** tr. scoff at; deride. —n. a scoff or taunt. □□**jeeringly** adv. [16th c.: orig. unkn.]

Jeez /dʒiːz/ int. sl. a mild expression of surprise, discovery, etc. (cf. GEE¹). [abbr. of JESUS]

jehad var. of JIHAD.

Jehovah /dʒəˈhəʊvə/ n. the Hebrew name of God in the Old Testament. □**Jehovah's Witness** a member of a millenarian Christian sect rejecting the supremacy of the State and religious institutions over personal conscience, faith, etc. [med.L Iehoua(h) f. Heb. YHVH (with the vowels of adonai 'my lord' included: see YAHWEH]

Jehovist /dʒəˈhəʊvɪst/ n. = YAHWIST.

jejune /dʒɪˈdʒuːn/ adj. **1** intellectually unsatisfying; shallow. **2** puerile. **3** (of ideas, writings, etc.) meagre, scanty; dry and uninteresting. **4** (of the land) barren, poor. □□**jejunely** adv. **jejuneness** n. [orig. = fasting, f. L jejunus]

jejunum /dʒɪˈdʒuːnəm/ n. Anat. the part of the small intestine between the duodenum and ileum. [L, neut. of jejunus fasting]

Jekyll and Hyde /ˌdʒekɪl ənd ˈhaɪd/ n. a person alternately displaying opposing good and evil personalities. [R. L. Stevenson's story The Strange Case of Dr Jekyll and Mr Hyde]

jell /dʒel/ v.intr. colloq. **1 a** set as a jelly. **b** (of ideas etc.) take a definite form. **2** (of two different things) cohere. [back-form. f. JELLY]

jellaba var. of DJELLABA.

jellify /ˈdʒelɪfaɪ/ v.tr. & intr. (-ies, -ied) turn into jelly; make or become like jelly. □□**jellification** /-fɪˈkeɪʃ(ə)n/ n.

jelly /ˈdʒelɪ/ n. & v. —n. (pl. -ies) **1 a** a soft stiffish semi-transparent preparation of boiled sugar and fruit-juice or milk etc., often cooled in a mould and eaten as a dessert. **b** a similar preparation of fruit-juice etc. for use as a jam or a condiment (redcurrant jelly). **c** a similar preparation derived from meat, bones, etc., and gelatin (marrowbone jelly). **2** any substance of a similar consistency. **3** Brit. sl. gelignite (cf. GELLY). —v. (-ies, -ied) **1** intr. & tr. set or cause to set as a jelly, congeal. **2** tr. set (food) in a jelly (jellied eels). □**jelly baby** Brit. a jelly-like sweet in the stylized shape of a baby. **jelly bag** a bag for straining juice for jelly. **jelly bean** a jelly-like sweet in the shape of a bean. □□**jelly-like** adj. [ME f. OF gelee frost, jelly, f. Rmc gelata f. L gelare freeze f. gelu frost]

jellyfish /ˈdʒelɪfɪʃ/ n. (pl. usu. same) **1** a marine coelenterate of the class Scyphozoa having an umbrella-shaped jelly-like body and stinging tentacles. **2** colloq. a feeble person.

jemmy /ˈdʒemɪ/ n. & v. (US **jimmi** /ˈdʒɪmɪ/) —n. (pl. -ies or **jimmis**) a burglar's short crowbar, usu. made in sections. —v.tr. (-ies, -ied) force open with a jemmy. [pet-form of the name James]

je ne sais quoi /ʒə nə seɪ ˈkwɑː, dʒə-/ n. an indefinable something. [F, = I do not know what]

jennet /ˈdʒenɪt/ n. a small Spanish horse. [F genet f. Sp. jinete light horseman f. Arab. zenāta Berber tribe famous as horsemen]

jenny /ˈdʒenɪ/ n. (pl. -ies) **1** hist. = spinning-jenny. **2** a female donkey or ass. **3** a locomotive crane. □**jenny-wren** a popular name for a female wren. [pet-form of the name Janet]

jeopardize /ˈdʒepədaɪz/ v.tr. (also -ise) endanger; put into jeopardy.

jeopardy /ˈdʒepədɪ/ n. **1** danger, esp. of severe harm or loss. **2** Law danger resulting from being on trial for a criminal offence. [ME iuparti f. OF ieu parti divided (i.e. even) game, f. L jocus game + partitus past part. of partire divide f. pars partis part]

Jer. abbr. Jeremiah (Old Testament).

jerbil var. of GERBIL.

jerboa /dʒɜːˈbəʊə/ n. any small desert rodent of the family Dipodidae with long hind legs and the ability to make large jumps. [mod.L f. Arab. yarbū' flesh of loins, jerboa]

jeremiad /ˌdʒerɪˈmaɪæd/ n. a doleful complaint or lamentation; a list of woes. [F jérémiade f. Jérémie Jeremiah f. eccl.L Jeremias, with ref. to the Lamentations of Jeremiah in the Old Testament]

Jeremiah /ˌdʒerɪˈmaɪə/ n. a dismal prophet, a denouncer of the times. [with ref. to Jeremiah (as JEREMIAD)]

jerk¹ /dʒɜːk/ n. & v. —n. **1** a sharp sudden pull, twist, twitch, start, etc. **2** a spasmodic muscular twitch. **3** (in pl.) Brit. colloq. exercises (physical jerks). **4** sl. a fool; a stupid person. —v. **1** intr. move with a jerk. **2** tr. pull, thrust, twist, etc., with a jerk. **3** tr. throw with a suddenly arrested motion. **4** tr. Weight-lifting raise (a weight) from shoulder-level to above the head. □**jerk off** coarse sl. masturbate. ¶ Usually considered a taboo use. □□**jerker** n. [16th c.: perh. imit.]

jerk² /dʒɜːk/ v.tr. cure (beef) by cutting it in long slices and drying it in the sun. [Amer. Sp. charquear f. charqui f. Quechua echarqui dried flesh]

jerkin /ˈdʒɜːkɪn/ n. **1** a sleeveless jacket. **2** hist. a man's close-fitting jacket, often of leather. [16th c.: orig. unkn.]

jerky /ˈdʒɜːkɪ/ adj. (**jerkier**, **jerkiest**) **1** having sudden abrupt movements. **2** spasmodic. □□**jerkily** adv. **jerkiness** n.

jeroboam /ˌdʒerəˈbəʊəm/ n. a wine bottle of 4-12 times the ordinary size. [Jeroboam king of Israel (1 Kings 11:28, 14:16)]

Jerry /ˈdʒerɪ/ n. (pl. -ies) Brit. sl. **1** a German (esp. in military contexts). **2** the Germans collectively. [prob. alt. of German]

jerry /ˈdʒerɪ/ n. (pl. -ies) Brit. sl. a chamber-pot.

jerry-builder /ˈdʒerɪˌbɪldə(r)/ n. a builder of unsubstantial houses with poor-quality materials. □□ **jerry-building** n. **jerry-built** adj.

jerrycan /ˈdʒerɪˌkæn/ n. (also **jerrican**) a kind of (orig. German) petrol- or water-can. [JERRY + CAN²]

jerrymander var. of GERRYMANDER.

jersey /'dʒɜːzɪ/ n. (pl. **-eys**) **1 a** a knitted usu. woollen pullover or similar garment. **b** a plain-knitted (orig. woollen) fabric. **2 (Jersey)** a light brown dairy cow from Jersey. [*Jersey*, largest of the Channel Islands]

Jerusalem artichoke /dʒəˈruːsələm/ n. **1** a species of sunflower, *Helianthus tuberosus*, with edible underground tubers. **2** this tuber used as a vegetable. [corrupt. of It. *girasole* sunflower]

jess /dʒes/ n. & v. —n. a short strap of leather, silk, etc., put round the leg of a hawk in falconry. —v.tr. put jesses on (a hawk etc.). [ME *ges* f. OF *ges*, *get* ult. f. L *jactus* a throw f. *jacere jact-* to throw]

jessamin (also **jessamine**) var. of JASMINE.

jest /dʒest/ n. & v. —n. **1 a** a joke. **b** fun. **2 a** raillery, banter. **b** an object of derision (*a standing jest*). —v.intr. **1** joke; make jests. **2** fool about; play or act triflingly. □**in jest** in fun. □□**jestful** adj. [orig. = exploit, f. OF *geste* f. L *gesta* neut. pl. past part. of *gerere* do]

jester /'dʒestə(r)/ n. a professional joker or 'fool' at a medieval court etc., traditionally wearing a cap and bells and carrying a 'sceptre'.

Jesuit /'dʒezjʊɪt/ n. a member of the Society of Jesus, a Roman Catholic order founded by St Ignatius Loyola and others in 1534. [F *jésuite* or mod.L *Jesuita* f. *Jesus*: see JESUS]

Jesuitical /ˌdʒezjʊˈɪtɪk(ə)l/ adj. **1** of or concerning the Jesuits. **2** often *offens*. dissembling or equivocating, in the manner once associated with Jesuits. □□**Jesuitically** adv.

Jesus /'dʒiːzəs/ int. colloq. an exclamation of surprise, dismay, etc. [name of the founder of the Christian religion d. *c.* AD 30]

jet¹ /dʒet/ n. & v. —n. **1** a stream of water, steam, gas, flame, etc. shot out esp. from a small opening. **2** a spout or nozzle for emitting water etc. in this way. **3 a** a jet engine. **b** an aircraft powered by one or more jet engines. —v. (**jetted, jetting**) **1** intr. spurt out in jets. **2** tr. & intr. colloq. send or travel by jet plane. □**jet engine** an engine using jet propulsion for forward thrust, esp. of an aircraft. **jet lag** extreme tiredness and other bodily effects felt after a long flight involving marked differences of local time. **jet-propelled 1** having jet propulsion. **2** (of a person etc.) very fast. **jet propulsion** propulsion by the backward ejection of a high-speed jet of gas etc. **jet set** colloq. wealthy people frequently travelling by air, esp. for pleasure. **jet-setter** colloq. a member of the jet set. **jet stream 1** a narrow current of very strong winds encircling the globe several miles above the earth. **2** the stream from a jet engine. [earlier as verb (in sense 1): F *jeter* throw ult. f. L *jactare* frequent. of *jacere jact-* throw]

jet² /dʒet/ n. **1 a** a hard black variety of lignite capable of being carved and highly polished. **b** (*attrib.*) made of this. **2** (in full **jet-black**) a deep glossy black colour. [ME f. AF *geet*, OF *jaiet* f. L *gagates* f. Gk *gagatēs* f. *Gagai* in Asia Minor]

jeté /ʒeˈteɪ/ n. Ballet a spring or leap with one leg forward and the other stretched backwards. [F, past part. of *jeter* throw: see JET¹]

jetsam /'dʒetsəm/ n. discarded material washed ashore, esp. that thrown overboard to lighten a ship etc. (cf. FLOTSAM). [contr. of JETTISON]

jettison /'dʒetɪs(ə)n, -z(ə)n/ v. & n. —v.tr. **1 a** throw (esp. heavy material) overboard to lighten a ship, hot-air balloon, etc. **b** drop (goods) from an aircraft. **2** abandon; get rid of (something no longer wanted). —n. the act of jettisoning. [ME f. AF *getteson*, OF *getaison* f. L *jactatio -onis* f. *jactare* throw: see JET¹]

jetton /'dʒet(ə)n/ n. a counter with a stamped or engraved design esp. for insertion like a coin to operate a machine etc. [F *jeton* f. *jeter* throw, add up accounts: see JET¹]

jetty /'dʒetɪ/ n. (pl. **-ies**) **1** a pier or breakwater constructed to protect or defend a harbour, coast, etc. **2** a landing-pier. [ME f. OF *jetee*, fem. past part. of *jeter* throw: see JET¹]

jeu d'esprit /ˌʒɜː deˈspriː/ n. (pl. **jeux d'esprit** pronunc. same) a witty or humorous (usu. literary) trifle. [F, = game of the spirit]

jeunesse dorée /ˌʒɜːnes ˈdɔːreɪ/ n. = gilded youth (see GILD¹). [F]

Jew /dʒuː/ n. & v. —n. **1** a person of Hebrew descent or whose religion is Judaism. **2** sl. offens. (as a stereotype) a person considered to be parsimonious or to drive a hard bargain in trading. ¶ The stereotype, which is now deeply offensive, arose from historical associations of Jews as moneylenders in medieval England. —v.tr. (**jew**) sl. offens. get a financial advantage over. □**jew's harp** a small lyre-shaped musical instrument held between the teeth and struck with the finger. [ME f. OF *giu* f. L *judaeus* f. Gk *ioudaios* ult. f. Heb. *yᵉhûḏî* f. *yᵉhûḏâh* Judah]

jewel /'dʒuːəl/ n. & v. —n. **1 a** a precious stone. **b** this as used for its hardness as a bearing in watchmaking. **2** a personal ornament containing a jewel or jewels. **3** a precious person or thing. —v.tr. (**jewelled, jewelling**; US **jeweled, jeweling**) **1** (esp. as **jewelled** adj.) adorn or set with jewels. **2** (in watchmaking) set with jewels. □**jewel-fish** a scarlet and green tropical cichlid fish, *Hemichromis bimaculatus*. □□**jewelly** adj. [ME f. AF *juel, jeuel*, OF *joel*, of uncert. orig.]

jeweller /'dʒuːələ(r)/ n. (US **jeweler**) a maker of or dealer in jewels or jewellery. □**jeweller's rouge** finely ground rouge for polishing. [ME f. AF *jueler*, OF *juelier* (as JEWEL)]

jewellery /'dʒuːəlrɪ/ n. (also **jewelry** /'dʒuːəlrɪ/) jewels or other ornamental objects, esp. for personal adornment, regarded collectively. [ME f. OF *juelerie* and f. JEWEL, JEWELLER]

Jewess /'dʒuːes/ n. a female Jew.

jewfish /'dʒuːfɪʃ/ n. **1** a grouper, *Epinephelus itajara*, of N. American, Atlantic, and Pacific coasts. **2** any of various large Australian fish used as food, esp. the mulloway.

Jewish /'dʒuːɪʃ/ adj. **1** of or relating to Jews. **2** of Judaism. □□**Jewishly** adv. **Jewishness** n.

Jewry /'dʒʊərɪ/ n. (pl. **-ies**) **1** Jews collectively. **2** hist. a Jews' quarter in a town etc. [ME f. AF *juerie*, OF *juierie* (as JEW)]

Jezebel /'dʒezəˌbel/ n. a shameless or immoral woman. [*Jezebel*, wife of Ahab in the Old Testament (1 Kings 16, 19, 21)]

jib¹ /dʒɪb/ n. & v. —n. **1** a triangular staysail from the outer end of the jib-boom to the top of the foremast or from the bowsprit to the masthead. **2** the projecting arm of a crane. —v.tr. & intr. (**jibbed, jibbing**) (of a sail etc.) pull or swing round from one side of the ship to the other; gybe. □**jib-boom** a spar run out from the end of the bowsprit. [17th c.: orig. unkn.]

jib² /dʒɪb/ v.intr. (**jibbed, jibbing**) **1 a** (of an animal, esp. a horse) stop and refuse to go on; move backwards or sideways instead of going on. **b** (of a person) refuse to continue. **2** (foll. by *at*) show aversion to (a person or course of action). □□**jibber** n. [19th c.: orig. unkn.]

jibba /'dʒɪbə/ n. (also **jibbah**) a long coat worn by Muslim men. [Egypt. var. of Arab. *jubba*]

jibe¹ var. of GIBE.

jibe² US var. of GYBE.

jibe³ /dʒaɪb/ v.intr. (usu. foll. by *with*) US colloq. agree; be in accord. [19th c.: orig. unkn.]

jiff /dʒɪf/ n. (also **jiffy**, pl. **-ies**) colloq. a short time; a moment (*in a jiffy; half a jiff*). [18th c.: orig. unkn.]

Jiffy bag /'dʒɪfɪ/ n. propr. a type of padded envelope for postal use.

jig /dʒɪg/ n. & v. —n. **1 a** a lively dance with leaping movements. **b** the music for this, usu. in triple time. **2** a device that holds a piece of work and guides the tools operating on it. —v. (**jigged, jigging**) **1** intr. dance a jig. **2** tr. & intr. move quickly and jerkily up and down. **3** *tr.* work on or equip with a jig or jigs. □**jig about** fidget. [16th c.: orig. unkn.]

jigger[1] /'dʒɪgə(r)/ *n.* **1** *Naut.* **a** a small tackle consisting of a double and single block with a rope. **b** a small sail at the stern. **c** a small smack having this. **2** *sl.* a gadget. **3** *Golf* an iron club with a narrow face. **4** *Billiards colloq.* a cue-rest. **5 a** a measure of spirits etc. **b** a small glass holding this. **6** a person or thing that jigs.

jigger[2] /'dʒɪgə(r)/ *n.* **1** = CHIGOE. **2** *US* = CHIGGER 2. [corrupt.]

jiggered /'dʒɪgəd/ *adj. colloq.* (as a mild oath) confounded (*I'll be jiggered*). [euphem.]

jiggery-pokery /ˌdʒɪgərɪ'pəʊkərɪ/ *n. Brit. colloq.* deceitful or dishonest dealing, trickery. [cf. Sc. *joukery-pawkery* f. *jouk* dodge, skulk]

jiggle /'dʒɪg(ə)l/ *v.* (often foll. by *about* etc.) **1** *tr.* shake lightly; rock jerkily. **2** *intr.* fidget. □□**jiggly** *adj.* [JIG or JOGGLE[1]]

jigsaw /'dʒɪgsɔː/ *n.* **1 a** (in full **jigsaw puzzle**) a puzzle consisting of a picture on board or wood etc. cut into irregular interlocking pieces to be reassembled. **b** a mental puzzle resolvable by assembling various pieces of information. **2** a machine saw with a fine blade enabling it to cut curved lines in a sheet of wood, metal, etc.

jihad /dʒɪ'hæd, -'hɑːd/ *n.* (also **jehad**) a holy war undertaken by Muslims against unbelievers. [Arab. *jihād*]

jill var. of GILL[4].

jilt /dʒɪlt/ *v. & n.* —*v.tr.* abruptly reject or abandon (a lover etc.). —*n.* a person (esp. a woman) who jilts a lover. [17th c.: orig. unkn.]

Jim Crow /dʒɪm 'krəʊ/ *n. US* **1** the practice of segregating Blacks. **2** *offens.* a Black. **3** an implement for straightening iron bars or bending rails by screw pressure. □□ **Jim Crowism** *n.* (in sense 1). [nickname]

jim-jams /'dʒɪmdʒæmz/ *n.pl.* **1** *sl.* = *delirium tremens*. **2** *colloq.* a fit of depression or nervousness. [fanciful redupl.]

jimmy *US* var. of JEMMY.

jimson /'dʒɪms(ə)n/ *n.* (in full **jimson weed**) *US* a highly poisonous tall weed, *Datura stramonium*, with large trumpet-shaped flowers. [*Jamestown* in Virginia]

jingle /'dʒɪŋg(ə)l/ *n. & v.* —*n.* **1** a mixed noise as of bells or light metal objects being shaken together. **2 a** a repetition of the same sound in words, esp. as an aid to memory or to attract attention. **b** a short verse of this kind used in advertising etc. —*v.* **1** *intr. & tr.* make or cause to make a jingling sound. **2** *intr.* (of writing) be full of alliterations, rhymes, etc. □□ **jingly** *adj.* (**jinglier**, **jingliest**). [ME: imit.]

jingo /'dʒɪŋgəʊ/ *n.* (*pl.* **-oes**) a supporter of policy favouring war; a blustering patriot. □**by jingo!** a mild oath. □□**jingoism** *n.* **jingoist** *n.* **jingoistic** /-'ɪstɪk/ *adj.* [17th c.: orig. a conjuror's word: polit. sense from use of *by jingo* in a popular song, then applied to patriots]

jink /dʒɪŋk/ *v. & n.* —*v.* **1** *intr.* move elusively; dodge. **2** *tr.* elude by dodging. —*n.* an act of dodging or eluding. [orig. Sc.: prob. imit. of nimble motion]

jinnee /dʒɪ'niː/ *n.* (also **jinn**, **djinn** /dʒɪn/) (*pl.* **jinn** or **djinn**) (in Muslim mythology) an intelligent being lower than the angels, able to appear in human and animal forms, and having power over people. [Arab. *jinnī*, pl. *jinn*: cf. GENIE]

jinx /dʒɪŋks/ *n. & v. colloq.* —*n.* a person or thing that seems to cause bad luck. —*v.tr.* (often in *passive*) subject (a person) to an unlucky force. [perh. var. of *jynx* wryneck, charm]

jitter /'dʒɪtə(r)/ *n. & v. colloq.* —*n.* (**the jitters**) extreme nervousness. —*v.intr.* be nervous; act nervously. □□**jittery** *adj.* **jitteriness** *n.* [20th c.: orig. unkn.]

jitterbug /'dʒɪtəbʌg/ *n. & v.* —*n.* **1** a nervous person. **2** *hist.* **a** a fast popular dance. **b** a person fond of

dancing this. —*v.intr.* (**-bugged**, **-bugging**) dance the jitterbug.

jiu-jitsu var. of JU-JITSU.

jive /dʒaɪv/ *n. & v.* —*n.* **1** a jerky lively style of dance esp. popular in the 1950s. **2** music for this. —*v.intr.* **1** dance the jive. **2** play jive music. □□**jiver** *n.* [20th c.: orig. uncert.]

jizz /dʒɪz/ *n.* the characteristic impression given by an animal or plant. [20th c.: orig. unkn.]

Jnr. *abbr.* Junior.

jo /dʒəʊ/ *n.* (*pl.* **joes**) *Sc.* a sweetheart or beloved. [var. of JOY]

job[1] /dʒɒb/ *n. & v.* —*n.* **1** a piece of work, esp. one done for hire or profit. **2** a paid position of employment. **3** *colloq.* anything one has to do. **4** *colloq.* a difficult task (*had a job to find them*). **5** a product of work, esp. if well done. **6** *Computing* an item of work regarded separately. **7** *sl.* a crime, esp. a robbery. **8** a transaction in which private advantage prevails over duty or public interest. **9** a state of affairs or set of circumstances (*is a bad job*). —*v.* (**jobbed**, **jobbing**) **1** *intr.* do jobs; do piece-work. **2 a** *intr.* deal in stocks. **b** *tr.* buy and sell (stocks or goods) as a middleman. **3 a** *intr.* turn a position of trust to private advantage. **b** *tr.* deal corruptly with (a matter). **4** *tr. US sl.* swindle. □**job-control language** *Computing* a language enabling the user to determine the tasks to be undertaken by the operating system. **job-hunt** *colloq.* seek employment. **job lot** a miscellaneous group of articles, esp. bought together. **jobs for the boys** *colloq.* profitable situations etc. to reward one's supporters. **job-sharing** an arrangement by which a full-time job is done jointly by several part-time employees who share the remuneration. **just the job** *colloq.* exactly what is wanted. **make a job** (or **good job**) **of** do thoroughly or successfully. **on the job** *colloq.* **1** at work; in the course of doing a piece of work. **2** engaged in sexual intercourse. **out of a job** unemployed. [16th c.: orig. unkn.]

job[2] /dʒɒb/ *v. & n.* —*v.* (**jobbed**, **jobbing**) **1** *tr.* prod; stab slightly. **2** *intr.* (foll. by *at*) thrust. —*n.* a prod or thrust; a jerk at a horse's bit. [ME, app. imit.: cf. JAB]

jobber /'dʒɒbə(r)/ *n.* **1** *Brit.* a principal or wholesaler dealing on the Stock Exchange. ¶ Up to Oct. 1986 permitted to deal only with brokers, not directly with the public. From Oct. 1986 the name has ceased to be in official use (see BROKER 2). **2** *US* **a** a wholesaler. **b** *derog.* a broker (see BROKER 2). **3** a person who jobs. [JOB[1]]

jobbery /'dʒɒbərɪ/ *n.* corrupt dealing.

jobbing /'dʒɒbɪŋ/ *adj.* working on separate or occasional jobs (esp. of a computer, gardener, or printer).

jobcentre /'dʒɒbˌsentə(r)/ *n. Brit.* any of several government offices displaying information about available jobs.

jobless /'dʒɒblɪs/ *adj.* without a job; unemployed. □□ **joblessness** *n.*

Job's comforter /dʒəʊbz/ *n.* a person who under the guise of comforting aggravates distress. [the patriarch *Job* in the Old Testament (Job 16:2)]

jobsheet /'dʒɒbʃiːt/ *n.* a sheet for recording details of jobs done.

Job's tears /dʒəʊbz/ *n.pl.* the seeds of a grass, *Coix lacryma-jobi*, used as beads. [the patriarch *Job* in the Old Testament]

jobwork /'dʒɒbwɜːk/ *n.* work done and paid for by the job.

Jock /dʒɒk/ *n. sl.* a Scotsman. [Sc. form of the name *Jack* (see JACK[1])]

jock /dʒɒk/ *n. colloq.* a jockey. [abbr.]

jockey /'dʒɒkɪ/ *n. & v.* —*n.* (*pl.* **-eys**) a rider in horse-races, esp. a professional one. —*v.* (**-eys**, **-eyed**) **1** *tr.* **a** trick or cheat (a person). **b** outwit. **2** *tr.* (foll. by *away*, *out*, *in*, etc.) draw (a person) by trickery. **3** *intr.* cheat. □**jockey cap** a cap with a long peak, as worn by jockeys. **jockey for position** try to gain an advantageous position esp. by skilful manœuvring or unfair action. □□**jockeydom** *n*. **jockeyship** *n*. [dimin. of JOCK]

jockstrap /'dʒɒkstræp/ *n*. a support or protection for the male genitals, worn esp. by sportsmen. [sl. *jock* genitals + STRAP]

jocose /dʒə'kəʊs/ *adj*. **1** playful in style. **2** fond of joking, jocular. □□**jocosely** *adv*. **jocoseness** *n*. **jocosity** /-'kɒsɪtɪ/ *n*. (*pl.* -ies). [L *jocosus* f. *jocus* jest]

jocular /'dʒɒkjʊlə(r)/ *adj*. **1** merry; fond of joking. **2** of the nature of a joke; humorous. □□**jocularity** /-'lærɪtɪ/ *n*. (*pl.* -ies). **jocularly** *adv*. [L *jocularis* f. *joculus* dimin. of *jocus* jest]

jocund /'dʒɒkənd/ *adj*. *literary* merry, cheerful, sprightly. □□**jocundity** /dʒə'kʌndɪtɪ/ *n*. (*pl.* -ies). **jocundly** *adv*. [ME f. OF f. L *jocundus, jucundus* f. *juvare* delight]

jodhpurs /'dʒɒdpəz/ *n.pl.* long breeches for riding etc., close-fitting from the knee to the ankle. [*Jodhpur* in India]

Joe Bloggs /dʒəʊ 'blɒgz/ *n. Brit. colloq.* a hypothetical average man.

Joe Blow /dʒəʊ 'bləʊ/ *n. US colloq.* = JOE BLOGGS.

joey /'dʒəʊɪ/ *n.* (*pl.* -eys) *Austral.* **1** a young kangaroo. **2** a young animal. [Aboriginal *joè*]

jog /dʒɒg/ *v. & n.* —*v.* (**jogged, jogging**) **1** *intr.* run at a slow pace, esp. as physical exercise. **2** *intr.* (of a horse) move at a jogtrot. **3** *intr.* (often foll. by *on, along*) proceed laboriously; trudge. **4** *intr.* go on one's way. **5** *intr.* proceed; get through the time (*we must jog on somehow*). **6** *intr.* move up and down with an unsteady motion. **7** *tr.* nudge (a person), esp. to arouse attention. **8** *tr.* shake with a push or jerk. **9** *tr.* stimulate (a person's or one's own memory). —*n.* **1** a shake, push, or nudge. **2** a slow walk or trot. [ME: app. imit.]

jogger /'dʒɒgə(r)/ *n.* a person who jogs, esp. one who runs for physical exercise.

joggle¹ /'dʒɒg(ə)l/ *v. & n.* —*v.tr. & intr.* shake or move by or as if by repeated jerks. —*n.* **1** a slight shake. **2** the act or action of joggling. [frequent. of JOG]

joggle² /'dʒɒg(ə)l/ *n. & v.* —*n.* **1** a joint of two pieces of stone or timber, contrived to prevent their sliding on one another. **2** a notch in one of the two pieces, a projection in the other, or a small piece let in between the two, for this purpose. —*v.tr.* join with a joggle. [perh. f. *jog* = JAG¹]

jogtrot /'dʒɒgtrɒt/ *n.* **1** a slow regular trot. **2** a monotonous progression.

john /dʒɒn/ *n. US sl.* a lavatory. [the name *John*]

John Bull /dʒɒn 'bʊl/ *n.* a personification of England or the typical Englishman. [the name of a character repr. the English nation in J. Arbuthnot's satire *Law is a Bottomless Pit* (1712)]

John Dory /dʒɒn 'dɔːrɪ/ *n.* (*pl.* -ies) a European marine fish, *Zeus faber*, with a laterally flattened body and a black spot on each side.

johnny /'dʒɒnɪ/ *n.* (*pl.* -ies) *Brit. colloq.* a fellow; a man. □**johnny-come-lately** *colloq.* a recently arrived person. [familiar form of the name *John*]

Johnsonian /dʒɒn'səʊnɪən/ *adj.* **1** of or relating to Samuel Johnson, English man of letters and lexicographer (d. 1784). **2** typical of his style of writing.

joie de vivre /ˌʒwɑː də 'viːvrə/ *n.* a feeling of healthy and exuberant enjoyment of life. [F, = joy of living]

join /dʒɔɪn/ *v. & n.* —*v.* **1** *tr.* (often foll. by *to, together*) put together; fasten, unite (one thing or person to another or several together). **2** *tr.* connect (points) by a line etc. **3** *tr.* become a member of (an association, society, organization, etc.). **4** *tr.* take one's place with or in (a company, group, procession, etc.). **5** *tr.* **a** come into the company of (a person). **b** (foll. by *in*) take part with (others) in an activity etc. (*joined me in condemnation of the outrage*). **c** (foll. by *for*) share the company of for a specified occasion

(*may I join you for lunch?*). **6** *intr.* (often foll. by *with, to*) come together; be united. **7** *intr.* (often foll. by *in*) take part with others in an activity etc. **8** *tr.* be or become connected or continuous with (*the Inn joins the Danube at Passau*). —*n.* a point, line, or surface at which two or more things are joined. □**join battle** begin fighting. **join forces** combine efforts. **join hands 1 a** clasp each other's hands. **b** clasp one's hands together. **2** combine in an action or enterprise. **join up 1** enlist for military service. **-2** (often foll. by *with*) unite, connect. □□**joinable** *adj*. [ME f. OF *joindre* (stem *joign-*) f. L *jungere junct-* join: cf. YOKE]

joinder /'dʒɔɪndə(r)/ *n. Law* the act of bringing together. [AF f. OF *joindre* to join]

joiner /'dʒɔɪnə(r)/ *n.* **1** a person who makes furniture and light woodwork. **2** *colloq.* a person who readily joins societies etc. □□**joinery** *n.* (in sense 1). [ME f. AF *joignour*, OF *joigneor* (as JOIN)]

joint /dʒɔɪnt/ *n., adj., & v.* —*n.* **1 a** a place at which two things are joined together. **b** a point at which, or a contrivance by which, two parts of an artificial structure are joined. **2** a structure in an animal body by which two bones are fitted together. **3 a** any of the parts into which an animal carcass is divided for food. **b** any of the parts of which a body is made up. **4** *sl.* a place of meeting for drinking etc. **5** *sl.* a marijuana cigarette. **6** the part of a stem from which a leaf or branch grows. **7** a piece of flexible material forming the hinge of a book-cover. **8** *Geol.* a fissure in a mass of rock. —*adj.* **1** held or done by, or belonging to, two or more persons etc. in conjunction (*a joint mortgage; joint action*). **2** sharing with another in some action, state, etc. (*joint author; joint favourite*). —*v.tr.* **1** connect by joints. **2** divide (a body or member) at a joint or into joints. **3** fill up the joints of (masonry etc.) with mortar etc.; trim the surface of (a mortar joint). **4** prepare (a board etc.) for being joined to another by planing its edge. □**joint account** a bank account held by more than one person, each of whom has the right to deposit and withdraw funds. **joint and several** (of a bond etc.) signed by more than one person, of whom each is liable for the whole sum. **joint stock** capital held jointly; a common fund. **joint-stock company** one formed on the basis of a joint stock. **out of joint 1** (of a bone) dislocated. **2** out of order. □□**jointless** *adj*. **jointly** *adv*. [ME f. OF, past part. of *joindre* JOIN]

jointer /'dʒɔɪntə(r)/ *n.* **1 a** a plane for jointing. **b** a tool for jointing or pointing masonry. **2** a worker employed in jointing wires, pipes, etc.

jointress /'dʒɔɪntrɪs/ *n.* a widow who holds a jointure. [obs. *jointer* joint possessor]

jointure /'dʒɔɪntʃə(r)/ *n. & v.* —*n.* an estate settled on a wife for the period during which she survives her husband. —*v.tr.* provide (a wife) with a jointure. [ME f. OF f. L *junctura* (as JOIN)]

joist /dʒɔɪst/ *n.* each of a series of parallel supporting beams of timber, steel, etc., used in floors, ceilings, etc. □□**joisted** *adj*. [ME f. OF *giste* ult. f. L *jacēre* lie]

jojoba /həʊ'həʊbə/ *n.* a plant, *Simmondsia chinensis*, with seeds yielding an oily extract used in cosmetics etc. [Mex. Sp.]

joke /dʒəʊk/ *n. & v.* —*n.* **1 a** a thing said or done to excite laughter. **b** a witticism or jest. **2** a ridiculous thing, person, or circumstance. —*v.* **1** *intr.* make jokes. **2** *tr.* poke fun at; banter. □**no joke** *colloq.* a serious matter. □□**jokingly** *adv*. **joky** *adj*. (also **jokey**). **jokily** *adv*. **jokiness** *n*. [17th c. (*joque*), orig. sl.: perh. f. L *jocus* jest]

joker /'dʒəʊkə(r)/ *n.* **1** a person who jokes. **2** *sl.* a fellow; a man. **3** a playing-card usu. with a figure of a jester, used in some games esp. as a wild card. **4** *US* a clause unobtrusively inserted in a bill or document and affecting its operation in a way not immediately apparent. **5** an unexpected factor or resource. □**the joker in the pack** an unpredictable factor or participant.

jolie laide /ˌʒɒliːˈleɪd/ *n.* (*pl.* **jolies laides** *pronunc.* same) = BELLE LAIDE. [F f. *jolie* pretty + *laide* ugly]

jollify /ˈdʒɒlɪˌfaɪ/ *v.tr.* & *intr.* (**-ies**, **-ied**) make or be merry, esp. in drinking. □□ **jollification** /-fɪˈkeɪʃ(ə)n/ *n.*

jollity /ˈdʒɒlɪtɪ/ *n.* (*pl.* **-ies**) **1** merrymaking; festiveness. **2** (in *pl.*) festivities. [ME f. OF *joliveté* (as JOLLY¹)]

jolly¹ /ˈdʒɒlɪ/ *adj.*, *adv.*, *v.*, & *n.* —*adj.* (**jollier**, **jolliest**) **1** cheerful and good-humoured; merry. **2** festive, jovial. **3** slightly drunk. **4** *colloq.* (of a person or thing) very pleasant, delightful (often *iron.*: *a jolly shame*). —*adv. colloq.* very (*they were jolly unlucky*). —*v.tr.* (**-ies**, **-ied**) **1** (usu. foll. by *along*) *colloq.* coax or humour (a person) in a friendly way. **2** chaff, banter. —*n.* (*pl.* **-ies**) *colloq.* a party or celebration. □ **Jolly Roger** a pirates' black flag, usu. with the skull and crossbones. □□ **jollily** *adv.* **jolliness** *n.* [ME f. OF *jolif* gay, pretty, perh. f. ON *jól* YULE]

jolly² /ˈdʒɒlɪ/ *n.* (*pl.* **-ies**) (in full **jolly boat**) a clinker-built ship's boat smaller than a cutter. [18th c.: orig. unkn.: perh. rel. to YAWL]

jolt /dʒəʊlt, dʒɒlt/ *v.* & *n.* —*v.* **1** *tr.* disturb or shake from the normal position (esp. in a moving vehicle) with a jerk. **2** *tr.* give a mental shock to; perturb. **3** *intr.* (of a vehicle) move along with jerks, as on a rough road. —*n.* **1** such a jerk. **2** a surprise or shock. □□ **jolty** *adj.* (**joltier**, **joltiest**). [16th c.: orig. unkn.]

Jon. *abbr.* **1** Jonah (Old Testament). **2** Jonathan.

Jonah /ˈdʒəʊnə/ *n.* a person who seems to bring bad luck. [*Jonah* in the Old Testament]

jongleur /ʒɔ̃ˈɡlɜː(r)/ *n. hist.* an itinerant minstrel. [F, var. of *jougleur* JUGGLER]

jonquil /ˈdʒɒŋkwɪl/ *n.* a bulbous plant, *Narcissus jonquilla*, with clusters of small fragrant yellow flowers. [mod.L *jonquilla* or F *jonquille* f. Sp. *junquillo* dimin. of *junco*: see JUNCO]

Jordanian /dʒɔːˈdeɪnɪən/ *adj.* & *n.* —*adj.* of or relating to the kingdom of Jordan in the Middle East. —*n.* **1** a native or national of Jordan. **2** a person of Jordanian descent. [*Jordan*, river flowing into the Dead Sea]

jorum /ˈdʒɔːrəm/ *n.* **1** a large drinking-bowl. **2** its contents, esp. punch. [perh. f. *Joram* (2 Sam. 8:10)]

Jos. *abbr.* Joseph.

Josh. *abbr.* Joshua (Old Testament).

josh /dʒɒʃ/ *n.* & *v. sl.* —*n.* a good-natured or teasing joke. —*v.* **1** *tr.* tease or banter. **2** *intr.* indulge in ridicule. □□ **josher** *n.* [19th c.: orig. unkn.]

joss /dʒɒs/ *n.* a Chinese idol. □ **joss-house** a Chinese temple. **joss-stick** a stick of fragrant tinder mixed with clay, burnt as incense. [perh. ult. f. Port. *deos* f. L *deus* god]

josser /ˈdʒɒsə(r)/ *n. Brit. sl.* **1** a fool. **2** a fellow. [JOSS + -ER¹: cf. Austral. sense 'clergyman']

jostle /ˈdʒɒs(ə)l/ *v.* & *n.* —*v.* **1** *tr.* push against; elbow. **2** *tr.* (often foll. by *away*, *from*, etc.) push (a person) abruptly or roughly. **3** *intr.* (foll. by *against*) knock or push, esp. in a crowd. **4** *intr.* (foll. by *with*) struggle; have a rough exchange. —*n.* **1** the act or an instance of jostling. **2** a collision. [ME: earlier *justle* f. JOUST + -LE⁴]

jot /dʒɒt/ *v.* & *n.* —*v.tr.* (**jotted**, **jotting**) (usu. foll. by *down*) write briefly or hastily. —*n.* (usu. with *neg.* expressed or implied) a very small amount (*not one jot*). [earlier as noun: L f. Gk *iōta*: see IOTA]

jotter /ˈdʒɒtə(r)/ *n.* a small pad or notebook for making notes etc.

jotting /ˈdʒɒtɪŋ/ *n.* (usu. in *pl.*) a note; something jotted down.

joule /dʒuːl/ *n.* the SI unit of work or energy equal to the work done by a force of one newton when its point of application moves one metre in the direction of action of the force, equivalent to a watt-second. ¶ Symb.: **J**. [J. P. *Joule*, Engl. physicist d. 1889]

jounce /dʒaʊns/ *v.tr.* & *intr.* bump, bounce, jolt. [ME: orig. unkn.]

journal /ˈdʒɜːn(ə)l/ *n.* **1** a newspaper or periodical. **2** a daily record of events. **3** *Naut.* a logbook. **4** a book in which business transactions are entered, with a statement of the accounts to which each is to be debited and credited. **5** the part of a shaft or axle that rests on bearings. **6** (**the Journals**) *Parl.* a record of daily proceedings. [ME f. OF *jurnal* f. LL *diurnalis* DIURNAL]

journalese /ˌdʒɜːnəˈliːz/ *n.* a hackneyed style of language characteristic of some newspaper writing.

journalism /ˈdʒɜːnəˌlɪz(ə)m/ *n.* the business or practice of writing and producing newspapers.

journalist /ˈdʒɜːnəlɪst/ *n.* a person employed to write for or edit a newspaper or journal. □□ **journalistic** /-ˈlɪstɪk/ *adj.* **journalistically** /-ˈlɪstɪkəlɪ/ *adv.*

journalize /ˈdʒɜːnəˌlaɪz/ *v.tr.* (also **-ise**) record in a private journal.

journey /ˈdʒɜːnɪ/ *n.* & *v.* —*n.* (*pl.* **-eys**) **1** an act of going from one place to another, esp. at a long distance. **2** the distance travelled in a specified time (*a day's journey*). **3** the travelling of a vehicle along a route at a stated time. —*v.intr.* (**-eys**, **-eyed**) make a journey. □□ **journeyer** *n.* [ME f. OF *jornee* day, day's work or travel, ult. f. L *diurnus* daily]

journeyman /ˈdʒɜːnɪmən/ *n.* (*pl.* **-men**) **1** a qualified mechanic or artisan who works for another. **2** *derog.* **a** a reliable but not outstanding worker. **b** a mere hireling. [JOURNEY in obs. sense 'day's work' + MAN]

joust /dʒaʊst/ *n.* & *v. hist.* —*n.* a combat between two knights on horseback with lances. —*v.intr.* engage in a joust. □□ **jouster** *n.* [ME f. OF *juster* bring together ult. f. L *juxta* near]

Jove /dʒəʊv/ *n.* (in Roman mythology) Jupiter. □ **by Jove!** an exclamation of surprise or approval. [ME f. L *Jovis* genit. of OL *Jovis* used as genit. of JUPITER]

jovial /ˈdʒəʊvɪəl/ *adj.* **1** merry. **2** convivial. **3** hearty and good-humoured. □□ **joviality** /-ˈælɪtɪ/ *n.* **jovially** *adv.* [F f. LL *jovialis* of Jupiter (as JOVE), with ref. to the supposed influence of the planet Jupiter on those born under it]

Jovian /ˈdʒəʊvɪən/ *adj.* **1** (in Roman mythology) of or like Jupiter. **2** of the planet Jupiter.

jowar /dʒaʊˈwɑː(r)/ *n.* = DURRA. [Hindi *jawār*]

jowl¹ /dʒaʊl/ *n.* **1** the jaw or jawbone. **2** the cheek (*cheek by jowl*). □□ **-jowled** *adj.* (in *comb.*). [ME *chavel* jaw f. OE *ceafl*]

jowl² /dʒaʊl/ *n.* **1** the external loose skin on the throat or neck when prominent. **2** the dewlap of oxen, wattle of a bird, etc. □□ **jowly** *adj.* [ME *cholle* neck f. OE *ceole*]

joy /dʒɔɪ/ *n.* & *v.* —*n.* **1** (often foll. by *at*, *in*) a vivid emotion of pleasure; extreme gladness. **2** a thing that causes joy. **3** *Brit. colloq.* satisfaction, success (*got no joy*). —*v.* esp. *poet.* **1** *intr.* rejoice. **2** *tr.* gladden. □ **joy-bells** bells rung on festive occasions. **wish a person joy of** *iron.* be gladly rid of (what that person has to deal with). □□ **joyless** *adj.* **joylessly** *adv.* [ME f. OF *joie* ult. f. L *gaudium* f. *gaudēre* rejoice]

Joycean /ˈdʒɔɪsɪən/ *adj.* & *n.* —*adj.* of or characteristic of James Joyce, Irish poet and novelist (d. 1941) or his writings. —*n.* a specialist in or admirer of Joyce's works.

joyful /ˈdʒɔɪfʊl/ *adj.* full of, showing, or causing joy. □□ **joyfully** *adv.* **joyfulness** *n.*

joyous /ˈdʒɔɪəs/ *adj.* (of an occasion, circumstance, etc.) characterized by pleasure or joy; joyful. □□ **joyously** *adv.* **joyousness** *n.*

joyride /ˈdʒɔɪraɪd/ *n.* & *v. colloq.* —*n.* a ride for pleasure in a motor car, esp. without the owner's permission. —*v.intr.* (*past* **-rode** /-rəʊd/; *past part.* **-ridden** /-rɪd(ə)n/) go for a joyride. □□ **joyrider** *n.*

joystick /ˈdʒɔɪstɪk/ *n.* **1** *colloq.* the control column of an aircraft. **2** a lever that can be moved in several directions to control the movement of an image on a VDU screen.

JP *abbr.* Justice of the Peace.

Jr. *abbr.* Junior.

jt. *abbr.* joint.

jube /dʒuːb/ n. Austral. & NZ = JUJUBE 2. [abbr.]

jubilant /'dʒuːbɪlənt/ adj. exultant, rejoicing, joyful. □□**jubilance** n. **jubilantly** adv. [L jubilare jubilant- shout for joy]

jubilate /'dʒuːbɪˌleɪt/ v.intr. exult; be joyful. □□ **jubilation** /-'leɪʃ(ə)n/ n. [L jubilare (as JUBILANT)]

jubilee /'dʒuːbɪˌliː/ n. **1** a time or season of rejoicing. **2** an anniversary, esp. the 25th or 50th. **3** Jewish Hist. a year of emancipation and restoration, kept every 50 years. **4** RC Ch. a period of remission from the penal consequences of sin, granted under certain conditions for a year usu. at intervals of 25 years. **5** exultant joy. [ME f. OF jubilé f. LL jubilaeus (annus) (year) of jubilee ult. f. Heb. yōḇēl, orig. = ram, ram's-horn trumpet]

Jud. abbr. Judith (Apocrypha).

Judaeo- /dʒuː'diːəʊ/ comb. form (US **Judeo-**) Jewish; Jewish and. [L judaeus Jewish]

Judaic /dʒuː'deɪɪk/ adj. of or characteristic of the Jews or Judaism. [L Judaicus f. Gk Ioudaïkos f. Ioudaios JEW]

Judaism /'dʒuːdeɪˌɪz(ə)m/ n. **1** the religion of the Jews, with a belief in one God and a basis in Mosaic and rabbinical teachings. **2** the Jews collectively. □□ **Judaist** n. [ME f. LL Judaismus f. Gk Ioudaïsmos (as JUDAIC)]

Judaize /'dʒuːdeɪˌaɪz/ v. (also **-ise**) **1** intr. follow Jewish customs or rites. **2** tr. **a** make Jewish. **b** convert to Judaism. □□ **Judaization** /-'zeɪʃ(ə)n/ n. [LL judaizare f. Gk ioudaïzō (as JUDAIC)]

Judas /'dʒuːdəs/ n. **1** a person who betrays a friend. **2** (**judas**) a peep-hole in a door. □**Judas-tree** a Mediterranean tree, Cercis siliquastrum, with purple flowers usu. appearing before the leaves. [Judas Iscariot who betrayed Christ (Luke 22)]

judder /'dʒʌdə(r)/ v. & n. esp. Brit. —v.intr. **1** (esp. of a mechanism) vibrate noisily or violently. **2** (of a singer's voice) oscillate in intensity. —n. an instance of juddering. [imit.: cf. SHUDDER]

Judeo- US var. of JUDAEO-.

Judg. abbr. Judges (Old Testament).

judge /dʒʌdʒ/ n. & v. —n. **1** a public officer appointed to hear and try causes in a court of justice. **2** a person appointed to decide a dispute or contest. **3 a** a person who decides a question. **b** a person regarded in terms of capacity to decide on the merits of a thing or question (am no judge of that; a good judge of art). **4** Jewish Hist. a leader having temporary authority in Israel in the period between Joshua and the Kings. —v. **1** tr. **a** try (a cause) in a court of justice. **b** pronounce sentence on (a person). **2** tr. form an opinion about; estimate, appraise. **3** tr. act as a judge of (a dispute or contest). **4** tr. (often foll. by to + infin. or that + clause) conclude, consider, or suppose. **5** intr. **a** form a judgement. **b** act as judge. □**Judge Advocate General** an officer in supreme control of the courts martial in the armed forces. **Judges' Rules** Brit. rules regarding the admissibility of an accused's statements as evidence. □□**judgelike** adj. **judgeship** n. [ME f. OF juge (n.), juger (v.) f. L judex judicis f. jus law + -dicus speaking]

judgement /'dʒʌdʒmənt/ n. (also **judgment**) **1** the critical faculty; discernment (an error of judgement). **2** good sense. **3** an opinion or estimate (in my judgement). **4** the sentence of a court of justice; a decision by a judge. **5** often joc. a misfortune viewed as a deserved recompense (it is a judgement on you for getting up late). **6** criticism. □**against one's better judgement** contrary to what one really feels to be advisable. **judgement by default** see DEFAULT. **Judgement Day** the day on which the Last Judgement is believed to take place. **judgement-seat** a judge's seat; a tribunal. **the Last Judgement** (in some beliefs) the judgement of mankind expected to take place at the end of the world. [ME f. OF jugement (as JUDGE)]

judgemental /dʒʌdʒ'ment(ə)l/ adj. (also **judgmental**) **1** of or concerning or by way of judgement. **2** condemning, critical. □□ **judgementally** adv.

judicature /'dʒuːdɪkətʃə(r), -'dɪkətʃə(r)/ n. **1** the administration of justice. **2** a judge's office or term of office. **3** judges collectively. **4** a court of justice. [med.L judicatura f. L judicare to judge]

judicial /dʒuː'dɪʃ(ə)l/ adj. **1** of, done by, or proper to a court of law. **2** having the function of judgement (a judicial assembly). **3** of or proper to a judge. **4** expressing a judgement; critical. **5** impartial. **6** regarded as a divine judgement. □**judicial factor** Sc. an official receiver. **judicial separation** the separation of man and wife by decision of a court. □□**judicially** adv. [ME f. L judicialis f. judicium judgement f. judex JUDGE]

judiciary /dʒuː'dɪʃ(ə)rɪ/ n. (pl. **-ies**) the judges of a State collectively. [L judiciarius (as JUDICIAL)]

judicious /dʒuː'dɪʃəs/ adj. **1** sensible, prudent. **2** sound in discernment and judgement. □□ **judiciously** adv. **judiciousness** n. [F judicieux f. L judicium (as JUDICIAL)]

judo /'dʒuːdəʊ/ n. a sport of unarmed combat derived from ju-jitsu. □□**judoist** n. [Jap. f. jū gentle + dō way]

Judy /'dʒuːdɪ/ n. (pl. **-ies**) **1** see PUNCH¹. **2** (also **judy**) sl. a woman. [pet-form of the name Judith]

jug /dʒʌg/ n. & v. —n. **1 a** a deep vessel for holding liquids, with a handle and often with a spout or lip shaped for pouring. **b** the contents of this; a jugful. **2** US a large jar with a narrow mouth. **3** sl. prison. **4** (in pl.) US coarse sl. a woman's breasts. —v.tr. (**jugged, jugging**) **1** (usu. as **jugged** adj.) stew or boil (a hare or rabbit) in a covered vessel. **2** sl. imprison. □□**jugful** n. (pl. **-fuls**). [perh. f. Jug, pet-form of the name Joan etc.]

Jugendstil /'juːgəntˌʃtiːl/ n. the German name for art nouveau. [G f. Jugend youth + Stil style]

juggernaut /'dʒʌgəˌnɔːt/ n. **1** esp. Brit. a large heavy motor vehicle, esp. an articulated lorry. **2** a huge or overwhelming force or object. **3** (**Juggernaut**) an institution or notion to which persons blindly sacrifice themselves or others. [Hindi Jagannath f. Skr. Jagannātha = lord of the world: name of an idol of Krishna in Hindu mythol., carried in procession on a huge cart under which devotees are said to have formerly thrown themselves]

juggins /'dʒʌgɪnz/ n. Brit. sl. a simpleton. [perh. f. proper name Juggins (as JUG): cf. MUGGINS]

juggle /'dʒʌg(ə)l/ v. & n. —v. **1 a** intr. (often foll. by with) perform feats of dexterity, esp. by tossing objects in the air and catching them, keeping several in the air at the same time. **b** tr. perform such feats with. **2** tr. continue to deal with (several activities) at once, esp. with ingenuity. **3** intr. (foll. by with) & tr. **a** deceive or cheat. **b** misrepresent (facts). **c** rearrange adroitly. —n. **1** a piece of juggling. **2** a fraud. [ME, back-form. f. JUGGLER or f. OF jogler, jugler f. L joculari jest f. joculus dimin. of jocus jest]

juggler /'dʒʌglə(r)/ n. **1 a** a person who juggles. **b** a conjuror. **2** a trickster or impostor. □□ **jugglery** n. [ME f. OF jouglere -eor f. L joculator -oris (as JUGGLE)]

Jugoslav var. of YUGOSLAV.

jugular /'dʒʌgjʊlə(r)/ adj. & n. —adj. **1** of the neck or throat. **2** (of fish) having ventral fins in front of the pectoral fins. —n. = jugular vein. □**jugular vein** any of several large veins of the neck which carry blood from the head. [LL jugularis f. L jugulum collar-bone, throat, dimin. of jugum YOKE]

jugulate /'dʒʌgjuːˌleɪt/ v.tr. **1** kill by cutting the throat. **2** arrest the course of (a disease etc.) by a powerful remedy. [L jugulare f. jugulum (as JUGULAR)]

juice /dʒuːs/ n. **1** the liquid part of vegetables or fruits. **2** the fluid part of an animal body or substance, esp. a secretion (gastric juice). **3** the essence or spirit of anything. **4** colloq. petrol or electricity as a source of power. □□**juiceless** adj. [ME f. OF jus f. L jus broth, juice]

juicy /'dʒuːsɪ/ adj. (**juicier**, **juiciest**) **1** full of juice; succulent. **2** colloq. substantial or interesting; racy, scandalous. **3** colloq. profitable. □□**juicily** adv. **juiciness** n.

ju-jitsu /dʒuːˈdʒɪtsuː/ n. (also **jiu-jitsu**, **ju-jutsu**) a Japanese system of unarmed combat and physical training. [Jap. jūjutsu f. jū gentle + jutsu skill]

ju-ju /'dʒuːdʒuː/ n. **1** a charm or fetish of some W. African peoples. **2** a supernatural power attributed to this. [perh. f. F joujou toy]

jujube /'dʒuːdʒuːb/ n. **1 a** any plant of the genus Zizyphus bearing edible acidic berry-like fruits. **b** this fruit. **2** a lozenge of gelatin etc. flavoured with or imitating this. [F jujube or med.L jujuba ult. f. Gk zizuphon]

ju-jutsu var. of JU-JITSU.

jukebox /'dʒuːkbɒks/ n. a machine that automatically plays a selected musical recording when a coin is inserted. [Gullah juke disorderly + BOX¹]

Jul. abbr. July.

julep /'dʒuːlep/ n. **1 a** a sweet drink, esp. as a vehicle for medicine. **b** a medicated drink as a mild stimulant etc. **2** US iced and flavoured spirits and water (mint julep). [ME f. OF f. Arab. julāb f. Pers. gulāb f. gul rose + āb water]

Julian /'dʒuːlɪən/ adj. of or associated with Julius Caesar. □**Julian calendar** a calendar introduced by Julius Caesar, in which the year consisted of 365 days, every fourth year having 366 (cf. GREGORIAN CALENDAR). [L Julianus f. Julius]

julienne /ˌdʒuːlɪˈen/ n. & adj. —n. foodstuff, esp. vegetables, cut into short thin strips. —adj. cut into thin strips. [F f. the name Jules or Julien]

Juliet cap /'dʒuːlɪət/ n. a small network ornamental cap worn by brides etc. [the heroine of Shakesp. Romeo & Juliet]

July /dʒuːˈlaɪ/ n. (pl. **Julys**) the seventh month of the year. [ME f. AF julie f. L Julius (mensis month), named after Julius Caesar]

jumble /'dʒʌmb(ə)l/ v. & n. —v. **1** tr. (often foll. by up) confuse; mix up. **2** intr. move about in disorder. —n. **1** a confused state or heap; a muddle. **2** Brit. articles collected for a jumble sale. □**jumble sale** Brit. a sale of miscellaneous usu. second-hand articles, esp. for charity. □□**jumbly** adj. [prob. imit.]

jumbo /'dʒʌmbəʊ/ n. & adj. colloq. —n. (pl. **-os**) **1** a large animal (esp. an elephant), person, or thing. **2** (in full **jumbo jet**) a large airliner with capacity for several hundred passengers. ¶ Usu. applied specifically to the Boeing 747. —adj. **1** very large of its kind. **2** extra large (jumbo packet). [19th c. (orig. of a person): orig. unkn.: popularized as the name of a zoo elephant sold in 1882]

jumbuck /'dʒʌmbʌk/ n. Austral. colloq. a sheep. [Aboriginal]

jump /dʒʌmp/ v. & n. —v. **1** intr. move off the ground or other surface (usu. upward, at least initially) by sudden muscular effort in the legs. **2** intr. (often foll. by up, from, in, out, etc.) move suddenly or hastily in a specified way (we jumped into the car). **3** intr. give a sudden bodily movement from shock or excitement etc. **4** intr. undergo a rapid change, esp. an advance in status. **5** intr. (often foll. by about) change or move rapidly from one idea or subject to another. **6 a** intr. rise or increase suddenly (prices jumped). **b** tr. cause to do this. **7** tr. **a** pass over (an obstacle, barrier, etc.) by jumping. **b** move or pass over (an intervening thing) to a point beyond. **8** tr. skip or pass over (a passage in a book etc.). **9** tr. cause (a thing, or an animal, esp. a horse) to jump. **10** intr. (foll. by to, at) reach a conclusion hastily. **11** tr. (of a train) leave (the rails) owing to a fault. **12** tr. ignore and pass (a red traffic-light etc.). **13** tr. get on or off (a train etc.) quickly, esp. illegally or dangerously. **14** tr. pounce on or attack (a person) unexpectedly. **15** tr. take summary possession of (a claim allegedly abandoned or forfeit by the former occupant). —n. **1** the act or an

instance of jumping. **2 a** a sudden bodily movement caused by shock or excitement. **b** (**the jumps**) colloq. extreme nervousness or anxiety. **3** an abrupt rise in amount, price, value, status, etc. **4** an obstacle to be jumped, esp. by a horse. **5 a** a sudden transition. **b** a gap in a series, logical sequence, etc. □**get** (or **have**) **the jump on** colloq. get (or have) an advantage over (a person) by prompt action. **jump at** accept eagerly. **jump bail** see BAIL¹. **jump down a person's throat** colloq. reprimand or contradict a person fiercely. **jumped-up** colloq. upstart; presumptuously arrogant. **jump the gun** see GUN. **jumping-off place** (or **point** etc.) the place or point of starting. **jump-jet** a jet aircraft that can take off and land vertically. **jump-lead** a cable for conveying current from the battery of a motor vehicle to boost (or recharge) another. **jump-off** a deciding round in a showjumping competition. **jump on** colloq. attack or criticize severely and without warning. **jump out of one's skin** colloq. be extremely startled. **jump the queue 1** push forward out of one's turn. **2** take unfair precedence over others. **jump-rope** US a skipping-rope. **jump seat** US a folding extra seat in a motor vehicle. **jump ship** (of a seaman) desert. **jump-start** v.tr. start (a motor vehicle) by pushing it or with jump-leads. —n. the action of jump-starting. **jump suit** a one-piece garment for the whole body, of a kind orig. worn by paratroopers. **jump to it** colloq. act promptly and energetically. **one jump ahead** one stage further on than a rival etc. **on the jump** colloq. on the move; in a hurry. □□**jumpable** adj. [16th c.: prob. imit.]

jumper¹ /'dʒʌmpə(r)/ n. **1** a knitted pullover. **2** a loose outer jacket of canvas etc. worn by sailors. **3** US a pinafore dress. [prob. f. (17th-c., now dial.) jump short coat perh. f. F jupe f. Arab. jubba]

jumper² /'dʒʌmpə(r)/ n. **1** a person or animal that jumps. **2** Electr. a short wire used to make or break a circuit. **3** a rope made fast to keep a yard, mast, etc., from jumping. **4** a heavy chisel-ended iron bar for drilling blast-holes.

jumping bean /'dʒʌmpɪŋ/ n. the seed of a Mexican plant that jumps with the movement of the larva inside.

jumping jack /'dʒʌmpɪŋ/ n. **1** a small firework producing repeated explosions. **2** a toy figure of a man, with movable limbs.

jumpy /'dʒʌmpɪ/ adj. (**jumpier**, **jumpiest**) **1** nervous; easily startled. **2** making sudden movements, esp. of nervous excitement. □□**jumpily** adv. **jumpiness** n.

Jun. abbr. **1** June. **2** Junior.

junco /'dʒʌŋkəʊ/ n. (pl. **-os** or **-oes**) any small American finch of the genus Junco. [Sp. f. L juncus rush plant]

junction /'dʒʌŋkʃ(ə)n/ n. **1** a point at which two or more things are joined. **2** a place where two or more railway lines or roads meet, unite, or cross. **3** the act or an instance of joining. **4** Electronics a region of transition in a semiconductor between regions where conduction is mainly by electrons and regions where it is mainly by holes. □**junction box** a box containing a junction of electric cables etc. [L junctio (as JOIN)]

juncture /'dʒʌŋktʃə(r)/ n. **1** a critical convergence of events; a critical point of time (at this juncture). **2** a place where things join. **3** an act of joining. [ME f. L junctura (as JOIN)]

June /dʒuːn/ n. the sixth month of the year. [ME f. OF juin f. L Junius var. of Junonius sacred to Juno]

Jungian /'jʊŋɪən/ adj. & n. —adj. of the Swiss psychologist Carl Jung (d. 1961) or his system of analytical psychology. —n. a supporter of Jung or of his system.

jungle /'dʒʌŋg(ə)l/ n. **1 a** land overgrown with underwood or tangled vegetation, esp. in the tropics. **b** an area of such land. **2** a wild tangled mass. **3** a place of bewildering complexity or confusion, or of a struggle for survival (blackboard jungle). □**jungle**

fever a severe form of malaria. **law of the jungle** a state of ruthless competition. ▢▢**jungled** adj. **jungly** adj. [Hindi jangal f. Skr. jangala desert, forest]

junior /'dʒuːnɪə(r)/ adj. & n. —adj. **1** less advanced in age. **2** (foll. by to) inferior in age, standing, or position. **3** the younger (esp. appended to a name for distinction from an older person of the same name). **4** of less or least standing; of the lower or lowest position (junior partner). **5** Brit. (of a school) having pupils in a younger age-range, usu. 7–11. **6** US of the year before the final year at university, high school, etc. —n. **1** a junior person. **2** one's inferior in length of service etc. **3** a junior student. **4** a barrister who is not a QC. **5** US colloq. a young male child, esp. in relation to his family. ▢**junior college** US a college offering a two-year course esp. in preparation for completion at senior college. **junior common (or combination) room** Brit. **1** a room for social use by the junior members of a college. **2** the junior members collectively. **junior lightweight** see LIGHTWEIGHT. **junior middleweight** see MIDDLE-WEIGHT. ▢▢**juniority** /-'ɒrɪtɪ/ n. [L, compar. of juvenis young]

juniper /'dʒuːnɪpə(r)/ n. any evergreen shrub or tree of the genus Juniperus, esp. J. communis with prickly leaves and dark purple berry-like cones. ▢**oil of juniper** oil from juniper cones used in medicine and in flavouring gin etc. [ME f. L juniperus]

junk[1] /dʒʌŋk/ n. & v. —n. **1** discarded articles; rubbish. **2** anything regarded as of little value. **3** sl. a narcotic drug, esp. heroin. **4** old cables or ropes cut up for oakum etc. **5** Brit. a lump or chunk. **6** Naut. hard salt meat. **7** a lump of fibrous tissue in the sperm whale's head, containing spermaceti. —v.tr. discard as junk. ▢**junk food** food with low nutritional value. **junk mail** unsolicited advertising matter sent by post. **junk shop** a shop selling cheap second-hand goods or antiques. [ME: orig. unkn.]

junk[2] /dʒʌŋk/ n. a flat-bottomed sailing vessel used in the China seas, with a prominent stem and lugsails. [obs. F juncque, Port. junco, or Du. jonk, f. Jav. djong]

junker /'jʊŋkə(r)/ n. hist. **1** a young German nobleman. **2** a member of an exclusive (Prussian) aristocratic party. ▢▢**junkerdom** n. [G, earlier Junkher f. OHG (as YOUNG, HERR)]

junket /'dʒʌŋkɪt/ n. & v. —n. **1** a dish of sweetened and flavoured curds, often served with fruit or cream. **2** a feast. **3** a pleasure outing. **4** US an official's tour at public expense. —v.intr. (junketed, junketing) feast, picnic. ▢▢**junketing** n. [ME jonket f. OF jonquette rush-basket (used to carry junket) f. jonc rush f. L juncus]

junkie /'dʒʌŋkɪ/ n. sl. a drug addict.

Junr. abbr. Junior.

junta /'dʒʌntə/ n. **1 a** a political or military clique or faction taking power after a revolution or coup d'état. **b** a secretive group; a cabal. **2** a deliberative or administrative council in Spain or Portugal. [Sp. & Port. f. L juncta, fem. past part. (as JOIN)]

Jupiter /'dʒuːpɪtə(r)/ n. the largest planet of the solar system, orbiting about the sun between Mars and Saturn. [ME f. L Jupiter king of the gods f. OL Jovis pater]

jural /'dʒʊər(ə)l/ adj. **1** of law. **2** of rights and obligations. [L jus juris law, right]

Jurassic /dʒʊə'ræsɪk/ adj. & n. Geol. —adj. of or relating to the second period of the Mesozoic era with evidence of many large dinosaurs, the first birds (including Archaeopteryx), and mammals. ¶ Cf. Appendix II. —n. this era or system. [F jurassique f. Jura (Mountains): cf. Triassic]

jurat[1] /'dʒʊəræt/ n. Brit. **1** a municipal officer (esp. of the Cinque Ports) holding a position similar to that of an alderman. **2** an honorary judge or magistrate in the Channel Islands. [ME f. med.L juratus past part. of L jurare swear]

jurat[2] /'dʒʊəræt/ n. a statement of the circumstances in which an affidavit was made. [L juratum neut. past part. (as JURAT[1])]

juridical /dʒʊə'rɪdɪk(ə)l/ n. **1** of judicial proceedings. **2** relating to the law. ▢▢**juridically** adv. [L juridicus f. jus juris law + -dicus saying f. dicere say]

jurisconsult /ˌdʒʊərɪskən'sʌlt/ n. a person learned in law; a jurist. [L jurisconsultus f. jus juris law + consultus skilled: see CONSULT]

jurisdiction /ˌdʒʊərɪs'dɪkʃ(ə)n/ n. **1** (often foll. by over, of) the administration of justice. **2** a legal or other authority. **b** the extent of this; the territory it extends over. ▢▢**jurisdictional** adj. [ME juris-diccioun f. OF jurediction, juridiction, L jurisdictio f. jus juris law + dictio DICTION]

jurisprudence /ˌdʒʊərɪs'pruːd(ə)ns/ n. **1** the science or philosophy of law. **2** skill in law. ▢▢**jurisprudent** adj. & n. **jurisprudential** /-'denʃ(ə)l/ adj. [LL juris-prudentia f. L jus juris law + prudentia knowledge: see PRUDENT]

jurist /'dʒʊərɪst/ n. **1** an expert in law. **2** a legal writer. **3** US a lawyer. ▢▢**juristic** /-'rɪstɪk/ adj. **juristical** /-'rɪstɪk(ə)l/ adj. [F juriste or med.L jurista f. jus juris law]

juror /'dʒʊərə(r)/ n. **1** a member of a jury. **2** a person who takes an oath (cf. NONJUROR). [ME f. AF jurour, OF jureor f. L jurator -oris f. jurare jurat- swear]

jury /'dʒʊərɪ/ n. (pl. -ies) **1** a body of usu. twelve persons sworn to render a verdict on the basis of evidence submitted to them in a court of justice. **2** a body of persons selected to award prizes in a competition. ▢**jury-box** the enclosure for the jury in a lawcourt. [ME f. AF & OF juree oath, inquiry, f. jurata fem. past part. of L jurare swear]

juryman /'dʒʊərɪmən/ n. (pl. -men) a member of a jury.

jury-rigged /'dʒʊərɪrɪgd/ n. Naut. having temporary makeshift rigging. [perh. ult. f. OF ajurie aid]

jurywoman /'dʒʊərɪˌwʊmən/ n. (pl. -women) a woman member of a jury.

jussive /'dʒʌsɪv/ adj. Gram. expressing a command. [L jubēre juss- command]

just /dʒʌst/ adj. & adv. —adj. **1** acting or done in accordance with what is morally right or fair. **2** (of treatment etc.) deserved (a just reward). **3** (of feelings, opinions, etc.) well-grounded (just resentment). **4** right in amount etc.; proper. —adv. **1** exactly (just what I need). **2** exactly or nearly at this or that moment; a little time ago (I have just seen them). **3** colloq. simply, merely (we were just good friends; it just doesn't make sense). **4** barely; no more than (I just managed it; just a minute). **5** colloq. positively (it is just splendid). **6** quite (not just yet; it is just as well that I checked). **7** colloq. really, indeed (won't I just tell him!). **8** in questions, seeking precise information (just how did you manage?). ▢**just about** colloq. almost exactly; almost completely. **just in case** as a precaution. **just now 1** at this moment. **2** a little time ago. **just so 1** exactly arranged (they like everything just so). **2** it is exactly as you say. ▢▢ **justly** adv. **justness** n. [ME f. OF juste f. L justus f. jus right]

justice /'dʒʌstɪs/ n. **1** just conduct. **2** fairness. **3** the exercise of authority in the maintenance of right. **4** judicial proceedings (was duly brought to justice; the Court of Justice). **5 a** a magistrate. **b** a judge, esp. (in England) of the Supreme Court of Judicature. ▢**do justice to** treat fairly or appropriately; show due appreciation of. **do oneself justice** perform in a manner worthy of one's abilities. **in justice to** out of fairness to. **Justice of the Peace** an unpaid lay magistrate appointed to preserve the peace in a county, town, etc., hear minor cases, grant licenses, etc. **Mr (or Mrs) Justice** Brit. a form of address or reference to a Supreme Court Judge. **with justice** reasonably. ▢▢**justiceship** n. (in sense 5). [ME f. OF f. L justitia (as JUST)]

justiciable /dʒʌˈstɪʃəb(ə)l/ adj. liable to legal consideration. [OF f. justicier bring to trial f. med.L justitiare (as JUSTICE)]

justiciary /dʒʌˈstɪʃjərɪ/ n. & adj. —n. (pl. -ies) an administrator of justice. —adj. of the administration of justice. [med.L justitiarius f. L justitia: see JUSTICE]

justifiable /ˈdʒʌstɪˌfaɪəb(ə)l/ adj. that can be justified or defended. □justifiable homicide killing regarded as lawful and without criminal guilt, esp. the execution of a death sentence. □□justifiability /-ˈbɪlɪtɪ/ n. justifiableness n. justifiably adv. [F f. justifier: see JUSTIFY]

justify /ˈdʒʌstɪˌfaɪ/ v.tr. (-ies, -ied) 1 show the justice or rightness of (a person, act, etc.). 2 demonstrate the correctness of (an assertion etc.). 3 adduce adequate grounds for (conduct, a claim, etc.). 4 a (esp. in passive) (of circumstances) be such as to justify. b vindicate. 5 (as justified adj.) just, right (am justified in assuming). 6 Theol. declare (a person) righteous. 7 Printing adjust (a line of type) to fill a space evenly. □□justification /-fɪˈkeɪʃ(ə)n/ n. justificatory /-fɪˌkeɪtərɪ/ adj. justifier n. [ME f. F justifier f. LL justificare do justice to f. L justus JUST]

jut /dʒʌt/ v. & n. —v.intr. (jutted, jutting) (often foll. by out, forth) protrude, project. —n. a projection; a protruding point. [var. of JET¹]

Jute /dʒuːt/ n. a member of a Low-German tribe that settled in Britain in the 5th-6th c. □□Jutish adj. [repr. med.L Jutae, Juti, in OE Eotas, Iotas = Icel. Iótar people of Jutland in Denmark]

jute /dʒuːt/ n. 1 a rough fibre made from the bark of E. Indian plants of the genus Corchorus, used for making twine and rope, and woven into sacking, mats, etc. 2 either of two plants Corchorus capsularis or C. olitorius yielding this fibre. [Bengali jhōṭo f. Skr. jūṭa = jaṭā braid of hair]

juvenescence /ˌdʒuːvɪˈnes(ə)ns/ n. 1 youth. 2 the transition from infancy to youth. □□juvenescent adj. [L juvenescere reach the age of youth f. juvenis young]

juvenile /ˈdʒuːvəˌnaɪl/ adj. & n. —adj. 1 a young, youthful. b of or for young persons. 2 suited to or characteristic of youth. 3 often derog. immature (behaving in a very juvenile way). —n. 1 a young person. 2 Commerce a book intended for young people. 3 an actor playing the part of a youthful person. □juvenile court a court for the trial of children under 17. juvenile delinquency offences committed by a person or persons below the age of legal responsibility. juvenile delinquent such an offender. □□juvenilely adv. juvenility /-ˈnɪlɪtɪ/ n. [L juvenilis f. juvenis young]

juvenilia /ˌdʒuːvəˈnɪlɪə/ n.pl. works produced by an author or artist in youth. [L, neut. pl. of juvenilis (as JUVENILE)]

juxtapose /ˌdʒʌkstəˈpəʊz/ v.tr. 1 place (things) side by side. 2 (foll. by to, with) place (a thing) beside another. □□juxtaposition /-pəˈzɪʃ(ə)n/ n. juxtapositional /-pəˈzɪʃən(ə)l/ adj. [F juxtaposer f. L juxta next: see POSE¹]

K

K¹ /keɪ/ *n.* (also **k**) (*pl.* **Ks** or **K's**) the eleventh letter of the alphabet.

K² *abbr.* (also **K.**) **1** kelvin(s). **2** King, King's. **3** Köchel (catalogue of Mozart's works). **4** (also **k**) (prec. by a numeral) **a** *Computing* a unit of 1,024 (i.e. 2¹⁰) bytes or bits, or loosely 1,000. **b** 1,000. [sense 4 as abbr. of KILO-]

K³ *symb. Chem.* the element potassium.

k *abbr.* **1** kilo-. **2** knot(s).

Kaaba /'kɑːəbə/ *n.* (also **Caaba**) a sacred building at Mecca, the Muslim Holy of Holies containing the sacred black stone. [Arab. *Ka'ba*]

kabbala var. of CABBALA.

kabuki /kə'buːkɪ/ *n.* a form of popular traditional Japanese drama with highly stylized song, acted by males only. [Jap. f. *ka* song + *bu* dance + *ki* art]

kachina /kə'tʃiːnə/ *n.* **1** an American Indian ancestral spirit. **2** (in full **kachina dancer**) a person who represents a kachina in ceremonial dances. □ **kachina doll** a wooden doll representing a kachina. [Hopi, = supernatural]

Kaddish /'kædɪʃ/ *n.* **1** a Jewish mourner's prayer. **2** a doxology in the synagogue service. [Aram. *ḳaddīš* holy]

kadi var. of CADI.

Kaffir /'kæfə(r)/ *n.* **1 a** a member of the Xhosa-speaking peoples of S. Africa. **b** the language of these peoples. **2** *S.Afr. offens.* any Black African. [Arab. *kāfir* infidel f. *kafara* not believe]

kaffiyeh var. of KEFFIYEH.

Kafir /'kæfə(r)/ *n.* a native of the Hindu Kush mountains of NE Afghanistan. [formed as KAFFIR]

Kafkaesque /ˌkæfkə'esk/ *adj.* (of a situation, atmosphere, etc.) impenetrably oppressive, nightmarish, in a manner characteristic of the fictional world of Franz Kafka, German-speaking novelist (d. 1924).

kaftan var. of CAFTAN.

kai /kaɪ/ *n. NZ colloq.* food. [Maori]

kail var. of KALE.

kailyard var. of KALEYARD.

kaiser /'kaɪzə(r)/ *n. hist.* an emperor, esp. the German Emperor, the Emperor of Austria, or the head of the Holy Roman Empire. □□ **kaisership** *n.* [in mod. Eng. f. G *Kaiser* and Du. *keizer*; in ME f. OE *cāsere* f. Gmc adoption (through Gk *kaisar*) of L *Caesar*: see CAESAR]

kaka /'kɑːkɑː/ *n.* (*pl.* **kakas**) a large New Zealand parrot, *Nestor meridionalis*, with olive-brown plumage. [Maori]

kakapo /'kɑːkəˌpəʊ/ *n.* (*pl.* **-os**) an owl-like flightless New Zealand parrot, *Strigops habroptilus*. [Maori, = night kaka]

kakemono /ˌkækɪ'məʊnəʊ/ *n.* (*pl.* **-os**) a vertical Japanese wall-picture, usu. painted or inscribed on paper or silk and mounted on rollers. [Jap. f. *kake*-hang + *mono* thing]

kala-azar /ˌkɑːləˈzɑː(r)/ *n.* a tropical disease caused by the parasitic protozoan *Leishmania donovani*, which is transmitted to man by sandflies. [Assamese f. *kālā* black + *āzār* disease]

kale /keɪl/ *n.* (also **kail**) **1** a variety of cabbage, esp. one with wrinkled leaves and no compact head. Also called **curly kale**. **2** *US sl.* money. [ME, northern form of COLE]

kaleidoscope /kə'laɪdəˌskəʊp/ *n.* **1** a tube containing mirrors and pieces of coloured glass or paper, whose reflections produce changing patterns when the tube is rotated. **2** a constantly changing group of bright or interesting objects. □□ **kaleidoscopic** /-'skɒpɪk/ *adj.* **kaleidoscopical** /-'skɒpɪk(ə)l/ *adj.* [Gk *kalos* beautiful + *eidos* form + -SCOPE]

kalends var. of CALENDS.

kaleyard /'keɪljɑːd/ *n.* (also **kailyard**) *Sc.* a kitchen garden. □ **kaleyard school** a group of 19th-c. fiction writers including J. M. Barrie, who described local town life in Scotland in a romantic vein and with much use of the vernacular. [KALE + YARD²]

kali /'kælɪ, 'keɪlɪ/ *n.* a glasswort, *Salsola kali*, with fleshy jointed stems, having a high soda content. [Arab. *kalī* ALKALI]

kalmia /'kælmɪə/ *n.* a N. American evergreen shrub of the genus *Kalmia*, esp. *K. latifolia*, with showy pink flowers. [mod.L f. P. *Kalm*, Sw. botanist d. 1779]

Kalmuck /'kælmʌk/ *adj. & n.* —*adj.* of a Buddhist Mongolian people living in the western USSR. —*n.* **1** a member of this people. **2** the Ural-Altaic language of this people. [Russ. *kalmyk*]

kalong /'kɑːlɒŋ/ *n.* any of various fruit-eating bats of the family Pteropodidae, esp. *Pteropus edulis*; a flying fox. [Malay]

kalpa /'kælpə/ *n. Hinduism & Buddhism* the period between the beginning and the end of the world considered as the day of Brahma (4,320 million human years). [Skr.]

Kama /'kɑːmə/ *n.* the Hindu god of love. □ **Kama Sutra** /'suːtrə/ an ancient Sanskrit treatise on the art of erotic love. [Skr.]

kame /keɪm/ *n.* a short ridge of sand and gravel deposited from the water of a melted glacier. [Sc. form of COMB]

kamikaze /ˌkæmɪ'kɑːzɪ/ *n. & adj.* —*n. hist.* **1** a Japanese aircraft loaded with explosives and deliberately crashed by its pilot on its target. **2** the pilot of such an aircraft. —*adj.* **1** of or relating to a kamikaze. **2** reckless, dangerous, potentially self-destructive. [Jap. f. *kami* divinity + *kaze* wind]

kampong /'kæmpɒŋ/ *n.* a Malayan enclosure or village. [Malay: cf. COMPOUND²]

Kampuchean /ˌkæmpʊ'tʃɪən/ *n. & adj.* = CAMBODIAN. [*Kampuchea*, native name for Cambodia]

Kan. *abbr.* Kansas.

kana /'kɑːnə/ *n.* any of various Japanese syllabaries. [Jap.]

kanaka /kə'nækə, -'nɑːkə/ *n.* a South Sea Islander, esp. (formerly) one employed in forced labour in Australia. [Hawaiian, = man]

Kanarese /ˌkænə'riːz/ *n.* (*pl.* same) **1** a member of a Dravidian people living in western India. **2** the language of this people. [*Kanara* in India]

kangaroo /ˌkæŋgə'ruː/ *n.* a plant-eating marsupial of the genus *Macropus*, native to Australia and New Guinea, with a long tail and strongly developed hind quarters enabling it to travel by jumping. □ **kangaroo closure** *Brit. Parl.* a closure involving the chairperson of a committee selecting some amendments for discussion and excluding others. **kangaroo court** an improperly constituted or illegal court held by strikers etc. **kangaroo mouse** any small rodent of the genus *Microdipodops*, native to N. America, with long hind legs for hopping. **kangaroo paw** any plant of the genus *Angiozanthos*, with green and red woolly flowers. **kangaroo-rat** any burrowing rodent of the genus *Dipodomys*, having elongated hind feet. **kangaroo vine** an evergreen climbing plant, *Cissus antarctica*, with tooth-edged leaves. [Aboriginal name]

kanji /'kændʒɪ/ *n.* Japanese writing using Chinese characters. [Jap. f. *kan* Chinese + *ji* character]

Kannada /'kænədə/ n. the Kanarese language. [Kanarese *kannaḍa*]

kanoon /kə'nu:n/ n. an instrument like a zither, with fifty to sixty strings. [Pers. or Arab. *ḳānūn*]

Kans. abbr. Kansas.

KANU /'ka:nu:/ abbr. Kenya African National Union.

kaolin /'keɪəlɪn/ n. a fine soft white clay produced by the decomposition of other clays or feldspar, used esp. for making porcelain and in medicines. Also called *china clay*. □□ **kaolinic** /-'lɪnɪk/ adj. **kaolinize** v.tr. (also **-ise**). [F f. Chin. *gaoling* the name of a mountain f. *gao* high + *ling* hill]

kaon /'keɪɒn/ n. Physics a meson having a mass several times that of a pion. [*ka* repr. the letter *K* (as symbol for the particle) + -ON]

kapellmeister /kə'pel,maɪstə(r)/ n. (pl. same) the conductor of an orchestra, opera, choir, etc., esp. in German contexts. [G f. *Kapelle* court orchestra f. It. *cappella* CHAPEL + *Meister* master]

kapok /'keɪpɒk/ n. a fine fibrous cotton-like substance found surrounding the seeds of a tropical tree, *Ceiba pentandra*, used for stuffing cushions, soft toys, etc. [ult. f. Malay *kāpoq*]

kappa /'kæpə/ n. the tenth letter of the Greek alphabet (*K*, κ). [Gk]

kaput /kæ'pʊt/ predic.adj. sl. broken, ruined; done for. [G *kaputt*]

karabiner /,kærə'bi:nə(r)/ n. a coupling link with safety closure, used by mountaineers. [G, lit. 'carbine']

karakul /'kærə,kʊl/ n. (also **caracul**) 1 a variety of Asian sheep with a dark curled fleece when young. 2 fur made from or resembling this. Also called *Persian lamb*. [Russ.]

karat US var. of CARAT 2.

karate /kə'ra:tɪ/ n. a Japanese system of unarmed combat using the hands and feet as weapons. [Jap. f. *kara* empty + *te* hand]

karma /'ka:mə/ n. Buddhism & Hinduism 1 the sum of a person's actions in previous states of existence, viewed as deciding his or her fate in future existences. 2 destiny. □□ **karmic** adj. [Skr., = action, fate]

Karoo /kə'ru:/ n. (also **Karroo**) an elevated semi-desert plateau in S. Africa. [Afrik. f. Hottentot *karo* dry]

karri /'kærɪ/ n. (pl. **karris**) 1 a tall W. Australian tree, *Eucalyptus diversicolor*, with a hard red wood. 2 the timber from this. [Aboriginal]

Karroo var. of KAROO.

karst /ka:st/ n. a limestone region with underground drainage and many cavities and passages caused by the dissolution of the rock. [the *Karst*, a limestone region in NW Yugoslavia]

karyo- /'kærɪəʊ/ comb. form Biol. denoting the nucleus of a cell. [Gk *karuon* kernel]

karyokinesis /,kærɪəʊkɪ'ni:sɪs/ n. Biol. the division of a cell nucleus during mitosis. [KARYO- + Gk *kinēsis* movement f. *kineō* move]

karyotype /'kærɪə,taɪp/ n. the number and structure of the chromosomes in the nucleus of a cell.

kasbah /'kæzba:/ n. (also **casbah**) 1 the citadel of a N. African city. 2 an Arab quarter near this. [F *casbah* f. Arab. *kas(a)ba* citadel]

katabatic /,kætə'bætɪk/ adj. Meteorol. (of wind) caused by air flowing downwards (cf. ANABATIC). [Gk *katabatikos* f. *katabainō* go down]

katabolism var. of CATABOLISM.

katakana /,kætə'ka:nə/ n. an angular form of Japanese kana. [Jap., = side kana]

kathode var. of CATHODE.

katydid /'keɪtɪdɪd/ n. any of various green grasshoppers of the family Tettigoniidae, native to the US. [imit. of the sound it makes]

kauri /kaʊ'rɪ/ n. (pl. **kauris**) a coniferous New Zealand tree, *Agathis australis*, which produces valuable timber and a resin. □ **kauri-gum** this resin. [Maori]

kava /'ka:və/ n. 1 a Polynesian shrub, *Piper methysticum*. 2 an intoxicating drink made from the crushed roots of this. [Polynesian]

kawa-kawa /'ka:wə,ka:wə/ n. a New Zealand shrub, *Macropiper excelsum*, with aromatic leaves. [Maori]

kayak /'kaɪæk/ n. 1 an Eskimo one-man canoe consisting of a light wooden frame covered with sealskins. 2 a small covered canoe resembling this. [Eskimo]

kayo /keɪ'əʊ/ v. & n. colloq. —v.tr. (-oes, -oed) knock out; stun by a blow. —n. (pl. -os) a knockout. [repr. pronunc. of KO]

kazoo /kə'zu:/ n. a toy musical instrument into which the player sings or hums. [19th c., app. with ref. to the sound produced]

KB abbr. (in the UK) King's Bench.

KBE abbr. (in the UK) Knight Commander of the Order of the British Empire.

KC abbr. 1 King's College. 2 King's Counsel.

kc abbr. kilocycle(s).

KCB abbr. (in the UK) Knight Commander of the Order of the Bath.

KCMG abbr. (in the UK) Knight Commander of the Order of St Michael and St George.

kc/s abbr. kilocycles per second.

KCVO abbr. (in the UK) Knight Commander of the Royal Victorian Order.

KE abbr. kinetic energy.

kea /'ki:ə, 'keɪə/ n. a parrot, *Nestor notabilis*, of New Zealand, with brownish-green and red plumage. [Maori, imit.]

kebab /kɪ'bæb/ n. (usu. in pl.) small pieces of meat, vegetables, etc., packed closely and cooked on a skewer. [Urdu f. Arab. *kabāb*]

kedge /kedʒ/ v. & n. —v. 1 tr. move (a ship) by means of a hawser attached to a small anchor. 2 intr. (of a ship) move in this way. —n. (in full **kedge-anchor**) a small anchor for this purpose. [perh. a specific use of obs. *cagge*, dial. *cadge* bind, tie]

kedgeree /'kedʒərɪ, -'ri:/ n. 1 an Indian dish of rice, split pulse, onions, eggs, etc. 2 a European dish of fish, rice, hard-boiled eggs, etc. [Hindi *khichṛī*, Skr. *k'rsara* dish of rice and sesame]

keek /ki:k/ v. & n. Sc. —v.intr. peep. —n. a peep. [ME *kike*: cf. MDu., MLG *kīken*]

keel[1] /ki:l/ n. & v. —n. 1 the lengthwise timber or steel structure along the base of a ship, airship, or some aircraft, on which the framework of the whole is built up. 2 poet. a ship. 3 a ridge along the breastbone of many birds; a carina. 4 Bot. a prow-shaped pair of petals in a corolla etc. —v. 1 (often foll. by over) **a** intr. turn over or fall down. **b** tr. cause to do this. 2 tr. & intr. turn keel upwards. □□ **keelless** adj. [ME *kele* f. ON *kjölr* f. Gmc]

keel[2] /ki:l/ n. Brit. hist. 1 a flat-bottomed vessel, esp. of the kind formerly used on the River Tyne etc. for loading coal-ships. 2 an amount carried by such a vessel. [ME *kele* f. MLG *kēl*, MDu. *kiel* ship, boat, f. Gmc]

keelhaul /'ki:lhɔ:l/ v.tr. 1 drag (a person) through the water under the keel of a ship as a punishment. 2 scold or rebuke severely.

keelson /'ki:ls(ə)n/ n. (also **kelson** /'kels(ə)n/) a line of timber fastening a ship's floor-timbers to its keel. [ME *kelswayn*, perh. f. LG *kielswīn* f. *kiel* KEEL[1] + (prob.) *swīn* SWINE used as the name of a timber]

keen[1] /ki:n/ adj. 1 (of a person, desire, or interest) eager, ardent (*a keen sportsman*). 2 (foll. by *on*) much attracted by; fond of or enthusiastic about. 3 (of the senses) sharp; highly sensitive. 4 intellectually acute. 5 **a** having a sharp edge or point. **b** (of an edge etc.) sharp. 6 (of a sound, light, etc.) penetrating, vivid, strong. 7 (of a wind, frost, etc.) piercingly cold. 8 (of a pain etc.) acute, bitter. 9 Brit. (of a price) competitive. 10 colloq. excellent. □□ **keenly** adv. **keenness** n. [OE *cēne* f. Gmc]

keen[2] /ki:n/ n. & v. —n. an Irish funeral song

accompanied with wailing. —*v.* **1** *intr.* utter the keen. **2** *tr.* bewail (a person) in this way. **3** *tr.* utter in a wailing tone. □□ **keener** *n.* [Ir. *caoine* f. *caoinim* wail]

keep /kiːp/ *v.* & *n.* —*v.* (*past* and *past part.* **kept** /kept/) **1** *tr.* have continuous charge of; retain possession of. **2** *tr.* (foll. by *for*) retain or reserve for a future occasion or time (*will keep it for tomorrow*). **3** *tr.* & *intr.* retain or remain in a specified condition, position, course, etc. (*keep cool; keep off the grass; keep them happy*). **4** *tr.* put or store in a regular place (*knives are kept in this drawer*). **5** *tr.* (foll. by *from*) cause to avoid or abstain from something (*will keep you from going too fast*). **6** *tr.* detain; cause to be late (*what kept you?*). **7** *tr.* **a** observe or pay due regard to (a law, custom, etc.) (*keep one's word*). **b** honour or fulfil (a commitment, undertaking, etc.). **c** respect the commitment implied by (a secret etc.). **d** act fittingly on the occasion of (*keep the sabbath*). **8** *tr.* own and look after (animals) for amusement or profit (*keeps bees*). **9** *tr.* **a** provide for the sustenance of (a person, family, etc.). **b** (foll. by *in*) maintain (a person) with a supply of. **10** *tr.* carry on; manage (a shop, business, etc.). **11 a** *tr.* maintain (accounts, a diary, etc.) by making the requisite entries. **b** *tr.* maintain (a house) in proper order. **12** *tr.* have (a commodity) regularly on sale (*do you keep buttons?*). **13** *tr.* guard or protect (a person or place, a goal in football, etc.). **14** *tr.* preserve in being; continue to have (*keep order*). **15** *intr.* (foll. by verbal noun) continue or do repeatedly or habitually (*why do you keep saying that?*). **16** *tr.* continue to follow (a way or course). **17** *intr.* **a** (esp. of perishable commodities) remain in good condition. **b** (of news or information etc.) admit of being withheld for a time. **18** *tr.* remain in (one's bed, room, house, etc.). **19** *tr.* retain one's place in (a seat or saddle, one's ground, etc.) against opposition or difficulty. **20** *tr.* maintain (a person) in return for sexual favours (*a kept woman*). —*n.* **1** maintenance or the essentials for this (esp. food) (*hardly earn your keep*). **2** charge or control (*is in your keep*). **3** *hist.* a tower or stronghold. □ **for keeps** *colloq.* (esp. of something received or won) permanently, indefinitely. **how are you keeping?** how are you? **keep at** persist or cause to persist with. **keep away** (often foll. by *from*) **1** avoid being near. **2** prevent from being near. **keep back 1** remain or keep at a distance. **2** retard the progress of. **3** conceal; decline to disclose. **4** retain, withhold (*kept back £50*). **keep one's balance 1** remain stable; avoid falling. **2** retain one's composure. **keep down 1** hold in subjection. **2** keep low in amount. **3** lie low; stay hidden. **4** manage not to vomit (food eaten). **keep one's feet** manage not to fall. **keep-fit** regular exercises to promote personal fitness and health. **keep one's hair on** see HAIR. **keep one's hand in** see HAND. **keep in 1** confine or restrain (one's feelings etc.). **2** remain or confine indoors. **3** keep (a fire) burning. **keep in with** remain on good terms with. **keep off 1** stay or cause to stay away from. **2** ward off; avert. **3** abstain from. **4** avoid (a subject) (*let's keep off religion*). **keep on 1** continue to do something; do continually (*kept on laughing*). **2** continue to use or employ. **3** (foll. by *at*) pester or harass. **keep out 1** keep or remain outside. **2** exclude. **keep state 1** maintain one's dignity. **2** be difficult of access. **keep to 1** adhere to (a course, schedule, etc.). **2** observe (a promise). **3** confine oneself to. **keep to oneself 1** avoid contact with others. **2** refuse to disclose or share. **keep together** remain or keep in harmony. **keep track of** see TRACK¹. **keep under** hold in subjection. **keep up 1** maintain (progress etc.). **2** prevent (prices, one's spirits, etc.) from sinking. **3** keep in repair, in an efficient or proper state, etc. **4** carry on (a correspondence etc.). **5** prevent (a person) from going to bed, esp. when late. **6** (often foll. by *with*) manage not to fall behind. **keep up with the Joneses** strive

to compete socially with one's neighbours. **keep one's word** see WORD. □□ **keepable** *adj.* [OE *cēpan*, of unkn. orig.]

keeper /ˈkiːpə(r)/ *n.* **1** a person who keeps or looks after something or someone. **2** a custodian of a museum, art gallery, forest, etc. **3 a** = GAMEKEEPER. **b** a person in charge of animals in a zoo. **4 a** = *wicket-keeper*. **b** = GOALKEEPER. **5** a fruit etc. that remains in good condition. **6** a bar of soft iron across the poles of a horseshoe magnet to maintain its strength. **7 a** a plain ring to preserve a hole in a pierced ear lobe; a sleeper. **b** a ring worn to guard against the loss of a more valuable one.

keeping /ˈkiːpɪŋ/ *n.* **1** custody, charge (*in safe keeping*). **2** agreement, harmony (esp. *in* or *out of keeping*).

keepsake /ˈkiːpseɪk/ *n.* a thing kept for the sake of or in remembrance of the giver.

keeshond /ˈkeɪshɒnd/ *n.* **1** a dog of a Dutch breed with long thick hair like a large Pomeranian. **2** this breed. [Du.]

kef /kef/ *n.* (also **kif** /kɪf/) **1** a drowsy state induced by marijuana etc. **2** the enjoyment of idleness. **3** a substance smoked to produce kef. [Arab. *kayf* enjoyment, well-being]

keffiyeh /keˈfiːjeɪ/ *n.* (also **kaffiyeh**) a Bedouin Arab's kerchief worn as a head-dress. [Arab. *keffiya*, *kūfiyya*, perh. f. LL *cofea* COIF]

keg /keg/ *n.* a small barrel, usu. of less than 10 gallons or (in the US) 30 gallons. □ **keg beer** beer supplied from a sealed metal container. [ME *cag* f. ON *kaggi*, of unkn. orig.]

keister /ˈkiːstə(r), ˈkaɪstə(r)/ *n. US sl.* **1** the buttocks. **2** a suitcase, satchel, handbag, etc. [orig. unkn.]

keloid /ˈkiːlɔɪd/ *n.* fibrous tissue formed at the site of a scar or injury. [Gk *khēlē* claw + -OID]

kelp /kelp/ *n.* **1** any of several large broad-fronded brown seaweeds esp. of the genus *Laminaria*, suitable for use as manure. **2** the calcined ashes of seaweed formerly used in glass-making and soap manufacture because of their high content of sodium, potassium, and magnesium salts. [ME *cŭlp(e)*, of unkn. orig.]

kelpie /ˈkelpɪ/ *n. Sc.* **1** a water-spirit, usu. in the form of a horse, reputed to delight in the drowning of travellers etc. **2** an Australian sheepdog orig. bred from a Scottish collie. [18th c.: orig. unkn.]

kelson var. of KEELSON.

Kelt var. of CELT.

kelt /kelt/ *n.* a salmon or sea trout after spawning. [ME: orig. unkn.]

kelter var. of KILTER.

kelvin /ˈkelvɪn/ *n.* the SI unit of thermodynamic temperature, equal in magnitude to the degree celsius. ¶ Abbr.: **K**. □ **Kelvin scale** a scale of temperature with absolute zero as zero. [Lord *Kelvin*, Brit. physicist d. 1907]

kemp /kemp/ *n.* coarse hair in wool. □□ **kempy** *adj.* [ME f. ON *kampr* beard, whisker]

kempt /kempt/ *adj.* combed; neatly kept. [past part. of (now dial.) *kemb* COMB *v.* f. OE *cemban* f. Gmc]

ken /ken/ *n.* & *v.* —*n.* range of sight or knowledge (*it's beyond my ken*). —*v.tr.* (**kenning**; *past* and *past part.* **kenned** or **kent**) *Sc.* & *N.Engl.* **1** recognize at sight. **2** know. [OE *cennan* f. Gmc]

kendo /ˈkendəʊ/ *n.* a Japanese form of fencing with two-handed bamboo swords. [Jap., = sword-way]

kennel /ˈken(ə)l/ *n.* & *v.* —*n.* **1** a small shelter for a dog. **2** (in *pl.*) a breeding or boarding establishment for dogs. **3** a mean dwelling. —*v.* (**kennelled**, **kennelling**; *US* **kenneled**, **kenneling**) **1** *tr.* put into or keep in a kennel. **2** *intr.* live in or go to a kennel. [ME f. OF *chenil* f. med.L *canile* (unrecorded) f. L *canis* dog]

kenning /ˈkenɪŋ/ *n.* a compound expression in Old English and Old Norse poetry, e.g. *oar-steed* = ship. [ME, = 'teaching' etc. f. KEN]

kenosis /kɪˈnəʊsɪs/ *n. Theol.* the renunciation of the divine nature, at least in part, by Christ in the

Incarnation. □□ **kenotic** /-'nɒtɪk/ adj. [Gk. kenōsis f. kenoō to empty f. kenos empty]

kenspeckle /'ken,spek(ə)l/ adj. Sc. conspicuous. [kenspeck of Scand. orig.: rel. to KEN]

kent past and past part. of KEN.

Kentish /'kentɪʃ/ adj. of Kent in England. □**Kentish fire** Brit. a prolonged volley of rhythmic applause or a demonstration of dissent. [OE Centisc f. Cent f. L Cantium]

kentledge /'kentlɪdʒ/ n. Naut. pig-iron etc. used as permanent ballast. [F quintelage ballast, with assim. to kentle obs. var. of QUINTAL]

Kenyan /'kenjən, 'ki:njən/ adj. & n. —adj. of or relating to Kenya in E. Africa. —n. 1 a native or national of Kenya. 2 a person of Kenyan descent.

kepi /'kepɪ, 'keɪpɪ/ n. (pl. **kepis**) a French military cap with a horizontal peak. [F képi f. Swiss G käppi dimin. of kappe cap]

Kepler's laws /'kepləz/ n.pl. three theorems describing orbital motion. □□ **Keplerian** /-'lɪərɪən/ adj. [J. Kepler, Ger. astronomer d. 1630]

kept past and past part. of KEEP.

keratin /'kerətɪn/ n. a fibrous protein which occurs in hair, feathers, hooves, claws, horns, etc. [Gk keras keratos horn + -IN]

keratinize /'kerətɪ,naɪz/ v.tr. & intr. (also **-ise**) cover or become covered with a deposit of keratin. □□ **keratinization** /-'zeɪʃ(ə)n/ n.

keratose /'kerə,təʊs/ adj. (of sponge) composed of a horny substance. [Gk keras keratos horn + -OSE[1]]

kerb /kɜːb/ n. Brit. a stone edging to a pavement or raised path. □**kerb-crawler** a person who indulges in kerb-crawling. **kerb-crawling** the practice of driving slowly along the edge of a road, soliciting passers-by. **kerb drill** precautions, esp. looking to right and left, before crossing a road. [var. of CURB]

kerbstone /'kɜːbstəʊn/ n. each of a series of stones forming a kerb.

kerchief /'kɜːtʃiːf, -tʃɪf/ n. 1 a cloth used to cover the head. 2 poet. a handkerchief. □□ **kerchiefed** adj. [ME curchef f. AF courchef, OF couvrechief f. couvrir COVER + CHIEF head]

kerf /kɜːf/ n. 1 a slit made by cutting, esp. with a saw. 2 the cut end of a felled tree. [OE cyrf f. Gmc (as CARVE)]

kerfuffle /kə'fʌf(ə)l/ n. esp. Brit. colloq. a fuss or commotion. [Sc. curfuffle f. fuffle to disorder: imit.]

kermes /'kɜːmɪz/ n. 1 the female of a bug, Kermes ilicis, with a berry-like appearance. 2 (in full **kermes oak**) an evergreen oak, Quercus coccifera, of S. Europe and N. Africa, on which this insect feeds. 3 a red dye made from the dried bodies of these insects. 4 (in full **kermes mineral**) a bright red hydrous trisulphide of antimony. [F kermès f. Arab. & Pers. ḳirmiz: rel. to CRIMSON]

kermis /'kɜːmɪs/ n. 1 a periodical country fair, esp. in the Netherlands. 2 US a charity bazaar. [Du., orig. = mass on the anniversary of the dedication of a church, when yearly fair was held: f. kerk formed as CHURCH + mis, misse MASS[2]]

kern[1] /kɜːn/ n. Printing the part of a metal type projecting beyond its body or shank. □□ **kerned** adj. [perh. f. F carne corner f. OF charne f. L cardo cardinis hinge]

kern[2] /kɜːn/ n. (also **kerne**) 1 hist. a light-armed Irish foot-soldier. 2 a peasant; a boor. [ME f. Ir. ceithern]

kernel /'kɜːn(ə)l/ n. 1 a central, softer, usu. edible part within a hard shell of a nut, fruit stone, seed, etc. 2 the whole seed of a cereal. 3 the nucleus or essential part of anything. [OE cyrnel, dimin. of CORN[1]]

kerosine /'kerə,si:n/ n. (also **kerosene**) esp. US a fuel oil suitable for use in jet engines and domestic heating boilers; paraffin oil. [Gk kēros wax + -ENE]

Kerry /'kerɪ/ n. (pl. **-ies**) 1 an animal of a breed of small black dairy cattle. 2 this breed. [Kerry in Ireland]

Kerry blue /'kerɪ/ n. 1 a terrier of a breed with a silky blue-grey coat. 2 this breed.

kersey /'kɜːzɪ/ n. (pl. **-eys**) 1 a kind of coarse narrow cloth woven from long wool, usu. ribbed. 2 a variety of this. [ME, prob. f. Kersey in Suffolk]

kerseymere /'kɜːzɪmɪə(r)/ n. a twilled fine woollen cloth. [alt. of cassimere, var. of CASHMERE, assim. to KERSEY]

keskidee var. of KISKADEE.

kestrel /'kestr(ə)l/ n. any small falcon, esp. Falco tinnunculus, which hovers whilst searching for its prey. [ME castrell, perh. f. F dial. casserelle, F créc(er)elle, perh. imit. of its cry]

ketch /ketʃ/ n. a two-masted fore-and-aft rigged sailing-boat with a mizen-mast stepped forward of the rudder and smaller than its foremast. [ME catche, prob. f. CATCH]

ketchup /'ketʃʌp/ n. (also **catchup** /'kætʃʌp/) a spicy sauce made from tomatoes, mushrooms, vinegar, etc., used as a condiment. [Chin. dial. kōechiap pickled-fish brine]

ketone /'ki:təʊn/ n. any of a class of organic compounds in which two hydrocarbon groups are linked by a carbonyl group, e.g. propanone (acetone). □**ketone body** Biochem. any of several ketones produced in the body during the metabolism of fats. □□ **ketonic** /kɪ'tɒnɪk/ adj. [G Keton alt. of Aketon ACETONE]

ketonuria /,ki:təʊ'njʊərɪə/ n. the excretion of abnormally large amounts of ketone bodies in the urine.

ketosis /kɪ'təʊsɪs/ n. a condition characterized by raised levels of ketone bodies in the body, associated with fat metabolism and diabetes. □□ **ketotic** /-'tɒtɪk/ adj.

kettle /'ket(ə)l/ n. a vessel, usu. of metal with a lid, spout, and handle, for boiling water in. □**kettle hole** a depression in the ground in a glaciated area. **a pretty kettle of fish** an awkward state of affairs. □□ **kettleful** n. (pl. **-fuls**). [ME f. ON ketill ult. f. L catillus dimin. of catinus deep food-vessel]

kettledrum /'ket(ə)l,drʌm/ n. a large drum shaped like a bowl with a membrane adjustable for tension (and so pitch) stretched across. □□ **kettledrummer** n.

keV abbr. kilo-electronvolt.

Kevlar /'kevlə(r)/ n. propr. a synthetic fibre of high tensile strength used esp. as a reinforcing agent in the manufacture of rubber products, e.g. tyres.

kewpie /'kju:pɪ/ n. a small chubby doll with wings and a curl or topknot. [CUPID + -IE]

key[1] /ki:/ n. & v. —n. (pl. **keys**) 1 an instrument, usu. of metal, for moving the bolt of a lock forwards or backwards to lock or unlock. 2 a similar implement for operating a switch in the form of a lock. 3 an instrument for grasping screws, pegs, nuts, etc., esp. one for winding a clock etc. 4 a lever depressed by the finger in playing the organ, piano, flute, concertina, etc. 5 (often in pl.) each of several buttons for operating a typewriter, word processor, or computer terminal, etc. 6 what gives or precludes the opportunity for or access to something. 7 (attrib.) essential; of vital importance (the key element in the problem). 8 a place that by its position gives control of a sea, territory, etc. 9 a a solution or explanation. b a word or system for solving a cipher or code. c an explanatory list of symbols used in a map, table, etc. d a book of solutions to mathematical problems etc. e a literal translation of a book written in a foreign language. f the first move in a chess-problem solution. 10 Mus. a system of notes definitely related to each other, based on a particular note, and predominating in a piece of music (a study in the key of C major). 11 a tone or style of thought or expression. 12 a piece of wood or metal inserted between others to secure them. 13 the part of a first coat of wall plaster that passes between the laths and so secures the rest. 14 the roughness of a surface, helping the adhesion of plaster etc. **15** the samara of a sycamore etc. **16** a mechanical device for making or breaking an electric circuit, e.g. in telegraphy. —*v.tr.* (**keys, keyed**) **1** (foll. by *in, on,* etc.) fasten with a pin, wedge, bolt, etc. **2** (often foll. by *in*) enter (data) by means of a keyboard. **3** roughen (a surface) to help the adhesion of plaster etc. **4** (foll. by *to*) align or link (one thing to another). **5** regulate the pitch of the strings of (a violin etc.). **6** word (an advertisement in a particular periodical) so that answers to it can be identified (usu. by varying the form of address given). □**key industry** an industry essential to the carrying on of others, e.g. coal-mining, dyeing. **key map** a map in bare outline, to simplify the use of a full map. **key money** *Brit.* a payment demanded from an incoming tenant for the provision of a key to the premises. **key-ring** a ring for keeping keys on. **key signature** *Mus.* any of several combinations of sharps or flats after the clef at the beginning of each staff indicating the key of a composition. **key up** (often foll. by *to,* or *to* + infin.) make (a person) nervous or tense; excite. □□ **keyer** *n.* **keyless** *adj.* [OE *cǣg,* of unkn. orig.]

key² /kiː/ *n.* a low-lying island or reef, esp. in the W. Indies (cf. CAY). [Sp. *cayo* shoal, reef, infl. by QUAY]

keyboard /ˈkiːbɔːd/ *n. & v.* —*n.* a set of keys on a typewriter, computer, piano, etc. —*v.tr.* enter (data) by means of a keyboard. □□ **keyboarder** *n.*

keyhole /ˈkiːhəʊl/ *n.* a hole by which a key is put into a lock.

Keynesian /ˈkeɪnzɪən/ *adj. & n.* —*adj.* of or relating to the economic theories of J. M. Keynes (d. 1946), esp. regarding State control of the economy through money and taxation. —*n.* an adherent of these theories. □□ **Keynesianism** *n.*

keynote /ˈkiːnəʊt/ *n.* **1** a prevailing tone or idea (*the keynote of the whole occasion*). **2** (*attrib.*) intended to set the prevailing tone at a meeting or conference (*keynote address*). **3** *Mus.* the note on which a key is based.

keypad /ˈkiːpæd/ *n.* a miniature keyboard or set of buttons for operating a portable electronic device, telephone, etc.

keypunch /ˈkiːpʌntʃ/ *n. & v.* —*n.* a device for transferring data by means of punched holes or notches on a series of cards or paper tape. —*v.tr.* transfer (data) by means of a keypunch. □□ **keypuncher** *n.*

keystone /ˈkiːstəʊn/ *n.* **1** the central principle of a system, policy, etc., on which all the rest depends. **2** a central stone at the summit of an arch locking the whole together.

keystroke /ˈkiːstrəʊk/ *n.* a single depression of a key on a keyboard, esp. as a measure of work.

keyway /ˈkiːweɪ/ *n.* a slot for receiving a machined key.

keyword /ˈkiːwɜːd/ *n.* **1** the key to a cipher etc. **2 a** a word of great significance. **b** a significant word used in indexing.

KG *abbr.* (in the UK) Knight of the Order of the Garter.

kg *abbr.* kilogram(s).

KGB /ˌkeɪdʒiːˈbiː/ *n.* the State security police of the USSR since 1954. [Russ., abbr. of *Komitet gosudarstvennoĭ bezopasnosti* committee of State security]

Kgs. *abbr.* Kings (Old Testament).

khaddar /ˈkædə(r)/ *n.* Indian homespun cloth. [Hindi]

khaki /ˈkɑːkɪ/ *adj. & n.* —*adj.* dust-coloured; dull brownish-yellow. —*n.* (*pl.* **khakis**) **1** khaki fabric of twilled cotton or wool, used esp. in military dress. **2** the dull brownish-yellow colour of this. [Urdu *kākī* dust-coloured f. *kāk* dust]

khalasi /kəˈlæsɪ/ *n.* (*pl.* **khalasis**) a native Indian servant or labourer, esp. one employed as a seaman. [Hind.]

khamsin /ˈkæmsɪn/ *n.* (also **hamsin** /ˈhæ-/) an oppressive hot south or south-east wind occurring in Egypt for about 50 days in March, April, and May. [Arab. *ḳamsīn* f. *ḳamsūn* fifty]

khan¹ /kɑːn, kæn/ *n.* **1** a title given to rulers and officials in Central Asia, Afghanistan, etc. **2** *hist.* **a** the supreme ruler of the Turkish, Tartar, and Mongol tribes. **b** the emperor of China in the Middle Ages. □□ **khanate** *n.* [Turki *ḳān* lord]

khan² /kɑːn, kæn/ *n.* a caravanserai. [Arab. *ḳān* inn]

Khedive /kɪˈdiːv/ *n. hist.* the title of the viceroy of Egypt under Turkish rule 1867-1914. □□ **Khedival** *adj.* **Khedivial** *adj.* [F *khédive,* ult. f. Pers. *ḳadīv* prince]

Khmer /kmeə(r)/ *n. & adj.* —*n.* **1** a native of the ancient Khmer kingdom in SE Asia, or of modern Cambodia. **2** the language of this people. —*adj.* of the Khmers or their language. [native name]

kHz *abbr.* kilohertz.

kiang /kɪˈæŋ/ *n.* a wild Tibetan ass, *Equus hemionus kiang,* with a thick furry coat. [Tibetan *kyang*]

kibble¹ /ˈkɪb(ə)l/ *v.tr.* grind coarsely. [18th c.: orig. unkn.]

kibble² /ˈkɪb(ə)l/ *n. Brit.* an iron hoisting-bucket used in mines. [G *Kübel* (cf. OE *cyfel*) f. med.L *cupellus,* corn-measure, dimin. of *cuppa* cup]

kibbutz /kɪˈbʊts/ *n.* (*pl.* **kibbutzim** /-ˈtsiːm/) a communal esp. farming settlement in Israel. [mod.Heb. *ḳibbūṣ* gathering]

kibbutznik /kɪˈbʊtsnɪk/ *n.* a member of a kibbutz. [Yiddish (as KIBBUTZ)]

kibe /kaɪb/ *n.* an ulcerated chilblain, esp. on the heel. [ME, prob. f. Welsh *cibi*]

kibitka /kɪˈbɪtkə/ *n.* **1** a type of Russian hooded sledge. **2 a** a Tartar's circular tent, covered with felt. **b** a Tartar household. [Russ. f. Tartar *kibitz*]

kibitz /ˈkɪbɪts/ *v.intr. colloq.* act as a kibitzer. [Yiddish f. G *kiebitzen* (as KIBITZER)]

kibitzer /ˈkɪbɪtsə(r), kɪˈbɪtsə(r)/ *n. colloq.* **1** an onlooker at cards etc., esp. one who offers unwanted advice. **2** a busybody, a meddler. [Yiddish *kibitser* f. G *Kiebitz* lapwing, busybody]

kiblah /ˈkɪblə/ *n.* (also **qibla**) **1** the direction of the Kaaba (the sacred building at Mecca), to which Muslims turn at prayer. **2** = MIHRAB. [Arab. *ḳibla* that which is opposite]

kibosh /ˈkaɪbɒʃ/ *n.* (also **kybosh**) *sl.* nonsense. □**put the kibosh on** put an end to; finally dispose of. [19th c.: orig. unkn.]

kick¹ /kɪk/ *v. & n.* —*v.* **1** *tr.* strike or propel forcibly with the foot or hoof etc. **2** *intr.* (usu. foll. by *at, against*) **a** strike out with the foot. **b** express annoyance at or dislike of (treatment, a proposal, etc.); rebel against. **3** *tr. sl.* give up (a habit). **4** *tr.* (often foll. by *out* etc.) expel or dismiss forcibly. **5** *refl.* be annoyed with oneself (*I'll kick myself if I'm wrong*). **6** *tr. Football* score (a goal) by a kick. **7** *intr. Cricket* (of a ball) rise sharply from the pitch. —*n.* **1 a** a blow with the foot or hoof etc. **b** the delivery of such a blow. **2** *colloq.* **a** a sharp stimulant effect, esp. of alcohol (*has some kick in it*; *a cocktail with a kick in it*). **b** (often in *pl.*) a pleasurable thrill (*did it just for kicks*; *got a kick out of flying*). **3** strength, resilience (*have no kick left*). **4** *colloq.* a specified temporary interest or enthusiasm (*on a jogging kick*). **5** the recoil of a gun when discharged. **6** *Brit. Football colloq.* a player of specified kicking ability (*is a good kick*). □**kick about** (or **around**) *colloq.* **1 a** drift idly from place to place. **b** be unused or unwanted. **2 a** treat roughly or scornfully. **b** discuss (an idea) unsystematically. **kick against the pricks** see PRICK. **kick the bucket** *sl.* die. **kick-down** a device for changing gear in a motor vehicle by full depression of the accelerator. **kick one's heels** see HEEL. **kick in 1** knock down (a door etc.) by kicking. **2** esp. *US sl.* contribute (esp. money); pay one's share. **kick in the pants** (or **teeth**) *colloq.* a humiliating punishment or set-back. **kick off 1 a** *Football* begin or resume a match. **b** *colloq.* begin. **2** remove (shoes etc.) by kicking. **kick-off 1** *Football* the start or resumption of a match. **2** (in **for a kick-off**) *colloq.* for a start (*that's wrong for a kick-off*). **kick over the traces** see TRACE². **kick-pleat** a pleat in a narrow skirt to allow freedom of movement. **kick-turn** a standing turn in skiing. **kick up** (or **kick up a fuss, dust,** etc.) create a disturbance; object or register strong disapproval. **kick up one's heels** frolic. **kick a person upstairs** shelve a person by giving him or her promotion or a title. □□ **kickable** *adj.* **kicker** *n.* [ME *kike*, of unkn. orig.]

kick² /kɪk/ *n.* an indentation in the bottom of a glass bottle. [19th c.: orig. unkn.]

kickback /ˈkɪkbæk/ *n. colloq.* **1** the force of a recoil. **2** payment for collaboration, esp. collaboration for profit.

kickshaw /ˈkɪkʃɔː/ *n.* **1** *archaic,* usu. *derog.* a fancy dish in cookery. **2** something elegant but insubstantial; a toy or trinket. [F *quelque chose* something]

kicksorter /ˈkɪkˌsɔːtə(r)/ *n. colloq.* a device for analysing electrical pulses according to amplitude.

kickstand /ˈkɪkstænd/ *n.* a rod attached to a bicycle or motor cycle and kicked into a vertical position to support the vehicle when stationary.

kick-start /ˈkɪkstɑːt/ *n. & v.* —*n.* (also **kick-starter**) a device to start the engine of a motor cycle etc. by the downward thrust of a pedal. —*v.tr.* start (a motor cycle etc.) in this way.

kid¹ /kɪd/ *n. & v.* —*n.* **1** a young goat. **2** the leather made from its skin. **3** *sl.* a child or young person. —*v.intr.* (**kidded, kidding**) (of a goat) give birth. □ **handle with kid gloves** handle in a gentle, delicate, or gingerly manner. **kid brother** (or **sister**) *sl.* a younger brother or sister. **kid-glove** (*attrib.*) dainty or delicate. **kids' stuff** *sl.* something very simple. [ME *kide* f. ON *kith* f. Gmc]

kid² /kɪd/ *v.* (**kidded, kidding**) *colloq.* **1** *tr. & refl.* deceive, trick (*don't kid yourself; kidded his mother that he was ill*). **2** *tr. & intr.* tease (*only kidding*). □ **no kidding** (or **kid**) *sl.* that is the truth. □□ **kidder** *n.* **kiddingly** *adv.* [perh. f. KID¹]

kid³ /kɪd/ *n. hist.* a small wooden tub, esp. a sailor's mess tub for grog or rations. [perh. var. of KIT¹]

Kidderminster carpet /ˈkɪdəˌmɪnstə(r)/ *n.* a carpet made of two cloths of different colours woven together so that the carpet is reversible. [*Kidderminster* in S. England]

kiddie /ˈkɪdɪ/ *n.* (also **kiddy**) (*pl.* **-ies**) *sl.* = KID¹ n. 3.

kiddle /ˈkɪd(ə)l/ *n.* **1** a barrier in a river with an opening fitted with nets etc. to catch fish. **2** an arrangement of fishing-nets hung on stakes along the seashore. [ME f. AF *kidel,* OF *quidel, guidel*]

kiddo /ˈkɪdəʊ/ *n.* (*pl.* **-os**) *sl.* = KID¹ n. 3.

kiddy var. of KIDDIE.

kidnap /ˈkɪdnæp/ *v.tr.* (**kidnapped, kidnapping;** *US* **kidnaped, kidnaping**) **1** carry off (a person etc.) by illegal force or fraud esp. to obtain a ransom. **2** steal (a child). □□ **kidnapper** *n.* [back-form. f. *kidnapper* f. KID¹ + *nap* = NAB]

kidney /ˈkɪdnɪ/ *n.* (*pl.* **-eys**) **1** either of a pair of organs in the abdominal cavity of mammals, birds, and reptiles, which remove nitrogenous wastes from the blood and excrete urine. **2** the kidney of a sheep, ox, or pig as food. **3** temperament, nature, kind (*a man of that kidney; of the right kidney*). □ **kidney bean 1** a dwarf French bean. **2** a scarlet runner bean. **kidney dish** a kidney-shaped dish, esp. one used in surgery. **kidney machine** = *artificial kidney.* **kidney-shaped** shaped like a kidney, with one side concave and the other convex. **kidney vetch** a herbaceous plant, *Anthyllis vulneraria:* also called *lady's finger.* [ME *kidnei,* pl. *kidneiren,* app. partly f. *ei* EGG¹]

kidskin /ˈkɪdskɪn/ *n.* = KID¹ n. 2.

kiekie /ˈkiːkiː/ *n.* a New Zealand climbing plant with edible bracts, and leaves which are used for basket-making etc. [Maori]

kieselguhr /ˈkiːz(ə)lˌɡʊə(r)/ *n.* diatomaceous earth forming deposits in lakes and ponds and used as a filter, filler, insulator, etc., in various manufacturing processes. [G f. *Kiesel* gravel + dial. *Guhr* earthy deposit]

kif var. of KEF.

kike /kaɪk/ *n.* esp. *US sl. offens.* a Jew. [20th c.: orig. uncert.]

Kikuyu /kɪˈkuːjuː/ *n. & adj.* —*n.* (*pl.* same or **Kikuyus**) **1** a member of an agricultural Negro people, the largest Bantu-speaking group in Kenya. **2** the language of this people. —*adj.* of or relating to this people or their language. [native name]

kilderkin /ˈkɪldəkɪn/ *n.* **1** a cask for liquids etc., holding 16 or 18 gallons. **2** this measure. [ME, alt. of *kinderkin* f. MDu. *kinde(r)kin, kinneken,* dimin. of *kintal* QUINTAL]

kill /kɪl/ *v. & n.* —*v.tr.* **1 a** deprive of life or vitality; put to death; cause the death of. **b** (*absol.*) cause or bring about death (*must kill to survive*). **2** destroy; put an end to (feelings etc.) (*overwork killed my enthusiasm*). **3** *refl.* (often foll. by pres. part.) *colloq.* **a** overexert oneself (*don't kill yourself lifting them all at once*). **b** laugh heartily. **4** *colloq.* overwhelm (a person) with amusement, delight, etc. (*the things he says really kill me*). **5** switch off (a spotlight, engine, etc.). **6** *colloq.* delete (a line, paragraph, etc.) from a computer file. **7** *colloq.* cause pain or discomfort to (*my feet are killing me*). **8** pass (time, or a specified amount of it) usu. while waiting for a specific event (*had an hour to kill before the interview*). **9** defeat (a bill in Parliament). **10** *colloq.* consume the entire contents of (a bottle of wine etc.). **11 a** *Tennis* etc. hit (the ball) so skilfully that it cannot be returned. **b** stop (the ball) dead. **12** neutralize or render ineffective (taste, sound, colour, etc.) (*thick carpet killed the sound of footsteps*). —*n.* **1** an act of killing (esp. an animal). **2** an animal or animals killed, esp. by a sportsman. **3** *colloq.* the destruction or disablement of an enemy aircraft, submarine, etc. □ **dressed to kill** dressed showily, alluringly, or impressively. **in at the kill** present at or benefiting from the successful conclusion of an enterprise. **kill off 1** get rid of or destroy completely (esp. a number of persons or things). **2** (of an author) bring about the death of (a fictional character). **kill or cure** (usu. *attrib.*) drastic, extreme. **kill two birds with one stone** achieve two aims at once. **kill with kindness** spoil (a person) with overindulgence. [ME *cülle, kille,* perh. ult. rel. to QUELL]

killdeer /ˈkɪldɪə(r)/ *n.* a large American plover, *Charadrius vociferus,* with a plaintive song. [imit.]

killer /ˈkɪlə(r)/ *n.* **1 a** a person, animal, or thing that kills. **b** a murderer. **2** *colloq.* **a** an impressive, formidable, or excellent thing (*this one is quite difficult, but the next one is a real killer*). **b** a hilarious joke. **c** a decisive blow (*his brilliant header proved to be the killer*). □ **killer instinct 1** an innate tendency to kill. **2** a ruthless streak. **killer whale** a voracious cetacean, *Orcinus orca,* with a white belly and prominent dorsal fin.

killick /ˈkɪlɪk/ *n.* **1** a heavy stone used by small craft as an anchor. **2** a small anchor. **3** *Brit. naval sl.* a leading seaman. [17th c.: orig. unkn.]

killifish /ˈkɪlɪfɪʃ/ *n.* **1** any small fresh- or brackish-water fish of the family Cyprinodontidae, many of which are brightly coloured. **2** a brightly-coloured tropical aquarium fish, *Pterolebias peruensis.* [perh. f. *kill* stream f. Du. *kil* + FISH¹]

killing /ˈkɪlɪŋ/ *n. & adj.* —*n.* **1 a** the causing of death. **b** an instance of this. **2** a great (esp. financial) success (*make a killing*). —*adj. colloq.* **1** overwhelmingly funny. **2** exhausting; very strenuous. □ **killing-bottle** a bottle containing poisonous vapour to kill insects collected as specimens. □□ **killingly** *adv.*

killjoy /ˈkɪldʒɔɪ/ *n.* a person who throws gloom over or prevents other people's enjoyment.

kiln /kɪln/ *n.* a furnace or oven for burning, baking, or drying, esp. for calcining lime or firing pottery etc. [OE *cylene* f. L *culina* kitchen]

kiln-dry /'kɪlndraɪ/ *v.tr.* (**-ies**, **-ied**) dry in a kiln.

kilo /'kiːləʊ/ *n.* (*pl.* **-os**) **1** a kilogram. **2** a kilometre. [F: abbr.]

kilo- /'kɪləʊ/ *comb. form* denoting a factor of 1,000 (esp. in metric units). ¶ Abbr.: **k**, or **K** in *Computing*. [F f. Gk *khilioi* thousand]

kilobyte /'kɪləˌbaɪt/ *n. Computing* 1,024 (i.e. 2^{10}) bytes as a measure of memory size.

kilocalorie /'kɪləˌkæləri/ *n.* = CALORIE 2.

kilocycle /'kɪləˌsaɪk(ə)l/ *n.* a former measure of frequency, equivalent to 1 kilohertz. ¶ Abbr.: **kc**.

kilogram /'kɪləˌgræm/ *n.* (also **-gramme**) the SI unit of mass, equivalent to the international standard kept at Sèvres near Paris (approx. 2.205 lb.). ¶ Abbr.: **kg**. [F *kilogramme* (as KILO, GRAM[1])]

kilohertz /'kɪləˌhɜːts/ *n.* a measure of frequency equivalent to 1,000 cycles per second. ¶ Abbr.: **kHz**.

kilojoule /'kɪləˌdʒuːl/ *n.* 1,000 joules, esp. as a measure of the energy value of foods. ¶ Abbr.: **kJ**.

kilolitre /'kɪləˌliːtə(r)/ *n.* (*US* **-liter**) 1,000 litres (equivalent to 220 imperial gallons). ¶ Abbr.: **kl**.

kilometre /'kɪləˌmiːtə(r), *disp.* kɪ'lɒmɪtə(r)/ *n.* (*US* **kilometer**) a metric unit of measurement equal to 1,000 metres (approx. 0.62 miles). ¶ Abbr.: **km**. □□ **kilometric** /ˌkɪlə'metrɪk/ *adj.* [F *kilomètre* (as KILO-, METRE[1])]

kiloton /'kɪləˌtʌn/ *n.* (also **kilotonne**) a unit of explosive power equivalent to 1,000 tons of TNT.

kilovolt /'kɪləˌvɒlt/ *n.* 1,000 volts. ¶ Abbr.: **kV**.

kilowatt /'kɪləˌwɒt/ *n.* 1,000 watts. ¶ Abbr.: **kW**.

kilowatt-hour /ˌkɪləwɒt'aʊə(r)/ *n.* a measure of electrical energy equivalent to a power consumption of 1,000 watts for one hour. ¶ Abbr.: **kWh**.

kilt /kɪlt/ *n. & v.* —*n.* **1** a skirtlike garment, usu. of pleated tartan cloth and reaching to the knees, as traditionally worn by Highland men. **2** a similar garment worn by women and children. —*v.tr.* **1** tuck up (skirts) round the body. **2** (esp. as **kilted** *adj.*) gather in vertical pleats. □□ **kilted** *adj.* [orig. as verb: ME, of Scand. orig.]

kilter /'kɪltə(r)/ *n.* (also **kelter** /'kel-/) good working order (esp. *out of kilter*). [17th c.: orig. unkn.]

kiltie /'kɪltɪ/ *n.* a wearer of a kilt, esp. a kilted Highland soldier.

kimberlite /'kɪmbəˌlaɪt/ *n. Mineral.* a rare igneous blue-tinged rock sometimes containing diamonds, found in South Africa and Siberia. Also called *blue ground* (see BLUE[1]). [*Kimberley* in S. Africa]

kimono /kɪ'məʊnəʊ/ *n.* (*pl.* **-os**) **1** a long loose Japanese robe worn with a sash. **2** a European dressing-gown modelled on this. □□ **kimonoed** *adj.* [Jap.]

kin /kɪn/ *n. & adj.* —*n.* one's relatives or family. —*predic.adj.* (of a person) related (*we are kin*; *he is kin to me*) (see also AKIN). □**kith and kin** see KITH. **near of kin** closely related by blood, or in character. **next of kin** see NEXT. □□ **kinless** *adj.* [OE *cynn* f. Gmc]

-kin /kɪn/ *suffix* forming diminutive nouns (*catkin*; *manikin*). [from or after MDu. *-kijn*, *-ken*, OHG *-chin*]

kina /'kiːnə/ *n.* the monetary unit of Papua New Guinea. [Papuan]

kinaesthesia /ˌkɪnəs'θiːzɪə/ *n.* (*US* **kinesthesia**) a sense of awareness of the position and movement of the voluntary muscles of the body. □□ **kinaesthetic** /-'θetɪk/ *adj.* [Gk *kineō* move + *aisthēsis* sensation]

kincob /'kɪnkɒb/ *n.* a rich Indian fabric embroidered with gold or silver. [Urdu f. Pers. *kamk̲āb* f. *kamk̲ā* damask]

kind[1] /kaɪnd/ *n.* **1 a** a race or species (*human kind*). **b** a natural group of animals, plants, etc. (*the wolf kind*). **2** class, type, sort, variety (*what kind of cars are you looking for?*). ¶ In sense 2, *these* (or *those*) *kind* is often encountered when followed by a plural, as in *I don't like these kind of things*, but *this kind* and *these kinds* are usually preferred. **3** each of the elements of the Eucharist (*communion under* (or *in*) *both kinds*). **4** the manner or fashion natural to a person etc. (*act after their kind*; *true to kind*). □**kind of** *colloq.* to some extent (*felt kind of sorry*; *I kind of expected it*). **a kind of** used to imply looseness, vagueness, exaggeration, etc., in the term used (*a kind of Jane Austen of our times*; *I suppose he's a kind of doctor*). **in kind 1** in the same form, likewise (*was insulted and replied in kind*). **2** (of payment) in goods or labour as opposed to money (*received their wages in kind*). **3** character, quality (*differ in degree but not in kind*). **law of kind** *archaic* nature in general; the natural order. **nothing of the kind 1** not at all like the thing in question. **2** (expressing denial) not at all. **of its kind** within the limitations of its own class (*good of its kind*). **of a kind 1** *derog.* scarcely deserving the name (*a choir of a kind*). **2** similar in some important respect (*they're two of a kind*). **one's own kind** those with whom one has much in common. **something of the kind** something like the thing in question. [OE *cynd(e)*, *gecynd(e)* f. Gmc]

kind[2] /kaɪnd/ *adj.* **1** of a friendly, generous, benevolent, or gentle nature. **2** (usu. foll. by *to*) showing friendliness, affection, or consideration. **3 a** affectionate. **b** *archaic* loving. [OE *gecynde* (as KIND[1]): orig. = 'natural, native']

kinda /'kaɪndə/ *colloq.* = *kind of*. [corrupt.]

kindergarten /'kɪndəˌgɑːt(ə)n/ *n.* an establishment for preschool learning. [G, = children's garden]

kind-hearted /kaɪnd'hɑːtɪd/ *adj.* of a kind disposition. □□ **kind-heartedly** *adv.* **kind-heartedness** *n.*

kindle /'kɪnd(ə)l/ *v.* **1** *tr.* light or set on fire (a flame, fire, substance, etc.). **2** *intr.* catch fire, burst into flame. **3** *tr.* arouse or inspire (*kindle enthusiasm for the project*; *kindle jealousy in a rival*). **4** *intr.* (usu. foll. by *to*) respond, react (to a person, an action, etc.) (*kindle to his courage*). **5** *intr.* become animated, glow with passion etc. (*her imagination kindled*). **6** *tr. & intr.* make or become bright (*kindle the embers to a glow*). □□ **kindler** *n.* [ME f. ON *kynda*, kindle: cf. ON *kindill* candle, torch]

kindling /'kɪndlɪŋ/ *n.* small sticks etc. for lighting fires.

kindly[1] /'kaɪndlɪ/ *adv.* **1** in a kind manner (*spoke to the child kindly*). **2** often *iron.* used in a polite request or demand (*kindly acknowledge this letter*; *kindly leave me alone*). □**look kindly upon** regard sympathetically. **take a thing kindly** like or be pleased by it. **take kindly to** be pleased by or endeared to (a person or thing). **thank kindly** thank very much. [OE *gecyndelīce* (as KIND[2])]

kindly[2] /'kaɪndlɪ/ *adj.* (**kindlier**, **kindliest**) **1** kind, kind-hearted. **2** (of climate etc.) pleasant, genial. **3** *archaic* native-born (*a kindly Scot*). □□ **kindlily** *adv.* **kindliness** *n.* [OE *gecyndelic* (as KIND[1])]

kindness /'kaɪndnɪs/ *n.* **1** the state or quality of being kind. **2** a kind act.

kindred /'kɪndrɪd/ *n. & adj.* —*n.* **1** one's relations, referred to collectively. **2** a relationship by blood. **3** a resemblance or affinity in character. —*adj.* **1** related by blood or marriage. **2** allied or similar in character (*other kindred symptoms*). □**kindred spirit** a person whose character and outlook have much in common with one's own. [ME f. KIN + *-red* f. OE *rǣden* condition]

kine /kaɪn/ *archaic pl.* of COW[1].

kinematics /ˌkɪnɪ'mætɪks, ˌkaɪ-/ *n.pl.* (usu. treated as *sing.*) the branch of mechanics concerned with the motion of objects without reference to the forces which cause the motion. □□ **kinematic** *adj.* **kinematically** *adv.* [Gk *kinēma -matos* motion f. *kineō* move + -ICS]

kinematograph var. of CINEMATOGRAPH.

kinesics /kɪ'niːsɪks/ *n.pl.* (usu. treated as *sing.*) **1** the study of body movements and gestures which contribute to communication. **2** these movements; body language. [Gk *kinēsis* motion (as KINETIC)]

kinesiology /kɪ,niːsɪ'ɒlədʒɪ/ *n.* the study of the mechanics of body movements.

kinesthesia *US* var. of KINAESTHESIA.

kinetic /kɪ'netɪk, kaɪ-/ *adj.* of or due to motion. □**kinetic art** a form of art that depends on movement for its effect. **kinetic energy** the energy of motion. **kinetic theory** a theory which explains the physical properties of matter in terms of the motions of its constituent particles. □□**kinetically** *adv.* [Gk *kinētikos* f. *kineō* move]

kinetics /kɪ'netɪks, kaɪ-/ *n.pl.* **1** = DYNAMICS 1a. **2** (usu. treated as *sing.*) the branch of physical chemistry concerned with measuring and studying the rates of chemical reactions.

kinetin /'kaɪnɪtɪn/ *n.* *Biochem.* a synthetic kinin used to stimulate cell division in plants. [as KINETIC + -IN]

kinfolk *US* var. of KINSFOLK.

king /kɪŋ/ *n. & v.* **1** (as a title usu. **King**) a male sovereign, esp. the hereditary ruler of an independent State. **2** a person or thing pre-eminent in a specified field or class (*railway king*). **3** a large (or the largest) kind of plant, animal, etc. (*king penguin*). **4** *Chess* the piece on each side which the opposing side has to checkmate to win. **5** a piece in draughts with extra capacity of moving, made by crowning an ordinary piece that has reached the opponent's baseline. **6** a court-card bearing a representation of a king and usu. ranking next below an ace. **7** (**the King**) (in the UK) the national anthem when there is a male sovereign. **8** (**Kings** or **Books of Kings**) two Old Testament books dealing with history, esp. of the kingdom of Judah. —*v.tr.* make (a person) king. □**King Charles spaniel** a spaniel of a small black and tan breed. **king cobra** a large and venomous hooded Indian snake, *Ophiophagus hannah*. **king-crab 1** = *horseshoe crab*. **2** *US* any of various large edible spider crabs. **king-fish** any of various large fish, esp. the opah or mulloway. **king it 1** play or act the king. **2** (usu. foll. by *over*) govern, control. **King James Bible** (or **Version**) = *Authorized Version* (see AUTHORIZE). **King of Arms** *Heraldry* (in the UK) a chief herald (at the College of Arms: Garter, Clarenceux, and Norroy and Ulster; in Scotland: Lyon). **king of beasts** the lion. **king of birds** the eagle. **King of the Castle** a children's game consisting of trying to displace a rival from a mound. **King of Kings 1** God. **2** the title assumed by many eastern kings. **king-post** an upright post from the tie-beam of a roof to the apex of a truss. **King's Bench** see BENCH. **king's bishop, knight,** etc. *Chess* (of pieces which exist in pairs) the piece starting on the king's side of the board. **King's bounty** see BOUNTY. **King's colour** see COLOUR. **King's Counsel** see COUNSEL. **King's English** see ENGLISH. **King's evidence** see EVIDENCE. **king's evil** *hist.* scrofula, formerly held to be curable by the royal touch. **King's Guide** see GUIDE. **King's highway** see HIGHWAY. **king-size** (or **-sized**) larger than normal; very large. **King's Messenger** see MESSENGER. **king's pawn** *Chess* the pawn in front of the king at the beginning of a game. **King's Proctor** see PROCTOR. **king's ransom** a fortune. **King's Scout** see SCOUT¹. **King's speech** see SPEECH. □□ **kinghood** *n.* **kingless** *adj.* **kinglike** *adj.* **kingly** *adj.* **kingliness** *n.* **kingship** *n.* [OE *cyning, cyng* f. Gmc]

kingbird /'kɪŋbɜːd/ *n.* any flycatcher of the genus *Tyrannus*, with olive-grey plumage and long pointed wings.

kingbolt /'kɪŋbəʊlt/ *n.* = KINGPIN.

kingcraft /'kɪŋkrɑːft/ *n.* *archaic* the skilful exercise of kingship.

kingcup /'kɪŋkʌp/ *n.* *Brit.* a marsh marigold.

kingdom /'kɪŋdəm/ *n.* **1** an organized community headed by a king. **2** the territory subject to a king. **3 a** the spiritual reign attributed to God (*Thy kingdom come*). **b** the sphere of this (*kingdom of heaven*). **4** a domain belonging to a person, animal, etc. **5** a province of nature (*the vegetable kingdom*). **6** a specified mental or emotional province (*kingdom of the heart; kingdom of fantasy*). **7** *Biol.* the highest category in taxonomic classification. □**come into** (or **to**) **one's kingdom** achieve recognition or supremacy. **kingdom come** *sl.* eternity; the next world. **till kingdom come** *sl.* for ever. □□ **kingdomed** *adj.* [OE *cyningdōm* (as KING)]

kingfisher /'kɪŋ,fɪʃə(r)/ *n.* any bird of the family Alcedinidae esp. *Alcedo atthis* with a long sharp beak and brightly coloured plumage, which dives for fish in rivers etc.

kinglet /'kɪŋlɪt/ *n.* **1** a petty king. **2** *US* any of various small birds of the family Regulidae, esp. the goldcrest.

kingmaker /'kɪŋ,meɪkə(r)/ *n.* a person who makes kings, leaders, etc., through the exercise of political influence, orig. with ref. to the Earl of Warwick in the reign of Henry VI of England.

kingpin /'kɪŋpɪn/ *n.* **1 a** a main or large bolt in a central position. **b** a vertical bolt used as a pivot. **2** an essential person or thing, esp. in a complex system.

kinin /'kaɪnɪn/ *n.* **1** any of a group of polypeptides present in the blood after tissue damage. **2** any of a group of compounds which promote cell division and inhibit ageing in plants. [Gk *kineō* move + -IN]

kink /kɪŋk/ *n. & v.* —*n.* **1 a** a short backward twist in wire or tubing etc. such as may cause an obstruction. **b** a tight wave in human or animal hair. **2** a mental twist or quirk. —*v.intr. & tr.* form or cause to form a kink. [MLG *kinke* (v.) prob. f. Du. *kinken*]

kinkajou /'kɪŋkə,dʒuː/ *n.* a Central and S. American nocturnal fruit-eating mammal, *Potos flavus*, with a prehensile tail and living in trees. [F *quincajou* f. N.Amer. Ind.: cf. Algonquin *kwingwaage* wolverine]

kinky /'kɪŋkɪ/ *adj.* (**kinkier, kinkiest**) **1** *colloq.* **a** given to or involving abnormal sexual behaviour. **b** (of clothing etc.) bizarre in a sexually provocative way. **2** strange, eccentric. **3** having kinks or twists. □□ **kinkily** *adv.* **kinkiness** *n.* [KINK + -Y¹]

kino /'kiːnəʊ/ *n.* (*pl.* -os) a catechu-like gum produced by various trees and used in medicine and tanning as an astringent. [W. Afr.]

-kins /kɪnz/ *suffix* = -KIN, often with suggestions of endearment (*babykins*).

kinsfolk /'kɪnzfəʊk/ *n.pl.* (*US* **kinfolk**) one's relations by blood.

kinship /'kɪnʃɪp/ *n.* **1** blood relationship. **2** the sharing of characteristics or origins.

kinsman /'kɪnzmən/ *n.* (*pl.* -men; *fem.* **kinswoman,** *pl.* -women) **1** a blood relation or *disp.* a relation by marriage. **2** a member of one's own tribe or people.

kiosk /'kiːɒsk/ *n.* **1** a light open-fronted booth or cubicle from which food, newspapers, tickets, etc. are sold. **2** a telephone box. **3** *Austral.* a building in which refreshments are served in a park, zoo, etc. **4** a light open pavilion in Turkey and Iran. [F *kiosque* f. Turk. *kiūshk* pavilion f. Pers. *guš*]

kip¹ /kɪp/ *n. & v. Brit. sl.* —*n.* **1** a sleep or nap. **2** a bed or cheap lodging-house. **3** (also **kip-house** or **-shop**) a brothel. —*v.intr.* (**kipped, kipping**) sleep, take a nap. [cf. Da. *kippe* mean hut]

kip² /kɪp/ *n.* the hide of a young or small animal as used for leather. [ME: orig. unkn.]

kip³ /kɪp/ *n.* (*pl.* same or **kips**) the basic monetary unit of Laos. [Thai]

kip⁴ /kɪp/ *n. Austral. sl.* a small piece of wood from which coins are spun in the game of two-up. [perh. f. E dial.: cf. *keper* a flat piece of wood preventing a horse from eating the corn, or Ir. dial. *kippeen* f. Ir. *cipín* a little stick]

kipper /'kɪpə(r)/ *n. & v.* —*n.* **1** a kippered fish, esp. herring. **2** a male salmon in the spawning season. —*v.tr.* cure (a herring etc.) by splitting open, salting, and drying in the open air or smoke. [ME: orig. uncert.]

kipsie /'kɪpsɪ/ n. (also **kipsy**) (pl. **-ies**) Austral. sl. a house, home, lean-to, or shelter. [perh. f. KIP¹]

kir /kɜː(r)/ n. a drink made from dry white wine and crème de cassis. [Canon Felix Kir d. 1968, said to have invented the recipe]

kirby-grip /'kɜːbɪgrɪp/ n. (also **Kirbigrip** propr.) a type of sprung hairgrip. [Kirby, part of orig. manufacturer's name]

Kirghiz /kɪə'gɪz, 'kɜːgɪz/ n. & adj. —n. (pl. same) 1 a member of a Mongol people living in central Asia between the Volga and the Irtysh rivers. 2 the language of this people. —adj. of or relating to this people or their language. [Kirghiz]

kirk /kɜːk/ n. Sc. & N.Engl. 1 a church. 2 (**the Kirk** or **the Kirk of Scotland**) the Church of Scotland as distinct from the Church of England or from the Episcopal Church in Scotland. □**Kirk-session 1** the lowest court in the Church of Scotland. **2** hist. the lowest court in other Presbyterian Churches, composed of ministers and elders. [ME f. ON kirkja f. OE cir(i)ce CHURCH]

kirkman /'kɜːkmən/ n. (pl. **-men**) Sc. & N.Engl. a member of the Church of Scotland.

kirsch /kɪəʃ/ n. (also **kirschwasser** /'kɪəʃˌvasə(r)/) a brandy distilled from the fermented juice of cherries. [G Kirsche cherry, Wasser water]

kirtle /'kɜːt(ə)l/ n. archaic 1 a woman's gown or outer petticoat. 2 a man's tunic or coat. [OE cyrtel f. Gmc, ult. perh. f. L curtus short]

kiskadee /ˌkɪskə'diː/ n. (also **keskidee** /ˌkeskɪ'diː/) a tyrant flycatcher, Pitangus sulphuratus, of Central and S. America with brown and yellow plumage. [imit. of its cry]

kismet /'kɪsmet, 'kɪz-/ n. destiny, fate. [Turk. f. Arab. ḳisma(t) f. ḳasama divide]

kiss /kɪs/ v. & n. —v. 1 tr. touch with the lips, esp. as a sign of love, affection, greeting, or reverence. 2 tr. express (greeting or farewell) in this way. 3 absol. (of two persons) touch each others' lips in this way. 4 tr. (also absol.) (of a snooker ball etc. in motion) lightly touch (another ball). —n. 1 a touch with the lips in kissing. 2 the slight impact when one snooker ball etc. lightly touches another. 3 a small sweetmeat or piece of confectionery. □**kiss and tell** recount one's sexual exploits. **kiss a person's arse** coarse sl. act obsequiously towards a person. **kiss away** remove (tears etc.) by kissing. **kiss-curl** a small curl of hair on the forehead, at the nape, or in front of the ear. **kiss the dust** submit abjectly; be overthrown. **kiss goodbye to** colloq. accept the loss of. **kiss the ground** prostrate oneself as a token of homage. **kissing cousin** (or **kin** or **kind**) a distant relative (given a formal kiss on occasional meetings). **kissing-gate** Brit. a gate hung in a V- or U-shaped enclosure, to let one person through at a time. **kiss of death** an apparently friendly act which causes ruin. **kiss off** sl. **1** dismiss, get rid of. **2** go away, die. **kiss of life** mouth-to-mouth resuscitation. **kiss of peace** Eccl. a ceremonial kiss, esp. during the Eucharist, as a sign of unity. **kiss the rod** accept chastisement submissively. □□**kissable** adj. [OE cyssan f. Gmc]

kisser /'kɪsə(r)/ n. **1** a person who kisses. **2** (orig. Boxing) sl. the mouth; the face.

kissogram /'kɪsəˌgræm/ n. (also **Kissagram** propr.) a novelty telegram or greetings message delivered with a kiss.

kissy /'kɪsɪ/ adj. colloq. given to kissing (not the kissy type).

kist var. of CIST¹.

Kiswahili /ˌkɪswɑː'hiːlɪ/ n. one of the six languages preferred for use in Africa by the Organization for African Unity. [Swahili ki- prefix for an abstract or inanimate object]

kit¹ /kɪt/ n. & v. —n. **1** a set of articles, equipment, or clothing needed for a specific purpose (first-aid

kit; bicycle-repair kit). **2** the clothing etc. needed for any activity, esp. sport (football kit). **3** a set of all the parts needed to assemble an item, e.g. a piece of furniture, a model, etc. **4** Brit. a wooden tub. —v.tr. (**kitted**, **kitting**) (often foll. by out, up) equip with the appropriate clothing or tools. [ME f. MDu. kitte wooden vessel, of unkn. orig.]

kit² /kɪt/ n. **1** a kitten. **2** a young fox, badger, etc. [abbr.]

kit³ /kɪt/ n. hist. a small fiddle esp. as used by a dancing-master. [perh. f. L cithara; see CITTERN]

kitbag /'kɪtbæg/ n. a large, usu. cylindrical bag used for carrying a soldier's, traveller's, or sportsman's equipment.

kit-cat /'kɪtkæt/ n. (in full **kit-cat portrait**) a portrait of less than half length, but including one hand; usu. 36 × 28 in. [named after a series of portraits of the members of the Kit-Cat Club, an early 18th-c. Whig society]

kitchen /'kɪtʃɪn, -tʃ(ə)n/ n. **1** the room or area where food is prepared and cooked. **2** (attrib.) of or belonging to the kitchen (kitchen knife; kitchen table). **3** sl. the percussion section of an orchestra. □**everything but the kitchen sink** everything imaginable. **kitchen cabinet** a group of unofficial advisers thought to be unduly influential. **kitchen garden** a garden where vegetables and sometimes fruit or herbs are grown. **kitchen midden** a prehistoric refuse-heap which marks an ancient settlement, chiefly containing bones, seashells, etc. **kitchen-sink** (in art forms) depicting extreme realism, esp. drabness or sordidness (kitchen-sink school of painting; kitchen-sink drama). **kitchen tea** Austral. & NZ a party held before a wedding to which female guests bring items of kitchen equipment as presents. [OE cycene f. L coquere cook]

Kitchener bun /'kɪtʃɪnə(r)/ n. Austral. a cream-filled bun coated with cinnamon and sugar. [1st Earl Kitchener d. 1916]

kitchenette /ˌkɪtʃɪ'net, -tʃə'net/ n. a small kitchen or part of a room fitted as a kitchen.

kitchenware /'kɪtʃɪnˌweə(r), 'kɪtʃ(ə)n-/ n. the utensils used in the kitchen.

kite /kaɪt/ n. & v. —n. **1** a toy consisting of a light framework with thin material stretched over it, flown in the wind at the end of a long string. **2** any of various soaring birds of prey esp. of the genus Milvus with long wings and usu. a forked tail. **3** Brit. sl. an aeroplane. **4** sl. a fraudulent cheque, bill, or receipt. **5** Geom. a quadrilateral figure symmetrical about one diagonal. **6** sl. a letter or note, esp. one that is illicit or surreptitious. **7** (in pl.) the highest sail of a ship, set only in a light wind. **8** archaic a dishonest person, a sharper. —v. **1** intr. soar like a kite. **2** tr. (also absol.) originate or pass (fraudulent cheques, bills, or receipts). **3** tr. (also absol.) raise (money by dishonest means) (kite a loan). □**kite balloon** a sausage-shaped captive balloon for military observations. **kite-flying** fraudulent practice. [OE cȳta, of unkn. orig.]

Kitemark /'kaɪtmɑːk/ n. (in the UK) the official kite-shaped mark on goods approved by the British Standards Institution.

kith /kɪθ/ n. □**kith and kin** friends and relations. [OE cȳthth f. Gmc]

kitsch /kɪtʃ/ n. (often attrib.) garish, pretentious, or sentimental art, usu. vulgar and worthless (kitsch plastic models of the royal family). □□**kitschy** adj. (**kitschier**, **kitschiest**). **kitschiness** n. [G]

kitten /'kɪt(ə)n/ n. & v. —n. **1** a young cat. **2** a young ferret etc. —v.intr. & tr. (of a cat etc.) give birth or give birth to. □**have kittens** Brit. colloq. be extremely upset, anxious, or nervous. [ME kito(u)n, ketoun f. OF chitoun, chetoun dimin. of chat CAT]

kittenish /'kɪtənɪʃ/ adj. **1** like a young cat; playful and lively. **2** flirtatious. □□**kittenishly** adv. **kittenishness** n. [KITTEN]

kittiwake /'kɪtɪˌweɪk/ n. either of two small gulls,

b but d dog f few g get h he j yes k cat l leg m man n no p pen r red s sit t top v voice

Rissa tridactyla and *R. brevirostris*, nesting on sea cliffs. [imit. of its cry]

kittle /'kɪt(ə)l/ *adj.* (also **kittle-cattle** /'kɪt(ə)l ˌkæt(ə)l/) **1** (of a person) capricious, rash, or erratic in behaviour. **2** difficult to deal with. [ME (now Sc. & dial.) *kittle* tickle, prob. f. ON *kitla*]

kitty[1] /'kɪtɪ/ *n.* (*pl.* **-ies**) **1** a fund of money for communal use. **2** the pool in some card-games. **3** the jack in bowls. [19th c.: orig. unkn.]

kitty[2] /'kɪtɪ/ *n.* (*pl.* **-ies**) a pet-name or a child's name for a kitten or cat.

kiwi /'kiːwiː/ *n.* (*pl.* **kiwis**) **1** a flightless New Zealand bird of the genus *Apteryx* with hairlike feathers and a long bill. Also called APTERYX. **2** (**Kiwi**) *colloq.* a New Zealander, esp. a soldier or member of a national sports team. □**kiwi fruit** (or **berry**) the fruit of a climbing plant, *Actinidia chinensis*, having a thin hairy skin, green flesh, and black seeds: also called *Chinese gooseberry*. [Maori]

kJ *abbr.* kilojoule(s).

KKK *abbr. US* Ku Klux Klan.

kl *abbr.* kilolitre(s).

Klaxon /'klæks(ə)n/ *n. propr.* a horn or warning hooter, orig. on a motor vehicle. [name of the manufacturing company]

Kleenex /'kliːneks/ *n.* (*pl.* same or **Kleenexes**) orig. *US propr.* an absorbent disposable paper tissue, used esp. as a handkerchief.

Klein bottle /'klaɪn/ *n. Math.* a closed surface with only one side, formed by passing the neck of a tube through the side of the tube to join the hole in the base. [F. *Klein*, Ger. mathematician d. 1925]

klepht /kleft/ *n.* **1** a member of the original body of Greeks who refused to submit to the Turks in the 15th c. **2** any of their descendants. **3** a brigand or bandit. [mod. Gk *klephtēs* f. Gk *kleptēs* thief]

kleptomania /ˌkleptəʊ'meɪnɪə/ *n.* a recurrent urge to steal, usu. without regard for need or profit. □□ **kleptomaniac** /-nɪˌæk/ *n.* & *adj.* [Gk *kleptēs* thief + -MANIA]

klieg /kliːg/ *n.* (also **klieg light**) a powerful lamp in a film studio etc. [A. T. & J. H. *Kliegl*, Amer. inventors d. 1927, 1959]

klipspringer /'klɪpˌsprɪŋə(r)/ *n.* a S. African dwarf antelope, *Oreotragus oreotragus*, which can bound up and down rocky slopes. [Afrik. f. *klip* rock + *springer* jumper]

Klondike /'klɒndaɪk/ *n.* a source of valuable material. [*Klondike* in Yukon, Canada, where gold was found in 1896]

kloof /kluːf/ *n.* a steep-sided ravine or valley in S. Africa. [Du., = cleft]

kludge /klʌdʒ/ *n.* orig. *US sl.* **1** an ill-assorted collection of poorly matching parts. **2** *Computing* a machine, system, or program that has been badly put together.

klystron /'klaɪstrɒn/ *n.* an electron tube that generates or amplifies microwaves by velocity modulation. [Gk *kluzō klus-* wash over]

km *abbr.* kilometre(s).

K-meson /keɪ'mezɒn, -'miːzɒn/ *n.* = KAON. [K (see KAON) + MESON]

kn. *abbr. Naut.* knot(s).

knack /næk/ *n.* **1** an acquired or intuitive faculty of doing a thing adroitly. **2** a trick or habit of action or speech etc. (*has a knack of offending people*). **3** *archaic* an ingenious device (see KNICK-KNACK). [ME, prob. identical with *knack* sharp blow or sound f. LG, ult. imit.]

knacker /'nækə(r)/ *n.* & *v. Brit.* —*n.* **1** a buyer of useless horses for slaughter. **2** a buyer of old houses, ships, etc. for the materials. —*v.tr. sl.* **1** kill. **2** (esp. as **knackered** *adj.*) exhaust, wear out. [19th c.: orig. unkn.]

knackery /'nækərɪ/ *n.* (*pl.* **-ies**) a knacker's yard or business.

knag /næg/ *n.* **1** a knot in wood; the base of a branch.

2 a short dead branch. **3** a peg for hanging things on. □□ **knaggy** *adj.* [ME, perh. f. LG *Knagge*]

knap[1] /næp/ *n.* chiefly *dial.* the crest of a hill or of rising ground. [OE *cnæp(p)*, perh. rel. to ON *knappr* knob]

knap[2] /næp/ *v.tr.* (**knapped**, **knapping**) **1** break (stones for roads or building, flints, or *Austral.* ore) with a hammer. **2** *archaic* knock, rap, snap asunder. □□ **knapper** *n.* [ME, imit.]

knapsack /'næpsæk/ *n.* a soldier's or hiker's bag with shoulder-straps, carried on the back, and usu. made of canvas or weatherproof material. [MLG, prob. f. *knappen* bite + SACK[1]]

knapweed /'næpwiːd/ *n.* any of various plants of the genus *Centaurea*, having thistle-like purple flowers. [ME, orig. *knopweed* f. KNOP + WEED]

knar /nɑː(r)/ *n.* a knot or protuberance in a tree trunk, root, etc. [ME *knarre*, rel. to MLG, M.Du., MHG *knorre* knobbed protuberance]

knave /neɪv/ *n.* **1** a rogue, a scoundrel. **2** = JACK[1] *n.* 2. □□ **knavery** *n.* (*pl.* **-ies**). **knavish** *adj.* **knavishly** *adv.* **knavishness** *n.* [OE *cnafa* boy, servant, f. WG]

knawel /'nɔːəl/ *n.* any low-growing plant of the genus *Scleranthus*. [G *Knauel*]

knead /niːd/ *v.tr.* **1 a** work (a yeast mixture, clay, etc.) into dough, paste, etc. by pummelling. **b** make (bread, pottery, etc.) in this way. **2** blend or weld together (*kneaded them into a unified group*). **3** massage (muscles etc.) as if kneading. □□ **kneadable** *adj.* **kneader** *n.* [OE *cnedan* f. Gmc]

knee /niː/ *n.* & *v.* —*n.* **1 a** (often *attrib.*) the joint between the thigh and the lower leg in humans. **b** the corresponding joint in other animals. **c** the area around this. **d** the upper surface of the thigh of a sitting person; the lap (*held her on his knee*). **2** the part of a garment covering the knee. **3** anything resembling a knee in shape or position, esp. a piece of wood or iron bent at an angle, a sharp turn in a graph, etc. —*v.tr.* (**knees**, **kneed**, **kneeing**) **1** touch or strike with the knee (*kneed the ball past him*; *kneed him in the groin*). **2** *colloq.* cause (trousers) to bulge at the knee. □**bend** (or **bow**) **the knee** kneel, esp. in submission. **bring a person to his** or **her knees** reduce a person to submission. **knee-bend** the action of bending the knee, esp. as a physical exercise in which the body is raised and lowered without the use of the hands. **knee-breeches** close-fitting trousers reaching to or just below the knee. **knee-deep 1** (usu. foll. by *in*) **a** immersed up to the knees. **b** deeply involved. **2** so deep as to reach the knees. **knee-high** so high as to reach the knees. **knee-hole** a space for the knees, esp. under a desk. **knee-jerk 1** a sudden involuntary kick caused by a blow on the tendon just below the knee. **2** (*attrib.*) predictable, automatic, stereotyped. **knee-joint 1** = senses 1a, b of *n.* **2** a joint made of two pieces hinged together. **knee-length** reaching the knees. **knee-pan** the kneecap. **knees-up** *Brit. colloq.* a lively party or gathering. **on** (or **on one's**) **bended knee** (or **knees**) kneeling, esp. in supplication, submission, or worship. [OE *cnēo(w)*]

kneecap /'niːkæp/ *n.* & *v.* —*n.* **1** the convex bone in front of the knee-joint. **2** a protective covering for the knee. —*v.tr.* (**-capped**, **-capping**) *colloq.* shoot (a person) in the knee or leg as a punishment, esp. for betraying a terrorist group. □□ **kneecapping** *n.*

kneel /niːl/ *v.intr.* (*past* and *past part.* **knelt** /nelt/ or esp. *US* **kneeled**) fall or rest on the knees or a knee. [OE *cnēowlian* (as KNEE)]

kneeler /'niːlə(r)/ *n.* **1** a hassock or cushion used for kneeling, esp. in church. **2** a person who kneels.

knell /nel/ *n.* & *v.* —*n.* **1** the sound of a bell, esp. when rung solemnly for a death or funeral. **2** an announcement, event, etc., regarded as a solemn warning of disaster. —*v.* **1** *intr.* **a** (of a bell) ring solemnly, esp. for a death or funeral. **b** make a doleful or ominous sound. **2** *tr.* proclaim by or as by a knell (*knelled the death of all their hopes*). □**ring**

the knell of announce or herald the end of. [OE *cnyll, cnyllan:* perh. infl. by *bell*]

knelt *past* and *past part.* of KNEEL.

Knesset /'knesɪt/ *n.* the parliament of modern Israel. [Heb., lit. gathering]

knew *past* of KNOW.

knickerbocker /'nɪkə,bɒkə(r)/ *n.* **1** (in *pl.*) loose-fitting breeches gathered at the knee or calf. **2** (**Knickerbocker**) **a** a New Yorker. **b** a descendant of the original Dutch settlers in New York. □ **Knickerbocker Glory** ice-cream served with other ingredients in a tall glass. [Diedrich *Knickerbocker*, pretended author of W. Irving's *History of New York* (1809)]

knickers /'nɪkəz/ *n.pl.* **1** *Brit.* a woman's or girl's undergarment covering the body from the waist or hips to the top of the thighs and having leg-holes or separate legs. **2** esp. *US* **a** knickerbockers. **b** a boy's short trousers. **3** (as *int.*) *Brit. sl.* an expression of contempt. [abbr. of KNICKERBOCKER]

knick-knack /'nɪknæk/ *n.* **1** a useless and usu. worthless ornament; a trinket. **2** a small, dainty article of furniture, dress, etc. □□ **knick-knackery** *n.* **knick-knackish** *adj.* [redupl. of *knack* in obs. sense 'trinket']

knife /naɪf/ *n. & v.* —*n.* (*pl.* **knives** /naɪvz/) **1 a** a metal blade used as a cutting tool with usu. one long sharp edge fixed rigidly in a handle or hinged (cf. PENKNIFE). **b** a similar tool used as a weapon. **2** a cutting-blade forming part of a machine. **3** (as **the knife**) a surgical operation or operations. —*v.tr.* **1** cut or stab with a knife. **2** *sl.* bring about the defeat of (a person) by underhand means. □ **at knife-point** threatened with a knife or an ultimatum etc. **before you can say knife** *colloq.* very quickly or suddenly. **get one's knife into** treat maliciously or vindictively, persecute. **knife-board** a board on which knives are cleaned. **knife-edge 1** the edge of a knife. **2** a position of extreme danger or uncertainty. **3** a steel wedge on which a pendulum etc. oscillates. **4** = ARÊTE. **knife-grinder 1** a travelling sharpener of knives etc. **2** a person who grinds knives etc. during their manufacture. **knife-machine** a machine for cleaning knives. **knife-pleat** a narrow flat pleat on a skirt etc., usu. overlapping another. **knife-rest** a metal or glass support for a carving-knife or -fork at table. **knife-throwing** a circus etc. act in which knives are thrown at targets. **that one could cut with a knife** *colloq.* (of an accent, atmosphere, etc.) very obvious, oppressive, etc. □□ **knifelike** *adj.* **knifer** *n.* [OE *cnīf* f. ON *knífr* f. Gmc]

knight /naɪt/ *n. & v.* —*n.* **1** a man awarded a non-hereditary title (*Sir*) by a sovereign in recognition of merit or service. **2** *hist.* **a** a man, usu. noble, raised esp. by a sovereign to honourable military rank after service as a page and squire. **b** a military follower or attendant, esp. of a lady as her champion in a war or tournament. **3** a man devoted to the service of a woman, cause, etc. **4** *Chess* a piece usu. shaped like a horse's head. **5 a** *Rom.Hist.* a member of the class of *equites*, orig. the cavalry of the Roman army. **b** *Gk Hist.* a citizen of the second class in Athens. **6** (in full **knight of the shire**) *hist.* a gentleman representing a shire or county in parliament. —*v.tr.* confer a knighthood on. □ **knight bachelor** (*pl.* **knights bachelor**) a knight not belonging to a special order. **knight commander** see COMMANDER. **knight errant 1** a medieval knight wandering in search of chivalrous adventures. **2** a man of a chivalrous or quixotic nature. **knight-errantry** the practice or conduct of a knight errant. **Knight Hospitaller** (*pl.* **Knights Hospitaller**) a member of an order of monks with a military history, founded at Jerusalem *c.*1050. **knight marshal** *hist.* an officer of the royal household with judicial functions. **knight of the road** *colloq.* **1** a highwayman. **2** a commercial traveller. **3** a tramp. **4** a lorry driver or taxi driver. **knight-service**

hist. the tenure of land by military service. **Knight Templar** (*pl.* **Knights Templar**) a member of a religious and military order for the protection of pilgrims to the Holy Land, suppressed in 1312. □□ **knighthood** *n.* **knightlike** *adj.* **knightly** *adj.* & *adv. poet.* **knightliness** *n.* [OE *cniht* boy, youth, hero f. WG]

knightage /'naɪtɪdʒ/ *n.* **1** knights collectively. **2** a list and account of knights.

knish /knɪʃ/ *n.* a dumpling of flaky dough filled with cheese etc. and baked or fried. [Yiddish f. Russ.]

knit /nɪt/ *v. & n.* —*v.* (**knitting**; *past* and *past part.* **knitted** or (esp. in senses 2–4) **knit**) **1** *tr.* (also *absol.*) **a** make (a garment, blanket, etc.) by interlocking loops of esp. wool with knitting-needles. **b** make (a garment etc.) with a knitting machine. **c** make (a plain stitch) in knitting (*knit one, purl one*). **2 a** *tr.* contract (the forehead) in vertical wrinkles. **b** *intr.* (of the forehead) contract; frown. **3** *tr. & intr.* (often foll. by *together*) make or become close or compact esp. by common interests etc. (*a close-knit group*). **4** *intr.* (often foll. by *together*) (of parts of a broken bone) become joined; heal. —*n.* knitted material or a knitted garment. □ **knit up 1** make or repair by knitting. **2** conclude, finish, or end. □□ **knitter** *n.* [OE *cnyttan* f. WG: cf. KNOT[1]]

knitting /'nɪtɪŋ/ *n.* **1** a garment etc. in the process of being knitted. **2 a** the act of knitting. **b** an instance of this. □ **knitting-machine** a machine used for mechanically knitting garments etc. **knitting-needle** a thin pointed rod of steel, wood, plastic, etc., used esp. in pairs for knitting.

knitwear /'nɪtweə(r)/ *n.* knitted garments.

knives *pl.* of KNIFE.

knob /nɒb/ *n. & v.* —*n.* **1 a** a rounded protuberance, esp. at the end or on the surface of a thing. **b** a handle of a door, drawer, etc., shaped like a knob. **c** a knob-shaped attachment for pulling, turning, etc. (*press the knob under the desk*). **2** a small, usu. round, piece (of butter, coal, sugar, etc.). —*v.* (**knobbed**, **knobbing**) **1** *tr.* provide with knobs. **2** *intr.* (usu. foll. by *out*) bulge. □ **with knobs on** *Brit. sl.* that and more (used as a retort to an insult, in emphatic agreement, etc.) (*and the same to you with knobs on*). □□ **knobby** *adj.* **knoblike** *adj.* [ME f. MLG *knobbe* knot, knob, bud: cf. KNOP, NOB[2], NUB]

knobble /'nɒb(ə)l/ *n.* a small knob. □□ **knobbly** *adj.* [ME, dimin. of KNOB: cf. Du. & LG *knobbel*]

knobkerrie /'nɒb,kerɪ/ *n.* a short stick with a knobbed head used as a weapon esp. by S. African tribes. [after Afrik. *knopkierie*]

knobstick /'nɒbstɪk/ *n.* **1** = KNOBKERRIE. **2** *archaic* = BLACKLEG.

knock /nɒk/ *v. & n.* —*v.* **1 a** *tr.* strike (a hard surface) with an audible sharp blow (*knocked the table three times*). **b** *intr.* strike, esp. a door to gain admittance (*can you hear someone knocking?*; *knocked at the door*). **2** *tr.* make (a hole, a dent, etc.) by knocking (*knock a hole in the fence*). **3** *tr.* (usu. foll. by *in, out, off*, etc.) drive (a thing, a person, etc.) by striking (*knocked the ball into the hole*; *knocked those ideas out of his head*; *knocked her hand away*). **4** *tr. sl.* criticize. **5** *intr.* **a** (of a motor or other engine) make a thumping or rattling noise esp. as the result of a loose bearing. **b** = PINK[3]. **6** *tr. Brit. sl.* make a strong impression on, astonish. **7** *tr. Brit. coarse sl.* offens. = *knock off* 7. —*n.* **1** an act of knocking. **2 a** sharp rap, esp. at a door. **3** an audible sharp blow. **4** the sound of knocking in esp. a motor engine. **5** *Cricket colloq.* an innings. □ **knock about** (or **around**) **1** strike repeatedly; treat roughly (*knocked her about*). **2** lead a wandering adventurous life; wander aimlessly. **3** be present without design or volition (*there's a cup knocking about somewhere*). **4** (usu. foll. by *with*) be associated socially (*knocks about with his brother*). **knock against 1** collide with. **2** come across casually. **knock back 1** *Brit. sl.* eat or drink, esp. quickly. **2** *Brit. sl.* disconcert. **3**

Austral. & NZ colloq. refuse, rebuff. **knock-back** *n. Austral. & NZ colloq.* a refusal, a rebuff. **knock the bottom out of** see BOTTOM. **knock down 1** strike (esp. a person) to the ground with a blow. **2** demolish. **3** (usu. foll. by *to*) (at an auction) dispose of (an article) to a bidder by a knock with a hammer (*knocked the Picasso down to him for a million*). **4** *colloq.* lower the price of (an article). **5** take (machinery, furniture, etc.) to pieces for transportation. **6** *US sl.* steal. **7** *Austral. & NZ sl.* spend (a pay cheque etc.) freely. **knock-down** *attrib.adj.* **1** (of a blow, misfortune, argument, etc.) overwhelming. **2** *Brit.* (of a price) very low. **3** (of a price at auction) reserve. **4** (of furniture etc.) easily dismantled and reassembled. —*n. Austral. & NZ sl.* an introduction (to a person). **knock for knock agreement** an agreement between insurance companies by which each pays its own policyholder regardless of liability. **knock one's head against** come into collision with (unfavourable facts or conditions). **knocking-shop** *Brit. sl.* a brothel. **knock into a cocked hat** see COCK[1]. **knock into the middle of next week** *colloq.* send (a person) flying, esp. with a blow. **knock into shape** see SHAPE. **knock-kneed** having knock knees. **knock knees** an abnormal condition with the legs curved inwards at the knee. **knock off 1** strike off with a blow. **2** *colloq.* **a** finish work (*knocked off at 5.30*). **b** finish (work) (*knocked off work early*). **3** *colloq.* dispatch (business). **4** *colloq.* rapidly produce (a work of art, verses, etc.). **5** (often foll. by *from*) deduct (a sum) from a price, bill, etc. **6** *sl.* steal. **7** *Brit. coarse sl. offens.* have sexual intercourse with (a woman). **8** *sl.* kill. **knock on** *Rugby Football* drive (a ball) with the hand or arm towards the opponents' goal-line. **knock-on** *n.* an act of knocking on. **knock-on effect** a secondary, indirect, or cumulative effect. **knock on the head 1** stun or kill (a person) by a blow on the head. **2** *colloq.* put an end to (a scheme etc.). **knock on** (or **knock**) **wood** *US* = *touch wood*. **knock out 1** make (a person) unconscious by a blow on the head. **2** knock down (a boxer) for a count of 10, thereby winning the contest. **3** defeat, esp. in a knockout competition. **4** *sl.* astonish. **5** (*refl.*) *colloq.* exhaust (*knocked themselves out swimming*). **6** *colloq.* make or write (a plan etc.) hastily. **7** empty (a tobacco-pipe) by tapping. **8** *Austral., NZ, & US sl.* earn. **knock sideways** *colloq.* disconcert; astonish. **knock spots off** defeat easily. **knock together** put together or assemble hastily or roughly. **knock under** submit. **knock up 1** make or arrange hastily. **2** drive upwards with a blow. **3 a** become exhausted or ill. **b** exhaust or make ill. **4** *Brit.* arouse (a person) by a knock at the door. **5** *Cricket* score (runs) rapidly. **6** esp. *US sl.* make pregnant. **7** practise a ball game before formal play begins. **knock-up** *n.* a practice at tennis etc. **take a** (or **the**) **knock** be hard hit financially or emotionally. [ME f. OE *cnocian*: prob. imit.]

knockabout /'nɒkəˌbaʊt/ *adj. & n.* —*attrib.adj.* **1** (of comedy) boisterous; slapstick. **2** (of clothes) suitable for rough use. **3** *Austral.* of a farm or station handyman. —*n.* **1** *Austral.* a farm or station handyman. **2** a knockabout performer or performance.

knocker /'nɒkə(r)/ *n.* **1** a metal or wooden instrument hinged to a door for knocking to call attention. **2** a person or thing that knocks. **3** (in *pl.*) *coarse sl.* a woman's breasts. **4** a person who buys or sells door to door. □**knocker-up** *Brit. hist.* a person employed to rouse early workers by knocking at their doors or windows. **on the knocker 1 a** (buying or selling) from door to door. **b** (obtained) on credit. **2** *Austral. & NZ colloq.* promptly. **up to the knocker** *Brit. sl.* in good condition; to perfection.

knockout /'nɒkaʊt/ *n.* **1** the act of making unconscious by a blow. **2** *Boxing* etc. a blow that knocks an opponent out. **3** a competition in which the loser in each round is eliminated (also *attrib.: a knockout round*). **4** *colloq.* an outstanding or irresistible person or thing. □**knockout drops** a drug added to a drink to cause unconsciousness.

knoll[1] /nəʊl/ *n.* a small hill or mound. [OE *cnoll* hilltop, rel. to MDu., MHG *knolle* clod, ON *knollr* hilltop]

knoll[2] /nəʊl/ *v. & n. archaic* —*v.* **1** *tr. & intr.* = KNELL. **2** *tr.* summon by the sound of a bell. —*n.* = KNELL. [ME, var. of KNELL: perh. imit.]

knop /nɒp/ *n.* **1** a knob, esp. ornamental. **2** an ornamental loop or tuft in yarn. **3** *archaic* a flower-bud. [ME f. MLG, MDu. *knoppe*]

knopkierie /'knɒpˌkɪəri/ *n. S.Afr.* = KNOBKERRIE. [Afrik.]

knot[1] /nɒt/ *n. & v.* —*n.* **1 a** an intertwining of a rope, string, tress of hair, etc., with another, itself, or something else to join or fasten together. **b** a set method of tying a knot (*a reef knot*). **c** a ribbon etc. tied as an ornament and worn on a dress etc. **d** a tangle in hair, knitting, etc. **2 a** a unit of a ship's or aircraft's speed equivalent to one nautical mile per hour (see *nautical mile*). **b** a division marked by knots on a log-line, as a measure of speed. **c** *colloq.* a nautical mile. **3** (usu. foll. by *of*) a group or cluster (*a small knot of journalists at the gate*). **4** something forming or maintaining a union; a bond or tie, esp. of wedlock. **5** a hard lump of tissue in an animal or human body. **6 a** a knob or protuberance in a stem, branch, or root. **b** a hard mass formed in a tree trunk at the intersection with a branch. **c** a round cross-grained piece in timber where a branch has been cut through. **d** a node on the stem of a plant. **7** a difficulty; a problem. **8** a central point in a problem or the plot of a story etc. **9** (in full **porter's knot**) *Brit. hist.* a double shoulder-pad and forehead-loop used for carrying loads. —*v.* (**knotted, knotting**) **1** *tr.* tie (a string etc.) in a knot. **2** *tr.* entangle. **3** *tr.* knit (the brows). **4** *tr.* unite closely or intricately (*knotted together in intrigue*). **5 a** *intr.* make knots for fringing. **b** *tr.* make (a fringe) with knots. □**at a rate of knots** *colloq.* very fast. **get knotted!** *sl.* an expression of disbelief, annoyance, etc. **knot-garden** an intricately designed formal garden. **knot-hole** a hole in a piece of timber where a knot has fallen out (sense 6). **tie in knots** *colloq.* baffle or confuse completely. □□**knotless** *adj.* **knotter** *n.* **knotting** *n.* (esp. in sense 5 of *v.*). [OE *cnotta* f. WG]

knot[2] /nɒt/ *n.* a small sandpiper, *Calidris canutus.* [ME: orig. unkn.]

knotgrass /'nɒtgrɑːs/ *n.* **1** a common weed, *Polygonum aviculare,* with creeping stems and small pink flowers. **2** = POLYGONUM. Also called KNOTWEED.

knotty /'nɒtɪ/ *adj.* (**knottier, knottiest**) **1** full of knots. **2** hard to explain; puzzling (*a knotty problem*). □□**knottily** *adv.* **knottiness** *n.*

knotweed /'nɒtwiːd/ *n.* = POLYGONUM.

knotwork /'nɒtwɜːk/ *n.* ornamental work representing or consisting of intertwined cords.

knout /naʊt, nuːt/ *n. & v.* —*n. hist.* a scourge used in imperial Russia, often causing death. —*v.tr.* flog with a knout. [F f. Russ. *knut* f. Icel. *knútr,* rel. to KNOT[1]]

know /nəʊ/ *v. & n.* —*v.* (*past* **knew** /njuː/; *past part.* **known** /nəʊn/) **1** *tr.* (often foll. by *that, how, what,* etc.) **a** have in the mind; have learnt; be able to recall (*knows a lot about cars; knows what to do*). **b** (also *absol.*) be aware of (a fact) (*he knows I am waiting; I think he knows*). **c** have a good command of (a subject or language) (*knew German; knows his tables*). **2** *tr.* be acquainted or friendly with (a person or thing). **3** *tr.* **a** recognize; identify (*I knew him at once; knew him for an American*). **b** (foll. by *to* + infin.) be aware of (a person or thing) as being or doing what is specified (*knew them to be rogues*). **c** (foll. by *from*) be able to distinguish (one from another) (*did not know him from Adam*). **4** *tr.* be subject to (*her joy knew no bounds*). **5** *tr.* have personal experience of (fear etc.). **6** *tr.* (as **known**

adj.) **a** publicly acknowledged (*a known thief; a known fact*). **b** *Math.* (of a quantity etc.) having a value that can be stated. **7** *intr.* have understanding or knowledge. **8** *tr. archaic* have sexual intercourse with. —*n.* (in phr. **in the know**) *colloq.* well-informed; having special knowledge. □**all one knows** (or **knows how**) **1** all one can (*did all he knew to stop it*). **2** to the utmost of one's power (*tried all she knew*). **before one knows where one is** with baffling speed. **be not to know** **1** have no way of learning (*wasn't to know they'd arrive late*). **2** be not to be told (*she's not to know about the party*). **don't I know it!** *colloq.* an expression of rueful assent. **don't you know** *colloq.* or *joc.* an expression used for emphasis (*such a bore, don't you know*). **for all** (or **aught**) **I know** so far as my knowledge extends. **have been known to** be known to have done (*they have been known to not turn up*). **I knew it!** I was sure that this would happen. **I know what** I have a new idea, suggestion, etc. **know about** have information about. **know-all** *colloq.* a person who seems to know everything. **know best** be or claim to be better informed etc. than others. **know better than** (foll. by *that*, or *to* + infin.) be wise, well-informed, or well-mannered enough to avoid (specified behaviour etc.). **know by name 1** have heard the name of. **2** be able to give the name of. **know by sight** recognize the appearance (only) of. **know how** know the way to do something. **know-how** *n.* **1** practical knowledge; technique, expertise. **2** natural skill or invention. **know-it-all** = *know-all.* **know-nothing** *n.* **1** an ignorant person. **2** an agnostic. **know of** be aware of; have heard of (*not that I know of*). **know one's own mind** be decisive, not vacillate. **know the ropes** (or **one's stuff**) be fully knowledgeable or experienced. **know a thing or two** be experienced or shrewd. **know what's what** have adequate knowledge of the world, life, etc. **know who's who** be aware of who or what each person is. **not if I know it** only against my will. **not know that . . .** *colloq.* be fairly sure that . . . not (*I don't know that I want to go*). **not know what hit one** be suddenly injured, killed, disconcerted, etc. **not want to know** refuse to take any notice of. **what do you know** (or **know about that**)? *colloq.* an expression of surprise. **you know** *colloq.* **1** an expression implying something generally known or known to the hearer (*you know, the pub on the corner*). **2** an expression used as a gap-filler in conversation. **you know something** (or **what**)? I am going to tell you something. **you-know-what** (or **-who**) a thing or person unspecified but understood. **you never know** nothing in the future is certain. □□ **knowable** *adj.* **knower** *n.* [OE (*ge*)*cnāwan*, rel. to CAN[1], KEN]

knowing /ˈnəʊɪŋ/ *n.* & *adj.* —*n.* the state of being aware or informed of any thing. —*adj.* **1** usu. *derog.* cunning; sly. **2** showing knowledge; shrewd. □**there is no knowing** no one can tell. □□ **knowingness** *n.*

knowingly /ˈnəʊɪŋlɪ/ *adv.* **1** consciously; intentionally (*had never knowingly injured him*). **2** in a knowing manner (*smiled knowingly*).

knowledge /ˈnɒlɪdʒ/ *n.* **1 a** (usu. foll. by *of*) awareness or familiarity gained by experience (of a person, fact, or thing) (*have no knowledge of that*). **b** a person's range of information (*is not within his knowledge*). **2 a** (usu. foll. by *of*) a theoretical or practical understanding of a subject, language, etc. (*has a good knowledge of Greek*). **b** the sum of what is known (*every branch of knowledge*). **3** *Philos.* true, justified belief; certain understanding, as opp. to opinion. **4** = *carnal knowledge.* □**come to one's knowledge** become known to one. **to my knowledge** **1** so far as I know. **2** as I know for certain. [ME *knaulege*, with earlier *knawlechen* (v.) formed as KNOW + OE -*lēcan* f. *lāc* as in WEDLOCK]

knowledgeable /ˈnɒlɪdʒəb(ə)l/ *adj.* (also **knowledgable**) well-informed; intelligent. □□

knowledgeability /-ˈbɪlɪtɪ/ *n.* **knowledgeableness** *n.* **knowledgeably** *adv.*

known *past part.* of KNOW.

Knt. *abbr.* Knight.

knuckle /ˈnʌk(ə)l/ *n.* & *v.* —*n.* **1** the bone at a finger-joint, esp. that adjoining the hand. **2 a** a projection of the carpal or tarsal joint of a quadruped. **b** a joint of meat consisting of this with the adjoining parts, esp. of bacon or pork. —*v.tr.* strike, press, or rub with the knuckles. □**go the knuckle** *Austral. sl.* fight, punch. **knuckle-bone 1** bone forming a knuckle. **2** the bone of a sheep or other animal corresponding to or resembling a knuckle. **3** a knuckle of meat. **knuckle-bones 1** animal knuckle-bones used in the game of jacks. **2** the game of jacks. **knuckle down** (often foll. by *to*) **1** apply oneself seriously (to a task etc.). **2** (also **knuckle under**) give in; submit. **knuckle sandwich** *sl.* a punch in the mouth. **rap on** (or **over**) **the knuckles** see RAP[1]. □□ **knuckly** *adj.* [ME *knokel* f. MLG, MDu. *knökel*, dimin. of *knoke* bone]

knuckleduster /ˈnʌk(ə)lˌdʌstə(r)/ *n.* a metal guard worn over the knuckles in fighting, esp. to increase the effect of the blows.

knur /nɜː(r)/ *n.* (also **knurr**) **1** a hard excrescence on the trunk of a tree. **2** a hard concretion. [ME *knorre*, var. of KNAR]

knurl /nɜːl/ *n.* a small projecting knob, ridge, etc. □□ **knurled** /nɜːld/ *adj.* [KNUR]

KO *abbr.* **1** knockout. **2** kick-off.

koa /ˈkəʊə/ *n.* **1** a Hawaiian tree, *Acacia koa*, which produces dark red wood. **2** this wood. [Hawaiian]

koala /kəʊˈɑːlə/ *n.* (in full **koala bear**) an Australian bearlike marsupial, *Phascolarctos cinereus*, having thick grey fur and feeding on eucalyptus leaves. [Aboriginal *kūl(l)a*]

koan /ˈkəʊæn/ *n.* a riddle used in Zen Buddhism to demonstrate the inadequacy of logical reasoning. [Jap., = public matter (for thought)]

kobold /ˈkəʊbɒld/ *n.* (in Germanic mythology): **1** a familiar spirit; a brownie. **2** an underground spirit in mines etc. [G]

Köchel number /ˈkɜːx(ə)l/ *n. Mus.* a number given to each of Mozart's compositions in the complete catalogue of his works compiled by Köchel and his successors. [L. von *Köchel*, Austrian scientist d. 1877]

KO'd /keɪˈəʊd/ *adj.* knocked out. [abbr.]

Kodiak /ˈkəʊdɪˌæk/ *n.* (in full **Kodiak bear**) a large Alaskan brown bear, *Ursus arctos middendorffi*. [*Kodiak* Island, Alaska]

koel /ˈkəʊəl/ *n.* a dark-coloured cuckoo, *Eudynamys scolopacea*. [Hindi *kōīl* f. Skr. *kokila*]

kohl /kəʊl/ *n.* a black powder, usu. antimony sulphide or lead sulphide, used as eye make-up esp. in Eastern countries. [Arab. *kuḥl*]

kohlrabi /kəʊlˈrɑːbɪ/ *n.* (*pl.* **kohlrabies**) a variety of cabbage with an edible turnip-like swollen stem. [G f. It. *cavoli rape* (pl.) f. med.L *caulorapa* (as COLE, RAPE[2])]

koine /ˈkɔɪnɪ/ *n.* **1** the common language of the Greeks from the close of the classical period to the Byzantine era. **2** a common language shared by various peoples; a lingua franca. [Gk *koinē* (*dialektos*) common (language)]

kola var. of COLA.

kolinsky /kəˈlɪnskɪ/ *n.* (*pl.* -**ies**) **1** the Siberian mink, *Mustela sibirica*, having a brown coat in winter. **2** the fur of this. [Russ. *kolinskiĭ* f. *Kola* in NW Russia]

kolkhoz /ˈkɒlkɒz, kʌlˈxɔːz/ *n.* a collective farm in the USSR. [Russ. f. *kollektivnoe khozyaĭstvo* collective farm]

komitadji (also **komitaji**) var. of COMITADJI.

komodo dragon /kəˈməʊdəʊ/ *n.* (also **komodo lizard**) a large monitor lizard, *Varanus komodoensis*, native to the E. Indies. [*Komodo* Island in Indonesia]

Komsomol /ˈkɒmsəˌmɒl/ *n.* **1** an organization for Communist youth in the Soviet Union. **2** a member of this. [Russ. f. *Kommunisticheskiĭ soyuz molodezhi* Communist League of Youth]

koodoo var. of KUDU.

kook /kuːk/ *n. & adj. US sl.* —*n.* a crazy or eccentric person. —*adj.* crazy; eccentric. [20th c.: prob. f. CUCKOO]

kookaburra /ˈkʊkəˌbʌrə/ *n.* any Australian king-fisher of the genus *Dacelo*, esp. *D. novaeguineae*, which makes a strange laughing cry. Also called *laughing jackass.* [Aboriginal]

kooky /ˈkuːkɪ/ *adj.* (**kookier, kookiest**) *sl.* crazy. □□ **kookily** *adv.* **kookiness** *n.*

kop /kɒp/ *n.* **1** *S.Afr.* a prominent hill or peak. **2** (**Kop**) *Football* a high bank of terracing for standing spectators, esp. supporting the home side. [Afrik. f. Du., = head: cf. COP²]

kopek (also **kopeck**) var. of COPECK.

kopi /ˈkəʊpɪ/ *n. Austral.* powdered gypsum. [Aboriginal]

koppie /ˈkɒpɪ/ *n.* (also **kopje**) *S.Afr.* a small hill. [Afrik. *koppie*, Du. *kopje*, dimin. of *kop* head]

koradji /kəˈrædʒɪ/ *n.* (*pl.* **koradjis**) *Austral.* an Aboriginal medicine man. [Aboriginal]

Koran /kɔːˈrɑːn, kə-/ *n.* (also **Qur'an** /kə-/) the Islamic sacred book, believed to be the word of God as dictated to Muhammad and written down in Arabic. □□ **Koranic** /-ˈrænɪk, -ˈrɑːnɪk/ *adj.* [Arab. *ḳurʾān* recitation f. *ḳaraʾa* read]

Korean /kəˈriːən/ *n. & adj.* —*n.* **1** a native or national of N. or S. Korea in SE Asia. **2** the language of Korea. —*adj.* of or relating to Korea or its people or language.

korfball /ˈkɔːfbɔːl/ *n.* a game like basketball played by two teams consisting of 6 men and 6 women each. [Du. *korfbal* f. *korf* basket + *bal* ball]

kosher /ˈkəʊʃə(r), ˈkɒʃ-/ *adj. & n.* —*adj.* **1** (of food or premises in which food is sold, cooked, or eaten) fulfilling the requirements of Jewish law. **2** *colloq.* correct; genuine; legitimate. —*n.* **1** kosher food. **2** a kosher shop. [Heb. *kāšēr* proper]

koto /ˈkəʊtəʊ/ *n.* (*pl.* **-os**) a Japanese musical instrument with 13 long esp. silk strings. [Jap.]

kotow var. of KOWTOW.

koumiss /ˈkuːmɪs/ *n.* (also **kumiss, kumis**) a fermented liquor prepared from esp. mare's milk, used by Asian nomads and medicinally. [Tartar *kumiz*]

kourbash /ˈkʊəbæʃ/ *n.* (also **kurbash**) a whip, esp. of hippopotamus hide, used as an instrument of punishment in Turkey and Egypt. [Arab. *kurbāj* f. Turk. *kırbāç* whip]

kowhai /ˈkəʊwaɪ/ *n.* any of several trees or shrubs of the genus *Sophora*, esp. *S. microphylla* native to New Zealand, with pendant clusters of yellow flowers. [Maori]

kowtow /kaʊˈtaʊ/ *n. & v.* (also **kotow** /kəʊˈtaʊ/) *hist.* —*n.* the Chinese custom of kneeling and touching the ground with the forehead in worship or submission. —*v.intr.* **1** perform the kowtow. **2** (usu. foll. by *to*) act obsequiously. [Chin. *ketou* f. *ke* knock + *tou* head]

KP *n. US Mil. colloq.* **1** enlisted men detailed to help the cooks. **2** kitchen duty. [abbr. of *kitchen police*]

k.p.h. *abbr.* kilometres per hour.

Kr *symb. Chem.* the element krypton.

kraal /krɑːl/ *n. S.Afr.* **1** a village of huts enclosed by a fence. **2** an enclosure for cattle or sheep. [Afrik. f. Port. *curral*, of Hottentot orig.]

kraft /krɑːft/ *n.* (in full **kraft paper**) a kind of strong smooth brown wrapping paper. [G f. Sw., = strength]

krait /kraɪt/ *n.* any venomous snake of the genus *Bungarus* of E. Asia. [Hindi *karait*]

kraken /ˈkrɑːkən/ *n.* a large mythical sea-monster said to appear off the coast of Norway. [Norw.]

krans /krɑːns/ *n. S.Afr.* a precipitous or overhanging wall of rocks. [Afrik. f. Du. *krans* coronet]

Kraut /kraʊt/ *n. sl. offens.* a German. [shortening of SAUERKRAUT]

kremlin /ˈkremlɪn/ *n.* **1** a citadel within a Russian town. **2** (**the Kremlin**) **a** the citadel in Moscow. **b** the USSR Government housed within it. [F, f. Russ. *Kreml'*, of Tartar orig.]

kriegspiel /ˈkriːgspiːl/ *n.* **1** a war-game in which blocks representing armies etc. are moved about on maps. **2** a form of chess with an umpire, in which each player has only limited information about the opponent's moves. [G f. *Krieg* war + *Spiel* game]

krill /krɪl/ *n.* tiny planktonic crustaceans found in the seas around the Antarctic and eaten by baleen whales. [Norw. *kril* tiny fish]

krimmer /ˈkrɪmə(r)/ *n.* a grey or black fur obtained from the wool of young Crimean lambs. [G f. *Krim* Crimea]

kris /kriːs/ *n.* (also **crease, creese**) a Malay or Indonesian dagger with a wavy blade. [ult. f. Malay *k(i)rīs*]

Krishnaism /ˈkrɪʃnəˌɪz(ə)m/ *n. Hinduism* the worship of Krishna as an incarnation of Vishnu.

kromesky /krəˈmeskɪ/ *n.* (*pl.* **-ies**) a croquette of minced meat or fish, rolled in bacon and fried. [app. f. Pol. *kromeczka* small slice]

krona /ˈkrəʊnə/ *n.* **1** (*pl.* **kronor** /ˈkrəʊnə(r)/) the chief monetary unit of Sweden. **2** (*pl.* **kronur** /ˈkrəʊnə(r)/) the chief monetary unit of Iceland. [Sw. & Icel., = CROWN]

krone /ˈkrəʊnə/ *n.* (*pl.* **kroner** /ˈkrəʊnə(r)/) the chief monetary unit of Denmark and of Norway. [Da. & Norw., = CROWN]

Kroo var. of KRU.

Kru /kruː/ *n. & adj.* (also **Kroo**) —*n.* (*pl.* same) a member of a Black seafaring people on the coast of Liberia. —*adj.* of or concerning the Kru. [W. Afr.]

krugerrand /ˈkruːgəˌrænd, -ˌrɑːnt/ *n.* a S. African gold coin depicting President Kruger. [S. J. P. *Kruger*, S. Afr. statesman d. 1904, + RAND¹]

krummhorn /ˈkrʌmhɔːn/ *n.* (also **crumhorn**) a medieval wind instrument with a double reed and a curved end. [G f. *krumm* crooked + *Horn* HORN]

krypton /ˈkrɪptɒn/ *n. Chem.* an inert gaseous element of the noble gas group, forming a small portion of the earth's atmosphere and used in fluorescent lamps etc. ¶ Symb.: **Kr**. [Gk *krupton*, neut. adj. f. *kruptō* hide]

KS *abbr.* **1** *US* Kansas (in official postal use). **2** *Brit.* King's Scholar.

Kshatriya /ˈkʃætrɪə, ˈkʃɑ-/ *n.* a member of the second of the four great Hindu castes, the military caste. [Skr. f. *kshatra* rule]

K. St. J. *abbr.* Knight of the Order of St John.

KT *abbr.* **1** Knight Templar. **2** (in the UK) Knight of the Order of the Thistle.

Kt. *abbr.* Knight.

kt. *abbr.* knot.

Ku *symb. Chem.* the element kurchatovium.

kudos /ˈkjuːdɒs/ *n. colloq.* glory; renown. [Gk]

kudu /ˈkuːduː/ *n.* (also **koodoo**) either of two African antelopes, *Tragelaphus strepsiceros* or *T. imberbis*, with white stripes and corkscrew-shaped ridged horns. [Xhosa-Kaffir *iqudu*]

kudzu /ˈkʌdzuː/ *n.* (in full **kudzu vine**) a quick-growing climbing plant, *Pueraria thunbergiana*, with reddish-purple flowers. [Jap. *kuzu*]

Kufic /ˈkjuːfɪk/ *n. & adj.* (also **Cufic**) —*n.* an early angular form of the Arabic alphabet found chiefly in decorative inscriptions. —*adj.* of or in this type of script. [*Cufa*, a city S. of Baghdad in Iraq]

Ku Klux Klan /ˌkuːklʌksˈklæn, ˌkjuː-/ *n.* a secret society of White people in the southern States of the US, orig. formed after the Civil War and dedicated to persecuting and terrorizing Blacks. □□ **Ku Klux Klansman** *n.* (*pl.* **-men**). [perh. f. Gk *kuklos* circle + CLAN]

kukri /ˈkʊkrɪ/ *n.* (*pl.* **kukris**) a curved knife broadening towards the point, used by Gurkhas. [Hindi *kukṛī*]

kulak /'ku:læk/ n. hist. a peasant working for personal profit in Soviet Russia. [Russ., = fist, tight-fisted person]

kulan /'ku:lən/ n. a wild ass of SW Asia, closely related to the kiang. [Tartar]

kultur /kʊl'tʊə(r)/ n. esp. derog. German civilization and culture, seen as racist, authoritarian, and militaristic. [G f. L cultura CULTURE]

kulturkampf /kʊl'tʊəkæmpf/ n. hist. the conflict in 19th-c. Germany between the civil and ecclesiastical authorities esp. as regards the control of schools. [G (as KULTUR, Kampf struggle)]

kumara /'ku:mərə/ n. NZ a sweet potato. [Maori]

kumis (also **kumiss**) var. of KOUMISS.

kümmel /'kʊm(ə)l/ n. a sweet liqueur flavoured with caraway and cumin seeds. [G (as CUMIN)]

kumquat /'kʌmkwɒt/ n. (also **cumquat**) 1 an orange-like fruit with a sweet rind and acid pulp, used in preserves. 2 any shrub or small tree of the genus Fortunella yielding this. [Cantonese var. of Chin. kin kü golden orange]

kung fu /kʊŋ 'fu:, kʌŋ/ n. the Chinese form of karate. [Chin. gongfu f. gong merit + fu master]

kurbash var. of KOURBASH.

kurchatovium /ˌkɜːtʃə'təʊvɪəm/ n. Chem. = RUTHERFORDIUM. ¶ Symb.: **Ku**. [I. V. Kurchatov, Russ. physicist d. 1960]

Kurd /kɜːd/ n. a member of a mainly pastoral Aryan Islamic people living in Kurdistan (contiguous areas of Iraq, Iran, and Turkey). [Kurdish]

kurdaitcha /kə'daɪtʃə/ n. Austral. 1 the tribal use of a bone in spells intended to cause sickness or death. 2 a man empowered to point the bone at a victim. [Aboriginal]

Kurdish /'kɜːdɪʃ/ adj. & n. —adj. of or relating to the Kurds or their language. —n. the Iranian language of the Kurds.

kurrajong /'kʌrəˌdʒɒŋ/ n. (also **currajong**) an Australian tree, Brachychiton populneum, which produces a tough bast fibre. [Aboriginal]

kursaal /'kʊəzɑːl/ n. 1 a building for the use of visitors at a health resort, esp. at a German spa. 2 a casino. [G f. Kur CURE + Saal room]

kurta /'kɜːtə/ n. (also **kurtha**) a loose shirt or tunic worn by esp. Hindu men and women. [Hind.]

kurtosis /kɜː'təʊsɪs/ n. Statistics the sharpness of the peak of a frequency-distribution curve. [mod.L f. Gk kurtōsis bulging f. kurtos convex]

kV abbr. kilovolt(s).

kvass /kvɑːs/ n. a fermented beverage, low in alcohol, made from rye-flour or bread with malt in the Soviet Union. [Russ. kvas]

kW abbr. kilowatt(s).

KWAC /kwæk/ n. Computing etc. keyword and context. [abbr.]

kwacha /'kwɑːtʃə/ n. the chief monetary unit of Zambia. [native word, = dawn]

kwashiorkor /ˌkwɒʃɪ'ɔːkɔː(r)/ n. a form of malnutrition caused by a protein deficiency of diet, esp. in young children in the tropics. [native name in Ghana]

kWh abbr. kilowatt-hour(s).

KWIC /kwɪk/ n. Computing etc. keyword in context. [abbr.]

KWOC /kwɒk/ n. Computing etc. keyword out of context. [abbr.]

KY abbr. US Kentucky (in official postal use).

Ky. abbr. Kentucky.

kyanite /'kaɪəˌnaɪt/ n. a blue crystalline mineral of aluminium silicate. □□ **kyanitic** /-'nɪtɪk/ adj. [Gk kuanos dark blue]

kyanize /'kaɪəˌnaɪz/ v.tr. (also **-ise**) treat (wood) with a solution of corrosive sublimate to prevent decay. [J. H. Kyan, Engl. inventor d. 1850]

kybosh var. of KIBOSH.

kyle /kaɪl/ n. (in Scotland) a narrow channel between islands or between an island and the mainland. [Gael. caol strait]

kylie /'kaɪlɪ/ n. W. Austral. a boomerang. [Aboriginal]

kylin /'ki:lɪn/ n. a mythical composite animal figured on Chinese and Japanese ceramics. [Chin. qilin f. qi male + lin female]

kyloe /'kaɪləʊ/ n. Brit. 1 an animal of a breed of small usu. black long-horned highland cattle. 2 this breed. [Kyloe in Northumberland]

kymograph /'kaɪməˌgrɑːf/ n. an instrument for recording variations in pressure, e.g. in sound waves or in blood within blood-vessels. □□ **kymographic** /-'græfɪk/ adj. [Gk kuma wave + -GRAPH]

kyphosis /kaɪ'fəʊsɪs/ n. Med. excessive outward curvature of the spine, causing hunching of the back (opp. LORDOSIS). □□ **kyphotic** /-'fɒtɪk/ adj. [mod.L f. Gk kuphōsis f. kuphos bent]

Kyrie /'kɪərɪˌeɪ/ (in full **Kyrie eleison** /ɪ'leɪɪˌzɒn, -ˌsɒn, eɪ'leɪ-/) n. 1 **a** a short repeated invocation used in the RC and Greek Orthodox Churches, esp. at the beginning of the mass. **b** a response sometimes used in the Anglican Communion Service. 2 a musical setting of the Kyrie. [ME f. med.L f. Gk Kurie eleēson Lord, have mercy]

L

L¹ /el/ *n.* (also **l**) (*pl.* **Ls** or **L's**) **1** the twelfth letter of the alphabet. **2** (as a Roman numeral) 50. **3** a thing shaped like an L, esp. a joint connecting two pipes at right angles.

L² *abbr.* (also **L.**) **1** Lake. **2** *Brit.* learner driver (cf. L-PLATE). **3** Liberal. **4** Licentiate. **5** *Biol.* Linnaeus. **6** Lire.

l *abbr.* (also **l.**) **1** left. **2** line. **3** litre(s). **4** length. **5** *archaic* pound(s) (money).

£ *abbr.* (preceding a numeral) pound or pounds (of money). [L *libra*]

LA *abbr.* **1** Library Association. **2** Los Angeles. **3** *US* Louisiana (in official postal use).

La *symb. Chem.* the element lanthanum.

La. *abbr.* Louisiana.

la var. of LAH.

laager /ˈlɑːgə(r)/ *n. & v.* —*n.* **1** esp. *S.Afr.* a camp or encampment, esp. formed by a circle of wagons. **2** *Mil.* a park for armoured vehicles. —*v.* **1** *tr.* **a** form (vehicles) into a laager. **b** encamp (people) in a laager. **2** *intr.* encamp. [Afrik. f. Du. *leger*: see LEAGUER²]

Lab. *abbr.* **1** Labour. **2** Labrador.

lab /læb/ *n. colloq.* a laboratory. [abbr.]

labarum /ˈlæbərəm/ *n.* **1** a symbolic banner. **2** Constantine the Great's imperial standard, with Christian symbols added to Roman military symbols. [LL: orig. unkn.]

labdanum var. of LADANUM.

labefaction /ˌlæbɪˈfækʃ(ə)n/ *n. literary* a shaking, weakening, or downfall. [L *labefacere* weaken f. *labi* fall + *facere* make]

label /ˈleɪb(ə)l/ *n. & v.* —*n.* **1** **a** usu. small piece of paper, card, linen, metal, etc., for attaching to an object and giving its name, information about it, instructions for use, etc. **2** esp. *derog.* a short classifying phrase or name applied to a person, a work of art, etc. **3 a** a small fabric label sewn into a garment bearing the maker's name. **b** the logo, title, or trademark of esp. a fashion or recording company (*brought it out under his own label*). **c** the piece of paper in the centre of a gramophone record describing its contents etc. **4** an adhesive stamp on a parcel etc. **5** a word placed before, after, or in the course of a dictionary definition etc. to specify its subject, register, nationality, etc. **6** *Archit.* a dripstone. **7** *Heraldry* the mark of an eldest son, consisting of a superimposed horizontal bar with usu. three downward projections. —*v.tr.* (**labelled**, **labelling**) **1** attach a label to. **2** (usu. foll. by *as*) assign to a category (*labelled them as irresponsible*). **3 a** replace (an atom) by an atom of a usu. radioactive isotope as a means of identification. **b** replace an atom in (a molecule) or atoms in the molecules of (a substance). **4** (as **labelled** *adj.*) made identifiable by the replacement of atoms. □□ **labeller** *n.* [ME f. OF, = ribbon, prob. f. Gmc (as LAP¹)]

labia *pl.* of LABIUM.

labial /ˈleɪbɪəl/ *adj. & n.* —*adj.* **1 a** of the lips. **b** *Zool.* of, like, or serving as a lip, a liplike part, or a labium. **2** *Dentistry* designating the surface of a tooth adjacent to the lips. **3** *Phonet.* (of a sound) requiring partial or complete closure of the lips (e.g. *p*, *b*, *f*, *v*, *m*, *w*; and vowels in which lips are rounded, e.g. *oo* in moon). —*n. Phonet.* a labial sound. □ **labial pipe** *Mus.* an organ-pipe having lips; a flue-pipe. □□ **labialism** *n.* **labialize** *v.tr.* (also **-ise**) **labially** *adv.* [med.L *labialis* f. L *labia* lips]

labiate /ˈleɪbɪət/ *n. & adj.* —*n.* any plant of the family Labiatae, including mint and rosemary, having square stems and a corolla or calyx divided into two parts suggesting lips. —*adj.* **1** *Bot.* of or relating to the Labiatae. **2** *Bot. & Zool.* like a lip or labium. [mod.L *labiatus* (as LABIUM)]

labile /ˈleɪbaɪl, -bɪl/ *adj. Chem.* (of a compound) unstable; liable to displacement or change esp. if an atom or group is easily replaced by other atoms or groups. □□ **lability** /ləˈbɪlɪtɪ/ *n.* [ME f. LL *labilis* f. *labi* to fall]

labio- /ˈleɪbɪəʊ/ *comb. form* of the lips. [as LABIUM]

labiodental /ˌleɪbɪəʊˈdent(ə)l/ *adj.* (of a sound) made with the lips and teeth, e.g. *f* and *v*.

labiovelar /ˌleɪbɪəʊˈviːlə(r)/ *adj.* (of a sound) made with the lips and soft palate, e.g. *w*.

labium /ˈleɪbɪəm/ *n.* (*pl.* **labia** /-bɪə/) **1** (usu. in *pl.*) *Anat.* each of the two pairs of skin folds that enclose the vulva. **2** the lower lip in the mouth-parts of an insect or crustacean. **3** a lip, esp. the lower one of a labiate plant's corolla. □ **labia majora** /məˈdʒɔːrə/ the larger outer pair of labia (in sense 1). **labia minora** /mɪˈnɔːrə/ the smaller inner pair of labia (in sense 1, sing. = lip) [L = lip]

labor etc. *US & Austral.* var. of LABOUR etc.

laboratory /ləˈbɒrətərɪ/ *n.* (*pl.* **-ies**) a room or building fitted out for scientific experiments, research, teaching, or the manufacture of drugs and chemicals. [med.L *laboratorium* f. L *laborare* LABOUR]

laborious /ləˈbɔːrɪəs/ *adj.* **1** needing hard work or toil (*a laborious task*). **2** (esp. of literary style) showing signs of toil; pedestrian; not fluent. □□ **laboriously** *adv.* **laboriousness** *n.* [ME f. OF *laborieus* f. L *laboriosus* (as LABOUR)]

labour /ˈleɪbə(r)/ *n. & v.* (*US, Austral.* **labor**) —*n.* **1 a** physical or mental work; exertion; toil. **b** such work considered as supplying the needs of a community. **2 a** workers, esp. manual, considered as a class or political force (*a dispute between capital and labour*). **b** (**Labour**) the Labour Party. **3** the process of childbirth, esp. the period from the start of uterine contractions to delivery (*has been in labour for three hours*). **4** a particular task, esp. of a difficult nature. —*v.* **1** *intr.* work hard; exert oneself. **2** *intr.* (usu. foll. by *for*, or foll. by + infin.) strive for a purpose (*laboured to fulfil his promise*). **3** *tr.* **a** treat at excessive length; elaborate needlessly (*I will not labour the point*). **b** (as **laboured** *adj.*) done with great effort; not spontaneous or fluent. **4** *intr.* (often foll. by *under*) suffer under (a disadvantage or delusion) (*laboured under universal disapproval*). **5** *intr.* proceed with trouble or difficulty (*laboured slowly up the hill*). **6** *intr.* (of a ship) roll or pitch heavily. **7** *tr. archaic* or *poet.* till (the ground). □ **labour camp** a prison camp enforcing a regime of hard labour. **Labour Day** May 1 (or in the US and Canada the first Monday in September), celebrated in honour of working people. **Labour Exchange** *Brit. colloq.* or *hist.* an employment exchange; a jobcentre. **labour force** the body of workers employed, esp. at a single plant. **labouring man** a labourer. **labour-intensive** (of a form of work) needing a large work force. **labour in vain** make a fruitless effort. **labour-market** the supply of labour with reference to the demand on it. **labour of Hercules** a task needing enormous strength or effort. **labour of love** a task done for pleasure, not reward. **Labour Party 1** a British political party formed to represent the interests of ordinary working people. **2** any similar political party in other countries. **labour-saving** (of an appliance etc.) designed to reduce or eliminate work. **labour union** *US* a trade union. **lost labour** fruitless effort. [ME f. OF *labo(u)r*, *labourer* f. L *labor*, *-oris*, *laborare*]

labourer /'leɪbərə(r)/ *n.* (*US* **laborer**) **1** a person doing unskilled, usu. manual, work for wages. **2** a person who labours. [ME f. OF *laboureur* (as LABOUR)]

Labourite /'leɪbə‚raɪt/ *n.* (also **Laborite**) a member or follower of the Labour Party.

labra *pl.* of LABRUM.

Labrador /'læbrə‚dɔː(r)/ *n.* (in full **Labrador dog** or **retriever**) **1** a retriever of a breed with a black or golden coat often used as a gun dog or as a guide for a blind person. **2** this breed. [*Labrador* in Canada]

labret /'læbrɪt/ *n.* a piece of shell, bone, etc., inserted in the lip as an ornament. [LABRUM]

labrum /'leɪbrəm/ *n.* (*pl.* **labra** /-brə/) the upper lip in the mouth-parts of an insect. [L, = lip: rel. to LABIUM]

laburnum /lə'bɜːnəm/ *n.* any small tree of the genus *Laburnum* with racemes of golden flowers yielding poisonous seeds. Also called *golden chain*. [L]

labyrinth /'læbərɪnθ/ *n.* **1** a complicated irregular network of passages or paths etc.; a maze. **2** an intricate or tangled arrangement. **3** *Anat.* the complex arrangement of bony and membranous canals and chambers of the inner ear which constitute the organs of hearing and balance. □ **labyrinth fish** = GOURAMI. □□ **labyrinthian** /-'rɪnθɪən/ *adj.* **labyrinthine** /-'rɪnθaɪn/ *adj.* [F *labyrinthe* or L *labyrinthus* f. Gk *laburinthos*]

LAC *abbr.* Leading Aircraftman.

lac¹ /læk/ *n.* a resinous substance secreted as a protective covering by the lac insect, and used to make varnish and shellac. □ **lac insect** an Asian scale insect, *Laccifer lacca*, living in trees. [ult. f. Hind. *lākh* f. Prakrit *lakkha* f. Skr. *lākṣā*]

lac² var. of LAKH.

laccolith /'lækəlɪθ/ *n. Geol.* a lens-shaped intrusion of igneous rock which thrusts the overlying strata into a dome. [Gk *lakkos* reservoir + -LITH]

lace /leɪs/ *n. & v.* —*n.* **1** a fine open fabric, esp. of cotton or silk, made by weaving thread in patterns and used esp. to trim blouses, underwear, etc. **2** a cord or leather strip passed through eyelets or hooks on opposite sides of a shoe, corsets, etc., pulled tight and fastened. **3** braid used for trimming esp. dress uniform (*gold lace*). —*v.* **1** *tr.* (usu. foll. by *up*) **a** fasten or tighten (a shoe, corsets, etc.) with a lace or laces. **b** compress the waist of (a person) with a laced corset. **2** *tr.* flavour or fortify (coffee, beer, etc.) with a dash of spirits. **3** *tr.* (usu. foll. by *with*) **a** streak (a sky etc.) with colour (*cheek laced with blood*). **b** interlace or embroider (fabric) with thread etc. **4** *tr.* & (foll. by *into*) *intr. colloq.* lash, beat, defeat. **5** *tr.* (often foll. by *through*) pass (a shoelace etc.) through. **6** *tr.* trim with lace. □ **lace-glass** Venetian glass with lacelike designs. **lace-pillow** a cushion placed on the lap and providing support in lacemaking. **lace-up** —*n.* a shoe fastened with a lace. —*attrib.adj.* (of a shoe etc.) fastened by a lace or laces. [ME f. OF *laz*, *las*, *lacier* ult. f. L *laqueus* noose]

lacemaker /'leɪs‚meɪkə(r)/ *n.* a person who makes lace, esp. professionally. □□ **lacemaking** *n.*

lacerate /'læsə‚reɪt/ *v.tr.* **1** mangle or tear (esp. flesh or tissue). **2** distress or cause pain to (the feelings, the heart, etc.). □□ **lacerable** *adj.* **laceration** /-'reɪʃ(ə)n/ *n.* [L *lacerare* f. *lacer* torn]

lacertian /lə'sɜːtɪən/ *n. & adj.* (also **lacertilian** /‚læsə'tɪlɪən/, **lacertine** /'læsə‚taɪn/) —*n.* any reptile of the suborder Lacertilia, including lizards. —*adj.* of or relating to the Lacertilia; lizard-like, saurian. [L *lacerta* lizard]

lacewing /'leɪswɪŋ/ *n.* a neuropterous insect.

lacewood /'leɪswʊd/ *n.* the timber of the plane tree.

laches /'lætʃɪz, 'leɪ-/ *n. Law* delay in performing a legal duty, asserting a right, claiming a privilege, etc. [ME f. AF *laches(se)*, OF *laschesse* f. *lasche* ult. f. L *laxus* loose]

lachryma Christi /‚lækrɪmə 'krɪstɪ/ *n.* any of various wines from the slopes of Mt. Vesuvius. [L, = Christ's tear]

lachrymal /'lækrɪm(ə)l/ *adj. & n.* (also **lacrimal**, **lacrymal**) —*adj.* **1** *literary* of or for tears. **2** (usu. as **lacrimal**) *Anat.* concerned in the secretion of tears (*lacrimal canal*; *lacrimal duct*). —*n.* **1** = *lachrymal vase*. **2** (in *pl.*) (usu. as **lacrimals**) the lacrimal organs. □ **lachrymal vase** *hist.* a phial holding the tears of mourners at a funeral. [ME f. med.L *lachrymalis* f. L *lacrima* tear]

lachrymation /‚lækrɪ'meɪʃ(ə)n/ *n.* (also **lacrimation**, **lacrymation**) *formal* the flow of tears. [L *lacrimatio* f. *lacrimare* weep (as LACHRYMAL)]

lachrymator /'lækrɪ‚meɪtə(r)/ *n.* an agent irritating the eyes, causing tears.

lachrymatory /'lækrɪmətərɪ/ *adj. & n.* —*adj. formal* of or causing tears. —*n.* (*pl.* **-ies**) a name applied to phials of a kind found in ancient Roman tombs and thought to be lachrymal vases.

lachrymose /'lækrɪ‚məʊs/ *adj. formal* given to weeping; tearful. □□ **lachrymosely** *adv.* [L *lacrimosus* f. *lacrima* tear]

lacing /'leɪsɪŋ/ *n.* **1** lace trimming, esp. on a uniform. **2** a laced fastening on a shoe or corsets. **3** *colloq.* beating. **4** a dash of spirits in a beverage. □ **lacing course** a strengthening course built into an arch or wall.

laciniate /lə'sɪnɪət/ *adj.* (also **laciniated** /-‚eɪtɪd/) *Bot.* & *Zool.* divided into deep narrow irregular segments; fringed. □□ **laciniation** /-'eɪʃ(ə)n/ *n.* [L *lacinia* flap of a garment]

lack /læk/ *n. & v.* —*n.* (usu. foll. by *of*) an absence, want, or deficiency (*a lack of talent*; *felt the lack of warmth*). —*v.tr.* be without or deficient in (*lacks courage*). □ **for lack of** owing to the absence of (*went hungry for lack of money*). **lack for** lack. [ME *lac*, *lacen*, corresp. to MDu., MLG *lak* deficiency, MDu. *laken* to lack]

lackadaisical /‚lækə'deɪzɪk(ə)l/ *adj.* **1** unenthusiastic; listless; idle. **2** feebly sentimental and affected. □□ **lackadaisically** *adv.* **lackadaisicalness** *n.* [archaic *lackaday*, *-daisy* (int.): see ALACK]

lacker var. of LACQUER.

lackey /'lækɪ/ *n. & v.* (also **lacquey**) —*n.* (*pl.* **-eys**) *derog.* **a** a servile political follower. **b** an obsequious parasitical person. **2 a** a (usu. liveried) footman or manservant. **b** a servant. —*v.tr.* (**-eys**, **-eyed**) *archaic* behave servilely to; dance attendance on. □ **lackey moth** a moth, *Malacosoma neustria*, developing from a brightly striped caterpillar. [F *laquais*, obs. *alaquais* f. Cat. *alacay* = Sp. ALCALDE]

lacking /'lækɪŋ/ *adj.* **1** absent or deficient (*money was lacking*; *is lacking in determination*). **2** *colloq.* deficient in intellect; mentally subnormal.

lackland /'læklənd/ *n. & adj.* —*n.* **1** a person having no land. **2** (**Lackland**) a nickname for King John of England. —*adj.* having no land.

lacklustre /'læk‚lʌstə(r)/ *adj.* (*US* **lackluster**) **1** lacking in vitality, force, or conviction. **2** (of the eye) dull.

Laconian /lə'kəʊnɪən/ *n. & adj.* —*n.* an inhabitant or the dialect of ancient Laconia. —*adj.* of the Laconian dialect or people; Spartan. [L *Laconia* Sparta f. Gk *Lakōn* Spartan]

laconic /lə'kɒnɪk/ *adj.* **1** (of a style of speech or writing) brief; concise; terse. **2** (of a person) laconic in speech etc. □□ **laconically** *adv.* **laconicism** /-ɪ‚sɪz(ə)m/ *n.* [L f. Gk *Lakōnikos* f. *Lakōn* Spartan, the Spartans being known for their terse speech]

laconism /'lækə‚nɪz(ə)m/ *n.* **1** brevity of speech. **2** a short pithy saying. [Gk *lakōnismos* f. *lakōnizō* behave like a Spartan: see LACONIC]

lacquer /'lækə(r)/ *n. & v.* (also **lacker**) —*n.* **1** a

---

b *but*   d *dog*   f *few*   g *get*   h *he*   j *yes*   k *cat*   l *leg*   m *man*   n *no*   p *pen*   r *red*   s *sit*   t *top*   v *voice*

lacquey

661

sometimes coloured liquid made of shellac dissolved in alcohol, or of synthetic substances, that dries to form a hard protective coating for wood, brass, etc. **2** a chemical substance sprayed on hair to keep it in place. **3** the sap of the lacquer-tree used to varnish wood etc. —*v.tr.* coat with lacquer. □**lacquer-tree** an E. Asian tree, *Rhus verniciflua*, the sap of which is used as a hard-wearing varnish for wood. □□ **lacquerer** *n.* [obs. F *lacre* sealing-wax, f. unexpl. var. of Port. *laca* LAC¹]

lacquey var. of LACKEY.

lacrimal var. of LACHRYMAL.

lacrimation var. of LACHRYMATION.

lacrosse /lə'krɒs/ *n.* a game like hockey, but with a ball driven by, caught, and carried in a crosse. [F f. *la* the + CROSSE]

lacrymal var. of LACHRYMAL.

lacrymation var. of LACHRYMATION.

lactase /'lækteɪz, -teɪs/ *n. Biochem.* any of a group of enzymes which catalyse the hydrolysis of lactose to glucose and galactose. [F f. *lactose* LACTOSE]

lactate¹ /læk'teɪt/ *v.intr.* (of mammals) secrete milk. [as LACTATION]

lactate² /'lækteɪt/ *n. Chem.* any salt or ester of lactic acid.

lactation /læk'teɪʃ(ə)n/ *n.* **1** the secretion of milk by the mammary glands. **2** the suckling of young. [L *lactare* suckle f. *lac lactis* milk]

lacteal /'læktɪəl/ *adj. & n.* —*adj.* **1** of milk. **2** conveying chyle or other milky fluid. —*n.* (in *pl.*) the lymphatic vessels of the small intestine which absorb digested fats. [L *lacteus* f. *lac lactis* milk]

lactescence /læk'tes(ə)ns/ *n.* **1** a milky form or appearance. **2** a milky juice. [L *lactescere* f. *lactēre* be milky (as LACTIC)]

lactescent /læk'tes(ə)nt/ *adj.* **1** milky. **2** yielding a milky juice.

lactic /'læktɪk/ *adj. Chem.* of, relating to, or obtained from milk. □**lactic acid** a clear odourless syrupy carboxylic acid formed in sour milk, and produced in the muscle tissues during strenuous exercise. [L *lac lactis* milk]

lactiferous /læk'tɪfərəs/ *adj.* yielding milk or milky fluid. [LL *lactifer* (as LACTIC)]

lacto- /'læktəʊ/ *comb. form* milk. [L *lac lactis* milk]

lactobacillus /ˌlæktəʊbə'sɪləs/ *n.* (*pl.* -**bacilli** /-laɪ/) *Biol.* any Gram-positive rod-shaped bacterium of the genus *Lactobacillus*, producing lactic acid from the fermentation of carbohydrates.

lactometer /læk'tɒmɪtə(r)/ *n.* an instrument for testing the density of milk.

lactone /'læktəʊn/ *n. Chem.* any of a class of cyclic esters formed by the elimination of water from a hydroxy-carboxylic acid. [G *Lacton*]

lactoprotein /ˌlæktəʊ'prəʊtiːn/ *n.* the albuminous constituent of milk.

lactose /'læktəʊs, -təʊz/ *n. Chem.* a sugar that occurs in milk, and is less sweet than sucrose. [as LACTO-]

lacuna /lə'kjuːnə/ *n.* (*pl.* **lacunae** /-niː/ or **lacunas**) **1** a hiatus, blank, or gap. **2** a missing portion or empty page, esp. in an ancient MS, book, etc. **3** *Anat.* a cavity or depression, esp. in bone. □□ **lacunal** *adj.* **lacunar** *adj.* **lacunary** *adj.* **lacunose** *adj.* [L, = pool, f. *lacus* LAKE¹]

lacustrine /lə'kʌstraɪn/ *adj. formal* **1** of or relating to lakes. **2** living or growing in or beside a lake. [L *lacus* LAKE¹, after *palustris* marshy]

LACW *abbr.* Leading Aircraftwoman.

lacy /'leɪsɪ/ *adj* (**lacier**, **laciest**) of or resembling lace fabric. □□ **lacily** *adv.* **laciness** *n.*

lad /læd/ *n.* **1 a** a boy or youth. **b** a young son. **2** (esp. in *pl.*) *colloq.* a man; a fellow, esp. a workmate, drinking companion, etc. (*he's one of the lads*). **3** *colloq.* a high-spirited fellow; a rogue (*he's a bit of a lad*). **4** *Brit.* a stable-worker (regardless of age). □**lad's love** = SOUTHERNWOOD. [ME *ladde*, of unkn. orig.]

ladanum /'lædənəm/ *n.* (also **labdanum**

/'læbdənəm/) a gum resin from plants of the genus *Cistus*, used in perfumery etc. [L f. Gk *ladanon* f. *lēdon* mastic]

ladder /'lædə(r)/ *n. & v.* —*n.* **1** a set of horizontal bars of wood or metal fixed between two uprights and used for climbing up or down. **2** *Brit.* a vertical strip of unravelled fabric in a stocking etc. resembling a ladder. **3 a** a hierarchical structure. **b** such a structure as a means of advancement, promotion, etc. —*v. Brit.* **1** *intr.* (of a stocking etc.) develop a ladder. **2** *tr.* cause a ladder in (a stocking etc.). □**ladder-back** an upright chair with a back resembling a ladder. **ladder-stitch** transverse bars in embroidery. **ladder tournament** a sporting contest with each participant listed and entitled to a higher place by defeating the one above. [OE *hlǣd(d)er*, ult. f. Gmc: cf. LEAN¹]

laddie /'lædɪ/ *n. colloq.* a young boy or lad.

lade /leɪd/ *v.* (*past part.* **laden** /'leɪd(ə)n/) **1** *tr.* **a** put cargo on board (a ship). **b** ship (goods) as cargo. **2** *intr.* (of a ship) take on cargo. **3** *tr.* (as **laden** *adj.*) (usu. foll. by *with*) **a** (of a vehicle, donkey, person, tree, table, etc.) heavily loaded. **b** (of the conscience, spirit, etc.) painfully burdened with sin, sorrow, etc. [OE *hladan*]

la-di-da /ˌlɑːdɪ'dɑː/ *adj. & n. colloq.* —*adj.* pretentious or snobbish, esp. in manner or speech. —*n.* **1** a la-di-da person. **2** la-di-da speech or manners. [imit. of an affected manner of speech]

ladies *pl.* of LADY.

ladify var. of LADYFY.

Ladin /lə'diːn/ *n.* the Rhaeto-Romanic dialect of the Engadine in Switzerland. [Romansh, f. L *latinus* LATIN]

lading /'leɪdɪŋ/ *n.* **1** a cargo. **2** the act or process of lading.

Ladino /lə'diːnəʊ/ *n.* (*pl.* -**os**) **1** the Spanish dialect of the Sephardic Jews. **2** a mestizo or Spanish-speaking white person in Central America. [Sp., orig. = Latin, f. L (as LADIN)]

ladle /'leɪd(ə)l/ *n. & v.* —*n.* **1** a large long-handled spoon with a cup-shaped bowl used for serving esp. soups and gravy. **2** a vessel for transporting molten metal in a foundry. —*v.tr.* (often foll. by *out*) transf (liquid) from one receptacle to another. □**ladle out** distribute, esp. lavishly. □□ **ladleful** *n.* (*pl.* -**fuls**). **ladler** *n.* [OE *hlædel* f. *hladan* LADE]

lady /'leɪdɪ/ *n.* (*pl.* -**ies**) **1 a** a woman regarded as being of superior social status or as having the refined manners associated with this (cf. GENTLEMAN). **b** (**Lady**) a title used by peeresses, female relatives of peers, the wives and widows of knights, etc. **2** (often *attrib.*) a woman; a female person or animal (*ask that lady over there*; *lady butcher*; *lady dog*). **3** *colloq.* **a** a wife. **b** a man's girlfriend. **4** a ruling woman (*lady of the house*; *lady of the manor*). **5** (in *pl.* as a form of address) a female audience or the female part of an audience. **6** *hist.* a woman to whom a man, esp. a knight, is chivalrously devoted; a mistress. □**find the lady** = *three-card trick.* **the Ladies** (or **Ladies'**) *Brit.* a women's public lavatory. **ladies' chain** a figure in a quadrille etc. **ladies' fingers** = OKRA (cf. *lady's finger*). **Ladies' Gallery** a public gallery in the House of Commons, reserved for women. **ladies'** (or **lady's**) **man** a man fond of female company; a seducer. **ladies' night** a function at a men's club etc. to which women are invited. **ladies' room** a women's lavatory in a hotel, office, etc. **Lady altar** the altar in a Lady chapel. **Lady Bountiful** a patronizingly generous lady of the manor etc. (a character in Farquhar's *The Beaux' Stratagem*). **Lady chapel** a chapel in a large church or cathedral, usu. to the E. of the high altar, dedicated to the Virgin Mary. **Lady Day** the Feast of the Annunciation, 25 Mar. **lady-fern** a slender fern, *Athyrium filix-femina.* **lady-in-waiting** a lady attending a queen or princess. **lady-killer** a practised and habitual seducer. **lady-love** a man's sweetheart.

w *we* z zoo ʃ *she* ʒ decision θ *thin* ð *this* ŋ *ring* x lo*ch* tʃ *chip* dʒ jar (*see over for vowels*)

Lady Mayoress the wife of a Lord Mayor. **Lady Muck** *sl. derog.* a socially pretentious woman. **lady of the bedchamber** = *lady-in-waiting*. **lady of easy virtue** a sexually promiscuous woman; a prostitute. **lady's bedstraw** a yellow-flowered herbaceous plant, *Galium verum*. **lady's companion** a roll containing cottons etc. **lady's finger 1** = *kidney vetch*. **2** = LADYFINGER (cf. *ladies' fingers*). **lady's maid** a lady's personal maidservant. **lady's mantle** any rosaceous plant of the genus *Alchemilla* with yellowish-green clustered flowers. **lady-smock** = *cuckoo flower* 1. **lady's slipper** any orchidaceous plant of the genus *Cypripedium*, with a usu. yellow slipper-shaped lip on its flowers. **lady's tresses** any white-flowered orchid of the genus *Spiranthes*. **Lady Superior** the head of a convent or nunnery in certain orders. **my lady** a form of address used chiefly by servants etc. to holders of the title 'Lady'. **my lady wife** *joc.* my wife. **old lady** *colloq.* **1** a mother. **2** a wife or mistress. **Our Lady** the Virgin Mary. □□ **ladyhood** *n.* [OE *hlǣfdige* f. *hlāf* LOAF¹ + (unrecorded) *dig-* knead, rel. to DOUGH): in *Lady Day* etc. f. OE genit. *hlǣfdigan* (Our) Lady's]

ladybird /'leɪdɪˌbɜːd/ *n.* a coleopterous insect of the family Coccinellidae, with wing-covers usu. of a reddish-brown colour with black spots.

ladybug /'leɪdɪˌbʌg/ *n.* *US* = LADYBIRD.

ladyfinger /'leɪdɪˌfɪŋgə(r)/ *n.* *US* a finger-shaped sponge cake.

ladyfy /'leɪdɪˌfaɪ/ *v.tr.* (also **ladify**) (-ies, -ied) **1** make a lady of. **2** call (a person) 'lady'. **3** (as **ladyfied** *adj.*) having the manner of a fine lady.

ladylike /'leɪdɪˌlaɪk/ *adj.* **1 a** with the modesty, manners, etc., of a lady. **b** befitting a lady. **2** (of a man) effeminate.

ladyship /'leɪdɪˌʃɪp/ *n. archaic* being a lady. □**her** (or **your** or **their**) **ladyship** (or **ladyships**) **1** a respectful form of reference or address to a Lady or Ladies. **2** *iron.* a form of reference or address to a woman thought to be giving herself airs.

laevo- /'liːvəʊ/ *comb. form* (also **levo-**) on or to the left. [L *laevus* left]

laevorotatory /ˌliːvəʊˈrəʊtətərɪ/ *adj.* (*US* **levorotatory**) *Chem.* having the property of rotating the plane of a polarized light ray to the left (anti-clockwise facing the oncoming radiation).

laevulose /'liːvjʊˌləʊs, -ˌləʊz/ *n.* (*US* **levulose**) = FRUCTOSE. [LAEVO- + -ULE + -OSE²]

lag¹ /læg/ *v. & n.* —*v.intr.* (**lagged**, **lagging**) **1** (often foll. by *behind*) fall behind; not keep pace. **2** *US Billiards* make the preliminary strokes that decide which player shall begin. —*n.* **1** a delay. **2** *Physics* **a** retardation in a current or movement. **b** the amount of this. □**lag of tide** the interval by which a tide falls behind mean time at the 1st and 3rd quarters of the moon (cf. PRIMING²). □□ **lagger** *n.* [orig. = hindmost person, hang back: perh. f. a fanciful distortion of LAST¹ in a children's game (*fog, seg, lag,* = 1st, 2nd, last, in dial.)]

lag² /læg/ *v. & n.* —*v.tr.* (**lagged**, **lagging**) enclose or cover in lagging. —*n.* **1** the non-heat-conducting cover of a boiler etc.; lagging. **2** a piece of this. [prob. f. Scand.: cf. ON *lögg* barrel-rim, rel. to LAY¹]

lag³ /læg/ *n. & v. sl.* —*n.* (esp. as **old lag**) a habitual convict. —*v.tr.* (**lagged**, **lagging**) **1** send to prison. **2** apprehend; arrest. [19th c.: orig. unkn.]

lagan /'lægən/ *n.* goods or wreckage lying on the bed of the sea, sometimes with a marking buoy etc. for later retrieval. [OF, perh. of Scand. orig., f. root of LIE¹, LAY¹]

lager /'lɑːgə(r)/ *n.* a kind of beer, effervescent and light in colour and body. □**lager lout** *colloq.* a youth who behaves badly as a result of excessive drinking. [G *Lagerbier* beer brewed for keeping f. *Lager* store]

laggard /'lægəd/ *n. & adj.* —*n.* a dawdler; a person who lags behind. —*adj.* dawdling; slow. □□ **laggardly** *adj. & adv.* **laggardness** *n.* [LAG¹]

lagging /'lægɪŋ/ *n.* material providing heat insulation for a boiler, pipes, etc. [LAG²]

lagomorph /'lægəˌmɔːf/ *n. Zool.* any mammal of the order Lagomorpha, including hares and rabbits. [Gk *lagōs* hare + *morphē* form]

lagoon /ləˈguːn/ *n.* **1** a stretch of salt water separated from the sea by a low sandbank, coral reef, etc. **2** the enclosed water of an atoll. **3** *US, Austral., & NZ* a small freshwater lake near a larger lake or river. **4** an artificial pool for the treatment of effluent or to accommodate an overspill from surface drains during heavy rain. [F *lagune* or It. & Sp. *laguna* f. L *lacuna*: see LACUNA]

lah /lɑː/ *n.* (also **la**) *Mus.* **1** (in tonic sol-fa) the sixth note of a major scale. **2** the note A in the fixed-doh system. [ME f. L *labii*: see GAMUT]

lahar /'lɑːhɑː(r)/ *n.* a mud-flow composed mainly of volcanic debris. [Jav.]

laic /'leɪɪk/ *adj. & n.* —*adj.* non-clerical; lay; secular; temporal. —*n. formal* a lay person; a non-cleric. □□ **laical** *adj.* **laically** *adv.* [LL f. Gk *laïkos* f. *laos* people]

laicity /leɪˈɪsɪtɪ/ *n.* the status or influence of the laity.

laicize /'leɪɪˌsaɪz/ *v.tr.* (also **-ise**) **1** make (an office etc.) tenable by lay people. **2** subject (a school or institution) to the control of lay people. **3** secularize. □□ **laicization** /-ˈzeɪʃ(ə)n/ *n.*

laid *past and past part.* of LAY¹.

lain *past part.* of LIE¹.

lair¹ /leə(r)/ *n. & v.* —*n.* **1 a** a wild animal's resting-place. **b** a person's hiding-place; a den (*tracked him to his lair*). **2** a place where domestic animals lie down. **3** *Brit.* a shed or enclosure for cattle on the way to market. —*v.* **1** *intr.* go to or rest in a lair. **2** *tr.* place (an animal) in a lair. □□ **lairage** *n.* [OE *leger* f. Gmc: cf. LIE¹]

lair² /leə(r)/ *n. & v. Austral. sl.* —*n.* a youth or man who dresses flashily and shows off. —*v.intr.* (often foll. by *up* or *dress*) behave or dress like a lair. □□ **lairy** *adj.* [*lair* back-form. f. *lairy,* alt. f. LEERY]

laird /leəd/ *n. Sc.* a landed proprietor. □□ **lairdship** *n.* [Sc. form of LORD]

laissez-aller /ˌleseɪˈæleɪ/ *n.* (also **laisser-aller**) unconstrained freedom; an absence of constraint. [F, = let go]

laissez-faire /ˌleseɪˈfeə(r)/ *n.* (also **laisser-faire**) the theory or practice of governmental abstention from interference in the workings of the market etc. [F, = let act]

laissez-passer /ˌleseɪˈpæseɪ/ *n.* (also **laisser-passer**) a document allowing the holder to pass; a permit. [F, = let pass]

laity /'leɪɪtɪ/ *n.* (usu. prec. by *the*; usu. treated as *pl.*) **1** lay people, as distinct from the clergy. **2** non-professionals. [ME f. LAY² + -ITY]

lake¹ /leɪk/ *n.* a large body of water surrounded by land. □**the Great Lakes** the Lakes Superior, Huron, Michigan, Erie, and Ontario, along the boundary of the US and Canada. **Lake District** (or **the Lakes**) the region of the English lakes in Cumbria. **lake-dweller** a prehistoric inhabitant of lake-dwellings. **lake-dwellings** prehistoric huts built on piles driven into the bed or shore of a lake. **Lake Poets** Coleridge, Southey, and Wordsworth, who lived in and were inspired by the Lake District. □□ **lakeless** *adj.* **lakelet** *n.* [ME f. OF *lac* f. L *lacus* basin, pool, lake]

lake² /leɪk/ *n.* **1** a reddish colouring orig. made from lac (*crimson lake*). **2** a complex formed by the action of dye and mordants applied to fabric to fix colour. **3** any insoluble product of a soluble dye and mordant. [var. of LAC¹]

Lakeland /'leɪklənd/ *n.* = *Lake District.* □**Lakeland terrier 1** a terrier of a small stocky breed originating in the Lake District. **2** this breed.

lakeside /'leɪksaɪd/ *attrib.adj.* beside a lake.

lakh /læk, lɑːk/ *n.* (also **lac**) *Ind.* (usu. foll. by *of*) a hundred thousand (rupees etc.). [Hind. *lākh* f. Skr. *lakṣa*]

Lallan /ˈlælən/ *n.* & *adj. Sc.* —*n.* (now usu. **Lallans**) a Lowland Scots dialect, esp. as a literary language. —*adj.* of or concerning the Lowlands of Scotland. [var. of LOWLAND]

lallation /læˈleɪʃ(ə)n/ *n.* **1** the pronunciation of *r* as *l.* **2** imperfect speech, esp. that of young children. [L *lallare lallat-* sing a lullaby]

lallygag /ˈlælɪˌgæg/ *v.intr.* (**lallygagged, lallygagging**) *US sl.* **1** loiter. **2** cuddle amorously. [20th c.: orig. unkn.]

Lam. *abbr.* Lamentations (Old Testament).

lam[1] /læm/ *v.* (**lammed, lamming**) *sl.* **1** *tr.* thrash; hit. **2** *intr.* (foll. by *into*) hit (a person etc.) hard with a stick etc. [perh. f. Scand.: cf. ON *lemja* beat so as to LAME]

lam[2] /læm/ *n.* □**on the lam** *US sl.* in flight, esp. from the police. [20th c.: orig. unkn.]

lama /ˈlɑːmə/ *n.* a Tibetan or Mongolian Buddhist monk. □□ **Lamaism** *n.* **Lamaist** *n.* & *adj.* [Tibetan *blama* (with silent *b*)]

Lamarckism /ləˈmɑːkɪz(ə)m/ *n.* the theory of evolution devised by Lamarck, French botanist and zoologist (d. 1829), based on the inheritance of acquired characteristics. □□ **Lamarckian** *n.* & *adj.*

lamasery /ˈlɑːməsərɪ, ləˈmɑːsərɪ/ *n.* (*pl.* -**ies**) a monastery of lamas. [F *lamaserie* irreg. f. *lama* LAMA]

lamb /læm/ *n.* & *v.* —*n.* **1** a young sheep. **2** the flesh of a lamb as food. **3** a mild or gentle person, esp. a young child. —*v.* **1 a** *tr.* (in *passive*) (of a lamb) be born. **b** *intr.* (of a ewe) give birth to lambs. **2** *tr.* tend (lambing ewes). □**The Lamb** (or **The Lamb of God**) a name for Christ (see John 1:29) (cf. AGNUS DEI). **lamb's fry** lamb's testicles or other offal as food. **lamb's lettuce** a plant, *Valerianella locusta*, used in salad. **lamb's-tails** catkins from the hazel tree. **like a lamb** meekly, obediently. □□ **lamber** *n.* **lambhood** *n.* **lambkin** *n.* **lamblike** *adj.* [OE *lamb* f. Gmc]

lambaste /læmˈbeɪst/ *v.tr.* (also **lambast** /-ˈbæst/) *colloq.* **1** thrash; beat. **2** criticize severely. [LAM[1] + BASTE[3]]

lambda /ˈlæmdə/ *n.* **1** the eleventh letter of the Greek alphabet (*Λ, λ*). **2** (as λ) the symbol for wavelength. [ME f. Gk *la(m)bda*]

lambent /ˈlæmbənt/ *adj.* **1** (of a flame or a light) playing on a surface with a soft radiance but without burning. **2** (of the eyes, sky, etc.) softly radiant. **3** (of wit etc.) lightly brilliant. □□ **lambency** *n.* **lambently** *adv.* [L *lambere lambent-* lick]

lambert /ˈlæmbət/ *n.* a former unit of luminance, equal to the emission or reflection of one lumen per square centimetre. [J. H. *Lambert*, Ger. physicist d. 1777]

lambrequin /ˈlæmbrɪkɪn, ˈlæmbə-/ *n.* **1** *US* a short piece of drapery hung over the top of a door or a window or draped on a mantelpiece. **2** *Heraldry* = MANTLING. [F f. Du. (unrecorded) *lamperkin*, dimin. of *lamper* veil]

lambskin /ˈlæmskɪn/ *n.* a prepared skin from a lamb with the wool on or as leather.

lambswool /ˈlæmzwʊl/ *n.* (also **lamb's-wool**) soft fine wool from a young sheep used in knitted garments etc.

lame /leɪm/ *adj.* & *v.* —*adj.* **1** disabled, esp. in the foot or leg; limping; unable to walk normally (*lame in his right leg*). **2 a** (of an argument, story, excuse, etc.) unconvincing; unsatisfactory; weak. **b** (of verse etc.) halting. —*v.tr.* **1** make lame; disable. **2** harm permanently. □**lame-brain** *US colloq.* a stupid person. **lame duck 1** a disabled or weak person. **2** a defaulter on the Stock Exchange. **3** a firm etc. in financial difficulties. **4** *US* an official (esp. the President) in the final period of office, after the election of a successor. □□ **lamely** *adv.* **lameness** *n.* **lamish** *adj.* [OE *lama* f. Gmc]

lamé /ˈlɑːmeɪ/ *n.* & *adj.* —*n.* a fabric with gold or silver threads interwoven. —*adj.* (of fabric, a dress, etc.) having such threads. [F]

lamella /ləˈmelə/ *n.* (*pl.* **lamellae** /-liː/) **1** a thin layer, membrane, scale, or platelike tissue or part, esp. in bone tissue. **2** *Bot.* a membranous fold in a chloroplast. □□ **lamellar** *adj.* **lamellate** /ˈlæməˌleɪt/ *adj.* **lamelliform** *adj.* **lamellose** /-ləʊs/ *adj.* [L, dimin. of *lamina*: see LAMINA]

lamellibranch /ləˈmelɪˌbræŋk/ *n.* any aquatic mollusc having a shell formed of two pieces or valves, e.g. a mussel or oyster. Also called BIVALVE. [LAMELLA + Gk *bragkhia* gills]

lamellicorn /ləˈmelɪˌkɔːn/ *n.* & *adj.* —*n.* any beetle of the family Lamellicornia, having lamelliform antennae, including the stag beetle, cockchafer, dung-beetle, etc. —*adj.* having lamelliform antennae. [mod.L *lamellicornis* f. L *lamella* (see LAMELLA) + *cornu* horn]

lament /ləˈment/ *n.* & *v.* —*n.* **1** a passionate expression of grief. **2** a song or poem of mourning or sorrow. —*v.tr.* (also *absol.*) **1** express or feel grief for or about; regret (*lamented the loss of his ticket*). **2** (as **lamented** *adj.*) a conventional expression referring to a recently dead person (*your late lamented father*). □**lament for** (or **over**) mourn or regret. □□ **lamenter** *n.* **lamentingly** *adv.* [L *lamentum*]

lamentable /ˈlæməntəb(ə)l/ *adj.* **1** (of an event, fate, condition, character, etc.) deplorable; regrettable. **2** *archaic* mournful. □□ **lamentably** *adv.* [ME f. OF *lamentable* or L *lamentabilis* (as LAMENT)]

lamentation /ˌlæmənˈteɪʃ(ə)n/ *n.* **1** the act or an instance of lamenting. **2** a lament. □**Lamentations of Jeremiah** an Old Testament book concerning the destruction of Jerusalem in the 6th c. BC. [ME f. OF *lamentation* or L *lamentatio* (as LAMENT)]

lamina /ˈlæmɪnə/ *n.* (*pl.* **laminae** /-ˌniː/) a thin plate or scale, e.g. of bone, stratified rock, or vegetable tissue. □□ **laminose** *adj.* [L]

laminar /ˈlæmɪnə(r)/ *adj.* **1** consisting of laminae. **2** *Physics* (of a flow) taking place along constant streamlines, not turbulent.

laminate *v., n.,* & *adj.* —*v.* /ˈlæmɪˌneɪt/ **1** *tr.* beat or roll (metal) into thin plates. **2** *tr.* overlay with metal plates, a plastic layer, etc. **3** *tr.* manufacture by placing layer on layer. **4** *tr.* & *intr.* split or be split into layers or leaves. —*n.* /ˈlæmɪnət/ a laminated structure or material, esp. of layers fixed together to form rigid or flexible material. —*adj.* /ˈlæmɪnət/ in the form of lamina or laminae. □□ **lamination** /-ˈneɪʃ(ə)n/ *n.* **laminator** *n.* [LAMINA + -ATE[2], -ATE[3]]

Lammas /ˈlæməs/ *n.* (in full **Lammas Day**) the first day of August, formerly observed as harvest festival. [OE *hlāfmæsse* (as LOAF[1], MASS[2])]

lammergeyer /ˈlæməˌgaɪə(r)/ *n.* a large vulture, *Gypaetus barbatus*, with a very large wingspan (often of 3 m) and dark beardlike feathers on either side of its beak. [G *Lämmergeier* f. *Lämmer* lambs + *Geier* vulture]

lamp /læmp/ *n.* & *v.* —*n.* **1** a device for producing a steady light, esp.: **a** an electric bulb, and usu. its holder and shade or cover (*bedside lamp*; *bicycle lamp*). **b** an oil-lamp. **c** a usu. glass holder for a candle. **d** a gas-jet and mantle. **2** a source of spiritual or intellectual inspiration. **3** *poet.* the sun, the moon, or a star. **4** a device producing esp. ultraviolet or infrared radiation as a treatment for various complaints. —*v.* **1** *intr. poet.* shine. **2** *tr.* supply with lamps; illuminate. **3** *tr. US sl.* look at. □**lamp-chimney** a glass cylinder enclosing and making a draught for an oil-lamp flame. **lamp-holder** a device for supporting a lamp, esp. an electric one. **lamp standard** = LAMPPOST. □□ **lampless** *adj.* [ME f. OF *lampe* f. LL *lampada* f. accus. of L *lampas* torch f. Gk]

lampblack /ˈlæmpblæk/ *n.* a pigment made from soot.

lamplight /ˈlæmplaɪt/ n. light given by a lamp or lamps.

lamplighter /ˈlæmpˌlaɪtə(r)/ n. **1** hist. a person who lights street lamps. **2** US a spill for lighting lamps. □like a lamplighter with great speed.

lampoon /læmˈpuːn/ n. & v. —n. a satirical attack on a person etc. —v.tr. satirize. □□**lampooner** n. **lampoonery** n. **lampoonist** n. [F lampon, conjectured to be f. lampons let us drink f. lamper gulp down f. laper LAP³]

lamppost /ˈlæmppəʊst/ n. a tall post supporting a street-light.

lamprey /ˈlæmprɪ/ n. (pl. -eys) any eel-like aquatic vertebrate of the family Petromyzonidae, without scales, paired fins, or jaws, but having a sucker mouth with horny teeth and a rough tongue. [ME f. OF lampreie f. med.L lampreda: cf. LL lampetra perh. f. L lambere lick + petra stone]

lampshade /ˈlæmpʃeɪd/ n. a translucent cover for a lamp used to soften or direct its light.

Lancastrian /læŋˈkæstrɪən/ n. & adj. —n. **1** a native of Lancashire or Lancaster in NW England. **2** hist. a follower of the House of Lancaster or of the Red Rose party supporting it in the Wars of the Roses (cf. YORKIST). —adj. of or concerning Lancashire or Lancaster, or the House of Lancaster.

lance /lɑːns/ n. & v. —n. **1 a** a long weapon with a wooden shaft and a pointed steel head, used by a horseman in charging. **b** a similar weapon used for spearing a fish, killing a harpooned whale, etc. **2** a metal pipe supplying oxygen to burn metal. **3** = LANCER. —v.tr. **1** Surgery prick or cut open with a lancet. **2** pierce with a lance. **3** poet. fling; launch. □break a lance (usu. foll. by for, with) argue. **lance-bombardier** a rank in the Royal Artillery corresponding to lance-corporal in the infantry. **lance-corporal** the lowest rank of NCO in the Army. **lance-jack** Brit. sl. a lance-corporal or lance-bombardier. **lance-sergeant** a corporal acting as sergeant. **lance-snake** = FER DE LANCE. [ME f. OF lancier f. L lancea: lance-corporal on analogy of obs. lancepesade lowest grade of NCO ult. f. It. lancia spezzata broken lance]

lancelet /ˈlɑːnslɪt/ n. any small non-vertebrate fish-like chordate of the family Branchiostomidae, that burrows in sand. [LANCE n. + -LET, with ref. to its thin form]

lanceolate /ˈlɑːnsɪələt/ adj. shaped like a lance-head, tapering to each end. [LL lanceolatus f. lanceola dimin. of lancea lance]

lancer /ˈlɑːnsə(r)/ n. **1** hist. a soldier of a cavalry regiment armed with lances. **2** (in pl.) **a** a quadrille for 8 or 16 pairs. **b** the music for this. [F lancier (as LANCE)]

lancet /ˈlɑːnsɪt/ n. a small broad two-edged surgical knife with a sharp point. □lancet arch (or light or window) a narrow arch or window with a pointed head. □□**lanceted** adj. [ME f. OF lancette (as LANCE)]

lancewood /ˈlɑːnswʊd/ n. a tough elastic wood from a W. Indian tree Oxandra lanceolata, used for carriage-shafts, fishing-rods, etc.

Lancs. abbr. Lancashire.

Land /lʌnt/ n. (pl. **Länder** /ˈlendə(r)/) **1** a province of the Federal Republic of Germany. **2** a province of Austria. [G (as LAND)]

land /lænd/ n. & v. —n. **1** the solid part of the earth's surface (opp. SEA, WATER, AIR). **2 a** an expanse of country; ground; soil. **b** such land in relation to its use, quality, etc., or (often prec. by the) as a basis for agriculture (building land; this is good land; works on the land). **3** a country, nation, or State (land of hope and glory). **4 a** landed property. **b** (in pl.) estates. **5** the space between the rifling-grooves in a gun. **6** Sc. a building containing several dwellings. **7** S.Afr. ground fenced off for tillage. **8** a strip of plough or pasture land parted from others by drain-furrows. —v. **1 a** tr. & intr. set or go ashore. **b** intr. (often foll. by at) disembark (landed at the harbour). **2** tr. bring (an aircraft, its passengers, etc.) to the ground or the surface of water. **3** intr. (of an aircraft, bird, parachutist, etc.) alight on the ground or water. **4** tr. bring (a fish) to land. **5** tr. & intr. (also refl.; often foll. by up) colloq. bring to, reach, or find oneself in a certain situation, place, or state (landed himself in jail; landed up in France; landed her in trouble; landed up penniless). **6** tr. colloq. **a** deal (a person etc.) a blow etc. (landed him one in the eye). **b** (foll. by with) present (a person) with (a problem, job, etc.). **7** tr. set down (a person, cargo, etc.) from a vehicle, ship, etc. **8** tr. colloq. win or obtain (a prize, job, etc.) esp. against strong competition. □how the land lies what is the state of affairs. in the land of the living joc. still alive. **land-agency 1** the stewardship of an estate. **2** an agency for the sale etc. of estates. **land-agent 1** the steward of an estate. **2** an agent for the sale of estates. **land-bank** a bank issuing banknotes on the securities of landed property. **land breeze** a breeze blowing towards the sea from the land, esp. at night. **land-bridge** a neck of land joining two large land masses. **land-crab** a crab, Cardisoma guanhumi, that lives in burrows inland and migrates in large numbers to the sea to breed. **land force** (or **forces**) armies, not naval or air forces. **land-form** a natural feature of the earth's surface. **land-girl** Brit. a woman doing farm work, esp. in wartime. **land-grabber** an illegal seizer of land, esp. a person who took the land of an evicted Irish tenant. **land-law** (usu. in pl.) the law of landed property. **land-line** a means of telecommunication over land. **land-locked** almost or entirely enclosed by land. **land mass** a large area of land. **land-mine 1** an explosive mine laid in or on the ground. **2** a parachute mine. **land of cakes** Scotland. **land office** US an office recording dealings in public land. **land-office business** US enormous trade. **land of Nod** sleep (with pun on the phr. in Gen. 4:16). **land on one's feet** attain a good position, job, etc., by luck. **Land's End** the westernmost point of Cornwall and of England. **land-tax** hist. a tax assessed on landed property. **land-tie** a rod, beam, or piece of masonry securing or supporting a wall etc. by connecting it with the ground. **land-wind** a wind blowing seaward from the land. **land yacht** a vehicle with wheels and sails for recreational use on a beach etc. □□**lander** n. **landless** adj. **landward** adj. & adv. **landwards** adv. [OE f. Gmc]

landau /ˈlændɔː/ n. a four-wheeled enclosed carriage with a removable front cover and a back cover that can be raised and lowered. [Landau near Karlsruhe in Germany, where it was first made]

landaulet /ˌlændɔːˈlet/ n. **1** a small landau. **2** hist. a car with a folding hood over the rear seats.

landed /ˈlændɪd/ adj. **1** owning land (landed gentry). **2** consisting of, including, or relating to land (landed property).

Länder pl. of LAND.

landfall /ˈlændfɔːl/ n. the approach to land, esp. for the first time on a sea or air journey.

landfill /ˈlændfɪl/ n. **1** waste material etc. used to landscape or reclaim areas of ground. **2** the process of disposing of rubbish in this way.

landgrave /ˈlændgreɪv/ n. (fem. **landgravine** /-grəˌviːn/) hist. **1** a count having jurisdiction over a territory. **2** the title of certain German princes. □□ **landgraviate** /-ˈgreɪvɪət/ n. [MLG landgrave, MHG lantgrāve (as LAND, G Graf COUNT²)]

landholder /ˈlændˌhəʊldə(r)/ n. the proprietor or, esp., the tenant of land.

landing /ˈlændɪŋ/ n. **1 a** the act or process of coming to land. **b** an instance of this. **c** (also **landing-place**) a place where ships etc. land. **2 a** a platform between two flights of stairs, or at the top or bottom of a flight. **b** a passage leading to upstairs rooms. □landing-craft any of several types of craft esp. designed for putting troops and equipment ashore. **landing-gear** the undercarriage of an aircraft.

b *but* d *dog* f *few* g *get* h *he* j *yes* k *cat* l *leg* m *man* n *no* p *pen* r *red* s *sit* t *top* v *voice*

landing-net a net for landing a large fish which has been hooked. **landing-stage** a platform, often floating, on which goods and passengers are disembarked. **landing-strip** an airstrip.

landlady /ˈlænd͵leɪdɪ/ n. (pl. **-ies**) **1** a woman who lets land, a building, part of a building, etc., to a tenant. **2** a woman who keeps a public house, boarding-house, or lodgings.

ländler /ˈlendlə(r)/ n. **1** an Austrian dance in triple time, a precursor of the waltz. **2** the music for a ländler. [G f. *Landl* Upper Austria]

landloper /ˈlænd͵ləʊpə(r)/ n. esp. *Sc.* a vagabond. [MDu. *landlooper* (as LAND, *loopen* run, formed as LEAP)]

landlord /ˈlændlɔːd/ n. **1** a man who lets land, a building, part of a building, etc., to a tenant. **2** a man who keeps a public house, boarding-house, or lodgings.

landlubber /ˈlænd͵lʌbə(r)/ n. a person unfamiliar with the sea or sailing.

landmark /ˈlændmɑːk/ n. **1 a** a conspicuous object in a district etc. **b** an object marking the boundary of an estate, country, etc. **2** an event, change, etc. marking a stage or turning-point in history etc.

landocracy /lænˈdɒkrəsɪ/ n. (pl. **-ies**) *joc.* the landed class. □□ **landocrat** /ˈlændə͵kræt/ n.

landowner /ˈlænd͵əʊnə(r)/ n. an owner of land. □□ **landowning** adj. & n.

landrail /ˈlændreɪl/ n. = CORNCRAKE.

landscape /͵lændskeɪp, ˈlæns-/ n. & v. —n. **1** natural or imaginary scenery, as seen in a broad view. **2** (often *attrib.*) a picture representing this; the genre of landscape painting. **3** (in graphic design etc.) a format in which the width of an illustration etc. is greater than the height (cf. PORTRAIT). —v.tr. (also *absol.*) improve (a piece of land) by landscape gardening. □ **landscape gardener** (or **architect**) a person who plans the layout of landscapes, esp. extensive grounds. **landscape gardening** (or **architecture**) the laying out of esp. extensive grounds to resemble natural scenery. **landscape-marble** marble with treelike markings. **landscape-painter** an artist who paints landscapes. □□ **landscapist** n. [MDu. *landscap* (as LAND, -SHIP)]

landslide /ˈlændslaɪd/ n. **1** the sliding down of a mass of land from a mountain, cliff, etc. **2** an overwhelming majority for one side in an election.

landslip /ˈlændslɪp/ n. = LANDSLIDE 1.

landsman /ˈlændzmən/ n. (pl. **-men**) a non-sailor.

lane /leɪn/ n. **1** a narrow, often rural, road, street, or path. **2** a division of a road for a stream of traffic (*three-lane highway*). **3** a strip of track or water for a runner, rower, or swimmer in a race. **4** a path or course prescribed for or regularly followed by a ship, aircraft, etc. (*ocean lane*). **5** a gangway between crowds of people, objects, etc. □ **it's a long lane that has no turning** change is inevitable. [OE: orig. unkn.]

langlauf /ˈlæŋlaʊf/ n. cross-country skiing; a cross-country skiing race. [G, = long run]

langouste /lɑ̃ˈguːst, ˈlɒŋguːst/ n. a crawfish or spiny lobster. [F]

langoustine /͵lɑ̃guːˈstiːn, ˈlɒŋguː͵stiːn/ n. = NORWAY LOBSTER. [F]

lang syne /læŋ ˈsaɪn/ adv. & n. *Sc.* —adv. in the distant past. —n. the old days (cf. AULD LANG SYNE). [= long since]

language /ˈlæŋgwɪdʒ/ n. **1** the method of human communication, either spoken or written, consisting of the use of words in an agreed way. **2** the language of a particular community or country etc. (*speaks several languages*). **3 a** the faculty of speech. **b** a style or the faculty of expression; the use of words, etc. (*his language was poetic*; *hasn't the language to express it*). **c** (also **bad language**) coarse, crude, or abusive speech (*didn't like his language*). **4** a system of symbols and rules for writing computer programs or algorithms. **5** any method of expression (*the*

language of mime; *sign language*). **6** a professional or specialized vocabulary. **7** literary style. □ **language laboratory** a room equipped with tape recorders etc. for learning a foreign language. **language of flowers** a set of symbolic meanings attached to different flowers. **speak the same language** have a similar outlook, manner of expression, etc. [ME f. OF *langage* ult. f. L *lingua* tongue]

langue de chat /͵lɑ̃g də ˈʃɑː/ n. a very thin finger-shaped crisp biscuit or piece of chocolate. [F, = cat's tongue]

langue d'oc /lɑ̃g ˈdɒk/ n. the form of medieval French spoken south of the Loire, the basis of modern Provençal. [OF *langue* language f. L *lingua* tongue + *de* of + *oc* (f. L *hoc*) the form for *yes*]

langue d'oïl /lɑ̃g ˈdɔɪl/ n. medieval French as spoken north of the Loire, the basis of modern French. [as LANGUE D'OC + *oïl* (f. L *hoc ille*) the form for *yes*]

languid /ˈlæŋgwɪd/ adj. **1** lacking vigour; idle; inert; apathetic. **2** (of ideas etc.) lacking force; uninteresting. **3** (of trade etc.) slow-moving; sluggish. **4** faint; weak. □□ **languidly** adv. **languidness** n. [F *languide* or L *languidus* (as LANGUISH)]

languish /ˈlæŋgwɪʃ/ v.intr. **1** be or grow feeble; lose or lack vitality. **2** put on a sentimentally tender or languid look. □ **languish for** droop or pine for. **languish under** suffer under (esp. depression, confinement, etc.). □□ **languisher** n. **languishingly** adv. **languishment** n. [ME f. OF *languir*, ult. f. L *languēre*, rel. to LAX]

languor /ˈlæŋgə(r)/ n. **1** lack of energy or alertness; inertia; idleness; dullness. **2** faintness; fatigue. **3** a soft or tender mood or effect. **4** an oppressive stillness (of the air etc.). □□ **languorous** adj. **languorously** adv. [ME f. OF f. L *languor -oris* (as LANGUISH)]

langur /lʌŋˈgʊːə(r)/ n. any of various Asian long-tailed monkeys esp. of the genus *Presbytis*. [Hindi]

laniary /ˈlænɪərɪ/ adj. & n. —adj. (of a tooth) adapted for tearing; canine. —n. (pl. **-ies**) a laniary tooth. [L *laniarius* f. *lanius* butcher f. *laniare* to tear]

laniferous /ləˈnɪfərəs/ adj. (also **lanigerous** /ləˈnɪdʒərəs/) wool-bearing. [L *lanifer*, *-ger* f. *lana* wool]

lank /læŋk/ adj. **1** (of hair, grass, etc.) long, limp, and straight. **2** thin and tall. **3** shrunken; spare. □□ **lankly** adv. **lankness** n. [OE *hlanc* f. Gmc: cf. FLANK, LINK[1]]

lanky /ˈlæŋkɪ/ adj. (**lankier**, **lankiest**) (of limbs, a person, etc.) ungracefully thin and long or tall. □□ **lankily** adv. **lankiness** n.

lanner /ˈlænə(r)/ n. a S. European falcon, *Falco biarmicus*, esp. the female. [ME f. OF *lanier* perh. f. OF *lanier* cowardly, orig. = weaver f. L *lanarius* wool-merchant f. *lana* wool]

lanneret /ˈlænərɪt/ n. a male lanner, smaller than the female. [ME f. OF *laneret* (as LANNER)]

lanolin /ˈlænəlɪn/ n. a fat found naturally on sheep's wool and used purified for cosmetics etc. [G f. L *lana* wool + *oleum* oil]

lansquenet /ˈlænskənət/ n. **1** a card-game of German origin. **2** a German mercenary soldier in the 16th–17th c. [F f. G *Landsknecht* (as LAND, *Knecht* soldier f. OHG *kneht*: see KNIGHT)]

lantana /lænˈteɪnə/ n. any evergreen shrub of the genus *Lantana*, with usu. yellow or orange flowers. [mod.L]

lantern /ˈlænt(ə)n/ n. **1 a** a lamp with a transparent usu. glass case protecting a candle flame etc. **b** a similar electric etc. lamp. **c** its case. **2 a** a raised structure on a dome, room, etc., glazed to admit light. **b** a similar structure for ventilation etc. **3** the light-chamber of a lighthouse. **4** = *magic lantern*. □ **lantern fish** any marine fish of the family Myctophidae, having small light organs on the head and body. **lantern-fly** (pl. **-flies**) any tropical homopterous insect of the family Fulgoridae, formerly thought to be luminous. **lantern-jawed** having lantern jaws. **lantern jaws** long thin jaws and chin, giving a hollow look to the face. **lantern-slide** a slide for projection by a magic lantern etc. (see SLIDE *n.* 5b). **lantern-wheel** a lantern-shaped gearwheel; a trundle. [ME f. OF *lanterne* f. L *lanterna* f. Gk *lamptēr* torch, lamp]

lanthanide /'lænθəˌnaɪd/ *n. Chem.* an element of the lanthanide series. □**lanthanide series** a series of 15 metallic elements from lanthanum to lutetium in the periodic table, having similar chemical properties: also called *rare earths* (see RARE[1]). [G *Lanthanid* (as LANTHANUM)]

lanthanum /'lænθənəm/ *n. Chem.* a silvery metallic element of the lanthanide series which occurs naturally and is used in the manufacture of alloys. ¶ Symb.: **La**. [Gk *lanthanō* escape notice, from having remained undetected in cerium oxide]

lanugo /lə'nju:gəʊ/ *n.* fine soft hair, esp. that which covers the body and limbs of a human foetus. [L, = down f. *lana* wool]

lanyard /'lænjəd, -jɑ:d/ *n.* **1** a cord hanging round the neck or looped round the shoulder, esp. of a Scout or sailor etc., to which a knife, a whistle, etc., may be attached. **2** *Naut.* a short rope or line used for securing, tightening, etc. **3** a cord attached to a breech mechanism for firing a gun. [ME f. OF *laniere*, *lasniere*: assim. to YARD[1]]

Laodicean /ˌleɪəʊdɪ'si:ən/ *adj. & n.* —*adj.* lukewarm or half-hearted, esp. in religion or politics. —*n.* such a person. [L *Laodicea* in Asia Minor (with ref. to the early Christians there: see Rev. 3:16)]

Laotian /'laʊʃɪən, lɑ:'əʊʃɪən/ *n. & adj.* —*n.* **1 a** a native or national of Laos in SE Asia. **b** a person of Laotian descent. **2** the language of Laos. —*adj.* of or relating to Laos or its people or language.

lap[1] /læp/ *n.* **1 a** the front of the body from the waist to the knees of a sitting person (*sat on her lap*; *caught it in his lap*). **b** the clothing, esp. a skirt, covering the lap. **c** the front of a skirt held up to catch or contain something. **2** a hollow among hills. **3 a** hanging flap on a garment, a saddle, etc. □**in** (or **on**) **a person's lap** as a person's responsibility. **in the lap of the gods** (of an event etc.) open to chance; beyond human control. **in the lap of luxury** in extremely luxurious surroundings. **lap-dog** a small pet dog. **lap robe** *US* a travelling-rug. □□**lapful** *n.* (*pl.* **-fuls**). [OE *læppa* fold, flap]

lap[2] /læp/ *n. & v.* —*n.* **1 a** one circuit of a racetrack etc. **b** a section of a journey etc. (*finally we were on the last lap*). **2 a** an amount of overlapping. **b** an overlapping or projecting part. **3 a a** layer or sheet (of cotton etc. being made) wound on a roller. **b** a single turn of rope, silk, thread, etc., round a drum or reel. **4** a rotating disk for polishing a gem or metal. —*v.* (**lapped**, **lapping**) **1** *tr.* lead or overtake (a competitor in a race) by one or more laps. **2** *tr.* (often foll. by *about*, *round*) coil, fold, or wrap (a garment etc.) round esp. a person. **3** *tr.* (usu. foll. by *in*) enfold or swathe (a person) in wraps etc. **4** *tr.* (as **lapped** *adj.*) (usu. foll. by *in*) protectively encircled; enfolded caressingly. **5** *tr.* surround (a person) with an influence etc. **6** *intr.* (usu. foll. by *over*) project; overlap. **7** *tr.* cause to overlap. **8** *tr.* polish (a gem etc.) with a lap. □**half-lap** = *lap joint*. **lap joint** the joining of rails, shafts, etc., by halving the thickness of each at the joint and fitting them together. **lap of honour** a ceremonial circuit of a football pitch, a track, etc., by a winner or winners. **lap-strake** *n.* a clinker-built boat. —*adj.* clinker-built. **lap-weld** *v.tr.* weld with overlapping edges. —*n.* such a weld. [ME, prob. f. LAP[1]]

lap[3] /læp/ *v. & n.* —*v.* (**lapped**, **lapping**) **1** *tr.* **a** (also *absol.*) (usu. of an animal) drink (liquid) with the tongue. **b** (usu. foll. by *up*, *down*) consume (liquid) greedily. **c** (usu. foll. by *up*) consume (gossip, praise, etc.) greedily. **2 a** *tr.* (of water) move or beat upon (a shore) with a rippling sound as of lapping. **b** *intr.* (of waves etc.) move in ripples; make a lapping sound. —*n.* **1 a** the process or an act of lapping. **b** the amount of liquid taken up. **2** the sound of wavelets

on a beach. **3** liquid food for dogs. **4** *sl.* **a** a weak beverage. **b** any liquor. [OE *lapian* f. Gmc]

laparoscope /'læpərəˌskəʊp/ *n. Surgery* a fibre optic instrument inserted through the abdominal wall to give a view of the organs in the abdomen. □□ **laparoscopy** /-'rɒskəpɪ/ *n.* (*pl.* **-ies**). [Gk *lapara* flank + -SCOPE]

laparotomy /ˌlæpə'rɒtəmɪ/ *n.* (*pl.* **-ies**) a surgical incision into the abdominal cavity for exploration or diagnosis. [Gk *lapara* flank + -TOMY]

lapel /lə'pel/ *n.* the part of a coat, jacket, etc., folded back against the front round the neck opening. □□ **lapelled** *adj.* [LAP[1] + -EL]

lapicide /'læpɪˌsaɪd/ *n.* a person who cuts or engraves on stone. [L *lapicida* irreg. f. *lapis* -*idis* stone: see -CIDE]

lapidary /'læpɪdərɪ/ *adj. & n.* —*adj.* **1** concerned with stone or stones. **2** engraved upon stone. **3** (of writing style) dignified and concise, suitable for inscriptions. —*n.* (*pl.* **-ies**) a cutter, polisher, or engraver of gems. [ME f. L *lapidarius* f. *lapis* -*idis* stone]

lapilli /lə'pɪlaɪ/ *n.pl.* stone fragments ejected from volcanoes. [It. f. L, pl. dimin. of *lapis* stone]

lapis lazuli /ˌlæpɪs 'læzjʊˌlɪ, -ˌlaɪ/ *n.* **1** a blue mineral containing sodium aluminium silicate and sulphur, used as a gemstone. **2** a bright blue pigment formerly made from this. **3** its colour. [ME f. L *lapis* stone + med.L *lazuli* genit. of *lazulum* f. Pers. (as AZURE)]

Laplander /'læpˌlændə(r)/ *n.* **1** a native or national of Lapland. **2** a person of this descent. [*Lapland* f. Sw. *Lappland* (as LAPP, LAND)]

Lapp /læp/ *n. & adj.* —*n.* **1** a member of a nomadic Mongol people of N. Scandinavia. **2** the language of this people. —*adj.* of or relating to the Lapps or their language. [Sw. *Lapp*, perh. orig. a term of contempt: cf. MHG *lappe* simpleton]

lappet /'læpɪt/ *n.* **1** a small flap or fold of a garment etc. **2** a hanging or loose piece of flesh, such as a lobe or wattle. □□ **lappeted** *adj.* [LAP[1] + -ET[1]]

Lappish /'læpɪʃ/ *adj. & n.* —*adj.* = LAPP *adj.* —*n.* the Lapp language.

lapse /læps/ *n. & v.* —*n.* **1** a slight error; a slip of memory etc. **2** a weak or careless decline into an inferior state. **3** (foll. by *of*) an interval or passage of time (*after a lapse of three years*). **4** *Law* the termination of a right or privilege through disuse or failure to follow appropriate procedures. —*v.intr.* **1** fail to maintain a position or standard. **2** (foll. by *into*) fall back into an inferior or previous state. **3** (of a right or privilege etc.) become invalid because it is not used or claimed or renewed. **4** (as **lapsed** *adj.*) (of a person or thing) that has lapsed. □**lapse rate** *Meteorol.* the rate at which the temperature falls with increasing altitude. □□ **lapser** *n.* [L *lapsus* f. *labi laps-* glide, slip, fall]

lapstone /'læpstəʊn/ *n.* a shoemaker's stone held in the lap and used to beat leather on.

lapsus calami /ˌlæpsəs 'kæləˌmaɪ/ *n.* (*pl.* same) a slip of the pen. [L: see LAPSE]

lapsus linguae /ˌlæpsəs 'lɪŋgwaɪ/ *n.* a slip of the tongue. [L: see LAPSE]

laptop /'læptɒp/ *n.* (*attrib.*) (of a microcomputer) portable and suitable for use while travelling.

lapwing /'læpwɪŋ/ *n.* a plover, *Vanellus vanellus*, with black and white plumage, crested head, and a shrill cry. [OE *hlēapewince* f. *hlēapan* LEAP + WINK: assim. to LAP[1], WING]

larboard /'lɑ:bəd/ *n. & adj. Naut. archaic* = PORT[3]. [ME *lade-*, *ladde-*, *lathe-* (perh. = LADE + BOARD): later assim. to *starboard*]

larceny /'lɑ:sənɪ/ *n.* (*pl.* **-ies**) the theft of personal property. ¶ In 1968 replaced as a statutory crime in English law by *theft*. □□ **larcener** *n.* **larcenist** *n.* **larcenous** *adj.* [OF *larcin* f. L *latrocinium* f. *latro* robber, mercenary f. Gk *latreus*]

larch /lɑ:tʃ/ *n.* **1** a deciduous coniferous tree of the genus *Larix*, with bright foliage and producing tough timber. **2** (in full **larchwood**) its wood. [MHG *larche* ult. f. L *larix -icis*]

lard /lɑːd/ *n. & v.* —*n.* the internal fat of the abdomen of pigs, esp. when rendered and clarified for use in cooking and pharmacy. —*v.tr.* **1** insert strips of fat or bacon in (meat etc.) before cooking. **2** (foll. by *with*) embellish (talk or writing) with foreign or technical terms. [ME f. OF *lard* bacon f. L *lardum, laridum*, rel. to Gk *larinos* fat]

larder /'lɑːdə(r)/ *n.* **1** a room or cupboard for storing food. **2** a wild animal's store of food, esp. for winter. [ME f. OF *lardier* f. med.L *lardarium* (as LARD)]

lardon /'lɑːd(ə)n/ *n.* (also **lardoon** /-'duːn/) a strip of fat bacon used to lard meat. [ME f. F *lardon* (as LARD)]

lardy /'lɑːdɪ/ *adj.* like or with lard. ▫**lardy-cake** *Brit.* a cake made with lard, currants, etc.

lares /'lɑːriːz/ *n.pl. Rom.Hist.* the household gods. ▫**lares and penates** the home. [L]

large /lɑːdʒ/ *adj. & n.* —*adj.* **1** of considerable or relatively great size or extent. **2** of the larger kind (*the large intestine*). **3** of wide range; comprehensive. **4** pursuing an activity on a large scale (*large farmer*). —*n.* (**at large**) **1** at liberty. **2** as a body or whole (*popular with the people at large*). **3** (of a narration etc.) at full length and with all details. **4** without a specific target (*scatters insults at large*). **5** *US* representing a whole area and not merely a part of it (*congressman at large*). ▫**in large** on a large scale. **large as life** see LIFE. **large-minded** liberal; not narrow-minded. **larger than life** see LIFE. **large-scale** made or occurring on a large scale or in large amounts. ▫▫**largeness** *n.* **largish** *adj.* [ME f. OF f. fem. of L *largus* copious]

largely /'lɑːdʒlɪ/ *adv.* to a great extent; principally (*is largely due to laziness*).

largesse /lɑː'ʒes/ *n.* (also **largess**) **1** money or gifts freely given, esp. on an occasion of rejoicing, by a person in high position. **2** generosity, beneficence. [ME f. OF *largesse* ult. f. L *largus* copious]

larghetto /lɑː'getəʊ/ *adv., adj., & n. Mus.* —*adv. & adj.* in a fairly slow tempo. —*n.* (*pl.* **-os**) a larghetto passage or movement. [It., dimin. of LARGO]

largo /'lɑːgəʊ/ *adv., adj., & n. Mus.* —*adv. & adj.* in a slow tempo and dignified in style. —*n.* (*pl.* **-os**) a largo passage or movement. [It., = broad]

lariat /'lærɪət/ *n.* **1** a lasso. **2** a tethering-rope, esp. used by cowboys. [Sp. *la reata* f. *reatar* tie again (as RE-, L *aptare* adjust f. *aptus* APT, fit)]

lark[1] /lɑːk/ *n.* **1** any small bird of the family Alaudidae with brown plumage, elongated hind claw, and tuneful song, esp. the skylark. **2** any of various similar birds such as the meadow lark. [OE *lāferce, lǽwerce*, of unkn. orig.]

lark[2] /lɑːk/ *n. & v. colloq.* —*n.* **1** a frolic or spree; an amusing incident; a joke. **2** *Brit.* a type of activity, affair, etc. (*fed up with this digging lark*). —*v.intr.* (foll. by *about*) play tricks; frolic. ▫▫**larky** *adj.* **larkiness** *n.* [19th c.: orig. uncert.]

larkspur /'lɑːkspɜː(r)/ *n.* any of various plants of the genus *Consolida*, with a spur-shaped calyx.

larn /lɑːn/ *v. colloq.* or *joc.* **1** *intr.* = LEARN. **2** *tr.* teach (*that'll larn you*). [dial. form of LEARN]

larrikin /'lærɪkɪn/ *n. Austral.* a hooligan. [also Engl. dial.: perh. f. the name *Larry* (pet-form of *Lawrence*) + -KIN]

larrup /'lærəp/ *v.tr.* (**larruped, larruping**) *colloq.* thrash. [dial.: perh. f. LATHER]

Larry /'lærɪ/ *n.* ▫**as happy as Larry** *colloq.* extremely happy. [20th c.: orig. uncert.: cf. LARRIKIN]

larva /'lɑːvə/ *n.* (*pl.* **larvae** /-viː/) **1** the stage of development of an insect between egg and pupa, e.g. a caterpillar. **2** an immature form of other animals that undergo some metamorphosis, e.g. a tadpole. ▫▫**larval** *adj.* **larvicide** /'lɑːvɪˌsaɪd/ *n.* [L, = ghost, mask]

laryngeal /ləˈrɪndʒɪəl/ *adj.* **1** of or relating to the larynx. **2** *Phonet.* (of a sound) made in the larynx.

laryngitis /ˌlærɪnˈdʒaɪtɪs/ *n.* inflammation of the larynx. ▫▫**laryngitic** /-'dʒɪtɪk/ *adj.*

laryngoscope /ləˈrɪŋgəˌskəʊp/ *n.* an instrument for examining the larynx, or for inserting a tube through it.

laryngotomy /ˌlærɪŋˈgɒtəmɪ/ *n.* (*pl.* **-ies**) a surgical incision of the larynx, esp. to provide an air passage when breathing is obstructed.

larynx /'lærɪŋks/ *n.* (*pl.* **larynges** /ləˈrɪndʒiːz/) the hollow muscular organ forming an air passage to the lungs and holding the vocal cords in humans and other mammals. [mod.L f. Gk *larugx -ggos*]

lasagne /ləˈsænjə, -ˈsɑːnjə/ *n.* pasta in the form of sheets or wide ribbons, esp. as cooked and served with minced meat and cheese sauce. [It., pl. of *lasagna* f. L *lasanum* cooking-pot]

Lascar /'læskə(r)/ *n.* an E. Indian seaman. [ult. f. Urdu & Pers. *laškar* army]

lascivious /ləˈsɪvɪəs/ *adj.* **1** lustful. **2** inciting to or evoking lust. ▫▫**lasciviously** *adv.* **lasciviousness** *n.* [ME f. LL *lasciviosus* f. L *lascivia* lustfulness f. *lascivus* sportive, wanton]

lase /leɪz/ *v.intr.* **1** function as or in a laser. **2** (of a substance) undergo the physical processes employed in a laser. [back-form. f. LASER]

laser /'leɪzə(r)/ *n.* a device that generates an intense beam of coherent monochromatic radiation in the infrared, visible, or ultraviolet region of the electromagnetic spectrum, by stimulated emission of photons from an excited source. [*light amplification by stimulated emission of radiation*: cf. MASER]

laservision /'leɪzəˌvɪʒ(ə)n/ *n.* a system for the reproduction of video signals recorded on a disc with a laser. [LASER + VISION, after TELEVISION]

lash /læʃ/ *v. & n.* —*v.* **1** *intr.* make a sudden whiplike movement with a limb or flexible instrument. **2** *tr.* beat with a whip, rope, etc. **3** *intr.* pour or rush with great force. **4** *intr.* (foll. by *at, against*) strike violently. **5** *tr.* castigate in words. **6** *tr.* urge on as with a lash. **7** *tr.* (foll. by *down, together*, etc.) fasten with a cord, rope, etc. **8** *tr.* (of rain, wind, etc.) beat forcefully upon. —*n.* **1 a** a sharp blow made by a whip, rope, etc. **b** (prec. by *the*) punishment by beating with a whip etc. **2** the flexible end of a whip. **3** (usu. in *pl.*) an eyelash. ▫**lash out 1** speak or hit out angrily. **2** spend money extravagantly, be lavish. **lash-up** a makeshift or improvised structure or arrangement. ▫▫**lasher** *n.* **lashingly** *adv.* (esp. in senses 4-5 of *v.*). **lashless** *adj.* [ME: prob. imit.]

lashing /'læʃɪŋ/ *n.* **1** a beating. **2** cord used for lashing.

lashings /'læʃɪŋz/ *n.pl. Brit. colloq.* (foll. by *of*) plenty; an abundance.

lass /læs/ *n.* esp. *Sc. & N.Engl.* or *poet.* a girl or young woman. [ME *lasce* ult. f. ON *laskwa* unmarried (fem.)]

Lassa fever /'læsə/ *n.* an acute and often fatal febrile viral disease of tropical Africa. [*Lassa* in Nigeria, where first reported]

lassie /'læsɪ/ *n. colloq.* = LASS.

lassitude /'læsɪˌtjuːd/ *n.* **1** languor, weariness. **2** disinclination to exert or interest oneself. [F *lassitude* or L *lassitudo* f. *lassus* tired]

lasso /læˈsuː, ˈlæsəʊ/ *n. & v.* —*n.* (*pl.* **-os** or **-oes**) a rope with a noose at one end, used esp. in N. America for catching cattle etc. —*v.tr.* (**-oes, -oed**) catch with a lasso. ▫▫**lassoer** *n.* [Sp. *lazo* LACE]

last[1] /lɑːst/ *adj., adv., & n.* —*adj.* **1** after all others; coming at or belonging to the end. **2 a** most recent; next before a specified time (*last Christmas; last week*). **b** preceding; previous in a sequence (*got on at the last station*). **3** only remaining (*the last biscuit; our last chance*). **4** (prec. by *the*) least likely or suitable (*the last person I'd want; the last thing I'd have expected*). **5** the lowest in rank (*the last place*). —*adv.* **1** after all others (esp. in *comb.*: *last-mentioned*). **2** on the last occasion before the present (*when did you last see him?*). **3** (esp. in enumerating)

lastly. —*n.* **1** a person or thing that is last, last-mentioned, most recent, etc. **2** (prec. by *the*) the last mention or sight etc. (*shall never hear the last of it*). **3** the last performance of certain acts (*breathed his last*). **4** (prec. by *the*) **a** the end or last moment. **b** death. □at last (or long last) in the end; after much delay. last agony the pangs of death. last ditch a place of final desperate defence (often (with hyphen) *attrib.*). Last Judgement see JUDGEMENT. last minute (or moment) the time just before an important event (often (with hyphen) *attrib.*). last name surname. last post see POST³. last rites sacred rites for a person about to die. the last straw a slight addition to a burden or difficulty that makes it finally unbearable. the Last Supper that of Christ and his disciples on the eve of the Crucifixion, as recorded in the New Testament. last thing *adv.* very late, esp. as a final act before going to bed. the last word **1** a final or definitive statement (*always has the last word*; *is the last word on this subject*). **2** (often foll. by *in*) the latest fashion. on one's last legs see LEG. pay one's last respects see RESPECT. to (or till) the last till the end; esp. till death. [OE *latost* superl.: see LATE]

last² /lɑːst/ *v.intr.* **1** remain unexhausted or adequate or alive for a specified or considerable time; suffice (*enough food to last us a week*; *the battery lasts and lasts*). **2** continue for a specified time (*the journey lasts an hour*). □last out remain adequate or in existence for the whole of a period previously stated or implied. [OE *lǣstan* f. Gmc]

last³ /lɑːst/ *n.* a shoemaker's model for shaping or repairing a shoe or boot. □stick to one's last not meddle with what one does not understand. [OE *lǣste* last, *lǣst* boot, *lǣst* footprint f. Gmc]

lasting /ˈlɑːstɪŋ/ *adj.* **1** continuing, permanent. **2** durable. □□ lastingly *adv.* lastingness *n.*

lastly /ˈlɑːstlɪ/ *adv.* finally; in the last place.

lat. *abbr.* latitude.

latch /lætʃ/ *n. & v.* —*n.* **1** a bar with a catch and lever used as a fastening for a gate etc. **2** a spring-lock preventing a door from being opened from the outside without a key after being shut. —*v.tr. & intr.* fasten or be fastened with a latch. □latch on (often foll. by *to*) *colloq.* **1** attach oneself (to). **2** understand. on the latch fastened by the latch only, not locked. [prob. f. (now dial.) *latch* (v.) seize f. OE *læccan* f. Gmc]

latchkey /ˈlætʃkiː/ *n.* (*pl.* **-eys**) a key of an outer door. □latchkey child a child who is alone at home after school until a parent returns from work.

late /leɪt/ *adj. & adv.* —*adj.* **1** after the due or usual time; occurring or done after the proper time (*late for dinner*; *a late milk delivery*). **2 a** far on in the day or night or in a specified time or period. **b** far on in development. **3** flowering or ripening towards the end of the season (*late strawberries*). **4** (prec. by *the* or *my*, *his*, etc.) no longer alive or having the specified status (*my late husband*; *the late president*). **5** of recent date (*the late storms*). —*adv.* **1** after the due or usual time (*arrived late*). **2** far on in time (*this happened later on*). **3** at or till a late hour. **4** at a late stage of development. **5** formerly but not now (*late of the Scillies*). □at the latest as the latest time envisaged (*will have done it by six at the latest*). late in the day *colloq.* at a late stage in the proceedings, esp. too late to be useful. late Latin Latin of about AD 200–600. the latest the most recent news, fashion, etc. (*have you heard the latest?*). □□ lateness *n.* [OE *læt* (adj.), *late* (adv.) f. Gmc]

latecomer /ˈleɪtkʌmə(r)/ *n.* a person who arrives late.

lateen /ləˈtiːn/ *adj.* (of a ship) rigged with a lateen sail. □lateen sail a triangular sail on a long yard at an angle of 45° to the mast. [F (*voile*) *latine* Latin (sail), because common in the Mediterranean]

lately /ˈleɪtlɪ/ *adv.* not long ago; recently; in recent times. [OE *lætlīce* (as LATE, -LY²)]

La Tène /lɑː ˈten/ *adj.* of or relating to the second Iron-Age culture of central and W. Europe. [*La Tène* in Switzerland, where remains of it were first identified]

latent /ˈleɪt(ə)nt/ *adj.* **1** concealed, dormant. **2** existing but not developed or manifest. □latent heat *Physics* the heat required to convert a solid into a liquid or vapour, or a liquid into a vapour, without change of temperature. latent image *Photog.* an image not yet made visible by developing. □□ latency *n.* latently *adv.* [L *latēre latent-* be hidden]

-later /lətə(r)/ *comb. form* denoting a person who worships a particular thing or person (*idolater*). [Gk: see LATRIA]

lateral /ˈlætər(ə)l/ *adj. & n.* —*adj.* **1** of, at, towards, or from the side or sides. **2** descended from a brother or sister of a person in direct line. —*n.* a side part etc., esp. a lateral shoot or branch. □lateral line *Zool.* a visible line along the side of a fish consisting of a series of sense organs acting as vibration receptors. lateral thinking a method of solving problems indirectly or by apparently illogical methods. □□ laterally *adv.* [L *lateralis* f. *latus lateris* side]

laterite /ˈlætəraɪt/ *n.* a red or yellow ferruginous clay, friable and hardening in air, used for making roads in the tropics. □□ lateritic /-ˈrɪtɪk/ *adj.* [L *later* brick + -ITE¹]

latex /ˈleɪteks/ *n.* (*pl.* **latexes** or **latices** /-tɪˌsiːz/) **1** a milky fluid of mixed composition found in various plants and trees, esp. the rubber tree, and used for commercial purposes. **2** a synthetic product resembling this. [L, = liquid]

lath /lɑːθ/ *n. & v.* —*n.* (*pl.* **laths** /lɑːðz, lɑːðz/) a thin flat strip of wood, esp. each of a series forming a framework or support for plaster etc. —*v.tr.* attach laths to (a wall or ceiling). □lath and plaster a common material for interior walls and ceilings etc. [OE *lætt*]

lathe /leɪð/ *n.* a machine for shaping wood, metal, etc., by means of a rotating drive which turns the piece being worked on against changeable cutting tools. [prob. rel. to ODa. *lad* structure, frame, f. ON *hlath*, rel. to *hlatha* LADE]

lather /ˈlɑːðə(r), ˈlæðə(r)/ *n. & v.* —*n.* **1** a froth produced by agitating soap etc. and water. **2** frothy sweat, esp. of a horse. **3** a state of agitation. —*v.* **1** *intr.* (of soap etc.) form a lather. **2** *tr.* cover with lather. **3** *intr.* (of a horse etc.) develop or become covered with lather. **4** *tr. colloq.* thrash. □□ lathery *adj.* [OE *lēathor* (n.), *lēthran* (v.)]

lathi /ˈlɑːtɪ/ *n.* (*pl.* **lathis**) (in India) a long heavy iron-bound bamboo stick used as a weapon, esp. by police. [Hindi *lāṭhī*]

latices *pl.* of LATEX.

Latin /ˈlætɪn/ *n. & adj.* —*n.* **1** the Italic language of ancient Rome and its empire, originating in Latium. **2** *Rom.Hist.* an inhabitant of ancient Latium in Central Italy. —*adj.* **1** of or in Latin. **2** of the countries or peoples (e.g. France and Spain) using languages developed from Latin. **3** *Rom.Hist.* of or relating to ancient Latium or its inhabitants. **4** of the Roman Catholic Church. □Latin America the parts of Central and S. America where Spanish or Portuguese is the main language. Latin American *n.* a native of Latin America. —*adj.* of or relating to Latin America. Latin Church the Western Church. □□ Latinism *n.* Latinist *n.* [ME f. OF *Latin* or L *Latinus* f. *Latium*]

Latinate /ˈlætɪˌneɪt/ *adj.* having the character of Latin.

Latinize /ˈlætɪˌnaɪz/ *v.* (also **-ise**) **1** *tr.* give a Latin or Latinate form to. **2** *tr.* translate into Latin. **3** *tr.* make conformable to the ideas, customs, etc., of the ancient Romans, Latin peoples, or Latin Church. **4** *intr.* use Latin forms, idioms, etc. □□ Latinization /-ˈzeɪʃ(ə)n/ *n.* Latinizer *n.* [LL *latinizare* (as LATIN)]

latish /ˈleɪtɪʃ/ *adj. & adv.* fairly late.

latitude /ˈlætɪˌtjuːd/ n. **1** Geog. **a** the angular distance on a meridian north or south of the equator, expressed in degrees and minutes. **b** (usu. in pl.) regions or climes, esp. with reference to temperature (warm latitudes). **2** freedom from narrowness; liberality of interpretation. **3** tolerated variety of action or opinion (was allowed much latitude). **4** Astron. the angular distance of a celestial body or point from the ecliptic. □**high latitudes** regions near the poles. **low latitudes** regions near the equator. □□ **latitudinal** /-ˈtjuːdɪn(ə)l/ adj. **latitudinally** /-ˈtjuːdɪnəlɪ/ adv. [ME, = breadth, f. L latitudo -dinis f. latus broad]

latitudinarian /ˌlætɪˌtjuːdɪˈneərɪən/ adj. & n. —adj. allowing latitude esp. in religion; showing no preference among varying creeds and forms of worship. —n. a person with a latitudinarian attitude. □□ **latitudinarianism** n. [L latitudo -dinis breadth + -ARIAN]

latria /ˈleɪtrɪə/ n. Theol. supreme worship allowed to God alone. [LL f. Gk latreia worship f. latreuō serve]

latrine /ləˈtriːn/ n. a communal lavatory, esp. in a camp, barracks, etc. [F f. L latrina, shortening of lavatrina f. lavare wash]

-latry /lətrɪ/ comb. form denoting worship (idolatry). [Gk latreia: see LATRIA]

latten /ˈlæt(ə)n/ n. an alloy of copper and zinc, often rolled into sheets, and formerly used for monumental brasses and church articles. [ME latoun f. OF laton, leiton]

latter /ˈlætə(r)/ adj. **1 a** denoting the second-mentioned of two, or disp. the last-mentioned of three or more. **b** (prec. by the; usu. absol.) the second- or last-mentioned person or thing. **2** nearer to the end (the latter part of the year). **3** recent. **4** belonging to the end of a period, of the world, etc. □**latter-day** modern, newfangled. **Latter-day Saints** the Mormons' name for themselves. [OE lætra, compar. of læt LATE]

latterly /ˈlætəlɪ/ adv. **1** in the latter part of life or of a period. **2** recently.

lattice /ˈlætɪs/ n. **1 a** a structure of crossed laths or bars with spaces between, used as a screen, fence, etc. **b** (in full **lattice-work**) laths arranged in lattice formation. **2** Crystallog. a regular periodic arrangement of atoms, ions, or molecules in a crystalline solid. □**lattice frame** (or **girder**) a girder or truss made of top and bottom members connected by struts usu. crossing diagonally. **lattice window** a window with small panes set in diagonally crossing strips of lead. □□ **latticed** adj. **latticing** n. [ME f. OF lattis f. latte lath f. WG]

Latvian /ˈlætvɪən/ n. & adj. —n. **1 a** a native of Latvia, a Baltic republic of the USSR. **b** a person of Latvian descent. **2** the language of Latvia. —adj. of or relating to Latvia or its people or language.

laud /lɔːd/ v. & n. —v.tr. praise or extol, esp. in hymns. —n. **1** literary praise; a hymn of praise. **2** (in pl.) the traditional morning prayer of the Roman Catholic Church. [ME: (n.) f. OF laude, (v.) f. L laudare, f. L laus laudis praise]

laudable /ˈlɔːdəb(ə)l/ adj. commendable, praiseworthy. □□ **laudability** /-ˈbɪlɪtɪ/ n. **laudably** adv. [ME f. L laudabilis (as LAUD)]

laudanum /ˈlɔːdnəm, ˈlɒd-/ n. a solution containing morphine and prepared from opium, formerly used as a narcotic painkiller. [mod.L, the name given by Paracelsus to a costly medicament, later applied to preparations containing opium: perh. var. of LADANUM]

laudation /lɔːˈdeɪʃ(ə)n/ n. formal praise. [L laudatio -onis (as LAUD)]

laudatory /ˈlɔːdətərɪ/ adj. (also **laudative** /-tɪv/) expressing praise.

laugh /lɑːf/ v. & n. —v. **1** intr. make the spontaneous sounds and movements usual in expressing lively amusement, scorn, derision, etc. **2** tr. express by laughing. **3** tr. bring (a person) into a certain state

by laughing (laughed them into agreeing). **4** intr. (foll. by at) ridicule, make fun of (laughed at us for going). **5** intr. (**be laughing**) colloq. be in a fortunate or successful position. **6** intr. esp. poet. make sounds reminiscent of laughing. —n. **1** the sound or act or manner of laughing. **2** colloq. a comical or ridiculous thing. □**have the last laugh** be ultimately the winner. **laugh in a person's face** show open scorn for a person. **laugh off** get rid of (embarrassment or humiliation) with a jest. **laugh on the other side of one's face** change from enjoyment or amusement to displeasure, shame, apprehension, etc. **laugh out of court** deprive of a hearing by ridicule. **laugh up one's sleeve** be secretly or inwardly amused. □□ **laugher** n. [OE hlæhhan, hliehhan f. Gmc]

laughable /ˈlɑːfəb(ə)l/ adj. ludicrous; highly amusing. □□ **laughably** adv.

laughing /ˈlɑːfɪŋ/ n. & adj. —n. laughter. —adj. in senses of LAUGH v. □**laughing-gas** nitrous oxide as an anaesthetic, formerly used without oxygen and causing an exhilarating effect when inhaled. **laughing hyena** see HYENA. **laughing jackass** = KOOKABURRA. **laughing-stock** a person or thing open to general ridicule. **no laughing matter** something serious. □□ **laughingly** adv.

laughter /ˈlɑːftə(r)/ n. the act or sound of laughing. [OE hleahtor f. Gmc]

launce /lɑːns, læns/ n. a sand eel. [perh. f. LANCE: cf. garfish]

launch¹ /lɔːntʃ/ v. & n. —v. **1** tr. set (a vessel) afloat. **2** tr. hurl or send forth (a weapon, rocket, etc.). **3** tr. start or set in motion (an enterprise, a person on a course of action, etc.). **4** tr. formally introduce (a new product) with publicity etc. **5** intr. (often foll. by out, into, etc.) **a** make a start, esp. on an ambitious enterprise. **b** burst into strong language etc. —n. the act or an instance of launching. □**launch** (or **launching**) **pad** a platform with a supporting structure, from which rockets are launched. [ME f. AF launcher, ONF lancher, OF lancier LANCE v.]

launch² /lɔːntʃ/ n. **1** a large motor boat, used esp. for pleasure. **2** a man-of-war's largest boat. [Sp. lancha pinnace perh. f. Malay lancharan f. lanchār swift]

launcher /ˈlɔːntʃə(r)/ n. a structure or device to hold a rocket during launching.

launder /ˈlɔːndə(r)/ v. & n. —v.tr. **1** wash and iron (clothes, linen, etc.). **2** colloq. transfer (funds) to conceal a dubious or illegal origin. —n. a channel for conveying liquids, esp. molten metal. □□ **launderer** n. [ME launder (n.) washer of linen, contr. of lavander f. OF lavandier ult. f. L lavanda things to be washed, neut. pl. gerundive of lavare wash]

launderette /lɔːnˈdret/ n. (also **laundrette**) an establishment with coin-operated washing-machines and driers for public use.

laundress /ˈlɔːndrɪs/ n. a woman who launders clothes, linen, etc., esp. professionally.

laundry /ˈlɔːndrɪ/ n. (pl. -ies) **1** an establishment for washing clothes or linen. **2** clothes or linen for laundering or newly laundered. [contr. f. lavendry (f. OF lavanderie) after LAUNDER]

laureate /ˈlɒrɪət, ˈlɔː-/ adj. & n. —adj. **1** wreathed with laurel as a mark of honour. **2** consisting of laurel; laurel-like. —n. **1** a person who is honoured for outstanding creative or intellectual achievement (Nobel laureate). **2** = Poet Laureate. □□ **laureateship** n. [L laureatus f. laurea laurel-wreath f. laurus laurel]

laurel /ˈlɒr(ə)l/ n. & v. —n. **1** = BAY². **2 a** (in sing. or pl.) the foliage of the bay-tree used as an emblem of victory or distinction in poetry usu. formed into a wreath or crown. **b** (in pl.) honour or distinction. **3** any plant with dark-green glossy leaves like a bay-tree, e.g. cherry-laurel, mountain laurel, spurge laurel. —v.tr. (**laurelled, laurelling**; US **laureled, laureling**) wreathe with laurel. □**look to one's laurels** beware of losing one's pre-eminence. **rest**

on one's laurels be satisfied with what one has done and not seek further success. [ME *lorer* f. OF *lorier* f. Prov. *laurier* f. *laur* f. L *laurus*]

laurustinus /ˌlɔrəˈstaɪnəs/ *n.* an evergreen winter-flowering shrub, *Viburnum tinus*, with dense glossy green leaves and white or pink flowers. [mod.L f. L *laurus* laurel + *tinus* wild laurel]

lav /læv/ *n. Brit. colloq.* lavatory. [abbr.]

lava /ˈlɑːvə/ *n.* **1** the molten matter which flows from a volcano. **2** the solid substance which it forms on cooling. [It. f. *lavare* wash f. L]

lavabo /ləˈvɑːbəʊ/ *n.* (*pl.* **-os**) **1** *RC Ch.* **a** the ritual washing of the celebrant's hands at the offertory of the Mass. **b** a towel or basin used for this. **2** a monastery washing-trough. **3** a wash-basin. [L, = I will wash, first word of Psalm 26:6]

lavage /ˈlævɪdʒ/ *n. Med.* the washing-out of a body cavity, such as the colon or stomach, with water or a medicated solution. [F f. *laver* wash: see LAVE]

lavation /ləˈveɪʃ(ə)n/ *n. formal* washing. [L *lavatio* f. *lavare* wash]

lavatorial /ˌlævəˈtɔːrɪəl/ *adj.* (esp. of humour) relating to lavatories and their use.

lavatory /ˈlævətərɪ/ *n.* (*pl.* **-ies**) **1** a large receptacle for urine and faeces, usu. with running water and a flush mechanism as a means of disposal. **2** a room or compartment containing one or more of these. □**lavatory paper** = *toilet paper.* [ME, = washing vessel, f. LL *lavatorium* f. L *lavare lavat-* wash]

lave /leɪv/ *v.tr. literary* **1** wash, bathe. **2** (of water) wash against; flow along. [ME f. OF *laver* f. L *lavare* wash, perh. coalescing with OE *lafian*]

lavender /ˈlævɪndə(r)/ *n. & v.* —*n.* **1 a** any small evergreen shrub of the genus *Lavandula*, with narrow leaves and blue, purple, or pink aromatic flowers. **b** its flowers and stalks dried and used to scent linen, clothes, etc. **2** a pale blue colour with a trace of red. —*v.tr.* put lavender among (linen etc.). □**lavender-water** a perfume made from distilled lavender, alcohol, and ambergris. [ME f. AF *lavendre*, ult. f. med.L *lavandula*]

laver[1] /ˈleɪvə(r), ˈlɑː-/ *n.* any of various edible seaweeds, esp. *Porphyra umbilicalis*, having sheet-like fronds. □**laver bread** a Welsh dish of laver which is boiled, dipped in oatmeal, and fried. [L]

laver[2] /ˈleɪvə(r)/ *n.* **1** *Bibl.* a large brass vessel for Jewish priests' ritual ablutions. **2** *archaic* a washing or fountain basin; a font. [ME *lavo(u)r* f. OF *laveo(i)r* f. LL (as LAVATORY)]

lavish /ˈlævɪʃ/ *adj. & v.* —*adj.* **1** giving or producing in large quantities; profuse. **2** generous, unstinting. **3** excessive, over-abundant. —*v.tr.* (often foll. by *on*) bestow or spend (money, effort, praise, etc.) abundantly. □□**lavishly** *adv.* **lavishness** *n.* [ME f. obs. *lavish, lavas* (n.) profusion f. OF *lavasse* deluge of rain f. *laver* wash]

law /lɔː/ *n.* **1 a** a rule enacted or customary in a community and recognized as enjoining or prohibiting certain actions and enforced by the imposition of penalties. **b** a body of such rules (*the law of the land; forbidden under Scots law*). **2** the controlling influence of laws; a state of respect for laws (*law and order*). **3** laws collectively as a social system or subject of study (*was reading law*). **4** (with defining word) any of the specific branches or applications of law (*commercial law; law of contract*). **5** binding force or effect (*their word is law*). **6** (prec. by *the*) **a** the legal profession. **b** *colloq.* the police. **7** the statute and common law (opp. EQUITY). **8** (in *pl.*) jurisprudence. **9 a** the judicial remedy; litigation. **b** the lawcourts as providing this (*go to law*). **10** a rule of action or procedure, e.g. in a game, social context, form of art, etc. **11** a regularity in natural occurrences, esp. as formulated or propounded in particular instances (*the laws of nature; the law of gravity; Parkinson's law*). **12 a** divine commandments as expressed in the Bible or other sources. **b** (**Law of Moses**) the precepts of the Pentateuch. □**at** (or **in**) **law** according to the laws. **be a law unto oneself** do what one feels is right; disregard custom. **go to law** take legal action; make use of the lawcourts. **law-abiding** obedient to the laws. **law-abidingness** obedience to the laws. **law agent** (in Scotland) a solicitor. **law centre** *Brit.* an independent publicly-funded advisory service on legal matters. **Law Lord** a member of the House of Lords qualified to perform its legal work. **law of diminishing returns** see DIMINISH. **law of nature** = *natural law.* **laws of war** the limitations on belligerents' action recognized by civilized nations. **law term** a period appointed for the sitting of lawcourts. **lay down the law** be dogmatic or authoritarian. **take the law into one's own hands** redress a grievance by one's own means, esp. by force. [OE *lagu* f. ON *lag* something 'laid down' or fixed, rel. to LAY[1]]

lawbreaker /ˈlɔːˌbreɪkə(r)/ *n.* a person who breaks the law. □□**lawbreaking** *n. & adj.*

lawcourt /ˈlɔːkɔːt/ *n.* a court of law.

lawful /ˈlɔːfʊl/ *adj.* conforming with, permitted by, or recognized by law; not illegal or (of a child) illegitimate. □□**lawfully** *adv.* **lawfulness** *n.*

lawgiver /ˈlɔːˌgɪvə(r)/ *n.* a person who lays down laws.

lawless /ˈlɔːlɪs/ *adj.* **1** having no laws or enforcement of them. **2** disregarding laws. **3** unbridled, uncontrolled. □□**lawlessly** *adv.* **lawlessness** *n.*

lawmaker /ˈlɔːˌmeɪkə(r)/ *n.* a legislator.

lawman /ˈlɔːmæn/ *n.* (*pl.* **-men**) *US* a law-enforcement officer, esp. a sheriff or policeman.

lawn[1] /lɔːn/ *n.* a piece of grass kept mown and smooth in a garden, park, etc. □**lawn tennis** the usual form of tennis, played with a soft ball on outdoor grass or a hard court. [ME *laund* glade f. OF *launde* f. OCelt., rel. to LAND]

lawn[2] /lɔːn/ *n.* a fine linen or cotton fabric used for clothes. □□**lawny** *adj.* [ME, prob. f. *Laon* in France]

lawnmower /ˈlɔːnˌməʊə(r)/ *n.* a machine for cutting the grass on a lawn.

lawrencium /ləˈrensɪəm/ *n. Chem.* an artificially made transuranic radioactive metallic element. ¶ Symb.: **Lw.** [E. O. *Lawrence*, Amer. physicist d. 1958]

lawsuit /ˈlɔːsuːt, -sjuːt/ *n.* the process or an instance of making a claim in a lawcourt.

lawyer /ˈlɔɪə(r), ˈlɔːjə(r)/ *n.* a member of the legal profession, esp. a solicitor. □□**lawyerly** *adj.* [ME *law(i)er* f. LAW]

lax /læks/ *adj.* **1** lacking care, concern, or firmness. **2** loose, relaxed; not compact. **3** *Phonet.* pronounced with the vocal muscles relaxed. □□**laxity** *n.* **laxly** *adv.* **laxness** *n.* [ME, = loose, f. L *laxus*: rel. to SLACK[1]]

laxative /ˈlæksətɪv/ *adj. & n.* —*adj.* tending to stimulate or facilitate evacuation of the bowels. —*n.* a laxative medicine. [ME f. OF *laxatif -ive* or LL *laxativus* f. L *laxare* loosen (as LAX)]

lay[1] /leɪ/ *v. & n.* —*v.* (*past* and *past part.* **laid** /leɪd/) **1** *tr.* place on a surface, esp. horizontally or in the proper or specified place. **2** *tr.* put or bring into a certain or the required position or state (*laid my hand on her arm; lay a carpet*). **3** *intr. dial.* or *erron.* lie. ¶ This use, incorrect in standard English, is probably partly encouraged by confusion with *lay* as the past of *lie*, as in *the dog lay on the floor* which is correct; *the dog is laying on the floor* is not correct. **4** *tr.* make by laying (*lay the foundations*). **5** *tr.* (often *absol.*) (of a hen bird) produce (an egg). **6** *tr.* a cause to subside or lie flat. **b** deal with to remove (a ghost, fear, etc.). **7** *tr.* place or present for consideration (a case, proposal, etc.). **8** *tr.* set down as a basis or starting-point. **9** *tr.* (usu. foll. by *on*) attribute or impute (blame etc.). **10** *tr.* locate (a scene etc.) in a certain place. **11** *tr.* prepare or make ready (a plan or a trap). **12** *tr.* prepare (a table) for a meal. **13** *tr.* place or arrange the material for (a fire). **14** *tr.* put down as a wager; stake. **15** *tr.* (foll. by *with*) coat or strew (a surface). **16** *tr. sl. offens.* have sexual intercourse with (esp. a woman). —*n.* **1** the way, position, or direction in which something lies. **2** *sl. offens.* a partner (esp. female) in sexual intercourse. **3** the direction or amount of twist in rope-strands. □**in lay** (of a hen) laying eggs regularly. **laid-back** *colloq.* relaxed, unbothered, easygoing. **laid paper** paper with the surface marked in fine ribs. **laid up** confined to bed or the house. **lay about one 1** hit out on all sides. **2** criticize indiscriminately. **lay aside 1** put to one side. **2** cease to practise or consider. **3** save (money etc.) for future needs. **lay at the door of** see DOOR. **lay back** cause to slope back from the vertical. **lay bare** expose, reveal. **lay a charge** make an accusation. **lay claim to** claim as one's own. **lay down 1** put on the ground. **2** relinquish; give up (an office). **3** formulate (a rule or principle). **4** pay or wager (money). **5** begin to construct (a ship or railway). **6** store (wine) in a cellar. **7** set down on paper. **8** sacrifice (one's life). **9** convert (land) into pasture. **10** record (esp. popular music). **lay down the law** see LAW. **lay one's hands on** obtain, acquire, locate. **lay hands on 1** seize or attack. **2** place one's hands on or over, esp. in confirmation, ordination, or spiritual healing. **lay hold of** seize or grasp. **lay in** provide oneself with a stock of. **lay into** *colloq.* punish or scold heavily. **lay it on thick** (or **with a trowel**) *colloq.* flatter or exaggerate grossly. **lay low** overthrow, kill, or humble. **lay off 1** discharge (workers) temporarily because of a shortage of work. **2** *colloq.* desist. **lay-off** *n.* **1** a temporary discharge of workers. **2** a period when this is in force. **lay on 1** provide (a facility, amenity, etc.). **2** impose (a penalty, obligation, etc.). **3** inflict (blows). **4** spread on (paint etc.). **lay on the table** see TABLE. **lay open 1** break the skin of. **2** (foll. by *to*) expose (to criticism etc.). **lay out 1** spread out. **2** expose to view. **3** prepare (a corpse) for burial. **4** *colloq.* knock unconscious. **5** dispose (grounds etc.) according to a plan. **6** expend (money). **7** *refl.* (foll. by *to* + infin.) take pains (to do something) (*laid themselves out to help*). **lay store by** see STORE. **lay to rest** bury in a grave. **lay up 1** store, save. **2** put (a ship etc.) out of service. **lay waste** see WASTE. [OE *lecgan* f. Gmc]

lay² /leɪ/ *adj.* **1 a** non-clerical. **b** not ordained into the clergy. **2 a** not professionally qualified, esp. in law or medicine. **b** of or done by such persons. □**lay brother** (or **sister**) a person who has taken the vows of a religious order but is not ordained and is employed in ancillary or manual work. **lay reader** a lay person licensed to conduct some religious services. [ME f. OF *lai* f. eccl.L *laicus* f. Gk *laïkos* LAIC]

lay³ /leɪ/ *n.* **1** a short lyric or narrative poem meant to be sung. **2** a song. [ME f. OF *lai*, Prov. *lais*, of unkn. orig.]

lay⁴ *past* of LIE.

layabout /'leɪəˌbaʊt/ *n.* a habitual loafer or idler.

lay-by /'leɪbaɪ/ *n.* (*pl.* **lay-bys**) **1** *Brit.* an area at the side of an open road where vehicles may stop. **2** a similar arrangement on a canal or railway. **3** *Austral.* & *NZ* a system of paying a deposit to secure an article for later purchase.

layer /'leɪə(r)/ *n.* & *v.* —*n.* **1** a thickness of matter, esp. one of several, covering a surface. **2** a person or thing that lays. **3** a hen that lays eggs. **4** a shoot fastened down to take root while attached to the parent plant. —*v.tr.* **1 a** arrange in layers. **b** cut (hair) in layers. **2** propagate (a plant) as a layer. □**layer-out** a person who prepares a corpse for burial. □□ **layered** *adj.* [ME f. LAY¹ + -ER¹]

layette /leɪ'et/ *n.* a set of clothing, toilet articles, and bedclothes for a newborn child. [F, dimin. of OF *laie* drawer f. MDu. *laege*]

lay figure /leɪ/ *n.* **1** a dummy or jointed figure of a human body used by artists for arranging drapery on etc. **2** an unrealistic character in a novel etc. **3** a

person lacking in individuality. [*lay* f. obs. *layman* f. Du. *leeman* f. obs. *led* joint]

layman /'leɪmən/ *n.* (*pl.* **-men**; *fem.* **laywoman**, *pl.* **-women**) **1** any non-ordained member of a Church. **2** a person without professional or specialized knowledge in a particular subject.

layout /'leɪaʊt/ *n.* **1** the disposing or arrangement of a site, ground, etc. **2** the way in which plans, printed matter, etc., are arranged or set out. **3** something arranged or set out in a particular way. **4** the make-up of a book, newspaper, etc.

layover /'leɪˌəʊvə(r)/ *n.* a period of rest or waiting before a further stage in a journey etc.; a stopover.

layshaft /'leɪʃɑːft/ *n.* a second or intermediate transmission shaft in a machine.

lazar /'læzə(r)/ *n. archaic* a poor and diseased person, esp. a leper. [ME f. med.L *lazarus* f. the name in Luke 16:20]

lazaret /ˌlæzə'ret/ *n.* (also **lazaretto** /-'retəʊ/) (*pl.* **lazarets** or **lazarettos**) **1** a hospital for diseased people, esp. lepers. **2** a building or ship for quarantine. **3** the after part of a ship's hold, used for stores. [(F *lazaret*) f. It. *lazzaretto* f. *lazzaro* LAZAR]

laze /leɪz/ *v.* & *n.* —*v.* **1** *intr.* spend time lazily or idly. **2** *tr.* (often foll. by *away*) pass (time) in this way. —*n.* a spell of lazing. [back-form. f. LAZY]

lazuli /'læzjuːlɪ, -ˌlaɪ/ *n.* = LAPIS LAZULI. [abbr.]

lazy /'leɪzɪ/ *adj.* (**lazier**, **laziest**) **1** disinclined to work, doing little work. **2** of or inducing idleness. **3** (of a river) slow-moving. □□ **lazily** *adv.* **laziness** *n.* [earlier *laysie*, *lasie*, *laesy*, perh. f. LG: cf. LG *lasich* idle]

lazybones /'leɪzɪˌbəʊnz/ *n.* (*pl.* same) *colloq.* a lazy person.

lb. *abbr.* a pound or pounds (weight). [L *libra*]

l.b. *abbr. Cricket* leg-bye(s), leg-byed.

LBC *abbr.* London Broadcasting Company.

L/Bdr *abbr.* Lance-Bombardier.

l.b.w. *abbr. Cricket* leg before wicket.

l.c. *abbr.* **1** in the passage etc. cited. **2** lower case. **3** letter of credit. [sense 1 f. L *loco citato*]

LCC *abbr. hist.* London County Council.

LCD *abbr.* **1** liquid crystal display. **2** lowest (or least) common denominator.

LCM *abbr.* lowest (or least) common multiple.

L/Cpl *abbr.* Lance-Corporal.

LD *abbr.* lethal dose, usu. with a following numeral indicating the percentage of a group of animals killed by such a dose (*LD₅₀*).

Ld. *abbr.* Lord.

Ldg. *abbr.* Leading (Seaman etc.).

LDS *abbr.* Licentiate in Dental Surgery.

-le¹ /(ə)l/ *suffix* forming nouns, esp.: **1** names of appliances or instruments (*handle*; *thimble*). **2** names of animals and plants (*beetle*; *thistle*). ¶ The suffix has ceased to be syllabic in *fowl*, *snail*, *stile*. [ult. from or repr. OE *-el* etc. f. Gmc, with many IE cognates]

-le² /(ə)l/ *suffix* (also **-el**) forming nouns with (or orig. with) diminutive sense, or = -AL (*angle*; *castle*; *mantle*; *syllable*; *novel*; *tunnel*). [ME *-el*, *-elle* f. OF ult. f. L forms *-ellus*, *-ella*, etc.]

-le³ /(ə)l/ *suffix* forming adjectives, often with (or orig. with) the sense 'apt or liable to' (*brittle*; *fickle*; *little*; *nimble*). [ME f. OE *-el* etc. f. Gmc, corresp. to L *-ulus*]

-le⁴ /(ə)l/ *suffix* forming verbs, esp. expressing repeated action or movement or having diminutive sense (*bubble*; *crumple*; *wriggle*). ¶ Examples from OE are *handle*, *nestle*, *startle*, *twinkle*. [OE *-lian* f. Gmc]

LEA *abbr.* (in the UK) Local Education Authority.

lea /liː/ *n. poet.* a piece of meadow or pasture or arable land. [OE *lēa(h)* f. Gmc]

leach /liːtʃ/ *v.* **1** *tr.* make (a liquid) percolate through some material. **2** *tr.* subject (bark, ore, ash, or soil) to the action of percolating fluid. **3** *tr.* & *intr.* (foll. by *away*, *out*) remove (soluble matter) or be removed in this way. □□ **leacher** *n.* [prob. repr. OE *leccan* to water, f. WG]

lead[1] /liːd/ v. & n. —v. (past and past part. **led** /led/) **1** tr. cause to go with one, esp. by guiding or showing the way or by going in front and taking a person's hand or an animal's halter etc. **2** tr. **a** direct the actions or opinions of. **b** (often foll. by *to*, or *to* + infin.) guide by persuasion or example or argument (*what led you to that conclusion?*; *was led to think you may be right*). **3** tr. (also *absol.*) provide access to; bring to a certain position or destination (*this door leads you into a small room*; *the road leads to Lincoln*; *the path leads uphill*). **4** tr. pass or go through (a life etc. of a specified kind) (*led a miserable existence*). **5** tr. **a** have the first place in (*lead the dance*; *leads the world in sugar production*). **b** (*absol.*) go first; be ahead in a race or game. **c** (*absol.*) be pre-eminent in some field. **6** tr. be in charge of (*leads a team of researchers*). **7** tr. **a** direct by example. **b** set (a fashion). **c** be the principal player of (a group of musicians). **8** tr. (also *absol.*) begin a round of play at cards by playing (a card) or a card of (a particular suit). **9** intr. (foll. by *to*) have as an end or outcome; result in (*what does all this lead to?*). **10** intr. (foll. by *with*) Boxing make an attack (with a particular blow). **11 a** intr. (foll. by *with*) (of a newspaper) use a particular item as the main story (*led with the Stock Market crash*). **b** tr. (of a story) be the main feature of (a newspaper or part of it) (*the royal wedding will lead the front page*). **12** tr. (foll. by *through*) make (a liquid, strip of material, etc.) pass through a pulley, channel, etc. —n. **1** guidance given by going in front; example. **2 a** a leading place; the leadership (*is in the lead*; *take the lead*). **b** the amount by which a competitor is ahead of the others (*a lead of ten yards*). **3** a clue, esp. an early indication of the resolution of a problem (*is the first real lead in the case*). **4** a strap or cord for leading a dog etc. **5** a conductor (usu. a wire) conveying electric current from a source to an appliance. **6 a** the chief part in a play etc. **b** the person playing this. **7** (in full **lead story**) the item of news given the greatest prominence in a newspaper or magazine. **8 a** the act or right of playing first in a game or round of cards. **b** the card led. **9** the distance advanced by a screw in one turn. **10 a** an artificial watercourse, esp. one leading to a mill. **b** a channel of water in an ice-field. □**lead astray** see ASTRAY. **lead by the nose** cajole (a person) into compliance. **lead a person a dance** see DANCE. **lead-in 1** an introduction, opening, etc. **2** a wire leading in from outside, esp. from an aerial to a receiver or transmitter. **lead off 1** begin; make a start. **2** *colloq.* lose one's temper. **lead-off** n. an action beginning a process. **lead on 1** entice into going further than was intended. **2** mislead or deceive. **lead time** the time between the initiation and completion of a production process. **lead up the garden path** *colloq.* mislead. **lead the way** see WAY. □□**leadable** adj. [OE *lǣdan* f. Gmc]

lead[2] /led/ n. & v. —n. **1** *Chem.* a heavy bluish-grey soft ductile metallic element occurring naturally in galena and used in building and the manufacture of alloys. ¶ Symb.: **Pb**. **2 a** graphite. **b** a thin length of this for use in a pencil. **3** a lump of lead used in sounding water. **4** (in *pl.*) *Brit.* **a** strips of lead covering a roof. **b** a piece of lead-covered roof. **5** (in *pl.*) *Brit.* lead frames holding the glass of a lattice or stained-glass window. **6** *Printing* a blank space between lines of print (orig. with ref. to the metal strip used to give this space). **7** (*attrib.*) made of lead. —v.tr. **1** cover, weight, or frame (a roof or window panes) with lead. **2** *Printing* separate lines of (printed matter) with leads. **3** add a lead compound to (petrol etc.). □**lead acetate** a white crystalline compound of lead that dissolves in water to form a sweet-tasting solution. **lead-free** (of petrol) without added tetraethyl lead. **lead pencil** a pencil of graphite enclosed in wood. **lead-poisoning** acute or chronic poisoning by absorption of lead into the body. **lead shot** = SHOT[1] 3b. **lead tetraethyl** = TETRAETHYL

LEAD. **lead wool** a fibrous form of lead, used for jointing water pipes. □□**leadless** adj. [OE *lēad* f. WG]

leaden /'led(ə)n/ adj. **1** of or like lead. **2** heavy, slow, burdensome (*leaden limbs*). **3** inert, depressing (*leaden rule*). **4** lead-coloured (*leaden skies*). □**leaden seal** a stamped piece of lead holding the ends of a wire used as a fastening. □□**leadenly** adv. **leadenness** n. [OE *lēaden* (as LEAD[2])]

leader /'liːdə(r)/ n. **1 a** a person or thing that leads. **b** a person followed by others. **2 a** the principal player in a music group or of the first violins in an orchestra. **b** *US* a conductor of an orchestra. **3** *Brit.* = *leading article*. **4** a short strip of non-functioning material at each end of a reel of film or recording tape for connection to the spool. **5** (in full **Leader of the House**) *Brit.* a member of the government officially responsible for initiating business in Parliament. **6** a shoot of a plant at the apex of a stem or of the main branch. **7** (in *pl.*) *Printing* a series of dots or dashes across the page to guide the eye, esp. in tabulated material. **8** the horse placed at the front in a team or pair. □□**leaderless** adj. **leadership** n. [OE *lǣdere* (as LEAD[1])]

leading[1] /'liːdɪŋ/ adj. & n. —adj. chief; most important. —n. guidance, leadership. □**leading aircraftman** the rank above aircraftman in the RAF. **leading article** a newspaper article giving the editorial opinion. **leading counsel** the senior barrister of two or more in a case. **leading edge 1** the foremost edge of an aerofoil, esp. a wing or propeller blade. **2** *Electronics* the part of a pulse in which the amplitude increases (opp. *trailing edge*). **leading lady** the actress playing the principal part. **leading light** a prominent and influential person. **leading man** the actor playing the principal part. **leading note** *Mus.* = SUBTONIC. **leading question** a question that prompts the answer wanted. **leading seaman** the rank next below NCO in the Royal Navy. **leading-strings** (or **-reins**) **1** strings for guiding children learning to walk. **2** oppressive supervision or control. **leading tone** *US Mus.* = *leading note*.

leading[2] /'ledɪŋ/ n. *Printing* = LEAD[2] n. 6.

leadwort /'ledwɜːt/ n. = PLUMBAGO 2.

leaf /liːf/ n. & v. —n. (*pl.* **leaves** /liːvz/) **1 a** each of several flattened usu. green structures of a plant, usu. on the side of a stem or branch and the main organ of photosynthesis. **b** other similar plant structures, e.g. bracts, sepals, and petals (*floral leaf*). **2 a** foliage regarded collectively. **b** the state of having leaves out (*a tree in leaf*). **3** the leaves of tobacco or tea. **4** a single thickness of paper, esp. in a book with each side forming a page. **5** a very thin sheet of metal, esp. gold or silver. **6 a** the hinged part or flap of a door, shutter, table, etc. **b** an extra section inserted to extend a table. —v. **1** intr. put forth leaves. **2** tr. (foll. by *through*) turn over the pages of (a book etc.). □**leaf-green** the colour of green leaves. **leaf insect** any insect of the family Phylliidae, having a flattened body leaflike in appearance. **leaf-miner** any of various larvae burrowing in leaves, esp. moth caterpillars of the family Gracillariidae. **leaf-monkey** a langur. **leaf-mould** soil consisting chiefly of decayed leaves. **leaf spring** a spring made of strips of metal. **leaf-stalk** a petiole. □□**leafage** n. **leafed** adj. (also in *comb.*). **leafless** adj. **leaflessness** n. **leaflike** adj. [OE *lēaf* f. Gmc]

leafhopper /'liːfhɒpə(r)/ n. any homopterous insect of the family Cicadellidae, which sucks the sap of plants and often causes damage and spreads disease.

leaflet /'liːflɪt/ n. & v. —n. **1** a young leaf. **2** *Bot.* any division of a compound leaf. **3** a sheet of (usu. printed) paper (sometimes folded but not stitched) giving information, esp. for free distribution. —v.tr. (**leafleted**, **leafleting**) distribute leaflets to.

leafy /'liːfɪ/ adj. (**leafier**, **leafiest**) **1** having many leaves. **2** resembling a leaf. □□**leafiness** n.

league[1] /liːg/ *n. & v.* —*n.* **1** a collection of people, countries, groups, etc., combining for a particular purpose, esp. mutual protection or cooperation. **2** an agreement to combine in this way. **3** a group of sports clubs which compete over a period for a championship. **4** a class of contestants. —*v.intr.* (**leagues, leagued, leaguing**) (often foll. by *together*) join in a league. □**in league** allied, conspiring. **league football** *Austral.* Rugby League or Australian Rules football played in leagues. **league table 1** a listing of competitors as a league, showing their ranking according to performance. **2** any list of ranking order. [F *ligue* or It. *liga,* var. of *lega* f. *legare* bind f. L *ligare*]

league[2] /liːg/ *n. archaic* a varying measure of travelling-distance by land, usu. about three miles. [ME, ult. f. LL *leuga, leuca,* of Gaulish orig.]

leaguer[1] /ˈliːgə(r)/ *n.* esp. *US* a member of a league.

leaguer[2] /ˈliːgə(r)/ *n. & v.* = LAAGER. [Du. *leger* camp, rel. to LAIR[1]]

leak /liːk/ *n. & v.* —*n.* **1 a** a hole in a vessel, pipe, or container etc. caused by wear or damage, through which matter, esp. liquid or gas, passes accidentally in or out. **b** the matter passing in or out through this. **c** the act or an instance of leaking. **2 a** a similar escape of electrical charge. **b** the charge that escapes. **3** the intentional disclosure of secret information. —*v.* **1 a** *intr.* (of liquid, gas, etc.) pass in or out through a leak. **b** *tr.* lose or admit (liquid, gas, etc.) through a leak. **2** *tr.* intentionally disclose (secret information). **3** *intr.* (often foll. by *out*) (of a secret, secret information) become known. □**have** (or **take**) **a leak** *sl.* urinate. □□**leaker** *n.* [ME prob. f. LG]

leakage /ˈliːkɪdʒ/ *n.* **1** the action or result of leaking. **2** what leaks in or out. **3** an intentional disclosure of secret information.

leaky /ˈliːkɪ/ *adj.* (**leakier, leakiest**) **1** having a leak or leaks. **2** given to letting out secrets. □□**leakiness** *n.*

leal /liːl/ *adj. Sc.* loyal, honest. [ME f. AF *leal,* OF *leel, loial* (as LOYAL)]

lean[1] /liːn/ *v. & n.* —*v.* (*past* and *past part.* **leaned** /liːnd, lent/ or **leant** /lent/) **1** *intr. & tr.* (often foll. by *across, back, over,* etc.) be or place in a sloping position; incline from the perpendicular. **2** *intr. & tr.* (foll. by *against, on, upon*) rest or cause to rest for support against etc. **3** *intr.* (foll. by *on, upon*) rely on; derive support from. **4** *intr.* (foll. by *to, towards*) be inclined or partial to; have a tendency towards. —*n.* a deviation from the perpendicular; an inclination (*has a decided lean to the right*). □**lean on** *colloq.* put pressure on (a person) to act in a certain way. **lean over backwards** see BACKWARDS. **lean-to** (*pl.* **-tos**) a building with its roof leaning against a larger building or a wall. [OE *hleonian, hlinian* f. Gmc]

lean[2] /liːn/ *adj. & n.* —*adj.* **1** (of a person or animal) thin; having no superfluous fat. **2** (of meat) containing little fat. **3 a** meagre; of poor quality (*lean crop*). **b** not nourishing (*lean diet*). **4** unremunerative. —*n.* the lean part of meat. □**lean years** years of scarcity. □□**leanly** *adv.* **leanness** *n.* [OE *hlǽne* f. Gmc]

leaning /ˈliːnɪŋ/ *n.* a tendency or partiality.

leap /liːp/ *v. & n.* —*v.* (*past* and *past part.* **leaped** /liːpt, lept/ or **leapt** /lept/) **1** *intr.* jump or spring forcefully. **2** *tr.* jump across. **3** *intr.* (of prices etc.) increase dramatically. —*n.* a forceful jump. □**by leaps and bounds** with startlingly rapid progress. **leap in the dark** a daring step or enterprise whose consequences are unpredictable. **leap to the eye** be immediately apparent. **leap year** a year, occurring once in four, with 366 days (including 29th Feb. as an intercalary day). □□**leaper** *n.* [OE *hlȳp, hlēapan* f. Gmc: *leap year* prob. refers to the fact that feast-days after Feb. in such a year fall two days later (instead of the normal one day later) than in the previous year]

leap-frog /ˈliːpfrɒg/ *n. & v.* —*n.* a game in which players in turn vault with parted legs over another who is bending down. —*v.* (**-frogged, -frogging**) **1** *intr.* (foll. by *over*) perform such a vault. **2** *tr.* vault over in this way. **3** *tr. & intr.* (of two or more people, vehicles, etc.) overtake alternately.

learn /lɜːn/ *v.* (*past* and *past part.* **learned** /lɜːnt, lɜːnd/ or **learnt** /lɜːnt/) **1** *tr.* gain knowledge of or skill in by study, experience, or being taught. **2** *tr.* (foll. by *to* + infin.) acquire or develop a particular ability (*learn to swim*). **3** *tr.* commit to memory (*will try to learn your names*). **4** *intr.* (foll. by *of*) be informed about. **5** *tr.* (foll. by *that, how,* etc. + clause) become aware of by information or from observation. **6** *intr.* receive instruction; acquire knowledge or skill. **7** *tr. archaic* or *sl.* teach. □**learn one's lesson** see LESSON. □□**learnable** *adj.* **learnability** /-nəˈbɪlɪtɪ/ *n.* [OE *leornian* f. Gmc: cf. LORE[1]]

learned /ˈlɜːnɪd/ *adj.* **1** having much knowledge acquired by study. **2** showing or requiring learning (*a learned work*). **3** studied or pursued by learned persons. **4** concerned with the interests of learned persons; scholarly (*a learned journal*). **5** *Brit.* as a courteous description of a lawyer in certain formal contexts (*my learned friend*). □□**learnedly** *adv.* **learnedness** *n.* [ME f. LEARN in the sense 'teach']

learner /ˈlɜːnə(r)/ *n.* **1** a person who is learning a subject or skill. **2** (in full **learner driver**) a person who is learning to drive a motor vehicle and has not yet passed a driving test.

learning /ˈlɜːnɪŋ/ *n.* knowledge acquired by study. [OE *leornung* (as LEARN)]

lease /liːs/ *n. & v.* —*n.* an agreement by which the owner of a building or land allows another to use it for a specified time, usu. in return for payment. —*v.tr.* grant or take on lease. □**a new lease of** (*US* **on**) **life** a substantially improved prospect of living, or of use after repair. □□**leasable** *adj.* **leaser** *n.* [ME f. AF *les,* OF *lais, leis* f. *lesser, laissier* leave f. L *laxare* make loose (*laxus*)]

leaseback /ˈliːsbæk/ *n.* the leasing of a property back to the vendor.

leasehold /ˈliːshəʊld/ *n. & adj.* —*n.* **1** the holding of property by lease. **2** property held by lease. —*adj.* held by lease. □□**leaseholder** *n.*

leash /liːʃ/ *n. & v.* —*n.* a thong for holding a dog; a dog's lead. —*v.tr.* **1** put a leash on. **2** restrain. □**straining at the leash** eager to begin. [ME f. OF *lesse, laisse* f. specific use of *laisser* let run on a slack lead: see LEASE]

least /liːst/ *adj., n., & adv.* —*adj.* **1** smallest, slightest, most insignificant. **2** (prec. by *the;* esp. with *neg.*) any at all (*it does not make the least difference*). **3** (of a species or variety) very small (*least tern*). —*n.* the least amount. —*adv.* in the least degree. □**at least 1** at all events; anyway; even if there is doubt about a more extended statement. **2** (also **at the least**) not less than. **in the least** (or **the least**) (usu. with *neg.*) in the smallest degree; at all (*not in the least offended*). **least common denominator, multiple** see DENOMINATOR, MULTIPLE. **to say the least** (or **the least of it**) used to imply the moderation of a statement (*that is doubtful to say the least*). [OE *lǽst, lǽsest* f. Gmc]

leastways /ˈliːstweɪz/ *adv.* (also **leastwise** /-waɪz/) *dial.* or at least, or rather.

leat /liːt/ *n. Brit.* an open watercourse conducting water to a mill etc. [OE *-gelǣt* (as Y- + root of LET[1])]

leather /ˈleðə(r)/ *n. & v.* —*n.* **1 a** material made from the skin of an animal by tanning or a similar process. **b** (*attrib.*) made of leather. **2** a piece of leather for polishing with. **3** the leather part or parts of something. **4** *sl.* a cricket-ball or football. **5** (in *pl.*) leather clothes, esp. leggings, breeches, or clothes for wearing on a motor cycle. **6** a thong (*stirrup-leather*). —*v.tr.* **1** cover with leather. **2** polish or wipe with a leather. **3** beat, thrash (orig. with a leather thong). □**leather-jacket 1** *Brit.* a crane-fly

grub with a tough skin. **2** any of various tough-skinned marine fish of the family Monacanthidae.
leather-neck *Naut. sl.* a soldier or (esp. *US*) a marine (with reference to the leather stock formerly worn by them). [OE *lether* f. Gmc]
leatherback /'leðə,bæk/ *n.* a large marine turtle, *Dermochelys coriacea*, having a thick leathery carapace.
leathercloth /'leðə,klɒθ/ *n.* strong fabric coated to resemble leather.
leatherette /,leðə'ret/ *n.* imitation leather.
leathern /'leð(ə)n/ *n. archaic* made of leather.
leathery /'leðərɪ/ *adj.* **1** like leather. **2** (esp. of meat etc.) tough. ▫▫ **leatheriness** *n.*
leave[1] /liːv/ *v. & n.* —*v.* (*past* and *past part.* **left** /left/) **1 a** *tr.* go away from; cease to remain in or on (*left him quite well an hour ago*; *leave the track*; *leave here*). **b** *intr.* (often foll. by *for*) depart (*we leave tomorrow*; *has just left for London*). **2** *tr.* cause to or let remain; depart without taking (*has left his gloves*; *left a slimy trail*; *left a bad impression*; *six from seven leaves one*). **3** *tr.* (also *absol.*) cease to reside at or attend or belong to or work for (*has left the school*; *I am leaving for another firm*). **4** *tr.* abandon, forsake, desert. **5** *tr.* have remaining after one's death (*leaves a wife and two children*). **6** *tr.* bequeath. **7** *tr.* (foll. by *to* + infin.) allow (a person or thing) to do something without interference or assistance (*leave the future to take care of itself*). **8** *tr.* (foll. by *to*) commit or refer to another person (*leave that to me*; *nothing was left to chance*). **9** *tr.* **a** abstain from consuming or dealing with. **b** (in *passive*; often foll. by *over*) remain over. **10** *tr.* **a** deposit or entrust (a thing) to be attended to, collected, delivered, etc., in one's absence (*left a message with his secretary*). **b** depute (a person) to perform a function in one's absence. **11** *tr.* allow to remain or cause to be in a specified state or position (*left the door open*; *the performance left them unmoved*; *left nothing that was necessary undone*). **12** *tr.* pass (an object) so that it is in a specified relative direction (*leave the church on the left*). —*n.* the position in which a player leaves the balls in billiards, croquet, etc. ▫ **be left with 1** retain (a feeling etc.). **2** be burdened with (a responsibility etc.). **be well left** be well provided for by a legacy etc. **get left** *colloq.* be deserted or worsted. **have left** have remaining (*has no friends left*). **leave alone 1** refrain from disturbing, not interfere with. **2** not have dealings with. **leave be** *colloq.* refrain from disturbing, not interfere with. **leave behind 1** go away without. **2** leave as a consequence or a visible sign of passage. **3** pass. **leave a person cold** (or **cool**) not impress or excite a person. **leave go** *colloq.* relax one's hold. **leave hold of** cease holding. **leave it at that** *colloq.* abstain from comment or further action. **leave much** (or **a lot** etc.) **to be desired** be highly unsatisfactory. **leave off 1** come to or make an end. **2** discontinue (*leave off work*; *leave off talking*). **3** cease to wear. **leave out** omit, not include. **leave over** *Brit.* leave to be considered, settled, or used later. **leave a person to himself** or **herself 1** not attempt to control a person. **2** leave a person solitary. **left at the post** beaten from the start of a race. **left for dead** abandoned as being beyond rescue. **left luggage** *Brit.* luggage deposited for later retrieval, esp. at a railway station. ▫▫ **leaver** *n.* [OE *lǽfan* f. Gmc]
leave[2] /liːv/ *n.* **1** (often foll. by *to* + infin.) permission. **2 a** (in full **leave of absence**) permission to be absent from duty. **b** the period for which this lasts. ▫ **by** (or **with**) **your leave** often *iron.* an expression of apology for taking a liberty or making an unwelcome statement. **on leave** legitimately absent from duty. **take one's leave** bid farewell. **take one's leave of** bid farewell to. **take leave of one's senses** see SENSE. **take leave to** venture or presume to. [OE *léaf* f. WG: cf. LIEF, LOVE]
leaved /liːvd/ *adj.* **1** having leaves. **2** (in *comb.*)

having a leaf or leaves of a specified kind or number (*four-leaved clover*).
leaven /'lev(ə)n/ *n. & v.* —*n.* **1** a substance added to dough to make it ferment and rise, esp. yeast, or fermenting dough reserved for the purpose. **2 a** a pervasive transforming influence (cf. Matt. 13:33). **b** (foll. by *of*) a tinge or admixture of a specified quality. —*v.tr.* **1** ferment (dough) with leaven. **2 a** permeate and transform. **b** (foll. by *with*) modify with a tempering element. ▫ **the old leaven** traces of the unregenerate state (cf. 1 Cor. 5:6-8). [ME f. OF *levain* f. Gallo-Roman spec. use of L *levamen* relief f. *levare* lift]
leaves *pl.* of LEAF.
leavings /'liːvɪŋz/ *n.pl.* things left over, esp. as worthless.
Lebanese /,lebə'niːz/ *adj. & n.* —*adj.* of or relating to Lebanon in the Middle East. —*n.* (*pl.* same) **1** a native or national of Lebanon. **2** a person of Lebanese descent.
Lebensraum /'leɪbənz,raʊm/ *n.* the territory which a State or nation believes is needed for its natural development. [G, = living-space (orig. with reference to Germany, esp. in the 1930s)]
lech /letʃ/ *v. & n. colloq.* —*v.intr.* feel lecherous; behave lustfully. —*n.* **1** a strong desire, esp. sexual. **2** a lecher. [back-form. f. LECHER: (n.) perh. f. *letch* longing]
lecher /'letʃə(r)/ *n.* a lecherous man; a debauchee. [ME f. OF *lecheor* etc. f. *lechier* live in debauchery or gluttony f. Frank., rel. to LICK]
lecherous /'letʃərəs/ *adj.* lustful, having strong or excessive sexual desire. ▫▫ **lecherously** *adv.* **lecherousness** *n.* [ME f. OF *lecheros* etc. f. *lecheur* LECHER]
lechery /'letʃərɪ/ *n.* unrestrained indulgence of sexual desire. [ME f. OF *lecherie* f. *lecheur* LECHER]
lecithin /'lesɪθɪn/ *n.* **1** any of a group of phospholipids found naturally in animals, egg-yolk, and some higher plants. **2** a preparation of this used to emulsify foods etc. [Gk *lekithos* egg-yolk + -IN]
lectern /'lektɜːn, -t(ə)n/ *n.* **1** a stand for holding a book in a church or chapel, esp. for a bible from which lessons are to be read. **2** a similar stand for a lecturer etc. [ME *lettorne* f. OF *let(t)run*, med.L *lectrum* f. *legere lect-* read]
lection /'lekʃ(ə)n/ *n.* a reading of a text found in a particular copy or edition. [L *lectio* reading (as LECTERN)]
lectionary /'lekʃənərɪ/ *n.* (*pl.* -**ies**) **1** a list of portions of Scripture appointed to be read at divine service. **2** a book containing such portions. [ME f. med.L *lectionarium* (as LECTION)]
lector /'lektɔː(r)/ *n.* **1** a reader, esp. of lessons in a church service. **2** (*fem.* **lectrice** /lek'triːs/) a lecturer or reader, esp. one employed in a foreign university to give instruction in his or her native language. [L f. *legere lect-* read]
lecture /'lektʃə(r)/ *n. & v.* —*n.* **1** a discourse giving information about a subject to a class or other audience. **2** a long serious speech esp. as a scolding or reprimand. —*v.* **1** *intr.* (often foll. by *on*) deliver a lecture or lectures. **2** *tr.* talk seriously or reprovingly to (a person). **3** *tr.* instruct or entertain (a class or other audience) by a lecture. [ME f. OF *lecture* or med.L *lectura* f. L (as LECTOR)]
lecturer /'lektʃərə(r)/ *n.* a person who lectures, esp. as a teacher in higher education.
lectureship /'lektʃəʃɪp/ *n.* the office of lecturer. ¶ The form *lecturership*, which is strictly more regular, is in official use at Oxford University and elsewhere, but is not widely current.
lecythus /'lesɪθəs/ *n.* (*pl.* **lecythi** /-,θaɪ/) *Gk Antiq.* a thin narrow-necked vase or flask. [Gk *lēkuthos*]
LED *abbr.* light-emitting diode.
led *past* and *past part.* of LEAD[1].
lederhosen /'leɪdə,həʊz(ə)n/ *n.pl.* leather shorts as worn by men in Bavaria etc. [G, = leather trousers]

ledge /ledʒ/ *n.* **1** a narrow horizontal surface projecting from a wall etc. **2** a shelflike projection on the side of a rock or mountain. **3** a ridge of rocks, esp. below water. **4** *Mining* a stratum of metal-bearing rock. □□ **ledged** *adj.* **ledgy** *adj.* [perh. f. ME *legge* LAY[1]]

ledger /ˈledʒə(r)/ *n.* **1** a tall narrow book in which a firm's accounts are kept, esp. one which is the principal book of a set and contains debtor-and-creditor accounts. **2** a flat gravestone. **3** a horizontal timber in scaffolding, parallel to the face of the building. □ **ledger line** *Mus.* = LEGER LINE. **ledger-tackle** a kind of fishing tackle in which a lead weight keeps the bait on the bottom. [ME f. senses of Du. *ligger* and *legger* (f. *liggen* LIE[1],· *leggen* LAY[1])· & pronunc. of ME *ligge, legge*]

lee /liː/ *n.* **1** shelter given by a neighbouring object (*under the lee of*). **2** (in full **lee side**) the sheltered side, the side away from the wind (opp. *weather side*). □ **lee-board** a plank frame fixed to the side of a flat-bottomed vessel and let down into the water to diminish leeway. **lee shore** the shore to leeward of a ship. [OE *hlēo* f. Gmc]

leech[1] /liːtʃ/ *n.* **1** any freshwater or terrestrial annelid worm of the class *Hirudinea* with suckers at both ends, esp. *Hirudo medicinalis*, a bloodsucking parasite of vertebrates formerly much used medicinally. **2** a person who extorts profit from or sponges on others. □ **like a leech** persistently or clingingly present. [OE *lǣce*, assim. to LEECH[2]]

leech[2] /liːtʃ/ *n. archaic* or *joc.* a physician; a healer. [OE *lǣce* f. Gmc]

leech[3] /liːtʃ/ *n.* **1** a perpendicular or sloping side of a square sail. **2** the side of a fore-and-aft sail away from the mast or stay. [ME, perh. rel. to ON *lik*, a nautical term of uncert. meaning]

leechcraft /ˈliːtʃkrɑːft/ *n. archaic* the art of healing. [OE *lǣcecræft* (as LEECH[2], CRAFT)]

leek /liːk/ *n.* **1** an alliaceous plant, *Allium porrum*, with flat overlapping leaves forming an elongated cylindrical bulb, used as food. **2** this as a Welsh national emblem. [OE *lēac* f. Gmc]

leer[1] /lɪə(r)/ *v. & n.* —*v.intr.* look slyly or lasciviously or maliciously. —*n.* a leering look. □□ **leeringly** *adv.* [perh. f. obs. *leer* cheek f. OE *hlēor*, as though 'to glance over one's cheek']

leer[2] *var. of* LEHR.

leery /ˈlɪərɪ/ *adj.* (**leerier, leeriest**) *sl.* **1** knowing, sly. **2** (foll. by *of*) wary. □□ **leeriness** *n.* [perh. f. obs. *leer* looking askance f. LEER[1] + -Y[1]]

lees /liːz/ *n.pl.* **1** the sediment of wine etc. (*drink to the lees*). **2** dregs, refuse. [pl. of ME *lie* f. OF *lie* f. med.L *lia* f. Gaulish]

leet[1] /liːt/ *n. hist.* **1** (in full **Court leet**) a yearly or half-yearly court of record that lords of certain manors might hold. **2** its jurisdiction or district. [ME f. AF *lete* (= AL *leta*), of unkn. orig.]

leet[2] /liːt/ *n. Sc.* a selected list of candidates for some office. □ **short leet** = *short list*. [ME *lite* etc., prob. f. AF & OF *lit(t)e*, var. of *liste* LIST[1]]

leeward /ˈliːwəd, *Naut.* ˈluːəd/ *adj., adv., & n.* —*adj. & adv.* on or towards the side sheltered from the wind (opp. WINDWARD). —*n.* the leeward region, side, or direction (*to leeward; on the leeward of*).

leewardly /ˈliːwədlɪ, ˈluːədlɪ/ *adj.* (of a ship) apt to drift to leeward.

leeway /ˈliːweɪ/ *n.* **1** the sideways drift of a ship to leeward of the desired course. **2 a** allowable deviation or freedom of action. **b** *US* margin of safety. □ **make up leeway** struggle out of a bad position, recover lost time, etc.

left[1] /left/ *adj., adv., & n.* (opp. RIGHT). —*adj.* **1** on or towards the side of the human body which corresponds to the position of west if one regards oneself as facing north. **2** on or towards the part of an object which is analogous to a person's left side or (with opposite sense) which is nearer to an observer's left hand. **3** (also **Left**) *Polit.* of the Left.

—*adv.* on or to the left side. —*n.* **1** the left-hand part or region or direction. **2** *Boxing* **a** the left hand. **b** a blow with this. **3 a** (often **Left**) *Polit.* a group or section favouring radical socialism (orig. the more radical section of a continental legislature, seated on the president's left); such radicals collectively. **b** the more advanced or innovative section of any group. **4** the side of a stage which is to the left of a person facing the audience. **5** (esp. in marching) the left foot. **6** the left wing of an army. □ **have two left feet** be clumsy. **left and right** = *right and left*. **left bank** the bank of a river on the left facing downstream. **left bower** see BOWER[3]. **left field** *Baseball* the part of the outfield to the left of the batter as he or she faces the pitcher. **left hand 1** the hand of the left side. **2** (usu. prec. by *at, on, to*) the region or direction on the left side of a person. **left-hand** *adj.* **1** on or towards the left side of a person or thing (*left-hand drive*). **2** done with the left hand (*left-hand blow*). **3 a** (of rope) twisted counter-clockwise. **b** (of a screw) = LEFT-HANDED. **left turn** a turn that brings one's front to face as one's left side did before. **left wing 1** the radical or socialist section of a political party. **2** the left side of a football etc. team on the field. **3** the left side of an army. **left-wing** *adj.* socialist, radical. **left-winger** a person on the left wing. **marry with the left hand** marry morganatically (see LEFT-HANDED). □□ **leftish** *adj.* [ME *lüft, lift, left,* f. OE, orig. sense 'weak, worthless']

left[2] *past and past part.* of LEAVE[1].

left-handed /left'hændɪd/ *adj.* **1** using the left hand by preference as more serviceable than the right. **2** (of a tool etc.) made to be used with the left hand. **3** (of a blow) struck with the left hand. **4 a** turning to the left; towards the left. **b** (of a racecourse) turning anticlockwise. **c** (of a screw) advanced by turning to the left (anticlockwise). **5** awkward, clumsy. **6 a** (of a compliment) ambiguous. **b** of doubtful sincerity or validity. **7** (of a marriage) morganatic (from a German custom by which the bridegroom gave the bride his left hand in such marriages). □□ **left-handedly** *adv.* **left-handedness** *n.*

left-hander /left'hændə(r)/ *n.* **1** a left-handed person. **2** a left-handed blow.

leftie *var. of* LEFTY.

leftism /ˈleftɪz(ə)m/ *n. Polit.* the principles or policy of the left. □□ **leftist** *n. & adj.*

leftmost /ˈleftməʊst/ *adj.* furthest to the left.

leftovers /ˈleftˌəʊvəz/ *n.pl.* items (esp. of food) remaining after the rest has been used.

leftward /ˈleftwəd/ *adv. & adj.* —*adv.* (also **leftwards** /-wədz/) towards the left. —*adj.* going towards or facing the left.

lefty /ˈleftɪ/ *n.* (also **leftie**) (*pl.* -**ies**) *colloq.* **1** *Polit.* a left-winger. **2** a left-handed person.

leg /leg/ *n. & v.* —*n.* **1 a** each of the limbs on which a person or animal walks and stands. **b** the part of this from the hip to the ankle. **2** a leg of an animal or bird as food. **3** an artificial leg (*wooden leg*). **4** a part of a garment covering a leg or part of a leg. **5 a** a support of a chair, table, bed, etc. **b** a long thin support or prop, esp. a pole. **6** *Cricket* the half of the field (as divided lengthways through the pitch) in which the striker's feet are placed (opp. OFF). **7 a** a section of a journey. **b** a section of a relay race. **c** a stage in a competition. **d** one of two or more games constituting a round. **8** one branch of a forked object. **9** *Naut.* a run made on a single tack. **10** *archaic* an obeisance made by drawing back one leg and bending it while keeping the front leg straight. —*v.tr.* (**legged, legging**) propel (a boat) through a canal tunnel by pushing with one's legs against the tunnel sides. □ **feel** (or **find**) **one's legs** become able to stand or walk. **give a person a leg up** help a person to mount a horse etc. or get over an obstacle or difficulty. **have the legs of** be able to go further than. **have no legs** *colloq.* (of a golf ball etc.) have not enough momentum to reach the desired point. **keep one's legs** not fall. **leg before wicket** *Cricket* (of a batsman) out because of illegally obstructing the ball with a part of the body other than the hand. **leg break** *Cricket* **1** a ball which deviates from the leg side after bouncing. **2** such deviation. **leg-bye** see BYE[1]. **leg-cutter** *Cricket* a fast leg break. **leg-iron** a shackle or fetter for the leg. **leg it** *colloq.* walk or run hard. **leg-of-mutton sail** a triangular mainsail. **leg-of-mutton sleeve** a sleeve which is full and loose on the upper arm but close-fitting on the forearm. **leg-pull** *colloq.* a hoax. **leg-rest** a support for a seated invalid's leg. **leg-room** space for the legs of a seated person. **leg-show** a theatrical performance by scantily-dressed women. **leg slip** *Cricket* a fielder stationed for a ball glancing off the bat to the leg side behind the wicket. **leg spin** *Cricket* a type of spin which causes the ball to deviate from the leg side after bouncing. **leg stump** *Cricket* the stump on the leg side. **leg theory** *Cricket* bowling to leg with fielders massed on that side. **leg trap** *Cricket* a group of fielders near the wicket on the leg side. **leg warmer** either of a pair of tubular knitted garments covering the leg from ankle to thigh. **not have a leg to stand on** be unable to support one's argument by facts or sound reasons. **on one's last legs** near death or the end of one's usefulness etc. **on one's legs 1** (also **on one's hind legs**) standing esp. to make a speech. **2** well enough to walk about. **take to one's legs** run away. □□ **legged** /legd, 'legɪd/ *adj.* (also in *comb.*). **legger** *n.* [ME f. ON *leggr* f. Gmc]

legacy /'legəsɪ/ *n.* (*pl.* -ies) **1** a gift left in a will. **2** something handed down by a predecessor (*legacy of corruption*). □**legacy-hunter** a person who pays court to another to secure a legacy. [ME f. OF *legacie* legateship f. med.L *legatia* f. L *legare* bequeath]

legal /'li:g(ə)l/ *adj.* **1** of or based on law; concerned with law; falling within the province of law. **2** appointed or required by law. **3** permitted by law, lawful. **4** recognized by law, as distinct from equity. **5** *Theol.* **a** of the Mosaic law. **b** of salvation by works rather than by faith. □**legal aid** payment from public funds allowed, in cases of need, to help pay for legal advice or proceedings. **legal fiction** an assertion accepted as true (though probably fictitious) to achieve a useful purpose, esp. in legal matters. **legal holiday** *US* a public holiday established by law. **legal proceedings** see PROCEEDING. **legal separation** see SEPARATION. **legal tender** currency that cannot legally be refused in payment of a debt (usu. up to a limited amount for coins not made of gold). □□ **legally** *adv.* [F *légal* or L *legalis* f. *lex legis* law: cf. LEAL, LOYAL]

legalese /ˌli:gə'li:z/ *n.* *colloq.* the technical language of legal documents.

legalism /'li:gəˌlɪz(ə)m/ *n.* **1** excessive adherence to law or formula. **2** *Theol.* adherence to the Law rather than to the Gospel, the doctrine of justification by works. □□ **legalist** *n.* **legalistic** /-'lɪstɪk/ *adj.* **legalistically** /-'lɪstɪkəlɪ/ *adv.*

legality /lɪ'gælɪtɪ, li:'g-/ *n.* (*pl.* -ies) **1** lawfulness. **2** legalism. **3** (in *pl.*) obligations imposed by law. [F *légalité* or med.L *legalitas* (as LEGAL)]

legalize /'li:gəˌlaɪz/ *v.tr.* (also -ise) **1** make lawful. **2** bring into harmony with the law. □□ **legalization** /-'zeɪʃ(ə)n/ *n.*

legate /'legət/ *n.* **1** a member of the clergy representing the Pope. **2** *Rom.Hist.* **a** a deputy of a general. **b** a governor or deputy governor of a province. **3** *archaic* an ambassador or delegate. □**legate a latere** /ɑː 'læteˌreɪ/ a papal legate of the highest class, with full powers. □□ **legateship** *n.*

legatine /-tɪn/ *adj.* [OE f. OF *legat* f. L *legatus* past part. of *legare* depute, delegate]

legatee /ˌlegə'ti:/ *n.* the recipient of a legacy. [as LEGATOR + -EE]

legation /lɪ'geɪʃ(ə)n/ *n.* **1** a body of deputies. **2 a** the

office and staff of a diplomatic minister (esp. when not having ambassadorial rank). **b** the official residence of a diplomatic minister. **3** a legateship. **4** the sending of a legate or deputy. [ME f. OF *legation* or L *legatio* (as LEGATE[1])]

legato /lɪ'gɑːtəʊ/ *adv., adj., & n. Mus.* —*adv. & adj.* in a smooth flowing manner, without breaks between notes (cf. STACCATO, TENUTO). —*n.* (*pl.* -os) **1** a legato passage. **2** legato playing. [It., = bound, past part. of *legare* f. L *ligare* bind]

legator /lɪ'geɪtə(r)/ *n.* the giver of a legacy. [archaic *legate* bequeath f. L *legare* (as LEGACY)]

legend /'ledʒ(ə)nd/ *n.* **1 a** a traditional story sometimes popularly regarded as historical but unauthenticated; a myth. **b** such stories collectively. **c** a popular but unfounded belief. **d** *colloq.* a subject of such beliefs (*became a legend in his own lifetime*). **2 a** an inscription, esp. on a coin or medal. **b** *Printing* a caption. **c** wording on a map etc. explaining the symbols used. **3** *hist.* **a** the story of a saint's life. **b** a collection of lives of saints or similar stories. □□ **legendry** *n.* [ME (in sense 3) f. OF *legende* f. med.L *legenda* what is to be read, neut. pl. gerundive of L *legere* read]

legendary /'ledʒəndərɪ/ *adj.* **1** of or connected with legends. **2** described in a legend. **3** *colloq.* remarkable enough to be a subject of legend. **4** based on a legend. □□ **legendarily** *adv.* [med.L *legendarius* (as LEGEND)]

legerdemain /ˌledʒədə'meɪn/ *n.* **1** sleight of hand; conjuring or juggling. **2** trickery, sophistry. [ME f. F *léger de main* light of hand, dextrous]

leger line /'ledʒə(r)/ *n. Mus.* a short line added for notes above or below the range of a staff. [var. of LEDGER]

legging /'legɪŋ/ *n.* (usu. in *pl.*) a stout protective outer covering for the leg from the knee to the ankle.

leggy /'legɪ/ *adj.* (**leggier, leggiest**) **1 a** long-legged. **b** (of a woman) having attractively long legs. **2** long-stemmed. □□ **legginess** *n.*

leghorn /'leghɔːn, lɪ'gɔːn/ *n.* **1 a** a fine plaited straw. **b** a hat of this. **2** (**Leghorn**) **a** a bird of a small hardy breed of domestic fowl. **b** this breed. [*Leghorn* (Livorno) in Italy, from where the straw and fowls were imported]

legible /'ledʒɪb(ə)l/ *adj.* (of handwriting, print, etc.) clear enough to read; readable. □□ **legibility** /-'bɪlɪtɪ/ *n.* **legibly** *adv.* [ME f. LL *legibilis* f. *legere* read]

legion /'li:dʒ(ə)n/ *n. & adj.* —*n.* **1** a division of 3,000–6,000 men, including a complement of cavalry, in the ancient Roman army. **2** a large organized body. **3** a vast host, multitude, or number. —*predic.adj.* great in number (*his good works have been legion*). □**American Legion** (in the US) an association of ex-servicemen formed in 1919. **foreign legion** a body of foreign volunteers in a modern, esp. French, army. **Legion of Honour** a French order of distinction founded in 1802. **Royal British Legion** (in the UK) an association of ex-servicemen (and now women) formed in 1921. [ME f. OF f. L *legio -onis* f. *legere* choose]

legionary /'li:dʒənərɪ/ *adj. & n.* —*adj.* of a legion or legions. —*n.* (*pl.* -ies) a member of a legion. [L *legionarius* (as LEGION)]

legioned /'li:dʒ(ə)nd/ *adj. poet.* arrayed in legions.

legionella /ˌli:dʒə'nelə/ *n.* the bacterium *Legionella pneumophila*, which causes legionnaires' disease.

legionnaire /ˌli:dʒə'neə(r)/ *n.* **1** a member of a foreign legion. **2** a member of the American Legion or the Royal British Legion. □**legionnaires' disease** a form of bacterial pneumonia first identified after an outbreak at an American Legion meeting in 1976 (cf. LEGIONELLA). [F *légionnaire* (as LEGION)]

legislate /'ledʒɪsˌleɪt/ *v.intr.* **1** make laws. **2** (foll. by *for*) make provision by law. [back-form. f. LEGISLATION]

legislation /ˌledʒɪs'leɪʃ(ə)n/ *n.* **1** the process of making laws. **2** laws collectively. [LL *legis latio* f. *lex*

b *but* d *dog* f *few* g *get* h *he* j *yes* k *cat* l *leg* m *man* n *no* p *pen* r *red* s *sit* t *top* v *voice*

legis law + *latio* proposing f. *lat-* past part. stem of *ferre* bring]

legislative /'ledʒɪslətɪv/ *adj.* of or empowered to make legislation. □□ **legislatively** *adv.*

legislator /'ledʒɪsˌleɪtə(r)/ *n.* **1** a member of a legislative body. **2** a lawgiver. [L (as LEGISLATION)]

legislature /'ledʒɪsˌleɪtʃə(r), -lətʃə(r)/ *n.* the legislative body of a State.

legit /lɪ'dʒɪt/ *adj.* & *n. colloq.* —*adj.* legitimate. —*n.* **1** legitimate drama. **2** an actor in legitimate drama. [abbr.]

legitimate *adj.* & *v.* —*adj.* /lɪ'dʒɪtɪmət/ **1 a** (of a child) born of parents lawfully married to each other. **b** (of a parent, birth, descent, etc.) with, of, through, etc., a legitimate child. **2** lawful, proper, regular, conforming to the standard type. **3** logically admissible. **4 a** (of a sovereign's title) based on strict hereditary right. **b** (of a sovereign) having a legitimate title. **5** constituting or relating to serious drama as distinct from musical comedy, revue, etc. —*v.tr.* /lɪ'dʒɪtɪˌmeɪt/ **1** make legitimate by decree, enactment, or proof. **2** justify, serve as a justification for. □□ **legitimacy** /-məsɪ/ *n.* **legitimately** /-mətlɪ/ *adv.* **legitimation** /-'meɪʃ(ə)n/ *n.* [med.L *legitimare* f. L *legitimus* lawful f. *lex legis* law]

legitimatize /lɪ'dʒɪtɪməˌtaɪz/ *v.tr.* (also **-ise**) legitimize. □□ **legitimatization** /-'zeɪʃ(ə)n/ *n.*

legitimism /lɪ'dʒɪtɪˌmɪz(ə)m/ *n.* adherence to a sovereign or pretender whose claim is based on direct descent (esp. in French and Spanish history). □□ **legitimist** *n.* & *adj.* [F *légitimisme* f. *légitime* LEGITIMATE]

legitimize /lɪ'dʒɪtɪˌmaɪz/ *v.tr.* (also **-ise**) **1** make legitimate. **2** serve as a justification for. □□ **legitimization** /-'zeɪʃ(ə)n/ *n.*

legless /'leglɪs/ *adj.* **1** having no legs. **2** *sl.* drunk, esp. too drunk to stand.

legman /'legmæn/ *n.* (*pl.* **-men**) a person employed to go about gathering news or running errands etc.

Lego /'legəʊ/ *n. propr.* a construction toy consisting of interlocking plastic building blocks. [Da. *legetøj* toys f. *lege* to play]

legume /'legjuːm/ *n.* **1** the seed pod of a leguminous plant. **2** any seed, pod, or other edible part of a leguminous plant used as food. [F *légume* f. L *legumen* -minis f. *legere* pick, because pickable by hand]

leguminous /lɪ'gjuːmɪnəs/ *adj.* of or like the family Leguminosae, including peas and beans, having seeds in pods and usu. root nodules able to fix nitrogen. [mod.L *leguminosus* (as LEGUME)]

legwork /'legwɜːk/ *n.* work which involves a lot of walking, travelling, or physical activity.

lehr /lɪə(r)/ *n.* (also **leer**) a furnace used for the annealing of glass. [17th c.: orig. unkn.]

lei[1] /'leɪiː, leɪ/ *n.* a Polynesian garland of flowers. [Hawaiian]

lei[2] *pl.* of LEU.

Leibnizian /laɪb'nɪtsɪən/ *adj.* & *n.* —*adj.* of or relating to the philosophy of G. W. Leibniz, German philosopher (d. 1716), esp. regarding matter as a multitude of monads and assuming a pre-established harmony between spirit and matter. —*n.* a follower of this philosophy.

Leicester /'lestə(r)/ *n.* a kind of mild firm cheese, usu. orange-coloured and orig. made in Leicestershire.

Leics. *abbr.* Leicestershire.

leishmaniasis /ˌliːʃmə'naɪəsɪs/ *n.* any of several diseases caused by parasitic protozoans of the genus *Leishmania* transmitted by the bite of sandflies. [W. B. *Leishman*, Brit. physician d. 1926]

leister /'liːstə(r)/ *n.* & *v.* —*n.* a pronged salmon-spear. —*v.tr.* pierce with a leister. [ON *ljóstr* f. *ljósta* to strike]

leisure /'leʒə(r)/ *n.* **1** free time; time at one's own disposal. **2** enjoyment of free time. **3** (usu. foll. by *for*, or *to* + infin.) opportunity afforded by free time. □**at leisure 1** not occupied. **2** in an unhurried manner. **at one's leisure** when one has time. □□ **leisureless** *adj.* [ME f. AF *leisour*, OF *leisir* ult. f. L *licēre* be allowed]

leisured /'leʒəd/ *adj.* having ample leisure.

leisurely /'leʒəlɪ/ *adj.* & *adv.* —*adj.* having leisure; acting or done at leisure; unhurried, relaxed. —*adv.* without hurry. □□ **leisureliness** *n.*

leisurewear /'leʒəˌweə(r)/ *n.* informal clothes, especially tracksuits and other sportswear.

leitmotif /'laɪtməʊˌtiːf/ *n.* (also **leitmotiv**) a recurrent theme associated throughout a musical, literary, etc. composition with a particular person, idea, or situation. [G *Leitmotiv* (as LEAD[1], MOTIVE)]

lek[1] /lek/ *n.* the chief monetary unit of Albania. [Albanian]

lek[2] /lek/ *n.* a patch of ground used by groups of certain birds during the breeding season as a setting for the males' display and their meeting with the females. [perh. f. Sw. *leka* to play]

LEM *abbr.* lunar excursion module.

leman /'lemən/ *n.* (*pl.* **lemans**) *archaic* **1** a lover or sweetheart. **2** an illicit lover, esp. a mistress. [ME *leofman* (as LIEF, MAN)]

lemma /'lemə/ *n.* **1** an assumed or demonstrated proposition used in an argument or proof. **2 a** a heading indicating the subject or argument of a literary composition, a dictionary entry, etc. **b** (*pl.* **lemmata** /-mətə/) a heading indicating the subject or argument of an annotation. **3** a motto appended to a picture etc. [L f. Gk *lēmma* -*matos* thing assumed, f. the root of *lambanō* take]

lemme /'lemɪ/ *colloq.* let me. [corrupt.]

lemming /'lemɪŋ/ *n.* any small arctic rodent of the genus *Lemmus*, esp. *L. lemmus* of Norway which is reputed to rush headlong into the sea and drown during migration. [Norw.]

lemon /'lemən/ *n.* **1 a** a pale-yellow thick-skinned oval citrus fruit with acidic juice. **b** a tree of the species *Citrus limon* which produces this fruit. **2** a pale-yellow colour. **3** *colloq.* a person or thing regarded as feeble or unsatisfactory or disappointing. □**lemon balm** a bushy plant, *Melissa officinalis*, with leaves smelling and tasting of lemon. **lemon curd** (or **cheese**) a conserve made from lemons, butter, eggs, and sugar, with the consistency of cream cheese. **lemon drop** a boiled sweet flavoured with lemon. **lemon geranium** a lemon-scented pelargonium, *Pelargonium crispum*. **lemon grass** any fragrant tropical grass of the genus *Cymbopogon*, yielding an oil smelling of lemon. **lemon squash** *Brit.* a soft drink made from lemons and other ingredients, often sold in concentrated form. **lemon-squeezer** a device for extracting the juice from a lemon. **lemon thyme** a herb, *Thymus citriodorus*, with lemon-scented leaves used for flavouring. **lemon verbena** (or **plant**) a shrub, *Lippia citriodora*, with lemon-scented leaves. □□ **lemony** *adj.* [ME f. OF *limon* f. Arab. *līma*: cf. LIME[2]]

lemonade /ˌlemə'neɪd/ *n.* **1** an effervescent or still drink made from lemon juice. **2** a synthetic substitute for this.

lemon sole /'lemən/ *n.* a flat-fish, *Microstomus kitt*, of the plaice family. [F *limande*]

lemur /'liːmə(r)/ *n.* any arboreal primate of the family Lemuridae native to Madagascar, with a pointed snout and long tail. [mod.L f. L *lemures* (pl.) spirits of the dead, from its spectre-like face]

lend /lend/ *v.tr.* (*past* and *past part.* **lent** /lent/) **1** (usu. foll. by *to*) grant (to a person) the use of (a thing) on the understanding that it or its equivalent shall be returned. **2** allow the use of (money) at interest. **3** bestow or contribute (something temporary) (*lend assistance*; *lends a certain charm*). □**lend an ear** (or **one's ears**) listen. **lend a hand** = *give a hand* (see HAND). **lending library** a library from which books may be temporarily taken away with or *Brit.* without direct payment. **lend itself to** (of a thing) be suitable for. **Lend-Lease** *hist.* an arrangement made in 1941 whereby the US supplied equipment etc. to the UK and its allies, orig. as a loan in return for the use of British-owned military bases. **lend oneself to** accommodate oneself to (a policy or purpose). □□ **lendable** adj. **lender** n. **lending** n. [ME, earlier lēne(n) f. OE lænan f. læn LOAN[1]]

length /leŋθ, leŋkθ/ n. **1** measurement or extent from end to end; the greater of two or the greatest of three dimensions of a body. **2** extent in, of, or with regard to, time (a stay of some length; the length of a speech). **3** the distance a thing extends (at arm's length; ships a cable's length apart). **4** the length of a horse, boat, etc., as a measure of the lead in a race. **5** a long stretch or extent (a length of hair). **6** a degree of thoroughness in action (went to great lengths; prepared to go to any length). **7** a piece of material of a certain length (a length of cloth). **8** Prosody the quantity of a vowel or syllable. **9** Cricket **a** the distance from the batsman at which the ball pitches (the bowler keeps a good length). **b** the proper amount of this. **10** the extent of a garment in a vertical direction when worn. **11** the full extent of one's body. □**at length 1** (also **at full** or **great** etc. **length**) in detail, without curtailment. **2** after a long time, at last. [OE lengthu f. Gmc (as LONG[1])]

lengthen /'leŋθ(ə)n, 'leŋkθ(ə)n/ v. **1** tr. & intr. make or become longer. **2** tr. make (a vowel) long. □□ **lengthener** n.

lengthman /'leŋθmən/ n. (pl. -men) Brit. a person employed to maintain a section of railway or road.

lengthways /'leŋθweɪz, 'leŋkθ-/ adv. in a direction parallel with a thing's length.

lengthwise /'leŋθwaɪz, 'leŋkθ-/ adv. & adj. —adv. lengthways. —adj. lying or moving lengthways.

lengthy /'leŋθɪ, 'leŋkθɪ/ adj. (**lengthier, lengthiest**) **1** of unusual length. **2** (of speech, writing, style, a speaker, etc.) tedious, prolix. □□ **lengthily** adv. **lengthiness** n.

lenient /'li:nɪənt/ adj. **1** merciful, tolerant, not disposed to severity. **2** (of punishment etc.) mild. **3** archaic emollient. □□ **lenience** n. **leniency** n. **leniently** adv. [L lenire lenit- soothe f. lenis gentle]

Leninism /'lenɪnɪz(ə)m/ n. Marxism as interpreted and applied by Lenin. □□ **Leninist** n. & adj. **Leninite** n. & adj. [V. I. Lenin (name assumed by V. I. Ulyanov), Russian statesman d. 1924]

lenition /li:'nɪʃ(ə)n/ n. (in Celtic languages) the process or result of articulating a consonant softly. [L lenis soft, after G lenierung]

lenitive /'lenɪtɪv/ adj. & n. —adj. Med. soothing. —n. **1** Med. a soothing drug or appliance. **2** a palliative. [ME f. med.L lenitivus (as LENIENT)]

lenity /'lenɪtɪ/ n. (pl. -ies) literary **1** mercifulness, gentleness. **2** an act of mercy. [F lénité or L lenitas f. lenis gentle]

leno /'li:nəʊ/ n. (pl. -os) an open-work fabric with the warp threads twisted in pairs before weaving. [F linon f. lin flax f. L linum]

lens /lenz/ n. **1** a piece of a transparent substance with one or (usu.) both sides curved for concentrating or dispersing light-rays esp. in optical instruments. **2** a combination of lenses used in photography. **3** Anat. = crystalline lens. **4** Physics a device for focusing or otherwise modifying the direction of movement of light, sound, electrons, etc. □□ **lensed** adj. **lensless** adj. [L lens lentis lentil (from the similarity of shape)]

Lent /lent/ n. **1** Eccl. the period from Ash Wednesday to Holy Saturday, of which the 40 weekdays are devoted to fasting and penitence in commemoration of Christ's fasting in the wilderness. **2** (in pl.) the boat races held at Cambridge in the Lent term. □**Lent lily** Brit. a daffodil, esp. a wild one. **Lent term** Brit. the term at a university etc. in which Lent falls. [ME f. LENTEN]

lent past and past part. of LEND.

-lent /lənt/ suffix forming adjectives (pestilent; violent) (cf. -ULENT). [L -lentus -ful]

Lenten /'lent(ə)n/ adj. of, in, or appropriate to, Lent. □**Lenten fare** food without meat. [orig. as noun, = spring, f. OE lencten f. Gmc, rel. to LONG[1], perh. with ref. to lengthening of the day in spring: now regarded as adj. f. LENT + -EN[2]]

lenticel /'lentɪˌsel/ n. Bot. any of the raised pores in the stems of woody plants that allow gas exchange between the atmosphere and the internal tissues. [mod.L lenticella dimin. of L lens: see LENS]

lenticular /len'tɪkjʊlə(r)/ adj. **1** shaped like a lentil or a biconvex lens. **2** of the lens of the eye. [L lenticularis (as LENTIL)]

lentil /'lentɪl/ n. **1** a leguminous plant, Lens culinaris, yielding edible biconvex seeds. **2** this seed, esp. used as food with the husk removed. [ME f. OF lentille f. L lenticula (as LENS)]

lento /'lentəʊ/ adj. & adv. Mus. —adj. slow. —adv. slowly. [It.]

lentoid /'lentɔɪd/ adj. = LENTICULAR 1. [L lens (see LENS) + -OID]

Leo /'li:əʊ/ n. (pl. -os) **1** a constellation, traditionally regarded as contained in the figure of a lion. **2 a** the fifth sign of the zodiac (the Lion). **b** a person born when the sun is in this sign. [OE f. L, = LION]

Leonid /'li:ənɪd/ n. any of the meteors that seem to radiate from the direction of the constellation Leo. [L leo (see LEO) leonis + -ID[3]]

Leonine /'li:əˌnaɪn/ adj. & n. —adj. of Pope Leo; made or invented by Pope Leo. —n. (in pl.) leonine verse. □**Leonine City** the part of Rome round the Vatican fortified by Pope Leo IV. **leonine verse 1** medieval Latin verse in hexameter or elegiac metre with internal rhyme. **2** English verse with internal rhyme. [the name Leo (as LEONINE)]

leonine /'li:əˌnaɪn/ adj. **1** like a lion. **2** of or relating to lions. [ME f. OF leonin -ine or L leoninus f. leo leonis lion]

leopard /'lepəd/ n. (fem. **leopardess** /-dɪs/) **1** any large African or Asian flesh-eating cat, Panthera pardus, with either a black-spotted yellowish-fawn or all black coat. Also called PANTHER. **2** Heraldry a lion passant guardant as in the arms of England. **3** (attrib.) spotted like a leopard (leopard moth). □**leopard's bane** any plant of the genus Doronicum, with large yellow daisy-like flowers. [ME f. OF f. LL f. late Gk leopardos (as LION, PARD)]

leotard /'li:əˌtɑːd/ n. a close-fitting one-piece garment worn by ballet-dancers, acrobats, etc. [J. Léotard, French trapeze artist d. 1870]

leper /'lepə(r)/ n. **1** a person suffering from leprosy. **2** a person shunned on moral grounds. [ME, prob. attrib. use of leper leprosy f. OF lepre f. L lepra f. Gk, fem. of lepros scaly f. lepos scale]

lepidopterous /ˌlepɪ'dɒptərəs/ adj. of the order Lepidoptera of insects, with four scale-covered wings often brightly coloured, including butterflies and moths. □□ **lepidopteran** adj. & n. **lepidopterist** n. [Gk lepis -idos scale + pteron wing]

leporine /'lepəˌraɪn/ adj. of or like hares. [L leporinus f. lepus -oris hare]

leprechaun /'leprəˌkɔːn/ n. a small mischievous sprite in Irish folklore. [OIr. luchorpán f. lu small + corp body]

leprosy /'leprəsɪ/ n. **1** a contagious bacterial disease that affects the skin, mucous membranes, and nerves, causing disfigurement. Also called HANSEN's DISEASE. **2** moral corruption or contagion. [LEPROUS + -Y[3]]

leprous /'leprəs/ adj. **1** suffering from leprosy. **2** like or relating to leprosy. [ME f. OF f. LL leprosus f. lepra: see LEPER]

lepta pl. of LEPTON[1].

lepto- /'leptəʊ/ comb. form small, narrow. [Gk leptos fine, small, thin, delicate]

leptocephalic /ˌleptəsɪ'fælɪk/ adj. (also **leptocephalous** /-'sefələs/) narrow-skulled.

leptodactyl /ˌleptəʊˈdæktɪl/ *adj.* & *n.* —*adj.* having long slender toes. —*n.* a bird having these.

lepton[1] /ˈlept(ə)n/ *n.* (*pl.* **lepta** /-tə/) a Greek coin worth one-hundredth of a drachma. [Gk *lepton* (*nomisma* coin) neut. of *leptos* small]

lepton[2] /ˈlept(ə)n/ *n.* (*pl.* **leptons**) *Physics* any of a class of elementary particles which do not undergo strong interaction, e.g. an electron, muon, or neutrino. [LEPTO- + -ON]

leptospirosis /ˌleptəspɪˈrəʊsɪs/ *n.* an infectious disease caused by bacteria of the genus *Leptospira*, that occurs in rodents, dogs, and other mammals, and can be transmitted to man. [LEPTO- + SPIRO-[1] + -OSIS]

leptotene /ˈleptəˌtiːn/ *n.* *Biol.* the first stage of the prophase of meiosis in which each chromosome is apparent as two fine chromatids. [LEPTO- + Gk *tainia* band]

lesbian /ˈlezbɪən/ *n.* & *adj.* —*n.* a homosexual woman. —*adj.* **1** of homosexuality in women. **2** (**Lesbian**) of Lesbos. ◻◻ **lesbianism** *n.* [L *Lesbius* f. Gk *Lesbios* f. *Lesbos*, island in the Aegean Sea, home of Sappho (see SAPPHIC)]

lese-majesty /ˈliːz ˈmædʒɪstɪ/ *n.* (also **lèse-majesté** /leɪz ˈmæʒeˌsteɪ/) **1** treason. **2** an insult to a sovereign or ruler. **3** presumptuous conduct. [F *lèse-majesté* f. L *laesa majestas* injured sovereignty f. *laedere laesinjure* + *majestas* MAJESTY]

lesion /ˈliːʒ(ə)n/ *n.* **1** damage. **2** injury. **3** *Med.* a morbid change in the functioning or texture of an organ etc. [ME f. OF f. L *laesio -onis* f. *laedere laesinjure*]

less /les/ *adj.*, *adv.*, *n.*, & *prep.* —*adj.* **1** smaller in extent, degree, duration, number, etc. (*of less importance*; *in a less degree*). **2** of smaller quantity, not so much (opp. MORE) (*find less difficulty*; *eat less meat*). **3** *disp.* fewer (*eat less biscuits*). **4** of lower rank etc. (*no less a person than*; *James the Less*). —*adv.* to a smaller extent, in a lower degree. —*n.* a smaller amount or quantity or number (*cannot take less*; *for less than £10*; *is little less than disgraceful*). —*prep.* minus (*made £1,000 less tax*). ◻ **in less than no time** *joc.* very quickly or soon. **much** (or **still**) **less** with even greater force of denial (*do not suspect him of negligence, much less of dishonesty*). [OE *lǣssa* (adj.), *lǣs* (adv.), f. Gmc]

-less /lɪs/ *suffix* forming adjectives and adverbs: **1** from nouns, meaning 'not having, without, free from' (*doubtless*; *powerless*). **2** from verbs, meaning 'not affected by or doing the action of the verb' (*fathomless*; *tireless*). ◻◻ **-lessly** *suffix* forming adverbs. **-lessness** *suffix* forming nouns. [OE *-lēas* f. *lēas* devoid of]

lessee /leˈsiː/ *n.* (often foll. by *of*) a person who holds a property by lease. ◻◻ **lesseeship** *n.* [ME f. AF past part., OF *lessé* (as LEASE)]

lessen /ˈles(ə)n/ *v.tr.* & *intr.* make or become less, diminish.

lesser /ˈlesə(r)/ *adj.* (usu. *attrib.*) not so great as the other or the rest (*the lesser evil*; *the lesser celandine*). [double compar., f. LESS + -ER[3]]

lesson /ˈles(ə)n/ *n.* & *v.* —*n.* **1 a** an amount of teaching given at one time. **b** the time assigned to this. **2** (in *pl.*; foll. by *in*) systematic instruction (*gives lessons in dancing*; *took lessons in French*). **3** a thing learnt or to be learnt by a pupil. **4 a** an occurrence, example, rebuke, or punishment, that serves or should serve to warn or encourage (*let that be a lesson to you*). **b** a thing inculcated by experience or study. **5** a passage from the Bible read aloud during a church service, esp. either of two readings at morning and evening prayer in the Church of England. —*v.tr. archaic* **1** instruct. **2** admonish, rebuke. ◻ **learn one's lesson** profit from or bear in mind a particular (usu. unpleasant) experience. **teach a person a lesson** punish a person, esp. as a deterrent. [ME f. OF *leçon* f. L *lectio -onis*: see LECTION]

lessor /leˈsɔː(r)/ *n.* a person who lets a property by lease. [AF f. *lesser*: see LEASE]

lest /lest/ *conj.* **1** in order that not, for fear that (*lest we forget*). **2** that (*afraid lest we should be late*). [OE *thȳ lǣs the* whereby less that, later *the lǣste*, ME *lest(e)*]

let[1] /let/ *v.* & *n.* —*v.* (**letting**; *past* and *past part.* **let**) **1** *tr.* **a** allow to, not prevent or forbid (*we let them go*). **b** cause to (*let me know*; *let it be known*). **2** *tr.* (foll. by *into*) **a** allow to enter. **b** make acquainted with (a secret etc.). **c** inlay in. **3** *tr. Brit.* grant the use of (rooms, land, etc.) for rent or hire (*was let to the new tenant for a year*). **4** *tr.* allow or cause (liquid or air) to escape (*let blood*). **5** *tr.* award (a contract for work). **6** *aux.* supplying the first and third persons of the imperative in exhortations (*let us pray*), commands (*let it be done at once*; *let there be light*), assumptions (*let AB be equal to CD*), and permission or challenge (*let him do his worst*). —*n. Brit.* the act or an instance of letting a house, room, etc. (*a long let*). ◻ **let alone 1** not to mention, far less or more (*hasn't got a television, let alone a video*). **2** = *let be*. **let be** not interfere with, attend to, or do. **let down 1** lower. **2** fail to support or satisfy, disappoint. **3** lengthen (a garment). **4** deflate (a tyre). **let-down** *n.* a disappointment. **let down gently** avoid humiliating abruptly. **let drop** (or **fall**) **1** drop (esp. a word or hint) intentionally or by accident. **2** (foll. by *on, upon, to*) *Geom.* draw (a perpendicular) from an outside point to a line. **let fly 1** (often foll. by *at*) attack physically or verbally. **2** discharge (a missile). **let go 1** release, set at liberty. **2 a** (often foll. by *of*) lose or relinquish one's hold. **b** lose hold of. **3** cease to think or talk about. **let oneself go 1** give way to enthusiasm, impulse, etc. **2** cease to take trouble, neglect one's appearance or habits. **let in 1** allow to enter (*let the dog in*; *let in a flood of light*; *this would let in all sorts of evils*). **2** (usu. foll. by *for*) involve (a person, often oneself) in loss or difficulty. **3** (foll. by *on*) allow (a person) to share privileges, information, etc. **4** inlay (a thing) in another. **let oneself in** enter a building by means of a latchkey. **let loose** release or unchain (a dog, fury, a maniac, etc.). **let me see** see SEE[1]. **let off 1 a** fire (a gun). **b** explode (a bomb or firework). **2** allow or cause (steam, liquid, etc.) to escape. **3** allow to alight from a vehicle etc. **4 a** not punish or compel. **b** (foll. by *with*) punish lightly. **5** *Brit.* let (part of a house etc.). **let-off** *n.* being allowed to escape something. **let off steam** see STEAM. **let on** *colloq.* **1** reveal a secret. **2** pretend (*let on that he had succeeded*). **let out 1** allow to go out, esp. through a doorway. **2** release from restraint. **3** (often foll. by *that* + clause) reveal (a secret etc.). **4** make (a garment) looser esp. by adjustment at a seam. **5** put out to rent esp. to several tenants, or to contract. **6** exculpate. **let-out** *n. colloq.* an opportunity to escape. **let rip** see RIP[1]. **let slip** see SLIP[1]. **let through** allow to pass. **let up** *colloq.* **1** become less intense or severe. **2** relax one's efforts. **let-up** *n. colloq.* **1** a reduction in intensity. **2** a relaxation of effort. **to let** available for rent. [OE *lǣtan* f. Gmc, rel. to LATE]

let[2] /let/ *n.* & *v.* —*n.* **1** (in lawn tennis, squash, etc.) an obstruction of a ball or a player in certain ways, requiring the ball to be served again. **2** (*archaic* except in **without let or hindrance**) obstruction, hindrance. —*v.tr.* (**letting**; *past* and *past part.* **letted** or **let**) *archaic* hinder, obstruct. [OE *lettan* f. Gmc, rel. to LATE]

-let /lɪt, lət/ *suffix* forming nouns, usu. diminutives (*flatlet*; *leaflet*) or denoting articles of ornament or dress (*anklet*). [orig. corresp. (in *bracelet, crosslet*, etc.) to F *-ette* added to nouns in *-el*]

lethal /ˈliːθ(ə)l/ *adj.* causing or sufficient to cause death. ◻ **lethal chamber** a chamber in which animals may be killed painlessly with gas. **lethal dose** the amount of a toxic compound or drug that causes death in humans or animals. ◻◻ **lethality** /lɪˈθælɪtɪ/ *n.* **lethally** *adv.* [L *let(h)alis* f. *letum* death]

lethargy /ˈleθədʒɪ/ *n.* **1** lack of energy or vitality; a torpid, inert, or apathetic state. **2** *Med.* morbid

drowsiness or prolonged and unnatural sleep. ▢▢
lethargic /lɪˈθɑːdʒɪk/ *adj.* **lethargically** /lɪ
ˈθɑːdʒɪkəlɪ/ *adv.* [ME f. OF *litargie* f. LL *lethargia* f. Gk
lēthargia f. *lēthargos* forgetful f. *lēth-, lanthanomai*
forget]
Lethe /ˈliːθiː/ *n.* **1** (in Greek mythology) a river in
Hades producing forgetfulness of the past. **2** such
forgetfulness. ▢▢ **Lethean** /liːˈθiːən/ *adj.* [L, use of Gk
lēthē forgetfulness (as LETHARGY)]
let's /lets/ *contr.* let us (*let's go now*).
Lett /let/ *n. archaic* = LATVIAN *n.* [G *Lette* f. Lettish
Latvi]
letter /ˈletə(r)/ *n. & v.* —*n.* **1 a** a character representing one or more of the simple or compound
sounds used in speech, any of the alphabetic symbols.
b (in *pl.*) *colloq.* the initials of a degree etc. after the
holder's name. **c** *US* a school or college initial as a
mark of proficiency in games etc. **2 a** a written,
typed, or printed communication, usu. sent by post
or messenger. **b** (in *pl.*) an addressed legal or formal
document for any of various purposes. **3** the precise
terms of a statement, the strict verbal interpretation
(opp. SPIRIT *n.* 6) (*according to the letter of the law*). **4**
(in *pl.*) **a** literature. **b** acquaintance with books,
erudition. **c** authorship (*the profession of letters*). **5**
Printing **a** types collectively. **b** a fount of type. —*v.*
tr. **1 a** inscribe letters on. **b** impress a title etc. on
(a book-cover). **2** classify with letters. ▢**letter-bomb**
a terrorist explosive device in the form of a posted
packet. **letter-box** esp. *Brit.* a box or slot into which
letters are posted or delivered. **letter-card** a folded
card with a gummed edge for posting as a letter.
letter-heading = LETTERHEAD. **letter of comfort**
an assurance about a debt, short of a legal guarantee,
given to a bank by a third party. **letter of credence**
see CREDENCE. **letter of credit** see CREDIT.
letter-perfect *Theatr.* knowing one's part perfectly.
letter-quality of the quality of printing suitable for
a business letter; producing print of this quality. **letters missive** see MISSIVE. **letters of
administration** authority to administer the estate of
an intestate. **letters of marque** see MARQUE[2]. **letters
patent** see PATENT. **letter-writer 1** a person who
writes letters. **2** a book giving guidance on writing
letters. **man of letters** a scholar or author. **to the
letter** with adherence to every detail. ▢▢ **letterer**
n. **letterless** *adj.* [ME f. OF *lettre* f. L *litera, littera*
letter of alphabet, (in pl.) epistle, literature]
lettered /ˈletəd/ *adj.* well read or educated.
letterhead /ˈletəˌhed/ *n.* **1** a printed heading on
stationery. **2** stationery with this.
lettering /ˈletərɪŋ/ *n.* **1** the process of inscribing
letters. **2** letters inscribed.
letterpress /ˈletəˌpres/ *n.* **1 a** the contents of an
illustrated book other than the illustrations. **b**
printed matter relating to illustrations. **2** printing
from raised type, not from lithography or other
planographic processes.
Lettic /ˈletɪk/ *adj. & n. archaic* —*adj.* **1** = LATVIAN
adj. **2** of or relating to the Baltic branch of languages.
—*n.* = LATVIAN *n.* 2.
Lettish /ˈletɪʃ/ *adj. & n. archaic* = LATVIAN.
lettuce /ˈletɪs/ *n.* **1** a composite plant, *Lactuca sativa*,
with crisp edible leaves used in salads. **2** any of
various plants resembling this. [ME *letus(e)*, rel. to
OF *laituë* f. L *lactuca* f. *lac lactis* milk, with ref. to its
milky juice]
leu /ˈleruː/ *n.* (*pl.* **lei** /leɪ/) the basic monetary unit of
Romania. [Romanian, = lion]
leucine /ˈluːsiːn/ *n. Biochem.* an amino acid present
in protein and essential in the diet of vertebrates. [F
f. Gk *leukos* white + -IN]
leuco- /ˈluːkəʊ/ *comb. form* white. [Gk *leukos* white]
leucocyte /ˈluːkəˌsaɪt/ *n.* (also **leukocyte**) **1** a white
blood cell. **2** any blood cell that contains a nucleus.
▢▢ **leucocytic** /-ˈsɪtɪk/ *adj.*
leucoma /luːˈkəʊmə/ *n.* a white opacity in the cornea
of the eye.

leucorrhoea /ˌluːkəˈriːə/ *n.* a whitish or yellowish
discharge of mucus from the vagina.
leucotomy /luːˈkɒtəmɪ/ *n.* (*pl.* **-ies**) the surgical
lesions of white nerve fibres within the brain, formerly used in psychosurgery.
leukaemia /luːˈkiːmɪə/ *n.* (*US* **leukemia**) *Med.* any
of a group of malignant diseases in which the
bone-marrow and other blood-forming organs produce increased numbers of leucocytes. ▢▢
leukaemic *adj.* [mod.L f. G *Leukämie* f. Gk *leukos*
white + *haima* blood]
leukocyte var. of LEUCOCYTE.
Lev. *abbr.* Leviticus (Old Testament).
Levant /lɪˈvænt/ *n.* (prec. by *the*) the eastern part of
the Mediterranean with its islands and neighbouring
countries. ▢**Levant morocco** high-grade large-
grained morocco leather. [F, pres. part. of *lever* rise,
used as noun = point of sunrise, east]
levant /lɪˈvænt/ *v.intr. Brit.* abscond or bolt, esp.
with betting or gaming losses unpaid. [perh. f.
LEVANT]
levanter[1] /lɪˈvæntə(r)/ *n.* **1** a strong easterly Mediterranean wind. **2** (**Levanter**) a native or inhabitant of the Levant in the eastern Mediterranean.
levanter[2] /lɪˈvæntə(r)/ *n.* a person who levants.
Levantine /lɪˈvæntaɪn, ˈlevən-/ *adj. & n.* —*adj.* of or
trading to the Levant. —*n.* a native or inhabitant of
the Levant.
levator /lɪˈveɪtə(r)/ *n.* a muscle that lifts the structure
into which it is inserted. [L, = one who lifts f. *levare*
raise]
levee[1] /ˈlevɪ/ *n.* **1** *archaic* or *US* an assembly of
visitors or guests, esp. at a formal reception. **2** *hist.*
(in the UK) an assembly held by the sovereign or
sovereign's representative at which men only were
received. **3** *hist.* a reception of visitors on rising from
bed. [F *levé* var. of *lever* rising f. *lever* to rise: see
LEVY]
levee[2] /ˈlevɪ, lɪˈviː/ *n. US* **1** an embankment against
river floods. **2** a natural embankment built up by a
river. **3** a landing-place, a quay. [F *levée* fem. past
part. of *lever* raise: see LEVY]
level /ˈlev(ə)l/ *n., adj., & v.* —*n.* **1** a horizontal line
or plane. **2** a height or value reached, a position on a
real or imaginary scale (*eye level; sugar level in the
blood; danger level*). **3** a social, moral, or intellectual
standard. **4** a plane of rank or authority (*discussions
at Cabinet level*). **5 a** an instrument giving a line
parallel to the plane of the horizon for testing
whether things are horizontal. **b** *Surveying* an instrument for giving a horizontal line of sight. **6** a
more or less level surface. **7** a flat tract of land.
—*adj.* **1** having a flat and even surface; not bumpy.
2 horizontal; perpendicular to the plumb-line. **3**
(often foll. by *with*) **a** on the same horizontal plane
as something else. **b** having equality with something
else. **c** (of a spoonful etc.) with the contents flat with
the brim. **4** even, uniform, equable, or well-balanced
in quality, style, temper, judgement, etc. **5** (of a race)
having the leading competitors close together. —*v.*
(**levelled, levelling**; *US* **leveled, leveling**) **1** *tr.*
make level, even, or uniform. **2** *tr.* (often foll. by *to*
(or *with*) *the ground, in the dust*) raze or demolish. **3**
tr. (also *absol.*) aim (a missile or gun). **4** *tr.* (also
absol.; foll. by *at, against*) direct (an accusation,
criticism, or satire). **5** *tr.* abolish (distinctions). **6**
intr. (usu. foll. by *with*) *sl.* be frank or honest. **7** *tr.*
place on the same level. **8** *tr.* (also *absol.*) *Surveying*
ascertain differences in the height of (land). ▢**do
one's level best** *colloq.* do one's utmost; make all
possible efforts. **find one's level 1** reach the right
social, intellectual, etc. place in relation to others. **2**
(of a liquid) reach the same height in receptacles or
regions which communicate with each other. **level
crossing** *Brit.* a crossing of a railway and a road, or
two railways, at the same level. **level down** bring
down to a standard. **levelling-screw** a screw for
adjusting parts of a machine etc. to an exact level.

level off make or become level or smooth. **level out** make or become level, remove differences from. **level pegging** *Brit.* equality of scores or achievements. **level up** bring up to a standard. **on the level** *colloq. adv.* honestly, without deception. —*adj.* honest, truthful. **on a level with 1** in the same horizontal plane as. **2** equal with. □□ **levelly** *adv.* **levelness** *n.* [ME f. OF *livel* ult. f. L *libella* dimin. of *libra* scales, balance]

level-headed /ˌlev(ə)l'hedɪd/ *adj.* mentally well-balanced, cool, sensible. □□ **level-headedly** *adv.* **level-headedness** *n.*

leveller /'levələ(r)/ *n.* (*US* **leveler**) **1** a person who advocates the abolition of social distinctions. **2** (**Leveller**) *hist.* an extreme radical dissenter in 17th-c. England. **3** a person or thing that levels.

lever /'liːvə(r)/ *n. & v.* —*n.* **1** a bar resting on a pivot, used to help lift a heavy or firmly fixed object. **2** *Mech.* a simple machine consisting of a rigid bar pivoted about a fulcrum (fixed point) which can be acted upon by a force (effort) in order to move a load. **3** a projecting handle moved to operate a mechanism. **4** a means of exerting moral pressure. —*v.* **1** *intr.* use a lever. **2** *tr.* (often foll. by *away, out, up,* etc.) lift, move, or act on with a lever. □ **lever escapement** a mechanism connecting the escape wheel and the balance wheel using two levers. **lever watch** a watch with a lever escapement. [ME f. OF *levier, leveor* f. *lever* raise: see LEVY]

leverage /'liːvərɪdʒ/ *n.* **1** the action of a lever; a way of applying a lever. **2** the power of a lever; the mechanical advantage gained by use of a lever. **3** a means of accomplishing a purpose; power, influence. **4** a set or system of levers. **5** *US Commerce* gearing. □ **leveraged buyout** esp. *US* the buyout of a company by its management using outside capital.

leveret /'levərɪt/ *n.* a young hare, esp. one in its first year. [ME f. AF, dimin. of *levre,* OF *lievre* f. L *lepus leporis* hare]

leviable see LEVY.

leviathan /lɪ'vaɪəθ(ə)n/ *n.* **1** *Bibl.* a sea-monster. **2** anything very large or powerful, esp. a ship. **3** an autocratic monarch or State (in allusion to a book by Hobbes, 1651). [ME f. LL f. Heb. *liwyāṭān*]

levigate /'leviˌgeɪt/ *v.tr.* **1** reduce to a fine smooth powder. **2** make a smooth paste of. □□ **levigation** /-'geɪʃ(ə)n/ *n.* [L *levigare levigat-* f. *levis* smooth]

levin /'levɪn/ *n. archaic* **1** lightning. **2** a flash of lightning. [ME *leven(e),* prob. f. ON]

levirate /'liːvɪrət, 'lev-/ *n.* a custom of the ancient Jews and some other peoples by which a man is obliged to marry his brother's widow. □□ **leviratic** /-'rætɪk/ *adj.* **leviratical** /-'rætɪk(ə)l/ *adj.* [L *levir* brother-in-law + -ATE[1]]

Levis /'liːvaɪz/ *n.pl. propr.* a type of (orig. blue) denim jeans or overalls reinforced with rivets. [*Levi* Strauss, orig. US manufacturer in 1860s]

levitate /'levɪˌteɪt/ *v.* **1** *intr.* rise and float in the air (esp. with reference to spiritualism). **2** *tr.* cause to do this. □□ **levitation** /-'teɪʃ(ə)n/ *n.* **levitator** *n.* [L *levis* light, after GRAVITATE]

Levite /'liːvaɪt/ *n.* a member of the tribe of Levi, esp. of that part of it which provided assistants to the priests in the worship in the Jewish temple. [ME f. LL *levita* f. Gk *leuitēs* f. *Leui* f. Heb. *lēwi* Levi]

Levitical /lɪ'vɪtɪk(ə)l/ *adj.* **1** of the Levites or the tribe of Levi. **2** of the Levites' ritual. **3** of Leviticus. [LL *leviticus* f. Gk *leuitikos* (as LEVITE)]

levity /'levɪtɪ/ *n.* **1** lack of serious thought, frivolity, unbecoming jocularity. **2** inconstancy. **3** undignified behaviour. **4** *archaic* lightness of weight. [L *levitas* f. *levis* light]

levo- *US* var. of LAEVO-.

levodopa /ˌliːvə'dəupə/ *n.* laevorotatory dopa.

levulose *US* var. of LAEVULOSE.

levy /'levɪ/ *v. & n.* —*v.tr.* (-ies, -ied) **1 a** impose (a rate or toll). **b** raise (contributions or taxes). **c** (also *absol.*) raise (a sum of money) by legal execution or

process (*the debt was levied on the debtor's goods*). **d** seize (goods) in this way. **e** extort (*levy blackmail*). **2** enlist or enrol (troops etc.). **3** (usu. foll. by *upon, against*) wage, proceed to make (war). —*n.* (*pl.* -ies) **1 a** the collecting of a contribution, tax, etc., or of property to satisfy a legal judgement. **b** a contribution, tax, etc., levied. **2 a** the act or an instance of enrolling troops etc. **b** (in *pl.*) men enrolled. **c** a body of men enrolled. **d** the number of men enrolled. □□ **leviable** *adj.* [ME f. OF *levee* fem. past part. of *lever* f. L *levare* raise f. *levis* light]

lewd /ljuːd/ *adj.* **1** lascivious. **2** indecent, obscene. □□ **lewdly** *adv.* **lewdness** *n.* [OE *lǣwede* LAY[2], of unkn. orig.]

lewis /'luːɪs/ *n.* an iron contrivance for gripping heavy blocks of stone or concrete for lifting. [18th c.: orig. unkn.]

Lewis gun /'luːɪs/ *n.* a light machine-gun with a magazine, air cooling, and operation by gas from its own firing. [I. N. *Lewis,* Amer. soldier d. 1931, its inventor]

lewisite /'luːɪˌsaɪt/ *n.* an irritant gas that produces blisters, developed for use in chemical warfare. [W. L. *Lewis,* Amer. chemist d. 1943 + -ITE[1]]

lex domicilii /ˌleks dɒmɪ'sɪlɪˌaɪ/ *n. Law* the law of the country in which a person is domiciled. [L]

lexeme /'leksiːm/ *n. Linguistics* a basic lexical unit of a language comprising one or several words, the elements of which do not separately convey the meaning of the whole. [LEXICON + -EME]

lex fori /leks 'fɔːraɪ/ *n. Law* the law of the country in which an action is brought. [L]

lexical /'leksɪk(ə)l/ *adj.* **1** of the words of a language. **2** of or as of a lexicon. □□ **lexically** *adv.* [Gk *lexikos, lexikon:* see LEXICON]

lexicography /ˌleksɪ'kɒgrəfɪ/ *n.* the compiling of dictionaries. □□ **lexicographer** *n.* **lexicographic** /-kə'græfɪk/ *adj.* **lexicographical** /-kə'græfɪk(ə)l/ *adj.* **lexicographically** /-kə'græfɪkəlɪ/ *adv.*

lexicology /ˌleksɪ'kɒlədʒɪ/ *n.* the study of the form, history, and meaning of words. □□ **lexicological** /-kə'lɒdʒɪk(ə)l/ *adj.* **lexicologically** /-kə'lɒdʒɪkəlɪ/ *adv.* **lexicologist** *n.*

lexicon /'leksɪkən/ *n.* **1** a dictionary, esp. of Greek, Hebrew, Syriac, or Arabic. **2** the vocabulary of a person, language, branch of knowledge, etc. [mod.L f. Gk *lexikon* (*biblion* book), neut. of *lexikos* f. *lexis* word f. *legō* speak]

lexigraphy /lek'sɪgrəfɪ/ *n.* a system of writing in which each character represents a word. [Gk *lexis* (see LEXICON) + -GRAPHY]

lexis /'leksɪs/ *n.* **1** words, vocabulary. **2** the total stock of words in a language. [Gk: see LEXICON]

lex loci /leks 'ləusaɪ/ *n. Law* the law of the country in which a transaction is performed, a tort is committed, or a property is situated. [L]

lex talionis /ˌleks tælɪ'əunɪs/ *n.* the law of retaliation, whereby a punishment resembles the offence committed, in kind and degree. [L]

ley[1] /leɪ/ *n.* a field temporarily under grass. □ **ley farming** alternate growing of crops and grass. [ME (orig. adj.), perh. f. OE, rel. to LAY[1], LIE[1]]

ley[2] /liː, leɪ/ *n.* the supposed straight line of a prehistoric track, usu. between hilltops. [var. of LEA]

Leyden jar /'laɪd(ə)n/ *n.* an early form of capacitor consisting of a glass jar with layers of metal foil on the outside and inside. [*Leyden* (now *Leiden*) in Holland, where it was invented (1745)]

LF *abbr.* low frequency.

LH *abbr. Biochem.* luteinizing hormone.

l.h. *abbr.* left hand.

LI *abbr.* **1** Light Infantry. **2** *US* Long Island.

Li *symb. Chem.* the element lithium.

liability /ˌlaɪə'bɪlɪtɪ/ *n.* (*pl.* -ies) **1** the state of being liable. **2** a person or thing that is troublesome as an unwelcome responsibility; a handicap. **3** what a person is liable for, esp. (in *pl.*) debts or pecuniary obligations.

---

w *we*   z *zoo*   ʃ *she*   ʒ *decision*   θ *thin*   ð *this*   ŋ *ring*   x *loch*   tʃ *chip*   dʒ *jar*   (*see over for vowels*)

liable /ˈlaɪəb(ə)l/ *predic.adj.* **1** legally bound. **2** (foll. by *to*) subject to (a tax or penalty). **3** (foll. by *to* + infin.) under an obligation. **4** (foll. by *to*) exposed or open to (something undesirable). **5** (foll. by *to* + infin.) *disp.* apt, likely (*it is liable to rain*). **6** (foll. by *for*) answerable. [ME perh. f. AF f. OF *lier* f. L *ligare* bind]

liaise /lɪˈeɪz/ *v.intr.* (foll. by *with, between*) *colloq.* establish cooperation, act as a link. [back-form. f. LIAISON]

liaison /lɪˈeɪzɒn/ *n.* **1** communication or cooperation, esp. between military forces or units. **2** an illicit sexual relationship. **3** the binding or thickening agent of a sauce. **4** the sounding of an ordinarily silent final consonant before a word beginning with a vowel (or a mute *h* in French). □**liaison officer** an officer acting as a link between allied forces or units of the same force. [F f. *lier* bind f. L *ligare*]

liana /lɪˈɑːnə/ *n.* (also **liane** /-ˈɑːn/) any of several climbing and twining plants of tropical forests. [F *liane, lierne* clematis, of uncert. orig.]

liar /ˈlaɪə(r)/ *n.* a person who tells a lie or lies, esp. habitually. □**liar dice** a game with poker dice in which the result of a throw may be announced falsely. [OE *lēogere* (as LIE², -AR⁴)]

lias /ˈlaɪəs/ *n.* **1** (Lias) *Geol.* the lower strata of the Jurassic system of rocks, consisting of shales and limestones rich in fossils. **2** a blue limestone rock found in SW England. □□**liassic** /laɪˈæsɪk/ *adj.* (in sense 1). [ME f. OF *liois* hard limestone, prob. f. Gmc]

Lib. *abbr.* Liberal.

lib /lɪb/ *n. colloq.* liberation (*women's lib*). [abbr.]

libation /laɪˈbeɪʃ(ə)n, lɪ-/ *n.* **1 a** the pouring out of a drink-offering to a god. **b** such a drink-offering. **2** *joc.* a potation. [ME f. L *libatio* f. *libare* pour as offering]

libber /ˈlɪbə(r)/ *n. colloq.* an advocate of women's liberation.

libel /ˈlaɪb(ə)l/ *n. & v.* —*n.* **1** *Law* **a** a published false statement damaging to a person's reputation (cf. SLANDER). **b** the act of publishing this. **2 a** a false and defamatory written statement. **b** (foll. by *on*) a thing that brings discredit by misrepresentation etc. (*the portrait is a libel on him; the book is a libel on human nature*). **3 a** (in civil and ecclesiastical law) the plaintiff's written declaration. **b** *Sc. Law* a statement of the grounds of a charge. **4** (in full **public libel**) *Law* the publication of a libel that also involves the criminal law. —*v.tr.* (**libelled, libelling**; *US* **libeled, libeling**) **1** defame by libellous statements. **2** accuse falsely and maliciously. **3** *Law* publish a libel against. **4** (in ecclesiastical law) bring a suit against. □**criminal libel** *Law* a deliberate defamatory statement in a permanent form. □□**libeller** *n.* [ME f. OF f. L *libellus* dimin. of *liber* book]

libellous /ˈlaɪbələs/ *adj.* containing or constituting a libel. □□**libellously** *adv.*

liber /ˈlaɪbə(r)/ *n.* bast. [L, = bark]

liberal /ˈlɪbər(ə)l/ *adj. & n.* —*adj.* **1** given freely; ample, abundant. **2** (often foll. by *of*) giving freely, generous, not sparing. **3** open-minded, not prejudiced. **4** not strict or rigorous; (of interpretation) not literal. **5** for general broadening of the mind, not professional or technical (*liberal studies*). **6 a** favouring individual liberty, free trade, and moderate political and social reform. **b** (**Liberal**) of or characteristic of Liberals or a Liberal Party. **7** *Theol.* regarding many traditional beliefs as dispensable, invalidated by modern thought, or liable to change (*liberal Protestant; liberal Judaism*). —*n.* **1** a person of liberal views. **2** (**Liberal**) a supporter or member of a Liberal Party. □**liberal arts 1** *US* the arts as distinct from science and technology. **2** *hist.* the medieval trivium and quadrivium. **Liberal Democrat** (in the UK) a member of a party (formerly the *Social and Liberal Democrats*) formed from the Liberal Party and members of the Social Democratic Party. **Liberal Party** a political party advocating liberal policies. ¶In the UK the name was discontinued in official use in 1988, when the party regrouped with others to form the Social and Liberal Democrats (see *Liberal Democrat*). □□**liberalism** *n.* **liberalist** *n.* **liberalistic** /-ˈlɪstɪk/ *adj.* **liberally** *adv.* **liberalness** *n.* [ME, orig. = befitting a free man, f. OF f. L *liberalis* f. *liber* free (man)]

liberality /ˌlɪbəˈrælɪtɪ/ *n.* **1** free giving, munificence. **2** freedom from prejudice, breadth of mind. [ME f. OF *liberalite* or L *liberalitas* (as LIBERAL)]

liberalize /ˈlɪbərəˌlaɪz/ *v.tr. & intr.* (also **-ise**) make or become more liberal or less strict. □□**liberalization** /-ˈzeɪʃ(ə)n/ *n.* **liberalizer** *n.*

liberate /ˈlɪbəˌreɪt/ *v.tr.* **1** (often foll. by *from*) set at liberty, set free. **2** free (a country etc.) from an oppressor or an enemy occupation. **3** (often as **liberated** *adj.*) free (a person) from rigid social conventions, esp. in sexual behaviour. **4** *sl.* steal. **5** *Chem.* release (esp. a gas) from a state of combination. □□**liberator** *n.* [L *liberare liberat-* f. *liber* free]

liberation /ˌlɪbəˈreɪʃ(ə)n/ *n.* the act or an instance of liberating; the state of being liberated. □**liberation theology** a theory which interprets liberation from social, political, and economic oppression as an anticipation of ultimate salvation. □□**liberationist** *n.* [ME f. L *liberatio* f. *liberare*: see LIBERATE]

libertarian /ˌlɪbəˈteərɪən/ *n. & adj.* —*n.* **1** an advocate of liberty. **2** a believer in free will (opp. NECESSITARIAN). —*adj.* believing in free will. □□**libertarianism** *n.*

libertine /ˈlɪbəˌtiːn, -tɪn, -ˌtaɪn/ *n. & adj.* —*n.* **1** a dissolute or licentious person. **2** a free thinker on religion. **3** a person who follows his or her own inclinations. —*adj.* **1** licentious, dissolute. **2** free-thinking. **3** following one's own inclinations. □□**libertinage** *n.* **libertinism** *n.* [L *libertinus* freedman f. *libertus* made free f. *liber* free]

liberty /ˈlɪbətɪ/ *n.* (*pl.* **-ies**) **1 a** freedom from captivity, imprisonment, slavery, or despotic control. **b** a personification of this. **2 a** the right or power to do as one pleases. **b** (foll. by *to* + infin.) right, power, opportunity, permission. **c** *Philos.* freedom from control by fate or necessity. **3 a** (usu. in *pl.*) a right, privilege, or immunity, enjoyed by prescription or grant. **b** (in *sing.* or *pl.*) *hist.* an area having such privileges etc., esp. a district controlled by a city though outside its boundary or an area outside a prison where some prisoners might reside. **4** setting aside of rules or convention. □**at liberty 1** free, not imprisoned (*set at liberty*). **2** (foll. by *to* + infin.) entitled, permitted. **3** available, disengaged. **Liberty Bell** (in the US) a bell in Philadelphia rung at the adoption of the Declaration of Independence. **liberty boat** *Brit. Naut.* a boat carrying liberty men. **liberty bodice** a close-fitting under-bodice. **liberty hall** a place where one may do as one likes. **liberty horse** a horse performing in a circus without a rider. **liberty man** *Brit. Naut.* a sailor with leave to go ashore. **liberty of the subject** the rights of a subject under constitutional rule. **Liberty ship** *hist.* a prefabricated US-built freighter of the war of 1939–45. **take liberties 1** (often foll. by *with*) behave in an unduly familiar manner. **2** (foll. by *with*) deal freely or superficially with rules or facts. **take the liberty** (foll. by *to* + infin., or *of* + verbal noun) presume, venture. [ME f. OF *liberté* f. L *libertas -tatis* f. *liber* free]

libidinous /lɪˈbɪdɪnəs/ *adj.* lustful. □□**libidinously** *adv.* **libidinousness** *n.* [ME f. L *libidinosus* f. *libido -dinis* lust]

libido /lɪˈbiːdəʊ, lɪˈbaɪdəʊ/ *n.* (*pl.* **-os**) *Psychol.* psychic drive or energy, esp. that associated with sexual desire. □□**libidinal** /lɪˈbɪdɪn(ə)l/ *adj.* **libidinally** *adv.* [L: see LIBIDINOUS]

Lib-Lab /lɪbˈlæb, ˈlɪb-/ *adj. Brit. hist.* Liberal and Labour. [abbr.]

Libra /'liːbrə, 'lɪb-, 'laɪb-/ *n.* **1** a constellation, traditionally regarded as contained in the figure of scales. **2 a** the seventh sign of the zodiac (the Balance or Scales). **b** a person born when the sun is in this sign. □□ **Libran** *n.* & *adj.* [ME f. L, orig. = pound weight]

librarian /laɪˈbreərɪən/ *n.* a person in charge of, or an assistant in, a library. □□ **librarianship** *n.* [L *librarius*: see LIBRARY]

library /'laɪbrərɪ/ *n.* (*pl.* **-ies**) **1 a** a collection of books etc. for use by the public or by members of a group. **b** a person's collection of books. **2** a room or building containing a collection of books (for reading or reference rather than for sale). **3 a** a similar collection of films, records, computer routines, etc. **b** the place where these are kept. **4** a series of books issued by a publisher in similar bindings etc., usu. as a set. **5** a public institution charged with the care of a collection of books, films, etc. □ **library edition** a strongly bound edition. **library school** a college or a department in a university or polytechnic teaching librarianship. **library science** the study of librarianship. [ME f. OF *librairie* f. L *libraria* (*taberna* shop), fem. of *librarius* bookseller's, of books, f. *liber libri* book]

libration /laɪˈbreɪʃ(ə)n/ *n.* an apparent oscillation of a heavenly body, esp. the moon, by which the parts near the edge of the disc are alternately in view and out of view. [L *libratio* f. *librare* f. *libra* balance]

libretto /lɪˈbretəʊ/ *n.* (*pl.* **libretti** /-tɪ/ or **-os**) the text of an opera or other long musical vocal work. □□ **librettist** *n.* [It., dimin. of *libro* book f. L *liber libri*]

Librium /'lɪbrɪəm/ *n. propr.* a white crystalline drug used as a tranquillizer.

Libyan /'lɪbɪən, 'lɪbjən/ *adj.* & *n.* —*adj.* **1** of or relating to modern Libya in N. Africa. **2** of ancient N. Africa west of Egypt. **3** of or relating to the Berber group of languages. —*n.* **1 a** a native or national of modern Libya. **b** a person of Libyan descent. **2** an ancient language of the Berber group.

lice *pl.* of LOUSE.

licence /'laɪs(ə)ns/ *n.* (*US* **license**) **1** a permit from an authority to own or use something (esp. a dog, gun, television set, or vehicle), do something (esp. marry, print something, preach, or drive on a public road), or carry on a trade (esp. in alcoholic liquor). **2** leave, permission (*have I your licence to remove the fence?*). **3 a** liberty of action, esp. when excessive; disregard of law or propriety, abuse of freedom. **b** licentiousness. **4** a writer's or artist's irregularity in grammar, metre, perspective, etc., or deviation from fact, esp. for effect (*poetic licence*). **5** a university certificate of competence in a faculty. □ **license plate** *US* the number plate of a licensed vehicle. [ME f. OF f. L *licentia* f. *licēre* be lawful: *-se* by confusion with LICENSE]

license /'laɪs(ə)ns/ *v.tr.* (also **licence**) **1** grant a licence to (a person). **2** authorize the use of (premises) for a certain purpose, esp. the sale and consumption of alcoholic liquor. **3** authorize the publication of (a book etc.) or the performance of (a play). **4** *archaic* allow. □ **licensed victualler** see VICTUALLER. □□ **licensable** *adj.* **licenser** *n.* **licensor** *n.* [ME f. LICENCE: *-se* on analogy of the verbs PRACTISE, PROPHESY, perh. after ADVISE, where the sound differs from the corresp. noun]

licensee /ˌlaɪsənˈsiː/ *n.* the holder of a licence, esp. to sell alcoholic liquor.

licentiate /laɪˈsenʃɪət, -ʃət/ *n.* **1** a holder of a certificate of competence to practise a certain profession, or of a university licence. **2** a licensed preacher not yet having an appointment, esp. in a Presbyterian church. [ME f. med.L *licentiatus* past part. of *licentiare* f. L *licentia*: see LICENCE]

licentious /laɪˈsenʃəs/ *adj.* **1** immoral in sexual relations. **2** *archaic* disregarding accepted rules or conventions. □□ **licentiously** *adv.* **licentiousness** *n.* [L *licentiosus* f. *licentia*: see LICENCE]

lichee var. of LYCHEE.

lichen /'laɪkən, 'lɪtʃ(ə)n/ *n.* **1** any plant organism of the group Lichenes, composed of a fungus and an alga in symbiotic association, usu. of green, grey, or yellow tint and growing on and colouring rocks, tree-trunks, roofs, walls, etc. **2** any of several types of skin disease in which small round hard lesions occur close together. □□ **lichened** *adj.* (in sense 1). **lichenology** /-'nɒlədʒɪ/ *n.* (in sense 1). **lichenous** *adj.* (in sense 2). [L f. Gk *leikhēn*]

lich-gate /'lɪtʃɡeɪt/ *n.* (also **lych-gate**) a roofed gateway to a churchyard where a coffin awaits the clergyman's arrival. [ME f. OE *līc* corpse f. Gmc + GATE[1]]

licit /'lɪsɪt/ *adj.* not forbidden; lawful. □□ **licitly** *adv.* [L *licitus* past part. of *licēre* be lawful]

lick /lɪk/ *v.* & *n.* —*v.tr.* & *intr.* **1** *tr.* pass the tongue over, esp. to taste, moisten, or (of animals) clean. **2** *tr.* bring into a specified condition or position by licking (*licked it all up*; *licked it clean*). **3 a** *tr.* (of a flame, waves, etc.) touch; play lightly over. **b** *intr.* move gently or caressingly. **4** *colloq.* **a** defeat, excel. **b** surpass the comprehension of (*has got me licked*). **5** *colloq.* thrash. —*n.* **1** an act of licking with the tongue. **2** = *salt-lick*. **3** *colloq.* a fast pace (*at a lick*; *at full lick*). **4** *colloq.* **a** a small amount, quick treatment with (foll. by *of*: *a lick of paint*). **b** a quick wash. **5** a smart blow with a stick etc. □ **a lick and a promise** *colloq.* a hasty performance of a task, esp. of washing oneself. **lick a person's boots** (or **shoes**) toady; be servile. **lick into shape** see SHAPE. **lick one's lips** (or **chops**) **1** look forward with relish. **2** show one's satisfaction. **lick one's wounds** be in retirement after defeat. □□ **licker** *n.* (also in *comb.*). [OE *liccian* f. WG]

lickerish /'lɪkərɪʃ/ *adj.* (also **liquorish**) **1** lecherous. **2 a** fond of fine food. **b** greedy, longing. [ME *lickerous* f. OF *lecheros*: see LECHER]

lickety-split /ˌlɪkətɪˈsplɪt/ *adv. colloq.* at full speed; headlong. [prob. f. LICK (cf. *at full lick*) + SPLIT]

licking /'lɪkɪŋ/ *n. colloq.* **1** a thrashing. **2** a defeat.

lickspittle /'lɪkˌspɪt(ə)l/ *n.* a toady.

licorice var. of LIQUORICE.

lictor /'lɪktɔː(r)/ *n.* (usu. in *pl.*) *Rom.Hist.* an officer attending the consul or other magistrate, bearing the fasces, and executing sentence on offenders. [ME f. L, perh. rel. to *ligare* bind]

lid /lɪd/ *n.* **1** a hinged or removable cover, esp. for the top of a container. **2** = EYELID. **3** the operculum of a shell or a plant. **4** *sl.* a hat. □ **put the lid** (or **tin lid**) **on** *Brit. colloq.* **1** be the culmination of. **2** put a stop to. **take the lid off** *colloq.* expose (a scandal etc.). □□ **lidded** *adj.* (also in *comb.*). **lidless** *adj.* [OE *hlid* f. Gmc]

lido /'liːdəʊ, 'laɪ-/ *n.* (*pl.* **-os**) a public open-air swimming-pool or bathing-beach. [It. f. *Lido*, the name of a bathing-beach near Venice, f. L *litus* shore]

lie[1] /laɪ/ *v.* & *n.* —*v.intr.* (**lying** /'laɪɪŋ/; *past* **lay** /leɪ/; *past part.* **lain** /leɪn/) **1** be in or assume a horizontal position on a supporting surface; be at rest on something. **2** (of a thing) rest flat on a surface (*snow lay on the ground*). **3** (of abstract things) remain undisturbed or undiscussed etc. (*let matters lie*). **4 a** be kept or remain or be in a specified, esp. concealed, state or place (*lie hidden*; *lie in wait*; *malice lay behind those words*; *they lay dying*; *the books lay unread*; *the money is lying in the bank*). **b** (of abstract things) exist, reside; be in a certain position or relation (foll. by *in*, *with*, etc.: *the answer lies in education*; *my sympathies lie with the family*). **5 a** be situated or stationed (*the village lay to the east*; *the ships are lying off the coast*). **b** (of a road, route, etc.) lead (*the road lies over mountains*). **c** be spread out to view (*the desert lay before us*). **6** (of the dead) be buried in a grave. **7** (foll. by *with*) *archaic* have sexual intercourse. **8** *Law* be admissible or sustainable (*the objection will not lie*). **9** (of a game-bird) not rise. —*n.* **1 a** the way or direction or position in which a thing lies. **b** *Golf* the position of a golf ball when about to be struck. **2** the place of cover of an animal or a bird. □**as far as in me lies** to the best of my power. **let lie** not raise (a controversial matter etc.) for discussion etc. **lie about** (or **around**) be left carelessly out of place. **lie ahead** be going to happen; be in store. **lie back** recline so as to rest. **lie down** assume a lying position; have a short rest. **lie-down** *n.* a short rest. **lie down under** accept (an insult etc.) without protest. **lie heavy** cause discomfort or anxiety. **lie in 1** remain in bed in the morning. **2** *archaic* be brought to bed in childbirth. **lie-in** *n.* a prolonged stay in bed in the morning. **lie in state** (of a deceased great personage) be laid in a public place of honour before burial. **lie low 1** keep quiet or unseen. **2** be discreet about one's intentions. **lie off** *Naut.* stand some distance from shore or from another ship. **the lie of the land** the current state of affairs. **lie over** be deferred. **lie to** *Naut.* come almost to a stop facing the wind. **lie up** (of a ship) go into dock or be out of commission. **lie with** (often foll. by *to* + infin.) be the responsibility of (a person) (*it lies with you to answer*). **take lying down** (usu. with *neg.*) accept (defeat, rebuke, etc.) without resistance or protest etc. [OE *licgan* f. Gmc]

lie² /laɪ/ *n. & v.* —*n.* **1** an intentionally false statement (*tell a lie*; *pack of lies*). **2** imposture; false belief (*live a lie*). —*v.intr. & tr.* (**lies, lied, lying** /ˈlaɪɪŋ/) **1** *intr.* **a** tell a lie or lies (*they lied to me*). **b** (of a thing) be deceptive (*the camera cannot lie*). **2** *tr.* (usu. *refl.*; foll. by *into, out of*) get (oneself) into or out of a situation by lying (*lied themselves into trouble*; *lied my way out of danger*). □**give the lie to** serve to show the falsity of (a supposition etc.). **lie-detector** an instrument for determining whether a person is telling the truth by testing for physiological changes considered to be symptomatic of lying. [OE *lyge lēogan* f. Gmc]

Liebfraumilch /ˈliːbfraʊmɪlx/ *n.* a light white wine from the Rhine region. [G f. *Liebfrau* the Virgin Mary, the patroness of the convent where it was first made + *Milch* milk]

lied /liːd, liːt/ *n.* (*pl.* **lieder** /ˈliːdə(r)/) a type of German song, esp. of the Romantic period, usu. for solo voice with piano accompaniment. [G]

lief /liːf/ *adv. archaic* gladly, willingly. (usu. **had lief, would lief**) [orig. as adj. f. OE *lēof* dear, pleasant, f. Gmc, rel. to LEAVE², LOVE]

liege /liːdʒ/ *adj. & n.* usu. *hist.* —*adj.* (of a superior) entitled to receive or (of a vassal) bound to give feudal service or allegiance. —*n.* **1** (in full **liege lord**) a feudal superior or sovereign. **2** (usu. in *pl.*) a vassal or subject. [ME f. OF *lige, liege* f. med.L *laeticus*, prob. f. Gmc]

liegeman /ˈliːdʒmæn/ *n.* (*pl.* **-men**) *hist.* a sworn vassal; a faithful follower.

lien /ˈliːən/ *n. Law* a right over another's property to protect a debt charged on that property. [F f. OF *loien* f. L *ligamen* bond f. *ligare* bind]

lierne /lɪˈɜːn/ *n. Archit.* (in vaulting) a short rib connecting the bosses and intersections of the principal ribs. [ME f. F: see LIANA]

lieu /ljuː/ *n.* □**in lieu 1** instead. **2** (foll. by *of*) in the place of. [ME f. F f. L *locus* place]

Lieut. *abbr.* Lieutenant.

lieutenant /lefˈtenənt/ *n.* **1** a deputy or substitute acting for a superior. **2 a** an army officer next in rank below captain. **b** a naval officer next in rank below lieutenant commander. **3** *US* a police officer next in rank below captain. □**lieutenant colonel** (or **commander** or **general**) officers ranking next below colonel, commander, or general. **lieutenant-governor** the acting or deputy governor of a State, province, etc., under a governor or Governor-General. **Lieutenant of the Tower** the acting

commandant of the Tower of London. □□ **lieutenancy** *n.* (*pl.* **-ies**). [ME f. OF (as LIEU, TENANT)]

life /laɪf/ *n.* (*pl.* **lives** /laɪvz/) **1** the condition which distinguishes active animals and plants from inorganic matter, including the capacity for growth, functional activity, and continual change preceding death. **2 a** living things and their activity (*insect life*; *is there life on Mars?*). **b** human presence or activity (*no sign of life*). **3 a** the period during which life lasts, or the period from birth to the present time or from the present time to death (*have done it all my life*; *will regret it all my life*; *life membership*). **b** the duration of a thing's existence or of its ability to function; validity, efficacy, etc. (*the battery has a life of two years*). **4 a** a person's state of existence as a living individual (*sacrificed their lives*; *took many lives*). **b** a living person (*many lives were lost*). **5 a** an individual's occupation, actions, or fortunes; the manner of one's existence (*that would make life easy*; *start a new life*). **b** a particular aspect of this (*love-life*; *private life*). **6** the active part of existence; the business and pleasures of the world (*travel is the best way to see life*). **7** man's earthly or supposed future existence. **8 a** energy, liveliness, animation (*full of life*; *put some life into it!*). **b** an animating influence (*was the life of the party*). **9** the living, esp. nude, form or model (*taken from the life*). **10** a written account of a person's life; a biography. **11** *colloq.* a sentence of imprisonment for life (*they were all serving life*). **12** a chance; a fresh start (*cats have nine lives*; *gave the player three lives*). □**come to life 1** emerge from unconsciousness or inactivity; begin operating. **2** (of an inanimate object) assume an imaginary animation. **for dear** (or **one's**) **life** as if or in order to escape death; as a matter of extreme urgency (*hanging on for dear life*; *run for your life*). **for life** for the rest of one's life. **for the life of me** (foll. by pers. pron.) even if (one's) life depended on it (*cannot for the life of me remember*). **give one's life 1** (foll. by *for*) die; sacrifice oneself. **2** (foll. by *to*) dedicate oneself. **large as life** *colloq.* in person, esp. prominently (*stood there large as life*). **larger than life 1** exaggerated. **2** (of a person) having an exuberant personality. **life-and-death** vitally important; desperate (*a life-and-death struggle*). **life cycle** the series of changes in the life of an organism including reproduction. **life expectancy** the average period that a person at a specified age may expect to live. **life-force** inspiration or a driving force or influence. **life-form** an organism. **life-giving** that sustains life or uplifts and revitalizes. **Life Guards** (in the UK) a regiment of the royal household cavalry. **life history** the story of a person's life, esp. told at tedious length. **life insurance** insurance for a sum to be paid on the death of the insured person. **life-jacket** a buoyant or inflatable jacket for keeping a person afloat in water. **life peer** *Brit.* a peer whose title lapses on death. **life-preserver 1** a short stick with a heavily loaded end. **2** a life-jacket etc. **life-raft** an inflatable or timber etc. raft for use in an emergency instead of a boat. **life-saver** *colloq.* **1** a thing that saves one from serious difficulty. **2** *Austral. & NZ* = LIFEGUARD. **life sciences** biology and related subjects. **life sentence 1** a sentence of imprisonment for life. **2** an illness or commitment etc. perceived as a continuing threat to one's freedom. **life-size** (or **-sized**) of the same size as the person or thing represented. **life-support** *adj.* (of equipment) allowing vital functions to continue in an adverse environment or during severe disablement. **life-support machine** *Med.* a ventilator or respirator. **life's-work** a task etc. pursued throughout one's lifetime. **lose one's life** be killed. **a matter of life and death** a matter of vital importance. **not on your life** *colloq.* most certainly not. **save a person's life 1** prevent a person's death. **2** save a person from serious difficulty. **take one's life in one's hands**

take a crucial personal risk. **to the life** true to the original. [OE *līf* f. Gmc]

lifebelt /ˈlaɪfbelt/ *n.* a belt of buoyant or inflatable material for keeping a person afloat in water.

lifeblood /ˈlaɪfblʌd/ *n.* **1** the blood, as being necessary to life. **2** the vital factor or influence.

lifeboat /ˈlaɪfbəʊt/ *n.* **1** a specially constructed boat launched from land to rescue those in distress at sea. **2** a ship's small boat for use in emergency.

lifebuoy /ˈlaɪfbɔɪ/ *n.* a buoyant support (usu. a ring) for keeping a person afloat in water.

lifeguard /ˈlaɪfgɑːd/ *n.* an expert swimmer employed to rescue bathers from drowning.

lifeless /ˈlaɪflɪs/ *adj.* **1** lacking life; no longer living. **2** unconscious. **3** lacking movement or vitality. □□ **lifelessly** *adv.* **lifelessness** *n.* [OE *līflēas* (as LIFE, -LESS)]

lifelike /ˈlaɪflaɪk/ *adj.* closely resembling the person or thing represented. □□ **lifelikeness** *n.*

lifeline /ˈlaɪflaɪn/ *n.* **1 a** a rope etc. used for lifesaving, e.g. that attached to a lifebuoy. **b** a diver's signalling line. **2** a sole means of communication or transport. **3** a fold in the palm of the hand, regarded as significant in palmistry. **4** an emergency telephone counselling service.

lifelong /ˈlaɪflɒŋ/ *adj.* lasting a lifetime.

lifer /ˈlaɪfə(r)/ *n. sl.* a person serving a life sentence.

lifestyle /ˈlaɪfstaɪl/ *n.* the particular way of life of a person or group.

lifetime /ˈlaɪftaɪm/ *n.* **1** the duration of a person's life. **2** the duration of a thing or its usefulness. **3** *colloq.* an exceptionally long time. □ **of a lifetime** such as does not occur more than once in a person's life (*the chance of a lifetime*; *the journey of a lifetime*).

lift /lɪft/ *v.* & *n.* —*v.* **1** *tr.* (often foll. by *up, off, out,* etc.) raise or remove to a higher position. **2** *intr.* go up; be raised; yield to an upward force (*the window will not lift*). **3** *tr.* give an upward direction to (the eyes or face). **4** *tr.* **a** elevate to a higher plane of thought or feeling (*the news lifted their spirits*). **b** make less heavy or dull; add interest to (something esp. artistic). **c** enhance, improve (*lifted their game after half-time*). **5** *intr.* (of a cloud, fog, etc.) rise, disperse. **6** *tr.* remove (a barrier or restriction). **7** *tr.* transport supplies, troops, etc. by air. **8** *tr. colloq.* **a** steal. **b** plagiarize (a passage of writing etc.). **9** *Phonet.* **a** *tr.* make louder; raise the pitch of. **b** *intr.* (of the voice) rise. **10** *tr.* dig up (esp. potatoes etc. at harvest). **11** *intr.* (of a floor) swell upwards, bulge. **12** *tr.* hold or have on high (*the church lifts its spire*). **13** *tr.* hit (a cricket-ball) into the air. **14** *tr.* (usu. in *passive*) perform cosmetic surgery on (esp. the face or breasts) to reduce sagging. —*n.* **1** the act of lifting or process of being lifted. **2** a free ride in another person's vehicle (*gave them a lift*). **3 a** *Brit.* a platform or compartment housed in a shaft for raising and lowering persons or things to different floors of a building or different levels of a mine etc. **b** a similar apparatus for carrying persons up or down a mountain etc. (see *ski-lift*). **4 a** transport by air (see AIRLIFT *n.*). **b** a quantity of goods transported by air. **5** the upward pressure which air exerts on an aerofoil to counteract the force of gravity. **6** a supporting or elevating influence; a feeling of elation. **7** a layer of leather in the heel of a boot or shoe, esp. to correct shortening of a leg or increase height. **8 a** a rise in the level of the ground. **b** the extent to which water rises in a canal lock. □ **lift down** pick up and bring to a lower position. **lift a finger** (or **hand** etc.) (in *neg.*) make the slightest effort (*didn't lift a finger to help*). **lift off** (of a spacecraft or rocket) rise from the launching pad. **lift-off** *n.* the vertical take-off of a spacecraft or rocket. **lift up one's head** hold one's head high with pride. **lift up one's voice** sing out. □□ **liftable** *adj.* **lifter** *n.* [ME f. ON *lypta* f. Gmc]

ligament /ˈlɪgəmənt/ *n.* **1** *Anat.* **a** a short band of tough flexible fibrous connective tissue linking bones together. **b** any membranous fold keeping an organ

in position. **2** *archaic* a bond of union. □□ **ligamental** /-ˈment(ə)l/ *adj.* **ligamentary** /-ˈmentərɪ/ *adj.* **ligamentous** /-ˈmentəs/ *adj.* [ME f. L *ligamentum* bond f. *ligare* bind]

ligand /ˈlɪgənd/ *n. Chem.* an ion or molecule attached to a metal atom by covalent bonding in which both electrons are supplied by one atom. [L *ligandus* gerundive of *ligare* bind]

ligate /lɪˈgeɪt/ *v.tr. Surgery* tie up (a bleeding artery etc.). □□ **ligation** *n.* [L *ligare ligat-*]

ligature /ˈlɪgətʃə(r)/ *n.* & *v.* —*n.* **1** a tie or bandage, esp. in surgery for a bleeding artery etc. **2** *Mus.* a slur; a tie. **3** *Printing* two or more letters joined, e.g. æ. **4** a bond; a thing that unites. **5** the act of tying or binding. —*v.tr.* bind or connect with a ligature. [ME f. LL *ligatura* f. L *ligare ligat-* tie, bind]

liger /ˈlaɪgə(r)/ *n.* the offspring of a lion and a tigress (cf. TIGON). [portmanteau word f. LION + TIGER]

light¹ /laɪt/ *n.*, *v.*, & *adj.* —*n.* **1** the natural agent (electromagnetic radiation of wavelength between about 390 and 740 mm) that stimulates sight and makes things visible. **2** the medium or condition of the space in which this is present. **3** an appearance of brightness (*saw a distant light*). **4 a** a source of light, e.g. the sun, or a lamp, fire, etc. **b** (in *pl.*) illuminations. **5** (often in *pl.*) a traffic-light (*went through a red light*; *stop at the lights*). **6 a** the amount or quality of illumination in a place (*bad light stopped play*). **b** one's fair or usual share of this (*you are standing in my light*). **7 a** a flame or spark serving to ignite (*struck a light*). **b** a device producing this (*have you got a light?*). **8** the aspect in which a thing is regarded or considered (*appeared in a new light*). **9 a** mental illumination; elucidation, enlightenment. **b** hope, happiness; a happy outcome. **c** spiritual illumination by divine truth. **10** vivacity, enthusiasm, or inspiration visible in a person's face, esp. in the eyes. **11** (in *pl.*) a person's mental powers or ability (*according to one's lights*). **12** an eminent person (*a leading light*). **13 a** the bright part of a thing; a highlight. **b** the bright parts of a picture etc. esp. suggesting illumination (*light and shade*). **14 a** a window or opening in a wall to let light in. **b** the perpendicular division of a mullioned window. **c** a pane of glass esp. in the side or roof of a greenhouse. **15** (in a crossword etc.) each of the items filling a space and to be deduced from the clues. **16** *Law* the light falling on windows, the obstruction of which by a neighbour is illegal. —*v.* (*past* lit /lɪt/; *past part.* lit or (*attrib.*) lighted) **1** *tr.* & *intr.* set burning or begin to burn; ignite. **2** *tr.* provide with light or lighting. **3** *tr.* show (a person) the way or surroundings with a light. **4** *intr.* (usu. foll. by *up*) (of the face or eyes) brighten with animation. —*adj.* **1** well provided with light; not dark. **2** (of a colour) pale (*light blue*; *a light-blue ribbon*). □ **bring** (or **come**) **to light** reveal or be revealed. **festival of lights 1** = HANUKKAH. **2** = DIWALI. **in a good** (or **bad**) **light** giving a favourable (or unfavourable) impression. **in the light of** having regard to; drawing information from. **light-bulb** a glass bulb containing an inert gas and a metal filament, providing light when an electric current is passed through. **lighting-up time** the time during or after which vehicles on the road must show the prescribed lights. **light meter** an instrument for measuring the intensity of the light, esp. to show the correct photographic exposure. **light of day 1** daylight, sunlight. **2** general notice; public attention. **light of one's life** usu. *joc.* a much-loved person. **light-pen** (or **-gun**) **1** a penlike or gunlike photosensitive device held to the screen of a computer terminal for passing information on to it. **2** a light-emitting device used for reading bar-codes. **light show** a display of changing coloured lights for entertainment. **light up 1** *colloq.* begin to smoke a cigarette etc. **2** switch on lights or lighting; illuminate a scene. **light-year 1** *Astron.* the distance light travels in one year, nearly 6 million million miles. **2** (in *pl.*) *colloq.* a long distance or great amount. **lit up** *colloq.* drunk. **out like a light** deeply asleep or unconscious. **throw** (or **shed**) **light on** help to explain. □□ **lightish** *adj.* **lightless** *adj.* **lightness** *n.* [OE *lēoht*, *līht*, *līhtan* f. Gmc]

light² /laɪt/ *adj., adv., & v.* **1** of little weight; not heavy; easy to lift. **2 a** relatively low in weight, amount, density, intensity, etc. (*light arms*; *light traffic*; *light metal*; *light rain*; *a light breeze*). **b** deficient in weight (*light coin*). **c** (of an isotope etc.) having not more than the usual mass. **3 a** carrying or suitable for small loads (*light aircraft*; *light railway*). **b** (of a ship) unladen. **c** carrying only light arms, armaments, etc. (*light brigade*; *light infantry*). **d** (of a locomotive) with no train attached. **4 a** (of food, a meal, etc.) small in amount; easy to digest (*had a light lunch*). **b** (of drink) not heavy on the stomach or strongly alcoholic. **5 a** (of entertainment, music, etc.) intended for amusement, rather than edification; not profound. **b** frivolous, thoughtless, trivial (*a light remark*). **6** (of sleep or a sleeper) easily disturbed. **7** easily borne or done (*light duties*). **8** nimble; quick-moving (*a light step*; *light of foot*; *a light rhythm*). **9** (of a building etc.) graceful, elegant, delicate. **10** (of type) not heavy or bold. **11 a** free from sorrow; cheerful (*a light heart*). **b** giddy (*light in the head*). **12** (of soil) not dense; porous. **13** (of pastry, sponge, etc.) fluffy and well-aerated during cooking and with the fat fully absorbed. **14** (of a woman) unchaste or wanton; fickle. *—adv.* **1** in a light manner (*tread light*; *sleep light*). **2** with a minimum load or minimum luggage (*travel light*). *—v.intr.* (*past* and *past part.* **lit** /lɪt/ or **lighted**) **1** (foll. by *on*, *upon*) come upon or find by chance. **2** *archaic* **a** alight, descend. **b** (foll. by *on*) land on (shore etc.). □ **lighter-than-air** (of an aircraft) weighing less than the air it displaces. **light-fingered** given to stealing. **light flyweight** see FLYWEIGHT. **light-footed** nimble. **light-footedly** nimbly. **light-headed** giddy, frivolous, delirious. **light-headedly** in a light-headed manner. **light-headedness** being light-headed. **light-hearted** **1** cheerful. **2** (unduly) casual, thoughtless. **light-heartedly** in a light-hearted manner. **light-heartedness** being light-hearted. **light heavyweight** see HEAVYWEIGHT. **light industry** the manufacture of small or light articles. **light into** *colloq.* attack. **light middleweight** see MIDDLEWEIGHT. **light out** *colloq.* depart. **light touch** delicate or tactful treatment. **light welterweight** see WELTERWEIGHT. **make light of** treat as unimportant. **make light work of** do a thing quickly and easily. □□ **lightish** *adj.* **lightness** *n.* [OE *lēoht*, *līht*, *līhtan* f. Gmc, the verbal sense from the idea of relieving a horse etc. of weight]

lighten¹ /laɪt(ə)n/ *v.* **1 a** *tr. & intr.* make or become lighter in weight. **b** *tr.* reduce the weight or load of. **2** *tr.* bring relief to (the heart, mind, etc.). **3** *tr.* mitigate (a penalty).

lighten² /laɪt(ə)n/ *v.* **1 a** *tr.* shed light on. **b** *tr. & intr.* make or grow bright. **2** *intr.* **a** shine brightly; flash. **b** emit lightning (*it is lightening*).

lightening /laɪtənɪŋ/ *n.* a drop in the level of the womb during the last weeks of pregnancy.

lighter¹ /laɪtə(r)/ *n.* a device for lighting cigarettes etc.

lighter² /laɪtə(r)/ *n.* a boat, usu. flat-bottomed, for transferring goods from a ship to a wharf or another ship. [ME f. MDu. *lichter* (as LIGHT² in the sense 'unload')]

lighterage /laɪtərɪdʒ/ *n.* **1** the transference of cargo by means of a lighter. **2** a charge made for this.

lighterman /laɪtəmən/ *n.* (*pl.* **-men**) a person who works on a lighter.

lighthouse /laɪthaʊs/ *n.* a tower or other structure containing a beacon light to warn or guide ships at sea.

lighting /laɪtɪŋ/ *n.* **1** equipment in a room or street etc. for producing light. **2** the arrangement or effect of lights.

lightly /laɪtlɪ/ *adv.* in a light (esp. frivolous or unserious) manner. □ **get off lightly** escape with little or no punishment. **take lightly** not be serious about (a thing).

lightning /laɪtnɪŋ/ *n. & adj.* *—n.* a flash of bright light produced by an electric discharge between clouds or between clouds and the ground. *—attrib.adj.* very quick (*with lightning speed*). □ **lightning-conductor** (or **-rod**) a metal rod or wire fixed to an exposed part of a building or to a mast to divert lightning into the earth or sea. **lightning strike** a strike by workers at short notice, esp. without official union backing. [ME, differentiated from *lightening*, verbal noun f. LIGHTEN²]

lightproof /laɪtpruːf/ *adj.* able to resist the harmful effects of (esp. excessive) light.

lights /laɪts/ *n.pl.* the lungs of sheep, pigs, bullocks, etc., used as a food esp. for pets. [ME, noun use of LIGHT²: cf. LUNG]

lightship /laɪtʃɪp/ *n.* a moored or anchored ship with a beacon light.

lightsome /laɪtsəm/ *adj.* gracefully light; nimble; merry. □□ **lightsomely** *adv.* **lightsomeness** *n.*

lightweight /laɪtweɪt/ *adj. & n.* *—adj.* **1** (of a person, vehicle, garment, etc.) of below average weight. **2** of little importance or influence. *—n.* **1** a lightweight person, animal, or thing. **2 a** a weight in certain sports intermediate between featherweight and welterweight, in the amateur boxing scale 57-60 kg but differing for professionals, wrestlers, and weightlifters. **b** a sportsman of this weight. □ **junior lightweight** **1** a weight in professional boxing of 57.1-59 kg. **2** a professional boxer of this weight.

lightwood /laɪtwʊd/ *n.* **1** a tree with a light wood. **2** *US* wood or a tree with wood that burns with a bright flame.

ligneous /lɪgnɪəs/ *adj.* **1** (of a plant) woody (opp. HERBACEOUS). **2** of the nature of wood. [L *ligneus* (as LIGNI-)]

ligni- /lɪgnɪ/ *comb. form* wood. [L *lignum* wood]

lignify /lɪgnɪˌfaɪ/ *v.tr. & intr.* (**-ies**, **-ied**) *Bot.* make or become woody by the deposition of lignin.

lignin /lɪgnɪn/ *n. Bot.* a complex organic polymer deposited in the cell-walls of many plants making them rigid and woody. [as LIGNI- + -IN]

lignite /lɪgnaɪt/ *n.* a soft brown coal showing traces of plant structure, intermediate between bituminous coal and peat. □□ **lignitic** /-nɪtɪk/ *adj.* [F (as LIGNI-, -ITE¹)]

lignocaine /lɪgnəˌkeɪn/ *n. Pharm.* a local anaesthetic for the gums, mucous membranes, or skin, usu. given by injection. [*ligno-* (as LIGNI-) for XYLO- + COCA + -INE⁴]

lignum vitae /ˌlɪgnəm vaɪtɪ, viːtaɪ/ *n.* = GUAIACUM 2a. [L, = wood of life]

ligroin /lɪgrəʊɪn/ *n. Chem.* a volatile hydrocarbon mixture obtained from petroleum and used as a solvent. [20th c.: orig. unkn.]

ligulate /lɪgjʊlət/ *adj. Bot.* having strap-shaped florets. [formed as LIGULE + -ATE²]

ligule /lɪgjuːl/ *n. Bot.* a narrow projection from the top of a leaf-sheath of a grass. [L *ligula* strap, spoon f. *lingere* lick]

ligustrum /lɪˈgʌstrəm/ *n.* = PRIVET. [L]

likable var. of LIKEABLE.

like¹ /laɪk/ *adj., prep., adv., conj., & n.* *—adj.* (often governing a noun as if a transitive participle such as *resembling*) (**more like**, **most like**) **1 a** having some or all of the qualities of another or each other or an original; alike (*in like manner*; *as like as two peas*; *is very like her brother*). **b** resembling in some way, such as; in the same class as (*good writers like Dickens*). **c** (usu. in pairs correlatively) as one is so will the other be (*like mother, like daughter*). **2** characteristic of (*it is not like them to be late*). **3** in a suitable state or mood for (doing or having something) (*felt like working; felt like a cup of tea*). —*prep.* in the manner of; to the same degree as (*drink like a fish; sell like hot cakes; acted like an idiot*). —*adv.* **1** *archaic* likely (*they will come, like enough*). **2** *archaic* in the same manner (foll. by *as*: *sang like as a nightingale*). **3** *sl.* so to speak (*did a quick getaway, like; as I said, like, I'm no Shakespeare*). **4** *colloq.* likely, probably (*as like as not*). —*conj. colloq. disp.* **1** as (*cannot do it like you do*). **2** as if (*ate like they were starving*). —*n.* **1** a counterpart; an equal; a similar person or thing (*shall not see its like again; compare like with like*). **2** (prec. by *the*) a thing or things of the same kind (*will never do the like again*). □**and the like** and similar things; et cetera (*music, painting, and the like*). **be nothing like** (usu. with compl.) be in no way similar or comparable or adequate. **like anything** see ANYTHING. **like (or as like) as not** probably. **like-minded** having the same tastes, opinions, etc. **like-mindedly** in accordance with the same tastes etc. **like-mindedness** being like-minded. **like so** *colloq.* like this; in this manner. **the likes of** *colloq.* a person such as. **more like it** *colloq.* nearer what is required. [ME *līc, līk,* shortened form of OE *gelīc* ALIKE]

like² /laɪk/ *v. & n.* —*v.tr.* **1 a** find agreeable or enjoyable or satisfactory (*like reading; like the sea; like to dance*). **b** be fond of (a person). **2 a** choose to have; prefer (*like my coffee black; do not like such things discussed*). **b** wish for or be inclined to (*would like a cup of tea; should like to come*). **3** (usu. in *interrog.*; prec. by *how*) feel about; regard (*how would you like it if it happened to you?*). —*n.* (in *pl.*) the things one likes or prefers. □**I like that!** *iron.* as an exclamation expressing affront. **like it or not** *colloq.* whether it is acceptable or not. [OE *līcian* f. Gmc]

-like /laɪk/ *comb. form* forming adjectives from nouns, meaning 'similar to, characteristic of' (*doglike; shell-like; tortoise-like*). ¶ In formations intended as nonce-words, or not generally current, the hyphen should be used. It may be omitted when the first element is of one syllable, but nouns in *-l* always require it.

likeable /'laɪkəb(ə)l/ *adj.* (also **likable**) pleasant; easy to like. □□**likeableness** *n.* **likeably** /-blɪ/ *adv.*

likelihood /'laɪklɪˌhʊd/ *n.* probability; being likely. □**in all likelihood** very probably.

likely /'laɪklɪ/ *adj. & adv.* —*adj.* **1** probable; such as well might happen or be true (*it is not likely that they will come; the most likely place is London; a likely story*). **2** (foll. by *to* + infin.) to be reasonably expected (*he is not likely to come now*). **3** promising; apparently suitable (*this is a likely spot; three likely lads*). —*adv.* probably (*is very likely true*). □**as likely as not** probably. **not likely!** *colloq.* certainly not, I refuse. □□**likeliness** *n.* [ME f. ON *líkligr* (as LIKE¹, -LY¹)]

liken /'laɪkən/ *v.tr.* (foll. by *to*) point out the resemblance of (a person or thing to another). [ME f. LIKE¹ + -EN¹]

likeness /'laɪknɪs/ *n.* **1** (foll. by *between, to*) resemblance. **2** (foll. by *of*) a semblance or guise (*in the likeness of a ghost*). **3** a portrait or representation (*is a good likeness*). [OE *gelīknes* (as LIKE¹, -NESS)]

likewise /'laɪkwaɪz/ *adv.* **1** also, moreover, too. **2** similarly (*do likewise*). [for *in like wise*]

liking /'laɪkɪŋ/ *n.* **1** what one likes; one's taste (*is it to your liking?*). **2** (foll. by *for*) regard or fondness; taste or fancy (*had a liking for toffee*). [OE *līcung* (as LIKE², -ING)]

lilac /'laɪlək/ *n. & adj.* —*n.* **1** any shrub or small tree of the genus *Syringa,* esp. *S. vulgaris* with fragrant pale pinkish-violet or white blossoms. **2** a pale pinkish-violet colour. —*adj.* of this colour. [obs. F f. Sp. f. Arab. *līlāk* f. Pers. *līlak,* var. of *nīlak* bluish f. *nīl* blue]

liliaceous /ˌlɪlɪ'eɪʃəs/ *adj.* **1** of or relating to the

family Liliaceae of plants with elongated leaves growing from a corm, bulb, or rhizome, e.g. tulip, lily, or onion. **2** lily-like. [LL *liliaceus* f. L *lilium* lily]

lilliputian /ˌlɪlɪ'pjuːʃ(ə)n/ *n. & adj.* —*n.* a diminutive person or thing. —*adj.* diminutive. [*Lilliput* in Swift's *Gulliver's Travels*]

Lilo /'laɪləʊ/ *n.* (*pl.* **-os**) *propr.* a type of inflatable mattress. [f. *lie low*]

lilt /lɪlt/ *n. & v.* —*n.* **1 a** a light springing rhythm or gait. **b** a song or tune marked by this. **2** (of the voice) a characteristic cadence or inflection; a pleasant accent. —*v.intr.* (esp. as **lilting** *adj.*) move or speak etc. with a lilt (*a lilting step; a lilting melody*). [ME *lilte, lülte,* of unkn. orig.]

lily /'lɪlɪ/ *n.* (*pl.* **-ies**) **1 a** any bulbous plant of the genus *Lilium* with large trumpet-shaped often spotted flowers on a tall slender stem, e.g. the madonna lily and tiger lily. **b** any of several other plants of the family Liliaceae with similar flowers, e.g. the African lily. **c** the water lily. **2** a person or thing of special whiteness or purity. **3** a heraldic fleur-de-lis. **4** (*attrib.*) **a** delicately white (*a lily hand*). **b** pallid. □**lily-livered** cowardly. **lily of the valley** any liliaceous plant of the genus *Convallaria,* with oval leaves in pairs and racemes of white bell-shaped fragrant flowers. **lily-pad** a floating leaf of a water lily. **lily-white 1** as white as a lily. **2** innocent. □□ **lilied** *adj.* [OE *lilie* f. L *lilium* prob. f. Gk *leirion*]

lima bean /'liːmə/ *n.* **1** a tropical American bean plant, *Phaseolus limensis,* having large flat white edible seeds. **2** the seed of this plant. [*Lima* in Peru]

limb¹ /lɪm/ *n.* **1** any of the projecting parts of a person's or animal's body used for contact or movement. **2** a large branch of a tree. **3** a branch of a cross. **4** a spur of a mountain. **5** a clause of a sentence. □**out on a limb 1** isolated, stranded. **2** at a disadvantage. **tear limb from limb** violently dismember. **with life and limb** (esp. escape) without grave injury. □□**limbed** *adj.* (also in *comb.*). **limbless** *adj.* [OE *lim* f. Gmc]

limb² /lɪm/ *n.* **1** *Astron.* **a** a specified edge of the sun, moon, etc. (*eastern limb; lower limb*). **b** the graduated edge of a quadrant etc. **2** *Bot.* the broad part of a petal, sepal, or leaf. [F *limbe* or L *limbus* hem, border]

limber¹ /'lɪmbə(r)/ *adj. & v.* —*adj.* **1** lithe, agile, nimble. **2** flexible. —*v.* (usu. foll. by *up*) **1** *tr.* make (oneself or a part of the body etc.) supple. **2** *intr.* warm up in preparation for athletic etc. activity. □□ **limberness** *n.* [16th c.: orig. uncert.]

limber² /'lɪmbə(r)/ *n. & v.* —*n.* the detachable front part of a gun-carriage, consisting of two wheels, axle, pole, and ammunition-box. —*v.* **1** *tr.* attach a limber to (a gun etc.). **2** *intr.* fasten together the two parts of a gun-carriage. [ME *limo(u)r,* app. rel. to med.L *limonarius* f. *limo -onis* shaft]

limbo¹ /'lɪmbəʊ/ *n.* (*pl.* **-os**) **1** (in some Christian beliefs) the supposed abode of the souls of unbaptized infants, and of the just who died before Christ. **2** an intermediate state or condition of awaiting a decision etc. **3** prison, confinement. **4** a state of neglect or oblivion. [ME f. med.L phr. *in limbo,* f. *limbus:* see LIMB²]

limbo² /'lɪmbəʊ/ *n.* (*pl.* **-os**) a W. Indian dance in which the dancer bends backwards to pass under a horizontal bar which is progressively lowered to a position just above the ground. [a W. Indian word, perh. = LIMBER¹]

Limburger /'lɪmˌbɜːgə(r)/ *n.* a soft white cheese with a characteristic strong smell, orig. made in Limburg. [Du. f. *Limburg* in Belgium]

lime¹ /laɪm/ *n. & v.* —*n.* **1** (in full **quicklime**) a white caustic alkaline substance (calcium oxide) obtained by heating limestone and used for making mortar or as a fertilizer or bleach etc. **2** = BIRDLIME. —*v.tr.* **1** treat (wood, skins, land, etc.) with lime. **2** *archaic* catch (a bird etc.) with birdlime. □**lime water** an aqueous solution of calcium hydroxide used esp. to detect the presence of carbon dioxide.

□□**limeless** *adj.* **limy** *adj.* (**limier, limiest**). [OE *līm* f. Gmc, rel. to LOAM]

lime² /laɪm/ *n.* **1 a** a round citrus fruit like a lemon but greener, smaller, and more acid. **b** the tree, *Citrus aurantifolia*, bearing this. **2** (in full **lime-juice**) the juice of limes as a drink and formerly esp. as a cure for scurvy. **3** (in full **lime-green**) a pale green colour like a lime. [F f. mod.Prov. *limo*, Sp. *lima* f. Arab. *līma*: cf. LEMON]

lime³ /laɪm/ *n.* **1** (in full **lime-tree**) any ornamental tree of the genus *Tilia*, esp. *T. europaea* with heart-shaped leaves and fragrant yellow blossom. Also called LINDEN. **2** the wood of this. [alt. of *line* = OE *lind* = LINDEN]

limekiln /ˈlaɪmkɪln/ *n.* a kiln for heating limestone to produce quicklime.

limelight /ˈlaɪmlaɪt/ *n.* **1** an intense white light obtained by heating a cylinder of lime in an oxy-hydrogen flame, used formerly in theatres. **2** (prec. by *the*) the full glare of publicity; the focus of attention.

limepit /ˈlaɪmpɪt/ *n.* a pit containing lime for steeping hides to remove hair.

limerick /ˈlɪmərɪk/ *n.* a humorous or comic form of five-line stanza with a rhyme-scheme *aabba*. [said to be from the chorus 'will you come up to Limerick?' sung between improvised verses at a gathering: f. *Limerick* in Ireland]

limestone /ˈlaɪmstəʊn/ *n. Geol.* a sedimentary rock composed mainly of calcium carbonate, used as building material and in the making of cement.

limewash /ˈlaɪmwɒʃ/ *n.* a mixture of lime and water for coating walls.

Limey /ˈlaɪmɪ/ *n.* (*pl.* **-eys**) *US sl. offens.* a British person (orig. a sailor) or ship. [LIME², because of the former enforced consumption of lime-juice in the British Navy]

limit /ˈlɪmɪt/ *n. & v.* —*n.* **1** a point, line, or level beyond which something does not or may not extend or pass. **2** (often in *pl.*) the boundary of an area. **3** the greatest or smallest amount permissible or possible (*upper limit; lower limit*). **4** *Math.* a quantity which a function or sum of a series can be made to approach as closely as desired. —*v.tr.* (**limited, limiting**) **1** set or serve as a limit to. **2** (foll. by *to*) restrict. □**be the limit** *colloq.* be intolerable or extremely irritating. **off limits** *US* out of bounds. **within limits** moderately; with some degree of freedom. **without limit** with no restriction. □□ **limitable** *adj.* **limitative** /-tətɪv/ *adj.* **limiter** *n.* [ME f. L *limes limitis* boundary, frontier]

limitary /ˈlɪmɪtərɪ/ *adj.* **1** subject to restriction. **2** of, on, or serving as a limit.

limitation /ˌlɪmɪˈteɪʃ(ə)n/ *n.* **1** the act or an instance of limiting; the process of being limited. **2** a condition of limited ability (often in *pl.*: *know one's limitations*). **3** a limiting rule or circumstance (often in *pl.*: *has its limitations*). **4** a legally specified period beyond which an action cannot be brought, or a property right is not to continue. [ME f. L *limitatio* (as LIMIT)]

limited /ˈlɪmɪtɪd/ *adj.* **1** confined within limits. **2** not great in scope or talents (*has limited experience*). **3 a** few, scanty, restricted (*limited accommodation*). **b** restricted to a few examples (*limited edition*). □**limited** (or **limited liability**) **company** a company whose owners are legally responsible only to a limited amount for its debts. **limited liability** *Brit.* the status of being legally responsible only to a limited amount for debts of a trading company. □□ **limitedly** *adv.* **limitedness** *n.*

limitless /ˈlɪmɪtlɪs/ *adj.* **1** extending or going on indefinitely (*a limitless expanse*). **2** unlimited (*limitless generosity*). □□ **limitlessly** *adv.* **limitlessness** *n.*

limn /lɪm/ *v.tr.* **1** *archaic* paint (esp. a miniature portrait). **2** *hist.* illuminate (manuscripts). □□ **limner** *n.* [obs. *lumine* illuminate f. OF *luminer* f. L *luminare*: see LUMEN]

limnology /lɪmˈnɒlədʒɪ/ *n.* the study of the physical phenomena of lakes and other fresh waters. □□ **limnological** /-nəˈlɒdʒɪk(ə)l/ *adj.* **limnologist** *n.* [Gk *limnē* lake + -LOGY]

limo /ˈlɪməʊ/ *n.* (*pl.* **-os**) *US colloq.* a limousine. [abbr.]

limousine /ˈlɪmuˌziːn, ˌlɪmuˈziːn, ˈlɪməˌziːn/ *n.* a large luxurious motor car, often with a partition behind the driver. [F, orig. a caped cloak worn in the former French province of *Limousin*]

limp¹ /lɪmp/ *v. & n.* —*v.intr.* **1** walk lamely. **2** (of a damaged ship, aircraft, etc.) proceed with difficulty. **3** (of verse) be defective. —*n.* a lame walk. □□ **limper** *n.* **limpingly** *adv.* [rel. to obs. *limphalt* lame, OE *lemp-healt*]

limp² /lɪmp/ *adj.* **1** not stiff or firm; easily bent. **2** without energy or will. **3** (of a book) having a soft cover. □□ **limply** *adv.* **limpness** *n.* [18th c.: orig. unkn.: perh. rel. to LIMP¹ in the sense 'hanging loose']

limpet /ˈlɪmpɪt/ *n.* **1** any of various marine gastropod molluscs, esp. the common limpet *Patella vulgata*, with a shallow conical shell and a broad muscular foot that sticks tightly to rocks. **2** a clinging person. □**limpet mine** a mine designed to be attached to a ship's hull and set to explode after a certain time. [OE *lempedu* f. med.L *lampreda* limpet, LAMPREY]

limpid /ˈlɪmpɪd/ *adj.* **1** (of water, eyes, etc.) clear, transparent. **2** (of writing) clear and easily comprehended. □□ **limpidity** /-ˈpɪdɪtɪ/ *n.* **limpidly** *adv.* **limpidness** *n.* [F *limpide* or L *limpidus*, perh. rel. to LYMPH]

linage /ˈlaɪnɪdʒ/ *n.* **1** the number of lines in printed or written matter. **2** payment by the line.

linchpin /ˈlɪntʃpɪn/ *n.* **1** a pin passed through an axle-end to keep a wheel in position. **2** a person or thing vital to an enterprise, organization, etc. [ME *linch* f. OE *lynis* + PIN]

Lincoln green /ˈlɪŋkən/ *n.* a bright green cloth of a kind once made at Lincoln in E. England.

Lincs. *abbr.* Lincolnshire.

linctus /ˈlɪŋktəs/ *n.* a syrupy medicine, esp. a soothing cough mixture. [L f. *lingere* lick]

lindane /ˈlɪndeɪn/ *n. Chem.* a colourless crystalline chlorinated derivative of cyclohexane used as an insecticide. [T. van der *Linden*, Du. chemist b. 1884]

linden /ˈlɪnd(ə)n/ *n.* a lime-tree. [(orig. adj.) f. OE *lind* lime-tree: cf. LIME³]

line¹ /laɪn/ *n. & v.* —*n.* **1** a continuous mark or band made on a surface (*drew a line*). **2** use of lines in art, esp. draughtsmanship or engraving (*boldness of line*). **3** a thing resembling such a mark esp. a furrow or wrinkle. **4** *Mus.* **a** each of (usu. five) horizontal marks forming a stave in musical notation. **b** a sequence of notes or tones forming an instrumental or vocal melody. **5 a** a straight or curved continuous extent of length without breadth. **b** the track of a moving point. **6 a** a contour or outline, esp. as a feature of design (*admired the sculpture's clean lines; this year's line is full at the back; the ship's lines*). **b** a facial feature (*the cruel line of his mouth*). **7 a** (on a map or graph) a curve connecting all points having a specified common property. **b** (**the Line**) the Equator. **8 a** a limit or boundary. **b** a mark limiting the area of play, the starting or finishing point in a race, etc. **c** the boundary between a credit and a debit in an account. **9 a** a row of persons or things. **b** a direction as indicated by them (*line of march*). **c** *US* a queue. **10 a** a row of printed or written words. **b** a portion of verse written in one line. **11** (in *pl.*) **a** a piece of poetry. **b** the words of an actor's part. **c** a specified amount of text etc. to be written out as a school punishment. **12** a short letter or note (*drop me a line*). **13** (in *pl.*) = *marriage lines*. **14** a length of cord, rope, wire, etc., usu. serving a specified purpose, esp. a fishing-line or clothes-line. **15 a** a wire or cable for a telephone or telegraph. **b** a connection by means of this (*am trying to get a line*). **16 a** a single track of a railway. **b** one branch or route of a railway system, or the whole system under one management. **17 a** a regular succession of buses, ships, aircraft, etc., plying between certain places. **b** a company conducting this (*shipping line*). **18** a connected series of persons following one another in time (esp. several generations of a family); stock, succession (*a long line of craftsmen; next in line to the throne*). **19 a** a course or manner of procedure, conduct, thought, etc. (*did it along these lines; don't take that line with me*). **b** policy (*the party line*). **c** conformity (*bring them into line*). **20** a direction, course, or channel (*lines of communication*). **21** a department of activity; a province; a branch of business (*not in my line*). **22** a class of commercial goods (*a new line in hats*). **23** *colloq.* a false or exaggerated account or story; a dishonest approach (*gave me a line about missing the bus*). **24 a** a connected series of military fieldworks, defences, etc. (*behind enemy lines*). **b** an arrangement of soldiers or ships side by side; a line of battle (*ship of the line*). **c** (prec. by *the*) regular army regiments (not auxiliary forces or Guards). **25** each of the very narrow horizontal sections forming a television picture. **26** a narrow range of the spectrum that is noticeably brighter or darker than the adjacent parts. **27** the level of the base of most letters in printing and writing. **28** (as a measure) one twelfth of an inch. —*v.* **1** *tr.* mark with lines. **2** *tr.* cover with lines (*a face lined with pain*). **3** *tr.* & *intr.* position or stand at intervals along (*crowds lined the route*). □**all along the line** at every point. **bring into line** make conform. **come into line** conform. **end of the line** the point at which further effort is unproductive or one can go no further. **get a line on** *colloq.* learn something about. **in line for** likely to receive. **in the line of** in the course of (esp. duty). **in** (or **out of**) **line with** in (or not in) accordance with. **lay** (or **put**) **it on the line** speak frankly. **line-drawing** a drawing in which images are produced from variations of lines. **line of fire** the expected path of gunfire, a missile, etc. **line of force** *Physics* an imaginary line which represents the strength and direction of a magnetic, gravitational, or electric field at any point. **line of march** the route taken in marching. **line of vision** the straight line along which an observer looks. **line-out** (in Rugby Football) parallel lines of opposing forwards at right angles to the touchline for the throwing in of the ball. **line printer** a machine that prints output from a computer a line at a time rather than character by character. **line up 1** arrange or be arranged in a line or lines. **2** have ready; organize (*had a job lined up*). **line-up** *n.* **1** a line of people for inspection. **2** an arrangement of persons in a team or nations etc. in an alliance. **on the line 1** at risk (*put my reputation on the line*). **2** speaking on the telephone. **3** (of a picture in an exhibition) hung with its centre about level with the spectator's eye. **out of line** not in alignment; discordant. [ME *line, ligne* f. OF *ligne* ult. f. L *linea* f. *linum* flax, & f. OE *line* rope, series]

line[2] /laɪn/ *v.tr.* **1 a** cover the inside surface of (a garment, box, etc.) with a layer of usu. different material. **b** serve as a lining for. **2** cover as if with a lining (*shelves lined with books*). **3** *colloq.* fill, esp. plentifully. □**line one's pocket** (or **purse**) make money, usu. by corrupt means. [ME f. obs. *line* flax, with ref. to the use of linen for linings]

lineage /ˈlɪnɪɪdʒ/ *n.* lineal descent; ancestry, pedigree. [ME f. OF *linage, lignage* f. Rmc f. L *linea* LINE[1]]

lineal /ˈlɪnɪəl/ *adj.* **1** in the direct line of descent or ancestry. **2** linear; of or in lines. □□**lineally** *adv.* [ME f. OF f. LL *linealis* (as LINE[1])]

lineament /ˈlɪnɪəmənt/ *n.* (usu. in *pl.*) a distinctive feature or characteristic, esp. of the face. [ME f. L *lineamentum* f. *lineare* make straight f. *linea* LINE[1]]

linear /ˈlɪnɪə(r)/ *adj.* **1 a** of or in lines; in lines rather than masses (*linear development*). **b** of length (*linear

extent*). **2** long and narrow and of uniform breadth. **3** involving one dimension only. □**linear accelerator** *Physics* an accelerator in which particles travel in straight lines, not in closed orbits. **Linear B** a form of Bronze Age writing found in Crete and parts of Greece and recording a form of Mycenaean Greek: an earlier undeciphered form (**Linear A**) also exists. **linear equation** an equation between two variables that gives a straight line when plotted on a graph. **linear motor** a motor producing straight-line (not rotary) motion by means of a magnetic field. □□ **linearity** /-ˈærɪtɪ/ *n.* **linearize** *v.tr.* (also **-ise**). **linearly** *adv.* [L *linearis* f. *linea* LINE[1]]

lineation /ˌlɪnɪˈeɪʃ(ə)n/ *n.* **1** a marking with or drawing of lines. **2** a division into lines. [ME f. L *lineatio* f. *lineare* make straight]

lineman /ˈlaɪnmən/ *n.* (*pl.* **-men**) **1 a** a person who repairs and maintains telephone or electrical etc. lines. **b** a person who tests the safety of railway lines. **2** *US Football* a player in the line formed before a scrimmage.

linen /ˈlɪnɪn/ *n.* & *adj.* —*n.* **1 a** a cloth woven from flax. **b** a particular kind of this. **2** (*collect.*) articles made or orig. made of linen, calico, etc., as sheets, cloths, shirts, undergarments, etc. —*adj.* made of linen or flax (*linen cloth*). □**linen basket** a basket for soiled clothes. **wash one's dirty linen in public** be indiscreet about one's domestic quarrels etc. [OE *linen* f. WG, rel. to obs. *line* flax]

linenfold /ˈlɪnɪnˌfəʊld/ *n.* (often *attrib.*) a carved or moulded ornament representing a fold or scroll of linen (*linenfold panelling*).

liner[1] /ˈlaɪnə(r)/ *n.* a ship or aircraft etc. carrying passengers on a regular line. □**liner train** a fast goods train with detachable containers on permanently coupled wagons.

liner[2] /ˈlaɪnə(r)/ *n.* a removable lining.

-liner /ˈlaɪnə(r)/ *comb. form* (prec. by a numeral, usu. *one* or *two*) *colloq.* a spoken passage of a specified number of lines in a play etc. (*a one-liner*).

linesman /ˈlaɪnzmən/ *n.* (*pl.* **-men**) **1** (in games played on a pitch or court) an umpire's or referee's assistant who decides whether a ball falls within the playing area or not. **2** *Brit.* = LINEMAN 1.

ling[1] /lɪŋ/ *n.* a long slender marine fish, *Molva molva*, of N. Europe, used as food. [ME *leng(e)*, prob. f. MDu, rel. to LONG[1]]

ling[2] /lɪŋ/ *n.* any of various heathers, esp. *Calluna vulgaris*. □□ **lingy** *adj.* [ME f. ON *lyng*]

-ling[1] /lɪŋ/ *suffix* **1** denoting a person or thing: **a** connected with (*hireling; sapling*). **b** having the property of being (*weakling; underling*) or undergoing (*starveling*). **2** denoting a diminutive (*duckling*), often derogatory (*lordling*). [OE (as -LE[1] + -ING[3])· sense 2 f. ON]

-ling[2] /lɪŋ/ *suffix* forming adverbs and adjectives (*darkling; grovelling*) (cf. -LONG). [OE f. Gmc]

linga /ˈlɪŋgə/ *n.* (also **lingam** /ˈlɪŋgæm/) a phallus, esp. as the Hindu symbol of Siva. [Skr. *lingam*, lit. 'mark']

linger /ˈlɪŋgə(r)/ *v.intr.* **1 a** be slow or reluctant to depart. **b** stay about. **c** (foll. by *over, on,* etc.) dally (*lingered over dinner; lingered on what they said*). **2** (esp. of an illness) be protracted. **3** (foll. by *on*) (of a dying person or custom) be slow in dying; drag on feebly. □□ **lingerer** *n.* **lingeringly** *adv.* [ME *lenger*, frequent. of *leng* f. OE *lengan* f. Gmc, rel. to LENGTHEN]

lingerie /ˈlæʒərɪ/ *n.* women's underwear and nightclothes. [F f. *linge* linen]

lingo /ˈlɪŋgəʊ/ *n.* (*pl.* **-os** or **-oes**) *colloq.* **1** a foreign language. **2** the vocabulary of a special subject or group of people. [prob. f. Port. *lingoa* f. L *lingua* tongue]

lingua franca /ˌlɪŋgwə ˈfræŋkə/ *n.* (*pl.* **lingua francas**) **1** a language adopted as a common language between speakers whose native languages are different. **2** a system for mutual understanding. **3**

hist. a mixture of Italian with French, Greek, Arabic, and Spanish, used in the Levant. [It., = Frankish tongue]

lingual /'lɪŋgw(ə)l/ *adj.* **1** of or formed by the tongue. **2** of speech or languages. □□ **lingualize** *v.tr.* (also **-ise**). **lingually** *adv.* [med.L *lingualis* f. L *lingua* tongue, language]

linguiform /'lɪŋgwɪˌfɔːm/ *adj.* Bot., Zool., & Anat. tongue-shaped. [L *lingua* tongue + -FORM]

linguist /'lɪŋgwɪst/ *n.* a person skilled in languages or linguistics. [L *lingua* language]

linguistic /lɪŋ'gwɪstɪk/ *adj.* of or relating to language or the study of languages. □□ **linguistically** *adv.*

linguistics /lɪŋ'gwɪstɪks/ *n.* the scientific study of languages and their structure. □□ **linguistician** /-'stɪʃ(ə)n/ *n.* [F *linguistique* or G *Linguistik* (as LINGUIST)]

linguodental /ˌlɪŋgwəʊ'dent(ə)l/ *adj.* (of a sound) made with the tongue and teeth. [L *lingua* tongue + DENTAL]

liniment /'lɪnɪmənt/ *n.* an embrocation, usu. made with oil. [LL *linimentum* f. L *linire* smear]

lining /'laɪnɪŋ/ *n.* **1** a layer of material used to line a surface etc. **2** an inside layer or surface etc. (*stomach lining*).

link¹ /lɪŋk/ *n. & v.* —*n.* **1** one loop or ring of a chain etc. **2 a** a connecting part, esp. a thing or person that unites or provides continuity; one in a series. **b** a state or means of connection. **3** a means of contact by radio or telephone between two points. **4** a means of travel or transport between two places. **5** = *cuff-link* (see CUFF¹). **6** a measure equal to one-hundredth of a surveying chain (7.92 inches). —*v.* **1** *tr.* (foll. by *together, to, with*) connect or join (two things or one to another). **2** *tr.* clasp or intertwine (hands or arms). **3** *intr.* (foll. by *on, to, in to*) be joined; attach oneself to (a system, company, etc.). □ **link up** (foll. by *with*) connect or combine. **link-up** *n.* an act or result of linking up. [ME f. ON f. Gmc]

link² /lɪŋk/ *n. hist.* a torch of pitch and tow for lighting the way in dark streets. [16th c.: perh. f. med.L *li(n)chinus* wick f. Gk *lukhnos* light]

linkage /'lɪŋkɪdʒ/ *n.* **1** a connection. **2** a system of links; a linking or link.

linkman /'lɪŋkmæn/ *n.* (*pl.* **-men**) **1** a person providing continuity in a broadcast programme. **2** a player between the forwards and half-backs or strikers and backs in football etc.

links /lɪŋks/ *n.pl.* **1** (treated as *sing.* or *pl.*) a golf-course, esp. one having undulating ground, coarse grass, etc. **2** *Sc. dial.* level or undulating sandy ground near a seashore, with turf and coarse grass. [pl. of *link* 'rising ground' f. OE *hlinc*]

linn /lɪn/ *n. Sc.* **1 a** a waterfall. **b** a pool below this. **2** a precipice; a ravine. [Gael. *linne*]

Linnaean /lɪ'niːən, lɪ'neɪən/ *adj. & n.* —*adj.* of or relating to the Swedish naturalist Linnaeus (Linné, d. 1778) or his system of binary nomenclature in the classification of plants and animals. —*n.* a follower of Linnaeus. ¶ Spelt *Linnean* in *Linnean Society*.

linnet /'lɪnɪt/ *n.* a finch, *Acanthis cannabina*, with brown and grey plumage. [OF *linette* f. *lin* flax (the bird feeding on flax-seeds)]

lino /'laɪnəʊ/ *n.* (*pl.* **-os**) linoleum. [abbr.]

linocut /'laɪnəʊˌkʌt/ *n.* **1** a design or form carved in relief on a block of linoleum. **2** a print made from this. □□ **linocutting** *n.*

linoleum /lɪ'nəʊlɪəm/ *n.* a material consisting of a canvas backing thickly coated with a preparation of linseed oil and powdered cork etc., used esp. as a floor-covering. □□ **linoleumed** *adj.* [L *linum* flax + *oleum* oil]

Linotype /'laɪnəʊˌtaɪp/ *n. Printing propr.* a composing-machine producing lines of words as single strips of metal, used esp. for newspapers. [= *line o' type*]

linsang /'lɪnsæŋ/ *n.* any of various civet-like cats, esp. of the genus *Poiana* of Africa. [Jav.]

linseed /'lɪnsiːd/ *n.* the seed of flax. □ **linseed cake** pressed linseed used as cattle-food. **linseed meal** ground linseed. **linseed oil** oil extracted from linseed and used in paint and varnish. [OE *līnsǣd* f. *līn* flax + *sǣd* seed]

linsey-woolsey /ˌlɪnzɪ'wʊlzɪ/ *n.* a fabric of coarse wool woven on a cotton warp. [ME f. *linsey* coarse linen, prob. f. *Lindsey* in Suffolk + WOOL, with jingling ending]

linstock /'lɪnstɒk/ *n. hist.* a match-holder used to fire cannon. [earlier *lintstock* f. Du. *lontstok* f. *lont* match + *stok* stick, with assim. to LINT]

lint /lɪnt/ *n.* **1** a fabric, orig. of linen, with a raised nap on one side, used for dressing wounds. **2** fluff. **3** *Sc.* flax. □□ **linty** *adj.* [ME *lyn(n)et*, perh. f. OF *linette* linseed f. *lin* flax]

lintel /'lɪnt(ə)l/ *n. Archit.* a horizontal supporting piece of timber, stone, etc., across the top of a door or window. □□ **lintelled** *adj.* (*US* **linteled**). [ME f. OF *lintel* threshold f. Rmc *limitale* (unrecorded), infl. by LL *liminare* f. L *limen* threshold]

linter /'lɪntə(r)/ *n. US* **1** a machine for removing the short fibres from cotton seeds after ginning. **2** (in *pl.*) these fibres. [LINT + -ER¹]

liny /'laɪnɪ/ *adj.* (**linier, liniest**) marked with lines; wrinkled.

lion /'laɪən/ *n.* **1** (*fem.* **lioness** /-nɪs/) a large flesh-eating cat, *Panthera leo*, of Africa and S. Asia, with a tawny coat and, in the male, a flowing shaggy mane. **2** (**the Lion**) the zodiacal sign or constellation Leo. **3** a brave or celebrated person. **4** the lion as a national emblem of Great Britain or as a representation in heraldry. □ **lion-heart** a courageous person (esp. as a sobriquet of Richard I of England). **lion-hearted** brave and generous. **the lion's share** the largest or best part. □□ **lionhood** *n.* **lion-like** *adj.* [ME f. AF *liun* f. L *leo -onis* f. Gk *leōn leontos*]

lionize /'laɪəˌnaɪz/ *v.tr.* (also **-ise**) treat as a celebrity. □□ **lionization** /-'zeɪʃ(ə)n/ *n.* **lionizer** *n.*

lip /lɪp/ *n. & v.* —*n.* **1 a** either of the two fleshy parts forming the edges of the mouth-opening. **b** a thing resembling these. **c** = LABIUM. **2** the edge of a cup, vessel, etc., esp. the part shaped for pouring from. **3** *colloq.* impudent talk (*that's enough of your lip!*). —*v.tr.* (**lipped, lipping**) **1 a** touch with the lips; apply the lips to. **b** touch lightly. **2** *Golf* **a** hit a ball just to the edge of (a hole). **b** (of a ball) reach the edge of (a hole) but fail to drop in. □ **bite one's lip** repress an emotion; stifle laughter, a retort, etc. **curl one's lip** express scorn. **hang on a person's lips** listen attentively to a person. **lick one's lips** see LICK. **lip-read** (*past* and *past part.* **-read** /-red/) (esp. of a deaf person) understand (speech) entirely from observing a speaker's lip-movements. **lip-reader** a person who lip-reads. **lip-service** an insincere expression of support etc. **pass a person's lips** be eaten, drunk, spoken, etc. **smack one's lips** part the lips noisily in relish or anticipation, esp. of food. □□ **lipless** *adj.* **liplike** *adj.* **lipped** *adj.* (also in *comb.*). [OE *lippa* f. Gmc]

lipase /'laɪpeɪz, -peɪs/ *n. Biochem.* an enzyme that catalyses the decomposition of fats. [Gk *lipos* fat + -ASE]

lipid /'lɪpɪd/ *n. Chem.* any of a group of organic compounds that are insoluble in water but soluble in organic solvents, including fatty acids, oils, waxes, and steroids. [F *lipide* (as LIPASE)]

lipidosis /ˌlɪpɪ'dəʊsɪs/ *n.* (also **lipoidosis** /ˌlɪpɔɪ-/) (*pl.* **-doses** /-siːz/) any disorder of lipid metabolism in the body tissues.

Lipizzaner var. of LIPIZANER.

lipography /lɪ'pɒgrəfɪ/ *n.* the omission of letters or words in writing. [Gk *lip-* stem of *leipō* omit + -GRAPHY]

lipoid /'lɪpɔɪd/ *adj.* resembling fat.

lipoprotein /ˌlaɪpəʊ'prəʊtiːn/ *n. Biochem.* any of a

group of proteins that are combined with fats or other lipids. [Gk *lipos* fat + PROTEIN]

liposome /ˈlaɪpəʊˌsəʊm/ *n. Biochem.* a minute artificial spherical sac usu. of a phospholipid membrane enclosing an aqueous core. [G. *Liposom*: see LIPID]

Lippizaner /ˌlɪpɪtˈsɑːnə(r)/ *n.* (also **Lipizzaner**) **1** a horse of a fine white breed used esp. in displays of dressage. **2** this breed. [G f. *Lippiza* in Yugoslavia]

lippy /ˈlɪpɪ/ *adj.* (**lippier, lippiest**) *colloq.* **1** insolent, impertinent. **2** talkative.

lipsalve /ˈlɪpsælv/ *n.* **1** a preparation, usu. in stick form, to prevent or relieve sore lips. **2** flattery.

lipstick /ˈlɪpstɪk/ *n.* a small stick of cosmetic for colouring the lips.

liquate /lɪˈkweɪt/ *v.tr.* separate or purify (metals) by liquefying. □□ **liquation** /-ˈkweɪʃ(ə)n/ *n.* [L *liquare* melt, rel. to LIQUOR]

liquefy /ˈlɪkwɪˌfaɪ/ *v.tr. & intr.* (also **liquify**) (**-ies, -ied**) *Chem.* make or become liquid. □□ **liquefacient** /-ˈfeɪʃ(ə)nt/ *adj. & n.* **liquefaction** /-ˈfækʃ(ə)n/ *n.* **liquefactive** /-ˈfæktɪv/ *adj.* **liquefiable** *adj.* **liquefier** *n.* [F *liquéfier* f. L *liquefacere* f. *liquēre* be liquid]

liquescent /lɪˈkwes(ə)nt/ *adj.* becoming or apt to become liquid. [L *liquescere* (as LIQUEFY)]

liqueur /lɪˈkjʊə(r)/ *n.* any of several strong sweet alcoholic spirits, variously flavoured, usu. drunk after a meal. [F, = LIQUOR]

liquid /ˈlɪkwɪd/ *adj. & n.* —*adj.* **1** having a consistency like that of water or oil, flowing freely but of constant volume. **2** having the qualities of water in appearance; translucent (*liquid blue*; *a liquid lustre*). **3** (of a gas, e.g. air, hydrogen) reduced to a liquid state by intense cold. **4** (of sounds) clear and pure; harmonious, fluent. **5** (of assets) easily converted into cash. **6** not fixed; fluid (*liquid opinions*). —*n.* **1** a liquid substance. **2** *Phonet.* the sound of *l* or *r*. □ **liquid crystal** a turbid liquid with some order in its molecular arrangement. **liquid crystal display** a form of visual display in electronic devices, in which the reflectivity of a matrix of liquid crystals changes as a signal is applied. **liquid measure** a unit for measuring the volume of liquids. **liquid paraffin** *Pharm.* a colourless odourless oily liquid obtained from petroleum and used as a laxative. □□ **liquidly** *adv.* **liquidness** *n.* [ME f. L *liquidus* f. *liquēre* be liquid]

liquidambar /ˌlɪkwɪˈdæmbə(r)/ *n.* **1** any tree of the genus *Liquidambar* yielding a resinous gum. **2** this gum. [mod.L app. f. L *liquidus* (see LIQUID) + med.L *ambar* amber]

liquidate /ˈlɪkwɪˌdeɪt/ *v.* **1 a** *tr.* wind up the affairs of (a company or firm) by ascertaining liabilities and apportioning assets. **b** *intr.* (of a company) be liquidated. **2** *tr.* clear or pay off (a debt). **3** *tr.* put an end to or get rid of (esp. by violent means). [med.L *liquidare* make clear (as LIQUID)]

liquidation /ˌlɪkwɪˈdeɪʃ(ə)n/ *n.* the process of liquidating a company etc. □ **go into liquidation** (of a company etc.) be wound up and have its assets apportioned.

liquidator /ˈlɪkwɪˌdeɪtə(r)/ *n.* a person called in to wind up the affairs of a company etc.

liquidity /lɪˈkwɪdɪtɪ/ *n.* (*pl.* **-ies**) **1** the state of being liquid. **2 a** availability of liquid assets. **b** (in *pl.*) liquid assets. [F *liquidité* or med.L *liquiditas* (as LIQUID)]

liquidize /ˈlɪkwɪˌdaɪz/ *v.tr.* (also **-ise**) reduce (esp. food) to a liquid or puréed state.

liquidizer /ˈlɪkwɪˌdaɪzə(r)/ *n.* a machine for liquidizing.

liquify var. of LIQUEFY.

liquor /ˈlɪkə(r)/ *n. & v.* —*n.* **1** an alcoholic (esp. distilled) drink. **2** water used in brewing. **3** other liquid, esp. that produced in cooking. **4** *Pharm.* a solution of a specified drug in water. —*v.tr.* **1** dress (leather) with grease or oil. **2** steep (malt etc.) in water. [ME f. OF *lic(o)ur* f. L *liquor -oris* (as LIQUID)]

liquorice /ˈlɪkərɪs, -rɪʃ/ *n.* (also **licorice**) **1** a black root extract used as a sweet and in medicine. **2** the leguminous plant *Glycyrrhiza glabra* from which it is obtained. [ME f. AF *lycorys*, OF *licoresse* f. LL *liquiritia* f. Gk *glukurrhiza* f. *glukus* sweet + *rhiza* root]

liquorish /ˈlɪkərɪʃ/ *adj.* **1** = LICKERISH. **2** fond of or indicating a fondness for liquor. □□ **liquorishly** *adv.* **liquorishness** *n.* [var. of LICKERISH, misapplied]

lira /ˈlɪərə/ *n.* (*pl.* **lire** /ˈlɪəreɪ, ˈlɪərɪ/) **1** the chief monetary unit of Italy. **2** the chief monetary unit of Turkey. [It. f. Prov. *liura* f. L *libra* pound (weight etc.)]

lisle /laɪl/ *n.* (in full **lisle thread**) a fine smooth cotton thread for stockings etc. [*Lisle*, former spelling of *Lille* in France, where orig. made]

lisp /lɪsp/ *n. & v.* —*n.* **1** a speech defect in which *s* is pronounced like *th* in *thick* and *z* is pronounced like *th* in *this*. **2** a rippling of waters; a rustling of leaves. —*v.intr. & tr.* speak or utter with a lisp. □□ **lisper** *n.* **lispingly** *adv.* [OE *wlispian* (recorded in *āwlyspian*) f. *wlisp* (adj.) lisping, of uncert. orig.]

lissom /ˈlɪsəm/ *adj.* (also **lissome**) lithe, supple, agile. □□ **lissomly** *adv.* **lissomness** *n.* [ult. f. LITHE + -SOME[1]]

list[1] /lɪst/ *n. & v.* —*n.* **1** a number of connected items, names, etc., written or printed together usu. consecutively to form a record or aid to memory (*shopping list*). **2** (in *pl.*) **a** palisades enclosing an area for a tournament. **b** the scene of a contest. **3** *Brit.* **a** a selvage or edge of cloth, usu. of different material from the main body. **b** such edges used as a material. —*v.* **1** *tr.* make a list of. **2** *tr.* enter in a list. **3** *tr.* (as **listed** *adj.*) **a** (of securities) approved for dealings on the Stock Exchange. **b** (of a building in the UK) officially designated as being of historical importance and having protection from demolition or major alterations. **4** *tr. & intr. archaic* enlist. □ **enter the lists** issue or accept a challenge. **list price** the price of something as shown in a published list. □□ **listable** *adj.* [OE *liste* border, strip f. Gmc]

list[2] /lɪst/ *v. & n.* —*v.intr.* (of a ship etc.) lean over to one side, esp. owing to a leak or shifting cargo (cf. HEEL[2]). —*n.* the process or an instance of listing. [17th c.: orig. unkn.]

listen /ˈlɪs(ə)n/ *v.intr.* **1 a** make an effort to hear something. **b** attentively hear a person speaking. **2** (foll. by *to*) **a** give attention with the ear (*listened to my story*). **b** take notice of; respond to advice or a request or to the person expressing it. **3** (also **listen out**) (often foll. by *for*) seek to hear or be aware of by waiting alertly. □ **listen in 1** tap a telephonic communication. **2** use a radio receiving set. **listening-post 1 a** a point near an enemy's lines for detecting movements by sound. **b** a station for intercepting electronic communications. **2** a place for the gathering of information from reports etc. [OE *hlysnan* f. WG]

listenable /ˈlɪsənəb(ə)l/ *adj.* easy or pleasant to listen to. □□ **listenability** /-əˈbɪlɪtɪ/ *n.*

listener /ˈlɪsənə(r)/ *n.* **1** a person who listens. **2** a person receiving broadcast radio programmes.

lister /ˈlɪstə(r)/ *n. US* a plough with a double mould-board. [*list* prepare land for a crop + -ER[1]]

listeria /lɪˈstɪərɪə/ *n.* any motile rodlike bacterium of the genus *Listeria*, esp. *L. monocytogenes* infecting humans and animals eating contaminated food. [mod.L f. J. *Lister*, Engl. surgeon d. 1912]

listing /ˈlɪstɪŋ/ *n.* **1** a list or catalogue (see LIST[1] 1). **2** the drawing up of a list. **3** *Brit.* selvage (see LIST[1] *n.* 3).

listless /ˈlɪstlɪs/ *adj.* lacking energy or enthusiasm; disinclined for exertion. □□ **listlessly** *adv.* **listlessness** *n.* [ME f. obs. *list* inclination + -LESS]

lit *past* and *past part.* of LIGHT[1], LIGHT[2].

litany /ˈlɪtənɪ/ *n.* (*pl.* **-ies**) **1 a** a series of petitions for use in church services or processions, usu. recited by the clergy and responded to in a recurring formula by the people. **b** (**the Litany**) that contained in the Book of Common Prayer. **2** a tedious recital (*a litany of woes*). [ME f. OF *letanie* f. eccl.L *litania* f. Gk *litaneia* prayer f. *litē* supplication]

litchi var. of LYCHEE.

-lite /laɪt/ *suffix* forming names of minerals (*rhyolite*; *zeolite*). [F f. Gk *lithos* stone]

liter *US* var. of LITRE.

literacy /'lɪtərəsɪ/ *n.* the ability to read and write. [LITERATE + -ACY after *illiteracy*]

literae humaniores /ˌlɪtəˌraɪ huːˌmænɪ'ɔːrez/ *n. Brit.* the name of the school of classics and philosophy at Oxford University. [L, = the more humane studies]

literal /'lɪtər(ə)l/ *adj. & n.* —*adj.* **1** taking words in their usual or primary sense without metaphor or allegory (*literal interpretation*). **2** following the letter, text, or exact or original words (*literal translation*; *a literal transcript*). **3** (in full **literal-minded**) (of a person) prosaic; matter of fact. **4 a** not exaggerated (*the literal truth*). **b** so called without exaggeration (*a literal extermination*). **5** *colloq. disp.* so called with some exaggeration or using metaphor (*a literal avalanche of mail*). **6** of, in, or expressed by a letter or the letters of the alphabet. **7** *Algebra* not numerical. —*n. Printing* a misprint of a letter. □□ **literality** /-'rælɪtɪ/ *n.* **literalize** *v.tr.* (also **-ise**). **literally** *adv.* **literalness** *n.* [ME f. OF *literal* or LL *litteralis* f. L *littera* (as LETTER)]

literalism /'lɪtərəˌlɪz(ə)m/ *n.* insistence on a literal interpretation; adherence to the letter. □□ **literalist** *n.* **literalistic** /-'lɪstɪk/ *adj.*

literary /'lɪtərərɪ/ *adj.* **1** of, constituting, or occupied with books or literature or written composition, esp. of the kind valued for quality of form. **2** well informed about literature. **3** (of a word or idiom) used chiefly in literary works or other formal writing. □ **literary executor** see EXECUTOR. **literary history** the history of the treatment of a subject in literature. □□ **literarily** *adv.* **literariness** *n.* [L *litterarius* (as LETTER)]

literate /'lɪtərət/ *adj. & n.* —*adj.* able to read and write. —*n.* a literate person. □□ **literately** *adv.* [ME f. L *litteratus* (as LETTER)]

literati /ˌlɪtə'rɑːtiː/ *n.pl.* **1** men of letters. **2** the learned class. [L, pl. of *literatus* (as LETTER)]

literatim /ˌlɪtə'rɑːtɪm/ *adv.* letter for letter; textually, literally. [med.L]

literation /ˌlɪtə'reɪʃ(ə)n/ *n.* the representation of sounds etc. by a letter or group of letters. [L *litera* LETTER]

literature /'lɪtərətʃə(r), 'lɪtrə-/ *n.* **1** written works, esp. those whose value lies in beauty of language or in emotional effect. **2** the realm of letters. **3** the writings of a country or period. **4** literary production. **5** *colloq.* printed matter, leaflets, etc. **6** the material in print on a particular subject (*there is a considerable literature on geraniums*). [ME, = literary culture, f. L *litteratura* (as LITERATE)]

-lith /lɪθ/ *suffix* denoting types of stone (*laccolith*; *monolith*). [Gk *lithos* stone]

litharge /'lɪθɑːdʒ/ *n.* a usu. red crystalline form of lead monoxide. [ME f. OF *litarge* f. L *lithargyrus* f. Gk *litharguros* f. *lithos* stone + *arguros* silver]

lithe /laɪð/ *adj.* flexible, supple. □□ **lithely** *adv.* **litheness** *n.* **lithesome** *adj.* [OE *lithe* f. Gmc]

lithia /'lɪθɪə/ *n.* lithium oxide. □ **lithia water** water containing lithium salts and used against gout. [mod.L, alt. of earlier *lithion* f. Gk neut. of *litheios* f. *lithos* stone, after *soda* etc.]

lithic /'lɪθɪk/ *adj.* **1** of, like, or made of stone. **2** *Med.* of a calculus. [Gk *lithikos* (as LITHIA)]

lithium /'lɪθɪəm/ *n. Chem.* a soft silver-white metallic element, the lightest metal, used in alloys and in batteries. ¶ Symb.: **Li**. [LITHIA + -IUM]

litho /'laɪθəʊ/ *n. & v. colloq.* —*n.* = LITHOGRAPHY. —*v.tr.* (**-oes**, **-oed**) produce by lithography. [abbr.]

litho- /'lɪθəʊ, 'laɪθəʊ/ *comb. form* stone. [Gk *lithos* stone]

lithograph /'lɪθəˌɡrɑːf, 'laɪθə-/ *n. & v.* —*n.* a lithographic print. —*v.tr.* **1** print by lithography. **2** write or engrave on stone. [back-form. f. LITHOGRAPHY]

lithography /lɪ'θɒɡrəfɪ/ *n.* a process of obtaining prints from a stone or metal surface so treated that what is to be printed can be inked but the remaining area rejects ink. □□ **lithographer** *n.* **lithographic** /ˌlɪθə'ɡræfɪk/ *adj.* **lithographically** /ˌlɪθə'ɡræfɪkəlɪ/ *adv.* [G *Lithographie* (as LITHO-, -GRAPHY)]

lithology /lɪ'θɒlədʒɪ/ *n.* the science of the nature and composition of rocks. □□ **lithological** /-θə'lɒdʒɪk(ə)l/ *adj.*

lithophyte /'lɪθəˌfaɪt/ *n. Bot.* a plant that grows on stone.

lithopone /'lɪθəˌpəʊn/ *n.* a white pigment of zinc sulphide, barium sulphate, and zinc oxide. [LITHO- + Gk *ponos* work]

lithosphere /'lɪθəˌsfɪə(r)/ *n.* **1** the layer including the earth's crust and upper mantle. **2** solid earth (opp. HYDROSPHERE, ATMOSPHERE). □□ **lithospheric** /-'sferɪk/ *adj.*

lithotomy /lɪ'θɒtəmɪ/ *n.* (*pl.* **-ies**) the surgical removal of a stone from the urinary tract, esp. the bladder. □□ **lithotomist** *n.* **lithotomize** *v.tr.* (also **-ise**). [LL f. Gk *lithotomia* (as LITHO-, -TOMY)]

lithotripsy /'lɪθəˌtrɪpsɪ/ *n.* (*pl.* **-ies**) a treatment using ultrasound to shatter a stone in the bladder into small particles that can be passed through the urethra. □□ **lithotripter** *n.* **lithotriptic** *adj.* [LITHO- + Gk *tripsis* rubbing f. *tribo* rub]

Lithuanian /ˌlɪθjuː'eɪnɪən, ˌlɪθuː-/ *n. & adj.* —*n.* **1 a** a native of Lithuania, a Baltic republic of the USSR. **b** a person of Lithuanian descent. **2** the language of Lithuania. —*adj.* of or relating to Lithuania or its people or language.

litigant /'lɪtɪɡənt/ *n. & adj.* —*n.* a party to a lawsuit. —*adj.* engaged in a lawsuit. [F (as LITIGATE)]

litigate /'lɪtɪˌɡeɪt/ *v.* **1** *intr.* go to law; be a party to a lawsuit. **2** *tr.* contest (a point) in a lawsuit. □□ **litigable** /'lɪtɪɡəb(ə)l/ *adj.* **litigation** /-'ɡeɪʃ(ə)n/ *n.* **litigator** *n.* [L *litigare litigat-* f. *lis litis* lawsuit]

litigious /lɪ'tɪdʒəs/ *adj.* **1** given to litigation; unreasonably fond of going to law. **2** disputable in a lawcourt; offering matter for a lawsuit. **3** of lawsuits. □□ **litigiously** *adv.* **litigiousness** *n.* [ME f. OF *litigieux* or L *litigiosus* f. *litigium* litigation: see LITIGATE]

litmus /'lɪtməs/ *n.* a dye obtained from lichens that is red under acid conditions and blue under alkaline conditions. □ **litmus paper** a paper stained with litmus to be used as a test for acids or alkalis. [ME f. ONorw. *litmosi* f. ON *litr* dye + *mosi* moss]

litotes /laɪ'təʊtiːz/ *n.* ironical understatement, esp. the expressing of an affirmative by the negative of its contrary (e.g. *I shan't be sorry for I shall be glad*). [LL f. Gk *litotēs* f. *litos* plain, meagre]

litre /'liːtə(r)/ *n.* (*US* **liter**) a metric unit of capacity, formerly defined as the volume of one kilogram of water under standard conditions, now equal to 1 cubic decimetre (about 1.75 pints). □□ **litreage** /'liːtərɪdʒ/ *n.* [F f. *litron*, an obs. measure of capacity, f. med.L f. Gk *litra* a Sicilian monetary unit]

Litt.D. *abbr.* Doctor of Letters. [L *Litterarum Doctor*]

litter /'lɪtə(r)/ *n. & v.* —*n.* **1 a** refuse, esp. paper, discarded in an open or public place. **b** odds and ends lying about. **c** (*attrib.*) for disposing of litter (*litter-bin*). **2** a state of untidiness, disorderly accumulation of papers etc. **3** the young animals brought forth at a birth. **4** a vehicle containing a couch shut in by curtains and carried on men's shoulders or by beasts of burden. **5** a framework with a couch for transporting the sick and wounded. **6 a** straw, rushes, etc., as bedding, esp. for animals. **b** straw and dung in a farmyard. —*v.tr.* **1** make (a place) untidy with litter. **2** scatter untidily and leave lying about. **3** give birth to (whelps etc.). **4** (often foll. by *down*) **a** provide (a horse etc.) with litter as bedding. **b** spread litter or straw on (a floor) or in (a stable). □**litter-lout** = LITTERBUG. □□**littery** *adj.* (in senses 1, 2 of *n.*). [ME f. AF *litere*, OF *litiere* f. med.L *lectaria* f. L *lectus* bed]

littérateur /ˌlɪtərɑːˈtɜː(r)/ *n.* a literary person. [F]

litterbug /ˈlɪtəˌbʌg/ *n.* a person who carelessly leaves litter in a public place.

little /ˈlɪt(ə)l/ *adj., n.,* & *adv.* —*adj.* (**littler, littlest**; **less** /les/ or **lesser** /ˈlesə(r)/; **least** /liːst/) **1** small in size, amount, degree, etc.; not great or big: often used to convey affectionate or emotional overtones, or condescension, not implied by *small* (*a friendly little chap*; *a silly little fool*; *a nice little car*). **2 a** short in stature (*a little man*). **b** of short distance or duration (*will go a little way with you*; *wait a little while*). **3** (prec. by *a*) a certain though small amount of (*give me a little butter*). **4** trivial; relatively unimportant (*exaggerates every little difficulty*). **5** not much; inconsiderable (*gained little advantage from it*). **6** operating on a small scale (*the little shopkeeper*). **7** as a distinctive epithet: **a** of a smaller or the smallest size etc. (*little finger*). **b** that is the smaller or smallest of the name (*little auk*; *little grebe*). **8** young or younger (*a little boy*; *my little sister*). **9** as of a child, evoking tenderness, condescension, amusement, etc. (*we know their little ways*). **10** mean, paltry, contemptible (*you little sneak*). —*n.* **1** not much; only a small amount (*got very little out of it*; *did what little I could*). **2** (usu. prec. by *a*) **a** a certain but no great amount (*knows a little of everything*; *every little helps*). **b** a short time or distance (*after a little*). —*adv.* (**less, least**) **1** to a small extent only (*little-known authors*; *is little more than speculation*). **2** not at all; hardly (*they little thought*). **3** (prec. by *a*) somewhat (*is a little deaf*). □**in little** on a small scale. **the Little Bear** see BEAR². **little by little** by degrees; gradually. **little end** the smaller end of a connecting-rod, attached to the piston. **little finger** the smallest finger, at the outer end of the hand. **little man** esp. *joc.* (as a form of address) a boy. **little ones** young children or animals. **little or nothing** hardly anything. **the little people** fairies. **Little Russian** *hist. n.* a Ukrainian. —*adj.* Ukrainian. **little slam** *Bridge* the winning of 12 tricks. **the little woman** *colloq.* often *derog.* one's wife. **no little** considerable, a good deal of (*took no little trouble over it*). **not a little** *n.* much; a great deal. —*adv.* extremely (*not a little concerned*). □□ **littleness** *n.* [OE *lȳtel* f. Gmc]

littoral /ˈlɪtər(ə)l/ *adj.* & *n.* —*adj.* of or on the shore of the sea, a lake, etc. —*n.* a region lying along a shore. [L *littoralis* f. *litus litoris* shore]

liturgical /lɪˈtɜːdʒɪk(ə)l/ *adj.* of or related to liturgies or public worship. □□ **liturgically** *adv.* **liturgist** /ˈlɪtədʒɪst/ *n.* [med.L f. Gk *leitourgikos* (as LITURGY)]

liturgy /ˈlɪtədʒɪ/ *n.* (*pl.* -**ies**) **1 a** a form of public worship. **b** a set of formularies for this. **c** public worship in accordance with a prescribed form. **2** (**the Liturgy**) the Book of Common Prayer. **3** the Communion office of the Orthodox Church. **4** *Gk Antiq.* a public office or duty performed voluntarily by a rich Athenian. [F *liturgie* or LL *liturgia* f. Gk *leitourgia* public worship f. *leitourgos* minister f. *leit-* public + *ergon* work]

livable var. of LIVEABLE.

live¹ /lɪv/ *v.* **1** *intr.* have (esp. animal) life; be or remain alive. **2** *intr.* (foll. by *on*) subsist or feed (*lives on fruit*). **3** *intr.* (foll. by *on, off*) depend for subsistence (*lives off the family*; *lives on income from investments*). **4** *intr.* (foll. by *on, off*) sustain one's position or repute (*live on their reputation*; *lives by his wits*). **5** *tr.* **a** (with compl.) spend, pass, experience (*lived a happy life*). **b** express in one's life (*was living a lie*). **6** *intr.* conduct oneself in a specified way (*live quietly*). **7** *intr.* arrange one's habits, expenditure, feeding, etc. (*live modestly*). **8** *intr.* make or have one's abode. **9** *intr.* (foll. by *in*) spend the daytime (*the room does not seem to be lived in*). **10** *intr.* (of a

person or thing) survive. **11** *intr.* (of a ship) escape destruction. **12** *intr.* enjoy life intensely or to the full (*you haven't lived till you've drunk champagne*). □**live and let live** condone others' failings so as to be similarly tolerated. **live down** (usu. with *neg.*) cause (past guilt, embarrassment, etc.) to be forgotten by different conduct over a period of time (*you'll never live that down!*). **live in** *Brit.* (of a domestic employee) reside on the premises of one's work. **live-in** *attrib.adj.* (of a sexual partner) cohabiting. **live it up** *colloq.* live gaily and extravagantly. **live out 1** survive (a danger, difficulty, etc.). **2** (of a domestic employee) reside away from one's place of work. **live through** survive; remain alive at the end of. **live to** survive and reach (*lived to a great age*). **live to oneself** live in isolation. **live together** (esp. of a man and woman not married to each other) share a home and have a sexual relationship. **live up to** honour or fulfil; put into practice (principles etc.). **live with 1** share a home with. **2** tolerate; find congenial. **long live . . . !** an exclamation of loyalty (to a person etc. specified). [OE *libban, lifian,* f. Gmc]

live² /laɪv/ *adj.* **1** (*attrib.*) that is alive; living. **2** (of a broadcast) heard or seen at the time of its performance, not from a recording. **3** full of power, energy, or importance; not obsolete or exhausted (*disarmament is still a live issue*). **4** expending or still able to expend energy in various forms, esp.: **a** (of coals) glowing, burning. **b** (of a shell) unexploded. **c** (of a match) unkindled. **d** (of a wire etc.) connected to a source of electrical power. **5** (of rock) not detached, seeming to form part of the earth's frame. **6** (of a wheel or axle etc. in machinery) moving or imparting motion. □**live bait** small fish used to entice prey. **live load** the weight of persons or goods in a building or vehicle. **live oak** an American evergreen tree, *Quercus virginiana.* **live wire** an energetic and forceful person. [aphetic form of ALIVE]

liveable /ˈlɪvəb(ə)l/ *adj.* (also **livable**) **1** (of a house, room, climate, etc.) fit to live in. **2** (of a life) worth living. **3** (of a person) companionable; easy to live with. □□ **liveability** /-ˈbɪlɪtɪ/ *n.* **liveableness** *n.*

livelihood /ˈlaɪvlɪˌhʊd/ *n.* a means of living; sustenance. [OE *līflād* f. *līf* LIFE + *lād* course (see LOAD): assim. to obs. *livelihood* liveliness]

livelong¹ /ˈlɪvlɒŋ/ *adj. poet.* or *rhet.* in its entire length or apparently so (*the livelong day*). [ME *lefe longe* (as LIEF, LONG¹): assim. to LIVE¹]

livelong² /ˈlɪvlɒŋ/ *n.* an orpine. [LIVE¹ + LONG¹]

lively /ˈlaɪvlɪ/ *adj.* **1** full of life; vigorous, energetic. **2** brisk (*a lively pace*). **3** vivid, stimulating (*a lively discussion*). **4** vivacious, jolly, sociable. **5** *joc.* exciting, dangerous, difficult (*the press is making things lively for them*). **6** (of a colour) bright and vivid. **7** lifelike, realistic (*a lively description*). **8** (of a boat etc.) rising lightly to the waves. □□ **livelily** *adv.* **liveliness** *n.* [OE *līflic* (as LIFE, -LY¹)]

liven /ˈlaɪv(ə)n/ *v.tr.* & *intr.* (often foll. by *up*) *colloq.* brighten, cheer.

liver¹ /ˈlɪvə(r)/ *n.* **1 a** a large lobed glandular organ in the abdomen of vertebrates, functioning in many metabolic processes including the regulation of toxic materials in the blood, secreting bile, etc. **b** a similar organ in other animals. **2** the flesh of an animal's liver as food. **3** (in full **liver-colour**) a dark reddish-brown. □**liver chestnut** see CHESTNUT. **liver fluke** either of two types of fluke, esp. *Fasciola hepatica,* the adults of which live within the liver tissues of vertebrates, and the larvae within snails. **liver of sulphur** a liver-coloured mixture of potassium sulphides etc., used as a lotion in skin disease. **liver salts** *Brit.* salts to cure dyspepsia or biliousness. **liver sausage** a sausage containing cooked liver etc. □□ **liverless** *adj.* [OE *lifer* f. Gmc]

liver² /ˈlɪvə(r)/ *n.* a person who lives in a specified way (*a clean liver*).

liverish /ˈlɪvərɪʃ/ *adj.* **1** suffering from a disorder of the liver. **2** peevish, glum. □□ **liverishly** *adv.* **liverishness** *n.*

Liverpudlian /ˌlɪvəˈpʌdlɪən/ *n. & adj.* —*n.* a native of Liverpool in NW England. —*adj.* of or relating to Liverpool. [joc. f. *Liverpool* + PUDDLE]

liverwort /ˈlɪvəˌwɜːt/ *n.* any small leafy or thalloid bryophyte of the class Hepaticae, of which some have liver-shaped parts.

livery¹ /ˈlɪvərɪ/ *n.* (*pl.* -**ies**) **1 a** a distinctive clothing worn by a member of a City Company or by a servant. **b** membership of a City livery company. **2** a distinctive guise or marking or outward appearance (*birds in their winter livery*). **3** a distinctive colour scheme in which the vehicles, aircraft, etc., of a particular company or line are painted. **4** *US* a place where horses can be hired. **5** *hist.* a provision of food or clothing for retainers etc. **6** *Law* **a** the legal delivery of property. **b** a writ allowing this. □ **at livery** (of a horse) kept for the owner and fed and groomed for a fixed charge. **livery company** *Brit.* one of the London City Companies that formerly had a distinctive costume. **livery stable** a stable where horses are kept at livery or let out for hire. □□ **liveried** *adj.* (esp. in senses 1, 2). [ME f. AF *liveré*, OF *livrée*, fem. past part. of *livrer* DELIVER]

livery² /ˈlɪvərɪ/ *adj.* **1** of the consistency or colour of liver. **2** *Brit.* (of soil) tenacious. **3** *colloq.* liverish.

liveryman /ˈlɪvərɪmən/ *n.* (*pl.* -**men**) **1** *Brit.* a member of a livery company. **2** a keeper of or attendant in a livery stable.

lives *pl.* of LIFE.

livestock /ˈlaɪvstɒk/ *n.* (usu. treated as *pl.*) animals, esp. on a farm, regarded as an asset.

livid /ˈlɪvɪd/ *adj.* **1** *colloq.* furiously angry. **2 a** of a bluish leaden colour. **b** discoloured as by a bruise. □□ **lividity** /lɪˈvɪdɪtɪ/ *n.* **lividly** *adv.* **lividness** *n.* [F *livide* or L *lividus* f. *livēre* be bluish]

living /ˈlɪvɪŋ/ *n. & adj.* —*n.* **1** a livelihood or means of maintenance (*made my living as a journalist*; *what does she do for a living?*). **2** *Brit. Eccl.* a position as a vicar or rector with an income or property. —*adj.* **1** contemporary; now existent (*the greatest living poet*). **2** (of a likeness or image of a person) exact. **3** (of a language) still in vernacular use. **4** (of water) perennially flowing. **5** (of rock etc.) = LIVE² 5. □ **living death** a state of hopeless misery. **living-room** a room for general day use. **within living memory** within the memory of people still living.

lixiviate /lɪˈksɪvɪˌeɪt/ *v.tr.* separate (a substance) into soluble and insoluble constituents by the percolation of liquid. □□ **lixiviation** /-ˈeɪʃ(ə)n/ *n.* [L *lixivius* made into lye f. *lix* lye]

lizard /ˈlɪzəd/ *n.* any reptile of the suborder Lacertilia, having usu. a long body and tail, four legs, movable eyelids, and a rough or scaly hide. [ME f. OF *lesard*(*e*) f. L *lacertus*]

LJ *abbr.* (*pl.* **L JJ**) (in the UK) Lord Justice.

LL *abbr.* Lord Lieutenant.

ll. *abbr.* lines.

'll *v.* (usu. after pronouns) shall, will (*I'll*; *that'll*). [abbr.]

llama /ˈlɑːmə/ *n.* **1** a S. American ruminant, *Lama glama*, kept as a beast of burden and for its soft woolly fleece. **2** the wool from this animal, or cloth made from it. [Sp., prob. f. Quechua]

llanero /ljɑːˈneərəʊ/ *n.* (*pl.* -**os**) an inhabitant of the llanos. [Sp.]

llano /ˈlɑːnəʊ, ˈljɑː-/ *n.* (*pl.* -**os**) a treeless grassy plain or steppe, esp. in S. America. [Sp. f. L *planum* plain]

LL B *abbr.* Bachelor of Laws. [L *legum baccalaureus*]

LL D *abbr.* Doctor of Laws. [L *legum doctor*]

LL M *abbr.* Master of Laws. [L *legum magister*]

Lloyd's /lɔɪdz/ *n.* an incorporated society of underwriters in London. □ **Lloyd's List** a daily publication devoted to shipping news. **Lloyd's Register 1** an annual alphabetical list of ships assigned to various classes. **2** a society that produces this. [after

the orig. meeting in a coffee-house established in 1688 by Edward *Lloyd*]

LM *abbr.* **1** long metre. **2** lunar module.

lm *abbr.* lumen(s).

ln *abbr.* natural logarithm. [mod.L *logarithmus naturalis*]

lo /ləʊ/ *int. archaic* calling attention to an amazing sight. □ **lo and behold** *joc.* a formula introducing a surprising or unexpected fact. [OE *lā* int. of surprise etc., & ME *lō* = *lōke* LOOK]

loach /ləʊtʃ/ *n.* any small edible freshwater fish of the family Cobitidae. [ME f. OF *loche*, of unkn. orig.]

load /ləʊd/ *n. & v.* —*n.* **1 a** what is carried or is to be carried; a burden. **b** an amount usu. or actually carried (often in *comb.*: *a busload of tourists*; *a lorry-load of bricks*). **2** a unit of measure or weight of certain substances. **3** a burden or commitment of work, responsibility, care, grief, etc. **4** (in *pl.*; often foll. by *of*) *colloq.* plenty; a lot. **5 a** *Electr.* the amount of power supplied by a generating system at any given time. **b** *Electronics* an impedance or circuit that receives or develops the output of a transistor or other device. **6** the weight or force borne by the supporting part of a structure. **7** a material object or force acting as a weight or clog. **8** the resistance of machinery to motive power. —*v.* **1** *tr.* **a** put a load on or aboard (a person, vehicle, ship, etc.). **b** place (a load or cargo) aboard a ship, on a vehicle, etc. **2** *intr.* (often foll. by *up*) (of a ship, vehicle, or person) take a load aboard, pick up a load. **3** *tr.* (often foll. by *with*) **a** add weight to; be a weight or burden upon. **b** oppress (*a stomach loaded with food*). **4** *tr.* strain the bearing-capacity of (*a table loaded with food*). **5** *tr.* (also **load up**) (foll. by *with*) **a** supply overwhelmingly (*loaded us with work*). **b** assail overwhelmingly (*loaded us with abuse*). **6** *tr.* charge (a firearm) with ammunition. **7** *tr.* insert (the required operating medium) in a device, e.g. film in a camera, magnetic tape in a tape recorder, a program into a computer, etc. **8** *tr.* add an extra charge to (an insurance premium) in the case of a poorer risk. **9** *tr.* **a** weight with lead. **b** give a bias to (dice, a roulette wheel, etc.) with weights. □ **get a load of** *sl.* listen attentively to; notice. **load-displacement** (or -**draught**) the displacement of a ship when laden. **load line** a Plimsoll line. [OE *lād* way, journey, conveyance, f. Gmc: rel. to LEAD¹, LODE]

loaded /ˈləʊdɪd/ *adj.* **1** bearing or carrying a load. **2** *sl.* **a** wealthy. **b** drunk. **c** *US* drugged. **3** (of dice etc.) weighted or given a bias. **4** (of a question or statement) charged with some hidden or improper implication.

loader /ˈləʊdə(r)/ *n.* **1** a loading-machine. **2** (in *comb.*) a gun, machine, lorry, etc., loaded in a specified way (*breech-loader*). **3** an attendant who loads guns at a shoot. □□ -**loading** *adj.* (in sense 2).

loading /ˈləʊdɪŋ/ *n.* **1** *Electr.* the maximum current or power taken by an appliance. **2** an increase in an insurance premium due to a factor increasing the risk involved (see LOAD *v.* 8). **3** *Austral.* an increment added to a basic wage for special skills etc.

loadstar var. of LODESTAR.

loadstone var. of LODESTONE.

loaf¹ /ləʊf/ *n.* (*pl.* **loaves** /ləʊvz/) **1** a portion of baked bread, usu. of a standard size or shape. **2** a quantity of other food formed into a particular shape (*sugar loaf*; *meat loaf*). **3** *sl.* the head, esp. as a source of common sense (*use your loaf*). □ **loaf sugar** a sugar loaf as a whole or cut into lumps. [OE *hlāf* f. Gmc]

loaf² /ləʊf/ *v. & n.* —*v.* **1** *intr.* (often foll. by *about*, *around*) spend time idly; hang about. **2** *tr.* (foll. by *away*) waste (time) idly (*loafed away the morning*). **3** *intr.* saunter. —*n.* an act or spell of loafing. [prob. a back-form. f. LOAFER]

loafer /ˈləʊfə(r)/ *n.* **1** an idle person. **2** (**Loafer**) *propr.* a leather shoe shaped like a moccasin with a flat heel. [perh. f. G *Landläufer* vagabond]

loam /ləʊm/ *n.* **1** a fertile soil of clay and sand

containing decayed vegetable matter. **2** a paste of clay and water with sand, chopped straw, etc., used in making bricks, plastering, etc. □□ **loamy** *adj*. **loaminess** *n*. [OE *lām* f. WG, rel. to LIME¹]

loan¹ /ləʊn/ *n. & v.* —*n.* **1** something lent, esp. a sum of money to be returned normally with interest. **2** the act of lending or state of being lent. **3** funds acquired by the State, esp. from individuals, and regarded as a debt. **4** a word, custom, etc., adopted by one people from another. —*v.tr.* lend (esp. money). □ **loan shark** *colloq.* a person who lends money at exorbitant rates of interest. **loan-translation** an expression adopted by one language from another in a more or less literally translated form. **on loan** acquired or given as a loan. □□ **loanable** *adj*. **loanee** /ləʊˈniː/ *n*. **loaner** *n*. [ME *lan* f. ON *lán* f. Gmc: cf. LEND]

loan² /ləʊn/ *n.* (also **loaning** /ˈləʊnɪŋ/) *Sc.* **1** a lane. **2** an open place where cows are milked. [ME var. of LANE]

loanholder /ˈləʊnˌhəʊldə(r)/ *n.* **1** a person holding securities for a loan. **2** a mortgagee.

loanword /ˈləʊnwɜːd/ *n.* a word adopted, usu. with little modification, from a foreign language.

loath /ləʊθ/ *predic.adj.* (also **loth**) (usu. foll. by *to* + infin.) disinclined, reluctant, unwilling (*was loath to admit it*). □ **nothing loath** *adj.* quite willing. [OE *lāth* f. Gmc]

loathe /ləʊð/ *v.tr.* regard with disgust; abominate, detest. □□ **loather** *n*. **loathing** *n*. [OE *lāthian* f. Gmc, rel. to LOATH]

loathsome /ˈləʊðsəm/ *adj.* arousing hatred or disgust; offensive, repulsive. □□ **loathsomely** *adv.* **loathsomeness** *n*. [ME f. *loath* disgust f. LOATHE]

loaves *pl.* of LOAF¹.

lob /lɒb/ *v. & n.* —*v.tr.* (**lobbed**, **lobbing**) **1** hit or throw (a ball or missile etc.) slowly or in a high arc. **2** send (an opponent) a lobbed ball. —*n.* **1 a** a ball struck in a high arc. **b** a stroke producing this result. **2** *Cricket* a slow underarm ball. [earlier as noun, prob. f. LG or Du.]

lobar /ˈləʊbə(r)/ *adj.* **1** of the lungs (*lobar pneumonia*). **2** of, relating to, or affecting a lobe.

lobate /ˈləʊbeɪt/ *adj. Biol.* having a lobe or lobes. □□ **lobation** /-ˈbeɪʃ(ə)n/ *n*.

lobby /ˈlɒbɪ/ *n. & v.* —*n.* (*pl.* **-ies**) **1** a porch, ante-room, entrance-hall, or corridor. **2 a** (in the House of Commons) a large hall used esp. for interviews between MPs and members of the public. **b** (also **division lobby**) each of two corridors to which MPs retire to vote. **3 a** a body of persons seeking to influence legislators on behalf of a particular interest (*the anti-abortion lobby*). **b** an organized attempt by members of the public to influence legislators (*a lobby of MPs*). **4** (prec. by *the*) (in the UK) a group of journalists who receive unattributable briefings from the government (*lobby correspondent*). —*v.* (**-ies**, **-ied**) **1** *tr.* solicit the support of (an influential person). **2** *tr.* (of members of the public) seek to influence (the members of a legislature). **3** *intr.* frequent a parliamentary lobby. **4** *tr.* (foll. by *through*) get (a bill etc.) through a legislature, by interviews etc. in the lobby. □□ **lobbyer** *n*. **lobbyism** *n*. **lobbyist** *n*. [med.L *lobia*, *lobium* LODGE]

lobe /ləʊb/ *n.* **1** a roundish and flattish projecting or pendulous part, often each of two or more such parts divided by a fissure (*lobes of the brain*). **2** = ear lobe (see EAR¹). □□ **lobed** *adj*. **lobeless** *adj*. [LL f. Gk *lobos* lobe, pod]

lobectomy /ləˈbektəmɪ/ *n.* (*pl.* **-ies**) *Surgery* the excision of a lobe of an organ such as the thyroid gland, lung, etc.

lobelia /ləˈbiːlɪə/ *n.* any plant of the genus *Lobelia*, with blue, scarlet, white, or purple flowers having a deeply cleft corolla. [M. de *Lobel*, Flemish botanist in England d. 1616]

lobotomy /ləˈbɒtəmɪ/ *n.* (*pl.* **-ies**) *Surgery* = LEUCOTOMY. [LOBE + -TOMY]

lobscouse /ˈlɒbskaʊs/ *n.* a sailor's dish of meat stewed with vegetables and ship's biscuit. [18th c.: orig. unkn.: cf. Du. *lapskous*, Da., Norw., G *Lapskaus*]

lobster /ˈlɒbstə(r)/ *n. & v.* —*n.* **1** any large marine crustacean of the family Nephropidae, with stalked eyes and two pincer-like claws as the first pair of ten limbs. **2** its flesh as food. —*v.intr.* catch lobsters. □ **lobster-pot** a basket in which lobsters are trapped. **lobster thermidor** /ˈθɜːmɪdɔː(r)/ a mixture of lobster meat, mushrooms, cream, egg yolks, and sherry, cooked in a lobster shell. [OE *lopustre*, corrupt. of L *locusta* crustacean, locust: *thermidor* f. the name of the 11th month of the Fr. revolutionary calendar]

lobule /ˈlɒbjuːl/ *n.* a small lobe. □□ **lobular** *adj*. **lobulate** /-lət/ *adj*. [LOBE]

lobworm /ˈlɒbwɜːm/ *n.* **1** a large earthworm used as fishing-bait. **2** = LUGWORM. [LOB in obs. sense 'pendulous object']

local /ˈləʊk(ə)l/ *adj. & n.* —*adj.* **1** belonging to or existing in a particular place or places. **2** peculiar to or only encountered in a particular place or places. **3** of or belonging to the neighbourhood (*the local doctor*). **4** of or affecting a part and not the whole, esp. of the body (*local pain; a local anaesthetic*). **5** in regard to place. —*n.* a local person or thing, esp.: **1** an inhabitant of a particular place regarded with reference to that place. **2** a local train, bus, etc. **3** (often prec. by *the*) *Brit. colloq.* a local public house. **4** a local anaesthetic. **5** *US* a local branch of a trade union. □ **local authority** *Brit.* an administrative body in local government. **local Derby** see DERBY. **local government** a system of administration of a county, district, parish, etc., by the elected representatives of those who live there. **local option** (or **veto**) esp. *US* a system whereby the inhabitants of a district may prohibit the sale of alcoholic liquor there. **local preacher** a Methodist lay person authorized to conduct services in a particular circuit. **local time 1** time measured from the sun's transit over the meridian of a place. **2** the time as reckoned in a particular place, esp. with reference to an event recorded there. **local train** a train stopping at all the stations on its route. □□ **locally** *adv.* **localness** *n*. [ME f. OF f. LL *localis* f. L *locus* place]

locale /ləʊˈkɑːl/ *n.* a scene or locality, esp. with reference to an event or occurrence taking place there. [F *local* (n.) (as LOCAL), respelt to indicate stress: cf. MORALE]

localism /ˈləʊkəˌlɪz(ə)m/ *n.* **1** preference for what is local. **2** a local idiom, custom, etc. **3 a** attachment to a place. **b** a limitation of ideas etc. resulting from this.

locality /ləʊˈkælɪtɪ/ *n.* (*pl.* **-ies**) **1** a district or neighbourhood. **2** the site or scene of something, esp. in relation to its surroundings. **3** the position of a thing; the place where it is. [F *localité* or LL *localitas* (as LOCAL)]

localize /ˈləʊkəˌlaɪz/ *v.tr.* (also **-ise**) **1** restrict or assign to a particular place. **2** invest with the characteristics of a particular place. **3** attach to districts; decentralize. □□ **localizable** *adj*. **localization** /-ˈzeɪʃ(ə)n/ *n*.

locate /ləʊˈkeɪt/ *v.* **1** *tr.* discover the exact place or position of (*locate the enemy's camp*). **2** *tr.* establish in a place or in its proper place. **3** *tr.* state the locality of. **4** *tr.* (in *passive*) be situated. **5** *intr.* (often foll. by *in*) *US* take up residence or business (in a place). □□ **locatable** *adj*. **locator** *n*. [L *locare locat-* f. *locus* place]

location /ləʊˈkeɪʃ(ə)n/ *n.* **1** a particular place; the place or position in which a person or thing is. **2** the act of locating or process of being located. **3** an actual place or natural setting featured in a film or broadcast, as distinct from a simulation in a studio (*filmed entirely on location*). **4** *S.Afr.* an area where

Blacks are obliged to live, usu. on the outskirts of a town or city. [L *locatio* (as LOCATE)]

locative /'lɒkətɪv/ *n.* & *adj. Gram.* —*n.* the case of nouns, pronouns, and adjectives, expressing location. —*adj.* of or in the locative. [formed as LOCATE + -IVE, after *vocative*]

loc. cit. *abbr.* in the passage already cited. [L *loco citato*]

loch /lɒk, lɒx/ *n. Sc.* **1** a lake. **2** an arm of the sea, esp. when narrow or partially land-locked. [ME f. Gael.]

lochia /'lɒkɪə, 'ləʊ-/ *n.* a discharge from the uterus after childbirth. □□ **lochial** *adj.* [mod.L f. Gk *lokhia* neut. pl. of *lokhios* of childbirth]

loci *pl.* of LOCUS.

loci classici *pl.* of LOCUS CLASSICUS.

lock¹ /lɒk/ *n.* & *v.* —*n.* **1** a mechanism for fastening a door, lid, etc., with a bolt that requires a key of a particular shape, or a combination of movements (see *combination lock*), to work it. **2** a confined section of a canal or river where the level can be changed for raising and lowering boats between adjacent sections by the use of gates and sluices. **3 a** the turning of the front wheels of a vehicle to change its direction of motion. **b** (in full **full lock**) the maximum extent of this. **4** an interlocked or jammed state. **5** *Wrestling* a hold that keeps an opponent's limb fixed. **6** (in full **lock forward**) *Rugby Football* a player in the second row of a scrum. **7** an appliance to keep a wheel from revolving or slewing. **8** a mechanism for exploding the charge of a gun. **9** = *airlock* 2. —*v.* **1 a** *tr.* fasten with a lock. **b** *tr.* (foll. by *up*) shut and secure (esp. a building) by locking. **c** *intr.* (of a door, window, box, etc.) have the means of being locked. **2** *tr.* (foll. by *up, in, into*) enclose (a person or thing) by locking or as if by locking. **3** *tr.* (often foll. by *up, away*) store or allocate inaccessibly (*capital locked up in land*). **4** *tr.* (foll. by *in*) hold fast (in sleep or enchantment etc.). **5** *tr.* (usu. in *passive*) (of land, hills, etc.) enclose. **6** *tr.* & *intr.* make or become rigidly fixed or immovable. **7** *intr.* & *tr.* become or cause to become jammed or caught. **8** *tr.* (often in *passive*; foll. by *in*) entangle in an embrace or struggle. **9** *tr.* provide (a canal etc.) with locks. **10** *tr.* (foll. by *up, down*) convey (a boat) through a lock. **11** *intr.* go through a lock on a canal etc. □ **lock-keeper** a keeper of a lock on a river or canal. **lock-knit** knitted with an interlocking stitch. **lock-nut** *Mech.* a nut screwed down on another to keep it tight. **lock on to** locate or cause to locate by radar etc. and then track. **lock out 1** keep (a person) out by locking the door. **2** (of an employer) submit (employees) to a lockout. **lock step** marching with each person as close as possible to the one in front. **lock stitch** a stitch made by a sewing-machine by firmly locking together two threads or stitches. **lock, stock, and barrel** *n.* the whole of a thing. —*adv.* completely. **under lock and key** securely locked up. □□ **lockable** *adj.* **lockless** *adj.* [OE *loc* f. Gmc]

lock² /lɒk/ *n.* **1 a** a portion of hair that coils or hangs together. **b** (in *pl.*) the hair of the head. **2** a tuft of wool or cotton. □□ **-locked** *adj.* (in *comb.*). [OE *locc* f. Gmc]

lockage /'lɒkɪdʒ/ *n.* **1** the amount of rise and fall effected by canal locks. **2** a toll for the use of a lock. **3** the construction or use of locks. **4** locks collectively; the aggregate of locks constructed.

locker /'lɒkə(r)/ *n.* **1** a small lockable cupboard or compartment, esp. each of several for public use. **2** *Naut.* a chest or compartment for clothes, stores, ammunition, etc. **3** a person or thing that locks. □ **locker-room** a room containing lockers (in sense 1), esp. in a pavilion or sports centre.

locket /'lɒkɪt/ *n.* **1** a small ornamental case holding a portrait, lock of hair, etc., and usu. hung from the neck. **2** a metal plate or band on a scabbard. [OF *locquet* dimin. of *loc* latch, lock, f. WG (as LOCK¹)]

lockfast /'lɒkfɑːst/ *adj. Sc.* secured with a lock.

lockjaw /'lɒkdʒɔː/ *n.* = TRISMUS. ¶ Not in technical use.

lockout /'lɒkaʊt/ *n.* the exclusion of employees by their employer from their place of work until certain terms are agreed to.

locksman /'lɒksmən/ *n.* (*pl.* **-men**) a lock-keeper.

locksmith /'lɒksmɪθ/ *n.* a maker and mender of locks.

lock-up /'lɒkʌp/ *n.* & *adj.* —*n.* **1** a house or room for the temporary detention of prisoners. **2** *Brit.* non-residential premises etc. that can be locked up, esp. a small shop or storehouse. **3 a** the locking up of premises for the night. **b** the time of doing this. **4 a** the unrealizable state of invested capital. **b** an amount of capital locked up. —*attrib.adj. Brit.* that can be locked up (*lock-up shop*).

loco¹ /'ləʊkəʊ/ *n.* (*pl.* **-os**) *colloq.* a locomotive engine. [abbr.]

loco² /'ləʊkəʊ/ *adj.* & *n.* —*adj. sl.* crazy. —*n.* (*pl.* **-oes** or **-os**) (in full **loco-weed**) a poisonous leguminous plant of the US causing brain disease in cattle eating it. [Sp., = insane]

locomotion /ˌləʊkə'məʊʃ(ə)n/ *n.* **1** motion or the power of motion from one place to another. **2** travel; a means of travelling, esp. an artificial one. [L *loco* ablat. of *locus* place + *motio* MOTION]

locomotive /ˌləʊkə'məʊtɪv/ *n.* & *adj.* —*n.* (in full **locomotive engine**) an engine powered by steam, diesel fuel, or electricity, used for pulling trains. —*adj.* **1** of or relating to or effecting locomotion (*locomotive power*). **2** having the power of or given to locomotion; not stationary.

locomotor /ˌləʊkə'məʊtə(r)/ *adj.* of or relating to locomotion. [LOCOMOTION + MOTOR]

loculus /'lɒkjʊləs/ *n.* (*pl.* **loculi** /-ˌlaɪ/) *Zool., Anat.,* & *Bot.* each of a number of small separate cavities. □□ **locular** *adj.* [L, dimin. of *locus*: see LOCUS]

locum /'ləʊkəm/ *n. colloq.* = LOCUM TENENS. [abbr.]

locum tenens /ˌləʊkəm 'tiːnenz, 'tenenz/ *n.* (*pl.* **locum tenentes** /ˌləʊkəm tɪ'nentiːz/) a deputy acting esp. for a cleric or doctor. □□ **locum tenency** /ˌləʊkəm 'tenənsɪ/ *n.* [med.L, one holding a place: see LOCUS, TENANT]

locus /'ləʊkəs, 'lɒkəs/ *n.* (*pl.* **loci** /-saɪ, -kaɪ, -kiː/) **1** a position or point, esp. in a text, treatise, etc. **2** *Math.* a curve etc. formed by all the points satisfying a particular equation of the relation between co-ordinates, or by a point, line, or surface moving according to mathematically defined conditions. **3** *Biol.* the position of a gene, mutation, etc. on a chromosome. [L, = place]

locus classicus /ˌləʊkəs 'klæsɪkəs, ˌlɒkəs/ *n.* (*pl.* **loci classici** /ˌləʊsaɪ 'klæsɪˌsaɪ, ˌlɒkiː 'klæsɪˌkiː/) the best known or most authoritative passage on a subject. [L]

locus standi /ˌləʊkəs 'stændaɪ, ˌlɒkəs/ *n.* a recognized or identifiable place (esp. legal) status.

locust /'ləʊkəst/ *n.* **1** any of various African and Asian grasshoppers of the family Acrididae, migrating in swarms and destroying vegetation. **2** *US* a cicada. **3** (in full **locust bean**) a carob. **4** (in full **locust tree**) **a** a carob tree. **b** = ACACIA 3. **c** = KOWHAI. □ **locust-bird** (or **-eater**) any of various birds feeding on locusts. [ME f. OF *locuste* f. L *locusta* lobster, locust]

locution /lək'juːʃ(ə)n/ *n.* **1** a word or phrase, esp. considered in regard to style or idiom. **2** style of speech. [ME f. OF *locution* or L *locutio* f. *loqui locut-* speak]

lode /ləʊd/ *n.* a vein of metal ore. [var. of LOAD]

loden /'ləʊd(ə)n/ *n.* **1** a thick waterproof woollen cloth. **2** the dark green colour in which this is often made. [G]

lodestar /'ləʊdstɑː(r)/ *n.* (also **loadstar**) **1** a star that a ship etc. is steered by, esp. the polestar. **2 a** a guiding principle. **b** an object of pursuit. [LODE in obs. sense 'way, journey' + STAR]

b *but* d *dog* f *few* g *get* h *he* j *yes* k *cat* l *leg* m *man* n *no* p *pen* r *red* s *sit* t *top* v *voice*

lodestone /ˈləʊdstəʊn/ n. (also **loadstone**) **1** magnetic oxide of iron, magnetite. **2 a** a piece of this used as a magnet. **b** a thing that attracts.

lodge /lɒdʒ/ n. & v. —n. **1** a small house at the gates of a park or in the grounds of a large house, occupied by a gatekeeper, gardener, etc. **2** any large house or hotel, esp. in a resort. **3** a house occupied in the hunting or shooting season. **4 a** a porter's room or quarters at the gate of a college or other large building. **b** the residence of a head of a college, esp. at Cambridge. **5** the members or the meeting-place of a branch of a society such as the Freemasons. **6** a local branch of a trade union. **7** a beaver's or otter's lair. **8** a N. American Indian's tent or wigwam. —v. **1** tr. deposit in court or with an official a formal statement of (complaint or information). **2** tr. deposit (money etc.) for security. **3** tr. bring forward (an objection etc.). **4** tr. (foll. by in, with) place (power etc.) in a person or group. **5** tr. & intr. make or become fixed or caught without further movement (the bullet lodged in his brain; the tide lodges mud in the cavities). **6** tr. **a** provide with sleeping quarters. **b** receive as a guest or inmate. **c** establish as a resident in a house or room or rooms. **7** intr. reside or live, esp. as a guest paying for accommodation. **8** tr. serve as a habitation for; contain. **9** tr. (in passive; foll. by in) be contained in. **10 a** tr. (of wind or rain) flatten (crops). **b** intr. (of crops) be flattened in this way. [ME loge f. OF loge arbour, hut, f. med.L laubia, lobia (see LOBBY) f. Gmc]

lodgement /ˈlɒdʒm(ə)nt/ n. **1** the act of lodging or process of being lodged. **2** the depositing or a deposit of money. **3** an accumulation of matter intercepted in fall or transit. [F logement (as LODGE)]

lodger /ˈlɒdʒə(r)/ n. a person receiving accommodation in another's house for payment.

lodging /ˈlɒdʒɪŋ/ n. **1** temporary accommodation (a lodging for the night). **2** (in pl.) a room or rooms (other than in a hotel) rented for lodging in. **3** a dwelling-place. **4** (in pl.) the residence of a head of a college at Oxford. □**lodging-house** a house in which lodgings are let.

lodicule /ˈlɒdɪˌkjuːl/ n. Bot. a small green or white scale below the ovary of a grass flower. [L lodicula dimin. of lodix coverlet]

loess /ˈləʊɪs, lɜːs/ n. a deposit of fine light-coloured wind-blown dust found esp. in the basins of large rivers and very fertile when irrigated. □□ **loessial** /ləʊˈesɪəl, ˈlɜːsɪəl/ adj. [G Löss f. Swiss G lösch loose f. lösen loosen]

loft /lɒft/ n. & v. —n. **1** the space under the roof of a house, above the ceiling of the top floor; an attic. **2** a room over a stable, esp. for hay and straw. **3** a gallery in a church or hall (organ-loft). **4** US an upstairs room. **5** a pigeon-house. **6** Golf **a** a backward slope in a club-head. **b** a lofting stroke. —v.tr. **1 a** send (a ball etc.) high up. **b** clear (an obstacle) in this way. **2** (esp. as **lofted** adj.) give a loft to (a golf club). [OE f. ON lopt air, sky, upper room, f. Gmc (as LIFT)]

lofter /ˈlɒftə(r)/ n. a golf club for lofting the ball.

lofty /ˈlɒftɪ/ adj. (**loftier**, **loftiest**) **1** literary (of things) of imposing height, towering, soaring (lofty heights). **2** consciously haughty, aloof, or dignified (lofty contempt). **3** exalted or noble; sublime (lofty ideals). □□ **loftily** adv. **loftiness** n. [ME f. LOFT as in aloft]

log¹ /lɒg/ n. & v. —n. **1** an unhewn piece of a felled tree, or a similar rough mass of wood, esp. cut for firewood. **2 a** a float attached to a line wound on a reel for gauging the speed of a ship. **b** any other apparatus for the same purpose. **3** a record of events occurring during and affecting the voyage of a ship or aircraft (including the rate of a ship's progress shown by a log: see sense 2). **4** any systematic record of things done, experienced, etc. **5** = LOGBOOK. —v.tr. (**logged**, **logging**) **1 a** enter (the distance made or other details) in a ship's logbook. **b** enter details about (a person or event) in a logbook. **c** (of a ship)

achieve (a certain distance). **2 a** enter (information) in a regular record. **b** attain (a cumulative total of time etc. recorded in this way) (logged 50 hours on the computer). **3** cut into logs. □**like a log 1** in a helpless or stunned state (fell like a log under the left hook). **2** without stirring (slept like a log). **log cabin** a hut built of logs. **log in** = log on. **log-jam 1** a crowded mass of logs in a river. **2** a deadlock. **log-line** a line to which a ship's log (see sense 2a of n.) is attached. **log on** (or **off**) go through the procedures to begin (or conclude) use of a computer system. [ME: orig. unkn.]

log² /lɒg/ n. a logarithm (esp. prefixed to a number or algebraic symbol whose logarithm is to be indicated). [abbr.]

-log US var. of -LOGUE.

logan /ˈləʊgən/ n. (in full **logan-stone**) a poised heavy stone rocking at a touch. [= logging f. dial. log to rock + STONE]

loganberry /ˈləʊgənbərɪ/ n. (pl. **-ies**) **1** a hybrid, Rubus loganobaccus, between a blackberry and a raspberry with dull red acid fruits. **2** the fruit of this plant. [J. H. Logan, Amer. horticulturalist d. 1928 + BERRY]

logarithm /ˈlɒgəˌrɪð(ə)m/ n. **1** one of a series of arithmetic exponents tabulated to simplify computation by making it possible to use addition and subtraction instead of multiplication and division. **2** the power to which a fixed number or base (see BASE¹ 7) must be raised to produce a given number (the logarithm of 1000 to base 10 is 3). ¶ Abbr.: **log**. □**common logarithm** a logarithm to the base 10. **natural** (or **Napierian**) **logarithm** a logarithm to the base e (2.71828.....). ¶ Abbr.: **ln** or $\log_e$. □□ **logarithmic** /-ˈrɪðmɪk/ adj. **logarithmically** /-ˈrɪðmɪkəlɪ/ adv. [mod.L logarithmus f. Gk logos reckoning, ratio + arithmos number]

logbook /ˈlɒgbʊk/ n. **1** a book containing a detailed record or log. **2** Brit. a document recording the registration details of a motor vehicle. ¶ Now officially called vehicle registration document.

loge /ləʊʒ/ n. a private box or enclosure in a theatre. [F]

log$_e$ /lɒgˈiː/ abbr. natural logarithm.

-loger /lədʒə(r)/ comb. form forming nouns, = -LOGIST. [after astrologer]

logger /ˈlɒgə(r)/ n. US a lumberjack.

loggerhead /ˈlɒgəˌhed/ n. **1** an iron instrument with a ball at the end heated for melting pitch etc. **2** any of various large-headed animals, esp. a turtle (Caretta caretta) or shrike (Lanius ludovicianus). **3** archaic a blockhead or fool. □**at loggerheads** (often foll. by with) disagreeing or disputing. [prob. f. dial. logger block of wood for hobbling a horse + HEAD]

loggia /ˈləʊdʒə, ˈlɒ-/ n. **1** an open-sided gallery or arcade. **2** an open-sided extension of a house. [It., = LODGE]

logging /ˈlɒgɪŋ/ n. the work of cutting and preparing forest timber.

logia pl. of LOGION.

logic /ˈlɒdʒɪk/ n. **1 a** the science of reasoning, proof, thinking, or inference. **b** a particular scheme of or treatise on this. **2 a** a chain of reasoning (I don't follow your logic). **b** the correct or incorrect use of reasoning (your logic is flawed). **c** ability in reasoning (argues with great learning and logic). **d** arguments (is not governed by logic). **3 a** the inexorable force or compulsion of a thing (the logic of events). **b** the necessary consequence of (an argument, decision, etc.). **4 a** a system or set of principles underlying the arrangements of elements in a computer or electronic device so as to perform a specified task. **b** logical operations collectively. □□ **logician** /ləˈdʒɪʃ(ə)n/ n. [ME f. OF logique f. LL logica f. Gk logikē (tekhnē) (art) of reason: see LOGOS]

-logic /ˈlɒdʒɪk/ comb. form (also **-logical**) forming

adjectives corresponding esp. to nouns in *-logy* (*pathological*; *theological*). [from or after Gk *-logikos*: see -IC, -ICAL]

logical /'lɒdʒɪk(ə)l/ *adj.* **1** of logic or formal argument. **2** not contravening the laws of thought, correctly reasoned. **3** deducible or defensible on the ground of consistency; reasonably to be believed or done. **4** capable of correct reasoning. □**logical atomism** *Philos.* the theory that all propositions can be analysed into simple independent elements. **logical necessity** the compulsion to believe that of which the opposite is inconceivable. **logical positivism** (or **empiricism**) a form of positivism in which symbolic logic is used and linguistic problems of meaning are emphasized. □□ **logicality** /-'kælɪtɪ/ *n.* **logically** *adv.* [med.L *logicalis* f. LL *logica* (as LOGIC)]

logion /'ləʊgɪɒn/ *n.* (*pl.* **logia** /-gɪə/) a saying attributed to Christ, esp. one not recorded in the canonical Gospels. [Gk, = oracle f. *logos* word]

-logist /lədʒɪst/ *comb. form* forming nouns denoting a person skilled or involved in a branch of study etc. with a name in *-logy* (*archaeologist*; *etymologist*).

logistics /lə'dʒɪstɪks/ *n.pl.* **1** the organization of moving, lodging, and supplying troops and equipment. **2** the detailed organization and implementation of a plan or operation. □□ **logistic** *adj.* **logistical** *adj.* **logistically** *adv.* [F *logistique* f. *loger* lodge]

logo /'ləʊgəʊ, 'lɒgəʊ/ *n.* (*pl.* **-os**) *colloq.* = LOGOTYPE 2. [abbr.]

logogram /'lɒgəˌgræm/ *n.* a sign or character representing a word, esp. in shorthand. [Gk *logos* word + -GRAM]

logomachy /lə'gɒməkɪ/ *n.* (*pl.* **-ies**) *literary* a dispute about words; controversy turning on merely verbal points. [Gk *logomakhia* f. *logos* word + *makhia* fighting]

logorrhoea /ˌlɒgə'rɪə/ *n.* (*US* **logorrhea**) an excessive flow of words esp. in mental illness. [Gk *logos* word + *rhoia* flow]

Logos /'lɒgɒs/ *n.* the Word of God, or Second Person of the Trinity. [Gk, = word, reason]

logotype /'lɒgəˌtaɪp/ *n.* **1** *Printing* a single piece of type that prints a word or group of separate letters. **2 a** an emblem or device used as the badge of an organization in display material. **b** *Printing* a single piece of type that prints this. [Gk *logos* word + TYPE]

logrolling /'lɒgˌrəʊlɪŋ/ *n.* US **1** *colloq.* the practice of exchanging favours, esp. (in politics) of exchanging votes to mutual benefit. **2** a sport in which two contestants stand on a floating log and try to knock each other off. □□ **logroll** *v.intr.* & *tr.* **logroller** *n.* [polit. sense f. phr. *you roll my log and I'll roll yours*]

-logue /lɒg/ *comb. form* (*US* **-log**) **1** forming nouns denoting talk (*dialogue*) or compilation (*catalogue*). **2** = -LOGIST (*ideologue*). [from or after F *-logue* f. Gk *-logos, -logon*]

logwood /'lɒgwʊd/ *n.* **1** a W. Indian tree, *Haematoxylon campechianum.* **2** the wood of this, producing a substance used in dyeing.

-logy /lədʒɪ/ *comb. form* forming nouns denoting: **1** (usu. as **-ology**) a subject of study or interest (*archaeology*; *zoology*). **2** a characteristic of speech or language (*tautology*). **3** discourse (*trilogy*). [F *-logie* or med.L *-logia* f. Gk (as LOGOS)]

loin /lɔɪn/ *n.* **1** (in *pl.*) the part of the body on both sides of the spine between the false ribs and the hip-bones. **2** a joint of meat that includes the loin vertebrae. [ME f. OF *loigne* ult. f. L *lumbus*]

loincloth /'lɔɪnklɒθ/ *n.* a cloth worn round the loins, esp. as a sole garment.

loiter /'lɔɪtə(r)/ *v.* **1** *intr.* hang about; linger idly. **2** *intr.* travel indolently and with long pauses. **3** *tr.* (foll. by *away*) pass (time etc.) in loitering. □**loiter with intent** hang about in order to commit a felony. □□ **loiterer** *n.* [ME f. MDu. *loteren* wag about]

loll /lɒl/ *v.* **1** *intr.* stand, sit, or recline in a lazy attitude. **2** *intr.* (foll. by *out*) (of the tongue) hang

out. **3** *tr.* (foll. by *out*) hang (one's tongue) out. **4** *tr.* let (one's head or limbs) rest lazily on something. □□ **loller** *n.* [ME: prob. imit.]

Lollard /'lɒləd/ *n.* any of the followers of the 14th-c. religious reformer John Wyclif. □□ **Lollardism** *n.* [MDu. *lollaerd* f. *lollen* mumble]

lollipop /'lɒlɪˌpɒp/ *n.* a large usu. flat rounded boiled sweet on a small stick. □**lollipop man** (or **lady** or **woman**) *Brit. colloq.* an official using a circular sign on a stick to stop traffic for children to cross the road, esp. near a school. [perh. f. dial. *lolly* tongue + POP¹]

lollop /'lɒləp/ *v.intr.* (**lolloped, lolloping**) *colloq.* **1** flop about. **2** move or proceed in a lounging or ungainly way. [prob. f. LOLL, assoc. with TROLLOP]

lolly /'lɒlɪ/ *n.* (*pl.* **-ies**) **1** *colloq.* **a** a lollipop. **b** *Austral.* a sweet. **c** *Brit.* = ice lolly. **2** *Brit. sl.* money. [abbr. of LOLLIPOP]

Lombard /'lɒmbɑːd/ *n. & adj.* — *n.* **1** a member of a Germanic people who conquered Italy in the 6th c. **2** a native of Lombardy in N. Italy. **3** the dialect of Lombardy. — *adj.* of or relating to the Lombards or Lombardy. □□ **Lombardic** /-'bɑːdɪk/ *adj.* [ME f. OF *lombard* or MDu. *lombaerd*, f. It. *lombardo* f. med.L *Longobardus* f. L *Langobardus* f. Gmc]

Lombardy poplar /'lɒmbədɪ/ *n.* a variety of poplar with an especially tall slender form.

loment /'ləʊmənt/ *n. Bot.* a kind of pod that breaks up when mature into one-seeded joints. □□ **lomentaceous** /-'teɪʃ(ə)s/ *adj.* [L *lomentum* bean-meal (orig. cosmetic) f. *lavare* wash]

London clay /'lʌnd(ə)n/ *n.* a geological formation in the lower division of Eocene in SE England. [*London*, capital of the UK]

Londoner /'lʌndənə(r)/ *n.* a native or inhabitant of London.

London plane /'lʌnd(ə)n/ *n.* a hybrid plane-tree resistant to smoke and therefore often planted in streets.

London pride /'lʌnd(ə)n/ *n.* a pink-flowered saxifrage, *Saxifraga urbium.*

lone /ləʊn/ *attrib.adj.* **1** (of a person) solitary; without a companion or supporter. **2** (of a place) unfrequented, uninhabited, lonely. **3** *literary* feeling or causing to feel lonely. □**lone hand 1** a hand played or a player playing against the rest at quadrille and euchre. **2** a person or action without allies. **lone wolf** a person who prefers to act alone. [ME, f. ALONE]

lonely /'ləʊnlɪ/ *adj.* (**lonelier, loneliest**) **1** solitary, companionless, isolated. **2** (of a place) unfrequented. **3** sad because without friends or company. □**lonely heart** a lonely person (in sense 3). □□ **loneliness** *n.*

loner /'ləʊnə(r)/ *n.* a person or animal that prefers not to associate with others.

lonesome /'ləʊnsəm/ *adj.* **1** solitary, lonely. **2** feeling lonely or forlorn. **3** causing such a feeling. □**by** (or **on**) **one's lonesome** all alone. □□ **lonesomely** *adv.* **lonesomeness** *n.*

long¹ /lɒŋ/ *adj., n., & adv.* — *adj.* (**longer** /'lɒŋgə(r)/; **longest** /'lɒŋgɪst/) **1** measuring much from end to end in space or time; not soon traversed or finished (*a long line*; *a long journey*; *a long time ago*). **2** (following a measurement) in length or duration (*2 metres long*; *the vacation is two months long*). **3** relatively great in extent or duration (*a long meeting*). **4 a** consisting of a large number of items (*a long list*). **b** seemingly more than the stated amount; tedious, lengthy (*ten long miles*; *tired after a long day*). **5** of elongated shape. **6 a** lasting or reaching far back or forward in time (*a long friendship*). **b** (of a person's memory) retaining things for a long time. **7** far-reaching; acting at a distance; involving a great interval or difference. **8** *Phonet. & Prosody* of a vowel or syllable: **a** having the greater of the two recognized durations. **b** stressed. **c** (of a vowel in English) having the pronunciation shown in the name of the letter (as in *pile* and *cute* which have a long *i* and *u*, as distinct from *pill* and *cut*) (cf. SHORT *adj.* 6). **9** (of odds or a chance) reflecting or representing a low level of probability. **10** *Stock Exch.* **a** (of stocks) bought in large quantities in advance, with the expectation of a rise in price. **b** (of a broker etc.) buying etc. on this basis. **11** (of a bill of exchange) maturing at a distant date. **12** (of a cold drink) large and refreshing. **13** *colloq.* (of a person) tall. **14** (foll. by *on*) *colloq.* well supplied with. —*n.* **1** a long interval or period (*shall not be away for long; it will not take long*). **2** *Phonet.* **a** a long syllable or vowel. **b** a mark indicating that a vowel is long. **3 a** a long-dated stock. **b** a person who buys this. —*adv.* (**longer** /ˈlɒŋɡə(r)/; **longest** /ˈlɒŋɡɪst/) **1** by or for a long time (*long before; long ago; long live the king!*). **2** (following nouns of duration) throughout a specified time (*all day long*). **3** (in *compar.*; with *neg.*) after an implied point of time (*shall not wait any longer*). ▫**as** (or **so**) **long as 1** during the whole time that. **2** provided that; only if. **at long last** see LAST[1]. **before long** fairly soon (*shall see you before long*). **be long** (often foll. by *pres. part.* or *in* + verbal noun) take a long time; be slow (*was long finding it out; the chance was long in coming; I shan't be long*). **by a long chalk** see CHALK. **in the long run 1** over a long period. **2** eventually; finally. **long ago** in the distant past. **long-ago** *adj.* that is in the distant past. **the long and the short of it 1** all that can or need be said. **2** the eventual outcome. **long-case clock** a grandfather clock. **long-chain** (of a molecule) containing a chain of many carbon atoms. **long-dated** (of securities) not due for early payment or redemption. **long-day** (of a plant) needing a long daily period of light to cause flowering. **long-distance 1** (of a telephone call, public transport, etc.) between distant places. **2** (of a weather forecast) long-range. **long division** division of numbers with details of the calculations written down. **long dozen** thirteen. **long-drawn** (or **-drawn-out**) prolonged, esp. unduly. **long face** a dismal or disappointed expression. **long-faced** with a long face. **long field** *Cricket* **1** = *long off.* **2** = *long on.* **3** the part of the field behind the bowler. **long figure** (or *price*) a heavy cost. **long haul 1** the transport of goods or passengers over a long distance. **2** a prolonged effort or task. **long-headed** shrewd, far-seeing, sagacious. **long-headedness** being long-headed. **long hop** a short-pitched easily hit ball in cricket. **long hundredweight** see HUNDRED-WEIGHT. **long in the tooth** rather old (orig. of horses, from the recession of the gums with age). **long johns** *colloq.* underpants with full-length legs. **long-jump** an athletic contest of jumping as far as possible along the ground in one leap. **long leg** *Cricket* **1** a fielder far behind the batsman on the leg side. **2** this position. **long-legged** speedy. **long-life** (of consumable goods) treated to preserve freshness. **long-lived** having a long life; durable. **long measure** a measure of length (metres, miles, etc.). **long metre 1** a hymn stanza of four lines with eight syllables each. **2** a quatrain of iambic tetrameters with alternate lines rhyming. **long off** (or **on**) *Cricket* **1** a fielder far behind the bowler and towards the off (or on) side. **2** his position. **long-player** a long-playing record. **long-playing** (of a gramophone record) playing for about 20–30 minutes on each side. **long-range 1** (of a missile etc.) having a long range. **2** of or relating to a period of time far into the future. **long-running** continuing for a long time. **long ship** *hist.* a long narrow warship with many rowers, used esp. by the Vikings. **long shot 1** a wild guess or venture. **2** a bet at long odds. **3** *Cinematog.* a shot including objects at a distance. **long sight** the ability to see clearly only what is comparatively distant. **long-sleeved** with sleeves reaching to the wrist. **long-standing** that has long existed; not recent. **long-suffering** bearing provocation patiently. **long-sufferingly** in a long-suffering manner. **long suit**

1 many cards of one suit in a hand (esp. more than 3 or 4 in a hand of 13). **2** a thing at which one excels. **long-term** occurring in or relating to a long period of time (*long-term plans*). **long-time** that has been such for a long time. **long ton** see TON[1]. **long tongue** loquacity. **long vacation** *Brit.* the summer vacation of lawcourts and universities. **long waist** a low or deep waist of a dress or body. **long wave** a radio wave of frequency less than 300 kHz. **not by a long shot** by no means. ▫▫ **longish** *adj.* [OE *long, lang*]

long[2] /lɒŋ/ *v.intr.* (foll. by *for* or *to* + infin.) have a strong wish or desire for. [OE *langian* seem long to]

long. *abbr.* longitude.

-long /lɒŋ/ *comb. form* forming adjectives and adverbs: **1** for the duration of (*lifelong*). **2** = -LING[2] (*headlong*).

longboard /ˈlɒŋbɔːd/ *n.* US a type of surfboard.

longboat /ˈlɒŋbəʊt/ *n.* a sailing ship's largest boat.

longbow /ˈlɒŋbəʊ/ *n.* a bow drawn by hand and shooting a long feathered arrow.

longe var. of LUNGE[2].

longeron /ˈlɒndʒərən/ *n.* a longitudinal member of a plane's fuselage. [F, = girder]

longevity /lɒnˈdʒevɪtɪ/ *n.* long life. [LL *longaevitas* f. L *longus* life + *aevum* age]

longhair /ˈlɒŋheə(r)/ *n.* a person characterized by the associations of long hair, esp. a hippie or intellectual.

longhand /ˈlɒŋhænd/ *n.* ordinary handwriting (as opposed to shorthand or typing or printing).

longhorn /ˈlɒŋhɔːn/ *n.* **1** one of a breed of cattle with long horns. **2** any beetle of the family Cerambycidae with long antennae.

longhouse /ˈlɒŋhaʊs/ *n.* a tribal communal dwelling, esp. in N. America and the Far East.

longicorn /ˈlɒndʒɪ‚kɔːn/ *n.* a longhorn beetle. [mod.L *longicornis* f. L *longus* long + *cornu* horn]

longing /ˈlɒŋɪŋ/ *n.* & *adj.* —*n.* a feeling of intense desire. —*adj.* having or showing this feeling. ▫▫ **longingly** *adv.*

longitude /ˈlɒŋgɪ‚tjuːd, ˈlɒndʒ-/ *n.* **1** *Geog.* the angular distance east or west from a standard meridian such as Greenwich to the meridian of any place. ¶ Symb.: λ. **2** *Astron.* the angular distance of a celestial body north or south of the ecliptic measured along a great circle through the body and the poles of the ecliptic. [ME f. L *longitudo -dinis* f. *longus* long]

longitudinal /‚lɒŋgɪˈtjuːdɪn(ə)l, ‚lɒndʒ-/ *adj.* **1** of or in length. **2** running lengthwise. **3** of longitude. ▫**longitudinal wave** a wave vibrating in the direction of propagation. ▫▫ **longitudinally** *adv.*

longshore /ˈlɒŋʃɔː(r)/ *adj.* **1** existing on or frequenting the shore. **2** directed along the shore. [*along shore*]

longshoreman /ˈlɒŋʃɔːmən/ *n.* (*pl.* **-men**) US a docker.

long-sighted /lɒŋˈsaɪtɪd, ˈlɒŋ-/ *adj.* **1** having long sight. **2** having imagination or foresight. ▫▫ **long-sightedly** *adv.* **long-sightedness** *n.*

longstop /ˈlɒŋstɒp/ *n.* **1** *Cricket* **a** a position directly behind the wicket-keeper. **b** a fielder in this position. **2** a last resort.

longueur /lɔ̃ˈgɜː(r)/ *n.* **1** a tedious passage in a book etc. **2** a tedious stretch of time. [F, = length]

longways /ˈlɒŋweɪz/ *adv.* (also **longwise** /ˈlɒŋwaɪz/) = LENGTHWAYS.

long-winded /lɒŋˈwɪndɪd/ *adj.* **1** (of speech or writing) tediously lengthy. **2** able to run a long distance without rest. ▫▫ **long-windedly** *adv.* **long-windedness** *n.*

lonicera /ləˈnɪsərə/ *n.* **1** a dense evergreen shrub, *Lonicera nitidum*, much used as hedging. **2** = HONEYSUCKLE. [A. *Lonicerus*, Ger. botanist d. 1586]

loo[1] /luː/ *n.* *Brit.* *colloq.* a lavatory. [20th c.: orig. uncert.]

loo[2] /luː/ *n.* **1** a round card-game with penalties paid to the pool. **2** this penalty. ▫**loo table** a kind of circular table. [abbr. of obs. *lanterloo* f. F *lanturlu*, refrain of a song]

loof var. of LUFF.

loofah /'luːfə/ n. (also **luffa** /'lʌfə/) **1** a climbing gourdlike plant, *Luffa cylindrica*, native to Asia, producing edible marrow-like fruits. **2** the dried fibrous vascular system of this fruit used as a sponge. [Egypt. Arab. *lūfa*, the plant]

look /lʊk/ v., n., & int. —v. **1 a** intr. (often foll. by *at*) use one's sight; turn one's eyes in some direction. **b** tr. turn one's eyes on; contemplate or examine (*looked me in the eyes*). **2** intr. **a** make a visual or mental search (*I'll look in the morning*). **b** (foll. by *at*) consider, examine (*we must look at the facts*). **3** intr. (foll. by *for*) **a** search for. **b** hope or be on the watch for. **c** expect. **4** intr. inquire (*when one looks deeper*). **5** intr. have a specified appearance; seem (*look a fool*; *look foolish*). **6** intr. (foll. by *to*) **a** consider; take care of; be careful about (*look to the future*). **b** rely on (a person or thing) (*you can look to me for support*). **c** expect; count on; aim at. **7** intr. (foll. by *into*) investigate or examine. **8** tr. (foll. by *what, where*, etc. + clause) ascertain or observe by sight (*look where we are*). **9** intr. (of a thing) face or be turned, or have or afford an outlook, in a specified direction. **10** tr. express, threaten, or show (an emotion etc.) by one's looks. **11** intr. (foll. by *that* + clause) take care; make sure. **12** intr. (foll. by *to* + infin.) expect (*am looking to finish this today*). —n. **1** an act of looking; the directing of the eyes to look at a thing or person; a glance (*a scornful look*). **2** (in *sing.* or *pl.*) the appearance of a face; a person's expression or personal aspect. **3** the (esp. characteristic) appearance of a thing (*the place has a European look*). —int. (also **look here!**) calling attention, expressing a protest, etc. □**look after 1** attend to; take care of. **2** follow with the eye. □**look for. look one's age** appear to be as old as one really is. **look-alike** a person or thing closely resembling another (*a Prince Charles look-alike*). **look alive** (or **lively**) *colloq.* be brisk and alert. **look as if** suggest by appearance the belief that (*it looks as if he's gone*). **look back 1** (foll. by *on, upon, to*) turn one's thoughts to (something past). **2** (usu. with *neg.*) cease to progress (*since then we have never looked back*). **3** *Brit.* make a further visit later. **look before you leap** avoid precipitate action. **look daggers** see DAGGER. **look down on** (or **upon** or **look down one's nose at**) regard with contempt or a feeling of superiority. **look for trouble** see TROUBLE. **look forward to** await (an expected event) eagerly or with specified feelings. **look in** make a short visit or call. **look-in** n. *colloq.* **1** an informal call or visit. **2** a chance of participation or success (*never gets a look-in*). **look a person in the eye** (or **eyes** or **face**) look directly and unashamedly at him or her. **look like 1** have the appearance of. **2** *Brit.* seem to be (*they look like winning*). **3** threaten or promise (*it looks like rain*). **4** indicate the presence of (*it looks like woodworm*). **look on 1** (often foll. by *as*) regard (*looks on you as a friend*; *looked on them with disfavour*). **2** be a spectator; avoid participation. **look oneself** appear in good health (esp. after illness etc.). **look out 1** direct one's sight or put one's head out of a window etc. **2** (often foll. by *for*) be vigilant or prepared. **3** (foll. by *on, over*, etc.) have or afford a specified outlook. **4** search for and produce (*shall look one out for you*). **look over 1** inspect or survey (*looked over the house*). **2** examine (a document etc.) esp. cursorily (*shall look it over*). **look round 1** look in every or another direction. **2** examine the objects of interest in a place (*you must come and look round sometime*). **3** examine the possibilities etc. with a view to deciding on a course of action. **look-see** *colloq.* a survey or inspection. **look sharp** act promptly; make haste (orig. = keep strict watch). **look small** see SMALL. **look through 1** examine the contents of, esp. cursorily. **2** penetrate (a pretence or pretender) with insight. **3** ignore by pretending not to see (*I waved, but you just looked through me*).

look up 1 search for (esp. information in a book). **2** *colloq.* go to visit (a person) (*had intended to look them up*). **3** raise one's eyes (*looked up when I went in*). **4** improve, esp. in price, prosperity, or well-being (*things are looking up all round*). **look a person up and down** scrutinize a person keenly or contemptuously. **look up to** respect or venerate. **not like the look of** find alarming or suspicious. □□**-looking** adj. (in *comb.*). [OE *lōcian* f. WG]

looker /'lʊkə(r)/ n. **1** a person having a specified appearance (*a good-looker*). **2** *colloq.* an attractive woman. □**looker-on** a person who is a mere spectator.

looking-glass /'lʊkɪŋˌglɑːs/ n. a mirror for looking at oneself.

lookout /'lʊkaʊt/ n. **1** a watch or looking out (*on the lookout for bargains*). **2 a** a post of observation. **b** a person or party or boat stationed to keep watch. **3** a view over a landscape. **4** a prospect of luck (*it's a bad lookout for them*). **5** *colloq.* a person's own concern.

loom[1] /luːm/ n. an apparatus for weaving yarn or thread into fabric. [ME *lōme* f. OE *gelōma* tool]

loom[2] /luːm/ v. & n. —v.intr. (often foll. by *up*) **1** come into sight dimly, esp. as a vague and often magnified or threatening shape. **2** (of an event or prospect) be ominously close. —n. a vague often exaggerated first appearance of land at sea etc. [prob. f. LG or Du.: cf. E Fris. *lōmen* move slowly, MHG *lüemen* be weary]

loon /luːn/ n. **1** *US* any aquatic diving bird of the family Gaviidae, with a long slender body and a sharp bill; a diver. **2** *colloq.* a crazy person (cf. LOONY). [alt. f. *loom* f. ON *lómr*]

loony /'luːnɪ/ n. & adj. *sl.* —n. (*pl.* **-ies**) a mad or silly person; a lunatic. —adj. (**loonier, looniest**) crazy, silly. □**loony-bin** *sl.* a mental home or hospital. □□**looniness** n. [abbr. of LUNATIC]

loop /luːp/ n. & v. —n. **1 a** a figure produced by a curve, or a doubled thread etc., that crosses itself. **b** anything forming this figure. **2** a similarly shaped attachment or ornament formed of cord or thread etc. and fastened at the crossing. **3** a ring or curved piece of material as a handle etc. **4** a contraceptive coil. **5** (in full **loop-line**) a railway or telegraph line that diverges from a main line and joins it again. **6** a manœuvre in which an aeroplane describes a vertical loop. **7** *Skating* a manœuvre describing a curve that crosses itself, made on a single edge. **8** *Electr.* a complete circuit for a current. **9** an endless strip of tape or film allowing continuous repetition. **10** *Computing* a programmed sequence of instructions that is repeated until or while a particular condition is satisfied. —v. **1** tr. form (thread etc.) into a loop or loops. **2** tr. enclose with or as with a loop. **3** tr. (often foll. by *up, back, together*) fasten or join with a loop or loops. **4** intr. **a** form a loop. **b** move in looplike patterns. **5** intr. (also **loop the loop**) *Aeron.* perform an aerobatic loop. [ME: orig. unkn.]

looper /'luːpə(r)/ n. **1** a caterpillar of the geometer moth which progresses by arching itself into loops. **2** a device for making loops.

loophole /'luːphəʊl/ n. & v. —n. **1** a means of evading a rule etc. without infringing the letter of it. **2** a narrow vertical slit in a wall for shooting or looking through or to admit light or air. —v.tr. make loopholes in (a wall etc.). [ME *loop* in the same sense + HOLE]

loopy /'luːpɪ/ adj. (**loopier, loopiest**) **1** *sl.* crazy. **2** having many loops.

loose /luːs/ adj., n., & v. —adj. **1 a** not or no longer held by bonds or restraint. **b** (of an animal) not confined or tethered etc. **2** detached or detachable from its place (*has come loose*). **3** not held together or contained or fixed. **4** not specially fastened or packaged (*loose papers*; *had her hair loose*). **5** hanging partly free (*a loose end*). **6** slack, relaxed; not tense or tight. **7** not compact or dense (*loose soil*). **8** (of language, concepts, etc.) inexact; conveying only the general sense. **9** (preceding an agent noun) doing the expressed action in a loose or careless manner (*a loose thinker*). **10** morally lax; dissolute (*loose living*). **11** (of the tongue) likely to speak indiscreetly. **12** (of the bowels) tending to diarrhoea. **13** *Sport* **a** (of a ball) in play but not in any player's possession. **b** (of play etc.) with the players not close together. **14** *Cricket* **a** (of bowling) inaccurately pitched. **b** (of fielding) careless or bungling. **15** (in *comb.*) loosely (*loose-flowing*; *loose-fitting*). —*n.* **1** a state of freedom or unrestrainedness. **2** loose play in football (*in the loose*). **3** free expression. —*v.tr.* **1** release; set free; free from constraint. **2** untie or undo (something that constrains). **3** detach from moorings. **4** relax (*loosed my hold on it*). **5** discharge (a gun or arrow etc.). □**at a loose end** (*US* **at loose ends**) (of a person) unoccupied, esp. temporarily. **loose box** a compartment for a horse, in a stable or vehicle, in which it can move about. **loose change** money as coins in the pocket etc. for casual use. **loose cover** *Brit.* a removable cover for a chair or sofa etc. **loose-leaf** *adj.* (of a notebook, manual, etc.) with each leaf separate and removable. —*n.* a loose-leaf notebook etc. **loose-limbed** having supple limbs. **loose order** an arrangement of soldiers etc. with wide intervals. **on the loose 1** escaped from captivity. **2** having a free enjoyable time. □□ **loosely** *adv.* **looseness** *n.* **loosish** *adj.* [ME *lōs* f. ON *lauss* f. Gmc]

loosen /ˈluːs(ə)n/ *v.* **1** *tr.* & *intr.* make or become less tight or compact or firm. **2** *tr.* make (a regime etc.) less severe. **3** *tr.* release (the bowels) from constipation. **4** *tr.* relieve (a cough) from dryness. □**loosen a person's tongue** make a person talk freely. **loosen up** = *limber up* (see LIMBER¹). □□ **loosener** *n.*

loosestrife /ˈluːsstraɪf/ *n.* **1** any marsh plant of the genus *Lysimachia*, esp. the golden or yellow loosestrife, *L. vulgaris*. **2** any plant of the genus *Lythrum*, esp. the purple loosestrife *L. salicaria*, with racemes of star-shaped purple flowers. [LOOSE + STRIFE, taking the Gk name *lusimakhion* (f. *Lusimakhos*, its discoverer) as if directly f. *luō* undo + *makhē* battle]

loot /luːt/ *n.* & *v.* —*n.* **1** goods taken from an enemy; spoil. **2** booty; illicit gains made by an official. **3** *sl.* money. —*v.tr.* **1** rob (premises) or steal (goods) left unprotected, esp. after riots or other violent events. **2** plunder or sack (a city, building, etc.). **3** carry off as booty. □□ **looter** *n.* [Hindi *lūṭ*]

lop¹ /lɒp/ *v.* & *n.* —*v.* (**lopped, lopping**) **1** *tr.* **a** (often foll. by *off*, *away*) cut or remove (a part or parts) from a whole, esp. branches from a tree. **b** remove branches from (a tree). **2** *tr.* (often foll. by *off*, *away*) remove (items) as superfluous. **3** *intr.* (foll. by *at*) make lopping strokes on (a tree etc.). —*n.* parts lopped off, esp. branches and twigs of trees. □**lop and top** (or **crop**) the trimmings of a tree. □□ **lopper** *n.* [ME f. OE *loppian* (unrecorded): cf. obs. *lip* to prune]

lop² /lɒp/ *v.* (**lopped, lopping**) **1** *intr.* & *tr.* hang limply. **2** *intr.* (foll. by *about*) slouch, dawdle; hang about. **3** *intr.* move with short bounds. **4** *tr.* (of an animal) let (the ears) hang. □**lop-ears** drooping ears. **lop-eared** (of an animal) having drooping ears. □□ **loppy** *adj.* [rel. to LOB]

lope /ləʊp/ *v.* & *n.* —*v.intr.* (esp. of animals) run with a long bounding stride. —*n.* a long bounding stride. [ME, var. of Sc. *loup* f. ON *hlaupa* LEAP]

lopho- /ˈlɒfəʊ, ˈlɒfəʊ/ *comb. form Zool.* crested. [Gk *lophos* crest]

lophobranch /ˈləʊfəˌbræŋk, ˈlɒf-/ *adj.* (of a fish) having the gills arranged in tufts. [LOPHO- + BRANCHIA]

lophodont /ˈləʊfəˌdɒnt, ˈlɒf-/ *n.* & *adj.* —*adj.* having transverse ridges on the grinding surface of molar

teeth. —*n.* an animal with these teeth. [LOPHO- + Gk *odous odont-* tooth]

lophophore /ˈləʊfəˌfɔː(r), ˈlɒf-/ *n.* a tentacled disc at the mouth of bryozoans and brachiopods.

lopolith /ˈlɒpəʊlɪθ/ *n. Geol.* a large saucer-shaped intrusion of igneous rock. [Gk *lopas* basin + -LITH]

lopsided /lɒpˈsaɪdɪd/ *adj.* with one side lower or smaller than the other; unevenly balanced. □□ **lopsidedly** *adv.* **lopsidedness** *n.* [LOP² + SIDE]

loquacious /ləˈkweɪʃəs/ *adj.* **1** talkative. **2** (of birds or water) chattering, babbling. □□ **loquaciously** *adv.* **loquaciousness** *n.* **loquacity** /-ˈkwæsɪtɪ/ *n.* [L *loquax -acis* f. *loqui* talk]

loquat /ˈləʊkwɒt/ *n.* **1** a rosaceous tree, *Eriobotrya japonica*, bearing small yellow egg-shaped fruits. **2** this fruit. [Chin. dial. *luh kwat* rush orange]

loquitur /ˈlɒkwɪtə(r)/ *v.intr.* (he or she) speaks (with the speaker's name following, as a stage direction or to inform the reader). [L]

lor /lɔː(r)/ *int. Brit. sl.* an exclamation of surprise or dismay. [abbr. of LORD]

loran /ˈlɔːrən/ *n.* a system of long-distance navigation in which position is determined from the intervals between signal pulses received from widely spaced radio transmitters. [*long-range navigation*]

lord /lɔːd/ *n., int., & v.* —*n.* **1** a master or ruler. **2** *hist.* a feudal superior, esp. of a manor. **3** a peer of the realm or a person entitled to the title *Lord*, esp. a marquess, earl, viscount, or baron. **4** (**Lord**) (often prec. by *the*) a name for God or Christ. **5** (**Lord**) **a** prefixed as the designation of a marquis, earl, viscount, or baron. **b** prefixed to the Christian name of the younger son of a duke or marquis. **c** (**the Lords**) = *House of Lords*. **6** *Astrol.* the ruling planet (of a sign, house, or chart). —*int.* (**Lord**) expressing surprise, dismay, etc. —*v.tr.* confer the title of Lord upon. □**live like a lord** live sumptuously. **Lord Advocate** the principal law-officer of the Crown in Scotland. **Lord Bishop** the ceremonious title of any bishop. **Lord Chamberlain** see CHAMBERLAIN. **Lord** (or **Lord High**) **Chancellor** (in the UK) the highest officer of the Crown, presiding in the House of Lords etc. **Lord Chief Justice** (in the UK) the president of the Queen's Bench Division. **lord it over** domineer. **Lord Lieutenant 1** (in the UK) the chief executive authority and head of magistrates in each county. **2** *hist.* the viceroy of Ireland. **Lord Mayor** the title of the mayor in London and some other large cities. **Lord Ordinary** see ORDINARY *n.* 5. **lord over** (usu. in *passive*) domineer, rule over. **Lord President of the Council** (in the UK) the cabinet minister presiding at the Privy Council. **Lord Privy Seal** (in the UK) a senior cabinet minister without official duties. **Lord Provost** the head of a municipal corporation or borough in certain Scottish cities. **lords and ladies** wild arum. **Lords Commissioners** the members of a board performing the duties of a high State office put in commission. **Lord's Day** Sunday. **Lords of Session** the judges of the Scottish Court of Session. **Lord's Prayer** the Our Father, the prayer taught by Christ to his disciples. **Lords spiritual** the bishops in the House of Lords. **Lord's Supper** the Eucharist. **Lords temporal** the members of the House of Lords other than the bishops. **Our Lord** a name for Christ. **Sea Lord** a naval member of the Admiralty Board. □□ **lordless** *adj.* **lordlike** *adj.* [OE *hlāford* f. *hlāfweard* = bread-keeper (as LOAF¹, WARD)]

lordling /ˈlɔːdlɪŋ/ *n.* usu. *derog.* a minor lord.

lordly /ˈlɔːdlɪ/ *adj.* (**lordlier, lordliest**) **1** haughty, imperious. **2** suitable for a lord. □□ **lordliness** *n.* [OE *hlāfordlic* (as LORD)]

lordosis /lɔːˈdəʊsɪs/ *n. Med.* inward curvature of the spine (opp. KYPHOSIS). □□ **lordotic** /-ˈdɒtɪk/ *adj.* [mod.L f. Gk *lordōsis* f. *lordos* bent backwards]

lordship /ˈlɔːdʃɪp/ *n.* **1** (usu. **Lordship**) a title used in addressing or referring to a man with the rank of Lord or a judge or a bishop (*Your Lordship*; *His*

Lordship). **2** (foll. by *of, over*) dominion, rule, or ownership. **3** the condition of being a lord. [OE *hlāfordscipe* (as LORD, -SHIP)]

Lordy /'lɔːdɪ/ *int.* = LORD *int.*

lore¹ /lɔː(r)/ *n.* a body of traditions and knowledge on a subject or held by a particular group (*herbal lore; gypsy lore*). [OE *lār* f. Gmc, rel. to LEARN]

lore² /lɔː(r)/ *n. Zool.* a straplike surface between the eye and upper mandible in birds, or between the eye and nostril in snakes. [L *lorum* strap]

lorgnette /lɔːˈnjet/ *n.* (in *sing.* or *pl.*) a pair of eyeglasses or opera-glasses held by a long handle. [F f. *lorgner* to squint]

loricate /'lɒrɪkət/ *adj. & n. Zool.* —*adj.* having a defensive armour of bone, plates, scales, etc. —*n.* an animal with this. [L *loricatus* f. *lorica* breastplate f. *lorum* strap]

lorikeet /'lɒrɪˌkiːt/ *n.* any of various small brightly coloured parrots of the subfamily Loriinae, including the rainbow lorikeet. [dimin. of LORY, after *parakeet*]

loris /'lɔːrɪs/ *n.* (*pl.* same) either of two small tailless nocturnal primates, *Loris tardigradus* of S. India (**slender loris**), and *Nycticebus coucang* of the E. Indies (**slow loris**). [F perh. f. obs. Du. *loeris* clown]

lorn /lɔːn/ *adj. literary* desolate, forlorn, abandoned. [past part. of obs. *leese* f. OE *-lēosan* lose]

lorry /'lɒrɪ/ *n. Brit.* (*pl.* -**ies**) **1** a large strong motor vehicle for transporting goods etc. **2** a long flat low wagon. **3** a truck used on railways and tramways. [19th c.: orig. uncert.]

lory /'lɔːrɪ/ *n.* (*pl.* -**ies**) any of various brightly-coloured Australasian parrots of the subfamily Loriinae. [Malay *lūrī*]

lose /luːz/ *v.* (*past* and *past part.* **lost** /lɒst/) **1** *tr.* be deprived of or cease to have, esp. by negligence or misadventure. **2** *tr.* **a** be deprived of (a person, esp. a close relative) by death. **b** suffer the loss of (a baby) in childbirth. **3** *tr.* become unable to find; fail to keep in sight or follow or mentally grasp (*lose one's way*). **4** *tr.* let or have pass from one's control or reach (*lose one's chance; lose one's bearings*). **5** *tr.* be defeated in (a game, race, lawsuit, battle, etc.). **6** *tr.* evade; get rid of (*lost our pursuers*). **7** *tr.* fail to obtain, catch, or perceive (*lose a train; lose a word*). **8** *tr.* forfeit (a stake, deposit, right to a thing, etc.). **9** *tr.* spend (time, efforts, etc.) to no purpose (*lost no time in raising the alarm*). **10** *intr.* **a** suffer loss or detriment; incur a disadvantage. **b** be worse off, esp. financially. **11** *tr.* cause (a person) the loss of (*will lose you your job*). **12** *intr. & tr.* (of a timepiece) become slow; become slow by (a specified amount of time). **13** *tr.* (in *passive*) disappear, perish; be dead (*was lost in the war; is a lost art*). □**be lost** (or **lose oneself**) **in** be engrossed in. **be lost on** be wasted on, or not noticed or appreciated by. **be lost to** be no longer affected by or accessible to (*is lost to pity; is lost to the world*). **be lost without** have great difficulty if deprived of (*am lost without my diary*). **get lost** *sl.* (usu. in *imper.*) go away. **lose one's balance 1** fail to remain stable; fall. **2** fail to retain one's composure. **lose one's cool** *colloq.* lose one's composure. **lose face** be humiliated; lose one's credibility. **lose ground** see GROUND¹. **lose one's head** see HEAD. **lose heart** be discouraged. **lose one's heart** see HEART. **lose one's nerve** become timid or irresolute. **lose out** (often foll. by *on*) *colloq.* be unsuccessful; not get a fair chance or advantage (in). **lose one's temper** become angry. **lose time** allow time to pass with something unachieved etc. **lose touch** see TOUCH. **lose track of** see TRACK¹. **lose the** (or **one's**) **way** become lost; fail to reach one's destination. **losing battle** a contest or effort in which failure seems certain. **lost cause 1** an enterprise etc. with no chance of success. **2** a person one can no longer hope to influence. **lost generation 1** a generation with many of its men killed in war, esp. that of 1914-18. **2** an emotionally and culturally

unstable generation coming to maturity, esp. in 1915-25. □□ **losable** *adj.* [OE *losian* perish, destroy f. *los* loss]

loser /'luːzə(r)/ *n.* **1** a person or thing that loses or has lost (esp. a contest or game) (*is a poor loser; the loser pays*). **2** *colloq.* a person who regularly fails.

loss /lɒs/ *n.* **1** the act or an instance of losing; the state of being lost. **2** a person, thing, or amount lost. **3** the detriment or disadvantage resulting from losing (*that is no great loss*). □**at a loss** (sold etc.) for less than was paid for it. **be at a loss** be puzzled or uncertain. **be at a loss for words** not know what to say. **loss adjuster** an insurance agent who assesses the amount of compensation arising from a loss. **loss-leader** an item sold at a loss to attract customers. [ME *los, loss* prob. back-form. f. *lost*, past part. of LOSE]

lost *past* and *past part.* of LOSE.

lot /lɒt/ *n. & v.* —*n.* **1** *colloq.* (prec. by *a* or in *pl.*) **a** a large number or amount (*a lot of people; lots of chocolate*). **b** *colloq.* much (*a lot warmer; smiles a lot; is lots better*). **2 a** each of a set of objects used in making a chance selection. **b** this method of deciding (*chosen by lot*). **3** a share, or the responsibility resulting from it. **4** a person's destiny, fortune, or condition. **5** esp. *US* a plot; an allotment of land (*parking lot*). **6** an article or set of articles for sale at an auction etc. **7** a number or quantity of associated persons or things. —*v.tr.* (**lotted, lotting**) divide into lots. □**bad lot** a person of bad character. **cast** (or **draw**) **lots** decide by means of lots. **throw in one's lot with** decide to share the fortunes of. **the** (or **the whole**) **lot** the whole number or quantity. **a whole lot** *colloq.* very much (*is a whole lot better*). [OE *hlot* portion, choice f. Gmc]

loth var. of LOATH.

Lothario /lə'θɑːrɪəʊ, -'θeərɪəʊ/ *n.* (*pl.* -**os**) a rake or libertine. [a character in Rowe's *Fair Penitent* (1703)]

lotion /'ləʊʃ(ə)n/ *n.* a medicinal or cosmetic liquid preparation applied externally. [ME f. OF *lotion* or L *lotio* f. *lavare lot-* wash]

lottery /'lɒtərɪ/ *n.* (*pl.* -**ies**) **1** a means of raising money by selling numbered tickets and giving prizes to the holders of numbers drawn at random. **2** an enterprise, process, etc., whose success is governed by chance (*life is a lottery*). [prob. f. Du. *loterij* (as LOT)]

lotto /'lɒtəʊ/ *n.* a game of chance like bingo, but with numbers drawn instead of called. [It.]

lotus /'ləʊtəs/ *n.* **1** (in Greek mythology) a legendary plant inducing luxurious languor when eaten. **2 a** any water lily of the genus *Nelumbo*, esp. *N. nucifera* of India, with large pink flowers. **b** this flower used symbolically in Hinduism and Buddhism. **3** an Egyptian water lily, *Nymphaea lotus*, with white flowers. **4** any plant of the genus *Lotus*, e.g. bird's foot trefoil. □**lotus-eater** a person given to indolent enjoyment. **lotus-land** a place of indolent enjoyment. **lotus position** a cross-legged position of meditation with the feet resting on the thighs. [L f. Gk *lōtos*, of Semitic orig.]

louche /luːʃ/ *adj.* disreputable, shifty. [F, = squinting]

loud /laʊd/ *adj. & adv.* —*adj.* **1 a** strongly audible, esp. noisily or oppressively so. **b** able or liable to produce loud sounds (*a loud engine*). **c** clamorous, insistent (*loud complaints*). **2** (of colours, design, etc.) gaudy, obtrusive. **3** (of behaviour) aggressive and noisy. —*adv.* in a loud manner. □**loud hailer** an electronic device for amplifying the sound of the voice so that it can be heard at a distance. **loud-mouth** *colloq.* a loud-mouthed person. **loud-mouthed** *colloq.* noisily self-assertive; vociferous. **out loud** aloud. **2** loudly (*laughed out loud*). □□**louden** *v.tr. & intr.* **loudish** *adj.* **loudly** *adv.* **loudness** *n.* [OE *hlūd* f. WG]

loudspeaker /laʊd'spiːkə(r)/ *n.* an apparatus that converts electrical impulses into sound, esp. music and voice.

lough /lɒk, lɒx/ n. Ir. = LOCH. [Ir. *loch* LOCH, assim. to the related obs. ME form *lough*]

louis /'luːɪ/ n. (pl. same /'luːɪz/) hist. (in full **louis d'or** /-'dɔː(r)/) a former French gold coin worth about 20 francs. [*Louis*, the name of kings of France]

lounge /laʊndʒ/ v. & n. —v.intr. 1 recline comfortably and casually; loll. 2 stand or move about idly. —n. 1 a place for lounging, esp.: **a** a public room (e.g. in a hotel). **b** a place in an airport etc. with seats for waiting passengers. **c** a sitting-room in a house. 2 a spell of lounging. □**lounge bar** *Brit.* a more comfortable room for drinking in a public house. **lounge lizard** *colloq.* an idler in fashionable society. **lounge suit** *Brit.* a man's formal suit for ordinary day wear. [perh. f. obs. *lungis* lout]

lounger /'laʊndʒə(r)/ n. 1 a person who lounges. 2 a piece of furniture for relaxing on. 3 a casual garment for wearing when relaxing.

loupe /luːp/ n. a small magnifying glass used by jewellers etc. [F]

lour /'laʊə(r)/ v. & n. (also **lower**) —v.intr. 1 frown; look sullen. 2 (of the sky etc.) look dark and threatening. —n. 1 a scowl. 2 a gloomy look (of the sky etc.). □□**louringly** adv. **loury** adj. [ME *loure*, of unkn. orig.]

louse /laʊs/ n. & v. —n. 1 (pl. **lice** /laɪs/) **a** a parasitic insect, *Pediculus humanus*, infesting the human hair and skin and transmitting various diseases. **b** any insect of the order Anoplura or Mallophaga parasitic on mammals, birds, fish, or plants. 2 *sl.* (pl. **louses**) a contemptible or unpleasant person. —v.tr. remove lice from. □**louse up** *sl.* make a mess of. [OE *lūs*, pl. *lȳs*]

lousewort /'laʊswɜːt/ n. any plant of the genus *Pedicularis* with purple-pink flowers found in marshes and wet places.

lousy /'laʊzɪ/ adj. (**lousier**, **lousiest**) 1 infested with lice. 2 *colloq.* very bad; disgusting (also as a term of general disparagement). 3 *colloq.* (often foll. by *with*) well supplied, teeming (with). □□**lousily** adv. **lousiness** n.

lout /laʊt/ n. a rough, crude, or ill-mannered person (usu. a man). □□**loutish** adj. **loutishly** adv. **loutishness** n. [perh. f. archaic *lout* to bow]

louvre /'luːvə(r)/ n. (also **louver**) 1 each of a set of overlapping slats designed to admit air and some light and exclude rain. 2 a domed structure on a roof with side openings for ventilation etc. □**louvre-boards** the slats or boards making up a louvre. □□**louvred** adj. [ME f. OF *lover*, *lovier* skylight, prob. f. Gmc]

lovable /'lʌvəb(ə)l/ adj. (also **loveable**) inspiring or deserving love or affection. □□**lovability** /-'bɪlɪtɪ/ n. **lovableness** n. **lovably** adv.

lovage /'lʌvɪdʒ/ n. 1 a S. European herb, *Levisticum officinale*, used for flavouring etc. 2 a white-flowered umbelliferous plant, *Ligusticum scoticum*. [ME *loveache* alt. f. OF *levesche* f. LL *levisticum* f. L *ligusticum* neut. of *ligusticus* Ligurian]

lovat /'lʌvət/ n. (also *attrib.*) a muted green colour found esp. in tweed and woollen garments. [*Lovat* in Scotland]

love /lʌv/ n. & v. —n. 1 an intense feeling of deep affection or fondness for a person or thing; great liking. 2 sexual passion. 3 sexual relations. 4 **a** a beloved one; a sweetheart (often as a form of address). **b** *Brit. colloq.* a form of address regardless of affection. 5 *colloq.* a person of whom one is fond. 6 affectionate greetings (*give him my love*). 7 (often **Love**) a representation of Cupid. 8 (in some games) no score; nil. —v.tr. 1 (also *absol.*) feel love or deep fondness for. 2 delight in; admire; greatly cherish. 3 *colloq.* like very much (*loves books*). 4 (foll. by verbal noun, or *to* + infin.) be inclined, esp. as a habit; greatly enjoy; find pleasure in (*children love dressing up*; *loves to find fault*). □**fall in love** (often foll. by *with*) develop a great (esp. sexual) love (for). **for love** for pleasure not profit. **for the love of** for the sake of. **in love** (often foll. by *with*) deeply

enamoured (of). **love affair** a romantic or sexual relationship between two people in love. **love-apple** *archaic* a tomato. **love-bird** any of various African and Madagascan parrots, esp. *Agapornis personata*. **love-child** an illegitimate child. **love-feast** 1 a meal affirming brotherly love among early Christians. 2 a religious service of Methodists, etc., imitating this. **love game** a game in which the loser makes no score. **love-hate relationship** an intensely emotional relationship in which one or each party has ambivalent feelings of love and hate for the other. **love-in-a-mist** a blue-flowered garden plant, *Nigella damascena*, with many delicate green bracts. **love-letter** a letter expressing feelings of sexual love. **love-lies-bleeding** a garden plant, *Amaranthus caudatus*, with drooping spikes of purple-red blooms. **love-match** a marriage made for love's sake. **love-nest** a place of intimate lovemaking. **love-seat** an armchair or small sofa for two. **make love** (often foll. by *to*) 1 have sexual intercourse (with). 2 *archaic* pay amorous attention (to). **not for love or money** *colloq.* not in any circumstances. **out of love** no longer in love. □□ **loveworthy** adj. [OE *lufu* f. Gmc]

loveable var. of LOVABLE.

loveless /'lʌvlɪs/ adj. without love; unloving or unloved or both. □□**lovelessly** adv. **lovelessness** n.

lovelock /'lʌvlɒk/ n. a curl or lock of hair worn on the temple or forehead.

lovelorn /'lʌvlɔːn/ adj. pining from unrequited love.

lovely /'lʌvlɪ/ adj. & n. —adj. (**lovelier**, **loveliest**) 1 exquisitely beautiful. 2 *colloq.* pleasing, delightful. —n. (pl. **-ies**) *colloq.* a pretty woman. □**lovely and** *colloq.* delightfully (*lovely and warm*). □□**lovelily** adv. **loveliness** n. [OE *luflic* (as LOVE)]

lovemaking /'lʌv,meɪkɪŋ/ n. 1 amorous sexual activity, esp. sexual intercourse. 2 *archaic* courtship.

lover /'lʌvə(r)/ n. 1 a person in love with another. 2 a person with whom another is having sexual relations. 3 (in *pl.*) a couple in love or having sexual relations. 4 a person who likes or enjoys something specified (*a music lover*; *a lover of words*). □□ **loverless** adj.

lovesick /'lʌvsɪk/ adj. languishing with romantic love. □□**lovesickness** n.

lovesome /'lʌvsəm/ adj. *literary* lovely, lovable.

lovey /'lʌvɪ/ n. (pl. **-eys**) *colloq.* love, sweetheart (esp. as a form of address).

lovey-dovey /,lʌvɪ'dʌvɪ/ adj. fondly affectionate, esp. unduly sentimental.

loving /'lʌvɪŋ/ adj. & n. —adj. feeling or showing love; affectionate. —n. affection; active love. □**loving-cup** a two-handled drinking-cup passed round at banquets. **loving-kindness** tenderness and consideration. □□**lovingly** adv. **lovingness** n. [OE *lufiende* (as LOVE)]

low¹ /ləʊ/ adj., n., & adv. —adj. 1 of less than average height; not high or tall or reaching far up (*a low wall*). 2 **a** situated close to ground or sea level etc.; not elevated in position (*low altitude*). **b** (of the sun) near the horizon. **c** (of latitude) near the equator. 3 of or in humble rank or position (*of low birth*). 4 of small or less than normal amount or extent or intensity (*low price*; *low temperature*; *low in calories*). 5 small or reduced in quantity (*stocks are low*). 6 coming below the normal level (*a dress with a low neck*). 7 **a** dejected; lacking vigour (*feeling low*; *in low spirits*). **b** poorly nourished; indicative of poor nutrition. 8 (of a sound) not shrill or loud or high-pitched. 9 not exalted or sublime; commonplace. 10 unfavourable (*a low opinion*). 11 abject, mean, vulgar (*low cunning*; *low slang*). 12 (in *compar.*) situated on less high land or to the south. 13 (of a geographical period) earlier. —n. 1 a low or the lowest level or number (*the dollar has reached a new low*). 2 an area of low pressure. —adv. 1 in or to a low position or state. 2 in a low tone (*speak low*). 3 (of a sound) at or to a low pitch. □**low-born** of humble birth. **Low Church** the section of the Church of England giving a low place to ritual, priestly authority, and the sacraments. **low-class** of low quality or social class. **low comedy** that in which the subject and the treatment border on farce. **Low Countries** the Netherlands, Belgium, and Luxemburg. **low-cut** (of a dress etc.) made with a low neckline. **low-down** *adj.* abject, mean, dishonourable. *—n. colloq.* (usu. foll. by *on*) the relevant information (about). **lowest common denominator**, **multiple** see DENOMINATOR, MULTIPLE. **low frequency** (in radio) 30-300 kilohertz. **low gear** see GEAR. **Low German** see GERMAN. **low-grade** of low quality or strength. **low-key** lacking intensity or prominence; restrained. **Low Latin** medieval and later forms of Latin. **low-level** *Computing* (of a programming language) close in form to machine language. **low-loader** a lorry with a low floor and no sides, for heavy loads. **low-lying** at low altitude (above sea level etc.). **low mass** see MASS². **low-pitched 1** (of a sound) low. **2** (of a roof) having only a slight slope. **low pressure 1** little demand for activity or exertion. **2** an atmospheric condition with pressure below average. **low profile** avoidance of attention or publicity. **low-profile** *adj.* (of a motor-vehicle tyre) having a greater width than usual in relation to height. **low relief** see RELIEF 6a. **low-rise** (of a building) having few storeys. **low season** the period of fewest visitors at a resort etc. **low-spirited** dejected, dispirited. **low-spiritedness** dejection, depression. **low spirits** dejection, depression. **Low Sunday** the Sunday after Easter. **low tide** the time or level of the tide at its ebb. **low water** the tide at its lowest. **low-water mark 1** the level reached at low water. **2** a minimum recorded level or value etc. **Low Week** the week beginning with Low Sunday. □□ **lowish** *adj.* **lowness** *n.* [ME *lāh* f. ON *lágr* f. Gmc]

low² /ləʊ/ *n. & v. —n.* a sound made by cattle; a moo. *—v.intr.* utter this sound. [OE *hlōwan* f. Gmc]

lowboy /ˈləʊbɔɪ/ *n. US* a low chest or table with drawers and short legs.

lowbrow /ˈləʊbraʊ/ *adj. & n. —adj.* not highly intellectual or cultured. *—n.* a lowbrow person. □□ **lowbrowed** *adj.*

lower¹ /ˈləʊə(r)/ *adj. & adv. —adj.* (*compar.* of LOW¹). **1** less high in position or status. **2** situated below another part (*lower lip*; *lower atmosphere*). **3 a** situated on less high land (*Lower Egypt*). **b** situated to the South (*Lower California*). **4** (of a mammal, plant, etc.) evolved to only a slight degree (e.g. a platypus or fungus). *—adv.* in or to a lower position, status, etc. □ **lower case** see CASE². **lower class** working-class people and their families. **lower-class** *adj.* of the lower class. **lower deck 1** the deck of a ship situated immediately over the hold. **2** the petty officers and men of a ship collectively. **Lower House** the larger and usu. elected body in a legislature, esp. the House of Commons. **lower regions** (or **world**) hell; the realm of the dead. □□ **lowermost** *adj.*

lower² /ˈləʊə(r)/ *v.* **1** *tr.* let or haul down. **2** *tr. & intr.* make or become lower. **3** *tr.* reduce the height or pitch or elevation of (*lower your voice*; *lower one's eyes*). **4** *tr.* degrade. **5** *tr. & intr.* diminish.

lower³ var. of LOUR.

lowland /ˈləʊlənd/ *n. & adj. —n.* **1** (usu. in *pl.*) low-lying country. **2** (**Lowland**) (usu. in *pl.*) the region of Scotland lying south and east of the Highlands. *—adj.* of or in lowland or the Scottish Lowlands. □□ **lowlander** *n.* (also **Lowlander**).

lowlight /ˈləʊlaɪt/ *n.* **1** a monotonous or dull period; a feature of little prominence (*one of the lowlights of the evening*). **2** (usu. in *pl.*) a dark tint in the hair produced by dyeing. [after HIGHLIGHT]

lowly /ˈləʊlɪ/ *adj.* (**lowlier, lowliest**) **1** humble in feeling, behaviour, or status. **2** modest, unpretentious. **3** (of an organism) evolved to only a slight degree. □□ **lowlily** *adv.* **lowliness** *n.*

low-minded /ləʊˈmaɪndɪd/ *adj.* vulgar or ignoble in mind or character. □□ **low-mindedness** *n.*

lox¹ /lɒks/ *n.* liquid oxygen. [abbr.]

lox² /lɒks/ *n. US* smoked salmon. [Yiddish *laks*]

loyal /ˈlɔɪəl/ *adj.* **1** (often foll. by *to*) true or faithful (to duty, love, or obligation). **2** steadfast in allegiance; devoted to the legitimate sovereign or government of one's country. **3** showing loyalty. □ **loyal toast** a toast to the sovereign. □□ **loyally** *adv.* [F f. OF *loial* etc. f. L *legalis* LEGAL]

loyalist /ˈlɔɪəlɪst/ *n.* **1** a person who remains loyal to the legitimate sovereign etc., esp. in the face of rebellion or usurpation. **2** (**Loyalist**) a supporter of Parliamentary union between Great Britain and Northern Ireland. □□ **loyalism** *n.*

loyalty /ˈlɔɪəltɪ/ *n.* (*pl.* **-ies**) **1** the state of being loyal. **2** (often in *pl.*) a feeling or application of loyalty.

lozenge /ˈlɒzɪndʒ/ *n.* **1** a rhombus or diamond figure. **2** a small sweet or medicinal tablet, orig. lozenge-shaped, for dissolving in the mouth. **3** a lozenge-shaped pane in a window. **4** *Heraldry* a lozenge-shaped device. **5** the lozenge-shaped facet of a cut gem. □□ **lozenged** *adj.* (in sense 4). **lozengy** *adj.* [ME f. OF *losenge*, ult. of Gaulish or Iberian orig.]

LP *abbr.* **1** long-playing (gramophone record). **2** low pressure.

LPG *abbr.* liquefied petroleum gas.

L-plate /ˈelpleɪt/ *n. Brit.* a sign bearing the letter L, attached to the front and rear of a motor vehicle to indicate that it is being driven by a learner.

LPO *abbr.* London Philharmonic Orchestra.

LSD *abbr.* lysergic acid diethylamide.

l.s.d. /ˌelesˈdiː/ *n.* (also **£.s.d.**) *Brit.* **1** pounds, shillings, and pence (in former British currency). **2** money, riches. [L *librae, solidi, denarii*]

LSE *abbr.* London School of Economics.

LSO *abbr.* London Symphony Orchestra.

Lt. *abbr.* **1** Lieutenant. **2** light.

LTA *abbr.* Lawn Tennis Association.

Ltd. *abbr.* Limited.

Lu *symb. Chem.* the element lutetium.

lubber /ˈlʌbə(r)/ *n.* a big clumsy fellow; a lout. □ **lubber line** *Naut.* a line marked on a compass, showing the ship's forward direction. □□ **lubberlike** *adj.* **lubberly** *adj. & adv.* [ME, perh. f. OF *lobeor* swindler, parasite f. *lober* deceive]

lubra /ˈluːbrə/ *n. Austral.* sometimes *derog.* an Aboriginal woman. [F *loubra* f. Tasmanian]

lubricant /ˈluːbrɪkənt/ *n. & adj. —n.* a substance used to reduce friction. *—adj.* lubricating.

lubricate /ˈluːbrɪˌkeɪt/ *v.tr.* **1** reduce friction in (machinery etc.) by applying oil or grease etc. **2** make slippery or smooth with oil or grease. □□ **lubrication** /-ˈkeɪʃ(ə)n/ *n.* **lubricative** /-kətɪv/ *adj.* **lubricator** *n.* [L *lubricare lubricat-* f. *lubricus* slippery]

lubricious /luːˈbrɪʃəs/ *adj.* (also **lubricous** /ˈluːbrɪkəs/) **1** slippery, smooth, oily. **2** lewd, prurient, evasive. □□ **lubricity** *n.* [L *lubricus* slippery]

Lucan /ˈluːkən/ *adj.* of or relating to St Luke. [eccl.L *Lucas* f. Gk *Loukas* Luke]

luce /luːs/ *n.* a pike (fish), esp. when full-grown. [ME f. OF *lus, luis* f. LL *lucius*]

lucent /ˈluːs(ə)nt/ *adj. literary* **1** shining, luminous. **2** translucent. □□ **lucency** *n.* **lucently** *adv.* [L *lucēre* shine (as LUX)]

lucerne /luːˈsɜːn/ *n.* (also **lucern**) *Brit.* = ALFALFA. [F *luzerne* f. mod. Prov. *luzerno* glow-worm, with ref. to its shiny seeds]

lucid /ˈluːsɪd/ *adj.* **1** expressing or expressed clearly; easy to understand. **2** of or denoting intervals of sanity between periods of insanity or dementia. **3** *Bot.* with a smooth shining surface. **4** *poet.* bright. □□ **lucidity** /-ˈsɪdɪtɪ/ *n.* **lucidly** *adv.* **lucidness** *n.* [L *lucidus* (perh. through F *lucide* or It. *lucido*) f. *lucēre* shine (as LUX)]

Lucifer /ˈluːsɪfə(r)/ *n.* **1** Satan. **2** *poet.* the morning star (the planet Venus). **3** (**lucifer**) *archaic* a friction match. [OE f. L, = light-bringing, morning-star (as LUX, *-fer* f. *ferre* bring)]

luck /lʌk/ *n.* **1** chance regarded as the bringer of good or bad fortune. **2** circumstances of life (beneficial or not) brought by this. **3** good fortune; success due to chance (*in luck*; *out of luck*). □**for luck** to bring good fortune. **good luck 1** good fortune. **2** an omen of this. **hard luck** worse fortune than one deserves. **no such luck** *colloq.* unfortunately not. **try one's luck** make a venture. **with luck** if all goes well. **worse luck** *colloq.* unfortunately. [ME f. LG *luk* f. MLG *geluke*]

luckily /ˈlʌkɪlɪ/ *adv.* **1** (qualifying a whole sentence or clause) fortunately (*luckily there was enough food*). **2** in a lucky or fortunate manner.

luckless /ˈlʌklɪs/ *adj.* having no luck; unfortunate. □□**lucklessly** *adv.* **lucklessness** *n.*

lucky /ˈlʌkɪ/ *adj.* (**luckier, luckiest**) **1** having or resulting from good luck, esp. as distinct from skill or design or merit. **2** bringing good luck (*a lucky mascot*). **3** fortunate, appropriate (*a lucky guess*). □**lucky dip** *Brit.* a tub containing different articles concealed in wrapping or bran etc., and chosen at random by participants. □□**luckiness** *n.*

lucrative /ˈluːkrətɪv/ *adj.* profitable, yielding financial gain. □□**lucratively** *adv.* **lucrativeness** *n.* [ME f. L *lucrativus* f. *lucrari* to gain]

lucre /ˈluːkə(r)/ *n.* *derog.* financial profit or gain. □**filthy lucre** see FILTHY. [ME f. F *lucre* or L *lucrum*]

lucubrate /ˈluːkjʊˌbreɪt/ *v.intr. literary* **1** write or study, esp. by night. **2** express one's meditations in writing. □□**lucubrator** *n.* [L *lucubrare lucubrat-* work by lamplight (as LUX)]

lucubration /ˌluːkjʊˈbreɪʃ(ə)n/ *n.* *literary* **1** nocturnal study or meditation. **2** (usu. in *pl.*) literary writings, esp. of a pedantic or elaborate character. [L *lucubratio* (as LUCUBRATE)]

Lucullan /luːˈkʌlən, lʊ-/ *adj.* profusely luxurious. [L. Licinius *Lucullus*, Roman general of 1st c. BC famous for his lavish banquets]

lud /lʌd/ *n.* *Brit.* □**m'lud** (or **my lud**) a form of address to a judge in a court of law. [corrupt. of LORD]

Luddite /ˈlʌdaɪt/ *n. & adj.* —*n.* **1** *hist.* a member of any of the bands of English artisans who rioted against mechanization and destroyed machinery (1811–16). **2** a person opposed to increased industrialization or new technology. —*adj.* of the Luddites or their beliefs. □□**Luddism** *n.* **Luddism** *n.* [perh. f. Ned *Lud*, who destroyed machinery *c.*1779]

ludicrous /ˈluːdɪkrəs/ *adj.* absurd or ridiculous; laughable. □□**ludicrously** *adv.* **ludicrousness** *n.* [L *ludicrus* prob. f. *ludicrum* stage play]

ludo /ˈluːdəʊ/ *n.* *Brit.* a simple board game in which counters are moved round according to the throw of dice. [L, = I play]

lues /ˈluːiːz/ *n.* (in full **lues venerea** /vɪˈnɪərɪə/) syphilis. □□**luetic** /luːˈetɪk/ *adj.* [L]

luff /lʌf/ *n. & v.* (also **loof** /luːf/) *Naut.* —*n.* **1** the edge of the fore-and-aft sail next to the mast or stay. **2** *Brit.* the broadest part of the ship's bow where the sides begin to curve in. —*v.tr.* (also *absol.*) **1** steer (a ship) nearer to the wind. **2** turn (the helm) so as to achieve this. **3** obstruct (an opponent in yacht-racing) by sailing closer to the wind. **4** raise or lower (the jib of a crane or derrick). [ME *lo(o)f* f. OF *lof*, prob. f. LG]

luffa var. of LOOFAH.

Luftwaffe /ˈlʊftˌvæfə/ *n.* *hist.* the German Air Force. [G f. *Luft* air + *Waffe* weapon]

lug¹ /lʌg/ *v. & n.* —*v.* (**lugged, lugging**) **1** *tr.* **a** drag or tug (a heavy object) with effort or violence. **b** (usu. foll. by *round, about*) carry (something heavy) around with one. **2** *tr.* (usu. foll. by *in, into*) introduce (a subject etc.) irrelevantly. **3** *tr.* (usu. foll. by *along, to*) force (a person) to join in an activity. **4** *intr.* (usu.

foll. by *at*) pull hard. —*n.* **1** a hard or rough pull. **2** (in *pl.*) *US* affectation (*put on lugs*). [ME, prob. f. Scand.: cf. Sw. *lugga* pull a person's hair f. *lugg* forelock]

lug² /lʌg/ *n.* **1** *Sc.* or *colloq.* an ear. **2** a projection on an object by which it may be carried, fixed in place, etc. **3** esp. *US sl.* a lout; a sponger; a stupid person. [prob. of Scand. orig.: cf. LUG¹]

lug³ /lʌg/ *n.* = LUGWORM. [17th c.: orig. unkn.]

lug⁴ /lʌg/ *n.* = LUGSAIL. [abbr.]

luge /luːʒ/ *n. & v.* —*n.* a light toboggan for one or two people, ridden in the sitting position. —*v.intr.* ride on a luge. [Swiss F]

Luger /ˈluːgə(r)/ *n.* a type of German automatic pistol. [G. *Luger*, German firearms expert d. 1922]

luggage /ˈlʌgɪdʒ/ *n.* suitcases, bags, etc. to hold a traveller's belongings. □**luggage-van** *Brit.* a railway carriage for travellers' luggage. [LUG¹ + -AGE]

lugger /ˈlʌgə(r)/ *n.* a small ship carrying two or three masts with a lugsail on each. [LUGSAIL + -ER¹]

lughole /ˈlʌghəʊl, ˈlʌgəʊl/ *n. sl.* the ear orifice. [LUG² + HOLE]

lugsail /ˈlʌgseɪl, -s(ə)l/ *n.* *Naut.* a quadrilateral sail which is bent on and hoisted from a yard. [prob. f. LUG²]

lugubrious /luːˈguːbrɪəs, lʊ-/ *adj.* doleful, mournful, dismal. □□**lugubriously** *adv.* **lugubriousness** *n.* [L *lugubris* f. *lugēre* mourn]

lugworm /ˈlʌgwɜːm/ *n.* any polychaete worm of the genus *Arenicola*, living in muddy sand and leaving characteristic worm-casts on lower shores, and often used as bait by fishermen. [LUG³]

lukewarm /luːkˈwɔːm, ˈluːk-/ *adj.* **1** moderately warm; tepid. **2** unenthusiastic, indifferent. □□**lukewarmly** *adv.* **lukewarmness** *n.* [ME f. (now dial.) *luke, lew* f. OE]

lull /lʌl/ *v. & n.* —*v.* **1** *tr.* soothe or send to sleep gently. **2** *tr.* (usu. foll. by *into*) deceive (a person) into confidence (*lulled into a false sense of security*). **3** *tr.* allay (suspicions etc.) usu. by deception. **4** *intr.* (of noise, a storm, etc.) abate or fall quiet. —*n.* a temporary quiet period in a storm or in any activity. [ME, imit. of sounds used to quieten a child]

lullaby /ˈlʌləˌbaɪ/ *n. & v.* —*n.* (*pl.* **-ies**) **1** a soothing song to send a child to sleep. **2** the music for this. —*v.tr.* (**-ies, -ied**) sing to sleep. [as LULL + *-by* as in BYE-BYE²]

lulu /ˈluːluː/ *n. sl.* a remarkable or excellent person or thing. [19th c., perh. f. *Lulu*, pet form of *Louise*]

lumbago /lʌmˈbeɪgəʊ/ *n.* rheumatic pain in the muscles of the lower back. [L f. *lumbus* loin]

lumbar /ˈlʌmbə(r)/ *adj.* *Anat.* relating to the loin, esp. the lower back area. □**lumbar puncture** the withdrawal of spinal fluid from the lower back with a hollow needle, usu. for diagnosis. [med.L *lumbaris* f. L *lumbus* loin]

lumber¹ /ˈlʌmbə(r)/ *v.intr.* (usu. foll. by *along, past, by*, etc.) move in a slow clumsy noisy way. □□**lumbering** *adj.* [ME *lomere*, perh. imit.]

lumber² /ˈlʌmbə(r)/ *n. & v.* —*n.* **1** disused articles of furniture etc. inconveniently taking up space. **2** useless or cumbersome objects. **3** *US* partly prepared timber. —*v.* **1** *tr.* **a** (usu. foll. by *with*) leave (a person etc.) with something unwanted or unpleasant (*always lumbering me with the cleaning*). **b** (as **lumbered** *adj.*) in an unwanted or inconvenient situation (*afraid of being lumbered*). **2** *tr.* (usu. foll. by *together*) heap or group together carelessly. **3** *tr.* (usu. foll. by *up*) obstruct. **4** *intr.* cut and prepare forest timber for transport. □**lumber-jacket** a jacket, usu. of warm checked material, of the kind worn by lumberjacks. **lumber-room** a room where disused or cumbrous things are kept. □□**lumberer** *n.* (in sense 4 of *v.*). **lumbering** *n.* (in sense 4 of *v.*). [perh. f. LUMBER¹: later assoc. with obs. *lumber* pawnbroker's shop]

lumberjack /ˈlʌmbəˌdʒæk/ *n.* (also **lumberman** *pl.*

-men) esp. *US* one who fells, prepares, or conveys lumber.

lumbersome /ˈlʌmbəsəm/ *adj.* unwieldy, awkward.

lumbrical muscle /ˈlʌmbrɪk(ə)l/ *n.* any of the muscles flexing the fingers or toes. [mod.L *lumbricalis* f. L *lumbricus* earthworm, with ref. to its shape]

lumen /ˈluːmen/ *n.* **1** *Physics* the SI unit of luminous flux, equal to the amount of light emitted per second in a unit solid angle of one steradian from a uniform source of one candela. ¶ Abbr.: **lm.** **2** *Anat.* (*pl.* **lumina** /-mɪnə/) a cavity within a tube, cell, etc. □□ **luminal** /ˈluːmɪn(ə)l/ *adj.* [L *lumen luminis* a light, an opening]

Luminal /ˈluːmɪn(ə)l/ *n. propr.* phenobarbitone. [as LUMEN + -*al* as in *veronal*]

luminance /ˈluːmɪnəns/ *n. Physics* the intensity of light emitted from a surface per unit area in a given direction. [L *luminare* illuminate (as LUMEN)]

luminary /ˈluːmɪnərɪ/ *n.* (*pl.* **-ies**) **1** *literary* a natural light-giving body, esp. the sun or moon. **2** a person as a source of intellectual light or moral inspiration. **3** a prominent member of a group or gathering (*a host of show-business luminaries*). [ME f. OF *luminarie* or LL *luminarium* f. L LUMEN]

luminescence /ˌluːmɪˈnes(ə)ns/ *n.* the emission of light by a substance other than as a result of incandescence. □□ **luminescent** *adj.* [as LUMEN + -ESCENCE (see -ESCENT)]

luminiferous /ˌluːmɪˈnɪfərəs, ˌljuː-/ *adj.* producing or transmitting light.

luminous /ˈluːmɪnəs, ˈljuː-/ *adj.* **1** full of or shedding light; radiant, bright, shining. **2** phosphorescent, visible in darkness (*luminous paint*). **3** (esp. of a writer or a writer's work) throwing light on a subject. **4** of visible radiation (*luminous intensity*). □□ **luminosity** /-ˈnɒsɪtɪ/ *n.* **luminously** *adj.* **luminousness** *n.* [ME f. OF *lumineux* or L *luminosus*]

lumme /ˈlʌmɪ/ *int. Brit. sl.* an expression of surprise or interest. [= (*Lord*) *love me*]

lummox /ˈlʌməks/ *n. US colloq.* a clumsy or stupid person. [19th c. in US & dial.: orig. unkn.]

lump¹ /lʌmp/ *n. & v.* —*n.* **1** a compact shapeless or unshapely mass. **2** *sl.* a quantity or heap. **3** a tumour, swelling, or bruise. **4** a heavy, dull, or ungainly person. **5** (prec. by *the*) *Brit.* casual workers in the building and other trades. —*v.* **1** *tr.* (usu. foll. by *together*, *with*, *in with*, *under*, etc.) mass together or group indiscriminately. **2** *tr.* carry or throw carelessly (*lumping crates round the yard*). **3** *intr.* become lumpy. **4** *intr.* (usu. foll. by *along*) proceed heavily or awkwardly. **5** *intr.* (usu. foll. by *down*) sit down heavily. □ **in the lump** taking things as a whole; in a general manner. **lump in the throat** a feeling of pressure there, caused by emotion. **lump sugar** sugar shaped into lumps or cubes. **lump sum 1** a sum covering a number of items. **2** money paid down at once (opp. INSTALMENT). □□ **lumper** *n.* (in sense 2 of v.). [ME, perh. of Scand. orig.]

lump² /lʌmp/ *v.tr. colloq.* endure or suffer (a situation) ungraciously. □ **like it or lump it** put up with something whether one likes it or not. [imit.: cf. *dump*, *grump*, etc.]

lumpectomy /lʌmˈpektəmɪ/ *n.* (*pl.* **-ies**) the surgical removal of a usu. cancerous lump from the breast.

lumpenproletariat /ˈlʌmpənˌprəʊlɪˈteərɪət/ *n.* (esp. in Marxist terminology) the unorganized and unpolitical lower orders of society, not interested in revolutionary advancement. □□ **lumpen** *adj.* [G f. *Lumpen* rag, rogue: see PROLETARIAT]

lumpfish /ˈlʌmpfɪʃ/ *n.* (*pl.* **-fishes** or **-fish**) a spiny-finned fish, *Cyclopterus lumpus*, of the N. Atlantic with modified pelvic fins for clinging to objects. [MLG *lumpen*, MDu. *lumpe* (perh. = LUMP¹) + FISH¹]

lumpish /ˈlʌmpɪʃ/ *adj.* **1** heavy and clumsy. **2** stupid, lethargic. □□ **lumpishly** *adv.* **lumpishness** *n.*

lumpsucker /ˈlʌmpˌsʌkə(r)/ *n.* = LUMPFISH.

lumpy /ˈlʌmpɪ/ *adj.* (**lumpier, lumpiest**) **1** full of or covered with lumps. **2** (of water) cut up by the wind into small waves. □□ **lumpily** *adv.* **lumpiness** *n.*

lunacy /ˈluːnəsɪ/ *n.* (*pl.* **-ies**) **1** insanity (orig. of the intermittent kind attributed to changes of the moon); the state of being a lunatic. **2** *Law* such mental unsoundness as interferes with civil rights or transactions. **3** great folly or eccentricity; a foolish act.

luna moth /ˈluːnə/ *n.* a N. American moth, *Actias luna*, with crescent-shaped spots on its pale green wings. [L *luna*, = moon (from its markings)]

lunar /ˈluːnə(r), ˈljuː-/ *adj.* **1** of, relating to, or determined by the moon. **2** concerned with travel to the moon and related research. **3** (of light, glory, etc.) pale, feeble. **4** crescent-shaped, lunate. **5** of or containing silver (from alchemists' use of *luna* (= moon) for 'silver'). □ **lunar caustic** silver nitrate, esp. in stick form. **lunar cycle** = METONIC CYCLE. **lunar distance** the angular distance of the moon from the sun, a planet, or a star, used in finding longitude at sea. **lunar module** a small craft used for travelling between the moon's surface and a spacecraft in orbit around the moon. **lunar month 1** the period of the moon's revolution, esp. the interval between new moons of about 29½ days. **2** (in general use) a period of four weeks. **lunar nodes** the points at which the moon's orbit cuts the ecliptic. **lunar observation** the finding of longitude by lunar distance. **lunar orbit 1** the orbit of the moon round the earth. **2** an orbit round the moon. **lunar year** a period of 12 lunar months. [L *lunaris* f. *luna* moon]

lunate /ˈluːneɪt, ˈljuː-/ *adj. & n.* —*adj.* crescent-shaped. —*n.* a crescent-shaped prehistoric implement etc. □ **lunate bone** a crescent-shaped bone in the wrist. [L *lunatus* f. *luna* moon]

lunatic /ˈluːnətɪk/ *n. & adj.* —*n.* **1** an insane person. **2** someone foolish or eccentric. —*adj.* mad, foolish. □ **lunatic asylum** *hist.* a mental home or hospital. **lunatic fringe** an extreme or eccentric minority group. [ME f. OF *lunatique* f. LL *lunaticus* f. L *luna* moon]

lunation /luːˈneɪʃ(ə)n, ˈljuː-/ *n.* the interval between new moons, about 29½ days. [ME f. med.L *lunatio* (as LUNATIC)]

lunch /lʌntʃ/ *n. & v.* —*n.* **1** the meal eaten in the middle of the day. **2** a light meal eaten at any time. —*v.* **1** *intr.* eat one's lunch. **2** *tr.* provide lunch for. □ **lunch-box** a container for a packed meal. **lunch-hour** (or **-time**) a break from work, when lunch is eaten. □□ **luncher** *n.* [LUNCHEON]

luncheon /ˈlʌntʃ(ə)n/ *n. formal* lunch. □ **luncheon meat** a usu. tinned block of ground meat ready to cut and eat. **luncheon voucher** *Brit.* a voucher or ticket issued to employees and exchangeable for food at many restaurants and shops. [17th c.: orig. unkn.]

luncheonette /ˌlʌntʃəˈnet/ *n.* orig. *US* a small restaurant or snack bar serving light lunches.

lune /luːn/ *n. Geom.* a crescent-shaped figure formed on a sphere or plane by two arcs intersecting at two points. [F f. L *luna* moon]

lunette /luːˈnet/ *n.* **1** an arched aperture in a domed ceiling to admit light. **2** a crescent-shaped or semicircular space or alcove which contains a painting, statue, etc. **3** a watch-glass of flattened shape. **4** a ring through which a hook is placed to attach a vehicle to the vehicle towing it. **5** a temporary fortification with two faces forming a salient angle, and two flanks. **6** *RC Ch.* a holder for the consecrated host in a monstrance. [F, dimin. of *lune* (see LUNE)]

lung /lʌŋ/ *n.* either of the pair of respiratory organs which bring air into contact with the blood in humans and many other vertebrates. □ **lung-power** the power of one's voice. □□ **lunged** *adj.* **lungful** *n.* (*pl.* **-fuls**). **lungless** *adj.* [OE *lungen* f. Gmc, rel. to LIGHT²]

lunge¹ /lʌndʒ/ *n. & v.* —*n.* **1** a sudden movement forward. **2** a thrust with a sword etc., esp. the basic attacking move in fencing. **3** a movement forward by bending the front leg at the knee while keeping the back leg straight. —*v.* **1** *intr.* make a lunge. **2** *intr.* (usu. foll. by *at*, *out*) deliver a blow from the shoulder in boxing. **3** *tr.* drive (a weapon etc.) violently in some direction. [earlier *allonge* f. F *allonger* lengthen f. *à* to + *long* LONG¹]

lunge² /lʌndʒ, lju:-/ *n. & v.* (also **longe**) —*n.* **1** a long rope on which a horse is held and made to move in a circle round its trainer. **2** a circular exercise-ground for training horses. —*v.tr.* exercise (a horse) with or in a lunge. [F *longe*, *allonge* (as LUNGE¹)]

lungfish /ˈlʌŋfɪʃ/ *n.* any freshwater fish of the order Dipnoi, having gills and a modified swim bladder used as lungs, and able to aestivate to survive drought.

lungi /ˈlʊŋgi:/ *n.* (*pl.* **lungis**) a length of cotton cloth, usu. worn as a loincloth in India, or as a skirt in Burma (now Myanmar) where it is the national dress for both sexes. [Urdu]

lungwort /ˈlʌŋwɜːt/ *n.* **1** any herbaceous plant of the genus *Pulmonaria*, esp. *P. officinalis* with white-spotted leaves likened to a diseased lung. **2** a lichen, *Lobaria pulmonaria*, used as a remedy for lung disease.

lunisolar /ˌluːnɪˈsəʊlə(r)/ *adj.* of or concerning the sun and moon. □**lunisolar period** a period of 532 years between the repetitions of both solar and lunar cycles. **lunisolar year** a year with divisions regulated by changes of the moon and an average length made to agree with the solar year. [L *luna* moon + *sol* sun]

lunula /ˈluːnjʊlə/ *n.* (*pl.* **lunulae** /-ˌliː/) **1** a crescent-shaped mark, esp. the white area at the base of the fingernail. **2** a crescent-shaped Bronze-Age ornament. [L, dimin. of *luna* moon]

lupin /ˈluːpɪn/ *n.* (also **lupine** /-pɪn/) **1** any plant of the genus *Lupinus*, with long tapering spikes of blue, purple, pink, white, or yellow flowers. **2** (in *pl.*) seeds of the lupin. [ME f. L *lupinus*]

lupine /ˈluːpaɪn/ *adj.* of or like a wolf or wolves. [L *lupinus* f. *lupus* wolf]

lupus /ˈluːpəs/ *n.* any of various ulcerous skin diseases, esp. tuberculosis of the skin. □**lupus vulgaris** /vʌlˈgeərɪs/ tuberculosis with dark red patches on the skin, usu. due to direct inoculation of the tuberculosis bacillus into the skin. □□**lupoid** *adj.* **lupous** *adj.* [L, = wolf]

lur /lʊə(r)/ *n.* (also **lure** /ljʊə(r)/) a bronze S-shaped trumpet of prehistoric times, still used in Scandinavia to call cattle. [Da. & Norw.]

lurch¹ /lɜːtʃ/ *n. & v.* —*n.* a stagger, a sudden unsteady movement or leaning. —*v.intr.* stagger, move suddenly and unsteadily. [orig. Naut., *lee-lurch* alt. of *lee-latch* drifting to leeward]

lurch² /lɜːtʃ/ *n.* □**leave in the lurch** desert (a friend etc.) in difficulties. [orig. = a severe defeat in a game, f. F *lourche* (also the game itself, like backgammon)]

lurcher /ˈlɜːtʃə(r)/ *n.* **1** *Brit.* a cross-bred dog, usu. a retriever, collie, or sheepdog crossed with a greyhound, used esp. for hunting and by poachers. **2** *archaic* a petty thief, swindler, or spy. [f. obs. *lurch* (v.) var. of LURK]

lure¹ /ljʊə(r), lʊə(r)/ *v. & n.* —*v.tr.* **1** (usu. foll. by *away*, *into*) entice (a person, an animal, etc.) usu. with some form of bait. **2** attract back again or recall (a person, animal, etc.) with the promise of a reward. —*n.* **1** a thing used to entice. **2** (usu. foll. by *of*) the attractive or compelling qualities (of a pursuit etc.). **3** a falconer's apparatus for recalling a hawk, consisting of a bunch of feathers attached to a thong, within which the hawk finds food while being trained. □□**luring** *adj.* **luringly** *adv.* [ME f. OE *luere* f. Gmc]

lure² var. of LUR.

Lurex /ˈljʊəreks/ *n. propr.* **1** a type of yarn which incorporates a glittering metallic thread. **2** fabric made from this yarn.

lurid /ˈljʊərɪd, ˈlʊə-/ *adj.* **1** vivid or glowing in colour (*lurid orange*). **2** of an unnatural glare (*lurid nocturnal brilliance*). **3** sensational, horrifying, or terrible (*lurid details*). **4** showy, gaudy (*paperbacks with lurid covers*). **5** ghastly, wan (*lurid complexion*). **6** *Bot.* of a dingy yellowish brown. □**cast a lurid light on** explain or reveal (facts or character) in a horrific, sensational, or shocking way. □□**luridly** *adv.* **luridness** *n.* [L *luridus* f. *luror* wan or yellow colour]

lurk /lɜːk/ *v. & n.* —*v.intr.* **1** linger furtively or unobtrusively. **2 a** lie in ambush. **b** (usu. foll. by *in*, *under*, *about*, etc.) hide, esp. for sinister purposes. **3** (as **lurking** *adj.*) latent, semi-conscious (*a lurking suspicion*). —*n.* *Austral. sl.* a dodge, racket, or scheme; a method of profitable business. □□**lurker** *n.* [ME perh. f. LOUR with frequent. -*k* as in TALK]

luscious /ˈlʌʃəs/ *adj.* **1 a** richly sweet in taste or smell. **b** *colloq.* delicious. **2** (of literary style, music, etc.) over-rich in sound, imagery, or voluptuous suggestion. **3** voluptuously attractive. □□**lusciously** *adv.* **lusciousness** *n.* [ME perh. alt. of obs. *licious* f. DELICIOUS]

lush¹ /lʌʃ/ *adj.* **1** (of vegetation, esp. grass) luxuriant and succulent. **2** luxurious. □□**lushly** *adv.* **lushness** *n.* [ME, perh. var. of obs. *lash* soft, f. OF *lasche* lax (see LACHES): assoc. with LUSCIOUS]

lush² /lʌʃ/ *n. & v.* esp. *US sl.* —*n.* **1** alcohol, liquor. **2** an alcoholic, a drunkard. —*v.* **1** *tr. & intr.* drink (alcohol). **2** *tr.* ply with alcohol. [18th c.: perh. joc. use of LUSH¹]

lust /lʌst/ *n. & v.* —*n.* **1** strong sexual desire. **2 a** (usu. foll. by *for*, *of*) a passionate desire for (*a lust for power*). **b** (usu. foll. by *of*) a passionate enjoyment of (*the lust of battle*). **3** (usu. in *pl.*) a sensuous appetite regarded as sinful (*the lusts of the flesh*). —*v.intr.* (usu. foll. by *after*, *for*) have a strong or excessive (esp. sexual) desire. □□**lustful** *adj.* **lustfully** *adv.* **lustfulness** *n.* [OE f. Gmc]

luster *US* var. of LUSTRE¹.

lustra *pl.* of LUSTRUM.

lustral /ˈlʌstr(ə)l/ *adj.* relating to or used in ceremonial purification. [L *lustralis* (as LUSTRUM)]

lustrate /ˈlʌstreɪt/ *v.tr.* purify by expiatory sacrifice, ceremonial washing, or other such rite. □□**lustration** /-ˈstreɪʃ(ə)n/ *n.* [L *lustrare* (as LUSTRUM)]

lustre¹ /ˈlʌstə(r)/ *n. & v.* (*US* **luster**) —*n.* **1** gloss, brilliance, or sheen. **2** a shining or reflective surface. **3 a** a thin metallic coating giving an iridescent glaze to ceramics. **b** = LUSTREWARE. **4** a radiance or attractiveness; splendour, glory, distinction (of achievements etc.) (*add lustre to*; *shed lustre on*). **5 a** a prismatic glass pendant on a chandelier etc. **b** a cut-glass chandelier or candelabra. **6 a** *Brit.* a thin dress-material with a cotton warp, woollen weft, and a glossy surface. **b** any fabric with a sheen or gloss. —*v.tr.* put lustre on (pottery, a cloth, etc.). □□**lustreless** *adj.* (*US* **lusterless**). **lustrous** *adj.* **lustrously** *adv.* **lustrousness** *n.* [F f. It. *lustro* f. *lustrare* f. L *lustrare* illuminate]

lustre² /ˈlʌstə(r)/ *n.* (*US* **luster**) = LUSTRUM. [ME, Anglicized f. LUSTRUM]

lustreware /ˈlʌstəˌweə(r)/ *n.* (*US* **lusterware**) ceramics with an iridescent glaze. [LUSTRE¹]

lustrum /ˈlʌstrəm/ *n.* (*pl.* **lustra** /-strə/ or **lustrums**) a period of five years. [L, an orig. purificatory sacrifice after a quinquennial census]

lusty /ˈlʌstɪ/ *adj.* (**lustier**, **lustiest**) **1** healthy and strong. **2** vigorous or lively. □□**lustily** *adv.* **lustiness** *n.* [ME f. LUST + -Y¹]

lusus /ˈljuːsəs, ˈluː-/ *n.* (in full ***lusus naturae*** /nəˈtjʊəriː, -ˈtʊəraɪ/) a freak of nature. [L]

lutanist var. of LUTENIST.

lute¹ /luːt, ljuːt/ *n.* a guitar-like instrument with a long neck and a pear-shaped body, much used in the 14th–17th c. [ME f. F *lut*, *leüt*, prob. f. Prov. *laüt* f. Arab. *al-'ūd*]

lute² /luːt, ljuːt/ *n. & v.* —*n.* **1** clay or cement used to stop a hole, make a joint airtight, coat a crucible, protect a graft, etc. **2** a rubber seal for a jar etc. —*v.tr.* apply lute to. [ME f. OF *lut* f. L *lutum* mud, clay]

lutecium var. of LUTETIUM.

lutein /'luːtɪɪn, 'ljuː-/ *n. Chem.* a pigment of a deep yellow colour found in egg-yolk etc. [L *luteum* yolk of egg, neut. of *luteus* yellow]

luteinizing hormone /'luːtəˌnaɪzɪŋ/ *n. Biochem.* a hormone secreted by the anterior pituitary gland that in females stimulates ovulation and in males stimulates the synthesis of androgen. ¶ Abbr.: **LH.** [LUTEIN]

lutenist /'luːtənɪst, 'ljuː-/ *n.* (also **lutanist**) a lute-player. [med.L *lutanista* f. *lutana* LUTE[1]]

luteo- /'luːtɪəʊ, 'ljuː-/ *comb. form* orange-coloured. [as LUTEOUS + -O-]

luteofulvous /ˌluːtɪəʊˈfʌlvəs, ˌljuː-/ *adj.* orange-tawny.

luteous /'luːtɪəs, 'ljuː-/ *adj.* of a deep orange yellow or greenish yellow. [L *luteus* f. *lutum* WELD[2]]

lutestring /'luːtstrɪŋ, 'ljuː-/ *n. archaic* a glossy silk fabric. [app. f. *lustring* f. F *lustrine* or It. *lustrino* f. *lustro* LUSTRE[1]]

lutetium /luːˈtiːʃəm, ljuː-/ *n.* (also **lutecium**) *Chem.* a silvery metallic element of the lanthanide series. ¶ Symb.: **Lu.** [F *lutécium* f. L *Lutetia* the ancient name of Paris]

Lutheran /'luːθərən, 'ljuː-/ *n. & adj.* —*n.* **1** a follower of Martin Luther, Ger. religious reformer d. 1546. **2** a member of the Church which accepts the Augsburg confession of 1530, with justification by faith alone as a cardinal doctrine. —*adj.* of or characterized by the theology of Martin Luther. □□ **Lutheranism** *n.* **Lutheranize** *v.tr. & intr.* (also **-ise**).

Lutine bell /'luːtiːn/ *n.* a bell kept at Lloyd's in London and rung whenever there is an important announcement to be made to the underwriters. [HMS *Lutine*, which sank in 1799, whose bell it was]

luting /'luːtɪŋ/ *n.* = LUTE[2] *n.*

lutz /lʊts/ *n.* a jump in ice-skating in which the skater takes off from the outside back edge of one skate and lands, after a complete rotation in the air, on the outside back edge of the opposite skate. [prob. f. Gustave *Lussi* b. 1898, who invented it]

lux /lʌks/ *n.* (*pl.* same) *Physics* the SI unit of illumination, equivalent to one lumen per square metre. ¶ Abbr.: **lx.** [L *lux lucis* light]

luxe /lʊks, lʌks/ *n.* luxury (cf. DE LUXE). [F f. L *luxus*]

Luxemburger /'lʌksəmˌbɜːgə(r)/ *n.* **1** a native or national of Luxemburg. **2** a person of Luxemburg descent.

luxuriant /lʌgˈzjʊərɪənt, lʌkˈsj-, lʌgˈʒʊə-/ *adj.* **1** (of vegetation etc.) lush, profuse in growth. **2** prolific, exuberant, rank (*luxuriant imagination*). **3** (of literary or artistic style) florid, richly ornate. □□ **luxuriance** *n.* **luxuriantly** *adv.* [L *luxuriare* grow rank f. *luxuria* LUXURY]

luxuriate /lʌgˈzjʊərɪˌeɪt, lʌkˈsj-, lʌgˈʒʊə-/ *v.intr.* **1** (foll. by *in*) take self-indulgent delight in, enjoy in a luxurious manner. **2** take one's ease, relax in comfort.

luxurious /lʌgˈzjʊərɪəs, lʌkˈsj-, lʌgˈʒʊə-/ *adj.* **1** supplied with luxuries. **2** extremely comfortable. **3** fond of luxury, self-indulgent, voluptuous. □□ **luxuriously** *adv.* **luxuriousness** *n.* [ME f. OF *luxurios* f. L *luxuriosus* (as LUXURY)]

luxury /'lʌkʃərɪ/ *n.* (*pl.* **-ies**) **1** choice or costly surroundings, possessions, food, etc.; luxuriousness (*a life of luxury*). **2** something desirable for comfort or enjoyment, but not indispensable. **3** (*attrib.*) providing great comfort, expensive (*a luxury flat; a luxury holiday*). [ME f. OF *luxurie, luxure* f. L *luxuria* f. *luxus* abundance]

LV *abbr. Brit.* luncheon voucher.

Lw *symb. Chem.* the element lawrencium.

LWM *abbr.* low-water mark.

lx *abbr.* lux.

LXX *abbr.* Septuagint.

-ly[1] /lɪ/ *suffix* forming adjectives esp. from nouns, meaning: **1** having the qualities of (*princely; manly*). **2** recurring at intervals of (*daily; hourly*). [from or after OE *-lic* f. Gmc, rel. to LIKE[1]]

-ly[2] /lɪ/ *suffix* forming adverbs from adjectives, denoting esp. manner or degree (*boldly; happily; miserably; deservedly; amusingly*). [from or after OE *-līce* f. Gmc (as -LY[1])]

lycanthrope /'laɪkənˌθrəʊp/ *n.* **1** a werewolf. **2** an insane person who believes that he or she is an animal, esp. a wolf. [mod.L *lycanthropus* f. Gk (as LYCANTHROPY)]

lycanthropy /laɪˈkænθrəpɪ/ *n.* **1** the mythical transformation of a person into a wolf (see also WEREWOLF). **2** a form of madness involving the delusion of being a wolf, with changed appetites, voice, etc. [mod.L *lycanthropia* f. Gk *lukanthrōpia* f. *lukos* wolf + *anthrōpos* man]

lycée /'liːseɪ/ *n.* (*pl.* **lycées**) a State secondary school in France. [F f. L (as LYCEUM)]

Lyceum /laɪˈsiːəm/ *n.* **1 a** the garden at Athens in which Aristotle taught philosophy. **b** Aristotelian philosophy and its followers. **2** (**lyceum**) *US hist.* a literary institution, lecture-hall, or teaching-place. [L f. Gk *Lukeion* neut. of *Lukeios* epithet of Apollo (from whose neighbouring temple the Lyceum was named)]

lychee /'laɪtʃɪ, 'liː-/ *n.* (also **litchi, lichee**) **1** a sweet fleshy fruit with a thin spiny skin. **2** the tree, *Nephelium litchi*, orig. from China, bearing this. [Chin. *lizhi*]

lych-gate var. of LICH-GATE.

lychnis /'lɪknɪs/ *n.* any herbaceous plant of the genus *Lychnis*, including ragged robin. [L f. Gk *lukhnis* a red flower f. *lukhnos* lamp]

lycopod /'laɪkəˌpɒd/ *n.* any of various club-mosses, esp. of the genus *Lycopodium*. [Anglicized form of LYCOPODIUM]

lycopodium /ˌlaɪkəˈpəʊdɪəm/ *n.* **1** = LYCOPOD. **2** a fine powder of spores from this, used as an absorbent in surgery, and in making fireworks etc. [mod.L f. Gk *lukos* wolf + *pous podos* foot]

Lycra /'laɪkrə/ *n. propr.* an elastic polyurethane fibre or fabric used esp. for close-fitting sports clothing.

Lydian /'lɪdɪən/ *adj. & n.* —*n.* **1** a native or inhabitant of ancient Lydia in W. Asia Minor. **2** the language of this people. —*adj.* of or relating to the people of Lydia or their language. □ **Lydian mode** *Mus.* the mode represented by the natural diatonic scale F–F. [L *Lydius* f. Gk *Ludios* of Lydia]

lye /laɪ/ *n.* **1** water that has been made alkaline by lixiviation of vegetable ashes. **2** any strong alkaline solution, esp. of potassium hydroxide used for washing or cleansing. [OE *lēag* f. Gmc: cf. LATHER]

lying[1] /'laɪɪŋ/ *pres. part.* of LIE[1]. —*n.* a place to lie (*a dry lying*).

lying[2] /'laɪɪŋ/ *pres. part.* of LIE[2]. —*adj.* deceitful, false. □□ **lyingly** *adv.*

lyke-wake /'laɪkweɪk/ *n. Brit.* a night-watch over a dead body. [perh. f. ON: cf. LICH(-GATE), WAKE[1]]

lymph /lɪmf/ *n.* **1** *Physiol.* a colourless fluid containing white blood cells, drained from the tissues and conveyed through the body in the lymphatic system. **2** this fluid used as a vaccine. **3** exudation from a sore etc. **4** *poet.* pure water. □ **lymph gland** (or **node**) a small mass of tissue in the lymphatic system where lymph is purified and lymphocytes are formed. □□ **lymphoid** *adj.* **lymphous** *adj.* [F *lymphe* or L *lympha, limpa* water]

lymphatic /lɪmˈfætɪk/ *adj. & n.* —*adj.* **1** of or secreting or conveying lymph (*lymphatic gland*). **2** (of a person) pale, flabby, or sluggish. —*n.* a veinlike vessel conveying lymph. □ **lymphatic system** a network of vessels conveying lymph. [orig. = frenzied, f. L *lymphaticus* mad f. Gk *numpholēptos* seized by nymphs: now assoc. with LYMPH (on the analogy of *spermatic* etc.)]

lymphocyte /'lɪmfə,saɪt/ n. a form of leucocyte occurring in the blood, in lymph, etc. □□ **lymphocytic** /-'sɪtɪk/ adj.

lymphoma /lɪm'fəʊmə/ n. (pl. **lymphomata** /-mətə/) any malignant tumour of the lymph nodes, excluding leukaemia.

lyncean /lɪn'si:ən/ adj. lynx-eyed, keen-sighted. [L lynceus f. Gk lugkeios f. lugx LYNX]

lynch /lɪntʃ/ v.tr. (of a body of people) put (a person) to death for an alleged offence without a legal trial. □**lynch law** the procedure of a self-constituted illegal court that punishes or executes. □□ **lyncher** n. **lynching** n. [Lynch's law, after Capt. W. Lynch of Virginia c.1780]

lynchet /'lɪntʃɪt/ n. (in the UK) a ridge or ledge formed by ancient ploughing on a slope. [linch f. OE hlinc: cf. LINKS]

lynchpin var. of LINCHPIN.

lynx /lɪŋks/ n. 1 a medium-sized cat, Felis lynx, with short tail, spotted fur, and tufted ear-tips. 2 its fur. □**lynx-eyed** keen-sighted. □□ **lynxlike** adj. [ME f. L f. Gk lugx]

Lyon /'laɪən/ n. (in full **Lord Lyon** or **Lyon King of Arms**) the chief herald of Scotland. □**Lyon Court** the court over which he presides. [archaic form. of LION: named f. the lion on the royal shield]

lyophilic /,laɪə'fɪlɪk/ adj. (of a colloid) readily dispersed by a solvent. [Gk luō loosen, dissolve + Gk philos loving]

lyophilize /laɪ'ɒfɪ,laɪz/ v.tr. (also **-ise**) freeze-dry.

lyophobic /,laɪə'fəʊbɪk/ adj. (of a colloid) not lyophilic. [Gk luō loosen, dissolve + -PHOBIC (see -PHOBIA)]

lyrate /'laɪərət/ adj. Biol. lyre-shaped.

lyre /'laɪə(r)/ n. Gk Antiq. an ancient stringed instrument like a small U-shaped harp, played usu. with a plectrum and accompanying the voice. □**lyre-bird** any Australian bird of the family Menuridae, the male of which has a lyre-shaped tail display. **lyre-flower** a bleeding heart. [ME f. OF lire f. L lyra f. Gk lura]

lyric /'lɪrɪk/ adj. & n. —adj. 1 (of poetry) expressing the writer's emotions, usu. briefly and in stanzas or recognized forms. 2 (of a poet) writing in this manner. 3 of or for the lyre. 4 meant to be sung, fit to be expressed in song, songlike (lyric drama; lyric opera). —n. 1 a lyric poem or verse. 2 (in pl.) lyric verses. 3 (usu. in pl.) the words of a song. [F lyrique or L lyricus f. Gk lurikos (as LYRE)]

lyrical /'lɪrɪk(ə)l/ adj. 1 = LYRIC. 2 resembling, couched in, or using language appropriate to, lyric poetry. 3 colloq. highly enthusiastic (wax lyrical about). □□ **lyrically** adv. **lyricalness** n.

lyricism /'lɪrɪ,sɪz(ə)m/ n. 1 the character or quality of being lyric or lyrical. 2 a lyrical expression. 3 high-flown sentiments.

lyricist /'lɪrɪsɪst/ n. a person who writes the words to a song.

lyrist n. 1 /'laɪərɪst/ a person who plays the lyre. 2 /'lɪrɪst/ a lyric poet. [L lyrista f. Gk luristēs f. lura lyre]

lyse /laɪs/ v.tr. & intr. bring about or undergo lysis. [back-form. f. LYSIS]

lysergic acid /laɪ'sɜ:dʒɪk/ n. a crystalline acid extracted from ergot or prepared synthetically. □**lysergic acid diethylamide** /,daɪə'θaɪlə,maɪd/ a powerful hallucinogenic drug. ¶ Abbr.: **LSD**. [hydrolysis + ergot + -IC]

lysin /'laɪsɪn/ n. a protein in the blood able to cause lysis. [G Lysine]

lysine /'laɪsi:n/ n. Biochem. an amino acid present in protein and essential in the diet of vertebrates. [G Lysin, ult. f. LYSIS]

lysis /'laɪsɪs/ n. (pl. **lyses** /-si:z/) the disintegration of a cell. [L f. Gk lusis loosening f. luō loosen]

-lysis /lɪsɪs/ comb. form forming nouns denoting disintegration or decomposition (electrolysis; haemolysis).

Lysol /'laɪsɒl/ n. propr. a mixture of cresols and soft soap, used as a disinfectant. [LYSIS + -OL²]

lysosome /'laɪsə,səʊm/ n. a cytoplasmic organelle in eukaryotic cells containing degradative enzymes enclosed in a membrane. [LYSIS + -SOME³]

lysozyme /'laɪsə,zaɪm/ n. Biochem. an enzyme found in tears and egg-white which catalyses the destruction of cell walls of certain bacteria. [LYSIS + ENZYME]

lytic /'lɪtɪk/ adj. of, relating to, or causing lysis.

-lytic /'lɪtɪk/ comb. form forming adjectives corresponding to nouns in -lysis. [Gk lutikos (as LYSIS)]

M

M¹ /em/ n. (pl. **Ms** or **M's**) **1** the thirteenth letter of the alphabet. **2** (as a Roman numeral) 1,000.

M² abbr. (also **M.**) **1** Master. **2** (in titles) Member of. **3** *Monsieur*. **4** (in the UK in road designations) motorway. **5** mega-. **6** *Chem*. molar.

m abbr. (also **m.**) **1 a** masculine. **b** male. **2** married. **3** *Cricket* maiden (over). **4** mile(s). **5** metre(s). **6** million(s). **7** minute(s). **8** *Currency* mark(s). **9** mare. **10** milli-.

m' adj. = MY (*m'lud*).

'm n. colloq. madam (in *yes'm* etc.).

MA abbr. **1** Master of Arts. **2** *US* Massachusetts (in official postal use).

ma /mɑː/ n. colloq. mother. [abbr. of MAMMA¹]

ma'am /mæm, mɑːm, məm/ n. madam (used esp. in addressing royalty). [contr.]

Mac /mæk/ n. colloq. **1** a Scotsman. **2** *US* man (esp. as a form of address). [*Mac-* as a patronymic prefix in many Scottish and Irish surnames]

mac /mæk/ n. (also **mack**) *Brit. colloq.* mackintosh. [abbr.]

macabre /məˈkɑːbr/ adj. grim, gruesome. [ME f. OF *macabré* perh. f. *Macabé* a Maccabee, with ref. to a miracle play showing the slaughter of the Maccabees]

macadam /məˈkædəm/ n. **1** material for road-making with successive layers of compacted broken stone. **2** = TARMACADAM. □□ **macadamize** v.tr. (also **-ise**) [J. L. *McAdam*, Brit. surveyor d. 1836, who advocated using this material]

macadamia /ˌmækəˈdeɪmɪə/ n. any Australian evergreen tree of the genus *Macadamia*, esp. *M. ternifolia*, bearing edible nutlike seeds. [J. *Macadam*, Austral. chemist d. 1865]

macaque /məˈkæk/ n. any monkey of the genus *Macaca*, including the rhesus monkey and Barbary ape, having prominent cheek pouches and usu. a long tail. [F f. Port. *macaco* f. Fiot *makaku* some monkeys f. *kaku* monkey]

macaroni /ˌmækəˈrəʊnɪ/ n. **1** a tubular variety of pasta. **2** (pl. **macaronies**) hist. an 18th-c. British dandy affecting Continental fashions. [It. *maccaroni* f. late Gk *makaria* food made from barley]

macaronic /ˌmækəˈrɒnɪk/ n. & adj. —n. (in pl.) burlesque verses containing Latin (or other foreign) words and vernacular words with Latin etc. terminations. —adj. (of verse) of this kind. [mod.L *macaronicus* f. obs. It. *macaronico*, joc. formed as MACARONI]

macaroon /ˌmækəˈruːn/ n. a small light cake or biscuit made with white of egg, sugar, and ground almonds or coconut. [F *macaron* f. It. (as MACARONI)]

Macassar /məˈkæsə(r)/ n. (in full **Macassar oil**) a kind of oil formerly used as a dressing for the hair. [*Macassar*, now in Indonesia, from where its ingredients were said to come]

macaw /məˈkɔː/ n. any long-tailed brightly coloured parrot of the genus *Ara* or *Anodorhynchus*, native to S. and Central America. [Port. *macao*, of unkn. orig.]

Macc. abbr. Maccabees (Apocrypha).

Maccabees /ˈmækəˌbiːz/ n.pl. (in full **Books of the Maccabees**) four books of Jewish history and theology, of which the first and second are in the Apocrypha. □□ **Maccabean** /-ˈbiːən/ adj. [the name of a Jewish family that led a revolt *c*.170 BC under Judas *Maccabaeus*]

McCarthyism /məˈkɑːθɪˌɪz(ə)m/ n. (esp. in the US) the policy of hunting out suspected or known Communists and removing them esp. from government departments. [J. R. *McCarthy*, US senator d. 1957]

McCoy /məˈkɔɪ/ n. colloq. □ **the** (or **the real**) **McCoy** the real thing; the genuine article. [19th c.: orig. uncert.]

mace¹ /meɪs/ n. **1** a staff of office, esp. the symbol of the Speaker's authority in the House of Commons. **2** hist. a heavy club usu. having a metal head and spikes. **3** a stick used in the game of bagatelle. **4** = *mace-bearer*. □ **mace-bearer** an official who carries a mace on ceremonial occasions. [ME f. OF *mace*, *masse* f. Rmc *mattea* (unrecorded) club]

mace² /meɪs/ n. the dried outer covering of the nutmeg, used as a spice. [ME *macis* (taken as pl.) f. OF *macis* f. L *macir* a red spicy bark]

macédoine /ˈmæsɪˌdwɑːn/ n. mixed vegetables or fruit, esp. cut up small or in jelly. [F, = Macedonia, with ref. to the mixture of peoples there]

macer /ˈmeɪsə(r)/ n. a mace-bearer, esp. *Sc.* an official keeping order in a lawcourt. [ME f. OF *massier* f. *masse*: see MACE¹]

macerate /ˈmæsəˌreɪt/ v. **1** tr. & intr. make or become soft by soaking. **2** intr. waste away by fasting. □□ **maceration** /-ˈreɪʃ(ə)n/ n. **macerator** n. [L *macerare macerat-*]

Mach /mɑːk, mæk/ n. (in full **Mach number**) the ratio of the speed of a body to the speed of sound in the surrounding medium. □ **Mach one** (or **two** etc.) the speed (or twice the speed) of sound. [E. *Mach*, Austrian physicist d. 1916]

machete /məˈtʃetɪ, məˈʃetɪ/ n. (also **matchet** /ˈmætʃɪt/) a broad heavy knife used in Central America and the W. Indies as an implement and weapon. [Sp. f. *macho* hammer f. LL *marcus*]

machiavellian /ˌmækɪəˈvelɪən/ adj. elaborately cunning; scheming, unscrupulous. □□ **machiavellianism** n. [N. dei *Machiavelli*, Florentine statesman and political writer d. 1527, who advocated resort to morally questionable methods in the interests of the State]

machicolate /məˈtʃɪkəˌleɪt/ v.tr. (usu. as **machicolated** adj.) furnish (a parapet etc.) with openings between supporting corbels for dropping stones etc. on attackers. □□ **machicolation** /-ˈleɪʃ(ə)n/ n. [OF *machicoler*, ult. f. Prov. *machacol* f. *macar* crush + *col* neck]

machinable /məˈʃiːnəb(ə)l/ adj. capable of being cut by machine tools. □□ **machinability** /-ˈbɪlɪtɪ/ n.

machinate /ˈmækɪˌneɪt, ˈmæʃ-/ v.intr. lay plots; intrigue. □□ **machination** /-ˈneɪʃ(ə)n/ n. **machinator** n. [L *machinari* contrive (as MACHINE)]

machine /məˈʃiːn/ n. & v. —n. **1** an apparatus using or applying mechanical power, having several parts each with a definite function and together performing certain kinds of work. **2** a particular kind of machine, esp. a vehicle, a piece of electrical or electronic apparatus, etc. **3** an instrument that transmits a force or directs its application. **4** the controlling system of an organization etc. (*the party machine*). **5** a person who acts mechanically and with apparent lack of emotion. —v.tr. make or operate on with a machine (esp. in sewing or printing). □ **machine code** (or **language**) a computer language that a particular computer can respond to directly. **machine-readable** in a form that a computer can process. **machine tool** a mechanically operated tool for working on metal, wood, or plastics. **machine-tooled 1** shaped by a machine tool. **2** (of artistic presentation etc.) precise, slick, esp. excessively so. [F f. L *machina* f. Gk *makhana* Doric form of *mēkhanē* f. *mēkhos* contrivance]

machine-gun /məˈʃiːnˌgʌn/ n. & v. —n. an automatic gun giving continuous fire. —v.tr. (**-gunned**,

-gunning) shoot at with a machine-gun. □□
machine-gunner *n.*

machinery /mə'ʃiːnəri/ *n.* (*pl.* **-ies**) **1** machines collectively. **2** the components of a machine; a mechanism. **3** (foll. by *of*) an organized system. **4** (foll. by *for*) the means devised or available (*the machinery for decision-making*).

machinist /mə'ʃiːnɪst/ *n.* **1** a person who operates a machine, esp. a sewing-machine or a machine tool. **2** a person who makes machinery.

machismo /mə'tʃɪzməʊ, -'kɪzməʊ/ *n.* exaggeratedly assertive manliness; a show of masculinity. [Sp. f. *macho* MALE f. L *masculus*]

Machmeter /'mɑːkˌmiːtə(r), 'mæk-/ *n.* an instrument indicating air speed in the form of a Mach number.

macho /'mætʃəʊ/ *adj.* & *n.* —*adj.* showily manly or virile. —*n.* (*pl.* **-os**) **1** a macho man. **2** = MACHISMO. [MACHISMO]

machtpolitik /'mɑːxtpɒlɪˌtiːk/ *n.* power politics. [G]

macintosh var. of MACKINTOSH.

mack var. of MAC.

mackerel /'mæk(ə)l/ *n.* (*pl.* same or **mackerels**) a N. Atlantic marine fish, *Scomber scombrus*, with a greenish-blue body, used for food. □ **mackerel shark** a porbeagle. **mackerel sky** a sky dappled with rows of small white fleecy clouds, like the pattern on a mackerel's back. [ME f. AF *makerel*, OF *maquerel*]

mackintosh /'mækɪnˌtɒʃ/ *n.* (also **macintosh**) **1** *Brit.* a waterproof coat or cloak. **2** cloth waterproofed with rubber. [C. *Macintosh*, Sc. inventor d. 1843, who orig. patented the cloth]

mackle /'mæk(ə)l/ *n.* a blurred impression in printing. [F *macule* f. L *macula* blemish: see MACULA]

macle /'mæk(ə)l/ *n.* **1** a twin crystal. **2** a dark spot in a mineral. [F f. L (as MACKLE)]

McNaughten rules /mək'nɔːt(ə)n/ *n.pl.* (also **M'Naghten rules**) *Brit.* rules governing the decision as to the criminal responsibility of an insane person. [*McNaughten* or *McNaughtan*, name of a 19th-c. accused person]

macramé /mə'krɑːmɪ/ *n.* **1** the art of knotting cord or string in patterns to make decorative articles. **2** articles made in this way. [Turk. *makrama* bedspread f. Arab. *miḳrama*]

macro /'mækrəʊ/ *n.* (also **macro-instruction**) *Computing* a series of abbreviated instructions expanded automatically when required.

macro- /'mækrəʊ/ *comb. form* **1** long. **2** large, large-scale. [Gk *makro-* f. *makros* long, large]

macrobiotic /ˌmækrəʊbaɪ'ɒtɪk/ *adj.* & *n.* —*adj.* relating to or following a diet intended to prolong life, comprising pure vegetable foods, brown rice, etc. —*n.* (in *pl.*; treated as *sing.*) the use or theory of such a dietary system.

macrocarpa /ˌmækrəʊ'kɑːpə/ *n.* an evergreen tree, *Cupressus macrocarpa*, often cultivated for hedges or wind-breaks. [mod.L f. Gk MACRO- + *karpos* fruit]

macrocephalic /ˌmækrəʊsɪ'fælɪk/ *adj.* (also **macrocephalous** /-'sefələs/) having a long or large head. □□ **macrocephaly** /-'sefəlɪ/ *n.*

macrocosm /'mækrəʊˌkɒz(ə)m/ *n.* **1** the universe. **2** the whole of a complex structure. □□ **macrocosmic** /-'kɒzmɪk/ *adj.* **macrocosmically** /-'kɒzmɪkəlɪ/ *adv.*

macroeconomics /ˌmækrəʊˌiːkə'nɒmɪks/ *n.* the study of large-scale or general economic factors, e.g. national productivity. □□ **macroeconomic** *adj.*

macromolecule /ˌmækrəʊ'mɒlɪˌkjuːl/ *n.* *Chem.* a molecule containing a very large number of atoms. □□ **macromolecular** /-mə'lekjʊlə(r)/ *adj.*

macron /'mækrɒn/ *n.* a written or printed mark (¯) over a long or stressed vowel. [Gk *makron* neut. of *makros* large]

macrophage /'mækrəʊˌfeɪdʒ/ *n.* a large phagocytic white blood cell usu. occurring at points of infection.

macrophotography /ˌmækrəʊfə'tɒɡrəfɪ/ *n.* photography producing photographs larger than life.

macropod /'mækrəʊˌpɒd/ *n.* any plant-eating mammal of the family Macropodidae native to Australia

and New Guinea, including kangaroos and wallabies. [MACRO- + Gk *pous podos* foot]

macroscopic /ˌmækrəʊ'skɒpɪk/ *adj.* **1** visible to the naked eye. **2** regarded in terms of large units. □□ **macroscopically** *adv.*

macula /'mækjʊlə/ *n.* (*pl.* **maculae** /-ˌliː/) **1** a dark spot, esp. a permanent one, in the skin. **2** (in full **macula lutea** /'luːtɪə/) the region of greatest visual acuity in the retina. □□ **macular** *adj.* **maculation** /-'leɪʃ(ə)n/ *n.* [L, = spot, mesh]

mad /mæd/ *adj.* & *v.* —*adj.* (**madder, maddest**) **1** insane; having a disordered mind. **2** (of a person, conduct, or an idea) wildly foolish. **3** (often foll. by *about, on*) wildly excited or infatuated (*mad about football*; *is chess-mad*). **4** *colloq.* angry. **5** (of an animal) rabid. **6** wildly light-hearted. —*v.* (**madded, madding**) **1** *tr.* *US* make angry. **2** *intr.* *archaic* be mad; act madly (*the madding crowd*). □ **like mad** *colloq.* with great energy, intensity, or enthusiasm. **mad keen** *colloq.* extremely eager. □□ **madness** *n.* [OE *gemǣded* part. form f. *gemād* mad]

madam /'mædəm/ *n.* **1** a polite or respectful form of address or mode of reference to a woman. **2** *Brit. colloq.* a conceited or precocious girl or young woman. **3** a woman brothel-keeper. [ME f. OF *ma dame* my lady]

Madame /mə'dɑːm, 'mædəm/ *n.* **1** (*pl.* **Mesdames** /meɪ'dɑːm, -'dæm/) a title or form of address used of or to a French-speaking woman, corresponding to Mrs or madam. **2** (**madame**) = MADAM 1. [F (as MADAM)]

madcap /'mædkæp/ *adj.* & *n.* —*adj.* **1** wildly impulsive. **2** undertaken without forethought. —*n.* a wildly impulsive person.

madden /'mæd(ə)n/ *v.* **1** *tr.* & *intr.* make or become mad. **2** *tr.* irritate intensely. □□ **maddening** *adj.* **maddeningly** *adv.*

madder /'mædə(r)/ *n.* **1** a herbaceous plant, *Rubia tinctorum*, with yellowish flowers. **2** a red dye obtained from the root of the madder, or its synthetic substitute. [OE *mædere*]

made /meɪd/ **1** *past* and *past part.* of MAKE. **2** *adj.* (usu. in *comb.*) **a** (of a person or thing) built or formed (*well-made*; *strongly-made*). **b** successful (*a self-made man*). □ **have it made** *colloq.* be sure of success. **made for** ideally suited to. **made of** consisting of. **made of money** *colloq.* very rich.

Madeira /mə'dɪərə/ *n.* **1** a fortified white wine from the island of Madeira off the coast of N. Africa. **2** (in full **Madeira cake**) a kind of rich sponge cake.

madeleine /'mædəˌleɪn/ *n.* a small fancy sponge cake. [F]

Mademoiselle /ˌmædəmwə'zel/ *n.* (*pl.* **Mesdemoiselles** /ˌmeɪdm-/) **1** a title or form of address used of or to an unmarried French-speaking woman, corresponding to Miss or madam. **2** (**mademoiselle**) **a** a young Frenchwoman. **b** a French governess. [F f. *ma* my + *demoiselle* DAMSEL]

madhouse /'mædhaʊs/ *n.* **1** *archaic* or *colloq.* a mental home or hospital. **2** *colloq.* a scene of extreme confusion or uproar.

madly /'mædlɪ/ *adv.* **1** in a mad manner. **2** *colloq.* **a** passionately. **b** extremely.

madman /'mædmən/ *n.* (*pl.* **-men**) a man who is mad.

Madonna /mə'dɒnə/ *n.* *Eccl.* **1** (prec. by *the*) a name for the Virgin Mary. **2** (usu. **madonna**) a picture or statue of the Madonna. □ **madonna lily** the white *Lilium candidum*, as shown in many pictures of the Madonna. [It. f. *ma* = *mia* my + *donna* lady f. L *domina*]

madras /mə'drɑːs/ *n.* a strong cotton fabric with coloured or white stripes, checks, etc. [*Madras* in India]

madrepore /'mædrɪˌpɔː(r)/ *n.* **1** any perforated coral of the genus *Madrepora*. **2** the animal producing this. □□ **madreporic** /-'pɒrɪk/ *adj.* [F *madrépore* or mod.L *madrepora* f. It. *madrepora* f. *madre* mother + *poro* PORE¹]

madrigal /'mædrɪg(ə)l/ *n.* **1** a usu. 16th-c. or 17th-c. part-song for several voices, usu. arranged in elaborate counterpoint and without instrumental accompaniment. **2** a short love poem. □□ **madrigalian** /-'geɪlɪən/ *adj.* **madrigalesque** /-gə'lesk/ *adj.* **madrigalist** *n.* [It. *madrigale* f. med.L *matricalis* mother (church), formed as MATRIX]

madwoman /'mæd,wʊmən/ *n.* (*pl.* -women) a woman who is mad.

Maecenas /maɪ'siːnəs/ *n.* a generous patron of literature or art. [Gaius *Maecenas*, Roman statesman d. 8 BC, the patron of Horace and Virgil]

maelstrom /'meɪlstrəm/ *n.* **1** a great whirlpool. **2** a state of confusion. [early mod. Du. f. *malen* grind, whirl + *stroom* STREAM]

maenad /'miːnæd/ *n.* **1** a bacchante. **2** a frenzied woman. □□ **maenadic** /-'nædɪk/ *adj.* [L *Maenas Maenad-* f. Gk *Mainas -ados* f. *mainomai* rave]

maestoso /maɪ'stəʊzəʊ/ *adj.*, *adv.*, & *n. Mus.* —*adj.* & *adv.* to be performed majestically. —*n.* (*pl.* -os) a piece of music to be performed in this way. [It.]

maestro /'maɪstrəʊ/ *n.* (*pl.* **maestri** /-strɪ/ or -os) (often as a respectful form of address) **1** a distinguished musician, esp. a conductor or performer. **2** a great performer in any sphere, esp. artistic. [It., = master]

Mae West /meɪ 'west/ *n.* an inflatable life-jacket. [the name of an American film actress d. 1980, noted for her large bust]

Mafia /'mæfɪə, 'mɑː-/ *n.* **1** an organized international body of criminals, orig. in Sicily, now also in Italy and the US. **2** (**mafia**) a group regarded as exerting a hidden sinister influence. [It. dial. (Sicilian), = bragging]

Mafioso /,mæfɪ'əʊsəʊ, ,mɑː-/ *n.* (*pl.* **Mafiosi** /-sɪ/) a member of the Mafia. [It. (as MAFIA)]

mag /mæg/ *n. colloq.* a magazine (periodical). [abbr.]

mag. *abbr.* **1** magnesium. **2** magneto. **3** magnetic.

magazine /,mægə'ziːn/ *n.* **1** a periodical publication containing articles, stories, etc., usu. with photographs, illustrations, etc. **2** a chamber for holding a supply of cartridges to be fed automatically to the breech of a gun. **3** a similar device feeding a camera, slide projector, etc. **4** a store for arms, ammunition, and provisions for use in war. **5** a store for explosives. [F *magasin* f. It. *magazzino* f. Arab. *maḵāzin* pl. of *maḵzan* storehouse f. *ḵazana* store up]

magdalen /'mægdəlɪn/ *n.* **1** a reformed prostitute. **2** a home for reformed prostitutes. [Mary *Magdalen* of Magdala in Galilee (Luke 8:2), identified (prob. wrongly) with the sinner of Luke 7:37: f. eccl.L *Magdalena* f. Gk *Magdalēnē*]

Magdalenian /,mægdə'liːnɪən/ *adj.* & *n. Archaeol.* —*adj.* of the latest palaeolithic period in Europe, characterized by horn and bone tools. —*n.* the culture of this period. [F *Magdalénien* of La *Madeleine*, Dordogne, France, where remains were found]

mage /meɪdʒ/ *n. archaic* **1** a magician. **2** a wise and learned person. [ME, Anglicized f. MAGUS]

Magellanic cloud /,mædʒɪ'lænɪk/ *n.* each of two galaxies visible in the southern sky. [F. *Magellan*, Port. explorer d. 1521]

magenta /mə'dʒentə/ *n.* & *adj.* —*n.* **1** a brilliant mauvish-crimson shade. **2** an aniline dye of this colour; fuchsine. —*adj.* of or coloured with magenta. [*Magenta* in N. Italy, site of a battle (1859) fought shortly before the dye was discovered]

maggot /'mægət/ *n.* **1** a larva, esp. of the cheese-fly or bluebottle. **2** a whimsical fancy. □□ **maggoty** *adj.* [ME perh. alt. f. *maddock*, earlier *mathek* f. ON *mathkr*: cf. MAWKISH]

magi *pl.* of MAGUS.

magian /'meɪdʒɪən/ *adj.* & *n.* —*adj.* of the magi or Magi. —*n.* **1** a magus or Magus. **2** a magician. □□ **magianism** *n.* [L *magus*: see MAGUS]

magic /'mædʒɪk/ *n.*, *adj.*, & *v.* —*n.* **1 a** the supposed art of influencing the course of events by the occult control of nature or of the spirits. **b** witchcraft. **2** conjuring tricks. **3** an inexplicable or remarkable influence producing surprising results. **4** an enchanting quality or phenomenon. —*adj.* **1** of or resulting from magic. **2** producing surprising results. **3** *colloq.* wonderful, exciting. —*v.tr.* (**magicked**, **magicking**) change or create by magic, or apparently so. □ **like magic** very rapidly. **magic away** cause to disappear as if by magic. **magic carpet** a mythical carpet able to transport a person on it to any desired place. **magic eye 1** a photoelectric device used in equipment for detection, measurement, etc. **2** a small cathode-ray tube used to indicate the correct tuning of a radio receiver. **magic lantern** a simple form of image-projector using slides. **magic mushroom** a mushroom producing psilocybin. **magic square** a square divided into smaller squares each containing a number such that the sums of all vertical, horizontal, or diagonal rows are equal. [ME f. OF *magique* f. L *magicus* adj., LL *magica* n., f. Gk *magikos* (as MAGUS)]

magical /'mædʒɪk(ə)l/ *adj.* **1** of or relating to magic. **2** resembling magic; produced as if by magic. **3** wonderful, enchanting. □□ **magically** *adv.*

magician /mə'dʒɪʃ(ə)n/ *n.* **1** a person skilled in or practising magic. **2** a conjuror. **3** a person with exceptional skill. [ME f. OF *magicien* f. LL *magica* (as MAGIC)]

magilp var. of MEGILP.

Maginot line /'mæʒɪ,nəʊ/ *n.* **1** a line of fortifications along the NE border of France begun in 1929, overrun in 1940. **2** a line of defence on which one relies blindly. [A. *Maginot*, Fr. minister of war d. 1932]

magisterial /,mædʒɪ'stɪərɪəl/ *adj.* **1** imperious. **2** invested with authority. **3** of or conducted by a magistrate. **4** (of a work, opinion, etc.) highly authoritative. □□ **magisterially** *adv.* [med.L *magisterialis* f. LL *magisterius* f. L *magister* MASTER]

magisterium /,mædʒɪ'stɪərɪəm/ *n. RC Ch.* the official teaching of a bishop or pope. [L, = the office of a master (as MAGISTERIAL)]

magistracy /'mædʒɪstrəsɪ/ *n.* (*pl.* -ies) **1** the office or authority of a magistrate. **2** magistrates collectively.

magistral /mə'dʒɪstr(ə)l/ *adj.* **1** of a master or masters. **2** *Pharm.* (of a remedy etc.) devised and made up for a particular case (cf. OFFICINAL). [F *magistral* or L *magistralis* f. *magister* MASTER]

magistrate /'mædʒɪstrət, -,streɪt/ *n.* **1** a civil officer administering the law. **2** an official conducting a court for minor cases and preliminary hearings (*magistrates' court*). □□ **magistrateship** *n.* **magistrature** /-trə,tjʊə(r)/ *n.* [ME f. L *magistratus* (as MAGISTRAL)]

Maglemosian /,mægəl'məʊzɪən/ *n.* & *adj.* —*n.* a N. European mesolithic culture, characterized by bone and stone implements. —*adj.* of or relating to this culture. [*Maglemose* in Denmark, where articles from it were found]

maglev /'mæglev/ *n.* (usu. *attrib.*) magnetic levitation, a system in which trains glide above the track in a magnetic field. [abbr.]

magma /'mægmə/ *n.* (*pl.* **magmata** /-mətə/ or **magmas**) **1** fluid or semifluid material from which igneous rock is formed by cooling. **2** a crude pasty mixture of mineral or organic matter. □□ **magmatic** /-'mætɪk/ *adj.* [ME, = a solid residue f. L f. Gk *magma -atos* f. the root of *massō* knead]

Magna Carta /,mægnə 'kɑːtə/ *n.* (also **Magna Charta**) **1** a charter of liberty and political rights obtained from King John of England in 1215. **2** any similar document of rights. [med.L, = great charter]

magnanimous /mæg'nænɪməs/ *adj.* nobly generous; not petty in feelings or conduct. □□ **magnanimity** /,mægnə'nɪmɪtɪ/ *n.* **magnanimously** *adv.* [L *magnanimus* f. *magnus* great + *animus* soul]

magnate /'mægneɪt, -nɪt/ *n.* a wealthy and influential

b *but*   d *dog*   f *few*   g *get*   h *he*   j *yes*   k *cat*   l *leg*   m *man*   n *no*   p *pen*   r *red*   s *sit*   t *top*   v *voice*

person, esp. in business (*shipping magnate*; *financial magnate*). [ME f. LL *magnas -atis* f. L *magnus* great]

magnesia /mæg'ni:ʒə, -ʃə, -zjə/ *n.* **1** *Chem.* magnesium oxide. **2** (in general use) hydrated magnesium carbonate, a white powder used as an antacid and laxative. □□ **magnesian** *adj.* [ME f. med.L f. Gk *Magnēsia* (*lithos*) (stone) of Magnesia in Asia Minor, orig. referring to loadstone]

magnesite /'mægnɪˌsaɪt/ *n.* a white or grey mineral form of magnesium carbonate.

magnesium /mæg'ni:zɪəm/ *n.* *Chem.* a silvery metallic element occurring naturally in magnesite and dolomite, used for making light alloys and important as an essential element in living organisms. ¶ Symb.: **Mg.** □ **magnesium flare** (or **light**) a blinding white light produced by burning magnesium wire.

magnet /'mægnɪt/ *n.* **1** a piece of iron, steel, alloy, ore, etc., usu. in the form of a bar or horseshoe, having properties of attracting or repelling iron. **2** a lodestone. **3** a person or thing that attracts. [ME f. L *magnes magnetis* f. Gk *magnēs* = *Magnēs -ētos* (*lithos*) (stone) of Magnesia: cf. MAGNESIA]

magnetic /mæg'netɪk/ *adj.* **1 a** having the properties of a magnet. **b** producing, produced by, or acting by magnetism. **2** capable of being attracted by or acquiring the properties of a magnet. **3** very attractive or alluring (*a magnetic personality*). □ **magnetic compass** = COMPASS 1. **magnetic disk** see DISC. **magnetic equator** an imaginary line, near the equator, on which a magnetic needle has no dip. **magnetic field** a region of variable force around magnets, magnetic materials, or current-carrying conductors. **magnetic inclination** = DIP *n.* 8. **magnetic mine** a submarine mine detonated by the proximity of a magnetized body such as that of a ship. **magnetic moment** the property of a magnet that interacts with an applied field to give a mechanical moment. **magnetic needle** a piece of magnetized steel used as an indicator on the dial of a compass and in magnetic and electrical apparatus, esp. in telegraphy. **magnetic north** the point indicated by the north end of a compass needle. **magnetic pole** **1** each of the points near the extremities of the axis of rotation of the earth or another body where a magnetic needle dips vertically. **2** each of the regions of an artificial or natural magnet, from which the magnetic forces appear to originate. **magnetic storm** a disturbance of the earth's magnetic field caused by charged particles from the sun etc. **magnetic tape** a tape coated with magnetic material for recording sound or pictures or for the storage of information. □□ **magnetically** *adv.* [LL *magneticus* (as MAGNET)]

magnetism /'mægnɪˌtɪz(ə)m/ *n.* **1 a** magnetic phenomena and their study. **b** the property of producing these phenomena. **2** attraction; personal charm. [mod.L *magnetismus* (as MAGNET)]

magnetite /'mægnɪˌtaɪt/ *n.* magnetic iron oxide. [G *Magnetit* (as MAGNET)]

magnetize /'mægnɪˌtaɪz/ *v.tr.* (also **-ise**) **1** give magnetic properties to. **2** make into a magnet. **3** attract as or like a magnet. □□ **magnetizable** *adj.* **magnetization** /-'zeɪʃ(ə)n/ *n.* **magnetizer** *n.*

magneto /mæg'ni:təʊ/ *n.* (*pl.* **-os**) an electric generator using permanent magnets and producing high voltage, esp. for the ignition of an internal-combustion engine. [abbr. of MAGNETO-ELECTRIC]

magneto- /mæg'ni:təʊ/ *comb. form* indicating a magnet or magnetism. [Gk *magnēs*: see MAGNET]

magneto-electric /mæg,ni:təʊɪ'lektrɪk/ *adj.* (of an electric generator) using permanent magnets. □□ **magneto-electricity** /-'trɪsɪtɪ/ *n.*

magnetograph /mæg'ni:təˌɡrɑ:f/ *n.* an instrument for recording measurements of magnetic quantities.

magnetometer /ˌmægnɪ'tɒmɪtə(r)/ *n.* an instrument measuring magnetic forces, esp. the earth's magnetism. □□ **magnetometry** *n.*

magnetomotive /mæg,ni:təʊ'məʊtɪv/ *adj.* (of a

force) being the sum of the magnetizing forces along a circuit.

magneton /'mægnɪˌtɒn/ *n.* a unit of magnetic moment in atomic and nuclear physics. [F *magnéton* (as MAGNETIC)]

magnetosphere /mæg'ni:təˌsfɪə(r)/ *n.* the region surrounding a planet, star, etc. in which its magnetic field is effective.

magnetron /'mægnɪˌtrɒn/ *n.* an electron tube for amplifying or generating microwaves, with the flow of electrons controlled by an external magnetic field. [MAGNET + -TRON]

magnificat /mæg'nɪfɪˌkæt/ *n.* **1** a song of praise. **2** (**Magnificat**) the hymn of the Virgin Mary (Luke 1: 46-55) used as a canticle. [f. the opening words *magnificat anima mea Dominum* my soul magnifies the Lord]

magnification /ˌmægnɪfɪ'keɪʃ(ə)n/ *n.* **1** the act or an instance of magnifying; the process of being magnified. **2** the amount or degree of magnification. **3** the apparent enlargement of an object by a lens.

magnificent /mæg'nɪfɪs(ə)nt/ *adj.* **1** splendid, stately. **2** sumptuously constructed or adorned. **3** splendidly lavish. **4** *colloq.* fine, excellent. □□ **magnificence** *n.* **magnificently** *adv.* [F *magnificent* or L *magnificus* f. *magnus* great]

magnifico /mæg'nɪfɪˌkəʊ/ *n.* (*pl.* **-oes**) a magnate or grandee. [It., = MAGNIFICENT: orig. with ref. to Venice]

magnify /'mægnɪˌfaɪ/ *v.tr.* (**-ies, -ied**) **1** make (a thing) appear larger than it is, as with a lens. **2** exaggerate. **3** intensify. **4** *archaic* extol, glorify. □ **magnifying glass** a lens used to produce an enlarged image. □□ **magnifiable** *adj.* **magnifier** *n.* [ME f. OF *magnifier* or L *magnificare* (as MAGNIFICENT)]

magniloquent /mæg'nɪləkwənt/ *adj.* **1** grand or grandiose in speech. **2** boastful. □□ **magniloquence** *n.* **magniloquently** *adv.* [L *magniloquus* f. *magnus* great + *-loquus* -speaking]

magnitude /'mægnɪˌtjuːd/ *n.* **1** largeness. **2** size. **3** importance. **4 a** the degree of brightness of a star (see also *absolute magnitude, apparent magnitude*). **b** a class of stars arranged according to this (*of the third magnitude*). □ **of the first magnitude** very important. [ME f. L *magnitudo* f. *magnus* great]

magnolia /mæg'nəʊlɪə/ *n.* **1** any tree or shrub of the genus *Magnolia*, cultivated for its dark-green foliage and large waxlike flowers in spring. **2** a pale creamy-pink colour. [mod.L f. P. *Magnol*, Fr. botanist d. 1715]

magnox /'mægnɒks/ *n.* any of various magnesium-based alloys used to enclose uranium fuel elements in a nuclear reactor. [*magnesium no oxidation*]

magnum /'mægnəm/ *n.* (*pl.* **magnums**) **1** a wine bottle of about twice the standard size. **2 a** a cartridge or shell that is especially powerful or large. **b** (often *attrib.*) a cartridge or gun adapted so as to be more powerful than its calibre suggests. [L, neut. of *magnus* great]

magnum opus /ˌmægnəm 'əʊpəs/ *n.* **1** a great and usu. large work of art, literature, etc. **2** the most important work of an artist, writer, etc. [L, = great work: see OPUS]

magpie /'mægpaɪ/ *n.* **1** a European and American crow, *Pica pica*, with a long pointed tail and black and white plumage. **2** any of various birds with plumage like a magpie, esp. *Gymnorhina tibicen* of Australia. **3** an idle chatterer. **4** a person who collects things indiscriminately. **5 a** the division of a circular target next to the outer one. **b** a rifle shot which strikes this. [*Mag*, abbr. of *Margaret* + PIE²]

maguey /'mæɡweɪ/ *n.* an agave plant, esp. one yielding pulque. [Sp. f. Haitian]

magus /'meɪɡəs/ *n.* (*pl.* **magi** /'meɪdʒaɪ/) **1** a member of a priestly caste of ancient Persia. **2** a sorcerer. **3** (**the** (**three**) **Magi**) the 'wise men' from the East who brought gifts to the infant Christ (Matt. 2:1). [ME f. L f. Gk *magos* f. OPers. *magus*]

Magyar /'mægjɑ:(r)/ *n. & adj.* —*n.* **1** a member of a Ural-Altaic people now predominant in Hungary. **2** the language of this people. —*adj.* of or relating to this people or language. [native name]

maharaja /ˌmɑːhə'rɑːdʒə/ *n.* (also **maharajah**) *hist.* a title of some Indian princes. [Hindi *mahārājā* f. *mahā* great + RAJA]

maharanee /ˌmɑːhə'rɑːnɪ/ *n.* (also **maharani**) *hist.* a maharaja's wife or widow. [Hindi *mahārānī* f. *mahā* great + RANEE]

maharishi /ˌmɑːhə'rɪʃɪ/ *n.* a great Hindu sage or spiritual leader. [Hindi f. *mahā* great + RISHI]

mahatma /mə'hætmə/ *n.* **1 a** (in India etc.) a person regarded with reverence. **b** a sage. **2** each of a class of persons in India and Tibet supposed by some to have preternatural powers. [Skr. *mahātman* f. *mahā* great + *ātman* soul]

Mahayana /ˌmɑːhə'jɑːnə/ *n.* a school of Buddhism practised in China, Japan, and Tibet. [Skr. f. *mahā* great + *yāna* vehicle]

Mahdi /'mɑːdɪ/ *n.* (*pl.* **Mahdis**) **1** a spiritual and temporal messiah expected by Muslims. **2** esp. *hist.* a leader claiming to be this Messiah. □□ **Mahdism** *n.* **Mahdist** *n.* [Arab. *mahdīy* he who is guided right, past part. of *hadā* guide]

mah-jong /mɑː'dʒɒŋ/ *n.* (also **mah-jongg**) a Chinese game for four resembling rummy and played with 136 or 144 pieces called tiles. [Chin. dial. *ma-tsiang*, lit. sparrows]

mahlstick var. of MAULSTICK.

mahogany /mə'hɒgənɪ/ *n.* (*pl.* **-ies**) **1 a** a reddish-brown wood used for furniture. **b** the colour of this. **2** any tropical tree of the genus *Swietenia*, esp. *S. mahagoni*, yielding this wood. [17th c.: orig. unkn.]

mahonia /mə'həʊnɪə/ *n.* any evergreen shrub of the genus *Mahonia*, with yellow bell-shaped or globular flowers. [F *mahonne*, Sp. *mahona*, It. *maona*, Turk. *māwuna*]

mahout /mə'haʊt/ *n.* (in India etc.) an elephant-driver or -keeper. [Hindi *mahāut* f. Skr. *mahāmātra* high official, lit. 'great in measure']

Mahratta var. of MARATHA.

Mahratti var. of MARATHI.

mahseer /'mɑːsɪə(r)/ *n.* either of two freshwater Indian fish, *Barbus putitora* or *B. tor*, used as food. [Hindi *mahāsir*]

maid /meɪd/ *n.* **1** a female domestic servant. **2** *archaic* or *poet.* a girl or young woman. □ **maid of honour 1** an unmarried lady attending a queen or princess. **2** a kind of small custard tart. **3** esp. *US* a principal bridesmaid. □□ **maidish** *adj.* [ME, abbr. of MAIDEN]

maidan /maɪ'dɑːn/ *n.* *Anglo-Ind.* **1** an open space in or near a town. **2** a parade-ground. [Urdu f. Arab. *maydān*]

maiden /'meɪd(ə)n/ *n.* **1 a** *archaic* or *poet.* a girl; a young unmarried woman. **b** (*attrib.*) unmarried (*maiden aunt*). **2** *Cricket* = **maiden over**. **3** (*attrib.*) (of a female animal) unmated. **4** (often *attrib.*) **a** a horse that has never won a race. **b** a race open only to such horses. **5** (*attrib.*) being or involving the first attempt or occurrence (*maiden speech*; *maiden voyage*). □ **maiden name** a wife's surname before marriage. **maiden over** *Cricket* an over in which no runs are scored off the bat. □□ **maidenhood** *n.* **maidenish** *adj.* **maidenlike** *adj.* **maidenly** *adj.* [OE *mægden*, dimin. f. *mægeth* f. Gmc]

maidenhair /'meɪd(ə)n,heə(r)/ *n.* (in full **maidenhair fern**) a fern of the genus *Adiantum*, esp. *A. capillus-veneris*, with fine hairlike stalks and delicate fronds. □ **maidenhair tree** = GINKGO.

maidenhead /'meɪd(ə)n,hed/ *n.* **1** virginity. **2** the hymen.

maidservant /'meɪd,sɜːv(ə)nt/ *n.* a female domestic servant.

maieutic /meɪ'uːtɪk/ *adj.* (of the Socratic mode of enquiry) serving to bring a person's latent ideas into clear consciousness. [Gk *maieutikos* f. *maieuomai* act as a midwife f. *maia* midwife]

maigre /'meɪgə(r)/ *adj.* *RC Ch.* **1** (of a day) on which abstinence from meat is ordered. **2** (of food) suitable for eating on maigre days. [F, lit. lean: cf. MEAGRE]

mail[1] /meɪl/ *n. & v.* —*n.* **1 a** letters and parcels etc. conveyed by post. **b** the postal system. **c** one complete delivery or collection of mail. **d** one delivery of letters to one place, esp. to a business on one occasion. **2** a vehicle carrying mail. **3** *hist.* a bag of letters for conveyance by post. —*v.tr.* esp. *US* send (a letter etc.) by post. □ **mail-boat** a boat carrying mail. **mail carrier** *US* a postman or postwoman. **mail cart** *Brit. hist.* **1** a cart for carrying mail by road. **2** a light vehicle for carrying children. **mail coach** a railway coach or *hist.* stagecoach used for carrying mail. **mail drop** *US* a receptacle for mail. **mailing list** a list of people to whom advertising matter, information, etc., is to be posted. **mail order** an order for goods sent by post. **mail-order firm** a firm doing business by post. **mail train** a train carrying mail. [ME f. OF *male* wallet f. WG]

mail[2] /meɪl/ *n. & v.* —*n.* **1** armour made of rings, chains, or plates, joined together flexibly. **2** the protective shell, scales, etc., of an animal. —*v.tr.* clothe with or as if with mail. □ **coat of mail** a jacket covered with mail or composed of mail. **mailed fist** physical force. □□ **mailed** *adj.* [ME f. OF *maille* f. L *macula* spot, mesh]

mailable /'meɪləb(ə)l/ *adj.* acceptable for conveyance by post.

mailbag /'meɪlbæg/ *n.* a large sack or bag for carrying mail.

mailbox /'meɪlbɒks/ *n.* *US* a letter-box.

maillot /'mæ'jəʊ/ *n.* **1** tights for dancing, gymnastics, etc. **2** a woman's one-piece bathing-suit. **3** a jersey. [F]

mailman /'meɪlmən/ *n.* (*pl.* **-men**) *US* a postman.

maim /meɪm/ *v.tr.* **1** cripple, disable, mutilate. **2** harm, impair (*emotionally maimed by neglect*). [ME *maime* etc. f. OF *mahaignier* etc., of unkn. orig.]

main[1] /meɪn/ *adj. & n.* —*adj.* **1** chief in size, importance, extent, etc.; principal (*the main part*; *the main point*). **2** exerted to the full (*by main force*). —*n.* **1** a principal channel, duct, etc., for water, sewage, etc. (*water main*). **2** (usu. in *pl.*; prec. by *the*) **a** the central distribution network for electricity, gas, water, etc. **b** a domestic electricity supply as distinct from batteries. **3** *archaic* or *poet.* **a** the ocean or oceans (*the Spanish Main*). **b** the mainland. □ **in the main** for the most part. **main brace** *Naut.* the brace attached to the main yard. **the main chance** one's own interests. **main course 1** the chief course of a meal. **2** *Naut.* the mainsail. **main deck** *Naut.* **1** the deck below the spar-deck in a man-of-war. **2** the upper deck between the poop and the forecastle in a merchantman. **main line 1** a chief railway line. **2** *sl.* a principal vein, esp. as a site for a drug injection (cf. MAINLINE). **3** *US* a chief road or street. **main stem** *US colloq.* = **main street**. **main street** the principal street of a town. **Main Street** *US* materialistic philosophy (after Sinclair Lewis's novel, 1920). **main yard** *Naut.* the yard on which the mainsail is extended. **with might and main** with all one's force. [ME, partly f. ON *megenn*, *megn* (adj.), partly f. OE *mægen-* f. Gmc: (n.) orig. = physical force]

main[2] /meɪn/ *n.* **1** (in the game of hazard) a number (5, 6, 7, 8, or 9) called by a player before dice are thrown. **2** a match between fighting-cocks. [16th c.: prob. orig. *main chance*: see MAIN[1]]

mainframe /'meɪnfreɪm/ *n.* **1** the central processing unit and primary memory of a computer. **2** (often *attrib.*) a large computer system.

mainland /'meɪnlənd/ *n.* **1** a large continuous extent of land, excluding neighbouring islands etc. **2** (**Mainland**) the largest island in Orkney and in Shetland. □□ **mainlander** *n.*

mainline /'meɪnlaɪn/ v. sl. **1** intr. take drugs intravenously. **2** tr. inject (drugs) intravenously. □□ **mainliner** n.

mainly /'meɪnlɪ/ adv. for the most part; chiefly.

mainmast /'meɪnmɑːst/ n. Naut. the principal mast of a ship.

mainplane /'meɪnpleɪn/ n. the principal supporting surface of an aircraft (cf. TAILPLANE).

mainsail /'meɪnseɪl, -s(ə)l/ n. Naut. **1** (in a square-rigged vessel) the lowest sail on the mainmast. **2** (in a fore-and-aft rigged vessel) a sail set on the after part of the mainmast.

mainspring /'meɪnsprɪŋ/ n. **1** the principal spring of a mechanical watch, clock, etc. **2** a chief motive power; an incentive.

mainstay /'meɪnsteɪ/ n. **1** a chief support (has been his mainstay since his trouble). **2** Naut. a stay from the maintop to the foot of the foremast.

mainstream /'meɪnstriːm/ n. **1** (often attrib.) the prevailing trend in opinion, fashion, etc. **2** a type of jazz based on the 1930s swing style and consisting esp. of solo improvisation on chord sequences. **3** the principal current of a river.

maintain /meɪn'teɪn/ v.tr. **1** cause to continue; keep up, preserve (a state of affairs, an activity, etc.) (maintained friendly relations). **2** (often foll. by in; often refl.) support (life, a condition, etc.) by work, nourishment, expenditure, etc. (maintained him in comfort; maintained themselves by fishing). **3** (often foll. by that + clause) assert (an opinion, statement, etc.) as true (maintained that she was the best; his story was true, he maintained). **4** preserve or provide for the preservation of (a building, machine, road, etc.) in good repair. **5** give aid to (a cause, party, etc.). **6** provide means for (a garrison etc. to be equipped). □ **maintained school** Brit. a school supported from public funds. □□ **maintainable** adj. **maintainability** /-'bɪlɪtɪ/ n. [ME f. OF maintenir ult. f. L manu tenēre hold in the hand]

maintainer /meɪn'teɪnə(r)/ n. **1** a person or thing that maintains. **2** (also **maintainor**) Law hist. a person guilty of maintenance (see MAINTENANCE 3).

maintenance /'meɪntənəns/ n. **1** the process of maintaining or being maintained. **2 a** the provision of the means to support life, esp. by work etc. **b** (also **separate maintenance**) a husband's or wife's provision for a spouse after separation or divorce; alimony. **3** Law hist. the offence of aiding a party in litigation without lawful cause. [ME f. OF f. maintenir: see MAINTAIN]

maintop /'meɪntɒp/ n. Naut. a platform above the head of the lower mainmast.

maintopmast /meɪn'tɒpməst/ n. Naut. a mast above the head of the lower mainmast.

maiolica /mə'jɒlɪkə/ n. a white tin-glazed earthenware decorated with metallic colours, orig. popular in the Mediterranean area during the Renaissance (see also MAJOLICA). [It. f. former name of Majorca]

maisonette /ˌmeɪzə'net/ n. (also **maisonnette**) **1** a part of a house, block of flats, etc., forming separate living accommodation, usu. on two floors and having a separate entrance. **2** a small house. [F maisonnette dimin. of maison house]

maître d'hôtel /ˌmetrə dəʊ'tel, ˌmeɪt-/ n. **1** the manager, head steward, etc., of a hotel. **2** a head waiter. [F, = master of (the) house]

maize /meɪz/ n. **1** a cereal plant, Zea mays, native to N. America, yielding large grains set in rows on a cob. **2** the cobs or grains of this (see CORN¹). [F maïs or Sp. maiz, of Carib orig.]

Maj. abbr. Major.

majestic /mə'dʒestɪk/ adj. showing majesty; stately and dignified; grand, imposing. □□ **majestically** adv.

majesty /'mædʒɪstɪ/ n. (pl. **-ies**) **1** impressive stateliness, dignity, or authority, esp. of bearing, language, the law, etc. **2 a** royal power. **b** (**Majesty**) part of several titles given to a sovereign or a

sovereign's wife or widow or used in addressing them (Your Majesty; Her Majesty the Queen Mother). **3** a picture of God or Christ enthroned within an aureole. □ **Her** (or **His**) **Majesty's** part of the title of several State institutions (Her Majesty's Stationery Office). [ME f. OF majesté f. L majestas -tatis (as MAJOR)]

Majlis /'mædʒlɪs/ n. Polit. the parliament of various N. African or Middle Eastern countries, esp. Iran. [Pers., = assembly]

majolica /mə'jɒlɪkə, mə'dʒɒl-/ n. (also **maiolica** /mə'jɒl-/) **1 a** 19th-c. trade name for earthenware with coloured decoration on an opaque white glaze. **2** = MAIOLICA. [alt. f. MAIOLICA]

major /'meɪdʒə(r)/ adj., n., & v. —adj. **1** important, large, serious, significant (a major road; a major war; the major consideration must be their health). **2** (of an operation) serious or life-threatening. **3** Mus. **a** (of a scale) having intervals of a semitone between the third and fourth, and seventh and eighth degrees. **b** (of an interval) greater by a semitone than a minor interval (major third). **c** (of a key) based on a major scale, tending to produce a bright or joyful effect (D major). **4** of full age. **5** Brit. (appended to a surname, esp. in public schools) the elder of two brothers or the first to enter the school (Smith major). **6** Logic **a** (of a term) occurring in the predicate or conclusion of a syllogism. **b** (of a premiss) containing a major term. —n. **1** Mil. **a** an army officer next below lieutenant-colonel and above captain. **b** an officer in charge of a section of band instruments (drum major; pipe major). **2** a person of full age. **3** US **a** a student's special subject or course. **b** a student specializing in a specified subject (a philosophy major). **4** Logic a major term or premiss. —v.intr. (foll. by in) US study or qualify in a subject (majored in theology). □ **major axis** the axis of a conic, passing through its foci. **major-general** an officer next below a lieutenant-general. **major league** US a league of major importance in baseball etc. **major part** (often foll. by of) the majority. **major piece** Chess a rook or queen. **major planet** Jupiter, Saturn, Uranus, or Neptune. **major prophet** Isaiah, Jeremiah, Ezekiel, or Daniel. **major suit** Bridge spades or hearts. □□ **majorship** n. [ME f. L, compar. of magnus great]

major-domo /ˌmeɪdʒə'dəʊməʊ/ n. (pl. **-os**) **1** the chief official of an Italian or Spanish princely household. **2** a house-steward; a butler. [orig. mayordome f. Sp. mayordomo, It. maggiordomo f. med.L major domus highest official of the household (as MAJOR, DOME)]

majorette /ˌmeɪdʒə'ret/ n. = drum majorette. [abbr.]

majority /mə'dʒɒrɪtɪ/ n. (pl. **-ies**) **1** (usu. foll. by of) the greater number or part. ¶ Strictly used only with countable nouns, e.g. a majority of people, and not with mass nouns, e.g. a majority of the work. **2** Polit. **a** the number by which the votes cast for one party, candidate, etc. exceed those of the next in rank (won by a majority of 151). **b** a party etc. receiving the greater number of votes. **3** full legal age (attained his majority). **4** the rank of major. □ **the great majority 1** much the greater number. **2** euphem. the dead (has joined the great majority). **in the majority** esp. Polit. belonging to or constituting a majority party etc. **majority rule** the principle that the greater number should exercise greater power. **majority verdict** a verdict given by more than half of the jury, but not unanimous. [F majorité f. med.L majoritas -tatis (as MAJOR)]

majuscule /'mædʒəˌskjuːl/ n. & adj. —n. Palaeog. **1** a large letter, whether capital or uncial. **2** large lettering. —adj. of, written in, or concerning majuscules. □□ **majuscular** /mə'dʒʌskjʊlə(r)/ adj. [F f. L majuscula (littera letter), dimin. of MAJOR]

make /meɪk/ v. & n. —v. (past and past part. **made** /meɪd/) **1** tr. construct; create; form from parts or other substances (made a table; made it out of cardboard; made him a sweater). **2** tr. (foll. by to + infin.) cause or compel (a person etc.) to do something (*make him repeat it; was made to confess*). **3** *tr.* **a** cause to exist; create; bring about (*made a noise; made an enemy*). **b** cause to become or seem (*made an exhibition of myself; made him angry*). **c** appoint; designate (*made him a Cardinal*). **4** *tr.* compose; prepare; draw up (*made her will; made a film about Japan*). **5** *tr.* constitute; amount to (*makes a difference; 2 and 2 make 4; this makes the tenth time*). **6** *tr.* **a** undertake or agree to (an aim or purpose) (*made a promise; make an effort*). **b** execute or perform (a bodily movement, a speech, etc.) (*made a face; made a bow*). **7** *tr.* gain, acquire, procure (money, a profit, etc.) (*made £20,000 on the deal*). **8** *tr.* prepare (tea, coffee, a dish, etc.) for consumption (*made egg and chips*). **9** *tr.* **a** arrange bedclothes tidily on (a bed) ready for use. **b** arrange and light materials for (a fire). **10** *intr.* **a** proceed (*made towards the river*). **b** (foll. by *to* + infin.) begin an action (*he made to go*). **11** *tr. colloq.* **a** arrive at (a place) or in time for (a train etc.) (*made the border before dark; made the six o'clock train*). **b** manage to attend; manage to attend on (a certain day) or at (a certain time) (*couldn't make the meeting last week; can make any day except Friday*). **c** achieve a place in (*made the first eleven; made the six o'clock news*). **d** *US* achieve the rank of (*made colonel in three years*). **12** *tr.* establish or enact (a distinction, rule, law, etc.). **13** *tr.* consider to be; estimate as (*what do you make the time?; do you make that a 1 or a 7?*). **14** *tr.* secure the success or advancement of (*his mother made him; it made my day*). **15** *tr.* accomplish (a distance, speed, score, etc.) (*made 60 m.p.h. on the motorway*). **16** *tr.* **a** become by development or training (*made a great leader*). **b** serve as (*a log makes a useful seat*). **17** *tr.* (usu. foll. by *out*) represent as; cause to appear as (*makes him out a liar*). **18** *tr.* form in the mind; feel (*I make no judgement*). **19** *tr.* (foll. by *it* + compl.) **a** determine, establish, or choose (*let's make it Tuesday; made it my business to know*). **b** bring to (a chosen value etc.) (*decided to make it a dozen*). **20** *tr. sl.* have sexual relations with. **21** *tr. Cards* **a** win (a trick). **b** play (a card) to advantage. **c** win the number of tricks that fulfils (a contract). **d** shuffle (a pack of cards) for dealing. **22** *tr. Cricket* score (runs). **23** *tr. Electr.* complete or close (a circuit) (opp. BREAK). **24** *intr.* (of the tide) begin to flow or ebb. —*n.* **1** (esp. of a product) a type, origin, brand, etc. of manufacture (*different make of car; our own make*). **2** a kind of mental, moral, or physical structure or composition. **3** an act of shuffling cards. **4** *Electr.* **a** the making of contact. **b** the position in which this is made. □**be made for** be ideally suited to. **be made of** consist of (*cake made of marzipan*). **have it made** *colloq.* be sure of success. **made dish** a dish prepared from several separate foods. **made man** a man who has attained success. **made of money** *colloq.* very rich. **made road** a properly surfaced road of tarmac, concrete, etc. **made to measure** (of a suit etc.) made to a specific customer's measurements. **made to order** see ORDER. **make after** *archaic* pursue. **make against** be unfavourable to. **make as if** (or **though**) (foll. by *to* + infin. or conditional) act as if the specified circumstances applied (*made as if to leave; made as if he would hit me; made as if I had not noticed*). **make away** (or **off**) depart hastily. **make away with 1** get rid of; kill. **2** squander. **make-believe** (or **-belief**) **1** pretence. **2** pretended. **make believe** pretend. **make conversation** talk politely. **make a day** (or **night** etc.) **of it** devote a whole day (or night etc.) to an activity. **make do 1** manage with the limited or inadequate means available. **2** (foll. by *with*) manage with (something) as an inferior substitute. **make an example of** punish as a warning to others. **make a fool of** see FOOL¹. **make for 1** tend to result in (happiness etc.). **2** proceed towards (a place). **3** assault; attack. **4** confirm (an opinion). **make friends** (often foll. by *with*) become friendly. **make fun of** see FUN. **make**

good see GOOD. **make a habit of** see HABIT. **make a hash of** see HASH¹. **make hay** see HAY¹. **make head or tail of** see HEAD. **make a House** *Polit.* secure the presence of enough members for a quorum or support in the House of Commons. **make it** *colloq.* **1** succeed in reaching, esp. in time. **2** be successful. **3** (usu. foll. by *with*) *sl.* have sexual intercourse (with). **make it up 1** be reconciled, esp. after a quarrel. **2** fill in a deficit. **make it up to** remedy negligence, an injury, etc. to (a person). **make light of** see LIGHT². **make love** see LOVE. **make a meal of** see MEAL¹. **make merry** see MERRY. **make money** acquire wealth or an income. **make the most of** see MOST. **make much** (or **little** or **the best**) **of 1** derive much (or little etc.) advantage from. **2** give much (or little etc.) attention, importance, etc., to. **make a name for oneself** see NAME. **make no bones about** see BONE. **make nothing of 1** do without hesitation. **2** treat as a trifle. **3** be unable to understand, use, or deal with. **make of 1** construct from. **2** conclude to be the meaning or character of (*can you make anything of it?*). **make off** = *make away*. **make off with** carry away; steal. **make oneself scarce** see SCARCE. **make or break** (or **mar**) cause the success or ruin of. **make out 1 a** distinguish by sight or hearing. **b** decipher (handwriting etc.). **2** understand (*can't make him out*). **3** assert; pretend (*made out he liked it*). **4** *colloq.* make progress; fare (*how did you make out?*). **5** (usu. foll. by *to, in favour of*) draw up; write out (*made out a cheque to her*). **6** prove or try to prove (*how do you make that out?*). **make over 1** transfer the possession of (a thing) to a person. **2** refashion (a garment etc.). **make a point of** see POINT. **make sail** *Naut.* **1** spread a sail or sails. **2** start a voyage. **make shift** see SHIFT. **make so bold as to** see BOLD. **make time 1** (usu. foll. by *for* or *to* + infin.) find an occasion when time is available. **2** (usu. foll. by *with*) esp. *US sl.* make sexual advances (to a person). **make-up 1** cosmetics for the face etc., either generally or to create an actor's appearance or disguise. **2** the appearance of the face etc. when cosmetics have been applied (*his make-up was not convincing*). **3** *Printing* the making up of a type. **4** *Printing* the type made up. **5** a person's character, temperament, etc. **6** the composition or constitution (of a thing). **make up 1** serve or act to overcome (a deficiency). **2** complete (an amount, a party, etc.). **3** compensate. **4** be reconciled. **5** put together; compound; prepare (*made up the medicine*). **6** sew (parts of a garment etc.) together. **7** get (a sum of money, a company, etc.) together. **8** concoct (a story). **9** (of parts) compose (a whole). **10 a** apply cosmetics. **b** apply cosmetics to. **11** settle (a dispute). **12** prepare (a bed) for use with fresh sheets etc. **13** *Printing* arrange (type) in pages. **14** compile (a list, an account, a document, etc.). **15** arrange (a marriage etc.). **make up one's mind** decide, resolve. **make up to** curry favour with; court. **make water 1** urinate. **2** (of a ship) take in water. **make way 1** (often foll. by *for*) allow room for others to proceed. **2** achieve progress. **make one's way** proceed. **make with** *US colloq.* supply; perform; proceed with (*made with the feet and left in a hurry*). **on the make** *colloq.* **1** intent on gain. **2** looking for sexual partners. **self-made man** etc. a man etc. who has succeeded by his own efforts. □□ **makable** *adj.* [OE *macian* f. WG: rel. to MATCH¹]

maker /ˈmeɪkə(r)/ *n.* **1** (often in *comb.*) a person or thing that makes. **2** (**our, the,** etc. **Maker**) God. **3** *archaic* a poet.

makeshift /ˈmeɪkʃɪft/ *adj. & n.* —*adj.* temporary; serving for the time being (*a makeshift arrangement*). —*n.* a temporary substitute or device.

makeweight /ˈmeɪkweɪt/ *n.* **1** a small quantity or thing added to make up the full weight. **2** an unimportant extra person. **3** an unimportant point added to make an argument seem stronger.

making /ˈmeɪkɪŋ/ *n.* **1** in senses of MAKE *v.* **2** (in *pl.*) **a** earnings; profit. **b** (foll. by *of*) essential qualities or ingredients (*has the makings of a general*; *we have the makings of a meal*). **c** *US & Austral. colloq.* paper and tobacco for rolling a cigarette. □**be the making of** ensure the success or favourable development of. **in the making** in the course of being made or formed. [OE *macung* (as MAKE)]

mako[1] /ˈmækəʊ/ *n.* (*pl.* **-os**) a blue shark, *Isurus oxyrinchus*. [Maori]

mako[2] /ˈmækəʊ/ *n.* (*pl.* **-os**) a small New Zealand tree, *Aristotelia serrata*, with clusters of dark-red berries and large racemes of pink flowers. Also called WINEBERRY. [Maori]

Mal. *abbr.* Malachi (Old Testament).

mal- /mæl/ *comb. form* **1 a** bad, badly (*malpractice*; *maltreat*). **b** faulty, faultily (*malfunction*). **2** not (*maladroit*). [F *mal* badly f. L *male*]

malabsorption /ˌmæləbˈsɔːpʃ(ə)n/ *n.* imperfect absorption of food material by the small intestine.

malacca /məˈlækə/ *n.* (in full **malacca cane**) a rich-brown cane from the stem of the palm-tree *Calamus scipionum*, used for walking-sticks etc. [*Malacca* in Malaysia]

malachite /ˈmæləˌkaɪt/ *n.* a bright-green mineral of hydrous copper carbonate, taking a high polish and used for ornament. [OF *melochite* f. L *molochites* f. Gk *molokhitis* f. *molokhē* = *malakhē* mallow]

malaco- /ˈmæləkəʊ/ *comb. form* soft. [Gk *malakos* soft]

malacology /ˌmæləˈkɒlədʒɪ/ *n.* the study of molluscs.

malacostracan /ˌmæləˈkɒstrəkən/ *n. & adj.* —*n.* any crustacean of the class Malacostraca, including crabs, shrimps, lobsters, and krill. —*adj.* of or relating to this class. [MALACO- + Gk *ostrakon* shell]

maladaptive /ˌmæləˈdæptɪv/ *adj.* (of an individual, species, etc.) failing to adjust adequately to the environment, and undergoing emotional, behavioural, physical, or mental repercussions. □□ **maladaptation** /ˌmælædæpˈteɪʃ(ə)n/ *n.*

maladjusted /ˌmæləˈdʒʌstɪd/ *adj.* **1** not correctly adjusted. **2** (of a person) unable to adapt to or cope with the demands of a social environment. □□ **maladjustment** *n.*

maladminister /ˌmælədˈmɪnɪstə(r)/ *v.tr.* manage or administer inefficiently, badly, or dishonestly. □□ **maladministration** /-ˈstreɪʃ(ə)n/ *n.*

maladroit /ˌmæləˈdrɔɪt, ˈmæl-/ *adj.* clumsy; bungling. —**maladroitly** *adv.* **maladroitness** *n.* [F (as MAL-, ADROIT)]

malady /ˈmælədɪ/ *n.* (*pl.* **-ies**) **1** an ailment; a disease. **2** a morbid or depraved condition; something requiring a remedy. [ME f. OF *maladie* f. *malade* sick ult. f. L *male* ill + *habitus* past part. of *habēre* have]

mala fide /ˌmeɪlə ˈfaɪdɪ/ *adj. & adv.* —*adj.* acting or done in bad faith. —*adv.* in bad faith. [L]

Malaga /ˈmæləgə/ *n.* a sweet fortified wine from Málaga in S. Spain.

Malagasy /ˌmæləˈgæsɪ/ *adj. & n.* —*adj.* of or relating to Madagascar, an island in the Indian Ocean. —*n.* the language of Madagascar. [orig. *Malegass*, *Madegass* f. *Madagascar*]

malagueña /ˌmæləˈgenjə/ *n.* **1** a Spanish dance resembling the fandango. **2** a piece of music for or in the style of a fandango. [Sp. (as MALAGA)]

malaise /məˈleɪz/ *n.* **1** a nonspecific bodily discomfort not associated with the development of a disease. **2** a feeling of uneasiness. [F f. OF *mal* bad + *aise* EASE]

malamute /ˈmæləˌmjuːt/ *n.* (also **malemute**) an Eskimo dog. [name of an Alaskan Eskimo tribe]

malanders var. of MALLENDERS.

malapert /ˈmæləˌpɜːt/ *adj. & n. archaic* —*adj.* impudent; saucy. —*n.* an impudent or saucy person. [ME f. OF (as MAL-, *apert* = *espert* EXPERT)]

malapropism /ˈmæləprɒpˌɪz(ə)m/ *n.* (also **malaprop** /ˈmæləˌprɒp/) the use of a word in mistake for one sounding similar, to comic effect, e.g. *allegory* for *alligator*. [Mrs *Malaprop* (f. MALAPROPOS) in Sheridan's *The Rivals* (1775)]

malapropos /ˌmælæprəˈpəʊ/ *adv., adj., & n.* —*adv.* inopportunely; inappropriately. —*adj.* inopportune; inappropriate. —*n.* something inappropriately said, done, etc. [F *mal à propos* f. *mal* ill: see APROPOS]

malar /ˈmeɪlə(r)/ *adj. & n.* —*adj.* of the cheek. —*n.* a bone of the cheek. [mod.L *malaris* f. L *mala* jaw]

malaria /məˈleərɪə/ *n.* **1** an intermittent and remittent fever caused by a protozoan parasite of the genus *Plasmodium*, introduced by the bite of a mosquito. **2** *archaic* an unwholesome atmosphere caused by the exhalations of marshes, to which this fever was formerly attributed. □□ **malarial** *adj.* **malarian** *adj.* **malarious** *adj.* [It. *mal'aria* bad air]

malarkey /məˈlɑːkɪ/ *n. colloq.* humbug; nonsense. [20th c.: orig. unkn.]

malathion /ˌmæləˈθaɪən/ *n.* an insecticide containing phosphorus, with low toxicity to plants. [diethyl *maleate* + *thio-* acid + -ON]

Malay /məˈleɪ/ *n. & adj.* —*n.* **1 a** a member of a people predominating in Malaysia and Indonesia. **b** a person of Malay descent. **2** the language of this people, the official language of Malaysia. —*adj.* of or relating to this people or language. □□ **Malayan** *n. & adj.* [Malay *malāyu*]

Malayalam /ˌmæləˈjɑːləm/ *n.* the Dravidian language of the State of Kerala in S. India. [native]

Malayo- /məˈleɪjəʊ/ *comb. form* Malayan and (*Malayo-Chinese*). [MALAY]

malcontent /ˈmælkənˌtent/ *n. & adj.* —*n.* a discontented person; a rebel. —*adj.* discontented or rebellious. [F (as MAL-, CONTENT[1])]

mal de mer /ˌmæl də ˈmeə(r)/ *n.* seasickness. [F, = sickness of (the) sea]

male /meɪl/ *adj. & n.* —*adj.* **1** of the sex that can beget offspring by fertilization or insemination (*male child*; *male dog*). **2** of men or male animals, plants, etc.; masculine (*the male sex*; *a male-voice choir*). **3 a** (of plants or their parts) containing only fertilizing organs. **b** (of plants) thought of as male because of colour, shape, etc. **4** (of parts of machinery etc.) designed to enter or fill the corresponding female part (*a male screw*). —*n.* a male person or animal. □**male chauvinist** a man who is prejudiced against women or regards women as inferior. **male fern** a common lowland fern, *Dryopteris filixmas*. **male menopause** a crisis of potency, confidence, etc., supposed to afflict men in middle life. □□ **maleness** *n.* [ME f. OF *ma(s)le*, f. L *masculus* f. *mas* a male]

malediction /ˌmælɪˈdɪkʃ(ə)n/ *n.* **1** a curse. **2** the utterance of a curse. □□ **maledictive** *adj.* **maledictory** *adj.* [ME f. L *maledictio* f. *maledicere* speak evil of f. *male* ill + *dicere* dict- speak]

malefactor /ˈmælɪˌfæktə(r)/ *n.* a criminal; an evil-doer. □□ **malefaction** /-ˈfækʃ(ə)n/ *n.* [ME f. L f. *malefacere* malefact- f. *male* ill + *facere* do]

malefic /məˈlefɪk/ *adj. literary* (of magical arts etc.) harmful; baleful. [L *maleficus* f. *male* ill]

maleficent /məˈlefɪs(ə)nt/ *adj. literary* **1** (often foll. by *to*) hurtful. **2** criminal. □□ **maleficence** *n.* [*maleficence* formed as MALEFIC after *malevolence*]

maleic acid /məˈleɪɪk/ *n.* a colourless crystalline organic acid used in making synthetic resins. [F *maléique* (as MALIC ACID)]

malemute var. of MALAMUTE.

malevolent /məˈlevələnt/ *adj.* wishing evil to others. □□ **malevolence** *n.* **malevolently** *adv.* [OF *malivolent* or f. L *malevolens* f. *male* ill + *volens* willing, part. of *velle*]

malfeasance /mælˈfiːz(ə)ns/ *n. Law* evil-doing. □□ **malfeasant** *n. & adj.* [AF *malfaisance* f. OF *malfaisant* (as MAL-, *faisant* part. of *faire* do f. L *facere*): cf. MISFEASANCE]

malformation /ˌmælfɔːˈmeɪʃ(ə)n/ *n.* faulty formation. □□ **malformed** /-ˈfɔːmd/ *adj.*

malfunction /mælˈfʌŋkʃ(ə)n/ *n. & v.* —*n.* a failure to function in a normal or satisfactory manner. —*v.intr.* fail to function normally or satisfactorily.

mali /'mɑːlɪ/ n. (pl. **malis**) Ind. a member of the gardener caste; a gardener. [Hindi]

malic acid /'mælɪk/ n. an organic acid found in unripe apples and other fruits. [F malique f. L malum apple]

malice /'mælɪs/ n. **1 a** the intention to do evil. **b** a desire to tease, esp. cruelly. **2** Law wrongful intention, esp. as increasing the guilt of certain offences. □**malice aforethought** (or **prepense**) Law the intention to commit a crime, esp. murder. [ME f. OF f. L malitia f. malus bad]

malicious /mə'lɪʃəs/ adj. characterized by malice; intending or intended to do harm. □□**maliciously** adv. **maliciousness** n. [OF malicius f. L malitiosus (as MALICE)]

malign /mə'laɪn/ adj. & v. —adj. **1** (of a thing) injurious. **2** (of a disease) malignant. **3** malevolent. —v. tr. speak ill of; slander. □□**maligner** n. **malignity** /mə'lɪgnɪtɪ/ n. (pl. **-ies**). **malignly** adv. [ME f. OF malin maligne, malignier f. LL malignare contrive maliciously f. L malignus f. malus bad: cf. BENIGN]

malignant /mə'lɪgnənt/ adj. **1 a** (of a disease) very virulent or infectious (malignant cholera). **b** (of a tumour) tending to invade normal tissue and recur after removal; cancerous. **2** harmful; feeling or showing intense ill will. □**malignant pustule** a form of anthrax. □□**malignancy** n. (pl. **-ies**). **malignantly** adv. [LL malignare (as MALIGN)]

malinger /mə'lɪŋgə(r)/ v.intr. exaggerate or feign illness in order to escape duty, work, etc. □□ **malingerer** n. [back-form. f. malingerer app. f. F malingre, perh. formed as MAL- + haingre weak]

mall /mæl, mɔːl/ n. **1** a sheltered walk or promenade. **2** an enclosed shopping precinct. **3** hist. **a** = PALL-MALL. **b** an alley used for this. [var. of MAUL: applied to The Mall in London (orig. a pall-mall alley)]

mallard /'mælɑːd/ n. (pl. same or **mallards**) **1** a wild duck or drake, Anas platyrhynchos, of the northern hemisphere. **2** the flesh of the mallard. [ME f. OF prob. f. maslart (unrecorded, as MALE)]

malleable /'mælɪəb(ə)l/ adj. **1** (of metal etc.) able to be hammered or pressed permanently out of shape without breaking or cracking. **2** adaptable; pliable, flexible. □□ **malleability** /-'bɪlɪtɪ/ n. **malleably** adv. [ME f. OF f. med.L malleabilis f. L malleare to hammer f. malleus hammer]

mallee /'mælɪ/ n. Austral. **1** any of several types of eucalyptus, esp. Eucalyptus dumosa, that flourish in arid areas. **2** a scrub formed by mallee. □**mallee-bird** (or **-fowl** or **-hen**) a megapode, Leipoa ocellata, resembling a turkey. [Aboriginal]

mallei pl. of MALLEUS.

mallemuck var. of MOLLYMAWK.

mallenders /'mæləndəz/ n.pl. (also **malanders**) a dry scabby eruption behind a horse's knee. [ME f. OF malandre (sing.) f. L malandria (pl.) neck-pustules]

malleolus /mə'liːələs/ n. (pl. **malleoli** /-ˌlaɪ/) Anat. a bone with the shape of a hammer-head, esp. each of those forming a projection on either side of the ankle. [L, dimin. of malleus hammer]

mallet /'mælɪt/ n. **1** a hammer, usu. of wood. **2** a long-handled wooden hammer for striking a croquet or polo ball. [ME f. OF maillet f. mailler to hammer f. mail hammer f. L malleus]

malleus /'mælɪəs/ n. (pl. **mallei** /-lɪˌaɪ/) Anat. a small bone in the middle ear transmitting the vibrations of the tympanum to the incus. [L, = hammer]

mallow /'mæləʊ/ n. **1** any plant of the genus Malva, esp. M. sylvestris, with hairy stems and leaves and pink or purple flowers. **2** any of several other plants of the family Malvaceae, including marsh mallow and tree mallow. [OE meal(u)we f. L malva]

malm /mɑːm/ n. **1** a soft chalky rock. **2** a loamy soil produced by the disintegration of this rock. **3** a fine-quality brick made originally from malm, marl, or a similar chalky clay. [OE mealm- (in compounds) f. Gmc]

malmsey /'mɑːmzɪ/ n. a strong sweet wine orig. from Greece, now chiefly from Madeira. [ME f. MDu., MLG malmesie, -eye, f. Monemvasia in S. Greece: cf. MALVOISIE]

malnourished /mæl'nʌrɪʃt/ adj. suffering from malnutrition. □□ **malnourishment** n.

malnourishment /mæl'nʌrɪʃmənt/ n. = MAL-NUTRITION.

malnutrition /ˌmælnjuː'trɪʃ(ə)n/ n. a dietary condition resulting from the absence of some foods or essential elements necessary for health; insufficient nutrition.

malodorous /mæl'əʊdərəs/ adj. evil-smelling.

Malpighian layer /mæl'pɪgɪən/ n. a layer of proliferating cells in the epidermis. [M. Malpighi, It. physician d. 1694]

malpractice /mæl'præktɪs/ n. **1** improper or negligent professional treatment, esp. by a medical practitioner. **2 a** criminal wrongdoing; misconduct. **b** an instance of this.

malt /mɔːlt, mɒlt/ n. & v. —n. **1** barley or other grain that is steeped, germinated, and dried, esp. for brewing or distilling and vinegar-making. **2** colloq. malt whisky; malt liquor. —v. **1** tr. convert (grain) into malt. **2** intr. (of seeds) become malt when germination is checked by drought. □**malted milk 1** a hot drink made from dried milk and a malt preparation. **2** the powdered mixture from which this is made. **malt-house** a building used for preparing and storing malt. **malt liquor** alcoholic liquor made from malt by fermentation, not distillation, e.g. beer, stout. **malt whisky** whisky made from malted barley. [OE m(e)alt f. Gmc, rel. to MELT]

Maltese /mɔːl'tiːz, mɒl-/ n. & adj. —n. **1** (pl. same) **a** a native or national of Malta, an island in the W. Mediterranean. **b** a person of Maltese descent. **2** the language of Malta. —adj. of or relating to Malta or its people or language. □**Maltese cross** a cross with arms of equal length broadening from the centre, often indented at the ends. **Maltese dog** (or **terrier**) a small breed of spaniel or terrier.

maltha /'mælθə/ n. a cement made of pitch and wax or other ingredients. [L f. Gk]

Malthusian /mæl'θjuːzɪən/ adj. & n. —adj. of or relating to T. R. Malthus, English clergyman and economist (d. 1834) or his theories, esp. that sexual restraint should be exercised as a means of preventing an increase of the population beyond its means of subsistence. —n. a follower of Malthus. □□ **Malthusianism** n.

malting /'mɔːltɪŋ, 'mɒl-/ n. **1** the process or an instance of brewing or distilling with malt. **2** = malt-house.

maltose /'mɔːltəʊz/ n. Chem. a sugar produced by the hydrolysis of starch under the action of the enzymes in malt, saliva, etc. [F (as MALT)]

maltreat /mæl'triːt/ v.tr. ill-treat. □□ **maltreater** n. **maltreatment** n. [F maltraiter (as MAL-, TREAT)]

maltster /'mɔːltstə(r), 'mɒl-/ n. a person who makes malt.

malty /'mɔːltɪ, 'mɒl-/ adj. (**maltier**, **maltiest**) of, containing, or resembling malt. □□ **maltiness** n.

malvaceous /mæl'veɪʃəs/ adj. Bot. of or relating to the genus Malva or the family Malvaceae, which includes mallow. [L malvaceus f. malva MALLOW]

malversation /ˌmælvə'seɪʃ(ə)n/ n. formal **1** corrupt behaviour in a position of trust. **2** (often foll. by of) corrupt administration (of public money etc.). [F f. malverser f. L male badly + versari behave]

malvoisie /ˌmælvwə'ziː/ n. = MALMSEY. [ME f. OF malvesie f. F form of Monemvasia: see MALMSEY]

mam /mæm/ n. colloq. mother. [formed as MAMA]

mama /'mæmə, mə'mɑː/ n. colloq. (esp. as a child's term) = MAMMA.

mamba /'mæmbə/ n. any venomous African snake of the genus Dendroaspis, esp. the green mamba (D. angusticeps) or black mamba (D. polylepis). [Zulu imamba]

mambo /ˈmæmbəʊ/ n. & v. —n. (pl. -os) **1** a Latin American dance like the rumba. **2** the music for this. —v.intr. (-oes, -oed) perform the mambo. [Amer. Sp. prob. f. Haitian]

mamelon /ˈmæmələn/ n. a small rounded hillock. [F, = nipple f. mamelle breast f. L MAMILLA]

Mameluke /ˈmæməˌluːk/ n. hist. a member of the military class (orig. Caucasian slaves) that ruled Egypt 1254-1811. [F mameluk, ult. f. Arab. mamlūk slave f. malaka possess]

mamilla /məˈmɪlə/ n. (US **mammilla**) (pl. **mamillae** /-liː/) **1** the nipple of a woman's breast. **2** a nipple-shaped organ etc. □□ **mamillary** /ˈmæmɪləri/ adj. **mamillate** /ˈmæmɪˌleɪt/ adj. [L, dimin. of MAMMA²]

mamma¹ /ˈmæmə/ n. (also **momma** /ˈmɒmə/) colloq. (esp. as a child's term) mother. [imit. of child's ma, ma]

mamma² /ˈmæmə/ n. (pl. **mammae** /-miː/) **1** a milk-secreting organ of female mammals. **2** a corresponding non-secretory structure in male mammals. □□ **mammiform** adj. [OE f. L]

mammal /ˈmæm(ə)l/ n. any vertebrate of the class Mammalia, usu. a warm-blooded quadruped with hair or fur, the females of which possess milk-secreting mammae for the nourishment of the young, and including human beings, dogs, rabbits, whales, etc. □□ **mammalian** /-ˈmeɪlɪən/ adj. & n. **mammalogy** /-ˈmælədʒɪ/ n. [mod.L mammalia neut. pl. of L mammalis (as MAMMA²)]

mammaliferous /ˌmæməˈlɪfərəs/ adj. Geol. containing mammalian remains.

mammary /ˈmæməri/ adj. of the human female breasts or milk-secreting organs of other mammals. □ **mammary gland** the milk-producing gland of female mammals. [MAMMA² + -ARY¹]

mammee /mæˈmiː/ n. a tropical American tree, Mammea americana, with large red-rinded yellow-pulped fruit. [Sp. mamei f. Haitian]

mammilla US var. of MAMILLA.

mammography /mæˈmɒɡrəfɪ/ n. Med. an X-ray technique of diagnosing and locating abnormalities (esp. tumours) of the breasts. [MAMMA² + -GRAPHY]

Mammon /ˈmæmən/ n. **1** wealth regarded as a god or as an evil influence. **2** the worldly rich. □□ **Mammonish** adj. **Mammonism** n. **Mammonite** n. Mammonite n. [ME f. LL Mam(m)ona f. Gk mamōnas f. Aram. māmōn riches: see Matt. 6:24, Luke 16:9-13]

mammoth /ˈmæməθ/ n. & adj. —n. any large extinct elephant of the genus Mammuthus, with a hairy coat and curved tusks. —adj. huge. [Russ. mamo(n)t]

mammy /ˈmæmɪ/ n. (pl. **-ies**) colloq. **1** a child's word for mother. **2** US a Black nursemaid or nanny in charge of White children. [formed as MAMMA¹]

Man. abbr. Manitoba.

man /mæn/ n. & v. —n. (pl. **men** /men/) **1** an adult human male, esp. as distinct from a woman or boy. **2 a** a human being; a person (no man is perfect). **b** human beings in general; the human race (man is mortal). **3** a person showing characteristics associated with males (she's more of a man than he is). **4 a** a worker; an employee (the manager spoke to the men). **b** a manservant or valet. **c** hist. a vassal. **5 a** (usu. in pl.) soldiers, sailors, etc., esp. non-officers (was in command of 200 men). **b** an individual, usu. male, person (fought to the last man). **c** (usu. prec. by the, or poss. pron.) a person regarded as suitable or appropriate in some way; a person fulfilling requirements (I'm your man; not the man for the job). **6 a** a husband (man and wife). **b** colloq. a boyfriend or lover. **7 a** a human being of a specified historical period or character (Renaissance man). **b** a type of prehistoric man named after the place where the remains were found (Peking man; Piltdown man). **8** any one of a set of pieces used in playing chess, draughts, etc. **9** (as second element in comb.) a man of a specified nationality, profession, skill, etc.

(Dutchman; clergyman; horseman; gentleman). **10 a** an expression of impatience etc. used in addressing a male (nonsense, man!). **b** colloq. a general mode of address among hippies etc. (blew my mind, man!). **11** (prec. by a) a person; one (what can a man do?). **12 a** person pursued; an opponent etc. (the police have so far not caught their man). **13 (the Man)** US sl. **a** the police. **b** Black sl. White people. **14** (in comb.) a ship of a specified type (merchantman; Indiaman). —v.tr. (**manned, manning**) **1** supply (a ship, fort, factory, etc.) with a person or people for work or defence etc. **2** work or service or defend (a specified piece of equipment, a fortification, etc.) (man the pumps). **3** Naut. place men at (a part of a ship). **4** fill (a post or office). **5** (usu. refl.) fortify the spirits or courage of (manned herself for the task). □**as one man** in unison; in agreement. **be a man** be courageous; not show fear. **be one's own man 1** be free to act; be independent. **2** be in full possession of one's faculties etc. **man about town** a fashionable man of leisure. **man and boy** from childhood. **man-at-arms** (pl. **men-at-arms**) archaic a soldier, esp. when heavily armed and mounted. **man Friday** see FRIDAY. **man-hour** (or **day** etc.) an hour (or day etc.) regarded in terms of the amount of work that could be done by one person within this period. **man in the moon** the semblance of a face seen on the surface of a full moon. **man in** (US **on**) **the street** an ordinary average person, as distinct from an expert. **man-made** (esp. of a textile fibre) made by man, artificial, synthetic. **man of God 1** a clergyman. **2** a male saint. **man of honour** a man whose word can be trusted. **man of the house** the male head of a household. **man of letters** a scholar; an author. **man of the moment** a man of importance at a particular time. **man of straw 1** an insubstantial person; an imaginary person set up as an opponent. **2** a stuffed effigy. **3** a person undertaking a financial commitment without adequate means. **4** a sham argument set up to be defeated. **man-of-war** an armed ship, esp. of a specified country. **man of the world** see WORLD. **man-size** (or **-sized**) **1** of the size of a man; very large. **2** big enough for a man. **man to man** with candour; honestly. **men's** (or **men's room**) a usu. public lavatory for men. **my** (or **my good**) **man** a patronizing mode of address to a man. **separate** (or **sort out**) **the men from the boys** colloq. find those who are truly virile, competent, etc. **to a man** all without exception. □□ **manless** adj. [OE man(n), pl. menn, mannian, f. Gmc]

mana /ˈmɑːnə/ n. **1** power; authority; prestige. **2** supernatural or magical power. [Maori]

manacle /ˈmænək(ə)l/ n. & v. —n. (usu. in pl.) **1** a fetter or shackle for the hand; a handcuff. **2** a restraint. —v.tr. fetter with manacles. [ME f. OF manicle handcuff f. L manicula dimin. of manus hand]

manage /ˈmænɪdʒ/ v. & n. —v. **1** tr. organize; regulate; be in charge of (a business, household, team, a person's career, etc.). **2** tr. (often foll. by to + infin.) succeed in achieving; contrive (managed to arrive on time; managed a smile; managed to ruin the day). **3** intr. **a** (often foll. by with) succeed in one's aim, esp. against heavy odds (managed with one assistant). **b** meet one's needs with limited resources etc. (just about manages on a pension). **4** tr. gain influence with or maintain control over (a person etc.) (cannot manage their teenage son). **5** tr. (also absol.; often prec. by can, be able to) **a** cope with; make use of (couldn't manage another bite; can you manage by yourself?). **b** be free to attend on (a certain day) or at (a certain time) (can you manage Thursday?). **6** tr. handle or wield (a tool, weapon, etc.). **7** tr. take or have charge or control of (an animal or animals, esp. cattle). —n. archaic **1 a** the training of a horse. **b** the trained movements of a horse. **2** a riding-school (cf. MANÈGE). [It. maneggiare, maneggio ult. f. L manus hand]

manageable /'mænɪdʒəb(ə)l/ *adj.* able to be easily managed, controlled, or accomplished etc. □□ **manageability** /-'bɪlɪtɪ/ *n.* **manageableness** *n.* **manageably** *adv.*

management /'mænɪdʒmənt/ *n.* **1** the process or an instance of managing or being managed. **2 a** the professional administration of business concerns, public undertakings, etc. **b** the people engaged in this. **c** (prec. by *the*) a governing body; a board of directors or the people in charge of running a business, regarded collectively. **3** (usu. foll. by *of*) *Med.* the technique of treating a disease etc. **4** trickery; deceit.

manager /'mænɪdʒə(r)/ *n.* **1** a person controlling or administering a business or part of a business. **2** a person controlling the affairs, training, etc. of a person or team in sports, entertainment, etc. **3** *Brit. Parl.* a member of either House of Parliament appointed with others for some duty in which both Houses are concerned. **4** a person regarded in terms of skill in household or financial or other management (*a good manager*). □□ **managerial** /,mænɪ'dʒɪərɪəl/ *adj.* **managerially** /-'dʒɪərɪəlɪ/ *adv.* **managership** *n.*

manageress /,mænɪdʒə'res/ *n.* a woman manager, esp. of a shop, hotel, theatre, etc.

managing /'mænɪdʒɪŋ/ *adj.* **1** (in *comb.*) having executive control or authority (*managing director*). **2** (*attrib.*) fond of controlling affairs etc. **3** *archaic* economical.

manakin /'mænəkɪn/ *n.* any small bird of the family Pipridae of Central and S. America, the males of which are often brightly coloured. [var. of MANIKIN]

mañana /mæn'jɑːnə/ *adv.* & *n.* —*adv.* in the indefinite future (esp. to indicate procrastination). —*n.* an indefinite future time. [Sp., = tomorrow]

manatee /,mænə'tiː/ *n.* any large aquatic plant-eating mammal of the genus *Trichechus*, with paddle-like forelimbs, no hind limbs, and a powerful tail. [Sp. *manati* f. Carib *manattoui*]

manchineel /,mæntʃɪ'niːl/ *n.* a W. Indian tree, *Hippomane mancinella*, with a poisonous and caustic milky sap and acrid apple-like fruit. [F *mancenille* f. Sp. *manzanilla* dimin. of *manzana* apple]

Manchu /mæn'tʃuː/ *n.* & *adj.* —*n.* **1** a member of a people in China, descended from a Tartar people, who formed the last imperial dynasty (1644-1912). **2** the language of the Manchus, now spoken in part of NE China. —*adj.* of or relating to the Manchu people or their language. [Manchu, = pure]

manciple /'mænsɪp(ə)l/ *n.* an officer who buys provisions for a college, an Inn of Court, etc. [ME f. AF & OF f. L *mancipium* purchase f. *manceps* buyer f. *manus* hand + *capere* take]

Mancunian /mæŋ'kjuːnɪən/ *n.* & *adj.* —*n.* a native of Manchester in NW England. —*adj.* of or relating to Manchester. [L *Mancunium* Manchester]

-mancy /mænsɪ/ *comb. form* forming nouns meaning 'divination by' (*geomancy*; *necromancy*). □□ **-mantic** *comb. form* forming adjectives. [OF *-mancie* f. LL *-mantia* f. Gk *manteia* divination]

Mandaean /mæn'diːən/ *n.* & *adj.* —*n.* **1** a member of a Gnostic sect surviving in Iraq and claiming descent from John the Baptist. **2** the language of this sect. —*adj.* of or concerning the Mandaeans or their language. [Aram. *mandaiia* Gnostics f. *manda* knowledge]

mandala /'mændələ/ *n.* **1** a symbolic circular figure representing the universe in various religions. **2** *Psychol.* such a symbol in a dream, representing the dreamer's search for completeness and self-unity. [Skr. *máṇḍala* disc]

mandamus /mæn'deɪməs/ *n.* *Law* a judicial writ issued as a command to an inferior court, or ordering a person to perform a public or statutory duty. [L, = we command]

mandarin[1] /'mændərɪn/ *n.* **1** (**Mandarin**) the most widely spoken form of Chinese and the official language of China. **2** *hist.* a Chinese official in any of nine grades of the pre-Communist civil service. **3 a** a party leader; a bureaucrat. **b** a powerful member of the establishment. **4 a** a nodding Chinese figure, usu. of porcelain. **b** porcelain etc. decorated with Chinese figures in mandarin dress. □ **mandarin collar** a small close-fitting upright collar. **mandarin duck** a small Chinese duck, *Aix galericulata*, noted for its bright plumage. **mandarin sleeve** a wide loose sleeve. □□ **mandarinate** *n.* [Port. *mandarim* f. Malay f. Hindi *mantrī* f. Skr. *mantrin* counsellor]

mandarin[2] /'mændərɪn/ *n.* (also **mandarine** /-,riːn/) (in full **mandarin orange**) **1** a small flattish deep-coloured orange with a loose skin. **2** the tree, *Citrus reticulata*, yielding this. Also called TANGERINE. [F *mandarine* (perh. as MANDARIN[1], with ref. to the official's yellow robes)]

mandatary /'mændətərɪ/ *n.* (*pl.* **-ies**) esp. *hist.* a person or State receiving a mandate. [LL *mandatarius* (as MANDATE)]

mandate /'mændeɪt/ *n.* & *v.* —*n.* **1** an official command or instruction by an authority. **2** support for a policy or course of action, regarded by a victorious party, candidate, etc., as derived from the wishes of the people in an election. **3** a commission to act for another. **4** *Law* a commission by which a party is entrusted to perform a service, often gratuitously and with indemnity against loss by that party. **5** *hist.* a commission from the League of Nations to a member State to administer a territory. **6** a papal decree or decision. —*v.tr.* **1** instruct (a delegate) to act or vote in a certain way. **2** (usu. foll. by *to*) *hist.* commit (a territory etc.) to a mandatary. □□ **mandator** *n.* [L *mandatum*, neut. past part. of *mandare* command f. *manus* hand + *dare* give: sense 2 of n. after F *mandat*]

mandatory /'mændətərɪ/ *adj.* & *n.* —*adj.* **1** of or conveying a command. **2** compulsory. —*n.* (*pl.* **-ies**) = MANDATARY. □□ **mandatorily** *adv.* [LL *mandatorius* f. L (as MANDATE)]

mandible /'mændɪb(ə)l/ *n.* **1** the jaw, esp. the lower jaw in mammals and fishes. **2** the upper or lower part of a bird's beak. **3** either half of the crushing organ in an arthropod's mouth-parts. □□ **mandibular** /-'dɪbjʊlə(r)/ *adj.* **mandibulate** /-'dɪbjʊlət/ *adj.* [ME f. OF *mandible* or LL *mandibula* f. *mandere* chew]

mandolin /,mændə'lɪn/ *n.* (also **mandoline**) a musical instrument resembling a lute, having paired metal strings plucked with a plectrum. □□ **mandolinist** *n.* [F *mandoline* f. It. *mandolino* dimin. of MANDOLA]

mandorla /mæn'dɔːlə/ *n.* = VESICA 2. [It., = almond]

mandragora /mæn'drægərə/ *n.* *hist.* the mandrake, esp. as a type of narcotic (Shakesp. *Othello* III. iii. 334). [OE f. med.L f. L f. Gk *mandragoras*]

mandrake /'mændreɪk/ *n.* a poisonous plant, *Mandragora officinarum*, with white or purple flowers and large yellow fruit, having emetic and narcotic properties and possessing a root once thought to resemble the human form and to shriek when plucked. [ME *mandrag(g)e*, prob. f. MDu. *mandrag(r)e* f. med.L (as MANDRAGORA): assoc. with MAN + *drake* dragon (cf. DRAKE[1])]

mandrel /'mændr(ə)l/ *n.* **1 a** a shaft in a lathe to which work is fixed while being turned. **b** a cylindrical rod round which metal or other material is forged or shaped. **2** *Brit.* a miner's pick. [16th c.: orig. unkn.]

mandrill /'mændrɪl/ *n.* a large W. African baboon, *Papio sphinx*, the adult of which has a brilliantly coloured face and blue-coloured buttocks. [prob. f. MAN + DRILL[3]]

manducate /'mændjʊleɪt/ *v.tr.* *literary* chew; eat. □□ **manducation** /-'keɪʃ(ə)n/ *n.* **manducatory** /-kətərɪ, -'keɪtərɪ/ *adj.* [L *manducare manducat-* chew f. *manduco* guzzler f. *mandere* chew]

mane /meɪn/ *n.* **1** long hair growing in a line on the neck of a horse, lion, etc. **2** *colloq.* a person's long hair. □□ **maned** *adj.* (also in *comb.*). **maneless** *adj.* [OE *manu* f. Gmc]

manège /mæˈneɪʒ/ *n.* (also **manege**) **1** a riding-school. **2** the movements of a trained horse. **3** horsemanship. [F *manège* f. It. (as MANAGE)]

manes /ˈmɑːneɪz, ˈmeɪniːz/ *n.pl.* **1** the deified souls of dead ancestors. **2** (as *sing.*) the revered ghost of a dead person. [ME f. L]

maneuver *US* var. of MANŒUVRE.

manful /ˈmænfʊl/ *adj.* brave; resolute. □□ **manfully** *adv.* **manfulness** *n.*

mangabey /ˈmæŋɡəˌbeɪ/ *n.* any small long-tailed W. African monkey of the genus *Cercocebus*. [*Mangabey*, a region of Madagascar]

manganese /ˈmæŋɡəˌniːz/ *n.* **1** *Chem.* a grey brittle metallic transition element used with steel to make alloys. ¶ Symb.: **Mn**. **2** (in full **manganese oxide**) the black mineral oxide of this used in the manufacture of glass. □□ **manganic** /-ˈɡænɪk/ *adj.* **manganous** /ˈmæŋɡənəs/ *adj.* [F *manganèse* f. It. *manganese*, alt. f. MAGNESIA]

mange /meɪndʒ/ *n.* a skin disease in hairy and woolly animals, caused by an arachnid parasite and occasionally communicated to man. [ME *mangie*, *maniewe* f. OF *manjue*, *mangeue* itch f. *mangier manju-* eat f. L *manducare* chew]

mangel /ˈmæŋɡ(ə)l/ *n.* (also **mangold** /ˈmæŋɡ(ə)ld/) (in full **mangel-wurzel**, **mangold-wurzel** /-ˈwɜːz(ə)l/) a large kind of beet, *Beta vulgaris*, used as cattle food. [G *Mangoldwurzel* f. *Mangold* beet + *Wurzel* root]

manger /ˈmeɪndʒə(r)/ *n.* a long open box or trough in a stable etc., for horses or cattle to eat from. [ME f. OF *mangeoire*, *mangeure* ult. f. L (as MANDUCATE)]

mange-tout /ˈmɑ̃ʒtuː, -ˈtuː/ *n.* the sugar-pea. [F, = eat-all]

mangle[1] /ˈmæŋɡ(ə)l/ *n.* & *v.* esp. *Brit. hist.* —*n.* a machine having two or more cylinders usu. turned by a handle, between which wet clothes etc. are squeezed and pressed. —*v.tr.* press (clothes etc.) in a mangle. [Du. *mangel(stok)* f. *mangelen* to mangle, ult. f. Gk *magganon* + *stok* staff, STOCK]

mangle[2] /ˈmæŋɡ(ə)l/ *v.tr.* **1** hack, cut about, or mutilate by blows etc. **2** spoil (a quotation, text, etc.) by misquoting, mispronouncing, etc. **3** cut roughly so as to disfigure. □□ **mangler** *n.* [AF *ma(ha)ngler*, app. frequent. of *mahaignier* MAIM]

mango /ˈmæŋɡəʊ/ *n.* (*pl.* **-oes** or **-os**) **1** a fleshy yellowish-red fruit, eaten ripe or used green for pickles etc. **2** the Indian evergreen tree, *Mangifera indica*, bearing this. [Port. *manga* f. Malay *mangā* f. Tamil *mānkāy* f. *mān* mango-tree + *kāy* fruit]

mangold (also **mangold-wurzel**) var. of MANGEL.

mangonel /ˈmæŋɡən(ə)l/ *n.* *Mil. hist.* a military engine for throwing stones etc. [ME f. OF *mangonel(le)*, f. med.L *manganellus* dimin. of LL *manganum* f. Gk *magganon*]

mangosteen /ˈmæŋɡəˌstiːn/ *n.* **1** a white juicy-pulped fruit with a thick reddish-brown rind. **2** the E. Indian tree, *Garcinia mangostana*, bearing this. [Malay *manggustan*]

mangrove /ˈmæŋɡrəʊv/ *n.* any tropical tree or shrub of the genus *Rhizophora*, growing in shore-mud with many tangled roots above ground. [17th c.: orig. uncert.: assim. to GROVE]

mangy /ˈmeɪndʒɪ/ *adj.* (**mangier**, **mangiest**) **1** (esp. of a domestic animal) having mange. **2** squalid; shabby. □□ **mangily** *adv.* **manginess** *n.*

manhandle /ˈmænˌhænd(ə)l/ *v.tr.* **1** move (heavy objects) by human effort. **2** *colloq.* handle (a person) roughly.

manhattan /mænˈhæt(ə)n/ *n.* a cocktail made of vermouth, whisky, etc. [*Manhattan*, borough of New York City]

manhole /ˈmænhəʊl/ *n.* a covered opening in a floor, pavement, sewer, etc. for workmen to gain access.

manhood /ˈmænhʊd/ *n.* **1** the state of being a man

rather than a child or woman. **2 a** manliness; courage. **b** a man's sexual potency. **3** the men of a country etc. **4** the state of being human.

manhunt /ˈmænhʌnt/ *n.* an organized search for a person, esp. a criminal.

mania /ˈmeɪnɪə/ *n.* **1** *Psychol.* mental illness marked by periods of great excitement and violence. **2** (often foll. by *for*) excessive enthusiasm; an obsession (*has a mania for jogging*). [ME f. LL f. Gk, = madness f. *mainomai* be mad, rel. to MIND]

-mania /ˈmeɪnɪə/ *comb. form* **1** *Psychol.* denoting a special type of mental abnormality or obsession (*megalomania*; *nymphomania*). **2** denoting extreme enthusiasm or admiration (*bibliomania*; *Anglomania*).

maniac /ˈmeɪnɪˌæk/ *n.* & *adj.* —*n.* **1** *colloq.* a person exhibiting extreme symptoms of wild behaviour etc.; a madman. **2** *colloq.* an obsessive enthusiast. **3** *Psychol.* archaic a person suffering from mania. —*adj.* of or behaving like a maniac. □□ **maniacal** /məˈnaɪək(ə)l/ *adj.* **maniacally** /məˈnaɪəkəlɪ/ *adv.* [LL *maniacus* f. late Gk *maniakos* (as MANIA)]

-maniac /ˈmeɪnɪæk/ *comb. form* forming adjectives and nouns meaning 'affected with -mania' or 'a person affected with -mania' (*nymphomaniac*).

manic /ˈmænɪk/ *adj.* of or affected by mania. □ **manic-depressive** *Psychol. adj.* affected by or relating to a mental disorder with alternating periods of elation and depression. —*n.* a person having such a disorder. □□ **manically** *adv.*

Manichee /ˈmænɪkiː/ *n.* **1** an adherent of a religious system of the 3rd-5th c., representing Satan in a state of everlasting conflict with God. **2** *Philos.* a dualist (see DUALISM). □□ **Manichean** /-ˈkiːən/ *adj.* & *n.* (also **Manichaean**). **Manicheism** /-ˈkiːɪz(ə)m/ *n.* (also **Manichaeism**). [LL *Manichaeus* f. late Gk *Manikhaios*, f. *Manes* or *Manichaeus* Persian founder of the sect]

manicure /ˈmænɪˌkjʊə(r)/ *n.* & *v.* —*n.* **1** a usu. professional cosmetic treatment of the hands and fingernails. **2** = MANICURIST. —*v.tr.* apply a manicure to (the hands or a person). [F f. L *manus* hand + *cura* care]

manicurist /ˈmænɪˌkjʊərɪst/ *n.* a person who manicures hands and fingernails professionally.

manifest[1] /ˈmænɪˌfest/ *adj.* & *v.* —*adj.* clear or obvious to the eye or mind (*his distress was manifest*). —*v.* **1** *tr.* display or show (a quality, feeling, etc.) by one's acts etc. **2** *tr.* show plainly to the eye or mind. **3** *tr.* be evidence of; prove. **4** *refl.* (of a thing) reveal itself. **5** *intr.* (of a ghost) appear. □□ **manifestation** /-ˈsteɪʃ(ə)n/ *n.* **manifestative** /-ˈfestətɪv/ *adj.* **manifestly** *adv.* [ME f. OF *manifeste* (adj.), *manifester* (v.) or L *manifestus*, *manifestare* f. *manus* hand + *festus* (unrecorded) struck]

manifest[2] /ˈmænɪˌfest/ *n.* & *v.* —*n.* **1** a cargo-list for the use of customs officers. **2** a list of passengers in an aircraft or of trucks etc. in a goods train. —*v.tr.* record (names, cargo, etc.) in a manifest. [It. *manifesto*: see MANIFESTO]

manifesto /ˌmænɪˈfestəʊ/ *n.* (*pl.* **-os**) a public declaration of policy and aims esp. issued before an election by a political party, candidate, government, etc. [It. f. *manifestare* f. L (as MANIFEST[1])]

manifold /ˈmænɪˌfəʊld/ *adj.* & *n.* —*adj. literary* **1** many and various (*manifold vexations*). **2** having various forms, parts, applications, etc. **3** performing several functions at once. —*n.* **1** a thing with many different forms, parts, applications, etc. **2** *Mech.* a pipe or chamber branching into several openings. □□ **manifoldly** *adv.* **manifoldness** *n.* [OE *manigfeald* (as MANY, -FOLD)]

manikin /ˈmænɪkɪn/ *n.* (also **mannikin**) **1** a little man; a dwarf. **2** an artist's lay figure. **3** an anatomical model of the body. **4** (usu. **mannikin**) any small finchlike bird of the genus *Lonchura*, native to Africa and Australasia. [Du. *manneken*, dimin. of *man* MAN]

Manila /məˈnɪlə/ *n.* (also **Manilla**) **1** a cigar or cheroot made in Manila. **2** (in full **Manila hemp**) the strong fibre of a Philippine tree, *Musa textilis*, used for rope etc. **3** (also **manila**) a strong brown paper made from Manila hemp or other material and used for wrapping paper, envelopes, etc. [*Manila* in the Philippines]

manilla /mə'nɪlə/ *n.* a metal bracelet used by African tribes as a medium of exchange. [Sp., prob. dimin. of *mano* hand f. L *manus*]

manille /mə'nɪl/ *n.* the second best trump or honour in ombre or quadrille. [F f. Sp. *malilla* dimin. of *mala* bad f. L *malus*]

manioc /'mænɪˌɒk/ *n.* **1** cassava. **2** the flour made from it. [Tupi *mandioca*]

maniple /'mænɪp(ə)l/ *n.* **1** *Rom.Hist.* a subdivision of a legion, containing 120 or 60 men. **2** a Eucharistic vestment consisting of a strip hanging from the left arm. [OF *maniple* or L *manipulus* handful, troop f. *manus* hand]

manipulate /mə'nɪpjʊˌleɪt/ *v.tr.* **1** handle, treat, or use, esp. skilfully (a tool, question, material, etc.). **2** manage (a person, situation, etc.) to one's own advantage, esp. unfairly or unscrupulously. **3** manually examine and treat (a part of the body). **4** *Computing* alter, edit, or move (text, data, etc.). **5** stimulate (the genitals). □□ **manipulable** /-ləb(ə)l/ *adj.* **manipulability** /-lə'bɪlɪtɪ/ *n.* **manipulatable** *adj.* **manipulation** /-'leɪʃ(ə)n/ *n.* **manipulator** *n.* **manipulatory** /-lətərɪ/ *adj.* [back-form. f. *manipulation* f. F *manipulation* f. mod.L *manipulatio* (as MANIPLE), after F *manipuler*]

manipulative /mə'nɪpjʊlətɪv/ *adj.* **1** characterized by unscrupulous exploitation of a situation, person, etc., for one's own ends. **2** of or concerning manipulation. □□ **manipulatively** *adv.* **manipulativeness** *n.*

Manit. *abbr.* Manitoba.

manitou /'mænɪˌtuː/ *n. Amer. Ind.* **1** a good or evil spirit as an object of reverence. **2** something regarded as having supernatural power. [Algonquin *manito*, *-tu* he has surpassed]

mankind *n.* **1** /mæn'kaɪnd/ the human species. **2** /'mænkaɪnd/ male people, as distinct from female.

manky /'mæŋkɪ/ *adj.* (**mankier, mankiest**) *colloq.* **1** bad, inferior, defective. **2** dirty. [obs. *mank* mutilated, defective]

manlike /'mænlaɪk/ *adj.* **1** having the qualities of a man. **2** (of a woman) mannish. **3** (of an animal, shape, etc.) resembling a human being.

manly /'mænlɪ/ *adj.* (**manlier, manliest**) **1** having qualities regarded as admirable in a man, such as courage, frankness, etc. **2** (of a woman) mannish. **3** (of things, qualities, etc.) befitting a man. □□ **manliness** *n.*

manna /'mænə/ *n.* **1** the substance miraculously supplied as food to the Israelites in the wilderness (Exod. 16). **2** an unexpected benefit (esp. *manna from heaven*). **3** spiritual nourishment, esp. the Eucharist. **4** the sweet dried juice from the manna-ash and other plants, used as a mild laxative. □ **manna-ash** an ash tree native to S. Europe, *Fraxinus ornus*. [OE f. LL f. Gk f. Aram. *mannā* f. Heb. *mān*, explained as = *mān hū?* what is it?, but prob. = Arab. *mann* exudation of common tamarisk (*Tamarix gallica*)]

manned /mænd/ *adj.* (of an aircraft, spacecraft, etc.) having a human crew. [past part. of MAN]

mannequin /'mænɪkɪn/ *n.* **1** a model employed by a dressmaker etc. to show clothes to customers. **2** a window dummy. [F, = MANIKIN]

manner /'mænə(r)/ *n.* **1** a way a thing is done or happens (*always dresses in that manner*). **2** (in *pl.*) **a** social behaviour (*it is bad manners to stare*). **b** polite or well-bred behaviour (*he has no manners*). **c** modes of life; conditions of society. **3** a person's outward bearing, way of speaking, etc. (*has an imperious manner*). **4 a** a style in literature, art, etc. (*in the manner of Rembrandt*). **b** = MANNERISM 2a. **5** *archaic* a kind or sort (*what manner of man is he?*). □ **all**

manner of many different kinds of. **comedy of manners** satirical portrayal of social behaviour, esp. of the upper classes. **in a manner of speaking** in some sense; to some extent; so to speak. **manner of means** see MEANS. **to the manner born** *colloq.* naturally at ease in a specified job, situation, etc. **2** destined by birth to follow a custom or way of life (Shakesp. *Hamlet* I. iv. 17). □□ **mannerless** *adj.* (in sense 2b of *n.*). [ME f. AF *manere*, OF *maniere* ult. f. L *manuarius* of the hand (*manus*)]

mannered /'mænəd/ *adj.* **1** (in *comb.*) behaving in a specified way (*ill-mannered*; *well-mannered*). **2** (of a style, artist, writer, etc.) showing idiosyncratic mannerisms. **3** (of a person) eccentrically affected in behaviour.

mannerism /'mænəˌrɪz(ə)m/ *n.* **1** a habitual gesture or way of speaking etc.; an idiosyncrasy. **2 a** excessive addiction to a distinctive style in art or literature. **b** a stylistic trick. **3** a style of Italian art preceding the Baroque, characterized by lengthened figures. □□ **mannerist** *n.* **manneristic** /-'rɪstɪk/ *adj.* **manneristical** /-'rɪstɪk(ə)l/ *adj.* **manneristically** /-'rɪstɪkəlɪ/ *adv.* [MANNER]

mannerly /'mænəlɪ/ *adj.* & *adv.* —*adj.* well-mannered; polite. —*adv.* politely. □□ **mannerliness** *n.*

mannikin var. of MANIKIN.

mannish /'mænɪʃ/ *adj.* **1** usu. *derog.* (of a woman) masculine in appearance or manner. **2** characteristic of a man. □□ **mannishly** *adv.* **mannishness** *n.* [OE *mennisc* f. (and assim. to) MAN]

manœuvre /mə'nuːvə(r)/ *n.* & *v.* (US **maneuver**) —*n.* **1** a planned and controlled movement or series of moves. **2** (in *pl.*) a large-scale exercise of troops, warships, etc. **3 a** an often deceptive planned or controlled action designed to gain an objective. **b** a skilful plan. —*v.* **1** *intr.* & *tr.* perform or cause to perform a manœuvre (*manœuvred the car into the space*). **2** *intr.* & *tr.* perform or cause (troops etc.) to perform military manœuvres. **3 a** *tr.* (usu. foll. by *into*, *out*, *away*) force, drive, or manipulate (a person, thing, etc.) by scheming or adroitness. **b** *intr.* use artifice. □□ **manœuvrable** *adj.* **manœuvrability** /-vrə'bɪlɪtɪ/ *n.* **manœuvrer** *n.* [F *manœuvre*, *manœuvrer* f. med.L *manuoperare* f. L *manus* hand + *operari* to work]

manometer /mə'nɒmɪtə(r)/ *n.* a pressure gauge for gases and liquids. □□ **manometric** /ˌmænə'metrɪk/ *adj.* [F *manomètre* f. Gk *manos* thin]

ma non troppo see TROPPO[1].

manor /'mænə(r)/ *n.* **1** (also **manor-house**) **a** a large country house with lands. **b** the house of the lord of the manor. **2** *Brit.* **a** a unit of land consisting of a lord's demesne and lands rented to tenants etc. **b** *hist.* a feudal lordship over lands. **3** *Brit. colloq.* the district covered by a police station. □□ **manorial** /mə'nɔːrɪəl/ *adj.* [ME f. AF *maner*, OF *maneir*, f. L *manēre* remain]

manpower /'mænˌpaʊə(r)/ *n.* **1** the power generated by a man working. **2** the number of people available for work, service, etc.

manqué /'mɒŋkeɪ/ *adj.* (placed after noun) that might have been but is not; unfulfilled (*a comic actor manqué*). [F, past part. of *manquer* lack]

mansard /'mænsɑːd/ *n.* a roof which has four sloping sides, each of which becomes steeper halfway down. [F *mansarde* f. F. Mansard, Fr. architect d. 1666]

manse /mæns/ *n.* the house of a minister, esp. a Scottish Presbyterian. □ **son** (or **daughter**) **of the manse** the child of a Presbyterian etc. minister. [ME f. med.L *mansus*, *-sa*, *-sum*, house f. *manēre* mans- remain]

manservant /'mænˌsɜːv(ə)nt/ *n.* (*pl.* **menservants**) a male servant.

-manship /mənʃɪp/ *suffix* forming nouns denoting skill in a subject or activity (*craftsmanship*; *gamesmanship*).

mansion /'mænʃ(ə)n/ *n.* **1** a large house. **2** (usu.

in *pl.*) *Brit.* a large building divided into flats. □**mansion-house** *Brit.* the house of a lord mayor or a landed proprietor. **the Mansion House** the official residence of the Lord Mayor of London. [ME f. OF f. L *mansio -onis* a staying (as MANSE)]

manslaughter /ˈmænˌslɔːtə(r)/ *n.* **1** the killing of a human being. **2** *Law* the unlawful killing of a human being without malice aforethought.

mansuetude /ˈmænswɪˌtjuːd/ *n.* *archaic* meekness, docility, gentleness. [ME f. OF *mansuetude* or L *mansuetudo* f. *mansuetus* gentle, tame f. *manus* hand + *suetus* accustomed]

manta /ˈmæntə/ *n.* any large ray of the family Mobulidae, esp. *Manta birostris*, having winglike pectoral fins and a whiplike tail. [Amer. Sp., = large blanket]

mantel /ˈmænt(ə)l/ *n.* **1** = MANTELPIECE 1. **2** = MANTELSHELF. [var. of MANTLE]

mantelet /ˈmæntəlɪt/ *n.* (also **mantlet** /ˈmæntlɪt/) **1** *hist.* a woman's short loose sleeveless mantle. **2** a bulletproof screen for gunners. [ME f. OF, dimin. of *mantel* MANTLE]

mantelpiece /ˈmænt(ə)lˌpiːs/ *n.* **1** a structure of wood, marble, etc. above and around a fireplace. **2** = MANTELSHELF.

mantelshelf /ˈmænt(ə)lˌʃelf/ *n.* a shelf above a fireplace.

mantic /ˈmæntɪk/ *adj.* *formal* of or concerning divination or prophecy. [Gk *mantikos* f. *mantis* prophet]

mantid /ˈmæntɪd/ *n.* = MANTIS.

mantilla /mænˈtɪlə/ *n.* a lace scarf worn by Spanish women over the hair and shoulders. [Sp., dimin. of *manta* MANTLE]

mantis /ˈmæntɪs/ *n.* (*pl.* same or **mantises**) any insect of the family Mantidae, feeding on other insects etc. □**praying mantis** a mantis, *Mantis religiosa*, that holds its forelegs in a position suggestive of hands folded in prayer, while waiting to pounce on its prey. [Gk, = prophet]

mantissa /mænˈtɪsə/ *n.* the part of a logarithm after the decimal point. [L, = makeweight]

mantle /ˈmænt(ə)l/ *n.* & *v.* —*n.* **1** a loose sleeveless cloak, esp. of a woman. **2** a covering (*a mantle of snow*). **3** a spiritual influence or authority (see 2 Kings 2:13). **4** a fragile lacelike tube fixed round a gas-jet to give an incandescent light. **5** an outer fold of skin enclosing a mollusc's viscera. **6** a bird's back, scapulars, and wing-coverts, esp. if of a distinctive colour. **7** the region between the crust and the core of the earth. —*v.* **1** *tr.* clothe in or as if in a mantle; cover, conceal, envelop. **2** *intr.* **a** (of the blood) suffuse the cheeks. **b** (of the face) glow with a blush. **3** *intr.* (of a liquid) become covered with a coating or scum. [ME f. OF f. L *mantellum* cloak]

mantlet var. of MANTELET.

mantling /ˈmæntlɪŋ/ *n.* *Heraldry* **1** ornamental drapery etc. behind and around a shield. **2** a representation of this. [MANTLE + ING¹]

mantra /ˈmæntrə/ *n.* **1** a word or sound repeated to aid concentration in meditation, orig. in Hinduism and Buddhism. **2** a Vedic hymn. [Skr., = instrument of thought f. *man* think]

mantrap /ˈmæntræp/ *n.* a trap for catching poachers, trespassers, etc.

mantua /ˈmæntjʊə/ *n.* *hist.* a woman's loose gown of the 17th-18th c. [corrupt. of *manteau* (F, as MANTLE) after *Mantua* in Italy]

manual /ˈmænjʊəl/ *adj.* & *n.* —*adj.* **1** of or done with the hands (*manual labour*). **2** (of a machine etc.) worked by hand, not automatically. —*n.* **1 a** a book of instructions, esp. for operating a machine or learning a subject; a handbook (*a computer manual*). **b** any small book. **2** an organ keyboard played with the hands not the feet. **3** *Mil.* an exercise in handling a rifle etc. **4** *hist.* a book of the forms to be used by priests in the administration of the Sacraments. □**manual alphabet** sign language. □□**manually**

adv. [ME f. OF *manuel*, f. (and later assim. to) L *manualis* f. *manus* hand]

manufactory /ˌmænjʊˈfæktərɪ/ *n.* (*pl.* -ies) *archaic* = FACTORY. [MANUFACTURE, after *factory*]

manufacture /ˌmænjʊˈfæktʃə(r)/ *n.* & *v.* —*n.* **1 a** the making of articles esp. in a factory etc. **b** a branch of an industry (*woollen manufacture*). **2** esp. *derog.* the merely mechanical production of literature, art, etc. —*v.tr.* **1** make (articles), esp. on an industrial scale. **2** invent or fabricate (evidence, a story, etc.). **3** esp. *derog.* make or produce (literature, art, etc.) in a mechanical way. □□**manufacturable** *adj.* **manufacturability** /-tʃərəˈbɪlɪtɪ/ *n.* **manufacturer** *n.* [F f. It. *manifattura* & L *manufactum* made by hand]

manuka /mæˈnuːkə, ˈmɑːnəkə/ *n.* *Austral.* & *NZ* a small tree, *Leptospermum scoparium*, with aromatic leaves and hard timber. [Maori]

manumit /ˌmænjʊˈmɪt/ *v.tr.* (**manumitted**, **manumitting**) *hist.* set (a slave) free. □□ **manumission** /-ˈmɪʃ(ə)n/ *n.* [ME f. L *manumittere manumiss-* f. *manus* hand + *emittere* send forth]

manure /məˈnjʊə(r)/ *n.* & *v.* —*n.* **1** animal dung, esp. of horses, used for fertilizing land. **2** any compost or artificial fertilizer. —*v.tr.* (also *absol.*) apply manure to (land etc.). □□**manurial** *adj.* [ME f. AF *mainoverer* = OF *manouvrer* MANŒUVRE]

manuscript /ˈmænjʊskrɪpt/ *n.* & *adj.* —*n.* **1** a book, document, etc. written by hand. **2** an author's handwritten or typed text, submitted for publication. **3** handwritten form (*produced in manuscript*). —*adj.* written by hand. [med.L *manuscriptus* f. *manu* by hand + *scriptus* past part. of *scribere* write]

Manx /mæŋks/ *adj.* & *n.* —*adj.* of or relating to the Isle of Man. —*n.* **1** *Language hist.* the now extinct Celtic language formerly spoken in the Isle of Man. **2** (prec. by *the*; treated as *pl.*) the Manx people. □**Manx cat** a tailless cat. [ON f. OIr. *Manu* Isle of Man]

Manxman /ˈmæŋksmən/ *n.* (*pl.* -men; *fem.* **Manxwoman**, *pl.* -women) a native of the Isle of Man.

many /ˈmenɪ/ *adj.* & *n.* —*adj.* (**more** /mɔː(r)/; **most** /məʊst/) great in number; numerous (*many times*; *many people*; *many a person*; *his reasons were many*). —*n.* (as *pl.*) **1** a large number (*many like skiing*; *many went*). **2** (prec. by *the*) the multitude of people, working people. □**as many** the same number of (*six mistakes in as many lines*). **as many again** the same number additionally (*sixty here and as many again there*). **be too** (or **one too**) **many for** outwit, baffle. **a good** (or **great**) **many** a large number. **many-sided** having many sides, aspects, interests, capabilities, etc. **many-sidedness** *n.* the fact or state of being many-sided. **many's the time** often (*many's the time we saw it*). **many a time** many times. [OE *manig*, ult. f. Gmc]

manzanilla /ˌmænzəˈnɪlə/ *n.* a pale very dry Spanish sherry. [Sp., lit. 'camomile']

manzanita /ˌmænzəˈniːtə/ *n.* any of several evergreen shrubs of the genus *Arctostaphylos*, esp. *A. manzanita*, native to California. [Sp., dimin. of *manzana* apple]

Maoism /ˈmaʊɪz(ə)m/ *n.* the Communist doctrines of Mao Zedong (d. 1976), Chinese statesman. □□ **Maoist** *n.* & *adj.*

Maori /ˈmaʊrɪ/ *n.* & *adj.* —*n.* (*pl.* same or **Maoris**) **1** a member of the Polynesian aboriginal people of New Zealand. **2** the language of the Maori. —*adj.* of or concerning the Maori or their language. [native name]

map /mæp/ *n.* & *v.* —*n.* **1 a** a usu. flat representation of the earth's surface, or part of it, showing physical features, cities, etc. (cf. GLOBE). **b** a diagrammatic representation of a route etc. (*drew a map of the journey*). **2** a two-dimensional representation of the stars, the heavens, etc., or of the surface of a planet, the moon, etc. **3** a diagram showing the arrangement

aʊ how eɪ day əʊ no eə hair ɪə near ɔɪ boy ʊə poor aɪə fire aʊə sour (*see over for consonants*)

or components of a thing. **4** *sl.* the face. *—v.tr.* (**mapped, mapping**) **1** represent (a country etc.) on a map. **2** *Math.* associate each element of (a set) with one element of another set. □**map out** arrange in detail; plan (a course of conduct etc.). **off the map** *colloq.* **1** of no account; obsolete. **2** very distant. **on the map** *colloq.* prominent, important. **wipe off the map** *colloq.* obliterate. □□ **mapless** *adj.* **mappable** *adj.* **mapper** *n.* [L *mappa* napkin: in med.L *mappa* (*mundi*) map (of the world)]

maple /'meɪp(ə)l/ *n.* **1** any tree or shrub of the genus *Acer* grown for shade, ornament, wood, or its sugar. **2** the wood of the maple. □**maple-leaf** the leaf of the maple, used as an emblem of Canada. **maple sugar** a sugar produced by evaporating the sap of the sugar maple etc. **maple syrup** a syrup produced from the sap of the sugar maple etc. [ME *mapul* etc. f. OE *mapeltrēow, mapulder*]

maquette /mə'ket/ *n.* **1** a sculptor's small preliminary model in wax, clay, etc. **2** a preliminary sketch. [F f. It. *machietta* dimin. of *macchia* spot]

maquillage /,mæki'jɑːʒ/ *n.* **1** make-up; cosmetics. **2** the application of make-up. [F f. *maquiller* make up f. OF *masquiller* stain]

Maquis /mæ'kiː/ *n.* **1** the French resistance movement during the German occupation (1940-45). **2** a member of this. [F, = brushwood, f. Corsican It. *macchia* thicket]

Mar. *abbr.* March.

mar /mɑː(r)/ *v.tr.* (**marred, marring**) **1** ruin. **2** impair the perfection of; spoil; disfigure. [OE *merran* hinder]

marabou /'mærəˌbuː/ *n.* (also **marabout**) **1** a large W. African stork, *Leptoptilos crumeniferus.* **2** a tuft of down from the wing or tail of the marabou used as a trimming for hats etc. [F f. Arab. *murābiṭ* holy man (see MARABOUT), the stork being regarded as holy]

marabout /'mærəˌbuːt/ *n.* **1** a Muslim hermit or monk, esp. in N. Africa. **2** a shrine marking a marabout's burial-place. [F f. Port. *marabuto* f. Arab. *murābiṭ* holy man f. *ribāṭ* frontier station, where he acquired merit by combat against the infidel]

maraca /mə'rækə/ *n.* a hollow clublike gourd or gourd-shaped container filled with beans etc. and usu. shaken in pairs as a percussion instrument in Latin American music. [Port. *maracá*, prob. f. Tupi]

maraschino /,mærə'skiːnəʊ/ *n.* (*pl.* **-os**) a strong sweet liqueur made from a small black Dalmatian cherry. □**maraschino cherry** a cherry preserved in maraschino and used to decorate cocktails etc. [It. f. *marasca* small black cherry, for *amarasca* f. *amaro* bitter f. L *amarus*]

marasmus /mə'ræzməs/ *n.* a wasting away of the body. □□ **marasmic** *adj.* [mod.L f. Gk *marasmos* f. *mainō* wither]

Maratha /mə'rɑːtə, -'rætə/ *n.* (also **Mahratta**) a member of a warrior people native to the modern Indian State of Maharashtra. [Hindi *Marhaṭṭa* f. Skr. *Māhārāṣṭra* great kingdom]

Marathi /mə'rɑːtɪ, -'rætɪ/ *n.* (also **Mahratti**) the language of the Marathas. [MARATHA]

marathon /'mærəθ(ə)n/ *n.* **1** a long-distance running race, usu. of 26 miles 385 yards (42.195 km). **2** a long-lasting or difficult task, operation, etc. (often *attrib.: a marathon shopping expedition*). □□ **marathoner** *n.* [*Marathon* in Greece, scene of a victory over the Persians in 490 BC: a messenger was said to have run to Athens with the news, but the account has no authority]

maraud /mə'rɔːd/ *v.* **1** *intr.* **a** make a plundering raid. **b** pilfer systematically; plunder. **2** *tr.* plunder (a place). □□ **marauder** *n.* [F *marauder* f. *maraud* rogue]

marble /'mɑːb(ə)l/ *n. & v.* *—n.* **1** limestone in a metamorphic crystalline (or granular) state, and capable of taking a polish, used in sculpture and architecture. **2** (often *attrib.*) **a** anything made of marble (*a marble clock*). **b** anything resembling marble in hardness, coldness, durability, etc. (*her features were marble*). **3 a** a small ball of marble, glass, clay, etc., used as a toy. **b** (in *pl.*; treated as *sing.*) a game using these. **4** (in *pl.*) *sl.* one's mental faculties (*he's lost his marbles*). **5** (in *pl.*) a collection of sculptures (*Elgin Marbles*). *—v.tr.* **1** (esp. as **marbled** *adj.*) stain or colour (paper, the edges of a book, soap, etc.) to look like variegated marble. **2** (as **marbled** *adj.*) (of meat) streaked with alternating layers of lean and fat. □**marble cake** a cake with a mottled appearance, made of light and dark sponge. □□ **marbly** *adj.* [ME f. OF *marbre, marble*, f. L *marmor* f. Gk *marmaros* shining stone]

marbling /'mɑːblɪŋ/ *n.* **1** colouring or marking like marble. **2** streaks of fat in lean meat.

marc /mɑːk/ *n.* **1** the refuse of pressed grapes etc. **2** a brandy made from this. [F f. *marcher* tread, MARCH¹]

Marcan /'mɑːkən/ *adj.* of or relating to St Mark. [L *Marcus* Mark]

marcasite /'mɑːkəˌsaɪt/ *n.* **1** a yellowish crystalline iron sulphide mineral. **2** these bronze-yellow crystals used in jewellery. [ME f. med.L *marcasita*, f. Arab. *marḳašīṭā* f. Pers.]

marcato /mɑː'kɑːtəʊ/ *adv. & adj.* *Mus.* played with emphasis. [It., = marked]

marcel /mɑː'sel/ *n. & v.* *—n.* (in full **marcel wave**) a deep wave in the hair. *—v.tr.* (**marcelled, marcelling**) wave (hair) with a deep wave. [*Marcel* Grateau, Paris hairdresser d. 1936, who invented the method]

marcescent /mɑː'ses(ə)nt/ *adj.* (of part of a plant) withering but not falling. □□ **marcescence** *n.* [L *marcescere* incept. of *marcēre* wither]

March /mɑːtʃ/ *n.* the third month of the year. □**March hare** a hare in the breeding season, characterized by excessive leaping, strange behaviour, etc. (*mad as a March hare*). [ME f. OF *march(e)*, dial. var. of *marz, mars*, f. L *Martius* (*mensis*) (month) of Mars]

march¹ /mɑːtʃ/ *v. & n.* *—v.* **1** *intr.* (usu. foll. by *away, off, out*, etc.) walk in a military manner with a regular measured tread. **2** *tr.* (often foll. by *away, on, off*, etc.) cause to march or walk (*marched the army to Moscow; marched him out of the room*). **3** *intr.* **a** walk or proceed steadily, esp. across country. **b** (of events etc.) continue unrelentingly (*time marches on*). **4** *intr.* take part in a protest march. *—n.* **1 a** the act or an instance of marching. **b** the uniform step of troops etc. (*a slow march*). **2 a** a long difficult walk. **3** a procession as a protest or demonstration. **4** (usu. foll. by *of*) progress or continuity (*the march of events*). **5 a** a piece of music composed to accompany a march. **b** a composition of similar character and form. □**marching order** *Mil.* equipment or a formation for marching. **marching orders** *Mil.* the direction for troops to depart for war etc. **2** a dismissal (*gave him his marching orders*). **march on 1** advance towards (a military objective). **2** proceed. **march past** *n.* the marching of troops past a saluting-point at a review. *—v.intr.* (of troops) carry out a march past. **on the march 1** marching. **2** in steady progress. □□ **marcher** *n.* [F *marche* (n.), *marcher* (v.), f. LL *marcus* hammer]

march² /mɑːtʃ/ *n. & v.* *—n. hist.* **1** (usu. in *pl.*) a boundary, a frontier (esp. of the borderland between England and Scotland or Wales). **2** a tract of often disputed land between two countries. *—v.intr.* (foll. by *upon, with*) (of a country, an estate, etc.) have a common frontier with, border on. [ME f. OF *marche, marchir* ult. f. Gmc: cf. MARK¹]

marcher /'mɑːtʃə(r)/ *n.* an inhabitant of a march or border district.

marchioness /,mɑːʃə'nes, 'mɑː-/ *n.* **1** the wife or widow of a marquess. **2** a woman holding the rank of marquess in her own right (cf. MARQUISE). [med.L *marchionissa* f. *marchio -onis* captain of the marches (as MARCH²)]

marchpane /ˈmɑːtʃpeɪn/ *archaic* var. of MARZIPAN.

Mardi Gras /ˌmɑːdɪ ˈɡrɑː/ *n.* **1 a** Shrove Tuesday in some Catholic countries. **b** merrymaking on this day. **2** the last day of a carnival etc. **3** *Austral.* a carnival or fair at any time. [F, = fat Tuesday]

mardy /ˈmɑːdɪ/ *adj. dial.* sulky, whining, spoilt. [dial. *mard* spoilt, alt. of *marred* f. MAR]

mare¹ /meə(r)/ *n.* **1** the female of any equine animal, esp. the horse. **2** *sl. derog.* a woman. □**mare's nest** an illusory discovery. **mare's tail 1** a tall slender marsh plant, *Hippuris vulgaris.* **2** (in *pl.*) long straight streaks of cirrus cloud. [ME f. OE *mearh* horse f. Gmc: cf. MARSHAL]

mare² /ˈmɑːreɪ/ *n.* (*pl.* **maria** /ˈmɑːrɪə/ or **mares**) **1** (in full **mare clausum** /ˈklaʊsʊm/) *Law* the sea under the jurisdiction of a particular country. **2** (in full **mare liberum** /ˈliːbəˌrʊm/) *Law* the sea open to all nations. **3 a** any of a number of large dark flat areas on the surface of the moon, once thought to be seas. **b** a similar area on Mars. [L, = sea]

maremma /məˈremə/ *n.* (*pl.* **maremme** /-mɪ/) low marshy unhealthy land near a seashore. [It. f. L *maritima* (as MARITIME)]

margarine /ˌmɑːdʒəˈriːn, ˌmɑːɡə-, ˈmɑː-/ *n.* a butter-substitute made from vegetable oils or animal fats with milk etc. [F, misapplication of a chem. term, f. *margarique* f. Gk *margaron* pearl]

margay /ˈmɑːɡeɪ/ *n.* a small wild S. American cat, *Felis wiedii.* [F f. Tupi *mbaracaia*]

marge¹ /mɑːdʒ/ *n. Brit. colloq.* margarine. [abbr.]

marge² /mɑːdʒ/ *n. poet.* a margin or edge. [F f. L *margo* (as MARGIN)]

margin /ˈmɑːdʒɪn/ *n. & v.* —*n.* **1** the edge or border of a surface. **2 a** the blank border on each side of the print on a page etc. **b** a line ruled esp. on exercise paper, marking off a margin. **3** an amount (of time, money, etc.) by which a thing exceeds, falls short, etc. (*won by a narrow margin; a margin of profit*). **4** the lower limit of possibility, success, etc. (*his effort fell below the margin*). **5** *Austral.* an increment to a basic wage, paid for skill. **6** a sum deposited with a stockbroker to cover the risk of loss on a transaction on account. —*v.tr.* (**margined, margining**) provide with a margin or marginal notes. □**margin of error** a usu. small difference allowed for miscalculation, change of circumstances, etc. **margin release** a device on a typewriter allowing a word to be typed beyond the margin normally set. [ME f. L *margo -ginis*]

marginal /ˈmɑːdʒɪn(ə)l/ *adj.* **1 a** of or written in a margin. **b** having marginal notes. **2 a** of or at the edge; not central. **b** not significant or decisive (*the work is of merely marginal interest*). **3** *Brit.* (of a parliamentary seat or constituency) having a small majority at risk in an election. **4** close to the limit, esp. of profitability. **5** (of the sea) adjacent to the shore of a State. **6** (of land) difficult to cultivate; unprofitable. **7** barely adequate; unprovided for. □**marginal cost** the cost added by making one extra copy etc. □□**marginality** /-ˈnælɪtɪ/ *n.* **marginally** *adv.* [med.L *marginalis* (as MARGIN)]

marginalia /ˌmɑːdʒɪˈneɪlɪə/ *n.pl.* marginal notes. [med.L, neut. pl. of *marginalis*]

marginalize /ˈmɑːdʒɪnəˌlaɪz/ *v.tr.* (also **-ise**) make or treat as insignificant. □□**marginalization** /-ˈzeɪʃ(ə)n/ *n.*

marginate *v. & adj.* —*v.tr.* /ˈmɑːdʒɪˌneɪt/ **1** = MARGINALIZE. **2** provide with a margin or border. —*adj.* /ˈmɑːdʒɪnət/ *Biol.* having a distinct margin or border. □□**margination** /-ˈneɪʃ(ə)n/ *n.*

margrave /ˈmɑːɡreɪv/ *n. hist.* the hereditary title of some princes of the Holy Roman Empire (orig. of a military governor of a border province). □□ **margravate** /ˈmɑːɡrəvət/ *n.* [MDu. *markgrave* border count (as MARK¹, *grave* COUNT² f. OLG *grēve*)]

margravine /ˈmɑːɡrəˌviːn/ *n. hist.* the wife of a margrave. [Du. *markgravin* (as MARGRAVE)]

marguerite /ˌmɑːɡəˈriːt/ *n.* an ox-eye daisy. [F f. L *margarita* f. Gk *margarītēs* f. *margaron* pearl]

maria *pl.* of MARE².

mariage de convenance /ˌmærɪˌɑːʒ də ˌkɔ̃vəˈnɑ̃s/ *n.* = *marriage of convenience.* [F]

Marian /ˈmeərɪən/ *adj. RC Ch.* of or relating to the Virgin Mary (*Marian vespers*). [L *Maria* Mary]

marigold /ˈmærɪˌɡəʊld/ *n.* any plant of the genus *Calendula* or *Tagetes,* with golden or bright yellow flowers. [ME f. *Mary* (prob. the Virgin) + dial. *gold,* OE *golde,* prob. rel. to GOLD]

marijuana /ˌmærɪˈhwɑːnə/ *n.* (also **marihuana**) **1** the dried leaves, flowering tops, and stems of the hemp, used as a hallucinogenic drug usu. smoked in cigarettes. **2** the plant yielding these (cf. HEMP). [Amer. Sp.]

marimba /məˈrɪmbə/ *n.* **1** a xylophone played by natives of Africa and Central America. **2** a modern orchestral instrument derived from this. [Congo]

marina /məˈriːnə/ *n.* a specially designed harbour with moorings for pleasure-yachts etc. [It. & Sp. fem. adj. f. *marino* f. L (as MARINE)]

marinade /ˌmærɪˈneɪd, ˈmæ-/ *n. & v.* —*n.* **1** a mixture of wine, vinegar, oil, spices, etc., in which meat, fish, etc., is soaked before cooking. **2** meat, fish, etc., soaked in this liquid. —*v.tr.* soak (meat, fish, etc.) in a marinade. [F f. Sp. *marinada* f. *marinar* pickle in brine f. *marino* (as MARINE)]

marinate /ˈmærɪˌneɪt/ *v.tr.* = MARINADE. □□ **marination** /-ˈneɪʃ(ə)n/ *n.* [It. *marinare* or F *mariner* (as MARINE)]

marine /məˈriːn/ *adj. & n.* —*adj.* **1** of, found in, or produced by the sea. **2 a** of or relating to shipping or naval matters (*marine insurance*). **b** for use at sea. —*n.* **1** a country's shipping, fleet, or navy (*mercantile marine; merchant marine*). **2** a member of a body of troops trained to serve on land or sea. **3** a picture of a scene at sea. □**marine stores** new or old ships' material etc. sold as merchandise. **marine trumpet** a large single-stringed viol with a trumpet-like tone. **tell that to the marines** (or **horse marines**) *colloq.* an expression of disbelief. [ME f. OF *marin marine* f. L *marinus* f. *mare* sea]

mariner /ˈmærɪnə(r)/ *n.* a seaman. □**mariner's compass** a compass showing magnetic or true north and the bearings from it. [ME f. AF *mariner,* OF *marinier* f. med.L *marinarius* f. L (as MARINE)]

Mariolatry /ˌmeərɪˈɒlətrɪ/ *n. derog.* idolatrous worship of the Virgin Mary. [L *Maria* Mary + -LATRY, after *idolatry*]

marionette /ˌmærɪəˈnet/ *n.* a puppet worked by strings. [F *marionnette* f. *Marion* dimin. of *Marie* Mary]

Marist /ˈmɑːrɪst/ *n.* a member of the Roman Catholic Society of Mary. [F *Mariste* f. *Marie* Mary]

marital /ˈmærɪt(ə)l/ *adj.* **1** of marriage or the relations between husband and wife. **2** of or relating to a husband. □□**maritally** *adv.* [L *maritalis* f. *maritus* husband]

maritime /ˈmærɪˌtaɪm/ *adj.* **1** connected with the sea or seafaring (*maritime insurance*). **2** living or found near the sea. [L *maritimus* f. *mare* sea]

marjoram /ˈmɑːdʒərəm/ *n.* either of two aromatic herbs, *Origanum vulgare* (**wild marjoram**) or *Majorana hortensis* (**sweet marjoram**), the fresh or dried leaves of which are used as a flavouring in cookery. [ME & OF *majorane* f. med.L *majorana,* of unkn. orig.]

mark¹ /mɑːk/ *n. & v.* —*n.* **1** a trace, sign, stain, scar, etc., on a surface, face, page, etc. **2** (esp. in *comb.*) **a** a written or printed symbol (*exclamation mark; question mark*). **b** a numerical or alphabetical award denoting excellence, conduct, proficiency, etc. (*got a good mark for effort; gave him a black mark; gained 46 marks out of 50*). **3** (usu. foll. by *of*) a sign or indication of quality, character, feeling, etc. (*took off* *his hat as a mark of respect).* **4 a** a sign, seal, etc., used for distinction or identification. **b** a cross etc. made in place of a signature by an illiterate person. **5 a** a target, object, goal, etc. (*missed the mark with his first play*). **b** a standard for attainment (*his work falls below the mark*). **6** a line etc. indicating a position; a marker. **7** (usu. **Mark**) (followed by a numeral) a particular design, model, etc., of a car, aircraft, etc. (*this is the Mark 2 model*). **8** a runner's starting-point in a race. **9** *Naut.* a piece of material etc. used to indicate a position on a sounding-line. **10 a** *Rugby Football* a heel-mark on the ground made by a player who has caught the ball direct from a kick, knock-on, or throw-forward by an opponent. **b** *Austral. Rules* the catching before it reaches the ground of a ball kicked at least ten metres; the spot from which the subsequent kick is taken. **11** *sl.* the intended victim of a swindler etc. **12** *Boxing* the pit of the stomach. **13** *hist.* a tract of land held in common by a Teutonic or medieval German village community. — *v.tr.* **1 a** make a mark on (a thing or person), esp. by writing, cutting, scraping, etc. **b** put a distinguishing or identifying mark, initials, name, etc., on (clothes etc.) (*marked the tree with their initials*). **2 a** allot marks to; correct (a student's work etc.). **b** record (the points gained in games etc.). **3** attach a price to (goods etc.) (*marked the doll at 50p*). **4** (often foll. by *by*) show or manifest (displeasure etc.) (*marked his anger by leaving early*). **5** notice or observe (*she marked his agitation*). **6 a** characterize or be a feature of (*the day was marked by storms*). **b** acknowledge, recognize, celebrate (*marked the occasion with a toast*). **7** name or indicate (a place on a map, the length of a syllable, etc.) by a sign or mark. **8** characterize (a person or a thing) as (*marked them as weak*). **9 a** *Brit.* keep close to so as to prevent the free movement of (an opponent in sport). **b** *Austral. Rules* catch (the ball). **10** (as **marked** *adj.*) having natural marks (*is marked with silver spots*). **11** (of a graduated instrument) show, register (so many degrees etc.). **12** *US & Austral.* castrate (a lamb). □**one's mark** *colloq.* **1** what one prefers. **2** an opponent, object, etc., of one's own size, calibre, etc. (*the little one's more my mark*). **beside** (or **off** or **wide of**) **the mark 1** not to the point; irrelevant. **2** not accurate. **make one's mark** attain distinction. **mark down 1** mark (goods etc.) at a lower price. **2** make a written note of. **3** choose (a person) as one's victim. **mark-down** *n.* a reduction in price. **mark off** (often foll. by *from*) separate (one thing from another) by a boundary etc. (*marked off the subjects for discussion*). **mark of mouth** a depression in a horse's incisor indicating age. **mark out 1** plan (a course of action etc.). **2** destine (*marked out for success*). **3** trace out boundaries, a course, etc. **mark time 1** *Mil.* march on the spot, without moving forward. **2** act routinely; go through the motions. **3** await an opportunity to advance. **mark up 1** mark (goods etc.) at a higher price. **2** mark or correct (text etc.) for typesetting or alteration. **mark-up** *n.* **1** the amount added to the cost price of goods to cover overhead charges, profit, etc. **2** the corrections made in marking up text. **mark you** please note (*without obligation, mark you*). **off the mark 1** having made a start. **2** = *beside the mark*. **of mark** noteworthy. **on the mark** ready to start. **on your mark** (or **marks**) (as an instruction) get ready to start (esp. a race). **up to the mark** reaching the usual or normal standard, esp. of health. [OE *me(a)rc* (n.), *mearcian* (v.), f. Gmc]

mark² /maːk/ *n.* **1 a** = DEUTSCHE MARK. **b** = OSTMARK. **2** *hist.* **a** a denomination of weight for gold and silver. **b** English money of account. [OE *marc*, prob. rel. to med.L *marca, marcus*]

marked /maːkt/ *adj.* **1** having a visible mark. **2** clearly noticeable; evident (*a marked difference*). **3** (of playing-cards) having distinctive marks on their backs to assist cheating. □**marked man 1** a person

whose conduct is watched with suspicion or hostility. **2** a person destined to succeed. □□ **markedly** /-kɪdlɪ/ *adv.* **markedness** /-kɪdnɪs/ *n.* [OE (past part. of MARK¹)]

marker /'maːkə(r)/ *n.* **1** a stone, post, etc., used to mark a position, place reached, etc. **2** a person or thing that marks. **3** a felt-tipped pen with a broad tip. **4** a person who records a score, esp. in billiards. **5** a flare etc. used to direct a pilot to a target. **6** a bookmark. **7** *US sl.* a promissory note; an IOU.

market /'maːkɪt/ *n. & v.* — *n.* **1 a** the gathering of people for the purchase and sale of provisions, livestock, etc., esp. with a number of different vendors. **b** the time of this. **2** an open space or covered building used for this. **3** (often foll. by *for*) a demand for a commodity or service (*goods find a ready market*). **4** a place or group providing such a demand. **5** conditions as regards, or opportunity for, buying or selling. **6** the rate of purchase and sale, market value (*the market fell*). **7** (prec. by *the*) the trade in a specified commodity (*the corn market*). **8** (**the Market**) *Brit.* the European Economic Community. — *v.* (**marketed, marketing**) **1** *tr.* sell. **2** *tr.* offer for sale. **3** *intr.* buy or sell goods in a market. □**be in the market for** wish to buy. **be on** (or **come into**) **the market** be offered for sale. **make a market** *Stock Exch.* induce active dealing in a stock or shares. **market cross** a structure erected in a market-place, orig. a stone cross, later an arcaded building. **market-day** a day on which a market is regularly held, usu. weekly. **market garden** a place where vegetables and fruit are grown for the market etc. **market gardener** a person who owns or is employed in a market garden. **market maker** *Brit.* a member of the Stock Exchange granted certain privileges and trading to prescribed regulations. **market-place 1** an open space where a market is held in a town. **2** the scene of actual dealings. **market price** the price in current dealings. **market research** the study of consumers' needs and preferences. **market town** *Brit.* a town where a market is held. **market value** value as a saleable thing (opp. *book value*). **put on the market** offer for sale. □□ **marketer** *n.* **marketing** *n.* [ME ult. f. L *mercatus* f. *mercari* buy: see MERCHANT]

marketable /'maːkɪtəb(ə)l/ *adj.* able or fit to be sold. □□ **marketability** /-'bɪlɪtɪ/ *n.*

marketeer /ˌmaːkɪ'tɪə(r)/ *n.* **1** a supporter of the EEC and British membership of it. **2** a marketer.

markhor /'maːkɔː(r)/ *n.* a large spiral-horned wild goat, *Capra falconeri*, of N. India. [Pers. *mār-ḵwār* f. *mār* serpent + *ḵwār* -eating]

marking /'maːkɪŋ/ *n.* (usu. in *pl.*) **1** an identification mark, esp. a symbol on an aircraft. **2** the colouring of an animal's fur, feathers, skin, etc. □**marking-ink** indelible ink for marking linen etc.

marksman /'maːksmən/ *n.* (*pl.* **-men**) a person skilled in shooting, esp. with a pistol or rifle. □□ **marksmanship** *n.*

marl¹ /maːl/ *n. & v.* — *n.* soil consisting of clay and lime, with fertilizing properties. — *v.tr.* apply marl to (the ground). □□ **marly** *adj.* [ME f. OF *marle* f. med.L *margila* f. L *marga*]

marl² /maːl/ *n.* **1** a mottled yarn of differently coloured threads. **2** the fabric made from this. [shortening of *marbled*: see MARBLE]

marlin /'maːlɪn/ *n.* *US* any of various large long-nosed marine fish of the family *Istophoridae*, esp. the blue marlin *Makaira nigricans*. [MARLINSPIKE, with ref. to its pointed snout]

marline /'maːlɪn/ *n.* *Naut.* a thin line of two strands. □**marline-spike** = MARLINSPIKE. [ME f. Du. *marlijn* f. *marren* bind + *lijn* LINE¹]

marlinspike /'maːlɪnˌspaɪk/ *n.* *Naut.* a pointed iron tool used to separate strands of rope or wire. [orig. app. *marling-spike* f. *marl* fasten with marline (f. Du. *marlen* frequent. of MDu. *marren* bind) + -ING¹ + SPIKE¹]

marlite /'mɑːlaɪt/ n. a kind of marl that is not reduced to powder by the action of the air.

marmalade /'mɑːməˌleɪd/ n. a preserve of citrus fruit, usu. bitter oranges, made like jam. □ **marmalade cat** a cat with orange fur. [F *marmelade* f. Port. *marmelada* quince jam f. *marmelo* quince f. L *melimelum* f. Gk *melimēlon* f. *meli* honey + *mēlon* apple]

Marmite /'mɑːmaɪt/ n. **1** *Brit. propr.* a preparation made from yeast extract and vegetable extract, used in sandwiches and for flavouring. **2** (**marmite**) /also mɑːˈmiːt/ an earthenware cooking vessel. [F, = cooking-pot]

marmoreal /mɑːˈmɔːrɪəl/ adj. *poet.* of or like marble. □□ **marmoreally** adv. [L *marmoreus* (as MARBLE)]

marmoset /'mɑːməˌzet/ n. any of several small tropical American monkeys of the family Callitricidae, having a long bushy tail. [OF *marmouset* grotesque image, of unkn. orig.]

marmot /'mɑːmət/ n. any burrowing rodent of the genus *Marmota*, with a heavy-set body and short bushy tail. [F *marmotte* prob. f. Romansh *murmont* f. L *murem* (nominative *mus*) *montis* mountain mouse]

marocain /'mærəˌkeɪn/ n. a dress-fabric of ribbed crêpe. [F, = Moroccan f. *Maroc* Morocco]

Maronite /'mærəˌnaɪt/ n. a member of a sect of Syrian Christians dwelling chiefly in Lebanon. [med.L *Maronita* f. *Maro* the 5th-c. Syrian founder]

maroon[1] /məˈruːn/ adj. & n. —adj. brownish-crimson. —n. **1** this colour. **2** an explosive device giving a loud report. [F *marron* chestnut f. It. *marrone* f. med.Gk *maraon*]

maroon[2] /məˈruːn/ v. & n. —v.tr. **1** leave (a person) isolated in a desolate place (esp. an island). **2** (of a person or a natural phenomenon) cause (a person) to be unable to leave a place. —n. **1** a person descended from a group of fugitive slaves in the remoter parts of Surinam and the W. Indies. **2** a marooned person. [F *marron* f. Sp. *cimarrón* wild f. *cima* peak]

marque[1] /mɑːk/ n. a make of motor car, as distinct from a specific model (*the Jaguar marque*). [F, = MARK[1]]

marque[2] /mɑːk/ n. *hist.* □ **letters of marque** (or **marque and reprisal**) **1** a licence to fit out an armed vessel and employ it in the capture of an enemy's merchant shipping. **2** (in *sing.*) a ship carrying such a licence. [ME f. F f. Prov. *marca* f. *marcar* seize as a pledge]

marquee /mɑːˈkiː/ n. **1** a large tent used for social or commercial functions. **2** *US* a canopy over the entrance to a large building. [MARQUISE, taken as pl. & assim. to -EE]

marquess /'mɑːkwɪs/ n. a British nobleman ranking between a duke and an earl (cf. MARQUIS). □□ **marquessate** /-sət/ n. [var. of MARQUIS]

marquetry /'mɑːkɪtrɪ/ n. (also **marqueterie**) inlaid work in wood, ivory, etc. [F *marqueterie* f. *marqueter* variegate f. MARQUE[1]]

marquis /'mɑːkwɪs/ n. a foreign nobleman ranking between a duke and a count (cf. MARQUESS). □□ **marquisate** /-sət/ n. [ME f. OF *marchis* f. Rmc (as MARCH[2], -ESE)]

marquise /mɑːˈkiːz/ n. **1 a** the wife or widow of a marquis. **b** a woman holding the rank of marquis in her own right (cf. MARCHIONESS). **2** a finger-ring set with an oval pointed cluster of gems. **3** *archaic* = MARQUEE. [F, fem. of MARQUIS]

marquisette /ˌmɑːkɪˈzet/ n. a fine light cotton, rayon, or silk fabric for net curtains etc. [F, dimin. of MARQUISE]

marram /'mærəm/ n. a shore grass, *Ammophila arenaria*, that binds sand with its tough rhizomes. [ON *marálmr* f. *marr* sea + *hálmr* HAULM]

marriage /'mærɪdʒ/ n. **1** the legal union of a man and a woman in order to live together and often to have children. **2** an act or ceremony establishing this union. **3** one particular union of this kind (*by a previous marriage*). **4** an intimate union (*the marriage of true minds*). **5** *Cards* the union of a king and queen of the same suit. □ **by marriage** as a result of a marriage (*related by marriage*). **in marriage** as husband or wife (*give in marriage*; *take in marriage*). **marriage bureau** an establishment arranging introductions between persons wishing to marry. **marriage certificate** a certificate certifying the completion of a marriage ceremony. **marriage guidance** counselling of couples who have problems in married life. **marriage licence** a licence to marry. **marriage lines** *Brit.* a marriage certificate. **marriage of convenience** a marriage concluded to achieve some practical purpose, esp. financial or political. **marriage settlement** an arrangement securing property between spouses. [ME f. OF *mariage* f. *marier* MARRY[1]]

marriageable /'mærɪdʒəb(ə)l/ adj. **1** fit for marriage, esp. old or rich enough to marry. **2** (of age) fit for marriage. □□ **marriageability** /-ˈbɪlɪtɪ/ n.

married /'mærɪd/ adj. & n. —adj. **1** united in marriage. **2** of or relating to marriage (*married name*; *married life*). —n. (usu. in *pl.*) a married person (*young marrieds*).

marron glacé /ˌmærɒn ˈglɑːseɪ/ n. (pl. **marrons glacés** *pronunc.* same) a chestnut preserved in and coated with sugar. [F, = iced chestnut: cf. GLACÉ]

marrow /'mærəʊ/ n. **1** (in full **vegetable marrow**) **a** a large usu. white-fleshed edible gourd used as food. **b** the plant, *Cucurbita pepo*, yielding this. **2** a soft fatty substance in the cavities of bones, often taken as typifying vitality. **3** the essential part. □ **to the marrow** right through. □□ **marrowless** adj. **marrowy** adj. [OE *mearg*, *mærg* f. Gmc]

marrowbone /'mærəʊˌbəʊn/ n. a bone containing edible marrow.

marrowfat /'mærəʊˌfæt/ n. a kind of large pea.

marry[1] /'mærɪ/ v. (-ies, -ied) **1** tr. **a** take as one's wife or husband in marriage. **b** (often foll. by *to*) (of a priest etc.) join (persons) in marriage. **c** (of a parent or guardian) give (a son, daughter, etc.) in marriage. **2** intr. **a** enter into marriage. **b** (foll. by *into*) become a member of (a family) by marriage. **3** tr. **a** unite intimately. **b** correlate (things) as a pair. **c** *Naut.* splice (rope-ends) together without increasing their girth. □ **marry off** find a wife or husband for. [ME f. OF *marier* f. L *maritare* f. *maritus* husband]

marry[2] /'mærɪ/ int. *archaic* expressing surprise, asseveration, indignation, etc. [ME, = (the Virgin) *Mary*]

marrying /'mærɪɪŋ/ adj. likely or inclined to marry (*not a marrying man*).

Mars /mɑːz/ n. a reddish planet, fourth in order of distance from the sun and next beyond the earth. [L *Mars Martis* the Roman god of war]

Marsala /mɑːˈsɑːlə/ n. a dark sweet fortified dessert wine. [*Marsala* in Sicily, where orig. made]

Marseillaise /ˌmɑːseɪˈjeɪz, ˌmɑːsəˈleɪz/ n. the national anthem of France, first sung in Paris by Marseilles patriots. [F, fem. adj. f. *Marseille* Marseilles]

marsh /mɑːʃ/ n. **1** low land flooded in wet weather and usu. watery at all times. **2** (*attrib.*) of or inhabiting marshland. □ **marsh fever** malaria. **marsh gas** methane. **marsh-harrier** a European harrier, *Circus aeruginosus* (see HARRIER[3]). **marsh mallow** a shrubby herbaceous plant, *Althaea officinalis*, the roots of which were formerly used to make marshmallow. **marsh marigold** a golden-flowered ranunculaceous plant, *Caltha palustris*, growing in moist meadows etc.: also called KINGCUP. **marsh tit** a grey tit, *Parus palustris*, inhabiting marshland. **marsh trefoil** the buckbean. □□ **marshy** adj. (**marshier**, **marshiest**). **marshiness** n. [OE *mer(i)sc* f. WG]

marshal /'mɑːʃ(ə)l/ n. & v. —n. **1** (**Marshal**) **a** a high-ranking officer in the armed forces (*Air Marshal*; *Field Marshal*; *Marshal of France*). **b** a high-ranking officer of state (*Earl Marshal*). **2** an officer arranging ceremonies, controlling procedure at races, etc. **3** *US* the head of a police or fire department. **4** (in full **judge's marshal**) *Brit.* an official accompanying a judge on circuit, with secretarial and social duties. —*v.* (**marshalled, marshalling**; *US* **marshaled, marshaling**) **1** *tr.* arrange (soldiers, facts, one's thoughts, etc.) in due order. **2** *tr.* (often foll. by *into, to*) conduct (a person) ceremoniously. **3** *tr. Heraldry* combine (coats of arms). **4** *intr.* take up positions in due arrangement. □**marshalling yard** a railway yard in which goods trains etc. are assembled. **Marshal of the Royal Air Force** an officer of the highest rank in the Royal Air Force. □□**marshaller** *n.* **marshalship** *n.* [ME f. OF *mareschal* f. LL *mariscalcus* f. Gmc, lit. 'horse-servant']

marshland /ˈmɑːʃlənd/ *n.* land consisting of marshes.

marshmallow /mɑːʃˈmæləʊ/ *n.* a soft sweet made of sugar, albumen, gelatin, etc.

marsupial /mɑːˈsuːpɪəl/ *n.* & *adj.* —*n.* any mammal of the order Marsupialia, characterized by being born incompletely developed and usu. carried and suckled in a pouch on the mother's belly. —*adj.* **1** of or belonging to this order. **2** of or like a pouch (*marsupial muscle*). [mod.L *marsupialis* f. L *marsupium* f. Gk *marsupion* pouch, dimin. of *marsipos* purse]

mart /mɑːt/ *n.* **1** a trade centre. **2** an auction-room. **3 a** a market. **b** a market-place. [ME f. obs. Du. *mart*, var. of *markt* MARKET]

martagon /ˈmɑːtəgən/ *n.* a lily, *Lilium martagon*, with small purple turban-like flowers. [F f. Turk. *martagān* a form of turban]

Martello /mɑːˈteləʊ/ *n.* (*pl.* **-os**) (also **Martello tower**) a small circular fort, usu. on the coast to prevent a hostile landing. [alt. f. Cape *Mortella* in Corsica, where such a tower proved difficult to capture in 1794]

marten /ˈmɑːtɪn/ *n.* any weasel-like carnivore of the genus *Martes*, having valuable fur. [ME f. MDu. *martren* f. OF (*peau*) *martrine* marten (fur) f. *martre* f. WG]

martensite /ˈmɑːtɪnˌzaɪt/ *n.* the chief constituent of hardened steel. [A. *Martens*, German metallurgist d. 1914 + -ITE[1]]

martial /ˈmɑːʃ(ə)l/ *adj.* **1** of or appropriate to warfare. **2** warlike, brave; fond of fighting. □**martial arts** fighting sports such as judo and karate. **martial law** military government, involving the suspension of ordinary law. □□**martially** *adv.* [ME f. OF *martial* or L *martialis* of the Roman god Mars: see MARS]

Martian /ˈmɑːʃ(ə)n/ *adj.* & *n.* —*adj.* of the planet Mars. —*n.* a hypothetical inhabitant of Mars. [ME f. OF *martien* or L *Martianus* f. *Mars*: see MARS]

martin /ˈmɑːtɪn/ *n.* any of several swallows of the family Hirundinidae, esp. the house-martin and sand-martin. [prob. f. St *Martin*: see MARTINMAS]

martinet /ˌmɑːtɪˈnet/ *n.* a strict (esp. military or naval) disciplinarian. □□**martinettish** *adj.* (also **martinetish**). [J. *Martinet*, 17th-c. French drill-master]

martingale /ˈmɑːtɪŋˌgeɪl/ *n.* **1** a strap, or set of straps, fastened at one end to the noseband of a horse and at the other end to the girth, to prevent rearing etc. **2** *Naut.* a rope for holding down the jib-boom. **3** a gambling system of continually doubling the stakes in the hope of an eventual win that must yield a net profit. [F, of uncert. orig.]

Martini /mɑːˈtiːnɪ/ *n.* **1** *propr.* a type of vermouth. **2** a cocktail made of gin and French vermouth, and sometimes orange bitters etc. [*Martini & Rossi*, Italian firm selling vermouth]

Martinmas /ˈmɑːtɪnməs/ *n.* St Martin's day, 11 Nov. [ME f. St *Martin*, bishop of Tours in the 4th c., + MASS[2]]

martlet /ˈmɑːtlɪt/ *n.* **1** *Heraldry* an imaginary footless bird borne as a charge. **2** *archaic* **a** a swift. **b** a

house-martin. [F *martelet* alt. f. *martinet* dimin. f. MARTIN]

martyr /ˈmɑːtə(r)/ *n.* & *v.* —*n.* **1 a** a person who is put to death for refusing to renounce a faith or belief. **b** a person who suffers for adhering to a principle, cause, etc. **2** (foll. by *to*) a constant sufferer from (an ailment). —*v.tr.* **1** put to death as a martyr. **2** torment. □**make a martyr of oneself** accept or pretend to accept unnecessary discomfort etc. [OE *martir* f. eccl.L *martyr* f. Gk *martur*, *martus* -*uros* witness]

martyrdom /ˈmɑːtədəm/ *n.* **1** the sufferings and death of a martyr. **2** torment. [OE *martyrdōm* (as MARTYR, -DOM)]

martyrize /ˈmɑːtəˌraɪz/ *v.tr.* & *refl.* (also **-ise**) make a martyr of. □□**martyrization** /-ˈzeɪʃ(ə)n/ *n.*

martyrology /ˌmɑːtəˈrɒlədʒɪ/ *n.* (*pl.* **-ies**) **1** a list or register of martyrs. **2** the history of martyrs. □□ **martyrological** /-rəˈlɒdʒɪk(ə)l/ *adj.* **martyrologist** *n.* [med.L *martyrologium* f. eccl.Gk *marturologion* (as MARTYR, *logos* account)]

martyry /ˈmɑːtərɪ/ *n.* (*pl.* **-ies**) a shrine or church erected in honour of a martyr. [ME f. med.L *martyrium* f. Gk *marturion* martyrdom (as MARTYR)]

marvel /ˈmɑːv(ə)l/ *n.* & *v.* —*n.* **1** a wonderful thing. **2** (foll. by *of*) a wonderful example of (a quality). —*v.intr.* (**marvelled, marvelling**; *US* **marveled, marveling**) *literary* **1** (foll. by *at*, or *that* + clause) feel surprise or wonder. **2** (foll. by *how, why*, etc. + clause) wonder. □**marvel of Peru** a showy garden plant, *Mirabilis jalapa*, with flowers opening in the afternoon. □□**marveller** *n.* [ME f. OF *merveille*, *merveiller* f. LL *mirabilia* neut. pl. of L *mirabilis* f. *mirari* wonder at: see MIRACLE]

marvellous /ˈmɑːvələs/ *adj.* (*US* **marvelous**) **1** astonishing. **2** excellent. **3** extremely improbable. □□**marvellously** *adv.* **marvellousness** *n.* [ME f. OF *merveillos* f. *merveille* (as MARVEL)]

Marxism /ˈmɑːksɪz(ə)m/ *n.* the political and economic theories of Karl Marx, Ger. political philosopher (d. 1883), predicting the overthrow of capitalism and the eventual attainment of a classless society with the State controlling the means of production. □**Marxism-Leninism** Marxism as developed by Lenin. □□**Marxist** *n.* & *adj.* **Marxist-Leninist** *n.* & *adj.*

marzipan /ˈmɑːzɪˌpæn, -ˈpæn/ *n.* & *v.* —*n.* **1** a paste of ground almonds, sugar, etc., made up into small cakes etc., or used to coat large cakes. **2** a piece of marzipan. —*v.tr.* (**marzipanned, marzipanning**) cover with or as with marzipan. [G f. It. *marzapane*]

Masai /ˈmɑːsaɪ/ *n.* & *adj.* —*n.* (*pl.* same or **Masais**) **1 a** a pastoral people of mainly Hamitic stock living in Kenya and Tanzania. **b** a member of this people. **2** the Nilotic language of the Masai. —*adj.* of or relating to the Masai or their language. [Bantu]

mascara /mæˈskɑːrə/ *n.* a cosmetic for darkening the eyelashes. [It. *mascara*, *maschera* MASK]

mascle /ˈmæsk(ə)l/ *n. Heraldry* a lozenge voided, with a central lozenge-shaped aperture. [ME f. AF f. AL *ma(s)cula* f. L MACULA]

mascon /ˈmæskɒn/ *n. Astron.* a concentration of dense matter below the moon's surface, producing a gravitational pull. [*mass concentration*]

mascot /ˈmæskɒt/ *n.* a person, animal, or thing that is supposed to bring good luck. [F *mascotte* f. mod. Prov. *mascotto* fem. dimin. of *masco* witch]

masculine /ˈmæskjʊlɪn, ˈmɑːs-/ *adj.* & *n.* —*adj.* **1** of or characteristic of men. **2** manly, vigorous. **3** (of a woman) having qualities considered appropriate to a man. **4** *Gram.* of or denoting the gender proper to men's names. —*n. Gram.* the masculine gender; a masculine word. □□**masculinely** *adv.* **masculineness** *n.* **masculinity** /-ˈlɪnɪtɪ/ *n.* [ME f. OF *masculin -ine* f. L *masculinus* (as MALE)]

maser /ˈmeɪzə(r)/ *n.* a device using the stimulated emission of radiation by excited atoms to amplify or generate coherent monochromatic electromagnetic

---

b *but* d *dog* f *few* g *get* h *he* j *yes* k *cat* l *leg* m *man* n *no* p *pen* r *red* s *sit* t *top* v *voice*

radiation in the microwave range (cf. LASER). [*mi-crowave* amplification by the *s*timulated *e*mission of radiation]

mash /mæʃ/ *n. & v.* —*n.* **1** a soft mixture. **2** a mixture of boiled grain, bran, etc., given warm to horses etc. **3** *Brit. colloq.* mashed potatoes (*sausage and mash*). **4** a mixture of malt and hot water used to form wort for brewing. **5** a soft pulp made by crushing, mixing with water, etc. —*v.tr.* **1** reduce (potatoes etc.) to a uniform mass by crushing. **2** crush or pound to a pulp. **3** mix (malt) with hot water to form wort. □□ **masher** *n.* [OE *māsc* f. WG, perh. rel. to MIX]

mashie /ˈmæʃɪ/ *n.* Golf an iron formerly used for lofting or for medium distances. [perh. f. F *massue* club]

mask /mɑːsk/ *n. & v.* —*n.* **1** a covering for all or part of the face: **a** worn as a disguise, or to appear grotesque and amuse or terrify. **b** made of wire, gauze, etc., and worn for protection (e.g. by a fencer) or by a surgeon to prevent infection of a patient. **c** worn to conceal the face at balls etc. and usu. made of velvet or silk. **2** a respirator used to filter inhaled air or to supply gas for inhalation. **3** a likeness of a person's face, esp. one made by taking a mould from the face (*death-mask*). **4** a disguise or pretence (*throw off the mask*). **5** a hollow model of a human head worn by ancient Greek and Roman actors. **6** *Photog.* a screen used to exclude part of an image. **7** the face or head of an animal, esp. a fox. **8** = *face-pack*. **9** *archaic* a masked person. —*v.tr.* **1** cover (the face etc.) with a mask. **2** disguise or conceal (a taste, one's feelings, etc.). **3** protect from a process. **4** *Mil.* **a** conceal (a battery etc.) from the enemy's view. **b** hinder (an army etc.) from action by observing with adequate force. **c** hinder (a friendly force) by standing in its line of fire. □ **masking tape** adhesive tape used in painting to cover areas on which paint is not wanted. □□ **masker** *n.* [F *masque* f. It. *maschera* f. Arab. *maskara* buffoon f. *sakira* to ridicule]

masked /mɑːskt/ *adj.* wearing or disguised with a mask. □ **masked ball** a ball at which masks are worn.

maskinonge /ˈmæskɪˌnɒndʒ, -ˈnɒndʒɪ/ *n.* a large N. American pike, *Esox masquinongy*, esp. in the Great Lakes. [ult. f. Ojibwa, = great fish]

masochism /ˈmæsəˌkɪz(ə)m/ *n.* **1** a form of (esp. sexual) perversion characterized by gratification derived from one's own pain or humiliation (cf. SADISM). **2** *colloq.* the enjoyment of what appears to be painful or tiresome. □□ **masochist** *n.* **masochistic** /-ˈkɪstɪk/ *adj.* **masochistically** /-ˈkɪstɪkəlɪ/ *adv.* [L. von Sacher-*Masoch*, Austrian novelist d. 1895, who described cases of it]

mason /ˈmeɪs(ə)n/ *n. & v.* —*n.* **1** a person who builds with stone. **2** (**Mason**) a Freemason. —*v.tr.* build or strengthen with masonry. □ **mason's mark** a device carved on stone by the mason who dressed it. [ME f. OF *masson*, *maçonner*, ONF *machun*, prob. ult. f. Gmc]

Mason–Dixon line /ˌmeɪs(ə)nˈdɪks(ə)n/ *n.* (in the US) the boundary between Maryland and Pennsylvania, taken as the northern limit of the slave-owning States before the abolition of slavery. [C. *Mason* & J. *Dixon*, 18th-c. English astronomers who surveyed it]

Masonic /məˈsɒnɪk/ *adj.* of or relating to Freemasons.

masonry /ˈmeɪsənrɪ/ *n.* **1 a** the work of a mason. **b** stonework. **2** (**Masonry**) Freemasonry. [ME f. OF *maçonerie* (as MASON)]

Masorah /ˈmæsərə/ *n.* (also **Massorah**) a body of traditional information and comment on the text of the Hebrew Bible. [Heb. *māsōret*, perh. = bond]

Masorete /ˈmæsəˌriːt/ *n.* (also **Massorete**) a Jewish scholar contributing to the Masorah. □□ **Masoretic** /-ˈretɪk/ *adj.* [F *Massoret* & mod.L *Masoreta*, orig. a misuse of Heb. (see MASORAH), assim. to -ETE]

masque /mɑːsk/ *n.* **1** a dramatic and musical entertainment esp. of the 16th and 17th c., orig. of pantomime, later with metrical dialogue. **2** a dramatic composition for this. □□ **masquer** *n.* [var. of MASK]

masquerade /ˌmɑːskəˈreɪd, ˌmæs-/ *n. & v.* —*n.* **1** a false show or pretence. **2** a masked ball. —*v.intr.* (often foll. by *as*) appear in disguise, assume a false appearance. □□ **masquerader** *n.* [F *mascarade* f. Sp. *mascarada* f. *máscara* mask]

Mass. *abbr.* Massachusetts.

mass[1] /mæs/ *n., v., & adj.* —*n.* **1** a coherent body of matter of indefinite shape. **2** a dense aggregation of objects (*a mass of fibres*). **3** (in *sing.* or *pl.*; foll. by *of*) a large number or amount. **4** (usu. foll. by *of*) an unbroken expanse (of colour etc.). **5** (foll. by *of*) covered or abounding in (*was a mass of cuts and bruises*). **6** a main portion (of a painting etc.) as perceived by the eye. **7** (prec. by *the*) **a** the majority. **b** (in *pl.*) the ordinary people. **8** *Physics* the quantity of matter a body contains. **9** (*attrib.*) relating to, done by, or affecting large numbers of people or things; large-scale (*mass audience*; *mass action*; *mass murder*). —*v.tr. & intr.* **1** assemble into a mass or as one body (*massed bands*). **2** *Mil.* (with ref. to troops) concentrate or be concentrated. □ **centre of mass** a point representing the mean position of matter in a body or system. **in the mass** in the aggregate. **law of mass action** the principle that the rate of a chemical reaction is proportional to the masses of the reacting substances. **mass defect** the difference between the mass of an isotope and its mass number. **mass energy** a body's ability to do work according to its mass. **mass media** = MEDIA[1] 2. **mass noun** *Gram.* a noun that is not countable and cannot be used with the indefinite article or in the plural (e.g. *bread*). **mass number** the total number of protons and neutrons in a nucleus. **mass observation** *Brit.* the study and recording of the social habits and opinions of ordinary people. **mass-produce** produce by mass production. **mass production** the production of large quantities of a standardized article by a standardized mechanical process. **mass spectrograph** an apparatus separating isotopes, molecules, and molecular fragments according to mass by their passage in ionic form through electric and magnetic fields. **mass spectrometer** a device similar to a mass spectrograph but employing electrical detection. **mass spectrum** the distribution of ions shown by the use of a mass spectrograph or mass spectrometer. □□ **massless** *adj.* [ME f. OF *masse*, *masser* f. L *massa* f. Gk *maza* barley-cake: perh. rel. to *massō* knead]

mass[2] /mæs, mɑːs/ *n.* (often **Mass**) **1** the Eucharist, esp. in the Roman Catholic Church. **2** a celebration of this. **3** the liturgy used in the mass. **4** a musical setting of parts of this. □ **high mass** mass with incense, music, and usu. the assistance of a deacon and subdeacon. **low mass** mass with no music and a minimum of ceremony. [OE *mæsse* f. eccl.L *missa* f. L *mittere miss-* dismiss, perh. f. the concluding dismissal *Ite, missa est* Go, it is the dismissal]

massacre /ˈmæsəkə(r)/ *n. & v.* —*n.* **1** a general slaughter (of persons, occasionally of animals). **2** an utter defeat or destruction. —*v.tr.* **1** make a massacre of. **2** murder (esp. a large number of people) cruelly or violently. [OF, of unkn. orig.]

massage /ˈmæsɑːʒ, -sɑːdʒ/ *n. & v.* —*n.* **1** the rubbing, kneading, etc., of muscles and joints of the body with the hands, to stimulate their action, cure strains, etc. **2** an instance of this. —*v.tr.* **1** apply massage to. **2** manipulate (statistics) to give an acceptable result. □ **massage parlour** **1** an establishment providing massage. **2** *euphem.* a brothel. □□ **massager** *n.* [F f. *masser* treat with massage, perh. f. Port. *amassar* knead, f. *massa* dough: see MASS[1]]

massasauga /ˌmæsəˈsɔːgə/ *n.* a small N. American

rattlesnake, *Sistrurus catenatus*. [irreg. f. *Missisauga* River, Ontario]

massé /ˈmæseɪ/ *n. Billiards* a stroke made with the cue held nearly vertical. [F, past part. of *masser* make such a stroke (as MACE[1])]

masseter /mæˈsiːtə(r)/ *n.* either of two chewing-muscles which run from the temporal bone to the lower jaw. [Gk *masētēr* f. *masaomai* chew]

masseur /mæˈsɜː(r)/ *n.* (*fem.* **masseuse** /mæˈsɜːz/) a person who provides massage professionally. [F f. *masser*: see MASSAGE]

massicot /ˈmæsɪkət/ *n.* yellow lead monoxide, used as a pigment. [F, perh. rel. to It. *marzacotto* unguent prob. f. Arab. *mashakūnyā*]

massif /ˈmæsiːf, mæˈsiːf/ *n.* a compact group of mountain heights. [F *massif* used as noun: see MASSIVE]

massive /ˈmæsɪv/ *adj.* **1** large and heavy or solid. **2** (of the features, head, etc.) relatively large; of solid build. **3** exceptionally large (*took a massive overdose*). **4** substantial, impressive (*a massive reputation*). **5** *Mineral.* not visibly crystalline. **6** *Geol.* without structural divisions. □□ **massively** *adv.* **massiveness** *n.* [ME f. F *massif -ive* f. OF *massiz* ult. f. L *massa* MASS[1]]

Massorah var. of MASORAH.

Massorete var. of MASORETE.

mast[1] /mɑːst/ *n. & v. —n.* **1** a long upright post of timber, iron, etc., set up on a ship's keel, esp. to support sails. **2** a post or lattice-work upright for supporting a radio or television aerial. **3** a flag-pole (*half-mast*). **4** (in full **mooring-mast**) a strong steel tower to the top of which an airship can be moored. —*v.tr.* furnish (a ship) with masts. □ **before the mast** serving as an ordinary seaman (quartered in the forecastle). □□ **masted** *adj.* (also in *comb.*). **master** *n.* (also in *comb.*). [OE *mæst* f. WG]

mast[2] /mɑːst/ *n.* the fruit of the beech, oak, chestnut, and other forest-trees, esp. as food for pigs. [OE *mæst* f. WG, prob. rel. to MEAT]

mastaba /ˈmæstəbə/ *n.* **1** *Archaeol.* an ancient Egyptian tomb with sloping sides and a flat roof. **2** a bench, usu. of stone, attached to a house in Islamic countries. [Arab. *maṣṭabah*]

mastectomy /mæsˈtektəmi/ *n.* (*pl.* -ies) *Surgery* the amputation of a breast. [Gk *mastos* breast + -ECTOMY]

master /ˈmɑːstə(r)/ *n., adj., & v. —n.* **1 a** a person having control of persons or things. **b** an employer. **c** a male head of a household (*master of the house*). **d** the owner of a dog, horse, etc. **e** the owner of a slave. **f** *Naut.* the captain of a merchant ship. **g** *Hunting* the person in control of a pack of hounds etc. **2 a** a male teacher or tutor, esp. a schoolmaster. **3 a** the head of a college, school, etc. **b** the presiding officer of a livery company, Masonic lodge, etc. **4** a person who has or gets the upper hand (*we shall see which of us is master*). **5** a person skilled in a particular trade and able to teach others (often *attrib.*: *master carpenter*). **6** a holder of a university degree orig. giving authority to teach in the university (*Master of Arts; Master of Science*). **7 a** a revered teacher in philosophy etc. **b** (**the Master**) Christ. **8** a great artist. **9** *Chess* etc. a player of proved ability at international level. **10** an original version (e.g. of a film or gramophone record) from which a series of copies can be made. **11** (**Master**) **a** a title prefixed to the name of a boy not old enough to be called *Mr* (*Master T. Jones; Master Tom*). **b** *archaic* a title for a man of high rank, learning, etc. **12** (in England and Wales) an official of the Supreme Court. **13** a machine or device directly controlling another (cf. SLAVE). **14** (**Master**) a courtesy title of the eldest son of a Scottish viscount or baron (*the Master of Falkland*). —*adj.* **1** commanding, superior (*a master spirit*). **2** main, principal (*master bedroom*). **3** controlling others (*master plan*). —*v.tr.* **1** overcome, defeat. **2** reduce to subjection. **3** acquire complete knowledge of (a subject) or facility in using (an instrument etc.). **4** rule as a master. □ **be master of** **1** have at one's

disposal. **2** know how to control. **be one's own master** be independent or free to do as one wishes. **make oneself master of** acquire a thorough knowledge of or facility in using. **Master Aircrew** an RAF rank equivalent to warrant-officer. **master-at-arms** (*pl.* **masters-at-arms**) the chief police officer on a man-of-war or a merchant ship. **master-class** a class given by a person of distinguished skill, esp. in music. **master-hand 1** a person having commanding power or great skill. **2** the action of such a person. **master-key** a key that opens several locks, each of which also has its own key. **master mariner 1** the captain of a merchant ship. **2** a seaman certified competent to be captain. **master mason 1** a skilled mason, or one in business on his or her own account. **2** a fully qualified Freemason, who has passed the third degree. **Master of Ceremonies** see CEREMONY. **Master of the Rolls** (in England and Wales) a judge who presides over the Court of Appeal and was formerly in charge of the Public Record Office. **master-stroke** an outstandingly skilful act of policy etc. **master-switch** a switch controlling the supply of electricity etc. to an entire system. **master touch** a masterly manner of dealing with something. **master-work** a masterpiece. □□ **masterdom** *n.* **masterhood** *n.* **masterless** *adj.* [OE *mægester* (later also f. OF *maistre*) f. L *magister*, prob. rel. to *magis* more]

masterful /ˈmɑːstəfʊl/ *adj.* **1** imperious, domineering. **2** masterly. ¶ Normally used of a person, whereas *masterly* is used of achievements, abilities, etc. □□ **masterfully** *adv.* **masterfulness** *n.*

masterly /ˈmɑːstəlɪ/ *adj.* worthy of a master; very skilful (*a masterly piece of work*). □□ **masterliness** *n.*

mastermind /ˈmɑːstəmaɪnd/ *n. & v. —n.* **1 a** a person with an outstanding intellect. **b** such an intellect. **2** the person directing an intricate operation. —*v.tr.* plan and direct (a scheme or enterprise).

masterpiece /ˈmɑːstəpiːs/ *n.* **1** an outstanding piece of artistry or workmanship. **2** a person's best work.

mastership /ˈmɑːstəʃɪp/ *n.* **1** the position or function of a master, esp. a schoolmaster. **2** dominion, control.

mastersinger /ˈmɑːstəsɪŋə(r)/ *n.* = MEISTERSINGER.

mastery /ˈmɑːstərɪ/ *n.* **1** dominion, sway. **2** masterly skill. **3** (often foll. by *of*) comprehensive knowledge or use of a subject or instrument. **4** (prec. by *the*) upper hand. [ME f. OF *maistrie* (as MASTER)]

masthead /ˈmɑːsthed/ *n. & v. —n.* **1** the highest part of a ship's mast, esp. that of a lower mast as a place of observation or punishment. **2** the title of a newspaper etc. at the head of the front or editorial page. —*v.tr.* **1** send (a sailor) to the masthead. **2** raise (a sail) to its position on the mast.

mastic /ˈmæstɪk/ *n.* **1** a gum or resin exuded from the bark of the mastic tree, used in making varnish. **2** (in full **mastic tree**) the evergreen tree, *Pistacia lentiscus*, yielding this. **3** a waterproof filler and sealant used in building. **4** a liquor flavoured with mastic gum. [ME f. OF f. LL *mastichum* f. L *mastiche* f. Gk *mastikhē*, perh. f. *mastikhaō* (see MASTICATE) with ref. to its use as chewing-gum]

masticate /ˈmæstɪkeɪt/ *v.tr.* grind or chew (food) with one's teeth. □□ **mastication** /-ˈkeɪʃ(ə)n/ *n.* **masticator** *n.* **masticatory** *adj.* [LL *masticare masticat-* f. Gk *mastikhaō* gnash the teeth]

mastiff /ˈmæstɪf, ˈmɑːs-/ *n.* **1** a dog of a large strong breed with drooping ears and pendulous lips. **2** this breed of dog. [ME ult. f. OF *mastin* ult. f. L *mansuetus* tame; see MANSUETUDE]

mastitis /mæˈstaɪtɪs/ *n.* an inflammation of the mammary gland (the breast or udder). [Gk *mastos* breast + -ITIS]

mastodon /ˈmæstədɒn/ *n.* a large extinct mammal of the genus *Mammut*, resembling the elephant but having nipple-shaped tubercles on the crowns of its molar teeth. □□ **mastodontic** /-'dɒntɪk/ *adj.* [mod.L f. Gk *mastos* breast + *odous odontos* tooth]

mastoid /'mæstɔɪd/ *adj. & n.* —*adj.* shaped like a woman's breast. —*n.* **1** = *mastoid process.* **2** *colloq.* mastoiditis. □**mastoid process** a conical prominence on the temporal bone behind the ear, to which muscles are attached. [F *mastoïde* or mod.L *mastoides* f. Gk *mastoeidēs* f. *mastos* breast]

mastoiditis /ˌmæstɔɪ'daɪtɪs/ *n.* inflammation of the mastoid process.

masturbate /'mæstə,beɪt/ *v.intr. & tr.* arouse oneself sexually or cause (another person) to be aroused by manual stimulation of the genitals. □□ **masturbation** /-'beɪʃ(ə)n/ *n.* **masturbator** *n.* **masturbatory** *adj.* [L *masturbari masturbat-*]

mat[1] /mæt/ *n. & v.* —*n.* **1** a piece of coarse material for wiping shoes on, esp. a doormat. **2** a piece of cork, rubber, plastic, etc., to protect a surface from the heat or moisture of an object placed on it. **3** a piece of resilient material for landing on in gymnastics, wrestling, etc. **4** a piece of coarse fabric of plaited rushes, straw, etc., for lying on, packing furniture, etc. **5** a small rug. —*v.* (**matted, matting**) **1 a** *tr.* (esp. as **matted** *adj.*) entangle in a thick mass (*matted hair*). **b** *intr.* become matted. **2** *tr.* cover or furnish with mats. □**on the mat** *sl.* being reprimanded (orig. in the army, on the orderly-room mat before the commanding officer). [OE *m(e)att(e)* f. WG f. LL *matta*]

mat[2] var. of MATT.

mat[3] /mæt/ *n.* = MATRIX 1. [abbr.]

matador /'mætə,dɔː(r)/ *n.* **1** a bullfighter whose task is to kill the bull. **2** a principal card in ombre, quadrille, etc. **3** a domino game in which the piece played must make a total of seven. [Sp. f. *matar* kill f. Pers. *māt* dead]

Mata Hari /ˌmɑːtɑː 'hɑːrɪ/ *n.* a beautiful and seductive female spy. [name taken by M. G. Zelle, d. 1917, f. Malay *mata* eye + *hari* day]

match[1] /mætʃ/ *n. & v.* —*n.* **1** a contest or game of skill etc. in which persons or teams compete against each other. **2 a** a person able to contend with another as an equal (*meet one's match*; *be more than a match for*). **b** a person equal to another in some quality (*we shall never see his match*). **c** a person or thing exactly like or corresponding to another. **3** a marriage. **4** a person viewed in regard to his or her eligibility for marriage, esp. as to rank or fortune (*an excellent match*). —*v.* **1 a** *tr.* be equal to or harmonious with; correspond to in some essential respect (*the curtains match the wallpaper*). **b** *intr.* (often foll. by *with*) correspond; harmonize (*his socks do not match*; *does the ribbon match with your hat?*). **2** *tr.* (foll. by *against, with*) place (a person etc.) in conflict, contest, or competition with (another). **3** *tr.* find material etc. that matches (another) (*can you match this silk?*). **4** *tr.* find a person or thing suitable for another (*matching unemployed workers with vacant posts*). **5** *tr.* prove to be a match for. **6** *tr. Electronics* produce or have an adjustment of (circuits) such that maximum power is transmitted between them. **7** *tr.* (usu. foll. by *with*) *archaic* join (a person) with another in marriage. □**make a match** bring about a marriage. **match play** *Golf* play in which the score is reckoned by counting the holes won by each side (cf. *stroke play*). **match point 1** *Tennis* etc. **a** the state of a game when one side needs only one more point to win the match. **b** this point. **2** *Bridge* a unit of scoring in matches and tournaments. **to match** corresponding in some essential respect with what has been mentioned (*yellow dress with gloves to match*). **well-matched** fit to contend with each other, live together, etc., on equal terms. □□ **matchable** *adj.* [OE *gemæcca* mate, companion, f. Gmc]

match[2] /mætʃ/ *n.* **1** a short thin piece of wood, wax, etc., tipped with a composition that can be ignited by friction. **2** a piece of wick, cord, etc., designed to burn at a uniform rate, for firing a cannon etc. [ME f. OF *mesche, meiche*, perh. f. L *myxa* lamp-nozzle]

matchboard /'mætʃbɔːd/ *n.* a board with a tongue cut along one edge and a groove along another, so as to fit with similar boards.

matchbox /'mætʃbɒks/ *n.* a box for holding matches.

matchet var. of MACHETE.

matchless /'mætʃlɪs/ *adj.* without an equal, incomparable. □□ **matchlessly** *adv.*

matchlock /'mætʃlɒk/ *n. hist.* **1** an old type of gun with a lock in which a match was placed for igniting the powder. **2** such a lock.

matchmaker /'mætʃ,meɪkə(r)/ *n.* a person fond of scheming to bring about marriages. □□ **matchmaking** *n.*

matchstick /'mætʃstɪk/ *n.* the stem of a match.

matchwood /'mætʃwʊd/ *n.* **1** wood suitable for matches. **2** minute splinters. □**make matchwood of** smash utterly.

mate[1] /meɪt/ *n. & v.* —*n.* **1** a friend or fellow worker. **2** *colloq.* a general form of address, esp. to another man. **3 a** each of a pair, esp. of birds. **b** *colloq.* a partner in marriage. **c** (in *comb.*) a fellow member or joint occupant of (*team-mate*; *room-mate*). **4** *Naut.* an officer on a merchant ship subordinate to the master. **5** an assistant to a skilled worker (*plumber's mate*). —*v.* (often foll. by *with*) **1 a** *tr.* bring (animals or birds) together for breeding. **b** *intr.* (of animals or birds) come together for breeding. **2 a** *tr.* join (persons) in marriage. **b** *intr.* (of persons) be joined in marriage. **3** *intr. Mech.* fit well. □□ **mateless** *adj.* [ME f. MLG *mate* f. *gemate* messmate f. WG, rel. to MEAT]

mate[2] /meɪt/ *n. & v.tr. Chess* = CHECKMATE. □**fool's mate** a series of moves in which the first player is mated at the second player's second move. **scholar's mate** a series of moves in which the second player is mated at the first player's fourth move. [ME f. F *mat(er)*: see CHECKMATE]

maté /'mæteɪ/ *n.* **1** an infusion of the leaves of a S. American shrub, *Ilex paraguayensis.* **2** this shrub, or its leaves. **3** a vessel in which these leaves are infused. [Sp. *mate* f. Quechua *mati*]

matelot /'mætləʊ/ *n.* (also **matlow, matlo**) *Brit. sl.* a sailor. [F *matelot*]

matelote /'mætə,ləʊt/ *n.* a dish of fish etc. with a sauce of wine and onions. [F (as MATELOT)]

mater /'meɪtə(r)/ *n. Brit. sl.* mother. ¶ Now only in jocular or affected use. [L]

materfamilias /ˌmeɪtəfə'mɪlɪˌæs/ *n.* the woman head of a family or household (cf. PATERFAMILIAS). [L f. *mater* mother + *familia* FAMILY]

material /mə'tɪərɪəl/ *n. & adj.* —*n.* **1** the matter from which a thing is made. **2** cloth, fabric. **3** (in *pl.*) things needed for an activity (*building materials*; *cleaning materials*; *writing materials*). **4** a person or thing of a specified kind or suitable for a purpose (*officer material*). **5** (in *sing.* or *pl.*) information etc. to be used in writing a book etc. (*experimental material*; *materials for a biography*). **6** (in *sing.* or *pl.*, often foll. by *of*) the elements or constituent parts of a substance. —*adj.* **1** of matter; corporeal. **2** concerned with bodily comfort etc. (*material well-being*). **3** (of conduct, points of view, etc.) not spiritual. **4** (often foll. by *to*) important, essential, relevant (*at the material time*). **5** concerned with the matter, not the form, of reasoning. □□ **materiality** /-ɪ'ælɪtɪ/ *n.* [ME f. OF *materiel, -al*, f. LL *materialis* f. L (as MATTER)]

materialism /mə'tɪərɪəˌlɪz(ə)m/ *n.* **1** a tendency to prefer material possessions and physical comfort to spiritual values. **2** *Philos.* **a** the opinion that nothing exists but matter and its movements and modifications. **b** the doctrine that consciousness and will are wholly due to material agency. **3** *Art* a tendency to lay stress on the material aspect of objects. □□ **materialist** *n.* **materialistic** /-'lɪstɪk/ *adj.* **materialistically** /-'lɪstɪkəlɪ/ *adv.*

aʊ h**ow** eɪ d**ay** əʊ n**o** eə h**air** ɪə n**ear** ɔɪ b**oy** ʊə p**oor** aɪə f**ire** aʊə s**our** (*see over for consonants*)

materialize /məˈtɪərɪəˌlaɪz/ v. (also **-ise**) **1** intr. become actual fact. **2 a** tr. cause (a spirit) to appear in bodily form. **b** intr. (of a spirit) appear in this way. **3** intr. colloq. appear or be present when expected. **4** tr. represent or express in material form. **5** tr. make materialistic. □□ **materialization** /-ˈzeɪʃ(ə)n/ n.

materially /məˈtɪərɪəlɪ/ adv. **1** substantially, considerably. **2** in respect of matter.

materia medica /məˌtɪərɪə ˈmedɪkə/ n. **1** the remedial substances used in the practice of medicine. **2** the study of the origin and properties of these substances. [mod.L, transl. Gk hulē iatrikē healing material]

matériel /məˌtɪərɪˈel/ n. available means, esp. materials and equipment in warfare (opp. PERSONNEL). [F (as MATERIAL)]

maternal /məˈtɜːn(ə)l/ adj. **1** of or like a mother. **2** motherly. **3** related through the mother (maternal uncle). **4** of the mother in pregnancy and childbirth. □□ **maternalism** n. **maternalistic** /-ˈlɪstɪk/ adj. **maternally** adv. [ME f. OF maternel or L maternus f. mater mother]

maternity /məˈtɜːnɪtɪ/ n. **1** motherhood. **2** motherliness. **3** (attrib.) **a** for women during and just after childbirth (maternity hospital; maternity leave). **b** suitable for a pregnant woman (maternity dress; maternity wear). [F maternité f. med.L maternitas -tatis f. L maternus f. mater mother]

mateship /ˈmeɪtʃɪp/ n. Austral. companionship, fellowship.

matey /ˈmeɪtɪ/ adj. & n. (also **maty**) —adj. (**matier**, **matiest**) (often foll. by with) sociable; familiar and friendly. —n. Brit. (pl. **-eys**) colloq. (usu. as a form of address) mate, companion. □□ **mateyness** n. (also **matiness**). **matily** adv.

math /mæθ/ n. US colloq. mathematics (cf. MATHS). [abbr.]

mathematical /ˌmæθɪˈmætɪk(ə)l/ adj. **1** of or relating to mathematics. **2** (of a proof etc.) rigorously precise. □ **mathematical induction** = INDUCTION 3b. **mathematical tables** tables of logarithms and trigonometric values etc. □□ **mathematically** adv. [F mathématique or L mathematicus f. Gk mathēmatikos f. mathēma -matos science f. manthanō learn]

mathematics /ˌmæθɪˈmætɪks/ n.pl. **1** (also treated as sing.) the abstract science of number, quantity, and space studied in its own right (**pure mathematics**), or as applied to other disciplines such as physics, engineering, etc. (**applied mathematics**). **2** (as pl.) the use of mathematics in calculation etc. □□ **mathematician** /-məˈtɪʃ(ə)n/ n. [prob. f. F mathématiques pl. f. L mathematica f. Gk mathēmatika: see MATHEMATICAL]

maths /mæθs/ n. Brit. colloq. mathematics (cf. MATH). [abbr.]

Matilda /məˈtɪldə/ n. Austral. sl. a bushman's bundle; a swag. □ **waltz** (or **walk**) **Matilda** carry a swag. [the name Matilda]

matinée /ˈmætɪˌneɪ/ n. (US **matinee**) an afternoon performance in the theatre, cinema, etc. □ **matinée coat** (or **jacket**) a baby's short coat. **matinée idol** a handsome actor admired chiefly by women. [F, = what occupies a morning f. matin morning (as MATINS)]

matins /ˈmætɪnz/ n. (also **mattins**) (as sing or pl.) **1 a** a service of morning prayer in the Church of England. **b** the office of one of the canonical hours of prayer, properly a night office, but also recited with lauds at daybreak or on the previous evening. **2** (also **matin**) poet. the morning song of birds. [ME f. OF matines f. eccl.L matutinas, accus. fem. pl. adj. f. L matutinus of the morning f. Matuta dawn-goddess]

matlo (also **matlow**) var. of MATELOT.

matrass /ˈmætrəs/ n. hist. a long-necked glass vessel with a round or oval body, used for distilling etc. [F matras, of uncert. orig.]

matriarch /ˈmeɪtrɪˌɑːk/ n. a woman who is the head of a family or tribe. □□ **matriarchal** /-ˈɑːk(ə)l/ adj. [L mater mother, on the false analogy of PATRIARCH]

matriarchy /ˈmeɪtrɪˌɑːkɪ/ n. (pl. **-ies**) a form of social organization in which the mother is the head of the family and descent is reckoned through the female line.

matric /məˈtrɪk/ n. Brit. colloq. matriculation. [abbr.]

matrices pl. of MATRIX.

matricide /ˈmeɪtrɪˌsaɪd/ n. **1** the killing of one's mother. **2** a person who does this. □□ **matricidal** adj. [L matricida, matricidium f. mater matris mother]

matriculate /məˈtrɪkjʊˌleɪt/ v. **1** intr. be enrolled at a college or university. **2** tr. admit (a student) to membership of a college or university. □□ **matriculatory** adj. [med.L matriculare matriculatenrol f. LL matricula register, dimin. of L MATRIX]

matriculation /məˌtrɪkjʊˈleɪʃ(ə)n/ n. **1** the act or an instance of matriculating. **2** an examination to qualify for this.

matrilineal /ˌmætrɪˈlɪnɪəl/ adj. of or based on kinship with the mother or the female line. □□ **matrilineally** adv. [L mater matris mother + LINEAL]

matrilocal /ˌmætrɪˈləʊk(ə)l/ adj. of or denoting a custom in marriage where the husband goes to live with the wife's community. [L mater matris mother + LOCAL]

matrimony /ˈmætrɪmənɪ/ n. (pl. **-ies**) **1** the rite of marriage. **2** the state of being married. **3 a** a card-game. **b** the combination of king and queen of trumps in some card-games. □□ **matrimonial** /-ˈməʊnɪəl/ adj. **matrimonially** /-ˈməʊnɪəlɪ/ adv. [ME f. AF matrimonie, OF matremoi(g)ne f. L matrimonium f. mater matris mother]

matrix /ˈmeɪtrɪks/ n. (pl. **matrices** /-ˌsiːz/ or **matrixes**) **1** a mould in which a thing is cast or shaped, such as a gramophone record, printing type, etc. **2 a** an environment or substance in which a thing is developed. **b** a womb. **3** a mass of fine-grained rock in which gems, fossils, etc., are embedded. **4** Math. a rectangular array of elements in rows and columns that is treated as a single element. **5** Biol. the substance between cells or in which structures are embedded. **6** Computing a gridlike array of interconnected circuit elements. □ **matrix printer** = dot matrix printer (see DOT[1]). [L, = breeding-female, womb, register f. mater matris mother]

matron /ˈmeɪtrən/ n. **1** a married woman, esp. a dignified and sober one. **2** a woman managing the domestic arrangements of a school etc. **3** Brit. a woman in charge of the nursing in a hospital. ¶ Now usu. called senior nursing officer. □ **matron of honour** a married woman attending the bride at a wedding. □□ **matronhood** n. [ME f. OF matrone f. L matrona f. mater matris mother]

matronly /ˈmeɪtrənlɪ/ adj. like or characteristic of a matron, esp. in respect of staidness or portliness.

Matt. abbr. Matthew (esp. in the New Testament).

matt /mæt/ adj., n., & v. (also **mat**) —adj. (of a colour, surface, etc.) dull, without lustre. —n. **1** a border of dull gold round a framed picture. **2** (in full **matt paint**) paint formulated to give a dull flat finish (cf. GLOSS[1]). **3** the appearance of unburnished gold. —v.tr. (**matted**, **matting**) **1** make (gilding etc.) dull. **2** frost (glass). [F mat, mater, identical with mat MATE[2]]

matte[1] /mæt/ n. an impure product of the smelting of sulphide ores, esp. those of copper or nickel. [F]

matte[2] /mæt/ n. Cinematog. a mask to obscure part of an image and allow another image to be superimposed, giving a combined effect. [F]

matter /ˈmætə(r)/ n. & v. —n. **1 a** physical substance in general, as distinct from mind and spirit. **b** that which has mass and occupies space. **2** a particular substance (colouring matter). **3** (prec. by the; often foll. by with) the thing that is amiss (what is the matter?; there is something the matter with him). **4**

material for thought or expression. **5 a** the substance of a book, speech, etc., as distinct from its manner or form. **b** *Logic* the particular content of a proposition, as distinct from its form. **6** a thing or things of a specified kind (*printed matter; reading matter*). **7** an affair or situation being considered, esp. in a specified way (*a serious matter; a matter for concern; the matter of your overdraft*). **8** *Physiol.* **a** any substance in or discharged from the body (*faecal matter; grey matter*). **b** pus. **9** (foll. by *of, for*) what is or may be a good reason for (complaint, regret, etc.). **10** *Printing* the body of a printed work, as type or as printed sheets. —*v.intr.* **1** (often foll. by *to*) be of importance; have significance (*it does not matter to me when it happened*). **2** secrete or discharge pus. □ **as a matter of fact** in reality (esp. to correct a falsehood or misunderstanding). **for that matter** (or **for the matter of that**) **1** as far as that is concerned. **2** and indeed also. **in the matter of** as regards. **a matter of 1** approximately (*for a matter of 40 years*). **2** a thing that relates to, depends on, or is determined by (*a matter of habit; only a matter of time before they agree*). **a matter of course** see COURSE. **a matter of fact 1** what belongs to the sphere of fact as distinct from opinion etc. **2** *Law* the part of a judicial inquiry concerned with the truth of alleged facts (see also MATTER-OF-FACT). **a matter of form** a mere routine. **a matter of law** *Law* the part of a judicial inquiry concerned with the interpretation of the law. **a matter of record** see RECORD. **no matter 1** (foll. by *when, how*, etc.) regardless of (*will do it no matter what the consequences*). **2** it is of no importance. **what is the matter with** surely there is no objection to. **what matter?** that need not worry us. [ME f. AF *mater(i)e*, OF *matiere* f. L *materia* timber, substance, subject of discourse]

matter-of-fact /ˌmætərəˈfækt/ *adj.* (see also MATTER). **1** unimaginative, prosaic. **2** unemotional. □□ **matter-of-factly** *adv.* **matter-of-factness** *n.*

matting /ˈmætɪŋ/ *n.* **1** fabric of hemp, bast, grass, etc., for mats (*coconut matting*). **2** in senses of MAT¹ *v.*

mattins var. of MATINS.

mattock /ˈmætək/ *n.* an agricultural tool shaped like a pickaxe, with an adze and a chisel edge as the ends of the head. [OE *mattuc*, of unkn. orig.]

mattoid /ˈmætɔɪd/ *n.* a person of erratic mind, a mixture of genius and fool. [It. *mattoide* f. *matto* insane]

mattress /ˈmætrɪs/ *n.* a fabric case stuffed with soft, firm, or springy material, or a similar case filled with air or water, used on or as a bed. [ME f. OF *materas* f. It. *materasso* f. Arab. *almaṭraḥ* the place, the cushion f. *ṭaraḥa* throw]

maturate /ˈmætjʊˌreɪt/ *v.intr.* *Med.* (of a boil etc.) come to maturation. [L *maturatus* (as MATURE *v.*)]

maturation /ˌmætjʊˈreɪʃ(ə)n/ *n.* **1 a** the act or an instance of maturing; the state of being matured. **b** the ripening of fruit. **2** *Med.* **a** the formation of purulent matter. **b** the causing of this. □□ **maturative** /məˈtjʊərətɪv/ *adj.* [ME f. F *maturation* or med.L *maturatio* f. L (as MATURE *v.*)]

mature /məˈtjʊə(r)/ *adj.* & *v.* —*adj.* (**maturer, maturest**) **1** with fully developed powers of body and mind, adult. **2** complete in natural development, ripe. **3** (of thought, intentions, etc.) duly careful and adequate. **4** (of a bill etc.) due for payment. —*v.* **1 a** *tr.* & *intr.* develop fully. **b** *tr.* & *intr.* ripen. **c** *intr.* come to maturity. **2** *tr.* perfect (a plan etc.). **3** *intr.* (of a bill etc.) become due for payment. □ **mature student** an adult student who is older than most students. □□ **maturely** *adv.* **matureness** *n.* **maturity** *n.* [ME f. L *maturus* timely, early]

matutinal /ˌmætjuːˈtaɪn(ə)l, məˈtjuːtɪn(ə)l/ *adj.* **1** of or occurring in the morning. **2** early. [LL *matutinalis* f. L *matutinus*: see MATINS]

maty var. of MATEY.

matzo /ˈmɑːtsəʊ/ *n.* (*pl.* **-os** or **matzoth** /-əʊt/) **1** a

wafer of unleavened bread for the Passover. **2** such bread collectively. [Yiddish f. Heb. *maṣṣāh*]

maud /mɔːd/ *n.* **1** a Scots shepherd's grey striped plaid. **2** a travelling-rug like this. [18th c.: orig. unkn.]

maudlin /ˈmɔːdlɪn/ *adj.* & *n.* —*adj.* weakly or tearfully sentimental, esp. in a tearful and effusive stage of drunkenness. —*n.* weak or mawkish sentiment. [ME f. OF *Madeleine* f. eccl.L *Magdalena* MAGDALEN, with ref. to pictures of Mary Magdalen weeping]

maul /mɔːl/ *v.* & *n.* —*v.tr.* **1** beat and bruise. **2** handle roughly or carelessly. **3** damage by criticism. —*n.* **1** *Rugby Football* a loose scrum with the ball off the ground. **2** a brawl. **3** a special heavy hammer, commonly of wood, esp. for driving piles. □□ **mauler** *n.* [ME f. OF *mail* f. L *malleus* hammer]

maulstick /ˈmɔːlstɪk/ *n.* (also **mahlstick**) a light stick with a padded leather ball at one end, held by a painter in one hand to support the other hand. [Du. *maalstok* f. *malen* to paint + *stok* stick]

maunder /ˈmɔːndə(r)/ *v.intr.* **1** talk in a dreamy or rambling manner. **2** move or act listlessly or idly. [perh. f. obs. *maunder* beggar, to beg]

Maundy /ˈmɔːndɪ/ *n.* (in the UK) the distribution of money on the Thursday before Easter (see below). □ **Maundy money** specially minted silver coins distributed by the British sovereign on Maundy Thursday. **Maundy Thursday** the Thursday before Easter. [ME f. OF *mandé* f. L *mandatum* MANDATE, commandment (see John 13:34)]

mausoleum /ˌmɔːsəˈliːəm/ *n.* a large and grand tomb. [L f. Gk *Mausōleion* f. *Mausōlos* Mausolus king of Caria (4th c. BC), to whose tomb the name was orig. applied]

mauve /məʊv/ *adj.* & *n.* —*adj.* pale purple. —*n.* **1** this colour. **2** a bright but delicate pale purple dye from coal-tar aniline. □□ **mauvish** *adj.* [F, lit. = mallow, f. L *malva*]

maven /ˈmeɪv(ə)n/ *n.* *US colloq.* an expert or connoisseur. [Heb. *mēḇīn*]

maverick /ˈmævərɪk/ *n.* **1** *US* an unbranded calf or yearling. **2** an unorthodox or independent-minded person. [S. A. *Maverick*, Texas engineer and rancher d. 1870, who did not brand his cattle]

mavis /ˈmeɪvɪs/ *n.* *poet.* or *dial.* a song thrush. [ME f. OF *mauvis*, of uncert. orig.]

maw /mɔː/ *n.* **1 a** the stomach of an animal. **b** the jaws or throat of a voracious animal. **2** *colloq.* the stomach of a greedy person. [OE *maga* f. Gmc]

mawkish /ˈmɔːkɪʃ/ *adj.* **1** sentimental in a feeble or sickly way. **2** having a faint sickly flavour. □□ **mawkishly** *adv.* **mawkishness** *n.* [obs. *mawk* maggot f. ON *mathkr* f. Gmc]

max. *abbr.* maximum.

maxi /ˈmæksɪ/ *n.* (*pl.* **maxis**) *colloq.* a maxi-coat, -skirt, etc. [abbr.]

maxi- /ˈmæksɪ/ *comb. form* very large or long (*maxi-coat*). [abbr. of MAXIMUM: cf. MINI-]

maxilla /mækˈsɪlə/ *n.* (*pl.* **maxillae** /-liː/) **1** the jaw or jawbone, esp. the upper jaw in most vertebrates. **2** the mouth-part of many arthropods used in chewing. □□ **maxillary** *adj.* [L, = jaw]

maxim /ˈmæksɪm/ *n.* a general truth or rule of conduct expressed in a sentence. [ME f. F *maxime* or med.L *maxima* (*propositio*), fem. adj. (as MAXIMUM)]

maxima *pl.* of MAXIMUM.

maximal /ˈmæksɪm(ə)l/ *adj.* being or relating to a maximum; the greatest possible in size, duration, etc. □□ **maximally** *adv.*

maximalist /ˈmæksɪməlɪst/ *n.* a person who rejects compromise and expects a full response to (esp. political) demands. [MAXIMAL, after Russ. *maksimalist*]

maximize /ˈmæksɪˌmaɪz/ *v.tr.* (also **-ise**) increase or enhance to the utmost. □□ **maximization** /-ˈzeɪʃ(ə)n/ *n.* **maximizer** *n.* [L *maximus*: see MAXIMUM]

maximum /ˈmæksɪməm/ *n.* & *adj.* —*n.* (*pl.* **maxima** /-mə/) the highest possible or attainable amount.

—*adj.* that is a maximum. [mod.L, neut. of L *maximus*, superl. of *magnus* great]

maxwell /'mækswel/ *n.* a unit of magnetic flux in the c.g.s. system, equal to that induced through one square centimetre by a perpendicular magnetic field of one gauss. [J. C. *Maxwell*, Brit. physicist d. 1879]

May /meɪ/ *n.* **1** the fifth month of the year. **2** (**may**) the hawthorn or its blossom. **3** *poet.* bloom, prime. □**may-apple** an American herbaceous plant, *Podophyllum peltatum*, bearing a yellow egg-shaped fruit in May. **May-bug** a cockchafer. **May Day** 1 May esp. as a festival with dancing, or as an international holiday in honour of workers. **May queen** a girl chosen to preside over celebrations on May Day. **Queen of the May** = *May queen*. [ME f. OF *mai* f. L *Maius* (*mensis*) (month) of the goddess *Maia*]

may /meɪ/ *v.aux.* (*3rd sing. present* **may**; *past* **might** /maɪt/) **1** (often foll. by *well* for emphasis) expressing possibility (*it may be true*; *I may have been wrong*; *you may well lose your way*). **2** expressing permission (*you may not go*; *may I come in?*). ¶ Both *can* and *may* are used to express permission; in more formal contexts *may* is usual since *can* also denotes capability (*can I move?* = am I physically able to move?; *may I move?* = am I allowed to move?). **3** expressing a wish (*may he live to regret it*). **4** expressing uncertainty or irony in questions (*who may you be?*; *who are you, may I ask?*). **5** in purpose clauses and after *wish, fear*, etc. (*take such measures as may avert disaster*; *hope he may succeed*). □**be that as it may** (or **that is as may be**) that may or may not be so (implying that there are other factors) (*be that as it may, I still want to go*). [OE *mæg* f. Gmc, rel. to MAIN[1], MIGHT[2]]

Maya /'mɑːjə/ *n.* **1** (*pl.* same or **Mayas**) a member of an ancient Indian people of Central America. **2** the language of this people. □□**Mayan** *adj.* & *n.* [native name]

maya /'mɑːjə/ *n. Hinduism* a marvel or illusion, esp. in the phenomenal universe. [Skr. *māyā*]

maybe /'meɪbiː/ *adv.* perhaps, possibly. [ME f. *it may be*]

mayday /'meɪdeɪ/ *n.* an international radio distress-signal used esp. by ships and aircraft. [repr. pronunc. of F *m'aidez* help me]

mayest /'meɪɪst/ *archaic* = MAYST.

mayflower /'meɪˌflaʊə(r)/ *n.* any of various flowers that bloom in May, esp. the trailing arbutus, *Epigaea repens*.

mayfly /'meɪflaɪ/ *n.* (*pl.* -**flies**) **1** any insect of the order Ephemeroptera, living briefly in spring in the adult stage. **2** an imitation mayfly used by anglers.

mayhap /meɪˈhæp, 'meɪ-/ *adv. archaic* perhaps, possibly. [ME f. *it may hap*]

mayhem /'meɪhem/ *n.* **1** violent or damaging action. **2** *hist.* the crime of maiming a person so as to render him or her partly or wholly defenceless. [AF *mahem*, OF *mayhem* (as MAIM)]

maying /'meɪɪŋ/ *n.* & *adj.* participation in May Day festivities. [ME f. MAY]

mayn't /'meɪənt/ *contr.* may not.

mayonnaise /ˌmeɪəˈneɪz/ *n.* **1** a thick creamy dressing made of egg-yolks, oil, vinegar, etc. **2** a (usu. specified) dish dressed with this (*chicken mayonnaise*). [F, perh. f. *mahonnais -aise* of Port *Mahon* on Minorca]

mayor /meə(r)/ *n.* **1** the head of the municipal corporation of a city or borough. **2** (in England, Wales, and N. Ireland) the head of a district council with the status of a borough. □□**mayoral** *adj.* **mayorship** *n.* [ME f. OF *maire* f. L (as MAJOR)]

mayoralty /'meərəltɪ/ *n.* (*pl.* -**ies**) **1** the office of mayor. **2** a mayor's period of office. [ME f. OF *mairalté* (as MAYOR)]

mayoress /'meərɪs/ *n.* **1** a woman holding the office of mayor. **2** the wife of a mayor. **3** a woman fulfilling the ceremonial duties of a mayor's wife.

maypole /'meɪpəʊl/ *n.* a pole painted and decked with flowers and ribbons, for dancing round on May Day.

mayst /meɪst/ *archaic 2nd sing. present* of MAY.

mayweed /'meɪwiːd/ *n.* the stinking camomile, *Anthemis cotula*. [earlier *maidwede* f. obs. *maithe(n)* f. OE *magothe, mægtha* + WEED]

mazard /'mæzəd/ *n.* (also **mazzard**) **1** the wild sweet cherry, *Prunus avium*, of Europe. **2** *archaic* a head or face. [alt. of MAZER]

mazarine /ˌmæzəˈriːn/ *n.* & *adj.* a rich deep blue. [17th c., perh. f. the name of Cardinal *Mazarin*, French statesman d. 1661, or Duchesse de *Mazarin*, French noblewoman d. 1699]

maze /meɪz/ *n.* & *v.* —*n.* **1** a network of paths and hedges designed as a puzzle for those who try to penetrate it. **2** a complex network of paths or passages; a labyrinth. **3** confusion, a confused mass, etc. —*v.tr.* (esp. as **mazed** *adj.*) bewilder, confuse. □□**mazy** *adj.* (**mazier, maziest**). [ME, orig. as *mased* (adj.): rel. to AMAZE]

mazer /'meɪzə(r)/ *n. hist.* a hardwood drinking-bowl, usu. silver-mounted. [ME f. OF *masere* f. Gmc]

mazurka /məˈzɜːkə/ *n.* **1** a usu. lively Polish dance in triple time. **2** the music for this. [F *mazurka* or G *Masurka*, f. Pol. *mazurka* woman of the province *Mazovia*]

mazzard var. of MAZARD.

MB *abbr.* **1** Bachelor of Medicine. **2** *Computing* megabyte. [sense 1 f. L *Medicinae Baccalaureus*]

MBA *abbr.* Master of Business Administration.

MBE *abbr.* Member of the Order of the British Empire.

MC *abbr.* **1** Master of Ceremonies. **2** (in the UK) Military Cross. **3** (in the US) Member of Congress.

Mc *abbr.* megacycle(s).

MCC *abbr.* Marylebone Cricket Club.

McCarthyism, McCoy see at MACC-.

M.Ch. *abbr.* (also **M.Chir.**) Master of Surgery. [L *Magister Chirurgiae*]

mCi *abbr.* millicurie(s).

McNaughten see at MACN-.

M.Com. *abbr.* Master of Commerce.

MCP *abbr. colloq.* male chauvinist pig.

MCR *abbr. Brit.* Middle Common Room.

Mc/s *abbr.* megacycles per second.

MD *abbr.* **1** Doctor of Medicine. **2** Managing Director. **3** *US* Maryland (in official postal use). **4** mentally deficient. [sense 1 f. L *Medicinae Doctor*]

Md *symb. Chem.* the element mendelevium.

Md. *abbr.* Maryland.

MDMA *abbr.* methylenedioxymethamphetamine, an amphetamine-based drug that causes euphoric and hallucinatory effects, originally produced as an appetite suppressant (see ECSTASY 3).

MDT *abbr. US* Mountain Daylight Time.

ME *abbr.* **1** *US* Maine (in official postal use). **2** myalgic encephalomyelitis, an obscure disease with symptoms like those of influenza and prolonged periods of tiredness and depression.

Me. *abbr.* **1** Maine. **2** *Maître* (title of a French advocate).

me[1] /miː, mɪ/ *pron.* **1** *objective case* of I[2] (*he saw me*). **2** *colloq.* = I[2] (*it's me all right*; *is taller than me*). **3** *US colloq.* myself, to or for myself (*I got me a gun*). **4** *colloq.* used in exclamations (*ah me!*; *dear me!*; *silly me!*). □**me and mine** me and my relatives. [OE *me*, *mē* accus. & dative of I[2] f. Gmc]

me[2] /miː/ *n.* (also **mi**) *Mus.* **1** (in tonic sol-fa) the third note of a major scale. **2** the note E in the fixed-doh system. [ME f. L *mira*: see GAMUT]

mea culpa /ˌmiːə ˈkʌlpə, ˌmeɪə ˈkʊlpə/ *n.* & *int.* —*n.* an acknowledgement of one's fault or error. —*int.* expressing such an acknowledgement. [L, = by my fault]

mead[1] /miːd/ *n.* an alcoholic drink of fermented honey and water. [OE *me(o)du* f. Gmc]

æ *cat* ɑː *arm* e *bed* ɜː *her* ɪ *sit* iː *see* ɒ *hot* ɔː *saw* ʌ *run* ʊ *put* uː *too* ə *ago* aɪ *my*

mead[2] /miːd/ *n. poet.* or *archaic* = MEADOW. [OE *mæd* f. Gmc, rel. to MOW[1]]

meadow /'medəʊ/ *n.* **1** a piece of grassland, esp. one used for hay. **2** a piece of low well-watered ground, esp. near a river. □ **meadow brown** a common brown butterfly, *Maniola jurtina*. **meadow-grass** a perennial creeping grass, *Poa pratensis*. **meadow lark** *US* any songbird of the genus *Sturnella*, esp. the yellow-breasted *S. magna* of N. America. **meadow pipit** a common pipit, *Anthus pratensis*, native to Europe, Asia, and Africa. **meadow rue** any ranunculaceous plant of the genus *Thalictrum*, esp. *T. flavum* with small yellow flowers. **meadow saffron** a perennial plant, *Colchicum autumnale*, abundant in meadows, with lilac flowers: also called *autumn crocus*. □□ **meadowy** *adj.* [OE *mædwe*, oblique case of *mæd*: see MEAD[2]]

meadowsweet /'medəʊˌswiːt/ *n.* **1** a rosaceous plant, *Filipendula ulmaria*, common in meadows and damp places, with creamy-white fragrant flowers. **2** any of several rosaceous plants of the genus *Spiraea*, native to N. America.

meagre /'miːgə(r)/ *adj.* (*US* **meager**) **1** lacking in amount or quality (*a meagre salary*). **2** (of literary composition, ideas, etc.) lacking fullness, unsatisfying. **3** (of a person or animal) lean, thin. □□ **meagrely** *adv.* **meagreness** *n.* [ME f. AF *megre*, OF *maigre* f. L *macer*]

meal[1] /miːl/ *n.* **1** an occasion when food is eaten. **2** the food eaten on one occasion. □ **make a meal of 1** treat (a task etc.) too laboriously or fussily. **2** consume as a meal. **meals on wheels** *Brit.* a service by which meals are delivered to old people, invalids, etc. **meal-ticket 1** a ticket entitling one to a meal, esp. at a specified place with reduced cost. **2** a person or thing that is a source of food or income. [OE *mæl* mark, fixed time, meal f. Gmc]

meal[2] /miːl/ *n.* **1** the edible part of any grain or pulse (usu. other than wheat) ground to powder. **2** *Sc.* oatmeal. **3** *US* maize flour. **4** any powdery substance made by grinding. □ **meal-beetle** an insect, *Tenebrio molitor*, infesting granaries etc. **meal-worm** the larva of the meal-beetle. [OE *melu* f. Gmc]

mealie /'miːlɪ/ *n.* (also **mielie**) *S.Afr.* **1** (usu. in *pl.*) maize. **2** a corn-cob. [Afrik. *mielie* f. Port. *milho* maize, millet f. L *milium*]

mealtime /'miːltaɪm/ *n.* any of the usual times of eating.

mealy /'miːlɪ/ *adj.* (**mealier, mealiest**) **1 a** of or like meal; soft and powdery. **b** containing meal. **2** (of a complexion) pale. **3** (of a horse) spotty. **4** (in full **mealy-mouthed**) not outspoken; afraid to use plain expressions. □ **mealy bug** any insect of the genus *Pseudococcus*, infesting vines etc., whose body is covered with white powder. □□ **mealiness** *n.*

mean[1] /miːn/ *v.tr.* (*past* and *past part.* **meant** /ment/) **1 a** (often foll. by *to* + infin.) have as one's purpose or intention; have in mind (*they really mean mischief*; *I didn't mean to break it*). **b** (foll. by *by*) have as a motive in explanation (*what do you mean by that?*). **2** (often in *passive*) design or destine for a purpose (*mean it to be used*; *mean it for a stopgap*; *is meant to be a gift*). **3** intend to convey or indicate or refer to (a particular thing or notion) (*I mean we cannot go*; *I mean Richmond in Surrey*). **4** entail, involve (*it means catching the early train*). **5** (often foll. by *that* + clause) portend, signify (*this means trouble*; *your refusal means that we must look elsewhere*). **6** (of a word) have as its explanation in the same language or its equivalent in another language. **7** (foll. by *to*) be of some specified importance to (a person), esp. as a source of benefit or object of affection etc. (*that means a lot to me*). □ **mean business** be in earnest. **mean it** not be joking or exaggerating. **mean to say** really admit (usu. in *interrog.*: *do you mean to say you have lost it?*). **mean well** (often foll. by *to*, *towards*, *by*) have good intentions. [OE *mænan* f. WG, rel. to MIND]

mean[2] /miːn/ *adj.* **1** niggardly; not generous or liberal. **2** (of an action) ignoble, small-minded. **3** (of a person's capacity, understanding, etc.) inferior, poor. **4** (of housing) not imposing in appearance; shabby. **5 a** malicious, ill-tempered. **b** *US* vicious or aggressive in behaviour. **6** *colloq.* skilful, formidable (*is a mean fighter*). **7** *colloq.* ashamed (*feel mean*). □ **no mean** a very good (*that is no mean achievement*). **mean White** = *poor White*. □□ **meanly** *adv.* **meanness** *n.* [OE *mæne, gemæne* f. Gmc]

mean[3] /miːn/ *n. & adj. —n.* **1** a condition, quality, virtue, or course of action equally removed from two opposite (usu. unsatisfactory) extremes. **2** *Math.* **a** the term or one of the terms midway between the first and last terms of an arithmetical or geometrical etc. progression (*2 and 8 have the arithmetic mean 5 and the geometric mean 4*). **b** the quotient of the sum of several quantities and their number, the average. *—adj.* **1** (of a quantity) equally far from two extremes. **2** calculated as a mean. □ **mean free path** the average distance travelled by a gas molecule etc. between collisions. **mean sea level** the sea level halfway between the mean levels of high and low water. **mean sun** an imaginary sun moving in the celestial equator at the mean rate of the real sun, used in calculating solar time. **mean time** the time based on the movement of the mean sun. [ME f. AF *meen* f. OF *meien, moien* f. L *medianus* MEDIAN]

meander /mɪ'ændə(r)/ *v. & n. —v.intr.* **1** wander at random. **2** (of a stream) wind about. *—n.* **1** (in *pl.*) **a** the sinuous windings of a river. **b** winding paths. **2** a circuitous journey. **3** an ornamental pattern of lines winding in and out; a fret. [L *maeander* f. Gk *Maiandros*, the name of a winding river in Phrygia]

meandrine /mɪ'ændrɪn/ *adj.* full of windings (esp. of corals of the genus *Meandrina*, with a surface like a human brain). [MEANDER + -INE[1]]

meanie /'miːnɪ/ *n.* (also **meany**) (*pl.* **-ies**) *colloq.* a mean, niggardly, or small-minded person.

meaning /'miːnɪŋ/ *n. & adj. —n.* **1** what is meant by a word, action, idea, etc. **2** significance. **3** importance. *—adj.* expressive, significant (*a meaning glance*). □□ **meaningly** *adv.*

meaningful /'miːnɪŋfʊl/ *adj.* **1** full of meaning; significant. **2** *Logic* able to be interpreted. □□ **meaningfully** *adv.* **meaningfulness** *n.*

meaningless /'miːnɪŋlɪs/ *adj.* having no meaning or significance. □□ **meaninglessly** *adv.* **meaninglessness** *n.*

means /miːnz/ *n.pl.* **1** (often treated as *sing.*) that by which a result is brought about (*a means of quick travel*). **2 a** money resources (*live beyond one's means*). **b** wealth (*a man of means*). □ **by all means** (or **all manner of means**) **1** certainly. **2** in every possible way. **3** at any cost. **by means of** by the agency or instrumentality of (a thing or action). **by no means** (or **no manner of means**) not at all; certainly not. **means test** an official inquiry to establish need before financial assistance from public funds is given. [pl. of MEAN[3]]

meant *past* and *past part.* of MEAN[1].

meantime /'miːntaɪm/ *adv. & n. —adv.* = MEANWHILE. ¶ Less usual than *meanwhile. —n.* the intervening period (esp. *in the meantime*). [MEAN[3] + TIME]

meanwhile /'miːnwaɪl/ *adv. & n. —adv.* **1** in the intervening period of time. **2** at the same time. *—n.* the intervening period (esp. *in the meanwhile*). [MEAN[3] + WHILE]

meany var. of MEANIE.

measles /'miːz(ə)lz/ *n.pl.* (also treated as *sing.*) **1 a** an acute infectious viral disease marked by red spots on the skin. **b** the spots of measles. **2** a tapeworm disease of pigs. [ME *masele(s)* prob. f. MLG *masele*, MDu. *masel* pustule (cf. Du. *mazelen* measles), OHG *masala*: change of form prob. due to assim. to ME *meser* leper]

measly /'miːzlɪ/ *adj.* (**measlier, measliest**) **1** *colloq.*

inferior, contemptible, worthless. **2** of or affected with measles. **3** (of pork) infested with tapeworms. [MEASLES + -Y¹]

measurable /'meʒərəb(ə)l/ *adj.* that can be measured. □**within a measurable distance of** getting near (something undesirable). □□ **measurability** /-'bɪlɪtɪ/ *n.* **measurably** *adv.* [ME f. OF *mesurable* f. LL *mensurabilis* f. L *mensurare* (as MEASURE)]

measure /'meʒə(r)/ *n. & v.* —*n.* **1** a size or quantity found by measuring. **2** a system of measuring (*liquid measure; linear measure*). **3** a rod or tape etc. for measuring. **4** a vessel of standard capacity for transferring or determining fixed quantities of liquids etc. (*a pint measure*). **5 a** the degree, extent, or amount of a thing. **b** (foll. by *of*) some degree of (*there was a measure of wit in her remark*). **6** a unit of capacity, e.g. a bushel (*20 measures of wheat*). **7** a factor by which a person or thing is reckoned or evaluated (*their success is a measure of their determination*). **8** (usu. in *pl.*) suitable action to achieve some end (*took measures to ensure a good profit*). **9** a legislative enactment. **10** a quantity contained in another an exact number of times. **11** a prescribed extent or quantity. **12** *Printing* the width of a page or column of type. **13 a** poetical rhythm; metre. **b** a metrical group of a dactyl or two iambuses, trochees, spondees, etc. **14** *US Mus.* a bar or the time-content of a bar. **15** *archaic* a dance. **16** a mineral stratum (*coal measures*). —*v.* **1** *tr.* ascertain the extent or quantity of (a thing) by comparison with a fixed unit or with an object of known size. **2** *intr.* be of a specified size (*it measures six inches*). **3** *tr.* ascertain the size and proportion of (a person) for clothes. **4** *tr.* estimate (a quality, person's character, etc.) by some standard or rule. **5** *tr.* (often foll. by *off*) mark (a line etc. of a given length). **6** *tr.* (foll. by *out*) deal or distribute (a thing) in measured quantities. **7** *tr.* (foll. by *with, against*) bring (oneself or one's strength etc.) into competition with. **8** *tr. poet.* traverse (a distance). □**beyond measure** excessively. **for good measure** as something beyond the minimum; as a finishing touch. **in a** (or **some**) **measure** partly. **made to measure** *Brit.* (of clothes) made from measurements taken. **measure up 1 a** determine the size etc. of by measurement. **b** take comprehensive measurements. **2** (often foll. by *to*) have the necessary qualifications (for). **measuring-jug** (or **-cup**) a jug or cup marked to measure its contents. **measuring-tape** a tape marked to measure length. **measuring-worm** caterpillar of the geometer moth. [ME f. OF *mesure* f. L *mensura* f. *metiri mens-* measure]

measured /'meʒəd/ *adj.* **1** rhythmical; regular in movement (*a measured tread*). **2** (of language) carefully considered. □□ **measuredly** *adv.*

measureless /'meʒələs/ *adj.* not measurable; infinite. □□ **measurelessly** *adv.*

measurement /'meʒəmənt/ *n.* **1** the act or an instance of measuring. **2** an amount determined by measuring. **3** (in *pl.*) detailed dimensions.

meat /miːt/ *n.* **1** the flesh of animals (esp. mammals) as food. **2** (foll. by *of*) the essence or chief part of. **3** *US* the edible part of fruits, nuts, eggs, shellfish, etc. **4** *archaic* a food of any kind; a meal. □**meat and drink** a source of great pleasure. **meat-axe** a butcher's cleaver. **meat-fly** (*pl.* **-flies**) a fly that breeds in meat. **meat loaf** minced or chopped meat moulded into the shape of a loaf and baked. **meat safe** a cupboard for storing meat, usu. of wire gauze etc. □□ **meatless** *adj.* [OE *mete* food f. Gmc]

meatball /'miːtbɔːl/ *n.* minced meat compressed into a small round ball.

meatus /mɪ'eɪtəs/ *n.* (*pl.* same or **meatuses**) *Anat.* a channel or passage in the body or its opening. [L, = passage f. *meare* flow, run]

meaty /'miːtɪ/ *adj.* (**meatier, meatiest**) **1** full of

meat; fleshy. **2** of or like meat. **3** full of substance. □□ **meatily** *adv.* **meatiness** *n.*

Mecca /'mekə/ *n.* **1** a place one aspires to visit. **2** the birthplace of a faith, policy, pursuit, etc. [*Mecca* in Arabia, birthplace of Muhammad and chief place of Muslim pilgrimage]

mechanic /mɪ'kænɪk/ *n.* a skilled worker, esp. one who makes or uses or repairs machinery. [ME (orig. as adj.) f. OF *mecanique* or L *mechanicus* f. Gk *mēkhanikos* (as MACHINE)]

mechanical /mɪ'kænɪk(ə)l/ *adj.* **1** of or relating to machines or mechanisms. **2** working or produced by machinery. **3** (of a person or action) like a machine; automatic; lacking originality. **4 a** (of an agency, principle, etc.) belonging to mechanics. **b** (of a theory etc.) explaining phenomena by the assumption of mechanical action. **5** of or relating to mechanics as a science. □**mechanical advantage** the ratio of exerted to applied force in a machine. **mechanical drawing** a scale drawing of machinery etc. done with precision instruments. **mechanical engineer** a person skilled in the branch of engineering dealing with the design, construction, and repair of machines. **mechanical equivalent of heat** the conversion factor between heat energy and mechanical energy. □□ **mechanicalism** *n.* (in sense 4). **mechanically** *adv.* **mechanicalness** *n.* [ME f. L *mechanicus* (as MECHANIC)]

mechanician /ˌmekə'nɪʃ(ə)n/ *n.* a person skilled in constructing machinery.

mechanics /mɪ'kænɪks/ *n.pl.* (usu. treated as *sing.*) **1** the branch of applied mathematics dealing with motion and tendencies to motion. **2** the science of machinery. **3** the method of construction or routine operation of a thing.

mechanism /'mekəˌnɪz(ə)m/ *n.* **1** the structure or adaptation of parts of a machine. **2** a system of mutually adapted parts working together in or as in a machine. **3** the mode of operation of a process. **4** *Art* mechanical execution; technique. **5** *Philos.* the doctrine that all natural phenomena, including life, allow mechanical explanation by physics and chemistry. [mod.L *mechanismus* f. Gk (as MACHINE)]

mechanist /'mekənɪst/ *n.* **1** a mechanician. **2** an expert in mechanics. **3** *Philos.* a person who holds the doctrine of mechanism. □□ **mechanistic** /-'nɪstɪk/ *adj.* **mechanistically** /-'nɪstɪkəlɪ/ *adv.*

mechanize /'mekəˌnaɪz/ *v.tr.* (also **-ise**) **1** give a mechanical character to. **2** introduce machines in. **3** *Mil.* equip with tanks, armoured cars, etc. (orig. as a substitute for horse-drawn vehicles and cavalry). □□ **mechanization** /-'zeɪʃ(ə)n/ *n.* **mechanizer** *n.*

mechano- /'mekənəʊ/ *comb. form* mechanical. [Gk *mēkhano-* f. *mēkhanē* machine]

mechanoreceptor /ˌmekənəʊrɪ'septə(r)/ *n. Biol.* a sensory receptor that responds to mechanical stimuli such as touch or sound.

mechatronics /ˌmekə'trɒnɪks/ *n.* the science of the combination of electronics and mechanics in developing new manufacturing techniques. [*mech*-anics + *electronics*]

Mechlin /'meklɪn/ *n.* (in full **Mechlin lace**) lace made at Mechlin (now Mechelen or Malines) in Belgium.

M.Econ. *abbr.* Master of Economics.

meconium /mɪ'kəʊnɪəm/ *n. Med.* a dark substance forming the first faeces of a newborn infant. [L, lit. poppy-juice, f. Gk *mēkōnion* f. *mēkōn* poppy]

Med /med/ *n. colloq.* the Mediterranean Sea. [abbr.]

med. *abbr.* medium.

M.Ed. *abbr.* Master of Education.

medal /'med(ə)l/ *n.* a piece of metal, usu. in the form of a disc, struck or cast with an inscription or device to commemorate an event etc., or awarded as a distinction to a soldier, scholar, athlete, etc., for services rendered, for proficiency, etc. □**medal play** *Golf* = *stroke play.* □□ **medalled** *adj.* **medallic**

/mɪ'dælɪk/ *adj.* [F *médaille* f. It. *medaglia* ult. f. L *metallum* METAL]

medallion /mɪ'dæljən/ *n.* **1** a large medal. **2** a thing shaped like this, e.g. a decorative panel or tablet, portrait, etc. [F *médaillon* f. It. *medaglione* augment. of *medaglia* (as MEDAL)]

medallist /'medəlɪst/ *n.* (*US* **medalist**) **1** a recipient of a (specified) medal (*gold medallist*). **2** an engraver or designer of medals.

meddle /'med(ə)l/ *v.intr.* (often foll. by *with*, *in*) interfere in or busy oneself unduly with others' concerns. □□ **meddler** *n.* [ME f. OF *medler*, var. of *mesler* ult. f. L *miscēre* mix]

meddlesome /'medəlsəm/ *adj.* fond of meddling; interfering. □□ **meddlesomely** *adv.* **meddlesomeness** *n.*

Mede /miːd/ *n. hist.* a member of an Indo-European people which established an empire in Media in Persia (modern Iran) in the 7th c. BC. □□ **Median** *adj.* [ME f. L *Medi* (pl.) f. Gk *Mēdoi*]

media[1] /'miːdɪə/ *n.pl.* **1** *pl.* of MEDIUM. **2** (usu. prec. by *the*) the main means of mass communication (esp. newspapers and broadcasting) regarded collectively. ¶ Use as a mass noun with a singular verb is common (e.g. *the media is on our side*), but is generally disfavoured (cf. AGENDA, DATA). □ **media event** an event primarily intended to attract publicity.

media[2] /'miːdɪə/ *n.* (*pl.* **mediae** /-dɪˌiː/) **1** *Phonet.* a voiced stop, e.g. *g*, *b*, *d*. **2** *Anat.* a middle layer of the wall of an artery or other vessel. [L, fem. of *medius* middle]

mediaeval var. of MEDIEVAL.

medial /'miːdɪəl/ *adj.* **1** situated in the middle. **2** of average size. □□ **medially** *adv.* [LL *medialis* f. L *medius* middle]

median /'miːdɪən/ *adj.* & *n.* —*adj.* situated in the middle. —*n.* **1** *Anat.* a median artery, vein, nerve, etc. **2** *Geom.* a straight line drawn from any vertex of a triangle to the middle of the opposite side. **3** *Math.* the middle value of a series of values arranged in order of size. □□ **medianly** *adv.* [F *médiane* or L *medianus* (as MEDIAL)]

mediant /'miːdɪənt/ *n. Mus.* the third note of a diatonic scale of any key. [F *médiante* f. It. *mediante* part. of obs. *mediare* come between, f. L (as MEDIATE)]

mediastinum /ˌmiːdɪə'stiːnəm/ *n.* (*pl.* **mediastina** /-nə/) *Anat.* a membranous middle septum, esp. between the lungs. □□ **mediastinal** *adj.* [mod.L f. med.L *mediastinus* medial, after L *mediastinus* drudge f. *medius* middle]

mediate *v.* & *adj.* —*v.* /'miːdɪˌeɪt/ **1** *intr.* (often foll. by *between*) intervene (between parties in a dispute) to produce agreement or reconciliation. **2** *tr.* be the medium for bringing about (a result) or for conveying (a gift etc.). **3** *tr.* form a connecting link between. —*adj.* /'miːdɪət/ **1** connected not directly but through some other person or thing. **2** involving an intermediate agency. □□ **mediately** /-ətlɪ/ *adv.* **mediation** /-'eɪʃ(ə)n/ *n.* **mediator** /'miːdɪˌeɪtə(r)/ *n.* **mediatory** /'miːdɪətərɪ/ *adj.* [LL *mediare mediat-* f. L *medius* middle]

medic[1] /'medɪk/ *n. colloq.* a medical practitioner or student. [L *medicus* physician f. *medēri* heal]

medic[2] var. of MEDICK.

medicable /'medɪkəb(ə)l/ *adj.* admitting of remedial treatment. [L *medicabilis* (as MEDICATE)]

Medicaid /'medɪˌkeɪd/ *n.* (in the US) a Federal system of health insurance for those requiring financial assistance. [MEDICAL + AID]

medical /'medɪk(ə)l/ *adj.* & *n.* —*adj.* **1** of or relating to the science of medicine in general. **2** of or relating to conditions requiring medical and not surgical treatment (*medical ward*). —*n. colloq.* a medical examination. □ **medical certificate** a certificate of fitness or unfitness to work etc. **medical examination** an examination to determine a person's physical fitness. **medical jurisprudence** the law relating to medicine. **medical officer** *Brit.* a person

in charge of the health services of a local authority or other organization. **medical practitioner** a physician or surgeon. □□ **medically** *adv.* [F *médical* or med.L *medicalis* f. L *medicus*: see MEDIC[1]]

medicament /mɪ'dɪkəmənt, 'medɪkəmənt/ *n.* a substance used for medical treatment. [F *médicament* or L *medicamentum* (as MEDICATE)]

Medicare /'medɪˌkeə(r)/ *n.* (in the US) a Federal system of health insurance for persons over 65 years of age. [MEDICAL + CARE]

medicate /'medɪˌkeɪt/ *v.tr.* **1** treat medically. **2** impregnate with a medicinal substance. □□ **medicative** /'medɪkətɪv/ *adj.* [L *medicari medicat-* administer remedies to f. *medicus*: see MEDIC[1]]

medication /ˌmedɪ'keɪʃ(ə)n/ *n.* **1** a substance used for medical treatment. **2** treatment using drugs.

Medicean /ˌmedɪ'siːən/ *adj.* of the Medici family, rulers of Florence in the 15th c. [mod.L *Mediceus* f. It. *Medici*]

medicinal /mɪ'dɪsɪn(ə)l/ *adj.* & *n.* —*adj.* (of a substance) having healing properties. —*n.* a medicinal substance. □□ **medicinally** *adv.* [ME f. OF f. L *medicinalis* (as MEDICINE)]

medicine /'medsɪn, -dɪsɪn/ *n.* **1** the science or practice of the diagnosis, treatment, and prevention of disease, esp. as distinct from surgical methods. **2** any drug or preparation used for the treatment or prevention of disease, esp. one taken by mouth. **3** a spell, charm, or fetish which is thought to cure afflictions. □ **a dose** (or **taste**) **of one's own medicine** treatment such as one is accustomed to giving others. **medicine ball** a stuffed leather ball thrown and caught for exercise. **medicine chest** a box containing medicines etc. **medicine man** a person believed to have magical powers of healing, esp. among N. American Indians. **take one's medicine** submit to something disagreeable. [ME f. OF *medecine* f. L *medicina* f. *medicus*: see MEDIC[1]]

medick /'miːdɪk/ *n.* (also **medic**) any leguminous plant of the genus *Medicago*, esp. alfalfa. [ME f. L *medica* f. Gk *Mēdikē poa* Median grass]

medico /'medɪˌkəʊ/ *n.* (*pl.* **-os**) *colloq.* a medical practitioner or student. [It. f. L (as MEDIC[1])]

medico- /'medɪkəʊ/ *comb. form* medical; medical and (*medico-legal*). [L *medicus* (as MEDIC[1])]

medieval /ˌmedɪ'iːv(ə)l/ *adj.* (also **mediaeval**) **1** of, or in the style of, the Middle Ages. **2** *colloq.* old-fashioned, archaic. □ **medieval history** the history of the 5th-15th c. **medieval Latin** Latin of about AD 600-1500. □□ **medievalism** *n.* **medievalist** *n.* **medievalize** *v.tr.* & *intr.* (also **-ise**). **medievally** *adv.* [mod.L *medium aevum* f. L *medius* middle + *aevum* age]

mediocre /ˌmiːdɪ'əʊkə(r)/ *adj.* **1** of middling quality, neither good nor bad. **2** second-rate. [F *médiocre* or f. L *mediocris* of middle height or degree f. *medius* middle + *ocris* rugged mountain]

mediocrity /ˌmiːdɪ'ɒkrɪtɪ/ *n.* (*pl.* **-ies**) **1** the state of being mediocre. **2** a mediocre person or thing.

meditate /'medɪˌteɪt/ *v.* **1** *intr.* a exercise the mind in (esp. religious) contemplation. **b** (usu. foll. by *on*, *upon*) focus on a subject in this manner. **2** *tr.* plan mentally; design. □□ **meditation** /-'teɪʃ(ə)n/ *n.* **meditator** *n.* [L *meditari* contemplate]

meditative /'medɪtətɪv/ *adj.* **1** inclined to meditate. **2** indicative of meditation. □□ **meditatively** *adv.* **meditativeness** *n.*

Mediterranean /ˌmedɪtə'reɪnɪən/ *n.* & *adj.* —*n.* **1** a large landlocked sea bordered by S. Europe, SW Asia, and N. Africa. **2** a native of a country bordering on the Mediterranean. —*adj.* **1** of or characteristic of the Mediterranean or its surrounding region (*Mediterranean climate*; *Mediterranean cookery*). **2** (of a person) dark-complexioned and not tall. [L *mediterraneus* inland f. *medius* middle + *terra* land]

medium /'miːdɪəm/ *n.* & *adj.* —*n.* (*pl.* **media** or **mediums**) **1** the middle quality, degree, etc. between extremes (*find a happy medium*). **2** the means by which something is communicated (*the medium of sound*; *the medium of television*). **3** the intervening substance through which impressions are conveyed to the senses etc. (*light passing from one medium into another*). **4** *Biol.* the physical environment or conditions of growth, storage, or transport of a living organism (*the shape of a fish is ideal for its fluid medium*; *growing mould on the surface of a medium*). **5** an agency or means of doing something (*the medium through which money is raised*). **6** the material or form used by an artist, composer, etc. (*language as an artistic medium*). **7** the liquid (e.g. oil or gel) with which pigments are mixed for use in painting. **8** (*pl.* **mediums**) a person claiming to be in contact with the spirits of the dead and to communicate between the dead and the living. —*adj.* **1** between two qualities, degrees, etc. **2** average; moderate (*of medium height*). □**medium bowler** *Cricket* a bowler who bowls at a medium pace. **medium dry** (of sherry, wine, etc.) having a flavour intermediate between dry and sweet. **medium frequency** a radio frequency between 300 kHz and 3 MHz. **medium of circulation** something that serves as an instrument of commercial transactions, e.g. coin. **medium-range** (of an aircraft, missile, etc.) able to travel a medium distance. **medium wave** a radio wave of medium frequency. □□**mediumism** *n.* (in sense 8 of *n.*). **mediumistic** /-'mɪstɪk/ *adj.* (in sense 8 of *n.*). **mediumship** *n.* (in sense 8 of *n.*). [L, = middle, neut. of *medius*]

medlar /'medlə(r)/ *n.* **1** a rosaceous tree, *Mespilus germanica*, bearing small brown apple-like fruits. **2** the fruit of this tree which is eaten when decayed. [ME f. OF *medler* f. L *mespila* f. Gk *mespilē*, *-on*]

medley /'medlɪ/ *n.*, *adj.*, & *v.* —*n.* (*pl.* **-eys**) **1** a varied mixture; a miscellany. **2** a collection of musical items from one work or various sources arranged as a continuous whole. —*adj.* *archaic* mixed; motley. —*v.tr.* **-eys**, **-eyed**) *archaic* make a medley of; intermix. □**medley relay** a relay race between teams in which each member runs a different distance, swims a different stroke, etc. [ME f. OF *medlee* var. of *meslee* f. Rmc (as MEDDLE)]

Medoc /mer'dɒk, 'medɒk/ *n.* a fine red claret from the Médoc region of SW France.

medulla /mɪ'dʌlə/ *n.* **1** the inner region of certain organs or tissues usu. when it is distinguishable from the outer region or cortex, as in hair or a kidney. **2** the myelin layer of certain nerve fibres. **3** the soft internal tissue of plants. □**medulla oblongata** /ˌɒblɒŋ'gɑːtə/ the continuation of the spinal cord within the skull, forming the lowest part of the brain stem. □□**medullary** *adj.* [L, = pith, marrow, prob. rel. to *medius* middle]

medusa /mɪ'djuːsə/ *n.* (*pl.* **medusae** /-siː/ or **medusas**) **1** a jellyfish. **2** a free-swimming form of any coelenterate, having tentacles round the edge of a usu. umbrella-shaped jelly-like body, e.g. a jellyfish. □□**medusan** *adj.* [L f. Gk *Medousa*, name of a Gorgon with snakes instead of hair]

meed /miːd/ *n.* *literary* or *archaic* **1** reward. **2** merited portion (of praise etc.). [OE *mēd* f. WG, rel. to Goth. *mizdō*, Gk *misthos* reward]

meek /miːk/ *adj.* **1** humble and submissive; suffering injury etc. tamely. **2** piously gentle in nature. □□**meekly** *adv.* **meekness** *n.* [ME *me(o)c* f. ON *mjúkr* soft, gentle]

meerkat /'mɪəkæt/ *n.* the suricate. [Du., = sea-cat]

meerschaum /'mɪəʃəm/ *n.* **1** a soft white form of hydrated magnesium silicate, chiefly found in Turkey, which resembles clay. **2** a tobacco-pipe with the bowl made from this. [G, = sea-foam f. *Meer* sea + *Schaum* foam, transl. Pers. *kef-i-daryā*, with ref. to its frothiness]

meet¹ /miːt/ *v.* & *n.* —*v.* (*past* and *past part.* **met** /met/) **1 a** *tr.* encounter (a person or persons) by accident or design; come face to face with. **b** *intr.* (of two or more people) come into each other's company

by accident or design (*decided to meet on the bridge*). **2** *tr.* go to a place to be present at the arrival of (a person, train, etc.). **3 a** *tr.* (of a moving object, line, feature of landscape, etc.) come together or into contact with (*where the road meets the flyover*). **b** *intr.* come together or into contact (*where the sea and the sky meet*). **4 a** *tr.* make the acquaintance of (*delighted to meet you*). **b** *intr.* (of two or more people) make each other's acquaintance. **5** *intr.* & *tr.* come together or come into contact with for the purposes of conference, business, worship, etc. (*the committee meets every week*; *the union met management yesterday*). **6** *tr.* **a** (of a person or a group) deal with or answer (a demand, objection, etc.) (*met the original proposal with hostility*). **b** satisfy or conform with (proposals, deadlines, a person, etc.) (*agreed to meet the new terms*; *did my best to meet them on that point*). **7** *tr.* pay (a bill etc.); provide the funds required by (a cheque etc.) (*meet the cost of the move*). **8** *tr.* & (foll. by *with*) *intr.* experience, encounter, or receive (success, disaster, a difficulty, etc.) (*met their death*; *met with many problems*). **9** *tr.* oppose in battle, contest, or confrontation. **10** *intr.* (of clothes, curtains, etc.) join or fasten correctly (*my jacket won't meet*). —*n.* **1** the assembly of riders and hounds for a hunt. **2** the assembly of competitors for various sporting activities, esp. athletics. □**make ends meet** see END. **meet the case** be adequate. **meet the eye** (or **the ear**) be visible (or audible). **meet a person's eye** check if another person is watching and look into his or her eyes in return. **meet a person half way** make a compromise, respond in a friendly way to the advances of another person. **meet up** *colloq.* happen to meet. **meet with 1** see sense 8 of *v.* **2** receive (a reaction) (*met with the committee's approval*). **3** esp. *US* = sense 1a of *v.* **more in it than meets the eye** hidden qualities or complications. □□ **meeter** *n.* [OE *mētan* f. Gmc: cf. MOOT]

meet² /miːt/ *adj.* *archaic* suitable, fit, proper. □□ **meetly** *adv.* **meetness** *n.* [ME (*i*)*mete* repr. OE *gemǣte* f. Gmc, rel. to METE¹]

meeting /'miːtɪŋ/ *n.* **1** in senses of MEET¹. **2** an assembly of people, esp. the members of a society, committee, etc., for discussion or entertainment. **3** = *race meeting*. **4** an assembly (esp. of Quakers) for worship. **5** the persons assembled (*address the meeting*). □**meeting-house** a place of worship, esp. of Quakers etc.

mega- /'megə/ *comb. form* **1** large. **2** denoting a factor of one million (10^6) in the metric system of measurement. ¶ Abbr.: **M**. [Gk f. *megas* great]

megabuck /'megə,bʌk/ *n.* *US* *colloq.* a million dollars.

megabyte /'megə,baɪt/ *n.* *Computing* 1,048,576 (i.e. 2^{20}) bytes as a measure of data capacity, or loosely 1,000,000. ¶ Abbr.: **MB**.

megadeath /'megə,deθ/ *n.* the death of one million people (esp. as a unit in estimating the casualties of war).

megahertz /'megə,hɜːts/ *n.* one million hertz, esp. as a measure of frequency of radio transmissions. ¶ Abbr.: **MHz**.

megalith /'megəlɪθ/ *n.* *Archaeol.* a large stone, esp. one placed upright as a monument or part of one. [MEGA- + Gk *lithos* stone]

megalithic /ˌmegə'lɪθɪk/ *adj.* *Archaeol.* made of or marked by the use of large stones.

megalo- /'megələʊ/ *comb. form* great (*megalomania*). [Gk f. *megas megal-* great]

megalomania /ˌmegələ'meɪnɪə/ *n.* **1** a mental disorder producing delusions of grandeur. **2** a passion for grandiose schemes. □□ **megalomaniac** *adj.* & *n.* **megalomaniacal** /-mə'naɪək(ə)l/ *adj.* **megalomanic** /-'mænɪk/ *adj.*

megalopolis /ˌmegə'lɒpəlɪs/ *n.* **1** a great city or its way of life. **2** an urban complex consisting of a city and its environs. □□ **megalopolitan** /-lə'pɒlɪt(ə)n/ *adj.* & *n.* [MEGA- + Gk *polis* city]

megalosaurus /ˌmegələˈsɔːrəs/ n. a large flesh-eating dinosaur of the genus *Megalosaurus*, with stout hind legs and small forelimbs. [MEGALO- + Gk *sauros* lizard]

megaphone /ˈmegəˌfəʊn/ n. a large funnel-shaped device for amplifying the sound of the voice.

megapode /ˈmegəˌpəʊd/ n. (also **megapod** /-ˌpɒd/) any bird of the family Megapodidae, native to Australasia, that builds a mound of debris for the incubation of its eggs, e.g. a mallee fowl. [mod.L *Megapodius* (genus-name) formed as MEGA- + Gk *pous podos* foot]

megaron /ˈmegəˌrɒn/ n. the central hall of a large Mycenaean house. [Gk, = hall]

megaspore /ˈmegəˌspɔː(r)/ n. the larger of the two kinds of spores produced by some ferns (cf. MICROSPORE).

megastar /ˈmegəˌstɑː(r)/ n. a very famous person, esp. in the world of entertainment.

megaton /ˈmegəˌtʌn/ n. (also **megatonne**) a unit of explosive power equal to one million tons of TNT.

megavolt /ˈmegəˌvəʊlt/ n. one million volts, esp. as a unit of electromotive force. ¶ Abbr.: **MV**.

megawatt /ˈmegəˌwɒt/ n. one million watts, esp. as a measure of electrical power as generated by power stations. ¶ Abbr.: **MW**.

Megger /ˈmegə(r)/ n. *Electr. propr.* an instrument for measuring electrical insulation resistance. [cf. MEGOHM]

megilp /məˈgɪlp/ n. (also **magilp**) a mixture of mastic resin and linseed oil, added to oil paints, much used in the 19th c. [18th c.: orig. unkn.]

megohm /ˈmegəʊm/ n. *Electr.* one million ohms. [MEGA- + OHM]

megrim[1] /ˈmiːgrɪm/ n. **1** *archaic* migraine. **2** a whim, a fancy. **3** (in *pl.*) **a** depression; low spirits. **b** staggers, vertigo in horses etc. [ME *mygrane* f. OF MIGRAINE]

megrim[2] /ˈmiːgrɪm/ n. any deep-water flat-fish of the family *Lepidorhombus*, esp. *L. whiffiagonis*. Also called *sail-fluke*. [19th c.: orig. unkn.]

meiosis /maɪˈəʊsɪs/ n. **1** *Biol.* a type of cell division that results in daughter cells with half the chromosome number of the parent cell (cf. MITOSIS). **2** = LITOTES. □□ **meiotic** /-ˈɒtɪk/ *adj.* **meiotically** /-ˈɒtɪkəlɪ/ *adv.* [mod.L f. Gk *meiōsis* f. *meioō* lessen f. *meiōn* less]

Meissen /ˈmaɪs(ə)n/ n. a hard-paste porcelain made since 1710. [*Meissen* near Dresden in Germany]

Meistersinger /ˈmaɪstəˌsɪŋə(r)/ n. (*pl.* same) a member of one of the 14th-16th-c. German guilds for lyric poets and musicians. [G f. *Meister* MASTER + *Singer* SINGER (see SING)]

melamine /ˈmeləˌmiːn/ n. **1** a white crystalline compound that can be copolymerized with methanal to give thermosetting resins. **2** (in full **melamine resin**) a plastic made from melamine and used esp. for laminated coatings. [*melam* (arbitrary) + AMINE]

melancholia /ˌmelənˈkəʊlɪə/ n. a mental illness marked by depression and ill-founded fears. [LL: see MELANCHOLY]

melancholy /ˈmelənkəlɪ/ n. & adj. —n. (*pl.* -ies) **1** a pensive sadness. **2 a** mental depression. **b** a habitual or constitutional tendency to this. **3** *hist.* one of the four humours; black bile (see HUMOUR n. 5). —adj. (of a person) sad, gloomy; (of a thing) saddening, depressing; (of words, a tune, etc.) expressing sadness. □□ **melancholic** /-ˈkɒlɪk/ *adj.* **melancholically** /-ˈkɒlɪkəlɪ/ *adv.* [ME f. OF *melancolie* f. LL *melancholia* f. Gk *melagkholia* f. *melas* *melanos* black + *kholē* bile]

Melanesian /ˌmeləˈniːzɪən, -ʃ(ə)n/ n. & adj. —n. **1** a member of the dominant Negroid people of Melanesia, an island group in the W. Pacific. **2** the language of this people. —adj. of or relating to this people or their language. [*Melanesia* f. Gk *melas* black + *nēsos* island]

mélange /meɪˈlɑːʒ/ n. a mixture, a medley. [F f. *mêler* mix (as MEDDLE)]

melanin /ˈmelənɪn/ n. a dark-brown to black pigment occurring in the hair, skin, and iris of the eye, that is responsible for tanning of the skin when exposed to sunlight. [Gk *melas melanos* black + -IN]

melanism /ˈmeləˌnɪz(ə)m/ n. an unusual darkening of body tissues caused by excessive production of melanin.

melanoma /ˌmeləˈnəʊmə/ n. a malignant tumour of melanin-forming cells, usu. in the skin. [MELANIN + -OMA]

melanosis /ˌmeləˈnəʊsɪs/ n. **1** = MELANISM. **2** a disorder in the body's production of melanin. □□ **melanotic** /-ˈnɒtɪk/ *adj.* [mod.L f. Gk (as MELANIN)]

Melba /ˈmelbə/ n. □**do a Melba** *Austral. sl.* **1** return from retirement. **2** make several farewell appearances. **Melba sauce** a sauce made from puréed raspberries thickened with icing sugar. **Melba toast** very thin crisp toast. **peach Melba** a dish of ice-cream and peaches with liqueur or sauce. [Dame Nellie *Melba*, Austral. operatic soprano d. 1931]

meld[1] /meld/ v. & n. —v.tr. (also *absol.*) (in rummy, canasta, etc.) lay down or declare (one's cards) in order to score points. —n. a completed set or run of cards in any of these games. [G *melden* announce]

meld[2] /meld/ v.tr. & intr. orig. *US* merge, blend, combine. [perh. f. MELT + WELD[1]]

mêlée /ˈmeleɪ/ n. (*US* **melee**) **1** a confused fight, skirmish, or scuffle. **2** a muddle. [F (as MEDLEY)]

melic /ˈmelɪk/ adj. (of a poem, esp. a Gk lyric) meant to be sung. [L *melicus* f. Gk *melikos* f. *melos* song]

meliorate /ˈmiːlɪəˌreɪt/ v.tr. & intr. *literary* improve (cf. AMELIORATE). □□ **melioration** /-ˈreɪʃ(ə)n/ n. **meliorative** /-rətɪv/ *adj.* [LL *meliorare* (as MELIORISM)]

meliorism /ˈmiːlɪəˌrɪz(ə)m/ n. a doctrine that the world may be made better by human effort. □□ **meliorist** n. [L *melior* better + -ISM]

melisma /mɪˈlɪzmə/ n. (*pl.* **melismata** /-mətə/ or **melismas**) *Mus.* a group of notes sung to one syllable of text. □□ **melismatic** /-ˈmætɪk/ *adj.* [Gk]

melliferous /mɪˈlɪfərəs/ adj. yielding or producing honey. [L *mellifer* f. *mel* honey]

mellifluous /mɪˈlɪflʊəs/ adj. (of a voice or words) pleasing, musical, flowing. □□ **mellifluence** n. **mellifluent** adj. **mellifluously** adv. **mellifluousness** n. [ME f. OF *melliflue* or LL *mellifluus* f. *mel* honey + *fluere* flow]

mellow /ˈmeləʊ/ adj. & v. —adj. **1** (of sound, colour, light) soft and rich, free from harshness. **2** (of character) softened or matured by age or experience. **3** genial, jovial. **4** partly intoxicated. **5** (of fruit) soft, sweet, and juicy. **6** (of wine) well-matured, smooth. **7** (of earth) rich, loamy. —v.tr. & intr. make or become mellow. □□ **mellowly** adv. **mellowness** n. [ME, perh. f. attrib. use of OE *melu, melw-* MEAL[2]]

melodeon /mɪˈləʊdɪən/ n. (also **melodion**) **1** a small organ popular in the 19th c., similar to the harmonium. **2** a small German accordion, played esp. by folk musicians. [MELODY + HARMONIUM with Graecized ending]

melodic /mɪˈlɒdɪk/ adj. **1** of or relating to melody. **2** having or producing melody. □**melodic minor** a scale with the sixth and seventh degrees raised when ascending and lowered when descending. □□ **melodically** adv. [F *mélodique* f. LL *melodicus* f. Gk *melōidikos* (as MELODY)]

melodious /mɪˈləʊdɪəs/ adj. **1** of, producing, or having melody. **2** sweet-sounding. □□ **melodiously** adv. **melodiousness** n. [ME f. OF *melodieus* (as MELODY)]

melodist /ˈmelədɪst/ n. **1** a composer of melodies. **2** a singer.

melodize /ˈmeləˌdaɪz/ v. (also **-ise**) **1** intr. make a melody or melodies; make sweet music. **2** tr. make melodious. □□ **melodizer** n.

melodrama /ˈmeləˌdrɑːmə/ n. **1** a sensational dramatic piece with crude appeals to the emotions and usu. a happy ending. **2** the genre of drama of this type. **3** language, behaviour, or an occurrence suggestive of this. **4** *hist.* a play with songs interspersed and with orchestral music accompanying the action. □□ **melodramatic** /-drə'mætɪk/ *adj.* **melodramatically** /-drə'mætɪkəlɪ/ *adv.* **melodramatist** /-'dræmətɪst/ *n.* **melodramatize** /-'dræmə,taɪz/ *v.tr.* (also **-ise**). [earlier *melodrame* f. F *mélodrame* f. Gk *melos* music + F *drame* DRAMA]

melodramatics /,melədrə'mætɪks/ *n.pl.* melodramatic behaviour, action, or writing.

melody /'melədɪ/ *n.* (*pl.* **-ies**) **1** an arrangement of single notes in a musically expressive succession. **2** the principal part in harmonized music. **3** a musical arrangement of words. **4** sweet music, tunefulness. [ME f. OF *melodie* f. LL *melodia* f. Gk *melōidia* f. *melos* song]

melon /'melən/ *n.* **1** the sweet fruit of various gourds. **2** the gourd producing this (*honeydew melon*; *water melon*). □ **cut the melon 1** decide a question. **2** share abundant profits among a number of people. [ME f. OF f. LL *melo -onis* abbr. of L *melopepo* f. Gk *mēlopepōn* f. *mēlon* apple + *pepōn* gourd f. *pepōn* ripe]

melt /melt/ *v. & n.* —*v.* **1** *intr.* become liquefied by heat. **2** *tr.* change to a liquid condition by heat. **3** *tr.* (as **molten** *adj.*) (usu. of materials that require a great deal of heat to melt them) liquefied by heat (*molten lava*; *molten lead*). **4 a** *intr. & tr.* dissolve. **b** *intr.* (of food) be easily dissolved in the mouth. **5** *intr.* **a** (of a person, feelings, the heart, etc.) be softened as a result of pity, love, etc. **b** dissolve into tears. **6** *tr.* soften (a person, feelings, the heart, etc.) (*a look to melt a heart of stone*). **7** *intr.* (usu. foll. by *into*) change or merge imperceptibly into another form or state (*night melted into dawn*). **8** *intr.* (often foll. by *away*) (of a person) leave or disappear unobtrusively (*melted into the background*; *melted away into the crowd*). **9** *intr.* (usu. as **melting** *adj.*) (of sound) be soft and liquid (*melting chords*). **10** *intr. colloq.* (of a person) suffer extreme heat (*I'm melting in this thick jumper*). —*n.* **1** liquid metal etc. **2** an amount melted at any one time. **3** the process or an instance of melting. □ **melt away** disappear or make disappear by liquefaction. **melt down 1** melt (esp. metal articles) in order to reuse the raw material. **2** become liquid and lose structure (cf. MELTDOWN). **melting-point** the temperature at which any given solid will melt. **melting-pot 1** a pot in which metals etc. are melted and mixed. **2** a place where races, theories, etc. are mixed, or an imaginary pool where ideas are mixed together. **melt water** water formed by the melting of snow and ice, esp. from a glacier. □□ **meltable** *adj. & n.* **melter** *n.* **meltingly** *adv.* [OE *meltan, mieltan* f. Gmc, rel. to MALT]

meltdown /'meltdaʊn/ *n.* the melting of (and consequent damage to) a structure, esp. the overheated core of a nuclear reactor.

melton /'melt(ə)n/ *n.* cloth with a close-cut nap, used for overcoats etc. [*Melton Mowbray* in central England]

member /'membə(r)/ *n.* **1** a person belonging to a society, team, etc. **2** (**Member**) a person formally elected to take part in the proceedings of certain organizations (*Member of Parliament*; *Member of Congress*). **3** (also *attrib.*) a part or branch of a political body (*member State*; *a member of the EEC*). **4** a constituent portion of a complex structure. **5** a part of a sentence, equation, group of figures, mathematical set, etc. **6 a** any part or organ of the body, esp. a limb. **b** = PENIS. **7** used in the title awarded to a person admitted to (usu. the lowest grade of) certain honours (*Member of the British Empire*). □□ **membered** *adj.* (also in *comb.*). **memberless** *adj.* [ME f. OF *membre* f. L *membrum* limb]

membership /'membəʃɪp/ *n.* **1** being a member. **2** the number of members. **3** the body of members.

membrane /'membreɪn/ *n.* **1** any pliable sheetlike structure acting as a boundary, lining, or partition in an organism. **2** a thin pliable sheet or skin of various kinds. □□ **membranaceous** /,membrə'neɪʃəs/ *adj.* **membraneous** /mem'breɪnɪəs/ *adj.* **membranous** /'membrənəs/ *adj.* [L *membrana* skin of body, parchment (as MEMBER)]

membrum virile /,membrəm vɪ'raɪlɪ/ *n. archaic* the penis. [L, = male member]

memento /mɪ'mentəʊ/ *n.* (*pl.* **-oes** or **-os**) an object kept as a reminder or a souvenir of a person or an event. [L, imper. of *meminisse* remember]

memento mori /mɪ,mentəʊ 'mɔːrɪ, -raɪ/ *n.* a warning or reminder of death (e.g. a skull). [L, = remember you must die]

memo /'meməʊ/ *n.* (*pl.* **-os**) *colloq.* memorandum. [abbr.]

memoir /'memwɑː(r)/ *n.* **1** a historical account or biography written from personal knowledge or special sources. **2** (in *pl.*) an autobiography or a written account of one's memory of certain events or people. **3 a** an essay on a learned subject specially studied by the writer. **b** (in *pl.*) the proceedings or transactions of a learned society (*Memoirs of the American Mathematical Society*). □□ **memoirist** *n.* [F *mémoire* (masc.), special use of *mémoire* (fem.) MEMORY]

memorabilia /,memərə'bɪlɪə/ *n.pl.* **1** souvenirs of memorable events. **2** *archaic* memorable or noteworthy things. [L, neut. pl. (as MEMORABLE)]

memorable /'memərəb(ə)l/ *adj.* **1** worth remembering, not to be forgotten. **2** easily remembered. □□ **memorability** /-'bɪlɪtɪ/ *n.* **memorableness** *n.* **memorably** *adv.* [ME f. F *mémorable* or L *memorabilis* f. *memorare* bring to mind f. *memor* mindful]

memorandum /,memə'rændəm/ *n.* (*pl.* **memoranda** /-də/ or **memorandums**) **1** a note or record made for future use. **2** an informal written message, esp. in business, diplomacy, etc. **3** *Law* a document recording the terms of a contract or other legal details. [ME f. L neut. sing. gerundive of *memorare*: see MEMORABLE]

memorial /mɪ'mɔːrɪəl/ *n. & adj.* —*n.* **1** an object, institution, or custom established in memory of a person or event (*the Albert Memorial*). **2** (often in *pl.*) *hist.* a statement of facts as the basis of a petition etc.; a record; an informal diplomatic paper. —*adj.* intending to commemorate a person or thing (*memorial service*). □ **Memorial Day** *US* a day on which those who died on active service are remembered, usu. the last Monday in May. □□ **memorialist** *n.* [ME f. OF *memorial* or L *memorialis* (as MEMORY)]

memorialize /mɪ'mɔːrɪə,laɪz/ *v.tr.* (also **-ise**) **1** commemorate. **2** address a memorial to (a person or body).

memoria technica /mɪ,mɔːrɪə 'teknɪkə/ *n.* a system or contrivance used to assist the memory. [mod.L, = artificial memory]

memorize /'memə,raɪz/ *v.tr.* (also **-ise**) commit to memory. □□ **memorizable** *adj.* **memorization** /-'zeɪʃ(ə)n/ *n.* **memorizer** *n.*

memory /'memərɪ/ *n.* (*pl.* **-ies**) **1** the faculty by which things are recalled to or kept in the mind. **2 a** this faculty in an individual (*my memory is beginning to fail*). **b** one's store of things remembered (*buried deep in my memory*). **3** a recollection or remembrance (*the memory of better times*). **4** the storage capacity of a computer or other electronic machinery. **5** the remembrance of a person or thing (*his mother's memory haunted him*). **6 a** the reputation of a dead person (*his memory lives on*). **b** in formulaic phrases used of a dead sovereign etc. (*of blessed memory*). **7** the length of time over which the memory or memories of any given person or group extends (*within living memory*; *within the memory of anyone still working here*). **8** the act of remembering (*a deed worthy of memory*). □ **commit to memory** learn (a thing) so as to be able to recall it. **from memory** without verification in books etc. **in memory of** to keep alive the remembrance of. **memory bank** (or **board**) the memory device of a computer etc. **memory lane** (usu. prec. by *down, along*) an imaginary and sentimental journey into the past. **memory mapping** *Computing* the allocation of peripheral devices to appear located within the main memory of a computer. [ME f. OF *memorie, memoire* f. L *memoria* f. *memor* mindful, remembering, rel. to MOURN]

memsahib /'mem,saːɪb, -saːb/ *n. Anglo-Ind. hist.* a European married woman in India, as spoken of or to by Indians. [MA'AM + SAHIB]

men *pl.* of MAN.

menace /'menɪs/ *n. & v.* —*n.* **1** a threat. **2** a dangerous or obnoxious thing or person. **3** *joc.* a pest, a nuisance. —*v.tr. & intr.* threaten, esp. in a malignant or hostile manner. □□ **menacer** *n.* **menacingly** *adv.* [ME ult. f. L *minax -acis* threatening f. *minari* threaten]

ménage /meɪˈnaːʒ/ *n.* the members of a household. [OF *manaige* ult. f. L (as MANSION)]

ménage à trois /meɪˌnaːʒ ɑː ˈtrwaː/ *n.* an arrangement in which three people live together, usu. a married couple and the lover of one of them. [F, = household of three (as MÉNAGE)]

menagerie /mɪˈnædʒərɪ/ *n.* **1** a collection of wild animals in captivity for exhibition etc. **2** the place where these are housed. [F *ménagerie* (as MÉNAGE)]

menaquinone /ˌmenəˈkwɪnəʊn/ *n.* one of the K vitamins, produced by bacteria found in the large intestine, essential for the blood-clotting process. Also called *vitamin K₂*. [chem. deriv. of *methylnaphthoquinone*]

menarche /meˈnaːkɪ/ *n.* the onset of first menstruation. [mod.L formed as MENO- + Gk *arkhē* beginning]

mend /mend/ *v. & n.* —*v.* **1** *tr.* restore to a sound condition; repair (a broken article, a damaged road, torn clothes, etc.). **2** *intr.* regain health. **3** *tr.* improve (*mend matters*). **4** *tr.* add fuel to (a fire). —*n.* a darn or repair in material etc. (*a mend in my shirt*). □**mend one's fences** make peace with a person. **mend one's manners** improve one's behaviour. **mend or end** improve or abolish. **mend one's pace** go faster; alter one's pace to another's. **mend one's ways** reform, improve one's habits. **on the mend** improving in health or condition. □□ **mendable** *adj.* **mender** *n.* [ME f. AF *mender* f. *amender* AMEND]

mendacious /menˈdeɪʃəs/ *adj.* lying, untruthful. □□ **mendaciously** *adv.* **mendacity** /-ˈdæsɪtɪ/ *n.* (*pl.* **-ies**). [L *mendax -dacis* perh. f. *mendum* fault]

mendelevium /ˌmendəˈliːvɪəm/ *n. Chem.* an artificially made transuranic radioactive metallic element. ¶ Symb.: **Md**. [D. I. *Mendeleev*, Russ. chemist d. 1907]

Mendelism /'mendə,lɪz(ə)m/ *n.* the theory of heredity based on the recurrence of certain inherited characteristics transmitted by genes. □□ **Mendelian** /-ˈdiːlɪən/ *adj. & n.* [G. J. *Mendel*, Austrian botanist d. 1884 + -ISM]

mendicant /'mendɪkənt/ *adj. & n.* —*adj.* **1** begging. **2** (of a friar) living solely on alms. —*n.* **1** a beggar. **2** a mendicant friar. □□ **mendicancy** *n.* **mendicity** /-ˈdɪsɪtɪ/ *n.* [L *mendicare* beg f. *mendicus* beggar f. *mendum* fault]

mending /'mendɪŋ/ *n.* **1** the action of a person who mends. **2** things, esp. clothes, to be mended.

menfolk /'menfəʊk/ *n.pl.* **1** men in general. **2** the men of one's family.

menhaden /menˈheɪd(ə)n/ *n.* any large herring-like fish of the genus *Brevoortia*, of the E. coast of N. America, yielding valuable oil and used for manure. [Algonquian: cf. Narragansett *munnawhatteaûg*]

menhir /'menhɪə(r)/ *n. Archaeol.* a tall upright usu. prehistoric monumental stone. [Breton *men* stone + *hir* long]

menial /'miːnɪəl/ *adj. & n.* —*adj.* **1** (esp. of unskilled domestic work) degrading, servile. **2** usu. *derog.* (of a servant) domestic. —*n.* **1** a menial servant. **2** a servile person. □□ **menially** *adv.* [ME f. OF *meinee* household]

meningitis /ˌmenɪnˈdʒaɪtɪs/ *n.* an inflammation of the meninges due to infection by viruses or bacteria. □□ **meningitic** /-ˈdʒɪtɪk/ *adj.*

meninx /'miːnɪŋks/ *n.* (*pl.* **meninges** /mɪˈnɪndʒiːz/) (usu. in *pl.*) any of the three membranes that line the skull and vertebral canal and enclose the brain and spinal cord (dura mater, arachnoid, pia mater). □□ **meningeal** /mɪˈnɪndʒɪəl/ *adj.* [mod.L f. Gk *mēnigx -iggos* membrane]

meniscus /mɪˈnɪskəs/ *n.* (*pl.* **menisci** /-saɪ/) **1** *Physics* the curved upper surface of a liquid in a tube. **2** a lens that is convex on one side and concave on the other. **3** *Math.* a crescent-shaped figure. □□ **meniscoid** *adj.* [mod.L f. Gk *mēniskos* crescent, dimin. of *mēnē* moon]

Mennonite /'menə,naɪt/ *n.* a member of a Protestant sect originating in Friesland in the 16th c., emphasizing adult baptism and rejecting Church organization, military service, and public office. [*Menno* Simons, its founder, d. 1561]

meno- /'menəʊ/ *comb. form* menstruation. [Gk *mēn mēnos* month]

menology /mɪˈnɒlədʒɪ/ *n.* (*pl.* **-ies**) a calendar, esp. that of the Greek Church, with biographies of the saints. [mod.L *menologium* f. eccl.Gk *mēnologion* f. *mēn* month + *logos* account]

menopause /'menə,pɔːz/ *n.* **1** the ceasing of menstruation. **2** the period in a woman's life (usu. between 45 and 50) when this occurs (see also *male menopause*). □□ **menopausal** /-ˈpɔːz(ə)l/ *adj.* [mod.L *menopausis* (as MENO-, PAUSE)]

menorah /mɪˈnɔːrə/ *n.* a seven-armed candelabrum used in Jewish worship, esp. as a symbol of Judaism. [Heb., = candlestick]

menorrhagia /ˌmenəˈreɪdʒɪə/ *n.* abnormally heavy bleeding at menstruation. [MENO- + stem of Gk *rhēgnumi* burst]

menorrhoea /ˌmenəˈrɪə/ *n.* ordinary flow of blood at menstruation. [MENO- + Gk *rhoia* f. *rheō* flow]

menses /'mensiːz/ *n.pl.* **1** blood and other materials discharged from the uterus at menstruation. **2** the time of menstruation. [L, pl. of *mensis* month]

Menshevik /'menʃəvɪk/ *n. hist.* a member of the non-Leninist wing of the Russian Social Democratic Workers' Party (cf. BOLSHEVIK). [Russ. *Men'shevik* a member of the minority (*men'she* less)]

mens rea /menz ˈriːə/ *n.* criminal intent; the knowledge of wrongdoing. [L, = guilty mind]

menstrual /'menstrʊəl/ *adj.* of or relating to the menses or menstruation. □**menstrual cycle** the process of ovulation and menstruation in female primates. [ME f. L *menstrualis* f. *mensis* month]

menstruate /'menstrʊ,eɪt/ *v.intr.* undergo menstruation. [LL *menstruare menstruat-* (as MENSTRUAL)]

menstruation /ˌmenstrʊˈeɪʃ(ə)n/ *n.* the process of discharging blood and other materials from the uterus in sexually mature non-pregnant women at intervals of about one lunar month until the menopause.

menstruous /'menstrʊəs/ *adj.* **1** of or relating to the menses. **2** menstruating. [ME f. OF *menstrueus* or LL *menstruosus* (as MENSTRUAL)]

menstruum /'menstrʊəm/ *n.* (*pl.* **menstrua** /-strʊə/) a solvent. [ME f. L, neut. of *menstruus* monthly f. *mensis* month f. the alchemical parallel between transmutation into gold and the supposed action of menses on the ovum]

mensurable /'mensjʊrəb(ə)l/ *adj.* **1** measurable, having fixed limits. **2** *Mus.* = MENSURAL 2. [F *mensurable* or LL *mensurabilis* f. *mensurare* to measure f. L *mensura* MEASURE]

mensural /'mensjʊr(ə)l/ *adj.* **1** of or involving measure. **2** *Mus.* of or involving a fixed rhythm or notes of definite duration (cf. PLAINSONG). [L *mensuralis* f. *mensura* MEASURE]

mensuration /ˌmensjʊəˈreɪʃ(ə)n/ *n*. **1** measuring. **2** *Math*. the measuring of geometric magnitudes such as the lengths of lines, areas of surfaces, and volumes of solids. [LL *mensuratio* (as MENSURABLE)]

menswear /ˈmenzweə(r)/ *n*. clothes for men.

-ment /mənt/ *suffix* **1** forming nouns expressing the means or result of the action of a verb (*abridgement*; *embankment*). **2** forming nouns from adjectives (*merriment*; *oddment*). [from or after F f. L *-mentum*]

mental /ˈment(ə)l/ *adj*. & *n*. —*adj*. **1** of or in the mind. **2** done by the mind. **3** *colloq*. **a** insane. **b** crazy, wild, eccentric (*is mental about pop music*). —*n*. *colloq*. a mental patient. □**mental age** the degree of a person's mental development expressed as an age at which the same degree is attained by an average person. **mental arithmetic** arithmetic performed in the mind. **mental asylum** (or **home** or **hospital** or **institution**) an establishment for the care of mental patients. **mental cruelty** the infliction of suffering on another's mind, esp. *Law* as grounds for divorce. **mental defective** esp. *US* a person with impaired mental abilities. **mental deficiency** imperfect mental development leading to abnormally low intelligence. **mental illness** a disorder of the mind. **mental nurse** a nurse dealing with mentally ill patients. **mental patient** a sufferer from mental illness. **mental reservation** a qualification tacitly added in making a statement etc. □□ **mentally** *adv*. [ME f. OF *mental* or LL *mentalis* f. L *mens -ntis* mind]

mentalism /ˈmentəˌlɪz(ə)m/ *n*. **1** *Philos*. the theory that physical and psychological phenomena are ultimately only explicable in terms of a creative and interpretative mind. **2** *Psychol*. the primitive tendency to personify in spirit form the forces of nature, or endow inert objects with the quality of 'soul'. □□ **mentalist** *n*. **mentalistic** /-ˈlɪstɪk/ *adj*.

mentality /menˈtælɪtɪ/ *n*. (*pl*. **-ies**) **1** mental character or disposition. **2** kind or degree of intelligence. **3** what is in or of the mind.

mentation /menˈteɪʃ(ə)n/ *n*. **1** mental action. **2** state of mind. [L *mens -ntis* mind]

menthol /ˈmenθɒl/ *n*. a mint-tasting organic alcohol found in oil of peppermint etc., used as a flavouring and to relieve local pain. [G f. L *mentha* MINT¹]

mentholated /ˈmenθəˌleɪtɪd/ *adj*. treated with or containing menthol.

mention /ˈmenʃ(ə)n/ *v*. & *n*. —*v.tr*. **1** refer to briefly. **2** specify by name. **3** reveal or disclose (*do not mention this to anyone*). **4** (in dispatches) award (a person) a minor honour for meritorious, usu. gallant, military service. —*n*. **1** a reference, esp. by name, to a person or thing. **2** (in dispatches) a military honour awarded for outstanding conduct. □**don't mention it** said in polite dismissal of an apology or thanks. **make mention** (or **no mention**) **of** refer (or not refer) to. **not to mention** introducing a fact or thing of secondary or (as a rhetorical device) of primary importance. □□ **mentionable** *adj*. [OF f. L *mentio -onis* f. the root of *mens* mind]

mentor /ˈmentɔː(r)/ *n*. an experienced and trusted adviser. [F f. L f. Gk *Mentōr* adviser of the young Telemachus in Homer's *Odyssey* and Fénelon's *Télémaque*]

menu /ˈmenjuː/ *n*. **1 a** a list of dishes available in a restaurant etc. **b** a list of items to be served at a meal. **2** *Computing* a list of options showing the commands or facilities available. □**menu-driven** (of a program or computer) used by making selections from menus. [F, = detailed list, f. L *minutus* MINUTE²]

meow var. of MIAOW.

MEP *abbr*. Member of the European Parliament.

mepacrine /ˈmepəkrɪn/ *n*. *Brit*. quinacrine. [*methyl* + *paludism* (malaria) + *acridine*]

Mephistopheles /ˌmefɪˈstɒfɪˌliːz/ *n*. **1** an evil spirit to whom Faust, in the German legend, sold his soul.

2 a fiendish person. □□ **Mephistophelean** /-ˈliːən/ *adj*. **Mephistophelian** /-ˈfiːlɪən/ *adj*. [G (16th c.), of unkn. orig.]

mephitis /mɪˈfaɪtɪs/ *n*. **1** a noxious emanation, esp. from the earth. **2** a foul-smelling or poisonous stench. □□ **mephitic** /-ˈfɪtɪk/ *adj*. [L]

-mer /mə(r)/ *comb. form* denoting a substance of a specified class, esp. a polymer (*dimer*; *isomer*; *tautomer*). [Gk *meros* part, share]

meranti /məˈræntɪ/ *n*. a white, red, or yellow hardwood timber from any of various Malayan trees of the genus *Shorea*. [Malay]

mercantile /ˈmɜːkənˌtaɪl/ *adj*. **1** of trade, trading. **2** commercial. **3** mercenary, fond of bargaining. □**mercantile marine** shipping employed in commerce not war. [F f. It. f. *mercante* MERCHANT]

mercantilism /ˈmɜːkəntɪˌlɪz(ə)m/ *n*. an old economic theory that money is the only form of wealth. □□ **mercantilist** *n*.

mercaptan /mɜːˈkæpt(ə)n/ *n*. = THIOL. [mod.L *mercurium captans* capturing mercury]

Mercator projection /mɜːˈkeɪtə/ *n*. (also **Mercator's projection**) a projection of a map of the world on to a cylinder so that all the parallels of latitude have the same length as the equator, first published in 1569 and used esp. for marine charts and certain climatological maps. [G. *Mercator* (Latinized f. Kremer), Flemish-born geographer d. 1594]

mercenary /ˈmɜːsɪnərɪ/ *adj*. & *n*. —*adj*. primarily concerned with money or other reward (*mercenary motives*). —*n*. (*pl*. **-ies**) a hired soldier in foreign service. □□ **mercenariness** *n*. [ME f. L *mercenarius* f. *merces -edis* reward]

mercer /ˈmɜːsə(r)/ *n*. *Brit*. a dealer in textile fabrics, esp. silk and other costly materials. □□ **mercery** *n*. (*pl*. **-ies**). [ME f. AF *mercer*, OF *mercier* ult. f. L *merx mercis* goods]

mercerize /ˈmɜːsəˌraɪz/ *v.tr*. (also **-ise**) treat (cotton fabric or thread) under tension with caustic alkali to give greater strength and impart lustre. [J. *Mercer*, alleged inventor of the process d. 1866]

merchandise /ˈmɜːtʃənˌdaɪz/ *n*. & *v*. —*n*. goods for sale. —*v*. **1** *intr*. trade, traffic. **2** *tr*. trade or traffic in. **3** *tr*. **a** put on the market, promote the sale of (goods etc.). **b** advertise, publicize (an idea or person). □□ **merchandisable** *adj*. **merchandiser** *n*. [ME f. OF *marchandise* f. *marchand*: see MERCHANT]

merchant /ˈmɜːtʃ(ə)nt/ *n*. **1** a wholesale trader, esp. with foreign countries. **2** esp. *US* & *Sc*. a retail trader. **3** *colloq*. usu. *derog*. a person showing a partiality for a specified activity or practice (*speed merchant*). □**merchant bank** esp. *Brit*. a bank dealing in commercial loans and finance. **merchant banker** a member of a merchant bank. **merchant marine** *US* = *merchant navy*. **merchant navy** a nation's commercial shipping. **merchant prince** a wealthy merchant. **merchant ship** = MERCHANTMAN. [ME f. OF *marchand*, *marchant* ult. f. L *mercari* trade f. *merx mercis* merchandise]

merchantable /ˈmɜːtʃəntəb(ə)l/ *adj*. saleable, marketable. [ME f. *merchant* (v.) f. OF *marchander* f. *marchand*: see MERCHANT]

merchantman /ˈmɜːtʃəntmən/ *n*. (*pl*. **-men**) a ship conveying merchandise.

merciful /ˈmɜːsɪˌfʊl/ *adj*. having or showing or feeling mercy. □□ **mercifulness** *n*.

mercifully /ˈmɜːsɪˌfʊlɪ/ *adv*. **1** in a merciful manner. **2** (qualifying a whole sentence) fortunately (*mercifully, the sun came out*).

merciless /ˈmɜːsɪləs/ *adj*. **1** pitiless. **2** showing no mercy. □□ **mercilessly** *adv*. **mercilessness** *n*.

mercurial /mɜːˈkjʊərɪəl/ *adj*. & *n*. —*adj*. **1** (of a person) sprightly, ready-witted, volatile. **2** of or containing mercury. **3** (**Mercurial**) of the planet Mercury. —*n*. a drug containing mercury. □□ **mercurialism** *n*. **mercuriality** /-ˈælɪtɪ/ *n*. **mercurially** *adv*. [ME f. OF *mercuriel* or L *mercurialis* (as MERCURY)]

mercury /ˈmɜːkjʊrɪ/ n. **1** Chem. a silvery-white heavy liquid metallic element occurring naturally in cinnabar and used in barometers, thermometers, and amalgams; quicksilver. ¶ Symb.: **Hg**. **2** (**Mercury**) the planet nearest to the sun. **3** any plant of the genus Mercurialis, esp. M. perenne. □**mercury vapour lamp** a lamp in which light is produced by an electric discharge through mercury vapour. □□ **mercuric** /-ˈkjʊərɪk/ adj. **mercurous** adj. [ME f. L Mercurius messenger of the gods and god of traders f. merx mercis merchandise]

mercy /ˈmɜːsɪ/ n. & int. —n. (pl. -**ies**) **1** compassion or forbearance shown to enemies or offenders in one's power. **2** the quality of compassion. **3** an act of mercy. **4** (attrib.) administered or performed out of mercy or pity for a suffering person (mercy killing). **5** something to be thankful for (small mercies). —int. expressing surprise or fear. □**at the mercy of 1** wholly in the power of. **2** liable to danger or harm from. **have mercy on** (or **upon**) show mercy to. **mercy flight** the transporting by air of an injured or sick person from a remote area to a hospital. [ME f. OF merci f. L merces -edis reward, in LL pity, thanks]

mere¹ /mɪə(r)/ attrib.adj. (**merest**) that is solely or no more or better than what is specified (a mere boy; no mere theory). □**mere right** Law a right in theory. □□ **merely** adv. [ME f. AF meer, OF mier f. L merus unmixed]

mere² /mɪə(r)/ n. archaic or poet. a lake or pond. [OE f. Gmc]

mere³ /ˈmerɪ/ n. a Maori war-club, esp. one made of greenstone. [Maori]

meretricious /ˌmerɪˈtrɪʃəs/ adj. **1** (of decorations, literary style, etc.) showily but falsely attractive. **2** of or befitting a prostitute. □□ **meretriciously** adv. **meretriciousness** n. [L meretricius f. meretrix -tricis prostitute f. merēri be hired]

merganser /mɜːˈɡænsə(r)/ n. any of various diving fish-eating northern ducks of the genus Mergus, with a long narrow serrated hooked bill. Also called SAWBILL. [mod.L f. L mergus diver f. mergere dive + anser goose]

merge /mɜːdʒ/ v. **1** tr. & intr. (often foll. by with) **a** combine or be combined. **b** join or blend gradually. **2** intr. & tr. (foll. by in) lose or cause to lose character and identity in (something else). **3** tr. (foll. by in) embody (a title or estate) in (a larger one). □□ **mergence** n. [L mergere mers- dip, plunge, partly through legal AF merger]

merger /ˈmɜːdʒə(r)/ n. **1** the combining of two commercial companies etc. into one. **2** a merging, esp. of one estate in another. **3** Law the absorbing of a minor offence in a greater one. [AF (as MERGE)]

meridian /məˈrɪdɪən/ n. & adj. —n. **1** a circle passing through the celestial poles and zenith of any place on the earth's surface. **2** **a** a circle of constant longitude, passing through a given place and the terrestrial poles. **b** the corresponding line on a map. **3** archaic the point at which a sun or star attains its highest altitude. **4** prime; full splendour. —adj. **1** of noon. **2** of the period of greatest splendour, vigour, etc. [ME f. OF meridien or L meridianus (adj.) f. meridies midday f. medius middle + dies day]

meridional /məˈrɪdɪən(ə)l/ adj. & n. —adj. **1** of or in the south (esp. of Europe). **2** of or relating to a meridian. —n. an inhabitant of the south (esp. of France). [ME f. OF f. LL meridionalis irreg. f. L meridies: see MERIDIAN]

meringue /məˈræŋ/ n. **1** a confection of sugar, the white of eggs, etc., baked crisp. **2** a small cake or shell of this, usu. decorated or filled with whipped cream etc. [F, of unkn. orig.]

merino /məˈriːnəʊ/ n. (pl. -**os**) **1** (in full **merino sheep**) a variety of sheep with long fine wool. **2** a soft woollen or wool-and-cotton material like cashmere, orig. of merino wool. **3** a fine woollen yarn. [Sp., of uncert. orig.]

meristem /ˈmerɪˌstem/ n. Bot. a plant tissue consisting of actively dividing cells forming new tissue. □□ **meristematic** /-stəˈmætɪk/ adj. [Gk meristos divisible f. merizō divide f. meros part, after xylem]

merit /ˈmerɪt/ n. & v. —n. **1** the quality of deserving well. **2** excellence, worth. **3** (usu. in pl.) **a** a thing that entitles one to reward or gratitude. **b** esp. Law intrinsic rights and wrongs (the merits of a case). **4** Theol. good deeds as entitling to a future reward. —v.tr. (**merited, meriting**) deserve or be worthy of (reward, punishment, consideration, etc.). □**make a merit of** regard or represent (one's own conduct) as praiseworthy. **on its merits** with regard only to its intrinsic worth. **Order of Merit** Brit. an order founded in 1902, for distinguished achievement. [ME f. OF merite f. L meritum price, value, = past part. of merēri earn, deserve]

meritocracy /ˌmerɪˈtɒkrəsɪ/ n. (pl. -**ies**) **1** government by persons selected competitively according to merit. **2** a group of persons selected in this way. **3** a society governed by meritocracy.

meritorious /ˌmerɪˈtɔːrɪəs/ adj. **1** (of a person or act) having merit; deserving reward, praise, or gratitude. **2** deserving commendation for thoroughness etc. □□ **meritoriously** adv. **meritoriousness** n. [ME f. L meritorius f. merēri merit- earn]

merle /mɜːl/ n. Sc. or archaic a blackbird. [ME f. F f. L merula]

merlin /ˈmɜːlɪn/ n. a small European or N. American falcon, Falco columbarius, that hunts small birds. [ME f. AF merilun f. OF esmerillon augment. f. esmeril f. Frank.]

merlon /ˈmɜːlɒn/ n. the solid part of an embattled parapet between two embrasures. [F f. It. merlone f. merlo battlement]

mermaid /ˈmɜːmeɪd/ n. an imaginary half-human sea creature, with the head and trunk of a woman and the tail of a fish. [ME f. MERE² in obs. sense 'sea' + MAID]

merman /ˈmɜːmæn/ n. (pl. -**men**) the male equivalent of a mermaid.

mero- /ˈmerəʊ/ comb. form partly, partial. [Gk meros part]

-merous /mərəs/ comb. form esp. Bot. having so many parts (dimerous; 5-merous). [Gk (as MERO-)]

Merovingian /ˌmerəʊˈvɪndʒɪən/ adj. & n. —adj. of or relating to the Frankish dynasty founded by Clovis and reigning in Gaul and Germany c.500–750. —n. a member of this dynasty. [F mérovingien f. med.L Merovingi f. L Meroveus name of the reputed founder]

merriment /ˈmerɪmənt/ n. **1** exuberant enjoyment; being merry. **2** mirth, fun.

merry /ˈmerɪ/ adj. (**merrier, merriest**) **1 a** joyous. **b** full of laughter or gaiety. **2** Brit. colloq. slightly drunk. □**make merry 1** be festive; enjoy oneself. **2** (foll. by over) make fun of. **merry andrew** a mountebank's assistant; a clown or buffoon. **merry thought** esp. Brit. the wishbone of a bird. **play merry hell with** see HELL. □□ **merrily** adv. **merriness** n. [OE myrige f. Gmc]

merry-go-round /ˈmerɪɡəʊˌraʊnd/ n. **1** a revolving machine with wooden horses or cars for riding on at a fair etc. **2** a cycle of bustling activities.

merrymaking /ˈmerɪˌmeɪkɪŋ/ n. festivity, fun. □□ **merrymaker** n.

mesa /ˈmeɪsə/ n. US an isolated flat-topped hill with steep sides, found in landscapes with horizontal strata. [Sp., lit. table, f. L mensa]

mésalliance /meɪˈzælɪˌɑ̃s/ n. a marriage with a person of a lower social position. [F (as MIS-², ALLIANCE)]

mescal /ˈmeskæl/ n. **1 a** maguey. **b** liquor obtained from this. **2** a peyote cactus. □**mescal buttons** disc-shaped dried tops from the peyote cactus, eaten or chewed as an intoxicant. [Sp. mezcal f. Nahuatl mexcalli]

mescaline /ˈmeskəˌliːn/ n. (also **mescalin** /-lɪn/) a hallucinogenic alkaloid present in mescal buttons.

Mesdames *pl.* of MADAME.

Mesdemoiselles *pl.* of MADEMOISELLE.

mesembryanthemum /mɪˌzembrɪˈænθɪməm/ *n.* any of various succulent plants of the genus *Mesembryanthemum* of S. Africa, having daisy-like flowers in a wide range of bright colours that fully open in sunlight. [mod.L f. Gk *mesembria* noon + *anthemon* flower]

mesencephalon /ˌmesenˈsefəˌlɒn/ *n.* the part of the brain developing from the middle of the primitive or embryonic brain. Also called MIDBRAIN. [Gk *mesos* middle + *encephalon* brain: see ENCEPHALIC]

mesentery /ˈmesəntərɪ/ *n.* (*pl.* -ies) a double layer of peritoneum attaching the stomach, small intestine, pancreas, spleen, and other abdominal organs to the posterior wall of the abdomen. □□ **mesenteric** /-ˈterɪk/ *adj.* **mesenteritis** /-ˈraɪtɪs/ *n.* [med.L *mesenterium* f. Gk *mesenterion* (as MESO-, *enteron* intestine)]

mesh /meʃ/ *n.* & *v.* —*n.* **1** a network fabric or structure. **2** each of the open spaces or interstices between the strands of a net or sieve etc. **3** (in *pl.*) **a** a network. **b** a snare. **4** (in *pl.*) *Physiol.* an interlaced structure. —*v.* **1** *intr.* (often foll. by *with*) (of the teeth of a wheel) be engaged (with others). **2** *intr.* be harmonious. **3** *tr.* catch in a net. □ **in mesh** (of the teeth of wheels) engaged. [earlier *meish* etc. f. MDu. *maesche* f. Gmc]

mesial /ˈmiːzɪəl/ *adj. Anat.* of, in, or directed towards the middle line of a body. □□ **mesially** *adv.* [irreg. f. Gk *mesos* middle]

mesmerism /ˈmezməˌrɪz(ə)m/ *n.* **1** *Psychol.* **a** a hypnotic state produced in a person by another's influence over the will and nervous system. **b** a doctrine concerning this. **c** an influence producing this. **2** fascination. □□ **mesmeric** /mezˈmerɪk/ *adj.* **mesmerically** /-ˈmerɪkəlɪ/ *adv.* **mesmerist** *n.* [F. A. *Mesmer*, Austrian physician d. 1815]

mesmerize /ˈmezməˌraɪz/ *v.tr.* (also -**ise**) **1** *Psychol.* hypnotize; exercise mesmerism on. **2** fascinate, spellbind. □□ **mesmerization** /-ˈzeɪʃ(ə)n/ *n.* **mesmerizer** *n.* **mesmerizingly** *adv.*

mesne /miːn/ *adj. Law* intermediate. □ **mesne lord** *hist.* a lord holding an estate from a superior feudal lord. **mesne process** proceedings in a suit intervening between a primary and final process. **mesne profits** profits received from an estate by a tenant between two dates. [ME f. law F, var. of AF *meen*, MEAN³: cf. DEMESNE]

meso- /ˈmesəʊ, ˈmez-/ *comb. form* middle, intermediate. [Gk *mesos* middle]

mesoblast /ˈmesəʊˌblæst/ *n. Biol.* the middle germ-layer of an embryo.

mesoderm /ˈmesəʊˌdɜːm/ *n. Biol.* = MESOBLAST. [MESO- + Gk *derma* skin]

mesolithic /ˌmezəʊˈlɪθɪk/ *adj. Archaeol.* of or concerning the Stone Age between the palaeolithic and neolithic periods. [MESO- + Gk *lithos* stone]

mesomorph /ˈmesəʊˌmɔːf/ *n.* a person with a compact and muscular build of body (cf. ECTOMORPH, ENDOMORPH). □□ **mesomorphic** /-ˈmɔːfɪk/ *adj.* [MESO- + Gk *morphē* form]

meson /ˈmezɒn, ˈmiːzɒn/ *n. Physics* any of a class of elementary particles believed to participate in the forces that hold nucleons together in the atomic nucleus. □□ **mesic** /ˈmezɪk, ˈmiːz-/ *adj.* **mesonic** /mɪˈzɒnɪk/ *adj.* [earlier *mesotron*: cf. MESO-, -ON]

mesophyll /ˈmesəʊfɪl/ *n.* the inner tissue of a leaf. [MESO- + Gk *phullon* leaf]

mesophyte /ˈmesəʊˌfaɪt/ *n.* a plant needing only a moderate amount of water.

mesosphere /ˈmesəʊˌsfɪə(r)/ *n.* the region of the atmosphere extending from the top of the stratosphere to an altitude of about 50 miles.

Mesozoic /ˌmesəʊˈzəʊɪk/ *adj.* & *n. Geol.* —*adj.* of or relating to an era of geological time marked by the development of dinosaurs, and with evidence of the first mammals, birds, and flowering plants. ¶ Cf. Appendix II. —*n.* this era (cf. CENOZOIC, PALAEOZOIC). [MESO- + Gk *zōion* animal]

mesquite /ˈmeskiːt/ *n.* (also **mesquit**) any N. American leguminous tree of the genus *Prosopis*, esp. *P. juliflora*. □ **mesquite bean** a pod from the mesquite, used as fodder. [Mex. Sp. *mezquite*]

mess /mes/ *n.* & *v.* —*n.* **1** a dirty or untidy state of things (*the room is a mess*). **2** a state of confusion, embarrassment, or trouble. **3** something causing a mess, e.g. spilt liquid etc. **4** a domestic animal's excreta. **5 a** a company of persons who take meals together, esp. in the armed forces. **b** a place where such meals or recreation take place communally. **c** a meal taken there. **6** *derog.* a disagreeable concoction or medley. **7** a liquid or mixed food for hounds etc. **8** a portion of liquid or pulpy food. —*v.* **1** *tr.* (often foll. by *up*) **a** make a mess of; dirty. **b** muddle; make into a state of confusion. **2** *intr.* (foll. by *with*) interfere with. **3** *intr.* take one's meals. **4** *intr. colloq.* defecate. □ **make a mess of** bungle (an undertaking). **mess about** (or **around**) **1** act desultorily. **2** *colloq.* make things awkward for; cause arbitrary inconvenience to (a person). **mess-hall** a military dining area. **mess-jacket** a short close-fitting coat worn at the mess. **mess kit** a soldier's cooking and eating utensils. **mess of pottage** a material comfort etc. for which something higher is sacrificed (Gen. 25:29-34). **mess tin** a small container as part of a mess kit. [ME f. OF *mes* portion of food f. LL *missus* course at dinner, past part. of *mittere* send]

message /ˈmesɪdʒ/ *n.* & *v.* —*n.* **1** an oral or written communication sent by one person to another. **2** an inspired or significant communication from a prophet, writer, or preacher. **3** a mission or errand. **4** (in *pl.*) *Sc.* & *N.Engl.* things bought; shopping. —*v.tr.* **1** send as a message. **2** transmit (a plan etc.) by signalling etc. □ **get the message** *colloq.* understand what is meant. **message stick** *Austral.* a stick carved with significant marks, carried as identification by Aboriginal messengers. [ME f. OF ult. f. L *mittere miss-* send]

Messeigneurs pl. of MONSEIGNEUR.

messenger /ˈmesɪndʒə(r)/ *n.* **1** a person who carries a message. **2** a person employed to carry messages. □ **King's** (or **Queen's**) **Messenger** a courier in the diplomatic service. **messenger RNA** a form of RNA carrying genetic information from DNA to a ribosome. ¶ Abbr.: **mRNA**. [ME & OF *messager* (as MESSAGE): -*n*- as in *harbinger*, *passenger*, etc.]

Messiah /mɪˈsaɪə/ *n.* **1** a liberator or would-be liberator of an oppressed people or country. **2 a** the promised deliverer of the Jews. **b** Christ regarded as this. □□ **Messiahship** *n.* [ME f. OF *Messie* ult. f. Heb. *māšíaḥ* anointed]

Messianic /ˌmesɪˈænɪk/ *adj.* **1** of the Messiah. **2** inspired by hope or belief in a Messiah. □□ **Messianism** /mɪˈsaɪəˌnɪz(ə)m/ *n.* [F *messianique* (as MESSIAH) after *rabbinique* rabbinical]

Messieurs pl. of MONSIEUR.

messmate /ˈmesmeɪt/ *n.* a person with whom one regularly takes meals, esp. in the armed forces.

Messrs /ˈmesəz/ *pl.* of MR. [abbr. of MESSIEURS]

messuage /ˈmeswɪdʒ/ *n. Law* a dwelling-house with outbuildings and land assigned to its use. [ME f. AF: perh. an alternative form of *mesnage* dwelling]

messy /ˈmesɪ/ *adj.* (**messier**, **messiest**) **1** untidy or dirty. **2** causing or accompanied by a mess. **3** difficult to deal with; full of awkward complications. □□ **messily** *adv.* **messiness** *n.*

mestizo /meˈstiːzəʊ/ *n.* (*pl.* -**os**; *fem.* **mestiza** /-zə/, *pl.* -**as**) a Spaniard or Portuguese of mixed race, esp. the offspring of a Spaniard and an American Indian. [Sp. ult. f. L *mixtus* past part. of *miscēre* mix]

met¹ *past and past part.* of MEET¹.

met² /met/ *adj. colloq.* **1** meteorological. **2** metropolitan. **3** (**the Met**) **a** (in full **the Met Office**) (in the UK) the Meteorological Office. **b** the Metropolitan

Police in London. **c** the Metropolitan Opera House in New York. [abbr.]

meta- /ˈmetə/ *comb. form* (usu. **met-** before a vowel or *h*) **1** denoting change of position or condition (*metabolism*). **2** denoting position: **a** behind. **b** after or beyond (*metaphysics; metacarpus*). **c** of a higher or second-order kind (*metalanguage*). **3** *Chem.* **a** relating to two carbon atoms separated by one other in a benzene ring. **b** relating to a compound formed by dehydration (*metaphosphate*). [Gk *meta-*, *met-*, *meth-* f. *meta* with, after]

metabolism /mɪˈtæbəˌlɪz(ə)m/ *n.* all the chemical processes that occur within a living organism, resulting in energy production (**destructive metabolism**) and growth (**constructive metabolism**). □□ **metabolic** /ˌmetəˈbɒlɪk/ *adj.* **metabolically** /ˌmetəˈbɒlɪkəlɪ/ *adv.* [Gk *metabolē* change (as META-, *bolē* f. *ballō* throw)]

metabolite /mɪˈtæbəˌlaɪt/ *n. Physiol.* a substance formed in or necessary for metabolism.

metabolize /mɪˈtæbəˌlaɪz/ *v.tr. & intr.* (also **-ise**) process or be processed by metabolism. □□ **metabolizable** *adj.*

metacarpus /ˌmetəˈkɑːpəs/ *n.* (*pl.* **metacarpi** /-paɪ/) **1** the set of five bones of the hand that connects the wrist to the fingers. **2** this part of the hand. □□ **metacarpal** *adj.* [mod.L f. Gk *metakarpon* (as META-, CARPUS)]

metacentre /ˈmetəˌsentə(r)/ *n.* (*US* **metacenter**) the point of intersection between a line (vertical in equilibrium) through the centre of gravity of a floating body and a vertical line through the centre of pressure after a slight angular displacement, which must be above the centre of gravity to ensure stability. □□ **metacentric** /-ˈsentrɪk/ *adj.* [F *métacentre* (as META-, CENTRE)]

metage /ˈmiːtɪdʒ/ *n.* **1** the official measuring of a load of coal etc. **2** the duty paid for this. [METE[1] + -AGE]

metagenesis /ˌmetəˈdʒenɪsɪs/ *n.* the alternation of generations between sexual and asexual reproduction. □□ **metagenetic** /-dʒɪˈnetɪk/ *adj.* [mod.L (as META-, GENESIS)]

metal /ˈmet(ə)l/ *n., adj., & v.* —*n.* **1 a** any of a class of chemical elements such as gold, silver, iron, and tin, usu. lustrous ductile solids and good conductors of heat and electricity and forming basic oxides. **b** an alloy of any of these. **2** material used for making glass, in a molten state. **3** *Heraldry* gold or silver as tincture. **4** (in *pl.*) the rails of a railway line. **5** = *road-metal* (see ROAD[1]). —*adj.* made of metal. —*v.tr.* (**metalled**, **metalling**; *US* **metaled**, **metaling**) **1** provide or fit with metal. **2** *Brit.* make or mend (a road) with road-metal. □ **metal detector** an electronic device giving a signal when it locates metal. **metal fatigue** fatigue (see FATIGUE *n.* 2) in metal. [ME f. OF *metal* or L *metallum* f. Gk *metallon* mine]

metalanguage /ˈmetəˌlæŋgwɪdʒ/ *n.* **1** a form of language used to discuss a language. **2** a system of propositions about propositions.

metallic /mɪˈtælɪk/ *adj.* **1** of, consisting of, or characteristic of metal or metals. **2** sounding sharp and ringing, like struck metal. **3** having the sheen or lustre of metals. □□ **metallically** *adv.* [L *metallicus* f. Gk *metallikos* (as METAL)]

metalliferous /ˌmetəˈlɪfərəs/ *adj.* bearing or producing metal. [L *metallifer* (as METAL, -FEROUS)]

metallize /ˈmetəˌlaɪz/ *v.tr.* (also **-ise**; *US* **metalize**) **1** render metallic. **2** coat with a thin layer of metal. □□ **metallization** /-ˈzeɪʃ(ə)n/ *n.*

metallography /ˌmetəˈlɒgrəfɪ/ *n.* the descriptive science of the structure and properties of metals. □□ **metallographic** /ˌmetæləˈgræfɪk/ *adj.* **metallographical** /ˌmetæləˈgræfɪk(ə)l/ *adj.* **metallographically** /ˌmetæləˈgræfɪkəlɪ/ *adv.*

metalloid /ˈmetəˌlɔɪd/ *adj. & n.* —*adj.* having the form or appearance of a metal. —*n.* any element

intermediate in properties between metals and non-metals, e.g. boron, silicon, and germanium.

metallurgy /mɪˈtælədʒɪ, ˈmetəˌlɜːdʒɪ/ *n.* the science concerned with the production, purification, and properties of metals and their application. □□ **metallurgic** /ˌmetəˈlɜːdʒɪk/ *adj.* **metallurgical** /ˌmetəˈlɜːdʒɪk(ə)l/ *adj.* **metallurgically** /ˌmetəˈlɜːdʒɪkəlɪ/ *adv.* **metallurgist** *n.* [Gk *metallon* metal + -*ourgia* working]

metalwork /ˈmet(ə)lwɜːk/ *n.* **1** the art of working in metal. **2** metal objects collectively. □□ **metalworker** *n.*

metamere /ˈmetəˌmɪər/ *n. Zool.* each of several similar segments, that contain the same internal structures, of an animal body. [META- + Gk *meros* part]

metameric /ˌmetəˈmerɪk/ *adj.* **1** *Chem.* having the same proportional composition and molecular weight, but different functional groups and chemical properties. **2** *Zool.* of or relating to metameres. □□ **metamer** /ˈmetəmə(r)/ *n.* **metamerism** /meˈtæməˌrɪz(ə)m/ *n.*

metamorphic /ˌmetəˈmɔːfɪk/ *adj.* **1** of or marked by metamorphosis. **2** *Geol.* (of rock) that has undergone transformation by natural agencies such as heat and pressure. □□ **metamorphism** *n.* [META- + Gk *morphē* form]

metamorphose /ˌmetəˈmɔːfəʊz/ *v.tr.* **1** change in form. **2** (foll. by *to, into*) **a** turn (into a new form). **b** change the nature of. [F *métamorphoser* f. *métamorphose* METAMORPHOSIS]

metamorphosis /ˌmetəˈmɔːfəsɪs, ˌmetəmɔːˈfəʊsɪs/ *n.* (*pl.* **metamorphoses** /-ˌsiːz/) **1** a change of form (by natural or supernatural means). **2** a changed form. **3** a change of character, conditions, etc. **4** *Zool.* the transformation between an immature form and an adult form, e.g. from a pupa to an insect, or from a tadpole to a frog. [L f. Gk *metamorphōsis* f. *metamorphoō* transform (as META-, *morphoō* f. *morphē* form)]

metaphase /ˈmetəˌfeɪz/ *n. Biol.* the stage of meiotic or mitotic cell division when the chromosomes become attached to the spindle fibres.

metaphor /ˈmetəˌfɔː(r)/ *n.* **1** the application of a name or descriptive term or phrase to an object or action to which it is imaginatively but not literally applicable (e.g. *a glaring error*). **2** an instance of this. □□ **metaphoric** /-ˈfɒrɪk/ *adj.* **metaphorical** /-ˈfɒrɪk(ə)l/ *adj.* **metaphorically** /-ˈfɒrɪkəlɪ/ *adv.* [F *métaphore* or L *metaphora* f. Gk *metaphora* f. *metapherō* transfer]

metaphrase /ˈmetəˌfreɪz/ *n. & v.* —*n.* literal translation. —*v.tr.* put into other words. □□ **metaphrastic** /-ˈfræstɪk/ *adj.* [mod.L *metaphrasis* f. Gk *metaphrasis* f. *metaphrazō* translate]

metaphysic /ˌmetəˈfɪzɪk/ *n.* a system of metaphysics. **metaphysical** /ˌmetəˈfɪzɪk(ə)l/ *adj. & n.* —*adj.* **1** of or relating to metaphysics. **2** based on abstract general reasoning. **3** excessively subtle or theoretical. **4** incorporeal; supernatural. **5** visionary. **6** (of poetry, esp. in the 17th c. in England) characterized by subtlety of thought and complex imagery. —*n.* (**the Metaphysicals**) the metaphysical poets. □□ **metaphysically** *adv.*

metaphysics /ˌmetəˈfɪzɪks/ *n.pl.* (usu. treated as *sing.*) **1** the theoretical philosophy of being and knowing. **2** the philosophy of mind. **3** *colloq.* abstract or subtle talk; mere theory. □□ **metaphysician** /-ˈzɪʃ(ə)n/ *n.* **metaphysicize** /-ˈfɪzɪˌsaɪz/ *v.intr.* [ME *metaphysic* f. OF *metaphysique* f. med.L *metaphysica* ult. f. Gk *ta meta ta phusika* the things after the Physics, from the sequence of Aristotle's works]

metaplasia /ˌmetəˈpleɪzɪə/ *n. Physiol.* an abnormal change in the nature of a tissue. □□ **metaplastic** /-ˈplæstɪk/ *adj.* [mod.L f. G *Metaplase* f. Gk *metaplasis* (as META-, *plasis* f. *plassō* to mould)]

metapsychology /ˌmetəsaɪˈkɒlədʒɪ/ *n.* the study of the nature and functions of the mind beyond

what can be studied experimentally. □□
metapsychological /-kə'lɒdʒɪk(ə)l/ *adj.*

metastable /ˌmetə'steɪb(ə)l/ *adj.* **1** (of a state of equilibrium) stable only under small disturbances. **2** passing to another state so slowly as to seem stable. □□ **metastability** /-stə'bɪlɪtɪ/ *n.*

metastasis /me'tæstəsɪs/ *n.* (*pl.* **metastases** /-ˌsiːz/) *Physiol.* **1** the transference of a bodily function, disease, etc., from one part or organ to another. **2** the transformation of chemical compounds into others in the process of assimilation by an organism. □□ **metastasize** *v.intr.* (also **-ise**). **metastatic** /ˌmetə'stætɪk/ *adj.* [LL f. Gk f. *methistēmi* change]

metatarsus /ˌmetə'tɑːsəs/ *n.* (*pl.* **metatarsi** /-saɪ/) **1** the part of the foot between the ankle and the toes. **2** the set of bones in this. □□ **metatarsal** *adj.* [mod.L (as META-, TARSUS)]

metathesis /mɪ'tæθɪsɪs/ *n.* (*pl.* **metatheses** /-ˌsiːz/) **1** *Gram.* the transposition of sounds or letters in a word. **2** *Chem.* the interchange of atoms or groups of atoms between two molecules. **3** an instance of either of these. □□ **metathetic** /ˌmetə'θetɪk/ *adj.* **metathetical** /ˌmetə'θetɪk(ə)l/ *adj.* [LL f. Gk *metatithēmi* transpose]

metazoan /ˌmetə'zəʊən/ *n.* & *adj. Zool.* —*n.* any animal of the subkingdom Metazoa, having multicellular and differentiated tissues. —*adj.* of or relating to the Metazoans. [*Metazoa* f. Gk META- + *zōia* pl. of *zōion* animal]

mete¹ /miːt/ *v.tr.* **1** (usu. foll. by *out*) *literary* apportion or allot (a punishment or reward). **2** *poet.* or *Bibl.* measure. □ **mete-wand** (or **-yard**) a standard of estimation. [OE *metan* f. Gmc., rel. to MEET¹]

mete² /miːt/ *n.* a boundary or boundary stone. [ME f. OF f. L *meta* boundary, goal]

metempsychosis /ˌmetempsaɪ'kəʊsɪs/ *n.* (*pl.* **-psychoses** /-ˌsiːz/) **1** the supposed transmigration of the soul of a human being or animal at death into a new body of the same or a different species. **2** an instance of this. □□ **metempsychosist** *n.* [LL f. Gk *metempsukhōsis* (as META-, EN-², *psukhē* soul)]

meteor /'miːtɪə(r)/ *n.* **1** a small body of matter from outer space that becomes incandescent as a result of friction with the earth's atmosphere. **2** a streak of light emanating from a meteor. □ **meteor shower** a group of meteors appearing to come from one point in the sky. [ME f. mod.L *meteorum* f. Gk *meteōron* neut. of *meteōros* lofty, (as META-, *aeirō* raise)]

meteoric /ˌmiːtɪ'ɒrɪk/ *adj.* **1 a** of or relating to the atmosphere. **b** dependent on atmospheric conditions. **2** of meteors. **3** rapid like a meteor; dazzling, transient (*meteoric rise to fame*). □ **meteoric stone** a meteorite. □□ **meteorically** *adv.*

meteorite /'miːtɪəˌraɪt/ *n.* a fallen meteor, or fragment of natural rock or metal, that reaches the earth's surface from outer space. □□ **meteoritic** /-'rɪtɪk/ *adj.*

meteorograph /'miːtɪərəˌɡrɑːf/ *n.* an apparatus that records several meteorological phenomena at the same time. [F *météorographe* (as METEOR, -GRAPH)]

meteoroid /'miːtɪəˌrɔɪd/ *n.* any small body moving in the solar system that becomes visible as it passes through the earth's atmosphere as a meteor. □□ **meteoroidal** /-'rɔɪd(ə)l/ *adj.*

meteorology /ˌmiːtɪə'rɒlədʒɪ/ *n.* **1** the study of the processes and phenomena of the atmosphere, esp. as a means of forecasting the weather. **2** the atmospheric character of a region. □□ **meteorological** /-rə'lɒdʒɪk(ə)l/ *adj.* **meteorologically** /-rə'lɒdʒɪkəlɪ/ *adv.* **meteorologist** *n.* [Gk *meteōrologia* (as METEOR)]

meter¹ /'miːtə(r)/ *n.* & *v.* —*n.* **1** a person or thing that measures, esp. an instrument for recording a quantity of gas, electricity, etc. supplied, present, or needed. **2** = *parking-meter* (see PARK). —*v.tr.* measure by means of a meter. [ME f. METE¹ + -ER¹]

meter² *US* var. of METRE¹.

meter³ *US* var. of METRE².

-meter /miːtə(r), mɪ:tə(r)/ *comb. form* **1** forming nouns denoting measuring instruments (*barometer*). **2** *Prosody* forming nouns denoting lines of poetry with a specified number of measures (*pentameter*).

methadone /'meθəˌdəʊn/ *n.* a potent narcotic analgesic drug used to relieve severe pain, as a linctus to suppress coughs, and as a substitute for morphine or heroin. [6-di*methyl*amino-4,4-di*phenyl*-3-heptan*one*]

methamphetamine /ˌmeθæm'fetəmɪn, -ˌmiːn/ *n.* an amphetamine derivative with quicker and longer action, used as a stimulant. [METHYL + AMPHETAMINE]

methanal /'meθəˌnæl/ *n. Chem.* = FORMALDEHYDE. [METHANE + ALDEHYDE]

methane /'meθeɪn, 'miːθeɪn/ *n. Chem.* a colourless odourless inflammable gaseous hydrocarbon, the simplest in the alkane series, and the main constituent of natural gas. ¶ Chem. formula: CH_4. [METHYL + -ANE²]

methanoic acid /ˌmeθə'nəʊɪk/ *n. Chem.* = FORMIC ACID. [METHANE + -IC]

methanol /'meθəˌnɒl/ *n. Chem.* a colourless volatile inflammable liquid, used as a solvent. ¶ Chem. formula: CH_3OH. Also called *methyl alcohol*. [METHANE + ALCOHOL]

methinks /mɪ'θɪŋks/ *v.intr.* (*past* **methought** /mɪ'θɔːt/) *archaic* it seems to me. [OE *mē thyncth* f. *mē* dative of ME¹ + *thyncth* 3rd sing. of *thyncan* seem, THINK]

methionine /me'θaɪəˌniːn/ *n. Biochem.* an amino acid containing sulphur and an important constituent of proteins. [METHYL + Gk *theion* sulphur]

metho /'meθəʊ/ *n.* (*pl.* **-os**) *Austral. sl.* **1** methylated spirit. **2** a person addicted to drinking methylated spirit. [abbr.]

method /'meθəd/ *n.* **1** a special form of procedure esp. in any branch of mental activity. **2** orderliness; regular habits. **3** the orderly arrangement of ideas. **4** a scheme of classification. **5** *Theatr.* a technique of acting based on the actor's thorough emotional identification with the character. □ **method in one's madness** sense in what appears to be foolish or strange behaviour. [F *méthode* or L *methodus* f. Gk *methodos* pursuit of knowledge (as META-, *hodos* way)]

methodical /mɪ'θɒdɪk(ə)l/ *adj.* (also **methodic**) characterized by method or order. □□ **methodically** *adv.* [LL *methodicus* f. Gk *methodikos* (as METHOD)]

Methodist /'meθədɪst/ *n.* **1** a member of any of several Protestant religious bodies (now united) originating in the 18th-c. evangelistic movement of Charles and John Wesley and George Whitefield. **2** (**methodist**) a person who follows or advocates a particular method or system of procedure. □□ **Methodism** *n.* **Methodistic** /-'dɪstɪk/ *adj.* **Methodistical** /-'dɪstɪk(ə)l/ *adj.* [mod.L *methodista* (as METHOD): sense 1 prob. from following a specified 'method' of devotional study]

methodize /'meθəˌdaɪz/ *v.tr.* (also **-ise**) **1** reduce to order. **2** arrange in an orderly manner. □□ **methodizer** *n.*

methodology /ˌmeθə'dɒlədʒɪ/ *n.* (*pl.* **-ies**) **1** the science of method. **2** a body of methods used in a particular branch of activity. □□ **methodological** /-də'lɒdʒɪk(ə)l/ *adj.* **methodologically** /-də'lɒdʒɪkəlɪ/ *adv.* **methodologist** *n.* [mod.L *methodologia* or F *méthodologie* (as METHOD)]

methought *past* of METHINKS.

meths /meθs/ *n. Brit. colloq.* methylated spirit. [abbr.]

Methuselah /mɪ'θjuːzələ/ *n.* **1** a very old person or thing. **2** (**methuselah**) a wine bottle of about eight times the standard size. [ME: the name of a patriarch said to have lived 969 years (Gen. 5:27)]

methyl /'meθɪl, 'miːθaɪl/ *n. Chem.* the univalent hydrocarbon radical CH_3, present in many organic compounds. □ **methyl alcohol** = METHANOL. **methyl benzene** = TOLUENE. □□ **methylic** /mɪ'θɪlɪk/

methylate *adj.* [G *Methyl* or F *méthyle*, back-form. f. G *Methylen*, F *méthylène*: see METHYLENE]

methylate /'meθɪˌleɪt/ *v.tr.* **1** mix or impregnate with methanol. **2** introduce a methyl group into (a molecule or compound). □ **methylated spirit** (or **spirits**) alcohol impregnated with methanol to make it unfit for drinking and exempt from duty. □□ **methylation** /-'leɪʃ(ə)n/ *n.*

methylene /'meθɪˌliːn/ *n.* *Chem.* the highly reactive divalent group of atoms CH₂. [F *méthylène* f. Gk *methu* wine + *hulē* wood + -ENE]

metic /'metɪk/ *n.* *Gk Antiq.* an alien living in a Greek city with some privileges of citizenship. [irreg. f. Gk *metoikos* (as META-, *oikos* dwelling)]

meticulous /mə'tɪkjʊləs/ *adj.* **1** giving great or excessive attention to details. **2** very careful and precise. □□ **meticulously** *adv.* **meticulousness** *n.* [L *meticulosus* f. *metus* fear]

métier /'metjeɪ/ *n.* **1** one's trade, profession, or department of activity. **2** one's forte. [F ult. f. L *ministerium* service]

metis /mer'tiːs/ *n.* (*pl.* **metis**; *fem.* **metisse**, *pl.* **metisses**) a person of mixed race, esp. the offspring of a White person and an American Indian in Canada. [F *métis* OF *mestis* f. Rmc, rel. to MESTIZO]

metol /'metɒl/ *n.* a white soluble powder used as a photographic developer. [G, arbitrary name]

Metonic cycle /mɪ'tɒnɪk/ *n.* a period of 19 years (235 lunar months) covering all the changes of the moon's position relative to the sun and the earth. [Gk *Metōn*, Athenian astronomer of the 5th c. BC]

metonym /'metənɪm/ *n.* a word used in metonymy. [back-form. f. METONYMY, after *synonym*]

metonymy /mɪ'tɒnɪmɪ/ *n.* the substitution of the name of an attribute or adjunct for that of the thing meant (e.g. *Crown* for *king*, *the turf* for *horse-racing*). □□ **metonymic** /ˌmetə'nɪmɪk/ *adj.* **metonymical** /ˌmetə'nɪmɪk(ə)l/ *adj.* [LL *metonymia* f. Gk *metōnumia* (as META-, *onoma, onuma* name)]

metope /'metəʊp/ *n.* *Archit.* a square space between triglyphs in a Doric frieze. [L *metopa* f. Gk *metopē* (as META-, *opē* hole for a beam-end)]

metre¹ /'miːtə(r)/ *n.* (*US* **meter**) a metric unit and the base SI unit of linear measure, equal to about 39.4 inches, and reckoned as the length of the path travelled by light in a vacuum during ¹/₂₉₉,₇₉₂,₄₅₈ of a second. □ **metre-kilogram-second** denoting a system of measure using the metre, kilogram, and second as the basic units of length, mass, and time. ¶ Abbr.: **mks.** □□ **metreage** /'miːtərɪdʒ/ *n.* [F *mètre* f. Gk *metron* measure]

metre² /'miːtə(r)/ *n.* (*US* **meter**) **1 a** any form of poetic rhythm, determined by the number and length of feet in a line. **b** a metrical group or measure. **2** the basic pulse and rhythm of a piece of music. [OF *metre* f. L *metrum* f. Gk *metron* MEASURE]

metric /'metrɪk/ *adj.* of or based on the metre. □ **metric system** the decimal measuring system with the metre, litre, and gram (or kilogram) as units of length, volume, and mass (see also SI). **metric ton** (or **tonne**) 1,000 kilograms (2205 lb.). [F *métrique* (as METRE¹)]

-metric /'metrɪk/ *comb. form* (also **-metrical** /-k(ə)l/) forming adjectives corresponding to nouns in *-meter* and *-metry* (*thermometric*; *geometric*). □□ **-metrically** *comb. form* forming adverbs. [from or after F *métrique* f. L (as METRICAL)]

metrical /'metrɪk(ə)l/ *adj.* **1** of, relating to, or composed in metre (*metrical psalms*). **2** of or involving measurement (*metrical geometry*). □□ **metrically** *adv.* [ME f. L *metricus* f. Gk *metrikos* (as METRE²)]

metricate /'metrɪˌkeɪt/ *v.intr.* & *tr.* change or adapt to a metric system of measurement. □□ **metrication** /-'keɪʃ(ə)n/ *n.* **metricize** /-ˌsaɪz/ *v.tr.* (also **-ise**)

metritis /mɪ'traɪtɪs/ *n.* inflammation of the womb. [Gk *mētra* womb + -ITIS]

metro /'metrəʊ/ *n.* (*pl.* **-os**) an underground railway system in a city, esp. Paris. [F *métro*, abbr. of *métropolitain* METROPOLITAN]

metrology /mɪ'trɒlədʒɪ/ *n.* the scientific study of measurement. □□ **metrologic** /ˌmetrə'lɒdʒɪk/ *adj.* **metrological** /ˌmetrə'lɒdʒɪk(ə)l/ *adj.* [Gk *metron* measure + -LOGY]

metronome /'metrəˌnəʊm/ *n.* *Mus.* an instrument marking time at a selected rate by giving a regular tick. □□ **metronomic** /-'nɒmɪk/ *adj.* [Gk *metron* measure + *nomos* law]

metronymic /ˌmetrə'nɪmɪk/ *adj.* & *n.* —*adj.* (of a name) derived from the name of a mother or female ancestor. —*n.* a metronymic name. [Gk *mētēr mētros* mother, after *patronymic*]

metropolis /mɪ'trɒpəlɪs/ *n.* **1** the chief city of a country; a capital city. **2** a metropolitan bishop's see. **3** a centre of activity. [LL f. Gk *mētropolis* parent State f. *mētēr mētros* mother + *polis* city]

metropolitan /ˌmetrə'pɒlɪt(ə)n/ *adj.* & *n.* —*adj.* **1** of or relating to a metropolis, esp. as distinct from its environs (*metropolitan New York*). **2** belonging to, forming or forming part of, a mother country as distinct from its colonies etc. (*metropolitan France*). **3** of an ecclesiastical metropolis. —*n.* **1** (in full **metropolitan bishop**) a bishop having authority over the bishops of a province, in the Western Church equivalent to archbishop, in the Orthodox Church ranking above archbishop and below patriarch. **2** an inhabitant of a metropolis. □ **metropolitan county** *hist.* (in England) each of six units of local government centred on a large urban area (in existence 1974–86). **metropolitan magistrate** *Brit.* a paid professional magistrate in London (cf. *stipendiary magistrate*). □□ **metropolitanate** *n.* (in sense 1 of *n.*). **metropolitanism** *n.* [ME f. LL *metropolitanus* f. Gk *mētropolitēs* (as METROPOLIS)]

metrorrhagia /ˌmiːtrəʊ'reɪdʒɪə/ *n.* abnormal bleeding from the womb. [mod.L f. Gk *mētra* womb + -*rrhage* as HAEMORRHAGE]

-metry /mɪtrɪ/ *comb. form* forming nouns denoting procedures and systems corresponding to instruments in *-meter* (*calorimetry*; *thermometry*). [after *geometry* etc. f. Gk *-metria* f. *-metrēs* measurer]

mettle /'met(ə)l/ *n.* **1** the quality of a person's disposition or temperament (*a chance to show your mettle*). **2** natural ardour. **3** spirit, courage. □ **on one's mettle** incited to do one's best. □□ **mettled** *adj.* (also in *comb.*). **mettlesome** *adj.* [var. OF METAL *n.*]

meu /mjuː/ *n.* (also **mew**) = BALDMONEY. [irreg. f. L *meum* f. Gk *mēon*]

meunière /mɜː'njeə(r)/ *adj.* (esp. of fish) cooked or served in lightly browned butter with lemon juice and parsley (*sole meunière*). [F (*à la*) *meunière* (in the manner of) a miller's wife]

MeV *abbr.* mega-electronvolt(s).

mew¹ /mjuː/ *v.* & *n.* —*v.intr.* (of a cat, gull, etc.) utter its characteristic cry. —*n.* this sound, esp. of a cat. [ME: imit.]

mew² /mjuː/ *n.* a gull, esp. the common gull, *Larus canus*. [OE *mæw* f. Gmc]

mew³ /mjuː/ *n.* & *v.* —*n.* a cage for hawks, esp. while moulting. —*v.tr.* **1** put (a hawk) in a cage. **2** (often foll. by *up*) shut up; confine. [ME f. OF *mue* f. *muer* moult f. L *mutare* change]

mew⁴ var. of MEU.

mewl /mjuːl/ *v.intr.* (also **mule**) **1** cry feebly; whimper. **2** mew like a cat. [imit.: cf. MIAUL]

mews /mjuːz/ *n.* *Brit.* a set of stabling round an open yard or along a lane, now often converted into dwellings. [pl. (now used as sing.) of MEW³, orig. of the royal stables on the site of hawks' mews at Charing Cross]

Mexican /'meksɪkən/ *n.* & *adj.* —*n.* **1 a** a native or national of Mexico in Central America. **b** a person of Mexican descent. **2** a language spoken in Mexico, esp. Nahuatl. —*adj.* **1** of or relating to Mexico or its people. **2** of Mexican descent. [Sp. *mexicano*]

mezereon /mɪˈzɪərɪən/ *n.* a small European and Asian shrub, *Daphne mezereum*, with fragrant purplish red flowers and red berries. [med.L f. Arab. *māzaryūn*]

mezuzah /meˈzuːzə/ *n.* (*pl.* **mezuzoth** /-zəʊθ/) a parchment inscribed with religious texts and attached in a case to the doorpost of a Jewish house as a sign of faith. [Heb. *mᵉzūzāh* doorpost]

mezzanine /ˈmetsəˌniːn, ˈmez-/ *n.* **1** a low storey between two others (usu. between the ground and first floors). **2** *Brit. Theatr.* **a** a floor or space beneath the stage. **b** *US* a dress circle. [F f. It. *mezzanino* dimin. of *mezzano* middle f. L *medianus* MEDIAN]

mezza voce /ˌmetsə ˈvəʊtʃeɪ/ *adv. Mus.* with less than the full strength of the voice or sound. [It., = half voice]

mezzo /ˈmetsəʊ/ *adv. & n. Mus.* —*adv.* half, moderately. —*n.* (in full **mezzo-soprano**) (*pl.* **-os**) **1 a** a female singing-voice between soprano and contralto. **b** a singer with this voice. **2** a part written for mezzo-soprano. □**mezzo forte** fairly loud. **mezzo piano** fairly soft. [It., f. L *medius* middle]

mezzo-rilievo /ˈmetsəʊrɪˈljeɪvəʊ/ *n.* a raised surface in the form of half-relief, in which the figures project half their true proportions. [It., = half-relief]

mezzotint /ˈmetsəʊtɪnt/ *n. & v.* —*n.* **1** a method of printing or engraving in which the surface of a plate is roughened by scraping so that it produces tones and half-tones. **2** a print produced by this process. —*v.tr.* engrave in mezzotint. □□ **mezzotinter** *n.* [It. *mezzotinto* f. *mezzo* half + *tinto* tint]

MF *abbr.* medium frequency.

mf *abbr.* mezzo forte.

MFH *abbr. Brit.* Master of Foxhounds.

MG *abbr.* **1** machine-gun. **2** Morris Garages (as a make of car).

Mg *symb. Chem.* the element manganese.

mg *abbr.* milligram(s).

Mgr. *abbr.* **1** Manager. **2** *Monseigneur.* **3** Monsignor.

mho /məʊ/ *n.* (*pl.* **-os**) *Electr.* the reciprocal of an ohm, a former unit of conductance. [OHM reversed]

MHR *abbr.* (in the US and Australia) Member of the House of Representatives.

MHz *abbr.* megahertz.

MI *abbr.* **1** *US* Michigan (in official postal use). **2** *Brit. hist.* Military Intelligence.

mi var. of ME².

mi. *abbr. US* mile(s).

M.I.5 *abbr.* (in the UK) the department of Military Intelligence concerned with State security. ¶ Not in official use.

M.I.6 *abbr.* (in the UK) the department of Military Intelligence concerned with espionage. ¶ Not in official use.

miaow /mɪˈaʊ/ *n. & v.* (also **meow**) —*n.* the characteristic cry of a cat. —*v.intr.* make this cry. [imit.]

miasma /mɪˈæzmə, maɪ-/ *n.* (*pl.* **miasmata** /-mətə/ or **miasmas**) *archaic* an infectious or noxious vapour. □□ **miasmal** *adj.* **miasmatic** /-ˈmætɪk/ *adj.* **miasmic** *adj.* **miasmically** *adv.* [Gk, = defilement, f. *miainō* pollute]

miaul /mɪˈɔːl/ *v.intr.* cry like a cat; mew. [F *miauler*: imit.]

Mic. *abbr.* Micah (Old Testament).

mica /ˈmaɪkə/ *n.* any of a group of silicate minerals with a layered structure, esp. muscovite. □**mica-schist** (or **slate**) a fissile rock containing quartz and mica. □□ **micaceous** /-ˈkeɪʃəs/ *adj.* [L, = crumb]

mice *pl.* of MOUSE.

micelle /mɪˈsel, maɪˈsel/ *n. Chem.* an aggregate of molecules in a colloidal solution, as occurs e.g. when soap dissolves in water. [mod.L *micella* dimin. of L *mica* crumb]

Mich. *abbr.* **1** Michaelmas. **2** Michigan.

Michaelmas /ˈmɪkəlməs/ *n.* the feast of St Michael,

29 September. □**Michaelmas daisy** an autumn-flowering aster. **Michaelmas term** *Brit.* (in some universities) the autumn term. [OE *sancte Micheles mæsse* Saint Michael's mass: see MASS²]

mick /mɪk/ *n. sl. offens.* **1** an Irishman. **2** a Roman Catholic. [pet-form of the name *Michael*]

mickey /ˈmɪkɪ/ *n.* (also **micky**) □**take the mickey** (often foll. by *out of*) *sl.* tease, mock, ridicule. [20th c.: orig. uncert.]

Mickey Finn /ˌmɪkɪ ˈfɪn/ *n. sl.* **1** a strong alcoholic drink, esp. adulterated with a narcotic or laxative. **2** the adulterant itself. [20th c.: orig. uncert.]

mickle /ˈmɪk(ə)l/ *adj. & n.* (also **muckle** /ˈmʌk(ə)l/) *archaic* or *Sc.* —*adj.* much, great. —*n.* a large amount. □**many a little makes a mickle** (orig. *erron.* **many a mickle makes a muckle**) many small amounts accumulate to make a large amount. [ME f. ON *mikell* f. Gmc]

micky var. of MICKEY.

micro /ˈmaɪkrəʊ/ *n.* (*pl.* **-os**) *colloq.* **1** = MICRO-COMPUTER. **2** = MICROPROCESSOR.

micro- /ˈmaɪkrəʊ/ *comb. form* **1** small (*microchip*). **2** denoting a factor of one millionth (10^{-6}) (*microgram*). ¶ *Symb.*: μ. [Gk *mikro-* f. *mikros* small]

microanalysis /ˌmaɪkrəʊəˈnælɪsɪs/ *n.* the quantitative analysis of chemical compounds using a sample of a few milligrams.

microbe /ˈmaɪkrəʊb/ *n.* a minute living being; a micro-organism (esp. bacteria causing disease and fermentation). □□ **microbial** /-ˈkrəʊbɪəl/ *adj.* **microbic** /-ˈkrəʊbɪk/ *adj.* [F f. Gk *mikros* small + *bios* life]

microbiology /ˌmaɪkrəʊbaɪˈɒlədʒɪ/ *n.* the scientific study of micro-organisms, e.g. bacteria, viruses, and fungi. □□ **microbiological** /-ˌbaɪəˈlɒdʒɪk(ə)l/ *adj.* **microbiologically** /-ˌbaɪəˈlɒdʒɪkəlɪ/ *adv.* **microbiologist** *n.*

microburst /ˈmaɪkrəʊˌbɜːst/ *n.* a particularly violent wind shear, esp. during a thunderstorm.

microcephaly /ˌmaɪkrəʊˈsefəlɪ/ *n.* an abnormal smallness of the head in relation to the rest of the body. □□ **microcephalic** /-sɪˈfælɪk/ *adj. & n.* **microcephalous** /-ˈsefələs/ *adj.*

microchip /ˈmaɪkrəʊtʃɪp/ *n.* a small piece of semiconductor (usu. silicon) used to carry electronic circuits.

microcircuit /ˈmaɪkrəʊˌsɜːkɪt/ *n.* an integrated circuit on a microchip. □□ **microcircuitry** *n.*

microclimate /ˈmaɪkrəʊˌklaɪmɪt/ *n.* the climate of a small local area, e.g. inside a greenhouse. □□ **microclimatic** /-ˈmætɪk/ *adj.* **microclimatically** /-ˈmætɪkəlɪ/ *adv.*

microcode /ˈmaɪkrəʊˌkəʊd/ *n.* **1** = MICRO-INSTRUCTION. **2** = MICROPROGRAM.

microcomputer /ˈmaɪkrəʊkəmˌpjuːtə(r)/ *n.* a small computer that contains a microprocessor as its central processor.

microcopy /ˈmaɪkrəʊˌkɒpɪ/ *n. & v.* —*n.* (*pl.* **-ies**) a copy of printed matter that has been reduced by microphotography. —*v.tr.* (**-ies**, **-ied**) make a microcopy of.

microcosm /ˈmaɪkrəˌkɒz(ə)m/ *n.* **1** (often foll. by *of*) a miniature representation. **2** mankind viewed as the epitome of the universe. **3** any community or complex unity viewed in this way. □□ **microcosmic** /-ˈkɒzmɪk/ *adj.* **microcosmically** /-ˈkɒzmɪkəlɪ/ *adv.* [ME f. F *microcosme* or med.L *microcosmus* f. Gk *mikros kosmos* little world]

microdot /ˈmaɪkrəʊˌdɒt/ *n.* a microphotograph of a document etc. reduced to the size of a dot.

micro-economics /ˌmaɪkrəʊˌiːkəˈnɒmɪks/ *n.* the branch of economics dealing with individual commodities, producers, etc.

micro-electronics /ˌmaɪkrəʊɪlekˈtrɒnɪks/ *n.* the design, manufacture, and use of microchips and microcircuits.

microfiche /ˈmaɪkrəʊˌfiːʃ/ *n.* (*pl.* same or **microfiches**) a flat rectangular piece of film bearing microphotographs of the pages of a printed text or document.

microfilm /'maɪkrəʊfɪlm/ *n. & v.* —*n.* a length of film bearing microphotographs of documents etc. —*v.tr.* photograph (a document etc.) on microfilm.

microfloppy /'maɪkrəʊ,flɒpɪ/ *n.* (*pl.* -**ies**) (in full **microfloppy disk**) *Computing* a floppy disk with a diameter of less than 5¼ inches (usu. 3½ inches).

microform /'maɪkrəʊ,fɔːm/ *n.* microphotographic reproduction on film or paper of a manuscript etc.

microgram /'maɪkrəʊ,græm/ *n.* one-millionth of a gram.

micrograph /'maɪkrəʊ,grɑːf/ *n.* a photograph taken by means of a microscope.

microgroove /'maɪkrəʊ,gruːv/ *n.* a very narrow groove on a long-playing gramophone record.

microinstruction /,maɪkrəʊɪn'strʌkʃ(ə)n/ *n.* a machine-code instruction that effects a basic operation in a computer system.

microlight /'maɪkrəʊ,laɪt/ *n.* a kind of motorized hang-glider.

microlith /'maɪkrəʊlɪθ/ *n. Archaeol.* a minute worked flint usu. as part of a composite tool. □□ **microlithic** /-'lɪθɪk/ *adj.*

micromesh /'maɪkrəʊ,meʃ/ *n.* (often *attrib.*) material, esp. nylon, consisting of a very fine mesh.

micrometer /maɪ'krɒmɪtə(r)/ *n.* a gauge for accurately measuring small distances, thicknesses, etc. □□ **micrometry** *n.*

micrometre /'maɪkrəʊ,miːtə(r)/ *n.* one-millionth of a metre.

microminiaturization /,maɪkrəʊ,mɪnɪtʃəraɪ'zeɪʃ(ə)n/ *n.* (also -**isation**) the manufacture of very small electronic devices by using integrated circuits.

micron /'maɪkrɒn/ *n.* one-millionth of a metre. [Gk *mikron* neut. of *mikros* small: cf. MICRO-]

Micronesian /,maɪkrə'niːʒ(ə)n/ *adj. & n.* —*adj.* of or relating to Micronesia, an island-group in the W. Pacific. —*n.* a native of Micronesia. [*Micronesia*, formed as MICRO- + Gk *nēsos* island]

micro-organism /,maɪkrəʊ'ɔːgə,nɪz(ə)m/ *n.* any of various microscopic organisms, including algae, bacteria, fungi, protozoa, and viruses.

microphone /'maɪkrə,fəʊn/ *n.* an instrument for converting sound waves into electrical energy variations which may be reconverted into sound after transmission by wire or radio or after recording. □□ **microphonic** /-'fɒnɪk/ *adj.*

microphotograph /,maɪkrəʊ'fəʊtə,grɑːf/ *n.* a photograph reduced to a very small size.

microphyte /'maɪkrəʊ,faɪt/ *n.* a microscopic plant.

microprocessor /,maɪkrəʊ'prəʊsesə(r)/ *n.* an integrated circuit that contains all the functions of a central processing unit of a computer.

microprogram /,maɪkrəʊ'prəʊgræm/ *n.* a microinstruction program that controls the functions of a central processing unit of a computer.

micropyle /'maɪkrəʊ,paɪl/ *n. Bot.* a small opening in the surface of an ovule, through which pollen passes. [MICRO- + Gk *pulē* gate]

microscope /'maɪkrə,skəʊp/ *n.* an instrument magnifying small objects by means of a lens or lenses so as to reveal details invisible to the naked eye. [mod.L *microscopium* (as MICRO-, -SCOPE)]

microscopic /,maɪkrə'skɒpɪk/ *adj.* **1** so small as to be visible only with a microscope. **2** extremely small. **3** regarded in terms of small units. **4** of the microscope. □□ **microscopical** *adj.* (in sense 4). **microscopically** *adv.*

microscopy /maɪ'krɒskəpɪ/ *n.* the use of the microscope. □□ **microscopist** *n.*

microsecond /'maɪkrəʊ,sekənd/ *n.* one-millionth of a second.

Microsoft /'maɪkrəʊ,sɒft/ *n. propr.* an operating system for microcomputers. [the name of the developing company]

microsome /'maɪkrəʊ,səʊm/ *n. Biol.* a small particle

of organelle fragments obtained by centrifugation of homogenized cells. [MICRO- + -SOME³]

microspore /'maɪkrəʊ,spɔː(r)/ *n.* the smaller of the two kinds of spore produced by some ferns.

microstructure /'maɪkrəʊ,strʌktʃə(r)/ *n.* (in a metal or other material) the arrangement of crystals etc. which can be made visible and examined with a microscope.

microsurgery /'maɪkrəʊ,sɜːdʒərɪ/ *n.* intricate surgery performed using microscopes, enabling the tissue to be operated on with miniaturized precision instruments. □□ **microsurgical** /-'sɜːdʒɪk(ə)l/ *adj.*

microswitch /'maɪkrəʊswɪtʃ/ *n.* a switch that can be operated rapidly by a small movement.

microtome /'maɪkrəʊ,təʊm/ *n.* an instrument for cutting extremely thin sections of material for examination under a microscope. [MICRO- + -TOME]

microtone /'maɪkrəʊ,təʊn/ *n. Mus.* an interval smaller than a semitone.

microtubule /,maɪkrəʊ'tjuːbjuːl/ *n. Biol.* a minute protein filament occurring in cytoplasm and involved in forming the spindles during cell division etc.

microwave /'maɪkrəʊ,weɪv/ *n.* **1** an electromagnetic wave with a wavelength in the range 0.001–0.3m. **2** (in full **microwave oven**) an oven that uses microwaves to cook or heat food quickly.

micrurgy /'maɪkrɜːdʒɪ/ *n.* the manipulation of individual cells etc. under a microscope. [MICRO- + Gk *-ourgia* work]

micturition /,mɪktjʊə'rɪʃ(ə)n/ *n. formal* urination. [L *micturire micturit-*, desiderative f. *mingere micturinate*]

mid¹ /mɪd/ *attrib.adj.* **1** (usu. in *comb.*) that is the middle of (*in mid-air; from mid-June to mid-July*). **2** that is in the middle; medium, half. **3** *Phonet.* (of a vowel) pronounced with the tongue neither high nor low. [OE *midd* (recorded only in oblique cases), rel. to L *medius*, Gk *mesos*]

mid² /mɪd/ *prep. poet.* = AMID. [abbr. f. AMID]

Midas touch /'maɪdəs/ *n.* the ability to turn one's activities to financial advantage. [*Midas*, king of Phrygia, whose touch was said to turn all things to gold]

midbrain /'mɪdbreɪn/ *n.* the part of the brain developing from the middle of the primitive or embryonic brain.

midday /'mɪddeɪ/ *n.* the middle of the day; noon. [OE *middæg* (as MID¹, DAY)]

midden /'mɪd(ə)n/ *n.* **1** a dunghill. **2** a refuse heap near a dwelling. **3** = *kitchen midden*. [ME *myddyng*, of Scand. orig.: cf. Da. *mødding* muck heap]

middle /'mɪd(ə)l/ *adj., n., & v.* —*attrib.adj.* **1** at an equal distance from the extremities of a thing. **2** (of a member of a group) so placed as to have the same number of members on each side. **3** intermediate in rank, quality, etc. **4** average (*of middle height*). **5** (of a language) of the period between the old and modern forms. **6** *Gram.* designating the voice of (esp. Greek) verbs that expresses reciprocal or reflexive action. —*n.* **1** (often foll. by *of*) the middle point or position or part. **2** a person's waist. **3** *Gram.* the middle form or voice of a verb. **4** = *middle term.* —*v.tr.* **1** place in the middle. **2** *Football* return (the ball) from the wing to the midfield. **3** *Cricket* strike (the ball) with the middle of the bat. **4** *Naut.* fold in the middle. □ **in the middle of** (often foll. by *verbal noun*) in the process of; during. **middle age** the period between youth and old age, about 45 to 60. **middle-aged** in middle age. **the Middle Ages** the period of European history from the fall of the Roman Empire in the West (5th c.) to the fall of Constantinople (1453), or more narrowly from *c.*1000 to 1453. **middle-age** (or **-aged**) **spread** the increased bodily girth often associated with middle age. **Middle America 1** Mexico and Central America. **2** the middle class in the US, esp. as a conservative political force. **middle C** *Mus.* the C near the middle of the piano keyboard, the note between the treble and bass staves, at about

260 Hz. **middle class** the class of society between the upper and the lower, including professional and business workers and their families. **middle-class** *adj.* of the middle class. **middle common room** *Brit.* a common room for the use of graduate members of a college who are not Fellows. **middle course** a compromise between two extremes. **middle distance 1** (in a painted or actual landscape) the part between the foreground and the background. **2** *Athletics* a race distance of esp. 400 or 800 metres. **middle ear** the cavity of the central part of the ear behind the drum. **the Middle East** the area covered by countries from Egypt to Iran inclusive. **Middle Eastern** of or in the Middle East. **Middle English** the English language from *c.*1150 to 1500. **middle finger** the finger next to the forefinger. **middle game** the central phase of a chess game, when strategies are developed. **middle name 1** a person's name placed after the first name and before the surname. **2** a person's most characteristic quality (*sobriety is my middle name*). **middle-of-the-road** (of a person, course of action, etc.) moderate; avoiding extremes. **middle passage** the sea journey between W. Africa and the W. Indies (with ref. to the slave trade). **middle school** *Brit.* a school for children from about 9 to 13 years old. **middle-sized** of medium size. **Middle Temple** one of the two Inns of Court on the site of the Temple in London (cf. *Inner Temple*). **middle term** *Logic* the term common to both premisses of a syllogism. **middle watch** the watch from midnight to 4 a.m. **middle way 1** = *middle course*. **2** the eightfold path of Buddhism between indulgence and asceticism. **Middle West** (in the US) the region adjoining the northern Mississippi. [OE *middel* f. Gmc]

middlebrow /ˈmɪd(ə)lˌbraʊ/ *adj. & n. colloq.* —*adj.* claiming to be or regarded as only moderately intellectual. —*n.* a middlebrow person.

middleman /ˈmɪd(ə)lˌmæn/ *n.* (*pl.* **-men**) **1** any of the traders who handle a commodity between its producer and its consumer. **2** an intermediary.

middleweight /ˈmɪd(ə)lˌweɪt/ *n.* **1** a weight in certain sports intermediate between welterweight and light heavyweight, in the amateur boxing scale 71-5 kg but differing for professionals, wrestlers, and weightlifters. **2** a sportsman of this weight. □**junior middleweight 1** a weight in professional boxing of 66.7-69.8 kg. **2** a professional boxer of this weight. **light middleweight 1** a weight in amateur boxing of 67-71 kg. **2** an amateur boxer of this weight.

middling /ˈmɪdlɪŋ/ *adj., n., & adv.* —*adj.* **1 a** moderately good (esp. *fair to middling*). **b** *colloq.* (of a person's health) fairly well. **c** second-rate. **2** (of goods) of the second of three grades. —*n.* (in *pl.*) middling goods, esp. flour of medium fineness. —*adv.* fairly or moderately (*middling good*). □□ **middlingly** *adv.* [ME, of Sc. orig.: prob. f. MID¹ + -LING²]

Middx. *abbr.* Middlesex.

middy¹ /ˈmɪdɪ/ *n.* (*pl.* **-ies**) **1** *colloq.* a midshipman. **2** (in full **middy blouse**) a woman's or child's loose blouse with a collar like that worn by sailors.

middy² /ˈmɪdɪ/ *n.* (*pl.* **-ies**) *Austral. sl.* a measure of beer of varying size. [20th c.: orig. unkn.]

Mideast /ˈmɪdiːst/ *n.* *US* = *Middle East.*

midfield /ˈmɪdfiːld/ *n.* *Football* the central part of the pitch, away from the goals. □□ **midfielder** *n.*

midge /mɪdʒ/ *n.* **1** *colloq.* **a** a gnatlike insect. **b** a small person. **2 a** any dipterous non-biting insect of the family *Chironomidae*. **b** any similar insect of the family *Ceratopogonidae* with piercing mouthparts for sucking blood or eating smaller insects. [OE *mycg(e)* f. Gmc]

midget /ˈmɪdʒɪt/ *n.* **1** an extremely small person or thing. **2** (*attrib.*) very small. [MIDGE + -ET¹]

midgut /ˈmɪdɡʌt/ *n.* the middle part of the alimentary canal, including the small intestine.

midi /ˈmɪdɪ/ *n.* (*pl.* **midis**) a garment of medium length, usu. reaching to mid-calf. [MID¹ after MINI]

midibus /ˈmɪdɪˌbʌs/ *n.* a bus seating up to about 25 passengers.

midinette /ˌmɪdɪˈnet/ *n.* a Parisian shop-girl, esp. a milliner's assistant. [F f. *midi* midday + *dinette* light dinner]

midiron /ˈmɪdˌaɪən/ *n.* *Golf* an iron giving medium lift.

midland /ˈmɪdlənd/ *n. & adj.* —*n.* **1** (**the Midlands**) the inland counties of central England. **2** the middle part of a country. —*adj.* **1** of or in the midland or Midlands. **2** Mediterranean. □□ **midlander** *n.*

mid-life /ˈmɪdlaɪf/ *n.* middle age. □**mid-life crisis** an emotional crisis of self-confidence that can occur in early middle age.

midline /ˈmɪdlaɪn/ *n.* a median line, or plane of bilateral symmetry.

midmost /ˈmɪdməʊst/ *adj. & adv.* in the very middle.

midnight /ˈmɪdnaɪt/ *n.* **1** the middle of the night; 12 o'clock at night. **2** intense darkness. □**midnight blue** a very dark blue. **midnight sun** the sun visible at midnight during the summer in polar regions. [OE *midniht* (as MID¹, NIGHT)]

mid-off /mɪdˈɒf/ *n.* *Cricket* the position of the fielder near the bowler on the off side.

mid-on /mɪdˈɒn/ *n.* *Cricket* the position of the fielder near the bowler on the on side.

Midrash /ˈmɪdræʃ/ *n.* (*pl.* **Midrashim** /-ˈʃɪm/) an ancient commentary on part of the Hebrew scriptures. [Bibl. Heb. *miḏrāš* commentary]

midrib /ˈmɪdrɪb/ *n.* the central rib of a leaf.

midriff /ˈmɪdrɪf/ *n.* **1 a** the region of the front of the body between the thorax and abdomen. **b** the diaphragm. **2** a garment or part of a garment covering the abdomen. [OE *midhrif* (as MID¹,· *hrif* belly)]

midship /ˈmɪdʃɪp/ *n.* the middle part of a ship or boat.

midshipman /ˈmɪdʃɪpmən/ *n.* (*pl.* **-men**) **1** *Brit.* a naval officer of rank between naval cadet and sub-lieutenant. **2** *US* a naval cadet.

midships /ˈmɪdʃɪps/ *adv.* = AMIDSHIPS.

midst /mɪdst/ *prep. & n.* —*prep. poet.* amidst. —*n.* middle (now only in phrases as below). □**in the midst of** among; in the middle of. **in our** (or **your** or **their**) **midst** among us (or you or them). [ME *middest, middes* f. *in middes*, f. *in middan* (as IN, MID¹)]

midsummer /mɪdˈsʌmə(r), ˈmɪd-/ *n.* the period of or near the summer solstice, about 21 June. □**Midsummer** (or **Midsummer's**) **Day** 24 June. **midsummer madness** extreme folly. [OE *midsumor* (as MID¹, SUMMER¹)]

midtown /ˈmɪdtaʊn/ *n.* *US* the central part of a city between the downtown and uptown areas.

midway /ˈmɪdweɪ/ *adv.* in or towards the middle of the distance between two points.

Midwest /mɪdˈwest/ *n.* = *Middle West.*

midwicket /mɪdˈwɪkɪt/ *n.* *Cricket* the position of a fielder on the leg side opposite the middle of the pitch.

midwife /ˈmɪdwaɪf/ *n.* (*pl.* **-wives** /-waɪvz/) a person (usu. a woman) trained to assist women in childbirth. □□ **midwifery** /-ˌwɪfrɪ/ *n.* [ME, prob. f. obs. prep. *mid* with + WIFE woman, in the sense of 'one who is with the mother']

midwinter /mɪdˈwɪntə(r)/ *n.* the period of or near the winter solstice, about 22 Dec. [OE (as MID¹, WINTER)]

mielie var. of MEALIE.

mien /miːn/ *n.* *literary* a person's look or bearing, as showing character or mood. [prob. f. obs. *demean* f. DEMEAN²,· assim. to F *mine* expression]

miff /mɪf/ *v. & n. colloq.* —*v.tr.* (usu. in *passive*) put out of humour; offend. —*n.* **1** a petty quarrel. **2** a huff. [perh. imit.: cf. G *muff*, exclam. of disgust]

might¹ /maɪt/ *past* of MAY, used esp.: **1** in reported speech, expressing possibility (*said he might come*) or permission (*asked if I might leave*) (cf. MAY 1, 2). **2** (foll. by perfect infin.) expressing a possibility based on a condition not fulfilled (*if you'd looked you might have found it*; *but for the radio we might not have known*). **3** (foll. by present infin. or perfect infin.) expressing complaint that an obligation or expectation is not or has not been fulfilled (*he might offer to help*; *they might have asked*; *you might have known they wouldn't come*). **4** expressing a request (*you might call in at the butcher's*). **5** *colloq.* **a** = MAY 1 (*it might be true*). **b** (in tentative questions) = MAY 2 (*might I have the pleasure of this dance?*). **c** = MAY 4 (*who might you be?*). □**might as well** expressing that it is probably at least as desirable to do a thing as not to do it (*finished the work and decided they might as well go to lunch*; *won't win but might as well try*). **might-have-been** *colloq.* **1** a past possibility that no longer applies. **2** a person who could have been more eminent.

might² /maɪt/ *n.* **1** great bodily or mental strength. **2** power to enforce one's will (usu. in contrast with *right*). □**with all one's might** to the utmost of one's power. **with might and main** see MAIN¹. [OE *miht*, *mieht* f. Gmc, rel. to MAY¹]

mightn't /'maɪt(ə)nt/ *contr.* might not.

mighty /'maɪtɪ/ *adj.* & *adv.* —*adj.* (**mightier**, **mightiest**) **1** powerful or strong, in body, mind, or influence. **2** massive, bulky. **3** *colloq.* great, considerable. —*adv.* *colloq.* very (*a mighty difficult task*). □□**mightily** *adv.* **mightiness** *n.* [OE *mihtig* (as MIGHT²)]

mignonette /ˌmɪnjə'net/ *n.* **1 a** any of various plants of the genus *Reseda*, esp. *R. odorata*, with fragrant grey-green flowers. **b** the colour of these. **2** a light fine narrow pillow-lace. [F *mignonnette* dimin. of *mignon* small]

migraine /'miːɡreɪn, 'maɪ-/ *n.* a recurrent throbbing headache that usually affects one side of the head, often accompanied by nausea and disturbance of vision. □□**migrainous** *adj.* [F f. LL *hemicrania* f. Gk *hēmikrania* (as HEMI-, CRANIUM): orig. of a headache confined to one side of the head]

migrant /'maɪɡrənt/ *adj.* & *n.* —*adj.* that migrates. —*n.* a migrant person or animal, esp. a bird.

migrate /maɪ'ɡreɪt/ *v.intr.* **1** (of people) move from one place of abode to another, esp. in a different country. **2** (of a bird or fish) change its area of habitation with the seasons. **3** move under natural forces. □□**migration** /-'ɡreɪʃ(ə)n/ *n.* **migrational** /-'ɡreɪʃ(ə)l/ *adj.* **migrator** *n.* **migratory** *adj.* [L *migrare migrat-*]

mihrab /'miːrɑːb/ *n.* a niche or slab in a mosque, used to show the direction of Mecca. [Arab. *miḥrāb* praying-place]

mikado /mɪ'kɑːdəʊ/ *n.* (*pl.* **-os**) *hist.* the emperor of Japan. [Jap. f. *mi* august + *kado* door]

Mike /maɪk/ *n.* *sl.* □**for the love of Mike** an exclamation of entreaty or dismay. [abbr. of the name *Michael*]

mike¹ /maɪk/ *n.* *colloq.* a microphone. [abbr.]

mike² /maɪk/ *v.* & *n.* *Brit.* *sl.* —*v.intr.* shirk work; idle. —*n.* an act of shirking. [19th c.: orig. unkn.]

mil /mɪl/ *n.* one-thousandth of an inch, as a unit of measure for the diameter of wire etc. [L *millesimum* thousandth f. *mille* thousand]

milady /mɪ'leɪdɪ/ *n.* (*pl.* **-ies**) **1** an English noblewoman or great lady. **2** a form used in speaking of or to such a person. [F f. E *my lady*: cf. MILORD]

milage var. of MILEAGE.

Milanese /ˌmɪlə'niːz/ *adj.* & *n.* —*adj.* of or relating to Milan in N. Italy. —*n.* (*pl.* same) a native of Milan. □**Milanese silk** a finely woven silk or rayon.

milch /mɪltʃ/ *adj.* (of a domestic mammal) giving or kept for milk. □**milch cow** a source of easy profit, esp. a person. [ME *m(i)elche* repr. OE *mielce* (unrecorded) f. Gmc: see MILK]

mild /maɪld/ *adj.* **1** (esp. of a person) gentle and conciliatory. **2** (of a rule, punishment, illness, feeling, etc.) moderate; not severe. **3** (of the weather, esp. in winter) moderately warm. **4 a** (of food, tobacco, etc.)

not sharp or strong in taste etc. **b** *Brit.* (of beer) not strongly flavoured with hops (cf. BITTER). **5** (of medicine) operating gently. **6** tame, feeble; lacking energy or vivacity. □**mild steel** steel containing a small percentage of carbon, strong and tough but not readily tempered. □□**milden** *v.tr.* & *intr.* **mildish** *adj.* **mildness** *n.* [OE *milde* f. Gmc]

mildew /'mɪldjuː/ *n.* & *v.* —*n.* **1** a destructive growth of minute fungi on plants. **2** a similar growth on paper, leather, etc. exposed to damp. —*v.tr.* & *intr.* taint or be tainted with mildew. □□**mildewy** *adj.* [OE *mildēaw* f. Gmc]

mildly /'maɪldlɪ/ *adv.* in a mild fashion. □**to put it mildly** as an understatement (implying the reality is more extreme).

mile /maɪl/ *n.* **1** (also **statute mile**) a unit of linear measure equal to 1,760 yards (approx. 1.609 kilometres). **2** *hist.* a Roman measure of 1,000 paces (approx. 1,620 yards). **3** (in *pl.*) *colloq.* a great distance or amount (*miles better*; *beat them by miles*). **4** a race extending over a mile. [OE *mīl* ult. f. L *mil(l)ia* pl. of *mille* thousand (see sense 2)]

mileage /'maɪlɪdʒ/ *n.* (also **milage**) **1 a** a number of miles travelled, covered, etc. **b** the number of miles travelled by a vehicle per unit of fuel. **2** travelling expenses (per mile). **3** *colloq.* benefit, profit, advantage.

milepost /'maɪlpəʊst/ *n.* a post one mile from the finishing-post of a race etc.

miler /'maɪlə(r)/ *n.* *colloq.* a person or horse qualified or trained specially to run a mile.

milestone /'maɪlstəʊn/ *n.* **1** a stone set up beside a road to mark a distance in miles. **2** a significant event or stage in a life, history, project, etc.

milfoil /'mɪlfɔɪl/ *n.* the common yarrow, *Achillea millefolium*, with small white flowers and finely divided leaves. [ME f. OF f. L *millefolium* f. *mille* thousand + *folium* leaf, after Gk *muriophullon*]

miliary /'mɪlɪərɪ/ *adj.* **1** like a millet-seed in size or form. **2** (of a disease) having as a symptom a rash with lesions resembling millet-seed. [L *miliarius* f. *milium* millet]

milieu /mɪ'ljɜː, 'miːljɜː/ *n.* (*pl.* **milieux** or **milieus** /-ljɜːz/) one's environment or social surroundings. [F f. *mi* MID¹ + *lieu* place]

militant /'mɪlɪt(ə)nt/ *adj.* & *n.* —*adj.* **1** combative; aggressively active esp. in support of a (usu. political) cause. **2** engaged in warfare. —*n.* a militant person, esp. a political activist. □□**militancy** *n.* **militantly** *adv.* [ME f. OF f. L (as MILITATE)]

militarism /'mɪlɪtə‚rɪz(ə)m/ *n.* **1** the spirit or tendencies of a professional soldier. **2** undue prevalence of the military spirit or ideals. □□**militaristic** /-'rɪstɪk/ *adj.* **militaristically** /-'rɪstɪkəlɪ/ *adv.* [F *militarisme* (as MILITARY)]

militarist /'mɪlɪtərɪst/ *n.* **1** a person dominated by militaristic ideas. **2** a student of military science.

militarize /'mɪlɪtə‚raɪz/ *v.tr.* (also **-ise**) **1** equip with military resources. **2** make military or warlike. **3** imbue with militarism. □□**militarization** /-'zeɪʃ(ə)n/ *n.*

military /'mɪlɪtərɪ/ *adj.* & *n.* —*adj.* of, relating to, or characteristic of soldiers or armed forces. —*n.* (as *sing.* or *pl.*; prec. by *the*) members of the armed forces, as distinct from civilians and the police. □**military honours** marks of respect paid by troops at the burial of a soldier, to royalty, etc. **military police** a corps responsible for police and disciplinary duties in the army. **military policeman** a member of the military police. □□**militarily** *adv.* **militariness** *n.* [F *militaire* or L *militaris* f. *miles militis* soldier]

militate /'mɪlɪ‚teɪt/ *v.intr.* (usu. foll. by *against*) (of facts or evidence) have force or effect (*what you say militates against our opinion*). ¶ Often confused with *mitigate*. [L *militare militat-* f. *miles militis* soldier]

militia /mɪ'lɪʃə/ *n.* a military force, esp. one raised from the civil population and supplementing a regular army in an emergency. [L, = military service f. *miles militis* soldier]

militiaman /mɪˈlɪʃəmən/ *n.* (*pl.* **-men**) a member of a militia.

milk /mɪlk/ *n.* & *v.* —*n.* **1** an opaque white fluid secreted by female mammals for the nourishment of their young. **2** the milk of cows, goats, or sheep as food. **3** the milklike juice of plants, e.g. in the coconut. **4** a milklike preparation of herbs, drugs, etc. —*v.tr.* **1** draw milk from (a cow, ewe, goat, etc.). **2 a** exploit (a person) esp. financially. **b** get all possible advantage from (a situation). **3** extract sap, venom, etc. from. **4** *sl.* tap (telegraph or telephone wires etc.). □**cry over spilt milk** lament an irremediable loss or error. **in milk** secreting milk. **milk and honey** abundant means of prosperity. **milk and water** a feeble or insipid or mawkish discourse or sentiment. **milk bar** a snack bar selling milk drinks and other refreshments. **milk chocolate** chocolate for eating, made with milk. **milk float** *Brit.* a small usu. electric vehicle used in delivering milk. **milk-leg** a painful swelling, esp. of the legs, after childbirth. **milk-loaf** a loaf of bread made with milk. **milk of human kindness** kindness regarded as natural to humanity. **Milk of Magnesia** *Brit. propr.* a white suspension of magnesium hydroxide usu. in water as an antacid or laxative. **milk of sulphur** the amorphous powder of sulphur formed by precipitation. **milk-powder** milk dehydrated by evaporation. **milk pudding** a pudding of rice, sago, tapioca, etc., baked with milk in a dish. **milk round 1** a fixed route on which milk is delivered regularly. **2** a regular trip or tour involving calls at several places. **milk run** a routine expedition or service journey. **milk shake** a drink of milk, flavouring, etc., mixed by shaking or whisking. **milk sugar** lactose. **milk tooth** a temporary tooth in young mammals. **milk-vetch** any leguminous yellow-flowered plant of the genus *Astragalus*. **milk-white** white like milk. □□ **milker** *n.* [OE *milc, milcian* f. Gmc]

milkmaid /ˈmɪlkmeɪd/ *n.* a girl or woman who milks cows or works in a dairy.

milkman /ˈmɪlkmən/ *n.* (*pl.* **-men**) a person who sells or delivers milk.

milksop /ˈmɪlksɒp/ *n.* a spiritless man or youth.

milkweed /ˈmɪlkwiːd/ *n.* any of various wild plants with milky juice.

milkwort /ˈmɪlkwɜːt/ *n.* any plant of the genus *Polygala*, formerly supposed to increase women's milk.

milky /ˈmɪlkɪ/ *adj.* (**milkier, milkiest**) **1** of, like, or mixed with milk. **2** (of a gem or liquid) cloudy; not clear. **3** effeminate; weakly amiable. □**Milky Way** a faintly luminous band of light emitted by countless stars encircling the heavens; the Galaxy. □□ **milkiness** *n.*

mill¹ /mɪl/ *n.* & *v.* —*n.* **1 a** a building fitted with a mechanical apparatus for grinding corn. **b** such an apparatus. **2** an apparatus for grinding any solid substance to powder or pulp (*pepper-mill*). **3 a** a building fitted with machinery for manufacturing processes etc. (*cotton-mill*). **b** such machinery. **4 a** a boxing-match. **b** a fist fight. —*v.* **1** *tr.* grind (corn), produce (flour), or hull (seeds) in a mill. **2** *tr.* produce regular ribbed markings on the edge of (a coin). **3** *tr.* cut or shape (metal) with a rotating tool. **4** *intr.* (often foll. by *about, around*) (of people or animals) move in an aimless manner, esp. in a confused mass. **5** *tr.* thicken (cloth etc.) by fulling. **6** *tr.* beat (chocolate etc.) to froth. **7** *tr. sl.* beat, strike, fight. □**go** (or **put**) **through the mill** undergo (or cause to undergo) intensive work or training etc. **mill-dam** a dam put across a stream to make it usable by a mill. **mill-hand** a worker in a mill or factory. **mill-race** a current of water that drives a mill-wheel. **mill-wheel** a wheel used to drive a water-mill. □□

millable *adj.* [OE *mylen* ult. f. LL *molinum* f. L *mola* grindstone, mill f. *molere* grind]

mill² /mɪl/ *n.* *US* one-thousandth of a dollar as money of account. [L *millesimum* thousandth: cf. CENT]

millboard /ˈmɪlbɔːd/ *n.* stout pasteboard for bookbinding etc.

millefeuille /miːlˈfɜːj/ *n.* a rich confection of puff pastry split and filled with jam, cream, etc. [F, = thousand-leaf]

millenarian /ˌmɪlɪˈneərɪən/ *adj.* & *n.* —*adj.* **1** of or related to the millennium. **2** believing in the millennium. —*n.* a person who believes in the millennium. [as MILLENARY]

millenary /mɪˈlenərɪ/ *n.* & *adj.* —*n.* (*pl.* **-ies**) **1** a period of 1,000 years. **2** the festival of the 1,000th anniversary of a person or thing. **3** a person who believes in the millennium. —*adj.* of or relating to a millenary. [LL *millenarius* consisting of a thousand f. *milleni* distrib. of *mille* thousand]

millennium /mɪˈlenɪəm/ *n.* (*pl.* **millenniums** or **millennia** /-nɪə/) **1** a period of 1,000 years, esp. that of Christ's prophesied reign in person on earth (Rev. 20:1-5). **2** a period of good government, great happiness, and prosperity. □□ **millennial** *adj.* **millennialist** *n.* & *adj.* [mod.L f. L *mille* thousand after BIENNIUM]

millepede var. of MILLIPEDE.

millepore /ˈmɪlɪpɔː(r)/ *n.* a reef-building coral of the order Milleporina, with polyps protruding through pores in the calcareous exoskeleton. [F *millépore* or mod.L *millepora* f. L *mille* thousand + *porus* PORE¹]

miller /ˈmɪlə(r)/ *n.* **1** the proprietor or tenant of a corn-mill. **2** a person who works or owns a mill. □**miller's thumb** a small spiny freshwater fish, *Cottus gobio*: also called BULLHEAD. [ME *mylnere*, prob. f. MLG, MDu. *molner, mulner*, OS *mulineri* f. LL *molinarius* f. *molina* MILL¹,· assim. to MILL¹]

millesimal /mɪˈlesɪm(ə)l/ *adj.* & *n.* —*adj.* **1** thousandth. **2** of or belonging to a thousandth. **3** of or dealing with thousandths. —*n.* a thousandth part. □□ **millesimally** *adv.* [L *millesimus* f. *mille* thousand]

millet /ˈmɪlɪt/ *n.* **1** any of various cereal plants, esp. *Panicum miliaceum*, bearing a large crop of small nutritious seeds. **2** the seed of this. □**millet-grass** a tall woodland grass, *Milium effusum*. [ME f. F, dimin. of *mil* f. L *milium*]

milli- /ˈmɪlɪ/ *comb. form* a thousand, esp. denoting a factor of one thousandth. ¶ Abbr.: **m.** [L *mille* thousand]

milliammeter /ˌmɪlɪˈæmɪtə(r)/ *n.* an instrument for measuring electrical current in milliamperes.

milliampere /ˌmɪlɪˈæmpeə(r)/ *n.* one thousandth of an ampere, a measure for small electrical currents.

milliard /ˈmɪljəd, -jɑːd/ *n.* *Brit.* one thousand million. ¶ Now largely superseded by *billion*. [F f. *mille* thousand]

millibar /ˈmɪlɪbɑː(r)/ *n.* one-thousandth of a bar, the cgs unit of atmospheric pressure equivalent to 100 pascals.

milligram /ˈmɪlɪgræm/ *n.* one-thousandth of a gram.

millilitre /ˈmɪlɪliːtə(r)/ *n.* one-thousandth of a litre (0.002 pint).

millimetre /ˈmɪlɪmiːtə(r)/ *n.* one-thousandth of a metre (0.039 in.).

milliner /ˈmɪlɪnə(r)/ *n.* a person who makes or sells women's hats. □□ **millinery** *n.* [orig. = vendor of goods from *Milan*]

million /ˈmɪljən/ *n.* & *adj.* —*n.* (*pl.* same or (in sense 2) **millions**) (in *sing.* prec. by *a* or *one*) **1** a thousand thousand. **2** (in *pl.*) *colloq.* a very large number (*millions of years*). **3** (prec. by *the*) the bulk of the population. **4 a** *Brit.* a million pounds. **b** *US* a million dollars. —*adj.* that amount to a million. □**gone a million** *Austral. sl.* completely defeated. □□ **millionfold** *adj.* & *adv.* **millionth** *adj.* & *n.* [ME f. OF, prob. f. It. *millione* f. *mille* thousand + *-one* augment. suffix]

---

b *but* d *dog* f *few* ɡ *get* h *he* j *yes* k *cat* l *leg* m *man* n *no* p *pen* r *red* s *sit* t *top* v *voice*

millionaire /ˌmɪljəˈneə(r)/ n. (fem. **millionairess** /-rɪs/) **1** a person whose assets are worth at least one million pounds, dollars, etc. **2** a person of great wealth. [F millionnaire (as MILLION)]

millipede /ˈmɪlɪˌpiːd/ n. (also **millepede**) any arthropod of the class Diplopoda, having a long segmented body with two pairs of legs on each segment. [L millepeda wood-louse f. mille thousand + pes pedis foot]

millisecond /ˈmɪlɪˌsekənd/ n. one-thousandth of a second.

millpond /ˈmɪlpɒnd/ n. a pool of water retained by a mill-dam for the operation of a mill. □**like a millpond** (of a stretch of water) very calm.

Mills bomb /mɪlz/ n. an oval hand-grenade. [invented by Sir W. Mills d. 1932]

millstone /ˈmɪlstəʊn/ n. **1** each of two circular stones used for grinding corn. **2** a heavy burden or responsibility (cf. Matt. 18:6).

millwright /ˈmɪlraɪt/ n. a person who designs or builds mills.

milometer /maɪˈlɒmɪtə(r)/ n. an instrument for measuring the number of miles travelled by a vehicle.

milord /mɪˈlɔːd/ n. hist. an Englishman travelling in Europe in aristocratic style. [F f. E my lord: cf. MILADY]

milt /mɪlt/ n. **1** the spleen in mammals. **2** an analogous organ in other vertebrates. **3** a sperm-filled reproductive gland of a male fish. [OE milt(e) f. Gmc, perh. rel. to MELT]

milter /ˈmɪltə(r)/ n. a male fish in spawning-time.

mimbar /ˈmɪmbɑː(r)/ n. (also **minbar** /ˈmɪn-/) a stepped platform for preaching in a mosque. [Arab. minbar]

mime /maɪm/ n. & v. —n. **1** the theatrical technique of suggesting action, character, etc. by gesture and expression without using words. **2** a theatrical performance using this technique. **3** Gk & Rom. Antiq. a simple farcical drama including mimicry. **4** (also **mime artist**) a practitioner of mime. —v. **1** tr. (also absol.) convey (an idea or emotion) by gesture without words. **2** intr. (often foll. by to) (of singers etc.) mouth the words of a song etc. along with a soundtrack (mime to a record). □□ **mimer** n. [L mimus f. Gk mimos]

mimeograph /ˈmɪmɪəˌɡrɑːf/ n. & v. —n. **1** (often attrib.) a duplicating machine which produces copies from a stencil. **2** a copy produced in this way. —v.tr. reproduce (text or diagrams) by this process. [irreg. f. Gk mimeomai imitate: see -GRAPH]

mimesis /mɪˈmiːsɪs, maɪ-/ n. Biol. a close external resemblance of an animal to another that is distasteful or harmful to predators of the first. [Gk mimēsis imitation]

mimetic /mɪˈmetɪk/ adj. **1** relating to or habitually practising imitation or mimicry. **2** Biol. of or exhibiting mimesis. □□ **mimetically** adv. [Gk mimētikos imitation (as MIMESIS)]

mimic /ˈmɪmɪk/ v., n., & adj. —v.tr. (**mimicked**, **mimicking**) **1** imitate (a person, gesture, etc.) esp. to entertain or ridicule. **2** copy minutely or servilely. **3** (of a thing) resemble closely. —n. a person skilled in imitation. —adj. having an aptitude for mimicry; imitating; imitative, esp. for amusement. □□ **mimicker** n. [L mimicus f. Gk mimikos (as MIME)]

mimicry /ˈmɪmɪkrɪ/ n. (pl. -**ies**) **1** the act or art of mimicking. **2** a thing that mimics another. **3** Zool. mimesis.

miminy-piminy /ˌmɪmɪnɪ ˈpɪmɪnɪ/ adj. overrefined, finical (cf. NIMINY-PIMINY & NAMBY-PAMBY). [imit.]

mimosa /mɪˈməʊzə/ n. **1** any leguminous shrub of the genus Mimosa, esp. M. pudica, having globular usu. yellow flowers and sensitive leaflets which droop when touched. **2** any of various acacia plants with showy yellow flowers. [mod.L, app. f. L (as

MIME, from being as sensitive as animals) + -osa fem. suffix]

mimulus /ˈmɪmjʊləs/ n. any flowering plant of the genus Mimulus, including musk and the monkey flower. [mod.L, app. dimin. of L (as MIME, perh. with ref. to its masklike flowers)]

Min /mɪn/ n. any of the Chinese languages or dialects spoken in the Fukien province in SE China. [Chin.]

Min. abbr. **1** Minister. **2** Ministry.

min. abbr. **1** minute(s). **2** minimum. **3** minim (fluid measure).

mina var. of MYNA.

minaret /ˌmɪnəˈret/ n. a slender turret connected with a mosque and having a balcony from which the muezzin calls at hours of prayer. □□ **minareted** adj. [F minaret or Sp. minarete f. Turk. minare f. Arab. manār(a) lighthouse, minaret f. nār fire, light]

minatory /ˈmɪnətərɪ/ adj. threatening, menacing. [LL minatorius f. minari minat- threaten]

minbar var. of MIMBAR.

mince /mɪns/ v. & n. —v. **1** tr. cut up or grind (esp. meat) into very small pieces. **2** tr. (usu. with neg.) restrain (one's words etc.) within the bounds of politeness. **3** intr. (usu. as **mincing** adj.) speak or walk with an affected delicacy. —n. esp. Brit. minced meat. □**mince matters** (usu. with neg.) use polite expressions etc. **mince pie** a usu. small round pie containing mincemeat. □□ **mincer** n. **mincingly** adv. (in sense 3 of v.). [ME f. OF mincier ult. f. L (as MINUTIA)]

mincemeat /ˈmɪnsmiːt/ n. a mixture of currants, raisins, sugar, apples, candied peel, spices, and often suet. □**make mincemeat of** utterly defeat (a person, argument, etc.).

mind /maɪnd/ n. & v. —n. **1 a** the seat of consciousness, thought, volition, and feeling. **b** attention, concentration (my mind keeps wandering). **2** the intellect; intellectual powers. **3** remembrance, memory (it went out of my mind; I can't call it to mind). **4** one's opinion (we're of the same mind). **5** a way of thinking or feeling (shocking to the Victorian mind). **6** the focus of one's thoughts or desires (put one's mind to it). **7** the state of normal mental functioning (lose one's mind; in one's right mind). **8** a person as embodying mental faculties (a great mind). —v.tr. (usu. with neg. or interrog.) object to (do you mind if I smoke?; I don't mind your being late). **2 a** remember; take care to (mind you come on time). **b** (often foll. by out) take care; be careful. **3** have charge of temporarily (mind the house while I'm away). **4** apply oneself to, concern oneself with (business, affairs, etc.) (I try to mind my own business). **5** give heed to; notice (mind the step; don't mind the expense; mind how you go). **6** US & Ir. be obedient to (mind what your mother says). □**be in two minds** be undecided. **cast one's mind back** think back; recall an earlier time. **come into a person's mind** be remembered. **come to mind** (of a thought, idea, etc.) suggest itself. **don't mind me** iron. do as you please. **do you mind!** iron. an expression of annoyance. **give a person a piece of one's mind** scold or reproach a person. **have a good** (or **great** or **half a**) **mind to** (often as a threat, usu. unfulfilled) feel tempted to (I've a good mind to report you). **have** (**it**) **in mind** intend. **have a mind of one's own** be capable of independent opinion. **have on one's mind** be troubled by the thought of. **in one's mind's eye** in one's imagination or mental view. **mind-bending** colloq. (esp. of a psychedelic drug) influencing or altering one's state of mind. **mind-blowing** sl. **1** confusing, shattering. **2** (esp. of drugs etc.) inducing hallucinations. **mind-boggling** colloq. overwhelming, startling. **mind out for** guard against, avoid. **mind over matter** the power of the mind asserted over the physical universe. **mind one's Ps & Qs** be careful in one's behaviour. **mind-read** discern the thoughts of (another person). **mind-reader** a person capable of mind-reading.

mind-set habits of mind formed by earlier events. **mind the shop** have charge of affairs temporarily. **mind you** an expression used to qualify a previous statement (*I found it quite quickly; mind you, it wasn't easy*). **mind your back** (or **backs**) *colloq.* an expression to indicate that a person wants to get past. **never mind 1** an expression used to comfort or console. **2** (also **never you mind**) an expression used to evade a question. **open** (or **close**) **one's mind to** be receptive (or unreceptive) to (changes, new ideas, etc.). **put a person in mind of** remind a person of. **put** (or **set**) **a person's mind at rest** reassure a person. **put a person or thing out of one's mind** deliberately forget. **read a person's mind** discern a person's thoughts. **to my mind** in my opinion. [ME *mynd* f. OE *gemynd* f. Gmc]

minded /'maɪndɪd/ *adj.* **1** (in *comb.*) **a** inclined to think in some specified way (*mathematically minded*; *fair-minded*). **b** having a specified kind of mind (*high-minded*). **c** interested in or enthusiastic about a specified thing (*car-minded*). **2** (usu. foll. by *to* + infin.) disposed or inclined (to an action).

minder /'maɪndə(r)/ *n.* **1 a** a person whose job it is to attend to a person or thing. **b** (in *comb.*) (*child-minder; machine-minder*). **2** *sl.* **a** a bodyguard, esp. a person employed to protect a criminal. **b** a thief's assistant.

mindful /'maɪndfʊl/ *adj.* (often foll. by *of*) taking heed or care; being conscious. □□ **mindfully** *adv.* **mindfulness** *n.*

mindless /'maɪndlɪs/ *adj.* **1** lacking intelligence; stupid. **2** not requiring thought or skill (*totally mindless work*). **3** (usu. foll. by *of*) heedless (of advice etc.). □□ **mindlessly** *adv.* **mindlessness** *n.*

mine[1] /maɪn/ *poss.pron.* **1** the one or ones belonging to or associated with me (*it is mine; mine are over there*). **2** (*attrib.* before a vowel) *archaic* = MY (*mine eyes have seen; mine host*). □ **of mine** of or belonging to me (*a friend of mine*). [OE *mīn* f. Gmc]

mine[2] /maɪn/ *n.* & *v.* —*n.* **1** an excavation in the earth for extracting metal, coal, salt, etc. **2** an abundant source (of information etc.). **3** a receptacle filled with explosive and placed in the ground or in the water for destroying enemy personnel, ships, etc. **4 a** a subterranean gallery in which explosive is placed to blow up fortifications. **b** *hist.* a subterranean passage under the wall of a besieged fortress. —*v.tr.* **1** obtain (metal, coal, etc.) from a mine. **2** (also *absol.*, often foll. by *for*) dig in (the earth etc.) for ore etc. **3 a** dig or burrow in (usu. the earth). **b** make (a hole, passage, etc.) underground. **4** lay explosive mines under or in. **5** = UNDERMINE. □ **mine-detector** an instrument for detecting the presence of mines. □□ **mining** *n.* [ME f. OF *mine*, *miner*, perh. f. Celt.]

minefield /'maɪnfiːld/ *n.* **1** an area planted with explosive mines. **2** a subject or situation presenting unseen hazards.

minelayer /'maɪnˌleɪə(r)/ *n.* a ship or aircraft for laying mines.

miner /'maɪnə(r)/ *n.* **1** a person who works in a mine. **2** any burrowing insect or grub. □ **miner's right** *Austral.* a licence to dig for gold etc. on private or public land. [ME f. OF *minĕor*, *minour* (as MINE[2])]

mineral /'mɪnər(ə)l/ *n.* & *adj.* —*n.* **1** any of the species into which inorganic substances are classified. **2** a substance obtained by mining. **3** (often in *pl.*) *Brit.* an artificial mineral water or other effervescent drink. —*adj.* **1** of or containing a mineral or minerals. **2** obtained by mining. □ **mineral oil** petroleum or one of its distillation products. **mineral water 1** water found in nature with some dissolved salts present. **2** an artificial imitation of this, esp. soda water. **3** any effervescent non-alcoholic drink. **mineral wax** a fossil resin, esp. ozocerite. **mineral wool** a wool-like substance made from inorganic material, used for packing etc.

[ME f. OF *mineral* or med.L *mineralis* f. *minera* ore f. OF *miniere* mine]

mineralize /'mɪnərəˌlaɪz/ *v.* (also **-ise**) **1** *v.tr.* & *intr.* change wholly or partly into a mineral. **2** *v.tr.* impregnate (water etc.) with a mineral substance.

mineralogy /ˌmɪnəˈrælədʒɪ/ *n.* the scientific study of minerals. □□ **mineralogical** /-rəˈlɒdʒɪk(ə)l/ *adj.* **mineralogist** *n.*

minestrone /ˌmɪnɪˈstrəʊnɪ/ *n.* a soup containing vegetables and pasta, beans, or rice. [It.]

minesweeper /'maɪnˌswiːpə(r)/ *n.* a ship for clearing away floating and submarine mines.

minever var. of MINIVER.

mineworker /'maɪnˌwɜːkə(r)/ *n.* a person who works in a mine, esp. a coalmine.

Ming /mɪŋ/ *n.* **1** the dynasty ruling China 1368-1644. **2** Chinese porcelain made during the rule of this dynasty. [Chin.]

mingle /'mɪŋg(ə)l/ *v.tr.* & *intr.* mix, blend. □ **mingle their** etc. **tears** *literary* weep together. **mingle with** go about among. □□ **mingler** *n.* [ME *mengel* f. obs. *meng* f. OE *mengan*, rel. to AMONG]

mingy /'mɪndʒɪ/ *adj.* (**mingier**, **mingiest**) *Brit. colloq.* mean, stingy. □□ **mingily** *adv.* [perh. f. MEAN[2] and STINGY]

mini /'mɪnɪ/ *n.* (*pl.* **minis**) **1** *colloq.* a miniskirt, minidress, etc. **2** (**Mini**) *propr.* a make of small car. [abbr.]

mini- /'mɪnɪ/ *comb. form* miniature; very small or minor of its kind (*minibus; mini-budget*). [abbr. of MINIATURE]

miniature /'mɪnɪtʃə(r)/ *adj.*, *n.*, & *v.* —*adj.* **1** much smaller than normal. **2** represented on a small scale. —*n.* **1** any object reduced in size. **2** a small-scale minutely finished portrait. **3** this branch of painting (*portrait in miniature*). **4** a picture or decorated letters in an illuminated manuscript. —*v.tr.* represent on a smaller scale. □ **in miniature** on a small scale. **miniature camera** a camera producing small negatives. □□ **miniaturist** *n.* (in senses 2 and 3 of *n.*). [It. *miniatura* f. med.L *miniatura* f. L *miniare* rubricate, illuminate f. L *minium* red lead, vermilion]

miniaturize /'mɪnɪtʃəˌraɪz/ *v.tr.* (also **-ise**) produce in a smaller version; make small. □□ **miniaturization** /-ˈzeɪʃ(ə)n/ *n.*

minibus /'mɪnɪˌbʌs/ *n.* a small bus for about twelve passengers.

minicab /'mɪnɪˌkæb/ *n.* *Brit.* a car used as a taxi, but not licensed to ply for hire.

minicomputer /'mɪnɪkəmˌpjuːtə(r)/ *n.* a computer of medium power, more than a microcomputer but less than a mainframe.

minikin /'mɪnɪkɪn/ *adj.* & *n.* —*adj.* **1** diminutive. **2** affected, mincing. —*n.* a diminutive creature. [obs. Du. *minneken* f. *minne* love + *-ken*, *-kijn* -KIN]

minim /'mɪnɪm/ *n.* **1** *Mus.* a note having the time value of two crotchets or half a semibreve and represented by a hollow ring with a stem. Also called *half-note*. **2** one-sixtieth of a fluid drachm, about a drop. **3** an object or portion of the smallest size or importance. **4** a single down-stroke of the pen. [ME f. L *minimus* smallest]

minima *pl.* of MINIMUM.

minimal /'mɪnɪm(ə)l/ *adj.* **1** very minute or slight. **2** being or related to a minimum. **3** the least possible in size, duration, etc. **4** *Art* etc. characterized by the use of simple or primary forms or structures etc., often geometric or massive (*huge minimal forms in a few colours*). □□ **minimalism** *n.* (in sense 4). **minimally** *adv.* (in senses 1-3). [L *minimus* smallest]

minimalist /'mɪnɪməlɪst/ *n.* **1** (also *attrib.*) a person advocating small or moderate reform in politics (opp. MAXIMALIST). **2** = MENSHEVIK. **3** a person who advocates or practises minimal art. □□ **minimalism** *n.*

minimax /'mɪnɪˌmæks/ *n.* **1** *Math.* the lowest of a set of maximum values. **2** (usu. *attrib.*) **a** a strategy that minimizes the greatest risk to a participant in a game etc. **b** the theory that in a game with two players, a player's smallest possible maximum loss is equal to the same player's greatest possible minimum gain. [MINIMUM + MAXIMUM]

minimize /ˈmɪnɪˌmaɪz/ v. (also **-ise**) **1** tr. reduce to, or estimate at, the smallest possible amount or degree. **2** tr. estimate or represent at less than the true value or importance. **3** intr. attain a minimum value. □□ **minimization** /-ˈzeɪʃ(ə)n/ n. **minimizer** n.

minimum /ˈmɪnɪməm/ n. & adj. (pl. **minima** /-mə/) —n. the least possible or attainable amount (reduced to a minimum). —adj. that is a minimum. □ **minimum lending rate** the announced minimum percentage at which a central bank will discount bills (cf. base rate (see BASE¹)). ¶ Abolished in the UK in 1981. **minimum wage** the lowest wage permitted by law or special agreement. [L, neut. of minimus least]

minion /ˈmɪnjən/ n. derog. **1** a servile agent; a slave. **2** a favourite servant, animal, etc. **3** a favourite of a sovereign etc. [F mignon, OF mignot, of Gaulish orig.]

minipill /ˈmɪnɪpɪl/ n. a contraceptive pill containing a progestogen only (not oestrogen).

miniseries /ˈmɪnɪˌsɪərɪz/ n. a short series of television programmes on a common theme.

miniskirt /ˈmɪnɪˌskɜːt/ n. a very short skirt.

minister /ˈmɪnɪstə(r)/ n. & v. —n. **1** a head of a government department. **2** (in full **minister of religion**) a member of the clergy, esp. in the Presbyterian and Nonconformist Churches. **3** a diplomatic agent, usu. ranking below an ambassador. **4** (usu. foll. by of) a person employed in the execution of (a purpose, will, etc.) (a minister of justice). **5** (in full **minister general**) the superior of some religious orders. —v. **1** intr. (usu. foll. by to) render aid or service (to a person, cause, etc.). **2** tr. (usu. foll. by with) archaic furnish, supply, etc. □ **ministering angel** a kind-hearted person, esp. a woman, who nurses or comforts others (with ref. to Mark 1:13). **Minister of the Crown** Brit. Parl. a member of the Cabinet. **Minister of State** a government minister, in the UK usu. regarded as holding a rank below that of Head of Department. **Minister without Portfolio** a government minister who has Cabinet status, but is not in charge of a specific Department of State. □□ **ministrable** adj. [ME f. OF ministre f. L minister servant f. minus less]

ministerial /ˌmɪnɪˈstɪərɪəl/ adj. **1** of a minister of religion or a minister's office. **2** instrumental or subsidiary in achieving a purpose (ministerial in bringing about a settlement). **3 a** of a government minister. **b** siding with the Ministry against the Opposition. □□ **ministerialist** n. (in sense 3b). **ministerially** adv. [F ministériel or LL ministerialis f. L (as MINISTRY)]

ministration /ˌmɪnɪˈstreɪʃ(ə)n/ n. **1** (usu. in pl.) aid or service (the kind ministrations of his neighbours). **2** ministering, esp. in religious matters. **3** (usu. foll. by of) the supplying (of help, justice, etc.). □□ **ministrant** /ˈmɪnɪstrənt/ adj. & n. **ministrative** /ˈmɪnɪstrətɪv/ adj. [ME f. OF ministration or L ministratio (as MINISTER)]

ministry /ˈmɪnɪstrɪ/ n. (pl. **-ies**) **1 a** a government department headed by a minister. **b** the building which it occupies (the Ministry of Defence). **2 a** (prec. by the) the vocation or profession of a religious minister (called to the ministry). **b** the office of a religious minister, priest, etc. **c** the period of tenure of this. **3** (prec. by the) the body of ministers of a government or of a religion. **4** a period of government under one Prime Minister. **5** ministering, ministration. [ME f. L ministerium (as MINISTER)]

miniver /ˈmɪnɪvə(r)/ n. (also **minever**) plain white fur used in ceremonial costume. [ME f. AF menuver, OF menu vair (as MENU, VAIR)]

mink /mɪŋk/ n. **1** either of two small semi-aquatic stoatlike animals of the genus Mustela, M. vison of N. America and M. intreola of Europe. **2** the thick brown fur of these. **3** a coat made of this. [cf. Sw. mänk, menk]

minke /ˈmɪŋkə/ n. a small baleen whale, Balaenoptera acutorostrata, with a pointed snout. [prob. f. Meincke, the name of a Norw. whaler]

Minn. abbr. Minnesota.

minnesinger /ˈmɪnɪˌsɪŋə(r)/ n. a German lyric poet and singer of the 12th–14th c. [G, = love-singer]

minnow /ˈmɪnəʊ/ n. any of various small freshwater fish of the carp family, esp. Phoxinus phoxinus. [late ME menow, perh. repr. OE mynwe (unrecorded), myne: infl. by ME menuse, menise f. OF menuise, ult. rel. to MINUTIA]

Minoan /mɪˈnəʊən/ adj. & n. Archaeol. —adj. of or relating to the Bronze Age civilization centred on Crete (c.3000–1100 BC). —n. **1** an inhabitant of Minoan Crete or the Minoan world. **2** the language or scripts associated with the Minoans. [named after the legendary Cretan king Minos (Gk Mīnōs), to whom the palace excavated at Knossos was attributed]

minor /ˈmaɪnə(r)/ adj., n., & v. —adj. **1** lesser or comparatively small in size or importance (minor poet; minor operation). **2** Mus. **a** (of a scale) having intervals of a semitone between the second and third, fifth and sixth, and seventh and eighth degrees. **b** (of an interval) less by a semitone than a major interval. **c** (of a key) based on a minor scale, tending to produce a melancholy effect. **3** Brit. (in schools) indicating the younger of two children from the same family or the second to enter the school (usu. put after the name). **4** Logic **a** (of a term) occurring as the subject of the conclusion of a categorical syllogism. **b** (of a premiss) containing the minor term in a categorical syllogism. —n. **1** a person under the legal age limit or majority (no unaccompanied minors). **2** Mus. a minor key etc. **3** US a student's subsidiary subject or course (cf. MAJOR). **4** Logic a minor term or premiss. —v.intr. (foll. by in) US (of a student) undertake study in (a subject) as a subsidiary to a main subject. □ **in a minor key** (of novels, events, people's lives, etc.) understated, uneventful. **minor axis** Geom. (of a conic) the axis perpendicular to the major axis. **minor canon** a cleric who is not a member of the chapter, who assists in daily cathedral services. **minor league** US (in baseball, football, etc.) a league of professional clubs other than the major leagues. **minor orders** see ORDER. **minor piece** Chess a bishop or a knight. **minor planet** an asteroid. **minor prophet** any of the prophets from Hosea to Malachi, whose surviving writings are not lengthy. **minor suit** Bridge diamonds or clubs. [L, = smaller, less, rel. to minuere lessen]

minority /maɪˈnɒrɪtɪ/ n. (pl. **-ies**) **1** (often foll. by of) a smaller number or part, esp. within a political party or structure. **2** the number of votes cast for this (a minority of two). **3** the state of having less than half the votes or of being supported by less than half of the body of opinion (in the minority). **4** a relatively small group of people differing from others in the society of which they are a part in race, religion, language, political persuasion, etc. **5** (attrib.) relating to or done by the minority (minority interests). **6 a** the state of being under full legal age. **b** the period of this. [F minorité or med.L minoritas f. L minor: see MINOR]

Minotaur /ˈmaɪnəˌtɔː(r)/ n. (in Greek mythology) a man with a bull's head, kept in a Cretan labyrinth and fed with human flesh. [ME f. OF f. L Minotaurus f. Gk Mīnōtauros f. Mīnōs, legendary king of Crete (see MINOAN) + tauros bull]

minster /ˈmɪnstə(r)/ n. **1** a large or important church (York Minster). **2** the church of a monastery. [OE mynster f. eccl.L monasterium f. Gk monastērion MONASTERY]

minstrel /ˈmɪnstr(ə)l/ n. **1** a medieval singer or

musician, esp. singing or reciting poetry. **2** *hist.* a person who entertained patrons with singing, buffoonery, etc. **3** (usu. in *pl.*) a member of a band of public entertainers with blackened faces etc., performing songs and music ostensibly of Negro origin. [ME f. OF *menestral* entertainer, servant, f. Prov. *menest(ai)ral* officer, employee, musician, f. LL *ministerialis* official, officer: see MINISTERIAL]

minstrelsy /'mɪnstr(ə)lsɪ/ *n.* (*pl.* **-ies**) **1** the minstrel's art. **2** a body of minstrels. **3** minstrel poetry. [ME f. OF *menestralsie* (as MINSTREL)]

mint[1] /mɪnt/ *n.* **1** any aromatic plant of the genus *Mentha*. **2** a peppermint sweet or lozenge. □**mint julep** *US* a sweet iced alcoholic drink of bourbon flavoured with mint. **mint sauce** chopped mint in vinegar and sugar, usu. eaten with lamb. □□**minty** *adj.* (**mintier**, **mintiest**). [OE *minte* ult. f. L *ment(h)a* f. Gk *minthē*]

mint[2] /mɪnt/ *n.* & *v.* —*n.* **1** a place where money is coined, usu. under State authority. **2** a vast sum of money (*making a mint*). **3** a source of invention etc. (*a mint of ideas*). —*v.tr.* **1** make (coin) by stamping metal. **2** invent, coin (a word, phrase, etc.). □**in mint condition** (or **state**) freshly minted; (of books etc.) as new. **mint-mark** a mark on a coin to indicate the mint at which it was struck. **mint-master** the superintendent of coinage at a mint. **mint par** (in full **mint parity**) **1** the ratio between the gold equivalents of currency in two countries. **2** their rate of exchange based on this. □□**mintage** *n.* [OE *mynet* f. WG f. L *moneta* MONEY]

minuend /'mɪnjʊˌend/ *n. Math.* a quantity or number from which another is to be subtracted. [L *minuendus* gerundive of *minuere* diminish]

minuet /ˌmɪnjʊ'et/ *n.* & *v.* —*n.* **1** a slow stately dance for two in triple time. **2** *Mus.* the music for this, or music in the same rhythm and style, often as a movement in a suite, sonata, or symphony. —*v.intr.* (**minueted**, **minueting**) dance a minuet. [F *menuet*, orig. adj. = fine, delicate, dimin. of *menu*: see MENU]

minus /'maɪnəs/ *prep.*, *adj.*, & *n.* —*prep.* **1** with the subtraction of (*7 minus 4 equals 3*). ¶ Symb.: -. **2** (of temperature) below zero (*minus 2°*). **3** *colloq.* lacking; deprived of (*returned minus their dog*). —*adj.* **1** *Math.* negative. **2** *Electronics* having a negative charge. —*n.* **1** = minus sign. **2** *Math.* a negative quantity. **3** a disadvantage. □**minus sign** the symbol -, indicating subtraction or a negative value. [L, neut. of *minor* less]

minuscule /'mɪnəˌskjuːl/ *n.* & *adj.* —*n.* **1** *Palaeog.* a kind of cursive script developed in the 7th c. **2** a lower-case letter. —*adj.* **1** lower-case. **2** *colloq.* extremely small or unimportant. □□**minuscular** /mɪ'nʌskjʊlə(r)/ *adj.* [F f. L *minuscula* (*littera* letter) dimin. of *minor*: see MINOR]

minute[1] /'mɪnɪt/ *n.* & *v.* —*n.* **1** the sixtieth part of an hour. **2** a distance covered in one minute (*twenty minutes from the station*). **3 a** a moment; an instant; a point of time (*expecting her any minute*; *the train leaves in a minute*). **b** (prec. by *the*) *colloq.* the present time (*what are you doing at the minute?*). **c** (foll. by *clause*) as soon as (*call me the minute you get back*). **4** the sixtieth part of an angular degree. **5** (in *pl.*) a brief summary of the proceedings at a meeting. **6** an official memorandum authorizing or recommending a course of action. —*v.tr.* **1** record (proceedings) in the minutes. **2** send the minutes to (a person). □**just** (or **wait**) **a minute 1** a request to wait for a short time. **2** as a prelude to a query or objection. **minute-gun** a gun fired at intervals of a minute at funerals etc. **minute hand** the hand on a watch or clock which indicates minutes. **minute steak** a thin slice of steak to be cooked quickly. **up to the minute** completely up to date. [ME f. OF f. LL *minuta* (n.), f. fem. of *minutus* MINUTE[2]: senses 1 & 4 of noun f. med.L *pars minuta prima* first minute part (cf.

SECOND[2]): senses 5 & 6 perh. f. med.L *minuta scriptura* draft in small writing]

minute[2] /maɪ'njuːt/ *adj.* (**minutest**) **1** very small. **2** trifling, petty. **3** (of an inquiry, inquirer, etc.) accurate, detailed, precise. □□**minutely** *adv.* **minuteness** *n.* [ME f. L *minutus* past part. of *minuere* lessen]

Minuteman /'mɪnɪtˌmæn/ *n.* (*pl.* **-men**) *US* **1** a political watchdog or activist. **2** a type of three-stage intercontinental ballistic missile. **3** *hist.* an American militiaman of the revolutionary period (ready to march at a minute's notice).

minutia /maɪ'njuːʃɪə, mɪ-/ *n.* (*pl.* **-iae** /-ʃɪˌiː/) (usu. in *pl.*) a precise, trivial, or minor detail. [L, = smallness, in pl. trifles f. *minutus*: see MINUTE[2]]

minx /mɪŋks/ *n.* a pert, sly, or playful girl. □□ **minxish** *adj.* **minxishly** *adv.* [16th c.: orig. unkn.]

Miocene /'maɪəˌsiːn/ *adj.* & *n. Geol.* —*adj.* of or relating to the fourth epoch of the Tertiary period with evidence for the diversification of primates, including early apes. ¶ Cf. Appendix II. —*n.* this epoch or system. [irreg. f. Gk *meiōn* less + *kainos* new]

miosis /maɪ'əʊsɪs/ *n.* (also **myosis**) excessive constriction of the pupil of the eye. □□**miotic** /maɪ'ɒtɪk/ *adj.* [Gk *muō* shut the eyes + -OSIS]

mirabelle /ˌmɪrə'bel/ *n.* **1 a** a European variety of plum-tree, *Prunus insititia*, bearing small round yellow fruit. **b** a fruit from this tree. **2** a liqueur distilled from this fruit. [F]

miracle /'mɪrək(ə)l/ *n.* **1** an extraordinary event attributed to some supernatural agency. **2 a** any remarkable occurrence. **b** a remarkable development in some specified area (*an economic miracle*; *the German miracle*). **3** (usu. foll. by *of*) a remarkable or outstanding specimen (*the plan was a miracle of ingenuity*). □**miracle drug** a drug which represents a breakthrough in medical science. **miracle play** a medieval play based on the Bible or the lives of the saints. [ME f. OF f. L *miraculum* object of wonder f. *mirari* wonder f. *mirus* wonderful]

miraculous /mɪ'rækjʊləs/ *adj.* **1** of the nature of a miracle. **2** supernatural. **3** remarkable, surprising. □□**miraculously** *adv.* **miraculousness** *n.* [F *miraculeux* or med.L *miraculosus* f. L (as MIRACLE)]

mirador /ˌmɪrə'dɔː(r)/ *n.* a turret or tower etc. attached to a building, and commanding an excellent view. [Sp. f. *mirar* to look]

mirage /'mɪrɑːʒ/ *n.* **1** an optical illusion caused by atmospheric conditions, esp. the appearance of a sheet of water in a desert or on a hot road from the reflection of light. **2** an illusory thing. [F f. *se mirer* be reflected, f. L *mirare* look at]

MIRAS /'maɪræs/ *abbr.* (also **Miras**) mortgage interest relief at source.

mire /'maɪə(r)/ *n.* & *v.* —*n.* **1** a stretch of swampy or boggy ground. **2** mud, dirt. —*v.* **1** *tr.* & *intr.* plunge or sink in a mire. **2** *tr.* involve in difficulties. □**in the mire** in difficulties. [ME f. ON *mȳrr* f. Gmc, rel. to MOSS]

mirepoix /mɪə'pwɑː/ *n.* sautéd chopped vegetables, used in sauces etc. [F, f. Duc de *Mirepoix*, Fr. general d. 1757]

mirk var. of MURK.

mirky var. of MURKY.

mirror /'mɪrə(r)/ *n.* & *v.* —*n.* **1** a polished surface, usu. of amalgam-coated glass or metal, which reflects an image; a looking-glass. **2** anything regarded as giving an accurate reflection or description of something else. —*v.tr.* reflect as in a mirror. □**mirror carp** a breed of carp with large shiny scales. **mirror finish** a reflective surface. **mirror image** an identical image, but with the structure reversed, as in a mirror. **mirror symmetry** symmetry as of an object and its reflection. **mirror writing** backwards writing, like ordinary writing reflected in a mirror. [ME f. OF *mirour* ult. f. L *mirare* look at]

mirth /mɜːθ/ *n.* merriment, laughter. □□**mirthful** *adj.* **mirthfully** *adv.* **mirthfulness** *n.* **mirthless**

adj. **mirthlessly** *adv.* **mirthlessness** *n.* [OE *myrgth* (as MERRY)]

MIRV *abbr.* multiple independently-targeted re-entry vehicle (a type of missile).

mis-¹ /mɪs/ *prefix* added to verbs and verbal derivatives: meaning 'amiss', 'badly', 'wrongly', 'unfavourably' (*mislead*; *misshapen*; *mistrust*). [OE f. Gmc]

mis-² /mɪs/ *prefix* occurring in a few words adopted from French meaning 'badly', 'wrongly', 'amiss', 'ill-', or having a negative force (*misadventure*; *mischief*). [OF *mes-* ult. f. L *minus* (see MINUS): assim. to MIS-¹]

misaddress /ˌmɪsə'dres/ *v.tr.* **1** address (a letter etc.) wrongly. **2** address (a person) wrongly, esp. impertinently.

misadventure /ˌmɪsəd'ventʃə(r)/ *n.* **1** *Law* an accident without concomitant crime or negligence (*death by misadventure*). **2** bad luck. **3** a misfortune. [ME f. OF *mesaventure* f. *mesavenir* turn out badly (as MIS-², ADVENT: cf. ADVENTURE)]

misalign /ˌmɪsə'laɪn/ *v.tr.* give the wrong alignment to. □□ **misalignment** *n.*

misalliance /ˌmɪsə'laɪəns/ *n.* an unsuitable alliance, esp. an unsuitable marriage. □□ **misally** *v.tr.* (-ies, -ied). [MIS-¹ + ALLIANCE, after MÉSALLIANCE]

misanthrope /'mɪzən,θrəʊp, 'mɪs-/ *n.* (also **misanthropist** /mɪ'zænθrəpɪst/) **1** a person who hates mankind. **2** a person who avoids human society. □□ **misanthropic** /-'θrɒpɪk/ *adj.* **misanthropical** /-'θrɒpɪk(ə)l/ *adj.* **misanthropically** /-'θrɒpɪkəlɪ/ *adv.* **misanthropy** /mɪ'zænθrəpɪ/ *n.* **misanthropize** /mɪ'zænθrə,paɪz/ *v.intr.* (also **-ise**). [F f. Gk *misanthrōpos* f. *misos* hatred + *anthrōpos* man]

misapply /ˌmɪsə'plaɪ/ *v.tr.* (-ies, -ied) apply (esp. funds) wrongly. □□ **misapplication** /mɪs,æplɪ'keɪʃ(ə)n/ *n.*

misapprehend /ˌmɪsæprɪ'hend/ *v.tr.* misunderstand (words, a person). □□ **misapprehension** /-'henʃ(ə)n/ *n.* **misapprehensive** *adj.*

misappropriate /ˌmɪsə'prəʊprɪ,eɪt/ *v.tr.* apply (usu. another's money) to one's own use, or to a wrong use. □□ **misappropriation** /-prɪ'eɪʃ(ə)n/ *n.*

misbegotten /ˌmɪsbɪ'gɒt(ə)n/ *adj.* **1** illegitimate, bastard. **2** contemptible, disreputable.

misbehave /ˌmɪsbɪ'heɪv/ *v.intr.* & *refl.* (of a person or machine) behave badly. □□ **misbehaver** *n.* **misbehaviour** *n.*

misbelief /ˌmɪsbɪ'li:f/ *n.* **1** wrong or unorthodox religious belief. **2** a false opinion or notion.

misc. *abbr.* miscellaneous.

miscalculate /mɪs'kælkjʊ,leɪt/ *v.tr.* (also *absol.*) calculate (amounts, results, etc.) wrongly. □□ **miscalculation** /-'leɪʃ(ə)n/ *n.*

miscall /mɪs'kɔ:l/ *v.tr.* **1** call by a wrong or inappropriate name. **2** *archaic* or *dial.* call (a person) names.

miscarriage /'mɪs,kærɪdʒ, mɪs'kærɪdʒ/ *n.* **1** a spontaneous abortion, esp. before the 28th week of pregnancy. **2** *Brit.* the failure (of a plan, letter, etc.) to reach completion or its destination. □ **miscarriage of justice** any failure of the judicial system to attain the ends of justice. [MISCARRY, after CARRIAGE]

miscarry /mɪs'kærɪ/ *v.intr.* (-ies, -ied) **1** (of a woman) have a miscarriage. **2** *Brit.* (of a letter etc.) fail to reach its destination. **3** (of a business, plan, etc.) fail, be unsuccessful.

miscast /mɪs'kɑ:st/ *v.tr.* (*past* and *past part.* **-cast**) allot an unsuitable part to (an actor).

miscegenation /ˌmɪsɪdʒɪ'neɪʃ(ə)n/ *n.* the interbreeding of races, esp. of Whites and non-Whites. [irreg. f. L *miscēre* mix + *genus* race]

miscellanea /ˌmɪsə'leɪnɪə/ *n.pl.* **1** a literary miscellany. **2** a collection of miscellaneous items. [L neut. pl. (as MISCELLANEOUS)]

miscellaneous /ˌmɪsə'leɪnɪəs/ *adj.* **1** of mixed composition or character. **2** (foll. by pl. noun) of various

kinds. **3** (of a person) many-sided. □□ **miscellaneously** *adv.* **miscellaneousness** *n.* [L *miscellaneus* f. *miscellus* mixed f. *miscēre* mix]

miscellany /mɪ'selənɪ/ *n.* (*pl.* **-ies**) **1** a mixture, a medley. **2** a book containing a collection of stories etc., or various literary compositions. □□ **miscellanist** *n.* [F *miscellanées* (fem. pl.) or L MISCELLANEA]

mischance /mɪs'tʃɑ:ns/ *n.* **1** bad luck. **2** an instance of this. [ME f. OF *mesch(e)ance* f. *mescheoir* (as MIS-², CHANCE)]

mischief /'mɪstʃɪf/ *n.* **1** conduct which is troublesome, but not malicious, esp. in children. **2** pranks, scrapes (*get into mischief*; *keep out of mischief*). **3** playful malice, archness, satire (*eyes full of mischief*). **4** harm or injury caused by a person or thing. **5** a person or thing responsible for harm or annoyance (*that loose connection is the mischief*). **6** (prec. by *the*) the annoying part or aspect (*the mischief of it is that* etc.). □ **do a person a mischief** wound or kill a person. **get up to** (or **make**) **mischief** create discord. **mischief-maker** one who encourages discord, esp. by gossip etc. [ME f. OF *meschief* f. *meschever* (as MIS-², *chever* come to an end f. *chef* head: see CHIEF)]

mischievous /'mɪstʃɪvəs/ *adj.* **1** (of a person) disposed to mischief. **2** (of conduct) playfully malicious. **3** (of a thing) having harmful effects. □□ **mischievously** *adv.* **mischievousness** *n.* [ME f. AF *meschevous* f. OF *meschever*: see MISCHIEF]

misch metal /mɪʃ/ *n.* an alloy of lanthanide metals, usu. added to iron to improve its malleability. [G *mischen* mix + *Metall* metal]

miscible /'mɪsɪb(ə)l/ *adj.* (often foll. by *with*) capable of being mixed. □□ **miscibility** /-'bɪlɪtɪ/ *n.* [med.L *miscibilis* f. L *miscēre* mix]

misconceive /ˌmɪskən'si:v/ *v.* **1** *intr.* (often foll. by *of*) have a wrong idea or conception. **2** *tr.* (as **misconceived** *adj.*) badly planned, organized, etc. **3** *tr.* misunderstand (a word, person, etc.). □□ **misconceiver** *n.* **misconception** /-'sepʃ(ə)n/ *n.*

misconduct *n.* & *v.* —*n.* /mɪs'kɒndʌkt/ **1** improper or unprofessional behaviour. **2** bad management. —*v.* /ˌmɪskən'dʌkt/ **1** *refl.* misbehave. **2** *tr.* mismanage.

misconstrue /ˌmɪskən'stru:/ *v.tr.* (-construes, -construed, -construing) **1** interpret (a word, action, etc.) wrongly. **2** mistake the meaning of (a person). □□ **misconstruction** /-'strʌkʃ(ə)n/ *n.*

miscopy /mɪs'kɒpɪ/ *v.tr.* (-ies, -ied) copy (text etc.) incorrectly.

miscount /mɪs'kaʊnt/ *v.* & *n.* —*v.tr.* (also *absol.*) count wrongly. —*n.* a wrong count.

miscreant /'mɪskrɪənt/ *n.* & *adj.* —*n.* **1** a vile wretch, a villain. **2** *archaic* a heretic. —*adj.* **1** depraved, villainous. **2** *archaic* heretical. [ME f. OF *mescreant* (as MIS-², *creant* part. of *croire* f. L *credere* believe)]

miscue /mɪs'kju:/ *n.* & *v.* —*n.* (in snooker etc.) the failure to strike the ball properly with the cue. —*v.intr.* (-cues, -cued, -cueing or -cuing) make a miscue.

misdate /mɪs'deɪt/ *v.tr.* date (an event, a letter, etc.) wrongly.

misdeal /mɪs'di:l/ *v.* & *n.* —*v.tr.* (also *absol.*) (*past* and *past part.* **-dealt** /-'delt/) make a mistake in dealing (cards). —*n.* **1** a mistake in dealing cards. **2** a misdealt hand.

misdeed /mɪs'di:d/ *n.* an evil deed, a wrongdoing; a crime. [OE *misdǣd* (as MIS-¹, DEED)]

misdemeanant /ˌmɪsdɪ'mi:nənt/ *n.* a person convicted of a misdemeanour or guilty of misconduct. [archaic *misdemean* misbehave]

misdemeanour /ˌmɪsdɪ'mi:nə(r)/ *n.* (*US* **misdemeanor**) **1** an offence, a misdeed. **2** *Law* an indictable offence, (in the UK formerly) less heinous than a felony.

misdiagnose /ˌmɪs'daɪəg,nəʊz/ *v.tr.* diagnose incorrectly. □□ **misdiagnosis** /-'nəʊsɪs/ *n.*

misdial /mɪsˈdaɪəl/ v.tr. (also absol.) (-dialled, -dialling; US -dialed, -dialing) dial (a telephone number etc.) incorrectly.

misdirect /ˌmɪsdaɪˈrekt, -dɪˈrekt/ v.tr. 1 direct (a person, letter, blow, etc.) wrongly. 2 (of a judge) instruct (the jury) wrongly. □□ **misdirection** n.

misdoing /mɪsˈduːɪŋ/ n. a misdeed.

misdoubt /mɪsˈdaʊt/ v.tr. 1 have doubts or misgivings about the truth or existence of. 2 be suspicious about; suspect that.

miseducation /mɪsˌedjʊˈkeɪʃ(ə)n/ n. wrong or faulty education. □□ **miseducate** /-ˈedjʊˌkeɪt/ v.tr.

mise en scène /ˌmiːz ɑ̃ ˈsen/ n. 1 Theatr. the scenery and properties of a play. 2 the setting or surroundings of an event. [F]

misemploy /ˌmɪsɪmˈplɔɪ/ v.tr. employ or use wrongly or improperly. □□ **misemployment** n.

miser /ˈmaɪzə(r)/ n. 1 a person who hoards wealth and lives miserably. 2 an avaricious person. [L, = wretched]

miserable /ˈmɪzərəb(ə)l/ adj. 1 wretchedly unhappy or uncomfortable (felt miserable; a miserable hovel). 2 contemptible, mean. 3 causing wretchedness or discomfort (miserable weather). 4 Sc., Austral., & NZ stingy, mean. □□ **miserableness** n. **miserably** adv. [ME f. F misérable f. L miserabilis pitiable f. miserari to pity f. miser wretched]

misère /mɪˈzeə(r)/ n. Cards (in solo whist etc.) a declaration undertaking to win no tricks. [F, = poverty, MISERY]

miserere /ˌmɪzəˈreərɪ, -ˈrɪərɪ/ n. 1 a cry for mercy. 2 = MISERICORD 1. [ME f. L, imper. of miserēri have mercy (as MISER); first word of Ps. 51 in Latin]

misericord /mɪˈzerɪˌkɔːd/ n. 1 a shelving projection on the under side of a hinged seat in a choir stall serving (when the seat is turned up) to help support a person standing. 2 an apartment in a monastery in which some relaxations of discipline are permitted. 3 a dagger for dealing the death stroke. [ME f. OF misericorde f. L misericordia f. misericors compassionate f. stem of miserēri pity + cor cordis heart]

miserly /ˈmaɪzəlɪ/ adj. like a miser, niggardly. □□ **miserliness** n. [MISER]

misery /ˈmɪzərɪ/ n. (pl. -ies) 1 a wretched state of mind, or of outward circumstances. 2 a thing causing this. 3 colloq. a constantly depressed or discontented person. 4 = MISÈRE. □**put out of its** etc. **misery** 1 release (a person, animal, etc.) from suffering or suspense. 2 kill (an animal in pain). [ME f. OF misere or L miseria (as MISER)]

misfeasance /mɪsˈfiːz(ə)ns/ n. Law a transgression, esp. the wrongful exercise of lawful authority. [ME f. OF mesfaisance f. mesfaire misdo (as MIS-², faire do f. L facere): cf. MALFEASANCE]

misfield /mɪsˈfiːld/ v. & n. —v.tr. (also absol.) (in cricket, baseball, etc.) field (the ball) badly. —n. an instance of this.

misfire /mɪsˈfaɪə(r)/ v. & n. —v.intr. 1 (of a gun, motor engine, etc.) fail to go off or start or function regularly. 2 (of an action etc.) fail to have the intended effect. —n. a failure of function or intention.

misfit /ˈmɪsfɪt/ n. 1 a person unsuited to a particular kind of environment, occupation, etc. 2 a garment etc. that does not fit. □**misfit stream** Geog. a stream not corresponding in size to its valley.

misfortune /mɪsˈfɔːtʃuːn, -tjuːn/ n. 1 bad luck. 2 an instance of this.

misgive /mɪsˈɡɪv/ v.tr. (past **-gave** /-ˈɡeɪv/; past part. **-given** /-ˈɡɪv(ə)n/) (often foll. by about, that) (of a person's mind, heart, etc.) fill (a person) with suspicion or foreboding.

misgiving /mɪsˈɡɪvɪŋ/ n. (usu. in pl.) a feeling of mistrust or apprehension.

misgovern /mɪsˈɡʌv(ə)n/ v.tr. govern (a State etc.) badly. □□ **misgovernment** n.

misguide /mɪsˈɡaɪd/ v.tr. 1 (as **misguided** adj.) mistaken in thought or action. 2 mislead, misdirect.

□□ **misguidance** n. **misguidedly** adv. **misguidedness** n.

mishandle /mɪsˈhænd(ə)l/ v.tr. 1 deal with incorrectly or ineffectively. 2 handle (a person or thing) roughly or rudely; ill-treat.

mishap /ˈmɪshæp/ n. an unlucky accident.

mishear /mɪsˈhɪə(r)/ v.tr. (past and past part. **-heard** /-ˈhɜːd/) hear incorrectly or imperfectly.

mishit v. & n. —v.tr. /mɪsˈhɪt/ (**-hitting**; past and past part. **-hit**) hit (a ball etc.) faultily. —n. /ˈmɪshɪt/ a faulty or bad hit.

mishmash /ˈmɪʃmæʃ/ n. a confused mixture. [ME, reduplication of MASH]

Mishnah /ˈmɪʃnə/ n. a collection of precepts forming the basis of the Talmud, and embodying Jewish oral law. □□ **Mishnaic** /-ˈneɪɪk/ adj. [Heb. mišnāh (teaching by) repetition]

misidentify /ˌmɪsaɪˈdentɪˌfaɪ/ v.tr. (**-ies**, **-ied**) identify erroneously. □□ **misidentification** /-fɪˈkeɪʃ(ə)n/ n.

misinform /ˌmɪsɪnˈfɔːm/ v.tr. give wrong information to, mislead. □□ **misinformation** /-fəˈmeɪʃ(ə)n/ n.

misinterpret /ˌmɪsɪnˈtɜːprɪt/ v.tr. (**-interpreted**, **-interpreting**) 1 interpret wrongly. 2 draw a wrong inference from. □□ **misinterpretation** /-ˈteɪʃ(ə)n/ n. **misinterpreter** n.

misjudge /mɪsˈdʒʌdʒ/ v.tr. (also absol.) 1 judge wrongly. 2 have a wrong opinion of. □□ **misjudgement** n. (also **misjudgment**).

miskey /mɪsˈkiː/ v.tr. (**-keys**, **-keyed**) key (data) wrongly.

miskick v. & n. —v.tr. /mɪsˈkɪk/ (also absol.) kick a ball etc.) badly or wrongly. —n. /ˈmɪskɪk/ an instance of this.

mislay /mɪsˈleɪ/ v.tr. (past and past part. **-laid** /-leɪd/) 1 unintentionally put (a thing) where it cannot readily be found. 2 euphem. lose.

mislead /mɪsˈliːd/ v.tr. (past and past part. **-led** /-ˈled/) 1 cause (a person) to go wrong, in conduct, belief, etc. 2 lead astray or in the wrong direction. □□ **misleader** n.

misleading /mɪsˈliːdɪŋ/ adj. causing to err or go astray; imprecise, confusing. □□ **misleadingly** adv. **misleadingness** n.

mislike /mɪsˈlaɪk/ v.tr. & n. archaic dislike. [OE mislīcian (as MIS-¹, LIKE²)]

mismanage /mɪsˈmænɪdʒ/ v.tr. manage badly or wrongly. □□ **mismanagement** n.

mismarriage /mɪsˈmærɪdʒ/ n. an unsuitable marriage or alliance. [MIS-¹ + MARRIAGE]

mismatch v. & n. —v.tr. /mɪsˈmætʃ/ match unsuitably or incorrectly, esp. in marriage. —n. /ˈmɪsmætʃ/ a bad match.

mismated /mɪsˈmeɪtɪd/ adj. 1 (of people) not suited to each other, esp. in marriage. 2 (of objects) not matching.

mismeasure /mɪsˈmeʒə(r)/ v.tr. measure or estimate incorrectly. □□ **mismeasurement** n.

misname /mɪsˈneɪm/ v.tr. = MISCALL.

misnomer /mɪsˈnəʊmə(r)/ n. 1 a name or term used wrongly. 2 the wrong use of a name or term. [ME f. AF f. OF mesnom(m)er (as MIS-², nommer name f. L nominare formed as NOMINATE]

misogamy /mɪˈsɒɡəmɪ/ n. the hatred of marriage. □□ **misogamist** n. [Gk misos hatred + gamos marriage]

misogyny /mɪˈsɒdʒɪnɪ/ n. the hatred of women. □□ **misogynist** n. **misogynous** adj. [Gk misos hatred + gunē woman]

mispickel /ˈmɪsˌpɪk(ə)l/ n. Mineral. arsenical pyrites. [G]

misplace /mɪsˈpleɪs/ v.tr. 1 put in the wrong place. 2 bestow (affections, confidence, etc.) on an inappropriate object. 3 time (words, actions, etc.) badly. □□ **misplacement** n.

misplay /mɪsˈpleɪ/ v. & n. —v.tr. play (a ball, card, etc.) in a wrong or ineffective manner. —n. an instance of this.

æ cat ɑː arm e bed ɜː her ɪ sit iː see ɒ hot ɔː saw ʌ run ʊ put uː too ə ago aɪ my

misprint *n.* & *v.* —*n.* /'mɪsprɪnt/ a mistake in printing. —*v.tr.* /mɪs'prɪnt/ print wrongly.
misprision[1] /mɪs'prɪʒ(ə)n/ *n. Law* **1** (in full **misprision of a felony** or **of treason**) the deliberate concealment of one's knowledge of a crime, treason, etc. **2** a wrong action or omission. [ME f. AF *mesprisioun* f. OF *mesprison* error f. *mesprendre* to mistake (as MIS-[2], *prendre* take)]
misprision[2] /mɪs'prɪʒ(ə)n/ *n.* **1** a misreading, misunderstanding, etc. **2** (usu. foll. by *of*) a failure to appreciate the value of a thing. **3** *archaic* contempt. [MISPRIZE after MISPRISION[1]]
misprize /mɪs'praɪz/ *v.tr. literary* despise, scorn; fail to appreciate. [ME f. OF *mesprisier* (as MIS-[1], PRIZE[1])]
mispronounce /ˌmɪsprə'naʊns/ *v.tr.* pronounce (a word etc.) wrongly. □□ **mispronunciation** /-ˌnʌnsɪ'eɪʃ(ə)n/ *n.*
misquote /mɪs'kwəʊt/ *v.tr.* quote wrongly. □□ **misquotation** /-'teɪʃ(ə)n/ *n.*
misread /mɪs'riːd/ *v.tr.* (*past* and *past part.* -read /-'red/) read or interpret (text, a situation, etc.) wrongly.
misremember /ˌmɪsrɪ'membə(r)/ *v.tr.* remember imperfectly or incorrectly.
misreport /ˌmɪsrɪ'pɔːt/ *v.* & *n.* —*v.tr.* give a false or incorrect report of. —*n.* a false or incorrect report.
misrepresent /ˌmɪsreprɪ'zent/ *v.tr.* represent wrongly; give a false or misleading account or idea of. □□ **misrepresentation** /-'teɪʃ(ə)n/ *n.* **misrepresentative** *adj.*
misrule /mɪs'ruːl/ *n.* & *v.* —*n.* bad government; disorder. —*v.tr.* govern badly.
Miss. *abbr.* Mississippi.
miss[1] /mɪs/ *v.* & *n.* —*v.* **1** *tr.* (also *absol.*) fail to hit, reach, find, catch, etc. (an object or goal). **2** *tr.* fail to catch (a bus, train, etc.). **3** *tr.* fail to experience, see, or attend (an occurrence or event). **4** *tr.* fail to meet (a person); fail to keep (an appointment). **5** *tr.* fail to seize (an opportunity etc.) (*I missed my chance*). **6** *tr.* fail to hear or understand (*I'm sorry, I missed what you said*). **7** *tr.* **a** regret the loss or absence of (a person or thing) (*did you miss me while I was away?*). **b** notice the loss or absence of (an object) (*bound to miss the key if it isn't there*). **8** *tr.* avoid (*go early to miss the traffic*). **9** *tr.* = **miss out** 1. **10** *intr.* (of an engine etc.) fail, misfire. —*n.* **1** a failure to hit, reach, attain, connect, etc. **2** *colloq.* = MISCARRIAGE 1. □ **be missing** not have (see also MISSING *adj.*). **give (a thing) a miss** avoid, leave alone (*gave the party a miss*). **miss the boat** (or **bus**) lose an opportunity. **miss fire** (of a gun) fail to go off or hit the mark (cf. MISFIRE). **a miss is as good as a mile** the fact of failure or escape is not affected by the narrowness of the margin. **miss out 1** omit, leave out (*missed out my name from the list*). **2** (usu. foll. by *on*) *colloq.* fail to get or experience (*always misses out on the good times*). **not miss much** be alert. **not miss a trick** never fail to seize an opportunity, advantage, etc. □□ **missable** *adj.* [OE *missan* f. Gmc]
miss[2] /mɪs/ *n.* **1** a girl or unmarried woman. **2** (Miss) **a** the title of an unmarried woman or girl, or of a married woman retaining her maiden name for professional purposes. **b** the title of a beauty queen (*Miss World*). **3** usu. *derog.* or *joc.* a girl, esp. a schoolgirl, with implications of silliness etc. **4** the title used to address a female schoolteacher, shop assistant, etc. □□ **missish** *adj.* (in sense 3). [abbr. of MISTRESS]
missal /'mɪs(ə)l/ *n. RC Ch.* **1** a book containing the texts used in the service of the Mass throughout the year. **2** a book of prayers, esp. an illuminated one. [ME f. med.L *missale* neut. of eccl.L *missalis* of the mass f. *missa* MASS[2]]
missel-thrush var. of MISTLE-THRUSH.
misshape /mɪs'ʃeɪp/ *v.tr.* give a bad shape or form to; distort.
misshapen /mɪs'ʃeɪpən/ *adj.* ill-shaped, deformed, distorted. □□ **misshapenly** *adv.* **misshapenness** *n.*

missile /'mɪsaɪl/ *n.* **1** an object or weapon suitable for throwing at a target or for discharge from a machine. **2** a weapon, esp. a nuclear weapon, directed by remote control or automatically. □□ **missilery** /-lrɪ/ *n.* [L *missilis* f. *mittere miss-* send]
missing /'mɪsɪŋ/ *adj.* **1** not in its place; lost. **2** (of a person) not yet traced or confirmed as alive but not known to be dead. **3** not present. □ **missing link 1** a thing lacking to complete a series. **2** a hypothetical intermediate type, esp. between humans and apes.
mission /'mɪʃ(ə)n/ *n.* **1 a** a particular task or goal assigned to a person or group. **b** a journey undertaken as part of this. **c** a person's vocation (*mission in life*). **2** a military or scientific operation or expedition for a particular purpose. **3** a body of persons sent, esp. to a foreign country, to conduct negotiations etc. **4 a** a body sent to propagate a religious faith. **b** a field of missionary activity. **c** a missionary post or organization. **d** a place of worship attached to a mission. **5** a particular course or period of preaching, services, etc., undertaken by a parish or community. [F *mission* or L *missio* f. *mittere miss-* send]
missionary /'mɪʃənərɪ/ *adj.* & *n.* —*adj.* of, concerned with, or characteristic of, religious missions. —*n.* (*pl.* -ies) a person doing missionary work. □ **missionary position** *colloq.* a position for sexual intercourse with the woman lying on her back and the man lying on top and facing her. [mod.L *missionarius* f. L (as MISSION)]
missioner /'mɪʃənə(r)/ *n.* **1** a missionary. **2** a person in charge of a religious mission.
missis /'mɪsɪz/ *n.* (also **missus** /-səz/) *sl.* or *joc.* **1** a form of address to a woman. **2** a wife. □ **the missis** my or your wife. [corrupt. of MISTRESS: cf. MRS]
missive /'mɪsɪv/ *n.* **1** *joc.* a letter, esp. a long and serious one. **2** an official letter. **letter** (or **letters**) **missive** a letter from a sovereign to a dean and chapter nominating a person to be elected bishop. [ME f. med.L *missivus* f. L (as MISSION)]
misspell /mɪs'spel/ *v.tr.* (*past* and *past part.* -spelt or -spelled) spell wrongly.
misspelling /mɪs'spelɪŋ/ *n.* a wrong spelling.
misspend /mɪs'spend/ *v.tr.* (*past* and *past part.* -spent /-'spent/) (esp. as **misspent** *adj.*) spend amiss or wastefully.
misstate /mɪs'steɪt/ *v.tr.* state wrongly or inaccurately.
misstatement /mɪs'steɪtmənt/ *n.* a wrong or inaccurate statement.
misstep /mɪs'step/ *n.* **1** a wrong step or action. **2** a *faux pas.*
missus var. of MISSIS.
missy /'mɪsɪ/ *n.* (*pl.* -ies) an affectionate or derogatory form of address to a young girl.
mist /mɪst/ *n.* & *v.* —*n.* **1 a** water vapour near the ground in minute droplets limiting visibility. **b** condensed vapour settling on a surface and obscuring glass etc. **2** dimness or blurring of the sight caused by tears etc. **3** a cloud of particles resembling mist. —*v.tr.* & *intr.* (usu. foll. by *up*, *over*) cover or become covered with mist or as with mist. □□ **mistful** *adj.* **mistlike** *adj.* [OE f. Gmc]
mistake /mɪ'steɪk/ *n.* & *v.* —*n.* **1** an incorrect idea or opinion; a thing incorrectly done or thought. **2** an error of judgement. —*v.tr.* (*past* **mistook** /-'stʊk/; *past part.* **mistaken** /-'steɪkən/) **1** misunderstand the meaning or intention of (a person, a statement, etc.). **2** (foll. by *for*) wrongly take or identify (*mistook me for you*). **3** choose wrongly (*mistake one's vocation*). □ **and** (or **make**) **no mistake** *colloq.* undoubtedly. **by mistake** accidentally; in error. **there is no mistaking** one is sure to recognize (a person or thing). □□ **mistakable** *adj.* **mistakably** *adv.* [ME f. ON *mistaka* (as MIS-[1], TAKE)]
mistaken /mɪ'steɪkən/ *adj.* **1** wrong in opinion or judgement. **2** based on or resulting from this

(*mistaken loyalty; mistaken identity*). □□ **mistakenly** *adv.* **mistakenness** *n.*

misteach /mɪsˈtiːtʃ/ *v.tr.* (*past* and *past part.* **-taught** /-ˈtɔːt/) teach wrongly or incorrectly.

mister /ˈmɪstə(r)/ *n.* **1** a man without a title of nobility etc. (*a mere mister*). **2** *sl.* or *joc.* a form of address to a man. [weakened form of MASTER in unstressed use before a name: cf. MR]

mistigris /ˈmɪstɪɡrɪs/ *n. Cards* **1** a blank card used as a wild card in a form of draw poker. **2** this game. [F *mistigri* jack of clubs]

mistime /mɪsˈtaɪm/ *v.tr.* say or do at the wrong time. [OE *mistīmian* (as MIS-¹, TIME)]

mistitle /mɪsˈtaɪt(ə)l/ *v.tr.* give the wrong title or name to.

mistle thrush /ˈmɪs(ə)l/ *n.* (also **missel thrush**) a large thrush, *Turdus viscivorus*, with a spotted breast, that feeds on mistletoe berries. [OE *mistel* basil, mistletoe, of unkn. orig.]

mistletoe /ˈmɪs(ə)l,təʊ/ *n.* **1** a parasitic plant, *Viscum album*, growing on apple and other trees and bearing white glutinous berries in winter. **2** a similar plant, *Phoradendron flavescens*, native to N. America. [OE *misteltān* (as MISTLE (THRUSH), *tān* twig)]

mistook *past* of MISTAKE.

mistral /ˈmɪstrɑːl, mɪˈstrɑːl/ *n.* a cold northerly wind that blows down the Rhône valley and S. France into the Mediterranean. [F & Prov. f. L (as MAGISTRAL)]

mistranslate /ˌmɪstrænzˈleɪt, ˌmɪstrɑː-, -sˈleɪt/ *v.tr.* translate incorrectly. □□ **mistranslation** *n.*

mistreat /mɪsˈtriːt/ *v.tr.* treat badly. □□ **mistreatment** *n.*

mistress /ˈmɪstrɪs/ *n.* **1** a female head of a household. **2 a** a woman in authority over others. **b** the female owner of a pet. **3** a woman with power to control etc. (often foll. by *of*: *mistress of the situation*). **4** *Brit.* **a** a female teacher (*music mistress*). **b** a female head of a college etc. **5 a** a woman (other than his wife) with whom a married man has a (usu. prolonged) sexual relationship. **b** *archaic* or *poet.* a woman loved and courted by a man. **6** *archaic* or *dial.* (as a title) = MRS. □ **Mistress of the Robes** a lady in charge of the Queen's wardrobe. [ME f. OF *maistresse* f. *maistre* MASTER]

mistrial /mɪsˈtraɪəl/ *n.* **1** a trial rendered invalid through some error in the proceedings. **2** *US* a trial in which the jury cannot agree on a verdict.

mistrust /mɪsˈtrʌst/ *v.* & *n.* —*v.tr.* **1** be suspicious of. **2** feel no confidence in (a person, oneself, one's powers, etc.). —*n.* **1** suspicion. **2** lack of confidence.

mistrustful /mɪsˈtrʌstfʊl/ *adj.* **1** (foll. by *of*) suspicious. **2** lacking confidence or trust. □□ **mistrustfully** *adv.* **mistrustfulness** *n.*

misty /ˈmɪstɪ/ *adj.* (**mistier, mistiest**) **1** of or covered with mist. **2** indistinct or dim in outline. **3** obscure, vague (*a misty idea*). □□ **mistily** *adv.* **mistiness** *n.* [OE *mistig* (as MIST)]

mistype /mɪsˈtaɪp/ *v.tr.* type wrongly. [MIS-¹ + TYPE]

misunderstand /ˌmɪsʌndəˈstænd/ *v.tr.* (*past* and *past part.* **-understood** /-ˈstʊd/) **1** fail to understand correctly. **2** (usu. as **misunderstood** *adj.*) misinterpret the words or actions of (a person).

misunderstanding /ˌmɪsʌndəˈstændɪŋ/ *n.* **1** a failure to understand correctly. **2** a slight disagreement or quarrel.

misusage /mɪsˈjuːsɪdʒ/ *n.* **1** wrong or improper usage. **2** ill-treatment.

misuse *v.* & *n.* —*v.tr.* /mɪsˈjuːz/ **1** use wrongly; apply to the wrong purpose. **2** ill-treat. —*n.* /mɪsˈjuːs/ wrong or improper use or application. □□ **misuser** *n.*

MIT *abbr.* Massachusetts Institute of Technology.

mite¹ /maɪt/ *n.* any small arachnid of the order Acari, having four pairs of legs when adult. □□ **mity** *adj.* [OE *mīte* f. Gmc]

mite² /maɪt/ *n.* & *adv.* —*n.* **1** *hist.* a Flemish copper coin of small value. **2** any small monetary unit. **3** a small object or person, esp. a child. **4** a modest

contribution; the best one can do (*offered my mite of comfort*). —*adv.* (usu. prec. by *a*) *colloq.* somewhat (*is a mite shy*). [ME f. MLG, MDu. *mīte* f. Gmc: prob. the same as MITE¹]

miter *US* var. of MITRE.

Mithraism /ˈmɪθreɪ,ɪz(ə)m/ *n.* the cult of the ancient Persian god Mithras associated with the sun. □□ **Mithraic** /-ˈθreɪɪk/ *adj.* **Mithraist** *n.* [L *Mithras* f. Gk *Mithras* f. OPers. *Mithra* f. Skr. *Mitra*]

mithridatize /mɪˈθrɪdə,taɪz/ *v.tr.* (also **-ise**) render proof against a poison by administering gradually increasing doses of it. □□ **mithridatic** /-ˈdætɪk/ *adj.* **mithridatism** /-də,tɪz(ə)m/ *n.* [f. *mithridate* a supposed universal antidote attributed to *Mithridates* VI, king of Pontus d. 63 BC]

mitigate /ˈmɪtɪ,ɡeɪt/ *v.tr.* make milder or less intense or severe; moderate (*your offer certainly mitigated their hostility*). ¶ Often confused with *militate*. □ **mitigating circumstances** *Law* circumstances permitting greater leniency. □□ **mitigable** *adj.* **mitigation** /-ˈɡeɪʃ(ə)n/ *n.* **mitigator** *n.* **mitigatory** *adj.* [ME f. L *mitigare mitigat-* f. *mitis* mild]

mitochondrion /ˌmaɪtəˈkɒndrɪən/ *n.* (*pl.* **mitochondria** /-drɪə/) *Biol.* an organelle found in most eukaryotic cells, containing enzymes for respiration and energy production. [mod.L f. Gk *mitos* thread + *khondrion* dimin. of *khondros* granule]

mitosis /mɪˈtəʊsɪs, maɪ-/ *n. Biol.* a type of cell division that results in two daughter cells each having the same number and kind of chromosomes as the parent nucleus (cf. MEIOSIS). □□ **mitotic** /-ˈtɒtɪk/ *adj.* [mod.L f. Gk *mitos* thread]

mitral /ˈmaɪtr(ə)l/ *adj.* of or like a mitre. □ **mitral valve** a two-cusped valve between the left atrium and the left ventricle of the heart. [mod.L *mitralis* f. L *mitra* girdle]

mitre /ˈmaɪtə(r)/ *n.* & *v.* (*US* **miter**) —*n.* **1** a tall deeply-cleft head-dress worn by bishops and abbots, esp. as a symbol of office. **2** the joint of two pieces of wood or other material at an angle of 90°, such that the line of junction bisects this angle. **3** a diagonal join of two pieces of fabric that meet at a corner, made by folding. —*v.* **1** *tr.* bestow the mitre on. **2** *tr.* & *intr.* join with a mitre. □ **mitre-block** (or **board** or **box**) a guide for a saw in cutting mitre-joints. **mitre-wheels** a pair of bevelled cog-wheels with teeth set at 45° and axes at right angles. □□ **mitred** *adj.* [ME f. OF f. L *mitra* f. Gk *mitra* girdle, turban]

mitt /mɪt/ *n.* **1** = MITTEN 1. **2** a glove leaving the fingers and thumb-tip exposed. **3** *sl.* a hand or fist. **4** a baseball glove for catching the ball. [abbr. of MITTEN]

mitten /ˈmɪt(ə)n/ *n.* **1** a glove with two sections, one for the thumb and the other for all four fingers. **2** *sl.* (in *pl.*) boxing gloves. □□ **mittened** *adj.* [ME f. OF *mitaine* ult. f. L *medietas* half: see MOIETY]

mittimus /ˈmɪtɪməs/ *n.* a warrant committing a person to prison. [ME f. L, = we send]

mitzvah /ˈmɪtsvɑː/ *n.* (*pl.* **mitzvoth** /-vɒt/) in Judaism: **1** a precept or commandment. **2** a good deed done from religious duty. [Heb. *miṣwāh* commandment]

mix /mɪks/ *v.* & *n.* —*v.* **1** *tr.* combine or put together (two or more substances or things) so that the constituents of each are diffused among those of the other(s). **2** *tr.* prepare (a compound, cocktail, etc.) by combining the ingredients. **3** *tr.* combine an activity etc. with another simultaneously (*mix business and pleasure*). **4** *intr.* **a** join, be mixed, or combine, esp. readily (*oil and water will not mix*). **b** be compatible. **c** be sociable (*must learn to mix*). **5** *intr.* **a** (foll. by *with*) (of a person) be harmonious or sociable with; have regular dealings with. **b** (foll. by *in*) participate in. **6** *tr.* drink different kinds of (alcoholic liquor) in close succession. —*n.* **1 a** the act or an instance of mixing; a mixture. **b** the proportion of materials etc. in a mixture. **2** *colloq.* a group of persons of different types (*social mix*). **3** the ingredients prepared commercially for making a cake etc. or for a process such as making concrete. **4** the merging of film pictures or sound. □**be mixed up in** (or **with**) be involved in or with (esp. something undesirable). **mix in** be harmonious or sociable. **mix it** *colloq.* start fighting. **mix up 1** mix thoroughly. **2** confuse; mistake the identity of. **mix-up** *n.* a confusion, misunderstanding, or mistake. □□**mixable** *adj.* [back-form. f. MIXED (taken as past part.)]

mixed /mɪkst/ *adj.* **1** of diverse qualities or elements. **2** containing persons from various backgrounds etc. **3** for or involving persons of both sexes (*a mixed school; mixed bathing*). □**mixed bag** (or **bunch**) a diverse assortment of things or persons. **mixed blessing** a thing having advantages and disadvantages. **mixed crystal** one formed from more than one substance. **mixed doubles** *Tennis* a doubles game with a man and a woman as partners on each side. **mixed economy** an economic system combining private and State enterprise. **mixed farming** farming of both crops and livestock. **mixed feelings** a mixture of pleasure and dismay about something. **mixed grill** a dish of various grilled meats and vegetables etc. **mixed marriage** a marriage between persons of different races or religions. **mixed metaphor** a combination of inconsistent metaphors (e.g. *this tower of strength will forge ahead*). **mixed number** an integer and a proper fraction. **mixed-up** *colloq.* mentally or emotionally confused; socially ill-adjusted. □□**mixedness** /-ɪdnɪs/ *n.* [ME *mixt* f. OF *mixte* f. L *mixtus* past part. of *miscēre* mix]

mixer /ˈmɪksə(r)/ *n.* **1** a device for mixing foods etc. or for processing other materials. **2** a person who manages socially in a specified way (*a good mixer*). **3** a (usu. soft) drink to be mixed with another. **4** *Broadcasting & Cinematog.* **a** a device for merging input signals to produce a combined output in the form of sound or pictures. **b** a person who operates this. □**mixer tap** a tap through which mixed hot and cold water is drawn by means of separate controls.

mixture /ˈmɪkstʃə(r)/ *n.* **1** the process of mixing or being mixed. **2** the result of mixing; something mixed; a combination. **3** *Chem.* the product of the random distribution of one substance through another without any chemical reaction taking place between the components, as distinct from a chemical compound. **4** ingredients mixed together to produce a substance, esp. a medicine (*cough mixture*). **5** a person regarded as a combination of qualities and attributes. **6** gas or vaporized petrol or oil mixed with air, forming an explosive charge in an internal-combustion engine. □**the mixture as before** the same treatment repeated. [ME f. F *mixture* or L *mixtura* (as MIXED)]

mizen /ˈmɪz(ə)n/ *n.* (also **mizzen**) *Naut.* (in full **mizen-sail**) the lowest fore-and-aft sail of a fully rigged ship's mizen-mast. □**mizen-mast** the mast next aft of the mainmast. **mizen yard** that on which the mizen is extended. [ME f. F *misaine* f. It. *mezzana* mizen-sail, fem. of *mezzano* middle: see MEZZANINE]

mizzle[1] /ˈmɪz(ə)l/ *v.intr.* drizzle. □□**mizzly** *adj.* [ME, prob. f. LG *miseln*: cf. MDu. *miezelen*]

mizzle[2] /ˈmɪz(ə)l/ *v.intr.* *Brit. sl.* run away; decamp. [18th c.: orig. unkn.]

Mk. *abbr.* **1** the German mark. **2** Mark (esp. in the New Testament).

mks *abbr.* metre-kilogram-second.

Mkt. *abbr.* Market.

ml *abbr.* **1** millilitre(s). **2** mile(s).

MLA *abbr.* **1** Member of the Legislative Assembly. **2** Modern Language Association (of America).

MLC *abbr.* Member of the Legislative Council.

MLD *abbr.* minimum lethal dose.

MLF *abbr.* multilateral nuclear force.

M.Litt. *abbr.* Master of Letters. [L *Magister Litterarum*]

Mlle *abbr.* (*pl.* **Mlles**) *Mademoiselle.*

MLR *abbr.* minimum lending rate.

MM *abbr.* **1** *Messieurs.* **2** (in the UK) Military Medal. **3** Maelzel's metronome.

mm *abbr.* millimetre(s).

Mme *abbr.* (*pl.* **Mmes**) *Madame.*

m.m.f. *abbr.* magnetomotive force.

M.Mus. *abbr.* Master of Music.

MN *abbr.* **1** *Brit.* Merchant Navy. **2** *US* Minnesota (in official postal use).

Mn *symb. Chem.* the element manganese.

M'Naghten rules var. of MCNAUGHTEN RULES (see at MACN-).

mnemonic /nɪˈmɒnɪk/ *adj. & n.* —*adj.* of or designed to aid the memory. —*n.* a mnemonic device. □□**mnemonically** *adv.* **mnemonist** /ˈniːmənɪst/ *n.* [med.L *mnemonicus* f. Gk *mnēmonikos* f. *mnēmōn* mindful]

mnemonics /nɪˈmɒnɪks/ *n.pl.* (usu. treated as *sing.*) **1** the art of improving memory. **2** a system for this.

MO *abbr.* **1** Medical Officer. **2** money order. **3** *US* Missouri (in official postal use).

Mo *symb. Chem.* the element molybdenum.

Mo. *abbr.* Missouri.

mo /məʊ/ *n.* (*pl.* **mos**) *colloq.* a moment (*wait a mo*). [abbr.]

mo. *abbr.* *US* month.

moa /ˈməʊə/ *n.* (*pl.* **moas**) any extinct flightless New Zealand bird of the family Dinornithidae, resembling the ostrich. [Maori]

moan /məʊn/ *n. & v.* —*n.* **1** a long murmur expressing physical or mental suffering. **2** a low plaintive sound of wind etc. **3** a complaint; a grievance. —*v.* **1** *intr.* make a moan or moans. **2** *intr. colloq.* complain or grumble. **3** *tr.* a utter with moans. **b** lament. □□**moaner** *n.* **moanful** *adj.* **moaningly** *adv.* [ME f. OE *mān* (unrecorded) f. Gmc]

moat /məʊt/ *n. & v.* —*n.* a deep defensive ditch round a castle, town, etc., usu. filled with water. —*v.tr.* surround with or as with a moat. [ME *mot(e)* f. OF *mote, motte* mound]

mob /mɒb/ *n. & v.* —*n.* **1** a disorderly crowd; a rabble. **2** (prec. by *the*) usu. *derog.* the populace. **3** *colloq.* a gang; an associated group of persons. **4** *Austral.* a flock or herd. —*v.tr. & intr.* (**mobbed, mobbing**) **1** *tr.* **a** crowd round in order to attack or admire. **b** (of a mob) attack. **c** *US* crowd into (a building). **2** *intr.* assemble in a mob. □**mob law** (or **rule**) law or rule imposed and enforced by a mob. □□**mobber** *n. & adj.* [abbr. of *mobile*, short for L *mobile vulgus* excitable crowd: see MOBILE]

mob-cap /ˈmɒbkæp/ *n. hist.* a woman's large indoor cap covering all the hair, worn in the 18th and early 19th c. [obs. (18th-c.) *mob*, orig. = slut + CAP]

mobile /ˈməʊbaɪl/ *adj. & n.* —*adj.* **1** movable; not fixed; able to move or flow easily. **2** (of the face etc.) readily changing its expression. **3** (of a shop, library, etc.) accommodated in a vehicle so as to serve various places. **4** (of a person) able to change his or her social status. —*n.* a decorative structure that may be hung so as to turn freely. □**mobile home** a large caravan permanently parked and used as a residence. **mobile sculpture** a sculpture having moving parts. □□**mobility** /məˈbɪlɪti/ *n.* [ME f. F f. L *mobilis* f. *movēre* move]

mobilize /ˈməʊbɪˌlaɪz/ *v.* (also **-ise**) **1 a** *tr.* organize for service or action (esp. troops in time of war). **b** *intr.* be organized in this way. **2** *tr.* render movable; bring into circulation. □□**mobilizable** *adj.* **mobilization** /-ˈzeɪʃ(ə)n/ *n.* **mobilizer** *n.* [F *mobiliser* (as MOBILE)]

Möbius strip /ˈmɜːbɪəs/ *n. Math.* a one-sided surface formed by joining the ends of a rectangle after twisting one end through 180°. [A. F. *Möbius*, Ger. mathematician d. 1868]

mobocracy /mɒˈbɒkrəsɪ/ n. (pl. -ies) colloq. **1** rule by a mob. **2** a ruling mob.

mobster /ˈmɒbstə(r)/ n. sl. a gangster.

moccasin /ˈmɒkəsɪn/ n. **1** a type of soft leather slipper or shoe with combined sole and heel, as orig. worn by N. American Indians. **2** (in full **water moccasin**) US a poisonous American snake of the genus Agkistrodon piscivorus. [Amer. Ind. mockasin, makisin]

mocha /ˈmɒkə/ n. **1** a coffee of fine quality. **2** a beverage or flavouring made with this, often with chocolate added. **3** a soft kind of sheepskin. [Mocha, a port on the Red Sea, from where the coffee first came]

mock /mɒk/ v., adj., & n. —v. **1 a** tr. ridicule; scoff at. **b** intr. (foll. by at) act with scorn or contempt for. **2** tr. mimic contemptuously. **3** tr. jeer, defy, or delude contemptuously. —attrib.adj. sham, imitation (esp. without intention to deceive); pretended (a mock battle; mock cream). —n. **1** a thing deserving scorn. **2** (in pl.) colloq. mock examinations. □**make mock** (or **a mock**) **of** ridicule. **mock-heroic** adj. (of a literary style) burlesquing a heroic style. —n. such a style. **mock moon** paraselene. **mock orange** a white-flowered heavy-scented shrub, Philadelphus coronarius. **mock sun** parhelion. **mock turtle soup** soup made from a calf's head etc. to resemble turtle soup. **mock-up** an experimental model or replica of a proposed structure etc. □□**mockable** adj. **mockingly** adv. [ME mokke, mocque f. OF mo(c)quer deride f. Rmc]

mocker /ˈmɒkə(r)/ n. a person who mocks. □**put the mockers on** sl. **1** bring bad luck to. **2** put a stop to.

mockery /ˈmɒkərɪ/ n. (pl. -ies) **1 a** derision, ridicule. **b** a subject or occasion of this. **2** (often foll. by of) a counterfeit or absurdly inadequate representation. **3** a ludicrously or insultingly futile action etc. [ME f. OF moquerie (as MOCK)]

mockingbird /ˈmɒkɪŋˌbɜːd/ n. a bird that mimics the notes of other birds, esp. the American songbird Mimus polyglottos.

MOD abbr. (in the UK) Ministry of Defence.

mod¹ /mɒd/ adj. & n. colloq. —adj. modern, esp. in style of dress. —n. Brit. a young person (esp. in the 1960s) of a group aiming at sophistication and smart modern dress. □**mod cons** modern conveniences. [abbr.]

mod² /mɒd/ prep. Math. = MODULO. [abbr.]

mod³ /mɒd/ n. a Highland Gaelic meeting for music and poetry. [Gael. mōd]

modal /ˈməʊd(ə)l/ adj. **1** of or relating to mode or form as opposed to substance. **2** Gram. **a** of or denoting the mood of a verb. **b** (of an auxiliary verb, e.g. would) used to express the mood of another verb. **c** (of a particle) denoting manner. **3** Statistics of or relating to a mode; occurring most frequently in a sample or population. **4** Mus. denoting a style of music using a particular mode. **5** Logic (of a proposition) in which the predicate is affirmed of the subject with some qualification, or which involves the affirmation of possibility, impossibility, necessity, or contingency. □□**modally** adv. [med.L modalis f. L (as MODE)]

modality /məˈdælɪtɪ/ n. (pl. -ies) **1** the state of being modal. **2** (in sing. or pl.) a prescribed method of procedure. [med.L modalitas (as MODAL)]

mode /məʊd/ n. **1** a way or manner in which a thing is done; a method of procedure. **2** a prevailing fashion or custom. **3** Computing a way of operating or using a system (print mode). **4** Statistics the value that occurs most frequently in a given set of data. **5** Mus. **a** each of the scale systems that result when the white notes of the piano are played consecutively over an octave (Lydian mode). **b** each of the two main modern scale systems, the major and minor (minor mode). **6** Logic **a** the character of a modal proposition. **b** = MOOD². **7** Physics any of the distinct

kinds or patterns of vibration of an oscillating system. **8** US Gram. = MOOD². [F mode and L modus measure]

model /ˈmɒd(ə)l/ n. & v. —n. **1** a representation in three dimensions of an existing person or thing or of a proposed structure, esp. on a smaller scale (often attrib.: a model train). **2** a simplified (often mathematical) description of a system etc., to assist calculations and predictions. **3** a figure in clay, wax, etc., to be reproduced in another material. **4** a particular design or style of a structure or commodity, esp. of a car. **5 a** an exemplary person or thing (a model of self-discipline). **b** (attrib.) ideal, exemplary (a model student). **6** a person employed to pose for an artist or photographer or to display clothes etc. by wearing them. **7** a garment etc. by a well-known designer, or a copy of this. —v. (**modelled**, **modelling**; US **modeled**, **modeling**) **1** tr. **a** fashion or shape (a figure) in clay, wax, etc. **b** (foll. by after, on, etc.) form (a thing in imitation of). **2 a** intr. act or pose as a model. **b** tr. (of a person acting as a model) display (a garment). **3** tr. devise a (usu. mathematical) model of (a phenomenon, system, etc.). **4** tr. Painting cause to appear three-dimensional. □□**modeller** n. [F modelle f. It. modello ult. f. L modulus: see MODULUS]

modem /ˈməʊdem/ n. a combined device for modulation and demodulation, e.g. between a computer and a telephone line. [modulator + demodulator]

moderate adj., n., & v. —adj. /ˈmɒdərət/ **1** avoiding extremes; temperate in conduct or expression. **2** fairly or tolerably large or good. **3** (of the wind) of medium strength. **4** (of prices) fairly low. —n. /ˈmɒdərət/ a person who holds moderate views, esp. in politics. —v. /ˈmɒdəˌreɪt/ **1** tr. & intr. make or become less violent, intense, rigorous, etc. **2** tr. (also absol.) act as a moderator of or to. **3** tr. Physics retard (neutrons) with a moderator. □□**moderately** /-rətlɪ/ adv. **moderateness** /-rətnəs/ n. **moderatism** /ˈmɒdərəˌtɪz(ə)m/ n. [ME f. L moderatus past part. of moderare reduce, control: rel. to MODEST]

moderation /ˌmɒdəˈreɪʃ(ə)n/ n. **1** the process or an instance of moderating. **2** the quality of being moderate. **3** Physics the retardation of neutrons by a moderator (see MODERATOR 5). **4** (in pl.) (**Moderations**) the first public examination in some faculties for the Oxford BA degree. □**in moderation** in a moderate manner or degree. [ME f. OF f. L moderatio -onis (as MODERATE)]

moderato /ˌmɒdəˈrɑːtəʊ/ adj., adv., & n. Mus. —adj. & adv. performed at a moderate pace. —n. (pl. -os) a piece of music to be performed in this way. [It. (as MODERATE)]

moderator /ˈmɒdəˌreɪtə(r)/ n. **1** an arbitrator or mediator. **2** a presiding officer. **3** Eccl. a Presbyterian minister presiding over an ecclesiastical body. **4** an examiner for Moderations. **5** Physics a substance used in a nuclear reactor to retard neutrons. □□**moderatorship** n. [ME f. L (as MODERATE)]

modern /ˈmɒd(ə)n/ adj. & n. —adj. **1** of the present and recent times. **2** in current fashion; not antiquated. —n. (usu. in pl.) a person living in modern times. □**modern English** English from about 1500 onwards. **modern history** history from the end of the Middle Ages to the present day. □□**modernity** /-ˈdɜːnɪtɪ/ n. **modernly** adv. **modernness** n. [F moderne or LL modernus f. L modo just now]

modernism /ˈmɒdəˌnɪz(ə)m/ n. **1 a** modern ideas or methods. **b** the tendency of religious belief to harmonize with modern ideas. **2** a modern term or expression. □□**modernist** n. **modernistic** /-ˈnɪstɪk/ adj. **modernistically** /-ˈnɪstɪkəlɪ/ adv.

modernize /ˈmɒdəˌnaɪz/ v. (also -ise) **1** tr. make modern; adapt to modern needs or habits. **2** intr. adopt modern ways or views. □□**modernization** /-ˈzeɪʃ(ə)n/ n. **modernizer** n.

modest /ˈmɒdɪst/ adj. **1** having or expressing a humble or moderate estimate of one's own merits or achievements. **2** diffident, bashful, retiring. **3** decorous in manner and conduct. **4** moderate or restrained in amount, extent, severity, etc.; not excessive or exaggerated (*a modest sum*). **5** (of a thing) unpretentious in appearance etc. □□ **modestly** *adv.* [F *modeste* f. L *modestus* keeping due measure]

modesty /ˈmɒdɪstɪ/ *n.* the quality of being modest.

modicum /ˈmɒdɪkəm/ *n.* (foll. by *of*) a small quantity. [L, = short distance or time, neut. of *modicus* moderate f. *modus* measure]

modification /ˌmɒdɪfɪˈkeɪʃ(ə)n/ *n.* **1** the act or an instance of modifying or being modified. **2** a change made. [F or f. L *modificatio* (as MODIFY)]

modifier /ˈmɒdɪˌfaɪə(r)/ *n.* **1** a person or thing that modifies. **2** *Gram.* a word, esp. an adjective or noun used attributively, that qualifies the sense of another word (e.g. *good* and *family* in *a good family house*).

modify /ˈmɒdɪˌfaɪ/ *v.tr.* (-ies, -ied) **1** make less severe or extreme; tone down (*modify one's demands*). **2** make partial changes in; make different. **3** *Gram.* qualify or expand the sense of (a word etc.). **4** *Phonet.* change (a vowel) by umlaut. **5** *Chem.* change or replace all the substituent radicals of a polymer, thereby changing its physical properties such as solubility etc. (*modified starch*). □□ **modifiable** *adj.* **modificatory** /-fɪˌkeɪtərɪ/ *adj.* [ME f. OF *modifier* f. L *modificare* (as MODE)]

modillion /məˈdɪljən/ *n. Archit.* a projecting bracket under the corona of a cornice in the Corinthian and other orders. [F *modillon* f. It. *modiglione* ult. f. L *mutulus* mutule]

modish /ˈməʊdɪʃ/ *adj.* fashionable. □□ **modishly** *adv.* **modishness** *n.*

modiste /mɒˈdiːst/ *n.* a milliner; a dressmaker. [F (as MODE)]

Mods /mɒdz/ *n.pl. colloq.* Moderations (see MODERATION 4). [abbr.]

modular /ˈmɒdjʊlə(r)/ *adj.* of or consisting of modules or moduli. □□ **modularity** /-ˈlærɪtɪ/ *n.* [mod.L *modularis* f. L *modulus*: see MODULUS]

modulate /ˈmɒdjʊˌleɪt/ *v.* **1** *tr.* **a** regulate or adjust. **b** moderate. **2** *tr.* adjust or vary the tone or pitch of (the speaking voice). **3** *tr.* alter the amplitude or frequency of (a wave) by a wave of a lower frequency to convey a signal. **4** *intr.* & *tr. Mus.* (often foll. by *from*, *to*) change or cause to change from one key to another. □□ **modulation** /-ˈleɪʃ(ə)n/ *n.* **modulator** *n.* [L *modulari modulat-* to measure f. *modus* measure]

module /ˈmɒdjuːl/ *n.* **1** a standardized part or independent unit used in construction, esp. of furniture, a building, or an electronic system. **2** an independent self-contained unit of a spacecraft (*lunar module*). **3** a unit or period of training or education. **4 a** a standard or unit of measurement. **b** *Archit.* a unit of length for expressing proportions, e.g. the semidiameter of a column at the base. [F *module* or L *modulus*: see MODULUS]

modulo /ˈmɒdjʊˌləʊ/ *prep.* & *adj. Math.* using, or with respect to, a modulus (see MODULUS 2). [L, ablat. of *modulus*]

modulus /ˈmɒdjʊləs/ *n.* (*pl.* **moduli** /-ˌlaɪ/) *Math.* **1 a** the magnitude of a real number without regard to its sign. **b** the positive square root of the sum of the squares of the real and imaginary parts of a complex number. **2** a constant factor or ratio. **3** (in number theory) a number used as a divisor for considering numbers in sets giving the same remainder when divided by it. **4** a constant indicating the relation between a physical effect and the force producing it. [L, = measure, dimin. of *modus*]

modus operandi /ˌməʊdəs ˌɒpəˈrændɪ/ *n.* (*pl.* ***modi operandi*** /ˌməʊdɪ/) **1** the particular way in which a person performs a task or action. **2** the way a thing operates. [L, = way of operating: see MODUS]

modus vivendi /ˌməʊdəs vɪˈvɛndɪ/ *n.* (*pl.* ***modi vivendi*** /ˌməʊdɪ/) **1** a way of living or coping. **2 a** an arrangement whereby those in dispute can carry on pending a settlement. **b** an arrangement between

people who agree to differ. [L, = way of living: see MODE]

mofette /məˈfɛt/ *n.* **1** a fumerole. **2** an exhalation of vapour from this. [F *mofette* or Neapolitan It. *mofetta*]

mog /mɒɡ/ *n.* (also **moggie** /ˈmɒɡɪ/) *Brit. sl.* a cat. [20th c.: of dial. orig.]

Mogadon /ˈmɒɡəˌdɒn/ *n. propr.* a hypnotic drug used to treat insomnia.

mogul /ˈməʊɡ(ə)l/ *n.* **1** *colloq.* an important or influential person. **2** (**Mogul**) *hist.* **a** = MUGHAL. **b** (often **the Great Mogul**) any of the emperors of Delhi in the 16th-19th c. [Pers. *muġūl*: see MUGHAL]

MOH *abbr.* Medical Officer of Health.

mohair /ˈməʊhɛə(r)/ *n.* **1** the hair of the angora goat. **2** a yarn or fabric from this, either pure or mixed with wool or cotton. [ult. f. Arab. *muḵayyar*, lit. choice, select]

Mohammedan var. of MUHAMMADAN.

Mohawk /ˈməʊhɔːk/ *n.* **1 a** a member of a tribe of N. American Indians. **b** the language of this tribe. **2** *Skating* a step from either edge of the skate to the same edge on the other foot in the opposite direction. [native name]

Mohican /məʊˈhiːkən/ *n.* & *adj.* —*n.* a member of a N. American Indian people of Connecticut. —*adj.* **1** of or relating to this people. **2** (of a hairstyle) resembling that of the Mohicans, with the head shaved except for a strip of hair from the middle of the forehead to the back of the neck, often worn in long spikes. [native name]

moho /ˈməʊhəʊ/ *n.* (*pl.* **-os**) *Geol.* a boundary of discontinuity separating the earth's crust and mantle. [A. *Mohorovičić*, Yugoslav seismologist d. 1936]

moidore /ˈmɔɪdɔː(r)/ *n. hist.* a Portuguese gold coin, current in England in the 18th c. [Port. *moeda d'ouro* money of gold]

moiety /ˈmɔɪətɪ/ *n.* (*pl.* **-ies**) *Law* or *literary* **1** a half. **2** each of the two parts into which a thing is divided. [ME f. OF *moité*, *moitié* f. L *medietas -tatis* middle f. *medius* (adj.) middle]

moil /mɔɪl/ *v.* & *n. archaic* —*v.intr.* drudge (esp. *toil and moil*). —*n.* drudgery. [ME f. OF *moillier* moisten, paddle in mud, ult. f. L *mollis* soft]

moire /mwɑː(r)/ *n.* (in full **moire antique**) watered fabric, orig. mohair, now usu. silk. [F (earlier *mouaire*) f. MOHAIR]

moiré /ˈmwɑːreɪ/ *adj.* & *n.* —*adj.* **1** (of silk) watered. **2** (of metal) having a patterned appearance like watered silk. —*n.* **1** this patterned appearance. **2** = MOIRE. [F, past part. of *moirer* (as MOIRE)]

moist /mɔɪst/ *adj.* **1 a** slightly wet; damp. **b** (of the season etc.) rainy. **2** (of a disease) marked by a discharge of matter etc. □□ **moistly** *adv.* **moistness** *n.* [ME f. OF *moiste*, ult. from or rel. to L *mucidus* (see MUCUS) and *musteus* fresh (see MUST²)]

moisten /ˈmɔɪs(ə)n/ *v.tr.* & *intr.* make or become moist.

moisture /ˈmɔɪstʃə(r)/ *n.* water or other liquid diffused in a small quantity as vapour, or within a solid, or condensed on a surface. □□ **moistureless** *adj.* [ME f. OF *moistour* (as MOIST)]

moisturize /ˈmɔɪstʃəˌraɪz/ *v.tr.* (also **-ise**) make less dry (esp. the skin by use of a cosmetic). □□ **moisturizer** *n.*

moke /məʊk/ *n. sl.* **1** *Brit.* a donkey. **2** *Austral.* a very poor horse. [19th c.: orig. unkn.]

moksa /ˈmɒksə/ *n. Hinduism* etc. release from the cycle of rebirth. [Skr. *mokṣa*]

mol /məʊl/ *abbr.* = MOLE⁴.

molal /ˈməʊl(ə)l/ *adj. Chem.* (of a solution) containing one mole of solute per kilogram of solvent. □□ **molality** /məˈlælɪtɪ/ *n.* [MOLE⁴ + -AL]

molar¹ /ˈməʊlə(r)/ *adj.* & *n.* —*adj.* (usu. of a mammal's back teeth) serving to grind. —*n.* a molar tooth. [L *molaris* f. *mola* millstone]

molar² /ˈməʊlə(r)/ *adj.* **1** of or relating to mass. **2**

acting on or by means of large masses or units. [L *moles* mass]

molar[3] /'məʊlə(r)/ *adj. Chem.* **1** of a mass of substance usu. per mole (*molar latent heat*). **2** (of a solution) containing one mole of solute per litre of solvent. □□ **molarity** /mə'lærɪtɪ/ *n.* [MOLE[4] + -AR[1]]

molasses /mə'læsɪz/ *n.pl.* (treated as *sing.*) **1** uncrystallized syrup extracted from raw sugar during refining. **2** *US* treacle. [Port. *melaço* f. LL *mellaceum* MUST[2] f. *mel* honey]

mold *US* var. of MOULD[1], MOULD[2], MOULD[3].

molder *US* var. of MOULDER.

molding *US* var. of MOULDING.

moldy *US* var. of MOULDY.

mole[1] /məʊl/ *n.* **1** any small burrowing insect-eating mammal of the family Talpidae, esp. *Talpa europaea*, with dark velvety fur and very small eyes. **2** *colloq.* **a** a spy established deep within an organization and usu. dormant for a long period while attaining a position of trust. **b** a betrayer of confidential information. [ME *molle*, prob. f. MDu. *moll(e)*, *mol*, MLG *mol*, *mul*]

mole[2] /məʊl/ *n.* a small often slightly raised dark blemish on the skin caused by a high concentration of melanin. [OE *māl* f. Gmc]

mole[3] /məʊl/ *n.* **1** a massive structure serving as a pier, breakwater, or causeway. **2** an artificial harbour. [F *môle* f. L *moles* mass]

mole[4] /məʊl/ *n. Chem.* the SI unit of amount of substance equal to the quantity containing as many elementary units as there are atoms in 0.012 kg of carbon-12. [G *Mol* f. *Molekül* MOLECULE]

mole[5] /məʊl/ *n. Med.* an abnormal mass of tissue in the uterus. [F *môle* f. L *mola* millstone]

molecular /mə'lekjʊlə(r)/ *adj.* of, relating to, or consisting of molecules. □**molecular biology** the study of the structure and function of large molecules associated with living organisms. **molecular sieve** a crystalline substance with pores of molecular dimensions which permit the entry of certain molecules but are impervious to others. **molecular weight** = *relative molecular mass*. □□ **molecularity** /-'lærɪtɪ/ *n.* **molecularly** *adv.*

molecule /'mɒlɪˌkjuːl/ *n.* **1** *Chem.* the smallest fundamental unit (usu. a group of atoms) of a chemical compound that can take part in a chemical reaction. **2** (in general use) a small particle. [F *molécule* f. mod.L *molecula* dimin. of L *moles* mass]

molehill /'məʊlhɪl/ *n.* a small mound thrown up by a mole in burrowing. □**make a mountain out of a molehill** exaggerate the importance of a minor difficulty.

moleskin /'məʊlskɪn/ *n.* **1** the skin of a mole used as fur. **2 a** a kind of cotton fustian with its surface shaved before dyeing. **b** (in *pl.*) clothes, esp. trousers, made of this.

molest /mə'lest/ *v.tr.* **1** annoy or pester (a person) in a hostile or injurious way. **2** attack or interfere with (a person), esp. sexually. □□ **molestation** /ˌmɒle'steɪʃ(ə)n, ˌməʊl-/ *n.* **molester** *n.* [OF *molester* or L *molestare* annoy f. *molestus* troublesome]

moline /mə'laɪn/ *adj. Heraldry* (of a cross) having each extremity broadened and curved back. [prob. f. AF *moliné* f. *molin* MILL[1],· because of the resemblance to the iron support of a millstone]

moll /mɒl/ *n. sl.* **1** a gangster's female companion. **2** a prostitute. [pet-form of the name *Mary*]

mollify /'mɒlɪˌfaɪ/ *v.tr.* (-ies, -ied) **1** appease, pacify. **2** reduce the severity of; soften. □□ **mollification** /-fɪ'keɪʃ(ə)n/ *n.* **mollifier** *n.* [ME f. F *mollifier* or L *mollificare* f. *mollis* soft]

mollusc /'mɒləsk/ *n.* (*US* **mollusk**) any invertebrate of the phylum Mollusca, with a soft body and usu. a hard shell, including limpets, snails, cuttlefish, oysters, mussels, etc. □□ **molluscan** /mə'lʌskən/ *adj.* **molluscoid** /mə'lʌskɔɪd/ *adj.* **molluscous** /mə'lʌskəs/ *adj.* [mod.L *mollusca* neut. pl. of L *molluscus* f. *mollis* soft]

mollycoddle /'mɒlɪˌkɒd(ə)l/ *v.* & *n.* —*v.tr.* coddle, pamper. —*n.* an effeminate man or boy; a milksop. [formed as MOLL + CODDLE]

mollymawk /'mɒlɪmɔːk/ *n.* (also **mallemuck** /'mælɪˌmʌk/) any of various small kinds of albatross or similar birds. [Du. *mallemok* f. *mal* foolish + *mok* gull]

Moloch /'məʊlɒk/ *n.* **1 a** a Canaanite idol to whom children were sacrificed. **b** a tyrannical object of sacrifices. **2** (**moloch**) the spiny slow-moving grotesque Australian reptile, *Moloch horridus*. [LL f. Gk *Molokh* f. Heb. *mōlekָ*]

Molotov cocktail /'mɒləˌtɒf/ *n.* a crude incendiary device usu. consisting of a bottle filled with inflammable liquid. [V. M. *Molotov*, Russian statesman d. 1986]

molt *US* var. of MOULT.

molten /'məʊlt(ə)n/ *adj.* melted, esp. made liquid by heat. [past part. of MELT]

molto /'mɒltəʊ/ *adv. Mus.* very (*molto sostenuto*; *allegro molto*). [It. f. L *multus* much]

moly /'məʊlɪ/ *n.* (*pl.* **-ies**) **1** an alliaceous plant, *Allium moly*, with small yellow flowers. **2** a mythical herb with white flowers and black roots, endowed with magic properties. [L f. Gk *mōlu*]

molybdenite /mə'lɪbdɪˌnaɪt/ *n.* molybdenum disulphide as an ore.

molybdenum /mə'lɪbdɪnəm/ *n. Chem.* a silver-white brittle metallic transition element occurring naturally in molybdenite and used in steel to give strength and resistance to corrosion. ¶ Symb.: **Mo**. [mod.L, earlier *molybdena*, orig. = molybdenite, lead ore: L *molybdena* f. Gk *molubdaina* plummet f. *molubdos* lead]

mom /mɒm/ *n. US colloq.* mother. [abbr. of MOMMA]

moment /'məʊmənt/ *n.* **1** a very brief portion of time; an instant. **2** a short period of time (*wait a moment*) (see also MINUTE[1]). **3** an exact or particular point of time (*at last the moment arrived*; *I came the moment you called*). **4** importance (*of no great moment*). **5** *Physics* & *Mech.* etc. **a** the turning effect produced by a force acting at a distance on an object. **b** this effect expressed as the product of the force and the distance from its line of action to a point. □**at the moment** at this time; now. **in a moment 1** very soon. **2** instantly. **man** (or **woman** etc.) **of the moment** the one of importance at the time in question. **moment of inertia** *Physics* the quantity by which the angular acceleration of a body must be multiplied to give corresponding torque. **moment of truth** a time of crisis or test (orig. the final sword-thrust in a bullfight). **not for a** (or **one**) **moment** never; not at all. **this moment** immediately; at once (*come here this moment*). [ME f. OF f. L *momentum*: see MOMENTUM]

momenta *pl.* of MOMENTUM.

momentarily /'məʊməntərɪlɪ, -'terɪlɪ, -trɪlɪ/ *adv.* **1** for a moment. **2** *US* **a** at any moment. **b** instantly.

momentary /'məʊməntərɪ, -trɪ/ *adj.* **1** lasting only a moment. **2** short-lived; transitory. □□ **momentariness** *n.* [L *momentarius* (as MOMENT)]

momently /'məʊməntlɪ/ *adv. literary* **1** from moment to moment. **2** every moment. **3** for a moment.

momentous /mə'mentəs/ *adj.* having great importance. □□ **momentously** *adv.* **momentousness** *n.*

momentum /mə'mentəm/ *n.* (*pl.* **momenta** /-tə/) **1** *Physics* the quantity of motion of a moving body, measured as a product of its mass and velocity. **2** the impetus gained by movement. **3** strength or continuity derived from an initial effort. [L f. *movimentum* f. *movēre* move]

momma /'mɒmə/ *n.* var. of MAMMA[1].

mommy /'mɒmɪ/ *n.* (*pl.* **-ies**) esp. *US* = MUMMY[1].

Mon. *abbr.* Monday.

monad /'mɒnæd, 'məʊ-/ *n.* **1** the number one; a unit. **2** *Philos.* any ultimate unit of being (e.g. a soul, an atom, a person, God). **3** *Biol.* a simple organism, e.g. one assumed as the first in the genealogy of living beings. □□ **monadic** /məˈnædɪk/ *adj.* **monadism** *n.* (in sense 2). [F *monade* or LL *monas monad-* f. Gk *monas -ados* unit f. *monos* alone]

monadelphous /ˌmɒnəˈdelfəs/ *adj. Bot.* **1** (of stamens) having filaments united into one bundle. **2** (of a plant) with such stamens. [Gk *monos* one + *adelphos* brother]

monadnock /məˈnædnɒk/ *n.* a steep-sided isolated hill resistant to erosion and rising above a plain. [Mount *Monadnock* in New Hampshire, US]

monandry /məˈnændrɪ/ *n.* **1** the custom of having only one husband at a time. **2** *Bot.* the state of having a single stamen. □□ **monandrous** *adj.* [MONO- after *polyandry*]

monarch /ˈmɒnək/ *n.* **1** a sovereign with the title of king, queen, emperor, empress, or the equivalent. **2** a supreme ruler. **3** a powerful or pre-eminent person. **4** a large orange and black butterfly, *Danaus plexippus.* □□ **monarchal** /məˈnɑːk(ə)l/ *adj.* **monarchic** /məˈnɑːkɪk/ *adj.* **monarchical** /məˈnɑːkɪk(ə)l/ *adj.* **monarchically** /məˈnɑːkɪkəlɪ/ *adv.* [ME f. F *monarque* or LL *monarcha* f. Gk *monarkhēs, -os,* f. *monos* alone + *arkhō* to rule]

monarchism /ˈmɒnəˌkɪz(ə)m/ *n.* the advocacy of the principles of monarchy. □□ **monarchist** *n.* [F *monarchisme* (as MONARCHY)]

monarchy /ˈmɒnəkɪ/ *n.* (*pl.* **-ies**) **1** a form of government with a monarch at the head. **2** a State with this. □□ **monarchial** /mɒˈnɑːkɪəl/ *adj.* [ME f. OF *monarchie* f. LL *monarchia* f. Gk *monarkhia* the rule of one (as MONARCH)]

monastery /ˈmɒnəstərɪ, -strɪ/ *n.* (*pl.* **-ies**) the residence of a religious community, esp. of monks living in seclusion. [ME f. eccl.L *monasterium* f. eccl.Gk *monastērion* f. *monazō* live alone f. *monos* alone]

monastic /məˈnæstɪk/ *adj. & n.* —*adj.* **1** of or relating to monasteries or the religious communities living in them. **2** resembling these or their way of life; solitary and celibate. —*n.* a monk or other follower of a monastic rule. □□ **monastically** *adv.* **monasticism** /-ˌsɪz(ə)m/ *n.* **monasticize** /-ˌsaɪz/ *v.tr.* (also **-ise**). [F *monastique* or LL *monasticus* f. Gk *monastikos* (as MONASTERY)]

monatomic /ˌmɒnəˈtɒmɪk/ *adj. Chem.* **1** (esp. of a molecule) consisting of one atom. **2** having one replaceable atom or radical.

monaural /mɒˈnɔːr(ə)l/ *adj.* **1** = MONOPHONIC. **2** of or involving one ear. □□ **monaurally** *adv.* [MONO- + AURAL]

monazite /ˈmɒnəˌzaɪt/ *n.* a phosphate mineral containing rare-earth elements and thorium. [G *Monazit* f. Gk *monazō* live alone (because of its rarity)]

mondaine /mɔ̃ˈden/ *adj. & n.* —*adj.* **1** of the fashionable world. **2** worldly. —*n.* a worldly or fashionable woman. [F, fem. of *mondain:* see MUNDANE]

Monday /ˈmʌndeɪ, -dɪ/ *n. & adv.* —*n.* the second day of the week, following Sunday. —*adv. colloq.* **1** on Monday. **2** (**Mondays**) on Monday; each Monday. [OE *mōnandæg* day of the moon, transl. LL *lunae dies*]

Monel /ˈməʊn(ə)l/ *n.* (in full **Monel metal**) *propr.* a nickel-copper alloy with high tensile strength and resisting corrosion. [A. *Monell,* US businessman d. 1921]

monetarism /ˈmʌnɪtəˌrɪz(ə)m/ *n.* the theory or practice of controlling the supply of money as the chief method of stabilizing the economy.

monetarist /ˈmʌnɪtərɪst/ *n. & adj.* —*n.* an advocate of monetarism. —*adj.* in accordance with the principles of monetarism.

monetary /ˈmʌnɪtərɪ/ *adj.* **1** of the currency in use. **2** of or consisting of money. □□ **monetarily** *adv.* [F *monétaire* or LL *monetarius* f. L (as MONEY)]

monetize /ˈmʌnɪˌtaɪz/ *v.tr.* (also **-ise**) **1** give a fixed value as currency. **2** put (a metal) into circulation as money. □□ **monetization** /-ˈzeɪʃ(ə)n/ *n.* [F *monétiser* f. L (as MONEY)]

money /ˈmʌnɪ/ *n.* **1 a** a current medium of exchange in the form of coins and banknotes. **b** a particular form of this (*silver money*). **2** (*pl.* **-eys** or **-ies**) (in *pl.*) sums of money. **3 a** wealth; property viewed as convertible into money. **b** wealth as giving power or influence (*money speaks*). **c** a rich person or family (*has married into money*). **4 a** money as a resource (*time is money*). **b** profit, remuneration (*in it for the money*). □**for my money** in my opinion or judgement; for my preference (*is too aggressive for my money*). **have money to burn** see BURN[1]. **in the money** *colloq.* having or winning a lot of money. **money box** a box for saving money dropped through a slit. **money-changer** a person whose business it is to change money, esp. at an official rate. **money for jam** (or **old rope**) *colloq.* profit for little or no trouble. **money-grubber** *colloq.* a person greedily intent on amassing money. **money-grubbing** *n.* this practice. —*adj.* given to this. **money market** *Stock Exch.* trade in short-term stocks, loans, etc. **money of account** see ACCOUNT. **money order** an order for payment of a specified sum, issued by a bank or Post Office. **money spider** a small household spider supposed to bring financial luck. **money-spinner** a thing that brings in a profit. **money's-worth** good value for one's money. **put money into** invest in. □□ **moneyless** *adj.* [ME f. OF *moneie* f. L *moneta* mint, money, orig. a title of Juno, in whose temple at Rome money was minted]

moneybags /ˈmʌnɪˌbægz/ *n.pl.* (treated as *sing.*) *colloq.* usu. *derog.* a wealthy person.

moneyed /ˈmʌnɪd/ *adj.* **1** having much money; wealthy. **2** consisting of money (*moneyed assistance*).

moneylender /ˈmʌnɪˌlendə(r)/ *n.* a person who lends money, esp. as a business, at interest. □□ **moneylending** *n. & adj.*

moneymaker /ˈmʌnɪˌmeɪkə(r)/ *n.* **1** a person who earns much money. **2** a thing, idea, etc., that produces much money. □□ **moneymaking** *n. & adj.*

moneywort /ˈmʌnɪˌwɜːt/ *n.* a trailing evergreen plant, *Lysimachia nummularia,* with round glossy leaves and yellow flowers.

monger /ˈmʌŋɡə(r)/ *n.* (usu. in *comb.*) **1** a dealer or trader (*fishmonger; ironmonger*). **2** usu. *derog.* a person who promotes or deals in something specified (*warmonger; scaremonger*). [OE *mangere* f. *mangian* to traffic f. Gmc, ult. f. L *mango* dealer]

Mongol /ˈmɒŋɡ(ə)l/ *adj. & n.* —*adj.* **1** of or relating to the Asian people now inhabiting Mongolia in Central Asia. **2** resembling this people, esp. in appearance. **3** (**mongol**) often *offens.* suffering from Down's syndrome. —*n.* **1** a Mongolian. **2** (**mongol**) often *offens.* a person suffering from Down's syndrome. [native name: perh. f. *mong* brave]

Mongolian /mɒŋˈɡəʊlɪən/ *n. & adj.* —*n.* a native or inhabitant of Mongolia; the language of Mongolia. —*adj.* of or relating to Mongolia or its people or language.

mongolism /ˈmɒŋɡəˌlɪz(ə)m/ *n.* = DOWN'S SYNDROME. ¶ The term *Down's syndrome* is now much preferred in medical circles. [MONGOL + -ISM, because its physical characteristics were thought to be reminiscent of Mongolians]

Mongoloid /ˈmɒŋɡəˌlɔɪd/ *adj. & n.* —*adj.* **1** characteristic of the Mongolians, esp. in having a broad flat yellowish face. **2** (**mongoloid**) often *offens.* having the characteristic symptoms of Down's syndrome. —*n.* a Mongoloid or mongoloid person.

mongoose /ˈmɒŋɡuːs/ *n.* (*pl.* **mongooses**) any of various small flesh-eating civet-like mammals of the family Viverridae, esp. of the genus *Herpestes.* [Marathi *mangūs*]

mongrel /ˈmʌŋɡr(ə)l, ˈmɒŋ-/ *n. & adj.* —*n.* **1** a dog of no definable type or breed. **2** any other animal or plant resulting from the crossing of different breeds or types. **3** *derog.* a person of mixed race. —*adj.* of mixed origin, nature, or character. □□ **mongrelism** *n.* **mongrelize** *v.tr.* (also **-ise**). **mongrelization**

/-'zeɪʃ(ə)n/ *n.* **mongrelly** *adj.* [earlier *meng-, mang-* f. Gmc: prob. rel. to MINGLE]

'mongst *poet.* var. of AMONGST. [see AMONG]

monial /'məʊnɪəl/ *n.* a mullion. [ME f. OF *moinel* middle f. *moien* MEAN³]

monicker var. of MONIKER.

monies see MONEY 2.

moniker /'mɒnɪkə(r)/ *n.* (also **monicker, monniker**) *sl.* a name. [19th c.: orig. unkn.]

moniliform /mə'nɪlɪˌfɔːm/ *adj.* with a form suggesting a string of beads. [F *moniliforme* or mod.L *moniliformis* f. L *monile* necklace]

monism /'mɒnɪz(ə)m, 'məʊn-/ *n.* **1** any theory denying the duality of matter and mind. **2** the doctrine that only one ultimate principle or being exists. □□ **monist** *n.* **monistic** /-'nɪstɪk/ *adj.* [mod.L *monismus* f. Gk *monos* single]

monition /mə'nɪʃ(ə)n/ *n.* **1** (foll. by *of*) *literary* a warning (of danger). **2** *Eccl.* a formal notice from a bishop or ecclesiastical court admonishing a person not to commit an offence. [ME f. OF f. L *monitio -onis* (as MONITOR)]

monitor /'mɒnɪt(ə)r/ *n. & v.* —*n.* **1** any of various persons or devices for checking or warning about a situation, operation, etc. **2** a school pupil with disciplinary or other special duties. **3 a** a television receiver used in a studio to select or verify the picture being broadcast. **b** = *visual display unit.* **4** a person who listens to and reports on foreign broadcasts etc. **5** a detector of radioactive contamination. **6** *Zool.* any tropical lizard of the genus *Varanus,* supposed to give warning of the approach of crocodiles. **7** a heavily armed shallow-draught warship. —*v.tr.* **1** act as a monitor of. **2** maintain regular surveillance over. **3** regulate the strength of (a recorded or transmitted signal). □□ **monitorial** /-'tɔːrɪəl/ *adj.* **monitorship** *n.* [L f. *monēre monit-* warn]

monitory /'mɒnɪtərɪ/ *adj. & n.* —*adj. literary* giving or serving as a warning. —*n.* (*pl.* **-ies**) *Eccl.* a letter of admonition from the pope or a bishop. [L *monitorius* (as MONITION)]

monk /mʌŋk/ *n.* a member of a religious community of men living under certain vows esp. of poverty, chastity, and obedience. □□ **monkish** *adj.* [OE *munuc* ult. f. Gk *monakhos* solitary f. *monos* alone]

monkey /'mʌŋkɪ/ *n. & v.* —*n.* (*pl.* **-eys**) **1** any of various New World and Old World primates esp. of the families Cebidae (including capuchins), Callitrichidae (including marmosets and tamarins), and Cercopithecidae (including baboons and apes). **2** a mischievous person, esp. a child (*young monkey*). **3** *sl.* **a** *Brit.* £500. **b** *US* $500. **4** (in full **monkey engine**) a machine hammer for pile-driving etc. —*v.* (**-eys, -eyed**) **1** *tr.* mimic or mock. **2** *intr.* (often foll. by *with*) tamper or play mischievous tricks. **3** *intr.* (foll. by *around, about*) fool around. □ **have a monkey on one's back** *sl.* be a drug addict. **make a monkey of** humiliate by making appear ridiculous. **monkey bread** the baobab tree or its fruit. **monkey business** *colloq.* mischief. **monkey flower** a mimulus, esp. *Mimulus cardinalis,* with bright yellow flowers. **monkey-jacket** a short close-fitting jacket worn by sailors etc. or at a mess. **monkey-nut** a peanut. **monkey-puzzle** a coniferous tree, *Araucaria araucaria,* native to Chile, with downward-pointing branches and small close-set leaves. **monkey-suit** *colloq.* evening dress. **monkey tricks** *colloq.* mischief. **monkey wrench** a wrench with an adjustable jaw. □□ **monkeyish** *adj.* [16th c.: orig. unkn. (perh. LG)]

monkeyshine /'mʌŋkɪˌʃaɪn/ *n.* (usu. in *pl.*) *US colloq.* = *monkey tricks.*

monkfish /'mʌŋkfɪʃ/ *n.* **1** an angler-fish, esp. *Lophius piscatorius,* often used as food. **2** a large cartilaginous fish, *Squatina squatina,* with a flattened body and large pectoral fins. Also called *angel-shark.*

monkshood /'mʌŋkshʊd/ *n. Bot.* a poisonous garden plant *Aconitum napellus,* with hood-shaped blue or purple flowers.

monniker var. of MONIKER.

mono /'mɒnəʊ/ *adj. & n. colloq.* —*adj.* monophonic. —*n.* (*pl.* **-os**) a monophonic record, reproduction, etc. [abbr.]

mono- /'mɒnəʊ/ *comb. form* (usu. **mon-** before a vowel) **1** one, alone, single. **2** *Chem.* (forming names of compounds) containing one atom or group of a specified kind. [Gk f. *monos* alone]

monoacid /ˌmɒnəʊ'æsɪd/ *adj. Chem.* (of a base) having one replaceable hydroxide ion.

monobasic /ˌmɒnəʊ'beɪsɪk/ *adj. Chem.* (of an acid) having one replaceable hydrogen atom.

monocarpic /ˌmɒnəʊ'kɑːpɪk/ *adj.* (also **monocarpous** /-'kɑːpəs/) *Bot.* bearing fruit only once. [MONO- + Gk *karpos* fruit]

monocausal /ˌmɒnəʊ'kɔːz(ə)l/ *adj.* in terms of a sole cause.

monocephalous /ˌmɒnəʊ'sefələs/ *adj. Bot.* having only one head.

monochord /'mɒnəˌkɔːd/ *n. Mus.* an instrument with a single string and a movable bridge, used esp. to determine intervals. [ME f. OF *monocorde* f. LL *monochordon* f. Gk *monokhordon* (as MONO-, CHORD¹)]

monochromatic /ˌmɒnəkrə'mætɪk/ *adj.* **1** *Physics* (of light or other radiation) of a single wavelength or frequency. **2** containing only one colour. □□ **monochromatically** *adv.*

monochromatism /ˌmɒnəʊ'krəʊməˌtɪz(ə)m/ *n.* complete colour-blindness in which all colours appear as shades of one colour.

monochrome /'mɒnəˌkrəʊm/ *n. & adj.* —*n.* a photograph or picture done in one colour or different tones of this, or in black and white only. —*adj.* having or using only one colour or in black and white only. □□ **monochromic** /-'krəʊmɪk/ *adj.* [ult. f. Gk *monokhrōmatos* (as MONO-, *khrōmatos* f. *khrōma* colour)]

monocle /'mɒnək(ə)l/ *n.* a single eyeglass. □□ **monocled** *adj.* [F, orig. adj. f. LL *monoculus* one-eyed (as MONO-, *oculus* eye)]

monocline /'mɒnəʊˌklaɪn/ *n. Geol.* a bend in rock strata that are otherwise uniformly dipping or horizontal. □□ **monoclinal** /-'klaɪn(ə)l/ *adj.* [MONO- + Gk *klinō* lean, dip]

monoclinic /ˌmɒnəʊ'klɪnɪk/ *adj.* (of a crystal) having one axial intersection oblique. [MONO- + Gk *klinō* lean, slope]

monoclonal /ˌmɒnəʊ'kləʊn(ə)l/ *adj.* forming a single clone; derived from a single individual or cell. □ **monoclonal antibodies** antibodies produced artificially by a single clone and consisting of identical antibody molecules.

monocoque /'mɒnəˌkɒk/ *n. Aeron.* an aircraft or vehicle structure in which the chassis is integral with the body. [F (as MONO-, *coque* shell)]

monocot /'mɒnəʊˌkɒt/ *n.* = MONOCOTYLEDON. [abbr.]

monocotyledon /ˌmɒnəˌkɒtɪ'liːd(ə)n/ *n. Bot.* any flowering plant with a single cotyledon. □□ **monocotyledonous** *adj.*

monocracy /mə'nɒkrəsɪ/ *n.* (*pl.* **-ies**) government by one person only. □□ **monocratic** /-'krætɪk/ *adj.*

monocular /mə'nɒkjʊlə(r)/ *adj.* with or for one eye. □□ **monocularly** *adj.* [LL *monoculus* having one eye]

monoculture /'mɒnəʊˌkʌltʃə(r)/ *n.* the cultivation of a single crop.

monocycle /'mɒnəˌsaɪk(ə)l/ *n.* = UNICYCLE.

monocyte /'mɒnəˌsaɪt/ *n. Biol.* a large type of leucocyte.

monodactylous /ˌmɒnə'dæktɪləs/ *adj.* having one finger, toe, or claw.

monodrama /'mɒnəʊˌdrɑːmə/ *n.* a dramatic piece for one performer.

monody /'mɒnədɪ/ *n.* (*pl.* **-ies**) **1** an ode sung by a single actor in a Greek tragedy. **2** a poem lamenting a person's death. **3** *Mus.* a composition with only

æ *cat* ɑː *arm* e *bed* ɜː *her* ɪ *sit* iː *see* ɒ *hot* ɔː *saw* ʌ *run* ʊ *put* uː *too* ə *ago* aɪ *my*

one melodic line. □□**monodic** /məˈnɒdɪk/ *adj.*
monodist *n.* [LL *monodia* f. Gk *monōidia* f. *monōidos* singing alone (as MONO-, ODE)]

monoecious /məˈniːʃəs/ *adj.* **1** *Bot.* with unisexual male and female organs on the same plant. **2** *Zool.* hermaphrodite. [mod.L *Monoecia* the class of such plants (Linnaeus) f. Gk *monos* single + *oikos* house]

monofilament /ˈmɒnəʊˌfɪləmənt/ *n.* **1** a single strand of man-made fibre. **2** a type of fishing line using this.

monogamy /məˈnɒgəmɪ/ *n.* **1** the practice or state of being married to one person at a time. **2** *Zool.* the habit of having only one mate at a time. □□**monogamist** *n.* **monogamous** *adj.* **monogamously** *adv.* [F *monogamie* f. eccl.L f. Gk *monogamia* (as MONO-, *gamos* marriage)]

monogenesis /ˌmɒnəʊˈdʒɛnɪsɪs/ *n.* (also **monogeny** /məˈnɒdʒɪnɪ/) **1** the theory of the development of all beings from a single cell. **2** the theory that mankind descended from one pair of ancestors. □□ **monogenetic** /-dʒɪˈnɛtɪk/ *adj.*

monoglot /ˈmɒnəˌglɒt/ *adj.* & *n.* —*adj.* using only one language. —*n.* a monoglot person.

monogram /ˈmɒnəˌgræm/ *n.* two or more letters, esp. a person's initials, interwoven as a device. □□**monogrammatic** /-grəˈmætɪk/ *adj.* **monogrammed** *adj.* [F *monogramme* f. LL *monogramma* f. Gk (as MONO-, -GRAM)]

monograph /ˈmɒnəˌgrɑːf/ *n.* & *v.* —*n.* a separate treatise on a single subject or an aspect of it. —*v.tr.* write a monograph on. □□**monographer** /məˈnɒgrəfə(r)/ *n.* **monographist** /məˈnɒgrəfɪst/ *n.* **monographic** /ˌmɒnəˈgræfɪk/ *adj.* [earlier *monography* f. mod.L *monographia* f. *monographus* writer on a single genus or species (as MONO-, -GRAPH, -GRAPHY)]

monogynous /məˈnɒdʒɪnəs/ *adj. Bot.* having only one pistil.

monogyny /məˈnɒdʒɪnɪ/ *n.* the custom of having only one wife at a time.

monohull /ˈmɒnəʊˌhʌl/ *n.* a boat with a single hull.

monohybrid /ˌmɒnəʊˈhaɪbrɪd/ *n.* a hybrid with respect to only one allele.

monohydric /ˌmɒnəʊˈhaɪdrɪk/ *adj. Chem.* containing one hydroxyl group.

monokini /məˈnɒˈkiːnɪ/ *n.* a woman's one-piece beach-garment equivalent to the lower half of a bikini. [MONO- + BIKINI, by false assoc. with BI-]

monolayer /ˈmɒnəʊˌleɪə(r)/ *n. Chem.* a layer only one molecule in thickness.

monolingual /ˌmɒnəʊˈlɪŋgw(ə)l/ *adj.* speaking or using only one language.

monolith /ˈmɒnəlɪθ/ *n.* **1** a single block of stone, esp. shaped into a pillar or monument. **2** a person or thing like a monolith in being massive, immovable, or solidly uniform. **3** a large block of concrete. □□ **monolithic** /-ˈlɪθɪk/ *adj.* [F *monolithe* f. Gk *monolithos* (as MONO-, *lithos* stone)]

monologue /ˈmɒnəˌlɒg/ *n.* **1 a** a scene in a drama in which a person speaks alone. **b** a dramatic composition for one performer. **2** a long speech by one person in a conversation etc. □□ **monologic** /-ˈlɒdʒɪk/ *adj.* **monological** /-ˈlɒdʒɪk(ə)l/ *adj.* **monologist** /məˈnɒlədʒɪst/ *n.* (also **-loguist**). **monologize** /məˈnɒləˌdʒaɪz/ *v.intr.* (also **-ise**). [F f. Gk *monologos* speaking alone (as MONO-, -LOGUE)]

monomania /ˌmɒnəˈmeɪnɪə/ *n.* obsession of the mind by one idea or interest. □□ **monomaniac** *n.* & *adj.* **monomaniacal** /-məˈnaɪək(ə)l/ *adj.* [F *monomanie* (as MONO-, -MANIA)]

monomark /ˈmɒnəʊˌmɑːk/ *n. Brit.* a combination of letters, with or without figures, registered as an identification mark for goods, articles, addresses, etc.

monomer /ˈmɒnəmə(r)/ *n. Chem.* **1** a unit in a dimer, trimer, or polymer. **2** a molecule or compound that can be polymerized. □□ **monomeric** /-ˈmɛrɪk/ *adj.*

monomial /məˈnəʊmɪəl/ *adj.* & *n. Math.* —*adj.* (of

an algebraic expression) consisting of one term. —*n.* a monomial expression. [MONO- after *binomial*]

monomolecular /ˌmɒnəʊməˈlɛkjʊlə(r)/ *adj. Chem.* (of a layer) only one molecule in thickness.

monomorphic /ˌmɒnəˈmɔːfɪk/ *adj.* (also **monomorphous** /-ˈmɔːfəs/) *Biochem.* not changing form during development. □□ **monomorphism** *n.*

mononucleosis /ˌmɒnəʊˌnjuːklɪˈəʊsɪs/ *n.* an abnormally high proportion of monocytes in the blood, esp. = *glandular fever*. [MONO- + NUCLEO- + -OSIS]

monopetalous /ˌmɒnəˈpɛtələs/ *adj. Bot.* having the corolla in one piece, or the petals united into a tube.

monophonic /ˌmɒnəˈfɒnɪk/ *adj.* **1** (of sound-reproduction) using only one channel of transmission (cf. STEREOPHONIC). **2** *Mus.* homophonic. □□ **monophonically** *adv.* [MONO- + Gk *phōnē* sound]

monophthong /ˈmɒnəfˌθɒŋ/ *n. Phonet.* a single vowel sound. □□ **monophthongal** /-ˈθɒŋg(ə)l/ *adj.* [Gk *monophthoggos* (as MONO-, *phthoggos* sound)]

Monophysite /məˈnɒfɪˌzaɪt, ˈmɒnə-/ *n.* a person who holds that there is only one nature (partly divine, partly and subordinately human) in the person of Christ. [eccl.L *monophysita* f. eccl.Gk *monophusitēs* (as MONO-, *phusis* nature)]

monoplane /ˈmɒnəˌpleɪn/ *n.* an aeroplane with one set of wings (cf. BIPLANE).

monopolist /məˈnɒpəlɪst/ *n.* a person who has or advocates a monopoly. □□ **monopolistic** /-ˈlɪstɪk/ *adj.*

monopolize /məˈnɒpəˌlaɪz/ *v.tr.* (also **-ise**) **1** obtain exclusive possession or control of (a trade or commodity etc.). **2** dominate or prevent others from sharing in (a conversation, person's attention, etc.). □□ **monopolization** /-ˈzeɪʃ(ə)n/ *n.* **monopolizer** *n.*

monopoly /məˈnɒpəlɪ/ *n.* (*pl.* **-ies**) **1 a** the exclusive possession or control of the trade in a commodity or service. **b** this conferred as a privilege by the State. **2 a** a commodity or service that is subject to a monopoly. **b** a company etc. that possesses a monopoly. **3** (foll. by *of*, *US on*) exclusive possession, control, or exercise. [L *monopolium* f. Gk *monopōlion* (as MONO-, *pōleō* sell)]

monorail /ˈmɒnəʊˌreɪl/ *n.* a railway in which the track consists of a single rail, usu. elevated with the train units suspended from it.

monosaccharide /ˌmɒnəʊˈsækəˌraɪd/ *n. Chem.* a sugar that cannot be hydrolysed to give a simpler sugar, e.g. glucose.

monosodium glutamate /ˌmɒnəʊˈsəʊdɪəm ˈgluːtəˌmeɪt/ *n. Chem.* a sodium salt of glutamic acid used to flavour food (cf. GLUTAMATE).

monospermous /ˌmɒnəˈspɜːməs/ *adj. Bot.* having one seed. [MONO- + Gk *sperma* seed]

monostichous /məˈnɒstɪkəs/ *adj. Bot. & Zool.* arranged in or consisting of one layer or row. [MONO- + Gk *stikhos* row]

monosyllabic /ˌmɒnəsɪˈlæbɪk/ *adj.* **1** (of a word) having one syllable. **2** (of a person or statement) using or expressed in monosyllables. □□ **monosyllabically** *adv.*

monosyllable /ˈmɒnəˌsɪləb(ə)l/ *n.* a word of one syllable. □**in monosyllables** in simple direct words.

monotheism /ˈmɒnəˌθiːɪz(ə)m/ *n.* the doctrine that there is only one God. □□ **monotheist** *n.* **monotheistic** /-ˈɪstɪk/ *adj.* **monotheistically** /-ˈɪstɪkəlɪ/ *adv.* [MONO- + Gk *theos* god]

monotint /ˈmɒnəʊˌtɪnt/ *n.* = MONOCHROME.

monotone /ˈmɒnəˌtəʊn/ *n.* & *adj.* —*n.* **1** a sound or utterance continuing or repeated on one note without change of pitch. **2** sameness of style in writing. —*adj.* without change of pitch. [mod.L *monotonus* f. late Gk *monotonos* (as MONO-, TONE)]

monotonic /ˌmɒnəˈtɒnɪk/ *adj.* **1** uttered in a monotone. **2** *Math.* (of a function or quantity) varying in such a way that it either never decreases or never increases. □□ **monotonically** *adv.*

monotonous /məˈnɒtənəs/ *adj.* **1** lacking in variety; tedious through sameness. **2** (of a sound or utterance) without variation in tone or pitch. □□ **monotonize** *v.tr.* (also **-ise**). **monotonously** *adv.* **monotonousness** *n.*

monotony /mə'nɒtənɪ/ *n.* **1** the state of being monotonous. **2** dull or tedious routine.

monotreme /'mɒnə,triːm/ *n.* any mammal of the order Monotremata, native to Australia and New Guinea, including the duckbill and spiny anteater, laying large yolky eggs through a common opening for urine, faeces, etc. [MONO- + Gk *trēma -matos* hole]

monotype /'mɒnə,taɪp/ *n.* **1** (**Monotype**) *Printing propr.* a typesetting machine that casts and sets up types in individual characters. **2** an impression on paper made from an inked design painted on glass or metal.

monotypic /,mɒnə'tɪpɪk/ *adj.* having only one type or representative.

monovalent /,mɒnə'veɪlənt/ *adj. Chem.* having a valency of one; univalent. □□ **monovalence** *n.* **monovalency** *n.*

monoxide /mə'nɒksaɪd/ *n. Chem.* an oxide containing one oxygen atom (*carbon monoxide*). [MONO- + OXIDE]

Monroe doctrine /mʌn'rəʊ/ *n.* the US policy of objecting to intervention by European powers in the affairs of Latin America. [J. *Monroe*, US President d. 1831, who formulated it]

Monseigneur /,mɒnsen'jɜː(r)/ *n.* (*pl.* **Messeigneurs** /,mesen'jɜː(r)/) a title given to an eminent French person, esp. a prince, cardinal, archbishop, or bishop. [F f. *mon* my + *seigneur* lord]

Monsieur /mə'sjɜː(r)/ *n.* (*pl.* **Messieurs** /me'sjɜː(r)/) **1** the title or form of address used of or to a French-speaking man, corresponding to Mr or sir. **2** a Frenchman. [F f. *mon* my + *sieur* lord]

Monsignor /mɒn'siːnjə(r), -'njɔː(r)/ *n.* (*pl.* **Monsignori** /-'njɔːrɪ/) the title of various Roman Catholic prelates, officers of the papal court, etc. [It., after MONSEIGNEUR: see SIGNOR]

monsoon /mɒn'suːn/ *n.* **1** a wind in S. Asia, esp. in the Indian Ocean, blowing from the south west in summer (**wet monsoon**) and the north east in winter (**dry monsoon**). **2** a rainy season accompanying a wet monsoon. **3** any other wind with periodic alternations. □□ **monsoonal** *adj.* [obs. Du. *monssoen* f. Port. *monção* f. Arab. *mawsim* fixed season f. *wasama* to mark]

mons pubis /mɒnz 'pjuːbɪs/ *n.* a rounded mass of fatty tissue lying over the joint of a man's pubic bones. [L, = mount of the pubes]

monster /'mɒnstə(r)/ *n.* **1** an imaginary creature, usu. large and frightening, compounded of incongruous elements. **2** an inhumanly cruel or wicked person. **3** a misshapen animal or plant. **4** a large hideous animal or thing (e.g. a building). **5** (*attrib.*) huge; extremely large of its kind. [ME f. OF *monstre* f. L *monstrum* portent, monster f. *monēre* warn]

monstera /mɒn'stɪərə/ *n.* any climbing plant of the genus *Monstera*, including Swiss cheese plant. [mod.L, perh. f. L *monstrum* monster (from the odd appearance of its leaves)]

monstrance /'mɒnstrəns/ *n. RC Ch.* a vessel in which the Host is exposed for veneration. [ME, = demonstration, f. med.L *monstrantia* f. L *monstrare* show]

monstrosity /mɒn'strɒsɪtɪ/ *n.* (*pl.* **-ies**) **1** a huge or outrageous thing. **2** monstrousness. **3** = MONSTER 3. [LL *monstrositas* (as MONSTROUS)]

monstrous /'mɒnstrəs/ *adj.* **1** like a monster; abnormally formed. **2** huge. **3 a** outrageously wrong or absurd. **b** atrocious. □□ **monstrously** *adv.* **monstrousness** *n.* [ME f. OF *monstreux* or L *monstrosus* (as MONSTER)]

mons Veneris /mɒnz 'venərɪs/ *n.* a rounded mass of fatty tissue on a woman's abdomen above the vulva. [L, = mount of Venus]

Mont. *abbr.* Montana.

montage /mɒn'tɑːʒ/ *n.* **1 a** a process of selecting,

editing, and piecing together separate sections of cinema or television film to form a continuous whole. **b** a sequence of such film as a section of a longer film. **2 a** the technique of producing a new composite whole from fragments of pictures, words, music, etc. **b** a composition produced in this way. [F f. *monter* MOUNT¹]

montane /'mɒnteɪn/ *adj.* of or inhabiting mountainous country. [L *montanus* (as MOUNT², -ANE¹)]

montbretia /mɒn'briːʃə/ *n.* a hybrid plant of the genus *Crocosmia*, with bright orange-yellow trumpet-shaped flowers. [mod.L f. A. F. E. Coquebert de *Montbret*, Fr. botanist d. 1801]

monte /'mɒntɪ/ *n. Cards* **1** a Spanish game of chance, played with 45 cards. **2** (in full **three-card monte**) a game of Mexican origin played with three cards, similar to three-card trick. [Sp., = mountain, heap of cards]

Monte Carlo method /,mɒntɪ 'kɑːləʊ/ *n. Statistics* a method of using the random sampling of numbers in order to estimate the solution to a numerical problem. [*Monte Carlo* in Monaco, famous for its gambling casino]

Montessori /,mɒntɪ'sɔːrɪ/ *n.* (usu. *attrib.*) a system of education (esp. of young children) that seeks to develop natural interests and activities rather than use formal teaching methods. [Maria *Montessori*, It. educationist d. 1952, who initiated it]

month /mʌnθ/ *n.* **1** (in full **calendar month**) **a** each of usu. twelve periods into which a year is divided. **b** a period of time between the same dates in successive calendar months. **2** a period of 28 days or of four weeks. **3** = *lunar month*. □ **month of Sundays** a very long period. [OE *mōnath* f. Gmc, rel. to MOON]

monthly /'mʌnθlɪ/ *adj., adv., & n.* —*adj.* done, produced, or occurring once a month. —*adv.* once a month; from month to month. —*n.* (*pl.* **-ies**) **1** a monthly periodical. **2** (in *pl.*) *colloq.* a menstrual period.

monticule /'mɒntɪ,kjuːl/ *n.* **1** a small hill. **2** a small mound caused by a volcanic eruption. [F f. LL *monticulus* dimin. of *mons* MOUNT²]

monument /'mɒnjʊmənt/ *n.* **1** anything enduring that serves to commemorate or make celebrated, esp. a structure or building. **2** a stone or other structure placed over a grave or in a church etc. in memory of the dead. **3** an ancient building or site etc. that has survived or been preserved. **4** (foll. by *of*, *to*) a typical or outstanding example (*a monument of indiscretion*). **5** a written record. [ME f. F f. L *monumentum* f. *monēre* remind]

monumental /,mɒnjʊ'ment(ə)l/ *adj.* **1 a** extremely great; stupendous (*a monumental achievement*). **b** (of a literary work) massive and permanent. **2** of or serving as a monument. □ **monumental mason** a maker of tombstones etc. □□ **monumentality** /-'tælɪtɪ/ *n.* **monumentally** *adv.*

monumentalize /,mɒnjʊ'mentə,laɪz/ *v.tr.* (also **-ise**) record or commemorate by or as by a monument.

-mony /mənɪ/ *suffix* forming nouns esp. denoting an abstract state or quality (*acrimony; testimony*). [L *-monia, -monium*, rel. to -MENT]

moo /muː/ *v. & n.* —*v.intr.* (**moos**, **mooed**) make the characteristic vocal sound of cattle; = LOW². —*n.* (*pl.* **moos**) this sound. □ **moo-cow** a childish name for a cow. [imit.]

mooch /muːtʃ/ *v. colloq.* **1** *intr.* loiter or saunter desultorily. **2** *tr.* esp. *US* **a** steal. **b** beg. □□ **moocher** *n.* [ME, prob. f. OF *muchier* hide, skulk]

mood¹ /muːd/ *n.* **1** a state of mind or feeling. **2** (in *pl.*) fits of melancholy or bad temper. **3** (*attrib.*) inducing a particular mood (*mood music*). □ **in the** (or **no**) **mood** (foll. by *for*, or *to* + infin.) inclined (or disinclined) (*was in no mood to agree*). [OE *mōd* mind, thought, f. Gmc]

mood² /muːd/ *n.* **1** *Gram.* **a** a form or set of forms of a verb serving to indicate whether it is to express fact, command, wish, etc. (*subjunctive mood*). **b** the distinction of meaning expressed by different moods. **2** *Logic* any of the classes into which each of the figures of a valid categorical syllogism is subdivided. [var. of MODE, assoc. with MOOD[1]]

moody /'mu:dɪ/ *adj.* & *n.* —*adj.* (**moodier, moodiest**) given to changes of mood; gloomy, sullen. —*n. colloq.* a bad mood; a tantrum. □□ **moodily** *adv.* **moodiness** *n.* [OE *mōdig* brave (as MOOD[1])]

Moog /muːg/ *n.* (in full **Moog synthesizer**) *propr.* an electronic instrument with a keyboard, for producing a wide variety of musical sounds: see SYNTHESIZER. [R. A. *Moog*, Amer. engineer b. 1934, who invented it]

moolah /'muːlə/ *n. sl.* money. [20th c.: orig. unkn.]

moolvi /'muːlvɪ/ *n.* (also **moolvie**) **1** a Muslim doctor of the law. **2** a learned person or teacher (esp. as a term of respect among Muslims in India). [Urdu *mulvī* f. Arab. *mawlawīy* judicial: cf. MULLAH]

moon /muːn/ *n.* & *v.* —*n.* **1 a** the natural satellite of the earth, orbiting it monthly, illuminated by the sun and reflecting some light to the earth. **b** this regarded in terms of its waxing and waning in a particular month (*new moon*). **c** the moon when visible (*there is no moon tonight*). **2** a satellite of any planet. **3** (prec. by *the*) something desirable but unattainable (*promised them the moon*). **4** *poet.* a month. —*v.* **1** *intr.* (often foll. by *about, around*, etc.) move or look listlessly. **2** *tr.* (foll. by *away*) spend (time) in a listless manner. **3** *intr.* (foll. by *over*) act aimlessly or inattentively from infatuation for (a person). □ **moon boot** a thickly-padded boot designed for low temperatures. **moon-faced** having a round face. **over the moon** extremely happy or delighted. □□ **moonless** *adj.* [OE *mōna* f. Gmc, rel. to MONTH]

moonbeam /'muːnbiːm/ *n.* a ray of moonlight.

mooncalf /'muːnkɑːf/ *n.* a born fool.

moonfish /'muːnfɪʃ/ *n.* = OPAH.

Moonie /'muːnɪ/ *n. sl.* a member of the Unification Church. [Sun Myung *Moon*, its founder]

moonlight /'muːnlaɪt/ *n.* & *v.* —*n.* **1** the light of the moon. **2** (*attrib.*) lighted by the moon. —*v.intr.* (**-lighted**) *colloq.* have two paid occupations, esp. one by day and one by night. □ **moonlight flit** a hurried departure by night, esp. to avoid paying a debt. □□ **moonlighter** *n.*

moonlit /'muːnlɪt/ *adj.* lighted by the moon.

moonquake /'muːnkweɪk/ *n.* a tremor of the moon's surface.

moonrise /'muːnraɪz/ *n.* **1** the rising of the moon. **2** the time of this.

moonscape /'muːnskeɪp/ *n.* **1** the surface or landscape of the moon. **2** an area resembling this; a wasteland.

moonset /'muːnset/ *n.* **1** the setting of the moon. **2** the time of this.

moonshee /'muːnʃiː/ *n.* (also *munshi*) a secretary or language-teacher in India. [Urdu *munshī* f. Arab. *munšī* writer]

moonshine /'muːnʃaɪn/ *n.* **1** foolish or unrealistic talk or ideas. **2** *sl.* illicitly distilled or smuggled alcoholic liquor.

moonshiner /'muːnʃaɪnə(r)/ *n. US sl.* an illicit distiller or smuggler of alcoholic liquor.

moonshot /'muːnʃɒt/ *n.* the launching of a spacecraft to the moon.

moonstone /'muːnstəʊn/ *n.* feldspar of pearly appearance.

moonstruck /'muːnstrʌk/ *adj.* mentally deranged.

moony /'muːnɪ/ *adj.* (**moonier, mooniest**) **1** listless; stupidly dreamy. **2** of or like the moon.

Moor /mʊə(r), mɔː(r)/ *n.* a member of a Muslim people of mixed Berber and Arab descent, inhabiting NW Africa. [ME f. OF *More* f. L *Maurus* f. Gk *Mauros* inhabitant of Mauretania, a region of N. Africa]

moor[1] /mʊə(r), mɔː(r)/ *n.* **1** a tract of open uncultivated upland, esp. when covered with heather. **2** a tract of ground preserved for shooting. **3** *US* a fen. □□

moorish *adj.* **moory** *adj.* [OE *mōr* waste land, marsh, mountain, f. Gmc]

moor[2] /mʊə(r), mɔː(r)/ *v.* **1** *tr.* make fast (a boat, buoy, etc.) by attaching a cable etc. to a fixed object. **2** *intr.* (of a boat) be moored. □□ **moorage** *n.* [ME *more*, prob. f. LG or MLG *mōren*]

moorcock /'mʊəkɒk, 'mɔː-/ *n.* a male moorfowl.

moorfowl /'mʊəfaʊl, 'mɔː-/ *n.* a red grouse.

moorhen /'mʊəhen, 'mɔː-/ *n.* **1** a small aquatic bird, *Gallinula chloropus*, with long legs and a short red-yellow bill. **2** a female moorfowl.

mooring /'mʊərɪŋ, 'mɔːrɪŋ/ *n.* **1 a** a fixed object to which a boat, buoy, etc., is moored. **b** (often in *pl.*) a place where a boat etc. is moored. **2** (in *pl.*) a set of permanent anchors and chains laid down for ships to be moored to.

Moorish /'mʊərɪʃ, 'mɔːrɪʃ/ *adj.* of or relating to the Moors. □ **Moorish idol** a brightly-coloured Pacific fish of the genus *Zanclus*.

moorland /'mʊələnd, 'mɔː-/ *n.* an extensive area of moor.

moose /muːs/ *n.* (*pl.* same) a N. American deer; an elk. [Narragansett *moos*]

moot /muːt/ *adj., v.,* & *n.* —*adj.* (orig. the noun used *attrib.*) **1** debatable, undecided (*a moot point*). **2** *US Law* having no practical significance. —*v.tr.* raise (a question) for discussion. —*n.* **1** *hist.* an assembly. **2** *Law* a discussion of a hypothetical case as an academic exercise. [OE *mōt*, and *mōtian* converse, f. Gmc, rel. to MEET[1]]

mop[1] /mɒp/ *n.* & *v.* —*n.* **1** a wad or bundle of cotton or synthetic material fastened to the end of a stick, for cleaning floors etc. **2** a similarly-shaped large or small implement for various purposes. **3** anything resembling a mop, esp. a thick mass of hair. **4** an act of mopping or being mopped (*gave it a mop*). —*v.tr.* (**mopped, mopping**) **1** wipe or clean with or as with a mop. **2 a** wipe tears or sweat etc. from (one's face or brow etc.). **b** wipe away (tears etc.). □ **mop up 1** wipe up with or as with a mop. **2** *colloq.* absorb (profits etc.). **3** dispatch; make an end of. **4** *Mil.* **a** complete the occupation of (a district etc.) by capturing or killing enemy troops left there. **b** capture or kill (stragglers). □□ **moppy** *adj.* [ME *mappe*, perh. ult. rel. to L *mappa* napkin]

mop[2] /mɒp/ *n. Brit. hist.* an autumn fair or gathering at which farm-hands and servants were formerly hired. [perh. = *mop-fair*, at which a mop was carried by a maidservant seeking employment]

mope /məʊp/ *v.* & *n.* —*v.intr.* be gloomily depressed or listless; behave sulkily. —*n.* **1** a person who mopes. **2** (**the mopes**) low spirits. □□ **moper** *n.* **mopy** *adj.* (**mopier, mopiest**). **mopily** *adv.* **mopiness** *n.* [16th c.: prob. rel. to *mope, mopp(e)* fool]

moped /'məʊped/ *n.* a motorized bicycle with an engine capacity below 50 cc. [Sw. (as MOTOR, PEDAL[1])]

mophead /'mɒphed/ *n.* a person with thick matted hair.

mopoke /'məʊpəʊk/ *n.* (also **morepork** /'mɔːpɔːk/) **1** a boobook. **2** an Australian nocturnal insect-eating bird, *Podargus strigoides*. Also called FROGMOUTH. [imit. of the bird's cry]

moppet /'mɒpɪt/ *n. colloq.* (esp. as a term of endearment) a baby or small child. [obs. *moppe* baby, doll]

moquette /mɒ'ket/ *n.* a thick pile or looped material used for carpets and upholstery. [F, perh. f. obs. It. *mocaiardo* mohair]

mor /mɔː(r)/ *n.* humus formed under acid conditions. [Da.]

moraine /mə'reɪn/ *n.* an area covered by rocks and debris carried down and deposited by a glacier. □□ **morainal** *adj.* **morainic** *adj.* [F f. It. dial. *morena* f. F dial. *mor(re)* snout f. Rmc]

moral /'mɒr(ə)l/ *adj.* & *n.* —*adj.* **1 a** concerned with goodness or badness of human character or behaviour, or with the distinction between right and wrong. **b** concerned with accepted rules and standards of human behaviour. **2 a** conforming to accepted standards of general conduct. **b** capable of moral action (*man is a moral agent*). **3** (of rights or duties etc.) founded on moral law. **4 a** concerned with morals or ethics (*moral philosophy*). **b** (of a literary work etc.) dealing with moral conduct. **5** concerned with or leading to a psychological effect associated with confidence in a right action (*moral courage*; *moral support*; *moral victory*). —*n.* **1 a** a moral lesson (esp. at the end) of a fable, story, event, etc. **b** a moral maxim or principle. **2** (in *pl.*) moral behaviour, e.g. in sexual conduct. □**moral certainty** probability so great as to allow no reasonable doubt. **moral law** the conditions to be satisfied by any right course of action. **moral majority** the majority of people, regarded as favouring firm moral standards (orig. *Moral Majority*, name of a right-wing US movement). **moral philosophy** the branch of philosophy concerned with ethics. **moral pressure** persuasion by appealing to a person's moral sense. **Moral Re-Armament 1** = OXFORD GROUP. **2** the beliefs of this organization, esp. as applied to international relations. **moral science** systematic knowledge as applied to morals. **moral sense** the ability to distinguish right and wrong. □□**morally** *adv.* [ME f. L *moralis* f. *mos moris* custom, pl. *mores* morals]

morale /məˈrɑːl/ *n.* the mental attitude or bearing of a person or group, esp. as regards confidence, discipline, etc. [F *moral* respelt to preserve the pronunciation]

moralism /ˈmɒrəˌlɪz(ə)m/ *n.* **1** a natural system of morality. **2** religion regarded as moral practice.

moralist /ˈmɒrəlɪst/ *n.* **1** a person who practises or teaches morality. **2** a person who follows a natural system of ethics. □□**moralistic** /-ˈlɪstɪk/ *adj.* **moralistically** /-ˈlɪstɪkəlɪ/ *adv.*

morality /məˈrælɪtɪ/ *n.* (*pl.* -**ies**) **1** the degree of conformity of an idea, practice, etc., to moral principles. **2** right moral conduct. **3** a lesson in morals. **4** the science of morals. **5** a particular system of morals (*commercial morality*). **6** (in *pl.*) moral principles; points of ethics. **7** (in full **morality play**) *hist.* a kind of drama with personified abstract qualities as the main characters and inculcating a moral lesson, popular in the 16th c. [ME f. OF *moralité* or LL *moralitas* f. L (as MORAL)]

moralize /ˈmɒrəˌlaɪz/ *v.* (also -**ise**) **1** *intr.* (often foll. by *on*) indulge in moral reflection or talk. **2** *tr.* interpret morally; point the moral of. **3** *tr.* make moral or more moral. □□**moralization** /-ˈzeɪʃ(ə)n/ *n.* **moralizer** *n.* **moralizingly** *adv.* [F *moraliser* or med.L *moralizare* f. L (as MORAL)]

morass /məˈræs/ *n.* **1** an entanglement; a disordered situation, esp. one impeding progress. **2** *literary* a bog or marsh. [Du. *moeras* (assim. to *moer* MOOR¹) f. MDu. *marasch* f. OF *marais* marsh f. med.L *mariscus*]

moratorium /ˌmɒrəˈtɔːrɪəm/ *n.* (*pl.* **moratoriums** or **moratoria** /-rɪə/) **1** (often foll. by *on*) a temporary prohibition or suspension (of an activity). **2 a** a legal authorization to debtors to postpone payment. **b** the period of this postponement. [mod.L, neut. of LL *moratorius* delaying f. L *morari morat-* to delay f. *mora* delay]

Moravian /məˈreɪvɪən/ *n.* & *adj.* —*n.* **1** a native of Moravia, now part of Czechoslovakia. **2** a member of a Protestant sect founded in Saxony by emigrants from Moravia, holding views derived from the Hussites and accepting the Bible as the only source of faith. —*adj.* of, relating to, or characteristic of Moravia or its people.

moray /ˈmɒreɪ/ *n.* any tropical eel-like fish of the family Muraenidae, esp. *Muraena helena* found in Mediterranean waters. [Port. *moreia* f. L f. Gk *muraina*]

morbid /ˈmɔːbɪd/ *adj.* **1 a** (of the mind, ideas, etc.) unwholesome, sickly. **b** given to morbid feelings. **2** *colloq.* melancholy. **3** *Med.* of the nature of or indicative of disease. □**morbid anatomy** the anatomy of diseased organs, tissues, etc. □□**morbidity** /-ˈbɪdɪtɪ/ *n.* **morbidly** *adv.* **morbidness** *n.* [L *morbidus* f. *morbus* disease]

morbific /mɔːˈbɪfɪk/ *adj.* causing disease. [F *morbifique* or mod.L *morbificus* f. L *morbus* disease]

morbilli /mɔːˈbɪlɪ/ *n.pl.* **1** measles. **2** the spots characteristic of measles. [L, pl. of *morbillus* pustule f. *morbus* disease]

mordant /ˈmɔːd(ə)nt/ *adj.* & *n.* —*adj.* **1** (of sarcasm etc.) caustic, biting. **2** pungent, smarting. **3** corrosive or cleansing. **4** (of a substance) serving to fix colouring-matter or gold leaf on another substance. —*n.* a mordant substance (in senses 3, 4 of *adj.*). □□ **mordancy** *n.* **mordantly** *adv.* [ME f. F, part. of *mordre* bite f. L *mordēre*]

mordent /ˈmɔːd(ə)nt/ *n. Mus.* **1** an ornament consisting of one rapid alternation of a written note with the note immediately below it. **2** a pralltriller. [G f. It. *mordente* part. of *mordēre* bite]

more /mɔː(r)/ *adj.*, *n.*, & *adv.* —*adj.* **1** existing in a greater or additional quantity, amount, or degree (*more problems than last time*; *bring some more water*). **2** greater in degree (*more's the pity*; *the more fool you*). —*n.* a greater quantity, number, or amount (*more than three people*; *more to it than meets the eye*). —*adv.* **1** in a greater degree (*do it more carefully*). **2** to a greater extent (*people like to walk more these days*). **3** forming the comparative of adjectives and adverbs, esp. those of more than one syllable (*more absurd*; *more easily*). **4** again (*once more*; *never more*). **5** moreover. □**more and more** in an increasing degree. **more like it** see LIKE¹. **more of** to a greater extent (*more of a poet than a musician*). **more or less 1** in a greater or less degree. **2** approximately; as an estimate. **more so** of the same kind to a greater degree. [OE *māra* f. Gmc]

moreen /mɒˈriːn/ *n.* a strong ribbed woollen or cotton material for curtains etc. [perh. fanciful f. MOIRE]

moreish /ˈmɔːrɪʃ/ *adj.* (also **morish**) *colloq.* pleasant to eat, causing a desire for more.

morel¹ /məˈrel/ *n.* an edible fungus, *Morchella esculenta*, with ridged mushroom caps. [F *morille* f. Du. *morilje*]

morel² /məˈrel/ *n.* nightshade. [ME f. OF *morele* fem. of *morel* dark brown ult. f. L *Maurus* MOOR]

morello /məˈreləʊ/ *n.* (*pl.* -**os**) a sour kind of dark cherry. [It. *morello* blackish f. med.L *morellus* f. L (as MOREL¹)]

moreover /mɔːˈrəʊvə(r)/ *adv.* (introducing or accompanying a new statement) further, besides.

morepork var. of MOPOKE.

mores /ˈmɔːreɪz, -riːz/ *n.pl.* customs or conventions regarded as essential to or characteristic of a community. [L, pl. of *mos* custom]

Moresco var. of MORISCO.

Moresque /mɒˈresk/ *adj.* (of art or architecture) Moorish in style or design. [F f. It. *moresco* f. *Moro* MOOR]

morganatic /ˌmɔːgəˈnætɪk/ *adj.* **1** (of a marriage) between a person of high rank and another of lower rank, the spouse and children having no claim to the possessions or title of the person of higher rank. **2** (of a wife) married in this way. □□**morganatically** *adv.* [F *morganatique* or G *morganatisch* f. med.L *matrimonium ad morganaticam* 'marriage with a morning gift', the husband's gift to the wife after consummation being his only obligation in such a marriage]

morgue /mɔːg/ *n.* **1** a mortuary. **2** (in a newspaper office) a room or file of miscellaneous information, esp. for future obituaries. [F, orig. the name of a Paris mortuary]

moribund /ˈmɒrɪˌbʌnd/ *adj.* **1** at the point of death. **2** lacking vitality. □□**moribundity** /-ˈbʌndɪtɪ/ *n.* [L *moribundus* f. *mori* die]

Morisco /məˈrɪskəʊ/ *n.* & *adj.* (also **Moresco**

/-'reskəʊ/) —n. (pl. -os or -oes) 1 a Moor, esp. in Spain. 2 a morris dance. —adj. Moorish. [Sp. f. *Moro* MOOR]

morish var. of MOREISH.

Mormon /'mɔːmən/ n. a member of the Church of Jesus Christ of Latter-Day Saints, a millenary religion founded in 1830 by Joseph Smith on the basis of revelations in the Book of Mormon. □□ **Mormonism** n.

morn /mɔːn/ n. *poet.* morning. [OE *morgen* f. Gmc]

mornay /'mɔːneɪ/ n. a cheese-flavoured white sauce. [20th c.: orig. uncert.]

morning /'mɔːnɪŋ/ n. & int. —n. 1 the early part of the day, esp. from sunrise to noon (*this morning*; *during the morning*; *morning coffee*). 2 this time spent in a particular way (*had a busy morning*). 3 sunrise, daybreak. 4 a time compared with the morning, esp. the early part of one's life etc. — int. = *good morning* (see GOOD adj. 14). □**in the morning** 1 during or in the course of the morning. 2 *colloq.* tomorrow. **morning after** *colloq.* a hangover. **morning-after pill** a contraceptive pill effective when taken some hours after intercourse. **morning coat** a coat with tails, and with the front cut away below the waist. **morning dress** a man's morning coat and striped trousers. **morning glory** any of various twining plants of the genus *Ipomoea*, with trumpet-shaped flowers. **morning-room** a sitting-room for the morning. **morning sickness** nausea felt in the morning in pregnancy. **morning star** a planet or bright star, usu. Venus, seen in the east before sunrise. **morning watch** *Naut.* the 4–8 a.m. watch. [ME *mor(we)ning* f. *morwen* MORN + -ING[1] after *evening*]

Moro /'mɔːrəʊ/ n. (pl. -os) a Muslim living in the Philippines. [Sp., = MOOR]

Moroccan /mə'rɒkən/ n. & adj. —n. 1 a native or national of Morocco in N. Africa. 2 a person of Moroccan descent. —adj. of or relating to Morocco.

morocco /mə'rɒkəʊ/ n. (pl. -os) 1 a fine flexible leather made (orig. in Morocco) from goatskins tanned with sumac, used esp. in bookbinding and shoemaking. 2 an imitation of this in grained calf etc.

moron /'mɔːrɒn/ n. 1 *colloq.* a very stupid or foolish person. 2 an adult with a mental age of about 8–12. □□ **moronic** /mə'rɒnɪk/ adj. **moronically** /mə'rɒnɪkəlɪ/ adv. **moronism** n. [Gk *mōron*, neut. of *mōros* foolish]

morose /mə'rəʊs/ adj. sullen and ill-tempered. □□ **morosely** adv. **moroseness** n. [L *morosus* peevish etc. f. *mos moris* manner]

morph /mɔːf/ n. = ALLOMORPH. [back-form.]

morpheme /'mɔːfiːm/ n. Linguistics 1 a morphological element considered in respect of its functional relations in a linguistic system. 2 a meaningful morphological unit of a language that cannot be further divided (e.g. *in*, *come*, *-ing*, forming *incoming*). □□ **morphemic** /-'fiːmɪk/ adj. **morphemically** /-'fiːmɪkəlɪ/ adv. [F *morphème* f. Gk *morphē* form, after PHONEME]

morphemics /mɔː'fiːmɪks/ n.pl. (usu. treated as sing.) Linguistics the study of word structure.

morphia /'mɔːfɪə/ n. (in general use) = MORPHINE.

morphine /'mɔːfiːn/ n. an analgesic and narcotic drug obtained from opium and used medicinally to relieve pain. □□ **morphinism** /-fɪ,nɪz(ə)m/ n. [G *Morphin* & mod.L *morphia* f. *Morpheus* god of sleep]

morphogenesis /,mɔːfə'dʒenɪsɪs/ n. Biol. the development of form in organisms. □□ **morphogenetic** /-dʒɪ'netɪk/ adj. **morphogenic** adj. [mod.L f. Gk *morphē* form + GENESIS]

morphology /mɔː'fɒlədʒɪ/ n. the study of the forms of things, esp.: 1 Biol. the study of the forms of organisms. 2 Philol. a the study of the forms of words. b the system of forms in a language. □□ **morphological** /,mɔːfə'lɒdʒɪk(ə)l/ adj. **morphologically** /-fə'lɒdʒɪkəlɪ/ adv. **morphologist** n. [Gk *morphē* form + -LOGY]

Morris chair /'mɒrɪs/ n. a type of plain easy chair with an adjustable back. [William *Morris*, Engl. poet and craftsman d. 1896]

morris dance /'mɒrɪs/ n. a traditional English dance by groups of people in fancy costume, usu. as characters in legend, with ribbons and bells. □□ **morris dancer** n. **morris dancing** n. [*morys*, var. of MOORISH]

morrow /'mɒrəʊ/ n. (usu. prec. by *the*) *literary* 1 the following day. 2 the time following an event. [ME *morwe*, *moru* (as MORN)]

Morse /mɔːs/ n. & v. —n. (in full **Morse code**) an alphabet or code in which letters are represented by combinations of long and short light or sound signals. —v.tr. & intr. signal by Morse code. [S. F. B. *Morse*, Amer. electrician d. 1872, who devised it]

morsel /'mɔːs(ə)l/ n. a mouthful; a small piece (esp. of food). [ME f. OF, dimin. of *mors* a bite f. *mordēre* *mors-* to bite]

mort /mɔːt/ n. *Hunting* a note sounded when the quarry is killed. [ME f. OF f. L *mors mortis* death]

mortadella /,mɔːtə'delə/ n. (pl. **mortadelle** /-'dele/) a large spiced pork sausage. [It. dimin., irreg. f. L *murtatum* seasoned with myrtle berries]

mortal /'mɔːt(ə)l/ adj. & n. —adj. 1 (of a living being, esp. a human) subject to death. 2 (often foll. by *to*) causing death; fatal. 3 (of a battle) fought to the death. 4 associated with death (*mortal agony*). 5 (of an enemy) implacable. 6 (of pain, fear, an affront, etc.) intense, very serious. 7 *colloq.* a very great (*in a mortal hurry*). b long and tedious (*for two mortal hours*). 8 *colloq.* conceivable, imaginable (*every mortal thing*; *of no mortal use*). —n. 1 a mortal being, esp. a human. 2 *joc.* a person described in some specified way (*a thirsty mortal*). □**mortal sin** *Theol.* a grave sin that is regarded as depriving the soul of divine grace. □□ **mortally** adv. [ME f. OF *mortal*, *mortel* or L *mortalis* f. *mors mortis* death]

mortality /mɔː'tælɪtɪ/ n. (pl. -ies) 1 the state of being subject to death. 2 loss of life on a large scale. 3 a the number of deaths in a given period etc. b (in full **mortality rate**) a death rate. [ME f. OF *mortalité* f. L *mortalitas* *-tatis* (as MORTAL)]

mortar /'mɔːtə(r)/ n. & v. —n. 1 a mixture of lime with cement, sand, and water, used in building to bond bricks or stones. 2 a short large-bore cannon for firing shells at high angles. 3 a contrivance for firing a lifeline or firework. 4 a vessel made of hard material, in which ingredients are pounded with a pestle. —v.tr. 1 plaster or join with mortar. 2 attack or bombard with mortar shells. □□ **mortarless** adj. (in sense 1). **mortary** adj. (in sense 1). [ME f. AF *morter*, OF *mortier* f. L *mortarium*: partly from LG]

mortarboard /'mɔːtə,bɔːd/ n. 1 an academic cap with a stiff flat square top. 2 a flat board with a handle on the under-surface, for holding mortar in bricklaying etc.

mortgage /'mɔːgɪdʒ/ n. & v. —n. 1 a a conveyance of property by a debtor to a creditor as security for a debt (esp. one incurred by the purchase of the property), on the condition that it shall be returned on payment of the debt within a certain period. b a deed effecting this. 2 a a debt secured by a mortgage. b a loan resulting in such a debt. —v.tr. 1 convey (a property) by mortgage. 2 (often foll. by *to*) pledge (oneself, one's powers, etc.). □**mortgage rate** the rate of interest charged by a mortgagee. □□ **mortgageable** adj. [ME f. OF, = dead pledge f. *mort* f. L *mortuus* dead + *gage* GAGE[1]]

mortgagee /,mɔːgɪ'dʒiː/ n. the creditor in a mortgage, usu. a bank or building society.

mortgager /'mɔːgɪdʒə(r)/ n. (also **mortgagor** /-'dʒɔː(r)/) the debtor in a mortgage.

mortice var. of MORTISE.

mortician /mɔː'tɪʃ(ə)n/ n. *US* an undertaker; a manager of funerals. [L *mors mortis* death + -ICIAN]

mortify /'mɔːtɪ,faɪ/ v. (-ies, -ied) 1 tr. a cause (a person) to feel shamed or humiliated. b wound (a person's feelings). **2** *tr.* bring (the body, the flesh, the passions, etc.) into subjection by self-denial or discipline. **3** *intr.* (of flesh) be affected by gangrene or necrosis. □□ **mortification** /-frˈkeɪʃ(ə)n/ *n.* **mortifying** *adj.* **mortifyingly** *adv.* [ME f. OF *mortifier* f. eccl.L *mortificare* kill, subdue f. *mors mortis* death]

mortise /ˈmɔːtɪs/ *n.* & *v.* (also **mortice**) —*n.* a hole in a framework designed to receive the end of another part, esp. a tenon. —*v.tr.* **1** join securely, esp. by mortise and tenon. **2** cut a mortise in. □**mortise lock** a lock recessed into a mortise in the frame of a door or window etc. [ME f. OF *mortoise* f. Arab. *murtazz* fixed in]

mortmain /ˈmɔːtmeɪn/ *n.* *Law* **1** the status of lands or tenements held inalienably by an ecclesiastical or other corporation. **2** the land or tenements themselves. [ME f. AF, OF *mortemain* f. med.L *mortua manus* dead hand, prob. in allusion to impersonal ownership]

mortuary /ˈmɔːtjʊərɪ/ *n.* & *adj.* —*n.* (*pl.* **-ies**) a room or building in which dead bodies may be kept until burial or cremation. —*adj.* of or concerning death or burial. [ME f. AF *mortuarie* f. med.L *mortuarium* f. L *mortuarius* f. *mortuus* dead]

morula /ˈmɔːrʊlə/ *n.* (*pl.* **morulae** /-ˌliː/) a fully segmented ovum from which a blastula is formed. [mod.L, dimin. of L *morum* mulberry]

morwong /ˈmɔːwɒŋ/ *n.* any of various fish of the family Cheilodactylidae, native to Australasia, used as food. [Aboriginal]

Mosaic /məʊˈzeɪɪk/ *adj.* of or associated with Moses (in the Hebrew Bible). □**Mosaic Law** the laws attributed to Moses and listed in the Pentateuch. [F *mosaïque* or mod.L *Mosaicus* f. *Moses* f. Heb. *Mōšeh*]

mosaic /məʊˈzeɪɪk/ *n.* & *v.* —*n.* **1 a** a picture or pattern produced by an arrangement of small variously coloured pieces of glass or stone etc. **b** work of this kind as an art form. **2** a diversified thing. **3** an arrangement of photosensitive elements in a television camera. **4** *Biol.* a chimera. **5** (in full **mosaic disease**) a virus disease causing leaf-mottling in plants, esp. tobacco, maize, and sugar cane. **6** (*attrib.*) **a** of or like a mosaic. **b** diversified. —*v.tr.* (**mosaicked, mosaicking**) **1** adorn with mosaics. **2** combine into or as into a mosaic. □**mosaic gold 1** tin disulphide. **2** an alloy of copper and zinc used in cheap jewellery etc. □□ **mosaicist** /-ɪsɪst/ *n.* [ME f. F *mosaïque* f. It. *mosaico* f. med.L *mosaicus, musaicus* f. Gk *mous(e)ion* mosaic work f. *mousa* MUSE[1]]

mosasaurus /ˌməʊsəˈsɔːrəs/ *n.* any large extinct marine reptile of the genus *Mosasaurus*, with a long slender body and flipper-like limbs. [mod.L f. *Mosa* river Meuse (near which it was first discovered) + Gk *sauros* lizard]

moschatel /ˌmɒskəˈtel/ *n.* a small plant, *Adoxa moschatellina*, with pale-green flowers and a musky smell. [F *moscatelle* f. It. *moscatella* f. *moscato* musk]

moselle /məʊˈzel/ *n.* a light medium-dry white wine produced in the valley of the river Moselle in Germany.

mosey /ˈməʊzɪ/ *v.intr.* (**-eys, -eyed**) (often foll. by *along*) *sl.* walk in a leisurely or aimless manner. [19th c.: orig. unkn.]

moshav /məʊˈʃɑːv/ *n.* (*pl.* **moshavim**) a cooperative association of Israeli smallholders. [Heb. *mošāḇ*, lit. 'dwelling']

Moslem var. of MUSLIM.

mosque /mɒsk/ *n.* a Muslim place of worship. [F *mosquée* f. It. *moschea* f. Arab. *masjid*]

mosquito /mɒsˈkiːtəʊ/ *n.* (*pl.* **-oes**) any of various slender biting insects, esp. of the genus *Culex*, *Anopheles*, or *Aedes*, the female of which punctures the skin of humans and other animals with a long proboscis to suck their blood and transmits diseases such as filariasis and malaria. □**mosquito-boat** *US* a motor torpedo-boat. **mosquito-net** a net to keep

off mosquitoes. [Sp. & Port., dimin. of *mosca* f. L *musca* fly]

moss /mɒs/ *n.* & *v.* —*n.* **1** any small cryptogamous plant of the class Musci, growing in dense clusters on the surface of the ground, in bogs, on trees, stones, etc. **2** *Sc.* & *N.Engl.* a bog, esp. a peatbog. —*v.tr.* cover with moss. □**moss agate** agate with mosslike dendritic markings. **moss-grown** overgrown with moss. **moss-hag** *Sc.* broken ground from which peat has been taken. **moss-stitch** alternate plain and purl in knitting. □□ **mosslike** *adj.* [OE *mos* bog, moss f. Gmc]

mosso /ˈmɒsəʊ/ *adv.* *Mus.* with animation or speed. [It., past part. of *muovere* move]

mosstrooper /ˈmɒsˌtruːpə(r)/ *n.* a freebooter of the Scottish Border in the 17th c.

mossy /ˈmɒsɪ/ *adj.* (**mossier, mossiest**) **1** covered in or resembling moss. **2** *US sl.* antiquated, old-fashioned. □□ **mossiness** *n.*

most /məʊst/ *adj., n.,* & *adv.* —*adj.* **1** existing in the greatest quantity or degree (*you have made most mistakes*; *see who can make the most noise*). **2** the majority of; nearly all of (*most people think so*). —*n.* **1** the greatest quantity or number (*this is the most I can do*). **2** (**the most**) *sl.* the best of all. **3** the majority (*most of them are missing*). —*adv.* **1** in the highest degree (*this is most interesting*; *what most annoys me*). **2** forming the superlative of adjectives and adverbs, esp. those of more than one syllable (*most certain*; *most easily*). **3** *US colloq.* almost. □**at most** no more or better than (*this is at most a makeshift*). **at the most 1** as the greatest amount. **2** not more than. **for the most part 1** as regards the greater part. **2** usually. **make the most of 1** employ to the best advantage. **2** represent at its best or worst. **Most Honourable** a title given to marquises and to members of the Privy Council and the Order of the Bath. **Most Reverend** a title given to archbishops and to Roman Catholic bishops. [OE *mǣst* f. Gmc]

-most /məʊst/ *suffix* forming superlative adjectives and adverbs from prepositions and other words indicating relative position (*foremost*; *uttermost*). [OE -*mest* f. Gmc]

mostly /ˈməʊstlɪ/ *adv.* **1** as regards the greater part. **2** usually.

MOT *abbr.* **1** (in the UK) Ministry of Transport. **2** (in full **MOT test**) a compulsory annual test of motor vehicles of more than a specified age.

mot /məʊ/ *n.* (*pl.* **mots** pronunc. same) a witty saying. □**mot juste** /ˈʒuːst/ (*pl.* **mots justes** pronunc. same) the most appropriate expression. [F, = word, ult. f. L *muttum* uttered sound f. *muttire* murmur]

mote /məʊt/ *n.* a speck of dust. [OE *mot*, corresp. to Du. *mot* dust, sawdust, of unkn. orig.]

motel /məʊˈtel/ *n.* a roadside hotel providing accommodation for motorists and parking for their vehicles. [portmanteau word f. MOTOR + HOTEL]

motet /məʊˈtet/ *n.* *Mus.* a short sacred choral composition. [ME f. OF, dimin. of *mot*: see MOT]

moth /mɒθ/ *n.* **1** any usu. nocturnal insect of the order Lepidoptera excluding butterflies, having a stout body and without clubbed antennae. **2** any small lepidopterous insect of the family Tineidae breeding in cloth etc., on which its larva feeds. □**moth-eaten 1** damaged or destroyed by moths. **2** antiquated, time-worn. [OE *moththe*]

mothball /ˈmɒθbɔːl/ *n.* & *v.* —*n.* a ball of naphthalene etc. placed in stored clothes to keep away moths. —*v.tr.* **1** place in mothballs. **2** leave unused. □**in mothballs** stored unused for a considerable time.

mother /ˈmʌðə(r)/ *n.* & *v.* —*n.* **1 a** a woman in relation to a child or children to whom she has given birth. **b** (in full **adoptive mother**) a woman who has continuous care of a child, esp. by adoption. **2** any female animal in relation to its offspring. **3** a quality or condition etc. that gives rise to another (*necessity is the mother of invention*). **4** (in full **Mother Superior**) the head of a female religious community.

5 *archaic* (esp. as a form of address) an elderly woman. **6** (*attrib.*) **a** designating an institution etc. regarded as having maternal authority (*Mother Church*; *mother earth*). **b** designating the main ship, spacecraft, etc., in a convoy or mission (*the mother craft*). —*v.tr.* **1** give birth to; be the mother of. **2** protect as a mother. **3** give rise to; be the source of. **4** acknowledge or profess oneself the mother of. □**Mother Carey's chicken** = *storm petrel* 1. **mother country** a country in relation to its colonies. **mother-figure** an older woman who is regarded as a source of nurture, support, etc. **Mother Goose rhyme** *US* a nursery rhyme. **mother-in-law** (*pl.* **mothers-in-law**) the mother of one's husband or wife. **mother-in-law's tongue** a plant, *Sansevieria trifasciata*, with long erect pointed leaves. **mother-lode** *Mining* the main vein of a system. **mother naked** stark naked. **mother-of-pearl** a smooth iridescent substance forming the inner layer of the shell of some molluscs. **Mother's Day 1** *Brit.* = MOTHERING SUNDAY. **2** *US* an equivalent day on the second Sunday in May. **mother's ruin** *colloq.* gin. **mother's son** *colloq.* a man (*every mother's son of you*). **mother tongue 1** one's native language. **2** a language from which others have evolved. **mother wit** native wit; common sense. □□ **motherhood** *n.* **motherless** *adj.* **motherlessness** *n.* **motherlike** *adj. & adv.* [OE *mōdor* f. Gmc]

mothercraft /ˈmʌðəˌkrɑːft/ *n.* skill in or knowledge of looking after children as a mother.

Mothering Sunday /ˈmʌðərɪŋ/ *n. Brit.* the fourth Sunday in Lent, traditionally a day for honouring mothers with gifts.

motherland /ˈmʌðəˌlænd/ *n.* one's native country.

motherly /ˈmʌðəlɪ/ *adj.* **1** like or characteristic of a mother in affection, care, etc. **2** of or relating to a mother. □□ **motherliness** *n.* [OE *mōdorlic* (as MOTHER)]

mothproof /ˈmɒθpruːf/ *adj. & v.* —*adj.* (of clothes) treated so as to repel moths. —*v.tr.* treat (clothes) in this way.

mothy /ˈmɒθɪ/ *adj.* (**mothier**, **mothiest**) infested with moths.

motif /məʊˈtiːf/ *n.* **1** a distinctive or dominant idea in artistic or literary composition. **2** *Mus.* = FIGURE *n.* 10. **3** an ornament of lace etc. sewn separately on a garment. **4** an ornament on a vehicle identifying the maker, model, etc. [F (as MOTIVE)]

motile /ˈməʊtaɪl/ *adj. Zool. & Bot.* capable of motion. □□ **motility** /-ˈtɪlɪtɪ/ *n.* [L *motus* motion (as MOVE)]

motion /ˈməʊʃ(ə)n/ *n. & v.* —*n.* **1** the act or process of moving or of changing position. **2** a particular manner of moving the body in walking etc. **3** a change of posture. **4** a gesture. **5** a formal proposal put to a committee, legislature, etc. **6** *Law* an application for a rule or order of court. **7 a** an evacuation of the bowels. **b** (in *sing.* or *pl.*) faeces. **8** a piece of moving mechanism. —*v.* (often foll. by *to* + infin.) **1** *tr.* direct (a person) by a sign or gesture. **2** *intr.* (often foll. by *to* a person) make a gesture directing (*motioned to me to leave*). □**go through the motions 1** make a pretence; do something perfunctorily or superficially. **2** simulate an action by gestures. **in motion** moving; not at rest. **motion picture** (often with hyphen) *attrib.*) a film (see FILM *n.* 3) with the illusion of movement. **put** (or **set**) **in motion** set going or working. □□ **motional** *adj.* **motionless** *adj.* [ME f. OF f. L *motio -onis* (as MOVE)]

motivate /ˈməʊtɪˌveɪt/ *v.tr.* **1** supply a motive to; be the motive of. **2** cause (a person) to act in a particular way. **3** stimulate the interest of (a person in an activity). □□ **motivation** /-ˈveɪʃ(ə)n/ *n.* **motivational** /-ˈveɪʃən(ə)l/ *adj.* **motivationally** /-ˈveɪʃənəlɪ/ *adv.*

motive /ˈməʊtɪv/ *n., adj., & v.* —*n.* **1** a factor or circumstance that induces a person to act in a particular way. **2** = MOTIF. —*adj.* **1** tending to initiate movement. **2** concerned with movement.

—*v.tr.* = MOTIVATE. □**motive power** a moving or impelling power, esp. a source of energy used to drive machinery. □□ **motiveless** *adj.* **motivelessly** *adv.* **motivelessness** *n.* **motivity** /-ˈtɪvɪtɪ/ *n.* [ME f. OF *motif* (adj. & n.) f. LL *motivus* (adj.) (as MOVE)]

motley /ˈmɒtlɪ/ *adj. & n.* —*adj.* (**motlier**, **motliest**) **1** diversified in colour. **2** of varied character (*a motley crew*). —*n.* **1** an incongruous mixture. **2** *hist.* the particoloured costume of a jester. □**wear motley** play the fool. [ME *mottelay*, perh. ult. rel. to MOTE]

moto-cross /ˈməʊtəʊˌkrɒs/ *n.* cross-country racing on motor cycles. [MOTOR + CROSS-]

moto perpetuo /ˌməʊtəʊ pəˈpetjuəʊ/ *n. Mus.* a usu. fast-moving instrumental composition consisting mainly of notes of equal value. [It., = perpetual motion]

motor /ˈməʊtə(r)/ *n. & v.* —*n.* **1** a thing that imparts motion. **2** a machine (esp. one using electricity or internal combustion) supplying motive power for a vehicle etc. or for some other device with moving parts. **3** *Brit.* = *motor car.* **4** (*attrib.*) **a** giving, imparting, or producing motion. **b** driven by a motor (*motor-mower*). **c** of or for motor vehicles. **d** *Anat.* relating to muscular movement or the nerves activating it. —*v.intr.* & *tr. Brit.* go or convey in a motor vehicle. □**motor area** the part of the frontal lobe of the brain associated with the initiation of muscular action. **motor bicycle** a motor cycle or moped. **motor bike** *colloq.* = *motor cycle.* **motor boat** a motor-driven boat. **motor car** *Brit.* see CAR 1. **motor cycle** a two-wheeled motor-driven road vehicle without pedal propulsion. **motor cyclist** a rider of a motor cycle. **motor mouth** *US sl.* a person who talks incessantly and trivially. **motor nerve** a nerve carrying impulses from the brain or spinal cord to a muscle. **motor scooter** see SCOOTER. **motor vehicle** a road vehicle powered by an internal-combustion engine. □□ **motorial** /məʊˈtɔːrɪəl/ *adj.* (in sense 4a of *n.*). **motory** *adj.* (in sense 4a of *n.*). [L, = mover (as MOVE)]

motorable /ˈməʊtərəb(ə)l/ *adj.* (of a road) that can be used by motor vehicles.

motorcade /ˈməʊtəˌkeɪd/ *n.* a procession of motor vehicles. [MOTOR, after *cavalcade*]

motorist /ˈməʊtərɪst/ *n.* the driver of a motor car.

motorize /ˈməʊtəˌraɪz/ *v.tr.* (also **-ise**) **1** equip (troops etc.) with motor transport. **2** provide with a motor for propulsion etc. □□ **motorization** /-ˈzeɪʃ(ə)n/ *n.*

motorman /ˈməʊtəˌmæn/ *n.* (*pl.* **-men**) the driver of an underground train, tram, etc.

motorway /ˈməʊtəˌweɪ/ *n. Brit.* a main road with separate carriageways and limited access, specially constructed and controlled for fast motor traffic.

Motown /ˈməʊtaʊn/ *n.* music with rhythm and blues elements, associated with Detroit. [shortening of *Motor Town*, a name for Detroit]

motte /mɒt/ *n.* a mound forming the site of a castle, camp, etc. [ME f. OF *mote* (as MOAT)]

mottle /ˈmɒt(ə)l/ *v. & n.* —*v.tr.* (esp. as **mottled** *adj.*) mark with spots or smears of colour. —*n.* **1** an irregular arrangement of spots or patches of colour. **2** any of these spots or patches. [prob. back-form. f. MOTLEY]

motto /ˈmɒtəʊ/ *n.* (*pl.* **-oes**) **1** a maxim adopted as a rule of conduct. **2** a phrase or sentence accompanying a coat of arms or crest. **3** a sentence inscribed on some object and expressing an appropriate sentiment. **4** verses etc. in a paper cracker. **5** a quotation prefixed to a book or chapter. **6** *Mus.* a recurrent phrase having some symbolical significance. [It. (as MOT)]

moue /muː/ *n.* = POUT[1] *n.* [F]

moufflon /ˈmuːflɒn/ *n.* (also **mouflon**) a wild mountain sheep, *Ovis musimon*, of S. Europe. [F *mouflon* f. It. *muflone* f. Rmc]

mouillé /ˈmuːjeɪ/ *adj. Phonet.* (of a consonant) palatalized. [F, = wetted]

moujik var. of MUZHIK.

mould[1] /məʊld/ *n. & v.* (*US* **mold**) —*n.* **1** a hollow container into which molten metal etc. is poured or soft material is pressed to harden into a required shape. **2 a** a metal or earthenware vessel used to give shape to puddings etc. **b** a pudding etc. made in this way. **3** a form or shape, esp. of an animal body. **4** *Archit.* a moulding or group of mouldings. **5** a frame or template for producing mouldings. **6** character or disposition (*in heroic mould*). —*v.tr.* **1** make (an object) in a required shape or from certain ingredients (*was moulded out of clay*). **2** give a shape to. **3** influence the formation or development of (*consultation helps to mould policies*). **4** (esp. of clothing) fit closely to (*the gloves moulded his hands*). □□ **mouldable** *adj.* **moulder** *n.* [ME *mold(e)*, app. f. OF *modle* f. L *modulus*: see MODULUS]

mould² /məʊld/ *n.* (*US* **mold**) a woolly or furry growth of minute fungi occurring esp. in moist warm conditions. [ME prob. f. obs. *mould* adj.; past part. of *moul* grow mouldy f. ON *mygla*]

mould³ /məʊld/ *n.* (*US* **mold**) **1** loose earth. **2** the upper soil of cultivated land, esp. when rich in organic matter. □ **mould-board** the board in a plough that turns over the furrow-slice. [OE *molde* f. Gmc., rel. to MEAL²]

moulder /ˈməʊldə(r)/ *v.intr.* (*US* **molder**) **1** decay to dust. **2** (foll. by *away*) rot or crumble. **3** deteriorate. [perh. f. MOULD³, but cf. Norw. dial. *muldra* crumble]

moulding /ˈməʊldɪŋ/ *n.* (*US* **molding**) **1 a** an ornamentally shaped outline as an architectural feature, esp. in a cornice. **b** a strip of material in wood or stone etc. for use as moulding. **2** similar material in wood or plastic etc. used for other decorative purposes, e.g. in picture-framing.

mouldy /ˈməʊldɪ/ *adj.* (*US* **moldy**) (**-ier, -iest**) **1** covered with mould. **2** stale; out of date. **3** *colloq.* (as a general term of disparagement) dull, miserable, boring. □□ **mouldiness** *n.*

moulin /ˈmuːlæ̃/ *n.* a nearly vertical shaft in a glacier, formed by surface water percolating through a crack in the ice. [F, lit. = mill]

moult /məʊlt/ *v. & n.* (*US* **molt**) —*v.* **1** *intr.* shed feathers, hair, a shell, etc., in the process of renewing plumage, a coat, etc. **2** *tr.* (of an animal) shed (feathers, hair, etc.). —*n.* the act or an instance of moulting (*is in moult once a year*). □□ **moulter** *n.* [ME *moute* f. OE *mutian* (unrecorded) f. L *mutare* change: *-l-* after *fault* etc.]

mound¹ /maʊnd/ *n. & v.* —*n.* **1** a raised mass of earth, stones, or other compacted material. **2** a heap or pile. **3** a hillock. —*v.tr.* **1** heap up in a mound or mounds. **2** enclose with mounds. [16th c. (orig. = hedge or fence): orig. unkn.]

mound² /maʊnd/ *n. Heraldry* a ball of gold etc. representing the earth, and usu. surmounting a crown. [ME f. OF *monde* f. L *mundus* world]

mount¹ /maʊnt/ *v. & n.* —*v.* **1** *tr.* ascend or climb (a hill, stairs, etc.). **2** *tr.* **a** get up on (an animal, esp. a horse) to ride it. **b** set (a person) on horseback. **c** provide (a person) with a horse. **d** (as **mounted** *adj.*) serving on horseback (*mounted police*). **3** *tr.* go up or climb on to (a raised surface). **4** *intr.* **a** move upwards. **b** (often foll. by *up*) increase, accumulate. **c** (of a feeling) become stronger or more intense (*excitement was mounting*). **d** (of the blood) rise into the cheeks. **5** *tr.* (esp. of a male animal) get on to (a female) to copulate. **6** *tr.* (often foll. by *on*) place (an object) on an elevated support. **7** *tr.* **a** set in or attach to a backing, setting, or other support. **b** attach (a picture etc.) to a mount or frame. **c** fix (an object for viewing) on a microscope slide. **8** *tr.* **a** arrange (a play, exhibition, etc.) or present for public view or display. **b** take action to initiate (a programme, campaign, etc.). **9** *tr.* prepare (specimens) for preservation. **10** *tr.* **a** bring into readiness for operation. **b** raise (guns) into position on a fixed mounting. **11** *intr.* rise to a higher level of rank, power, etc. —*n.* **1** a backing, setting, or other support on which a

picture etc. is set for display. **2** the margin surrounding a picture or photograph. **3 a** a horse available for riding. **b** an opportunity to ride a horse, esp. as a jockey. **4** = *stamp-hinge* (see HINGE). □ **mount guard** (often foll. by *over*) perform the duty of guarding; take up sentry duty. □□ **mountable** *adj.* **mounter** *n.* [ME f. OF *munter, monter* ult. f. L (as MOUNT²)]

mount² /maʊnt/ *n. archaic* (except before a name): mountain, hill (*Mount Everest; Mount of Olives*). [ME f. OE *munt* & OF *mont* f. L *mons montis* mountain]

mountain /ˈmaʊntɪn/ *n.* **1** a large natural elevation of the earth's surface rising abruptly from the surrounding level; a large or high and steep hill. **2** a large heap or pile; a huge quantity (*a mountain of work*). **3** a large surplus stock of a commodity (*butter mountain*). □ **make a mountain out of a molehill** see MOLEHILL. **mountain ash 1** a tree, *Sorbus aucuparia*, with delicate pinnate leaves and scarlet berries: also called ROWAN. **2** any of several Australian eucalypts. **mountain chain** a connected series of mountains. **mountain goat** a white goatlike animal, *Oreamnos americanus*, of the Rocky Mountains etc. **mountain laurel** a N. American shrub, *Kalmia latifolia.* **mountain lion** a puma. **mountain panther** = OUNCE². **mountain range** a line of mountains connected by high ground. **mountain sickness** a sickness caused by the rarefaction of the air at great heights. **Mountain Time** *US* the standard time of parts of Canada and the US in or near the Rocky Mountains. **move mountains 1** achieve spectacular results. **2** make every possible effort. □□ **mountainy** *adj.* [ME f. OF *montaigne* ult. f. L (as MOUNT²)]

mountaineer /ˌmaʊntɪˈnɪə(r)/ *n. & v.* —*n.* **1** a person skilled in mountain-climbing. **2** a person living in an area of high mountains. —*v.intr.* climb mountains as a sport. □□ **mountaineering** *n.*

mountainous /ˈmaʊntɪnəs/ *adj.* **1** (of a region) having many mountains. **2** huge.

mountainside /ˈmaʊntɪnˌsaɪd/ *n.* the slope of a mountain below the summit.

mountebank /ˈmaʊntɪˌbæŋk/ *n.* **1** a swindler; a charlatan. **2** a clown. **3** *hist.* an itinerant quack appealing to an audience from a platform. □□ **mountebankery** *n.* [It. *montambanco = monta in banco* climb on bench: see MOUNT¹, BENCH]

Mountie /ˈmaʊntɪ/ *n. colloq.* a member of the Royal Canadian Mounted Police.

mounting /ˈmaʊntɪŋ/ *n.* **1** = MOUNT¹ *n.* 1. **2** in senses of MOUNT¹ *v.* □ **mounting-block** a block of stone placed to help a rider mount a horse.

mourn /mɔːn/ *v.* **1** *tr.* **a** (foll. by *for*) *intr.* feel or show deep sorrow or regret for (a dead person, a lost thing, a past event, etc.). **2** *intr.* show conventional signs of grief for a period after a person's death. [OE *murnan*]

mourner /ˈmɔːnə(r)/ *n.* **1** a person who mourns, esp. at a funeral. **2** a person hired to attend a funeral.

mournful /ˈmɔːnfʊl/ *adj.* **1** doleful, sad, sorrowing. **2** expressing or suggestive of mourning. □□ **mournfully** *adv.* **mournfulness** *n.*

mourning /ˈmɔːnɪŋ/ *n.* **1** the expression of deep sorrow, esp. for a dead person, by the wearing of solemn dress. **2** the clothes worn in mourning. □ **in mourning** assuming the signs of mourning, esp. in dress. **mourning-band** a band of black crape etc. round a person's sleeve or hat as a token of mourning. **mourning dove** an American dove with a plaintive note, *Zenaida macroura.* **mourning-paper** notepaper with a black edge. **mourning-ring** a ring worn as a memorial of a deceased person.

mousaka var. of MOUSSAKA.

mouse /maʊs/ *n. & v.* (*pl.* **mice** /maɪs/) **1 a** any of various small rodents of the family Muridae, esp. of the genus *Mus.* **b** any of several similar rodents such as a small shrew or vole. **2** a timid or feeble person. **3** *Computing* a small hand-held

device which controls the cursor on a VDU screen. **4**
sl. a black eye. —*v.intr.* /also maʊz/ **1** (esp. of a cat,
owl, etc.) hunt for or catch mice. **2** (foll. by *about*)
search industriously; prowl about as if searching.
□ **mouse-coloured 1** dark-grey with a yellow tinge.
2 nondescript light brown. **mouse deer** a chevrotain.
mouse hare a pika. □□ **mouselike** *adj.* & *adv.*
mouser *n.* [OE *mūs*, pl. *mȳs* f. Gmc]

mousetrap /ˈmaʊstræp/ *n.* **1** a sprung trap with bait
for catching and usu. killing mice. **2** (often *attrib.*)
cheese of poor quality.

moussaka /mʊˈsɑːkə, ˌmuːsəˈkɑː/ *n.* (also **mousaka**)
a Greek dish of minced meat, aubergine, etc. with a
cheese sauce. [mod. Gk or Turk.]

mousse /muːs/ *n.* **1 a** a dessert of whipped cream,
eggs, etc., usu. flavoured with fruit or chocolate. **b** a
meat or fish purée made with whipped cream etc. **2**
a preparation applied to the hair enabling it to be
styled more easily. [F, = moss, froth]

mousseline /muːˈsliːn/ *n.* **1** a muslin-like fabric of
silk etc. **2** a sauce of seasoned or sweet eggs and
cream. [F: see MUSLIN]

moustache /məˈstɑːʃ/ *n.* (*US* **mustache**) **1** hair left
to grow on a man's upper lip. **2** a similar growth
round the mouth of some animals. □ **moustache
cup** a cup with a partial cover to protect the
moustache when drinking. □□ **moustached** *adj.* [F
f. It. *mostaccio* f. Gk *mustax -akos*]

Mousterian /muːˈstɪərɪən/ *adj. Archaeol.* of or relating to the flint workings of the middle palaeolithic
epoch, dated to *c.*70,000–30,000 BC, and attributed to
Neanderthal peoples. [F *moustérien* f. *Le Moustier* in
SW France, where remains were found]

mousy /ˈmaʊsɪ/ *adj.* (**mousier**, **mousiest**) **1** of or
like a mouse. **2** (of a person) shy or timid; ineffectual.
3 = *mouse-coloured*. □□ **mousily** *adv.* **mousiness** *n.*

mouth *n.* & *v.* —*n.* /maʊθ/ (*pl.* **mouths** /maʊðz/) **1**
a an external opening in the head, through which
most animals admit food and emit communicative
sounds. **b** (in humans and some animals) the cavity
behind it containing the means of biting and chewing
and the vocal organs. **2 a** the opening of a container
such as a bag or sack. **b** the opening of a cave,
volcano, etc. **c** the open end of a woodwind or brass
instrument. **d** the muzzle of a gun. **3** the place where
a river enters the sea. **4** *colloq.* **a** talkativeness. **b**
impudent talk; cheek. **5** an individual regarded as
needing sustenance (*an extra mouth to feed*). **6** a
horse's readiness to feel and obey the pressure of
the bit. —*v.* /maʊð/ **1** *tr.* & *intr.* utter or speak
solemnly or with affectations; rant, declaim (*mouth-
ing platitudes*). **2** *tr.* utter very distinctly. **3** *intr.* **a**
move the lips silently. **b** grimace. **4** *tr.* take (food) in
the mouth. **5** *tr.* touch with the mouth. **6** *tr.* train the
mouth of (a horse). □ **give mouth** (of a dog) bark,
bay. **keep one's mouth shut** *colloq.* not reveal
a secret. **mouth-organ** = HARMONICA.
mouth-to-mouth (of resuscitation) in which a person breathes into a subject's lungs through the
mouth. **mouth-watering 1** (of food etc.) having a
delicious smell or appearance. **2** tempting, alluring.
put words into a person's mouth represent a
person as having said something in a particular way.
take the words out of a person's mouth say what
another was about to say. □□ **mouthed** /maʊðd/ *adj.*
(also in *comb.*). **mouther** /ˈmaʊðə(r)/ *n.* **mouthless**
/ˈmaʊθlɪs/ *adj.* [OE *mūth* f. Gmc]

mouthful /ˈmaʊθfʊl/ *n.* (*pl.* **-fuls**) **1** a quantity, esp.
of food, that fills the mouth. **2** a small quantity. **3** a
long or complicated word or phrase. **4** *US colloq.*
something important said.

mouthpiece /ˈmaʊθpiːs/ *n.* **1 a** the part of a musical
instrument placed between or against the lips. **b** the
part of a telephone for speaking into. **c** the part of a
tobacco-pipe placed between the lips. **2 a** a person
who speaks for another or others. **b** *colloq.* a lawyer.
3 a part attached as an outlet.

mouthwash /ˈmaʊθwɒʃ/ *n.* **1** a liquid antiseptic etc.
for rinsing the mouth or gargling. **2** *colloq.* nonsense.

mouthy /ˈmaʊðɪ/ *adj.* (**mouthier**, **mouthiest**) **1**
ranting, railing. **2** bombastic.

movable /ˈmuːvəb(ə)l/ *adj.* & *n.* (also **moveable**)
—*adj.* **1** that can be moved. **2** *Law* (of property) of
the nature of a chattel, as distinct from land or buildings. **3** (of a feast or festival) variable in date from year
to year. —*n.* **1** an article of furniture that may be
removed from a house, as distinct from a fixture. **2**
(in *pl.*) personal property. □ **movable-doh** *Mus.*
applied to a system of sight-singing in which doh is
the keynote of any major scale (cf. *fixed-doh*). □□
movability /-ˈbɪlɪtɪ/ *n.* **movableness** *n.* **movably**
adv. [ME f. OF (as MOVE)]

move /muːv/ *v.* & *n.* —*v.* **1** *intr.* & *tr.* change one's
position or posture, or cause to do this. **2** *tr.* & *intr.*
put or keep in motion; rouse, stir. **3 a** *intr.* make a
move in a board-game. **b** *tr.* change the position of (a
piece) in a board-game. **4** *intr.* (often foll. by *about*,
away, etc.) go or pass from place to place. **5** *intr.*
take action, esp. promptly (*moved to reduce unemployment*). **6** *intr.* make progress (*the project is
moving fast*). **7** *intr.* **a** change one's place of residence.
b (of a business etc.) change to new premises (also
tr.: *move house*; *move offices*). **8** *intr.* (foll. by *in*) live
or be socially active in (a specified place or group
etc.) (*moves in the best circles*). **9** *tr.* affect (a person)
with (usu. tender or sympathetic) emotion. **10** *tr.* **a**
(foll. by *in*) stimulate (laughter, anger, etc., in a
person). **b** (foll. by *to*) provoke (a person to laughter
etc.). **11** *tr.* (foll. by *to*, or *to* + infin.) prompt or
incline (a person to a feeling or action). **12 a** *tr.* cause
(the bowels) to be evacuated. **b** *intr.* (of the bowels)
be evacuated. **13** *tr.* (often foll. by *that* + clause)
propose in a meeting, deliberative assembly, etc. **14**
intr. (foll. by *for*) make a formal request or application. **15** *intr.* (of merchandise) be sold. —*n.* **1** the
act or an instance of moving. **2** a change of house,
business premises, etc. **3** a step taken to secure some
action or effect; an initiative. **4 a** the changing of the
position of a piece in a board-game. **b** a player's turn
to do this. □ **get a move on** *colloq.* **1** hurry up. **2**
make a start. **make a move** take action. **move
along** (or **on**) change to a new position, esp. to avoid
crowding, getting in the way, etc. **move heaven
and earth** see HEAVEN. **move in 1** take possession
of a new house. **2** get into a position of influence,
interference, etc. **3** get into a position of readiness
or proximity (for an offensive action etc.). **move
mountains** see MOUNTAIN. **move out 1** leave one's
home; change one's place of residence. **2** leave a
position, job, etc. **move over** (or **up**) adjust one's
position to make room for another. **on the move 1**
progressing. **2** moving about. [ME f. AF *mover*, OF
moveir f. L *movēre mot-*]

moveable var. of MOVABLE.

movement /ˈmuːvmənt/ *n.* **1** the act or an instance
of moving or being moved. **2 a** the moving parts of a
mechanism (esp. a clock or watch). **b** a particular
group of these. **3 a** a body of persons with a
common object (*the peace movement*). **b** a campaign
undertaken by such a body. **4** (usu. in *pl.*) a person's
activities and whereabouts, esp. at a particular time.
5 *Mus.* a principal division of a longer musical work,
self-sufficient in terms of key, tempo, structure, etc.
6 the progressive development of a poem, story, etc.
7 motion of the bowels. **8 a** an activity in a market
for some commodity. **b** a rise or fall in price. **9** a
mental impulse. **10** a development of position by a
military force or unit. [ME f. OF f. med.L *movimentum* (as MOVE)]

mover /ˈmuːvə(r)/ *n.* **1** a person or thing that moves.
2 a person who moves a proposition. **3** *US* a remover
of furniture. **4** the author of a fruitful idea.

movie /ˈmuːvɪ/ *n.* esp. *US colloq.* **1** a motion-picture
film. **2** (in full **movie-house**) a cinema.

moving /ˈmuːvɪŋ/ *adj.* **1** that moves or causes to

aʊ how eɪ day əʊ no eə hair ɪə near ɔɪ boy ʊə poor aɪə fire aʊə sour (*see over for consonants*)

move. **2** affecting with emotion. □**moving pavement** a structure like a conveyor belt for pedestrians. **moving picture** a continuous picture of events obtained by projecting a sequence of photographs taken at very short intervals. **moving staircase** an escalator. □□ **movingly** adv. (in sense 2).

mow[1] /məʊ/ v.tr. (past part. **mowed** or **mown**) **1** cut down (grass, hay, etc.) with a scythe or machine. **2** cut down the produce of (a field) or the grass etc. of (a lawn) by mowing. □**mow down** kill or destroy randomly or in great numbers. □□ **mowable** adj. **mower** n. [OE māwan f. Gmc, rel. to MEAD[2]]

mow[2] /məʊ/ n. US or dial. **1** a stack of hay, corn, etc. **2** a place in a barn where hay etc. is heaped. [OE mūga]

moxa /'mɒksə/ n. a downy substance from the dried leaves of Artemisia moxa etc., burnt on the skin in oriental medicine as a counterirritant. [Jap. mogusa f. moe kusa burning herb]

mozzarella /ˌmɒtsə'relə/ n. an Italian curd cheese orig. of buffalo milk. [It.]

MP abbr. **1** Member of Parliament. **2 a** military police. **b** military policeman.

mp abbr. mezzo piano.

m.p. abbr. melting-point.

m.p.g. abbr. miles per gallon.

m.p.h. abbr. miles per hour.

M.Phil. abbr. Master of Philosophy.

MPS abbr. Member of the Pharmaceutical Society.

MR abbr. Master of the Rolls.

Mr /'mɪstə(r)/ n. (pl. **Messrs**) **1** the title of a man without a higher title (Mr Jones). **2** a title prefixed to a designation of office etc. (Mr President; Mr Speaker). □**Mr Right** joc. a woman's destined husband. [abbr. of MISTER]

MRA abbr. Moral Re-Armament.

MRBM abbr. medium-range ballistic missile.

MRC abbr. (in the UK) Medical Research Council.

MRCA abbr. multi-role combat aircraft.

mRNA abbr. Biol. messenger RNA.

Mrs /'mɪsɪz/ n. (pl. same or **Mesdames**) the title of a married woman without a higher title (Mrs Jones). [abbr. of MISTRESS: cf. MISSIS]

MS abbr. **1** manuscript. **2** Master of Science. **3** Master of Surgery. **4** US Mississippi (in official postal use). **5** US motor ship. **6** multiple sclerosis.

Ms /mɪz, məz/ n. the title of a woman without a higher title, used regardless of marital status. [combination of MRS, MISS[2]]

MSC abbr. (in the UK) Manpower Services Commission.

M.Sc. abbr. Master of Science.

MS-DOS /ˌemes'dɒs/ abbr. Computing Microsoft disk operating system.

MSF abbr. (in the UK) Manufacturing, Science, and Finance (Union).

Msgr. abbr. US **1** Monseigneur. **2** Monsignor.

MSS /em'esɪz/ abbr. manuscripts.

MST abbr. (in Canada and the US) Mountain Standard Time.

MT abbr. **1** mechanical transport. **2** US Montana (in official postal use).

Mt. abbr. Mount.

MTB abbr. motor torpedo-boat.

M.Tech. abbr. Master of Technology.

mu /mjuː/ n. **1** the twelfth Greek letter (M, μ). **2** (μ, as a symbol) = MICRO- 2. □**mu-meson** = MUON. [Gk]

much /mʌtʃ/ adj., n., & adv. —adj. **1** existing or occurring in a great quantity (much trouble; not much rain; too much noise). **2** (prec. by as, how, that, etc.) with relative rather than distinctive sense (I don't know how much money you want). —n. **1** a great quantity (much of that is true). **2** (prec. by as, how, that, etc.) with relative rather than distinctive sense (we do not need that much). **3** (usu. in neg.) a noteworthy or outstanding example (not much to look at; not much of a party). —adv. **1 a** in a great degree (much to my surprise; is much the same). **b**

(qualifying a verb or past participle) greatly (they much regret the mistake; I was much annoyed). ¶ Much implies a strong verbal element in the participle, whereas very implies a strong adjectival element: compare the second example above with I was very annoyed. **c** qualifying a comparative or superlative adjective (much better; much the most likely). **2** for a large part of one's time (is much away from home). □**as much** the extent or quantity just specified; the idea just mentioned (I thought as much; as much as that?). **a bit much** colloq. somewhat excessive or immoderate. **make much of** see MAKE. **much as** even though (cannot come, much as I would like to). **much less** see LESS. **much obliged** see OBLIGE. **not much** colloq. **1** iron. very much. **2** certainly not. **not much in it** see IN. **too much** colloq. an intolerable situation etc. (that really is too much). **too much for 1** more than a match for. **2** beyond what is endurable by. □□ **muchly** adv. joc. [ME f. muchel MICKLE: for loss of el cf. BAD, WENCH]

muchness /'mʌtʃnɪs/ n. greatness in quantity or degree. □**much of a muchness** very nearly the same or alike.

mucilage /'mjuːsɪlɪdʒ/ n. **1** a viscous substance obtained from plant seeds etc. by maceration. **2** US a solution of gum. □□ **mucilaginous** /-'lædʒɪnəs/ adj. [ME f. F f. LL mucilago -ginis musty juice (MUCUS)]

muck /mʌk/ n. & v. —n. **1** farmyard manure. **2** colloq. dirt or filth; anything disgusting. **3** colloq. an untidy state; a mess. —v.tr. **1** (usu. foll. by up) Brit. colloq. bungle (a job). **2** (foll. by out) remove muck from. **3** make dirty. **4** manure with muck. □**make a muck of** colloq. bungle. **muck about** (or **around**) Brit. colloq. **1** potter or fool about. **2** (foll. by with) fool or interfere with. **muck in** Brit. (often foll. by with) share tasks etc. equally. **muck sweat** Brit. colloq. a profuse sweat. [ME muk prob. f. Scand.: cf. ON myki dung, rel. to MEEK]

mucker /'mʌkə(r)/ n. sl. **1** a friend or companion. **2** US a rough or coarse person. **3** Brit. a heavy fall. □□ **muckerish** adj. (in senses 1 and 2). [prob. f. muck in: see MUCK]

muckle var. of MICKLE.

muckrake /'mʌkreɪk/ v.intr. search out and reveal scandal, esp. among famous people. □□ **muckraker** n. **muckraking** n.

mucky /'mʌkɪ/ adj. (**muckier, muckiest**) **1** covered with muck. **2** dirty. □□ **muckiness** n.

muco- /'mjuːkəʊ/ comb. form Biochem. mucus, mucous.

mucopolysaccharide /ˌmjuːkəʊˌpɒlɪ'sækəˌraɪd/ n. Biochem. any of a group of polysaccharides whose molecules contain sugar residues and are often found as components of connective tissue.

mucosa /mjuː'kəʊsə/ n. (pl. **mucosae** /-siː/) a mucous membrane. [mod.L, fem. of mucosus: see MUCOUS]

mucous /'mjuːkəs/ adj. of or covered with mucus. □**mucous membrane** a mucus-secreting epithelial tissue lining many body cavities and tubular organs. □□ **mucosity** /-'kɒsɪtɪ/ n. [L mucosus (as MUCUS)]

mucro /'mjuːkrəʊ/ n. (pl. **mucrones** /-'krəʊniːz/) Bot. & Zool. a sharp-pointed part or organ. □□ **mucronate** /-krənət/ adj. [L mucro -onis sharp point]

mucus /'mjuːkəs/ n. **1** a slimy substance secreted by a mucous membrane. **2** a gummy substance found in all plants. **3** a slimy substance exuded by some animals, esp. fishes. [L]

mud /mʌd/ n. **1** wet soft earthy matter. **2** hard ground from the drying of an area of this. **3** what is worthless or polluting. □**as clear as mud** colloq. not at all clear. **fling** (or **sling** or **throw**) **mud** speak disparagingly or slanderously. **here's mud in your eye!** colloq. a drinking-toast. **mud-bath 1** a bath in the mud of mineral springs, esp. to relieve rheumatism etc. **2** a muddy scene or occasion. **mud-brick** a brick made from baked mud. **mud-flat** a stretch of muddy land left uncovered at low tide. **mud pack** a cosmetic paste applied thickly to the face. **mud pie**

mud made into a pie shape by a child. **mud puppy** *US* a large nocturnal salamander, *Necturus maculosus*, of eastern USA. **mud skipper** any of various gobies of the family Periophthalmidae, able to leave the water and leap on the mud. **mud-slinger** *colloq.* one given to making abusive or disparaging remarks. **mud-slinging** *colloq.* abuse, disparagement. **mud volcano** a volcano discharging mud. **one's name is mud** one is unpopular or in disgrace. [ME *mode*, *mudde*, prob. f. MLG *mudde*, MHG *mot* bog]

muddle /'mʌd(ə)l/ *v. & n.* —*v.* **1** *tr.* (often foll. by *up*, *together*) bring into disorder. **2** *tr.* bewilder, confuse. **3** *tr.* mismanage (an affair). **4** *tr. US* crush and mix (the ingredients for a drink). **5** *intr.* (often foll. by *with*) busy oneself in a confused and ineffective way. —*n.* **1** disorder. **2** a muddled condition. □**make a muddle of 1** bring into disorder. **2** bungle. **muddle along** (or **on**) progress in a haphazard way. **muddle-headed** stupid, confused. **muddle-headedness** stupidity; a confused state. **muddle through** succeed by perseverance rather than skill or efficiency. **muddle up** confuse (two or more things). □□**muddler** *n.* **muddlingly** *adv.* [perh. f. MDu. *moddelen*, frequent. of *modden* dabble in mud (as MUD)]

muddy /'mʌdɪ/ *adj. & v.* —*adj.* (**muddier**, **muddiest**) **1** like mud. **2** covered in or full of mud. **3** (of liquid) turbid. **4** mentally confused. **5** obscure. **6** (of light) dull. **7** (of colour) impure. —*v.tr.* (**-ies**, **-ied**) make muddy. □□**muddily** *adv.* **muddiness** *n.*

mudfish /'mʌdfɪʃ/ *n.* any fish that burrows in mud, esp. the bowfin.

mudflap /'mʌdflæp/ *n.* a flap hanging behind the wheel of a vehicle, to catch mud and stones etc. thrown up from the road.

mudguard /'mʌdgɑːd/ *n.* a curved strip or cover over a wheel of a bicycle or motor cycle to reduce the amount of mud etc. thrown up from the road.

mudlark /'mʌdlɑːk/ *n.* **1** *hist.* a destitute child searching in river mud for objects of value. **2** *hist.* a street urchin.

mudstone /'mʌdstəʊn/ *n.* a dark clay rock.

muesli /'muːzlɪ, 'mjuː-/ *n.* a breakfast food of crushed cereals, dried fruits, nuts, etc., eaten with milk. [Swiss G]

muezzin /muː'ɛzɪn/ *n.* a Muslim crier who proclaims the hours of prayer usu. from a minaret. [Arab. *mu'aḏḏin* part. of *'aḏḏana* proclaim]

muff[1] /mʌf/ *n.* a fur or other covering, usu. in the form of a tube with an opening at each end for the hands to be inserted for warmth. [Du. *mof*, MDu. *moffel*, *muffel* f. med.L *muff(u)la*, of unkn. orig.]

muff[2] /mʌf/ *v. & n.* —*v.tr.* **1** bungle; deal clumsily with. **2** fail to catch or receive (a ball etc.). **3** blunder in (a theatrical part etc.). —*n.* **1** a person who is awkward or stupid, orig. in some athletic sport. **2** a failure, esp. to catch a ball at cricket etc. □□**muffish** *adj.* [19th c.: orig. unkn.]

muffin /'mʌfɪn/ *n.* **1** *Brit.* a light flat round spongy cake, eaten toasted and buttered. **2** *US* a similar round cake made from batter or dough. □**muffin-man** *Brit.* (formerly) a seller of muffins in the street. [18th c.: orig. unkn.]

muffle[1] /'mʌf(ə)l/ *v. & n.* —*v.tr.* **1** (often foll. by *up*) wrap or cover for warmth. **2** cover or wrap up (a source of sound) to reduce its loudness. **3** (usu. as **muffled** *adj.*) stifle (an utterance, e.g. a curse). **4** prevent from speaking. —*n.* **1** a receptacle in a furnace where substances may be heated without contact with combustion products. **2** a similar chamber in a kiln for baking painted pottery. [ME: (n.) f. OF *moufle* thick glove; (v.) perh. f. OF *enmoufler* f. *moufle*]

muffle[2] /'mʌf(ə)l/ *n.* the thick part of the upper lip and nose of ruminants and rodents. [F *mufle*, of unkn. orig.]

muffler /'mʌflə(r)/ *n.* **1** a wrap or scarf worn for

warmth. **2** any of various devices used to deaden sound in musical instruments. **3** *US* the silencer of a motor vehicle.

mufti[1] /'mʌftɪ/ *n.* a Muslim legal expert empowered to give rulings on religious matters. [Arab. *muftī*, part. of *'aftā* decide a point of law]

mufti[2] /'mʌftɪ/ *n.* plain clothes worn by a person who also wears (esp. military) uniform (*in mufti*). [19th c.: perh. f. MUFTI[1]]

mug[1] /mʌg/ *n. & v.* —*n.* **1 a** a drinking-vessel, usu. cylindrical and with a handle and used without a saucer. **b** its contents. **2** *sl.* the face or mouth of a person. **3** *Brit. sl.* **a** a simpleton. **b** a gullible person. **4** *US sl.* a hoodlum or thug. —*v.* (**mugged**, **mugging**) **1** *tr.* rob (a person) with violence esp. in a public place. **2** *tr.* thrash. **3** *tr.* strangle. **4** *intr. sl.* make faces, esp. before an audience, a camera, etc. □**a mug's game** *Brit. colloq.* a foolish or unprofitable activity. **mug shot** *sl.* a photograph of a face, esp. for official purposes. □□**mugger** *n.* (esp. in sense 1 of *v.*). **mugful** *n.* (*pl.* **-fuls**). **mugging** *n.* (in sense 1 of *v.*). [prob. f. Scand.: sense 2 of *n.* prob. f. the representation of faces on mugs, and sense 3 prob. from this]

mug[2] /mʌg/ *v.tr.* (**mugged**, **mugging**) *Brit.* (usu. foll. by *up*) *sl.* learn (a subject) by concentrated study. [19th c.: orig. unkn.]

mugger[1] see MUG[1].

mugger[2] /'mʌgə(r)/ *n.* a broad-nosed Indian crocodile, *Crocodylus palustris*, venerated by many Hindus. [Hindi *magar*]

muggins /'mʌgɪnz/ *n.* (*pl.* same or **mugginses**) **1** *colloq.* **a** a simpleton. **b** a person who is easily outwitted (often with allusion to oneself: *so muggins had to pay*). **2** a card-game like snap. [perh. the surname *Muggins*, with allusion to MUG[1]]

muggy /'mʌgɪ/ *adj.* (**muggier**, **muggiest**) (of the weather, a day, etc.) oppressively damp and warm; humid. □□**mugginess** *n.* [dial. *mug* mist, drizzle f. ON *mugga*]

Mughal /'muːgɑːl/ *n.* **1** a Mongolian. **2** (*attrib.*) denoting the Muslim dynasty in India in the 16th-19th c. (cf. MOGUL 2b). [Pers. *mugūl* MONGOL]

mugwort /'mʌgwɜːt/ *n.* any of various plants of the genus *Artemisia*, esp. *A. vulgaris*, with silver-grey aromatic foliage. [OE *mucgwyrt* (as MIDGE, WORT)]

mugwump /'mʌgwʌmp/ *n. US* **1** a great man; a boss. **2** a person who holds aloof, esp. from party politics. [Algonquin *mugquomp* great chief]

Muhammadan //mə'hæməd(ə)n// *n. & adj.* (also **Mohammedan**) = MUSLIM. ¶ A term not used or favoured by Muslims, and often regarded as *offens.* □□**Muhammadanism** *n.* [*Muhammad*, Arabian prophet d. 632]

mujahidin /ˌmuːdʒɑːhɪ'diːn/ *n.pl.* (also **mujahedin**, **-deen**) guerrilla fighters in Islamic countries, esp. supporting Muslim fundamentalism. [Pers. & Arab. *mujāhidīn* pl. of *mujāhid* one who fights a JIHAD]

mulatto /mjuː'lætəʊ/ *n. & adj.* —*n.* (*pl.* **-os** or **-oes**) a person of mixed White and Black parentage. —*adj.* of the colour of mulattos; tawny. [Sp. *mulato* young mule, *mulatto*, irreg. f. *mulo* MULE[1]]

mulberry /'mʌlbərɪ/ *n.* (*pl.* **-ies**) **1** any deciduous tree of the genus *Morus*, grown originally for feeding silkworms, and now for its fruit and ornamental qualities. **2** its dark-red or white berry. **3** a dark-red or purple colour. [ME *mol-*, *mool-*, *mulberry*, dissim. f. *murberie* f. OE *mōrberie*, f. L *morum*: see BERRY]

mulch /mʌltʃ, mʌlʃ/ *n. & v.* —*n.* a mixture of wet straw, leaves, etc., spread around or over a plant to enrich or insulate the soil. —*v.tr.* treat with mulch. [prob. use as noun of *mulsh* soft: cf. dial. *melsh* mild f. OE *melsc*]

mulct /mʌlkt/ *v. & n.* —*v.tr.* **1** extract money from by fine or taxation. **2 a** (often foll. by *of*) deprive by fraudulent means; swindle. **b** obtain by swindling. —*n.* a fine. [earlier *mult(e)* f. L *multa*, *mulcta*: (v.) through F *mulcter* & L *mulctare*]

mule[1] /mjuːl/ *n.* **1** the offspring (usu. sterile) of a male donkey and a female horse, or (in general use) of a female donkey and a male horse (cf. HINNY[1]), used as a beast of burden. **2** a stupid or obstinate person. **3** (often *attrib.*) a hybrid and usu. sterile plant or animal (*mule canary*). **4** (in full **spinning mule**) a kind of spinning-machine producing yarn on spindles. [ME f. OF *mul(e)* f. L *mulus mula*]

mule[2] /mjuːl/ *n.* a light shoe or slipper without a back. [F]

mule[3] var. of MEWL.

muleteer /ˌmjuːlɪˈtɪə(r)/ *n.* a mule-driver. [F *muletier* f. *mulet* dimin. of OF *mul* MULE[1]]

mulga /ˈmʌlgə/ *n.* *Austral.* **1** a small spreading tree, *Acacia aneura.* **2** the wood of this tree. **3** scrub or bush. **4** *colloq.* the outback. [Aboriginal]

muliebrity /ˌmjuːlɪˈebrɪtɪ/ *n.* *literary* **1** womanhood. **2** the normal characteristics of a woman. **3** softness, effeminacy. [LL *muliebritas* f. L *mulier* woman]

mulish /ˈmjuːlɪʃ/ *adj.* **1** like a mule. **2** stubborn. □□ **mulishly** *adv.* **mulishness** *n.*

mull[1] /mʌl/ *v.tr.* & *intr.* (often foll. by *over*) ponder or consider. [perh. f. *mull* grind to powder, ME *mul* dust f. MDu.]

mull[2] /mʌl/ *v.tr.* warm (wine or beer) with added sugar, spices, etc. [17th c.: orig. unkn.]

mull[3] /mʌl/ *n.* *Sc.* a promontory. [ME: cf. Gael. *maol*, Icel. *múli*]

mull[4] /mʌl/ *n.* humus formed under non-acid conditions. [G f. Da. *muld*]

mull[5] /mʌl/ *n.* a thin soft plain muslin. [abbr. of *mulmull* f. Hindi *malmal*]

mullah /ˈmʌlə/ *n.* a Muslim learned in Islamic theology and sacred law. [Pers., Turk., Urdu *mullā* f. Arab. *mawlā*]

mullein /ˈmʌlɪn/ *n.* any herbaceous plant of the genus *Verbascum*, with woolly leaves and yellow flowers. [ME f. OF *moleine* f. Gaulish]

muller /ˈmʌlə(r)/ *n.* a stone or other heavy weight used for grinding material on a slab. [ME, perh. f. AF *moldre* grind]

mullet /ˈmʌlɪt/ *n.* any fish of the family Mullidae (**red mullet**) or Mugilidae (**grey mullet**), usu. with a thick body and a large blunt-nosed head, commonly used as food. [ME f. OF *mulet* dimin. of L *mullus* red mullet f. Gk *mollos*]

mulligatawny /ˌmʌlɪgəˈtɔːnɪ/ *n.* a highly seasoned soup orig. from India. [Tamil *milagutannir* pepper-water]

mullion /ˈmʌljən/ *n.* (also **munnion** /ˈmʌn-/) a vertical bar dividing the lights in a window (cf. TRANSOM). □□ **mullioned** *adj.* [prob. an altered form of MONIAL]

mullock /ˈmʌlək/ *n.* **1** *Austral.* or *dial.* refuse, rubbish. **2** *Austral.* **a** rock containing no gold. **b** refuse from which gold has been extracted. **3** *Austral.* ridicule. [ME dimin. of *mul* dust, rubbish, f. MDu.]

mulloway /ˈmʌləweɪ/ *n.* *Austral.* a large marine fish, *Sciaena antarctica*, used as food. [19th c.: orig. unkn.]

multangular /mʌlˈtæŋgjʊlə(r)/ *adj.* having many angles. [med.L *multangularis* (as MULTI-, ANGULAR)]

multi- /ˈmʌltɪ/ *comb. form* many; more than one. [L f. *multus* much, many]

multi-access /ˌmʌltɪˈækses/ *n.* (often *attrib.*) the simultaneous connection to a computer of a number of terminals.

multiaxial /ˌmʌltɪˈæksɪəl/ *adj.* of or involving several axes.

multicellular /ˌmʌltɪˈseljʊlə(r)/ *adj.* *Biol.* having many cells.

multichannel /ˌmʌltɪˈtʃæn(ə)l/ *adj.* employing or possessing many communication or television channels.

multicolour /ˈmʌltɪˌkʌl(ə)r/ *adj.* (also **multicoloured**) of many colours.

multicultural /ˌmʌltɪˈkʌltʃər(ə)l/ *adj.* of or relating to or constituting several cultural or ethnic groups within a society. □□ **multiculturally** *adv.*

multidimensional /ˌmʌltɪdaɪˈmenʃən(ə)l/ *adj.* of or involving more than three dimensions. □□ **multidimensionality** /-ˈnælɪtɪ/ *n.* **multidimensionally** *adv.*

multidirectional /ˌmʌltɪdaɪˈrekʃən(ə)l/ *adj.* of, involving, or operating in several directions.

multifaceted /ˌmʌltɪˈfæsɪtɪd/ *adj.* having several facets.

multifarious /ˌmʌltɪˈfeərɪəs/ *adj.* **1** (foll. by pl. noun) many and various. **2** having great variety. □□ **multifariously** *adv.* **multifariousness** *n.* [L *multifarius*]

multifid /ˈmʌltɪfɪd/ *adj.* *Bot.* & *Zool.* divided into many parts. [L *multifidus* (as MULTI-, *fid-* stem of *findere* cleave)]

multifoil /ˈmʌltɪˌfɔɪl/ *n.* *Archit.* an ornament consisting of more than five foils.

multiform /ˈmʌltɪˌfɔːm/ *n.* (usu. *attrib.*) **1** having many forms. **2** of many kinds. □□ **multiformity** /-ˈfɔːmɪtɪ/ *n.*

multifunctional /ˌmʌltɪˈfʌŋkʃən(ə)l/ *adj.* having or fulfilling several functions.

multigrade /ˈmʌltɪˌgreɪd/ *n.* (usu. *attrib.*) an engine oil etc. meeting the requirements of several standard grades.

multilateral /ˌmʌltɪˈlætər(ə)l/ *adj.* **1 a** (of an agreement, treaty, conference, etc.) in which three or more parties participate. **b** performed by more than one party (*multilateral disarmament*). **2** having many sides. □□ **multilaterally** *adv.*

multilingual /ˌmʌltɪˈlɪŋgw(ə)l/ *adj.* in or using several languages. □□ **multilingually** *adv.*

multimillion /ˈmʌltɪˌmɪljən/ *attrib.adj.* costing or involving several million (pounds, dollars, etc.) (*multimillion dollar fraud*).

multimillionaire /ˌmʌltɪˌmɪljəˈneə(r)/ *n.* a person with a fortune of several millions.

multinational /ˌmʌltɪˈnæʃən(ə)l/ *adj.* & *n.* —*adj.* **1** (of a business organization) operating in several countries. **2** relating to or including several nationalities or ethnic groups. —*n.* a multinational company. □□ **multinationally** *adv.*

multinomial /ˌmʌltɪˈnəʊmɪəl/ *adj.* & *n.* *Math.* = POLYNOMIAL. [MULTI-, after *binomial*]

multiparous /mʌlˈtɪpərəs/ *adj.* **1** bringing forth many young at a birth. **2** having borne more than one child. [MULTI- + -PAROUS]

multipartite /ˌmʌltɪˈpɑːtaɪt/ *adj.* divided into many parts.

multiphase /ˈmʌltɪˌfeɪz/ *n.* *Electr.* = POLYPHASE.

multiple /ˈmʌltɪp(ə)l/ *adj.* & *n.* —*adj.* **1** having several or many parts, elements, or individual components. **2** (foll. by pl. noun) many and various. **3** *Bot.* (of fruit) collective. —*n.* **1** a number that may be divided by another a certain number of times without a remainder (*56 is a multiple of 7*). **2** a multiple shop or store. □**least** (or **lowest**) **common multiple** the least quantity that is a multiple of two or more given quantities. **multiple-choice** (of a question in an examination) accompanied by several possible answers from which the correct one has to be chosen. **multiple personality** *Psychol.* the apparent existence of two or more distinct personalities in one individual. **multiple sclerosis** see SCLEROSIS. **multiple shop** (or **store**) *Brit.* a shop or store with branches in several places. **multiple standard** see STANDARD. **multiple star** several stars so close as to seem one, esp. when forming a connected system. □□ **multiply** *adv.* [F f. LL *multiplus* f. L (as MULTIPLEX)]

multiplex /ˈmʌltɪˌpleks/ *adj.* & *v.* —*adj.* **1** manifold; of many elements. **2** involving simultaneous transmission of several messages along a single channel of communication. —*v.tr.* incorporate into a multiplex signal or system. □□ **multiplexer** *n.* (also **multiplexor**). [L (as MULTI-, *-plex -plicis* -fold)]

multipliable /'mʌltɪˌplaɪəb(ə)l/ *adj.* that can be multiplied.

multiplicable /'mʌltɪˌplɪkəb(ə)l/ *adj.* = MULTI-PLIABLE. [OF *multiplicable* or med.L *multiplicabilis* f. L (as MULTIPLY)]

multiplicand /ˌmʌltɪplɪ'kænd/ *n.* a quantity to be multiplied by a multiplier. [med.L *multiplicandus* gerundive of L *multiplicare* (as MULTIPLY)]

multiplication /ˌmʌltɪplɪ'keɪʃ(ə)n/ *n.* **1** the arithmetical process of multiplying. **2** the act or an instance of multiplying. □**multiplication sign** the sign (×) to indicate that one quantity is to be multiplied by another, as in 2 × 3 = 6. **multiplication table** a list of multiples of a particular number, usu. from 1 to 12. □□ **multiplicative** /-'plɪkətɪv/ *adj.* [ME f. OF *multiplication* or L *multiplicatio* (as MULTIPLY)]

multiplicity /ˌmʌltɪ'plɪsɪtɪ/ *n.* (*pl.* **-ies**) **1** manifold variety. **2** (foll. by *of*) a great number. [LL *multiplicitas* (as MULTIPLEX)]

multiplier /'mʌltɪˌplaɪə(r)/ *n.* **1** a quantity by which a given number is multiplied. **2** *Econ.* a factor by which an increment of income exceeds the resulting increment of saving or investment. **3** *Electr.* an instrument for increasing by repetition the intensity of a current, force, etc.

multiply /'mʌltɪˌplaɪ/ *v.* (**-ies, -ied**) **1** *tr.* (also *absol.*) obtain from (a number) another that is a specified number of times its value (*multiply 6 by 4 and you get 24*). **2** *intr.* increase in number esp. by procreation. **3** *tr.* produce a large number of (instances etc.). **4** *tr.* **a** breed (animals). **b** propagate (plants). [ME f. OF *multiplier* f. L *multiplicare* (as MULTIPLEX)]

multipolar /ˌmʌltɪ'pəʊlə(r)/ *adj.* having many poles (see POLE²).

multiprocessing /ˌmʌltɪ'prəʊsesɪŋ/ *n. Computing* processing by a number of processors sharing a common memory and common peripherals.

multiprogramming /ˌmʌltɪ'prəʊgræmɪŋ/ *n. Computing* the execution of two or more independent programs concurrently.

multi-purpose /ˌmʌltɪ'pɜːpəs/ *n.* (*attrib.*) having several purposes.

multiracial /ˌmʌltɪ'reɪʃ(ə)l/ *adj.* relating to or made up of many human races. □□ **multiracially** *adv.*

multi-role /ˌmʌltɪ'rəʊl/ *n.* (*attrib.*) having several roles or functions.

multi-stage /'mʌltɪˌsteɪdʒ/ *n.* (*attrib.*) (of a rocket etc.) having several stages of operation.

multi-storey /ˌmʌltɪ'stɔːrɪ/ *n.* (*attrib.*) (of a building) having several (esp. similarly designed) storeys.

multitude /'mʌltɪˌtjuːd/ *n.* **1** (often foll. by *of*) a great number. **2** a large gathering of people; a crowd. **3** (**the multitude**) the common people. **4** the state of being numerous. [ME f. OF f. L *multitudo -dinis* f. *multus* many]

multitudinous /ˌmʌltɪ'tjuːdɪnəs/ *adj.* **1** very numerous. **2** consisting of many individuals or elements. **3** (of an ocean etc.) vast. □□ **multitudinously** *adv.* **multitudinousness** *n.* [L (as MULTITUDE)]

multi-user /ˌmʌltɪ'juːzə(r)/ *n.* (*attrib.*) (of a computer system) having a number of simultaneous users (cf. MULTI-ACCESS).

multivalent /ˌmʌltɪ'veɪlənt/ *adj. Chem.* **1** having a valency of more than two. **2** having a variable valency. □□ **multivalency** *n.*

multivalve /'mʌltɪˌvælv/ *n.* (*attrib.*) (of a shell etc.) having several valves.

multiversity /ˌmʌltɪ'vɜːsɪtɪ/ *n.* (*pl.* **-ies**) a large university with many different departments. [MULTI- + UNIVERSITY]

multivocal /mʌl'tɪvək(ə)l/ *adj.* having many meanings.

multi-way /'mʌltɪˌweɪ/ *n.* (*attrib.*) having several paths of communication etc.

mum¹ /mʌm/ *n. Brit. colloq.* mother. [abbr. of MUMMY¹]

mum² /mʌm/ *adj. colloq.* silent (*keep mum*). □**mum's the word** say nothing. [ME: imit. of closed lips]

mum³ /mʌm/ *v.intr.* (**mummed, mumming**) act in a traditional masked mime. [cf. MUM² and MLG *mummen*]

mumble /'mʌmb(ə)l/ *v. & n.* —*v.* **1** *intr. & tr.* speak or utter indistinctly. **2** *tr.* bite or chew with or as with toothless gums. —*n.* an indistinct utterance. □□ **mumbler** *n.* **mumblingly** *adv.* [ME *momele*, as MUM²: cf. LG *mummelen*]

mumbo-jumbo /ˌmʌmbəʊ'dʒʌmbəʊ/ *n.* (*pl.* **-jumbos**) **1** meaningless or ignorant ritual. **2** language or action intended to mystify or confuse. **3** an object of senseless veneration. [*Mumbo Jumbo*, a supposed African idol]

mummer /'mʌmə(r)/ *n.* **1** an actor in a traditional masked mime. **2** *archaic or derog.* an actor in the theatre. [ME f. OF *momeur* f. *momer* MUM³]

mummery /'mʌmərɪ/ *n.* (*pl.* **-ies**) **1** ridiculous (esp. religious) ceremonial. **2** a performance by mummers. [OF *momerie* (as MUMMER)]

mummify /'mʌmɪˌfaɪ/ *v.tr.* (**-ies, -ied**) **1** embalm and preserve (a body) in the form of a mummy (see MUMMY²). **2** (usu. as **mummified** *adj.*) shrivel or dry up (tissues etc.). □□ **mummification** /-fɪ'keɪʃ(ə)n/ *n.*

mummy¹ /'mʌmɪ/ *n.* (*pl.* **-ies**) *Brit. colloq.* mother. [imit. of a child's pronunc.: cf. MAMMA¹]

mummy² /'mʌmɪ/ *n.* (*pl.* **-ies**) **1** a body of a human being or animal embalmed for burial, esp. in ancient Egypt. **2** a dried-up body. **3** a pulpy mass (*beat it to a mummy*). **4** a rich brown pigment. [F *momie* f. med.L *mumia* f. Arab. *mūmiyā* f. Pers. *mūm* wax]

mumps /mʌmps/ *n.pl.* **1** (treated as *sing.*) a contagious and infectious viral disease with swelling of the parotid salivary glands in the face. **2** a fit of sulks. □□ **mumpish** *adj.* (in sense 2). [archaic *mump* be sullen]

munch /mʌntʃ/ *v.tr.* eat steadily with a marked action of the jaws. [ME, imit.: cf. CRUNCH]

mundane /mʌn'deɪn/ *adj.* **1** dull, routine. **2** of this world; worldly. □□ **mundanely** *adv.* **mundaneness** *n.* **mundanity** /-'dænɪtɪ/ *n.* (*pl.* **-ies**). [ME f. OF *mondain* f. LL *mundanus* f. L *mundus* world]

mung /mʌŋ/ *n.* (in full **mung bean**) a leguminous plant, *Phaseolus aureus*, native to India and used as food. [Hindi *mūng*]

mungo /'mʌŋgəʊ/ *n.* (*pl.* **-os**) the short fibres recovered from heavily felted material. [19th c.: orig. uncert.]

municipal /mjuː'nɪsɪp(ə)l/ *adj.* of or concerning a municipality or its self-government. □□ **municipalize** *v.tr.* (also **-ise**). **municipalization** /-'zeɪʃ(ə)n/ *n.* **municipally** *adv.* [L *municipalis* f. *municipium* free city f. *municeps -cipis* citizen with privileges f. *munia* civic offices + *capere* take]

municipality /mjuːˌnɪsɪ'pælɪtɪ/ *n.* (*pl.* **-ies**) **1** a town or district having local government. **2** the governing body of this area. [F *municipalité* f. *municipal* (as MUNICIPAL)]

munificent /mjuː'nɪfɪs(ə)nt/ *adj.* (of a giver or a gift) splendidly generous, bountiful. □□ **munificence** *n.* **munificently** *adv.* [L *munificent-*, var. stem of *munificus* f. *munus* gift]

muniment /'mjuːnɪmənt/ *n.* (usu. in *pl.*) **1** a document kept as evidence of rights or privileges etc. **2** an archive. [ME f. OF f. L *munimentum* defence, in med.L title-deed f. *munire munit-* fortify]

munition /mjuː'nɪʃ(ə)n/ *n. & v.* —*n.* (usu. in *pl.*) military weapons, ammunition, equipment, and stores. —*v.tr.* supply with munitions. [F f. L *munitio -onis* fortification (as MUNIMENT)]

munitioner /mjuː'nɪʃənə(r)/ *n.* a person who makes or supplies munitions.

munnion var. of MULLION.

munshi var. of MOONSHEE.

munt /mʊnt/ *n. S.Afr. sl. offens.* a Black African. [Bantu *umuntu* person]

muntjac /'mʌntdʒæk/ *n.* (also **muntjak**) any small

deer of the genus *Muntiacus* native to SE Asia, the male having tusks and small antlers. [Sundanese *minchek*]

Muntz metal /mʌnts/ *n.* an alloy (60% copper, 40% zinc) used for sheathing ships etc. [G. F. *Muntz*, Engl. manufacturer d. 1857]

muon /'mjuːɒn/ *n. Physics* an unstable elementary particle like an electron, but with a much greater mass. [μ (MU), as the symbol for it]

murage /'mjʊərɪdʒ/ *n. hist.* a tax levied for building or repairing the walls of a town. [ME f. OF, in med.L *muragium* f. OF *mur* f. L *murus* wall]

mural /'mjʊər(ə)l/ *n. & adj.* —*n.* a painting executed directly on a wall. —*adj.* **1** of or like a wall. **2** on a wall. □ **mural crown** *Rom. Antiq.* a crown or garland given to the soldier who was first to scale the wall of a besieged town. □□ **muralist** *n.* [F f. L *muralis* f. *murus* wall]

murder /'mɜːdə(r)/ *n. & v.* —*n.* **1** the unlawful premeditated killing of a human being by another (cf. MANSLAUGHTER). **2** *colloq.* an unpleasant, troublesome, or dangerous state of affairs (*it was murder here on Saturday*). —*v.tr.* **1** kill (a human being) unlawfully, esp. wickedly or inhumanly. **2** *Law* kill (a human being) with a premeditated motive. **3** *colloq.* utterly defeat or spoil by a bad performance, mispronunciation etc. (*murdered the soliloquy in the second act*). □ **cry blue murder** *sl.* make an extravagant outcry. **get away with murder** *colloq.* do whatever one wishes and escape punishment. **murder will out** murder cannot remain undetected. □□ **murderer** *n.* **murderess** *n.* [OE *morthor* & OF *murdre* f. Gmc]

murderous /'mɜːdərəs/ *adj.* (of a person, weapon, action, etc.) capable of, intending, or involving murder or great harm. □□ **murderously** *adv.* **murderousness** *n.*

mure /mjʊə(r)/ *v.tr. archaic* **1** immure. **2** (foll. by *up*) wall up or shut up in an enclosed space. [ME f. OF *murer* f. *mur*: see MURAGE]

murex /'mjʊərəks/ *n.* (*pl.* **murices** /-rɪˌsiːz/ or **murexes**) any gastropod mollusc of the genus *Murex*, yielding a purple dye. [L]

murine /'mjʊəˌraɪn/ *adj.* of or like a mouse or mice. [L *murinus* f. *mus muris* mouse]

murk /mɜːk/ *n. & adj.* (also **mirk**) —*n.* **1** darkness, poor visibility. **2** air obscured by fog etc. —*adj. archaic* (of night, day, place, etc.) = MURKY. [prob. f. Scand.: cf. ON *myrkr*]

murky /'mɜːkɪ/ *adj.* (also **mirky**) (**-ier, -iest**) **1** dark, gloomy. **2** (of darkness) thick, dirty. **3** suspiciously obscure (*murky past*). □□ **murkily** *adv.* **murkiness** *n.*

murmur /'mɜːmə(r)/ *n. & v.* —*n.* **1** a subdued continuous sound, as made by waves, a brook, etc. **2** a softly spoken or nearly inarticulate utterance. **3** *Med.* a recurring sound heard in the auscultation of the heart and usu. indicating abnormality. **4** a subdued expression of discontent. —*v.* **1** *intr.* make a subdued continuous sound. **2** *tr.* utter (words) in a low voice. **3** *intr.* (usu. foll. by *at, against*) complain in low tones, grumble. □□ **murmurer** *n.* **murmuringly** *adv.* **murmurous** *adj.* [ME f. OF *murmurer* f. L *murmurare*: cf. Gk *mormurō* (of water) roar, Skr. *marmaras* noisy]

murphy /'mɜːfɪ/ *n.* (*pl.* **-ies**) *sl.* a potato. [Ir. surname]

Murphy's Law /'mɜːfɪz/ *n. joc.* any of various maxims about the perverseness of things.

murrain /'mʌrɪn/ *n.* **1** an infectious disease of cattle, carried by parasites. **2** *archaic* a plague, esp. the potato blight during the Irish famine in the mid-19th c. [ME f. AF *moryn*, OF *morine* f. *morir* f. L *mori* die]

murrey /'mʌrɪ/ *n. & adj. archaic* —*n.* the colour of a mulberry; a deep red or purple. —*adj.* of this colour. [ME f. OF *moré* f. med.L *moratus* f. *morum* mulberry]

murther /'mɜːðə(r)/ *archaic* var. of MURDER.

Mus.B. *abbr.* (also **Mus. Bac.**) Bachelor of Music. [L *Musicae Baccalaureus*]

Muscadet /'mʌskəˌdeɪ/ *n.* **1** a white wine from the Loire region of France. **2** a variety of grape from which the wine is made. [*Muscadet* variety of grape]

muscadine /'mʌskədɪn, -ˌdaɪn/ *n.* a variety of grape with a musk flavour, used chiefly in wine-making. [perh. Engl. form f. Prov. MUSCAT]

muscarine /'mʌskərɪn/ *n.* a poisonous alkaloid from the fungus *Amanita muscaria*. [L *muscarius* f. *musca* fly]

muscat /'mʌskət/ *n.* **1** a sweet fortified white wine made from muscadines. **2** a muscadine. [F f. Prov. *muscat muscade* (adj.) f. *musc* MUSK]

muscatel /ˌmʌskə'tel/ *n.* (also **muscadel** /-'del/) **1** = MUSCAT. **2** a raisin from a muscadine grape. [ME f. OF f. Prov. dimin. of *muscat*: see MUSCAT]

muscle /'mʌs(ə)l/ *n. & v.* —*n.* **1** a fibrous tissue with the ability to contract, producing movement in or maintaining the position of an animal body. **2** the part of an animal body that is composed of muscles. **3** physical power or strength. —*v.intr.* (usu. foll. by *in*) *colloq.* force oneself on others; intrude by forceful means. □ **muscle-bound** with muscles stiff and inelastic through excessive exercise or training. **muscle-man** a man with highly developed muscles, esp. one employed as an intimidator. **not move a muscle** be completely motionless. □□ **muscled** *adj.* (usu. in *comb.*). **muscleless** *adj.* **muscly** *adj.* [F f. L *musculus* dimin. of *mus* mouse, from the fancied mouselike form of some muscles]

muscology /mʌs'kɒlədʒɪ/ *n.* the study of mosses. □□ **muscologist** *n.* [mod.L *muscologia* f. L *muscus* moss]

muscovado /ˌmʌskə'vɑːdəʊ/ *n.* (*pl.* **-os**) an unrefined sugar made from the juice of sugar cane by evaporation and draining off the molasses. [Sp. *mascabado* (sugar) of the lowest quality]

Muscovite /'mʌskəˌvaɪt/ *n. & adj.* —*n.* **1** a native or citizen of Moscow. **2** *archaic* a Russian. —*adj.* **1** of or relating to Moscow. **2** *archaic* of or relating to Russia. [mod.L *Muscovita* f. *Muscovia* = MUSCOVY]

muscovite /'mʌskəˌvaɪt/ *n.* a silver-grey form of mica with a sheetlike crystalline structure that is used in the manufacture of electrical equipment etc. [obs. MUSCOVY *glass* (in the same sense) + -ITE[1]]

Muscovy /'mʌskəvɪ/ *n. archaic* Russia. □ **Muscovy duck** a tropical American duck, *Cairina moschata*, having a small crest and red markings on its head. [obs. F *Muscovie* f. mod.L *Moscovia* f. Russ. *Moskva* Moscow]

muscular /'mʌskjʊlə(r)/ *adj.* **1** of or affecting the muscles. **2** having well-developed muscles. □ **muscular Christianity** a Christian life of cheerful physical activity as described in the writings of Charles Kingsley. **muscular dystrophy** see DYSTROPHY. **muscular rheumatism** = MYALGIA. **muscular stomach** see STOMACH. □□ **muscularity** /-'lærɪtɪ/ *n.* **muscularly** *adv.* [earlier *musculous* (as MUSCLE)]

musculature /'mʌskjʊlətʃə(r)/ *n.* the muscular system of a body or organ. [F f. L (as MUSCLE)]

Mus.D. *abbr.* (also **Mus. Doc.**) Doctor of Music. [L *Musicae Doctor*]

muse[1] /mjuːz/ *n.* **1** (as **the Muses**) (in Greek and Roman mythology) nine goddesses, the daughters of Zeus and Mnemosyne, who inspire poetry, music, drama, etc. **2** (usu. prec. by *the*) **a** a poet's inspiring goddess. **b** a poet's genius. [ME f. OF *muse* or L *musa* f. Gk *mousa*]

muse[2] /mjuːz/ *v. & n. literary* —*v.* **1** *intr.* **a** (usu. foll. by *on, upon*) ponder, reflect. **b** (usu. foll. by *on*) gaze meditatively (on a scene etc.). **2** *tr.* say meditatively. —*n. archaic* a fit of abstraction. [ME f. OF *muser* to waste time f. Rmc perh. f. med.L *musum* muzzle]

musette /mjuː'zet/ *n.* **1** **a** a kind of small bagpipe with bellows, common in the French court in the 17th-18th c. **b** a tune imitating the sound of this. **2** a small oboe-like double-reed instrument in 19th-c. France. **3** a popular dance in the courts of Louis XIV and XV. **4** *US* a small knapsack. [ME f. OF, dimin. of *muse* bagpipe]

museum /mjuːˈzɪəm/ *n.* a building used for storing and exhibiting objects of historical, scientific, or cultural interest. □**museum piece 1** a specimen of art etc. fit for a museum. **2** *derog.* an old-fashioned or quaint person or object. □□**museology** /-ˈɒlədʒɪ/ *n.* [L f. Gk *mouseion* seat of the Muses: see MUSE¹]

mush¹ /mʌʃ/ *n.* **1** soft pulp. **2** feeble sentimentality. **3** *US* maize porridge. □□**mushy** *adj.* (**mushier, mushiest**). **mushily** *adv.* **mushiness** *n.* [app. var. of MASH]

mush² /mʌʃ/ *v. & n. US* —*v.intr.* **1** (in *imper.*) used as a command to dogs pulling a sledge to urge them forward. **2** go on a journey across snow with a dog-sledge. —*n.* a journey across snow with a dog-sledge. [prob. corrupt. f. F *marchons* imper. of *marcher* advance]

mushroom /ˈmʌʃrʊm, -ruːm/ *n. & v.* —*n.* **1** the usu. edible spore-producing body of various fungi, esp. *Agaricus campestris*, with a stem and domed cap, proverbial for its rapid growth. **2** the pinkish-brown colour of this. **3** any item resembling a mushroom in shape (*darning mushroom*). **4** (usu. *attrib.*) something that appears or develops suddenly or is ephemeral; an upstart. —*v.intr.* **1** appear or develop rapidly. **2** expand and flatten like a mushroom cap. **3** gather mushrooms. □**mushroom cloud** a cloud suggesting the shape of a mushroom, esp. from a nuclear explosion. **mushroom growth 1** a sudden development or expansion. **2** anything undergoing this. □□**mushroomy** *adj.* [ME f. OF *mousseron* f. LL *mussirio -onis*]

music /ˈmjuːzɪk/ *n.* **1** the art of combining vocal or instrumental sounds (or both) to produce beauty of form, harmony, and expression of emotion. **2** the sounds so produced. **3** musical compositions. **4** the written or printed score of a musical composition. **5** certain pleasant sounds, e.g. birdsong, the sound of a stream, etc. □**music box** *US* = musical box. **music centre** equipment combining radio, record-player, tape recorder, etc. **music drama** Wagnerian-type opera without formal arias etc. and governed by dramatic considerations. **music-hall** *Brit.* **1** variety entertainment, popular *c.*1850–1914, consisting of singing, dancing, and novelty acts. **2** a theatre where this took place. **music of the spheres** see SPHERE. **music-paper** paper printed with staves for writing music. **music stand** a rest or frame on which sheet music or a score is supported. **music stool** a stool for a pianist, usu. with adjustable height. **music theatre** in late 20th-c. music, the combination of elements from music and drama in new forms distinct from traditional opera, esp. as designed for small groups of performers. **music to one's ears** something very pleasant to hear. [ME f. OF *musique* f. L *musica* f. Gk *mousikē* (*tekhnē* art) of the Muses (*mousa* Muse: see MUSE¹)]

musical /ˈmjuːzɪk(ə)l/ *adj. & n.* —*adj.* **1** of or relating to music. **2** (of sounds, a voice, etc.) melodious, harmonious. **3** fond of or skilled in music (*the musical one of the family*). **4** set to or accompanied by music. —*n.* a musical film or comedy. □**musical box** *Brit.* a mechanical instrument playing a tune by causing a toothed cylinder to strike a comblike metal plate within a box. **musical bumps** a game similar to musical chairs, with players sitting on the floor and the one left standing eliminated. **musical chairs 1** a party game in which the players compete in successive rounds for a decreasing number of chairs. **2** a series of changes or political manœuvring etc. after the manner of the game. **musical comedy** a light dramatic entertainment of songs, dialogue, and dancing, connected by a slender plot. **musical film** a film in which music is an important feature. **musical glasses** an instrument in which notes are produced by rubbing graduated glass bowls or tubes. **musical saw** a bent saw played with a violin bow. □□**musicality** /-ˈkælɪtɪ/ *n.* **musicalize** *v.tr.* (also -**ise**). **musically** *adv.* **musicalness** *n.* [ME f. OF f. med.L *musicalis* f. L *musica*: see MUSIC]

musicale /ˌmjuːzɪˈkɑːl/ *n. US* a musical party. [F fem. adj. (as MUSICAL)]

musician /mjuːˈzɪʃ(ə)n/ *n.* a person who plays a musical instrument, esp. professionally, or is otherwise musically gifted. □□**musicianly** *adj.* **musicianship** *n.* [ME f. OF *musicien* f. *musique* (as MUSIC, -ICIAN)]

musicology /ˌmjuːzɪˈkɒlədʒɪ/ *n.* the study of music other than that directed to proficiency in performance or composition. □□**musicologist** *n.* **musicological** /-kəˈlɒdʒɪk(ə)l/ *adj.* [F *musicologie* or MUSIC + -LOGY]

musique concrète /mjuːˌziːk kɔ̃ˈkret/ *n.* = *concrete music.* [F]

musk /mʌsk/ *n.* **1** a strong-smelling reddish-brown substance produced by a gland in the male musk deer and used as an ingredient in perfumes. **2** the plant, *Mimulus moschatus*, with pale-green ovate leaves and yellow flowers (orig. with a smell of musk which is no longer perceptible in modern varieties). □**musk deer** any small Asian deer of the genus *Moschus*, having no antlers and in the male having long protruding canine teeth. **musk duck** the Australian duck *Biziura lobata*, having a musky smell. **musk melon** the common yellow or green melon, *Cucumis melo*, usu. with a raised network of markings on the skin. **musk ox** a large goat-antelope, *Ovibos moschatus*, native to N. America, with a thick shaggy coat and small curved horns. **musk-rose** a rambling rose, *Rosa moschata*, with large white flowers smelling of musk. **musk thistle** a nodding thistle, *Carduus nutans*, whose flowers have a musky fragrance. **musk-tree** (or -**wood**) an Australian tree, *Olearia argophylla*, with a musky smell. □□**musky** *adj.* (**muskier, muskiest**). **muskiness** *n.* [ME f. LL *muscus* f. Pers. *mušk*, perh. f. Skr. *muṣka* scrotum (from the shape of the musk deer's gland)]

muskeg /ˈmʌskeg/ *n.* a level swamp or bog in Canada. [Cree]

muskellunge /ˈmʌskəˌlʌndʒ/ *n.* = MASKINONGE. [Algonquian]

musket /ˈmʌskɪt/ *n. hist.* an infantryman's (esp. smooth-bored) light gun, often supported on the shoulder. □**musket-shot 1** a shot fired from a musket. **2** the range of this shot. [F *mousquet* f. It. *moschetto* crossbow bolt f. *mosca* fly]

musketeer /ˌmʌskɪˈtɪə(r)/ *n. hist.* a soldier armed with a musket.

musketry /ˈmʌskɪtrɪ/ *n.* **1** muskets, or soldiers armed with muskets, referred to collectively. **2** the knowledge of handling muskets.

muskrat /ˈmʌskræt/ *n.* **1** a large aquatic rodent, *Ondatra zibethica*, native to N. America, having a musky smell. Also called MUSQUASH. **2** the fur of this.

Muslim /ˈmʊzlɪm, ˈmʌ-/ *n. & adj.* (also **Moslem** /ˈmɒzləm/) —*n.* a follower of the Islamic religion. —*adj.* of or relating to the Muslims or their religion. [Arab. *muslim*, part. of *aslama*: see ISLAM]

muslin /ˈmʌzlɪn/ *n.* **1** a fine delicately woven cotton fabric. **2** *US* a cotton cloth in plain weave. □□**muslined** *adj.* [F *mousseline* f. It. *mussolina* f. *Mussolo* Mosul in Iraq, where it was made]

musmon /ˈmʌzmən/ *n. Zool.* = MOUFFLON. [L *musimo* f. Gk *mousmōn*]

muso /ˈmjuːzəʊ/ *n.* (*pl.* -**os**) *sl.* a musician, esp. a professional. [abbr.]

musquash /ˈmʌskwɒʃ/ *n.* = MUSKRAT. [Algonquian]

muss /mʌs/ *v. & n. US colloq.* —*v.tr.* (often foll. by *up*) disarrange; throw into disorder. —*n.* a state of confusion; untidiness, mess. □□**mussy** *adj.* [app. var. of MESS]

mussel /ˈmʌs(ə)l/ *n.* **1** any bivalve mollusc of the genus *Mytilus*, living in sea water and often used for food. **2** any similar freshwater mollusc of the genus *Margaritifer* or *Anodonta*, forming pearls. [ME f. OE *mus(c)le* & MLG *mussel*, ult. rel. to L *musculus* (as MUSCLE)]

Mussulman /ˈmʌsəlmən/ *n. & adj. archaic* —*n.* (*pl.* -**mans** or -**men**) a Muslim. —*adj.* of or concerning Muslims. [Pers. *musulmān* orig. adj. f. *muslim* (as MUSLIM)]

must[1] /mʌst/ *v. & n.* —*v.aux.* (*3rd sing. present* **must**; *past* **had to** or in indirect speech **must**) (foll. by infin., or *absol.*) **1 a** be obliged to (*you must go to school*; *must we leave now?*; *said he must go*; *I must away*). ¶The negative (i.e. lack of obligation) is expressed by *not have to* or *need not*; *must not* denotes positive forbidding, as in *you must not smoke*. **b** in ironic questions (*must you slam the door?*). **2** be certain to (*we must win in the end*; *you must be her sister*; *he must be mad*; *they must have left by now*; *seemed as if the roof must blow off*). **3** ought to (*we must see what can be done*; *it must be said that*). **4** expressing insistence (*I must ask you to leave*). **5** (foll. by *not* + infin.) **a** not be permitted to, be forbidden to (*you must not smoke*). **b** ought not; need not (*you mustn't think he's angry*; *you must not worry*). **c** expressing insistence that something should not be done (*they must not be told*). **6** (as past or historic present) expressing the perversity of destiny (*what must I do but break my leg*). —*n. colloq.* a thing that cannot or should not be overlooked or missed (*if you go to London St Paul's is a must*). □**I must say** often *iron.* I cannot refrain from saying (*I must say he made a good attempt*; *a fine way to behave*, *I must say*). **must needs** see NEEDS. [OE *mōste* past of *mōt* may]

must[2] /mʌst/ *n.* grape-juice before fermentation is complete. [OE f. L *mustum* neut. of *mustus* new]

must[3] /mʌst/ *n.* mustiness, mould. [back-form. f. MUSTY]

must[4] /mʌst/ *adj. & n.* (also **musth**) —*adj.* (of a male elephant or camel) in a state of frenzy. —*n.* this state. [Urdu f. Pers. *mast* intoxicated]

mustache *US* var. of MOUSTACHE.

mustachio /məˈstɑːʃɪəʊ/ *n.* (*pl.* -**os**) (often in *pl.*) *archaic* a moustache. □□**mustachioed** *adj.* [Sp. *mostacho* & It. *mostaccio* (as MOUSTACHE)]

mustang /ˈmʌstæŋ/ *n.* a small wild horse native to Mexico and California. □**mustang grape** a grape from the wild vine *Vitis candicans*, of the southern US, used for making wine. [Sp. *mestengo* f. *mesta* company of graziers, & Sp. *mostrenco*]

mustard /ˈmʌstəd/ *n.* **1 a** any of various plants of the genus *Brassica* with slender pods and yellow flowers, esp. *B. nigra*. **b** any of various plants of the genus *Sinapis*, esp. *S. alba*, eaten at the seedling stage, often with cress. **2** the seeds of these which are crushed, made into a paste, and used as a spicy condiment. **3** the brownish-yellow colour of this condiment. **4** *sl.* a thing which adds piquancy or zest. □**mustard gas** a colourless oily liquid, whose vapour is a powerful irritant and vesicant. **mustard plaster** a poultice made with mustard. **mustard seed 1** the seed of the mustard plant. **2** a small thing capable of great development (Matt. 13:31). [ME f. OF *mo(u)starde*: orig. the condiment as prepared with MUST[2]]

muster /ˈmʌstə(r)/ *v. & n.* —*v.* **1** *tr.* collect (orig. soldiers) for inspection, to check numbers, etc. **2** *tr.* & *intr.* collect, gather together. **3** *tr. Austral.* round up (livestock). —*n.* **1** the assembly of persons for inspection. **2** an assembly, a collection. **3** *Austral.* a rounding up of livestock. **4** *Austral. sl.* attendance (at a meeting, etc.) (*had a good muster*). □**muster-book** a book for registering military personnel. **muster in** *US* enrol (recruits). **muster out** *US* discharge (soldiers etc.). **muster-roll** an official list of officers and men in a regiment or ship's company. **muster up** collect or summon (courage, strength, etc.). **pass muster** be accepted as adequate.

□□**musterer** *n.* (in sense 3 of *n.* & *v.*). [ME f. OF *mo(u)stre* ult. f. L *monstrare* show]

musth var. of MUST[4].

mustn't /ˈmʌs(ə)nt/ *contr.* must not.

musty /ˈmʌstɪ/ *adj.* (**mustier**, **mustiest**) **1** mouldy. **2** of a mouldy or stale smell or taste. **3** stale, antiquated (*musty old books*). □□**mustily** *adv.* **mustiness** *n.* [perh. alt. f. *moisty* (MOIST) by assoc. with MUST[2]]

mutable /ˈmjuːtəb(ə)l/ *adj. literary* **1** liable to change. **2** fickle. □□**mutability** /-ˈbɪlɪtɪ/ *n.* [L *mutabilis* f. *mutare* change]

mutagen /ˈmjuːtədʒ(ə)n/ *n.* an agent promoting mutation, e.g. radiation. □□**mutagenic** /-ˈdʒenɪk/ *adj.* **mutagenesis** /-ˈdʒenɪsɪs/ *n.* [MUTATION + -GEN]

mutant /ˈmjuːt(ə)nt/ *adj. & n.* —*adj.* resulting from mutation. —*n.* a mutant form. [L *mutant-* part. f. *mutare* change]

mutate /mjuːˈteɪt/ *v.intr. & tr.* undergo or cause to undergo mutation. [back-form. f. MUTATION]

mutation /mjuːˈteɪʃ(ə)n/ *n.* **1** the process or an instance of change or alteration. **2** a genetic change which, when transmitted to offspring, gives rise to heritable variations. **3** a mutant. **4 a** an umlaut. **b** (in a Celtic language) a change of a consonant etc. determined by a preceding word. □□**mutational** *adj.* **mutationally** *adv.* [ME f. L *mutatio* f. *mutare* change]

mutatis mutandis /muːˌtɑːtɪs muːˈtændɪs, mjuː:-, -ɪs/ *adv.* (in comparing cases) making the necessary alterations. [L]

mutch /mʌtʃ/ *n. dial.* a woman's or child's linen cap. [ME f. MDu. *mutse* MHG *mütze* f. med.L *almucia* AMICE]

mute /mjuːt/ *adj., n., & v.* —*adj.* **1** silent, refraining from or temporarily bereft of speech. **2** not emitting articulate sound. **3** (of a person or animal) dumb. **4** not expressed in speech (*mute protest*). **5 a** (of a letter) not pronounced. **b** (of a consonant) plosive. **6** (of hounds) not giving tongue. —*n.* **1** a dumb person (*a deaf mute*). **2** *Mus.* **a** a clamp for damping the resonance of the strings of a violin etc. **b** a pad or cone for damping the sound of a wind instrument. **3** an unsounded consonant. **4** an actor whose part is in a dumb show. **5** a dumb servant in oriental countries. **6** a hired mourner. —*v.tr.* **1** deaden, muffle, or soften the sound of (a thing, esp. a musical instrument). **2 a** tone down, make less intense. **b** (as **muted** *adj.*) (of colours etc.) subdued (*a muted green*). □**mute button** a device on a telephone etc. to temporarily prevent the caller from hearing what is being said at the receiver's end. **mute swan** the common white swan. □□**mutely** *adv.* **muteness** *n.* [ME f. OF *muet*, dimin. of *mu* f. L *mutus*, assim. to L]

mutilate /ˈmjuːtɪˌleɪt/ *v.tr.* **1 a** deprive (a person or animal) of a limb or organ. **b** destroy the use of (a limb or organ). **2** render (a book etc.) imperfect by excision or some act of destruction. □□**mutilation** /-ˈleɪʃ(ə)n/ *n.* **mutilative** /-lətɪv/ *adj.* **mutilator** *n.* [L *mutilare* f. *mutilus* maimed]

mutineer /ˌmjuːtɪˈnɪə(r)/ *n.* a person who mutinies. [F *mutinier* f. *mutin* rebellious f. *muete* movement ult. f. L *movēre* move]

mutinous /ˈmjuːtɪnəs/ *adj.* rebellious; tending to mutiny. □□**mutinously** *adv.* [obs. *mutine* rebellion f. F *mutin*: see MUTINEER]

mutiny /ˈmjuːtɪnɪ/ *n. & v.* —*n.* (*pl.* -**ies**) an open revolt against constituted authority, esp. by soldiers or sailors against their officers. —*v.intr.* (-**ies**, -**ied**) (often foll. by *against*) revolt; engage in mutiny. [obs. *mutine* (as MUTINOUS)]

mutism /ˈmjuːtɪz(ə)m/ *n.* muteness; silence; dumbness. [F *mutisme* f. L (as MUTE)]

muton /ˈmjuːtɒn/ *n. Biol.* the smallest element of genetic material capable of giving rise to a mutant individual.

mutt /mʌt/ *n.* **1** *sl.* an ignorant, stupid, or blundering person. **2** *derog.* a dog. [abbr. of *mutton-head*]

mutter /'mʌtə(r)/ v. & n. —v. 1 intr. speak low in a barely audible manner. 2 intr. (often foll. by against, at) murmur or grumble about. 3 tr. utter (words etc.) in a low tone. 4 tr. say in secret. —n. 1 muttered words or sounds. 2 muttering. □□ **mutterer** n. **mutteringly** adv. [ME, rel. to MUTE]

mutton /'mʌt(ə)n/ n. 1 the flesh of sheep used for food. 2 joc. a sheep. □ **mutton-bird** Austral. 1 any bird of the genus Puffinus, esp. the short-tailed shearwater, P. tenuirostris. 2 any of various petrels. **mutton chop** 1 a piece of mutton, usu. the rib and half vertebra to which it is attached. 2 (in full **mutton chop whisker**) a side whisker shaped like this. **mutton dressed as lamb** colloq. a usu. middle-aged or elderly woman dressed or made up to appear younger. **mutton-head** colloq. a dull, stupid person. **mutton-headed** colloq. dull, stupid. □□ **muttony** adj. [ME f. OF moton f. med.L multo -onis prob. f. Gaulish]

mutual /'mju:tʃʊəl, -tjʊəl/ adj. 1 (of feelings, actions, etc.) experienced or done by each of two or more parties with reference to the other or others (mutual affection). 2 colloq. disp. common to two or more persons (a mutual friend; a mutual interest). 3 standing in (a specified) relation to each other (mutual well-wishers; mutual beneficiaries). □ **mutual fund** US a unit trust. **mutual inductance** the property of an electric circuit that causes an electromotive force to be generated in it by change in the current flowing through a magnetically linked circuit. **mutual induction** the production of an electromotive force between adjacent circuits that are magnetically linked. **mutual insurance** insurance in which some or all of the profits are divided among the policyholders. □□ **mutuality** /-'ælɪtɪ/ n. **mutually** adv. [ME f. OF mutuel f. L mutuus mutual, borrowed, rel. to mutare change]

mutualism /'mju:tʃʊə,lɪz(ə)m, 'mju:tjʊ-/ n. 1 the doctrine that mutual dependence is necessary to social well-being. 2 mutually beneficial symbiosis. □□ **mutualist** n. & adj. **mutualistic** /-'lɪstɪk/ adj. **mutualistically** /-'lɪstɪkəlɪ/ adv.

mutuel /'mju:tjʊəl/ n. esp. US a totalizator; a pari-mutuel. [abbr. of PARI-MUTUEL]

mutule /'mju:tju:l/ n. Archit. a block derived from the ends of wooden beams projecting under a Doric cornice. [F f. L mutulus]

muu-muu /'mu:mu:/ n. a woman's loose brightly-coloured dress. [Hawaiian]

Muzak /'mju:zæk/ n. 1 propr. a system of music transmission for playing in public places. 2 (**muzak**) recorded light background music. [alt. f. MUSIC]

muzhik /'mu:ʒɪk/ n. (also **moujik**) hist. a Russian peasant. [Russ. muzhik]

muzzle /'mʌz(ə)l/ n. & v. —n. 1 the projecting part of an animal's face, including the nose and mouth. 2 a guard, usu. made of straps or wire, fitted over an animal's nose and mouth to stop it biting or feeding. 3 the open end of a firearm. —v.tr. 1 put a muzzle on (an animal etc.). 2 impose silence upon. 3 Naut. take in (a sail). □ **muzzle-loader** a gun that is loaded through the muzzle. **muzzle velocity** the velocity with which a projectile leaves the muzzle of a gun. □□ **muzzler** n. [ME f. OF musel ult. f. med.L musum: cf. MUSE[2]]

muzzy /'mʌzɪ/ adj. (**muzzier**, **muzziest**) 1 a mentally hazy; dull, spiritless. b stupid from drinking alcohol. 2 blurred, indistinct. □□ **muzzily** adv. **muzziness** n. [18th c.: orig. unkn.]

MV abbr. 1 motor vessel. 2 muzzle velocity. 3 megavolt(s).

MVO abbr. (in the UK) Member of the Royal Victorian Order.

MW abbr. 1 megawatt(s). 2 medium wave.

mW abbr. milliwatt(s).

Mx. abbr. 1 maxwell(s). 2 Middlesex (a former county in England).

MY abbr. motor yacht.

my /maɪ/ poss.pron. (attrib.) 1 of or belonging to me or myself (my house; my own business). 2 as a form of address in affectionate, sympathetic, jocular, or patronizing contexts (my dear boy). 3 in various expressions of surprise (my God!; oh my!). 4 Brit. colloq. indicating the speaker's husband, wife, child, etc. (my Johnny's ill again). □ **my Lady** (or **Lord**) the form of address to certain titled persons. [ME mī, reduced f. mīn MINE[1]]

my- comb. form var. of MYO-.

myalgia /maɪ'ældʒə/ n. a pain in a muscle or group of muscles. □□ **myalgic** adj. [mod.L f. Gk mus muscle]

myalism /'maɪə,lɪz(ə)m/ n. a kind of sorcery akin to obeah, practised esp. in the W. Indies. [myal, prob. of W.Afr. orig.]

myall /'maɪəl/ n. 1 a any tree of the genus Acacia, esp. A. pendula, native to Australia. b the hard scented wood of this, used for fences and tobacco-pipes. 2 an Aboriginal living in a traditional way. [Aboriginal maiāl]

myasthenia /,maɪəs'θi:nɪə/ n. a condition causing abnormal weakness of certain muscles. [mod.L f. Gk mus muscle: cf. ASTHENIA]

mycelium /maɪ'si:lɪəm/ n. (pl. **mycelia** /-lɪə/) the vegetative part of a fungus, consisting of microscopic threadlike hyphae. □□ **mycelial** adj. [mod.L f. Gk mukēs mushroom, after EPITHELIUM]

Mycenaean /,maɪsɪ'ni:ən/ adj. & n. —adj. Archaeol. of or relating to the late Bronze Age civilization in Greece (c.1500–1100 BC), depicted in the Homeric poems and represented by finds at Mycenae and elsewhere. —n. an inhabitant of Mycenae or the Mycenaean world. [L Mycenaeus]

-mycin /'maɪsɪn/ comb. form used to form the names of antibiotic compounds derived from fungi. [Gk mukēs fungus + -IN]

mycology /maɪ'kɒlədʒɪ/ n. 1 the study of fungi. 2 the fungi of a particular region. □□ **mycological** /-kə'lɒdʒɪk(ə)l/ adj. **mycologically** /-kə'lɒdʒɪkəlɪ/ adv. **mycologist** n. [Gk mukēs mushroom + -LOGY]

mycorrhiza /,maɪkə'raɪzə/ n. (pl. **mycorrhizae** /-zi:/) a symbiotic association of a fungus and the roots of a plant. □□ **mycorrhizal** adj. [mod.L f. Gk mukēs mushroom + rhiza root]

mycosis /maɪ'kəʊsɪs/ n. any disease caused by a fungus, e.g. ringworm. □□ **mycotic** /-'kɒtɪk/ adj. [Gk mukēs mushroom + -OSIS]

mycotoxin /,maɪkə'tɒksɪn/ n. any toxic substance produced by a fungus.

mycotrophy /maɪ'kɒtrəfɪ/ n. the condition of a plant which has mycorrhizae and is perhaps helped to assimilate nutrients as a result. [G Mykotrophie f. Gk mukēs mushroom + trophē nourishment]

mydriasis /mɪ'draɪəsɪs/ n. excessive dilation of the pupil of the eye. [L f. Gk mudriasis]

myelin /'maɪɪlɪn/ n. a white substance which forms a sheath around certain nerve-fibres. □□ **myelination** /-'neɪʃ(ə)n/ n. [Gk muelos marrow + -IN]

myelitis /,maɪə'laɪtɪs/ n. inflammation of the spinal cord. [mod.L f. Gk muelos marrow]

myeloid /'maɪɪ,lɔɪd/ adj. of or relating to bone marrow or the spinal cord. [Gk muelos marrow]

myeloma /,maɪɪ'ləʊmə/ n. (pl. **myelomas** or **myelomata** /-mətə/) a malignant tumour of the bone marrow. [mod.L, as MYELITIS + -OMA]

mylodon /'maɪləd(ə)n/ n. an extinct gigantic ground sloth of the genus Mylodon, with cylindrical teeth and found in deposits formed during the ice age of the Pleistocene epoch in South America. [mod.L f. Gk mulē mill, molar + odous odontos tooth]

myna /'maɪnə/ n. (also **mynah**, **mina**) any of various SE Asian starlings, esp. Gracula religiosa able to mimic the human voice. [Hindi mainā]

myo- /'maɪəʊ/ comb. form (also **my-** before a vowel) muscle. [Gk mus muos muscle]

myocardium /,maɪəʊ'kɑːdɪəm/ n. (pl. **myocardia** /-dɪə/) the muscular tissue of the heart. □□

myocardiac adj. **myocardial** adj. [MYO- + Gk *kardia* heart]

myofibril /ˌmaɪəʊˈfaɪbrɪl/ n. any of the elongated contractile threads found in striated muscle cells.

myogenic /ˌmaɪəˈdʒenɪk/ adj. originating in muscle tissue.

myoglobin /ˌmaɪəʊˈgləʊbɪn/ n. an oxygen-carrying protein containing iron and found in muscle cells.

myology /maɪˈɒlədʒɪ/ n. the study of the structure and function of muscles.

myope /ˈmaɪəʊp/ n. a short-sighted person. [F f. LL *myops* f. Gk *muōps* f. *muō* shut + *ōps* eye]

myopia /maɪˈəʊpɪə/ n. **1** short-sightedness. **2** lack of imagination or intellectual insight. □□ **myopic** /-ˈɒpɪk/ adj. **myopically** /-ˈɒpɪkəlɪ/ adv. [mod.L (as MYOPE)]

myosis var. of MIOSIS.

myosotis /ˌmaɪəˈsəʊtɪs/ n. (also **myosote** /ˈmaɪəˌsəʊt/) any plant of the genus *Myosotis* with blue, pink, or white flowers, esp. a forget-me-not. [L f. Gk *muosōtis* f. *mus muos* mouse + *ous ōtos* ear]

myotonia /ˌmaɪəˈtəʊnɪə/ n. the inability to relax voluntary muscle after vigorous effort. □□ **myotonic** /-ˈtɒnɪk/ adj. [MYO- + Gk *tonos* tone]

myriad /ˈmɪrɪəd/ n. & adj. *literary* —n. **1** an indefinitely great number. **2** ten thousand. —adj. of an indefinitely great number. [LL *mirias miriad-* f. Gk *murias -ados* f. *murioi* 10,000]

myriapod /ˈmɪrɪəˌpɒd/ n. & adj. —n. any land-living arthropod of the group Myriapoda, with numerous leg-bearing segments, e.g. centipedes and millipedes. —adj. of or relating to this group. [mod.L *Myriapoda* (as MYRIAD, Gk *pous podos* foot)]

myrmidon /ˈmɜːmɪd(ə)n/ n. **1** a hired ruffian. **2** a base servant. [L *Myrmidones* (pl.) f. Gk *Murmidones*, warlike Thessalian people who went with Achilles to Troy]

myrobalan /maɪˈrɒbələn/ n. **1** (in full **myrobalan plum**) = *cherry plum*. **2** (in full **myrobalan nut**) the fruit of an Asian tree, *Terminalia chebula*, used in medicines, for tanning leather, and to produce inks and dyes. [F *myrobolan* or L *myrobalanum* f. Gk *murobalanos* f. *muron* unguent + *balanos* acorn]

myrrh[1] /mɜː(r)/ n. a gum resin from several trees of the genus *Commiphora* used, esp. in the Near East, in perfumery, medicine, incense, etc. □□ **myrrhic** adj. **myrrhy** adj. [OE *myrra, myrre* f. L *myrr(h)a* f. Gk *murra*, of Semitic orig.]

myrrh[2] /mɜː(r)/ n. = *sweet cicely*. [L *myrris* f. Gk *murris*]

myrtaceous /mɜːˈteɪʃ(ə)s/ adj. of or relating to the plant family Myrtaceae, including myrtles.

myrtle /ˈmɜːt(ə)l/ n. **1** an evergreen shrub of the genus *Myrtus* with aromatic foliage and white flowers, esp. *M. communis*, bearing purple-black ovoid berries. **2** US = PERIWINKLE[1]. [ME f. med.L *myrtilla, -us* dimin. of L *myrta, myrtus* f. Gk *murtos*]

myself /maɪˈself/ pron. **1** emphat. form of I[2] or ME[1] (*I saw it myself; I like to do it myself*). **2** refl. form of ME[1] (*I was angry with myself; able to dress myself; as bad as myself*). **3** in my normal state of body and mind (*I'm not myself today*). **4** poet. = I[2]. □ **by myself** see *by oneself*. **I myself** I for my part (*I myself am doubtful*). [ME[1] + SELF: *my-* partly after *herself* with *her* regarded as poss. pron.]

mysterious /mɪˈstɪərɪəs/ adj. **1** full of or wrapped in mystery. **2** (of a person) delighting in mystery. □□ **mysteriously** adv. **mysteriousness** n. [F *mystérieux* f. *mystère* f. OF (as MYSTERY[1])]

mystery[1] /ˈmɪstərɪ/ n. (pl. **-ies**) **1** a secret, hidden, or inexplicable matter (*the reason remains a mystery*). **2** secrecy or obscurity (*wrapped in mystery*). **3** (attrib.) secret, undisclosed (*mystery guest*). **4** the practice of making a secret of (esp. unimportant) things (*engaged in mystery and intrigue*). **5** (in full **mystery story**) a fictional work dealing with a

puzzling event, esp. a crime (*a well-known mystery writer*). **6 a** a religious truth divinely revealed, esp. one beyond human reason. **b** *RC Ch.* a decade of the rosary. **7** (in pl.) **a** the secret religious rites of the ancient Greeks, Romans, etc. **b** *archaic* the Eucharist. □ **make a mystery of** treat as an impressive secret. **mystery play** a miracle play. **mystery tour** (or **trip**) a pleasure excursion to an unspecified destination. [ME f. OF *mistere* or L *mysterium* f. Gk *mustērion*, rel. to MYSTIC]

mystery[2] /ˈmɪstərɪ/ n. (pl. **-ies**) *archaic* a handicraft or trade, esp. as referred to in indentures etc. (*art and mystery*). [ME f. med.L *misterium* contr. of *ministerium* MINISTRY, assoc. with MYSTERY[1]]

mystic /ˈmɪstɪk/ n. & adj. —n. a person who seeks by contemplation and self-surrender to obtain unity or identity with or absorption into the Deity or the ultimate reality, or who believes in the spiritual apprehension of truths that are beyond the understanding. —adj. **1** mysterious and awe-inspiring. **2** spiritually allegorical or symbolic. **3** occult, esoteric. **4** of hidden meaning. □□ **mysticism** /-ˌsɪz(ə)m/ n. [ME f. OF *mystique* or L *mysticus* f. Gk *mustikos* f. *mustēs* initiated person f. *muō* close the eyes or lips, initiate]

mystical /ˈmɪstɪk(ə)l/ adj. of mystics or mysticism. □□ **mystically** adv.

mystify /ˈmɪstɪˌfaɪ/ v.tr. (**-ies**, **-ied**) **1** bewilder, confuse. **2** hoax, take advantage of the credulity of. **3** wrap up in mystery. □□ **mystification** /-fɪˈkeɪʃ(ə)n/ n. [F *mystifier* (irreg. formed as MYSTIC or MYSTERY[1])]

mystique /mɪˈstiːk/ n. **1** an atmosphere of mystery and veneration attending some activity or person. **2** any skill or technique impressive or mystifying to the layman. [F f. OF (as MYSTIC)]

myth /mɪθ/ n. **1** a traditional narrative usu. involving supernatural or imaginary persons and embodying popular ideas on natural or social phenomena etc. **2** such narratives collectively. **3** a widely held but false notion. **4** a fictitious person, thing, or idea. **5** an allegory (*the Platonic myth*). □□ **mythic** adj. **mythical** adj. **mythically** adv. [mod.L *mythus* f. LL *mythos* f. Gk *muthos*]

mythi pl. of MYTHUS.

mythicize /ˈmɪθɪˌsaɪz/ v.tr. (also **-ise**) treat (a story etc.) as mythical; interpret mythically. □□ **mythicism** /-ˌsɪz(ə)m/ n. **mythicist** /-sɪst/ n.

mytho- /ˈmɪθəʊ/ comb. form myth.

mythogenesis /ˌmɪθəʊˈdʒenɪsɪs/ n. the production of myths.

mythographer /mɪˈθɒɡrəfə(r)/ n. a compiler of myths.

mythography /mɪˈθɒɡrəfɪ/ n. the representation of myths in plastic art.

mythology /mɪˈθɒlədʒɪ/ n. (pl. **-ies**) **1** a body of myths (*Greek mythology*). **2** the study of myths. □□ **mythologer** n. **mythologic** /-θəˈlɒdʒɪk/ adj. **mythological** /-θəˈlɒdʒɪk(ə)l/ adj. **mythologically** /-θəˈlɒdʒɪkəlɪ/ adv. **mythologist** n. **mythologize** v.tr. & intr. (also **-ise**). **mythologizer** n. [ME f. F *mythologie* or LL *mythologia* f. Gk *muthologia* (as MYTHO-, -LOGY)]

mythomania /ˌmɪθəʊˈmeɪnɪə/ n. an abnormal tendency to exaggerate or tell lies. □□ **mythomaniac** /-ˌæk/ n. & adj.

mythopoeia /ˌmɪθəʊˈpiːə/ n. the making of myths. □□ **mythopoeic** adj. (also **mythopoetic** /-pəʊˈetɪk/).

mythus /ˈmɪθəs/ n. (pl. **mythi** /-θaɪ/) *literary* a myth. [mod.L: see MYTH]

myxo- /ˈmɪksəʊ/ comb. form (also **myx-** before a vowel) mucus. [Gk *muxa* mucus]

myxoedema /ˌmɪksəˈdiːmə/ n. (US **myxedema**) a syndrome caused by hypothyroidism, resulting in thickening of the skin, weight gain, mental dullness, loss of energy, and sensitivity to cold.

myxoma /mɪkˈsəʊmə/ n. (pl. **myxomas** or **myxomata** /-mətə/) a benign tumour of mucous or gelatinous tissue. □□ **myxomatous** /-'sɒmətəs/ *adj.* [mod.L (as MYXO-, -OMA)]

myxomatosis /ˌmɪksəmə'təʊsɪs/ *n.* an infectious usu. fatal viral disease in rabbits, causing swelling of the mucous membranes.

myxomycete /ˌmɪksəʊmaɪ'siːt/ *n.* any of a group of small acellular organisms inhabiting damp areas.

myxovirus /'mɪksəʊˌvaɪərəs/ *n.* any of a group of viruses including the influenza virus.

N

N¹ /en/ *n.* (also **n**) (*pl.* **Ns** or **N's**) **1** the fourteenth letter of the alphabet. **2** *Printing* en. **3** *Math.* an indefinite number. □**to the nth** (or **nth degree**) **1** *Math.* to any required power. **2** to any extent; to the utmost.

N² *abbr.* (also **N.**) **1** North; Northern. **2** newton(s). **3** *Chess* knight. **4** New. **5** nuclear.

N³ *symb. Chem.* the element nitrogen.

n *abbr.* (also **n.**) **1** name. **2** nano-. **3** neuter. **4** noon. **5** note. **6** noun.

'n *conj.* (also **'n'**) *colloq.* and. [abbr.]

-n¹ *suffix* see -EN².

-n² *suffix* see -EN³.

Na *symb. Chem.* the element sodium.

na /nə/ *adv. Sc.* (in *comb.*; usu. with an auxiliary verb) = NOT (*I canna do it*; *they didna go*).

n/a *abbr.* **1** not applicable. **2** not available.

NAAFI /'næfɪ/ *abbr. Brit.* **1** Navy, Army, and Air Force Institutes. **2** a canteen for servicemen run by the NAAFI.

nab /næb/ *v.tr.* (**nabbed**, **nabbing**) *sl.* **1** arrest; catch in wrongdoing. **2** seize, grab. [17th c., also *napp*, as in KIDNAP: orig. unkn.]

nabob /'neɪbɒb/ *n.* **1** *hist.* a Muslim official or governor under the Mughal empire. **2** (formerly) a conspicuously wealthy person, esp. one returned from India with a fortune. [Port. *nababo* or Sp. *nabab*, f. Urdu (as NAWAB)]

nacarat /'nækə,ræt/ *n.* a bright orange-red colour. [F, perh. f. Sp. & Port. *nacardo* (*nacar* NACRE).]

nacelle /nə'sel/ *n.* **1** the outer casing of the engine of an aircraft. **2** the car of an airship. [F, f. LL *navicella* dimin. of L *navis* ship]

nacho /'nætʃəʊ/ *n.* (*pl.* **-os**) (usu. in *pl.*) a tortilla chip, usu. topped with melted cheese and spices etc. [20th c.: orig. uncert.]

NACODS /'neɪkɒdz/ *abbr.* (in the UK) National Association of Colliery Overmen, Deputies, and Shotfirers.

nacre /'neɪkə(r)/ *n.* mother-of-pearl from any shelled mollusc. □□ **nacred** *adj.* **nacreous** /'neɪkrɪəs/ *adj.* **nacrous** /-krəs/ *adj.* [F]

nadir /'neɪdɪə(r), 'næd-/ *n.* **1** the part of the celestial sphere directly below an observer (opp. ZENITH). **2** the lowest point in one's fortunes; a time of deep despair. [ME f. OF f. Arab. *naẓīr* (*as-samt*) opposite (to the zenith)]

naevus /'niːvəs/ *n.* (*US* **nevus**) (*pl.* **naevi** /-vaɪ/) **1** a birthmark in the form of a raised red patch on the skin. **2** = MOLE². □□ **naevoid** *adj.* [L]

naff¹ /næf/ *v.intr. sl.* **1** (in *imper.*, foll. by *off*) go away. **2** (as **naffing** *adj.*) used as an intensive to express annoyance etc. [prob. euphem. for FUCK: cf. EFF]

naff² /næf/ *adj. sl.* **1** unfashionable; socially awkward. **2** worthless, rubbishy. [20th c.: orig. unkn.]

Naffy /'næfɪ/ *n. sl.* = NAAFI. [phonet. sp.]

nag¹ /næg/ *v. & n.* —*v.* (**nagged**, **nagging**) **1 a** *tr.* annoy or irritate (a person) with persistent fault-finding or continuous urging. **b** (often foll. by *at*) find fault, complain, or urge, esp. persistently. **2** *intr.* (of a pain) ache dully but persistently. **3 a** *tr.* worry or preoccupy (a person, the mind, etc.) (*his mistake nagged him*). **b** *intr.* (often foll. by *at*) worry or gnaw. —*n.* a persistently nagging person. □□ **nagger** *n.* **naggingly** *adv.* [of dial., perh. Scand. or LG, orig.: cf. Norw. & Sw. *nagga* gnaw, irritate, LG (*g*)*naggen* provoke]

nag² /næg/ *n.* **1** *colloq.* a horse. **2** a small riding-horse or pony. [ME: orig. unkn.]

Nah. *abbr.* Nahum (Old Testament).

Nahuatl /naː'wɑːt(ə)l, 'nɑː-/ *n. & adj.* —*n.* **1** a member of a group of peoples native to S. Mexico and Central America, including the Aztecs. **2** the language of these people. —*adj.* of or concerning the Nahuatl peoples or language. □□ **Nahuatlan** *adj.* [Sp. f. Nahuatl]

naiad /'naɪæd/ *n.* (*pl.* **naiads** or **-des** /-ə,diːz/) **1** *Mythol.* a water-nymph. **2** the larva of a dragonfly etc. **3** any aquatic plant of the genus *Najas*, with narrow leaves and small flowers. [L *Naïas Naïad-* f. Gk *Naias -ados* f. *naō* flow]

nail /neɪl/ *n. & v.* —*n.* **1** a small usu. sharpened metal spike with a broadened flat head, driven in with a hammer to join things together or to serve as a peg, protection (cf. HOBNAIL), or decoration. **2 a** a horny covering on the upper surface of the tip of the human finger or toe. **b** a claw or talon. **c** a hard growth on the upper mandible of some soft-billed birds. **3** *hist.* a measure of cloth length (equal to 2¼ inches). —*v.tr.* **1** fasten with a nail or nails (*nailed it to the beam*; *nailed the planks together*). **2** fix or keep (a person, attention, etc.) fixed. **3 a** secure, catch, or get hold of (a person or thing). **b** expose or discover (a lie or a liar). □**hard as nails 1** callous; unfeeling. **2** in good physical condition. **nail-biting** causing severe anxiety or tension. **nail-brush** a small brush for cleaning the nails. **nail one's colours to the mast** persist; refuse to give in. **nail down 1** bind (a person) to a promise etc. **2** define precisely. **3** fasten (a thing) with nails. **nail enamel** *US* = *nail polish*. **nail-file** a roughened metal or emery strip used for smoothing the nails. **nail-head** *Archit.* an ornament like the head of a nail. **nail in a person's coffin** something thought to increase the risk of death. **nail polish** a varnish applied to the nails to colour them or make them shiny. **nail-punch** (or **-set**) a tool for sinking the head of a nail below a surface. **nail-scissors** small curved scissors for trimming the nails. **nail up 1** close (a door etc.) with nails. **2** fix (a thing) at a height with nails. **nail varnish** *Brit.* = *nail polish*. **on the nail** (esp. of payment) without delay (*cash on the nail*). □□ **nailed** *adj.* (also in *comb.*). **nailless** *adj.* [OE *nægel*, *næglan* f. Gmc]

nailer /'neɪlə(r)/ *n.* a nail-maker. □□ **nailery** *n.*

nainsook /'neɪnsʊk/ *n.* a fine soft cotton fabric, orig. Indian. [Hindi *nainsukh* f. *nain* eye + *sukh* pleasure]

naira /'naɪrə/ *n.* the chief monetary unit of Nigeria. [contr. of *Nigeria*]

naïve /nɑː'iːv, naɪ'iːv/ *adj.* (also **naive**) **1** artless; innocent; unaffected. **2** foolishly credulous; simple. □□ **naïvely** *adv.* **naïveness** *n.* [F, fem. of *naïf* f. L *nativus* NATIVE]

naïvety /nɑː'iːvtɪ, naɪ-/ *n.* (also **naivety**, *naïveté* /nɑː'iːvteɪ/) (*pl.* **-ies** or **naïvetés**) **1** the state or quality of being naïve. **2** a naïve action. [F *naïveté* (as NAÏVE)]

naked /'neɪkɪd/ *adj.* **1** without clothes; nude. **2** plain; undisguised; exposed (*the naked truth*; *his naked soul*). **3** (of a light, flame, etc.) unprotected from the wind etc.; unshaded. **4** defenceless. **5** without addition, comment, support, evidence, etc. (*his naked word*; *naked assertion*). **6 a** (of landscape) barren; treeless. **b** (of rock) exposed; without soil etc. **7** (of a sword etc.) unsheathed. **8** (usu. foll. by *of*) devoid; without. **9** without leaves, hairs, scales, shell, etc. **10** (of a room, wall, etc.) without decoration, furnishings, etc.; empty, plain. □**naked boys** (or **lady** or **ladies**) the meadow saffron, which flowers while leafless: also called *autumn crocus*. **the naked eye**

unassisted vision, e.g. without a telescope, microscope, etc. □□ **nakedly** *adv.* **nakedness** *n.* [OE *nacod* f. Gmc]

naker /'neɪkə(r)/ *n. hist.* a kettledrum. [ME f. OF *nacre nacaire* f. Arab. *naḳḳāra* drum]

NALGO /'nælɡəʊ/ *abbr. Brit.* National and Local Government Officers' Association.

namby-pamby /ˌnæmbɪ'pæmbɪ/ *adj. & n.* —*adj.* **1** lacking vigour or drive; weak. **2** insipidly pretty or sentimental. —*n.* (*pl.* **-ies**) **1** a namby-pamby person. **2** namby-pamby talk. [fanciful formulation on name of *Ambrose* Philips, Engl. pastoral writer d. 1749]

name /neɪm/ *n. & v.* —*n.* **1 a** the word by which an individual person, animal, place, or thing is known, spoken of, etc. (*mentioned him by name; her name is Joanna*). **b** all who go under one name; a family, clan, or people in terms of its name (*the Scottish name*). **2 a** a usu. abusive term used of a person etc. (*called him names*). **b** a word denoting an object or esp. a class of objects, ideas, etc. (*what is the name of that kind of vase?; that sort of behaviour has no name*). **3** a famous person (*many great names were there*). **4** a reputation, esp. a good one (*has a name for honesty; their name is guarantee enough*). **5** something existing only nominally (opp. FACT, REALITY). **6** (*attrib.*) widely known (*a name brand of shampoo*). —*v.tr.* **1** give a usu. specified name to (*named the dog Spot*). **2** call (a person or thing) by the right name (*named the man in the photograph*). **3** mention; specify; cite (*named his requirements*). **4** nominate; appoint, etc. (*was named the new chairman*). **5** specify as something desired (*named it as her dearest wish*). **6** *Brit. Parl.* (of the Speaker) mention (an MP) as disobedient to the chair. □ **by name** called (*Tom by name*). **have to one's name** possess. **in all but name** virtually. **in name** (or **name only**) as a mere formality; hardly at all (*is the leader in name only*). **in a person's name** = *in the name of*. **in the name of** calling to witness; invoking (*in the name of goodness*). **in one's own name** independently; without authority. **make a name for oneself** become famous. **name after** (*US* **for**) call (a person) by the name of (a specified person) (*named him after his uncle Roger*). **name-calling** abusive language. **name-child** (usu. foll. by *of*) one named after another person. **name-day 1** the feast-day of a saint after whom a person is named. **2** *Brit.* = *ticket-day.* **name the day** arrange a date (esp. of a woman fixing the date for her wedding). **name-drop** (**-dropped**, **-dropping**) indulge in name-dropping. **name-dropper** a person who name-drops. **name-dropping** the familiar mention of famous people as a form of boasting. **name names** mention specific names, esp. in accusation. **name of the game** *colloq.* the purpose or essence of an action etc. **name-part** the title role in a play etc. **name-plate** a plate or panel bearing the name of an occupant of a room etc. **name-tape** a tape fixed to a garment etc. and bearing the name of the owner. **of** (or **by**) **the name of** called. **put one's name down for 1** apply for. **2** promise to subscribe (a sum). **what's in a name?** names are arbitrary labels. **you name it** *colloq.* no matter what; whatever you like. □□ **nameable** *adj.* [OE *nama, noma,* (*ge*)*namian* f. Gmc, rel. to L *nomen,* Gk *onoma*]

nameless /'neɪmlɪs/ *adj.* **1** having no name or name-inscription. **2** inexpressible; indefinable (*a nameless sensation*). **3** unnamed; anonymous, esp. deliberately (*our informant, who shall be nameless*). **4** too loathsome or horrific to be named (*nameless vices*). **5** obscure; inglorious. **6** illegitimate. □□ **namelessly** *adv.* **namelessness** *n.*

namely /'neɪmlɪ/ *adv.* that is to say; in other words.

namesake /'neɪmseɪk/ *n.* a person or thing having the same name as another (*was her aunt's namesake*). [prob. f. phr. *for the name's sake*]

namma var. of GNAMMA.

nan /næn/ *n.* (also **nana, nanna** /'nænə/) *Brit. colloq.* grandmother. [childish pronunc.]

nana /'nɑːnə/ *n. sl.* a silly person; a fool. [perh. f. BANANA]

nancy /'nænsɪ/ *n. & adj.* (also **nance** /næns/) *sl.* —*n.* (*pl.* **-ies**) (in full **nancy boy**) an effeminate man, esp. a homosexual. —*adj.* effeminate. [pet-form of the name *Ann*]

nankeen /næŋ'kiːn, næn-/ *n.* **1** a yellowish cotton cloth. **2** a yellowish buff colour. **3** (in *pl.*) trousers of nankeen. [*Nankin*(*g*) in China, where orig. made]

nanna var. of NAN.

nanny /'nænɪ/ *n. & v.* —*n.* (*pl.* **-ies**) **1 a** a child's nurse. **b** an unduly protective person, institution, etc. (*the nanny State*). **2** = NAN. **3** (in full **nanny-goat**) a female goat. —*v.tr.* (**-ies, -ied**) be unduly protective towards. [formed as NANCY]

nano- /'nænəʊ, 'neɪnəʊ/ *comb. form* denoting a factor of 10^{-9} (*nanosecond*). [L f. Gk *nanos* dwarf]

nanometre /'nænəʊˌmiːt(ə)r/ *n.* one thousand-millionth of a metre.

nanosecond /'nænəʊˌsekənd/ *n.* one thousand-millionth of a second.

naos /'neɪɒs/ *n.* (*pl.* **naoi** /'neɪɔɪ/) *Gk Hist.* the inner part of a temple. [Gk, = temple]

nap[1] /næp/ *v. & n.* —*v.intr.* (**napped, napping**) sleep lightly or briefly. —*n.* a short sleep or doze, esp. by day (*took a nap*). □ **catch a person napping 1** find a person asleep or off guard. **2** detect in negligence or error. [OE *hnappian,* rel. to OHG (*h*)*naffezan* to slumber]

nap[2] /næp/ *n. & v.* —*n.* **1** the raised pile on textiles, esp. velvet. **2** a soft downy surface. **3** *Austral. colloq.* blankets, bedding, swag. —*v.tr.* (**napped, napping**) raise a nap on (cloth). □□ **napless** *adj.* [ME *noppe* f. MDu., MLG *noppe* nap, *noppen* trim nap from]

nap[3] /næp/ *n. & v.* —*n.* **1 a** a form of whist in which players declare the number of tricks they expect to take, up to five. **b** a call of five in this game. **2 a** the betting of all one's money on one horse etc. **b** a tipster's choice for this. —*v.tr.* (**napped, napping**) name (a horse etc.) as a probable winner. □ **go nap 1** attempt to take all five tricks in nap. **2** risk everything in one attempt. **3** win all the matches etc. in a series. **nap hand** a good winning position worth risking in a venture. **not go nap on** *Austral. colloq.* not be too keen on; not care much for. [abbr. of orig. name of game NAPOLEON]

napa var. of NAPPA.

napalm /'neɪpɑːm/ *n. & v.* —*n.* **1** a thickening agent produced from naphthenic acid, other fatty acids, and aluminium. **2** a jellied petrol made from this, used in incendiary bombs. —*v.tr.* attack with napalm bombs. [NAPHTHENIC + *palmitic acid* in coconut oil]

nape /neɪp/ *n.* the back of the neck. [ME: orig. unkn.]

napery /'neɪpərɪ/ *n. Sc.* or *archaic* household linen, esp. table linen. [ME f. OF *naperie* f. *nape* (as NAPKIN)]

naphtha /'næfθə/ *n.* an inflammable oil obtained by the dry distillation of organic substances such as coal, shale, or petroleum. [L f. Gk, = inflammable volatile liquid issuing from the earth, of Oriental origin]

naphthalene /'næfθəˌliːn/ *n.* a white crystalline aromatic substance produced by the distillation of coal tar and used in mothballs and the manufacture of dyes etc. □□ **naphthalic** /-'θælɪk/ *adj.* [NAPHTHA + -ENE]

naphthene /'næfθiːn/ *n.* any of a group of cyclo-alkanes. [NAPHTHA + -ENE]

naphthenic /næf'θiːnɪk/ *adj.* of a naphthene or its radical. □ **naphthenic acid** any carboxylic acid resulting from the refining of petroleum.

Napierian logarithm /neɪ'pɪərɪən/ *n.* see LOG-ARITHM. [J. *Napier,* Sc. mathematician d. 1617]

napkin /'næpkɪn/ *n.* **1** (in full **table napkin**) a square piece of linen, paper, etc. used for wiping the lips, fingers, etc. at meals, or serving fish etc. on; a serviette. **2** *Brit.* a baby's nappy. **3** a small towel.

□**napkin-ring** a ring used to hold (and distinguish) a person's table napkin when not in use. [ME f. OF *nappe* f. L *mappa* (MAP)]

napoleon /nə'pəʊlɪən/ *n.* **1** *hist.* a gold twenty-franc piece minted in the reign of Napoleon I. **2** *hist.* a 19th-c. high boot. **3** = NAP³. **4** *US* = MILLEFEUILLE. □**double napoleon** *hist.* a forty-franc piece. [F *napoléon* f. *Napoléon*, name of 19th-c. French emperors]

Napoleonic /nə,pəʊlɪ'ɒnɪk/ *adj.* of, relating to, or characteristic of Napoleon I or his time.

nappa /'næpə/ *n.* (also **napa**) a soft leather made by a special process from the skin of sheep or goats. [*Napa* in California]

nappe /næp/ *n. Geol.* a sheet of rock that has moved sideways over neighbouring strata, usu. as a result of overthrust. [F *nappe* tablecloth]

napper /'næpə(r)/ *n. Brit. sl.* the head. [18th c.: orig. uncert.]

nappy /'næpɪ/ *n.* (*pl.* **-ies**) *Brit.* a piece of towelling or other absorbent material wrapped round a baby to absorb or retain urine and faeces. □**nappy rash** inflammation of a baby's skin, caused by prolonged contact with a damp nappy. [abbr. of NAPKIN]

narceine /'nɑːsɪ,iːn/ *n.* a narcotic alkaloid obtained from opium. [F *narcéine* f. Gk *narkē* numbness]

narcissism /'nɑːsɪ,sɪz(ə)m, nɑː'sɪs-/ *n. Psychol.* excessive or erotic interest in oneself, one's physical features, etc. □□**narcissist** *n.* **narcissistic** /-'sɪstɪk/ *adj.* **narcissistically** /-'sɪstɪkəlɪ/ *adv.* [*Narcissus* (Gk *Narkissos*), youth who fell in love with his reflection in water]

narcissus /nɑː'sɪsəs/ *n.* (*pl.* **narcissi** /-saɪ/ or **narcissuses**) any bulbous plant of the genus *Narcissus*, esp. *N. poeticus* bearing a heavily scented single flower with an undivided corona edged with crimson and yellow. [L f. Gk *narkissos*, perh. f. *narkē* numbness, with ref. to its narcotic effects]

narcolepsy /'nɑːkə,lepsɪ/ *n. Med.* a disease with fits of sleepiness and drowsiness. □□**narcoleptic** /-'leptɪk/ *adj. & n.* [Gk *narkoō* make numb, after EPILEPSY]

narcosis /nɑː'kəʊsɪs/ *n.* **1** *Med.* the working or effects of soporific narcotics. **2** a state of insensibility. [Gk *narkōsis* f. *narkoō* make numb]

narcotic /nɑː'kɒtɪk/ *adj. & n.* —*adj.* **1** (of a substance) inducing drowsiness, sleep, stupor, or insensibility. **2** (of a drug) affecting the mind. **3** of or involving narcosis. **4** soporific. —*n.* a narcotic substance, drug, or influence. □□**narcotically** *adv.* **narcotism** /'nɑːkə,tɪz(ə)m/ *n.* **narcotize** /'nɑːkə,taɪz/ *v.tr.* (also **-ise**). **narcotization** /,nɑːkətaɪ'zeɪʃ(ə)n/ *n.* [ME f. OF *narcotique* or med.L f. Gk *narkōtikos* (as NARCOSIS)]

nard /nɑːd/ *n.* **1** any of various plants yielding an aromatic balsam used by the ancients. **2** = SPIKENARD. [ME f. L *nardus* f. Gk *nardos* f. Semitic word]

nardoo /nɑː'duː/ *n.* **1** a clover-like plant, *Marsilea drummondii*, native to Australia. **2** a food made from the spores of this plant. [Aboriginal]

nares /'neərɪz/ *n.pl. Anat.* the nostrils. □□**narial** *adj.* [pl. of L *naris*]

narghile /'nɑːgɪlɪ/ *n.* an oriental tobacco-pipe with the smoke drawn through water; a hookah. [Pers. *nārgīleh* (*nārgīl* coconut)]

nark /nɑːk/ *n. & v. Brit. sl.* —*n.* **1** a police informer or decoy. **2** *Austral.* an annoying person or thing. —*v.tr.* (usu. in *passive*) annoy; infuriate (*was narked by their attitude*). □**nark it!** stop that! [Romany *nāk* nose]

narky /'nɑːkɪ/ *adj.* (**narkier**, **narkiest**) *sl.* bad-tempered, irritable. [NARK]

narrate /nə'reɪt/ *v.tr.* (also *absol.*) **1** give a continuous story or account of. **2** provide a spoken commentary or accompaniment for (a film etc.). □□**narratable** *adj.* **narration** /nə'reɪʃ(ə)n/ *n.* [L *narrare narrat-*]

narrative /'nærətɪv/ *n. & adj.* —*n.* **1** a spoken or written account of connected events in order of

happening. **2** the practice or art of narration. —*adj.* in the form of, or concerned with, narration (*narrative verse*). □□**narratively** *adv.* [F *narratif -ive* f. LL *narrativus* (as NARRATE)]

narrator /nə'reɪtə(r)/ *n.* **1** an actor, announcer, etc. who delivers a commentary in a film, broadcast, etc. **2** a person who narrates. [L (as NARRATE)]

narrow /'nærəʊ/ *adj., n., & v.* —*adj.* (**narrower**, **narrowest**) **1 a** of small width in proportion to length; lacking breadth. **b** confined or confining; constricted (*within narrow bounds*). **2** of limited scope; restricted (*in the narrowest sense*). **3** with little margin (*a narrow escape*). **4** searching; precise; exact (*a narrow examination*). **5** = NARROW-MINDED. **6** (of a vowel) tense. **7** of small size. —*n.* **1** (usu. in *pl.*) the narrow part of a strait, river, sound, etc. **2** a narrow pass or street. —*v.* **1** *intr.* become narrow; diminish; contract; lessen. **2** *tr.* make narrow; constrict; restrict. □**narrow boat** *Brit.* a canal boat, esp. one less than 7 ft. (2.1 metres) wide. **narrow circumstances** poverty. **narrow cloth** cloth less than 52 inches wide. **narrow gauge** a railway track that has a smaller gauge than the standard one. **narrow seas** the English Channel and the Irish Sea. **narrow squeak** **1** a narrow escape. **2** a success barely attained. □□**narrowish** *adj.* **narrowly** *adv.* **narrowness** *n.* [OE *nearu nearw-* f. Gmc]

narrow-minded /,nærəʊ'maɪndɪd/ *adj.* rigid or restricted in one's views, intolerant, prejudiced, illiberal. □□**narrow-mindedly** *adv.* **narrow-mindedness** *n.*

narthex /'nɑːθeks/ *n.* **1** a railed-off antechamber or porch etc. at the western entrance of some early Christian churches, used by catechumens, penitents, etc. **2** a similar antechamber in a modern church. [L f. Gk *narthēx* giant fennel, stick, casket, narthex]

narwhal /'nɑːw(ə)l/ *n.* an Arctic white whale, *Monodon monoceros*, the male of which has a long straight spirally fluted tusk developed from one of its teeth. Also called BELUGA. [Du. *narwal* f. Da. *narhval* f. *hval* whale: cf. ON *náhvalr* (perh. f. *nár* corpse, with ref. to its skin-colour)]

nary /'neərɪ/ *adj. colloq.* or *dial.* not a; no (*nary a one*). [f. *ne'er a*]

NAS *abbr. Brit.* Noise Abatement Society.

NASA /'næsə/ *abbr.* (in the US) National Aeronautics and Space Administration.

nasal /'neɪz(ə)l/ *adj. & n.* —*adj.* **1** of, for, or relating to the nose. **2** *Phonet.* (of a letter or a sound) pronounced with the breath passing through the nose, e.g. *m*, *n*, *ng*, or French *en*, *un*, etc. **3** (of the voice or speech) having an intonation caused by breathing through the nose. —*n.* **1** *Phonet.* a nasal letter or sound. **2** *hist.* a nose-piece on a helmet. □□ **nasality** /-'zælɪtɪ/ *n.* **nasalize** *v.intr. & tr.* (also **-ise**). **nasalization** /-'zeɪʃ(ə)n/ *n.* **nasally** *adv.* [F *nasal* or med.L *nasalis* f. L *nasus* nose]

nascent /'næs(ə)nt, 'neɪs-/ *adj.* **1** in the act of being born. **2** just beginning to be; not yet mature. **3** *Chem.* just being formed and therefore unusually reactive (*nascent hydrogen*). □□**nascency** /'næsənsɪ/ *n.* [L *nasci nascent-* be born]

naseberry /'neɪzbərɪ/ *n.* (*pl.* **-ies**) a sapodilla. [Sp. & Port. *néspera* medlar f. L (see MEDLAR): assim. to BERRY]

naso- /'neɪzəʊ/ *comb. form* nose. [L *nasus* nose]

naso-frontal /,neɪzəʊ'frʌnt(ə)l/ *adj.* of or relating to the nose and forehead.

nastic /'næstɪk/ *adj. Bot.* (of the movement of plant parts) not determined by an external stimulus. [Gk *nastos* squeezed together f. *nassō* to press]

nasturtium /nə'stɜːʃəm/ *n.* **1** (in general use) a trailing plant, *Tropaeolum majus*, with rounded edible leaves and bright orange, yellow, or red flowers. **2** any cruciferous plant of the genus *Nasturtium*, including watercress. [L]

nasty /'nɑːstɪ/ *adj.* (**nastier**, **nastiest**) **1 a** highly unpleasant (*a nasty experience*). **b** annoying; objectionable (*the car has a nasty habit of breaking down*). **2** difficult to negotiate; dangerous, serious (*a nasty fence*; *a nasty question*; *a nasty illness*). **3** (of a person or animal) ill-natured, ill-tempered, spiteful; violent, offensive (*nasty to his mother*; *turns nasty when he's drunk*). **4** (of the weather) foul, wet, stormy. **5 a** disgustingly dirty, filthy. **b** unpalatable; disagreeable (*nasty smell*). **c** (of a wound) septic. **6 a** obscene. **b** delighting in obscenity. □**a nasty bit** (or **piece**) **of work** *colloq.* an unpleasant or contemptible person. **a nasty one 1** a rebuff; a snub. **2** an awkward question. **3** a disabling blow etc. □□ **nastily** *adv.* **nastiness** *n.* [ME: orig. unkn.]

NAS/UWT *abbr.* (in the UK) National Association of Schoolmasters and Union of Women Teachers.

Nat. *abbr.* **1** National. **2** Nationalist. **3** Natural.

natal /ˈneɪt(ə)l/ *adj.* of or from one's birth. [ME f. L *natalis* (as NATION)]

natality /nəˈtælɪtɪ/ *n.* (*pl.* **-ies**) birth rate. [F *natalité* (as NATAL)]

natation /nəˈteɪʃ(ə)n/ *n. formal* or *literary* the act or art of swimming. [L *natatio* f. *natare* swim]

natatorial /ˌneɪtəˈtɔːrɪəl, ˌnæ-/ *adj.* (also **natatory** /ˈneɪtətərɪ, nəˈteɪtərɪ/) *formal* **1** swimming. **2** of or concerning swimming. [LL *natatorius* f. L *natator* swimmer (as NATATION)]

natatorium /ˌneɪtəˈtɔːrɪəm/ *n. US* a swimming-pool, esp. indoors. [LL neut. of *natatorius* (see NATATORIAL)]

natch /nætʃ/ *adv. colloq.* = NATURALLY. [abbr.]

nates /ˈneɪtiːz/ *n.pl. Anat.* the buttocks. [L]

NATFHE *abbr.* (in the UK) National Association of Teachers in Further and Higher Education.

nathless /ˈneɪθlɪs/ *adv.* (also **natheless**) *archaic* nevertheless. [ME f. OE *nā* not (f. *ne* not + *ā* ever) + THE + *læs* LESS]

nation /ˈneɪʃ(ə)n/ *n.* **1** a community of people of mainly common descent, history, language, etc., forming a State or inhabiting a territory. **2** a tribe or confederation of tribes of N. American Indians. □**law of nations** *Law* international law. □□ **nationhood** *n.* [ME f. OF f. L *natio -onis* f. *nasci nat-* be born]

national /ˈnæʃən(ə)l/ *adj. & n.* —*adj.* **1** of or common to a nation or the nation. **2** peculiar to or characteristic of a particular nation. —*n.* **1** a citizen of a specified country, usu. entitled to hold that country's passport (*French nationals*). **2** a fellow countryman. **3** (**the National**) = Grand National. □**national anthem** a song adopted by a nation, expressive of its identity etc. and intended to inspire patriotism. **National Assembly 1** an elected house of legislature in various countries. **2** *hist.* the elected legislature in France 1789-91. **National Assistance** *hist.* **1** (in Britain) the former official name for supplementary benefits under National Insurance. **2** such benefits. **national bank** *US* a bank chartered under the federal government. **national convention** *US* a convention of a major political party, nominating candidates for the presidency etc. **national debt** the money owed by a State because of loans to it. **national football** *Austral.* Australian Rules football. **National Front** a UK political party with extreme reactionary views on immigration etc. **national grid** *Brit.* **1** the network of high-voltage electric power lines between major power stations. **2** the metric system of geographical coordinates used in maps of the British Isles. **National Guard** (in the US) the primary reserve force partly maintained by the States but available for federal use. **National Health** (or **Health Service**) (in the UK) a system of national medical care paid for mainly by taxation and started in 1948. **national income** the total money earned within a nation. **National Insurance** (in the UK) the system of compulsory payments by employed persons (supplemented by employers) to provide State assistance in sickness, unemployment, retirement, etc. **national park** an area of natural beauty protected by the State for the use of the general public. **national service** *Brit. hist.* service in the army etc. under conscription. **National Socialism** *hist.* the doctrines of nationalism, racial purity, etc., adopted by the Nazis. **National Socialist** *hist.* a member of the fascist party implementing National Socialism in Germany, 1933-45. **National Trust** (in the UK, Australia, etc.) an organization for maintaining and preserving historic buildings etc. □□ **nationally** *adv.* [F (as NATION)]

nationalism /ˈnæʃənəˌlɪz(ə)m/ *n.* **1 a** patriotic feeling, principles, etc. **b** an extreme form of this; chauvinism. **2** a policy of national independence. □□ **nationalist** *n. & adj.* **nationalistic** /-ˈlɪstɪk/ *adj.* **nationalistically** /-ˈlɪstɪkəlɪ/ *adv.*

nationality /ˌnæʃəˈnælɪtɪ/ *n.* (*pl.* **-ies**) **1 a** the status of belonging to a particular nation (*what is your nationality?*; *has British nationality*). **b** a nation (*people of all nationalities*). **2** the condition of being national; distinctive national qualities. **3** an ethnic group forming a part of one or more political nations. **4** existence as a nation; nationhood. **5** patriotic sentiment.

nationalize /ˈnæʃənəˌlaɪz/ *v.tr.* (also **-ise**) **1** take over (railways, coal-mines, the steel industry, land, etc.) from private ownership on behalf of the State. **2 a** make national. **b** make into a nation. **3** naturalize (a foreigner). □□ **nationalization** /-ˈzeɪʃ(ə)n/ *n.* **nationalizer** *n.* [F *nationaliser* (as NATIONAL)]

nationwide /ˈneɪʃ(ə)nˌwaɪd/ *adj.* extending over the whole nation.

native /ˈneɪtɪv/ *n. & adj.* —*n.* **1 a** (usu. foll. by *of*) a person born in a specified place, or whose parents are domiciled in that place at the time of the birth (*a native of Bristol*). **b** a local inhabitant. **2** often *offens.* **a** a member of a non-White indigenous people, as regarded by the colonial settlers. **b** *S.Afr.* a Black person. **3** (usu. foll. by *of*) an indigenous animal or plant. **4** an oyster reared in British waters, esp. in artificial beds (*a Whitstable native*). **5** *Austral.* a White person born in Australia. —*adj.* **1** (usu. foll. by *to*) belonging to a person or thing by nature; inherent; innate (*spoke with the facility native to him*). **2** of one's birth or birthplace (*native dress*; *native country*). **3** belonging to one by right of birth. **4** (usu. foll. by *to*) belonging to a specified place (*the anteater is native to S. America*). **5 a** (esp. of a non-European) indigenous; born in a place. **b** of the natives of a place (*native customs*). **6** unadorned; simple; artless. **7** *Geol.* (of metal etc.) found in a pure or uncombined state. **8** *Austral. & NZ* resembling an animal or plant familiar elsewhere (*native rabbit*). □**go native** (of a settler) adopt the local way of life, esp. in a non-European country. **native bear** *Austral. & NZ* = KOALA. **native rock** rock in its original place. □□ **natively** *adv.* **nativeness** *n.* [ME (earlier as adj.) f. OF *natif -ive* or L *nativus* f. *nasci nat-* be born]

nativism /ˈneɪtɪˌvɪz(ə)m/ *n. Philos.* the doctrine of innate ideas. □□ **nativist** *n.*

nativity /nəˈtɪvɪtɪ/ *n.* (*pl.* **-ies**) **1** (esp. **the Nativity**) **a** the birth of Christ. **b** the festival of Christ's birth; Christmas. **2** a picture of the Nativity. **3** birth. **4** the horoscope at a person's birth. **5 a** the birth of the Virgin Mary or St John the Baptist. **b** the festival of the nativity of the Virgin (8 Sept.) or St John (24 June). □**nativity play** a play usu. performed by children at Christmas dealing with the birth of Christ. [ME f. OF *nativité* f. LL *nativitas -tatis* f. L (as NATIVE)]

NATO /ˈneɪtəʊ/ *abbr.* (also **Nato**) North Atlantic Treaty Organization.

natron /ˈneɪtrən/ *n.* a mineral form of hydrated sodium salts found in dried lake beds. [F f. Sp. *natrón* f. Arab. *naṭrūn* f. Gk *nitron* NITRE]

NATSOPA /ˈnætˈsəʊpə/ *abbr.* (in the UK) National Society of Operative Printers, Graphical and Media Personnel (orig. Printers and Assistants).

w *we* z *zoo* ʃ *she* ʒ *decision* θ *thin* ð *this* ŋ *ring* x *loch* tʃ *chip* dʒ *jar* (*see over for vowels*)

natter /'nætə(r)/ v. & n. colloq. —v.intr. **1** chatter idly. **2** grumble; talk fretfully. —n. **1** aimless chatter. **2** grumbling talk. □□ **natterer** n. [orig. Sc., imit.]

natterjack /'nætə,dʒæk/ n. a toad, *Bufo calamita*, with a bright yellow stripe down its back, and moving by running not hopping. [perh. f. NATTER, from its loud croak, + JACK¹]

nattier blue /'nætɪə(r)/ n. a soft shade of blue. [much used by J. M. *Nattier*, Fr. painter d. 1766]

natty /'nætɪ/ adj. (**nattier**, **nattiest**) colloq. **1 a** smartly or neatly dressed, dapper. **b** spruce; trim; smart (*a natty blouse*). **2** deft. □□ **nattily** adv. **nattiness** n. [orig. sl., perh. rel. to NEAT¹]

natural /'nætʃər(ə)l/ adj. & n. —adj. **1 a** existing in or caused by nature; not artificial (*natural landscape*). **b** uncultivated; wild (*existing in its natural state*). **2** in the course of nature; not exceptional or miraculous (*died of natural causes; a natural occurrence*). **3** (of human nature etc.) not surprising; to be expected (*natural for her to be upset*). **4 a** (of a person or a person's behaviour) unaffected, easy, spontaneous. **b** (foll. by *to*) spontaneous, easy (*friendliness is natural to him*). **5 a** (of qualities etc.) inherent; innate (*a natural talent for music*). **b** (of a person) having such qualities (*a natural linguist*). **6** not disguised or altered (as by make-up etc.). **7** lifelike; as if in nature (*the portrait looked very natural*). **8** likely by its or their nature to be such (*natural enemies; the natural antithesis*). **9** having a physical existence as opposed to what is spiritual, intellectual, etc. (*the natural world*). **10 a** related by nature, out of wedlock, esp. in a specified manner (*her natural son*). **b** illegitimate (*a natural child*). **11** based on the innate moral sense; instinctive (*natural justice*). **12** Mus. **a** (of a note) not sharpened or flattened (*B natural*). **b** (of a scale) not containing any sharps or flats. **13** not enlightened or communicated by revelation (*the natural man*). —n. **1** colloq. (usu. foll. by *for*) a person or thing naturally suitable, adept, expert, etc. (*a natural for the championship*). **2** archaic a person mentally deficient from birth. **3** Mus. **a** a sign (♮) denoting a return to natural pitch after a sharp or a flat. **b** a natural note. **c** a white key on a piano. **4 a** Cards a hand making 21 in the first deal in pontoon. **b** a throw of 7 or 11 at craps. **5** a pale fawn colour. □ **natural-born** having a character or position by birth. **natural childbirth** Med. childbirth with minimal medical or technological intervention. **natural classification** a scientific classification according to natural features. **natural death** death by age or disease, not by accident, poison, violence, etc. **natural food** food without preservatives etc. **natural gas** an inflammable mainly methane gas found in the earth's crust, not manufactured. **natural historian** a writer or expert on natural history. **natural history 1** the study of animals or plants esp. as set forth for popular use. **2** an aggregate of the facts concerning the flora and fauna etc. of a particular place or class (*a natural history of the Isle of Wight*). **natural key** (or **scale**) Mus. a key or scale having no sharps or flats, i.e. C major and A minor. **natural language** a language that has developed naturally. **natural law 1** Philos. unchanging moral principles common to all people by virtue of their nature as human beings. **2** a correct statement of an invariable sequence between specified conditions and a specified phenomenon. **3** the laws of nature; regularity in nature (*where they saw chance, we see natural law*). **natural life** the duration of one's life on earth. **natural logarithm** see LOGARITHM. **natural magic** magic involving the supposed invocation of impersonal spirits. **natural note** Mus. a note that is neither sharp nor flat. **natural numbers** the integers 1, 2, 3, etc. **natural philosopher** archaic a physicist. **natural philosophy** archaic physics. **natural religion** a religion based on reason (opp. *revealed religion*); deism. **natural resources** materials or conditions occurring in nature and capable of

economic exploitation. **natural science** the sciences used in the study of the physical world, e.g. physics, chemistry, geology, biology, botany. **natural selection** the Darwinian theory of the survival and propagation of organisms best adapted to their environment. **natural theology** the knowledge of God as gained by the light of natural reason. **natural uranium** unenriched uranium. **natural virtues** Philos. justice, prudence, temperance, fortitude. **natural year** the time taken by one revolution of the earth round the sun, 365 days 5 hours 48 minutes. □□ **naturalness** n. [ME f. OF naturel f. L naturalis (as NATURE)]

naturalism /'nætʃərə,lɪz(ə)m/ n. **1** the theory or practice in art and literature of representing nature, character, etc. realistically and in great detail. **2 a** Philos. a theory of the world that excludes the supernatural or spiritual. **b** any moral or religious system based on this theory. **3** action based on natural instincts. **4** indifference to conventions. [NATURAL, in Philos. after F *naturalisme*]

naturalist /'nætʃərəlɪst/ n. & adj. —n. **1** an expert in natural history. **2** a person who believes in or practises naturalism. —adj. = NATURALISTIC.

naturalistic /,nætʃərə'lɪstɪk/ adj. **1** imitating nature closely; lifelike. **2** of or according to naturalism. **3** of natural history. □□ **naturalistically** adv.

naturalize /'nætʃərə,laɪz/ v. (also -**ise**) **1** tr. admit (a foreigner) to the citizenship of a country. **2** tr. introduce (an animal, plant, etc.) into another region so that it flourishes in the wild. **3** tr. adopt (a foreign word, custom, etc.). **4** intr. become naturalized. **5** tr. Philos. exclude from the miraculous; explain naturalistically. **6** tr. free from conventions; make natural. **7** tr. cause to appear natural. **8** intr. study natural history. □□ **naturalization** /-'zeɪʃ(ə)n/ n. [F *naturaliser* (as NATURAL)]

naturally /'nætʃərəlɪ/ adv. **1** in a natural manner. **2** as a natural result. **3** (qualifying a whole sentence) as might be expected; of course.

nature /'neɪtʃə(r)/ n. **1** a thing's or person's innate or essential qualities or character (*not in their nature to be cruel; is the nature of iron to rust*). **2** (often **Nature**) **a** the physical power causing all the phenomena of the material world (*Nature is the best physician*). **b** these phenomena, including plants, animals, landscape, etc. (*nature gives him comfort*). **3** a kind, sort, or class (*things of this nature*). **4** = human nature. **5 a** a specified element of human character (*the rational nature; our animal nature*). **b** a person of a specified character (*even strong natures quail*). **6 a** an uncultivated or wild area, condition, community, etc. **b** the countryside, esp. when picturesque. **7** inherent impulses determining character or action. **8** heredity as an influence on or determinant of personality (opp. NURTURE). **9** a living thing's vital functions or needs (*such a diet will not support nature*). □ **against nature** unnatural; immoral. **against** (or **contrary to**) **nature** miraculous; miraculously. **back to nature** returning to a pre-civilized or natural state. **by nature** innately. **from nature** Art using natural objects as models. **human nature** general human characteristics, feelings, etc. **in nature 1** actually existing. **2** anywhere; at all. **in** (or **of**) **the nature of** characteristically resembling or belonging to the class of (*the answer was in the nature of an excuse*). **in a state of nature 1** in an uncivilized or uncultivated state. **2** totally naked. **3** in an unregenerate state. **law of nature** = natural law 2. **nature cure** = NATUROPATHY. **nature-printing** a method of producing a print of leaves etc. by pressing them on a prepared plate. **nature reserve** a tract of land managed so as to preserve its flora, fauna, physical features, etc. **nature study** the practical study of plant and animal life etc. as a school subject. **nature trail** a signposted path through the countryside

æ cat ɑ: arm e bed ɜ: her ɪ sit iː see ɒ hot ɔ: saw ʌ run ʊ put uː too ə ago aɪ my

designed to draw attention to natural phenomena. [ME f. OF f. L *natura* f. *nasci nat-* be born]

natured /'neɪtʃəd/ *adj.* (in *comb.*) having a specified disposition (*good-natured*; *ill-natured*).

naturism /'neɪtʃə,rɪz(ə)m/ *n.* **1** nudism. **2** naturalism in regard to religion. **3** the worship of natural objects. □□ **naturist** *n.*

naturopathy /,neɪtʃə'rɒpəθɪ/ *n.* **1** the treatment of disease etc. without drugs, usu. involving diet, exercise, massage, etc. **2** this regimen used preventively. □□ **naturopath** /'neɪtʃərə,pæθ/ *n.* **naturopathic** /,neɪtʃərə'pæθɪk/ *adj.*

naught /nɔːt/ *n. & adj.* —*n.* **1** archaic or literary nothing, nought. **2** *US* = NOUGHT. —*adj.* (usu. *predic.*) archaic or literary worthless; useless. □ **bring to naught** ruin; baffle. **come to naught** be ruined or baffled. **set at naught** disregard; despise. [OE *nāwiht, -wuht* f. *nā* (see NO²) + *wiht* WIGHT]

naughty /'nɔːtɪ/ *adj.* (**naughtier, naughtiest**) **1** (esp. of children) disobedient; badly behaved. **2** *colloq. joc.* indecent. **3** archaic wicked. □□ **naughtily** *adv.* **naughtiness** *n.* [ME f. NAUGHT + -Y¹]

nauplius /'nɔːplɪəs/ *n.* (*pl.* **nauplii** /-plɪ,aɪ/) the first larval stage of some crustaceans. [L, = a kind of shellfish, or f. Gk *Nauplios* son of Poseidon]

nausea /'nɔːzɪə, -sɪə/ *n.* **1** a feeling of sickness with an inclination to vomit. **2** loathing; revulsion. [L f. Gk *nausia* f. *naus* ship]

nauseate /'nɔːzɪ,eɪt, -sɪ,eɪt/ *v.* **1** *tr.* affect with nausea (*was nauseated by the smell*). **2** *intr.* (usu. foll. by *at*) loathe food, an occupation, etc.; feel sick. □□ **nauseating** *adj.* **nauseatingly** *adv.* [L *nauseare* (as NAUSEA)]

nauseous /'nɔːzɪəs, -sɪəs/ *adj.* **1** causing nausea. **2** offensive to the taste or smell. **3** disgusting; loathsome. □□ **nauseously** *adv.* **nauseousness** *n.* [L *nauseosus* (as NAUSEA)]

nautch /nɔːtʃ/ *n.* a performance of professional Indian dancing-girls. □ **nautch-girl** a professional Indian dancing-girl. [Urdu (Hindi) *nāch* f. Prakrit *nachcha* f. Skr. *nritja* dancing]

nautical /'nɔːtɪk(ə)l/ *adj.* of or concerning sailors or navigation; naval; maritime. □ **nautical almanac** a yearbook containing astronomical and tidal information for navigators etc. **nautical mile** a unit of approx. 2,025 yards (1,852 metres): also called *sea mile*. □□ **nautically** *adv.* [F *nautique* or f. L *nauticus* f. Gk *nautikos* f. *nautēs* sailor f. *naus* ship]

nautilus /'nɔːtɪləs/ *n.* (*pl.* **nautiluses** or **nautili** /-,laɪ/) **1** any cephalopod of the genus *Nautilus* with a light brittle spiral shell, esp. (**pearly nautilus**) one having a chambered shell with nacreous septa. **2** (in full **paper nautilus**) any small floating octopus of the genus *Argonauta*, of which the female has a very thin shell and webbed sail-like arms. [L f. Gk *nautilos*, lit. sailor (as NAUTICAL)]

Navajo /'nævə,həʊ/ *n.* (also **Navaho**) (*pl.* **-os**) **1** a member of an American Indian people native to New Mexico and Arizona. **2** the language of this people. [Sp., = pueblo]

naval /'neɪv(ə)l/ *adj.* **1** of, in, for, etc. the navy or a navy. **2** of or concerning ships (*a naval battle*). □ **naval academy** a college for training naval officers. **naval architect** a designer of ships. **naval architecture** the designing of ships. **naval officer** an officer in a navy. **naval stores** all materials used in shipping. □□ **navally** *adv.* [L *navalis* f. *navis* ship]

navarin /'nævə,ræ̃/ *n.* a casserole of mutton or lamb with vegetables. [F]

nave¹ /neɪv/ *n.* the central part of a church, usu. from the west door to the chancel and excluding the side aisles. [med.L *navis* f. L *navis* ship]

nave² /neɪv/ *n.* the hub of a wheel. [OE *nafu, nafa* f. Gmc, rel. to NAVEL]

navel /'neɪv(ə)l/ *n.* **1** a depression in the centre of the belly caused by the detachment of the umbilical cord. **2** a central point. □ **navel orange** a large

seedless orange with a navel-like formation at the top. [OE *nafela* f. Gmc, rel. to NAVE²]

navelwort /'neɪvəl,wɜːt/ *n.* a pennywort.

navicular /nə'vɪkjʊlə(r)/ *adj. & n.* —*adj.* boat-shaped. —*n.* (in full **navicular bone**) a boat-shaped bone in the foot or hand. □ **navicular disease** an inflammatory disease of the navicular bone in horses, causing lameness. [F *naviculaire* or LL *navicularis* f. L *navicula* dimin. of *navis* ship]

navigable /'nævɪgəb(ə)l/ *adj.* **1** (of a river, the sea, etc.) affording a passage for ships. **2** (of a ship etc.) seaworthy (*in navigable condition*). **3** (of a balloon, airship, etc.) steerable. □□ **navigability** /-'bɪlɪtɪ/ *n.* [F *navigable* or L *navigabilis* (as NAVIGATE)]

navigate /'nævɪ,geɪt/ *v.* **1** *tr.* manage or direct the course of (a ship, aircraft, etc.). **2** *tr.* **a** sail on (a sea, river, etc.). **b** travel or fly through (the air). **3** *intr.* (of a passenger in a vehicle) assist the driver by map-reading etc. **4** *intr.* sail a ship; sail in a ship. **5** *tr.* (often *refl.*) *colloq.* steer (oneself, a course, etc.) through a crowd etc. [L *navigare* f. *navis* ship + *agere* drive]

navigation /,nævɪ'geɪʃ(ə)n/ *n.* **1** the act or process of navigating. **2** any of several methods of determining or planning a ship's or aircraft's position and course by geometry, astronomy, etc. **3** a voyage. □ **inland navigation** communication by canals and rivers. **navigation light** a light on a ship or aircraft at night, indicating its position and direction. □□ **navigational** *adj.* [F or f. L *navigatio* (as NAVIGATE)]

navigator /'nævɪ,geɪtə(r)/ *n.* **1** a person skilled or engaged in navigation. **2** an explorer by sea. [L (as NAVIGATE)]

navvy /'nævɪ/ *n. & v. Brit.* —*n.* (*pl.* **-ies**) a labourer employed in building or excavating roads, canals, etc. —*v.intr.* (**-ies, -ied**) work as a navvy. [abbr. of NAVIGATOR]

navy /'neɪvɪ/ *n.* (*pl.* **-ies**) **1** (often **the Navy**) **a** the whole body of a State's ships of war, including crews, maintenance systems, etc. **b** the officers and men of a navy. **2** (in full **navy blue**) a dark-blue colour as used in naval uniform. **3** *poet.* a fleet of ships. □ **Navy Department** *US* the government department in charge of the navy. **Navy List** *Brit.* an official list containing the names of all naval officers etc. **navy yard** *US* a government shipyard with civilian labour. [ME, = fleet f. OF *navie* ship, fleet f. Rmc & pop.L *navia* ship f. L *navis*]

nawab /nə'wɑːb, -'wɔːb/ *n.* **1** the title of a distinguished Muslim in Pakistan. **2** *hist.* the title of a governor or nobleman in India. [Urdu *nawwāb* pl. f. Arab. *nā'ib* deputy: cf. NABOB]

nay /neɪ/ *adv. & n.* —*adv.* **1** or rather; and even; and more than that (*impressive, nay, magnificent*). **2** *archaic* = NO² *adv.* 1. —*n.* **1** the word 'nay'. **2** a negative vote (*counted 16 nays*). [ME f. ON *nei* f. *ne* not + *ei* AYE²]

naysay /'neɪseɪ/ *v.* (*3rd sing. present* **-says**; *past* and *past part.* **-said**) esp. *US* **1** *intr.* utter a denial or refusal. **2** *tr.* refuse or contradict. □□ **naysayer** *n.*

Nazarene /,næzə'riːn, 'næ-/ *n. & adj.* —*n.* **1 a** (prec. by *the*) Christ. **b** (esp. in Jewish or Muslim use) a Christian. **2** a native or inhabitant of Nazareth. **3** a member of an early Jewish-Christian sect. —*adj.* of or concerning Nazareth, the Nazarenes, etc. [ME f. LL *Nazarenus* f. Gk *Nazarēnos* f. *Nazaret* Nazareth]

Nazarite /'næzə,raɪt/ *n.* (also **Nazirite**) *hist.* a Hebrew who had taken certain vows of abstinence; an ascetic (Num. 6). [LL *Nazaraeus* f. Heb. *nāzîr* f. *nāzar* to separate or consecrate oneself]

Nazi /'nɑːtsɪ, 'nɑːzɪ/ *n. & adj.* —*n.* (*pl.* **Nazis**) **1** *hist.* a member of the German National Socialist party. **2** *derog.* a person holding extreme racist or authoritarian views or behaving brutally. **3** a person belonging to any organization similar to the Nazis. —*adj.* of or concerning the Nazis, Nazism, etc. □□ **Nazidom** *n.* **Nazify** /-,faɪ/ *v.tr.* (**-ies, -ied**). **Naziism**

/-iː,ɪz(ə)m/ *n.* **Nazism** /ˈnɑːtsɪz(ə)m/ *n.* [repr. pronunc. of *Nati-* in G *Nationalsozialist*]

Nazirite var. of NAZARITE.

NB *abbr.* **1** *US* Nebraska (in official postal use). **2** New Brunswick. **3** no ball. **4** Scotland (North Britain). **5** *nota bene.*

Nb *symb. Chem.* the element niobium.

NBC *abbr.* (in the US) National Broadcasting Company.

N. by E. *abbr.* North by East.

N. by W. *abbr.* North by West.

NC *abbr.* North Carolina (also in official postal use).

NCB *abbr. hist.* (in the UK) National Coal Board. ¶ Since 1987 officially called *British Coal.*

NCO *abbr.* non-commissioned officer.

NCU *abbr.* (in the UK) National Communications Union.

ND *abbr. US* North Dakota (in official postal use).

Nd *symb. Chem.* the element neodymium.

n.d. *abbr.* no date.

-nd[1] *suffix* forming nouns (*fiend*; *friend*). [OE *-ond*, orig. part. ending]

-nd[2] *suffix* see -AND, -END.

N.Dak. *abbr.* North Dakota.

NE *abbr.* **1** north-east. **2** north-eastern.

Ne *symb. Chem.* the element neon.

né /neɪ/ *adj.* born (indicating a man's previous name) (*Lord Beaconsfield, né Benjamin Disraeli*). [F, past part. of *naître* be born: cf. NÉE]

Neanderthal /nɪˈændə,tɑːl/ *adj.* of or belonging to the type of human widely distributed in palaeolithic Europe, with a retreating forehead and massive brow-ridges. [*Neanderthal*, a region in W. Germany where remains were found]

neap /niːp/ *n. & v.* —*n.* (in full **neap tide**) a tide just after the first and third quarters of the moon when there is least difference between high and low water. —*v.* **1** *intr.* (of a tide) tend towards or reach the highest point of a neap tide. **2** *tr.* (in *passive*) (of a ship) be kept aground, in harbour, etc., by a neap tide. [OE *nēpflōd* (cf. FLOOD), of unkn. orig.]

Neapolitan /nɪəˈpɒlɪt(ə)n/ *n. & adj.* —*n.* a native or citizen of Naples in Italy. —*adj.* of or relating to Naples. □**Neapolitan ice-cream** ice-cream made in layers of different colours. **Neapolitan violet** a sweet-scented double viola. [ME f. L *Neapolitanus* f. L *Neapolis* Naples f. Gk f. *neos* new + *polis* city]

near /nɪə(r)/ *adv., prep., adj., & v.* —*adv.* **1** (often foll. by *to*) to or at a short distance in space or time; close by (*the time drew near; dropped near to them*). **2** closely (*as near as one can guess*). **3** *archaic* almost, nearly (*very near died*). **4** *archaic* parsimoniously; meanly (*lives very near*). —*prep.* (compar. & superl. also used) **1** to or at a short distance (in space, time, condition, or resemblance) from (*stood near the back; occurs nearer the end; the sun is near setting*). **2** (in *comb.*) **a** that is almost (*near-hysterical; a near-Communist*). **b** intended as a substitute for; resembling (*near-beer*). —*adj.* **1** (usu. *predic.*) close at hand; close to, in place or time (*the man nearest you; in the near future*). **2 a** closely related (*a near relation*). **b** intimate (*a near friend*). **3** (of a part of a vehicle, animal, or road) left (*the near fore leg; near side front wheel* (orig. of the side from which one mounted)) (opp. OFF). **4** close; narrow (*a near escape; a near guess*). **5** (of a road or way) direct. **6** niggardly, mean. —*v.* **1** *tr.* approach; draw near to (*neared the harbour*). **2** *intr.* draw near (*could distinguish them as they neared*). □**come** (or **go**) **near** (foll. by verbal noun, or *to* + verbal noun) be on the point of, almost succeed in (*came near to falling*). **go near** (foll. by *to* + infin.) narrowly fail. **near at hand 1** within easy reach. **2** in the immediate future. **the Near East** the region comprising the countries of the eastern Mediterranean. **Near Eastern** of the Near East. **near go** *colloq.* a narrow escape. **near the knuckle** *colloq.* verging on the indecent. **near miss 1** (of a bomb etc.) close to the target. **2** a situation in which

a collision is narrowly avoided. **3** (of an attempt) almost but not quite successful. **near sight** esp. *US* = *short sight.* **near thing** a narrow escape. **near upon** *archaic* not far in time from. □□ **nearish** *adj.* **nearness** *n.* [ME f. ON *nær*, orig. compar. of *ná* = OE *nēah* NIGH]

nearby *adj. & adv.* —*adj.* /ˈnɪəbaɪ/ situated in a near position (*a nearby hotel*). —*adv.* /nɪəˈbaɪ/ close; not far away.

Nearctic /nɪˈɑːktɪk/ *adj.* of or relating to the Arctic and the temperate parts of N. America as a zoogeographical region. [NEO- + ARCTIC]

nearly /ˈnɪəlɪ/ *adv.* **1** almost (*we are nearly there*). **2** closely (*they are nearly related*). □**not nearly** nothing like; far from (*not nearly enough*).

nearside /ˈnɪəsaɪd/ *n.* (often *attrib.*) esp. *Brit.* the left side of a vehicle, animal, etc. (cf. OFFSIDE *n.*).

near-sighted /nɪəˈsaɪtɪd/ *n.* esp. *US* = SHORT-SIGHTED. □□ **near-sightedly** *adv.* **near-sightedness** *n.*

neat[1] /niːt/ *adj.* **1** tidy and methodical. **2** elegantly simple in form etc.; well-proportioned. **3** (of language, style, etc.) brief, clear, and pointed; epigrammatic. **4 a** cleverly executed (*a neat piece of work*). **b** deft; dextrous. **5** (of esp. alcoholic liquor) undiluted. **6** *US sl.* (as a general term of approval) good, pleasing, excellent. □□ **neatly** *adv.* **neatness** *n.* [F *net* f. L *nitidus* shining f. *nitēre* shine]

neat[2] /niːt/ *n. archaic* **1** a bovine animal. **2** (as *pl.*) cattle. □**neat's-foot oil** oil made from boiled cow-heel and used to dress leather. [OE *nēat* f. Gmc]

neaten /ˈniːt(ə)n/ *v.tr.* make neat.

neath /niːθ/ *prep. poet.* beneath. [BENEATH]

NEB *abbr.* **1** (in the UK) National Enterprise Board. **2** New English Bible.

Neb. *abbr.* Nebraska.

neb /neb/ *n. Sc. & N.Engl.* **1** a beak or bill. **2** a nose; a snout. **3** a tip, spout, or point. [OE *nebb* ult. f. Gmc: cf. NIB]

nebbish /ˈnebɪʃ/ *n. & adj. colloq.* —*n.* a submissive or timid person. —*adj.* submissive; timid. [Yiddish *nebach* poor thing!]

Nebr. *abbr.* Nebraska.

Nebuchadnezzar /,nebjuːkədˈnezə(r)/ *n.* a wine bottle of about 20 times the standard size. [name of a king of Babylon (6th c. BC)]

nebula /ˈnebjʊlə/ *n.* (*pl.* **nebulae** /-,liː/ or **nebulas**) **1** *Astron.* **a** a cloud of gas and dust, sometimes glowing and sometimes appearing as a dark silhouette against other glowing matter. **b** a bright area caused by a galaxy, or a large cloud of distant stars. **2** *Med.* a clouded spot on the cornea causing defective vision. [L, = mist]

nebular /ˈnebjʊlə(r)/ *adj.* of or relating to a nebula or nebulae. □**nebular theory** (or **hypothesis**) the theory that the solar and stellar systems were developed from a primeval nebula.

nebulous /ˈnebjʊləs/ *adj.* **1** cloudlike. **2 a** formless, clouded. **b** hazy, indistinct, vague (*put forward a few nebulous ideas*). **3** *Astron.* of or like a nebula or nebulae. □**nebulous star** a small cluster of indistinct stars, or a star in a luminous haze. □□ **nebulosity** /-ˈlɒsɪtɪ/ *n.* **nebulously** *adv.* **nebulousness** *n.* [ME f. F *nébuleux* or L *nebulosus* (as NEBULA)]

nebuly /ˈnebjʊlɪ/ *adj. Heraldry* wavy in form; cloudlike. [F *nébulé* f. med.L *nebulatus* f. L NEBULA]

necessarian /,nesɪˈseərɪən/ *n. & adj.* = NECESSITARIAN. □□ **necessarianism** *n.*

necessarily /ˈnesəsərɪlɪ, -ˈserɪlɪ/ *adv.* as a necessary result; inevitably.

necessary /ˈnesəsərɪ/ *adj. & n.* —*adj.* **1** requiring to be done, achieved, etc.; requisite, essential (*it is necessary to work; lacks the necessary documents*). **2** determined, existing, or happening by natural laws, predestination, etc., not by free will; inevitable (*a necessary evil*). **3** *Philos.* (of a concept or a mental process) inevitably resulting from or produced by the nature of things etc., so that the contrary is impossible. **4** *Philos.* (of an agent) having no independent volition. —*n.* (*pl.* **-ies**) (usu. in *pl.*) any of the basic requirements of life, such as food, warmth, etc. □**the necessary** *colloq.* **1** money. **2** an action, item, etc., needed for a purpose (*they will do the necessary*). [ME f. OF *necessaire* f. L *necessarius* f. *necesse* needful]

necessitarian /nɪˌsesɪˈteərɪən/ *n. & adj. Philos.* —*n.* a person who holds that all action is predetermined and free will is impossible. —*adj.* of or concerning such a person or theory (opp. LIBERTARIAN). □□ **necessitarianism** *n.*

necessitate /nɪˈsesɪˌteɪt/ *v.tr.* **1** make necessary (esp. as a result) (*will necessitate some sacrifice*). **2** *US* (usu. foll. by *to* + infin.) force or compel (a person) to do something. [med.L *necessitare* compel (as NECESSITY)]

necessitous /nɪˈsesɪtəs/ *adj.* poor; needy. [F *nécessiteux* or f. NECESSITY + -OUS]

necessity /nɪˈsesɪtɪ/ *n.* (*pl.* **-ies**) **1 a** an indispensible thing; a necessary (*central heating is a necessity*). **b** (usu. foll. by *of*) indispensability (*the necessity of a warm overcoat*). **2** a state of things or circumstances enforcing a certain course (*there was a necessity to hurry*). **3** imperative need (*necessity is the mother of invention*). **4** want; poverty; hardship (*stole because of necessity*). **5** constraint or compulsion regarded as a natural law governing all human action. □**of necessity** unavoidably. [ME f. OF *necessité* f. L *necessitas -tatis* f. *necesse* needful]

neck /nek/ *n. & v.* —*n.* **1 a** the part of the body connecting the head to the shoulders. **b** the part of a shirt, dress, etc. round or close to the neck. **2 a** something resembling a neck, such as the narrow part of a cavity or vessel, a passage, channel, pass, isthmus, etc. **b** the narrow part of a bottle near the mouth. **3** the part of a violin etc. bearing the finger-board. **4** the length of a horse's head and neck as a measure of its lead in a race. **5** the flesh of an animal's neck (*neck of lamb*). **6** *Geol.* solidified lava or igneous rock in an old volcano crater or pipe. **7** *Archit.* the lower part of a capital. **8** *sl.* impudence (*you've got a neck, asking that*). —*v.* **1** *intr. & tr. colloq.* kiss and caress amorously. **2 a** *tr.* form a narrowed part in. **b** *intr.* form a narrowed part. □**get it in the neck** *colloq.* **1** receive a severe reprimand or punishment. **2** suffer a fatal or severe blow. **neck and neck** running level in a race etc. **neck of the woods** *colloq.* a usu. remote locality. **neck or nothing** risking everything on success. **up to one's neck** (often foll. by *in*) *colloq.* very deeply involved; very busy. □□ **necked** *adj.* (also in *comb.*). **necker** *n.* (in sense 1 of *v.*). **neckless** *adj.* [OE *hnecca* ult. f. Gmc]

neckband /ˈnekbænd/ *n.* a strip of material round the neck of a garment.

neckcloth /ˈnekklɒθ/ *n. hist.* a cravat.

neckerchief /ˈnekətʃɪf/ *n.* a square of cloth worn round the neck.

necking /ˈnekɪŋ/ *n. Archit.* = NECK *n.* 7.

necklace /ˈnekləs, -lɪs/ *n. & v.* —*n.* **1** a chain or string of beads, precious stones, links, etc., worn as an ornament round the neck. **2** *S.Afr.* a tyre soaked or filled with petrol, placed round a victim's neck, and set alight. —*v.tr. S.Afr.* kill with a 'necklace'.

necklet /ˈneklɪt/ *n.* **1** = NECKLACE *n.* 1. **2** a strip of fur worn round the neck.

neckline /ˈneklaɪn/ *n.* the edge or shape of the opening of a garment at the neck (*a square neckline*).

necktie /ˈnektaɪ/ *n.* esp. *US* = TIE *n.* 2. □**necktie party** *sl.* a lynching or hanging.

neckwear /ˈnekweə(r)/ *n.* collars, ties, etc.

necro- /ˈnekrəʊ/ *comb. form* corpse. [from or after Gk *nekro-* f. *nekros* corpse]

necrobiosis /ˌnekrəʊbaɪˈəʊsɪs/ *n.* decay in the tissues of the body, esp. swelling of the collagen bundles in the dermis. □□ **necrobiotic** /-ˈɒtɪk/ *adj.*

necrolatry /neˈkrɒlətrɪ/ *n.* worship of, or excessive reverence towards, the dead.

necrology /neˈkrɒlədʒɪ/ *n.* (*pl.* **-ies**) **1** a list of recently dead people. **2** an obituary notice. □□ **necrological** /-rəˈlɒdʒɪk(ə)l/ *adj.*

necromancy /ˈnekrəʊˌmænsɪ/ *n.* **1** the prediction of the future by the supposed communication with the dead. **2** witchcraft. □□ **necromancer** *n.* **necromantic** /-ˈmæntɪk/ *adj.* [ME f. OF *nigromancie* f. med.L *nigromantia* changed (by assoc. with L *niger nigri* black) f. LL *necromantia* f. Gk *nekromanteia* (as NECRO-, -MANCY)]

necrophilia /ˌnekrəˈfɪlɪə/ *n.* (also **necrophily** /nɪˈkrɒfɪlɪ/) a morbid and esp. erotic attraction to corpses. □□ **necrophil** /ˈnek-/ *n.* **necrophile** /ˈnekrəˌfaɪl/ *n.* **necrophiliac** /-ˈfɪlɪˌæk/ *n.* **necrophilic** *adj.* **necrophilism** /-ˈkrɒfɪˌlɪz(ə)m/ *n.* **necrophilist** /-ˈkrɒfɪlɪst/ *n.* [NECRO- + Gk *-philia* loving]

necrophobia /ˌnekrəˈfəʊbɪə/ *n.* an abnormal fear of death or dead bodies.

necropolis /neˈkrɒpəlɪs/ *n.* an ancient cemetery or burial place.

necropsy /ˈnekrɒpsɪ/ *n.* (also **necroscopy** /-ˈkrɒskəpɪ/) (*pl.* **-ies**) = AUTOPSY 1. [NECRO- after AUTOPSY, or + -SCOPY]

necrosis /neˈkrəʊsɪs/ *n. Med. & Physiol.* the death of tissue caused by disease or injury, esp. as one of the symptoms of gangrene or pulmonary tuberculosis. □□ **necrose** /-ˈkrəʊs/ *v.intr.* **necrotic** /-ˈkrɒtɪk/ *adj.* **necrotize** /ˈnekrəˌtaɪz/ *v.intr.* (also **-ise**). [mod.L f. Gk *nekrōsis* (as NECRO-, -OSIS)]

nectar /ˈnektə(r)/ *n.* **1** a sugary substance produced by plants and made into honey by bees. **2** (in Greek and Roman mythology) the drink of the gods. **3** a drink compared to this. □□ **nectarean** /-ˈteərɪən/ *adj.* **nectareous** /-ˈteərɪəs/ *adj.* **nectariferous** /-ˈrɪfərəs/ *adj.* **nectarous** *adj.* [L f. Gk *nektar*]

nectarine /ˈnektərɪn, -ˌriːn/ *n.* **1** a variety of peach with a thin brightly-coloured smooth skin and firm flesh. **2** the tree bearing this. [orig. as adj., = nectar-like, f. NECTAR + -INE[4]]

nectary /ˈnektərɪ/ *n.* (*pl.* **-ies**) the nectar-secreting organ of a flower or plant. [mod.L *nectarium* (as NECTAR)]

NEDC *abbr.* (in the UK) National Economic Development Council.

neddy /ˈnedɪ/ *n.* (*pl.* **-ies**) *colloq.* **1** a donkey. **2** (**Neddy**) = NEDC. [dimin. of *Ned*, pet-form of the name *Edward*]

née /neɪ/ *adj.* (*US* **nee**) (used in adding a married woman's maiden name after her surname) born (*Mrs Ann Smith, née Jones*). [F, fem. past part. of *naitre* be born]

need /niːd/ *v. & n.* —*v.* **1** *tr.* stand in want of; require (*needs a new coat*). **2** *tr.* (foll. by *to* + infin.; *3rd sing. present neg. or interrog.* **need** without *to*) be under the necessity or obligation (*it needs to be done carefully; he need not come; need you ask?*). **3** *intr. archaic* be necessary. —*n.* **1 a** a want or requirement (*my needs are few; the need for greater freedom*). **b** a thing wanted (*my greatest need is a car*). **2** circumstances requiring some course of action; necessity (*there is no need to worry; if need arise*). **3** destitution; poverty. **4** a crisis; an emergency (*failed them in their need*). □**at need** in time of need. **had need** *archaic* ought to (*had need remember*). **have need of** require; want. **have need to** require to (*has need to be warned*). **in need** requiring help. **in need of** requiring. **need not have** did not need to (but did). [OE *nēodian*, *nēd* f. Gmc]

needful /ˈniːdfʊl/ *adj.* **1** requisite; necessary; indispensable. **2** (prec. by *the*) **a** what is necessary. **b** *colloq.* money or action needed for a purpose. □□ **needfully** *adv.* **needfulness** *n.*

needle /ˈniːd(ə)l/ *n. & v.* —*n.* **1 a** a very thin small piece of smooth steel etc. pointed at one end and with a slit (eye) for thread at the other, used in sewing. **b** a larger plastic, wooden, etc. slender stick without an eye, used in knitting. **c** a slender hooked stick used in crochet. **2** a pointer on a dial (see *magnetic needle*). **3** any of several small thin pointed instruments, esp.: **a** a surgical instrument for stitching. **b** the end of a hypodermic syringe. **c** = STYLUS. **d** an etching tool. **e** a steel pin exploding the cartridge of a breech-loading gun. **4 a** an obelisk (*Cleopatra's Needle*). **b** a pointed rock or peak. **5** the leaf of a fir or pine tree. **6** a beam used as a temporary support during underpinning. **7** *Brit. sl.* a fit of bad temper or nervousness (*got the needle while waiting*). —*v.tr.* **1** *colloq.* incite or irritate; provoke (*the silence needled him*). **2** sew, pierce, or operate on with a needle. □**needle game** (or **match** etc.) *Brit.* a contest that is very close or arouses personal grudges. **needle in a haystack** something almost impossible to find because it is concealed by so many other things etc. **needle-lace** lace made with needles not bobbins. **needle-point 1** a very sharp point. **2** = *needle-lace*. **3** = GROS or PETIT POINT. **needle's eye** (or **eye of a needle**) the least possible aperture, esp. with ref. to Matt. 19:24. **needle time** an agreed maximum allowance of time for broadcasting music from records. **needle valve** a valve closed by a thin tapering part. [OE *nǣdl* f. Gmc]

needlecord /ˈniːd(ə)lˌkɔːd/ *n.* a fine-ribbed corduroy fabric.

needlecraft /ˈniːd(ə)lˌkrɑːft/ *n.* skill in needlework.

needlefish /ˈniːd(ə)lfɪʃ/ *n.* a garfish.

needleful /ˈniːd(ə)lˌfʊl/ *n.* (*pl.* **-fuls**) the length of thread etc. put into a needle at one time.

needless /ˈniːdlɪs/ *adj.* **1** unnecessary. **2** uncalled for; gratuitous. □**needless to say** of course; it goes without saying. □□**needlessly** *adv.* **needlessness** *n.*

needlewoman /ˈniːd(ə)lˌwʊmən/ *n.* (*pl.* **-women**) **1** a seamstress. **2** a woman or girl with specified sewing skill (*a good needlewoman*).

needlework /ˈniːd(ə)lˌwɜːk/ *n.* sewing or embroidery.

needs /niːdz/ *adv. archaic* (usu. prec. or foll. by *must*) of necessity (*must needs decide*). [OE *nēdes* (as NEED, -s³)]

needy /ˈniːdɪ/ *adj.* (**needier**, **neediest**) **1** (of a person) poor; destitute. **2** (of circumstances) characterized by poverty. □□**neediness** *n.*

neep /niːp/ *n. Sc.* & *N.Engl.* a turnip. [OE *nǣp* f. L *napus*]

ne'er /neə(r)/ *adv. poet.* = NEVER. □**ne'er-do-well** *n.* a good-for-nothing person. —*adj.* good-for-nothing. [ME contr. of NEVER]

nefarious /nɪˈfeərɪəs/ *adj.* wicked; iniquitous. □□ **nefariously** *adv.* **nefariousness** *n.* [L *nefarius* f. *nefas* wrong f. *ne-* not + *fas* divine law]

neg. *abbr.* negative.

negate /nɪˈɡeɪt/ *v.tr.* **1** nullify; invalidate. **2** imply, involve, or assert the non-existence of. **3** be the negation of. □□**negator** *n.* [L *negare negat-* deny]

negation /nɪˈɡeɪʃ(ə)n/ *n.* **1** the absence or opposite of something actual or positive. **2 a** the act of denying. **b** an instance of this. **3** (usu. foll. by *of*) a refusal, contradiction, or denial. **4** a negative statement or doctrine. **5** a negative or unreal thing; a nonentity. **6** *Logic* the assertion that a certain proposition is false. □□**negatory** /ˈneɡətərɪ/ *adj.* [F *negation* or L *negatio* (as NEGATE)]

negative /ˈneɡətɪv/ *adj., n.* & *v.* —*adj.* **1** expressing or implying denial, prohibition, or refusal (*a negative vote; a negative answer*). **2** (of a person or attitude): **a** lacking positive attributes; apathetic; pessimistic. **b** opposing or resisting; uncooperative. **3** marked by the absence of qualities (*a negative reaction; a negative result from the test*). **4** of the opposite nature to a thing regarded as positive (*debt is negative capital*). **5** *Algebra* (of a quantity) less than zero, to be subtracted from others or from zero (opp. POSITIVE). **6** *Electr.* **a** of the kind of charge carried by electrons (opp. POSITIVE). **b** containing or producing such a

charge. —*n.* **1** a negative statement, reply, or word (*hard to prove a negative*). **2** *Photog.* **a** an image with black and white reversed or colours replaced by complementary ones, from which positive pictures are obtained. **b** a developed film or plate bearing such an image. **3** a negative quality; an absence of something. **4** (prec. by *the*) a position opposing the affirmative. **5** *Logic* = NEGATION 6. —*v.tr.* **1** refuse to accept or countenance; veto; reject. **2** disprove (an inference or hypothesis). **3** contradict (a statement). **4** neutralize (an effect). □**in the negative** with negative effect; so as to reject a proposal etc.; no (*the answer was in the negative*). **negative evidence** (or **instance**) evidence of the non-occurrence of something. **negative feedback 1** the return of part of an output signal to the input, tending to decrease the amplification etc. **2** feedback that tends to diminish or counteract the process giving rise to it. **negative geotropism** see GEOTROPISM. **negative income tax** an amount credited as allowance to a taxed income, and paid as benefit when it exceeds debited tax. **negative pole** the south-seeking pole of a magnet. **negative proposition** *Logic* = NEGATION 6. **negative quantity** *joc.* nothing. **negative sign** a symbol (−) indicating subtraction or a value less than zero. **negative virtue** abstention from vice. □□**negatively** *adv.* **negativeness** *n.* **negativity** /-ˈtɪvɪtɪ/ *n.* [ME f. OF *negatif -ive* or LL *negativus* (as NEGATE)]

negativism /ˈneɡətɪˌvɪz(ə)m/ *n.* **1** a negative position or attitude; extreme scepticism, criticism, etc. **2** denial of accepted beliefs. □□**negativist** *n.* **negativistic** /-ˈvɪstɪk/ *adj.*

neglect /nɪˈɡlekt/ *v.* & *n.* —*v.tr.* **1** fail to care for or to do; be remiss about (*neglected their duty; neglected his children*). **2** (foll. by verbal noun, or *to* + infin.) fail; overlook or forget the need to (*neglected to inform them; neglected telling them*). **3** not pay attention to; disregard (*neglected the obvious warning*). —*n.* **1** lack of caring; negligence (*the house suffered from neglect*). **2 a** the act of neglecting. **b** the state of being neglected (*the house fell into neglect*). **3** (usu. foll. by *of*) disregard. □□**neglectful** *adj.* **neglectfully** *adv.* **neglectfulness** *n.* [L *neglegere neglect-* f. *neg-* not + *legere* choose, pick up]

negligee /ˈneɡlɪˌʒeɪ/ *n.* (also **negligee**, **négligé**) **1** (usu. **negligee**) a woman's dressing-gown of thin fabric. **2** unceremonious or informal attire. [F, past part. of *négliger* NEGLECT]

negligence /ˈneɡlɪdʒ(ə)ns/ *n.* **1 a** a lack of proper care and attention; carelessness. **b** an act of carelessness. **2** *Law* = contributory negligence. **3** *Art* freedom from restraint or artificiality. □□**negligent** *adj.* **negligently** *adv.* [ME f. OF *negligence* or L *negligentia* f. *negligere* = *neglegere*: see NEGLECT]

negligible /ˈneɡlɪdʒɪb(ə)l/ *adj.* not worth considering; insignificant. □**negligible quantity** a person etc. that need not be considered. □□**negligibility** /-ˈbɪlɪtɪ/ *n.* **negligibly** *adv.* [obs. F f. *négliger* NEGLECT]

negotiable /nɪˈɡəʊʃəb(ə)l/ *adj.* **1** open to discussion or modification. **2** able to be negotiated. □□ **negotiability** /-ˈbɪlɪtɪ/ *n.*

negotiate /nɪˈɡəʊʃɪˌeɪt/ *v.* **1** intr. (usu. foll. by *with*) confer with others in order to reach a compromise or agreement. **2** tr. arrange (an affair) or bring about (a result) by negotiating (*negotiated a settlement*). **3** tr. find a way over, through, etc. (an obstacle, difficulty, fence, etc.). **4** tr. **a** transfer (a cheque etc.) to another for a consideration. **b** convert (a cheque etc.) into cash or notes. **c** get or give value for (a cheque etc.) in money. □□**negotiant** /-ʃɪənt/ *n.* **negotiation** /-ʃɪˈeɪʃ(ə)n, -sɪˈeɪʃ(ə)n/ *n.* **negotiator** *n.* [L *negotiari* f. *negotium* business f. *neg-* not + *otium* leisure]

Negress /ˈniːɡrɪs/ *n.* a female Negro.

Negrillo /nɪˈɡrɪləʊ/ *n.* (*pl.* **-os**) a member of a very small Negroid people native to Central and S. Africa. [Sp., dimin. of NEGRO]

Negrito /nɪˈgriːtəʊ/ n. (pl. -os) a member of a small Negroid people native to the Malayo-Polynesian region. [as NEGRILLO]

Negritude /ˈniːgrɪˌtjuːd/ n. 1 the quality or state of being a Negro. 2 the affirmation or consciousness of the value of Negro culture. [F négritude NIGRITUDE]

Negro /ˈniːgrəʊ/ n. & adj. —n. (pl. -oes) a member of a dark-skinned race orig. native to Africa. ¶ Now often considered offens.; the term Black is usually preferred. —adj. 1 of or concerning Negroes. 2 (as **negro**) Zool. black or dark (negro ant). □**Negro spiritual** a religious song derived from the musical traditions of Black people in the southern US. [Sp. & Port., f. L niger nigri black]

Negroid /ˈniːgrɔɪd/ adj. & n. —adj. 1 (of features etc.) characterizing a member of the Negro race, esp. in having dark skin, tightly curled hair, and a broad flattish nose. 2 of or concerning Negroes. —n. a Negro. [NEGRO]

Negus /ˈniːgəs/ n. hist. the title of the ruler of Ethiopia. [Amh. n'gus king]

negus /ˈniːgəs/ n. hist. a hot drink of port, sugar, lemon, and spice. [Col. F. Negus d. 1732, its inventor]

Neh. abbr. Nehemiah (Old Testament).

neigh /neɪ/ n. & v. —n. 1 the high whinnying sound of a horse. 2 any similar sound, e.g. a laugh. —v. 1 intr. make such a sound. 2 tr. say, cry, etc. with such a sound. [OE hnægan, of imit. orig.]

neighbour /ˈneɪbə(r)/ n. & v. (US neighbor) —n. 1 a person living next door to or near or nearest another (my next-door neighbour; his nearest neighbour is 12 miles away; they are neighbours). 2 a a person regarded as having the duties or claims of friendliness, consideration, etc., of a neighbour. b a fellow human being, esp. as having claims on friendship. 3 a person or thing near or next to another (my neighbour at dinner). 4 (attrib.) neighbouring. —v. 1 tr. border on; adjoin. 2 intr. (often foll. by on, upon) border; adjoin. □□ **neighbouring** adj. **neighbourless** adj. **neighbourship** n. [OE nēahgebūr (as NIGH: gebūr, cf. BOOR)]

neighbourhood /ˈneɪbəˌhʊd/ n. (US **neighborhood**) 1 a a district, esp. one forming a community within a town or city. b the people of a district; one's neighbours. 2 neighbourly feeling or conduct. □**in the neighbourhood of** roughly; about (paid in the neighbourhood of £100). **neighbourhood watch** systematic local vigilance by householders to discourage crime, esp. against property.

neighbourly /ˈneɪbəlɪ/ adj. (US **neighborly**) characteristic of a good neighbour; friendly; kind. □□ **neighbourliness** (n).

neither /ˈnaɪðə(r), ˈniːð-/ adj., pron., adv., & conj. —adj. & pron. (foll. by sing. verb) 1 not the one nor the other (of two things); not either (neither of the accusations is true; neither of them knows; neither wish was granted; neither went to the fair). 2 disp. none of any number of specified things. —adv. 1 not either; not on the one hand (foll. by nor; introducing the first of two or more things in the negative: neither knowing nor caring; would neither come in nor go out; neither the teachers nor the parents nor the children). 2 not either; also not (if you do not, neither shall I). 3 (with neg.) disp. either (I don't know that neither). —conj. archaic nor yet; nor (I know not, neither can I guess). [ME naither, neither f. OE nowther contr. of nōhwæther (as NO², WHETHER): assim. to EITHER]

nek /nek/ n. S.Afr. = COL 1. [Du., = NECK]

nekton /ˈnektən/ n. Zool. any aquatic animal able to swim and move independently. [G f. Gk nēkton neut. of nēktos swimming f. nēkhō swim]

nelly /ˈnelɪ/ n. (pl. -ies) a silly or effeminate person. □**not on your nelly** Brit. sl. certainly not. [perh. f. the name Nelly: idiom f. rhyming sl. Nelly Duff = puff = breath: cf. not on your life]

nelson /ˈnels(ə)n/ n. a wrestling-hold in which one arm is passed under the opponent's arm from behind and the hand is applied to the neck (half nelson), or both arms and hands are applied (full nelson). [app. f. the name Nelson]

nelumbo /nɪˈlʌmbəʊ/ n. (pl. -os) any water lily of the genus Nelumbo, native to India and China, bearing small pink flowers. Also called LOTUS. [mod.L f. Sinh. neḷum(bu)]

nematocyst /nɪˈmætəsɪst, ˈnemə-/ n. a specialized cell in a jellyfish etc. containing a coiled thread that can be projected as a sting. [as NEMATODE + CYST]

nematode /ˈnemətəʊd/ n. any parasitic or free-living worm of the phylum Nematoda, with a slender unsegmented cylindrical shape. Also called ROUNDWORM. [Gk nēma -matos thread + -ODE¹]

Nembutal /ˈnembjuˌtɑːl/ n. propr. a sodium salt of pentobarbitone, used as a sedative and anticonvulsant. [Na (= sodium) + 5-ethyl-5-(1-methylbutyl) barbiturate + -AL]

nem. con. abbr. with no one dissenting. [L nemine contradicente]

nemertean /nɪˈmɜːtɪən/ n. & adj. (also **nemertine** /-taɪn/) —n. any marine ribbon worm of the phylum Nemertea, often very long and brightly coloured, found in tangled knots in coastal waters of Europe and the Mediterranean. —adj. of or relating to this class. [mod.L Nemertes f. Gk Nēmertēs name of a sea nymph]

nemesia /nɪˈmiːzə/ n. any S. African plant of the genus Nemesia, cultivated for its variously coloured and irregular flowers. [mod.L f. Gk nemesion, the name of a similar plant]

nemesis /ˈnemɪsɪs/ n. (pl. **nemeses** /-ˌsiːz/) 1 retributive justice. 2 a a downfall caused by this. b an agent of such a downfall. [Gk, = righteous indignation, personified as goddess of retribution f. nemō give what is due]

neo- /ˈniːəʊ/ comb. form 1 new, modern. 2 a new or revived form of. [Gk f. neos new]

neoclassical /ˌniːəʊˈklæsɪk(ə)l/ adj. (also **neoclassic** /-sɪk/) of or relating to a revival of a classical style or treatment in art, literature, music, etc. □□ **neoclassicism** /-ˌsɪz(ə)m/ n. **neoclassicist** /-sɪst/ n.

neocolonialism /ˌniːəʊkəˈləʊnɪəˌlɪz(ə)m/ n. the use of economic, political, or other pressures to control or influence other countries, esp. former dependencies. □□ **neocolonialist** n. & adj.

neodymium /ˌniːəˈdɪmɪəm/ n. Chem. a silver-grey naturally-occurring metallic element of the lanthanide series used in colouring glass etc. ¶ Symb.: Nd. [NEO- + DIDYMIUM]

neolithic /ˌniːəˈlɪθɪk/ adj. of or relating to the later Stone Age, when ground or polished stone weapons and implements prevailed. [NEO- + Gk lithos stone]

neologism /niːˈɒlədʒˌɪz(ə)m/ n. 1 a new word or expression. 2 the coining or use of new words. □□ **neologist** n. **neologize** /-ˌdʒaɪz/ v.intr. (also -ise). [F néologisme (as NEO-, -LOGY, -ISM)]

neomycin /ˌniːəʊˈmaɪsɪn/ n. an antibiotic related to streptomycin.

neon /ˈniːɒn/ n. Chem. an inert gaseous element occurring in traces in the atmosphere and giving an orange glow when electricity is passed through it in a sealed low-pressure tube, used in lights and illuminated advertisements (neon light; neon sign). ¶ Symb.: Ne. [Gk, neut. of neos new]

neonate /ˈniːəˌneɪt/ n. a newborn child. □□ **neonatal** /-ˈneɪt(ə)l/ adj. [mod.L neonatus (as NEO-, L nasci natus be born)]

neophyte /ˈniːəˌfaɪt/ n. 1 a new convert, esp. to a religious faith. 2 RC Ch. a a novice of a religious order. b a newly ordained priest. 3 a beginner; a novice. [eccl.L neophytus f. NT Gk neophutos newly planted (as NEO- phuton plant)]

neoplasm /ˈniːəʊˌplæz(ə)m/ n. a new and abnormal growth of tissue in some part of the body, esp. a tumour. □□ **neoplastic** /-'plæstɪk/ *adj.* [NEO- + Gk *plasma* formation: see PLASMA]

Neoplatonism /ˌniːəʊˈpleɪtəˌnɪz(ə)m/ *n.* a philosophical and religious system developed by the followers of Plotinus in the third c., combining Platonic thought with oriental mysticism. □□ **Neoplatonic** /-pləˈtɒnɪk/ *adj.* **Neoplatonist** *n.*

neoprene /ˈniːəʊˌpriːn/ *n.* a synthetic rubber-like polymer. [NEO- + *chloroprene* etc. (perh. f. PROPYL + -ENE)]

neoteny /nɪˈɒtɪnɪ/ *n.* the retention of juvenile features in the adult form of some animals, e.g. an axolotl. □□ **neotenic** /-ˈtenɪk/ *adj.* **neotenous** *adj.* [G *Neotenie* (as NEO- + Gk *teinō* extend)]

neoteric /ˌniːəˈterɪk/ *adj. literary* recent; newfangled; modern. [LL *neotericus* f. Gk *neōterikos* (*neōteros* compar. of *neos* new)]

neotropical /ˌniːəʊˈtrɒpɪk(ə)l/ *adj.* of or relating to tropical and S. America as a biogeographical region.

Nepalese /ˌnepəˈliːz/ *adj. & n.* (*pl.* same) = NEPALI.

Nepali /nɪˈpɔːlɪ/ *n. & adj.* —*n.* (*pl.* same or **Nepalis**) **1 a** a native or national of Nepal in Central Asia. **b** a person of Nepali descent. **2** the language of Nepal. —*adj.* of or relating to Nepal or its language or people.

nepenthe /nɪˈpenθɪ/ *n.* = NEPENTHES 1. [var. of NEPENTHES, after It. *nepente*]

nepenthes /nɪˈpenθiːz/ *n.* **1** *poet.* a drug causing forgetfulness of grief. **2** any pitcher-plant of the genus *Nepenthes*. [L f. Gk *nēpenthes* (*pharmakon* drug), neut. of *nēpenthēs* f. *nē-* not + *penthos* grief]

nephew /ˈnevjuː, ˈnef-/ *n.* a son of one's brother or sister, or of one's brother-in-law or sister-in-law. [ME f. OF *neveu* f. L *nepos nepotis* grandson, nephew]

nephology /nɪˈfɒlədʒɪ/ *n.* the study of clouds. [Gk *nephos* cloud + -LOGY]

nephrite /ˈnefraɪt/ *n.* a green, yellow, or white calcium magnesium silicate form of jade. [G *Nephrit* f. Gk *nephros* kidney, with ref. to its supposed efficacy in treating kidney disease]

nephritic /nɪˈfrɪtɪk/ *adj.* **1** of or in the kidneys; renal. **2** of or relating to nephritis. [LL *nephriticus* f. Gk *nephritikos* (as NEPHRITIS)]

nephritis /nɪˈfraɪtɪs/ *n.* inflammation of the kidneys. Also called *Bright's disease*. [LL f. Gk *nephros* kidney]

nephro- /ˈnefrəʊ/ *comb. form* (usu. **nephr-** before a vowel) kidney. [Gk f. *nephros* kidney]

ne plus ultra /ˌneɪ plʊs ˈʊltrɑː/ *n.* **1** the furthest attainable point. **2** the culmination, acme, or perfection. [L, = not further beyond, the supposed inscription on the Pillars of Hercules (the Strait of Gibraltar) prohibiting passage by ships]

nepotism /ˈnepəˌtɪz(ə)m/ *n.* favouritism shown to relatives in conferring offices or privileges. □□ **nepotist** *n.* **nepotistic** /-ˈtɪstɪk/ *adj.* [F *népotisme* f. It. *nepotismo* f. *nepote* NEPHEW: orig. with ref. to popes with illegitimate sons called nephews]

Neptune /ˈneptjuːn/ *n.* a distant planet of the solar system, eighth from the sun, discovered in 1846 from mathematical computations. [ME f. F *Neptune* or L *Neptunus* god of the sea]

neptunium /nepˈtjuːnɪəm/ *n. Chem.* a radioactive transuranic metallic element produced when uranium atoms absorb bombarding neutrons. ¶ Symb.: **Np**. [NEPTUNE, as the next planet beyond Uranus, + -IUM]

NERC *abbr.* (in the UK) Natural Environment Research Council.

nerd /nɜːd/ *n.* (also **nurd**) esp. *US sl.* a foolish, feeble, or uninteresting person. □□ **nerdy** *adj.* [20th c.: orig. uncert.]

nereid /ˈnɪərɪɪd/ *n. Mythol.* a sea-nymph. [L *Nereïs Nereïd-* f. Gk *Nērēis -idos* daughter of the sea-god Nereus]

nerine /nɪˈraɪnɪ/ *n.* any S. African plant of the genus *Nerine*, bearing flowers with usu. six narrow strap-shaped petals, often crimped and twisted. [mod.L f. the L name of a water-nymph]

neroli /ˈnɪərəlɪ/ *n.* (in full **neroli oil**) an essential oil from the flowers of the Seville orange, used in perfumery. [F *néroli* f. It. *neroli*, perh. f. the name of an Italian princess]

nervate /ˈnɜːveɪt/ *adj.* (of a leaf) having veins. □□ **nervation** /-ˈveɪʃ(ə)n/ *n.* [NERVE + -ATE²]

nerve /nɜːv/ *n. & v.* —*n.* **1 a** a fibre or bundle of fibres that transmits impulses of sensation or motion between the brain or spinal cord and other parts of the body. **b** the material constituting these. **2 a** coolness in danger; bravery; assurance. **b** *colloq.* impudence, audacity (*they've got a nerve*). **3** (in *pl.*) the bodily state in regard to physical sensitiveness and the interaction between the brain and other parts. **b** a state of heightened nervousness or sensitivity; a condition of mental or physical stress (*need to calm my nerves*). **4** a rib of a leaf, esp. the midrib. **5** *poet. archaic* a sinew or tendon. —*v.tr.* **1** (usu. *refl.*) brace (oneself) to face danger, suffering, etc. **2** give strength, vigour, or courage to. □**get on a person's nerves** irritate or annoy a person. **have nerves of iron** (or **steel**) (of a person etc.) be not easily upset or frightened. **nerve-cell** an elongated branched cell transmitting impulses in nerve tissue. **nerve-centre 1** a group of closely connected nerve cells associated in performing some function. **2** the centre of control of an organization etc. **nerve gas** a poisonous gas affecting the nervous system. **nerve-racking** stressful, frightening; straining the nerves. □□ **nerved** *adj.* (also in *comb.*). [ME, = sinew, f. L *nervus*, rel. to Gk *neuron*]

nerveless /ˈnɜːvlɪs/ *adj.* **1** inert, lacking vigour or spirit. **2** confident; not nervous. **3** (of style) diffuse. **4** *Bot. & Entomol.* without nervures. **5** *Anat. & Zool.* without nerves. □□ **nervelessly** *adv.* **nervelessness** *n.*

nervine /ˈnɜːvaɪn/ *adj. & n.* —*adj.* relieving nerve-disorders. —*n.* a nervine drug. [F *nervin* (as NERVE)]

nervo- /ˈnɜːvəʊ/ *comb. form* (also **nerv-** before a vowel) a nerve or the nerves.

nervous /ˈnɜːvəs/ *adj.* **1** having delicate or disordered nerves. **2** timid or anxious. **3 a** excitable; highly strung; easily agitated. **b** resulting from this temperament (*nervous tension*; *a nervous headache*). **4** affecting or acting on the nerves. **5** (foll. by *of* + verbal noun) reluctant, afraid (*am nervous of meeting them*). □**nervous breakdown** a period of mental illness, usu. resulting from severe depression or anxiety. **nervous system** the body's network of specialized cells which transmit nerve impulses between parts of the body (cf. *central nervous system*, *peripheral nervous system*). **nervous wreck** *colloq.* a person suffering from mental stress, exhaustion, etc. □□ **nervously** *adv.* **nervousness** *n.* [ME f. L *nervosus* (as NERVE)]

nervure /ˈnɜːvjʊə(r)/ *n.* **1** each of the hollow tubes that form the framework of an insect's wing; a venule. **2** the principal vein of a leaf. [F *nerf* nerve]

nervy /ˈnɜːvɪ/ *adj.* (**nervier**, **nerviest**) **1** nervous; easily excited or disturbed. **2** *US* bold, impudent. **3** *archaic* sinewy, strong. □□ **nervily** *adv.* **nerviness** *n.*

nescient /ˈnesɪənt/ *adj. literary* (foll. by *of*) lacking knowledge; ignorant. □□ **nescience** *n.* [LL *nescientia* f. L *nescire* not know f. *ne-* not + *scire* know]

ness /nes/ *n.* a headland or promontory. [OE *næs*, rel. to OE *nasu* NOSE]

-ness /nɪs/ *suffix* forming nouns from adjectives, expressing: **1** state or condition, or an instance of this (*bitterness*; *conceitedness*; *happiness*; *a kindness*). **2** something in a certain state (*wilderness*). [OE *-nes*, *-ness* f. Gmc]

nest /nest/ *n. & v.* —*n.* **1** a structure or place where a bird lays eggs and shelters its young. **2** an animal's or insect's breeding-place or lair. **3** a snug or secluded retreat or shelter. **4** (often foll. by *of*) a place fostering something undesirable (*a nest of vice*). **5** a brood or swarm. **6** a group or set of similar objects, often of different sizes and fitting together for storage (*a nest of tables*). —*v.* **1** *intr.* use or build a nest. **2** *intr.* take wild birds' nests or eggs. **3** *intr.* (of objects) fit together or one inside another. **4** *tr.* (usu. as **nested** *adj.*) establish in or as in a nest. □**nest egg 1** a sum of money saved for the future. **2** a real or artificial egg left in a nest to induce hens to lay eggs there. □□ **nestful** *n.* (*pl.* **-fuls**). **nesting** *n.* (in sense 2 of *v.*). **nestlike** *adj.* [OE *nest*]

nestle /ˈnes(ə)l/ *v.* **1** *intr.* (often foll. by *down*, *in*, etc.) settle oneself comfortably. **2** *intr.* press oneself against another in affection etc. **3** *tr.* (foll. by *in*, *into*, etc.) push (a head or shoulder etc.) affectionately or snugly. **4** *intr.* lie half hidden or embedded. [OE *nestlian* (as NEST)]

nestling /ˈneslɪŋ, ˈnest-/ *n.* a bird that is too young to leave its nest.

net[1] /net/ *n. & v.* —*n.* **1** an open-meshed fabric of cord, rope, fibre, etc. **2** a piece of net used esp. to restrain, contain, or delimit, or to catch fish or other animals. **3** a structure with net to enclose an area of ground, esp. in sport. **4 a** a structure with net used in various games, esp. forming the goal in football, netball, etc., and dividing the court in tennis etc. **b** (often in *pl.*) a practice-ground in cricket, surrounded by nets. **5** a system or procedure for catching or entrapping a person or persons. **6** = NETWORK. —*v.* (**netted**, **netting**) **1** *tr.* **a** cover, confine, or catch with a net. **b** procure as with a net. **2** *tr.* hit (a ball) into the net, esp. of a goal. **3** *intr.* make netting. **4** *tr.* make (a purse, hammock, etc.) by knotting etc. threads together to form a net. **5** *tr.* fish with nets, or set nets, in (a river). **6** *tr.* (usu. as **netted** *adj.*) mark with a netlike pattern; reticulate. □□ **netful** *n.* (*pl.* **-fuls**). [OE *net*, *nett*]

net[2] /net/ *adj. & v.* (also **nett**) —*adj.* **1** (esp. of money) remaining after all necessary deductions, or free from deductions. **2** (of a price) to be paid in full; not reducible. **3** (of a weight) excluding that of the packaging or container etc. **4** (of an effect, result, etc.) ultimate, effective. —*v.tr.* (**netted**, **netting**) gain or yield (a sum) as net profit. □**net profit** the effective profit; the actual gain after working expenses have been paid. **net ton** see TON[1]. [F *net* NEAT[1]]

netball /ˈnetbɔːl/ *n.* a team game in which goals are scored by throwing a ball through a high horizontal ring with a net suspended from it.

nether /ˈneðə(r)/ *adj. archaic* = LOWER[1]. □**nether regions** (or **world**) hell; the underworld. □□ **nethermost** *adj.* [OE *nithera* etc. f. Gmc]

Netherlander /ˈneðələndə(r)/ *n.* **1** a native or national of the Netherlands. **2** a person of Dutch descent. □□ **Netherlandish** *adj.* [Du. *Nederlander*, *Nederlandsch*]

Netherlands /ˈneðələndz/ *n.* **1** (usu. prec. by *the*) Holland. **2** *hist.* the Low Countries. [Du. *Nederland* (as NETHER, LAND)]

netsuke /ˈnetsʊkɪ/ *n.* (*pl.* same or **netsukes**) (in Japan) a carved button-like ornament, esp. of ivory or wood, formerly worn to suspend articles from a girdle. [Jap.]

nett var. of NET[2].

netting /ˈnetɪŋ/ *n.* **1** netted fabric. **2** a piece of this.

nettle /ˈnet(ə)l/ *n. & v.* —*n.* **1** any plant of the genus *Urtica*, esp. *U. dioica*, with jagged leaves covered with stinging hairs. **2** any of various plants resembling this. —*v.tr.* **1** irritate, provoke, annoy. **2** sting with nettles. □**nettle-rash** a skin eruption like nettle stings. [OE *netle*, *netele*]

network /ˈnetwɜːk/ *n. & v.* —*n.* **1** an arrangement of intersecting horizontal and vertical lines, like the structure of a net. **2** a complex system of railways, roads, canals, etc. **3** a group of people who exchange information, contacts, and experience for professional or social purposes. **4** a chain of interconnected computers, machines, or operations. **5** a system of connected electrical conductors. **6** a

group of broadcasting stations connected for a simultaneous broadcast of a programme. —*v.* **1** *tr.* broadcast on a network. **2** *intr.* establish a network. **3** *tr.* link (machines, esp. computers) to operate interactively. **4** *intr.* be a member of a network (see sense 3 of *n.*).

networker /ˈnetˌwɜːkə(r)/ *n.* **1** *Computing* a member of an organization or computer network who operates from home or from an external office. **2** a member of a professional or social network.

neume /njuːm/ *n.* (also **neum**) *Mus.* a sign in plainsong indicating a note or group of notes to be sung to a syllable. [ME f. OF *neume* f. med.L *neu(p)ma* f. Gk *pneuma* breath]

neural /ˈnjʊər(ə)l/ *adj.* of or relating to a nerve or the central nervous system. □□ **neurally** *adv.* [Gk *neuron* nerve]

neuralgia /njʊəˈrældʒə/ *n.* an intense intermittent pain along the course of a nerve, esp. in the head or face. □□ **neuralgic** *adj.* [as NEURAL + -ALGIA]

neurasthenia /ˌnjʊərəsˈθiːnɪə/ *n.* a general term for fatigue, anxiety, listlessness, etc. (not in medical use). □□ **neurasthenic** /-ˈθenɪk/ *adj. & n.* [Gk *neuron* nerve + ASTHENIA]

neuritis /njʊəˈraɪtɪs/ *n.* inflammation of a nerve or nerves. □□ **neuritic** /-ˈrɪtɪk/ *adj.* [formed as NEURO- + -ITIS]

neuro- /ˈnjʊərəʊ/ *comb. form* a nerve or the nerves. [Gk *neuron* nerve]

neurogenesis /ˌnjʊərəʊˈdʒenɪsɪs/ *n.* the growth and development of nervous tissue.

neurogenic /ˌnjʊərəʊˈdʒenɪk/ *adj.* caused by or arising in nervous tissue.

neuroglia /njʊəˈrɒɡlɪə/ *n.* the connective tissue supporting the central nervous system. [NEURO- + Gk *glia* glue]

neurohormone /ˌnjʊərəʊˈhɔːməʊn/ *n.* a hormone produced by nerve-cells and secreted into the circulation.

neurology /njʊəˈrɒlədʒɪ/ *n.* the scientific study of nerve systems. □□ **neurological** /-rəˈlɒdʒɪk(ə)l/ *adj.* **neurologically** /-rəˈlɒdʒɪkəlɪ/ *adv.* **neurologist** *n.* [mod.L *neurologia* f. mod. Gk (as NEURO-, -LOGY)]

neuroma /njʊəˈrəʊmə/ *n.* (*pl.* **neuromas** or **neuromata** /-mətə/) a tumour on a nerve or in nerve-tissue. [Gk *neuron* nerve + -OMA]

neuromuscular /ˌnjʊərəʊˈmʌskjʊlə(r)/ *adj.* of or relating to nerves and muscles.

neuron /ˈnjʊərɒn/ *n.* (also **neurone** /-rəʊn/) a specialized cell transmitting nerve impulses; a nerve-cell. □□ **neuronal** /-ˈrəʊn(ə)l/ *adj.* **neuronic** /-ˈrɒnɪk/ *adj.* [Gk *neuron* nerve]

neuropath /ˈnjʊərəʊˌpæθ/ *n.* a person affected by nervous disease, or with an abnormally sensitive nervous system. □□ **neuropathic** /-ˈpæθɪk/ *adj.* **neuropathy** /-ˈrɒpəθɪ/ *n.*

neuropathology /ˌnjʊərəʊpəˈθɒlədʒɪ/ *n.* the pathology of the nervous system. □□ **neuropathologist** *n.*

neurophysiology /ˌnjʊərəʊˌfɪzɪˈɒlədʒɪ/ *n.* the physiology of the nervous system. □□ **neurophysiological** /-zɪəˈlɒdʒɪk(ə)l/ *adj.* **neurophysiologist** *n.*

neuropteran /njʊəˈrɒptərən/ *n.* any insect of the order Neuroptera, including lacewings, having four finely-veined membranous leaflike wings. □□ **neuropterous** *adj.* [NEURO- + Gk *pteron* wing]

neurosis /njʊəˈrəʊsɪs/ *n.* (*pl.* **neuroses** /-siːz/) a mental illness characterized by irrational or depressive thought or behaviour, caused by a disorder of the nervous system usu. without organic change. [mod.L (as NEURO-, -OSIS)]

neurosurgery /ˌnjʊərəʊˈsɜːdʒərɪ/ *n.* surgery performed on the nervous system, esp. the brain and spinal cord. □□ **neurosurgeon** *n.* **neurosurgical** *adj.*

neurotic /njʊəˈrɒtɪk/ *adj. & n.* —*adj.* **1** caused by or relating to neurosis. **2** (of a person) suffering from neurosis. **3** *colloq.* abnormally sensitive or obsessive. —*n.* a neurotic person. □□**neurotically** *adv.* **neuroticism** /-,sɪz(ə)m/ *n.*

neurotomy /njʊəˈrɒtəmɪ/ *n.* (*pl.* **-ies**) the operation of cutting a nerve, esp. to produce sensory loss.

neurotransmitter /ˈnjʊərəʊtrænsˌmɪtə(r)/ *n.* *Biochem.* a chemical substance released from a nerve fibre that effects the transfer of an impulse to another nerve or muscle.

neuter /ˈnjuːtə(r)/ *adj.*, *n.*, & *v.* —*adj.* **1** *Gram.* (of a noun etc.) neither masculine nor feminine. **2** (of a plant) having neither pistils nor stamen. **3** (of an insect) sexually undeveloped. —*n.* **1** *Gram.* a neuter word. **2 a** a non-fertile insect, esp. a worker bee or ant. **b** a castrated animal. —*v.tr.* castrate or spay. [ME f. OF *neutre* or L *neuter* neither f. *ne-* not + *uter* either]

neutral /ˈnjuːtr(ə)l/ *adj.* & *n.* —*adj.* **1** not helping or supporting either of two opposing sides, esp. States at war or in dispute; impartial. **2** belonging to a neutral party, State, etc. (*neutral ships*). **3** indistinct, vague, indeterminate. **4** (of a gear) in which the engine is disconnected from the driven parts. **5** (of colours) not strong or positive; grey or beige. **6** *Chem.* neither acid nor alkaline. **7** *Electr.* neither positive nor negative. **8** *Biol.* sexually undeveloped; asexual. —*n.* **1 a** a neutral State or person. **b** a subject of a neutral State. **2** a neutral gear. □□**neutrality** /-ˈtrælɪtɪ/ *n.* **neutrally** *adv.* [ME f. obs. F *neutral* or L *neutralis* of neuter gender (as NEUTER)]

neutralism /ˈnjuːtrəˌlɪz(ə)m/ *n.* a policy of political neutrality. □□**neutralist** *n.*

neutralize /ˈnjuːtrəˌlaɪz/ *v.tr.* (also **-ise**) **1** make neutral. **2** counterbalance; render ineffective by an opposite force or effect. **3** exempt or exclude (a place) from the sphere of hostilities. □□**neutralization** /-ˈzeɪʃ(ə)n/ *n.* **neutralizer** *n.* [F *neutraliser* f. med.L *neutralizare* (as NEUTRAL)]

neutrino /njuːˈtriːnəʊ/ *n.* (*pl.* **-os**) any of a group of stable elementary particles with zero electric charge and probably zero mass, which travel at the speed of light. [It., dimin. of *neutro* neutral (as NEUTER)]

neutron /ˈnjuːtrɒn/ *n.* an elementary particle of about the same mass as a proton but without an electric charge, present in all atomic nuclei except those of ordinary hydrogen. □**neutron bomb** a bomb producing neutrons and little blast, causing damage to life but little destruction to property. **neutron star** a very dense star composed mainly of neutrons. [NEUTRAL + -ON]

Nev. *abbr.* Nevada.

névé /ˈneveɪ/ *n.* an expanse of granular snow not yet compressed into ice at the head of a glacier. [Swiss F, = glacier, ult. f. L *nix nivis* snow]

never /ˈnevə(r)/ *adv.* **1 a** at no time; on no occasion; not ever (*have never been to Paris; never saw them again*). **b** *colloq.* as an emphatic negative (*I never heard you come in*). **2** not at all (*never fear*). **3** *colloq.* (expressing surprise) surely not (*you never left the key in the lock!*). □**never-never** (often prec. by *the*) *Brit. colloq.* hire purchase. **never-never land** an imaginary utopian place. **never a one** none. **never say die** see DIE¹. **well I never!** expressing great surprise. [OE *nǣfre* f. *ne* not + *ǣfre* EVER]

nevermore /ˌnevəˈmɔː(r)/ *adv.* at no future time.

nevertheless /ˌnevəðəˈles/ *adv.* in spite of that; notwithstanding; all the same.

nevus *US* var. of NAEVUS.

new /njuː/ *adj.* & *adv.* —*adj.* **1 a** of recent origin or arrival. **b** made, invented, discovered, acquired, or experienced recently or now for the first time (*a new star; has many new ideas*). **2** in original condition; not worn or used. **3 a** renewed or reformed (*a new life; the new order*). **b** reinvigorated (*felt like a new person*). **4** different from a recent previous one (*has a new job*). **5** in addition to others already existing (*have you been to the new supermarket?*). **6** (often foll. by *to*) unfamiliar or strange (*a new sensation; the*

idea was new to me). **7** (often foll. by *at*) (of a person) inexperienced, unaccustomed (to doing something) (*am new at this business*). **8** (usu. prec. by *the*) often *derog.* **a** later, modern. **b** newfangled. **c** given to new or modern ideas (*the new man*). **d** recently affected by social change (*the new rich*). **9** (often prec. by *the*) advanced in method or theory (*the new formula*). **10** (in place-names) discovered or founded later than and named after (*New York; New Zealand*). —*adv.* (usu. in *comb.*) **1** newly, recently (*new-found; new-baked*). **2** anew, afresh. □**new birth** *Theol.* spiritual regeneration. **new broom** see BROOM. **new deal** new arrangements or conditions, esp. when better than the earlier ones. **new-laid** (of an egg) freshly laid. **new look** a new or revised appearance or presentation, esp. of something familiar. **the new mathematics** (or **maths**) a system of teaching mathematics to children, with emphasis on investigation by them and on set theory. **new moon 1** the moon when first seen as a crescent after conjunction with the sun. **2** the time of its appearance. **a new one** (often foll. by *on*) *colloq.* an account or idea not previously encountered (by a person). **new potatoes** the earliest potatoes of a new crop. **new star** a nova. **new style** dating reckoned by the Gregorian Calendar. **New Testament** the part of the Bible concerned with the life and teachings of Christ and his earliest followers. **new town** *Brit.* a town established as a completely new settlement with government sponsorship. **new wave 1** = NOUVELLE VAGUE. **2** a style of rock music popular in the 1970s. **New World** North and South America regarded collectively in relation to Europe. **new year 1** the calendar year just begun or about to begin. **2** the first few days of a year. **New Year's Day** 1 January. **New Year's Eve** 31 December. □□ **newish** *adj.* **newness** *n.* [OE *nīwe* f. Gmc]

newborn /njuːˈbɔːn, ˈnjuːbɔːn/ *adj.* **1** (of a child etc.) recently born. **2** spiritually reborn; regenerated.

newcomer /ˈnjuːˌkʌmə(r)/ *n.* **1** a person who has recently arrived. **2** a beginner in some activity.

newel /ˈnjuːəl/ *n.* **1** the supporting central post of winding stairs. **2** the top or bottom supporting post of a stair-rail. [ME f. OF *noel, nouel*, knob f. med.L *nodellus* dimin. of L *nodus* knot]

newfangled /njuːˈfæŋg(ə)ld/ *adj. derog.* different from what one is used to; objectionably new. [ME *newfangle* (now dial.) liking what is new f. *newe* new *adv.* + *-fangel* f. OE *fangol* (unrecorded) inclined to take]

Newfoundland /njuːˈfaʊndlənd/ *n.* (in full **Newfoundland dog**) **1** a dog of a very large breed with a thick coarse coat. **2** this breed. [the name of a Canadian province, an island at the mouth of the St Lawrence river]

newly /ˈnjuːlɪ/ *adv.* **1** recently (*a friend newly arrived; a newly-discovered country*). **2** afresh, anew (*newly painted*). **3** in a new or different manner (*newly arranged*). □**newly-wed** a recently married person.

Newmarket /ˈnjuːˌmɑːkɪt/ *n.* a gambling card-game in which players seek to play cards that match those on the table. [*Newmarket* in S. England]

news /njuːz/ *n.pl.* (usu. treated as *sing.*) **1** information about important or interesting recent events, esp. when published or broadcast. **2** (prec. by *the*) a broadcast report of news. **3** newly received or noteworthy information. **4** (foll. by *to*) *colloq.* information not previously known (to a person) (*that's news to me*). □**news agency** an organization that collects and distributes news items. **news bulletin** a collection of items of news, esp. for broadcasting. **news conference** a press conference. **news-gatherer** *n.* a person who researches news items esp. for broadcast or publication. **news-gathering** this process. **news room** a room in a newspaper or broadcasting office where news is processed. **news-sheet** a simple form of newspaper; a newsletter. **news-stand** a stall for the sale of newspapers.

æ *cat* ɑː *arm* e *bed* ɜː *her* ɪ *sit* iː *see* ɒ *hot* ɔː *saw* ʌ *run* ʊ *put* uː *too* ə *ago* aɪ *my*

news-vendor a newspaper-seller. □□ **newsless** adj. [ME, pl. of NEW after OF noveles or med.L nova neut. pl. of novus new]

newsagent /ˈnjuːzˌeɪdʒ(ə)nt/ n. Brit. a seller of or shop selling newspapers and usu. related items, e.g. stationery.

newsboy /ˈnjuːzbɔɪ/ n. a boy who sells or delivers newspapers.

newsbrief /ˈnjuːzbriːf/ n. a short item of news, esp. on television; a newsflash.

newscast /ˈnjuːzkɑːst/ n. a radio or television broadcast of news reports.

newscaster /ˈnjuːzˌkɑːstə(r)/ n. = NEWSREADER.

newsdealer /ˈnjuːzˌdiːlə(r)/ n. US = NEWSAGENT.

newsflash /ˈnjuːzflæʃ/ n. a single item of important news broadcast separately and often interrupting other programmes.

newsgirl /ˈnjuːzɡɜːl/ n. a girl who sells or delivers newspapers.

newsletter /ˈnjuːzˌletə(r)/ n. an informal printed report issued periodically to the members of a society, business, organization, etc.

newsman /ˈnjuːzmæn/ n. (pl. **-men**) a newspaper reporter; a journalist.

newsmonger /ˈnjuːzˌmʌŋɡə(r)/ n. a gossip.

newspaper /ˈnjuːsˌpeɪpə(r)/ n. 1 a printed publication (usu. daily or weekly) containing news, advertisements, correspondence, etc. 2 the sheets of paper forming this (wrapped in newspaper).

newspaperman /ˈnjuːspeɪpəˌmæn/ n. (pl. **-men**) a journalist.

Newspeak /ˈnjuːspiːk/ n. ambiguous euphemistic language used esp. in political propaganda. [an artificial official language in George Orwell's Nineteen Eighty-Four (1949)]

newsprint /ˈnjuːzprɪnt/ n. a type of low-quality paper on which newspapers are printed.

newsreader /ˈnjuːzˌriːdə(r)/ n. a person who reads out broadcast news bulletins.

newsreel /ˈnjuːzriːl/ n. a short cinema film of recent events.

newsworthy /ˈnjuːzˌwɜːðɪ/ adj. topical; noteworthy as news. □□ **newsworthiness** n.

newsy /ˈnjuːzɪ/ adj. (**newsier**, **newsiest**) colloq. full of news.

newt /njuːt/ n. any of various small amphibians, esp. of the genus Triturus, having a well-developed tail. [ME f. ewt, with n from an (cf. NICKNAME): var. of evet EFT]

newton /ˈnjuːt(ə)n/ n. Physics the SI unit of force that, acting on a mass of one kilogram, increases its velocity by one metre per second every second along the direction that it acts. ¶ Abbr.: **N**. [Sir Isaac Newton, Engl. scientist d. 1727]

Newtonian /njuːˈtəʊnɪən/ adj. of or devised by Isaac Newton (see NEWTON). □ **Newtonian mechanics** the system of mechanics which relies on Newton's laws of motion concerning the relations between forces acting and motions occurring. **Newtonian telescope** a reflecting telescope with a small secondary mirror at 45° to the main beam of light to reflect it into a magnifying eyepiece.

New Zealander /ˈziːləndə(r)/ n. 1 a native or national of New Zealand, an island group in the Pacific. 2 a person of New Zealand descent.

next /nekst/ adj., adv., n., & prep. —adj. 1 (often foll. by to) being or positioned or living nearest (in the next house; the chair next to the fire). 2 the nearest in order of time; the first or soonest encountered or considered (next Friday; ask the next person you see). —adv. 1 (often foll. by to) in the nearest place or degree (put it next to mine; came next to last). 2 on the first or soonest occasion (when we next meet). —n. the next person or thing. —prep. colloq. next to. □ **next-best** the next in order of preference. **next door** see DOOR. **next of kin** the closest living relative or relatives. **next to** almost (next to nothing left).

the next world see WORLD. [OE nēhsta superl. (as NIGH)]

nexus /ˈneksəs/ n. (pl. same) 1 a connected group or series. 2 a bond; a connection. [L f. nectere nex- bind]

NF abbr. (in the UK) National Front.

Nfld abbr. (also **NF**) Newfoundland.

NFU abbr. (in the UK) National Farmers' Union.

n.g. abbr. no good.

NGA abbr. (in the UK) National Graphical Association.

ngaio /ˈnaɪəʊ/ n. (pl. **-os**) a small New Zealand tree, Myoporum laetum, with edible fruit and light white timber. [Maori]

NGO abbr. non-governmental organization.

NH abbr. US New Hampshire (also in official postal use).

NHI abbr. (in the UK) National Health Insurance.

NHS abbr. (in the UK) National Health Service.

NI abbr. 1 (in the UK) National Insurance. 2 Northern Ireland.

Ni symb. Chem. the element nickel.

niacin /ˈnaɪəsɪn/ n. = NICOTINIC ACID. [nicotinic acid + -IN]

nib /nɪb/ n. & v. —n. 1 the point of a pen, which touches the writing surface. 2 (in pl.) shelled and crushed coffee or cocoa beans. 3 the point of a tool etc. —v. (**nibbed**, **nibbing**) 1 tr. provide with a nib. 2 tr. mend the nib of. 3 tr. & intr. nibble. [prob. f. MDu. nib or MLG nibbe, var. of nebbe NEB]

nibble /ˈnɪb(ə)l/ v. & n. —v. 1 tr. & (foll. by at) intr. a take small bites at. b eat in small amounts. c bite at gently or cautiously or playfully. 2 intr. (foll. by at) show cautious interest in. —n. 1 an instance of nibbling. 2 a very small amount of food. 3 Computing half a byte, i.e. 4 bits. □□ **nibbler** n. [prob. of LG or Du. orig.: cf. LG nibbeln gnaw]

niblick /ˈnɪblɪk/ n. Golf an iron with a large round heavy head, used esp. for playing out of bunkers. [19th c.: orig. unkn.]

nibs /nɪbz/ n. □ **his nibs** joc. colloq. a mock title used with reference to an important or self-important person. [19th c.: orig. unkn. (cf. earlier nabs)]

nice /naɪs/ adj. 1 pleasant, agreeable, satisfactory. 2 (of a person) kind, good-natured. 3 iron. bad or awkward (a nice mess you've made). 4 a fine or subtle (a nice distinction). b requiring careful thought or attention (a nice problem). 5 fastidious; delicately sensitive. 6 punctilious, scrupulous (were not too nice about their methods). 7 (foll. by an adj., often with and) satisfactory or adequate in terms of the quality described (a nice long time; nice and warm). □ **nice work** a task well done. □□ **nicely** adv. **niceness** n. **nicish** adj. (also **niceish**). [ME, = stupid, wanton f. OF, = silly, simple f. L nescius ignorant (as nescience: see NESCIENT)]

Nicene Creed /naɪˈsiːn, ˈnaɪ-/ n. a formal statement of Christian belief based on that adopted at the first Council of Nicaea in 325. [Nicene ME f. LL Nicenus of Nicaea in Asia Minor]

nicety /ˈnaɪsɪtɪ/ n. (pl. **-ies**) 1 a subtle distinction or detail. 2 precision, accuracy. 3 intricate or subtle quality (a point of great nicety). 4 (in pl.) a minutiae; fine details. b refinements, trimmings. □ **to a nicety** with exactness. [ME f. OF niceté (as NICE)]

niche /nɪtʃ, niːʃ/ n. & v. —n. 1 a shallow recess, esp. in a wall to contain a statue etc. 2 a comfortable or suitable position in life or employment. 3 an appropriate combination of conditions for a species to thrive. —v.tr. (often as **niched** adj.) 1 place in a niche. 2 ensconce (esp. oneself) in a recess or corner. [F f. nicher make a nest, ult. f. L nidus nest]

Nichrome /ˈnaɪkrəʊm/ n. propr. a group of nickel-chromium alloys used for making wire in heating elements etc. [NICKEL + CHROME]

Nick /nɪk/ n. □ **Old Nick** the Devil. [prob. f. a pet-form of the name Nicholas]

nick[1] /nɪk/ n. & v. —n. 1 a small cut or notch. 2 Brit. sl. a a prison. b a police station. 3 (prec. by in with adj.) *Brit. colloq.* condition (*in reasonable nick*). **4** the junction between the floor and walls in a squash court. —*v.tr.* **1** make a nick or nicks in. **2** *Brit. sl.* **a** steal. **b** arrest, catch. □**in the nick of time** only just in time; just at the right moment. [ME: orig. uncert.]

nick² /nɪk/ *v.intr. Austral. sl.* (foll. by *off*, *in*, etc.) move quickly or furtively. [19th c.: orig. uncert. (cf. NIP¹ 4)]

nickel /ˈnɪk(ə)l/ *n. & v.* —*n.* **1** *Chem.* a malleable ductile silver-white metallic transition element, occurring naturally in various minerals and used in special steels, in magnetic alloys, and as a catalyst. ¶ Symb.: **Ni**. **2** *colloq.* a US five-cent coin. —*v.tr.* (**nickelled**, **nickelling**; *US* **nickeled**, **nickeling**) coat with nickel. □**nickel brass** an alloy of copper, zinc, and a small amount of nickel. **nickel-plated** coated with nickel by plating. **nickel silver** = *German silver*. **nickel steel** a type of stainless steel with chromium and nickel. □□**nickelic** *adj.* **nickelous** *adj.* [abbr. of G *Kupfernickel* copper-coloured ore, from which nickel was first obtained, f. *Kupfer* copper + *Nickel* demon, with ref. to the ore's failure to yield copper]

nickelodeon /ˌnɪkəˈləʊdɪən/ *n. US colloq.* a jukebox. [NICKEL + MELODEON]

nicker /ˈnɪkə(r)/ *n.* (*pl.* same) *Brit. sl.* a pound (in money). [20th c.: orig. unkn.]

nick-nack var. of KNICK-KNACK.

nickname /ˈnɪkneɪm/ *n. & v.* —*n.* a familiar or humorous name given to a person or thing instead of or as well as the real name. —*v.tr.* **1** give a nickname to. **2** call (a person or thing) by a nickname. [ME f. *eke-name*, with *n* from *an* (cf. NEWT): *eke* = addition, f. OE *ēaca* (as EKE)]

nicol /ˈnɪk(ə)l/ *n.* (in full **nicol prism**) a device for producing plane-polarized light, consisting of two pieces of cut calcite cemented together with Canada balsam. [W. *Nicol*, Sc. physicist d. 1851, its inventor]

nicotine /ˈnɪkəˌtiːn/ *n.* a colourless poisonous alkaloid present in tobacco. □□**nicotinism** *n.* **nicotinize** *v.tr.* (also **-ise**). [F f. mod.L *nicotiana* (*herba*) tobacco-plant, f. J. *Nicot*, Fr. diplomat & introducer of tobacco into France in the 16th c.]

nicotinic acid /ˌnɪkəˈtɪnɪk/ *n.* a vitamin of the B complex, found in milk, liver, and yeast, a deficiency of which causes pellagra. Also called NIACIN.

nictitate /ˈnɪktɪˌteɪt/ *v.intr.* close and open the eyes; blink or wink. □**nictitating membrane** a clear membrane forming a third eyelid in amphibians, birds, and some other animals, that can be drawn across the eye to give protection without loss of vision. □□**nictitation** /-ˈteɪʃ(ə)n/ *n.* [med.L *nictitare* frequent. of L *nictare* blink]

nide /naɪd/ *n.* (*Brit.* **nye** /naɪ/) a brood of pheasants. [F *nid* or L *nidus*: see NIDUS]

nidificate /ˈnɪdɪfɪˌkeɪt/ *v.intr.* = NIDIFY.

nidify /ˈnɪdɪˌfaɪ/ *v.intr.* (**-ies**, **-ied**) (of a bird) build a nest. □□**nidification** /-fɪˈkeɪʃ(ə)n/ *n.* [L *nidificare* f. NIDUS nest]

nidus /ˈnaɪdəs/ *n.* (*pl.* **nidi** /-daɪ/ or **niduses**) **1** a place in which an insect etc. deposits its eggs, or in which spores or seeds develop. **2** a place in which something is nurtured or developed. [L, rel. to NEST]

niece /niːs/ *n.* a daughter of one's brother or sister, or of one's brother-in-law or sister-in-law. [ME f. OF ult. f. L *neptis* granddaughter]

niello /nɪˈeləʊ/ *n.* (*pl.* **nielli** /-liː/ or **-os**) **1** a black composition of sulphur with silver, lead, or copper, for filling engraved lines in silver or other metal. **2 a** such ornamental work. **b** an object decorated with this. □□**nielloed** *adj.* [It. f. L *nigellus* dimin. of *niger* black]

niff /nɪf/ *n. & v. Brit. colloq.* —*n.* a smell, esp. an unpleasant one. —*v.intr.* smell, stink. □□**niffy** *adj.* (**niffier**, **niffiest**). [orig. dial.]

nifty /ˈnɪftɪ/ *adj.* (**niftier**, **niftiest**) *colloq.* **1** clever,

adroit. **2** smart, stylish. □□**niftily** *adv.* **niftiness** *n.* [19th c.: orig. uncert.]

niggard /ˈnɪgəd/ *n. & adj.* —*n.* a mean or stingy person. —*adj. archaic* = NIGGARDLY. [ME, alt. f. earlier (obs.) *nigon*, prob. of Scand. orig.: cf. NIGGLE]

niggardly /ˈnɪgədlɪ/ *adj. & adv.* —*adj.* **1** stingy, parsimonious. **2** meagre, scanty. —*adv.* in a stingy or meagre manner. □□**niggardliness** *n.*

nigger /ˈnɪgə(r)/ *n. offens.* **1** a Black person. **2** a dark-skinned person. □**a nigger in the woodpile** a hidden cause of trouble or inconvenience. [earlier *neger* f. F *nègre* f. Sp. *negro* NEGRO]

niggle /ˈnɪg(ə)l/ *v. & n.* —*v.* **1** *intr.* be over-attentive to details. **2** *intr.* find fault in a petty way. **3** *tr. colloq.* irritate; nag pettily. —*n.* a trifling complaint or criticism; a worry or annoyance. [app. of Scand. orig.: cf. Norw. *nigla*]

niggling /ˈnɪglɪŋ/ *adj.* **1** troublesome or irritating in a petty way. **2** trifling or petty. □□**nigglingly** *adv.*

nigh /naɪ/ *adv., prep., & adj. archaic* or *dial.* near. [OE *nēh*, *nēah*]

night /naɪt/ *n.* **1** the period of darkness between one day and the next; the time from sunset to sunrise. **2** nightfall (*shall not reach home before night*). **3** the darkness of night (*as black as night*). **4** a night or evening appointed for some activity, or spent or regarded in a certain way (*last night of the Proms*; *a great night out*). □**night-blindness** = NYCTALOPIA. **night fighter** an aeroplane used for interception at night. **night-hawk 1** a nocturnal prowler, esp. a thief. **2** a nightjar. **night-life** entertainment available at night in a town. **night-light** a dim light kept on in a bedroom at night. **night-long** throughout the night. **night nurse** a nurse on duty during the night. **night-owl** *colloq.* a person active at night. **night safe** a safe with access from the outer wall of a bank for the deposit of money etc. when the bank is closed. **night school** an institution providing evening classes for those working by day. **night shift** a shift of workers employed during the night. **night-soil** the contents of cesspools etc. removed at night, esp. for use as manure. **night-time** the time of darkness. **night-watchman 1** a person whose job is to keep watch by night. **2** *Cricket* an inferior batsman sent in when a wicket falls near the close of a day's play. □□**nightless** *adj.* [OE *neaht*, *niht* f. Gmc]

nightbird /ˈnaɪtbɜːd/ *n.* a person who habitually goes about at night.

nightcap /ˈnaɪtkæp/ *n.* **1** *hist.* a cap worn in bed. **2** a hot or alcoholic drink taken at bedtime.

nightclothes /ˈnaɪtkləʊðz/ *n.* clothes worn in bed.

nightclub /ˈnaɪtklʌb/ *n.* a club that is open at night and provides refreshment and entertainment.

nightdress /ˈnaɪtdres/ *n.* a woman's or child's loose garment worn in bed.

nightfall /ˈnaɪtfɔːl/ *n.* the onset of night; the end of daylight.

nightgown /ˈnaɪtgaʊn/ *n.* **1** = NIGHTDRESS. **2** *hist.* a dressing-gown.

nightie /ˈnaɪtɪ/ *n. colloq.* a nightdress. [abbr.]

nightingale /ˈnaɪtɪŋˌgeɪl/ *n.* any small reddish-brown bird of the genus *Luscinia*, esp. *L. megarhynchos*, of which the male sings melodiously, esp. at night. [OE *nihtegala* (whence obs. *nightgale*) f. Gmc: for *-n-* cf. FARTHINGALE]

nightjar /ˈnaɪtdʒɑː(r)/ *n.* any nocturnal bird of the family Caprimulgidae, having a characteristic harsh cry.

nightly /ˈnaɪtlɪ/ *adj. & adv.* —*adj.* **1** happening, done, or existing in the night. **2** recurring every night. —*adv.* every night. [OE *nihtlic* (as NIGHT)]

nightmare /ˈnaɪtmeə(r)/ *n.* **1** a frightening or unpleasant dream. **2** *colloq.* a terrifying or very unpleasant experience or situation. **3** a haunting or obsessive fear. □□**nightmarish** *adj.* **nightmarishly** *adv.* [an evil spirit (incubus) once thought to lie on and suffocate sleepers: OE *mære* incubus]

nightshade /'naɪtʃeɪd/ *n.* any of various poisonous plants, esp. of the genus *Solanum*, including *S. nigrum* (**black nightshade**) with black berries, and *S. dulcamara* (**woody nightshade**) with red berries. □**deadly nightshade** = BELLADONNA. [OE *nihtscada* app. formed as NIGHT + SHADE, prob. with ref. to its poisonous properties]

nightshirt /'naɪtʃɜːt/ *n.* a long shirt worn in bed.

nightspot /'naɪtspɒt/ *n.* a nightclub.

nightstick /'naɪtstɪk/ *n.* *US* a policeman's truncheon.

nigrescent /nɪ'gres(ə)nt/ *adj.* blackish. □□ **nigrescence** *n.* [L *nigrescere* grow black f. *niger nigri* black]

nigritude /'nɪgrɪˌtjuːd/ *n.* blackness. [L *nigritudo* (as NIGRESCENT)]

nihilism /'naɪɪˌlɪz(ə)m, 'naɪhɪˌlɪz(ə)m/ *n.* **1** the rejection of all religious and moral principles. **2** an extreme form of scepticism maintaining that nothing has a real existence. □□ **nihilist** *n.* **nihilistic** /-'lɪstɪk/ *adj.* [L *nihil* nothing]

nihility /naɪ'hɪlɪtɪ/ *n.* (*pl.* **-ies**) **1** non-existence, nothingness. **2** a mere nothing; a trifle. [med.L *nihilitas* (as NIHILISM)]

nihil obstat /ˌnaɪhɪl 'ɒbstæt/ *n.* **1** *RC Ch.* a certificate that a book is not open to objection on doctrinal or moral grounds. **2** an authorization or official approval. [L, = nothing hinders]

-nik /nɪk/ *suffix* forming nouns denoting a person associated with a specified thing or quality (*beatnik; refusenik*). [Russ. (as SPUTNIK) and Yiddish]

nil /nɪl/ *n.* nothing; no number or amount (esp. as a score in games). [L, = *nihil* nothing]

Nile /naɪl/ *n.* & *adj.* (in full **Nile-blue**, **Nile-green**) pale greenish blue or green. [the river *Nile* in NE Africa]

nilgai /'niːlɡaɪ/ *n.* a large short-horned Indian antelope, *Boselaphus tragocamelus*. [Hindi *nīlgāī* f. *nīl* blue + *gāī* cow]

Nilotic /naɪ'lɒtɪk/ *adj.* **1** of or relating to the Nile or the Nile region of Africa. **2** of or relating to a group of E. African Negroid peoples, or the languages spoken by them. [L *Niloticus* f. Gk *Neilōtikos* f. *Neilos* Nile]

nim /nɪm/ *n.* a game in which two players must alternately take one or more objects from one of several heaps and seek either to avoid taking or to take the last remaining object. [20th c.: perh. f. archaic *nim* take (as NIMBLE), or G *nimm* imper. of *nehmen* take]

nimble /'nɪmb(ə)l/ *adj.* (**nimbler**, **nimblest**) **1** quick and light in movement or action; agile. **2** (of the mind) quick to comprehend; clever, versatile. □□ **nimbleness** *n.* **nimbly** *adv.* [OE *nǣmel* quick to seize f. *niman* take f. Gmc, with *-b-* as in THIMBLE]

nimbostratus /ˌnɪmbəʊ'streɪtəs, -'strɑːtəs/ *n.* (*pl.* **nimbostrati** /-taɪ/) *Meteorol.* a low dark-grey layer of cloud. [mod.L, f. NIMBUS + STRATUS]

nimbus /'nɪmbəs/ *n.* (*pl.* **nimbi** /-baɪ/ or **nimbuses**) **1 a** a bright cloud or halo investing a deity or person or thing. **b** the halo of a saint etc. **2** *Meteorol.* a rain-cloud. □□ **nimbused** *adj.* [L, = cloud, aureole]

niminy-piminy /ˌnɪmɪnɪ'pɪmɪnɪ/ *adj.* feeble, affected; lacking in vigour. [cf. MIMINY-PIMINY, NAMBY-PAMBY]

Nimrod /'nɪmrɒd/ *n.* a great hunter or sportsman. [Heb. *Nimrōd* valiant: see Gen. 10:8–9]

nincompoop /'nɪŋkəmˌpuːp/ *n.* a simpleton; a fool. [17th c.: orig. unkn.]

nine /naɪn/ *n.* & *adj.* —*n.* **1** one more than eight, or one less than ten; the sum of five units and four units. **2** a symbol for this (9, ix, IX). **3** a size etc. denoted by nine. **4** a set or team of nine individuals. **5** the time of nine o'clock (*is it nine yet?*). **6** a card with nine pips. **7** (**the Nine**) the nine muses. —*adj.* that amount to nine. □**dressed up to the nines**

dressed very elaborately. **nine days' wonder** a person or thing that is briefly famous. **nine times out of ten** nearly always. **nine to five** a designation of typical office hours. [OE *nigon* f. Gmc]

ninefold /'naɪnfəʊld/ *adj.* & *adv.* **1** nine times as much or as many. **2** consisting of nine parts.

ninepin /'naɪnpɪn/ *n.* **1** (in *pl.*; usu. treated as *sing.*) a game in which nine pins are set up at the end of an alley and bowled at in an attempt to knock them down. **2** a pin used in this game.

nineteen /naɪn'tiːn/ *n.* & *adj.* —*n.* **1** one more than eighteen, nine more than ten. **2** the symbol for this (19, xix, XIX). **3** a size etc. denoted by nineteen. —*adj.* that amount to nineteen. □**talk nineteen to the dozen** see DOZEN. □□ **nineteenth** *adj.* & *n.* [OE *nigontȳne*]

ninety /'naɪntɪ/ *n.* & *adj.* —*n.* (*pl.* **-ies**) **1** the product of nine and ten. **2** a symbol for this (90, xc, XC). **3** (in *pl.*) the numbers from 90 to 99, esp. the years of a century or of a person's life. —*adj.* that amount to ninety. □**ninety-first**, **-second**, etc. the ordinal numbers between ninetieth and a hundredth. **ninety-one**, **-two**, etc. the cardinal numbers between ninety and a hundred. □□ **ninetieth** *adj.* & *n.* **ninetyfold** *adj.* & *adv.* [OE *nigontig*]

ninja /'nɪndʒə/ *n.* a person skilled in ninjutsu. [Jap.]

ninjutsu /nɪn'dʒʊtsuː/ *n.* one of the Japanese martial arts, characterized by stealthy movement and camouflage. [Jap.]

ninny /'nɪnɪ/ *n.* (*pl.* **-ies**) a foolish or simple-minded person. [perh. f. *innocent*]

ninon /'niːnɒ̃/ *n.* a lightweight silk dress fabric. [F]

ninth /naɪnθ/ *n.* & *adj.* —*n.* **1** the position in a sequence corresponding to the number 9 in the sequence 1–9. **2** something occupying this position. **3** each of nine equal parts of a thing. **4** *Mus.* **a** an interval or chord spanning nine consecutive notes in the diatonic scale (e.g. C to D an octave higher). **b** a note separated from another by this interval. —*adj.* that is the ninth. □□ **ninthly** *adv.*

niobium /naɪ'əʊbɪəm/ *n.* *Chem.* a rare grey-blue metallic transition element occurring naturally in several minerals and used in alloys for superconductors. ¶ Symb.: **Nb**. Also called COLUMBIUM. □□ **niobic** *adj.* **niobous** *adj.* [*Niobe* daughter of Tantalus: so called because first found in TANTALITE]

Nip /nɪp/ *n.* *sl. offens.* a Japanese person. [abbr. of NIPPONESE]

nip[1] /nɪp/ *v.* & *n.* —*v.* (**nipped**, **nipping**) **1** *tr.* pinch, squeeze, or bite sharply. **2** *tr.* (often foll. by *off*) remove by pinching etc. **3** *tr.* (of the cold, frost, etc.) cause pain or harm to. **4** *intr.* (foll. by *in*, *out*, etc.) *Brit. colloq.* go nimbly or quickly. **5** *tr.* *US sl.* steal, snatch. —*n.* **1 a** a pinch, a sharp squeeze. **b** a bite. **2 a** biting cold. **b** a check to vegetation caused by this. □**nip and tuck** *US* neck and neck. **nip in the bud** suppress or destroy (esp. an idea) at an early stage. □□ **nipping** *adj.* [ME, prob. of LG or Du. orig.]

nip[2] /nɪp/ *n.* & *v.* —*n.* a small quantity of spirits. —*v.intr.* (**nipped**, **nipping**) drink spirits. [prob. abbr. of *nipperkin* small measure: cf. LG, Du. *nippen* to sip]

nipa /'niːpə/ *n.* **1** an E. Indian palm-tree, *Nipa fruticans*, with a creeping trunk and large feathery leaves. **2** an alcoholic drink made from its sap. [Sp. & Port. f. Malay *nīpah*]

nipper /'nɪpə(r)/ *n.* **1** a person or thing that nips. **2** the claw of a crab, lobster, etc. **3** *Brit. colloq.* a young child. **4** (in *pl.*) any tool for gripping or cutting, e.g. forceps or pincers.

nipple /'nɪp(ə)l/ *n.* **1** a small projection in which the mammary ducts of either sex of mammals terminate and from which in females milk is secreted for the young. **2** the teat of a feeding-bottle. **3** a device like a nipple in function, e.g. the tip of a grease-gun. **4** a nipple-like protuberance. **5** *US* a short section of pipe with a screw-thread at each end for coupling. [16th c., also *neble*, *nible*, perh. dimin. f. *neb*]

w *we*   z *zoo*   ʃ *she*   ʒ *decision*   θ *thin*   ð *this*   ŋ *ring*   x *loch*   tʃ *chip*   dʒ *jar*   (*see over for vowels*)

nipplewort /'nɪp(ə)l₁wɜːt/ *n.* a yellow-flowered weed, *Lapsana communis*.

Nipponese /₁nɪpə'niːz/ *n.* & *adj.* —*n.* (*pl.* same) a Japanese person. —*adj.* Japanese. [Jap. *Nippon* Japan, lit. 'land of the rising sun']

nippy /'nɪpɪ/ *adj.* (**nippier, nippiest**) *colloq.* **1** quick, nimble, active. **2** chilly, cold. □□ **nippily** *adv.* [NIP¹ + -Y¹]

NIREX /'naɪreks/ *abbr.* (in the UK) Nuclear Industry Radioactive Waste Executive.

nirvana /nɜː'vɑːnə, nɪə-/ *n.* (in Buddhism) perfect bliss and release from karma, attained by the extinction of individuality. [Skr. *nirvāṇa* f. *nirvā* be extinguished f. *nis* out + *vā-* to blow]

nisei /niː'seɪ/ *n. US* an American whose parents were immigrants from Japan. [Jap., lit. 'second generation']

nisi /'naɪsaɪ/ *adj. Law* that takes effect only on certain conditions (*decree nisi*). [L, = 'unless']

Nissen hut /'nɪs(ə)n/ *n.* a tunnel-shaped hut of corrugated iron with a cement floor. [P. N. *Nissen*, British engineer d. 1930, its inventor]

nit¹ /nɪt/ *n.* **1** the egg or young form of a louse or other parasitic insect esp. of human head-lice or body-lice. **2** *Brit. sl.* a stupid person. □ **nit-pick** *colloq.* indulge in nit-picking. **nit-picker** *colloq.* a person who nit-picks. **nit-picking** *n.* & *adj. colloq.* fault-finding in a petty manner. [OE *hnitu* f. WG]

nit² /nɪt/ *int. Austral. sl.* used as a warning that someone is approaching. □ **keep nit** keep watch; act as guard. [19th c.: orig. unkn.: cf. NIX³]

niter *US* var. of NITRE.

nitinol /'nɪtɪ₁nɒl/ *n.* an alloy of nickel and titanium. [*Ni* + *Ti* + *Naval Ordnance Laboratory*, Maryland, US]

nitrate *n.* & *v.* —*n.* /'naɪtreɪt/ **1** any salt or ester of nitric acid. **2** potassium or sodium nitrate when used as a fertilizer. —*v.tr.* /naɪ'treɪt/ *Chem.* treat, combine, or impregnate with nitric acid. □□ **nitration** /-'treɪʃ(ə)n/ *n.* [F (as NITRE, -ATE¹)]

nitre /'naɪtə(r)/ *n.* (*US* **niter**) saltpetre, potassium nitrate. [ME f. OF f. L *nitrum* f. Gk *nitron*, of Semitic orig.]

nitric /'naɪtrɪk/ *adj.* of or containing nitrogen, esp. in the quinquevalent state. □ **nitric acid** a colourless corrosive poisonous liquid. ¶ Chem. formula: HNO_3. **nitric oxide** a colourless gas. ¶ Chem. formula: NO. [F *nitrique* (as NITRE)]

nitride /'naɪtraɪd/ *n. Chem.* a binary compound of nitrogen with a more electropositive element. [NITRE + -IDE]

nitrify /'naɪtrɪ₁faɪ/ *v.tr.* (-**ies**, -**ied**) **1** impregnate with nitrogen. **2** convert (nitrogen, usu. in the form of ammonia) into nitrites or nitrates. □□ **nitrifiable** *adj.* **nitrification** /-fɪ'keɪʃ(ə)n/ *n.* [F *nitrifier* (as NITRE)]

nitrile /'naɪtraɪl/ *n. Chem.* an organic compound consisting of an alkyl radical bound to a cyanide radical.

nitrite /'naɪtraɪt/ *n.* any salt or ester of nitrous acid.

nitro- /'naɪtrəʊ/ *comb. form* **1** of or containing nitric acid, nitre, or nitrogen. **2** made with or by use of any of these. **3** of or containing the monovalent -NO_2 group (*the nitro groups in TNT*). [Gk (as NITRE)]

nitrobenzene /₁naɪtrəʊ'benziːn/ *n.* a yellow oily liquid made by the nitration of benzene and used to make aniline etc.

nitrocellulose /₁naɪtrəʊ'seljʊ₁ləʊz, -₁ləʊs/ *n.* a highly flammable material made by treating cellulose with concentrated nitric acid, used in the manufacture of explosives and celluloid.

nitrogen /'naɪtrədʒ(ə)n/ *n. Chem.* a colourless tasteless odourless gaseous element that forms four-fifths of the atmosphere and is an essential constituent of proteins and nucleic acids. ¶ Symb.: N. □ **nitrogen cycle** the interconversion of nitrogen and its compounds, usu. in the form of nitrates, in nature. **nitrogen fixation** a chemical process in which atmospheric nitrogen is assimilated into organic compounds in living organisms and hence into the nitrogen cycle. □□ **nitrogenous** /-'trɒdʒɪnəs/ *adj.* [F *nitrogène* (as NITRO-, -GEN)]

nitroglycerine /₁naɪtrəʊ'glɪsərɪn/ *n.* (also **nitroglycerin**) an explosive yellow liquid made by reacting glycerol with a mixture of concentrated sulphuric and nitric acids.

nitrous /'naɪtrəs/ *adj.* of, like, or impregnated with nitrogen, esp. in the tervalent state. □ **nitrous acid** a weak acid existing only in solution and in the gas phase. ¶ Chem. formula: HNO_2. **nitrous oxide** a colourless gas used as an anaesthetic (= *laughing-gas*) and as an aerosol propellant. ¶ Chem. formula: N_2O. [L *nitrosus* (as NITRE), partly through F *nitreux*]

nitty-gritty /₁nɪtɪ'grɪtɪ/ *n. sl.* the realities or practical details of a matter. [20th c.: orig. uncert.]

nitwit /'nɪtwɪt/ *n. colloq.* a stupid person. □□ **nitwittery** /-'wɪtərɪ/ *n.* [perh. f. NIT¹ + WIT¹]

nitwitted /'nɪtwɪtɪd/ *adj.* stupid. □□ **nitwittedness** /-'wɪtɪdnɪs/ *n.*

nix¹ /nɪks/ *n.* & *v. sl.* —*n.* **1** nothing. **2** a denial or refusal. —*v.tr.* **1** cancel. **2** reject. [G, colloq. var. of *nichts* nothing]

nix² /nɪks/ *n.* (*fem.* **nixie** /'nɪksɪ/) a water-elf. [G (fem. *Nixe*)]

nix³ /nɪks/ *int. Brit. sl.* giving warning to confederates etc. that a person in authority is approaching. [19th c.: perh. = NIX¹]

NJ *abbr. US* New Jersey (also in official postal use).

NM *abbr. US* New Mexico (in official postal use).

n.m. *abbr.* nautical mile.

N.Mex. *abbr.* New Mexico.

NMR *abbr.* (also **nmr**) nuclear magnetic resonance.

NNE *abbr.* north-north-east.

NNW *abbr.* north-north-west.

No¹ *symb. Chem.* the element nobelium.

No² var. of NOH.

No. *abbr.* **1** number. **2** *US* North. [sense 1 f. L *numero*, ablat. of *numerus* number]

no¹ /nəʊ/ *adj.* **1** not any (*there is no excuse*; *no circumstances could justify it*; *no two of them are alike*). **2** not a, quite other than (*is no fool*; *is no part of my plan*; *caused no slight inconvenience*). **3** hardly any (*is no distance*; *did it in no time*). **4** used elliptically as a slogan, notice, etc., to forbid, reject, or deplore the thing specified (*no parking*; *no surrender*). □ **by no means** see MEANS. **no-account** unimportant, worthless. **no-ball** *Cricket n.* an unlawfully delivered ball (counting one to the batting side if not otherwise scored from). —*v.tr.* pronounce (a bowler) to have bowled a no-ball. **no-claim** (or -**claims**) **bonus** a reduction of the insurance premium charged when the insured has not made a claim under the insurance during an agreed preceding period. **no date** (of a book etc.) not bearing a date of publication etc. **no dice** see DICE. **no doubt** see DOUBT. **no end** see END. **no entry** (of a notice) prohibiting vehicles or persons from entering a road or place. **no-fault** *US* (of insurance) valid regardless of the allocation of blame for an accident etc. **no fear** see FEAR. **no-frills** lacking ornament or embellishment. **no go** impossible, hopeless. **no-go area** an area forbidden to unauthorized people. **no good** see GOOD. **no-good** see GOOD. **no-hitter** *US Baseball* a game in which a team does not get a player to first base. **no-hoper** *Austral. sl.* a useless person. **no joke** see JOKE. **no joy** see JOY n. **3. no little** see LITTLE. **no man** no person, nobody. **no man's land 1** *Mil.* the space between two opposing armies. **2** an area not assigned to any owner. **3** an area not clearly belonging to any one subject etc. **no-no** *colloq.* a thing not possible or acceptable. **no-nonsense** serious, without flippancy. **no place** *US* nowhere. **no-show** a person who has reserved a seat etc. but neither uses it nor cancels the reservation. **no side** *Rugby Football* **1** the end of a game. **2** the referee's announcement of this. **no**

small see SMALL. **no sweat** *colloq.* no bother, no trouble. **no thoroughfare** an indication that passage along a street, path, etc., is blocked or prohibited. **no time** see TIME. **no trumps** (or **trump**) *Bridge* a declaration or bid involving playing without a trump suit. **no-trumper** *Bridge* a hand on which a no-trump bid can suitably be, or has been, made. **no way** *colloq.* **1** it is impossible. **2** I will not agree etc. **no whit** see WHIT. **no-win** of or designating a situation in which success is impossible. **no wonder** see WONDER. . . . **or no** . . . regardless of the . . . (*rain or no rain, I shall go out*). **there is no . . .ing** it is impossible to . . . (*there is no accounting for tastes*; *there was no mistaking what he meant*). [ME f. *nān*, *nōn* NONE[1],· orig. only before consonants]

no[2] /nəʊ/ *adv. & n.* —*adv.* **1** equivalent to a negative sentence: the answer to your question is negative, your request or command will not be complied with, the statement made or course of action intended or conclusion arrived at is not correct or satisfactory, the negative statement made is correct. **2** (foll. by *compar.*) by no amount; not at all (*no better than before*). **3** *Sc.* not (*will ye no come back again?*). —*n.* (*pl.* **noes**) **1** an utterance of the word *no*. **2** a denial or refusal. **3** a negative vote. **□is no more** has died or ceased to exist. **no better than she should be** morally suspect; sexually promiscuous. **no can do** *colloq.* I am unable to do it. **the noes have it** the negative voters are in the majority. **no less** (often foll. by *than*) **1** as much (*gave me £50, no less*; *gave me no less than £50*; *is no less than a scandal*; *a no less fatal victory*). **2** as important (*no less a person than the President*). **3** *disp.* no fewer (*no less than ten people have told me*). **no longer** not now or henceforth as formerly. **no more** *n.* nothing further (*have no more to say*; *want no more of it*). —*adj.* not any more (*no more wine?*). —*adv.* **1** no longer. **2** never again. **3** to no greater extent (*is no more a lord than I am*; *could no more do it than fly in the air*). **4** just as little, neither (*you did not come, and no more did he*). **no, no** an emphatic equivalent of a negative sentence (cf. sense 1 of *adv.*). **no-see-em** (or **-um**) *US* a small bloodsucking insect, esp. a midge of the family *Ceratopogonidae*. **no sooner . . . than** see SOON. **not take no for an answer** persist in spite of refusals. **or no** or not (*pleasant or no, it is true*). **whether or no 1** in either case. **2** (as an indirect question) which of a case and its negative (*tell me whether or no*). [OE *nō*, *nā* f. *ne* not + *ō*, *ā* ever]

n.o. *abbr. Cricket* not out.

Noah's ark /ˈnəʊəz, nɔːz/ *n.* **1 a** the ship in which (according to the Bible) Noah, his family, and the animals were saved. **b** an imitation of this as a child's toy. **2** a large or cumbrous or old-fashioned trunk or vehicle. **3** a small bivalve mollusc, *Arca tetragona*, with a boat-shaped shell. [*Noah*, Hebrew patriarch in Gen. 6]

nob[1] /nɒb/ *n. Brit. sl.* a person of wealth or high social position. [orig. Sc. *knabb*, *nab*; 18th c., of unkn. orig.]

nob[2] /nɒb/ *n. sl.* the head. **□his nob** *Cribbage* a score of one point for holding the jack of the same suit as a card turned up by the dealer. [perh. var. of KNOB]

nobble /ˈnɒb(ə)l/ *v.tr. Brit. sl.* **1** tamper with (a racehorse) to prevent its winning. **2** get hold of (money etc.) dishonestly. **3** catch (a criminal). **4** secure the support of or weaken (a person) esp. by underhand means. **5** seize, grab. [prob. = dial. *knobble*, *knubble* knock, beat, f. KNOB]

nobbler /ˈnɒblə(r)/ *n. Austral. sl.* a glass or drink of liquor. [19th c.: orig. unkn.]

Nobelist /nəʊˈbelɪst/ *n. US* a winner of a Nobel prize.

nobelium /nəʊˈbiːlɪəm/ *n. Chem.* a radioactive trans-uranic metallic element. ¶ Symb.: **No**. [*Nobel* (see NOBEL PRIZE) + -IUM]

Nobel prize /ˈnəʊbel, -ˈbel/ *n.* any of six international prizes awarded annually for physics, chemistry, physiology or medicine, literature, economics, and the promotion of peace. [Alfred *Nobel* (d. 1896), Swedish chemist and engineer, who endowed them]

nobiliary /nəˈbɪljərɪ/ *adj.* of the nobility. **□nobiliary particle** a preposition forming part of a title of nobility (e.g. French *de*, German *von*). [F *nobiliaire* (as NOBLE)]

nobility /nəʊˈbɪlɪtɪ/ *n.* (*pl.* **-ies**) **1** nobleness of character, mind, birth, or rank. **2** (prec. by *a*, *the*) a class of nobles, an aristocracy. [ME f. OF *nobilité* or L *nobilitas* (as NOBLE)]

noble /ˈnəʊb(ə)l/ *adj. & n.* —*adj.* (**nobler**, **noblest**) **1** belonging by rank, title, or birth to the aristocracy. **2** of excellent character; having lofty ideals; free from pettiness and meanness, magnanimous. **3** of imposing appearance, splendid, magnificent, stately. **4** excellent, admirable (*noble horse*; *noble cellar*). —*n.* **1** a nobleman or noblewoman. **2** *hist.* a former English gold coin first issued in 1351. **□noble gas** any gaseous element of a group that almost never combine with other elements. **noble metal** a metal (e.g. gold, silver, or platinum) that resists chemical action, does not corrode or tarnish in air or water, and is not easily attacked by acids. **noble savage** primitive man idealized as in Romantic literature. **the noble science** boxing. **□□nobleness** *n.* **nobly** *adv.* [ME f. OF f. L (*g*)*nobilis*, rel. to KNOW]

nobleman /ˈnəʊbəlmən/ *n.* (*pl.* **-men**) a man of noble rank or birth, a peer.

noblesse /nəʊˈbles/ *n.* the class of nobles (esp. of a foreign country). **□noblesse oblige** /ɒˈbliːʒ/ privilege entails responsibility. [ME = nobility, f. OF (as NOBLE)]

noblewoman /ˈnəʊbəl‚wʊmən/ *n.* (*pl.* **-women**) a woman of noble rank or birth, a peeress.

nobody /ˈnəʊbədɪ/ *pron. & n.* —*pron.* no person. —*n.* (*pl.* **-ies**) a person of no importance, authority, or position. **□like nobody's business** see BUSINESS. **nobody's fool** see FOOL. [ME f. NO[1] + BODY (= person)]

nock /nɒk/ *n. & v.* —*n.* **1** a notch at either end of a bow for holding the string. **2 a** a notch at the butt-end of an arrow for receiving the bowstring. **b** a notched piece of horn serving this purpose. —*v.tr.* set (an arrow) on the string. [ME, perh. = *nock* forward upper corner of some sails, f. MDu. *nocke*]

noctambulist /nɒkˈtæmbjʊlɪst/ *n.* a sleepwalker. **□□noctambulism** *n.* [L *nox noctis* night + *ambulare* walk]

noctule /ˈnɒktjuːl/ *n.* a large W. European bat, *Nyctalus noctula*. [F f. It. *nottola* bat]

nocturn /ˈnɒktɜːn/ *n. RC Ch.* a part of matins orig. said at night. [ME f. OF *nocturne* or eccl.L *nocturnum* neut. of L *nocturnus*: see NOCTURNAL]

nocturnal /nɒkˈtɜːn(ə)l/ *adj.* of or in the night; done or active by night. **□nocturnal emission** involuntary emission of semen during sleep. **□□nocturnally** *adv.* [LL *nocturnalis* f. L *nocturnus* of the night f. *nox noctis* night]

nocturne /ˈnɒktɜːn/ *n.* **1** *Mus.* a short composition of a romantic nature, usu. for piano. **2** a picture of a night scene. [F (as NOCTURN)]

nocuous /ˈnɒkjʊəs/ *adj. literary* noxious, harmful. [L *nocuus* f. *nocēre* hurt]

nod /nɒd/ *v. & n.* —*v.* (**nodded**, **nodding**) **1** *intr.* incline one's head slightly and briefly in greeting, assent, or command. **2** *intr.* let one's head fall forward in drowsiness; be drowsy. **3** *tr.* incline (one's head). **4** *tr.* signify (assent etc.) by a nod. **5** *intr.* (of flowers, plumes, etc.) bend downwards and sway, or move up and down. **6** *intr.* make a mistake due to a momentary lack of alertness or attention. **7** *intr.* (of a building etc.) incline from the perpendicular (*nodding to its fall*). —*n.* a nodding of the head. **□get the nod** *US* be chosen or approved. **nodding acquaintance** (usu. foll. by *with*) a very slight acquaintance with a person or subject. **nod off** *colloq.* fall asleep. **nod through** *colloq.* **1** approve on the nod. **2** *Brit. Parl.* formally count (a Member of

Parliament) as if having voted when unable to do so. **on the nod** *colloq.* **1** with merely formal assent and no discussion. **2** on credit. □□ **noddingly** *adv.* [ME *nodde*, of unkn. orig.]

noddle[1] /'nɒd(ə)l/ *n. colloq.* the head. [ME *nodle*, of unkn. orig.]

noddle[2] /'nɒd(ə)l/ *v.tr.* nod or wag (one's head). [NOD + -LE[4]]

noddy /'nɒdɪ/ *n. (pl.* **-ies**) **1** a simpleton. **2** any of various tropical sea birds of the genus *Anous*, resembling terns. [prob. f. obs. *noddy* foolish, which is perh. f. NOD]

node /nəʊd/ *n.* **1** *Bot.* **a** the part of a plant stem from which one or more leaves emerge. **b** a knob on a root or branch. **2** *Anat.* a natural swelling or bulge in an organ or part of the body. **3** *Astron.* either of two points at which a planet's orbit intersects the plane of the ecliptic or the celestial equator. **4** *Physics* a point of minimum disturbance in a standing wave system. **5** *Electr.* a point of zero current or voltage. **6** *Math.* **a** a point at which a curve intersects itself. **b** a vertex in a graph. **7** a component in a computer network. □□ **nodal** *adj.* **nodical** *adj.* (in sense 3). [L *nodus* knot]

nodi *pl.* of NODUS.

nodose /nə'dəʊs/ *adj.* knotty, knotted. □□ **nodosity** /-'dɒsɪtɪ/ *n.* [L *nodosus* (as NODE)]

nodule /'nɒdjuːl/ *n.* **1** a small rounded lump of anything, e.g. flint in chalk, carbon in cast iron, or a mineral on the seabed. **2** a small swelling or aggregation of cells, e.g. a small tumour, node, or ganglion, or a swelling on a root of a legume containing bacteria. □□ **nodular** *adj.* **nodulated** *adj.* **nodulation** /-'leɪʃ(ə)n/ *n.* **nodulose** *adj.* **nodulous** *adj.* [L *nodulus* dimin. of *nodus:* see NODUS]

nodus /'nəʊdəs/ *n. (pl.* **nodi** /-daɪ/) a knotty point, a difficulty, a complication in the plot of a story etc. [L, = knot]

Noel /nəʊ'el/ *n.* Christmas (esp. as a refrain in carols). [F f. L (as NATAL)]

noetic /nəʊ'etɪk, nəʊ'iːtɪk/ *adj. & n.* —*adj.* **1** of the intellect. **2** purely intellectual or abstract. **3** given to intellectual speculation. —*n.* (in *sing.* or *pl.*) the science of the intellect. [Gk *noētikos* f. *noētos* intellectual f. *noeō* apprehend]

nog[1] /nɒg/ *n. & v.* —*n.* **1** a small block or peg of wood. **2** a snag or stump on a tree. **3** nogging. —*v.tr.* (**nogged, nogging**) **1** secure with nogs. **2** build in the form of nogging. [17th c.: orig. unkn.]

nog[2] /nɒg/ *n.* **1** *Brit.* a strong beer brewed in East Anglia. **2** an egg-flip. [17th c.: orig. unkn.]

noggin /'nɒgɪn/ *n.* **1** a small mug. **2** a small measure, usu. ¼ pint, of spirits. **3** *sl.* the head. [17th c.: orig. unkn.]

nogging /'nɒgɪŋ/ *n.* brickwork or timber braces in a timber frame. [NOG[1] + -ING[1]]

Noh /nəʊ/ *n.* (also **No**) traditional Japanese drama with dance and song, evolved from Shinto rites. [Jap. *nō*]

nohow /'nəʊhaʊ/ *adv.* **1** *US* in no way; by no means. **2** *dial.* out of order; out of sorts.

noil /nɔɪl/ *n.* (in *sing.* or *pl.*) short wool-combings. [perh. f. OF *noel* f. med.L *nodellus* dimin. of L *nodus* knot]

noise /nɔɪz/ *n. & v.* —*n.* **1** a sound, esp. a loud or unpleasant or undesired one. **2** a series of loud sounds, esp. shouts; a confused sound of voices and movements. **3** irregular fluctuations accompanying a transmitted signal but not relevant to it. **4** (in *pl.*) conventional remarks, or speechlike sounds without actual words (*made sympathetic noises*). —*v.* **1** *tr.* (usu. in *passive*) make public; spread abroad (a person's fame or a fact). **2** *intr. archaic* make much noise. □ **make a noise 1** (usu. foll. by *about*) talk or complain much. **2** be much talked of; attain notoriety. **noise-maker** a device for making a loud noise at a festivity etc. **noise pollution** harmful or annoying noise. **noises off** sounds made off stage to be heard

by the audience of a play. [ME f. OF, = outcry, disturbance, f. L *nausea*: see NAUSEA]

noiseless /'nɔɪzlɪs/ *adj.* **1** silent. **2** making no avoidable noise. □□ **noiselessly** *adv.* **noiselessness** *n.*

noisette /nwɑː'zet/ *n.* a small round piece of meat etc. [F, dimin. of *noix* nut]

noisome /'nɔɪsəm/ *adj. literary* **1** harmful, noxious. **2** evil-smelling. **3** objectionable, offensive. □□ **noisomeness** *n.* [ME f. obs. *noy* f. ANNOY]

noisy /'nɔɪzɪ/ *adj.* (**noisier, noisiest**) **1** full of or attended with noise. **2** making or given to making much noise. **3** clamorous, turbulent. **4** (of a colour, garment, etc.) loud, conspicuous. □□ **noisily** *adv.* **noisiness** *n.*

nolens volens /ˌnəʊlenz 'vəʊlenz/ *adv. literary* willy-nilly, perforce. [L participles, = unwilling, willing]

nolle prosequi /ˌnɒlɪ 'prɒsɪˌkwaɪ/ *n. Law* **1** the relinquishment by a plaintiff or prosecutor of all or part of a suit. **2** the entry of this on record. [L, = refuse to pursue]

nom. *abbr.* nominal.

nomad /'nəʊmæd/ *n. & adj.* —*n.* **1** a member of a tribe roaming from place to place for pasture. **2** a wanderer. —*adj.* **1** living as a nomad. **2** wandering. □□ **nomadic** /-'mædɪk/ *adj.* **nomadically** /-'mædɪkəlɪ/ *adv.* **nomadism** *n.* **nomadize** *v.intr.* (also **-ise**). [F *nomade* f. L *nomas nomad-* f. Gk *nomas -ados* f. *nemō* to pasture]

nombril /'nɒmbrɪl/ *n. Heraldry* the point halfway between fess point and the base of the shield. [F, = navel]

nom de guerre /ˌnɒm də 'geə(r)/ *n. (pl.* **noms de guerre** *pronunc.* same) an assumed name under which a person fights, plays, writes, etc. [F, = war-name]

nom de plume /ˌnɒm də 'pluːm/ *n. (pl.* **noms de plume** *pronunc.* same) an assumed name under which a person writes. [formed in E of F words, = pen-name, after NOM DE GUERRE]

nomen /'nəʊmen/ *n.* an ancient Roman's second name, indicating the gens, as in Marcus *Tullius* Cicero. [L, = name]

nomenclature /nəʊ'menklətʃə(r), 'nəʊmənˌkleɪtʃə(r)/ *n.* **1** a person's or community's system of names for things. **2** the terminology of a science etc. **3** systematic naming. **4** a catalogue or register. □□ **nomenclative** *adj.* **nomenclatural** /-'klætʃər(ə)l/ *adj.* [F f. L *nomenclatura* f. *nomen + calare* call]

nominal /'nɒmɪn(ə)l/ *adj.* **1** existing in name only; not real or actual (*nominal and real prices; nominal ruler*). **2** (of a sum of money, rent, etc.) virtually nothing; much below the actual value of a thing. **3** of or in names (*nominal and essential distinctions*). **4** consisting of or giving the names (*nominal list of officers*). **5** of or as or like a noun. □ **nominal definition** a statement of all that is connoted in the name of a concept. **nominal value** the face value (of a coin, shares, etc.). □□ **nominally** *adv.* [ME f. F *nominal* or L *nominalis* f. *nomen -inis* name]

nominalism /'nɒmɪnəˌlɪz(ə)m/ *n. Philos.* the doctrine that universals or general ideas are mere names (opp. REALISM). □□ **nominalist** *n.* **nominalistic** /-'lɪstɪk/ *adj.* [F *nominalisme* (as NOMINAL)]

nominalize /'nɒmɪnəˌlaɪz/ *v.tr.* (also **-ise**) form a noun from (a verb, adjective, etc.), e.g. *output, truth,* from *put out, true.* □□ **nominalization** /-'zeɪʃ(ə)n/ *n.*

nominate /'nɒmɪˌneɪt/ *v.tr.* **1** propose (a candidate) for election. **2** appoint to an office (*a board of six nominated and six elected members*). **3** name or appoint (a date or place). **4** mention by name. **5** call by the name of, designate. □□ **nominator** *n.* [L *nominare nominat-* (as NOMINAL)]

nomination /ˌnɒmɪ'neɪʃ(ə)n/ *n.* **1** the act or an instance of nominating; the state of being nominated. **2** the right of nominating for an appointment (*have a nomination at your disposal*). [ME f. OF *nomination* or L *nominatio* (as NOMINATE)]

---

nominative /'nɒmɪnətɪv/ n. & adj. —n. Gram. 1 the case of nouns, pronouns, and adjectives, expressing the subject of a verb. 2 a word in this case. —adj. 1 Gram. of or in this case. 2 /-neɪtɪv/ of, or appointed by, nomination (as distinct from election). □□ **nominatival** /-'taɪv(ə)l/ adj. [ME f. OF nominatif -ive or L nominativus (as NOMINATE), transl. Gk onomastikē (ptōsis case)]

nominee /ˌnɒmɪ'niː/ n. 1 a person who is nominated for an office or as the recipient of a grant etc. 2 Commerce a person (not necessarily the owner) in whose name a stock etc. is registered. [NOMINATE]

nomogram /'nɒməˌgræm, 'nəʊm-/ n. (also **nomograph** /-ˌgrɑːf/) a graphical presentation of relations between quantities whereby the value of one may be found by simple geometrical construction (e.g. drawing a straight line) from those of others. □□ **nomographic** /-'græfɪk/ adj. **nomographically** /-'græfɪkəlɪ/ adv. **nomography** /nə'mɒgrəfɪ/ n. [Gk nomo- f. nomos law + -GRAM]

nomothetic /ˌnɒmə'θetɪk, ˌnəʊm-/ adj. 1 stating (esp. scientific) laws. 2 legislative. [obs. nomothete legislator f. Gk nomothetēs]

-nomy /nəmɪ/ comb. form denoting an area of knowledge or the laws governing it (aeronomy; economy).

non- /nɒn/ prefix giving the negative sense of words with which it is combined, esp.: 1 not doing or having or involved with (non-attendance; non-payment; non-productive). 2 a not of the kind or class described (non-alcoholic; non-member; non-event). b forming terms used adjectivally (non-union; non-party). 3 a lack of (non-access). 4 (with adverbs) not in the way described (non-aggressively). 5 forming adjectives from verbs, meaning 'that does not' or 'that is not meant to (or to be)' (non-skid; non-iron). 6 used to form a neutral negative sense when a form in in- or un- has a special sense or (usu. unfavourable) connotation (non-controversial; non-effective; non-human). ¶ The number of words that can be formed with this prefix is unlimited; consequently only a selection, considered the most current or semantically noteworthy, can be given here. [from or after ME no(u)n- f. AF noun-, OF non-, nom- f. L non not]

nona- /'nɒnə/ comb. form nine. [L f. nonus ninth]

non-abstainer /ˌnɒnəb'steɪnə(r)/ n. a person who does not abstain (esp. from alcohol).

non-acceptance /ˌnɒnək'sept(ə)ns/ n. a lack of acceptance.

non-access /nɒn'ækses/ n. a lack of access.

non-addictive /ˌnɒnə'dɪktɪv/ adj. (of a drug, habit, etc.) not causing addiction.

nonage /'nəʊnɪdʒ, 'nɒn-/ n. 1 hist. the state of being under full legal age, minority. 2 a period of immaturity. [ME f. AF nounage, OF nonage (as NON-, AGE)]

nonagenarian /ˌnəʊnədʒɪ'neərɪən, ˌnɒn-/ n. & adj. —n. a person from 90 to 99 years old. —adj. of this age. [L nonagenarius f. nonageni distributive of nonaginta ninety]

non-aggression /ˌnɒnə'greʃ(ə)n/ n. lack of or restraint from aggression (often attrib.: non-aggression pact).

nonagon /'nɒnəgən/ n. a plane figure with nine sides and angles. [L nonus ninth, after HEXAGON]

non-alcoholic /ˌnɒnælkə'hɒlɪk/ adj. & n. (of a drink etc.) not containing alcohol.

non-aligned /ˌnɒnə'laɪnd/ adj. (of States etc.) not aligned with another (esp. major) power. □□ **non-alignment** n.

non-allergic /ˌnɒnə'lɜːdʒɪk/ adj. not causing allergy; not allergic.

non-ambiguous /ˌnɒnæm'bɪgjʊəs/ adj. not ambiguous. ¶ Neutral in sense: see NON- 6, UNAMBIGUOUS.

non-appearance /ˌnɒnə'pɪərəns/ n. failure to appear or be present.

non-art /nɒn'ɑːt/ n. something that avoids the normal forms of art.

nonary /'nəʊnərɪ/ adj. & n. —adj. Math. (of a scale of notation) having nine as its base. —n. (pl. -ies) a group of nine. [L nonus ninth]

non-Aryan /nɒn'eɪrɪən/ adj. & n. —adj. (of a person or language) not Aryan or of Aryan descent. —n. a non-Aryan person.

non-attached /ˌnɒnə'tætʃd/ adj. that is not attached. ¶ Neutral in sense: see NON- 6, UNATTACHED.

non-attendance /ˌnɒnə'tend(ə)ns/ n. failure to attend.

non-attributable /ˌnɒnə'trɪbjʊtəb(ə)l/ adj. that cannot or may not be attributed to a particular source etc. □□ **non-attributably** adv.

non-availability /ˌnɒnəˌveɪlə'bɪlɪtɪ/ n. a state of not being available.

non-believer /ˌnɒnbɪ'liːvə(r)/ n. a person who does not believe or has no (esp. religious) faith.

non-belligerency /ˌnɒnbə'lɪdʒərənsɪ/ n. a lack of belligerency.

non-belligerent /ˌnɒnbə'lɪdʒərənt/ adj. & n. —adj. not engaged in hostilities. —n. a non-belligerent nation, State, etc.

non-biological /ˌnɒnbaɪə'lɒdʒɪk(ə)l/ adj. not concerned with biology or living organisms.

non-Black /nɒn'blæk/ adj. & n. —adj. 1 (of a person) not Black. 2 of or relating to non-Black people. —n. a non-Black person.

non-breakable /nɒn'breɪkəb(ə)l/ adj. not breakable.

non-capital /nɒn'kæpɪt(ə)l/ adj. (of an offence) not punishable by death.

non-Catholic /nɒn'kæθəlɪk, -'kæθlɪk/ adj. & n. —adj. not Roman Catholic. —n. a non-Catholic person.

nonce /nɒns/ n. □ **for the nonce** for the time being; for the present occasion. **nonce-word** a word coined for one occasion. [ME for than anes (unrecorded) = for the one, altered by wrong division (cf. NEWT)]

nonchalant /'nɒnʃələnt/ adj. calm and casual, unmoved, unexcited, indifferent. □□ **nonchalance** n. **nonchalantly** adv. [F, part. of nonchaloir f. chaloir be concerned]

non-Christian /nɒn'krɪstjən, -'krɪstʃ(ə)n/ adj. & n. —adj. not Christian. —n. a non-Christian person.

non-citizen /nɒn'sɪtɪz(ə)n/ n. a person who is not a citizen (of a particular State, town, etc.).

non-classified /nɒn'klæsɪˌfaɪd/ adj. (esp. of information) that is not classified. ¶ Neutral in sense: see NON- 6, UNCLASSIFIED.

non-clerical /nɒn'klerɪk(ə)l/ adj. not doing or involving clerical work.

non-collegiate /ˌnɒnkə'liːdʒət/ adj. 1 not attached to a college. 2 not having colleges.

non-com /'nɒnkɒm/ n. colloq. a non-commissioned officer. [abbr.]

non-combatant /nɒn'kɒmbət(ə)nt/ n. a person not fighting in a war, esp. a civilian, army chaplain, etc.

non-commissioned /ˌnɒnkə'mɪʃ(ə)nd/ adj. Mil. (of an officer) not holding a commission.

noncommittal /ˌnɒnkə'mɪt(ə)l/ adj. avoiding commitment to a definite opinion or course of action. □□ **noncommittally** adv.

non-communicant /ˌnɒnkə'mjuːnɪkənt/ n. a person who is not a communicant (esp. in the religious sense).

non-communicating /ˌnɒnkə'mjuːnɪˌkeɪtɪŋ/ adj. that does not communicate.

non-communist /nɒn'kɒmjʊnɪst/ adj. & n. (also **non-Communist** with ref. to a particular party) —adj. not advocating or practising communism. —n. a non-communist person.

non-compliance /ˌnɒnkəm'plaɪəns/ n. failure to comply; a lack of compliance.

non compos mentis /ˌnɒn kɒmpɒs 'mentɪs/ adj. (also **non compos**) not in one's right mind. [L, = not having control of one's mind]

non-conductor /ˌnɒnkən'dʌktə(r)/ n. a substance

that does not conduct heat or electricity. □□ **non-conducting** *adj.*

non-confidential /ˌnɒnkɒnfɪ'denʃ(ə)l/ *adj.* not confidential. □□ **non-confidentially** *adv.*

nonconformist /ˌnɒnkən'fɔːmɪst/ *n.* **1** a person who does not conform to the doctrine or discipline of an established Church, esp. (**Nonconformist**) a member of a (usu. Protestant) sect dissenting from the Anglican Church. **2** a person who does not conform to a prevailing principle. □□ **nonconformism** *n.* **Nonconformism** *n.*

nonconformity /ˌnɒnkən'fɔːmɪtɪ/ *n.* **1 a** nonconformists as a body, esp. (**Nonconformity**) Protestants dissenting from the Anglican Church. **b** the principles or practice of nonconformists, esp. (**Nonconformity**) Protestant dissent. **2** (usu. foll. by *to*) failure to conform to a rule etc. **3** lack of correspondence between things.

non-contagious /ˌnɒnkən'teɪdʒəs/ *adj.* not contagious.

non-content /'nɒnkən,tent/ *n. Brit.* a negative voter in the House of Lords.

non-contentious /ˌnɒnkən'tenʃəs/ *adj.* not contentious.

non-contributory /ˌnɒnkən'trɪbjʊtərɪ/ *adj.* not contributing or (esp. of a pension scheme) involving contributions.

non-controversial /ˌnɒn,kɒntrə'vɜːʃ(ə)l/ *adj.* not controversial. ¶ Neutral in sense: see NON- 6, UNCONTROVERSIAL.

non-cooperation /ˌnɒnkəʊ,ɒpə'reɪʃ(ə)n/ *n.* failure to cooperate; a lack of cooperation.

non-delivery /ˌnɒndɪ'lɪvərɪ/ *n.* failure to deliver.

non-denominational /ˌnɒndɪ,nɒmɪ'neɪʃən(ə)l/ *adj.* not restricted as regards religious denomination.

nondescript /'nɒndɪskrɪpt/ *adj.* & *n.* —*adj.* lacking distinctive characteristics, not easily classified, neither one thing nor another. —*n.* a nondescript person or thing. □□ **nondescriptly** *adv.* **nondescriptness** *n.* [NON- + *descript* described f. L *descriptus* (as DESCRIBE)]

non-destructive /ˌnɒndɪ'strʌktɪv/ *adj.* that does not involve destruction or damage.

non-drinker /nɒn'drɪŋkə(r)/ *n.* a person who does not drink alcoholic liquor.

non-driver /nɒn'draɪvə(r)/ *n.* a person who does not drive a motor vehicle.

none[1] /nʌn/ *pron., adj.,* & *adv.* —*pron.* **1** (foll. by *of*) **a** not any of (*none of this concerns me*; *none of them have found it*; *none of your impudence!*). **b** not any one of (*none of them has come*). ¶ The verb following *none* in this sense can be singular or plural according to the sense. **2 a** no persons (*none but fools have ever believed it*). **b** no person (*none can tell*). —*adj.* (usu. with a preceding noun implied) **1** no; not any (*you have money and I have none*; *would rather have a bad reputation than none at all*). **2** not to be counted in a specified class (*his understanding is none of the clearest*; *if a linguist is wanted, I am none*). —*adv.* (foll. by *the* + compar., or *so, too*) by no amount; not at all (*am none the wiser*; *are none too fond of him*). □**none the less** nevertheless. **none other** (usu. foll. by *than*) no other person. **none-so-pretty** London Pride. [OE *nān* f. *ne* not + *ān* ONE]

none[2] /nəʊn/ *n.* (also in *pl.*) **1** the office of the fifth of the canonical hours of prayer, orig. said at the ninth hour (3 p.m.). **2** this hour. [F f. L *nona* fem. sing. of *nonus* ninth: cf. NOON]

non-earning /nɒn'ɜːnɪŋ/ *adj.* not earning (esp. a regular wage or salary).

non-effective /ˌnɒnɪ'fektɪv/ *adj.* that does not have an effect. ¶ Neutral in sense: see NON- 6, INEFFECTIVE.

non-ego /nɒn'iːgəʊ/ *n. Philos.* all that is not the conscious self.

nonentity /nɒ'nentɪtɪ/ *n.* (*pl.* **-ies**) **1** a person or thing of no importance. **2 a** non-existence. **b** a non-existent thing, a figment. [med.L *nonentitas* non-existence]

nones /nəʊnz/ *n.pl.* in the ancient Roman calendar, the ninth day before the ides by inclusive reckoning, i.e. the 7th day of March, May, July, October, the 5th of other months. [OF *nones* f. L *nonae* fem. pl. of *nonus* ninth]

non-essential /ˌnɒnɪ'senʃ(ə)l/ *adj.* not essential. ¶ Neutral in sense: see NON- 6, INESSENTIAL.

nonesuch var. of NONSUCH.

nonet /nəʊ'net/ *n.* **1** *Mus.* **a** a composition for nine voices or instruments. **b** the performers of such a piece. **2** a group of nine. [It. *nonetto* f. *nono* ninth f. L *nonus*]

nonetheless var. of *none the less*.

non-Euclidean /ˌnɒnjuː'klɪdɪən/ *adj.* denying or going beyond Euclidean principles in geometry.

non-European /ˌnɒnjʊərə'pɪən/ *adj.* & *n.* —*adj.* not European. —*n.* a non-European person.

non-event /ˌnɒnɪ'vent/ *n.* an unimportant or anti-climactic occurrence.

non-existent /ˌnɒnɪg'zɪst(ə)nt/ *adj.* not existing. □□ **non-existence** *n.*

non-explosive /ˌnɒnɪk'spləʊsɪv/ *adj.* (of a substance) that does not explode.

non-fattening /nɒn'fætənɪŋ/ *adj.* (of food) that does not fatten.

nonfeasance /nɒn'fiːz(ə)ns/ *n.* failure to perform an act required by law. [NON-: see MISFEASANCE]

non-ferrous /nɒn'ferəs/ *adj.* (of a metal) other than iron or steel.

non-fiction /nɒn'fɪkʃ(ə)n/ *n.* literary work other than fiction, including biography and reference books. □□ **non-fictional** *adj.*

non-flam /nɒn'flæm/ *adj.* = NON-FLAMMABLE.

non-flammable /nɒn'flæməb(ə)l/ *adj.* not in-flammable.

non-fulfilment /ˌnɒnfʊl'fɪlmənt/ *n.* failure to fulfil (an obligation).

non-functional /nɒn'fʌŋkʃən(ə)l/ *adj.* not having a function.

nong /nɒŋ/ *n. Austral. sl.* a foolish or stupid person. [20th c.: orig. unkn.]

non-governmental /ˌnɒngʌvən'ment(ə)l/ *adj.* not belonging to or associated with a government.

non-human /nɒn'hjuːmən/ *adj.* & *n.* —*adj.* (of a being) not human. —*n.* a non-human being. ¶ Neutral in sense: see NON- 6, INHUMAN, UNHUMAN.

non-infectious /ˌnɒnɪn'fekʃəs/ *adj.* (of a disease) not infectious.

non-inflected /ˌnɒnɪn'flektɪd/ *adj.* (of a language) not having inflections.

non-interference /ˌnɒnɪntə'fɪərəns/ *n.* a lack of interference.

non-intervention /ˌnɒnɪntə'venʃ(ə)n/ *n.* the principle or practice of not becoming involved in others' affairs, esp. by one State in regard to another.

non-intoxicating /ˌnɒnɪn'tɒksɪ,keɪtɪŋ/ *adj.* (of drink) not causing intoxication.

non-iron /nɒn'aɪən/ *adj.* (of a fabric) that needs no ironing.

nonjoinder /nɒn'dʒɔɪndə(r)/ *n. Law* the failure of a partner etc. to become a party to a suit.

nonjuror /nɒn'dʒʊərə(r)/ *n.* a person who refuses to take an oath, esp. *hist.* a member of the clergy refusing to take the oath of allegiance to William and Mary in 1689. □□ **nonjuring** *adj.*

non-jury /nɒn'dʒʊərɪ/ *adj.* (of a trial) without a jury.

non-linear /nɒn'lɪnɪə(r)/ *adj.* not linear, esp. with regard to dimension.

non-literary /nɒn'lɪtərərɪ/ *adj.* (of writing, a text, etc.) not literary in character.

non-logical /nɒn'lɒdʒɪk(ə)l/ *adj.* not involving logic. ¶ Neutral in sense: see NON- 6, ILLOGICAL. □□ **non-logically** *adv.*

non-magnetic /ˌnɒnmæg'netɪk/ *adj.* (of a substance) not magnetic.

non-member /nɒn'membə(r)/ *n.* a person who is not a member (of a particular association, club, etc.). □□ **non-membership** *n.*

non-metal /nɒn'met(ə)l/ *adj.* not made of metal. □□ **non-metallic** /-mɪ'tælɪk/ *adj.*

non-militant /nɒn'mɪlɪt(ə)nt/ *adj.* not militant.

non-military /nɒn'mɪlɪtərɪ/ *adj.* not military; not involving armed forces, civilian.

non-ministerial /ˌnɒnmɪnɪ'stɪərɪəl/ *adj.* not ministerial (esp. in political senses).

non-moral /nɒn'mɒr(ə)l/ *adj.* not concerned with morality. ¶ Neutral in sense: see NON- 6, AMORAL, IMMORAL. □□ **non-morally** *adv.*

non-natural /nɒn'nætʃər(ə)l/ *adj.* not involving natural means or processes. ¶ Neutral in sense: see NON- 6, UNNATURAL.

non-negotiable /ˌnɒnnɪ'gəʊʃəb(ə)l/ *adj.* that cannot be negotiated (esp. in financial senses).

non-net /nɒn'net/ *adj.* (of a book) not subject to a minimum selling price.

non-nuclear /nɒn'njuːklɪə(r)/ *adj.* **1** not involving nuclei or nuclear energy. **2** (of a State etc.) not having nuclear weapons.

non-observance /ˌnɒnəb'zɜːv(ə)ns/ *n.* failure to observe (esp. an agreement, requirement, etc.).

non-operational /ˌnɒnɒpə'reɪʃən(ə)l/ *adj.* **1** that does not operate. **2** out of order.

non-organic /ˌnɒnɔː'gænɪk/ *adj.* not organic. ¶ Neutral in sense: see NON- 6, INORGANIC.

nonpareil /'nɒnpər(ə)l, ˌnɒnpə'reɪl/ *adj. & n.* —*adj.* unrivalled or unique. —*n.* such a person or thing. [F f. *pareil* equal f. pop.L *pariculus* dimin. of L *par*]

non-participating /ˌnɒnpɑː'tɪsɪˌpeɪtɪŋ/ *adj.* not taking part.

non-partisan /ˌnɒnpɑː'tɪ'zæn/ *adj.* not partisan.

non-party /nɒn'pɑːtɪ/ *adj.* independent of political parties.

non-payment /nɒn'peɪmənt/ *n.* failure to pay; a lack of payment.

non-person /'nɒn,pɜːs(ə)n/ *n.* a person regarded as non-existent or insignificant (cf. UNPERSON).

non-personal /nɒn'pɜːsən(ə)l/ *adj.* not personal. ¶ Neutral in sense: see NON- 6, IMPERSONAL.

non-physical /nɒn'fɪzɪk(ə)l/ *adj.* not physical. □□ **non-physically** *adv.*

non placet /nɒn 'pleɪset/ *n.* a negative vote in a Church or university assembly. [L, = it does not please]

non-playing /nɒn'pleɪɪŋ/ *adj.* that does not play or take part (in a game etc.).

nonplus /nɒn'plʌs/ *v. & n.* —*v.tr.* (**nonplussed**, **nonplussing**) completely perplex. —*n.* a state of perplexity, a standstill (*at a nonplus*; *reduce to a nonplus*). [L *non plus* not more]

non-poisonous /nɒn'pɔɪzənəs/ *adj.* (of a substance) not poisonous.

non-political /ˌnɒnpə'lɪtɪk(ə)l/ *adj.* not political; not involved in politics.

non-porous /nɒn'pɔːrəs/ *adj.* (of a substance) not porous.

non possumus /nɒn 'pɒsjuməs/ *n.* a statement of inability to act in a matter. [L, = we cannot]

non-productive /ˌnɒnprə'dʌktɪv/ *adj.* not productive. ¶ Neutral in sense: see NON- 6, UNPRODUCTIVE. □□ **non-productively** *adv.*

non-professional /ˌnɒnprə'feʃən(ə)l/ *adj.* not professional (esp. in status). ¶ Neutral in sense: see NON- 6, UNPROFESSIONAL.

non-profit /nɒn'prɒfɪt/ *adj.* not involving or making a profit.

non-profit-making /nɒn'prɒfɪt,meɪkɪŋ/ *adj.* (of an enterprise) not conducted primarily to make a profit.

non-proliferation /ˌnɒnprə,lɪfə'reɪʃ(ə)n/ *n.* the prevention of an increase in something, esp. possession of nuclear weapons.

non-racial /nɒn'reɪʃ(ə)l/ *adj.* not involving race or racial factors.

non-reader /nɒn'riːdə(r)/ *n.* a person who cannot read.

non-resident /nɒn'rezɪd(ə)nt/ *adj. & n.* —*adj.* **1** not residing in a particular place, esp. (of a member of the clergy) not residing where his or her duties require. **2** (of a post) not requiring the holder to reside at the place of work. —*n.* a non-resident person, esp. a person using some of the facilities of a hotel. □□ **non-residence** *n.* **non-residential** /-'denʃ(ə)l/ *adj.*

non-resistance /ˌnɒnrɪ'zɪst(ə)ns/ *n.* failure to resist; a lack of resistance.

non-returnable /ˌnɒnrɪ'tɜːnəb(ə)l/ *adj.* that may or need or will not be returned.

non-rigid /nɒn'rɪdʒɪd/ *adj.* (esp. of materials) not rigid.

non-scientific /nɒn,saɪən'tɪfɪk/ *adj.* not involving science or scientific methods. ¶ Neutral in sense: see NON- 6, UNSCIENTIFIC. □□ **non-scientist** /-'saɪəntɪst/ *n.*

non-sectarian /ˌnɒnsek'teərɪən/ *adj.* not sectarian.

nonsense /'nɒns(ə)ns/ *n.* **1 a** (often as *int.*) absurd or meaningless words or ideas; foolish or extravagant conduct. **b** an instance of this. **2** a scheme, arrangement, etc., that one disapproves of. **3** (often *attrib.*) a form of literature meant to amuse by absurdity (*nonsense verse*). □□ **nonsensical** /-'sensɪk(ə)l/ *adj.* **nonsensicality** /nɒn,sensɪ'kælɪtɪ/ *n.* (*pl.* -**ies**). **nonsensically** /-'sensɪkəlɪ/ *adv.*

non sequitur /nɒn 'sekwɪtə(r)/ *n.* a conclusion that does not logically follow from the premisses. [L, = it does not follow]

non-sexual /nɒn'seksjʊəl, -ʃʊəl/ *adj.* not based on or involving sex. □□ **non-sexually** *adv.*

non-skid /nɒn'skɪd/ *adj.* **1** that does not skid. **2** that inhibits skidding.

non-slip /nɒn'slɪp/ *adj.* **1** that does not slip. **2** that inhibits slipping.

non-smoker /nɒn'sməʊkə(r)/ *n.* **1** a person who does not smoke. **2** a train compartment etc. in which smoking is forbidden. □□ **non-smoking** *adj. & n.*

non-soluble /nɒn'sɒljʊb(ə)l/ *adj.* (esp. of a substance) not soluble. ¶ Neutral in sense: see NON- 6, INSOLUBLE.

non-specialist /nɒn'speʃəlɪst/ *n.* a person who is not a specialist (in a particular subject).

non-specific /ˌnɒnspɪ'sɪfɪk/ *adj.* that cannot be specified.

non-standard /nɒn'stændəd/ *adj.* not standard.

non-starter /nɒn'stɑːtə(r)/ *n.* **1** a person or animal that does not start in a race. **2** *colloq.* a person or thing that is unlikely to succeed or be effective.

non-stick /nɒn'stɪk/ *adj.* **1** that does not stick. **2** that does not allow things to stick to it.

non-stop /nɒn'stɒp/ *adj., adv., & n.* —*adj.* **1** (of a train etc.) not stopping at intermediate places. **2** (of a journey, performance, etc.) done without a stop or intermission. —*adv.* without stopping or pausing. —*n.* a non-stop train etc.

non-subscriber /ˌnɒnsəb'skraɪbə(r)/ *n.* a person who is not a subscriber.

nonsuch /'nʌnsʌtʃ/ *n.* (also **nonesuch**) **1** a person or thing that is unrivalled, a paragon. **2** a leguminous plant, *Medicago lupulina*, with black pods. [NONE[1] + SUCH, usu. now assim. to NON-]

nonsuit /nɒn'sjuːt, -'suːt/ *n. & v. Law* —*n.* the stoppage of a suit by the judge when the plaintiff fails to make out a legal case or to bring sufficient evidence. —*v.tr.* subject (a plaintiff) to a nonsuit. [ME f. AF *no(u)nsuit*]

non-swimmer /nɒn'swɪmə(r)/ *n.* a person who cannot swim.

non-technical /nɒn'teknɪk(ə)l/ *adj.* **1** not technical. **2** without technical knowledge.

non-toxic /nɒn'tɒksɪk/ *adj.* not toxic.

non-transferable /ˌnɒntræns'fɜːrəb(ə)l/ *adj.* that may not be transferred.

non-U /nɒn'juː/ *adj. colloq.* not characteristic of the upper class. [NON- + U[2]]

non-uniform /nɒn'juːnɪˌfɔːm/ *adj.* not uniform.

non-union /nɒn'juːnɪən/ *adj.* **1** not belonging to a

trade union. **2** not done or produced by members of a trade union.

non-usage /nɒn'juːzɪdʒ, -'juːsɪdʒ/ *n.* failure to use.

non-use /nɒn'juːs/ *n.* failure to use.

non-user /nɒn'juːzə(r)/ *n. Law* the failure to use a right, by which it may be lost. [AF *nounuser* (unrecorded) (as NON-, USER)]

non-verbal /nɒn'vɜːb(ə)l/ *adj.* not involving words or speech. □□ **non-verbally** *adv.*

non-vintage /nɒn'vɪntɪdʒ/ *adj.* (of wine etc.) not vintage.

non-violence /nɒn'vaɪələns/ *n.* the avoidance of violence, esp. as a principle. □□ **non-violent** *adj.*

non-volatile /nɒn'vɒlə,taɪl/ *adj.* (esp. of a substance) not volatile.

non-voting /nɒn'vəʊtɪŋ/ *adj.* not having or using a vote. □□ **non-voter** *n.*

non-White /nɒn'waɪt/ *adj. & n.* —*adj.* **1** (of a person) not White. **2** of or relating to non-White people. —*n.* a non-White person.

non-word /nɒnwɜːd/ *n.* an unrecorded or unused word.

noodle[1] /'nuːd(ə)l/ *n.* a strip or ring of pasta. [G *Nudel*]

noodle[2] /'nuːd(ə)l/ *n.* **1** a simpleton. **2** *sl.* the head. [18th c.: orig. unkn.]

nook /nʊk/ *n.* a corner or recess; a secluded place. [ME *nok(e)* corner, of unkn. orig.]

nooky /'nʊkɪ/ *n.* (also **nookie**) *sl.* sexual intercourse. [20th c.: perh. f. NOOK]

noon /nuːn/ *n.* **1** twelve o'clock in the day, midday. **2** the culminating point. [OE *nōn* f. L *nona (hora)* ninth hour: orig. = 3 p.m. (cf. NONE[2])]

noonday /'nuːndeɪ/ *n.* midday.

no one /'nəʊ wʌn/ *n.* no person; nobody.

noontide /'nuːntaɪd/ *n.* (also **noontime** /-taɪm/) midday.

noose /nuːs/ *n. & v.* —*n.* **1** a loop with a running knot, tightening as the rope or wire is pulled, esp. in a snare, lasso, or hangman's halter. **2** a snare or bond. **3** *joc.* the marriage tie. —*v.tr.* **1** catch with or enclose in a noose, ensnare. **2 a** make a noose on (a cord). **b** (often foll. by *round*) arrange (a cord) in a noose. □ **put one's head in a noose** bring about one's own downfall. [ME *nose*, perh. f. OF *no(u)s* f. L *nodus* knot]

nopal /'nəʊp(ə)l/ *n.* any American cactus of the genus *Nopalea*, esp. *N. cochinellifera* grown in plantations for breeding cochineal. [F & Sp. f. Nahuatl *nopalli* cactus]

nope /nəʊp/ *adv. colloq.* = NO[2] *adv.* 1. [NO[2]]

nor /nɔː(r), nə(r)/ *conj.* **1** and not; and not either (*neither one thing nor the other; not a man nor a child was to be seen; I said I had not seen it, nor had I; all that is true, nor must we forget ...; can neither read nor write*). **2** and no more; neither ('*I cannot go*'—'*Nor can I*'). □ **nor ... nor** *poet.* or *archaic* neither ... nor ... [ME, contr. f. obs. *nother* f. OE *nawther, nāhwæther* (as NO[2], WHETHER)]

nor' /nɔː(r)/ *n. & adj. & adv.* (esp. in compounds) = NORTH (*nor'ward; nor'wester*). [abbr.]

noradrenalin /,nɔːrə'drenəlɪn/ *n.* (also **noradrenaline**) a hormone released by the adrenal medulla and by sympathetic nerve endings as a neurotransmitter. [*normal* + ADRENALIN]

Nordic /'nɔːdɪk/ *adj. & n.* —*adj.* **1** of or relating to the tall blond dolichocephalic Germanic people found in N. Europe, esp. in Scandinavia. **2** of or relating to Scandinavia or Finland. **3** (of skiing) with cross-country work and jumping. —*n.* a Nordic person, esp. a native of Scandinavia or Finland. [F *nordique* f. *nord* north]

Norfolk jacket /'nɔːfək/ *n.* a man's loose belted jacket, with box pleats. [*Norfolk* in S. England]

nork /nɔːk/ *n.* (usu. in *pl.*) *Austral. sl.* a woman's breast. [20th c.: orig. uncert.]

norland /'nɔːlənd/ *n. Brit.* a northern region. [contr. of NORTHLAND]

norm /nɔːm/ *n.* **1** a standard or pattern or type. **2** a standard quantity to be produced or amount of work to be done. **3** customary behaviour etc. [L *norma* carpenter's square]

normal /'nɔːm(ə)l/ *adj. & n.* —*adj.* **1** conforming to a standard; regular, usual, typical. **2** free from mental or emotional disorder. **3** *Geom.* (of a line) at right angles, perpendicular. **4** *Chem.* (of a solution) containing one gram-equivalent of solute per litre. —*n.* **1 a** the normal value of a temperature etc., esp. blood-heat. **b** the usual state, level, etc. **2** *Geom.* a line at right angles. □ **normal distribution** *Statistics* a function that represents the distribution of many random variables as a symmetrical bell-shaped graph. **normal school** (in the US, France, etc.) a school or college for training teachers. □□ **normalcy** *n.* esp. *US.* **normality** /-'mælɪtɪ/ *n.* [F *normal* or L *normalis* (as NORM)]

normalize /'nɔːmə,laɪz/ *v.* (also **-ise**) **1** *tr.* make normal. **2** *intr.* become normal. **3** *tr.* cause to conform. □□ **normalization** /-'zeɪʃ(ə)n/ *n.* **normalizer** *n.*

normally /'nɔːməlɪ/ *adv.* **1** in a normal manner. **2** usually.

Norman /'nɔːmən/ *n. & adj.* —*n.* **1** a native or inhabitant of Normandy. **2** a descendant of the people of mixed Scandinavian and Frankish origin established there in the 10th c., who conquered England in 1066. **3** Norman French. **4** *Archit.* the style of Romanesque architecture found in Britain under the Normans. **5** any of the English kings from William I to Stephen. —*adj.* **1** of or relating to the Normans. **2** of or relating to the Norman style of architecture. □ **Norman Conquest** see CONQUEST. **Norman English** English as spoken or influenced by the Normans. **Norman French** French as spoken by the Normans or (after 1066) in English lawcourts. □□ **Normanesque** /-'nesk/ *adj.* **Normanism** *n.* **Normanize** *v.tr. & intr.* (also **-ise**). [OF *Normans* pl. of *Normant* f. ON *Northmathr* (as NORTH, MAN)]

normative /'nɔːmətɪv/ *adj.* of or establishing a norm. □□ **normatively** *adv.* **normativeness** *n.* [F *normatif -ive* f. L *norma* (see NORM)]

Norn /nɔːn/ *n.* any of three goddesses of destiny in Scandinavian mythology. [ON: orig. unkn.]

Norroy /'nɒrɔɪ/ *n.* (in full **Norroy and Ulster**) *Heraldry* (in the UK) the title given to the third King of Arms, with jurisdiction north of the Trent and (since 1943) in N. Ireland (cf. CLARENCEUX, *King of Arms*). [ME f. AF *norroi* (unrecorded) f. OF *nord* north, *roi* king]

Norse /nɔːs/ *n. & adj.* —*n.* **1 a** the Norwegian language. **b** the Scandinavian language-group. **2** (prec. by *the*; treated as *pl.*) **a** the Norwegians. **b** the Vikings. —*adj.* of ancient Scandinavia, esp. Norway. □ **Old Norse 1** the Germanic language from which the Scandinavian languages are derived. **2** the language of Norway and its colonies until the 14th c. □□ **Norseman** *n.* (*pl.* **-men**). [Du. *noor(d)sch* f. *noord* north]

north /nɔːθ/ *n., adj., & adv.* —*n.* **1 a** the point of the horizon 90° anticlockwise from east. **b** the compass point corresponding to this. **c** the direction in which this lies. **2** (usu. **the North**) **a** the part of the world or a country or a town lying to the north, esp. = *north country* or *Northern States*. **b** the Arctic. **c** the industrialized nations. **3** (**North**) *Bridge* a player occupying the position designated 'north'. —*adj.* **1** towards, at, near, or facing north. **2** coming from the north (*north wind*). —*adv.* **1** towards, at, or near the north. **2** (foll. by *of*) further north than. □ **North American** *adj.* of North America. —*n.* a native or inhabitant of North America, esp. a citizen of the US or Canada. **north and south** lengthwise along a line from north to south. **north by east** (or **west**) between north and north-north-east (or north-north-west). **north country** the northern part of England (north of the Humber). **North-countryman** (*pl.* **-men**) a native of the north country. **north-east** *n.* **1** the point of the horizon midway between north and east. **2** the compass point corresponding to this. **3** the direction in which this lies. —*adj.* of, towards, or coming from the north-east. —*adv.* towards, at, or near the north-east. **North-East** the part of a country or town lying to the north-east. **north-easterly** *adj.* & *adv.* = *north-east.* **north-eastern** lying on the north-east side. **north-east passage** a passage for ships along the northern coast of Europe and Asia, formerly thought of as a possible route to the East. **north light** light from the north, esp. as desired by painters and in factory design. **north-north-east** the point or direction midway between north and north-east. **north-north-west** the point or direction midway between north and north-west. **North Pole 1** the northernmost point of the earth's axis of rotation. **2** the northernmost point about which the stars appear to revolve. **North Sea** the sea between Britain, the Netherlands, Germany, and Scandinavia. **North Star** the polestar. **north-west** *n.* **1** the point of the horizon midway between north and west. **2** the compass point corresponding to this. **3** the direction in which this lies. —*adj.* of, towards, or coming from the north-west. —*adv.* towards, at, or near the north-west. **North-West** the part of a country or town lying to the north-west. **north-westerly** *adj.* & *adv.* = *north-west.* **north-western** lying on the north-west side. **north-west passage** a passage for ships along the northern coast of America, formerly thought of as a possible route from the Atlantic to the Pacific. **to the north** (often foll. by *of*) in a northerly direction. [OE f. Gmc]

Northants /nɔːˈθænts/ *abbr.* Northamptonshire.

northbound /ˈnɔːθbaʊnd/ *adj.* travelling or leading northwards.

northeaster /nɔːˈθiːstə(r)/ *n.* a north-east wind.

norther /ˈnɔːðə(r)/ *n.* US a strong cold north wind blowing in autumn and winter over Texas, Florida, and the Gulf of Mexico.

northerly /ˈnɔːðəlɪ/ *adj.*, *adv.*, & *n.* —*adj.* & *adv.* **1** in a northern position or direction. **2** (of wind) blowing from the north. —*n.* (*pl.* **-ies**) (usu. in *pl.*) a wind blowing from the north.

northern /ˈnɔːð(ə)n/ *adj.* **1** of or in the north; inhabiting the north. **2** lying or directed towards the north. □**Northern hemisphere** the half of the earth north of the equator. **northern lights** the aurora borealis. **Northern States** the States in the north of the US. □□**northernmost** *adj.* [OE *northerne* (as NORTH, -ERN)]

northerner /ˈnɔːðənə(r)/ *n.* a native or inhabitant of the north.

northing /ˈnɔːθɪŋ/ *n.* Naut. the distance travelled or measured northward.

Northland /ˈnɔːθlənd/ *n.* poet. the northern lands; the northern part of a country. [OE (as NORTH, LAND)]

Northman /ˈnɔːθmən/ *n.* (*pl.* **-men**) a native of Scandinavia, esp. of Norway. [OE]

Northumb. *abbr.* Northumberland.

Northumbrian /nɔːˈθʌmbrɪən/ *adj.* & *n.* —*adj.* of or relating to ancient Northumbria (England north of the Humber) or modern Northumberland. —*n.* **1** a native of ancient Northumbria or modern Northumberland. **2** the dialect of ancient Northumbria or modern Northumberland. [obs. *Northumber*, persons living beyond the Humber, f. OE *Northhymbre*]

northward /ˈnɔːθwəd/ *adj.*, *adv.*, & *n.* —*adj.* & *adv.* (also **northwards**) towards the north. —*n.* a northward direction or region.

northwester /nɔːˈθwestə(r)/ *n.* a north-west wind.

Norway lobster /ˈnɔːweɪ/ *n.* a small European lobster, *Nephrops norvegicus*. [*Norway* in N. Europe]

Norway rat /ˈnɔːweɪ/ *n.* the common brown rat, *Rattus norvegicus*.

Norwegian /nɔːˈwiːdʒ(ə)n/ *n.* & *adj.* —*n.* **1 a** a native

or national of Norway. **b** a person of Norwegian descent. **2** the language of Norway. —*adj.* of or relating to Norway or its people or language. [med.L *Norvegia* f. ON *Norvegr* (as NORTH, WAY), assim. to *Norway*]

nor'-wester /nɔːˈwestə(r)/ *n.* **1** a northwester. **2** a glass of strong liquor. **3** an oilskin hat, a sou'wester. [contr.]

Nos. *abbr.* numbers. [cf. No.]

nose /nəʊz/ *n.* & *v.* —*n.* **1** an organ above the mouth on the face or head of a human or animal, containing nostrils and used for smelling and breathing. **2 a** the sense of smell (*dogs have a good nose*). **b** the ability to detect a particular thing (*a nose for scandal*). **3** the odour or perfume of wine, tea, tobacco, hay, etc. **4** the open end or nozzle of a tube, pipe, pair of bellows, retort, etc. **5 a** the front end or projecting part of a thing, e.g. of a car or aircraft. **b** = NOSING. **6** *sl.* an informer of the police. —*v.* **1** *tr.* (often foll. by *out*) **a** perceive the smell of, discover by smell. **b** detect. **2** *tr.* thrust or rub one's nose against or into, esp. in order to smell. **3** *intr.* (usu. foll. by *about*, *around*, etc.) pry or search. **4 a** *intr.* make one's way cautiously forward. **b** *tr.* make (one's or its way). □**as plain as the nose on your face** easily seen. **by a nose** by a very narrow margin (*won the race by a nose*). **count noses** count those present, one's supporters, etc.; decide a question by mere numbers. **cut off one's nose to spite one's face** disadvantage oneself in the course of trying to disadvantage another. **get up a person's nose** *sl.* annoy a person. **keep one's nose clean** *sl.* stay out of trouble, behave properly. **keep one's nose to the grindstone** see GRINDSTONE. **nose-cone** the cone-shaped nose of a rocket etc. **nose-flute** a musical instrument blown with the nose in Fiji etc. **nose leaf** a fleshy part on the nostrils of some bats, used for echo location. **nose-monkey** the proboscis monkey. **nose-piece 1** = NOSEBAND. **2** the part of a helmet etc. protecting the nose. **3** the part of a microscope to which the object-glass is attached. **nose-rag** *sl.* a pocket handkerchief. **nose-to-tail** (of vehicles) moving or stationary one close behind another, esp. in heavy traffic. **nose-wheel** a landing-wheel under the nose of an aircraft. **on the nose 1** US *sl.* precisely. **2** *Austral. sl.* annoying. **put a person's nose out of joint** *colloq.* embarrass, disconcert, frustrate, or supplant a person. **rub a person's nose in it** see RUB. **see no further than one's nose** be short-sighted, esp. in foreseeing the consequences of one's actions etc. **speak through one's nose** pronounce words with a nasal twang. **turn up one's nose** (usu. foll. by *at*) *colloq.* show disdain. **under a person's nose** *colloq.* right before a person (esp. of defiant or unnoticed actions). **with one's nose in the air** haughtily. □□ **nosed** *adj.* (also in *comb.*). **noseless** *adj.* [OE *nosu*]

nosebag /ˈnəʊzbæg/ *n.* a bag containing fodder, hung on a horse's head.

noseband /ˈnəʊzbænd/ *n.* the lower band of a bridle, passing over the horse's nose.

nosebleed /ˈnəʊzbliːd/ *n.* an instance of bleeding from the nose.

nosedive /ˈnəʊzdaɪv/ *n.* & *v.* —*n.* **1** a steep downward plunge by an aeroplane. **2** a sudden plunge or drop. —*v.intr.* make a nosedive.

nosegay /ˈnəʊzgeɪ/ *n.* a bunch of flowers, esp. a sweet-scented posy. [NOSE + GAY in obs. use = ornament]

nosepipe /ˈnəʊzpaɪp/ *n.* a piece of piping used as a nozzle.

nosering /ˈnəʊzrɪŋ/ *n.* a ring fixed in the nose of an animal (esp. a bull) for leading it, or of a person for ornament.

nosey var. of NOSY.

nosh /nɒʃ/ *v.* & *n.* *sl.* —*v.tr.* & *intr.* **1** eat or drink. **2** US eat between meals. —*n.* **1** food or drink. **2** US a snack. □**nosh-up** Brit. a large meal. [Yiddish]

noshery /ˈnɒʃərɪ/ n. (pl. -ies) sl. a restaurant or snack bar.

nosing /ˈnəʊzɪŋ/ n. a rounded edge of a step, moulding, etc., or a metal shield for it.

nosography /nəˈsɒgrəfɪ/ n. the systematic description of diseases. [Gk nosos disease + -GRAPHY]

nosology /nəˈsɒlədʒɪ/ n. the branch of medical science dealing with the classification of diseases. □□ **nosological** /ˌnɒsəˈlɒdʒɪk(ə)l/ adj. [Gk nosos disease + -LOGY]

nostalgia /nɒˈstældʒɪə, -dʒə/ n. 1 (often foll. by for) sentimental yearning for a period of the past. 2 regretful or wistful memory of an earlier time. 3 severe homesickness. □□ **nostalgic** adj. **nostalgically** adv. [mod.L f. Gk nostos return home]

nostoc /ˈnɒstɒk/ n. any gelatinous blue-green unicellular alga of the genus Nostoc, that can fix nitrogen from the atmosphere. [name invented by Paracelsus]

Nostradamus /ˌnɒstrəˈdɑːməs/ n. a person who claims to foretell future events. [Latinized form of the name of M. de Nostredame, French astrologer and physician d. 1566]

nostril /ˈnɒstrɪl/ n. either of two external openings of the nasal cavity in vertebrates that admit air to the lungs and smells to the olfactory nerves. □□ **nostrilled** adj. (also in comb.). [OE nosthyrl, nosterl f. nosu NOSE + thȳr(e)l hole: cf. THRILL]

nostrum /ˈnɒstrəm/ n. 1 a quack remedy, a patent medicine, esp. one prepared by the person recommending it. 2 a pet scheme, esp. for political or social reform. [L, neut. of noster our, used in sense 'of our own make']

nosy /ˈnəʊzɪ/ adj. & n. (also **nosey**) —adj. (**nosier**, **nosiest**) 1 colloq. inquisitive, prying. 2 having a large nose. 3 having a distinctive (good or bad) smell. —n. (pl. -ies) a person with a large nose. □ **Nosy Parker** esp. Brit. colloq. a busybody. □□ **nosily** adv. **nosiness** n.

not /nɒt/ adv. expressing negation, esp.: 1 (also **n't** joined to a preceding verb) following an auxiliary verb or be or (in a question) the subject of such a verb (I cannot say; she isn't there; didn't you tell me?; am I not right?; aren't we smart?). ¶ Use with other verbs is now archaic (I know not; fear not), except with participles and infinitives (not knowing, I cannot say; we asked them not to come). 2 used elliptically for a negative sentence or verb or phrase (Is she coming?—I hope not; Do you want it?—Certainly not!). 3 used to express the negative of other words (not a single one was left; Are they pleased?—Not they; he is not my cousin, but my nephew). □ **not at all** (in polite reply to thanks) there is no need for thanks. **not but what** archaic 1 all the same; nevertheless (I cannot do it; not but what a stronger man might). 2 not such ... or so ... that ... not (not such a fool but what he can see it). **not half** see HALF. **not least** with considerable importance, notably. **not much** see MUCH. **not quite** 1 almost (am not quite there). 2 noticeably not (not quite proper). **not that** (foll. by clause) it is not to be inferred that (if he said so—not that he ever did—he lied). **not a thing** nothing at all. **not very** see VERY. [ME contr. of NOUGHT]

nota bene /ˌnəʊtə ˈbeneɪ/ v.tr. (as imper.) observe what follows, take notice (usu. drawing attention to a following qualification of what has preceded). [L, = note well]

notability /ˌnəʊtəˈbɪlɪtɪ/ n. (pl. -ies) 1 the state of being notable (names of no historical notability). 2 a prominent person. [ME f. OF notabilité or LL notabilitas (as NOTABLE)]

notable /ˈnəʊtəb(ə)l/ adj. & n. —adj. worthy of note; striking, remarkable, eminent. —n. an eminent person. □□ **notableness** n. **notably** adv. [ME f. OF f. L notabilis (as NOTE)]

notarize /ˈnəʊtəˌraɪz/ v.tr. (also **-ise**) US certify (a document) as a notary.

notary /ˈnəʊtərɪ/ n. (pl. -ies) (in full **notary public**)

a person authorized to perform certain legal formalities, esp. to draw up or certify contracts, deeds, etc. □□ **notarial** /nəʊˈteərɪəl/ adj. **notarially** /nəʊˈteərɪəlɪ/ adv. [ME f. L notarius secretary (as NOTE)]

notate /nəʊˈteɪt/ v.tr. write in notation. [back-form. f. NOTATION]

notation /nəʊˈteɪʃ(ə)n/ n. 1 a the representation of numbers, quantities, pitch and duration etc. of musical notes, etc. by symbols. b any set of such symbols. 2 a set of symbols used to represent chess moves, dance steps, etc. 3 US a a note or annotation. b a record. 3 colloq. a step or degree (move up a notch). 4 US a deep gorge. —v.tr. 1 make notches in. 2 (foll. by up) record or score with or as with notches. 3 secure or insert by notches. □□ **notational** adj. [F notation or L notatio (as NOTE)]

notch /nɒtʃ/ n. & v. —n. 1 a V-shaped indentation on an edge or surface. 2 a nick made on a stick etc. in order to keep count. 3 colloq. a step or degree (move up a notch). 4 US a deep gorge. —v.tr. 1 make notches in. 2 (foll. by up) record or score with or as with notches. 3 secure or insert by notches. □□ **notched** adj. **notcher** n. **notchy** adj. (**notchier**, **notchiest**). [AF noche perh. f. a verbal form nocher (unrecorded), of uncert. orig.]

note /nəʊt/ n. & v. —n. 1 a brief record of facts, topics, thoughts, etc., as an aid to memory, for use in writing, public speaking, etc. (often in pl.: make notes; spoke without notes). 2 an observation, usu. unwritten, of experiences etc. (compare notes). 3 a short or informal letter. 4 a formal diplomatic or parliamentary communication. 5 a short annotation or additional explanation in a book etc.; a footnote. 6 a Brit. = BANKNOTE (a five-pound note). b a written promise or notice of payment of various kinds. 7 a notice, attention (worthy of note). b distinction, eminence (a person of note). 8 a a written sign representing the pitch and duration of a musical sound. b a single tone of definite pitch made by a musical instrument, the human voice, etc. c a key of a piano etc. 9 a a bird's song or call. b a single tone in this. 10 a quality or tone of speaking, expressing mood or attitude etc. (sound a note of warning; ended on a note of optimism). 11 a characteristic; a distinguishing feature. —v.tr. 1 observe, notice; give or draw attention to. 2 (often foll. by down) record as a thing to be remembered or observed. 3 (in passive; often foll. by for) be famous or well known (for a quality, activity, etc.) (were noted for their generosity). □ **hit** (or **strike**) **the right note** speak or act in exactly the right manner. **of note** important, distinguished (a person of note). **take note** (often foll. by of) observe; pay attention (to). □□ **noted** adj. (in sense 3 of v.). **noteless** adj. [ME f. OF note (n.), noter (v.) f. L nota mark]

notebook /ˈnəʊtbʊk/ n. a small book for making or taking notes.

notecase /ˈnəʊtkeɪs/ n. a wallet for holding banknotes.

notelet /ˈnəʊtlɪt/ n. a small folded sheet of paper, usu. with a decorative design, for an informal letter.

notepaper /ˈnəʊtˌpeɪpə(r)/ n. paper for writing letters.

noteworthy /ˈnəʊtˌwɜːðɪ/ adj. worthy of attention; remarkable. □□ **noteworthiness** n.

nothing /ˈnʌθɪŋ/ n. & adv. —n. 1 not anything (nothing has been done; have nothing to do). 2 no thing (often foll. by compl.: I see nothing that I want; can find nothing useful). 3 a a person or thing of no importance or concern; a trivial event or remark (was nothing to me; the little nothings of life). b (attrib.) colloq. of no value; indeterminate (a nothing sort of day). 4 non-existence; what does not exist. 5 (in calculations) no amount; nought (a third of nothing is nothing). —adv. 1 not at all, in no way (helps us nothing; is nothing like enough). 2 US colloq. not at all (Is he ill?—Ill nothing, he's dead.). □ **be nothing to** 1 not concern. 2 not compare with. **be** (or **have**) **nothing to do with** 1 have no connection with. 2 not be involved or associated with. **for**

nothing 1 at no cost; without payment. 2 to no purpose. **have nothing on** 1 be naked. 2 have no engagements. **no nothing** *colloq.* (concluding a list of negatives) nothing at all. **nothing doing** *colloq.* 1 **a** there is no prospect of success or agreement. **b** I refuse. 2 nothing is happening. **nothing** (or **nothing else**) **for it** (often foll. by *but to* + infin.) no alternative (*nothing for it but to pay up*). **nothing** (or **not much**) **in it** (or **to it**) 1 untrue or unimportant. 2 simple to do. 3 no (or little) advantage to be seen in one possibility over another. **nothing less than** at least (*nothing less than a disaster*). **think nothing of it** do not apologize or feel bound to show gratitude. [OE *nān thing* (as NO[1], THING)]

nothingness /'nʌθɪŋnɪs/ *n.* 1 non-existence; the non-existent. 2 worthlessness, triviality, insignificance.

notice /'nəʊtɪs/ *n. & v.* —*n.* 1 attention, observation (*it escaped my notice*). 2 a displayed sheet etc. bearing an announcement or other information. 3 **a** an intimation or warning, esp. a formal one to allow preparations to be made (*give notice; at a moment's notice*). **b** (often foll. by *to* + infin.) a formal announcement or declaration of intention to end an agreement or leave employment at a specified time (*hand in one's notice; notice to quit*). 4 a short published review or comment about a new play, book, etc. —*v.tr.* 1 (often foll. by *that, how,* etc. + clause) perceive, observe; take notice of. 2 remark upon; speak of. □**at short** (or **a moment's**) **notice** with little warning. **notice-board** *Brit.* a board for displaying notices. **take notice** (or **no notice**) show signs (or no signs) of interest. **take notice of** 1 observe; pay attention to. 2 act upon. **under notice** served with a formal notice. [ME f. OF f. L *notitia* being known f. *notus* past part. of *noscere* know]

noticeable /'nəʊtɪsəb(ə)l/ *adj.* 1 easily seen or noticed; perceptible. 2 noteworthy. □**noticeably** *adv.*

notifiable /'nəʊtɪˌfaɪəb(ə)l/ *adj.* (of a disease) that must be notified to the health authorities.

notify /'nəʊtɪˌfaɪ/ *v.tr.* (-**ies**, -**ied**) 1 (often foll. by *of,* or *that* + clause) inform or give notice to (a person). 2 make known; announce or report (a thing). □□ **notification** /-frˈkeɪʃ(ə)n/ *n.* [ME f. OF *notifier* f. L *notificare* f. *notus* known: see NOTICE]

notion /'nəʊʃ(ə)n/ *n.* 1 **a** a concept or idea; a conception (*it was an absurd notion*). **b** an opinion (*has the notion that people are honest*). **c** a vague view or understanding (*have no notion what you mean*). 2 an inclination, impulse, or intention (*has no notion of conforming*). 3 (in *pl.*) small, useful articles, esp. haberdashery. [L *notio* idea f. *notus* past part. of *noscere* know]

notional /'nəʊʃən(ə)l/ *adj.* 1 **a** hypothetical, imaginary. **b** (of knowledge etc.) speculative; not based on experiment etc. 2 *Gram.* (of a verb) conveying its own meaning, not auxiliary. □□ **notionally** *adv.* [obs. F *notional* or med.L *notionalis* (as NOTION)]

notochord /'nəʊtəˌkɔːd/ *n.* a cartilaginous skeletal rod supporting the body in all embryo and some adult chordate animals. [Gk *nōton* back + CHORD[2]]

notorious /nəʊˈtɔːrɪəs/ *adj.* well known, esp. unfavourably (*a notorious criminal; notorious for its climate*). □□ **notoriety** /-təˈraɪətɪ/ *n.* **notoriously** *adv.* [med.L *notorius* f. L *notus* (as NOTION)]

notornis /nəʊˈtɔːnɪs/ *n.* a rare flightless New Zealand bird, *Porphyrio mantelli,* with a large bill and brightly coloured plumage. Also called TAKAHE. [Gk *notos* south + *ornis* bird]

Notts. /nɒts/ *abbr.* Nottinghamshire.

notwithstanding /ˌnɒtwɪθˈstændɪŋ, -wɪðˈstændɪŋ/ *prep., adv., & conj.* —*prep.* in spite of; without prevention by (*notwithstanding your objections; this fact notwithstanding*). —*adv.* nevertheless; all the same. —*conj.* (usu. foll. by *that* + clause) although. [ME, orig. absol. part. f. NOT + WITHSTAND + -ING[2]]

nougat /'nuːgɑː/ *n.* a sweet made from sugar or honey, nuts, and egg-white. [F f. Prov. *nogat* f. *noga* nut]

nought /nɔːt/ *n.* 1 the digit 0; a cipher. 2 *poet.* or *archaic* (in certain phrases) nothing (cf. NAUGHT). □**noughts and crosses** a paper-and-pencil game with a square grid of nine squares, in which players seek to complete a row of three noughts or three crosses entered alternately. [OE *nōu̯iht* f. *ne* not + *ōwiht* var. of *āwiht* AUGHT[1]]

noun /naʊn/ *n. Gram.* a word (other than a pronoun) or group of words used to name or identify any of a class of persons, places, or things (**common noun**), or a particular one of these (**proper noun**). □□ **nounal** *adj.* [ME f. AF f. L *nomen* name]

nourish /'nʌrɪʃ/ *v.tr.* 1 **a** sustain with food. **b** enrich; promote the development of (the soil etc.). **c** provide with intellectual or emotional sustenance or enrichment. 2 foster or cherish (a feeling etc.). □□ **nourisher** *n.* [ME f. OF *norir* f. L *nutrire*]

nourishing /'nʌrɪʃɪŋ/ *adj.* (esp. of food) containing much nourishment; sustaining. □□ **nourishingly** *adv.*

nourishment /'nʌrɪʃmənt/ *n.* sustenance, food.

nous /naʊs/ *n.* 1 *colloq.* common sense; gumption. 2 *Philos.* the mind or intellect. [Gk]

nouveau riche /ˌnuːvəʊ ˈriːʃ/ *n.* (*pl.* **nouveaux riches** *pronunc.* same) a person who has recently acquired (usu. ostentatious) wealth. [F, = new rich]

nouvelle cuisine /ˌnuːvel kwɪˈziːn/ *n.* a modern style of cookery avoiding heaviness and emphasizing presentation. [F, = new cookery]

nouvelle vague /ˌnuːvel ˈvɑːg/ *n.* a new trend, esp. in French film-making of the early 1960s. [F, fem. of *nouveau* new + *vague* wave]

Nov. *abbr.* November.

nova /'nəʊvə/ *n.* (*pl.* **novae** /-viː/ or **novas**) a star showing a sudden large increase of brightness and then subsiding. [L, fem. of *novus* new, because orig. thought to be a new star]

novel[1] /'nɒv(ə)l/ *n.* 1 a fictitious prose story of book length. 2 (prec. by *the*) this type of literature. [It. *novella* (*storia* story) fem. of *novello* new f. L *novellus* f. *novus*]

novel[2] /'nɒv(ə)l/ *adj.* of a new kind or nature; strange; previously unknown. □□ **novelly** *adv.* [ME f. OF f. L *novellus* f. *novus* new]

novelese /ˌnɒvəˈliːz/ *n. derog.* a style characteristic of inferior novels.

novelette /ˌnɒvəˈlet/ *n.* 1 **a** a short novel. **b** *Brit. derog.* a light romantic novel. 2 *Mus.* a piano piece in free form with several themes.

novelettish /ˌnɒvəˈletɪʃ/ *adj. derog.* in the style of a light romantic novel; sentimental.

novelist /'nɒvəlɪst/ *n.* a writer of novels. □□ **novelistic** /-ˈlɪstɪk/ *adj.*

novelize /'nɒvəˌlaɪz/ *v.tr.* (also -**ise**) make into a novel. □□ **novelization** /-ˈzeɪʃ(ə)n/ *n.*

novella /nəˈvelə/ *n.* (*pl.* **novellas**) a short novel or narrative story; a tale. [It.: see NOVEL[1]]

novelty /'nɒvəltɪ/ *n. & adj.* —*n.* (*pl.* -**ies**) 1 **a** newness; new character. **b** originality. 2 a new or unusual thing or occurrence. 3 a small toy or decoration etc. of novel design. 4 (*attrib.*) having novelty (*novelty toys*). [ME f. OF *novelté* (as NOVEL[2])]

November /nəˈvembə(r)/ *n.* the eleventh month of the year. [ME f. OF *novembre* f. L *November* f. *novem* nine (orig. the ninth month of the Roman year)]

novena /nəˈviːnə/ *n. RC Ch.* a devotion consisting of special prayers or services on nine successive days. [med.L f. L *novem* nine]

novice /'nɒvɪs/ *n.* 1 **a** a probationary member of a religious order, before the taking of vows. **b** a new convert. 2 a beginner; an inexperienced person. 3 an animal that has not won a major prize in a competition. [ME f. OF f. L *novicius* f. *novus* new]

noviciate /nəˈvɪʃɪət/ *n.* (also **novitiate**) 1 the period of being a novice. 2 a religious novice. 3 novices' quarters. [F *noviciat* or med.L *noviciatus* (as NOVICE)]

Novocaine /'nəʊvəˌkeɪn/ *n.* (also **novocaine**) *propr.* a local anaesthetic derived from benzoic acid. [L *novus* new + COCAINE]

now /naʊ/ *adv., conj., & n.* —*adv.* **1** at the present or mentioned time. **2** immediately (*I must go now*). **3** by this or that time (*it was now clear*). **4** under the present circumstances (*I cannot now agree*). **5** on this further occasion (*what do you want now?*). **6** in the immediate past (*just now*). **7** (esp. in a narrative or discourse) then, next (*the police now arrived; now to consider the next point*). **8** (without reference to time, giving various tones to a sentence) surely, I insist, I wonder, etc. (*now what do you mean by that?; oh come now!*). —*conj.* (often foll. by *that* + clause) as a consequence of the fact (*now that I am older; now you mention it*). —*n.* this time; the present (*should be there by now; has happened before now*). □**as of now** from or at this time. **for now** until a later time (*goodbye for now*). **now and again** (or **then**) from time to time; intermittently. **now or never** an expression of urgency. [OE *nū*]

nowadays /'naʊəˌdeɪz/ *adv. & n.* —*adv.* at the present time or age; in these times. —*n.* the present time.

noway /'nəʊweɪ/ *adv.* = NOWISE; (see *no way*).

Nowel (also **Nowell**) *archaic* var. of NOEL.

nowhere /'nəʊweə(r)/ *adv. & pron.* —*adv.* in or to no place. —*pron.* no place. □**be** (or **come in**) **nowhere** be unplaced in a race or competition. **come from nowhere** be suddenly evident or successful. **get nowhere** make or cause to make no progress. **in the middle of nowhere** *colloq.* remote from urban life. **nowhere near** not nearly. [OE *nāhwǣr* (as NO¹, WHERE)]

nowise /'nəʊwaɪz/ *adv.* in no manner; not at all.

nowt /naʊt/ *n. colloq.* or *dial.* nothing. [var. of NOUGHT]

noxious /'nɒkʃəs/ *adj.* harmful, unwholesome. □□ **noxiously** *adv.* **noxiousness** *n.* [f. L *noxius* f. *noxa* harm]

noyau /'nwɑːjəʊ/ *n.* (*pl.* **noyaux** /-jəʊz/) a liqueur of brandy flavoured with fruit-kernels. [F, = kernel, ult. f. L *nux nucis* nut]

nozzle /'nɒz(ə)l/ *n.* a spout on a hose etc. from which a jet issues. [NOSE + -LE²]

NP *abbr.* Notary Public.

Np *symb. Chem.* the element neptunium.

n.p. *abbr.* **1** new paragraph. **2** no place of publication.

NPA *abbr.* (in the UK) Newspaper Publishers' Association.

NPL *abbr.* (in the UK) National Physical Laboratory.

nr. *abbr.* near.

NS *abbr.* **1** new style. **2** new series. **3** Nova Scotia.

NSB *abbr.* (in the UK) National Savings Bank.

NSC *abbr.* (in the US) National Security Council.

NSF *abbr.* (in the US) National Science Foundation.

NSPCC *abbr.* (in the UK) National Society for the Prevention of Cruelty to Children.

NSW *abbr.* New South Wales.

NT *abbr.* **1** New Testament. **2** Northern Territory (of Australia). **3** no trumps.

n't /ənt/ *adv.* (in *comb.*) = NOT (usu. with *is, are, have, must*, and the auxiliary verbs *can, do, should, would: isn't; mustn't*) (see also CAN'T, DON'T, WON'T). [contr.]

Nth. *abbr.* North.

nth see N¹.

NTP *abbr.* normal temperature and pressure.

nu /njuː/ *n.* the thirteenth letter of the Greek alphabet (N, ν). [Gk]

nuance /'njuːɑːs/ *n. & v.* —*n.* a subtle difference in or shade of meaning, feeling, colour, etc. —*v.tr.* give a nuance or nuances to. [F f. *nuer* to shade, ult. f. L *nubes* cloud]

nub /nʌb/ *n.* **1** the point or gist (of a matter or story). **2** a small lump, esp. of coal. **3** a stub; a small residue. □□ **nubby** *adj.* [app. var. of *knub*, f. MLG *knubbe, knobbe* KNOB]

nubble /'nʌb(ə)l/ *n.* a small knob or lump. □□ **nubbly** *adj.* [dimin. of NUB]

nubile /'njuːbaɪl/ *adj.* (of a woman) marriageable or sexually attractive. □□ **nubility** /-'bɪlɪtɪ/ [L *nubilis* f. *nubere* become the wife of]

nuchal /'njuːk(ə)l/ *adj.* of or relating to the nape of the neck. [*nucha* nape f. med.L *nucha* medulla oblongata f. Arab. *nuḵa'* spinal marrow]

nuci- /njuː'sɪ/ *comb. form* nut. [L *nux nucis* nut]

nuciferous /njuː'sɪfərəs/ *adj. Bot.* bearing nuts.

nucivorous /njuː'sɪvərəs/ *adj.* nut-eating.

nuclear /'njuːklɪə(r)/ *adj.* **1** of, relating to, or constituting a nucleus. **2** using nuclear energy (*nuclear reactor*). **3** having nuclear weapons. □ **nuclear bomb** a bomb involving the release of energy by nuclear fission or fusion or both. **nuclear disarmament** the renunciation of nuclear weapons. **nuclear energy** energy obtained by nuclear fission or fusion. **nuclear family** a couple and their children, regarded as a basic social unit. **nuclear fission** a nuclear reaction in which a heavy nucleus splits spontaneously or on impact with another particle, with the release of energy. **nuclear force** a strong attractive force between nucleons in the atomic nucleus that holds the nucleus together. **nuclear-free** free from nuclear weapons, power, etc. **nuclear fuel** a substance that will sustain a fission chain reaction so that it can be used as a source of nuclear energy. **nuclear fusion** a nuclear reaction in which atomic nuclei of low atomic number fuse to form a heavier nucleus with the release of energy. **nuclear magnetic resonance** the absorption of electromagnetic radiation by a nucleus having a magnetic moment when in an external magnetic field, used mainly as an analytical technique and in body imaging for diagnosis. ¶ Abbr.: **NMR, nmr. nuclear physics** the physics of atomic nuclei and their interactions, esp. in the generation of nuclear energy. **nuclear power 1** electric or motive power generated by a nuclear reactor. **2** a country that has nuclear weapons. **nuclear reactor** a device in which a nuclear fission chain reaction is sustained and controlled in order to produce energy. **nuclear umbrella** supposed protection afforded by an alliance with a country possessing nuclear weapons. **nuclear warfare** warfare in which nuclear weapons are used. **nuclear waste** any radioactive waste material from the reprocessing of spent nuclear fuel. **nuclear winter** obstruction of sunlight as a potential result of nuclear warfare, causing extreme cold. [NUCLEUS + -AR¹]

nuclease /'njuːklɪˌeɪz/ *n.* an enzyme that catalyses the breakdown of nucleic acids.

nucleate /'njuːklɪˌeɪt/ *adj. & v.* —*adj.* having a nucleus. —*v.intr. & tr.* form or form into a nucleus. □□ **nucleation** /-'eɪʃ(ə)n/ *n.* [LL *nucleare* nucleat- form a kernel (as NUCLEUS)]

nuclei *pl.* of NUCLEUS.

nucleic acid /njuː'kliːɪk, -'kleɪɪk/ *n.* either of two complex organic molecules (DNA and RNA), consisting of many nucleotides linked in a long chain, and present in all living cells.

nucleo- /'njuːklɪəʊ/ *comb. form* nucleus; nucleic acid (*nucleo-protein*).

nucleolus /njuː'kliːələs, -klɪ'əʊləs/ *n.* (*pl.* **nucleoli** /-laɪ/) a small dense spherical structure within a non-dividing nucleus. □□ **nucleolar** *adj.* [LL, dimin. of L *nucleus*: see NUCLEUS]

nucleon /'njuːklɪˌɒn/ *n. Physics* a proton or neutron.

nucleonics /ˌnjuːklɪ'ɒnɪks/ *n.pl.* (treated as *sing.*) the branch of science and technology concerned with atomic nuclei and nucleons, esp. the exploitation of nuclear power. □□ **nucleonic** *adj.* [NUCLEAR, after *electronics*]

nucleoprotein /ˌnjuːklɪəʊ'prəʊtiːn/ *n.* a complex of nucleic acid and protein.

nucleoside /'njuːklɪəˌsaɪd/ *n. Biochem.* an organic

compound consisting of a purine or pyrimidine base linked to a sugar, e.g. adenosine.

nucleotide /'njuːklɪəˌtaɪd/ n. Biochem. an organic compound consisting of a nucleoside linked to a phosphate group.

nucleus /'njuːklɪəs/ n. (pl. **nuclei** /-lɪ,aɪ/) **1 a** the central part or thing round which others are collected. **b** the kernel of an aggregate or mass. **2** an initial part meant to receive additions. **3** Astron. the solid part of a comet's head. **4** Physics the positively charged central core of an atom that contains most of its mass. **5** Biol. a large dense organelle of eukaryotic cells, containing the genetic material. **6** a discrete mass of grey matter in the central nervous system. [L, = kernel, inner part, dimin. of nux nucis nut]

nuclide /'njuːklaɪd/ n. Physics a certain type of atom characterized by the number of protons and neutrons in its nucleus. □□ **nuclidic** /njuːˈklɪdɪk/ adj. [NUCLEUS + Gk eidos form]

nude /njuːd/ adj. & n. —adj. naked, bare, unclothed. —n. **1** a painting, sculpture, photograph, etc. of a nude human figure; such a figure. **2** a nude person. **3** (prec. by the) **a** an unclothed state. **b** the representation of an undraped human figure as a genre in art. □ **nude contract** Law = bare contract. [L nudus]

nudge /nʌdʒ/ v. & n. —v.tr. **1** prod gently with the elbow to attract attention. **2** push gently or gradually. **3** give a gentle reminder or encouragement to (a person). —n. the act or an instance of nudging; a gentle push. □□ **nudger** n. [17th c.: orig. unkn.: cf. Norw. dial. nugga, nyggja to push, rub]

nudist /'njuːdɪst/ n. a person who advocates or practises going unclothed. □□ **nudism** n.

nudity /'njuːdɪtɪ/ n. the state of being nude; nakedness.

nugatory /'njuːgətərɪ/ adj. **1** futile, trifling, worthless. **2** inoperative; not valid. [L nugatorius f. nugari to trifle f. nugae jests]

nugget /'nʌgɪt/ n. **1 a** a lump of gold, platinum, etc., as found in the earth. **b** a lump of anything compared to this. **2** something valuable for its size (often abstract in sense: a little nugget of information). [app. f. dial. nug lump etc.]

nuisance /'njuːs(ə)ns/ n. **1** a person, thing, or circumstance causing trouble or annoyance. **2** anything harmful or offensive to the community or a member of it and for which a legal remedy exists. □ **nuisance value** an advantage resulting from the capacity to harass or frustrate. [ME f. OF, = hurt, f. nuire nuis- f. L nocēre to hurt]

NUJ abbr. (in the UK) National Union of Journalists.

nuke /njuːk/ n. & v. colloq. —n. a nuclear weapon. —v.tr. bomb or destroy with nuclear weapons. [abbr.]

null /nʌl/ adj. & n. —adj. **1** (esp. **null and void**) invalid; not binding. **2** non-existent; amounting to nothing. **3** having or associated with the value zero. **4** Computing **a** empty; having no elements (null list). **b** all the elements of which are zeros (null matrix). **5** without character or expression. —n. a dummy letter in a cipher. □ **null character** Computing a character denoting nothing, usu. represented by a zero. **null hypothesis** a hypothesis suggesting that the difference between statistical samples does not imply a difference between populations. **null instrument** an instrument used by adjustment to give a reading of zero. **null link** Computing a reference incorporated into the last item in a list to indicate there are no further items in the list. [F nul nulle or L nullus none f. ne not + ullus any]

nullah /'nʌlə/ n. Anglo-Ind. a dry river-bed or ravine. [Hindi nālā]

nulla-nulla /'nʌlə,nʌlə/ n. (also **nulla**) Austral. a hardwood club used by Aborigines. [Aboriginal]

nullify /'nʌlɪ,faɪ/ v.tr. (-ies, -ied) make null; neutralize, invalidate, cancel. □□ **nullification** /-fɪˈkeɪʃ(ə)n/ n. **nullifier** n.

nullipara /nʌˈlɪpərə/ n. a woman who has never borne a child. □□ **nulliparous** adj. [mod.L f. L nullus none + -para fem. of -parus f. parere bear children]

nullipore /'nʌlɪˌpɔː(r)/ n. any of various seaweeds able to secrete lime. [L nullus none + PORE[1]]

nullity /'nʌlɪtɪ/ n. (pl. -ies) **1** Law **a** being null; invalidity, esp. of marriage. **b** an act, document, etc., that is null. **2 a** nothingness. **b** a mere nothing; a nonentity. [F nullité or med.L nullitas f. L nullus none]

NUM abbr. (in the UK) National Union of Mineworkers.

Num. abbr. Numbers (Old Testament).

numb /nʌm/ adj. & v. —adj. (often foll. by with) deprived of feeling or the power of motion (numb with cold). —v.tr. **1** make numb. **2** stupefy, paralyse. □ **numb-fish** = electric ray. □□ **numbly** adv. **numbness** n. [ME nome(n) past part. of nim take: for -b cf. THUMB]

numbat /'nʌmbæt/ n. a small Australian marsupial, Myrmecobius fasciatus, with a bushy tail and black and white striped back. [Aboriginal]

number /'nʌmbə(r)/ n. & v. —n. **1 a** an arithmetical value representing a particular quantity and used in counting and making calculations. **b** a word, symbol, or figure representing this; a numeral. **c** an arithmetical value showing position in a series esp. for identification, reference, etc. (registration number). **2** (often foll. by of) the total count or aggregate (the number of accidents has decreased; twenty in number). **3 a** the study of the behaviour of numbers; numerical reckoning (the laws of number). **b** (in pl.) arithmetic (not good at numbers). **4 a** (in sing. or pl.) a quantity or amount; a total; a count (a large number of people; only in small numbers). **b** (in pl.) numerical preponderance (force of numbers; there is safety in numbers). **5 a** a person or thing having a place in a series, esp. a single issue of a magazine, an item in a programme, etc. **b** a song, dance, musical item, etc. **6** company, collection, group (among our number). **7** Gram. **a** the classification of words by their singular or plural forms. **b** a particular such form. **8** colloq. a person or thing regarded familiarly or affectionately (usu. qualified in some way: an attractive little number). **9** (**Numbers**) the Old Testament book containing a census. —v.tr. **1** include (I number you among my friends). **2** assign a number or numbers to. **3** have or amount to (a specified number). **4 a** count. **b** include. □ **by numbers** following simple instructions (as if) identified by numbers. **one's days are numbered** one does not have long to live. **have a person's number** colloq. understand a person's real motives, character, etc. **have a person's number on it** (of a bomb, bullet, etc.) be destined to hit a specified person. **number cruncher** Computing & Math. sl. a machine capable of complex calculations etc. **number crunching** the act or process of making these calculations. **one's number is up** colloq. one is finished or doomed to die. **a number of** some, several. ¶ Use with a plural verb is now standard: a number of problems remain. **number one** n. colloq. oneself (always takes care of number one). —adj. most important (the number one priority). **number-plate** a plate on a vehicle displaying its registration number. **numbers game 1** usu. derog. action involving only arithmetical work. **2** US a lottery based on the occurrence of unpredictable numbers in the results of races etc. **Number Ten** 10 Downing Street, the official London home of the British Prime Minister. **number two** a second in command. **without number** innumerable. [ME f. OF nombre (n.), nombrer (v.) f. L numerus, numerare]

numberless /'nʌmbəlɪs/ adj. innumerable.

numbles /'nʌmb(ə)lz/ n.pl. Brit. archaic a deer's entrails. [ME f. OF numbles, nombles loin etc., f. L lumbulus dimin. of lumbus loin: cf. UMBLES]

numbskull var. of NUMSKULL.

numdah /'nʌmdɑ:/ n. an embroidered felt rug from India etc. [Urdu namdā f. Pers. namad carpet]

numen /'nju:men/ n. (pl. **numina** /-mɪnə/) a presiding deity or spirit. [L numen -minis]

numerable /'nju:mərəb(ə)l/ adj. that can be counted. □□ **numerably** adv. [L numerabilis f. numerare NUMBER v.]

numeral /'nju:mər(ə)l/ n. & adj. —n. a word, figure, or group of figures denoting a number. —adj. of or denoting a number. [LL numeralis f. L (as NUMBER)]

numerate /'nju:mərət/ adj. acquainted with the basic principles of mathematics. □□ **numeracy** n. [L numerus number + -ATE² after literate]

numeration /,nju:mə'reɪʃ(ə)n/ n. **1 a** a method or process of numbering or computing. **b** calculation. **2** the expression in words of a number written in figures. [ME f. L numeratio payment, in LL numbering (as NUMBER)]

numerator /'nju:mə,reɪtə(r)/ n. **1** the number above the line in a vulgar fraction showing how many of the parts indicated by the denominator are taken (e.g. 2 in ⅔). **2** a person or device that numbers. [F numérateur or LL numerator (as NUMBER)]

numerical /nju:'merɪk(ə)l/ adj. (also **numeric**) of or relating to a number or numbers (numerical superiority). □ **numerical analysis** the branch of mathematics that deals with the development and use of numerical methods for solving problems. □□ **numerically** adv. [med.L numericus (as NUMBER)]

numerology /,nju:mə'rɒlədʒɪ/ n. (pl. **-ies**) the study of the supposed occult significance of numbers. □□ **numerological** /-rə'lɒdʒɪk(ə)l/ adj. **numerologist** n. [L numerus number + -LOGY]

numerous /'nju:mərəs/ adj. **1** (with pl.) great in number (received numerous gifts). **2** consisting of many (a numerous family). □□ **numerously** adv. **numerousness** n. [L numerosus (as NUMBER)]

numina pl. of NUMEN.

numinous /'nju:mɪnəs/ adj. **1** indicating the presence of a divinity. **2** spiritual. **3** awe-inspiring. [L numen: see NUMEN]

numismatic /,nju:mɪz'mætɪk/ adj. of or relating to coins or medals. □□ **numismatically** adv. [F numismatique f. L numisma f. Gk nomisma -atos current coin f. nomizō use currently]

numismatics /,nju:mɪz'mætɪks/ n.pl. (usu. treated as sing.) the study of coins or medals. □□ **numismatist** /-'mɪzmətɪst/ n.

numismatology /nju:,mɪzmə'tɒlədʒɪ/ n. = NUMISMATICS.

nummulite /'nʌmjʊ,laɪt/ n. a disc-shaped fossil shell of a foraminiferous protozoan found in Tertiary strata. [L nummulus dimin. of nummus coin]

numnah /'nʌmnə/ n. a saddle-cloth or pad placed under a saddle. [Urdu namdā: see NUMDAH]

numskull /'nʌmskʌl/ n. (also **numbskull**) a stupid or foolish person. [NUMB + SKULL]

nun /nʌn/ n. a member of a community of women living apart under religious vows. □□ **nunhood** n. **nunlike** adj. **nunnish** adj. [ME f. OE nunne and OF nonne f. eccl.L nonna fem. of nonnus monk, orig. a title given to an elderly person]

nunatak /'nʌnə,tæk/ n. an isolated peak of rock projecting above a surface of land ice or snow e.g. in Greenland. [Eskimo]

nun-buoy /'nʌnbɔɪ/ n. a buoy circular in the middle and tapering to each end. [obs. nun child's top + BUOY]

nunc dimittis /,nʌŋk dɪ'mɪtɪs/ n. the Song of Simeon (Luke 2:29-32) used as a canticle. [f. the opening words nunc dimittis now let (your servant) depart]

nunciature /'nʌnʃə,tjʊə(r)/ n. RC Ch. the office or tenure of a nuncio. [It. nunziatura (as NUNCIO)]

nuncio /'nʌnʃɪəʊ, -sɪəʊ/ n. (pl. **-os**) RC Ch. a papal ambassador. [It. f. L nuntius messenger]

nuncupate /'nʌŋkju,peɪt/ v.tr. declare (a will or testament) orally, not in writing. □□ **nuncupation**

/-'peɪʃ(ə)n/ n. **nuncupative** /-pətɪv/ adj. [L nuncupare nuncupat- name]

nunnery /'nʌnərɪ/ n. (pl. **-ies**) a religious house of nuns; a convent.

NUPE /'nju:pɪ/ abbr. (in the UK) National Union of Public Employees.

nuptial /'nʌpʃ(ə)l/ adj. & n. —adj. of or relating to marriage or weddings. —n. (usu. in pl.) a wedding. [F nuptial or L nuptialis f. nuptiae wedding f. nubere nupt- wed]

NUR abbr. (in the UK) National Union of Railwaymen.

nurd var. of NERD.

nurse /nɜ:s/ n. & v. —n. **1** a person trained to assist doctors in caring for the sick or infirm. **2** a person employed or trained to take charge of young children. **3** archaic = wet-nurse. **4** Forestry a tree planted as a shelter to others. **5** Zool. a sexually imperfect bee, ant, etc., caring for a young brood; a worker. —v. **1 a** intr. work as a nurse. **b** tr. attend to (a sick person). **c** tr. give medical attention to (an illness or injury). **2** tr. & intr. feed or be fed at the breast. **3** tr. (in passive; foll. by in) be brought up in (a specified condition) (nursed in poverty). **4** tr. hold or treat carefully or caressingly (sat nursing my feet). **5** tr. **a** foster; promote the development of (the arts, plants, etc.). **b** harbour or nurture (a grievance, hatred, etc.). **c** pay special attention to (nursed the voters). **6** tr. Billiards keep (the balls) together for a series of cannons. [reduced f. ME and OF norice, nurice f. LL nutricia fem. of L nutricius f. nutrix -icis f. nutrire NOURISH]

nurseling var. of NURSLING.

nursemaid /'nɜ:smeɪd/ n. **1** a woman in charge of a child or children. **2** a person who watches over or guides another carefully.

nursery /'nɜ:sərɪ/ n. (pl. **-ies**) **1 a** a room or place equipped for young children. **b** = day nursery. **2** a place where plants, trees, etc., are reared for sale or transplantation. **3** any sphere or place in or by which qualities or types of people are fostered or bred. **4** Billiards **a** grouped balls (see NURSE v. 6). **b** (in full **nursery cannon**) a cannon on three close balls. □ **nursery nurse** a person trained to take charge of babies and young children. **nursery rhyme** a simple traditional song or story in rhyme for children. **nursery school** a school for children between the ages of three and five. **nursery slopes** Skiing gentle slopes suitable for beginners. **nursery stakes** a race for two-year-old horses.

nurseryman /'nɜ:sərɪmən/ n. (pl. **-men**) an owner of or worker in a plant nursery.

nursing /'nɜ:sɪŋ/ n. **1** the practice or profession of caring for the sick as a nurse. **2** (attrib.) concerned with or suitable for nursing the sick or elderly etc. (nursing home; nursing sister). □ **nursing officer** a senior nurse (see senior nursing officer).

nursling /'nɜ:slɪŋ/ n. (also **nurseling**) an infant that is being suckled.

nurture /'nɜ:tʃə(r)/ n. & v. —n. **1** the process of bringing up or training (esp. children); fostering care. **2** nourishment. **3** sociological factors as an influence on or determinant of personality (opp. NATURE). —v.tr. **1** bring up; rear. **2** nourish. □□ **nurturer** n. [ME f. OF nour(e)ture (as NOURISH)]

NUS abbr. **1** (in the UK) National Union of Seamen. **2** (in the UK) National Union of Students.

NUT abbr. (in the UK) National Union of Teachers.

nut /nʌt/ n. & v. —n. **1 a** a fruit consisting of a hard or tough shell around an edible kernel. **b** this kernel. **2** a pod containing hard seeds. **3** a small usu. square or hexagonal flat piece of metal or other material with a threaded hole through it for screwing on the end of a bolt to secure it. **4** sl. a person's head. **5** sl. **a** a crazy or eccentric person. **b** an obsessive enthusiast or devotee (a health-food nut). **6** a small lump of coal, butter, etc. **7 a** a device fitted to the bow of a violin for adjusting its tension. **b** the fixed ridge on the neck of a stringed instrument over which the strings pass. **8** (in *pl.*) *coarse sl.* the testicles. —*v.intr.* (**nutted, nutting**) seek or gather nuts (*go nutting*). □**do one's nut** *sl.* be extremely angry or agitated. **for nuts** *colloq.* even tolerably well (*cannot sing for nuts*). **nut cutlet** a cutlet-shaped portion of meat-substitute, made from nuts etc. **nut-house** *sl.* a mental home or hospital. **nut-oil** an oil obtained from hazelnuts and walnuts and used in paints and varnishes. **nuts and bolts** *colloq.* the practical details. **nut-tree** any tree bearing nuts, esp. a hazel. **off one's nut** *sl.* crazy. □□ **nutlike** *adj.* [OE *hnutu* f. Gmc]

nutant /ˈnjuːt(ə)nt/ *adj. Bot.* nodding, drooping. [L *nutare* nod]

nutation /njuːˈteɪʃ(ə)n/ *n.* **1** the act or an instance of nodding. **2** *Astron.* a periodic oscillation of the earth's poles. **3** oscillation of a spinning top. **4** the spiral movement of a plant organ during growth. [L *nutatio* (as NUTANT)]

nutcase /ˈnʌtkeɪs/ *n. sl.* a crazy or foolish person.

nutcracker /ˈnʌtˌkrækə(r)/ *n.* (usu. in *pl.*) a device for cracking nuts.

nutgall /ˈnʌtɡɔːl/ *n.* a gall found on dyer's oak, used as a dyestuff.

nuthatch /ˈnʌthætʃ/ *n.* any small bird of the family Sittidae, climbing up and down tree-trunks and feeding on nuts, insects, etc. [NUT + *hatch* rel. to HATCH[2]]

nutlet /ˈnʌtlɪt/ *n.* a small nut or nutlike fruit.

nutmeg /ˈnʌtmeɡ/ *n.* **1** an evergreen E. Indian tree, *Myristica fragrans*, yielding a hard aromatic spheroidal seed. **2** the seed of this used as a spice and in medicine. □ **nutmeg-apple** the fruit of this tree, yielding mace and nutmeg. [ME: partial transl. of OF *nois mug(u)ede* ult. f. L *nux* nut + LL *muscus* MUSK]

nutria /ˈnjuːtrɪə/ *n.* the skin or fur of a coypu. [Sp., = otter]

nutrient /ˈnjuːtrɪənt/ *n. & adj.* —*n.* any substance that provides essential nourishment for the maintenance of life. —*adj.* serving as or providing nourishment. [L *nutrire* nourish]

nutriment /ˈnjuːtrɪmənt/ *n.* **1** nourishing food. **2** an intellectual or artistic etc. nourishment or stimulus. □□ **nutrimental** /-ˈment(ə)l/ *adj.* [L *nutrimentum* (as NUTRIENT)]

nutrition /njuːˈtrɪʃ(ə)n/ *n.* **1 a** the process of providing or receiving nourishing substances. **b** food, nourishment. **2** the study of nutrients and nutrition. □□ **nutritional** *adj.* [F *nutrition* or LL *nutritio* (as NUTRIENT)]

nutritionist /njuːˈtrɪʃənɪst/ *n.* a person who studies or is an expert on the processes of human nourishment.

nutritious /njuːˈtrɪʃəs/ *adj.* efficient as food; nourishing. □□ **nutritiously** *adv.* **nutritiousness** *n.* [L *nutritius* (as NURSE)]

nutritive /ˈnjuːtrɪtɪv/ *adj. & n.* —*adj.* **1** of or concerned in nutrition. **2** serving as nutritious food. —*n.* a nutritious article of food. [ME f. F *nutritif -ive* f. med.L *nutritivus* (as NUTRIENT)]

nuts /nʌts/ *adj. & int.* —*adj. sl.* crazy, mad, eccentric. —*int. sl.* an expression of contempt or derision (*nuts to you*). □**be nuts about** (or **on**) *colloq.* be enthusiastic about or very fond of.

nutshell /ˈnʌtʃel/ *n.* the hard exterior covering of a nut. □**in a nutshell** in a few words.

nutter /ˈnʌtə(r)/ *n. Brit. sl.* a crazy or eccentric person.

nutty /ˈnʌtɪ/ *adj.* (**nuttier, nuttiest**) **1 a** full of nuts. **b** tasting like nuts. **2** *sl.* = NUTS *adj.* □□ **nuttiness** *n.*

nux vomica /nʌks ˈvɒmɪkə/ *n.* **1** an E. Indian tree, *Strychnos nux-vomica*, yielding a poisonous fruit. **2** the seeds of this tree, containing strychnine. [med.L f. L *nux* nut + *vomicus* f. *vomere* vomit]

nuzzle /ˈnʌz(ə)l/ *v.* **1** *tr.* prod or rub gently with the nose. **2** *intr.* (foll. by *into, against, up to*) press the nose gently. **3** *tr.* (also *refl.*) nestle; lie snug. [ME f. NOSE + -LE[4]]

NV *abbr. US* Nevada (in official postal use).

NW *abbr.* **1** north-west. **2** north-western.

NY *abbr. US* New York (also in official postal use).

nyala var. of INYALA.

NYC *abbr.* New York City.

nyctalopia /ˌnɪktəˈləʊpɪə/ *n.* the inability to see in dim light or at night. Also called *night-blindness*. [LL f. Gk *nuktalōps* f. *nux nuktos* night + *alaos* blind + *ōps* eye]

nyctitropic /ˌnɪktɪˈtrəʊpɪk/ *adj. Bot.* (of plant movements) occurring at night and caused by changes in light and temperature. [Gk *nukti-* comb. form of *nux nuktos* night + *tropos* turn]

nye var. of NIDE.

nylghau /ˈnɪlɡɔː/ *n.* = NILGAI. [Hind. f. Pers. *nīlgāw* f. *nīl* blue + *gāw* cow]

nylon /ˈnaɪlɒn/ *n.* **1** any of various synthetic polyamide fibres having a protein-like structure, with tough, lightweight, elastic properties, used in industry and for textiles etc. **2** a nylon fabric. **3** (in *pl.*) stockings made of nylon. [invented word, after *cotton, rayon*]

nymph /nɪmf/ *n.* **1** any of various mythological semi-divine spirits regarded as maidens and associated with aspects of nature, esp. rivers and woods. **2** *poet.* a beautiful young woman. **3 a** an immature form of some insects. **b** a young dragonfly or damselfly. □□ **nymphal** *adj.* **nymphean** /-ˈfiːən/ *adj.* **nymphlike** *adj.* [ME f. OF *nimphe* f. L *nympha* f. Gk *numphē*]

nymphae /ˈnɪmfiː/ *n.pl. Anat.* the labia minora. [L, pl. of *nympha*: see NYMPH]

nymphet /ˈnɪmfet, -ˈfet/ *n.* **1** a young nymph. **2** *colloq.* a sexually attractive young woman.

nympho /ˈnɪmfəʊ/ *n.* (*pl.* **-os**) *colloq.* a nymphomaniac. [abbr.]

nympholepsy /ˈnɪmfəˌlepsɪ/ *n.* ecstasy or frenzy caused by desire of the unattainable. [NYMPHOLEPT after *epilepsy*]

nympholept /ˈnɪmfəˌlept/ *n.* a person inspired by violent enthusiasm esp. for an ideal. □□ **nympholeptic** /-ˈleptɪk/ *adj.* [Gk *numpholēptos* caught by nymphs (as NYMPH, *lambanō* take)]

nymphomania /ˌnɪmfəˈmeɪnɪə/ *n.* excessive sexual desire in women. □□ **nymphomaniac** *n. & adj.* [mod.L (as NYMPH, -MANIA)]

nystagmus /nɪˈstæɡməs/ *n.* rapid involuntary movements of the eyes. □□ **nystagmic** *adj.* [Gk *nustagmos* nodding f. *nustazō* nod]

NZ *abbr.* New Zealand.

O

O[1] /əʊ/ n. (also **o**) (pl. **Os** or **O's**) **1** the fifteenth letter of the alphabet. **2** (**0**) nought, zero (in a sequence of numerals esp. when spoken). **3** a human blood type of the ABO system.

O[2] abbr. (also **O.**) Old.

O[3] symb. Chem. the element oxygen.

O[4] /əʊ/ int. **1** var. of OH[1]. **2** prefixed to a name in the vocative (*O God*). [ME, natural excl.]

O' /əʊ, ə/ prefix of Irish patronymic names (*O'Connor*). [Ir. ó, ua, descendant]

o' /ə/ prep. of, on (esp. in phrases: *o'clock*; *will-o'-the-wisp*). [abbr.]

-o /əʊ/ suffix forming usu. sl. or colloq. variants or derivatives (*beano*; *wino*). [perh. OH[1] as joc. suffix]

-o- /əʊ/ suffix the terminal vowel of combining forms (*spectro-*; *chemico-*; *Franco-*). ¶ Often elided before a vowel, as in *neuralgia*. [orig. Gk]

oaf /əʊf/ n. (pl. **oafs**) **1** an awkward lout. **2** a stupid person. □□ **oafish** adj. **oafishly** adv. **oafishness** n. [orig. = elf's child, var. of obs. *auf* f. ON *álfr* elf]

oak /əʊk/ n. **1** any tree or shrub of the genus *Quercus* usu. having lobed leaves and bearing acorns. **2** the durable wood of this tree, used esp. for furniture and in building. **3** (attrib.) made of oak (*oak table*). **4** a heavy outer door of a set of university college rooms. **5** (**the Oaks**) (treated as sing.) an annual race at Epsom for three-year-old fillies (from the name of a nearby estate). □ **oak-apple** (or **-gall**) an apple-like gall containing larvae of certain wasps, found on oak trees. □□ **oaken** adj. [OE *āc* f. Gmc]

oakum /əʊkəm/ n. a loose fibre obtained by picking old rope to pieces and used esp. in caulking. [OE *ǣcumbe*, *ācumbe*, lit. 'off-combings']

O. & M. abbr. organization and methods.

OAP abbr. Brit. old-age pensioner.

oar /ɔ:(r)/ n. **1** a pole with a blade used for rowing or steering a boat by leverage against the water. **2** a rower. □ **put one's oar in** interfere, meddle. **rest** (*US* **lay**) **on one's oars** relax one's efforts. □□ **oared** adj. (also in comb.). **oarless** adj. [OE *ār* f. Gmc, perh. rel. to Gk *eretmos* oar]

oarfish /ɔ:fɪʃ/ n. a ribbonfish, *Regalecus glesne*.

oarlock /ɔ:lɒk/ n. *US* a rowlock.

oarsman /ɔ:zmən/ n. (pl. **-men**; fem. **oarswoman**, pl. **-women**) a rower. □□ **oarsmanship** n.

oarweed /ɔ:wi:d/ n. (also **oreweed**) any large marine alga esp. of the genus *Laminaria*, often growing along shores.

OAS abbr. **1** Organization of American States. **2** on active service.

oasis /əʊˈeɪsɪs/ n. (pl. **oases** /-si:z/) **1** a fertile spot in a desert, where water is found. **2** an area or period of calm in the midst of turbulence. [LL f. Gk, app. of Egypt. orig.]

oast /əʊst/ n. a kiln for drying hops. □ **oast-house** a building containing this. [OE *āst* f. Gmc]

oat /əʊt/ n. **1 a** a cereal plant, *Avena sativa*, cultivated in cool climates. **b** (in pl.) the grain yielded by this, used as food. **2** any other cereal of the genus *Avena*, esp. the wild oat, *A. fatua*. **3** poet. the oat-stem used as a musical pipe by shepherds etc., usu. in pastoral or bucolic poetry. **4** (in pl.) sl. sexual gratification. □ **feel one's oats** colloq. **1** be lively. **2** *US* feel self-important. **oat-grass** any of various grasses, esp. of the genus *Arrhenatherum*. **off one's oats** colloq. not hungry. **sow one's oats** (or **wild oats**) indulge in youthful excess or promiscuity. □□ **oaten** adj. [OE *āte*, pl. *ātan*, of unkn. orig.]

oatcake /əʊtkeɪk/ n. a thin unleavened biscuit-like food made of oatmeal, common in Scotland and N. England.

oath /əʊθ/ n. (pl. **oaths** /əʊðz/) **1** a solemn declaration or undertaking (often naming God) as to the truth of something or as a commitment to future action. **2** a statement or promise contained in an oath (*oath of allegiance*). **3** a profane or blasphemous utterance; a curse. □ **on** (or **under**) **oath** having sworn a solemn oath. **take** (or **swear**) **an oath** make such a declaration or undertaking. [OE *āth* f. Gmc]

oatmeal /əʊtmi:l/ n. **1** meal made from ground oats used esp. in porridge and oatcakes. **2** a greyish-fawn colour flecked with brown.

OAU abbr. Organization of African Unity.

OB abbr. Brit. outside broadcast.

ob. abbr. he or she died. [L *obiit*]

ob- /ɒb/ prefix (also **oc-** before *c*, **of-** before *f*, **op-** before *p*) occurring mainly in words of Latin origin, meaning: **1** exposure, openness (*object*; *obverse*). **2** meeting or facing (*occasion*; *obvious*). **3** direction (*oblong*; *offer*). **4** opposition, hostility, or resistance (*obstreperous*; *opponent*; *obstinate*). **5** hindrance, blocking, or concealment (*obese*; *obstacle*; *occult*). **6** finality or completeness (*obsolete*; *occupy*). **7** (in modern technical words) inversely; in a direction or manner contrary to the usual (*obconical*; *obovate*). [L f. *ob* towards, against, in the way of]

Obad. abbr. Obadiah (Old Testament).

obbligato /ˌɒblɪˈɡɑːtəʊ/ n. (pl. **-os**) Mus. an accompaniment, usu. special and unusual in effect, forming an integral part of a composition (*with violin obbligato*). [It., = obligatory, f. L *obligatus* past part. (as OBLIGE)]

obconical /ɒbˈkɒnɪk(ə)l/ adj. (also **obconic**) in the form of an inverted cone.

obcordate /ɒbˈkɔːdeɪt/ adj. Biol. in the shape of a heart and attached at the pointed end.

obdurate /ˈɒbdjʊrət/ adj. **1** stubborn. **2** hardened against persuasion or influence. □□ **obduracy** n. **obdurately** adv. **obdurateness** n. [ME f. L *obduratus* past part. of *obdurare* (as OB-, *durare* harden f. *durus* hard)]

OBE abbr. (in the UK) Officer of the Order of the British Empire.

obeah /əʊbɪə/ n. (also **obi** /əʊbɪ/) a kind of sorcery practised esp. in the West Indies. [W. Afr.]

obeche /əʊˈbiːtʃɪ/ n. **1** a West African tree, *Triplochiton scleroxylon*. **2** the light-coloured timber from this. [Nigerian name]

obedience /əʊˈbiːdɪəns/ n. **1** obeying as an act or practice or quality. **2** submission to another's rule or authority. **3** compliance with a law or command. **4** Eccl. **a** compliance with a monastic rule. **b** a sphere of authority (*the Roman obedience*). □ **in obedience to** actuated by or in accordance with. [ME f. OF f. L *obedientia* (as OBEY)]

obedient /əʊˈbiːdɪənt/ adj. **1** obeying or ready to obey. **2** (often foll. by *to*) submissive to another's will; dutiful (*obedient to the law*). □□ **obediently** adv. [ME f. OF f. L *obediens -entis* (as OBEY)]

obeisance /əʊˈbeɪs(ə)ns/ n. **1** a bow, curtsey, or other respectful or submissive gesture (*make an obeisance*). **2** homage, submission, deference (*pay obeisance*). □□ **obeisant** adj. **obeisantly** adv. [ME f. OF *obeissance* (as OBEY)]

obeli pl. of OBELUS.

obelisk /ˈɒbəlɪsk/ n. **1 a** a tapering usu. four-sided stone pillar set up as a monument or landmark etc. **b** a mountain, tree, etc., of similar shape. **2** = OBELUS. [L *obeliscus* f. Gk *obeliskos* dimin. of *obelos* SPIT[2]]

b *but*   d *dog*   f *few*   g *get*   h *he*   j *yes*   k *cat*   l *leg*   m *man*   n *no*   p *pen*   r *red*   s *sit*   t *top*   v *voice*

obelize /'ɒbəˌlaɪz/ v.tr. (also -ise) mark with an obelus as spurious etc. [Gk obelizō f. obelos: see OBELISK]

obelus /'ɒbələs/ n. (pl. obeli /-ˌlaɪ/) 1 a dagger-shaped reference mark in printed matter. 2 a mark (− or ÷) used in ancient manuscripts to mark a word or passage, esp. as spurious. [L f. Gk obelos SPIT²]

obese /əʊ'biːs/ adj. very fat; corpulent. □□ **obeseness** n. **obesity** n. [L obesus (as OB-, edere eat)]

obey /əʊ'beɪ/ v. 1 tr. a carry out the command of (you will obey me). b carry out (a command) (obey orders). 2 intr. do what one is told to do. 3 tr. be actuated by (a force or impulse). □□ **obeyer** n. [ME f. OF obeir f. L obedire (as OB-, audire hear)]

obfuscate /'ɒbfʌˌskeɪt/ v.tr. 1 obscure or confuse (a mind, topic, etc.). 2 stupefy, bewilder. □□ **obfuscation** /-'keɪʃ(ə)n/ n. **obfuscatory** adj. [LL obfuscare (as OB-, fuscus dark)]

obi¹ var. of OBEAH.

obi² /'əʊbɪ/ n. (pl. **obis**) a broad sash worn with a Japanese kimono. [Jap. obi belt]

obit /'ɒbɪt, 'əʊbɪt/ n. colloq. an obituary. [abbr.]

obiter dictum /ˌɒbɪtə 'dɪktəm/ n. (pl. **obiter dicta** /-tə/) 1 a judge's expression of opinion uttered in court or giving judgement, but not essential to the decision and therefore without binding authority. 2 an incidental remark. [L f. obiter by the way + dictum a thing said]

obituary /ə'bɪtjʊərɪ/ n. (pl. **-ies**) 1 a notice of a death or deaths esp. in a newspaper. 2 an account of the life of a deceased person. 3 (attrib.) of or serving as an obituary. □□ **obituarial** /-tjʊ'eərɪəl/ adj. **obituarist** n. [med.L obituarius f. L obitus death f. obire obit- die (as OB-, ire go)]

object n. & v. —n. /'ɒbdʒɪkt/ 1 a material thing that can be seen or touched. 2 (foll. by of) a person or thing to which action or feeling is directed (the object of attention; the object of our study). 3 a thing sought or aimed at; a purpose. 4 Gram. a noun or its equivalent governed by an active transitive verb or by a preposition. 5 Philos. a thing external to the thinking mind or subject. 6 derog. a person or thing of esp. a pathetic or ridiculous appearance. 7 Computing a package of information and a description of its manipulation. —v. /əb'dʒekt/ 1 intr. (often foll. by to, against) express or feel opposition, disapproval, or reluctance; protest (I object to being treated like this; objecting against government policies). 2 tr. (foll. by that + clause) state as an objection (objected that they were kept waiting). 3 tr. (foll. by to, against, or that + clause) adduce (a quality or fact) as contrary or damaging (to a case). □**no object** not forming an important or restricting factor (money no object). **object-ball** Billiards etc. that at which a player aims the cue-ball. **object-glass** the lens in a telescope etc. nearest to the object observed. **object language** 1 a language described by means of another language (see METALANGUAGE). 2 Computing a language into which a program is translated by means of a compiler or assembler. **object-lesson** a striking practical example of some principle. **object of the exercise** the main point of an activity. □□ **objectless** /'ɒbdʒɪktlɪs/ adj. **objector** /əb'dʒektə(r)/ n. [ME f. med.L objectum thing presented to the mind, past part. of L objicere (as OB-, jacere ject-throw)]

objectify /ɒb'dʒektɪˌfaɪ/ v.tr. (**-ies**, **-ied**) 1 make objective; embody. 2 present as an object of perception. □□ **objectification** /-fɪ'keɪʃ(ə)n/ n.

objection /əb'dʒekʃ(ə)n/ n. 1 an expression or feeling of opposition or disapproval. 2 the act of objecting. 3 an adverse reason or statement. [ME f. OF objection or LL objectio (as OBJECT)]

objectionable /əb'dʒekʃ(ə)nəb(ə)l/ adj. 1 open to objection. 2 unpleasant, offensive. □□ **objectionableness** n. **objectionably** /-blɪ/ adv.

objective /əb'dʒektɪv/ adj. & n. —adj. 1 external to the mind; actually existing; real. 2 (of a person, writing, art, etc.) dealing with outward things or exhibiting facts uncoloured by feelings or opinions; not subjective. 3 Gram. (of a case or word) constructed as or appropriate to the object of a transitive verb or preposition (cf. ACCUSATIVE). 4 aimed at (objective point). 5 (of symptoms) observed by another and not only felt by the patient. —n. 1 something sought or aimed at; an objective point. 2 Gram. the objective case. 3 = object-glass. □□ **objectival** /ˌɒbdʒek'taɪv(ə)l/ adj. **objectively** adv. **objectiveness** n. **objectivity** /ˌɒbdʒek'tɪvɪtɪ/ n. **objectivize** /əb'dʒektɪˌvaɪz/ v.tr. (also -ise). **objectivization** /əbˌdʒektɪvaɪ'zeɪʃ(ə)n/ n. [med.L objectivus (as OBJECT)]

objectivism /əb'dʒektɪˌvɪz(ə)m/ n. 1 the tendency to lay stress on what is objective. 2 Philos. the belief that certain things (esp. moral truths) exist apart from human knowledge or perception of them. □□ **objectivist** n. **objectivistic** /-'vɪstɪk/ adj.

objet d'art /ˌɒbʒeɪ 'dɑː/ n. (pl. **objets d'art** pronunc. same) a small decorative object. [F, lit. 'object of art']

objurgate /'ɒbdʒəˌgeɪt/ v.tr. literary chide or scold. □□ **objurgation** /-'geɪʃ(ə)n/ n. **objurgatory** /ɒb'dʒɜːgətərɪ/ adj. [L objurgare objurgat- (as OB-, jurgare quarrel f. jurgium strife)]

oblanceolate /ɒb'lɑːnsɪələt/ adj. Bot. (esp. of leaves) lanceolate with the more pointed end at the base.

oblate¹ /'ɒbleɪt/ n. a person dedicated to a monastic or religious life or work. [F f. med.L oblatus f. offere oblat- offer (as OB-, ferre bring)]

oblate² /'ɒbleɪt/ adj. Geom. (of a spheroid) flattened at the poles (cf. PROLATE). [mod.L oblatus (as OBLATE¹)]

oblation /əʊ'bleɪʃ(ə)n/ n. Relig. 1 a thing offered to a divine being. 2 the presentation of bread and wine to God in the Eucharist. □□ **oblational** adj. **oblatory** /'ɒblətərɪ/ adj. [ME f. OF oblation or LL oblatio (as OBLATE¹)]

obligate v. & adj. —v.tr. /'ɒblɪˌgeɪt/ 1 (usu. in passive; foll. by to + infin.) bind (a person) legally or morally. 2 US commit (assets) as security. —adj. /'ɒblɪgət/ Biol. that has to be as described (obligate parasite). □□ **obligator** n. [L obligare obligat- (as OBLIGE)]

obligation /ˌɒblɪ'geɪʃ(ə)n/ n. 1 the constraining power of a law, precept, duty, contract, etc. 2 a duty; a burdensome task. 3 a binding agreement, esp. one enforceable under legal penalty; a written contract or bond. 4 a a service or benefit (repay an obligation). b indebtedness for this (be under an obligation). □**day of obligation** Eccl. a day on which all are required to attend Mass or Communion. **of obligation** obligatory. □□ **obligational** adj. [ME f. OF f. L obligatio -onis (as OBLIGE)]

obligatory /ə'blɪgətərɪ/ adj. 1 legally or morally binding. 2 compulsory and not merely permissive. 3 constituting an obligation. □□ **obligatorily** adv. [ME f. LL obligatorius (as OBLIGE)]

oblige /ə'blaɪdʒ/ v. 1 tr. (foll. by to + infin.) constrain, compel. 2 tr. be binding on. 3 tr. a make indebted by conferring a favour. b (foll. by with, or by + verbal noun) gratify (oblige me by leaving). c perform a service for (often absol.: will you oblige?). 4 tr. (in passive; foll. by to) be indebted (am obliged to you for your help). 5 intr. colloq. (foll. by with) make a contribution of a specified kind (Doris obliged with a song). 6 tr. archaic or Law (foll. by to, or to + infin.) bind by oath, promise, contract, etc. □**much obliged** an expression of thanks. □□ **obliger** n. [ME f. OF obliger f. L obligare (as OB-, ligare bind)]

obligee /ˌɒblɪ'dʒiː/ n. Law a person to whom another is bound by contract or other legal procedure (cf. OBLIGOR).

obliging /ə'blaɪdʒɪŋ/ adj. courteous, accommodating; ready to do a service or kindness. □□ **obligingly** adv. **obligingness** n.

obligor /ˌɒblɪ'gɔː(r)/ n. Law a person who is bound to another by contract or other legal procedure (cf. OBLIGEE).

oblique /ə'bliːk/ adj., n., & v. —adj. 1 a slanting;

declining from the vertical or horizontal. **b** diverging from a straight line or course. **2** not going straight to the point; roundabout, indirect. **3** *Geom.* **a** (of a line, plane figure, or surface) inclined at other than a right angle. **b** (of an angle) acute or obtuse. **c** (of a cone, cylinder, etc.) with an axis not perpendicular to the plane of its base. **4** *Anat.* neither parallel nor perpendicular to the long axis of a body or limb. **5** *Bot.* (of a leaf) with unequal sides. **6** *Gram.* denoting any case other than the nominative or vocative. —*n.* **1** an oblique stroke (/). **2** an oblique muscle. —*v.intr.* (**obliques, obliqued, obliquing**) esp. *Mil.* advance obliquely. □**oblique oration** (or **speech**) = *reported speech* (see REPORT). **oblique sphere** see SPHERE. □□ **obliquely** *adv.* **obliqueness** *n.* **obliquity** /ə'blɪkwɪtɪ/ *n.* [ME f. F f. L *obliquus*]

obliterate /ə'blɪtə‚reɪt/ *v.tr.* **1 a** blot out; efface, erase, destroy. **b** leave no clear traces of. **2** deface (a postage stamp etc.) to prevent further use. □□ **obliteration** /-'reɪʃ(ə)n/ *n.* **obliterative** /-rətɪv/ *adj.* **obliterator** *n.* [L *obliterare* (as OB-, *litera* LETTER)]

oblivion /ə'blɪvɪən/ *n.* **1 a** the state of having or being forgotten. **b** disregard; an unregarded state. **2** an amnesty or pardon. □**fall into oblivion** be forgotten or disused. [ME f. OF f. L *oblivio -onis* f. *oblivisci* forget]

oblivious /ə'blɪvɪəs/ *adj.* **1** (often foll. by *of*) forgetful, unmindful. **2** (foll. by *to, of*) unaware or unconscious of. □□ **obliviously** *adv.* **obliviousness** *n.* [ME f. L *obliviosus* (as OBLIVION)]

oblong /'ɒblɒŋ/ *adj. & n.* —*adj.* **1** deviating from a square form by having one long axis, esp. rectangular with adjacent sides unequal. **2** greater in breadth than in height. —*n.* an oblong figure or object. [ME f. L *oblongus* longish (as OB-, *longus* long)]

obloquy /'ɒbləkwɪ/ *n.* **1** the state of being generally ill spoken of. **2** abuse, detraction. [ME f. LL *obloquium* contradiction f. L *obloqui* deny (as OB-, *loqui* speak)]

obnoxious /əb'nɒkʃəs/ *adj.* offensive, objectionable, disliked. □□ **obnoxiously** *adv.* **obnoxiousness** *n.* [orig. = vulnerable (to harm), f. L *obnoxiosus* or *obnoxius* (as OB-, *noxa* harm: assoc. with NOXIOUS)]

oboe /'əʊbəʊ/ *n.* **1 a** a woodwind double-reed instrument of treble pitch and plaintive incisive tone. **b** its player. **2** an organ stop with a quality resembling an oboe. □**oboe d'amore** /dæ'mɔːreɪ/ an oboe with a pear-shaped bell and mellow tone, pitched a minor third below a normal oboe, commonly used in baroque music. □□ **oboist** /'əʊbəʊɪst/ *n.* [It. *oboe* or F *hautbois* f. *haut* high + *bois* wood: *d'amore* = of love]

obol /'ɒb(ə)l/ *n.* an ancient Greek coin, equal to one-sixth of a drachma. [L *obolus* f. Gk *obolos*, var. of *obelos* OBELUS]

obovate /ɒb'əʊveɪt/ *adj. Biol.* (of a leaf) ovate with the narrower end at the base.

obscene /əb'siːn/ *adj.* **1** offensively or repulsively indecent, esp. by offending accepted sexual morality. **2** *colloq.* highly offensive or repugnant (*an obscene accumulation of wealth*). **3** *Brit. Law* (of a publication) tending to deprave or corrupt. □□ **obscenely** *adv.* **obsceneness** *n.* [F *obscène* or L *obsc(a)enus* ill-omened, abominable]

obscenity /əb'senɪtɪ/ *n.* (*pl.* -ies) **1** the state or quality of being obscene. **2** an obscene action, word, etc. [L *obscaenitas* (as OBSCENE)]

obscurantism /‚ɒbskjʊə'ræntɪz(ə)m/ *n.* opposition to knowledge and enlightenment. □□ **obscurant** /əb'skjʊərənt/ *n.* **obscurantist** *n.* [*obscurant* f. G f. L *obscurans* f. *obscurare*: see OBSCURE]

obscure /əb'skjʊə(r)/ *adj. & v.* —*adj.* **1** not clearly expressed or easily understood. **2** unexplained, doubtful. **3** dark, dim. **4** indistinct; not clear. **5** hidden; remote from observation. **6 a** unnoticed. **b** (of a person) undistinguished, hardly known. **7** (of a colour) dingy, dull, indefinite. —*v.tr.* **1** make obscure, dark, indistinct, or unintelligible. **2** dim the glory of; outshine. **3** conceal from sight. □**obscure**

vowel = *indeterminate vowel.* □□ **obscuration** /-'reɪʃ(ə)n/ *n.* **obscurely** *adv.* [ME f. OF *obscur* f. L *obscurus* dark]

obscurity /əb'skjʊərɪtɪ/ *n.* (*pl.* -ies) **1** the state of being obscure. **2** an obscure person or thing. [F *obscurité* f. L *obscuritas* (as OBSCURE)]

obsecration /‚ɒbsɪ'kreɪʃ(ə)n/ *n.* earnest entreaty. [ME f. L *obsecratio* f. *obsecrare* entreat (as OB-, *sacrare* f. *sacer sacri* sacred)]

obsequies /'ɒbsɪkwɪz/ *n.pl.* **1** funeral rites. **2** a funeral. □□ **obsequial** /əb'siːkwɪəl/ *adj.* [ME, pl. of obs. *obsequy* f. AF *obsequie*, OF *obseque* f. med.L *obsequiae* f. L *exsequiae* funeral rites (see EXEQUIES): assoc. with *obsequium* (see OBSEQUIOUS)]

obsequious /əb'siːkwɪəs/ *adj.* servilely obedient or attentive. □□ **obsequiously** *adv.* **obsequiousness** *n.* [ME f. L *obsequiosus* f. *obsequium* compliance (as OB-, *sequi* follow)]

observance /əb'zɜːv(ə)ns/ *n.* **1** the act or process of keeping or performing a law, duty, custom, ritual, etc. **2** an act of a religious or ceremonial character; a customary rite. **3** the rule of a religious order. **4** *archaic* respect, deference. [ME f. OF f. L *observantia* (as OBSERVE)]

observant /əb'zɜːv(ə)nt/ *adj. & n.* —*adj.* **1** acute or diligent in taking notice. **2** attentive in esp. religious observances (*an observant few*). —*n.* (**Observant**) a member of the branch of the Franciscan order that observes the strict rule. □□ **observantly** *adv.* [F (as OBSERVE)]

observation /‚ɒbzə'veɪʃ(ə)n/ *n.* **1** the act or an instance of noticing; the condition of being noticed. **2** perception; the faculty of taking notice. **3** a remark or statement, esp. one that is of the nature of a comment. **4 a** the accurate watching and noting of phenomena as they occur in nature with regard to cause and effect or mutual relations. **b** the noting of the symptoms of a patient, the behaviour of a suspect, etc. **5** the taking of the sun's or another heavenly body's altitude to find a latitude or longitude. **6** *Mil.* the watching of a fortress or hostile position or movements. □**observation car** esp. *US* a carriage in a train built so as to afford good views. **observation post** *Mil.* a post for watching the effect of artillery fire etc. **under observation** being watched. □□ **observational** *adj.* **observationally** *adv.* [ME f. L *observatio* (as OBSERVE)]

observatory /əb'zɜːvətərɪ/ *n.* (*pl.* -ies) a room or building equipped for the observation of natural, esp. astronomical or meteorological, phenomena. [mod.L *observatorium* f. L *observare* (as OBSERVE)]

observe /əb'zɜːv/ *v.* **1** *tr.* (often foll. by *that, how* + clause) perceive, note; take notice of; become conscious of. **2** *tr.* watch carefully. **3** *tr.* **a** follow or adhere to (a law, command, method, principle, etc.). **b** keep or adhere to (an appointed time). **c** maintain (silence). **d** duly perform (a rite). **e** celebrate (an anniversary). **4** *tr.* examine and note (phenomena) without the aid of experiment. **5** *tr.* (often foll. by *that* + clause) say, esp. by way of comment. **6** *intr.* (foll. by *on*) make a remark or remarks about. □□ **observable** *adj.* **observably** *adv.* [ME f. OF *observer* f. L *observare* watch (as OB-, *servare* keep)]

observer /əb'zɜːvə(r)/ *n.* **1** a person who observes. **2** an interested spectator. **3** a person who attends a conference etc. to note the proceedings but does not participate. **4 a** a person trained to notice and identify aircraft. **b** a person carried in an aeroplane to note the enemy's position etc.

obsess /əb'ses/ *v.tr.* (often in *passive*) preoccupy, haunt; fill the mind of (a person) continually. □□ **obsessive** *adj.* & *n.* **obsessively** *adv.* **obsessiveness** *n.* [L *obsidēre obsess-* (as OB-, *sedēre* sit)]

obsession /əb'seʃ(ə)n/ *n.* **1** the act of obsessing or the state of being obsessed. **2** a persistent idea or thought dominating a person's mind. **3** a condition in which such ideas are present. □□ **obsessional** *adj.*

obsessionalism *n.* **obsessionally** *adv.* [L *obsessio* (as OBSESS)]

obsidian /əb'sɪdɪən/ *n.* a dark glassy volcanic rock formed from hardened lava. [L *obsidianus*, error for *obsianus* f. *Obsius*, the name (in Pliny) of the discoverer of a similar stone]

obsolescent /ˌɒbsə'les(ə)nt/ *adj.* becoming obsolete; going out of use or date. □□ **obsolescence** *n.* [L *obsolescere obsolescent-* (as OB-, *solēre* be accustomed)]

obsolete /'ɒbsəˌliːt/ *adj.* **1** disused, discarded, antiquated. **2** *Biol.* less developed than formerly or than in a cognate species; rudimentary. □□ **obsoletely** *adv.* **obsoleteness** *n.* **obsoletism** *n.* [L *obsoletus* past part. (as OBSOLESCENT)]

obstacle /'ɒbstək(ə)l/ *n.* a person or thing that obstructs progress. □ **obstacle-race** a race in which various obstacles have to be negotiated. [ME f. OF f. L *obstaculum* f. *obstare* impede (as OB-, *stare* stand)]

obstetric /əb'stetrɪk/ *adj.* (also **obstetrical**) of or relating to childbirth and associated processes. □□ **obstetrically** *adv.* **obstetrician** /-stə'trɪʃ(ə)n/ *n.* [mod.L *obstetricus* for L *obstetricius* f. *obstetrix* midwife f. *obstare* be present (as OB-, *stare* stand)]

obstetrics /əb'stetrɪks/ *n.pl.* (treated as *sing.*) the branch of medicine and surgery concerned with childbirth and midwifery.

obstinate /'ɒbstɪnət/ *adj.* **1** stubborn, intractable. **2** firmly adhering to one's chosen course of action or opinion despite dissuasion. **3** inflexible, self-willed. **4** unyielding; not readily responding to treatment etc. □□ **obstinacy** *n.* **obstinately** *adv.* [ME f. L *obstinatus* past part. of *obstinare* persist (as OB-, *stare* stand)]

obstreperous /əb'strepərəs/ *adj.* **1** turbulent, unruly; noisily resisting control. **2** noisy, vociferous. □□ **obstreperously** *adv.* **obstreperousness** *n.* [L *obstreperus* f. *obstrepere* (as OB-, *strepere* make a noise)]

obstruct /əb'strʌkt/ *v.tr.* **1** block up; make hard or impossible to pass. **2** prevent or retard the progress of; impede. □□ **obstructor** *n.* [L *obstruere obstruct-* (as OB-, *struere* build)]

obstruction /əb'strʌkʃ(ə)n/ *n.* **1** the act or an instance of blocking; the state of being blocked. **2** the act of making or the state of becoming more or less impassable. **3** an obstacle or blockage. **4** the retarding of progress by deliberate delays, esp. of Parliamentary business. **5** *Sport* the act of unlawfully obstructing another player. **6** *Med.* a blockage in a bodily passage, esp. in an intestine. □□ **obstructionism** *n.* (in sense 4). **obstructionist** *n.* (in sense 4). [L *obstructio* (as OBSTRUCT)]

obstructive /əb'strʌktɪv/ *adj.* & *n.* —*adj.* causing or intended to cause an obstruction. —*n.* an obstructive person or thing. □□ **obstructively** *adv.* **obstructiveness** *n.*

obtain /əb'teɪn/ *v.* **1** *tr.* acquire, secure; have granted to one. **2** *intr.* be prevalent or established or in vogue. □□ **obtainable** *adj.* **obtainability** /-'bɪlɪtɪ/ *n.* **obtainer** *n.* **obtainment** *n.* **obtention** /əb'tenʃ(ə)n/ *n.* [ME f. OF *obtenir* f. L *obtinēre obtent-* keep (as OB-, *tenēre* hold)]

obtrude /əb'truːd/ *v.* **1** *intr.* be or become obtrusive. **2** *tr.* (often foll. by *on, upon*) thrust forward (oneself, one's opinion, etc.) importunately. □□ **obtruder** *n.* **obtrusion** /-'truːʒ(ə)n/ *n.* [L *obtrudere obtrus-* (as OB-, *trudere* push)]

obtrusive /əb'truːsɪv/ *adj.* **1** unpleasantly or unduly noticeable. **2** obtruding oneself. □□ **obtrusively** *adv.* **obtrusiveness** *n.* [as OBTRUDE]

obtund /əb'tʌnd/ *v.tr.* blunt or deaden (a sense or faculty). [ME f. L *obtundere obtus-* (as OB-, *tundere* beat)]

obtuse /əb'tjuːs/ *adj.* **1** dull-witted; slow to understand. **2** of blunt form; not sharp-pointed or sharp-edged. **3** (of an angle) more than 90° and less than 180°. **4** (of pain or the senses) dull; not acute. □□

obtusely *adv.* **obtuseness** *n.* **obtusity** *n.* [L *obtusus* past part. (as OBTUND)]

obverse /'ɒbvɜːs/ *n.* & *adj.* —*n.* **1 a** the side of a coin or medal etc. bearing the head or principal design. **b** this design (cf. REVERSE). **2** the front or proper or top side of a thing. **3** the counterpart of a fact or truth. —*adj.* **1** *Biol.* narrower at the base or point of attachment than at the apex or top (see OB- 7). **2** answering as the counterpart to something else. □□ **obversely** *adv.* [L *obversus* past part. (as OBVERT)]

obvert /əb'vɜːt/ *v.tr. Logic* alter (a proposition) so as to infer another proposition with a contradictory predicate, e.g. *no men are immortal* to *all men are mortal*. □□ **obversion** *n.* [L *obvertere obvers-* (as OB-, *vertere* turn)]

obviate /'ɒbvɪˌeɪt/ *v.tr.* get round or do away with (a need, inconvenience, etc.). □□ **obviation** /-'eɪʃ(ə)n/ *n.* [LL *obviare* oppose (as OB-, *via* way)]

obvious /'ɒbvɪəs/ *adj.* easily seen or recognized or understood; palpable, indubitable. □□ **obviously** *adv.* **obviousness** *n.* [L *obvius* f. *ob viam* in the way]

OC *abbr.* Officer Commanding.

oc- /ɒk/ *prefix* assim. form of OB- before *c*.

ocarina /ˌɒkə'riːnə/ *n.* a small egg-shaped ceramic (usu. terracotta) or metal wind instrument. [It. f. *oca* goose (from its shape)]

Occam's razor /ˌɒkəmz/ *n.* the principle attributed to the English philosopher William of Occam (d. *c.*1350) that the fewest possible assumptions are to be made in explaining a thing.

occasion /ə'keɪʒ(ə)n/ *n.* & *v.* —*n.* **1 a** a special or noteworthy event or happening (*dressed for the occasion*). **b** the time or occurrence of this (*on the occasion of their marriage*). **2** (often foll. by *for*, or *to* + infin.) a reason, ground, or justification (*there is no occasion to be angry*). **3** a juncture suitable for doing something; an opportunity. **4** an immediate but subordinate or incidental cause (*the assassination was the occasion of the war*). —*v.tr.* **1** be the occasion or cause of; bring about esp. incidentally. **2** (foll. by *to* + infin.) cause (a person or thing to do something). □ **on occasion** now and then; when the need arises. **rise to the occasion** produce the necessary will, energy, ability, etc., in unusually demanding circumstances. **take occasion** (foll. by *to* + infin.) make use of the opportunity. [ME f. OF *occasion* or L *occasio* juncture, reason, f. *occidere occas-* go down (as OB-, *cadere* fall)]

occasional /ə'keɪʒən(ə)l/ *adj.* **1** happening irregularly and infrequently. **2** made or meant for, or associated with, a special occasion. **3** acting on a special occasion. □ **occasional cause** a secondary cause; an occasion (see OCCASION *n.* 4). **occasional table** a small table for irregular and varied use. □□ **occasionality** /-'nælɪtɪ/ *n.* **occasionally** *adv.*

Occident /'ɒksɪd(ə)nt/ *n. poet.* or *rhet.* **1** (prec. by *the*) the West. **2** western Europe. **3** Europe, America, or both, as distinct from the Orient. **4** European in contrast to Oriental civilization. [ME f. OF f. L *occidens -entis* setting, sunset, west (as OCCASION)]

occidental /ˌɒksɪ'dent(ə)l/ *adj.* & *n.* —*adj.* **1** of the Occident. **2** western. **3** of Western nations. —*n.* (**Occidental**) a native of the Occident. □□ **occidentalism** *n.* **occidentalist** *n.* **occidentalize** *v.tr.* (also **-ise**). **occidentally** *adv.* [ME f. OF *occidental* or L *occidentalis* (as OCCIDENT)]

occipito- /ɒk'sɪpɪtəʊ/ *comb. form* the back of the head. [as OCCIPUT]

occiput /'ɒksɪpʌt/ *n.* the back of the head. □□ **occipital** /-'sɪpɪt(ə)l/ *adj.* [ME f. L *occiput* (as OB-, *caput* head)]

Occitan /'ɒksɪt(ə)n/ *n.* (also *attrib.*) the Provençal language. □□ **Occitanian** /-'teɪnɪən/ *n.* & *adj.* [F: cf. LANGUE D'OC]

occlude /ə'kluːd/ *v.tr.* **1** stop up or close (pores or an orifice). **2** *Chem.* absorb and retain (gases or impurities). □ **occluded front** *Meteorol.* a front resulting from occlusion. [L *occludere occlus-* (as OB-, *claudere* shut)]

occlusion /əˈkluːʒ(ə)n/ *n.* **1** the act or process of occluding. **2** *Meteorol.* a phenomenon in which the cold front of a depression overtakes the warm front, causing upward displacement of warm air between them. **3** *Dentistry* the position of the teeth when the jaws are closed. **4** the blockage or closing of a hollow organ etc. (*coronary occlusion*). **5** *Phonet.* the momentary closure of the vocal passage. □□ **occlusive** *adj.*

occult *adj.* & *v.* —*adj.* /ɒˈkʌlt, ˈɒkʌlt/ **1** involving the supernatural; mystical, magical. **2** kept secret; esoteric. **3** recondite, mysterious; beyond the range of ordinary knowledge. **4** *Med.* not obvious on inspection. —*v.tr.* /ɒˈkʌlt/ *Astron.* (of a concealing body much greater in size than the concealed body) hide from view by passing in front; conceal by being in front. □ **the occult** occult phenomena generally. **occulting light** a lighthouse light that is cut off at regular intervals. □□ **occultation** /-ˈteɪʃ(ə)n/ *n.* **occultism** *n.* **occultist** *n.* **occultly** *adv.* **occultness** *n.* [L *occulere occult-* (as OB-, *celare* hide)]

occupant /ˈɒkjʊpənt/ *n.* **1** a person who occupies, resides in, or is in a place etc. (*both occupants of the car were unhurt*). **2** a person holding property, esp. land, in actual possession. **3** a person who establishes a title by taking possession of something previously without an established owner. □□ **occupancy** *n.* (*pl.* -ies). [F *occupant* or L *occupans -antis* (as OCCUPY)]

occupation /ˌɒkjʊˈpeɪʃ(ə)n/ *n.* **1** what occupies one; a means of passing one's time. **2** a person's temporary or regular employment; a business, calling, or pursuit. **3** the act of occupying or state of being occupied. **4 a** the act of taking or holding possession of (a country, district, etc.) by military force. **b** the state or time of this. **5** tenure, occupancy. **6** (*attrib.*) for the sole use of the occupiers of the land concerned (*occupation road*). [ME f. AF *ocupacioun*, OF *occupation* f. L *occupatio -onis* (as OCCUPY)]

occupational /ˌɒkjʊˈpeɪʃən(ə)l/ *adj.* **1** of or in the nature of an occupation or occupations. **2** (of a disease, hazard, etc.) rendered more likely by one's occupation. □ **occupational therapy** mental or physical activity designed to assist recovery from disease or injury.

occupier /ˈɒkjʊˌpaɪə(r)/ *n.* *Brit.* a person residing in a property as its owner or tenant.

occupy /ˈɒkjʊˌpaɪ/ *v.tr.* (-ies, -ied) **1** reside in; be the tenant of. **2** take up or fill (space or time or a place). **3** hold (a position or office). **4** take military possession of (a country, region, town, strategic position). **5** place oneself in (a building etc.) forcibly or without authority. **6** (usu. in *passive*; often foll. by *in*, *with*) keep busy or engaged. [ME f. OF *occuper* f. L *occupare* seize (as OB-, *capere* take)]

occur /əˈkɜː(r)/ *v.intr.* (**occurred**, **occurring**) **1** come into being as an event or process at or during some time; happen. **2** exist or be encountered in some place or conditions. **3** (foll. by *to*; usu. foll. by *that* + clause) come into the mind of, esp. as an unexpected or casual thought (*it occurred to me that you were right*). [L *occurrere* go to meet, present itself (as OB-, *currere* run)]

occurrence /əˈkʌrəns/ *n.* **1** the act or an instance of occurring. **2** an incident or event. □ **of frequent occurrence** often occurring. [*occurrent* that occurs f. F f. L *occurrens -entis* (as OCCUR)]

ocean /ˈəʊʃ(ə)n/ *n.* **1 a** a large expanse of sea, esp. each of the main areas called the Atlantic, Pacific, Indian, Arctic, and Antarctic Oceans. **b** these regarded cumulatively as the body of water surrounding the land of the globe. **2** (usu. prec. by *the*) the sea. **3** (often in *pl.*) a very large expanse or quantity of anything (*oceans of time*). □ **ocean-going** (of a ship) able to cross oceans. **ocean tramp** a merchant ship, esp. a steamer, running on no regular line or route. □□ **oceanward** *adv.* (also **-wards**). [ME f. OF *occean* f. L *oceanus* f. Gk *ōkeanos* stream encircling the earth's disc, Atlantic]

oceanarium /ˌəʊʃəˈneərɪəm/ *n.* (*pl.* **oceanariums** or **-ria** /-rɪə/) a large seawater aquarium for keeping sea animals. [OCEAN + -ARIUM, after *aquarium*]

Oceania /ˌəʊsɪˈɑːnɪə/ *n.* the islands of the Pacific and adjacent seas. □□ **Oceanian** *adj.* & *n.* [mod.L f. F *Océanie* f. L (as OCEAN)]

oceanic /ˌəʊʃɪˈænɪk, ˌəʊsɪ-/ *adj.* **1** of, like, or near the ocean. **2** (of a climate) governed by the ocean. **3** of the part of the ocean distant from the continents. **4** (**Oceanic**) of Oceania.

Oceanid /əʊˈsiːənɪd/ *n.* (*pl.* **Oceanids** or **-ides** /ˌəʊsɪˈænɪˌdiːz/) (in Greek mythology) an ocean nymph. [Gk *ōkeanis -idos* daughter of Oceanus]

oceanography /ˌəʊʃəˈnɒɡrəfɪ/ *n.* the study of the oceans. □□ **oceanographer** *n.* **oceanographic** /-nəˈɡræfɪk/ *adj.* **oceanographical** /-nəˈɡræfɪk(ə)l/ *adj.*

ocellus /ɒˈseləs/ *n.* (*pl.* **ocelli** /-laɪ/) **1** each of the simple, as opposed to compound, eyes of insects etc. **2** a spot of colour surrounded by a ring of a different colour on the wing of a butterfly etc. □□ **ocellar** *adj.* **ocellate** /ˈɒsɪlət/ *adj.* **ocellated** /ˈɒsɪˌleɪtɪd/ *adj.* [L, dimin. of *oculus* eye]

ocelot /ˈɒsɪˌlɒt/ *n.* **1** a medium-sized cat, *Felis pardalis*, native to S. and Central America, having a deep yellow or orange coat with black striped and spotted markings. **2** its fur. [F f. Nahuatl *ocelotl* jaguar]

och /ɒx/ *int.* *Sc.* & *Ir.* expressing surprise or regret. [Gael. & Ir.]

oche /ˈɒkɪ/ *n.* (also **hockey** /ˈɒkɪ, ˈhɒkɪ/) *Darts* the line behind which the players stand when throwing. [20th c.: orig. uncert. (perh. connected with OF *ochen* cut a deep notch in)]

ocher *US* var. of OCHRE.

ochlocracy /ɒkˈlɒkrəsɪ/ *n.* (*pl.* -ies) mob rule. □□ **ochlocrat** /ˈɒkləˌkræt/ *n.* **ochlocratic** /ˌɒkləˈkrætɪk/ *adj.* [F *ochlocratie* f. Gk *okhlokratia* f. *okhlos* mob]

ochone /ɒˈxəʊn/ *int.* (also **ohone**) *Sc.* & *Ir.* expressing regret or lament. [Gael. & Ir. *ochóin*]

ochre /ˈəʊkə(r)/ *n.* (*US* **ocher**) **1** a mineral of clay and ferric oxide, used as a pigment varying from light yellow to brown or red. **2** a pale brownish yellow. □□ **ochreish** *adj.* **ochreous** /ˈəʊkrɪəs/ *adj.* **ochrous** /ˈəʊkrəs/ *adj.* **ochry** /ˈəʊkrɪ/ *adj.* [ME f. OF *ocre* f. L *ochra* f. Gk *ōkhra* yellow ochre]

-ock /ək/ *suffix* forming nouns orig. with diminutive sense (*hillock*; *bullock*). [from or after OE *-uc*, *-oc*]

ocker /ˈɒkə(r)/ *n.* *Austral. sl.* a boorish or aggressive Australian (esp. as a stereotype). [20th c.: orig. uncert.]

o'clock /əˈklɒk/ *adv.* of the clock (used to specify the hour) (*6 o'clock*).

OCR *abbr.* optical character recognition.

Oct. *abbr.* October.

oct. *abbr.* octavo.

oct- /ɒkt/ *comb. form* assim. form of OCTA-, OCTO- before a vowel.

octa- /ˈɒktə/ *comb. form* (also **oct-** before a vowel) eight. [Gk *okta-* f. *oktō* eight]

octad /ˈɒktæd/ *n.* a group of eight. [LL *octas octad-* f. Gk *oktas -ados* f. *oktō* eight]

octagon /ˈɒktəgən/ *n.* **1** a plane figure with eight sides and angles. **2** an object or building with this cross-section. □□ **octagonal** /-ˈtægən(ə)l/ *adj.* **octagonally** /-ˈtægənəlɪ/ *adv.* [L *octagonos* f. Gk *oktagōnos* (as OCTA-, -GON)]

octahedron /ˌɒktəˈhiːdrən, -ˈhedrən/ *n.* (*pl.* **octahedrons** or **octahedra** /-drə/) **1** a solid figure contained by eight (esp. triangular) plane faces. **2** a body, esp. a crystal, in the form of a regular octahedron. □ **regular octahedron** an octahedron contained by equal and equilateral triangles. □□ **octahedral** *adj.* [Gk *oktaedron* (as OCTA-, -HEDRON)]

octal /'ɒkt(ə)l/ adj. reckoning or proceeding by eights (octal scale).

octamerous /ɒk'tæmərəs/ adj. 1 esp. Bot. having eight parts. 2 Zool. having organs arranged in eights.

octane /'ɒkteɪn/ n. a colourless inflammable hydrocarbon of the alkane series. ¶ Chem. formula: C_8H_{18}. □**high-octane** (of fuel used in internal-combustion engines) having good antiknock properties, not detonating readily during the power stroke. **octane number** (or **rating**) a figure indicating the antiknock properties of a fuel. [OCT- + -ANE]

octant /'ɒkt(ə)nt/ n. 1 an arc of a circle equal to one eighth of the circumference. 2 such an arc with two radii, forming an area equal to one eighth of the circle. 3 each of eight parts into which three planes intersecting (esp. at right angles) at a point divide the space or the solid body round it. 4 Astron. a point in a body's apparent course 45° distant from a given point, esp. a point at which the moon is 45° from conjunction or opposition with the sun. 5 an instrument in the form of a graduated eighth of a circle, used in astronomy and navigation. [L octans octant- half-quadrant f. octo eight]

octaroon var. of OCTOROON.

octastyle /'ɒktə,staɪl/ adj. & n. —adj. having eight columns at the end or in front. —n. an octastyle portico or building. [L octastylus f. Gk oktastulos (as OCTA- + stulos pillar)]

octavalent /,ɒktə'veɪlənt/ adj. Chem. having a valency of eight. [OCTA- + VALENCE[1]]

octave /'ɒktɪv/ n. 1 Mus. a a series of eight notes occupying the interval between (and including) two notes, one having twice or half the frequency of vibration of the other. b this interval. c each of the two notes at the extremes of this interval. d these two notes sounding together. 2 a group or stanza of eight lines; an octet. 3 a the seventh day after a festival. b a period of eight days including a festival and its octave. 4 a group of eight. 5 the last of eight parrying positions in fencing. 6 Brit. a wine-cask holding an eighth of a pipe. [ME f. OF f. L octava dies eighth day (reckoned inclusively)]

octavo /ɒk'teɪvəʊ, ɒk'tɑːvəʊ/ n. (pl. -os) 1 a size of book or page given by folding a standard sheet three times to form a quire of eight leaves. 2 a book or sheet of this size. ¶ Abbr.: **8vo**. [L in octavo in an eighth f. octavus eighth]

octennial /ɒk'tenɪəl/ adj. 1 lasting eight years. 2 occurring every eight years. [LL octennium period of eight years (as OCT-, annus year)]

octet /ɒk'tet/ n. (also **octette**) 1 Mus. a a composition for eight voices or instruments. b the performers of such a piece. 2 a group of eight. 3 the first eight lines of a sonnet. 4 Chem. a stable group of eight electrons. [It. ottetto or G Oktett: assim. to OCT-, DUET, QUARTET]

octo- /'ɒktəʊ/ comb. form (also **oct-** before a vowel) eight. [L octo or Gk oktō eight]

October /ɒk'təʊbə(r)/ n. the tenth month of the year. [OE f. L (as OCTO-): cf. DECEMBER, SEPTEMBER]

Octobrist /ɒk'təʊbrɪst/ n. hist. a member of the moderate party in the Russian Duma, supporting the Imperial Constitutional Manifesto of 30 Oct. 1905. [OCTOBER, after Russ. oktyabríst]

octocentenary /,ɒktəʊsen'tiːnərɪ/ n. & adj. —n. (pl. -ies) 1 an eight-hundredth anniversary. 2 a celebration of this. —adj. of or relating to an octocentenary.

octodecimo /,ɒktəʊ'desɪ,məʊ/ n. (pl. -os) 1 a size of book or page given by folding a standard sheet into eighteen leaves. 2 a book or sheet of this size. [in octodecimo f. L octodecimus eighteenth]

octogenarian /,ɒktəʊdʒɪ'neərɪən/ n. & adj. —n. a person from 80 to 89 years old. —adj. of this age. [L octogenarius f. octogeni distributive of octoginta eighty]

octopod /'ɒktə,pɒd/ n. any cephalopod of the order Octopoda, with eight arms usu. having suckers,

and a round saclike body, including octopuses. [Gk oktōpous -podos f. oktō eight + pous foot]

octopus /'ɒktəpəs/ n. (pl. **-es**) 1 any cephalopod mollusc of the genus Octopus having eight suckered arms, a soft saclike body, and strong beaklike jaws. 2 an organized and usu. harmful ramified power or influence. [Gk oktōpous: see OCTOPOD]

octoroon /,ɒktə'ruːn/ n. (also **octaroon**) the offspring of a quadroon and a White, a person of one-eighth Negro blood. [OCTO- after QUADROON]

octosyllabic /,ɒktəʊsɪ'læbɪk/ adj. & n. —adj. having eight syllables. —n. an octosyllabic verse. [LL octosyllabus (as OCTO-, SYLLABLE)]

octosyllable /,ɒktə'sɪləb(ə)l/ n. & adj. —n. an octosyllabic verse or word. —adj. = OCTOSYLLABIC.

octroi /'ɒktrwɑː/ n. 1 a duty levied in some European countries on goods entering a town. 2 a the place where this is levied. b the officials by whom it is levied. [F f. octroyer grant, f. med.L auctorizare: see AUTHORIZE]

octuple /'ɒktjʊp(ə)l/ adj., n., & v. —adj. eightfold. —n. an eightfold amount. —v.tr. & intr. multiply by eight. [F octuple or L octuplus (adj.) f. octo eight: cf. DOUBLE]

ocular /'ɒkjʊlə(r)/ adj. & n. —adj. of or connected with the eyes or sight; visual. —n. the eyepiece of an optical instrument. □**ocular spectrum** see SPECTRUM. □□ **ocularly** adv. [F oculaire f. LL ocularis f. L oculus eye]

ocularist /'ɒkjʊlərɪst/ n. a maker of artificial eyes. [F oculariste (as OCULAR)]

oculate /'ɒkjʊlət/ adj. = OCELLATE (see OCELLUS). [L oculatus f. oculus eye]

oculist /'ɒkjʊlɪst/ n. a person who specializes in the medical treatment of eye disorders or defects. □□ **oculistic** /-'lɪstɪk/ adj. [F oculiste f. L oculus eye]

oculo- /'ɒkjʊləʊ/ comb. form eye (oculo-nasal). [L oculus eye]

OD[1] abbr. ordnance datum.

OD[2] /əʊ'diː/ n. & v. esp. US sl. —n. an overdose, esp. of a narcotic drug. —v.intr. (**OD's, OD'd, OD'ing**) take an overdose. [abbr.]

od[1] /ɒd/ n. a hypothetical power once thought to pervade nature and account for various scientific phenomena. [arbitrary term coined in G by Baron von Reichenbach, Ger. scientist d. 1869]

od[2] /ɒd/ n. (as int. or in oaths) archaic = GOD. [corruption]

o.d. abbr. outer diameter.

odal var. of UDAL.

odalisque /'əʊdəlɪsk/ n. hist. an Eastern female slave or concubine, esp. in the Turkish Sultan's seraglio. [F f. Turk. odalik f. oda chamber + lik function]

odd /ɒd/ adj. & n. —adj. 1 extraordinary, strange, queer, remarkable, eccentric. 2 casual, occasional, unconnected (odd jobs; odd moments). 3 not normally noticed or considered; unpredictable (in some odd corner; picks up odd bargains). 4 additional; beside the reckoning (earned the odd pound). 5 a (of numbers such as 3 and 5) not integrally divisible by two. b (of things or persons numbered consecutively) bearing such a number (no parking on odd dates). 6 left over when the rest have been distributed or divided into pairs (have got an odd sock). 7 detached from a set or series (a few odd volumes). 8 (appended to a number, sum, weight, etc.) somewhat more than (forty odd; forty-odd people). 9 by which a round number, given sum, etc., is exceeded (we have 102—what shall we do with the odd 2?). —n. Golf a handicap of one stroke at each hole. □**odd job** a casual isolated piece of work. **odd job man** (or **odd jobber**) Brit. a person who does odd jobs. **odd man out** 1 a person or thing differing from all the others in a group in some respect. 2 a method of selecting one of three or more persons e.g. by tossing a coin. □□ **oddish** adj. **oddly** adv. **oddness** n. [ME f. ON odda- in odda-mathr third man, odd man, f. oddi angle]

oddball /'ɒdbɔːl/ n. colloq. 1 an odd or eccentric person. 2 (attrib.) strange, bizarre.

Oddfellow /'ɒdfeˌləʊ/ n. a member of a fraternity similar to the Freemasons.

oddity /'ɒdɪtɪ/ n. (pl. -ies) 1 a strange person, thing, or occurrence. 2 a peculiar trait. 3 the state of being odd.

oddment /'ɒdmənt/ n. 1 an odd article; something left over. 2 (in pl.) miscellaneous articles. 3 Brit. Printing matter other than the main text.

odds /ɒdz/ n.pl. 1 the ratio between the amounts staked by the parties to a bet, based on the expected probability either way. 2 the chances or balance of probability in favour of or against some result (the odds are against it; the odds are that it will rain). 3 the balance of advantage (the odds are in your favour; won against all the odds). 4 an equalizing allowance to a weaker competitor. 5 a difference giving an advantage (it makes no odds). □ at odds (often foll. by with) in conflict or at variance. by all odds certainly. lay (or give) odds offer a bet with odds favourable to the other better. odds and ends miscellaneous articles or remnants. odds-on a state when success is more likely than failure, esp. as indicated by the betting odds. over the odds above a generally agreed price etc. take odds offer a bet with odds unfavourable to the other better. what's the odds? colloq. what does it matter? [app. pl. of ODD n.: cf. NEWS]

ode /əʊd/ n. 1 a lyric poem, usu. rhymed and in the form of an address, in varied or irregular metre. 2 hist. a poem meant to be sung. [F f. LL oda f. Gk ōidē Attic form of aoidē song f. aeidō sing]

-ode[1] /əʊd/ suffix forming nouns meaning 'thing of the nature of' (geode; trematode). [Gk -ōdēs adj. ending]

-ode[2] /əʊd/ comb. form Electr. forming names of electrodes, or devices having them (cathode; diode). [Gk hodos way]

odeum /'əʊdɪəm/ n. (pl. odeums or odea /-dɪə/) a building for musical performances, esp. among the ancient Greeks and Romans. [F odéum or L odeum f. Gk ōideion (as ODE)]

odious /'əʊdɪəs/ adj. hateful, repulsive. □□ odiously adv. odiousness n. [ME f. OF odieus f. L odiosus (as ODIUM)]

odium /'əʊdɪəm/ n. a general or widespread dislike or reprobation incurred by a person or associated with an action. [L, = hatred f. odi to hate]

odometer /əʊ'dɒmɪtə(r)/ n. (also hodometer /hɒ-/) an instrument for measuring the distance travelled by a wheeled vehicle. □□ odometry n. [F odomètre f. Gk hodos way: see -METER]

odonto- /əʊ'dɒntəʊ/ comb. form tooth. [Gk odous odont- tooth]

odontoglossum /əʊˌdɒntə'glɒsəm/ n. any of various orchids bearing flowers with jagged edges like toothmarks. [ODONTO- + Gk glōssa tongue]

odontoid /əʊ'dɒntɔɪd/ adj. toothlike. □ odontoid process a projection from the second cervical vertebra. [Gk odontoeidēs (as ODONTO- + Gk eidos form)]

odontology /ˌəʊdɒn'tɒlədʒɪ/ n. the scientific study of the structure and diseases of teeth. □□ odontological /-tə'lɒdʒɪk(ə)l/ adj. odontologist n.

odor US var. of ODOUR.

odoriferous /ˌəʊdə'rɪfərəs/ adj. diffusing a scent, esp. an agreeable one; fragrant. □□ odoriferously adv. [ME f. L odorifer (as ODOUR)]

odorous /'əʊdərəs/ adj. 1 having a scent. 2 = ODORIFEROUS. □□ odorously adv. [L odorus fragrant (as ODOUR)]

odour /'əʊdə(r)/ n. (US odor) 1 the property of a substance that has an effect on the nasal sense of smell. 2 a lasting quality or trace attaching to something (an odour of intolerance). 3 regard, repute (in bad odour). □□ odourless adj. (in sense 1). [ME f. AF odour, OF odor f. L odor -oris smell, scent]

odyssey /'ɒdɪsɪ/ n. (pl. -eys) a series of wanderings; a long adventurous journey. □□ **Odyssean** adj. [L Odyssea f. Gk Odusseia, title of an epic poem attributed to Homer describing the adventures of Odysseus (Ulysses) on his journey home from Troy]

OECD abbr. Organization for Economic Cooperation and Development.

OED abbr. Oxford English Dictionary.

oedema /ɪ'diːmə/ n. (US edema) a condition characterized by an excess of watery fluid collecting in the cavities or tissues of the body. Also called DROPSY. □□ **oedematose** adj. **oedematous** adj. [LL f. Gk oidēma -atos f. oideō swell]

Oedipus complex /'iːdɪpəs/ n. Psychol. (according to Freud etc.) the complex of emotions aroused in a young (esp. male) child by a subconscious sexual desire for the parent of the opposite sex and wish to exclude the parent of the same sex. □□ **Oedipal** adj. [Gk Oidipous, legendary king of Thebes who unknowingly killed his father and married his mother]

oenology /iː'nɒlədʒɪ/ n. (US enology) the study of wines. □□ **oenological** /ˌiːnə'lɒdʒɪk(ə)l/ adj. **oenologist** n. [Gk oinos wine]

oenophile /'iːnəfaɪl/ n. a connoisseur of wines. □□ **oenophilist** /iː'nɒfɪlɪst/ n. [as OENOLOGY]

o'er /'əʊə(r)/ adv. & prep. poet. = OVER. [contr.]

oersted /'ɜːstɛd/ n. a unit of magnetic field strength equivalent to 79.58 amperes per metre. [H. C. Oersted, Da. physicist d. 1851]

oesophagus /iː'sɒfəgəs/ n. (US esophagus) (pl. oesophagi /-ˌdʒaɪ/ or -guses) the part of the alimentary canal from the mouth to the stomach; the gullet. □□ **oesophageal** /iːˌsɒfə'dʒiːəl, ˌiːsə'fædʒɪəl/ adj. [ME f. Gk oisophagos]

oestrogen /'iːstrədʒ(ə)n/ n. (US estrogen) 1 any of various steroid hormones developing and maintaining female characteristics of the body. 2 this hormone produced artificially for use in oral contraceptives etc. □□ **oestrogenic** /-'dʒenɪk/ adj. **oestrogenically** /-'dʒenɪkəlɪ/ adv. [OESTRUS + -GEN]

oestrus /'iːstrəs/ n. (also oestrum, US estrus, estrum) a recurring period of sexual receptivity in many female mammals; heat. □□ **oestrous** adj. [Gk oistros gadfly, frenzy]

œuvre /'ɜːvr/ n. the works of an author, painter, composer, etc., esp. regarded collectively. [F, = work, f. L opera]

of /ɒv, əv/ prep. connecting a noun (often a verbal noun) or pronoun with a preceding noun, adjective, adverb, or verb, expressing a wide range of relations broadly describable as follows: 1 origin, cause, or authorship (paintings of Turner; people of Rome; died of malnutrition). 2 the material or substance constituting or identifying a thing (a house of cards; was built of bricks). 3 belonging, connection, or possession (a thing of the past; articles of clothing; the head of the business; the tip of the iceberg). 4 identity or close relation (the city of Rome; a pound of apples; a fool of a man). 5 removal, separation, or privation (north of the city; got rid of them; robbed us of £1000). 6 reference, direction, or respect (beware of the dog; suspected of lying; very good of you; short of money; the selling of goods). 7 objective relation (love of music; in search of peace). 8 partition, classification, or inclusion (no more of that; part of the story; a friend of mine; this sort of book; some of us will stay). 9 description, quality, or condition (the hour of prayer; a person of tact; a girl of ten; on the point of leaving). 10 US time in relation to the following hour (a quarter of three). □ be of possess intrinsically; give rise to (is of great interest). of all designating the (nominally) least likely or expected example (you of all people!). of all the nerve (or cheek etc.) an exclamation of indignation at a person's impudence etc. of an evening (or morning etc.) colloq. 1 on most evenings (or mornings etc.). 2 at some time in the evenings (or mornings etc.).

of late recently. **of old** formerly; long ago. [OE, unaccented form of *æf*, f. Gmc]

of- /ɒf/ *prefix* assim. form of OB- before *f*.

ofay /ˈəʊfeɪ/ *n. US sl. offens.* a White person (esp. used by Blacks). [20th c.: prob. of Afr. orig.]

Off. *abbr.* 1 Office. 2 Officer.

off /ɒf/ *adv., prep., adj., & n. —adv.* 1 away; at or to a distance (*drove off*; *is three miles off*). 2 out of position; not on or touching or attached; loose, separate, gone (*has come off*; *take your coat off*). 3 so as to be rid of (*sleep it off*). 4 so as to break continuity or continuance; discontinued, stopped (*turn off the radio*; *take a day off*; *the game is off*). 5 not available as a choice, e.g. on a menu (*chips are off*). 6 to the end; entirely; so as to be clear (*clear off*; *finish off*; *pay off*). 7 situated as regards money, supplies, etc. (*is badly off*; *is not very well off*). 8 off-stage (*noises off*). 9 (of food etc.) beginning to decay. 10 (with preceding numeral) denoting a quantity produced or made at one time (esp. *one-off*). —*prep.* 1 a from; away or down or up from (*fell off the chair*; *took something off the price*; *jumped off the edge*). b not on (*was already off the pitch*). 2 a (temporarily) relieved of or abstaining from (*off duty*; *am off my diet*). b not attracted by for the time being (*off their food*; *off smoking*). c not achieving or doing one's best in (*off form*; *off one's game*). 3 using as a source or means of support (*live off the land*). 4 leading from; not far from (*a street off the Strand*). 5 at a short distance to sea from (*sank off Cape Horn*). —*adj.* 1 far, further (*the off side of the wall*). 2 (of a part of a vehicle, animal, or road) right (*the off front wheel*). 3 *Cricket* designating the half of the field (as divided lengthways through the pitch) to which the striker's feet are pointed. —*n.* 1 *Cricket* the off side. 2 the start of a race. □**a bit off** *Brit. colloq.* 1 rather annoying or unfair. 2 somewhat unwell (*am feeling a bit off*). **off and on** intermittently; now and then. **off-centre** not quite coinciding with a central position. **the off chance** see CHANCE. **off colour** 1 not in good health. 2 *US* somewhat indecent. **off the cuff** see CUFF¹. **off-day** a day when one is not at one's best. **off-drive** *Cricket* drive (the ball) to the off side. **off one's feet** see FOOT. **off form** see FORM. **off guard** see GUARD. **off one's hands** see HAND. **off one's head** see HEAD. **off-key** 1 out of tune. 2 not quite suitable or fitting. **off-licence** *Brit.* 1 a shop selling alcoholic drink for consumption elsewhere. 2 a licence for this. **off limits** see LIMIT. **off-line** *Computing* (of a computer terminal or process) not directly controlled by or connected to a central processor. **off of** *sl. disp.* = OFF *prep.* (*picked it off of the floor*). **off-peak** used or for use at times other than those of greatest demand. **off the peg** see PEG. **off-piste** (of skiing) away from prepared ski runs. **off the point** *adj.* irrelevant. —*adv.* irrelevantly. **off-putting** *Brit.* disconcerting; repellent. **off the record** see RECORD. **off-road** *attrib.adj.* 1 away from the road, on rough terrain. 2 (of a vehicle etc.) designed for rough terrain or for cross-country driving. **off-season** a time when business etc. is slack. **off-stage** *adj. & adv.* not on the stage and so not visible or audible to the audience. **off-street** (esp. of parking vehicles) other than on a street. **off-time** a time when business etc. is slack. **off-the-wall** *sl.* crazy, absurd, outlandish. **off-white** white with a grey or yellowish tinge. [orig. var. of OF, to distinguish the sense]

offal /ˈɒf(ə)l/ *n.* 1 the less valuable edible parts of a carcass, esp. the entrails and internal organs. 2 refuse or waste stuff. 3 carrion; putrid flesh. [ME f. MDu. *afval* f. *af* OFF + *vallen* FALL]

offbeat *adj. & n. —adj.* /ˈɒfbiːt, ɒfˈbiːt/ 1 not coinciding with the beat. 2 eccentric, unconventional. —*n.* /ˈɒfbiːt/ any of the unaccented beats in a bar.

offcut /ˈɒfkʌt/ *n.* a remnant of timber, paper, etc., after cutting.

offence /əˈfens/ *n.* (*US* **offense**) 1 an illegal act; a transgression or misdemeanour. 2 a wounding of the feelings; resentment or umbrage (*no offence was meant*). 3 the act of attacking or taking the offensive; aggressive action. □**give offence** cause hurt feelings. **take offence** suffer hurt feelings. □□ **offenceless** *adj.* [orig. = stumbling, stumbling-block: ME & OF *offens* f. L *offensus* annoyance, and ME & F *offense* f. L *offensa* a striking against, hurt, displeasure, both f. *offendere* (as OB-, *fendere fens-* strike)]

offend /əˈfend/ *v.* 1 *tr.* cause offence to or resentment in; wound the feelings of. 2 *tr.* displease or anger. 3 *intr.* (often foll. by *against*) do wrong; transgress. □□ **offendedly** *adv.* **offender** *n.* **offending** *adj.* [ME f. OF *offendre* f. L (as OFFENCE)]

offense *US* var. of OFFENCE.

offensive /əˈfensɪv/ *adj. & n. —adj.* 1 giving or meant or likely to give offence; insulting (*offensive language*). 2 disgusting, foul-smelling, nauseous, repulsive. 3 a aggressive, attacking. b (of a weapon) meant for use in attack. —*n.* 1 an aggressive action or attitude (*take the offensive*). 2 an attack, an offensive campaign or stroke. 3 aggressive or forceful action in pursuit of a cause (*a peace offensive*). □□ **offensively** *adv.* **offensiveness** *n.* [F *offensif -ive* or med.L *offensivus* (as OFFENCE)]

offer /ˈɒfə(r)/ *v. & n. —v.* 1 *tr.* present for acceptance or refusal or consideration (*offered me a drink*; *was offered a lift*; *offer one's services*; *offer no apology*). 2 *intr.* (foll. by *to* + infin.) express readiness or show intention (*offered to take the children*). 3 *tr.* provide; give an opportunity for. 4 *tr.* make available for sale. 5 *tr.* (of a thing) present to one's attention or consideration (*each day offers new opportunities*). 6 *tr.* present (a sacrifice, prayer, etc.) to a deity. 7 *intr.* present itself; occur (*as opportunity offers*). 8 *tr.* give an opportunity for (battle) to an enemy. 9 *tr.* attempt, or try to show (violence, resistance, etc.). —*n.* 1 an expression of readiness to do or give if desired, or to buy or sell (for a certain amount). 2 an amount offered. 3 a proposal (esp. of marriage). 4 a bid. □**on offer** for sale at a certain (esp. reduced) price. □□ **offerer** *n.* **offeror** *n.* [OE *offrian* in religious sense, f. L *offerre* (as OB-, *ferre* bring)]

offering /ˈɒfərɪŋ/ *n.* 1 a contribution, esp. of money, to a Church. 2 a thing offered as a religious sacrifice or token of devotion. 3 anything, esp. money, contributed or offered.

offertory /ˈɒfətəri, -trɪ/ *n.* (*pl.* **-ies**) 1 *Eccl.* a the offering of the bread and wine at the Eucharist. b an anthem accompanying this. 2 a the collection of money at a religious service. b the money collected. [ME f. eccl.L *offertorium* offering f. LL *offert-* for L *oblat-* past part. stem of *offerre* OFFER]

offhand *adj. & adv. —adj.* /ɒfˈhænd, ˈɒfhænd/ curt or casual in manner. —*adv.* /ɒfˈhænd/ 1 in an offhand manner. 2 without preparation or premeditation. □□ **offhanded** *adj.* **offhandedly** *adv.* **offhandedness** *n.*

office /ˈɒfɪs/ *n.* 1 a room or building used as a place of business, esp. for clerical or administrative work. 2 a room or department or building for a particular kind of business (*ticket office*; *post office*). 3 the local centre of a large business (*our London office*). 4 *US* the consulting-room of a professional person. 5 a position with duties attached to it; a place of authority or trust or service, esp. of a public nature. 6 tenure of an official position, esp. that of a minister of State or of the party forming the Government (*hold office*; *out of office for 13 years*). 7 (**Office**) the quarters or staff or collective authority of a Government department etc. (*Foreign Office*). 8 a duty attaching to one's position; a task or function. 9 (usu. in *pl.*) a piece of kindness or attention; a service (esp. *through the good offices of*). 10 *Eccl.* a an authorized form of worship (*Office for the Dead*). b (in full **divine office**) the daily service of the Roman Catholic breviary (*say the office*). 11 a ceremonial duty. 12 (in *pl.*) *Brit.* the parts of a house devoted to household work, storage, etc. 13 *sl.* a hint or signal. □**the last offices**

rites due to the dead. **office-bearer** an official or officer. **office block** a large building designed to contain business offices. **office boy** (or **girl**) a young man (or woman) employed to do minor jobs in a business office. **office hours** the hours during which business is normally conducted. **office of arms** the College of Arms, or a similar body in another country. **office-worker** an employee in a business office. [ME f. OF f. L *officium* performance of a task (in med.L also office, divine service), f. *opus* work + *facere fic-* do]

officer /'ɒfɪsə(r)/ *n. & v. —n.* **1** a person holding a position of authority or trust, esp. one with a commission in the armed services, in the mercantile marine, or on a passenger ship. **2** a policeman or policewoman. **3** a holder of a post in a society (e.g. the president or secretary). **4** a holder of a public, civil, or ecclesiastical office; a sovereign's minister; an appointed or elected functionary (usu. with a qualifying word: *medical officer*; *probation officer*; *returning officer*). **5** a bailiff (*the sheriff's officer*). **6** a member of the grade below commander in the Order of the British Empire etc. —*v.tr.* **1** provide with officers. **2** act as the commander of. □**officer of arms** a herald or pursuivant. [ME f. AF *officer*, OF *officier* f. med.L *officiarius* f. L *officium*: see OFFICE]

official /ə'fɪʃ(ə)l/ *adj. & n. —adj.* **1** of or relating to an office (see OFFICE n. 5, 6) or its tenure or duties. **2** characteristic of officials and bureaucracy. **3** emanating from or attributable to a person in office; properly authorized. **4** holding office; employed in a public capacity. **5** *Med.* according to the pharmacopoeia, officinal. —*n.* **1** a person holding office or engaged in official duties. **2** (in full **official principal**) the presiding officer or judge of an archbishop's, bishop's, or esp. archdeacon's court. □**official birthday** *Brit.* a day in June chosen for the observance of the sovereign's birthday. **official secrets** confidential information involving national security. □□ **officialdom** *n.* **officialism** *n.* **officially** *adv.* [ME (as noun) f. OF f. L *officialis* (as OFFICE)]

officialese /ə,fɪʃə'li:z/ *n. derog.* the formal precise language characteristic of official documents.

officiant /ə'fɪʃɪənt/ *n.* a person who officiates at a religious ceremony.

officiate /ə'fɪʃɪˌeɪt/ *v.intr.* **1** act in an official capacity, esp. on a particular occasion. **2** perform a divine service or ceremony. □□ **officiation** *n.* **officiator** *n.* [med.L *officiare* perform a divine service (*officium*): see OFFICE]

officinal /ˌɒfɪ'si:n(ə)l, ə'fɪsɪn(ə)l/ *adj.* **1 a** (of a medicine) kept ready for immediate dispensing. **b** made from the pharmacopoeia recipe (cf. MAGISTRAL). **c** (of a name) adopted in the pharmacopoeia. **2** (of a herb or drug) used in medicine. □□ **officinally** *adv.* [med.L *officinalis* f. L *officina* workshop]

officious /ə'fɪʃəs/ *adj.* **1** asserting one's authority aggressively; domineering. **2** intrusive or excessively enthusiastic in offering help etc.; meddlesome. **3** *Diplomacy* informal, unofficial. □□ **officiously** *adv.* **officiousness** *n.* [L *officiosus* obliging f. *officium*: see OFFICE]

offing /'ɒfɪŋ/ *n.* the more distant part of the sea in view. □**in the offing** not far away; likely to appear or happen soon. [perh. f. OFF + -ING¹]

offish /'ɒfɪʃ/ *adj. colloq.* inclined to be aloof. □□ **offishly** *adv.* **offishness** *n.* [OFF: cf. *uppish*]

offload /'ɒfləʊd, ɒf'ləʊd/ *v.tr.* get rid of (esp. something unpleasant) by giving it to someone else.

off-price /'ɒfpraɪs/ *adj.* US involving merchandise sold at a lower price than that recommended by the manufacturer.

offprint /'ɒfprɪnt/ *n.* a printed copy of an article etc. originally forming part of a larger publication.

offscreen /'ɒfskri:n/ *adj. & adv. —adj.* not appearing on a cinema, television, or VDU screen. —*adv.* **1** without use of a screen. **2** outside the view presented by a cinema-film scene.

offset *n. & v. —n.* /'ɒfset/ **1** a side-shoot from a plant serving for propagation. **2** an offshoot or scion. **3** a compensation; a consideration or amount diminishing or neutralizing the effect of a contrary one. **4** *Archit.* a sloping ledge in a wall etc. where the thickness of the part above is diminished. **5** a mountain-spur. **6** a bend in a pipe etc. to carry it past an obstacle. **7** (often *attrib.*) a method of printing in which ink is transferred from a plate or stone to a uniform rubber surface and from there to paper etc. (*offset litho*). **8** *Surveying* a short distance measured perpendicularly from the main line of measurement. —*v.tr.* /'ɒfset, ɒf'set/ (-**setting**; *past* and *past part.* -**set**) **1** counterbalance, compensate. **2** place out of line. **3** print by the offset process.

offshoot /'ɒfʃu:t/ *n.* **1** a side-shoot or branch. **2** something derivative.

offshore /'ɒfʃɔ:(r)/ *adj.* **1** situated at sea some distance from the shore. **2** (of the wind) blowing seawards. **3** (of goods, funds, etc.) made or registered abroad.

offside *adj. & n. —adj.* /ɒf'saɪd/ *Sport* (of a player in a field game) in a position, usu. ahead of the ball, that is not allowed if it affects play. —*n.* /'ɒfsaɪd/ (often *attrib.*) esp. *Brit.* the right side of a vehicle, animal, etc. (cf. NEARSIDE).

offsider /ɒf'saɪdə(r)/ *n. Austral. colloq.* a partner, assistant, or deputy.

offspring /'ɒfsprɪŋ/ *n.* (*pl.* same) **1** a person's child or children or descendant(s). **2** an animal's young or descendant(s). **3** a result. [OE *ofspring* f. OF from + *springan* SPRING *v.*]

oft /ɒft/ *adv. archaic* or *literary* often (usu. in *comb.*: *oft-recurring*). □**oft-times** often. [OE]

often /'ɒf(ə)n, 'ɒft(ə)n/ *adv.* (**oftener**, **oftenest**) **1 a** frequently; many times. **b** at short intervals. **2** in many instances. □**as often as not** in roughly half the instances. [ME: extended f. OFT, prob. after *selden* = SELDOM]

ogam var. of OGHAM.

ogdoad /'ɒgdəʊˌæd/ *n.* a group of eight. [LL *ogdoas ogdoad-* f. Gk *ogdoas -ados* f. *ogdoos* eighth f. *oktō* eight]

ogee /'əʊdʒi:, -'dʒi:/ *adj. & n. Archit. —adj.* showing in section a double continuous S-shaped curve. —*n.* an S-shaped line or moulding. □**ogee arch** an arch with two ogee curves meeting at the apex. □□ **ogee'd** *adj.* [app. f. OGIVE, as being the usu. moulding in groin-ribs]

ogham /'ɒgəm/ *n.* (also **ogam**) **1** an ancient British and Irish alphabet of twenty characters formed by parallel strokes on either side of or across a continuous line. **2** an inscription in this alphabet. **3** each of its characters. [OIr. *ogam*, referred to *Ogma*, its supposed inventor]

ogive /'əʊdʒaɪv, -'dʒaɪv/ *n.* **1** a pointed or Gothic arch. **2** one of the diagonal groins or ribs of a vault. **3** an S-shaped line. **4** *Statistics* a cumulative frequency graph. □□ **ogival** *adj.* [ME f. F, of unkn. orig.]

ogle /'əʊg(ə)l/ *v. & n. —v.* **1** *tr.* eye amorously or lecherously. **2** *intr.* look amorously. —*n.* an amorous or lecherous look. □□ **ogler** *n.* [prob. LG or Du.: cf. LG *oegeln*, frequent. of *oegen* look at]

ogre /'əʊgə(r)/ *n.* (*fem.* **ogress** /-grɪs/) **1** a man-eating giant in folklore etc. **2** a terrifying person. □□ **ogreish** *adj.* (also **ogrish**). [F, first used by Perrault in 1697, of unkn. orig.]

OH *abbr.* US Ohio (in official postal use).

oh¹ /əʊ/ *int.* (also **O**) expressing surprise, pain, entreaty, etc. (*oh, what a mess*; *oh for a holiday*). □**oh boy** expressing surprise, excitement, etc. **oh well** expressing resignation. [var. of O¹]

oh² /əʊ/ *n.* = O¹ 2.

o.h.c. *abbr.* overhead camshaft.

ohm /əʊm/ *n. Electr.* the SI unit of resistance, transmitting a current of one ampere when subjected to a potential difference of one volt. ¶ *Symb.:* Ω. □□ **ohmage** *n.* [G. S. *Ohm*, Ger. physicist d. 1854]

b *but* d *dog* f *few* g *get* h *he* j *yes* k *cat* l *leg* m *man* n *no* p *pen* r *red* s *sit* t *top* v *voice*

ohmmeter /'əʊm,miːtə(r)/ n. an instrument for measuring electrical resistance.

OHMS abbr. on Her (or His) Majesty's Service.

Ohm's law /əʊmz/ n. Electr. a law stating that current is proportional to voltage and inversely proportional to resistance. [see OHM]

oho /əʊ'həʊ/ int. expressing surprise or exultation. [ME f. O⁴ + HO]

ohone var. of OCHONE.

o.h.v. abbr. overhead valve.

oi /ɔɪ/ int. calling attention or expressing alarm etc. [var. of HOY¹]

-oid /ɔɪd/ suffix forming adjectives and nouns, denoting form or resemblance (asteroid; rhomboid; thyroid). □□ **-oidal** suffix forming adjectives. **-oidally** suffix forming adverbs. [mod.L -oides f. Gk -oeidēs f. eidos form]

oidium /əʊ'ɪdɪəm/ n. (pl. **oidia** /-dɪə/) spores formed by the breaking up of fungal hyphae into cells. [mod.L f. Gk ōion egg + -idion dimin. suffix]

oil /ɔɪl/ n. & v. —n. 1 any of various thick, viscous, usu. inflammable liquids insoluble in water but soluble in organic solvents (see also essential oil, fixed oil, mineral oil, volatile oil). 2 US petroleum. 3 (in comb.) using oil as fuel (oil-heater). 4 a (usu. in pl.) = oil-paint. b colloq. a picture painted in oil-paints. 5 (in pl.) = OILSKIN. —v. 1 tr. apply oil to; lubricate. 2 tr. impregnate or treat with oil (oiled silk). 3 tr. & intr. supply with or take on oil as fuel. 4 tr. & intr. make (butter, grease, etc.) into or (of butter etc.) become an oily liquid. □**oil-bird** a guacharo. **oil drum** a metal drum used for transporting oil. **oiled silk** silk made waterproof with oil. **oil engine** an engine driven by the explosion of vaporized oil mixed with air. **oil-fired** using oil as fuel. **oil a person's hand** (or **palm**) bribe a person. **oil-lamp** a lamp using oil as fuel. **oil-meal** ground oilcake. **oil of vitriol** see VITRIOL. **oil-paint** (or **-colour**) a mix of ground colour pigment and oil. **oil-painting 1** the art of painting in oil-paints. **2** a picture painted in oil-paints. **oil-palm** either of two trees, Elaeis guineensis of W. Africa, or E. oleifera of the US, from which palm oil is extracted. **oil-pan** an engine sump. **oil-paper** a paper made transparent or waterproof by soaking in oil. **oil-press** an apparatus for pressing oil from seeds etc. **oil rig** a structure with equipment for drilling an oil well. **oil-sand** a stratum of porous rock yielding petroleum. **oil-seed** any of various seeds from cultivated crops yielding oil, e.g. rape, peanut, or cotton. **oil-shale** a fine-grained rock from which oil can be extracted. **oil-slick** a smooth patch of oil, esp. one on the sea. **oil-tanker** a ship designed to carry oil in bulk. **oil one's tongue** say flattering or glib things. **oil well** a well from which mineral oil is drawn. **oil the wheels** help make things go smoothly. **well oiled** colloq. very drunk. □□ **oilless** adj. [ME oli, oile f. AF, ONF olie = OF oile etc. f. L oleum (olive) oil f. olea olive]

oilcake /'ɔɪlkeɪk/ n. a mass of compressed linseed etc. left after oil has been extracted, used as fodder or manure.

oilcan /'ɔɪlkæn/ n. a can containing oil, esp. one with a long nozzle for oiling machinery.

oilcloth /'ɔɪlklɒθ/ n. 1 a fabric waterproofed with oil. 2 an oilskin. 3 a canvas coated with linseed or other oil and used to cover a table or floor.

oiler /'ɔɪlə(r)/ n. 1 an oilcan for oiling machinery. 2 an oil-tanker. 3 US a an oil well. b (in pl.) oilskin.

oilfield /'ɔɪlfiːld/ n. an area yielding mineral oil.

oilman /'ɔɪlmən/ n. (pl. -men) a person who deals in oil.

oilskin /'ɔɪlskɪn/ n. 1 cloth waterproofed with oil. 2 a a garment made of this. b (in pl.) a suit made of this.

oilstone /'ɔɪlstəʊn/ n. a fine-grained flat stone used with oil for sharpening flat tools, e.g. chisels, planes, etc. (cf. WHETSTONE).

oily /'ɔɪlɪ/ adj. (**oilier, oiliest**) 1 of, like, or containing much oil. 2 covered or soaked with oil. 3 (of a manner etc.) fawning, insinuating, unctuous. □□ **oilily** adv. **oiliness** n.

oink /ɔɪŋk/ v.intr. (of a pig) make its characteristic grunt. [imit.]

ointment /'ɔɪntmənt/ n. a smooth greasy healing or cosmetic preparation for the skin. [ME oignement, ointment, f. OF oignement ult. f. L (as UNGUENT): oint-after obs. oint anoint f. OF, past part. of oindre ANOINT]

Oireachtas /'ɪərəx,θæs/ n. the legislature of the Irish Republic: the President, Dáil, and Seanad. [Ir.]

OK¹ /əʊ'keɪ/ adj., adv., n., & v. (also **okay**) colloq. —adj. (often as int. expressing agreement or acquiescence) all right; satisfactory. —adv. well, satisfactorily (that worked out OK). —n. (pl. **OKs**) approval, sanction. —v.tr. (**OK's, OK'd, OK'ing**) give an OK to; approve, sanction. [orig. US: prob. abbr. of orl (or oll) korrect, joc. form of 'all correct']

OK² abbr. US Oklahoma (in official postal use).

okapi /əʊ'kɑːpɪ/ n. (pl. same or **okapis**) a ruminant mammal, Okapia johnstoni, native to N. and NE Zaïre, with a head resembling that of a giraffe and a body resembling that of a zebra, having a dark chestnut coat and transverse stripes on the hindquarters and upper legs only. [Mbuba]

okay var. of OK¹.

okey-dokey /,əʊkɪ'dəʊkɪ/ adj. & adv. (also **okey-doke** /-'dəʊk/) sl. = OK¹. [redupl.]

Okla. abbr. Oklahoma.

okra /'əʊkrə, 'ɒkrə/ n. 1 a malvaceous African plant, Abelmoschus esculentus, yielding long ridged seed-pods. 2 the seed-pods eaten as a vegetable and used to thicken soups and stews. Also called GUMBO, ladies' fingers. [W.Afr. native name]

-ol¹ /ɒl/ suffix Chem. the termination of alcohol, used in names of alcohols or analogous compounds (methanol; phenol).

-ol² /ɒl/ comb. form = -OLE. [L oleum oil]

old /əʊld/ adj. (**older, oldest**) (cf. ELDER, ELDEST). 1 a advanced in age; far on in the natural period of existence. b not young or near its beginning. 2 made long ago. 3 long in use. 4 worn or dilapidated or shabby from the passage of time. 5 having the characteristics (experience, feebleness, etc.) of age (the child has an old face). 6 practised, inveterate (an old offender; old in crime). 7 belonging only or chiefly to the past; lingering on; former (old times; haunted by old memories). 8 dating from far back; long established or known; ancient, primeval (old as the hills; old friends; an old family). 9 (appended to a period of time) of age (is four years old; a four-year-old boy; a four-year-old). 10 (of language) as used in former or earliest times. 11 colloq. as a term of affection or casual reference (good old Charlie; old shipmate). 12 the former or first of two or more similar things (our old house; wants his old job back). □**old age** the later part of normal life. **old-age pension** = retirement pension. **old-age pensioner** a person receiving this. **Old Bailey** the Central Criminal Court in London. **Old Bill** Brit. sl. the police. **old bird** a wary person. **old boy 1** a former male pupil of a school. **2** colloq. **a** an elderly man. **b** an affectionate form of address to a boy or man. **old boy network** Brit. colloq. preferment in employment of those from a similar social background, esp. fellow ex-pupils of public schools. **the old country** the native country of colonists etc. **Old English** the English language up to c.1150. **old-fashioned** in or according to a fashion or tastes no longer current; antiquated. **Old French** the French language of the period before c.1400. **old fustic** see FUSTIC. **old girl 1** a former female pupil of a school. **2** colloq. **a** an elderly woman. **b** an affectionate term of address to a girl or woman. **Old Glory** US the US national flag. **old gold** a dull brownish-gold colour. **old guard** the original or past or conservative members of a group. **old hand** a person with much experience. **old hat** *colloq.* something tediously familiar or out of date. **Old High German** High German (see GERMAN) up to *c.*1200. **old lady** *colloq.* one's mother or wife. **old lag** see LAG³. **old maid 1** *derog.* an elderly unmarried woman. **2** a prim and fussy person. **3** a card-game in which players try not to be left with an unpaired queen. **old-maidish** like an old maid. **old man** *colloq.* **1** one's husband or father. **2** one's employer or other person in authority over one. **3** an affectionate form of address to a boy or man. **old man's beard** a wild clematis, *Clematis vitalba*, with grey fluffy hairs round the seeds: also called *traveller's joy* (see TRAVELLER). **old master 1** a great artist of former times, esp. of the 13th-17th c. in Europe. **2** a painting by such a painter. **old moon** the moon in its last quarter, before the new moon. **Old Nick** *colloq.* the Devil. **Old Norse** see NORSE. **an old one** a familiar joke. **Old Pals Act** *Brit.* the principle that friends should always help one another. **Old Pretender** James Stuart (1688-1766), son of James II and claimant to the British throne. **old retainer** see RETAINER 3b. **old school 1** traditional attitudes. **2** people having such attitudes. **old school tie** *Brit.* **1** a necktie with a characteristic pattern worn by the pupils of a particular (usu. public) school. **2** the principle of excessive loyalty to traditional values. **old soldier** an experienced person, esp. in an arduous activity. **old stager** an experienced person, an old hand. **old style** of a date reckoned by the Julian calendar. **Old Testament** the part of the Christian Bible containing the scriptures of the Hebrews. **old-time** belonging to former times. **old-timer** *US* a person with long experience or standing. **old wives' tale** a foolish or unscientific tradition or belief. **old woman** *colloq.* **1** one's wife or mother. **2** a fussy or timid man. **old-womanish** fussy and timid. **Old World** Europe, Asia, and Africa. **old-world** belonging to or associated with old times. **old year** the year just ended or about to end. □□ **oldish** *adj.* **oldness** *n.* [OE *ald* f. WG]

olden /ˈəʊld(ə)n/ *adj.* archaic of old; of a former age (esp. *in olden times*).

oldie /ˈəʊldɪ/ *n.* *colloq.* an old person or thing.

oldster /ˈəʊldstə(r)/ *n.* an old person. [OLD + -STER, after *youngster*]

-ole /əʊl/ *comb. form* forming names of esp. heterocyclic compounds (*indole*). [L *oleum* oil]

oleaceous /ˌəʊlɪˈeɪʃəs/ *adj.* of the plant family Oleaceae, including olive and jasmine. [mod.L *Oleaceae* f. L *olea* olive-tree]

oleaginous /ˌəʊlɪˈædʒɪnəs/ *adj.* **1** having the properties of or producing oil. **2** oily, greasy. **3** obsequious, ingratiating. [F *oléagineux* f. L *oleaginus* f. *oleum* oil]

oleander /ˌəʊlɪˈændə(r)/ *n.* an evergreen poisonous shrub, *Nerium oleander*, native to the Mediterranean and bearing clusters of white, pink, or red flowers. [med.L]

oleaster /ˌəʊlɪˈæstə(r)/ *n.* any of various trees of the genus *Elaeagnus*, often thorny and with evergreen leathery foliage, esp. *E. angustifolia* bearing olive-shaped yellowish fruits. Also called *Russian olive*. [ME f. L f. *olea* olive-tree: see -ASTER]

olecranon /əʊˈlekrənɒn, ˌəʊlɪˈkreɪnən/ *n.* a bony prominence on the upper end of the ulna at the elbow. [Gk *ōle(no)kranon* f. *ōlenē* elbow + *kranion* head]

olefin /ˈəʊlɪfɪn/ *n.* (also **olefine**) *Chem.* = ALKENE. [F *oléfiant* oil-forming (with ref. to oily ethylene dichloride)]

oleic acid /əʊˈliːɪk/ *n.* an unsaturated fatty acid present in many fats and soaps. □□ **oleate** /ˈəʊlɪət/ *n.* [L *oleum* oil]

oleiferous /ˌəʊlɪˈɪfərəs/ *adj.* yielding oil. [L *oleum* oil + -FEROUS]

oleo- /ˈəʊlɪəʊ/ *comb. form* oil. [L *oleum* oil]

oleograph /ˈəʊlɪəˌgrɑːf/ *n.* a print made to resemble an oil-painting.

oleomargarine /ˌəʊlɪəʊˌmɑːdʒəˈriːn, -ˈmɑːdʒərɪn, -ˌmɑːgəˈriːn/ *n.* **1** a fatty substance extracted from beef fat and often used in margarine. **2** *US* a margarine made from vegetable oils.

oleometer /ˌəʊlɪˈɒmɪtə(r)/ *n.* an instrument for determining the density and purity of oils.

oleo-resin /ˌəʊlɪəʊˈrezɪn/ *n.* a natural or artificial mixture of essential oils and a resin, e.g. balsam.

oleum /ˈəʊlɪəm/ *n.* concentrated sulphuric acid containing excess sulphur trioxide in solution forming a dense corrosive liquid. [L, = oil]

O level /əʊ/ *n. Brit. hist.* = *ordinary level*. [abbr.]

olfaction /ɒlˈfækʃ(ə)n/ *n.* the act or capacity of smelling; the sense of smell. □□ **olfactive** *adj.* [L *olfactus* a smell f. *olēre* to smell + *facere fact-* make]

olfactory /ɒlˈfæktərɪ/ *adj.* of or relating to the sense of smell (*olfactory nerves*). [L *olfactare* frequent. of *olfacere* (as OLFACTION)]

olibanum /ɒˈlɪbənəm/ *n.* an aromatic gum resin from any tree of the genus *Boswellia*, used as incense. [ME f. med.L f. LL *libanus* f. Gk *libanos* frankincense, of Semitic orig.]

oligarch /ˈɒlɪgɑːk/ *n.* a member of an oligarchy. [Gk *oligarkhēs* f. *oligoi* few + *arkhō* to rule]

oligarchy /ˈɒlɪgɑːkɪ/ *n.* (*pl.* **-ies**) **1** government by a small group of people. **2** a State governed in this way. **3** the members of such a government. □□ **oligarchic** /-ˈgɑːkɪk/ *adj.* **oligarchical** /-ˈgɑːkɪk(ə)l/ *adj.* **oligarchically** /-ˈgɑːkɪkəlɪ/ *adv.* [F *oligarchie* f. med.L *oligarchia* f. Gk *oligarkhia* (as OLIGARCH)]

oligo- /ˈɒlɪgəʊ/ *comb. form* few, slight. [Gk *oligos* small, *oligoi* few]

Oligocene /ˈɒlɪgəˌsiːn/ *adj. & n. Geol.* —*adj.* of or relating to the third epoch of the Tertiary period, with evidence of the first primates. ¶ Cf. Appendix II. —*n.* this epoch or system. [as OLIGO- + Gk *kainos* new]

oligopoly /ˌɒlɪˈgɒpəlɪ/ *n.* (*pl.* **-ies**) a state of limited competition between a small number of producers or sellers. □□ **oligopolist** *n.* **oligopolistic** /-ˈlɪstɪk/ *adj.* [OLIGO-, after MONOPOLY]

oligosaccharide /ˌɒlɪgəʊˈsækəˌraɪd/ *n.* any carbohydrate whose molecules are composed of a relatively small number of monosaccharide units.

oligotrophic /ˌɒlɪgəʊˈtrəʊfɪk/ *adj.* (of a lake etc.) relatively poor in plant nutrients. □□ **oligotrophy** /ˌɒlɪˈgɒtrəfɪ/ *n.*

olio /ˈəʊlɪəʊ/ *n.* (*pl.* **-os**) **1** a mixed dish; a stew of various meats and vegetables. **2** a hotchpotch or miscellany. [Sp. *olla* stew f. L *olla* cooking-pot]

olivaceous /ˌɒlɪˈveɪʃəs/ *adj.* olive-green; of a dusky yellowish green.

olivary /ˈɒlɪvərɪ/ *adj. Anat.* olive-shaped; oval. [L *olivarius* (as OLIVE)]

olive /ˈɒlɪv/ *n. & adj.* —*n.* **1** (in full **olive tree**) any evergreen tree of the genus *Olea*, having dark-green lance-shaped leathery leaves with silvery undersides, esp. *O. europaea* of the Mediterranean, and *O. africana* native to S. Africa. **2** the small oval fruit of this, having a hard stone and bitter flesh, green when unripe and bluish-black when ripe. **3** (in full **olive-green**) the greyish-green colour of an unripe olive. **4** the wood of the olive tree. **5** *Anat.* each of a pair of olive-shaped swellings in the medulla oblongata. **6 a** any olive-shaped gastropod of the genus *Oliva*. **b** the shell of this. **7** a slice of beef or veal made into a roll with stuffing inside and stewed. —*adj.* **1** coloured like an unripe olive. **2** (of the complexion) yellowish-brown, sallow. □ **olive branch 1** the branch of an olive tree as a symbol of peace. **2** a gesture of reconciliation or friendship. **olive crown** a garland of olive leaves as a sign of victory. **olive drab** the dull olive colour of US army uniforms. **olive oil** an oil extracted from olives used esp. in cookery. [ME f. OF f. L *oliva* f. Gk *elaia* f. *elaion* oil]

olivine /'ɒlɪ,viːn/ n. Mineral. a naturally occurring form of magnesium-iron silicate, usu. olive-green and found in igneous rocks.

olla podrida /,ɒlə pə'driːdə/ n. = OLIO. [Sp., lit. 'rotten pot' (as OLIO + L putridus: cf. PUTRID)]

olm /ɒlm/ n. a blind cave-dwelling salamander, Proteus anguinus, native to SE Europe, usu. transparent but turning brown in light and having external gills. [G]

-ology /'ɒlədʒɪ/ comb. form see -LOGY.

oloroso /,ɒlə'rəʊsəʊ/ n. (pl. -os) a heavy dark medium-sweet sherry. [Sp., lit. 'fragrant']

Olympiad /ə'lɪmpɪ,æd/ n. **1 a** a period of four years between Olympic games, used by the ancient Greeks in dating events. **b** a four-yearly celebration of the ancient Olympic Games. **2** a celebration of the modern Olympic Games. **3** a regular international contest in chess etc. [ME f. F Olympiade f. L Olympias Olympiad- f. Gk Olumpias Olumpiad- f. Olumpios: see OLYMPIAN, OLYMPIC]

Olympian /ə'lɪmpɪən/ adj. & n. —adj. **1 a** of or associated with Mount Olympus in NE Greece, traditionally the home of the Greek gods. **b** celestial, godlike. **2** (of manners etc.) magnificent, condescending, superior. **3 a** of or relating to ancient Olympia in S. Greece. **b** = OLYMPIC. —n. **1** any of the pantheon of twelve gods regarded as living on Olympus. **2** a person of great attainments or of superhuman calm and detachment. [L Olympus or Olympia: see OLYMPIC]

Olympic /ə'lɪmpɪk/ adj. & n. —adj. of ancient Olympia or the Olympic games. —n. **(the Olympics)** the Olympic games. □**Olympic games 1** an ancient Greek festival held at Olympia every four years, with athletic, literary, and musical competitions. **2** a modern international revival of this as a sports festival held every four years since 1896 in different venues. [L Olympicus f. Gk Olumpikos of Olympus or Olympia (the latter being named from the games in honour of Zeus of Olympus)]

OM abbr. (in the UK) Order of Merit.

-oma /'əʊmə/ n. forming nouns denoting tumours and other abnormal growths (carcinoma). [mod.L f. Gk -ōma suffix denoting the result of verbal action]

omasum /əʊ'meɪsəm/ n. (pl. omasa /-sə/) the third stomach of a ruminant. [L, = bullock's tripe]

ombre /'ɒmbə(r)/ n. a card-game for three, popular in Europe in the 17th-18th c. [Sp. hombre man, with ref. to one player seeking to win the pool]

ombré /'ɔ̃breɪ/ adj. (of a fabric etc.) having gradual shading of colour from light to dark. [F, past part. of ombrer to shadow (as UMBER)]

ombro- /'ɒmbrəʊ/ comb. form rain. [Gk ombros rain-shower]

ombudsman /'ɒmbʊdzmən/ n. (pl. -men) an official appointed by a government to investigate individuals' complaints against public authorities etc. [Sw., = legal representative]

-ome /əʊm/ suffix forming nouns denoting objects or parts of a specified nature (rhizome; trichome). [var. of -OMA]

omega /'əʊmɪgə/ n. **1** the last (24th) letter of the Greek alphabet (Ω, ω). **2** the last of a series; the final development. [Gk, ō mega = great O]

omelette /'ɒmlɪt/ n. (also **omelet**) a dish of beaten eggs cooked in a frying-pan and served plain or with a savoury or sweet filling. [F omelette, obs. amelette by metathesis f. alumette var. of alumelle f. lemele knife-blade f. L lamella: see LAMELLA]

omen /'əʊmən, -men/ n. & v. —n. **1** an occurrence or object regarded as portending good or evil. **2** prophetic significance (of good omen). —v.tr. (usu. in passive) portend; foreshow. □□ **omened** adj. (also in comb.). [L omen ominis]

omentum /əʊ'mentəm/ n. (pl. omenta /-tə/) a fold of peritoneum connecting the stomach with other abdominal organs. □□ **omental** adj. [L]

omertà /,əʊmeə'tɑː/ n. a code of silence, esp. as practised by the Mafia. [It., = conspiracy of silence]

omicron /ə'maɪkrən/ n. the fifteenth letter of the Greek alphabet (O, ο). [Gk, o mikron = small o]

ominous /'ɒmɪnəs/ adj. **1** threatening; indicating disaster or difficulty. **2** of evil omen; inauspicious. **3** giving or being an omen. □□ **ominously** adv. **ominousness** n. [L ominosus (as OMEN)]

omission /ə'mɪʃ(ə)n/ n. **1** the act or an instance of omitting or being omitted. **2** something that has been omitted or overlooked. □□ **omissive** adj. [ME f. OF omission or LL omissio (as OMIT)]

omit /ə'mɪt/ v.tr. (**omitted**, **omitting**) **1** leave out; not insert or include. **2** leave undone. **3** (foll. by verbal noun or to + infin.) fail or neglect (omitted saying anything; omitted to say). □□ **omissible** adj. [ME f. L omittere omiss- (as OB-, mittere send)]

ommatidium /,ɒmə'tɪdɪəm/ n. (pl. **ommatidia** /-dɪə/) a structural element in the compound eye of an insect. [mod.L f. Gk ommatidion dimin. of omma ommat- eye]

omni- /'ɒmnɪ/ comb. form **1** all; of all things. **2** in all ways or places. [L f. omnis all]

omnibus /'ɒmnɪbəs/ n. & adj. —n. **1** formal = BUS. **2** a volume containing several novels etc. previously published separately. —adj. **1** serving several purposes at once. **2** comprising several items. [F f. L (dative pl. of omnis), = for all]

omnicompetent /,ɒmnɪ'kɒmpɪt(ə)nt/ adj. **1** able to deal with all matters. **2** having jurisdiction in all cases. □□ **omnicompetence** n.

omnidirectional /,ɒmnɪdɪ'rekʃən(ə)l/ adj. (of an aerial etc.) receiving or transmitting in all directions.

omnifarious /,ɒmnɪ'feərɪəs/ adj. of all sorts or varieties. [LL omnifarius (as OMNI-): cf. MULTIFARIOUS]

omnipotent /ɒm'nɪpət(ə)nt/ adj. **1** having great or absolute power. **2** having great influence. □□ **omnipotence** n. **omnipotently** adv. [ME f. OF f. L omnipotens (as OMNI-, POTENT¹)]

omnipresent /,ɒmnɪ'prez(ə)nt/ adj. **1** present everywhere at the same time. **2** widely or constantly encountered. □□ **omnipresence** n. [med.L omnipraesens (as OMNI-, PRESENT¹)]

omniscient /ɒm'nɪsɪənt, -ʃɪənt/ adj. knowing everything or much. □□ **omniscience** n. **omnisciently** adv. [med.L omnisciens -entis (as OMNI-, scire know)]

omnium gatherum /,ɒmnɪəm 'gæðərəm/ n. colloq. a miscellany or strange mixture. [mock L f. L omnium of all + GATHER]

omnivorous /ɒm'nɪvərəs/ adj. **1** feeding on many kinds of food, esp. on both plants and flesh. **2** making use of everything available. □□ **omnivore** /'ɒmnɪ,vɔː(r)/ n. **omnivorously** adv. **omnivorousness** n. [L omnivorus (as OMNI-, -VOROUS)]

omphalo- /'ɒmfələʊ/ comb. form navel. [Gk (as OMPHALOS)]

omphalos /'ɒmfə,lɒs/ n. Gk Antiq. **1** a conical stone (esp. that at Delphi) representing the navel of the earth. **2** a boss on a shield. **3** a centre or hub. [Gk, = navel, boss, hub]

on /ɒn/ prep., adv., adj., & n. —prep. **1** (so as to be) supported by or attached to or covering or enclosing (sat on a chair; stuck on the wall; rings on her fingers; leaned on his elbow). **2** carried with; about the person of (have you a pen on you?). **3** (of time) exactly at; during; contemporaneously with (on 29 May; on the hour; on schedule; working on Tuesday). **4** immediately after or before (I saw them on my return). **5** as a result of (on further examination I found this). **6** (so as to be) having membership etc. of or residence at or in (she is on the board of directors; lives on the continent). **7** supported financially by (lives on £50 a week; lives on his wits). **8** close to; just by (a house on the sea; lives on the main road). **9** in the direction of; against. **10** so as to threaten; touching or striking (advanced on him; pulled a knife on me; a punch on *the nose).* **11** having as an axis or pivot (*turned on his heels*). **12** having as a basis or motive (*works on a ratchet; arrested on suspicion*). **13** having as a standard, confirmation, or guarantee (*had it on good authority; did it on purpose; I promise on my word*). **14** concerning or about (*writes on frogs*). **15** using or engaged with (*is on the pill; here on business*). **16** so as to affect (*walked out on her*). **17** at the expense of (*the drinks are on me; the joke is on him*). **18** added to (*disaster on disaster; ten pence on a pint of beer*). **19** in a specified manner or style (often foll. by *the* + adj. or noun: *on the cheap; on the run*). —*adv.* **1** (so as to be) covering or in contact with something, esp. of clothes (*put your boots on*). **2** in the appropriate direction; towards something (*look on*). **3** further forward; in an advanced position or state (*time is getting on; it happened later on*). **4** with continued movement or action (*went plodding on; keeps on complaining*). **5** in operation or activity (*the light is on; the chase was on*). **6** due to take place as planned (*is the party still on?*). **7** *colloq.* **a** (of a person) willing to participate or approve, or make a bet. **b** (of an idea, proposal, etc.) practicable or acceptable (*that's just not on*). **8** being shown or performed (*a good film on tonight*). **9** (of an actor) on stage. **10** (of an employee) on duty. **11** forward (*head on*). —*adj. Cricket* designating the part of the field on the striker's side and in front of the wicket. —*n. Cricket* the on side. ▫ **be on about** refer to or discuss esp. tediously or persistently (*what are they on about?*). **be on at** *colloq.* nag or grumble at. **be on to 1** realize the significance or intentions of. **2** get in touch with (esp. by telephone). **on and off** intermittently; now and then. **on and on** continually; at tedious length. **on-line** *Computing* (of equipment or a process) directly controlled by or connected to a central processor. **on-off 1** (of a switch) having two positions, 'on' and 'off'. **2** = *on and off.* **on-stage** *adj. & adv.* on the stage; visible to the audience. **on-street** (with ref. to parking vehicles) at the side of a street. **on time** punctual, punctually. **on to** to a position or state on or in contact with (cf. ONTO). [OE *on, an* f. Gmc]

-on /ɒn/ *suffix Physics, Biochem., & Chem.* forming nouns denoting: **1** elementary particles (*meson; neutron*). **2** quanta (*photon*). **3** molecular units (*codon*). **4** substances (*interferon; parathion*). [ION, orig. in *electron*]

onager /ˈɒnəgə(r)/ *n.* **1** a wild ass, esp. *Equus hemionus* of Central Asia. **2** *hist.* an ancient military engine for throwing rocks. [ME f. L f. Gk *onagros* f. *onos* ass + *agrios* wild]

onanism /ˈəʊnə,nɪz(ə)m/ *n.* **1** masturbation. **2** coitus interruptus. ▫▫ **onanist** *n.* **onanistic** /-ˈnɪstɪk/ *adj.* [F *onanisme* or mod.L *onanismus* f. *Onan* (Gen. 38: 9)]

ONC *abbr.* (in the UK) Ordinary National Certificate.

once /wʌns/ *adv., conj., & n.* —*adv.* **1** on one occasion or for one time only (*did not once say please; have read it once*). **2** at some point or period in the past (*could once play chess*). **3** ever or at all (*if you once forget it*). **4** multiplied by one; by one degree. —*conj.* as soon as (*once they have gone we can relax*). —*n.* one time or occasion (*just the once*). ▫ **all at once 1** without warning; suddenly. **2** all together. **at once 1** immediately. **2** simultaneously. **for once** on this (or that) occasion, even if at no other. **once again** (or **more**) another time. **once and for all** (or **once for all**) (done) in a final or conclusive manner, esp. so as to end hesitation or uncertainty. **once** (or **every once**) **in a while** from time to time; occasionally. **once or twice** a few times. **once-over** *colloq.* a rapid preliminary inspection or piece of work. **once upon a time** at some vague time in the past. [ME *ānes, ōnes*, genit. of ONE]

oncer /ˈwʌnsə(r)/ *n.* **1** *Brit. hist. sl.* a one-pound note. **2** *colloq.* a thing that occurs only once. **3** *Austral.*

colloq. an election of an MP likely to serve only one term.

onco- /ˈɒŋkəʊ/ *comb. form Med.* tumour. [Gk *ogkos* mass]

oncogene /ˈɒnkə,dʒiːn/ *n.* a gene which can transform a cell into a tumour cell. ▫▫ **oncogenic** /-ˈdʒenɪk/ *adj.* **oncogenous** /-ˈkɒdʒɪnəs/ *adj.*

oncology /ɒŋˈkɒlədʒɪ/ *n. Med.* the study of tumours.

oncoming /ˈɒn,kʌmɪŋ/ *adj. & n.* —*adj.* approaching from the front. —*n.* an approach or onset.

oncost /ˈɒnkɒst/ *n. Brit.* an overhead expense.

OND *abbr.* (in the UK) Ordinary National Diploma.

on dit /ɔ̃ ˈdiː/ *n.* (*pl.* **on dits** *pronunc.* same) a piece of gossip or hearsay. [F, = they say]

one /wʌn/ *adj., n., & pron.* —*adj.* **1** single and integral in number. **2** (with a noun implied) a single person or thing of the kind expressed or implied (*one of the best; a nasty one*). **3 a** particular but undefined, esp. as contrasted with another (*that is one view; one thing after another*). **b** *colloq.* (as an emphatic) a noteworthy example of (*that is one difficult question*). **4** only such (*the one man who can do it*). **5** forming a unity (*one and undivided*). **6** identical; the same (*of one opinion*). —*n.* **1 a** the lowest cardinal number. **b** a thing numbered with it. **2** unity; a unit (*one is half of two; came in ones and twos*). **3 a** single thing or person or example (often referring to a noun previously expressed or implied: *the big dog and the small one*). **4** *colloq.* an alcoholic drink (*have a quick one; have one on me*). **5** a story or joke (*the one about the frog*). —*pron.* **1** a person of a specified kind (*loved ones; like one possessed*). **2** any person, as representing people in general (*one is bound to lose in the end*). **3** I, me (*one would like to help*). ¶ Often regarded as an affectation. ▫ **all one** (often foll. by *to*) a matter of indifference. **at one** in agreement. **for one** being one, even if the only one (*I for one do not believe it*). **for one thing** as a single consideration, ignoring others. **one another** each the other or others (as a formula of reciprocity: *love one another*). **one-armed bandit** *colloq.* a fruit machine worked by a long handle at the side. **one by one** singly, successively. **one day 1** on an unspecified day. **2** at some unspecified future date. **one-horse 1** using a single horse. **2** *colloq.* small, poorly equipped. **one-liner** *colloq.* a single brief sentence, often witty or apposite. **one-man** involving, done, or operated by only one man. **one-night stand 1** a single performance of a play etc. in a place. **2** *colloq.* a sexual liaison lasting only one night. **one-off** *colloq.* made or done as the only one; not repeated. **one or two** see OR[1]. **one-piece** (of a bathing-suit etc.) made as a single garment. **one-sided 1** favouring one side in a dispute; unfair, partial. **2** having or occurring on one side only. **3** larger or more developed on one side. **one-sidedly** in a one-sided manner. **one-sidedness** the act or state of being one-sided. **one-time** former. **one-to-one** with one member of one group corresponding to one of another. **one-track mind** a mind preoccupied with one subject. **one-two** *colloq.* **1** *Boxing* the delivery of two punches in quick succession. **2** *Football* etc. a series of reciprocal passes between two advancing players. **one-up** *colloq.* having a particular advantage. **one-upmanship** *colloq.* the art of maintaining a psychological advantage. **one-way** allowing movement or travel in one direction only. [OE *ān* f. Gmc]

-one /əʊn/ *suffix Chem.* forming nouns denoting various compounds, esp. ketones (*acetone*). [Gk *-ōnē* fem. patronymic]

onefold /ˈwʌnfəʊld/ *adj.* consisting of only one member or element; simple.

oneiric /əˈnaɪərɪk/ *adj.* of or relating to dreams or dreaming. [Gk *oneiros* dream]

oneiro- /əˈnaɪrəʊ/ *comb. form* dream. [Gk *oneiros* dream]

oneiromancy /əˈnaɪrə,mænsɪ/ *n.* the interpretation of dreams.

oneness /'wʌnnɪs/ *n*. **1** the fact or state of being one; singleness. **2** uniqueness. **3** agreement; unity of opinion. **4** identity, sameness.

oner /'wʌnə(r)/ *n. Brit. sl.* **1** one pound (of money). **2** a remarkable person or thing.

onerous /'ɒnərəs, 'əʊn-/ *adj*. **1** burdensome; causing or requiring trouble. **2** *Law* involving heavy obligations. □□ **onerously** *adv*. **onerousness** *n*. [ME f. OF *onereus* f. L *onerosus* f. *onus oneris* burden]

oneself /wʌn'self/ *pron*. the reflexive and (in apposition) emphatic form of *one* (*kill oneself; one has to do it oneself*).

onestep /'wʌnstep/ *n*. a vigorous kind of foxtrot in duple time.

onflow /'ɒnfləʊ/ *n*. an onward flow.

onglaze /'ɒnɡleɪz/ *adj*. (of painting etc.) done on a glazed surface.

ongoing /'ɒnɡəʊɪŋ/ *adj*. **1** continuing to exist or be operative etc. **2** that is or are in progress (*ongoing discussions*). □□ **ongoingness** *n*.

onion /'ʌnjən/ *n*. **1** a liliaceous plant, *Allium cepa*, having a short stem and bearing greenish-white flowers. **2** the swollen bulb of this with many concentric skins used in cooking, pickling, etc. □**know one's onions** be fully knowledgeable or experienced. **onion dome** a bulbous dome on a church, palace, etc. **onion-skin 1** the brown outermost skin or any outer skin of an onion. **2** thin smooth translucent paper. □□ **oniony** *adj*. [ME f. AF *union*, OF *oignon* ult. f. L *unio -onis*]

onlooker /'ɒn,lʊkə(r)/ *n*. a non-participating observer; a spectator. □□ **onlooking** *adj*.

only /'əʊnlɪ/ *adv., adj., & conj.* —*adv*. **1** solely, merely, exclusively; and no one or nothing more besides (*I only want to sit down; will only make matters worse; needed six only; is only a child*). **2** no longer ago than (*saw them only yesterday*). **3** not until (*arrives only on Tuesday*). **4** with no better result than (*hurried home only to find her gone*). ¶ In informal English *only* is usually placed between the subject and verb regardless of what it refers to (e.g. *I only want to talk to you*); in more formal English it is often placed more exactly, esp. to avoid ambiguity (e.g. *I want to talk only to you*). In speech, intonation usually serves to clarify the sense. —*attrib.adj.* **1** existing alone of its or their kind (*their only son*). **2** best or alone worth knowing (*the only place to eat*). —*conj. colloq.* **1** except that; but for the fact that (*I would go, only I feel ill*). **2** but then (as an extra consideration) (*he always makes promises, only he never keeps them*). □**only-begotten** *literary* begotten as the only child. **only too** extremely (*is only too willing*). [OE *ānlic, ǣnlic*, ME *onliche* (as ONE, -LY²)]

o.n.o. *abbr. Brit.* or near offer.

onomastic /,ɒnə'mæstɪk/ *adj*. relating to names or nomenclature. [Gk *onomastikos* f. *onoma* name]

onomastics /,ɒnə'mæstɪks/ *n.pl.* (treated as *sing.*) the study of the origin and formation of (esp. personal) proper names.

onomatopoeia /,ɒnə,mætə'pi:ə/ *n*. **1** the formation of a word from a sound associated with what is named (e.g. *cuckoo, sizzle*). **2** the use of such words. □□ **onomatopoeic** *adj*. **onomatopoeically** *adv*. [LL f. Gk *onomatopoiia* word-making f. *onoma -matos* name + *poieō* make]

onrush /'ɒnrʌʃ/ *n*. an onward rush.

onscreen /'ɒnskri:n/ *adj. & adv.* —*adj*. appearing on a cinema, television, or VDU screen. —*adv*. **1** on or by means of a screen. **2** within the view presented by a cinema-film scene.

onset /'ɒnset/ *n*. **1** an attack. **2** a beginning, esp. an energetic or determined one.

onshore /'ɒnʃɔ:(r)/ *adj*. **1** on the shore. **2** (of the wind) blowing from the sea towards the land.

onside /'ɒnsaɪd, ɒn'saɪd/ *adj*. (of a player in a field game) in a lawful position; not offside.

onslaught /'ɒnslɔ:t/ *n*. a fierce attack. [earlier *anslaight* f. MDu. *aenslag* f. *aen* on + *slag* blow, with assim. to obs. *slaught* slaughter]

Ont. *abbr*. Ontario.

-ont /ɒnt/ *comb. form Biol.* denoting an individual of a specified type (*symbiont*). [Gk *ōn ont-* being]

onto /'ɒntu:/ *prep. disp.* to a position or state on or in contact with (cf. *on to*). ¶ The form *onto* is still not fully accepted in the way that *into* is, although it is in wide use. It is however useful in distinguishing sense as between *we drove on to the beach* (i.e. in that direction) and *we drove onto the beach* (i.e. in contact with it).

ontogenesis /,ɒntə'dʒenɪsɪs/ *n*. the origin and development of an individual (cf. PHYLOGENESIS). □□ **ontogenetic** /-tə'nɛtɪk/ *adj*. **ontogenetically** /-dʒɪ'netɪkəlɪ/ *adv*. [formed as ONTOGENY + Gk *genesis* birth]

ontogeny /ɒn'tɒdʒənɪ/ *n*. = ONTOGENESIS. □□ **ontogenic** /-tə'dʒenɪk/ *adj*. **ontogenically** /-tə'dʒenɪkəlɪ/ *adv*. [Gk *ōn ont-* being, pres. part. of *eimi* be + -GENY]

ontology /ɒn'tɒlədʒɪ/ *n*. the branch of metaphysics dealing with the nature of being. □□ **ontological** /-tə'lɒdʒɪk(ə)l/ *adj*. **ontologically** /-tə'lɒdʒɪkəlɪ/ *adv*. **ontologist** *n*. [mod.L *ontologia* f. Gk *ōn ont-* being + -LOGY]

onus /'əʊnəs/ *n*. (*pl*. **onuses**) a burden, duty, or responsibility. [L]

onward /'ɒnwəd/ *adv. & adj.* —*adv*. (also **onwards**) **1** further on. **2** towards the front. **3** with advancing motion. —*adj*. directed onwards.

onyx /'ɒnɪks/ *n*. a semiprecious variety of agate with different colours in layers. □**onyx marble** banded calcite etc. used as a decorative material. [ME f. OF *oniche, onix* f. L f. Gk *onux* fingernail, onyx]

oo- /'əʊə/ *comb. form* (US **oö-**) *Biol.* egg, ovum. [Gk *ōion* egg]

oocyte /'əʊə,saɪt/ *n*. an immature ovum in an ovary.

oodles /'u:d(ə)lz/ *n.pl. colloq.* a very great amount. [19th-c. US: orig. unkn.]

oof /u:f/ *n. sl.* money, cash. [Yiddish *ooftisch*, G *auf dem Tische* on the table (of money in gambling)]

oofy /'u:fɪ/ *adj. sl.* rich, wealthy. □□ **oofiness** *n*.

oogamous /əʊ'ɒɡəməs/ *adj*. reproducing by the union of mobile male and immobile female cells. □□ **oogamy** *n*.

oogenesis /,əʊə'dʒenɪsɪs/ *n*. the production or development of an ovum.

ooh /u:/ *int*. expressing surprise, delight, pain, etc. [natural exclam.]

oolite /'əʊə,laɪt/ *n*. **1** a sedimentary rock, usu. limestone, consisting of rounded grains made up of concentric layers. **2** = OOLITH. □□ **oolitic** /-'lɪtɪk/ *adj*. [F *oölithe* (as OO-, -LITE)]

oolith /'əʊəlɪθ/ *n*. any of the rounded grains making up oolite.

oology /əʊ'ɒlədʒɪ/ *n*. the study or collecting of birds' eggs. □□ **oological** /,əʊə'lɒdʒɪk(ə)l/ *adj*. **oologist** *n*.

oolong /'u:lɒŋ/ *n*. a dark kind of cured China tea. [Chin. *wulong* black dragon]

oomiak var. of UMIAK.

oompah /'ʊmpɑ:/ *n. colloq.* the rhythmical sound of deep-toned brass instruments in a band. [imit.]

oomph /ʊmf/ *n. sl.* **1** energy, enthusiasm. **2** attractiveness, esp. sexual appeal. [20th c.: orig. uncert.]

-oon /u:n/ *suffix* forming nouns, orig. from French words in stressed *-on* (*balloon; buffoon*). ¶ Replaced by *-on* in recent borrowings and those with unstressed *-on* (*baron*). [L *-o -onis*, sometimes via It. *-one*]

oops /u:ps, ʊps/ *int. colloq.* expressing surprise or apology, esp. on making an obvious mistake. [natural exclam.]

oosperm /'əʊə,spɜ:m/ *n*. a fertilized ovum.

ooze¹ /u:z/ *v. & n.* —*v*. **1** *intr*. (of fluid) pass slowly through the pores of a body. **2** *intr*. trickle or leak slowly out. **3** *intr*. (of a substance) exude moisture.

4 *tr.* exude or exhibit (a feeling) liberally (*oozed sympathy*). —*n.* **1** a sluggish flow or exudation. **2** an infusion of oak-bark or other vegetable matter, used in tanning. □□**oozy** *adj.* **oozily** *adv.* **ooziness** *n.* [orig. as noun (sense 2), f. OE *wōs* juice, sap]

ooze² /uːz/ *n.* **1** a deposit of wet mud or slime, esp. at the bottom of a river, lake, or estuary. **2** a bog or marsh; soft muddy ground. □□ **oozy** *adj.* [OE *wāse*]

OP *abbr.* **1** *RC Ch.* Order of Preachers (Dominican). **2** observation post. **3** opposite prompt.

op /ɒp/ *n. colloq.* operation (in surgical and military senses).

op. /ɒp/ *abbr.* **1** *Mus.* opus. **2** operator.

op- /ɒp/ *prefix* assim. form of OB- before *p*.

o.p. *abbr.* **1** out of print. **2** overproof.

opacify /əʊˈpæsɪˌfaɪ/ *v.tr.* & *intr.* (-ies, -ied) make or become opaque. □□ **opacifier** *n.*

opacity /əˈpæsɪtɪ/ *n.* **1** the state of being opaque. **2** obscurity of meaning. **3** obtuseness of understanding. [F *opacité* f. L *opacitas -tatis* (as OPAQUE)]

opah /ˈəʊpə/ *n.* a large rare deep-sea fish, *Lampris guttatus*, usu. having a silver-blue back with white spots and crimson fins. Also called MOONFISH. [W. Afr. name]

opal /ˈəʊp(ə)l/ *n.* a quartzlike form of hydrated silica, usu. white or colourless and sometimes showing changing colours, often used as a gemstone. □**opal glass** a semi-translucent white glass. [F *opale* or L *opalus* prob. ult. f. Skr. *upalas* precious stone]

opalescent /ˌəʊpəˈles(ə)nt/ *adj.* showing changing colours like an opal. □□ **opalesce** *v.intr.* **opalescence** *n.*

opaline /ˈəʊpəˌlaɪn/ *adj.* & *n.* —*adj.* opal-like, opalescent, iridescent. —*n.* opal glass.

opaque /əʊˈpeɪk/ *adj.* & *n.* —*adj.* (**opaquer**, **opaquest**) **1** not transmitting light. **2** impenetrable to sight. **3** obscure; not lucid. **4** obtuse, dull-witted. —*n.* **1** an opaque thing or substance. **2** a substance for producing opaque areas on negatives. □□ **opaquely** *adv.* **opaqueness** *n.* [ME *opak* f. L *opacus*: spelling now assim. to F]

op art /ɒp/ *n. colloq.* = *optical art.* [abbr.]

op. cit. *abbr.* in the work already quoted. [L *opere citato*]

OPEC /ˈəʊpek/ *abbr.* Organization of Petroleum Exporting Countries.

open /ˈəʊpən/ *adj.*, *v.*, & *n.* —*adj.* **1** not closed or locked or blocked up; allowing entrance or passage or access. **2 a** (of a room, field, or other area) having its door or gate in a position allowing access, or part of its confining boundary removed. **b** (of a container) not fastened or sealed; in a position or with the lid etc. in a position allowing access to the inside part. **3** unenclosed, unconfined, unobstructed (*the open road; open views*). **4 a** uncovered, bare, exposed (*open drain; open wound*). **b** *Sport* (of a goal mouth or other object of attack) unprotected, vulnerable. **5** undisguised, public, manifest; not exclusive or limited (*open scandal; open hostilities*). **6** expanded, unfolded, or spread out (*had the map open on the table*). **7** (of a fabric) not close; with gaps or intervals. **8 a** (of a person) frank and communicative. **b** (of the mind) accessible to new ideas; unprejudiced or undecided. **9 a** (of an exhibition, shop, etc.) accessible to visitors or customers; ready for business. **b** (of a meeting) admitting all, not restricted to members etc. **10 a** (of a race, competition, scholarship, etc.) unrestricted as to who may compete. **b** (of a champion, scholar, etc.) having won such a contest. **11** (of government) conducted in an informative manner receptive to enquiry, criticism, etc., from the public. **12** (foll. by *to*) **a** willing to receive (*is open to offers*). **b** (of a choice, offer, or opportunity) still available (*there are three courses open to us*). **c** likely to suffer from or be affected by (*open to abuse*). **13 a** (of the mouth) with lips apart, esp. in surprise or incomprehension. **b** (of the ears or eyes) eagerly attentive. **14** *Mus.* **a** (of a string) allowed to vibrate

along its whole length. **b** (of a pipe) unstopped at each end. **c** (of a note) sounded from an open string or pipe. **15** (of an electrical circuit) having a break in the conducting path. **16** (of the bowels) not constipated. **17** (of a return ticket) not restricted as to day of travel. **18** (of a cheque) not crossed. **19** (of a boat) without a deck. **20** (of a river or harbour) free of ice. **21** (of the weather or winter) free of frost. **22** *Phonet.* **a** (of a vowel) produced with a relatively wide opening of the mouth. **b** (of a syllable) ending in a vowel. **23** (of a town, city, etc.) not defended even if attacked. —*v.* **1** *tr.* & *intr.* make or become open or more open. **2 a** *tr.* change from a closed or fastened position so as to allow access (*opened the door; opened the box*). **b** *intr.* (of a door, lid, etc.) have its position changed to allow access (*the door opened slowly*). **3** *tr.* remove the sealing or fastening element of (a container) to get access to the contents (*opened the envelope*). **4** *intr.* (foll. by *into, on to*, etc.) (of a door, room, etc.) afford access as specified (*opened on to a large garden*). **5 a** *tr.* start or establish or set going (a business, activity, etc.). **b** *intr.* be initiated; make a start (*the session opens tomorrow; the story opens with a murder*). **c** *tr.* (of a counsel in a lawcourt) make a preliminary statement in (a case) before calling witnesses. **6** *tr.* **a** spread out or unfold (a map, newspaper, etc.). **b** (often *absol.*) refer to the contents of (a book). **7** *intr.* (often foll. by *with*) (of a person) begin speaking, writing, etc. (*he opened with a warning*). **8** *intr.* (of a prospect) come into view; be revealed. **9** *tr.* reveal or communicate (one's feelings, intentions, etc.). **10** *tr.* make (one's mind, heart, etc.) more sympathetic or enlightened. **11** *tr.* ceremonially declare (a building etc.) to be completed and in use. **12** *tr.* break up (ground) with a plough etc. **13** *tr.* cause evacuation of (the bowels). **14** *Naut.* **a** *tr.* get a view of by change of position. **b** *intr.* come into full view. —*n.* **1** (prec. by *the*) **a** open space or country or air. **b** public notice or view; general attention (esp. *into the open*). **2** an open championship, competition, or scholarship. □**be open with** speak frankly to. **keep open house** see HOUSE. **open air** (usu. prec. by *the*) a free or unenclosed space outdoors. **open-air** (*attrib.*) out of doors. **open-and-shut** (of an argument, case, etc.) straightforward and conclusive. **open-armed** cordial; warmly receptive. **open book** a person who is easily understood. **open day** a day when the public may visit a place normally closed to them. **open door** free admission of foreign trade and immigrants. **open-door** *adj.* open, accessible, public. **open the door to** see DOOR. **open-ended** having no predetermined limit or boundary. **open a person's eyes** see EYE. **open-eyed 1** with the eyes open. **2** alert, watchful. **open-faced** having a frank or ingenuous expression. **open-handed** generous. **open-handedly** generously. **open-handedness** generosity. **open-hearted** frank and kindly. **open-heartedness** an open-hearted quality. **open-hearth process** a process of steel manufacture, using a shallow reverberatory furnace. **open-heart surgery** surgery with the heart exposed and the blood made to bypass it. **open house** welcome or hospitality for all visitors. **open ice** ice through which navigation is possible. **open letter** a letter, esp. of protest, addressed to an individual and published in a newspaper or journal. **open market** an unrestricted market with free competition of buyers and sellers. **open-minded** accessible to new ideas; unprejudiced. **open-mindedly** in an open-minded manner. **open-mindedness** the quality of being open-minded. **open-mouthed** with the mouth open, esp. in surprise. **open out 1** unfold; spread out. **2** develop, expand. **3** become communicative. **4** accelerate. **open-plan** (usu. *attrib.*) (of a house, office, etc.) having large undivided rooms. **open prison** a prison with the minimum of physical restraints on prisoners. **open question** a matter on which differences of opinion are legitimate. **open-reel** (of a tape recorder) having reels of tape requiring individual threading, as distinct from a cassette. **open sandwich** a sandwich without a top slice of bread. **open sea** an expanse of sea away from land. **open season** the season when restrictions on the killing of game etc. are lifted. **open secret** a supposed secret that is known to many people. **open sesame** see SESAME. **open shop 1** a business etc. where employees do not have to be members of a trade union (opp. *closed shop*). **2** this system. **open society** a society with wide dissemination of information and freedom of belief. **Open University** (in the UK) a university that teaches mainly by broadcasting and correspondence, and is open to those without formal academic qualifications. **open up 1** unlock (premises). **2** make accessible. **3** reveal; bring to notice. **4** accelerate esp. a motor vehicle. **5** begin shooting or sounding. **open verdict** a verdict affirming that a crime has been committed but not specifying the criminal or (in case of violent death) the cause. **with open arms** see ARM¹. □□ **openable** *adj.* **openness** *n.* [OE *open*]

opencast /ˈəʊpənˌkɑːst/ *adj. Brit.* (of a mine or mining) with removal of the surface layers and working from above, not from shafts.

opener /ˈəʊpənə(r), ˈəʊpnə(r)/ *n.* **1** a device for opening tins, bottles, etc. **2** *colloq.* the first item on a programme etc. **3** *Cricket* an opening batsman. □ **for openers** *colloq.* to start with.

opening /ˈəʊpənɪŋ, ˈəʊpnɪŋ/ *n. & adj.* —*n.* **1** an aperture or gap, esp. allowing access. **2** a favourable situation or opportunity. **3** a beginning; an initial part. **4** *Chess* a recognized sequence of moves at the beginning of a game. **5** a counsel's preliminary statement of a case in a lawcourt. —*adj.* initial, first. □ **opening-time** *Brit.* the time at which public houses may legally open for custom.

openly /ˈəʊpənlɪ/ *adv.* **1** frankly, honestly. **2** publicly; without concealment. [OE *openlīce* (as OPEN, -LY²)]

openwork /ˈəʊpənˌwɜːk/ *n.* a pattern with intervening spaces in metal, leather, lace, etc.

opera¹ /ˈɒpərə, ˈɒprə/ *n.* **1 a** a dramatic work in one or more acts, set to music for singers (usu. in costume) and instrumentalists. **b** this as a genre. **2** a building for the performance of opera. □ **opera-glasses** small binoculars for use at the opera or theatre. **opera-hat** a man's tall collapsible hat. **opera-house** a theatre for the performance of opera. [It. f. L, = labour, work]

opera² *pl.* of OPUS.

operable /ˈɒpərəb(ə)l/ *adj.* **1** that can be operated. **2** suitable for treatment by surgical operation. □□ **operability** /-ˈbɪlɪtɪ/ *n.* [LL *operabilis* f. L (as OPERATE)]

opera buffa /ˌɒpərə ˈbuːfə/ *n.* (esp. Italian) comic opera, esp. with characters drawn from everyday life. [It.]

opéra comique /ˌɒpeˌrɑː kɒˈmiːk/ *n.* (esp. French) opera on a light-hearted theme, with spoken dialogue. [F]

operand /ˈɒpəˌrænd/ *n. Math.* the quantity etc. on which an operation is to be done. [L *operandum* neut. gerundive of *operari*: see OPERATE]

opera seria /ˌɒpərə ˈsɪərɪə/ *n.* (esp. 18th-c. Italian) opera on a serious, usu. classical or mythological theme. [It.]

operate /ˈɒpəˌreɪt/ *v.* **1** *tr.* manage, work, control; put or keep in a functional state. **2** *intr.* be in action; function. **3** *intr.* produce an effect; exercise influence (*the tax operates to our disadvantage*). **4** *intr.* (often foll. by *on*) **a** perform a surgical operation. **b** conduct a military or naval action. **c** be active in business etc., esp. dealing in stocks and shares. **5** *intr.* (foll. by *on*) influence or affect (feelings etc.). **6** *tr.* bring about; accomplish. □ **operating system** the basic software that enables the running of a computer program. **operating theatre** (or **room**) a room for surgical operations. [L *operari* to work f. *opus operis* work]

operatic /ˌɒpəˈrætɪk/ *adj.* **1** of or relating to opera. **2** resembling or characteristic of opera. □□ **operatically** *adv.* [irreg. f. OPERA¹, after *dramatic*]

operatics /ˌɒpəˈrætɪks/ *n.pl.* the production and performance of operas.

operation /ˌɒpəˈreɪʃ(ə)n/ *n.* **1 a** the action or process or method of working or operating. **b** the state of being active or functioning (*not yet in operation*). **c** the scope or range of effectiveness of a thing's activity. **2** an active process; a discharge of a function (*the operation of breathing*). **3** a piece of work, esp. one in a series (often in *pl.*: *begin operations*). **4** an act of surgery performed on a patient. **5 a** a strategic movement of troops, ships, etc. for military action. **b** preceding a code-name (*Operation Overlord*). **6** a financial transaction. **7** *Math.* the subjection of a number or quantity or function to a process affecting its value or form, e.g. multiplication, differentiation. □ **operations research** = *operational research*. [ME f. OF f. L *operatio -onis*]

operational /ˌɒpəˈreɪʃən(ə)l/ *adj.* **1 a** of or used for operations. **b** engaged or involved in operations. **2** able or ready to function. □ **operational research** the application of scientific principles to business management, providing a quantitative basis for complex decisions. □□ **operationally** *adv.*

operative /ˈɒpərətɪv/ *adj. & n.* —*adj.* **1** in operation; having effect. **2** having the principal relevance (*'may' is the operative word*). **3** of or by surgery. **4** *Law* expressing an intent to perform a transaction. —*n.* **1** a worker, esp. a skilled one. **2** *US* a private detective. □□ **operatively** *adv.* **operativeness** *n.* [LL *operativus* f. L (as OPERATE)]

operator /ˈɒpəˌreɪtə(r)/ *n.* **1** a person operating a machine etc., esp. making connections of lines in a telephone exchange. **2** a person operating or engaging in business. **3** *colloq.* a person acting in a specified way (*a smooth operator*). **4** *Math.* a symbol or function denoting an operation (e.g. ×, +). [LL f. L *operari* (as OPERATE)]

operculum /əˈpɜːkjʊləm, əʊ-/ *n.* (*pl.* **opercula** /-lə/) **1** *Zool.* **a** a flaplike structure covering the gills in a fish. **b** a platelike structure closing the aperture of a gastropod mollusc's shell when the organism is retracted. **c** any of various other parts covering or closing an aperture, such as a flap over the nostrils in some birds. **2** *Bot.* a lidlike structure of the spore-containing capsule of mosses. □□ **opercular** *adj.* **operculate** /-lət/ *adj.* **operculi-** *comb. form.* [L f. *operire* cover]

operetta /ˌɒpəˈretə/ *n.* **1** a one-act or short opera. **2** a light opera. [It., dimin. of *opera*: see OPERA]

ophicleide /ˈɒfɪˌklaɪd/ *n.* **1** an obsolete usu. bass brass wind instrument developed from the serpent. **2** a powerful organ reed-stop. [F *ophicléide* f. Gk *ophis* serpent + *kleis kleidos* key]

ophidian /əʊˈfɪdɪən/ *n. & adj.* —*n.* any reptile of the suborder Serpentes (formerly Ophidia), including snakes. —*adj.* **1** of or relating to this group. **2** snakelike. [mod.L Ophidia f. Gk *ophis* snake]

ophio- /ˈɒfɪəʊ/ *comb. form* snake. [Gk *ophis* snake]

ophthalmia /ɒfˈθælmɪə/ *n.* an inflammation of the eye, esp. conjunctivitis. [LL f. Gk f. *ophthalmos* eye]

ophthalmic /ɒfˈθælmɪk/ *adj.* of or relating to the eye and its diseases. □ **ophthalmic optician** an optician qualified to prescribe as well as dispense spectacles and contact lenses. [L *ophthalmicus* f. Gk *ophthalmikos* (as OPHTHALMIA)]

ophthalmo- /ɒfˈθælməʊ/ *comb. form Optics* denoting the eye. [Gk *ophthalmos* eye]

ophthalmology /ˌɒfθælˈmɒlədʒɪ/ *n.* the scientific study of the eye. □□ **ophthalmological** /-məˈlɒdʒɪk(ə)l/ *adj.* **ophthalmologist** *n.*

ophthalmoscope /ɒfˈθælməˌskəʊp/ *n.* an instrument for inspecting the retina and other parts of the eye. □□ **ophthalmoscopic** /-ˈskɒpɪk/ *adj.*

-opia /ˈəʊpɪə/ *comb. form* denoting a visual disorder (*myopia*). [Gk f. *ōps* eye]

opiate *adj., n.,* & *v.* —*adj.* /ˈəʊpɪət/ **1** containing opium. **2** narcotic, soporific. —*n.* /ˈəʊpɪət/ **1** a drug containing opium, usu. to ease pain or induce sleep. **2** a thing which soothes or stupefies. —*v.tr.* /ˈəʊpɪˌeɪt/ **1** mix with opium. **2** stupefy. [med.L *opiatus, -um, opiare* f. L *opium*: see OPIUM]

opine /əʊˈpaɪn/ *v.tr.* (often foll. by *that* + clause) hold or express as an opinion. [L *opinari* think, believe]

opinion /əˈpɪnjən/ *n.* **1** a belief or assessment based on grounds short of proof. **2** a view held as probable. **3** (often foll. by *on*) what one thinks about a particular topic or question (*my opinion on capital punishment*). **4 a** a formal statement of professional advice (*will get a second opinion*). **b** *Law* a formal statement of reasons for a judgement given. **5** an estimation (*had a low opinion of it*). □ **be of the opinion that** believe or maintain that. **in one's opinion** according to one's view or belief. **a matter of opinion** a disputable point. **opinion poll** = GALLUP POLL. **public opinion** views generally prevalent, esp. on moral questions. [ME f. OF f. L *opinio -onis* (as OPINE)]

opinionated /əˈpɪnjəˌneɪtɪd/ *adj.* conceitedly assertive or dogmatic in one's opinions. □□ **opinionatedly** *adv.* **opinionatedness** *n.* [obs. *opinionate* in the same sense f. OPINION]

opium /ˈəʊpɪəm/ *n.* **1** a reddish-brown heavy-scented addictive drug prepared from the juice of the opium poppy, used in medicine as an analgesic and narcotic. **2** anything regarded as soothing or stupefying. □ **opium den** a haunt of opium-smokers. **opium poppy** a poppy, *Papaver somniferum,* native to Europe and E. Asia, with white, red, pink, or purple flowers. [ME f. L f. Gk *opion* poppy-juice f. *opos* juice]

opopanax /əʊˈpɒpəˌnæks/ *n.* **1 a** an umbelliferous plant, *Opopanax chironium,* with yellow flowers. **b** a resinous gum obtained from the roots of this plant and used in perfume. **2** = *sponge tree.* [ME f. L f. Gk f. *opos* juice + *panax* formed as PANACEA]

opossum /əˈpɒsəm/ *n.* **1 a** any mainly tree-living marsupial of the family Didelphidae, native to America, having a prehensile tail and hind feet with an opposable thumb. **b** (in full **water opossum**) an opossum, *Chironectes minimus,* suited to an aquatic habitat and having webbed hind feet. Also called YAPOK. **2** *Austral.* & *NZ* = POSSUM 2. [Virginian Ind. *āpassūm*]

opp. *abbr.* opposite.

oppo /ˈɒpəʊ/ *n.* (pl. **-os**) *Brit. colloq.* a colleague or friend. [*opposite number*]

opponent /əˈpəʊnənt/ *n.* & *adj.* —*n.* a person who opposes or belongs to an opposing side. —*adj.* opposing, contrary, opposed. □ **opponent muscle** a muscle enabling the thumb to be placed front to front against a finger of the same hand. □□ **opponency** *n.* [L *opponere opponent-* (as OB-, *ponere* place)]

opportune /ˈɒpəˌtjuːn/ *adj.* **1** (of a time) well-chosen or especially favourable or appropriate (*an opportune moment*). **2** (of an action or event) well-timed; done or occurring at a favourable or useful time. □□ **opportunely** *adv.* **opportuneness** *n.* [ME f. OF *opportun -une* f. L *opportunus* (as OB-, *portus* harbour), orig. of the wind driving towards the harbour]

opportunism /ˌɒpəˈtjuːnɪz(ə)m, ˈɒpə-/ *n.* **1** the adaptation of policy or judgement to circumstances or opportunity, esp. regardless of principle. **2** the seizing of opportunities when they occur. □□ **opportunist** *n.* **opportunistic** /-ˈnɪstɪk/ *adj.* **opportunistically** /-ˈnɪstɪkəlɪ/ *adv.* [OPPORTUNE after It. *opportunismo* and F *opportunisme* in political senses]

opportunity /ˌɒpəˈtjuːnɪtɪ/ *n.* (pl. **-ies**) **1** a good chance; a favourable occasion. **2** a chance or opening offered by circumstances. **3** good fortune. □ **opportunity knocks** an opportunity occurs. [ME

f. OF *opportunité* f. L *opportunitas -tatis* (as OPPORTUNE)]

opposable /əˈpəʊzəb(ə)l/ *adj.* **1** able to be opposed. **2** *Zool.* (of the thumb in primates) capable of facing and touching the other digits on the same hand.

oppose /əˈpəʊz/ *v.tr.* (often *absol.*) **1** set oneself against; resist, argue against. **2** be hostile to. **3** take part in a game, sport, etc., against (another competitor or team). **4** (foll. by *to*) place in opposition or contrast. □ **as opposed to** in contrast with. □□ **opposer** *n.* [ME f. OF *opposer* f. L *opponere*: see OPPONENT]

opposite /ˈɒpəzɪt/ *adj., n., adv.,* & *prep.* —*adj.* **1** (often foll. by *to*) having a position on the other or further side, facing or back to back. **2** (often foll. by *to, from*) **a** of a contrary kind; diametrically different. **b** being the other of a contrasted pair. **3** (of angles) between opposite sides of the intersection of two lines. **4** *Bot.* (of leaves etc.) placed at the same height on the opposite sides of the stem, or placed straight in front of another organ. —*n.* an opposite thing or person or term. —*adv.* **1** in an opposite position (*the tree stands opposite*). **2** (of a leading theatrical etc. part) in a complementary role to (another performer). —*prep.* in a position opposite to (*opposite the house is a tree*). □ **opposite number** a person holding an equivalent position in another group or organization. **opposite prompt** the side of a theatre stage usually to an actor's right. **the opposite sex** women in relation to men or vice versa. □□ **oppositely** *adv.* **oppositeness** *n.* [ME f. OF f. L *oppositus* past part. of *opponere*: see OPPONENT]

opposition /ˌɒpəˈzɪʃ(ə)n/ *n.* **1** resistance, antagonism. **2** the state of being hostile or in conflict or disagreement. **3** contrast or antithesis. **4 a** a group or party of opponents or competitors. **b** (**the Opposition**) *Brit.* the principal parliamentary party opposed to that in office. **5** the act of opposing or placing opposite. **6 a** diametrically opposite position. **b** *Astrol.* & *Astron.* the position of two heavenly bodies when their longitude differs by 180°, as seen from the earth. □□ **oppositional** *adj.* [ME f. OF f. L *oppositio* (as OB-, POSITION)]

oppress /əˈpres/ *v.tr.* **1** keep in subservience by coercion. **2** govern or treat harshly or with cruel injustice. **3** weigh down (with cares or unhappiness). □□ **oppressor** *n.* [ME f. OF *oppresser* f. med.L *oppressare* (as OB-, PRESS[1])]

oppression /əˈpreʃ(ə)n/ *n.* **1** the act or an instance of oppressing; the state of being oppressed. **2** prolonged harsh or cruel treatment or control. **3** mental distress. [OF f. L *oppressio* (as OPPRESS)]

oppressive /əˈpresɪv/ *adj.* **1** oppressing; harsh or cruel. **2** difficult to endure. **3** (of weather) close and sultry. □□ **oppressively** *adv.* **oppressiveness** *n.* [F *oppressif -ive* f. med.L *oppressivus* (as OPPRESS)]

opprobrious /əˈprəʊbrɪəs/ *adj.* (of language) severely scornful; abusive. □□ **opprobriously** *adv.* [ME f. LL *opprobriosus* (as OPPROBRIUM)]

opprobrium /əˈprəʊbrɪəm/ *n.* **1** disgrace or bad reputation attaching to some act or conduct. **2** a cause of this. [L f. *opprobrum* (as OB-, *probrum* disgraceful act)]

oppugn /əˈpjuːn/ *v.tr. literary* call into question; controvert. □□ **oppugner** *n.* [ME f. L *oppugnare* attack, besiege (as OB-, L *pugnare* fight)]

oppugnant /əˈpʌgnənt/ *adj. formal* attacking; opposing. □□ **oppugnance** *n.* **oppugnancy** *n.* **oppugnation** /-ˈneɪʃ(ə)n/ *n.*

opsimath /ˈɒpsɪˌmæθ/ *n. literary* a person who learns only late in life. □□ **opsimathy** /-ˈsɪməθɪ/ *n.* [Gk *opsimathēs* f. *opse* late + *math-* learn]

opsonin /ˈɒpsənɪn/ *n.* an antibody which assists the action of phagocytes. □□ **opsonic** /ɒpˈsɒnɪk/ *adj.* [Gk *opsōnion* victuals + -IN]

opt /ɒpt/ *v.intr.* (usu. foll. by *for, between*) exercise an option; make a choice. □ **opt out** (often foll. by *of*) choose not to participate (*opted out of the race*). [F *opter* f. L *optare* choose, wish]

optant /'ɒpt(ə)nt/ n. **1** a person who may choose one of two nationalities. **2** a person who chooses or has chosen.

optative /ɒp'teɪtɪv, 'ɒptətɪv/ adj. & n. Gram. —adj. expressing a wish. —n. the optative mood. □**optative mood** a set of verb-forms expressing a wish etc., distinct esp. in Sanskrit and Greek. □□ **optatively** adv. [F *optatif -ive* f. LL *optativus* (as OPT)]

optic /'ɒptɪk/ adj. & n. —adj. of or relating to the eye or vision (*optic nerve*). —n. **1** a lens etc. in an optical instrument. **2** *archaic* or *joc.* the eye. **3** (**Optic**) *Brit. propr.* a device fastened to the neck of a bottle for measuring out spirits etc. □**optic angle** the angle formed by notional lines from the extremities of an object to the eye, or by lines from the eyes to a given point. **optic axis 1** a line passing through the centre of curvature of a lens or spherical mirror and parallel to the axis of symmetry. **2** the direction in a doubly refracting crystal for which no double refraction occurs. **optic lobe** the dorsal lobe in the brain from which the optic nerve arises. [F *optique* or med.L *opticus* f. Gk *optikos* f. *optos* seen]

optical /'ɒptɪk(ə)l/ adj. **1** of sight; visual. **2 a** of or concerning sight or light in relation to each other. **b** belonging to optics. **3** (esp. of a lens) constructed to assist sight or on the principles of optics. □**optical activity** *Chem.* the property of rotating the plane of polarization of plane-polarized light. **optical art** a style of painting that gives the illusion of movement by the precise use of pattern and colour. **optical brightener** any fluorescent substance used to produce a whitening effect on laundry. **optical character recognition** the identification of printed characters using photoelectric devices. **optical disc** see DISC. **optical fibre** thin glass fibre through which light can be transmitted. **optical glass** a very pure kind of glass used for lenses etc. **optical illusion 1** a thing having an appearance so resembling something else as to deceive the eye. **2** an instance of mental misapprehension caused by this. **optical microscope** a microscope using the direct perception of light (cf. *electron microscope*). □□ **optically** adv.

optician /ɒp'tɪʃ(ə)n/ n. **1** a maker or seller of optical instruments, esp. spectacles and contact lenses. **2** a person trained in the detection and correction of poor eyesight (see OPTOMETRIST). [F *opticien* f. med.L *optica* (as OPTIC)]

optics /'ɒptɪks/ n.pl. (treated as *sing.*) the scientific study of sight and the behaviour of light, or of other radiation or particles (*electron optics*).

optima pl. of OPTIMUM.

optimal /'ɒptɪm(ə)l/ adj. best or most favourable, esp. under a particular set of circumstances. □□ **optimally** adv. [L *optimus* best]

optimism /'ɒptɪˌmɪz(ə)m/ n. **1** an inclination to hopefulness and confidence (opp. PESSIMISM). **2** *Philos.* **a** the doctrine, esp. as set forth by Leibniz, that this world is the best of all possible worlds. **b** the theory that good must ultimately prevail over evil in the universe. □□ **optimist** n. **optimistic** /-'mɪstɪk/ adj. **optimistically** /-'mɪstɪkəlɪ/ adv. [F *optimisme* f. L OPTIMUM]

optimize /'ɒptɪˌmaɪz/ v. (also **-ise**) **1** tr. make the best or most effective use of (a situation, an opportunity, etc.). **2** intr. be an optimist. □□ **optimization** /-'zeɪʃ(ə)n/ n. [L *optimus* best]

optimum /'ɒptɪməm/ n. & adj. —n. (pl. **optima** /-mə/ or **optimums**) **1 a** the most favourable conditions (for growth, reproduction, etc.). **b** the best or most favourable situation. **2** the best possible compromise between opposing tendencies. —adj. = OPTIMAL. [L, neut. (as n.) of *optimus* best]

option /'ɒpʃ(ə)n/ n. **1 a** the act or an instance of choosing; a choice. **b** a thing that is or may be chosen (*those are the options*). **2** the liberty of choosing;

freedom of choice. **3** *Stock Exch.* etc. the right, obtained by payment, to buy, sell, etc. specified stocks etc. at a specified price within a set time. □**have no option but to** must. **keep** (or **leave) one's options open** not commit oneself. [F or f. L *optio*, stem of *optare* choose]

optional /'ɒpʃən(ə)l/ adj. being an option only; not obligatory. □□ **optionality** /-'nælɪtɪ/ n. **optionally** adv.

optometer /ɒp'tɒmɪtə(r)/ n. an instrument for testing the refractive power and visual range of the eye. □□ **optometric** /ˌɒptə'metrɪk/ adj. **optometry** n. [Gk *optos* seen + -METER]

optometrist /ɒp'tɒmɪtrɪst/ n. esp. *US* **1** a person who practises optometry. **2** = *ophthalmic optician*.

optophone /'ɒptəˌfəʊn/ n. an instrument converting light into sound, and so enabling the blind to read print etc. by ear. [Gk *optos* seen + -PHONE]

opulent /'ɒpjʊlənt/ adj. **1** ostentatiously rich; wealthy. **2** luxurious (*opulent surroundings*). **3** abundant; profuse. □□ **opulence** n. **opulently** adv. [L *opulens, opulent-* f. *opes* wealth]

opuntia /əʊ'pʌnʃɪə/ n. any cactus of the genus *Opuntia*, with jointed cylindrical or elliptical stems and barbed bristles. Also called *prickly pear*. [L plant-name f. *Opus -untis* in Locris in ancient Greece]

opus /'əʊpəs, 'ɒp-/ n. (pl. **opuses** or **opera** /'ɒpərə/) **1** *Mus.* **a** a separate musical composition or set of compositions of any kind. **b** (also **op.**) used before a number given to a composer's work, usu. indicating the order of publication (*Beethoven, op. 15*). **2** any artistic work (cf. MAGNUM OPUS). □**opus Dei** /'deɪiː/ *Eccl.* **1** liturgical worship regarded as man's primary duty to God. **2** (**Opus Dei**) a Roman Catholic organization of laymen and priests founded in Spain in 1928 with the aim of re-establishing Christian ideals in society. [L, = work]

opuscule /ə'pʌskju:l/ n. (also **opusculum** /ə'pʌskjʊləm/) (pl. **opuscules** or **opuscula** /-lə/) a minor (esp. musical or literary) work. [F f. L *opusculum* dimin. of OPUS]

OR abbr. **1** operational research. **2** *US* Oregon (in official postal use). **3** other ranks.

or[1] /ɔː(r), ə(r)/ conj. **1 a** introducing the second of two alternatives (*white or black*). **b** introducing all but the first, or only the last, of any number of alternatives (*white or grey or black; white, grey, or black*). **2** (often prec. by *either*) introducing the only remaining possibility or choice given (*take it or leave it; either come in or go out*). **3** (prec. by *whether*) introducing the second part of an indirect question or conditional clause (*ask him whether he was there or not; must go whether I like or dislike it*). **4** introducing a synonym or explanation of a preceding word etc. (*suffered from vertigo or giddiness*). **5** introducing a significant afterthought (*he must know—or is he bluffing?*). **6** = *or else* (*run or you'll be late*). **7** *poet.* each of two; either (*or in the heart or in the head*). □**not A or B** not A, and also not B. **one or two** (or **two or three** etc.) *colloq.* a few. **or else 1** otherwise (*do it now, or else you will have to do it tomorrow*). **2** *colloq.* expressing a warning or threat (*hand over the money or else*). **or rather** introducing a rephrasing or qualification of a preceding statement etc. (*he was there, or rather I heard that he was*). **or so** (after a quantity or a number) or thereabouts (*send me ten or so*). [reduced form of obs. *other* conj. (which superseded OE *oththe* or), of uncert. orig.]

or[2] /ɔː(r)/ n. & adj. Heraldry —n. a gold or yellow colour. —adj. (usu. following noun) gold or yellow (*a crescent or*). [F f. L *aurum* gold]

-or[1] /ə(r)/ suffix forming nouns denoting a person or thing performing the action of a verb, or an agent more generally (*actor; escalator; tailor*) (see also -ATOR, -ITOR). [L -or, -ator, etc., sometimes via AF -eour, OF -ëor, -ëur]

-or[2] /ə(r)/ suffix forming nouns denoting state or

condition (*error*; *horror*). [L *-or -oris*, sometimes via (or after) OF *-or*, *-ur*]

-or[3] /ə(r)/ *suffix* forming adjectives with comparative sense (*major*; *senior*). [AF *-our* f. L *-or*]

-or[4] /ə(r)/ *suffix US* = -OUR[1].

orache /ˈɒrɪtʃ/ *n.* (also **orach**) an edible plant, *Atriplex hortensis*, with red, yellow, or green leaves sometimes used as a substitute for spinach or sorrel. Also called SALTBUSH. [ME *arage* f. AF *arasche* f. L *atriplex* f. Gk *atraphaxus*]

oracle /ˈɒrək(ə)l/ *n.* **1 a** a place at which advice or prophecy was sought from the gods in classical antiquity. **b** the usu. ambiguous or obscure response given at an oracle. **c** a prophet or prophetess at an oracle. **2 a** a person or thing regarded as an infallible guide to future action etc. **b** a saying etc. regarded as infallible guidance. **3** divine inspiration or revelation. **4 (Oracle)** *Brit. propr.* a teletext service provided by Independent Television. [ME f. OF f. L *oraculum* f. *orare* speak]

oracular /əˈrækjʊlə(r)/ *adj.* **1** of or concerning an oracle or oracles. **2** (esp. of advice etc.) mysterious or ambiguous. **3** prophetic. □□ **oracularity** /-ˈlærɪtɪ/ *n.* **oracularly** *adv.* [L (as ORACLE)]

oracy /ˈɔːrəsɪ/ *n.* the ability to express oneself fluently in speech. [L *os oris* mouth, after *literacy*]

oral /ˈɔːr(ə)l/ *adj. & n.* —*adj.* **1** by word of mouth; spoken; not written (*the oral tradition*). **2** done or taken by the mouth (*oral contraceptive*). **3** of the mouth. **4** *Psychol.* of or concerning a supposed stage of infant emotional and sexual development, in which the mouth is of central interest. —*n. colloq.* a spoken examination, test, etc. □**oral sex** sexual activity in which the genitals of one partner are stimulated by the mouth of the other. **oral society** a society that has not reached the stage of literacy. □□ **orally** *adv.* [LL *oralis* f. L *os oris* mouth]

Orange /ˈɒrɪndʒ/ *adj.* of or relating to Orangemen or their activities. □□ **Orangeism** *n.*

orange /ˈɒrɪndʒ/ *n. & adj.* —*n.* **1 a** a large roundish juicy citrus fruit with a bright reddish-yellow tough rind. **b** any of various trees or shrubs of the genus *Citrus*, esp. *C. sinensis* or *C. aurantium*, bearing fragrant white flowers and yielding this fruit. **2 a** fruit or plant resembling this. **3 a** the reddish-yellow colour of an orange. **b** orange pigment. —*adj.* orange-coloured; reddish-yellow. □**orange blossom** the flowers of the orange tree, traditionally worn by the bride at a wedding. **orange flower water** a solution of neroli in water. **orange peel 1** the skin of an orange. **2** a rough surface resembling this. **orange pekoe** tea made from very small leaves. **orange squash** *Brit.* a soft drink made from oranges and other ingredients, often sold in concentrated form. **orange-stick** a thin stick, pointed at one end and usu. of orange wood, for manicuring the fingernails. **orange-wood** the wood of the orange tree. [ME f. OF *orenge*, ult. f. Arab. *nāranj* f. Pers. *nārang*]

orangeade /ˌɒrɪndʒˈeɪd/ *n.* a usu. fizzy non-alcoholic drink flavoured with orange.

Orangeman /ˈɒrɪndʒmən/ *n.* (*pl.* **-men**) a member of a political society formed in 1795 to support Protestantism in Ireland. [after William of *Orange* (William III)]

orangery /ˈɒrɪndʒərɪ/ *n.* (*pl.* **-ies**) a place, esp. a special structure, where orange-trees are cultivated.

orang-utan /ɔːˌræŋuːˈtæn/ *n.* (also **orang-outang** /-uːˈtæŋ/) a large red long-haired tree-living ape, *Pongo pygmaeus*, native to Borneo and Sumatra, with characteristic long arms and hooked hands and feet. [Malay *ōrang ūtan* wild man]

orate /ɔːˈreɪt/ *v.intr.* esp. *joc.* or *derog.* make a speech or speak, esp. pompously or at length. [back-form. f. ORATION]

oration /ɔːˈreɪʃ(ə)n, ə-/ *n.* **1** a formal speech, discourse, etc., esp. when ceremonial. **2** *Gram.* a way of

speaking; language. [ME f. L *oratio* discourse, prayer f. *orare* speak, pray]

orator /ˈɒrətə(r)/ *n.* **1 a** a person making a speech. **b** an eloquent public speaker. **2** (in full **public orator**) an official speaking for a university on ceremonial occasions. □□ **oratorial** /-ˈtɔːrɪəl/ *adj.* [ME f. AF *oratour*, OF *orateur* f. L *orator -oris* speaker, pleader (as ORATION)]

oratorio /ˌɒrəˈtɔːrɪəʊ/ *n.* (*pl.* **-os**) a semi-dramatic work for orchestra and voices esp. on a sacred theme, performed without costume, scenery, or action. □□ **oratorial** *adj.* [It. f. eccl.L *oratorium*, orig. of musical services at church of Oratory of St Philip Neri in Rome]

oratory /ˈɒrətərɪ/ *n.* (*pl.* **-ies**) **1** the art or practice of formal speaking, esp. in public. **2** exaggerated, eloquent, or highly coloured language. **3** a small chapel, esp. for private worship. **4 (Oratory)** *RC Ch.* **a** a religious society of priests without vows founded in Rome in 1564 and providing plain preaching and popular services. **b** a branch of this in England etc. □□ **oratorian** /-ˈtɔːrɪən/ *adj. & n.* **oratorical** /-ˈtɒrɪk(ə)l/ *adj.* [senses 1 and 2 f. L *ars oratoria* art of speaking; senses 3 and 4 ME f. AF *oratorie*, OF *oratoire* f. eccl.L *oratorium*: both f. L *oratorius* f. *orare* pray, speak]

orb /ɔːb/ *n. & v.* —*n.* **1** a globe surmounted by a cross esp. carried by a sovereign at a coronation. **2 a** sphere; a globe. **3** *poet.* a heavenly body. **4** *poet.* an eyeball; an eye. —*v.* **1** *tr.* enclose in (an orb); encircle. **2** *intr.* form or gather into an orb. [L *orbis* ring]

orbicular /ɔːˈbɪkjʊlə(r)/ *adj. formal* **1** circular and flat; disc-shaped; ring-shaped. **2** spherical; globular; rounded. **3** forming a complete whole. □□ **orbicularity** /-ˈlærɪtɪ/ *n.* **orbicularly** *adv.* [ME f. LL *orbicularis* f. L *orbiculus* dimin. of *orbis* ring]

orbiculate /ɔːˈbɪkjʊlət/ *adj. Bot.* (of a leaf etc.) almost circular.

orbit /ˈɔːbɪt/ *n. & v.* —*n.* **1 a** the curved, usu. closed course of a planet, satellite, etc. **b** (prec. by *in*, *into*, *out of*, etc.) the state of motion in an orbit. **c** one complete passage around an orbited body. **2** the path of an electron round an atomic nucleus. **3** a range or sphere of action. **4 a** the eye socket. **b** the area around the eye of a bird or insect. —*v.* (**orbited**, **orbiting**) **1** *intr.* **a** (of a satellite etc.) go round in orbit. **b** fly in a circle. **2** *tr.* move in orbit round. **3** *tr.* put into orbit. □□ **orbiter** *n.* [L *orbita* course, track (in med.L eye-cavity): fem. of *orbitus* circular f. *orbis* ring]

orbital /ˈɔːbɪt(ə)l/ *adj. & n.* —*adj.* **1** *Anat., Astron., & Physics* of an orbit or orbits. **2** (of a road) passing round the outside of a town. —*n. Physics* a state or function representing the possible motion of an electron round an atomic nucleus. □**orbital sander** a sander having a circular and not oscillating motion.

orca /ˈɔːkə/ *n.* **1** any of various whales, esp. the killer whale. **2** any other large sea-animal or monster. [F *orque* or L *orca* a kind of whale]

Orcadian /ɔːˈkeɪdɪən/ *adj. & n.* —*adj.* of or relating to the Orkney Islands off the N. coast of Scotland. —*n.* a native of the Orkney Islands. [L *Orcades* Orkney Islands]

orch. *abbr.* **1** orchestrated by. **2** orchestra.

orchard /ˈɔːtʃəd/ *n.* a piece of enclosed land with fruit-trees. □□ **orchardist** *n.* [OE *ortgeard* f. L *hortus* garden + YARD[2]]

orcharding /ˈɔːtʃədɪŋ/ *n.* the cultivation of fruit-trees.

orchardman /ˈɔːtʃədmən/ *n.* (*pl.* **-men**) a fruit-grower.

orchestra /ˈɔːkɪstrə/ *n.* **1** a usu. large group of instrumentalists, esp. combining strings, wood-winds, brass, and percussion (*symphony orchestra*). **2 a** (in full **orchestra pit**) the part of a theatre, opera house, etc., where the orchestra plays, usu. in front of the stage and on a lower level. **b** *US* the stalls in a theatre. **3** the semicircular space in front of an ancient Greek theatre-stage where the chorus danced and sang. □**orchestra stalls** the front of the stalls. □□**orchestral** /-'kestr(ə)l/ *adj.* **orchestrally** /-'kestrəlɪ/ *adv.* [L f. Gk *orkhēstra* f. *orkheomai* to dance (see sense 3)]

orchestrate /'ɔ:kɪˌstreɪt/ *v.tr.* **1** arrange, score, or compose for orchestral performance. **2** combine, arrange, or build up (elements of a situation etc.) for maximum effect. □□**orchestration** /-'streɪʃ(ə)n/ *n.* **orchestrator** *n.*

orchid /'ɔ:kɪd/ *n.* **1** any usu. epiphytic plant of the family Orchidaceae, bearing flowers in fantastic shapes and brilliant colours, usu. having one petal larger than the others and variously spurred, lobed, pouched, etc. **2** a flower of any of these plants. □□**orchidaceous** /-'deɪʃəs/ *adj.* **orchidist** *n.* **orchidology** /-'dɒlədʒɪ/ *n.* [mod.L *Orchid(ac)eae* irreg. f. L *orchis*: see ORCHIS]

orchil /'ɔ:tʃɪl/ *n.* (also **orchilla** /ɔ:'tʃɪlə/, **archil** /'ɑ:tʃɪl/) **1** a red or violet dye from lichen, esp. from *Roccella tinctoria*, often used in litmus. **2** the tropical lichen yielding this. [ME f. OF *orcheil* etc. perh. ult. f. L *herba urceolaris* a plant for polishing glass pitchers]

orchis /'ɔ:kɪs/ *n.* **1** any orchid of the genus *Orchis*, with a tuberous root and an erect fleshy stem having a spike of usu. purple or red flowers. **2** any of various wild orchids. [L f. Gk *orkhis*, orig. = testicle (with ref. to the shape of its tuber)]

orchitis /ɔ:'kaɪtɪs/ *n.* inflammation of the testicles. [mod.L f. Gk *orkhis* testicle]

orcin /'ɔ:sɪn/ *n.* (also **orcinol** /'ɔ:sɪˌnɒl/) a crystalline substance, becoming red in air, extracted from any of several lichens and used to make dyes. [mod.L *orcina* f. It. *orcello* orchil]

ord. *abbr.* ordinary.

ordain /ɔ:'deɪn/ *v.tr.* **1** confer holy orders on; appoint to the Christian ministry (*ordained him priest; was ordained in 1970*). **2 a** (often foll. by *that* + clause) decree (*ordained that he should go*). **b** (of God, fate, etc.) destine; appoint (*has ordained us to die*). □□ **ordainer** *n.* **ordainment** *n.* [ME f. AF *ordeiner*, OF *ordein-* stressed stem of *ordener* f. L *ordinare* f. *ordo -inis* order]

ordeal /ɔ:'di:l/ *n.* **1** a painful or horrific experience; a severe trial. **2** *hist.* an ancient esp. Germanic test of guilt or innocence by subjection of the accused to severe pain or torture, survival of which was taken as divine proof of innocence. □**ordeal tree** the tanghin. [OE *ordāl, ordēl* f. Gmc: cf. DEAL¹]

order /'ɔ:də(r)/ *n. & v.* —*n.* **1 a** the condition in which every part, unit, etc. is in its right place; tidiness (*restored some semblance of order*). **b** a usu. specified sequence, succession, etc. (*alphabetical order; the order of events*). **2** (in *sing.* or *pl.*) an authoritative command, direction, instruction, etc. (*only obeying orders; gave orders for it to be done; the judge made an order*). **3** a state of peaceful harmony under a constituted authority (*order was restored; law and order*). **4** (esp. in *pl.*) a social class, rank, etc., constituting a distinct group in society (*the lower orders; the order of baronets*). **5** a kind; a sort (*talents of a high order*). **6 a** a usu. written direction to a manufacturer, tradesman, waiter, etc. to supply something. **b** the quantity of goods etc. supplied. **7** the constitution or nature of the world, society, etc. (*the moral order; the order of things*). **8** *Biol.* a taxonomic rank below a class and above a family. **9** (esp. **Order**) a fraternity of monks and friars, or formerly of knights, bound by a common rule of life (*the Franciscan order; the order of Templars*). **10 a** any of the grades of the Christian ministry. **b** (in *pl.*) the status of a member of the clergy (*Anglican orders*). **11 a** any of the five classical styles of architecture (Doric, Ionic, Corinthian, Tuscan, and Composite) based on the proportions of columns, amount of decoration, etc. **b** any style or mode of architecture subject to uniform established proportions. **12** (esp. **Order**) **a** a company of distinguished people instituted esp. by a sovereign to which appointments are made as an honour or reward (*Order of the Garter; Order of Merit*). **b** the insignia worn by members of an order. **13** *Math.* **a** a degree of complexity of a differential equation (*equation of the first order*). **b** the order of the highest derivative in the equation. **14** *Math.* **a** the size of a matrix. **b** the number of elements of a finite group. **15** *Eccl.* the stated form of divine service (*the order of confirmation*). **16** the principles of procedure, decorum, etc., accepted by a meeting, legislative assembly, etc. or enforced by its president. **17** *Mil.* a style of dress and equipment (*review order*). **b** (prec. by *the*) the position of a company etc. with arms ordered (see *order arms*). **18** a Masonic or similar fraternity. **19** any of the nine grades of angelic beings (seraphim, cherubim, thrones, dominations, principalities, powers, virtues, archangels, angels). **20** a pass admitting the bearer to a theatre, museum, private house, etc. free or cheap or as a privilege. —*v.tr.* **1** (usu. foll. by *to* + infin., or *that* + clause) command; bid; prescribe (*ordered him to go; ordered that they should be sent*). **2** command or direct (a person) to a specified destination (*was ordered to Singapore; ordered them home*). **3** direct a manufacturer, waiter, tradesman, etc. to supply (*ordered a new suit; ordered dinner*). **4** put in order; regulate (*ordered her affairs*). **5** (of God, fate, etc.) ordain (*fate ordered it otherwise*). **6** *US* command (a thing) done or (a person) dealt with (*ordered it settled; ordered him expelled*). □**by order** according to the proper authority. **holy orders** the status of a member of the clergy, esp. the grades of bishop, priest, and deacon. **in bad** (or **good** etc.) **order** not working (or working properly etc.). **in order 1** one after another according to some principle. **2** ready or fit for use. **3** according to the rules (of procedure at a meeting etc.). **in order that** with the intention; so that. **in order to** with the purpose of doing; with a view to. **keep order** enforce orderly behaviour. **made to order 1** made according to individual requirements, measurements, etc. (opp. *ready-made*). **2** exactly what is wanted. **minor orders** *RC Ch. hist.* the grades of members of the clergy below that of deacon. **not in order** not working properly. **of** (or **in** or **on**) **the order of 1** approximately. **2** having the order of magnitude specified by (*of the order of one in a million*). **on order** (of goods etc.) ordered but not yet received. **order about 1** dominate; command officiously. **2** send hither and thither. **order arms** *Mil.* hold a rifle with its butt on the ground close to one's right side. **order book 1** a book in which a tradesman enters orders. **2** the level of incoming orders. **order-form** a printed form in which details are entered by a customer. **Order in Council** *Brit.* a sovereign's order on an administrative matter given by the advice of the Privy Council. **Order of the Bath** (or **Garter** or **Merit**) each of several honours conferred by the sovereign for services etc. to the State. **order of the day 1** the prevailing state of things. **2** a principal topic of action or a procedure decided upon. **3** business set down for treatment; a programme. **order of magnitude** a class in a system of classification determined by size, usu. by powers of 10. **Order! Order!** *Parl.* a call for silence or calm, esp. by the Speaker of the House of Commons. **order-paper** esp. *Parl.* a written or printed order of the day; an agenda. **order to view** a house-agent's request for a client to be allowed to inspect premises. **out of order 1** not working properly. **2** not according to the rules (of a meeting, organization, etc.). **take orders 1** accept commissions. **2** accept and carry out commands. **3** (also **take holy orders**) be ordained. □□**orderer** *n.* [ME f. OF *ordre* f. L *ordo ordinis* row, array, degree, command, etc.]

orderly /'ɔ:dəlɪ/ *adj. & n.* —*adj.* **1** methodically arranged; regular. **2** obedient to discipline; well-behaved; not unruly. **3** *Mil.* **a** of or concerned with orders. **b** charged with the conveyance or execution of orders. —*n.* (*pl.* **-ies**) **1** an esp. male cleaner in a hospital. **2** a soldier who carries orders for an officer etc. □**orderly book** *Brit. Mil.* a regimental or company book for entering orders. **orderly officer** *Brit. Mil.* the officer of the day. **orderly room** *Brit. Mil.* a room in a barracks used for company business. □□ **orderliness** *n.*

ordinal /ˈɔːdɪn(ə)l/ *n. & adj.* —*n.* **1** (in full **ordinal number**) a number defining a thing's position in a series, e.g. 'first', 'second', 'third', etc. (cf. CARDINAL). **2** *Eccl.* a service-book, esp. one with the forms of service used at ordinations. —*adj.* **1 a** of or relating to an ordinal number. **b** defining a thing's position in a series etc. **2** *Biol.* of or concerning an order (see ORDER *n.* 8). [ME f. LL *ordinalis* & med.L *ordinale* neut. f. L (as ORDER)]

ordinance /ˈɔːdɪnəns/ *n.* **1** an authoritative order; a decree. **2** an enactment by a local authority. **3** a religious rite. **4** *archaic* = ORDONNANCE. [ME f. OF *ordenance* f. med.L *ordinantia* f. L *ordinare*: see ORDAIN]

ordinand /ˈɔːdɪnænd/ *n. Eccl.* a candidate for ordination. [L *ordinandus*, gerundive of *ordinare* ORDAIN]

ordinary /ˈɔːdɪnərɪ/ *adj. & n.* —*adj.* **1 a** regular, normal, customary, usual (*in the ordinary course of events*). **b** boring; commonplace (*an ordinary little man*). **2** *Brit. Law* (esp. of a judge) having immediate or *ex officio* jurisdiction, not deputed. —*n.* (*pl.* **-ies**) **1** *Brit. Law* a person, esp. a judge, having immediate or *ex officio* jurisdiction. **2** (**the Ordinary**) **a** an archbishop in a province. **b** a bishop in a diocese. **3** (usu. **Ordinary**) *RC Ch.* **a** those parts of a service, esp. the mass, which do not vary from day to day. **b** a rule or book laying down the order of divine service. **4** *Heraldry* a charge of the earliest, simplest, and commonest kind (esp. chief, pale, bend, fess, bar, chevron, cross, saltire). **5** (**Ordinary**) (also **Lord Ordinary**) any of the judges of the Court of Session in Scotland, constituting the Outer House. **6** esp. *US hist.* an early type of bicycle with one large and one very small wheel; a penny-farthing. **7** *Brit. hist.* **a** a public meal provided at a fixed time and price at an inn etc. **b** an establishment providing this. **8** *US* **a** tavern. □**in ordinary** *Brit.* by permanent appointment (esp. to the royal household) (*physician in ordinary*). **in the ordinary way** if the circumstances are or were not exceptional. **ordinary level** *Brit. hist.* the lowest of the three levels of the GCE examination. **ordinary scale** = *decimal scale.* **ordinary seaman** a sailor of the lowest rank, that below able-bodied seaman. **ordinary shares** *Brit.* shares entitling holders to a dividend from net profits (cf. *preference shares*). **out of the ordinary** unusual. □□ **ordinarily** *adv.* **ordinariness** *n.* [ME f. L *ordinarius* orderly (as ORDER)]

ordinate /ˈɔːdɪnɪt/ *n. Math.* a straight line from any point drawn parallel to one coordinate axis and meeting the other, usually a coordinate measured parallel to the vertical (cf. ABSCISSA). [L *linea ordinata applicata* line applied parallel f. *ordinare*: see ORDAIN]

ordination /ˌɔːdɪˈneɪʃ(ə)n/ *n.* **1 a** the act of conferring holy orders esp. on a priest or deacon. **b** the admission of a priest etc. to church ministry. **2** the arrangement of things etc. in ranks; classification. **3** the act of decreeing or ordaining. [ME f. OF *ordination* or L *ordinatio* (as ORDAIN)]

ordnance /ˈɔːdnəns/ *n.* **1** mounted guns; cannon. **2** a branch of government service dealing esp. with military stores and materials. □**ordnance datum** *Brit.* mean sea level as defined for Ordnance Survey. **Ordnance map** *Brit.* a map produced by Ordnance Survey. **Ordnance Survey** *Brit.* (in the UK) an official survey organization, orig. under the Master of the Ordnance, preparing large-scale detailed maps of the whole country. [ME var. of ORDINANCE]

ordonnance /ˈɔːdənəns/ *n.* the systematic arrangement esp. of literary or architectural work. [F f. OF *ordenance*: see ORDINANCE]

Ordovician /ˌɔːdəˈvɪsɪən, ˌɔːdəʊˈvɪʃɪən/ *adj. & n. Geol.* —*adj.* of or relating to the second period of the Palaeozoic era, with evidence of the first vertebrates and an abundance of marine invertebrates. ¶ Cf. Appendix II. —*n.* this period or system. [L *Ordovices* ancient British tribe in N. Wales]

ordure /ˈɔːdjʊə(r)/ *n.* **1** excrement; dung. **2** obscenity; filth; foul language. [ME f. OF f. *ord* foul f. L *horridus*: see HORRID]

Ore. *abbr.* Oregon.

ore /ɔː(r)/ *n.* a naturally occurring solid material from which metal or other valuable minerals may be extracted. [OE *ōra* unwrought metal, *ār* bronze, rel. to L *aes* crude metal, bronze]

öre /ˈvərə/ *n.* (also **øre**) a Scandinavian monetary unit equal to one-hundredth of a krona or krone. [Swedish]

oread /ˈɔːrɪˌæd/ *n.* (in Greek and Roman mythology) a mountain nymph. [ME f. L *oreas -ados* f. Gk *oreias* f. *oros* mountain]

orectic /əˈrektɪk/ *adj. Philos. & Med.* of or concerning desire or appetite. [Gk *orektikos* f. *oregō* stretch out]

Oreg. *abbr.* Oregon.

oregano /ˌɒrɪˈɡɑːnəʊ/ *n.* the dried leaves of wild marjoram used as a culinary herb (cf. MARJORAM). [Sp., = ORIGANUM]

oreography var. of OROGRAPHY.

oreweed var. of OARWEED.

orfe /ɔːf/ *n.* a golden-coloured ide. [G & F: cf. L *orphus* f. Gk *orphos* sea-perch]

organ /ˈɔːɡən/ *n.* **1 a a** usu. large musical instrument having pipes supplied with air from bellows, sounded by keys, and distributed into sets or stops which form partial organs, each with a separate keyboard (*choir organ*; *pedal organ*). **b** a smaller instrument without pipes, producing similar sounds electronically. **c** a smaller keyboard wind instrument with metal reeds; a harmonium. **d** = *barrel-organ.* **2 a** a usu. self-contained part of an organism having a special vital function (*vocal organs*; *digestive organs*). **b** esp. *joc.* the penis. **3** a medium of communication, esp. a newspaper, sectarian periodical, etc. **4** *archaic* a professionally trained singing voice. **5** *Phrenol. archaic* a region of the brain held to be the seat of a particular faculty. □**organ-blower** a person or mechanism working the bellows of an organ. **organ-grinder** the player of a barrel-organ. **organ-loft** a gallery in a church or concert-room for an organ. **organ of Corti** see CORTI. **organ-pipe** any of the pipes on an organ. **organ-screen** an ornamental screen usu. between the choir and the nave of a church, cathedral, etc., on which the organ is placed. **organ-stop 1** a set of pipes of a similar tone in an organ. **2** the handle of the mechanism that brings it into action. [ME f. OE *organa* & OF *organe*, f. L *organum* f. Gk *organon* tool]

organdie /ˈɔːɡəndɪ, -ˈɡændɪ/ *n.* (*US* **organdy**) (*pl.* **-ies**) a fine translucent cotton muslin, usu. stiffened. [F *organdi*, of unkn. orig.]

organelle /ˌɔːɡəˈnel/ *n. Biol.* any of various organized or specialized structures which form part of a cell. [mod.L *organella* dimin.; see ORGAN, -LE]

organic /ɔːˈɡænɪk/ *adj.* **1 a** *Physiol.* of or relating to a bodily organ or organs. **b** *Med.* (of a disease) affecting the structure of an organ. **2** (of a plant or animal) having organs or an organized physical structure. **3** *Agriculture* produced or involving production without the use of chemical fertilizers, pesticides, etc. (*organic crop*; *organic farming*). **4** *Chem.* (of a compound etc.) containing carbon (opp. INORGANIC). **5 a** structural, inherent. **b** constitutional, fundamental. **6** organized, systematic, coordinated (*an organic whole*). □**organic chemistry** the chemistry of carbon compounds. **organic law** a law stating the formal constitution of a country. □□ **organically**

adv. [F *organique* f. L *organicus* f. Gk *organikos* (as ORGAN)]

organism /ˈɔːgəˌnɪz(ə)m/ *n.* **1** a living individual consisting of a single cell or of a group of interdependent parts sharing the life processes. **2 a** an individual live plant or animal. **b** the material structure of this. **3** a whole with interdependent parts compared to a living being. [F *organisme* (as ORGANIZE)]

organist /ˈɔːgənɪst/ *n.* the player of an organ.

organization /ˌɔːgənaɪˈzeɪʃ(ə)n/ *n.* (also **-isation**) **1** the act or an instance of organizing; the state of being organized. **2** an organized body, esp. a business, government department, charity, etc. **3** systematic arrangement; tidiness. □**organization man** a man who subordinates his individuality and his personal life to the organization he serves. □□ **organizational** *adj.* **organizationally** *adv.*

organize /ˈɔːgəˌnaɪz/ *v.tr.* (also **-ise**) **1 a** give an orderly structure to, systematize. **b** bring the affairs of (another person or oneself) into order; make arrangements for (a person). **2 a** arrange for or initiate (a scheme etc.). **b** provide; take responsibility for (*organized some sandwiches*). **3** (often *absol.*) **a** enrol (new members) in a trade union, political party, etc. **b** form (a trade union or other political group). **4 a** form (different elements) into an organic whole. **b** form (an organic whole). **5** (esp. as **organized** *adj.*) make organic; make into a living being or tissue. □□ **organizable** *adj.* **organizer** *n.* [ME f. OF *organiser* f. med.L *organizare* f. L (as ORGAN)]

organo- /ˈɔːgənəʊ/ *comb. form* **1** esp. *Biol.* organ. **2** *Chem.* organic. [Gk (as ORGAN)]

organoleptic /ˌɔːgənəʊˈlɛptɪk/ *adj.* affecting the organs of sense. [ORGANO- + Gk *lēptikos* disposed to take f. *lambanō* take]

organometallic /ɔːˌgænəʊmɪˈtælɪk/ *adj.* (of a compound) organic and containing a metal.

organon /ˈɔːgəˌnɒn/ *n.* (also **organum** /ˈɔːgənəm/) an instrument of thought, esp. a means of reasoning or a system of logic. [Gk *organon* & L *organum* (as ORGAN): *Organon* was the title of Aristotle's logical writings, and *Novum* (new) *Organum* that of Bacon's]

organotherapy /ˌɔːgənəʊˈθɛrəpɪ/ *n.* the treatment of disease with extracts of organs.

organza /ɔːˈgænzə/ *n.* a thin stiff transparent silk or synthetic dress fabric. [prob. f. *Lorganza* (US trade name)]

organzine /ˈɔːgənˌziːn, -ˈgænziːn/ *n.* a silk thread in which the main twist is in a contrary direction to that of the strands. [F *organsin* f. It. *organzino*, of unkn. orig.]

orgasm /ˈɔːgæz(ə)m/ *n.* & *v.* — *n.* **1 a** the climax of sexual excitement, esp. during sexual intercourse. **b** an instance of this. **2** violent excitement; rage. — *v.intr.* experience a sexual orgasm. □□ **orgasmic** /-ˈgæzmɪk/ *adj.* **orgasmically** /-ˈgæzmɪkəlɪ/ *adv.* **orgastic** /-ˈgæstɪk/ *adj.* **orgastically** /-ˈgæstɪkəlɪ/ *adv.* [F *orgasme* or mod.L f. Gk *orgasmos* f. *orgaō* swell, be excited]

orgeat /ˈɔːdʒɪˌæt, ˈɔːʒɑː/ *n.* a cooling drink made from barley or almonds and orange-flower water. [F f. Prov. *orjat* f. *ordi* barley f. L *hordeum*]

orgiastic /ˌɔːdʒɪˈæstɪk/ *adj.* of or resembling an orgy. □□ **orgiastically** *adv.* [Gk *orgiastikos* f. *orgiastēs* agent-noun f. *orgiazō* hold an orgy]

orgulous /ˈɔːgjʊləs/ *adj. archaic* haughty; splendid. [ME f. OF *orguillus* f. *orguill* pride f. Frank.]

orgy /ˈɔːdʒɪ/ *n.* (*pl.* **-ies**) **1** a wild drunken festivity at which indiscriminate sexual activity takes place. **2** excessive indulgence in an activity. **3** (usu. in *pl.*) *Gk & Rom. Hist.* secret rites used in the worship of esp. Bacchus, celebrated with dancing, drunkenness, singing, etc. [orig. pl., f. F *orgies* f. L *orgia* f. Gk *orgia* secret rites]

oribi /ˈɒrɪbɪ/ *n.* (*pl.* same or **oribis**) a small S. African grazing antelope, *Ourebia ourebi*, having a reddish fawn back and white underparts. [prob. Khoisan]

oriel /ˈɔːrɪəl/ *n.* **1** a large polygonal recess built from usu. from an upper storey and supported from the ground or on corbels. **2** (in full **oriel window**) **a** any of the windows in an oriel. **b** the projecting window of an upper storey. [ME f. OF *oriol* gallery, of unkn. orig.]

orient /ˈɔːrɪənt/ *n., adj.,* & *v.* — *n.* **1** (**the Orient**) **a** *poet.* the east. **b** the countries E. of the Mediterranean, esp. E. Asia. **2** an orient pearl. — *adj.* **1** *poet.* oriental. **2** (of precious stones and esp. the finest pearls coming orig. from the East) lustrous; sparkling; precious. **3** *archaic* **a** radiant. **b** (of the sun, daylight, etc.) rising. — *v.* /ˈɔːrɪˌɛnt, ˈɒr-/ **1** *tr.* **a** place or exactly determine the position of with the aid of a compass; settle or find the bearings of. **b** (often foll. by *towards*) bring (oneself, different elements, etc.) into a clearly understood position or relationship; direct. **2** *tr.* **a** place or build (a church, building, etc.) facing towards the East. **b** bury (a person) with the feet towards the East. **3** *intr.* turn eastward or in a specified direction. □**orient oneself** determine how one stands in relation to one's surroundings. [ME f. OF *orient, orienter* f. L *oriens -entis* rising, sunrise, east, f. *oriri* rise]

oriental /ˌɔːrɪˈɛnt(ə)l, ˌɒr-/ *adj.* & *n.* — *adj.* **1** (often **Oriental**) **a** of or characteristic of Eastern civilization etc. **b** of or concerning the East, esp. E. Asia. **2** (of a pearl etc.) orient. — *n.* (esp. **Oriental**) a native of the Orient. □□ **orientalism** *n.* **orientalist** *n.* **orientalize** *v.intr.* & *tr.* (also **-ise**). **orientally** *adv.* [ME f. OF *oriental* or L *orientalis* (as ORIENT)]

orientate /ˈɒrɪɛnˌteɪt, ˈɔːr-/ *v.tr.* & *intr.* = ORIENT *v.* [prob. back-form. f. ORIENTATION]

orientation /ˌɒrɪɛnˈteɪʃ(ə)n, ˌɔːr-/ *n.* **1** the act or an instance of orienting; the state of being oriented. **2 a** a relative position. **b** a person's attitude or adjustment in relation to circumstances, esp. politically or psychologically. **3** an introduction to a subject or situation; a briefing. **4** the faculty by which birds etc. find their way home from a distance. □**orientation course** esp. *US* a course giving information to newcomers to a university etc. □□ **orientational** *adj.* [app. f. ORIENT]

orienteering /ˌɔːrɪɛnˈtɪərɪŋ, ˌɒr-/ *n.* a competitive sport in which runners cross open country with a map, compass, etc. □□ **orienteer** *n.* & *v.intr.* [Sw. *orientering*]

orifice /ˈɒrɪfɪs/ *n.* an opening, esp. the mouth of a cavity, a bodily aperture, etc. [F f. LL *orificium* f. *os oris* mouth + *facere* make]

oriflamme /ˈɒrɪˌflæm/ *n.* **1** *hist.* the sacred scarlet silk banner of St Denis given to early French kings by the abbot of St Denis on setting out for war. **2** a standard, a principle, or an ideal as a rallying-point in a struggle. **3** a bright conspicuous object, colour, etc. [ME f. OF f. L *aurum* gold + *flamma* flame]

origami /ˌɒrɪˈgɑːmɪ/ *n.* the Japanese art of folding paper into decorative shapes and figures. [Jap. f. *ori* fold + *kami* paper]

origan /ˈɒrɪgən/ *n.* (also **origanum** /əˈrɪgənəm/) any plant of the genus *Origanum*, esp. wild marjoram (see MARJORAM). [(ME f. OF *origan*) f. L *origanum* f. Gk *origanon*]

origin /ˈɒrɪdʒɪn/ *n.* **1** a beginning or starting-point; a derivation; a source (*a word of Latin origin*). **2** (often in *pl.*) a person's ancestry (*what are his origins?*). **3** *Anat.* **a** a place at which a muscle is firmly attached. **b** a place where a nerve or blood vessel begins or branches from a main nerve or blood vessel. **4** *Math.* a fixed point from which coordinates are measured. [F *origine* or f. L *origo -ginis* f. *oriri* rise]

original /əˈrɪdʒɪn(ə)l/ *adj.* & *n.* — *adj.* **1** existing from the beginning; innate. **2** novel; inventive; creative (*has an original mind*). **3** serving as a pattern; not derivative or imitative; firsthand (*in the original Greek*; *has an original Rembrandt*). — *n.* **1**

an original model, pattern, picture, etc. from which another is copied or translated (*kept the copy and destroyed the original*). **2** an eccentric or unusual person. **3 a** a garment specially designed for a fashion collection. **b** a copy of such a garment made to order. □**original instrument** a musical instrument, or a copy of one, dating from the time the music played on it was composed. **original print** a print made directly from an artist's own woodcut, etching, etc., and printed under the artist's supervision. **original sin** the innate depravity of all mankind held to be a consequence of the Fall. □□**originally** *adv.* [ME f. OF *original* or L *originalis* (as ORIGIN)]

originality /ə,rɪdʒɪ'nælɪtɪ/ *n.* (*pl.* **-ies**) **1** the power of creating or thinking creatively. **2** newness or freshness (*this vase has originality*). **3** an original act, thing, trait, etc.

originate /ə'rɪdʒɪ,neɪt/ *v.* **1** *tr.* cause to begin; initiate. **2** *intr.* (usu. foll. by *from*, *in*, *with*) have as an origin; begin. □□**origination** /-'neɪʃ(ə)n/ *n.* **originative** /-nətɪv/ *adj.* **originator** *n.* [med. L *originare* (as ORIGIN)]

orinasal /,ɒrɪ'neɪz(ə)l/ *adj.* (esp. of French nasalized vowels) sounded with both the mouth and the nose. [L *os oris* mouth + NASAL]

o-ring /'əʊrɪŋ/ *n.* a gasket in the form of a ring with a circular cross-section.

oriole /'ɔːrɪəʊl/ *n.* **1** any Old World bird of the genus *Oriolus*, many of which have brightly coloured plumage (see *golden oriole*). **2** any New World bird of the genus *Icterus*, with similar coloration. [med.L *oriolus* f. OF *oriol* f. L *aureolus* dimin. of *aureus* golden f. *aurum* gold]

Orion /ə'raɪən/ *n.* a brilliant constellation on the celestial equator visible from most parts of the earth. □**Orion's belt** three bright stars in a short line across the middle of the constellation. **Orion's hound** Sirius. [ME f. L f. Gk *ōriōn*, name of a legendary hunter]

orison /'ɒrɪz(ə)n/ *n.* (usu. in *pl.*) *archaic* a prayer. [ME f. AF *ureison*, OF *oreison* f. L (as ORATION)]

-orium /'ɔːrɪəm/ *suffix* forming nouns denoting a place for a particular function (*auditorium*; *crematorium*). [L, neut. of adjectives in *-orius*: see -ORY¹]

Oriya /ɔː'riːə/ *n.* **1** a native of the State of Orissa in India. **2** the Indo-European language of this people. [Hindi]

orle /ɔːl/ *n.* *Heraldry* a narrow band or border of charges near the edge of a shield. [F *o(u)rle* f. *ourler* to hem, ult. f. L *ora* edge]

Orlon /'ɔːlɒn/ *n. propr.* a man-made fibre and fabric for textiles and knitwear. [invented word, after NYLON]

orlop /'ɔːlɒp/ *n.* the lowest deck of a ship with three or more decks. [ME f. MDu. *overloop* covering f. *overloopen* run over (as OVER-, LEAP)]

ormer /'ɔːmə(r)/ *n.* an edible univalve mollusc, *Haliotis tuberculata*, having a flattened shell with a series of holes of increasing size along the outer margin. Also called *sea-ear*. [Channel Islands F f. F *ormier* f. L *auris maris* ear of sea]

ormolu /'ɔːmə,luː/ *n.* **1** (often *attrib.*) **a** a gilded bronze or gold-coloured alloy of copper, zinc, and tin used to decorate furniture, make ornaments, etc. **b** articles made of or decorated with these. **2** showy trash. [F *or moulu* powdered gold (for use in gilding)]

ornament /'ɔːnəmənt/ *n.* & *v.* —*n.* **1 a** a thing used or serving to adorn, esp. a small trinket, vase, figure, etc. (*a mantelpiece crowded with ornaments*; *her only ornament was a brooch*). **b** a quality or person conferring adornment, grace, or honour (*an ornament to her profession*). **2** decoration added to embellish esp. a building (*a tower rich in ornament*). **3** (in *pl.*) *Mus.* embellishments and decorations made to a melody. **4** (usu. in *pl.*) the accessories of worship, e.g. the altar, chalice, sacred vessels, etc. —*v.tr.* /'ɔːnə,ment/ adorn; beautify. □□**ornamentation**

/-men'teɪʃ(ə)n/ *n.* [ME f. AF *urnement*, OF *o(u)r-nement* f. L *ornamentum* equipment f. *ornare* adorn]

ornamental /,ɔːnə'ment(ə)l/ *adj.* & *n.* —*adj.* serving as an ornament; decorative. —*n.* a thing considered to be ornamental, esp. a cultivated plant. □□**ornamentalism** *n.* **ornamentalist** *n.* **ornamentally** *adv.*

ornate /ɔː'neɪt/ *adj.* **1** elaborately adorned; highly decorated. **2** (of literary style) convoluted; flowery. □□**ornately** *adv.* **ornateness** *n.* [ME f. L *ornatus* past part. of *ornare* adorn]

ornery /'ɔːnərɪ/ *adj.* *US colloq.* **1** cantankerous; unpleasant. **2** of poor quality. □□**orneriness** *n.* [var. of ORDINARY]

ornithic /ɔː'nɪθɪk/ *adj.* of or relating to birds. [Gk *ornithikos* birdlike (as ORNITHO-)]

ornitho- /'ɔːnɪθəʊ/ *comb. form* bird. [Gk f. *ornis ornithos* bird]

ornithology /,ɔːnɪ'θɒlədʒɪ/ *n.* the scientific study of birds. □□**ornithological** /-θə'lɒdʒɪk(ə)l/ *adj.* **ornithologically** /-θə'lɒdʒɪkəlɪ/ *adv.* **ornithologist** *n.* [mod.L *ornithologia* f. Gk *ornithologos* treating of birds (as ORNITHO-, -LOGY)]

ornithorhynchus /,ɔːnɪθəʊ'rɪŋkəs/ *n.* = PLATYPUS. [ORNITHO- + Gk *rhugkhos* bill]

oro- /'ɔːrəʊ/ *comb. form* mountain. [Gk *oros* mountain]

orogeny /ɔː'rɒdʒɪnɪ/ *n.* (also **orogenesis** /,ɔːrəʊ'dʒɛnɪsɪs/) the process of the formation of mountains. □□**orogenetic** /,ɔːrəʊdʒɪ'netɪk/ *adj.* **orogenic** /,ɔːrəʊ'dʒɛnɪk/ *adj.*

orography /ɒ'rɒɡrəfɪ, ɔː-/ *n.* (also **oreography** /,ɒrɪ'ɒɡrəfɪ/) the branch of physical geography dealing with mountains. □□**orographic** /-rə'ɡræfɪk/ *adj.* **orographical** /-'ɡræfɪk(ə)l/ *adj.*

orotund /'ɒrə,tʌnd, 'ɔːr-/ *adj.* **1** (of the voice or phrasing) full, round; imposing. **2** (of writing, style, expression, etc.) pompous; pretentious. [L *ore rotundo* with rounded mouth]

orphan /'ɔːf(ə)n/ *n.* & *v.* —*n.* (often *attrib.*) **1** a child bereaved of a parent or usu. both parents. **2** a person bereft of previous protection, advantages, etc. —*v.tr.* bereave (a child) of its parents or a parent. □□**orphanhood** *n.* **orphanize** *v.tr.* (also **-ise**). [ME f. LL *orphanus* f. Gk *orphanos* bereaved]

orphanage /'ɔːfənɪdʒ/ *n.* **1** a usu. residential institution for the care and education of orphans. **2** orphanhood.

Orphean /ɔː'fiːən/ *adj.* like the music of Orpheus, a legendary Greek poet and lyre-player; melodious; entrancing. [L *Orpheus* (adj.) f. Gk *Orpheios* f. *Orpheus*]

Orphic /'ɔːfɪk/ *adj.* **1** of or concerning Orpheus or the mysteries, doctrines, etc. associated with him; oracular; mysterious. **2** = ORPHEAN. □□**Orphism** *n.* [L *Orphicus* f. Gk *Orphikos* f. *Orpheus*]

orphrey /'ɔːfrɪ/ *n.* (*pl.* **-eys**) an ornamental stripe or border or separate piece of ornamental needlework, esp. on ecclesiastical vestments. [ME *orfreis* (taken as pl.) (gold) embroidery f. OF f. med.L *aurifrisium* etc. f. L *aurum* gold + *Phrygius* Phrygian, also 'embroidered']

orpiment /'ɔːpɪmənt/ *n.* **1** a mineral form of arsenic trisulphide, formerly used as a dye and artist's pigment. Also called *yellow arsenic*. **2** (in full **red orpiment**) = REALGAR. [ME f. OF f. L *auripigmentum* f. *aurum* gold + *pigmentum* pigment]

orpine /'ɔːpɪn/ *n.* (also **orpin**) a succulent herbaceous purple-flowered plant, *Sedum telephium*. Also called LIVELONG². [ME f. OF *orpine*, prob. alt. of ORPIMENT, orig. of a yellow-flowered species of the same genus]

orra /'ɒrə/ *adj.* *Sc.* **1** not matched; odd. **2** occasional; extra. [18th c.: orig. unkn.]

orrery /'ɒrərɪ/ *n.* (*pl.* **-ies**) a clockwork model of the solar system. [named after the fourth Earl of *Orrery*, for whom one was made]

orris /'ɒrɪs/ *n.* **1** any plant of the genus *Iris*, esp. *I. florentina*. **2** = ORRISROOT. □**orris-powder** powdered orrisroot. [16th c.: app. an unexpl. alt. of IRIS]

orrisroot /ˈɒrɪsˌruːt/ n. the fragrant rootstock of the orris, used in perfumery and formerly in medicine.

ortanique /ˈɔːtəˌniːk/ n. a citrus fruit produced by crossing an orange and a tangerine. [*orange* + *tangerine* + un*ique*]

ortho- /ˈɔːθəʊ/ *comb. form* **1 a** straight, rectangular, upright. **b** right, correct. **2** *Chem.* **a** relating to two adjacent carbon atoms in a benzene ring. **b** relating to acids and salts (e.g. *orthophosphates*) giving *meta*-compounds on removal of water. [Gk *orthos* straight]

orthocephalic /ˌɔːθəʊsɪˈfælɪk/ adj. having a head with a medium ratio of breadth to height.

orthochromatic /ˌɔːθəʊkrəʊˈmætɪk/ adj. giving fairly correct relative intensity to colours in photography by being sensitive to all except red.

orthoclase /ˈɔːθəʊˌkleɪs/ n. a common alkali feldspar usu. occurring as variously coloured crystals, used in ceramics and glass-making. [ORTHO- +Gk *klasis* breaking]

orthodontics /ˌɔːθəˈdɒntɪks/ n.pl. (treated as *sing.*) (also **orthodontia** /-ˈdɒntɪə/) the treatment of irregularities in the teeth and jaws. □□ **orthodontic** adj. **orthodontist** n. [ORTHO- + Gk *odous odont-* tooth]

orthodox /ˈɔːθəˌdɒks/ adj. **1 a** holding correct or currently accepted opinions, esp. on religious doctrine, morals, etc. **b** not independent-minded; unoriginal; unheretical. **2** (of religious doctrine, standards of morality, etc.) generally accepted as right or true; authoritatively established; conventional. **3** (also **Orthodox**) (of Judaism) strictly keeping to traditional doctrine and ritual. □ **Orthodox Church** the Eastern Church, separated from the Western Church in the 11th c., having the Patriarch of Constantinople as its head, and including the national Churches of Russia, Romania, Greece, etc. □□ **orthodoxly** adv. [eccl.L *orthodoxus* f. Gk *orthodoxos* f. *doxa* opinion]

orthodoxy /ˈɔːθəˌdɒksɪ/ n. (pl. **-ies**) **1** the state of being orthodox. **2 a** the orthodox practice of Judaism. **b** the body of orthodox Jews. **3** esp. *Relig.* an authorized or generally accepted theory, doctrine, etc. [LL *orthodoxia* f. late Gk *orthodoxia* sound doctrine (as ORTHODOX)]

orthoepy /ˈɔːθəʊˌɪpɪ, ɔːˈθəʊɪpɪ/ n. the scientific study of the correct pronunciation of words. □□ **orthoepic** /-ˈepɪk/ adj. **orthoepist** n. [Gk *orthoepeia* correct speech (as ORTHO-, *epos* word)]

orthogenesis /ˌɔːθəʊˈdʒenɪsɪs/ n. a theory of evolution which proposes that variations follow a defined direction and are not merely sporadic and fortuitous. □□ **orthogenetic** /-dʒɪˈnetɪk/ adj. **orthogenetically** /-dʒɪˈnetɪkəlɪ/ adv.

orthognathous /ɔːˈθɒɡnəθəs/ adj. (of mammals, including man) having a jaw which does not project forwards and a facial angle approaching a right angle. [ORTHO- + Gk *gnathos* jaw]

orthogonal /ɔːˈθɒɡən(ə)l/ adj. of or involving right angles. [F f. *orthogone* (as ORTHO-, -GON)]

orthography /ɔːˈθɒɡrəfɪ/ n. (pl. **-ies**) **1 a** correct or conventional spelling. **b** spelling with reference to its correctness (*dreadful orthography*). **c** the study or science of spelling. **2 a** perspective projection used in maps and elevations in which the projection lines are parallel. **b** a map etc. so projected. □□ **orthographer** n. **orthographic** /-ˈɡræfɪk/ adj. **orthographical** /-ˈɡræfɪk(ə)l/ adj. **orthographically** /-ˈɡræfɪkəlɪ/ adv. [ME f. OF *ortografie* f. L *orthographia* f. Gk *orthographia* (as ORTHO-, -GRAPHY)]

orthopaedics /ˌɔːθəˈpiːdɪks/ n.pl. (treated as *sing.*) (*US* **-pedics**) the branch of medicine dealing with the correction of deformities of bones or muscles, orig. in children. □□ **orthopaedic** adj. **orthopaedist** n. [F *orthopédie* (as ORTHO-, *pédie* f. Gk *paideia* rearing of children)]

orthopteran /ɔːˈθɒptərən/ n. any insect of the order Orthoptera, with straight narrow forewings, and hind legs modified for jumping etc., including grasshoppers and crickets. □□ **orthopterous** adj. [ORTHO- + Gk *pteros* wing]

orthoptic /ɔːˈθɒptɪk/ adj. relating to the correct or normal use of the eyes. □□ **orthoptist** n. [ORTHO- + Gk *optikos* of sight: see OPTIC]

orthoptics /ɔːˈθɒptɪks/ n. *Med.* the study or treatment of irregularities of the eyes, esp. with reference to the eye-muscles.

orthorhombic /ˌɔːθəˈrɒmbɪk/ adj. *Crystallog.* (of a crystal) characterized by three mutually perpendicular axes which are unequal in length, as in topaz and talc.

orthotone /ˈɔːθəˌtəʊn/ adj. & n. —adj. (of a word) having an independent stress pattern, not enclitic nor proclitic. —n. a word of this kind.

ortolan /ˈɔːtələn/ n. (in full **ortolan bunting**) *Zool.* a small European bird, *Emberiza hortulana*, eaten as a delicacy. [F f. Prov., lit. gardener, f. L *hortulanus* f. *hortulus* dimin. of *hortus* garden]

Orwellian /ɔːˈwelɪən/ adj. of or characteristic of the writings of George Orwell (E. A. Blair), English writer d. 1950, esp. with reference to the totalitarian development of the State as depicted in *1984* and *Animal Farm*.

-ory[1] /ərɪ/ suffix forming nouns denoting a place for a particular function (*dormitory*; *refectory*). □□ **-orial** /ˈɔːrɪəl/ suffix forming adjectives. [L *-oria*, *-orium*, sometimes via ONF and AF *-orie*, OF *-oire*]

-ory[2] /ərɪ/ suffix forming adjectives (and occasionally nouns) relating to or involving a verbal action (*accessory*; *compulsory*; *directory*). [L *-orius*, sometimes via AF *-ori(e)*, OF *-oir(e)*]

oryx /ˈɒrɪks/ n. any large straight-horned antelope of the genus *Oryx*, native to Africa and Arabia. [ME f. L f. Gk *orux* stonemason's pickaxe, f. its pointed horns]

OS abbr. **1** old style. **2** ordinary seaman. **3** (in the UK) Ordnance Survey. **4** outsize. **5** out of stock.

Os symb. *Chem.* the element osmium.

Osage orange /ˈəʊseɪdʒ/ n. **1** a hardy thorny tree, *Maclura pomifera*, of the US, bearing inedible wrinkled orange-like fruit. **2** the durable orange-coloured timber from this. [name of a N. American Indian tribe]

Oscan /ˈɒskən/ n. & adj. —n. the ancient language of Campania in Italy, related to Latin and surviving only in inscriptions. —adj. relating to or written in Oscan. [L *Oscus*]

Oscar /ˈɒskə(r)/ n. any of the statuettes awarded by the US Academy of Motion Picture Arts and Sciences for excellence in film acting, directing, etc. [the name *Oscar*]

oscillate /ˈɒsɪˌleɪt/ v. **1** intr. & tr. **a** swing to and fro like a pendulum. **b** move to and fro between points. **2** intr. vacillate; vary between extremes of opinion, action, etc. **3** intr. *Physics* move with periodic regularity. **4** intr. *Electr.* (of a current) undergo high-frequency alternations as across a spark-gap or in a valve-transmitter circuit. **5** intr. (of a radio receiver) radiate electromagnetic waves owing to faulty operation. □□ **oscillation** /-ˈleɪʃ(ə)n/ n. **oscillator** n. **oscillatory** /ɒˈsɪlətərɪ, ˈɒsɪˌleɪtərɪ/ adj. [L *oscillare oscillat-* swing]

oscillo- /əˈsɪləʊ/ comb. form oscillation, esp. of electric current.

oscillogram /əˈsɪləˌɡræm/ n. a record obtained from an oscillograph.

oscillograph /əˈsɪləˌɡrɑːf/ n. a device for recording oscillations. □□ **oscillographic** /-ˈɡræfɪk/ adj. **oscillography** /-ˈlɒɡrəfɪ/ n.

oscilloscope /əˈsɪləˌskəʊp/ n. a device for viewing oscillations by a display on the screen of a cathode-ray tube. □□ **oscilloscopic** /-ˈskɒpɪk/ adj.

oscine /ˈɒsɪn/ adj. (also **oscinine** /ˈɒsɪˌniːn/) of or relating to the suborder Oscines of passerine birds including many of the songbirds. [L *oscen -cinis* songbird (as OB-, *canere* sing)]

oscitation /ˌɒsɪ'teɪʃ(ə)n/ n. formal **1** yawning; drowsiness. **2** inattention; negligence. [L oscitatio f. oscitare gape f. os mouth + citare move]

oscula pl. of OSCULUM.

oscular /'ɒskjʊlə(r)/ adj. **1** of or relating to the mouth. **2** of or relating to kissing. [L osculum mouth, kiss, dimin. of os mouth]

osculate /'ɒskjʊˌleɪt/ v. **1** tr. Math. (of a curve or surface) have contact of at least the second order with; have two branches with a common tangent, with each branch extending in both directions of the tangent. **2** v.intr. & tr. joc. kiss. **3** intr. Biol. (of a species etc.) be related through an intermediate species; have common characteristics with another or with each other. □□ **osculant** adj. **osculation** /-'leɪʃ(ə)n/ n. **osculatory** /'ɒskjʊlətərɪ/ adj. [L osculari kiss (as OSCULAR)]

osculum /'ɒskjʊləm/ n. (pl. **oscula** /-lə/) a mouthlike aperture, esp. of a sponge. [L: see OSCULAR]

-ose[1] /əʊs/ suffix forming adjectives denoting possession of a quality (grandiose; verbose). □□ **-osely** suffix forming adverbs. **-oseness** suffix forming nouns (cf. -OSITY). [from or after L -osus]

-ose[2] /əʊs/ suffix Chem. forming names of carbohydrates (cellulose; sucrose). [after GLUCOSE]

osier /'əʊzɪə(r)/ n. **1** any of various willows, esp. Salix viminalis, with long flexible shoots used in basketwork. **2** a shoot of a willow. □ **osier-bed** a place where osiers are grown. [ME f. OF: cf. med.L auseria osier-bed]

-osis /'əʊsɪs/ suffix (pl. **-oses** /'əʊsiːz/) denoting a process or condition (apotheosis; metamorphosis), esp. a pathological state (acidosis; neurosis; thrombosis). [L f. Gk -ōsis suffix of verbal nouns]

-osity /'ɒsɪtɪ/ suffix forming nouns from adjectives in -ose (see -OSE[1]) and -ous (verbosity; curiosity). [F -osité or L -ositas -ositatis: cf. -ITY]

Osmanli /ɒz'mænlɪ, ɒs-/ adj. & n. = OTTOMAN. [Turk. f. Osman f. Arab. 'uṭmān (see OTTOMAN) + -li adj. suffix]

osmic /'ɒzmɪk/ adj. of or relating to odours or the sense of smell. □□ **osmically** adv. [Gk osmē smell, odour]

osmium /'ɒzmɪəm/ n. Chem. a hard bluish-white transition element, the heaviest known metal, occurring naturally in association with platinum and used in certain alloys. ¶ Symb.: Os. [Gk osmē smell (from the pungent smell of its tetroxide)]

osmosis /ɒz'məʊsɪs/ n. **1** Biochem. the passage of a solvent through a semi-permeable partition into a more concentrated solution. **2** any process by which something is acquired by absorption. □□ **osmotic** /-'mɒtɪk/ adj. **osmotically** /-'mɒtɪkəlɪ/ adv. [orig. osmose, after F f. Gk ōsmos push]

osmund /'ɒzmənd/ n. (also **osmunda** /-də/) any fern of the genus Osmunda, esp. the royal fern, having large divided fronds. [ME f. AF, of uncert. orig.]

osprey /'ɒspreɪ, -prɪ/ n. (pl. **-eys**) **1** a large bird of prey, Pandion haliaetus, with a brown back and white markings, feeding on fish. Also called fish-hawk. **2** a plume on a woman's hat. [ME f. OF ospres app. ult. f. L ossifraga osprey f. os bone + frangere break]

ossein /'ɒsɪɪn/ n. the collagen of bones. [L osseus (as OSSEOUS)]

osseous /'ɒsɪəs/ adj. **1** consisting of bone. **2** having a bony skeleton. **3** ossified. [L osseus f. os ossis bone]

ossicle /'ɒsɪk(ə)l/ n. **1** Anat. any small bone, esp. of the middle ear. **2** a small piece of bonelike substance. [L ossiculum dimin. (as OSSEOUS)]

Ossie var. of AUSSIE.

ossify /'ɒsɪˌfaɪ/ v.tr. & intr. (-ies, -ied) **1** turn into bone; harden. **2** make or become rigid, callous, or unprogressive. □□ **ossific** /ɒ'sɪfɪk/ adj. **ossification** /-fɪ'keɪʃ(ə)n/ n. [F ossifier f. L os ossis bone]

osso bucco /ˌɒsəʊ 'bʊkəʊ/ n. shin of veal containing marrowbone stewed in wine with vegetables. [It., = marrowbone]

ossuary /'ɒsjʊərɪ/ n. (pl. **-ies**) **1** a receptacle for the bones of the dead; a charnel-house; a bone-urn. **2** a cave in which ancient bones are found. [LL ossuarium irreg. f. os ossis bone]

osteitis /ˌɒstɪ'aɪtɪs/ n. inflammation of the substance of a bone. [Gk osteon bone + -ITIS]

ostensible /ɒ'stensɪb(ə)l/ adj. concealing the real; professed (his ostensible function was that of interpreter). □□ **ostensibly** adv. [F f. med.L ostensibilis f. L ostendere ostens- stretch out to view (as OB-, tendere stretch)]

ostensive /ɒ'stensɪv/ adj. **1** directly demonstrative. **2** (of a definition) indicating by direct demonstration that which is signified by a term. □□ **ostensively** adv. **ostensiveness** n. [LL ostensivus (as OSTENSIBLE)]

ostensory /ɒ'stensərɪ/ n. (pl. **-ies**) RC Ch. a receptacle for displaying the host to the congregation; a monstrance. [med.L ostensorium (as OSTENSIBLE)]

ostentation /ˌɒsten'teɪʃ(ə)n/ n. **1** a pretentious and vulgar display esp. of wealth and luxury. **2** the attempt or intention to attract notice; showing off. □□ **ostentatious** adj. **ostentatiously** adv. [ME f. OF f. L ostentatio -onis f. ostentare frequent. of ostendere: see OSTENSIBLE]

osteo- /'ɒstɪəʊ/ comb. form bone. [Gk osteon]

osteoarthritis /ˌɒstɪəʊɑː'θraɪtɪs/ n. a degenerative disease of joint cartilage, esp. in the elderly. □□ **osteoarthritic** /-'θrɪtɪk/ adj.

osteogenesis /ˌɒstɪəʊ'dʒenɪsɪs/ n. the formation of bone. □□ **osteogenetic** /-dʒɪ'netɪk/ adj.

osteology /ˌɒstɪ'ɒlədʒɪ/ n. the study of the structure and function of the skeleton and bony structures. □□ **osteological** /-ə'lɒdʒɪk(ə)l/ adj. **osteologically** /-ə'lɒdʒɪkəlɪ/ adv. **osteologist** n.

osteomalacia /ˌɒstɪəʊmə'leɪʃɪə/ n. softening of the bones, often through a deficiency of vitamin D and calcium. □□ **osteomalacic** /-'læsɪk/ adj. [mod.L (as OSTEO-, Gk malakos soft)]

osteomyelitis /ˌɒstɪəʊmaɪɪ'laɪtɪs/ n. inflammation of the bone or of bone marrow, usu. due to infection.

osteopathy /ˌɒstɪ'ɒpəθɪ/ n. the treatment of disease through the manipulation of bones, esp. the spine, displacement of these being the supposed cause. □□ **osteopath** /'ɒstɪəˌpæθ/ n. **osteopathic** /ˌɒstɪə'pæθɪk/ adj.

osteoporosis /ˌɒstɪəʊpə'rəʊsɪs/ n. a condition of brittle and fragile bones caused by loss of bony tissue, esp. as a result of hormonal changes, or deficiency of calcium or vitamin D. [OSTEO- + Gk poros passage, pore]

ostinato /ˌɒstɪ'nɑːtəʊ/ n. (pl. **-os**) (often attrib.) Mus. a persistent phrase or rhythm repeated through all or part of a piece. [It., = OBSTINATE]

ostler /'ɒslə(r)/ n. Brit. hist. a stableman at an inn. [f. earlier HOSTLER, hosteler f. AF hostiler, OF (h)ostelier (as HOSTEL)]

Ostmark /'ɒstmɑːk/ n. the chief monetary unit of the Democratic Republic of Germany. [G, = east mark: see MARK[2]]

Ostpolitik /'ɒstpɒlɪˌtiːk/ n. the foreign policy of many western European countries with reference to the Communist bloc. [G f. Ost east + Politik politics]

ostracize /'ɒstrəˌsaɪz/ v.tr. (also **-ise**) **1** exclude (a person) from a society, favour, common privileges, etc.; refuse to associate with. **2** (esp. in ancient Athens) banish (a powerful or unpopular citizen) for five or ten years by popular vote. □□ **ostracism** /-ˌsɪz(ə)m/ n. [Gk ostrakizō f. ostrakon shell, potsherd (used to write a name on in voting)]

ostrich /'ɒstrɪtʃ/ n. **1** a large African swift-running flightless bird, Struthio camelus, with long legs and two toes on each foot. **2** a person who refuses to accept facts (from the belief that ostriches bury their heads in the sand when pursued). □ **ostrich-farm** a place that breeds ostriches for their feathers. **ostrich-plume** a feather or bunch of feathers of an ostrich. [ME f. OF ostric(h)e f. L avis bird + LL *struthio* f. Gk *strouthiōn* ostrich f. *strouthos* sparrow, ostrich]

Ostrogoth /ˈɒstrəˌgɒθ/ *n. hist.* a member of the Eastern branch of the Goths, who conquered Italy in the 5th-6th c. □□ **Ostrogothic** /-ˈgɒθɪk/ *adj.* [LL *Ostrogothi* (pl.) f. Gmc *austro-* (unrecorded) east + LL *Gothi* Goths: see GOTH]

OT *abbr.* Old Testament.

-ot[1] /ət/ *suffix* forming nouns, orig. diminutives (*ballot*; *chariot*; *parrot*). [F]

-ot[2] /ət/ *suffix* forming nouns denoting persons (*patriot*), e.g. natives of a place (*Cypriot*). [F *-ote*, L *-ota*, Gk *-ōtēs*]

OTC *abbr.* (in the UK) Officers' Training Corps.

other /ˈʌðə(r)/ *adj., n.* or *pron., & adv.* —*adj.* **1** not the same as one or some already mentioned or implied; separate in identity or distinct in kind (*other people*; *use other means*; *I assure you, my reason is quite other*). **2 a** further; additional (*a few other examples*). **b** alternative of two (*open your other eye*) (cf. *every other*). **3** (prec. by *the*) that remains after all except the one or ones in question have been considered, eliminated, etc. (*must be in the other pocket*; *where are the other two?*; *the other three men left*). **4** (foll. by *than*) apart from; excepting (*any person other than you*). —*n.* or *pron.* (orig. an ellipt. use of the adj., now with pl. in *-s*) **1** an additional, different, or extra person, thing, example, etc. (*one or other of us will be there*; *some others have come*) (see also ANOTHER, *each other*). **2** (in *pl.*; prec. by *the*) the ones remaining (*where are the others?*). —*adv.* (usu. foll. by *than*) *disp.* otherwise (*cannot react other than angrily*). ¶ In this sense *otherwise* is standard except in less formal use. □ **no other** *archaic* nothing else (*I can do no other*). **of all others** out of the many possible or likely (*on this night of all others*). **on the other hand** see HAND. **the other day** (or **night** or **week** etc.) a few days etc. ago (*heard from him the other day*). **other-directed** governed by external circumstances and trends. **other half** *colloq.* one's wife or husband. **the other place** *Brit. joc.* Oxford University as regarded by Cambridge, and vice versa. **other ranks** soldiers other than commissioned officers. **the other thing** esp. *joc.* an unexpressed alternative (*if you don't like it, do the other thing*). **other things being equal** if conditions are or were alike in all but the point in question. **the other woman** a married man's mistress. **the other world** see WORLD. **someone** (or **something** or **somehow** etc.) **or other** some unspecified person, thing, manner, etc. [OE *ōther* f. Gmc]

otherness /ˈʌðənɪs/ *n.* **1** the state of being different; diversity. **2** a thing or existence other than the thing mentioned and the thinking subject.

otherwhere /ˈʌðəˌweə(r)/ *adj. archaic* or *poet.* elsewhere.

otherwise /ˈʌðəˌwaɪz/ *adv. & adj.* —*adv.* **1** else; or else; in the circumstances other than those considered etc. (*bring your umbrella, otherwise you will get wet*). **2** in other respects (*he is untidy, but otherwise very suitable*). **3** (often foll. by *than*) in a different way (*could not have acted otherwise; cannot react otherwise than angrily*). **4** as an alternative (*otherwise known as Jack*). —*adj.* **1** (*predic.*) in a different state (*the matter is quite otherwise*). **2** *archaic* that would otherwise exist (*their otherwise dullness*). □ **and** (or **or**) **otherwise** the negation or opposite (of a specified thing) (*the merits or otherwise of the Bill; experiences pleasant and otherwise*). [OE *on ōthre wisan* (as OTHER, WISE[2])]

other-worldly /ˌʌðəˈwɜːldlɪ/ *adj.* **1** unworldly; impractical. **2** concerned with life after death etc. □□ **other-worldliness** *n.*

otic /ˈəʊtɪk/ *adj.* of or relating to the ear. [Gk *ōtikos* f. *ous ōtos* ear]

-otic /ˈɒtɪk/ *suffix* forming adjectives and nouns corresponding to nouns in *-osis*, meaning 'affected with or producing or resembling a condition in *-osis*' or 'a person affected with this' (*narcotic*; *neurotic*; *osmotic*). □□ **-otically** *suffix* forming adverbs. [from or after F *-otique* f. L f. Gk *-ōtikos* adj. suffix]

otiose /ˈəʊʃɪəʊs, ˈəʊt-, -əʊz/ *adj.* **1** serving no practical purpose; not required; functionless. **2** *archaic* indolent; futile. □□ **otiosely** *adv.* **otioseness** *n.* [L *otiosus* f. *otium* leisure]

otitis /əˈtaɪtɪs/ *n.* inflammation of the ear. [mod.L (as OTO-)]

oto- /ˈəʊtəʊ/ *comb. form* ear. [Gk *ōto-* f. *ous ōtos* ear]

otolaryngology /ˌəʊtəˌlærɪnˈgɒlədʒɪ/ *n.* the study of diseases of the ear and throat. □□ **otolaryngological** /-gəˈlɒdʒɪk(ə)l/ *adj.* **otolaryngologist** *n.*

otolith /ˈəʊtəlɪθ/ *n.* any of the small particles of calcium carbonate in the inner ear. □□ **otolithic** /-ˈlɪθɪk/ *adj.*

otology /əʊˈtɒlədʒɪ/ *n.* the study of the anatomy and diseases of the ear. □□ **otological** /-təˈlɒdʒɪk(ə)l/ *adj.* **otologist** *n.*

otorhinolaryngology /ˌəʊtəˌraɪnəʊˌlærɪnˈgɒlədʒɪ/ *n.* the study of diseases of the ear, nose, and throat.

otoscope /ˈəʊtəˌskəʊp/ *n.* an apparatus for examining the eardrum and the passage leading to it from the ear. □□ **otoscopic** /-ˈskɒpɪk/ *adj.*

ottava rima /ɒˌtɑːvə ˈriːmə/ *n.* a stanza of eight lines of 10 or 11 syllables, rhyming *abab.abcc*. [It., lit. eighth rhyme]

otter /ˈɒtə(r)/ *n.* **1 a** any of several aquatic fish-eating mammals of the family Mustelidae, esp. of the genus *Lutra*, having strong claws and webbed feet. **b** its fur or pelt. **2** = *sea otter*. **3** a piece of board used to carry fishing-bait in water. **4** a type of paravane, esp. as used on non-naval craft. □ **otter-board** a device for keeping the mouth of a trawl-net open. **otter-dog** (or **-hound**) a dog of a breed used in otter-hunting. [OE *otr, ot(t)or* f. Gmc]

otto var. of ATTAR.

Ottoman /ˈɒtəmən/ *adj. & n.* —*adj. hist.* **1** of or concerning the dynasty of Osman or Othman I, the branch of the Turks to which he belonged, or the empire ruled by his descendants. **2** Turkish. —*n.* (*pl.* **Ottomans**) an Ottoman person; a Turk. □ **the Ottoman Porte** see PORTE. [F f. Arab. *'utmānī* adj. of Othman (*'utmān*)]

ottoman /ˈɒtəmən/ *n.* (*pl.* **ottomans**) **1 a** an upholstered seat, usu. square and without a back or arms, sometimes a box with a padded top. **b** a footstool of similar design. **2** a heavy silken fabric with a mixture of cotton or wool. [F *ottomane* fem. (as OTTOMAN)]

OU *abbr. Brit.* **1** Open University. **2** Oxford University.

oubliette /ˌuːblɪˈet/ *n.* a secret dungeon with access only through a trapdoor. [F f. *oublier* forget]

ouch /aʊtʃ/ *int.* expressing pain or annoyance. [imit.: cf. G *autsch*]

ought[1] /ɔːt/ *v.aux.* (usu. foll. by *to* + infin.; present and past indicated by the following infin.) **1** expressing duty or rightness (*we ought to love our neighbours*). **2** expressing shortcoming (*it ought to have been done long ago*). **3** expressing advisability or prudence (*you ought to go for your own good*). **4** expressing esp. strong probability (*he ought to be there by now*). □ **ought not** the negative form of *ought* (*he ought not to have stolen it*). [OE *āhte*, past of *āgan* OWE]

ought[2] /ɔːt/ *n.* (also **aught**) *colloq.* a figure denoting nothing; nought. [perh. f. *an ought* for a NOUGHT; cf. ADDER]

ought[3] var. of AUGHT[1].

oughtn't /ˈɔːt(ə)nt/ *contr.* ought not.

Ouija /ˈwiːdʒə/ *n.* (in full **Ouija board**) *propr.* a board having letters or signs at its rim to which a planchette, movable pointer, or upturned glass points in answer to questions from attenders at a seance etc. [F *oui* yes + G *ja* yes]

ounce[1] /aʊns/ *n.* **1 a** a unit of weight of one-sixteenth of a pound avoirdupois (approx. 28 grams). ¶ Abbr.: **oz**. **b** a unit of one-twelfth of a pound troy or apothecaries' measure, equal to 480 grains (approx. 31 grams). **2** a small quantity. □**fluid ounce** *Brit*. **1** a unit of capacity equal to one-twentieth of a pint (approx. 0.028 litre). **2** *US* a unit of capacity equal to one-sixteenth of a pint (approx. 0.034 litre). [ME & OF *unce* f. L *uncia* twelfth part of pound or foot: cf. INCH[1]]

ounce[2] /aʊns/ *n*. an Asian wild cat, *Panthera uncia*, with leopard-like markings on a cream-coloured coat. Also called *mountain panther, snow leopard*. [ME f. OF *once* (earlier *lonce*) = It. *lonza* ult. f. L *lynx*: see LYNX]

OUP *abbr*. Oxford University Press.

our /'aʊə(r)/ *poss.pron*. (*attrib*.) **1** of or belonging to us or ourselves (*our house; our own business*). **2** of or belonging to all people (*our children's future*). **3** (esp. as **Our**) of Us the king or queen, emperor or empress, etc. (*given under Our seal*). **4** of us, the editorial staff of a newspaper etc. (*a foolish adventure in our view*). **5** *Brit. colloq*. indicating a relative, acquaintance, or colleague of the speaker (*our Barry works there*). □**Our Father 1** the Lord's Prayer. **2** God. **Our Lady** the Virgin Mary. **Our Lord 1** Jesus Christ. **2** God. **Our Saviour** Jesus Christ. [OE *ūre* orig. genit. pl. of 1st pers. pron. = of us, later treated as possessive adj.]

-our[1] /ə(r)/ *suffix* var. of -OR[2] surviving in some nouns (*ardour; colour; valour*).

-our[2] /ə(r)/ *suffix* var. of -OR[1] (*saviour*).

ours /'aʊəz/ *poss.pron*. the one or ones belonging to or associated with us (*it is ours; ours are over there*). □**of ours** of or belonging to us (*a friend of ours*).

ourself /aʊə'self/ *pron. archaic* a word formerly used instead of *myself* by a sovereign, newspaper editorial staff, etc. (cf. OUR 3, 4).

ourselves /aʊə'selvz/ *pron*. **1 a** *emphat. form* of WE or US (*we ourselves did it; made it ourselves; for our friends and ourselves*). **b** *refl. form* of US (*are pleased with ourselves*). **2** in our normal state of body or mind (*not quite ourselves today*). □**be ourselves** act in our normal unconstrained manner. **by ourselves** see *by oneself*.

-ous /əs/ *suffix* **1** forming adjectives meaning 'abounding in, characterized by, of the nature of' (*envious; glorious; mountainous; poisonous*). **2** *Chem*. denoting a state of lower valence than the corresponding word in *-ic* (*ferrous*). □□**-ously** *suffix* forming adverbs. **-ousness** *suffix* forming nouns. [from or after AF *-ous*, OF *-eus*, f. L *-osus*]

ousel var. of OUZEL.

oust /aʊst/ *v.tr*. **1** (usu. foll. by *from*) drive out or expel, esp. by forcing oneself into the place of. **2** (usu. foll. by *of*) *Law* put (a person) out of possession; deprive. [AF *ouster*, OF *oster* take away, f. L *obstare* oppose, hinder (as OB-, *stare* stand)]

ouster /'aʊstə(r)/ *n*. **1** ejection as a result of physical action, judicial process, or political upheaval. **2** esp. *US* dismissal, expulsion.

out /aʊt/ *adv., prep., n., adj., int., & v*. —*adv*. **1** away from or not in or at a place etc. (*keep him out; get out of here; my son is out in Canada*). **2** (forming part of phrasal verbs) **a** indicating dispersal away from a centre etc. (*hire out; share out; board out*). **b** indicating coming or bringing into the open for public attention etc. (*call out; send out; shine out; stand out*). **c** indicating a need for attentiveness (*watch out; look out; listen out*). **3** not in one's house, office, etc. (*went out for a walk*). **4** to or at an end; completely (*tired out; die out; out of bananas; fight it out; typed it out*). **5** (of a fire, candle, etc.) not burning. **6** in error (*was 3% out in my calculations*). **7** *colloq*. unconscious (*she was out for five minutes*). **8 a** (of a tooth) extracted. **b** (of a joint, bone, etc.) dislocated (*put his shoulder out*). **9** (of a party, politician, etc.) not in office. **10** (of a jury) considering its verdict in secrecy. **11** (of workers) on strike. **12** (of a secret) revealed. **13** (of a flower) blooming, open. **14** (of a book) published. **15** (of a star) visible after dark. **16** unfashionable (*turn-ups are out*). **17** (of a batsman, batter, etc.) no longer taking part as such, having been caught, stumped, etc. **18** not worth considering; rejected (*that idea is out*). **19** *colloq*. (prec. by *superl*.) known to exist (*the best game out*). **20** (of a stain, mark, etc.) not visible, removed (*painted out the sign*). **21** (of time) not spent working (*took five minutes out*). **22** (of a rash, bruise, etc.) visible. **23** (of the tide) at the lowest point. **24** *Boxing* unable to rise from the floor (*out for the count*). **25** *archaic* (of a young upper-class woman) introduced into society. **26** (in a radio conversation etc.) transmission ends (*over and out*). —*prep*. **1** out of (*looked out the window*). **2** *archaic* outside; beyond the limits of. —*n*. **1** *colloq*. a way of escape; an excuse. **2** (**the outs**) the political party out of office. —*adj*. **1** (of a match) played away. **2** (of an island) away from the mainland. —*int*. a peremptory dismissal, reproach, etc. (*out, you scoundrel!*). —*v*. **1** *tr*. **a** put out. **b** *colloq*. eject forcibly. **2** *intr*. come or go out; emerge (*murder will out*). **3** *tr. Boxing* knock out. □**at outs** at variance or enmity. **not out** *Cricket* (of a side or a batsman) not having been caught, bowled, etc. **out and about** (of a person, esp. after an illness) engaging in normal activity. **out and away** by far. **out and out 1** thorough; surpassing. **2** thoroughly; surpassingly. **out at elbows** see ELBOW. **out for** having one's interest or effort directed to; intent on. **out of 1** from within (*came out of the house*). **2** not within (*I was never out of England*). **3** from among (*nine people out of ten; must choose out of these*). **4** beyond the range of (*is out of reach*). **5** without or so as to be without (*was swindled out of his money; out of breath; out of sugar*). **6** from (*get money out of him*). **7** owing to; because of (*asked out of curiosity*). **8** by the use of (material) (*what did you make it out of?*). **9** at a specified distance from (a town, port, etc.) (*seven miles out of Liverpool*). **10** beyond (*something out of the ordinary*). **11** *Racing* (of an animal, esp. a horse) born of. **out of bounds** see BOUND[2]. **out of date** see DATE[1]. **out of doors** see DOOR. **out of drawing** see DRAWING. **out of hand** see HAND. **out of it** not included; forlorn. **out of order** see ORDER. **out of pocket** see POCKET. **out of the question** see QUESTION. **out of sorts** see SORT. **out of temper** see TEMPER. **out of this world** see WORLD. **out of the way** see WAY. **out to** keenly striving to do. **out to lunch** *colloq*. crazy, mad. **out with** an exhortation to expel or dismiss (an unwanted person). **out with it** say what you are thinking. [OE *ūt*, OHG *ūz*, rel. to Skr. *ud-*]

out- /aʊt/ *prefix* added to verbs and nouns, meaning: **1** so as to surpass or exceed (*outdo; outnumber*). **2** external, separate (*outline; outhouse; outdoors*). **3** out of; away from; outward (*outspread; outgrowth*).

out-act /aʊt'ækt/ *v.tr*. surpass in acting or performing.

outage /'aʊtɪdʒ/ *n*. a period of time during which a power-supply etc. is not operating.

out-and-outer /ˌaʊtənd'aʊtə(r)/ *n. sl*. **1** a thorough or supreme person or thing. **2** an extremist.

outback /'aʊtbæk/ *n*. esp. *Austral*. the remote and usu. uninhabited inland districts. □□**outbacker** *n*.

outbalance /aʊt'bæləns/ *v.tr*. **1** count as more important than. **2** outweigh.

outbid /aʊt'bɪd/ *v.tr*. (**-bidding**; *past* and *past part*. **-bid**) **1** bid higher than (another person) at an auction. **2** surpass in exaggeration etc.

outblaze /aʊt'bleɪz/ *v*. **1** *intr*. blaze out or outwards. **2** *tr*. blaze more brightly than.

outboard /'aʊtbɔːd/ *adj., adv., & n*. —*adj*. **1** (of a motor) portable and attachable to the outside of the stern of a boat. **2** (of a boat) having an outboard motor. —*adj. & adv*. on, towards, or near the outside of esp. a ship, an aircraft, etc. —*n*. **1** an outboard engine. **2** a boat with an outboard engine.

outbound /'aʊtbaʊnd/ *adj*. outward bound.

æ *cat* ɑː *arm* e *bed* ɜː *her* ɪ *sit* iː *see* ɒ *hot* ɔː *saw* ʌ *run* ʊ *put* uː *too* ə *ago* aɪ *my*

outbrave /aʊt'breɪv/ v.tr. **1** outdo in bravery. **2** face defiantly.

outbreak /'aʊtbreɪk/ n. **1** a usu. sudden eruption of anger, war, disease, rebellion, etc. **2** an outcrop.

outbreeding /'aʊt,briːdɪŋ/ n. the theory or practice of breeding from animals not closely related. □□ **outbreed** v.intr. & tr. (past and past part. **-bred**).

outbuilding /'aʊt,bɪldɪŋ/ n. a detached shed, barn, garage, etc. within the grounds of a main building; an outhouse.

outburst /'aʊtbɜːst/ n. **1** an explosion of anger etc., expressed in words. **2** an act or instance of bursting out. **3** an outcrop.

outcast /'aʊtkɑːst/ n. & adj. —n. **1** a person cast out from or rejected by his or her home, country, society, etc. **2** a tramp or vagabond. —adj. rejected; homeless; friendless.

outcaste n. & v. —n. /'aʊtkɑːst/ (also attrib.) **1** a person who has no caste, esp. in Hindu society. **2** a person who has lost his or her caste. —v.tr. /-'kɑːst/ cause (a person) to lose his or her caste.

outclass /aʊt'klɑːs/ v.tr. **1** belong to a higher class than. **2** defeat easily.

outcome /'aʊtkʌm/ n. a result; a visible effect.

outcrop /'aʊtkrɒp/ n. & v. —n. **1 a** the emergence of a stratum, vein, or rock, at the surface. **b** a stratum etc. emerging. **2** a noticeable manifestation or occurrence. —v.intr. (**-cropped**, **-cropping**) appear as an outcrop; crop out.

outcry /'aʊtkraɪ/ n. (pl. **-ies**) **1** the act or an instance of crying out. **2** an uproar. **3** a noisy or prolonged public protest.

outdance /aʊt'dɑːns/ v.tr. surpass in dancing.

outdare /aʊt'deə(r)/ v.tr. **1** outdo in daring. **2** overcome by daring.

outdated /aʊt'deɪtɪd/ adj. out of date; obsolete.

outdistance /aʊt'dɪst(ə)ns/ v.tr. leave (a competitor) behind completely.

outdo /aʊt'duː/ v.tr. (3rd sing. present **-does**; past **-did**; past part. **-done**) exceed or excel in doing or performance; surpass.

outdoor /'aʊtdɔː(r)/ adj. done, existing, or used out of doors.

outdoors /aʊt'dɔːz/ adv. & n. —adv. in or into the open air; out of doors. —n. the world outside buildings; the open air.

outer /'aʊtə(r)/ adj. & n. —adj. **1** outside; external (pierced the outer layer). **2** farther from the centre or inside; relatively far out. **3** objective or physical, not subjective or psychical. —n. **1 a** the division of a target furthest from the bull's-eye. **b** a shot that strikes this. **2** an outer garment or part of one. **3** Austral. sl. the part of a racecourse outside the enclosure. **4** an outer container for transport or display. □ **the outer bar** see BAR¹. **outer garments** clothes worn over other clothes or outdoors. **Outer House** Sc. Law the hall where judges of the Court of Session sit singly. **outer man** (or **woman**) personal appearance; dress. **outer planet** a planet with an orbit outside the earth's. **outer space** the universe beyond the earth's atmosphere. **the outer world** people outside one's own circle. [ME f. OUT, replacing UTTER¹]

outermost /'aʊtə,məʊst/ adj. furthest from the inside; the most far out.

outerwear /'aʊtə,weə(r)/ n. = outer garments.

outface /aʊt'feɪs/ v.tr. disconcert or defeat by staring or by a display of confidence.

outfall /'aʊtfɔːl/ n. the mouth of a river, drain, etc., where it empties into the sea etc.

outfield /'aʊtfiːld/ n. **1** the outer part of a cricket or baseball field. **2** outlying land. □□ **outfielder** n.

outfight /aʊt'faɪt/ v.tr. fight better than; beat in a fight.

outfit /'aʊtfɪt/ n. & v. —n. **1** a set of clothes worn or esp. designed to be worn together. **2** a complete set of equipment etc. for a specific purpose. **3** colloq. a group of people regarded as a unit, organization,

etc.; a team. —v.tr. (also refl.) (**-fitted**, **-fitting**) provide with an outfit, esp. of clothes.

outfitter /'aʊt,fɪtə(r)/ n. a supplier of equipment, esp. of men's clothing; a haberdasher.

outflank /aʊt'flæŋk/ v.tr. **1 a** extend one's flank beyond that of (an enemy). **b** outmanœuvre (an enemy) in this way. **2** get the better of; confound (an opponent).

outflow /'aʊtfləʊ/ n. **1** an outward flow. **2** the amount that flows out.

outfly /aʊt'flaɪ/ v.tr. (**-flies**; past **-flew**; past part. **-flown**) **1** surpass in flying. **2** fly faster or farther than.

outfox /aʊt'fɒks/ v.tr. colloq. outwit.

outgeneral /aʊt'dʒenər(ə)l/ v.tr. (**-generalled**, **-generalling**; US **-generaled**, **-generaling**) **1** outdo in generalship. **2** get the better of by superior strategy or tactics.

outgo /aʊt'gəʊ/ v. & n. —v.tr. (3rd sing. present **-goes**; past **-went**; past part. **-gone**) archaic go faster than; surpass. —n. /'aʊtgəʊ/ (pl. **-goes**) expenditure of money, effort, etc.

outgoing /'aʊt,gəʊɪŋ/ adj. & n. —adj. **1** friendly; sociable; extrovert. **2** retiring from office. **3** going out or away. —n. **1** (in pl.) expenditure. **2** the act or an instance of going out.

outgrow /aʊt'grəʊ/ v.tr. (past **-grew**; past part. **-grown**) **1** grow too big for (one's clothes). **2** leave behind (a childish habit, taste, ailment, etc.) as one matures. **3** grow faster or taller than (a person, plant, etc.). □ **outgrow one's strength** become lanky and weak through too rapid growth.

outgrowth /'aʊtgrəʊθ/ n. **1** something that grows out. **2** an offshoot; a natural product. **3** the process of growing out.

outguess /aʊt'ges/ v.tr. guess correctly what is intended by (another person).

outgun /aʊt'gʌn/ v.tr. (**-gunned**, **-gunning**) **1** surpass in military or other power or strength. **2** shoot better than.

outhouse /'aʊthaʊs/ n. **1** a building, esp. a shed, lean-to, barn, etc. built next to or in the grounds of a house. **2** US an outdoor lavatory.

outing /'aʊtɪŋ/ n. **1** a short holiday away from home, esp. of one day or part of a day; a pleasure-trip, an excursion. **2** any brief journey from home. **3** an appearance in an outdoor match, race, etc. [OUT v. = put out, go out + -ING¹]

outjockey /aʊt'dʒɒkɪ/ v.tr. (**-eys**, **-eyed**) outwit by adroitness or trickery.

outjump /aʊt'dʒʌmp/ v.tr. surpass in jumping.

outlander /'aʊt,lændə(r)/ n. a foreigner, alien, or stranger.

outlandish /aʊt'lændɪʃ/ adj. **1** looking or sounding foreign. **2** bizarre, strange, unfamiliar. □□ **outlandishly** adv. **outlandishness** n. [OE ūtlendisc f. ūtland foreign country f. OUT + LAND]

outlast /aʊt'lɑːst/ v.tr. last longer than (a person, thing, or quality) (outlasted its usefulness).

outlaw /'aʊtlɔː/ n. & v. —n. **1** a fugitive from the law. **2** hist. a person deprived of the protection of the law. —v.tr. **1** declare (a person) an outlaw. **2** make illegal; proscribe (a practice etc.). □ **outlaw strike** an unofficial strike. □□ **outlawry** n. [OE ūtlaga, ūtlagian f. ON útlagi f. útlagr outlawed, rel. to OUT, LAW]

outlay /'aʊtleɪ/ n. what is spent on something.

outlet /'aʊtlet, -lɪt/ n. **1** a means of exit or escape. **2** (usu. foll. by for) a means of expression (of a talent, emotion, etc.) (find an outlet for tension). **3** an agency, distributor, or market for goods (a new retail outlet in China). **4** US a power point. [ME f. OUT- + LET¹]

outlier /'aʊt,laɪə(r)/ n. **1** (also attrib.) an outlying part or member. **2** Geol. a younger rock formation isolated in older rocks. **3** Statistics a result differing greatly from others in the same sample.

outline /'aʊtlaɪn/ n. & v. —n. **1** a rough draft of a diagram, plan, proposal, etc. **2 a** a précis of a proposed novel, article, etc. **b** a verbal description of essential parts only; a summary. **3** a sketch containing only contour lines. **4** (in *sing.* or *pl.*) **a** lines enclosing or indicating an object (*the outline of a shape under the blankets*). **b** a contour. **c** an external boundary. **5** (in *pl.*) the main features or general principles (*the outlines of a plan*). **6** the representation of a word in shorthand. —*v.tr.* **1** draw or describe in outline. **2** mark the outline of. □**in outline** sketched or represented as an outline.

outlive /aʊtˈlɪv/ *v.tr.* **1** live longer than (another person). **2** live beyond (a specified date or time). **3** live through (an experience).

outlook /ˈaʊtlʊk/ *n.* **1** the prospect for the future (*the outlook is bleak*). **2** one's mental attitude or point of view (*narrow in their outlook*). **3** what is seen on looking out.

outlying /ˈaʊtˌlaɪɪŋ/ *adj.* situated far from a centre; remote.

outmanœuvre /ˌaʊtməˈnuːvə(r)/ *v.tr.* (*US* -**maneuver**) **1** use skill and cunning to secure an advantage over (a person). **2** outdo in manœuvring.

outmatch /aʊtˈmætʃ/ *v.tr.* be more than a match for (an opponent etc.); surpass.

outmeasure /aʊtˈmeʒə(r)/ *v.tr.* exceed in quantity or extent.

outmoded /aʊtˈməʊdɪd/ *adj.* **1** no longer in fashion. **2** obsolete. □□ **outmodedly** *adv.* **outmodedness** *n.*

outmost /ˈaʊtməʊst/ *adj.* **1** outermost, furthest. **2** uttermost. [ME, var. of *utmost* UTMOST]

outnumber /aʊtˈnʌmbə(r)/ *v.tr.* exceed in number.

outpace /aʊtˈpeɪs/ *v.tr.* **1** go faster than. **2** outdo in a contest.

out-patient /ˈaʊtˌpeɪʃ(ə)nt/ *n.* a hospital patient who is resident at home but attends regular appointments in hospital.

outperform /ˌaʊtpəˈfɔːm/ *v.tr.* **1** perform better than. **2** surpass in a specified field or activity. □□ **outperformance** *n.*

outplacement /ˈaʊtˌpleɪsmənt/ *n.* the act or process of finding new employment for esp. executive workers who have been dismissed or made redundant.

outplay /aʊtˈpleɪ/ *v.tr.* surpass in playing; play better than.

outpoint /aʊtˈpɔɪnt/ *v.tr.* (in various sports, esp. boxing) score more points than.

outport /ˈaʊtpɔːt/ *n.* **1** a subsidiary port. **2** *Can.* a small remote fishing village.

outpost /ˈaʊtpəʊst/ *n.* **1** a detachment set at a distance from the main body of an army, esp. to prevent surprise. **2** a distant branch or settlement. **3** the furthest territory of an (esp. the British) empire.

outpouring /ˈaʊtˌpɔːrɪŋ/ *n.* **1** (usu. in *pl.*) a copious spoken or written expression of emotion. **2** what is poured out.

output /ˈaʊtpʊt/ *n. & v.* —*n.* **1** the product of a process, esp. of manufacture, or of mental or artistic work. **2** the quantity or amount of this. **3** the printout, results, etc. supplied by a computer. **4** the power etc. delivered by an apparatus. **5** a place where energy, information, etc. leaves a system. —*v.tr.* (-**putting**; *past* and *past part.* -**put** or -**putted**) **1** put or send out. **2** (of a computer) supply (results etc.).

outrage /ˈaʊtreɪdʒ/ *n. & v.* —*n.* **1** an extreme or shocking violation of others' rights, sentiments, etc. **2** a gross offence or indignity. **3** fierce anger or resentment (*a feeling of outrage*). —*v.tr.* **1** subject to outrage. **2** injure, insult, etc. flagrantly. **3** shock and anger. [ME f. OF *outrage* f. *outrer* exceed f. *outre* f. L *ultra* beyond]

outrageous /aʊtˈreɪdʒəs/ *adj.* **1** immoderate. **2** shocking. **3** grossly cruel. **4** immoral, offensive. □□ **outrageously** *adv.* **outrageousness** *n.* [ME f. OF *outrageus* (as OUTRAGE)]

outran *past* of OUTRUN.

outrange /aʊtˈreɪndʒ/ *v.tr.* (of a gun or its user) have a longer range than.

outrank /aʊtˈræŋk/ *v.tr.* **1** be superior in rank to. **2** take priority over.

outré /ˈuːtreɪ/ *adj.* **1** outside the bounds of what is usual or proper. **2** eccentric or indecorous. [F, past part. of *outrer*: see OUTRAGE]

outreach *v. & n.* —*v.tr.* /aʊtˈriːtʃ/ **1** reach further than. **2** surpass. **3** *poet.* stretch out (one's arms etc.). —*n.* /ˈaʊtriːtʃ/ **1 a** any organization's involvement with or influence in the community, esp. in the context of social welfare. **b** the extent of this. **2** the extent or length of reaching out (*an outreach of 38 metres*).

out-relief /ˈaʊtrɪˌliːf/ *n.* *Brit. hist.* assistance given to very poor people not living in a workhouse etc.; outdoor relief.

outride /aʊtˈraɪd/ *v.tr.* (*past* -**rode**; *past part.* -**ridden**) **1** ride better, faster, or further than. **2** (of a ship) come safely through (a storm etc.).

outrider /ˈaʊtˌraɪdə(r)/ *n.* **1** a mounted attendant riding ahead of, or with, a carriage etc. **2** a motor cyclist acting as a guard in a similar manner. **3** *US* a herdsman keeping cattle within bounds. □□ **outriding** *n.*

outrigged /ˈaʊtrɪgd/ *adj.* (of a boat etc.) having outriggers.

outrigger /ˈaʊtˌrɪgə(r)/ *n.* **1** a beam, spar, or framework, rigged out and projecting from or over a ship's side for various purposes. **2** a similar projecting beam etc. in a building. **3** a log etc. fixed parallel to a canoe to stabilize it. **4 a** an extension of the splinter-bar of a carriage etc. to enable another horse to be harnessed outside the shafts. **b** a horse harnessed in this way. **5 a** an iron bracket bearing a rowlock attached horizontally to a boat's side to increase the leverage of the oar. **b** a boat fitted with these. [OUT- + RIG¹: perh. partly after obs. (Naut.) *outligger*]

outright *adv. & adj.* —*adv.* /aʊtˈraɪt/ **1** altogether, entirely (*proved outright*). **2** not gradually, nor by degrees, nor by instalments (*bought it outright*). **3** without reservation, openly (*denied the charge outright*). —*adj.* /ˈaʊtraɪt/ **1** downright, direct, complete (*their resentment turned to outright anger*). **2** undisputed, clear (*the outright winner*). □□ **outrightness** *n.*

outrival /aʊtˈraɪv(ə)l/ *v.tr.* (-**rivalled**, -**rivalling**; *US* -**rivaled**, -**rivaling**) outdo as a rival.

outrode *past* of OUTRIDE.

outrun *v. & n.* —*v.tr.* /aʊtˈrʌn/ (-**running**; *past* -**ran**; *past part.* -**run**) **1 a** run faster or farther than. **b** escape from. **2** go beyond (a specified point or limit). —*n.* /ˈaʊtrʌn/ *Austral.* a sheep-run distant from its homestead.

outrush /ˈaʊtrʌʃ/ *n.* **1** a rushing out. **2** a violent overflow.

outsail /aʊtˈseɪl/ *v.tr.* sail better or faster than.

outsat *past* and *past part.* of OUTSIT.

outsell /aʊtˈsel/ *v.tr.* (*past* and *past part.* -**sold**) **1** sell more than. **2** be sold in greater quantities than.

outset /ˈaʊtset/ *n.* the start, beginning. □**at** (or **from**) **the outset** from the beginning.

outshine /aʊtˈʃaɪn/ *v.tr.* (*past* and *past part.* -**shone**) shine brighter than; surpass in ability, excellence, etc.

outshoot /aʊtˈʃuːt/ *v.tr.* (*past* and *past part.* -**shot**) **1** shoot better or further than (another person). **2** esp. *US* score more goals, points, etc. than (another player or team).

outside *n., adj., adv., & prep.* —*n.* /aʊtˈsaɪd, ˈaʊtsaɪd/ **1** the external side or surface; the outer parts (*painted blue on the outside*). **2** the external appearance; the outward aspect of a building etc. **3** (of a path) the side away from the wall or next to the road. **4** (also *attrib.*) all that is without; the world as distinct from the thinking subject (*learn about the outside world*; *viewed from the outside the problem is simple*). **5** a position on the outer side (*the gate opens from the outside*). **6** *colloq.* the highest computation (*it is a mile at the outside*). **7** an outside player in football

etc. **8** (in *pl.*) the outer sheets of a ream of paper.
—*adj.* /'autsaid/ **1** of or on or nearer the outside;
outer. **2 a** not of or belonging to some circle or institution (*outside help; outside work*). **b** (of a broker)
not a member of the Stock Exchange. **3** (of a chance
etc.) remote; very unlikely. **4** (of an estimate etc.)
the greatest or highest possible (*the outside price*). **5**
(of a player in football etc.) positioned nearest to the
edge of the field. —*adv.* /aut'said/ **1** on or to the
outside. **2** in or to the open air. **3** not within or
enclosed or included. **4** *sl.* not in prison. —*prep.*
/aut'said/ (also *disp.* foll. by *of*) **1** not in; to or at the
exterior of (*meet me outside the post office*). **2** external
to, not included in, beyond the limits of (*outside the
law*). □**at the outside** (of an estimate etc.) at the
most. **get outside of** *sl.* eat or drink. **outside and
in** outside and inside. **outside broadcast** *Brit.* a
broadcast made on location and not in a studio.
outside edge (on an ice-skate) each of the edges
facing outwards when both feet are together. **outside
in** = *inside out*. **outside interest** a hobby; an
interest not connected with one's work or normal
way of life. **outside seat** a seat nearer the end of a
row. **outside track** the outside lane of a sports track
etc. which is longer because of the curve.

outsider /aut'saidə(r)/ *n.* **1 a** a non-member of some
circle, party, profession, etc. **b** an uninitiated person,
a layman. **2** a person without special knowledge,
breeding, etc., or not fit to mix with good society. **3** a
competitor, applicant, etc. thought to have little
chance of success.

outsit /aut'sit/ *v.tr.* (**-sitting**; *past* and *past part.*
-sat) sit longer than (another person or thing).

outsize /'autsaiz/ *adj.* & *n.* —*adj.* **1** unusually large.
2 (of garments etc.) of an exceptionally large size.
—*n.* an exceptionally large person or thing, esp.
a garment. □□ **outsizeness** *n.*

outskirts /'autskɜːts/ *n.pl.* the outer border or fringe
of a town, district, subject, etc.

outsmart /aut'smɑːt/ *v.tr. colloq.* outwit, be cleverer
than.

outsold *past* and *past part.* of OUTSELL.

outspan /'autspæn/ *v.* & *n.* *S.Afr.* —*v.* (**-spanned**,
-spanning) **1** *tr.* (also *absol.*) unharness (animals)
from a cart, plough, etc. **2** *intr.* break a wagon
journey. —*n.* a place for grazing or encampment.
[S.Afr. Du. *uitspannen* unyoke]

outspend /aut'spend/ *v.tr.* (*past* and *past part.*
-spent) spend more than (one's resources or another
person).

outspoken /aut'spəukən/ *adj.* given to or involving
plain speaking; frank in stating one's opinions. □□
outspokenly *adv.* **outspokenness** *n.*

outspread *adj.* & *v.* —*adj.* /aut'spred, 'autspred/
spread out; fully extended or expanded. —*v.tr.* &
intr. /aut'spred/ (*past* and *past part.* **-spread**) spread
out; expand.

outstanding /aut'stændiŋ/ *adj.* **1 a** conspicuous,
eminent, esp. because of excellence. **b** (usu. foll. by
at, in) remarkable in (a specified field). **2** (esp. of a
debt) not yet settled (*£200 still outstanding*). □□
outstandingly *adv.*

outstare /aut'steə(r)/ *v.tr.* **1** outdo in staring. **2** abash
by staring.

outstation /'aut,steiʃ(ə)n/ *n.* **1** a branch of an
organization, enterprise, or business in a remote
area or at a considerable distance from headquarters.
2 esp. *Austral.* & *NZ* part of a farming estate separate
from the main estate.

outstay /aut'stei/ *v.tr.* **1** stay beyond the limit of
(one's welcome, invitation, etc.). **2** stay or endure
longer than (another person etc.).

outstep /aut'step/ *v.tr.* (**-stepped**, **-stepping**) step
outside or beyond.

outstretch /'autstretʃ, aut'stretʃ/ *v.tr.* **1** (usu. as
outstretched *adj.*) reach out or stretch out (esp.
one's hands or arms). **2** reach or stretch further
than.

outstrip /aut'strip/ *v.tr.* (**-stripped**, **-stripping**) **1**
pass in running etc. **2** surpass in competition or
relative progress or ability.

out-swinger /'aut,swiŋə(r)/ *n.* a ball that swings
away from the batsman.

out-take /'autteik/ *n.* a length of film or tape rejected
in editing.

out-talk /aut'tɔːk/ *v.tr.* outdo or overcome in talking.

out-think /aut'θiŋk/ *v.tr.* (*past* and *past part.*
-thought) outwit; outdo in thinking.

out-thrust *adj.*, *v.*, & *n.* —*adj.* /'autθrʌst/ extended;
projected (*ran forward with out-thrust arms*). —*v.tr.*
/aut'θrʌst/ (*past* and *past part.* **-thrust**) thrust out.
—*n.* /'autθrʌst/ **1** the act or an instance of thrusting
forcibly outward. **2** the act or an instance of becoming
prominent or noticeable.

out-top /aut'tɒp/ *v.tr.* (**-topped**, **-topping**) surmount,
surpass in height, extent, etc.

out-tray /'auttrei/ *n.* a tray for outgoing documents,
letters, etc.

out-turn /'auttɜːn/ *n.* **1** the quantity produced. **2** the
result of a process or sequence of events.

outvalue /aut'væljuː/ *v.tr.* (**-values**, **-valued**,
-valuing) be of greater value than.

outvote /aut'vəut/ *v.tr.* defeat by a majority of votes.

outwalk /aut'wɔːk/ *v.tr.* **1** outdo in walking. **2** walk
beyond.

outward /'autwəd/ *adj.*, *adv.*, & *n.* —*adj.* **1** situated
on or directed towards the outside. **2** going out (*on
the outward voyage*). **3** bodily, external, apparent,
superficial (*in all outward respects*). **4** *archaic* visible
(*the outward man*). —*adv.* (also **outwards**) in an
outward direction; towards the outside. —*n.* the
outward appearance of something; the exterior.
□**outward bound 1** (of a ship, passenger, etc.) going
away from home. **2** (**Outward Bound**) (in the UK)
a movement to provide adventure training, naval
training, and other outdoor activities for young
people. **outward form** appearance. **outward
things** the world around us. **to outward seeming**
apparently. □□ **outwardly** *adv.* [OE *ūtweard* (as OUT,
-WARD)]

outwardness /'autwədnis/ *n.* **1** external existence;
objectivity. **2** an interest or belief in outward things,
objective-mindedness.

outwards var. of OUTWARD *adv.*

outwash /'autwɒʃ/ *n.* the material carried from a
glacier by melt water and deposited beyond the
moraine.

outwatch /aut'wɒtʃ/ *v.tr.* **1** watch more than or
longer than. **2** *archaic* keep awake beyond the end of
(night etc.).

outwear *v.* & *n.* —*v.tr.* /aut'weə(r)/ (*past* **-wore**;
past part. **-worn**) **1** exhaust; wear out; wear away. **2**
live or last beyond the duration of. **3** (as **outworn**
adj.) out of date, obsolete. —*n.* /'autweə(r)/ outer
clothing.

outweigh /aut'wei/ *v.tr.* exceed in weight, value,
importance, or influence.

outwent *past* of OUTGO.

outwit /aut'wit/ *v.tr.* (**-witted**, **-witting**) be too
clever or crafty for; deceive by greater ingenuity.

outwith /aut'wiθ/ *prep.* *Sc.* outside, beyond.

outwore *past* of OUTWEAR.

outwork /'autwɜːk/ *n.* **1** an advanced or detached
part of a fortification. **2** work done outside the shop
or factory which supplies it. □□ **outworker** *n.* (in
sense 2).

outworn *past part.* of OUTWEAR.

ouzel /'uːz(ə)l/ *n.* (also **ousel**) **1** = *ring ouzel* (see
RING[1]). **2** = *water ouzel*. **3** *archaic* a blackbird. [OE
ōsle blackbird, of unkn. orig.]

ouzo /'uːzəu/ *n.* (*pl.* **-os**) a Greek aniseed-flavoured
spirit. [mod.Gk]

ova *pl.* of OVUM.

oval /'əuv(ə)l/ *adj.* & *n.* —*adj.* **1** egg-shaped, ellipsoidal. **2** having the outline of an egg, elliptical. —*n.*
1 an egg-shaped or elliptical closed curve. **2** any

object with an oval outline. **3** *Austral.* a ground for Australian Rules football. □**Oval Office** the office of the US President in the White House. □□**ovality** /-ˈvælɪtɪ/ *n.* **ovally** *adv.* **ovalness** *n.* [med.L *ovalis* (as OVUM)]

ovary /ˈəʊvərɪ/ *n.* (*pl.* **-ies**) **1** each of the female reproductive organs in which ova are produced. **2** the hollow base of the carpel of a flower, containing one or more ovules. □□**ovarian** /əˈveərɪən/ *adj.* **ovariectomy** /-rɪˈektəmɪ/ *n.* (*pl.* **-ies**) (in sense 1). **ovariotomy** /-rɪˈɒtəmɪ/ *n.* (*pl.* **-ies**) (in sense 1). **ovaritis** /-ˈraɪtɪs/ *n.* (in sense 1). [mod.L *ovarium* (as OVUM)]

ovate /ˈəʊveɪt/ *adj. Biol.* egg-shaped as a solid or in outline; oval. [L *ovatus* (as OVUM)]

ovation /əʊˈveɪʃ(ə)n/ *n.* **1** an enthusiastic reception, esp. spontaneous and sustained applause. **2** *Rom. Antiq.* a lesser form of triumph. □**standing ovation** prolonged applause during which the crowd or audience rise to their feet. □□**ovational** *adj.* [L *ovatio* f. *ovare* exult]

oven /ˈʌv(ə)n/ *n.* **1** an enclosed compartment of brick, stone, or metal for cooking food. **2** a chamber for heating or drying. **3** a small furnace or kiln used in chemistry, metallurgy, etc. □**oven-ready** (of food) prepared before sale so as to be ready for immediate cooking in the oven. [OE *ofen* f. Gmc]

ovenbird /ˈʌv(ə)n,bɜːd/ *n.* any Central or S. American bird of the family Furnariidae, many of which make domed nests.

ovenproof /ˈʌv(ə)n,pruːf/ *adj.* suitable for use in an oven; heat-resistant.

ovenware /ˈʌv(ə)n,weə(r)/ *n.* dishes that can be used for cooking food in the oven.

over /ˈəʊvə(r)/ *adv., prep., n., & adj.* —*adv.* expressing movement or position or state above or beyond something stated or implied: **1** outward and downward from a brink or from any erect position (*knocked the man over*). **2** so as to cover or touch a whole surface (*paint it over*). **3** so as to produce a fold, or reverse a position; with the effect of being upside down. **4 a** across a street or other space (*decided to cross over; came over from America*). **b** for a visit etc. (*invited them over last night*). **5** with transference or change from one hand or part to another (*went over to the enemy; swapped them over*). **6** with motion above something; so as to pass across something (*climb over; fly over; boil over*). **7** from beginning to end with repetition or detailed concentration (*think it over; did it six times over*). **8** in excess; more than is right or required (*left over*). **9** for or until a later time (*hold it over*). **10** at an end; settled (*the crisis is over; all is over between us*). **11** (in full **over to you**) (as *int.*) (in radio conversations etc.) said to indicate that it is the other person's turn to speak. **12** (as *int.*) *Cricket* an umpire's call to change ends. —*prep.* **1** above, in, or to a position higher than; upon. **2** out and down from; down from the edge of (*fell over the cliff*). **3** so as to cover (*a hat over his eyes*). **4** above and across; so as to clear (*flew over the North Pole; a bridge over the Thames*). **5** concerning; engaged with; as a result of; while occupied with (*laughed over a good joke; fell asleep over the newspaper*). **6 a** in superiority of; superior to; in charge of (*a victory over the enemy; reign over three kingdoms*). **b** in preference to. **7** divided by. **8 a** throughout; covering the extent of (*travelled over most of Africa; a blush spread over his face*). **b** so as to deal with completely (*went over the plans*). **9 a** for the duration of (*stay over Saturday night*). **b** at any point during the course of (*I'll do it over the weekend*). **10** beyond; more than (*bids of over £50; are you over 18?*). **11** transmitted by (*heard it over the radio*). **12** in comparison with (*gained 20% over last year*). **13** having recovered from (*am now over my cold; will get over it in time*). —*n. Cricket* **1** a sequence of balls (now usu. six), bowled from one end of the pitch. **2** play resulting from this (*a maiden over*). —*adj.* (see

also OVER-). **1** upper, outer. **2** superior. **3** extra. □**begin** (or **start** etc.) **over** *US* begin again. **get it over with** do or undergo something unpleasant etc. so as to be rid of it. **give over** (usu. as *int.*) *colloq.* stop talking. **not over** not very; not at all (*not over friendly*). **over again** once again, again from the beginning. **over against** in an opposite situation to; adjacent to, in contrast with. **over-age** over a certain age limit. **over all** taken as a whole. **over and above** in addition to; not to mention (*£100 over and above the asking price*). **over and over** so that the same thing or the same point comes up again and again (*said it over and over; rolled it over and over*). **over the fence** *Austral.* & *NZ sl.* unreasonable; unfair; indecent. **over one's head** see HEAD. **over the hill** see HILL. **over the moon** see MOON. **over-the-top** *colloq.* (esp. of behaviour, dress, etc.) outrageous, excessive. **over the way** (in a street etc.) facing or opposite. [OE *ofer* f. Gmc]

over- /ˈəʊvə(r)/ *prefix* added to verbs, nouns, adjectives, and adverbs, meaning: **1** excessively; to an unwanted degree (*overheat; overdue*). **2** upper, outer, extra (*overcoat; overtime*). **3** 'over' in various senses (*overhang; overshadow*). **4** completely, utterly (*overawe; overjoyed*).

over-abundant /ˌəʊvərəˈbʌnd(ə)nt/ *adj.* in excessive quantity. □□**over-abound** /-ˈbaʊnd/ *v.intr.* **over-abundance** *n.* **over-abundantly** *adv.*

overachieve /ˌəʊvərəˈtʃiːv/ *v.* **1** *intr.* do more than might be expected (esp. scholastically). **2** *tr.* achieve more than (an expected goal or objective etc.). □□ **overachievement** *n.* **overachiever** *n.*

overact /ˌəʊvərˈækt/ *v.tr.* & *intr.* act in an exaggerated manner.

over-active /ˌəʊvərˈæktɪv/ *adj.* excessively active. □□**over-activity** /-ˈtɪvɪtɪ/ *n.*

overage /ˈəʊvərɪdʒ/ *n.* a surplus or excess, esp. an amount greater than estimated.

overall *adj., adv., & n.* —*adj.* /ˈəʊvər,ɔːl/ **1** from end to end (*overall length*). **2** total, inclusive of all (*overall cost*). —*adv.* /ˌəʊvərˈɔːl/ in all parts; taken as a whole (*overall, the performance was excellent*). —*n.* /ˈəʊvər,ɔːl/ **1** *Brit.* an outer garment worn to keep out dirt, wet, etc. **2** (in *pl.*) protective trousers, dungarees, or a combination suit, worn by workmen etc. **3** *Brit.* close-fitting trousers worn as part of army uniform. □□**overalled** /ˈəʊvər,ɔːld/ *adj.*

overambitious /ˌəʊvəræmˈbɪʃəs/ *adj.* excessively ambitious. □□**overambition** *n.* **overambitiously** *adv.*

over-anxious /ˌəʊvərˈæŋkʃəs/ *adj.* excessively anxious. □□**over-anxiety** /-ænˈzaɪɪtɪ/ *n.* **over-anxiously** *adv.*

overarch /ˌəʊvərˈɑːtʃ/ *v.tr.* form an arch over. □□ **overarching** *adj.*

overarm /ˈəʊvər,ɑːm/ *adj. & adv.* **1** *Cricket & Tennis* etc. with the hand above the shoulder (*bowl it overarm; an overarm service*). **2** *Swimming* with one or both arms lifted out of the water during a stroke.

overate *past of* OVEREAT.

overawe /ˌəʊvərˈɔː/ *v.tr.* **1** restrain by awe. **2** keep in awe.

overbalance /ˌəʊvəˈbæləns/ *v. & n.* —*v.* **1** *tr.* cause (a person or thing) to lose its balance and fall. **2** *intr.* fall over, capsize. **3** *tr.* outweigh. —*n.* **1** an excess. **2** the amount of this.

overbear /ˌəʊvəˈbeə(r)/ *v.tr.* (*past* -**bore**; *past part.* -**borne**) **1** (as **overbearing** *adj.*) **a** domineering, masterful. **b** overpowering. **2** bear down; upset by weight, force, or emotional pressure. **3** put down or repress by power or authority. **4** surpass in importance etc., outweigh. □□**overbearingly** *adv.* **overbearingness** *n.*

overbid *v. & n.* —*v.* /ˌəʊvəˈbɪd/ (-**bidding**; *past* and *past part.* -**bid**) **1** *tr.* make a higher bid than. **2** *tr.* (also *absol.*) *Bridge* **a** bid more on (one's hand) than warranted. **b** overcall. —*n.* /ˈəʊvəbɪd/ a bid that is higher than another, or higher than is justified. □□ **overbidder** *n.*

overblouse /ˈəʊvəˌblaʊz/ *n.* a garment like a blouse, but worn without tucking it into a skirt or trousers.

overblown /ˌəʊvəˈbləʊn/ *adj.* **1** excessively inflated or pretentious. **2** (of a flower or a woman's beauty etc.) past its prime.

overboard /ˈəʊvəˌbɔːd/ *adv.* from on a ship into the water (*fall overboard*). □**go overboard 1** be highly enthusiastic. **2** behave immoderately; go too far. **throw overboard** abandon, discard.

overbold /ˌəʊvəˈbəʊld/ *adj.* excessively bold.

overbook /ˌəʊvəˈbʊk/ *v.tr.* (also *absol.*) make too many bookings for (an aircraft, hotel, etc.).

overboot /ˈəʊvəˌbuːt/ *n.* a boot worn over another boot or shoe.

overbore *past* of OVERBEAR.

overborne *past part.* of OVERBEAR.

overbought *past* and *past part.* of OVERBUY.

overbrim /ˌəʊvəˈbrɪm/ *v.* (**-brimmed**, **-brimming**) **1** *tr.* flow over the brim of. **2** *intr.* (of a vessel or liquid) overflow at the brim.

overbuild /ˌəʊvəˈbɪld/ *v.tr.* (*past* and *past part.* **-built**) **1** build over or upon. **2** place too many buildings on (land etc.).

overburden /ˌəʊvəˈbɜːd(ə)n/ *v.* & *n.* —*v.tr.* burden (a person, thing, etc.) to excess. —*n.* **1** rock etc. that must be removed prior to mining the mineral deposit beneath it. **2** an excessive burden. □□ **overburdensome** *adj.*

overbusy /ˌəʊvəˈbɪzɪ/ *adj.* excessively busy.

overbuy /ˌəʊvəˈbaɪ/ *v.tr.* & *intr.* (*past* and *past part.* **-bought**) buy (a commodity etc.) in excess of immediate need.

overcall *v.* & *n.* —*v.tr.* /ˌəʊvəˈkɔːl/ (also *absol.*) *Bridge* **1** make a higher bid than (a previous bid or opponent). **2** *Brit.* = OVERBID *v.* 2a. —*n.* /ˈəʊvəˌkɔːl/ an act or instance of overcalling.

overcame *past* of OVERCOME.

overcapacity /ˌəʊvəkəˈpæsɪtɪ/ *n.* a state of saturation or an excess of productive capacity.

overcapitalize /ˌəʊvəˈkæpɪtəˌlaɪz/ *v.tr.* (also **-ise**) fix or estimate the capital of (a company etc.) too high.

overcareful /ˌəʊvəˈkeəfʊl/ *adj.* excessively careful. □□ **overcarefully** *adv.*

overcast *adj.*, *v.*, & *n.* —*adj.* /ˈəʊvəˌkɑːst/ **1** (of the sky, weather, etc.) covered with cloud; dull and gloomy. **2** (in sewing) edged with stitching to prevent fraying. —*v.tr.* /ˌəʊvəˈkɑːst/ (*past* and *past part.* **-cast**) **1** cover (the sky etc.) with clouds or darkness. **2** stitch over (a raw edge etc.) to prevent fraying. —*n.* /ˈəʊvəˌkɑːst/ a cloud covering part of the sky.

overcautious /ˌəʊvəˈkɔːʃəs/ *adj.* excessively cautious. □□ **overcaution** *n.* **overcautiously** *adv.* **overcautiousness** *n.*

overcharge /ˌəʊvəˈtʃɑːdʒ/ *v.* & *n.* —*v.tr.* **1 a** charge too high a price to (a person) or for (a thing). **b** charge (a specified sum) beyond the right price. **2** put too much charge into (a battery, gun, etc.). **3** put exaggerated or excessive detail into (a description, picture, etc.). —*n.* an excessive charge (of explosive, money, etc.).

overcheck /ˈəʊvəˌtʃek/ *n.* **1** a combination of two different-sized check patterns. **2** a cloth with this pattern.

overcloud /ˌəʊvəˈklaʊd/ *v.tr.* **1** cover with cloud. **2** mar, spoil, or dim, esp. as the result of anxiety etc. (*overclouded by uncertainties*). **3** make obscure.

overcoat /ˈəʊvəˌkəʊt/ *n.* **1** a heavy coat, esp. one worn over indoor clothes for warmth outdoors in cold weather. **2** a protective coat of paint etc.

overcome /ˌəʊvəˈkʌm/ *v.* (*past* **-came**; *past part.* **-come**) **1** *tr.* prevail over, master, conquer. **2** *tr.* (as **overcome** *adj.*) **a** exhausted, made helpless. **b** (usu. foll. by *with*, *by*) affected by (emotion etc.). **3** *intr.* be victorious. [OE *ofercuman* (as OVER-, COME)]

overcompensate /ˌəʊvəˈkɒmpenˌseɪt/ *v.* **1** *tr.* (usu. foll. by *for*) compensate excessively for (something).

2 *intr. Psychol.* strive for power etc. in an exaggerated way, esp. to make allowance or amends for a real or fancied grievance, defect, handicap, etc. □□ **overcompensation** /-penˈseɪʃ(ə)n/ *n.* **overcompensatory** /-ˈseɪtərɪ/ *adj.*

overconfident /ˌəʊvəˈkɒnfɪd(ə)nt/ *adj.* excessively confident. □□ **overconfidence** *n.* **overconfidently** *adv.*

overcook /ˌəʊvəˈkʊk/ *v.tr.* cook too much or for too long. □□ **overcooked** *adj.*

overcritical /ˌəʊvəˈkrɪtɪk(ə)l/ *adj.* excessively critical; quick to find fault.

overcrop /ˌəʊvəˈkrɒp/ *v.tr.* (**-cropped**, **-cropping**) exhaust (the land) by the continuous growing of crops.

overcrowd /ˌəʊvəˈkraʊd/ *v.tr.* fill (a space, object, etc.) beyond what is usual or comfortable. □□ **overcrowding** *n.*

over-curious /ˌəʊvəˈkjʊərɪəs/ *adj.* excessively curious. □□ **over-curiosity** /ˌəʊvəˌkjʊərɪˈɒsɪtɪ/ *n.* **over-curiously** *adv.*

over-delicate /ˌəʊvəˈdelɪkət/ *adj.* excessively delicate. □□ **over-delicacy** *n.*

overdevelop /ˌəʊvədɪˈveləp/ *v.tr.* (**-developed**, **-developing**) **1** develop too much. **2** *Photog.* treat with developer for too long.

overdo /ˌəʊvəˈduː/ *v.tr.* (*3rd sing. present* **-does**; *past* **-did**; *past part.* **-done**) **1** carry to excess, go too far, exaggerate (*I think you overdid the sarcasm*). **2** (esp. as **overdone** *adj.*) overcook. □**overdo it** (or **things**) exhaust oneself. [OE *oferdōn* (as OVER-, DO¹)]

overdose /ˈəʊvəˌdəʊs/ *n.* & *v.* —*n.* an excessive dose (of a drug etc.). —*v.tr.* give an excessive dose of (a drug etc.) or to (a person). □□ **overdosage** /ˌəʊvəˈdəʊsɪdʒ/ *n.*

overdraft /ˈəʊvəˌdrɑːft/ *n.* **1** a deficit in a bank account caused by drawing more money than is credited to it. **2** the amount of this.

overdraw /ˌəʊvəˈdrɔː/ *v.* (*past* **-drew**; *past part.* **-drawn**) **1** *tr.* **a** draw a sum of money in excess of the amount credited to (one's bank account). **b** (as **overdrawn** *adj.*) having overdrawn one's account. **2** *intr.* overdraw one's account. **3** *tr.* exaggerate in describing or depicting. □□ **overdrawer** *n.* (in senses 1 & 2).

overdress *v.* & *n.* —*v.* /ˌəʊvəˈdres/ **1** *tr.* dress with too much display or formality. **2** *intr.* overdress oneself. —*n.* /ˈəʊvəˌdres/ a dress worn over another dress or a blouse etc.

overdrink /ˌəʊvəˈdrɪŋk/ *v.intr.* & *refl.* (*past* **-drank**; *past part.* **-drunk**) drink too much.

overdrive /ˈəʊvəˌdraɪv/ *n.* **1 a** a mechanism in a motor vehicle providing a gear ratio higher than that of the usual gear. **b** an additional speed-increasing gear. **2** (usu. prec. by *in*, *into*) a state of high or excessive activity.

overdub *v.* & *n.* —*v.tr.* /ˌəʊvəˈdʌb/ (**-dubbed**, **-dubbing**) (also *absol.*) impose (additional sounds) on an existing recording. —*n.* /ˈəʊvəˌdʌb/ the act or an instance of overdubbing.

overdue /ˌəʊvəˈdjuː/ *adj.* **1** past the time when due or ready. **2** not yet paid, arrived, born, etc., though after the expected time. **3** (of a library book etc.) retained longer than the period allowed.

overeager /ˌəʊvərˈiːgə(r)/ *adj.* excessively eager. □□ **overeagerly** *adv.* **overeagerness** *n.*

overeat /ˌəʊvərˈiːt/ *v.intr.* & *refl.* (*past* **-ate**; *past part.* **-eaten**) eat too much.

overelaborate /ˌəʊvərˈlæbərət/ *adj.* excessively elaborate. □□ **overelaborately** *adv.*

over-emotional /ˌəʊvərˈməʊʃən(ə)l/ *adj.* excessively emotional. □□ **over-emotionally** *adv.*

overemphasis /ˌəʊvərˈemfəsɪs/ *n.* excessive emphasis. □□ **overemphasize** /-fəˌsaɪz/ *v.tr.* & *intr.* (also **-ise**).

overenthusiasm /ˌəʊvərɪnˈθjuːzɪˌæz(ə)m, -ˈθuːzɪˌæz(ə)m/ *n.* excessive enthusiasm. □□

overenthusiastic /-'æstɪk/ *adj.*
overenthusiastically /-'æstɪkəlɪ/ *adv.*

overestimate /,əʊvər'estɪ,meɪt/ *v. & n.* —*v.tr.* (also *absol.*) form too high an estimate of (a person, ability, cost, etc.). —*n.* too high an estimate. □□ **overestimation** /-'meɪʃ(ə)n/ *n.*

overexcite /,əʊvərɪk'saɪt/ *v.tr.* excite excessively. □□ **overexcitement** *n.*

over-exercise /,əʊvər'eksə,saɪz/ *v. & n.* —*v.* **1** *tr.* use or exert (a part of the body, one's authority, etc.) too much. **2** *intr.* take too much exercise; overexert oneself. —*n.* excessive exercise.

overexert /,əʊvərɪg'zɜːt/ *v.tr. & refl.* exert too much. □□ **overexertion** /-ɪg'zɜːʃ(ə)n/ *n.*

overexpose /,əʊvərɪk'spəʊz/ *v.tr.* (also *absol.*) **1** expose too much, esp. to the public eye. **2** *Photog.* expose (film) for too long a time. □□ **overexposure** *n.*

overextend /,əʊvərɪk'stend/ *v.tr.* **1** extend (a thing) too far. **2** (also *refl.*) take on (oneself) or impose on (another person) an excessive burden of work.

overfall /'əʊvə,fɔːl/ *n.* **1** a turbulent stretch of sea etc. caused by a strong current or tide over a submarine ridge, or by a meeting of currents. **2** a place provided on a dam, weir, etc. for the overflow of surplus water.

overfamiliar /,əʊvəfə'mɪlɪə(r)/ *adj.* excessively familiar.

overfatigue /,əʊvəfə'tiːg/ *n.* excessive fatigue.

overfeed /,əʊvə'fiːd/ *v.tr.* (*past* and *past part.* **-fed**) feed excessively.

overfill /,əʊvə'fɪl/ *v.tr. & intr.* fill to excess or to overflowing.

overfine /,əʊvə'faɪn/ *adj.* excessively fine; too precise.

overfish /,əʊvə'fɪʃ/ *v.tr.* deplete (a stream etc.) by too much fishing.

overflow *v. & n.* —*v.* /,əʊvə'fləʊ/ **1** *tr.* **a** flow over (the brim, limits, etc.). **b** flow over the brim or limits of. **2** *intr.* **a** (of a receptacle etc.) be so full that the contents overflow it (*until the cup was overflowing*). **b** (of contents) overflow a container. **3** *tr.* (of a crowd etc.) extend beyond the limits of (a room etc.). **4** *tr.* flood (a surface or area). **5** *intr.* (foll. by *with*) be full of. **6** *intr.* (of kindness, a harvest, etc.) be very abundant. —*n.* /'əʊvə,fləʊ/ (also *attrib.*) **1** what overflows or is superfluous (*mop up the overflow*; *put the overflow audience in another room*). **2** an instance of overflowing (*overflow occurs when both systems are run together*). **3** (esp. in a bath or sink) an outlet for excess water etc. **4** *Computing* the generation of a number having more digits than the assigned location. □ **overflow meeting** a meeting for those who cannot be accommodated at the main gathering. [OE *oferflōwan* (as OVER-, FLOW)]

overfly /,əʊvə'flaɪ/ *v.tr.* (**-flies**; *past* **-flew**; *past part.* **-flown**) fly over or beyond (a place or territory). □□ **overflight** /'əʊvə,flaɪt/ *n.*

overfold /'əʊvə,fəʊld/ *n.* a series of strata folded so that the middle part is upside down.

overfond /,əʊvə'fɒnd/ *adj.* (often foll. by *of*) having too great an affection or liking (for a person or thing) (*overfond of chocolate*; *an overfond parent*). □□ **overfondly** *adv.* **overfondness** *n.*

overfulfil /,əʊvəfʊl'fɪl/ *v.tr.* (US **-fulfill**) (**-fulfilled**, **-fulfilling**) fulfil (a plan, quota, etc.) beyond expectation or before the appointed time. □□ **overfulfilment** *n.*

overfull /,əʊvə'fʊl/ *adj.* filled excessively or to overflowing.

overgeneralize /,əʊvə'dʒenrə,laɪz/ *v.* (also **-ise**) **1** *intr.* draw general conclusions from inadequate data etc. **2** *intr.* argue more widely than is justified by the available evidence, by circumstances, etc. **3** *tr.* draw an over-general conclusion from (data, circumstances, etc.). □□ **overgeneralization** /-'zeɪʃ(ə)n/ *n.*

overgenerous /,əʊvə'dʒenərəs/ *adj.* excessively generous. □□ **overgenerously** *adv.*

overglaze /'əʊvə,gleɪz/ *n. & adj.* —*n.* **1** a second glaze applied to ceramic ware. **2** decoration on a glazed surface. —*adj.* (of painting etc.) done on a glazed surface.

overground /'əʊvə,graʊnd/ *adj.* **1** raised above the ground. **2** not underground.

overgrow /,əʊvə'grəʊ/ *v.tr.* (*past* **-grew**; *past part.* **-grown**) **1** (as **overgrown** *adj.* /,əʊvə'grəʊn, 'əʊvə,grəʊn/) **a** abnormally large (*a great overgrown child*). **b** wild; grown over with vegetation (*an overgrown pond*). **2** grow over, overspread, esp. so as to choke (*nettles have overgrown the pathway*). **3** grow too big for (one's strength etc.). □□ **overgrowth** *n.*

overhand /'əʊvə,hænd/ *adj. & adv.* **1** (in cricket, tennis, baseball, etc.) thrown or played with the hand above the shoulder. **2** *Swimming* = OVERARM. **3 a** with the palm of the hand downward or inward. **b** with the hand above the object held. □ **overhand knot** a simple knot made by forming a loop and passing the free end through it.

overhang *v. & n.* —*v.* /,əʊvə'hæŋ/ (*past* and *past part.* **-hung**) **1** *tr. & intr.* project or hang over. **2** *tr.* menace, preoccupy, threaten. —*n.* /'əʊvə,hæŋ/ **1** the overhanging part of a structure or rock-formation. **2** the amount by which this projects.

overhaste /,əʊvə'heɪst/ *n.* excessive haste. □□ **overhasty** *adj.* **overhastily** *adv.*

overhaul *v. & n.* —*v.tr.* /,əʊvə'hɔːl/ **1 a** take to pieces in order to examine. **b** examine the condition of (and repair if necessary). **2** overtake. —*n.* /'əʊvə,hɔːl/ a thorough examination, with repairs if necessary. [orig. Naut., = release (rope-tackle) by slackening]

overhead *adv., adj., & n.* —*adv.* /,əʊvə'hed/ **1** above one's head. **2** in the sky or in the storey above. —*adj.* /'əʊvəhed/ **1** (of a driving mechanism etc.) above the object driven. **2** (of expenses) arising from general running costs, as distinct from particular business transactions. —*n.* /'əʊvə,hed/ (in *pl.* or US in *sing.*) overhead expenses.

overhear /,əʊvə'hɪə(r)/ *v.tr.* (*past* and *past part.* **-heard**) (also *absol.*) hear as an eavesdropper or as an unperceived or unintentional listener.

overheat /,əʊvə'hiːt/ *v.* **1** *tr. & intr.* make or become too hot; heat to excess. **2** *tr.* (as **overheated** *adj.*) too passionate about a matter.

overindulge /,əʊvərɪn'dʌldʒ/ *v.tr. & intr.* indulge to excess. □□ **overindulgence** *n.* **overindulgent** *adj.*

overinsure /,əʊvərɪn'ʃʊə(r)/ *v.tr.* insure (property etc.) for more than its real value; insure excessively. □□ **overinsurance** *n.*

overissue /,əʊvər'ɪʃuː, -'ɪsjuː/ *v. & n.* —*v.tr.* (**-issues**, **-issued**, **-issuing**) issue (notes, shares, etc.) beyond the authorized amount, or the ability to pay. —*n.* the notes, shares, etc., or the amount so issued.

overjoyed /,əʊvə'dʒɔɪd/ *adj.* (often foll. by *at, to hear*, etc.) filled with great joy.

overkill *n. & v.* —*n.* /'əʊvəkɪl/ **1** the amount by which destruction or the capacity for destruction exceeds what is necessary for victory or annihilation. **2** excess; excessive behaviour. —*v.tr. & intr.* /'əʊvəkɪl, ,əʊvə'kɪl/ kill or destroy to a greater extent than necessary.

overladen /,əʊvə'leɪd(ə)n/ *adj.* bearing or carrying too large a load.

overlaid *past* and *past part.* of OVERLAY[1].

overlain *past part.* of OVERLIE.

overland /'əʊvə,lænd/ *adj., adv., & v.* —*adj. & adv.* /also ,əʊvə'lænd/ **1** by land. **2** not by sea. —*v. Austral.* **1** *tr.* drive (livestock) overland. **2** *intr.* go a long distance overland.

overlander /'əʊvə,lændə(r)/ *n. Austral. & NZ* **1** a person who drives livestock overland. **2** *sl.* a tramp, a sundowner.

overlap *v. & n.* —*v.* /,əʊvə'læp/ (**-lapped**, **-lapping**) **1** *tr.* (of part of an object) partly cover (another object). **2** *tr.* cover and extend beyond. **3** *intr.* (of two things) partly coincide; not be completely separate (*where psychology and philosophy overlap*). —*n.* /'əʊvəˌlæp/ **1** an instance of overlapping. **2** the amount of this.

over-large /ˌəʊvə'lɑːdʒ/ *adj.* too large.

overlay[1] *v. & n.* —*v.tr.* /ˌəʊvə'leɪ/ (*past* and *past part.* **-laid**) **1** lay over. **2** (foll. by *with*) cover the surface of (a thing) with (a coating etc.). **3** overlie. —*n.* /'əʊvəˌleɪ/ **1** a thing laid over another. **2** (in printing, mapreading, etc.) a transparent sheet to be superimposed on another sheet. **3** *Computing* **a** the process of transferring a block of data etc. to replace what is already stored. **b** a section so transferred. **4** a coverlet, small tablecloth, etc.

overlay[2] *past* of OVERLIE.

overleaf /ˌəʊvə'liːf/ *adv.* on the other side of the leaf (of a book) (*see the diagram overleaf*).

overleap /ˌəʊvə'liːp/ *v.tr.* (*past* and *past part.* **-leaped** or **-leapt**) **1** leap over, surmount. **2** omit, ignore. [OE *oferhlēapan* (as OVER, LEAP)]

overlie /ˌəʊvə'laɪ/ *v.tr.* (**-lying**; *past* **-lay**; *past part.* **-lain**) **1** lie on top of. **2** smother (a child etc.) by lying on top.

overload *v. & n.* —*v.tr.* /ˌəʊvə'ləʊd/ load excessively; force (a person, thing, etc.) beyond normal or reasonable capacity. —*n.* /'əʊvəˌləʊd/ an excessive quantity; a demand etc. which surpasses capability or capacity.

over-long /ˌəʊvə'lɒŋ/ *adj. & adv.* too or excessively long.

overlook *v. & n.* —*v.tr.* /ˌəʊvə'lʊk/ **1** fail to notice; ignore, condone (an offence etc.). **2** have a view from above, be higher than. **3** supervise, oversee. **4** bewitch with the evil eye. —*n.* /'əʊvəˌlʊk/ *US* a commanding position or view. □□ **overlooker** /'əʊvəˌlʊkə(r)/ *n.*

overlord /'əʊvəˌlɔːd/ *n.* a supreme lord. □□ **overlordship** *n.*

overly /'əʊvəlɪ/ *adv.* esp. *US & Sc.* excessively; too.

overlying *pres. part.* of OVERLIE.

overman *v. & n.* —*v.tr.* /ˌəʊvə'mæn/ (**-manned**, **-manning**) provide with too large a crew, staff, etc. —*n.* /'əʊvəˌmæn/ (*pl.* **-men**) **1** an overseer in a colliery. **2** *Philos.* = SUPERMAN.

overmantel /'əʊvəˌmænt(ə)l/ *n.* ornamental shelves etc. over a mantelpiece.

over-many /ˌəʊvə'menɪ/ *adj.* too many; an excessive number.

overmaster /ˌəʊvə'mɑːstə(r)/ *v.tr.* master completely; conquer. □□ **overmastering** *adj.* **overmastery** *n.*

overmatch /ˌəʊvə'mætʃ/ *v.tr.* be more than a match for; defeat by superior strength etc.

overmeasure /'əʊvəˌmeʒə(r)/ *n.* an amount beyond what is proper or sufficient.

over-much /ˌəʊvə'mʌtʃ/ *adv. & adj.* —*adv.* to too great an extent; excessively. —*adj.* excessive; superabundant.

over-nice /ˌəʊvə'naɪs/ *adj.* excessively fussy, punctilious, particular, etc. □□ **over-niceness** *n.* **over-nicety** *n.*

overnight /ˌəʊvə'naɪt/ *adv. & adj.* —*adv.* **1** for the duration of a night (*stay overnight*). **2** during the course of a night. **3** suddenly, immediately (*the situation changed overnight*). —*adj.* **1** for use overnight (*an overnight bag*). **2** done etc. overnight (*an overnight stop*).

overnighter /ˌəʊvə'naɪtə(r)/ *n.* **1** a person who stops at a place overnight. **2** an overnight bag.

overpaid *past* and *past part.* of OVERPAY.

overparted /ˌəʊvə'pɑːtɪd/ *adj. Theatr.* having too demanding a part to play; cast beyond one's ability.

over-particular /ˌəʊvəpə'tɪkjʊlə(r)/ *adj.* excessively particular or fussy.

overpass *n. & v.* —*n.* /'əʊvəˌpɑːs/ a road or railway line that passes over another by means of a bridge. —*v.tr.* /ˌəʊvə'pɑːs/ **1** pass over or across or beyond. **2** get to the end of; surmount. **3** (as **overpassed** or **overpast** *adj.*) that has gone by, past.

overpay /ˌəʊvə'peɪ/ *v.tr.* (*past* and *past part.* **-paid**) recompense (a person, service, etc.) too highly. □□ **overpayment** *n.*

overpitch /ˌəʊvə'pɪtʃ/ *v.tr.* **1** *Cricket* bowl (a ball) so that it pitches or would pitch too near the stumps. **2** exaggerate.

overplay /ˌəʊvə'pleɪ/ *v.tr.* play (a part) to excess; give undue importance to; overemphasize. □ **overplay one's hand** be unduly optimistic about one's capabilities. **2** spoil a good case by exaggerating its value.

overplus /'əʊvəˌplʌs/ *n.* a surplus, a superabundance. [ME, partial transl. of AF *surplus* or med.L *su(pe)rplus*]

overpopulated /ˌəʊvə'pɒpjʊˌleɪtɪd/ *adj.* having too large a population. □□ **overpopulation** /-'leɪʃ(ə)n/ *n.*

overpower /ˌəʊvə'paʊə(r)/ *v.tr.* **1** reduce to submission, subdue. **2** make (a thing) ineffective or imperceptible by greater intensity. **3** (of heat, emotion, etc.) be too intense for, overwhelm. □□ **overpowering** *adj.* **overpoweringly** *adv.*

overprice /ˌəʊvə'praɪs/ *v.tr.* price (a thing) too highly.

overprint *v. & n.* —*v.tr.* /ˌəʊvə'prɪnt/ **1** print further matter on (a surface already printed, esp. a postage stamp). **2** print (further matter) in this way. **3** *Photog.* print (a positive) darker than was intended. **4** (also *absol.*) print too many copies of (a work). —*n.* /'əʊvəprɪnt/ **1** the words etc. overprinted. **2** an overprinted postage stamp.

overproduce /ˌəʊvəprə'djuːs/ *tr.* (usu. *absol.*) **1** produce more of (a commodity) than is wanted. **2** produce to an excessive degree. □□ **overproduction** *n.*

overproof /'əʊvəˌpruːf/ *adj.* containing more alcohol than proof spirit does.

overqualified /ˌəʊvə'kwɒlɪˌfaɪd/ *adj.* too highly qualified (esp. for a particular job etc.).

overran *past* of OVERRUN.

overrate /ˌəʊvə'reɪt/ *v.tr.* assess too highly.

overreach /ˌəʊvə'riːtʃ/ *v.tr.* circumvent, outwit; get the better of by cunning or artifice. □ **overreach oneself 1** strain oneself by reaching too far. **2** defeat one's object by going too far.

overreact /ˌəʊvərɪ'ækt/ *v.intr.* respond more forcibly etc. than is justified. □□ **overreaction** *n.*

overrefine /ˌəʊvərɪ'faɪn/ *v.tr.* (also *absol.*) **1** refine too much. **2** make too subtle distinctions in (an argument etc.).

override *v. & n.* —*v.tr.* /ˌəʊvə'raɪd/ (*past* **-rode**; *past part.* **-ridden**) **1** have or claim precedence or superiority over (*an overriding consideration*). **2 a** intervene and make ineffective. **b** interrupt the action of (an automatic device) esp. to take manual control. **3 a** trample down or underfoot. **b** supersede arrogantly. **4** extend over, esp. (of a part of a fractured bone) overlap (another part). **5** ride over (enemy country). **6** exhaust (a horse etc.) by hard riding. —*n.* /'əʊvəˌraɪd/ **1** the action or process of suspending an automatic function. **2** a device for this.

overrider /'əʊvəˌraɪdə(r)/ *n. Brit.* each of a pair of projecting pieces on the bumper of a car.

overripe /ˌəʊvə'raɪp/ *adj.* (esp. of fruit etc.) past its best; excessively ripe; full-blown.

overrode *past* of OVERRIDE.

overruff *v. & n.* —*v.tr.* /ˌəʊvə'rʌf/ (also *absol.*) overtrump. —*n.* /'əʊvəˌrʌf/ an instance of this.

overrule /ˌəʊvə'ruːl/ *v.tr.* **1** set aside (a decision, argument, proposal, etc.) by exercising a superior authority. **2** annul a decision by or reject a proposal of (a person) in this way.

overrun *v. & n.* —*v.tr.* /ˌəʊvə'rʌn/ (**-running**; *past* **-ran**; *past part.* **-run**) **1** (of vermin, weeds, etc.) swarm or spread over. **2** conquer or ravage (territory) by force. **3** (of time, expenditure, production, etc.) exceed (a fixed limit). **4** *Printing* carry over (a word etc.) to the next line or page. **5** *Mech.* rotate faster than. **6** flood (land). —*n.* /'əʊvə,rʌn/ **1** an instance of overrunning. **2** the amount of this. **3** the movement of a vehicle at a speed greater than is imparted by the engine. [OE *oferyrnan* (as OVER-, RUN)]

oversailing /,əʊvə'seɪlɪŋ/ *adj.* (of a part of a building) projecting beyond what is below. [OVER + F *saillir* SALLY¹]

oversaw *past* of OVERSEE.

overscrupulous /,əʊvə'skruːpjʊləs/ *adj.* excessively scrupulous or particular.

overseas *adv.* & *adj.* —*adv.* /,əʊvə'siːz/ (also **oversea**) abroad (*was sent overseas for training*; *came back from overseas*). —*adj.* /'əʊvə,siːz/ (also **oversea**) **1** foreign; across or beyond the sea. **2** of or connected with movement or transport over the sea (*overseas postage rates*).

oversee /,əʊvə'siː/ *v.tr.* (**-sees**; *past* **-saw**; *past part.* **-seen**) officially supervise (workers, work, etc.). [OE *ofersēon* look at from above (as OVER-, SEE¹)]

overseer /'əʊvə,siːə(r)/ *n.* a person who supervises others, esp. workers. □**overseer of the poor** *Brit. hist.* a parish official who administered funds to the poor. [OVERSEE]

oversell /,əʊvə'sel/ *v.tr.* (*past* and *past part.* **-sold**) (also *absol.*) **1** sell more of (a commodity etc.) than one can deliver. **2** exaggerate the merits of.

over-sensitive /,əʊvə'sensɪtɪv/ *adj.* excessively sensitive; easily hurt by, or too quick to react to, outside influences. □□**over-sensitiveness** *n.* **over-sensitivity** /-'tɪvɪtɪ/ *n.*

overset /,əʊvə'set/ *v.tr.* (**-setting**; *past* and *past part.* **-set**) **1** overturn, upset. **2** *Printing* set up (type) in excess of the available space.

oversew /'əʊvə,səʊ/ *v.tr.* (*past part.* **-sewn** or **-sewed**) **1** sew (two edges) with every stitch passing over the join. **2** join the sections of (a book) by a stitch of this type.

oversexed /,əʊvə'sekst/ *adj.* having unusually strong sexual desires.

overshadow /,əʊvə'ʃædəʊ/ *v.tr.* **1** appear much more prominent or important than. **2** cast into the shade; shelter from the sun. [OE *ofersceadwian* (as OVER-, SHADOW)]

overshoe /'əʊvə,ʃuː/ *n.* a shoe of rubber, felt, etc., worn over another as protection from wet, cold, etc.

overshoot *v.* & *n.* —*v.tr.* /,əʊvə'ʃuːt/ (*past* and *past part.* **-shot**) **1** pass or send beyond (a target or limit). **2** (of an aircraft) fly beyond or taxi too far along (the runway) when landing or taking off. —*n.* /'əʊvə,ʃuːt/ **1** the act of overshooting. **2** the amount of this. □**overshoot the mark** go beyond what is intended or proper; go too far. **overshot wheel** a waterwheel operated by the weight of water falling into buckets attached to its periphery.

overside /,əʊvə'saɪd/ *adv.* over the side of a ship (into a smaller boat, or into the sea).

oversight /'əʊvə,saɪt/ *n.* **1** a failure to notice something. **2** an inadvertent mistake. **3** supervision.

oversimplify /,əʊvə'sɪmplɪ,faɪ/ *v.tr.* (**-ies**, **-ied**) (also *absol.*) distort (a problem etc.) by stating it in too simple terms. □□**oversimplification** /-fɪ'keɪʃ(ə)n/ *n.*

oversize /'əʊvə,saɪz/ *adj.* (also **-sized** /-,saɪzd/) of more than the usual size.

overskirt /'əʊvə,skɜːt/ *n.* an outer or second skirt.

overslaugh /'əʊvə,slɔː/ *n.* & *v.* —*n. Brit. Mil.* the passing over of one's turn of duty. —*v.tr.* **1** *Brit. Mil.* pass over (one's duty) in consideration of another duty that takes precedence. **2** *US* pass over in favour of another. **3** *US* omit to consider. [Du. *overslag* (n.) f. *overslaan* omit (as OVER, *slaan* strike)]

oversleep /,əʊvə'sliːp/ *v.intr.* & *refl.* (*past* and *past part.* **-slept**) **1** continue sleeping beyond the intended time of waking. **2** sleep too long.

oversleeve /'əʊvə,sliːv/ *n.* a protective sleeve covering an ordinary sleeve.

oversold *past* and *past part.* of OVERSELL.

oversolicitous /,əʊvəsə'lɪsɪtəs/ *adj.* excessively worried, anxious, eager, etc. □□**oversolicitude** *n.*

oversoul /'əʊvə,səʊl/ *n.* God as a spirit animating the universe and including all human souls.

overspecialize /,əʊvə'speʃə,laɪz/ *v.intr.* (also **-ise**) concentrate too much on one aspect or area. □□**overspecialization** /-'zeɪʃ(ə)n/ *n.*

overspend /,əʊvə'spend/ *v.* (*past* and *past part.* **-spent**) **1** *intr.* & *refl.* spend too much. **2** *tr.* spend more than (a specified amount).

overspill /'əʊvə,spɪl/ *n.* **1** what is spilt over or overflows. **2** the surplus population leaving a country or city to live elsewhere.

overspread /,əʊvə'spred/ *v.tr.* (*past* and *past part.* **-spread**) **1** become spread or diffused over. **2** cover or occupy the surface of. **3** (as **overspread** *adj.*) (usu. foll. by *with*) covered (*high mountains overspread with trees*). [OE *ofersprædan* (as OVER-, SPREAD)]

overstaff /,əʊvə'stɑːf/ *v.tr.* provide with too large a staff.

overstate /,əʊvə'steɪt/ *v.tr.* **1** state (esp. a case or argument) too strongly. **2** exaggerate. □□**overstatement** *n.*

overstay /,əʊvə'steɪ/ *v.tr.* stay longer than (one's welcome, a time limit, etc.).

oversteer /'əʊvə,stɪə(r)/ *v.* & *n.* —*v.intr.* (of a motor vehicle) have a tendency to turn more sharply than was intended. —*n.* this tendency.

overstep /,əʊvə'step/ *v.tr.* (**-stepped**, **-stepping**) **1** pass beyond (a boundary or mark). **2** violate (certain standards of behaviour etc.).

overstock /,əʊvə'stɒk/ *v.tr.* stock excessively.

overstrain /,əʊvə'streɪn/ *v.tr.* strain too much.

overstress /,əʊvə'stres/ *v.* & *n.* —*v.tr.* stress too much. —*n.* an excessive degree of stress.

overstretch /,əʊvə'stretʃ/ *v.tr.* **1** stretch too much. **2** (esp. as **overstretched** *adj.*) make excessive demands on (resources, a person, etc.).

overstrung *adj.* **1** /,əʊvə'strʌŋ/ (of a person, disposition, etc.) intensely strained, highly strung. **2** /'əʊvə,strʌŋ/ (of a piano) with strings in sets crossing each other obliquely.

overstudy /,əʊvə'stʌdɪ/ *v.tr.* (**-ies**, **-ied**) **1** study beyond what is necessary or desirable. **2** (as **overstudied** *adj.*) excessively deliberate; affected.

overstuff /,əʊvə'stʌf/ *v.tr.* **1** stuff more than is necessary. **2** (as **overstuffed** *adj.*) (of furniture) made soft and comfortable by thick upholstery.

oversubscribe /,əʊvəsəb'skraɪb/ *v.tr.* (usu. as **oversubscribed** *adj.*) subscribe for more than the amount available of (a commodity offered for sale etc.) (*the offer was oversubscribed*).

oversubtle /,əʊvə'sʌt(ə)l/ *adj.* excessively subtle; not plain or clear.

oversupply /,əʊvəsə'plaɪ/ *v.* & *n.* —*v.tr.* (**-ies**, **-ied**) supply with too much. —*n.* an excessive supply.

oversusceptible /,əʊvəsə'septɪb(ə)l/ *adj.* too susceptible or vulnerable.

overt /əʊ'vɜːt, 'əʊvɜːt/ *adj.* unconcealed; done openly. □□**overtly** *adv.* **overtness** *n.* [ME f. OF past part. of *ovrir* open f. L *aperire*]

overtake /,əʊvə'teɪk/ *v.tr.* (*past* **-took**; *past part.* **-taken**) **1** (also *absol.*) catch up with and pass in the same direction. **2** (of a storm, misfortune, etc.) come suddenly or unexpectedly upon. **3** become level with and exceed (a compared value etc.).

overtask /,əʊvə'tɑːsk/ *v.tr.* **1** give too heavy a task to. **2** be too heavy a task for.

overtax /,əʊvə'tæks/ *v.tr.* **1** make excessive demands on (a person's strength etc.). **2** tax too heavily.

overthrow *v.* & *n.* —*v.tr.* /,əʊvə'θrəʊ/ (*past* **-threw**; *past part.* **-thrown**) **1** remove forcibly from power. **2** put an end to (an institution etc.). **3** conquer, overcome. **4** knock down, upset. —*n.* /'əʊvə,θrəʊ/ **1** a defeat or downfall. **2** *Cricket* **a** a fielder's return of the ball, not stopped near the wicket and so allowing further runs. **b** such a run. **3** *Archit.* a panel of decorated wrought-iron work in an arch or gateway.

overthrust /'əʊvə,θrʌst/ *n. Geol.* the thrust of esp.

overtime /'əʊvə,taɪm/ *n. & adv.* —*n.* **1** the time during which a person works at a job in addition to the regular hours. **2** payment for this. **3** *US Sport* = *extra time.* —*adv.* in addition to regular hours.

overtire /,əʊvə'taɪə(r)/ *v.tr. & refl.* exhaust or wear out (esp. an invalid etc.).

overtone /'əʊvə,təʊn/ *n.* **1** *Mus.* any of the tones above the lowest in a harmonic series. **2** a subtle or elusive quality or implication (*sinister overtones*). [OVER- + TONE, after G *Oberton*]

overtop /,əʊvə'tɒp/ *v.tr.* (**-topped, -topping**) **1** be or become higher than. **2** surpass.

overtrain /,əʊvə'treɪn/ *v.tr. & intr.* subject to or undergo too much (esp. athletic) training with a consequent loss of proficiency.

overtrick /'əʊvətrɪk/ *n. Bridge* a trick taken in excess of one's contract.

overtrump /,əʊvə'trʌmp/ *v.tr.* (also *absol.*) play a higher trump than (another player).

overture /'əʊvə,tjʊə(r)/ *n.* **1** an orchestral piece opening an opera etc. **2** a one-movement composition in this style. **3** (usu. in *pl.*) **a** an opening of negotiations. **b** a formal proposal or offer (esp. *make overtures to*). **4** the beginning of a poem etc. [ME f. OF f. L *apertura* APERTURE]

overturn *v. & n.* —*v.* /,əʊvə'tɜːn/ **1** *tr.* cause to fall down or over; upset. **2** *tr.* reverse; subvert; abolish; invalidate. **3** *intr.* fall down; fall over. —*n.* /'əʊvə,tɜːn/ a subversion, an act of upsetting.

overuse *v. & n.* —*v.tr.* /,əʊvə'juːz/ use too much. —*n.* /,əʊvə'juːs/ excessive use.

overvalue /,əʊvə'væljuː/ *v.tr.* (**-values, -valued, -valuing**) value too highly; have too high an opinion of.

overview /'əʊvə,vjuː/ *n.* a general survey.

overweening /,əʊvə'wiːnɪŋ/ *adj.* arrogant, presumptuous, conceited, self-confident. □□ **overweeningly** *adv.* **overweeningness** *n.*

overweight *adj., n., & v.* —*adj.* /,əʊvə'weɪt/ beyond an allowed or suitable weight. —*n.* /'əʊvə,weɪt/ excessive or extra weight; preponderance. —*v.tr.* /,əʊvə'weɪt/ (usu. foll. by *with*) load unduly.

overwhelm /,əʊvə'welm/ *v.tr.* **1** overpower with emotion. **2** (often foll. by *with*) overpower with an excess of business etc. **3** bring to sudden ruin or destruction; crush. **4** bury or drown beneath a huge mass, submerge utterly.

overwhelming /,əʊvə'welmɪŋ/ *adj.* irresistible by force of numbers, influence, amount, etc. □□ **overwhelmingly** *adv.* **overwhelmingness** *n.*

overwind *v. & n.* —*v.tr.* /,əʊvə'waɪnd/ (*past* and *past part.* **-wound**) wind (a mechanism, esp. a watch) beyond the proper stopping point. —*n.* /'əʊvə,waɪnd/ an instance of this.

overwinter /,əʊvə'wɪntə(r)/ *v.* **1** *intr.* (usu. foll. by *at, in*) spend the winter. **2** *intr.* (of insects, fungi, etc.) live through the winter. **3** *tr.* keep (animals, plants, etc.) alive through the winter.

overwork /,əʊvə'wɜːk/ *v. & n.* —*v.* **1** *intr.* work too hard. **2** *tr.* cause (another person) to work too hard. **3** *tr.* weary or exhaust with too much work. **4** *tr.* make excessive use of. —*n.* excessive work.

overwound *past* and *past part.* of OVERWIND.

overwrite /,əʊvə'raɪt/ *v.* (*past* **-wrote**; *past part.* **-written**) **1** *tr.* write on top of (other writing). **2** *tr. Computing* destroy (data) in (a file etc.) by entering new data. **3** *intr.* (esp. as **overwritten** *adj.*) write too elaborately or too ornately. **4** *intr. & refl.* write too much; exhaust oneself by writing. **5** *tr.* write too much about. **6** *intr.* (esp. as **overwriting** *n.*) in shipping insurance, accept more risk than the premium income limits allow.

overwrought /,əʊvə'rɔːt/ *adj.* **1** overexcited, nervous, distraught. **2** overdone; too elaborate.

overzealous /,əʊvə'zeləs/ *adj.* too zealous in one's

attitude, behaviour, etc.; excessively enthusiastic. □□ **overzeal** /-'ziːl/ *n.*

ovi-[1] /'əʊvɪ/ *comb. form* egg, ovum. [L *ovum* egg]

ovi-[2] /'əʊvɪ/ *comb. form* sheep. [L *ovis* sheep]

ovibovine /,əʊvɪ'bəʊvaɪn/ *adj. & n. Zool.* —*adj.* having characteristics intermediate between a sheep and an ox. —*n.* such an animal, e.g. a musk-ox.

oviduct /'əʊvɪ,dʌkt/ *n.* the tube through which an ovum passes from the ovary. □□ **oviducal** /-'djuːk(ə)l/ *adj.* **oviductal** /-'dʌkt(ə)l/ *adj.*

oviform /'əʊvɪ,fɔːm/ *adj.* egg-shaped.

ovine /'əʊvaɪn/ *adj.* of or like sheep. [LL *ovinus* f. L *ovis* sheep]

oviparous /əʊ'vɪpərəs/ *adj. Zool.* producing young by means of eggs expelled from the body before they are hatched (cf. VIVIPAROUS). □□ **oviparity** /-'pærɪtɪ/ *n.* **oviparously** *adv.*

oviposit /,əʊvɪ'pɒzɪt/ *v.intr.* (**oviposited, ovipositing**) lay an egg or eggs, esp. with an ovipositor. □□ **oviposition** /-pə'zɪʃ(ə)n/ *n.* [OVI-[1] + L *ponere posit-* to place]

ovipositor /,əʊvɪ'pɒzɪtə(r)/ *n.* a pointed tubular organ with which a female insect deposits her eggs. [mod.L f. OVI-[1] + L *positor* f. *ponere posit-* to place]

ovoid /'əʊvɔɪd/ *adj. & n.* —*adj.* **1** (of a solid or of a surface) egg-shaped. **2** oval, with one end more pointed than the other. —*n.* an ovoid body or surface. [F *ovoïde* f. mod.L *ovoides* (as OVUM)]

ovolo /'əʊvə,ləʊ/ *n.* (*pl.* **ovoli** /-,liː/) *Archit.* a rounded convex moulding. [It. dimin. of *ovo* egg f. L OVUM]

ovotestis /,əʊvə'testɪs/ *n.* (*pl.* **-testes** /-tiːz/) *Zool.* an organ producing both ova and spermatozoa. [OVUM + TESTIS]

ovoviviparous /,əʊvəʊvɪ'vɪpərəs/ *adj. Zool.* producing young by means of eggs hatched within the body (cf. OVIPAROUS, VIVIPAROUS). □□ **ovoviviparity** /-'pærɪtɪ/ *n.* [OVUM + VIVIPAROUS]

ovulate /'ɒvjʊ,leɪt/ *v.intr.* produce ova or ovules, or discharge them from the ovary. □□ **ovulation** /-'leɪʃ(ə)n/ *n.* **ovulatory** *adj.* [mod.L *ovulum* (as OVULE)]

ovule /'əʊvjuːl/ *n.* the part of the ovary of seed plants that contains the germ cell; an unfertilized seed. □□ **ovular** *adj.* [F f. med.L *ovulum*, dimin. of OVUM]

ovum /'əʊvəm/ *n.* (*pl.* **ova** /'əʊvə/) **1** a mature reproductive cell of female animals, produced by the ovary. **2** the egg cell of plants. [L, = egg]

ow /aʊ/ *int.* expressing sudden pain. [natural exclam.]

owe /əʊ/ *v.tr.* **1 a** be under obligation (to a person etc.) to pay or repay (money etc.) (*we owe you five pounds*; *owe more than I can pay*). **b** (*absol.*, usu. foll. by *for*) be in debt (*still owe for my car*). **2** (often foll. by *to*) render (gratitude etc., a person honour, gratitude, etc.) (*owe grateful thanks to*). **3** (usu. foll. by *to*) be indebted to a person or thing for (*we owe to Newton the principle of gravitation*). □ **owe a person a grudge** cherish resentment against a person. **owe it to oneself** (often foll. by *to* + infin.) need (to do) something to protect one's own interests. [OE *āgan* (see OUGHT[1]) f. Gmc]

owing /'əʊɪŋ/ *predic.adj.* **1** owed; yet to be paid (*the balance owing*). **2** (foll. by *to*) **a** caused by; attributable to (*the cancellation was owing to ill health*). **b** (as *prep.*) because of (*trains are delayed owing to bad weather*).

owl /aʊl/ *n.* **1** any nocturnal bird of prey of the order Strigiformes, with large eyes and a hooked beak, including barn owls, tawny owls, etc. **2** *colloq.* a person compared to an owl, esp. in looking solemn or wise. □ **owl-light** dusk, twilight. **owl-monkey** (*pl.* **-eys**) a douroucouli. □□ **owlery** *n.* (*pl.* **-ies**). **owlish** *adj.* **owlishly** *adv.* **owlishness** *n.* (in sense 2). **owl-like** *adj.* [OE *ūle* f. Gmc]

owlet /'aʊlɪt/ *n.* a small or young owl.

own /əʊn/ *adj. & v.* —*adj.* (prec. by possessive) **1 a** belonging to oneself or itself; not another's (*saw it with my own eyes*). **b** individual, peculiar, particular (*a charm all of its own*). **2** used to emphasize identity rather than possession (*cooks his own meals*). **3** (*absol.*) **a** private property (*is it your own?*). **b** kindred (*among my own*). —*v.* **1** *tr.* have as property; possess. **2 a** *tr.* confess; admit as valid, true, etc. (*own their faults*; *owns he did not know*). **b** *intr.* (foll. by *to*) confess to (*owned to a prejudice*). **3** *tr.* acknowledge paternity, authorship, or possession of. □**come into one's own 1** receive one's due. **2** achieve recognition. **get one's own back** (often foll. by *on*) *colloq.* get revenge. **hold one's own** maintain one's position; not be defeated or lose strength. **of one's own** belonging to oneself alone. **on one's own 1** alone. **2** independently, without help. **own brand** (often *attrib.*) goods manufactured specially for a retailer and bearing the retailer's name. **own goal 1** a goal scored (usu. by mistake) against the scorer's own side. **2** an act or initiative that has the unintended effect of harming one's own interests. **own up** (often foll. by *to*) confess frankly. □□**-owned** *adj.* (in *comb.*). [OE *āgen*, *āgnian*: see OWE]

owner /'əʊnə(r)/ *n.* **1** a person who owns something. **2** *sl.* the captain of a ship. □**owner-occupier** a person who owns the house etc. he or she lives in. □□**ownerless** *adj.* **ownership** *n.*

owt /aʊt/ *n. colloq.* or *dial.* anything. [var. of AUGHT¹]

ox /ɒks/ *n.* (*pl.* **oxen** /'ɒks(ə)n/) **1** any bovine animal, esp. a large usu. horned domesticated ruminant used for draught, for supplying milk, and for eating as meat. **2** a castrated male of a domesticated species of cattle, *Bos taurus*. □**ox-fence** a strong fence for keeping in cattle, consisting of railings, a hedge, and often a ditch. **ox-pecker** any African bird of the genus *Buphagus*, feeding on skin parasites living on animals. [OE *oxa* f. Gmc]

ox- var. of OXY-².

oxalic acid /ɒk'sælɪk/ *n. Chem.* a very poisonous and sour acid found in sorrel and rhubarb leaves. ¶ Chem. formula: (COOH)₂. □□**oxalate** /'ɒksəˌleɪt/ *n.* [F *oxalique* f. L *oxalis* f. Gk *oxalis* wood sorrel]

oxalis /'ɒksəlɪs/ *n.* any plant of the genus *Oxalis*, with trifoliate leaves and white or pink flowers. [L f. Gk f. *oxus* sour]

oxbow /'ɒksbəʊ/ *n.* **1** a U-shaped collar of an ox-yoke. **2 a** a loop formed by a horseshoe bend in a river. **b** a lake formed when the river cuts across the narrow end of the loop.

Oxbridge /'ɒksbrɪdʒ/ *n. Brit.* **1** (also *attrib.*) Oxford and Cambridge universities regarded together, esp. in contrast to newer institutions. **2** (often *attrib.*) the characteristics of these universities. [portmanteau word f. *Ox*(ford) + (*Cam*)*bridge*]

oxen *pl.* of ox.

oxer /'ɒksə(r)/ *n.* an ox-fence.

ox-eye /'ɒksaɪ/ *n.* a plant with a flower like the eye of an ox. □**ox-eye daisy** *n.* a daisy, *Leucanthemum vulgare*, having flowers with white petals and a yellow centre: also called *white ox-eye*. □□**ox-eyed** *adj.*

Oxf. *abbr.* Oxford.

Oxfam /'ɒksfæm/ *abbr.* Oxford Committee for Famine Relief.

Oxford bags /'ɒksfəd/ *n.* wide baggy trousers. [*Oxford* in S. England]

Oxford blue /'ɒksfəd/ *n.* & *adj.* —*n.* a dark blue, sometimes with a purple tinge. —*adj.* of this colour.

Oxford Group /'ɒksfəd/ *n.* a religious movement founded at Oxford in 1921, with discussion of personal problems by groups.

Oxford Movement /'ɒksfəd/ *n.* an Anglican High-Church movement started in Oxford in 1833, advocating traditional forms of worship.

oxherd /'ɒkshɜːd/ *n.* a cowherd.

oxhide /'ɒkshaɪd/ *n.* **1** the hide of an ox. **2** leather made from this.

oxidant /'ɒksɪd(ə)nt/ *n.* an oxidizing agent. □□ **oxidation** /-'deɪʃ(ə)n/ *n.* **oxidational** /-'deɪʃən(ə)l/ *adj.* **oxidative** /-ˌdeɪtɪv/ *adj.* [F, part. of *oxider* (as OXIDE)]

oxide /'ɒksaɪd/ *n.* a binary compound of oxygen. [F f. *oxygène* OXYGEN + -*ide* after *acide* ACID]

oxidize /'ɒksɪˌdaɪz/ *v.* (also -**ise**) **1** *intr.* & *tr.* combine or cause to combine with oxygen. **2** *tr.* & *intr.* cover (metal) or (of metal) become covered with a coating of oxide; make or become rusty. **3** *intr.* & *tr.* undergo or cause to undergo a loss of electrons. □**oxidized silver** the popular name for silver covered with a dark coat of silver sulphide. **oxidizing agent** *Chem.* a substance that brings about oxidation by being reduced and gaining electrons. □□**oxidizable** *adj.* **oxidization** /-'zeɪʃ(ə)n/ *n.* **oxidizer** *n.*

oxlip /'ɒkslɪp/ *n.* **1** a woodland primula, *Primula elatior*. **2** (in general use) a natural hybrid between a primrose and a cowslip.

Oxon. /'ɒks(ə)n/ *abbr.* **1** Oxfordshire. **2** of Oxford University or the diocese of Oxford. [abbr. of med.L *Oxoniensis* f. *Oxonia*: see OXONIAN]

Oxonian /ɒk'səʊnɪən/ *adj.* & *n.* —*adj.* of or relating to Oxford or Oxford University. —*n.* **1** a member of Oxford University. **2** a native or inhabitant of Oxford. [*Oxonia* Latinized name of *Ox*(*en*)*ford*]

oxtail /'ɒksteɪl/ *n.* the tail of an ox, often used in making soup.

oxter /'ɒkstə(r)/ *n. Sc.* & *N.Engl.* the armpit. [OE *ōhsta*, *ōxta*]

oxtongue /'ɒkstʌŋ/ *n.* **1** the tongue of an ox, esp. cooked as food. **2** any composite plant of the genus *Picris*, with bright yellow flowers.

oxy-¹ /'ɒksɪ/ *comb. form* denoting sharpness (*oxytone*). [Gk *oxu-* f. *oxus* sharp]

oxy-² /'ɒksɪ/ *comb. form* (also **ox-** /ɒks/) *Chem.* oxygen (*oxyacetylene*). [abbr.]

oxyacetylene /ˌɒksɪə'setɪˌliːn/ *adj.* of or using a mixture of oxygen and acetylene, esp. in cutting or welding metals (*oxyacetylene burner*).

oxyacid /'ɒksɪˌæsɪd/ *n. Chem.* an acid containing oxygen.

oxygen /'ɒksɪdʒ(ə)n/ *n. Chem.* a colourless tasteless odourless gaseous element, occurring naturally in air, water, and most minerals and organic substances, and essential to plant and animal life. ¶ Symb.: **O**. □**oxygen mask** a mask placed over the nose and mouth to supply oxygen for breathing. **oxygen tent** a tentlike enclosure supplying a patient with air rich in oxygen. □□ **oxygenous** /ɒk'sɪdʒɪnəs/ *adj.* [F *oxygène* acidifying principle (as OXY- 2): it was at first held to be the essential principle in the formation of acids]

oxygenate /'ɒksɪdʒəˌneɪt, ɒk'sɪ-/ *v.tr.* **1** supply, treat, or mix with oxygen; oxidize. **2** charge (blood) with oxygen by respiration. □□ **oxygenation** /-'neɪʃ(ə)n/ *n.* [F *oxygéner* (as OXYGEN)]

oxygenator /'ɒksɪdʒəˌneɪtə(r)/ *n.* an apparatus for oxygenating the blood.

oxygenize /'ɒksɪdʒəˌnaɪz, ɒk'sɪ-/ (also -**ise**) *v.tr.* = OXYGENATE.

oxyhaemoglobin /ˌɒksɪˌhiːmə'gləʊbɪn/ *n. Biochem.* a bright red complex formed when haemoglobin combines with oxygen.

oxymoron /ˌɒksɪ'mɔːrɒn/ *n. rhet.* a figure of speech in which apparently contradictory terms appear in conjunction (e.g. *faith unfaithful kept him falsely true*). [Gk *oxumōron* neut. of *oxumōros* pointedly foolish f. *oxus* sharp + *mōros* foolish]

oxytocin /ˌɒksɪ'təʊsɪn/ *n.* **1** a hormone released by the pituitary gland that causes increased contraction of the womb during labour and stimulates the ejection of milk into the ducts of the breasts. **2** a synthetic form of this used to induce labour etc. [*oxytocic* accelerating parturition f. Gk *oxutokia* sudden delivery (as OXY-¹, *tokos* childbirth)]

oxytone /'ɒksɪˌtəʊn/ *adj.* & *n.* —*adj.* (esp. in ancient Greek) having an acute accent on the last syllable. —*n.* a word of this kind. [Gk *oxutonos* (as OXY-¹, *tonos* tone)]

oyer and terminer /ˌɔɪə(r) ənd 'tɜːmɪnə(r)/ *n. hist.* a commission issued to judges on a circuit to hold courts. [ME f. AF *oyer et terminer* f. L *audire* hear + *et* and + *terminare* determine]

oyez /əʊˈjes, -ˈjez/ *int.* (also **oyes**) uttered, usu. three times, by a public crier or a court officer to command silence and attention. [ME f. AF, OF *oiez*, *oyez*, imper. pl. of *oïr* hear f. L *audire*]

oyster /ˈɔɪstə(r)/ *n.* **1** any of various bivalve molluscs of the family Ostreidae or Aviculidae, esp. an edible kind, *Ostrea edulus*, of European waters. **2** an oyster-shaped morsel of meat in a fowl's back. **3** something regarded as containing all that one desires (*the world is my oyster*). **4** (in full **oyster-white**) a white colour with a grey tinge. □**oyster-bank** (or **-bed**) a part of the sea-bottom where oysters breed or are bred. **oyster-catcher** any usu. coastal wading bird of the genus *Haematopus*, with a strong orange-coloured bill, feeding on shellfish. **oyster-farm** an area of the seabed used for breeding oysters. **oyster-plant 1** = SALSIFY. **2** a blue-flowered plant,

Mertensia maritima, growing on beaches. [ME & OF *oistre* f. L *ostrea*, *ostreum* f. Gk *ostreon*]

Oz /ɒz/ *n.* *Austral.* *sl.* Australia. [abbr.]

oz. *abbr.* ounce(s). [It. f. *onza* ounce]

ozocerite /əʊˈzəʊkəˌraɪt/ *n.* (also **ozokerite**) a wax-like fossil paraffin used for candles, insulation, etc. [G *Ozokerit* f. Gk *ozō* smell + *kēros* wax]

ozone /ˈəʊzəʊn/ *n.* **1** *Chem.* a colourless unstable gas with a pungent odour and powerful oxidizing properties, used for bleaching etc. ¶ Chem. formula: O_3. **2** *colloq.* **a** invigorating air at the seaside etc. **b** exhilarating influence. □**ozone-friendly** (of manufactured articles) containing chemicals that are not destructive to the ozone layer. **ozone layer** a layer of ozone in the stratosphere that absorbs most of the sun's ultraviolet radiation. □□ **ozonic** /əʊˈzɒnɪk/ *adj.* **ozonize** *v.tr.* (also **-ise**). **ozonization** /-ˈzeɪʃ(ə)n/ *n.* **ozonizer** *n.* [G *Ozon* f. Gk, neut. pres. part. of *ozō* smell]

Ozzie var. of AUSSIE.

P

P¹ /piː/ n. (also **p**) (pl. **Ps** or **P's**) the sixteenth letter of the alphabet.

P² abbr. (also **P.**) **1** (on road signs) parking. **2** Chess pawn. **3** Physics poise (unit). **4** (also Ⓟ) proprietary.

P³ symb. Chem. the element phosphorus.

p abbr. (also **p.**) **1** Brit. penny, pence. **2** page. **3** pico-. **4** piano (softly).

PA abbr. **1** personal assistant. **2** public address (esp. PA system). **3** Press Association. **4** US Pennsylvania (in official postal use).

Pa symb. Chem. the element protactinium.

pa /pɑː/ n. colloq. father. [abbr. of PAPA]

p.a. abbr. per annum.

pabulum /ˈpæbjʊləm/ n. food, esp. for the mind (mental pabulum). [L f. pascere feed]

PABX abbr. Brit. private automatic branch exchange.

paca /ˈpækə/ n. any tailless rodent of the genus Cuniculus, esp. the spotted cavy of S. and Central America. [Sp. & Port., f. Tupi]

pace¹ /peɪs/ n. & v. —n. **1 a** a single step in walking or running. **b** the distance covered in this (about 75 cm or 30 in.). **c** the distance between two successive stationary positions of the same foot in walking. **2** speed in walking or running. **3** Theatr. & Mus. speed or tempo in theatrical or musical performance (played with great pace). **4** a rate of progression. **5 a** a manner of walking or running; a gait. **b** any of various gaits, esp. of a trained horse etc. (rode at an ambling pace). —v. **1** intr. **a** walk (esp. repeatedly or methodically) with a slow or regular pace (pacing up and down). **b** (of a horse) = AMBLE. **2** tr. traverse by pacing. **3** tr. set the pace for (a rider, runner, etc.). **4** tr. (foll. by out) measure (a distance) by pacing. □keep pace (often foll. by with) advance at an equal rate (as). pace bowler Cricket a bowler who delivers the ball at high speed without spin. pace-setter **1** a leader. **2** = PACEMAKER 1. put a person through his (or her) paces test a person's qualities in action etc. set the pace determine the speed, esp. by leading. stand (or stay) the pace be able to keep up with others. □□ -paced adj. pacer n. [ME f. OF pas f. L passus f. pandere pass- stretch]

pace² /ˈpɑːtʃeɪ, ˈpeɪsɪ/ prep. (in stating a contrary opinion) with due deference to (the person named). [L, ablat. of pax peace]

pacemaker /ˈpeɪsˌmeɪkə(r)/ n. **1** a competitor who sets the pace in a race. **2** a natural or artificial device for stimulating the heart muscle and determining the rate of its contractions.

pacha var. of PASHA.

pachinko /pəˈtʃɪŋkəʊ/ n. a Japanese form of pinball. [Jap.]

pachisi /pəˈtʃiːzɪ/ n. a four-handed Indian board-game with six cowries used like dice. [Hindi, = of 25 (the highest throw)]

pachyderm /ˈpækɪˌdɜːm/ n. any thick-skinned mammal, esp. an elephant or rhinoceros. □□ **pachydermatous** /-ˈdɜːmətəs/ adj. [F pachyderme f. Gk pakhudermos f. pakhus thick + derma -matos skin]

pacific /pəˈsɪfɪk/ adj. & n. —adj. **1** characterized by or tending to peace; tranquil. **2** (**Pacific**) of or adjoining the Pacific. —n. (**the Pacific**) the generally placid expanse of ocean between America to the east and Asia to the west. □**Pacific Time** the standard time used in the Pacific region of Canada and the US. □□ **pacifically** adv. [F pacifique or L pacificus f. pax pacis peace]

pacification /ˌpæsɪfɪˈkeɪʃ(ə)n/ n. the act of pacifying

or the process of being pacified. □□ **pacificatory** /pəˈsɪfɪkətərɪ/ adj. [F f. L pacificatio -onis (as PACIFY)]

pacifier /ˈpæsɪˌfaɪə(r)/ n. **1** a person or thing that pacifies. **2** US a baby's dummy.

pacifism /ˈpæsɪˌfɪz(ə)m/ n. the belief that war and violence are morally unjustified and that all disputes can be settled by peaceful means. □□ **pacifist** n. & adj. [F pacifisme f. pacifier PACIFY]

pacify /ˈpæsɪˌfaɪ/ v.tr. (**-ies**, **-ied**) **1** appease (a person, anger, etc.). **2** bring (a country etc.) to a state of peace. [ME f. OF pacifier or L pacificare (as PACIFIC)]

pack¹ /pæk/ n. & v. —n. **1 a** a collection of things wrapped up or tied together for carrying. **b** = BACKPACK. **2** a set of items packaged for use or disposal together. **3** usu. derog. a lot or set (of similar things or persons) (a pack of lies; a pack of thieves). **4** Brit. a set of playing cards. **5 a** a group of hounds esp. for foxhunting. **b** a group of wild animals, esp. wolves, hunting together. **6** an organized group of Cub Scouts or Brownies. **7** Rugby Football a team's forwards. **8 a** a medicinal or cosmetic substance applied to the skin; = face-pack. **b** a hot or cold pad of absorbent material for treating a wound etc. **9** = pack ice. **10** a quantity of fish, fruit, etc., packed in a season etc. **11** Med. **a** the wrapping of a body or part of a body in a wet sheet etc. **b** a sheet etc. used for this. —v. **1** tr. (often foll. by up) **a** fill (a suitcase, bag, etc.) with clothes and other items. **b** put (things) together in a bag or suitcase, esp. for travelling. **2** intr. & tr. come or put closely together; crowd or cram (packed a lot into a few hours; passengers packed like sardines). **3** tr. (in passive; often foll. by with) be filled (with); contain extensively (the restaurant was packed; the book is packed with information). **4** tr. fill (a hall, theatre, etc.) with an audience etc. **5** tr. cover (a thing) with something pressed tightly round. **6** intr. be suitable for packing. **7** tr. colloq. **a** carry (a gun etc.). **b** be capable of delivering (a punch) with skill or force. **8** intr. (of animals or Rugby forwards) form a pack. □**pack-animal** an animal for carrying packs. **pack-drill** a military punishment of marching up and down carrying full equipment. **packed lunch** a lunch carried in a bag, box, etc., esp. to work, school, etc. **packed out** colloq. full, crowded. **pack ice** an area of large crowded pieces of floating ice in the sea. **pack it in** (or **up**) colloq. end or stop it. **pack off** send (a person) away, esp. abruptly or promptly. **pack-rat** US a large hoarding rodent. **pack-saddle** a saddle adapted for supporting packs. **pack up** colloq. **1** (esp. of a machine) stop functioning; break down. **2** retire from an activity, contest, etc. **send packing** colloq. dismiss (a person) summarily. □□ **packable** adj. [ME f. MDu., MLG pak, pakken, of unkn. orig.]

pack² /pæk/ v.tr. select (a jury etc.) or fill (a meeting) so as to secure a decision in one's favour. [prob. f. obs. verb pact f. PACT]

package /ˈpækɪdʒ/ n. & v. —n. **1 a** a bundle of things packed. **b** a parcel, box, etc., in which things are packed. **2** (in full **package deal**) a set of proposals or items offered or agreed to as a whole. **3** Computing a piece of software suitable for various applications rather than one which is custom-built. **4** colloq. = package holiday. —v.tr. make up into or enclose in a package. □**package holiday** (or **tour** etc.) a holiday or tour etc. with all arrangements made at an inclusive price. □□ **packager** n. [PACK¹ + -AGE]

packaging /ˈpækɪdʒɪŋ/ n. **1** a wrapping or container for goods. **2** the process of packing goods.

æ cat ɑː arm e bed ɜː her ɪ sit iː see ɒ hot ɔː saw ʌ run ʊ put uː too ə ago aɪ my

packer /'pækə(r)/ n. a person or thing that packs, esp. a dealer who prepares and packs food for transportation and sale.

packet /'pækɪt/ n. **1** a small package. **2** colloq. a large sum of money won, lost, or spent. **3** (in full **packet-boat**) hist. a mail-boat or passenger ship. [PACK¹ + -ET¹]

packhorse /'pækhɔːs/ n. a horse for carrying loads.

packing /'pækɪŋ/ n. **1** the act or process of packing. **2** material used as padding to pack esp. fragile articles. **3** material used to seal a join or assist in lubricating an axle. □**packing-case** a case (usu. wooden) or framework for packing goods in.

packthread /'pækθred/ n. stout thread for sewing or tying up packs.

pact /pækt/ n. an agreement or a treaty. [ME f. OF pact(e) f. L pactum, neut. past part. of pacisci agree]

pad¹ /pæd/ n. & v. —n. **1** a piece of soft material used to reduce friction or jarring, fill out hollows, hold or absorb liquid, etc. **2** a number of sheets of blank paper fastened together at one edge, for writing or drawing on. **3** = ink-pad. **4** the fleshy underpart of an animal's foot or of a human finger. **5** a guard for the leg and ankle in sports. **6** a flat surface for helicopter take-off or rocket-launching. **7** colloq. a lodging, esp. a bedsitter or flat. **8** the floating leaf of a water lily. —v.tr. (**padded, padding**) **1** provide with a pad or padding; stuff. **2** (foll. by out) lengthen or fill out (a book etc.) with unnecessary material. □**padded cell** a room with padded walls in a mental hospital. [prob. of LG or Du. orig.]

pad² /pæd/ v. & n. —v. (**padded, padding**) **1** intr. walk with a soft dull steady step. **2 a** tr. tramp along (a road etc.) on foot. **b** intr. travel on foot. —n. the sound of soft steady steps. [LG padden tread, pad PATH]

padding /'pædɪŋ/ n. soft material used to pad or stuff with.

paddle¹ /'pæd(ə)l/ n. & v. —n. **1** a short broad-bladed oar used without a rowlock. **2** a paddle-shaped instrument. **3** Zool. a fin or flipper. **4** each of the boards fitted round the circumference of a paddle-wheel or mill-wheel. **5** the action or a spell of paddling. —v. **1** intr. & tr. move on water or propel a boat by means of paddles. **2** intr. & tr. row gently. **3** tr. esp. US colloq. spank. □**paddle-boat** (or **-steamer** etc.) a boat, steamer, etc., propelled by a paddle-wheel. **paddle-wheel** a wheel for propelling a ship, with boards round the circumference so as to press backwards against the water. □□**paddler** n. [15th c.: orig. unkn.]

paddle² /'pæd(ə)l/ v. & n. —v.intr. walk barefoot or dabble the feet or hands in shallow water. —n. the action or a spell of paddling. □□**paddler** n. [prob. of LG or Du. orig.: cf. LG paddeln tramp about]

paddock /'pædək/ n. **1** a small field, esp. for keeping horses in. **2** a turf enclosure adjoining a racecourse where horses or cars are assembled before a race. **3** Austral. & NZ a field; a plot of land. [app. var. of (now dial.) parrock (OE pearruc): see PARK]

Paddy /'pædɪ/ n. (pl. **-ies**) colloq. often offens. an Irishman. [pet-form of the Irish name Padraig (= Patrick)]

paddy¹ /'pædɪ/ n. (pl. **-ies**) **1** (in full **paddy-field**) a field where rice is grown. **2** rice before threshing or in the husk. [Malay pādī]

paddy² /'pædɪ/ n. (pl. **-ies**) Brit. colloq. a rage; a fit of temper. [PADDY]

pademelon /'pædɪ,melən/ n. any small wallaby of the genus Thylogale, inhabiting the coastal scrub of Australia. [corrupt. of an Aboriginal name]

padlock /'pædlɒk/ n. & v. —n. a detachable lock hanging by a pivoted hook on the object fastened. —v.tr. secure with a padlock. [ME f. LOCK¹: first element unexpl.]

padouk /pə'duːk/ n. **1** any timber tree of the genus Pterocarpus, esp. P. indicus. **2** the wood of this tree, resembling rosewood. [Burmese]

padre /'pɑːdrɪ, -dreɪ/ n. a chaplain in any of the armed services. [It., Sp., & Port., = father, priest, f. L pater patris father]

padsaw /'pædsɔː/ n. a saw with a narrow blade, for cutting curves.

paean /'piːən/ n. (US **pean**) a song of praise or triumph. [L f. Doric Gk paian hymn of thanksgiving to Apollo (under the name of Paian)]

paederast var. of PEDERAST.

paederasty var. of PEDERASTY.

paediatrics /,piːdɪ'ætrɪks/ n.pl. (treated as sing.) (US **pediatrics**) the branch of medicine dealing with children and their diseases. □□**paediatric** adj. **paediatrician** /-ə'trɪʃ(ə)n/ n. [PAEDO- + Gk iatros physician]

paedo- /'piːdəʊ/ comb. form (US **pedo-**) child. [Gk pais paid- child]

paedophile /'piːdə,faɪl/ n. (US **pedophile**) a person who displays paedophilia.

paedophilia /,piːdə'fɪlɪə/ n. (US **pedophilia**) sexual desire directed towards children.

paella /paɪ'elə, pɑː-/ n. a Spanish dish of rice, saffron, chicken, seafood, etc., cooked and served in a large shallow pan. [Catalan f. OF paele f. L patella pan]

paeon /'piːən/ n. a metrical foot of one long syllable and three short syllables in any order. □□**paeonic** /piː'ɒnɪk/ adj. [L f. Gk paiōn, the Attic form of paian PAEAN]

paeony var. of PEONY.

pagan /'peɪgən/ n. & adj. —n. a person not subscribing to any of the main religions of the world, esp. formerly regarded by Christians as unenlightened or heathen. —adj. **1 a** of or relating to or associated with pagans. **b** irreligious. **2** identifying divinity or spirituality in nature; pantheistic. □□**paganish** adj. **paganism** n. **paganize** v.tr. & intr. (also **-ise**). [ME f. L paganus villager, rustic f. pagus country district: in Christian L = civilian, heathen]

page¹ /peɪdʒ/ n. & v. —n. **1 a** a leaf of a book, periodical, etc. **b** each side of this. **c** what is written or printed on this. **2 a** an episode that might fill a page in written history etc.; a record. **b** a memorable event. —v.tr. paginate. [F f. L pagina f. pangere fasten]

page² /peɪdʒ/ n. & v. —n. **1** a boy or man, usu. in livery, employed to run errands, attend to a door, etc. **2** a boy employed as a personal attendant of a person of rank, a bride, etc. **3** hist. a boy in training for knighthood and attached to a knight's service. —v.tr. **1** (in hotels, airports, etc.) summon by making an announcement or by sending a messenger. **2** summon by means of a pager. □**page-boy 1** = PAGE² n. 2. **2** a woman's hairstyle with the hair reaching to the shoulder and rolled under at the ends. [ME f. OF, perh. f. It. paggio f. Gk paidion, dimin. of pais paidos boy]

pageant /'pædʒ(ə)nt/ n. **1 a** a brilliant spectacle, esp. an elaborate parade. **b** a spectacular procession, or play performed in the open, illustrating historical events. **c** a tableau etc. on a fixed stage or moving vehicle. **2** an empty or specious show. [ME pagyn, of unkn. orig.]

pageantry /'pædʒəntrɪ/ n. (pl. **-ies**) **1** elaborate or sumptuous show or display. **2** an instance of this.

pager /'peɪdʒə(r)/ n. a radio device with a bleeper, activated from a central point to alert the person wearing it.

paginal /'pædʒɪn(ə)l/ adj. **1** of pages (of books etc.). **2** corresponding page for page. □□**paginary** adj. [LL paginalis (as PAGE¹)]

paginate /'pædʒɪ,neɪt/ v.tr. assign numbers to the pages of a book etc. □□**pagination** /-'neɪʃ(ə)n/ n. [F paginer f. L pagina PAGE¹]

pagoda /pə'gəʊdə/ n. **1** a Hindu or Buddhist temple or sacred building, esp. a many-tiered tower, in India and the Far East. **2** an ornamental imitation of this. □**pagoda-tree** any of various trees, esp. Sophora *japonica*, resembling a pagoda in shape. [Port. *pagode*, prob. ult. f. Pers. *butkada* idol temple]

pah /pɑː/ *int.* expressing disgust or contempt. [natural utterance]

Pahlavi /'pɑːləvɪ/ *n.* (also **Pehlevi** /'peɪləvɪ/) the writing system of Persia from the 2nd c. BC to the advent of Islam in the 7th c. AD. [Pers. *pahlawī* f. *pahlav* f. *parthava* Parthia]

paid *past* and *past part.* of PAY[1].

pail /peɪl/ *n.* **1** a bucket. **2** an amount contained in this. □□ **pailful** *n.* (*pl.* -**fuls**) [OE *pægel* gill (cf. MDu. *pegel* gauge), assoc. with OF *paelle*: see PAELLA]

paillasse var. of PALLIASSE.

paillette /pæ'ljet, paɪ'jet/ *n.* **1** a piece of bright metal used in enamel painting. **2** a spangle. [F, dimin. of *paille* f. L *palea* straw, chaff]

pain /peɪn/ *n.* & *v.* —*n.* **1 a** the range of unpleasant bodily sensations produced by illness or by harmful physical contact etc. **b** a particular kind or instance of this (often in *pl.*: *suffering from stomach pains*). **2** mental suffering or distress. **3** (in *pl.*) careful effort; trouble taken (*take pains*; *got nothing for my pains*). **4** (also **pain in the neck**) *colloq.* a troublesome person or thing; a nuisance. —*v.tr.* **1** cause pain to. **2** (as **pained** *adj.*) expressing pain (*a pained expression*). □ **in pain** suffering pain. **on** (or **under**) **pain of** with (death etc.) as the penalty. [ME f. OF *peine* f. L *poena* penalty]

painful /'peɪnfʊl/ *adj.* **1** causing bodily or mental pain or distress. **2** (esp. of part of the body) suffering pain. **3** causing trouble or difficulty; laborious (*a painful climb*). □□ **painfully** *adv.* **painfulness** *n.*

painkiller /'peɪn,kɪlə(r)/ *n.* a medicine or drug for alleviating pain. □□ **painkilling** *adj.*

painless /'peɪnlɪs/ *adj.* not causing or suffering pain. □□ **painlessly** *adv.* **painlessness** *n.*

painstaking /'peɪnz,teɪkɪŋ/ *adj.* careful, industrious, thorough. □□ **painstakingly** *adv.* **painstakingness** *n.*

paint /peɪnt/ *n.* & *v.* —*n.* **1 a** colouring matter, esp. in liquid form for imparting colour to a surface. **b** this as a dried film or coating (*the paint peeled off*). **2** *joc.* or *archaic* cosmetic make-up, esp. rouge or nail varnish. —*v.tr.* **1 a** cover the surface of (a wall, object, etc.) with paint. **b** apply paint of a specified colour to (*paint the door green*). **2** depict (an object, scene, etc.) with paint; produce (a picture) by painting. **3** describe vividly as if by painting (*painted a gloomy picture of the future*). **4** *joc.* or *archaic* **a** apply liquid or cosmetic to (the face, skin, etc.). **b** apply (a liquid to the skin etc.). □ **painted lady** an orange-red butterfly, esp. *Cynthia cardui*, with black and white spots. **paint out** efface with paint. **paint shop** the part of a factory where goods are painted, esp. by spraying. **paint-stick** a stick of water-soluble paint used like a crayon. **paint the town red** *colloq.* enjoy oneself flamboyantly. □□ **paintable** *adj.* [ME f. *peint* past part. of OF *peindre* f. L *pingere pict-* paint]

paintbox /'peɪntbɒks/ *n.* a box holding dry paints for painting pictures.

paintbrush /'peɪntbrʌʃ/ *n.* a brush for applying paint.

painter[1] /'peɪntə(r)/ *n.* a person who paints, esp. an artist or decorator. [ME f. OF *peintour* ult. f. L *pictor* (as PAINT)]

painter[2] /'peɪntə(r)/ *n.* a rope attached to the bow of a boat for tying it to a quay etc. [ME, prob. f. OF *penteur* rope from a masthead: cf. G *Pentertakel* f. *pentern* fish the anchor]

painterly /'peɪntəlɪ/ *adj.* **1 a** using paint well; artistic. **b** characteristic of a painter or paintings. **2** (of a painting) lacking clearly defined outlines.

painting /'peɪntɪŋ/ *n.* **1** the process or art of using paint. **2** a painted picture.

paintwork /'peɪntwɜːk/ *n.* **1** a painted surface or area in a building etc. **2** the work of painting.

painty /'peɪntɪ/ *adj.* (**paintier**, **paintiest**) **1** of or

covered in paint. **2** (of a picture etc.) overcharged with paint.

pair /peə(r)/ *n.* & *v.* —*n.* **1** a set of two persons or things used together or regarded as a unit (*a pair of gloves*; *a pair of eyes*). **2** an article (e.g. scissors, trousers, or pyjamas) consisting of two joined or corresponding parts not used separately. **3 a** an engaged or married couple. **b** a mated couple of animals. **4** two horses harnessed side by side (*a coach and pair*). **5** the second member of a pair in relation to the first (*cannot find its pair*). **6** two playing cards of the same denomination. **7** *Parl.* either or both of two MPs etc. on opposite sides absenting themselves from voting by mutual arrangement. —*v.tr.* & *intr.* **1** (often foll. by *off*) arrange or be arranged in couples. **2 a** join or be joined in marriage. **b** (of animals) mate. **3** *Parl.* form a pair. □ **in pairs** in twos. **pair production** *Physics* the conversion of a radiation quantum into an electron and a positron. **pair royal** a set of three cards of the same denomination. [ME f. OF *paire* f. L *paria* neut. pl. of *par* equal]

paisa /'paɪzə/ *n.* (*pl.* **paise** /-zeɪ or -zə/) a coin and monetary unit of India, Pakistan, Nepal, and Bangladesh, equal to one-hundredth of a rupee or taka. [Hindi]

Paisley /'peɪzlɪ/ *n.* (often *attrib.*) **1** a distinctive detailed pattern of curved feather-shaped figures. **2** a soft woollen garment having this pattern. [*Paisley* in Scotland]

pajamas *US* var. of PYJAMAS.

pakeha /'pɑːkɪ,hɑː/ *n.* *NZ* a White person as opposed to a Maori. [Maori]

Paki /'pækɪ/ *n.* (*pl.* **Pakis**) *Brit. sl. offens.* a Pakistani, esp. an immigrant in Britain. [abbr.]

Pakistani /,pɑːkɪ'stɑːnɪ, ,pækɪ-/ *n.* & *adj.* —*n.* **1** a native or national of Pakistan. **2** a person of Pakistani descent. —*adj.* of or relating to Pakistan. [Hindu]

pakora /pə'kɔːrə/ *n.* a piece of cauliflower, carrot, or other vegetable, coated in seasoned batter and deep-fried. [Hind.]

pal /pæl/ *n.* & *v.* —*n.* *colloq.* a friend, mate, or comrade. —*v.intr.* (**palled**, **palling**) (usu. foll. by *up*) associate; form a friendship. [Romany = brother, mate, ult. f. Skr. *bhrātr* BROTHER]

palace /'pælɪs/ *n.* **1** the official residence of a sovereign, president, archbishop, or bishop. **2** a splendid mansion; a spacious building. □ **palace revolution** (or **coup**) the (usu. non-violent) overthrow of a sovereign, government, etc. at the hands of senior officials. [ME f. OF *palais* f. L *Palatium* Palatine (hill) in Rome where the house of the emperor was situated]

paladin /'pælədɪn/ *n.* *hist.* **1** any of the twelve peers of Charlemagne's court, of whom the Count Palatine was the chief. **2** a knight errant; a champion. [F *paladin* f. It. *paladino* f. L *palatinus*: see PALATINE[1]]

Palaearctic /,pælɪ'ɑːktɪk/ *adj.* *Zool.* of the Arctic and temperate parts of the old world. [PALAEO- + ARCTIC]

palaeo- /'pælɪəʊ, 'peɪlɪəʊ/ *comb. form* (*US* **paleo-**) ancient, old; of ancient (esp. prehistoric) times. [Gk *palaios* ancient]

palaeobotany /,pælɪəʊ'bɒtənɪ/ *n.* the study of fossil plants.

Palaeocene /'pælɪə,siːn/ *adj.* & *n.* (*US* **Paleocene**) *Geol.* —*adj.* of or relating to the earliest epoch of the Tertiary period with evidence of the emergence and development of mammals. —*n.* this epoch or system. ¶ Cf. Appendix II. [PALAEO- + Gk *kainos* new]

palaeoclimatology /,pælɪəʊ,klaɪmə'tɒlədʒɪ, ,peɪlɪəʊ-/ *n.* (*US* **paleoclimatology**) the study of the climate in geologically past times.

palaeogeography /,pælɪəʊdʒɪ'ɒgrəfɪ, ,peɪlɪəʊ-/ *n.* (*US* **paleogeography**) the study of the geographical features at periods in the geological past.

palaeography /,pælɪ'ɒgrəfɪ/ *n.* (*US* **paleography**) the study of writing and documents from the past. □□ **palaeographer** *n.* **palaeographic** /-ə'græfɪk/

palaeographical /-ə'græfɪk(ə)l/ *adj.* **palaeographically** /-ə'græfɪkəlɪ/ *adv.* [F *paléographie* f. mod.L *palaeographia* (as PALAEO-, -GRAPHY)]

palaeolithic /ˌpælɪəʊ'lɪθɪk/ *adj.* (*US* **paleolithic**) *Archaeol.* of or relating to the early part of the Stone Age. [PALAEO- + Gk *lithos* stone]

palaeomagnetism /ˌpælɪəʊ'mægnɪˌtɪz(ə)m/ *n.* (*US* **paleomagnetism**) the study of the magnetism remaining in rocks.

palaeontology /ˌpælɪɒn'tɒlədʒɪ, ˌpælɪ-/ *n.* (*US* **paleontology**) the study of life in the geological past. □□ **palaeontological** /-tə'lɒdʒɪkəl/ *adj.* **palaeontologist** *n.* [PALAEO- + Gk *onta* neut. pl. of *ōn* being, part. of *eimi* be + -LOGY]

Palaeozoic /ˌpælɪəʊ'zəʊɪk/ *adj.* & *n.* (also **Paleozoic**) *Geol.* —*adj.* of or relating to an era of geological time marked by the appearance of marine and terrestrial plants and animals, esp. invertebrates. Cf. Appendix II. —*n.* this era (cf. CENOZOIC, MESOZOIC). [PALAEO- + Gk *zōē* life, *zōos* living]

palaestra /pə'li:strə, -'laɪstrə/ *n.* (also **palestra** /-'lestrə/) *Gk* & *Rom. Antiq.* a wrestling-school or gymnasium. [ME f. L *palaestra* f. Gk *palaistra* f. *palaiō* wrestle]

palais /'pæleɪ/ *n. colloq.* a public hall for dancing. [F *palais* (*de danse*) (dancing hall)]

palanquin /ˌpælən'ki:n/ *n.* (also **palankeen**) (in India and the East) a covered litter for one passenger. [Port. *palanquim*: cf. Hindi *pālkī* f. Skr. *palyanka* bed, couch]

palatable /'pælətəb(ə)l/ *adj.* **1** pleasant to taste. **2** (of an idea, suggestion, etc.) acceptable, satisfactory. □□ **palatability** /-'bɪlɪtɪ/ *n.* **palatableness** *n.* **palatably** *adv.*

palatal /'pælət(ə)l/ *adj.* & *n.* —*adj.* **1** of the palate. **2** (of a sound) made by placing the surface of the tongue against the hard palate (e.g. *y* in *yes*). —*n.* a palatal sound. □□ **palatalize** *v.tr.* (also **-ise**). **palatalization** /-'zeɪʃ(ə)n/ *n.* **palatally** *adv.* [F (as PALATE)]

palate /'pælət/ *n.* **1** a structure closing the upper part of the mouth cavity in vertebrates. **2** the sense of taste. **3** a mental taste or inclination; liking. [ME f. L *palatum*]

palatial /pə'leɪʃ(ə)l/ *adj.* (of a building) like a palace, esp. spacious and splendid. □□ **palatially** *adv.* [L (as PALACE)]

palatinate /pə'lætɪˌneɪt/ *n.* territory under the jurisdiction of a count Palatine.

palatine[1] /'pæləˌtaɪn/ *adj.* (also **Palatine**) *hist.* **1** (of an official or feudal lord) having local authority that elsewhere belongs only to a sovereign (*Count Palatine*). **2** (of a territory) subject to this authority. [ME f. F *palatin -ine* f. L *palatinus* of the PALACE]

palatine[2] /'pæləˌtaɪn/ *adj.* & *n.* —*adj.* of or connected with the palate. —*n.* (in full **palatine bone**) each of two bones forming the hard palate. [F *palatin -ine* (as PALATE)]

palaver /pə'lɑːvə(r)/ *n.* & *v.* —*n.* **1** fuss and bother, esp. prolonged and tedious. **2** profuse or idle talk. **3** cajolery. **4** *colloq.* an affair or business. **5** esp. *hist.* a parley between African or other natives and traders. —*v.* **1** *intr.* talk profusely. **2** *tr.* flatter, wheedle. [Port. *palavra* word f. L (as PARABLE)]

pale[1] /peɪl/ *adj.* & *v.* —*adj.* **1** (of a person or complexion) of a whitish or ashen appearance. **2 a** (of a colour) faint; not dark or deep. **b** faintly coloured. **3** of faint lustre; dim. —*v.* **1** *intr.* & *tr.* grow or make pale. **2** *intr.* (often foll. by *before, beside*) become feeble in comparison (with). □□ **palely** *adv.* **paleness** *n.* **palish** *adj.* [ME f. OF *pale, palir* f. L *pallidus* f. *pallēre* be pale]

pale[2] /peɪl/ *n.* **1** a pointed piece of wood for fencing etc.; a stake. **2** a boundary or enclosed area. **3** *Heraldry* a vertical stripe in the middle of a shield. □ **beyond the pale** outside the bounds of acceptable behaviour. **in pale** *Heraldry* arranged vertically. [ME f. OF *pal* f. L *palus* stake]

palea /'peɪlɪə/ *n.* (*pl.* **paleae** /-lɪˌiː/) *Bot.* a chafflike bract, esp. in a flower of grasses. [L, = chaff]

paled /peɪld/ *adj.* having palings.

paleface /'peɪlfeɪs/ *n.* a name supposedly used by the N. American Indians for the White man.

paleo- *comb. form US* var. of PALAEO-.

Paleocene *US* var. of PALAEOCENE.

Paleozoic *US* var. of PALAEOZOIC.

Palestinian /ˌpælɪ'stɪnɪən/ *adj.* & *n.* —*adj.* of or relating to Palestine, a region (in ancient and modern times) and former mandated territory on the E. Mediterranean coast. —*n.* **1** a native of Palestine in ancient or modern times. **2** an Arab, or a descendant of one, born or living in the area formerly called Palestine.

palestra var. of PALAESTRA.

palette /'pælɪt/ *n.* **1** a thin board or slab or other surface, usu. with a hole for the thumb, on which an artist lays and mixes colours. **2** the range of colours used by an artist. □ **palette-knife 1** a thin steel blade with a handle for mixing colours or applying or removing paint. **2** a kitchen knife with a long blunt round-ended flexible blade. [F, dimin. of *pale* shovel f. L *pala* spade]

palfrey /'pɔːlfrɪ/ *n.* (*pl.* **-eys**) *archaic* a horse for ordinary riding, esp. for women. [ME f. OF *palefrei* f. med.L *palefredus*, LL *paraveredus* f. Gk *para* beside, extra, + L *veredus* light horse, of Gaulish orig.]

Pali /'pɑːlɪ/ *n.* an Indic language used in the canonical books of Buddhists. [Skr. *pāli-bhāsā* f. *pāli* canon + *bhāsā* language]

palimony /'pælɪmənɪ/ *n.* esp. *US colloq.* an allowance made by one member of an unmarried couple to the other after separation. [PAL + ALIMONY]

palimpsest /'pælɪmpˌsest/ *n.* **1** a piece of writing-material or manuscript on which the original writing has been effaced to make room for other writing. **2** a monumental brass turned and re-engraved on the reverse side. [L *palimpsestus* f. Gk *palimpsēstos* f. *palin* again + *psēstos* rubbed smooth]

palindrome /'pælɪnˌdrəʊm/ *n.* a word or phrase that reads the same backwards as forwards (e.g. *rotator, nurses run*). □□ **palindromic** /-'drɒmɪk/ *adj.* **palindromist** *n.* [Gk *palindromos* running back again f. *palin* again + *drom-* run]

paling /'peɪlɪŋ/ *n.* **1** a fence of pales. **2** a pale.

palingenesis /ˌpælɪn'dʒenɪsɪs/ *n. Biol.* the exact reproduction of ancestral characteristics in ontogenesis. □□ **palingenetic** /-dʒə'netɪk/ *adj.* [Gk *palin* again + *genesis* birth, GENESIS]

palinode /'pælɪˌnəʊd/ *n.* **1** a poem in which the writer retracts a view or sentiment expressed in a former poem. **2** a recantation. [F *palinode* or LL *palinodia* f. Gk *palinōidia* f. *palin* again + *ōidē* song]

palisade /ˌpælɪ'seɪd/ *n.* & *v.* —*n.* **1 a** a fence of pales or iron railings. **b** a strong pointed wooden stake used in a close row for defence. **2** *US* (in *pl.*) a line of high cliffs. —*v.tr.* enclose or provide with a palisade. □ **palisade layer** *Bot.* a layer of elongated cells below the epidermis. [F *palissade* f. Prov. *palissada* f. *palissa* paling ult. f. L *palus* stake]

pall[1] /pɔːl/ *n.* **1** a cloth spread over a coffin, hearse, or tomb. **2** a shoulder-band with pendants, worn as an ecclesiastical vestment and sign of authority. **3** a dark covering (*a pall of darkness; a pall of smoke*). **4** *Heraldry* a Y-shaped bearing charged with crosses representing the front of an ecclesiastical pall. [OE *pæll*, f. L *pallium* cloak]

pall[2] /pɔːl/ *v.* **1** *intr.* (often foll. by *on*) become uninteresting (to). **2** *tr.* satiate, cloy. [ME, f. APPAL]

palladia *pl.* of PALLADIUM[2].

Palladian /pə'leɪdɪən/ *adj. Archit.* in the neoclassical style of Palladio. □□ **Palladianism** *n.* [A. *Palladio*, It. architect d. 1580]

palladium[1] /pə'leɪdɪəm/ *n. Chem.* a white ductile

metallic element occurring naturally in various ores and used in chemistry as a catalyst and for making jewellery. ¶ Symb.: **Pd**. [mod.L f. *Pallas*, an asteroid discovered (1803) just before the element, + -IUM; cf. CERIUM]

palladium[2] /pə'leɪdɪəm/ *n.* (*pl.* **palladia** /-dɪə/) a safeguard or source of protection. [ME f. L f. Gk *palladion* image of Pallas (Athene), a protecting deity]

pallbearer /'pɔːl‚beərə(r)/ *n.* a person helping to carry or officially escorting a coffin at a funeral.

pallet[1] /'pælɪt/ *n.* **1** a straw mattress. **2** a mean or makeshift bed. [ME *pailet, paillet* f. AF *paillete* straw f. OF *paille* f. L *palea*]

pallet[2] /'pælɪt/ *n.* **1** a flat wooden blade with a handle, used in ceramics to shape clay. **2** = PALETTE. **3** a portable platform for transporting and storing loads. **4** a projection transmitting motion from an escapement to a pendulum etc. **5** a projection on a machine-part, serving to change the mode of motion of a wheel. □□ **palletize** *v.tr.* (also **-ise**) (in sense 3). [F *palette*: see PALETTE]

pallia *pl.* of PALLIUM.

palliasse /'pælɪ‚æs/ *n.* (also **paillasse**) a straw mattress. [F *paillasse* f. It. *pagliaccio* ult. f. L *palea* straw]

palliate /'pælɪ‚eɪt/ *v.tr.* **1** alleviate (disease) without curing it. **2** excuse, extenuate. □□ **palliation** /-'eɪʃ(ə)n/ *n.* **palliator** *n.* [LL *palliare* to cloak f. *pallium* cloak]

palliative /'pælɪətɪv/ *n. & adj.* —*n.* anything used to alleviate pain, anxiety, etc. —*adj.* serving to alleviate. □□ **palliatively** *adv.* [F *palliatif -ive* or med.L *palliativus* (as PALLIATE)]

pallid /'pælɪd/ *adj.* pale, esp. from illness. □□ **pallidity** /-'lɪdɪtɪ/ *n.* **pallidly** *adv.* **pallidness** *n.* [L *pallidus* PALE[1]]

pallium /'pælɪəm/ *n.* (*pl.* **palliums** or **pallia** /-lɪə/) **1** an ecclesiastical pall, esp. that sent by the Pope to an archbishop as a symbol of authority. **2** *hist.* a man's large rectangular cloak esp. as worn in antiquity. **3** *Zool.* the mantle of a mollusc or brachiopod. [L]

pall-mall /pæl'mæl, pel'mel/ *n. hist.* a game in which a ball was driven through an iron ring suspended in a long alley. [obs. F *pallemaille* f. It. *pallamaglio* f. *palla* ball + *maglio* mallet]

pallor /'pælə(r)/ *n.* pallidness, paleness. [L f. *pallēre* be pale]

pally /'pælɪ/ *adj.* (**pallier, palliest**) *colloq.* like a pal; friendly.

palm[1] /pɑːm/ *n.* **1** any usu. tropical tree of the family Palmae, with no branches and a mass of large pinnate or fan-shaped leaves at the top. **2** the leaf of this tree as a symbol of victory. **3 a** supreme excellence. **b** a prize for this. **4** a branch of various trees used instead of a palm in non-tropical countries, esp. in celebrating Palm Sunday. □ **palm oil** oil from the fruit of any of various palms. **Palm Sunday** the Sunday before Easter, celebrating Christ's entry into Jerusalem. **palm wine** an alcoholic drink made from fermented palm sap. □□ **palmaceous** /pæl'meɪʃəs/ *adj.* [OE *palm(a)* f. Gmc f. L *palma* PALM[2], its leaf being likened to a spread hand]

palm[2] /pɑːm/ *n. & v.* —*n.* **1** the inner surface of the hand between the wrist and fingers. **2** the part of a glove that covers this. **3** the palmate part of an antler. —*v.tr.* conceal in the hand. □ **in the palm of one's hand** under one's control or influence. **palm off 1** (often foll. by *on*) **a** impose or thrust fraudulently (on a person). **b** cause a person to accept unwillingly or unknowingly (*palmed my old typewriter off on him*). **2** (often foll. by *with*) cause (a person) to accept unwillingly or unknowingly (*palmed him off with my old typewriter*). □□ **palmar** /'pælmə(r)/ *adj.* **palmed** *adj.* **palmful** *n.* (*pl.* **-fuls**). [ME *paume* f. OF *paume* f. L *palma*: later assim. to L]

palmate /'pælmeɪt/ *adj.* **1** shaped like an open hand.

2 having lobes etc. like spread fingers. [L *palmatus* (as PALM[2])]

palmer /'pɑːmə(r)/ *n.* **1** *hist.* **a** a pilgrim returning from the Holy Land with a palm branch or leaf. **b** an itinerant monk under a vow of poverty. **2** a hairy artificial fly used in angling. **3** (in full **palmer-worm**) a destructive hairy caterpillar of a European moth, *Euproctis chrysorrhoea*. [ME f. AF *palmer*, OF *palmier* f. med.L *palmarius* pilgrim]

palmette /pæl'met/ *n. Archaeol.* an ornament of radiating petals like a palm-leaf. [F, dimin. of *palme* PALM[1]]

palmetto /pæl'metəʊ/ *n.* (*pl.* **-os**) a small palm tree, e.g. any of various fan palms of the genus *Sabal* or *Chamaerops*. [Sp. *palmito*, dimin. of *palma* PALM[1], assim. to It. words in *-etto*]

palmiped /'pælmɪ‚ped/ *adj. & n.* (also **palmipede** /-‚piːd/) —*adj.* web-footed. —*n.* a web-footed bird. [L *palmipes -pedis* (as PALM[2], *pes pedis* foot)]

palmistry /'pɑːmɪstrɪ/ *n.* supposed divination from lines and other features on the palm of the hand. □□ **palmist** *n.* [ME (orig. *palmestry*) f. PALM[2]: second element unexpl.]

palmy /'pɑːmɪ/ *adj.* (**palmier, palmiest**) **1** of or like or abounding in palms. **2** triumphant, flourishing (*palmy days*).

palmyra /pæl'maɪərə/ *n.* an Asian palm, *Borassus flabellifer*, with fan-shaped leaves used for matting etc. [Port. *palmeira* palm-tree, assim. to *Palmyra* in Syria]

palomino /‚pælə'miːnəʊ/ *n.* (*pl.* **-os**) a golden or cream-coloured horse with a light-coloured mane and tail, orig. bred in the south-western US. [Amer. Sp. f. Sp. *palomino* young pigeon f. *paloma* dove f. L *palumba*]

paloverde /‚pæləʊ'vɜːdɪ/ *n.* any yellow-flowered thorny tree of the genus *Cercidium* in Arizona etc. [Amer. Sp., = green tree]

palp /pælp/ *n.* (also **palpus** /'pælpəs/) (*pl.* **palps** or **palpi** /-paɪ/) a segmented sense-organ at the mouth of an arthropod; a feeler. □□ **palpal** *adj.* [L *palpus* f. *palpare* feel]

palpable /'pælpəb(ə)l/ *adj.* **1** that can be touched or felt. **2** readily perceived by the senses or mind. □□ **palpability** /-'bɪlɪtɪ/ *n.* **palpably** *adv.* [ME f. LL *palpabilis* (as PALPATE)]

palpate /pæl'peɪt/ *v.tr.* examine (esp. medically) by touch. □□ **palpation** /-'peɪʃ(ə)n/ *n.* [L *palpare palpat-* touch gently]

palpebral /'pælpɪbr(ə)l/ *adj.* of or relating to the eyelids. [LL *palpebralis* f. L *palpebra* eyelid]

palpitate /'pælpɪ‚teɪt/ *v.intr.* **1** pulsate, throb. **2** tremble. □□ **palpitant** *adj.* [L *palpitare* frequent. of *palpare* touch gently]

palpitation /‚pælpɪ'teɪʃ(ə)n/ *n.* **1** throbbing, trembling. **2** (often in *pl.*) increased activity of the heart due to exertion, agitation, or disease. [L *palpitatio* (as PALPITATE)]

palpus var. of PALP.

palsgrave /'pɔːlzgreɪv/ *n.* a Count Palatine. [Du. *paltsgrave* f. *palts* palatinate + *grave* count]

palstave /'pɔːlsteɪv/ *n. Archaeol.* a type of chisel made of bronze etc. shaped to fit into a split handle. [Da. *paalstav* f. ON *pálstavr* f. *páll* hoe (cf. L *palus* stake) + *stafr* STAFF[1]]

palsy /'pɔːlzɪ, 'pɒl-/ *n. & v.* —*n.* (*pl.* **-ies**) **1** paralysis, esp. with involuntary tremors. **2 a** a condition of utter helplessness. **b** a cause of this. —*v.tr.* (**-ies, -ied**) **1** affect with palsy. **2** render helpless. [ME *pa(r)lesi* f. OF *paralisie* ult. f. L *paralysis*: see PARALYSIS]

palter /'pɔːltə(r), 'pɒl-/ *v.intr.* **1** haggle or equivocate. **2** trifle. □□ **palterer** *n.* [16th c.: orig. unkn.]

paltry /'pɔːltrɪ, 'pɒl-/ *adj.* (**paltrier, paltriest**) worthless, contemptible, trifling. □□ **paltriness** *n.* [16th c.: f. *paltry* trash app. f. *palt, pelt* rubbish + -RY (cf. *trumpery*): cf. LG *paltrig* ragged]

paludal /pə'ljuːd(ə)l, 'pæl-/ *adj.* **1** of a marsh. **2**

malarial. □□ **paludism** *n.* (in sense 2). [L *palus -udis* marsh + -AL]

paly /'peɪlɪ/ *adj. Heraldry* divided into equal vertical shapes. [OF *palé* f. *pal* PALE²]

palynology /ˌpælɪ'nɒlədʒɪ/ *n.* the study of pollen, spores, etc., for rock-dating and the study of past environments. □□ **palynological** /-nə'lɒdʒɪk(ə)l/ *adj.* **palynologist** *n.* [Gk *palunō* sprinkle + -LOGY]

pampas /'pæmpəs/ *n.pl.* large treeless plains in S. America. □**pampas-grass** a tall grass, *Cortaderia selloana*, from S. America, with silky flowering plumes. [Sp. f. Quechua *pampa* plain]

pamper /'pæmpə(r)/ *v.tr.* **1** overindulge (a person, taste, etc.), cosset. **2** spoil (a person) with luxury. □□ **pamperer** *n.* [ME, prob. of LG or Du. orig.]

pampero /pæm'peərəʊ/ *n.* (*pl.* -os) a strong cold SW wind in S. America, blowing from the Andes to the Atlantic. [Sp. (as PAMPAS)]

pamphlet /'pæmflɪt/ *n.* & *v.* —*n.* a small, usu. unbound booklet or leaflet containing information or a short treatise. —*v.tr.* (**pamphleted**, **pamphleting**) distribute pamphlets to. [ME f. *Pamphilet*, the familiar name of the 12th-c. Latin love poem *Pamphilus seu de Amore*]

pamphleteer /ˌpæmflɪ'tɪə(r)/ *n.* & *v.* —*n.* a writer of (esp. political) pamphlets. —*v.intr.* write pamphlets.

pan¹ /pæn/ *n.* & *v.* —*n.* **1 a** a vessel of metal, earthenware, or plastic, usu. broad and shallow, used for cooking and other domestic purposes. **b** the contents of this. **2** a panlike vessel in which substances are heated etc. **3** any similar shallow container such as the bowl of a pair of scales or that used for washing gravel etc. to separate gold. **4** *Brit.* the bowl of a lavatory. **5** part of the lock that held the priming in old guns. **6** a hollow in the ground (*salt-pan*). **7** a hard substratum of soil. **8** *US sl.* the face. —*v.* (**panned, panning**) **1** *tr. colloq.* criticize severely. **2 a** *tr.* (foll. by *off, out*) wash (gold-bearing gravel) in a pan. **b** *intr.* search for gold by panning gravel. **c** *intr.* (foll. by *out*) (of gravel) yield gold. □**pan out** (of an action etc.) turn out in a specified way. □□ **panful** *n.* (*pl.* -**fuls**). **panlike** *adj.* [OE *panne*, perh. ult. f. L *patina* dish]

pan² /pæn/ *v.* & *n.* —*v.* (**panned, panning**) **1** *tr.* swing (a cine-camera) horizontally to give a panoramic effect or to follow a moving object. **2** *intr.* (of a cine-camera) be moved in this way. —*n.* a panning movement. [abbr. of PANORAMA]

pan³ /pɑːn/ *n. Bot.* **1** a leaf of the betel. **2** this enclosing lime and areca-nut parings, chewed in India etc. [Hindi f. Skr. *parna* feather, leaf]

pan- /pæn/ *comb. form* **1** all; the whole of. **2** relating to the whole or all the parts of a continent, racial group, religion, etc. (*pan-American*; *pan-African*; *pan-Hellenic*; *pan-Anglican*). [Gk f. *pan* neut. of *pas* all]

panacea /ˌpænə'siːə/ *n.* a universal remedy. □□ **panacean** *adj.* [L f. Gk *panakeia* f. *panakēs* all-healing (as PAN-, *akos* remedy)]

panache /pə'næʃ/ *n.* **1** assertiveness or flamboyant confidence of style or manner. **2** *hist.* a tuft or plume of feathers, esp. as a head-dress or on a helmet. [F f. It. *pennacchio* f. LL *pinnaculum* dimin. of *pinna* feather]

panada /pə'nɑːdə/ *n.* **1** a thick paste of flour etc. **2** bread boiled to a pulp and flavoured. [Sp. ult. f. L *panis* bread]

panama /'pænəmɑː/ *n.* a hat of strawlike material made from the leaves of a pine-tree. [*Panama* in Central America]

Panamanian /ˌpænə'meɪnɪən/ *n.* & *adj.* —*n.* **1** a native or national of the Republic of Panama in Central America. **2** a person of Panamanian descent. —*adj.* of or relating to Panama.

panatella /ˌpænə'telə/ *n.* a long thin cigar. [Amer. Sp. *panatela*, = long thin biscuit f. It. *panatella* dimin. of *panata* (as PANADA)]

pancake /'pænkeɪk, 'pæŋ-/ *n.* & *v.* —*n.* **1** a thin flat

cake of batter usu. fried and turned in a pan and rolled up with a filling. **2** a flat cake of make-up etc. —*v.* **1** *intr.* make a pancake landing. **2** *tr.* cause (an aircraft) to pancake. □**flat as a pancake** completely flat. **Pancake Day** Shrove Tuesday (on which pancakes are traditionally eaten). **pancake landing** an emergency landing by an aircraft with its undercarriage still retracted, in which the pilot attempts to keep the aircraft in a horizontal position throughout. [ME f. PAN¹ + CAKE]

panchayat /pʌn'tʃaɪət/ *n.* a village council in India. [Hindi f. Skr. *pancha* five]

Panchen lama /'pæntʃ(ə)n ˌlɑːmə/ *n.* a Tibetan lama ranking next after the Dalai lama. [Tibetan *panchen* great learned one]

panchromatic /ˌpænkrəʊ'mætɪk/ *adj. Photog.* (of a film etc.) sensitive to all visible colours of the spectrum.

pancreas /'pæŋkrɪəs/ *n.* a gland near the stomach supplying the duodenum with digestive fluid and secreting insulin into the blood. □□ **pancreatic** /-'ætɪk/ *adj.* **pancreatitis** /-'taɪtɪs/ *n.* [mod.L f. Gk *pagkreas* (as PAN-, *kreas -atos* flesh)]

pancreatin /'pæŋkrɪətɪn/ *n.* a digestive extract containing pancreatic enzymes, prepared from animal pancreases.

panda /'pændə/ *n.* **1** (also **giant panda**) a large bearlike mammal, *Ailuropoda melanoleuca*, native to China and Tibet, having characteristic black and white markings. **2** (also **red panda**) a Himalayan racoon-like mammal, *Ailurus fulgens*, with reddish-brown fur and a long bushy tail. □**panda car** *Brit.* a police patrol car (orig. white with black stripes on the doors). [Nepali name]

pandect /'pændekt/ *n.* (usu. in *pl.*) **1** a complete body of laws. **2** *hist.* a compendium in 50 books of the Roman civil law made by order of Justinian in the 6th c. [F *pandecte* or L *pandecta pandectes* f. Gk *pandektēs* all-receiver (as PAN-, *dektēs* f. *dekhomai* receive)]

pandemic /pæn'demɪk/ *adj.* & *n.* —*adj.* (of a disease) prevalent over a whole country or the world. —*n.* a pandemic disease. [Gk *pandēmos* (as PAN-, *dēmos* people)]

pandemonium /ˌpændɪ'məʊnɪəm/ *n.* **1** uproar; utter confusion. **2** a scene of this. [mod.L (place of all demons in Milton's *Paradise Lost*) f. PAN- + Gk *daimōn* DEMON]

pander /'pændə(r)/ *v.* & *n.* —*v.intr.* (foll. by *to*) gratify or indulge a person, a desire or weakness, etc. —*n.* **1** a go-between in illicit love affairs; a procurer. **2** a person who encourages coarse desires. [*Pandare*, a character in Boccaccio and in Chaucer's *Troilus and Criseyde*, f. L *Pandarus* f. Gk *Pandaros*]

pandit var. of PUNDIT 1.

P. & O. *abbr.* Peninsular and Oriental Shipping Company (or Line).

Pandora's box /pæn'dɔːrəz/ *n.* a process that once activated will generate many unmanageable problems. [in Gk Mythol. the box from which the ills of mankind were released, Hope alone remaining: f. Gk *Pandōra* all-gifted (as PAN-, *dōron* gift)]

p. & p. *abbr. Brit.* postage and packing.

pane /peɪn/ *n.* **1** a single sheet of glass in a window or door. **2** a rectangular division of a chequered pattern etc. [ME f. OF *pan* f. L *pannus* piece of cloth]

panegyric /ˌpænɪ'dʒɪrɪk/ *n.* a laudatory discourse; a eulogy. □□ **panegyrical** *adj.* [F *panégyrique* f. L *panegyricus* f. Gk *panēgurikos* of public assembly (as PAN-, *ēguris* = *agora* assembly)]

panegyrize /'pænɪdʒɪˌraɪz/ *v.tr.* (also -**ise**) speak or write in praise of; eulogize. □□ **panegyrist** /-'dʒɪrɪst/ *n.* [Gk *panēgurizō* (as PANEGYRIC)]

panel /'pæn(ə)l/ *n.* & *v.* —*n.* **1 a** a distinct, usu. rectangular, section of a surface (e.g. of a wall, door, or vehicle). **b** a control panel (see CONTROL *n.* 5). **c** = *instrument panel*. **2** a strip of material as part of a garment. **3** a group of people forming a team in a broadcast game, discussion, etc. **4** *Brit. hist.* a list of medical practitioners registered in a district as accepting patients under the National Insurance Act. **5 a** a list of available jurors; a jury. **b** *Sc.* a person or persons accused of a crime. —*v.tr.* (**panelled, panelling;** *US* **paneled, paneling**) **1** fit or provide with panels. **2** cover or decorate with panels. □ **panel-beater** one whose job is to beat out the metal panels of motor vehicles. **panel game** a broadcast quiz etc. played by a panel. **panel heating** the heating of rooms by panels in the wall etc. containing the sources of heat. **panel pin** a thin nail with a very small head. **panel saw** a saw with small teeth for cutting thin wood for panels. **panel truck** *US* a small enclosed delivery truck. [ME & OF, = piece of cloth, ult. f. L *pannus*: see PANE]

panelling /ˈpænəlɪŋ/ *n.* (*US* **paneling**) **1** panelled work. **2** wood for making panels.

panellist /ˈpænəlɪst/ *n.* (*US* **panelist**) a member of a panel (esp. in broadcasting).

pang /pæŋ/ *n.* (often in *pl.*) a sudden sharp pain or painful emotion. [16th c.: var. of earlier *prange* pinching f. Gmc]

panga /ˈpæŋgə/ *n.* a bladed African tool like a machete. [native name in E. Africa]

pangolin /ˈpæŋgəlɪn/ *n.* any scaly anteater of the genus *Manis*, native to Asia and Africa, having a small head with elongated snout and tongue, and a tapering tail. [Malay *peng-gōling* roller (from its habit of rolling itself up)]

panhandle /ˈpænˌhænd(ə)l/ *n. & v. US* —*n.* a narrow strip of territory extending from one State into another. —*v.tr. & intr. colloq.* beg for money in the street. □□ **panhandler** *n.*

panic[1] /ˈpænɪk/ *n. & v.* —*n.* **1 a** sudden uncontrollable fear or alarm. **b** (*attrib.*) characterized or caused by panic (*panic buying*). **2** infectious apprehension or fright esp. in commercial dealings. —*v.tr. & intr.* (**panicked, panicking**) (often foll. by *into*) affect or be affected with panic (*was panicked into buying*). □ **panic button** a button for summoning help in an emergency. **panic-monger** a person who fosters a panic. **panic stations** a state of emergency. **panic-stricken** (or **-struck**) affected with panic; very apprehensive. □□ **panicky** *adj.* [F *panique* f. mod.L *panicus* f. Gk *panikos* f. *Pan* a rural god causing terror]

panic[2] /ˈpænɪk/ *n.* any grass of the genus *Panicum*, including millet and other cereals. [OE f. L *panicum* f. *panus* thread on bobbin, millet-ear f. Gk *pēnos* web]

panicle /ˈpænɪk(ə)l/ *n. Bot.* a loose branching cluster of flowers, as in oats. □□ **panicled** *adj.* [L *paniculum* dimin. of *panus* thread]

panjandrum /pænˈdʒændrəm/ *n.* **1** a mock title for an important person. **2** a pompous or pretentious official etc. [app. invented in nonsense verse by S. Foote 1755]

panne /pæn/ *n.* (in full **panne velvet**) a velvet-like fabric of silk or rayon with a flattened pile. [F]

pannier /ˈpænɪə(r)/ *n.* **1** a basket, esp. one of a pair carried by a beast of burden. **2** each of a pair of bags or boxes on either side of the rear wheel of a bicycle or motor cycle. **3** *hist.* **a** part of a skirt looped up round the hips. **b** a frame supporting this. [ME f. OF *panier* f. L *panarium* bread-basket f. *panis* bread]

pannikin /ˈpænɪkɪn/ *n. Brit.* **1** a small metal drinking-cup. **2** the contents of this. [PAN[1] + -KIN, after *cannikin*]

panoply /ˈpænəplɪ/ *n.* (*pl.* **-ies**) **1** a complete or splendid array. **2** a complete suit of armour. □□ **panoplied** *adj.* [F *panoplie* or mod.L *panoplia* full armour f. Gk (as PAN-, *oplia* f. *hopla* arms)]

panoptic /pænˈɒptɪk/ *adj.* showing or seeing the whole at one view. [Gk *panoptos* seen by all, *panoptēs* all-seeing]

panorama /ˌpænəˈrɑːmə/ *n.* **1** an unbroken view of a surrounding region. **2** a complete survey or presentation of a subject, sequence of events, etc. **3** a picture or photograph containing a wide view. **4** a continuous passing scene. □□ **panoramic** /-ˈræmɪk/ *adj.* **panoramically** /-ˈræmɪkəlɪ/ *adv.* [PAN- + Gk *horama* view f. *horaō* see]

pan-pipes /ˈpænpaɪps/ *n.pl.* a musical instrument orig. associated with the Greek rural god Pan, made of a series of short pipes graduated in length and fixed together with the mouthpieces in line.

pansy /ˈpænzɪ/ *n.* (*pl.* **-ies**) **1** any garden plant of the genus *Viola*, with flowers of various rich colours. **2** *colloq. derog.* **a** an effeminate man. **b** a male homosexual. [F *pensée* thought, pansy f. *penser* think f. L *pensare* frequent. of *pendere pens-* weigh]

pant /pænt/ *v. & n.* —*v.* **1** *intr.* breathe with short quick breaths. **2** *tr.* (often foll. by *out*) utter breathlessly. **3** *intr.* (often foll. by *for*) yearn or crave. **4** *intr.* (of the heart etc.) throb violently. —*n.* **1** a panting breath. **2** a throb. □□ **pantingly** *adv.* [ME f. OF *pantaisier* ult. f. Gk *phantasioō* cause to imagine (as FANTASY)]

pantalets /ˌpæntəˈlets/ *n.pl.* (also **pantalettes**) *hist.* **1** long underpants worn by women and girls in the 19th c., with a frill at the bottom of each leg. **2** women's cycling trousers. [dimin. of PANTALOON]

pantaloon /ˌpæntəˈluːn/ *n.* **1** (in *pl.*) **a** *hist.* men's close-fitting breeches fastened below the calf or at the foot. **b** esp. *US* trousers. **2** (**Pantaloon**) a character in Italian comedy wearing pantaloons (in sense 1a). [F *pantalon* f. It. *pantalone*, a character in Italian comedy]

pantechnicon /pænˈteknɪkən/ *n. Brit.* a large van for transporting furniture. [PAN- + TECHNIC orig. as the name of a bazaar and then a furniture warehouse]

pantheism /ˈpænθɪˌɪz(ə)m/ *n.* **1** the belief that God is identifiable with the forces of nature and with natural substances. **2** worship that admits or tolerates all gods. □□ **pantheist** *n.* **pantheistic** /-ˈɪstɪk/ *adj.* **pantheistical** /-ˈɪstɪk(ə)l/ *adj.* **pantheistically** /-ˈɪstɪkəlɪ/ *adv.* [PAN- + Gk *theos* god]

pantheon /ˈpænθɪən/ *n.* **1** a building in which illustrious dead are buried or have memorials. **2** the deities of a people collectively. **3** a temple dedicated to all the gods, esp. the circular one at Rome. [ME f. L f. Gk *pantheion* (as PAN-, *theion* holy f. *theos* god)]

panther /ˈpænθə(r)/ *n.* **1** a leopard, esp. with black fur. **2** *US* a puma. [ME f. OF *pantere* f. L *panthera* f. Gk *panthēr*]

pantie-girdle /ˈpæntɪˌɡɜːd(ə)l/ *n.* a woman's girdle with a crotch shaped like pants.

panties /ˈpæntɪz/ *n.pl. colloq.* short-legged or legless underpants worn by women and girls. [dimin. of PANTS]

pantihose /ˈpæntɪˌhəʊz/ *n.* (*US* **panty hose**) (usu. treated as *pl.*) women's tights. [PANTIES + HOSE]

pantile /ˈpæntaɪl/ *n.* a roof-tile curved to form an S-shaped section, fitted to overlap. [PAN[1] + TILE]

panto /ˈpæntəʊ/ *n.* (*pl.* **-os**) *Brit. colloq.* = PANTOMIME 1. [abbr.]

panto- /ˈpæntəʊ/ *comb. form* all, universal. [Gk *pas pantos* all]

pantograph /ˈpæntəˌɡrɑːf/ *n.* **1** *Art & Painting* an instrument for copying a plan or drawing etc. on a different scale by a system of jointed rods. **2** a jointed framework conveying a current to an electric vehicle from overhead wires. □□ **pantographic** /-ˈɡræfɪk/ *adj.* [PANTO- + Gk *-graphos* writing]

pantomime /ˈpæntəˌmaɪm/ *n.* **1** *Brit.* a theatrical entertainment based on a fairy tale, with music, topical jokes, etc., usu. produced about Christmas. **2** the use of gestures and facial expression to convey meaning, esp. in drama and dance. **3** *colloq.* an absurd or outrageous piece of behaviour. □□ **pantomimic** /-ˈmɪmɪk/ *adj.* [F *pantomime* or L *pantomimus* f. Gk *pantomimos* (as PANTO-, MIME)]

pantothenic acid /ˌpæntəˈθenɪk/ *n.* a vitamin of the B complex, found in rice, bran, and many other foods, and essential for the oxidation of fats and carbohydrates. [Gk *pantothen* from every side]

pantry /'pæntrɪ/ *n.* (*pl.* -ies) **1** a small room or cupboard in which crockery, cutlery, table linen, etc., are kept. **2** a larder. [ME f. AF *panetrie*, OF *paneterie* f. *panetier* baker ult. f. LL *panarius* bread-seller f. L *panis* bread]

pantryman /'pæntrɪmən/ *n.* (*pl.* -men) a butler or a butler's assistant.

pants /pænts/ *n.pl. colloq.* **1** *Brit.* underpants or knickers. **2** *US* trousers or slacks. □**bore** (or **scare** etc.) **the pants off** *colloq.* bore, scare, etc., to an intolerable degree. **pants** (or **pant**) **suit** esp. *US* a trouser suit. **with one's pants down** *colloq.* in an embarrassingly unprepared state. [abbr. of PANTALOONS]

panty hose *US* var. of PANTIHOSE.

panzer /'pæntsə(r), 'pænz-/ *n.* **1** (in *pl.*) armoured troops. **2** (*attrib.*) heavily armoured (*panzer division*). [G, = coat of mail]

pap[1] /pæp/ *n.* **1 a** soft or semi-liquid food for infants or invalids. **b** a mash or pulp. **2** light or trivial reading matter; nonsense. □□**pappy** *adj.* [ME prob. f. MLG, MDu. *pappe*, prob. ult. f. L *pappare* eat]

pap[2] /pæp/ *n. archaic* or *dial.* the nipple of a breast. [ME, of Scand. orig.: ult. imit. of sucking]

papa /pə'pɑ:/ *n. archaic* father (esp. as a child's word). [F f. LL f. Gk *papas*]

papabile /pə'pɑ:bɪˌleɪ/ *adj.* suitable for high office. [It., = suitable to be pope, f. L *papa* pope]

papacy /'peɪpəsɪ/ *n.* (*pl.* -ies) **1** a pope's office or tenure. **2** the papal system. [ME f. med.L *papatia* f. *papa* pope]

papain /pə'peɪɪn/ *n.* an enzyme obtained from unripe pawpaws, used to tenderize meat and as a food supplement to aid digestion. [PAPAYA + -IN]

papal /'peɪp(ə)l/ *adj.* of or relating to a pope or to the papacy. □**Papal States** *hist.* the temporal dominions belonging to the Pope, esp. in central Italy. □□ **papally** *adv.* [ME f. OF f. med.L *papalis* f. eccl.L *papa* POPE[1]]

paparazzo /ˌpæpə'rɑːtsəʊ/ *n.* (*pl.* **paparazzi** /-tsɪ/) a freelance photographer who pursues celebrities to get photographs of them. [It.]

papaverous /pə'peɪvərəs/ *adj.* like or related to the poppy. □□ **papaveraceous** /-'reɪʃəs/ *adj.* [L *papaver* poppy]

papaw var. of PAWPAW.

papaya /pə'paɪə/ *n.* = PAWPAW 1. [earlier form of PAWPAW]

paper /'peɪpə(r)/ *n. & v.* —*n.* **1** a material manufactured in thin sheets from the pulp of wood or other fibrous substances, used for writing or drawing or printing on, or as wrapping material etc. **2** (*attrib.*) **a** made of or using paper. **b** flimsy like paper. **3** = NEWSPAPER. **4 a** a document printed on paper. **b** (in *pl.*) documents attesting identity or credentials. **c** (in *pl.*) documents belonging to a person or relating to a matter. **5** *Commerce* **a** negotiable documents, e.g. bills of exchange. **b** (*attrib.*) recorded on paper though not existing (*paper profits*). **6 a** a set of questions to be answered at one session in an examination. **b** the written answers to these. **7** = WALLPAPER. **8** an essay or dissertation, esp. one read to a learned society or published in a learned journal. **9** a piece of paper, esp. as a wrapper etc. **10** *Theatr. sl.* free tickets or the people admitted by them (*the house is full of paper*). —*v.tr.* **1** apply paper to, esp. decorate (a wall etc.) with wallpaper. **2** (foll. by *over*) **a** cover (a hole or blemish) with paper. **b** disguise or try to hide (a fault etc.). **3** *Theatr. sl.* fill (a theatre) by giving free passes. □**on paper 1** in writing. **2** in theory; to judge from written or printed evidence. **paper-boy** (or **-girl**) a boy or girl who delivers or sells newspapers. **paper-chase** a cross-country run in which the runners follow a trail marked by torn-up paper. **paper-clip** a clip of bent wire or of plastic for holding several sheets of paper together.

paper-hanger a person who decorates with wallpaper, esp. professionally. **paper-knife** a blunt knife for opening letters etc. **paper-mill** a mill in which paper is made. **paper money** money in the form of banknotes. **paper mulberry** a small Asiatic tree, *Broussonetia papyrifera*, of the mulberry family, whose bark is used for making paper and cloth. **paper nautilus** see NAUTILUS 2. **paper round 1** a job of regularly delivering newspapers. **2** a route taken doing this. **paper tape** *Computing* tape made of paper, esp. that on which data or instructions are represented by means of holes punched in it, for conveying to a processor etc. **paper tiger** an apparently threatening, but ineffectual, person or thing. □□ **paperer** *n.* **paperless** *adj.* [ME f. AF *papir*, = OF *papier* f. L *papyrus*: see PAPYRUS]

paperback /'peɪpəˌbæk/ *adj. & n.* —*adj.* (of a book) bound in stiff paper not boards. —*n.* a paperback book.

paperweight /'peɪpəˌweɪt/ *n.* a small heavy object for keeping loose papers in place.

paperwork /'peɪpəˌwɜːk/ *n.* routine clerical or administrative work.

papery /'peɪpərɪ/ *adj.* like paper in thinness or texture.

papier mâché /ˌpæpjeɪ 'mæʃeɪ/ *n.* paper pulp used for moulding into boxes, trays, etc. [F, = chewed paper]

papilionaceous /pəˌpɪljə'neɪʃəs/ *adj.* (of a plant) with a corolla like a butterfly. [mod.L *papilionaceus* f. L *papilio -onis* butterfly]

papilla /pə'pɪlə/ *n.* (*pl.* **papillae** /-liː/) **1** a small nipple-like protuberance in a part or organ of the body. **2** *Bot.* a small fleshy projection on a plant. □□ **papillary** *adj.* **papillate** /'pæpɪˌleɪt/ *adj.* **papillose** /'pæpɪˌləʊs/ *adj.* [L, = nipple, dimin. of *papula*: see PAPULA]

papilloma /ˌpæpɪ'ləʊmə/ *n.* (*pl.* **papillomas** or **papillomata** /-mətə/) a wartlike usu. benign tumour.

papillon /pə'pɪljən/ *n.* **1** a toy dog of a breed with ears suggesting the form of a butterfly. **2** this breed. [F, = butterfly, f. L *papilio -onis*]

papist /'peɪpɪst/ *n. & adj.* often *derog.* —*n.* **1** a Roman Catholic. **2** *hist.* an advocate of papal supremacy. —*adj.* of or relating to Roman Catholics. □□ **papistic** /pə'pɪstɪk/ *adj.* **papistical** /pə'pɪstɪk(ə)l/ *adj.* **papistry** *n.* [F *papiste* or mod.L *papista* f. eccl.L *papa* POPE[1]]

papoose /pə'puːs/ *n.* a N. American Indian young child. [Algonquin]

pappus /'pæpəs/ *n.* (*pl.* **pappi** /-paɪ/) a group of hairs on the fruit of thistles, dandelions, etc. □□ **pappose** *adj.* [L f. Gk *pappos*]

paprika /'pæprɪkə, pə'priːkə/ *n.* **1** *Bot.* a red pepper. **2** a condiment made from it. [Magyar]

pap test /pæp/ *n.* a test done by a cervical smear. [abbr. of G. N. *Papanicolaou*, US scientist d. 1962]

papula /'pæpjʊlə/ *n.* (also **papule** /-pjuːl/) (*pl.* **papulae** /-ˌliː/) **1** a pimple. **2** a small fleshy projection on a plant. □□ **papular** *adj.* **papulose** *adj.* **papulous** *adj.* [L]

papyrology /ˌpæpɪ'rɒlədʒɪ/ *n.* the study of ancient papyri. □□ **papyrological** /-rə'lɒdʒɪk(ə)l/ *adj.* **papyrologist** *n.*

papyrus /pə'paɪərəs/ *n.* (*pl.* **papyri** /-raɪ/) **1** an aquatic plant, *Cyperus papyrus*, with dark green stems topped with fluffy inflorescences. **2 a** a writing-material prepared in ancient Egypt from the pithy stem of this. **b** a document written on this. [ME f. L *papyrus* f. Gk *papuros*]

par[1] /pɑː(r)/ *n.* **1** the average or normal amount, degree, condition, etc. (*feel below par*; *be up to par*). **2** equality; an equal status or footing (*on a par with*). **3** *Golf* the number of strokes a first-class player should normally require for a hole or course. **4** *Stock Exch.* the face value of stocks and shares etc. (*at par*). **5** (in full **par of exchange**) the recognized value of one country's currency in terms of another's. □**above** (or **below**) **par** *Stock Exch.* at a premium (or discount). **at par** *Stock Exch.* at face value. **par for the course** *colloq.* what is normal or expected in any given circumstances. [L (adj. & n.) = equal, equality]

par² /pɑ:(r)/ *n. Brit.* esp. *Journalism colloq.* paragraph. [abbr.]

par. *abbr.* (also **para.**) paragraph.

par- /pər, pær, pɑ:/ *prefix* var. of PARA-¹ before a vowel or *h*; (*paraldehyde*; *parody*; *parhelion*).

para /'pærə/ *n. colloq.* **1** a paratrooper. **2** a paragraph. [abbr.]

para-¹ /'pærə/ *prefix* (also **par-**) **1** beside (*para-military*). **2** beyond (*paranormal*). **3** *Chem.* **a** modification of (*paraldehyde*). **b** relating to diametrically opposite carbon atoms in a benzene ring (*paradichlorobenzene*). [from or after Gk *para-* f. *para* beside, past, beyond]

para-² /'pærə/ *comb. form* protect, ward off (*parachute*; *parasol*). [F f. It. f. L *parare* defend]

parabiosis /ˌpærəbaɪ'əʊsɪs/ *n. Biol.* the natural or artificial joining of two individuals. □□**parabiotic** /-'ɒtɪk/ *adj.* [mod.L, formed as PARA-¹ + Gk *biōsis* mode of life f. *bios* life]

parable /'pærəb(ə)l/ *n.* **1** a narrative of imagined events used to illustrate a moral or spiritual lesson. **2** an allegory. [ME f. OF *parabole* f. LL sense 'allegory, discourse' of L *parabola* comparison]

parabola /pə'ræbələ/ *n.* an open plane curve formed by the intersection of a cone with a plane parallel to its side, resembling the path of a projectile under the action of gravity. [mod.L f. Gk *parabolē* placing side by side, comparison (as PARA-¹, *bolē* a throw f. *ballō*)]

parabolic /ˌpærə'bɒlɪk/ *adj.* **1** of or expressed in a parable. **2** of or like a parabola. □□**parabolically** *adv.* [LL *parabolicus* f. Gk *parabolikos* (as PARABOLA)]

parabolical /ˌpærə'bɒlɪk(ə)l/ *adj.* = PARABOLIC 1.

paraboloid /pə'ræbəˌlɔɪd/ *n.* **1** (in full **paraboloid of revolution**) a solid generated by the rotation of a parabola about its axis of symmetry. **2** a solid having two or more non-parallel parabolic cross-sections. □□**paraboloidal** *adj.*

paracetamol /ˌpærə'setəˌmɒl, -'si:təˌmɒl/ *n.* **1** a drug used to reduce pain and relieve fever. **2** a tablet of this. [*para-acetyl*am*inophenol*]

parachronism /pə'rækrəˌnɪz(ə)m/ *n.* an error in chronology, esp. by assigning too late a date. [PARA-¹ + Gk *khronos* time, perh. after *anachronism*]

parachute /'pærəˌʃu:t/ *n. & v.* —*n.* **1** a rectangular or umbrella-shaped apparatus allowing a person or heavy object attached to it to descend slowly from a height, esp. from an aircraft, or to retard motion in other ways. **2** (*attrib.*) dropped or to be dropped by parachute (*parachute troops*; *parachute flare*). —*v.tr. & intr.* convey or descend by parachute. [F (as PARA-², CHUTE¹)]

parachutist /'pærəˌʃuːtɪst/ *n.* **1** a person who uses a parachute. **2** (in *pl.*) parachute troops.

Paraclete /'pærəˌkli:t/ *n.* in the Holy Spirit as advocate or counsellor (John 14:16, 26, etc.). [ME f. OF *paraclet* f. LL *paracletus* f. Gk *paraklētos* called in aid (as PARA-¹, *klētos* f. *kaleō* call)]

parade /pə'reɪd/ *n. & v.* —*n.* **1 a** a formal or ceremonial muster of troops for inspection. **b** = *parade-ground*. **2** a public procession. **3** ostentatious display (*made a parade of their wealth*). **4** a public square, promenade, or row of shops. —*v.* **1** *intr.* assemble for parade. **2 a** *tr.* march through (streets etc.) in procession. **b** *intr.* march ceremonially. **3** *tr.* display ostentatiously. □**on parade 1** taking part in a parade. **2** on display. **parade-ground** a place for the muster of troops. □□**parader** *n.* [F, = show, f. Sp. *parada* and It. *parata* ult. f. L *parare* prepare, furnish]

paradiddle /'pærəˌdɪd(ə)l/ *n.* a drum roll with alternate beating of sticks. [imit.]

paradigm /'pærəˌdaɪm/ *n.* an example or pattern, esp. a representative set of the inflections of a noun, verb, etc. □□**paradigmatic** /-dɪg'mætɪk/ *adj.* **paradigmatically** /-dɪg'mætɪkəlɪ/ *adv.* [LL *paradigma* f. Gk *paradeigma* f. *paradeiknumi* show side by side (as PARA-¹, *deiknumi* show)]

paradise /'pærəˌdaɪs/ *n.* **1** (in some religions) heaven as the ultimate abode of the just. **2** a place or state of complete happiness. **3** (in full **earthly paradise**) the abode of Adam and Eve in the biblical account of the Creation; the garden of Eden. □□**paradisaical** /-dɪ'seɪɪk(ə)l/ *adj.* **paradisal** /'pærəˌdaɪs(ə)l/ *adj.* **paradisiacal** /-dɪ'saɪək(ə)l/ *adj.* **paradisical** /-'dɪsɪk(ə)l/ *adj.* [ME f. OF *paradis* f. LL *paradisus* f. Gk *paradeisos* f. Avestan *pairidaēza* park]

parados /'pærəˌdɒs, -ˌdəʊ/ *n.* an elevation of earth behind a fortified place as a protection against attack from the rear, esp. a mound along the back of a trench. [F (as PARA-², *dos* back f. L *dorsum*)]

paradox /'pærəˌdɒks/ *n.* **1 a** a seemingly absurd or contradictory statement, even if actually well-founded. **b** a self-contradictory or essentially absurd statement. **2** a person or thing conflicting with a preconceived notion of what is reasonable or possible. **3** a paradoxical quality or character. [orig. = a statement contrary to accepted opinion, f. LL *paradoxum* f. Gk *paradoxon* neut. adj. (as PARA-¹, *doxa* opinion)]

paradoxical /ˌpærə'dɒksɪk(ə)l/ *adj.* **1** of or like or involving paradox. **2** fond of paradox. □□**paradoxically** *adv.*

paraffin /'pærəfɪn/ *n.* **1** an inflammable waxy or oily substance obtained by distillation from petroleum or shale, used in liquid form (also **paraffin oil**) esp. as a fuel. **2** *Chem.* = ALKANE. □**paraffin wax** paraffin in its solid form. [G (1830) f. L *parum* little + *affinis* related, from the small affinity it has for other substances]

paragoge /ˌpærə'gəʊdʒɪ/ *n.* the addition of a letter or syllable to a word in some contexts or as a language develops (e.g. *t* in *peasant*). □□**paragogic** /-'gɒdʒɪk/ *adj.* [LL f. Gk *paragōgē* derivation (as PARA-¹, *agōgē* f. *agō* lead)]

paragon /'pærəgən/ *n.* **1 a** a model of excellence. **b** a supremely excellent person or thing. **2** (foll. by *of*) a model (of virtue etc.). **3** a perfect diamond of 100 carats or more. [obs. F f. It. *paragone* touchstone, med.Gk *parakonē* whetstone]

paragraph /'pærəˌgrɑ:f/ *n. & v.* —*n.* **1** a distinct section of a piece of writing, beginning on a new usu. indented line. **2** a symbol (usu. ¶) used to mark a new paragraph, and also as a reference mark. **3** a short item in a newspaper, usu. of only one paragraph. —*v.tr.* arrange (a piece of writing) in paragraphs. □□**paragraphic** /-'græfɪk/ *adj.* [F *paragraphe* or med.L *paragraphus* f. Gk *paragraphos* short stroke marking a break in sense (as PARA-¹, *graphō* write)]

parakeet /'pærəˌkiːt/ *n.* (*US* also **parrakeet**) any of various small usu. long-tailed parrots. [OF *paroquet*, It. *parrocchetto*, Sp. *periquito*, perh. ult. f. dimin. of *Pierre* etc. Peter: cf. PARROT]

paralanguage /'pærəˌlæŋgwɪdʒ/ *n.* elements or factors in communication that are ancillary to language proper, e.g. intonation and gesture.

paraldehyde /pə'rældɪˌhaɪd/ *n.* a cyclic polymer of acetaldehyde, used as a narcotic and sedative. [PARA-¹ + ALDEHYDE]

paralegal /ˌpærə'liːg(ə)l/ *adj. & n.* esp. *US* —*adj.* of or relating to auxiliary aspects of the law. —*n.* a person trained in subsidiary legal matters. [PARA-¹ + LEGAL]

paralipomena /ˌpærəlɪ'pɒmɪnə/ *n.pl.* (also **-leipomena** /-laɪ'pɒmɪnə/) **1** things omitted from a work and added as a supplement. **2** *Bibl.* the books of Chronicles in the Old Testament, containing particulars omitted from Kings. [ME f. eccl.L f. Gk *paraleipomena* f. *paraleipō* omit (as PARA-¹, *leipō* leave)]

paralipsis /ˌpærəˈlɪpsɪs/ *n.* (also **-leipsis** /-ˈlaɪpsɪs/) (*pl.* **-ses** /-siːz/) *Rhet.* **1** the device of giving emphasis by professing to say little or nothing of a subject, as in *not to mention their unpaid debts of several millions.* **2** an instance of this. [LL f. Gk *paraleipsis* passing over (as PARA-¹, *leipsis* f. *leipō* leave)]

parallax /ˈpærəˌlæks/ *n.* **1** the apparent difference in the position or direction of an object caused when the observer's position is changed. **2** the angular amount of this. □□ **parallactic** /-ˈlæktɪk/ *adj.* [F *parallaxe* f. mod.L *parallaxis* f. Gk *parallaxis* change f. *parallassō* to alternate (as PARA-¹, *allassō* exchange f. *allos* other)]

parallel /ˈpærəˌlel/ *adj., n.,* & *v.* —*adj.* **1 a** (of lines or planes) side by side and having the same distance continuously between them. **b** (foll. by *to, with*) (of a line or plane) having this relation (to another). **2** (of circumstances etc.) precisely similar, analogous, or corresponding. **3 a** (of processes etc.) occurring or performed simultaneously. **b** *Computing* involving the simultaneous performance of operations. —*n.* **1** a person or thing precisely analogous or equal to another. **2** a comparison (*drew a parallel between the two situations*). **3** (in full **parallel of latitude**) *Geog.* **a** each of the imaginary parallel circles of constant latitude on the earth's surface. **b** a corresponding line on a map (*the 49th parallel*). **4** *Printing* two parallel lines (‖) as a reference mark. —*v.tr.* (**paralleled, paralleling**) **1** be parallel to; correspond to. **2** represent as similar; compare. **3** adduce as a parallel instance. □**in parallel** (of electric circuits) arranged so as to join at common points at each end. **parallel bars** a pair of parallel rails on posts for gymnastics. □□ **parallelism** *n.* [F *parallèle* f. L *parallelus* f. Gk *parallēlos* (as PARA-¹, *allēlos* one another)]

parallelepiped /ˌpærəlelˈepɪˌped, -ləˈpaɪpɪd/ *n.* *Geom.* a solid body of which each face is a parallelogram. [Gk *parallēlepipedon* (as PARALLEL, *epipedon* plane surface)]

parallelogram /ˌpærəˈleləˌgræm/ *n.* *Geom.* a four-sided plane rectilinear figure with opposite sides parallel. □**parallelogram of forces 1** a parallelogram illustrating the theorem that if two forces acting at a point are represented in magnitude and direction by two sides of a parallelogram meeting at that point, their resultant is represented by the diagonal drawn from that point. **2** this theorem. [F *parallélogramme* f. LL *parallelogrammum* f. Gk *parallēlogrammon* (as PARALLEL, *grammē* line)]

paralogism /pəˈræləˌdʒɪz(ə)m/ *n.* *Logic* **1** a fallacy. **2** illogical reasoning (esp. of which the reasoner is unconscious). □□ **paralogist** *n.* **paralogize** *v.intr.* (also **-ise**). [F *paralogisme* f. LL *paralogismus* f. Gk *paralogismos* f. *paralogizomai* reason falsely f. *paralogos* contrary to reason (as PARA-¹, *logos* reason)]

paralyse /ˈpærəˌlaɪz/ *n.* (*US* **paralyze**) **1** affect with paralysis. **2** render powerless; cripple. □□ **paralysation** /-ˈzeɪʃ(ə)n/ *n.* **paralysingly** *adv.* [F *paralyser* f. *paralysie*: cf. PALSY]

paralysis /pəˈrælɪsɪs/ *n.* (*pl.* **paralyses** /-ˌsiːz/) **1** a nervous condition with impairment or loss of esp. the motor function of the nerves. **2** a state of utter powerlessness. [L f. Gk *paralusis* f. *paraluō* disable (as PARA-¹, *luō* loosen)]

paralytic /ˌpærəˈlɪtɪk/ *adj.* & *n.* —*adj.* **1** affected by paralysis. **2** *sl.* very drunk. —*n.* a person affected by paralysis. □□ **paralytically** *adv.* [ME f. OF *paralytique* f. L *paralyticus* f. Gk *paralutikos* (as PARALYSIS)]

paramagnetic /ˌpærəmægˈnetɪk/ *adj.* (of a body or substance) tending to become weakly magnetized so as to lie parallel to a magnetic field force. □□ **paramagnetism** /-ˈmægnɪˌtɪz(ə)m/ *n.*

paramatta var. of PARRAMATTA.

paramecium /ˌpærəˈmiːsɪəm/ *n.* (also **paramoecium**) any freshwater protozoan of the genus *Paramecium*, of a characteristic slipper-like shape covered with cilia. [mod.L f. Gk *paramēkēs* oval (as PARA-¹, *mēkos* length)]

paramedic /ˌpærəˈmedɪk/ *n.* a paramedical worker.

paramedical /ˌpærəˈmedɪk(ə)l/ *adj.* (of services etc.) supplementing and supporting medical work.

parameter /pəˈræmɪtə(r)/ *n.* **1** *Math.* a quantity constant in the case considered but varying in different cases. **2 a** an (esp. measurable or quantifiable) characteristic or feature. **b** (loosely) a constant element or factor, esp. serving as a limit or boundary. □□ **parametric** /ˌpærəˈmetrɪk/ *adj.* **parametrize** *v.tr.* (also **-ise**). [mod.L f. Gk *para* beside + *metron* measure]

paramilitary /ˌpærəˈmɪlɪtərɪ/ *adj.* (of forces) ancillary to and similarly organized to military forces.

paramnesia /ˌpærəmˈniːzɪə/ *n.* *Psychol.* = DÉJÀ VU. [PARA-¹ + AMNESIA]

paramo /ˈpærəˌməʊ/ *n.* (*pl.* **-os**) a high treeless plateau in tropical S. America. [Sp. & Port. f. L *paramus*]

paramoecium var. of PARAMECIUM.

paramount /ˈpærəˌmaʊnt/ *adj.* **1** supreme; requiring first consideration; pre-eminent (*of paramount importance*). **2** in supreme authority. □□ **paramountcy** *n.* **paramountly** *adv.* [AF *paramont* f. OF *par* by + *amont* above: cf. AMOUNT]

paramour /ˈpærəˌmʊə(r)/ *n.* archaic or derog. an illicit lover of a married person. [ME f. OF *par amour* by love]

parang /ˈpæræŋ/ *n.* a large heavy Malayan knife used for clearing vegetation etc. [Malay]

paranoia /ˌpærəˈnɔɪə/ *n.* **1** a mental disorder esp. characterized by delusions of persecution and self-importance. **2** an abnormal tendency to suspect and mistrust others. □□ **paranoiac** *adj.* & *n.* **paranoiacally** *adv.* **paranoic** /-ˈnəʊɪk, -ˈnɔɪɪk/ *adj.* **paranoically** /-ˈnəʊɪkəlɪ, -ˈnɔɪkəlɪ/ *adv.* **paranoid** /ˈpærəˌnɔɪd/ *adj.* & *n.* [mod.L f. Gk f. *paranoos* distracted (as PARA-¹, *noos* mind)]

paranormal /ˌpærəˈnɔːm(ə)l/ *adj.* beyond the scope of normal objective investigation or explanation. □□ **paranormally** *adv.*

parapet /ˈpærəpɪt/ *n.* **1** a low wall at the edge of a roof, balcony, etc., or along the sides of a bridge. **2** a defence of earth or stone to conceal and protect troops. □□ **parapeted** *adj.* [F *parapet* or It. *parapetto* breast-high wall (as PARA-², *petto* breast f. L *pectus*)]

paraph /ˈpærəf/ *n.* a flourish after a signature, orig. as a precaution against forgery. [ME f. F *paraphe* f. med.L *paraphus* for *paragraphus* PARAGRAPH]

paraphernalia /ˌpærəfəˈneɪlɪə/ *n.pl.* (also treated as *sing.*) miscellaneous belongings, items of equipment, accessories, etc. [orig. = property owned by a married woman, f. med.L *paraphernalia* f. LL *parapherna* f. Gk *parapherna* property apart from a dowry (as PARA-¹, *pherna* f. *phernē* dower)]

paraphrase /ˈpærəˌfreɪz/ *n.* & *v.* —*n.* a free rendering or rewording of a passage. —*v.tr.* express the meaning of (a passage) in other words. □□ **paraphrastic** /-ˈfræstɪk/ *adj.* [F *paraphrase* or L *paraphrasis* f. Gk *paraphrasis* f. *paraphrazō* (as PARA-¹ *phrazō* tell)]

paraplegia /ˌpærəˈpliːdʒə/ *n.* paralysis of the legs and part or the whole of the trunk. □□ **paraplegic** *adj.* & *n.* [mod.L f. Gk *paraplēgia* f. *paraplēssō* (as PARA-¹, *plēssō* strike)]

parapsychology /ˌpærəsaɪˈkɒlədʒɪ/ *n.* the study of mental phenomena outside the sphere of ordinary psychology (hypnosis, telepathy, etc.). □□ **parapsychological** /-ˌsaɪkəˈlɒdʒɪk(ə)l/ *adj.* **parapsychologist** *n.*

paraquat /ˈpærəˌkwɒt/ *n.* a quick-acting herbicide, becoming inactive on contact with the soil. [PARA-¹

+ QUATERNARY (from the position of the bond between the two parts of the molecule relative to quaternary nitrogen atom)]

parascending /ˈpærəˌsendɪŋ/ *n.* a sport in which participants wearing open parachutes are towed behind a vehicle or motor boat to gain height before release for a conventional descent, usu. towards a predetermined target. □□ **parascender** *n.*

paraselene /ˌpærəsɪˈliːnɪ/ *n.* (*pl.* **paraselenae** /-niː/) a bright spot, esp. an image of the moon, on a lunar halo. Also called *mock moon.* [mod.L (as PARA-[1], Gk *selēnē* moon)]

parasite /ˈpærəˌsaɪt/ *n.* **1** an organism living in or on another and benefiting at the expense of the other. **2** a person who lives off or exploits another or others. **3** *Philol.* an inorganic sound or letter developing from an adjacent one. □□ **parasitic** /-ˈsɪtɪk/ *adj.* **parasitical** /-ˈsɪtɪk(ə)l/ *adj.* **parasitically** /-ˈsɪtɪkəlɪ/ *adv.* **parasiticide** /-ˈsɪtɪˌsaɪd/ *n.* **parasitism** *n.* **parasitology** /-ˈtɒlədʒɪ/ *n.* **parasitologist** /-ˈtɒlədʒɪst/ *n.* [L *parasitus* f. Gk *parasitos* one who eats at another's table (as PARA-[1], *sitos* food)]

parasitize /ˈpærəsɪˌtaɪz/ *v.tr.* (also **-ise**) infest as a parasite. □□ **parasitization** /-ˈzeɪʃ(ə)n/ *n.*

parasol /ˈpærəˌsɒl/ *n.* a light umbrella used to give shade from the sun. [F f. It. *parasole* (as PARA-[2], *sole* sun f. L *sol*)]

parasympathetic /ˌpærəˌsɪmpəˈθetɪk/ *adj. Anat.* relating to the part of the nervous system that consists of nerves leaving the lower end of the spinal cord and connecting with those in or near the viscera (cf. SYMPATHETIC 9). [PARA-[1] + SYMPATHETIC, because some of these nerves run alongside sympathetic nerves]

parasynthesis /ˌpærəˈsɪnθɪsɪs/ *n. Philol.* a derivation from a compound, e.g. *black-eyed* from *black eye(s)* + *-ed.* □□ **parasynthetic** /-ˈθetɪk/ *adj.* [Gk *parasunthesis* (as PARA-[1], SYNTHESIS)]

parataxis /ˌpærəˈtæksɪs/ *n. Gram.* the placing of clauses etc. one after another, without words to indicate coordination or subordination, e.g. *Tell me, how are you?* □□ **paratactic** /-ˈtæktɪk/ *adj.* **paratactically** /-ˈtæktɪkəlɪ/ *adv.* [Gk *parataxis* (as PARA-[1], *taxis* arrangement f. *tassō* arrange)]

parathion /ˌpærəˈθaɪən/ *n.* a highly toxic agricultural insecticide. [PARA-[1] + THIO- + -ON]

parathyroid /ˌpærəˈθaɪrɔɪd/ *n. & adj. Anat.* —*n.* a gland next to the thyroid, secreting a hormone that regulates calcium levels in the body. —*adj.* of or associated with this gland.

paratroop /ˈpærəˌtruːp/ *n.* (*attrib.*) of or consisting of paratroops (*paratroop regiment*).

paratrooper /ˈpærəˌtruːpə(r)/ *n.* a member of a body of paratroops.

paratroops /ˈpærəˌtruːps/ *n.pl.* troops equipped to be dropped by parachute from aircraft. [contr. of PARACHUTE + TROOP]

paratyphoid /ˌpærəˈtaɪfɔɪd/ *n. & adj.* —*n.* a fever resembling typhoid but caused by various different though related bacteria. —*adj.* of, relating to, or caused by this fever.

paravane /ˈpærəˌveɪn/ *n.* a torpedo-shaped device towed at a depth regulated by its vanes or planes to cut the moorings of submerged mines.

par avion /ˌpɑːr æˈvjɔ̃/ *adv.* by airmail. [F, = by aeroplane]

parboil /ˈpɑːbɔɪl/ *v.tr.* partly cook by boiling. [ME f. OF *parbo(u)illir* f. LL *perbullire* boil thoroughly (as PER-, *bullire* boil: confused with PART)]

parbuckle /ˈpɑːˌbʌk(ə)l/ *n. & v.* —*n.* a rope arranged like a sling, for raising or lowering casks and cylindrical objects. —*v.tr.* raise or lower with this. [earlier *parbunkle*, of unkn. orig.: assoc. with BUCKLE]

parcel /ˈpɑːs(ə)l/ *n. & v.* —*n.* **1 a** goods etc. wrapped up in a single package. **b** a bundle of things wrapped up, usu. in paper. **2** a piece of land, esp. as part of an estate. **3** a quantity dealt with in one commercial transaction. **4** *archaic* part. —*v.tr.* (**parcelled,**

parcelling; *US* **parceled, parceling**) **1** (foll. by *up*) wrap as a parcel. **2** (foll. by *out*) divide into portions. **3** cover (rope) with strips of canvas. □**parcel post** the branch of the postal service dealing with parcels. [ME f. OF *parcelle* ult. f. L *particula* (as PART)]

parch /pɑːtʃ/ *v.* **1** *tr.* & *intr.* make or become hot and dry. **2** *tr.* roast (peas, corn, etc.) slightly. [ME *perch*, *parche*, of unkn. orig.]

parched /pɑːtʃt/ *adj.* **1** hot and dry; dried out with heat. **2** *colloq.* thirsty.

parchment /ˈpɑːtʃmənt/ *n.* **1 a** an animal skin, esp. that of a sheep or goat, prepared as a writing or painting surface. **b** a manuscript written on this. **2** (in full **vegetable parchment**) high-grade paper made to resemble parchment. [ME f. OF *parchemin*, ult. a blend of LL *pergamina* writing material from Pergamum (in Asia Minor) with *Parthica pellis* Parthian skin (leather)]

parclose /ˈpɑːkləʊz/ *n.* a screen or railing in a church, separating a side chapel. [ME f. OF *parclos -ose* past part. of *parclore* enclose]

pard /pɑːd/ *n. archaic* or *poet.* a leopard. [ME f. OF f. L *pardus* f. Gk *pardos*]

pardalote /ˈpɑːdəˌləʊt/ *n.* any small brightly-coloured Australian bird of the genus *Pardalotus*, with spotted plumage. Also called *diamond-bird.* [mod.L *Pardalotus* f. Gk *pardalōtos* spotted like a leopard (as PARD)]

pardner /ˈpɑːdnə(r)/ *n. US colloq.* a partner or comrade. [corrupt.]

pardon /ˈpɑːd(ə)n/ *n., v.,* & *int.* —*n.* **1** the act of excusing or forgiving an offence, error, etc. **2** (in full **free pardon**) a remission of the legal consequences of a crime or conviction. **3** *RC Ch.* an indulgence. —*v.tr.* **1** release from the consequences of an offence, error, etc. **2** forgive or excuse a person for (an offence etc.). **3** make (esp. courteous) allowances for; excuse. —*int.* (also **pardon me** or **I beg your pardon**) **1** a formula of apology or disagreement. **2** a request to repeat something said. □□ **pardonable** *adj.* **pardonably** *adv.* [ME f. OF *pardun, pardoner* f. med.L *perdonare* concede, remit (as PER-, *donare* give)]

pardoner /ˈpɑːdənə(r)/ *n. hist.* a person licensed to sell papal pardons or indulgences. [ME f. AF (as PARDON)]

pare /peə(r)/ *v.tr.* **1 a** trim or shave (esp. fruit and vegetables) by cutting away the surface or edge. **b** (often foll. by *off, away*) cut off (the surface or edge). **2** (often foll. by *away, down*) diminish little by little. □□ **parer** *n.* [ME f. OF *parer* adorn, peel (fruit), f. L *parare* prepare]

paregoric /ˌpærɪˈgɒrɪk/ *n.* (in full **paregoric elixir**) *hist.* a camphorated tincture of opium used to reduce pain. [LL *paregoricus* f. Gk *parēgorikos* soothing (as PARA-[1], *-agoros* speaking f. *agora* assembly)]

pareira /pəˈreərə/ *n.* a drug from the root of a Brazilian shrub, *Chondrodendron tomentosum*, used as a muscle relaxant in surgery etc. [Port. *parreira* vine trained against a wall]

parenchyma /pəˈreŋkɪmə/ *n.* **1** *Anat.* the functional part of an organ as distinguished from the connective and supporting tissue. **2** *Bot.* the cellular material, usu. soft and succulent, found esp. in the softer parts of leaves, pulp of fruits, bark and pith of stems, etc. □□ **parenchymal** *adj.* **parenchymatous** /-ˈkɪmətəs/ *adj.* [Gk *paregkhuma* something poured in besides (as PARA-[1], *egkhuma* infusion f. *egkheō* pour in)]

parent /ˈpeərənt/ *n. & v.* —*n.* **1** a person who has begotten or borne offspring; a father or mother. **2** a person who has adopted a child. **3** a forefather. **4** an animal or plant from which others are derived. **5** a source or origin. **6** an initiating organization or enterprise. —*v.tr.* (also *absol.*) be a parent of. □**parent company** a company of which other companies are subsidiaries. **parent-teacher association** a local organization of parents and

b *but* d *dog* f *few* g *get* h *he* j *yes* k *cat* l *leg* m *man* n *no* p *pen* r *red* s *sit* t *top* v *voice*

teachers for promoting closer relations and improving educational facilities at a school. □□
parental /pə'rent(ə)l/ *adj.* **parentally** /pə'rentəlɪ/ *adv.* **parenthood** *n.* [ME f. OF f. L *parens parentis* f. *parere* bring forth]

parentage /'peərəntɪdʒ/ *n.* lineage; descent from or through parents (*their parentage is unknown*). [ME f. OF (as PARENT)]

parenteral /pə'rentər(ə)l/ *adj. Med.* administered or occurring elsewhere than in the alimentary canal. □□ **parenterally** *adv.* [PARA-¹ + Gk *enteron* intestine]

parenthesis /pə'renθəsɪs/ *n.* (*pl.* **parentheses** /-ˌsiːz/) **1 a** a word, clause, or sentence inserted as an explanation or afterthought into a passage which is grammatically complete without it, and usu. marked off by brackets or dashes or commas. **b** (in *pl.*) a pair of round brackets () used for this. **2** an interlude or interval. □ **in parenthesis** as a parenthesis or afterthought. [LL f. Gk *parenthesis* f. *parentithēmi* put in beside]

parenthesize /pə'renθəˌsaɪz/ *v.tr.* (also **-ise**) **1** (also *absol.*) insert as a parenthesis. **2** put into brackets or similar punctuation.

parenthetic /ˌpærən'θetɪk/ *adj.* **1** of or by way of a parenthesis. **2** interposed. □□ **parenthetical** *adj.* **parenthetically** *adv.* [PARENTHESIS after *synthesis*, *synthetic*, etc.]

parenting /'peərəntɪŋ/ *n.* the occupation or concerns of parents.

parergon /pə'rɜːgən/ *n.* (*pl.* **parerga** /-gə/) **1** work subsidiary to one's main employment. **2** an ornamental accessory. [L f. Gk *parergon* (as PARA-¹, *ergon* work)]

paresis /pə'riːsɪs, 'pærɪsɪs/ *n.* (*pl.* **pareses** /-siːz/) *Med.* partial paralysis. □□ **paretic** /-'retɪk/ *adj.* [mod.L f. Gk f. *pariēmi* let go (as PARA-¹, *hiēmi* let go)]

par excellence /ˌpɑːr eksə'lɑ̃s/ *adv.* as having special excellence; being the supreme example of its kind (*the short story par excellence*). [F, = by excellence]

parfait /'pɑːfeɪ/ *n.* **1** a rich packed pudding of whipped cream, eggs, etc. **2** layers of ice-cream, meringue, etc., served in a tall glass. [F *parfait* PERFECT *adj.*]

pargana /pə'gʌnə/ *n.* (also **pergunnah**, **pergana**) (in India) a group of villages or a subdivision of a district. [Urdu *pargana* district]

parget /'pɑːdʒɪt/ *v.* & *n.* —*v.tr.* (**pargeted**, **pargeting**) **1** plaster (a wall etc.) esp. with an ornamental pattern. **2** roughcast. —*n.* **1** plaster applied in this way; ornamental plasterwork. **2** roughcast. [ME f. OF *pargeter, parjeter* f. *par* all over + *jeter* throw]

parhelion /pɑː'hiːlɪən/ *n.* (*pl.* **parhelia** /-lɪə/) a bright spot on the solar halo. Also called *mock sun, sun-dog*. □□ **parheliacal** /-hɪ'laɪək(ə)l/ *adj.* **parhelic** *adj.* [L *parelion* f. Gk (as PARA-¹, *hēlios* sun)]

pariah /pə'raɪə, 'pærɪə/ *n.* **1** a social outcast. **2** *hist.* a member of a low caste or of no caste in S. India. □ **pariah-dog** = PYE-DOG. [Tamil *paraiyar* pl. of *paraiyan* hereditary drummer f. *parai* drum]

parietal /pə'raɪət(ə)l/ *adj.* **1** *Anat.* of the wall of the body or any of its cavities. **2** *Bot.* of the wall of a hollow structure etc. **3** *US* relating to residence within a college. □ **parietal bone** either of a pair of bones forming the central part of the sides and top of the skull. [F *pariétal* or LL *parietalis* f. L *paries -etis* wall]

pari-mutuel /ˌpɑːriː'mjuːtjuːˌel/ *n.* **1** a form of betting in which those backing the first three places divide the losers' stakes (less the operator's commission). **2** a totalizator. [F, = mutual stake]

paring /'peərɪŋ/ *n.* a strip or piece cut off.

pari passu /ˌpɑːrɪ 'pæsuː, ˌpærɪ/ *adv.* **1** with equal speed. **2** simultaneously and equally. [L]

Paris commune see COMMUNE¹.

Paris green /'pærɪs/ *n.* a poisonous chemical used as a pigment and insecticide. [*Paris* in France]

parish /'pærɪʃ/ *n.* **1** an area having its own church

and clergy. **2** (in full **civil parish**) a district constituted for purposes of local government. **3** the inhabitants of a parish. **4** *US* a county in Louisiana. □ **parish clerk** an official performing various duties concerned with the church. **parish council** *Brit.* the administrative body in a civil parish. **parish pump** (often *attrib.*) a symbol of a parochial or restricted outlook. **parish register** a book recording christenings, marriages, and burials, at a parish church. [ME *paroche, parosse* f. OF *paroche, paroisse* f. eccl.L *parochia, paroechia* f. Gk *paroikia* sojourning f. *paroikos* (as PARA-¹, *-oikos* -dwelling f. *oikeō* dwell)]

parishioner /pə'rɪʃənə(r)/ *n.* an inhabitant of a parish. [obs. *parishen* f. ME f. OF *parossien*, formed as PARISH]

Parisian /pə'rɪzɪən/ *adj.* & *n.* —*adj.* of or relating to Paris in France. —*n.* **1** a native or inhabitant of Paris. **2** the kind of French spoken in Paris. [F *parisien*]

parison /'pærɪs(ə)n/ *n.* a rounded mass of glass formed by rolling immediately after taking it from the furnace. [F *paraison* f. *parer* prepare f. L *parare*]

parity¹ /'pærɪtɪ/ *n.* **1** equality or equal status, esp. as regards status or pay. **2** parallelism or analogy (*parity of reasoning*). **3** equivalence of one currency with another; being at par. **4** (of a number) the fact of being even or odd. **5** *Physics* (of a quantity) the fact of changing its sign or remaining unaltered under a given transformation of coordinates etc. [F *parité* or LL *paritas* (as PAR¹)]

parity² /'pærɪtɪ/ *n. Med.* **1** the fact or condition of having borne children. **2** the number of children previously borne. [formed as -PAROUS + -ITY]

park /pɑːk/ *n.* & *v.* —*n.* **1** a large public garden in a town, for recreation. **2** a large enclosed piece of ground, usu. with woodland and pasture, attached to a country house etc. **3 a** a large area of land kept in its natural state for public recreational use. **b** a large enclosed area of land used to accommodate wild animals in captivity (*wildlife park*). **4** an area for motor vehicles etc. to be left in (*car park*). **5** the gear position or function in automatic transmission in which the gears are locked, preventing the vehicle's movement. **6** an area devoted to a specified purpose (*industrial park*). **7 a** *US* a sports ground. **b** (usu. prec. by *the*) a football pitch. —*v.tr.* **1** (also *absol.*) leave (a vehicle) usu. temporarily, in a car park, by the side of the road, etc. **2** *colloq.* deposit and leave, usu. temporarily. □ **parking-light** a small light at the side of a vehicle, for use when the vehicle is parked at night. **parking-lot** *US* an outdoor area for parking vehicles. **parking-meter** a coin-operated meter which receives fees for vehicles parked in the street and indicates the time available. **parking-ticket** a notice, usu. attached to a vehicle, of a penalty imposed for parking illegally. **park oneself** *colloq.* sit down. [ME f. OF *parc* f. med.L *parricus* f. Gmc orig., rel. to *pearruc*: see PADDOCK]

parka /'pɑːkə/ *n.* **1** a skin jacket with hood, worn by Eskimos. **2** a similar windproof fabric garment worn by mountaineers etc. [Aleutian]

parkin /'pɑːkɪn/ *n. Brit.* a cake or biscuit made with oatmeal, ginger, and treacle or molasses. [perh. f. the name *Parkin*, dimin. of *Peter*]

Parkinsonism /'pɑːkɪnsəˌnɪz(ə)m/ *n.* = PARKINSON'S DISEASE.

Parkinson's disease /'pɑːkɪns(ə)nz/ *n.* a progressive disease of the nervous system with tremor, muscular rigidity, and emaciation. Also called PARKINSONISM. [J. *Parkinson*, Engl. surgeon d. 1824]

Parkinson's law /'pɑːkɪns(ə)nz/ *n.* the notion that work expands so as to fill the time available for its completion. [C. N. *Parkinson*, Engl. writer b. 1909]

parkland /'pɑːklænd/ *n.* open grassland with clumps of trees etc.

parkway /'pɑːkweɪ/ *n.* **1** *US* an open landscaped

highway. **2** *Brit.* a railway station with extensive parking facilities.

parky /'pɑːkɪ/ *adj.* (**parkier, parkiest**) *Brit. colloq.* chilly. [19th c.: orig. unkn.]

Parl. *abbr. Brit.* **1** Parliament. **2** Parliamentary.

parlance /'pɑːləns/ *n.* a particular way of speaking, esp. as regards choice of words, idiom, etc. [OF f. *parler* speak, ult. f. L *parabola* (see PARABLE): in LL = 'speech']

parlay /'pɑːleɪ/ *v. & n. US* —*v.tr.* **1** use (money won on a bet) as a further stake. **2** increase in value by or as if by parlaying. —*n.* **1** an act of parlaying. **2** a bet made by parlaying. [F *paroli* f. It. f. *paro* like f. L *par* equal]

parley /'pɑːlɪ/ *n. & v.* —*n.* (*pl.* **-eys**) a conference for debating points in a dispute, esp. a discussion of terms for an armistice etc. —*v.intr.* (**-leys, -leyed**) (often foll. by *with*) hold a parley. [perh. f. OF *parlee*, fem. past part. of *parler* speak: see PARLANCE]

parliament /'pɑːləmənt/ *n.* **1** (**Parliament**) **a** (in the UK) the highest legislature, consisting of the Sovereign, the House of Lords, and the House of Commons. **b** the members of this legislature for a particular period, esp. between one dissolution and the next. **2** a similar legislature in other nations and States. [ME f. OF *parlement* speaking (as PARLANCE)]

parliamentarian /ˌpɑːləmenˈteərɪən/ *n. & adj.* —*n.* **1** a member of a parliament, esp. one well-versed in its procedures. **2** *hist.* an adherent of Parliament in the English Civil War of the 17th c. —*adj.* = PARLIAMENTARY.

parliamentary /ˌpɑːləˈmentərɪ/ *adj.* **1** of or relating to a parliament. **2** enacted or established by a parliament. **3** (of language) admissible in a parliament; polite. ▫**Parliamentary Commissioner for Administration** the official name of the ombudsman in the UK. **parliamentary private secretary** a member of parliament assisting a government minister.

parlour /'pɑːlə(r)/ *n.* (*US* **parlor**) **1** a sitting-room in a private house. **2** a room in a hotel, convent, etc., for the private use of residents. **3** esp. *US* a shop providing specified goods or services (*beauty parlour; ice-cream parlour*). **4** a room or building equipped for milking cows. **5** (*attrib.*) *derog.* denoting support for political views by those who do not try to practise them (*parlour socialist*). ▫**parlour game** an indoor game, esp. a word game. **parlour-maid** *hist.* a maid who waits at table. [ME f. AF *parlur*, OF *parleor*, *parleur*: see PARLANCE]

parlous /'pɑːləs/ *adj. & adv. archaic* or *joc.* —*adj.* **1** dangerous or difficult. **2** hard to deal with. —*adv.* extremely. ▫▫**parlously** *adv.* **parlousness** *n.* [ME, = PERILOUS]

Parma violet /'pɑːmə/ *n.* a variety of sweet violet with heavy scent and lavender-coloured flowers often crystallized for food decoration. [*Parma* in Italy]

Parmesan /ˌpɑːmɪˈzæn, 'pɑː-/ *n.* a kind of hard dry cheese made orig. at Parma and used esp. in grated form. [F f. It. *parmegiano* of Parma in Italy]

Parnassian /pɑːˈnæsɪən/ *adj. & n.* —*adj.* **1** of Parnassus, a mountain in C. Greece, in antiquity sacred to the Muses. **2** poetic. **3** of or relating to a group of French poets in the late 19th c., emphasizing strictness of form, named from the anthology *Le Parnasse contemporain* (1866). —*n.* a member of this group.

parochial /pəˈrəʊkɪəl/ *adj.* **1** of or concerning a parish. **2** (of affairs, views, etc.) merely local, narrow or restricted in scope. ▫▫**parochialism** *n.* **parochiality** /-ˈælɪtɪ/ *n.* **parochially** *adv.* [ME f. AF *parochiel*, OF *parochial* f. eccl.L *parochialis* (as PARISH)]

parody /'pærədɪ/ *n. & v.* —*n.* (*pl.* **-ies**) **1** a humorous exaggerated imitation of an author, literary work, style, etc. **2** a feeble imitation; a travesty. —*v.tr.* (**-ies, -ied**) **1** compose a parody of. **2** mimic

humorously. ▫▫**parodic** /pəˈrɒdɪk/ *adj.* **parodist** *n.* [LL *parodia* or Gk *parōidia* burlesque poem (as PARA-[1], *ōidē* ode)]

parol /pəˈrəʊl/ *adj. & n. Law* —*adj.* **1** given orally. **2** (of a document) not given under seal. —*n.* an oral declaration. [OF *parole* (as PAROLE)]

parole /pəˈrəʊl/ *n. & v.* —*n.* **1 a** the release of a prisoner temporarily for a special purpose or completely before the expiry of a sentence, on the promise of good behaviour. **b** such a promise. **2** a word of honour. —*v.tr.* put (a prisoner) on parole. ▫**on parole** released on the terms of parole. ▫▫ **parolee** /-ˈliː/ *n.* [F, = word: see PARLANCE]

paronomasia /ˌpærənəˈmeɪzɪə/ *n.* a play on words; a pun. [L f. Gk *paronomasia* (as PARA-[1], *onomasia* naming f. *onomazō* to name f. *onoma* a name)]

paronym /'pærənɪm/ *n.* **1** a word cognate with another. **2** a word formed from a foreign word. ▫▫**paronymous** /pəˈrɒnɪməs/ *adj.* [Gk *parōnumon*, neut. of *parōnumos* (as PARA-[1], *onuma* name)]

parotid /pəˈrɒtɪd/ *adj. & n.* —*adj.* situated near the ear. —*n.* (in full **parotid gland**) a salivary gland in front of the ear. ▫**parotid duct** a duct opening from the parotid gland into the mouth. [F *parotide* or L *parotis parotid-* f. Gk *parōtis -idos* (as PARA-[1], *ous ōtos* ear)]

parotitis /ˌpærəˈtaɪtɪs/ *n.* **1** inflammation of the parotid gland. **2** mumps. [PAROTID + -ITIS]

-parous /pərəs/ *comb. form* bearing offspring of a specified number or kind (*multiparous; viviparous*). [L *-parus* -bearing f. *parere* bring forth]

Parousia /pəˈruːzɪə/ *n. Theol.* the supposed second coming of Christ. [Gk, = presence, coming]

paroxysm /'pærək‚sɪz(ə)m/ *n.* **1** (often foll. by *of*) a sudden attack or outburst (of rage, laughter, etc.). **2** a fit of disease. ▫▫**paroxysmal** /-ˈsɪzm(ə)l/ *adj.* [F *paroxysme* f. med.L *paroxysmus* f. Gk *paroxusmos* f. *paroxunō* exasperate (as PARA-[1], *oxunō* sharpen f. *oxus* sharp)]

paroxytone /pəˈrɒksɪˌtəʊn/ *adj. & n.* —*adj.* (esp. in ancient Greek) having an acute accent on the last syllable but one. —*n.* a word of this kind. [mod.L f. Gk *paroxutonos* (as PARA-[1], OXYTONE)]

parpen /'pɑːpən/ *n.* a stone passing through a wall from side to side, with two smooth vertical faces. [ME f. OF *parpain*, prob. ult. f. L *per* through + *pannus* piece of cloth, in Rmc 'piece of wall']

parquet /'pɑːkɪ, -keɪ/ *n. & v.* —*n.* **1** a flooring of wooden blocks arranged in a pattern. **2** *US* the stalls of a theatre. —*v.tr.* (**parqueted** /-keɪd/; **parqueting** /-keɪɪŋ/) furnish (a room) with a parquet floor. [F, = small compartment, floor, dimin. of *parc* PARK]

parquetry /'pɑːkɪtrɪ/ *n.* the use of wooden blocks to make floors or inlay for furniture.

parr /pɑː(r)/ *n.* a young salmon with blue-grey finger-like markings on its sides, younger than a smolt. [18th c.: orig. unkn.]

parrakeet *US* var. of PARAKEET.

parramatta /ˌpærəˈmætə/ *n.* (also **paramatta**) a light dress fabric of wool and silk or cotton. [*Parramatta* in New South Wales, Australia]

parricide /'pærɪˌsaɪd/ *n.* **1** the killing of a near relative, esp. of a parent. **2** an act of parricide. **3** a person who commits parricide. ▫▫**parricidal** /-ˈsaɪd(ə)l/ *adj.* [F *parricide* or L *parricida* (= sense 3), *parricidium* (= sense 1), of uncert. orig., assoc. in L with *pater* father and *parens* parent]

parrot /'pærət/ *n. & v.* —*n.* **1** any of various mainly tropical birds of the order Psittaciformes, with a short hooked bill, often having vivid plumage and able to mimic the human voice. **2** a person who mechanically repeats the words or actions of another. —*v.tr.* (**parroted, parroting**) repeat mechanically. ▫**parrot-fashion** (learning or repeating) mechanically without understanding. **parrot-fish** any fish of the genus *Scarus*, with a mouth like a parrot's bill and forming a protective mucous cocoon against predators. [prob. f. obs. or dial. F *perrot* parrot, dimin. of *Pierre* Peter: cf. PARAKEET]

parry /'pærɪ/ *v. & n.* —*v.tr.* (-**ies**, -**ied**) **1** avert or ward off (a weapon or attack), esp. with a countermove. **2** deal skilfully with (an awkward question etc.). —*n.* (*pl.* -**ies**) an act of parrying. [prob. repr. F *parez* imper. of *parer* f. It. *parare* ward off]

parse /pɑːz/ *v.tr.* **1** describe (a word in context) grammatically, stating its inflection, relation to the sentence, etc. **2** resolve (a sentence) into its component parts and describe them grammatically. □□ **parser** *n.* esp. *Computing* [perh. f. ME *pars* parts of speech f. OF *pars*, pl. of *part* PART, infl. by L *pars* part]

parsec /'pɑːsek/ *n.* a unit of stellar distance, equal to about 3.25 light years (3.08 × 10¹⁶ metres), the distance at which the mean radius of the earth's orbit subtends an angle of one second of arc. [PARALLAX + SECOND²]

Parsee /pɑːˈsiː/ *n.* **1** an adherent of Zoroastrianism. **2** a descendant of the Persians who fled to India from Muslim persecution in the 7th-8th c. **3** = PAHLAVI. □□ **Parseeism** *n.* [Pers. *pārsī* Persian f. *pārs* Persia]

parsimony /'pɑːsɪmənɪ/ *n.* **1** carefulness in the use of money or other resources. **2** meanness, stinginess. □ **law of parsimony** the assertion that no more causes or forces should be assumed than are necessary to account for the facts. □□ **parsimonious** /-ˈməʊnɪəs/ *adj.* **parsimoniously** /-ˈməʊnɪəslɪ/ *adv.* **parsimoniousness** /-ˈməʊnɪəsnɪs/ *n.* [ME f. L *parsimonia, parcimonia* f. *parcere pars-* spare]

parsley /'pɑːslɪ/ *n.* a biennial herb, *Petroselinum crispum*, with white flowers and crinkly aromatic leaves, used for seasoning and garnishing food. □ **parsley fern** a fern, *Cryptogramma crispa*, with leaves like parsley. **parsley-piert** a dwarf annual herb, *Aphanes arvensis*. [ME *percil, per(e)sil* f. OF *peresil*, and OE *petersilie* ult. f. L *petroselinum* f. Gk *petroselinon; parsley-piert* prob. corrupt. of F *perce-pierre* pierce stone]

parsnip /'pɑːsnɪp/ *n.* **1** a biennial umbelliferous plant, *Pastinaca sativa*, with yellow flowers and a large pale-yellow tapering root. **2** this root eaten as a vegetable. [ME *pas(se)nep* (with assim. to *nep* turnip) f. OF *pasnaie* f. L *pastinaca*]

parson /'pɑːs(ə)n/ *n.* **1** a rector. **2** a vicar or any beneficed member of the clergy. **3** *colloq.* any (esp. Protestant) member of the clergy. □ **parson's nose** the piece of fatty flesh at the rump of a fowl. □□ **parsonical** /-'sɒnɪk(ə)l/ *adj.* [ME *person(e), parson* f. OF *persone* f. L *persona* PERSON (in med.L rector)]

parsonage /'pɑːsənɪdʒ/ *n.* a church house provided for a parson.

part /pɑːt/ *n., v., & adv.* —*n.* **1** some but not all of a thing or number of things. **2** an essential member or constituent of anything (*part of the family*; *a large part of the job*). **3** a component of a machine etc. (*spare parts*; *needs a new part*). **4 a** a portion of a human or animal body. **b** (in *pl.*) = *private parts.* **5 a** a division of a book, broadcast serial, etc., esp. as much as is issued or broadcast at one time. **6** each of several equal portions of a whole (*the recipe has 3 parts sugar to 2 parts flour*). **7 a** a portion allotted; a share. **b** a person's share in an action or enterprise (*will have no part in it*). **c** one's duty (*was not my part to interfere*). **8 a** a character assigned to an actor on stage. **b** the words spoken by an actor on stage. **c** a copy of these. **9** *Mus.* a melody or other constituent of harmony assigned to a particular voice or instrument. **10** each of the sides in an agreement or dispute. **11** (in *pl.*) a region or district (*am not from these parts*). **12** (in *pl.*) abilities (*a man of many parts*). **13** *US* = PARTING 2. —*v.* **1** *tr. & intr.* divide or separate into parts (*the crowd parted to let them through*). **2** *intr.* **a** leave one another's company (*they parted the best of friends*). **b** (foll. by *from*) say goodbye to. **3** *tr.* cause to separate (*they fought hard and had to be parted*). **4** *intr.* (foll. by *with*) give up

possession of; hand over. **5** *tr.* separate (the hair of the head on either side of the parting) with a comb. —*adv.* to some extent; partly (*is part iron and part wood*; *a lie that is part truth*). □ **for the most part** see MOST. **for one's part** as far as one is concerned. **in part** (or **parts**) to some extent; partly. **look the part** appear suitable for a role. **on the part of** on the behalf or initiative of (*no objection on my part*). **part and parcel** (usu. foll. by *of*) an essential part. **part company** see COMPANY. **part-exchange** *n.* a transaction in which goods are given as part of the payment for other goods, with the balance in money. —*v.tr.* give (goods) in such a transaction. **part of speech** *n.* each of the categories to which words are assigned in accordance with their grammatical and semantic functions (in English esp. noun, pronoun, adjective, adverb, verb, preposition, conjunction, and interjection). **part-song** a song with three or more voice-parts, often without accompaniment, and harmonic rather than contrapuntal in character. **part time** less than the full time required by an activity. **part-time** *adj.* occupying or using only part of one's working time. **part-timer** a person employed in part-time work. **part-work** *Brit.* a publication appearing in several parts over a period of time. **play a part 1** be significant or contributory. **2** act deceitfully. **3** perform a theatrical role. **take in good part** see GOOD. **take part** (often foll. by *in*) assist or have a share (in). **take the part of** support; back up. **three parts** three quarters. [ME f. OF f. L *pars partis* (n.), *partire, partiri* (v.)]

partake /pɑːˈteɪk/ *v.intr.* (*past* **partook** /-ˈtʊk/; *past part.* **partaken** /-ˈteɪkən/) **1** (foll. by *of, in*) take a share or part. **2** (foll. by *of*) eat or drink some or *colloq.* all (of a thing). **3** (foll. by *of*) have some (of a quality etc.) (*their manner partook of insolence*). □□ **partakable** *adj.* **partaker** *n.* [16th c.: back-form. f. *partaker, partaking* = part-taker etc.]

parterre /pɑːˈteə(r)/ *n.* **1** a level space in a garden occupied by flower-beds arranged formally. **2** *US* the ground floor of a theatre auditorium, esp. the pit overhung by balconies. [F, = *par terre* on the ground]

parthenogenesis /ˌpɑːθɪnəʊˈdʒenɪsɪs/ *n. Biol.* reproduction by a male gamete without fertilization, esp. as a normal process in invertebrates and lower plants. □□ **parthenogenetic** /-dʒɪˈnetɪk/ *adj.* **parthenogenetically** /-dʒɪˈnetɪkəlɪ/ *adv.* [mod.L f. Gk *parthenos* virgin + *genesis* as GENESIS]

Parthian shot /'pɑːθɪən/ *n.* a remark or glance etc. reserved for the moment of departure. [*Parthia*, an ancient kingdom in W. Asia: from the custom of a retreating Parthian horseman firing a shot at the enemy]

partial /'pɑːʃ(ə)l/ *adj. & n.* —*adj.* **1** not complete; forming only part (*a partial success*). **2** biased, unfair. **3** (foll. by *to*) having a liking for. —*n. Mus.* any of the constituents of a musical sound. □ **partial eclipse** an eclipse in which only part of the luminary is covered or darkened. **partial verdict** a verdict finding a person guilty of part of a charge. □□ **partially** *adv.* **partialness** *n.* [ME f. OF *parcial* f. LL *partialis* (as PART)]

partiality /ˌpɑːʃɪˈælɪtɪ/ *n.* **1** bias, favouritism. **2** (foll. by *for*) fondness. [ME f. OF *parcialité* f. med.L *partialitas* (as PARTIAL)]

participant /pɑːˈtɪsɪpənt/ *n.* a participator.

participate /pɑːˈtɪsɪˌpeɪt/ *v.intr.* **1** (foll. by *in*) take a part or share (in). **2** *literary* or *formal* (foll. by *of*) have a certain quality (*the speech participated of wit*). □□ **participation** /-ˈpeɪʃ(ə)n/ *n.* **participator** *n.* **participatory** *adj.* [L *participare* f. *particeps -cipis* taking part, formed as PART + *-cip-* = *cap-* stem of *capere* take]

participle /'pɑːtɪˌsɪp(ə)l/ *n. Gram.* a word formed from a verb (e.g. *going, gone, being, been*) and used in compound verb-forms (e.g. *is going, has been*) or as an adjective (e.g. *working woman, burnt toast*). □□ **participial** /-ˈsɪpɪəl/ *adj.* **participially** /-ˈsɪpɪəlɪ/

adv. [ME f. OF, by-form of *participe* f. L *participium* (as PARTICIPATE)]

particle /ˈpɑːtɪk(ə)l/ *n.* **1** a minute portion of matter. **2** the least possible amount (*not a particle of sense*). **3** *Gram.* **a** a minor part of speech, esp. a short undeclinable one. **b** a common prefix or suffix such as *in-, -ness*. [ME f. L *particula* (as PART)]

particoloured /ˈpɑːtɪˌkʌləd/ *adj.* partly of one colour, partly of another or others. [PARTY² + COLOURED]

particular /pəˈtɪkjʊlə(r)/ *adj. & n. —adj.* **1** relating to or considered as one thing or person as distinct from others; individual (*in this particular instance*). **2** more than is usual; special, noteworthy (*took particular trouble*). **3** scrupulously exact; fastidious. **4** detailed (*a full and particular account*). **5** *Logic* (of a proposition) in which something is asserted of some but not all of a class (opp. UNIVERSAL). *—n.* **1** a detail; an item. **2** (in *pl.*) points of information; a detailed account. ▫**in particular** especially, specifically. [ME f. OF *particuler* f. L *particularis* (as PARTICLE)]

particularism /pəˈtɪkjʊləˌrɪz(ə)m/ *n.* **1** exclusive devotion to one party, sect, etc. **2** the principle of leaving political independence to each State in an empire or federation. **3** the theological doctrine of individual election or redemption. ▫▫**particularist** *n.* [F *particularisme*, mod.L *particularismus*, and G *Partikularismus* (as PARTICULAR)]

particularity /pəˌtɪkjʊˈlærɪtɪ/ *n.* **1** the quality of being individual or particular. **2** fullness or minuteness of detail in a description.

particularize /pəˈtɪkjʊləˌraɪz/ *v.tr.* (also **-ise**) *tr.* (also *absol.*) **1** name specially or one by one. **2** specify (items). ▫▫**particularization** /-ˈzeɪʃ(ə)n/ *n.* [F *particulariser* (as PARTICULAR)]

particularly /pəˈtɪkjʊləlɪ/ *adv.* **1** especially, very. **2** specifically (*they particularly asked for you*). **3** in a particular or fastidious manner.

particulate /pəˈtɪkjʊˌleɪt, -lət/ *adj. & n. —adj.* in the form of separate particles. *—n.* matter in this form. [L *particula* PARTICLE]

parting /ˈpɑːtɪŋ/ *n.* **1** a leave-taking or departure (often *attrib.*: *parting words*). **2** *Brit.* the dividing line of combed hair. **3** a division; an act of separating. ▫**parting shot** = PARTHIAN SHOT.

parti pris /ˌpɑːtɪ ˈpriː/ *n. & adj.* **1** a preconceived view; a bias. *—adj.* prejudiced, biased. [F, = side taken]

partisan /ˈpɑːtɪˌzæn, -ˈzæn/ *n. & adj. —n.* (also **partizan**) **1** a strong, esp. unreasoning, supporter of a party, cause, etc. **2** *Mil.* a guerrilla in wartime. *—adj.* **1** of or characteristic of partisans. **2** loyal to a particular cause; biased. ▫▫**partisanship** *n.* [F f. It. dial. *partigiano* etc. f. *parte* PART]

partita /pɑːˈtiːtə/ *n.* (*pl.* **partite** /-teɪ/) *Mus.* **1** a suite. **2** an air with variations. [It., fem. past part. of *partire* divide, formed as PART]

partite /ˈpɑːtaɪt/ *adj.* **1** divided (esp. in *comb.*: *tripartite*). **2** *Bot. & Zool.* divided to or nearly to the base. [L *partitus* past part. of *partiri* PART *v.*]

partition /pɑːˈtɪʃ(ə)n/ *n. & v. —n.* **1** division into parts, esp. *Polit.* of a country with separate areas of government. **2** a structure dividing a space into two parts, esp. a light interior wall. *—v.tr.* **1** divide into parts. **2** (foll. by *off*) separate (part of a room etc.) with a partition. ▫▫**partitioned** *adj.* **partitioner** *n.* **partitionist** *n.* [ME f. OF f. L *partitio -onis* (as PARTITE)]

partitive /ˈpɑːtɪtɪv/ *adj. & n. Gram. —adj.* (of a word, form, etc.) denoting part of a collective group or quantity. *—n.* a partitive word (e.g. *some, any*) or form. ▫**partitive genitive** a genitive used to indicate a whole divided into or regarded in parts, expressed in English by *of* as in *most of us*. ▫▫**partitively** *adv.* [F *partitif -ive* or med.L *partitivus* (as PARTITE)]

partizan var. of PARTISAN.

partly /ˈpɑːtlɪ/ *adv.* **1** with respect to a part or parts. **2** to some extent.

partner /ˈpɑːtnə(r)/ *n. & v. —n.* **1** a person who shares or takes part with another or others, esp. in a business firm with shared risks and profits. **2** a companion in dancing. **3** a player (esp. one of two) on the same side in a game. **4** either member of a married couple, or of an unmarried couple living together. *—v.tr.* **1** be the partner of. **2** associate as partners. ▫▫**partnerless** *adj.* [ME, alt. of *parcener* joint heir, after PART]

partnership /ˈpɑːtnəʃɪp/ *n.* **1** the state of being a partner or partners. **2** a joint business. **3** a pair or group of partners.

partook *past* of PARTAKE.

partridge /ˈpɑːtrɪdʒ/ *n.* (*pl.* same or **partridges**) **1** any game-bird of the genus *Perdix*, esp. *P. perdix* of Europe and Asia. **2** any other of various similar birds of the family Phasianidae, including the snow partridge. [ME *partrich* etc. f. OF *perdriz* etc. f. L *perdix -dicis*: for *-dge* cf. CABBAGE]

parturient /pɑːˈtjʊərɪənt/ *adj.* about to give birth. [L *parturire* be in labour, incept. f. *parere* part- bring forth]

parturition /ˌpɑːtjʊˈrɪʃ(ə)n/ *n. formal* the act of bringing forth young; childbirth. [LL *parturitio* (as PARTURIENT)]

party¹ /ˈpɑːtɪ/ *n. & v. —n.* (*pl.* **-ies**) **1** a social gathering, usu. of invited guests. **2** a body of persons engaged in an activity or travelling together (*fishing party*; *search party*). **3** a group of people united in a cause, opinion, etc., esp. a political group organized on a national basis. **4** a person or persons forming one side in an agreement or dispute. **5** (foll. by *to*) *Law* an accessory (to an action). **6** *colloq.* a person. *—v.tr. & intr.* (**-ies, -ied**) entertain at or attend a party. ▫**party line** **1** the policy adopted by a political party. **2** a telephone line shared by two or more subscribers. **party-wall** a wall common to two adjoining buildings or rooms. [ME f. OF *partie* ult. f. L *partire*: see PART]

party² /ˈpɑːtɪ/ *adj. Heraldry* divided into parts of different colours. [ME f. OF *parti* f. L (as PARTY¹)]

parvenu /ˈpɑːvəˌnuː/ *n. & adj. —n.* (*fem.* **parvenue**) **1** a person of obscure origin who has gained wealth or position. **2** an upstart. *—adj.* **1** associated with or characteristic of such a person. **2** upstart. [F, past part. of *parvenir* arrive f. L *pervenire* (as PER-, *venire* come)]

parvis /ˈpɑːvɪs/ *n.* (also **parvise**) **1** an enclosed area in front of a cathedral, church, etc. **2** a room over a church porch. [ME f. OF *parvis* ult. f. LL *paradisus* PARADISE, a court in front of St Peter's, Rome]

pas /pɑː/ *n.* (*pl.* same) a step in dancing, esp. in classical ballet. ▫***pas de chat*** /də ˈʃɑː/ a leap in which each foot in turn is raised to the opposite knee. ***pas de deux*** /də ˈdɜː/ a dance for two persons. ***pas glissé*** see GLISSÉ. ***pas seul*** /ˈsɜːl/ a solo dance. [F, = step]

pascal *n.* **1** /ˈpæsk(ə)l/ the SI unit of pressure, equal to one newton per square metre. **2** (**Pascal**) /ˈpæsˈkɑːl/ *Computing* a programming language esp. used in education. [B. *Pascal*, Fr. scientist d. 1662: sense 2 so named because he built a calculating machine]

paschal /ˈpæsk(ə)l/ *adj.* **1** of or relating to the Jewish Passover. **2** of or relating to Easter. ▫**paschal lamb** **1** a lamb sacrificed at Passover. **2** Christ. [ME f. OF *pascal* f. eccl.L *paschalis* f. *pascha* f. Gk *paskha* f. Aram. *pasḥa*, rel. to Heb. *pesaḥ* PASSOVER]

pash /pæʃ/ *n. sl.* a brief infatuation. [abbr. of PASSION]

pasha /ˈpɑːʃə/ *n.* (also **pacha**) *hist.* the title (placed after the name) of a Turkish officer of high rank, e.g. a military commander, the governor of a province, etc. [Turk. *paşa*, prob. = *başa* f. *baş* head, chief]

pashm /ˈpæʃəm/ *n.* the under-fur of some Tibetan animals, esp. that of goats as used for Cashmere shawls.

Pashto /ˈpʌʃtəʊ/ *n. & adj. —n.* the official language

---

b *but* d *dog* f *few* g *get* h *he* j *yes* k *cat* l *leg* m *man* n *no* p *pen* r *red* s *sit* t *top* v *voice*

of Afghanistan, also spoken in areas of Pakistan. —*adj.* of or in this language. [Pashto]

paso doble /ˌpæsəʊ ˈdəʊbleɪ/ *n.* **1** a ballroom dance based on a Latin American style of marching. **2** this style of marching. [Sp., = double step]

pasque-flower /ˈpæskˌflaʊə(r)/ *n.* a ranunculaceous plant, *Pulsatilla vulgaris*, with bell-shaped purple flowers and fernlike foliage. Also called ANEMONE. [earlier *passe-flower* f. F *passe-fleur*: assim. to *pasque* = obs. *pasch* (as PASCHAL), Easter]

pasquinade /ˌpæskwɪˈneɪd/ *n.* a lampoon or satire, orig. one displayed in a public place. [It. *pasquinata* f. *Pasquino*, a statue in Rome on which abusive Latin verses were annually posted]

pass[1] /pɑːs/ *v.* & *n.* —*v.* (*past part.* passed) (see also PAST). **1** *intr.* (often foll. by *along, by, down, on*, etc.) move onward; proceed, esp. past some point of reference (*saw the procession passing*). **2** *tr.* **a** go past; leave (a thing etc.) on one side or behind in proceeding. **b** overtake, esp. in a vehicle. **c** go across (a frontier, mountain range, etc.). **3** *intr.* & *tr.* be transferred or cause to be transferred from one person or place to another (*pass the butter; the title passes to his son*). **4** *tr.* surpass; be too great for (*it passes my comprehension*). **5** *intr.* get through; effect a passage. **6** *intr.* **a** be accepted as adequate; go uncensored (*let the matter pass*). **b** (foll. by *as, for*) be accepted or currently known as. **c** *US* (of a person with some Black ancestry) be accepted as White. **7** *tr.* move; cause to go (*passed her hand over her face; passed a rope round it*). **8 a** *intr.* (of a candidate in an examination) be successful. **b** *tr.* be successful in (an examination). **c** *tr.* (of an examiner) judge the performance of (a candidate) to be satisfactory. **9 a** *tr.* (of a bill) be examined and approved by (a parliamentary body or process). **b** *tr.* cause or allow (a bill) to proceed to further legislative processes. **c** *intr.* (of a bill or proposal) be approved. **10** *intr.* **a** occur, elapse (*the remark passed unnoticed; time passes slowly*). **b** happen; be done or said (*heard what passed between them*). **11 a** *intr.* circulate; be current. **b** *tr.* put into circulation (*was passing forged cheques*). **12** *tr.* spend or use up (a certain time or period) (*passed the afternoon reading*). **13** *tr.* (also *absol.*) (in field games) send (the ball) to another player of one's own side. **14** *intr.* forgo one's turn or chance in a game etc. **15** *intr.* (foll. by *to, into*) change from one form (to another). **16** *intr.* come to an end. **17** *tr.* discharge from the body as or with excreta. **18** *tr.* (foll. by *on, upon*) **a** utter (criticism) about. **b** pronounce (a judicial sentence) on. **19** *intr.* (often foll. by *on, upon*) adjudicate. **20** *tr.* not declare or pay (a dividend). **21** *tr.* cause (troops etc.) to go by esp. ceremonially. —*n.* **1** an act or instance of passing. **2 a** success in an examination. **b** *Brit.* the status of a university degree without honours. **3** written permission to pass into or out of a place, or to be absent from quarters. **4 a** a ticket or permit giving free entry or access etc. **b** = *free pass*. **5** (in field games) a transference of the ball to another player on the same side. **6** a thrust in fencing. **7** a juggling trick. **8** an act of passing the hands over anything, as in conjuring or hypnotism. **9** a critical position (*has come to a fine pass*). □**in passing** **1** by the way. **2** in the course of speech, conversation, etc. **make a pass at** *colloq.* make amorous or sexual advances to. **pass away 1** *euphem.* die. **2** cease to exist; come to an end. **pass by 1** go past. **2** disregard, omit. **passed pawn** *Chess* a pawn that has advanced beyond the pawns on the other side. **pass one's eye over** read (a document etc.) cursorily. **pass muster** see MUSTER. **pass off 1** (of feelings etc.) disappear gradually. **2** (of proceedings) be carried through (in a specified way). **3** (foll. by *as*) misrepresent (a person or thing) as something else. **4** evade or lightly dismiss (an awkward remark etc.). **pass on 1** proceed on one's way. **2** *euphem.* die. **3** transmit to the next person in a series. **pass out 1** become unconscious.

2 *Brit. Mil.* complete one's training as a cadet. **3** distribute. **pass over 1** omit, ignore, or disregard. **2** ignore the claims of (a person) to promotion or advancement. **3** *euphem.* die. **pass round 1** distribute. **2** send or give to each of a number in turn. **pass through** experience. **pass the time of day** see TIME. **pass up** *colloq.* refuse or neglect (an opportunity etc.). **pass water** urinate. □□ **passer** *n.* [ME f. OF *passer* ult. f. L *passus* PACE[1]]

pass[2] /pɑːs/ *n.* **1** a narrow passage through mountains. **2** a navigable channel, esp. at the mouth of a river. □**sell the pass** betray a cause. [ME, var. of PACE[1], infl. by F *pas* and by PASS[1]]

passable /ˈpɑːsəb(ə)l/ *adj.* **1** barely satisfactory; just adequate. **2** (of a road, pass, etc.) that can be passed. □□ **passableness** *n.* **passably** *adv.* [ME f. OF (as PASS[1])]

passacaglia /ˌpæsəˈkɑːlɪə/ *n. Mus.* an instrumental piece usu. with a ground bass. [It. f. Sp. *pasacalle* f. *pasar* pass + *calle* street: orig. often played in the streets]

passage[1] /ˈpæsɪdʒ/ *n.* **1** the process or means of passing; transit. **2** = PASSAGEWAY. **3** the liberty or right to pass through. **4 a** the right of conveyance as a passenger by sea or air. **b** a journey by sea or air. **5** a transition from one state to another. **6 a** a short extract from a book etc. **b** a section of a piece of music. **7** the passing of a bill etc. into law. **8** (in *pl.*) an interchange of words etc. **9** *Anat.* a duct etc. in the body. □**passage of** (or **at**) **arms** a fight or dispute. **work one's passage** earn a right (orig. of passage) by working for it. [ME f. OF (as PASS[1])]

passage[2] /ˈpæsɪdʒ/ *v.* **1** *intr.* (of a horse or rider) move sideways, by the pressure of the rein on the horse's neck and of the rider's leg on the opposite side. **2** *tr.* make (a horse) do this. [F *passager*, earlier *passéger* f. It. *passeggiare* to walk, pace f. *passeggio* walk f. L *passus* PACE[1]]

passageway /ˈpæsɪdʒˌweɪ/ *n.* a narrow way for passing along, esp. with walls on either side; a corridor.

passant /ˈpæs(ə)nt/ *adj. Heraldry* (of an animal) walking and looking to the dexter side, with three paws on the ground and the right forepaw raised. [ME f. OF, part. of *passer* PASS[1]]

passband /ˈpɑːsbænd/ *n.* a frequency band within which signals are transmitted by a filter without attenuation.

passbook /ˈpɑːsbʊk/ *n.* a book issued by a bank or building society etc. to an account-holder recording sums deposited and withdrawn.

passé /ˈpæseɪ/ *adj.* (*fem.* **passée**) **1** behind the times; out of date. **2** past its prime. [F, past part. of *passer* PASS[1]]

passementerie /ˈpæsməntrɪ/ *n.* a trimming of gold or silver lace, braid, beads, etc. [F f. *passement* gold lace etc. f. *passer* PASS[1]]

passenger /ˈpæsɪndʒə(r)/ *n.* **1** a traveller in or on a public or private conveyance (other than the driver, pilot, crew, etc.). **2** *colloq.* a member of a team, crew, etc., who does no effective work. **3** (*attrib.*) for the use of passengers (*passenger seat*). □**passenger-mile** one mile travelled by one passenger, as a unit of traffic. **passenger-pigeon** an extinct wild pigeon of N. America, capable of long flight. [ME f. OF *passager* f. OF *passager* (adj.) passing (as PASSAGE[1]): *-n-* as in *messenger* etc.]

passe-partout /ˌpæspɑːˈtuː, ˌpɑːs-/ *n.* **1** a master-key. **2** a picture-frame (esp. for mounted photographs) consisting of two pieces of glass stuck together at the edges with adhesive tape. **3** adhesive tape or paper used for this. [F, = passes everywhere]

passer-by /ˌpɑːsəˈbaɪ/ *n.* (*pl.* **passers-by**) a person who goes past, esp. by chance.

passerine /ˈpæsəˌriːn/ *n.* & *adj.* —*n.* any perching bird of the order Passeriformes, having feet with three toes pointing forward and one pointing backwards, including sparrows and most land birds.

w *we* z zoo ʃ *she* ʒ decision θ *thin* ð *this* ŋ *ring* x *loch* tʃ *chip* dʒ *jar* (*see over for vowels*)

—*adj.* **1** of or relating to this order. **2** of the size of a sparrow. [L *passer* sparrow]

passible /'pæsɪb(ə)l/ *adj.* Theol. capable of feeling or suffering. □□ **passibility** /-'bɪlɪtɪ/ *n.* [ME f. OF *passible* or LL *passibilis* f. L *pati pass-* suffer]

passim /'pæsɪm/ *adv.* (of allusions or references in a published work) to be found at various places throughout the text. [L f. *passus* scattered f. *pandere* spread]

passing /'pɑːsɪŋ/ *adj. & n.* —*adj.* **1** in senses of PASS *v.* **2** transient, fleeting (*a passing glance*). **3** cursory, incidental (*a passing reference*). —*n.* **1** in senses of PASS *v.* **2** euphem. the death of a person (*mourned his passing*). □**passing note** *Mus.* a note not belonging to the harmony but interposed to secure a smooth transition. **passing shot** *Tennis* a shot aiming the ball beyond and out of reach of the other player. □□ **passingly** *adv.*

passion /'pæʃ(ə)n/ *n.* **1** strong barely controllable emotion. **2** an outburst of anger (*flew into a passion*). **3** intense sexual love. **4 a** strong enthusiasm (*has a passion for football*). **b** an object arousing this. **5** (**the Passion**) **a** Relig. the suffering of Christ during his last days. **b** a narrative of this from the Gospels. **c** a musical setting of any of these narratives. □**passion-flower** any climbing plant of the genus *Passiflora*, with a flower that was supposed to suggest the instruments of the Crucifixion. **passion-fruit** the edible fruit of some species of passion-flower, esp. *Passiflora edulis*: also called GRANADILLA. **passion-play** a miracle play representing Christ's Passion. **Passion Sunday** the fifth Sunday in Lent. **Passion Week 1** the week between Passion Sunday and Palm Sunday. **2** = *Holy Week.* □□ **passionless** *adj.* [ME f. OF f. LL *passio -onis* f. L *pati pass-* suffer]

passional /'pæʃən(ə)l/ *adj. & n.* —*adj.* literary of or marked by passion. —*n.* a book of the sufferings of saints and martyrs.

passionate /'pæʃənət/ *adj.* **1** dominated by or easily moved to strong feeling, esp. love or anger. **2** showing or caused by passion. □□ **passionately** *adv.* **passionateness** *n.* [ME f. med.L *passionatus* (as PASSION)]

Passiontide /'pæʃ(ə)n,taɪd/ *n.* the last two weeks of Lent.

passivate /'pæsɪ,veɪt/ *v.tr.* make (esp. metal) passive (see PASSIVE). □□ **passivation** /-'veɪʃ(ə)n/ *n.*

passive /'pæsɪv/ *adj.* **1** suffering action; acted upon. **2** offering no opposition; submissive. **3 a** not active; inert. **b** (of a metal) abnormally unreactive. **4** *Gram.* designating the voice in which the subject undergoes the action of the verb (e.g. in *they were killed*). **5** (of a debt) incurring no interest payment. □**passive obedience 1** surrender to another's will without cooperation. **2** compliance with commands irrespective of their nature. **passive resistance** a non-violent refusal to cooperate. **passive smoking** the involuntary inhaling, esp. by a non-smoker, of smoke from others' cigarettes etc. □□ **passively** *adv.* **passiveness** *n.* **passivity** /-'sɪvɪtɪ/ *n.* [ME f. OF *passif -ive* or L *passivus* (as PASSION)]

passkey /'pɑːskiː/ *n.* **1** a private key to a gate etc. for special purposes. **2** a master-key.

passmark /'pɑːsmɑːk/ *n.* the minimum mark needed to pass an examination.

Passover /'pɑːs,əʊvə(r)/ *n.* **1** the Jewish spring festival commemorating the liberation of the Israelites from Egyptian bondage, held from the 14th to the 21st day of the seventh month of the Jewish year. **2** = *paschal lamb.* [*pass over* = pass without touching, with ref. to the exemption of the Israelites from the death of the first-born (Exod. 12)]

passport /'pɑːspɔːt/ *n.* **1** an official document issued by a government certifying the holder's identity and citizenship, and entitling the holder to travel under its protection to and from foreign countries. **2** (foll. by *to*) a thing that ensures admission or attainment (*a passport to success*). [F *passeport* (as PASS[1], PORT[1])]

password /'pɑːswɜːd/ *n.* a selected word or phrase securing recognition, admission, etc., when used by those to whom it is disclosed.

past /pɑːst/ *adj., n., prep., & adv.* —*adj.* **1** gone by in time and no longer existing (*in past years*; *the time is past*). **2** recently completed or gone by (*the past month*; *for some time past*). **3** relating to a former time (*past president*). **4** *Gram.* expressing a past action or state. —*n.* **1** (prec. by *the*) **a** past time. **b** what has happened in past time (*cannot undo the past*). **2** a person's past life or career, esp. if discreditable (*a man with a past*). **3** a past tense or form. —*prep.* **1** beyond in time or place (*is past two o'clock*; *ran past the house*). **2** beyond the range, duration, or compass of (*past belief*; *past endurance*). —*adv.* so as to pass by (*hurried past*). □**not put it past a person** believe it possible of a person. **past it** colloq. incompetent or unusable through age. **past master 1** a person who is especially adept or expert in an activity, subject, etc. **2** a person who has been a master in a guild, Freemason's lodge, etc. **past perfect** = PLUPERFECT. [past part. of PASS[1] *v.*]

pasta /'pæstə/ *n.* **1** a dried flour paste used in various shapes in cooking (e.g. lasagne, spaghetti). **2** a cooked dish made from this. [It., = PASTE]

paste /peɪst/ *n. & v.* —*n.* **1** any moist fairly stiff mixture, esp. of powder and liquid. **2** a dough of flour with fat, water, etc., used in baking. **3** an adhesive of flour, water, etc., esp. for sticking paper and other light materials. **4** an easily spread preparation of ground meat, fish, etc. (*anchovy paste*). **5** a hard vitreous composition used in making imitation gems. **6** a mixture of clay, water, etc., used in making ceramic ware, esp. a mixture of low plasticity used in making porcelain. —*v.tr.* **1** fasten or coat with paste. **2** *sl.* **a** beat or thrash. **b** bomb or bombard heavily. □**paste-up** a document prepared for copying etc. by combining and pasting various sections on a backing. □□ **pasting** *n.* (esp. in sense 2 of *v.*). [ME f. OF f. LL *pasta* small square medicinal lozenge f. Gk *pastē* f. *pastos* sprinkled]

pasteboard /'peɪstbɔːd/ *n.* **1** a sheet of stiff material made by pasting together sheets of paper. **2** (*attrib.*) **a** flimsy, unsubstantial. **b** fake.

pastel /'pæst(ə)l/ *n.* **1** a crayon consisting of powdered pigments bound with a gum solution. **2** a work of art in pastel. **3** a light and subdued shade of a colour. □□ **pastelist** *n.* **pastellist** *n.* [F *pastel* or It. *pastello*, dimin. of *pasta* PASTE]

pastern /'pæst(ə)n/ *n.* **1** the part of a horse's foot between the fetlock and the hoof. **2** a corresponding part in other animals. [ME *pastron* f. OF *pasturon* f. *pasture* hobble ult. f. L *pastorius* of a shepherd: see PASTOR]

pasteurize /'pɑːstjə,raɪz, -tʃə,raɪz, 'pæst-/ *v.tr.* (also **-ise**) subject (milk etc.) to the process of partial sterilization by heating. □□ **pasteurization** /-'zeɪʃ(ə)n/ *n.* **pasteurizer** *n.* [L. *Pasteur*, Fr. chemist d. 1895]

pasticcio /pæs'tɪtʃəʊ/ *n.* (*pl.* **-os**) = PASTICHE. [It.: see PASTICHE]

pastiche /pæs'tiːʃ/ *n.* **1** a medley, esp. a picture or a musical composition, made up from or imitating various sources. **2** a literary or other work of art composed in the style of a well-known author. [F f. It. *pasticcio* ult. f. LL *pasta* PASTE]

pastille /'pæstɪl/ *n.* **1** a small sweet or lozenge. **2** a small roll of aromatic paste burnt as a fumigator etc. □**pastille-burner** an ornamental ceramic container in which an aromatic pastille may be burnt. [F f. L *pastillus* little loaf, lozenge f. *panis* loaf]

pastime /'pɑːstaɪm/ *n.* **1** a pleasant recreation or hobby. **2** a sport or game. [PASS[1] + TIME]

pastis /'pæstɪs/ *n.* an aniseed-flavoured aperitif. [F]

pastor /'pɑːstə(r)/ *n.* **1** a minister in charge of a church or a congregation. **2** a person exercising spiritual guidance. **3** a pink starling, *Sturnus roseus*.

æ *cat* ɑː *arm* e *bed* ɜː *her* ɪ *sit* iː *see* ɒ *hot* ɔː *saw* ʌ *run* ʊ *put* uː *too* ə *ago* aɪ *my*

□□ **pastorship** *n*. [ME f. AF & OF *pastour* f. L *pastor*
-oris shepherd f. *pascere past-* feed, graze]

pastoral /'pɑːstər(ə)l/ *adj*. & *n*. —*adj*. **1** of, relating
to, or associated with shepherds or flocks and herds.
2 (of land) used for pasture. **3** (of a poem, picture,
etc.) portraying country life, usu. in a romantic or
idealized form. **4** of or appropriate to a pastor. —*n*.
1 a pastoral poem, play, picture, etc. **2** a letter from a
pastor (esp. a bishop) to the clergy or people.
□ **pastoral staff** a bishop's crosier. **pastoral**
theology that considering religious truth in relation
to spiritual needs. □□ **pastoralism** *n*. **pastorality**
/-'rælɪtɪ/ *n*. **pastorally** *adv*. [ME f. L *pastoralis* (as
PASTOR)]

pastorale /ˌpæstəˈrɑːl, -lɪ/ *n*. (*pl*. **pastorales** or
pastorali /-liː/) **1** a slow instrumental composition
in compound time, usu. with drone notes in the bass.
2 a simple musical play with a rural subject. [It. (as
PASTORAL)]

pastoralist /'pɑːstərəlɪst/ *n*. *Austral*. a farmer of
sheep or cattle.

pastorate /'pɑːstərət/ *n*. **1** the office or tenure of a
pastor. **2** a body of pastors.

pastrami /pæˈstrɑːmɪ/ *n*. seasoned smoked beef.
[Yiddish]

pastry /'peɪstrɪ/ *n*. (*pl*. **-ies**) **1** a dough of flour, fat,
and water baked and used as a base and covering for
pies etc. **2 a** food, esp. cake, made wholly or partly of
this. **b** a piece or item of this food. □ **pastry-cook** a
cook who specializes in pastry, esp. for public sale.
[PASTE after OF *pastaierie*]

pasturage /'pɑːstʃərɪdʒ/ *n*. **1** land for pasture. **2** the
process of pasturing cattle etc. [OF (as PASTURE)]

pasture /'pɑːstjə(r)/ *n*. & *v*. —*n*. **1** land covered with
grass etc. suitable for grazing animals, esp. cattle or
sheep. **2** herbage for animals. —*v*. **1** *tr*. put (animals)
to graze in a pasture. **2** *intr*. & *tr*. (of animals) graze.
[ME f. OF f. LL *pastura* (as PASTOR)]

pasty[1] /'pæstɪ/ *n*. (*pl*. **-ies**) a pastry case with a sweet
or savoury filling, baked without a dish to shape it.
[ME f. OF *pasté* ult. f. LL *pasta* PASTE]

pasty[2] /'peɪstɪ/ *adj*. (**pastier**, **pastiest**) **1** of or like
or covered with paste. **2** unhealthily pale (esp. in
complexion) (*pasty-faced*). □□ **pastily** *adv*. **pastiness**
n.

Pat /pæt/ *n*. a nickname for an Irishman. [abbr. of
the name *Patrick*]

Pat. *abbr*. Patent.

pat[1] /pæt/ *v*. & *n*. —*v*. (**patted**, **patting**) **1** *tr*. strike
gently with the hand or a flat surface. **2** *tr*. flatten or
mould by patting. **3** *tr*. strike gently with the inner
surface of the hand, esp. as a sign of affection,
sympathy, or congratulation. **4** *intr*. (foll. by *on*,
upon) beat lightly. —*n*. **1** a light stroke or tap, esp.
with the hand in affection etc. **2** the sound made by
this. **3** a small mass (esp. of butter) formed by patting.
□ **pat-a-cake** a child's game with the patting of hands
(the first words of a nursery rhyme). **pat on the**
back a gesture of approval or congratulation. **pat a**
person on the back congratulate a person. [ME,
prob. imit.]

pat[2] /pæt/ *adj*. & *adv*. —*adj*. **1** known thoroughly
and ready for any occasion. **2** apposite or opportune,
esp. unconvincingly so (*gave a pat answer*). —*adv*. **1**
in a pat manner. **2** appositely, opportunely. □ **have**
off pat know or have memorized perfectly. **stand**
pat esp. *US* **1** stick stubbornly to one's opinion or
decision. **2** *Poker* retain one's hand as dealt; not
draw other cards. □□ **patly** *adv*. **patness** *n*. [16th c.:
rel. to PAT[1]]

pat[3] /pæt/ *n*. □ **on one's pat** *Austral*. *sl*. on one's
own. [*Pat Malone*, rhyming slang for *own*]

patagium /ˌpætəˈdʒaɪəm/ *n*. (*pl*. **patagia** /-ˈdʒaɪə/)
Zool. **1** the wing-membrane of a bat or similar
animal. **2** a scale covering the wing-joint in moths
and butterflies. [med.L use of L *patagium* f. Gk
patageion gold edging]

patball /'pætbɔːl/ *n*. **1** a simple game of ball played
between two players. **2** *derog*. lawn tennis.

patch /pætʃ/ *n*. & *v*. —*n*. **1** a piece of material or
metal etc. used to mend a hole or as reinforcement.
2 a pad worn to protect an injured eye. **3** a dressing
etc. put over a wound. **4** a large or irregular
distinguishable area on a surface. **5** *colloq*. a period
of time in terms of its characteristic quality (*went*
through a bad patch). **6** a piece of ground. **7** *colloq*.
an area assigned to or patrolled by an authorized
person, esp. a police officer. **8** a number of plants
growing in one place (*brier patch*). **9** a scrap or
remnant. **10** a temporary electrical connection. **11**
hist. a small disc etc. of black silk attached to the
face, worn esp. by women in the 17th–18th c. for
adornment. **12** *Mil*. a piece of cloth on a uniform as
the badge of a unit. —*v.tr*. **1** (often foll. by *up*) repair
with a patch or patches; put a patch or patches on. **2**
(of material) serve as a patch to. **3** (often foll. by *up*)
put together, esp. hastily or in a makeshift way. **4**
(foll. by *up*) settle (a quarrel etc.) esp. hastily or
temporarily. □ **not a patch on** *colloq*. greatly inferior
to. **patch cord** an insulated lead with a plug at each
end, for use with a patchboard. **patch panel** =
PATCHBOARD. **patch pocket** one made of a piece of
cloth sewn on a garment. **patch test** a test for allergy
by applying to the skin patches containing allergenic
substances. □□ **patcher** *n*. [ME *pacche, patche*, perh.
var. of *peche* f. OF *pieche* dial. var. of *piece* PIECE]

patchboard /'pætʃbɔːd/ *n*. a board with electrical
sockets linked to enable changeable permutations of
connection.

patchouli /pəˈtʃuːlɪ, 'pætʃʊlɪ/ *n*. **1** a strongly scented
E. Indian plant, *Pogostemon cablin*. **2** the perfume
obtained from this. [a native name in Madras]

patchwork /'pætʃwɜːk/ *n*. **1** needlework using small
pieces of cloth with different designs, forming a
pattern. **2** a thing composed of various small pieces
or fragments.

patchy /'pætʃɪ/ *adj*. (**patchier**, **patchiest**) **1** uneven
in quality. **2** having or existing in patches. □□
patchily *adv*. **patchiness** *n*.

pate /peɪt/ *n*. *archaic* or *colloq*. the head, esp. representing the seat of intellect. [ME: orig. unkn.]

pâte /pɑːt/ *n*. the paste of which porcelain is made.
[F, = PASTE]

pâté /'pæteɪ/ *n*. a rich paste or spread of mashed and
spiced meat or fish etc. □ *pâté de foie gras* /də fwɑː
'grɑː/ a paste of fatted goose liver. [F f. OF *pasté* (as
PASTY[1])]

patella /pəˈtelə/ *n*. (*pl*. **patellae** /-liː/) the kneecap.
□□ **patellar** *adj*. **patellate** /-lət/ *adj*. [L, dimin. of
patina: see PATEN]

paten /'pæt(ə)n/ *n*. **1** a shallow dish used for the
bread at the Eucharist. **2** a thin circular plate of
metal. [ME ult. f. OF *patene* or L *patena, patina*
shallow dish f. Gk *patanē* a plate]

patent /'peɪt(ə)nt, 'pæt-/ *n*., *adj*., & *v*. —*n*. **1** a
government authority to an individual or organization conferring a right or title, esp. the sole
right to make or use or sell some invention. **2** a
document granting this authority. **3** an invention or
process protected by it. —*adj*. **1** /'peɪt(ə)nt/ obvious,
plain. **2** conferred or protected by patent. **3 a** made
and marketed under a patent; proprietary. **b** to
which one has a proprietary claim. **4** such as might
be patented; ingenious, well-contrived. **5** (of an
opening etc.) allowing free passage. —*v.tr*. obtain a
patent for (an invention). □ **letters patent** an open
document from a sovereign or government conferring a patent or other right. **patent leather**
leather with a glossy varnished surface. **patent**
medicine medicine made and marketed under a
patent and available without prescription. **patent**
office an office from which patents are issued. **patent**
Patent Roll (in the UK) a list of patents issued in
a year. □□ **patency** *n*. **patentable** *adj*. **patently**

/'peɪtəntlɪ/ *adv.* (in sense 1 of *adj.*). [ME f. OF *patent* and L *patēre* lie open]

patentee /ˌpeɪtən'tiː/ *n.* **1** a person who takes out or holds a patent. **2** a person for the time being entitled to the benefit of a patent.

patentor /'peɪtəntə(r)/ *n.* a person or body that grants a patent.

pater /'peɪtə(r)/ *n. Brit. colloq.* father. ¶ Now only in jocular or affected use. [L]

paterfamilias /ˌpeɪtəfə'mɪlɪˌæs/ *n.* the male head of a family or household. [L, = father of the family]

paternal /pə'tɜːn(ə)l/ *adj.* **1** of or like or appropriate to a father. **2** fatherly. **3** related through the father. **4** (of a government etc.) limiting freedom and responsibility by well-meant regulations. □□ **paternally** *adv.* [LL *paternalis* f. L *paternus* f. *pater* father]

paternalism /pə'tɜːnəˌlɪz(ə)m/ *n.* the policy of governing in a paternal way, or behaving paternally to one's associates or subordinates. □□ **paternalist** *n.* **paternalistic** /-'lɪstɪk/ *adj.* **paternalistically** /-'lɪstɪkəlɪ/ *adv.*

paternity /pə'tɜːnɪtɪ/ *n.* **1** fatherhood. **2** one's paternal origin. **3** the source or authorship of a thing. □ **paternity test** a blood test to determine whether a man may be or cannot be the father of a particular child. [ME f. OF *paternité* or LL *paternitas*]

paternoster /ˌpætə'nɒstə(r)/ *n.* **1 a** the Lord's Prayer, esp. in Latin. **b** a rosary bead indicating that this is to be said. **2** a lift consisting of a series of linked doorless compartments moving continuously on a circular belt. [OE f. L *pater noster* our father]

path /pɑːθ/ *n.* (*pl.* **paths** /pɑːðz/) **1** a way or track laid down for walking or made by continual treading. **2** the line along which a person or thing moves (*flight path*). **3** a course of action or conduct. **4** a sequence of movements or operations taken by a system. □□ **pathless** *adj.* [OE *pæth* f. WG]

-path /pæθ/ *comb. form* forming nouns denoting: **1** a practitioner of curative treatment (*homoeopath*; *osteopath*). **2** a person who suffers from a disease (*psychopath*). [back-form. f. -PATHY, or f. Gk *-pathēs* -sufferer (as PATHOS)]

Pathan /pə'tɑːn/ *n.* a member of a Pashto-speaking people inhabiting NW Pakistan and SE Afghanistan. [Hindi]

pathetic /pə'θetɪk/ *adj.* **1** arousing pity or sadness or contempt. **2** *Brit. colloq.* miserably inadequate. **3** *archaic* of the emotions. □ **pathetic fallacy** the attribution of human feelings and responses to inanimate things, esp. in art and literature. □□ **pathetically** *adv.* [F *pathétique* f. LL *patheticus* f. Gk *pathētikos* (as PATHOS)]

pathfinder /'pɑːθˌfaɪndə(r)/ *n.* **1** a person who explores new territory, investigates a new subject, etc. **2** an aircraft or its pilot sent ahead to locate and mark the target area for bombing.

patho- /'pæθəʊ/ *comb. form* disease. [Gk *pathos* suffering: see PATHOS]

pathogen /'pæθədʒ(ə)n/ *n.* an agent causing disease. □□ **pathogenic** /-'dʒenɪk/ *adj.* **pathogenous** /-'θɒdʒənəs/ *adj.* [PATHO- + -GEN]

pathogenesis /ˌpæθə'dʒenɪsɪs/ *n.* (also **pathogeny** /pə'θɒdʒənɪ/) the manner of development of a disease. □□ **pathogenetic** /-dʒɪ'netɪk/ *adj.*

pathological /ˌpæθə'lɒdʒɪk(ə)l/ *adj.* **1** of pathology. **2** of or caused by a physical or mental disorder (*a pathological fear of spiders*). □□ **pathologically** *adv.*

pathology /pə'θɒlədʒɪ/ *n.* **1** the science of bodily diseases. **2** the symptoms of a disease. □□ **pathologist** *n.* [F *pathologie* or mod.L *pathologia* (as PATHO-, -LOGY)]

pathos /'peɪθɒs/ *n.* a quality in speech, writing, events, etc., that excites pity or sadness. [Gk *pathos* suffering, rel. to *paskhō* suffer, *penthos* grief]

pathway /'pɑːθweɪ/ *n.* **1** a path or its course. **2** *Biochem.* etc. a sequence of reactions undergone in a living organism.

-pathy /pəθɪ/ *comb. form* forming nouns denoting: **1** curative treatment (*allopathy*; *homoeopathy*). **2** feeling (*telepathy*). [Gk *patheia* suffering]

patience /'peɪʃ(ə)ns/ *n.* **1** calm endurance of hardship, provocation, pain, delay, etc. **2** tolerant perseverance or forbearance. **3** the capacity for calm self-possessed waiting. **4** esp. *Brit.* a game for one player in which cards taken in random order have to be arranged in certain groups or sequences. □ **have no patience with 1** be unable to tolerate. **2** be irritated by. [ME f. OF f. L *patientia* (as PATIENT)]

patient /'peɪʃ(ə)nt/ *adj. & n.* —*adj.* having or showing patience. —*n.* a person receiving or registered to receive medical treatment. □□ **patiently** *adv.* [ME f. OF f. L *patiens -entis* pres. part. of *pati* suffer]

patina /'pætɪnə/ *n.* (*pl.* **patinas**) **1** a film, usu. green, formed on the surface of old bronze. **2** a similar film on other surfaces. **3** a gloss produced by age on woodwork. □□ **patinated** /-ˌneɪtɪd/ *adj.* **patination** /-'neɪʃ(ə)n/ *n.* [It. f. L *patina* dish]

patio /'pætɪəʊ/ *n.* (*pl.* **-os**) **1** a paved usu. roofless area adjoining and belonging to a house. **2** an inner court open to the sky in a Spanish or Spanish-American house. [Sp.]

patisserie /pə'tiːsərɪ/ *n.* **1** a shop where pastries are made and sold. **2** pastries collectively. [F *pâtisserie* f. med.L *pasticium* pastry f. *pasta* PASTE]

Patna rice /'pætnə/ *n.* a variety of rice with long firm grains. [*Patna* in India, where it was orig. grown]

patois /'pætwɑː/ *n.* (*pl.* same /-wɑːz/) the dialect of the common people in a region, differing fundamentally from the literary language. [F, = rough speech, perh. f. OF *patoier* treat roughly f. *patte* paw]

patrial /'peɪtrɪəl/ *adj. & n. Brit. hist.* —*adj.* having the right to live in the UK through the British birth of a parent or a grandparent. —*n.* a person with this right. □□ **patriality** /-'ælɪtɪ/ *n.* [obs. F *patrial* or med.L *patrialis* f. L *patria* fatherland f. *pater* father]

patriarch /'peɪtrɪˌɑːk/ *n.* **1** the male head of a family or tribe. **2** (often in *pl.*) *Bibl.* any of those regarded as fathers of the human race, esp. the sons of Jacob, or Abraham, Isaac, and Jacob, and their forefathers. **3** *Eccl.* **a** the title of a chief bishop, esp. those presiding over the Churches of Antioch, Alexandria, Constantinople, and (formerly) Rome; now also the title of the heads of certain autocephalous Orthodox Churches. **b** (in the Roman Catholic Church) a bishop ranking next above primates and metropolitans, and immediately below the pope. **c** the head of a Uniate community. **4 a** the founder of an order, science, etc. **b** a venerable old man. **c** the oldest member of a group. □□ **patriarchal** /-'ɑːk(ə)l/ *adj.* **patriarchally** /-'ɑːkəlɪ/ *adv.* [ME f. OF *patriarche* f. eccl.L *patriarcha* f. Gk *patriarkhēs* f. *patria* family f. *patēr* father + *-arkhēs* -ruler]

patriarchate /'peɪtrɪˌɑːkət/ *n.* **1** the office, see, or residence of an ecclesiastical patriarch. **2** the rank of a tribal patriarch. [med.L *patriarchatus* (as PATRIARCH)]

patriarchy /'peɪtrɪˌɑːkɪ/ *n.* (*pl.* **-ies**) a system of society, government, etc., ruled by a man and with descent through the male line. □□ **patriarchism** *n.* [med.L *patriarchia* f. Gk *patriarkhia* (as PATRIARCH)]

patrician /pə'trɪʃ(ə)n/ *n. & adj.* —*n.* **1** *hist.* a member of the ancient Roman nobility (cf. PLEBEIAN). **2** *hist.* a nobleman in some Italian republics. **3** an aristocrat. —*adj.* **1** noble, aristocratic. **2** *hist.* of the ancient Roman nobility. [ME f. OF *patricien* f. L *patricius* having a noble father f. *pater patris* father]

patriciate /pə'trɪʃɪət/ *n.* **1** a patrician order; an aristocracy. **2** the rank of patrician. [L *patriciatus* (as PATRICIAN)]

patricide /'pætrɪˌsaɪd/ *n.* = PARRICIDE (esp. with reference to the killing of one's own father). □□ **patricidal** /-'saɪd(ə)l/ *adj.* [LL *patricida, patricidium,* alt. of L *parricida, parricidium* (see PARRICIDE) after *pater* father]

b *but* d *dog* f *few* g *get* h *he* j *yes* k *cat* l *leg* m *man* n *no* p *pen* r *red* s *sit* t *top* v *voice*

patrilineal /ˌpætrɪˈlɪnɪəl/ adj. of or relating to, or based on kinship with, the father or descent through the male line. [L pater patris father + LINEAL]

patrimony /ˈpætrɪmənɪ/ n. (pl. -ies) 1 property inherited from one's father or ancestor. 2 a heritage. 3 the endowment of a church etc. □□ **patrimonial** /-ˈməʊnɪəl/ adj. [ME patrimoigne f. OF patrimoine f. L patrimonium f. pater patris father]

patriot /ˈpeɪtrɪət, ˈpæt-/ n. a person who is devoted to and ready to support or defend his or her country. □□ **patriotic** /-ˈɒtɪk/ adj. **patriotically** /-ˈɒtɪklɪ/ adv. **patriotism** n. [F patriote f. LL patriota f. Gk patriōtēs f. patrios of one's fathers f. patēr patros father]

patristic /pəˈtrɪstɪk/ adj. of the early Christian writers or their work. □□ **patristics** n.pl. (usu. treated as sing.). [G patristisch f. L pater patris father]

patrol /pəˈtrəʊl/ n. & v. —n. 1 the act of walking or travelling around an area, esp. at regular intervals, in order to protect or supervise it. 2 one or more persons or vehicles assigned or sent out on patrol, esp. a detachment of guards, police, etc. 3 a a detachment of troops sent out to reconnoitre. b such reconnaissance. 4 a routine operational voyage of a ship or aircraft. 5 a routine monitoring of astronomical or other phenomena. 6 Brit. an official controlling traffic where children cross the road. 7 a unit of six to eight Scouts or Guides. —v. (patrolled, patrolling) 1 tr. carry out a patrol of. 2 intr. act as a patrol. □ **patrol car** a police car used in patrolling roads and streets. **patrol wagon** esp. US a police van for transporting prisoners. □□ **patroller** n. [F patrouiller paddle in mud f. patte paw: (n.) f. G Patrolle f. F patrouille]

patrolman /pəˈtrəʊlmən/ n. (pl. -men) US a policeman of the lowest rank.

patrology /pəˈtrɒlədʒɪ/ n. (pl. -ies) 1 the study of the writings of the Fathers of the Church. 2 a collection of such writings. □□ **patrological** /ˌpætrəˈlɒdʒɪk(ə)l/ adj. **patrologist** n. [Gk patēr patros father]

patron /ˈpeɪtrən/ n. (fem. **patroness**) 1 a person who gives financial or other support to a person, cause, work of art, etc., esp. one who buys works of art. 2 a usu. regular customer of a shop etc. 3 Rom. Antiq. a the former owner of a freed slave. b the protector of a client. 4 Brit. a person who has the right of presenting a member of the clergy to a benefice. □ **patron saint** the protecting or guiding saint of a person, place, etc. [ME f. OF f. L patronus protector of clients, defender f. pater patris father]

patronage /ˈpætrənɪdʒ/ n. 1 the support, promotion, or encouragement given by a patron. 2 a patronizing or condescending manner. 3 Rom. Antiq. the rights and duties or position of a patron. 4 Brit. the right of presenting a member of the clergy to a benefice etc. 5 a customer's support for a shop etc. [ME f. OF (as PATRON)]

patronal /ˈpætrən(ə)l, ˈpeɪt-, pəˈtrəʊn(ə)l/ adj. of or relating to a patron saint (the patronal festival). [F patronal or LL patronalis (as PATRON)]

patronize /ˈpætrəˌnaɪz/ v.tr. (also -ise) 1 treat condescendingly. 2 act as a patron towards (a person, cause, artist, etc.); support; encourage. 3 frequent (a shop etc.) as a customer. □□ **patronization** /-ˈzeɪʃ(ə)n/ n. **patronizer** n. **patronizing** adj. **patronizingly** adv. [obs. F patroniser or med.L patronizare (as PATRON)]

patronymic /ˌpætrəˈnɪmɪk/ n. & adj. —n. a name derived from the name of a father or ancestor, e.g. Johnson, O'Brien, Ivanovich. —adj. (of a name) so derived. [LL patronymicus f. Gk patrōnumikos f. patrōnumos f. patēr patros father + onuma, onoma name]

patroon /pəˈtruːn/ n. US hist. a landowner with manorial privileges under the Dutch governments of New York and New Jersey. [Du., = PATRON]

patsy /ˈpætsɪ/ n. (pl. -ies) esp. US sl. a person who is deceived, ridiculed, tricked, etc. [20th c.: orig. unkn.]

pattée /ˈpæteɪ, -tɪ/ adj. (of a cross) having almost triangular arms becoming very broad at the ends so as to form a square. [F f. patte paw]

patten /ˈpæt(ə)n/ n. hist. a shoe or clog with a raised sole or set on an iron ring, for walking in mud etc. [ME f. OF patin f. patte paw]

patter[1] /ˈpætə(r)/ v. & n. —v. 1 intr. make a rapid succession of taps, as of rain on a window-pane. 2 intr. run with quick short steps. 3 tr. cause (water etc.) to patter. —n. a rapid succession of taps, short light steps, etc. [PAT[1]]

patter[2] /ˈpætə(r)/ n. & v. —n. 1 a the rapid speech used by a comedian or introduced into a song. b the words of a comic song. 2 the words used by a person selling or promoting a product; a sales pitch. 3 the special language or jargon of a profession, class, etc. —v. 1 tr. repeat (prayers etc.) in a rapid mechanical way. 2 intr. talk glibly or mechanically. [ME f. pater = PATERNOSTER]

pattern /ˈpæt(ə)n/ n. & v. —n. 1 a repeated decorative design on wallpaper, cloth, a carpet, etc. 2 a regular or logical form, order, or arrangement of parts (behaviour pattern; the pattern of one's daily life). 3 a model or design, e.g. of a garment, from which copies can be made. 4 an example of excellence; an ideal; a model (a pattern of elegance). 5 a wooden or metal figure from which a mould is made for a casting. 6 a sample (of cloth, wallpaper, etc.). 7 the marks made by shots, bombs, etc. on a target or target area. 8 a random combination of shapes or colours. —v.tr. 1 (usu. foll. by after, on) model (a thing) on a design etc. 2 decorate with a pattern. □ **pattern bombing** bombing over a large area, not on a single target. [ME patron (see PATRON): differentiated in sense and spelling since the 16th–17th c.]

patty /ˈpætɪ/ n. (pl. -ies) 1 a little pie or pastry. 2 US a small flat cake of minced meat etc. [F pâté PASTY[1]]

pattypan /ˈpætɪˌpæn/ n. a pan for baking a patty.

patulous /ˈpætjʊləs/ adj. 1 (of branches etc.) spreading. 2 formal open; expanded. □□ **patulously** adj. **patulousness** n. [L patulus f. patēre be open]

paua /ˈpaʊə/ n. 1 a large edible New Zealand shellfish of the genus Haliotis. 2 its ornamental shell. 3 a fish-hook made from this. [Maori]

paucity /ˈpɔːsɪtɪ/ n. smallness of number or quantity. [ME f. OF paucité or f. L paucitas f. paucus few]

Pauli exclusion principle /ˈpaʊlɪ/ n. Physics the assertion that no two fermions can have the same quantum number. [W. Pauli, Austrian physicist d. 1958]

Pauline /ˈpɔːlaɪn/ adj. of or relating to St Paul (the Pauline epistles). [ME f. med.L Paulinus f. L Paulus Paul]

Paul Jones /pɔːl ˈdʒəʊnz/ n. a ballroom dance in which partners are exchanged according to a pattern. [the name of an Amer. naval officer d. 1792]

paulownia /pɔːˈləʊnɪə/ n. any Chinese tree of the genus Paulownia, with fragrant purple flowers. [Anna Paulovna, Russian princess d. 1865]

paunch /pɔːntʃ/ n. & v. —n. 1 the belly or stomach, esp. when protruding. 2 a ruminant's first stomach; the rumen. 3 Naut. a thick strong mat. —v.tr. disembowel (an animal). □□ **paunchy** adj. (**paunchier**, **paunchiest**). **paunchiness** n. [ME f. AF pa(u)nche, ONF panche ult. f. L pantex panticis bowels]

pauper /ˈpɔːpə(r)/ n. 1 a person without means; a beggar. 2 hist. a recipient of poor-law relief. 3 Law a person who may sue in forma pauperis. □□ **pauperdom** /-dəm/ n. **pauperism** /-ˌrɪz(ə)m/ n. **pauperize** v.tr. (also -ise). **pauperization** /-ˈzeɪʃ(ə)n/ n. [L, = poor]

pause /pɔːz/ n. & v. —n. 1 an interval of inaction, esp. when due to hesitation; a temporary stop. 2 a break in speaking or reading; a silence. 3 Mus. a mark (⌢) over a note or rest that is to be lengthened by an unspecified amount. —v.intr. 1 make a pause; wait. 2 (usu. foll. by upon) linger over (a word etc.).

□**give pause to** cause (a person) to hesitate. [ME f. OF *pause* or L *pausa* f. Gk *pausis* f. *pauō* stop]

pavage /ˈpeɪvɪdʒ/ n. **1** paving. **2** a tax or toll towards the paving of streets. [ME f. OF f. *paver* PAVE]

pavane /pəˈvɑːn/ n. (also **pavan** /ˈpævˌ(ə)n/) *hist.* **1** a stately dance in elaborate clothing. **2** the music for this. [F *pavane* f. Sp. *pavana*, perh. f. *pavon* peacock]

pave /peɪv/ v.tr. **1 a** cover (a street, floor, etc.) with paving etc. **b** cover or strew (a floor etc.) with anything (*paved with flowers*). **2** prepare (*paved the way for her arrival*). □**paving-stone** a large flat usu. rectangular piece of stone etc. for paving. □□**paver** n. **paving** n. **pavior** /ˈpeɪvjə(r)/ n. (also **paviour**). [ME f. OF *paver*, back-form. (as PAVEMENT)]

pavé /ˈpæveɪ/ n. **1** a paved street, road, or path. **2** a setting of jewels placed closely together. [F, past part. of *paver*: see PAVE]

pavement /ˈpeɪvmənt/ n. **1** *Brit.* a paved path for pedestrians at the side of and a little higher than a road. **2** the covering of a street, floor, etc., made of tiles, wooden blocks, asphalt, and esp. of rectangular stones. **3** *US* a roadway. **4** *Zool.* a pavement-like formation of close-set teeth, scales, etc. □**pavement artist 1** *Brit.* an artist who draws on paving-stones with coloured chalks, hoping to be given money by passers-by. **2** *US* an artist who displays paintings for sale on a pavement. [ME f. OF f. L *pavimentum* f. *pavire* beat, ram]

pavilion /pəˈvɪljən/ n. & v. —n. **1** *Brit.* a building at a cricket or other sports ground used for changing, refreshments, etc. **2** a summerhouse or other decorative building in a garden. **3** a tent, esp. a large one with crenellated decorations at a show, fair, etc. **4** a building used for entertainments. **5** a temporary stand at an exhibition. **6** a detached building at a hospital. **7** a usu. highly decorated subdivision of a building. **8** the part of a cut gemstone below the girdle. —v.tr. enclose in or provide with a pavilion. [ME f. OF *pavillon* f. L *papilio -onis* butterfly, tent]

pavior, paviour see PAVE.

pavlova /pævˈləʊvə/ n. a meringue cake with cream and fruit. [A. *Pavlova*, Russ. ballerina d. 1931]

Pavlovian /pævˈləʊvɪən/ adj. of or relating to I. P. Pavlov, Russian physiologist d. 1936, or his work, esp. on conditioned reflexes.

pavonine /ˈpævənaɪn/ adj. of or like a peacock. [L *pavoninus* f. *pavo -onis* peacock]

paw /pɔː/ n. & v. —n. **1** a foot of an animal having claws or nails. **2** *colloq.* a person's hand. —v. **1** tr. strike or scrape with a paw or foot. **2** intr. scrape the ground with a paw or hoof. **3** tr. *colloq.* fondle awkwardly or indecently. [ME *pawe, powe* f. OF *poue* etc. ult. f. Frank.]

pawky /ˈpɔːkɪ/ adj. (**pawkier, pawkiest**) *Sc.* & *dial.* **1** drily humorous. **2** shrewd. □□**pawkily** adv. **pawkiness** n. [Sc. & N.Engl. dial. *pawk* trick, of unkn. orig.]

pawl /pɔːl/ n. & v. —n. **1** a lever with a catch for the teeth of a wheel or bar. **2** *Naut.* a short bar used to lock a capstan, windlass, etc., to prevent it from recoiling. —v.tr. secure (a capstan etc.) with a pawl. [perh. f. LG & Du. *pal*, rel. to *pal* fixed]

pawn¹ /pɔːn/ n. **1** *Chess* a piece of the smallest size and value. **2** a person used by others for their own purposes. [ME f. AF *poun*, OF *peon* f. med.L *pedo -onis* foot-soldier f. L *pes pedis* foot: cf. PEON]

pawn² /pɔːn/ v. & n. —v.tr. **1** deposit an object, esp. with a pawnbroker, as security for money lent. **2** pledge or wager (one's life, honour, word, etc.). —n. **1** an object left as security for money etc. lent. **2** anything or any person left with another as security etc. □**in** (or **at**) **pawn** (of an object etc.) held as security. [ME f. OF *pan, pand, pant*, pledge, security f. WG]

pawnbroker /ˈpɔːnˌbrəʊkə(r)/ n. a person who lends money at interest on the security of personal property pawned. □□**pawnbroking** n.

pawnshop /ˈpɔːnʃɒp/ n. a shop where pawnbroking is conducted.

pawpaw /ˈpɔːpɔː/ n. (also **papaw** /pəˈpɔː/, **papaya** /pəˈpaɪə/) **1 a** an elongated melon-shaped fruit with edible orange flesh and small black seeds. **b** a tropical tree, *Carica papaya*, bearing this and producing a milky sap from which papain is obtained. **2** *US* a N. American tree, *Asimina triloba*, with purple flowers and edible fruit. [earlier *papay(a)* f. Sp. & Port. *papaya*, of Carib orig.]

PAX abbr. private automatic (telephone) exchange.

pax /pæks/ n. **1** the kiss of peace. **2** (as int.) *Brit. sl.* a call for a truce (used esp. by schoolchildren). [ME f. L, = peace]

pay¹ /peɪ/ v. & n. —v.tr. (past and past part. **paid** /peɪd/) **1** (also absol.) give (a person etc.) what is due for services done, goods received, debts incurred, etc. (*paid him in full; I assure you I have paid*). **2 a** give (a usu. specified amount) for work done, a debt, a ransom, etc. (*they pay £6 an hour*). **b** (foll. by *to*) hand over the amount of (a debt, wages, recompense, etc.) to (*paid the money to the assistant*). **3 a** give, bestow, or express (attention, respect, a compliment, etc.) (*paid them no heed*). **b** make (a visit, a call, etc.) (*paid a visit to their uncle*). **4** (also absol.) (of a business, undertaking, attitude, etc.) be profitable or advantageous to (a person etc.). **5** reward or punish (*can never pay you for what you have done for us; I shall pay you for that*). **6** (usu. as **paid** adj.) recompense (work, time, etc.) (*paid holiday*). **7** (usu. foll. by *out, away*) let out (a rope) by slackening it. —n. wages; payment. □**in the pay of** employed by. **paid holidays** an agreed holiday period for which wages are paid as normal. **paid-up member** (esp. of a trade-union member) a person who has paid the subscriptions in full. **pay-as-you-earn** *Brit.* the deduction of income tax from wages at source. **pay-bed** a hospital bed for private patients. **pay-claim** a demand for an increase in pay, esp. by a trade union. **pay-day** a day on which payment, esp. of wages, is made or expected to be made. **pay dearly** (usu. foll. by *for*) **1** obtain at a high cost, great effort, etc. **2** suffer for a wrongdoing etc. **pay dirt** (or **gravel**) *US* **1** *Mineral.* ground worth working for ore. **2** a financially promising situation. **pay envelope** *US* = *pay-packet*. **pay for 1** hand over the price of. **2** bear the cost of. **3** suffer or be punished for (a fault etc.). **pay in** pay (money) into a bank account. **paying guest** a boarder. **pay its** (or **one's**) **way** cover costs; not be indebted. **pay one's last respects** show respect towards a dead person by attending the funeral. **pay off 1** dismiss (workers) with a final payment. **2** *colloq.* yield good results; succeed. **3** pay (a debt) in full. **4** (of a ship) turn to leeward through the movement of the helm. **pay-off** n. sl. **1** an act of payment. **2** a climax. **3** a final reckoning. **pay out** (or **back**) punish or be revenged on. **pay-packet** *Brit.* a packet or envelope containing an employee's wages. **pay phone** a coin-box telephone. **pay the piper and call the tune** pay for, and therefore have control over, a proceeding. **pay one's respects** make a polite visit. **pay station** *US* = *pay phone*. **pay through the nose** *colloq.* pay much more than a fair price. **pay up** pay the full amount, or the full amount of. **put paid to** *colloq.* **1** deal effectively with (a person). **2** terminate (hopes etc.). □□**payee** /peɪˈiː/ n. **payer** n. [ME f. OF *paie*, *payer* f. L *pacare* appease f. *pax pacis* peace]

pay² /peɪ/ v.tr. (past and past part. **payed**) *Naut.* smear (a ship) with pitch, tar, etc. as a defence against wet. [OF *peier* f. L *picare* f. *pix picis* PITCH²]

payable /ˈpeɪəb(ə)l/ adj. **1** that must be paid; due (*payable in April*). **2** that may be paid. **3** (of a mine etc.) profitable.

payback /ˈpeɪbæk/ n. **1** a financial return; a reward. **2** the profit from an investment etc., esp. one equal to the initial outlay. □**payback period** the length of time required for an investment to pay for itself in terms of profits or savings.

PAYE *abbr. Brit.* pay-as-you-earn.

payload /'peɪləʊd/ *n.* **1** the part of an aircraft's load from which revenue is derived. **2 a** the explosive warhead carried by an aircraft or rocket. **b** the instruments etc. carried by a spaceship.

paymaster /'peɪˌmɑːstə(r)/ *n.* **1** an official who pays troops, workmen, etc. **2** a person, organization, etc., to whom another owes duty or loyalty because of payment given. **3** (in full **Paymaster General**) *Brit.* the minister at the head of the Treasury department responsible for payments.

payment /'peɪmənt/ *n.* **1** the act or an instance of paying. **2** an amount paid. **3** reward, recompense. [ME f. OF *paiement* (as PAY[1])]

paynim /'peɪnɪm/ *n. archaic* **1** a pagan. **2** a non-Christian, esp. a Muslim. [ME f. OF *pai(e)nime* f. eccl.L *paganismus* heathenism (as PAGAN)]

payola /per'əʊlə/ *n.* esp. *US* **1** a bribe offered in return for unofficial promotion of a product etc. in the media. **2** the practice of such bribery. [PAY[1] + *-ola* as in *Victrola*, make of gramophone]

payroll /'peɪrəʊl/ *n.* a list of employees receiving regular pay.

paysage /per'zɑːʒ/ *n.* **1** a rural scene; a landscape. **2** landscape painting. □□ **paysagist** /'peɪzɑːdʒɪst/ *n.* [F f. *pays* country: see PEASANT]

Pb *symb. Chem.* the element lead. [L *plumbum*]

PBX *abbr.* private branch exchange (private telephone switchboard).

PC *abbr.* **1** (in the UK) police constable. **2** (in the UK) Privy Counsellor. **3** personal computer.

p.c. *abbr.* **1** per cent. **2** postcard.

PCB *abbr.* **1** *Computing* printed circuit board. **2** *Chem.* polychlorinated biphenyl, any of several toxic aromatic compounds containing two benzene molecules in which hydrogens have been replaced by chlorine atoms, formed as waste in industrial processes.

PCM *abbr.* pulse code modulation.

pct. *abbr. US* per cent.

PD *abbr. US* Police Department.

Pd *symb. Chem.* the element palladium.

pd. *abbr.* paid.

p.d.q. *abbr. colloq.* pretty damn quick.

PDT *abbr. US* Pacific Daylight Time.

PE *abbr.* physical education.

p/e *abbr.* price/earnings (ratio).

pea /piː/ *n.* **1 a** a hardy climbing plant, *Pisum sativum*, with seeds growing in pods and used for food. **b** its seed. **2** any of several similar plants (*sweet pea*; *chick-pea*). □ **pea-brain** *colloq.* a stupid or dim-witted person. **pea-green** bright green. **pea-souper** *Brit. colloq.* a thick yellowish fog. [back-form. f. PEASE (taken as pl.: cf. CHERRY)]

peace /piːs/ *n.* **1 a** quiet; tranquillity (*needs peace to work well*). **b** mental calm; serenity (*peace of mind*). **2 a** (often *attrib.*) freedom from or the cessation of war (*peace talks*). **b** (esp. **Peace**) a treaty of peace between two States etc. at war. **3** freedom from civil disorder. **4** *Eccl.* a ritual liturgical greeting. □ **at peace 1** in a state of friendliness. **2** serene. **3** *euphem.* dead. **hold one's peace** keep silence. **keep the peace** prevent, or refrain from, strife. **make one's peace** (often foll. by *with*) re-establish friendly relations. **make peace** bring about peace; reconcile. **the peace** (or **the queen's peace**) peace existing within a realm; civil order. **Peace Corps** *US* an organization sending young people to work as volunteers in developing countries. **peace-offering 1** a propitiatory or conciliatory gift. **2** *Bibl.* an offering presented as a thanksgiving to God. **peace-pipe** a tobacco-pipe as a token of peace among US Indians. [ME f. AF *pes*, OF *pais* f. L *pax pacis*]

peaceable /'piːsəb(ə)l/ *adj.* **1** disposed to peace; unwarlike. **2** free from disturbance; peaceful. □□

peaceableness *n.* **peaceably** *adv.* [ME f. OF *peisible, plaisible* f. LL *placibilis* pleasing f. L *placēre* please]

peaceful /'piːsfʊl/ *adj.* **1** characterized by peace; tranquil. **2** not violating or infringing peace (*peaceful coexistence*). **3** belonging to a state of peace. □□ **peacefully** *adv.* **peacefulness** *n.*

peacemaker /'piːsˌmeɪkə(r)/ *n.* a person who brings about peace. □□ **peacemaking** *n. & adj.*

peacetime /'piːstaɪm/ *n.* a period when a country is not at war.

peach[1] /piːtʃ/ *n.* **1 a** a round juicy stone-fruit with downy cream or yellow skin flushed with red. **b** the tree, *Prunus persica*, bearing it. **2** the yellowish-pink colour of a peach. **3** *colloq.* **a** a person or thing of superlative quality. **b** an attractive young woman. □ **peach-bloom** an oriental porcelain-glaze of reddish pink, usu. with green markings. **peach-blow 1** a delicate purplish-pink colour. **2** = *peach-bloom*. **peaches and cream** (of a complexion) creamy skin with downy pink cheeks. **peach Melba** see MELBA. □□ **peachy** *adj.* (**peachier, peachiest**). **peachiness** *n.* [ME f. OF *peche, pesche,* f. med.L *persica* f. L *persicum* (*malum*), lit. Persian apple]

peach[2] /piːtʃ/ *v.* **1** *intr.* (usu. foll. by *against, on*) *colloq.* turn informer; inform. **2** *tr. archaic* inform against. [ME f. *appeach* f. AF *enpecher,* OF *empechier* IMPEACH]

pea-chick /'piːtʃɪk/ *n.* a young peafowl. [formed as PEACOCK + CHICK[1]]

peacock /'piːkɒk/ *n.* **1** a male peafowl, having brilliant plumage and a tail (with eyelike markings) that can be expanded erect in display like a fan. **2** this type of ostentatious display. □ **peacock blue** the lustrous greenish blue of a peacock's neck. **peacock butterfly** a butterfly, *Inachis io*, with eyelike markings on its wings. [ME *pecock* f. OE *pēa* f. L *pavo* + COCK[1]]

peafowl /'piːfaʊl/ *n.* **1** a peacock or peahen. **2** a pheasant of the genus *Pavo*.

peahen /'piːhen/ *n.* a female peafowl.

pea-jacket /'piːˌdʒækɪt/ *n.* a sailor's short double-breasted overcoat of coarse woollen cloth. [prob. f. Du. *pijjakker* f. *pij* coat of coarse cloth + *jekker* jacket: assim. to JACKET]

peak[1] /piːk/ *n. & v.* — *n.* **1** a projecting usu. pointed part, esp.: **a** the pointed top of a mountain. **b** a mountain with a peak. **c** a stiff brim at the front of a cap. **d** a pointed beard. **e** the narrow part of a ship's hold at the bow or stern (*forepeak*; *after-peak*). **f** *Naut.* the upper outer corner of a sail extended by a gaff. **2 a** the highest point in a curve (*on the peak of the wave*). **b** the time of greatest success (in a career etc.). **c** the highest point on a graph etc. — *v.intr.* reach the highest value, quality, etc. (*output peaked in September*). □ **peak hour** the time of the most intense traffic etc. **peak-load** the maximum of electric power demand etc. □□ **peaked** *adj.* **peaky** *adj.* **peakiness** *n.* [prob. back-form. f. *peaked* var. of dial. *picked* pointed (PICK[2])]

peak[2] /piːk/ *v.intr.* **1** waste away. **2** (as **peaked** *adj.*) sharp-featured; pinched. [16th c.: orig. unkn.]

peaky /'piːkɪ/ *adj.* (**peakier, peakiest**) **1** sickly; puny. **2** white-faced.

peal[1] /piːl/ *n. & v.* — *n.* **1 a** the loud ringing of a bell or bells, esp. a series of changes. **b** a set of bells. **2 a** loud repeated sound, esp. of thunder, laughter, etc. — *v.* **1** *intr.* sound forth in a peal. **2** *tr.* utter sonorously. **3** *tr.* ring (bells) in peals. [ME *pele* f. *apele* APPEAL]

peal[2] /piːl/ *n.* a salmon grilse. [16th c.: orig. unkn.]

pean[1] /piːn/ *n. Heraldry* fur represented as sable spotted with or. [16th c.: orig. unkn.]

pean[2] *US* var. of PAEAN.

peanut /'piːnʌt/ *n.* **1** a leguminous plant, *Arachis hypogaea*, bearing pods that ripen underground and contain seeds used as food and yielding oil. **2** the seed of this plant. **3** (in *pl.*) *colloq.* a paltry or trivial thing or amount, esp. of money. □**peanut butter** a paste of ground roasted peanuts.

pear /peə(r)/ *n.* **1** a yellowish or brownish-green fleshy fruit, tapering towards the stalk. **2** any of various trees of the genus *Pyrus* bearing it, esp. *P. communis.* □**pear-drop** a small sweet with the shape of a pear. [OE *pere, peru* ult. f. L *pirum*]

pearl¹ /pɜːl/ *n. & v.* —*n.* **1 a** (often *attrib.*) a usu. white or bluish-grey hard mass formed within the shell of a pearl-oyster or other bivalve mollusc, highly prized as a gem for its lustre (*pearl necklace*). **b** an imitation of this. **c** (in *pl.*) a necklace of pearls. **d** = *mother-of-pearl* (cf. *seed-pearl*). **2** a precious thing; the finest example. **3** anything resembling a pearl, e.g. a dewdrop, tear, etc. —*v.* **1** *tr. poet.* **a** sprinkle with pearly drops. **b** make pearly in colour etc. **2** *tr.* reduce (barley etc.) to small rounded grains. **3** *intr.* fish for pearl-oysters. **4** *intr. poet.* form pearl-like drops. □**cast pearls before swine** offer a treasure to a person unable to appreciate it. **pearl ash** commercial potassium carbonate. **pearl barley** barley reduced to small round grains by grinding. **pearl bulb** a translucent electric light bulb. **pearl button** a button made of mother-of-pearl or an imitation of it. **pearl-diver** a person who dives for pearl-oysters. **pearl millet** a tall cereal, *Pennisetum typhoides.* **pearl onion** a very small onion used in pickles. **pearl-oyster** any of various marine bivalve molluscs of the genus *Pinctada,* bearing pearls. □□ **pearler** *n.* [ME f. OF *perle* prob. f. L *perna* leg (applied to leg-of-mutton-shaped bivalve)]

pearl² /pɜːl/ *n. Brit.* = PICOT. [var. of PURL¹]

pearled /pɜːld/ *adj.* **1** adorned with pearls. **2** formed into pearl-like drops or grains. **3** pearl-coloured.

pearlescent /pɜːˈles(ə)nt/ *adj.* having or producing the appearance of mother-of-pearl.

pearlite var. of PERLITE.

pearlized /ˈpɜːlaɪzd/ *adj.* treated so as to resemble mother-of-pearl.

pearlware /ˈpɜːlweə(r)/ *n.* a fine white glazed earthenware.

pearlwort /ˈpɜːlwɜːt/ *n. Bot.* any small herbaceous plant of the genus *Sagina,* inhabiting rocky and sandy areas.

pearly /ˈpɜːlɪ/ *adj. & n.* —*adj.* (**pearlier, pearliest**) **1** resembling a pearl; lustrous. **2** containing pearls or mother-of-pearl. **3** adorned with pearls. —*n.* (*pl.* -**ies**) (in *pl.*) *Brit.* **1** pearly kings and queens. **2** a pearly king's or queen's clothes or pearl buttons. □**Pearly Gates** *colloq.* the gates of Heaven. **pearly king** (or **queen**) *Brit.* a London costermonger (or his wife) wearing clothes covered with pearl buttons. **pearly nautilus** see NAUTILUS. □□ **pearliness** *n.*

pearmain /ˈpeəmeɪn, ˈpɜː-/ *n.* a variety of apple with firm white flesh. [ME, = warden pear, f. OF *parmain, permain,* prob. ult. f. L *parmensis* of *Parma* in Italy]

peart /pɜːt/ *adj. US* lively; cheerful. [var. of PERT.]

peasant /ˈpez(ə)nt/ *n.* **1** esp. *colloq.* a countryman or countrywoman; a rustic. **2 a** a worker on the land, esp. a labourer or smallholder. **b** *hist.* a member of an agricultural class dependent on subsistence farming. **3** *derog.* a lout; a boorish person. □□ **peasantry** *n.* (*pl.* -**ies**). **peasanty** *adj.* [ME f. AF *paisant,* OF *païsent,* earlier *païsence* f. *païs* country ult. f. L *pagus* canton]

pease /piːz/ *n.pl. archaic* peas. □**pease-pudding** boiled split peas (served esp. with boiled ham). [OE *pise* pea, pl. *pisan,* f. LL *pisa* f. L *pisum* f. Gk *pison:* cf. PEA]

peashooter /ˈpiːˌʃuːtə(r)/ *n.* a small tube for blowing dried peas through as a toy.

peat /piːt/ *n.* **1** vegetable matter decomposed in water and partly carbonized, used for fuel, in horticulture, etc. **2** a cut piece of this. □□ **peaty** *adj.* [ME f. AL *peta,* perh. f. Celt.: cf. PIECE]

peatbog /ˈpiːtbɒg/ *n.* a bog composed of peat.

peatmoss /ˈpiːtmɒs/ *n.* **1** a peatbog. **2** any of various mosses of the genus *Sphagnum,* which grow in damp conditions and form peat as they decay.

peau-de-soie /ˌpəʊdəˈswɑː/ *n.* a smooth finely-ribbed satiny fabric of silk or rayon. [F, = skin of silk]

pebble /ˈpeb(ə)l/ *n.* **1** a small smooth stone worn by the action of water. **2 a** a type of colourless transparent rock-crystal used for spectacles. **b** a lens of this. **c** (*attrib.*) *colloq.* (of a spectacle-lens) very thick and convex. **3** an agate or other gem, esp. when found as a pebble in a stream etc. □**not the only pebble on the beach** (esp. of a person) easily replaced. **pebble-dash** mortar with pebbles in it used as a coating for external walls. □□ **pebbly** *adj.* [OE *papel-stān* pebble-stone, *pyppelrīpig* pebble-stream, of unkn. orig.]

p.e.c. *abbr.* photoelectric cell.

pecan /ˈpiːkən/ *n.* **1** a pinkish-brown smooth nut with an edible kernel. **2** a hickory, *Carya illinoensis,* of the southern US, producing this. [earlier *paccan,* of Algonquian orig.]

peccable /ˈpekəb(ə)l/ *adj. formal* liable to sin. □□ **peccability** /-ˈbɪlɪtɪ/ *n.* [F, f. med.L *peccabilis* f. *peccare* sin]

peccadillo /ˌpekəˈdɪləʊ/ *n.* (*pl.* -**oes** or -**os**) a trifling offence; a venial sin. [Sp. *pecadillo,* dimin. of *pecado* sin f. L (as PECCANT)]

peccant /ˈpekənt/ *adj. formal* **1** sinning. **2** inducing disease; morbid. □□ **peccancy** *n.* [F *peccant* or L *peccare* sin]

peccary /ˈpekərɪ/ *n.* (*pl.* -**ies**) any American wild pig of the family Tayassuidae, esp. *Tayassu tajacu* and *T. pecari.* [Carib *pakira*]

peccavi /peˈkɑːvɪ/ *int. & n.* —*int.* expressing guilt. —*n.* (*pl.* **peccavis**) a confession of guilt. [L, = I have sinned]

pêche Melba /peʃ ˈmelbə/ *n.* = *peach Melba* (see MELBA). [F]

peck¹ /pek/ *v. & n.* —*v.tr.* **1** strike or bite (something) with a beak. **2** kiss (esp. a person's cheek) hastily or perfunctorily. **3 a** make (a hole) by pecking. **b** (foll. by *out, off*) remove or pluck out by pecking. **4** *colloq.* (also *absol.*) eat (food) listlessly; nibble at. **5** mark with short strokes. **6** (usu. foll. by *up, down*) break with a pick etc. —*n.* **1 a** a stroke or bite with a beak. **b** a mark made by this. **2** a hasty or perfunctory kiss. □**peck at 1** eat (food) listlessly; nibble. **2** carp at; nag. **3** strike (a thing) repeatedly with a beak. **pecking** (or **peck**) **order** a social hierarchy, orig. as observed among hens. [ME prob. f. MLG *pekken,* of unkn. orig.]

peck² /pek/ *n.* **1** a measure of capacity for dry goods, equal to 2 gallons or 8 quarts. **2** a vessel used to contain this amount. □**a peck of** a large number or amount of (troubles, dirt, etc.). [ME f. AF *pek,* of unkn. orig.]

pecker /ˈpekə(r)/ *n.* **1** a bird that pecks (*woodpecker*). **2** *US coarse sl.* the penis. □**keep your pecker up** *Brit. colloq.* remain cheerful.

peckish /ˈpekɪʃ/ *adj. colloq.* **1** hungry. **2** *US* irritable.

pecorino /ˌpekəˈriːnəʊ/ *n.* (*pl.* -**os**) an Italian cheese made from ewes' milk. [It. f. *pecorino* (adj.) f. *pecora* sheep]

pecten /ˈpektɪn/ *n.* (*pl.* **pectens** or **pectines** /-tɪˌniːz/) *Zool.* **1** a comblike structure of various kinds in animal bodies. **2** any bivalve mollusc of the genus *Pecten.* Also called SCALLOP. □□ **pectinate** /-nət/ *adj.* **pectinated** /-ˌneɪtɪd/ *adj.* **pectination** /-ˈneɪʃ(ə)n/ *n.* (all in sense 1). [L *pecten pectinis* comb]

pectin /ˈpektɪn/ *n. Biochem.* any of various soluble gelatinous polysaccharides found in ripe fruits etc. and used as a setting agent in jams and jellies. □□ **pectic** *adj.* [Gk *pēktos* congealed f. *pēgnumi* make solid]

pectoral /ˈpektər(ə)l/ *adj. & n.* —*adj.* **1** of or relating to the breast or chest; thoracic (*pectoral fin; pectoral muscle*). **2** worn on the chest (*pectoral cross*). —*n.* **1** (esp. in *pl.*) a pectoral muscle. **2** a pectoral fin. **3** an ornamental breastplate esp. of a Jewish high priest.

---

b *but* d *dog* f *few* g *get* h *he* j *yes* k *cat* l *leg* m *man* n *no* p *pen* r *red* s *sit* t *top* v *voice*

[ME f. OF f. L *pectorale* (n.), *pectoralis* (adj.) f. *pectus pectoris* breast, chest]

pectose /'pektəʊs/ *n. Biochem.* an insoluble polysaccharide derivative found in unripe fruits and converted into pectin by ripening, heating, etc. [*pectic* (see PECTIN) + -OSE²]

peculate /'pekjʊˌleɪt/ *v.tr.* & *intr.* embezzle (money). □□ **peculation** /-'leɪʃ(ə)n/ *n.* **peculator** *n.* [L *peculari* rel. to *peculium*: see PECULIAR]

peculiar /pɪ'kjuːlɪə(r)/ *adj.* & *n.* —*adj.* **1** strange; odd; unusual (*a peculiar flavour*; *is a little peculiar*). **2 a** (usu. foll. by *to*) belonging exclusively (*a fashion peculiar to the time*). **b** belonging to the individual (*in their own peculiar way*). **3** particular; special (*a point of peculiar interest*). —*n.* **1** a peculiar property, privilege, etc. **2** a parish or church exempt from the jurisdiction of the diocese in which it lies. [ME f. L *peculiaris* of private property f. *peculium* f. *pecu* cattle]

peculiarity /pɪˌkjuːlɪ'ærɪtɪ/ *n.* (*pl.* -ies) **1 a** idiosyncrasy; unusualness; oddity. **b** an instance of this. **2** a characteristic or habit (*meanness is his peculiarity*). **3** the state of being peculiar.

peculiarly /pɪ'kjuːlɪəlɪ/ *adv.* **1** more than usually; especially (*peculiarly annoying*). **2** oddly. **3** as regards oneself alone; individually (*does not affect him peculiarly*).

pecuniary /pɪ'kjuːnɪərɪ/ *adj.* **1** of, concerning, or consisting of, money (*pecuniary aid*; *pecuniary considerations*). **2** (of an offence) entailing a money penalty or fine. □□ **pecuniarily** *adv.* [L *pecuniarius* f. *pecunia* money f. *pecu* cattle]

pedagogue /'pedəˌɡɒɡ/ *n. archaic* or *derog.* a schoolmaster; a teacher. □□ **pedagogic** /-'ɡɒɡɪk, -'ɡɒdʒɪk/ *adj.* **pedagogical** /-'ɡɒɡɪk(ə)l, -'ɡɒdʒɪk(ə)l/ *adj.* **pedagogically** /-'ɡɒɡɪkəlɪ, -'ɡɒdʒɪkəlɪ/ *adv.* **pedagogism** *n.* (also **pedagoguism**). [ME f. L *paedagogus* f. Gk *paidagōgos* f. *pais paidos* boy + *agōgos* guide]

pedagogy /'pedəˌɡɒdʒɪ, -ˌɡɒɡɪ/ *n.* the science of teaching. □□ **pedagogics** /-'ɡɒdʒɪks, -'ɡəʊdʒɪks/ *n.* [F *pédagogie* f. Gk *paidagōgia* (as PEDAGOGUE)]

pedal¹ /'ped(ə)l/ *n.* & *v.* —*n.* **1** any of several types of foot-operated levers or controls for mechanisms, esp.: **a** either of a pair of levers for transmitting power to a bicycle or tricycle wheel etc. **b** any of the foot-operated controls in a motor vehicle. **c** any of the foot-operated keys of an organ used for playing notes, or for drawing out several stops at once etc. **d** each of the foot-levers on a piano etc. for making the tone fuller or softer. **e** each of the foot-levers on a harp for altering the pitch of the strings. **2** a note sustained in one part, usu. the bass, through successive harmonies, some of which are independent of it. —*v.* (**pedalled, pedalling**; *US* **pedaled, pedaling**) **1** *intr.* operate a cycle, organ, etc. by using the pedals. **2** *tr.* work (a bicycle etc.) with the pedals. □ **pedal cycle** a bicycle. [F *pédale* f. It. *pedale* f. L (as PEDAL²)]

pedal² /'ped(ə)l, 'piːd(ə)l/ *adj. Zool.* of the foot or feet (esp. of a mollusc). [L *pedalis* f. *pes pedis* foot]

pedalo /'pedəˌləʊ/ *n.* (*pl.* -os) a pedal-operated pleasure-boat.

pedant /'ped(ə)nt/ *n.* **1** a person who insists on strict adherence to formal rules or literal meaning at the expense of a wider view. **2** a person who rates academic learning or technical knowledge above everything. **3** a person who is obsessed by a theory; a doctrinaire. □□ **pedantic** /pɪ'dæntɪk/ *adj.* **pedantically** /pɪ'dæntɪkəlɪ/ *adv.* **pedantize** *v.intr.* & *tr.* (also -ise). **pedantry** *n.* (*pl.* -ies). [F *pédant* f. It. *pedante*: app. formed as PEDAGOGUE]

pedate /'pedeɪt/ *adj.* **1** *Zool.* having feet. **2** *Bot.* (of a leaf) having divisions like toes or a bird's claws. [L *pedatus* f. *pes pedis* foot]

peddle /'ped(ə)l/ *v.* **1** *tr.* **a** sell (goods), esp. in small quantities, as a pedlar. **b** advocate or promote (ideas, a philosophy, a way of life, etc.). **2** *tr.* sell (drugs)

illegally. **3** *intr.* engage in selling, esp. as a pedlar. [back-form. f. PEDLAR]

peddler /'pedlə(r)/ *n.* **1** a person who sells drugs illegally. **2** *US* var. of PEDLAR.

pederast /'pedəˌræst/ *n.* (also **paederast**) a man who performs pederasty.

pederasty /'pedəˌræstɪ/ *n.* (also **paederasty**) anal intercourse between a man and a boy. [mod.L *paederastia* f. Gk *paiderastia* f. *pais paidos* boy + *erastēs* lover]

pedestal /'pedɪst(ə)l/ *n.* & *v.* —*n.* **1** a base supporting a column or pillar. **2** the stone etc. base of a statue etc. **3** either of the two supports of a knee-hole desk or table, usu. containing drawers. —*v.tr.* (**pedestalled, pedestalling**; *US* **pedestaled, pedestaling**) set or support on a pedestal. □ **pedestal table** a table with a single central support. **put** (or **set**) **on a pedestal** regard as highly admirable, important, etc.; venerate. [F *piédestal* f. It. *piedestallo* f. *piè* foot f. L *pes pedis* + *di* of + *stallo* STALL¹]

pedestrian /pɪ'destrɪən/ *n.* & *adj.* —*n.* **1** (often *attrib.*) a person who is walking, esp. in a town (*pedestrian crossing*). **2** a person who walks competitively. —*adj.* prosaic; dull; uninspired. □ **pedestrian crossing** *Brit.* a specified part of a road where pedestrians have right of way to cross. **pedestrian precinct** an area of a town restricted to pedestrians. □□ **pedestrianism** *n.* **pedestrianize** *v.tr.* & *intr.* (also -ise). **pedestrianization** /-'zeɪʃ(ə)n/ *n.* [F *pédestre* or L *pedester -tris*]

pediatrics *US* var. of PAEDIATRICS.

pedicab /'pedɪˌkæb/ *n.* a pedal-operated rickshaw.

pedicel /'pedɪs(ə)l/ *n.* (also **pedicle** /'pedɪk(ə)l/) **1** a small (esp. subordinate) stalklike structure in a plant or animal (cf. PEDUNCLE). **2** *Surgery* part of a graft left temporarily attached to its original site. □□ **pedicellate** /-səˌleɪt/ *adj.* **pediculate** /pɪ'dɪkjʊlət/ *adj.* [mod.L *pedicellus* & L *pediculus* dimin. of *pes pedis* foot]

pedicular /pɪ'dɪkjʊlə(r)/ *adj.* (also **pediculous** /-ləs/) infested with lice. □□ **pediculosis** /-'ləʊsɪs/ *n.* [L *pedicularis, -losus* f. *pediculus* louse]

pedicure /'pedɪˌkjʊə(r)/ *n.* & *v.* —*n.* **1** the care or treatment of the feet, esp. of the toenails. **2** a person practising this, esp. professionally. —*v.tr.* treat (the feet) by removing corns etc. [F *pédicure* f. L *pes pedis* foot + *curare*: see CURE]

pedigree /'pedɪˌɡriː/ *n.* **1** (often *attrib.*) a recorded line of descent of a person or esp. a pure-bred domestic or pet animal. **2** the derivation of a word. **3** a genealogical table. **4** *colloq.* the 'life history' of a person, thing, idea, etc. □□ **pedigreed** *adj.* [ME *pedegru* etc. f. AF f. OF *pie de grue* (unrecorded) crane's foot, a mark denoting succession in pedigrees]

pediment /'pedɪmənt/ *n.* **1 a** the triangular front part of a building in Grecian style, surmounting esp. a portico of columns. **b** a similar part of a building in Roman or Renaissance style. **2** *Geol.* a broad flattish rock surface at the foot of a mountain slope. □□ **pedimental** /-'ment(ə)l/ *adj.* **pedimented** *adj.* [earlier *pedament, periment*, perh. corrupt. of PYRAMID]

pedlar /'pedlə(r)/ *n.* (*US* **peddler**) **1** a travelling seller of small items esp. carried in a pack etc. **2** (usu. foll. by *of*) a retailer of gossip etc. □□ **pedlary** *n.* [ME *pedlere* alt. of *pedder* f. *ped* pannier, of unkn. orig.]

pedo- *comb. form US* var. of PAEDO-.

pedology /pɪ'dɒlədʒɪ/ *n.* the scientific study of soil, esp. its formation, nature, and classification. □□ **pedological** /ˌpedə'lɒdʒɪk(ə)l/ *adj.* **pedologist** *n.* [Russ. *pedologiya* f. Gk *pedon* ground]

pedometer /pɪ'dɒmɪtə(r)/ *n.* an instrument for estimating the distance travelled on foot by recording the number of steps taken. [F *pédomètre* f. L *pes pedis* foot]

peduncle /pɪ'dʌŋk(ə)l/ *n.* **1** *Bot.* the stalk of a flower, fruit, or cluster, esp. a main stalk bearing a solitary flower or subordinate stalks (cf. PEDICEL). **2** *Zool.* a stalklike projection in an animal body. □□ **peduncular** /-kjʊlə(r)/ *adj.* **pedunculate** /-kjʊlət/ *adj.* [mod.L *pedunculus* f. L *pes pedis* foot: see -UNCLE]

pee /piː/ *v. & n. colloq.* —*v.* (**pees, peed**) **1** *intr.* urinate. **2** *tr.* pass (urine, blood, etc.) from the bladder. —*n.* **1** urination. **2** urine. [initial letter of PISS]

peek /piːk/ *v. & n.* —*v.intr.* (usu. foll. by *in, out, at*) look quickly or slyly; peep. —*n.* a quick or sly look. [ME *pike, pyke,* of unkn. orig.]

peekaboo /ˈpiːkəˌbuː/ *adj. & n.* —*adj.* **1** (of a garment etc.) transparent or having a pattern of small holes. **2** (of a hairstyle) concealing one eye with a fringe or wave. —*n. US* = BO-PEEP. [PEEK + BOO]

peel[1] /piːl/ *v. & n.* —*v.* **1** *tr.* **a** strip the skin, rind, bark, wrapping, etc. from (a fruit, vegetable, tree, etc.). **b** (usu. foll. by *off*) strip (skin, peel, wrapping, etc.) from a fruit etc. **2** *intr.* **a** (of a tree, an animal's or person's body, a painted surface, etc.) become bare of bark, skin, paint, etc. **b** (often foll. by *off*) (of bark, a person's skin, paint, etc.) flake off. **3** *intr.* (often foll. by *off*) *colloq.* (of a person) strip for exercise etc. **4** *tr. Croquet* send (another player's ball) through the hoops. —*n.* the outer covering of a fruit, vegetable, prawn, etc.; rind. □**peel off 1** veer away and detach oneself from a group of marchers, a formation of aircraft, etc. **2** *colloq.* strip off one's clothes. □□ **peeler** *n.* (in sense 1 of *v.*). [earlier *pill, pele* (orig. = plunder) f. ME *pilien* etc. f. OE *pilian* (unrecorded) f. L *pilare* f. *pilus* hair]

peel[2] /piːl/ *n.* a shovel, esp. a baker's shovel for bringing loaves etc. into or out of an oven. [ME & OF *pele* f. L *pala,* rel. to *pangere* fix]

peel[3] /piːl/ *n.* (also **pele**) *hist.* a small square tower built in the 16th c. in the border counties of England and Scotland for defence against raids. [ME *pel* stake, palisade, f. AF & OF *pel* f. L *palus* stake: cf. PALE²]

peeler /ˈpiːlə(r)/ *n. Brit. archaic sl.* or *dial.* a policeman. [Sir Robert *Peel,* Engl. statesman d. 1850]

peeling /ˈpiːlɪŋ/ *n.* a strip of the outer skin of a vegetable, fruit, etc. (*potato peelings*).

peen /piːn/ *n. & v.* —*n.* the wedge-shaped or thin or curved end of a hammer-head (opp. FACE *n.* 5a). —*v.tr.* **1** hammer with a peen. **2** treat (sheet metal) with a stream of metal shot in order to shape it. [17th c.: also *pane,* app. f. F *panne* f. Du. *pen* f. L *pinna* point]

peep[1] /piːp/ *v. & n.* —*v.intr.* **1** (usu. foll. by *at, in, out, into*) look through a narrow opening; look furtively. **2** (usu. foll. by *out*) **a** (of daylight, a flower beginning to bloom, etc.) come slowly into view; emerge. **b** (of a quality etc.) show itself unconsciously. —*n.* **1** a furtive or peering glance. **2** the first appearance (*at peep of day*). □**peep-bo** = BO-PEEP. **peep-hole** a small hole that may be looked through. **peeping Tom** a furtive voyeur. **peep-show** a small exhibition of pictures etc. viewed through a lens or hole set into a box etc. **peep-sight** the aperture backsight of some rifles. **peep-toe** (or -**toed**) (of a shoe) leaving the toes partly bare. [ME: cf. PEEK, PEER¹]

peep[2] /piːp/ *v. & n.* —*v.intr.* make a shrill feeble sound as of young birds, mice, etc.; squeak; chirp. —*n.* such a sound. [imit.: cf. CHEEP]

peeper /ˈpiːpə(r)/ *n.* **1** a person who peeps. **2** *colloq.* an eye. **3** *US sl.* a private detective.

peepul /ˈpiːp(ə)l/ *n.* (also **pipal**) = BO-TREE. [Hindi *pīpal* f. Skr. *pippala*]

peer[1] /pɪə(r)/ *v.intr.* **1** (usu. foll. by *into, at,* etc.) look keenly or with difficulty (*peered into the fog*). **2** appear; peep out. **3** *archaic* come into view. [var. of *pire,* LG *piren;* perh. partly f. APPEAR]

peer[2] /pɪə(r)/ *n. & v.* —*n.* **1 a** (*fem.* **peeress**) a member of one of the degrees of the nobility in Britain, i.e. a duke, marquis, earl, viscount, or baron. **b** a noble of any country. **2** a person who is equal in

ability, standing, rank, or value; a contemporary (*tried by a jury of his peers*). —*v.intr. & tr.* (usu. foll. by *with*) rank or cause to rank equally. □**peer group** a group of people of the same age, status, interests, etc. **peer of the realm** (or **the United Kingdom**) any of the class of peers whose adult members may all sit in the House of Lords. □□ **peerless** *adj.* [ME f. AF & OF *pe(e)r, perer* f. LL *pariare* f. L *par* equal]

peerage /ˈpɪərɪdʒ/ *n.* **1** peers as a class; the nobility. **2** the rank of peer or peeress (*was given a life peerage*). **3** a book containing a list of peers with their genealogy etc.

peeve /piːv/ *v. & n. colloq.* —*v.tr.* (usu. as **peeved** *adj.*) annoy; vex; irritate. —*n.* **1** a cause of annoyance. **2** vexation. [back-form. f. PEEVISH]

peevish /ˈpiːvɪʃ/ *adj.* querulous; irritable. □□ **peevishly** *adv.* **peevishness** *n.* [ME, = foolish, mad, spiteful, etc., of unkn. orig.]

peewit /ˈpiːwɪt/ *n.* (also **pewit**) **1** a lapwing. **2** its cry. [imit.]

peg /peg/ *n. & v.* —*n.* **1 a** a usu. cylindrical pin or bolt of wood or metal, often tapered at one end, and used for holding esp. two things together. **b** such a peg attached to a wall etc. and used for hanging garments etc. on. **c** a peg driven into the ground and attached to a rope for holding up a tent. **d** a bung for stoppering a cask etc. **e** each of several pegs used to tighten or loosen the strings of a violin etc. **f** a small peg, matchstick, etc. stuck into holes in a board for calculating the scores at cribbage. **2** *Brit.* = *clothes-peg.* **3** *Brit.* a measure of spirits or wine. —*v.tr.* (**pegged, pegging**) **1** (usu. foll. by *down, in, out,* etc.) fix (a thing) with a peg. **2** *Econ.* **a** stabilize (prices, wages, exchange rates, etc.). **b** prevent the price of (stock etc.) from falling or rising by freely buying or selling at a given price. **3** mark (the score) with pegs on a cribbage-board. □**off the peg** (of clothes) ready-made. **peg away** (often foll. by *at*) work consistently and esp. for a long period. **peg down** restrict (a person etc.) to rules, a commitment, etc. **peg-leg 1** an artificial leg. **2** a person with an artificial leg. **peg on** = *peg away.* **peg out 1** *sl.* die. **2** score the winning point at cribbage. **3** *Croquet* hit the peg with the ball as the final stroke in a game. **4** mark the boundaries of (land etc.). **a peg to hang an idea etc. on** a suitable occasion or pretext etc. for it. **a round** (or **square**) **peg in a square** (or **round**) **hole** a misfit. **take a person down a peg or two** humble a person. [ME, prob. of LG or Du. orig.: cf. MDu. *pegge,* Du. dial. *peg,* LG *pigge*]

pegboard /ˈpegbɔːd/ *n.* a board having a regular pattern of small holes for pegs, used for commercial displays, games, etc.

pegmatite /ˈpegməˌtaɪt/ *n.* a coarsely crystalline type of granite. [Gk *pēgma -atos* thing joined together f. *pēgnumi* fasten]

pegtop /ˈpegtɒp/ *n.* a pear-shaped spinning-top with a metal pin or peg forming the point, spun by the rapid uncoiling of a string wound round it.

Pehlevi var. of PAHLAVI.

PEI *abbr.* Prince Edward Island.

peignoir /ˈpeɪnwɑː(r)/ *n.* a woman's loose dressing-gown. [F f. *peigner* to comb]

pejorative /prɪˈdʒɒrətɪv, ˈpiːdʒə-/ *adj. & n.* —*adj.* (of a word, an expression, etc.) depreciatory. —*n.* a depreciatory word. □□ **pejoratively** *adv.* [F *péjoratif -ive* f. LL *pejorare* make worse (*pejor*)]

pekan /ˈpekən/ *n.* a N. American flesh-eating mammal, *Martes pennanti,* valued for its fur. [Can.F f. Abnaki *pékané*]

peke /piːk/ *n. colloq.* a Pekingese dog. [abbr.]

Pekingese /ˌpiːkɪˈniːz/ *n. & adj.* (also **Pekinese**) —*n.* (*pl.* same) **1 a** a lap-dog of a short-legged breed with long hair and a snub nose. **b** this breed. **2 a** citizen of Peking (Beijing) in China. **3** the form of the Chinese language used in Beijing. —*adj.* of or concerning Beijing or its language or citizens.

pekoe /ˈpiːkəʊ/ *n.* a superior kind of black tea. [Chin.

æ cat *ɑː* arm *e* bed *ɜː* her *ɪ* sit *iː* see *ɒ* hot *ɔː* saw *ʌ* run *ʊ* put *uː* too *ə* ago *aɪ* my dial. *pek-ho* f. *pek* white + *ho* down, leaves being picked young with down on them]

pelage /'pelɪdʒ/ *n.* the fur, hair, wool, etc. of a mammal. [F f. *poil* hair]

Pelagian /pɪ'leɪdʒɪən/ *adj.* & *n.* —*adj.* of or concerning the monk Pelagius (4th–5th c.) or his theory denying the doctrine of original sin. —*n.* a follower of Pelagius. □□ **Pelagianism** *n.* [eccl.L *Pelagianus* f. *Pelagius*]

pelagian /pɪ'leɪdʒɪən/ *adj.* & *n.* —*adj.* inhabiting the open sea. —*n.* an inhabitant of the open sea. [L *pelagius* f. Gk *pelagios* of the sea (*pelagos*)]

pelagic /pɪ'lædʒɪk/ *adj.* **1** of or performed on the open sea (*pelagic whaling*). **2** (of marine life) belonging to the upper layers of the open sea. [L *pelagicus* f. Gk *pelagikos* (as PELAGIAN)]

pelargonium /ˌpelɑ'gəʊnɪəm/ *n.* any plant of the genus *Pelargonium*, with red, pink, or white flowers and fragrant leaves. Also called GERANIUM. [mod.L f. Gk *pelargos* stork: cf. GERANIUM]

pele var. of PEEL³.

pelf /pelf/ *n. derog.* or *joc.* money; wealth. [ME f. ONF f. OF *pelfre, peufre* spoils, of unkn. orig.: cf. PILFER]

pelham /'peləm/ *n.* a horse's bit combining a curb and a snaffle. [the surname *Pelham*]

pelican /'pelɪkən/ *n.* any large gregarious waterfowl of the family Pelecanidae with a large bill and a pouch in the throat for storing fish. □ **pelican crossing** (in the UK) a pedestrian crossing with traffic lights operated by pedestrians. [OE *pellican* & OF *pelican* f. LL *pelicanus* f. Gk *pelekan* prob. f. *pelekus* axe, with ref. to its bill]

pelisse /pɪ'liːs/ *n. hist.* **1** a woman's cloak with armholes or sleeves, reaching to the ankles. **2** a fur-lined cloak, esp. as part of a hussar's uniform. [F f. med.L *pellicia* (*vestis*) (garment) of fur f. *pellis* skin]

pelite /'piːlaɪt/ *n.* a rock composed of claylike sediment. [Gk *pēlos* clay, mud]

pellagra /pɪ'lægrə, -'leɪgrə/ *n.* a disease caused by deficiency of nicotinic acid, characterized by cracking of the skin and often resulting in insanity. □□ **pellagrous** *adj.* [It. f. *pelle* skin, after PODAGRA]

pellet /'pelɪt/ *n.* & *v.* —*n.* **1** a small compressed ball of paper, bread, etc. **2** a pill. **3 a** a small mass of bones, feathers, etc. regurgitated by a bird of prey. **b** a small hard piece of animal, usu. rodent, excreta. **4 a** a piece of small shot. **b** an imitation bullet for a toy gun. —*v.tr.* (**pelleted, pelleting**) **1** make into a pellet or pellets. **2** hit with (esp. paper) pellets. □□ **pelletize** *v.tr.* (also -**ise**). [ME f. OF *pelote* f. L *pila* ball]

pellicle /'pelɪk(ə)l/ *n.* a thin skin, membrane, or film. □□ **pellicular** /-'lɪkjʊlə(r)/ *adj.* [F *pellicule* f. L *pellicula*, dimin. of *pellis* skin]

pellitory /'pelɪtərɪ/ *n.* any of several wild plants, esp.: **1** (in full **pellitory of Spain**) a composite plant, *Anacyclus pyrethrum*, with a pungent-flavoured root, used as a local irritant etc. **2** (in full **pellitory of the wall**) a low bushy plant, *Parietaria judaica*, with greenish flowers growing on or at the foot of walls. [(sense 1) alt. f. ME f. OF *peletre, peretre* f. L *pyrethrum* f. Gk *purethron* feverfew: (sense 2) ult. f. OF *paritaire* f. LL *parietaria* f. L *paries -etis* wall]

pell-mell /pel'mel/ *adv., adj.,* & *n.* —*adv.* **1** headlong, recklessly (*rushed pell-mell out of the room*). **2** in disorder or confusion (*stuffed the papers together pell-mell*). —*adj.* confused, tumultuous. —*n.* confusion; a mixture. [F *pêle-mêle*, OF *pesle mesle, mesle pesle*, etc., redupl. of *mesle* f. *mesler* mix]

pellucid /pɪ'luːsɪd, -'ljuːsɪd/ *adj.* **1** (of water, light, etc.) transparent, clear. **2** (of style, speech, etc.) not confused; clear. **3** mentally clear. □□ **pellucidity** /-'sɪdɪtɪ/ *n.* **pellucidly** *adv.* [L *pellucidus* f. *perlucēre* (as PER-, *lucēre* shine)]

Pelmanism /'pelməˌnɪz(ə)m/ *n.* **1** a system of

memory-training orig. devised by the Pelman Institute. **2** a card-game based on this. □□ **Pelmanize** *v.tr.* (also -**ise**).

pelmet /'pelmɪt/ *n.* a narrow border of cloth, wood, etc. above esp. a window, concealing the curtain rail. [prob. f. F PALMETTE]

pelorus /pɪ'lɔːrəs/ *n.* a sighting device like a ship's compass for taking bearings. [perh. f. *Pelorus*, reputed name of Hannibal's pilot]

pelota /pɪ'lɒtə, pɪ'ləʊtə/ *n.* a Basque or Spanish game played in a walled court with a ball and basket-like rackets attached to the hand. [Sp., = ball, augment. of *pella* f. L *pila*]

pelt¹ /pelt/ *v.* & *n.* —*v.* **1** *tr.* (usu. foll. by *with*) **a** hurl many small missiles at. **b** strike repeatedly with missiles. **c** assail (a person etc.) with insults, abuse, etc. **2** *intr.* (usu. foll. by *down*) (of rain etc.) fall quickly and torrentially. **3** *intr.* run fast. **4** *intr.* (often foll. by *at*) fire repeatedly. —*n.* the act or an instance of pelting. □**at full pelt** as fast as possible. [16th c.: orig. unkn.]

pelt² /pelt/ *n.* **1** the undressed skin of a fur-bearing mammal. **2** the skin of a sheep, goat, etc. with short wool, or stripped ready for tanning. **3** *joc.* the human skin. □□ **peltry** *n.* [ME f. obs. *pellet* skin, dimin. of *pel* f. AF *pell*, OF *pel*, or back-form. f. *peltry*, AF *pelterie*, OF *peleterie* f. *peletier* furrier, ult. f. L *pellis* skin]

pelta /'peltə/ *n.* (*pl.* **peltae** /-tiː/) **1** a small light shield used by the ancient Greeks, Romans, etc. **2** *Bot.* a shieldlike structure. □□ **peltate** *adj.* [L f. Gk *peltē*]

pelvic /'pelvɪk/ *adj.* of or relating to the pelvis. □**pelvic girdle** the bony or cartilaginous structure in vertebrates to which the posterior limbs are attached.

pelvis /'pelvɪs/ *n.* (*pl.* **pelvises** or **pelves** /-viːz/) **1** a basin-shaped cavity at the lower end of the torso of most vertebrates, formed from the innominate bone with the sacrum and other vertebrae. **2** the basin-like cavity of the kidney. [L, = basin]

Pembs. *abbr.* Pembrokeshire (a former county in Wales).

pemmican /'pemɪkən/ *n.* **1** a cake of dried pounded meat mixed with melted fat, orig. made by N. American Indians. **2** beef so treated and flavoured with currants etc. for use by Arctic travellers etc. [Cree *pimecan* f. *pime* fat]

pemphigus /'pemfɪgəs/ *n. Med.* the formation of watery blisters or eruptions on the skin. □□ **pemphigoid** *adj.* **pemphigous** *adj.* [mod.L f. Gk *pemphix -igos* bubble]

PEN *abbr.* International Association of Poets, Playwrights, Editors, Essayists, and Novelists.

Pen. *abbr.* Peninsula.

pen¹ /pen/ *n.* & *v.* —*n.* **1** an instrument for writing or drawing with ink, orig. consisting of a shaft with a sharpened quill or metal nib, now more widely applied. **2 a** (usu. prec. by *the*) the occupation of writing. **b** a style of writing. **3** *Zool.* the internal feather-shaped cartilaginous shell of certain cuttlefish, esp. squid. —*v.tr.* (**penned, penning**) **1** write. **2** compose and write. □**pen and ink** *n.* **1** the instruments of writing. **2** writing. **pen-and-ink** *adj.* drawn or written with ink. **pen-feather** a quill-feather of a bird's wing. **pen-friend** a friend communicated with by letter only. **pen-light** a small electric torch shaped like a fountain-pen. **pen-name** a literary pseudonym. **pen-pal** *colloq.* = *pen-friend*. **pen-pusher** *colloq. derog.* a clerical worker. **pen-pushing** *colloq. derog.* clerical work. **put pen to paper** begin writing. [ME f. OF *penne* f. L *penna* feather]

pen² /pen/ *n.* & *v.* —*n.* **1** a small enclosure for cows, sheep, poultry, etc. **2** a place of confinement. **3** an enclosure for sheltering submarines. **4** a Jamaican farm or plantation. —*v.tr.* (**penned, penning**) (often foll. by *in, up*) enclose or shut in a pen. [OE *penn*, of unkn. orig.]

aʊ *how* eɪ *day* əʊ *no* eə *hair* ɪə *near* ɔɪ *boy* ʊə *poor* aɪə *fire* aʊə *sour* (*see over for consonants*)

pen[3] /pen/ n. a female swan. [16th c.: orig. unkn.]

pen[4] /pen/ n. US sl. = PENITENTIARY n. 1. [abbr.]

penal /'piːn(ə)l/ adj. **1 a** of or concerning punishment or its infliction (*penal laws*; *a penal sentence*; *a penal colony*). **b** (of an offence) punishable, esp. by law. **2** extremely severe (*penal taxation*). □**penal servitude** hist. imprisonment with compulsory labour. □□**penally** adv. [ME f. OF *penal* or L *poenalis* f. *poena* PAIN]

penalize /'piːnəlaɪz/ v.tr. (also **-ise**) **1** subject (a person) to a penalty or comparative disadvantage. **2** make or declare (an action) penal. □□**penalization** /-'zeɪʃ(ə)n/ n.

penalty /'penəltɪ/ n. (pl. **-ies**) **1 a** a punishment, esp. a fine, for a breach of law, contract, etc. **b** a fine paid. **2** a disadvantage, loss, etc., esp. as a result of one's own actions (*paid the penalty for his carelessness*). **3 a** a disadvantage imposed on a competitor or side in a game etc. for a breach of the rules etc. **b** (attrib.) awarded against a side incurring a penalty (*penalty kick*; *penalty goal*). **4** *Bridge* etc. points gained by opponents when a contract is not fulfilled. □**penalty area** *Football* the ground in front of the goal in which a foul by defenders involves the award of a penalty kick. **penalty box** *Ice Hockey* an area reserved for penalized players and some officials. **the penalty of** a disadvantage resulting from (a quality etc.). **penalty rate** *Austral.* an increased rate of pay for overtime. **under** (or **on**) **penalty of** under the threat of (dismissal etc.). [AF *penalte* (unrecorded), F *pénalité* f. med.L *penalitas* (as PENAL)]

penance /'penəns/ n. & v. —n. **1** an act of self-punishment as reparation for guilt. **2 a** (in the RC and Orthodox Church) a sacrament including confession of and absolution for a sin. **b** a penalty imposed esp. by a priest, or undertaken voluntarily, for a sin. —v.tr. impose a penance on. □**do penance** perform a penance. [ME f. OF f. L *paenitentia* (as PENITENT)]

penannular /pen'ænjʊlə(r)/ adj. almost ringlike. [L *paene* almost + ANNULAR]

penates /pɪ'nɑːtiːz, -teɪz/ n.pl. (in Roman mythology) the household gods, esp. of the storeroom (see LARES). [L f. *penus* provision of food]

pence pl. of PENNY.

penchant /'pɑ̃ʃɑ̃/ n. an inclination or liking (*has a penchant for old films*). [F, pres. part. of *pencher* incline]

pencil /'pensɪl/ n. & v. —n. **1** (often *attrib.*). **a** an instrument for writing or drawing, usu. consisting of a thin rod of graphite etc. enclosed in a wooden cylinder (*a pencil sketch*). **b** a similar instrument with a metal or plastic cover and retractable lead. **c** a cosmetic in pencil form. **2** (attrib.) resembling a pencil in shape (*pencil skirt*). **3** *Optics* a set of rays meeting at a point. **4** *Geom.* a figure formed by a set of straight lines meeting at a point. **5** a draughtsman's art or style. —v.tr. (**pencilled, pencilling**; US **penciled, penciling**) **1** tint or mark with or as if with a pencil. **2** (usu. foll. by *in*) **a** write, esp. tentatively or provisionally (*have pencilled in the 29th for our meeting*). **b** (esp. as **pencilled** adj.) fill (an area) with soft pencil strokes (*pencilled in her eyebrows*). □**pencil-case** a container for pencils etc. **pencil-sharpener** a device for sharpening a pencil by rotating it against a cutting edge. □□**penciller** n. [ME f. OF *pincel* ult. f. L *penicillum* paintbrush, dimin. of *peniculus* brush, dimin. of *penis* tail]

pendant /'pend(ə)nt/ n. (also **pendent**) **1** a hanging jewel etc., esp. one attached to a necklace, bracelet, etc. **2** a light fitting, ornament, etc., hanging from a ceiling. **3** *Naut.* **a** a short rope hanging from the head of a mast etc., used for attaching tackles. **b** = PENNANT 1. **4** the shank and ring of a pocket-watch by which it is suspended. **5** /'pend(ə)nt, 'pɑ̃dɑ̃/ (usu. foll. by *to*) a match, companion, parallel, complement, etc. [ME f. OF f. *pendre* hang f. L *pendere*]

pendent /'pend(ə)nt/ adj. (also **pendant**) **1 a** hanging. **b** overhanging. **2** undecided; pending. **3** *Gram.* (esp. of a sentence) incomplete; not having a finite verb (*pendent nominative*). □□**pendency** n. [ME (as PENDANT)]

pendente lite /pen,denti 'laɪti/ adv. Law during the progress of a suit. [L]

pendentive /pen'dentɪv/ n. Archit. a curved triangle of vaulting formed by the intersection of a dome with its supporting arches. [F *pendentif -ive* (adj.) (as PENDANT)]

pending /'pendɪŋ/ adj. & prep. —predic.adj. **1** awaiting decision or settlement, undecided (*a settlement was pending*). **2** about to come into existence (*patent pending*). —prep. **1** during (*pending these negotiations*). **2** until (*pending his return*). □**pending-tray** a tray for documents, letters, etc., awaiting attention. [after F *pendant* (see PENDENT)]

pendragon /pen'drægən/ n. hist. an ancient British or Welsh prince (often as a title). [Welsh, = chief war-leader, f. *pen* head + *dragon* standard]

penduline /'pendjʊˌlaɪn/ adj. **1** (of a nest) suspended. **2** (of a bird) of a kind that builds such a nest. [F (as PENDULOUS)]

pendulous /'pendjʊləs/ adj. **1** (of ears, breasts, flowers, bird's nests, etc.) hanging down; drooping and esp. swinging. **2** oscillating. □□**pendulously** adv. [L *pendulus* f. *pendēre* hang]

pendulum /'pendjʊləm/ n. a weight suspended so as to swing freely, esp. a rod with a weighted end regulating the movement of a clock's works. □**swing of the pendulum** the tendency of public opinion to oscillate between extremes, esp. between political parties. [L neut. adj. (as PENDULOUS)]

peneplain /'piːnɪˌpleɪn/ n. Geol. a fairly flat area of land produced by erosion. [L *paene* almost + PLAIN[1]]

penetralia /ˌpenɪ'treɪlɪə/ n.pl. **1** innermost shrines or recesses. **2** secret or hidden parts; mysteries. [L, neut. pl. of *penetralis* interior (as PENETRATE)]

penetrate /'penɪˌtreɪt/ v. **1** tr. **a** find access into or through, esp. forcibly. **b** (usu. foll. by *with*) imbue (a person or thing) with; permeate. **2** tr. see into, find out, or discern (a person's mind, the truth, a meaning, etc.). **3** tr. see through (darkness, fog, etc.) (*could not penetrate the gloom*). **4** intr. be absorbed by the mind (*my hint did not penetrate*). **5** tr. (as **penetrating** adj.) **a** having or suggesting sensitivity or insight (*a penetrating remark*). **b** (of a voice etc.) easily heard through or above other sounds; piercing. **6** tr. (of a man) put the penis into the vagina of (a woman). **7** intr. (usu. foll. by *into*, *through*, *to*) make a way. □□**penetrable** /-trəb(ə)l/ adj. **penetrability** /-trə'bɪlɪtɪ/ n. **penetrant** adj. & n. **penetratingly** adv. **penetration** /-'treɪʃ(ə)n/ n. **penetrative** /-trətɪv/ adj. **penetrator** n. [L *penetrare* place or enter within f. *penitus* interior]

penguin /'peŋgwɪn/ n. any flightless sea bird of the family Spheniscidae of the southern hemisphere, with black upper-parts and white under-parts, and wings developed into scaly flippers for swimming underwater. [16th c., orig. = great auk: orig. unkn.]

penholder /'pen,həʊldə(r)/ n. the esp. wooden shaft of a pen with a metal nib.

penicillate /'penɪsɪlət, -'sɪlɪt/ adj. Biol. **1** having or forming a small tuft or tufts. **2** marked with streaks as of a pencil or brush. [L *penicillum*: see PENCIL]

penicillin /ˌpenɪ'sɪlɪn/ n. any of various antibiotics produced naturally by moulds of the genus *Penicillium*, or synthetically, and able to prevent the growth of certain disease-causing bacteria. [mod.L *Penicillium* genus name f. L *penicillum*: see PENCIL]

penile /'piːnaɪl/ adj. of or concerning the penis. [mod.L *penilis*]

penillion pl. of PENNILL.

peninsula /pɪ'nɪnsjʊlə/ n. a piece of land almost surrounded by water or projecting far into a sea or lake etc. □□**peninsular** adj. [L *paeninsula* f. *paene* almost + *insula* island]

b *but* d *dog* f *few* g *get* h *he* j *yes* k *cat* l *leg* m *man* n *no* p *pen* r *red* s *sit* t *top* v *voice*

penis /'piːnɪs/ *n.* (*pl.* **penises** or **penes** /-niːz/) **1** the male organ of copulation and (in mammals) urination. **2** the male copulatory organ in lower vertebrates. [L, = tail, penis]

penitent /'penɪt(ə)nt/ *adj. & n.* —*adj.* regretting and wishing to atone for sins etc.; repentant. —*n.* **1** a repentant sinner. **2** a person doing penance under the direction of a confessor. **3** (in *pl.*) various RC orders associated for mutual discipline etc. □□**penitence** *n.* **penitently** *adv.* [ME f. OF f. L *paenitens* f. *paenitēre* repent]

penitential /ˌpenɪ'tenʃ(ə)l/ *adj.* of or concerning penitence or penance. □**penitential psalms** seven psalms (6, 32, 38, 51, 102, 130, 143) expressing penitence. □□**penitentially** *adv.* [OF *penitencial* f. LL *paenitentialis* f. *paenitentia* penitence (as PENITENT)]

penitentiary /ˌpenɪ'tenʃərɪ/ *n. & adj.* —*n.* (*pl.* **-ies**) **1** *US* a reformatory prison. **2** an office in the papal court deciding questions of penance, dispensations, etc. —*adj.* **1** of or concerning penance. **2** of or concerning reformatory treatment. **3** *US* (of an offence) making a culprit liable to a prison sentence. □**Grand Penitentiary** a cardinal presiding over the penitentiary. [ME f. med.L *paenitentiarius* (adj. & n.) (as PENITENT)]

penknife /'pennaɪf/ *n.* a small folding knife, esp. for carrying in a pocket.

penman /'penmən/ *n.* (*pl.* **-men**) **1** a person who writes by hand with a specified skill (*a good penman*). **2** an author. □□**penmanship** *n.*

Penn. *abbr.* (also **Penna.**) Pennsylvania.

pennant /'penənt/ *n.* **1** *Naut.* a tapering flag, esp. that flown at the masthead of a vessel in commission. **2** = PENDANT 3a. **3** = PENNON. **4** *US* a flag denoting a sports championship etc. [blend of PENDANT and PENNON]

penniless /'penɪlɪs/ *adj.* having no money; destitute. □□**pennilessly** *adv.* **pennilessness** *n.*

pennill /'penɪl/ *n.* (*pl.* **penillion** /pe'nɪljən/) (usu. in *pl.*) an improvised stanza sung to a harp accompaniment at an eisteddfod etc. [Welsh f. *penn* head]

pennon /'penən/ *n.* **1** a long narrow flag, triangular or swallow-tailed, esp. as the military ensign of lancer regiments. **2** *Naut.* a long pointed streamer on a ship. **3** a flag. □□**pennoned** *adj.* [ME f. OF f. L *penna* feather]

penn'orth var. of PENNYWORTH.

Pennsylvania Dutch /ˌpensɪl'veɪnɪə/ *n.* **1** a dialect of High German spoken by descendants of 17th–18th-c. German and Swiss immigrants to Pennsylvania etc. **2** (as *pl.*) these settlers or their descendants.

Pennsylvanian /ˌpensɪl'veɪnɪən/ *n. & adj.* —*n.* **1** a native or inhabitant of Pennsylvania, a State of the US. **2** (prec. by *the*) esp. *US Geol.* the upper Carboniferous period or system. —*adj.* **1** of or relating to Pennsylvania. **2** esp. *US Geol.* of or relating to the upper Carboniferous period or system.

penny /'penɪ/ *n.* (*pl.* for separate coins **-ies**, for a sum of money **pence** /pens/) **1** a British coin and monetary unit equal to one-hundredth of a pound. ¶ Abbr.: **p**. **2** *hist.* a former British bronze coin and monetary unit equal to one-two-hundred-and-fortieth of a pound. ¶ Abbr.: **d**. **3** *US colloq.* a one-cent coin. **4** *Bibl.* a denarius. □**in for a penny, in for a pound** an exhortation to total commitment to an undertaking. **like a bad penny** continually returning when unwanted. **pennies from heaven** unexpected benefits. **penny black** the first adhesive postage stamp (1840, value one penny). **penny cress** *Bot.* a plant, *Thlaspi arvense*, with flat round pods. **penny dreadful** *Brit.* a cheap sensational comic or story-book. **the penny drops** *colloq.* one begins to understand at last. **penny farthing** *Brit.* an early type of bicycle with one large and one small wheel. **a penny for your thoughts** a request to a thoughtful person to confide in the speaker. **penny-in-the-slot** (of a machine) activated by a coin pushed into a slot. **penny-pincher** a niggardly person. **penny-pinching** *n.* meanness. —*adj.* mean. **penny post** *Brit. hist.* the system of carrying letters etc. at a standard charge of 1d. regardless of distance. **penny whistle** a tin pipe with six holes giving different notes. **penny wise** too careful in saving small amounts. **penny wise and pound foolish** mean in small expenditures but wasteful of large amounts. **a pretty penny** a large sum of money. **two a penny** almost worthless though easily obtained. [OE *penig*, *penning* f. Gmc, perh. rel. to PAWN[2]]

-penny /pənɪ/ *comb. form Brit.* forming attributive adjectives meaning 'costing . . . pence' (esp. in pre-decimal currency) (*fivepenny*).

pennyroyal /ˌpenɪ'rɔɪəl/ *n.* **1** a creeping mint, *Mentha pulegium*, cultivated for its supposed medicinal properties. **2** *US* an aromatic plant, *Hedeoma pulegioides*. [app. f. earlier *puliol(e) ryall* f. AF *puliol*, OF *pouliol* ult. f. L *pulegium* + real ROYAL]

pennyweight /'penɪweɪt/ *n.* a unit of weight, 24 grains or one-twentieth of an ounce troy.

pennywort /'penɪwɜːt/ *n.* any of several wild plants with rounded leaves, esp.: **1** (**wall pennywort**) *Umbilicus rupestris*, growing in crevices. **2** (**marsh** or **water pennywort**) *Hydrocotyle vulgaris*, growing in marshy places. [ME, f. PENNY + WORT]

pennyworth /'penɪwɜːθ/ *n.* (also **penn'orth** /'penəθ/) **1** as much as can be bought for a penny. **2** a bargain of a specified kind (*a bad pennyworth*). □**not a pennyworth** not the least bit.

penology /piː'nɒlədʒɪ/ *n.* the study of the punishment of crime and of prison management. □□**penological** /-nə'lɒdʒɪk(ə)l/ *adj.* **penologist** *n.* [L *poena* penalty + -LOGY]

pensée /pã'seɪ/ *n.* a thought or reflection put into literary form; an aphorism. [F]

pensile /'pensaɪl/ *adj.* **1** hanging down; pendulous. **2** (of a bird etc.) building a pensile nest. [L *pensilis* f. *pendēre pens-* hang]

pension[1] /'penʃ(ə)n/ *n. & v.* —*n.* **1 a** a regular payment made by a government to people above a specified age, to widows, or to the disabled. **b** similar payments made by an employer etc. on the retirement of an employee. **2 a** a pension paid to a scientist, artist, etc. for services to the state, or to fund work. **b** any pension paid esp. by a government on charitable grounds. —*v.tr.* **1** grant a pension to. **2** bribe with a pension. □**pension off 1** dismiss with a pension. **2** cease to employ or use. □□**pensionless** *adj.* [ME f. OF f. L *pensio -onis* payment f. *pendere pens-* pay]

pension[2] /pã'sjõ/ *n.* a European, esp. French, boarding-house providing full or half board at a fixed rate. □**en pension** /ã/ as a boarder. [F: see PENSION[1]]

pensionable /'penʃənəb(ə)l/ *adj.* **1** entitled to a pension. **2** (of a service, job, etc.) entitling an employee to a pension. □□**pensionability** /-'brlɪtɪ/ *n.*

pensionary /'penʃənərɪ/ *adj. & n.* —*adj.* of or concerning a pension. —*n.* (*pl.* **-ies**) **1** a pensioner. **2** a creature; a hireling. □**Grand Pensionary** *hist.* the first minister of Holland and Zealand (1619–1794). [med.L *pensionarius* (as PENSION[1])]

pensioner /'penʃənə(r)/ *n.* a recipient of a pension, esp. the retirement pension. [ME f. AF *pensionner*, OF *pensionnier* (as PENSION[1])]

pensive /'pensɪv/ *adj.* **1** deep in thought. **2** sorrowfully thoughtful. □□**pensively** *adv.* **pensiveness** *n.* [ME f. OF *pensif*, *-ive* f. *penser* think f. L *pensare* frequent. of *pendere pens-* weigh]

penstemon var. of PENTSTEMON.

penstock /'penstɒk/ *n.* **1** a sluice; a floodgate. **2** *US* a channel for conveying water to a water-wheel. [PEN[2] in sense 'mill-dam' + STOCK]

pent /pent/ *adj.* (often foll. by *in*, *up*) closely confined;

shut in (*pent up feelings*). [past part. of *pend* var. of
PEN² *v.*]

penta- /ˈpentə/ *comb. form* **1** five. **2** *Chem.* (forming
the names of compounds) containing five atoms or
groups of a specified kind (*pentachloride*; *pentoxide*).
[Gk f. *pente* five]

pentachord /ˈpentəˌkɔːd/ *n.* **1** a musical instrument
with five strings. **2** a series of five musical notes.

pentacle /ˈpentək(ə)l/ *n.* a figure used as a symbol,
esp. in magic, e.g. a pentagram. [med.L *pentaculum*
(as PENTA-)]

pentad /ˈpentæd/ *n.* **1** the number five. **2** a group of
five. [Gk *pentas -ados* f. *pente* five]

pentadactyl /ˌpentəˈdæktɪl/ *adj.* *Zool.* having five
toes or fingers.

pentagon /ˈpentəgən/ *n.* **1** a plane figure with five
sides and angles. **2** (**the Pentagon**) **a** the pentagonal
Washington headquarters of the US defence forces.
b the leaders of the US defence forces. □□ **pentagonal**
/-ˈtægən(ə)l/ *adj.* [F *pentagone* or f. LL *pentagonus* f.
Gk *pentagōnon* (as PENTA-, -GON)]

pentagram /ˈpentəˌgræm/ *n.* a five-pointed star
formed by extending the sides of a pentagon both
ways until they intersect, formerly used as a mystic
symbol. [Gk *pentagrammon* (as PENTA-, -GRAM)]

pentagynous /penˈtædʒɪnəs/ *adj.* *Bot.* having five
pistils.

pentahedron /ˌpentəˈhiːdrən/ *n.* a solid figure with
five faces. □□ **pentahedral** *adj.*

pentamerous /penˈtæmərəs/ *adj.* **1** *Bot.* having five
parts in a flower-whorl. **2** *Zool.* having five joints or
parts.

pentameter /penˈtæmɪtə(r)/ *n.* **1** a verse of five feet,
e.g. English iambic verse of ten syllables. **2** a form of
Gk or Latin dactylic verse composed of two halves
each of two feet and a long syllable, used in elegiac
verse. [L f. Gk *pentametros* (as PENTA-, -METER)]

pentandrous /penˈtændrəs/ *adj.* *Bot.* having five
stamens.

pentane /ˈpenteɪn/ *n.* *Chem.* a hydrocarbon of the
alkane series. ¶ *Chem.* formula: C_5H_{12}. [Gk *pente* five
+ ALKANE]

pentangle /ˈpenˌtæŋg(ə)l/ *n.* = PENTAGRAM. [ME
perh. f. med.L *pentaculum* PENTACLE, assim. to L
angulus ANGLE]

pentanoic acid /ˌpentəˈnəʊɪk/ *n.* *Chem.* a colourless
liquid carboxylic acid used in making perfumes.
[PENTANE]

pentaprism /ˈpentəˌprɪz(ə)m/ *n.* a five-sided prism
with two silvered surfaces used in a viewfinder to
obtain a constant deviation of all rays of light through
90°.

Pentateuch /ˈpentəˌtjuːk/ *n.* the first five books of
the Old Testament, traditionally ascribed to Moses.
□□ **pentateuchal** /-ˈtjuːk(ə)l/ *adj.* [eccl.L *pen-*
tateuchus f. eccl.Gk *pentateukhos* (as PENTA-, *teukhos*
implement, book)]

pentathlon /penˈtæθlən/ *n.* an athletic event comprising five different events for each competitor. □□
pentathlete /-ˈtæθliːt/ *n.* [Gk f. *pente* five + *athlon*
contest]

pentatonic /ˌpentəˈtɒnɪk/ *adj.* *Mus.* **1** consisting of
five notes. **2** relating to such a scale.

pentavalent /ˌpentəˈveɪlənt/ *adj.* *Chem.* having a
valency of five; quinquevalent.

Pentecost /ˈpentɪˌkɒst/ *n.* **1 a** Whit Sunday. **b** a
festival celebrating the descent of the Holy Spirit on
Whit Sunday. **2 a** the Jewish harvest festival, on the
fiftieth day after the second day of Passover (Lev. 23:
15–16). **b** a synagogue ceremony on the anniversary
of the giving of the Law on Mount Sinai. [OE
pentecosten & OF *pentecoste*, f. eccl.L *pentecoste* f. Gk
pentēkostē (*hēmera*) fiftieth (day)]

Pentecostal /ˌpentɪˈkɒst(ə)l/ *adj.* & *n.* —*adj.* (also
pentecostal) **1** of or relating to Pentecost. **2** of or
designating Christian sects and individuals who
emphasize the gifts of the Holy Spirit, are often
fundamentalist in outlook, and express religious

feelings by clapping, shouting, dancing, etc. —*n.*
a Pentecostalist. □□ **Pentecostalism** *n.*
Pentecostalist *adj.* & *n.*

penthouse /ˈpenthaʊs/ *n.* **1** a house or flat on the
roof or the top floor of a tall building. **2** a sloping
roof, esp. of an outhouse built on to another building.
3 an awning, a canopy. [ME *pentis* f. OF *apentis*, -*dis*,
f. med.L *appendicium*, in LL = appendage, f. L (as
APPEND): infl. by HOUSE]

pentimento /ˌpentɪˈmentəʊ/ *n.* (*pl.* **pentimenti**
/-tiː/) the phenomenon of earlier painting
showing through a layer or layers of paint on a
canvas. [It., = repentance]

pentobarbitone /ˌpentəʊˈbɑːbɪˌtəʊn/ *n.* (*US*
pentobarbital /-ˌtæl/) a narcotic and sedative barbiturate drug formerly used to relieve insomnia.
[PENTA-, BARBITONE, BARBITAL]

pentode /ˈpentəʊd/ *n.* a thermionic valve having five
electrodes. [Gk *pente* five + *hodos* way]

pentose /ˈpentəʊz/ *n.* *Biochem.* any monosaccharide
containing five carbon atoms, including ribose.
[PENTA- + -OSE²]

pent-roof /ˈpentruːf/ *n.* a roof sloping in one direction
only. [PENTHOUSE + ROOF]

pentstemon /pentˈstiːmən, ˈpentstəmən/ *n.* (also
penstemon /penˈstiːmən/) any American herbaceous plant of the genus *Penstemon*, with showy
flowers and five stamens, one of which is sterile.
[mod.L, irreg. f. PENTA- + Gk *stēmōn* warp, used for
'stamen']

pentyl /ˈpentɪl/ *n.* = AMYL. [PENTANE + -YL]

penult /pɪˈnʌlt, ˈpiːnʌlt/ *n.* & *adj.* —*n.* the last but
one (esp. syllable). —*adj.* last but one. [abbr. of L
paenultimus (see PENULTIMATE) or of PENULTIMATE]

penultimate /pɪˈnʌltɪmət/ *adj.* & *n.* —*adj.* last but
one. —*n.* **1** the last but one. **2** the last syllable but
one. [L *paenultimus* f. *paene* almost + *ultimus* last,
after *ultimate*]

penumbra /pɪˈnʌmbrə/ *n.* (*pl.* **penumbrae** /-briː/ or
penumbras) **1 a** the partly shaded region around
the shadow of an opaque body, esp. that around the
total shadow of the moon or earth in an eclipse. **b**
the less dark outer part of a sunspot. **2** a partial
shadow. □□ **penumbral** *adj.* [mod.L f. L *paene* almost
+ UMBRA shadow]

penurious /pɪˈnjʊərɪəs/ *adj.* **1** poor; destitute. **2**
stingy; grudging. **3** scanty. □□ **penuriously** *adv.*
penuriousness *n.* [med.L *penuriosus* (as PENURY)]

penury /ˈpenjʊrɪ/ *n.* (*pl.* -**ies**) **1** destitution; poverty.
2 a lack; scarcity. [ME f. L *penuria*, perh. rel. to *paene*
almost]

peon /ˈpiːən/ *n.* **1 a** a Spanish American day labourer
or farm-worker. **b** a poor or destitute South American. **2** /ˈpiːən, pjuːn/ an Indian office messenger,
attendant, or orderly. **3** a bullfighter's assistant. **4**
hist. a worker held in servitude in the southern US.
□□ **peonage** *n.* [Port. *peão* & Sp. *peon* f. med.L *pedo*
-*onis* walker f. L *pes pedis* foot: cf. PAWN¹]

peony /ˈpiːənɪ/ *n.* (also **paeony**) (*pl.* -**ies**) any herbaceous plant of the genus *Paeonia*, with large globular red, pink, or white flowers, often double in
cultivated varieties. [OE *peonie* f. L *peonia* f. Gk
paiōnia f. *Paiōn*, physician of the gods]

people /ˈpiːp(ə)l/ *n.* & *v.* —*n.* **1** (usu. as *pl.*) **a** persons
composing a community, tribe, race, nation, etc. (*the*
English people; *a warlike people*; *the peoples of the*
Commonwealth). **b** a group of persons of a usu.
specified kind (*the chosen people*; *these people here*;
right-thinking people). **2** (prec. by *the*; treated as *pl.*)
a the mass of people in a country etc. not having
special rank or position. **b** these considered as an
electorate (*the people will reject it*). **3** parents or other
relatives (*my people are French*). **4 a** subjects, armed
followers, a retinue, etc. **b** a congregation of a parish
priest etc. **5** persons in general (*people do not like*
rudeness). —*v.tr.* (usu. foll. by *with*) **1** fill with
people, animals, etc.; populate. **2** (esp. as **peopled**
adj.) inhabit; occupy; fill (*thickly peopled*). □**people's**

democracy a political system, esp. in E. Europe, with power regarded as invested in the people. [ME f. AF *poeple, people*, OF *pople, peuple*, f. L *populus*]

PEP *abbr. Brit.* **1** Political and Economic Planning. **2** Personal Equity Plan.

pep /pep/ *n. & v. colloq.* —*n.* vigour; go; spirit. —*v.tr.* (**pepped, pepping**) (usu. foll. by *up*) fill with vigour. □**pep pill** a pill containing a stimulant drug. **pep talk** a usu. short talk intended to enthuse, encourage, etc. [abbr. of PEPPER]

peperino /ˌpepəˈriːnəʊ/ *n.* a light porous (esp. brown) volcanic rock formed of small grains of sand, cinders, etc. [It. f. *pepere* pepper]

peperoni var. of PEPPERONI.

peplum /ˈpepləm/ *n.* **1** a short flounce etc. at waist level, esp. of a blouse or jacket over a skirt. **2** *Gk Antiq.* a woman's outer garment. [L f. Gk *peplos*]

pepo /ˈpiːpəʊ/ *n.* (*pl.* **-os**) any fleshy fruit of the melon or cucumber type, with numerous seeds and surrounded by a hard skin. [L, = pumpkin, f. Gk *pepōn sikuos* ripe gourd]

pepper /ˈpepə(r)/ *n. & v.* —*n.* **1 a** a hot aromatic condiment from the dried berries of certain plants used whole or ground. **b** any climbing vine of the genus *Piper*, esp. *P. nigrum*, yielding these berries. **2** anything hot or pungent. **3 a** any plant of the genus *Capsicum*, esp. *C. annuum*. **b** the fruit of this used esp. as a vegetable or salad ingredient. **4** = CAYENNE. —*v.tr.* **1** sprinkle or treat with or as if with pepper. **2 a** pelt with missiles. **b** hurl abuse etc. at. **3** punish severely. □**black pepper** the unripe ground or whole berries of *Piper nigrum* as a condiment. **green pepper** the unripe fruit of *Capsicum annuum*. **pepper-mill** a device for grinding pepper by hand. **pepper-pot 1** a small container with a perforated lid for sprinkling pepper. **2** a W. Indian dish of meat etc. stewed with cayenne pepper. **3** *colloq.* a Jamaican. **red** (or **yellow**) **pepper** the ripe fruit of *Capsicum annuum*. **sweet pepper** a pepper with a relatively mild taste. **white pepper** the ripe or husked ground or whole berries of *Piper nigrum* as a condiment. [OE *piper, pipor* f. L *piper* f. Gk *peperi* f. Skr. *pippalī* berry, peppercorn]

pepperbox /ˈpepəˌbɒks/ *n.* = *pepper-pot*.

peppercorn /ˈpepəkɔːn/ *n.* **1** the dried berry of *Piper nigrum* as a condiment. **2** (in full **peppercorn rent**) a nominal rent.

peppermint /ˈpepəmɪnt/ *n.* **1 a** a mint plant, *Mentha piperita*, grown for the strong-flavoured oil obtained from its leaves. **b** the oil from this. **2** a sweet flavoured with peppermint. **3** *Austral.* any of various eucalyptuses yielding oil with a similar flavour. □□ **pepperminty** *adj.*

pepperoni /ˌpepəˈrəʊnɪ/ *n.* (also **peperoni**) beef and pork sausage seasoned with pepper. [It. *peperone* chilli]

pepperwort /ˈpepəˌwɜːt/ *n.* any cruciferous plant of the genus *Lepidium*, esp. garden cress.

peppery /ˈpepərɪ/ *adj.* **1** of, like, or containing much, pepper. **2** hot-tempered. **3** pungent; stinging. □□ **pepperiness** *n.*

peppy /ˈpepɪ/ *adj.* (**peppier, peppiest**) *colloq.* vigorous, energetic, bouncy. □□ **peppily** *adv.* **peppiness** *n.*

pepsin /ˈpepsɪn/ *n.* an enzyme contained in the gastric juice, which hydrolyses proteins. [G f. Gk *pepsis* digestion]

peptic /ˈpeptɪk/ *adj.* concerning or promoting digestion. □**peptic glands** glands secreting gastric juice. **peptic ulcer** an ulcer in the stomach or duodenum. [Gk *peptikos* able to digest (as PEPTONE)]

peptide /ˈpeptaɪd/ *n. Biochem.* any of a group of organic compounds consisting of two or more amino acids bonded in sequence. [G *Peptid*, back-form. (as POLYPEPTIDE)]

peptone /ˈpeptəʊn/ *n.* a protein fragment formed by hydrolysis in the process of digestion. □□ **peptonize**

/-təˌnaɪz/ *v.tr.* (also **-ise**). [G *Pepton* f. Gk *peptos*, neut. *pepton* cooked]

per /pɜː(r)/ *prep.* **1** for each; for every (*two sweets per child; five miles per hour*). **2** by means of; by; through (*per post; per rail*). **3** (in full **as per**) in accordance with (*as per instructions*). **4** *Heraldry* in the direction of. □**as per usual** *colloq.* as usual. [L]

per- /pɜː(r), pə(r)/ *prefix* **1** forming verbs, nouns, and adjectives meaning: **a** through; all over (*perforate; perforation; pervade*). **b** completely; very (*perfervid; perturb*). **c** to destruction; to the bad (*pervert; perdition*). **2** *Chem.* having the maximum of some element in combination, esp.: **a** in the names of binary compounds in *-ide* (*peroxide*). **b** in the names of oxides, acids, etc. in *-ic* (*perchloric; permanganic*). **c** in the names of salts of these acids (*perchlorate; permanganate*). [L *per-* (as PER)]

peradventure /pərədˈventʃə(r), ˌper-/ *adv. & n. archaic* or *joc.* —*adv.* perhaps. —*n.* uncertainty; chance; conjecture; doubt (esp. *beyond* or *without peradventure*). [ME f. OF *per* or *par auenture* by chance (as PER, ADVENTURE)]

perambulate /pəˈræmbjʊˌleɪt/ *v.* **1** *tr.* walk through, over, or about (streets, the country, etc.). **2** *intr.* walk from place to place. **3** *tr.* **a** travel through and inspect (territory). **b** formally establish the boundaries of (a parish etc.) by walking round them. □□ **perambulation** /-ˈleɪʃ(ə)n/ *n.* **perambulatory** *adj.* [L *perambulare perambulat-* (as PER-, *ambulare* walk)]

perambulator /pəˈræmbjʊˌleɪtə(r)/ *n. Brit. formal* = PRAM. [PERAMBULATE]

per annum /pər ˈænəm/ *adv.* for each year. [L]

percale /pəˈkeɪl/ *n.* a closely woven cotton fabric like calico. [F, of uncert. orig.]

per capita /pə ˈkæpɪtə/ *adv. & adj.* (also **per caput** /ˈkæpʊt/) for each person. [L, = by heads]

perceive /pəˈsiːv/ *v.tr.* **1** apprehend, esp. through the sight; observe. **2** (usu. foll. by *that, how,* etc. + clause) apprehend with the mind; understand. **3** regard mentally in a specified manner (*perceives the universe as infinite*). □□ **perceivable** *adj.* **perceiver** *n.* [ME f. OF *perçoivre*, f. L *percipere* (as PER-, *capere* take)]

per cent /pə ˈsent/ *adv. & n.* (*US* **percent**) —*adv.* in every hundred. —*n.* **1** percentage. **2** one part in every hundred (*half a per cent*). **3** (in *pl.*) *Brit.* public securities yielding interest of so much per cent (*three per cents*).

percentage /pəˈsentɪdʒ/ *n.* **1** a rate or proportion per cent. **2** a proportion. **3** *colloq.* personal benefit or advantage.

percentile /pəˈsentaɪl/ *n. Statistics* one of 99 values of a variable dividing a population into 100 equal groups as regards the value of that variable.

percept /ˈpɜːsept/ *n. Philos.* **1** an object of perception. **2** a mental concept resulting from perceiving, esp. by sight. [L *perceptum* perceived (thing), neut. past part. of *percipere* PERCEIVE, after *concept*]

perceptible /pəˈseptɪb(ə)l/ *adj.* capable of being perceived by the senses or intellect. □□ **perceptibility** /-ˈbɪlɪtɪ/ *n.* **perceptibly** *adv.* [OF *perceptible* or LL *perceptibilis* f. L (as PERCEIVE)]

perception /pəˈsepʃ(ə)n/ *n.* **1 a** the faculty of perceiving. **b** an instance of this. **2** (often foll. by *of*) **a** the intuitive recognition of a truth, aesthetic quality, etc. **b** an instance of this (*a sudden perception of the true position*). **3** *Philos.* the ability of the mind to refer sensory information to an external object as its cause. □□ **perceptional** *adj.* **perceptual** /pəˈseptjʊəl/ *adj.* **perceptually** /pəˈseptjʊəlɪ/ *adv.* [ME f. L *perceptio* (as PERCEIVE)]

perceptive /pəˈseptɪv/ *adj.* **1** capable of perceiving. **2** sensitive; discerning; observant (*a perceptive remark*). □□ **perceptively** *adv.* **perceptiveness** *n.* **perceptivity** /-ˈtɪvɪtɪ/ *n.* [med.L *perceptivus* (as PERCEIVE)]

perch¹ /pɜːtʃ/ *n. & v.* —*n.* **1** a usu. horizontal bar, branch, etc. used by a bird to rest on. **2** a usu. high or precarious place for a person or thing to rest on. **3** a measure of length, esp. for land, of 5½ yards (see also ROD, POLE). —*v.intr. & tr.* (usu. foll. by *on*) settle or rest, or cause to settle or rest on or as if on a perch etc. (*the bird perched on a branch*; *a town perched on a hill*). □**knock a person off his perch 1** vanquish, destroy. **2** make less confident or secure. **square perch** 30¼ sq. yards. [ME f. OF *perche, percher* f. L *pertica* pole]

perch² /pɜːtʃ/ *n.* (*pl.* same or **perches**) any spiny-finned freshwater edible fish of the genus *Perca*, esp. *P. fluviatilis* of Europe. [ME f. OF *perche* f. L *perca* f. Gk *perkē*]

perchance /pəˈtʃɑːns/ *adv. archaic* or *poet.* **1** by chance. **2** possibly; maybe. [ME f. AF *par chance* f. *par* by, CHANCE]

percher /ˈpɜːtʃə(r)/ *n.* any bird with feet adapted for perching; a passerine.

percheron /ˈpeəʃəˌrɒ̃/ *n.* a powerful breed of cart-horse. [F, orig. bred in le *Perche*, a district of N. France]

perchlorate /pəˈklɔːreɪt/ *n. Chem.* a salt or ester of perchloric acid.

perchloric acid /pəˈklɔːrɪk/ *n. Chem.* a strong liquid acid containing heptavalent chlorine. [PER- + CHLORINE]

percipient /pəˈsɪpɪənt/ *adj. & n.* —*adj.* **1** able to perceive; conscious. **2** discerning; observant. —*n.* a person who perceives, esp. something outside the range of the senses. □□ **percipience** *n.* **percipiently** *adv.* [L (as PERCEIVE)]

percolate /ˈpɜːkəˌleɪt/ *v.* **1** intr. (often foll. by *through*) **a** (of liquid etc.) filter or ooze gradually (esp. through a porous surface). **b** (of an idea etc.) permeate gradually. **2** *tr.* prepare (coffee) by repeatedly passing boiling water through ground beans. **3** *tr.* ooze through; permeate. **4** *tr.* strain (a liquid, powder, etc.) through a fine mesh etc. □□ **percolation** /-ˈleɪʃ(ə)n/ *n.* [L *percolare* (as PER-, *colare* strain f. *colum* strainer)]

percolator /ˈpɜːkəˌleɪtə(r)/ *n.* a machine for making coffee by circulating boiling water through ground beans.

per contra /pɜː ˈkɒntrə/ *adv.* on the opposite side (of an account, assessment, etc.); on the contrary. [It.]

percuss /pəˈkʌs/ *v.tr. Med.* tap (a part of the body) gently with a finger or an instrument as part of a diagnosis. [L *percutere percuss-* strike (as PER-, *cutere = quatere* shake)]

percussion /pəˈkʌʃ(ə)n/ *n.* **1** *Mus.* **a** (often *attrib.*) the playing of music by striking instruments with sticks etc. (*a percussion band*). **b** the section of such instruments in an orchestra (*asked the percussion to stay behind*). **2** *Med.* the act or an instance of percussing. **3** the forcible striking of one esp. solid body against another. □**percussion cap** a small amount of explosive powder contained in metal or paper and exploded by striking, used esp. in toy guns and formerly in some firearms. □□ **percussionist** *n.* **percussive** *adj.* **percussively** *adv.* **percussiveness** *n.* [F *percussion* or L *percussio* (as PERCUSS)]

percutaneous /ˌpɜːkjuˈteɪnɪəs/ *adj.* esp. *Med.* made or done through the skin. [L *per cutem* through the skin]

per diem /pɜː ˈdiːem, ˈdaɪem/ *adv., adj. & n.* —*adv. & adj.* for each day. —*n.* an allowance or payment for each day. [L]

perdition /pəˈdɪʃ(ə)n/ *n.* eternal death; damnation. [ME f. OF *perdiciun* or eccl.L *perditio* f. L *perdere* destroy (as PER-, *dere dit- = dare* give)]

perdurable /pəˈdjʊərəb(ə)l/ *adj. formal* permanent; eternal; durable. □□ **perdurability** /-ˈbɪlɪtɪ/ *n.* **perdurably** *adv.* [ME f. OF f. LL *perdurabilis* (as PER-, DURABLE)]

père /peə(r)/ *n.* (added to a surname to distinguish a father from a son) the father, senior (cf. FILS). [F, = father]

Père David's deer /ˌpeə ˈdeɪvɪdz/ *n.* a large slender-antlered deer, *Elaphurus davidianus*. [after Father A. *David*, Fr. missionary d. 1900]

peregrinate /ˈperɪɡrɪˌneɪt/ *v.intr. archaic* or *joc.* travel; journey, esp. extensively or at leisure. □□ **peregrination** /-ˈneɪʃ(ə)n/ *n.* **peregrinator** *n.* [L *peregrinari* (as PEREGRINE)]

peregrine /ˈperɪɡrɪn/ *n. & adj.* —*n.* (in full **peregrine falcon**) a kind of falcon much used for hawking. —*adj. archaic* imported from abroad; foreign; outlandish. [L *peregrinus* f. *peregre* abroad f. *per* through + *ager* field]

peremptory /pəˈremptərɪ, ˈperɪm-/ *adj.* **1** (of a statement or command) admitting no denial or refusal. **2** (of a person, a person's manner, etc.) dogmatic; imperious; dictatorial. **3** *Law* not open to appeal or challenge; final. **4** absolutely fixed; essential. □**peremptory challenge** *Law* a defendant's objection to a proposed juror, made without needing to give a reason. □□ **peremptorily** *adv.* **peremptoriness** *n.* [AF *peremptorie*, OF *peremptoire* f. L *peremptorius* deadly, decisive, f. *perimere perempt-* destroy, cut off (as PER-, *emere* take, buy)]

perennial /pəˈrenɪəl/ *adj. & n.* —*adj.* **1** lasting through a year or several years. **2** (of a plant) lasting several years (cf. ANNUAL). **3** lasting a long time or for ever. **4** (of a stream) flowing through all seasons of the year. —*n.* a perennial plant (*a herbaceous perennial*). □□ **perenniality** /-ˈælɪtɪ/ *n.* **perennially** *adv.* [L *perennis* (as PER-, *annus* year)]

perestroika /ˌpereˈstrɔɪkə/ *n.* (in the Soviet Union) the policy or practice of restructuring or reforming the economic and political system. [Russ. *perestroĭka* = restructuring]

perfect /ˈpɜːfɪkt/ *adj., v., & n.* —*adj.* **1** complete; not deficient. **2** faultless (*a perfect diamond*). **3** very satisfactory (*a perfect evening*). **4** exact; precise (*a perfect circle*). **5** entire; unqualified (*a perfect stranger*). **6** *Math.* (of a number) equal to the sum of its divisors. **7** *Gram.* (of a tense) denoting a completed action or event in the past, formed in English with *have* or *has* and the past participle, as in *they have eaten*. **8** *Mus.* (of pitch) absolute. **9** *Bot.* **a** (of a flower) having all four types of whorl. **b** (of a fungus) in the stage where the sexual spores are formed. **10** (often foll. by *in*) thoroughly trained or skilled (*is perfect in geometry*). —*v.tr.* /pəˈfekt/ **1** make perfect; improve. **2** carry through; complete. **3** complete (a sheet) by printing the other side. —*n. Gram.* the perfect tense. □**perfect binding** a form of bookbinding in which the leaves are attached to the spine by gluing rather than sewing. **perfect interval** *Mus.* a fourth or fifth as it would occur in a major or minor scale starting on the lower note of the interval, or octave. **perfect pitch** = *absolute pitch* 1. □□ **perfecter** *n.* **perfectible** /pəˈfektɪb(ə)l/ *adj.* **perfectibility** /pəˌfektɪˈbɪlɪtɪ/ *n.* **perfectness** *n.* [ME and OF *parfit, perfet* f. L *perfectus* past part. of *perficere* complete (as PER-, *facere* do)]

perfecta /pəˈfektə/ *n. US* a form of betting in which the first two places in a race must be predicted in the correct order. [Amer. Sp. *quiniela perfecta* perfect quinella]

perfection /pəˈfekʃ(ə)n/ *n.* **1** the act or process of making perfect. **2** the state of being perfect; faultlessness, excellence. **3** a perfect person, thing, or example. **4** an accomplishment. **5** full development; completion. □**to perfection** exactly; completely. [ME f. OF f. L *perfectio -onis* (as PERFECT)]

perfectionism /pəˈfekʃəˌnɪz(ə)m/ *n.* **1** the uncompromising pursuit of excellence. **2** *Philos.* the belief that religious or moral perfection is attainable. □□ **perfectionist** *n. & adj.* [PERFECT]

perfective /pəˈfektɪv/ *adj. & n. Gram.* —*adj.* (of an aspect of a verb etc.) expressing the completion of an action (opp. IMPERFECTIVE). —*n.* the perfective aspect or form of a verb. [med.L *perfectivus* (as PERFECT)]

perfectly /'pɜːfɪktlɪ/ *adv.* **1** completely; absolutely (*I understand you perfectly*). **2** quite, completely (*is perfectly capable of doing it*). **3** in a perfect way.

perfecto /pə'fektəʊ/ *n.* (*pl.* **-os**) orig. *US* a large thick cigar pointed at each end. [Sp., = perfect]

perfervid /pə'fɜːvɪd/ *adj. literary* very fervid. □□ **perfervidly** *adv.* **perfervidness** *n.* [mod.L *perfervidus* (as PER-, FERVID)]

perfidy /'pɜːfɪdɪ/ *n.* breach of faith; treachery. □□ **perfidious** /-'fɪdɪəs/ *adj.* **perfidiously** /-'fɪdɪəslɪ/ *adv.* [L *perfidia* f. *perfidus* treacherous (as PER-, *fides* f. *fides* faith)]

perfoliate /pə'fəʊlɪət/ *adj.* (of a plant) having the stalk apparently passing through the leaf. [mod.L *perfoliatus* (as PER-, FOLIATE)]

perforate *v. & adj.* —*v.* /'pɜːfə,reɪt/ **1** *tr.* make a hole or holes through; pierce. **2** *tr.* make a row of small holes in (paper etc.) so that a part may be torn off easily. **3** *tr.* make an opening into; pass into or extend through. **4** *intr.* (usu. foll. by *into*, *through*, etc.) penetrate. —*adj.* /'pɜːfərət/ perforated. □□ **perforation** /-'reɪʃ(ə)n/ *n.* **perforative** /'pɜːfərətɪv/ *adj.* **perforator** /'pɜːfə,reɪtə(r)/ *n.* [L *perforare* (as PER-, *forare* pierce)]

perforce /pə'fɔːs/ *adv. archaic* unavoidably; necessarily. [ME f. OF *par force* by FORCE[1]]

perform /pə'fɔːm/ *v.* **1** *tr.* (also *absol.*) carry into effect; be the agent of; do (a command, promise, task, etc.). **2** *tr.* (also *absol.*) go through, execute (a public function, play, piece of music, etc.). **3** *intr.* act in a play; play music, sing, etc. (*likes performing*). **4** *intr.* (of a trained animal) execute tricks etc. at a public show. □□ **performable** *adj.* **performability** /-'bɪlɪtɪ/ *n.* **performatory** *adj. & n.* (*pl.* **-ies**). **performer** *n.* **performing** *adj.* [ME f. AF *parfourmer* f. OF *parfournir* (assim. to *forme* FORM) f. *par* PER- + *fournir* FURNISH]

performance /pə'fɔːməns/ *n.* **1** (usu. foll. by *of*) **a** the act or process of performing or carrying out. **b** the execution or fulfilment (of a duty etc.). **2** a staging or production (of a drama, piece of music, etc.) (*the afternoon performance*). **3** a person's achievement under test conditions etc. (*put up a good performance*). **4** *colloq.* a fuss; a scene; a public exhibition (*made such a performance about leaving*). **5 a** the capabilities of a machine, esp. a car or aircraft. **b** (*attrib.*) of high capability (*a performance car*).

performative /pə'fɔːmətɪv/ *adj. & n.* —*adj.* **1** of or relating to performance. **2** denoting an utterance that effects an action by being spoken or written (e.g. *I bet, I apologize*). —*n.* a performative utterance.

performing arts /pə'fɔːmɪŋ/ *n.pl.* the arts, such as drama, music, and dance, that require performance for their realization.

perfume /'pɜːfjuːm/ *n. & v.* —*n.* **1** a sweet smell. **2** fluid containing the essence of flowers etc.; scent. —*v.tr.* /also pə'fjuːm/ (usu. as **perfumed** *adj.*) impart a sweet scent to; impregnate with a sweet smell. □□ **perfumy** *adj.* [F *parfum, parfumer* f. obs. It. *parfumare, perfumare* (as PER-, *fumare* smoke, FUME): orig. of smoke from a burning substance]

perfumer /pə'fjuːmə(r)/ *n.* a maker or seller of perfumes. □□ **perfumery** *n.* (*pl.* **-ies**).

perfunctory /pə'fʌŋktərɪ/ *adj.* **1** done merely for the sake of getting through a duty. **2** superficial; mechanical. □□ **perfunctorily** *adv.* **perfunctoriness** *n.* [LL *perfunctorius* careless f. L *perfungi perfunct-* (as PER-, *fungi* perform)]

perfuse /pə'fjuːz/ *v.tr.* **1** (often foll. by *with*) **a** besprinkle (with water etc.). **b** cover or suffuse (with radiance etc.). **2** pour or diffuse (water etc.) through or over. **3** *Med.* cause a fluid to pass through (an organ etc.). □□ **perfusion** /-ʒ(ə)n/ *n.* **perfusive** /-sɪv/ *adj.* [L *perfundere perfus-* (as PER-, *fundere* pour)]

pergana var. of PARGANA.

pergola /'pɜːgələ/ *n.* an arbour or covered walk, formed of growing plants trained over trellis-work. [It. f. L *pergula* projecting roof f. *pergere* proceed]

pergunnah var. of PARGANA.

perhaps /pə'hæps/ *adv.* **1** it may be; possibly (*perhaps it is lost*). **2** introducing a polite request (*perhaps you would open the window?*). [PER + HAP]

peri /'pɪərɪ/ *n.* (*pl.* **peris**) **1** (in Persian mythology) a fairy; a good (orig. evil) genius. **2** a beautiful or graceful being. [Pers. *parī*]

peri- /'perɪ/ *prefix* **1** round, about. **2** *Astron.* the point nearest to (*perigee; perihelion*). [Gk *peri* around, about]

perianth /'perɪ,ænθ/ *n.* the outer part of a flower. [F *périanthe* f. mod.L *perianthium* (as PERI- + Gk *anthos* flower)]

periapt /'perɪ,æpt/ *n.* a thing worn as a charm; an amulet. [F *périapte* f. Gk *periapton* f. *haptō* fasten]

pericardium /,perɪ'kaːdɪəm/ *n.* (*pl.* **pericardia** /-dɪə/) the membranous sac enclosing the heart. □□ **pericardiac** /-dɪ,æk/ *adj.* **pericardial** *adj.* **pericarditis** /-'daɪtɪs/ *n.* [mod.L f. Gk *perikardion* (as PERI- + *kardia* heart)]

pericarp /'perɪ,kaːp/ *n.* the part of a fruit formed from the wall of the ripened ovary. [F *péricarpe* f. Gk *perikarpion* pod, shell (as PERI-, *karpos* fruit)]

perichondrium /,perɪ'kɒndrɪəm/ *n.* the membrane enveloping cartilage tissue (except at the joints). [PERI- + Gk *khondros* cartilage]

periclase /'perɪ,kleɪs/ *n.* a pale mineral consisting of magnesia. [mod.L *periclasia*, erron. f. Gk *peri* exceedingly + *klasis* breaking, from its perfect cleavage]

periclinal /,perɪ'klaɪn(ə)l/ *adj. Geol.* (of a mound etc.) sloping down in all directions from a central point. [Gk *periklinēs* sloping on all sides (as PERI-, CLINE)]

pericope /pə'rɪkəpɪ/ *n.* a short passage or paragraph, esp. a portion of Scripture read in public worship. [LL f. Gk *perikopē* (as PERI-, *kopē* cutting f. *koptō* cut)]

pericranium /,perɪ'kreɪnɪəm/ *n.* the membrane enveloping the skull. [mod.L f. Gk (as PERI-, *kranion* skull)]

peridot /'perɪ,dɒt/ *n.* a green variety of olivine, used esp. as a semiprecious stone. [ME f. OF *peritot*, of unkn. orig.]

perigee /'perɪ,dʒiː/ *n.* the point in a celestial body's orbit where it is nearest the earth (opp. APOGEE). □□ **perigean** /,perɪ'dʒiː,ən/ *adj.* [F *périgée* f. mod.L f. Gk *perigeion* round the earth (as PERI-, *gē* earth)]

periglacial /,perɪ'gleɪʃ(ə)l, -sɪəl/ *adj.* of or relating to a region adjoining a glacier.

perigynous /pə'rɪdʒɪnəs/ *adj.* (of stamens) situated around the pistil or ovary. [mod.L *perigynus* (as PERI-, -GYNOUS)]

perihelion /,perɪ'hiː,lɪən/ *n.* (*pl.* **perihelia** /-lɪə/) the point of a planet's or comet's orbit nearest to the sun's centre. [Graecized f. mod.L *perihelium* (as PERI-, Gk *hēlios* sun)]

peril /'perɪl/ *n. & v.* —*n.* serious and immediate danger. —*v.tr.* (**perilled, perilling**; *US* **periled, periling**) threaten; endanger. □**at one's peril** at one's own risk. **in peril of** with great risk to (*in peril of your life*). **peril point** *US Econ.* a critical threshold or limit. [ME f. OF f. L *peric(u)lum*]

perilous /'perɪləs/ *adj.* **1** full of risk; dangerous; hazardous. **2** exposed to imminent risk of destruction etc. □□ **perilously** *adv.* **perilousness** *n.* [ME f. OF *perillous* f. L *periculosus* f. *periculum*: see PERIL]

perilune /'perɪ,luːn, -,ljuːn/ *n.* the point in a body's lunar orbit where it is closest to the moon's centre (opp. APOLUNE). [PERI- + L *luna* moon, after *perigee*]

perilymph /'perɪlɪmf/ *n.* the fluid in the labyrinth of the ear.

perimeter /pə'rɪmɪtə(r)/ *n.* **1 a** the circumference or outline of a closed figure. **b** the length of this. **2 a** the outer boundary of an enclosed area. **b** a defended boundary. **3** an instrument for measuring a field of vision. □□ **perimetric** /,perɪ'metrɪk/ *adj.* [F *périmètre* or f. L *perimetrus* f. Gk *perimetros* (as PERI-, *metros* f. *metron* measure)]

---

w *we*   z *zoo*   ʃ *she*   ʒ *decision*   θ *thin*   ð *this*   ŋ *ring*   x *loch*   tʃ *chip*   dʒ *jar*   (*see over for vowels*)

perinatal /ˌperɪˈneɪt(ə)l/ *adj.* of or relating to the time immediately before and after birth.

perineum /ˌperɪˈniːəm/ *n.* the region of the body between the anus and the scrotum or vulva. □□ **perineal** *adj.* [LL f. Gk *perinaion*]

period /ˈpɪərɪəd/ *n. & adj.* —*n.* **1** a length or portion of time (*showers and bright periods*). **2** a distinct portion of history, a person's life, etc. (*the Georgian period; Picasso's Blue Period*). **3** *Geol.* a time forming part of a geological era (*the Quaternary period*). **4 a** an interval between recurrences of an astronomical or other phenomenon. **b** the time taken by a planet to rotate about its axis. **5** the time allowed for a lesson in school. **6** an occurrence of menstruation. **7 a** a complete sentence, esp. one consisting of several clauses. **b** (in *pl.*) rhetorical language. **8** esp. *US* **a** = *full stop* (see FULL¹). **b** used at the end of a sentence etc. to indicate finality, absoluteness, etc. (*we want the best, period*). **9 a** a set of figures marked off in a large number to assist in reading. **b** a set of figures repeated in a recurring decimal. **c** the smallest interval over which a function takes the same value. **10** *Chem.* a sequence of elements between two noble gases forming a row in the periodic table. —*adj.* belonging to or characteristic of some past period (*period furniture*). □**of the period** of the era under discussion (*the custom of the period*). **period piece** an object or work whose main interest lies in its historical etc. associations. [ME f. OF *periode* f. L *periodus* f. Gk *periodos* (as PERI-, *odos = hodos* way)]

periodate /pəˈraɪədeɪt/ *n. Chem.* a salt or ester of periodic acid.

periodic /ˌpɪərɪˈɒdɪk/ *adj.* **1** appearing or occurring at regular intervals. **2** of or concerning the period of a celestial body (*periodic motion*). **3** (of diction etc.) expressed in periods (see PERIOD *n.* 7a). □**periodic decimal** *Math.* a set of figures repeated in a recurring decimal. **periodic function** *Math.* a function returning to the same value at regular intervals. **periodic table** an arrangement of elements in order of increasing atomic number and in which elements of similar chemical properties appear at regular intervals. □□ **periodicity** /-rɪəˈdɪsɪtɪ/ *n.* [F *périodique* or L *periodicus* f. Gk *periodikos* (as PERIOD)]

periodic acid /ˌpɜːraɪˈɒdɪk/ *n. Chem.* a hygroscopic solid acid containing heptavalent iodine. [PER- + IODINE]

periodical /ˌpɪərɪˈɒdɪk(ə)l/ *n. & adj.* —*n.* a newspaper, magazine, etc. issued at regular intervals, usu. monthly or weekly. —*adj.* **1** published at regular intervals. **2** periodic, occasional. □□ **periodically** *adv.*

periodization /ˌpɪərɪədaɪˈzeɪʃ(ə)n/ *n.* the division of history into periods.

periodontics /ˌperɪəˈdɒntɪks/ *n.pl.* (treated as *sing.*) the branch of dentistry concerned with the structures surrounding and supporting the teeth. □□ **periodontal** *adj.* **periodontist** *n.* [PERI- + Gk *odous odont-* tooth]

periodontology /ˌperɪədɒnˈtɒlədʒɪ/ *n.* = PERIODONTICS.

periosteum /ˌperɪˈɒstɪəm/ *n.* (*pl.* **periostea** /-tɪə/) a membrane enveloping the bones where no cartilage is present. □□ **periosteal** *adj.* **periostitis** /-ˈstaɪtɪs/ *n.* [mod.L f. Gk *periosteon* (as PERI-, *osteon* bone)]

peripatetic /ˌperɪpəˈtetɪk/ *adj. & n.* —*adj.* **1** (of a teacher) working in more than one school or college etc. **2** going from place to place; itinerant. **3** (**Peripatetic**) Aristotelian (from Aristotle's habit of walking in the Lyceum whilst teaching). —*n.* a peripatetic person, esp. a teacher. □□ **peripatetically** *adv.* **peripateticism** /-sɪz(ə)m/ *n.* [ME f. OF *peripatetique* or L *peripateticus* f. Gk *peripatētikos* f. *peripateō* (as PERI-, *pateō* walk)]

peripeteia /ˌperɪpɪˈtaɪə, -ˈtiːə/ *n.* a sudden change of fortune in a drama or in life. [Gk (as PERI-, *pet-* f. *piptō* fall)]

peripheral /pəˈrɪfər(ə)l/ *adj. & n.* —*adj.* **1** of minor importance; marginal. **2** of the periphery; on the fringe. **3** *Anat.* near the surface of the body, with special reference to the circulation and nervous system. **4** (of equipment) used with a computer etc. but not an integral part of it. —*n.* a peripheral device or piece of equipment. □**peripheral nervous system** *Anat.* the nervous system outside the brain and spinal cord. □□ **peripherally** *adv.*

periphery /pəˈrɪfərɪ/ *n.* (*pl.* **-ies**) **1** the boundary of an area or surface. **2** an outer or surrounding region (*built on the periphery of the old town*). [LL *peripheria* f. Gk *periphereia* circumference (as PERI-, *phereia* f. *phero* bear)]

periphrasis /pəˈrɪfrəsɪs/ *n.* (*pl.* **periphrases** /-ˌsiːz/) **1** a roundabout way of speaking; circumlocution. **2** a roundabout phrase. [L f. Gk f. *periphrazō* (as PERI-, *phrazō* declare)]

periphrastic /ˌperɪˈfræstɪk/ *adj. Gram.* **1** of or involving periphrasis. **2** (of a case, tense, etc.) formed by combination of words rather than by inflection (e.g. *did go, of the people* rather than *went, the people's*). □□ **periphrastically** *adv.* [Gk *periphrastikos* (as PERIPHRASIS)]

peripteral /pəˈrɪptər(ə)l/ *adj.* (of a temple) surrounded by a single row of columns. [Gk *peripteron* (as PERI-, Gk *pteron* wing)]

periscope /ˈperɪskəʊp/ *n.* an apparatus with a tube and mirrors or prisms, by which an observer in a trench, submerged submarine, or at the rear of a crowd etc., can see things otherwise out of sight.

periscopic /ˌperɪˈskɒpɪk/ *adj.* of a periscope. □**periscopic lens** a lens allowing distinct vision over a wide angle. □□ **periscopically** *adv.*

perish /ˈperɪʃ/ *v.* **1** *intr.* be destroyed; suffer death or ruin. **2 a** *intr.* (esp. of rubber, a rubber object, etc.) lose its normal qualities; deteriorate, rot. **b** *tr.* cause to rot or deteriorate. **3** *tr.* (in *passive*) suffer from cold or exposure (*we were perished standing outside*). □**perish the thought** an exclamation of horror against an unwelcome idea. □□ **perishless** *adj.* [ME f. OF *perir* f. L *perire* pass away (as PER-, *ire* go)]

perishable /ˈperɪʃəb(ə)l/ *adj. & n.* —*adj.* liable to perish; subject to decay. —*n.* a thing, esp. a foodstuff, subject to speedy decay. □□ **perishability** /-ˈbɪlɪtɪ/ *n.* **perishableness** *n.*

perisher /ˈperɪʃə(r)/ *n. Brit. sl.* an annoying person.

perishing /ˈperɪʃɪŋ/ *adj. & adv. colloq.* —*adj.* **1** confounded. **2** freezing cold, extremely chilly. —*adv.* confoundedly. □□ **perishingly** *adv.*

perisperm /ˈperɪspɜːm/ *n.* a mass of nutritive material outside the embryo-sac in some seeds. [PERI- + Gk *sperma* seed]

peristalsis /ˌperɪˈstælsɪs/ *n.* an involuntary muscular wavelike movement by which the contents of the alimentary canal etc. are propelled along. □□ **peristaltic** *adj.* **peristaltically** *adv.* [mod.L f. Gk *peristellō* wrap around (as PERI-, *stellō* place)]

peristome /ˈperɪstəʊm/ *n.* **1** *Bot.* a fringe of small teeth around the mouth of a capsule in mosses and certain fungi. **2** *Zool.* the parts surrounding the mouth of various invertebrates. [mod.L *peristoma* f. PERI- + Gk *stoma* mouth]

peristyle /ˈperɪstaɪl/ *n.* a row of columns surrounding a temple, court, cloister, etc.; a space surrounded by columns. [F *péristyle* f. L *peristylum* f. Gk *peristulon* (as PERI-, *stulos* pillar)]

peritoneum /ˌperɪtəˈniːəm/ *n.* (*pl.* **peritoneums** or **peritonea** /-ˈniːə/) the double serous membrane lining the cavity of the abdomen. □□ **peritoneal** *adj.* [LL f. Gk *peritonaion* (as PERI-, *tonaion* f. *-tonos* stretched)]

peritonitis /ˌperɪtəˈnaɪtɪs/ *n.* an inflammatory disease of the peritoneum.

periwig /ˈperɪwɪg/ *n.* esp. *hist.* a wig. □□ **periwigged** *adj.* [alt. of PERUKE, with *-wi-* for F *-u-* sound]

periwinkle¹ /ˈperɪˌwɪŋk(ə)l/ *n.* **1** any plant of the genus *Vinca*, esp. an evergreen trailing plant with blue or white flowers. **2** a tropical shrub, *Catharanthus roseus*, native to Madagascar. [ME f. AF *pervenke*, OF *pervenche* f. LL *pervinca*, assim. to PERIWINKLE²]

periwinkle² /ˈperɪˌwɪŋk(ə)l/ *n.* = WINKLE. [16th c.: orig. unkn.]

perjure /ˈpɜːdʒə(r)/ *v.refl. Law* **1** wilfully tell an untruth when on oath. **2** (as **perjured** *adj.*) guilty of or involving perjury. □□ **perjurer** *n.* [ME f. OF *parjurer* f. L *perjurare* (as PER-, *jurare* swear)]

perjury /ˈpɜːdʒərɪ/ *n.* (*pl.* **-ies**) *Law* **1** a breach of an oath, esp. the act of wilfully telling an untruth when on oath. **2** the practice of this. □□ **perjurious** /-ˈdʒʊərɪəs/ *adj.* [ME f. AF *perjurie* f. OF *parjurie* f. L *perjurium* (as PERJURE)]

perk¹ /pɜːk/ *v. & adj.* —*v.tr.* raise (one's head etc.) briskly. —*adj.* perky; pert. □ **perk up** **1** recover confidence, courage, life, or zest. **2** restore confidence or courage or liveliness in (esp. another person). **3** smarten up. [ME, perh. f. var. of PERCH¹]

perk² /pɜːk/ *n. Brit. colloq.* a perquisite. [abbr.]

perk³ /pɜːk/ *v. colloq.* **1** *intr.* (of coffee) percolate, make a bubbling sound in the percolator. **2** *tr.* percolate (coffee). [abbr. of PERCOLATE]

perky /ˈpɜːkɪ/ *adj.* (**perkier, perkiest**) **1** self-assertive; saucy; pert. **2** lively; cheerful. □□ **perkily** *adv.* **perkiness** *n.*

perlite /ˈpɜːlaɪt/ *n.* (also **pearlite**) a glassy type of vermiculite, expandable to a solid form by heating, used for insulation etc. [F f. *perle* pearl]

perm¹ /pɜːm/ *n. & v.* —*n.* a permanent wave. —*v.tr.* give a permanent wave to (a person or a person's hair). [abbr.]

perm² /pɜːm/ *n. & v. colloq.* —*n.* a permutation. —*v.tr.* make a permutation of. [abbr.]

permafrost /ˈpɜːməˌfrɒst/ *n.* subsoil which remains below freezing-point throughout the year, as in polar regions. [PERMANENT + FROST]

permalloy /ˈpɜːməˌlɔɪ/ *n.* an alloy of nickel and iron that is easily magnetized and demagnetized. [PERMEABLE + ALLOY]

permanent /ˈpɜːmənənt/ *adj.* lasting, or intended to last or function, indefinitely (opp. TEMPORARY). □ **permanent magnet** a magnet retaining its magnetic properties without continued excitation. **Permanent Secretary** (or **Under-secretary** etc.) *Brit.* a senior grade in the Civil Service, often a permanent adviser to a minister. **permanent set 1** the irreversible deformation of a substance after being subjected to stress. **2** the amount of this. **permanent tooth** a tooth succeeding a milk tooth in a mammal, and lasting most of the mammal's life. **permanent wave** an artificial wave in the hair, intended to last for some time. **permanent way** *Brit.* the finished roadbed of a railway. □□ **permanence** *n.* **permanency** *n.* **permanentize** *v.tr.* (also **-ise**). **permanently** *adv.* [ME f. OF *permanent* or L *permanēre* (as PER-, *manēre* remain)]

permanganate /pɜːˈmæŋɡəˌneɪt, -nət/ *n. Chem.* any salt of permanganic acid, esp. potassium permanganate.

permanganic acid /ˌpɜːmæŋˈɡænɪk/ *n. Chem.* an acid containing heptavalent manganese. [PER- + MANGANIC: see MANGANESE]

permeability /ˌpɜːmɪəˈbɪlɪtɪ/ *n.* **1** the state or quality of being permeable. **2** a quantity measuring the influence of a substance on the magnetic flux in the region it occupies.

permeable /ˈpɜːmɪəb(ə)l/ *adj.* capable of being permeated. [L *permeabilis* (as PERMEATE)]

permeate /ˈpɜːmɪˌeɪt/ *v.* **1** *tr.* penetrate throughout; pervade; saturate. **2** *intr.* (usu. foll. by *through, among,* etc.) diffuse itself. □□ **permeance** *n.* **permeant** *adj.* **permeation** /-ˈeɪʃ(ə)n/ *n.* **permeator** *n.* [L *permeare permeat-* (as PER-, *meare* pass, go)]

Permian /ˈpɜːmɪən/ *adj. & n. Geol.* —*adj.* of or relating to the last period of the Palaeozoic era with evidence of the development of reptiles and amphibians, and deposits of sandstone. ¶ Cf. Appendix II. —*n.* this period or system. [*Perm* in Russia]

per mille /pɜː ˈmɪlɪ/ *adv.* (also **per mil** /mɪl/) in every thousand. [L]

permissible /pəˈmɪsɪb(ə)l/ *adj.* allowable. □□ **permissibility** /-ˈbɪlɪtɪ/ *n.* **permissibly** *adv.* [ME f. F or f. med.L *permissibilis* (as PERMIT)]

permission /pəˈmɪʃ(ə)n/ *n.* (often foll. by *to* + infin.) consent; authorization. [ME f. OF or f. L *permissio* (as PERMIT)]

permissive /pəˈmɪsɪv/ *adj.* **1** tolerant; liberal, esp. in sexual matters (*the permissive society*). **2** giving permission. □ **permissive legislation** legislation giving powers but not enjoining their use. □□ **permissively** *adv.* **permissiveness** *n.* [ME f. OF (-*if* -*ive*) or med.L *permissivus* (as PERMIT)]

permit *v. & n.* —*v.* /pəˈmɪt/ (**permitted, permitting**) **1** *tr.* give permission or consent to; authorize (*permit me to say*). **2 a** *tr.* allow; give an opportunity to (*permit the traffic to flow again*). **b** *intr.* give an opportunity (*circumstances permitting*). **3** *intr.* (foll. by *of*) admit; allow for. —*n.* /ˈpɜːmɪt/ **1 a** a document giving permission to act in a specified way (*was granted a work permit*). **b** a document etc. which allows entry into a specified zone. **2** *formal* permission. □□ **permittee** /ˌpɜːmɪˈtiː/ *n.* **permitter** *n.* [L *permittere* (as PER-, *mittere miss-* let go)]

permittivity /ˌpɜːmɪˈtɪvɪtɪ/ *n. Electr.* a quantity measuring the ability of a substance to store electrical energy in an electric field.

permutate /ˈpɜːmjʊˌteɪt/ *v.tr.* change the order or arrangement of. [as PERMUTE, or back-form. f. PERMUTATION]

permutation /ˌpɜːmjʊˈteɪʃ(ə)n/ *n.* **1 a** an ordered arrangement or grouping of a set of numbers, items, etc. **b** any one of the range of possible groupings. **2** any combination or selection of a specified number of things from a larger group, esp. *Brit.* matches in a football pool. □□ **permutational** *adj.* [ME f. OF or f. L *permutatio* (as PERMUTE)]

permute /pəˈmjuːt/ *v.tr.* alter the sequence or arrangement of. [ME f. L *permutare* (as PER-, *mutare* change)]

Permutit /ˈpɜːmjʊtɪt/ *n. propr.* an artificial zeolite used as an ion exchanger esp. for the softening of water. [G f. L *permutare* to exchange]

pernicious /pəˈnɪʃəs/ *adj.* destructive; ruinous; fatal. □ **pernicious anaemia** see ANAEMIA. □□ **perniciously** *adv.* **perniciousness** *n.* [L *perniciosus* f. *pernicies* ruin f. *nex necis* death]

pernickety /pəˈnɪkɪtɪ/ *adj. colloq.* **1** fastidious. **2** precise or over-precise. **3** ticklish, requiring tact or careful handling. [19th-c. Sc.: orig. unkn.]

pernoctate /pəˈnɒkteɪt/ *v.intr. formal* pass or spend the night. □□ **pernoctation** /-ˈteɪʃ(ə)n/ *n.* [LL *pernoctare pernoctat-* (as PER-, *noctare* f. *nox noctis* night)]

peroneal /ˌperəˈniːəl/ *adj. Anat.* relating to or near the fibula. [mod.L *peronaeus* peroneal muscle f. *perone* fibula f. Gk *peronē* pin, fibula]

perorate /ˈperəˌreɪt/ *v.intr.* **1** sum up and conclude a speech. **2** speak at length. [L *perorare perorat-* (as PER-, *orare* speak)]

peroration /ˌperəˈreɪʃ(ə)n/ *n.* the concluding part of a speech, forcefully summing up what has been said.

peroxidase /pəˈrɒksɪˌdeɪz, -ˌdeɪs/ *n. Biochem.* any of a class of enzymes found esp. in plants, which catalyze the oxidation of a substrate by hydrogen peroxide.

peroxide /pəˈrɒksaɪd/ *n. & v.* —*n. Chem.* **1 a** = *hydrogen peroxide.* **b** (often *attrib.*) a solution of hydrogen peroxide used to bleach the hair or as an antiseptic. **2** a compound of oxygen with another element containing the greatest possible proportion of oxygen. **3** any salt or ester of hydrogen peroxide. —*v.tr.* bleach (the hair) with peroxide. [PER- + OXIDE]

perpendicular /ˌpɜːpənˈdɪkjʊlə(r)/ *adj. & n.* —*adj.* **1 a** at right angles to the plane of the horizon. **b** (usu.

foll. by *to*) *Geom.* at right angles (to a given line, plane, or surface). **2** upright, vertical. **3** (of a slope etc.) very steep. **4** (**Perpendicular**) *Archit.* of the third stage of English Gothic (15th-16th c.) with vertical tracery in large windows. **5** *joc.* in a standing position. —*n.* **1** a perpendicular line. **2** a plumb-rule or a similar instrument. **3** (prec. by *the*) a perpendicular line or direction (*is out of the perpendicular*). □□ **perpendicularity** /-ˈlærɪtɪ/ *n.* **perpendicularly** *adv.* [ME f. L *perpendicularis* f. *perpendiculum* plumb-line f. PER- + *pendēre* hang]

perpetrate /ˈpɜːpɪˌtreɪt/ *v.tr.* commit or perform (a crime, blunder, or anything outrageous). □□ **perpetration** /-ˈtreɪʃ(ə)n/ *n.* **perpetrator** *n.* [L *perpetrare perpetrat-* (as PER-, *patrare* effect)]

perpetual /pəˈpetjʊəl/ *adj.* **1** eternal; lasting for ever or indefinitely. **2** continuous, uninterrupted. **3** *colloq.* frequent, much repeated (*perpetual interruptions*). **4** permanent during life (*perpetual secretary*). □ **perpetual calendar** a calendar which can be adjusted to show any combination of day, month, and year. **perpetual check** *Chess* the position of play when a draw is obtained by repeated checking of the king. **perpetual motion** the motion of a hypothetical machine which once set in motion would run for ever unless subject to an external force or to wear. □□ **perpetualism** *n.* **perpetually** *adv.* [ME f. OF *perpetuel* f. L *perpetualis* f. *perpetuus* f. *perpes -etis* continuous]

perpetuate /pəˈpetjʊˌeɪt/ *v.tr.* **1** make perpetual. **2** preserve from oblivion. □□ **perpetuance** *n.* **perpetuation** /-ˈeɪʃ(ə)n/ *n.* **perpetuator** *n.* [L *perpetuare* (as PERPETUAL)]

perpetuity /ˌpɜːpɪˈtjuːɪtɪ/ *n.* (*pl.* -**ies**) **1** the state or quality of being perpetual. **2** a perpetual annuity. **3** a perpetual possession or position. □ **in** (or **to** or **for**) **perpetuity** for ever. [ME f. OF *perpetuité* f. L *perpetuitas -tatis* (as PERPETUAL)]

perpetuum mobile /pɜːˌpetjuːəm ˈməʊbɪlɪ/ *n.* **1** = *perpetual motion*. **2** *Mus.* = MOTO PERPETUO. [L *perpetuus* continuous + *mobilis* movable, after PRIMUM MOBILE]

perplex /pəˈpleks/ *v.tr.* **1** puzzle, bewilder, or disconcert (a person, a person's mind, etc.). **2** complicate or confuse (a matter). **3** (as **perplexed** *adj.*) *archaic* entangled, intertwined. □□ **perplexedly** /-ɪdlɪ/ *adv.* **perplexingly** *adv.* [back-form. f. *perplexed* f. obs. *perplex* (adj.) f. OF *perplexe* or L *perplexus* (as PER-, *plexus* past part. of *plectere* plait)]

perplexity /pəˈpleksɪtɪ/ *n.* (*pl.* -**ies**) **1** bewilderment; the state of being perplexed. **2** a thing which perplexes. **3** *archaic* an entangled state. [ME f. OF *perplexité* or LL *perplexitas* (as PERPLEX)]

per pro. /pɜː ˈprəʊ/ *abbr.* through the agency of (used in signatures). ¶ The correct sequence is A *per pro.* B, where B is signing on behalf of A. [L *per procurationem*]

perquisite /ˈpɜːkwɪzɪt/ *n.* **1** an extra profit or allowance additional to a main income etc. **2** a customary extra right or privilege. **3** an incidental benefit attached to employment etc. **4** a thing which has served its primary use and to which a subordinate or servant has a customary right. [ME f. med.L *perquisitum* f. L *perquirere* search diligently for (as PER-, *quaerere* seek)]

Perrier /ˈperɪˌeɪ/ *n. propr.* an effervescent natural mineral water. [the name of a spring at Vergèze, France, its source]

perron /ˈperən/ *n.* an exterior staircase leading up to a main entrance to a church or other (usu. large) building. [ME f. OF ult. f. L *petra* stone]

perry /ˈperɪ/ *n.* (*pl.* -**ies**) *Brit.* a drink like cider, made from the fermented juice of pears. [ME *pereye* etc. f. OF *peré*, ult. f. L *pirum* pear]

per se /pɜː ˈseɪ/ *adv.* by or in itself; intrinsically. [L]

persecute /ˈpɜːsɪˌkjuːt/ *v.tr.* **1** subject (a person etc.) to hostility or ill-treatment, esp. on the grounds of political or religious belief. **2** harass; worry. **3** (often

foll. by *with*) bombard (a person) with questions etc. □□ **persecutor** *n.* **persecutory** *adj.* [ME f. OF *persecuter* back-form. f. *persecuteur* persecutor f. LL *persecutor* f. L *persequi* (as PER-, *sequi secut-* follow, pursue)]

persecution /ˌpɜːsɪˈkjuːʃ(ə)n/ *n.* the act or an instance of persecuting; the state of being persecuted. □ **persecution complex** (or **mania**) an irrational obsessive fear that others are scheming against one.

perseverance /ˌpɜːsɪˈvɪərəns/ *n.* **1** the steadfast pursuit of an objective. **2** (often foll. by *in*) constant persistence (in a belief etc.). [ME f. OF f. L *perseverantia* (as PERSEVERE)]

perseverate /pəˈsevəˌreɪt/ *v.intr.* **1** continue action etc. for an unusually or excessively long time. **2** *Psychol.* tend to prolong or repeat a response after the original stimulus has ceased. □□ **perseveration** /-ˈreɪʃ(ə)n/ *n.* [L *perseverare* (as PERSEVERE)]

persevere /ˌpɜːsɪˈvɪə(r)/ *v.intr.* (often foll. by *in*, *at*, *with*) continue steadfastly or determinedly; persist. [ME f. OF *perseverer* f. L *perseverare* persist f. *perseverus* very strict (as PER-, *severus* severe)]

Persian /ˈpɜːʃ(ə)n/ *n. & adj.* —*n.* **1 a** a native or inhabitant of ancient or modern Persia (now Iran). **b** a person of Persian descent. **2** the language of ancient Persia or modern Iran. ¶ With modern reference the preferred terms are *Iranian* and *Farsi*. **3** (in full **Persian cat**) **a** a cat of a breed with long silky hair and a thick tail. **b** this breed. —*adj.* of or relating to Persia or its people or language. □ **Persian carpet** (or **rug**) a carpet or rug of a traditional pattern made in Persia. **Persian lamb** the silky tightly curled fur of a young karakul, used in clothing. [ME f. OF *persien* f. med.L]

persiennes /ˌpɜːsɪˈenz/ *n.pl.* window shutters, or outside blinds, with louvres. [F, fem. pl. of obs. *persien* Persian]

persiflage /ˈpɜːsɪˌflɑːʒ/ *n.* light raillery, banter. [F *persifler* banter, formed as PER- + *siffler* whistle]

persimmon /pɜːˈsɪmən/ *n.* **1** any usu. tropical evergreen tree of the genus *Diospyros* bearing edible tomato-like fruits. **2** the fruit of this. [corrupt. of an Algonquian word]

persist /pəˈsɪst/ *v.intr.* **1** (often foll. by *in*) continue firmly or obstinately (in an opinion or a course of action) esp. despite obstacles, remonstrance, etc. **2** (of an institution, custom, phenomenon, etc.) continue in existence; survive. [L *persistere* (as PER-, *sistere* stand)]

persistent /pəˈsɪst(ə)nt/ *adj.* **1** continuing obstinately; persisting. **2** enduring. **3** constantly repeated (*persistent nagging*). **4** *Biol.* (of horns, leaves, etc.) remaining instead of falling off in the normal manner. □□ **persistence** *n.* **persistency** *n.* **persistently** *adv.*

person /ˈpɜːs(ə)n/ *n.* **1** an individual human being (*a cheerful and forthright person*). **2** the living body of a human being (*hidden about your person*). **3** *Gram.* any of three classes of personal pronouns, verbforms, etc.: the person speaking (**first person**); the person spoken to (**second person**); the person spoken of (**third person**). **4** (in *comb.*) used to replace *-man* in offices open to either sex (*salesperson*). **5** (in Christianity) God as Father, Son, or Holy Ghost (*three persons in one God*). **6** *euphem.* the genitals (*expose one's person*). **7** a character in a play or story. □ **in one's own person** oneself; as oneself. **in person** physically present. **person-to-person 1** between individuals. **2** (of a phone call) booked through the operator to a specified person. [ME f. OF *persone* f. L *persona* actor's mask, character in a play, human being]

persona /pɜːˈsəʊnə/ *n.* (*pl.* **personae** /-niː/) **1** an aspect of the personality as shown to or perceived by others (opp. ANIMA). **2** *Literary criticism* an author's assumed character in his or her writing. □ ***persona grata*** /ˈɡrɑːtə/ a person, esp. a diplomat, acceptable to certain others. ***persona non grata*** /nɒn, nəʊn 'grɑːtə/ a person not acceptable. [L (as PERSON)]

personable /'pɜːsənəb(ə)l/ *adj.* pleasing in appearance and behaviour. □□**personableness** *n.* **personably** *adv.*

personage /'pɜːsənɪdʒ/ *n.* **1** a person, esp. of rank or importance. **2** a character in a play etc. [ME f. PERSON + -AGE, infl. by med.L *personagium* effigy & F *personnage*]

personal /'pɜːsən(ə)l/ *adj.* **1** one's own; individual; private. **2** done or made in person (*made a personal appearance*; *my personal attention*). **3** directed to or concerning an individual (*a personal letter*). **4** referring (esp. in a hostile way) to an individual's private life or concerns (*making personal remarks*; *no need to be personal*). **5** of the body and clothing (*personal hygiene*; *personal appearance*). **6** existing as a person, not as an abstraction or thing (*a personal God*). **7** *Gram.* of or denoting one of the three persons (*personal pronoun*). □**personal column** the part of a newspaper devoted to private advertisements or messages. **personal computer** a computer designed for use by a single individual, esp. in an office or business environment. **personal equation 1** the allowance for an individual person's time of reaction in making observations, esp. in astronomy. **2** a bias or prejudice. **personal equity plan** a scheme for limited personal investment in shares, unit trusts, etc. **personal identification number** a number allocated to an individual, serving as a password esp. for a cash dispenser, computer, etc. **personal pronoun** a pronoun replacing the subject, object, etc., of a clause etc., e.g. *I, we, you, them, us*. **personal property** (or **estate**) *Law* all one's property except land and those interests in land that pass to one's heirs (cf. REAL¹ *adj.* 3). **personal service** individual service given to a customer. **personal stereo** a small portable audio cassette player, often with radio, or compact disc player, used with lightweight headphones. **personal touch** a way of treating a matter characteristic of or designed for an individual. [ME. OF f. L *personalis* (as PERSON)]

personality /ˌpɜːsə'nælɪtɪ/ *n.* (*pl.* **-ies**) **1** the distinctive character or qualities of a person, often as distinct from others (*an attractive personality*). **2** a famous person; a celebrity (*a TV personality*). **3** a person who stands out from others by virtue of his or her character (*is a real personality*). **4** personal existence or identity; the condition of being a person. **5** (usu. in *pl.*) personal remarks. □**have personality** have a lively character or noteworthy qualities. **personality cult** the extreme adulation of an individual. [ME f. OF *personalité* f. LL *personalitas -tatis* (as PERSONAL)]

personalize /'pɜːsənəˌlaɪz/ *v.tr.* (also **-ise**) **1** make personal, esp. by marking with one's name etc. **2** personify. □□**personalization** /-'zeɪʃ(ə)n/ *n.*

personally /'pɜːsənəlɪ/ *adv.* **1** in person (*see to it personally*). **2** for one's own part (*speaking personally*). **3** as a person (*a God existing personally*). **4** in a personal manner (*took the criticism personally*).

personalty /'pɜːsənəltɪ/ *n.* (*pl.* **-ies**) *Law* one's personal property or estate (opp. REALTY). [AF *personalté* (as PERSONAL)]

personate /'pɜːsəˌneɪt/ *v.tr.* **1** play the part of (a character in a drama etc.; another type of person). **2** pretend to be (another person), esp. for fraudulent purposes; impersonate. □□**personation** /-'neɪʃ(ə)n/ *n.* **personator** *n.* [LL *personare personat-* (as PERSON)]

personhood /'pɜːsənˌhʊd/ *n.* the quality or condition of being an individual person.

personification /pəˌsɒnɪfɪ'keɪʃ(ə)n/ *n.* **1** the act of personifying. **2** (foll. by *of*) a person or thing viewed as a striking example of (a quality etc.) (*the personification of ugliness*).

personify /pə'sɒnɪˌfaɪ/ *v.tr.* (**-ies, -ied**) **1** attribute a personal nature to (an abstraction or thing). **2** symbolize (a quality etc.) by a figure in human form.

3 (usu. as **personified** *adj.*) embody (a quality) in one's own person; exemplify typically (*has always been kindness personified*). □□**personifier** *n.* [F *personnifier* (as PERSON)]

personnel /ˌpɜːsə'nel/ *n.* a body of employees, persons involved in a public undertaking, armed forces, etc. □**personnel carrier** an armoured vehicle for transporting troops etc. **personnel department** etc. the part of an organization concerned with the appointment, training, and welfare of employees. [F, orig. adj. = personal]

perspective /pə'spektɪv/ *n. & adj.* —*n.* **1 a** the art of drawing solid objects on a two-dimensional surface so as to give the right impression of relative positions, size, etc. **b** a picture drawn in this way. **2** the apparent relation between visible objects as to position, distance, etc. **3** a mental view of the relative importance of things (*keep the right perspective*). **4** a geographical or imaginary prospect. —*adj.* of or in perspective. □**in perspective 1** drawn or viewed according to the rules of perspective. **2** correctly regarded in terms of relative importance. □□**perspectival** /-'taɪv(ə)l/ *adj.* **perspectively** *adv.* [ME f. med.L *perspectiva* (*ars* art) f. *perspicere perspect-* (as PER-, *specere spect-* look)]

Perspex /'pɜːspeks/ *n. propr.* a tough light transparent acrylic thermoplastic used instead of glass. [L *perspicere* look through (as PER-, *specere* look)]

perspicacious /ˌpɜːspɪ'keɪʃəs/ *adj.* having mental penetration or discernment. □□**perspicaciously** *adv.* **perspicaciousness** *n.* **perspicacity** /-'kæsɪtɪ/ *n.* [L *perspicax -acis* (as PERSPEX)]

perspicuous /pə'spɪkjʊəs/ *adj.* **1** easily understood; clearly expressed. **2** (of a person) expressing things clearly. □□**perspicuity** /-'kjuːɪtɪ/ *n.* **perspicuously** *adv.* **perspicuousness** *n.* [ME, = transparent f. L *perspicuus* (as PERSPECTIVE)]

perspiration /ˌpɜːspɪ'reɪʃ(ə)n/ *n.* **1** = SWEAT. **2** sweating. □□**perspiratory** /-'spɪrətərɪ/ *adj.* [F (as PERSPIRE)]

perspire /pə'spaɪə(r)/ *v.* **1** *intr.* sweat or exude perspiration, esp. as the result of heat, exercise, anxiety, etc. **2** *tr.* sweat or exude (fluid etc.). [F *perspirer* f. L *perspirare* (as PER-, *spirare* breathe)]

persuade /pə'sweɪd/ *v.tr. & refl.* **1** (often foll. by *of*, or *that* + clause) cause (another person or oneself) to believe; convince (*persuaded them that it would be helpful*; *tried to persuade me of its value*). **2 a** (often foll. by *to* + infin.) induce (another person or oneself) (*persuaded us to join them*; *managed to persuade them at last*). **b** (foll. by *away from, down to*, etc.) lure, attract, entice, etc. (*persuaded them away from the pub*). □□**persuadable** *adj.* **persuadability** /-də'bɪlɪtɪ/ *n.* **persuasible** *adj.* [L *persuadēre* (as PER-, *suadēre suas-* advise)]

persuader /pə'sweɪdə(r)/ *n.* **1** a person who persuades. **2** *sl.* a gun or other weapon.

persuasion /pə'sweɪʒ(ə)n/ *n.* **1** persuading (*yielded to persuasion*). **2** persuasiveness (*use all your persuasion*). **3** a belief or conviction (*my private persuasion*). **4** a religious belief, or the group or sect holding it (*of a different persuasion*). **5** *colloq.* any group or party (*the male persuasion*). [ME f. L *persuasio* (as PERSUADE)]

persuasive /pə'sweɪsɪv/ *adj.* able to persuade. □□**persuasively** *adv.* **persuasiveness** *n.* [F *persuasif -ive* or med.L *persuasivus* (as PERSUADE)]

PERT *abbr.* programme evaluation and review technique.

pert /pɜːt/ *adj.* **1** saucy or impudent, esp. in speech or conduct. **2** (of clothes etc.) neat and suggestive of jauntiness. **3** = PEART. □□**pertly** *adv.* **pertness** *n.* [ME f. OF *apert* f. L *apertus* past part. of *aperire* open & f. OF *aspert* f. L *expertus* EXPERT]

pertain /pə'teɪn/ *v.intr.* **1** (foll. by *to*) **a** relate or have reference to. **b** belong to as a part or appendage or accessory. **2** (usu. foll. by *to*) be appropriate to. [ME f. OF *partenir* f. L *pertinēre* (as PER-, *tenēre* hold)]

pertinacious /ˌpɜːtɪ'neɪʃəs/ *adj.* stubborn; persistent; obstinate (in a course of action etc.). □□ **pertinaciously** *adv.* **pertinaciousness** *n.*
pertinacity /-'næsɪtɪ/ *n.* [L *pertinax* (as PER-, *tenax* tenacious)]
pertinent /'pɜːtɪnənt/ *adj.* **1** (often foll. by *to*) relevant to the matter in hand; apposite. **2** to the point. □□ **pertinence** *n.* **pertinency** *n.* **pertinently** *adv.* [ME f. OF *pertinent* or L *pertinēre* (as PERTAIN)]
perturb /pə'tɜːb/ *v.tr.* **1** throw into confusion or disorder. **2** disturb mentally; agitate. **3** *Physics & Math.* subject (a physical system, or a set of equations, or its solution) to a perturbation. □□ **perturbable** *adj.* **perturbative** /pə'tɜːbətɪv, 'pɜːtəˌbeɪtɪv/ *adj.* **perturbingly** *adv.* [ME f. OF *pertourber* f. L (as PER-, *turbare* disturb)]
perturbation /ˌpɜːtə'beɪʃ(ə)n/ *n.* **1** the act or an instance of perturbing; the state of being perturbed. **2** a cause of disturbance or agitation. **3** *Physics* a slight alteration of a physical system, e.g. of the electrons in an atom, caused by a secondary influence. **4** *Astron.* a minor deviation in the course of a celestial body, caused by the attraction of a neighbouring body.
pertussis /pə'tʌsɪs/ *n.* whooping cough. [mod.L f. PER- + L *tussis* cough]
peruke /pə'ruːk/ *n.* *hist.* a wig. [F *perruque* f. It. *perrucca parrucca,* of unkn. orig.]
peruse /pə'ruːz/ *v.tr.* **1** (also *absol.*) read or study, esp. thoroughly or carefully. **2** examine (a person's face etc.) carefully. □□ **perusal** *n.* **peruser** *n.* [ME, orig. = use up, prob. f. AL f. Rmc (as PER-, USE)]
Peruvian /pə'ruːvɪən/ *n.* & *adj.* —*n.* **1** a native or national of Peru. **2** a person of Peruvian descent. —*adj.* of or relating to Peru. □**Peruvian bark** the bark of the cinchona tree. [mod.L *Peruvia* Peru]
perv /pɜːv/ *n.* & *v.* (also **perve**) *sl.* —*n.* **1** a sexual pervert. **2** *Austral.* an erotic gaze. —*v.intr.* **1** act like a sexual pervert. **2** (foll. by *at, on*) *Austral.* gaze with erotic interest. [abbr.]
pervade /pə'veɪd/ *v.tr.* **1** spread throughout, permeate. **2** (of influences etc.) become widespread among or in. **3** be rife among or through. □□ **pervasion** /-ʒ(ə)n/ *n.* [L *pervadere* (as PER-, *vadere vas-* go)]
pervasive /pə'veɪsɪv/ *adj.* **1** pervading. **2** able to pervade. □□ **pervasively** *adv.* **pervasiveness** *n.*
perve var. of PERV.
perverse /pə'vɜːs/ *adj.* **1** (of a person or action) deliberately or stubbornly departing from what is reasonable or required. **2** persistent in error. **3** wayward; intractable; peevish. **4** perverted; wicked. **5** (of a verdict etc.) against the weight of evidence or the judge's direction. □□ **perversely** *adv.* **perverseness** *n.* **perversity** *n.* (*pl.* -ies). [ME f. OF *pervers perverse* f. L *perversus* (as PERVERT)]
perversion /pə'vɜːʃ(ə)n/ *n.* **1** an act of perverting; the state of being perverted. **2** a perverted form of an act or thing. **3 a** preference for an abnormal form of sexual activity. **b** such an activity. [ME f. L *perversio* (as PERVERT)]
pervert *v.* & *n.* —*v.tr.* /pə'vɜːt/ **1** turn (a person or thing) aside from its proper use or nature. **2** misapply or misconstrue (words etc.). **3** lead astray (a person, a person's mind, etc.) from right opinion or conduct, or esp. religious belief. **4** (as **perverted** *adj.*) showing perversion. —*n.* /'pɜːvɜːt/ **1** a perverted person. **2** a person showing sexual perversion. □□ **perversive** /pə'vɜːsɪv/ *adj.* **pervertedly** /pə'vɜːtɪdlɪ/ *adv.* **perverter** /-'vɜːtə(r)/ *n.* [ME f. OF *pervertir* or f. L *pervertere* (as PER-, *vertere vers-* turn): cf. CONVERT]
pervious /'pɜːvɪəs/ *adj.* **1** permeable. **2** (usu. foll. by *to*) **a** affording passage. **b** accessible (to reason etc.). □□ **perviousness** *n.* [L *pervius* (as PER-, *vius* f. *via* way)]
Pesach /'peɪsɑːx/ *n.* the Passover festival. [Heb. *Pesaḥ*]
peseta /pə'seɪtə/ *n.* the chief monetary unit of Spain,

orig. a silver coin. [Sp., dimin. of *pesa* weight f. L *pensa* pl. of *pensum*: see POISE¹]
pesky /'peskɪ/ *adj.* (**peskier, peskiest**) esp. *US colloq.* troublesome; confounded; annoying. □□ **peskily** *adv.* **peskiness** *n.* [18th c.: perh. f. PEST]
peso /'peɪsəʊ/ *n.* (*pl.* -os) **1** the chief monetary unit of several Latin American countries and of the Philippines. **2** a note or coin worth one peso. [Sp., = weight, f. L *pensum*: see POISE¹]
pessary /'pesərɪ/ *n.* (*pl.* -ies) *Med.* **1** a device worn in the vagina to support the uterus or as a contraceptive. **2** a vaginal suppository. [ME f. LL *pessarium, pessulum* f. *pessum, pessus* f. Gk *pessos* oval stone]
pessimism /'pesɪˌmɪz(ə)m/ *n.* **1** a tendency to take the worst view or expect the worst outcome. **2** *Philos.* a belief that this world is as bad as it could be or that all things tend to evil (opp. OPTIMISM). □□ **pessimist** *n.* **pessimistic** /-'mɪstɪk/ *adj.* **pessimistically** /-'mɪstɪkəlɪ/ *adv.* [L *pessimus* worst, after OPTIMISM]
pest /pest/ *n.* **1** a troublesome or annoying person or thing; a nuisance. **2** a destructive animal, esp. an insect which attacks crops, livestock, etc. **3** *archaic* a pestilence; a plague. □**pest-house** *hist.* a hospital for sufferers from the plague etc. [F *peste* or L *pestis* plague]
pester /'pestə(r)/ *v.tr.* trouble or annoy, esp. with frequent or persistent requests. □□ **pesterer** *n.* [prob. f. *impester* f. F *empestrer* encumber: infl. by PEST]
pesticide /'pestɪˌsaɪd/ *n.* a substance used for destroying insects or other organisms harmful to cultivated plants or to animals. □□ **pesticidal** /-'saɪd(ə)l/ *adj.*
pestiferous /pe'stɪfərəs/ *adj.* **1** noxious; pestilent. **2** harmful; pernicious; bearing moral contagion. [L *pestifer, -ferus* (as PEST)]
pestilence /'pestɪləns/ *n.* a fatal epidemic disease, esp. bubonic plague. [ME f. OF f. L *pestilentia* (as PESTILENT)]
pestilent /'pestɪlənt/ *adj.* **1** destructive to life, deadly. **2** harmful or morally destructive. **3** *colloq.* troublesome; annoying. □□ **pestilently** *adv.* [L *pestilens, pestilentus* f. *pestis* plague]
pestilential /ˌpestɪ'lenʃ(ə)l/ *adj.* **1** of or relating to pestilence. **2** dangerous; troublesome; pestilent. □□ **pestilentially** *adv.* [ME f. med.L *pestilentialis* f. L *pestilentia* (as PESTILENT)]
pestle /'pes(ə)l/ *n.* & *v.* —*n.* **1** a club-shaped instrument for pounding substances in a mortar. **2** an appliance for pounding etc. —*v.* **1** *tr.* pound with a pestle or in a similar manner. **2** *intr.* use a pestle. [ME f. OF *pestel* f. L *pistillum* f. *pinsare pist-* to pound]
pestology /pe'stɒlədʒɪ/ *n.* the scientific study of pests (esp. harmful insects) and of methods of dealing with them. □□ **pestological** /-stə'lɒdʒɪk(ə)l/ *adj.* **pestologist** *n.*
Pet. *abbr.* Peter (New Testament).
pet¹ /pet/ *n., adj.,* & *v.* —*n.* **1** a domestic or tamed animal kept for pleasure or companionship. **2** a darling, a favourite (often as a term of endearment). —*attrib.adj.* **1** kept as a pet (*pet lamb*). **2** of or for pet animals (*pet food*). **3** often *joc.* favourite or particular (*pet aversion*). **4** expressing fondness or familiarity (*pet name*). —*v.tr.* (**petted, petting**) **1** treat as a pet. **2** (also *absol.*) fondle, esp. erotically. □□ **petter** *n.* [16th-c. Sc. & N.Engl. dial.: orig. unkn.]
pet² *n.* a feeling of petty resentment or ill-humour (esp. *be in a pet*). [16th c.: orig. unkn.]
peta- /'petə/ *comb. form* denoting a factor of 10^{15}. [perh. f. PENTA-]
petal /'pet(ə)l/ *n.* each of the parts of the corolla of a flower. □□ **petaline** /-ˌlaɪn, -lɪn/ *adj.* **petalled** *adj.* (also in *comb.*). **petal-like** *adj.* **petaloid** *adj.* [mod.L *petalum,* in LL metal plate f. Gk *petalon* leaf f. *petalos* outspread]
petard /pɪ'tɑːd/ *n.* *hist.* **1** a small bomb used to blast down a door etc. **2** a kind of firework or cracker. □**hoist with one's own petard** affected oneself by

one's schemes against others. [F *pétard* f. *péter* break wind]

petasus /'petəsəs/ *n.* **1** an ancient Greek hat with a low crown and broad brim, esp. (in Greek mythology) as worn by Hermes. **2** the winged hat of Hermes. [L f. Gk *petasos*]

petaurist /pə'tɔːrɪst/ *n.* any flying squirrel of the genus *Petaurista*, native to E. Asia. [Gk *petauristēs* performer on a springboard (*petauron*)]

Pete /piːt/ *n.* □for **Pete's sake** see SAKE¹. [abbr. of the name *Peter*]

petechia /pɪ'tiːkɪə/ *n.* (*pl.* **petechiae** /-kɪˌiː/) *Med.* a small red or purple spot as a result of bleeding into the skin. □□ **petechial** *adj.* [mod.L f. It. *petecchia* a freckle or spot on one's face]

peter¹ /'piːtə(r)/ *v.* & *n.* —*v.intr.* **1** (foll. by *out*) (orig. of a vein of ore etc.) diminish, come to an end. **2** *Bridge* play an echo. —*n. Bridge* an echo. [19th c.: orig. unkn.]

peter² /'piːtə(r)/ *n. sl.* **1** a prison cell. **2** a safe. [perh. f. the name *Peter*]

peterman /'piːtəmən/ *n.* (*pl.* **-men**) *sl.* a safe-breaker.

Peter Pan /ˌpiːtə 'pæn/ *n.* a person who retains youthful features, or who is immature. [hero of J. M. Barrie's play of the same name (1904)]

Peter Principle /'piːtə/ *n. joc.* the principle that members of a hierarchy are promoted until they reach the level at which they are no longer competent. [L. J. *Peter*, its propounder, b. 1919]

petersham /'piːtəʃəm/ *n.* thick corded silk ribbon used for stiffening in dressmaking etc. [Lord *Petersham*, Engl. army officer d. 1851]

Peter's pence /'piːtəz/ *n.pl. RC Ch.* **1** *hist.* an annual tax of one penny, formerly paid to the papal see. **2** (since 1860) a voluntary payment to the papal treasury. [St *Peter*, as first pope]

pethidine /'peθɪdiːn/ *n.* a synthetic soluble analgesic used esp. in childbirth. [perh. f. PIPERIDINE (from which the drug is derived) + ETHYL]

petiole /'petɪˌəʊl/ *n.* the slender stalk joining a leaf to a stem. □□ **petiolar** *adj.* **petiolate** /-lət/ *adj.* [F *pétiole* f. L *petiolus* little foot, stalk]

petit /'petɪ/ *adj.* esp. *Law* petty; small; of lesser importance. □ **petit jury** = *petty jury*. [ME f. OF, = small, f. Rmc, perh. imit. of child's speech]

petit bourgeois /ˌpetɪ 'buəʒwɑː, ˌpətɪ/ *n.* (*pl.* **petits bourgeois** *pronunc.* same) a member of the lower middle classes. [F]

petite /pə'tiːt/ *adj.* (of a woman) of small and dainty build. □ **petite bourgeoisie** /ˌbuəʒwɑː'ziː/ the lower middle classes. [F, fem. of PETIT]

petit four /ˌpetɪ 'fɔː(r), ˌpətɪ/ *n.* (*pl.* **petits fours** /'fɔːz/) a very small fancy cake, biscuit, or sweet. [F, = little oven]

petition /pɪ'tɪʃ(ə)n/ *n.* & *v.* —*n.* **1** a supplication or request. **2** a formal written request, esp. one signed by many people, appealing to authority in some cause. **3** *Law* an application to a court for a writ etc. —*v.* **1** *tr.* make or address a petition to (*petition your MP*). **2** *intr.* (often foll. by *for, to*) appeal earnestly or humbly. □ **Petition of Right 1** *hist.* a parliamentary declaration of rights and liberties of the people assented to by Charles I in 1628. **2** *Law* a common-law remedy against the crown for the recovery of property. □□ **petitionable** *adj.* **petitionary** *adj.* **petitioner** *n.* [ME f. OF f. L *petitio -onis*]

petitio principii /pɪˌtɪʃɪəʊ prɪn'kɪpɪˌaɪ/ *n.* a logical fallacy in which a conclusion is taken for granted in the premiss; begging the question. [L, = assuming a principle: see PETITION]

petit-maître /ˌpətɪ'meɪtr/ *n.* a dandy or coxcomb. [F, = little master]

petit mal /ˌpetɪ 'mæl, ˌpətɪ/ *n.* a mild form of epilepsy with only momentary loss of consciousness (cf. GRAND MAL). [F, = little sickness]

petit point /ˌpetɪ 'pwæ̃, ˌpətɪ 'pɔɪnt/ *n.* **1** embroidery on canvas using small stitches. **2** tent-stitch. [F, = little point]

petits pois /ˌpetɪ 'pwɑː, ˌpətɪ/ *n.pl.* small green peas. [F]

Petrarchan /pɪ'trɑːkən/ *adj.* denoting a sonnet of the kind used by the Italian poet Petrarch (d. 1374), with an octave rhyming abbaabba, and a sestet usu. rhyming cdcdcd or cdecde.

petrel /'petr(ə)l/ *n.* any of various sea birds of the family Procellariidae or Hydrobatidae, usu. flying far from land. [17th c. (also *pitteral*), of uncert. orig.: later assoc. with St Peter (Matt. 14:30)]

Petri dish /'petrɪ, 'piːt-/ *n.* a shallow covered dish used for the culture of bacteria etc. [J. R. *Petri*, Ger. bacteriologist d. 1921]

petrifaction /ˌpetrɪ'fækʃ(ə)n/ *n.* **1** the process of fossilization whereby organic matter is turned into a stony substance. **2** a petrified substance or mass. **3** a state of extreme fear or terror. [PETRIFY after *stupefaction*]

petrify /'petrɪˌfaɪ/ *v.* (**-ies, -ied**) **1** *tr.* paralyse with fear, astonishment, etc. **2** *tr.* change (organic matter) into a stony substance. **3** *intr.* become like stone. **4** *tr.* deprive (the mind, a doctrine, etc.) of vitality; deaden. [F *pétrifier* f. med.L *petrificare* f. L *petra* rock f. Gk]

petro- /'petrəʊ/ *comb. form* **1** rock. **2** petroleum (*petrochemistry*). [Gk *petros* stone or *petra* rock]

petrochemical /ˌpetrəʊ'kemɪk(ə)l/ *n.* & *adj.* —*n.* a substance industrially obtained from petroleum or natural gas. —*adj.* of or relating to petrochemistry or petrochemicals.

petrochemistry /ˌpetrəʊ'kemɪstrɪ/ *n.* **1** the chemistry of rocks. **2** the chemistry of petroleum.

petrodollar /'petrəʊˌdɒlə(r)/ *n.* a notional unit of currency earned by a petroleum-exporting country.

petroglyph /'petrəʊglɪf/ *n.* a rock-carving, esp. a prehistoric one. [PETRO- + Gk *glyphē* carving]

petrography /pe'trɒgrəfɪ/ *n.* the scientific description of the composition and formation of rocks. □□ **petrographer** *n.* **petrographic** /-'græfɪk/ *adj.* **petrographical** /-'græfɪk(ə)l/ *adj.*

petrol /'petr(ə)l/ *n. Brit.* **1** refined petroleum used as a fuel in motor vehicles, aircraft, etc. **2** (*attrib.*) concerned with the supply of petrol (*petrol pump*; *petrol station*). □ **petrol bomb** a simple bomb made of a petrol-filled bottle and a wick. [F *pétrole* f. med.L *petroleum*: see PETROLEUM]

petrolatum /ˌpetrə'leɪtəm/ *n. US* petroleum jelly. [mod.L f. PETROL + *-atum*]

petroleum /pɪ'trəʊlɪəm/ *n.* a hydrocarbon oil found in the upper strata of the earth, refined for use as a fuel for heating and in internal-combustion engines, for lighting, dry-cleaning, etc. □ **petroleum ether** a volatile liquid distilled from petroleum, consisting of a mixture of hydrocarbons. **petroleum jelly** a translucent solid mixture of hydrocarbons used as a lubricant, ointment, etc. [med.L f. L *petra* rock f. Gk + L *oleum* oil]

petrolic /pɪ'trɒlɪk/ *adj.* of or relating to petrol or petroleum.

petrology /pɪ'trɒlədʒɪ/ *n.* the study of the origin, structure, composition, etc., of rocks. □□ **petrologic** /ˌpetrə'lɒdʒɪk/ *adj.* **petrological** /ˌpetrə'lɒdʒɪk(ə)l/ *adj.* **petrologist** *n.*

petrous /'petrəs/ *adj.* **1** *Anat.* denoting the hard part of the temporal bone protecting the inner ear. **2** *Geol.* of, like, or relating to rock. [L *petrosus* f. L *petra* rock f. Gk]

petticoat /'petɪˌkəʊt/ *n.* **1** a woman's or girl's skirted undergarment hanging from the waist or shoulders. **2** *sl.* **a** a woman or girl. **b** (in *pl.*) the female sex. **3** (*attrib.*) often *derog.* feminine; associated with women (*petticoat pedantry*). □□ **petticoated** *adj.* **petticoatless** *adj.* [ME f. *petty coat*]

pettifog /'petɪfɒg/ *v.intr.* (**pettifogged, pettifogging**) **1** practise legal deception or trickery. **2** quibble or wrangle about petty points. [back-form. f. PETTIFOGGER]

pettifogger /'petɪˌfɒgə(r)/ *n.* **1** a rascally lawyer; an inferior legal practitioner. **2** a petty practitioner in any activity. □□**pettifoggery** *n.* **pettifogging** *adj.* [PETTY + *fogger* underhand dealer, prob. f. *Fugger* family of merchants in Augsburg in the 15th-16th c.]

pettish /'petɪʃ/ *adj.* peevish, petulant; easily put out. □□**pettishly** *adv.* **pettishness** *n.* [PET² + -ISH¹]

petty /'petɪ/ *adj.* (**pettier, pettiest**) **1** unimportant; trivial. **2** mean, small-minded; contemptible. **3** minor; inferior; on a small scale (*petty princes*). **4** *Law* (of a crime) of lesser importance (*petty sessions*) (cf. COMMON, GRAND). □**petty bourgeois** = PETIT BOURGEOIS. **petty bourgeoisie** = *petite bourgeoisie*. **petty cash** money from or for small items of receipt or expenditure. **petty jury** a jury of 12 persons who try the final issue of fact in civil or criminal cases and pronounce a verdict. **petty officer** a naval NCO. **petty treason** see TREASON. □□**pettily** *adv.* **pettiness** *n.* [ME *pety*, var. of PETIT]

petulant /'petjʊlənt/ *adj.* peevishly impatient or irritable. □□**petulance** *n.* **petulantly** *adv.* [F *pétulant* f. L *petulans -antis* f. *petere* seek]

petunia /pɪ'tju:nɪə/ *n.* **1** any plant of the genus *Petunia* with white, purple, red, etc., funnel-shaped flowers. **2** a dark violet or purple colour. [mod.L f. F *petun* f. Guarani *petỹ* tobacco]

petuntse /pɪ'tʊntsɪ, -'tʌntsɪ/ *n.* a white variable feldspathic mineral used for making porcelain. [Chin. *baidunzi* f. *bai* white + *dun* stone + suffix -*zi*]

pew /pju:/ *n. & v. —n.* **1** (in a church) a long bench with a back; an enclosed compartment. **2** *Brit. colloq.* a seat (esp. *take a pew*). —*v.tr.* furnish with pews. □□**pewage** *n.* **pewless** *adj.* [ME *pywe, puwe* f. OF *puye* balcony f. L *podia* pl. of PODIUM]

pewit var. of PEEWIT.

pewter /'pju:tə(r)/ *n.* **1** a grey alloy of tin with lead, copper, or antimony or various other metals. **2** utensils made of this. **3** *sl.* a tankard etc. as a prize. □□**pewterer** *n.* [ME f. OF *peutre, peualtre* f. Rmc, of unkn. orig.]

peyote /peɪ'əʊtɪ/ *n.* **1** any Mexican cactus of the genus *Lophophora*, esp. *L. williamsii* having no spines and button-like tops when dried. **2** a hallucinogenic drug containing mescaline prepared from this. [Amer. Sp. f. Nahuatl *peyotl*]

Pf. *abbr.* pfennig.

Pfc. *abbr. US* Private First Class.

pfennig /'pfenɪg, 'fenɪg/ *n.* a small German coin, worth one-hundredth of a mark. [G, rel. to PENNY]

PG *abbr.* **1** (of films) classified as suitable for children subject to parental guidance. **2** paying guest.

pH /pi:'eɪtʃ/ *n. Chem.* a logarithm of the reciprocal of the hydrogen-ion concentration in moles per litre of a solution, giving a measure of its acidity or alkalinity. [G, f. *Potenz* power + *H* (symbol for hydrogen)]

phaeton /'feɪt(ə)n/ *n.* **1** a light open four-wheeled carriage, usu. drawn by a pair of horses. **2** *US* a touring-car. [F *phaéton* f. L *Phaethon* f. Gk *Phaethōn*, son of Helios the sun god who was allowed to drive the sun-chariot for a day, with disastrous results]

phage /feɪdʒ, fɑ:ʒ/ *n.* = BACTERIOPHAGE. [abbr.]

phagocyte /'fæɡə,saɪt/ *n.* a type of cell capable of engulfing and absorbing foreign matter, esp. a leucocyte ingesting bacteria in the body. □□ **phagocytic** /-'sɪtɪk/ *adj.* [Gk *phag-* eat + -CYTE]

phagocytosis /,fæɡəsaɪ'təʊsɪs/ *n.* the ingestion of bacteria etc. by phagocytes. □□ **phagocytize** /'fæɡə-/ *v.tr.* (also -ise). **phagocytose** /'fæɡə-/ *v.tr.*

-phagous /fəɡəs/ *comb. form* that eats (as specified) (*ichthyophagous*). [L -*phagus* f. Gk -*phagos* f. *phagein* eat]

-phagy /fədʒɪ/ *comb. form* the eating of (specified food) (*ichthyophagy*). [Gk -*phagia* (as -PHAGOUS)]

phalange /'fælændʒ/ *n.* **1** *Anat.* = PHALANX 4. **2** (**Phalange**) a right-wing activist Maronite party in Lebanon (cf. FALANGE). [F f. L *phalanx*: see PHALANX]

phalangeal /fə'lændʒɪəl/ *adj. Anat.* of or relating to a phalanx.

phalanger /fə'lændʒə(r)/ *n.* any of various marsupials of the family Phalangeridae, including cuscuses and possums. [F f. Gk *phalaggion* spider's web, f. the webbed toes of its hind feet]

phalanx /'fælæŋks/ *n.* (*pl.* **phalanxes** or **phalanges** /'fælæn,dʒiːz/) **1** *Gk Antiq.* a line of battle, esp. a body of Macedonian infantry drawn up in close order. **2** a set of people etc. forming a compact mass, or banded for a common purpose. **3** a bone of the finger or toe. **4** *Bot.* a bundle of stamens united by filaments. [L f. Gk *phalagx -ggos*]

phalarope /'fælə,rəʊp/ *n.* any small wading or swimming bird of the subfamily Phalaropodidae, with a straight bill and lobed feet. [F f. mod.L *Phalaropus*, irreg. f. Gk *phalaris* coot + *pous podos* foot]

phalli *pl.* of PHALLUS.

phallic /'fælɪk/ *adj.* **1** of, relating to, or resembling a phallus. **2** *Psychol.* denoting the stage of male sexual development characterized by preoccupation with the genitals. □□**phallically** *adv.* [F *phallique* & Gk *phallikos* (as PHALLUS)]

phallocentric /,fæləʊ'sentrɪk/ *adj.* centred on the phallus or on male attitudes. □□**phallocentricity** /-'trɪsɪtɪ/ *n.* **phallocentrism** /-trɪz(ə)m/ *n.*

phallus /'fæləs/ *n.* (*pl.* **phalli** /-laɪ/ or **phalluses**) **1** the (esp. erect) penis. **2** an image of this as a symbol of generative power in nature. □□**phallicism** /-lɪ,sɪz(ə)m/ *n.* **phallism** *n.* [LL f. Gk *phallos*]

phanariot /fə'nærɪət/ *n. hist.* a member of a class of Greek officials in Constantinople under the Ottoman Empire. [mod.Gk *phanariōtēs* f. *Phanar* the part of the city where they lived f. Gk *phanarion* lighthouse (on the Golden Horn)]

phanerogam /'fænərə,ɡæm/ *n. Bot.* a plant that has stamens and pistils, a flowering plant (cf. CRYPTOGAM). □□**phanerogamic** /-'ɡæmɪk/ *adj.* **phanerogamous** /-'rɒɡəməs/ *adj.* [F *phanérogame* f. Gk *phaneros* visible + *gamos* marriage]

phantasize var. of FANTASIZE.

phantasm /'fæn,tæz(ə)m/ *n.* **1** an illusion, a phantom. **2** (usu. foll. by *of*) an illusory likeness. **3** a supposed vision of an absent (living or dead) person. □□ **phantasmal** /-'tæzm(ə)l/ *adj.* **phantasmic** /-'tæzmɪk/ *adj.* [ME f. OF *fantasme* f. L f. Gk *phantasma* f. *phantazō* make visible f. *phainō* show]

phantasmagoria /,fæntæzmə'ɡɔːrɪə/ *n.* **1** a shifting series of real or imaginary figures as seen in a dream. **2** an optical device for rapidly varying the size of images on a screen. □□**phantasmagoric** /-'ɡɒrɪk/ *adj.* **phantasmagorical** /-'ɡɒrɪk(ə)l/ *adj.* [prob. f. F *fantasmagorie* (as PHANTASM + fanciful ending)]

phantast var. of FANTAST.

phantasy var. of FANTASY.

phantom /'fæntəm/ *n. & adj. —n.* **1** a ghost; an apparition; a spectre. **2** a form without substance or reality; a mental illusion. **3** *Med.* a model of the whole or part of the body used to practise or demonstrate operative or therapeutic methods. —*adj.* merely apparent; illusory. □**phantom circuit** an arrangement of telegraph or other electrical wires equivalent to an extra circuit. **phantom limb** a continuing sensation of the presence of a limb which has been amputated. **phantom pregnancy** *Med.* the symptoms of pregnancy in a person not actually pregnant. [ME f. OF *fantosme* ult. f. Gk *phantasma* (as PHANTASM)]

Pharaoh /'feərəʊ/ *n.* **1** the ruler of ancient Egypt. **2** the title of this ruler. □**Pharaoh's serpent** an indoor firework burning and uncoiling in serpentine form. □□**Pharaonic** /,feəreɪ'ɒnɪk/ *adj.* [OE f. eccl.L *Pharao* f. Gk *Pharaō* f. Heb. *par'ōh* f. Egypt. *pr-'o* great house]

Pharisee /'færɪ,siː/ *n.* **1** a member of an ancient Jewish sect, distinguished by strict observance of the traditional and written law, and commonly held to have pretensions to superior sanctity. **2** a self-righteous person; a hypocrite. □□**Pharisaic** /,færɪ'seɪɪk/ *adj.* **Pharisaical** /,færɪ'seɪɪk(ə)l/ *adj.* **Pharisaism** /'færɪseɪ,ɪz(ə)m/ *n.* [OE *fariseus* & OF *pharise* f. eccl.L *pharisaeus* f. Gk *Pharisaios* f. Aram. *p'rišayyâ* pl. f. Heb. *pārûš* separated]

pharmaceutical /ˌfɑːməˈsjuːtɪk(ə)l/ *adj.* **1** of or engaged in pharmacy. **2** of the use or sale of medicinal drugs. □□ **pharmaceutically** *adv.* **pharmaceutics** *n.* [LL *pharmaceuticus* f. Gk *pharmakeutikos* f. *pharmakeutēs* druggist f. *pharmakon* drug]

pharmacist /ˈfɑːməsɪst/ *n.* a person qualified to prepare and dispense drugs.

pharmacognosy /ˌfɑːməˈkɒgnəsɪ/ *n.* the science of drugs, esp. relating to medicinal products in their natural or unprepared state. [Gk *pharmakon* drug + *gnōsis* knowledge]

pharmacology /ˌfɑːməˈkɒlədʒɪ/ *n.* the science of the action of drugs on the body. □□ **pharmacological** /-kəˈlɒdʒɪk(ə)l/ *adj.* **pharmacologically** /-kəˈlɒdʒɪkəlɪ/ *adv.* **pharmacologist** *n.* [mod.L *pharmacologia* f. Gk *pharmakon* drug]

pharmacopoeia /ˌfɑːməkəˈpiːə/ *n.* **1** a book, esp. one officially published, containing a list of drugs with directions for use. **2** a stock of drugs. □□ **pharmacopoeial** *adj.* [mod.L f. Gk *pharmakopoiia* f. *pharmakopoios* drug-maker (as PHARMACOLOGY + *-poios* making)]

pharmacy /ˈfɑːməsɪ/ *n.* (*pl.* **-ies**) **1** the preparation and the (esp. medicinal) dispensing of drugs. **2** a pharmacist's shop, a dispensary. [ME f. OF *farmacie* f. med.L *pharmacia* f. Gk *pharmakeia* practice of the druggist f. *pharmakeus* f. *pharmakon* drug]

pharos /ˈfeərɒs/ *n.* a lighthouse or a beacon to guide sailors. [L f. Gk *Pharos* island off Alexandria where a famous lighthouse stood]

pharyngo- /fəˈrɪŋgəʊ/ *comb. form* denoting the pharynx.

pharyngotomy /ˌfærɪŋˈgɒtəmɪ/ *n.* (*pl.* **-ies**) an incision into the pharynx.

pharynx /ˈfærɪŋks/ *n.* (*pl.* **pharynges** /-rɪŋˌdʒiːz/) a cavity, with enclosing muscles and mucous membrane, behind the nose and mouth, and connecting them to the oesophagus. □□ **pharyngal** /-ˈrɪŋg(ə)l/ *adj.* **pharyngeal** /-ˈdʒiːəl/ *adj.* **pharyngitis** /-ˈdʒaɪtɪs/ *n.* [mod.L f. Gk *pharugx -ggos*]

phase /feɪz/ *n. & v.* —*n.* **1** a distinct period or stage in a process of change or development. **2** each of the aspects of the moon or a planet, according to the amount of its illumination, esp. the new moon, the first quarter, the last quarter, and the full moon. **3** *Physics* a stage in a periodically recurring sequence, esp. of alternating electric currents or light vibrations. **4** a difficult or unhappy period, esp. in adolescence. **5** a genetic or seasonal variety of an animal's coloration etc. **6** *Chem.* a distinct and homogeneous form of matter separated by its surface from other forms. —*v.tr.* carry out (a programme etc.) in phases or stages. □**in phase** having the same phase at the same time. **out of phase** not in phase. **phase in** (or **out**) bring gradually into (or out of) use. **phase rule** *Chem.* a rule relating numbers of phases, constituents, and degrees of freedom. **three-phase** (of an electric generator, motor, etc.) designed to supply or use simultaneously three separate alternating currents of the same voltage, but with phases differing by a third of a period. □□ **phasic** *adj.* [F *phase* & f. earlier *phasis* f. Gk *phasis* appearance f. *phainō phan-* show]

phatic /ˈfætɪk/ *adj.* (of speech etc.) used to convey general sociability rather than to communicate a specific meaning, e.g. 'nice morning, isn't it?' [Gk *phatos* spoken f. *phēmi phan-* speak]

Ph.D. *abbr.* Doctor of Philosophy. [L *philosophiae doctor*]

pheasant /ˈfez(ə)nt/ *n.* any of several long-tailed game-birds of the family Phasianidae, orig. from Asia. □□ **pheasantry** *n.* (*pl.* **-ies**) [ME f. AF *fesaunt* f. OF *faisan* f. L *phasianus* f. Gk *phasianos* (bird) of the river *Phasis* in Asia Minor]

phenacetin /fɪˈnæsɪtɪn/ *n.* an acetyl derivative of

phenol used to treat fever etc. [PHENO- + ACETYL + -IN]

pheno- /ˈfiːnəʊ/ *comb. form* **1** *Chem.* derived from benzene (*phenol*; *phenyl*). **2** showing (*phenocryst*). [Gk *phainō* shine (with ref. to substances used for illumination), show]

phenobarbitone /ˌfiːnəʊˈbɑːbɪˌtəʊn/ *n.* (*US* **phenobarbital** /-t(ə)l/) a narcotic and sedative barbiturate drug used esp. to treat epilepsy.

phenocryst /ˈfiːnəkrɪst/ *n.* a large or conspicuous crystal in porphyritic rock. [F *phénocryste* (as PHENO-, CRYSTAL)]

phenol /ˈfiːnɒl/ *n. Chem.* **1** the monohydroxyl derivative of benzene used in dilute form as an antiseptic and disinfectant. Also called CARBOLIC. ¶ Chem. formula: C_6H_5OH. **2** any hydroxyl derivative of an aromatic hydrocarbon. □□ **phenolic** /fɪˈnɒlɪk/ *adj.* [F *phénole* f. *phène* benzene (formed as PHENO-)]

phenolphthalein /ˌfiːnɒlˈθeɪliːn/ *n. Chem.* a white crystalline solid used in solution as an acid-base indicator and medicinally as a laxative. [PHENOL + *phthal* f. NAPHTHALENE + -IN]

phenomena *pl.* of PHENOMENON.

phenomenal /fɪˈnɒmɪn(ə)l/ *adj.* **1** of the nature of a phenomenon. **2** extraordinary, remarkable, prodigious. **3** perceptible by, or perceptible only to, the senses. □□ **phenomenalize** *v.tr.* (also **-ise**). **phenomenally** *adv.*

phenomenalism /fɪˈnɒmɪnəˌlɪz(ə)m/ *n. Philos.* **1** the doctrine that human knowledge is confined to the appearances presented to the senses. **2** the doctrine that appearances are the foundation of all our knowledge. □□ **phenomenalist** *n.* **phenomenalistic** /-ˈlɪstɪk/ *adj.*

phenomenology /fɪˌnɒmɪˈnɒlədʒɪ/ *n. Philos.* **1** the science of phenomena. **2** the description and classification of phenomena. □□ **phenomenological** /-nəˈlɒdʒɪk(ə)l/ *adj.* **phenomenologically** /-nəˈlɒdʒɪkəlɪ/ *adv.*

phenomenon /fɪˈnɒmɪnən/ *n.* (*pl.* **phenomena** /-nə/) **1** a fact or occurrence that appears or is perceived, esp. one of which the cause is in question. **2** a remarkable person or thing. **3** *Philos.* the object of a person's perception; what the senses or the mind notice. [LL f. Gk *phainomenon* neut. pres. part. of *phainomai* appear f. *phainō* show]

phenotype /ˈfiːnəʊˌtaɪp/ *n. Biol.* a set of observable characteristics of an individual or group as determined by its genotype and environment. □□ **phenotypic** /-ˈtɪpɪk/ *adj.* **phenotypical** /-ˈtɪpɪk(ə)l/ *adj.* **phenotypically** /-ˈtɪpɪkəlɪ/ *adv.* [G *Phaenotypus* (as PHENO-, TYPE)]

phenyl /ˈfiːnaɪl, -nɪl/ *n. Chem.* the univalent radical formed from benzene by the removal of a hydrogen atom. [PHENO- + -YL]

phenylalanine /ˌfiːnaɪlˈæləˌniːn/ *n. Biochem.* an amino acid widely distributed in plant proteins and essential in the human diet. [PHENYL + ALANINE]

phenylketonuria /ˌfiːnaɪlˌkiːtəˈnjʊərɪə/ *n.* an inherited inability to metabolize phenylalanine, ultimately leading to mental deficiency if untreated. [PHENYL + KETONE + -URIA]

pheromone /ˈferəˌməʊn/ *n.* a chemical substance secreted and released by an animal for detection and response by another usu. of the same species. □□ **pheromonal** /-ˈməʊn(ə)l/ *adj.* [Gk *pherō* convey + HORMONE]

phew /fjuː/ *int.* an expression of impatience, discomfort, relief, astonishment, or disgust. [imit. of puffing]

phi /faɪ/ *n.* the twenty-first letter of the Greek alphabet (Φ, φ). □**Phi Beta Kappa** **1** (in the US) an intercollegiate honorary society to which distinguished scholars may be elected (from the initial letters of a Greek motto, = philosophy is the guide to life). **2** a member of this society. [Gk]

phial /ˈfaɪəl/ *n.* a small glass bottle, esp. for liquid medicine. [ME f. OF *fiole* f. L *phiola phiala* f. Gk *phialē*, a broad flat vessel: cf. VIAL]

Phil. *abbr.* **1** Philadelphia. **2** Philharmonic. **3** Philippians (New Testament). **4** Philosophy.

phil- *comb. form* var. of PHILO-.

-phil *comb. form* var. of -PHILE.

philabeg var. of FILIBEG.

philadelphus /ˌfɪləˈdelfəs/ *n.* any highly-scented deciduous flowering shrub of the genus *Philadelphus*, esp. the mock orange. [mod.L f. Gk *philadelphon*]

philander /fɪˈlændə(r)/ *v.intr.* (often foll. by *with*) flirt or have casual affairs with women; womanize. □□**philanderer** *n.* [*philander* (n.) used in Gk literature as the proper name of a lover, f. Gk *philandros* fond of men f. *anēr* male person: see PHIL-]

philanthrope /ˈfɪlənˌθrəʊp/ *n.* = PHILANTHROPIST (see PHILANTHROPY). [Gk *philanthrōpos* (as PHIL-, *anthrōpos* human being)]

philanthropic /ˌfɪlənˈθrɒpɪk/ *adj.* loving one's fellow men; benevolent. □□**philanthropically** *adv.* [F *philanthropique* (as PHILANTHROPE)]

philanthropy /fɪˈlænθrəpɪ/ *n.* **1** a love of mankind. **2** practical benevolence, esp. charity on a large scale. □□**philanthropism** *n.* **philanthropist** *n.* **philanthropize** *v.tr. & intr.* (also **-ise**). [LL *philanthropia* f. Gk *philanthrōpia* (as PHILANTHROPE)]

philately /fɪˈlætəlɪ/ *n.* the collection and study of postage stamps. □□**philatelic** /ˌfɪləˈtelɪk/ *adj.* **philatelically** /ˌfɪləˈtelɪkəlɪ/ *adv.* **philatelist** *n.* [F *philatélie* f. Gk *ateleia* exemption from payment f. *a-* not + *telos* toll, tax]

-phile /faɪl/ *comb. form* (also **-phil** /fɪl/) forming nouns and adjectives denoting fondness for what is specified (*bibliophile*; *Francophile*). [Gk *philos* dear, loving]

Philem. *abbr.* Philemon (New Testament).

philharmonic /ˌfɪlhɑːˈmɒnɪk/ *adj.* **1** fond of music. **2** used characteristically in the names of orchestras, choirs, etc. (*Royal Philharmonic Orchestra*). [F *philharmonique* f. It. *filarmonico* (as PHIL-, HARMONIC)]

philhellene /ˈfɪlheˌliːn, -ˈheliːn/ *n.* (often *attrib.*) **1** a lover of Greece and Greek culture. **2** *hist.* a supporter of the cause of Greek independence. □□**philhellenic** /-ˈliːnɪk/ *adj.* **philhellenism** /-ˈhelɪˌnɪz(ə)m/ *n.* **philhellenist** /-ˈhelɪnɪst/ *n.* [Gk *philellēn* (as PHIL-, HELLENE)]

-philia /ˈfɪlɪə/ *comb. form* **1** denoting (esp. abnormal) fondness or love for what is specified (*necrophilia*). **2** denoting undue inclination (*haemophilia*). □□ **-philiac** /-lɪˌæk/ *comb. form* forming nouns and adjectives. **-philic** *comb. form* forming adjectives. **-philous** *comb. form* forming adjectives. [Gk f. *philos* loving]

philippic /fɪˈlɪpɪk/ *n.* a bitter verbal attack or denunciation. [L *philippicus* f. Gk *philippikos* the name of Demosthenes' speeches against Philip II of Macedon and Cicero's against Mark Antony]

Philippine /ˈfɪlɪˌpiːn/ *adj.* of or relating to the Philippine Islands or their people; Filipino. [*Philip II of Spain*]

Philistine /ˈfɪlɪˌstaɪn/ *n. & adj.* —*n.* **1** a member of a people opposing the Israelites in ancient Palestine. **2** (usu. **philistine**) a person who is hostile or indifferent to culture, or one whose interests or tastes are commonplace or material. —*adj.* hostile or indifferent to culture, commonplace, prosaic. □□ **philistinism** /-stɪnɪz(ə)m/ *n.* [ME f. F *Philistin* f. LL *Philistinus* f. Gk *Philistinos* = *Palaistinos* f. Heb. *pᵉlištī*]

Phillips /ˈfɪlɪps/ *n.* (usu. *attrib.*) *propr.* denoting a screw with a cross-shaped slot for turning, or a corresponding screwdriver. [name of the original US manufacturer]

phillumenist /fɪˈljuːmənɪst, fɪˈluː-/ *n.* a collector of matchbox labels. □□**phillumeny** *n.* [PHIL- + L *lumen* light]

Philly /ˈfɪlɪ/ *n. US sl.* Philadelphia. [abbr.]

philo- /ˈfɪləʊ/ *comb. form* (also **phil-** before a vowel or *h*) denoting a liking for what is specified.

philodendron /ˌfɪləʊˈdendrən/ *n.* (*pl.* **philodendrons** or **philodendra** /-drə/) any tropical American climbing plant of the genus *Philodendron*, with bright foliage. [PHILO- + Gk *dendron* tree]

philogynist /fɪˈlɒdʒənɪst/ *n.* a person who likes or admires women. [PHILO- + Gk *gunē* woman]

philology /fɪˈlɒlədʒɪ/ *n.* **1** the science of language, esp. in its historical and comparative aspects. **2** the love of learning and literature. □□**philologian** /-ləˈləʊdʒ(ə)n/ *n.* **philologist** *n.* **philological** /-ləˈlɒdʒɪk(ə)l/ *adj.* **philologically** /-ləˈlɒdʒɪkəlɪ/ *adv.* **philologize** *v.intr.* (also **-ise**). [F *philologie* f. L *philologia* love of learning f. Gk (as PHILO-, -LOGY)]

Philomel /ˈfɪləˌmel/ *n.* (also **Philomela** /ˌfɪləˈmiːlə/) *poet.* the nightingale. [earlier *philomene* f. med.L *philomena* f. L *philomela* nightingale f. Gk *philomēla*: cap. with ref. to the myth of *Philomela*]

philoprogenitive /ˌfɪləʊprəʊˈdʒenɪtɪv/ *adj.* **1** prolific. **2** loving one's offspring.

philosopher /fɪˈlɒsəfə(r)/ *n.* **1** a person engaged or learned in philosophy or a branch of it. **2** a person who lives by philosophy. **3** a person who shows philosophic calmness in trying circumstances. □**philosophers'** (or **philosopher's**) **stone** the supreme object of alchemy, a substance supposed to change other metals into gold or silver. [ME f. AF *philosofre* var. of OF, *philosophe* f. L *philosophus* f. Gk *philosophos* (as PHILO-, *sophos* wise)]

philosophical /ˌfɪləˈsɒfɪk(ə)l/ *adj.* (also **philosophic**) **1** of or according to philosophy. **2** skilled in or devoted to philosophy or learning; learned (*philosophical society*). **3** wise; serene; temperate. **4** calm in adverse circumstances. □□ **philosophically** *adv.* [LL *philosophicus* f. L *philosophia* (as PHILOSOPHY)]

philosophize /fɪˈlɒsəˌfaɪz/ *v.* (also **-ise**) **1** *intr.* reason like a philosopher. **2** *intr.* moralize. **3** *intr.* speculate; theorize. **4** *tr.* render philosophic. □□**philosophizer** *n.* [app. f. F *philosopher*]

philosophy /fɪˈlɒsəfɪ/ *n.* (*pl.* **-ies**) **1** the use of reason and argument in seeking truth and knowledge of reality, esp. of the causes and nature of things and of the principles governing existence, the material universe, perception of physical phenomena, and human behaviour. **2 a** a particular system or set of beliefs reached by this. **b** a personal rule of life. **3** advanced learning in general (*doctor of philosophy*). **4** serenity; calmness; conduct governed by a particular philosophy. [ME f. OF *filosofie* f. L *philosophia* wisdom f. Gk (as PHILO-, *sophos* wise)]

philtre /ˈfɪltə(r)/ *n.* (*US* **philter**) a drink supposed to excite sexual love in the drinker. [F *philtre* f. L *philtrum* f. Gk *philtron* f. *phileō* to love]

-phily /ˈfɪlɪ/ *comb. form* = -PHILIA.

phimosis /faɪˈməʊsɪs/ *n.* a constriction of the foreskin, making it difficult to retract. □□**phimotic** /-ˈmɒtɪk/ *adj.* [mod.L f. Gk, = muzzling]

phiz /fɪz/ *n.* (also **phizog** /ˈfɪzɒg/) *Brit. colloq.* **1** the face. **2** the expression on a face. [abbr. of *phiznomy* = PHYSIOGNOMY]

phlebitis /flɪˈbaɪtɪs/ *n.* inflammation of the walls of a vein. □□**phlebitic** /-ˈbɪtɪk/ *adj.* [mod.L f. Gk f. *phleps phlebos* vein]

phlebotomy /flɪˈbɒtəmɪ/ *n.* **1** the surgical opening or puncture of a vein. **2** *esp. hist.* blood-letting as a medical treatment. □□**phlebotomist** *n.* **phlebotomize** *v.tr.* (also **-ise**). [ME f. OF *flebothomi* f. LL *phlebotomia* f. Gk f. *phleps phlebos* vein + -TOMY]

phlegm /flem/ *n.* **1** the thick viscous substance secreted by the mucous membranes of the respiratory passages, discharged by coughing. **2 a** coolness and calmness of disposition. **b** sluggishness or apathy (supposed to result from too much phlegm in the constitution). **3** *archaic* phlegm regarded as one of the four bodily humours. □□**phlegmy** *adj.*

æ cat ɑː arm e bed ɜː her ɪ sit iː see ɒ hot ɔː saw ʌ run ʊ put uː too ə ago aɪ my

[ME & OF *fleume* f. LL *phlegma* f. Gk *phlegma -atos* inflammation f. *phlegō* burn]

phlegmatic /fleg'mætɪk/ *adj.* stolidly calm; unexcitable, unemotional. □□ **phlegmatically** *adv.*

phloem /'fləʊem/ *n. Bot.* the tissue conducting food material in plants (cf. XYLEM). [Gk *phloos* bark]

phlogiston /flə'dʒɪst(ə)n, -'ɡɪst(ə)n/ *n.* a substance formerly supposed to exist in all combustible bodies, and to be released in combustion. [mod.L f. Gk *phlogizō* set on fire f. *phlox phlogos* flame]

phlox /flɒks/ *n.* any cultivated plant of the genus *Phlox*, with scented clusters of esp. white, blue, and red flowers. [L f. Gk *phlox*, the name of a plant (lit. flame)]

-phobe /fəʊb/ *comb. form* forming nouns and adjectives denoting fear or dislike of what is specified (*xenophobe*). [F f. L *-phobus* f. Gk *-phobos* f. *phobos* fear]

phobia /'fəʊbɪə/ *n.* an abnormal or morbid fear or aversion. □□ **phobic** *adj.* & *n.* [-PHOBIA used as a separate word]

-phobia /'fəʊbɪə/ *comb. form* forming abstract nouns denoting fear or aversion of what is specified (*agoraphobia*; *xenophobia*). □□ **-phobic** *comb. form* forming adjectives. [L f. Gk]

phoebe /'fiːbɪ/ *n.* any American flycatcher of the genus *Sayornis*. [imit.: infl. by the name]

Phoenician /fə'nɪʃ(ə)n, fə'niː-/ *n.* & *adj.* —*n.* a member of a Semitic people of ancient Phoenicia in S. Syria or of its colonies. —*adj.* of or relating to Phoenicia. [ME f. OF *phenicien* f. L *Phoenicia* f. L *Phoenice* f. Gk *Phoinikē* Phoenicia]

phoenix /'fiːnɪks/ *n.* **1** a mythical bird, the only one of its kind, that after living for five or six centuries in the Arabian desert, burnt itself on a funeral pyre and rose from the ashes with renewed youth to live through another cycle. **2** a unique person or thing. [OE & OF *fenix* f. L *phoenix* f. Gk *phoinix* Phoenician, purple, phoenix]

pholas /'fəʊlæs/ *n.* a piddock, esp. of the genus *Pholas*. [mod.L f. Gk *phōlas* that lurks in a hole (*phōleos*)]

phon /fɒn/ *n.* a unit of the perceived loudness of sounds. [Gk *phōnē* sound]

phonate /'fəʊneɪt/ *v.intr.* utter a vocal sound. □□ **phonation** /'neɪʃ(ə)n/ *n.* **phonatory** /'fəʊnətərɪ/ *adj.* [Gk *phōnē* voice]

phone[1] /fəʊn/ *n.* & *v.tr.* & *intr. colloq.* = TELEPHONE. □ **phone book** = *telephone directory.* **phone-in** *n.* a broadcast programme during which the listeners or viewers telephone the studio etc. and participate. [abbr.]

phone[2] /fəʊn/ *n.* a simple vowel or consonant sound. [formed as PHONEME]

-phone /fəʊn/ *comb. form* forming nouns and adjectives meaning: **1** an instrument using or connected with sound (*telephone*; *xylophone*). **2** a person who uses a specified language (*anglophone*). [Gk *phōnē* voice, sound]

phonecard /'fəʊnkɑːd/ *n.* a card containing prepaid units for use with a Cardphone.

phoneme /'fəʊniːm/ *n.* any of the units of sound in a specified language that distinguish one word from another (e.g. *p*, *b*, *d*, *t* as in pad, pat, bad, bat, in English). □□ **phonemic** /-'niːmɪk/ *adj.* **phonemics** /-'niːmɪks/ *n.* [F *phonème* f. Gk *phōnēma* sound, speech f. *phōneō* speak]

phonetic /fə'netɪk/ *adj.* **1** representing vocal sounds. **2** (of a system of spelling etc.) having a direct correspondence between symbols and sounds. **3** of or relating to phonetics. □□ **phonetically** *adv.* **phoneticism** /-sɪz(ə)m/ *n.* **phoneticist** /-sɪst/ *n.* **phoneticize** /-saɪz/ *v.tr.* (also **-ise**). [mod.L *phoneticus* f. Gk *phōnētikos* f. *phōneō* speak]

phonetics /fə'netɪks/ *n.pl.* (usu. treated as *sing.*) **1** vocal sounds and their classification. **2** the study of these. □□ **phonetician** /ˌfəʊnɪ'tɪʃ(ə)n/ *n.*

phonetist /'fəʊnɪtɪst/ *n.* **1** a person skilled in phonetics. **2** an advocate of phonetic spelling.

phoney /'fəʊnɪ/ *adj.* & *n.* (also **phony**) *colloq.* —*adj.* (**phonier, phoniest**) **1** sham; counterfeit. **2** fictitious; fraudulent. —*n.* (*pl.* **-eys** or **-ies**) a phoney person or thing. □□ **phonily** *adv.* **phoniness** *n.* [20th c.: orig. unkn.]

phonic /'fɒnɪk, 'fəʊ-/ *adj.* & *n.* —*adj.* of sound; acoustic; of vocal sounds. —*n.* (in *pl.*) a method of teaching reading based on sounds. □□ **phonically** *adv.* [Gk *phōnē* voice]

phono- /'fəʊnəʊ/ *comb. form* denoting sound. [Gk *phōnē* voice, sound]

phonogram /'fəʊnəˌgræm/ *n.* a symbol representing a spoken sound.

phonograph /'fəʊnəˌgrɑːf/ *n.* **1** *Brit.* an early form of gramophone using cylinders and able to record as well as reproduce sound. **2** *US* a gramophone.

phonography /fə'nɒgrəfɪ/ *n.* **1** writing in esp. shorthand symbols, corresponding to the sounds of speech. **2** the recording of sounds by phonograph. □□ **phonographic** /ˌfəʊnə'græfɪk/ *adj.*

phonology /fə'nɒlədʒɪ/ *n.* the study of sounds in a language. □□ **phonological** /ˌfəʊnə'lɒdʒɪk(ə)l, ˌfɒn-/ *adj.* **phonologically** /ˌfəʊnə'lɒdʒɪkəlɪ, ˌfɒn-/ *adv.* **phonologist** *n.*

phonon /'fəʊnɒn/ *n. Physics* a quantum of sound or elastic vibrations. [Gk *phōnē* sound, after PHOTON]

phony var. of PHONEY.

phooey /'fuːɪ/ *int.* an expression of disgust or disbelief. [imit.]

-phore /fɔː(r)/ *comb. form* forming nouns meaning 'bearer' (*ctenophore; semaphore*). □□ **-phorous** /fərəs/ *comb. form* forming adjectives. [mod.L f. Gk *-phoros -phoron* bearing, bearer f. *pherō* bear]

phoresy /fɒ'riːsɪ, 'fɒrəsɪ/ *n. Biol.* an association in which one organism is carried by another, without being a parasite. □□ **phoretic** /fɒ'retɪk/ *adj.* [F *phorésie* f. Gk *phorēsis* being carried]

phormium /'fɔːmɪəm/ *n.* **1** a liliaceous plant, *Phormium tenax*, yielding a leaf-fibre that is used commercially. **2** New Zealand flax. [mod.L f. Gk *phormion* a species of plant]

phosgene /'fɒzdʒiːn/ *n.* a colourless poisonous gas (carbonyl chloride), formerly used in warfare. ¶ Chem. formula: $COCl_2$. [Gk *phōs* light + -GEN, with ref. to its orig. production by the action of sunlight on chlorine and carbon monoxide]

phosphatase /'fɒsfəˌteɪz, -teɪs/ *n. Biochem.* any enzyme that catalyses the synthesis or hydrolysis of an organic phosphate.

phosphate /'fɒsfeɪt/ *n.* **1** any salt or ester of phosphoric acid, esp. used as a fertilizer. **2** an effervescent drink containing a small amount of phosphate. □□ **phosphatic** /-'fætɪk/ *adj.* [F f. *phosphore* PHOSPHORUS]

phosphene /'fɒsfiːn/ *n.* the sensation of rings of light produced by pressure on the eyeball due to irritation of the retina. [irreg. f. Gk *phōs* light + *phainō* show]

phosphide /'fɒsfaɪd/ *n. Chem.* a binary compound of phosphorus with another element or group.

phosphine /'fɒsfiːn/ *n. Chem.* a colourless ill-smelling gas, phosphorus trihydride. ¶ Chem. formula: PH_3. □□ **phosphinic** /-'fɪnɪk/ *adj.* [PHOSPHO- + -INE[4], after *amine*]

phosphite /'fɒsfaɪt/ *n. Chem.* any salt or ester of phosphorous acid. [F (as PHOSPHO-)]

phospho- /'fɒsfəʊ/ *comb. form* denoting phosphorus. [abbr.]

phospholipid /ˌfɒsfə'lɪpɪd/ *n. Biochem.* any lipid consisting of a phosphate group and one or more fatty acids.

phosphor /'fɒsfə(r)/ *n.* **1** = PHOSPHORUS. **2** a synthetic fluorescent or phosphorescent substance esp. used in cathode-ray tubes. □ **phosphor bronze** a tough hard bronze alloy containing a small amount of phosphorus, used esp. for bearings. [G f. L *phosphorus* PHOSPHORUS]

phosphorate /'fɒsfəˌreɪt/ *v.tr.* combine or impregnate with phosphorus.

phosphorescence /ˌfɒsfə'res(ə)ns/ *n.* **1** radiation similar to fluorescence but detectable after excitation ceases. **2** the emission of light without combustion or perceptible heat. □□**phosphoresce** *v.intr.* **phosphorescent** *adj.*

phosphorite /'fɒsfəˌraɪt/ *n.* a non-crystalline form of apatite.

phosphorus /'fɒsfərəs/ *n. Chem.* a non-metallic element occurring naturally in various phosphate rocks and existing in allotropic forms, esp. as a poisonous whitish waxy substance burning slowly at ordinary temperatures and so appearing luminous in the dark, and a reddish form used in matches, fertilizers, etc. ¶ Symb.: **P**. □□**phosphoric** /-'fɒrɪk/ *adj.* **phosphorous** *adj.* [L, = morning star, f. Gk *phôsphoros* f. *phôs* light + *-phoros* -bringing]

phosphorylate /fɒs'fɒrɪˌleɪt/ *v.tr. Chem.* introduce a phosphate group into (an organic molecule etc.). □□**phosphorylation** /-'leɪʃ(ə)n/ *n.*

phossy jaw /'fɒsɪ/ *n. colloq. hist.* gangrene of the jawbone caused by phosphorus poisoning. [abbr.]

phot /fɒt, fəʊt/ *n.* a unit of illumination equal to one lumen per square centimetre. [Gk *phôs phôtos* light]

photic /'fəʊtɪk/ *adj.* **1** of or relating to light. **2** (of ocean layers) reached by sunlight.

photism /'fəʊtɪz(ə)m/ *n.* a hallucinatory sensation or vision of light. [Gk *phôtismos* f. *phôtizô* shine f. *phôs phôtos* light]

photo /'fəʊtəʊ/ *n. & v.* —*n.* (*pl.* -os) = PHOTOGRAPH *n.* —*v.tr.* (-oes, -oed) = PHOTOGRAPH *v.* □**photo-call** an occasion on which theatrical performers, famous personalities, etc., pose for photographers by arrangement. **photo finish** a close finish of a race or contest, esp. one where the winner is only distinguishable on a photograph. [abbr.]

photo- /'fəʊtəʊ/ *comb. form* denoting: **1** light (*photosensitive*). **2** photography (*photocomposition*). [Gk *phôs phôtos* light, or as abbr. of PHOTOGRAPH]

photobiology /ˌfəʊtəʊbaɪ'ɒlədʒɪ/ *n.* the study of the effects of light on living organisms.

photocell /'fəʊtəʊˌsel/ *n.* = photoelectric cell.

photochemistry /ˌfəʊtəʊ'kemɪstrɪ/ *n.* the study of the chemical effects of light. □□**photochemical** *adj.*

photocomposition /ˌfəʊtəʊˌkɒmpə'zɪʃ(ə)n/ *n.* = FILMSETTING.

photoconductivity /ˌfəʊtəʊˌkɒndʌk'tɪvɪtɪ/ *n.* conductivity due to the action of light. □□ **photoconductive** /-kən'dʌktɪv/ *adj.* **photoconductor** /-kən'dʌktə(r)/ *n.*

photocopier /'fəʊtəʊˌkɒpɪə(r)/ *n.* a machine for producing photocopies.

photocopy /'fəʊtəʊˌkɒpɪ/ *n. & v.* —*n.* (*pl.* -ies) a photographic copy of printed or written material produced by a process involving the action of light on a specially prepared surface. —*v.tr.* (-ies, -ied) make a photocopy of. □□**photocopiable** *adj.*

photodiode /ˌfəʊtəʊ'daɪəʊd/ *n.* a semiconductor diode responding electrically to illumination.

photoelectric /ˌfəʊtəʊɪ'lektrɪk/ *adj.* marked by or using emissions of electrons from substances exposed to light. □**photoelectric cell** a device using this effect to generate current. □□**photoelectricity** /-'trɪsɪtɪ/ *n.*

photoelectron /ˌfəʊtəʊɪ'lektrɒn/ *n.* an electron emitted from an atom by interaction with a photon, esp. one emitted from a solid surface by the action of light.

photoemission /ˌfəʊtəʊɪ'mɪʃ(ə)n/ *n.* the emission of electrons from a surface by the action of light incident on it. □□**photoemitter** *n.*

photofit /'fəʊtəʊfɪt/ *n.* a reconstructed picture of a person (esp. one sought by the police) made from composite photographs of facial features (cf. IDENTIKIT).

photogenic /ˌfəʊtəʊ'dʒenɪk, -'dʒiːnɪk/ *adj.* **1** (esp. of a person) having an appearance that looks pleasing in photographs. **2** *Biol.* producing or emitting light. □□ **photogenically** *adv.*

photogram /'fəʊtəʊˌgræm/ *n.* **1** a picture produced with photographic materials but without a camera. **2** *archaic* a photograph.

photogrammetry /ˌfəʊtəʊ'græmɪtrɪ/ *n.* the use of photography for surveying. □□**photogrammetrist** *n.*

photograph /'fəʊtəˌgrɑːf/ *n. & v.* —*n.* a picture taken by means of the chemical action of light or other radiation on sensitive film. —*v.tr.* (also *absol.*) take a photograph of (a person etc.). □□**photographable** *adj.* **photographer** /fə'tɒgrəfə(r)/ *n.* **photographic** /-'græfɪk/ *adj.* **photographically** /-'græfɪkəlɪ/ *adv.*

photography /fə'tɒgrəfɪ/ *n.* the taking and processing of photographs.

photogravure /ˌfəʊtəʊgrə'vjʊə(r)/ *n.* **1** an image produced from a photographic negative transferred to a metal plate and etched in. **2** this process. [F (as PHOTO-, *gravure* engraving)]

photojournalism /ˌfəʊtəʊ'dʒɜːnəˌlɪz(ə)m/ *n.* the art or practice of relating news by photographs, with or without an accompanying text, esp. in magazines etc. □□**photojournalist** *n.*

photolithography /ˌfəʊtəʊlɪ'θɒgrəfɪ/ *n.* (also **photolitho** /-'laɪθəʊ/) lithography using plates made photographically. □□**photolithographer** *n.* **photolithographic** /-θə'græfɪk/ *adj.* **photolithographically** /-θə'græfɪkəlɪ/ *adv.*

photolysis /fəʊ'tɒlɪsɪs/ *n.* decomposition or dissociation of molecules by the action of light. □□ **photolyse** /'fəʊtəˌlaɪz/ *v.tr. & intr.* **photolytic** /-tə'lɪtɪk/ *adj.*

photometer /fəʊ'tɒmɪtə(r)/ *n.* an instrument for measuring light. □□**photometric** /ˌfəʊtəʊ'metrɪk/ *adj.* **photometry** /-'tɒmɪtrɪ/ *n.*

photomicrograph /ˌfəʊtəʊ'maɪkrəˌgrɑːf/ *n.* a photograph of an image produced by a microscope. □□ **photomicrography** /-'krɒgrəfɪ/ *n.*

photomontage /ˌfəʊtəʊmɒn'tɑːʒ/ *n.* **1** the technique of producing a montage (see MONTAGE 2) using photographs. **2** a composite picture produced in this way.

photon /'fəʊtɒn/ *n.* a quantum of electromagnetic radiation energy, proportional to the frequency of radiation. [Gk *phôs phôtos* light, after *electron*]

photo-offset /ˌfəʊtəʊ'ɒfset/ *n.* offset printing with plates made photographically.

photoperiod /ˌfəʊtəʊ'pɪərɪəd/ *n.* the period of daily illumination which an organism receives. □□ **photoperiodic** /-ɪ'ɒdɪk/ *adj.*

photoperiodism /ˌfəʊtəʊ'pɪərɪəˌdɪz(ə)m/ *n.* the response of an organism to changes in the lengths of the daily periods of light.

photophobia /ˌfəʊtəʊ'fəʊbɪə/ *n.* an abnormal fear of or aversion to light. □□**photophobic** *adj.*

photoreceptor /ˌfəʊtəʊrɪ'septə(r)/ *n.* any living structure that responds to incident light.

photosensitive /ˌfəʊtəʊ'sensɪtɪv/ *adj.* reacting chemically, electrically, etc., to light. □□ **photosensitivity** /-'tɪvɪtɪ/ *n.*

photosetting /'fəʊtəʊˌsetɪŋ/ *n.* = FILMSETTING. □□ **photoset** *v.tr.* (*past* and *past part.* -set). **photosetter** *n.*

photosphere /'fəʊtəʊˌsfɪə(r)/ *n.* the luminous envelope of a star from which its light and heat radiate. □□**photospheric** /-'sferɪk/ *adj.*

Photostat /'fəʊtəʊˌstæt/ *n. & v.* —*n. propr.* **1** a type of machine for making photocopies. **2** a copy made by this means. —*v.tr.* (**photostat**) (-statted, -statting) make a Photostat of. □□**photostatic** /-'stætɪk/ *adj.*

photosynthesis /ˌfəʊtəʊ'sɪnθɪsɪs/ *n.* the process in which the energy of sunlight is used by organisms, esp. green plants to synthesize carbohydrates from carbon dioxide and water. □□**photosynthesize** *v.tr. & intr.* (also -ise). **photosynthetic** /-'θetɪk/ *adj.* **photosynthetically** /-'θetɪkəlɪ/ *adv.*

phototransistor /ˌfəʊtəʊtræn'zɪstə(r), -trɑː'nzɪstə(r), -'sɪstə(r)/ *n.* a transistor that responds to incident light by generating and amplifying an electric current.

phototropism /ˌfəʊtəʊˈtrəʊpɪz(ə)m, fəˈtɒtrəˌpɪz(ə)m/ *n.* the tendency of a plant etc. to bend or turn towards or away from a source of light. □□ **phototropic** /-ˈtrɒpɪk/ *adj.*

photovoltaic /ˌfəʊtəʊvɒlˈteɪɪk/ *adj.* relating to the production of electric current at the junction of two substances exposed to light.

phrasal /ˈfreɪz(ə)l/ *adj. Gram.* consisting of a phrase. □**phrasal verb** an idiomatic phrase consisting of a verb and an adverb (e.g. *break down*) or a verb and a preposition (e.g. *see to*).

phrase /freɪz/ *n. & v.* —*n.* **1** a group of words forming a conceptual unit, but not a sentence. **2** an idiomatic or short pithy expression. **3** a manner or mode of expression (*a nice turn of phrase*). **4** *Mus.* a group of notes forming a distinct unit within a larger piece. —*v.tr.* **1** express in words (*phrased the reply badly*). **2** (esp. when reading aloud or speaking) divide (sentences etc.) into units so as to convey the meaning of the whole. **3** *Mus.* divide (music) into phrases etc. in performance. □**phrase book** a book for tourists etc. listing useful expressions with their equivalent in a foreign language. □□ **phrasing** *n.* [earlier *phrasis* f. L f. Gk f. *phrazō* declare, tell]

phraseogram /ˈfreɪzɪəˌgræm/ *n.* a written symbol representing a phrase, esp. in shorthand.

phraseology /ˌfreɪzɪˈɒlədʒɪ/ *n.* (*pl.* **-ies**) **1** a choice or arrangement of words. **2** a mode of expression. □□ **phraseological** /-zɪəˈlɒdʒɪk(ə)l/ *adj.* [mod.L *phraseologia* f. Gk *phraseōn* genit. pl. of *phrasis* PHRASE]

phreatic /frɪˈætɪk/ *adj. Geol.* **1** (of water) situated underground in the zone of saturation; ground water. **2** (of a volcanic eruption or explosion) caused by the heating and expansion of underground water. [Gk *phrear phreatos* well]

phrenetic /frɪˈnetɪk/ *adj.* **1** frantic. **2** fanatic. □□ **phrenetically** *adv.* [ME, var. of FRENETIC]

phrenic /ˈfrenɪk/ *adj. Anat.* of or relating to the diaphragm. [F *phrénique* f. Gk *phrēn phrenos* diaphragm, mind]

phrenology /frɪˈnɒlədʒɪ/ *n. hist.* the study of the shape and size of the cranium as a supposed indication of character and mental faculties. □□ **phrenological** /-nəˈlɒdʒɪk(ə)l/ *adj.* **phrenologist** *n.*

Phrygian /ˈfrɪdʒɪən/ *n. & adj.* —*n.* **1** a native or inhabitant of ancient Phrygia in central Asia Minor. **2** the language of this people. —*adj.* of or relating to Phrygia or its people or language. □**Phrygian bonnet** (or **cap**) an ancient conical cap with the top bent forwards, now identified with the cap of liberty. **Phrygian mode** *Mus.* the mode represented by the natural diatonic scale E–E.

phthalic acid /ˈfθælɪk/ *n. Chem.* one of three isomeric dicarboxylic acids derived from benzene. □□ **phthalate** /-leɪt/ *n.* [abbr. of NAPHTHALIC: see NAPHTHALENE]

phthisis /ˈfθaɪsɪs, ˈθaɪ-/ *n.* any progressive wasting disease, esp. pulmonary tuberculosis. □□ **phthisic** *adj.* **phthisical** *adj.* [L f. Gk f. *phthinō* to decay]

phut /fʌt/ *n.* a dull abrupt sound as of an impact or explosion. □**go phut** *colloq.* (esp. of a scheme or plan) collapse, break down. [perh. f. Hindi *phaṭnā* to burst]

phycology /faɪˈkɒlədʒɪ/ *n.* the study of algae. □□ **phycological** /-kəˈlɒdʒɪk(ə)l/ *adj.* **phycologist** *n.* [Gk *phukos* seaweed + -LOGY]

phycomycete /ˌfaɪkəʊˈmaɪsiːt/ *n.* any of various fungi which typically form non-septate mycelium. [Gk *phukos* seaweed + pl. of Gk *mukēs* mushroom]

phyla *pl.* of PHYLUM.

phylactery /frɪˈlæktərɪ/ *n.* (*pl.* **-ies**) **1** a small leather box containing Hebrew texts on vellum, worn by Jewish men at morning prayer as a reminder to keep the law. **2** an amulet; a charm. **3** a usu. ostentatious religious observance. **4** a fringe; a border. [ME f. OF

f. LL *phylacterium* f. Gk *phulaktērion* amulet f. *phulassō* guard]

phyletic /faɪˈletɪk/ *adj. Biol.* of or relating to the development of a species or other group. [Gk *phuletikos* f. *phuletēs* tribesman f. *phulē* tribe]

phyllo- /ˈfɪləʊ/ *comb. form* leaf. [Gk *phullo-* f. *phullon* leaf]

phyllode /ˈfɪləʊd/ *n.* a flattened leaf-stalk resembling a leaf. [mod.L *phyllodium* f. Gk *phullōdēs* leaflike (as PHYLLO-)]

phyllophagous /frˈlɒfəgəs/ *adj.* feeding on leaves.

phylloquinone /ˌfaɪləʊˈkwɪnəʊn/ *n.* one of the K vitamins, found in cabbage, spinach, and other leafy green vegetables, and essential for the blood clotting process. Also called *vitamin K$_1$*.

phyllostome /ˈfɪləʊˌstəʊm/ *n.* any bat of the family Phyllostomatidae having a nose leaf. [PHYLLO- + Gk *stoma* mouth]

phyllotaxis /ˌfɪləʊˈtæksɪs/ *n.* (also **phyllotaxy** /-ˈtæksɪ/) the arrangement of leaves on an axis or stem. □□ **phyllotactic** *adj.*

phylloxera /ˌfɪlɒkˈsɪərə, frˈlɒksərə/ *n.* any plant-louse of the genus *Phylloxera*, esp. of a species attacking vines. [mod.L f. Gk *phullon* leaf + *xēros* dry]

phylo- /ˈfaɪləʊ/ *comb. form Biol.* denoting a race or tribe. [Gk *phulon, phulē*]

phylogenesis /ˌfaɪləʊˈdʒenəsɪs/ *n.* (also **phylogeny** /faɪˈlɒdʒənɪ/) **1** the evolutionary development of an organism or groups of organisms. **2** a history of this. □□ **phylogenetic** /-dʒɪˈnetɪk/ *adj.* **phylogenic** /-ˈdʒenɪk/ *adj.*

phylum /ˈfaɪləm/ *n.* (*pl.* **phyla** /-lə/) *Biol.* a taxonomic rank below kingdom comprising a class or classes and subordinate taxa. [mod.L f. Gk *phulon* race]

physalis /faɪˈsælɪs/ *n.* any plant of the genus *Physalis*, bearing fruit surrounded by lantern-like calyxes (see *Chinese lantern* 2). [Gk *physallis* bladder, with ref. to the inflated calyx]

physic /ˈfɪzɪk/ *n. & v.* esp. *archaic.* —*n.* **1** a medicine (*a dose of physic*). **2** the art of healing. **3** the medical profession. —*v.tr.* (**physicked**, **physicking**) dose with physic. □**physic garden** a garden for cultivating medicinal herbs etc. [ME f. OF *fisique* medicine f. L *physica* f. Gk *phusikē* (*epistēmē*) (knowledge) of nature]

physical /ˈfɪzɪk(ə)l/ *adj. & n.* —*adj.* **1** of or concerning the body (*physical exercise*; *physical education*). **2** of matter; material (*both mental and physical force*). **3 a** of, or according to, the laws of nature (*a physical impossibility*). **b** belonging to physics (*physical science*). —*n.* (in full **physical examination**) a medical examination to determine physical fitness. □**physical chemistry** the application of physics to the study of chemical behaviour. **physical geography** geography dealing with natural features. **physical jerks** *colloq.* physical exercises. **physical science** the sciences used in the study of inanimate natural objects, e.g. physics, chemistry, astronomy, etc. **physical training** exercises promoting bodily fitness and strength. □□ **physicality** /-ˈkælɪtɪ/ *n.* **physically** *adv.* **physicalness** *n.* [ME f. med.L *physicalis* f. L *physica* (as PHYSIC)]

physician /frˈzɪʃ(ə)n/ *n.* **1 a** a person legally qualified to practise medicine and surgery. **b** a specialist in medical diagnosis and treatment. **c** any medical practitioner. **2** a healer (*work is the best physician*). [ME f. OF *fisicien* (as PHYSIC)]

physicist /ˈfɪzɪsɪst/ *n.* a person skilled or qualified in physics.

physico- /ˈfɪzɪkəʊ/ *comb. form* **1** physical (and). **2** of physics (and). [Gk *phusikos* (as PHYSIC)]

physico-chemical /ˌfɪzɪkəʊˈkemɪk(ə)l/ *adj.* relating to physics and chemistry or to physical chemistry.

physics /ˈfɪzɪks/ *n.* the science dealing with the properties and interactions of matter and energy.

w *we*   z *zoo*   ʃ *she*   ʒ *decision*   θ *thin*   ð *this*   ŋ *ring*   x *loch*   tʃ *chip*   dʒ *jar*   (*see over for vowels*)

[pl. of *physic* physical (thing), after L *physica*, Gk *phusika* natural things f. *phusis* nature]

physio /ˈfɪzɪəʊ/ *n.* (*pl.* **-os**) *colloq.* a physiotherapist. [abbr.]

physio- /ˈfɪzɪəʊ/ *comb. form* nature; what is natural. [Gk *phusis* nature]

physiocracy /ˌfɪzɪˈɒkrəsɪ/ *n.* (*pl.* **-ies**) *hist.* **1** government according to the natural order, esp. as advocated by some 18th-c. economists. **2** a society based on this. □□ **physiocrat** /ˈfɪzɪəˌkræt/ *n.* **physiocratic** /-ɪəˈkrætɪk/ *adj.* [F *physiocratie* (as PHYSIO-, -CRACY)]

physiognomy /ˌfɪzɪˈɒnəmɪ/ *n.* (*pl.* **-ies**) **1 a** the cast or form of a person's features, expression, body, etc. **b** the art of supposedly judging character from facial characteristics etc. **2** the external features of a landscape etc. **3** a characteristic, esp. moral, aspect. □□ **physiognomic** /-ɪəˈnɒmɪk/ *adj.* **physiognomical** /-ɪəˈnɒmɪk(ə)l/ *adj.* **physiognomically** /-ɪəˈnɒmɪkəlɪ/ *adv.* **physiognomist** *n.* [ME *fisnomie* etc. f. OF *phisonomie* f. med.L *phisonomia* f. Gk *phusiognōmonia* judging of a man's nature (by his features) (as PHYSIO-, *gnōmōn* judge)]

physiography /ˌfɪzɪˈɒɡrəfɪ/ *n.* the description of nature, of natural phenomena, or of a class of objects; physical geography. □□ **physiographer** *n.* **physiographic** /-ɪəˈɡræfɪk/ *adj.* **physiographical** /-ɪəˈɡræfɪk(ə)l/ *adj.* **physiographically** /-ɪəˈɡræfɪkəlɪ/ *adv.* [F *physiographie* (as PHYSIO-, -GRAPHY)]

physiological /ˌfɪzɪəˈlɒdʒɪk(ə)l/ *adj.* (also **physiologic**) of or concerning physiology. □**physiological salt solution** a saline solution having a concentration about equal to that of body fluids. □□ **physiologically** *adv.*

physiology /ˌfɪzɪˈɒlədʒɪ/ *n.* **1** the science of the functions of living organisms and their parts. **2** these functions. □□ **physiologist** *n.* [F *physiologie* or L *physiologia* f. Gk *phusiologia* (as PHYSIO-, -LOGY)]

physiotherapy /ˌfɪzɪəʊˈθerəpɪ/ *n.* the treatment of disease, injury, deformity, etc., by physical methods including manipulation, massage, infrared heat treatment, remedial exercise, etc., not by drugs. □□ **physiotherapist** *n.*

physique /fɪˈziːk/ *n.* the bodily structure, development, and organization of an individual (*an undernourished physique*). [F, orig. adj. (as PHYSIC)]

-phyte /faɪt/ *comb. form* forming nouns denoting a vegetable or plantlike organism (*saprophyte*; *zoophyte*). □□ **-phytic** /ˈfɪtɪk/ *comb. form* forming adjectives. [Gk *phuton* plant f. *phuō* come into being]

phyto- /ˈfaɪtəʊ/ *comb. form* denoting a plant.

phytochemistry /ˌfaɪtəʊˈkemɪstrɪ/ *n.* the chemistry of plant products. □□ **phytochemical** *adj.* **phytochemist** *n.*

phytochrome /ˈfaɪtəʊˌkrəʊm/ *n.* *Biochem.* a blue-green pigment found in many plants, and regulating various developmental processes according to the nature and timing of the light it absorbs. [PHYTO- + Gk *khrōma* colour]

phytogenesis /ˌfaɪtəʊˈdʒenɪsɪs/ *n.* (also **phytogeny** /-ˈtɒdʒɪnɪ/) the science of the origin or evolution of plants.

phytogeography /ˌfaɪtəʊdʒɪˈɒɡrəfɪ/ *n.* the geographical distribution of plants.

phytopathology /ˌfaɪtəʊpəˈθɒlədʒɪ/ *n.* the study of plant diseases.

phytophagous /faɪˈtɒfəɡəs/ *adj.* feeding on plants.

phytoplankton /ˌfaɪtəʊˈplæŋkt(ə)n/ *n.* plankton consisting of plants.

phytotomy /faɪˈtɒtəmɪ/ *n.* the dissection of plants.

phytotoxic /ˌfaɪtəʊˈtɒksɪk/ *adj.* poisonous to plants.

phytotoxin /ˌfaɪtəʊˈtɒksɪn/ *n.* **1** any toxin derived from a plant. **2** a substance poisonous or injurious to plants, esp. one produced by a parasite.

pi¹ /paɪ/ *n.* **1** the sixteenth letter of the Greek alphabet (Π, π). **2** (as π) the symbol of the ratio of the circumference of a circle to its diameter (approx. 3.14159). □**pi-meson** = PION. [Gk: sense 2 f. Gk *periphereia* circumference]

pi² /paɪ/ *adj. Brit. sl.* pious. □**pi jaw** a long moralizing lecture or reprimand. [abbr.]

pi³ *US* var. of PIE³.

piacular /paɪˈækjʊlə(r)/ *adj. formal* **1** expiatory. **2** needing expiation. [L *piacularis* f. *piaculum* expiation f. *piare* appease]

piaffe /pɪˈæf/ *v.intr.* (of a horse etc.) move as in a trot, but slower. [F *piaffer* to strut]

piaffer /pɪˈæfə(r)/ *n.* the action of piaffing.

pia mater /ˌpaɪə ˈmeɪtə(r)/ *n. Anat.* the delicate innermost membrane enveloping the brain and spinal cord (see MENINX). [med.L, = tender mother, transl. of Arab. *al-'umm al-raḳīḳa*: cf. DURA MATER]

piani *pl.* of PIANO².

pianism /ˈpiːəˌnɪz(ə)m/ *n.* **1** the art or technique of piano-playing. **2** the skill or style of a composer of piano music. □□ **pianistic** /-ˈnɪstɪk/ *adj.* **pianistically** /-ˈnɪstɪkəlɪ/ *adv.*

pianissimo /ˌpɪəˈnɪsɪˌməʊ/ *adj., adv., & n. Mus.* —*adj.* performed very softly. —*adv.* very softly. —*n.* (*pl.* **-os** or **pianissimi** /-mɪ/) a passage to be performed very softly. [It., superl. of PIANO²]

pianist /ˈpɪənɪst/ *n.* the player of a piano. [F *pianiste* (as PIANO¹)]

piano¹ /pɪˈænəʊ/ *n.* (*pl.* **-os**) a large musical instrument played by pressing down keys on a keyboard and causing hammers to strike metal strings, the vibration from which is stopped by dampers when the keys are released. □**piano-accordion** an accordion with the melody played on a small vertical keyboard like that of a piano. **piano organ** a mechanical piano constructed like a barrel-organ. **piano-player 1** a pianist. **2** a contrivance for playing a piano automatically. **piano roll** a roll of paper with perforations, used in a Pianola to reproduce music by allowing air to pass through the holes to depress the keys. [It., abbr. of PIANOFORTE]

piano² /ˈpjɑːnəʊ/ *adj., adv., & n.* —*adj.* **1** *Mus.* performed softly. **2** subdued. —*adv.* **1** *Mus.* softly. **2** in a subdued manner. —*n.* (*pl.* **-os** or **piani** /-nɪ/) *Mus.* a piano passage. [It. f. L *planus* flat, (of sound) soft]

pianoforte /ˌpɪænəʊˈfɔːtɪ/ *n. Mus. formal* or *archaic* a piano. [It., earlier *piano e forte* soft and loud, expressing its gradation of tone]

Pianola /pɪəˈnəʊlə/ *n.* **1** *propr.* a kind of automatic piano; a player-piano. **2** (**pianola**) *Bridge* an easy hand needing no skill. **3** (**pianola**) an easy task. [app. dimin. of PIANO¹]

piano nobile /ˌpjɑːnəʊ ˈnəʊbɪˌleɪ/ *n. Archit.* the main storey of a large house. [It., = noble floor]

piassava /ˌpiːəˈsɑːvə/ *n.* **1** a stout fibre obtained from the leaf-stalks of various American and African palm-trees. **2** any of these trees. [Port. f. Tupi *piaçaba*]

piastre /pɪˈæstə(r)/ *n.* (*US* **piaster**) a small coin and monetary unit of several Middle Eastern countries. [F *piastre* f. It. *piastra* (*d'argento*) plate (of silver), formed as PLASTER]

piazza /pɪˈætsə/ *n.* **1** a public square or market-place esp. in an Italian town. **2** *US* the veranda of a house. [It., formed as PLACE]

pibroch /ˈpiːbrɒx, -brɒk/ *n.* a series of esp. martial or funerary variations on a theme for the bagpipes. [Gael. *piobaireachd* art of piping f. *piobair* piper f. *piob* f. E PIPE]

pic /pɪk/ *n. colloq.* a picture, esp. a cinema film. [abbr.]

pica¹ /ˈpaɪkə/ *n. Printing* **1** a unit of type-size (⅙ inch). **2** a size of letters in typewriting (10 per inch). [AL *pica* 15th-c. book of rules about church feasts, perh. formed as PIE²]

pica² /ˈpaɪkə/ *n. Med.* the eating of substances other than normal food. [mod.L or med.L, = magpie]

picador /'pɪkə,dɔː(r)/ n. a mounted man with a lance who goads the bull in a bullfight. [Sp. f. *picar* prick]

picaresque /,pɪkə'resk/ adj. (of a style of fiction) dealing with the episodic adventures of rogues etc. [F f. Sp. *picaresco* f. *pícaro* rogue]

picaroon /,pɪkə'ruːn/ n. **1 a** a rogue. **b** a thief. **2 a** a pirate. **b** a pirate ship. [Sp. *picarón* (as PICARESQUE)]

picayune /,pɪkə'juːn/ n. & adj. *US* —n. **1** *colloq.* a small coin of little value, esp. a 5-cent piece. **2** an insignificant person or thing. —adj. mean; contemptible; petty. [F *picaillon* Piedmontese coin, cash, f. Prov. *picaioun*, of unkn. orig.]

piccalilli /,pɪkə'lɪlɪ/ n. (pl. **piccalillis**) a pickle of chopped vegetables, mustard, and hot spices. [18th c.: perh. f. PICKLE + CHILLI]

piccaninny /,pɪkə'nɪnɪ/ n. & adj. (*US* **pickaninny**) —n. (pl. **-ies**) often *offens.* a small Black or Australian Aboriginal child. —adj. *archaic* very small. [W.Ind. Negro f. Sp. *pequeño* or Port. *pequeno* little]

piccolo /'pɪkə,ləʊ/ n. (pl. **-os**) **1** a small flute sounding an octave higher than the ordinary one. **2** its player. [It., = small (flute)]

pichiciago /,pɪtʃɪsɪ'eɪɡəʊ/ n. (pl. **-os**) a small S. American armadillo, *Chlamyphorus truncatus*. [Sp. *pichiciego* perh. f. Guarani *pichey* armadillo + Sp. *ciego* blind f. L *caecus*]

pick¹ /pɪk/ v. & n. —v.tr. **1** (also *absol.*) choose carefully from a number of alternatives (*picked the pink one; picked a team; picked the right moment to intervene*). **2** detach or pluck (a flower, fruit, etc.) from a stem, tree, etc. **3 a** probe (the teeth, nose, ears, a pimple, etc.) with the finger, an instrument, etc. to remove unwanted matter. **b** clear (a bone, carcass, etc.) of scraps of meat etc. **4** (also *absol.*) (of a person) eat (food, a meal, etc.) in small bits; nibble without appetite. **5** (also *absol.*) esp. *US* pluck the strings of (a banjo etc.). **6** remove stalks etc. from (esp. soft fruit) before cooking. **7 a** select (a route or path) carefully over difficult terrain by foot. **b** place (one's steps etc.) carefully. **8** pull apart (*pick oakum*). **9** (of a bird) take up (grains etc.) in the beak. —n. **1** the act or an instance of picking. **2 a** a selection or choice. **b** the right to select (*had first pick of the prizes*). **3** (usu. foll. by *of*) the best (*the pick of the bunch*). □**pick and choose** select carefully or fastidiously. **pick at 1** eat (food) without interest; nibble. **2** = *pick on* 1 (see PICK¹). **pick a person's brains** extract ideas, information, etc., from a person for one's own use. **pick holes** (or **a hole**) **in 1** make holes in (material etc.) by plucking, poking, etc. **2** find fault with (an idea etc.). **pick a lock** open a lock with an instrument other than the proper key, esp. with intent to steal. **pick-me-up 1** a tonic for the nerves etc. **2** a good experience, good news, etc. that cheers. **pick off 1** pluck (leaves etc.) off. **2** shoot (people etc.) one by one without haste. **3** eliminate (opposition etc.) singly. **pick on 1** find fault with; nag at. **2** select. **pick out 1** take from a larger number (*picked him out from the others*). **2** distinguish from surrounding objects or at a distance (*can just pick out the church spire*). **3** play (a tune) by ear on the piano etc. **4** (often foll. by *in*, *with*) **a** highlight (a painting etc.) with touches of another colour. **b** accentuate (decoration, a painting, etc.) with a contrasting colour (*picked out the handles in red*). **5** make out (the meaning of a passage etc.). **pick over** select the best from. **pick a person's pockets** steal the contents of a person's pockets. **pick a quarrel** start an argument or a fight deliberately. **pick to pieces** = *take to pieces* (see PIECE). **pick up 1** grasp and raise (from the ground etc.) (*picked up his hat*). **2** gain or acquire by chance or without effort (*picked up a cold*). **3 a** fetch (a person, animal, or thing) left in another person's charge. **b** stop for and take along with one, esp. in a vehicle (*pick me up on the corner*). **4** make the acquaintance of (a person) casually, esp. as a sexual overture. **5** (of one's health, the weather, share prices, etc.) recover, prosper, improve. **6** (of a

motor engine etc.) recover speed; accelerate. **7** (of the police etc.) take into charge; arrest. **8** detect by scrutiny or with a telescope, searchlight, radio, etc. (*picked up most of the mistakes; picked up a distress signal*). **9** (often foll. by *with*) form or renew a friendship. **10** accept the responsibility of paying (a bill etc.). **11** (*refl.*) raise (oneself etc.) after a fall etc. **12** raise (the feet etc.) clear of the ground. **13** *Golf* pick up one's ball, esp. when conceding a hole. **pick-up 1** *sl.* a person met casually, esp. for sexual purposes. **2** a small open motor truck. **3 a** the part of a record-player carrying the stylus. **b** a detector of vibrations etc. **4 a** the act of picking up. **b** something picked up. **pick-your-own** (usu. *attrib.*) (of commercially grown fruit and vegetables) dug or picked by the customer at the place of production. **take one's pick** make a choice. □□**pickable** adj. [ME, earlier *pike*, of unkn. orig.]

pick² /pɪk/ n. & v. —n. **1** a long-handled tool having a usu. curved iron bar pointed at one or both ends, used for breaking up hard ground, masonry, etc. **2** *colloq.* a plectrum. **3** any instrument for picking, such as a toothpick. —v.tr. **1** break the surface of (the ground etc.) with or as if with a pick. **2** make (holes etc.) in this way. [ME, app. var. of PIKE²]

pickaback var. of PIGGYBACK.

pickaninny *US* var. of PICCANINNY.

pickaxe /'pɪkæks/ n. & v. (*US* **pickax**) —n. = PICK² n. 1. —v. **1** *tr.* break (the ground etc.) with a pickaxe. **2** *intr.* work with a pickaxe. [ME *pikois* f. OF *picois*, rel. to PIKE²: assim. to AXE]

pickelhaube /'pɪkəl,haʊbə/ n. *hist.* a German soldier's spiked helmet. [G]

picker /'pɪkə(r)/ n. **1** a person or thing that picks. **2** (often in *comb.*) a person who gathers or collects (*hop-picker; rag-picker*).

pickerel /'pɪkər(ə)l/ n. (pl. same or **pickerels**) a young pike. [ME, dimin. of PIKE¹]

picket /'pɪkɪt/ n. & v. —n. **1** a person or group of people outside a place of work, intending to persuade esp. workers not to enter during a strike etc. **2** a pointed stake or peg driven into the ground to form a fence or palisade, to tether a horse, etc. **3** (also **picquet, piquet**) *Mil.* **a** a small body of troops sent out to watch for the enemy, held in readiness, etc. **b** a party of sentries. **c** an outpost. **d** a camp-guard on police duty in a garrison town etc. —v. (**picketed, picketing**) **1 a** *tr.* & *intr.* station or act as a picket. **b** *tr.* beset or guard (a factory, workers, etc.) with a picket or pickets. **2** *tr.* secure (a place) with stakes. **3** *tr.* tether (an animal). □**picket line** a boundary established by workers on strike, esp. at the entrance to the place of work, which others are asked not to cross. □□**picketer** n. [F *piquet* pointed stake f. *piquer* prick, f. *pic* PICK²]

pickings /'pɪkɪŋz/ n.pl. **1** perquisites; pilferings (*rich pickings*). **2** remaining scraps; gleanings.

pickle /'pɪk(ə)l/ n. & v. —n. **1 a** (often in *pl.*) food, esp. vegetables, preserved in brine, vinegar, mustard, etc. and used as a relish. **b** the brine, vinegar, etc. in which food is preserved. **2** *colloq.* a plight (*a fine pickle we are in!*). **3** *Brit. colloq.* a mischievous child. **4** an acid solution for cleaning metal etc. —v.tr. **1** preserve in pickle. **2** treat with pickle. **3** (as **pickled** adj.) *sl.* drunk. [ME *pekille, pykyl*, f. MDu., MLG *pekel*, of unkn. orig.]

pickler /'pɪklə(r)/ n. **1** a person who pickles vegetables etc. **2** a vegetable suitable for pickling.

picklock /'pɪklɒk/ n. **1** a person who picks locks. **2** an instrument for this.

pickpocket /'pɪk,pɒkɪt/ n. a person who steals from the pockets of others.

Pickwickian /pɪk'wɪkɪən/ adj. **1** of or like Mr Pickwick in Dickens's *Pickwick Papers*, esp. in being jovial, plump, etc. **2** (of words or their sense) misunderstood or misused, esp. to avoid offence.

picky /'pɪkɪ/ adj. (**pickier, pickiest**) *colloq.* excessively fastidious; choosy. □□**pickiness** n.

picnic /'pɪknɪk/ n. & v. —n. **1** an outing or excursion including a packed meal eaten out of doors. **2** any meal eaten out of doors or without preparation, tables, chairs, etc. **3** (usu. with *neg.*) *colloq.* something agreeable or easily accomplished etc. (*it was no picnic organizing the meeting*). —v.intr. (**picnicked**, **picnicking**) take part in a picnic. □□ **picnicker** n. **picnicky** adj. *colloq.* [F *pique-nique*, of unkn. orig.]

pico- /'paɪkəʊ, 'pi:kəʊ/ *comb. form* denoting a factor of 10^{-12} (*picometre*). [Sp. *pico* beak, peak, little bit]

picot /'pi:kəʊ/ n. a small loop of twisted thread in a lace edging etc. [F, dimin. of *pic* peak, point]

picotee /ˌpɪkə'ti:/ n. a type of carnation of which the flowers have a light ground and dark-edged petals. [F *picoté -ée* past part. of *picoter* prick (as PICOT)]

picquet var. of PICKET 3.

picric acid /'pɪkrɪk/ n. a very bitter yellow compound used in dyeing and surgery and in explosives. □□ **picrate** /-reɪt/ n. [Gk *pikros* bitter]

Pict /pɪkt/ n. a member of an ancient people of N. Britain. □□ **Pictish** adj. [ME f. LL *Picti* perh. f. *pingere pict-* paint, tattoo]

pictograph /'pɪktəˌgrɑːf/ n. (also **pictogram** /'pɪktəˌgræm/) **1 a** a pictorial symbol for a word or phrase. **b** an ancient record consisting of these. **2** a pictorial representation of statistics etc. on a chart, graph, etc. □□ **pictographic** /-'græfɪk/ adj. **pictography** /-'tɒgrəfɪ/ n. [L *pingere pict-* paint]

pictorial /pɪk'tɔːrɪəl/ adj. & n. —adj. **1** of or expressed in a picture or pictures. **2** illustrated. **3** picturesque. —n. a journal, postage stamp, etc., with a picture or pictures as the main feature. □□ **pictorially** adv. [LL *pictorius* f. L *pictor* painter (as PICTURE)]

picture /'pɪktʃə(r)/ n. & v. —n. **1 a** (often *attrib.*) a painting, drawing, photograph, etc., esp. as a work of art (*picture frame*). **b** a portrait, esp. a photograph, of a person (*does not like to have her picture taken*). **c** a beautiful object (*her hat is a picture*). **2 a** a total visual or mental impression produced; a scene (*the picture looks bleak*). **b** a written or spoken description (*drew a vivid picture of moral decay*). **3 a** a film. **b** (in *pl.*) *Brit.* a showing of films at a cinema (*went to the pictures*). **c** (in *pl.*) films in general. **4** an image on a television screen. **5** *colloq.* **a** esp. *iron.* a person or thing exemplifying something (*he was the picture of innocence*). **b** a person or thing resembling another closely (*the picture of her aunt*). —v.tr. **1** represent in a picture. **2** (also *refl.*; often foll. by *to*) imagine, esp. visually or vividly (*pictured it to herself*). **3** describe graphically. □ **get the picture** *colloq.* grasp the tendency or drift of circumstances, information, etc. **in the picture** fully informed or noticed. **out of the picture** uninvolved, inactive; irrelevant. **picture-book** a book containing many illustrations. **picture-card** a court-card. **picture-gallery** a place containing an exhibition or collection of pictures. **picture-goer** a person who frequents the cinema. **picture hat** a woman's wide-brimmed highly decorated hat as in pictures by Reynolds and Gainsborough. **picture-moulding 1** woodwork etc. used for framing pictures. **2** a rail on a wall used for hanging pictures from. **picture-palace** (or **-theatre**) *Brit. archaic* a cinema. **picture postcard** a postcard with a picture on one side. **picture window** a very large window consisting of one pane of glass. **picture-writing** a mode of recording events etc. by pictorial symbols as in early hieroglyphics etc. [ME f. L *pictura* f. *pingere pict-* paint]

picturesque /ˌpɪktʃə'resk/ adj. **1** (of landscape etc.) beautiful or striking, as in a picture. **2** (of language etc.) strikingly graphic; vivid. □□ **picturesquely** adv. **picturesqueness** n. [F *pittoresque* f. It. *pittoresco* f. *pittore* painter f. L (as PICTORIAL): assim. to PICTURE]

piddle /'pɪd(ə)l/ v. & n. —v.intr. **1** *colloq.* urinate (used esp. to or by children). **2** work or act in a trifling way. **3** (as **piddling** adj.) *colloq.* trivial; trifling. —n. *colloq.* **1** urination. **2** urine (used esp.

to or by children). □□ **piddler** n. [sense 1 prob. f. PISS + PUDDLE: sense 2 perh. f. PEDDLE]

piddock /'pɪdək/ n. any rock-boring bivalve mollusc of the family Pholadidae, used for bait. [18th c.: orig. unkn.]

pidgin /'pɪdʒɪn/ n. a simplified language containing vocabulary from two or more languages, used for communication between people not having a common language. □ **pidgin English** a pidgin in which the chief language is English, used orig. between Chinese and Europeans. [corrupt. of *business*]

pi-dog var. of PYE-DOG.

pie¹ /paɪ/ n. **1** a baked dish of meat, fish, fruit, etc., usu. with a top and base of pastry. **2** anything resembling a pie in form (*a mud pie*). □ **easy as pie** very easy. **pie chart** a circle divided into sectors to represent relative quantities. **pie-eater** *Austral. sl.* a person of little account. **pie-eyed** *sl.* drunk. **pie in the sky** an unrealistic prospect of future happiness after present suffering; a misleading promise. [ME, perh. = PIE² f. miscellaneous contents compared to objects collected by a magpie]

pie² /paɪ/ n. *archaic* **1** a magpie. **2** a pied animal. [ME f. OF f. L *pica*]

pie³ /paɪ/ n. & v. (*US* **pi**) —n. **1** a confused mass of printers' type. **2** chaos. —v.tr. (**pieing**) muddle up (type). [perh. transl. F PÂTÉ = PIE¹]

pie⁴ /paɪ/ n. *hist.* a former monetary unit of India equal to one-twelfth of an anna. [Hind. etc. *pā'ī* f. Skr. *pad, padī* quarter]

piebald /'paɪbɔːld/ adj. & n. —adj. **1** (usu. of an animal, esp. a horse) having irregular patches of two colours, esp. black and white. **2** motley; mongrel. —n. a piebald animal, esp. a horse.

piece /pi:s/ n. & v. —n. **1 a** (often foll. by *of*) one of the distinct portions forming part of or broken off from a larger object; a bit; a part (*a piece of string*). **b** each of the parts of which a set or category is composed (*a five-piece band*; *a piece of furniture*). **2** a coin of specified value (*50p piece*). **3 a** a usu. short literary or musical composition or a picture. **b** a theatrical play. **4** an item, instance, or example (*a piece of impudence*; *a piece of news*). **5 a** any of the objects used to make moves in board-games. **b** a chessman (strictly, other than a pawn). **6** a definite quantity in which a thing is sold. **7** (often foll. by *of*) an enclosed portion (of land etc.). **8** *derog. sl.* a woman. **9** *US* (foll. by *of*) *sl.* a financial share or investment in (*has a piece of the new production*). —v.tr. **1** (usu. foll. by *together*) form into a whole; put together; join (*finally pieced his story together*). **2** (usu. foll. by *out*) **a** eke out. **b** form (a theory etc.) by combining parts etc. **3** (usu. foll. by *up*) patch. **4** join (threads) in spinning. □ **break to pieces** break into fragments. **by the piece** (paid) according to the quantity of work done. **go to pieces** collapse emotionally; suffer a breakdown. **in one piece 1** unbroken. **2** unharmed. **in pieces** broken. **of a piece** (often foll. by *with*) uniform, consistent, in keeping. **piece-goods** fabrics, esp. Lancashire cottons, woven in standard lengths. **a piece of cake** see CAKE. **a piece of eight** *hist.* a Spanish dollar, equivalent to 8 reals. **piece of goods** *sl. derog.* a woman. **a piece of one's mind** a sharp rebuke or lecture. **piece of water** a small lake etc. **piece of work** a thing made by working (cf. *nasty piece of work*). **piece-rates** a rate paid according to the amount produced. **piece-work** work paid for by the amount produced. **say one's piece** give one's opinion or make a prepared statement. **take to pieces 1** break up or dismantle. **2** criticize harshly. □□ **piecer** n. (in sense 4 of *v.*). [ME f. AF *pece*, OF *piece* f. Rmc, prob. of Gaulish orig.: cf. PEAT]

pièce de résistance /ˌpjes də reɪ'zi:stɑ̃s/ n. (*pl.* **pièces de résistance** pronunc. same) **1** the most important or remarkable item. **2** the most substantial dish at a meal. [F]

piecemeal /'pi:smi:l/ adv. & adj. —adv. piece by

piece; gradually. —*adj.* partial; gradual; unsystematic. [ME f. PIECE + -*meal* f. OE *mǽlum* (instr. dative pl. of *mǽl* MEAL¹)]

piecrust /ˈpaɪkrʌst/ *n.* the baked pastry crust of a pie. □**piecrust table** a table with an indented edge like a piecrust.

pied /paɪd/ *adj.* particoloured. □**Pied Piper** a person enticing followers esp. to their doom. [ME f. PIE², orig. of friars)

pied-à-terre /ˌpjeɪdɑːˈteə(r)/ *n.* (*pl.* **pieds-à-terre** pronunc. same) a usu. small flat, house, etc. kept for occasional use. [F, lit. 'foot to earth']

piedmont /ˈpiːdmɒnt/ *n.* a gentle slope leading from the foot of mountains to a region of flat land. [It. *piemonte* mountain foot, name of a region at the foot of the Alps]

pie-dog var. of PYE-DOG.

pieman /ˈpaɪmən/ *n.* (*pl.* **-men**) a pie seller.

pier /pɪə(r)/ *n.* **1 a** a structure of iron or wood raised on piles and leading out to sea, a lake, etc., used as a promenade and landing-stage, and often with entertainment arcades etc. **b** a breakwater; a mole. **2 a** a support of an arch or of the span of a bridge; a pillar. **b** solid masonry between windows etc. □**pier-glass** a large mirror, used orig. to fill wall-space between windows. [ME *per* f. AL *pera*, of unkn. orig.]

pierce /pɪəs/ *v.* **1** *tr.* **a** (of a sharp instrument etc.) penetrate the surface of. **b** (often foll. by *with*) prick with a sharp instrument, esp. to make a hole in. **c** make (a hole etc.) (*pierced a hole in the belt*). **d** (of cold, grief, etc.) affect keenly or sharply. **e** (of a light, glance, sound, etc.) penetrate keenly or sharply. **2** (as **piercing** *adj.*) (of a glance, intuition, high noise, bright light, etc.) keen, sharp, or unpleasantly penetrating. **3** *tr.* force (a way etc.) through or into (something) (*pierced their way through the jungle*). **4** *intr.* (usu. foll. by *through*, *into*) penetrate. □□ **piercer** *n.* **piercingly** *adv.* [ME f. OF *percer* f. L *pertundere* bore through (as PER-, *tundere tus-* thrust)]

pierrot /ˈpɪərəʊ, ˈpjerəʊ/ *n.* (*fem.* **pierrette** /pɪəˈret, pjeˈret/) *Theatr.* **1** a white-faced entertainer in pier shows etc. with a loose white clown's costume. **2** a French pantomime character so dressed. [F, dimin. of *Pierre* Peter]

pietà /ˌpjeɪˈtɑː/ *n.* a picture or sculpture of the Virgin Mary holding the dead body of Christ on her lap or in her arms. [It. f. L (as PIETY)]

pietas /ˈpaɪəˌtɑːs/ *n.* respect due to an ancestor, a forerunner, etc. [L: see PIETY]

pietism /ˈpaɪəˌtɪz(ə)m/ *n.* **1 a** pious sentiment. **b** an exaggerated or affected piety. **2** (esp. as **Pietism**) *hist.* a movement for the revival of piety in the Lutheran Church in the 17th c. □□ **pietist** *n.* **pietistic** /-ˈtɪstɪk/ *adj.* **pietistical** /-ˈtɪstɪk(ə)l/ *adj.* [G *Pietismus* (as PIETY)]

piety /ˈpaɪɪtɪ/ *n.* (*pl.* **-ies**) **1** the quality of being pious. **2** a pious act. [ME f. OF *pieté* f. L *pietas -tatis* dutifulness (as PIOUS)]

piezoelectricity /paɪˌiːzəʊˌlekˈtrɪsɪtɪ/ *n.* electric polarization in a substance resulting from the application of mechanical stress, esp. in certain crystals. □□ **piezoelectric** /-ɪˈlektrɪk/ *adj.* **piezoelectrically** /-ɪˈlektrɪkəlɪ/ *adv.* [Gk *piezō* press + ELECTRIC]

piezometer /ˌpaɪɪˈzɒmɪtə(r)/ *n.* an instrument for measuring the magnitude or direction of pressure.

piffle /ˈpɪf(ə)l/ *n.* & *v.* *colloq.* —*n.* nonsense; empty speech. —*v.intr.* talk or act feebly; trifle. □□ **piffler** *n.* [imit.]

piffling /ˈpɪflɪŋ/ *adj.* *colloq.* trivial; worthless.

pig /pɪg/ *n.* & *v.* —*n.* **1 a** any omnivorous hoofed bristly mammal of the family Suidae, esp. a domesticated kind, *Sus scrofa*. **b** *US* a young pig, a piglet. **c** (often in *comb.*) any similar animal (*guinea-pig*). **2** the flesh of esp. a young or sucking pig as food (*roast pig*). **3** *colloq.* **a** a greedy, dirty, obstinate, sulky, or annoying person. **b** an unpleasant, awkward, or difficult thing, task, etc. **4** an oblong mass of metal (esp. iron or lead) from a smelting-furnace. **5** *sl. derog.* a policeman. —*v.* (**pigged, pigging**) **1** *tr.* (also *absol.*) (of a sow) bring forth (piglets). **2** *tr. colloq.* eat (food) greedily. **3** *intr.* herd together or behave like pigs. □**bleed like a pig** (or **stuck pig**) bleed copiously. **buy a pig in a poke** buy, accept, etc. something without knowing its value or esp. seeing it. **in pig** (of a sow) pregnant. **in a pig's eye** *colloq.* certainly not. **make a pig of oneself** overeat. **make a pig's ear of** *colloq.* make a mess of; bungle. **pig in the middle** a person who is placed in an awkward situation between two others (after a ball game for three with one in the middle). **pig-iron** crude iron from a smelting-furnace. **Pig Island** *Austral.* & *NZ sl.* New Zealand. **pig it** live in a disorderly, untidy, or filthy fashion. **pig-jump** *Austral. sl. n.* a jump made by a horse from all four legs. —*v.intr.* (of a horse) jump in this manner. **pig Latin** a made-up jargon. **pig-meat** *Brit.* pork, ham, or bacon. **pig out** (often foll. by *on*) esp. *US sl.* eat gluttonously. **pigs might fly** *iron.* an expression of disbelief. **pig-sticker** a long sharp knife. **pig's wash** = PIGSWILL. □□ **piggish** *adj.* **piggishly** *adv.* **piggishness** *n.* **piglet** *n.* **piglike** *adj.* **pigling** *n.* [ME *pigge* f. OE *pigga* (unrecorded)]

pigeon¹ /ˈpɪdʒɪn, -dʒ(ə)n/ *n.* **1** any of several large usu. grey and white birds of the family Columbidae, esp. *Columba livia*, often domesticated and bred to carry messages etc.; a dove (cf. *rock-pigeon*). **2** a person easily swindled; a simpleton. □**pigeon-breast** (or **-chest**) a deformed human chest with a projecting breastbone. **pigeon-breasted** (or **-chested**) having a pigeon-breast. **pigeon-fancier** a person who keeps and breeds fancy pigeons. **pigeon-fancying** this pursuit. **pigeon-hawk** = MERLIN. **pigeon-hearted** cowardly. **pigeon-hole** *n.* **1** each of a set of compartments in a cabinet or on a wall for papers, letters, etc. **2** a small recess for a pigeon to nest in. —*v.tr.* **1** deposit (a document) in a pigeon-hole. **2** put (a matter) aside for future consideration or to forget it. **3** assign (a person or thing) to a preconceived category. **pigeon pair** *Brit.* **1** boy and girl twins. **2** a boy and girl as sole children. **pigeon's milk 1** a secretion from the oesophagus with which pigeons feed their young. **2** an imaginary article for which children are sent on a fool's errand. **pigeon-toed** (of a person) having the toes turned inwards. □□ **pigeonry** *n.* (*pl.* **-ies**). [ME f. OF *pijon* f. LL *pipio -onis* (imit.)]

pigeon² /ˈpɪdʒɪn, -dʒ(ə)n/ *n.* **1** = PIDGIN. **2** *colloq.* a particular concern, job, or business (*that's not my pigeon*).

piggery /ˈpɪgərɪ/ *n.* (*pl.* **-ies**) **1** a pig-breeding farm etc. **2** = PIGSTY. **3** piggishness.

piggy /ˈpɪgɪ/ *n.* & *adj.* —*n.* (also **piggie**) *colloq.* **1** a little pig. **2 a** a child's word for a pig. **b** a child's word for a toe. **3** *Brit.* the game of tipcat. —*adj.* (**piggier, piggiest**) **1** like a pig. **2** (of features etc.) like those of a pig (*little piggy eyes*). □**piggy bank** a pig-shaped money box. **piggy in the middle** = *pig in the middle*.

piggyback /ˈpɪgɪˌbæk/ *n.* & *adv.* (also **pickaback** /ˈpɪkəˌbæk/) —*n.* a ride on the back and shoulders of another person. —*adv.* **1** on the back and shoulders of another person. **2** on the back or top of a larger object. [16th c.: orig. unkn.]

pigheaded /pɪgˈhedɪd/ *adj.* obstinate. □□ **pigheadedly** *adv.* **pigheadedness** *n.*

pigment /ˈpɪgmənt/ *n.* & *v.* —*n.* **1** colouring-matter used as paint or dye, usu. as an insoluble suspension. **2** the natural colouring-matter of animal or plant tissue, e.g. chlorophyll, haemoglobin. —*v.tr.* colour with or as if with pigment. □□ **pigmental** /-ˈment(ə)l/ *adj.* **pigmentary** *adj.* [ME f. L *pigmentum* f. *pingere* paint]

pigmentation /ˌpɪgmənˈteɪʃ(ə)n/ *n.* **1** the natural

colouring of plants, animals, etc. **2** the excessive colouring of tissue by the deposition of pigment.

pigmy var. of PYGMY.

pignut /'pɪgnʌt/ n. = earth-nut.

pigpen /'pɪgpen/ n. US = PIGSTY.

pigskin /'pɪgskɪn/ n. **1** the hide of a pig. **2** leather made from this. **3** US a football.

pigsticking /'pɪg,stɪkɪŋ/ n. **1** the hunting of wild boar with a spear on horseback. **2** the butchering of pigs.

pigsty /'pɪgstaɪ/ n. (pl. -ies) **1** a pen or enclosure for a pig or pigs. **2** a filthy house, room, etc.

pigswill /'pɪgswɪl/ n. kitchen refuse and scraps fed to pigs.

pigtail /'pɪgteɪl/ n. **1** a plait of hair hanging from the back of the head, or either of a pair at the sides. **2** a thin twist of tobacco. □□ **pigtailed** adj.

pigwash /'pɪgwɒʃ/ n. = PIGSWILL.

pigweed /'pɪgwiːd/ n. any herb of the genus Amaranthus, grown for grain or fodder.

pika /'paɪkə/ n. any small rabbit-like mammal of the genus Ochotona, with small ears and no tail. [Tungus piika]

pike[1] /paɪk/ n. (pl. same) **1** a large voracious freshwater fish, Esox lucius, with a long narrow snout and sharp teeth. **2** any other fish of the family Esocidae. □ **pike-perch** any of various pikelike perches of the genus Lucioperca or Stizostedion. [ME, = PIKE[2] (because of its pointed jaw)]

pike[2] /paɪk/ n. & v. —n. **1** hist. an infantry weapon with a pointed steel or iron head on a long wooden shaft. **2** N.Engl. the peaked top of a hill, esp. in names of hills in the Lake District. —v.tr. thrust through or kill with a pike. □ **pike on** colloq. withdraw timidly from. [OE pīc point, prick: sense 2 perh. f. ON]

pike[3] /paɪk/ n. **1** a toll-gate; a toll. **2** a turnpike road. [abbr. of TURNPIKE]

pike[4] /paɪk/ n. a jackknife position in diving or gymnastics. [20th c.: orig. unkn.]

pikelet /'paɪklɪt/ n. N.Engl. a thin kind of crumpet. [Welsh (bara) pyglyd pitchy (bread)]

pikeman /'paɪkmən/ n. (pl. -men) the keeper of a turnpike.

piker /'paɪkə(r)/ n. a cautious, timid, or mean person.

pikestaff /'paɪkstɑːf/ n. **1** the wooden shaft of a pike. **2** a walking-stick with a metal point. □ **plain as a pikestaff** quite plain or obvious (orig. packstaff, a smooth staff used by a pedlar).

pilaster /pɪ'læstə(r)/ n. a rectangular column, esp. one projecting from a wall. □□ **pilastered** adj. [F pilastre f. It. pilastro f. med.L pilastrum f. L pila pillar]

pilau /pɪ'laʊ/ n. (also **pilaff** /pɪ'læf/, **pilaw** /pɪ'lɔː/) a Middle Eastern or Indian dish of spiced rice or wheat with meat, fish, vegetables, etc. [Turk. pilāv]

pilch /pɪltʃ/ n. archaic a baby's usu. waterproof garment worn over a nappy. [OE pyl(e)ce f. LL pellicia: see PELISSE]

pilchard /'pɪltʃəd/ n. a small marine fish, Sardinia pilchardus of the herring family (see SARDINE). [16th c. pilcher etc.: orig. unkn.]

pile[1] /paɪl/ n. & v. —n. **1** a heap of things laid or gathered upon one another (a pile of leaves). **2 a** a large imposing building (a stately pile). **b** a large group of tall buildings. **3** colloq. **a** a large quantity. **b** a large amount of money; a fortune (made his pile). **4 a** a series of plates of dissimilar metals laid one on another alternately to produce an electric current. **b** = atomic pile. **5** a funeral pyre. —v. **1** tr. **a** (often foll. by up, on) heap up (piled the plates on the table). **b** (foll. by with) load (piled the bed with coats). **2** intr. (usu. foll. by in, into, on, out of, etc.) crowd hurriedly or tightly (all piled into the car; piled out of the restaurant). □ **pile arms** hist. place (usu. four) rifles with their butts on the ground and the muzzles together. **pile it on** colloq. exaggerate. **pile on the agony** colloq. exaggerate for effect or to gain

sympathy etc. **pile up 1** accumulate; heap up. **2** colloq. run (a ship) aground or cause (a vehicle etc.) to crash. **pile-up** n. colloq. a multiple crash of road vehicles. [ME f. OF f. L pila pillar, pier, mole]

pile[2] /paɪl/ n. & v. —n. **1** a heavy beam driven vertically into the bed of a river, soft ground, etc., to support the foundations of a superstructure. **2** a pointed stake or post. **3** Heraldry a wedge-shaped device. —v.tr. **1** provide with piles. **2** drive (piles) into the ground etc. □ **pile-driver** a machine for driving piles into the ground. **pile-dwelling** a dwelling built on piles, esp. in a lake. [OE pīl f. L pilum javelin]

pile[3] /paɪl/ n. **1** the soft projecting surface on velvet, plush, etc., or esp. on a carpet; nap. **2** soft hair or down, or the wool of a sheep. [ME prob. f. AF pyle, peile, OF poil f. L pilus hair]

piles /paɪlz/ n.pl. colloq. haemorrhoids. [ME prob. f. L pila ball, f. the globular form of external piles]

pileus /'paɪlɪəs/ n. (pl. **pilei** /-lɪ,aɪ/) the caplike part of a mushroom or other fungus. □□ **pileate** /-lɪət/ adj. **pileated** /-lɪ,eɪtɪd/ adj. [L, = felt cap]

pilewort /'paɪlwɜːt/ n. the lesser celandine. [PILES, f. its reputed efficacy against piles]

pilfer /'pɪlfə(r)/ v.tr. (also absol.) steal (objects) esp. in small quantities. □□ **pilferage** /-rɪdʒ/ n. **pilferer** n. [ME f. AF & OF pelfrer pillage, of unkn. orig.: assoc. with archaic pill plunder: PELF]

pilgrim /'pɪlgrɪm/ n. & v. —n. **1** a person who journeys to a sacred place for religious reasons. **2** a person regarded as journeying through life etc. **3** a traveller. —v.intr. (**pilgrimed**, **pilgriming**) wander like a pilgrim. □ **Pilgrim Fathers** English Puritans who founded the colony of Plymouth, Massachusetts, in 1620. □□ **pilgrimize** v.intr. (also -ise). [ME pilegrim f. Prov. pelegrin f. L peregrinus stranger: see PEREGRINE]

pilgrimage /'pɪlgrɪmɪdʒ/ n. & v. —n. **1** a pilgrim's journey (go on a pilgrimage). **2** life viewed as a journey. **3** any journey taken for nostalgic or sentimental reasons. —v.intr. go on a pilgrimage. [ME f. Prov. pilgrinatge (as PILGRIM)]

Pilipino /,pɪlɪ'piːnəʊ/ n. the national language of the Philippines. [Tagalog f. Sp. Filipino]

pill /pɪl/ n. **1 a** solid medicine formed into a ball or a flat disc for swallowing whole. **b** (usu. prec. by the) colloq. a contraceptive pill. **2** an unpleasant or painful necessity; a humiliation (a bitter pill; must swallow the pill). **3** colloq. or joc. a ball, e.g. a football, a cannon-ball. □ **sugar** (or **sweeten**) **the pill** make an unpleasant necessity acceptable. [MDu., MLG pille prob. f. L pilula dimin. of pila ball]

pillage /'pɪlɪdʒ/ v. & n. —v.tr. (also absol.) plunder; sack (a place or a person). —n. the act or an instance of pillaging, esp. in war. □□ **pillager** n. [ME f. OF f. piller plunder]

pillar /'pɪlə(r)/ n. **1 a** a usu. slender vertical structure of wood, metal, or esp. stone used as a support for a roof etc. **b** a similar structure used for ornament. **c** a post supporting a structure. **2** a person regarded as a mainstay or support (a pillar of the faith; a pillar of strength). **3** an upright mass of air, water, rock, etc. (pillar of salt). **4** a solid mass of coal etc. left to support the roof of a mine. □ **from pillar to post** (driven etc.) from one place to another; to and fro. **pillar-box** Brit. a public postbox shaped like a pillar. **pillar-box red** a bright red colour, as of pillar-boxes. **Pillars of Hercules 1** two rocks on either side of the Strait of Gibraltar. **2** the ultimate limit. □□ **pillared** adj. **pillaret** n. [ME & AF piler, OF pilier ult. f. L pila pillar]

pillbox /'pɪlbɒks/ n. **1** a small shallow cylindrical box for holding pills. **2** a hat of a similar shape. **3** Mil. a small partly underground enclosed concrete fort used as an outpost.

pillion /'pɪljən/ n. **1** seating for a passenger behind a motor cyclist. **2** hist. **a** a woman's light saddle. **b** a cushion attached to the back of a saddle for a usu.

female passenger. □**ride pillion** travel seated behind a motor cyclist etc. [Gael. *pillean*, *pillin* dimin. of *pell* cushion f. L *pellis* skin]

pilliwinks /'pɪlɪwɪŋks/ *n. hist.* an instrument of torture used for squeezing the fingers. [ME *pyrwykes*, *pyrewinkes*, of unkn. orig.]

pillock /'pɪlək/ *n. Brit. sl.* a stupid person; a fool. [16th c., = penis (var. of *pillicock*): 20th c. in sense defined]

pillory /'pɪlərɪ/ *n. & v. —n.* (*pl.* -**ies**) *hist.* a wooden framework with holes for the head and hands, enabling the public to assault or ridicule a person so imprisoned. —*v.tr.* (-**ies**, -**ied**) **1** expose (a person) to ridicule or public contempt. **2** *hist.* put in the pillory. [ME f. AL *pillorium* f. OF *pilori* etc.: prob. f. Prov. *espilori* of uncert. orig.]

pillow /'pɪləʊ/ *n. & v. —n.* **1 a** a usu. oblong support for the head, esp. in bed, with a cloth cover stuffed with feathers, flock, foam rubber, etc. **b** any pillow-shaped block or support. **2** = *lace-pillow*. —*v.tr.* **1** rest (the head etc.) on or as if on a pillow (*pillowed his head on his arms*). **2** serve as a pillow for (*moss pillowed her head*). □**pillow-fight** a mock fight with pillows, esp. by children. **pillow-lace** lace made on a lace-pillow. **pillow lava** lava forming rounded masses. **pillow talk** romantic or intimate conversation in bed. □□**pillowy** *adj.* [OE *pyle*, *pylu*, ult. f. L *pulvinus* cushion]

pillowcase /'pɪləʊˌkeɪs/ *n.* a washable cotton etc. cover for a pillow.

pillowslip /'pɪləʊslɪp/ *n.* = PILLOWCASE.

pillule var. of PILULE.

pillwort /'pɪlwɜːt/ *n.* an aquatic fern, *Pilularia globulifera*, with small globular spore-producing bracts.

pilose /'paɪləʊz/ *adj.* (also **pilous** /'paɪləs/) covered with hair. □□ **pilosity** /paɪ'lɒsɪtɪ/ *n.* [L *pilosus* f. *pilus* hair]

pilot /'paɪlət/ *n. & v. —n.* **1** a person who operates the flying controls of an aircraft. **2** a person qualified to take charge of a ship entering or leaving harbour. **3** (usu. *attrib.*) an experimental undertaking or test, esp. in advance of a larger one (*a pilot project*). **4** a guide; a leader. **5** *archaic* a steersman. —*v.tr.* (**piloted**, **piloting**) **1** act as a pilot on (a ship) or of (an aircraft). **2** conduct, lead, or initiate as a pilot (*piloted the new scheme*). □**pilot balloon** a small balloon used to track air currents etc. **pilot-bird** a rare dark-brown Australian babbler, *Pycnoptilus floccosus*, with a distinctive loud cry. **pilot chute** a small parachute used to bring the main one into operation. **pilot-cloth** thick blue woollen cloth for seamen's coats etc. **pilot-fish** a small fish, *Naucrates ductor*, said to act as a pilot leading a shark to food. **pilot-house** = *wheel-house*. **pilot-jacket** = PEA-JACKET. **pilot-light 1** a small gas burner kept alight to light another. **2** an electric indicator light or control light. **pilot officer** *Brit.* the lowest commissioned rank in the RAF. □□ **pilotage** *n.* **pilotless** *adj.* [F *pilote* f. med.L *pilotus*, *pedot(t)a* f. Gk *pēdon* oar]

Pilsner /'pɪlznə(r)/, -snə(r)/ *n.* (also **Pilsener**) a lager beer brewed or like that brewed at *Pilsen* (Plzen) in Czechoslovakia.

pilule /'pɪljuːl/ *n.* (also **pillule**) a small pill. □□ **pilular** *adj.* **pilulous** *adj.* [F f. L *pilula*: see PILL]

pimento /pɪ'mentəʊ/ *n.* (*pl.* -**os**) **1** a small tropical tree, *Pimenta dioica*, native to Jamaica. **2** the unripe dried berries of this, usu. crushed for culinary use. Also called ALLSPICE. **3** = PIMIENTO. [Sp. *pimiento* (as PIMIENTO)]

pimiento /ˌpɪmɪ'entəʊ, pɪm'jentəʊ/ *n.* (*pl.* -**os**) = *sweet pepper* (see PEPPER). [Sp. f. L *pigmentum* PIGMENT, in med.L = spice]

pimp /pɪmp/ *n. & v. —n.* a man who lives off the earnings of a prostitute or a brothel; a pander; a ponce. —*v.intr.* act as a pimp. [17th c.: orig. unkn.]

pimpernel /'pɪmpəˌnel/ *n.* any plant of the genus *Anagallis*, esp. = *scarlet pimpernel*. [ME f. OF *pimpernelle*, *piprenelle* ult. f. L *piper* PEPPER]

pimping /'pɪmpɪŋ/ *adj.* **1** small or mean. **2** sickly. [17th c.: orig. unkn.]

pimple /'pɪmp(ə)l/ *n.* **1** a small hard inflamed spot on the skin. **2** anything resembling a pimple, esp. in relative size. □□ **pimpled** *adj.* **pimply** *adj.* [ME nasalized f. OE *piplian* break out in pustules]

PIN /pɪn/ *n.* personal identification number (as issued by a bank etc. to validate electronic transactions). [abbr.]

pin /pɪn/ *n. & v. —n.* **1 a** a small thin pointed piece of esp. steel wire with a round or flattened head used (esp. in sewing) for holding things in place, attaching one thing to another, etc. **b** any of several types of pin (*drawing-pin*; *safety pin*; *hairpin*). **c** a small brooch (*diamond pin*). **d** a badge fastened with a pin. **2** a peg of wood or metal for various purposes, e.g. a wooden skittle in bowling. **3** something of small value (*don't care a pin*; *for two pins I'd resign*). **4** (in *pl.*) *colloq.* legs (*quick on his pins*). **5** *Med.* a steel rod used to join the ends of fractured bones while they heal. **6** *Chess* a position in which a piece is pinned to another. **7** *Golf* a stick with a flag placed in a hole to mark its position. **8** *Mus.* a peg round which one string of a musical instrument is fastened. **9** a half-firkin cask for beer. —*v.tr.* (**pinned**, **pinning**) **1 a** (often foll. by *to*, *up*, *together*) fasten with a pin or pins (*pinned up the hem*; *pinned the papers together*). **b** transfix with a pin, lance, etc. **2** (usu. foll. by *on*) fix (blame, responsibility, etc.) on a person etc. (*pinned the blame on his friend*). **3** (often foll. by *against*, *on*, etc.) seize and hold fast. **4** *Chess* prevent (an opposing piece) from moving except by exposing a more valuable piece to capture. □**on pins and needles** in an agitated state of suspense. **pin down 1** (often foll. by *to*) bind (a person etc.) to a promise, arrangement, etc. **2** force (a person) to declare his or her intentions. **3** restrict the actions or movement of (an enemy etc.). **4** specify (a thing) precisely (*could not pin down his unease to a particular cause*). **5** hold (a person etc.) down by force. **pin one's faith** (or **hopes** etc.) **on** rely implicitly on. **pin-feather** *Zool.* an ungrown feather. **pin-high** *Golf* (of a ball) at the same distance ahead as the pin. **pin-money 1** *hist.* an allowance to a woman for dress etc. from her husband. **2** a very small sum of money, esp. for spending on inessentials (*only works for pin-money*). **pins and needles** a tingling sensation in a limb recovering from numbness. **pin-table** a table used in playing pinball. **pin-tuck** a very narrow ornamental tuck. **pin-up 1** a photograph of a popular or sexually attractive person, designed to be hung on the wall. **2** a person shown in such a photograph. **pin-wheel** a small Catherine wheel. **split pin** a metal cotter pin passed through a hole and held in place by its gaping split end. [OE *pinn* f. L *pinna* point etc., assoc. with *penna* PEN¹]

pina colada /ˌpiːnə kə'lɑːdə/ *n.* a drink made from pineapple juice, rum, and coconut. [Sp., lit. 'strained pineapple']

pinafore /'pɪnəˌfɔː(r)/ *n.* esp. *Brit.* **1 a** an apron, esp. with a bib. **b** a woman's sleeveless wraparound washable covering for the clothes, tied at the back. **2** (in full **pinafore dress**) a collarless sleeveless dress worn over a blouse or jumper. [PIN + AFORE (because orig. pinned on the front of a dress)]

pinaster /paɪ'næstə(r)/ *n.* = *cluster pine*. [L, = wild pine f. *pinus* pine + -ASTER]

pinball /'pɪnbɔːl/ *n.* a game in which small metal balls are shot across a board and score points by striking pins with lights etc.

pince-nez /'pænsneɪ, pæs'neɪ/ *n.* (*pl.* same) a pair of eyeglasses with a nose-clip instead of earpieces. [F, lit. = pinch-nose]

pincers /'pɪnsəz/ *n.pl.* **1** (also **pair of pincers**) a gripping-tool resembling scissors but with blunt usu. concave jaws to hold a nail etc. for extraction. **2** the front claws of lobsters and some other crustaceans. □**pincer movement** *Mil.* a movement by two wings of an army converging on the enemy. [ME *pinsers*, *pinsours* f. AF f. OF *pincier* PINCH]

pincette /pæˈset/ *n.* small pincers; tweezers. [F]

pinch /pɪntʃ/ *v. & n.* —*v.* **1** *tr.* **a** grip (esp. the skin of part of the body or of another person) tightly, esp. between finger and thumb (*pinched my finger in the door*; *stop pinching me*). **b** (often *absol.*) (of a shoe, garment, etc.) constrict (the flesh) painfully. **2** *tr.* (of cold, hunger, etc.) grip (a person) painfully (*she was pinched with cold*). **3** *tr. sl.* **a** steal; take without permission. **b** arrest (a person) (*pinched him for loitering*). **4** (as **pinched** *adj.*) (of the features) drawn, as with cold, hunger, worry, etc. **5 a** *tr.* (usu. foll. by *in*, *of*, *for*, etc.) stint (a person). **b** *intr.* be niggardly with money, food, etc. **6** *tr.* (usu. foll. by *out*, *back*, *down*) *Hort.* remove (leaves, buds, etc.) to encourage bushy growth. **7** *intr.* sail very close to the wind. —*n.* **1** the act or an instance of pinching etc. the flesh. **2** an amount that can be taken up with fingers and thumb (*a pinch of snuff*). **3** the stress or pain caused by poverty, cold, hunger, etc. **4** *sl.* **a** an arrest. **b** a theft. □**at** (or **in**) **a pinch** in an emergency; if necessary. **feel the pinch** experience the effects of poverty. **pinch-hitter** *US* **1** a baseball player who bats instead of another in an emergency. **2** a person acting as a substitute. [ME f. AF & ONF *pinchier* (unrecorded), OF *pincier*, ult. f. L *pungere* *punct-* prick]

pinchbeck /ˈpɪntʃbek/ *n. & adj.* —*n.* an alloy of copper and zinc resembling gold and used in cheap jewellery etc. —*adj.* **1** counterfeit; sham. **2** cheap; tawdry. [C. *Pinchbeck*, Engl. watchmaker d. 1732]

pinchpenny /ˈpɪntʃˌpeni/ *n.* (*pl.* -**ies**) (also *attrib.*) a miserly person.

pincushion /ˈpɪnˌkʊʃ(ə)n/ *n.* a small cushion for holding pins.

pine[1] /paɪn/ *n.* **1** any evergreen tree of the genus *Pinus* native to northern temperate regions, with needle-shaped leaves growing in clusters. **2** the soft timber of this, often used to make furniture. Also called DEAL[2]. **3** (*attrib.*) made of pine. **4** = PINEAPPLE. □**pine cone** the cone-shaped fruit of the pine tree. **pine marten** a weasel-like mammal, *Martes martes*, native to Europe and America, with a dark brown coat and white throat and stomach. **pine nut** the edible seed of various pine trees. □□**pinery** *n.* (*pl.* -**ies**). [ME f. OE *pīn* & OF *pin* f. L *pinus*]

pine[2] /paɪn/ *v.intr.* **1** (often foll. by *away*) decline or waste away, esp. from grief, disease, etc. **2** (usu. foll. by *for*, *after*, or *to* + infin.) long eagerly; yearn. [OE *pīnian*, rel. to obs. E *pine* punishment, f. Gmc f. med.L *pena*, L *poena*]

pineal /ˈpɪnɪəl, ˈpaɪ-/ *adj.* shaped like a pine cone. □**pineal body** (or **gland**) a pea-sized conical mass of tissue behind the third ventricle of the brain, secreting a hormone-like substance in some mammals. [F *pinéal* f. L *pinea* pine cone: see PINE[1]]

pineapple /ˈpaɪnˌæp(ə)l/ *n.* **1** a tropical plant, *Ananas comosus*, with a spiral of sword-shaped leaves and a thick stem bearing a large fruit developed from many flowers. **2** the fruit of this, consisting of yellow flesh surrounded by a tough segmented skin and topped with a tuft of stiff leaves. [PINE[1], from the fruit's resemblance to a pine cone]

pinetum /paɪˈniːtəm/ *n.* (*pl.* **pineta** /-tə/) a plantation of pine-trees or other conifers for scientific or ornamental purposes. [L f. *pinus* pine]

pinfold /ˈpɪnfəʊld/ *n. & v.* —*n.* a pound for stray cattle etc. —*v.tr.* confine (cattle) in a pinfold. [OE *pundfald* (as POUND[3], FOLD[2])]

ping /pɪŋ/ *n. & v.* —*n.* a single short high ringing sound. —*v.intr.* make a ping. [imit.]

pinger /ˈpɪŋə(r)/ *n.* **1** a device that transmits pings at short intervals for purposes of detection or measurement etc. **2** a device to ring a bell.

pingo /ˈpɪŋgəʊ/ *n.* (*pl.* -**os**) *Geol.* a dome-shaped mound found in permafrost areas. [Eskimo]

ping-pong /ˈpɪŋpɒŋ/ *n.* = *table tennis*. [imit. f. the sound of a bat striking a ball]

pinguid /ˈpɪŋgwɪd/ *adj. formal* or *joc.* fat, oily, or greasy. [L *pinguis* fat]

pinhead /ˈpɪnhed/ *n.* **1** the flattened head of a pin. **2** a very small thing. **3** *colloq.* a stupid or foolish person.

pinheaded /pɪnˈhedɪd/ *adj. colloq.* stupid, foolish. □□**pinheadedness** *n.*

pinhole /ˈpɪnhəʊl/ *n.* **1** a hole made by a pin. **2** a hole into which a peg fits. □**pinhole camera** a camera with a pinhole aperture and no lens.

pinion[1] /ˈpɪnjən/ *n. & v.* —*n.* **1** the outer part of a bird's wing, usu. including the flight feathers. **2** *poet.* a wing; a flight-feather. —*v.tr.* **1** cut off the pinion of (a wing or bird) to prevent flight. **2 a** bind the arms of (a person). **b** (often foll. by *to*) bind (the arms, a person, etc.) esp. to a thing. [ME f. OF *pignon* ult. f. L *pinna*: see PIN]

pinion[2] /ˈpɪnjən/ *n.* **1** a small cog-wheel engaging with a larger one. **2** a cogged spindle engaging with a wheel. [F *pignon* alt. f. obs. *pignol* f. L *pinea* pine-cone (as PINE[1])]

pink[1] /pɪŋk/ *n. & adj.* —*n.* **1** a pale red colour (*decorated in pink*). **2 a** any cultivated plant of the genus *Dianthus*, with sweet-smelling white, pink, crimson, etc. flowers. **b** the flower of this plant. **3** (prec. by *the*) the most perfect condition etc. (*the pink of elegance*). **4** (also **hunting-pink**) **a** a fox-hunter's red coat. **b** the cloth for this. **c** a fox-hunter. —*adj.* **1** (often in *comb.*) of a pale red colour of any of various shades (*rose-pink*; *salmon-pink*). **2** esp. *derog.* tending to socialism. □**in the pink** *colloq.* in very good health. **pink-collar** (usu. *attrib.*) (of a profession etc.) traditionally associated with women (cf. *white-collar*, *blue-collar* (see BLUE[1])). **pink disease** a disease of young children with pink discoloration of the extremities. **pink elephants** *colloq.* hallucinations caused by alcoholism. **pink-eye 1** a contagious fever in horses. **2** contagious ophthalmia in humans and some livestock. **pink-gin** gin flavoured with angostura bitters. □□**pinkish** *adj.* **pinkly** *adv.* **pinkness** *n.* **pinky** *adj.* [perh. f. dial. *pink-eyed* having small eyes]

pink[2] /pɪŋk/ *v.tr.* **1** pierce slightly with a sword etc. **2** cut a scalloped or zigzag edge on. **3** (often foll. by *out*) ornament (leather etc.) with perforations. **4** adorn; deck. □**pinking shears** (or **scissors**) a dressmaker's serrated shears for cutting a zigzag edge. [ME, perh. f. LG or Du.: cf. LG *pinken* strike, peck]

pink[3] /pɪŋk/ *v.intr.* (of a vehicle engine) emit a series of high-pitched explosive sounds caused by faulty combustion. [imit.]

pink[4] /pɪŋk/ *n. hist.* a sailing-ship, esp. with a narrow stern, orig. small and flat-bottomed. [ME f. MDu. *pin(c)ke*, of unkn. orig.]

pink[5] /pɪŋk/ *n.* a yellowish lake pigment made by combining vegetable colouring matter with a white base (*brown pink*; *French pink*). [17th c.: orig. unkn.]

pink[6] /pɪŋk/ *n. Brit.* **1** a young salmon. **2** *dial.* a minnow. [15th c. *penk*, of unkn. orig.]

pinkie /ˈpɪŋkɪ/ *n.* esp. *US & Sc.* the little finger. [cf. dial. *pink* small, half-shut (eye)]

Pinkster /ˈpɪŋkstə(r)/ *n. US* Whitsuntide. □**pinkster flower** the pink azalea, *Rhododendron nudiflorum*. [Du., = Pentecost]

pinna /ˈpɪnə/ *n.* (*pl.* **pinnae** /-niː/ or **pinnas**) **1** the auricle; the external part of the ear. **2** a primary division of a pinnate leaf. **3** a fin or finlike structure, feather, wing, etc. [L, = *penna* feather, wing, fin]

pinnace /ˈpɪnɪs/ *n. Naut.* a warship's or other ship's small boat, usu. motor-driven, orig. schooner-rigged or eight-oared. [F *pinnace*, *pinasse* ult. f. L *pinus* PINE[1]]

pinnacle /ˈpɪnək(ə)l/ *n. & v.* —*n.* **1** the culmination or climax (of endeavour, success, etc.). **2** a natural peak. **3** a small ornamental turret usu. ending in a pyramid or cone, crowning a buttress, roof, etc. —*v.tr.* **1** set on or as if on a pinnacle. **2** form the pinnacle of. **3** provide with pinnacles. [ME *pinacle* f. OF *pin(n)acle* f. LL *pinnaculum* f. *pinna* wing, point (as PIN, -CULE)]

pinnae *pl.* of PINNA.

pinnate /'pɪneɪt/ *adj.* **1** (of a compound leaf) having leaflets arranged on either side of the stem, usu. in pairs opposite each other. **2** having branches, tentacles, etc., on each side of an axis. □□ **pinnated** *adj.* **pinnately** *adv.* **pinnation** /-'neɪʃ(ə)n/ *n.* [L *pinnatus* feathered (as PINNA)]

pinni- /'pɪnɪ/ *comb. form* wing, fin. [L *pinna*]

pinniped /'pɪnɪˌped/ *adj. & n.* —*adj.* denoting any aquatic mammal with limbs ending in fins. —*n.* a pinniped mammal. [L *pinna* fin + *pes ped-* foot]

pinnule /'pɪnjuːl/ *n.* **1** the secondary division of a pinnate leaf. **2** a part or organ like a small wing or fin. □□ **pinnular** *adj.* [L *pinnula* dimin. of *pinna* fin, wing]

pinny /'pɪnɪ/ *n.* (*pl.* -**ies**) *colloq.* a pinafore. [abbr.]

pinochle /'piːˌnʌk(ə)l/ *n.* US **1** a card-game with a double pack of 48 cards (nine to ace only). **2** the combination of queen of spades and jack of diamonds in this game. [19th c.: orig. unkn.]

pinole /pɪ'nəʊlɪ/ *n.* US flour made from parched cornflour, esp. mixed with sweet flour made of mesquite beans, sugar, etc. [Amer. Sp. f. Aztec *pinolli*]

piñon /pɪ'njəʊn/ *n.* **1** a pine, *Pinus cembra*, bearing edible seeds. **2** the seed of this, a type of pine nut. [Sp. f. L *pinea* pine cone]

pinpoint /'pɪnpɔɪnt/ *n. & v.* —*n.* **1** the point of a pin. **2** something very small or sharp. **3** (*attrib.*) **a** very small. **b** precise, accurate. —*v.tr.* locate with precision (*pinpointed the target*).

pinprick /'pɪnprɪk/ *n.* **1** a prick caused by a pin. **2** a trifling irritation.

pinstripe /'pɪnstraɪp/ *n.* **1** a very narrow stripe in (esp. worsted or serge) cloth. **2** a fabric or garment with this.

pint /paɪnt/ *n.* **1** a measure of capacity for liquids etc., one-eighth of a gallon or 20 fluid oz. (0.568 litre). **2** *Brit. colloq.* a pint of beer. **b** a pint of a liquid, esp. milk. **3** *Brit.* a measure of shellfish, being the amount containable in a pint mug (*bought a pint of whelks*). □ **pint-pot** a pot, esp. of pewter, holding one pint, esp. of beer. **pint-sized** *colloq.* very small, esp. of a person. [ME f. OF *pinte*, of unkn. orig.]

pinta /'paɪntə/ *n. Brit. colloq.* a pint of milk. [corrupt. of *pint of*]

pintail /'pɪnteɪl/ *n.* a duck, esp. *Anas acuta*, or grouse with a pointed tail.

pintle /'pɪnt(ə)l/ *n.* a pin or bolt, esp. one on which some other part turns. [OE *pintel* penis, of unkn. orig.: cf. OFris. etc. *pint*]

pinto /'pɪntəʊ, 'piː-/ *adj. & n.* US —*adj.* piebald. —*n.* (*pl.* -**os**) a piebald horse. [Sp., = mottled, ult. f. L *pictus* past part. of *pingere* paint]

pinworm /'pɪnwɜːm/ *n.* a small parasitic nematode worm, *Enterobius vermicularis*, of which the female has a pointed tail.

piny /'paɪnɪ/ *adj.* of, like, or full of pines.

Pinyin /'pɪn'jɪn/ *n.* a system of romanized spelling for transliterating Chinese. [Chin. *pīn-yīn*, lit. 'spell sound']

piolet /pjəʊ'leɪ/ *n.* a two-headed ice-axe for mountaineering. [F]

pion /'paɪɒn/ *n. Physics* a meson having a mass approximately 270 times that of an electron. Also called *pi meson* (see PI[1]). □□ **pionic** /paɪ'ɒnɪk/ *adj.* [PI[1] (the letter used as a symbol for the particle) + -ON]

pioneer /ˌpaɪə'nɪə(r)/ *n. & v.* —*n.* **1** an initiator of a new enterprise, an inventor, etc. **2** an explorer or settler; a colonist. **3** *Mil.* a member of an infantry

group preparing roads, terrain, etc. for the main body of troops. —*v.* **1 a** *tr.* initiate or originate (an enterprise etc.). **b** *intr.* act or prepare the way as a pioneer. **2** *tr. Mil.* open up (a road etc.) as a pioneer. **3** *tr.* go before, lead, or conduct (another person or persons). [F *pionnier* foot-soldier, pioneer, OF *paonier, peon(n)ier* (as PEON)]

pious /'paɪəs/ *adj.* **1** devout; religious. **2** hypocritically virtuous; sanctimonious. **3** dutiful. □ **pious fraud** a deception intended to benefit those deceived, esp. religiously. □□ **piously** *adv.* **piousness** *n.* [L *pius* dutiful, pious]

pip[1] *n. & v.* —*n.* the seed of an apple, pear, orange, grape, etc. —*v.tr.* (**pipped, pipping**) remove the pips from (fruit etc.). □□ **pipless** *adj.* [abbr. of PIPPIN]

pip[2] /pɪp/ *n. Brit.* a short high-pitched sound, usu. mechanically produced, esp. as a radio time signal. [imit.]

pip[3] /pɪp/ *n.* **1** any of the spots on a playing-card, dice, or domino. **2** *Brit.* a star (1–3 according to rank) on the shoulder of an army officer's uniform. **3** a single blossom of a clustered head of flowers. **4** a diamond-shaped segment of the surface of a pineapple. **5** an image of an object on a radar screen. [16th c. *peep*, of unkn. orig.]

pip[4] /pɪp/ *n.* **1** a disease of poultry etc. causing thick mucus in the throat and white scale on the tongue. **2** *colloq.* a fit of disgust or bad temper (esp. *give one the pip*). [ME f. MDu. *pippe*, MLG *pip* prob. ult. f. corrupt. of L *pituita* slime]

pip[5] /pɪp/ *v.tr.* (**pipped, pipping**) *Brit. colloq.* **1** hit with a shot. **2** defeat. **3** blackball. □ **pip at the post** defeat at the last moment. **pip out** die. [PIP[2] or PIP[1]]

pipa /'pɪpə/ *n.* an aquatic toad, *Pipa pipa*, having a flat body with long webbed feet, the female of which carries her eggs and tadpoles in pockets on her back. Also called SURINAM TOAD. [Surinam Negro *pipál* (masc.), *pipá* (fem.)]

pipal var. of PEEPUL.

pipe /paɪp/ *n. & v.* —*n.* **1** a tube of metal, plastic, wood, etc. used to convey water, gas, etc. **2** (also **tobacco-pipe**) **a** a narrow wooden or clay etc. tube with a bowl at one end containing burning tobacco, the smoke from which is drawn into the mouth. **b** the quantity of tobacco held by this (*smoked a pipe*). **3** *Mus.* **a** a wind instrument consisting of a single tube. **b** any of the tubes by which sound is produced in an organ. **c** (in *pl.*) = BAGPIPES. **d** (in *pl.*) a set of pipes joined together, e.g. pan-pipes. **4** a tubal organ, vessel, etc. in an animal's body. **5** a high note or song, esp. of a bird. **6** a cylindrical vein of ore. **7** a cavity in cast metal. **8 a** a boatswain's whistle. **b** the sounding of this. **9** a cask for wine, esp. as a measure of two hogsheads, usu. equivalent to 105 gallons (about 477 litres). **10** *archaic* the voice, esp. in singing. —*v.tr.* **1** (also *absol.*) play (a tune etc.) on a pipe or pipes. **2 a** convey (oil, water, gas, etc.) by pipes. **b** provide with pipes. **3** transmit (music, a radio programme, etc.) by wire or cable. **4** (usu. foll. by *up, on, to*, etc.) *Naut.* **a** summon (a crew) to a meal, work, etc. **b** signal the arrival of (an officer etc.) on board. **5** utter in a shrill voice; whistle. **6 a** arrange (icing, cream, etc.) in decorative lines or twists on a cake etc. **b** ornament (a cake etc.) with piping. **7** trim (a dress etc.) with piping. **8** lead or bring (a person etc.) by the sound of a pipe. **9** propagate (pinks etc.) by taking cuttings at the joint of a stem. □ **pipe away** give a signal for (a boat) to start. **pipe-cleaner** a piece of flexible covered wire for cleaning a tobacco-pipe. **pipe down 1** *colloq.* be quiet or less insistent. **2** *Naut.* dismiss from duty. **pipe-fish** any of various long slender fish of the family Syngnathidae, with an elongated snout. **pipe-light** a spill for lighting a pipe. **pipe major** an NCO commanding regimental pipers. **pipe-organ** *Mus.* an organ using pipes instead of or as well as reeds. **pipe-rack** a rack for holding tobacco-pipes. **pipe-rolls** *hist.* the annual records of the British Exchequer from the 12th-19th

c. prob. because subsidiary documents were rolled in pipe form. **pipe-stem** the shaft of a tobacco-pipe. **pipe-stone** a hard red clay used by US Indians for tobacco-pipes. **pipe up** begin to play, sing, speak, etc. **put that in your pipe and smoke it** colloq. a challenge to another to accept something frank or unwelcome. □□**pipeful** n. (pl. **-fuls**). **pipeless** adj. **pipy** adj. [OE pīpe, pīpian & OF piper f. Gmc ult. f. L pipare peep, chirp]

pipeclay /'paɪpkleɪ/ n. & v. —n. a fine white clay used for tobacco-pipes, whitening leather, etc. —v.tr. **1** whiten (leather etc.) with this. **2** put in order.

pipedream /'paɪpdriːm/ n. an unattainable or fanciful hope or scheme. [orig. as experienced when smoking an opium pipe]

pipeline /'paɪplaɪn/ n. **1** a long, usu. underground, pipe for conveying esp. oil. **2** a channel supplying goods, information, etc. □**in the pipeline** awaiting completion or processing.

pip emma /pɪp 'emə/ adv. & n. Brit. colloq. = P.M. [formerly signallers' names for letters PM]

piper /'paɪpə(r)/ n. **1** a bagpipe-player. **2** a person who plays a pipe, esp. an itinerant musician. [OE pīpere (as PIPE)]

piperidine /pɪ'perɪˌdiːn/ n. Chem. a peppery-smelling liquid formed by the reduction of pyridine. [L piper pepper + -IDE + -INE⁴]

pipette /pɪ'pet/ n. & v. —n. a slender tube for transferring or measuring small quantities of liquids esp. in chemistry. —v.tr. transfer or measure (a liquid) using a pipette. [F, dimin. of PIPE]

piping /'paɪpɪŋ/ n. & adj. —n. **1** the act or an instance of piping, esp. whistling or singing. **2** a thin pipelike fold used to edge hems or frills on clothing, seams on upholstery, etc. **3** ornamental lines of icing, cream, potato, etc. on a cake or other dish. **4** lengths of pipe, or a system of pipes, esp. in domestic use. —adj. (of a noise) high; whistling. □**piping hot** very or suitably hot (esp. as required of food, water, etc.).

pipistrelle /ˌpɪpɪ'strel/ n. any bat of the genus Pipistrellus, native to temperate regions and feeding on insects. [F f. It. pipistrello, vip-, f. L vespertilio bat f. vesper evening]

pipit /'pɪpɪt/ n. **1** any of various birds of the family Motacillidae, esp. of the genus Anthus, found worldwide and having brown plumage often heavily streaked with a lighter colour. **2** = meadow pipit. [prob. imit.]

pipkin /'pɪpkɪn/ n. a small earthenware pot or pan. [16th c.: orig. unkn.]

pippin /'pɪpɪn/ n. **1 a** an apple grown from seed. **b** a red and yellow dessert apple. **2** colloq. an excellent person or thing; a beauty. [ME f. OF pepin, of unkn. orig.]

pipsqueak /'pɪpskwiːk/ n. colloq. an insignificant or contemptible person or thing. [imit.]

piquant /'piːkənt, -kɑːnt/ adj. **1** agreeably pungent, sharp, or appetizing. **2** pleasantly stimulating, or disquieting to the mind. □□**piquancy** n. **piquantly** adv. [F, pres. part. of piquer (as PIQUE¹)]

pique¹ /piːk/ v. & n. —v.tr. (**piques**, **piqued**, **piquing**) **1** wound the pride of, irritate. **2** arouse (curiosity, interest, etc.). **3** (refl.; usu. foll. by on) pride or congratulate oneself. —n. ill-feeling; enmity; resentment (in a fit of pique). [F piquer prick, irritate, f. Rmc]

pique² /piːk/ n. & v. —n. the winning of 30 points on cards and play in piquet before one's opponent scores anything. —v. (**piques**, **piqued**, **piquing**) **1** tr. score a pique against. **2** intr. score a pique. [F pic, of unkn. orig.]

piqué /'piːkeɪ/ n. a stiff ribbed cotton or other fabric. [F, past part. of piquer: see PIQUE¹]

piquet¹ /pɪ'ket/ n. a game for two players with a pack of 32 cards (seven to ace only). [F, of unkn. orig.]

piquet² var. of PICKET 3.

piracy /'paɪrəsɪ/ n. (pl. **-ies**) **1** the practice or an act of robbery of ships at sea. **2** a similar practice or act in other forms, esp. hijacking. **3** the infringement of copyright. [med.L piratia f. Gk pirateia (as PIRATE)]

piragua /pɪ'rægwə/ n. **1** a long narrow canoe made from a single tree-trunk. **2** a two-masted sailing barge. [Sp. f. Carib, = dug-out]

piranha /pɪ'rɑːnə, -'rɑːnjə/ n. (also **piraya** /-'rɑːjə/) any of various freshwater predatory fish of the genera Pygocentrus, Rooseveltiella, or Serrasalmus, native to S. America and having sharp cutting teeth. [Port. f. Tupi, var. of piraya scissors]

pirate /'paɪrət/ n. & v. —n. **1 a** a person who commits piracy. **b** a ship used by pirates. **2** a person who infringes another's copyright or other business rights; a plagiarist. **3** (often attrib.) a person, organization, etc., that broadcasts without official authorization (pirate radio station). —v.tr. **1** appropriate or reproduce (the work or ideas etc. of another) without permission, for one's own benefit. **2** plunder. □□**piratic** /-'rætɪk/ adj. **piratical** /-'rætɪk(ə)l/ adj. **piratically** /-'rætɪkəlɪ/ adv. [ME f. L pirata f. Gk peiratēs f. peiraō attempt, assault]

piraya var. of PIRANHA.

piripiri /ˌpɪrɪ'pɪrɪ/ n. (pl. **piripiris**) NZ a rosaceous plant, Acaena anserinifolia, native to New Zealand and having prickly burs. [Maori]

pirogue /pɪ'rəʊg/ n. = PIRAGUA. [F, prob. f. Galibi]

pirouette /ˌpɪru'et/ n. & v. —n. a dancer's spin on one foot or the point of the toe. —v.intr. perform a pirouette. [F, = spinning-top]

pis aller /ˌpiːz æ'leɪ/ n. a course of action followed as a last resort. [F f. pis worse + aller go]

piscary /'pɪskərɪ/ n. □**common of piscary** the right of fishing in another's water in common with the owner and others. [ME f. med.L piscaria neut. pl. of L piscarius f. piscis fish]

piscatorial /ˌpɪskə'tɔːrɪəl/ adj. = PISCATORY 1. □□**piscatorially** adv.

piscatory /'pɪskətərɪ/ adj. **1** of or concerning fishermen or fishing. **2** addicted to fishing. [L piscatorius f. piscator fisherman f. piscis fish]

Pisces /'paɪsiːz, 'pɪskiːz/ n. (pl. same) **1** a constellation, traditionally regarded as contained in the figure of fishes. **2 a** the twelfth sign of the zodiac (the Fishes). **b** a person born when the sun is in this sign. □□**Piscean** /'paɪsɪən/ n. & adj. [ME f. L, pl. of piscis fish]

pisciculture /'pɪsɪˌkʌltʃə(r)/ n. the artificial rearing of fish. □□**piscicultural** /-'kʌltʃər(ə)l/ adj. **pisciculturist** /-'kʌltʃərɪst/ n. [L piscis fish, after agriculture etc.]

piscina /pɪ'siːnə, -'saɪnə/ n. (pl. **piscinae** /-niː/ or **piscinas**) **1** a stone basin near the altar in RC and pre-Reformation churches for draining water used in the Mass. **2** a fish-pond. **3** hist. a Roman bathing-pond. [L f. piscis fish]

piscine¹ /'pɪsaɪn/ adj. of or concerning fish. [L piscis fish]

piscine² /pɪ'siːn/ n. a bathing-pool. [F (as PISCINA)]

piscivorous /pɪ'sɪvərəs/ adj. fish-eating. [L piscis fish + -VOROUS]

pish /pɪʃ/ int. an expression of contempt, impatience, or disgust. [imit.]

pisiform /'pɪsɪˌfɔːm/ adj. pea-shaped. □**pisiform bone** a small bone in the wrist in the upper row of the carpus. [mod.L pisiformis f. pisum pea]

pismire /'pɪsˌmaɪə(r)/ n. dial. an ant. [ME f. PISS (from smell of anthill) + obs. mire ant]

piss /pɪs/ v. & n. coarse sl. ¶ Usually considered a taboo word. —v. **1** intr. urinate. **2** tr. **a** discharge (blood etc.) when urinating. **b** wet with urine. **3** tr. (as **pissed** adj.) Brit. drunk. —n. **1** urine. **2** an act of urinating. □**piss about** fool or mess about. **piss artist 1** a drunkard. **2** a person who fools about. **3** a glib person. **piss down** rain heavily. **piss off** Brit. **1** go away. **2** (often as **pissed off** adj.) annoy; depress.

piss-pot a chamber-pot. **piss-taker** a person who mocks. **piss-taking** mockery. **piss-up** a drinking spree. **take the piss** (often foll. by *out of*) mock; deride. [ME f. OF *pisser* (imit.)]

pissoir /piːˈswɑːr/ *n.* a public urinal. [F]

pistachio /pɪˈstɑːʃɪəʊ/ *n.* (*pl.* **-os**) **1** an evergreen tree, *Pistacia vera*, bearing small brownish-green flowers and ovoid reddish fruit. **2** (in full **pistachio nut**) the edible pale-green seed of this. **3** a pale green colour. [It. *pistaccio* and Sp. *pistacho* f. L *pistacium* f. Gk *pistakion* f. Pers. *pistah*]

piste /piːst/ *n.* a ski-run of compacted snow. [F, = racetrack]

pistil /ˈpɪstɪl/ *n.* the female organs of a flower, comprising the stigma, style, and ovary. □□ **pistillary** *adj.* **pistilliferous** /-ˈlɪfərəs/ *adj.* **pistilline** /-ˌlaɪn/ *adj.* [F *pistile* or L *pistillum* PESTLE]

pistillate /ˈpɪstɪlət/ *adj.* **1** having pistils. **2** having pistils but no stamens.

pistol /ˈpɪst(ə)l/ *n. & v.* —*n.* **1** a small hand-held firearm. **2** anything of a similar shape. —*v.tr.* (**pistolled**, **pistolling**; *US* **pistoled**, **pistoling**) shoot with a pistol. □**hold a pistol to a person's head** coerce a person by threats. **pistol-grip** a handle shaped like a pistol-butt. **pistol-shot 1** the range of a pistol. **2** a shot fired from a pistol. **pistol-whip** (**-whipped**, **-whipping**) beat with a pistol. [obs. F f. G *Pistole* f. Czech *pišt'al*]

pistole /pɪˈstəʊl/ *n. hist.* a foreign (esp. Spanish) gold coin. [F *pistole* abbr. of *pistolet*, of uncert. orig.]

pistoleer /ˌpɪstəˈlɪə(r)/ *n.* a soldier armed with a pistol.

piston /ˈpɪst(ə)n/ *n.* **1** a disc or short cylinder fitting closely within a tube in which it moves up and down against a liquid or gas, used in an internal-combustion engine to impart motion, or in a pump to receive motion. **2** a sliding valve in a trumpet etc. □**piston-ring** a ring on a piston sealing the gap between the piston and the cylinder wall. **piston-rod** a rod or crankshaft attached to a piston to drive a wheel or to impart motion. [F f. It. *pistone* var. of *pestone* augment. of *pestello* PESTLE]

pit[1] /pɪt/ *n. & v.* —*n.* **1 a** a usu. large deep hole in the ground. **b** a hole made in digging for industrial purposes, esp. for coal (*chalk pit*; *gravel pit*). **c** a covered hole as a trap for esp. wild animals. **2 a** an indentation left after smallpox, acne, etc. **b** a hollow in a plant or animal body or on any surface. **3** *Brit. Theatr.* **a** = *orchestra pit.* **b** usu. *hist.* seating at the back of the stalls. **c** the people in the pit. **4 a** (**the pit** or **bottomless pit**) hell. **b** (**the pits**) *sl.* a wretched or the worst imaginable place, situation, person, etc. **5 a** an area at the side of a track where racing cars are serviced and refuelled. **b** a sunken area in a workshop floor for access to a car's underside. **6** *US* the part of the floor of an exchange allotted to special trading (*wheat-pit*). **7** = COCKPIT. **8** *Brit. sl.* a bed. —*v.* (**pitted**, **pitting**) **1** *tr.* (usu. foll. by *against*) a set (one's wits, strength, etc.) in opposition or rivalry. **b** set (a cock, dog, etc.) to fight, orig. in a pit, against another. **2** *tr.* (usu. as **pitted** *adj.*) make pits, esp. scars, in. **3** *intr.* (of the flesh etc.) retain the impression of a finger etc. when touched. **4** *tr. Hort.* put (vegetables etc. for storage) into a pit. □**dig a pit for** try to ensnare. **pit-head 1** the top of a mineshaft. **2** the area surrounding this. **pit of the stomach 1** the floor of the stomach. **2** the depression below the bottom of the breastbone. **pit pony** *hist.* a pony kept underground for haulage in coal-mines. **pit-prop** a balk of wood used to support the roof of a coal mine. **pit-saw** a large saw for use in a saw-pit. **pit viper** any US snake of the family Crotalidae with a pit between the eye and the nostril. [OE *pytt* ult. f. L *puteus* well]

pit[2] /pɪt/ *n. & v. US* —*n.* the stone of a fruit. —*v.tr.* (**pitted**, **pitting**) remove pits from (fruit). [perh. Du., rel. to PITH]

pita var. of PITTA.

pit-a-pat /ˈpɪtəˌpæt/ *adv. & n.* (also **pitter-patter** /ˈpɪtəˌpætə(r)/) —*adv.* **1** with a sound like quick light steps. **2** with a faltering sound (*heart went pit-a-pat*). —*n.* such a sound. [imit.]

pitch[1] /pɪtʃ/ *v. & n.* —*v.* **1** *tr.* (also *absol.*) erect and fix (a tent, camp, etc.). **2** *tr.* **a** throw; fling. **b** (in games) throw (a flat object) towards a mark. **3** *tr.* fix or plant (a thing) in a definite position. **4** *tr.* express in a particular style or at a particular level (*pitched his argument at the most basic level*). **5** *intr.* (often foll. by *against*, *into*, etc.) fall heavily, esp. headlong. **6** *intr.* (of a ship etc.) plunge in a longitudinal direction (cf. ROLL *v.* 8a). **7** *tr. Mus.* set at a particular pitch. **8** *intr.* (of a roof etc.) slope downwards. **9** *intr.* (often foll. by *about*) move with a vigorous jogging motion, as in a train, carriage, etc. **10** *Cricket* **a** *tr.* cause (a bowled ball) to strike the ground at a specified point etc. **b** *intr.* (of a bowled ball) strike the ground. **11** *tr. colloq.* tell (a yarn or a tale). **12** *tr. Golf* play (a ball) with a pitch shot. **13** *tr.* pave (a road) with stones. —*n.* **1 a** the area of play in a field-game. **b** *Cricket* the area between the creases. **2** height, degree, intensity, etc. (*the pitch of despair*; *nerves were strung to a pitch*). **3 a** the steepness of a slope, esp. of a roof, stratum, etc. **b** the degree of such a pitch. **4** *Mus.* **a** that quality of a sound which is governed by the rate of vibrations producing it; the degree of highness or lowness of a tone. **b** = *concert pitch.* **5** the pitching motion of a ship etc. **6** *Cricket* the act or mode of delivery in bowling, or the spot where the ball bounces. **7** *colloq.* a salesman's advertising or selling approach. **8** *Brit.* a place where a street vendor sells wares, has a stall, etc. **9** (also **pitch shot**) *Golf* a high approach shot with a short run. **10** *Mech.* the distance between successive corresponding points or lines, e.g. between the teeth of a cog-wheel etc. **11** the height to which a falcon etc. soars before swooping on its prey. **12** the delivery of a baseball by a pitcher. □**pitch-and-toss** a gambling game in which coins are pitched at a mark and then tossed. **pitched battle 1** a vigorous argument etc. **2** *Mil.* a battle planned beforehand and fought on chosen ground. **pitched roof** a sloping roof. **pitch in** *colloq.* set to work vigorously. **pitch into** *colloq.* **1** attack forcibly with blows, words, etc. **2** assail (food, work, etc.) vigorously. **pitch on** (or **upon**) happen to select. **pitch-pipe** *Mus.* a small pipe blown to set the pitch for singing or tuning. **pitch up** *Cricket* bowl (a ball) to bounce near the batsman. **pitch wickets** *Cricket* fix the stumps in the ground and place the bails. [ME *pic(c)he*, perh. f. OE *picc(e)an* (unrecorded: cf. *picung* stigmata)]

pitch[2] /pɪtʃ/ *n. & v.* —*n.* **1** a sticky resinous black or dark-brown substance obtained by distilling tar or turpentine, semi-liquid when hot, hard when cold, and used for caulking the seams of ships etc. **2** any of various bituminous substances including asphalt. —*v.tr.* cover, coat, or smear with pitch. □**pitch-black** (or **-dark**) very or completely dark. **pitch-pine** any of various pine-trees, esp. *Pinus rigida* or *P. palustris*, yielding much resin. [OE *pic* f. Gmc f. L *pix picis*]

pitchblende /ˈpɪtʃblend/ *n.* a mineral form of uranium oxide occurring in pitchlike masses and yielding radium. [G *Pechblende* (as PITCH[2], BLENDE)]

pitcher[1] /ˈpɪtʃə(r)/ *n.* **1** a large usu. earthenware jug with a lip and a handle, for holding liquids. **2** a modified leaf in pitcher form. **3** (in *pl.*) broken pottery crushed and reused. □**pitcher-plant** any of various plants, esp. of the family Nepenthaceae or Sarraceniaceae, with pitcher leaves that can hold liquids, trap insects, etc. □□ **pitcherful** *n.* (*pl.* **-fuls**). [ME f. OF *pichier*, *pechier*, f. Frank.]

pitcher[2] /ˈpɪtʃə(r)/ *n.* **1** a person or thing that pitches. **2** *Baseball* a player who delivers the ball to the batter. **3** a stone used for paving.

pitchfork /ˈpɪtʃfɔːk/ *n. & v.* —*n.* a long-handled two-pronged fork for pitching hay etc. —*v.tr.* **1**

throw with or as if with a pitchfork. **2** (usu. foll. by *into*) thrust (a person) forcibly into a position, office, etc. [in ME *pickfork*, prob. f. PICK¹ + FORK, assoc. with PITCH¹]

pitchstone /'pɪtʃstəʊn/ *n.* obsidian etc. resembling pitch.

pitchy /'pɪtʃɪ/ *adj.* (**pitchier, pitchiest**) of, like, or dark as pitch.

piteous /'pɪtɪəs/ *adj.* deserving or causing pity; wretched. □□ **piteously** *adv.* **piteousness** *n.* [ME *pito(u)s* etc. f. AF *pitous*, OF *pitos* f. Rmc (as PIETY)]

pitfall /'pɪtfɔːl/ *n.* **1** an unsuspected snare, danger, or drawback. **2** a covered pit for trapping animals etc.

pith /pɪθ/ *n. & v.* —*n.* **1** spongy white tissue lining the rind of an orange, lemon, etc. **2** the essential part; the quintessence (*came to the pith of his argument*). **3** *Bot.* the spongy cellular tissue in the stems and branches of dicotyledonous plants. **4 a** physical strength; vigour. **b** force; energy. **5** *archaic* spinal marrow. —*v.tr.* **1** remove the pith or marrow from. **2** slaughter or immobilize (an animal) by severing the spinal cord. □ **pith helmet** a lightweight sun-helmet made from the dried pith of the sola etc. □□ **pithless** *adj.* [OE *pitha* f. WG]

pithecanthrope /ˌpɪθɪ'kænθrəʊp/ *n.* any prehistoric apelike human of the extinct genus *Pithecanthropus*, now considered to be part of the genus *Homo* (see also JAVA MAN). [Gk *pithēkos* ape + *anthrōpos* man]

pithos /'pɪθɒs/ *n.* (*pl.* **pithoi** /-θɔɪ/) *Archaeol.* a large storage jar. [Gk]

pithy /'pɪθɪ/ *adj.* (**pithier, pithiest**) **1** (of style, speech, etc.) condensed, terse, and forcible. **2** of, like, or containing much pith. □□ **pithily** *adv.* **pithiness** *n.*

pitiable /'pɪtɪəb(ə)l/ *adj.* **1** deserving or causing pity. **2** contemptible. □□ **pitiableness** *n.* **pitiably** *adv.* [ME f. OF *piteable, pitoiable* (as PITY)]

pitiful /'pɪtɪfʊl/ *adj.* **1** causing pity. **2** contemptible. **3** *archaic* compassionate. □□ **pitifully** *adv.* **pitifulness** *n.*

pitiless /'pɪtɪlɪs/ *adj.* showing no pity (*the pitiless heat of the desert*). □□ **pitilessly** *adv.* **pitilessness** *n.*

pitman /'pɪtmən/ *n.* **1** (*pl.* -**men**) a collier. **2** *US* (*pl.* -**mans**) a connecting rod in machinery.

piton /'piːtɒn/ *n.* a peg or spike driven into a rock or crack to support a climber or a rope. [F, = eye-bolt]

Pitot tube /'piːtəʊ/ *n.* a device consisting of an open-ended right-angled tube used to measure the speed or flow of a fluid. [H. *Pitot*, Fr. physicist d. 1771]

pitpan /'pɪtpæn/ *n.* a Central American boat made from a tree-trunk. [Miskito]

pitta /'pɪtə/ *n.* (also **pita**) a flat hollow unleavened bread which can be split and filled with salad etc. [mod.Gk, = a cake]

pittance /'pɪt(ə)ns/ *n.* **1** a scanty or meagre allowance, remuneration, etc. (*paid him a mere pittance*). **2** a small number or amount. **3** *hist.* a pious bequest to a religious house for extra food etc. [ME f. OF *pitance* f. med.L *pi(e)tantia* f. L *pietas* PITY]

pitter-patter var. of PIT-A-PAT.

pittosporum /ˌpɪtəʊ'spɔːrəm/ *n.* any evergreen shrub of the family Pittosporaceae, chiefly native to Australasia with many species having fragrant foliage. [Gk *pitta* PITCH² + *sporos* seed]

pituitary /pɪ'tjuːɪtərɪ/ *n. & adj.* —*n.* (*pl.* -**ies**) (also **pituitary gland** or **body**) a small ductless gland at the base of the brain secreting various hormones essential for growth and other bodily functions. —*adj.* of or relating to this gland. [L *pituitarius* secreting phlegm f. *pituita* phlegm]

pity /'pɪtɪ/ *n. & v.* —*n.* (*pl.* -**ies**) **1** sorrow and compassion aroused by another's condition (*felt pity for the child*). **2** something to be regretted; grounds for regret (*what a pity!; the pity of it is that he didn't mean it*). —*v.tr.* (-**ies**, -**ied**) feel (often contemptuous) pity for (*they are to be pitied; I pity you if you think that*). □ **for pity's sake** an exclamation of urgent

supplication, anger, etc. **more's the pity** so much the worse. **take pity on** feel or act compassionately towards. □□ **pitying** *adj.* **pityingly** *adv.* [ME f. OF *pité* f. L *pietas* (as PIETY)]

pityriasis /ˌpɪtɪ'raɪəsɪs/ *n.* any of a group of skin diseases characterized by the shedding of branlike scales. [mod.L f. Gk *pituriasis* f. *pituron* bran]

più /pju/ *adv. Mus.* more (*più piano*). [It.]

pivot /'pɪvət/ *n. & v.* —*n.* **1** a short shaft or pin on which something turns or oscillates. **2** a crucial or essential person, point, etc., in a scheme or enterprise. **3** *Mil.* the man or men about whom a body of troops wheels. —*v.* (**pivoted, pivoting**) **1** *intr.* turn on or as if on a pivot. **2** *intr.* (foll. by *on, upon*) hinge on; depend on. **3** *tr.* provide with or attach by a pivot. □□ **pivotable** *adj.* **pivotability** /-'bɪlɪtɪ/ *n.* **pivotal** *adj.* [F, of uncert. orig.]

pix¹ /pɪks/ *n.pl. colloq.* pictures, esp. photographs. [abbr.: cf. PIC]

pix² var. of PYX.

pixel /'pɪks(ə)l/ *n. Electronics* any of the minute areas of uniform illumination of which an image on a display screen is composed. [abbr. of *picture element*: cf. PIX¹]

pixie /'pɪksɪ/ *n.* (also **pixy**) (*pl.* -**ies**) a being like a fairy; an elf. □ **pixie hat** (or **hood**) a child's hat with a pointed crown. [17th c.: orig. unkn.]

pixilated /'pɪksɪˌleɪtɪd/ *adj.* (also **pixillated**) **1** bewildered; crazy. **2** drunk. [var. of *pixie-led* (as PIXIE, LED)]

pizazz /pɪ'zæz/ *n.* (also **pizzazz, pzazz** etc.) *sl.* verve, energy, liveliness, sparkle.

pizza /'piːtsə/ *n.* a flat round base of dough with a topping of tomatoes, cheese, onions, etc. [It., = pie]

pizzeria /ˌpiːtsə'riːə/ *n.* a place where pizzas are made or sold. [It. (as PIZZA)]

pizzicato /ˌpɪtsɪ'kɑːtəʊ/ *adv., adj., & n. Mus.* —*adv.* plucking the strings of a violin etc. with the finger. —*adj.* (of a note, passage, etc.) performed pizzicato. —*n.* (*pl.* **pizzicatos** or **pizzicati** /-tɪ/) a note, passage, etc. played pizzicato. [It., past part. of *pizzicare* twitch f. *pizzare* f. *pizza* edge]

pizzle /'pɪz(ə)l/ *n.* esp. *Austral.* the penis of an animal, esp. a bull, formerly used as a whip. [LG *pesel*, dimin. of MLG *pēse*, MDu. *pēze*]

pk. *abbr.* **1** park. **2** peak. **3** peck(s).

pl. *abbr.* **1** plural. **2** place. **3** plate. **4** esp. *Mil.* platoon.

PLA *abbr.* (in the UK) Port of London Authority.

placable /'plækəb(ə)l/ *adj.* easily placated; mild; forgiving. □□ **placability** /-'bɪlɪtɪ/ *n.* **placably** *adv.* [ME f. OF *placable* or L *placabilis* f. *placare* appease]

placard /'plækɑːd/ *n. & v.* —*n.* a printed or handwritten poster esp. for advertising. —*v.tr.* /also plæ'kɑːd/ **1** set up placards on (a wall etc.). **2** advertise by placards. **3** display (a poster etc.) as a placard. [ME f. OF *placquart* f. *plaquier* to plaster f. MDu. *placken*]

placate /plə'keɪt, 'plæ-, 'pleɪ-/ *v.tr.* pacify; conciliate. □□ **placatingly** *adv.* **placation** /plə'keɪʃ(ə)n/ *n.* **placatory** /plə'keɪtərɪ/ *adj.* [L *placare placat-*]

place /pleɪs/ *n. & v.* —*n.* **1 a** a particular portion of space. **b** a portion of space occupied by a person or thing (*it has changed its place*). **c** a proper or natural position (*he is out of his place; take your places*). **2** a city, town, village, etc. (*was born in this place*). **3** a residence; a dwelling (*has a place in the country; come round to my place*). **4 a** a group of houses in a town etc., esp. a square. **b** a country house with its surroundings. **5** a person's rank or status (*know their place; a place in history*). **6** a space, esp. a seat, for a person (*two places in the coach*). **7** a building or area for a specific purpose (*place of worship; bathing-place*). **8 a** a point reached in a book etc. (*lost my place*). **b** a passage in a book. **9** a particular spot on a surface, esp. of the skin (*a sore place on his wrist*). **10 a** employment or office, esp. government employment (*lost his place at the Ministry*). **b** the duties or entitlements of office etc. (*is his place to* *hire staff*). **11** a position as a member of a team, a student in a college, etc. **12** *Brit.* any of the first three or sometimes four positions in a race, esp. other than the winner (*backed it for a place*). **13** the position of a figure in a series indicated in decimal or similar notation (*calculated to 50 decimal places*). —*v.tr.* **1** put (a thing etc.) in a particular place or state; arrange. **2** identify, classify, or remember correctly (*cannot place him*). **3** assign to a particular place; locate. **4 a** appoint (a person, esp. a member of the clergy) to a post. **b** find a situation, living, etc. for. **c** (usu. foll. by *with*) consign to a person's care etc. (*placed her with her aunt*). **5** assign rank, importance, or worth to (*place him among the best teachers*). **6 a** dispose of (goods) to a customer. **b** make (an order for goods etc.). **7** (often foll. by *in*, *on*, etc.) have (confidence etc.). **8** invest (money). **9** *Brit.* state the position of (any of the first three or sometimes four runners) in a race. **10** *tr.* (as placed *adj.*) **a** *Brit.* among the first three or sometimes four in a race. **b** *US* second in a race. **11** *Football* get (a goal) by a place-kick. ▫**all over the place** in disorder; chaotic. **give place to 1** make room for. **2** yield precedence to. **3** be succeeded by. **go places** *colloq.* be successful. **in place** in the right position; suitable. **in place of** in exchange for; instead of. **in places** at some places or in some parts, but not others. **keep a person in his** or **her place** suppress a person's pretensions. **out of place 1** in the wrong position. **2** unsuitable. **place-bet 1** *Brit.* a bet on a horse to come first, second, third, or sometimes fourth in a race. **2** *US* a bet on a horse to come second. **place-brick** an imperfectly burnt brick from the windward side of the kiln. **place card** a card marking a person's place at a table etc. **place in the sun** a favourable situation, position, etc. **place-kick** *Football* a kick made when the ball is previously placed on the ground. **place-mat** a small mat on a table underneath a person's plate. **place-name** the name of a town, village, hill, field, lake, etc. **place-setting** a set of plates, cutlery, etc. for one person at a meal. **put oneself in another's place** imagine oneself in another's position. **put a person in his** or **her place** deflate or humiliate a person. **take place** occur. **take one's place** go to one's correct position, be seated, etc. **take the place of** be substituted for; replace. ▫▫**placeless** *adj.* **placement** *n.* [ME f. OF f. L *platea* f. Gk *plateia* (*hodos*) broad (way)]

placebo /pləˈsiːbəʊ/ *n.* (*pl.* **-os**) **1 a** a pill, medicine, etc. prescribed for psychological reasons but having no physiological effect. **b** a placebo used as a control in testing new drugs etc. **c** a blank sample in a test. **2** *RC Ch.* the opening antiphon of the vespers for the dead. [L, = I shall be acceptable or pleasing f. *placēre* please, first word of Ps. 114:9]

placenta /pləˈsentə/ *n.* (*pl.* **placentae** /-tiː/ or **placentas**) **1** a flattened circular organ in the uterus of pregnant mammals nourishing and maintaining the foetus through the umbilical cord and expelled after birth. **2** (in flowers) part of the ovary wall carrying the ovules. ▫▫**placental** *adj.* [L f. Gk *plakous -ountos* flat cake f. the root of *plax plakos* flat plate]

placer /ˈpleɪsə(r), ˈplæsə(r)/ *n.* a deposit of sand, gravel, etc., in the bed of a stream etc., containing valuable minerals in particles. [Amer. Sp., rel. to *placel* sandbank f. *plaza* PLACE]

placet /ˈpleɪset/ *n.* an affirmative vote in a church or university assembly. [L, = it pleases]

placid /ˈplæsɪd/ *adj.* **1** (of a person) not easily aroused or disturbed; peaceful. **2** mild; calm; serene. ▫▫**placidity** /pləˈsɪdɪtɪ/ *n.* **placidly** *adv.* **placidness** *n.* [F *placide* or L *placidus* f. *placēre* please]

placket /ˈplækɪt/ *n.* **1** an opening or slit in a garment, for fastenings or access to a pocket. **2** the flap of fabric under this. [var. of PLACARD]

placoid /ˈplækɔɪd/ *adj.* & *n.* —*adj.* **1** (of a fish-scale) consisting of a hard base embedded in the skin and a spiny backward projection (cf. CTENOID). **2** (of a fish) covered with these scales. —*n.* a placoid fish, e.g. a shark. [Gk *plax plakos* flat plate]

plafond /plæˈfɔ̃/ *n.* **1 a** an ornately decorated ceiling. **b** such decoration. **2** an early form of contract bridge. [F f. *plat* flat + *fond* bottom]

plagal /ˈpleɪg(ə)l/ *adj. Mus.* (of a church mode) having sounds between the dominant and its octave (cf. AUTHENTIC). ▫**plagal cadence** (or **close**) a cadence in which the chord of the subdominant immediately precedes that of the tonic. [med.L *plagalis* f. *plaga* plagal mode f. L *plagius* f. med. Gk *plagios* (in anc. Gk = oblique) f. Gk *plagos* side]

plage /plɑːʒ/ *n.* **1** *Astron.* an unusually bright region on the sun. **2** a sea beach, esp. at a fashionable resort. [F, = beach]

plagiarism /ˈpleɪdʒəˌrɪz(ə)m/ *n.* **1** the act or an instance of plagiarizing. **2** something plagiarized. ▫▫ **plagiarist** *n.* **plagiaristic** /-ˈrɪstɪk/ *adj.*

plagiarize /ˈpleɪdʒəˌraɪz/ *v.tr.* (also **-ise**) (also *absol.*) **1** take and use (the thoughts, writings, inventions, etc. of another person) as one's own. **2** pass off the thoughts etc. of (another person) as one's own. ▫▫ **plagiarizer** *n.* [L *plagiarius* kidnapper f. *plagium* a kidnapping f. Gk *plagion*]

plagio- /ˈpleɪdʒɪəʊ/ *comb. form* oblique. [Gk *plagios* oblique f. *plagos* side]

plagioclase /ˈpleɪdʒɪəʊˌkleɪz/ *n.* a series of feldspar minerals forming glassy crystals. [PLAGIO- + Gk *klasis* cleavage]

plague /pleɪg/ *n.*, *v.*, & *int.* —*n.* **1** a deadly contagious disease spreading rapidly over a wide area. **2** (foll. by *of*) an unusual infestation of a pest etc. (*a plague of frogs*). **3 a** great trouble. **b** an affliction, esp. as regarded as divine punishment. **4** *colloq.* a nuisance. —*v.tr.* (**plagues**, **plagued**, **plaguing**) **1** affect with plague. **2** *colloq.* pester or harass continually. —*int. joc.* or *archaic* a curse etc. (*a plague on it!*). ▫▫ **plaguesome** *adj.* [ME f. L *plaga* stroke, wound prob. f. Gk *plaga*, *plēgē*]

plaice /pleɪs/ *n.* (*pl.* same) **1** a European flatfish, *Pleuronectes platessa*, having a brown back with orange spots and a white underside, much used for food. **2** (in full **American plaice**) a N. Atlantic fish, *Hippoglossoides platessoides*. [ME f. OF *plaiz* f. LL *platessa* app. f. Gk *platus* broad]

plaid /plæd/ *n.* **1** (often *attrib.*) chequered or tartan, esp. woollen, twilled cloth (*a plaid skirt*). **2** a long piece of plaid worn over the shoulder as part of Highland Scottish costume. ▫▫ **plaided** *adj.* [Gael. *plaide*, of unkn. orig.]

plain[1] /pleɪn/ *adj.*, *adv.*, & *n.* —*adj.* **1** clear; evident (*is plain to see*). **2** readily understood; simple (*in plain words*). **3 a** (of food, sewing, decoration, etc.) uncomplicated; not elaborate; unembellished; simple. **b** without a decorative pattern. **4** (esp. of a woman or girl) ugly. **5** outspoken; straightforward. **6** (of manners, dress, etc.) unsophisticated; homely (*a plain man*). **7** (of drawings etc.) not coloured (*penny plain, twopence coloured*). **8** not in code. —*adv.* **1** clearly; unequivocally (*to speak plain, I don't approve*). **2** simply (*that is plain stupid*). —*n.* **1** a level tract of esp. treeless country. **2** a basic knitting stitch made by putting the needle through the back of the stitch and passing the wool round the front of the needle (opp. PURL[1]). ▫**be plain with** speak bluntly to. **plain card** neither a trump nor a court-card. **plain chocolate** dark chocolate without added milk. **plain clothes** ordinary clothes worn esp. as a disguise by policemen etc. **plain-clothes** (*attrib.*) wearing plain clothes. **plain cook** a person competent in plain English cooking. **plain dealing** candour; straightforwardness. **plain flour** flour with no added raising agent. **plain sailing 1** sailing a straightforward course. **2** an uncomplicated situation or course of action. **plain service** *Eccl.* a church service without music. **plain-spoken**

outspoken; blunt. **plain suit** a suit that is not trumps. **plain text** a text not in cipher or code. **plain time** time not paid for at overtime rates. **plain weaving** weaving with the weft alternately over and under the warp. □□ **plainly** *adv.* **plainness** /'pleɪnnɪs/ *n.* [ME f. OF *plain* (adj. & n.) f. L *planus* (adj.), *planum* (n.)]

plain² /pleɪn/ *v.intr. archaic* or *poet.* **1** mourn. **2** complain. **3** make a plaintive sound. [ME f. OF *plaindre* (stem *plaign-*) f. L *plangere planct-* lament]

plainchant /'pleɪntʃɑːnt/ *n.* = PLAINSONG.

plainsman /'pleɪnzmən/ *n.* (*pl.* **-men**) a person who lives on a plain, esp. in N. America.

plainsong /'pleɪnsɒŋ/ *n.* unaccompanied church music sung in unison in medieval modes and in free rhythm corresponding to the accentuation of the words (cf. GREGORIAN CHANT).

plaint /pleɪnt/ *n.* **1** *Brit. Law* an accusation; a charge. **2** *literary* or *archaic* a complaint; a lamentation. [ME f. OF *plainte* fem. past part. of *plaindre*, and OF *plaint* f. L *planctus* (as PLAIN²)]

plaintiff /'pleɪntɪf/ *n. Law* a person who brings a case against another into court (opp. DEFENDANT). [ME f. OF *plaintif* (adj.) (as PLAINTIVE)]

plaintive /'pleɪntɪv/ *adj.* **1** expressing sorrow; mournful. **2** mournful-sounding. □□ **plaintively** *adv.* **plaintiveness** *n.* [ME f. OF (*-if*, *-ive*) f. *plainte* (as PLAINT)]

plait /plæt/ *n. & v.* —*n.* **1** a length of hair, straw, etc., in three or more interlaced strands. **2** = PLEAT. —*v.tr.* form (hair etc.) into a plait. [ME f. OF *pleit* fold ult. f. L *plicare* fold]

plan /plæn/ *n. & v.* —*n.* **1 a** a formulated and esp. detailed method by which a thing is to be done; a design or scheme. **b** an intention or proposed proceeding (*my plan was to distract them*; *plan of campaign*). **2** a drawing or diagram made by projection on a horizontal plane, esp. showing a building or one floor of a building (cf. ELEVATION). **3** a large-scale detailed map of a town or district. **4 a** a table etc. indicating times, places, etc. of intended proceedings. **b** a scheme or arrangement (*prepared the seating plan*). **5** an imaginary plane perpendicular to the line of vision and containing the objects shown in a picture. —*v.* (**planned**, **planning**) **1** *tr.* (often foll. by *that* + clause or *to* + infin.) arrange (a procedure etc.) beforehand; form a plan (*planned to catch the evening ferry*). **2** *tr.* **a** design (a building, new town, etc.). **b** make a plan of (an existing building, an area, etc.). **3** *tr.* (as **planned** *adj.*) in accordance with a plan (*his planned arrival*; *planned parenthood*). **4** *intr.* make plans. □ **planning permission** *Brit.* formal permission for building development etc., esp. from a local authority. **plan on** *colloq.* aim at doing; intend. □□ **planning** *n.* [F f. earlier *plant*, f. It. *pianta* plan of building: cf. PLANT]

planar /'pleɪnə(r)/ *adj. Math.* of, relating to, or in the form of a plane.

planarian /plə'neərɪən/ *n.* any flatworm of the class Turbellaria, usu. living in fresh water. [mod.L *Planaria* the genus-name, fem. of L *planarius* lying flat]

planchet /'plænʃɪt/ *n.* a plain metal disc from which a coin is made. [dimin. of *planch* slab of metal f. OF *planche*: see PLANK]

planchette /plɑːn'ʃet/ *n.* a small usu. heart-shaped board on castors with a pencil that is supposedly caused to write spirit messages when a person's fingers rest lightly on it. [F, dimin. of *planche* PLANK]

Planck's constant /plæŋks/ *n.* (also **Planck constant**) a fundamental constant, equal to the energy of quanta of electromagnetic radiation divided by its frequency, with a value of 6.626×10^{-34} joules. [M. *Planck*, Ger. physicist d. 1947]

plane¹ /pleɪn/ *n., adj., & v.* —*n.* **1 a** a flat surface on which a straight line joining any two points on it would wholly lie. **b** an imaginary flat surface through or joining etc. material objects. **2** a level surface. **3**

colloq. = AEROPLANE. **4** a flat surface producing lift by the action of air or water over and under it (usu. in *comb.*: *hydroplane*). **5** (often foll. by *of*) a level of attainment, thought, knowledge, etc. **6** a flat thin object such as a tabletop. —*adj.* **1** (of a surface etc.) perfectly level. **2** (of an angle, figure, etc.) lying in a plane. —*v.intr.* **1** (often foll. by *down*) travel or glide in an aeroplane. **2** (of a speedboat etc.) skim over water. **3** soar. □ **plane chart** a chart on which meridians and parallels of latitude are represented by equidistant straight lines, used in plane sailing. **plane polarization** a process restricting the vibrations of electromagnetic radiation, esp. light, to one direction. **plane sailing 1** the practice of determining a ship's position on the theory that she is moving on a plane. **2** = *plain sailing* (see PLAIN¹). **plane-table** a surveying instrument used for direct plotting in the field, with a circular drawing-board and pivoted alidade. [L *planum* flat surface, neut. of *planus* PLAIN¹ (different. f. PLAIN¹ in 17th c.): adj. after F *plan*, *plane*]

plane² /pleɪn/ *n. & v.* —*n.* **1** a tool consisting of a wooden or metal block with a projecting steel blade, used to smooth a wooden surface by paring shavings from it. **2** a similar tool for smoothing metal. —*v.tr.* **1** smooth (wood, metal, etc.) with a plane. **2** (often foll. by *away*, *down*) pare (irregularities) with a plane. **3** *archaic* level (*plane the way*). [ME f. OF var. of *plaine* f. LL *plana* f. L *planus* PLAIN¹]

plane³ /pleɪn/ *n.* (in full **plane-tree**) any tree of the genus *Platanus* often growing to great heights, with maple-like leaves and bark which peels in uneven patches. [ME f. OF f. L *platanus* f. Gk *platanos* f. *platus* broad]

planet /'plænɪt/ *n.* **1** a celestial body moving in an elliptical orbit round a star; the earth. **2** esp. *Astrol. hist.* a celestial body distinguished from the fixed stars by having an apparent motion of its own (including the moon and sun), esp. with reference to its supposed influence on people and events. □□ **planetology** /-'tɒlədʒɪ/ *n.* [ME f. OF *planete* f. LL *planeta*, *planetes* f. Gk *planētēs* wanderer, planet f. *planaomai* wander]

planetarium /ˌplænɪ'teərɪəm/ *n.* (*pl.* **planetariums** or **planetaria** /-rɪə/) **1** a domed building in which images of stars, planets, constellations, etc. are projected for public entertainment or education. **2** the device used for such projection. **3** = ORRERY. [mod.L (as PLANET)]

planetary /'plænɪtərɪ/ *adj.* **1** of or like planets (*planetary influence*). **2** terrestrial; mundane. **3** wandering; erratic. □ **planetary nebula** a ring-shaped nebula formed by an expanding shell of gas round a star. [LL *planetarius* (as PLANET)]

planetesimal /ˌplænɪ'tesɪməl/ *n.* any of a vast number of minute planets or planetary bodies. □ **planetesimal hypothesis** the theory that planets were formed by the accretion of planetesimals in a cold state. [PLANET, after *infinitesimal*]

planetoid /'plænɪˌtɔɪd/ *n.* = ASTEROID.

plangent /'plændʒ(ə)nt/ *adj.* **1** (of a sound) loud and reverberating. **2** (of a sound) plaintive; sad. □□ **plangency** *n.* [L *plangere plangent-* lament]

planimeter /plə'nɪmɪtə(r)/ *n.* an instrument for mechanically measuring the area of a plane figure. □□ **planimetric** /-'metrɪk/ *adj.* **planimetrical** /-'metrɪk(ə)l/ *adj.* **planimetry** *n.* [F *planimètre* f. L *planus* level]

planish /'plænɪʃ/ *v.tr.* flatten (sheet metal, coining-metal, etc.) with a smooth-faced hammer or between rollers. □□ **planisher** *n.* [ME f. OF *planir* smooth f. *plain* PLANE¹ *adj.*]

planisphere /'plænɪˌsfɪə(r)/ *n.* a map formed by the projection of a sphere or part of a sphere on a plane, esp. to show the appearance of the heavens at a specific time or place. □□ **planispheric** /-'sferɪk/ *adj.* [ME f. med.L *planisphaerium* (as PLANE¹, SPHERE): infl. by F *planisphère*]

plank /plæŋk/ n. & v. —n. **1** a long flat piece of timber used esp. in building, flooring, etc. **2** an item of a political or other programme (cf. PLATFORM). —v.tr. **1** provide, cover, or floor, with planks. **2** (usu. foll. by *down*; also *absol.*) esp. *US colloq.* **a** put (a thing, person, etc.) down roughly or violently. **b** pay (money) on the spot or abruptly (*planked down £5*). □**plank bed** a bed of boards without a mattress, esp. in prison. **walk the plank** *hist.* (of a pirate's captive etc.) be made to walk blindfold along a plank over the side of a ship to one's death in the sea. [ME f. ONF *planke*, OF *planche* f. LL *planca* board f. *plancus* flat-footed]

planking /'plæŋkɪŋ/ n. planks as flooring etc.

plankton /'plæŋkt(ə)n/ n. the chiefly microscopic organisms drifting or floating in the sea or fresh water (see BENTHOS, NEKTON). □□ **planktonic** /-'tɒnɪk/ adj. [G f. Gk *plagktos* wandering f. *plazomai* wander]

planner /'plænə(r)/ n. **1** a person who controls or plans the development of new towns, designs buildings, etc. **2** a person who makes plans. **3** a list, table, etc., with information helpful in planning.

plano- /'pleɪnəʊ/ comb. form level, flat. [L *planus* flat]

planoconcave /ˌpleɪnəʊ'kɒnkeɪv/ adj. (of a lens etc.) with one surface plane and the other concave.

planoconvex /ˌpleɪnəʊ'kɒnveks/ adj. (of a lens etc.) with one surface plane and the other convex.

planographic /ˌpleɪnə'græfɪk/ adj. relating to or produced by a process in which printing is done from a plane surface. □□ **planography** /plə'nɒgrəfɪ/ n.

planometer /plə'nɒmɪtə(r)/ n. a flat plate used as a gauge for plane surfaces in metalwork.

plant /plɑːnt/ n. & v. —n. **1 a** any living organism of the kingdom Plantae, usu. containing chlorophyll enabling it to live wholly on inorganic substances and lacking specialized sense organs and the power of voluntary movement. **b** a small organism of this kind, as distinguished from a shrub or tree. **2 a** machinery, fixtures, etc., used in industrial processes. **b** a factory. **3** *colloq.* something, esp. incriminating or compromising, positioned or concealed so as to be discovered later. —v.tr. **1** place (a seed, bulb, or growing thing) in the ground so that it may take root and flourish. **2** (often foll. by *in*, *on*, etc.) put or fix in position. **3** deposit (young fish, spawn, oysters, etc.) in a river or lake. **4** station (a person etc.), esp. as a spy or source of information. **5** *refl.* take up a position (*planted myself by the door*). **6** cause (an idea etc.) to be established esp. in another person's mind. **7** deliver (a blow, kiss, etc.) with a deliberate aim. **8** *sl.* position or conceal (something incriminating or compromising) for later discovery. **9 a** settle or people (a colony etc.). **b** found or establish (a city, community, etc.). **10** bury. □**plant-louse** a small insect that infests plants, esp. an aphis. **plant out** transfer (a plant) from a pot or frame to the open ground; set out (seedlings) at intervals. □□ **plantable** adj. **plantlet** n. **plantlike** adj. [OE *plante* & F *plante* f. L *planta* sprout, slip, cutting]

Plantagenet /plæn'tædʒɪnɪt/ adj. & n. —adj. of or relating to the kings of England from Henry II to Richard II. —n. any of these kings. [= sprig of broom (L *planta genista*) worn as a distinctive mark, the origin of their surname]

plantain[1] /'plæntɪn/ n. any shrub of the genus *Plantago*, with broad flat leaves spread out close to the ground and seeds used as food for birds and as a mild laxative. □**plantain lily** = HOSTA. [ME f. OF f. L *plantago -ginis* f. *planta* sole of the foot (from its broad prostrate leaves)]

plantain[2] /'plæntɪn/ n. **1** a banana plant, *Musa paradisiaca*, widely grown for its fruit. **2** the starchy fruit of this containing less sugar than a dessert banana and chiefly used in cooking. [earlier *platan* f. Sp. *plá(n)tano* plane-tree, prob. assim. f. Galibi *palatana* etc.]

plantar /'plæntə(r)/ adj. of or relating to the sole of the foot. [L *plantaris* f. *planta* sole]

plantation /plæn'teɪʃ(ə)n, plɑːn-/ n. **1** an estate on which cotton, tobacco, etc. is cultivated, esp. in former colonies, formerly by slave labour. **2** an area planted with trees etc. **3** *hist.* a colony; colonization. □**plantation song** a song of the kind formerly sung by Blacks on American plantations. [ME f. OF *plantation* or L *plantatio* (as PLANT)]

planter /'plɑːntə(r)/ n. **1** a person who cultivates the soil. **2** the manager or occupier of a coffee, cotton, tobacco, etc. plantation. **3** a large container for decorative plants. **4** a machine for planting seeds etc. (*potato-planter*).

plantigrade /'plæntɪˌgreɪd/ adj. & n. —adj. (of an animal) walking on the soles of its feet. —n. a plantigrade animal, e.g. humans or bears (cf. DIGITIGRADE). [F f. mod.L *plantigradus* f. L *planta* sole + *-gradus* -walking]

plaque /plæk, plɑːk/ n. **1** an ornamental tablet of metal, porcelain, etc., esp. affixed to a building in commemoration. **2** a deposit on teeth where bacteria proliferate. **3** *Med.* **a** a patch or eruption of skin etc. as a result of damage. **b** a fibrous lesion in atherosclerosis. **4** a small badge of rank in an honorary order. □□ **plaquette** /plæ'ket/ n. [F f. Du. *plak* tablet f. *plakken* stick]

plash[1] /plæʃ/ n. & v. —n. **1** a splash; a plunge. **2 a** a marshy pool. **b** a puddle. —v. **1** tr. & intr. splash. **2** tr. strike the surface of (water). □□ **plashy** adj. [OE *plæsc*, prob. imit.]

plash[2] /plæʃ/ v.tr. **1** bend down and interweave (branches, twigs, etc.) to form a hedge. **2** make or renew (a hedge) in this way. [ME f. OF *pla(i)ssier* ult. f. L *plectere* plait: cf. PLEACH]

plasma /'plæzmə/ n. (also **plasm** /'plæz(ə)m/) **1** the colourless fluid part of blood, lymph, or milk, in which corpuscles or fat-globules are suspended. **2** = PROTOPLASM. **3** a gas of positive ions and free electrons with an approximately equal positive and negative charge. **4** a green variety of quartz used in mosaic and for other decorative purposes. □□ **plasmatic** /-'mætɪk/ adj. **plasmic** adj. [LL, = mould f. Gk *plasma -atos* f. *plassō* to shape]

plasmodesma /ˌplæzmə'dezmə/ n. (pl. **plasmodesmata** /-mətə/) a narrow thread of cytoplasm that passes through cell walls and affords communication between plant cells. [PLASMA + Gk *desma* bond, fetter]

plasmodium /plæz'məʊdɪəm/ n. (pl. **plasmodia** /-dɪə/) **1** any parasitic protozoan of the genus *Plasmodium*, including those causing malaria in man. **2** a form within the life cycle of various micro-organisms including slime moulds, usu. consisting of a mass of naked protoplasm containing many nuclei. □□ **plasmodial** adj. [mod.L f. PLASMA[1] + -odium: see -ODE[1]]

plasmolyse /'plæzməˌlaɪz/ v.intr. & tr. (US **plasmolyze**) undergo or subject to plasmolysis.

plasmolysis /plæz'mɒlɪsɪs/ n. contraction of the protoplast of a plant cell as a result of loss of water from the cell. [mod.L (as PLASMA, -LYSIS)]

plaster /'plɑːstə(r)/ n. & v. —n. **1** a soft pliable mixture esp. of lime putty with sand or Portland cement etc. for spreading on walls, ceilings, etc., to form a smooth hard surface when dried. **2** *Brit.* = *sticking-plaster* (see STICK[2]). **3** *hist.* a curative or protective substance spread on a bandage etc. and applied to the body (*mustard plaster*). —v.tr. **1** cover (a wall etc.) with plaster or a similar substance. **2** (often foll. by *with*) coat thickly or to excess; bedaub (*plastered the bread with jam; the wall was plastered with slogans*). **3** stick or apply (a thing) thickly like plaster (*plastered glue all over it*). **4** (often foll. by *down*) make (esp. hair) smooth with water, cream, etc.; fix flat. **5** (as **plastered** adj.) *sl.* drunk. **6** apply a medical plaster or plaster cast to. **7** *sl.* bomb or shell heavily. □**plaster cast 1** a bandage stiffened with plaster of Paris and applied to a broken limb etc. **2** a statue or mould made of plaster. **plaster of Paris** fine white plaster made of gypsum and used for making plaster casts etc. **plaster saint** *iron.* a person regarded as being without moral faults or human frailty. □□ **plasterer** *n.* **plastery** *adj.* [ME f. OE & OF *plastre* or F *plastrer* f. med.L *plastrum* f. L *emplastrum* f. Gk *emplastron*]

plasterboard /ˈplɑːstəˌbɔːd/ *n.* two boards with a filling of plaster used to form or line the inner walls of houses etc.

plastic /ˈplæstɪk/ *n. & adj.* —*n.* **1** any of a number of synthetic polymeric substances that can be given any required shape. **2** (*attrib.*) made of plastic (*plastic bag*). —*adj.* **1** capable of being moulded; pliant; supple. **2** moulding or giving form to clay, wax, etc. **3** *Biol.* exhibiting an adaptability to environmental changes. **4** (esp. in philosophy) formative, creative. □ **plastic arts** art forms involving modelling or moulding, e.g. sculpture and ceramics, or art involving the representation of solid objects with three-dimensional effects. **plastic bomb** a bomb containing plastic explosive. **plastic explosive** a putty-like explosive capable of being moulded by hand. **plastic surgeon** a qualified practitioner of plastic surgery. **plastic surgery** the process of reconstructing or repairing parts of the body by the transfer of tissue, either in the treatment of injury or for cosmetic reasons. □□ **plastically** *adv.* **plasticity** /-ˈtɪsɪtɪ/ *n.* **plasticize** /-ˌsaɪz/ *v.tr.* (also **-ise**). **plasticization** /-saɪˈzeɪʃ(ə)n/ *n.* **plasticizer** /-ˌsaɪzə(r)/ *n.* **plasticky** *adj.* [F *plastique* or L *plasticus* f. Gk *plastikos* f. *plassō* mould]

Plasticine /ˈplæstɪˌsiːn/ *n. propr.* a soft plastic material used, esp. by children, for modelling. [PLASTIC + -INE⁴]

plastid /ˈplæstɪd/ *n.* any small organelle in the cytoplasm of a plant cell, containing pigment or food. [G f. Gk *plastos* shaped]

plastron /ˈplæstrən/ *n.* **1 a** a fencer's leather-covered breastplate. **b** a lancer's breast-covering of facings-cloth. **2 a** an ornamental front on a woman's bodice. **b** a man's starched shirt-front. **3 a** the ventral part of the shell of a tortoise or turtle. **b** the corresponding part in other animals. **4** *hist.* a steel breastplate. □□ **plastral** *adj.* [F f. It. *piastrone* augment. of *piastra* breastplate, f. L *emplastrum* PLASTER]

plat¹ /plæt/ *n.* US **1** a plot of land. **2** a plan of an area of land. [16th c.: collateral form of PLOT]

plat² /plæt/ *n. & v.* —*n.* = PLAIT *n.* 1. —*v.tr.* (**platted, platting**) = PLAIT *v.*

platan /ˈplæt(ə)n/ *n.* = PLANE³. [ME f. L *platanus*: see PLANE³]

plat du jour /ˌplɑ duː ˈʒuːə(r)/ *n.* a dish specially featured on a day's menu. [F, = dish of the day]

plate /pleɪt/ *n. & v.* —*n.* **1 a** a shallow vessel, usu. circular and of earthenware or china, from which food is eaten or served. **b** the contents of this (*ate a plate of sandwiches*). **2** a similar vessel usu. of metal or wood, used esp. for making a collection in a church etc. **3** US a main course of a meal, served on one plate. **4** *Austral. & NZ* a contribution of cakes, sandwiches, etc., to a social gathering. **5** (*collect.*) **a** utensils of silver, gold, or other metal. **b** objects of plated metal. **6** a piece of metal with a name or inscription for affixing to a door, container, etc. **7** an illustration on special paper in a book. **8** a thin sheet of metal, glass, etc., coated with a sensitive film for photography. **9** a flat thin usu. rigid sheet of metal etc. with an even surface and uniform thickness, often as part of a mechanism. **10 a** a smooth piece of metal etc. for engraving. **b** an impression made from this. **11 a** a silver or gold cup as a prize for a horse-race etc. **b** a race with this as a prize. **12 a** a thin piece of plastic material, moulded to the shape of the mouth and gums, to which artificial teeth or another orthodontic appliance are attached. **b** *colloq.* a complete denture or orthodontic appliance. **13**

Geol. each of several rigid sheets of rock thought to form the earth's outer crust. **14** *Biol.* a thin flat organic structure or formation. **15** a light shoe for a racehorse. **16** a stereotype, electrotype, or plastic cast of a page of composed movable types, or a metal or plastic copy of filmset matter, from which sheets are printed. **17** *US Baseball* a flat piece of whitened rubber marking the station of a batter or pitcher. **18** *US* the anode of a thermionic valve. **19** a horizontal timber laid along the top of a wall to support the ends of joists or rafters (*window-plate*). —*v.tr.* **1** apply a thin coat esp. of silver, gold, or tin to (another metal). **2** cover (esp. a ship) with plates of metal, esp. for protection. **3** make a plate of (type etc.) for printing. □ **on a plate** *colloq.* available with little trouble to the recipient. **on one's plate** for one to deal with or consider. **plate armour** armour of metal plates, for a man, ship, etc. **plate glass** thick fine-quality glass for shop windows etc., orig. cast in plates. **plate-rack** *Brit.* a rack in which plates are placed to drain. **plate tectonics** *Geol.* the study of the earth's surface based on the concept of moving 'plates' (see sense 13 of *n.*) forming its structure. **plate tracery** *Archit.* tracery with perforations in otherwise continuous stone. □□ **plateful** *n.* (*pl.* **-fuls**). **plateless** *adj.* **plater** *n.* [ME f. OF f. med.L *plata* plate armour f. *platus* (adj.) ult. f. Gk *platus* flat]

plateau /ˈplætəʊ/ *n. & v.* —*n.* (*pl.* **plateaux** /-təʊz/ or **plateaus**) **1** an area of fairly level high ground. **2** a state of little variation after an increase. —*v.intr.* (**plateaus, plateaued**) (often foll. by *out*) reach a level or stable state after an increase. [F f. OF *platel* dimin. of *plat* flat surface]

platelayer /ˈpleɪtˌleɪə(r)/ *n. Brit.* a person employed in fixing and repairing railway rails.

platelet /ˈpleɪtlɪt/ *n.* a small colourless disc of protoplasm found in blood and involved in clotting.

platen /ˈplæt(ə)n/ *n.* **1** a plate in a printing-press which presses the paper against the type. **2** a cylindrical roller in a typewriter against which the paper is held. [OF *platine* a flat piece f. *plat* flat]

plateresque /ˌplætəˈresk/ *adj.* richly ornamented in a style suggesting silverware. [Sp. *plateresco* f. *platero* silversmith f. *plata* silver]

platform /ˈplætfɔːm/ *n.* **1** a raised level surface; a natural or artificial terrace. **2** a raised surface from which a speaker addresses an audience. **3** *Brit.* a raised elongated structure along the side of a track in a railway station. **4** the floor area at the entrance to a bus. **5** a thick sole of a shoe. **6** the declared policy of a political party. □ **platform ticket** a ticket allowing a non-traveller access to a station platform. [F *plateforme* ground-plan f. *plate* flat + *forme* FORM]

plating /ˈpleɪtɪŋ/ *n.* **1** a coating of gold, silver, etc. **2** racing for plates.

platinic /pləˈtɪnɪk/ *adj.* of or containing (esp. tetravalent) platinum.

platinize /ˈplætɪˌnaɪz/ *v.tr.* (also **-ise**) coat with platinum. □□ **platinization** /-ˈzeɪʃ(ə)n/ *n.*

platinoid /ˈplætɪˌnɔɪd/ *n.* an alloy of copper, zinc, nickel, and tungsten.

platinum /ˈplætɪnəm/ *n. Chem.* a ductile malleable silvery-white metallic element occurring naturally in nickel and copper ores, unaffected by simple acids and fusible only at a very high temperature, used in making jewellery and laboratory apparatus. ¶ Symb.: **Pt.** □ **platinum black** platinum in powder form like lampblack. **platinum blonde** (or **blond**) *adj.* silvery-blond. —*n.* a person with silvery-blond hair. **platinum metal** any metallic element found with and resembling platinum e.g. osmium, iridium, and palladium. [mod.L f. earlier *platina* f. Sp., dimin. of *plata* silver]

platitude /ˈplætɪˌtjuːd/ *n.* **1** a trite or commonplace remark, esp. one solemnly delivered. **2** the use of platitudes; dullness, insipidity. □□ **platitudinize** /-ˈtjuːdɪˌnaɪz/ *v.intr.* (also **-ise**). **platitudinous**

/-'tjuːdɪnəs/ *adj.* [F *f. plat* flat, after *certitude, multitudinous,* etc.]

Platonic /plə'tɒnɪk/ *adj.* **1** of or associated with the Greek philosopher Plato (d. 347 BC) or his ideas. **2** (**platonic**) (of love or friendship) purely spiritual, not sexual. **3** (**platonic**) confined to words or theory; not leading to action; harmless. □**Platonic solid** (or **body**) any of the five regular solids (tetrahedron, cube, octahedron, dodecahedron, icosahedron). □□ **Platonically** *adv.* [L *Platonicus* f. Gk *Platōnikos* f. *Platōn* Plato]

Platonism /'pleɪtə,nɪz(ə)m/ *n.* the philosophy of Plato or his followers. □□ **Platonist** *n.*

platoon /plə'tuːn/ *n.* **1** *Mil.* a subdivision of a company, a tactical unit commanded by a lieutenant and usu. divided into three sections. **2** a group of persons acting together. [F *peloton* small ball, dimin. of *pelote*: see PELLET, -OON]

platteland /'plɑːtə,lɑːnt/ *n.* *S.Afr.* remote country districts. □□ **plattelander** *n.* [Afrik., = flat land]

platter /'plætə(r)/ *n.* **1** a large flat dish or plate, esp. for food. **2** *colloq.* a gramophone record. □**on a platter** = *on a plate* (see PLATE). [ME & AF *plater* f. AF *plat* PLATE]

platy- /'plætɪ/ *comb. form* broad, flat. [Gk *platu-* f. *platus* broad, flat]

platyhelminth /,plætɪ'helmɪnθ/ *n.* any invertebrate of the phylum Platyhelminthes, including flatworms, flukes, and tapeworms.

platypus /'plætɪpəs/ *n.* an Australian aquatic egg-laying mammal, *Ornithorhynchus anatinus,* having a pliable ducklike bill, webbed feet, and sleek grey fur. Also called DUCKBILL.

platyrrhine /'plætɪ,raɪn/ *adj.* & *n.* —*adj.* (of primates) having nostrils far apart and directed forwards or sideways (cf. CATARRHINE). —*n.* such an animal. [PLATY- + Gk *rhis rhin-* nose]

plaudit /'plɔːdɪt/ *n.* (usu. in *pl.*) **1** a round of applause. **2** an emphatic expression of approval. [shortened f. L *plaudite* applaud, imper. pl. of *plaudere plaus-* applaud, said by Roman actors at the end of a play]

plausible /'plɔːzɪb(ə)l/ *adj.* **1** (of an argument, statement, etc.) seeming reasonable or probable. **2** (of a person) persuasive but deceptive. □□ **plausibility** /-'bɪlɪtɪ/ *n.* **plausibly** *adv.* [L *plausibilis* (as PLAUDIT)]

play /pleɪ/ *v.* & *n.* —*v.* **1** *intr.* (often foll. by *with*) occupy or amuse oneself pleasantly with some recreation, game, exercise, etc. **2** *intr.* (foll. by *with*) act light-heartedly or flippantly (with feelings etc.). **3** *tr.* **a** perform on or be able to perform on (a musical instrument). **b** perform (a piece of music etc.). **c** cause (a record, record-player, etc.) to produce sounds. **4 a** *intr.* (foll. by *in*) perform a role in (a drama etc.). **b** *tr.* perform (a drama or role) on stage, or in a film or broadcast. **c** *tr.* give a dramatic performance at (a particular theatre or place). **5** *tr.* act in real life the part of (*play truant; play the fool*). **6** *tr.* (foll. by *on*) perform (a trick or joke etc.) on (a person). **7** *tr.* (foll. by *for*) regard (a person) as (something specified) (*played me for a fool*). **8** *tr.* *colloq.* participate, cooperate; do what is wanted (*they won't play*). **9** *intr.* gamble. **10** *tr.* gamble on. **11** *tr.* **a** take part in (a game or recreation). **b** compete with (another player or team) in a game. **c** occupy (a specified position) in a team for a game. **d** (foll. by *in, on, at,* etc.) assign (a player) to a position. **12** *tr.* move (a piece) or display (a playing-card) in one's turn in a game. **13** *tr.* (also *absol.*) strike (a ball etc.) or execute (a stroke) in a game. **14** *intr.* move about in a lively or unrestrained manner. **15** *intr.* (often foll. by *on*) **a** touch gently. **b** emit light, water, etc. (*fountains gently playing*). **16** *tr.* allow (a fish) to exhaust itself pulling against a line. **17** *intr.* (often foll. by *at*) **a** engage in a half-hearted way (in an activity). **b** pretend to be. **18** *intr.* (of a cricket ground etc.) be conducive to play as specified (*the pitch is playing fast*). **19** *intr.* *colloq.* act or behave (as specified) (*play fair*). **20** *tr.* (foll. by *in, out,* etc.) accompany (a person) with music (*were

played out with bagpipes*). —*n.* **1** recreation, amusement, esp. as the spontaneous activity of children and young animals. **2 a** the playing of a game. **b** the action or manner of this. **c** the status of the ball etc. in a game as being available to be played according to the rules (*in play; out of play*). **3** a dramatic piece for the stage etc. **4** activity or operation (*are in full play; brought into play*). **5 a** freedom of movement. **b** space or scope for this. **6** brisk, light, or fitful movement. **7** gambling. **8** an action or manœuvre, esp. in or as in a game. □**at play** engaged in recreation. **in play** for amusement; not seriously. **make play** act effectively. **make a play for** *colloq.* make a conspicuous attempt to acquire. **make play with** use ostentatiously. **play about** (or **around**) behave irresponsibly. **play along** pretend to cooperate. **play back** play (sounds recently recorded), esp. to monitor recording quality etc. **play-back** *n.* a playing back of a sound or sounds. **play ball** see BALL¹. **play by ear 1** perform (music) without the aid of a score. **2** (also **play it by ear**) proceed instinctively or step by step according to results and circumstances. **play one's cards right** (or **well**) make good use of opportunities; act shrewdly. **play down** minimize the importance of. **play ducks and drakes with** see DUCK¹. **played out** exhausted of energy or usefulness. **play false** act, or treat a (person), deceitfully or treacherously. **play fast and loose** act unreliably; ignore one's obligations. **play the field** see FIELD. **play for time** seek to gain time by delaying. **play the game** see GAME¹. **play God** see GOD. **play havoc with** see HAVOC. **play hell with** see HELL. **play hookey** see HOOKEY. **play into a person's hands** act so as to unwittingly to give a person an advantage. **play it cool** *colloq.* **1** affect indifference. **2** be relaxed or unemotional. **play the man** = *be a man* (see MAN). **play the market** speculate in stocks etc. **play off** (usu. foll. by *against*) **1** oppose (one person against another), esp. for one's own advantage. **2** play an extra match to decide a draw or tie. **play-off** *n.* a match played to decide a draw or tie. **play on 1** continue to play. **2** take advantage of (a person's feelings etc.). **play oneself in** become accustomed to the prevailing conditions in a game etc. **play on words** a pun. **play-pen** a portable enclosure for young children to play in. **play possum** see POSSUM. **play safe** (or **for safety**) avoid risks. **play-suit** a garment for a young child. **play to the gallery** see GALLERY. **play up 1** behave mischievously. **2** cause trouble; be irritating (*my rheumatism is playing up again*). **3** obstruct or annoy in this way (*played the teacher up*). **4** put all one's energy into a game. **play up to** flatter, esp. to win favour. **play with fire** take foolish risks. □□ **playable** *adj.* **playability** /-'bɪlɪtɪ/ *n.* [OE *plega* (n.), *pleg(i)an* (v.), orig. = (to) exercise]

playa /'plɑːjə/ *n.* a flat dried-up area, esp. a desert basin from which water evaporates quickly. [Sp., = beach, f. LL *plagia*]

play-act /'pleɪækt/ *v.* **1** *intr.* act in a play. **2** *intr.* behave affectedly or insincerely. **3** *tr.* act (a scene, part, etc.). □□ **play-acting** *n.* **play-actor** *n.*

playbill /'pleɪbɪl/ *n.* **1** a poster announcing a theatrical performance. **2** *US* a theatre programme.

playboy /'pleɪbɔɪ/ *n.* an irresponsible pleasure-seeking man, esp. a wealthy one.

player /'pleɪə(r)/ *n.* **1** a person taking part in a sport or game. **2** a person playing a musical instrument. **3** a person who plays a part on the stage; an actor. **4** = *record-player.* □**player-piano** a piano fitted with an apparatus enabling it to be played automatically. [OE *plegere* (as PLAY)]

playfellow /'pleɪ,feləʊ/ *n.* a playmate.

playful /'pleɪfʊl/ *adj.* **1** fond of or inclined to play. **2** done in fun; humorous, jocular. □□ **playfully** *adv.* **playfulness** *n.*

playgoer /'pleɪ,gəʊə(r)/ *n.* a person who goes often to the theatre.

w *we* z *zoo* ʃ *she* ʒ *decision* θ *thin* ð *this* ŋ *ring* x *loch* tʃ *chip* dʒ *jar* (*see over for vowels*)

playground /'pleɪgraʊnd/ *n.* an outdoor area for children to play on.

playgroup /'pleɪgruːp/ *n.* a group of preschool children who play regularly together at a particular place under supervision.

playhouse /'pleɪhaʊs/ *n.* **1** a theatre. **2** a toy house for children to play in.

playing-card /'pleɪɪŋˌkɑːd/ *n.* each of a set of usu. 52 oblong pieces of card or other material with an identical pattern on one side and different values represented by numbers and symbols on the other, used to play various games.

playing-field /'pleɪɪŋˌfiːld/ *n.* a field used for outdoor team games.

playlet /'pleɪlɪt/ *n.* a short play or dramatic piece.

playmate /'pleɪmeɪt/ *n.* a child's companion in play.

playschool /'pleɪskuːl/ *n.* a nursery for preschool children.

plaything /'pleɪθɪŋ/ *n.* **1** a toy or other thing to play with. **2** a person treated as a toy.

playtime /'pleɪtaɪm/ *n.* time for play or recreation.

playwright /'pleɪraɪt/ *n.* a person who writes plays.

plaza /'plɑːzə/ *n.* a market-place or open square (esp. in a Spanish town). [Sp., = place]

plc *abbr.* (also **PLC**) Public Limited Company.

plea /pliː/ *n.* **1** an earnest appeal or entreaty. **2** *Law* a formal statement by or on behalf of a defendant. **3** an argument or excuse. □**plea bargaining** *US* an arrangement between prosecutor and defendant whereby the defendant pleads guilty to a lesser charge in the expectations of leniency. [ME & AF *ple, plai,* OF *plait, plaid* agreement, discussion f. L *placitum* a decree, neut. past part. of *placēre* to please]

pleach /pliːtʃ/ *v.tr.* entwine or interlace (esp. branches to form a hedge). [ME *pleche* f. OF (as PLASH²)]

plead /pliːd/ *v.* (*past* and *past part.* **pleaded** or esp. *US, Sc.,* & *dial.* **pled** /pled/) **1** *intr.* (foll. by *with*) make an earnest appeal to. **2** *intr. Law* address a lawcourt as an advocate on behalf of a party. **3** *tr.* maintain (a cause) esp. in a lawcourt. **4** *tr. Law* declare to be one's state as regards guilt in or responsibility for a crime (*plead guilty; plead insanity*). **5** *tr.* offer or allege as an excuse (*pleaded forgetfulness*). **6** *intr.* make an appeal or entreaty. □□**pleadable** *adj.* **pleader** *n.* **pleadingly** *adv.* [ME f. AF *pleder,* OF *plaidier* (as PLEA)]

pleading /'pliːdɪŋ/ *n.* (usu. in *pl.*) a formal statement of the cause of an action or defence.

pleasance /'plez(ə)ns/ *n.* a secluded enclosure or part of a garden, esp. one attached to a large house. [ME f. OF *plaisance* (as PLEASANT)]

pleasant /'plez(ə)nt/ *adj.* (**pleasanter, pleasantest**) pleasing to the mind, feelings, or senses. □□ **pleasantly** *adv.* **pleasantness** *n.* [ME f. OF *plaisant* (as PLEASE)]

pleasantry /'plezəntrɪ/ *n.* (*pl.* **-ies**) **1** a pleasant or amusing remark, esp. made in casual conversation. **2** a humorous manner of speech. **3** jocularity. [F *plaisanterie* (as PLEASANT)]

please /pliːz/ *v.* **1** *tr.* (also *absol.*) be agreeable to; make glad; give pleasure to (*the gift will please them; anxious to please*). **2** *tr.* (in *passive*) **a** (foll. by *to* + infin.) be glad or willing to (*am pleased to help*). **b** (often foll. by *about, at, with*) derive pleasure or satisfaction (from). **3** *tr.* (with *it* as subject; usu. foll. by *to* + infin.) be the inclination or wish of (*it did not please them to attend*). **4** *intr.* think fit; have the will or desire (*take as many as you please*). **5** *tr.* (short for **may it please you**) used in polite requests (*come in, please*). □**if you please** if you are willing, esp. *iron.* to indicate unreasonableness (*then, if you please, we had to pay*). **pleased as Punch** see PUNCH⁴. **please oneself** do as one likes. □□ **pleased** *adj.* **pleasing** *adj.* **pleasingly** *adv.* [ME *plaise* f. OF *plaisir* f. L *placēre*]

pleasurable /'pleʒərəb(ə)l/ *adj.* causing pleasure;

agreeable. □□ **pleasurableness** *n.* **pleasurably** *adv.* [PLEASURE + -ABLE, after *comfortable*]

pleasure /'pleʒə(r)/ *n.* & *v.* —*n.* **1** a feeling of satisfaction or joy. **2** enjoyment. **3** a source of pleasure or gratification (*painting was my chief pleasure; it is a pleasure to talk to them*). **4** *formal* a person's will or desire (*what is your pleasure?*). **5** sensual gratification or enjoyment (*a life of pleasure*). **6** (*attrib.*) done or used for pleasure (*pleasure-ground*). —*v.* **1** *tr.* give (esp. sexual) pleasure to. **2** *intr.* (often foll. by *in*) take pleasure. □**take pleasure in** like doing. **with pleasure** gladly. [ME & OF *plesir, plaisir* PLEASE, used as a noun]

pleat /pliːt/ *n.* & *v.* —*n.* a fold or crease, esp. a flattened fold in cloth doubled upon itself. —*v.tr.* make a pleat or pleats in. [ME, var. of PLAIT]

pleb /pleb/ *n. colloq.* usu. *derog.* an ordinary insignificant person. □□ **plebby** *adj.* [abbr. of PLEBEIAN]

plebeian /plɪ'biːən/ *n.* & *adj.* —*n.* a commoner, esp. in ancient Rome. —*adj.* **1** of low birth; of the common people. **2** uncultured. **3** coarse, ignoble. □□ **plebeianism** *n.* [L *plebeius* f. *plebs plebis* the common people]

plebiscite /'plebɪsɪt, -ˌsaɪt/ *n.* **1** the direct vote of all the electors of a State etc. on an important public question, e.g. a change in the constitution. **2** the public expression of a community's opinion, with or without binding force. **3** *Rom.Hist.* a law enacted by the plebeians' assembly. □□ **plebiscitary** /-'bɪsɪtərɪ/ *adj.* [F *plébiscite* f. L *plebiscitum* f. *plebs plebis* the common people + *scitum* decree f. *sciscere* vote for]

plectrum /'plektrəm/ *n.* (*pl.* **plectrums** or **plectra** /-trə/) **1** a thin flat piece of plastic or horn etc. held in the hand and used to pluck a string, esp. of a guitar. **2** the corresponding mechanical part of a harpsichord etc. [L f. Gk *plēktron* f. *plēssō* strike]

pled see PLEAD.

pledge /pledʒ/ *n.* & *v.* —*n.* **1** a solemn promise or undertaking. **2** a thing given as security for the fulfilment of a contract, the payment of a debt, etc., and liable to forfeiture in the event of failure. **3** a thing put in pawn. **4** a thing given as a token of love, favour, or something to come. **5** the drinking of a person's health; a toast. **6** a solemn undertaking to abstain from alcohol (*sign the pledge*). **7** the state of being pledged (*goods lying in pledge*). —*v.tr.* **1 a** deposit as security. **b** pawn. **2** promise solemnly by the pledge of (one's honour, word, etc.). **3** (often *refl.*) bind by a solemn promise. **4** drink to the health of. □**pledge one's troth** see TROTH. □□ **pledgeable** *adj.* **pledger** *n.* **pledgor** *n.* [ME *plege* f. OF *plege* f. LL *plebium* f. *plebire* assure]

pledgee /ple'dʒiː/ *n.* a person to whom a pledge is given.

pledget /'pledʒɪt/ *n.* a small wad of lint etc. [16th c.: orig. unkn.]

pleiad /'plaɪəd/ *n.* a brilliant group of (usu. seven) persons or things. [named after PLEIADES]

Pleiades /'plaɪəˌdiːz/ *n.pl.* a cluster of stars in the constellation Taurus, usu. known as the 'Seven Sisters'. [ME f. L *Pleias* f. Gk *Plēias -ados*]

Pleistocene /'plaɪstəˌsiːn/ *adj.* & *n. Geol.* —*adj.* of or relating to the first epoch of the Quaternary period marked by great fluctuations in temperature with glacial periods followed by interglacial periods. —*n.* this epoch or system. Also called *Ice age*. ¶Cf. Appendix II. [Gk *pleistos* most + *kainos* new]

plenary /'pliːnərɪ/ *adj.* **1** entire, unqualified, absolute (*plenary indulgence*). **2** (of an assembly) to be attended by all members. [LL *plenarius* f. *plenus* full]

plenipotentiary /ˌplenɪpə'tenʃərɪ/ *n.* & *adj.* —*n.* (*pl.* **-ies**) a person (esp. a diplomat) invested with the full power of independent action. —*adj.* **1** having this power. **2** (of power) absolute. [med.L *plenipotentiarius* f. *plenus* full + *potentia* power]

plenitude /'plenɪˌtjuːd/ *n. literary* **1** fullness, completeness. **2** abundance. [ME f. OF f. LL *plenitudo* f. *plenus* full]

plenteous /'plentɪəs/ adj. poet. plentiful. □□
plenteously adv. **plenteousness** n. [ME f. OF
plentivous f. plentif -ive f. plenté PLENTY: cf. bounteous]
plentiful /'plentɪfʊl/ adj. abundant, copious. □□
plentifully adv. **plentifulness** n.
plenty /'plentɪ/ n., adj., & adv. —n. (often foll. by of)
a great or sufficient quantity or number (we have
plenty; plenty of time). —adj. colloq. existing in an
ample quantity. —adv. colloq. fully, entirely (it is
plenty large enough). [ME plenteth, plente f. OF
plentet f. L plenitas -tatis f. plenus full]
plenum /'pli:nəm/ n. **1** a full assembly of people or a
committee etc. **2** Physics space filled with matter. [L,
neut. of plenus full]
pleochroic /ˌpli:ə'krəʊɪk/ adj. showing different colours when viewed in different directions. □□
pleochroism n. [Gk pleiōn more + -khroos f. khrōs
colour]
pleomorphism /ˌpli:ə'mɔ:fɪz(ə)m/ n. Biol., Chem., &
Mineral. the occurrence of more than one distinct
form. □□ **pleomorphic** adj. [Gk pleiōn more + morphē form]
pleonasm /'pli:əˌnæz(ə)m/ n. the use of more words
than are needed to give the sense (e.g. see with one's
eyes). □□ **pleonastic** /-'næstɪk/ adj. **pleonastically**
/-'næstɪkəlɪ/ adv. [LL pleonasmus f. Gk pleonasmos f.
pleonazō be superfluous]
plesiosaurus /ˌpli:sɪə'sɔ:rəs/ n. (also **plesiosaur**
/'pli:sɪəˌsɔ:(r)/) any of a group of extinct marine
reptiles with a broad flat body, short tail, long flexible
neck, and large paddle-like limbs. [mod.L f. Gk plēsios
near + sauros lizard]
plessor var. of PLEXOR.
plethora /'pleθərə/ n. **1** an oversupply, glut, or
excess. **2** Med. **a** an abnormal excess of red corpuscles
in the blood. **b** an excess of any body fluid. □□
plethoric /also plɪ'θɒrɪk/ adj. **plethorically**
/plɪ'θɒrɪkəlɪ/ adv. [LL f. Gk plēthōrē f. plēthō be full]
pleura¹ /'plʊərə/ n. (pl. **pleurae** /-ri:/) **1** each of a
pair of serous membranes lining the thorax and
enveloping the lungs in mammals. **2** lateral extensions of the body-wall in arthropods. □□ **pleural**
adj. [med.L f. Gk, = side of the body, rib]
pleura² pl. of PLEURON.
pleurisy /'plʊərɪsɪ/ n. inflammation of the pleura,
marked by pain in the chest or side, fever, etc. □□
pleuritic /-'rɪtɪk/ adj. [ME f. OF pleurisie f. LL
pleurisis alt. f. L pleuritis f. Gk (as PLEURA¹)]
pleuro- /'plʊərəʊ/ comb. form **1** denoting the pleura.
2 denoting the side.
pleuron /'plʊərɒn/ n. (pl. **pleura** /-rə/) = PLEURA¹ 2.
[Gk, = side of the body, rib]
pleuropneumonia /ˌplʊərəʊnjuː'məʊnɪə/ n. pneumonia complicated with pleurisy.
Plexiglas /'pleksɪˌglɑːs/ n. propr. = PERSPEX. [formed
as PLEXOR + GLASS]
plexor /'pleksə(r)/ n. (also **plessor** /'plesə(r)/) Med. a
small hammer used to test reflexes and in percussing.
[irreg. f. Gk plēxis percussion + -OR¹]
plexus /'pleksəs/ n. (pl. same or **plexuses**) **1** Anat. a
network of nerves or vessels in an animal body
(gastric plexus). **2** any network or weblike formation.
□□ **plexiform** adj. [L f. plectere plex- plait]
pliable /'plaɪəb(ə)l/ adj. **1** bending easily; supple. **2**
yielding, compliant. □□ **pliability** /-'bɪlɪtɪ/ n.
pliableness n. **pliably** adv. [F f. plier bend: see
PLY¹]
pliant /'plaɪənt/ adj. = PLIABLE 1. □□ **pliancy** n.
pliantly adv. [ME f. OF (as PLIABLE)]
plicate /'plaɪkeɪt/ adj. Biol. & Geol. folded, crumpled,
corrugated. □□ **plicated** /plɪ'keɪtɪd/ adj. [L plicatus
past part. of plicare fold]
plication /plɪ'keɪʃ(ə)n/ n. **1** the act of folding. **2** a
fold; a folded condition. [ME f. med.L plicatio or L
plicare fold, after complication]
plié /'pli:eɪ/ n. Ballet a bending of the knees with the
feet on the ground. [F, past part. of plier bend: see
PLY¹]

pliers /'plaɪəz/ n.pl. pincers with parallel flat usu.
serrated surfaces for holding small objects, bending
wire, etc. [(dial.) ply bend (as PLIABLE)]
plight¹ /plaɪt/ n. a condition or state, esp. an unfortunate one. [ME & AF plit = OF pleit fold: see
PLAIT: -gh- by confusion with PLIGHT²]
plight² /plaɪt/ v. & n. archaic —v.tr. **1** pledge or
promise solemnly (one's faith, loyalty, etc.). **2** (foll.
by to) engage, esp. in marriage. —n. an engagement
or act of pledging. □**plight one's troth** see TROTH.
[orig. as noun, f. OE pliht danger f. Gmc]
plimsoll /'plɪms(ə)l/ n. (also **plimsole**) Brit. a
rubber-soled canvas sports shoe. [prob. from the
resemblance of the side of the sole to a PLIMSOLL
LINE]
Plimsoll line /'plɪms(ə)l/ n. (also **Plimsoll mark**)
a marking on a ship's side showing the limit of legal
submersion under various conditions. [S. Plimsoll,
Engl. politician d. 1898, promoter of the Merchant
Shipping Act of 1876]
plinth /plɪnθ/ n. **1** the lower square slab at the base
of a column. **2** a base supporting a vase or statue etc.
[F plinthe or L plinthus f. Gk plinthos tile, brick,
squared stone]
Pliocene /'plaɪəˌsi:n/ adj. & n. Geol. —adj. of or
relating to the last epoch of the Tertiary period with
evidence of the extinction of many mammals, and
the development of hominids. —n. this epoch or
system. ¶ Cf. Appendix II. [Gk pleiōn more + kainos
new]
plissé /'pli:seɪ/ adj. & n. —adj. (of cloth etc.) treated
so as to cause permanent puckering. —n. material
treated in this way. [F, past part. of plisser pleat]
PLO abbr. Palestine Liberation Organization.
plod /plɒd/ v. & n. —v. (**plodded**, **plodding**) **1** intr.
(often foll. by along, on, etc.) walk doggedly or
laboriously; trudge. **2** intr. (often foll. by at) work
slowly and steadily. **3** tr. tread or make (one's way)
laboriously. —n. the act or a spell of plodding. □□
plodder n. **ploddingly** adv. [16th c.: prob. imit.]
-ploid /plɔɪd/ comb. form Biol. forming adjectives
denoting the number of sets of chromosomes in a
cell (diploid; polyploid). [after HAPLOID]
ploidy /'plɔɪdɪ/ n. the number of sets of chromosomes
in a cell. [after DIPLOIDY, POLYPLOIDY, etc.]
plonk¹ /plɒŋk/ v. & n. —v.tr. **1** set down hurriedly
or clumsily. **2** (usu. foll. by down) set down firmly.
—n. **1** an act of plonking. **2** a heavy thud. [imit.]
plonk² /plɒŋk/ n. colloq. cheap or inferior wine.
[orig. Austral.: prob. corrupt. of blanc in F vin blanc
white wine]
plop /plɒp/ n., v., & adv. —n. **1** a sound as of a
smooth object dropping into water without a splash.
2 an act of falling with this sound. —v. (**plopped**,
plopping) intr. & tr. fall or drop with a plop. —adv.
with a plop. [19th c.: imit.]
plosion /'pləʊʒ(ə)n/ n. Phonet. the sudden release of
breath in the pronunciation of a stop consonant.
[EXPLOSION]
plosive /'pləʊsɪv/ adj. & n. Phonet. —adj. pronounced with a sudden release of breath. —n. a
plosive sound. [EXPLOSIVE]
plot /plɒt/ n. & v. —n. **1** a defined and usu. small
piece of ground. **2** the interrelationship of the main
events in a play, novel, film, etc. **3** a conspiracy or
secret plan, esp. to achieve an unlawful end. **4** esp.
US a graph or diagram. **5** a graph showing the
relation between two variables. —v. (**plotted**,
plotting) tr. **1** make a plan or map of (an existing
object, a place or thing to be laid out, constructed,
etc.). **2** (also absol.) plan or contrive secretly (a
crime, conspiracy, etc.). **3** mark (a point or course
etc.) on a chart or diagram. **4 a** mark out or allocate
(points) on a graph. **b** make (a curve etc.) by marking
out a number of points. □□ **plotless** adj. **plotlessness**
n. **plotter** n. [OE and f. OF complot secret plan: both
of unkn. orig.]
plough /plaʊ/ n. & v. (esp. US **plow**) —n. **1** an

implement with a cutting blade fixed in a frame drawn by a tractor or by horses, for cutting furrows in the soil and turning it up. **2** an implement resembling this and having a comparable function (*snowplough*). **3** ploughed land. **4** (**the Plough**) the constellation Ursa Major or its seven bright stars. —*v.* **1** *tr.* (also *absol.*) turn up (the earth) with a plough, esp. before sowing. **2** *tr.* (foll. by *out*, *up*, *down*, etc.) turn or extract (roots, weeds, etc.) with a plough. **3** *tr.* furrow or scratch (a surface) as if with a plough. **4** *tr.* produce (a furrow or line) in this way. **5** *intr.* (foll. by *through*) advance laboriously, esp. through work, a book, etc. **6** *intr.* (foll. by *through*, *into*) move like a plough violently. **7** *intr.* & *tr. Brit. colloq.* fail in an examination. □**plough back 1** plough (grass etc.) into the soil to enrich it. **2** reinvest (profits) in the business producing them. **Plough Monday** the first Monday after the Epiphany. **put one's hand to the plough** undertake a task (Luke 9:62). □□ **ploughable** *adj.* **plougher** *n.* [OE *plōh* f. ON *plógr* f. Gmc]

ploughman /ˈplaumən/ *n.* (*pl.* -**men**) a person who uses a plough. □**ploughman's lunch** a meal of bread and cheese with pickle or salad. **ploughman's spikenard** a composite fragrant plant, *Inula conyzae*, with purplish-yellow flowerheads.

ploughshare /ˈplauʃeə(r)/ *n.* the cutting blade of a plough.

plover /ˈplʌvə(r)/ *n.* any plump-breasted wading bird of the family Charadriidae, including the lapwing, usu. having a pigeon-like bill. [ME & AF f. OF *plo(u)vier* ult. f. L *pluvia* rain]

plow *US* var. of PLOUGH.

ploy /plɔɪ/ *n. colloq.* a stratagem; a cunning manœuvre to gain an advantage. [orig. Sc., 18th c.: orig. unkn.]

PLP *abbr.* (in the UK) Parliamentary Labour Party.

PLR *abbr.* (in the UK) Public Lending Right.

pluck /plʌk/ *v.* & *n.* —*v.* **1** *tr.* (often foll. by *out*, *off*, etc.) remove by picking or pulling out or away. **2** *tr.* strip (a bird) of feathers. **3** *tr.* pull at, twitch. **4** *intr.* (foll. by *at*) tug or snatch at. **5** *tr.* sound (the string of a musical instrument) with the finger or plectrum etc. **6** *tr.* plunder. **7** *tr.* swindle. —*n.* **1** courage, spirit. **2** an act of plucking; a twitch. **3** the heart, liver, and lungs of an animal as food. □**pluck up** summon up (one's courage, spirits, etc.). □□ **plucker** *n.* **pluckless** *adj.* [OE *ploccian*, *pluccian*, f. Gmc]

plucky /ˈplʌkɪ/ *adj.* (**pluckier**, **pluckiest**) brave, spirited. □□ **pluckily** *adv.* **pluckiness** *n.*

plug /plʌg/ *n.* & *v.* —*n.* **1** a piece of solid material fitting tightly into a hole, used to fill a gap or cavity or act as a wedge or stopper. **2 a** a device of metal pins in an insulated casing fitting into holes in a socket for making an electrical connection, esp. between an appliance and the mains. **b** *colloq.* an electric socket. **3** = *sparking-plug* (see SPARK[1]). **4** *colloq.* a piece of (often free) publicity for an idea, product, etc. **5** a mass of solidified lava filling the neck of a volcano. **6** a cake or stick of tobacco; a piece of this for chewing. **7** = *fire-plug*. —*v.* (**plugged**, **plugging**) **1** *tr.* (often foll. by *up*) stop (a hole etc.) with a plug. **2** *tr. sl.* shoot or hit (a person etc.). **3** *tr. colloq.* seek to popularize (an idea, product, etc.) by constant recommendation. **4** *intr. colloq.* (often foll. by *at*) work steadily away (at). □**plug in** connect electrically by inserting a plug in a socket. **plug-in** *adj.* able to be connected by means of a plug. **plug-ugly** *US sl. n.* (*pl.* -**ies**) a thug or ruffian. —*adj.* villainous-looking. □□ **plugger** *n.* [MDu. & MLG *plugge*, of unkn. orig.]

plum /plʌm/ *n.* **1 a** an oval fleshy fruit, usu. purple or yellow when ripe, with sweet pulp and a flattish pointed stone. **b** any deciduous tree of the genus *Prunus* bearing this. **2** a reddish-purple colour. **3** a dried grape or raisin used in cooking. **4** *colloq.* the best of a collection; something especially prized (often *attrib.*: *a plum job*). □**plum cake** a cake

containing raisins, currants, etc. **plum duff** a plain flour pudding with raisins or currants. **plum pudding** a rich boiled suet pudding with raisins, currants, spices, etc. [OE *plūme* f. med.L *pruna* f. L *prunum*]

plumage /ˈpluːmɪdʒ/ *n.* a bird's feathers. □□ **plumaged** *adj.* (usu. in *comb.*). [ME f. OF (as PLUME)]

plumassier /ˌpluːmæˈsɪə(r)/ *n.* a person who trades or works in ornamental feathers. [F f. *plumasse* augment. of *plume* (as PLUME)]

plumb¹ /plʌm/ *n.*, *adv.*, *adj.*, & *v.* —*n.* a ball of lead or other heavy material, esp. one attached to the end of a line for finding the depth of water or determining the vertical on an upright surface. —*adv.* **1** exactly (*plumb in the centre*). **2** vertically. **3** *US sl.* quite, utterly (*plumb crazy*). —*adj.* **1** vertical. **2** downright, sheer (*plumb nonsense*). **3** *Cricket* (of the wicket) level, true. —*v.tr.* **1 a** measure the depth of (water) with a plumb. **b** determine (a depth). **2** test (an upright surface) to determine the vertical. **3** reach or experience in extremes (*plumb the depths of fear*). **4** learn in detail the facts about (a matter). □**out of plumb** not vertical. **plumb-line** a line with a plumb attached. **plumb-rule** a mason's plumb-line attached to a board. [ME, prob. ult. f. L *plumbum* lead, assim. to OF *plomb* lead]

plumb² /plʌm/ *v.* **1** *tr.* provide (a building or room etc.) with plumbing. **2** *tr.* (often foll. by *in*) fit as part of a plumbing system. **3** *intr.* work as a plumber. [back-form. f. PLUMBER]

plumbago /plʌmˈbeɪgəʊ/ *n.* (*pl.* -**os**) **1** = GRAPHITE. **2** any plant of the genus *Plumbago*, with grey or blue flowers. Also called LEADWORT. [L f. *plumbum* LEAD²]

plumbeous /ˈplʌmbɪəs/ *adj.* **1** of or like lead. **2** lead-glazed. [L *plumbeus* f. *plumbum* LEAD²]

plumber /ˈplʌmə(r)/ *n.* a person who fits and repairs the apparatus of a water-supply, heating, etc. [ME *plummer* etc. f. OF *plommier* f. L *plumbarius* f. *plumbum* LEAD²]

plumbic /ˈplʌmbɪk/ *adj.* **1** *Chem.* containing lead esp. in its tetravalent form. **2** *Med.* due to the presence of lead. □□ **plumbism** *n.* (in sense 2). [L *plumbum* lead]

plumbing /ˈplʌmɪŋ/ *n.* **1** the system or apparatus of water-supply, heating, etc., in a building. **2** the work of a plumber. **3** *colloq.* lavatory installations.

plumbless /ˈplʌmlɪs/ *adj.* (of a depth of water etc.) that cannot be plumbed.

plumbous /ˈplʌmbəs/ *n. Chem.* containing lead in its divalent form.

plume /pluːm/ *n.* & *v.* —*n.* **1** a feather, esp. a large one used for ornament. **2** an ornament of feathers etc. attached to a helmet or hat or worn in the hair. **3** something resembling this (*a plume of smoke*). **4** *Zool.* a feather-like part or formation. —*v.* **1** *tr.* decorate or provide with a plume or plumes. **2** *refl.* (foll. by *on*, *upon*) pride (oneself on esp. something trivial). **3** *tr.* (of a bird) preen (itself or its feathers). □□ **plumeless** *adj.* **plumelike** *adj.* **plumery** *n.* [ME f. OF f. L *pluma* down]

plummet /ˈplʌmɪt/ *n.* & *v.* —*n.* **1** a plumb or plumb-line. **2** a sounding-line. **3** a weight attached to a fishing-line to keep the float upright. —*v.intr.* (**plummeted**, **plummeting**) fall or plunge rapidly. [ME f. OF *plommet* dimin. (as PLUMB¹)]

plummy /ˈplʌmɪ/ *adj.* (**plummier**, **plummiest**) **1** abounding or rich in plums. **2** *colloq.* (of a voice) sounding affectedly rich or deep in tone. **3** *colloq.* good, desirable.

plumose /ˈpluːməʊs/ *adj.* **1** feathered. **2** feather-like. [L *plumosus* (as PLUME)]

plump¹ /plʌmp/ *adj.* & *v.* —*adj.* (esp. of a person or animal or part of the body) having a full rounded shape; fleshy; filled out. —*v.tr.* & *intr.* (often foll. by *up*, *out*) make or become plump; fatten. □□ **plumpish** *adj.* **plumply** *adv.* **plumpness** *n.* **plumpy** *adj.* [ME *plompe* f. MDu. *plomp* blunt, MLG *plump*, *plomp* shapeless etc.]

plump[2] /plʌmp/ *v., n., adv.,* & *adj.* —*v.* **1** *intr.* & *tr.* (often foll. by *down*) drop or fall abruptly (*plumped down on the chair; plumped it on the floor*). **2** *intr.* (foll. by *for*) decide definitely in favour of (one of two or more possibilities). **3** *tr.* (often foll. by *out*) utter abruptly; blurt out. —*n.* an abrupt plunge; a heavy fall. —*adv. colloq.* **1** with a sudden or heavy fall. **2** directly, bluntly (*I told him plump*). —*adj. colloq.* direct, unqualified (*answered with a plump 'no'*). [ME f. MLG *plumpen*, MDu. *plompen*: orig. imit.]

plumule /ˈpluːmjuːl/ *n.* **1** the rudimentary shoot or stem of an embryo plant. **2** a down feather on a young bird. □□ **plumulaceous** /ˌpluːmjʊˈleɪʃəs/ *adj.* (in sense 2). **plumular** /ˈpluːmjʊlə(r)/ *adj.* (in sense 1). [F *plumule* or L *plumula*, dimin. (as PLUME)]

plumy /ˈpluːmɪ/ *adj.* (**plumier, plumiest**) **1** plume-like, feathery. **2** adorned with plumes.

plunder /ˈplʌndə(r)/ *v.* & *n.* —*v.tr.* **1** rob (a place or person) forcibly of goods, e.g. as in war. **2** rob systematically. **3** (also *absol.*) steal or embezzle (goods). —*n.* **1** the violent or dishonest acquisition of property. **2** property acquired by plundering. **3** *colloq.* profit, gain. □□ **plunderer** *n.* [LG *plündern* lit. 'rob of household goods' f. MHG *plunder* clothing etc.]

plunge /plʌndʒ/ *v.* & *n.* —*v.* **1** (usu. foll. by *in, into*) **a** *tr.* thrust forcefully or abruptly. **b** *intr.* dive; propel oneself forcibly. **c** *intr.* & *tr.* enter or cause to enter a certain condition or embark on a certain course abruptly or impetuously (*they plunged into a lively discussion; the room was plunged into darkness*). **2** *tr.* immerse completely. **3** *intr.* **a** move suddenly and dramatically downward. **b** (foll. by *down, into*, etc.) move with a rush (*plunged down the stairs*). **c** diminish rapidly (*share prices have plunged*). **4** *intr.* (of a horse) start violently forward. **5** *intr.* (of a ship) pitch. **6** *intr. colloq.* gamble heavily; run into debt. —*n.* a plunging action or movement; a dive. □ **plunging** (or **plunge**) **neckline** a low-cut neckline. **take the plunge** *colloq.* commit oneself to a (usu. risky) course of action. [ME f. OF *plungier* ult. f. L *plumbum* plummet]

plunger /ˈplʌndʒə(r)/ *n.* **1** a part of a mechanism that works with a plunging or thrusting movement. **2** a rubber cup on a handle for clearing blocked pipes by a plunging and sucking action. **3** *colloq.* a reckless gamble.

plunk /plʌŋk/ *n.* & *v.* —*n.* **1** the sound made by the sharply plucked string of a stringed instrument. **2** *US* a heavy blow. **3** *US* = PLONK[1] *n.* —*v.* **1** *intr.* & *tr.* sound or cause to sound with a plunk. **2** *tr. US* hit abruptly. **3** *tr. US* = PLONK[1] *v.* [imit.]

pluperfect /pluːˈpɜːfɪkt/ *adj.* & *n. Gram.* —*adj.* (of a tense) denoting an action completed prior to some past point of time specified or implied, formed in English by *had* and the past participle, as: *he had gone by then*. —*n.* the pluperfect tense. [mod.L *plusperfectum* f. L *plus quam perfectum* more than perfect]

plural /ˈplʊər(ə)l/ *adj.* & *n.* —*adj.* **1** more than one in number. **2** *Gram.* (of a word or form) denoting more than one, or (in languages with dual number) more than two. —*n. Gram.* **1** a plural word or form. **2** the plural number. □□ **plurally** *adv.* [ME f. OF *plurel* f. L *pluralis* f. *plus pluris* more]

pluralism /ˈplʊərəˌlɪz(ə)m/ *n.* **1** holding more than one office, esp. an ecclesiastical office or benefice, at a time. **2** a form of society in which the members of minority groups maintain their independent cultural traditions. **3** *Philos.* a system that recognizes more than one ultimate principle (cf. MONISM 2). □□ **pluralist** *n.* **pluralistic** /-ˈlɪstɪk/ *adj.* **pluralistically** /-ˈlɪstɪkəlɪ/ *adv.*

plurality /plʊəˈrælɪtɪ/ *n.* (*pl.* **-ies**) **1** the state of being plural. **2** = PLURALISM 1. **3** a large or the greater number. **4** *US* a majority that is not absolute. [ME f. OF *pluralité* f. LL *pluralitas* (as PLURAL)]

pluralize /ˈplʊərəˌlaɪz/ *v.* (also **-ise**) **1** *tr.* & *intr.* make

or become plural. **2** *tr.* express in the plural. **3** *intr.* hold more than one ecclesiastical office or benefice.

pluri- /ˈplʊərɪ/ *comb. form* several. [L *plus pluris* more, *plures* several]

plus /plʌs/ *prep., adj., n.,* & *conj.* —*prep.* **1** *Math.* with the addition of (*3 plus 4 equals 7*). ¶ Symbol: +. **2** (of temperature) above zero (*plus 2° C*). **3** *colloq.* with; having gained; newly possessing (*returned plus a new car*). —*adj.* **1** (after a number) at least (*fifteen plus*). **2** (after a grade etc.) rather better than (*beta plus*). **3** *Math.* positive. **4** having a positive electrical charge. **5** (*attrib.*) additional, extra (*plus business*). —*n.* **1** = *plus sign.* **2** *Math.* an additional or positive quantity. **3** an advantage (*experience is a definite plus*). —*conj. colloq. disp.* also; and furthermore (*they arrived late, plus they were hungry*). □ **plus sign** the symbol +, indicating addition or a positive value. [L, = more]

plus-fours /plʌsˈfɔːz/ *n.* long wide men's knickerbockers usu. worn for golf etc. [20th c.: so named because the overhang at the knee requires an extra four inches]

plush /plʌʃ/ *n.* & *adj.* —*n.* cloth of silk or cotton etc., with a long soft nap. —*adj.* **1** made of plush. **2** plushy. □□ **plushly** *adv.* **plushness** *n.* [obs. F *pluche* contr. f. *peluche* f. OF *peluchier* f. It. *peluzzo* dimin. of *pelo* f. L *pilus* hair]

plushy /ˈplʌʃɪ/ *adj.* (**plushier, plushiest**) *colloq.* stylish, luxurious. □□ **plushiness** *n.*

plutarchy /ˈpluːtɑːkɪ/ *n.* (*pl.* **-ies**) plutocracy. [Gk *ploutos* wealth + *-arkhia* -rule]

Pluto /ˈpluːtəʊ/ *n.* the outermost known planet of the solar system. [L f. Gk *Ploutōn* god of the underworld]

plutocracy /pluːˈtɒkrəsɪ/ *n.* (*pl.* **-ies**) **1 a** government by the wealthy. **b** a State governed in this way. **2 a** wealthy élite or ruling class. □□ **plutocratic** /ˌpluːtəˈkrætɪk/ *adj.* **plutocratically** /ˌpluːtəˈkrætɪkəlɪ/ *adv.* [Gk *ploutokratia* f. *ploutos* wealth + -CRACY]

plutocrat /ˈpluːtəˌkræt/ *n. derog.* or *joc.* **1** a member of a plutocracy or wealthy élite. **2** a wealthy and influential person.

pluton /ˈpluːt(ə)n/ *n. Geol.* a body of plutonic rock. [back-form. f. PLUTONIC]

Plutonian /pluːˈtəʊnɪən/ *adj.* **1** infernal. **2** of the infernal regions. [L *Plutonius* f. Gk *Ploutōnios* (as PLUTO)]

plutonic /pluːˈtɒnɪk/ *adj.* **1** *Geol.* (of rock) formed as igneous rock by solidification below the surface of the earth. **2** (**Plutonic**) = PLUTONIAN. [formed as PLUTONIAN]

plutonium /pluːˈtəʊnɪəm/ *n. Chem.* a dense silvery radioactive metallic transuranic element of the actinide series, used in some nuclear reactors and weapons. ¶ Symb.: Pu. [PLUTO (as the next planet beyond Neptune) + -IUM]

pluvial /ˈpluːvɪəl/ *adj.* & *n.* —*adj.* **1** of rain; rainy. **2** *Geol.* caused by rain. —*n.* a period of prolonged rainfall. □□ **pluvious** *adj.* (in sense 1). [L *pluvialis* f. *pluvia* rain]

pluviometer /ˌpluːvɪˈɒmɪtə(r)/ *n.* a rain-gauge. □□ **pluviometric** /-əˈmetrɪk/ *adj.* **pluviometrical** /-əˈmetrɪk(ə)l/ *adj.* **pluviometrically** /-əˈmetrɪkəlɪ/ *adv.* [L *pluvia* rain + -METER]

ply[1] /plaɪ/ *n.* (*pl.* **-ies**) **1** a thickness or layer of certain materials, esp. wood or cloth (*three-ply*). **2** a strand of yarn or rope etc. [ME f. F *pli* f. *plier, pleier* f. L *plicare* fold]

ply[2] /plaɪ/ *v.* (**-ies, -ied**) **1** *tr.* use or wield vigorously (a tool, weapon, etc.). **2** *tr.* work steadily at (one's business or trade). **3** *tr.* (foll. by *with*) **a** supply (a person) continuously (with food, drink, etc.). **b** approach repeatedly (with questions, demands, etc.). **4 a** *intr.* (often foll. by *between*) (of a vehicle etc.) travel regularly (to and fro between two points). **b** *tr.* work (a route) in this way. **5** *intr.* (of a taxi-driver, boatman, etc.) attend regularly for custom (*ply for trade*). **6** *intr.* sail to windward. [ME *plye*, f. APPLY]

Plymouth Brethren /'plɪməθ/ *n.pl.* a strict Calvinistic religious body formed at Plymouth in Devon *c.*1830, having no formal creed and no official order of ministers.

plywood /'plaɪwʊd/ *n.* a strong thin board consisting of two or more layers glued and pressed together with the direction of the grain alternating.

PM *abbr.* **1** Prime Minister. **2** post-mortem. **3** Provost Marshal.

Pm *symb. Chem.* the element promethium.

p.m. *abbr.* after noon. [L *post meridiem*]

PMG *abbr.* **1** Paymaster General. **2** Postmaster General.

PMT *abbr.* premenstrual tension.

PNdB *abbr.* perceived noise decibel(s).

pneumatic /nju:'mætɪk/ *adj.* & *n.* —*adj.* **1** of or relating to air or wind. **2** containing or operated by compressed air. **3** connected with or containing air cavities esp. in the bones of birds or in fish. □**pneumatic drill** a drill driven by compressed air, for breaking up a hard surface. **pneumatic trough** a shallow container used in laboratories to collect gases in jars over the surface of water or mercury. □□**pneumatically** *adv.* **pneumaticity** /ˌnju:mə'tɪsɪtɪ/ *n.* [F *pneumatique* or L *pneumaticus* f. Gk *pneumatikos* f. *pneuma* wind f. *pneō* breathe]

pneumatics /nju:'mætɪks/ *n.pl.* (treated as *sing.*) the science of the mechanical properties of gases.

pneumato- /'nju:mətəʊ/ *comb. form* denoting: **1** air. **2** breath. **3** spirit. [Gk f. *pneuma* (as PNEUMATIC)]

pneumatology /ˌnju:mə'tɒlədʒɪ/ *n.* **1** the branch of theology concerned with the Holy Ghost and other spiritual concepts. **2** *archaic* psychology. □□ **pneumatological** /-tə'lɒdʒɪk(ə)l/ *adj.*

pneumatophore /'nju:mətəˌfɔ:(r)/ *n.* **1** the gaseous cavity of various hydrozoa, such as the Portuguese man-of-war. **2** an aerial root specialized for gaseous exchange found in various plants growing in swampy areas.

pneumo- /'nju:məʊ/ *comb. form* denoting the lungs. [abbr. of *pneumono-* f. Gk *pneumōn* lung]

pneumoconiosis /ˌnju:məʊˌkɒnɪ'əʊsɪs/ *n.* a lung disease caused by inhalation of dust or small particles. [PNEUMO- + Gk *konis* dust]

pneumogastric /ˌnju:məʊ'gæstrɪk/ *adj.* of or relating to the lungs and stomach.

pneumonectomy /ˌnju:ju:mə'nektəmɪ/ *n.* (*pl.* **-ies**) *Surgery* the surgical removal of a lung or part of a lung.

pneumonia /nju:'məʊnɪə/ *n.* a bacterial inflammation of one lung (**single pneumonia**) or both lungs (**double pneumonia**) causing the air sacs to fill with pus and become solid. □□**pneumonic** /nju:'mɒnɪk/ *adj.* [L f. Gk f. *pneumōn* lung]

pneumonitis /ˌnju:mə'naɪtɪs/ *n.* inflammation of the lungs usu. caused by a virus.

pneumothorax /ˌnju:məʊ'θɔ:ræks/ *n.* the presence of air or gas in the cavity between the lungs and the chest wall.

PNG *abbr.* Papua New Guinea.

PO *abbr.* **1** Post Office. **2** postal order. **3** Petty Officer. **4** Pilot Officer.

Po *symb. Chem.* the element polonium.

po /pəʊ/ *n.* (*pl.* **pos**) *Brit. colloq.* a chamber-pot.

POA *abbr.* (in the UK) Prison Officers' Association.

poach[1] /pəʊtʃ/ *v.tr.* **1** cook (an egg) without its shell in or over boiling water. **2** cook (fish etc.) by simmering in a small amount of liquid. □□ **poacher** *n.* [ME f. OF *pochier* f. *poche* POKE[2]]

poach[2] /pəʊtʃ/ *v.* **1** *tr.* (also *absol.*) catch (game or fish) illegally. **2** *intr.* (often foll. by *on*) trespass or encroach (on another's property, ideas, etc.). **3** *tr.* appropriate illicitly or unfairly (a person, thing, idea, etc.). **4** *tr. Tennis* etc. take (a shot) in one's partner's portion of the court. **5 a** *tr.* trample or cut up (turf) with hoofs. **b** *intr.* (of land) become sodden by being trampled. □□ **poacher** *n.* [earlier *poche*, perh. f. F *pocher* put in a pocket (as POACH[1])]

pochard /'pəʊtʃəd/ *n.* any duck of the genus *Aythya*, esp. *A. ferina*, the male of which has a bright reddish-brown head and neck and a grey breast. [16th c.: orig. unkn.]

pochette /pɒ'ʃet/ *n.* a woman's envelope-shaped handbag. [F, dimin. of *poche* pocket: see POKE[2]]

pock /pɒk/ *n.* (also **pock-mark**) **1** a small pus-filled spot on the skin, esp. caused by chickenpox or smallpox. **2** a mark resembling this. □**pock-marked** bearing marks resembling or left by such spots. □□ **pocky** *adj.* [OE *poc* f. Gmc]

pocket /'pɒkɪt/ *n.* & *v.* —*n.* **1** a small bag sewn into or on clothing, for carrying small articles. **2** a pouchlike compartment in a suitcase, car door, etc. **3** one's financial resources (*it is beyond my pocket*). **4** an isolated group or area (*a few pockets of resistance remain*). **5 a** a cavity in the earth containing ore, esp. gold. **b** a cavity in rock, esp. filled with foreign matter. **6** a pouch at the corner or on the side of a billiard- or snooker-table into which balls are driven. **7** = *air pocket*. **8** (*attrib.*) **a** of a suitable size and shape for carrying in a pocket. **b** smaller than the usual size. —*v.tr.* (**pocketed, pocketing**) **1** put into one's pocket. **2** appropriate, esp. dishonestly. **3** confine as in a pocket. **4** submit to (an injury or affront). **5** conceal or suppress (one's feelings). **6** *Billiards* etc. drive (a ball) into a pocket. □**in pocket 1** having gained in a transaction. **2** (of money) available. **in a person's pocket 1** under a person's control. **2** close to or intimate with a person. **out of pocket** having lost in a transaction. **out-of-pocket expenses** the actual outlay of cash incurred. **pocket battleship** *hist.* a warship armoured and equipped like, but smaller than, a battleship. **pocket borough** *Brit. hist.* a borough in which the election of political representatives was controlled by one person or family. **pocket gopher** = GOPHER[1] 1. **pocket knife** a knife with a folding blade or blades, for carrying in the pocket. **pocket money 1** money for minor expenses. **2** *Brit.* an allowance of money made to a child. **put one's hand in one's pocket** spend or provide money. □□ **pocketable** *adj.* **pocketless** *adj.* **pockety** *adj.* (in sense 5 of *n.*). [ME f. AF *poket(e)* dimin. of *poke* POKE[2]]

pocketbook /'pɒkɪtˌbʊk/ *n.* **1** a notebook. **2** a booklike case for papers or money carried in a pocket. **3** *US* a purse or handbag. **4** *US* a paperback or other small book.

pocketful /'pɒkɪtˌfʊl/ *n.* (*pl.* **-fuls**) as much as a pocket will hold.

poco /'pəʊkəʊ/ *adv. Mus.* a little; rather (*poco adagio*). [It.]

pod[1] /pɒd/ *n.* & *v.* —*n.* **1** a long seed-vessel esp. of a leguminous plant, e.g. a pea. **2** the cocoon of a silkworm. **3** the case surrounding locust eggs. **4** a narrow-necked eel-net. **5** a compartment suspended under an aircraft for equipment etc. —*v.* (**podded, podding**) **1** *intr.* bear or form pods. **2** *tr.* remove (peas etc.) from pods. □**in pod** *colloq.* pregnant. [back-form. f. dial. *podware, podder* field crops, of unkn. orig.]

podagra /pə'dægrə, 'pɒdəgrə/ *n. Med.* gout of the foot, esp. the big toe. □□ **podagral** *adj.* **podagric** *adj.* **podagrous** *adj.* [L f. Gk *pous podos* foot + *agra* seizure]

podgy /'pɒdʒɪ/ *adj.* (**podgier, podgiest**) **1** (of a person) short and fat. **2** (of a face etc.) plump, fleshy. □□ **podginess** *n.* [19th c.: f. *podge* a short fat person]

podiatry /pə'daɪətrɪ/ *n. US* = CHIROPODY. □□ **podiatrist** *n.* [Gk *pous podos* foot + *iatros* physician]

podium /'pəʊdɪəm/ *n.* (*pl.* **podiums** or **podia** /-dɪə/) **1** a continuous projecting base or pedestal round a room or house etc. **2** a raised platform round the arena of an amphitheatre. **3** a platform or rostrum. [L f. Gk *podion* dimin. of *pous pod-* foot]

podzol /'pɒdzɒl/ *n.* (also **podsol** /-sɒl/) a soil with minerals leached from its surface layers into a lower stratum. □□ **podzolize** *v.tr.* & *intr.* (also **-ise**). [Russ. f. *pod* under, *zola* ashes]

poem /'pəʊɪm/ *n.* **1** a metrical composition, usu. concerned with feeling or imaginative description. **2** an elevated composition in verse or prose. **3** something with poetic qualities (*a poem in stone*). [F *poème* or L *poema* f. Gk *poēma* = *poiēma* f. *poieō* make]

poesy /'pəʊɪzɪ, -sɪ/ *n. archaic* **1** poetry. **2** the art or composition of poetry. [ME f. OF *poesie* ult. f. L *poesis* f. Gk *poēsis* = *poiēsis* making, poetry (as POEM)]

poet /'pəʊɪt/ *n.* (*fem.* **poetess**) **1** a writer of poems. **2** a person possessing high powers of imagination or expression etc. □**Poet Laureate** (in the UK) a poet appointed to write poems for State occasions. **Poets' Corner** part of Westminster Abbey where several poets are buried or commemorated. [ME f. OF *poete* f. L *poeta* f. Gk *poētēs* = *poiētēs* maker, poet (as POEM)]

poetaster /ˌpəʊɪ'tæstə(r)/ *n.* a paltry or inferior poet. [mod.L (as POET): see -ASTER]

poetic /pəʊ'etɪk/ *adj.* (also **poetical** /-tɪk(ə)l/) **1 a** of or like poetry or poets. **b** written in verse. **2** elevated or sublime in expression. □**poetic justice** well-deserved unforeseen retribution or reward. **poetic licence** a writer's or artist's transgression of established rules for effect. □□**poetically** *adv.* [F *poétique* f. L *poeticus* f. Gk *poētikos* (as POET)]

poeticize /pəʊ'etɪˌsaɪz/ *v.tr.* (also **-ise**) make (a theme) poetic.

poetics /pəʊ'etɪks/ *n.* **1** the art of writing poetry. **2** the study of poetry and its techniques.

poetize /'pəʊɪˌtaɪz/ *v.* (also **-ise**) **1** *intr.* play the poet. **2** *intr.* compose poetry. **3** *tr.* treat poetically. **4** *tr.* celebrate in poetry. [F *poétiser* (as POET)]

poetry /'pəʊɪtrɪ/ *n.* **1** the art or work of a poet. **2** poems collectively. **3** a poetic or tenderly pleasing quality. **4** anything compared to poetry. [ME f. med.L *poetria* f. L *poeta* POET, prob. after *geometry*]

po-faced /pəʊ'feɪsd/ *adj.* **1** solemn-faced, humourless. **2** smug. [20th c.: perh. f. PO, infl. by *poker-faced*]

pogo /'pəʊgəʊ/ *n.* (*pl.* **-os**) (also **pogo stick**) a toy consisting of a spring-loaded stick with rests for the feet, for springing about on. [20th c.: orig. uncert.]

pogrom /'pɒgrəm, -rɒm/ *n.* an organized massacre (orig. of Jews in Russia). [Russ., = devastation f. *gromit* destroy]

poignant /'pɔɪnjənt/ *adj.* **1** painfully sharp to the emotions or senses; deeply moving. **2** arousing sympathy. **3** sharp or pungent in taste or smell. **4** pleasantly piquant. □□**poignance** *n.* **poignancy** *n.* **poignantly** *adv.* [ME f. OF, pres. part. of *poindre* prick f. L *pungere*]

poikilotherm /'pɔɪkɪləˌθɜːm/ *n.* an organism that regulates its body temperature by behavioural means, such as basking or burrowing; a cold-blooded organism (cf. HOMOEOTHERM). □□**poikilothermal** /-'θɜːm(ə)l/ *adj.* **poikilothermia** /-'θɜːmɪə/ *n.* **poikilothermic** /-'θɜːmɪk/ *adj.* **poikilothermy** *n.* [Gk *poikilos* multicoloured, changeable + *thermē* heat]

poilu /pwɑ:'lu:/ *n. hist.* a French private soldier, esp. as a nickname. [F, lit. hairy f. *poil* hair]

poinciana /ˌpɔɪnsɪ'ɑːnə/ *n.* any tropical tree of the genus *Poinciana*, with bright showy red flowers. [mod.L f. M. de *Poinci*, 17th-c. governor in the West Indies + -*ana* fem. suffix]

poind /pɔɪnd/ *v.* & *n. Sc.* —*v.tr.* distrain upon; impound. —*n.* **1** an act of poinding. **2** an animal or chattel poinded. [ME f. OE *pyndan* impound]

poinsettia /pɔɪn'setɪə/ *n.* a shrub, *Euphorbia pulcherrima*, with large showy scarlet or pink bracts surrounding small yellow flowers. [mod.L f. J. R. *Poinsett*, Amer. diplomat d. 1851]

point /pɔɪnt/ *n.* & *v.* —*n.* **1** the sharp or tapered end of a tool, weapon, pencil, etc. **2** a tip or extreme end. **3** that which in geometry has position but not magnitude, e.g. the intersection of two lines. **4** a particular place or position (*Bombay and points east;*

point of contact). **5 a** a precise or particular moment (*at the point of death*). **b** the critical or decisive moment (*when it came to the point, he refused*). **6** a very small mark on a surface. **7 a** a dot or other punctuation mark, esp. = *full point* = FULL[1]. **b** a dot or small stroke used in Semitic languages to indicate vowels or distinguish consonants. **8** = *decimal point.* **9** a stage or degree in progress or increase (*abrupt to the point of rudeness; at that point we gave up*). **10** a level of temperature at which a change of state occurs (*freezing-point*). **11** a single item; a detail or particular (*we differ on these points; it is a point of principle*). **12 a** a unit of scoring in games or of measuring value etc. **b** an advantage or success in less quantifiable contexts such as an argument or discussion. **c** a unit of weight (2 mg) for diamonds. **d** a unit (of varying value) in quoting the price of stocks etc. **13 a** (usu. prec. by *the*) the significant or essential thing; what is actually intended or under discussion (*that was the point of the question*). **b** (usu. with *neg.* or *interrog.*; often foll. by *in*) sense or purpose; advantage or value (*saw no point in staying*). **c** (usu. prec. by *the*) a salient feature of a story, joke, remark, etc. (*don't see the point*). **14** a distinctive feature or characteristic (*it has its points; tact is not his good point*). **15** pungency, effectiveness (*their comments lacked point*). **16 a** each of 32 directions marked at equal distances round a compass. **b** the corresponding direction towards the horizon. **17** (usu. in *pl.*) *Brit.* a junction of two railway lines, with a pair of linked tapering rails that can be moved laterally to allow a train to pass from one line to the other. **18** *Brit.* = *power point.* **19** (usu. in *pl.*) each of a set of electrical contacts in the distributor of a motor vehicle. **20** *Cricket* **a** a fielder on the off side near the batsman. **b** this position. **21** the tip of the toe in ballet. **22** a promontory. **23** the prong of a deer's antler. **24** the extremities of a dog, horse, etc. **25** *Printing* a unit of measurement for type bodies (in the UK and US 0.0138 in., in Europe 0.0148 in.). **26** *Hunting* **a** a spot to which a straight run is made. **b** such a run. **27** *Heraldry* any of nine particular positions on a shield used for specifying the position of charges etc. **28** *Boxing* the tip of the chin as a spot for a knockout blow. **29** *Mil.* a small leading party of an advanced guard. **30** *hist.* a tagged lace for lacing a bodice, attaching a hose to a doublet, etc. **31** *Naut.* a short piece of cord at the lower edge of a sail for tying up a reef. **32** the act or position of a dog in pointing. —*v.* **1** (usu. foll. by *to, at*) **a** *tr.* direct or aim (a finger, weapon, etc.). **b** *intr.* direct attention in a certain direction (*pointed to the house across the road*). **2** *intr.* (foll. by *at, towards*) **a** aim or be directed to. **b** tend towards. **3** *intr.* (foll. by *to*) indicate; be evidence of (*it all points to murder*). **4** *tr.* give point or force to (words or actions). **5** *tr.* fill in or repair the joints of (brickwork) with smoothly finished mortar or cement. **6** *tr.* a punctuate. **b** insert points in (written Hebrew etc.). **c** mark (Psalms etc.) with signs for chanting. **7** *tr.* sharpen (a pencil, tool, etc.). **8** *tr.* (also *absol.*) (of a dog) indicate the presence of (game) by acting as pointer. □**at all points** in every part or respect. **at the point of** (often foll. by verbal noun) on the verge of; about to do (the action specified). **beside the point** irrelevant or irrelevantly. **case in point** an instance that is relevant or (prec. by *the*) under consideration. **have a point** be correct or effective in one's contention. **in point** apposite, relevant. **in point of fact** see FACT. **make** (or **prove**) **a** (or **one's**) **point** establish a proposition; prove one's contention. **make a point of** (often foll. by verbal noun) insist on; treat or regard as essential. **nine points** nine tenths, i.e. nearly the whole (esp. *possession is nine points of the law*). **on** (or **upon**) **the point of** (foll. by verbal noun) about to do (the action specified). **point-duty** the positioning of a police officer or traffic warden at a crossroad or other point to control traffic. **point** lace thread lace made wholly with a needle. **point of honour** an action or circumstance that affects one's reputation. **point of no return** a point in a journey or enterprise at which it becomes essential or more practical to continue to the end. **point of order** a query in a debate etc. as to whether correct procedure is being followed. **point-of-sale** (usu. *attrib.*) denoting publicity etc. associated with the place at which goods are retailed. **point of view 1** a position from which a thing is viewed. **2** a particular way of considering a matter. **point out** (often foll. by *that* + clause) indicate, show; draw attention to. **point-to-point** a steeplechase over a marked course for horses used regularly in hunting. **point up** emphasize; show as important. **score points off** get the better of in an argument etc. **take a person's point** concede that a person has made a valid contention. **to the point** relevant or relevantly. **up to a point** to some extent but not completely. **win on points** *Boxing* win by scoring more points, not by a knockout. [ME f. OF *point, pointer* f. L *punctum* f. *pungere punct-* prick]

point-blank /ˌpɔɪntˈblæŋk/ *adj. & adv.* —*adj.* **1 a** (of a shot) aimed or fired horizontally at a range very close to the target. **b** (of a distance or range) very close. **2** (of a remark, question, etc.) blunt, direct. —*adv.* **1** at very close range. **2** directly, bluntly. [prob. f. POINT + BLANK = white spot in the centre of a target]

pointed /ˈpɔɪntɪd/ *adj.* **1** sharpened or tapering to a point. **2** (of a remark etc.) having point; penetrating, cutting. **3** emphasized; made evident. □□ **pointedly** *adv.* **pointedness** *n.*

pointer /ˈpɔɪntə(r)/ *n.* **1** a thing that points, e.g. the index hand of a gauge etc. **2** a rod for pointing to features on a map, chart, etc. **3** *colloq.* a hint, clue, or indication. **4 a** a dog of a breed that on scenting game stands rigid looking towards it. **b** this breed. **5** (in *pl.*) two stars in the Great Bear in line with the pole star.

pointillism /ˈpwæntɪˌlɪz(ə)m/ *n. Art* a technique of impressionist painting using tiny dots of various pure colours, which become blended in the viewer's eye. □□ **pointillist** *n. & adj.* **pointillistic** /-ˈlɪstɪk/ *adj.* [F *pointillisme* f. *pointiller* mark with dots]

pointing /ˈpɔɪntɪŋ/ *n.* **1** cement or mortar filling the joints of brickwork. **2** facing produced by this. **3** the process of producing this.

pointless /ˈpɔɪntlɪs/ *adj.* **1** without a point. **2** lacking force, purpose, or meaning. **3** (in games) without a point scored. □□ **pointlessly** *adv.* **pointlessness** *n.*

pointsman /ˈpɔɪntsmən/ *n.* (*pl.* **-men**) *Brit.* **1** a person in charge of railway points. **2** a policeman or traffic warden on point-duty.

pointy /ˈpɔɪntɪ/ *adj.* (**pointier, pointiest**) having a noticeably sharp end; pointed.

poise[1] /pɔɪz/ *n. & v.* —*n.* **1** composure or self-possession of manner. **2** equilibrium; a stable state. **3** carriage (of the head etc.). —*v.* **1** *tr.* balance; hold suspended or supported. **2** *tr.* carry (one's head etc. in a specified way). **3** *intr.* be balanced; hover in the air etc. [ME f. OF *pois, peis, peser* ult. f. L *pensum* weight f. *pendere pens-* weigh]

poise[2] /pɔɪz/ *n. Physics* a unit of dynamic viscosity, such that a tangential force of one dyne per square centimetre causes a velocity change one centimetre per second between two parallel planes in a liquid separated by one centimetre. [J. L. M. *Poiseuille*, Fr. physician d. 1869]

poised /pɔɪzd/ *adj.* **1** composed, self-assured. **2** (often foll. by *for*, or *to* + infin.) ready for action.

poison /ˈpɔɪz(ə)n/ *n. & v.* —*n.* **1** a substance that when introduced into or absorbed by a living organism causes death or injury, esp. one that kills by rapid action even in a small quantity. **2** *colloq.* a harmful influence or principle etc. **3** *Physics & Chem.* a substance that interferes with the normal progress of a nuclear reaction, chain reaction, catalytic reaction, etc. —*v.tr.* **1** administer poison to (a person or animal). **2** kill or injure or infect with poison. **3** infect (air, water, etc.) with poison. **4** (esp. as **poisoned** *adj.*) treat (a weapon) with poison. **5** corrupt or pervert (a person or mind). **6** spoil or destroy (a person's pleasure etc.). **7** render (land etc.) foul and unfit for its purpose by a noxious application etc. □ **poison gas** = GAS *n.* 4. **poison ivy** a N. American climbing plant, *Rhus toxicodendron*, secreting an irritant oil from its leaves. **poison-pen letter** an anonymous libellous or abusive letter. □□ **poisoner** *n.* **poisonous** *adj.* **poisonously** *adv.* [ME f. OF *poison, poisonner* (as POTION)]

Poisson distribution /ˈpwʌsɔ̃/ *n. Statistics* a discrete frequency distribution which gives the probability of events occurring in a fixed time. [S. D. *Poisson*, French mathematician d. 1840]

poke[1] /pəʊk/ *v. & n.* —*v.* **1** (foll. by *in, up, down,* etc.) **a** *tr.* thrust or push with the hand, point of a stick, etc. **b** *intr.* be thrust forward. **2** *tr.* (foll. by *at* etc.) make thrusts with a stick etc. **3** *tr.* thrust the end of a finger etc. against. **4** *tr.* (foll. by *in*) produce (a hole etc. in a thing) by poking. **5** *tr.* thrust forward, esp. obtrusively. **6** *tr.* stir (a fire) with a poker. **7** *intr.* **a** (often foll. by *about, around*) move or act desultorily; potter. **b** (foll. by *about, into*) pry; search casually. **8** *tr. coarse sl.* have sexual intercourse with. **9** *tr.* (foll. by *up*) *colloq.* confine (esp. oneself) in a poky place. —*n.* **1** the act or an instance of poking. **2** a thrust or nudge. **3** a device fastened on cattle etc. to prevent them breaking through fences. **4 a** a projecting brim or front of a woman's bonnet or hat. **b** (in full **poke-bonnet**) a bonnet having this. □ **poke fun at** ridicule, tease. **poke one's nose into** *colloq.* pry or intrude into (esp. a person's affairs). [ME f. MDu. and MLG *poken*, of unkn. orig.]

poke[2] /pəʊk/ *n. dial.* a bag or sack. □ **buy a pig in a poke** see PIG. [ME f. ONF *poke, poque* = OF *poche*: cf. POUCH]

poker[1] /ˈpəʊkə(r)/ *n.* a stiff metal rod with a handle for stirring an open fire. □ **poker-work 1** the technique of burning designs on white wood etc. with a heated metal rod. **2** a design made in this way.

poker[2] /ˈpəʊkə(r)/ *n.* a card-game in which bluff is used as players bet on the value of their hands. □ **poker-dice** dice with card designs from ace to nine instead of spots. **poker-face** the impassive countenance appropriate to a poker-player. **2 a** person with this. **poker-faced** having a poker-face. [19th c.: orig. unkn.: cf. G *pochen* to brag, *Pochspiel* bragging game]

pokeweed /ˈpəʊkwiːd/ *n.* a tall hardy American plant, *Phytolacca americana*, with spikes of cream flowers and purple berries that yield emetics and purgatives. [*poke*, Amer. Ind. word + WEED]

pokey /ˈpəʊkɪ/ *n. US sl.* prison. [perh. f. POKY]

poky /ˈpəʊkɪ/ *adj.* (**pokier, pokiest**) (of a room etc.) small and cramped. □□ **pokily** *adv.* **pokiness** *n.* [POKE[1] (in colloq. sense 'confine') + -Y[1]]

polack /ˈpəʊlæk/ *n. US sl. offens.* a person of Polish origin. [F *Polaque* and G *Polack* f. Pol. *Polak*]

polar /ˈpəʊlə(r)/ **1** *adj.* **a** of or near a pole of the earth or a celestial body, or of the celestial sphere. **b** (of a species or variety) living in the north polar region. **2** having magnetic polarity. **3 a** (of a molecule) having a positive charge at one end and a negative charge at the other. **b** (of a compound) having electric charges. **4** *Geom.* of or relating to a pole. **5** directly opposite in character or tendency. □ **polar bear** a white bear, *Ursus maritimus*, of the Arctic regions. **polar body** a small cell produced from an oocyte during the formation of an ovum, which does not develop further. **polar circle** each of the circles parallel to the equator at a distance of 23° 27′ from either pole. **polar coordinates** a system by which a point can be located with reference to two angles.

polar curve a curve related in a particular way to a given curve and to a fixed point called a *pole*. **polar distance** the angular distance of a point on a sphere from the nearest pole. **polar star** = POLESTAR. □□ **polarly** *adv*. [F *polaire* or mod.L *polaris* (as POLE²)]

polari- /ˈpəʊləri/ *comb. form* polar. [mod.L *polaris* (as POLAR)]

polarimeter /ˌpəʊləˈrɪmɪtə(r)/ *n*. an instrument used to measure the polarization of light or the effect of a substance on the rotation of the plane of polarized light. □□ **polarimetric** /-ˈmetrɪk/ *adj*. **polarimetry** *n*.

polariscope /pəʊˈlærɪˌskəʊp/ *n*. = POLARIMETER. □□ **polariscopic** /-ˈskɒpɪk/ *adj*.

polarity /pəˈlærɪtɪ/ *n*. (*pl*. **-ies**) **1** the tendency of a lodestone, magnetized bar, etc., to point with its extremities to the magnetic poles of the earth. **2** the condition of having two poles with contrary qualities. **3** the state of having two opposite tendencies, opinions, etc. **4** the electrical condition of a body (positive or negative). **5** a magnetic attraction towards an object or person.

polarize /ˈpəʊləˌraɪz/ *v*. (also **-ise**) **1** *tr*. restrict the vibrations of (a transverse wave, esp. light) to one direction. **2** *tr*. give magnetic or electric polarity to (a substance or body). **3** *tr*. reduce the voltage of (an electric cell) by the action of electrolysis products. **4** *tr*. & *intr*. divide into two groups of opposing opinion etc. □□ **polarizable** *adj*. **polarization** /-ˈzeɪʃ(ə)n/ *n*. **polarizer** *n*.

polarography /ˌpəʊləˈrɒgrəfɪ/ *n*. *Chem*. the analysis by measurement of current-voltage relationships in electrolysis between mercury electrodes. □□ **polarographic** /-əˈgræfɪk/ *adj*.

Polaroid /ˈpəʊləˌrɔɪd/ *n. propr*. **1** material in thin plastic sheets that produces a high degree of plane polarization in light passing through it. **2** a type of camera with internal processing that produces a finished print rapidly after each exposure. **3** (in *pl*.) sunglasses with lenses made from Polaroid. [POLARI- + -OID]

polder /ˈpəʊldə(r)/ *n*. a piece of low-lying land reclaimed from the sea or a river, esp. in the Netherlands. [MDu. *polre*, Du. *polder*]

Pole /pəʊl/ *n*. **1** a native or national of Poland. **2** a person of Polish descent. [G f. Pol. *Polanie*, lit. field-dwellers f. *pole* field]

pole¹ /pəʊl/ *n*. & *v*. —*n*. **1** a long slender rounded piece of wood or metal, esp. with the end placed in the ground as a support etc. **2** a wooden shaft fitted to the front of a vehicle and attached to the yokes or collars of the draught animals. **3** = PERCH¹. —*v.tr*. **1** provide with poles. **2** (usu. foll. by *off*) push off (a punt etc.) with a pole. □ **pole position** the most favourable position at the start of a motor race (orig. next to the inside boundary-fence). **pole-vault** (or **-jump**) *n*. the athletic sport of vaulting over a high bar with the aid of a long flexible pole held in the hands and giving extra spring. —*v.intr*. take part in this sport. **pole-vaulter** a person who pole-vaults. **under bare poles** *Naut*. with no sail set. **up the pole** *sl*. **1** crazy, eccentric. **2** in difficulty. [OE *pāl* ult. f. L *palus* stake]

pole² /pəʊl/ *n*. **1** (in full **north pole**, **south pole**) a each of the two points in the celestial sphere about which the stars appear to revolve. **b** each of the extremities of the axis of rotation of the earth or another body. **c** see *magnetic pole*. ¶ The spelling is *North Pole* and *South Pole* when used as geographical designations. **2** each of the two opposite points on the surface of a magnet at which magnetic forces are strongest. **3** each of two terminals (positive and negative) of an electric cell or battery etc. **4** each of two opposed principles or ideas. **5** *Geom*. each of two points in which the axis of a circle cuts the surface of a sphere. **6** a fixed point to which others are referred. **7** *Biol*. an extremity of the main axis of any spherical or oval organ. □ **be poles apart** differ

greatly, esp. in nature or opinion. □□ **poleward** *adj*. **polewards** *adj*. & *adv*. [ME f. L *polus* f. Gk *polos* pivot, axis, sky]

poleaxe /ˈpəʊlæks/ *n*. & *v*. —*n*. **1** a battleaxe. **2** a butcher's axe. —*v.tr*. hit or kill with or as if with a poleaxe. [ME *pol(l)ax*, *-ex* f. MDu. *pol(l)aex*, MLG *pol(l)exe* (as POLL¹, AXE)]

polecat /ˈpəʊlkæt/ *n*. **1** *Brit*. a small European brownish-black fetid flesh-eating mammal, *Mustela putorius*, of the weasel family. **2** *US* a skunk. [*pole* (unexplained) + CAT]

polemic /pəˈlemɪk/ *n*. & *adj*. —*n*. **1** a controversial discussion. **2** *Polit*. a verbal or written attack, esp. on a political opponent. —*adj*. (also **polemical**) involving dispute; controversial. □□ **polemically** *adv*. **polemicist** /-sɪst/ *n*. **polemicize** *v.tr*. (also **-ise**). **polemize** /ˈpɒlɪˌmaɪz/ *v.tr*. (also **-ise**). [med.L *polemicus* f. Gk *polemikos* f. *polemos* war]

polemics /pəˈlemɪks/ *n.pl*. the art or practice of controversial discussion.

polenta /pəˈlentə/ *n*. porridge made of maize meal etc. [It. f. L, = pearl barley]

polestar /ˈpəʊlstɑː(r)/ *n*. **1** *Astron*. a star in Ursa Minor now about 1° distant from the celestial north pole. **2** a thing or principle serving as a guide. **b** a centre of attraction.

police /pəˈliːs/ *n*. & *v*. —*n*. **1** (usu. prec. by *the*) the civil force of a State, responsible for maintaining public order. **2** (as *pl*.) the members of a police force (*several hundred police*). **3** a force with similar functions of enforcing regulations (*military police*; *railway police*). —*v.tr*. **1** control (a country or area) by means of police. **2** provide with police. **3** keep order in; control. □ **police constable** see CONSTABLE. **police dog** a dog, esp. an Alsatian, used in police work. **police officer** a policeman or policewoman. **police State** a totalitarian State controlled by political police supervising the citizens' activities. **police station** the office of a local police force. [F f. med.L *politia* POLICY¹]

policeman /pəˈliːsmən/ *n*. (*pl*. **-men**; *fem*. **policewoman**, *pl*. **-women**) a member of a police force.

policy¹ /ˈpɒlɪsɪ/ *n*. (*pl*. **-ies**) **1** a course or principle of action adopted or proposed by a government, party, business, or individual etc. **2** prudent conduct; sagacity. [ME f. OF *policie* f. L *politia* f. Gk *politeia* citizenship f. *politēs* citizen f. *polis* city]

policy² /ˈpɒlɪsɪ/ *n*. (*pl*. **-ies**) **1** a contract of insurance. **2** a document containing this. [F *police* bill of lading, contract of insurance, f. Prov. *poliss(i)a* prob. f. med.L *apodissa*, *apodixa*, f. L *apodixis* f. Gk *apodeixis* evidence, proof (as APO-, *deiknumi* show)]

policyholder /ˈpɒlɪsɪˌhəʊldə(r)/ *n*. a person or body holding an insurance policy.

polio /ˈpəʊlɪəʊ/ *n*. = POLIOMYELITIS. [abbr.]

poliomyelitis /ˌpəʊlɪəʊˌmaɪɪˈlaɪtɪs/ *n*. *Med*. an infectious viral disease that affects the central nervous system and which can cause temporary or permanent paralysis. [mod.L f. Gk *polios* grey + *muelos* marrow]

Polish /ˈpəʊlɪʃ/ *adj*. & *n*. —*adj*. **1** of or relating to Poland. **2** of the Poles or their language. —*n*. the language of Poland. □ **Polish notation** *Math*. a system of formula notation without brackets and punctuation. [POLE + -ISH¹]

polish /ˈpɒlɪʃ/ *v*. & *n*. —*v*. **1** *tr*. & *intr*. make or become smooth or glossy by rubbing. **2** (esp. as **polished** *adj*.) refine or improve; add finishing touches to. —*n*. **1** a substance used for polishing. **2** smoothness or glossiness produced by friction. **3** the act or an instance of polishing. **4** refinement or elegance of manner, conduct, etc. □ **polish off** finish (esp. food) quickly. **polish up** revise or improve (a skill etc.). □□ **polishable** *adj*. **polisher** *n*. [ME f. OF *polir* f. L *polire polit-*]

politburo /ˈpɒlɪtˌbjʊərəʊ/ *n*. (*pl*. **-os**) the principal policy-making committee of a Communist party, esp.

in the USSR. [Rus. *politbyuro* f. *politícheskoe byuró* political bureau]

polite /pəˈlaɪt/ *adj.* (**politer**, **politest**) **1** having good manners; courteous. **2** cultivated, cultured. **3** refined, elegant (*polite letters*). □□ **politely** *adv.* **politeness** *n.* [L *politus* (as POLISH)]

politesse /ˌpɒlɪˈtes/ *n.* formal politeness. [F f. It. *politezza*, *pulitezza* f. *pulito* polite]

politic /ˈpɒlɪtɪk/ *adj.* & *v.* —*adj.* **1** (of an action) judicious, expedient. **2** (of a person) prudent, sagacious. **3** political (now only in *body politic*). —*v.intr.* (**politicked**, **politicking**) engage in politics. □□ **politicly** *adv.* [ME f. OF *politique* f. L *politicus* f. Gk *politikos* f. *politēs* citizen f. *polis* city]

political /pəˈlɪtɪk(ə)l/ *adj.* **1 a** of or concerning the State or its government, or public affairs generally. **b** of, relating to, or engaged in politics. **c** belonging to or forming part of a civil administration. **2** having an organized form of society or government. **3** taking or belonging to a side in politics. **4** relating to or affecting interests of status or authority in an organization rather than matters of principle (*a political decision*). □ **political asylum** see ASYLUM. **political economist** a student of or expert in political economy. **political economy** the study of the economic aspects of government. **political geography** that dealing with boundaries and the possessions of States. **political prisoner** a person imprisoned for political beliefs or actions. **political science** the study of the State and systems of government. **political scientist** a specialist in political science. □□ **politically** *adv.* [L *politicus* (as POLITIC)]

politician /ˌpɒlɪˈtɪʃ(ə)n/ *n.* **1** a person engaged in or concerned with politics, esp. as a practitioner. **2** a person skilled in politics. **3** *US derog.* a person with self-interested political concerns.

politicize /pəˈlɪtɪˌsaɪz/ *v.* (also **-ise**) **1** *tr.* **a** give a political character to. **b** make politically aware. **2** *intr.* engage in or talk politics. □□ **politicization** /-ˈzeɪʃ(ə)n/ *n.*

politico /pəˈlɪtɪˌkəʊ/ *n.* (*pl.* **-os**) *colloq.* a politician or political enthusiast. [Sp. or It. (as POLITIC)]

politico- /pəˈlɪtɪkəʊ/ *comb. form* **1** politically. **2** political and (*politico-social*). [Gk *politikos*: see POLITIC]

politics /ˈpɒlɪtɪks/ *n.pl.* **1** (treated as *sing.* or *pl.*) **a** the art and science of government. **b** public life and affairs as involving authority and government. **2** (usu. treated as *pl.*) **a** a particular set of ideas, principles, or commitments in politics (*what are their politics?*). **b** activities concerned with the acquisition or exercise of authority or government. **c** an organizational process or principle affecting authority, status, etc. (*the politics of the decision*).

polity /ˈpɒlɪtɪ/ *n.* (*pl.* **-ies**) **1** a form or process of civil government or constitution. **2** an organized society; a State as a political entity. [L *politia* f. Gk *politeia* f. *politēs* citizen f. *polis* city]

polka /ˈpɒlkə, ˈpəʊlkə/ *n.* & *v.* —*n.* **1** a lively dance of Bohemian origin in duple time. **2** the music for this. —*v.intr.* (**polkas**, **polkaed** /-kəd/ or **polka'd**, **polkaing** /-kəɪŋ/) dance the polka. □ **polka dot** a round dot as one of many forming a regular pattern on a textile fabric etc. [F and G f. Czech *půlka* half-step f. *půl* half]

poll[1] /pəʊl/ *n.* & *v.* —*n.* **1 a** the process of voting at an election. **b** the counting of votes at an election. **c** the result of voting. **d** the number of votes recorded (*a heavy poll*). **2** = GALLUP POLL, opinion poll. **3 a** a human head. **b** the part of this on which hair grows (*flaxen poll*). **4** a hornless animal, esp. one of a breed of hornless cattle. —*v.* **1** *tr.* **a** take the vote or votes of. **b** (in *passive*) have one's vote taken. **c** (of a candidate) receive (so many votes). **d** give (a vote). **2** *tr.* record the opinion of (a person or group) in an opinion poll. **3** *intr.* give one's vote. **4** *tr.* cut off the top of (a tree or plant), esp. make a pollard of. **5** *tr.*

(esp. as **polled** *adj.*) cut the horns off (cattle). **6** *tr. Computing* check the status of (a computer system) at intervals. □ **poll tax 1** *hist.* a tax levied on every adult. **2** = *community charge*. □□ **pollee** /pəʊˈliː/ *n.* (in sense 2 of *n.*). **pollster** *n.* [ME, perh. f. LG or Du.]

poll[2] /pɒl/ *n.* a tame parrot (*Pretty poll!*). □ **poll parrot** a user of conventional or clichéd phrases and arguments. [*Poll*, a conventional name for a parrot, alt. f. *Moll*, a familiar form of *Mary*]

pollack /ˈpɒlək/ *n.* (also **pollock**) a European marine fish, *Pollachius pollachius*, with a characteristic protruding lower jaw, used for food. [earlier (Sc.) *podlock*: orig. unkn.]

pollan /ˈpɒlən/ *n.* a freshwater fish, *Coregonus pollan*, found in Irish lakes. [perh. f. Ir. *poll* deep water]

pollard /ˈpɒləd/ *n.* & *v.* —*n.* **1** an animal that has lost or cast its horns; an ox, sheep, or goat of a hornless breed. **2** a tree whose branches have been cut off to encourage the growth of new young branches, esp. a riverside willow. **3 a** the bran sifted from flour. **b** a fine bran containing some flour. —*v.tr.* make (a tree) a pollard. [POLL[1] + -ARD]

pollen /ˈpɒlən/ *n.* the fine dustlike grains discharged from the male part of a flower containing the gamete that fertilizes the female ovule. □ **pollen analysis** = PALYNOLOGY. **pollen count** an index of the amount of pollen in the air, published esp. for the benefit of those allergic to it. □□ **pollenless** *adj.* **pollinic** /pəˈlɪnɪk/ *adj.* [L *pollen pollinis* fine flour, dust]

pollex /ˈpɒleks/ *n.* (*pl.* **pollices** /-lɪˌsiːz/) the innermost digit of a forelimb, usu. the thumb in primates. [L, = thumb or big toe]

pollie var. of POLLY[2].

pollinate /ˈpɒlɪˌneɪt/ *v.tr.* (also *absol.*) sprinkle (a stigma) with pollen. □□ **pollination** /-ˈneɪʃ(ə)n/ *n.* **pollinator** *n.*

polling /ˈpəʊlɪŋ/ *n.* the registering or casting of votes. □ **polling-booth** a compartment in which a voter stands to mark the ballot-paper. **polling-day** the day of a local or general election. **polling-station** a building, often a school, where voting takes place during an election.

pollinic see POLLEN.

polliniferous /ˌpɒlɪˈnɪfərəs/ *adj.* bearing or producing pollen.

polliwog /ˈpɒlɪˌwɒg/ *n.* (also **pollywog**) *US dial.* a tadpole. [earlier *polwigge*, *polwygle* f. POLL[1] + WIGGLE]

pollock var. of POLLACK.

pollute /pəˈluːt/ *v.tr.* **1** contaminate or defile (the environment). **2** make foul or filthy. **3** destroy the purity or sanctity of. □□ **pollutant** *adj.* & *n.* **polluter** *n.* **pollution** *n.* [ME f. L *polluere pollut-*]

polly[1] /ˈpɒlɪ/ *n.* (*pl.* **-ies**) *colloq.* a bottle or glass of Apollinaris water. [abbr.]

polly[2] /ˈpɒlɪ/ *n.* (also **pollie**) (*pl.* **-ies**) *Austral.* & *US* a politician. [abbr.]

Pollyanna /ˌpɒlɪˈænə/ *n.* a cheerful optimist; an excessively cheerful person. □□ **Pollyannaish** *adj.* **Pollyannaism** *n.* [character in a novel (1913) by E. Porter]

pollywog var. of POLLIWOG.

polo /ˈpəʊləʊ/ *n.* a game of Eastern origin like hockey played on horseback with a long-handled mallet. □ **polo-neck** a high round turned-over collar. **polo-stick** a mallet for playing polo. [Balti, = ball]

polonaise /ˌpɒləˈneɪz/ *n.* & *adj.* —*n.* **1** a dance of Polish origin in triple time. **2** the music for this. **3** *hist.* a woman's dress consisting of a bodice and a skirt open from the waist downwards to show an underskirt. —*adj.* cooked in a Polish style. [F, fem. of *polonais* Polish f. med.L *Polonia* Poland]

polonium /pəˈləʊnɪəm/ *n. Chem.* a rare radioactive metallic element, occurring naturally in uranium ores. ¶ Symb.: **Po**. [F & mod.L f. med.L *Polonia* Poland (the discoverer's native country) + -IUM]

polony /pə'ləʊnɪ/ n. (pl. -ies) Brit. = BOLOGNA SAUSAGE. [app. corrupt.]

poltergeist /'pɒltə,gaɪst/ n. a noisy mischievous ghost, esp. one manifesting itself by physical damage. [G f. poltern create a disturbance + Geist GHOST]

poltroon /pɒl'truːn/ n. a spiritless coward. □□ **poltroonery** n. [F poltron f. It. poltrone perh. f. poltro sluggard]

poly /'pɒlɪ/ n. (pl. polys) colloq. polytechnic. [abbr.]

poly-[1] /'pɒlɪ/ comb. form denoting many or much. [Gk polu- f. polus much, polloi many]

poly-[2] /'pɒlɪ/ comb. form Chem. polymerized (polyunsaturated). [POLYMER]

polyadelphous /,pɒlɪə'delfəs/ adj. Bot. having numerous stamens grouped into three or more bundles.

polyamide /,pɒlɪ'æmaɪd/ n. Chem. any of a class of condensation polymers produced from the interaction of an amino group of one molecule and a carboxylic acid group of another, and which includes many synthetic fibres such as nylon.

polyandry /'pɒlɪ,ændrɪ/ n. 1 polygamy in which a woman has more than one husband. 2 Bot. the state of having numerous stamens. □□ **polyandrous** /-'ændrəs/ adj. [POLY-[1] + andry f. Gk anēr andros male]

polyanthus /,pɒlɪ'ænθəs/ n. (pl. polyanthuses) a flower cultivated from hybridized primulas. [mod.L, formed as POLY-[1] + Gk anthos flower]

polycarbonate /,pɒlɪ'kɑːbə,neɪt/ n. any of a class of polymers in which the units are linked through a carbonate group, mainly used as moulding materials.

polychaete /'pɒlɪ,kiːt/ n. any aquatic annelid worm of the class Polychaeta, including lugworms and ragworms, having numerous bristles on the fleshy lobes of each body segment. □□ **polychaetan** /-'kiːt(ə)n/ adj. **polychaetous** /-'kiːtəs/ adj.

polychromatic /,pɒlɪkrəʊ'mætɪk/ adj. 1 many coloured. 2 (of radiation) containing more than one wavelength. □□ **polychromatism** /-'krəʊmə,tɪz(ə)m/ n.

polychrome /'pɒlɪ,krəʊm/ adj. & n. —adj. painted, printed, or decorated in many colours. —n. 1 a work of art in several colours, esp. a coloured statue. 2 varied colouring. □□ **polychromic** /-'krəʊmɪk/ adj. **polychromous** /-'krəʊməs/ adj. [F f. Gk polukhrōmos as POLY-[1], khrōma colour]

polychromy /'pɒlɪ,krəʊmɪ/ n. the art of painting in several colours, esp. as applied to ancient pottery, architecture, etc. [F polychromie (as POLYCHROME)]

polyclinic /'pɒlɪ,klɪnɪk/ n. a clinic devoted to various diseases; a general hospital.

polycrystalline /,pɒlɪ'krɪstə,laɪn/ adj. (of a solid substance) consisting of many crystalline parts at various orientations, e.g. a metal casting.

polycyclic /,pɒlɪ'saɪklɪk/ adj. Chem. having more than one ring of atoms in the molecule.

polydactyl /,pɒlɪ'dæktɪl/ adj. & n. —adj. (of an animal) having more than five fingers or toes. —n. a polydactyl animal.

polyester /,pɒlɪ'estə(r)/ n. any of a group of condensation polymers used to form synthetic fibres such as Terylene or to make resins.

polyethene /'pɒlɪ,eθiːn/ n. Chem. = POLYTHENE.

polyethylene /,pɒlɪ'eθɪ,liːn/ n. = POLYTHENE.

polygamous /pə'lɪgəməs/ adj. 1 having more than one wife or husband at the same time. 2 having more than one mate. 3 bearing some flowers with stamens only, some with pistils only, some with both, on the same or different plants. □□ **polygamic** /-'gæmɪk/ adj. **polygamist** n. **polygamously** adv. **polygamy** n. [Gk polugamos (as POLY-[1], -gamos marrying)]

polygene /'pɒlɪ,dʒiːn/ n. Biol. each of a group of independent genes that collectively affect a characteristic.

polygenesis /,pɒlɪ'dʒenɪsɪs/ n. the (usu. postulated) origination of a race or species from several independent stocks. □□ **polygenetic** /-dʒɪ'netɪk/ adj.

polygeny /pə'lɪgənɪ/ n. the theory that mankind originated from several independent pairs of ancestors. □□ **polygenism** n. **polygenist** n.

polyglot /'pɒlɪ,glɒt/ adj. & n. —adj. 1 of many languages. 2 (of a person) speaking or writing several languages. 3 (of a book, esp. the Bible) with the text translated into several languages. —n. 1 a polyglot person. 2 a polyglot book, esp. a Bible. □□ **polyglottal** /-'glɒt(ə)l/ adj. **polyglottic** /-'glɒtɪk/ adj. **polyglottism** n. [F polyglotte f. Gk poluglōttos (as POLY-[1], glōtta tongue)]

polygon /'pɒlɪgən, ,gɒn/ n. a plane figure with many (usu. a minimum of three) sides and angles. □**polygon of forces** a polygon that represents by the length and direction of its sides all the forces acting on a body or point. □□ **polygonal** /pə'lɪgən(ə)l/ adj. [LL polygonum f. Gk polugōnon (neut. adj.) (as POLY-[1] + -gōnos angled)]

polygonum /pə'lɪgənəm/ n. any plant of the genus Polygonum, with small bell-shaped flowers. Also called KNOTGRASS, KNOTWEED. [mod.L f. Gk polugonon]

polygraph /'pɒlɪ,grɑːf/ n. a machine designed to detect and record changes in physiological characteristics (e.g. rates of pulse and breathing), used esp. as a lie-detector.

polygyny /pə'lɪdʒɪnɪ/ n. polygamy in which a man has more than one wife. □□ **polygynous** /pə'lɪdʒɪnəs/ adj. [POLY-[1] + gyny f. Gk gunē woman]

polyhedron /,pɒlɪ'hiːdrən, -'hedrən/ n. (pl. **polyhedra** /-drə/) a solid figure with many (usu. more than six) faces. □□ **polyhedral** adj. **polyhedric** adj. [Gk poluedron neut. of poluedros (as POLY-[1], hedra base)]

polyhistor /,pɒlɪ'hɪstə(r)/ n. = POLYMATH.

polymath /'pɒlɪ,mæθ/ n. 1 a person of much or varied learning. 2 a great scholar. □□ **polymathic** /,pɒlɪ'mæθɪk/ adj. **polymathy** /pə'lɪməθɪ/ n. [Gk polumathēs (as POLY-[1], math- stem manthanō learn)]

polymer /'pɒlɪmə(r)/ n. a compound composed of one or more large molecules that are formed from repeated units of smaller molecules. □□ **polymeric** /-'merɪk/ adj. **polymerism** n. **polymerize** v.intr. & tr. (also -ise). **polymerization** /-'zeɪʃ(ə)n/ n. [G f. Gk polumeros having many parts (as POLY-[1], meros share)]

polymerous /pə'lɪmərəs/ adj. Biol. having many parts.

polymorphism /,pɒlɪ'mɔːfɪz(ə)m/ n. 1 a Biol. the existence of various different forms in the successive stages of the development of an organism. b = PLEOMORPHISM. 2 Chem. = ALLOTROPY. □□ **polymorphic** adj. **polymorphous** adj.

Polynesian /,pɒlɪ'niːʒ(ə)n/ adj. & n. —adj. of or relating to Polynesia, a group of Pacific islands including New Zealand, Hawaii, Samoa, etc. —n. 1 a a native of Polynesia. b a person of Polynesian descent. 2 the family of languages including Maori, Hawaiian, and Samoan. [as POLY-[1] + Gk nēsos island]

polyneuritis /,pɒlɪ,njʊə'raɪtɪs/ n. any disorder that affects many of the peripheral nerves. □□ **polyneuritic** /-'rɪtɪk/ adj.

polynomial /,pɒlɪ'nəʊmɪəl/ n. & adj. Math. —n. an expression of more than two algebraic terms, esp. the sum of several terms that contain different powers of the same variable(s). —adj. of or being a polynomial. [POLY-[1] after multinomial]

polynya /pə'lɪnjə/ n. a stretch of open water surrounded by ice, esp. in the Arctic seas. [Russ. f. pole field]

polyp /'pɒlɪp/ n. 1 Zool. an individual coelenterate. 2 Med. a small usu. benign growth protruding from a mucous membrane. [F polype (as POLYPUS)]

polypary /'pɒlɪpərɪ/ n. (pl. -ies) the common stem or support of a colony of polyps. [mod.L polyparium (as POLYPUS)]

polypeptide /,pɒlɪ'peptaɪd/ n. Biochem. a peptide

formed by the combination of about ten or more amino acids. [G *Polypeptid* (as POLY-², PEPTONE)]

polyphagous /pə'lıfəgəs/ *adj.* *Zool.* able to feed on various kinds of food.

polyphase /'pɒlɪˌfeɪz/ *adj.* *Electr.* (of a device or circuit) designed to supply or use simultaneously several alternating currents of the same voltage but with different phases.

polyphone /'pɒlɪˌfəʊn/ *n.* *Phonet.* a symbol or letter that represents several different sounds.

polyphonic /ˌpɒlɪ'fɒnɪk/ *adj.* **1** *Mus.* (of vocal music etc.) in two or more relatively independent parts; contrapuntal. **2** *Phonet.* (of a letter etc.) representing more than one sound. □□ **polyphonically** *adv.* [Gk *poluphōnos* (as POLY-¹, *phōnē* voice, sound)]

polyphony /pə'lɪfənɪ/ *n.* (*pl.* -ies) **1** *Mus.* **a** polyphonic style in musical composition; counterpoint. **b** a composition written in this style. **2** *Philol.* the symbolization of different vocal sounds by the same letter or character. □□ **polyphonous** *adj.*

polypi *pl.* of POLYPUS.

polyploid /'pɒlɪˌplɔɪd/ *n.* & *adj.* *Biol.* —*n.* a nucleus or organism that contains more than two sets of chromosomes. —*adj.* of or being a polyploid. □□ **polyploidy** *n.* [G (as POLY-¹, -PLOID)]

polypod /'pɒlɪˌpɒd/ *adj.* & *n.* *Zool.* —*adj.* having many feet. —*n.* a polypod animal. [F *polypode* (adj.) f. Gk (as POLYPUS)]

polypody /'pɒlɪˌpəʊdɪ/ *n.* (*pl.* -ies) any fern of the genus *Polypodium*, usu. found in woods growing on trees, walls, and stones. [ME f. L *polypodium* f. Gk *polupodion* (as POLYPUS)]

polypoid /'pɒlɪˌpɔɪd/ *adj.* of or like a polyp. □□ **polypous** /-pəs/ *adj.*

polypropene /ˌpɒlɪ'prəʊpiːn/ *n.* = POLYPROPYLENE.

polypropylene /ˌpɒlɪ'prəʊpɪˌliːn/ *n.* *Chem.* any of various polymers of propylene including thermoplastic materials used for films, fibres, or moulding materials. Also called POLYPROPENE.

polypus /'pɒlɪpəs/ *n.* (*pl.* **polypi** /-ˌpaɪ/ or **polypuses**) *Med.* = POLYP 2. [ME f. L *polypus* f. Gk *pōlupos*, *polupous* cuttlefish, polyp (as POLY-¹, *pous podos* foot)]

polysaccharide /ˌpɒlɪ'sækəˌraɪd/ *n.* any of a group of carbohydrates whose molecules consist of long chains of monosaccharides.

polysemy /ˌpɒlɪ'siːmɪ, 'pɒl-/ *n.* *Philol.* the existence of many meanings (of a word etc.). □□ **polysemic** /-'siːmɪk/ *adj.* **polysemous** /-'siːməs/ *adj.* [POLY-¹ + Gk *sēma* sign]

polystyrene /ˌpɒlɪ'staɪəˌriːn/ *n.* a thermoplastic polymer of styrene, usu. hard and colourless or expanded with a gas to produce a lightweight rigid white substance, used for insulation and in packaging.

polysyllabic /ˌpɒlɪsɪ'læbɪk/ *adj.* **1** (of a word) having many syllables. **2** characterized by the use of words of many syllables. □□ **polysyllabically** *adv.*

polysyllable /'pɒlɪˌsɪləb(ə)l/ *n.* a polysyllabic word.

polytechnic /ˌpɒlɪ'teknɪk/ *n.* & *adj.* —*n.* an institution of higher education offering courses in many (esp. vocational) subjects at degree level or below. —*adj.* dealing with or devoted to various vocational or technical subjects. [F *polytechnique* f. Gk *polutekhnos* (as POLY-¹ *tekhnē* art)]

polytetrafluoroethylene /ˌpɒlɪˌtetrəˌfluərəʊ'eθɪˌliːn/ *n.* *Chem.* a tough translucent polymer resistant to chemicals and used to coat cooking utensils etc. ¶ Abbr.: PTFE. [POLY-² + TETRA- + FLUORO- + ETHYLENE]

polytheism /'pɒlɪθiːˌɪz(ə)m/ *n.* the belief in or worship of more than one god. □□ **polytheist** *n.* **polytheistic** /-'ɪstɪk/ *adj.* [F *polythéisme* f. Gk *polutheos* of many gods (as POLY-¹, *theos* god)]

polythene /'pɒlɪˌθiːn/ *n.* *Chem.* a tough light thermoplastic polymer of ethylene, usu. translucent and flexible or opaque and rigid, used for packaging and insulating materials. Also called POLYETHYLENE, POLYETHENE.

polytonality /ˌpɒlɪtəʊ'nælɪtɪ/ *n.* *Mus.* the simultaneous use of two or more keys in a composition. □□ **polytonal** /-'təʊn(ə)l/ *adj.*

polyunsaturated /ˌpɒlɪʌn'sætʃəˌreɪtɪd, -tjʊˌreɪtɪd/ *adj.* *Chem.* (of a compound, esp. a fat or oil molecule) containing several double or triple bonds and therefore capable of further reaction.

polyurethane /ˌpɒlɪ'jʊərəˌθeɪn/ *n.* any polymer containing the urethane group, used in adhesives, paints, plastics, rubbers, foams, etc.

polyvalent /ˌpɒlɪ'veɪlənt/ *adj.* *Chem.* having a valency of more than two, or several valencies. □□ **polyvalence** *n.*

polyvinyl acetate /ˌpɒlɪ'vaɪnɪl/ *n.* *Chem.* a soft plastic polymer used in paints and adhesives. ¶ Abbr.: PVA.

polyvinyl chloride /ˌpɒlɪ'vaɪnɪl/ *n.* a tough transparent solid polymer of vinyl chloride, easily coloured and used for a wide variety of products including pipes, flooring, etc. ¶ Abbr.: PVC.

polyzoan /ˌpɒlɪ'zəʊən/ *n.* = BRYOZOAN.

pom /pɒm/ *n.* **1** a Pomeranian dog. **2** *Austral.* & *NZ sl. offens.* = POMMY. [abbr.]

pomace /'pʌmɪs/ *n.* **1** the mass of crushed apples in cider-making before or after the juice is pressed out. **2** the refuse of fish etc. after the oil has been extracted, generally used as a fertilizer. [ME f. med.L *pomacium* cider f. L *pomum* apple]

pomade /pə'mɑːd/ *n.* & *v.* —*n.* scented dressing for the hair and the skin of the head. —*v.tr.* anoint with pomade. [F *pommade* f. It. *pomata* f. med.L f. L *pomum* apple (from which it was orig. made)]

pomander /pə'mændə(r)/ *n.* **1** a ball of mixed aromatic substances placed in a cupboard etc. or *hist.* carried in a box, bag, etc. as a protection against infection. **2** a (usu. spherical) container for this. **3** a spiced orange etc. similarly used. [earlier *pom(e)amber* f. AF f. OF *pome d'embre* f. med.L *pomum de ambra* apple of ambergris]

pomatum /pə'mɑːtəm/ *n.* & *v.tr.* = POMADE. [mod.L f. L *pomum* apple]

pome /pəʊm/ *n.* a firm-fleshed fruit in which the carpels from the central core enclose the seeds, e.g. the apple, pear, and quince. □□ **pomiferous** /pə'mɪfərəs/ *adj.* [ME f. OF ult. f. *poma* pl. of L *pomum* fruit, apple]

pomegranate /'pɒmɪˌgrænɪt, 'pɒmˌgrænɪt/ *n.* **1 a** an orange-sized fruit with a tough golden-orange outer skin containing many seeds in a red pulp. **b** the tree bearing this fruit, *Punica granatum*, native to N. Africa and W. Asia. **2** an ornamental representation of a pomegranate. [ME f. OF *pome grenate* (as POME, L *granatum* having many seeds f. *granum* seed)]

pomelo /'pʌməˌləʊ/ *n.* (*pl.* -os) **1** = SHADDOCK. **2** *US* = GRAPEFRUIT. [19th c.: orig. unkn.]

Pomeranian /ˌpɒmə'reɪnɪən/ *n.* **1** a small dog with long silky hair, a pointed muzzle, and pricked ears. **2** this breed. [*Pomerania* in Germany and Poland]

pomfret /'pɒmfrɪt/ *n.* **1** any of various fish of the family Stromateidae of the Indian and Pacific Oceans. **2** a dark-coloured deep-bodied marine fish, *Brama brama*, used as food. [app. f. Port. *pampo*]

pomfret-cake /'pʌmfrɪt, 'pɒ-/ *n.* (also **Pontefract-cake** /'pɒntɪˌfrækt/) *Brit.* a small round flat liquorice sweetmeat orig. made at Pontefract (earlier *Pomfret*) in Yorkshire.

pomiculture /'pɒmɪˌkʌltʃə(r)/ *n.* fruit-growing. [L *pomum* fruit + CULTURE]

pommel /'pʌm(ə)l/ *n.* & *v.* —*n.* **1** a knob, esp. at the end of a sword-hilt. **2** the upward projecting front part of a saddle. —*v.tr.* (**pommelled, pommelling**; *US* **pommeled, pommeling**) = PUMMEL. □ **pommel horse** a vaulting horse fitted with a pair of curved handgrips. [ME f. OF *pomel* f. Rmc *pomellum* (unrecorded), dimin. of L *pomum* fruit, apple]

pommy /'pɒmɪ/ *n.* (also **pommie**) (*pl.* -ies) *Austral.* & *NZ sl. offens.* a British person, esp. a recent immigrant. [20th c.: orig. uncert.]

pomology /pə'mɒlədʒɪ/ n. the science of fruit-growing. □□ **pomological** /-mə'lɒdʒɪk(ə)l/ adj. **pomologist** n. [L pomum fruit + -LOGY]

pomp /pɒmp/ n. 1 a splendid display; splendour. 2 (often in pl.) vainglory (the pomps and vanities of this wicked world). [ME f. OF pompe f. L pompa f. Gk pompē procession, pomp f. pempō send]

pompadour /'pɒmpə,dʊə(r)/ n. a woman's hairstyle with the hair in a high turned-back roll round the face. [f. Marquise de Pompadour, the mistress of Louis XV of France d. 1764]

pompano /pɒm'pɑːnəʊ/ n. (pl. -os) any of various fish of the family Carangidae or Stromateidae of the Atlantic and Pacific Oceans, used as food. [Sp. pámpano]

pom-pom /'pɒmpɒm/ n. an automatic quick-firing gun esp. on a ship. [imit.]

pompon /'pɒmpɒn/ n. (also **pompom**) 1 an ornamental ball or bobble made of wool, silk, or ribbons, usu. worn on women's or children's hats or clothing. 2 the round tuft on a soldier's cap, the front of a shako, etc. 3 (often attrib.) a dahlia or chrysanthemum with small tightly-clustered petals. [F, of unkn. orig.]

pompous /'pɒmpəs/ n. 1 self-important, affectedly grand or solemn. 2 (of language) pretentious; unduly grand in style. 3 archaic magnificent; splendid. □□ **pomposity** /pɒm'pɒsɪtɪ/ n. (pl. -ies). **pompously** adv. **pompousness** n. [ME f. OF pompeux f. LL pomposus (as POMP)]

'pon /pɒn/ prep. archaic = UPON. [abbr.]

ponce /pɒns/ n. & v. Brit. sl. —n. 1 a man who lives off a prostitute's earnings; a pimp. 2 offens. a homosexual; an effeminate man. —v.intr. act as a ponce. □ **ponce about** move about effeminately or ineffectually. □□ **poncey** adj. (also **poncy**) (in sense 2 of n.). [perh. f. POUNCE[1]]

poncho /'pɒntʃəʊ/ n. (pl. -os) 1 a S. American cloak made of a blanket-like piece of cloth with a slit in the middle for the head. 2 a garment in this style. [S.Amer. Sp., f. Araucanian]

pond /pɒnd/ n. & v. —n. 1 a fairly small body of still water formed naturally or by hollowing or embanking. 2 joc. the sea. —v. 1 tr. hold back, dam up (a stream etc.). 2 intr. form a pond. □ **pond-life** animals (esp. invertebrates) that live in ponds. [ME var. of POUND[3]]

ponder /'pɒndə(r)/ v. 1 tr. weigh mentally; think over; consider. 2 intr. (usu. foll. by on, over) think; muse. [ME f. OF ponderer f. L ponderare f. pondus -eris weight]

ponderable /'pɒndərəb(ə)l/ adj. literary having appreciable weight or significance. □□ **ponderability** /-'bɪlɪtɪ/ n. [LL ponderabilis (as PONDER)]

ponderation /,pɒndə'reɪʃ(ə)n/ n. literary the act or an instance of weighing, balancing, or considering. [L ponderatio (as PONDER)]

ponderosa /,pɒndə'rəʊsə/ n. US 1 a N. American pine-tree, Pinus ponderosa. 2 the red timber of this tree. [mod.L, fem. of L ponderosus: see PONDEROUS]

ponderous /'pɒndərəs/ adj. 1 heavy; unwieldy. 2 laborious. 3 (of style etc.) dull; tedious. □□ **ponderosity** /-'rɒsɪtɪ/ n. **ponderously** adv. **ponderousness** n. [ME f. L ponderosus f. pondus -eris weight]

pondweed /'pɒndwiːd/ n. any of various aquatic plants, esp. of the genus Potamogeton, growing in still or running water.

pone[1] /pəʊn/ n. US 1 unleavened maize bread, esp. as made by N. American Indians. 2 a fine light bread made with milk, eggs, etc. 3 a cake or loaf of this. [Algonquian, = bread]

pone[2] /'pəʊnɪ/ n. the dealer's opponent in two-handed card games. [L, 2nd sing. imper. of ponere place]

pong /pɒŋ/ n. & v. Brit. colloq. —n. an unpleasant smell. —v.intr. stink. □□ **pongy** /'pɒŋɪ/ adj. (**pongier**, **pongiest**). [20th c.: orig. unkn.]

pongal /'pɒŋ(ə)l/ n. 1 the Tamil New Year festival at which new rice is cooked. 2 a dish of cooked rice. [Tamil poṅkal boiling]

pongee /pɒn'dʒiː, pʌn-/ n. 1 a soft usu. unbleached type of Chinese silk fabric. 2 an imitation of this in cotton etc. [perh. f. Chin. dial. pun-chī own loom, i.e. home-made]

pongid /'pɒndʒɪd/ n. & adj. any ape of the family Pongidae, including gorillas, chimpanzees, and orang-utans. —adj. of or relating to this family. [mod.L Pongidae f. Pongo the genus-name: see PONGO[1]]

pongo[1] /'pɒŋgəʊ/ n. (pl. -os) 1 an orang-utan. 2 Naut. sl. a soldier. [Congolese mpongo, orig. of African apes]

pongo[2] /'pɒŋgəʊ/ n. (pl. -os) Austral. & NZ sl. offens. an Englishman. [20th c.: orig. unkn.]

poniard /'pɒnjəd/ n. literary a small slim dagger. [F poignard f. OF poignal f. med.L pugnale f. L pugnus fist]

pons /pɒnz/ n. (pl. **pontes** /'pɒntiːz/) Anat. (in full **pons Varolii** /vəˈrəʊlɪ,aɪ/ the part of the brain stem that links the medulla oblongata and the thalamus. □ **pons asinorum** /,æsɪ'nɔːrəm/ any difficult proposition, orig. a rule of geometry from Euclid ('bridge of asses'). [L, = bridge: Varolii f. C. Varoli, It. anatomist d. 1575]

pont /pɒnt/ n. S.Afr. a flat-bottomed ferry-boat. [Du.]

Pontefract-cake var. of POMFRET-CAKE.

pontes pl. of PONS.

pontifex /'pɒntɪ,feks/ n. (pl. **pontifices** /pɒn'tɪfɪ,siːz/) 1 = PONTIFF. 2 Rom. Antiq. a member of the principal college of priests in Rome. □ **Pontifex Maximus** the head of this. [L pontifex -ficis f. pons pontis bridge + -fex f. facere make]

pontiff /'pɒntɪf/ n. RC Ch. (in full **sovereign** or **supreme pontiff**) the Pope. [F pontife (as PONTIFEX)]

pontifical /pɒn'tɪfɪk(ə)l/ adj. & n. —adj. 1 RC Ch. of or befitting a pontiff; papal. 2 pompously dogmatic; with an attitude of infallibility. —n. 1 an office-book of the Western Church containing rites to be performed by the Pope or bishops. 2 (in pl.) the vestments and insignia of a bishop, cardinal, or abbot. □ **pontifical mass** a high mass, usu. celebrated by a cardinal, bishop, etc. □□ **pontifically** adv. [ME f. F pontifical or L pontificalis (as PONTIFEX)]

pontificate v. & n. —v.intr. pontif /pɒn'tɪfɪ,keɪt/ 1 a play the pontiff; pretend to be infallible. b be pompously dogmatic. 2 RC Ch. officiate as bishop, esp. at mass. —n. /pɒn'tɪfɪkət/ 1 the office of pontifex, bishop, or pope. 2 the period of this. [L pontificatus (as PONTIFEX)]

pontifices pl. of PONTIFEX.

pontoon[1] /pɒn'tuːn/ n. Brit. 1 a card-game in which players try to acquire cards with a face value totalling 21 and no more. 2 = NATURAL n. 4a. [prob. corrupt.]

pontoon[2] /pɒn'tuːn/ n. & v. —n. 1 a flat-bottomed boat. 2 each of several boats, hollow metal cylinders, etc., used to support a temporary bridge. 3 = CAISSON 1,2. —v.tr. cross (a river) by means of pontoons. [F ponton f. L ponto -onis f. pons pontis bridge]

pony /'pəʊnɪ/ n. (pl. -ies) 1 a horse of any small breed. 2 a small drinking-glass. 3 (in pl.) sl. racehorses. 4 Brit. sl. £25. □ **pony-tail** a person's hair drawn back, tied, and hanging down like a pony's tail. **pony-trekker** a person who travels across country on a pony for pleasure. **pony-trekking** this as a hobby or activity. [perh. f. poulney (unrecorded) f. F poulenet dimin. of poulain foal]

pooch /puːtʃ/ n. esp. US sl. a dog. [20th c.: orig. unkn.]

poodle /'puːd(ə)l/ n. 1 a a dog of a breed with a curly coat that is usually clipped. b this breed. 2 a lackey or servile follower. [G Pudel(hund) f. LG pud(d)eln splash in water: cf. PUDDLE]

poof /puf, puːf/ n. (also **pouf**, **poove** /puːv/) Brit. sl. derog. 1 an effeminate man. 2 a male homosexual. □□ **poofy** /'pufɪ/ adj. [19th c.: cf. PUFF in sense 'braggart']

poofter /'puftə(r), 'puː-/ n. sl. derog. = POOF.

pooh /puː/ *int.* & *n.* —*int.* expressing impatience or contempt. —*n. sl.* excrement. [imit.]

Pooh-Bah /ˈpuːbɑː/ *n.* (also **pooh-bah**) a holder of many offices at once. [a character in W. S. Gilbert's *The Mikado* (1885)]

pooh-pooh /puːˈpuː/ *v.tr.* express contempt for; ridicule; dismiss (an idea etc.) scornfully. [redupl. of POOH]

pooja var. of PUJA.

pooka /ˈpuːkə/ *n. Ir.* a hobgoblin. [Ir. *púca*]

pool¹ /puːl/ *n.* & *v.* —*n.* **1** a small body of still water, usu. of natural formation. **2** a small shallow body of any liquid. **3** = *swimming-pool* (see SWIM). **4** a deep place in a river. —*v.* **1** *tr.* form into a pool. **2** *intr.* (of blood) become static. [OE *pōl*, MLG, MDu. *pōl*, OHG *pfuol* f. WG]

pool² /puːl/ *n.* & *v.* —*n.* **1 a** (often *attrib.*) a common supply of persons, vehicles, commodities, etc. for sharing by a group of people (*a typing pool*; *a pool car*). **b** a group of persons sharing duties etc. **2 a** the collective amount of players' stakes in gambling etc. **b** a receptacle for this. **3 a** a joint commercial venture, esp. an arrangement between competing parties to fix prices and share business to eliminate competition. **b** the common funding for this. **4 a** *US* a game on a billiard-table with usu. 16 balls. **b** *Brit.* a game on a billiard-table in which each player has a ball of a different colour with which he tries to pocket the others in fixed order, the winner taking all of the stakes. **5** a group of contestants who compete against each other in a tournament for the right to advance to the next round. —*v.tr.* **1** put (resources etc.) into a common fund. **2** share (things) in common. **3** (of transport or organizations etc.) share (traffic, receipts). **4** *Austral. sl.* **a** involve (a person) in a scheme etc., often by deception. **b** implicate, inform on. □**the pools** *Brit.* = *football pool.* [F *poule* (= hen) in same sense: assoc. with POOL¹]

poolroom /ˈpuːlruːm, -rʊm/ *n. US* **1** a betting shop. **2** a place for playing pool.

poon /puːn/ *n.* any E. Indian tree of the genus *Calophyllum.* □**poon oil** an oil from the seeds of this tree, used in medicine and for lamps. [Sinh. *pūna*]

poop¹ /puːp/ *n.* & *v.* —*n.* the stern of a ship; the aftermost and highest deck. —*v.tr.* **1** (of a wave) break over the stern of (a ship). **2** (of a ship) receive (a wave) over the stern. [ME f. OF *pupe*, *pope* ult. f. L *puppis*]

poop² /puːp/ *v.tr.* (esp. as **pooped** *adj.*) *US colloq.* exhaust; tire out. [20th c.: orig. unkn.]

poor /pʊə(r)/ *adj.* **1** lacking adequate money or means to live comfortably. **2** (foll. by *in*) deficient in (a possession or quality) (*the poor in spirit*). **3 a** scanty, inadequate (*a poor crop*). **b** less good than is usual or expected (*poor visibility*; *is a poor driver*; *in poor health*). **c** paltry; inferior (*poor condition*; *came a poor third*). **4 a** deserving pity or sympathy; unfortunate (*you poor thing*). **b** with reference to a dead person (*as my poor father used to say*). **5** spiritless; despicable (*is a poor creature*). **6** often *iron.* or *joc.* humble; insignificant (*in my poor opinion*). □**poor-box** a collection-box, esp. in church, for the relief of the poor. **poor law** *hist.* a law relating to the support of paupers. **poor man's** an inferior or cheaper substitute for. **poor man's weather-glass** the pimpernel. **poor-rate** *hist.* a rate or assessment for relief or support of the poor. **poor relation** an inferior or subordinate member of a family or any other group. **poor-spirited** timid; cowardly. **poor White** *offens.* (esp. used by Blacks) a member of a socially inferior group of White people. **take a poor view of** regard with disfavour or pessimism. [ME & OF *pov(e)re*, *poure* f. L *pauper*]

poorhouse /ˈpʊəhaʊs/ *n. hist.* = WORKHOUSE 1.

poorly /ˈpʊəlɪ/ *adv.* & *adj.* —*adv.* **1** scantily; defectively. **2** with no great success. **3** meanly; contemptibly. —*predic.adj.* unwell.

poorness /ˈpʊənɪs/ *n.* **1** defectiveness. **2** the lack of some good quality or constituent.

poove var. of POOF.

POP *abbr.* Post Office Preferred (size of envelopes etc.).

pop¹ /pɒp/ *n.*, *v.*, & *adv.* —*n.* **1 a** a sudden sharp explosive sound as of a cork when drawn. **2** *colloq.* an effervescent sweet drink. —*v.* (**popped**, **popping**) **1** *intr.* & *tr.* make or cause to make a pop. **2** *intr.* & *tr.* (foll. by *in*, *out*, *up*, *down*, etc.) go, move, come, or put unexpectedly or in a quick or hasty manner (*pop out to the shops*; *pop in for a visit*; *pop it on your head*). **3 a** *intr.* & *tr.* burst, making a popping sound. **b** *tr.* heat (popcorn etc.) until it pops. **4** *intr.* (often foll. by *at*) *colloq.* fire a gun (at birds etc.). **5** *tr. sl.* pawn. **6** *tr. sl.* inject (a drug etc.). **7** *intr.* (often foll. by *up*) (of a cricket-ball) rise sharply off the pitch. —*adv.* with the sound of a pop (*heard it go pop*). □**in pop** *Brit. sl.* in pawn. **pop off** *colloq.* **1** die. **2** quietly slip away (cf. sense 2 of *v.*). **pop the question** *colloq.* propose marriage. **pop-shop** *Brit. sl.* a pawnbroker's shop. **pop-up 1** (of a toaster etc.) operating so as to move the object (toast when ready etc.) quickly upwards. **2** (of a book, greetings card, etc.) containing three-dimensional figures, illustrations, etc., that rise up when the page is turned. **3** *Computing* (of a menu) able to be superimposed on the screen being worked on and suppressed rapidly. [ME: imit.]

pop² /pɒp/ *adj.* & *n. colloq.* —*adj.* **1** in a popular or modern style. **2** performing popular music etc. (*pop group*; *pop star*). —*n.* **1** pop music. **2** a pop record or song (*top of the pops*). □**pop art** based on modern popular culture and the mass media, esp. as a critical comment on traditional fine art values. **pop festival** a festival at which popular music etc. is performed. [abbr.]

pop³ /pɒp/ *n.* esp. *US colloq.* father. [abbr. of POPPA]

pop. *abbr.* population.

popadam var. of POPPADAM.

popcorn /ˈpɒpkɔːn/ *n.* **1** Indian corn which bursts open when heated. **2** these kernels when popped.

pope¹ /pəʊp/ *n.* **1** (as title usu. **Pope**) the head of the Roman Catholic Church (also called the Bishop of Rome). **2** the head of the Coptic Church. **3** = RUFF². □**pope's eye 1** a lymphatic gland surrounded with fat in the middle of a sheep's leg. **2** *Sc.* a cut of steak. □□**popedom** *n.* **popeless** *adj.* [OE f. eccl.L *pāpa* bishop, pope f. eccl.Gk *papas* = Gk *pappas* father: cf. PAPA]

pope² /pəʊp/ *n.* a parish priest of the Orthodox Church in Russia etc. [Russ. *pop* f. OSlav. *popŭ* f. WG f. eccl.Gk (as POPE¹)]

popery /ˈpəʊpərɪ/ *n. derog.* the papal system; the Roman Catholic Church.

pop-eyed /ˈpɒpaɪd/ *adj. colloq.* **1** having bulging eyes. **2** wide-eyed (with surprise etc.).

popgun /ˈpɒpgʌn/ *n.* **1** a child's toy gun which shoots a pellet etc. by the compression of air with a piston. **2** *derog.* an inefficient firearm.

popinjay /ˈpɒpɪndʒeɪ/ *n.* **1** a fop, a conceited person, a coxcomb. **2 a** *archaic* a parrot. **b** *hist.* a figure of a parrot on a pole as a mark to shoot at. [ME f. AF *papeiaye*, OF *papingay* etc. f. Sp. *papagayo* f. Arab. *babaġā*: assim. to JAY]

popish /ˈpəʊpɪʃ/ *adj. derog.* Roman Catholic. □□ **popishly** *adv.*

poplar /ˈpɒplə(r)/ *n.* **1** any tree of the genus *Populus*, with a usu. rapidly growing trunk and tremulous leaves. **2** *US* = *tulip-tree.* [ME f. AF *popler*, OF *poplier* f. *pople* f. L *populus*]

poplin /ˈpɒplɪn/ *n.* a plain-woven fabric usu. of cotton, with a corded surface. [obs. F *papeline* perh. f. It. *papalina* (fem.) PAPAL, f. the papal town Avignon where it was made]

popliteal /pɒpˈlɪtɪəl/ *adj.* of the hollow at the back of the knee. [mod.L *popliteus* f. L *poples -itis* this hollow]

poppa /ˈpɒpə/ *n. US colloq.* father (esp. as a child's word). [var. of PAPA]

poppadam /'pɒpədəm/ *n.* (also **poppadom**, **popadam**) *Ind.* a thin, crisp, spiced bread eaten with curry etc. [Tamil *pappaḍam*]

popper /'pɒpə(r)/ *n.* **1** *Brit. colloq.* a press-stud. **2** a person or thing that pops. **3** *colloq.* a small vial of amyl nitrite used for inhalation.

poppet /'pɒpɪt/ *n.* **1** *Brit. colloq.* (esp. as a term of endearment) a small or dainty person. **2** (in full **poppet-head**) the head of a lathe. **3** a small square piece of wood fitted inside the gunwale or washstrake of a boat. □**poppet-head** *Brit.* the frame at the top of a mine-shaft supporting pulleys for the ropes used in hoisting. **poppet-valve** *Engin.* a mushroom-shaped valve, lifted bodily from its seat rather than hinged. [ME *popet(te)*, ult. f. L *pup(p)a*: cf. PUPPET]

popping-crease /'pɒpɪŋˌkriːs/ *n.* *Cricket* a line four feet in front of and parallel to the wicket, within which the batsman must keep the bat or one foot grounded to avoid the risk of being stumped. [POP[1], perh. in obs. sense 'strike']

popple /'pɒp(ə)l/ *v.* & *n.* —*v.intr.* (of water) tumble about, toss to and fro. —*n.* the act or an instance of rolling, tossing, or rippling of water. □□**popply** *adj.* [ME prob. f. MDu. *popelen* murmur, quiver, of imit. orig.]

poppy /'pɒpɪ/ *n.* (*pl.* **-ies**) any plant of the genus *Papaver*, with showy often red flowers and a milky sap with narcotic properties. □**Poppy Day** = *Remembrance Sunday.* **poppy-head 1** the seed capsule of the poppy. **2** an ornamental top on the end of a church pew. □□**poppied** *adj.* [OE *popig, papæg*, etc. f. med.L *papauum* f. L *papaver*]

poppycock /'pɒpɪˌkɒk/ *n.* *sl.* nonsense. [Du. dial. *pappekak*]

popsy /'pɒpsɪ/ *n.* (also **popsie**) (*pl.* **-ies**) *colloq.* (usu. as a term of endearment) a young woman. [shortening of POPPET]

populace /'pɒpjʊləs/ *n.* **1** the common people. **2** *derog.* the rabble. [F f. It. *popolaccio* f. *popolo* people + *-accio* pejorative suffix]

popular /'pɒpjʊlə(r)/ *adj.* **1** liked or admired by many people or by a specified group (*popular teachers*; *a popular hero*). **2 a** of or carried on by the general public (*popular meetings*). **b** prevalent among the general public (*popular discontent*). **3** adapted to the understanding, taste, or means of the people (*popular science*; *popular medicine*). □**popular front** a party or coalition representing left-wing elements. **popular music** songs, folk tunes, etc., appealing to popular tastes. □□**popularism** *n.* **popularity** /-ˈlærɪtɪ/ *n.* **popularly** *adv.* [ME f. AF *populer*, OF *populeir* or L *popularis* f. *populus* people]

popularize /'pɒpjʊləˌraɪz/ *v.tr.* (also **-ise**) **1** make popular. **2** cause (a person, principle, etc.) to be generally known or liked. **3** present (a technical subject, specialized vocabulary, etc.) in a popular or readily understandable form. □□**popularization** /-ˈzeɪʃ(ə)n/ *n.* **popularizer** *n.*

populate /'pɒpjʊˌleɪt/ *v.tr.* **1** inhabit; form the population of (a town, country, etc.). **2** supply with inhabitants; people (*a densely populated district*). [med.L *populare populat-* (as PEOPLE)]

population /ˌpɒpjʊˈleɪʃ(ə)n/ *n.* **1 a** the inhabitants of a place, country, etc. referred to collectively. **b** any specified group within this (*the Irish population of Liverpool*). **2** the total number of any of these (*a population of eight million*; *the seal population*). **3** the act or process of supplying with inhabitants (*the population of forest areas*). **4** *Statistics* any finite or infinite collection of items under consideration. □**population explosion** a sudden large increase of population. [LL *populatio* (as PEOPLE)]

populist /'pɒpjʊlɪst/ *n.* & *adj.* —*n.* a member or adherent of a political party seeking support mainly from the ordinary people. —*adj.* of or relating to such a political party. □□**populism** *n.* **populistic** /-ˈlɪstɪk/ *adj.* [L *populus* people]

populous /'pɒpjʊləs/ *adj.* thickly inhabited. □□

populously *adv.* **populousness** *n.* [ME f. LL *populosus* (as PEOPLE)]

porbeagle /pɔː'biːg(ə)l/ *n.* a large shark, *Lamna nasus*, having a pointed snout. [18th-c. Corn. dial., of unkn. orig.]

porcelain /'pɔːsəlɪn/ *n.* **1** a hard vitrified translucent ceramic. **2** objects made of this. □**porcelain clay** kaolin. **porcelain-shell** cowrie. □□**porcellaneous** /ˌpɔːsəˈleɪnɪəs/ *adj.* **porcellanous** /pɔː'selənəs/ *adj.* [F *porcelaine* cowrie, porcelain f. It. *porcellana* f. *porcella* dimin. of *porca* sow (a cowrie being perh. likened to a sow's vulva) f. L *porca* fem. of *porcus* pig]

porch /pɔːtʃ/ *n.* **1** a covered shelter for the entrance of a building. **2** *US* a veranda. **3** (**the Porch**) = *the Stoa* (see STOA 2). □□**porched** *adj.* **porchless** *adj.* [ME f. OF *porche* f. L *porticus* (transl. Gk *stoa*) f. *porta* passage]

porcine /'pɔːsaɪn/ *adj.* of or like pigs. [F *porcin* or f. L *porcinus* f. *porcus* pig]

porcupine /'pɔːkjʊˌpaɪn/ *n.* **1** any rodent of the family Hystricidae native to Africa, Asia, and SE Europe, or the family Erethizontidae native to America, having defensive spines or quills. **2** (*attrib.*) denoting any of various animals or other organisms with spines. □**porcupine fish** a marine fish, *Diodon hystrix*, covered with sharp spines and often distending itself into a spherical shape. □□**porcupinish** *adj.* **porcupiny** *adj.* [ME f. OF *porc espin* f. Prov. *porc espi(n)* ult. f. L *porcus* pig + *spina* thorn]

pore[1] /pɔː(r)/ *n.* esp. *Biol.* a minute opening in a surface through which gases, liquids, or fine solids may pass. [ME f. OF f. L *porus* f. Gk *poros* passage, pore]

pore[2] /pɔː(r)/ *v.intr.* (foll. by *over*) **1** be absorbed in studying (a book etc.). **2** meditate on, think intently about (a subject). [ME *pure* etc. perh. f. OE *puriān* (unrecorded): cf. PEER[1]]

porgy /'pɔːgɪ/ *n.* (*pl.* **-ies**) *US* any usu. marine fish of the family Sparidae, used as food. Also called *sea bream*. [18th c.: orig. uncert.: cf. Sp. & Port. *pargo*]

porifer /'pɔːrɪfə(r)/ *n.* any aquatic invertebrate of the phylum Porifera, including sponges. [mod.L *Porifera* f. L *porus* PORE[1] + *-fer* bearing]

pork /pɔːk/ *n.* the (esp. unsalted) flesh of a pig, used as food. □**pork-barrel** *US colloq.* government funds as a source of political benefit. **pork-butcher** a person who slaughters pigs for sale, or who sells pork rather than other meats. **pork pie** a pie of minced pork etc. eaten cold. **pork pie hat** a hat with a flat crown and a brim turned up all round. [ME *porc* f. OF *porc* f. L *porcus* pig]

porker /'pɔːkə(r)/ *n.* **1** a pig raised for food. **2** a young fattened pig.

porkling /'pɔːklɪŋ/ *n.* a young or small pig.

porky[1] /'pɔːkɪ/ *adj.* (**porkier, porkiest**) **1** *colloq.* fleshy, fat. **2** of or like pork.

porky[2] /'pɔːkɪ/ *n.* (*pl.* **-ies**) *US colloq.* a porcupine. [abbr.]

porn /pɔːn/ *n.* *colloq.* pornography. [abbr.]

porno /'pɔːnəʊ/ *n.* & *adj.* *colloq.* —*n.* pornography. —*adj.* pornographic. [abbr.]

pornography /pɔː'nɒgrəfɪ/ *n.* **1** the explicit description or exhibition of sexual activity in literature, films, etc., intended to stimulate erotic rather than aesthetic or emotional feelings. **2** literature etc. characterized by this. □□**pornographer** *n.* **pornographic** /-nə'græfɪk/ *adj.* **pornographically** /-nə'græfɪkəlɪ/ *adv.* [Gk *pornographos* writing of harlots f. *pornē* prostitute + *graphō* write]

porous /'pɔːrəs/ *adj.* **1** full of pores. **2** letting through air, water, etc. **3** (of an argument, security system, etc.) leaky, admitting infiltration. □□**porosity** /pɔː'rɒsɪtɪ/ *n.* **porously** *adv.* **porousness** *n.* [ME f. OF *poreux* f. med.L *porosus* f. L *porus* PORE[1]]

porphyria /pɔː'fɪrɪə/ *n.* any of a group of genetic disorders associated with abnormal metabolism of various pigments. [mod.L f. *porphyrin* purple substance excreted by porphyria patients f. Gk *porphura* purple]

porphyry /'pɔːrfɪrɪ/ *n.* (*pl.* **-ies**) **1** a hard rock quarried in ancient Egypt, composed of crystals of white or red feldspar in a red matrix. **2** *Geol.* an igneous rock with large crystals scattered in a matrix of much smaller crystals. ◻◻ **porphyritic** /-'rɪtɪk/ *adj.* [ME ult. f. med.L *porphyreum* f. Gk *porphurītēs* f. *porphura* purple]

porpoise /'pɔːpəs/ *n.* any of various small toothed whales of the family Phocaenidae, esp. of the genus *Phocaena*, with a low triangular dorsal fin and a blunt rounded snout. [ME *porpays* etc. f. OF *po(u)rpois* etc. ult. f. L *porcus* pig + *piscis* fish]

porridge /'pɒrɪdʒ/ *n.* **1** a dish consisting of oatmeal or another meal or cereal boiled in water or milk. **2** *sl.* imprisonment. ◻◻ **porridgy** *adj.* [16th c.: alt. of POTTAGE]

porringer /'pɒrɪndʒə(r)/ *n.* a small bowl, often with a handle, for soup, stew, etc. [earlier *pottinger* f. OF *potager* f. *potage* (see POTTAGE): -n- as in *messenger* etc.]

port[1] /pɔːt/ *n.* **1** a harbour. **2** a place of refuge. **3** a town or place possessing a harbour, esp. one where customs officers are stationed. ◻**port of call** a place where a ship or a person stops on a journey. **Port of London Authority** the corporate body controlling the London harbour and docks. [OE f. L *portus* & ME prob. f. OF f. L *portus*]

port[2] /pɔːt/ *n.* (in full **port wine**) a strong, sweet, dark-red (occas. brown or white) fortified wine of Portugal. [shortened form of *Oporto*, city in Portugal from which port is shipped]

port[3] /pɔːt/ *n.* & *v.* —*n.* the left-hand side (looking forward) of a ship, boat, or aircraft (cf. STARBOARD). —*v.tr.* (also *absol.*) turn (the helm) to port. ◻**port tack** see TACK[1] 4. **port watch** see WATCH *n.* 3b. [prob. orig. the side turned towards PORT[1]]

port[4] /pɔːt/ *n.* **1 a** an opening in the side of a ship for entrance, loading, etc. **b** a porthole. **2** an aperture for the passage of steam, water, etc. **3** *Electr.* a socket or aperture in an electronic circuit, esp. in a computer network, where connections can be made with peripheral equipment. **4** an aperture in a wall etc. for a gun to be fired through. **5** esp. *Sc.* a gate or gateway, esp. of a walled town. [ME & OF *porte* f. L *porta*]

port[5] /pɔːt/ *v.* & *n.* —*v.tr.* *Mil.* carry (a rifle, or other weapon) diagonally across and close to the body with the barrel etc. near the left shoulder (esp. *port arms!*). —*n.* **1** *Mil.* this position. **2** external deportment; carriage; bearing. [ME f. OF *port* ult. f. L *portare* carry]

port[6] /pɔːt/ *n.* *Austral.* **1** a suitcase or travelling bag. **2** a shopping bag, sugar bag, etc. [abbr. of PORTMANTEAU]

portable /'pɔːtəb(ə)l/ *adj.* & *n.* —*adj.* **1** easily movable, convenient for carrying (*portable TV*; *portable computer*). **2** (of a right, privilege, etc.) capable of being transferred or adapted in altered circumstances (*portable pension*). —*n.* a portable object, e.g. a radio, typewriter, etc. (*decided to buy a portable*). ◻◻ **portability** /ˌpɔːtə'bɪlɪtɪ/ *n.* **portableness** *n.* **portably** *adv.* [ME f. OF *portable* or LL *portabilis* f. L *portare* carry]

portage /'pɔːtɪdʒ/ *n.* & *v.* —*n.* **1** the carrying of boats or goods between two navigable waters. **2** a place at which this is necessary. **3 a** the act or an instance of carrying or transporting. **b** the cost of this. —*v.tr.* convey (a boat or goods) between navigable waters. [ME f. OF f. *porter*: see PORT[5]]

Portakabin /'pɔːtəˌkæbɪn/ *n.* *propr.* a portable room or building designed for quick assembly. [PORTABLE + CABIN]

portal[1] /'pɔːt(ə)l/ *n.* a doorway or gate etc., esp. a large and elaborate one. [ME f. OF f. med.L *portale* (neut. adj.): see PORTAL[2]]

portal[2] /'pɔːt(ə)l/ *adj.* **1** of or relating to an aperture in an organ through which its associated vessels pass. **2** of or relating to the portal vein. ◻**portal vein** a vein conveying blood to the liver from the spleen, stomach, pancreas, and intestines. [mod.L *portalis* f. L *porta* gate]

portamento /ˌpɔːtə'mentəʊ/ *n.* (*pl.* **portamenti** /-tɪ/) *Mus.* **1** the act or an instance of gliding from one note to another in singing, playing the violin, etc. **2** piano-playing in a manner intermediate between legato and staccato. [It., = carrying]

portative /'pɔːtətɪv/ *adj.* **1** serving to carry or support. **2** *Mus. hist.* (esp. of a small pipe-organ) portable. [ME f. OF *portatif*, app. alt. of *portatil* f. med.L *portatilis* f. L *portare* carry]

portcullis /pɔːt'kʌlɪs/ *n.* **1** a strong heavy grating sliding up and down in vertical grooves, lowered to block a gateway in a fortress etc. **2** (**Portcullis**) *Heraldry* one of the four pursuivants of the English College of Arms, with this as a badge. ◻◻ **portcullised** *adj.* [ME f. OF *porte coleïce* sliding door f. *porte* door f. L *porta* + *col(e)ice* fem. of *couleïs* sliding ult. f. L *colare* filter]

Porte /pɔːt/ *n.* (in full the **Sublime** or **Ottoman Porte**) *hist.* the Ottoman court at Constantinople. [F (*la Sublime Porte* = the exalted gate), transl. of Turk. title of the central office of the Ottoman government]

porte-cochère /ˌpɔːtkɒ'ʃeə(r)/ *n.* **1** a porch large enough for vehicles to pass through, usu. into a courtyard. **2** *US* a roofed structure extending from the entrance of a building over a place where vehicles stop to discharge passengers. [F f. *porte* PORT[4] + *cochère* (fem. adj.) f. *coche* COACH]

portend /pɔː'tend/ *v.tr.* **1** foreshadow as an omen. **2** give warning of. [ME f. L *portendere portent-* f. por- PRO-[1] + *tendere* stretch]

portent /'pɔːtent, -t(ə)nt/ *n.* **1** an omen, a significant sign of something to come. **2** a prodigy; a marvellous thing. [L *portentum* (as PORTEND)]

portentous /pɔː'tentəs/ *adj.* **1** like or serving as a portent. **2** pompously solemn. ◻◻ **portentously** *adv.*

porter[1] /'pɔːtə(r)/ *n.* **1 a** a person employed to carry luggage etc., esp. a railway, airport, or hotel employee. **b** a hospital employee who moves equipment, trolleys, etc. **2** a dark-brown bitter beer brewed from charred or browned malt (app. orig. made esp. for porters). **3** *US* a sleeping-car attendant. ◻◻ **porterage** *n.* [ME f. OF *port(e)our* f. med.L *portator -oris* f. *portare* carry]

porter[2] /'pɔːtə(r)/ *n.* *Brit.* a gatekeeper or doorkeeper, esp. of a large building. [ME & AF, OF *portier* f. LL *portarius* f. *porta* door]

porterhouse /'pɔːtəˌhaʊs/ *n.* esp. *US* **1** *hist.* a house at which porter and other drinks were retailed. **2** a house where steaks, chops, etc. were served. ◻**porterhouse steak** a thick steak cut from the thick end of a sirloin.

portfire /'pɔːtˌfaɪə(r)/ *n.* a device for firing rockets, igniting explosives in mining, etc. [after F *porte-feu* f. *porter* carry + *feu* fire]

portfolio /pɔːt'fəʊlɪəʊ/ *n.* (*pl.* **-os**) **1** a case for keeping loose sheets of paper, drawings, etc. **2** a range of investments held by a person, a company, etc. **3** the office of a minister of State (cf. *minister without portfolio*). **4** samples of an artist's work. [It. *portafogli* f. *portare* carry + *foglio* leaf f. L *folium*]

porthole /'pɔːtˌhəʊl/ *n.* **1** an (esp. glazed) aperture in a ship's or aircraft's side for the admission of light. **2** *hist.* an aperture for pointing a cannon through.

portico /'pɔːtɪˌkəʊ/ *n.* (*pl.* **-oes** or **-os**) a colonnade; a roof supported by columns at regular intervals usu. attached as a porch to a building. [It. f. L *porticus* PORCH]

portière /ˌpɔːtɪ'eə(r)/ *n.* a curtain hung over a door or doorway. [F f. *porte* door f. L *porta*]

portion /'pɔːʃ(ə)n/ *n.* & *v.* —*n.* **1** a part or share. **2** the amount of food allotted to one person. **3** a specified or limited quantity. **4** one's destiny or lot.

5 a dowry. —*v.tr.* **1** divide (a thing) into portions. **2** (foll. by *out*) distribute. **3** give a dowry to. **4** (foll. by *to*) assign (a thing) to (a person). □□ **portionless** *adj.* (in sense 5 of *n.*). [ME f. OF *porcion* portion f. L *portio -onis*]

Portland cement /'pɔːtlənd/ *n.* a cement manufactured from chalk and clay which when hard resembles Portland stone in colour.

Portland stone /'pɔːtlənd/ *n.* a limestone from the Isle of Portland in Dorset, used in building.

portly /'pɔːtlɪ/ *adj.* (**portlier, portliest**) **1** corpulent; stout. **2** *archaic* of a stately appearance. □□ **portliness** *n.* [PORT⁵ (in the sense 'bearing') + -LY¹]

portmanteau /pɔːt'mæntəʊ/ *n.* (*pl.* **portmanteaus** /-təʊz/ or **portmanteaux** /-təʊz/) a leather trunk for clothes etc., opening into two equal parts. □ **portmanteau word** a word blending the sounds and combining the meanings of two others, e.g. *motel, Oxbridge.* [F *portmanteau* f. *porter* carry f. L *portare* + *manteau* MANTLE]

portolan /'pɔːtəˌlæn/ *n.* (also **portolano** /ˌpɔːtə'lɑːnəʊ/) (*pl.* **portolans** or **portolanos**) *hist.* a book of sailing directions with charts, descriptions of harbours, etc. [It. *portolano* f. *porto* PORT¹]

portrait /'pɔːtrɪt/ *n.* **1** a representation of a person or animal, esp. of the face, made by drawing, painting, photography, etc. **2** a verbal picture; a graphic description. **3** a person etc. resembling or typifying another (*is the portrait of his father*). **4** (in graphic design etc.) a format in which the height of an illustration etc. is greater than the width (cf. LANDSCAPE). [F, past part. of OF *portraire* PORTRAY]

portraitist /'pɔːtrɪtɪst/ *n.* a person who takes or paints portraits.

portraiture /'pɔːtrɪtʃə(r)/ *n.* **1** the art of painting or taking portraits. **2** graphic description. **3** a portrait. [ME f. OF (as PORTRAIT)]

portray /pɔː'treɪ/ *v.tr.* **1** make a likeness of. **2** describe graphically. □□ **portrayable** *adj.* **portrayal** *n.* **portrayer** *n.* [ME f. OF *portraire* f. *por-* = PRO-¹ + *traire* draw f. L *trahere*]

Port Salut /ˌpɔː sə'luː/ *n.* a pale mild type of cheese. [after the Trappist monastery in France where it was first produced]

Portuguese /ˌpɔːtjʊ'giːz, ˌpɔːtʃ-/ *n.* & *adj.* —*n.* (*pl.* same) **1 a** a native or national of Portugal. **b** a person of Portuguese descent. **2** the language of Portugal. —*adj.* of or relating to Portugal or its people or language. □ **Portuguese man-of-war** a dangerous tropical or sub-tropical marine hydrozoan of the genus *Physalia* with a large crest and a poisonous sting. [Port. *portuguez* f. med.L *portugalensis*]

POS *abbr.* point-of-sale.

pose¹ /pəʊz/ *v.* & *n.* —*v.* **1** *intr.* assume a certain attitude of body, esp. when being photographed or being painted for a portrait. **2** *intr.* (foll. by *as*) set oneself up as or pretend to be (another person etc.) (*posing as a celebrity*). **3** *intr.* behave affectedly in order to impress others. **4** *tr.* put forward or present (a question etc.). **5** *tr.* place (an artist's model etc.) in a certain attitude or position. —*n.* **1** an attitude of body or mind. **2** an attitude or pretence, esp. one assumed for effect (*his generosity is a mere pose*). [F *poser* (v.), *pose* (n.) f. LL *pausare* PAUSE: some senses by confusion with L *ponere* place (cf. COMPOSE)]

pose² /pəʊz/ *v.tr.* puzzle (a person) with a question or problem. [obs. *appose* f. OF *aposer* var. of *opposer* OPPOSE]

poser /'pəʊzə(r)/ *n.* **1** a person who poses (see POSE¹ *v.* 3). **2** a puzzling question or problem.

poseur /pəʊ'zɜː(r)/ *n.* (*fem.* **poseuse** /pəʊ'zɜːz/) a person who poses for effect or behaves affectedly. [F f. *poser* POSE¹]

posh /pɒʃ/ *adj.* & *adv. colloq.* —*adj.* **1** smart; stylish. **2** of or associated with the upper classes (*spoke with a posh accent*). —*adv.* in a stylish or upper-class way (*talk posh; act posh*). □ **posh up** smarten up. □□ **poshly** *adv.* **poshness** *n.* [20th c.: perh. f. sl. *posh* a

dandy: *port out starboard home* (referring to the more comfortable accommodation on ships to and from the East) is a later association and not the true origin]

posit /'pɒzɪt/ *v.* & *n.* —*v.tr.* (**posited, positing**) **1** assume as a fact, postulate. **2** put in place or position. —*n. Philos.* a statement which is made on the assumption that it will prove valid. [L *ponere posit-* place]

position /pə'zɪʃ(ə)n/ *n.* & *v.* —*n.* **1** a place occupied by a person or thing. **2** the way in which a thing or its parts are placed or arranged (*sitting in an uncomfortable position*). **3** the proper place (*in position*). **4** the state of being advantageously placed (*jockeying for position*). **5** a person's mental attitude; a way of looking at a question (*changed their position on nuclear disarmament*). **6** a person's situation in relation to others (*puts one in an awkward position*). **7** rank or status; high social standing. **8** paid employment. **9** a place where troops etc. are posted for strategical purposes (*the position was stormed*). **10** the configuration of chessmen etc. during a game. **11** a specific pose in ballet etc. (*hold first position*). **12** *Logic* **a** a proposition. **b** a statement of proposition. —*v.tr.* place in position. □ **in a position to** enabled by circumstances, resources, information, etc. to (do, state, etc.). **position paper** orig. *US* (in business etc.) a written report of attitude or intentions. **position vector** *Math.* a vector which determines the position of a point. □□ **positional** *adj.* **positionally** *adv.* **positioner** *n.* [ME f. OF *position* or L *positio -onis* (as POSIT)]

positive /'pɒzɪtɪv/ *adj.* & *n.* —*adj.* **1** formally or explicitly stated; definite, unquestionable (*positive proof*). **2** (of a person) convinced, confident, or overconfident in his or her opinion (*positive that I was not there*). **3 a** absolute; not relative. **b** *Gram.* (of an adjective or adverb) expressing a simple quality without comparison (cf. COMPARATIVE, SUPERLATIVE). **4** *colloq.* downright; complete (*it would be a positive miracle*). **5** constructive; directional (*positive criticism; positive thinking*). **6** marked by the presence rather than absence of qualities or *Med.* symptoms (*a positive reaction to the plan; the test was positive*). **7** esp. *Philos.* dealing only with matters of fact; practical (cf. POSITIVISM 1). **8** tending in a direction naturally or arbitrarily taken as that of increase or progress (*clockwise rotation is positive*). **9** greater than zero (*positive and negative integers*) (opp. NEGATIVE). **10** *Electr.* of, containing, or producing the kind of electrical charge produced by rubbing glass with silk; an absence of electrons. **11** (of a photographic image) showing lights and shades or colours true to the original (opp. NEGATIVE). —*n.* a positive adjective, photograph, quantity, etc. □ **positive discrimination** the practice of making distinctions in favour of groups considered to be underprivileged. **positive feedback 1** a constructive response to an experiment, questionnaire, etc. **2** *Electronics* the return of part of an output signal to the input, tending to increase the amplification etc. **positive geotropism** see GEOTROPISM. **positive pole** the north-seeking pole. **positive ray** *Physics* a canal ray. **positive sign** = *plus sign.* **positive vetting** *Brit.* an exhaustive inquiry into the background and character of a candidate for a post in the Civil Service that involves access to secret material. □□ **positively** *adv.* **positiveness** *n.* **positivity** /ˌpɒzɪ'tɪvɪtɪ/ *n.* [ME f. OF *positif -ive* or L *positivus* (as POSIT)]

positivism /'pɒzɪtɪˌvɪz(ə)m/ *n.* **1** *Philos.* the philosophical system of Auguste Comte, recognizing only non-metaphysical facts and observable phenomena, and rejecting metaphysics and theism. **2** a religious system founded on this. **3** = *logical positivism.* □□ **positivist** *n.* **positivistic** /-'vɪstɪk/ *adj.* **positivistically** /-'vɪstɪkəlɪ/ *adv.* [F *positivisme* (as POSITIVE)]

positron /'pɒzɪˌtrɒn/ n. Physics an elementary particle with a positive charge equal to the negative charge of an electron and having the same mass as an electron. [POSITIVE + -TRON]

posology /pə'sɒledʒɪ/ n. the study of the dosage of medicines. [F posologie f. Gk posos how much]

posse /'pɒsɪ/ n. 1 a strong force or company or assemblage. 2 (in full **posse comitatus** /ˌkɒmɪ'teɪtəs/) a a body of constables, law-enforcers, etc. b esp. US a body of men summoned by a sheriff etc. to enforce the law. [med.L, = power f. L posse be able: comitatus = of the county]

possess /pə'zes/ v.tr. 1 hold as property; own. 2 have a faculty, quality, etc. (they possess a special value for us). 3 (also refl.; foll. by in) maintain (oneself, one's soul, etc.) in a specified state (possess oneself in patience). 4 a (of a demon etc.) occupy; have power over (a person etc.) (possessed by the devil). b (of an emotion, infatuation, etc.) dominate, be an obsession of (possessed by fear). 5 have sexual intercourse with (esp. a woman). □ **be possessed of** own, have. **possess oneself of** take or get for one's own. **what possessed you?** an expression of incredulity. □□ **possessor** n. **possessory** adj. [OF possesser f. L possidēre possess- f. potis able + sedēre sit]

possession /pə'zeʃ(ə)n/ n. 1 the act or state of possessing or being possessed. 2 the thing possessed. 3 the act or state of actual holding or occupancy. 4 Law power or control similar to lawful ownership but which may exist separately from it (prosecuted for possession of narcotic drugs). 5 (in pl.) property, wealth, subject territory, etc. 6 Football etc. temporary control of the ball by a particular player. □ **in possession** 1 (of a person) possessing. 2 (of a thing) possessed. **in possession of** 1 having in one's possession. 2 maintaining control over (in possession of one's wits). **in the possession of** held or owned by. **possession order** an order made by a court directing that possession of a property be given to the owner. **take possession** (often foll. by of) become the owner or possessor (of a thing). □□ **possessionless** adj. [ME f. OF possession or L possessio -onis (as POSSESS)]

possessive /pə'zesɪv/ adj. & n. —adj. 1 showing a desire to possess or retain what one already owns. 2 showing jealous and domineering tendencies towards another person. 3 Gram. indicating possession. —n. (in full **possessive case**) Gram. the case of nouns and pronouns expressing possession. □ **possessive pronoun** each of the pronouns indicating possession (my, your, his, their, etc.) or the corresponding absolute forms (mine, yours, his, theirs, etc.). □□ **possessively** adv. **possessiveness** n. [L possessivus (as POSSESS), transl. Gk ktētikē (ptōsis case)]

posset /'pɒsɪt/ n. hist. a drink made of hot milk curdled with ale, wine, etc., often flavoured with spices, formerly much used as a remedy for colds etc. [ME poshote: orig. unkn.]

possibility /ˌpɒsɪ'bɪlɪtɪ/ n. (pl. -ies) 1 the state or fact of being possible, or an occurrence of this (outside the range of possibility; saw no possibility of going away). 2 a thing that may exist or happen (there are three possibilities). 3 (usu. in pl.) the capability of being used, improved, etc.; the potential of an object or situation (esp. have possibilities). [ME f. OF possibilité or LL possibilitas -tatis (as POSSIBLE)]

possible /'pɒsɪb(ə)l/ adj. & n. —adj. 1 capable of existing or happening; that may be managed, achieved, etc. (came as early as possible; did as much as possible). 2 that is likely to happen etc. (few thought their victory possible). 3 acceptable; potential (a possible way of doing it). —n. 1 a possible candidate, member of a team, etc. 2 (prec. by the) whatever is likely, manageable, etc. 3 the highest possible score, esp. in shooting etc. [ME f. OF possible or L possibilis f. posse be able]

possibly /'pɒsɪblɪ/ adv. 1 perhaps. 2 in accordance with possibility (cannot possibly refuse).

possum /'pɒsəm/ n. 1 colloq. = OPOSSUM 1. 2 Austral. & NZ colloq. a phalanger resembling an American opossum. □ **play possum** 1 pretend to be asleep or unconscious when threatened. 2 feign ignorance. [abbr.]

post¹ /pəʊst/ n. & v. —n. 1 a long stout piece of timber or metal set upright in the ground etc.: a to support something, esp. in building. b to mark a position, boundary, etc. c to carry notices. 2 a pole etc. marking the start or finish of a race. —v.tr. 1 (often foll. by up) a attach (a paper etc.) in a prominent place; stick up (post no bills). b announce or advertise by placard or in a published text. 2 publish the name of (a ship etc.) as overdue or missing. 3 placard (a wall etc.) with bills etc. 4 US achieve (a score in a game etc.). □ **post-mill** a windmill pivoted on a post and turning to catch the wind. [OE f. L postis: in ME also f. OF etc.]

post² /pəʊst/ n., v., & adv. —n. 1 Brit. the official conveyance of parcels, letters, etc. (send it by post). 2 Brit. a single collection, dispatch, or delivery of these; the letters etc. dispatched (has the post arrived yet?). 3 Brit. a place where letters etc. are dealt with; a post office or postbox (take it to the post). 4 hist. a one of a series of couriers who carried mail on horseback between fixed stages. b a letter-carrier; a mail cart. —v. 1 tr. put (a letter etc.) in the post. 2 tr. (esp. as **posted** adj.) (often foll. by up) supply a person with information (keep me posted). 3 tr. a enter (an item) in a ledger. b (often foll. by up) complete (a ledger) in this way. c carry (an entry) from an auxiliary book to a more formal one, or from one account to another. 4 intr. a travel with haste, hurry. b hist. travel with relays of horses. —adv. express; with haste. □ **post-chaise** hist. a travelling carriage hired from stage to stage or drawn by horses hired in this manner. **post exchange** US Mil. a shop at a military camp etc. **post-free** Brit. carried by post free of charge or with the postage prepaid. **post-haste** with great speed. **post-horn** a valveless horn formerly used to announce the arrival of the post. **Post Office** 1 the public department or corporation responsible for postal services and (in some countries) telecommunication. 2 (**post office**) a a room or building where postal business is carried on. b US = postman's knock. **post-office box** a numbered place in a post office where letters are kept until called for. **post-paid** on which postage has been paid. **post room** the department of a company that deals with incoming and outgoing mail. **post-town** a town with a post office, esp. one that is not a sub-office of another. [F poste (fem.) f. It. posta ult. f. L ponere posit- place]

post³ /pəʊst/ n. & v. —n. 1 a place where a soldier is stationed or which he patrols. 2 a place of duty. 3 a a position taken up by a body of soldiers. b a force occupying this. c a fort. 4 a situation, paid employment. 5 = trading post. 6 Naut. hist. a commission as an officer in command of a vessel of 20 guns or more. —v.tr. 1 place or station (soldiers, an employee, etc.). 2 appoint to a post or command. □ **first** (or **last**) **post** Brit. a bugle-call giving notice of the hour of retiring at night. **last post** Brit. a bugle-call blown at military funerals etc. [F poste (masc.) f. It. posto f. Rmc postum (unrecorded) f. L ponere posit- place]

post- /pəʊst/ prefix after in time or order. [from or after L post (adv. & prep.)]

postage /'pəʊstɪdʒ/ n. the amount charged for sending a letter etc. by post, usu. prepaid in the form of a stamp (£25 including postage & packing). □ **postage meter** US a franking-machine. **postage stamp** an official stamp affixed to or imprinted on a letter etc. indicating the amount of postage paid.

postal /'pəʊst(ə)l/ adj. & n. —adj. 1 of the post. 2 by post (postal vote). —n. US a postcard. □ **postal card**

US = POSTCARD. **postal code** = POSTCODE. **postal meter** a franking-machine. **postal note** *Austral.* & *NZ* = *postal order*. **postal order** a money order issued by the Post Office, payable to a specified person. **Postal Union** a union of the governments of various countries for the regulation of international postage. □□ **postally** *adv.* [F (*poste* POST²)]

postbag /ˈpəʊstbæg/ *n. Brit.* = MAILBAG.

postbox /ˈpəʊstbɒks/ *n. Brit.* a letter-box.

postcard /ˈpəʊstkɑːd/ *n.* a card, often with a photograph on one side, for sending a short message by post without an envelope.

post-classical /pəʊstˈklæsɪk(ə)l/ *adj.* (esp. of Greek and Roman literature) later than the classical period.

postcode /ˈpəʊstkəʊd/ *n.* a group of letters or letters and figures which are added to a postal address to assist sorting.

post-coital /pəʊstˈkəʊɪt(ə)l/ *adj.* occurring or existing after sexual intercourse. □□ **post-coitally** *adv.*

postdate *v.* & *n.* —*v.tr.* /pəʊstˈdeɪt/ affix or assign a date later than the actual one to (a document, event, etc.). —*n.* /ˈpəʊstdeɪt/ such a date.

post-doctoral /ˌpəʊstˈdɒktər(ə)l/ *adj.* of or relating to research undertaken after the completion of doctoral research.

post-entry /pəʊstˈentrɪ/ *n.* (*pl.* **-ies**) a late or subsequent entry, esp. in a race or in bookkeeping.

poster /ˈpəʊstə(r)/ *n.* **1** a placard in a public place. **2** a large printed picture. **3** a billposter. □ **poster paint** a gummy opaque paint.

poste restante /ˌpəʊst reˈstɑ̃t/ *n.* **1** a direction on a letter to indicate that it should be kept at a specified post office until collected by the addressee. **2** the department in a post office where such letters are kept. [F, = letter(s) remaining]

posterior /pɒˈstɪərɪə(r)/ *adj.* & *n.* —*adj.* **1** later; coming after in series, order, or time. **2** situated at the back. —*n.* (in *sing.* or *pl.*) the buttocks. □□ **posteriority** /pɒˌstɪərɪˈɒrɪtɪ/ *n.* **posteriorly** *adv.* [L, compar. of *posterus* following f. *post* after]

posterity /pɒˈsterɪtɪ/ *n.* **1** all succeeding generations. **2** the descendants of a person. [ME f. OF *posterité* f. L *posteritas -tatis* f. *posterus*: see POSTERIOR]

postern /ˈpɒst(ə)n, ˈpəʊ-/ *n.* **1** a back door. **2** a side way or entrance. [ME f. OF *posterne, posterle,* f. LL *posterula* dimin. of *posterus*: see POSTERIOR]

postfix *n.* & *v.* —*n.* /ˈpəʊstfɪks/ a suffix. —*v.tr.* /pəʊstˈfɪks/ append (letters) at the end of a word.

postglacial /pəʊstˈɡleɪʃ(ə)l, -sɪəl/ *adj.* & *n.* —*adj.* formed or occurring after a glacial period. —*n.* a postglacial period or deposit.

postgraduate /pəʊstˈɡrædjʊət/ *adj.* & *n.* —*adj.* **1** (of a course of study) carried on after taking a first degree. **2** of or relating to students following this course of study (*postgraduate accommodation*). —*n.* a postgraduate student.

posthumous /ˈpɒstjʊməs/ *adj.* **1** occurring after death. **2** (of a child) born after the death of its father. **3** (of a book etc.) published after the author's death. □□ **posthumously** *adv.* [L *postumus* last (superl. f. *post* after): in LL *posth-* by assoc. with *humus* ground]

postiche /pɒˈstiːʃ/ *n.* a coil of false hair, worn as an adornment. [F, = false, f. It. *posticcio*]

postie /ˈpəʊstɪ/ *n. colloq.* a postman or postwoman. [abbr.]

postil /ˈpɒstɪl/ *n. hist.* **1** a marginal note or comment, esp. on a text of Scripture. **2** a commentary. [ME f. OF *postille* f. med.L *postilla,* of uncert. orig.]

postilion /pɒˈstɪljən/ *n.* (also **postillion**) the rider on the near (left-hand side) horse drawing a coach etc. when there is no coachman. [F *postillon* f. It. *postiglione* post-boy f. *posta* POST²]

post-impressionism /ˌpəʊstɪmˈpreʃ(ə)nɪz(ə)m/ *n.* artistic aims and methods developed as a reaction against impressionism and intending to express the individual artist's conception of the objects represented rather than the ordinary observer's view. □□ **post-impressionist** *n.* & *adj.* **post-impressionistic** /-ˈnɪstɪk/ *adj.*

postindustrial /ˌpəʊstɪnˈdʌstrɪəl/ *adj.* relating to or characteristic of a society or economy which no longer relies on heavy industry.

postliminy /pəʊstˈlɪmɪnɪ/ *n.* **1** (in international law) the restoration to their former status of persons and things taken in war. **2** (in Roman law) the right of a banished person or captive to resume civic privileges on return from exile. [L *postliminium* (as POST-, *limen liminis* threshold)]

postlude /ˈpəʊstluːd/ *n. Mus.* a concluding voluntary. [POST-, after PRELUDE]

postman /ˈpəʊstmən/ *n.* (*pl.* **-men**; *fem.* **postwoman**, *pl.* **-women**) a person who is employed to deliver and collect letters etc. □ **postman's knock** *Brit.* a parlour game in which imaginary letters are delivered in exchange for kisses.

postmark /ˈpəʊstmɑːk/ *n.* & *v.* —*n.* an official mark stamped on a letter, esp. one giving the place, date, etc. of dispatch or arrival, and serving to cancel the stamp. —*v.tr.* mark (an envelope etc.) with this.

postmaster /ˈpəʊstˌmɑːstə(r)/ *n.* a man in charge of a post office. □ **postmaster general** the head of a country's postal service. ¶ The office was abolished in the UK in 1969.

post-millennial /ˌpəʊstmɪˈlenɪəl/ *adj.* following the millennium.

post-millennialism /ˌpəʊstmɪˈlenɪəˌlɪz(ə)m/ *n.* the doctrine that a second Advent will follow the millennium. □□ **post-millennialist** *n.*

postmistress /ˈpəʊstˌmɪstrɪs/ *n.* a woman in charge of a post office.

post-modern /pəʊstˈmɒd(ə)n/ *adj.* (in literature, architecture, the arts, etc.) denoting a movement reacting against modern tendencies, esp. by drawing attention to former conventions. □□ **post-modernism** *n.* **post-modernist** *n.* & *adj.*

post-mortem /pəʊstˈmɔːtəm/ *n., adv.,* & *adj.* —*n.* **1** (in full **post-mortem examination**) an examination made after death, esp. to determine its cause. **2** *colloq.* a discussion analysing the course and result of a game, election, etc. *adv.* & *adj.* after death. [L]

postnatal /pəʊstˈneɪt(ə)l/ *adj.* characteristic of or relating to the period after childbirth.

post-nuptial /pəʊstˈnʌpʃ(ə)l/ *adj.* after marriage.

post-obit /pəʊstˈəʊbɪt/ *n.* & *adj.* —*n.* a bond given to a lender by a borrower securing a sum for payment on the death of another person from whom the borrower expects to inherit. —*adj.* taking effect after death. [L *post obitum* f. *post* after + *obitus* decease f. *obire* die]

postoperative /pəʊstˈɒpərətɪv/ *adj.* relating to or occurring in a period after a surgical operation.

post-partum /pəʊstˈpɑːtəm/ *adj.* following parturition.

postpone /pəʊstˈpəʊn, pəˈspəʊn/ *v.tr.* cause or arrange (an event etc.) to take place at a later time. □□ **postponable** *adj.* **postponement** *n.* **postponer** *n.* [L *postponere* (as POST-, *ponere posit-* place)]

postposition /ˌpəʊstpəˈzɪʃ(ə)n/ *n.* **1** a word or particle, esp. an enclitic, placed after the word it modifies, e.g. -*ward* in *homeward* and *at* in *the books we looked at.* **2** the use of a postposition. □□ **postpositional** *adj.* & *n.* **postpositive** /pəʊstˈpɒzɪtɪv/ *adj.* & *n.* **postpositively** /-ˈpɒzɪtɪvlɪ/ *adv.* [LL *postpositio* (as POSTPONE)]

postprandial /pəʊstˈprændɪəl/ *adj. formal* or *joc.* after dinner or lunch. [POST- + L *prandium* a meal]

postscript /ˈpəʊstskrɪpt, ˈpəʊskrɪpt/ *n.* **1** an additional paragraph or remark, usu. at the end of a letter after the signature and introduced by 'PS'. **2** any additional information, action, etc. [L *postscriptum* neut. past part. of *postscribere* (as POST-, *scribere* write)]

post-tax /pəʊstˈtæks/ *adj.* (of income) after the deduction of taxes.

---

aʊ h*ow*　eɪ d*ay*　əʊ n*o*　eə h*air*　ɪə n*ear*　ɔɪ b*oy*　ʊə p*oor*　aɪə f*ire*　aʊə s*our*　(*see over for consonants*)

postulant /'pɒstjʊlənt/ n. a candidate, esp. for admission into a religious order. [F postulant or L postulans -antis (as POSTULATE)]

postulate v. & n. —v.tr. /'pɒstjʊˌleɪt/ **1** (often foll. by that + clause) assume as a necessary condition, esp. as a basis for reasoning; take for granted. **2** claim. **3** (in ecclesiastical law) nominate or elect to a higher rank. —n. /'pɒstjʊlət/ **1** a thing postulated. **2** a fundamental prerequisite or condition. **3** Math. an assumption used as a basis for mathematical reasoning. □□ **postulation** /ˌpɒstjʊˈleɪʃ(ə)n/ n. [L postulare postulat- demand]

postulator /'pɒstjʊˌleɪtə(r)/ n. **1** a person who postulates. **2** RC Ch. a person who presents a case for canonization or beatification.

posture /'pɒstʃə(r)/ n. & v. —n. **1** the relative position of parts, esp. of the body (in a reclining posture). **2** carriage or bearing (improved by good posture and balance). **3** a mental or spiritual attitude or condition. **4** the condition or state (of affairs etc.) (in more diplomatic postures). —v. **1** intr. assume a mental or physical attitude, esp. for effect (inclined to strut and posture). **2** tr. pose (a person). □□ **postural** adj. **posturer** n. [F f. It. postura f. L positura f. ponere posit- place]

postwar /'pəʊstˈwɔː(r), 'pəʊst-/ adj. occurring or existing after a war (esp. the most recent major war).

posy /'pəʊzɪ/ n. (pl. -ies) **1** a small bunch of flowers. **2** archaic a short motto, line of verse, etc., inscribed within a ring. □ **posy-ring** a ring with this inscription. [alt. f. POESY]

pot¹ /pɒt/ n. & v. —n. **1** a vessel, usu. rounded, of ceramic ware or metal or glass for holding liquids or solids or for cooking in. **2 a** a coffee-pot, flowerpot, glue-pot, jam-pot, teapot, etc. **b** = chimney-pot. **c** = lobster-pot. **3** a drinking vessel of pewter etc. **4** the contents of a pot (ate a whole pot of jam). **5** the total amount of the bet in a game etc. **6** colloq. a large sum (pots of money). **7** sl. a vessel given as a prize in an athletic contest, esp. a silver cup. **8** = pot-belly. —v.tr. (**potted, potting**) **1** place in a pot. **2** (usu. as **potted** adj.) preserve in a sealed pot (potted shrimps). **3** sit (a young child) on a chamber pot. **4** pocket (a ball) in billiards etc. **5** shoot at, hit, or kill (an animal) with a pot shot. **6** seize or secure. **7** abridge or epitomize (in a potted version; potted wisdom). □ **go to pot** colloq. deteriorate; be ruined. **pot-bellied** having a pot-belly. **pot-belly** (pl. -ies) **1** a protruding stomach. **2** a person with this. **3** a small bulbous stove. **pot-boiler 1** a work of literature or art done merely to make the writer or artist a living. **2** a writer or artist who does this. **pot-bound** (of a plant) having roots which fill the flowerpot, leaving no room to expand. **pot cheese** US cottage cheese. **pot-herb** any herb grown in a kitchen garden. **pot-hook 1** a hook over a hearth for hanging a pot etc. on, or for lifting a hot pot. **2** a curved stroke in handwriting, esp. as made in learning to write. **pot-hunter 1** a person who hunts for game at random. **2** a person who takes part in a contest merely for the sake of the prize. **pot luck** whatever (hospitality etc.) is available. **pot of gold** an imaginary reward; an ideal; a jackpot. **pot pie** a pie of meat etc. or fruit with a crust baked in a pot. **pot plant** a plant grown in a flowerpot. **pot roast** a piece of meat cooked slowly in a covered dish. **pot-roast** v.tr. cook (a piece of meat) in this way. **pot-shot 1** a random shot. **2** a shot aimed at an animal etc. within easy reach. **3** a shot at a game-bird etc. merely to provide a meal. **pot-valiant** courageous because of drunkenness. **pot-valour** this type of courage. □□ **potful** n. (pl. -fuls). [OE pott, corresp. to OFris., MDu., MLG pot, f. pop.L]

pot² /pɒt/ n. sl. marijuana. □ **pot-head** one who smokes this. [prob. f. Mex. Sp. potiguaya]

pot³ /pɒt/ n. & v. Austral. & NZ —n. a dropped goal in rugby football. —v.tr. (**potted, potting**) score (a dropped goal). [perh. f. pot-shot]

potable /'pəʊtəb(ə)l/ adj. drinkable. □□ **potability** /-ˈbɪlɪtɪ/ n. [F potable or LL potabilis f. L potare drink]

potage /pɒˈtɑːʒ/ n. thick soup. [F (as POTTAGE)]

potamic /pəˈtæmɪk/ adj. of rivers. □□ **potamology** /ˌpɒtəˈmɒlɪdʒɪ/ n. [Gk potamos river]

potash /'pɒtæʃ/ n. an alkaline potassium compound, usu. potassium carbonate or hydroxide. [17th-c. pot-ashes f. Du. pot-asschen (as POT¹, ASH¹): orig. obtained by leaching vegetable ashes and evaporating the solution in iron pots]

potassium /pəˈtæsɪəm/ n. Chem. a soft silver-white metallic element occurring naturally in seawater and various minerals, an essential element for living organisms, and forming many useful compounds used industrially. ¶ Symb.: **K**. □ **potassium chloride** a white crystalline solid used as a fertilizer and in photographic processing. **potassium cyanide** a highly toxic solid that can be hydrolysed to give poisonous hydrogen cyanide gas: also called CYANIDE. **potassium iodide** a white crystalline solid used as an additive to table salt to prevent iodine deficiency. **potassium permanganate** a purple crystalline solid that is used in solution as an oxidizing agent and disinfectant. □□ **potassic** adj. [POTASH + -IUM]

potation /pəˈteɪʃ(ə)n/ n. **1** a drink. **2** the act or an instance of drinking. **3** (usu. in pl.) the act or an instance of tippling. □□ **potatory** /pəʊˈteɪtərɪ/ adj. [ME f. OF potation or L potatio f. potare drink]

potato /pəˈteɪtəʊ/ n. (pl. -oes) **1** a starchy plant tuber that is cooked and used for food. **2** the plant, Solanum tuberosum, bearing this. **3** colloq. a hole in (esp. the heel of) a sock or stocking. □ **potato chip** = CHIP n. 3. **potato crisp** Brit. = CRISP n. 1. [Sp. patata var. of Taino batata]

pot-au-feu /ˌpɒtəʊˈfə/ n. **1** a large cooking pot of the kind common in France. **2** the soup or broth cooked in it. **3** the traditional French recipe associated with this. [F, = pot on the fire]

potch /pɒtʃ/ n. an opal of inferior quality. [19th c.: orig. unkn.]

poteen /pɒˈtiːn/ n. (also **potheen** /-ˈtʃiːn/) Ir. alcohol made illicitly, usu. from potatoes. [Ir. poitín dimin. of pota POT¹]

potent¹ /'pəʊt(ə)nt/ adj. **1** powerful; strong. **2** (of a reason) cogent; forceful. **3** (of a male) capable of sexual erection or orgasm. **4** literary mighty. **potence** n. **potency** n. **potently** adv. [L potens -entis pres. part. of posse be able]

potent² /'pəʊt(ə)nt/ adj. & n. Heraldry —adj. **1** having a crutch-head shape. **2** (of a fur) formed by a series of such shapes. —n. this fur. [ME f. OF potence crutch f. L potentia power (as POTENT¹)]

potentate /'pəʊtənˌteɪt/ n. a monarch or ruler. [ME f. OF potentat or L potentatus dominion (as POTENT²)]

potential /pəˈtenʃ(ə)l/ adj. & n. —adj. capable of coming into being or action; latent. —n. **1** the capacity for use or development; possibility (achieved its highest potential). **2** usable resources. **3** Physics the quantity determining the energy of mass in a gravitational field or of charge in an electric field. □ **potential barrier** a region of high potential impeding the movement of particles etc. **potential difference** the difference of electric potential between two points. **potential energy** a body's ability to do work by virtue of its position relative to others, stresses within itself, electric charge, etc. □□ **potentiality** /-ʃɪˈælɪtɪ/ n. **potentialize** v.tr. (also -**ise**). **potentially** adv. [ME f. OF potencial or LL potentialis f. potentia (as POTENT¹)]

potentiate /pəˈtenʃɪˌeɪt/ v.tr. **1** make more powerful, esp. increase the effectiveness of (a drug). **2** make possible. [as POTENT¹ after SUBSTANTIATE]

potentilla /ˌpəʊtənˈtɪlə/ n. any plant or shrub of the genus Potentilla; a cinquefoil. [med.L, dimin. of L potens POTENT¹]

potentiometer /pəˌtenʃɪˈɒmɪtə(r)/ n. an instrument for measuring or adjusting small electrical

potentials. □□ **potentiometric** /-ʃɪəˈmetrɪk/ *adj.*
potentiometry /-ʃɪˈɒmɪtrɪ/ *n.*
potheen var. of POTEEN.
pother /ˈpɒðə(r)/ *n. & v. literary* —*n.* a noise; commotion; fuss. —*v.* 1 *tr.* fluster, worry. 2 *intr.* make a fuss. [16th c.: orig. unkn.]
pothole /ˈpɒthəʊl/ *n. & v.* —*n.* 1 *Geol.* a deep hole or system of caves and underground river-beds formed by the erosion of rock esp. by the action of water. 2 a deep hole in the ground or a river-bed. 3 a hole in a road surface caused by wear or subsidence. —*v.intr. Brit.* explore potholes. □□ **potholer** *n.* **potholing** *n.*
potion /ˈpəʊʃ(ə)n/ *n.* a dose or quantity of medicine, a drug, poison, etc. [ME f. OF f. L *potio -onis* f. *potus* having drunk]
potlatch /ˈpɒtlætʃ/ *n.* (among N. American Indians) a ceremonial giving away or destruction of property to enhance status. [Chinook f. Nootka *patlatsh* gift]
potoroo /ˌpɒtəˈruː/ *n. Austral.* any small marsupial of the genus *Potorus*, native to Australia and Tasmania; a rat kangaroo. [Aboriginal]
pot-pourri /pəʊˈpʊərɪ, -riː/ *n.* 1 a mixture of dried petals and spices used to perfume a room etc. 2 a musical or literary medley. [F, = rotten pot]
potrero /pɒˈtreərəʊ/ *n.* (*pl.* **-os**) 1 (in the SW US and S. America) a paddock or pasture for horses or cattle. 2 (in the SW US) a narrow steep-sided plateau. [Sp. f. *potro* colt, pony]
potsherd /ˈpɒtʃɜːd/ *n.* a broken piece of ceramic material, esp. one found on an archaeological site.
pottage /ˈpɒtɪdʒ/ *n. archaic* soup, stew. [ME f. OF *potage* (as POT¹)]
potter¹ /ˈpɒtə(r)/ *v.* (*US* **putter** /ˈpʌtə(r)/) 1 *intr.* a (often foll. by *about, around*) work or occupy oneself in a desultory but pleasant manner (*likes pottering about in the garden*). b (often foll. by *at, in*) dabble in a subject or occupation. 2 *intr.* go slowly, dawdle, loiter (*pottered up to the pub*). 3 *tr.* (foll. by *away*) fritter away (one's time etc.). □□ **potterer** *n.* [frequent. of dial. *pote* push f. OE *potian*]
potter² /ˈpɒtə(r)/ *n.* a maker of ceramic vessels. □**potter's field** a burial place for paupers, strangers, etc. (after Matt. 27:7). **potter's wheel** a horizontal revolving disc to carry clay for making pots. [OE *pottere* (as POT¹)]
pottery /ˈpɒtərɪ/ *n.* (*pl.* **-ies**) 1 vessels etc. made of fired clay. 2 a potter's work. 3 a potter's workshop. □**the Potteries** a district in N. Staffordshire, where the English pottery industry is centred. [ME f. OF *poterie* f. *potier* POTTER²]
potting shed /ˈpɒtɪŋ/ *n.* a building in which plants are potted and tools etc. are stored.
pottle /ˈpɒt(ə)l/ *n.* 1 a small punnet or carton for strawberries etc. 2 *archaic* a a measure for liquids; a half gallon. b a pot etc. containing this. [ME f. OF *potel* (as POT¹)]
potto /ˈpɒtəʊ/ *n.* (*pl.* **-os**) 1 a W. African lemur-like mammal, *Perodicticus potto*. 2 a kinkajou. [perh. f. Guinea dial.]
Pott's fracture /pɒts/ *n.* a fracture of the lower end of the fibula, usu. with dislocation of the ankle. [P. *Pott*, Engl. surgeon d. 1788]
potty¹ /ˈpɒtɪ/ *adj.* (**pottier, pottiest**) *Brit. sl.* 1 foolish or crazy. 2 insignificant, trivial (esp. *potty little*). □□ **pottiness** *n.* [19th c.: orig. unkn.]
potty² /ˈpɒtɪ/ *n.* (*pl.* **-ies**) *colloq.* a chamber-pot, esp. for a child.
pouch /paʊtʃ/ *n. & v.* —*n.* 1 a small bag or detachable outside pocket. 2 a baggy area of skin underneath the eyes etc. 3 a a pocket-like receptacle in which marsupials carry their young during lactation. b any of several similar structures in various animals, e.g. in the cheeks of rodents. 4 a soldier's leather ammunition bag. 5 a lockable bag for mail or dispatches. 6 *Bot.* a baglike cavity, esp. the seed-vessel, in a plant. —*v.tr.* 1 put or make into a pouch. 2 take possession of; pocket. 3 make (part of a dress

etc.) hang like a pouch. □□ **pouched** *adj.* **pouchy** *adj.* [ME f. ONF *pouche*: cf. POKE²]
pouf var. of POOF.
pouffe /puːf/ *n.* (also **pouf**) a large firm cushion used as a low seat or footstool. [F *pouf*; ult. imit.]
poulard /puːˈlɑːd/ *n.* a domestic hen that has been spayed and fattened for eating. [F *poularde* f. *poule* hen]
poult¹ /pəʊlt/ *n.* a young domestic fowl, turkey, pheasant, etc. [ME, contr. f. PULLET]
poult² /puːlt/ *n.* (in full **poult-de-soie** /ˌpuːdəˈswɑː/) a fine corded silk or taffeta, usu. coloured. [F, of unkn. orig.]
poulterer /ˈpəʊltərə(r)/ *n.* a dealer in poultry and usu. game. [ME *poulter* f. OF *pouletier* (as PULLET)]
poultice /ˈpəʊltɪs/ *n. & v.* —*n.* a soft medicated and usu. heated mass applied to the body and kept in place with muslin etc., for relieving soreness and inflammation. —*v.tr.* apply a poultice to. [orig. *pultes* (pl.) f. L *puls pultis* pottage, pap, etc.]
poultry /ˈpəʊltrɪ/ *n.* domestic fowls (ducks, geese, turkeys, chickens, etc.), esp. as a source of food. [ME f. OF *pouletrie* (as POULTERER)]
pounce¹ /paʊns/ *v. & n.* —*v.intr.* 1 spring or swoop, esp. as in capturing prey. 2 (often foll. by *on, upon*) a make a sudden attack. b seize eagerly upon an object, remark, etc. (*pounced on what we said*). —*n.* 1 the act or an instance of pouncing. 2 the claw or talon of a bird of prey. □□ **pouncer** *n.* [perh. f. PUNCHEON¹]
pounce² /paʊns/ *n. & v.* —*n.* 1 a fine powder formerly used to prevent ink from spreading on unglazed paper. 2 powdered charcoal etc. dusted over a perforated pattern to transfer the design to the object beneath. —*v.tr.* 1 dust with pounce. 2 transfer (a design etc.) by use of pounce. 3 smooth (paper etc.) with pounce or pumice. □□ **pouncer** *n.* [F *ponce, poncer* f. L *pumex* PUMICE]
pouncet-box /ˈpaʊnsɪt/ *n. archaic* a small box with a perforated lid for perfumes etc. [16th c.: perh. orig. erron. f. *pounced* (= perforated) *box*]
pound¹ /paʊnd/ *n.* 1 a unit of weight equal to 16 oz. avoirdupois (0.4536 kg), or 12 oz. troy (0.3732 kg). 2 (in full **pound sterling**) (*pl.* same or **pounds**) the chief monetary unit of the UK and several other countries. □**pound cake** a rich cake containing a pound (or equal weights) of each chief ingredient. **pound coin** (or **note**) a coin or note worth one pound sterling. **pound of flesh** any legitimate but crippling demand. **pound Scots** *hist.* 1s. 8d. **pound sign** the sign £, representing a pound. [OE *pund* ult. f. L *pondo* Roman pound weight of 12 ounces]
pound² /paʊnd/ *v.* 1 *tr.* a crush or beat with repeated heavy blows. b thump or pummel, esp. with the fists. c grind to a powder or pulp. 2 *intr.* (foll. by *at, on*) deliver heavy blows or gunfire. 3 *intr.* (foll. by *along* etc.) make one's way heavily or clumsily. 4 *intr.* (of the heart) beat heavily. □**pound out** produce with or as if with heavy blows. □□ **pounder** *n.* [OE *pūnian*, rel. to Du. *puin*, LG *pün* rubbish]
pound³ /paʊnd/ *n. & v.* —*n.* 1 an enclosure where stray animals or officially removed vehicles are kept until redeemed. 2 a place of confinement. —*v.tr.* enclose (cattle etc.) in a pound. □**pound lock** a lock with two gates to confine water and often a side reservoir to maintain the water level. [ME f. OE *pund-* in *pundfald*: see PINFOLD]
poundage /ˈpaʊndɪdʒ/ *n.* 1 a commission or fee of so much per pound sterling or weight. 2 a percentage of the total earnings of a business, paid as wages. 3 a person's weight, esp. that which is regarded as excess.
poundal /ˈpaʊnd(ə)l/ *n. Physics* a unit of force equal to the force required to give a mass of one pound an acceleration of one foot per second per second. [POUND¹ + *-al* perh. after *quintal*]
pounder /ˈpaʊndə(r)/ *n.* (usu. in *comb.*) 1 a thing or person weighing a specified number of pounds (*a*

five-pounder). **2** a gun carrying a shell of a specified number of pounds. **3** a thing worth, or a person possessing, so many pounds sterling.

pour /pɔː(r)/ *v.* **1** *intr.* & *tr.* (usu. foll. by *down*, *out*, *over*, etc.) flow or cause to flow esp. downwards in a stream or shower. **2** *tr.* dispense (a drink, e.g. tea) by pouring. **3** *intr.* (of rain, or with *it*) fall heavily. **4** *intr.* (usu. foll. by *in*, *out*, etc.) come or go in profusion or rapid succession (*the crowd poured out*; *letters poured in*; *poems poured from her fertile mind*). **5** *tr.* discharge or send freely (*poured forth arrows*). **6** *tr.* (often foll. by *out*) utter at length or in a rush (*poured out their story*; *poured scorn on my attempts*). □ it never rains but it pours follows rarely come singly. **pour cold water on** see COLD. **pour oil on the waters** (or **on troubled waters**) calm a disagreement or disturbance, esp. with conciliatory words. □□ **pourable** *adj.* **pourer** *n.* [ME: orig. unkn.]

pourboire /pʊəˈbwɑː(r)/ *n.* a gratuity or tip. [F, = *pour boire* (money) for drinking]

poussin /ˈpuːsæ̃/ *n.* a young chicken bred for eating. [F]

pout[1] /paʊt/ *v.* & *n.* —*v.* **1** *intr.* **a** push the lips forward as an expression of displeasure or sulking. **b** (of the lips) be pushed forward. **2** *tr.* push (the lips) forward in pouting. —*n.* **1** such an action or expression. **2** (**the pouts**) a fit of sulking. □□ **pouter** *n.* **poutingly** *adv.* **pouty** *adj.* [ME, perh. f. OE *putian* (unrecorded) be inflated: cf. POUT[2]]

pout[2] /paʊt/ *n.* **1** = BIB[1] 3. **2** = EELPOUT. [OE *-puta* in *ælepūta* eelpout, f. WG]

pouter /ˈpaʊtə(r)/ *n.* **1** a person who pouts. **2** a kind of pigeon able to inflate its crop considerably.

poverty /ˈpɒvətɪ/ *n.* **1** the state of being poor; want of the necessities of life. **2** (often foll. by *of*, *in*) scarcity or lack. **3** inferiority, poorness, meanness. **4** *Eccl.* renunciation of the right to individual ownership of property. □ **poverty line** the minimum income level needed to secure the necessities of life. **poverty-stricken** extremely poor. **poverty trap** a situation in which an increase of income incurs a loss of State benefits, making real improvement impossible. [ME f. OF *poverte*, *poverté* f. L *paupertas -tatis* f. *pauper* poor]

POW *abbr.* prisoner of war.

pow /paʊ/ *int.* expressing the sound of a blow or explosion. [imit.]

powder /ˈpaʊdə(r)/ *n.* & *v.* —*n.* **1** a substance in the form of fine dry particles. **2** a medicine or cosmetic in this form. **3** = GUNPOWDER. —*v.tr.* **1 a** apply powder to (*powder one's nose*). **b** sprinkle or decorate with or as with powder. **2** (esp. as **powdered** *adj.*) reduce to a fine powder (*powdered milk*). □ **keep one's powder dry** be cautious and alert. **powder blue** pale blue. **powder-flask** *hist.* a small case for carrying gunpowder. **powder-keg** **1** a barrel of gunpowder. **2** a dangerous or volatile situation. **powder metallurgy** the production of metal as fine powders to make objects. **powder-monkey** *hist.* a boy employed on board ship to carry powder to the guns. **powder-puff** a soft pad for applying powder to the skin, esp. the face. **powder-room** a women's cloakroom or lavatory in a public building. **powder snow** loose dry snow on a ski-run etc. **take a powder** *sl.* depart quickly. □□ **powdery** *adj.* [ME f. OF *poudre* f. L *pulvis pulveris* dust]

power /ˈpaʊə(r)/ *n.* & *v.* —*n.* **1** the ability to do or act (*will do all in my power*; *has the power to change colour*). **2** a particular faculty of body or mind (*lost the power of speech*; *powers of persuasion*). **3 a** government, influence, or authority. **b** political or social ascendancy or control (*the party in power*; *Black Power*). **4** authorization; delegated authority (*power of attorney*; *police powers*). **5** (often foll. by *over*) personal ascendancy. **6** an influential person, group, or organization (*the press is a power in the land*). **7 a** military strength. **b** a state having

international influence, esp. based on military strength (*the leading powers*). **8** vigour, energy. **9** an active property or function (*has a high heating power*). **10** *colloq.* a large number or amount (*has done me a power of good*). **11** the capacity for exerting mechanical force or doing work (*horsepower*). **12** mechanical or electrical energy as distinct from hand-labour (often *attrib.*: *power tools*; *power steering*). **13 a** a public supply of (esp. electrical) energy. **b** a particular source or form of energy (*hydroelectric power*). **14** a mechanical force applied e.g. by means of a lever. **15** *Physics* the rate of energy output. **16** the product obtained when a number is multiplied by itself a certain number of times (*2 to the power of 3 = 8*). **17** the magnifying capacity of a lens. **18 a** a deity. **b** (in *pl.*) the sixth order of the ninefold celestial hierarchy. —*v.tr.* **1** supply with mechanical or electrical energy. **2** (foll. by *up*, *down*) increase or decrease the power supplied to (a device); switch on or off. □ **in the power of** under the control of. **more power to your elbow!** an expression of encouragement or approval. **power behind the throne** a person who asserts authority or influence without having formal status. **power block** a group of nations constituting an international political force. **power cut** a temporary withdrawal or failure of an electric power supply. **power-dive** *n.* a steep dive of an aircraft with the engines providing thrust. —*v.intr.* perform a power-dive. **power line** a conductor supplying electrical power, esp. one supported by pylons or poles. **power of attorney** see ATTORNEY. **power pack** **1** a unit for supplying power. **2** the equipment for converting an alternating current (from the mains) to a direct current at a different (usu. lower) voltage. **power play** **1** tactics involving the concentration of players at a particular point. **2** similar tactics in business, politics, etc., involving a concentration of resources, effort, etc. **power point** *Brit.* a socket in a wall etc. for connecting an electrical device to the mains. **power politics** political action based on power or influence. **power-sharing** a policy agreed between parties or within a coalition to share responsibility for decision-making and political action. **power station** a building where electrical power is generated for distribution. **the powers that be** those in authority (Rom. 13:1). **power stroke** the stroke of an internal-combustion engine, in which the piston is moved downward by the expansion of gases. □□ **powered** *adj.* (also in comb.). [ME & AF *poer* etc., OF *poeir* ult. f. L *posse* be able]

powerboat /ˈpaʊəˌbəʊt/ *n.* a powerful motor boat.

powerful /ˈpaʊəfʊl/ *adj.* **1** having much power or strength. **2** politically or socially influential. □□ **powerfully** *adv.* **powerfulness** *n.*

powerhouse /ˈpaʊəhaʊs/ *n.* **1** = *power station*. **2** a person or thing of great energy.

powerless /ˈpaʊəlɪs/ *adj.* **1** without power or strength. **2** (often foll. by *to* + infin.) wholly unable (*powerless to help*). □□ **powerlessly** *adv.* **powerlessness** *n.*

powerplant /ˈpaʊəˌplɑːnt/ *n.* an apparatus or an installation which provides power for industry, a machine, etc.

powwow /ˈpaʊwaʊ/ *n.* & *v.* —*n.* a conference or meeting for discussion (orig. among N. American Indians). —*v.tr.* hold a powwow. [Algonquian *powah*, *powwaw* magician (lit. 'he dreams')]

pox /pɒks/ *n.* **1** any virus disease producing a rash of pimples that become pus-filled and leave pock-marks on healing. **2** *colloq.* = SYPHILIS. **3** a plant disease that causes pocklike spots. □ **a pox on** *archaic* an exclamation of anger or impatience with (a person). [alt. spelling of *pocks* pl. of POCK]

poxy /ˈpɒksɪ/ *adj.* (**poxier**, **poxiest**) **1** infected by pox. **2** *sl.* of poor quality; worthless.

pozzolana /ˌpɒtsəˈlɑːnə/ n. (also **puzzolana**) a volcanic ash used for mortar or hydraulic cement. [It., f. *pozz(u)olano* (adj.) of *Pozzuoli* near Naples]

pp *abbr.* pianissimo.

pp. *abbr.* pages.

p.p. *abbr.* (also **pp**) *per pro.*

PPE *abbr. Brit.* philosophy, politics, and economics (as a degree course at Oxford University).

p.p.m. *abbr.* parts per million.

PPS *abbr. Brit.* **1** Parliamentary Private Secretary. **2** additional postscript.

PR *abbr.* **1** public relations. **2** proportional representation. **3** *US* Puerto Rico.

Pr *symb. Chem.* the element praseodymium.

pr. *abbr.* pair.

PRA *abbr.* (in the UK) President of the Royal Academy.

praam var. of PRAM².

practicable /ˈpræktɪkəb(ə)l/ *adj.* **1** that can be done or used. **2** possible in practice. □□ **practicability** /-ˈbɪlɪtɪ/ n. **practicableness** n. **practicably** *adv.* [F *praticable* f. *pratiquer* put into practice (as PRACTICAL)]

practical /ˈpræktɪk(ə)l/ *adj. & n. —adj.* **1** of or concerned with practice or use rather than theory. **2** suited to use or action; designed mainly to fulfil a function (*practical shoes*). **3** (of a person) inclined to action rather than speculation; able to make things function well. **4 a** that is such in effect though not nominally (*for all practical purposes*). **b** virtual (*in practical control*). **5** feasible; concerned with what is actually possible (*practical politics*). *—n.* a practical examination or lesson. □ **practical joke** a humorous trick played on a person. **practical joker** a person who plays practical jokes. □□ **practicality** /-ˈkælɪtɪ/ n. (*pl.* **-ies**). **practicalness** n. [earlier *practic* f. obs. F *practique* or LL *practicus* f. Gk *praktikos* f. *prassō* do, act]

practically /ˈpræktɪkəlɪ/ *adv.* **1** virtually, almost (*practically nothing*). **2** in a practical way.

practice /ˈpræktɪs/ n. & v. —n. **1** habitual action or performance (*the practice of teaching*; *makes a practice of saving*). **2** a habit or custom (*has been my regular practice*). **3 a** repeated exercise in an activity requiring the development of skill (*to sing well needs much practice*). **b** a session of this (*time for target practice*). **4** action or execution as opposed to theory. **5** the professional work or business of a doctor, lawyer, etc. (*has a practice in town*). **6** an established method of legal procedure. **7** procedure generally, esp. of a specified kind (*bad practice*). *—v.tr. & intr. US* var. of PRACTISE. □ **in practice 1** when actually applied; in reality. **2** skilful because of recent exercise in a particular pursuit. **out of practice** lacking a former skill from lack of recent practice. **put into practice** actually apply (an idea, method, etc.). [ME f. PRACTISE, after *advice*, *device*]

practician /prækˈtɪʃ(ə)n/ n. a worker; a practitioner. [obs. F *practicien* f. *practique* f. med.L *practica* f. Gk *praktikē* fem. of *praktikos*: see PRACTICAL]

practise /ˈpræktɪs/ v. (*US* **practice**) **1** tr. perform habitually; carry out in action (*practise the same method*; *practise what you preach*). **2** tr. & (foll. by *in*, *on*) intr. do repeatedly as an exercise to improve a skill; exercise oneself in or on (an activity requiring skill) (*had to practise in the art of speaking*; *practise your reading*). **3** tr. (as **practised** adj.) experienced, expert (*a practised liar*; *with a practised hand*). **4** tr. **a** pursue or be engaged in (a profession, religion, etc.). **b** (as **practising** adj.) currently active or engaged in (a profession or activity) (*a practising Christian*; *a practising lawyer*). **5** intr. (foll. by *on*, *upon*) take advantage of; impose upon. **6** intr. archaic scheme, contrive (*when first we practise to deceive*). □□ **practiser** n. [ME f. OF *pra(c)tiser* or med.L *practizare* alt. f. *practicare* (as PRACTICAL)]

practitioner /prækˈtɪʃənə(r)/ n. a person practising a profession, esp. medicine (*general practitioner*). [obs. *practitian* = PRACTICIAN]

prae- /priː/ *prefix* = PRE- (esp. in words regarded as Latin or relating to Roman antiquity). [L: see PRE-]

praecipe /ˈpriːsɪpɪ/ n. **1** a writ demanding action or an explanation of non-action. **2** an order requesting a writ. [L (the first word of the writ), imper. of *praecipere* enjoin: see PRECEPT]

praecocial /prɪˈkəʊʃ(ə)l/ *adj. & n.* (*US* **precocial**) *—adj.* (of a bird) having young that can feed themselves as soon as they are hatched. *—n.* a praecocial bird (cf. ALTRICIAL). [L *praecox -cocis* (as PRECOCIOUS)]

praemunire /ˌpriːmjuːˈnɪərɪ/ n. *hist.* a writ charging a sheriff to summon a person accused of asserting or maintaining papal jurisdiction in England. [med.L, = forewarn, for L *praemonēre* (as PRAE-, *monēre* warn): the words *praemunire facias* that you warn (a person to appear) occur in the writ]

praenomen /priːˈnəʊmen/ n. an ancient Roman's first or personal name (e.g. *Marcus* Tullius Cicero). [L f. *prae* before + *nomen* name]

praepostor /prɪˈpɒstə(r)/ n. (also **prepostor**) *Brit.* (at some public schools) a prefect or monitor. [*praepositor* alt. f. L *praepositus* past part. of *praeponere* set over (as PRAE-, *ponere posit-* place)]

praesidium var. of PRESIDIUM.

praetor /ˈpriːtə(r)/, -tɔː(r)/ n. (*US* **pretor**) *Rom. Hist.* each of two ancient Roman magistrates ranking below consul. □□ **praetorial** /-ˈtɔːrɪəl/ *adj.* **praetorship** n. [ME f. F *préteur* or L *praetor* (perh. as PRAE-, *ire it-* go)]

praetorian /priːˈtɔːrɪən/ *adj. & n.* (*US* **pretorian**) *Rom.Hist. —adj.* of or having the powers of a praetor. *—n.* a man of praetorian rank. □ **praetorian guard** the bodyguard of the Roman emperor. [ME f. L *praetorianus* (as PRAETOR)]

pragmatic /prægˈmætɪk/ *adj.* **1** dealing with matters with regard to their practical requirements or consequences. **2** treating the facts of history with reference to their practical lessons. **3** *hist.* of or relating to the affairs of a State. **4** (also **pragmatical**) **a** concerning pragmatism. **b** meddlesome. **c** dogmatic. □ **pragmatic sanction** *hist.* an imperial or royal ordinance issued as a fundamental law, esp. regarding a question of royal succession. □□ **pragmaticality** /-ˈkælɪtɪ/ n. **pragmatically** *adv.* [LL *pragmaticus* f. Gk *pragmatikos* f. *pragma -matos* deed]

pragmatics /prægˈmætɪks/ n.pl. (usu. treated as *sing.*) the branch of linguistics dealing with language in use.

pragmatism /ˈprægmətɪz(ə)m/ n. **1** a pragmatic attitude or procedure. **2** a philosophy that evaluates assertions solely by their practical consequences and bearing on human interests. □□ **pragmatist** n. **pragmatistic** /-ˈtɪstɪk/ *adj.* [Gk *pragma*: see PRAGMATIC]

pragmatize /ˈprægmətaɪz/ *v.tr.* (also **-ise**) **1** represent as real. **2** rationalize (a myth).

prahu var. of PROA.

prairie /ˈpreərɪ/ n. a large area of usu. treeless grassland esp. in N. America. □ **prairie chicken** (or **hen**) a N. American grouse, *Tympanuchus cupido*. **prairie dog** any N. American rodent of the genus *Cynomys*, living in burrows and making a barking sound. **prairie oyster** a seasoned raw egg, swallowed without breaking the yolk. **prairie schooner** *US* a covered wagon used by the 19th-c. pioneers in crossing the N. American prairies. **prairie wolf** = COYOTE. [F f. OF *praerie* ult. f. L *pratum* meadow]

praise /preɪz/ v. & n. —v.tr. **1** express warm approval or admiration of. **2** glorify (God) in words. —n. the act or an instance of praising; commendation (*won high praise*; *were loud in their praises*). □ **praise be!** an exclamation of pious gratitude. **sing the praises of** commend (a person) highly. □□ **praiseful** *adj.* [PRAGMATIC]

praiser n. [ME f. OF *preisier* price, prize, praise, f. LL *pretiare* f. L *pretium* price: cf. PRIZE¹]

praiseworthy /ˈpreɪzˌwɜːðɪ/ *adj.* worthy of praise; commendable. □□**praiseworthily** *adv.* **praiseworthiness** *n.*

Prakrit /ˈprɑːkrɪt/ *n.* any of the (esp. ancient or medieval) vernacular dialects of North and Central India existing alongside or derived from Sanskrit. [Skr. *prākṛta* unrefined: cf. SANSKRIT]

praline /ˈprɑːliːn/ *n.* a sweet made by browning nuts in boiling sugar. [F f. Marshal de Plessis-*Praslin*, Fr. soldier d. 1675, whose cook invented it]

pralltriller /ˈprɑːlˌtrɪlə(r)/ *n.* a musical ornament consisting of one rapid alternation of the written note with the note immediately above it. [G f. *prallen* rebound + *Triller* TRILL]

pram[1] /præm/ *n. Brit.* a four-wheeled carriage for a baby, pushed by a person on foot. [abbr. of PERAMBULATOR]

pram[2] /prɑːm/ *n.* (also **praam**) **1** a flat-bottomed gunboat or Baltic cargo-boat. **2** a Scandinavian ship's dinghy. [MDu. *prame*, *praem*, MLG *prām(e)*, f. OSlav. *pramŭ*]

prana /ˈprɑːnə/ *n.* **1** (in Hinduism) breath as a life-giving force. **2** the breath; breathing. [Skr.]

prance /prɑːns/ *v. & n.* —*v.intr.* **1** (of a horse) raise the forelegs and spring from the hind legs. **2** (often foll. by *about*) walk or behave in an elated or arrogant manner. —*n.* **1** the act of prancing. **2** a prancing movement. □□**prancer** *n.* [ME: orig. unkn.]

prandial /ˈprændɪəl/ *adj. formal* or *joc.* of dinner or lunch. [L *prandium* meal]

prang /præŋ/ *v. & n. Brit. sl.* —*v.tr.* **1** crash or damage (an aircraft or vehicle). **2** bomb (a target) successfully. —*n.* the act or an instance of pranging. [imit.]

prank /præŋk/ *n.* a practical joke; a piece of mischief. □□**prankful** *adj.* **prankish** *adj.* **pranksome** *adj.* [16th c.: orig. unkn.]

prankster /ˈpræŋkstə(r)/ *n.* a person fond of playing pranks.

prase /preɪz/ *n.* a translucent leek-green type of quartz. [F f. L *prasius* f. Gk *prasios* (adj.) leek-green f. *prason* leek]

praseodymium /ˌpreɪzɪəˈdɪmɪəm/ *n. Chem.* a soft silvery metallic element of the lanthanide series, occurring naturally in various minerals and used in catalyst mixtures. ¶ Symb.: **Pr**. [G *Praseodym* f. Gk *prasios* (see PRASE) from its green salts, + G *Didym* DIDYMIUM]

prat /præt/ *n. sl.* **1** *Brit.* a silly or foolish person. **2** the buttocks. [16th-c. cant (in sense 2): orig. unkn.]

prate /preɪt/ *v. & n.* —*v.* **1** *intr.* chatter; talk too much. **2** *intr.* talk foolishly or irrelevantly. **3** *tr.* tell or say in a prating manner. —*n.* prating; idle talk. □□**prater** *n.* **prating** *adj.* [ME f. MDu., MLG *praten*, prob. imit.]

pratfall /ˈprætfɔːl/ *n. US sl.* **1** a fall on the buttocks. **2** a humiliating failure.

pratie /ˈpreɪtɪ/ *n. esp. Ir.* a potato. [corrupt.]

pratincole /ˈprætɪŋˌkəʊl/ *n.* any of various birds of the subfamily Glareolinae, inhabiting sandy and stony areas and feeding on insects. [mod.L *pratincola* f. L *pratum* meadow + *incola* inhabitant]

pratique /ˈpræˈtiːk/ *n.* a licence to have dealings with a port, granted to a ship after quarantine or on showing a clean bill of health. [F, = practice, intercourse, f. It. *pratica* f. med.L *practica*: see PRACTICIAN]

prattle /ˈpræt(ə)l/ *v. & n.* —*v.intr. & tr.* chatter or say in a childish way. —*n.* **1** childish chatter. **2** inconsequential talk. □□**prattler** *n.* **prattling** *adj.* [MLG *pratelen* (as PRATE)]

prau var. of PROA.

prawn /prɔːn/ *n. & v.* —*n.* any of various marine crustaceans, resembling a shrimp but usu. larger. —*v.intr.* fish for prawns. □**come the raw prawn** see RAW. [ME *pra(y)ne*, of unkn. orig.]

praxis /ˈpræksɪs/ *n.* **1** accepted practice or custom. **2** the practising of an art or skill. [med.L f. Gk, = doing, f. *prassō* do]

pray /preɪ/ *v.* (often foll. by *for* or *to* + infin. or *that* + clause) **1** *intr.* (often foll. by *to*) say prayers (to God etc.); make devout supplication. **2 a** *tr.* entreat, beseech. **b** *tr. & intr.* ask earnestly (*prayed to be released*). **3** *tr.* (as *imper.*) archaic & *formal* please (*pray tell me*). □**praying mantis** see MANTIS. [ME f. OF *preier* f. LL *precare* f. L *precari* entreat]

prayer[1] /preə(r)/ *n.* **1 a** a solemn request or thanksgiving to God or an object of worship (*say a prayer*). **b** a formula or form of words used in praying (*the Lord's prayer*). **c** the act of praying (*be at prayer*). **d** a religious service consisting largely of prayers (*morning prayers*). **2 a** an entreaty to a person. **b** a thing entreated or prayed for. □**not have a prayer** *US colloq.* have no chance (of success etc.). **prayer-book** a book containing the forms of prayer in regular use, esp. the Book of Common Prayer. **prayer-mat** a small carpet used by Muslims when praying. **prayer-wheel** a revolving cylindrical box inscribed with or containing prayers, used esp. by Tibetan Buddhists. □□**prayerless** *adj.* [ME f. OF *preiere* ult. f. L *precarius* obtained by entreaty f. *prex precis* prayer]

prayer[2] /ˈpreɪə(r)/ *n.* a person who prays.

prayerful /ˈpreəˌfʊl/ *adj.* **1** (of a person) given to praying; devout. **2** (of speech, actions, etc.) characterized by or expressive of prayer. □□**prayerfully** *adv.* **prayerfulness** *n.*

pre- /priː/ *prefix* before (in time, place, order, degree, or importance). [from or after L *prae-* f. *prae* (adv. & prep.)]

preach /priːtʃ/ *v.* **1 a** *intr.* deliver a sermon or religious address. **b** *tr.* deliver (a sermon); proclaim or expound (the Gospel etc.). **2** *intr.* give moral advice in an obtrusive way. **3** *tr.* advocate or inculcate (a quality or practice etc.). □□**preachable** *adj.* [ME f. OF *prechier* f. L *praedicare* proclaim, in eccl.L *preach* (as PRAE-, *dicare* declare)]

preacher /ˈpriːtʃə(r)/ *n.* a person who preaches, esp. a minister of religion. [ME f. AF *prech(o)ur*, OF *prech(e)or* f. eccl.L *praedicator* (as PREACH)]

preachify /ˈpriːtʃɪˌfaɪ/ *v.intr.* (**-ies**, **-ied**) *colloq.* preach or moralize tediously.

preachment /ˈpriːtʃmənt/ *n.* usu. *derog.* preaching, sermonizing.

preachy /ˈpriːtʃɪ/ *adj.* (**preachier**, **preachiest**) *colloq.* inclined to preach or moralize. □□**preachiness** *n.*

preadolescent /ˌpriːædəˈles(ə)nt/ *adj. & n.* —*adj.* **1** (of a child) having nearly reached adolescence. **2** of or relating to the two or three years preceding adolescence. —*n.* a preadolescent child. □□**preadolescence** *n.*

preamble /priːˈæmb(ə)l, ˈpriː-/ *n.* **1** a preliminary statement or introduction. **2** the introductory part of a statute or deed etc. □□**preambular** /-ˈæmbjʊlə(r)/ *adj.* [ME f. OF *preambule* f. med.L *praeambulum* f. LL *praeambulus* (adj.) going before (as PRE-, AMBLE)]

pre-amp /ˈpriːæmp/ *n.* = PREAMPLIFIER. [abbr.]

preamplifier /priːˈæmplɪˌfaɪə(r)/ *n.* an electronic device that amplifies a very weak signal (e.g. from a microphone or pickup) and transmits it to a main amplifier. □□**preamplified** *adj.*

prearrange /ˌpriːəˈreɪndʒ/ *v.tr.* arrange beforehand. □□**prearrangement** *n.*

preatomic /ˌpriːəˈtɒmɪk/ *adj.* existing or occurring before the use of atomic energy.

Preb. *abbr.* Prebendary.

prebend /ˈprebənd/ *n.* **1** the stipend of a canon or member of chapter. **2** a portion of land or tithe from which this is drawn. □□**prebendal** *adj.* [ME f. OF *prebende* f. LL *praebenda* pension, neut.pl. gerundive of L *praebēre* grant f. *prae* forth + *habēre* hold]

prebendary /ˈprebəndərɪ/ *n.* (*pl.* **-ies**) **1** the holder of a prebend. **2** an honorary canon. □□

prebendaryship n. [ME f. med.L praebendarius (as PREBEND)]

Precambrian /priːˈkæmbriən/ adj. & n. Geol. —adj. of or relating to the earliest era of geological time from the formation of the earth to the first forms of life. ¶ Cf. Appendix II. —n. this era.

precarious /prɪˈkeəriəs/ adj. 1 uncertain; dependent on chance (makes a precarious living). 2 insecure, perilous (precarious health). □□ **precariously** adv. **precariousness** n. [L precarius: see PRAYER¹]

precast /priːˈkɑːst/ adj. (of concrete) cast in its final shape before positioning.

precative /ˈprekətɪv/ adj. (of a word or form) expressing a wish or request. [LL precativus f. precari pray]

precaution /prɪˈkɔːʃ(ə)n/ n. 1 an action taken beforehand to avoid risk or ensure a good result. 2 (in pl.) colloq. the use of contraceptives. □□ **precautionary** adj. [F précaution f. LL praecautio -onis f. L praecavēre (as PRAE-, cavēre caut- beware of)]

precede /prɪˈsiːd/ v.tr. **1 a** come or go before in time, order, importance, etc. (preceding generations; the preceding paragraph; sons of barons precede baronets). **b** walk etc. in front of (preceded by our guide). **2** (foll. by by) cause to be preceded (must precede this measure by milder ones). [OF preceder f. L praecedere (as PRAE-, cedere cess- go)]

precedence /ˈpresɪd(ə)ns/ n. (also **precedency**) **1** priority in time, order, or importance, etc. **2** the right of preceding others on formal occasions. □ **take precedence** (often foll. by over, of) have priority (over).

precedent n. & adj. —n. /ˈpresɪd(ə)nt/ a previous case or legal decision etc. taken as a guide for subsequent cases or as a justification. —adj. /prɪˈsiːd(ə)nt, ˈpresɪ-/ preceding in time, order, importance, etc. □□ **precedently** /ˈpriːsɪdəntlɪ, ˈpresɪ-/ adv. [ME f. OF (n. & adj.) (as PRECEDE)]

precedented /ˈpresɪˌdentɪd/ adj. having or supported by a precedent.

precent /prɪˈsent/ v. **1** intr. act as a precentor. **2** tr. lead the singing of (a psalm etc.). [back-form. f. PRECENTOR]

precentor /prɪˈsentə(r)/ n. **1** a person who leads the singing or (in a synagogue) the prayers of a congregation. **2** a minor canon who administers the musical life of a cathedral. □□ **precentorship** n. [F précenteur or L praecentor f. praecinere (as PRAE-, canere sing)]

precept /ˈpriːsept/ n. **1** a command; a rule of conduct. **2** moral instruction (example is better than precept). **3 a** a writ or warrant. **b** Brit. an order for collection or payment of money under a local rate. □□ **preceptive** /prɪˈseptɪv/ adj. [ME f. L praeceptum neut. past part. of praecipere praecept- warn, instruct (as PRAE-, capere take)]

preceptor /prɪˈseptə(r)/ n. a teacher or instructor. □□ **preceptorial** /ˌpriːsepˈtɔːriəl/ adj. **preceptorship** n. **preceptress** /-trɪs/ n. [L praeceptor (as PRECEPT)]

precession /prɪˈseʃ(ə)n/ n. the slow movement of the axis of a spinning body around another axis. □ **precession of the equinoxes 1** the slow retrograde motion of equinoctial points along the ecliptic. **2** the resulting earlier occurrence of equinoxes in each successive sidereal year. □□ **precessional** adj. [LL praecessio (as PRECEDE)]

pre-Christian /priːˈkrɪstiən/ adj. before Christ or the advent of Christianity.

precinct /ˈpriːsɪŋkt/ n. **1** an enclosed or clearly defined area, e.g. around a cathedral, college, etc. **2** a specially designated area in a town, esp. with the exclusion of traffic (shopping precinct). **3** (in pl.) **a** the surrounding area or environs. **b** the boundaries. **4** US **a** a subdivision of a county, city, etc., for police or electoral purposes. **b** (in pl.) a neighbourhood. [ME f. med.L praecinctum neut. past part. of praecingere encircle (as PRAE-, cingere gird)]

preciosity /ˌpreʃɪˈɒsɪtɪ/ n. overrefinement in art or language, esp. in the choice of words. [OF préciosité f. L pretiositas f. pretiosus (as PRECIOUS)]

precious /ˈpreʃəs/ adj. & adv. —adj. **1** of great value or worth. **2** beloved; much prized (precious memories). **3** affectedly refined, esp. in language or manner. **4** colloq. often iron. **a** considerable (a precious lot you know about it). **b** expressing contempt or disdain (you can keep your precious flowers). —adv. colloq. extremely, very (tried precious hard; had precious little left). □ **precious metals** gold, silver, and platinum. **precious stone** a piece of mineral having great value esp. as used in jewellery. □□ **preciously** adv. **preciousness** n. [ME f. OF precios f. L pretiosus f. pretium price]

precipice /ˈpresɪpɪs/ n. **1** a vertical or steep face of a rock, cliff, mountain, etc. **2** a dangerous situation. [F précipice or L praecipitium falling headlong, precipice (as PRECIPITOUS)]

precipitant /prɪˈsɪpɪt(ə)nt/ adj. & n. —adj. = PRECIPITATE adj. —n. Chem. a substance that causes another substance to precipitate. □□ **precipitance** n. **precipitancy** n. [obs. F précipitant pres. part. of précipiter (as PRECIPITATE)]

precipitate v., adj., & n. —v.tr. /prɪˈsɪpɪˌteɪt/ **1** hasten the occurrence of; cause to occur prematurely. **2** (foll. by into) send rapidly into a certain state or condition (were precipitated into war). **3** throw down headlong. **4** Chem. cause (a substance) to be deposited in solid form from a solution. **5** Physics **a** cause (dust etc.) to be deposited from the air on a surface. **b** condense (vapour) into drops and so deposit it. —adj. /prɪˈsɪpɪtət/ **1** headlong; violently hurried (precipitate departure). **2** (of a person or act) hasty, rash, inconsiderate. —n. /prɪˈsɪpɪtət/ **1** Chem. a substance precipitated from a solution. **2** Physics moisture condensed from vapour by cooling and depositing, e.g. rain or dew. □□ **precipitable** /prɪˈsɪpɪtəb(ə)l/ adj. **precipitability** /prɪˌsɪpɪtəˈbɪlɪtɪ/ n. **precipitately** /prɪˈsɪpɪtətlɪ/ adv. **precipitateness** /prɪˈsɪpɪtətnɪs/ n. **precipitator** /prɪˈsɪpɪˌteɪtə(r)/ n. [L praecipitare praecipitat- f. praeceps praecipitis headlong (as PRAE-, caput head)]

precipitation /prɪˌsɪpɪˈteɪʃ(ə)n/ n. **1** the act of precipitating or the process of being precipitated. **2** rash haste. **3 a** rain or snow etc. falling to the ground. **b** a quantity of this. [F précipitation or L praecipitatio (as PRECIPITATE)]

precipitous /prɪˈsɪpɪtəs/ adj. **1 a** of or like a precipice. **b** dangerously steep. **2** = PRECIPITATE adj. □□ **precipitously** adv. **precipitousness** n. [obs. F précipiteux f. L praeceps (as PRECIPITATE)]

précis /ˈpreɪsiː/ n. & v. —n. (pl. same /-siːz/) a summary or abstract, esp. of a text or speech. —v.tr. (**précises** /-siːz/; **précised** /-siːd/; **précising** /-siːɪŋ/) make a précis of. [F, = PRECISE (as n.)]

precise /prɪˈsaɪs/ adj. **1 a** accurately expressed. **b** definite, exact. **2** punctilious; scrupulous in being exact, observing rules, etc. **3** identical, exact (at that precise moment). □□ **preciseness** n. [F précis -ise f. L praecidere praecis- cut short (as PRAE-, caedere cut)]

precisely /prɪˈsaɪslɪ/ adv. **1** in a precise manner; exactly. **2** (as a reply) quite so; as you say.

precisian /prɪˈsɪʒ(ə)n/ n. a person who is rigidly precise or punctilious, esp. in religious observance. □□ **precisianism** n.

precision /prɪˈsɪʒ(ə)n/ n. **1** the condition of being precise; accuracy. **2** the degree of refinement in measurement etc. **3** (attrib.) marked by or adapted for precision (precision instruments; precision timing). □□ **precisionism** n. **precisionist** n. [F précision or L praecisio (as PRECISE)]

preclassical /priːˈklæsɪk(ə)l/ adj. before a period regarded as classical, esp. in music and literature.

preclinical /priːˈklɪnɪk(ə)l/ adj. **1** of or relating to the first, chiefly theoretical, stage of a medical education. **2** (of a stage in a disease) before symptoms can be identified.

preclude /prɪˈkluːd/ v.tr. 1 (foll. by from) prevent, exclude (precluded from taking part). 2 make impossible; remove (so as to preclude all doubt). □□ **preclusion** /-ˈkluːʒ(ə)n/ n. **preclusive** /-ˈkluːsɪv/ adj. [L praecludere praeclus- (as PRAE-, claudere shut)]

precocial US var. of PRAECOCIAL.

precocious /prɪˈkəʊʃəs/ adj. 1 often derog. (of a person, esp. a child) prematurely developed in some faculty or characteristic. 2 (of an action etc.) indicating such development. 3 (of a plant) flowering or fruiting early. □□ **precociously** adv. **precociousness** n. **precocity** /-ˈkɒsɪtɪ/ n. [L praecox -cocis f. praecoquere ripen fully (as PRAE-, coquere cook)]

precognition /ˌpriːkɒɡˈnɪʃ(ə)n/ n. 1 (supposed) foreknowledge, esp. of a supernatural kind. 2 Sc. the preliminary examination of witnesses etc., esp. to decide whether there is ground for a trial. □□ **precognitive** /-ˈkɒɡnɪtɪv/ adj. [LL praecognitio (as PRE-, COGNITION)]

precoital /priːˈkəʊɪt(ə)l/ adj. preceding sexual intercourse. □□ **precoitally** adv.

pre-Columbian /ˌpriːkəˈlʌmbɪən/ adj. before the discovery of America by Columbus.

preconceive /ˌpriːkənˈsiːv/ v.tr. form (an idea or opinion etc.) beforehand.

preconception /ˌpriːkənˈsepʃ(ə)n/ n. 1 a preconceived idea. 2 a prejudice.

preconcert /ˌpriːkənˈsɜːt/ v.tr. arrange or organize beforehand.

precondition /ˌpriːkənˈdɪʃ(ə)n/ n. & v. —n. a prior condition, that must be fulfilled before other things can be done. —v.tr. bring into a required condition beforehand.

preconize /ˈpriːkəˌnaɪz/ v.tr. (also -ise) 1 proclaim or commend publicly. 2 summon by name. 3 RC Ch. (of the Pope) approve publicly the appointment of (a bishop). □□ **preconization** /-ˈzeɪʃ(ə)n/ n. [ME f. med.L praeconizare f. L praeco -onis herald]

preconscious /priːˈkɒnʃəs/ adj. & n. Psychol. —adj. 1 preceding consciousness. 2 of or associated with a part of the mind below the level of immediate conscious awareness, from which memories and emotions can be recalled. —n. this part of the mind. □□ **preconsciousness** n.

precool /priːˈkuːl/ v.tr. cook in advance.

precool /priːˈkuːl/ v.tr. cool in advance.

precordial /priːˈkɔːdɪəl/ adj. in front of or about the heart.

precostal /priːˈkɒst(ə)l/ adj. in front of the ribs.

precursor /priːˈkɜːsə(r)/ n. 1 a a forerunner. b a person who precedes in office etc. 2 a harbinger. 3 a substance from which another is formed by decay or chemical reaction etc. [L praecursor f. praecurrere praecurs- (as PRAE-, currere run)]

precursory /prɪˈkɜːsərɪ/ adj. (also **precursive** /-sɪv/) 1 preliminary, introductory. 2 (foll. by of) serving as a harbinger (as L praecursorius (as PRECURSOR)]

precut /priːˈkʌt/ v.tr. (past and past part. -cut) cut in advance.

predacious /prɪˈdeɪʃəs/ adj. (also **predaceous**) 1 (of an animal) predatory. 2 relating to such animals (predacious instincts). □□ **predaciousness** n. **predacity** /-ˈdæsɪtɪ/ n. [L praeda booty: cf. audacious]

predate /priːˈdeɪt/ v.tr. exist or occur at a date earlier than.

predation /prɪˈdeɪʃ(ə)n/ n. 1 (usu. in pl.) = DE-PREDATION. 2 Zool. the natural preying of one animal on others. [L praedatio -onis taking of booty f. L praeda booty]

predator /ˈpredətə(r)/ n. 1 an animal naturally preying on others. 2 a person, State, etc., compared to this. [L praedator plunderer f. praedari seize as plunder f. praeda booty (as PREDACIOUS)]

predatory /ˈpredətərɪ/ adj. 1 (of an animal) preying naturally upon others. 2 (of a nation, State, or individual) plundering or exploiting others. □□

predatorily adv. **predatoriness** n. [L praedatorius (as PREDATOR)]

predecease /ˌpriːdɪˈsiːs/ v. & n. —v.tr. die earlier than (another person). —n. a death preceding that of another.

predecessor /ˈpriːdɪˌsesə(r)/ n. 1 a former holder of an office or position with respect to a later holder (my immediate predecessor). 2 an ancestor. 3 a thing to which another has succeeded (the new plan will share the fate of its predecessor). [ME f. OF predecesseur f. LL praedecessor (as PRAE-, decessor retiring officer, as DECEASE)]

pre-decimal /ˌpriːˈdesɪm(ə)l/ adj. of or relating to a time before the introduction of a decimal system, esp. of coinage.

predella /prɪˈdelə/ n. 1 an altar-step, or raised shelf at the back of an altar. 2 a painting or sculpture on this, or any picture forming an appendage to a larger one esp. beneath an altarpiece. [It., = stool]

predestinarian /prɪˌdestɪˈneərɪən/ n. & adj. —n. a person who believes in predestination. —adj. of or relating to predestination.

predestinate v. & adj. —v.tr. /prɪˈdestɪˌneɪt/ = PREDESTINE. —adj. /prɪˈdestɪnət/ predestined. [ME f. eccl.L praedestinare praedestinat- (as PRAE-, destinare establish)]

predestination /prɪˌdestɪˈneɪʃ(ə)n/ n. Theol. (as a belief or doctrine) the divine foreordaining of all that will happen, esp. with regard to the salvation of some and not others. [ME f. eccl.L praedestinatio (as PREDESTINATE)]

predestine /priːˈdestɪn/ v.tr. 1 determine beforehand. 2 ordain in advance by divine will or as if by fate. [ME f. OF predestiner or eccl.L praedestinare PREDESTINATE v.]

predetermine /ˌpriːdɪˈtɜːmɪn/ v.tr. 1 determine or decree beforehand. 2 predestine. □□ **predeterminable** adj. **predeterminate** /-nət/ adj. **predetermination** /-ˈneɪʃ(ə)n/ n. [LL praedeterminare (as PRAE-, DETERMINE)]

predial /ˈpriːdɪəl/ adj. & n. hist. —adj. 1 a of land or farms. b rural, agrarian. c (of a slave, tenant, etc.) attached to farms or the land. 2 (of a tithe) consisting of agricultural produce. —n. a predial slave. [med.L praedialis f. L praedium farm]

predicable /ˈpredɪkəb(ə)l/ adj. & n. —adj. that may be predicated or affirmed. —n. 1 a predicable thing. 2 (in pl.) Logic the five classes to which predicates belong: genus, species, difference, property, and accident. □□ **predicability** /-ˈbɪlɪtɪ/ n. [med.L praedicabilis that may be affirmed (as PREDICATE)]

predicament /prɪˈdɪkəmənt/ n. 1 a difficult, unpleasant, or embarrassing situation. 2 Philos. a category in (esp. Aristotelian) logic. [ME (in sense 2) f. LL praedicamentum thing predicated: see PREDICATE]

predicant /ˈpredɪkənt/ adj. & n. —adj. hist. (of a religious order, esp. the Dominicans) engaged in preaching. —n. 1 hist. a predicant person, esp. a Dominican friar. 2 S.Afr. = PREDIKANT. [L praedicans part. of praedicare (as PREDICATE)]

predicate v. & n. —v.tr. /ˈpredɪˌkeɪt/ 1 assert or affirm as true or existent. 2 (foll. by on) found or base (a statement etc.) on. —n. /ˈpredɪkət/ 1 Gram. what is said about the subject of a sentence etc. (e.g. went home in John went home). 2 Logic a what is predicated. b what is affirmed or denied of the subject by means of the copula (e.g. mortal in all men are mortal). □□ **predication** /-ˈkeɪʃ(ə)n/ n. [L praedicare praedicat- proclaim (as PRAE-, dicare declare)]

predicative /prɪˈdɪkətɪv/ adj. 1 Gram. (of an adjective or noun) forming or contained in the predicate, as old in the dog is old (but not in the old dog) and house in there is a large house (opp. ATTRIBUTIVE). 2 that predicates. □□ **predicatively** adv. [L praedicativus (as PREDICATE)]

predict /prɪˈdɪkt/ v.tr. (often foll. by that + clause) make a statement about the future; foretell,

prophesy. □□**predictive** adj. **predictively** adv.
predictor n. [L praedicere praedict- (as PRAE-, dicere say)]

predictable /prɪ'dɪktəb(ə)l/ adj. that can be predicted or is to be expected. □□**predictability** /-'bɪlɪtɪ/ n. **predictably** adv.

prediction /prɪ'dɪkʃ(ə)n/ n. **1** the art of predicting or the process of being predicted. **2** a thing predicted; a forecast. [L praedictio -onis (as PREDICT)]

predigest /ˌpriː'daɪ'dʒest/ v.tr. **1** render (food) easily digestible before being eaten. **2** make (reading matter) easier to read or understand. □□**predigestion** /-'dʒestʃ(ə)n/ n.

predikant /ˌpreɪdɪ'kɑːnt/ n. S.Afr. a minister of the Dutch Reformed Church. [Du. (as PREDICANT)]

predilection /ˌpriːdɪ'lekʃ(ə)n/ n. (often foll. by for) a preference or special liking. [F prédilection ult. f. L praediligere praedilect- prefer (as PRAE-, diligere select): see DILIGENT]

predispose /ˌpriːdɪ'spəʊz/ v.tr. **1** influence favourably in advance. **2** (foll. by to, or to + infin.) render liable or inclined beforehand. □□ **predisposition** /-pə'zɪʃ(ə)n/ n.

prednisone /'prednɪˌzəʊn/ n. a synthetic drug similar to cortisone, used to relieve rheumatic and allergic conditions and to treat leukaemia. [perh. f. pregnant + diene + cortisone]

predominant /prɪ'dɒmɪnənt/ adj. **1** predominating. **2** being the strongest or main element. □□ **predominance** n. **predominantly** adv.

predominate /prɪ'dɒmɪˌneɪt/ v.intr. **1** (foll. by over) have or exert control. **2** be superior. **3** be the strongest or main element; preponderate (a garden in which dahlias predominate). [med.L praedominari (as PRAE-, DOMINATE)]

predominately /prɪ'dɒmɪnətlɪ/ adv. = PRE-DOMINANTLY (see PREDOMINANT). [rare predominate (adj.) = PREDOMINANT]

predoom /priː'duːm/ v.tr. doom beforehand.

predorsal /priː'dɔːs(ə)l/ adj. in front of the dorsal region.

predynastic /ˌpriːdɪ'næstɪk/ adj. of or relating to a period before the normally recognized dynasties (esp. of ancient Egypt).

pre-echo /priː'ekəʊ/ n. (pl. -oes) **1** a faint copy heard just before an actual sound in a recording, caused by the accidental transfer of signals. **2** a foreshadowing.

pre-eclampsia /ˌpriːɪ'klæmpsɪə/ n. a condition of pregnancy characterized by high blood pressure and other symptoms associated with eclampsia. □□ **pre-eclamptic** adj. & n.

pre-elect /ˌpriːɪ'lekt/ v.tr. elect beforehand.

pre-election /ˌpriːɪ'lekʃ(ə)n/ n. **1** an election held beforehand. **2** (attrib.) (esp. of an act or undertaking) done or given before an election.

pre-embryo /priː'embrɪəʊ/ n. Med. a human embryo in the first fourteen days after fertilization. □□ **pre-embryonic** /-'ɒnɪk/ adj.

pre-eminent /priː'emɪnənt/ adj. **1** excelling others. **2** outstanding; distinguished in some quality. □□ **pre-eminence** n. **pre-eminently** adv. [ME f. L praeeminens (as PRAE-, EMINENT)]

pre-empt /priː'empt/ v. **1** tr. **a** forestall. **b** acquire or appropriate in advance. **2** tr. prevent (an attack) by disabling the enemy. **3** tr. obtain by pre-emption. **4** tr. US take for oneself (esp. public land) so as to have the right of pre-emption. **5** intr. Bridge make a pre-emptive bid. □□ **preemptor** n. **preemptory** adj. [back-form. f. PRE-EMPTION]

pre-emption /priː'empʃ(ə)n/ n. **1 a** the purchase or appropriation by one person or party before the opportunity is offered to others. **b** the right to purchase (esp. public land) in this way. **2** prior appropriation or acquisition. [med.L praeemptio (as PRAE-, emere empt- buy)]

pre-emptive /priː'emptɪv/ adj. **1** pre-empting; serving to pre-empt. **2** (of military action) intended to prevent attack by disabling the enemy (a pre-emptive

strike). **3** Bridge (of a bid) intended to be high enough to discourage further bidding.

preen /priːn/ v.tr. & refl. **1** (of a bird) tidy (the feathers or itself) with its beak. **2** (of a person) smarten or admire (oneself, one's hair, clothes, etc.). **3** (often foll. by on) congratulate or pride (oneself). □**preen gland** a gland situated at the base of a bird's tail and producing oil used in preening. □□ **preener** n. [ME, app. var. of earlier prune (perh. rel. to PRUNE²): assoc. with Sc. & dial. preen pierce, pin]

pre-engage /ˌpriːɪn'geɪdʒ/ v.tr. engage beforehand. □□ **pre-engagement** n.

pre-establish /ˌpriːɪ'stæblɪʃ/ v.tr. establish beforehand.

pre-exist /ˌpriːɪg'zɪst/ v.intr. exist at an earlier time. □□ **pre-existence** n. **pre-existent** adj.

pref. abbr. **1** prefix. **2** preface. **3 a** preference. **b** preferred.

prefab /'priːfæb/ n. Brit. colloq. a prefabricated building, esp. a small house. [abbr.]

prefabricate /priː'fæbrɪˌkeɪt/ v.tr. **1** manufacture sections of (a building etc.) prior to their assembly on a site. **2** produce in an artificially standardized way. □□ **prefabrication** /-'keɪʃ(ə)n/ n.

preface /'prefəs/ n. & v. —n. **1** an introduction to a book stating its subject, scope, etc. **2** the preliminary part of a speech. **3** Eccl. the introduction to the central part of the Eucharistic service. —v.tr. **1** (foll. by with) introduce or begin (a speech or event) (prefaced my remarks with a warning). **2** provide (a book etc.) with a preface. **3** (of an event etc.) lead up to (another). □□ **prefatorial** /-'tɔːrɪəl/ adj. **prefatory** /-tərɪ/ adj. [ME f. OF f. med.L praefatia for L praefatio f. praefari (as PRAE-, fari speak)]

prefect /'priːfekt/ n. **1** the chief administrative officer of certain departments, esp. in France. **2** esp. Brit. a senior pupil in a school etc. authorized to enforce discipline. **3** Rom. Antiq. a senior magistrate or military commander. □□ **prefectoral** /-'fektər(ə)l/ adj. **prefectorial** /-'tɔːrɪəl/ adj. [ME f. OF f. L praefectus past part. of praeficere set in authority over (as PRAE-, facere make)]

prefecture /'priːfektjʊə(r)/ n. **1** a district under the government of a prefect. **2 a** a prefect's office or tenure. **b** his official residence. □□ **prefectural** /prɪ'fektʃər(ə)l/ adj. [F préfecture or L praefectura (as PREFECT)]

prefer /prɪ'fɜː(r)/ v.tr. (**preferred**, **preferring**) **1** (often foll. by to, or to + infin.) choose rather; like better (would prefer to stay; prefers coffee to tea). **2** submit (information, an accusation, etc.) for consideration. **3** promote or advance (a person). □**preferred shares** (or **stock**) = preference shares or stock. [ME f. OF preferer f. L praeferre (as PRAE-, ferre lat- bear)]

preferable /'prefərəb(ə)l/ adj. **1** to be preferred. **2** more desirable. □□ **preferably** adv.

preference /'prefərəns/ n. **1** the act or an instance of preferring or being preferred. **2** a thing preferred. **3 a** the favouring of one person etc. before others. **b** Commerce the favouring of one country by admitting its products at a lower import duty. **4** Law a prior right, esp. to the payment of debts. □**in preference to** as a thing preferred over (another). **preference shares** (or **stock**) Brit. shares or stock whose entitlement to dividend takes priority over that of ordinary shares. [F préférence f. med.L praeferentia (as PREFER)]

preferential /ˌprefə'renʃ(ə)l/ adj. **1** of or involving preference (preferential treatment). **2** giving or receiving a favour. **3** Commerce (of a tariff etc.) favouring particular countries. **4** (of voting) in which the voter puts candidates in order of preference. □□ **preferentially** adv. [as PREFERENCE, after differential]

preferment /prɪ'fɜːmənt/ n. promotion to office.

prefigure /priː'fɪgə(r)/ v.tr. **1** represent beforehand by a figure or type. **2** imagine beforehand. □□

prefiguration /-'reɪʃ(ə)n/ n. **prefigurative** /-rətɪv/ adj. **prefigurement** n. [ME f. eccl.L praefigurare (as PRAE-, FIGURE)]

prefix /'priːfɪks/ n. & v. —n. **1** a verbal element placed at the beginning of a word to adjust or qualify its meaning (e.g. ex-, non-, re-) or (in some languages) as an inflectional formative. **2** a title placed before a name (e.g. Mr). —v.tr. (often foll. by to) **1** add as an introduction. **2** join (a word or element) as a prefix. □□ **prefixation** /-'seɪʃ(ə)n/ n. **prefixion** /-'fɪkʃ(ə)n/ n. [earlier as verb: ME f. OF prefixer (as PRE-, FIX): (n.) f. L praefixum]

preflight /'priːflaɪt/ attrib.adj. occurring or provided before an aircraft flight.

preform /priː'fɔːm/ v.tr. form beforehand. □□ **preformation** /-'meɪʃ(ə)n/ n.

preformative /priː'fɔːmətɪv/ adj. & n. —adj. **1** forming beforehand. **2** prefixed as the formative element of a word. —n. a preformative syllable or letter.

prefrontal /priː'frʌnt(ə)l/ adj. **1** in front of the frontal bone of the skull. **2** in the forepart of the frontal lobe of the brain.

preglacial /priː'gleɪʃ(ə)l, -sɪəl/ adj. before a glacial period.

pregnable /'pregnəb(ə)l/ adj. able to be captured etc.; not impregnable. [ME f. OF prenable takable: see IMPREGNABLE[1]]

pregnancy /'pregnənsɪ/ n. (pl. -ies) the condition or an instance of being pregnant.

pregnant /'pregnənt/ adj. **1** (of a woman or female animal) having a child or young developing in the uterus. **2** full of meaning; significant or suggestive (a pregnant pause). **3** (esp. of a person's mind) imaginative, inventive. **4** (foll. by with) plentifully provided (pregnant with danger). □ **pregnant construction** Gram. one in which more is implied than the words express (e.g. not have a chance implying of success etc.). □□ **pregnantly** adv. (in sense 2). [ME f. F prégnant or L praegnans -antis, earlier praegnas (prob. as PRAE-, (g)nasci be born)]

preheat /priː'hiːt/ v.tr. heat beforehand.

prehensile /priː'hensaɪl/ adj. Zool. (of a tail or limb) capable of grasping. □□ **prehensility** /-'sɪlɪtɪ/ n. [F préhensile f. L prehendere prehens- (as PRE-, hendere grasp)]

prehension /prɪ'henʃ(ə)n/ n. **1** grasping, seizing. **2** mental apprehension. [L prehensio (as PREHENSILE)]

prehistoric /,priːhɪ'stɒrɪk/ adj. **1** of or relating to the period before written records. **2** colloq. utterly out of date. □□ **prehistorian** /-'stɔːrɪən/ n. **prehistorically** adv. **prehistory** /-'hɪstərɪ/ n. [F préhistorique (as PRE-, HISTORIC)]

prehuman /priː'hjuːmən/ adj. existing before the time of man.

pre-ignition /,priːɪg'nɪʃ(ə)n/ n. the premature firing of the explosive mixture in an internal-combustion engine.

prejudge /priː'dʒʌdʒ/ v.tr. **1** form a premature judgement on (a person, issue, etc.). **2** pass judgement on (a person) before a trial or proper enquiry. □□ **prejudgement** n. **prejudication** /-,dʒuːdɪ'keɪʃ(ə)n/ n.

prejudice /'predʒʊdɪs/ n. & v. —n. **1 a** a preconceived opinion. **b** (foll. by against, in favour of) bias or partiality. **2** harm or injury that results or may result from some action or judgement (to the prejudice of). —v.tr. **1** impair the validity or force of (a right, claim, statement, etc.). **2** (esp. as **prejudiced** adj.) cause (a person) to have a prejudice. □ **without prejudice** (often foll. by to) without detriment to any existing right or claim). [ME f. OF prejudice f. L praejudicium (as PRAE-, judicium judgement)]

prejudicial /,predʒʊ'dɪʃ(ə)l/ adj. causing prejudice; detrimental. □□ **prejudicially** adv. [ME f. OF prejudiciel (as PREJUDICE)]

prelacy /'preləsɪ/ n. (pl. -ies) **1** church government by prelates. **2** (prec. by the) prelates collectively. **3**

the office or rank of prelate. [ME f. AF prelacie f. med.L prelatia (as PRELATE)]

prelapsarian /,priːlæp'seərɪən/ adj. before the Fall of man. [PRE- + L lapsus (as LAPSE)]

prelate /'prelət/ n. **1** a high ecclesiastical dignitary, e.g. a bishop. **2** hist. an abbot or prior. □□ **prelatic** /prɪ'lætɪk/ adj. **prelatical** /prɪ'lætɪk(ə)l/ adj. [ME f. OF prelat f. med.L praelatus past part.: see PREFER]

prelature /'prelətjʊə(r)/ n. **1** the office of prelate. **2** (prec. by the) prelates collectively. [F prélature f. med.L praelatura (as PRELATE)]

prelim /'priːlɪm, prɪ'lɪm/ n. colloq. **1** a preliminary examination, esp. at a university. **2** (in pl.) the pages preceding the text of a book. [abbr.]

preliminary /prɪ'lɪmɪnərɪ/ adj., n., & adv. —adj. introductory, preparatory. —n. (pl. -ies) (usu. in pl.) **1** a preliminary action or arrangement (dispense with the preliminaries). **2** a preliminary trial or contest. —adv. (foll. by to) preparatory to; in advance of (was completed preliminary to the main event). □□ **preliminarily** adv. [mod.L praeliminaris or F préliminaire (as PRE-, limen liminis threshold)]

preliterate /priː'lɪtərət/ adj. of or relating to a society or culture that has not developed the use of writing.

prelude /'preljuːd/ n. & v. —n. (often foll. by to) **1** an action, event, or situation serving as an introduction. **2** the introductory part of a poem etc. **3 a** an introductory piece of music, often preceding a fugue or forming the first piece of a suite or beginning an act of an opera. **b** a short piece of music of a similar type, esp. for the piano. —v.tr. **1** serve as a prelude to. **2** introduce with a prelude. □□ **preludial** /prɪ'ljuːdɪəl/ adj. [F prélude or med.L praeludium f. L praeludere praelus- (as PRAE-, ludere play)]

premarital /priː'mærɪt(ə)l/ adj. existing or (esp. of sexual relations) occurring before marriage. □□ **premaritally** adv.

premature /'premə,tjʊə(r), -'tjʊə(r)/ adj. **1 a** occurring or done before the usual or proper time; too early (a premature decision). **b** too hasty (must not be premature). **2** (of a baby, esp. a viable one) born (esp. three or more weeks) before the end of the full term of gestation. □□ **prematurely** adv. **prematureness** n. **prematurity** /-'tjʊərɪtɪ/ n. [L praematurus very early (as PRAE-, MATURE)]

premaxillary /,priː'mæk'sɪlərɪ/ adj. in front of the upper jaw.

premed /priː'med/ n. colloq. **1** = PREMEDICATION. **2** a premedical course or student. [abbr.]

premedical /priː'medɪk(ə)l/ adj. of or relating to study in preparation for a course in medicine.

premedication /,priːmedɪ'keɪʃ(ə)n/ n. medication to prepare for an operation or other treatment.

premeditate /priː'medɪ,teɪt/ v.tr. think out or plan (an action) beforehand (premeditated murder). □□ **premeditation** /-'teɪʃ(ə)n/ n. [L praemeditari (as PRAE-, MEDITATE)]

premenstrual /priː'menstrʊəl/ adj. of, occurring, or experienced before menstruation (premenstrual tension). □□ **premenstrually** adv.

premier /'premɪə(r)/ n. & adj. —n. a prime minister or other head of government. —adj. **1** first in importance, order, or time. **2** of earliest creation (premier earl). □□ **premiership** n. [ME f. OF = first, f. L (as PRIMARY)]

première /'premɪ,eə(r)/ n. & v. —n. the first performance or showing of a play or film. —v.tr. give a première of. [F, fem. of premier (adj.) (as PREMIER)]

premillennial /,priːmɪ'lenɪəl/ adj. existing or occurring before the millennium, esp. with reference to the supposed second coming of Christ. □□ **premillennialism** n. **premillennialist** n.

premise n. & v. —n. /'premɪs/ **1** Logic = PREMISS. **2** (in pl.) **a** a house or building with its grounds and appurtenances. **b** Law houses, lands, or tenements previously specified in a document etc. —v.tr. /prɪ'maɪz/ say or write by way of introduction. □ **on the premises** in the building etc. concerned. [ME f.

b but d dog f few g get h he j yes k cat l leg m man n no p pen r red s sit t top v voice

OF *premisse* f. med.L *praemissa* (*propositio*) (proposition) set in front f. L *praemittere praemiss-* (as PRAE-, *mittere* send)]

premiss /'premɪs/ *n. Logic* a previous statement from which another is inferred. [var. of PREMISE]

premium /'priːmɪəm/ *n.* **1** an amount to be paid for a contract of insurance. **2 a** a sum added to interest, wages, etc.; a bonus. **b** a sum added to ordinary charges. **3** a reward or prize. **4** (*attrib.*) (of a commodity) of best quality and therefore more expensive. □**at a premium 1** highly valued; above the usual or nominal price. **2** scarce and in demand. **Premium Bond** (or **Savings Bond**) *Brit.* a government security without interest but with a draw for cash prizes. **put a premium on 1** provide or act as an incentive to. **2** attach special value to. [L *praemium* booty, reward (as PRAE-, *emere* buy, take)]

premolar /priː'məʊlə(r)/ *adj. & n.* —*adj.* in front of a molar tooth. —*n.* (in an adult human) each of eight teeth situated in pairs between each of the four canine teeth and each first molar.

premonition /ˌpreməˈnɪʃ(ə)n, ˌpriː-/ *n.* a forewarning; a presentiment. □□**premonitor** /prɪ'mɒnɪtə(r)/ *n.* **premonitory** /prɪ'mɒnɪtəri/ *adj.* [F *prémonition* or LL *praemonitio* f. L *praemonēre praemonit-* (as PRAE-, *monēre* warn)]

Premonstratensian /ˌpriːmɒnstrəˈtensɪən/ *adj. & n. hist.* —*adj.* of or relating to an order of regular canons founded at Prémontré in France in 1120, or of the corresponding order of nuns. —*n.* a member of either of these orders. [med.L *Praemonstratensis* f. *Praemonstratus* the abbey of Prémontré (lit. = foreshown)]

premorse /priː'mɔːs/ *adj. Bot. & Zool.* with the end abruptly terminated. [L *praemordēre praemors-* bite off (as PRAE-, *mordēre* bite)]

prenatal /priː'neɪt(ə)l/ *adj.* of or concerning the period before childbirth. □□**prenatally** *adv.*

prentice /'prentɪs/ *n. & v. archaic* —*n.* = APPRENTICE. —*v.tr.* (as **prenticed** *adj.*) apprenticed. □**prentice hand** an inexperienced hand. □□ **prenticeship** *n.* [ME f. APPRENTICE]

preoccupation /priːˌɒkjʊ'peɪʃ(ə)n/ *n.* **1** the state of being preoccupied. **2** a thing that engrosses the mind. [F *préoccupation* or L *praeoccupatio* (as PREOCCUPY)]

preoccupy /priː'ɒkjʊˌpaɪ/ *v.tr.* (**-ies, -ied**) **1** (of a thought etc.) dominate or engross the mind of (a person) to the exclusion of other thoughts. **2** (as **preoccupied** *adj.*) otherwise engrossed; mentally distracted. **3** occupy beforehand. [PRE- + OCCUPY, after L *praeoccupare* seize beforehand]

preocular /priː'ɒkjʊlə(r)/ *adj.* in front of the eye.

preordain /ˌpriːɔː'deɪn/ *v.tr.* ordain or determine beforehand.

prep /prep/ *n. colloq.* **1** *Brit.* **a** the preparation of school work by a pupil. **b** the period when this is done. **2** *US* a student in a preparatory school. [abbr. of PREPARATION]

prep. *abbr.* preposition.

prepack /priː'pæk/ *v.tr.* (also **pre-package** /-'pækɪdʒ/) pack (goods) on the site of production or before retail.

prepaid *past* and *past part.* of PREPAY.

preparation /ˌprepə'reɪʃ(ə)n/ *n.* **1** the act or an instance of preparing; the process of being prepared. **2** (often in *pl.*) something done to make ready. **3** a specially prepared substance, esp. a food or medicine. **4** work done by school pupils to prepare for a lesson. **5** *Mus.* the sounding of the discordant note in a chord in the preceding chord where it is not discordant, lessening the effect of the discord. [ME f. OF f. L *praeparatio -onis* (as PREPARE)]

preparative /prɪ'pærətɪv/ *adj. & n.* —*adj.* preparatory. —*n.* **1** *Mil. & Naut.* a signal on a drum, bugle, etc., as an order to make ready. **2** a preparatory act. □□**preparatively** *adv.* [ME f. OF *preparatif -ive* f. med.L *praeparativus* (as PREPARE)]

preparatory /prɪ'pærətəri/ *adj. & adv.* —*adj.* (often

foll. by *to*) serving to prepare; introductory. —*adv.* (often foll. by *to*) in a preparatory manner (*was packing preparatory to departure*). □**preparatory school** a usu. private school preparing pupils for a higher school or *US* for college or university. □□ **preparatorily** *adv.* [ME f. LL *praeparatorius* (as PREPARE)]

prepare /prɪ'peə(r)/ *v.* **1** *tr.* make or get ready for use, consideration, etc. **2** *tr.* make ready or assemble (food, a meal, etc.) for eating. **3 a** *tr.* make (a person or oneself) ready or disposed in some way (*prepares students for university; prepared them for a shock*). **b** *intr.* put oneself or things in readiness, get ready (*prepare to jump*). **4** *tr.* make (a chemical product etc.) by a regular process. **5** *tr. Mus.* lead up to (a discord). □**be prepared** (often foll. by *for*, or *to* + *infin.*) be disposed or willing to. □□ **preparer** *n.* [ME f. F *préparer* or L *praeparare* (as PRAE-, *parare* make ready)]

preparedness /prɪ'peərɪdnɪs/ *n.* a state of readiness, esp. for war.

prepay /priː'peɪ/ *v.tr.* (*past* and *past part.* **prepaid**) **1** pay (a charge) in advance. **2** pay postage on (a letter or parcel etc.) before posting. □□ **prepayable** *adj.* **prepayment** *n.*

prepense /prɪ'pens/ *adj.* (usu. placed after noun) esp. *Law* deliberate, intentional (*malice prepense*). □□**prepensely** *adv.* [earlier *prepensed* past part. of obs. *prepense* (v.) alt. f. earlier *purpense* f. AF & OF *purpenser* (as PUR-, *penser*): see PENSIVE]

preplan /priː'plæn/ *v.tr.* (**preplanned, preplanning**) plan in advance.

preponderant /prɪ'pɒndərənt/ *adj.* surpassing in influence, power, number, or importance; predominant, preponderating. □□**preponderance** *n.* **preponderantly** *adv.*

preponderate /prɪ'pɒndəˌreɪt/ *v.intr.* (often foll. by *over*) **1 a** be greater in influence, quantity, or number. **b** predominate. **2 a** be of greater importance. **b** weigh more. [L *praeponderare* (as PRAE-, PONDER)]

preposition /ˌprepə'zɪʃ(ə)n/ *n. Gram.* a word governing (and usu. preceding) a noun or pronoun and expressing a relation to another word or element, as in: 'the man *on* the platform', 'came *after* dinner', 'what did you do it *for*?' □□**prepositional** *adj.* **prepositionally** *adv.* [ME f. L *praepositio* f. *praeponere praeposit-* (as PRAE-, *ponere* place)]

prepositive /priː'pɒzɪtɪv/ *adj. Gram.* (of a word, particle, etc.) that should be placed before or prefixed. [LL *praepositivus* (as PREPOSITION)]

prepossess /ˌpriːpə'zes/ *v.tr.* **1** (usu. in *passive*) (of an idea, feeling, etc.) take possession of (a person); imbue. **2 a** prejudice (usu. favourably and spontaneously). **b** (as **prepossessing** *adj.*) attractive, appealing. □□**prepossession** /-'zeʃ(ə)n/ *n.*

preposterous /prɪ'pɒstərəs/ *adj.* **1** utterly absurd; outrageous. **2** contrary to nature, reason, or common sense. □□**preposterously** *adv.* **preposterousness** *n.* [L *praeposterus* reversed, absurd (as PRAE-, *posterus* coming after)]

prepostor var. of PRAEPOSTOR.

prepotent /prɪ'pəʊt(ə)nt/ *adj.* **1** greater than others in power, influence, etc. **2 a** having a stronger fertilizing influence. **b** dominant in transmitting hereditary qualities. □□**prepotence** *n.* **prepotency** *n.* [ME f. L *praepotens -entis*, part. of *praeposse* (as PRAE-, *posse* be able)]

preppy /'prepɪ/ *n. & adj. US colloq.* —*n.* (*pl.* **-ies**) a person attending an expensive private school or who looks like such a person (with short hair, blazer, etc.). —*adj.* (**preppier, preppiest**) **1** like a preppy. **2** neat and fashionable. [PREP (SCHOOL) + -Y²]

preprandial /priː'prændɪəl/ *adj. formal* or *joc.* before dinner or lunch. [PRE- + L *prandium* a meal]

pre-preference /priː'prefərəns/ *adj. Brit.* (of shares, claims, etc.) ranking before preference shares etc.

preprint /'priːprɪnt/ *n.* a printed document issued in advance of general publication.

preprocessor /pri:'prəʊsesə(r)/ *n.* a computer program that modifies data to conform with the input requirements of another program.

prep school /prep/ *n.* = PREPARATORY SCHOOL. [abbr. of PREPARATORY]

prepublication /ˌpri:pʌblɪ'keɪʃ(ə)n/ *adj.* & *n.* —*attrib.adj.* produced or occurring before publication. —*n.* publication in advance or beforehand.

prepuce /'pri:pju:s/ *n.* **1** = FORESKIN. **2** the fold of skin surrounding the clitoris. □□ **preputial** /pri:'pju:ʃ(ə)l/ *adj.* [ME f. L *praeputium*]

prequel /'pri:kw(ə)l/ *n.* a story, film, etc., whose events or concerns precede those of an existing work. [PRE- + SEQUEL]

Pre-Raphaelite /pri:'ræfəlaɪt/ *n.* & *adj.* —*n.* a member of a group of English 19th-c. artists, including Holman Hunt, Millais, and D. G. Rossetti, emulating the work of Italian artists before the time of Raphael. —*adj.* **1** of or relating to the Pre-Raphaelites. **2** (**pre-Raphaelite**) (esp. of a woman) like a type painted by a Pre-Raphaelite (e.g. with long thick curly auburn hair). □ **Pre-Raphaelite Brotherhood** the chosen name of the Pre-Raphaelites. □□ **pre-Raphaelitism** *n.*

pre-record /ˌpri:rɪ'kɔ:d/ *v.tr.* record (esp. material for broadcasting) in advance.

prerequisite /pri:'rekwɪzɪt/ *adj.* & *n.* —*adj.* required as a precondition. —*n.* a prerequisite thing.

prerogative /prɪ'rɒgətɪv/ *n.* **1** a right or privilege exclusive to an individual or class. **2** (in full **royal prerogative**) *Brit.* the right of the sovereign, theoretically subject to no restriction. [ME f. OF *prerogative* or L *praerogativa* privilege (orig. to vote first) f. *praerogativus* asked first (as PRAE-, *rogare* ask)]

Pres. *abbr.* President.

presage *n.* & *v.* —*n.* /'presɪdʒ/ **1** an omen or portent. **2** a presentiment or foreboding. —*v.tr.* /'presɪdʒ, prɪ'seɪdʒ/ **1** portend, foreshadow. **2** give warning of (an event etc.) by natural means. **3** (of a person) predict or have a presentiment of. □□ **presageful** /prɪ'seɪdʒfʊl/ *adj.* **presager** *n.* [ME f. F *présage*, *présager* f. L *praesagium* f. *praesagire* forebode (as PRAE-, *sagire* perceive keenly)]

presbyopia /ˌprezbɪ'əʊpɪə/ *n.* long-sightedness caused by loss of elasticity of the eye lens, occurring esp. in middle and old age. □□ **presbyopic** /-'ɒpɪk/ *adj.* [mod.L f. Gk *presbus* old man + *ōps ōpos* eye]

presbyter /'prezbɪtə(r)/ *n.* **1** an elder in the early Christian Church. **2** (in the Episcopal Church) a minister of the second order; a priest. **3** (in the Presbyterian Church) an elder. □□ **presbyteral** /-'bɪtər(ə)l/ *adj.* **presbyterate** /-'bɪtərət/ *n.* **presbyterial** /-'tɪərɪəl/ *adj.* **presbytership** *n.* [eccl.L f. Gk *presbuteros* elder, compar. of *presbus* old]

Presbyterian /ˌprezbɪ'tɪərɪən/ *adj.* & *n.* —*adj.* (of a church) governed by elders all of equal rank, esp. with reference to the national Church of Scotland. —*n.* **1** a member of a Presbyterian Church. **2** an adherent of the Presbyterian system. □□ **Presbyterianism** *n.* [eccl.L *presbyterium* (as PRESBYTERY)]

presbytery /'prezbɪtərɪ/ *n.* (*pl.* -**ies**) **1** the eastern part of a chancel beyond the choir; the sanctuary. **2 a** a body of presbyters, esp. a court next above a Kirk-session. **b** a district represented by this. **3** the house of a Roman Catholic priest. [ME f. OF *presbiterie* f. eccl.L f. Gk *presbuterion* (as PRESBYTER)]

preschool /'pri:sku:l, pri:'sku:l/ *adj.* of or relating to the time before a child is old enough to go to school. □□ **preschooler** /-'sku:lə(r)/ *n.*

prescient /'presɪənt/ *adj.* having foreknowledge or foresight. □□ **prescience** *n.* **presciently** *adv.* [L *praescire praescient-* know beforehand (as PRAE-, *scire* know)]

prescind /prɪ'sɪnd/ *v.* **1** *tr.* (foll. by *from*) cut off (a part from a whole), esp. prematurely or abruptly. **2**

intr. (foll. by *from*) leave out of consideration. [L *praescindere* (as PRAE-, *scindere* cut)]

prescribe /prɪ'skraɪb/ *v.* **1** *tr.* **a** advise the use of (a medicine etc.), esp. by an authorized prescription. **b** recommend, esp. as a benefit (*prescribed a change of scenery*). **2** *tr.* lay down or impose authoritatively. **3** *intr.* (foll. by *to*, *for*) assert a prescriptive right or claim. □□ **prescriber** *n.* [L *praescribere praescript-* direct in writing (as PRAE-, *scribere* write)]

prescript /'pri:skrɪpt/ *n.* an ordinance, law, or command. [L *praescriptum* neut. past part.: see PRESCRIBE]

prescription /prɪ'skrɪpʃ(ə)n/ *n.* **1** the act or an instance of prescribing. **2 a** a doctor's (usu. written) instruction for the composition and use of a medicine. **b** a medicine prescribed. **3** (in full **positive prescription**) uninterrupted use or possession from time immemorial or for the period fixed by law as giving a title or right. **4 a** an ancient custom viewed as authoritative. **b** a claim founded on long use. □ **negative prescription** the time limit within which an action or claim can be raised. [ME f. OF f. L *praescriptio -onis* (as PRESCRIBE)]

prescriptive /prɪ'skrɪptɪv/ *adj.* **1** prescribing. **2** *Linguistics* concerned with or laying down rules of usage. **3** based on prescription (*prescriptive right*). **4** prescribed by custom. □□ **prescriptively** *adv.* **prescriptiveness** *n.* **prescriptivism** *n.* **prescriptivist** *n.* & *adj.* [LL *praescriptivus* (as PRESCRIBE)]

preselect /ˌpri:sɪ'lekt/ *v.tr.* select in advance. □□ **preselection** *n.*

preselective /ˌpri:sɪ'lektɪv/ *adj.* that can be selected or set in advance.

preselector /ˌpri:sɪ'lektə(r)/ *n.* any of various devices for selecting a mechanical or electrical operation in advance of its execution, e.g. a gear-change in a motor vehicle.

presence /'prez(ə)ns/ *n.* **1** the state or condition of being present (*your presence is requested*). **2 a** a place where a person is (*was admitted to their presence*). **3 a** a person's appearance or bearing, esp. when imposing (*an august presence*). **b** a person's force of personality (esp. *have presence*). **4** a person or thing that is present (*the royal presence*; *there was a presence in the room*). **5** representation for reasons of political influence (*maintained a presence*). □ **in the presence of** in front of; observed by. **presence chamber** a room in which a monarch or other distinguished person receives visitors. **presence of mind** calmness and self-command in sudden difficulty etc. [ME f. OF f. L *praesentia* (as PRESENT¹)]

present¹ /'prez(ə)nt/ *adj.* & *n.* —*adj.* **1** (usu. *predic.*) being in the place in question (*was present at the trial*). **2 a** now existing, occurring, or being such (*the present Duke*; *during the present season*). **b** now being considered or discussed etc. (*in the present case*). **3** *Gram.* expressing an action etc. now going on or habitually performed (*present participle*; *present tense*). —*n.* (prec. by *the*) **1** the time now passing (*no time like the present*). **2** *Gram.* the present tense. □ **at present** now. **by these presents** *Law* by this document (*know all men by these presents*). **for the present 1** just now. **2** as far as the present is concerned. **present company excepted** excluding those who are here now. **present-day** *adj.* of this time; modern. [ME f. OF f. L *praesens -entis* part. of *praeesse* be at hand (as PRAE-, *esse* be)]

present² /prɪ'zent/ *v.* & *n.* —*v.tr.* **1** introduce, offer, or exhibit, esp. for public attention or consideration. **2 a** (with a thing as object, foll. by *to*) offer or give as a gift (to a person), esp. formally or ceremonially. **b** (with a person as object, foll. by *with*) make available to; cause to have (*presented them with a new car*; *that presents us with a problem*). **3 a** (of a company, producer, etc.) put (a form of entertainment) before the public. **b** (of a performer, compère, etc.) introduce or put before an audience. **4** introduce (a person)

æ *cat* ɑ: *arm* e *bed* ɜ: *her* ɪ *sit* i: *see* ɒ *hot* ɔ: *saw* ʌ *run* ʊ *put* u: *too* ə *ago* aɪ *my*

formally (*may I present my fiancé?*; *was presented at court*). **5** offer, give (compliments etc.) (*may I present my card*; *present my regards to your family*). **6 a** (of a circumstance) reveal (some quality etc.) (*this presents some difficulty*). **b** exhibit (an appearance etc.) (*presented a rough exterior*). **7** (of an idea etc.) offer or suggest itself. **8** deliver (a cheque, bill, etc.) for acceptance or payment. **9 a** (usu. foll. by *at*) aim (a weapon). **b** hold out (a weapon) in a position for aiming. **10** (*refl.* or *absol.*) *Med.* (of a patient or illness etc.) come forward for or undergo initial medical examination. **11** (*absol.*) *Med.* (of a part of a foetus) be directed toward the cervix at the time of delivery. **12** (foll. by *to*) *Law* bring formally under notice, submit (an offence, complaint, etc.). **13** (foll. by *to*) *Eccl.* recommend (a clergyman) to a bishop for institution to a benefice. —*n.* the position of presenting arms in salute. □**present arms** hold a rifle etc. vertically in front of the body as a salute. **present oneself 1** appear. **2** come forward for examination etc. □□ **presenter** *n.* (in sense 3 of *v.*). [ME f. OF *presenter* f. L *praesentare* (as PRESENT[1])]

present[3] /ˈprez(ə)nt/ *n.* a gift; a thing given or presented. □**make a present of** give as a gift. [ME f. OF (as PRESENT[1]), orig. in phr. *mettre une chose en present à quelqu'un* put a thing into the presence of a person]

presentable /prɪˈzentəb(ə)l/ *adj.* **1** of good appearance; fit to be presented to other people. **2** fit for presentation. □□ **presentability** /-ˈbɪlɪtɪ/ *n.* **presentableness** *n.* **presentably** *adv.*

presentation /ˌprezənˈteɪʃ(ə)n/ *n.* **1 a** the act or an instance of presenting; the process of being presented. **b** a thing presented. **2** the manner or quality of presenting. **3** a demonstration or display of materials, information, etc.; a lecture. **4** an exhibition or theatrical performance. **5** a formal introduction. **6** the position of the foetus in relation to the cervix at the time of delivery. □□ **presentational** *adj.* **presentationally** *adv.* [ME f. OF f. LL *praesentatio -onis* (as PRESENT[2])]

presentationism /ˌprezənˈteɪʃəˌnɪz(ə)m/ *n. Philos.* the doctrine that in perception the mind has immediate cognition of the object. □□ **presentationist** *n.*

presentative /prɪˈzentətɪv/ *adj.* **1** *Philos.* subject to direct cognition. **2** *hist.* (of a benefice) to which a patron has the right of presentation. [prob. f. med.L (as PRESENTATION)]

presentee /ˌprezənˈtiː/ *n.* **1** the recipient of a present. **2** a person presented. [ME f. AF (as PRESENT[2])]

presentient /prɪˈsenʃ(ə)nt, -ˈzenʃ(ə)nt/ *adj.* (often foll. by *of*) having a presentiment. [L *praesentiens* (as PRAE-, SENTIENT)]

presentiment /prɪˈzentɪmənt, -ˈsentɪmənt/ *n.* a vague expectation; a foreboding (esp. of misfortune). [obs. F *présentiment* (as PRE-, SENTIMENT)]

presently /ˈprez(ə)ntlɪ/ *adv.* **1** soon; after a short time. **2** esp. *US & Sc.* at the present time; now.

presentment /prɪˈzentmənt/ *n.* the act of presenting information, esp. a statement on oath by a jury of a fact known to them. [ME f. OF *presentement* (as PRESENT[2])]

preservation /ˌprezəˈveɪʃ(ə)n/ *n.* **1** the act of preserving or process of being preserved. **2** a state of being well or badly preserved (*in an excellent state of preservation*). [ME f. OF f. med.L *praeservatio -onis* (as PRESERVE)]

preservationist /ˌprezəˈveɪʃənɪst/ *n.* a supporter or advocate of preservation, esp. of antiquities and historic buildings.

preservative /prɪˈzɜːvətɪv/ *n. & adj.* —*n.* a substance for preserving perishable foodstuffs, wood, etc. —*adj.* tending to preserve. [ME f. OF *preservatif -ive* f. med.L *praeservativus -um* (as PRESERVE)]

preserve /prɪˈzɜːv/ *v. & n.* —*v.tr.* **1 a** keep safe or free from harm, decay, etc. **b** keep alive (a name, memory, etc.). **2** maintain (a thing) in its existing

state. **3** retain (a quality or condition). **4 a** treat or refrigerate (food) to prevent decomposition or fermentation. **b** prepare (fruit) by boiling it with sugar, for long-term storage. **5** keep (game, a river, etc.) undisturbed for private use. —*n.* (in *sing.* or *pl.*) **1** preserved fruit; jam. **2** a place where game or fish etc. is preserved. **3** a sphere or area of activity regarded as a person's own. □**well-preserved** (of an elderly person) showing little sign of ageing. □□ **preservable** *adj.* **preserver** *n.* [ME f. OF *preserver* f. LL *praeservare* (as PRAE-, *servare* keep)]

pre-set /priːˈset/ *v.tr.* (**-setting**; *past* and *past part.* **-set**) **1** set or fix (a device) in advance of its operation. **2** settle or decide beforehand.

preshrunk /priːˈʃrʌŋk/ *adj.* (of a fabric or garment) treated so that it shrinks during manufacture and not in use.

preside /prɪˈzaɪd/ *v.intr.* **1** (often foll. by *at, over*) be in a position of authority, esp. as the chairperson or president of a meeting. **2 a** exercise control or authority. **b** (foll. by *at*) *colloq.* play an instrument in company (*presided at the piano*). [F *présider* f. L *praesidēre* (as PRAE-, *sedēre* sit)]

presidency /ˈprezɪdənsɪ/ *n.* (*pl.* **-ies**) **1** the office of president. **2** the period of this. [Sp. & Port. *presidencia*, It. *presidenza* f. med.L *praesidentia* (as PRESIDE)]

president /ˈprezɪd(ə)nt/ *n.* **1** the elected head of a republican State. **2** the head of a society or council etc. **3** the head of certain colleges. **4** *US* **a** the head of a university. **b** the head of a company, etc. **5** a person in charge of a meeting, council, etc. □□ **presidential** /-ˈdenʃ(ə)l/ *adj.* **presidentially** /-ˈdenʃəlɪ/ *adv.* **presidentship** *n.* [ME f. OF f. L (as PRESIDE)]

presidium /prɪˈsɪdɪəm, -ˈzɪdɪəm/ *n.* (also **praesidium**) a standing executive committee in a Communist country, esp. in the USSR. [Russ. *prezidium* f. L *praesidium* protection etc. (as PRESIDE)]

presocratic /ˌpriːsəˈkrætɪk/ *adj.* (of philosophy) of the time before Socrates.

press[1] /pres/ *v. & n.* —*v.* **1** *tr.* apply steady force to (a thing in contact) (*press a switch*; *pressed the two surfaces together*). **2** *tr.* **a** compress or apply pressure to a thing to flatten, shape, or smooth it, as by ironing (*got the curtains pressed*). **b** squeeze (a fruit etc.) to extract its juice. **c** manufacture (a gramophone record etc.) by moulding under pressure. **3** *tr.* (foll. by *out of, from*, etc.) squeeze (juice etc.). **4** *tr.* embrace or caress by squeezing (*pressed my hand*). **5** *intr.* (foll. by *on, against*, etc.) exert pressure. **6** *intr.* be urgent; demand immediate action (*time was pressing*). **7** *intr.* (foll. by *for*) make an insistent demand. **8** *intr.* (foll. by *up, round*, etc.) form a crowd. **9** *intr.* (foll. by *on, forward*, etc.) hasten insistently. **10** *tr.* (often in *passive*) (of an enemy etc.) bear heavily on. **11** *tr.* (often foll. by *for, or to* + infin.) urge or entreat (*pressed me to stay*; *pressed me for an answer*). **12** *tr.* (foll. by *on, upon*) **a** put forward or urge (an opinion, claim, or course of action). **b** insist on the acceptance of (an offer, a gift, etc.). **13** *tr.* insist on (*did not press the point*). **14** *intr.* (foll. by *on*) produce a strong mental or moral impression; oppress; weigh heavily. **15** *intr.* *Golf* try too hard for a long shot etc. and so strike the ball imperfectly. —*n.* **1** the act or an instance of pressing (*give it a slight press*). **2 a** a device for compressing, flattening, shaping, extracting juice, etc. (*trouser press*; *flower press*; *wine press*). **b** a machine that applies pressure to a workpiece by means of a tool, in order to punch shapes, bend it, etc. **3** = *printing-press*. **4** (prec. by *the*) **a** the art or practice of printing. **b** newspapers, journalists, etc., generally or collectively (*read it in the press*; *pursued by the press*). **5** a notice or piece of publicity in newspapers etc. (*got a good press*). **6** (**Press**) **a** a printing house or establishment. **b** a publishing company (*Athlone Press*). **7 a** crowding. **b** a crowd (of people etc.). **8** the pressure of affairs. **9** esp. *Ir. & Sc.* a large usu. shelved cupboard for clothes, books, etc., esp. in a recess. □**at** (or **in**) **press** (or **the press**) being printed. **be pressed for** have barely enough (time etc.). **go** (or **send**) **to press** go or send to be printed. **press agent** a person employed to attend to advertising and press publicity. **press-box** a reporters' enclosure esp. at a sports event. **press the button** **1** set machinery in motion. **2** *colloq*. take a decisive initial step. **press-button** *adj*. = *push-button*. **press conference** an interview given to journalists to make an announcement or answer questions. **press gallery** a gallery for reporters esp. in a legislative assembly. **press-on** (of a material) that can be pressed or ironed on. **press release** an official statement issued to newspapers for information. **press-stud** a small fastening device engaged by pressing its two halves together. **press-up** an exercise in which the prone downward-facing body is raised from the legs or trunk upwards by pressing down on the hands to straighten the arms. [ME f. OF *presser, presse* f. L *pressare* frequent. of *premere press-*]

press² /pres/ *v. & n.* —*v.tr.* **1** *hist.* force to serve in the army or navy. **2** bring into use as a makeshift (*was pressed into service*). —*n. hist.* compulsory enlistment esp. in the navy. [alt. f. obs. *prest* (v. & n.) f. OF *prest* loan, advance pay f. *prester* f. L *praestare* furnish (as PRAE-, *stare* stand)]

press-gang /ˈpresgæŋ/ *n. & v.* —*n.* **1** *hist.* a body of men employed to press men into service in the army or navy. **2** any group using similar coercive methods. —*v.tr.* force into service.

pressie /ˈprezi/ *n.* (also **prezzie**) *colloq.* a present or gift. [abbr.]

pressing /ˈpresɪŋ/ *adj. & n.* —*adj.* **1** urgent (*pressing business*). **2 a** urging strongly (*a pressing invitation*). **b** persistent, importunate (*since you are so pressing*). —*n.* **1** a thing made by pressing, esp. a gramophone record. **2** a series of these made at one time. **3** the act or an instance of pressing a thing, esp. a gramophone record or grapes etc. (*all at one pressing*). □□ **pressingly** *adv.*

pressman /ˈpresmən/ *n.* (*pl.* **-men**) **1** a journalist. **2** an operator of a printing-press.

pressmark /ˈpresmɑːk/ *n.* a library shelf-mark showing the location of a book etc.

pressure /ˈpreʃə(r)/ *n. & v.* —*n.* **1 a** the exertion of continuous force on or against a body by another in contact with it. **b** the force exerted. **c** the amount of this (expressed by the force on a unit area) (*atmospheric pressure*). **2** urgency; the need to meet a deadline etc. (*work under pressure*). **3** affliction or difficulty (*under financial pressure*). **4** constraining influence (*if pressure is brought to bear*). —*v.tr.* **1** apply (esp. moral) pressure to. **2 a** coerce. **b** (often foll. by *into*) persuade (*was pressured into attending*). □**pressure-cook** cook in a pressure-cooker. **pressure-cooker** an airtight pan for cooking quickly under steam pressure. **pressure gauge** a gauge showing the pressure of steam etc. **pressure group** a group or association formed to promote a particular interest or cause by influencing public policy. **pressure point** **1** a point where an artery can be pressed against a bone to inhibit bleeding. **2** a point on the skin sensitive to pressure. **3** a target for political pressure or influence. **pressure suit** an inflatable suit for flying at a high altitude. [ME f. L *pressura* (as PRESS¹)]

pressurize /ˈpreʃəraɪz/ *v.tr.* (also **-ise**) **1** (esp. as **pressurized** *adj.*) maintain normal atmospheric pressure in (an aircraft cabin etc.) at a high altitude. **2** raise to a high pressure. **3** pressure (a person). □**pressurized-water reactor** a nuclear reactor in which the coolant is water at high pressure. □□ **pressurization** /-ˈzeɪʃ(ə)n/ *n.*

Prestel /ˈprestel/ *n. propr.* (in the UK) the computerized visual information system operated by British Telecom. [PRESS¹ + TELECOMMUNICATION]

prestidigitator /ˌprestɪˈdɪdʒɪˌteɪtə(r)/ *n. formal* a

conjuror. □□ **prestidigitation** /-ˈteɪʃ(ə)n/ *n.* [F *prestidigitateur* f. *preste* nimble (as PRESTO) + L *digitus* finger]

prestige /preˈstiːʒ/ *n.* **1** respect, reputation, or influence derived from achievements, power, associations, etc. **2** (*attrib.*) having or conferring prestige. □□ **prestigeful** *adj.* [F, = illusion, glamour, f. LL *praestigium* (as PRESTIGIOUS)]

prestigious /preˈstɪdʒəs/ *adj.* having or showing prestige. □□ **prestigiously** *adv.* **prestigiousness** *n.* [orig. = deceptive, f. L *praestigiosus* f. *praestigiae* juggler's tricks]

prestissimo /preˈstɪsɪˌməʊ/ *adv. & n. Mus.* —*adv.* in a very quick tempo. —*n.* (*pl.* **-os**) a movement or passage played in this way. [It., superl. (as PRESTO 1)]

presto /ˈprestəʊ/ *adv. & n.* —*adv.* **1** *Mus.* in quick tempo. **2** (in a conjuror's formula in performing a trick) quickly (*hey presto!*). —*n.* (*pl.* **-os**) *Mus.* a movement to be played in a quick tempo. [It. f. LL *praestus* f. L *praesto* ready]

prestressed /priːˈstrest/ *adj.* strengthened by stressing in advance, esp. of concrete by means of stretched rods or wires put in during manufacture.

presumably /prɪˈzjuːməblɪ/ *adv.* as may reasonably be presumed.

presume /prɪˈzjuːm/ *v.* **1** *tr.* (often foll. by *that* + clause) suppose to be true; take for granted. **2** *tr.* (often foll. by *to* + infin.) **a** take the liberty; be impudent enough (*presumed to question their authority*). **b** dare, venture (*may I presume to ask?*). **3** *intr.* be presumptuous; take liberties. **4** *intr.* (foll. by *on, upon*) take advantage of or make unscrupulous use of (a person's good nature etc.). □□ **presumable** *adj.* **presumedly** *adv.* [ME f. OF *presumer* f. L *praesumere praesumpt-* anticipate, venture (as PRAE-, *sumere* take)]

presuming /prɪˈzjuːmɪŋ/ *adj.* presumptuous. □□ **presumingly** *adv.* **presumingness** *n.*

presumption /prɪˈzʌmpʃ(ə)n/ *n.* **1** arrogance; presumptuous behaviour. **2 a** the act of presuming a thing to be true. **b** a thing that is or may be presumed to be true. **3** a ground for presuming (*a strong presumption against their being guilty*). **4** *Law* an inference from known facts. [ME f. OF *presumpcion* f. L *praesumptio -onis* (as PRESUME)]

presumptive /prɪˈzʌmptɪv/ *adj.* giving grounds for presumption (*presumptive evidence*). □□ **presumptively** *adv.* [F *présomptif -ive* f. LL *praesumptivus* (as PRESUME)]

presumptuous /prɪˈzʌmptjʊəs/ *adj.* unduly or overbearingly confident and presuming. □□ **presumptuously** *adv.* **presumptuousness** *n.* [ME f. OF *presumptueux* f. LL *praesumptuosus, -tiosus* (as PRESUME)]

presuppose /ˌpriːsəˈpəʊz/ *v.tr.* (often foll. by *that* + clause) **1** assume beforehand. **2** imply. [ME f. OF *presupposer*, after med.L *praesupponere* (as PRE-, SUPPOSE)]

presupposition /ˌpriːsʌpəˈzɪʃ(ə)n/ *n.* **1** the act or an instance of presupposing. **2** a thing assumed beforehand as the basis of argument etc. [med.L *praesuppositio* (as PRAE-, *supponere* as SUPPOSE)]

pre-tax /priːˈtæks, ˈpriːtæks/ *adj.* (of income or profits) before the deduction of taxes.

pre-teen /priːˈtiːn/ *adj.* of or relating to a child before the age of thirteen.

pretence /prɪˈtens/ *n.* (*US* **pretense**) **1** pretending, make-believe. **2 a** a pretext or excuse (*on the slightest pretence*). **b** a false show of intentions or motives (*under the pretence of friendship*; *under false pretences*). **3** (foll. by *to*) a claim, esp. a false or ambitious one (*has no pretence to any great talent*). **4 a** affectation, display. **b** pretentiousness, ostentation (*stripped of all pretence*). [ME f. AF *pretense* ult. f. med.L *pretensus* pretended (as PRETEND)]

pretend /prɪˈtend/ *v. & adj.* —*v.* **1** *tr.* claim or assert falsely so as to deceive (*pretend knowledge*; *pretended that they were foreigners*). **2** *tr.* imagine to oneself in play (*pretended to be monsters*; *pretended it was night*). **3** *tr.* **a** profess, esp. falsely or extravagantly (*does not pretend to be a scholar*). **b** (as **pretended** *adj.*) falsely claim to be such (*a pretended friend*). **4** *intr.* (foll. by *to*) **a** lay claim to (a right or title etc.). **b** profess to have (a quality etc.). —*adj. colloq.* pretended; in pretence (*pretend money*). [ME f. F *prétendre* or f. L (as PRAE-, *tendere tent*-, later *tens*- stretch)]

pretender /prɪˈtendə(r)/ *n.* **1** a person who claims a throne or title etc. **2** a person who pretends.

pretense *US* var. of PRETENCE.

pretension /prɪˈtenʃ(ə)n/ *n.* **1** (often foll. by *to*) **a** an assertion of a claim. **b** a justifiable claim (*has no pretensions to the name*; *has some pretensions to be included*). **2** pretentiousness. [med.L *praetensio, -tio* (as PRETEND)]

pretentious /prɪˈtenʃəs/ *adj.* **1** making an excessive claim to great merit or importance. **2** ostentatious. □□ **pretentiously** *adv.* **pretentiousness** *n.* [F *prétentieux* (as PRETENSION)]

preter- /ˈpriːtə(r)/ *comb. form* more than. [L *praeter* (adv. & prep.), = past, beyond]

preterite /ˈpretərɪt/ *adj. & n.* (*US* **preterit**) *Gram.* —*adj.* expressing a past action or state. —*n.* a preterite tense or form. [ME f. OF *preterite* or L *praeteritus* past part. of *praeterire* pass (as PRETER-, *ire it-* go)]

preterm /priːˈtɜːm/ *adj. & adv.* born or occurring prematurely.

pretermit /ˌpriːtəˈmɪt/ *v.tr.* (**pretermitted**, **pretermitting**) *formal* **1** omit to mention (a fact etc.). **2** omit to do or perform; neglect. **3** leave off (a custom or continuous action) for a time. □□ **pretermission** /-ˈmɪʃ(ə)n/ *n.* [L *praetermittere* (as PRETER-, *mittere miss-* let go)]

preternatural /ˌpriːtəˈnætʃər(ə)l/ *adj.* outside the ordinary course of nature; supernatural. □□ **preternaturalism** *n.* **preternaturally** *adv.*

pretext /ˈpriːtekst/ *n.* **1** an ostensible or alleged reason or intention. **2** an excuse offered. □**on** (or **under**) **the pretext** (foll. by *of*, or *that* + clause) professing as one's object or intention. [L *praetextus* outward display f. *praetexere praetext-* (as PRAE-, *texere* weave)]

pretor *US* var. of PRAETOR.

pretorian *US* var. of PRAETORIAN.

prettify /ˈprɪtɪfaɪ/ *v.tr.* (**-ies**, **-ied**) make (a thing or person) pretty esp. in an affected way. □□ **prettification** /-fɪˈkeɪʃ(ə)n/ *n.* **prettifier** *n.*

pretty /ˈprɪtɪ/ *adj., n., v., & adv.* —*adj.* (**prettier**, **prettiest**) **1** attractive in a delicate way without being truly beautiful or handsome (*a pretty child*; *a pretty dress*; *a pretty tune*). **2** fine or good of its kind (*a pretty wit*). **3** *iron.* considerable, fine (*a pretty penny*; *a pretty mess you have made*). —*adv. colloq.* fairly, moderately (*am pretty well*; *find it pretty difficult*). —*n.* (*pl.* **-ies**) a pretty person (esp. as a form of address to a child). —*v.tr.* (**-ies**, **-ied**) (often foll. by *up*) make pretty or attractive. □**pretty much** (or **nearly** or **well**) *colloq.* almost; very nearly. **pretty-pretty** too pretty. **sitting pretty** *colloq.* in a favourable or advantageous position. □□ **prettily** *adv.* **prettiness** *n.* **prettyish** *adj.* **prettyism** *n.* [OE *prættig* f. WG]

pretzel /ˈprets(ə)l/ *n.* (also **bretzel** /ˈbret-/) a crisp knot-shaped or stick-shaped salted biscuit. [G]

prevail /prɪˈveɪl/ *v.intr.* **1** (often foll. by *against*, *over*) be victorious or gain mastery. **2** be the more usual or predominant. **3** exist or occur in general use or experience; be current. **4** (foll. by *on*, *upon*) persuade. □**prevailing wind** the wind that most frequently occurs at a place. □□ **prevailingly** *adv.* [ME f. L *praevalēre* (as PRAE-, *valēre* have power), infl. by AVAIL]

prevalent /ˈprevələnt/ *adj.* **1** generally existing or occurring. **2** predominant. □□ **prevalence** *n.* **prevalently** *adv.* [as PREVAIL]

prevaricate /prɪˈværɪkeɪt/ *v.intr.* **1** speak or act evasively or misleadingly. **2** quibble, equivocate. ¶ Often confused with *procrastinate.* □□ **prevarication** /-ˈkeɪʃ(ə)n/ *n.* **prevaricator** *n.* [L *praevaricari* walk crookedly, practise collusion, in eccl.L transgress (as PRAE-, *varicari* straddle f. *varus* bent, knock-kneed)]

prevenient /prɪˈviːnɪənt/ *adj. formal* preceding something else. [L *praeveniens* pres. part of *praevenire* (as PREVENT)]

prevent /prɪˈvent/ *v.tr.* **1** (often foll. by *from* + verbal noun) stop from happening or doing something; hinder; make impossible (*the weather prevented me from going*). **2** *archaic* go or arrive before, precede. □□ **preventable** *adj.* (also **preventible**). **preventability** /-təˈbɪlɪtɪ/ *n.* (also **preventibility**). **preventer** *n.* **prevention** *n.* [ME = anticipate, f. L *praevenire praevent-* come before, hinder (as PRAE-, *venire* come)]

preventative /prɪˈventətɪv/ *adj. & n.* = PREVENTIVE. □□ **preventatively** *adv.*

preventive /prɪˈventɪv/ *adj. & n.* —*adj.* serving to prevent, esp. preventing disease, breakdown, etc. (*preventive medicine*; *preventive maintenance*). —*n.* a preventive agent, measure, drug, etc. □**preventive detention** the imprisonment of a criminal for corrective training etc. □□ **preventively** *adv.*

preview /ˈpriːvjuː/ *n. & v.* —*n.* **1** the act of seeing in advance. **2 a** the showing of a film, play, exhibition, etc., before it is seen by the general public. **b** (*US* **prevue**) a film trailer. —*v.tr.* see or show in advance.

previous /ˈpriːvɪəs/ *adj. & adv.* —*adj.* **1** (often foll. by *to*) coming before in time or order. **2** done or acting hastily. —*adv.* (foll. by *to*) before (*had called previous to writing*). □**previous question** *Parl.* a motion concerning the vote on a main question. □□ **previously** *adv.* **previousness** *n.* [L *praevius* (as PRAE-, *via* way)]

previse /prɪˈvaɪz/ *v.tr. literary* foresee or forecast (an event etc.). □□ **prevision** /-ˈvɪʒ(ə)n/ *n.* **previsional** /-ˈvɪʒən(ə)l/ *adj.* [L *praevidēre praevis-* (as PRAE-, *vidēre* see)]

prevue *US* var. of PREVIEW *n.* 2b.

pre-war /priːˈwɔː(r), ˈpriːwɔː(r)/ *adj.* existing or occurring before a war (esp. the most recent major war).

prey /preɪ/ *n. & v.* —*n.* **1** an animal that is hunted or killed by another for food. **2** (often foll. by *to*) a person or thing that is influenced by or vulnerable to (something undesirable) (*became a prey to morbid fears*). **3** *Bibl.* or *archaic* plunder, booty, etc. —*v.intr.* (foll. by *on, upon*) **1** seek or take as prey. **2** make a victim of. **3** (of a disease, emotion, etc.) exert a harmful influence (*fear preyed on his mind*). □**beast** (or **bird**) **of prey** an animal (or bird) which hunts animals for food. □□ **preyer** *n.* [ME f. OF *preie* f. L *praeda* booty]

prezzie var. of PRESSIE.

priapic /praɪˈæpɪk/ *adj.* phallic. [*Priapos* (as PRIAPISM) + -IC]

priapism /ˈpraɪəpɪz(ə)m/ *n.* **1** lewdness, licentiousness. **2** *Med.* persistent erection of the penis. [F *priapisme* f. LL *priapismus* f. Gk *priapismos* f. *priapizō* be lewd f. *Priapos* god of procreation]

price /praɪs/ *n. & v.* —*n.* **1 a** the amount of money or goods for which a thing is bought or sold. **b** value or worth (*a pearl of great price*; *beyond price*). **2** what is or must be given, done, sacrificed, etc., to obtain or achieve something. **3** the odds in betting (*starting price*). —*v.tr.* **1** fix or find the price of (a thing for sale). **2** estimate the value of. □**above** (or **beyond**) or **without**) **price** so valuable that no price can be stated. **at any price** no matter what the cost, sacrifice, etc. (*peace at any price*). **at a price** at a high cost. **price-fixing** the maintaining of prices at a certain level by agreement between competing sellers. **price-list** a list of current prices of items on sale. **price on a person's head** a reward for a person's capture or death. **price oneself out of the market** lose to one's competitors by charging more than customers are willing to pay. **price-ring** a group of traders acting illegally to control certain prices. **price tag 1** the label on an item showing its price. **2** the cost of an enterprise or undertaking. **price war** fierce competition among traders cutting prices. **set a price on** declare the price of. **what price . . .?** (often foll. by verbal noun) *colloq.* **1** what is the chance of . . .? (*what price your finishing the course?*). **2** *iron.* the expected or much boasted . . . proves disappointing (*what price your friendship now?*). □□ **priced** *adj.* (also in *comb.*). **pricer** *n.* [(n.) ME f. OF *pris* f. L *pretium*: (v.) var. of *prise* = PRIZE¹]

priceless /ˈpraɪslɪs/ *adj.* **1** invaluable; beyond price. **2** *colloq.* very amusing or absurd. □□ **pricelessly** *adv.* **pricelessness** *n.*

pricey /ˈpraɪsɪ/ *adj.* (also **pricy**) (**pricier, priciest**) *colloq.* expensive. □□ **priciness** *n.*

prick /prɪk/ *v. & n.* —*v.* **1** *tr.* pierce slightly; make a small hole in. **2** *tr.* (foll. by *off, out*) mark (esp. a pattern) with small holes or dots. **3** *tr.* trouble mentally (*my conscience is pricking me*). **4** *intr.* feel a pricking sensation. **5** *intr.* (foll. by *at, into,* etc.) make a thrust as if to prick. **6** *tr.* (foll. by *in, off, out*) plant (seedlings etc.) in small holes pricked in the earth. **7** *tr. Brit. archaic* mark off (a name in a list, esp. to select a sheriff) by pricking. **8** *tr. archaic* spur or urge on (a horse etc.). —*n.* **1** the act or an instance of pricking. **2** a small hole or mark made by pricking. **3** a pain caused as by pricking. **4** a mental pain (*felt the pricks of conscience*). **5** *coarse sl.* **a** the penis. **b** *derog.* (as a term of contempt) a person. ¶ Usually considered a taboo use. **6** *archaic* a goad for oxen. □**kick against the pricks** persist in futile resistance. **prick up one's ears 1** (of a dog etc.) make the ears erect when on the alert. **2** (of a person) become suddenly attentive. □□ **pricker** *n.* [OE *pri-cian* (v.), *pricca* (n.)]

pricket /ˈprɪkɪt/ *n.* **1** *Brit.* a male fallow deer in its second year, having straight unbranched horns. **2** a spike for holding a candle. [ME f. AL *prikettus -um,* dimin. of PRICK]

prickle /ˈprɪk(ə)l/ *n. & v.* —*n.* **1 a** a small thorn. **b** *Bot.* a thornlike process developed from the epidermis of a plant. **2** a hard-pointed spine of a hedgehog etc. **3** a prickling sensation. —*v.tr. & intr.* affect or be affected with a sensation as of pricking. [OE *pricel* PRICK: v.) also dimin. of PRICK]

prickly /ˈprɪklɪ/ *adj.* (**pricklier, prickliest**) **1** (esp. in the names of plants and animals) having prickles. **2** (of a person) ready to take offence. **3** tingling. □**prickly heat** an itchy inflammation of the skin, causing a tingling sensation and common in hot countries. **prickly pear 1** any cactus of the genus *Opuntia,* native to arid regions of America, bearing barbed bristles and large pear-shaped prickly fruits. **2** its fruit. **prickly poppy** a tropical poppy-like plant, *Argemone mexicana,* with prickly leaves and yellow flowers. □□ **prickliness** *n.*

pricy var. of PRICEY.

pride /praɪd/ *n. & v.* —*n.* **1 a** a feeling of elation or satisfaction at achievements or qualities or possessions etc. that do one credit. **b** an object of this feeling. **2** a high or overbearing opinion of one's worth or importance. **3** (in full **proper pride**) a proper sense of what befits one's position; self-respect. **4** a group or company (of animals, esp. lions). **5** the best condition; the prime. —*v.refl.* (foll. by *on, upon*) be proud of. □**my, his,** etc. **pride and joy** a thing of which one is very proud. **pride of the morning** a mist or shower at sunrise, supposedly indicating a fine day to come. **pride of place** the most important or prominent position. **take pride (or a pride) in 1** be proud of. **2** maintain in good condition or appearance. □□ **prideful** *adj.* **pridefully** *adv.* **prideless** *adj.* [OE *prȳtu, prȳte, prȳde* f. *prūd* PROUD]

prie-dieu /priːˈdjɜː/ *n.* (*pl.* **prie-dieux** *pronunc.* same) a kneeling-desk for prayer. [F, = pray God]

priest /priːst/ *n.* **1** an ordained minister of the Roman Catholic or Orthodox Church, or of the Anglican Church (above a deacon and below a bishop), authorized to perform certain rites and administer certain sacraments. **2** an official minister of a non-Christian religion. □**priest's hole** *hist.* a hiding-place for a Roman Catholic priest during times of religious persecution. □□ **priestless** *adj.* **priestlike** *adj.* **priestling** *n.* [OE *prēost,* ult. f. eccl.L *presbyter*: see PRESBYTER]

priestcraft /ˈpriːstkrɑːft/ *n.* usu. *derog.* the work and influence of priests.

priestess /ˈpriːstɪs/ *n.* a female priest of a non-Christian religion.

priesthood /ˈpriːsthʊd/ *n.* (usu. prec. by *the*) **1** the office or position of priest. **2** priests in general.

priestly /ˈpriːstlɪ/ *adj.* of or associated with priests. □□ **priestliness** *n.* [OE *prēostlic* (as PRIEST)]

prig /prɪg/ *n.* a self-righteously correct or moralistic person. □□ **priggery** *n.* **priggish** *adj.* **priggishly** *adv.* **priggishness** *n.* [16th-c. cant, = tinker: orig. unkn.]

prim /prɪm/ *adj. & v.* —*adj.* (**primmer, primmest**) **1** (of a person or manner) stiffly formal and precise. **2** (of a woman or girl) demure. **3** prudish. —*v.tr.* (**primmed, primming**) **1** form (the face, lips, etc.) into a prim expression. **2** make prim. □□ **primly** *adv.* **primness** *n.* [17th c.: prob. orig. cant f. OF *prin prime* excellent f. L *primus* first]

prima ballerina /ˌpriːmə ˌbælə'riːnə/ *n.* the chief female dancer in a ballet or ballet company. [It.]

primacy /ˈpraɪməsɪ/ *n.* (*pl.* **-ies**) **1** pre-eminence. **2** the office of a primate. [ME f. OF *primatie* or med.L *primatia* (as PRIMATE)]

prima donna /ˌpriːmə ˈdɒnə/ *n.* (*pl.* **prima donnas**) **1** the chief female singer in an opera or opera company. **2** a temperamentally self-important person. □□ **prima donna-ish** *adj.* [It.]

primaeval var. of PRIMEVAL.

prima facie /ˌpraɪmə ˈfeɪʃiː/ *adv. & adj.* —*adv.* at first sight; from a first impression (*seems prima facie to be guilty*). —*adj.* (of evidence) based on the first impression (*can see a prima facie reason for it*). [ME f. L, fem. ablat. of *primus* first, *facies* FACE]

primal /ˈpraɪm(ə)l/ *adj.* **1** primitive, primeval. **2** chief, fundamental. □□ **primally** *adv.* [med.L *primalis* f. L *primus* first]

primary /ˈpraɪmərɪ/ *adj. & n.* —*adj.* **1 a** of the first importance; chief (*that is our primary concern*). **b** fundamental, basic. **2** earliest, original; first in a series. **3** of the first rank in a series; not derived (*the primary meaning of a word*). **4** designating any of the colours red, green, and blue, or for pigments red, blue, and yellow, from which all other colours can be obtained by mixing. **5** (of a battery or cell) generating electricity by irreversible chemical reaction. **6** (of education) for young children, esp. below the age of 11. **7** (**Primary**) *Geol.* of the lowest series of strata. **8** *Biol.* belonging to the first stage of development. **9** (of an industry or source of production) concerned with obtaining or using raw materials. **10** *Gram.* (of a tense in Latin and Greek) present, future, perfect, or future perfect (cf. HISTORIC). —*n.* (*pl.* **-ies**) **1** a thing that is primary. **2** (in full **primary election**) (in the US) a preliminary election to appoint delegates to a party conference or to select the candidates for a principal (esp. presidential) election. **3** = *primary planet.* **4** (**Primary**) *Geol.* the Primary period. **5** = *primary feather.* **6** = *primary coil.* □**primary coil** a coil to which current is supplied in a transformer. **primary feather** a large flight-feather of a bird's wing. **primary planet** a planet that directly orbits the sun (cf. *secondary planet*). **primary school** a school where young children are taught, esp. below the age of 11. □□ **primarily** /'praɪmərɪlɪ, -'meərɪlɪ/ *adv.* [ME f. L *primarius* f. *primus* first]

primate /'praɪmeɪt/ *n.* **1** any animal of the order Primates, the highest order of mammals, including tarsiers, lemurs, apes, monkeys, and man. **2** an archbishop. □**Primate of All England** the Archbishop of Canterbury. **Primate of England** the Archbishop of York. □□ **primatial** /-'meɪʃ(ə)l/ *adj.* **primatology** /-mə'tɒlədʒɪ/ *n.* (in sense 1). [ME f. OF *primat* f. L *primas -atis* (adj.) of the first rank f. *primus* first, in med.L = primate]

primavera /ˌpriːmə'veɪrə/ *n.* **1** a Central American tree, *Cybistax donnellsmithii*, bearing yellow blooms. **2** the hard light-coloured timber from this. [Sp., = spring (the season) f. L *primus* first + *ver* SPRING]

prime[1] /praɪm/ *adj. & n.* —*adj.* **1** chief, most important (*the prime agent; the prime motive*). **2** (esp. of cattle and provisions) first-rate, excellent. **3** primary, fundamental. **4** *Math.* **a** (of a number) divisible only by itself and unity (e.g. 2, 3, 5, 7, 11). **b** (of numbers) having no common factor but unity. —*n.* **1** the state of the highest perfection of something (*in the prime of life*). **2** (prec. by *the*; foll. by *of*) the best part. **3** the beginning or first age of anything. **4** *Eccl.* **a** the second canonical hour of prayer, appointed for the first hour of the day (i.e. 6 a.m.). **b** the office of this. **c** *archaic* this time. **5** a prime number. **6** *Printing* a symbol (′) added to a letter etc. as a distinguishing mark, or to a figure as a symbol for minutes or feet. **7** the first of eight parrying positions in fencing. □**prime cost** the direct cost of a commodity in terms of materials, labour, etc. **prime meridian** **1** the meridian from which longitude is reckoned, esp. that passing through Greenwich. **2** the corresponding line on a map. **prime minister** the head of an elected government; the principal minister of a sovereign or State. **prime mover** **1** an initial natural or mechanical source of motive power. **2** the author of a fruitful idea. **prime rate** the lowest rate at which money can be borrowed commercially. **prime time** the time at which a radio or television audience is expected to be at its highest. **prime vertical** the great circle of the heavens passing through the zenith and the E. and W. points of the horizon. □□ **primeness** *n.* [(n.) OE *prīm* f. L *prima* (*hora*) first (hour), & MF f. OF *prime*: (adj.) ME f. OF f. L *primus* first]

prime[2] /praɪm/ *v.tr.* **1** prepare (a thing) for use or action. **2** prepare (a gun) for firing or (an explosive) for detonation. **3 a** pour (a liquid) into a pump to prepare it for working. **b** inject petrol into (the cylinder or carburettor of an internal-combustion engine). **4** prepare (wood etc.) for painting by applying a substance that prevents paint from being absorbed. **5** equip (a person) with information etc. **6** ply (a person) with food or drink in preparation for something. [16th c.: orig. unkn.]

primer[1] /'praɪmə(r)/ *n.* **1** a substance used to prime wood etc. **2** a cap, cylinder, etc., used to ignite the powder of a cartridge etc.

primer[2] /'praɪmə(r)/ *n.* **1** an elementary textbook for teaching children to read. **2** an introductory book. [ME f. AF f. med.L *primarius -arium* f. L *primus* first]

primeval /praɪ'miːv(ə)l/ *adj.* (also **primaeval**) **1** of or relating to the first age of the world. **2** ancient, primitive. □□ **primevally** *adv.* [L *primaevus* f. *primus* first + *aevum* age]

primigravida /ˌpriːmɪ'grævɪdə, ˌpraɪmɪ-/ *n.* (*pl.* **primigravidae** /-ˌdiː/) a woman who is pregnant for the first time. [mod.L fem. f. L *primus* first + *gravidus* pregnant: see GRAVID]

priming[1] /'praɪmɪŋ/ *n.* **1** a mixture used by painters for a preparatory coat. **2** a preparation of sugar added to beer. **3 a** gunpowder placed in the pan of a firearm. **b** a train of powder connecting the fuse with the charge in blasting etc.

priming[2] /'praɪmɪŋ/ *n.* an acceleration of the tides

taking place from the neap to the spring tides. [*prime* (v.) f. PRIME[1] + -ING[1]]

primipara /praɪ'mɪpərə/ *n.* (*pl.* **primiparae** /-ˌriː/) a woman who is bearing a child for the first time. □□ **primiparous** *adj.* [mod.L fem. f. *primus* first + *-parus* f. *parere* bring forth]

primitive /'prɪmɪtɪv/ *adj. & n.* —*adj.* **1** early, ancient; at an early stage of civilization (*primitive man*). **2** undeveloped, crude, simple (*primitive methods*). **3** original, primary. **4** *Gram. & Philol.* (of words or language) radical; not derivative. **5** *Math.* (of a line, figure, etc.) from which another is derived, from which some construction begins, etc. **6** (of a colour) primary. **7** *Geol.* of the earliest period. **8** *Biol.* appearing in the earliest or a very early stage of growth or evolution. —*n.* **1 a** a painter of the period before the Renaissance. **b** a modern imitator of such. **c** an untutored painter with a direct naïve style. **d** a picture by such a painter. **2** a primitive word, line, etc. □**the Primitive Church** the Christian Church in its earliest times. □□ **primitively** *adv.* **primitiveness** *n.* [ME f. OF *primitif -ive* or L *primitivus* first of its kind f. *primitus* in the first place f. *primus* first]

primitivism /'prɪmɪtɪˌvɪz(ə)m/ *n.* **1** primitive behaviour. **2** belief in the superiority of what is primitive. **3** the practice of primitive art. □□ **primitivist** *n. & adj.*

primo /'priːməʊ/ *n.* (*pl.* **-os**) *Mus.* the leading or upper part in a duet etc.

primogenitor /ˌpraɪməʊ'dʒenɪtə(r)/ *n.* **1** the earliest ancestor of a people etc. **2** an ancestor. [var. of *progenitor*, after PRIMOGENITURE]

primogeniture /ˌpraɪməʊ'dʒenɪtʃə(r)/ *n.* **1** the fact or condition of being the first-born child. **2** (in full **right of primogeniture**) the right of succession belonging to the first-born, esp. the feudal rule by which the whole real estate of an intestate passes to the eldest son. □□ **primogenital** *adj.* **primogenitary** *adj.* [med.L *primogenitura* f. L *primo* first + *genitura* f. *gignere genit-* beget]

primordial /praɪ'mɔːdɪəl/ *adj.* **1** existing at or from the beginning, primeval. **2** original, fundamental. □□ **primordiality** /-'ælɪtɪ/ *n.* **primordially** *adv.* [ME f. LL *primordialis* (as PRIMORDIUM)]

primordium /praɪ'mɔːdɪəm/ *n.* (*pl.* **primordia** /-dɪə/) *Biol.* an organ or tissue in the early stages of development. [L, neut. of *primordius* original f. *primus* first + *ordiri* begin]

primp /prɪmp/ *v.tr.* **1** make (the hair, one's clothes, etc.) tidy. **2** *refl.* make (oneself) smart. [dial. var. of PRIM]

primrose /'prɪmrəʊz/ *n.* **1 a** any plant of the genus *Primula*, esp. *P. vulgaris*, bearing pale yellow flowers. **b** the flower of this. **2** a pale yellow colour. □**primrose path** the pursuit of pleasure, esp. with disastrous consequences (with ref. to Shakesp. *Hamlet* I. iii. 50). [ME *primerose*, corresp. to OF *primerose* and med.L *prima rosa*, lit. first rose: reason for the name unkn.]

primula /'prɪmjʊlə/ *n.* any plant of the genus *Primula*, bearing primrose-like flowers in a wide variety of colours during the spring, including primroses, cowslips, and polyanthuses. [med.L, fem. of *primulus* dimin. of *primus* first]

primum mobile /ˌpraɪmʊm 'məʊbɪlɪ/ *n.* **1** the central or most important source of motion or action. **2** *Astron.* in the medieval version of the Ptolemaic system, an outer sphere supposed to move round the earth in 24 hours carrying the inner spheres with it. [med.L, = first moving thing]

Primus /'praɪməs/ *n. propr.* a brand of portable stove burning vaporized oil for cooking etc. [L (as PRIMUS)]

primus /'praɪməs/ *n.* the presiding bishop of the Scottish Episcopal Church. [L, = first]

primus inter pares /ˌpriːməs ˌɪntə 'pɑːriːz/ *n.* a first among equals; the senior or representative member of a group. [L]

prince /prɪns/ n. (as a title usu. **Prince**) **1** a male member of a royal family other than a reigning king. **2** (in full **prince of the blood**) a son or grandson of a British monarch. **3** a ruler of a small State, actually or nominally subject to a king or emperor. **4** (as an English rendering of foreign titles) a noble usu. ranking next below a duke. **5** (as a courtesy title in some connections) a duke, marquis, or earl. **6** (often foll. by *of*) the chief or greatest (*the prince of novelists*). □**Prince Charming** an idealized young hero or lover. **prince consort 1** the husband of a reigning female sovereign who is himself a prince. **2** the title conferred on him. **Prince of Darkness** Satan. **Prince of Peace** Christ. **Prince of Wales** the heir apparent to the British throne, as a title conferred by the monarch. **Prince Regent** a prince who acts as regent, esp. George (afterwards IV) as regent 1811–20. **prince royal** the eldest son of the reigning monarch. **prince's feather** a tall plant, *Amaranthus hypochondriacus*, with feathery spikes of small red flowers. **prince's metal** a brasslike alloy of copper and zinc. □□ **princedom** n. **princelet** n. **princelike** adj. **princeship** n. [ME f. OF f. L *princeps principis* first, chief, from *primus* first + *capere* take]

princeling /ˈprɪnslɪŋ/ n. a young or petty prince.

princely /ˈprɪnslɪ/ adj. (**princelier**, **princeliest**) **1 a** of or worthy of a prince. **b** held by a prince. **2** sumptuous, generous, splendid. □□ **princeliness** n.

princess /prɪnˈses/ n. (as a title usu. **Princess** /ˈprɪnses/) **1** the wife of a prince. **2** a female member of a royal family other than a reigning queen. **3** (in full **princess of the blood**) a daughter or granddaughter of a British monarch. **4** a pre-eminent woman or thing personified as a woman. □**Princess Regent 1** a princess who acts as regent. **2** the wife of a Prince Regent. **Princess Royal** a monarch's eldest daughter, as a title conferred by the monarch. [ME f. OF *princesse* (as PRINCE)]

principal /ˈprɪnsɪp(ə)l/ adj. & n. —adj. **1** (usu. attrib.) first in rank or importance; chief (*the principal town of the district*). **2** main, leading (*a principal cause of my success*). **3** (of money) constituting the original sum invested or lent. —n. **1** a head, ruler, or superior. **2** the head of some schools, colleges, and universities. **3** the leading performer in a concert, play, etc. **4** a capital sum as distinguished from interest or income. **5** a person for whom another acts as agent etc. **6** (in the UK) a civil servant of the grade below Secretary. **7** the person actually responsible for a crime. **8** a person for whom another is surety. **9** each of the combatants in a duel. **10 a** a main rafter supporting purlins. **b** a main girder. **11** an organ stop sounding an octave above the diapason. **12** *Mus.* the leading player in each section of an orchestra. □**principal boy** (or **girl**) an actress who takes the leading male (or female) part in a pantomime. **principal clause** *Gram.* a clause to which another clause is subordinate. **principal in the first degree** a person directly responsible for a crime as its actual perpetrator. **principal in the second degree** a person directly responsible for a crime as aiding in its perpetration. **principal parts** *Gram.* the parts of a verb from which all other parts can be deduced. □□ **principalship** n. [ME f. OF f. L *principalis* first, original (as PRINCE)]

principality /ˌprɪnsɪˈpælɪtɪ/ n. (pl. **-ies**) **1** a State ruled by a prince. **2** the government of a prince. **3** (in pl.) the fifth order of the ninefold celestial hierarchy. **4** (**the Principality**) *Brit.* Wales. [ME f. OF *principalité* f. LL *principalitas -tatis* (as PRINCIPAL)]

principally /ˈprɪnsɪpəlɪ/ adv. for the most part; chiefly.

principate /ˈprɪnsɪpət/ n. **1** a State ruled by a prince. **2** *Rom.Hist.* the rule of the early emperors during which some republican forms were retained. [ME f. OF *principat* or L *principatus* first place]

principle /ˈprɪnsɪp(ə)l/ n. **1** a fundamental truth or

law as the basis of reasoning or action (*arguing from first principles*; *moral principles*). **2 a** a personal code of conduct (*a person of high principle*). **b** (in pl.) such rules of conduct (*has no principles*). **3** a general law in physics etc. (*the uncertainty principle*). **4** a law of nature forming the basis for the construction or working of a machine etc. **5** a fundamental source; a primary element (*held water to be the first principle of all things*). **6** *Chem.* a constituent of a substance, esp. one giving rise to some quality, etc. □**in principle** as regards fundamentals but not necessarily in detail. **on principle** on the basis of a moral attitude (*I refuse on principle*). [ME f. OF *principe* f. L *principium* source, (in pl.) foundations (as PRINCE)]

principled /ˈprɪnsɪp(ə)ld/ adj. based on or having (esp. praiseworthy) principles of behaviour.

prink /prɪŋk/ v. **1** tr. (usu. refl.) **a** make (oneself etc.) smart. **b** (foll. by *up*) smarten (oneself) up. **c** (of a bird) preen. **2** intr. dress oneself up. [16th c.: prob. f. *prank* dress, adorn, rel. to MLG *prank* pomp, Du. *pronk* finery]

print /prɪnt/ n. & v. —n. **1** an indentation or mark on a surface left by the pressure of a thing in contact with it (*fingerprint*; *footprint*). **2 a** printed lettering or writing (*large print*). **b** words in printed form. **c** a printed publication, esp. a newspaper. **d** the quantity of a book etc. printed at one time. **e** the state of being printed. **3** a picture or design printed from a block or plate. **4** *Photog.* a picture produced on paper from a negative. **5** a printed cotton fabric. —v.tr. **1 a** produce or reproduce (a book, picture, etc.) by applying inked types, blocks, or plates, to paper, vellum, etc. **b** (of an author, publisher, or editor) cause (a book or manuscript etc.) to be produced or reproduced in this way. **2** express or publish in print. **3 a** (often foll. by *on, in*) impress or stamp (a mark or figure on a surface). **b** (often foll. by *with*) impress or stamp (a soft surface, e.g. of butter or wax, with a seal, die, etc.). **4** (often absol.) write (words or letters) without joining, in imitation of typography. **5** (often foll. by *off, out*) *Photog.* produce (a picture) by the transmission of light through a negative. **6** (usu. foll. by *out*) (of a computer etc.) produce output in printed form. **7** mark (a textile fabric) with a decorative design in colours. **8** (foll. by *on*) impress (an idea, scene, etc. on the mind or memory). **9** transfer (a coloured or plain design) from paper etc. to the unglazed or glazed surface of ceramic ware. □**appear in print** have one's work published. **in print 1** (of a book etc.) available from the publisher. **2** in printed form. **out of print** no longer available from the publisher. **printed circuit** an electric circuit with thin strips of conductor on a flat insulating sheet, usu. made by a process like printing. □□ **printable** adj. **printability** /-təˈbɪlɪtɪ/ n. **printless** adj. (in sense 1 of n.). [ME f. OF *priente*, *preinte*, fem. past part. of *preindre* press f. L *premere*]

printer /ˈprɪntə(r)/ n. **1** a person who prints books, magazines, advertising matter, etc. **2** the owner of a printing business. **3** a device that prints, esp. as part of a computer system. □**printer's devil** an errand-boy in a printer's office. **printer's mark** a device used as a printer's trade mark. **printer's pie** = PIE³ n.

printery /ˈprɪntərɪ/ n. (pl. **-ies**) *US* a printer's office or works.

printhead /ˈprɪnthed/ n. the component in a printer (see PRINTER 3) that assembles and prints the characters on the paper.

printing /ˈprɪntɪŋ/ n. **1** the production of printed books etc. **2** a single impression of a book. **3** printed letters or writing imitating them. □**printing-press** a machine for printing from types or plates etc.

printmaker /ˈprɪntˌmeɪkə(r)/ n. a person who makes print. □□ **printmaking** n.

printout /ˈprɪntaʊt/ n. computer output in printed form.

printworks /ˈprɪntwɜːks/ n. a factory where fabrics are printed.

prior /ˈpraɪə(r)/ adj., adv., & n. —adj. **1** earlier. **2** (often foll. by to) coming before in time, order, or importance. —adv. (foll. by to) before (decided prior to their arrival). —n. **1** the superior officer of a religious house or order. **2** (in an abbey) the officer next under the abbot. □□ **priorate** /-rət/ n. **prioress** n. **priorship** n. [L, = former, elder, compar. of OL pri = L prae before]

priority /praɪˈɒrɪtɪ/ n. (pl. -ies) **1** the fact or condition of being earlier or antecedent. **2** precedence in rank etc. **3** an interest having prior claim to consideration. □□ **prioritize** v.tr. (also -ise). **prioritization** /-taɪˈzeɪʃ(ə)n/ n. [ME f. OF priorité f. med.L prioritas -tatis f. L prior (as PRIOR)]

priory /ˈpraɪərɪ/ n. (pl. -ies) a monastery governed by a prior or a nunnery governed by a prioress. [ME f. AF priorie, med.L prioria (as PRIOR)]

prise /praɪz/ v. & n. (also **prize**) —v.tr. force open or out by leverage (prised up the lid; prised the box open). —n. leverage, purchase. [ME & OF prise levering instrument (as PRIZE[1])]

prism /ˈprɪz(ə)m/ n. **1** a solid geometric figure whose two ends are similar, equal, and parallel rectilinear figures, and whose sides are parallelograms. **2** a transparent body in this form, usu. triangular with refracting surfaces at an acute angle with each other, which separates white light into a spectrum of colours. □□ **prismal** /ˈprɪzm(ə)l/ adj. [LL prisma f. Gk prisma prismatos thing sawn f. prizō to saw]

prismatic /prɪzˈmætɪk/ adj. **1** of, like, or using a prism. **2 a** (of colours) distributed by or as if by a transparent prism. **b** (of light) displayed in the form of a spectrum. □□ **prismatically** adv. [F prismatique f. Gk prisma (as PRISM)]

prismoid /ˈprɪzmɔɪd/ n. a body like a prism, with similar but unequal parallel polygonal ends. □□ **prismoidal** /-ˈmɔɪd(ə)l/ adj.

prison /ˈprɪz(ə)n/ n. & v. —n. **1** a place in which a person is kept in captivity, esp. a building to which persons are legally committed while awaiting trial or for punishment; a jail. **2** custody, confinement (in prison). —v.tr. poet. (**prisoned**, **prisoning**) put in prison. □ **prison-breaking** escape from prison. **prison camp** a camp for prisoners of war or of State. [ME f. OF prisun, -on f. L prensio -onis f. prehensio f. prehendere prehens- lay hold of]

prisoner /ˈprɪznə(r)/ n. **1** a person kept in prison. **2** (in full **prisoner at the bar**) a person in custody on a criminal charge and on trial. **3** a person or thing confined by illness, another's grasp, etc. **4** (in full **prisoner of war**) a person who has been captured in war. □ **prisoner of conscience** see CONSCIENCE. **prisoner of State** (or **State prisoner**) a person confined for political reasons. **prisoner's base** a game played by two parties of boys etc., each occupying a distinct base or home. **take prisoner** seize and hold as a prisoner. [ME f. AF prisoner, OF prisonier (as PRISON)]

prissy /ˈprɪsɪ/ adj. (**prissier**, **prissiest**) prim, prudish. □□ **prissily** adv. **prissiness** n. [perh. f. PRIM + SISSY]

pristine /ˈprɪstiːn, ˈprɪstaɪn/ adj. **1** in its original condition; unspoilt. **2** disp. spotless; fresh as if new. **3** ancient, primitive. [L pristinus former]

prithee /ˈprɪðiː/ int. archaic pray, please. [= I pray thee]

privacy /ˈprɪvəsɪ, ˈpraɪ-/ n. **1 a** the state of being private and undisturbed. **b** a person's right to this. **2** freedom from intrusion or public attention. **3** avoidance of publicity.

private /ˈpraɪvət, -vɪt/ adj. & n. —adj. **1** belonging to an individual; one's own; personal (private property). **2** confidential; not to be disclosed to others (private talks). **3** kept or removed from public knowledge or observation. **4 a** not open to the public. **b** for an individual's exclusive use (private room). **5** (of a place) secluded; affording privacy. **6** (of a person) not holding public office or an official position. **7** (of education or medical treatment) conducted outside the State system, at the individual's expense. —n. **1** a private soldier. **2** (in pl.) colloq. the genitals. □ **in private** privately; in private company or life. **private bill** a parliamentary bill affecting an individual or corporation only. **private company** Brit. a company with restricted membership and no issue of shares. **private detective** a detective engaged privately, outside an official police force. **private enterprise 1** a business or businesses not under State control. **2** individual initiative. **private eye** colloq. a private detective. **private first class** US a soldier ranking above an ordinary private but below officers. **private hotel** a hotel not obliged to take all comers. **private house** the dwelling-house of a private person, as distinct from a shop, office, or public building. **private law** a law relating to individual persons and private property. **private life** life as a private person, not as an official, public performer, etc. **private means** income from investments etc., apart from earned income. **private member** a member of a legislative body not holding a government office. **private member's bill** a bill introduced by a private member, not part of government legislation. **private parts** the genitals. **private patient** Brit. a patient treated by a doctor other than under the National Health Service. **private practice** Brit. medical practice that is not part of the National Health Service. **private press** a printing establishment operated by a private person or group not primarily for profit and usu. on a small scale. **private school 1** Brit. a school supported wholly by the payment of fees. **2** US a school not supported mainly by the State. **private secretary** a secretary dealing with the personal and confidential concerns of a businessman or businesswoman. **private sector** the part of the economy free of direct State control. **private soldier** an ordinary soldier other than the officers (and US other than recruits). **private view** the viewing of an exhibition (esp. of paintings) before it is open to the public. **private war 1** a feud between persons or families disregarding the law of murder etc. **2** hostilities against members of another State without the sanction of one's own government. **private wrong** an offence against an individual but not against society as a whole. □□ **privately** adv. [ME f. L privatus, orig. past part. of privare deprive]

privateer /ˌpraɪvəˈtɪə(r)/ n. **1** an armed vessel owned and officered by private individuals holding a government commission and authorized for war service. **2 a** a commander of such a vessel. **b** (in pl.) its crew. □□ **privateering** n. [PRIVATE, after volunteer]

privateersman /ˌpraɪvəˈtɪəzmən/ n. (pl. **-men**) = PRIVATEER 2.

privation /praɪˈveɪʃ(ə)n/ n. **1** lack of the comforts or necessities of life (suffered many privations). **2** (often foll. by of) loss or absence (of a quality). [ME f. L privatio (as PRIVATE)]

privative /ˈprɪvətɪv/ adj. **1** consisting in or marked by the loss or removal or absence of some quality or attribute. **2** (of a term) denoting the privation or absence of a quality etc. **3** Gram. (of a particle etc.) expressing privation, as Gk a- = 'not'. □□ **privatively** adv. [F privatif -ive or L privativus (as PRIVATION)]

privatize /ˈpraɪvəˌtaɪz, -vɪˌtaɪz/ v.tr. (also **-ise**) make private, esp. assign (a business etc.) to private as distinct from State control or ownership; denationalize. □□ **privatization** /-ˈzeɪʃ(ə)n/ n.

privet /ˈprɪvɪt/ n. any evergreen shrub of the genus Ligustrum, esp. L. vulgare bearing small white flowers and black berries, and much used for hedges. [16th c.: orig. unkn.]

privilege /ˈprɪvɪlɪdʒ/ n. & v. —n. **1 a** a right, advantage, or immunity, belonging to a person, class, or office. **b** the freedom of members of a legislative assembly when speaking at its meetings. **2** a special benefit or honour (*it is a privilege to meet you*). **3** a monopoly or patent granted to an individual, corporation, etc. **4** *US Stock Exch.* an option. —*v.tr.* **1** invest with a privilege. **2** (foll. by *to* + infin.) allow (a person) as a privilege (to do something). **3** (often foll. by *from*) exempt (a person from a liability etc.). □□ **privileged** *adj.* [ME f. OF *privilege* f. L *privilegium* bill or law affecting an individual, f. *privus* private + *lex legis* law]

privity /'prɪvɪtɪ/ *n.* (*pl.* **-ies**) **1** *Law* a relation between two parties that is recognized by law, e.g. that of blood, lease, or service. **2** (often foll. by *to*) the state of being privy (to plans etc.). [ME f. OF *priveté* f. med.L *privitas -tatis* f. L *privus* private]

privy /'prɪvɪ/ *adj.* & *n.* —*adj.* **1** (foll. by *to*) sharing in the secret of (a person's plans etc.). **2** *archaic* hidden, secret. —*n.* (*pl.* **-ies**) **1** *US* or *archaic* a lavatory. **2** *Law* a person having a part or interest in any action, matter, or thing. □ **Privy Council 1** (in the UK) a body of advisers appointed by the sovereign (now chiefly on an honorary basis and including present and former government ministers etc.). **2** usu. *hist.* a sovereign's or governor-general's private counsellors. **privy counsellor** (or **councillor**) a private adviser, esp. a member of a Privy Council. **privy purse** *Brit.* **1** an allowance from the public revenue for the monarch's private expenses. **2** the keeper of this. **privy seal** (in the UK) a seal formerly affixed to documents that are afterwards to pass the Great Seal or that do not require it. □□ **privily** *adv.* [ME f. OF *privé* f. L *privatus* PRIVATE]

prize[1] /praɪz/ *n.* & *v.* —*n.* **1** something that can be won in a competition or lottery etc. **2** a reward given as a symbol of victory or superiority. **3** something striven for or worth striving for (*missed all the great prizes of life*). **4** (*attrib.*) **a** to which a prize is awarded (*a prize bull; a prize poem*). **b** supremely excellent or outstanding of its kind. —*v.tr.* value highly (*a much prized possession*). □ **prize-giving** an award of prizes, esp. formally at a school etc. **prize-money** money offered as a prize. **prize-ring 1** an enclosed area (now usu. a square) for prizefighting. **2** the practice of prizefighting. [(n.) ME, var. of PRICE: (v.) ME f. OF *pris-* stem of *preisier* PRAISE]

prize[2] /praɪz/ *n.* & *v.* —*n.* **1** a ship or property captured in naval warfare. **2** a find or windfall. —*v.tr.* make a prize of. □ **prize-court** a department of an admiralty court concerned with prizes. [ME f. OF *prise* taking, booty, fem. past part. of *prendre* f. L *prehendere prehens-* seize: later identified with PRIZE[1]]

prize[3] var. of PRISE.

prizefight /'praɪzfaɪt/ *n.* a boxing-match fought for prize-money. □□ **prizefighter** *n.*

prizeman /'praɪzmən/ *n.* (*pl.* **-men**) a winner of a prize, esp. a specified academic one.

prizewinner /'praɪzˌwɪnə(r)/ *n.* a winner of a prize. □□ **prizewinning** *adj.*

PRO *abbr.* **1** Public Record Office. **2** public relations officer.

pro[1] /prəʊ/ *n.* & *adj. colloq.* —*n.* (*pl.* **-os**) a professional. —*adj.* professional. □ **pro-am** involving professionals and amateurs. [abbr.]

pro[2] /prəʊ/ *adj., n., & prep.* —*adj.* (of an argument or reason) for; in favour. —*n.* (*pl.* **-os**) a reason or argument for or in favour. —*prep.* in favour of. □ **pros and cons** reasons or considerations for and against a proposition etc. [L, = for, on behalf of]

pro-[1] /prəʊ/ *prefix* **1** favouring or supporting (*pro-government*). **2** acting as a substitute or deputy for (*proconsul*). **3** forwards (*produce*). **4** forwards and downwards (*prostrate*). **5** onwards (*proceed; progress*). **6** in front of (*protect*). [L *pro* in front (of), for, on behalf of, instead of, on account of]

pro-[2] /prəʊ/ *prefix* before in time, place, order, etc. (*problem; proboscis; prophet*). [Gk *pro* before]

proa /'prəʊə/ *n.* (also **prau, prahu** /'prɑːuː/) a Malay

boat, esp. with a large triangular sail and a canoe-like outrigger. [Malay *prāū, prāhū*]

proactive /prəʊ'æktɪv/ *adj.* **1** (of a person, policy, etc.) creating or controlling a situation by taking the initiative. **2** of or relating to mental conditioning or a habit etc. which has been learned. □□ **proaction** /-'ækʃ(ə)n/ *n.* **proactively** *adv.* **proactivity** /-'tɪvɪtɪ/ *n.* [PRO-[2], after REACTIVE]

probability /ˌprɒbə'bɪlɪtɪ/ *n.* (*pl.* **-ies**) **1** the state or condition of being probable. **2** the likelihood of something happening. **3** a probable or most probable event (*the probability is that they will come*). **4** *Math.* the extent to which an event is likely to occur, measured by the ratio of the favourable cases to the whole number of cases possible. □ **in all probability** most probably. [F *probabilité* or L *probabilitas* (as PROBABLE)]

probable /'prɒbəb(ə)l/ *adj.* & *n.* —*adj.* (often foll. by *that* + clause) that may be expected to happen or prove true; likely (*the probable explanation; it is probable that they forgot*). —*n.* a probable candidate, member of a team, etc. □□ **probably** *adv.* [ME f. OF f. L *probabilis* f. *probare* prove]

proband /'prəʊbænd/ *n.* a person forming the starting-point for the genetic study of a family etc. [L *probandus*, gerundive of *probare* test]

probang /'prəʊbæŋ/ *n. Surgery* a strip of flexible material with a sponge or button etc. at the end for introducing into the throat. [17th c. (named *provang* by its inventor): orig. unkn., perh. alt. after *probe*]

probate /'prəʊbeɪt, -bət/ *n.* & *v.* —*n.* **1** the official proving of a will. **2** a verified copy of a will with a certificate as handed to the executors. —*v.tr. US* establish the validity of (a will). [ME f. L *probatum* neut. past part. of *probare* PROVE]

probation /prə'beɪʃ(ə)n/ *n.* **1** *Law* a system of suspending the sentence on an offender subject to a period of good behaviour under supervision. **2** a process or period of testing the character or abilities of a person in a certain role, esp. of a new employee. **3** a moral trial or discipline. □ **on probation** undergoing probation, esp. legal supervision. **probation officer** an official supervising offenders on probation. □□ **probational** *adj.* **probationary** *adj.* [ME f. OF *probation* or L *probatio* (as PROVE)]

probationer /prə'beɪʃənə(r)/ *n.* **1** a person on probation, e.g. a newly appointed nurse, teacher, etc. **2** an offender on probation. □□ **probationership** *n.*

probative /'prəʊbətɪv/ *adj.* affording proof; evidential. [L *probativus* (as PROVE)]

probe /prəʊb/ *n.* & *v.* —*n.* **1** a penetrating investigation. **2** any small device, esp. an electrode, for measuring, testing, etc. **3** a blunt-ended surgical instrument usu. of metal for exploring a wound etc. **4** (in full **space probe**) an unmanned exploratory spacecraft transmitting information about its environment. —*v.tr.* **1** examine or enquire into closely. **2** explore (a wound or part of the body) with a probe. **3** penetrate with a sharp instrument. □□ **probeable** *adj.* **prober** *n.* **probingly** *adv.* [LL *proba* proof, in med.L = examination, f. L *probare* test]

probit /'prɒbɪt/ *n. Statistics* a unit of probability based on deviation from the mean of a standard distribution. [*probability unit*]

probity /'prəʊbɪtɪ, 'prɒ-/ *n.* uprightness, honesty. [F *probité* or L *probitas* f. *probus* good]

problem /'prɒbləm/ *n.* **1** a doubtful or difficult matter requiring a solution (*how to prevent it is a problem; the problem of ventilation*). **2** something hard to understand or accomplish or deal with. **3** (*attrib.*) **a** causing problems; difficult to deal with (*problem child*). **b** (of a play, novel, etc.) in which a social or other problem is treated. **4 a** *Physics & Math.* an inquiry starting from given conditions to investigate or demonstrate a fact, result, or law. **b** *Geom.* a proposition in which something has to be constructed (cf. THEOREM). **5 a** (in various games, esp. chess) an arrangement of men, cards, etc., in which the solver

---

æ *cat* ɑː *arm* e *bed* ɜː *her* ɪ *sit* iː *see* ɒ *hot* ɔː *saw* ʌ *run* ʊ *put* uː *too* ə *ago* aɪ *my*

has to achieve a specified result. **b** a puzzle or question for solution. [ME f. OF *probleme* or L *problema* f. Gk *problēma -matos* f. *proballō* (as PRO-², *ballō* throw)]

problematic /ˌprɒbləˈmætɪk/ *adj.* (also **problematical**) **1** attended by difficulty. **2** doubtful or questionable. **3** *Logic* enunciating or supporting what is possible but not necessarily true. □□ **problematically** *adv.* [F *problématique* or LL *problematicus* f. Gk *problēmatikos* (as PROBLEM)]

proboscidean /ˌprɒbəˈsɪdɪən/ *adj. & n.* (also **proboscidian**) —*adj.* **1** having a proboscis. **2** of or like a proboscis. **3** of the mammalian order Proboscidea, including elephants and their extinct allies. —*n.* a mammal of this order. [mod.L *Proboscidea* (as PROBOSCIS)]

proboscis /prəˈbɒsɪs/ *n.* **1** the long flexible trunk or snout of some mammals, e.g. an elephant or tapir. **2** the elongated mouth parts of some insects. **3** the sucking organ in some worms. **4** *joc.* the human nose. □**proboscis monkey** a monkey, *Nasalis larvatus*, native to Borneo, the male of which has a large pendulous nose. □□ **proboscidiferous** /-sɪˈdɪfərəs/ *adj.* **proboscidiform** /-ˈsɪdɪˌfɔːm/ *adj.* [L *proboscis -cidis* f. Gk *proboskis* f. *proboskō* (as PRO-², *boskō* feed)]

procaine /ˈprəʊkeɪn/ *n.* (also **procain**) a synthetic compound used as a local anaesthetic. [PRO-¹ + COCAINE]

procaryote var. of PROKARYOTE.

procedure /prəˈsiːdjə(r), -dʒə(r)/ *n.* **1** a way of proceeding, esp. a mode of conducting business or a legal action. **2** a mode of performing a task. **3** a series of actions conducted in a certain order or manner. **4** a proceeding. **5** *Computing* = SUBROUTINE. □□ **procedural** *adj.* **procedurally** *adv.* [F *procédure* (as PROCEED)]

proceed /prəˈsiːd, prəʊ-/ *v.intr.* **1** (often foll. by *to*) go forward or on further; make one's way. **2** (often foll. by *with*, or *to* + infin.) continue; go on with an activity (*proceeded with their work*; *proceeded to tell the whole story*). **3** (of an action) be carried on or continued (*the case will now proceed*). **4** adopt a course of action (*how shall we proceed?*). **5** go on to say. **6** (foll. by *against*) start a lawsuit (against a person). **7** (often foll. by *from*) come forth or originate (*shouts proceeded from the bedroom*). **8** (foll. by *to*) *Brit.* take the degree of (MA etc.). [ME f. OF *proceder* f. L *procedere* proces- (as PRO-¹, *cedere* go)]

proceeding /prəˈsiːdɪŋ/ *n.* **1** an action or piece of conduct (*a high-handed proceeding*). **2** (in *pl.*) (in full **legal proceedings**) an action at law; a lawsuit. **3** (in *pl.*) a published report of discussions or a conference.

proceeds /ˈprəʊsiːdz/ *n.pl.* money produced by a transaction or other undertaking. [pl. of obs. *proceed* (n.) f. PROCEED]

process¹ /ˈprəʊses/ *n. & v.* —*n.* **1** a course of action or proceeding, esp. a series of stages in manufacture or some other operation. **2** the progress or course of something (*in process of construction*). **3** a natural or involuntary operation or series of changes (*the process of growing old*). **4** an action at law; a summons or writ. **5** *Anat.*, *Zool.*, *& Bot.* a natural appendage or outgrowth on an organism. —*v.tr.* **1** handle or deal with by a particular process. **2** treat (food, esp. to prevent decay) (*processed cheese*). **3** *Computing* operate on (data) by means of a program. □**in process of time** as time goes on. **process server** a sheriff's officer who serves writs. □□ **processable** *adj.* [ME f. OF *proces* f. L *processus* (as PROCEED)]

process² /prəˈses/ *v.intr.* walk in procession. [back-form. f. PROCESSION]

procession /prəˈseʃ(ə)n/ *n.* **1** a number of people or vehicles etc. moving forward in orderly succession, esp. at a ceremony, demonstration, or festivity. **2** the movement of such a group (*go in procession*). **3** a race in which no competitor is able to overtake another. **4** *Theol.* the emanation of the Holy Spirit.

□□ **processionist** *n.* [ME f. OF f. L *processio -onis* (as PROCEED)]

processional /prəˈseʃ(ə)n(ə)l/ *adj. & n.* —*adj.* **1** of processions. **2** used, carried, or sung in processions. —*n.* *Eccl.* an office-book of processional hymns etc. [med.L *processionalis* (adj.), *-ale* (n.) (as PROCESSION)]

processor /ˈprəʊsesə(r)/ *n.* a machine that processes things, esp.: **1** = *central processor*. **2** = *food processor*.

procès-verbal /ˌprɒseɪvɛːˈbaːl/ *n.* (*pl.* **procès-verbaux** /-ˈbəʊ/) a written report of proceedings; minutes. [F]

prochronism /ˈprəʊkrəˌnɪz(ə)m/ *n.* the action of referring an event etc. to an earlier date than the true one. [PRO-² + Gk *khronos* time]

proclaim /prəˈkleɪm/ *v.tr.* **1** (often foll. by *that* + clause) announce or declare publicly or officially. **2** declare (a person) to be (a king, traitor, etc.). **3** reveal as being (*an accent that proclaims you a Scot*). □□ **proclaimer** *n.* **proclamation** /ˌprɒkləˈmeɪʃ(ə)n/ *n.* **proclamatory** /-ˈklæmətərɪ/ *adj.* [ME *proclame* f. L *proclamare* cry out (as PRO-¹, CLAIM)]

proclitic /prəˈklɪtɪk/ *adj. & n. Gram.* —*adj.* (of a monosyllable) closely attached in pronunciation to a following word and having itself no accent. —*n.* such a word, e.g. *at* in *at home*. □□ **proclitically** *adv.* [mod.L *procliticus* f. Gk *proklinō* lean forward, after LL *encliticus*: see ENCLITIC]

proclivity /prəˈklɪvɪtɪ/ *n.* (*pl.* **-ies**) a tendency or inclination. [L *proclivitas* f. *proclivis* inclined (as PRO-¹, *clivus* slope)]

proconsul /prəʊˈkɒns(ə)l/ *n.* **1** *Rom.Hist.* a governor of a province, in the later republic usu. an ex-consul. **2** a governor of a modern colony etc. **3** a deputy consul. □□ **proconsular** /-sjuːlə(r)/ *adj.* **proconsulate** /-sjʊlət/ *n.* **proconsulship** *n.* [ME f. L, earlier *pro consule* (one acting) for the consul]

procrastinate /prəʊˈkræstɪˌneɪt/ *v.intr.* defer action; be dilatory. ¶ Often confused with *prevaricate*. □□ **procrastination** /-ˈneɪʃ(ə)n/ *n.* **procrastinative** /-nətɪv/ *adj.* **procrastinator** *n.* **procrastinatory** *adj.* [L *procrastinare procrastinat-* (as PRO-¹, *crastinus* of tomorrow f. *cras* tomorrow)]

procreate /ˈprəʊkrɪˌeɪt/ *v.tr.* (often *absol.*) bring (offspring) into existence by the natural process of reproduction. □□ **procreant** /ˈprəʊkrɪənt/ *adj.* **procreative** *adj.* **procreation** /-ˈeɪʃ(ə)n/ *n.* **procreator** *n.* [L *procreare procreat-* (as PRO-¹, *creare* create)]

Procrustean /prəʊˈkrʌstɪən/ *adj.* seeking to enforce uniformity by forceful or ruthless methods. [Gk *Prokroustēs*, lit. stretcher, f. *prokrouō* beat out: the name of a legendary robber who fitted victims to a bed by stretching them or cutting off parts of them]

proctology /prɒkˈtɒlədʒɪ/ *n.* the branch of medicine concerned with the anus and rectum. □□ **proctological** /-təˈlɒdʒɪk(ə)l/ *adj.* **proctologist** *n.* [Gk *prōktos* anus + -LOGY]

proctor /ˈprɒktə(r)/ *n.* **1** *Brit.* an officer (usu. one of two) at certain universities, appointed annually and having mainly disciplinary functions. **2** *US* a supervisor of students in an examination etc. **3** *Law* a person managing causes in a court (now chiefly ecclesiastical) that administers civil or canon law. **4** a representative of the clergy in the Church of England convocation. □**Queen's** (or **King's**) **Proctor** (in the UK) an official who has the right to intervene in probate, divorce, and nullity cases when collusion or the suppression of facts is alleged. □□ **proctorial** /-ˈtɔːrɪəl/ *adj.* **proctorship** *n.* [ME, syncopation of PROCURATOR]

proctoscope /ˈprɒktəˌskəʊp/ *n.* a medical instrument for inspecting the rectum. [Gk *prōktos* anus + -SCOPE]

procumbent /prəˈkʌmbənt/ *adj.* **1** lying on the face; prostrate. **2** *Bot.* growing along the ground. [L *procumbere* fall forwards (as PRO-¹, *cumbere* lay oneself)]

procuration /ˌprɒkjʊˈreɪʃ(ə)n/ *n.* **1** *formal* the action of procuring, obtaining, or bringing about. **2** the function or an authorized action of an attorney. [ME f. OF *procuration* or L *procuratio* (as PROCURE)]

procurator /'prɒkjʊˌreɪtə(r)/ *n.* **1** an agent or proxy, esp. one who has power of attorney. **2** *Rom.Hist.* a treasury officer in an imperial province. □**procurator fiscal** (in Scotland) a local coroner and public prosecutor. □□ **procuratorial** /-rə'tɔːrɪəl/ *adj.* **procuratorship** *n.* [ME f. OF *procurateur* or L *procurator* administrator, finance-agent (as PROCURE)]

procure /prə'kjʊə(r)/ *v.tr.* **1** obtain, esp. by care or effort; acquire (*managed to procure a copy*). **2** bring about (*procured their dismissal*). **3** (also *absol.*) obtain (women) for prostitution. □□ **procurable** *adj.* **procural** *n.* **procurement** *n.* [ME f. OF *procurer* f. L *procurare* take care of, manage (as PRO-¹, *curare* see to)]

procurer /prə'kjʊərə(r)/ *n.* (*fem.* **procuress** /-rɪs/) a person who obtains women for prostitution. [ME f. AF *procurour*, OF *procureur* f. L *procurator*: see PROCURATOR]

prod /prɒd/ *v.* & *n.* —*v.* (**prodded, prodding**) **1** *tr.* poke with the finger or a pointed object. **2** *tr.* stimulate to action. **3** *intr.* (foll. by *at*) make a prodding motion. —*n.* **1** a poke or thrust. **2** a stimulus to action. **3** a pointed instrument. □□ **prodder** *n.* [16th c.: perh. imit.]

prodigal /'prɒdɪg(ə)l/ *adj.* & *n.* —*adj.* **1** recklessly wasteful. **2** (foll. by *of*) lavish. —*n.* **1** a prodigal person. **2** (in full **prodigal son**) a repentant wastrel, returned wanderer, etc. (Luke 15:11–32). □□ **prodigality** /-'gælɪtɪ/ *n.* **prodigally** *adv.* [med.L *prodigalis* f. L *prodigus* lavish]

prodigious /prə'dɪdʒəs/ *adj.* **1** marvellous or amazing. **2** enormous. **3** abnormal. □□ **prodigiously** *adv.* **prodigiousness** *n.* [L *prodigiosus* (as PRODIGY)]

prodigy /'prɒdɪdʒɪ/ *n.* (*pl.* **-ies**) **1** a person endowed with exceptional qualities or abilities, esp. a precocious child. **2** a marvellous thing, esp. one out of the ordinary course of nature. **3** (foll. by *of*) a wonderful example (of a quality). [L *prodigium* portent]

prodrome /'prəʊdrəʊm, 'prɒdrəʊm/ *n.* **1** a preliminary book or treatise. **2** *Med.* a premonitory symptom. □□ **prodromal** /'prɒdrəʊm(ə)l/ *adj.* **prodromic** /prə'drɒmɪk/ *adj.* [F f. mod.L f. Gk *prodromos* precursor (as PRO-², *dromos* running)]

produce *v.* & *n.* —*v.tr.* /prə'djuːs/ **1** bring forward for consideration, inspection, or use (*will produce evidence*). **2** manufacture (goods) from raw materials etc. **3** bear or yield (offspring, fruit, a harvest, etc.). **4** bring into existence. **5** cause or bring about (a reaction, sensation, etc.). **6** *Geom.* extend or continue (a line). **7 a** bring (a play, performer, book, etc.) before the public. **b** supervise the production of (a film, broadcast, etc.). —*n.* /'prɒdjuːs/ **1 a** what is produced, esp. agricultural and natural products collectively (*dairy produce*). **b** an amount of this. **2** (often foll. by *of*) a result (of labour, efforts, etc.). **3** a yield, esp. in the assay of ore. □□ **producible** /prə'djuːsɪb(ə)l/ *adj.* **producibility** /prəˌdjuːsɪ'bɪlɪtɪ/ *n.* [ME f. L *producere* (as PRO-¹, *ducere* duct- lead)]

producer /prə'djuːsə(r)/ *n.* **1** *Econ.* a person who produces goods or commodities. **2 a** a person generally responsible for the production of a film or play (apart from the direction of the acting). **b** *Brit.* the director of a play or broadcast programme. □**producer gas** a combustible gas formed by passing air, or air and steam, through red-hot carbon.

product /'prɒdʌkt/ *n.* **1** a thing or substance produced by natural process or manufacture. **2** a result (*the product of their labours*). **3** *Math.* a quantity obtained by multiplying quantities together. [ME f. L *productum*, neut. past part. of *producere* PRODUCE]

production /prə'dʌkʃ(ə)n/ *n.* **1** the act or an instance of producing; the process of being produced. **2** the process of being manufactured, esp. in large

quantities (*go into production*). **3** a total yield. **4** a thing produced, esp. a literary or artistic work, a film, play, etc. □**production line** a systematized sequence of mechanical or manual operations involved in producing a commodity. □□ **productional** *n.* [ME f. OF f. L *productio -onis* (as PRODUCT)]

productive /prə'dʌktɪv/ *adj.* **1** of or engaged in the production of goods. **2** producing much (*productive soil; a productive writer*). **3** *Econ.* producing commodities of exchangeable value (*productive labour*). **4** (foll. by *of*) producing or giving rise to (*productive of great annoyance*). □□ **productively** *adv.* **productiveness** *n.* [F *productif -ive* or LL *productivus* (as PRODUCT)]

productivity /ˌprɒdʌk'tɪvɪtɪ/ *n.* **1** the capacity to produce. **2** the quality or state of being productive. **3** the effectiveness of productive effort, esp. in industry. **4** production per unit of effort.

proem /'prəʊɪm/ *n.* **1** a preface or preamble to a book or speech. **2** a beginning or prelude. □□ **proemial** /-'iːmɪəl/ *adj.* [ME f. OF *proeme* or L *prooemium* f. Gk *prooimion* prelude (as PRO-², *oimē* song)]

Prof. *abbr.* Professor.

prof /prɒf/ *n. colloq.* a professor. [abbr.]

profane /prə'feɪn/ *adj.* & *v.* —*adj.* **1** not belonging to what is sacred or biblical; secular. **2** irreverent, blasphemous. **3** (of a rite etc.) heathen. **4** not initiated into religious rites or any esoteric knowledge. —*v.tr.* **1** treat (a sacred thing) with irreverence or disregard. **2** violate or pollute (what is entitled to respect). □□ **profanation** /ˌprɒfə'neɪʃ(ə)n/ *n.* **profanely** *adv.* **profaneness** *n.* **profaner** *n.* [ME *prophane* f. OF *prophane* or med.L *prophanus* f. L *profanus* before (i.e. outside) the temple, not sacred (as PRO-¹, *fanum* temple)]

profanity /prə'fænɪtɪ/ *n.* (*pl.* **-ies**) **1** a profane act. **2** profane language; blasphemy. [LL *profanitas* (as PROFANE)]

profess /prə'fes/ *v.* **1** *tr.* claim openly to have (a quality or feeling). **2** *tr.* (foll. by *to* + infin.) pretend. **3** *tr.* declare (*profess ignorance*). **4** *tr.* affirm one's faith in or allegiance to. **5** *tr.* receive into a religious order under vows. **6** *tr.* have as one's profession or business. **7 a** *tr.* teach (a subject) as a professor. **b** *intr.* perform the duties of a professor. [ME f. L *profitērī profess-* declare publicly (as PRO-¹, *fatērī* confess)]

professed /prə'fest/ *adj.* **1** self-acknowledged (*a professed Christian*). **2** alleged, ostensible. **3** claiming to be duly qualified. **4** (of a monk or nun) having taken the vows of a religious order. □□ **professedly** /-sɪdlɪ/ *adv.* (in senses 1, 2).

profession /prə'feʃ(ə)n/ *n.* **1** a vocation or calling, esp. one that involves some branch of advanced learning or science (*the medical profession*). **2** a body of people engaged in a profession. **3** a declaration or avowal. **4** a declaration of belief in a religion. **5 a** the declaration or vows made on entering a religious order. **b** the ceremony or fact of being professed in a religious order. □**the oldest profession** *colloq.* or *joc.* prostitution. □□ **professionless** *adj.* [ME f. OF f. L *professio -onis* (as PROFESS)]

professional /prə'feʃən(ə)l/ *adj.* & *n.* —*adj.* **1** of or belonging to or connected with a profession. **2 a** having or showing the skill of a professional, competent. **b** worthy of a professional (*professional conduct*). **3** engaged in a specified activity as one's main paid occupation (cf. AMATEUR) (*a professional boxer*). **4** *derog.* engaged in a specified activity regarded with disfavour (*a professional agitator*). —*n.* a professional person. □**professional foul** a deliberate foul in football etc., esp. to prevent an opponent from scoring. □□ **professionally** *adv.*

professionalism /prə'feʃənəˌlɪz(ə)m/ *n.* the qualities or typical features of a profession or of professionals, esp. competence, skill, etc. □□ **professionalize** *v.tr.* (also **-ise**).

professor /prə'fesə(r)/ *n.* **1 a** (often as a title) a university academic of the highest rank; the holder of a university chair. **b** *US* a university teacher. **2** a person who professes a religion. □□ **professorate** *n*. **professorial** /ˌprɒfɪˈsɔːrɪəl/ *adj*. **professorially** /ˌprɒfɪˈsɔːrɪəlɪ/ *adv*. **professoriate** /ˌprɒfɪˈsɔːrɪət/ *n*. **professorship** *n*. [ME f. OF *professeur* or L *professor* (as PROFESS)]

proffer /ˈprɒfə(r)/ *v. & n. —v.tr.* (esp. as **proffered** *adj.*) offer (a gift, services, a hand, etc.). *—n. literary* an offer or proposal. [ME f. AF & OF *proffrir* (as PRO-[1], *offrir* OFFER)]

proficient /prəˈfɪʃ(ə)nt/ *adj. & n. —adj.* (often foll. by *in, at*) adept, expert. *—n.* a person who is proficient. □□ **proficiency** /-sɪ/ *n.* **proficiently** *adv.* [L *proficiens proficient-* (as PROFIT)]

profile /ˈprəʊfaɪl/ *n. & v. —n.* **1 a** an outline (esp. of a human face) as seen from one side. **b** a representation of this. **2** a short biographical or character sketch. **3** *Statistics* a representation by a graph or chart of information (esp. on certain characteristics) recorded in a quantified form. **4** a characteristic personal manner or attitude. **5** a vertical cross-section of a structure. **6** a flat outline piece of scenery on stage. *—v.tr.* **1** represent in profile. **2** give a profile to. □ **in profile** as seen from one side. **keep a low profile** remain inconspicuous. □□ **profiler** *n.* **profilist** *n.* [obs. It. *profilo, profilare* (as PRO-[1], *filare* spin f. L *filare* thread)]

profit /ˈprɒfɪt/ *n. & v. —n.* **1** an advantage or benefit. **2** financial gain; excess of returns over outlay. *—v.* (**profited, profiting**) **1** *tr.* (also *absol.*) be beneficial to. **2** *intr.* obtain an advantage or benefit (*profited by the experience*). □ **at a profit** with financial gain. **profit and loss account** an account in which gains are credited and losses debited so as to show the net profit or loss at any time. **profit margin** the profit remaining in a business after costs have been deducted. **profit-sharing** the sharing of profits esp. between employer and employees. **profit-taking** the sale of shares etc. at a time when profit will accrue. □□ **profitless** *adj.* [ME f. OF f. L *profectus* progress, profit f. *proficere profect-* advance (as PRO-[1], *facere* do)]

profitable /ˈprɒfɪtəb(ə)l/ *adj.* **1** yielding profit; lucrative. **2** beneficial; useful. □□ **profitability** /-ˈbɪlɪtɪ/ *n.* **profitableness** *n.* **profitably** *adv.* [ME f. OF (as PROFIT)]

profiteer /ˌprɒfɪˈtɪə(r)/ *v. & n. —v.intr.* make or seek to make excessive profits, esp. illegally or in black market conditions. *—n.* a person who profiteers.

profiterole /prəˈfɪtəˌrəʊl/ *n.* a small hollow case of choux pastry usu. filled with cream and covered with chocolate sauce. [F, dimin. of *profit* PROFIT]

profligate /ˈprɒflɪgət/ *adj. & n. —adj.* **1** licentious; dissolute. **2** recklessly extravagant. *—n.* a profligate person. □□ **profligacy** /-gəsɪ/ *n.* **profligately** *adv.* [L *profligatus* dissolute, past part. of *profligare* overthrow, ruin (as PRO-[1], *fligere* strike down)]

pro forma /prəʊ ˈfɔːmə/ *adv., adj., n. —adv. & adj.* as or being a matter of form. *—n.* (in full **pro-forma invoice**) an invoice sent in advance of goods supplied. [L]

profound /prəˈfaʊnd/ *adj. & n. —adj.* (**profounder, profoundest**) **1 a** having or showing great knowledge or insight (*a profound treatise*). **b** demanding deep study or thought (*profound doctrines*). **2** (of a state or quality) deep, intense, unqualified (*a profound sleep; profound indifference*). **3** at or extending to a great depth (*profound crevasses*). **4** (of a sigh) deep-drawn. **5** (of a disease) deep-seated. *—n.* (prec. by *the*) *poet.* the vast depth (of the ocean, soul, etc.). □□ **profoundly** *adv.* **profoundness** *n.* **profundity** /prəˈfʌndɪtɪ/ *n.* (*pl.* **-ies**). [ME f. AF & OF *profund*, *profond* f. L *profundus* deep (as PRO-[1], *fundus* bottom)]

profuse /prəˈfjuːs/ *adj.* **1** (often foll. by *in, of*) lavish; extravagant (*was profuse in her generosity*). **2** (of a thing) exuberantly plentiful; abundant (*profuse bleeding; a profuse variety*). □□ **profusely** *adv.*

profuseness *n.* **profusion** /prəˈfjuːʒ(ə)n/ *n.* [ME f. L *profusus* past part. of *profundere profus-* (as PRO-[1], *fundere fus-* pour)]

progenitive /prəʊˈdʒenɪtɪv/ *adj.* capable of or connected with the production of offspring.

progenitor /prəʊˈdʒenɪtə(r)/ *n.* **1** the ancestor of a person, animal, or plant. **2** a political or intellectual predecessor. **3** the origin of a copy. □□ **progenitorial** /-ˈtɔːrɪəl/ *adj.* **progenitorship** *n.* [ME f. OF *progeniteur* f. L *progenitor -oris* f. *progignere progenit-* (as PRO-[1], *gignere* beget)]

progeniture /prəʊˈdʒenɪtjʊə(r)/ *n.* **1** the act or an instance of procreation. **2** young, offspring.

progeny /ˈprɒdʒɪnɪ/ *n.* **1** the offspring of a person or other organism. **2** a descendant or descendants. **3** an outcome or issue. [ME f. OF *progenie* f. L *progenies* f. *progignere* (as PROGENITOR)]

progesterone /prəʊˈdʒestəˌrəʊn/ *n.* a steroid hormone released by the corpus luteum which stimulates the preparation of the uterus for pregnancy (see also PROGESTOGEN). [*progestin* (as PRO-[2], GESTATION) + *luteosterone* f. CORPUS LUTEUM + STEROL]

progestogen /prəʊˈdʒestədʒɪn/ *n.* **1** any of a group of steroid hormones (including progesterone) that maintain pregnancy and prevent further ovulation during it. **2** a similar hormone produced synthetically.

proglottis /prəʊˈglɒtɪs/ *n.* (*pl.* **proglottides** /-ˌdiːz/) each segment in the strobile of a tapeworm that contains a complete reproductive system. [mod.L f. Gk *proglōssis* (as PRO-[2], *glōssis* f. *glōssa, glōtta* tongue), from its shape]

prognathous /prɒgˈneɪθəs, ˈprɒgnəθəs/ *adj.* **1** having a projecting jaw. **2** (of a jaw) projecting. □□ **prognathic** /prɒgˈnæθɪk/ *adj.* **prognathism** *n.* [PRO-[2] + Gk *gnathos* jaw]

prognosis /prɒgˈnəʊsɪs/ *n.* (*pl.* **prognoses** /-siːz/) **1** a forecast; a prognostication. **2** a forecast of the course of a disease. [LL f. Gk *prognōsis* (as PRO-[2], *gignōskō* know)]

prognostic /prɒgˈnɒstɪk/ *n. & adj. —n.* **1** (often foll. by *of*) an advance indication or omen, esp. of the course of a disease etc. **2** a prediction; a forecast. *—adj.* foretelling; predictive (*prognostic of a good result*). □□ **prognostically** *adv.* [ME f. OF *pronostique* f. L *prognosticum* f. Gk *prognōstikon* neut. of *prognōstikos* (as PROGNOSIS)]

prognosticate /prɒgˈnɒstɪˌkeɪt/ *v.tr.* **1** (often foll. by *that* + clause) foretell; foresee; prophesy. **2** (of a thing) betoken; indicate (future events etc.). □□ **prognosticable** /-kəb(ə)l/ *adj.* **prognostication** /-ˈkeɪʃ(ə)n/ *n.* **prognosticative** /-kətɪv/ *adj.* **prognosticator** *n.* **prognosticatory** *adj.* [med.L *prognosticare* (as PROGNOSTIC)]

programme /ˈprəʊgræm/ *n. & v.* (*US* **program**) *—n.* **1** a usu. printed list of a series of events, performers, etc. at a public function etc. **2** a radio or television broadcast. **3** a plan of future events (*the programme is dinner and an early night*). **4** a course or series of studies, lectures, etc.; a syllabus. **5** (usu. **program**) a series of coded instructions to control the operation of a computer or other machine. *—v.tr.* (**programmed, programming**; *US* **programed, programing**) **1** make a programme or definite plan of. **2** (usu. **program**) express (a problem) or instruct (a computer) by means of a program. □ **programme music** a piece of music intended to tell a story, evoke images, etc. □□ **programmable** *adj.* **programmability** /-ˈbɪlɪtɪ/ *n.* **programmatic** /-grəˈmætɪk/ *adj.* **programmatically** /-grəˈmætɪkəlɪ/ *adv.* **programmer** *n.* [LL *programma* f. Gk *programma -atos* f. *prographō* write publicly (as PRO-[2], *graphō* write): spelling after F *programme*]

progress /ˈprəʊgres/ *n. & v. —n.* **1** forward or onward movement towards a destination. **2** advance or development towards completion, betterment, etc.; improvement (*has made little progress this term; the progress of civilization*). **3** *Brit. archaic* a State journey or official tour, esp. by royalty. —v. **1** intr. /prə'gres/ move or be moved forward or onward; continue (the argument is progressing). **2** intr. /prə'gres/ advance or develop towards completion, improvement, etc. (science progresses). **3** tr. cause (work etc.) to make regular progress. □in progress in the course of developing; going on. **progress-chaser** a person employed to check the regular progress of manufacturing work. **progress report** an account of progress made. [ME f. L progressus f. progredi (as PRO-[1], gradi walk: (v.) readopted f. US after becoming obs. in Brit. use in the 17th c.]

progression /prə'greʃ(ə)n/ n. **1** the act or an instance of progressing (a mode of progression). **2** a succession; a series. **3** Math. **a** = arithmetic progression. **b** = geometric progression. **c** = harmonic progression. **4** Mus. passing from one note or chord to another. □□ **progressional** adj. [ME f. OF progression or L progressio (as PROGRESS)]

progressionist /prə'greʃənɪst/ n. **1** an advocate of or believer in esp. political or social progress. **2** a person who believes in the theory of gradual progression to higher forms of life.

progressive /prə'gresɪv/ adj. & n. —adj. **1** moving forward (progressive motion). **2** proceeding step by step; cumulative (progressive drug use). **3 a** (of a political party, government, etc.) favouring or implementing rapid progress or social reform. **b** modern; efficient (this is a progressive company). **4** (of disease, violence, etc.) increasing in severity or extent. **5** (of taxation) at rates increasing with the sum taxed. **6** (of a card-game, dance, etc.) with periodic changes of partners. **7** Gram. (of an aspect) expressing an action in progress, e.g. am writing, was writing. **8** (of education) informal and without strict discipline, stressing individual needs. —n. (also **Progressive**) an advocate of progressive political policies. □□ **progressively** adv. **progressiveness** n. **progressivism** n. **progressivist** n. & adj. [F progressif -ive or med.L progressivus (as PROGRESS)]

pro hac vice /ˌprəʊ hɑːk 'vaɪsɪ/ adv. for this occasion (only). [L]

prohibit /prə'hɪbɪt/ v.tr. (**prohibited, prohibiting**) (often foll. by from + verbal noun) **1** formally forbid, esp. by authority. **2** prevent; make impossible (his accident prohibits him from playing football). □ **prohibited degrees** degrees of blood relationship within which marriage is forbidden. □□ **prohibiter** n. **prohibitor** n. [ME f. L prohibēre (as PRO-[1], habēre hold)]

prohibition /ˌprəʊhɪ'bɪʃ(ə)n, ˌprəʊɪ'b-/ n. **1** the act or an instance of forbidding; a state of being forbidden. **2** Law **a** an edict or order that forbids. **b** a writ from a superior court forbidding an inferior court from proceeding in a suit deemed to be beyond its cognizance. **3** (usu. **Prohibition**) the prevention by law of the manufacture and sale of alcohol, esp. in the US (1920-33). □□ **prohibitionary** adj. **prohibitionist** n. [ME f. OF prohibition or L prohibitio (as PROHIBIT)]

prohibitive /prə'hɪbɪtɪv/ adj. **1** prohibiting. **2** (of prices, taxes, etc.) so high as to prevent purchase, use, abuse, etc. (published at a prohibitive price). □□ **prohibitively** adv. **prohibitiveness** n. **prohibitory** adj. [F prohibitif -ive or L prohibitivus (as PROHIBIT)]

project n. & v. —n. /'prɒdʒekt/ **1** a plan; a scheme. **2** a planned undertaking. **3** a usu. long-term task undertaken by a student to be submitted for assessment. —v. /prə'dʒekt/ **1** tr. plan or contrive (a course of action, scheme, etc.). **2** intr. protrude; jut out. **3** tr. throw; cast; impel (projected the stone into the water). **4** tr. extrapolate (results etc.) to a future time; forecast (I project that we shall produce two million next year). **5** tr. cause (light, shadow, images, etc.) to fall on a surface, screen, etc. **6** tr. cause (a sound, esp. the voice) to be heard at a distance. **7** tr.

(often refl. or absol.) express or promote (oneself or a positive image) forcefully or effectively. **8** tr. Geom. **a** draw straight lines from a centre or parallel lines through every point of (a given figure) to produce a corresponding figure on a surface or a line by intersecting it. **b** draw (such lines). **c** produce (such a corresponding figure). **9** tr. make a projection of (the earth, sky, etc.). **10** tr. Psychol. **a** (also absol.) attribute (an emotion etc.) to an external object or person, esp. unconsciously. **b** (refl.) project (oneself) into another's feelings, the future, etc. [ME f. L projectum neut. past part. of projicere (as PRO-[1], jacēre throw)]

projectile /prə'dʒektaɪl/ n. & adj. —n. **1** a missile, esp. fired by a rocket. **2** a bullet, shell, etc. fired from a gun. **3** any object thrown as a weapon. —adj. **1** capable of being projected by force, esp. from a gun. **2** projecting or impelling. [mod.L projectilis (adj.), -ile (n.) (as PROJECT)]

projection /prə'dʒekʃ(ə)n/ n. **1** the act or an instance of projecting; the process of being projected. **2** a thing that projects or obtrudes. **3** the presentation of an image etc. on a surface or screen. **4 a** a forecast or estimate based on present trends (a projection of next year's profits). **b** this process. **5 a** a mental image or preoccupation viewed as an objective reality. **b** the unconscious transfer of one's own impressions or feelings to external objects or persons. **6** Geom. the act or an instance of projecting a figure. **7** the representation on a plane surface of any part of the surface of the earth or a celestial sphere (Mercator projection). □□ **projectionist** n. (in sense 3). [L projectio (as PROJECT)]

projective /prə'dʒektɪv/ adj. **1** Geom. **a** relating to or derived by projection. **b** (of a property of a figure) unchanged by projection. **2** Psychol. mentally projecting or projected (a projective imagination). □ **projective geometry** the study of the projective properties of geometric figures. □□ **projectively** adv.

projector /prə'dʒektə(r)/ n. **1 a** an apparatus containing a source of light and a system of lenses for projecting slides or film on to a screen. **b** an apparatus for projecting rays of light. **2** a person who forms or promotes a project. **3** archaic a promoter of speculative companies.

prokaryote /prəʊ'kærɪət/ n. (also **procaryote**) an organism in which the chromosomes are not separated from the cytoplasm by a membrane; a bacterium (cf. EUKARYOTE). □□ **prokaryotic** /-'ɒtɪk/ adj. [PRO-[2] + KARYO- + -ote as in ZYGOTE]

prolactin /prəʊ'læktɪn/ n. a hormone released from the anterior pituitary gland that stimulates milk production after childbirth. [PRO-[1] + LACTATION]

prolapse /'prəʊlæps/ n. & v. —n. (also **prolapsus** /-'læpsəs/) **1** the forward or downward displacement of a part or organ. **2** the prolapsed part or organ, esp. the womb or rectum. —v.intr. undergo prolapse. [L prolabi prolaps- (as PRO-[1], labi slip)]

prolate /'prəʊleɪt/ adj. **1** Geom. (of a spheroid) lengthened in the direction of a polar diameter (cf. OBLATE[2]). **2** growing or extending in width. **3** widely spread. **4** Gram. = PROLATIVE. □□ **prolately** adv. [L prolatus past part. of proferre prolong (as PRO-[1], ferre carry)]

prolative /prə'leɪtɪv/ adj. Gram. serving to continue or complete a predication, e.g. go (prolative infinitive) in you may go.

prole /prəʊl/ adj. & n. derog. colloq. —adj. proletarian. —n. a proletarian. [abbr.]

proleg /'prəʊleg/ n. a fleshy abdominal limb of a caterpillar or other larva. [PRO-[1] + LEG]

prolegomenon /ˌprəʊlɪ'gɒmɪnən/ n. (pl. **prolegomena** /-nə/) (usu. in pl.) an introduction or preface to a book etc., esp. when critical or discursive. □□ **prolegomenary** adj. **prolegomenous** adj. [L f. Gk, neut. passive pres. part. of prolegō (as PRO-[2], legō say)]

prolepsis /prəʊ'lepsɪs, -'liːpsɪs/ n. (pl. **prolepses**

/-siːz/) **1** the anticipation and answering of possible objections in rhetorical speech. **2** anticipation. **3** the representation of a thing as existing before it actually does or did so, as in *he was a dead man when he entered*. **4** *Gram.* the anticipatory use of adjectives, as in *paint the town red*. □□ **proleptic** *adj.* [LL f. Gk *prolēpsis* f. *prolambanō* anticipate (as PRO-², *lambanō* take)]

proletarian /ˌprəʊlɪ'teərɪən/ *adj. & n.* —*adj.* of or concerning the proletariat. —*n.* a member of the proletariat. □□ **proletarianism** *n.* **proletarianize** *v.tr.* (also -**ise**). [L *proletarius* one who served the State not with property but with offspring (*proles*)]

proletariat /ˌprəʊlɪ'teərɪət/ *n.* (also **proletariate**) **1 a** *Econ.* wage-earners collectively, esp. those without capital and dependent on selling their labour. **b** esp. *derog.* the lowest class of the community, esp. when considered as uncultured. **2** *Rom.Hist.* the lowest class of citizens. [F *prolétariat* (as PROLETARIAN)]

pro-life /prəʊ'laɪf/ *adj.* in favour of preserving life, esp. in opposing abortion.

proliferate /prə'lɪfəˌreɪt/ *v.* **1** *intr.* reproduce; increase rapidly in numbers; grow by multiplication. **2** *tr.* produce (cells etc.) rapidly. □□ **proliferation** /-'reɪʃ(ə)n/ *n.* **proliferative** /-rətɪv/ *adj.* [back-form. f. *proliferation* f. F *prolifération* f. *prolifère* (as PROLIFEROUS)]

proliferous /prə'lɪfərəs/ *adj.* **1** (of a plant) producing many leaf or flower buds; growing luxuriantly. **2** growing or multiplying by budding. **3** spreading by proliferation. [L *proles* offspring + -FEROUS]

prolific /prə'lɪfɪk/ *adj.* **1** producing many offspring or much output. **2** (often foll. by *of*) abundantly productive. **3** (often foll. by *in*) abounding, copious. □□ **prolificacy** *n.* **prolifically** *adv.* **prolificness** *n.* [med.L *prolificus* (as PROLIFEROUS)]

prolix /'prəʊlɪks, prə'lɪks/ *adj.* (of speech, writing, etc.) lengthy; tedious. □□ **prolixity** /-'lɪksɪtɪ/ *n.* **prolixly** *adv.* [ME f. OF *prolixe* or L *prolixus* poured forth, extended (as PRO-¹, *liquēre* be liquid)]

prolocutor /'prəʊlə,kjʊtə(r), prə'lɒk-/ *n.* **1** *Eccl.* the chairperson esp. of the lower house of convocation of either province of the Church of England. **2** a spokesman. □□ **prolocutorship** *n.* [ME f. L f. *proloqui prolocut-* (as PRO-¹, *loqui* speak)]

prologize /'prəʊlə,gaɪz/ *v.intr.* (also **prologuize**, -**ise**) write or speak a prologue. [med.L *prologizare* f. Gk *prologizō* speak prologue (as PROLOGUE)]

prologue /'prəʊlɒg/ *n. & v.* —*n.* **1 a** a preliminary speech, poem, etc., esp. introducing a play (cf. EPILOGUE). **b** the actor speaking the prologue. **2** (usu. foll. by *to*) any act or event serving as an introduction. —*v.tr.* (**prologues, prologued, prologuing**) introduce with or provide with a prologue. [ME *prolog* f. OF *prologue* f. L *prologus* f. Gk *prologos* (as PRO-², *logos* speech)]

prolong /prə'lɒŋ/ *v.tr.* **1** extend (an action, condition, etc.) in time or space. **2** lengthen the pronunciation of (a syllable etc.). **3** (as **prolonged** *adj.*) lengthy, esp. tediously so. □□ **prolongation** /ˌprəʊlɒŋ'geɪʃ(ə)n/ *n.* **prolongedly** /-ɪdlɪ/ *adv.* **prolonger** *n.* [ME f. OF *prolonger* & f. LL *prolongare* (as PRO-¹, *longus* long)]

prolusion /prə'ljuːʒ(ə)n, -'luːʒ(ə)n/ *n.* *formal* **1** a preliminary essay or article. **2** a first attempt. □□ **prolusory** /-sərɪ/ *adj.* [L *prolusio* f. *proludere proslus-* practise beforehand (as PRO-¹, *ludere lus-* play)]

prom /prɒm/ *n. colloq.* **1** *Brit.* = PROMENADE *n.* 1a. **2** *Brit.* = *promenade concert*. **3** *US* = PROMENADE *n.* 3. [abbr.]

promenade /ˌprɒmə'nɑːd/ *n. & v.* —*n.* **1 a** *Brit.* a paved public walk along the sea front at a resort. **b** any paved public walk. **2** a walk, or sometimes a ride or drive, taken esp. for display, social intercourse, etc. **3** *US* a school or university ball or dance. **4** a march of dancers in country dancing etc. —*v.* **1** *intr.* make a promenade. **2** *tr.* lead (a person etc.) about a place esp. for display. **3** *tr.* make a promenade through (a place). □ **promenade concert** a concert

at which the audience, or part of it, can stand, sit on the floor, or move about. **promenade deck** an upper deck on a passenger ship where passengers may promenade. [F f. *se promener* walk, refl. of *promener* take for a walk]

promenader /ˌprɒmə'nɑːdə(r)/ *n.* **1** a person who promenades. **2** *Brit.* a person who attends a promenade concert, esp. regularly.

promethazine /prəʊ'meθəˌziːn/ *n.* an antihistamine drug used to treat allergies, motion sickness, etc. [PROPYL + di*methyl*amine + phenothi*azine*]

Promethean /prə'miːθɪən/ *adj.* daring or inventive like Prometheus, who in Greek myth was punished for stealing fire from the gods and giving it to the human race along with other skills.

promethium /prə'miːθɪəm/ *n.* *Chem.* a radioactive metallic element of the lanthanide series occurring in nuclear-waste material. ¶ Symb.: **Pm**. [*Prometheus*: see PROMETHEAN]

prominence /'prɒmɪnəns/ *n.* **1** the state of being prominent. **2** a prominent thing, esp. a jutting outcrop, mountain, etc. **3** *Astron.* a stream of incandescent gas projecting above the sun's chromosphere. [obs.F f. L *prominentia* jutting out (as PROMINENT)]

prominent /'prɒmɪnənt/ *adj.* **1** jutting out; projecting. **2** conspicuous. **3** distinguished; important. □□ **prominency** *n.* **prominently** *adv.* [L *prominēre* jut out: cf. EMINENT]

promiscuous /prə'mɪskjʊəs/ *adj.* **1 a** (of a person) having frequent and diverse sexual relationships, esp. transient ones. **b** (of sexual relationships) of this kind. **2** of mixed and indiscriminate composition or kinds; indiscriminate (*promiscuous hospitality*). **3** *colloq.* carelessly irregular; casual. □□ **promiscuity** /-'skjuːɪtɪ/ *n.* **promiscuously** *adv.* **promiscuousness** *n.* [L *promiscuus* (as PRO-¹, *miscēre* mix)]

promise /'prɒmɪs/ *n. & v.* —*n.* **1** an assurance that one will or will not undertake a certain action, behaviour, etc. (*a promise of help*; *gave a promise to be generous*). **2** a sign or signs of future achievements, good results, etc. (*a writer of great promise*). —*v.tr.* **1** (usu. foll. by *to* + infin., or *that* + clause; also *absol.*) make (a person) a promise, esp. to do, give, or procure (a thing) (*I promise you a fair hearing*; *they promise not to be late*; *promised that he would be there*; *cannot positively promise*). **2 a** afford expectations of (*the discussions promise future problems*; *promises to be a good cook*). **b** (foll. by *to* + infin.) seem likely to (*is promising to rain*). **3** *colloq.* assure, confirm (*I promise you, it will not be easy*). **4** (usu. in *passive*) *archaic* betroth (*she is promised to another*). □ **the promised land 1** *Bibl.* Canaan (Gen. 12:7 etc.). **2** any desired place, esp. heaven. **promise oneself** look forward to (a pleasant time etc.). **promise well** (or **ill** etc.) hold out good (or bad etc.) prospects. □□ **promisee** /-'siː/ *n.* esp. *Law.* **promiser** *n.* **promisor** *n.* esp. *Law.* [ME f. L *promissum* neut. past part. of *promittere* put forth, promise (as PRO-¹, *mittere* send)]

promising /'prɒmɪsɪŋ/ *adj.* likely to turn out well; hopeful; full of promise (*a promising start*). □□ **promisingly** *adv.*

promissory /'prɒmɪsərɪ/ *adj.* **1** conveying or implying a promise. **2** (often foll. by *of*) full of promise. □ **promissory note** a signed document containing a written promise to pay a stated sum to a specified person or the bearer at a specified date or on demand. [med.L *promissorius* f. L *promissor* (as PROMISE)]

promo /'prəʊməʊ/ *n. & adj. colloq.* —*n.* (*pl.* -**os**) **1** publicity, advertising. **2** a trailer for a television programme. —*adj.* promotional. [abbr.]

promontory /'prɒməntərɪ/ *n.* (*pl.* -**ies**) **1** a point of high land jutting out into the sea etc.; a headland. **2** *Anat.* a prominence or protuberance in the body. [med.L *promontorium* alt. (after *mons montis* mountain) f. L *promunturium* (perh. f. PRO-¹, *mons*)]

promote /prə'məʊt/ *v.tr.* **1** (often foll. by *to*) advance or raise (a person) to a higher office, rank, etc. (*was promoted to captain*). **2** help forward; encourage; support actively (a cause, process, desired result, etc.) (*promoted women's suffrage*). **3** publicize and sell (a product). **4** attempt to ensure the passing of (a private act of parliament). **5** *Chess* raise (a pawn) to the rank of queen etc. when it reaches the opponent's end of the board. □□ **promotable** *adj.* **promotability** /-'brlrtr/ *n.* **promotion** /-'məʊʃ(ə)n/ *n.* **promotional** /-'məʊʃən(ə)l/ *adj.* **promotive** *adj.* [ME f. L *promovēre promot-* (as PRO-[1], *movēre* move)]

promoter /prə'məʊtə(r)/ *n.* **1** a person who promotes. **2** a person who finances, organizes, etc. a sporting event, theatrical production, etc. **3** (in full **company promoter**) a person who promotes the formation of a joint-stock company. **4** *Chem.* an additive that increases the activity of a catalyst. [earlier *promotour* f. AF f. med.L *promotor* (as PROMOTE)]

prompt /prɒmpt/ *adj., adv., v., & n.* —*adj.* **1 a** acting with alacrity; ready. **b** made, done, etc. readily or at once (*a prompt reply*). **2 a** (of a payment) made forthwith. **b** (of goods) for immediate delivery and payment. —*adv.* punctually (*at six o'clock prompt*). —*v.tr.* **1** (usu. foll. by *to*, or *to* + infin.) incite; urge (*prompted them to action*). **2 a** (also *absol.*) supply a forgotten word, sentence, etc., to (an actor, reciter, etc.). **b** assist (a hesitating speaker) with a suggestion. **3** give rise to; inspire (a feeling, thought, action, etc.). —*n.* **1 a** an act of prompting. **b** a thing said to help the memory of an actor etc. **c** = PROMPTER 2. **d** *Computing* an indication or sign on a VDU screen to show that the system is waiting for input. **2** the time limit for the payment of an account, stated on a prompt note. □**prompt-book** a copy of a play for a prompter's use. **prompt-box** a box in front of the footlights beneath the stage where the prompter sits. **prompt-note** a note sent to a customer as a reminder of payment due. **prompt side** the side of the stage where the prompter sits, usu. to the actor's left. □□ **prompting** *n.* **promptitude** *n.* **promptly** *adv.* **promptness** *n.* [ME f. OF *prompt* or L *promptus* past part. of *promere prompt-* produce (as PRO-[1], *emere* take)]

prompter /'prɒmptə(r)/ *n.* **1** a person who prompts. **2** *Theatr.* a person seated out of sight of the audience who prompts the actors.

promulgate /'prɒməl,geɪt/ *v.tr.* **1** make known to the public; disseminate; promote (a cause etc.). **2** proclaim (a decree, news, etc.). □□ **promulgation** /-'geɪʃ(ə)n/ *n.* **promulgator** *n.* [L *promulgare* (as PRO-[1], *mulgēre* milk, cause to come forth)]

promulge /prəʊ'mʌldʒ/ *v.tr. archaic* = PROMULGATE. [PROMULGATE]

pronaos /prəʊ'neɪɒs/ *n.* (*pl.* **pronaoi** /-'neɪɔɪ/) *Gk Antiq.* the space in front of the body of a temple, enclosed by a portico and projecting side walls. [L f. Gk *pronaos* hall of a temple (as PRO-[2], NAOS)]

pronate /'prəʊneɪt/ *v.tr.* put (the hand, forearm, etc.) into a prone position (with the palm etc. downwards) (cf. SUPINATE). □□ **pronation** /-'neɪʃ(ə)n/ *n.* [back-form. f. *pronation* (as PRONE)]

pronator /prəʊ'neɪtə(r)/ *n. Anat.* any muscle producing or assisting in pronation.

prone /prəʊn/ *adj.* **1 a** lying face downwards (cf. SUPINE). **b** lying flat; prostrate. **c** having the front part downwards, esp. the palm of the hand. **2** (usu. foll. by *to*, or *to* + infin.) disposed or liable, esp. to a bad action, condition, etc. (*is prone to bite his nails*). **3** (usu. in *comb.*) more than usually likely to suffer (*accident-prone*). **4** *archaic* with a downward slope or direction. □□ **pronely** *adv.* **proneness** /'prəʊnnɪs/ *n.* [ME f. L *pronus* f. *pro* forwards]

proneur /prəʊ'nɜː(r)/ *n.* a person who extols; a flatterer. [F *prôneur* f. *prôner* eulogize f. *prône* place in church where addresses were delivered]

prong /prɒŋ/ *n. & v.* —*n.* each of two or more projecting pointed parts at the end of a fork etc. —*v.tr.* **1** pierce or stab with a fork. **2** turn up (soil)

with a fork. □**prong-buck** (or -**horn** or -**horned antelope**) a N. American deerlike ruminant, *Antilocapra americana*, the male of which has horns with forward-pointing prongs. **three-pronged attack** an attack on three separate points at once. □□ **pronged** *adj.* (also in *comb.*). [ME (also *prang*), perh. rel. to MLG *prange* pinching instrument]

pronominal /prəʊ'nɒmɪn(ə)l/ *adj.* of, concerning, or being, a pronoun. □□ **pronominalize** *v.tr.* (also -**ise**). **pronominally** *adv.* [LL *pronominalis* f. L *pronomen* (as PRO-[1], *nomen, nominis* noun)]

pronoun /'prəʊnaʊn/ *n.* a word used instead of and to indicate a noun already mentioned or known, esp. to avoid repetition (e.g. *we, their, this, ourselves*). [PRO-[1], + NOUN, after F *pronom*, L *pronomen* (as PRO-[1], *nomen* name)]

pronounce /prə'naʊns/ *v.* **1** *tr.* (also *absol.*) utter or speak (words, sounds, etc.) in a certain way. **2** *tr.* **a** utter or deliver (a judgement, sentence, curse, etc.) formally or solemnly. **b** proclaim or announce officially (*I pronounce you man and wife*). **3** *tr.* state or declare, as being one's opinion (*the apples were pronounced excellent*). **4** *intr.* (usu. foll. by *on, for, against, in favour of*) pass judgement; give one's opinion (*pronounced for the defendant*). □□ **pronounceable** /-səb(ə)l/ *adj.* **pronouncement** *n.* **pronouncer** *n.* [ME f. OF *pronuncier* f. L *pronuntiare* (as PRO-[1], *nuntiare* announce f. *nuntius* messenger)]

pronounced /prə'naʊnst/ *adj.* **1** (of a word, sound, etc.) uttered. **2** strongly marked; decided (*a pronounced flavour; a pronounced limp*). □□ **pronouncedly** /-'naʊnsɪdlɪ/ *adv.*

pronto /'prɒntəʊ/ *adv. colloq.* promptly, quickly. [Sp. f. L (as PROMPT)]

pronunciation /prə,nʌnsɪ'eɪʃ(ə)n/ *n.* **1** the way in which a word is pronounced, esp. with reference to a standard. **2** the act or an instance of pronouncing. **3** a person's way of pronouncing words etc. [ME f. OF *prononciation* or L *pronuntiatio* (as PRONOUNCE)]

proof /pruːf/ *n., adj., & v.* —*n.* **1** facts, evidence, argument, etc. establishing or helping to establish a fact (*proof of their honesty; no proof that he was there*). **2** *Law* the spoken or written evidence in a trial. **3** a demonstration or act of proving (*not capable of proof; in proof of my assertion*). **4** a test or trial (*put them to the proof; the proof of the pudding is in the eating*). **5** the standard of strength of distilled alcoholic liquors. **6** *Printing* a trial impression taken from type or film, used for making corrections before final printing. **7** the stages in the resolution of a mathematical or philosophical problem. **8** each of a limited number of impressions from an engraved plate before the ordinary issue is printed and usu. (in full **proof before letters**) before an inscription or signature is added. **9** a photographic print made for selection etc. **10** *Sc. Law* a trial before a judge instead of by a jury. —*adj.* **1** impervious to penetration, ill effects, etc. (*proof against the severest weather; his soul is proof against corruption*). **2** (in *comb.*) able to withstand damage or destruction by a specified agent (*soundproof; childproof*). **3** being of proof alcoholic strength. **4** (of armour) of tried strength. —*v.tr.* **1** make (something) proof, esp. make (fabric) waterproof. **2** make a proof of (a printed work, engraving, etc.). □**above proof** (of alcohol) having a stronger than standard strength. **proof-plane** a small flat conductor on an insulating handle for measuring the electrification of a body. **proof positive** absolutely certain proof. **proof-sheet** a sheet of printer's proof. **proof spirit** a mixture of alcohol and water having proof strength. □□ **proofless** *adj.* [ME *prōf prōve*, earlier *prēf* etc. f. OF *proeve, prueve* f. LL *proba* f. L *probare* (see PROVE); adj. and sometimes v. formed app. by ellipsis f. phr. *of proof* = proved to be impenetrable]

proofread /'pruːfriːd/ *v.tr.* (*past and past part.* -**read** /-red/) read (printer's proofs) and mark any errors. □□ **proofreader** *n.* **proofreading** *n.*

prop[1] /prɒp/ *n. & v.* —*n.* **1** a rigid support, esp. one not an integral part of the thing supported. **2** a person who supplies support, assistance, comfort, etc. **3** *Rugby Football* a forward at either end of the front row of a scrum. **4** esp. *Austral.* a horse's action of propping. —*v.* (**propped, propping**) **1** *tr.* (often foll. by *against, up,* etc.) support with or as if with a prop (*propped him against the wall; propped it up with a brick*). **2** *intr.* esp. *Austral.* (of a horse etc.) come to a dead stop with the forelegs rigid. [ME prob. f. MDu. *proppe*: cf. MLG, MDu. *proppen* (v.)]

prop[2] /prɒp/ *n. Theatr. colloq.* **1** = PROPERTY 3. **2** (in *pl.*) a property man or mistress. [abbr.]

prop[3] /prɒp/ *n. colloq.* an aircraft propeller. □**prop-jet** a turboprop. [abbr.]

prop. *abbr.* **1** proprietor. **2** proposition.

propaedeutic /ˌprəʊpɪˈdjuːtɪk/ *adj. & n.* —*adj.* serving as an introduction to higher study; introductory. —*n.* (esp. in *pl.*) preliminary learning; a propaedeutic subject, study, etc. □□ **propaedeutical** *adj.* [PRO-[2] + Gk *paideutikos* of teaching, after Gk *propaideuō* teach beforehand]

propaganda /ˌprɒpəˈɡændə/ *n.* **1 a** an organized programme of publicity, selected information, etc., used to propagate a doctrine, practice, etc. **b** usu. *derog.* the information, doctrines, etc., propagated in this way. **2** (**Propaganda**) *RC Ch.* a committee of cardinals responsible for foreign missions. [It. f. mod.L *congregatio de propaganda fide* congregation for propagation of the faith]

propagandist /ˌprɒpəˈɡændɪst/ *n.* a member or agent of a propaganda organization; a person who spreads propaganda. □□ **propagandism** *n.* /-ˈdɪstɪk/ *adj.* **propagandistically** /-ˈdɪstɪkəlɪ/ *adv.* **propagandize** *v.intr. & tr.* (also **-ise**).

propagate /ˈprɒpəˌɡeɪt/ *v.tr.* **1 a** breed specimens of (a plant, animal, etc.) by natural processes from the parent stock. **b** (*refl.* or *absol.*) (of a plant, animal, etc.) reproduce itself. **2** disseminate; spread (a statement, belief, theory, etc.). **3** hand down (a quality etc.) from one generation to another. **4** extend the operation of; transmit (a vibration, earthquake, etc.). □□ **propagation** /-ˈɡeɪʃ(ə)n/ *n.* **propagative** *adj.* [L *propagare propagat-* multiply plants from layers, f. *propago* (as PRO-[1], *pangere* fix, layer)]

propagator /ˈprɒpəˌɡeɪtə(r)/ *n.* **1** a person or thing that propagates. **2** a small box that can be heated, used for germinating seeds or raising seedlings.

propane /ˈprəʊpeɪn/ *n.* a gaseous hydrocarbon of the alkane series used as bottled fuel. ¶ Chem. formula: C_3H_8. [PROPIONIC (ACID) + -ANE]

propanoic acid /ˌprəʊpəˈnəʊɪk/ *n. Chem.* = PRO-PIONIC ACID. [PROPANE + -IC]

propanone /ˈprəʊpəˌnəʊn/ *n. Chem.* = ACETONE. [PROPANE + -ONE]

propel /prəˈpel/ *v.tr.* (**propelled, propelling**) **1** drive or push forward. **2** urge on; encourage. □**propelling pencil** a pencil with a replaceable lead moved upward by twisting the outer case. [ME, = expel, f. L *propellere* (as PRO-[1], *pellere puls-* drive)]

propellant /prəˈpelənt/ *n.* **1** a thing that propels. **2** an explosive that fires bullets etc. from a firearm. **3** a substance used as a reagent in a rocket engine etc. to provide thrust.

propellent /prəˈpelənt/ *adj.* propelling; capable of driving or pushing forward.

propeller /prəˈpelə(r)/ *n.* **1** a person or thing that propels. **2** a revolving shaft with blades, esp. for propelling a ship or aircraft (cf. *screw-propeller*). □**propeller shaft** a shaft transmitting power from an engine to a propeller or to the driven wheels of a motor vehicle. **propeller turbine** a turbo-propeller.

propene /ˈprəʊpiːn/ *n. Chem.* = PROPYLENE. [PROPANE + ALKENE]

propensity /prəˈpensɪtɪ/ *n.* (*pl.* **-ies**) an inclination or tendency (*has a propensity for wandering*). [*propense* f. L *propensus* inclined, past part. of *propendēre* (as PRO-[1], *pendēre* hang)]

proper /ˈprɒpə(r)/ *adj., adv., & n.* —*adj.* **1 a** accurate, correct (*in the proper sense of the word; gave him the proper amount*). **b** fit, suitable, right (*at the proper time; do it the proper way*). **2** decent; respectable, esp. excessively so (*not quite proper*). **3** (usu. foll. by *to*) belonging or relating exclusively or distinctively (*with the respect proper to them*). **4** (usu. placed after noun) strictly so called; real; genuine (*this is the crypt, not the cathedral proper*). **5** *colloq.* thorough; complete (*had a proper row about it*). **6** (usu. placed after noun) *Heraldry* in the natural, not conventional, colours (*a peacock proper*). **7** *archaic* (of a person) handsome; comely. **8** *archaic* own (*with my proper eyes*). —*adv. Brit. dial.* or *colloq.* **1** completely; very (*felt proper daft*). **2** (with reference to speech) in a genteel manner (*learn to talk proper*). —*n. Eccl.* the part of a service that varies with the season or feast. □**proper fraction** a fraction that is less than unity, with the numerator less than the denominator. **proper motion** *Astron.* the part of the apparent motion of a fixed star etc. that is due to its actual movement in space relative to the sun. **proper noun** (or **name**) *Gram.* a name used for an individual person, place, animal, country, title, etc., and spelt with a capital letter, e.g. Jane, London, Everest. **proper psalms** (or **lessons** etc.) psalms or lessons etc. appointed for a particular day. □□ **properness** *n.* [ME f. OF *propre* f. L *proprius* one's own, special]

properly /ˈprɒpəlɪ/ *adv.* **1** fittingly; suitably (*do it properly*). **2** accurately; correctly (*properly speaking*). **3** rightly (*he very properly refused*). **4** with decency; respectably (*behave properly*). **5** *colloq.* thoroughly (*they were properly ashamed*).

propertied /ˈprɒpətɪd/ *adj.* having property, esp. land.

property /ˈprɒpətɪ/ *n.* (*pl.* **-ies**) **1 a** something owned; a possession, esp. a house, land, etc. **b** *Law* the right to possession, use, etc. **c** possessions collectively, esp. real estate (*has money in property*). **2** an attribute, quality, or characteristic (*has the property of dissolving grease*). **3** a moveable object used on a theatre stage, in a film, etc. **4** *Logic* a quality common to a whole class but not necessary to distinguish it from others. □**common property** a thing known by most people. **property man** (or **mistress**) a man (or woman) in charge of theatrical properties. **property qualification** a qualification for office, or for the exercise of a right, based on the possession of property. **property tax** a tax levied directly on property. [ME through AF f. OF *propriété* f. L *proprietas -tatis* (as PROPER)]

prophase /ˈprəʊfeɪz/ *n. Biol.* the phase in cell division in which chromosomes contract and each becomes visible as two chromatids. [PRO-[2] + PHASE]

prophecy /ˈprɒfɪsɪ/ *n.* (*pl.* **-ies**) **1 a** a prophetic utterance, esp. Biblical. **b** a prediction of future events (*a prophecy of massive inflation*). **2** the faculty, function, or practice of prophesying (*the gift of prophecy*). [ME f. OF *profecie* f. LL *prophetia* f. Gk *prophēteia* (as PROPHET)]

prophesy /ˈprɒfɪˌsaɪ/ *v.* (**-ies, -ied**) **1** *tr.* (usu. foll. by *that, who,* etc.) foretell (an event etc.). **2** *intr.* speak as a prophet; foretell future events. **3** *intr. archaic* expound the Scriptures. □□ **prophesier** /-ˌsaɪə(r)/ *n.* [ME f. OF *profecier* (as PROPHECY)]

prophet /ˈprɒfɪt/ *n.* (*fem.* **prophetess** /-tɪs/) **1** a teacher or interpreter of the supposed will of God, esp. any of the Old Testament or Hebrew prophets. **2 a** a person who foretells events. **b** a person who advocates and speaks innovatively for a cause (*a prophet of the new order*). **3** (**the Prophet**) **a** Muhammad. **b** Joseph Smith, founder of the Mormons, or one of his successors. **c** (in *pl.*) the prophetic writings of the Old Testament. **4** *colloq.* a tipster. □□ **prophethood** *n.* **prophetism** *n.* **prophetship** *n.* [ME f. OF *prophete* f. L *propheta, prophetes* f. Gk

prophētēs spokesman (as PRO-[2], *phētēs* speaker f. *phēmi* speak)]

prophetic /prə'fetɪk/ *adj.* **1** (often foll. by *of*) containing a prediction; predicting. **2** of or concerning a prophet. □□ **prophetical** *adj.* **prophetically** *adv.* **propheticism** /-ˌsɪz(ə)m/ *n.* [F *prophétique* or LL *propheticus* f. Gk *prophētikos* (as PROPHET)]

prophylactic /ˌprɒfɪ'læktɪk/ *adj. & n.* —*adj.* tending to prevent disease. —*n.* **1** a preventive medicine or course of action. **2** esp. *US* a condom. [F *prophylactique* f. Gk *prophulaktikos* f. *prophulassō* (as PRO-[2], *phulassō* guard)]

prophylaxis /ˌprɒfɪ'læksɪs/ *n.* (*pl.* **prophylaxes** /-siːz/) preventive treatment against disease. [mod.L f. PRO-[2] + Gk *phulaxis* act of guarding]

propinquity /prə'pɪŋkwɪtɪ/ *n.* **1** nearness in space; proximity. **2** close kinship. **3** similarity. [ME f. OF *propinquité* or L *propinquitas* f. *propinquus* near f. *prope* near to]

propionic acid /ˌprəʊpɪ'ɒnɪk/ *n.* a colourless sharp-smelling liquid carboxylic acid used for inhibiting the growth of mould in bread. ¶ Chem. formula: C_2H_5COOH. Also called PROPANOIC ACID. □□ **propionate** /'prəʊpɪəˌneɪt/ *n.* [F *propionique*, formed as PRO-[2] + Gk *piōn* fat, as being the first in the series of 'true' fatty acids]

propitiate /prə'pɪʃɪˌeɪt/ *v.tr.* appease (an offended person etc.). □□ **propitiator** *n.* [L *propitiare* (as PROPITIOUS)]

propitiation /prəˌpɪʃɪ'eɪʃ(ə)n/ *n.* **1** appeasement. **2** *Bibl.* atonement, esp. Christ's. **3** *archaic* a gift etc. meant to propitiate. [ME f. LL *propitiatio* (as PROPITIATE)]

propitiatory /prə'pɪʃɪətərɪ/ *adj.* serving or intended to propitiate (*a propitiatory smile*). □□ **propitiatorily** *adv.* [ME f. LL *propitiatorius* (as PROPITIATE)]

propitious /prə'pɪʃəs/ *adj.* **1** (of an omen etc.) favourable. **2** (often foll. by *for*, of the weather, an occasion, etc.) suitable. **3** well-disposed (*the fates were propitious*). □□ **propitiously** *adv.* **propitiousness** *n.* [ME f. OF *propicieus* or L *propitius*]

propolis /'prɒpəlɪs/ *n.* a red or brown resinous substance collected by bees from buds for use in constructing hives. [L f. Gk *propolis* suburb, bee-glue, f. PRO-[2] + *polis* city]

proponent /prə'pəʊnənt/ *n. & adj.* —*n.* a person advocating a motion, theory, or proposal. —*adj.* proposing or advocating a theory etc. [L *proponere* (as PROPOUND)]

proportion /prə'pɔː'ʃ(ə)n/ *n. & v.* —*n.* **1 a** a comparative part or share (*a large proportion of the profits*). **b** a comparative ratio (*the proportion of births to deaths*). **2** the correct or pleasing relation of things or parts of a thing (*the house has fine proportions*; *exaggerated out of all proportion*). **3** (in *pl.*) dimensions; size (*large proportions*). **4** *Math.* an equality of ratios between two pairs of quantities, e.g. 3:5 and 9:15. **b** a set of such quantities. **c** *Math.* = *rule of three*; see also *direct proportion*, *inverse proportion*. —*v.tr.* (usu. foll. by *to*) make (a thing etc.) proportionate (*must proportion the punishment to the crime*). □ **in proportion 1** by the same factor. **2** without exaggerating (importance etc.) (*must get the facts in proportion*). □□ **proportioned** *adj.* (also in *comb.*). **proportionless** *adj.* **proportionment** *n.* [ME f. OF *proportion* or L *proportio* (as PRO-[1], PORTION)]

proportionable /prə'pɔː'ʃənəb(ə)l/ *adj.* = PROPORTIONAL. □□ **proportionably** *adv.*

proportional /prə'pɔː'ʃən(ə)l/ *adj. & n.* —*adj.* in due proportion; comparable (*a proportional increase in the expense*; *resentment proportional to his injuries*). —*n.* *Math.* each of the terms of a proportion. □ **proportional representation** an electoral system in which all parties gain seats in proportion to the number of votes cast for them. □□ **proportionality** /-'nælɪtɪ/ *n.* **proportionally** *adv.*

proportionalist /prə'pɔː'ʃənəlɪst/ *n.* an advocate of proportional representation.

proportionate /prə'pɔː'ʃənət/ *adj.* = PROPORTIONAL. □□ **proportionately** *adv.*

proposal /prə'pəʊz(ə)l/ *n.* **1 a** the act or an instance of proposing something. **b** a course of action etc. so proposed (*the proposal was never carried out*). **2** an offer of marriage.

propose /prə'pəʊz/ *v.* **1** *tr.* (also *absol.*) put forward for consideration or as a plan. **2** *tr.* (usu. foll. by *to* + infin., or verbal noun) intend; purpose (*propose to open a restaurant*). **3** *intr.* (usu. foll. by *to*) offer oneself in marriage. **4** *tr.* nominate (a person) as a member of a society, for an office, etc. **5** *tr.* offer (a person's health, a person, etc.) as a subject for a toast. □□ **proposer** *n.* [ME f. OF *proposer* f. L *proponere* (as PROPOUND)]

proposition /ˌprɒpə'zɪʃ(ə)n/ *n. & v.* —*n.* **1** a statement or assertion. **2** a scheme proposed; a proposal. **3** *Logic* a statement consisting of subject and predicate that is subject to proof or disproof. **4** *colloq.* a problem, opponent, prospect, etc. that is to be dealt with (*a difficult proposition*). **5** *Math.* a formal statement of a theorem or problem, often including the demonstration. **6 a** an enterprise etc. with regard to its likelihood of commercial etc. success. **b** a person regarded similarly. **7** *colloq.* a sexual proposal. —*v.tr. colloq.* make a proposal (esp. of sexual intercourse) to (*he propositioned her*). □ **not a proposition** unlikely to succeed. □□ **propositional** *adj.* [ME f. OF *proposition* or L *propositio* (as PROPOUND)]

propound /prə'paʊnd/ *v.tr.* **1** offer for consideration; propose. **2** *Law* produce (a will etc.) before the proper authority so as to establish its legality. □□ **propounder** *n.* [earlier *propoune*, *propone* f. L *proponere* (as PRO-[1], *ponere posit-* place): cf. *compound*, *expound*]

proprietary /prə'praɪətərɪ/ *adj.* **1 a** of, holding, or concerning property (*the proprietary classes*). **b** of or relating to a proprietor (*proprietary rights*). **2** held in private ownership. □ **proprietary medicine** any of several drugs, medicines, etc. produced by private companies under brand names. **proprietary name** (or **term**) a name of a product etc. registered by its owner as a trade mark and not usable by another without permission. [LL *proprietarius* (as PROPERTY)]

proprietor /prə'praɪətə(r)/ *n.* (*fem.* **proprietress**) **1** a holder of property. **2** the owner of a business etc., esp. of a hotel. □□ **proprietorial** /-'tɔːrɪəl/ *adj.* **proprietorially** /-'tɔːrɪəlɪ/ *adv.* **proprietorship** *n.*

propriety /prə'praɪɪtɪ/ *n.* (*pl.* **-ies**) **1** fitness; rightness (*doubt the propriety of refusing him*). **2** correctness of behaviour or morals (*highest standards of propriety*). **3** (in *pl.*) the details or rules of correct conduct (*must observe the proprieties*). [ME, = ownership, peculiarity f. OF *propriété* PROPERTY]

proprioceptive /ˌprəʊprɪə'septɪv/ *adj.* relating to stimuli produced and perceived within an organism, esp. relating to the position and movement of the body. [L *proprius* own + RECEPTIVE]

proptosis /prɒp'təʊsɪs/ *n. Med.* protrusion or displacement, esp. of an eye. [LL f. Gk *proptōsis* (as PRO-[2], *piptō* fall)]

propulsion /prə'pʌlʃ(ə)n/ *n.* **1** the act or an instance of driving or pushing forward. **2** an impelling influence. □□ **propulsive** /-'pʌlsɪv/ *adj.* [med.L *propulsio* f. L *propellere* (as PROPEL)]

propyl /'prəʊpɪl/ *n. Chem.* the univalent radical of propane. ¶ Chem. formula: C_3H_7-. [PROPIONIC (ACID) + -YL]

propyla *pl.* of PROPYLON.

propylaeum /ˌprɒpɪ'liːəm/ *n.* (*pl.* **propylaea** /-'liːə/) **1** the entrance to a temple. **2** (**the Propylaeum**) the entrance to the Acropolis at Athens. [L f. Gk *propulaion* (as PRO-[2], *pulē* gate)]

propylene /ˈprəʊpɪˌliːn/ n. Chem. a gaseous hydrocarbon of the alkene series used in the manufacture of chemicals. ¶ Chem. formula: C_3H_6.

propylon /ˈprɒpɪˌlɒn/ n. (pl. **propylons** or **propyla** /-lə/) = PROPYLAEUM. [L f. Gk propulon (as PRO-², pulē gate)]

pro rata /prəʊ ˈrɑːtə, ˈreɪtə/ adj. & adv. —adj. proportional. —adv. proportionally. [L, = according to the rate]

prorate /prəʊˈreɪt, ˈprəʊ-/ v.tr. allocate or distribute pro rata. □□ **proration** n.

prorogue /prəˈrəʊg/ v. (**prorogues, prorogued, proroguing**) **1** tr. discontinue the meetings of (a parliament etc.) without dissolving it. **2** intr. (of a parliament etc.) be prorogued. □□ **prorogation** /-rəˈgeɪʃ(ə)n/ n. [ME proroge f. OF proroger, -guer f. L prorogare prolong (as PRO-¹, rogare ask)]

pros- /prɒs/ prefix **1** to, towards. **2** in addition. [Gk f. pros (prep.)]

prosaic /prəˈzeɪɪk, prəʊ-/ adj. **1** like prose, lacking poetic beauty. **2** unromantic; dull; commonplace (took a prosaic view of life). □□ **prosaically** adv. **prosaicness** n. [F prosaïque or LL prosaicus (as PROSE)]

prosaist /ˈprəʊzeɪɪst/ n. **1** a prose-writer. **2** a prosaic person. □□ **prosaism** n. [F prosaïste f. L prosa PROSE]

proscenium /prəˈsiːnɪəm, prəʊ-/ n. (pl. **prosceniums** or **proscenia** /-nɪə/) **1** the part of the stage in front of the drop or curtain, usu. with the enclosing arch. **2** the stage of an ancient theatre. [L f. Gk proskēnion (as PRO-², skēnē stage)]

prosciutto /prəʊˈʃuːtəʊ/ n. (pl. **-os**) Italian ham, esp. cured and eaten as an hors-d'œuvre. [It.]

proscribe /prəˈskraɪb/ v.tr. **1** banish, exile (proscribed from the club). **2** put (a person) outside the protection of the law. **3** reject or denounce (a practice etc.) as dangerous etc. □□ **proscription** /-ˈskrɪpʃ(ə)n/ n. **proscriptive** /-ˈskrɪptɪv/ adj. [L proscribere (as PRO-¹, scribere script- write)]

prose /prəʊz/ n. & v. —n. **1** the ordinary form of the written or spoken language (opp. POETRY, VERSE) (Milton's prose works). **2** a passage of prose, esp. for translation into a foreign language. **3** a tedious speech or conversation. **4** a plain matter-of-fact quality (the prose of existence). **5** Eccl. = SEQUENCE 8. —v. **1** intr. (usu. foll. by about, away, etc.) talk tediously (was prosing away about his dog). **2** tr. turn (a poem etc.) into prose. □**prose idyll** a short description in prose of a picturesque, esp. rustic, incident, character, etc. **prose poem** (or **poetry**) a piece of imaginative poetic writing in prose. □□ **proser** n. [ME f. OF f. L prosa (oratio) straightforward (discourse), fem. of prosus, earlier prorsus direct]

prosector /prəˈsektə(r)/ n. a person who dissects dead bodies in preparation for an anatomical lecture etc. [LL = anatomist, f. prosecare prosect- (as PRO-¹, secare cut), perh. after F prosecteur]

prosecute /ˈprɒsɪˌkjuːt/ v.tr. **1** (also absol.) **a** institute legal proceedings against (a person). **b** institute a prosecution with reference to (a claim, crime, etc.) (decided not to prosecute). **2** follow up, pursue (an inquiry, studies, etc.). **3** carry on (a trade, pursuit, etc.). □□ **prosecutable** adj. [ME f. L prosequi prosecut- (as PRO-¹, sequi follow)]

prosecution /ˌprɒsɪˈkjuːʃ(ə)n/ n. **1 a** the institution and carrying on of a criminal charge in a court. **b** the carrying on of legal proceedings against a person. **c** the prosecuting party in a court case (the prosecution denied this). **2** the act or an instance of prosecuting (met her in the prosecution of his hobby). [OF prosecution or LL prosecutio (as PROSECUTE)]

prosecutor /ˈprɒsɪˌkjuːtə(r)/ n. (fem. **prosecutrix** /-trɪks/) a person who prosecutes, esp. in a criminal court. □□ **prosecutorial** /-ˈtɔːrɪəl/ adj.

proselyte /ˈprɒsɪˌlaɪt/ n. & v. —n. **1** a person converted, esp. recently, from one opinion, creed, party, etc., to another. **2** a Gentile convert to

Judaism. —v.tr. US = PROSELYTIZE. □□ **proselytism** /-lɪˌtɪz(ə)m/ n. [ME f. LL proselytus f. Gk prosēluthos stranger, convert (as PROS-, stem ēluth- of erkhomai come)]

proselytize /ˈprɒsɪlɪˌtaɪz/ v.tr. (also **-ise**) (also absol.) convert (a person or people) from one belief etc. to another, esp. habitually. □□ **proselytizer** n.

prosenchyma /prɒˈseŋkɪmə/ n. a plant tissue of elongated cells with interpenetrating tapering ends, occurring esp. in vascular tissue. □□ **prosenchymal** adj. **prosenchymatous** /-ˈkɪmətəs/ adj. [Gk pros toward + egkhuma infusion, after parenchyma]

prosify /ˈprəʊzɪˌfaɪ/ v.tr. (**-ies, -ied**) **1** tr. turn into prose. **2** tr. make prosaic. **3** intr. write prose.

prosit /ˈprəʊzɪt/ int. an expression used in drinking a person's health etc. [G f. L, = may it benefit]

prosody /ˈprɒsədɪ/ n. **1** the theory and practice of versification; the laws of metre. **2** the study of speech-rhythms. □□ **prosodic** /prəˈsɒdɪk/ adj. **prosodist** n. [ME f. L prosodia accent f. Gk prosōidia (as PROS-, ODE)]

prosopography /ˌprɒsəˈpɒgrəfɪ, ˌprɒsəʊ-/ n. (pl. **-ies**) **1** a description of a person's appearance, personality, social and family connections, career, etc. **2** the study of such descriptions, esp. in Roman history. □□ **prosopographer** n. **prosopographic** /-pəˈgræfɪk/ adj. **prosopographical** /-pəˈgræfɪk(ə)l/ adj. [mod.L prosopographia f. Gk prosōpon face, person]

prosopopoeia /ˌprɒsəpəˈpiːə/ n. the rhetorical introduction of a pretended speaker or the personification of an abstract thing. [L f. Gk prosōpopoiia f. prosōpon person + poieō make]

prospect /ˈprɒspekt/ n. & v. —n. **1 a** (often in pl.) an expectation, esp. of success in a career etc. (his prospects were brilliant; offers a gloomy prospect; no prospect of success). **b** something one has to look forward to (don't relish the prospect of meeting him). **2** an extensive view of landscape etc. (a striking prospect). **3** a mental picture (a new prospect in his mind). **4 a** a place likely to yield mineral deposits. **b** a sample of ore for testing. **c** the resulting yield. **5** a possible or probable customer, subscriber, etc. —v. /prəˈspekt/ **1** intr. (usu. foll. by for) **a** explore a region for gold etc. **b** look out for or search for something. **2** tr. **a** explore (a region) for gold etc. **b** work (a mine) experimentally. **c** (of a mine) promise (a specified yield). □**prospect well** (or **ill** etc.) (of a mine) promise well (or ill etc.). □□ **prospectless** adj. **prospector** /prəˈspektə(r)/ n. [ME f. L prospectus: see PROSPECTUS]

prospective /prəˈspektɪv/ adj. **1** concerned with or applying to the future (implies a prospective obligation) (cf. RETROSPECTIVE). **2** some day to be; expected; future (prospective bridegroom). □□ **prospectively** adv. **prospectiveness** n. [obs. F prospectif -ive or LL prospectivus (as PROSPECTUS)]

prospectus /prəˈspektəs/ n. a printed document advertising or describing a school, commercial enterprise, forthcoming book, etc. [L, = prospect f. prospicere (as PRO-¹, specere look)]

prosper /ˈprɒspə(r)/ v. **1** intr. succeed; thrive (nothing he touches prospers). **2** tr. make successful (Heaven prosper him). [ME f. OF prosperer or L prosperare (as PROSPEROUS)]

prosperity /prɒˈsperɪtɪ/ n. a state of being prosperous; wealth or success.

prosperous /ˈprɒspərəs/ adj. **1** successful; rich (a prosperous merchant). **2** flourishing; thriving (a prosperous enterprise). **3** auspicious (a prosperous wind). □□ **prosperously** adv. **prosperousness** n. [ME f. obs. F prospereus f. L prosper(us)]

prostaglandin /ˌprɒstəˈglændɪn/ n. any of a group of hormone-like substances causing contraction of the muscles in mammalian (esp. uterine) tissues etc. [G f. PROSTATE + GLAND¹ + -IN]

prostate /ˈprɒsteɪt/ n. (in full **prostate gland**) a gland surrounding the neck of the bladder in male mammals and releasing a fluid forming part of

aʊ how eɪ day əʊ no eə hair ɪə near ɔɪ boy ʊə poor aɪə fire aʊə sour (see over for consonants) the semen. □□ **prostatic** /-'stætɪk/ *adj.* [F f. mod.L *prostata* f. Gk *prostatēs* one that stands before (as PRO-², *statos* standing)]

prosthesis /'prɒsθɪsɪs, -'θiːsɪs/ *n.* (*pl.* **prostheses** /-ˌsiːz/) **1 a** an artificial part supplied to remedy a deficiency, e.g. a false breast, leg, tooth, etc. **b** the branch of surgery supplying and fitting prostheses. **2** *Gram.* the addition of a letter or syllable at the beginning of a word, e.g. *be-* in *beloved*. □□ **prosthetic** /-'θetɪk/ *adj.* **prosthetically** /-'θetɪkəlɪ/ *adv.* [LL f. Gk *prosthesis* f. *prostithēmi* (as PROS-, *tithēmi* place)]

prosthetics /prɒs'θetɪks/ *n.pl.* (usu. treated as *sing.*) = PROSTHESIS 1b.

prostitute /'prɒstɪˌtjuːt/ *n. & v.* —*n.* **1 a** a woman who engages in sexual activity for payment. **b** (usu. **male prostitute**) a man or boy who engages in sexual activity, esp. with homosexual men, for payment. **2** a person who debases himself or herself for personal gain. —*v.tr.* **1** (esp. *refl.*) make a prostitute of (esp. oneself). **2 a** misuse (one's talents, skills, etc.) for money. **b** offer (oneself, one's honour, etc.) for unworthy ends, esp. for money. □□ **prostitution** /-'tjuːʃ(ə)n/ *n.* **prostitutor** *n.* [L *prostituere prostitut-* offer for sale (as PRO-¹, *statuere* set up, place)]

prostrate *adj. & v.* —*adj.* /'prɒstreɪt/ **1 a** lying face downwards, esp. in submission. **b** lying horizontally. **2** overcome, esp. by grief, exhaustion, etc. (*prostrate with self-pity*). **3** *Bot.* growing along the ground. —*v.tr.* /prɒ'streɪt, prə-/ **1** lay (a person etc.) flat on the ground. **2** (*refl.*) throw (oneself) down in submission etc. **3** (of fatigue, illness, etc.) overcome; reduce to extreme physical weakness. □□ **prostration** /prɒ'streɪʃ(ə)n, prə-/ *n.* [ME f. L *prostratus* past part. of *prosternere* (as PRO-¹, *sternere strat-* lay flat)]

prostyle /'prəʊstaɪl/ *n. & adj.* —*n.* a portico with not more than four columns. —*adj.* (of a building) having such a portico. [L *prostylos* having pillars in front (as PRO-², STYLE)]

prosy /'prəʊzɪ/ *adj.* (**prosier**, **prosiest**) tedious; commonplace; dull (*prosy talk*). □□ **prosily** *adv.* **prosiness** *n.*

Prot. *abbr.* **1** Protectorate. **2** Protestant.

protactinium /ˌprəʊtæk'tɪnɪəm/ *n.* *Chem.* a radioactive metallic element whose chief isotope yields actinium by decay. ¶ Symb.: **Pa**. [G (as PROTO-, ACTINIUM)]

protagonist /prəʊ'tægənɪst/ *n.* **1** the chief person in a drama, story, etc. **2** the leading person in a contest etc.; a principal performer. **3** (usu. foll. by *of*, *for*) *disp.* an advocate or champion of a cause, course of action, etc. (*a protagonist of women's rights*). [Gk *prōtagōnistēs* (as PROTO-, *agōnistēs* actor)]

protamine /'prəʊtəˌmiːn/ *n.* any of a group of proteins found in association with chromosomal DNA in the sperm of birds and fish. [PROTO- + AMINE]

protasis /'prɒtəsɪs/ *n.* (*pl.* **protases** /-ˌsiːz/) the clause expressing the condition in a conditional sentence. □□ **protatic** /-'tætɪk/ *adj.* [L, f. Gk *protasis* proposition (as PRO-², *teinō* stretch)]

protea /'prəʊtɪə/ *n.* any shrub of the genus *Protea* native to S. Africa, with conelike flower-heads. [mod.L f. PROTEUS, with ref. to the many species]

protean /'prəʊtɪən, -'tiːən/ *adj.* **1** variable, taking many forms. **2** (of an artist, writer, etc.) versatile. [after *Proteus*: see PROTEUS]

protease /'prəʊtɪˌeɪs/ *n.* any enzyme able to hydrolyse proteins and peptides by proteolysis. [PROTEIN + -ASE]

protect /prə'tekt/ *v.tr.* **1** (often foll. by *from*, *against*) keep (a person, thing, etc.) safe; defend; guard (*goggles protected her eyes from dust*; *guards protected the queen*). **2** *Econ.* shield (home industry) from competition by imposing import duties on foreign goods. **3** *Brit.* provide funds to meet (a bill, draft, etc.). **4** provide (machinery etc.) with appliances to prevent injury from it. [L *protegere protect-* (as PRO-¹, *tegere* cover)]

protection /prə'tekʃ(ə)n/ *n.* **1 a** the act or an instance of protecting. **b** the state of being protected; defence (*affords protection against the weather*). **c** a thing, person, or animal that provides protection (*bought a dog as protection*). **2** (also **protectionism** /-ˌnɪz(ə)m/) *Econ.* the theory or practice of protecting home industries. **3** *colloq.* **a** immunity from molestation obtained by payment to gangsters etc. under threat of violence. **b** (in full **protection money**) the money so paid, esp. on a regular basis. **4** = *safe conduct*. **5** *archaic* the keeping of a woman as a mistress. □□ **protectionist** *n.* [ME f. OF *protection* or LL *protectio* (as PROTECT)]

protective /prə'tektɪv/ *adj. & n.* —*adj.* **1** protecting; intended or intending to protect. **2** (of food) protecting against deficiency diseases. —*n.* something that protects, esp. a condom. □ **protective clothing** clothing worn to shield the body from dangerous substances or a hostile environment. **protective colouring** colouring disguising or camouflaging a plant or animal. **protective custody** the detention of a person for his or her own protection. □□ **protectively** *adv.* **protectiveness** *n.*

protector /prə'tektə(r)/ *n.* (*fem.* **protectress** /-trɪs/) **1 a** a person who protects. **b** a guardian or patron. **2** *hist.* a regent in charge of a kingdom during the minority, absence, etc. of the sovereign. **3** (often in *comb.*) a thing or device that protects (*chest-protector*). **4** (**Protector**) (in full **Lord Protector of the Commonwealth**) *hist.* the title of Oliver Cromwell 1653-58 and his son Richard Cromwell 1658-59. □□ **protectoral** *adj.* **protectorship** *n.* [ME f. OF *protecteur* f. LL *protector* (as PROTECT)]

protectorate /prə'tektərət/ *n.* **1 a** a State that is controlled and protected by another. **b** such a relation of one State to another. **2** *hist.* **a** the office of the protector of a kingdom or State. **b** the period of this, esp. in England under the Cromwells 1653-59.

protégé /'prɒtɪˌʒeɪ, -teˌʒeɪ, 'prəʊ-/ *n.* (*fem.* **protégée** *pronunc.* same) a person under the protection, patronage, tutelage, etc. of another. [F, past part. of *protéger* f. L *protegere* PROTECT]

protein /'prəʊtiːn/ *n.* any of a group of organic compounds composed of one or more chains of amino acids and forming an essential part of all living organisms. □□ **proteinaceous** /-'neɪʃəs/ *adj.* **proteinic** /-'tiːnɪk/ *adj.* **proteinous** /-'tiːnəs, -'tiːɪnəs/ *adj.* [F *protéine*, G *Protein* f. Gk *prōteios* primary]

pro tem /prəʊ 'tem/ *adj. & adv. colloq.* = PRO TEMPORE. [abbr.]

pro tempore /prəʊ 'tempərɪ/ *adj. & adv.* for the time being. [L]

proteolysis /ˌprəʊtɪ'ɒlɪsɪs/ *n.* the splitting of proteins or peptides by the action of enzymes esp. during the process of digestion. □□ **proteolytic** /-ə'lɪtɪk/ *adj.* [mod.L f. PROTEIN + -LYSIS]

Proterozoic /ˌprəʊtərəʊ'zəʊɪk/ *adj. & n. Geol.* —*adj.* of or relating to the later part of the Precambrian era, characterized by the oldest forms of life. —*n.* this time. [Gk *proteros* former + *zōē* life, *zōos* living]

protest *n. & v.* —*n.* /'prəʊtest/ **1** a statement of dissent or disapproval; a remonstrance (*made a protest*). **2** (often *attrib.*) a usu. public demonstration of objection to government etc. policy (*marched in protest*; *protest demonstration*). **3** a solemn declaration. **4** *Law* a written declaration, usu. by a notary public, that a bill has been presented and payment or acceptance refused. —*v.* /prə'test/ **1** *intr.* (usu. foll. by *against*, *at*, *about*, etc.) make a protest against an action, proposal, etc. **2** *tr.* (often foll. by *that* + clause; also *absol.*) affirm (one's innocence etc.) solemnly, esp. in reply to an accusation etc. **3** *tr.* *Law* write or obtain a protest in regard to (a bill). **4** *tr.* *US* object to (a decision etc.). □ **under protest** unwillingly. □□ **protester** *n.* **protestingly** *adv.* **protestor** *n.* [ME f. OF *protest* (n.), *protester* (v.), f. L *protestari* (as PRO-¹, *testari* assert f. *testis* witness)]

Protestant /'prɒtɪst(ə)nt/ *n. & adj.* —*n.* **1** a member or follower of any of the western Christian Churches that are separate from the Roman Catholic Church in accordance with the principles of the Reformation. **2** (**protestant**) /'prɒtɪst(ə)nt, prə'test(ə)nt/ a protesting person. —*adj.* **1** of or relating to any of the Protestant Churches or their members etc. **2** (**protestant**) /also prə'testənt/ protesting. □□ **Protestantism** *n.* **Protestantize** *v.tr.* & *intr.* (also -**ise**). [mod.L *protestans*, part. of L *protestari* (see PROTEST)]

protestation /,prɒtɪ'steɪʃ(ə)n/ *n.* **1** a strong affirmation. **2** a protest. [ME f. OF *protestation* or LL *protestatio* (as PROTEST)]

Proteus /'prəʊtɪəs, -tju:s/ *n.* **1** a changing or inconstant person or thing. **2** (**proteus**) **a** any bacterium of the genus *Proteus*, usu. found in the intestines and faeces of animals. **b** = OLM. [L f. Gk *Prōteus* a sea-god able to take various forms at will]

prothalamium /,prəʊθə'leɪmɪəm/ *n.* (also **prothalamion** /-mɪən/) (*pl.* **prothalamia** /-mɪə/) a song or poem to celebrate a forthcoming wedding. [title of a poem by Spenser, after *epithalamium*]

prothallium /prəʊ'θælɪəm/ *n.* (*pl.* **prothallia** /-lɪə/) = PROTHALLUS. [mod.L f. PRO-² + Gk *thallion* dimin. of *thallos*: see PROTHALLUS]

prothallus /prəʊ'θæləs/ *n.* (*pl.* **prothalli** /-laɪ/) *Bot.* the gametophyte of certain plants, esp. a fern. [mod.L f. PRO-² + Gk *thallos* green shoot]

prothesis /'prɒθɪsɪs/ *n.* (*pl.* **protheses** /-,si:z/) **1** *Eccl.* **a** the placing of the Eucharistic elements on the credence table. **b** a credence table. **c** the part of a church where this stands. **2** *Gram.* = PROSTHESIS 2. □□ **prothetic** /prə'θetɪk/ *adj.* [Gk f. *protithēmi* (as PRO-², *tithēmi* place)]

prothonotary var. of PROTONOTARY.

protist /'prəʊtɪst/ *n.* any usu. unicellular organism of the kingdom Protista, with both plant and animal characteristics, including bacteria, fungi, algae, and protozoa. □□ **protistology** /-'tɒlədʒɪ/ *n.* [mod.L *Protista* f. Gk *prōtista* neut. pl. superl. f. *prōtos* first]

protium /'prəʊtɪəm/ *n.* the ordinary isotope of hydrogen as distinct from heavy hydrogen (cf. DEUTERIUM, TRITIUM). [mod.L f. PROTO- + -IUM]

proto- /'prəʊtəʊ/ *comb. form* **1** original, primitive (*proto-Germanic*; *proto-Slavic*). **2** first, original (*protomartyr*; *protophyte*). [Gk *prōto-* f. *prōtos* first]

protocol /,prəʊtə'kɒl/ *n.* & *v.* —*n.* **1 a** official, esp. diplomatic, formality and etiquette observed on State occasions etc. **b** the rules, formalities, etc. of any procedure, group, etc. **2** the original draft of a diplomatic document, esp. of the terms of a treaty agreed to in conference and signed by the parties. **3** a formal statement of a transaction. **4** the official formulae at the beginning and end of a charter, papal bull, etc. **5** *US* a record of experimental observations etc. —*v.* (**protocolled**, **protocolling**) **1** *intr.* draw up a protocol or protocols. **2** *tr.* record in a protocol. [orig. Sc. *prothocoll* f. OF *prothocole* f. med.L *protocollum* f. Gk *protokollon* flyleaf (as PROTO-, *kolla* glue)]

protomartyr /,prəʊtəʊ'mɑːtə(r)/ *n.* the first martyr in any cause, esp. the first Christian martyr St Stephen.

proton /'prəʊtɒn/ *n.* *Physics* a stable elementary particle with a positive electric charge, equal in magnitude to that of an electron, and occurring in all atomic nuclei. □□ **protonic** /prə'tɒnɪk/ *adj.* [Gk, neut. of *prōtos* first]

protonotary /,prəʊtə'nəʊtərɪ, prə'tɒnə-/ *n.* (*pl.* -**ies**) (also **prothonotary** /,prəʊθ-, prə'θɒnə-/) a chief clerk in some law courts, orig. in the Byzantine court. □**Protonotary Apostolic** (or **Apostolical**) a member of the college of prelates who register papal acts, direct the canonization of saints, etc. [med.L *protonotarius* f. late Gk *protonotarios* (as PROTO-, NOTARY)]

protopectin /,prəʊtə'pektɪn/ *n.* = PECTOSE.

protophyte /'prəʊtə,faɪt/ *n.* a unicellular plant bearing gametes.

protoplasm /'prəʊtə,plæz(ə)m/ *n.* the material comprising the living part of a cell, consisting of a nucleus embedded in membrane-enclosed cytoplasm. □□ **protoplasmal** /-'plæzm(ə)l/ *adj.* **protoplasmatic** /-'mætɪk/ *adj.* **protoplasmic** /-'plæzmɪk/ *adj.* [Gk *protoplasma* (as PROTO-, PLASMA)]

protoplast /'prəʊtə,plæst/ *n.* the protoplasm of one cell. □□ **protoplastic** /-'plæstɪk/ *adj.* [F *protoplaste* or LL *protoplastus* f. Gk *protoplastos* (as PROTO-, *plassō* mould)]

prototherian /,prəʊtəʊ'θɪərɪən/ *n.* & *adj.* —*n.* any mammal of the subclass Prototheria, including monotremes. —*adj.* of or relating to this subclass. [PROTO- + Gk *thēr* wild beast]

prototype /'prəʊtə,taɪp/ *n.* **1** an original thing or person of which or whom copies, imitations, improved forms, representations, etc. are made. **2** a trial model or preliminary version of a vehicle, machine, etc. □□ **prototypal** *adj.* **prototypic** /-'tɪpɪk/ *adj.* **prototypical** /-'tɪpɪk(ə)l/ *adj.* **prototypically** /-'tɪpɪkəlɪ/ *adv.* [F *prototype* or LL *prototypus* f. Gk *prototupos* (as PROTO-, TYPE)]

protozoan /,prəʊtə'zəʊən/ *n.* & *adj.* —*n.* (also **protozoon** /-'zəʊɒn/) (*pl.* **protozoa** /-'zəʊə/ or **protozoans**) any usu. unicellular and microscopic organism of the subkingdom Protozoa, including amoebae and ciliates. —*adj.* (also **protozoic** /-'zəʊɪk/) of or relating to this phylum. □□ **protozoal** *adj.* [mod.L (as PROTO-, Gk *zōion* animal)]

protract /prə'trækt/ *v.tr.* **1** prolong or lengthen in space or esp. time (*protracted their stay for some weeks*). **2** draw (a plan of ground etc.) to scale. □□ **protractedly** *adv.* **protractedness** *n.* [L *protrahere protract-* (as PRO-¹, *trahere* draw)]

protractile /prə'træktaɪl/ *adj.* (of a part of the body etc.) capable of being protruded or extended.

protraction /prə'trækʃ(ə)n/ *n.* **1** the act or an instance of protracting; the state of being protracted. **2** a drawing to scale. **3** the action of a protractor muscle. [F *protraction* or LL *protractio* (as PROTRACT)]

protractor /prə'træktə(r)/ *n.* **1** an instrument for measuring angles, usu. in the form of a graduated semicircle. **2** a muscle serving to extend a limb etc.

protrude /prə'tru:d/ *v.* **1** *intr.* extend beyond or above a surface; project. **2** *tr.* thrust or cause to thrust forth. □□ **protrudent** *adj.* **protrusible** *adj.* **protrusion** /-ʒ(ə)n/ *n.* **protrusive** *adj.* [L *protrudere* (as PRO-¹, *trudere trus-* thrust)]

protrusile /prə'tru:saɪl/ *adj.* (of a limb etc.) capable of being thrust forward. [PRO-¹ + EXTRUSILE: see EXTRUDE]

protuberant /prə'tju:bərənt/ *adj.* bulging out; prominent (*protuberant eyes*; *a protuberant fact*). □□ **protuberance** *n.* [LL *protuberare* (as PRO-¹, *tuber* bump)]

proud /praʊd/ *adj.* **1** feeling greatly honoured or pleased (*am proud to know him*; *proud of his friendship*). **2 a** (often foll. by *of*) valuing oneself, one's possessions, etc. highly, or esp. too highly; haughty; arrogant (*proud of his ancient name*). **b** (often in *comb.*) having a proper pride; satisfied (*house-proud*; *proud of a job well done*). **3 a** (of an occasion etc.) justly arousing pride (*a proud day for us*; *a proud sight*). **b** (of an action etc.) showing pride (*a proud wave of the hand*). **4** (of a thing) imposing; splendid. **5** slightly projecting from a surface etc. (*the nail stood proud of the plank*). **6** (of flesh) overgrown round a healing wound. **7** (of water) swollen in flood. □**do proud** *colloq.* **1** treat (a person) with lavish generosity or honour (*they did us proud on our anniversary*). **2** (*refl.*) act honourably or worthily. **proud-hearted** haughty; arrogant. □□ **proudly** *adv.* **proudness** *n.* [OE *prūt, prūd* f. OF *prud, prod* oblique case of *pruz* etc. valiant, ult. f. LL *prode* f. L *prodesse* be of value (as PRO-¹, *esse* be)]

Prov. *abbr.* **1** Proverbs (Old Testament). **2** Province. **3** Provençal.

prove /pruːv/ *v.* (*past part.* **proved** or **proven** /ˈpruːv(ə)n, ˈprəʊ-/) **1** *tr.* (often foll. by *that* + clause) demonstrate the truth of by evidence or argument. **2** *intr.* **a** (usu. foll. by *to* + infin.) be found (*it proved to be untrue*). **b** emerge incontrovertibly as (*will prove the winner*). **3** *tr. Math.* test the accuracy of (a calculation). **4** *tr.* establish the genuineness and validity of (a will). **5** *intr.* (of dough) rise in bread-making. **6** *tr.* = PROOF 6. **7** *tr.* subject (a gun etc.) to a testing process. **8** *tr. archaic* test the qualities of; try. □**not proven** (in Scottish Law) a verdict that there is insufficient evidence to establish guilt or innocence. **prove oneself** show one's abilities, courage, etc. □□ **provable** *adj.* **provability** /-ˈbɪlɪtɪ/ *n.* **provably** *adv.* [ME f. OF *prover* f. L *probare* test, approve, demonstrate f. *probus* good]

provenance /ˈprɒvɪnəns/ *n.* **1** the place of origin or history, esp. of a work of art etc. **2** origin. [F f. *provenir* f. L *provenire* (as PRO-¹, *venire* come)]

Provençal /ˌprɒvɒnˈsɑːl, ˌprɒvɑˈsæl/ *adj. & n.* —*adj.* of or concerning the language, inhabitants, landscape, etc. of Provence, a former province of SE France. —*n.* **1** a native of Provence. **2** the language of Provence. [F (as PROVINCIAL f. *provincia* as L colloq. name for southern Gaul under Roman rule)]

provender /ˈprɒvɪndə(r)/ *n.* **1** animal fodder. **2** *joc.* food for human beings. [ME f. OF *provendre, provende* ult. f. L *praebenda* (see PREBEND)]

provenience /prəˈviːnɪəns/ *n. US* = PROVENANCE. [L *provenire* f. *venire* come]

proverb /ˈprɒvɜːb/ *n.* **1** a short pithy saying in general use, held to embody a general truth. **2** a person or thing that is notorious (*he is a proverb for inaccuracy*). **3** (**Proverbs** or **Book of Proverbs**) a didactic poetic Old Testament book of maxims attributed to Solomon and others. [ME f. OF *proverbe* or L *proverbium* (as PRO-¹, *verbum* word)]

proverbial /prəˈvɜːbɪəl/ *adj.* **1** (esp. of a specific characteristic etc.) as well-known as a proverb; notorious (*his proverbial honesty*). **2** of or referred to in a proverb (*the proverbial ill wind*). □□ **proverbiality** /-bɪˈælɪtɪ/ *n.* **proverbially** *adv.* [ME f. L *proverbialis* (as PROVERB)]

provide /prəˈvaɪd/ *v.* **1** *tr.* supply; furnish (*provided them with food; provided food for them; provided a chance for escape*). **2** *intr.* **a** (usu. foll. by *for, against*) make due preparation (*provided for any eventuality; provided against invasion*). **b** (usu. foll. by *for*) prepare for the maintenance of a person etc. **3** *tr.* (also *refl.*) equip with necessities (*they had to provide themselves*). **4** *tr.* (usu. foll. by *that*) stipulate in a will, statute, etc. **5** *tr.* (usu. foll. by *to*) *Eccl. hist.* **a** appoint (an incumbent) to a benefice. **b** (of the Pope) appoint (a successor) to a benefice not yet vacant. [ME f. L *providēre* (as PRO-¹, *vidēre vis-* see)]

provided /prəˈvaɪdɪd/ *adj. & conj.* —*adj.* supplied, furnished. —*conj.* (often foll. by *that*) on the condition or understanding (that).

providence /ˈprɒvɪd(ə)ns/ *n.* **1** the protective care of God or nature. **2** (**Providence**) God in this aspect. **3** timely care or preparation; foresight; thrift. □**special providence** a particular instance of God's providence. [ME f. OF *providence* or L *providentia* (as PROVIDE)]

provident /ˈprɒvɪd(ə)nt/ *adj.* having or showing foresight; thrifty. □**Provident Society** *Brit.* = *Friendly Society.* □□ **providently** *adv.* [ME f. L (as PROVIDE)]

providential /ˌprɒvɪˈdenʃ(ə)l/ *adj.* **1** of or by divine foresight or interposition. **2** opportune, lucky. □□ **providentially** *adv.* [PROVIDENCE + -IAL, after *evidential* etc.]

provider /prəˈvaɪdə(r)/ *n.* **1** a person or thing that provides. **2** the breadwinner of a family etc.

providing /prəˈvaɪdɪŋ/ *conj.* = PROVIDED *conj.*

province /ˈprɒvɪns/ *n.* **1** a principal administrative division of a country etc. **2** (**the provinces**) the whole of a country outside the capital, esp. regarded as uncultured, unsophisticated, etc. **3** a sphere of action; business (*outside my province as a teacher*). **4** a branch of learning etc. (*in the province of aesthetics*). **5** *Eccl.* a district under an archbishop or a metropolitan. **6** *Rom.Hist.* a territory outside Italy under a Roman governor. [ME f. OF f. L *provincia* charge, province]

provincial /prəˈvɪnʃ(ə)l/ *adj. & n.* —*adj.* **1 a** of or concerning a province. **b** of or concerning the provinces. **2** unsophisticated or uncultured in manner, speech, opinion, etc. —*n.* **1** an inhabitant of a province or the provinces. **2** an unsophisticated or uncultured person. **3** *Eccl.* the head or chief of a province or of a religious order in a province. □□ **provinciality** /-ʃɪˈælɪtɪ/ *n.* **provincialize** *v.tr.* (also **-ise**). **provincially** *adv.* [ME f. OF f. L *provincialis* (as PROVINCE)]

provincialism /prəˈvɪnʃəˌlɪz(ə)m/ *n.* **1** provincial manners, fashion, mode of thought, etc., esp. regarded as restricting or narrow. **2** a word or phrase peculiar to a provincial region. **3** concern for one's local area rather than one's country. □□ **provincialist** *n.*

provision /prəˈvɪʒ(ə)n/ *n. & v.* —*n.* **1 a** the act or an instance of providing (*made no provision for his future*). **b** something provided (*a provision of bread*). **2** (in *pl.*) food, drink, etc., esp. for an expedition. **3 a** a legal or formal statement providing for something. **b** a clause of this. **4** *Eccl. hist.* an appointment to a benefice not yet vacant (cf. PROVIDE 5). —*v.tr.* supply (an expedition etc.) with provisions. □□ **provisioner** *n.* **provisionless** *adj.* **provisionment** *n.* [ME f. OF f. L *provisio -onis* (as PROVIDE)]

provisional /prəˈvɪʒən(ə)l/ *adj. & n.* —*adj.* **1** providing for immediate needs only; temporary. **2** (**Provisional**) designating the unofficial wing of the IRA established in 1970, advocating terrorism. —*n.* (**Provisional**) a member of the Provisional wing of the IRA. □□ **provisionality** /-ˈnælɪtɪ/ *n.* **provisionally** *adv.* **provisionalness** *n.*

proviso /prəˈvaɪzəʊ/ *n.* (*pl.* **-os**) **1** a stipulation. **2** a clause of stipulation or limitation in a document. [L, neut. ablat. past part. of *providēre* PROVIDE, in med.L phr. *proviso quod* it being provided that]

provisor /prəˈvaɪzə(r)/ *n. Eccl.* **1** a deputy of a bishop or archbishop. **2** *hist.* the holder of a provision (see PROVISION *n.* 4). [ME f. AF *provisour* f. L *provisor -oris* (as PROVIDE)]

provisory /prəˈvaɪzərɪ/ *adj.* **1** conditional; having a proviso. **2** making provision (*provisory care*). □□ **provisorily** *adv.* [F *provisoire* or med.L *provisorius* (as PROVISOR)]

Provo /ˈprəʊvəʊ/ *n.* (*pl.* **-os**) *colloq.* a member of the Provisional IRA. [abbr.]

provocation /ˌprɒvəˈkeɪʃ(ə)n/ *n.* **1** the act or an instance of provoking; a state of being provoked (*did it under severe provocation*). **2** a cause of annoyance. **3** *Law* an action, insult, etc. held to be likely to provoke physical retaliation. [ME f. OF *provocation* or L *provocatio* (as PROVOKE)]

provocative /prəˈvɒkətɪv/ *adj. & n.* —*adj.* **1** (usu. foll. by *of*) tending to provoke, esp. anger or sexual desire. **2** intentionally annoying. —*n.* a provocative thing. □□ **provocatively** *adv.* **provocativeness** *n.* [ME f. obs. F *provocatif -ive* f. LL *provocativus* (as PROVOKE)]

provoke /prəˈvəʊk/ *v.tr.* **1 a** (often foll. by *to*, or *to* + infin.) rouse or incite (*provoked him to fury*). **b** (as **provoking** *adj.*) exasperating; irritating. **2** call forth; instigate (indignation, an inquiry, a storm, etc.). **3** (usu. foll. by *into* + verbal noun) irritate or stimulate (a person) (*the itch provoked him into scratching*). **4** tempt; allure. **5** cause, give rise to (*will provoke fermentation*). □□ **provokable** *adj.* **provokingly** *adv.* [ME f. OF *provoquer* f. L *provocare* (as PRO-¹, *vocare* call)]

provost /'prɒvəst/ n. **1** Brit. the head of some colleges esp. at Oxford or Cambridge. **2** Eccl. **a** the head of a chapter in a cathedral. **b** hist. the head of a religious community. **3** Sc. the head of a municipal corporation or burgh. **4** the Protestant minister of the principal church of a town etc. in Germany etc. **5** US a high administrative officer in a university. **6** = provost marshal. □**provost guard** US a body of soldiers under a provost marshal. **provost marshal 1** the head of military police in camp or on active service. **2** the master-at-arms of a ship in which a court-martial is to be held. □□**provostship** n. [ME f. OE profost & AF provost, prevost f. med.L propositus for praepositus: see PRAEPOSTOR]

prow /praʊ/ n. **1** the fore-part or bow of a ship adjoining the stern. **2** a pointed or projecting front part. [F proue f. Prov. proa or It. dial. prua f. L prora f. Gk prōira]

prowess /'praʊɪs/ n. **1** skill; expertise. **2** valour; gallantry. [ME f. OF proesce f. prou valiant]

prowl /praʊl/ v. & n. —v. **1** tr. roam (a place) in search or as if in search of prey, plunder, etc. **2** intr. (often foll. by about, around) move about like a hunter. —n. the act or an instance of prowling. □**on the prowl** moving about secretively or rapaciously, esp. in search of sexual contact etc. **prowl car** US a police squad car. □□**prowler** n. [ME prolle, of unkn. orig.]

prox. abbr. proximo.

prox. acc. abbr. proxime accessit.

proxemics /prɒk'si:mɪks/ n. Sociol. the study of socially conditioned spatial factors in ordinary human relations. [PROXIMITY + -emics: cf. phonemics]

proximal /'prɒksɪm(ə)l/ adj. situated towards the centre of the body or point of attachment. □□**proximally** adv. [L proximus nearest]

proximate /'prɒksɪmət/ adj. **1** nearest or next before or after (in place, order, time, causation, thought process, etc.). **2** approximate. □□**proximately** adv. [L proximatus past part. of proximare draw near (as PROXIMAL)]

proxime accessit /ˌprɒksɪmɪ ək'sɪsɪt/ n. **1** second place in an examination etc. **2** a person gaining this. [L, = came very near]

proximity /prɒk'sɪmɪtɪ/ n. nearness in space, time, etc. (sat in close proximity to them). □**proximity fuse** an electronic device causing a projectile to explode when near its target. **proximity of blood** kinship. [ME f. F proximité or L proximitas (as PROXIMAL)]

proximo /'prɒksɪˌməʊ/ adj. Commerce of next month (the third proximo). [L proximo mense in the next month]

proxy /'prɒksɪ/ n. (pl. -ies) (also attrib.) **1** the authorization given to a substitute or deputy (a proxy vote; was married by proxy). **2** a person authorized to act as a substitute etc. **3 a** a document giving the power to act as a proxy, esp. in voting. **b** a vote given by this. [ME f. obs. procuracy f. med.L procuratia (as PROCURATION)]

PRS abbr. **1** (in the UK) President of the Royal Society. **2** Performing Rights Society.

prude /pruːd/ n. a person having or affecting an attitude of extreme propriety or modesty esp. in sexual matters. □□**prudery** n. (pl. -ies). **prudish** adj. **prudishly** adv. **prudishness** n. [F, back form. f. prudefemme fem. of prud'homme good man and true f. prou worthy]

prudent /'pruːd(ə)nt/ adj. **1** (of a person or conduct) careful to avoid undesired consequences; circumspect. **2** discreet. □□**prudence** n. **prudently** adv. [ME f. OF prudent or L prudens = providens PROVIDENT]

prudential /pruː'denʃ(ə)l/ adj. & n. —adj. of, involving, or marked by prudence (prudential motives). —n. (in pl.) **1** prudential considerations or matters. **2** US minor administrative or financial matters. □□

prudentialism n. **prudentialist** n. **prudentially** adv. [PRUDENT + -IAL, after evidential etc.]

pruinose /'pruːɪˌnəʊs/ adj. esp. Bot. covered with white powdery granules; frosted in appearance. [L pruinosus f. pruina hoar-frost]

prune¹ /pruːn/ n. **1** a dried plum. **2** colloq. a silly or disliked person. [ME f. OF ult. f. L prunum f. Gk prou(m)non plum]

prune² /pruːn/ v.tr. **1 a** (often foll. by down) trim (a tree etc.) by cutting away dead or overgrown branches etc. **b** (usu. foll. by off, away) lop (branches etc.) from a tree. **2** reduce (costs etc.) (must try to prune expenses). **3 a** (often foll. by of) clear (a book etc.) of superfluities. **b** remove (superfluities). □**pruning-hook** a long-handled hooked cutting tool used for pruning. □□**pruner** n. [ME prouyne f. OF pro(o)ignier ult. f. L rotundus ROUND]

prunella¹ /pruː'nelə/ n. any plant of the genus Prunella, esp. P. vulgaris, bearing pink, purple, or white flower spikes, and formerly thought to cure quinsy. Also called SELF HEAL. [mod.L, = quinsy: earlier brunella dimin. of med.L brunus brown]

prunella² /pruː'nelə/ n. a strong silk or worsted fabric used formerly for barristers' gowns, the uppers of women's shoes, etc. [perh. f. F prunelle, of uncert. orig.]

prurient /'prʊərɪənt/ adj. **1** having an unhealthy obsession with sexual matters. **2** encouraging such an obsession. □□**prurience** n. **pruriency** n. **pruriently** adv. [L prurire itch, be wanton]

prurigo /prʊə'raɪgəʊ/ n. a skin disease marked by severe itching. □□**pruriginous** /prʊə'rɪdʒɪnəs/ adj. [L prurigo -ginis f. prurire to itch]

pruritus /prʊə'raɪtəs/ n. severe itching of the skin. □□**pruritic** /-'rɪtɪk/ adj. [L, = itching (as PRURIGO)]

Prussian /'prʌʃ(ə)n/ adj. & n. —adj. of or relating to Prussia, a former German State, or relating to its rigidly militaristic tradition. —n. a native of Prussia. □**Old Prussian** the language spoken in Prussia until the 17th c. **Prussian blue** a deep blue pigment, ferric ferrocyanide, used in painting and dyeing.

prussic /'prʌsɪk/ adj. of or obtained from Prussian blue. □**prussic acid** hydrocyanic acid. [F prussique f. Prusse Prussia]

pry¹ /praɪ/ v.intr. (**pries, pried**) **1** (usu. foll. by into) inquire impertinently (into a person's private affairs etc.). **2** (usu. foll. by into, about, etc.) look or peer inquisitively. □□**prying** adj. **pryingly** adv. [ME prie, of unkn. orig.]

pry² /praɪ/ v.tr. (**pries, pried**) US (often foll. by out of, open, etc.) = PRISE. [PRISE taken as pries 3rd sing. pres.]

PS abbr. **1** Police Sergeant. **2** postscript. **3** private secretary. **4** prompt side.

Ps. abbr. (pl. **Pss.**) Psalm, Psalms (Old Testament).

psalm /sɑːm/ n. **1 a** (also **Psalm**) any of the sacred songs contained in the Book of Psalms, esp. when set for metrical chanting in a service. **b** (**the Psalms** or **the Book of Psalms**) the book of the Old Testament containing the Psalms. **2** a sacred song or hymn. □**psalm-book** a book containing the Psalms, esp. with metrical settings for worship. □□**psalmic** adj. [OE (p)sealm f. LL psalmus f. Gk psalmos song sung to a harp f. psallō pluck]

psalmist /'sɑːmɪst/ n. **1** the author or composer of a psalm. **2** (**the Psalmist**) David or the author of any of the Psalms. [LL psalmista (as PSALM)]

psalmody /'sɑːmədɪ, 'sæl-/ n. **1** the practice or art of singing psalms, hymns, etc., esp. in public worship. **2 a** the arrangement of psalms for singing. **b** the psalms so arranged. □□**psalmodic** /sæl'mɒdɪk/ adj. **psalmodist** n. **psalmodize** v.intr. (also -ise). [ME f. LL psalmodia f. Gk psalmōidia singing to a harp (as PSALM, ōidē song)]

psalter /'sɔːltə(r), 'spl-/ n. **1 a** the Book of Psalms. **b** a version of this (the English Psalter; Prayer-Book Psalter). **2** a copy of the Psalms, esp. for liturgical use. [ME f. AF sauter, OF sautier, & OE (p)saltere f.

psalterium f. Gk *psaltērion* stringed instrument (*psallō* pluck), in eccl.L Book of Psalms]

psalterium /sɔːlˈtɛrɪəm, sɒl-/ *n.* the third stomach of a ruminant, the omasum. [L (see PSALTER): named from its booklike form]

psaltery /ˈsɔːltərɪ, ˈsɒl-/ *n.* (*pl.* **-ies**) an ancient and medieval instrument like a dulcimer but played by plucking the strings with the fingers or a plectrum. [ME f. OF *sauterie* etc. f. L (as PSALTER)]

PSBR *abbr. Brit.* public sector borrowing requirement.

psephology /seˈfɒlədʒɪ, pse-/ *n.* the statistical study of elections, voting, etc. □□ **psephological** /-fəˈlɒdʒɪk(ə)l/ *adj.* **psephologically** /-fəˈlɒdʒɪkəlɪ/ *adv.* **psephologist** *n.* [Gk *psēphos* pebble, vote + -LOGY]

pseud /sjuːd/ *adj. & n. colloq.* —*adj.* intellectually or socially pretentious; not genuine. —*n.* such a person; a poseur. [abbr. of PSEUDO]

pseud- var. of PSEUDO-.

pseudepigrapha /ˌsjuːdɪˈpɪɡrəfə/ *n.pl.* **1** Jewish writings ascribed to various Old Testament prophets etc. but written during or just before the early Christian period. **2** spurious writings. □□ **pseudepigraphal** *adj.* **pseudepigraphic** /-ˈɡræfɪk/ *adj.* **pseudepigraphical** /-ˈɡræfɪk(ə)l/ *adj.* [neut. pl. of Gk *pseudepigraphos* with false title (as PSEUDO-, EPIGRAPH)]

pseudo /ˈsjuːdəʊ/ *adj. & n.* —*adj.* **1** sham; spurious. **2** insincere. —*n.* (*pl.* **-os**) a pretentious or insincere person. [see PSEUDO-]

pseudo- /ˈsjuːdəʊ/ *comb. form* (also **pseud-** before a vowel) **1** supposed or purporting to be but not really so; false; not genuine (*pseudo-intellectual*; *pseudepigrapha*). **2** resembling or imitating (often in technical applications) (*pseudo-language*; *pseudo-acid*). [Gk f. *pseudēs* false, *pseudos* falsehood]

pseudocarp /ˈsjuːdəʊˌkɑːp/ *n.* a fruit formed from parts other than the ovary, e.g. the strawberry or fig. [PSEUDO- + Gk *karpos* fruit]

pseudomorph /ˈsjuːdəˌmɔːf/ *n.* **1** a crystal etc. consisting of one mineral with the form proper to another. **2** a false form. □□ **pseudomorphic** /-ˈmɔːfɪk/ *adj.* **pseudomorphism** /-ˈmɔːfɪz(ə)m/ *n.* **pseudomorphous** /-ˈmɔːfəs/ *adj.* [PSEUDO- + Gk *morphē* form]

pseudonym /ˈsjuːdənɪm/ *n.* a fictitious name, esp. one assumed by an author. [F *pseudonyme* f. Gk *pseudōnumos* as PSEUDO-, *-ōnumos* f. *onoma* name)]

pseudonymous /sjuːˈdɒnɪməs/ *adj.* writing or written under a false name. □□ **pseudonymity** /-ˈnɪmɪtɪ/ *n.* **pseudonymously** *adv.*

pseudopod /ˈsjuːdəʊˌpɒd/ *n.* = PSEUDOPODIUM. [mod.L (as PSEUDOPODIUM)]

pseudopodium /ˌsjuːdəʊˈpəʊdɪəm/ *n.* (*pl.* **pseudopodia** /-dɪə/) (in amoeboid cells) a temporary protrusion of protoplasm for movement, feeding, etc. [mod.L (as PSEUDO-, PODIUM)]

pseudo-science /ˈsjuːdəʊˌsaɪəns/ *n.* a pretended or spurious science. □□ **pseudo-scientific** /-ˈtɪfɪk/ *adj.*

pshaw /pʃɔː, ʃɔː/ *int. archaic* an expression of contempt or impatience. [imit.]

psi /psaɪ/ *n.* **1** the twenty-third letter of the Greek alphabet (Ψ, ψ). **2** supposed parapsychological faculties, phenomena, etc. regarded collectively. [Gk]

p.s.i. *abbr.* pounds per square inch.

psilocybin /ˌsɪləˈsaɪbɪn/ *n.* a hallucinogenic alkaloid found in Mexican mushrooms of the genus *Psilocybe*. [*Psilocybe* f. Gk *psilos* bald + *kubē* head]

psilosis /saɪˈləʊsɪs/ *n.* = SPRUE². [Gk *psilōsis* f. *psilos* bare]

psittacine /ˈsɪtəˌsaɪn/ *adj.* of or relating to parrots; parrot-like. [L *psittacinus* f. *psittacus* f. Gk *psittakos* parrot]

psittacosis /ˌsɪtəˈkəʊsɪs/ *n.* a contagious viral disease of birds transmissible (esp. from parrots) to human beings as a form of pneumonia. [mod.L f. L *psittacus* (as PSITTACINE) + -OSIS]

psoas /ˈsəʊəs/ *n.* either of two muscles used in flexing the hip joint. [Gk, accus. pl. of *psoa*, taken as sing.]

psoriasis /səˈraɪəsɪs/ *n.* a skin disease marked by red scaly patches. □□ **psoriatic** /ˌsɔːrɪˈætɪk/ *adj.* [mod.L f. Gk *psōriasis* f. *psōriaō* have an itch f. *psōra* itch]

psst /pst/ *int.* (also **pst**) a whispered exclamation seeking to attract a person's attention surreptitiously. [imit.]

PST *abbr. US* Pacific Standard Time.

PSV *abbr. Brit.* public service vehicle.

psych /saɪk/ *v.tr. colloq.* **1** (usu. foll. by *up*; often *refl.*) prepare (oneself or another person) mentally for an ordeal etc. **2 a** (usu. foll. by *out*) analyse (a person's motivation etc.) for one's own advantage (*can't psych him out*). **b** subject to psychoanalysis. **3** (often foll. by *out*) influence a person psychologically, esp. negatively; intimidate, frighten. □ **psych out** break down mentally; become confused or deranged. [abbr.]

psyche /ˈsaɪkɪ/ *n.* **1** the soul; the spirit. **2** the mind. [L f. Gk *psukhē* breath, life, soul]

psychedelia /ˌsaɪkɪˈdiːlɪə/ *n.pl.* **1** psychedelic articles, esp. posters, paintings, etc. **2** psychedelic drugs.

psychedelic /ˌsaɪkɪˈdɛlɪk/ *adj. & n.* —*adj.* **1 a** expanding the mind's awareness etc., esp. through the use of hallucinogenic drugs. **b** (of an experience) hallucinatory; bizarre. **c** (of a drug) producing hallucinations. **2** *colloq.* **a** producing an effect resembling that of a psychedelic drug; having vivid colours or designs etc. **b** (of colours, patterns, etc.) bright, bold and often abstract. —*n.* a hallucinogenic drug. □□ **psychedelically** *adv.* [irreg. f. Gk (as PSYCHE, *dēlos* clear, manifest)]

psychiatry /saɪˈkaɪətrɪ/ *n.* the study and treatment of mental disease. □□ **psychiatric** /-kɪˈætrɪk/ *adj.* **psychiatrical** /-kɪˈætrɪk(ə)l/ *adj.* **psychiatrically** /-kɪˈætrɪkəlɪ/ *adv.* **psychiatrist** *n.* [as PSYCHE + *iatreia* healing f. *iatros* healer]

psychic /ˈsaɪkɪk/ *adj. & n.* —*adj.* **1 a** (of a person) considered to have occult powers, such as telepathy, clairvoyance, etc. **b** (of a faculty, phenomenon, etc.) inexplicable by natural laws. **2** of the soul or mind. **3** *Bridge* (of a bid) made on the basis of a hand not usually considered strong enough to support it. —*n.* **1** a person considered to have psychic powers; a medium. **2** *Bridge* a psychic bid. **3** (in *pl.*) the study of psychic phenomena. [Gk *psukhikos* (as PSYCHE)]

psychical /ˈsaɪkɪk(ə)l/ *adj.* **1** concerning psychic phenomena or faculties (*psychical research*). **2** of the soul or mind. □□ **psychically** *adv.* **psychicism** /-ɪˌsɪz(ə)m/ *n.* **psychicist** /-ɪˌsɪst/ *n.*

psycho /ˈsaɪkəʊ/ *n. & adj. colloq.* —*n.* (*pl.* **-os**) a psychopath. —*adj.* psychopathic. [abbr.]

psycho- /ˈsaɪkəʊ/ *comb. form* relating to the mind or psychology. [Gk *psukho-* as PSYCHE)]

psychoactive /ˌsaɪkəʊˈæktɪv/ *adj.* affecting the mind.

psychoanalysis /ˌsaɪkəʊəˈnælɪsɪs/ *n.* a therapeutic method of treating mental disorders by investigating the interaction of conscious and unconscious elements in the mind and bringing repressed fears and conflicts into the conscious mind. □□ **psychoanalyse** /-ˈænəˌlaɪz/ *v.tr.* **psychoanalyst** /-ˈænəlɪst/ *n.* **psychoanalytic** /-ˌænəˈlɪtɪk/ *adj.* **psychoanalytical** /-ˌænəˈlɪtɪk(ə)l/ *adj.* **psychoanalytically** /-ˌænəˈlɪtɪkəlɪ/ *adv.*

psychobabble /ˈsaɪkəʊˌbæb(ə)l/ *n. US colloq. derog.* jargon used in popular psychology.

psychodrama /ˈsaɪkəʊˌdrɑːmə/ *n.* **1** a form of psychotherapy in which patients act out events from their past. **2** a play or film etc. in which psychological elements are the main interest.

psychodynamics /ˌsaɪkəʊdaɪˈnæmɪks/ *n.pl.* (treated as *sing.*) the study of the activity of and the interrelation between the various parts of an individual's personality or psyche. □□ **psychodynamic** *adj.* **psychodynamically** *adv.*

b *but* d *dog* f *few* g *get* h *he* j *yes* k *cat* l *leg* m *man* n *no* p *pen* r *red* s *sit* t *top* v *voice*

psychogenesis /ˌsaɪkəʊ'dʒenɪsɪs/ *n.* the study of the origin of the mind's development.

psychokinesis /ˌsaɪkəʊki'ni:sɪs/ *n.* the movement of objects supposedly by mental effort without the action of natural forces.

psycholinguistics /ˌsaɪkəʊlɪŋ'gwɪstɪks/ *n.pl.* (treated as *sing.*) the study of the psychological aspects of language and language-learning. □□ **psycholinguist** /-'lɪŋgwɪst/ *n.* **psycholinguistic** *adj.*

psychological /ˌsaɪkə'lɒdʒɪk(ə)l/ *adj.* **1** of, relating to, or arising in the mind. **2** of or relating to psychology. **3** *colloq.* (of an ailment etc.) having a basis in the mind; imaginary (*her cold is psychological*). □ **psychological block** a mental inability or inhibition caused by emotional factors. **psychological moment** the most appropriate time for achieving a particular effect or purpose. **psychological warfare** a campaign directed at reducing an opponent's morale. □□ **psychologically** *adv.*

psychology /saɪ'kɒlədʒɪ/ *n.* (*pl.* **-ies**) **1** the scientific study of the human mind and its functions, esp. those affecting behaviour in a given context. **2** a treatise on or theory of this. **3 a** the mental characteristics or attitude of a person or group. **b** the mental factors governing a situation or activity (*the psychology of crime*). □□ **psychologist** *n.* **psychologize** *v.tr.* & *intr.* (also **-ise**). [mod.L *psychologia* (as PSYCHO-, -LOGY)]

psychometrics /ˌsaɪkəʊ'metrɪks/ *n.pl.* (treated as *sing.*) the science of measuring mental capacities and processes.

psychometry /saɪ'kɒmɪtrɪ/ *n.* **1** the supposed divination of facts about events, people, etc., from inanimate objects associated with them. **2** the measurement of mental abilities. □□ **psychometric** /-kə'metrɪk/ *adj.* **psychometrically** /-kə'metrɪkəlɪ/ *adv.* **psychometrist** *n.*

psychomotor /ˌsaɪkəʊ,məʊtə(r)/ *adj.* concerning the study of movement resulting from mental activity.

psychoneurosis /ˌsaɪkəʊnjʊə'rəʊsɪs/ *n.* neurosis, esp. with the indirect expression of emotions.

psychopath /'saɪkə,pæθ/ *n.* **1** a person suffering from chronic mental disorder esp. with abnormal or violent social behaviour. **2** a mentally or emotionally unstable person. □□ **psychopathic** /-'pæθɪk/ *adj.* **psychopathically** /-'pæθɪkəlɪ/ *adv.*

psychopathology /ˌsaɪkəʊpə'θɒlədʒɪ/ *n.* **1** the scientific study of mental disorders. **2** a mentally or behaviourally disordered state. □□ **psychopathological** /-ˌpæθə'lɒdʒɪk(ə)l/ *adj.*

psychopathy /saɪ'kɒpəθɪ/ *n.* psychopathic or psychologically abnormal behaviour.

psychophysics /ˌsaɪkəʊ'fɪzɪks/ *n.* the science of the relation between the mind and the body. □□ **psychophysical** *adj.*

psychophysiology /ˌsaɪkəʊ,fɪzɪ'ɒlədʒɪ/ *n.* the branch of physiology dealing with mental phenomena. □□ **psychophysiological** /-zɪə'lɒdʒɪk(ə)l/ *adj.*

psychosexual /ˌsaɪkəʊ'sekʃʊəl, -'sekʃʊəl/ *adj.* of or involving the psychological aspects of the sexual impulse. □□ **psychosexually** *adv.*

psychosis /saɪ'kəʊsɪs/ *n.* (*pl.* **psychoses** /-si:z/) a severe mental derangement, esp. when resulting in delusions and loss of contact with external reality. [Gk *psukhōsis* f. *psukhoō* give life to (as PSYCHE)]

psychosocial /ˌsaɪkəʊ'səʊʃ(ə)l/ *adj.* of or involving the influence of social factors or human interactive behaviour. □□ **psychosocially** *adv.*

psychosomatic /ˌsaɪkəʊsə'mætɪk/ *adj.* **1** (of an illness etc.) caused or aggravated by mental conflict, stress, etc. **2** of the mind and body together. □□ **psychosomatically** *adv.*

psychosurgery /ˌsaɪkəʊ'sɜːdʒərɪ/ *n.* brain surgery as a means of treating mental disorder. □□ **psychosurgical** *adj.*

psychotherapy /ˌsaɪkəʊ'θerəpɪ/ *n.* the treatment of mental disorder by psychological means. □□ **psychotherapeutic** /-'pju:tɪk/ *adj.* **psychotherapist** *n.*

psychotic /saɪ'kɒtɪk/ *adj.* & *n.* —*adj.* of or characterized by a psychosis. —*n.* a person suffering from a psychosis. □□ **psychotically** *adv.*

psychotropic /ˌsaɪkəʊ'trɒpɪk/ *n.* (of a drug) acting on the mind. [PSYCHO- + Gk *tropē* turning: see TROPIC]

psychrometer /saɪ'krɒmɪtə(r)/ *n.* a thermometer consisting of a dry bulb and a wet bulb for measuring atmospheric humidity. [Gk *psukhros* cold + -METER]

PT *abbr.* physical training.

Pt *symb. Chem.* the element platinum.

pt. *abbr.* **1** part. **2** pint. **3** point. **4** port.

PTA *abbr.* **1** parent-teacher association. **2** Passenger Transport Authority.

ptarmigan /'tɑːmɪgən/ *n.* any of various game-birds of the genus *Lagopus*, esp. *L. mutus*, with grouselike appearance and black or grey plumage in the summer and white in the winter. [Gael. *tàrmachan*: p- after Gk words in *pt-*]

PT boat *n. US* a motor torpedo-boat. [Patrol Torpedo]

Pte. *abbr.* Private (soldier).

pteridology /ˌterɪ'dɒlədʒɪ/ *n.* the study of ferns. □□ **pteridological** /-də'lɒdʒɪk(ə)l/ *adj.* **pteridologist** *n.* [Gk *pteris -idos* fern + -LOGY]

pteridophyte /'terɪdə,faɪt/ *n.* any flowerless plant of the division Pteridophyta, including ferns, clubmosses, and horsetails. [Gk *pteris -idos* fern + *phuton* plant]

ptero- /'terəʊ/ *comb. form* wing. [Gk *pteron* wing]

pterodactyl /ˌterə'dæktɪl/ *n.* a large extinct flying birdlike reptile with a long slender head and neck.

pteropod /'terə,pɒd/ *n.* a marine gastropod with the middle part of its foot expanded into a pair of winglike lobes. [PTERO- + Gk *pous podos* foot]

pterosaur /'terə,sɔ:(r)/ *n.* any of a group of extinct flying reptiles with large bat-like wings, including pterodactyls. [PTERO- + Gk *saura* lizard]

pteroylglutamic acid /ˌterəʊ,aɪlglu:'tæmɪk/ *n.* = FOLIC ACID. [*pteroic* acid + -YL + GLUTAMIC (ACID)]

pterygoid process /'terɪ,gɔɪd/ *adj.* each of a pair of processes from the sphenoid bone in the skull. [Gk *pterux -ugos* wing]

PTFE *abbr.* polytetrafluoroethylene.

ptisan /'tɪz(ə)n, tɪ'zæn/ *n.* a nourishing drink, esp. barley water. [ME & OF *tizanne* etc. f. L *ptisana* f. Gk *ptisanē* peeled barley]

PTO *abbr.* please turn over.

Ptolemaic /ˌtɒlɪ'meɪɪk/ *adj. hist.* **1** of or relating to Ptolemy, a 2nd-c. Alexandrian astronomer, or his theories. **2** of or relating to the Ptolemies, Macedonian rulers of Egypt from the death of Alexander the Great (323 BC) to the death of Cleopatra (30 BC). □ **Ptolemaic system** the theory that the earth is the stationary centre of the Universe (cf. COPERNICAN SYSTEM). [L *Ptolemaeus* f. Gk *Ptolemaios*]

ptomaine /'təʊmeɪn/ *n.* any of various amine compounds, some toxic, in putrefying animal and vegetable matter. □ **ptomaine poisoning** *archaic* food poisoning. [F *ptomaïne* f. It. *ptomaina* irreg. f. Gk *ptōma* corpse]

ptosis /'təʊsɪs/ *n.* a drooping of the upper eyelid due to paralysis etc. □□ **ptotic** /'təʊtɪk/ *adj.* [Gk *ptōsis* f. *piptō* fall]

Pty. *abbr. Austral., NZ,* & *S.Afr.* proprietary.

ptyalin /'taɪəlɪn/ *n.* an enzyme which hydrolyses certain carbohydrates and is found in the saliva of humans and some other animals. [Gk *ptualon* spittle]

Pu *symb. Chem.* the element plutonium.

pub /pʌb/ *n. colloq.* **1** *Brit.* a public house. **2** *Austral.* a hotel. □ **pub-crawl** *Brit. colloq.* a drinking tour of several pubs. [abbr.]

puberty /'pju:bətɪ/ *n.* the period during which adolescents reach sexual maturity and become capable of reproduction. □ **age of puberty** the age at which puberty begins, in law usu. 14 in boys and 12 in girls.

□□pubertal *adj.* [ME f. F *puberté* or L *pubertas* f. *puber* adult]

pubes[1] /'pju:bi:z/ *n.* (*pl.* same) the lower part of the abdomen at the front of the pelvis, covered with hair from puberty. [L]

pubes[2] *pl.* of PUBIS.

pubescence /pju:'bes(ə)ns/ *n.* 1 the time when puberty begins. 2 *Bot.* soft down on the leaves and stems of plants. 3 *Zool.* soft down on various parts of animals, esp. insects. □□**pubescent** *adj.* [F *pubescence* or med.L *pubescentia* f. L *pubescere* reach puberty]

pubic /'pju:bɪk/ *adj.* of or relating to the pubes or pubis.

pubis /'pju:bɪs/ *n.* (*pl.* **pubes** /-bi:z/) either of a pair of bones forming the two sides of the pelvis. [L *os pubis* bone of the PUBES]

public /'pʌblɪk/ *adj.* & *n.* —*adj.* 1 of or concerning the people as a whole (*a public holiday*; *the public interest*). 2 open to or shared by all the people (*public baths*; *public library*; *public meeting*). 3 done or existing openly (*made his views public*; *a public protest*). 4 a (of a service, funds, etc.) provided by or concerning local or central government (*public money*; *public records*; *public expenditure*). b (of a person) in government (*had a distinguished public career*). 5 well-known; famous (*a public institution*). 6 *Brit.* of, for, or acting for, a university (*public examination*). —*n.* 1 (as *sing.* or *pl.*) the community in general, or members of the community. 2 a section of the community having a particular interest or in some special connection (*the reading public*; *my public demands my loyalty*). 3 *Brit. colloq.* **a** = *public bar*. **b** = *public house*. □**go public** become a public company. **in public** openly, publicly. **in the public domain** belonging to the public as a whole, esp. not subject to copyright. **in the public eye** famous or notorious. **public act** an act of legislation affecting the public as a whole. **public-address system** loudspeakers, microphones, amplifiers, etc., used in addressing large audiences. **public bar** *Brit.* the least expensive bar in a public house. **public bill** a bill of legislation affecting the public as a whole. **public company** *Brit.* a company that sells shares to all buyers on the open market. **public enemy** a notorious wanted criminal. **public figure** a famous person. **public health** the provision of adequate sanitation, drainage, etc. by government. **public house** 1 *Brit.* an inn providing alcoholic drinks for consumption on the premises. 2 an inn. **public law** 1 the law of relations between individuals and the State. 2 = *public act.* **public lending right** the right of authors to payment when their books etc. are lent by public libraries. **public libel** a published libel. **public nuisance** 1 an illegal act against the public generally. 2 *colloq.* an obnoxious person. **public opinion** views, esp. moral, prevalent among the general public. **public ownership** the State ownership of the means of production, distribution, and exchange. **public prosecutor** a law officer conducting criminal proceedings on behalf of the State or in the public interest. **Public Record Office** an institution keeping official archives, esp. birth, marriage, and death certificates, for public inspection. **public relations** the professional maintenance of a favourable public image, esp. by a company, famous person, etc. **public relations officer** a person employed by a company etc. to promote a favourable public image. **public school** 1 *Brit.* a private fee-paying secondary school, esp. for boarders. 2 *US, Austral.,* & *Sc.* etc. any non-fee-paying school. **public sector** that part of an economy, industry, etc., that is controlled by the State. **public servant** a State official. **public spirit** a willingness to engage in community action. **public-spirited** having a public spirit. **public-spiritedly** in a public-spirited manner. **public-spiritedness** the quality of being public-spirited. **public transport**

buses, trains, etc., charging set fares and running on fixed routes, esp. when State-owned. **public utility** an organization supplying water, gas, etc. to the community. **public works** building operations etc. done by or for the State on behalf of the community. **public wrong** an offence against society as a whole. □□**publicly** *adv.* [ME f. OF *public* or L *publicus* f. *pubes* adult]

publican /'pʌblɪkən/ *n.* 1 a *Brit.* the keeper of a public house. b *Austral.* the keeper of a hotel. 2 *Rom.Hist.* & *Bibl.* a tax-collector or tax-farmer. [ME f. OF *publicain* f. L *publicanus* f. *publicum* public revenue (as PUBLIC)]

publication /,pʌblɪ'keɪʃ(ə)n/ *n.* 1 a the preparation and issuing of a book, newspaper, engraving, music, etc. to the public. b a book etc. so issued. 2 the act or an instance of making something publicly known. [ME f. OF f. L *publicatio -onis* (as PUBLISH)]

publicist /'pʌblɪsɪst/ *n.* 1 a publicity agent or public relations officer. 2 a journalist, esp. concerned with current affairs. 3 *archaic* a writer or other person skilled in international law. □□**publicism** *n.* **publicistic** /-'sɪstɪk/ *adj.* [F *publiciste* f. L (*jus*) *publicum* public law]

publicity /pʌb'lɪsɪtɪ/ *n.* 1 a the professional exploitation of a product, company, person, etc., by advertising or popularizing. b material or information used for this. 2 public exposure; notoriety. □**publicity agent** a person employed to produce or heighten public exposure. [F *publicité* (as PUBLIC)]

publicize /'pʌblɪsaɪz/ *v.tr.* (also **-ise**) advertise; make publicly known.

publish /'pʌblɪʃ/ *v.tr.* 1 (also *absol.*) (of an author, publisher, etc.) prepare and issue (a book, newspaper, engraving, etc.) for public sale. 2 make generally known. 3 announce (an edict etc.) formally; read (marriage banns). 4 *Law* communicate (a libel etc.) to a third party. □□**publishable** *adj.* [ME *puplise* etc. f. OF *puplier, publier* f. L *publicare* (as PUBLIC)]

publisher /'pʌblɪʃə(r)/ *n.* 1 a person or esp. a company that produces and distributes copies of a book, newspaper, etc. for sale. 2 *US* a newspaper proprietor. 3 a person or thing that publishes.

puce /pju:s/ *adj.* & *n.* dark red or purple-brown. [F, = flea(-colour) f. L *pulex -icis*]

puck[1] /pʌk/ *n.* a rubber disc used as a ball in ice hockey. [19th c.: orig. unkn.]

puck[2] /pʌk/ *n.* 1 a mischievous or evil sprite. 2 a mischievous child. □□**puckish** *adj.* **puckishly** *adv.* **puckishness** *n.* **pucklike** *adj.* [OE *pūca*: cf. Welsh *pwca,* Ir. *púca*]

pucka var. of PUKKA.

pucker /'pʌkə(r)/ *v.* & *n.* —*v.tr.* & *intr.* (often foll. by *up*) gather or cause to gather into wrinkles, folds, or bulges (*puckered her eyebrows*; *this seam is puckered up*). —*n.* such a wrinkle, bulge, fold, etc. □□**puckery** *adj.* [prob. frequent., formed as POKE[2], POCKET (cf. PURSE)]

pud /pʊd/ *n. colloq.* = PUDDING. [abbr.]

pudding /'pʊdɪŋ/ *n.* 1 a any of various sweet cooked dishes (*plum pudding*; *rice pudding*). b a savoury dish containing flour, suet, etc. (*Yorkshire pudding*; *steak and kidney pudding*). c the sweet course of a meal. d the intestines of a pig etc. stuffed with oatmeal, spices, blood, etc. (*black pudding*). 2 *colloq.* a person or thing resembling a pudding. 3 (*Naut.* = **puddening** /'pʊdənɪŋ/) a pad or tow binding to prevent chafing etc. □**in the pudding club** *sl.* pregnant. **pudding-cloth** a cloth used for tying up some puddings for boiling. **pudding face** *colloq.* a large fat face. **pudding-head** *colloq.* a stupid person. **pudding-stone** a conglomerate rock consisting of rounded pebbles in a siliceous matrix. □□**puddingy** *adj.* [ME *poding* f. OF *boudin* black pudding ult. f. L *botellus* sausage: see BOWEL]

puddle /'pʌd(ə)l/ *n.* & *v.* —*n.* 1 a small pool, esp. of rainwater on a road etc. 2 clay and sand mixed with water and used as a watertight covering for embankments etc. **3** a circular patch of disturbed water made by the blade of an oar at each stroke. —*v.* **1** *tr.* **a** knead (clay and sand) into puddle. **b** line (a canal etc.) with puddle. **2** *intr.* make puddle from clay etc. **3** *tr.* stir (molten iron) to produce wrought iron by expelling carbon. **4** *intr.* **a** dabble or wallow in mud or shallow water. **b** busy oneself in an untidy way. **5** *tr.* make (water etc.) muddy. **6** *tr.* work (mixed water and clay) to separate gold or opal. □□ **puddler** *n.* **puddly** *adj.* [ME *podel, puddel*, dimin. of OE *pudd* ditch]

pudency /'pju:dənsɪ/ *n. literary* modesty; shame. [LL *pudentia* (as PUDENDUM)]

pudendum /pju:'dendəm/ *n.* (*pl.* **pudenda** /-də/) (usu. in *pl.*) the genitals, esp. of a woman. □□ **pudendal** *adj.* **pudic** /'pju:dɪk/ *adj.* [L *pudenda* (*membra* parts), neut. pl. of gerundive of *pudēre* be ashamed]

pudgy /'pʌdʒɪ/ *adj.* (**pudgier, pudgiest**) *colloq.* (esp. of a person) plump, thickset. □□ **pudge** *n.* **pudgily** *adv.* **pudginess** *n.* [cf. PODGY]

pueblo /'pweblən/ *n.* (*pl.* **-os**) a town or village in Latin America, esp. an Indian settlement. [Sp., = people, f. L *populus*]

puerile /'pjʊəraɪl/ *adj.* **1** trivial, childish, immature. **2** of or like a child. □ **puerile breathing** breathing characterized by a loud pulmonary murmur as in children, a sign of disease in an adult. □□ **puerilely** *adv.* **puerility** /-'rɪlɪtɪ/ *n.* (*pl.* **-ies**). [F *puéril* or L *puerilis* f. *puer* boy]

puerperal /pju:'ɜ:pər(ə)l/ *adj.* of or caused by childbirth. □ **puerperal fever** fever following childbirth and caused by uterine infection. [L *puerperus* f. *puer* child + *-parus* bearing]

Puerto Rican /ˌpwɜ:təʊ 'ri:kən/ *n. & adj.* —*n.* **1** a native of Puerto Rico, an island of the Greater Antilles. **2** a person of Puerto Rican descent. —*adj.* of or relating to Puerto Rico or its inhabitants.

puff /pʌf/ *n. & v.* —*n.* **1 a** a short quick blast of breath or wind. **b** the sound of this; a similar sound. **c** a small quantity of vapour, smoke, etc., emitted in one blast (*went up in a puff of smoke*). **2** a cake etc. containing jam, cream, etc., and made of light esp. puff pastry. **3** a gathered mass of material in a dress etc. (*puff sleeve*). **4** a rolled protuberant mass of hair. **5 a** an extravagantly enthusiastic review of a book etc., esp. in a newspaper. **b** an advertisement for goods etc., esp. in a newspaper. **6** = *powder-puff*. **7** *US* an eiderdown. **8** *colloq.* one's life (*in all my puff*). —*v.* **1** *intr.* emit a puff of air or breath; blow with short blasts. **2** *intr.* (usu. foll. by *away, out*, etc.) (of a person smoking, a steam engine, etc.) emit or move with puffs (*puffing away at his cigar; a train puffed out of the station*). **3** *tr.* (usu. in *passive*; often foll. by *out*) put out of breath (*arrived somewhat puffed; completely puffed him out*). **4** *intr.* breathe hard; pant. **5** *tr.* utter pantingly ('*No more,*' he puffed). **6** *intr. & tr.* (usu. foll. by *up, out*) become or cause to become inflated; swell (*his eye was inflamed and puffed up; puffed up the balloon*). **7** *tr.* (usu. foll. by *out, up, away*) blow or emit (dust, smoke, a light object, etc.) with a puff. **8** *tr.* smoke (a pipe etc.) in puffs. **9** *tr.* (usu. as **puffed up** *adj.*) elate; make proud or boastful. **10** *tr.* advertise or promote (goods, a book, etc.) with exaggerated or false praise. □ **puff-adder** a large venomous African viper, *Bitis arietans*, which inflates the upper part of its body and hisses when excited. **puff and blow** = sense 4 of *v.* **puff-ball** any of various fungi having a ball-shaped spore case. **puff pastry** light flaky pastry. **puff-puff** *Brit.* a childish word for a steam-engine or train. **puff up** = sense 9 of *v.* [ME *puf, puffe*, perh. f. OE, imit. of the sound of breath]

puffer /'pʌfə(r)/ *n.* **1** a person or thing that puffs. **2** = *puff-puff*. □ **puffer-fish** = *globe-fish*.

puffin /'pʌfɪn/ *n.* any of various sea birds of the family Alcidae native to the N. Atlantic and N.

Pacific, esp. *Fratercula arctica*, having a large head with a brightly coloured triangular bill, and black and white plumage. [ME *poffin, pophyn*, of unkn. orig.]

puffy /'pʌfɪ/ *adj.* (**puffier, puffiest**) **1** swollen, esp. of the face etc. **2** fat. **3** gusty. **4** short-winded; puffed out. □□ **puffily** *adv.* **puffiness** *n.*

pug¹ /pʌɡ/ *n.* **1** (in full **pug-dog**) **a** a dwarf breed of dog like a bulldog with a broad flat nose and deeply wrinkled face. **b** a dog of this breed. **2** a fox. **3** *Brit.* a small locomotive for shunting etc. □ **pug-nose** a short squat or snub nose. **pug-nosed** having such a nose. □□ **puggish** *adj.* **puggy** *adj.* [16th c.: perh. f. LG or Du.]

pug² /pʌɡ/ *n. & v.* —*n.* loam or clay mixed and prepared for making bricks, pottery, etc. —*v.tr.* (**pugged, pugging**) **1** prepare (clay) thus. **2** pack (esp. the space under the floor to deaden sound) with pug, sawdust, etc. □ **pug-mill** a mill for preparing pug. □□ **pugging** *n.* [19th c.: orig. unkn.]

pug³ /pʌɡ/ *n. sl.* a boxer. [abbr. of PUGILIST]

pug⁴ /pʌɡ/ *n. & v.* —*n.* the footprint of an animal. —*v.tr.* (**pugged, pugging**) track by pugs. [Hindi *pag* footprint]

puggaree /'pʌɡərɪ/ *n.* **1** an Indian turban. **2** a thin muslin scarf tied round a sun-helmet etc. and shielding the neck. [Hindi *pagrī* turban]

pugilist /'pju:dʒɪlɪst/ *n.* a boxer, esp. a professional. □□ **pugilism** *n.* **pugilistic** /-'lɪstɪk/ *adj.* [L *pugil* boxer]

pugnacious /pʌɡ'neɪʃəs/ *adj.* quarrelsome; disposed to fight. □□ **pugnaciously** *adv.* **pugnaciousness** *n.* **pugnacity** /-'næsɪtɪ/ *n.* [L *pugnax -acis* f. *pugnare* fight f. *pugnus* fist]

puisne /'pju:nɪ/ *adj. Law* denoting a judge of a superior court inferior in rank to chief justices. [OF f. *puis* f. L *postea* afterwards + *né* born f. L *natus*: cf. PUNY]

puissance /'pju:ɪs(ə)ns, 'pwɪs-/ *n.* **1** /also pwi:'sɑ̃s/ a test of a horse's ability to jump large obstacles in showjumping. **2** *archaic* great power, might, or influence. [ME (in sense 2) f. OF (as PUISSANT)]

puissant /'pju:ɪs(ə)nt, 'pwɪːs-, 'pwɪs-/ *adj. literary* or *archaic* having great power or influence; mighty. □□ **puissantly** *adv.* [ME f. OF f. L *posse* be able: cf. POTENT¹]

puja /'pu:dʒə/ *n.* (also **pooja**) a Hindu rite of worship; a prayer. [Skr.]

puke /pju:k/ *v. & n. sl.* —*v.tr. & intr.* vomit. —*n.* vomit. □□ **pukey** *adj.* [16th c.: prob. imit.]

pukeko /'pu:keˌkəʊ/ *n.* (*pl.* **-os**) *Austral. & NZ* a rail, *Porphyrio porphyrio*, with blue, black, and white plumage. [Maori]

pukka /'pʌkə/ *adj.* (also **pukkah, pucka**) *Anglo-Ind.* **1** genuine. **2** of good quality; reliable (*did a pukka job*). **3** of full weight. [Hindi *pakkā* cooked, ripe, substantial]

pulchritude /'pʌlkrɪˌtjuːd/ *n. literary* beauty. □□ **pulchritudinous** /-'tjuːdɪnəs/ *adj.* [ME f. L *pulchritudo -dinis* f. *pulcher -chri* beautiful]

pule /pju:l/ *v.intr. literary* cry querulously or weakly; whine, whimper. [16th c.: prob. imit.: cf. F *piauler*]

Pulitzer prize /'pʊlɪtsə(r), 'pju:-/ *n.* each of 13 annual awards for achievements in American journalism, literature, and music. [J. *Pulitzer*, Amer. newspaper-publisher d. 1911]

pull /pʊl/ *v. & n.* —*v.* **1** *tr.* exert force upon (a thing) tending to move it to oneself or the origin of the force (*stop pulling my hair*). **2** *tr.* cause to move in this way (*pulled it nearer; pulled me into the room*). **3** *intr.* exert a pulling force (*the horse pulls well; the engine will not pull*). **4** *tr.* extract (a cork or tooth) by pulling. **5** *tr.* damage (a muscle etc.) by abnormal strain. **6** *tr.* move (a boat) by pulling on the oars. **b** *intr.* (of a boat etc.) be caused to move, esp. in a specified direction. **7** *intr.* (often foll. by *up*) proceed with effort (up a hill etc.). **8** *tr.* (foll. by *on*) bring out (a weapon) for use against (a person). **9 a** *tr.* check the speed of (a horse), esp. so as to make it lose the race. **b** *intr.* (of a horse) strain against the bit. **10** *tr.* attract or secure (custom or support). **11** *tr.* draw (liquor) from a barrel etc. **12** *intr.* (foll. by *at*) tear or pluck at. **13** *intr.* (often foll. by *on*, *at*) inhale deeply; draw or suck (on a pipe etc.). **14** *tr.* (often foll. by *up*) remove (a plant) by the root. **15** *tr.* **a** *Cricket* strike (the ball) to the leg side. **b** *Golf* strike (the ball) widely to the left. **16** *tr.* print (a proof etc.). **17** *tr. colloq.* achieve or accomplish (esp. something illicit). —*n.* **1** the act of pulling. **2** the force exerted by this. **3** a means of exerting influence; an advantage. **4** something that attracts or draws attention. **5** a deep draught of liquor. **6** a prolonged effort, e.g. in going up a hill. **7** a handle etc. for applying a pull. **8** a spell of rowing. **9** a printer's rough proof. **10** *Cricket & Golf* a pulling stroke. **11** a suck at a cigarette. □**pull about 1** treat roughly. **2** pull from side to side. **pull apart** (or **to pieces**) = *take to pieces* (see PIECE). **pull back** retreat or cause to retreat. **pull-back** *n.* **1** a retarding influence. **2** a withdrawal of troops. **pull down 1** demolish (esp. a building). **2** humiliate. **3** *colloq.* earn (a sum of money) as wages etc. **pull a face** assume a distinctive or specified (e.g. sad or angry) expression. **pull a fast one** see FAST[1]. **pull in 1** (of a bus, train, etc.) arrive to take passengers. **2** (of a vehicle) move to the side of or off the road. **3** earn or acquire. **4** *colloq.* arrest. **pull-in** *n. Brit.* a roadside café or other stopping-place. **pull a person's leg** deceive a person playfully. **pull off 1** remove by pulling. **2** succeed in achieving or winning. **pull oneself together** recover control of oneself. **pull the other one** *colloq.* expressing disbelief (with ref. to *pull a person's leg*). **pull out 1** take out by pulling. **2** depart. **3** withdraw from an undertaking. **4** (of a bus, train, etc.) leave with its passengers. **5** (of a vehicle) move out from the side of the road, or from its normal position to overtake. **pull-out** *n.* something that can be pulled out, esp. a section of a magazine. **pull over** (of a vehicle) pull in. **pull the plug on** *colloq.* defeat, discomfit. **pull one's punches** avoid using one's full force. **pull rank** take unfair advantage of one's seniority. **pull round** (or **through**) recover or cause to recover from an illness. **pull strings** exert (esp. clandestine) influence. **pull the strings** be the real actuator of what another does. **pull together** work in harmony. **pull up 1** stop or cause to stop moving. **2** pull out of the ground. **3** reprimand. **4** check oneself. **pull one's weight** do one's fair share of work. **pull wires** esp. *US* = *pull strings*. □□ **puller** *n.* [OE (*ā*)*pullian*, perh. rel. to LG *pūlen*, MDu. *polen* to shell]

pullet /ˈpʊlɪt/ *n.* a young hen, esp. one less than one year old. [ME f. OF *poulet* dimin. of *poule* ult. fem. of L *pullus* chicken]

pulley /ˈpʊlɪ/ *n. & v.* —*n.* (*pl.* -eys) **1** a grooved wheel or set of wheels for a cord etc. to pass over, set in a block and used for changing the direction of a force. **2** a wheel or drum fixed on a shaft and turned by a belt, used esp. to increase speed or power. —*v.tr.* (-eys, -eyed) **1** hoist or work with a pulley. **2** provide with a pulley. [ME f. OF *polie* prob. ult. f. med. Gk *polidion* (unrecorded) pivot, dimin. of *polos* POLE[2]]

Pullman /ˈpʊlmən/ *n.* **1** a railway carriage or motor coach affording special comfort. **2** a sleeping-car. [G. M. *Pullman*, Amer. designer d. 1897]

pullover /ˈpʊl,əʊvə(r)/ *n.* a knitted garment put on over the head and covering the top half of the body.

pullulate /ˈpʌljʊ,leɪt/ *v.intr.* **1** (of a seed, shoot, etc.) bud, sprout, germinate. **2** (esp. of an animal) swarm, throng; breed prolifically. **3** develop; spring up; come to life. **4** (foll. by *with*) abound. □□ **pullulant** *adj.* **pullulation** /-ˈleɪʃ(ə)n/ *n.* [L *pullulare* sprout f. *pullulus* dimin. of *pullus* young of an animal]

pulmonary /ˈpʌlmənərɪ/ *adj.* **1** of or relating to the lungs. **2** having lungs or lunglike organs. **3** affected with or susceptible to lung disease. □**pulmonary**

artery the artery conveying blood from the heart to the lungs. **pulmonary tuberculosis** a form of tuberculosis caused by inhaling the tubercle bacillus into the lungs. **pulmonary vein** the vein carrying oxygenated blood from the lungs to the heart. □□ **pulmonate** /-nət/ *adj.* [L *pulmonarius* f. *pulmo -onis* lung]

pulmonic /pʌlˈmɒnɪk/ *adj.* = PULMONARY 1. [F *pulmonique* or f. mod.L *pulmonicus* f. L *pulmo* (as PULMONARY)]

pulp /pʌlp/ *n. & v.* —*n.* **1** the soft fleshy part of fruit etc. **2** any soft thick wet mass. **3** a soft shapeless mass derived from rags, wood, etc., used in paper-making. **4** (often *attrib.*) poor quality (often sensational) writing orig. printed on rough paper (*pulp fiction*). **5** vascular tissue filling the interior cavity and root canals of a tooth. **6** *Mining* pulverized ore mixed with water. —*v.* **1** *tr.* reduce to pulp. **2** *tr.* withdraw (a publication) from the market, usu. recycling the paper. **3** *tr.* remove pulp from. **4** *intr.* become pulp. □□ **pulper** *n.* **pulpless** *adj.* **pulpy** *adj.* **pulpiness** *n.* [L *pulpa*]

pulpit /ˈpʊlpɪt/ *n.* **1** a raised enclosed platform in a church etc. from which the preacher delivers a sermon. **2** (prec. by *the*) preachers or preaching collectively. [ME f. L *pulpitum* scaffold, platform]

pulpwood /ˈpʌlpwʊd/ *n.* timber suitable for making pulp.

pulque /ˈpʊlkeɪ, ˈpʊlkɪ/ *n.* a Mexican fermented drink made from the sap of the maguey. □**pulque brandy** a strong intoxicant made from pulque. [17th c.: Amer. Sp., of unkn. orig.]

pulsar /ˈpʌlsɑː(r)/ *n. Astron.* a cosmic source of regular and rapid pulses of radiation usu. at radio frequencies, e.g. a rotating neutron star. [*pulsating* st*ar*, after *quasar*]

pulsate /pʌlˈseɪt, ˈpʌl-/ *v.intr.* **1** expand and contract rhythmically; throb. **2** vibrate, quiver, thrill. □□ **pulsation** /-ˈseɪʃ(ə)n/ *n.* **pulsator** /-ˈseɪtə(r)/ *n.* **pulsatory** /ˈpʌlsətərɪ/ *adj.* [L *pulsare* frequent. of *pellere puls-* drive, beat]

pulsatile /ˈpʌlsə,taɪl/ *adj.* **1** of or having the property of pulsation. **2** (of a musical instrument) played by percussion. [med.L *pulsatilis* (as PULSATE)]

pulsatilla /ˌpʌlsəˈtɪlə/ *n.* any plant of the genus *Pulsatilla*, esp. the pasque-flower. [mod.L dimin. of *pulsata* fem. past part. (as PULSATE), because it quivers in the wind]

pulse[1] /pʌls/ *n. & v.* —*n.* **1 a** a rhythmical throbbing of the arteries as blood is propelled through them, esp. as felt in the wrists, temples, etc. **b** each successive beat of the arteries or heart. **2** a throb or thrill of life or emotion. **3** a latent feeling. **4** a single vibration of sound, electric current, light, etc., esp. as a signal. **5** a musical beat. **6** any regular or recurrent rhythm, e.g. of the stroke of oars. —*v.intr.* **1** pulsate. **2** (foll. by *out*, *in*, etc.) transmit etc. by rhythmical beats. □**pulse code** coding information in pulses. **pulse code modulation** a pulse modulation technique of representing a signal by a sequence of binary codes. **pulse modulation** a type of modulation in which pulses are varied to represent a signal. □□ **pulseless** *adj.* [ME f. OF *pous* f. L *pulsus* f. *pellere puls-* drive, beat]

pulse[2] /pʌls/ *n.* (as *sing.* or *pl.*) **1** the edible seeds of various leguminous plants, e.g. chick-peas, lentils, beans, etc. **2** the plant or plants producing this. [ME f. OF *pols* f. L *puls pultis* porridge of meal etc.]

pulsimeter /pʌlˈsɪmɪtə(r)/ *n.* an instrument for measuring the rate or force of a pulse.

pulverize /ˈpʌlvə,raɪz/ *v.* (also **-ise**) **1** *tr.* reduce to fine particles. **2** *tr. & intr.* crumble to dust. **3** *colloq. tr.* **a** demolish. **b** defeat utterly. □□ **pulverizable** *adj.* **pulverization** /-ˈzeɪʃ(ə)n/ *n.* **pulverizator** *n.* **pulverizer** *n.* [ME f. LL *pulverizare* f. *pulvis pulveris* dust]

pulverulent /pʌlˈveruːlənt/ *adj.* **1** consisting of fine particles; powdery. **2** likely to crumble. [L *pul-verulentus* (as PULVERIZE)]

puma /ˈpjuːmə/ *n.* a wild American cat, *Felis concolor*, usu. with a plain greyish-black coat. Also called COUGAR, PANTHER, *mountain lion*. [Sp. f. Quechua]

pumice /ˈpʌmɪs/ *n. & v.* —*n.* (in full **pumice-stone**) **1** a light porous volcanic rock often used as an abrasive in cleaning or polishing substances. **2** a piece of this used for removing hard skin etc. —*v.tr.* rub or clean with a pumice. □□ **pumiceous** /pjuːˈmɪʃəs/ *adj.* [ME f. OF *pomis* f. L *pumex pumicis* (dial. *pom-*): cf. POUNCE²]

pummel /ˈpʌm(ə)l/ *v.tr.* (**pummelled, pummelling;** *US* **pummeled, pummeling**) strike repeatedly esp. with the fist. [alt. f. POMMEL]

pump¹ /pʌmp/ *n. & v.* —*n.* **1** a machine, usu. with rotary action or the reciprocal action of a piston, for raising or moving liquids, compressing gases, inflating tyres, etc. **2** an instance of pumping; a stroke of a pump. —*v.* **1** *tr.* (often foll. by *in, out, into, up,* etc.) raise or remove (liquid, gas, etc.) with a pump. **2** *tr.* (often foll. by *up*) fill (a tyre etc.) with air. **3** *tr.* remove (water etc.) with a pump. **4** *intr.* work a pump. **5** *tr.* (often foll. by *out*) cause to move, pour forth, etc., as if by pumping. **6** *tr.* elicit information from (a person) by persistent questioning. **7** *tr.* **a** move vigorously up and down. **b** shake (a person's hand) effusively. □**pump-brake** a handle of a pump, esp. with a transverse bar for several people to work at. **pump-handle** *colloq.* shake (a person's hand) effusively. **pump iron** *colloq.* exercise with weights. **pump-priming 1** introduce fluid etc. into a pump to prepare it for working. **2** esp. *US* the stimulation of commerce etc. by investment. **pump room 1** a room where fuel pumps etc. are stored or controlled. **2** a room at a spa etc. where medicinal water is dispensed. [ME *pumpe, pompe* (orig. Naut.): prob. imit.]

pump² /pʌmp/ *n.* **1** a plimsoll. **2** a light shoe for dancing etc. **3** *US* a court shoe. [16th c.: orig. unkn.]

pumpernickel /ˈpʌmpə,nɪk(ə)l, ˈpʊ-/ *n.* German wholemeal rye bread. [G, earlier = lout, bumpkin, of uncert. orig.]

pumpkin /ˈpʌmpkɪn/ *n.* **1** any of various plants of the genus *Cucurbita*, esp. *C. maxima*, with large lobed leaves and tendrils. **2** the large rounded yellow fruit of this with a thick rind and edible flesh. [alt. f. earlier *pompon, pumpion* f. obs. F *po(m)pon* f. L *pepo -onis* f. Gk *pepōn* large melon: see PEPO]

pun¹ /pʌn/ *n. & v.* —*n.* the humorous use of a word to suggest different meanings, or of words of the same sound and different meanings. —*v.intr.* (**punned, punning**) (foll. by *on*) make a pun or puns with (words). □□ **punningly** *adv.* [17th c.: perh. f. obs. *pundigrion,* a fanciful formation]

pun² /pʌn/ *v.tr.* (**punned, punning**) *Brit.* consolidate (earth or rubble) by pounding or ramming. □□ **punner** *n.* [dial. var. of POUND²]

puna /ˈpuːnə/ *n.* **1** a high plateau in the Peruvian Andes. **2** = *mountain sickness.* [Quechua, in sense 1]

punch¹ /pʌntʃ/ *v. & n.* —*v.tr.* **1** strike bluntly, esp. with a closed fist. **2** prod or poke with a blunt object. **3 a** pierce a hole in (metal, paper, a ticket, etc.) as or with a punch. **b** pierce (a hole) by punching. **4** *US* drive (cattle) by prodding with a stick etc. —*n.* **1** a blow with a fist. **2** the ability to deliver this. **3** *colloq.* vigour, momentum; effective force. □**punch** (or **punched**) **card** (or **tape**) a card or paper tape perforated according to a code, for conveying instructions or data to a data processor etc. **punch-drunk** stupefied from or as though from a series of heavy blows. **punching-bag** *US* a suspended stuffed bag used as a punchball. **punch-line** words giving the point of a joke or story. **punch-up** *Brit. colloq.* a fist-fight; a brawl. □□ **puncher** *n.* [ME, var. of POUNCE¹]

punch² /pʌntʃ/ *n.* **1** any of various devices or machines for punching holes in materials (e.g. paper,

leather, metal, plaster). **2** a tool or machine for impressing a design or stamping a die on a material. [perh. an abbr. of PUNCHEON¹, or f. PUNCH¹]

punch³ /pʌntʃ/ *n.* a drink of wine or spirits mixed with water, fruit juices, spices, etc., and usu. served hot. □**punch-bowl 1** a bowl in which punch is mixed. **2** a deep round hollow in a hill. [17th c.: orig. unkn.]

punch⁴ /pʌntʃ/ *n.* **1** (**Punch**) a grotesque humpbacked figure in a puppet-show called *Punch and Judy.* **2** (in full **Suffolk punch**) a short-legged thickset draught horse. □**as pleased as Punch** showing great pleasure. [abbr. of PUNCHINELLO]

punchball /ˈpʌntʃbɔːl/ *n.* **1** a stuffed or inflated ball suspended or mounted on a stand, for punching as a form of exercise. **2** *US* a ball game in which a rubber ball is punched with the fist or head.

puncheon¹ /ˈpʌntʃ(ə)n/ *n.* **1** a short post, esp. one supporting a roof in a coal-mine. **2** = PUNCH². [ME f. OF *poinson, po(i)nchon,* ult. f. L *pungere punct-* prick]

puncheon² /ˈpʌntʃ(ə)n/ *n. hist.* a large cask for liquids etc. holding from 72 to 120 gallons. [ME f. OF *poinson, po(i)nchon,* of unkn. orig. (prob. not the same as in PUNCHEON¹)]

Punchinello /ˌpʌntʃɪˈneləʊ/ *n.* (*pl.* **-os**) **1** the chief character in a traditional Italian puppet show. **2** a short stout person of comical appearance. [Neapolitan dial. *Polecenella,* It. *Pulcinella,* perh. dimin. of *pollecena,* young turkey-cock with a hooked beak f. *pulcino* chicken ult. f. L *pullus*]

punchy /ˈpʌntʃɪ/ *adj.* (**punchier, punchiest**) having punch or vigour; forceful. □□ **punchily** *adv.* **punchiness** *n.*

puncta *pl.* of PUNCTUM.

punctate /ˈpʌŋkteɪt/ *adj. Biol.* marked or studded with points, dots, spots, etc. □□ **punctation** /-ˈteɪʃ(ə)n/ *n.* [L *punctum* (as POINT)]

punctilio /pʌŋkˈtɪlɪəʊ/ *n.* (*pl.* **-os**) **1** a delicate point of ceremony or honour. **2** the etiquette of such points. **3** petty formality. [It. *puntiglio* & Sp. *puntillo* dimin. of *punto* POINT]

punctilious /pʌŋkˈtɪlɪəs/ *adj.* **1** attentive to formality or etiquette. **2** precise in behaviour. □□ **punctiliously** *adv.* **punctiliousness** *n.* [F *pointilleux* f. *pointille* f. It. (as PUNCTILIO)]

punctual /ˈpʌŋktjʊəl/ *adj.* **1** observant of the appointed time. **2** neither early nor late. **3** *Geom.* of a point. □□ **punctuality** /-ˈælɪtɪ/ *n.* **punctually** *adv.* [ME f. med.L *punctualis* f. L *punctum* POINT]

punctuate /ˈpʌŋktjʊ,eɪt/ *v.tr.* **1** insert punctuation marks in. **2** interrupt at intervals (*punctuated his tale with heavy sighs*). [med.L *punctuare punctuat-* (as PUNCTUAL)]

punctuation /ˌpʌŋktjʊˈeɪʃ(ə)n/ *n.* **1** the system or arrangement of marks used to punctuate a written passage. **2** the practice or skill of punctuating. □**punctuation mark** any of the marks (e.g. full stop and comma) used in writing to separate sentences and phrases etc. and to clarify meaning. [med.L *punctuatio* (as PUNCTUATE)]

punctum /ˈpʌŋktəm/ *n.* (*pl.* **puncta** /-tə/) *Biol.* a speck, dot, spot of colour, etc., or an elevation or depression on a surface. [L, = POINT]

puncture /ˈpʌŋktʃə(r)/ *n. & v.* —*n.* **1** a prick or pricking, esp. the accidental piercing of a pneumatic tyre. **2** a hole made in this way. —*v.* **1** *tr.* make a puncture in. **2** *intr.* undergo puncture. **3** *tr.* prick or pierce. [ME f. L *punctura* f. *pungere punct-* prick]

pundit /ˈpʌndɪt/ *n.* **1** (also **pandit**) a Hindu learned in Sanskrit and in the philosophy, religion, and jurisprudence of India. **2** often *iron.* a learned expert or teacher. □□ **punditry** *n.* [Hind. *paṇḍit* f. Skr. *paṇḍita* learned]

pungent /ˈpʌndʒ(ə)nt/ *adj.* **1** having a sharp or strong taste or smell, esp. so as to produce a pricking sensation. **2** (of remarks) penetrating, biting, caustic. **3** mentally stimulating. **4** *Biol.* having a sharp point.

□□**pungency** *n*. **pungently** *adv*. [L *pungent-* pres. part. of *pungere* prick]

Punic /'pjuːnɪk/ *adj*. & *n*. —*adj*. of or relating to ancient Carthage in N. Africa. —*n*. the language of Carthage, related to Phoenician. □**Punic faith** treachery. [L *Punicus, Poenicus* f. *Poenus* f. Gk *Phoinix* Phoenician]

punish /'pʌnɪʃ/ *v.tr*. **1** cause (an offender) to suffer for an offence. **2** inflict a penalty for (an offence). **3** *colloq*. inflict severe blows on (an opponent). **4 a** tax severely; subject to severe treatment. **b** abuse or treat improperly. □□**punishable** *adj*. **punisher** *n*. **punishing** *adj*. (in sense 4a). **punishingly** *adv*. [ME f. OF *punir* f. L *punire = poenire* f. *poena* penalty]

punishment /'pʌnɪʃmənt/ *n*. **1** the act or an instance of punishing; the condition of being punished. **2** the loss or suffering inflicted in this. **3** *colloq*. severe treatment or suffering. [ME f. AF & OF *punissement* f. *punir*]

punitive /'pjuːnɪtɪv/ *adj*. (also **punitory** /-tərɪ/) **1** inflicting or intended to inflict punishment. **2** (of taxation etc.) extremely severe. **3** *Law* (of damages etc.) = VINDICTIVE. □□**punitively** *adv*. [F *punitif -ive* or med.L *punitivus* (as PUNISHMENT)]

Punjabi /pʊn'dʒɑːbɪ/ *n*. & *adj*. —*n*. (*pl*. **Punjabis**) **1** a native of the Punjab in India. **2** the language of this people. —*adj*. of or relating to the Punjab. [Hindi *pañjābī*]

punk /pʌŋk/ *n*. & *adj*. —*n*. **1 a** a worthless person or thing (often as a general term of abuse). **b** nonsense. **2 a** (in full **punk rock**) a loud fast-moving form of rock music with crude and aggressive effects. **b** (in full **punk rocker**) a devotee of this. **3** *US* a hoodlum or ruffian. **4** *US* a passive male homosexual. **5** *US* an inexperienced person; a novice. **6** soft crumbly wood that has been attacked by fungus, used as tinder. —*adj*. **1** worthless, rotten. **2** denoting punk rock and its associations. □□**punky** *adj*. [18th c.: orig. unkn.: cf. SPUNK]

punkah /'pʌŋkə/ *n*. **1** (in India) a fan usu. made from the leaf of the palmyra. **2** a large swinging cloth fan on a frame worked by a cord or electrically. □**punkah-wallah** a person who works a punkah. [Hindi *paṅkhā* fan f. Skr. *pakṣaka* f. *pakṣa* wing]

punnet /'pʌnɪt/ *n*. *Brit*. a small light basket or container for fruit or vegetables. [19th c.: perh. dimin. of dial. *pun* POUND¹]

punster /'pʌnstə(r)/ *n*. a person who makes puns, esp. habitually.

punt¹ /pʌnt/ *n*. & *v*. —*n*. a long narrow flat-bottomed boat, square at both ends, used mainly for pleasure on rivers and propelled by a long pole. —*v*. **1** *tr*. propel (a punt) with a pole. **2** *intr*. & *tr*. travel or convey in a punt. □□**punter** *n*. [ME f. MLG *punte, punto* & MDu. *ponte* ferry-boat f. L *ponto* Gaulish transport vessel]

punt² /pʌnt/ *v*. & *n*. —*v.tr*. kick (a ball, esp. in rugby) after it has dropped from the hands and before it reaches the ground. —*n*. such a kick. □□**punter** *n*. [prob. f. dial. *punt* push forcibly: cf. BUNT³]

punt³ /pʌnt/ *v*. & *n*. —*v.intr*. **1** (in some card-games) lay a stake against the bank. **2** *Brit*. *colloq*. **a** bet on a horse etc. **b** speculate in shares etc. —*n*. **1** a bet. **2** a point in faro. [F *ponter* f. *ponte* player against the bank f. Sp. *punto* POINT]

punt⁴ /pʊnt/ *n*. the chief monetary unit of the Republic of Ireland. [Ir., = pound]

punter /'pʌntə(r)/ *n*. **1** a person who gambles or lays a bet. **2 a** *colloq*. a customer or client; a member of an audience. **b** *sl*. a prostitute's client. **3** a point in faro.

puny /'pjuːnɪ/ *adj*. (**punier, puniest**) **1** undersized. **2** weak, feeble. **3** petty. □□**punily** *adv*. **puniness** *n*. [phonetic spelling of PUISNE]

pup /pʌp/ *n*. & *v*. —*n*. **1** a young dog. **2** a young wolf, rat, seal, etc. **3** *Brit*. an unpleasant or arrogant young man. —*v.tr*. (**pupped, pupping**) (also *absol*.) (of a bitch etc.) bring forth (young). □**in pup** (of a bitch)

pregnant. **sell a person a pup** swindle a person, esp. by selling something worthless. [back-form. f. PUPPY as if a dimin. in -Y²]

pupa /'pjuːpə/ *n*. (*pl*. **pupae** /-piː/) an insect in the stage of development between larva and imago. □□ **pupal** *adj*. [mod.L f. L *pupa* girl, doll]

pupate /pjuː'peɪt/ *v.intr*. become a pupa. □□**pupation** *n*.

pupil¹ /'pjuːpɪl, -p(ə)l/ *n*. **1** a person who is taught by another, esp. a schoolchild or student in relation to a teacher. **2** *Sc. Law* a boy less than 14 or a girl less than 12 years in age. □□**pupillage** *n*. (also **pupilage**). **pupillary** *adj*. (also **pupilary**). [ME, orig. = orphan, ward f. OF *pupille* or L *pupillus, -illa,* dimin. of *pupus* boy, *pupa* girl]

pupil² /'pjuːpɪl, -p(ə)l/ *n*. the dark circular opening in the centre of the iris of the eye, varying in size to regulate the passage of light to the retina. □□ **pupillar** *adj*. (also **pupilar**). **pupillary** *adj*. (also **pupilary**). [OF *pupille* or L *pupilla,* dimin. of *pupa* doll (as PUPIL¹): so called from the tiny images visible in the eye]

pupiparous /pjuː'pɪpərəs/ *adj*. *Entomol*. bringing forth young which are already in a pupal state. [mod.L *pupipara* neut. pl. of *pupiparus* (as PUPA, *parere* bring forth)]

puppet /'pʌpɪt/ *n*. **1** a small figure representing a human being or animal and moved by various means as entertainment. **2** a person whose actions are controlled by another. □**puppet State** a country that is nominally independent but actually under the control of another power. □□**puppetry** *n*. [later form of POPPET]

puppeteer /ˌpʌpɪ'tɪə(r)/ *n*. a person who works puppets.

puppy /'pʌpɪ/ *n*. (*pl*. **-ies**) **1** a young dog. **2** a conceited or arrogant young man. □**puppy-fat** temporary fatness of a child or adolescent. **puppy love** = *calf-love* (see CALF¹). □□**puppyhood** *n*. **puppyish** *adj*. [ME perh. f. OF *po(u)pee* doll, plaything, toy f. Rmc (as POPPET)]

pur- /pɜː(r)/ *prefix* = PRO-¹ (*purchase*; *pursue*). [AF f. OF *por-, pur-, pour-* f. L *por-, pro-*]

Purana /puː'rɑːnə/ *n*. any of a class of Sanskrit sacred writings on Hindu mythology, folklore, etc. □□ **Puranic** *adj*. [Skr. *purāṇa* ancient legend, ancient, f. *purā* formerly]

Purbeck marble /'pɜːbek/ *n*. (also **Purbeck stone**) *Archit*. a hard usu. polished limestone from Purbeck in Dorset, used in pillars, effigies, etc.

purblind /'pɜːblaɪnd/ *adj*. **1** partly blind; dim-sighted. **2** obtuse, dim-witted. □□**purblindness** *n*. [ME *pur(e) blind* f. PURE orig. in sense 'utterly', with assim. to PUR-]

purchase /'pɜːtʃɪs, -tʃəs/ *v*. & *n*. —*v.tr*. **1** acquire by payment; buy. **2** obtain or achieve at some cost. **3** *Naut*. haul up (an anchor etc.) by means of a pulley, lever, etc. —*n*. **1** the act or an instance of buying. **2** something bought. **3** *Law* the acquisition of property by one's personal action and not by inheritance. **4 a** a firm hold on a thing to move it or to prevent it from slipping; leverage. **b** a device or tackle for moving heavy objects. **5** the annual rent or return from land. □**purchase tax** *Brit*. *hist*. a tax on goods bought, levied at higher rates for non-essential or luxury goods. □□**purchasable** *adj*. **purchaser** *n*. [ME f. AF *purchacer*, OF *pourchacier* seek to obtain (as PUR-, CHASE¹)]

purdah /'pɜːdə/ *n*. *Ind*. **1** a system in certain Muslim and Hindu societies of screening women from strangers by means of a veil or curtain. **2** a curtain in a house, used for this purpose. [Urdu & Pers. *pardah* veil, curtain]

pure /pjʊə(r)/ *adj*. **1** unmixed, unadulterated (*pure white; pure alcohol*). **2** of unmixed origin or descent (*pure-blooded*). **3** chaste. **4** morally or sexually undefiled; not corrupt. **5** guiltless. **6** sincere. **7** mere, simple, nothing but, sheer (*it was pure malice*). **8** (of a sound) not discordant, perfectly in tune. **9** (of a subject of study) dealing with abstract concepts and not practical application. **10 a** (of a vowel) not joined with another in a diphthong. **b** (of a consonant) not accompanied by another. □**pure science** a science depending on deductions from demonstrated truths (e.g. mathematics or logic), or one studied without practical applications. □□ **pureness** *n.* [ME f. OF *pur* pure f. L *purus*]

purée /'pjʊəreɪ/ *n. & v.* —*n.* a pulp of vegetables or fruit etc. reduced to a smooth cream. —*v.tr.* (**purées**, **puréed**) make a purée of. [F]

purely /'pjʊəlɪ/ *adv.* **1** in a pure manner. **2** merely, solely, exclusively.

purfle /'pɜːf(ə)l/ *n. & v.* —*n.* **1** an ornamental border, esp. on a violin etc. **2** *archaic* the ornamental or embroidered edge of a garment. —*v.tr.* **1** decorate with a purfle. **2** (often foll. by *with*) ornament (the edge of a building). **3** beautify. □□ **purfling** *n.* [ME f. OF *porfil, porfiler* ult. f. L *filum* thread]

purgation /pɜːˈgeɪʃ(ə)n/ *n.* **1** purification. **2** purging of the bowels. **3** spiritual cleansing, esp. (*RC Ch.*) of a soul in purgatory. **4** *hist.* the cleansing of oneself from accusation or suspicion by an oath or ordeal. [ME f. OF *purgation* or L *purgatio* (as PURGE)]

purgative /'pɜːgətɪv/ *adj. & n.* —*adj.* **1** serving to purify. **2** strongly laxative. —*n.* **1** a purgative thing. **2** a laxative. [ME f. OF *purgatif -ive* or LL *purgativus* (as PURGE)]

purgatory /'pɜːgətərɪ/ *n. & adj.* —*n.* (*pl.* **-ies**) **1** the condition or supposed place of spiritual cleansing, esp. (*RC Ch.*) of those dying in the grace of God but having to expiate venial sins etc. **2** a place or state of temporary suffering or expiation. —*adj.* purifying. □□ **purgatorial** /-'tɔːrɪəl/ *adj.* [ME f. AF *purgatorie*, OF *-oire* f. med.L *purgatorium*, neut. of LL *purgatorius* (as PURGE)]

purge /pɜːdʒ/ *v. & n.* —*v.tr.* **1** (often foll. by *of, from*) make physically or spiritually clean. **2** remove by a cleansing process. **3** rid (an organization, party, etc.) of persons regarded as undesirable. **4 a** empty (the bowels). **b** empty the bowels of. **5** *Law* atone for or wipe out (an offence, esp. contempt of court). —*n.* **1** the act or an instance of purging. **2** a purgative. □□ **purger** *n.* [ME f. OF *purg(i)er* f. L *purgare* purify f. *purus* pure]

purify /'pjʊərɪˌfaɪ/ *v.tr.* (**-ies, -ied**) **1** (often foll. by *of, from*) cleanse or make pure. **2** make ceremonially clean. **3** clear of extraneous elements. □□ **purification** /-fɪˈkeɪʃ(ə)n/ *n.* **purificatory** /-fɪˌkeɪtərɪ/ *adj.* **purifier** *n.* [ME f. OF *purifier* f. L *purificare* (as PURE)]

Purim /'pjʊərɪm, pjuːˈriːm/ *n.* a Jewish spring festival commemorating the defeat of Haman's plot to massacre the Jews (Esth. 9). [Heb., pl. of *pūr*, perh. = LOT *n.* 2]

purine /'pjʊəriːn/ *n.* **1** *Chem.* an organic nitrogenous base forming uric acid on oxidation. **2** any of a group of derivatives with purine-like structure, including the nucleotide constituents adenine and guanine. [G *Purin* L *purus* pure + *uricum* uric acid + *-in* -INE⁴]

purist /'pjʊərɪst/ *n.* a stickler for or advocate of scrupulous purity, esp. in language or art. □□ **purism** *n.* **puristic** /-'rɪstɪk/ *adj.* [F *puriste* f. *pur* PURE]

puritan /'pjʊərɪt(ə)n/ *n. & adj.* —*n.* **1** (**Puritan**) *hist.* a member of a group of English Protestants who regarded the Reformation of the Church under Elizabeth as incomplete and sought to simplify and regulate forms of worship. **2** a purist member of any party. **3** a person practising or affecting extreme strictness in religion or morals. —*adj.* **1** *hist.* of or relating to the Puritans. **2** scrupulous and austere in religion or morals. □□ **puritanism** *n.* [LL *puritas* (as PURITY) after earlier *Catharan* (as CATHAR)]

puritanical /ˌpjʊərɪˈtænɪk(ə)l/ *adj.* often *derog.* practising or affecting strict religious or moral behaviour. □□ **puritanically** *adv.*

purity /'pjʊərɪtɪ/ *n.* **1** pureness, cleanness. **2** freedom from physical or moral pollution. [ME f. OF *pureté*, with assim. to LL *puritas -tatis* f. L *purus* pure]

purl¹ /pɜːl/ *n. & v.* —*n.* **1 a** knitting stitch made by putting the needle through the front of the previous stitch and passing the yarn round the back of the needle. **2** a cord of twisted gold or silver wire for bordering. **3** a chain of minute loops; a picot. **4** the ornamental edges of lace, ribbon, etc. —*v.tr.* (also *absol.*) knit with a purl stitch. [orig. *pyrle, pirle* f. Sc. *pirl* twist: the knitting sense may be f. a different word]

purl² /pɜːl/ *v. & n.* —*v.intr.* (of a brook etc.) flow with a swirling motion and babbling sound. —*n.* this motion or sound. [16th c.: prob. imit.: cf. Norw. *purla* bubble up]

purler /'pɜːlə(r)/ *n. Brit. colloq.* a headlong fall. [*purl* upset, rel. to PURL¹]

purlieu /'pɜːljuː/ *n.* (*pl.* **purlieus**) **1** a person's bounds or limits. **2** a person's usual haunts. **3** *Brit. hist.* a tract on the border of a forest, esp. one earlier included in it and still partly subject to forest laws. **4** (in *pl.*) the outskirts; an outlying region. [ME *purlew*, prob. alt. after F *lieu* place f. AF *purale(e)*, OF *pouralée* a going round to settle the boundaries f. *po(u)raler* traverse]

purlin /'pɜːlɪn/ *n.* a horizontal beam along the length of a roof, resting on principals and supporting the common rafters or boards. [ME: orig. uncert.]

purloin /pəˈlɔɪn/ *v.tr. formal* or *joc.* steal, pilfer. □□ **purloiner** *n.* [ME f. AF *purloigner* put away, do away with (as PUR-, *loign* far f. L *longe*)]

purple /'pɜːp(ə)l/ *n., adj., & v.* —*n.* **1** a colour intermediate between red and blue. **2** (in full **Tyrian purple**) a crimson dye obtained from some molluscs. **3** a purple robe, esp. as the dress of an emperor or senior magistrate. **4** the scarlet official dress of a cardinal. **5** (prec. by *the*) a position of rank, authority, or privilege. —*adj.* of a purple colour. —*v.tr. & intr.* make or become purple. □**born in the purple 1** born into a reigning family. **2** belonging to the most privileged class. **purple emperor** a large butterfly, *Apatura iris*, with purple wings. **purple heart** *Brit. colloq.* a heart-shaped stimulant tablet, esp. of amphetamine. **Purple Heart** (in the US) a decoration for those wounded in action. **purple passage** (or **patch**) **1** an ornate or elaborate passage in a literary composition. **2** *Austral. colloq.* a piece of luck or success. □□ **purpleness** *n.* **purplish** *adj.* **purply** *adj.* [OE alt. f. *purpure purpuran* f. L *purpura* (as PURPURA)]

purport *v. & n.* —*v.tr.* /pəˈpɔːt/ **1** profess; be intended to seem (*purports to be the royal seal*). **2** (often foll. by *that* + clause) (of a document or speech) have as its meaning; state. —*n.* /'pɜːpɔːt/ **1** the ostensible meaning of something. **2** the sense or tenor (of a document or statement). □□ **purportedly** /pəˈpɔːtɪdlɪ/ *adv.* [ME f. AF & OF *purport, porport* f. *purporter* f. med.L *proportare* (as PRO-¹, *portare* carry)]

purpose /'pɜːpəs/ *n. & v.* —*n.* **1** an object to be attained; a thing intended. **2** the intention to act. **3** resolution, determination. —*v.tr.* have as one's purpose; design, intend. □**on purpose** intentionally. **purpose-built** (or **-made**) built or made for a specific purpose. **to no purpose** with no result or effect. **to the purpose 1** relevant. **2** useful. [ME f. OF *porpos, purpos* f. L *proponere* (as PROPOUND)]

purposeful /'pɜːpəsˌfʊl/ *adj.* **1** having or indicating purpose. **2** intentional. **3** resolute. □□ **purposefully** *adv.* **purposefulness** *n.*

purposeless /'pɜːpəslɪs/ *adj.* having no aim or plan. □□ **purposelessly** *adv.* **purposelessness** *n.*

purposely /'pɜːpəslɪ/ *adv.* on purpose; intentionally.

purposive /'pɜːpəsɪv/ *adj.* **1** having or serving a purpose. **2** done with a purpose. **3** (of a person or conduct) having purpose or resolution; purposeful. □□ **purposively** *adv.* **purposiveness** *n.*

purpura /'pɜːpjʊrə/ *n.* **1** a disease characterized by purple or livid spots on the skin, due to internal bleeding from small blood vessels. **2** any mollusc of the genus *Purpura*, some of which yield a purple dye. □□ **purpuric** /-'pjʊərɪk/ *adj.* [L f. Gk *porphura* purple]

purpure /'pɜːpjʊə(r)/ *n. & adj. Heraldry* purple. [OE *purpure* & OF *purpre* f. L *purpura* (as PURPURA)]

purpurin /'pɜːpjʊrɪn/ *n.* a red colouring-matter occurring naturally in madder roots, or manufactured synthetically.

purr /pɜː(r)/ *v. & n.* —*v.* **1** *intr.* (of a cat) make a low vibratory sound expressing contentment. **2** *intr.* (of machinery etc.) make a similar sound. **3** *intr.* (of a person) express pleasure. **4** *tr.* utter or express (words or contentment) in this way. —*n.* a purring sound. [imit.]

purse /pɜːs/ *n. & v.* —*n.* **1** a small pouch of leather etc. for carrying money on the person. **2** *US* a handbag. **3** a receptacle resembling a purse in form or purpose. **4** money, funds. **5** a sum collected as a present or given as a prize in a contest. —*v.* **1** *tr.* (often foll. by *up*) pucker or contract (the lips). **2** *intr.* become contracted and wrinkled. □ **hold the purse-strings** have control of expenditure. **the public purse** the national treasury. [OE *purs* f. med.L *bursa*, *byrsa* purse f. Gk *bursa* hide, leather]

purser /'pɜːsə(r)/ *n.* an officer on a ship who keeps the accounts, esp. the head steward in a passenger vessel. □□ **pursership** *n.*

purslane /'pɜːslɪn/ *n.* any of various plants of the genus *Portulaca*, esp. *P. oleracea*, with green or golden leaves, used as a herb and salad vegetable. [ME f. OF *porcelaine* (cf. PORCELAIN) alt. f. L *porcil(l)aca, portulaca*]

pursuance /pə'sjuːəns/ *n.* (foll. by *of*) the carrying out or observance (of a plan, idea, etc.).

pursuant /pə'sjuːənt/ *adj. & adv.* —*adj.* pursuing. —*adv.* (foll. by *to*) conforming to or in accordance with. □□ **pursuantly** *adv.* [ME, = prosecuting, f. OF *po(u)rsuiant* part. of *po(u)rsu(iv)ir* (as PURSUE): assim. to AF *pursuer* and PURSUE]

pursue /pə'sjuː/ *v.* (**pursues, pursued, pursuing**) **1** *tr.* follow with intent to overtake or capture or do harm to. **2** *tr.* continue or proceed along (a route or course of action). **3** *tr.* follow or engage in (study or other activity). **4** *tr.* proceed in compliance with (a plan etc.). **5** *tr.* seek after, aim at. **6** *tr.* continue to investigate or discuss (a topic). **7** *tr.* seek the attention or acquaintance of (a person) persistently. **8** *tr.* (of misfortune etc.) persistently assail. **9** *tr.* persistently attend, stick to. **10** *intr.* go in pursuit. □□ **pursuable** *adj.* **pursuer** *n.* [ME f. AF *pursiwer, -suer* = OF *porsivre* etc. ult. f. L *prosequi* follow after]

pursuit /pə'sjuːt/ *n.* **1** the act or an instance of pursuing. **2** an occupation or activity pursued. □ **in pursuit of** pursuing. [ME f. OF *poursuite* (as PUR-, SUIT)]

pursuivant /'pɜːsɪv(ə)nt/ *n.* **1** *Brit.* an officer of the College of Arms ranking below a herald. **2** *archaic* a follower or attendant. [ME f. OF *pursivant* pres. part. of *pursivre* (as PURSUE)]

pursy /'pɜːsɪ/ *adj.* **1** short-winded; puffy. **2** corpulent. □□ **pursiness** *n.* [ME, earlier *pursive* f. AF *porsif* f. OF *polsif* f. *polser* breathe with difficulty f. L *pulsare* (as PULSATE)]

purulent /'pjʊərʊlənt/ *adj.* **1** consisting of or containing pus. **2** discharging pus. □□ **purulence** *n.* **purulency** *n.* **purulently** *adv.* [F *purulent* or L *purulentus* (as PUS)]

purvey /pə'veɪ/ *v.* **1** *tr.* provide or supply (articles of food) as one's business. **2** *intr.* (often foll. by *for*) **a** make provision. **b** act as supplier. □□ **purveyor** *n.* [ME f. AF *purveier*, OF *porveiir* f. L *providēre* PROVIDE]

purveyance /pə'veɪəns/ *n.* **1** the act of purveying. **2** *Brit. hist.* the right of the sovereign to provisions etc. at a fixed price. [ME f. OF *porveance* f. L *providentia* PROVIDENCE]

purview /'pɜːvjuː/ *n.* **1** the scope or range of a document, scheme, etc. **2** the range of physical or mental vision. [ME f. AF *purveü*, OF *porveü* past part. of *porveiir* (as PURVEY)]

pus /pʌs/ *n.* a thick yellowish or greenish liquid produced from infected tissue. [L *pus puris*]

push /pʊʃ/ *v. & n.* —*v.* **1** *tr.* exert a force on (a thing) to move it away from oneself or from the origin of the force. **2** *tr.* cause to move in this direction. **3** *intr.* exert such a force (*do not push against the door*). **4** *intr. & tr.* **a** thrust forward or upward. **b** project or cause to project (*pushes out new roots; the cape pushes out into the sea*). **5** *intr.* move forward by force or persistence. **6** *tr.* make (one's way) by pushing. **7** *intr.* exert oneself, esp. to surpass others. **8** *tr.* (often foll. by *to, into,* or *to* + infin.) urge or impel. **9** *tr.* tax the abilities or tolerance of; press (a person) hard. **10** *tr.* pursue (a claim etc.). **11** *tr.* promote the use or sale or adoption of, e.g. by advertising. **12** *intr.* (foll. by *for*) demand persistently (*pushed hard for reform*). **13** *tr. colloq.* sell (a drug) illegally. —*n.* **1** the act or an instance of pushing; a shove or thrust. **2** the force exerted in this. **3** a vigorous effort. **4** a military attack in force. **5** enterprise, determination to succeed. **6** the use of influence to advance a person. **7** the pressure of affairs. **8** a crisis. □ **be pushed for** *colloq.* have very little of (esp. time). **get the push** *colloq.* be dismissed or sent away. **give a person the push** *colloq.* dismiss or send away a person. **push along** (often in *imper.*) *colloq.* depart, leave. **push around** *colloq.* bully. **push-bike** *Brit. colloq.* a bicycle worked by pedals. **push-button** **1** a button to be pushed esp. to operate an electrical device. **2** (*attrib.*) operated in this way. **push one's luck** take undue risks. **2** act presumptuously. **push off** **1** push with an oar etc. to get a boat out into a river etc. **2** (often in *imper.*) *colloq.* go away. **push-pull** **1** operated by pushing and pulling. **2** *Electr.* consisting of two valves etc. operated alternately. **push-start** *n.* the starting of a motor vehicle by pushing it to turn the engine. —*v.tr.* start (a vehicle) in this way. **push through** get (a scheme, proposal, etc.) completed or accepted quickly. **push-up** = *press-up*. [ME f. OF *pousser, pou(l)ser* f. L *pulsare* (as PULSATE)]

pushcart /'pʊʃkɑːt/ *n.* a handcart or barrow.

pushchair /'pʊʃtʃeə(r)/ *n. Brit.* a folding chair on wheels, for pushing a child in.

pusher /'pʊʃə(r)/ *n.* **1** *colloq.* an illegal seller of drugs. **2** *colloq.* a pushing or pushy person. **3** a child's utensil for pushing food onto a spoon etc.

pushful /'pʊʃfʊl/ *adj.* pushy; arrogantly self-assertive. □□ **pushfully** *adv.*

pushing /'pʊʃɪŋ/ *adj.* **1** pushy; aggressively ambitious. **2** *colloq.* having nearly reached (a specified age). □□ **pushingly** *adv.*

pushover /'pʊʃˌəʊvə(r)/ *n. colloq.* **1** something that is easily done. **2** a person who can easily be overcome, persuaded, etc.

pushrod /'pʊʃrɒd/ *n.* a rod operated by cams, that opens and closes the valves in an internal-combustion engine.

Pushtu /'pʌʃtuː/ *n. & adj.* = PASHTO. [Pers. *puštū*]

pushy /'pʊʃɪ/ *adj.* (**pushier, pushiest**) *colloq.* **1** excessively or unpleasantly self-assertive. **2** selfishly determined to succeed. □□ **pushily** *adv.* **pushiness** *n.*

pusillanimous /ˌpjuːsɪ'lænɪməs/ *adj.* lacking courage; timid. □□ **pusillanimity** /-lə'nɪmɪtɪ/ *n.* **pusillanimously** *adv.* [eccl.L *pusillanimis* f. *pusillus* very small + *animus* mind]

puss /pʊs/ *n. colloq.* **1** a cat (esp. as a form of address). **2** a playful or coquettish girl. **3** a hare. □ **puss moth** a large European moth, *Cerura vinula.* [prob. f. MLG *pūs*, Du. *poes*, of unkn. orig.]

pussy /'pʊsɪ/ *n.* (*pl.* **-ies**) **1** (also **pussy-cat**) *colloq.* a cat. **2** *coarse sl.* the vulva. ¶ Usually considered a taboo use. □ **pussy willow** any of various willows, esp. *Salix discolor*, with furry catkins.

pussyfoot /'pʊsɪˌfʊt/ *v.intr.* **1** move stealthily or

warily. **2** act cautiously or noncommittally. □□
pussyfooter *n.*

pustulate *v. & adj.* —*v.tr. & intr.* /'pʌstjʊˌleɪt/ form into pustules. —*adj.* /-lət/ of or relating to a pustule or pustules. □□ **pustulation** /-'leɪʃ(ə)n/ *n.* [LL *pustulare* f. *pustula*: see PUSTULE]

pustule /'pʌstjuːl/ *n.* a pimple containing pus. □□ **pustular** *adj.* **pustulous** *adj.* [ME f. OF *pustule* or L *pustula*]

put[1] /pʊt/ *v. & n.* —*v.* (**putting**; *past* and *past part.* **put**) **1** *tr.* move to or cause to be in a specified place or position (*put it in your pocket*; *put the children to bed*; *put your signature here*). **2** *tr.* bring into a specified condition, relation, or state (*puts me in great difficulty*; *an accident put the car out of action*). **3** *tr.* **a** (often foll. by *on*) impose or assign (*put a tax on beer*; *where do you put the blame?*). **b** (foll. by *on, to*) impose or enforce the existence of (*put a veto on it*; *put a stop to it*). **4** *tr.* **a** cause (a person) to go or be, habitually or temporarily (*put them at their ease*; *put them on the right track*). **b** *refl.* imagine (oneself) in a specified situation (*put yourself in my shoes*). **5** *tr.* (foll. by *for*) substitute (one thing for another). **6** *intr.* express (a thought or idea) in a specified way (*to put it mildly*). **7** *tr.* (foll. by *at*) estimate an amount etc. at a specified amount (*put the cost at £50*). **8** *tr.* (foll. by *into*) express or translate in (words, or another language). **9** *tr.* (foll. by *into*) invest (money in an asset, e.g. land). **10** *tr.* (foll. by *on*) stake (money) on (a horse etc.). **11** *tr.* (foll. by *to*) apply or devote to a use or purpose (*put it to good use*). **12** *tr.* (foll. by *to*) submit for consideration or attention (*let me put it to you another way*; *shall now put it to a vote*). **13** *tr.* (foll. by *to*) subject (a person) to (death, suffering, etc.). **14** *tr.* throw (esp. a shot or weight) as an athletic sport or exercise. **15** *tr.* (foll. by *to*) couple (an animal) with (another of the opposite sex) for breeding. **16** *intr.* (foll. by *back, off, out*, etc.) (of a ship etc.) proceed or follow a course in a specified direction. **17** *intr.* US (foll. by *in, out of*) (of a river) flow in a specified direction. —*n.* **1** a throw of the shot or weight. **2** *Stock Exch.* the option of selling stock at a fixed price at a given date. □**not know where to put oneself** feel deeply embarrassed. **put about 1** spread (information, rumour, etc.). **2** *Naut.* turn round; put (a ship) on the opposite tack. **3** trouble, distress. **put across 1** make acceptable or effective. **2** express in an understandable way. **3** (often in **put it (or one) across**) achieve by deceit. **put away 1** put (a thing) back in the place where it is normally kept. **2** lay (money etc.) aside for future use. **3 a** confine or imprison. **b** commit to a home or mental institution. **4** consume (food and drink), esp. in large quantities. **5** put (an old or sick animal) to death. **put back 1** restore to its proper or former place. **2** change (a planned event) to a later date or time. **3** move back the hands of (a clock or watch). **4** check the advance of. **put a bold** etc. **face on it** see FACE. **put the boot in** see BOOT. **put by** lay (money etc.) aside for future use. **put down 1** suppress by force or authority. **2** *colloq.* snub or humiliate. **3** record or enter in writing. **4** enter the name of (a person) on a list, esp. as a member or subscriber. **5** (foll. by *as, for*) account or reckon. **6** (foll. by *to*) attribute (*put it down to bad planning*). **7** put (an old or sick animal) to death. **8** preserve or store (eggs etc.) for future use. **9** pay (a specified sum) as a deposit. **10** put (a baby) to bed. **11** land (an aircraft). **12** stop to let (passengers) get off. **put-down** *n. colloq.* a snub or humiliating criticism. **put an end to** see END. **put one's foot down** see FOOT. **put one's foot in it** see FOOT. **put forth 1** (of a plant) send out (buds or leaves). **2** *formal* submit or put into circulation. **put forward 1** suggest or propose. **2** advance the hands of (a clock or watch). **3** (often *refl.*) put into a prominent position; draw attention to. **put in 1 a** enter or submit (a claim etc.). **b** (foll. by *for*) submit a claim for (a specified

thing. **2** (foll. by *for*) be a candidate for (an appointment, election, etc.). **3** spend (time). **4** perform (a spell of work) as part of a whole. **5** interpose (a remark, blow, etc.). **put a person in mind of** see MIND. **put it to a person** (often foll. by *that* + clause) challenge a person to deny. **put one's mind to** see MIND. **put off 1 a** postpone. **b** postpone an engagement with (a person). **2** (often foll. by *with*) evade (a person) with an excuse etc. **3** hinder or dissuade. **4** offend, disconcert; cause (a person) to lose interest in something. **put on 1** clothe oneself with. **2** cause (an electrical device, light, etc.) to function. **3** cause (transport) to be available. **4** stage (a play, show, etc.). **5** advance the hands of (a clock or watch). **6 a** pretend to be affected by (an emotion). **b** assume, take on (a character or appearance). **c** (**put it on**) exaggerate one's feelings etc. **7** increase one's weight by (a specified amount). **8** send (a cricketer) on to bowl. **9** (foll. by *to*) make aware of or put in touch with (*put us on to their new accountant*). **put-on** *n. colloq.* a deception or hoax. **put out 1 a** (often as **put out** *adj.*) disconcert or annoy. **b** (often *refl.*) inconvenience (*don't put yourself out*). **2** extinguish (a fire or light). **3** cause (a batsman or side) to be out. **4** dislocate (a joint). **5** exert (strength etc.). **6** lend (money) at interest. **7** allocate (work) to be done off the premises. **8** blind (a person's eyes). **put over 1** make acceptable or effective. **2** express in an understandable way. **3** US postpone. **4** US achieve by deceit. **put a sock in it** see SOCK[1]. **put store by** see STORE. **put through 1** carry out or complete (a task or transaction). **2** (often foll. by *to*) connect (a person) by telephone to another subscriber. **put to flight** see FLIGHT[2]. **put together 1** assemble (a whole) from parts. **2** combine (parts) to form a whole. **put under** render unconscious by anaesthetic etc. **put up 1** build or erect. **2** raise (a price etc.). **3** take or provide accommodation (*friends put me up for the night*). **4** engage in (a fight, struggle, etc.) as a form of resistance. **5** present (a proposal). **6 a** present oneself for election. **b** propose for election. **7** provide (money) as a backer in an enterprise. **8** display (a notice). **9** publish (banns). **10** offer for sale or competition. **11** cause (game) to rise from cover. **12** put (a sword) back in its sheath. **put-up** *adj.* fraudulently presented or devised. **put upon** *colloq.* make unfair or excessive demands on; take advantage of (a person). **put a person up to 1** inform or instruct a person about. **2** (usu. foll. by verbal noun) instigate a person in (*put them up to stealing the money*). **put up with** endure, tolerate; submit to. **put the wind up** see WIND[1]. **put a person wise** see WISE. **put words into a person's mouth** see MOUTH. □□ **putter** *n.* [ME f. an unrecorded OE form *putian*, of unkn. orig.]

put[2] var. of PUTT.

putative /'pjuːtətɪv/ *adj.* reputed, supposed (*his putative father*). □□ **putatively** *adv.* [ME f. OF *putatif* -*ive* or LL *putativus* f. L *putare* think]

putlog /'pʌtlɒg/ *n.* (also **putlock** /-lɒk/) a short horizontal timber projecting from a wall, on which scaffold floorboards rest. [17th c.: orig. uncert.]

put-put /'pʌtpʌt/ *n. & v.* —*n.* the rapid intermittent sound of a small petrol engine. —*v.intr.* (**put-putted, put-putting**) make this sound. [imit.]

putrefy /'pjuːtrɪˌfaɪ/ *v.* (**-ies, -ied**) **1** *intr. & tr.* become or make putrid; go bad. **2** *intr.* fester, suppurate. **3** *intr.* become morally corrupt. □□ **putrefacient** /-'feɪʃ(ə)nt/ *adj.* **putrefaction** /-'fækʃ(ə)n/ *n.* **putrefactive** /-'fæktɪv/ *adj.* [ME f. L *putrefacere* f. *puter putris* rotten]

putrescent /pjuː'tres(ə)nt/ *adj.* **1** in the process of rotting. **2** of or accompanying this process. □□ **putrescence** *n.* [L *putrescere* incept. of *putrēre* (as PUTRID)]

putrid /'pjuːtrɪd/ *adj.* **1** decomposed, rotten. **2** foul, noxious. **3** corrupt. **4** *sl.* of poor quality; contemptible; very unpleasant. □□ **putridity** /-'rɪdɪtɪ/ *n.* **putridly**

adv. **putridness** *n.* [L *putridus* f. *putrēre* to rot f. *puter putris* rotten]

putsch /pʊtʃ/ *n.* an attempt at political revolution; a violent uprising. [Swiss G, = thrust, blow]

putt /pʌt/ *v.* & *n.* (also **put**) —*v.tr.* (**putted, putting**) strike (a golf ball) gently to get it into or nearer to a hole on a putting-green. —*n.* a putting stroke. □**putting-green** (in golf) the smooth area of grass round a hole. [differentiated f. PUT¹]

puttee /'pʌtɪ/ *n.* **1** a long strip of cloth wound spirally round the leg from ankle to knee for protection and support. **2** *US* a leather legging. [Hindi *paṭṭī* band, bandage]

putter¹ /'pʌtə(r)/ *n.* **1** a golf club used in putting. **2** a golfer who putts.

putter² /'pʌtə(r)/ *n.* & *v.* = PUT-PUT. [imit.]

putter³ *US* var. of POTTER¹.

putto /'pʊtəʊ/ *n.* (*pl.* **putti** /-tɪ/) a representation of a naked child (esp. a cherub or a cupid) in (esp. Renaissance) art. [It., = boy, f. L *putus*]

putty /'pʌtɪ/ *n.* & *v.* —*n.* (*pl.* **-ies**) **1** a cement made from whiting and raw linseed oil, used for fixing panes of glass, filling holes in woodwork, etc. **2** a fine white mortar of lime and water, used in pointing brickwork, etc. **3** a polishing powder usu. made from tin oxide, used in jewellery work. —*v.tr.* (**-ies, -ied**) cover, fix, join, or fill up with putty. □**putty in a person's hands** someone who is overcompliant, or easily influenced. [F *potée*, lit. potful]

puy /pwiː/ *n.* a small extinct volcanic cone, esp. in the Auvergne, France. [F, = hill, f. L *podium*: see PODIUM]

puzzle /'pʌz(ə)l/ *n.* & *v.* —*n.* **1** a difficult or confusing problem; an enigma. **2** a problem or toy designed to test knowledge or ingenuity. —*v.* **1** *tr.* confound or disconcert mentally. **2** *intr.* (usu. foll. by *over* etc.) be perplexed (about). **3** *tr.* (usu. as **puzzling** *adj.*) require much thought to comprehend (*a puzzling situation*). **4** *tr.* (foll. by *out*) solve or understand by hard thought. □□**puzzlement** *n.* **puzzlingly** *adv.* [16th c.: orig. unkn.]

puzzler /'pʌzlə(r)/ *n.* a difficult question or problem.

puzzolana var. of POZZOLANA.

PVA *abbr.* polyvinyl acetate.

PVC *abbr.* polyvinyl chloride.

Pvt. *abbr.* **1** private. **2** *US* private soldier.

PW *abbr.* policewoman.

p.w. *abbr.* per week.

PWR *abbr.* pressurized-water reactor.

PX *abbr.* *US* post exchange.

pyaemia /paɪ'iːmɪə/ *n.* (*US* **pyemia**) blood-poisoning caused by the spread of pus-forming bacteria in the bloodstream from a source of infection. □□**pyaemic** *adj.* [mod.L f. Gk *puon* pus + *haima* blood]

pycnic var. of PYKNIC.

pye-dog /'paɪdɒɡ/ *n.* (also **pie-dog, pi-dog**) a vagrant mongrel, esp. in Asia. [Anglo-Ind. *pye, paë*, Hindi *pāhī* outsider + DOG]

pyelitis /,paɪə'laɪtɪs/ *n.* inflammation of the renal pelvis. [Gk *puelos* trough, basin + -ITIS]

pyemia *US* var. of PYAEMIA.

pygmy /'pɪɡmɪ/ *n.* (also **pigmy**) (*pl.* **-ies**) **1** a member of a dwarf people of equatorial Africa and parts of SE Asia. **2** a very small person, animal, or thing. **3** an insignificant person. **4** (*attrib.*) **a** of or relating to pygmies. **b** (of a person, animal, etc.) dwarf. □□ **pygmaean** /-'miːən/ *adj.* **pygmean** /-'miːən/ *adj.* [ME f. L *pygmaeus* f. Gk *pugmaios* dwarf f. *pugmē* the length from elbow to knuckles, fist]

pyjamas /pɪ'dʒɑːməz, pə-/ *n.pl.* (*US* **pajamas**) **1** a suit of loose trousers and jacket for sleeping in. **2** loose trousers tied round the waist, worn by both sexes in some Asian countries. **3** (**pyjama**) (*attrib.*) designating parts of a suit of pyjamas (*pyjama jacket; pyjama trousers*). [Urdu *pā(ē)jāma* f. Pers. *pae, pay* leg + Hindi *jāma* clothing]

pyknic /'pɪknɪk/ *adj.* & *n.* (also **pycnic**) *Anthropol.* —*adj.* characterized by a thick neck, large abdomen,

and relatively short limbs. —*n.* a person of this bodily type. [Gk *puknos* thick]

pylon /'paɪlən, -lɒn/ *n.* **1** a tall structure erected as a support (esp. for electric-power cables) or boundary or decoration. **2** a gateway, esp. of an ancient Egyptian temple. **3** a structure marking a path for aircraft. **4** a structure supporting an aircraft engine. [Gk *pulōn* f. *pulē* gate]

pylorus /paɪ'lɔːrəs/ *n.* (*pl.* **pylori** /-raɪ/) *Anat.* the opening from the stomach into the duodenum. □□ **pyloric** /-'lɒrɪk/ *adj.* [LL f. Gk *pulōros, pulouros* gatekeeper f. *pulē* gate + *ouros* warder]

pyorrhoea /,paɪə'riːə/ *n.* (*US* **pyorrhea**) **1** a disease of periodontal tissue causing shrinkage of the gums and loosening of the teeth. **2** any discharge of pus. [Gk *puo-* f. *puon* pus + *rhoia* flux f. *rheō* flow]

pyracantha /,paɪərə'kænθə/ *n.* any evergreen thorny shrub of the genus *Pyracantha*, having white flowers and bright red or yellow berries. [L f. Gk *purakantha*]

pyramid /'pɪrəmɪd/ *n.* **1** a monumental structure, usu. of stone, with a square base and sloping sides meeting centrally at an apex, esp. an ancient Egyptian royal tomb. **2** a solid of this type with a base of three or more sides. **3** a pyramid-shaped thing or pile of things. **4** (in *pl.*) a game played on a billiard-table with (usu. 15) coloured balls and a cue-ball. □**pyramid selling** a system of selling goods in which agency rights are sold to an increasing number of distributors at successively lower levels. □□ **pyramidal** /-'ræmɪd(ə)l/ *adj.* **pyramidally** /-'ræmɪdəlɪ/ *adv.* **pyramidic** /-'mɪdɪk/ *adj.* (also **pyramidical** /-'mɪdɪk(ə)l/). **pyramidically** /-'mɪdɪkəlɪ/ *adv.* **pyramidwise** *adj.* [ME f. L *pyramis* f. Gk *puramis -idos*]

pyre /'paɪə(r)/ *n.* a heap of combustible material esp. a funeral pile for burning a corpse. [L *pyra* f. Gk *pura* f. *pur* fire]

pyrethrin /paɪ'riːθrɪn/ *n.* any of several active constituents of pyrethrum flowers used in the manufacture of insecticides.

pyrethrum /paɪ'riːθrəm/ *n.* **1** any of several aromatic chrysanthemums of the genus *Tanacetum*, esp. *T. coccineum*. **2** an insecticide made from the dried flowers of these plants, esp. *Tanacetum cinerariifolium*. [L f. Gk *purethron* feverfew]

pyretic /paɪ'retɪk, pɪ-/ *adj.* of, for, or producing fever. [mod.L *pyreticus* f. Gk *puretos* fever]

Pyrex /'paɪəreks/ *n. propr.* a hard heat-resistant type of glass, often used for cookware. [invented word]

pyrexia /paɪ'reksɪə, pɪ-/ *n. Med.* = FEVER. □□ **pyrexial** *adj.* **pyrexic** *adj.* **pyrexical** *adj.* [mod.L f. Gk *purexis* f. *puressō* be feverish f. *pur* fire]

pyridine /'pɪrədiːn/ *n. Chem.* a colourless volatile odorous liquid, formerly obtained from coal tar, used as a solvent and in chemical manufacture. ¶ Chem. formula: C_5H_5N. [Gk *pur* fire + -ID⁴ + -INE⁴]

pyridoxine /,pɪrɪ'dɒksɪn/ *n.* a vitamin of the B complex occurring in yeast, and important in the body's use of unsaturated fatty acids. Also called *vitamin* B_6. [PYRIDINE + OX- + -INE⁴]

pyrimidine /pɪ'rɪmɪdiːn/ *n.* **1** *Chem.* an organic nitrogenous base. **2** any of a group of derivatives with similar structure, including the nucleotide constituents uracil, thymine, and cytosine. [G *Pyrimidin* f. *Pyridin* (as PYRIDINE, IMIDE)]

pyrite /'paɪəraɪt/ *n.* = PYRITES. [F *pyrite* or L (as PYRITES)]

pyrites /paɪ'raɪtiːz/ *n.* (in full **iron pyrites**) a yellow lustrous form of iron disulphide. □□ **pyritic** /-'rɪtɪk/ *adj.* **pyritiferous** /-rɪ'tɪfərəs/ *adj.* **pyritize** /'paɪrɪˌtaɪz/ *v.tr.* (also **-ise**). **pyritous** /'paɪrɪtəs/ *adj.* [L f. Gk *puritēs* of fire (*pur*)]

pyro /'paɪərəʊ/ *n. colloq.* = PYROGALLIC ACID.

pyro- /'paɪərəʊ/ *comb. form* **1** denoting fire. **2** *Chem.* denoting a new substance formed from another by elimination of water (*pyrophosphate*). **3** *Mineral.* denoting a mineral etc. showing some property or change under the action of heat, or having a fiery red or yellow colour. [Gk *puro-* f. *pur* fire]

pyroclastic /ˌpaɪərəʊˈklæstɪk/ *adj.* (of rocks etc.) formed as the result of a volcanic eruption. □□ **pyroclast** *n.*

pyroelectric /ˌpaɪərəʊɪˈlektrɪk/ *adj.* having the property of becoming electrically charged when heated. □□ **pyroelectricity** /-ˈtrɪsɪtɪ/ *n.*

pyrogallic acid /ˌpaɪərəʊˈgælɪk/ *n.* a weak acid used as a developer in photography, etc.

pyrogallol /ˌpaɪərəʊˈgælɒl/ *n.* = PYROGALLIC ACID.

pyrogenic /ˌpaɪərəʊˈdʒenɪk/ *adj.* (also **pyrogenous** /paɪˈrɒdʒɪnəs/) **1 a** producing heat, esp. in the body. **b** producing fever. **2** produced by combustion or volcanic processes.

pyrography /paɪˈrɒgrəfɪ/ *n.* = *poker-work* (see POKER[1]).

pyroligneous /ˌpaɪərəʊˈlɪgnɪəs/ *adj.* produced by the action of fire or heat on wood.

pyrolyse /ˈpaɪərəˌlaɪz/ *v.tr.* (*US* **pyrolyze**) decompose by pyrolysis. [PYROLYSIS after *analyse*]

pyrolysis /paɪˈrɒlɪsɪs/ *n.* chemical decomposition brought about by heat. □□ **pyrolytic** /ˌpaɪrəˈlɪtɪk/ *adj.*

pyromania /ˌpaɪərəʊˈmeɪnɪə/ *n.* an obsessive desire to set fire to things. □□ **pyromaniac** *n.*

pyrometer /paɪˈrɒmɪtə(r)/ *n.* an instrument for measuring high temperatures, esp. in furnaces and kilns. □□ **pyrometric** /-rəˈmetrɪk/ *adj.* **pyrometrically** /-rəˈmetrɪkəlɪ/ *adv.* **pyrometry** /-mɪtrɪ/ *n.*

pyrope /ˈpaɪərəʊp/ *n.* a deep red variety of garnet. [ME f. OF *pirope* f. L *pyropus* f. Gk *purōpos* gold-bronze, lit. fiery-eyed, f. *pur* fire + *ōps* eye]

pyrophoric /ˌpaɪərəʊˈfɒrɪk/ *adj.* (of a substance) liable to ignite spontaneously on exposure to air. [mod.L *pyrophorus* f. Gk *purophoros* fire-bearing f. *pur* fire + *pherō* bear]

pyrosis /paɪˈrəʊsɪs/ *n. Med.* a burning sensation in the lower part of the chest, combined with the return of gastric acid to the mouth. [mod.L f. Gk *purōsis* f. *puroō* set on fire f. *pur* fire]

pyrotechnic /ˌpaɪərəʊˈteknɪk/ *adj.* **1** of or relating to fireworks. **2** (of wit etc.) brilliant or sensational. □□ **pyrotechnical** *adj.* **pyrotechnist** *n.* **pyrotechny** /ˈpaɪrəʊ-/ *n.* [PYRO- f. Gk *tekhnē* art]

pyrotechnics /ˌpaɪərəʊˈteknɪks/ *n.pl.* **1** the art of making fireworks. **2** a display of fireworks. **3** any brilliant display.

pyroxene /paɪˈrɒksiːn/ *n.* any of a group of minerals commonly found as components of igneous rocks, composed of silicates of calcium, magnesium, and iron. [PYRO- + Gk *xenos* stranger (because supposed to be alien to igneous rocks)]

pyroxylin /paɪˈrɒksɪlɪn/ *n.* a form of nitrocellulose, soluble in ether and alcohol, used as a basis for lacquers, artificial leather, etc. [F *pyroxyline* (as PYRO-, Gk *xulon* wood)]

pyrrhic[1] /ˈpɪrɪk/ *adj.* (of a victory) won at too great a cost to be of use to the victor. [*Pyrrhus* of Epirus, who defeated the Romans at Asculum in 279 BC, but sustained heavy losses]

pyrrhic[2] /ˈpɪrɪk/ *n. & adj.* —*n.* a metrical foot of two short or unaccented syllables. —*adj.* written in or based on pyrrhics. [L *pyrrhichius* f. Gk *purrhikhios* (*pous*) pyrrhic (foot)]

Pyrrhonism /ˈpɪrəˌnɪz(ə)m/ *n.* **1** the philosophy of Pyrrho of Elis (*c.*300 BC), maintaining that certainty of knowledge is unattainable. **2** scepticism; philosophic doubt. □□ **Pyrrhonist** *n.* [Gk *Purrhōn* Pyrrho]

pyruvate /paɪˈruːveɪt/ *n. Biochem.* any salt or ester of pyruvic acid.

pyruvic acid /paɪˈruːvɪk/ *n.* an organic acid occurring as an intermediate in many stages of metabolism. [as PYRO- + L *uva* grape]

Pythagoras' theorem /paɪˈθægərəs/ *n.* the theorem attributed to Pythagoras (see PYTHAGOREAN) that the square on the hypotenuse of a right-angled triangle is equal to the sum of the squares on the other two sides.

Pythagorean /paɪˌθægəˈriːən/ *adj. & n.* —*adj.* of or relating to the Greek philosopher Pythagoras (6th c. BC) or his philosophy, esp. regarding the transmigration of souls. —*n.* a follower of Pythagoras.

Pythian /ˈpɪθɪən/ *adj.* of or relating to Delphi (in central Greece) or its ancient oracle of Apollo. [L *Pythius* f. Gk *Puthios* f. *Puthō*, an older name of Delphi]

python /ˈpaɪθ(ə)n/ *n.* any constricting snake of the family Pythonidae, esp. of the genus *Python*, found throughout the tropics in the Old World. □□ **pythonic** /-ˈθɒnɪk/ *adj.* [L f. Gk *Puthōn* a huge serpent or monster killed by Apollo]

pythoness /ˈpaɪθənɪs/ *n.* **1** the Pythian priestess. **2** a witch. [ME f. OF *phitonise* f. med.L *phitonissa* f. LL *pythonissa* fem. of *pytho* f. Gk *puthōn* soothsaying demon: cf. PYTHON]

pyuria /paɪˈjʊərɪə/ *n. Med.* the presence of pus in urine. [Gk *puon* pus + -URIA]

pyx /pɪks/ *n.* (also **pix**) **1** *Eccl.* the vessel in which the consecrated bread of the Eucharist is kept. **2** (in the UK) a box at the Royal Mint in which specimen gold and silver coins are deposited to be tested annually. [ME f. L (as PYXIS)]

pyxidium /pɪkˈsɪdɪəm/ *n.* (*pl.* **pyxidia** /-dɪə/) *Bot.* a seed-capsule with a top that comes off like the lid of a box. [mod.L f. Gk *puxidion*, dimin. of *puxis*: see PYXIS]

pyxis /ˈpɪksɪs/ *n.* (*pl.* **pyxides** /-ˌdiːz/) **1** a small box or casket. **2** = PYXIDIUM. [ME f. L f. Gk *puxis* f. *puxos* BOX[3]]

pzazz var. of PIZAZZ.

Q

Q¹ /kjuː/ *n.* (also **q**) (*pl.* **Qs** or **Q's**) the seventeenth letter of the alphabet.

Q² *abbr.* (also **Q.**) **1** Queen, Queen's. **2** question.

Qantas /ˈkwɒntəs/ *n.* the international airline of Australia. [abbr. of Queensland *and* Northern Territory Aerial Services]

QARANC *abbr.* Queen Alexandra's Royal Army Nursing Corps.

QB *abbr.* Queen's Bench.

QC *abbr. Law* Queen's Counsel.

QED *abbr. quod erat demonstrandum.*

Q fever /kjuː/ *n.* a mild febrile disease caused by rickettsiae. [Q = query]

qibla var. of KIBLAH.

Qld. *abbr.* Queensland.

QM *abbr.* quartermaster.

QMG *abbr.* Quartermaster General.

QMS *abbr.* Quartermaster Sergeant.

QPM *abbr.* (in the UK) Queen's Police Medal.

qr. *abbr.* quarter(s).

Q-ship /ˈkjuːʃɪp/ *n.* an armed and disguised merchant ship used as a decoy or to destroy submarines. [Q = query]

QSO *abbr.* quasi-stellar object, quasar.

qt. *abbr.* quart(s).

q.t. *n. colloq.* quiet (esp. *on the q.t.*). [abbr.]

qu. *abbr.* **1** query. **2** question.

qua /kwɑː/ *conj.* in the capacity of; as being (*Napoleon qua general*). [L, ablat. fem. sing. of *qui* who (rel. pron.)]

quack¹ /kwæk/ *v. & n.* —*n.* the harsh sound made by ducks. —*v.intr.* **1** utter this sound. **2** *colloq.* talk loudly and foolishly. [imit.: cf. Du. *kwakken*, G *quacken* croak, quack]

quack² /kwæk/ *n.* **1 a** an unqualified practiser of medicine. **b** (*attrib.*) of or characteristic of unskilled medical practice (*quack cure*). **2** a charlatan. **3** *sl.* any doctor or medical officer. □□ **quackery** *n.* **quackish** *adj.* [abbr. of *quacksalver* f. Du. (prob. f. obs. *quacken* prattle + *salf* SALVE¹)]

quad¹ /kwɒd/ *n. colloq.* a quadrangle. [abbr.]

quad² /kwɒd/ *n. colloq.* = QUADRUPLET 1. [abbr.]

quad³ /kwɒd/ *n. Printing* a piece of blank metal type used in spacing. [abbr. of earlier QUADRAT]

quad⁴ /kwɒd/ *n. & adj.* —*n.* quadraphony. —*adj.* quadraphonic. [abbr.]

quadragenarian /ˌkwɒdrədʒɪˈneərɪən/ *n. & adj.* —*n.* a person from 40 to 49 years old. —*adj.* of this age. [LL *quadragenarius* f. *quadrageni* distrib. of *quadraginta* forty]

Quadragesima /ˌkwɒdrəˈdʒesɪmə/ *n.* the first Sunday in Lent. [LL, fem. of L *quadragesimus* fortieth f. *quadraginta* forty, Lent having 40 days]

quadragesimal /ˌkwɒdrəˈdʒesɪm(ə)l/ *adj.* **1** (of a fast, esp. in Lent) lasting forty days. **2** Lenten.

quadrangle /ˈkwɒdˌræŋ(ə)l/ *n.* **1 a** four-sided plane figure, esp. a square or rectangle. **2 a** a four-sided court, esp. enclosed by buildings, as in some colleges. **b** a court with the buildings round it. □□ **quadrangular** /-ˈræŋjʊlə(r)/ *adj.* [ME f. OF f. LL *quadrangulum* square, neut. of *quadrangulus* (as QUADRI-, ANGLE¹)]

quadrant /ˈkwɒdrənt/ *n.* **1** a quarter of a circle's circumference. **2** a plane figure enclosed by two radii of a circle at right angles and the arc cut off by them. **3** a quarter of a sphere etc. **4 a** a thing, esp. a graduated strip of metal, shaped like a quarter-circle. **b** an instrument graduated (esp. through an arc of 90°) for taking angular measurements. □□ **quadrantal** /-ˈdrænt(ə)l/ *adj.* [ME f. L *quadrans -antis* quarter f. *quattuor* four]

quadraphonic /ˌkwɒdrəˈfɒnɪk/ *adj.* (also **quadrophonic**) (of sound reproduction) using four transmission channels. □□ **quadraphonically** *adv.* **quadraphonics** *n.pl.* **quadraphony** /-ˈrɒfənɪ/ *n.* [QUADRI- + STEREOPHONIC]

quadrat /ˈkwɒdrət/ *n. Ecol.* a small area marked out for study. [var. of QUADRATE]

quadrate *adj., n., & v.* —*adj.* /ˈkwɒdrət/ esp. *Anat.* & *Zool.* square or rectangular (*quadrate bone; quadrate muscle*). —*n.* /ˈkwɒdrət/ **1** a quadrate bone or muscle. **2** a rectangular object. —*v.* /kwɒˈdreɪt/ **1** *tr.* make square. **2** *intr. & tr.* (often foll. by *with*) conform or make conform. [ME f. L *quadrare quadrat-* make square f. *quattuor* four]

quadratic /kwɒˈdrætɪk/ *adj. & n. Math.* —*adj.* **1** involving the second and no higher power of an unknown quantity or variable (*quadratic equation*). **2** square. —*n.* **1** a quadratic equation. **2** (in *pl.*) the branch of algebra dealing with these. [F *quadratique* or mod.L *quadraticus* (as QUADRATE)]

quadrature /ˈkwɒdrətʃə(r)/ *n.* **1** *Math.* the process of constructing a square with an area equal to that of a figure bounded by a curve, e.g. a circle. **2** *Astron.* **a** each of two points at which the moon is 90° from the sun as viewed from earth. **b** the position of a heavenly body in relation to another 90° away. [F *quadrature* or L *quadratura* (as QUADRATE)]

quadrennial /kwɒˈdrenɪəl/ *adj.* **1** lasting four years. **2** recurring every four years. □□ **quadrennially** *adv.* [as QUADRENNIUM]

quadrennium /kwɒˈdrenɪəm/ *n.* (*pl.* **quadrenniums** or **quadrennia** /-nɪə/) a period of four years. [L *quadriennium* (as QUADRI-, *annus* year)]

quadri- /ˈkwɒdrɪ/ *comb. form* denoting four. [L f. *quattuor* four]

quadric /ˈkwɒdrɪk/ *adj. & n. Geom.* —*adj.* (of a surface) described by an equation of the second degree. —*n.* a quadric surface. [L *quadra* square]

quadriceps /ˈkwɒdrɪˌseps/ *n. Anat.* a four-headed muscle at the front of the thigh. [mod.L (as QUADRI-, BICEPS)]

quadrifid /ˈkwɒdrɪfɪd/ *adj. Bot.* having four divisions or lobes. [L *quadrifidus* (as QUADRI-, *findere fid-* cleave)]

quadrilateral /ˌkwɒdrɪˈlætər(ə)l/ *adj. & n.* —*adj.* having four sides. —*n.* a four-sided figure. [LL *quadrilaterus* (as QUADRI-, *latus lateris* side)]

quadrille¹ /kwɒˈdrɪl/ *n.* **1** a square dance containing usu. five figures. **2** the music for this. [F f. Sp. *cuadrilla* troop, company f. *cuadra* square or It. *quadriglia* f. *quadra* square]

quadrille² /kwɒˈdrɪl/ *n.* a card game for four players with forty cards, fashionable in the 18th c. [F, perh. f. Sp. *cuartillo* f. *cuarto* fourth, assim. to QUADRILLE¹]

quadrillion /kwɒˈdrɪljən/ *n.* (*pl.* same or **quadrillions**) a thousand raised to the fifth (or formerly, esp. *Brit.*, the eighth) power (10^{15} and 10^{24} respectively). [F (as QUADRI-, MILLION)]

quadrinomial /ˌkwɒdrɪˈnəʊmɪəl/ *n. & adj. Math.* —*n.* an expression of four algebraic terms. —*adj.* of or being a quadrinomial. [QUADRI- + Gk *nomos* part, portion]

quadripartite /ˌkwɒdrɪˈpɑːtaɪt/ *adj.* **1** consisting of four parts. **2** shared by or involving four parties.

quadriplegia /ˌkwɒdrɪˈpliːdʒɪə, -dʒə/ *n. Med.* paralysis of all four limbs. □□ **quadriplegic** *adj. & n.* [mod.L (as QUADRI-, Gk *plēgē* blow, strike)]

---

b *but* d *dog* f *few* g *get* h *he* j *yes* k *cat* l *leg* m *man* n *no* p *pen* r *red* s *sit* t *top* v *voice*

quadrivalent /ˌkwɒdrɪˈveɪlənt/ *adj. Chem.* having a valency of four.

quadrivium /kwɒˈdrɪvɪəm/ *n. hist.* a medieval university course of arithmetic, geometry, astronomy, and music. [L, = the place where four roads meet (as QUADRI-, *via* road)]

quadroon /kwɒˈdruːn/ *n.* the offspring of a White person and a mulatto; a person of one quarter Negro blood. [Sp. *cuarterón* f. *cuarto* fourth, assim. to QUADRI-]

quadrophonic var. of QUADRAPHONIC.

quadrumanous /kwɒˈdruːmənəs/ *adj.* (of primates other than humans) four-handed, i.e. with opposable digits on all four limbs. [mod.L *quadrumana* neut. pl. of *quadrumanus* (as QUADRI-, L *manus* hand)]

quadruped /ˈkwɒdrʊˌped/ *n. & adj.* —*n.* a four-footed animal, esp. a four-footed mammal. —*adj.* four-footed. □□ **quadrupedal** /-ˈruːpɪd(ə)l/ *adj.* [F *quadrupède* or L *quadrupes -pedis* f. *quadru-* var. of QUADRI- + L *pes ped-* foot]

quadruple /ˈkwɒdrʊp(ə)l/ *adj., n., & v.* —*adj.* 1 fourfold. 2 a having four parts. b involving four participants (*quadruple alliance*). 3 being four times as many or as much. 4 (of time in music) having four beats in a bar. —*n.* a fourfold number or amount. —*v.tr. & intr.* multiply by four; increase fourfold. □□ **quadruply** *adv.* [F f. L *quadruplus* (as QUADRI-, *-plus* as in *duplus* DUPLE)]

quadruplet /ˈkwɒdrʊplɪt, -ˈdruːplɪt/ *n.* 1 each of four children born at one birth. 2 a set of four things working together. 3 *Mus.* a group of four notes to be performed in the time of three. [QUADRUPLE, after *triplet*]

quadruplicate *adj. & v.* —*adj.* /kwɒˈdruːplɪkət/ 1 fourfold. 2 of which four copies are made. —*v.tr.* /kwɒˈdruːplɪˌkeɪt/ 1 multiply by four. 2 make four identical copies of. □ **in quadruplicate** in four identical copies. □□ **quadruplication** /-ˈkeɪʃ(ə)n/ *n.* [L *quadruplicare* f. *quadruplex -plicis* fourfold: cf. QUADRUPED, DUPLEX]

quadruplicity /ˌkwɒdrʊˈplɪsɪtɪ/ *n.* the state of being fourfold. [L *quadruplex -plicis* (see QUADRUPLICATE), after *duplicity*]

quaestor /ˈkwiːstə(r)/ *n.* either of two ancient Roman magistrates with mainly financial responsibilities. □□ **quaestorial** /-ˈstɔːrɪəl/ *adj.* **quaestorship** *n.* [ME f. L f. *quaerere* quaesit- seek]

quaff /kwɒf, kwɑːf/ *v. literary* 1 *tr. & intr.* drink deeply. 2 *tr.* drain (a cup etc.) in long draughts. □□ **quaffable** *adj.* **quaffer** *n.* [16th c.: perh. imit.]

quag /kwæg, kwɒg/ *n.* a marshy or boggy place. □□ **quaggy** *adj.* [rel. to dial. *quag* (v.) = shake: prob. imit.]

quagga /ˈkwægə/ *n.* an extinct zebra-like mammal, *Equus quagga*, formerly native to S. Africa, with yellowish-brown stripes on the head, neck, and forebody. [Xhosa-Kaffir *iqwara*]

quagmire /ˈkwɒgˌmaɪə(r), ˈkwæg-/ *n.* 1 a soft boggy or marshy area that gives way underfoot. 2 a hazardous or awkward situation. [QUAG + MIRE]

quahog /ˈkwɒːhɒg/ *n.* (*US* **quahaug** /-hɔːg/) any of various edible clams of the Atlantic coast of N. America. [Narraganset Indian]

quaich /kweɪx/ *n.* (also **quaigh**) *Sc.* a kind of drinking-cup, usu. of wood and with two handles. [Gael. *cuach* cup, prob. f. L *caucus*]

quail[1] /kweɪl/ *n.* (*pl.* same or **quails**) any small migratory bird of the genus *Coturnix*, with a short tail and allied to the partridge. [ME f. OF *quaille* f. med.L *coacula* (prob. imit.)]

quail[2] /kweɪl/ *v.intr.* flinch; be apprehensive with fear. [ME, of unkn. orig.]

quaint /kweɪnt/ *adj.* 1 piquantly or attractively unfamiliar or old-fashioned. 2 daintily odd. □□ **quaintly** *adv.* **quaintness** *n.* [earlier senses 'wise, cunning': ME f. OF *cointe* f. L *cognitus* past part. of *cognoscere* ascertain]

quake /kweɪk/ *v. & n.* —*v.intr.* 1 shake, tremble. 2 rock to and fro. 3 (of a person) shake or shudder (*was quaking with fear*). —*n.* 1 *colloq.* an earthquake. 2 an act of quaking. □ **quaking-grass** any grass of the genus *Briza*, having slender stalks and trembling in the wind: also called *dodder-grass.* □□ **quaky** *adj.* (**quakier, quakiest**). [OE *cwacian*]

Quaker /ˈkweɪkə(r)/ *n.* a member of the Society of Friends, a Christian movement devoted to peaceful principles and eschewing formal doctrine, sacraments, and ordained ministers. □□ **Quakerish** *adj.* **Quakerism** *n.* [QUAKE + -ER[1]]

qualification /ˌkwɒlɪfɪˈkeɪʃ(ə)n/ *n.* 1 the act or an instance of qualifying. 2 an accomplishment fitting a person for a position or purpose. 3 a a circumstance, condition, etc., that modifies or limits (*the statement had many qualifications*). b a thing that detracts from completeness or absoluteness (*their relief had one qualification*). 4 a condition that must be fulfilled before a right can be acquired etc. 5 an attribution of a quality (*the qualification of our policy as opportunist is unfair*). □□ **qualificatory** /ˈkwɒlɪfɪˌkeɪtərɪ/ *adj.* [F *qualification* or med.L *qualificatio* (as QUALIFY)]

qualify /ˈkwɒlɪˌfaɪ/ *v.* (**-ies, -ied**) 1 *tr.* make competent or fit for a position or purpose. 2 *tr.* make legally entitled. 3 *intr.* (foll. by *for*) (of a person) satisfy the conditions or requirements (for a position, award, competition, etc.). 4 *tr.* add reservations to; modify or make less absolute (a statement or assertion). 5 *tr. Gram.* (of a word, esp. an adjective) attribute a quality to another word, esp. a noun. 6 *tr.* moderate, mitigate; make less severe or extreme. 7 *tr.* alter the strength or flavour of. 8 *tr.* (foll. by *as*) attribute a specified quality to, describe as (*the idea was qualified as absurd*). 9 *tr.* (as **qualifying** *adj.*) serving to determine those that qualify (*qualifying examination*). □□ **qualifiable** *adj.* **qualifier** *n.* [F *qualifier* f. med.L *qualificare* f. L *qualis* such as]

qualitative /ˈkwɒlɪtətɪv, -ˌteɪtɪv/ *adj.* concerned with or depending on quality (*led to a qualitative change in society*). □ **qualitative analysis** *Chem.* detection of the constituents, as elements, functional groups, etc., present in a substance (opp. *quantitative analysis*). □□ **qualitatively** *adv.* [LL *qualitativus* (as QUALITY)]

quality /ˈkwɒlɪtɪ/ *n.* (*pl.* **-ies**) 1 the degree of excellence of a thing (*of good quality; poor in quality*). 2 a general excellence (*their work has quality*). b (*attrib.*) of high quality (*a quality product*). 3 a distinctive attribute or faculty; a characteristic trait. 4 the relative nature or kind or character of a thing (*is made in three qualities*). 5 the distinctive timbre of a voice or sound. 6 *archaic* high social standing (*people of quality*). 7 *Logic* the property of a proposition's being affirmative or negative. □ **quality control** a system of maintaining standards in manufactured products by testing a sample of the output against the specification. [ME f. OF *qualité* f. L *qualitas -tatis* f. *qualis* of what kind]

qualm /kwɑːm, kwɔːm/ *n.* 1 a misgiving; an uneasy doubt esp. about one's own conduct. 2 a scruple of conscience. 3 a momentary faint or sick feeling. □□ **qualmish** *adj.* [16th c.: orig. uncert.]

quandary /ˈkwɒndərɪ/ *n.* (*pl.* **-ies**) 1 a state of perplexity. 2 a difficult situation; a practical dilemma. [16th c.: orig. uncert.]

quango /ˈkwæŋgəʊ/ *n.* (*pl.* **-os**) a semi-public body with financial support from and senior appointments made by the government. [abbr. of *quasi* (or *quasi-*autonomous) *non-government(al) organization*]

quant /kwɒnt/ *n. & v.* —*n. Brit.* a punting-pole with a prong at the bottom to prevent it sinking into the mud, as used by Norfolk bargemen etc. —*v.tr.* (also *absol.*) propel (a boat) with a quant. [15th c.: perh. f. L *contus* f. Gk *kontos* boat-pole]

quanta *pl.* of QUANTUM.

quantal /ˈkwɒnt(ə)l/ *adj.* 1 composed of discrete units; varying in steps, not continuously. 2 of or relating to a quantum or quantum theory. □□ **quantally** adv. [L *quantus* how much]

quantic /'kwɒntɪk/ n. Math. a rational integral homogeneous function of two or more variables.

quantify /'kwɒntɪ,faɪ/ v.tr. (-ies, -ied) 1 determine the quantity of. 2 measure or express as a quantity. 3 Logic define the application of (a term or proposition) by the use of all, some, etc., e.g. 'for all x if x is A then x is B'. □□ **quantifiable** adj. **quantifiability** /-ə'bɪlɪtɪ/ n. **quantification** /,kwɒntɪfɪ'keɪʃ(ə)n/ n. **quantifier** n. [med.L *quantificare* (as QUANTAL)]

quantitative /'kwɒntɪtətɪv, -,teɪtɪv/ adj. 1 a concerned with quantity. b measured or measurable by quantity. 2 of or based on the quantity of syllables. □**quantitative analysis** Chem. measurement of the amounts of the constituents of a substance (opp. QUALITATIVE ANALYSIS). □□ **quantitatively** adv. [med.L *quantitativus* (as QUANTITY)]

quantitive /'kwɒntɪtɪv/ adj. = QUANTITATIVE. □□ **quantitively** adv.

quantity /'kwɒntɪtɪ/ n. (pl. -ies) 1 the property of things that is measurable. 2 the size or extent or weight or amount or number. 3 a specified or considerable portion or number or amount (buys in quantity; the quantity of heat in a body). 4 (in pl.) large amounts or numbers; an abundance (quantities of food; is found in quantities on the shore). 5 the length or shortness of vowel sounds or syllables. 6 Math. a a value, component, etc. that may be expressed in numbers. b the figure or symbol representing this. □**quantity mark** a mark put over a vowel etc. to indicate its length. **quantity surveyor** a person who measures and prices building work. **quantity theory** the hypothesis that prices correspond to changes in the monetary supply. [ME f. OF *quantité* f. L *quantitas -tatis* f. *quantus* how much]

quantize /'kwɒntaɪz/ v.tr. (also **-ise**) 1 form into quanta. 2 apply quantum mechanics to. □□ **quantization** /-'zeɪʃ(ə)n/ n.

quantum /'kwɒntəm/ n. (pl. **quanta** /-tə/) 1 Physics a a discrete quantity of energy proportional in magnitude to the frequency of radiation it represents. b an analogous discrete amount of any other physical quantity. 2 a a required or allowed amount. b a share or portion. □**quantum jump** (or **leap**) 1 a sudden large increase or advance. 2 Physics an abrupt transition in an atom or molecule from one quantum state to another. **quantum mechanics** (or **theory**) Physics a system or theory using the assumption that energy exists in discrete units. [L, neut. of *quantus* how much]

quaquaversal /,kweɪkwə'vɜːs(ə)l/ adj. Geol. pointing in every direction. [LL *quaquaversus* f. *quaqua* wheresoever + *versus* towards]

quarantine /'kwɒrən,tiːn/ n. & v. —n. 1 isolation imposed on persons or animals that have arrived from elsewhere or been exposed to, and might spread, infectious or contagious disease. 2 the period of this isolation. —v.tr. impose such isolation on, put in quarantine. [It. *quarantina* forty days f. *quaranta* forty]

quark[1] /kwɑːk/ n. Physics any of several postulated components of elementary particles. [invented word, assoc. with 'Three quarks for Muster Mark' in Joyce's *Finnegans Wake* (1939)]

quark[2] /kwɑːk/ n. a type of low-fat curd cheese. [G]

quarrel[1] /'kwɒr(ə)l/ n. & v. —n. 1 a violent contention or altercation between individuals or with others. 2 a rupture of friendly relations. 3 an occasion of complaint against a person, a person's actions, etc. —v.intr. (**quarrelled, quarrelling**; US **quarreled, quarreling**) 1 (often foll. by with) take exception; find fault. 2 fall out; have a dispute; break off friendly relations. □□ **quarreller** n. [ME f. OF *querele* f. L *querel(l)a* complaint f. *queri* complain]

quarrel[2] /'kwɒr(ə)l/ n. hist. a short heavy square-headed arrow or bolt used in a crossbow or arbalest. [ME f. OF *quar(r)el* ult. f. LL *quadrus* square]

quarrelsome /'kwɒrəlsəm/ adj. given to or characterized by quarrelling. □□ **quarrelsomely** adv. **quarrelsomeness** n.

quarrian /'kwɒrɪən/ n. (also **quarrion**) a cockatiel. [prob. Aboriginal]

quarry[1] /'kwɒrɪ/ n. & v. —n. (pl. -ies) 1 an excavation made by taking stone etc. for building etc. from its bed. 2 a place from which stone etc. may be extracted. 3 a source of information, knowledge, etc. —v. (-ies, -ied) 1 tr. extract (stone) from a quarry. 2 tr. extract (facts etc.) laboriously from books etc. 3 intr. laboriously search documents etc. [ME f. med.L *quare(r)ia* f. OF *quarriere* f. L *quadrum* square]

quarry[2] /'kwɒrɪ/ n. (pl. -ies) 1 the object of pursuit by a bird of prey, hounds, hunters, etc. 2 an intended victim or prey. [ME f. AF f. OF *cuiree, couree* (assim. to *cuir* leather and *curer* disembowel) ult. f. L *cor* heart: orig. = parts of deer placed on hide and given to hounds]

quarry[3] /'kwɒrɪ/ n. (pl. -ies) 1 a diamond-shaped pane of glass as used in lattice windows. 2 (in full **quarry tile**) an unglazed floor-tile. [a later form of QUARREL[2] in the same sense]

quarryman /'kwɒrɪmən/ n. (pl. -men) a worker in a quarry.

quart /'kwɔːt/ n. 1 a liquid measure equal to a quarter of a gallon; two pints. 2 a vessel containing this amount. 3 US a unit of dry measure, equivalent to one-thirty-second of a bushel (1.1 litre). 4 /kɑːt/ (also **quarte**) the fourth of eight parrying positions in fencing. □**a quart into a pint pot** 1 a large amount etc. fitted into a small space. 2 something difficult or impossible to achieve. [ME f. OF *quarte* f. L *quarta* fem. of *quartus* fourth f. *quattuor* four]

quartan /'kwɔːt(ə)n/ adj. (of a fever etc.) recurring every fourth day. [ME f. OF *quartaine* f. L (*febris*) *quartana* f. *quartus* fourth]

quarte var. of QUART 4.

quarter /'kwɔːtə(r)/ n. & v. —n. 1 each of four equal parts into which a thing is or might be divided. 2 a period of three months, usu. for which payments become due on the quarter day. 3 a point of time 15 minutes before or after any hour. 4 a school or US university term. 5 a 25 US or Canadian cents. b a coin of this denomination. 6 a part of a town, esp. as occupied by a particular class or group (residential quarter). 7 a a point of the compass. b a region at such a point. 8 the direction, district, or source of supply etc. (help from any quarter; came from all quarters). 9 (in pl.) a lodgings; an abode. b Mil. the living accommodation of troops etc. 10 a one fourth of a lunar month. b the moon's position between the first and second (**first quarter**) or third and fourth (**last quarter**) of these. 11 a each of the four parts into which an animal's or bird's carcass is divided, each including a leg or wing. b (in pl.) hist. the four parts into which a traitor etc. was cut after execution. c (in pl.) = HINDQUARTERS. 12 mercy offered or granted to an enemy in battle etc. on condition of surrender. 13 a Brit. a grain measure equivalent to 8 bushels. b one-fourth of a hundredweight (28 lb. or US 25 lb.). 14 a each of four divisions on a shield. b a charge occupying this, placed in chief. 15 either side of a ship abaft the beam. 16 (in American and Australian football) each of four equal periods into which a match is divided. —v.tr. 1 divide into quarters. 2 hist. divide (the body of an executed person) in this way. 3 a put (troops etc.) into quarters. b station or lodge in a specified place. 4 (foll. by on) impose (a person) on another as a lodger. 5 cut (a log) into quarters, and these into planks so as to show the grain well. 6 (esp. of a dog) range or traverse (the ground) in every direction. 7 Heraldry a place or bear (charges or coats of arms) on the four quarters of a shield's surface. b add (another's coat) to one's hereditary arms. **c** (foll. by *with*) place in alternate quarters with. **d** divide (a shield) into four or more parts by vertical and horizontal lines. ▫**quarter-binding** the type of bookbinding in which the spine is bound in one material (usu. leather) and the sides in another. **quarter day** one of four days on which quarterly payments are due, tenancies begin and end, etc. **quarter-final** a match or round preceding the semifinal. **quarter-hour 1** a period of 15 minutes. **2** = sense 3 of *n*. **quarter-light** *Brit.* a window in the side of a motor vehicle, closed carriage, etc. other than the main door-window. **quarter-line** *Rugby Football* a space enclosed by a line across the ground 22 metres from the goal-line. **quarter note** esp. *US Mus.* a crotchet. **quarter-plate 1** a photographic plate or film 8.3 × 10.8 cm. **2** a photograph reproduced from it. **quarter sessions** *hist.* (in the UK) a court of limited criminal and civil jurisdiction and of appeal, usu. held quarterly. **quarter-tone** *Mus.* half a semitone. [ME f. AF *quarter*, OF *quartier* f. L *quartarius* fourth part (of a measure) f. *quartus* fourth]

quarterage /ˈkwɔːtərɪdʒ/ *n*. **1** a quarterly payment. **2** a quarter's wages, allowance, pension, etc.

quarterback /ˈkwɔːtəˌbæk/ *n*. a player in American football who directs attacking play.

quarterdeck /ˈkwɔːtəˌdek/ *n*. **1** part of a ship's upper deck near the stern, usu. reserved for officers. **2** the officers of a ship or the navy.

quartering /ˈkwɔːtərɪŋ/ *n*. **1** (in *pl.*) the coats of arms marshalled on a shield to denote the alliances of a family with the heiresses of others. **2** the provision of quarters for soldiers. **3** the act or an instance of dividing, esp. into four equal parts. **4** timber sawn into lengths, used for high-quality floor-boards etc.

quarterly /ˈkwɔːtəlɪ/ *adj.*, *adv.*, & *n.* —*adj.* **1** produced or occurring once every quarter of a year. **2** (of a shield) quartered. —*adv.* **1** once every quarter of a year. **2** in the four, or in two diagonally opposite, quarters of a shield. —*n.* (*pl.* -**ies**) a quarterly review or magazine.

quartermaster /ˈkwɔːtəˌmɑːstə(r)/ *n*. **1** a regimental officer in charge of quartering, rations, etc. **2** a naval petty officer in charge of steering, signals, etc. ▫**Quartermaster General** the head of the army department in charge of quartering etc. **quartermaster sergeant** a sergeant assisting an army quartermaster.

quartern /ˈkwɔːt(ə)n/ *n*. *Brit.* *archaic* a quarter of a pint. ▫**quartern loaf** a four-pound loaf. [ME, = quarter f. AF *quartrun*, OF *quart(e)ron* f. QUART fourth or *quartier* QUARTER]

quarterstaff /ˈkwɔːtəˌstɑːf/ *n*. *hist.* a stout pole 6-8 feet long, formerly used as a weapon.

quartet /kwɔːˈtet/ *n*. (also **quartette**) **1** *Mus.* **a** a composition for four voices or instruments. **b** the performers of such a piece. **2** any group of four. [F *quartette* f. It. *quartetto* f. *quarto* fourth f. L *quartus*]

quartic /ˈkwɑːtɪk/ *adj.* & *n*. *Math.* —*adj.* involving the fourth and no higher power of an unknown quantity or variable. —*n.* a quartic equation. [L *quartus* fourth]

quartile /ˈkwɔːtaɪl/ *adj.* & *n*. *Astrol.* relating to the aspect of two celestial bodies 90° apart. —*n.* **1** a quartile aspect. **2** *Statistics* one of three values of a variable dividing a population into four equal groups as regards the value of that variable. [med.L *quartilis* f. L *quartus* fourth]

quarto /ˈkwɔːtəʊ/ *n*. (*pl.* -**os**) *Printing* **1** the size given by folding a (usu. specified) sheet of paper twice. **2** a book consisting of sheets folded in this way. ¶ Abbr.: **4to.** ▫**quarto paper** paper folded in this way and cut into sheets. [L (*in*) *quarto* (in) the fourth (of a sheet), ablat. of *quartus* fourth]

quartz /kwɔːts/ *n*. a mineral form of silica that crystallizes as hexagonal prisms. ▫**quartz clock** a clock operated by vibrations of an electrically driven

quartz crystal. **quartz lamp** a quartz tube containing mercury vapour and used as a light source. [G *Quarz* f. WSlav. *kwardy*]

quartzite /ˈkwɔːtsaɪt/ *n*. a metamorphic rock consisting mainly of quartz.

quasar /ˈkweɪzɑː(r), -sɑː(r)/ *n*. *Astron.* any of a class of starlike celestial objects having a spectrum with a large red-shift. [*quasi-stellar*]

quash /kwɒʃ/ *v.tr.* **1** annul; reject as not valid, esp. by a legal procedure. **2** suppress; crush (a rebellion etc.). [ME f. OF *quasser*, *casser* annul f. LL *cassare* f. *cassus* null, void or f. L *cassare* frequent. of *quatere* shake]

quasi /ˈkweɪzaɪ, ˈkwɑːzɪ/ *adv.* (introducing an exclamation) that is to say; as it were. [L, = as if, almost]

quasi- /ˈkweɪzaɪ, ˈkwɑːzɪ/ *comb. form* **1** seemingly; apparently but not really (*quasi-scientific*). **2** being partly or almost (*quasi-independent*). [L *quasi* as if, almost]

quassia /ˈkwɒʃə/ *n*. **1** an evergreen tree, *Quassia amara*, native to S. America. **2** the wood, bark, or root of this tree, yielding a bitter medicinal tonic and insecticide. [G. *Quassi*, 18th-c. Surinam slave, who discovered its medicinal properties]

quatercentenary /ˌkwætəsenˈtiːnərɪ/ *n.* & *adj.* —*n.* (*pl.* -**ies**) **1** a four-hundredth anniversary. **2** a festival marking this. —*adj.* of this anniversary. [L *quater* four times + CENTENARY]

quaternary /kwəˈtɜːnərɪ/ *adj.* & *n*. —*adj.* **1** having four parts. **2** (**Quaternary**) *Geol.* of or relating to the most recent period in the Cenozoic era with evidence of many species of present-day plants and animals (cf. PLEISTOCENE, HOLOCENE). ¶ Cf. Appendix II. —*n.* (*pl.* -**ies**) **1** a set of four things. **2** (**Quaternary**) *Geol.* the Quaternary period or system. [ME f. L *quaternarius* f. *quaterni* distrib. of *quattuor* four]

quaternion /kwəˈtɜːnɪən/ *n*. **1** a set of four. **2** *Math.* a complex number of the form $w + xi + yj + zk$, where w, x, y, z are real numbers and i, j, k are imaginary units that satisfy certain conditions. [ME f. LL *quaternio -onis* (as QUATERNARY)]

quatorzain /ˈkætəˌzeɪn/ *n*. any fourteen-line poem; an irregular sonnet. [F *quatorzaine* f. *quatorze* fourteen f. L *quattuordecim*]

quatorze /kəˈtɔːz/ *n*. a set of four aces, kings, queens, or jacks, in one hand at piquet, scoring fourteen. [F: see QUATORZAIN]

quatrain /ˈkwɒtreɪn/ *n*. a stanza of four lines, usu. with alternate rhymes. [F f. *quatre* four f. L *quattuor*]

quatrefoil /ˈkætrəˌfɔɪl/ *n*. a four-pointed or four-leafed figure, esp. as an ornament in architectural tracery, resembling a flower or clover leaf. [ME f. AF f. *quatre* four: see FOIL[2]]

quattrocento /ˌkwætrəʊˈtʃentəʊ/ *n*. the style of Italian art of the 15th c. ▫▫**quattrocentist** *n*. [It., = 400 used with reference to the years 1400-99]

quaver /ˈkweɪvə(r)/ *v.* & *n*. —*v.* **1** *intr.* **a** (esp. of a voice or musical sound) vibrate, shake, tremble. **b** use trills or shakes in singing. **2** *tr.* **a** sing (a note or song) with quavering. **b** (often foll. by *out*) say in a trembling voice. —*n.* **1** *Mus.* a note having the time value of an eighth of a semibreve or half a crotchet and represented by a large dot with a hooked stem. Also called *eighth. note.* **2** a trill in singing. **3** a tremble in speech. ▫▫**quaveringly** *adv.* [ME f. *quave*, perh. f. OE *cwafian* (unrecorded: cf. *cwacian* QUAKE)]

quavery /ˈkweɪvərɪ/ *adj.* (of a voice etc.) tremulous. ▫▫**quaveriness** *n*.

quay /kiː/ *n*. a solid stationary artificial landing-place lying alongside or projecting into water for loading and unloading ships. ▫▫**quayage** *n*. [ME *key(e)*, *kay* f. OF *kay* f. Gaulish *caio* f. OCelt.]

quayside /ˈkiːsaɪd/ *n*. the land forming or near a quay.

Que. *abbr.* Quebec.

quean /kwiːn/ *n. archaic* an impudent or ill-behaved girl or woman. [OE *cwene* woman: cf. QUEEN]

queasy /ˈkwiːzɪ/ *adj.* (-ier, -iest) **1 a** (of a person) feeling nausea. **b** (of a person's stomach) easily upset, weak of digestion. **2** (of the conscience etc.) overscrupulous, tender. □□ **queasily** *adv.* **queasiness** *n.* [ME *queysy, coisy* perh. f. AF & OF, rel. to OF *coisir* hurt]

Quechua /ˈketʃwə/ *n.* (also **Quichua** /ˈkɪ-/) a S. American Indian language widely spoken in Peru and neighbouring countries. □□ **Quechuan** *adj.* [Sp. f. Quechua]

queen /kwiːn/ *n. & v.* —*n.* **1** (as a title usu. **Queen**) a female sovereign, esp. the hereditary ruler of an independent State. **2** (in full **queen consort**) a king's wife. **3** a woman, country, or thing pre-eminent or supreme in a specified area or of its kind (*tennis queen*; *the queen of roses*). **4** the fertile female among ants, bees, etc. **5** the most powerful piece in chess. **6** a court card with a picture of a queen. **7** *sl.* a male homosexual, esp. an effeminate one. **8 a** an honoured female, e.g. the Virgin Mary (*Queen of Heaven*). **b** an ancient goddess (*Venus, Queen of love*). **9** a belle or mock sovereign on some occasion (*beauty queen*; *queen of the May*). **10** a person's sweetheart, wife, or mistress. **11** (**the Queen**) (in the UK) the national anthem when there is a female sovereign. —*v.tr.* **1** make (a woman) queen. **2** *Chess* convert (a pawn) into a queen when it reaches the opponent's side of the board. □ **Queen-Anne** in the style of English architecture, furniture, etc., in or about Queen Anne's time, the early 18th c. **Queen Anne's lace** cow-parsley. **queen bee 1** the fertile female in a hive. **2** the chief or controlling woman in an organization or social group. **queen-cake** a small soft cake often with raisins etc. **queen dowager** the widow of a king. **queen it** play the queen. **queen mother** the dowager who is mother of the sovereign. **queen of the meadows** meadowsweet. **queen of puddings** a pudding made with bread, jam, and meringue. **queen-post** one of two upright timbers between the tie-beam and principal rafters of a roof-truss. **Queen's bench** see BENCH. **queen's bishop, knight**, etc. *Chess* (of pieces which exist in pairs) the piece starting on the queen's side of the board. **Queen's bounty** see BOUNTY. **Queen's colour** see COLOUR. **Queen's Counsel** see COUNSEL. **the Queen's English** see ENGLISH. **Queen's evidence** see EVIDENCE. **Queen's Guide** see GUIDE. **Queen's highway** see HIGHWAY. **queen-size** (or **-sized**) of an extra-large size, usu. smaller than king-size. **Queen's Messenger** see MESSENGER. **queen's pawn** *Chess* the pawn in front of the queen at the beginning of a game. **Queen's Proctor** see PROCTOR. **Queen's Scout** see SCOUT¹. **Queen's speech** see SPEECH. **queen's-ware** cream-coloured Wedgwood. □□ **queendom** *n.* **queenhood** *n.* **queenless** *adj.* **queenlike** *adj.* **queenship** *n.* [OE *cwēn* f. Gmc; cf. QUEAN]

queenie /ˈkwiːnɪ/ *n. sl.* = QUEEN *n.* 7.

queenly /ˈkwiːnlɪ/ *adj.* (**queenlier, queenliest**) **1** fit for or appropriate to a queen. **2** majestic; queenlike. □□ **queenliness** *n.*

Queensberry Rules /ˈkwiːnzbərɪ/ *n.pl.* the standard rules, esp. of boxing. [the 8th Marquis of *Queensberry*, Engl. nobleman d. 1900, who supervised the preparation of boxing laws in 1867]

queer /kwɪə(r)/ *adj., n., & v.* —*adj.* **1** strange; odd; eccentric. **2** shady; suspect; of questionable character. **3 a** slightly ill; giddy; faint. **b** *Brit. sl.* drunk. **4** *derog. sl.* (esp. of a man) homosexual. —*n.* *derog. sl.* a homosexual. —*v.tr. sl.* spoil; put out of order. □ **in Queer Street** *sl.* in a difficulty, in debt or trouble or disrepute. **queer a person's pitch** spoil a person's chances, esp. secretly or maliciously. □□ **queerish** *adj.* **queerly** *adv.* **queerness** *n.* [perh. f. G *quer* oblique (as THWART)]

quell /kwel/ *v.tr.* **1 a** crush or put down (a rebellion

etc.). **b** reduce (rebels etc.) to submission. **2** suppress (fear, anger, etc.). □□ **queller** *n.* (also in *comb.*). [OE *cwellan* kill f. Gmc]

quench /kwentʃ/ *v.tr.* **1** satisfy (thirst) by drinking. **2** extinguish (a fire or light etc.). **3** cool, esp. with water (heat, a heated thing). **4** esp. *Metallurgy* cool (a hot substance) in cold water, air, oil, etc. **5 a** stifle or suppress (desire etc.). **b** *Physics & Electronics* inhibit or prevent (oscillation, luminescence, etc.) by counteractive means. **6** *sl.* reduce (an opponent) to silence. □□ **quenchable** *adj.* **quencher** *n.* **quenchless** *adj.* [ME f. OE *-cwencan* causative f. *-cwincan* be extinguished]

quenelle /kəˈnel/ *n.* a seasoned ball or roll of pounded fish or meat. [F, of unkn. orig.]

querist /ˈkwɪərɪst/ *n. literary* a person who asks questions; a questioner. [L *quaerere* ask]

quern /kwɜːn/ *n.* **1** a hand-mill for grinding corn. **2** a small hand-mill for pepper etc. □ **quern-stone** a millstone. [OE *cweorn(e)* f. Gmc]

querulous /ˈkwerʊləs/ *adj.* complaining, peevish. □□ **querulously** *adv.* **querulousness** *n.* [LL *querulosus* or L *querulus* f. *queri* complain]

query /ˈkwɪərɪ/ *n. & v.* —*n.* (*pl.* -ies) **1** a question, esp. expressing doubt or objection. **2** a question mark, or the word *query* spoken or written to question accuracy or as a mark of interrogation. —*v.* (-ies, -ied) **1** *tr.* (often foll. by *whether, if*, etc. + clause) ask or inquire. **2** *tr.* call (a thing) in question in speech or writing. **3** *tr.* dispute the accuracy of. **4** *intr.* put a question. [Anglicized form of *quaere* f. L *quaerere* ask, after INQUIRY]

quest /kwest/ *n. & v.* —*n.* **1** a search or the act of seeking. **2** the thing sought, esp. the object of a medieval knight's pursuit. —*v.* **1** *intr.* (often foll. by *about*) **a** (often foll. by *for*) go about in search of something. **b** (of a dog etc.) search about for game. **2** *tr. poet.* search for, seek out. □ **in quest of** seeking. □□ **quester** *n.* **questingly** *adv.* [ME f. OF *queste, quester* ult. f. L *quaerere quaest-* seek]

question /ˈkwestʃ(ə)n/ *n. & v.* —*n.* **1** a sentence worded or expressed so as to seek information. **2 a** doubt about or objection to a thing's truth, credibility, advisability, etc. (*allowed it without question*). **b** the raising of such doubt etc. **3** a matter to be discussed or decided or voted on. **4** a problem requiring an answer or solution. **5** (foll. by *of*) a matter or concern depending on conditions (*it's a question of money*). —*v.tr.* **1** ask questions of; interrogate. **2** subject (a person) to examination. **3** throw doubt upon; raise objections to. **4** seek information from the study of (phenomena, facts). □ **be a question of time** be certain to happen sooner or later. **beyond all question** undoubtedly. **come into question** be discussed; become of practical importance. **in question** that is being discussed or referred to (*the person in question*). **is not the question** is irrelevant. **out of the question** too impracticable etc. to be worth discussing; impossible. **put the question** require supporters and opponents of a proposal to record their votes, divide a meeting. **question mark** a punctuation mark (?) indicating a question. **question-master** *Brit.* a person who presides over a quiz game etc. **question time** *Parl.* a period during parliamentary proceedings when MPs may question ministers. □□ **questioner** *n.* **questioningly** *adv.* **questionless** *adj.* [ME f. AF *questiun*, OF *question, questionner* f. L *quaestio -onis* f. *quaerere quaest-* seek]

questionable /ˈkwestʃənəb(ə)l/ *adj.* **1** doubtful as regards truth or quality. **2** not clearly in accordance with honesty, honour, wisdom, etc. □□ **questionability** /ˌkwestʃənəˈbɪlɪtɪ/ *n.* **questionableness** *n.* **questionably** *adv.*

questionary /ˈkwestʃənərɪ/ *n.* (*pl.* -ies) = QUESTIONNAIRE. [med.L *quaestionarium* or F (as QUESTIONNAIRE)]

questionnaire /ˌkwestʃə'neə(r), ˌkestjə-/ n. **1** a formulated series of questions, esp. for statistical study. **2** a document containing these. [F f. *questionner* QUESTION + -*aire* -ARY[1]]

quetzal /'kwetz(ə)l/ n. **1** any of various brilliantly coloured birds of the family Trogonidae, esp. the Central and S. American *Pharomachrus mocinno*, the male of which has long green tail coverts. **2** the chief monetary unit of Guatemala. [Sp. f. Aztec f. *quetzalli* the bird's tail-feather]

queue /kju:/ n. & v. esp. Brit. —n. **1** a line or sequence of persons, vehicles, etc., awaiting their turn to be attended to or to proceed. **2** a pigtail or plait of hair. —v.intr. (**queues, queued, queuing** or **queueing**) (often foll. by *up*) (of persons etc.) form a queue; take one's place in a queue. □**queue-jump** Brit. push forward out of turn in a queue. [F f. L *cauda* tail]

quibble /'kwɪb(ə)l/ n. & v. —n. **1** a petty objection; a trivial point of criticism. **2** a play on words; a pun. **3** an evasion; an insubstantial argument which relies on an ambiguity etc. —v.intr. use quibbles. □□ **quibbler** n. **quibbling** adj. **quibblingly** adv. [dimin. of obs. *quib* prob. f. L *quibus* dative & ablat. pl. of *qui* who (familiar from use in legal documents)]

quiche /ki:ʃ/ n. an open flan or tart with a savoury filling. [F]

Quichua var. of QUECHUA.

quick /kwɪk/ adj., adv., & n. —adj. **1** taking only a short time (*a quick worker*). **2** arriving after a short time, prompt (*quick action*; *quick results*). **3** with only a short interval (*in quick succession*). **4** lively, intelligent. **5** acute, alert (*has a quick ear*). **6** (of a temper) easily roused. **7** archaic living, alive (*the quick and the dead*). —adv. **1** quickly, at a rapid rate. **2** (as *int.*) come, go, etc., quickly. —n. **1** the soft flesh below the nails, or the skin, or a sore. **2** the seat of feeling or emotion (*cut to the quick*). □**be quick** act quickly. **quick-fire 1** (of repartee etc.) rapid. **2** firing shots in quick succession. **quick-freeze** 1 freeze (food) rapidly so as to preserve its natural qualities. 2 this process. **quick march** Mil. **1** a march in quick time. **2** the command to begin this. **quick one** colloq. a drink taken quickly. **quick step** Mil. a step used in quick time (cf. QUICKSTEP). **quick time** Mil. marching at about 120 paces per minute. **quick trick** Bridge **1** a trick in the first two rounds of a suit. **2** the card that should win this. **quick with child** archaic at a stage of pregnancy when movements of the foetus have been felt. □□ **quickly** adv. **quickness** n. [OE *cwic(u)* alive f. Gmc]

quicken /'kwɪkən/ v. **1** tr. & intr. make or become quicker; accelerate. **2** tr. give life or vigour to; rouse; animate; stimulate. **3** intr. **a** (of a woman) reach a stage in pregnancy when movements of the foetus can be felt. **b** (of a foetus) begin to show signs of life. **4** tr. archaic kindle; make (a fire) burn brighter. **5** intr. come to life.

quickie /'kwɪkɪ/ n. colloq. **1** a thing done or made quickly or hastily. **2** a drink taken quickly.

quicklime /'kwɪklaɪm/ n. = LIME[1] n. 1.

quicksand /'kwɪksænd/ n. **1** loose wet sand that sucks in anything placed or falling into it. **2** a bed of this.

quickset /'kwɪkset/ adj. & n. —adj. (of a hedge) formed of slips of plants, esp. hawthorn set in the ground to grow. —n. **1** such slips. **2** a hedge formed in this way.

quicksilver /'kwɪkˌsɪlvə(r)/ n. & v. —n. **1** mercury. **2** mobility of temperament or mood. —v.tr. coat (a mirror-glass) with an amalgam of tin.

quickstep /'kwɪkstep/ n. & v. —n. a fast foxtrot (cf. *quick step*). —v.intr. (-**stepped**, -**stepping**) dance the quickstep.

quickthorn /'kwɪkθɔːn/ n. a common hawthorn, *Crataegus monogyna*.

quick-witted /kwɪk'wɪtɪd/ adj. quick to grasp a situation, make repartee, etc. □□ **quick-wittedness** n.

quid[1] /kwɪd/ n. (pl. same) Brit. sl. one pound sterling. □**not the full quid** Austral. sl. mentally deficient. **quids in** sl. in a position of profit. [prob. f. *quid* the nature of a thing f. L *quid* what, something]

quid[2] /kwɪd/ n. a lump of tobacco for chewing. [dial. var. of CUD]

quiddity /'kwɪdɪtɪ/ n. (pl. -**ies**) **1** Philos. the essence of a person or thing; what makes a thing what it is. **2** a quibble; a trivial objection. [med.L *quidditas* f. L *quid* what]

quidnunc /'kwɪdnʌŋk/ n. archaic a newsmonger, a person given to gossip. [L *quid* what + *nunc* now]

quid pro quo /ˌkwɪd prəʊ 'kwəʊ/ n. **1** a thing given as compensation. **2** return made (for a gift, favour, etc.). [L, = something for something]

quiescent /kwɪ'es(ə)nt/ adj. **1** motionless, inert. **2** silent, dormant. □□ **quiescence** n. **quiescency** n. **quiescently** adv. [L *quiescere* f. *quies* QUIET]

quiet /'kwaɪət/ adj., n., & v. —adj. (**quieter, quietest**) **1** with little or no sound or motion. **2** of gentle or peaceful disposition. **3** (of a colour, piece of clothing, etc.) unobtrusive; not showy. **4** not overt; private; disguised (*quiet resentment*). **5** undisturbed; uninterrupted; free or far from vigorous action (*a quiet time for prayer*). **6** informal; simple (*just a quiet wedding*). **7** enjoyed in quiet (*a quiet smoke*). **8** tranquil; not anxious or remorseful. —n. **1** silence; stillness. **2** an undisturbed state; tranquillity. **3** a state of being free from urgent tasks or agitation (*it is very quiet at work*). **4** a peaceful state of affairs (*all quiet along the frontier*). —v. **1** tr. sooth, make quiet. **2** intr. (often foll. by *down*) become quiet or calm. □**be quiet** (esp. in *imper.*) cease talking etc. **keep quiet 1** refrain from making a noise. **2** (often foll. by *about*) suppress or refrain from disclosing information etc. **on the quiet** unobtrusively; secretly. □□ **quietly** adv. **quietness** n. [ME f. AF *quiete* f. OF *quiet(e)*, *quieté* f. L *quietus* past part. of *quiescere*: see QUIESCENT]

quieten /'kwaɪət(ə)n/ v.tr. & intr. Brit. (often foll. by *down*) = QUIET v.

quietism /'kwaɪəˌtɪz(ə)m/ n. **1** a passive attitude towards life, with devotional contemplation and abandonment of the will, as a form of religious mysticism. **2** the principle of non-resistance. □□ **quietist** n. & adj. **quietistic** /-'tɪstɪk/ adj. [It. *quietismo* (as QUIET)]

quietude /'kwaɪɪˌtjuːd/ n. a state of quiet.

quietus /kwaɪ'iːtəs/ n. **1** something which quiets or represses. **2** discharge or release from life; death, final riddance. [med.L *quietus est* he is quit (QUIET) used as a form of receipt]

quiff /kwɪf/ n. Brit. **1** a man's tuft of hair, brushed upward from the forehead. **2** a curl plastered down on the forehead. [20th c.: orig. unkn.]

quill /kwɪl/ n. & v. —n. **1** (in full **quill-feather**) a large feather in a wing or tail. **2** the hollow stem of this. **3** (in full **quill pen**) a pen made of a quill. **4** (usu. in *pl.*) the spines of a porcupine. **5** a musical pipe made of a hollow stem. —v.tr. form into cylindrical quill-like folds; goffer. □**quill-coverts** the feathers covering the base of quill-feathers. □□ **quilling** n. [ME prob. f. (M)LG *quiele*]

quilt[1] /kwɪlt/ n. & v. —n. **1** a bed-covering made of padding enclosed between layers of cloth etc. and kept in place by cross lines of stitching. **2** a bedspread of similar design (*patchwork quilt*). —v.tr. **1** cover or line with padded material. **2** make or join together (pieces of cloth with padding between) after the manner of a quilt. **3** sew up (a coin, letter, etc.) between two layers of a garment etc. **4** compile (a literary work) out of extracts or borrowed ideas. □□ **quilter** n. **quilting** n. [ME f. OF *coilte, cuilte* f. L *culcita* mattress, cushion]

quilt[2] /kwɪlt/ v.tr. Austral. sl. thrash; clout. [perh. f. QUILT[1]]

quim /kwɪm/ *n. coarse sl.* the female genitals. [18th c.: orig. unkn.]

quin /kwɪn/ *n.* esp. *Brit. colloq.* a quintuplet. [abbr.]

quinacrine /'kwɪnə,kri:n, -krɪn/ *n.* an anti-malarial drug derived from acridine. [*quinine* + *acridine*]

quinary /'kwaɪnərɪ/ *adj.* **1** of the number five. **2** having five parts. [L *quinarius* f. *quini* distrib. of *quinque* five]

quinate /'kwaɪneɪt/ *adj. Bot.* (of a leaf) having five leaflets. [L *quini* (as QUINARY)]

quince /kwɪns/ *n.* **1** a hard acid pear-shaped fruit used as a preserve or flavouring. **2** any shrub or small tree of the genus *Cydonia*, esp. *C. oblonga*, bearing this fruit. [ME, orig. collect. pl. of obs. *quoyn*, *coyn*, f. OF *cooin* f. L *cotoneum* var. of *cydoneum* (apple) of *Cydonia* in Crete]

quincentenary /,kwɪnsen'ti:nərɪ/ *n. & adj.* —*n.* (*pl.* -**ies**) **1** a five-hundredth anniversary. **2** a festival marking this. —*adj.* of this anniversary. □□ **quincentennial** /-'tenɪəl/ *adj. & n.* [irreg. f. L *quinque* five + CENTENARY]

quincunx /'kwɪnkʌŋks/ *n.* **1** five objects set so that four are at the corners of a square or rectangle and the fifth is at its centre, e.g. the five on dice or cards. **2** this arrangement, esp. in planting trees. □□ **quincuncial** /kwɪn'kʌnʃ(ə)l/ *adj.* **quincuncially** /-'kʌnʃəlɪ/ *adv.* [L, = five-twelfths f. *quinque* five, *uncia* twelfth]

quinella /kwɪ'nelə/ *n.* a form of betting in which the better must select the first two place-winners in a race, not necessarily in the correct order. [Amer. Sp. *quiniela*]

quinine /'kwɪni:n, -'ni:n/ *n.* **1** an alkaloid found esp. in cinchona bark. **2** a bitter drug containing this, used as a tonic and to reduce fever. [*quina* cinchona bark f. Sp. *quina* f. Quecha *kina* bark]

quinol /'kwɪnɒl/ *n.* = HYDROQUINONE.

quinoline /'kwɪnə,li:n/ *n. Chem.* an oily amine obtained from the distillation of coal tar or by synthesis and used in the preparation of drugs etc.

quinone /'kwɪnəʊn, -'nəʊn/ *n. Chem.* **1** a yellow crystalline derivative of benzene with the hydrogen atoms on opposite carbon atoms replaced by two of oxygen. **2** any in a class of similar compounds.

quinquagenarian /,kwɪŋkwədʒɪ'neərɪən/ *n. & adj.* —*n.* a person from 50 to 59 years old. —*adj.* of or relating to this age. [L *quinquagenarius* f. *quinquageni* distrib. of *quinquaginta* fifty]

Quinquagesima /,kwɪŋkwə'dʒesɪmə/ *n.* (in full **Quinquagesima Sunday**) the Sunday before the beginning of Lent. [med.L, fem. of L *quinquagesimus* fiftieth f. *quinquaginta* fifty, after QUADRAGESIMA]

quinque- /'kwɪŋkwɪ/ *comb. form* five. [L f. *quinque* five]

quinquennial /kwɪn'kwenɪəl/ *adj.* **1** lasting five years. **2** recurring every five years. □□ **quinquennially** *adv.* [L *quinquennis* (as QUIN-QUENNIUM)]

quinquennium /kwɪn'kwenɪəm/ *n.* (*pl.* **quinquenniums** or **quinquennia** /-nɪə/) a period of five years. [L f. *quinque* five + *annus* year]

quinquereme /'kwɪŋkwɪ,ri:m/ *n.* an ancient Roman galley with five files of oarsmen on each side. [L *quinqueremis* (as QUINQUE-, *remus* oar)]

quinquevalent /'kwɪnkwə,veɪlənt/ *adj.* having a valency of five.

quinsy /'kwɪnzɪ/ *n.* an inflammation of the throat, esp. an abscess in the region around the tonsils. □□ **quinsied** *adj.* [ME f. OF *quinencie* f. med.L *quinancia* f. Gk *kunagkhē* f. *kun-* dog + *agkhō* throttle]

quint /kwɪnt/ *n.* **1** a sequence of five cards in the same suit in piquet etc. **2** *US* a quintuplet. □ **quint major** a quint headed by an ace. [F *quinte* f. L *quinta* fem. of *quintus* fifth f. *quinque* five]

quintain /'kwɪntɪn/ *n. hist.* **1** a post set up as a mark in tilting, and often provided with a sandbag to swing round and strike an unsuccessful tilter. **2** the medieval military exercise of tilting at such a mark.

[ME f. OF *quintaine* perh. ult. f. L *quintana* camp market f. *quintus* (*manipulus*) fifth (maniple)]

quintal /'kwɪnt(ə)l/ *n.* **1** a weight of about 100 lb. **2** a hundredweight (112 lb.). **3** a weight of 100 kg. [ME f. OF *quintal*, med.L *quintale* f. Arab. *ḳinṭār*]

quintan /'kwɪnt(ə)n/ *adj.* (of a fever etc.) recurring every fifth day. [L *quintanus* f. *quintus* fifth]

quinte /kæt/ *n.* the fifth of eight parrying positions in fencing. [F: see QUINT]

quintessence /kwɪn'tes(ə)ns/ *n.* **1** the most essential part of any substance; a refined extract. **2** (usu. foll. by *of*) the purest and most perfect, or most typical, form, manifestation, or embodiment of some quality or class. **3** (in Ancient Philosophy) a fifth substance (beside the four elements) forming heavenly bodies and pervading all things. □□ **quintessential** /,kwɪntɪ'senʃ(ə)l/ *adj.* **quintessentially** /,kwɪntɪ'senʃəlɪ/ *adv.* [ME (in sense 3) f. F f. med.L *quinta essentia* fifth ESSENCE]

quintet /kwɪn'tet/ *n.* (also **quintette**) **1** *Mus.* **a** a composition for five voices or instruments. **b** the performers of such a piece. **2** any group of five. [F *quintette* f. It. *quintetto* f. *quinto* fifth f. L *quintus*]

quintillion /kwɪn'tɪljən/ *n.* (*pl.* same or **quintillions**) a thousand raised to the sixth (or formerly, esp. *Brit.*, the tenth) power (10^{18} and 10^{30} respectively). □□ **quintillionth** *adj. & n.* [L *quintus* fifth + MILLION]

quintuple /'kwɪntjʊp(ə)l/ *adj., n., & v.* —*adj.* **1** fivefold; consisting of five parts. **2** involving five parties. **3** (of time in music) having five beats in a bar. —*n.* a fivefold number or amount. —*v.tr. & intr.* multiply by five; increase fivefold. □□ **quintuply** *adv.* [F *quintuple* f. L *quintus* fifth, after QUADRUPLE]

quintuplet /'kwɪntjʊplɪt, -'tju:plɪt/ *n.* **1** each of five children born at one birth. **2** a set of five things working together. **3** *Mus.* a group of five notes to be performed in the time of three or four. [QUINTUPLE, after QUADRUPLET, TRIPLET]

quintuplicate *adj. & v.* —*adj.* /kwɪn'tju:plɪkət/ **1** fivefold. **2** of which five copies are made. —*v.tr. & intr.* /kwɪn'tju:plɪ,keɪt/ multiply by five. □ **in quintuplicate** in five identical copies. **2** in groups of five. [F *quintuple* f. L *quintus* fifth, after QUADRUPLICATE]

quip /kwɪp/ *n. & v.* —*n.* **1** a clever saying; an epigram; a sarcastic remark etc. **2** a quibble; an equivocation. —*v.intr.* (**quipped**, **quipping**) make quips. □□ **quipster** *n.* [abbr. of obs. *quippy* perh. f. L *quippe* forsooth]

quipu /'ki:pu:, 'kwi:pu:/ *n.* the ancient Peruvians' substitute for writing by variously knotting threads of various colours. [Quechua, = knot]

quire /'kwaɪə(r)/ *n.* **1** four sheets of paper etc. folded to form eight leaves, as often in medieval manuscripts. **2** any collection of leaves one within another in a manuscript or book. **3** 25 (formerly 24) sheets of paper. □ **in quires** unbound; in sheets. [ME f. OF *qua(i)er* ult. f. L *quaterni* set of four (as QUATERNARY)]

quirk /kwз:k/ *n.* **1** a peculiarity of behaviour. **2** a trick of fate; a freak. **3** a flourish in writing. **4** (often *attrib.*) *Archit.* a hollow in a moulding. □□ **quirkish** *adj.* **quirky** *adj.* (**quirkier**, **quirkiest**). **quirkily** *adv.* **quirkiness** *n.* [16th c.: orig. unkn.]

quirt /kwз:t/ *n. & v.* —*n.* a short-handled riding-whip with a braided leather lash. —*v.tr.* strike with this. [Sp. *cuerda* CORD]

quisling /'kwɪzlɪŋ/ *n.* **1** a person cooperating with an occupying enemy; a collaborator or fifth-columnist. **2** a traitor. □□ **quislingite** *adj. & n.* [V. *Quisling*, renegade Norwegian Army officer d. 1945]

quit /kwɪt/ *v. & adj.* —*v.tr.* (**quitting**; *past and past part.* **quitted** or **quit**) **1** (also *absol.*) give up; let go; abandon (a task etc.). **2** *US* cease; stop (*quit grumbling*). **3 a** leave or depart from (a place, person, etc.). **b** (*absol.*) (of a tenant) leave occupied premises (esp. *notice to quit*). **4** (*refl.*) acquit; behave (*quit* *oneself well*). —*predic.adj*. (foll. by *of*) rid (*glad to be quit of the problem*). □**quit hold of** loose. [ME f. OF *quitte, quitter* f. med.L *quittus* f. L *quietus* QUIET]

quitch /kwɪtʃ/ *n*. (in full **quitch-grass**) = COUCH[2]. [OE *cwice*, perh. rel. to QUICK]

quite /kwaɪt/ *adv*. **1** completely; entirely; wholly; to the utmost extent; in the fullest sense. **2** somewhat; rather; to some extent. **3** (often foll. by *so*) said to indicate agreement. □**quite another** (or **other**) very different (*that's quite another matter*). **quite a few** *colloq*. a fairly large number of. **quite something** a remarkable thing. [ME f. obs. *quite* (adj.) = QUIT]

quits /kwɪts/ *predic.adj*. on even terms by retaliation or repayment (*then we'll be quits*). □**call it** (or **cry**) **quits** acknowledge that things are now even; agree not to proceed further in a quarrel etc. [perh. colloq. abbr. of med.L *quittus*: see QUIT]

quittance /ˈkwɪt(ə)ns/ *n. archaic* or *poet*. **1** (foll. by *from*) a release. **2** an acknowledgement of payment; a receipt. [ME f. OF *quitance* f. *quiter* QUIT]

quitter /ˈkwɪtə(r)/ *n*. **1** a person who gives up easily. **2** a shirker.

quiver[1] /ˈkwɪvə(r)/ *v. & n*. —*v*. **1** *intr*. tremble or vibrate with a slight rapid motion, esp.: **a** (usu. foll. by *with*) as the result of emotion (*quiver with anger*). **b** (usu. foll. by *in*) as the result of air currents etc. (*quiver in the breeze*). **2** *tr*. (of a bird, esp. a skylark) make (its wings) quiver. —*n*. a quivering motion or sound. □□**quiveringly** *adv*. **quivery** *adj*. [ME f. obs. *quiver* nimble: cf. QUAVER]

quiver[2] /ˈkwɪvə(r)/ *n*. a case for holding arrows. □**have an arrow** (or **shaft**) **left in one's quiver** not be resourceless. [ME f. OF *quivre* f. WG (cf. OE *cocor*)]

quiverful /ˈkwɪvəˌfʊl/ *n*. (*pl*. **-fuls**) **1** as much as a quiver can hold. **2** many children of one parent (Ps. 127:5). [QUIVER[2]]

qui vive /kiː ˈviːv/ *n*. □**on the qui vive** on the alert; watching for something to happen. [F, = lit. '(long) live who?', i.e. on whose side are you?, as a sentry's challenge]

quixotic /kwɪkˈsɒtɪk/ *adj*. **1** extravagantly and romantically chivalrous; regardless of material interests in comparison with honour or devotion. **2** visionary; pursuing lofty but unattainable ideals. □□ **quixotically** *adv*. **quixotism** /ˈkwɪksəˌtɪz(ə)m/ *n*. **quixotry** /ˈkwɪksətrɪ/ *n*. [Don *Quixote*, hero of Cervantes' romance f. Sp. *quixote* thigh armour]

quiz[1] /kwɪz/ *n. & v*. —*n*. (*pl*. **quizzes**) **1** a test of knowledge, esp. between individuals or teams as a form of entertainment. **2** an interrogation, examination, or questionnaire. —*v.tr*. (**quizzed, quizzing**) examine by questioning. □**quiz-master** a person who presides over a quiz. [19th-c. dial.: orig. unkn.]

quiz[2] /kwɪz/ *v. & n. archaic* —*v.tr*. (**quizzed, quizzing**) **1** look curiously at; observe the ways or oddities of; survey through an eyeglass. **2** make sport of; regard with a mocking air. —*n*. (*pl*. **quizzes**) **1** a hoax, a thing done to burlesque or expose another's oddities. **2 a** an odd or eccentric person; a person of ridiculous appearance. **b** a person given to quizzing. □□ **quizzer** *n*. [18th c.: orig. unkn.]

quizzical /ˈkwɪzɪk(ə)l/ *adj*. **1** expressing or done with mild or amused perplexity. **2** strange; comical. □□ **quizzicality** /-ˈkælɪtɪ/ *n*. **quizzically** *adv*. **quizzicalness** *n*.

quod /kwɒd/ *n. Brit. sl*. prison. [17th c.: orig. unkn.]

quod erat demonstrandum /kwɒd ˌeræt ˌdemənˈstrændəm/ (esp. at the conclusion of a proof etc.) which was the thing to be proved. ¶ Abbr.: **QED**. [L]

quodlibet /ˈkwɒdlɪˌbet/ *n*. **1** *hist*. **a** a topic for philosophical or theological discussion. **b** an exercise on this. **2** a light-hearted medley of well-known tunes. □□ **quodlibetarian** /-brˈteərɪən/ *n*. **quodlibetical** /-ˈbetɪk(ə)l/ *adj*. **quodlibetically** /-ˈbetɪkəlɪ/ *adv*. [ME f. L f. *quod* what + *libet* it pleases one]

quod vide /kwɒd ˈviːdeɪ/ which see (in cross-references etc.). ¶ Abbr.: **q.v.** [L]

quoin /kɔɪn/ *n. & v*. —*n*. **1** an external angle of a building. **2** a stone or brick forming an angle; a cornerstone. **3** a wedge used for locking type in a forme. **4** a wedge for raising the level of a gun, keeping the barrel from rolling, etc. —*v.tr*. secure or raise with quoins. □□ **quoining** *n*. [var. of COIN]

quoit /kɔɪt/ *n. & v*. —*n*. **1** a heavy flattish sharp-edged iron ring thrown to encircle an iron peg or to land as near as possible to the peg. **2** (in *pl*.) a game consisting of aiming and throwing these. **3** a ring of rope, rubber, etc. for use in a similar game. **4 a** the flat stone of a dolmen. **b** the dolmen itself. —*v.tr*. fling like a quoit. [ME: orig. unkn.]

quokka /ˈkwɒkə/ *n*. a small Australian short-tailed wallaby, *Setonix brachyurus*. [Aboriginal name]

quondam /ˈkwɒndæm/ *attrib.adj*. that once was; sometime; former. [L (adv.), = formerly]

Quonset /ˈkwɒnsɪt/ *n. US propr*. a prefabricated metal building with a semicylindrical corrugated roof. [*Quonset* Point, Rhode Island, where it was first made]

quorate /ˈkwɔːrət, -reɪt/ *adj. Brit*. (of a meeting) attended by a quorum. [QUORUM]

quorum /ˈkwɔːrəm/ *n*. the fixed minimum number of members that must be present to make the proceedings of an assembly or society valid. [L, = of whom (we wish that you be two, three, etc.), in the wording of commissions]

quota /ˈkwəʊtə/ *n*. **1** the share that an individual person or company is bound to contribute to or entitled to receive from a total. **2** a quantity of goods etc. which under official controls must be manufactured, exported, imported, etc. **3** the number of yearly immigrants allowed to enter a country, students allowed to enrol for a course, etc. [med.L *quota* (*pars*) how great (a part), fem. of *quotus* f. *quot* how many]

quotable /ˈkwəʊtəb(ə)l/ *adj*. worth, or suitable for, quoting. □□ **quotability** /-ˈbɪlɪtɪ/ *n*.

quotation /kwəʊˈteɪʃ(ə)n/ *n*. **1** the act or an instance of quoting or being quoted. **2** a passage or remark quoted. **3** *Mus*. a short passage or tune taken from one piece of music to another. **4** *Stock Exch*. an amount stated as the current price of stocks or commodities. **5** a contractor's estimate. □**quotation mark** each of a set of punctuation marks, single (' ') or double (" "), used to mark the beginning and end of a quoted passage, a book title, etc., or words regarded as slang or jargon. [med.L *quotatio* (as QUOTE)]

quote /kwəʊt/ *v. & n*. —*v.tr*. **1** cite or appeal to (an author, book, etc.) in confirmation of some view. **2** repeat a statement by (another person) or copy out a passage from (*don't quote me*). **3** (often *absol*.) **a** repeat or copy out (a passage) usu. with an indication that it is borrowed. **b** (foll. by *from*) cite (an author, book, etc.). **4** (foll. by *as*) cite (an author etc.) as proof, evidence, etc. **5 a** enclose (words) in quotation marks. **b** (as *int*.) (in dictation, reading aloud, etc.) indicate the presence of opening quotation marks (*he said, quote, 'I shall stay'*). **6** (often foll. by *at*) state the price of (a commodity, bet, etc.) (*quoted at 200 to 1*). **7** *Stock Exch*. regularly list the price of. —*n. colloq*. **1** a passage quoted. **2** a price quoted. **3** (usu. in *pl*.) quotation marks. [ME, earlier 'mark with numbers', f. med.L *quotare* f. *quot* how many, or as QUOTA]

quoth /kwəʊθ/ *v.tr*. (only in 1st and 3rd person) *archaic* said. [OE *cwæth* past of *cwethan* say f. Gmc]

quotidian /kwɒˈtɪdɪən/ *adj. & n*. —*adj*. **1** daily, of every day. **2** commonplace, trivial. —*n*. (in full **quotidian fever**) a fever recurring every day. [ME f. OF *cotidien* & L *cotidianus* f. *cotidie* daily]

quotient /ˈkwəʊʃ(ə)nt/ *n*. a result obtained by

dividing one quantity by another. [ME f. L *quotiens* how many times f. *quot* how many, by confusion with -ENT]

Qur'an var. of KORAN.

q.v. *abbr.* quod vide.

qwerty /ˈkwɜːtɪ/ *attrib.adj.* denoting the standard keyboard on English-language typewriters, word processors, etc., with *q, w, e, r, t,* and *y* as the first keys on the top row of letters.

qy. *abbr.* query.

R

R¹ /ɑː(r)/ n. (also r) (pl. **Rs** or **R's**) the eighteenth letter of the alphabet. □**the r months** the months with r in their names (September to April) as the season for oysters.

R² abbr. (also **R.**) **1** Regina (Elizabeth R). **2** Rex. **3** River. **4** (also ®) registered as a trademark. **5** (in names of societies etc.) Royal. **6** Chess rook. **7** Railway. **8** rand. **9** Regiment. **10** Réaumur. **11** radius. **12** roentgen.

r. abbr. (also r) **1** right. **2** recto. **3** run(s). **4** radius.

RA abbr. **1 a** (in the UK) Royal Academy. **b** (in the UK) Royal Academician. **2** (in the UK) Royal Artillery. **3** right ascension.

Ra symb. Chem. the element radium.

RAAF abbr. Royal Australian Air Force.

rabbet /'ræbɪt/ n. & v. —n. a step-shaped channel etc. cut along the edge or face or projecting angle of a length of wood etc., usu. to receive the edge or tongue of another piece. —v.tr. (**rabbeted**, **rabbeting**) **1** join or fix with a rabbet. **2** make a rabbet in. □**rabbet plane** a plane for cutting a groove along an edge. [ME f. OF rab(b)at abatement, recess f. rabattre REBATE]

rabbi /'ræbaɪ/ n. (pl. **rabbis**) **1** a Jewish scholar or teacher, esp. of the law. **2** a person appointed as a Jewish religious leader. □**Chief Rabbi** the religious head of the Jewish communities in Britain. □□ **rabbinate** /'ræbɪnət/ n. [ME & OE f. eccl.L f. Gk rhabbi f. Heb. rabbī my master f. raḇ master + pronominal suffix]

rabbinical /rə'bɪnɪk(ə)l/ adj. (also **rabbinic**) of or relating to rabbis, or to Jewish law or teaching. □□ **rabbinically** adv.

rabbit /'ræbɪt/ n. & v. —n. **1 a** any of various burrowing gregarious plant-eating mammals of the hare family, esp. Oryctolagus cuniculus, with long ears and a short tail, varying in colour from brown in the wild to black and white, and kept as a pet or for meat. **b** US a hare. **c** the fur of the rabbit. **2** Brit. colloq. a poor performer in any sport or game. —v. intr. (**rabbited**, **rabbiting**) **1** hunt rabbits. **2** (often foll. by on, away) Brit. colloq. talk excessively or pointlessly; chatter (rabbiting on about his holiday). □**rabbit punch** a short chop with the edge of the hand to the nape of the neck. **rabbit warren** an area in which rabbits have their burrows, or are kept for meat etc. □□ **rabbity** adj. [ME perh. f. OF: cf. F dial. rabotte, Walloon robète, Flem. robbe]

rabble¹ /'ræb(ə)l/ n. **1** a disorderly crowd; a mob. **2** a contemptible or inferior set of people. **3** (prec. by the) the lower or disorderly classes of the populace. □**rabble-rouser** a person who stirs up the rabble or a crowd of people in agitation for social or political change. **rabble-rousing** adj. tending to arouse the emotions of a crowd. —n. the act or process of doing this. [ME: orig. uncert.]

rabble² /'ræb(ə)l/ n. an iron bar with a bent end for stirring molten metal etc. [F râble f. med.L rotabulum, L rutabulum fire-shovel f. ruere rut-rake up]

Rabelaisian /,ræbə'leɪzɪən/ adj. & n. —adj. **1** of or like Rabelais or his writings. **2** marked by exuberant imagination and language, coarse humour, and satire. —n. an admirer or student of Rabelais. [F. Rabelais, Fr. satirist d. 1553]

rabid /'ræbɪd, 'reɪ-/ adj. **1** furious, violent (rabid hate). **2** unreasoning; headstrong; fanatical (a rabid anarchist). **3** (esp. of a dog) affected with rabies; mad. **4** of or connected with rabies. □□ **rabidity**

/rə'bɪdɪtɪ/ n. **rabidly** adv. **rabidness** n. [L rabidus f. rabere rave]

rabies /'reɪbiːz/ n. a contagious and fatal viral disease esp. of dogs, transmissible through the saliva to humans etc. and causing madness and convulsions; hydrophobia. [L f. rabere rave]

RAC abbr. **1** (in the UK) Royal Automobile Club. **2** (in the UK) Royal Armoured Corps.

raccoon var. of RACOON.

race¹ /reɪs/ n. & v. —n. **1** a contest of speed between runners, horses, vehicles, ships, etc. **2** (in pl.) a series of these for horses, dogs, etc. at a fixed time on a regular course. **3** a contest between persons to be first to achieve something. **4 a** a strong or rapid current flowing through a narrow channel in the sea or a river (a tide race). **b** the channel of a stream etc. (a mill-race). **5** each of two grooved rings in a ball-bearing or roller bearing. **6** Austral. a fenced passageway for drafting sheep etc. **7** a passageway along which football players etc. run to enter the field. **8** (in weaving) the channel along which the shuttle moves. **9** archaic **a** the course of the sun or moon. **b** the course of life (has run his race). —v. **1** intr. take part in a race. **2** tr. have a race with. **3** tr. try to surpass in speed. **4** intr. (foll. by with) compete in speed with. **5** tr. cause (a horse, car, etc.) to race. **6 a** intr. go at full or (of an engine, propeller, the pulse, etc.) excessive speed. **b** tr. cause (a person or thing) to do this (raced the bill through the House). **7** intr. (usu. as **racing** adj.) follow or take part in horse-racing (a racing man). □**not in the race** Austral. sl. having no chance. **race meeting** a sequence of horse-races at one place. **racing car** a motor car built for racing on a prepared track. [ME, = running, f. ON rás]

race² /reɪs/ n. **1** each of the major divisions of humankind, having distinct physical characteristics. **2** a tribe, nation, etc., regarded as of a distinct ethnic stock. **3** the fact or concept of division into races (discrimination based on race). **4** a genus, species, breed, or variety of animals, plants, or micro-organisms. **5** a group of persons, animals, or plants connected by common descent. **6** any great division of living creatures (the feathered race; the four-footed race). **7** descent; kindred (of noble race; separate in language and race). **8** a class of persons etc. with some common feature (the race of poets). □**race relations** relations between members of different races usu. in the same country. **race riot** an outbreak of violence due to racial antagonism. [F f. It. razza, of unkn. orig.]

race³ /reɪs/ n. a ginger root. [OF rais, raiz f. L radix radicis root]

racecard /'reɪskɑːd/ n. a programme of races.

racecourse /'reɪskɔːs/ n. a ground or track for horse-racing.

racegoer /'reɪsgəʊə(r)/ n. a person who frequents horse-races.

racehorse /'reɪshɔːs/ n. a horse bred or kept for racing.

racemate /'ræsɪmeɪt/ n. Chem. a racemic mixture.

raceme /rə'siːm/ n. Bot. a flower cluster with the separate flowers attached by short equal stalks at equal distances along a central stem (cf. CYME). [L racemus grape-bunch]

racemic /rə'siːmɪk, -'semɪk/ adj. Chem. composed of equal numbers of dextrorotatory and laevorotatory molecules of a compound. □□ **racemize** /'ræsɪmaɪz/ v.tr. & intr. (also **-ise**). [RACEME + -IC, orig. of tartaric acid in grape-juice]

racemose /'ræsɪ͵məʊs/ *adj.* **1** *Bot.* in the form of a raceme. **2** *Anat.* (of a gland etc.) clustered. [L *racemosus* (as RACEME)]

racer /'reɪsə(r)/ *n.* **1** a horse, yacht, bicycle, etc., of a kind used for racing. **2** a circular horizontal rail along which the traversing-platform of a heavy gun moves. **3** a person or thing that races.

racetrack /'reɪstræk/ *n.* **1** = RACECOURSE. **2** a track for motor-racing.

raceway /'reɪsweɪ/ *n.* **1** a track or channel along which something runs, esp.: **a** a channel for water. **b** a groove in which ball-bearings run. **c** a pipe or tubing enclosing electrical wires. **2** esp. *US* **a** a track for trotting, pacing, or harness racing. **b** a racecourse.

rachis /'reɪkɪs/ *n.* (*pl.* **rachides** /-kɪ͵diːz/) **1** *Bot.* **a** a stem of grass etc. bearing flower-stalks at short intervals. **b** the axis of a compound leaf or frond. **2** *Anat.* the vertebral column or the cord from which it develops. **3** *Zool.* a feather-shaft, esp. the part bearing the barbs. □□ **rachidial** /rə'kɪdɪəl/ *adj.* [mod.L f. Gk *rhakhis* spine: the E pl. *-ides* is erron.]

rachitis /rə'kaɪtɪs/ *n.* rickets. □□ **rachitic** /-'kɪtɪk/ *adj.* [mod.L f. Gk *rhakhitis* (as RACHIS)]

Rachmanism /'rækmə͵nɪz(ə)m/ *n.* *Brit.* the exploitation and intimidation of slum tenants by unscrupulous landlords. [P. *Rachman*, London landlord of the early 1960s]

racial /'reɪʃ(ə)l/ *adj.* **1** of or concerning race (*racial diversities*; *racial minority*). **2** on the grounds of or connected with difference in race (*racial discrimination*; *racial tension*). □□ **racially** *adv.*

racialism /'reɪʃə͵lɪz(ə)m/ *n.* = RACISM 1. □□ **racialist** *n. & adj.*

racism /'reɪsɪz(ə)m/ *n.* **1 a** a belief in the superiority of a particular race; prejudice based on this. **b** antagonism towards other races, esp. as a result of this. **2** the theory that human abilities etc. are determined by race. □□ **racist** *n. & adj.*

rack¹ /ræk/ *n. & v.* —*n.* **1 a** a framework usu. with rails, bars, hooks, etc., for holding or storing things. **b** a frame for holding animal fodder. **2** a cogged or toothed bar or rail engaging with a wheel or pinion etc., or using pegs to adjust the position of something. **3** *hist.* an instrument of torture stretching the victim's joints by the turning of rollers to which the wrists and ankles were tied. —*v.tr.* **1** (of disease or pain) inflict suffering on. **2** *hist.* torture (a person) on the rack. **3** place in or on a rack. **4** shake violently. **5** injure by straining. **6** oppress (tenants) by exacting excessive rent. **7** exhaust (the land) by excessive use. □ **on the rack** in distress or under strain. **rack one's brains** make a great mental effort (*racked my brains for something to say*). **rack-railway** a railway with a cogged rail between the bearing rails. **rack-rent** *n.* **1** a high rent, annually equalling the full value of the property to which it relates. **2** an extortionate rent. —*v.tr.* exact this from (a tenant) or for (land). **rack-renter** a tenant paying or a landlord exacting an extortionate rent. **rack-up** *US* achieve (a score etc.). **rack-wheel** a cog-wheel. [ME *rakke* f. MDu., MLG *rak, rek*, prob. f. *recken* stretch]

rack² /ræk/ *n.* destruction (esp. *rack and ruin*). [var. of WRACK, WRECK]

rack³ /ræk/ *n.* a joint of lamb etc. including the front ribs. [perh. f. RACK¹]

rack⁴ /ræk/ *v.tr.* (often foll. by *off*) draw off (wine, beer, etc.) from the lees. [ME f. Prov. *arracar* f. *raca* stems and husks of grapes, dregs]

rack⁵ /ræk/ *n. & v.* —*v.intr.* (of driving clouds. —*v.intr.* (of clouds) be driven before the wind. [ME, prob. f. Scand. orig.: cf. Norw. and Sw. dial. *rak* wreckage etc. f. *reka* drive]

rack⁶ /ræk/ *n. & v.* —*n.* a horse's gait between a trot and a canter. —*v.intr.* progress in this way.

racket¹ /'rækɪt/ *n.* (also **racquet**) **1** a bat with a round or oval frame strung with catgut, nylon, etc., used in tennis, squash, etc. **2** (in *pl.*) a ball game for

two or four persons played with rackets in a plain four-walled court. **3** a snow shoe resembling a racket. □ **racket-ball** a small hard orig. kid-covered ball of cork and string. **racket-press** a press for keeping rackets taut and in shape. **racket-tail** a S. American humming-bird, *Loddigesia mirabilis*, with a racket-shaped tail. [F *racquette* f. It. *racchetta* f. Arab. *rāḥa* palm of the hand]

racket² /'rækɪt/ *n.* **1 a** a disturbance; an uproar; a din. **b** social excitement; gaiety. **2** *sl.* **a** a scheme for obtaining money or attaining other ends by fraudulent and often violent means. **b** a dodge; a sly game. **3** *colloq.* an activity; a way of life; a line of business (*starting up a new racket*). □□ **rackety** *adj.* [16th c.: perh. imit.]

racketeer /͵rækɪ'tɪə(r)/ *n.* a person who operates a dishonest business. □□ **racketeering** *n.*

racon /'reɪkɒn/ *n.* esp. *US* a radar beacon that can be identified and located by its response to a radar signal from a ship etc. [*radar* + *bea*con]

raconteur /͵rækɒn'tɜː(r)/ *n.* (*fem.* **raconteuse** /-'tɜːz/) a teller of anecdotes. [F f. *raconter* relate, RECOUNT]

racoon /rə'kuːn/ *n.* (also **raccoon**) **1** any greyish-brown furry N. American nocturnal flesh-eating mammal of the genus *Procyon*, with a bushy tail and sharp snout. **2** the fur of the racoon. [Algonquian dial.]

racquet var. of RACKET¹.

racy /'reɪsɪ/ *adj.* (**racier, raciest**) **1** lively and vigorous in style. **2** risqué, suggestive. **3** having characteristic qualities in a high degree (*a racy flavour*). □□ **racily** *adv.* **raciness** *n.* [RACE² + -Y¹]

rad¹ /ræd/ *n.* (*pl.* same) radian. [abbr.]

rad² /ræd/ *n. sl.* a political radical. [abbr.]

rad³ /ræd/ *n.* *Physics* a unit of absorbed dose of ionizing radiation, corresponding to the absorption of 0.01 joule per kilogram of absorbing material. [*r*adiation *a*bsorbed *d*ose]

RADA /'rɑːdə/ *abbr.* (in the UK) Royal Academy of Dramatic Art.

radar /'reɪdɑː(r)/ *n.* **1** a system for detecting the direction, range, or presence of aircraft, ships, and other (usu. moving) objects, by sending out pulses of high frequency electromagnetic waves. **2** the apparatus used for this. □ **radar trap** the use of radar to detect vehicles exceeding a speed limit. [*ra*dio *d*etection *a*nd *r*anging]

RADC *abbr.* (in the UK) Royal Army Dental Corps.

raddle /'ræd(ə)l/ *n. & v.* —*n.* red ochre (often used to mark sheep). —*v.tr.* **1** colour with raddle or too much rouge. **2** (as **raddled** *adj.*) worn out; untidy, unkempt. [var. of RUDDLE]

radial /'reɪdɪəl/ *adj. & n.* —*adj.* **1** of, concerning, or in rays. **2 a** arranged like rays or radii; having the position or direction of a radius. **b** having spokes or radiating lines. **c** acting or moving along lines diverging from a centre. **3** *Anat.* relating to the radius (*radial artery*). **4** (in full **radial-ply**) (of a vehicle tyre) having the core fabric layers arranged radially at right angles to the circumference and the tread strengthened. —*n.* **1** *Anat.* the radial nerve or artery. **2** a radial-ply tyre. □ **radial engine** an engine having cylinders arranged along radii. **radial symmetry** symmetry occurring about any number of lines or planes passing through the centre of an organism etc. **radial velocity** esp. *Astron.* the speed of motion along a radial line, esp. between a star etc. and an observer. □□ **radially** *adv.* [med.L *radialis* (as RADIUS)]

radian /'reɪdɪən/ *n.* *Geom.* a unit of angle, equal to an angle at the centre of a circle the arc of which is equal in length to the radius. [RADIUS + -AN]

radiant /'reɪdɪənt/ *adj. & n.* —*adj.* **1** emitting rays of light. **2** (of eyes or looks) beaming with joy or hope or love. **3** (of beauty) splendid or dazzling. **4** (of light) issuing in rays. **5** operating radially. **6** extending radially; radiating. —*n.* **1** the point or object from which light or heat radiates, esp. in an electric or gas heater. **2** *Astron.* a radiant point. □**radiant heat** heat transmitted by radiation, not by conduction or convection. **radiant heater** a heater that works by this method. **radiant point 1** a point from which rays or radii proceed. **2** *Astron.* the apparent focal point of a meteor shower. □□ **radiance** *n.* **radiancy** *n.* **radiantly** *adv.* [ME f. L *radiare* (as RADIUS)]

radiate *v. & adj.* —*v.* /ˈreɪdɪˌeɪt/ **1** *intr.* **a** emit rays of light, heat, or other electromagnetic waves. **b** (of light or heat) be emitted in rays. **2** *tr.* emit (light, heat, or sound) from a centre. **3** *tr.* transmit or demonstrate (life, love, joy, etc.) (*radiates happiness*). **4** *intr. & tr.* diverge or cause to diverge or spread from a centre. **5** *tr.* (as **radiated** *adj.*) with parts arranged in rays. —*adj.* /ˈreɪdɪət/ having divergent rays or parts radially arranged. □□ **radiately** /-ətlɪ/ *adv.* **radiative** /-ətɪv/ *adj.* [L *radiare radiat-* (as RADIUS)]

radiation /ˌreɪdɪˈeɪʃ(ə)n/ *n.* **1** the act or an instance of radiating; the process of being radiated. **2** *Physics* **a** the emission of energy as electromagnetic waves or as moving particles. **b** the energy transmitted in this way, esp. invisibly. **3** (in full **radiation therapy**) treatment of cancer and other diseases using radiation, such as X-rays or ultraviolet light. □**radiation chemistry** the study of the chemical effects of radiation on matter. **radiation sickness** sickness caused by exposure to radiation, such as X-rays or gamma rays. □□ **radiational** *adj.* **radiationally** *adv.* [L *radiatio* (as RADIATE)]

radiator /ˈreɪdɪˌeɪtə(r)/ *n.* **1** a person or thing that radiates. **2 a** a device for heating a room etc., consisting of a metal case through which hot water or steam circulates. **b** a usu. portable oil or electric heater resembling this. **3** an engine-cooling device in a motor vehicle or aircraft with a large surface for cooling circulating water. □**radiator grille** a grille at the front of a motor vehicle allowing air to circulate to the radiator.

radical /ˈrædɪk(ə)l/ *adj. & n.* —*adj.* **1** of the root or roots; fundamental (*a radical error*). **2** far-reaching; thorough; going to the root (*radical change*). **3 a** advocating thorough reform; holding extreme political views; revolutionary. **b** (of a measure etc.) advanced by or according to principles of this kind. **4** forming the basis; primary (*the radical idea*). **5** *Math.* of the root of a number or quantity. **6** (of surgery etc.) seeking to ensure the removal of all diseased tissue. **7** of the roots of words. **8** *Mus.* belonging to the root of a chord. **9** *Bot.* of, or springing direct from, the root. **10** *hist.* belonging to an extreme section of the Liberal Party. **11** *US hist.* seeking extreme anti-South action at the time of the Civil War. —*n.* **1** a person holding radical views or belonging to a radical party. **2** *Chem.* **a** a free radical. **b** an element or atom or a group of these normally forming part of a compound and remaining unaltered during the compound's ordinary chemical changes. **3** the root of a word. **4** a fundamental principle; a basis. **5** *Math.* **a** a quantity forming or expressed as the root of another. **b** a radical sign. □**radical sign** √, ∛, etc., indicating the square, cube, etc., root of the number following. □□ **radicalism** *n.* **radicalize** *v.tr. & intr.* (also **-ise**). **radicalization** /-ˈzeɪʃ(ə)n/ *n.* **radically** *adv.* **radicalness** *n.* [ME f. LL *radicalis* f. L *radix radicis* root]

radicchio /rəˈdiːkɪəʊ/ *n.* (*pl.* **-os**) a variety of chicory with dark red-coloured leaves. [It., = chicory]

radices *pl.* of RADIX.

radicle /ˈrædɪk(ə)l/ *n.* **1** the part of a plant embryo that develops into the primary root; a rootlet. **2** a rootlike subdivision of a nerve or vein. □□ **radicular** /rəˈdɪkjʊlə(r)/ *adj.* [L *radicula* (as RADIX)]

radii *pl.* of RADIUS.

radio /ˈreɪdɪəʊ/ *n. & v.* —*n.* (*pl.* **-os**) **1** (often *attrib.*) **a** the transmission and reception of sound messages

etc. by electromagnetic waves of radio-frequency (cf. WIRELESS). **b** an apparatus for receiving, broadcasting, or transmitting radio signals. **c** a message sent or received by radio. **2 a** sound broadcasting in general (*prefers the radio*). **b** a broadcasting station or channel (*Radio One*). —*v.* (**-oes, -oed**) **1** *tr.* **a** send (a message) by radio. **b** send a message to (a person) by radio. **2** *intr.* communicate or broadcast by radio. □**radio astronomy** the branch of astronomy concerned with the radio-frequency range of the electromagnetic spectrum. **radio cab** (or **car**) a cab or car equipped with a two-way radio. **radio fix** the position of an aircraft, ship, etc., found by radio. **radio galaxy** a galaxy emitting radiation in the radio-frequency range of the electromagnetic spectrum. **radio ham** see HAM. **radio star** a small star etc. emitting strong radio waves. **radio telescope** a directional aerial system for collecting and analysing radiation in the radio-frequency range from stars etc. [short for *radio-telegraphy* etc.]

radio- /ˈreɪdɪəʊ/ *comb. form* **1** denoting radio or broadcasting. **2 a** connected with radioactivity. **b** denoting artificially prepared radioisotopes of elements (*radio-caesium*). **3** connected with rays or radiation. **4** *Anat.* belonging to the radius in conjunction with some other part (*radio-carpal*). [RADIUS + -O- or f. RADIO]

radioactive /ˌreɪdɪəʊˈæktɪv/ *adj.* of or exhibiting radioactivity. □□ **radioactively** *adv.*

radioactivity /ˌreɪdɪəʊækˈtɪvɪtɪ/ *n.* the spontaneous disintegration of atomic nuclei, with the emission of usu. penetrating radiation or particles.

radio-assay /ˌreɪdɪəʊˈseɪ/ *n.* an analysis of a substance based on radiation from a sample.

radiobiology /ˌreɪdɪəʊbaɪˈɒlədʒɪ/ *n.* the biology concerned with the effects of radiation on organisms and the application in biology of radiological techniques. □□ **radiobiological** /-ə'lɒdʒɪk(ə)l/ *adj.* **radiobiologically** /-ə'lɒdʒɪkəlɪ/ *adv.* **radiobiologist** *n.*

radiocarbon /ˌreɪdɪəʊˈkɑːbən/ *n.* a radioactive isotope of carbon. □**radiocarbon dating** = *carbon dating*.

radiochemistry /ˌreɪdɪəʊˈkemɪstrɪ/ *n.* the chemistry of radioactive materials. □□ **radiochemical** *adj.* **radiochemist** *n.*

radio-controlled /ˌreɪdɪəʊkən'trəʊld/ *adj.* (of a model aircraft etc.) controlled from a distance by radio.

radio-element /ˌreɪdɪəʊ'elɪmənt/ *n.* a natural or artificial radioactive element or isotope.

radio-frequency /ˈreɪdɪəʊˌfriːkwənsɪ/ *n.* (*pl.* **-ies**) the frequency band of telecommunication, ranging from 10^4 to 10^{11} or 10^{12} Hz.

radiogenic /ˌreɪdɪəʊ'dʒenɪk/ *adj.* **1** produced by radioactivity. **2** suitable for broadcasting by radio. □□ **radiogenically** *adv.*

radio-goniometer /ˌreɪdɪəʊˌɡəʊnɪ'ɒmɪtə(r)/ *n.* an instrument for finding direction using radio waves.

radiogram /ˈreɪdɪəʊˌɡræm/ *n.* **1** *Brit.* a combined radio and record-player. **2** a picture obtained by X-rays, gamma rays, etc. **3** a radio-telegram. [RADIO- + -GRAM, GRAMOPHONE]

radiograph /ˈreɪdɪəʊˌɡrɑːf/ *n. & v.* —*n.* **1** an instrument recording the intensity of radiation. **2** = RADIOGRAM 2. —*v.tr.* obtain a picture of by X-ray, gamma ray, etc. □□ **radiographer** /-'ɒɡrəfə(r)/ *n.* **radiographic** /-dɪə'ɡræfɪk/ *adj.* **radiographically** /-dɪə'ɡræfɪkəlɪ/ *adv.* **radiography** /-'ɒɡrəfɪ/ *n.*

radioimmunology /ˌreɪdɪəʊˌɪmjuː'nɒlədʒɪ/ *n.* the application of radiological techniques in immunology.

radioisotope /ˌreɪdɪəʊ'aɪsəˌtəʊp/ *n.* a radioactive isotope. □□ **radioisotopic** /-'tɒpɪk/ *adj.* **radioisotopically** /-'tɒpɪkəlɪ/ *adv.*

radiolarian /ˌreɪdɪəʊ'leərɪən/ *n.* any marine protozoan of the order Radiolaria, having a siliceous skeleton and radiating pseudopodia. [mod.L *radiolaria* f. L *radiolus* dimin. of RADIUS]

radiology /ˌreɪdɪˈɒlədʒɪ/ *n.* the scientific study of X-rays and other high-energy radiation, esp. as used in medicine. □□ **radiologic** /-əˈlɒdʒɪk/ *adj.* **radiological** /-əˈlɒdʒɪk(ə)l/ *adj.* **radiologist** *n.*

radiometer /ˌreɪdɪˈɒmɪtə(r)/ *n.* an instrument for measuring the intensity or force of radiation. □□ **radiometry** *n.*

radiometric /ˌreɪdɪəʊˈmetrɪk/ *adj.* of or relating to the measurement of radioactivity. □ **radiometric dating** a method of dating geological specimens by determining the relative proportions of the isotopes of a radioactive element present in a sample.

radionics /ˌreɪdɪˈɒnɪks/ *n.pl.* (usu. treated as *sing.*) the study and interpretation of radiation believed to be emitted from substances, esp. as a form of diagnosis. [RADIO- + -*onics*, after ELECTRONICS]

radionuclide /ˌreɪdɪəʊˈnjuːklaɪd/ *n.* a radioactive nuclide.

radiopaque /ˌreɪdɪəʊˈpeɪk/ *adj.* (also **radio-opaque**) opaque to X-rays or similar radiation. □□ **radiopacity** /-ˈpæsɪtɪ/ *n.* [RADIO- + OPAQUE]

radiophonic /ˌreɪdɪəʊˈfɒnɪk/ *adj.* of or relating to synthetic sound, esp. music, produced electronically.

radioscopy /ˌreɪdɪˈɒskəpɪ/ *n.* the examination by X-rays etc. of objects opaque to light. □□ **radioscopic** /-əˈskɒpɪk/ *adj.*

radiosonde /ˈreɪdɪəʊˌsɒnd/ *n.* a miniature radio transmitter broadcasting information about pressure, temperature, etc., from various levels of the atmosphere, carried esp. by balloon. [RADIO- + G *Sonde* probe]

radio-telegram /ˌreɪdɪəʊˈtelɪˌɡræm/ *n.* a telegram sent by radio, usu. from a ship to land.

radio-telegraphy /ˌreɪdɪəʊtɪˈlegrəfɪ/ *n.* telegraphy using radio transmission. □□ **radio-telegraph** /-ˈtelɪˌgrɑːf/ *n.*

radio-telephony /ˌreɪdɪəʊtɪˈlefənɪ/ *n.* telephony using radio transmission. □□ **radio-telephone** /-ˈtelɪˌfəʊn/ *n.* **radio-telephonic** /-ˌtelɪˈfɒnɪk/ *adj.*

radiotelex /ˌreɪdɪəʊˈteleks/ *n.* a telex sent usu. from a ship to land.

radiotherapy /ˌreɪdɪəʊˈθerəpɪ/ *n.* the treatment of disease by X-rays or other forms of radiation. □□ **radiotherapeutic** /-ˈpjuːtɪk/ *adj.* **radiotherapist** *n.*

radish /ˈrædɪʃ/ *n.* **1** a cruciferous plant, *Raphanus sativus*, with a fleshy pungent root. **2** this root, eaten esp. raw in salads etc. [OE *rædic* f. L *radix radicis* root]

radium /ˈreɪdɪəm/ *n. Chem.* a radioactive metallic element orig. obtained from pitchblende etc., used esp. in luminous materials and in radiotherapy. ¶ Symb.: **Ra**. □ **radium bomb** a container holding a large quantity of radium and used in radiotherapy as a source of gamma rays. **radium emanation** = RADON. **radium therapy** the treatment of disease by the use of radium. [L *radius* ray]

radius /ˈreɪdɪəs/ *n. & v.* —*n.* (*pl.* **radii** /-dɪˌaɪ/ or **radiuses**) **1** *Math.* **a** a straight line from the centre to the circumference of a circle or sphere. **b** a radial line from the focus to any point of a curve. **c** the length of the radius of a circle etc. **2** a usu. specified distance from a centre in all directions (*within a radius of 20 miles*; *has a large radius of action*). **3 a** the thicker and shorter of the two bones in the human forearm (cf. ULNA). **b** the corresponding bone in a vertebrate's foreleg or a bird's wing. **4** any of the five arm-like structures of a starfish. **5 a** any of a set of lines diverging from a point like the radii of a circle. **b** an object of this kind, e.g. a spoke. **6 a** the outer rim of a composite flower-head, e.g. a daisy. **b** a radiating branch of an umbel. —*v.tr.* give a rounded form to (an edge etc.). □ **radius vector** *Math.* a variable line drawn from a fixed point to an orbit or other curve, or to any point as an indication of the latter's position. [L, = staff, spoke, ray]

radix /ˈreɪdɪks/ *n.* (*pl.* **radices** /-dɪˌsiːz/) **1** *Math.* a number or symbol used as the basis of a numeration scale (e.g. ten in the decimal system). **2** (usu. foll. by *of*) a source or origin. [L, = root]

radome /ˈreɪdəʊm/ *n.* a dome or other structure, transparent to radio waves, protecting radar equipment, esp. on the outer surface of an aircraft. [*radar* + *dome*]

radon /ˈreɪdɒn/ *n. Chem.* a gaseous radioactive inert element arising from the disintegration of radium, and used in radiotherapy. ¶ Symb.: **Rn**. [RADIUM after argon etc.]

radula /ˈrædjʊlə/ *n.* (*pl.* **radulae** /-ˌliː/) a filelike structure in molluscs for scraping off food particles and drawing them into the mouth. □□ **radular** *adj.* [L, = scraper f. *radere* scrape]

RAF *abbr.* /*colloq.* ræf/ (in the UK) Royal Air Force.

Rafferty's rules /ˈræfətɪz/ *n. Austral. & NZ colloq.* no rules at all, esp. in boxing. [E dial. corrupt. of *refractory*]

raffia /ˈræfɪə/ *n.* (also **raphia**) **1** a palm-tree, *Raphia ruffia*, native to Madagascar, having very long leaves. **2** the fibre from its leaves used for making hats, baskets, etc., and for tying plants etc. [Malagasy]

raffinate /ˈræfɪˌneɪt/ *n. Chem.* a refined liquid oil produced by solvent extraction of impurities. [F *raffiner* + -ATE[1]]

raffish /ˈræfɪʃ/ *adj.* **1** disreputable; rakish. **2** tawdry. □□ **raffishly** *adv.* **raffishness** *n.* [as RAFT[2] + -ISH[1]]

raffle[1] /ˈræf(ə)l/ *n. & v.* —*n.* a fund-raising lottery with goods as prizes. —*v.tr.* (often foll. by *off*) dispose of by means of a raffle. [ME, a kind of dice-game, f. OF *raf(f)le*, of unkn. orig.]

raffle[2] /ˈræf(ə)l/ *n.* **1** rubbish; refuse. **2** lumber; debris. [ME, perh. f. OF *ne rifle, ne rafle* nothing at all]

raft[1] /rɑːft/ *n. & v.* —*n.* **1** a flat floating structure of timber or other materials for conveying persons or things. **2** a lifeboat or small (often inflatable) boat, esp. for use in emergencies. **3** a floating accumulation of trees, ice, etc. —*v.* **1** *tr.* transport as or on a raft. **2** *tr.* cross (water) on a raft. **3** *tr.* form into a raft. **4** *intr.* (often foll. by *across*) work a raft (across water etc.). [ME f. ON *raptr* RAFTER]

raft[2] /rɑːft/ *n. colloq.* **1** a large collection. **2** (foll. by *of*) a crowd. [*raff* rubbish, perh. of Scand. orig.]

rafter[1] /ˈrɑːftə(r)/ *n.* each of the sloping beams forming the framework of a roof. □□ **raftered** *adj.* [OE *ræfter*, rel. to RAFT[1]]

rafter[2] /ˈrɑːftə(r)/ *n.* **1** a person who rafts timber. **2** a person who travels by raft.

raftsman /ˈrɑːftsmən/ *n.* (*pl.* **-men**) a worker on a raft.

rag[1] /ræg/ *n.* **1 a** a torn, frayed, or worn piece of woven material. **b** one of the irregular scraps to which cloth etc. is reduced by wear and tear. **2** (in *pl.*) old or worn clothes. **3** (*collect.*) scraps of cloth used as material for paper, stuffing, etc. **4** *derog.* **a** a newspaper. **b** a flag, handkerchief, curtain, etc. **5** (usu. with *neg.*) the smallest scrap of cloth etc. (*not a rag to cover him*). **6** an odd scrap; an irregular piece. **7** a jagged projection, esp. on metal. □ **in rags 1** much torn. **2** in old torn clothes. **rag-and-bone man** *Brit.* an itinerant dealer in old clothes, furniture, etc. **rag-bag 1** a bag in which scraps of fabric etc. are kept for use. **2** a miscellaneous collection. **3** *sl.* a sloppily-dressed woman. **rag bolt** a bolt with barbs to keep it tight when it has been driven in. **rag book** a children's book made of untearable cloth. **rag doll** a stuffed doll made of cloth. **rag paper** paper made from rags. **rag-picker** a collector and seller of rags. **rags to riches** poverty to affluence. **rag trade** *colloq.* the business of designing, making, and selling women's clothes. [ME, prob. back-form. f. RAGGED]

rag[2] /ræg/ *n. & v. sl.* —*n. Brit.* **1** a fund-raising programme of stunts, parades, and entertainment organized by students. **2** *colloq.* a prank. **3 a** a rowdy celebration. **b** a noisy disorderly scene. —*v.* (**ragged**, **ragging**) **1** *tr.* tease; torment; play rough jokes on. **2** *tr.* scold; reprove severely. **3** *intr. Brit.* engage in rough play; be noisy and riotous. [18th c.: orig. unkn.: cf. BALLYRAG]

rag³ /ræg/ n. **1** a large coarse roofing-slate. **2** any of various kinds of hard coarse sedimentary stone that break into thick slabs. [ME: orig. unkn., but assoc. with RAG¹]

rag⁴ /ræg/ n. Mus. a ragtime composition or tune. [perh. f. RAGGED: see RAGTIME]

raga /ˈrɑːɡə/ n. (also **rag** /rɑːɡ/) Ind. Mus. **1** a pattern of notes used as a basis for improvisation. **2** a piece using a particular raga. [Skr., = colour, musical tone]

ragamuffin /ˈræɡəˌmʌfɪn/ n. a person in ragged dirty clothes, esp. a child. [prob. based on RAG¹: cf. 14th-c. ragamoffyn the name of a demon]

rage /reɪdʒ/ n. & v. —n. **1** fierce or violent anger. **2** a fit of this (flew into a rage). **3** the violent action of a natural force (the rage of the storm). **4** (foll. by for) **a** a vehement desire or passion. **b** a widespread temporary enthusiasm or fashion. **5** poet. poetic, prophetic, or martial enthusiasm or ardour. **6** sl. a lively frolic. —v.intr. **1** be full of anger. **2** (often foll. by at, against) speak furiously or madly; rave. **3** (of wind, battle, fever, etc.) be violent; be at its height; continue unchecked. **4** Austral. sl. seek enjoyment; go on a spree. □**all the rage** popular, fashionable. [ME f. OF rager ult. f. L RABIES]

ragee /rɑːˈɡiː/ n. (also **raggee**) a coarse cereal, Eleusine coracana, forming a staple food in parts of India etc. [Hindi rāgī]

ragged /ˈræɡɪd/ adj. **1** (of clothes etc.) torn; frayed. **2** rough; shaggy; hanging in tufts. **3** (of a person) in ragged clothes. **4** with a broken or jagged outline or surface. **5** faulty; imperfect. **6** lacking finish, smoothness, or uniformity (ragged rhymes). **7** exhausted (esp. be run ragged). □**ragged robin** a pink-flowered campion, Lychnis flos-cuculi, with tattered petals. □□ **raggedly** adv. **raggedness** n. **raggedy** adj. [ME f. ON roggvathr tufted]

ragee var. of RAGEE.

raggle-taggle /ˈræɡəlˌtæɡ(ə)l/ adj. (also **wraggle-taggle**) ragged; rambling, straggling. [app. fanciful var. of RAGTAG]

raglan /ˈræɡlən/ n. (often attrib.) an overcoat without shoulder seams, the sleeves running up to the neck. □**raglan sleeve** a sleeve of this kind. [Lord Raglan, Brit. commander d. 1855]

ragout /ræˈɡuː/ n. & v. —n. meat in small pieces stewed with vegetables and highly seasoned. —v.tr. cook (food) in this way. [F ragoût f. ragoûter revive the taste of]

ragstone /ˈræɡstəʊn/ n. = RAG³ 2.

ragtag /ˈræɡtæɡ/ n. (in full **ragtag and bobtail**) derog. the rabble or common people. [earlier tag-rag, tag and rag, f. RAG¹ + TAG¹]

ragtime /ˈræɡtaɪm/ n. & adj. —n. music characterized by a syncopated melodic line and regularly-accented accompaniment, evolved by American Black musicians in the 1890s and played esp. on the piano. —adj. sl. disorderly, disreputable, inferior (a ragtime army). [prob. f. RAG⁴]

raguly /ˈræɡjuːlɪ/ adj. Heraldry like a row of sawn-off branches. [perh. f. RAGGED after nebuly]

ragweed /ˈræɡwiːd/ n. **1** = RAGWORT. **2** US any plant of the genus Ambrosia, with allergenic pollen.

ragwort /ˈræɡwɜːt/ n. any yellow-flowered ragged-leaved plant of the genus Senecio.

rah /rɑː/ int. esp. US colloq. an expression of encouragement, approval, etc. [shortening of HURRAH]

raid /reɪd/ n. & v. —n. **1** a rapid surprise attack, esp.: **a** by troops, aircraft, etc. in warfare. **b** to commit a crime or do harm. **2** a surprise attack by police etc. to arrest suspected persons or seize illicit goods. **3** Stock Exch. an attempt to lower prices by the concerted selling of shares. **4** (foll. by on, upon) a forceful or insistent attempt to make a person or thing provide something. —v.tr. **1** make a raid on (a

person, place, or thing). **2** plunder, deplete. □□ **raider** n. [ME, Sc. form of OE rād ROAD]

rail¹ /reɪl/ n. & v. —n. **1** a level or sloping bar or series of bars: **a** used to hang things on. **b** running along the top of a set of banisters. **c** forming part of a fence or barrier as protection against contact, falling over, etc. **2** a steel bar or continuous line of bars laid on the ground, usu. as one of a pair forming a railway track. **3** (often attrib.) a railway (send it by rail; rail fares). **4** (in pl.) the inside boundary fence of a racecourse. **5** a horizontal piece in the frame of a panelled door etc. (cf. STILE²). —v.tr. **1** furnish with a rail or rails. **2** (usu. foll. by in, off) enclose with rails (a small space was railed off). **3** convey (goods) by rail. □**off the rails** disorganized; out of order; deranged. **over the rails** over the side of a ship. **rail fence** esp. US a fence made of posts and rails. **rail gun** an electromagnetic projectile launcher used esp. as an anti-missile weapon. □□ **railage** n. **railless** adj. [ME f. OF reille iron rod f. L regula RULE]

rail² /reɪl/ v.intr. (often foll. by at, against) complain using abusive language; rant. □□ **railer** n. **railing** n. & adj. [ME f. F railler f. Prov. ralhar jest, ult. f. L rugire bellow]

rail³ /reɪl/ n. any bird of the family Rallidae, often inhabiting marshes, esp. the corncrake and water rail. [ME f. ONF raille f. Rmc, perh. imit.]

railcar /ˈreɪlkɑː(r)/ n. a railway vehicle consisting of a single powered coach.

railcard /ˈreɪlkɑːd/ n. Brit. a pass entitling the holder to reduced rail fares.

railhead /ˈreɪlhed/ n. **1** the farthest point reached by a railway under construction. **2** the point on a railway at which road transport of goods begins.

railing /ˈreɪlɪŋ/ n. **1** (usu. in pl.) a fence or barrier made of rails. **2** the material for these.

raillery /ˈreɪlərɪ/ n. (pl. **-ies**) **1** good-humoured ridicule; rallying. **2** an instance of this. [F raillerie (as RAIL²)]

railman /ˈreɪlmən/ n. (pl. **-men**) = RAILWAYMAN.

railroad /ˈreɪlrəʊd/ n. & v. —n. esp. US = RAILWAY. —v.tr. **1** (often foll. by to, into, through, etc.) rush or coerce (a person or thing) (railroaded me into going too). **2** send (a person) to prison by means of false evidence.

railway /ˈreɪlweɪ/ n. **1** a track or set of tracks made of steel rails upon which goods trucks and passenger trains run. **2** such a system worked by a single company (Great Western Railway). **3** the organization and personnel required for its working. **4** a similar set of tracks for other vehicles etc. □**railway-yard** the area where rolling-stock is kept and made up into trains.

railwayman /ˈreɪlweɪmən/ n. (pl. **-men**) a railway employee.

raiment /ˈreɪmənt/ n. archaic clothing. [ME f. obs. arrayment (as ARRAY)]

rain /reɪn/ n. & v. —n. **1 a** the condensed moisture of the atmosphere falling visibly in separate drops. **b** the fall of such drops. **2** (in pl.) **a** rainfalls. **b** (prec. by the) the rainy season in tropical countries. **3 a** falling liquid or solid particles or objects. **b** the rainlike descent of these. **c** a large or overwhelming quantity (a rain of congratulations). —v. **1** intr. (prec. by it as subject) rain falls (it is raining; if it rains). **2 a** intr. fall in showers or like rain (tears rained down their cheeks; blows rain upon him). **b** tr. (prec. by it as subject) send in large quantities (it rained blood; it is raining invitations). **3** tr. send down like rain; lavishly bestow (rained benefits on us; rained blows upon him). **4** intr. (of the sky, the clouds, etc.) send down rain. □**rain cats and dogs** see CAT. **rain check** US **1** a ticket given for later use when a sporting fixture or other outdoor event is interrupted or postponed by rain. **2** a promise that an offer will be maintained though deferred.

rain-cloud a cloud bringing rain. **rain forest** luxuriant tropical forest with heavy rainfall. **rain-gauge** an instrument measuring rainfall. **rain-making** the action of attempting to increase rainfall by artificial means. **rain off** (or *US* **out**) (esp. in *passive*) cause (an event etc.) to be terminated or cancelled because of rain. **rain or shine** whether it rains or not. **rain-shadow** a region shielded from rain by mountains etc. **rain-wash** 1 loose material carried away by rain. 2 the movement of this. **rain-worm** the common earthworm. □□ **rainless** *adj.* **raintight** *adj.* [OE *regn, rēn, regnian* f. Gmc]

rainbird /ˈreɪnbɜːd/ *n.* a bird said to foretell rain by its cry, esp. the green woodpecker.

rainbow /ˈreɪnbəʊ/ *n.* & *adj.* —*n.* 1 an arch of colours (conventionally red, orange, yellow, green, blue, indigo, violet) formed in the sky (or across a cataract etc.) opposite the sun by reflection, twofold refraction, and dispersion of the sun's rays in falling rain or in spray or mist. 2 a similar effect formed by the moon's rays. —*adj.* many-coloured. □ **rainbow lorikeet** a small brightly coloured Polynesian parrot, *Trichoglossus haematodus.* **rainbow trout** a large trout, *Salmo gairdneri,* orig. of the Pacific coast of N. America. **secondary rainbow** an additional arch with the colours in reverse order formed inside or outside a rainbow by twofold reflection and twofold refraction. [OE *regnboga* (as RAIN, BOW[1])]

raincoat /ˈreɪnkəʊt/ *n.* a waterproof or water-resistant coat.

raindrop /ˈreɪndrɒp/ *n.* a single drop of rain. [OE *regndropa*]

rainfall /ˈreɪnfɔːl/ *n.* 1 a fall of rain. 2 the quantity of rain falling within a given area in a given time.

rainproof /ˈreɪnpruːf/ *adj.* (esp. of a building, garment, etc.) resistant to rainwater.

rainstorm /ˈreɪnstɔːm/ *n.* a storm with heavy rain.

rainwater /ˈreɪnˌwɔːtə(r)/ *n.* water obtained from collected rain, as distinct from a well etc.

rainy /ˈreɪnɪ/ *adj.* (**rainier, rainiest**) 1 (of weather, a climate, day, region, etc.) in or on which rain is falling or much rain usually falls. 2 (of cloud, wind, etc.) laden with or bringing rain. □ **rainy day** a time of special need in the future. □□ **rainily** *adv.* **raininess** *n.* [OE *rēnig* (as RAIN)]

raise /reɪz/ *v.* & *n.* —*v.tr.* 1 put or take into a higher position. 2 (often foll. by *up*) cause to rise or stand up or be vertical; set upright. 3 increase the amount or value or strength of (*raised their prices*). 4 (often foll. by *up*) construct or build up. 5 levy or collect or bring together (*raise money; raise an army*). 6 cause to be heard or considered (*raise a shout; raise an objection*). 7 set going or bring into being; rouse (*raise a protest; raise hopes*). 8 bring up; educate. 9 breed or grow (*raise one's own vegetables*). 10 promote to a higher rank. 11 (foll. by *to*) *Math.* multiply a quantity to a specified power. 12 cause (bread) to rise with yeast. 13 *Cards* **a** bet more than (another player). **b** increase (a stake). **c** *Bridge* make a bid contracting for more tricks in the same suit as (one's partner); increase (a bid) in this way. 14 abandon or force an enemy to abandon (a siege or blockade). 15 remove (a barrier or embargo). 16 cause (a ghost etc.) to appear (opp. LAY[1] 6b). 17 *colloq.* find (a person etc. wanted). 18 establish contact with (a person etc.) by radio or telephone. 19 (usu. as **raised** *adj.*) cause (pastry etc.) to stand without support (*a raised pie*). 20 *Naut.* come in sight of (land, a ship, etc.). 21 make a nap on (cloth). 22 extract from the earth. —*n.* 1 *Cards* an increase in a stake or bid (cf. sense 13 of *v.*). 2 esp. *US* an increase in salary. □ **raise Cain** see CAIN. **raised beach** *Geol.* a beach lying above water level owing to changes since its formation. **raise the devil** *colloq.* make a disturbance. **raise a dust** 1 cause turmoil. 2 obscure the truth. **raise one's eyebrows** see EYEBROW. **raise one's eyes** see EYE. **raise from the dead** restore to life. **raise one's glass to** drink the health of. **raise one's hand to**

make as if to strike (a person). **raise one's hat** (often foll. by *to*) remove it momentarily as a gesture of courtesy or respect. **raise hell** *colloq.* make a disturbance. **raise a laugh** cause others to laugh. **raise a person's spirits** give him or her new courage or cheerfulness. **raise one's voice** speak, esp. louder. **raise the wind** *Brit.* procure money for a purpose. □□ **raisable** *adj.* [ME f. ON *reisa,* rel. to REAR[2]]

raisin /ˈreɪz(ə)n/ *n.* a partially dried grape. □□ **raisiny** *adj.* [ME f. OF ult. f. L *racemus* grape-bunch]

raison d'être /ˌreɪzɒ̃ ˈdetr/ *n.* (*pl.* **raisons d'être** *pronunc.* same) a purpose or reason that accounts for or justifies or originally caused a thing's existence. [F, = reason for being]

raj /rɑːdʒ/ *n.* (prec. by *the*) *hist.* British sovereignty in India. [Hindi *rāj* reign]

raja /ˈrɑːdʒə/ *n.* (also **rajah**) *hist.* 1 an Indian king or prince. 2 a petty dignitary or noble in India. 3 a Malay or Javanese chief. □□ **rajaship** *n.* [Hindi *rājā* f. Skr. *rājan* king]

raja yoga /ˈrɑːdʒə/ *n.* a form of yoga intended to achieve control over the mind and emotions. [Skr. f. *rājan* king + YOGA]

Rajput /ˈrɑːdʒpʊt, -puːt/ *n.* (also **Rajpoot**) a member of a Hindu soldier caste claiming Kshatriya descent. [Hindi *rājpūt* f. Skr. *rājan* king + *putrá* son]

rake[1] /reɪk/ *n.* & *v.* —*n.* 1 **a** an implement consisting of a pole with a crossbar toothed like a comb at the end, or with several tines held together by a crosspiece, for drawing together hay etc. or smoothing loose soil or gravel. **b** a wheeled implement for the same purpose. 2 a similar implement used for other purposes, e.g. by a croupier drawing in money at a gaming-table. —*v.* 1 *tr.* collect or gather or remove with or as with a rake. 2 *tr.* make tidy or smooth with a rake (*raked it level*). 3 *intr.* use a rake. 4 *tr.* & *intr.* search with or as with a rake, search thoroughly, ransack. 5 *tr.* **a** direct gunfire along (a line) from end to end. **b** sweep with the eyes. **c** (of a window etc.) have a commanding view of. 6 *tr.* scratch or scrape. □ **rake in** *colloq.* amass (profits etc.). **rake-off** *colloq.* a commission or share, esp. in a disreputable deal. **rake up** (or **over**) revive the memory of (past quarrels, grievances, etc.). □□ **raker** *n.* [OE *raca, racu* f. Gmc, partly f. ON *raka* scrape, rake]

rake[2] /reɪk/ *n.* a dissolute man of fashion. □ **rake's progress** a progressive deterioration, esp. through self-indulgence (the title of a series of engravings by Hogarth 1735). [short for archaic *rakehell* in the same sense]

rake[3] /reɪk/ *v.* & *n.* —*v.* 1 *tr.* & *intr.* set or be set at a sloping angle. 2 *intr.* **a** (of a mast or funnel) incline from the perpendicular towards the stern. **b** (of a ship or its bow or stern) project at the upper part of the bow or stern beyond the keel. —*n.* 1 a raking position or build. 2 the amount by which a thing rakes. 3 the slope of the stage or the auditorium in a theatre. 4 the slope of a seat-back etc. 5 the angle of the edge or face of a cutting tool. [17th c.: prob. rel. to G *ragen* project, of unkn. orig.]

raki /rəˈkiː, ˈrækɪ/ *n.* (*pl.* **rakis**) any of various spirits made in E. Europe and the Middle East. [Turk. *raqi*]

rakish[1] /ˈreɪkɪʃ/ *adj.* of or like a rake (see RAKE[2]); dashing; jaunty. □□ **rakishly** *adv.* **rakishness** *n.*

rakish[2] /ˈreɪkɪʃ/ *adj.* (of a ship) smart and fast-looking, seemingly built for speed and therefore open to suspicion of piracy. [RAKE[3], assoc. with RAKE[2]]

raku /ˈrɑːkuː/ *n.* a kind of Japanese earthenware, usu. lead-glazed. [Jap., lit. enjoyment]

rale /rɑːl/ *n.* an abnormal rattling sound heard in the auscultation of unhealthy lungs. [F f. *râler* to rattle]

rall. /ræl/ *adv.* & *adj.* & *n.* = RALLENTANDO. [abbr.]

rallentando /ˌrælənˈtændəʊ/ *adv.*, *adj.*, & *n. Mus.* —*adv.* & *adj.* with a gradual decrease of speed.

—*n.* (*pl.* **-os** or **rallentandi** /-dɪ/) a passage to be performed in this way. [It.]

ralli car /ˈrælɪ/ *n.* (also **ralli cart**) *hist.* a light two-wheeled horse-drawn vehicle for four persons. [*Ralli*, name of the first purchaser 1885]

ralline /ˈrælaɪn/ *adj.* of the bird-family Rallidae (see RAIL³). [mod.L *rallus* RAIL³]

rally¹ /ˈrælɪ/ *v. & n.* —*v.* (**-ies, -ied**) **1** *tr. & intr.* (often foll. by *round, behind, to*) bring or come together as support or for concentrated action. **2** *tr. & intr.* bring or come together again after a rout or dispersion. **3 a** *intr.* renew a conflict. **b** *tr.* cause to do this. **4 a** *tr.* revive (courage etc.) by an effort of will. **b** *tr.* rouse (a person or animal) to fresh energy. **c** *intr.* pull oneself together. **5** *intr.* recover after illness or prostration or fear, regain health or consciousness, revive. **6** *intr.* (of share-prices etc.) increase after a fall. —*n.* (*pl.* **-ies**) **1** an act of reassembling forces or renewing conflict; a reunion for fresh effort. **2** a recovery of energy after or in the middle of exhaustion or illness. **3** a mass meeting of supporters or persons having a common interest. **4** a competition for motor vehicles, usu. over public roads. **5** (in lawn tennis etc.) an extended exchange of strokes between players. □ **rally-cross** motor racing over roads and cross-country. □□ **rallier** *n.* [F *rallier* (as RE-, ALLY¹)]

rally² /ˈrælɪ/ *v.tr.* (**-ies, -ied**) subject to good-humoured ridicule. [F *railler*: see RAIL²]

RAM *abbr.* **1** (in the UK) Royal Academy of Music. **2** *Computing* random-access memory.

ram /ræm/ *n. & v.* —*n.* **1** an uncastrated male sheep, a tup. **2** (**the Ram**) the zodiacal sign or constellation Aries. **3** *hist.* **a** = *battering ram* (see BATTER¹). **b** a beak projecting from the bow of a battleship, for piercing the sides of other ships. **c** a battleship with such a beak. **4** the falling weight of a pile-driving machine. **5 a** a hydraulic water-raising or lifting machine. **b** the piston of a hydrostatic press. **c** the plunger of a force-pump. —*v.tr.* (**rammed, ramming**) **1** force or squeeze into place by pressure. **2** (usu. foll. by *down, in, into*) beat down or drive in by heavy blows. **3** (of a ship, vehicle, etc.) strike violently, crash against. **4** (foll. by *against, at, on, into*) dash or violently impel. □ **ram home** stress forcefully (an argument, lesson, etc.). □□ **rammer** *n.* [OE *ram(m)*, perh. rel. to ON *rammr* strong]

Ramadan /ˈræmə͵dæn/ *n.* (also **Ramadhan** /-͵zæn/) the ninth month of the Muslim year, during which strict fasting is observed from sunrise to sunset. [Arab. *ramaḍān* f. *ramaḍa* be hot; reason for name uncert.]

ramal /ˈreɪm(ə)l/ *adj. Bot.* of or proceeding from a branch. [L *ramus* branch]

Raman effect /ˈrɑːmən/ *n.* the change of frequency in the scattering of radiation in a medium, used in spectroscopic analysis. [Sir C. V. *Raman*, Ind. physicist d. 1970]

ramble /ˈræmb(ə)l/ *v. & n.* —*v.intr.* **1** walk for pleasure, with or without a definite route. **2** wander in discourse, talk or write disconnectedly. —*n.* a walk taken for pleasure. [prob. f. MDu. *rammelen* (of an animal) wander about in sexual excitement, frequent. of *rammen* copulate with, rel. to RAM]

rambler /ˈræmblə(r)/ *n.* **1** a person who rambles. **2** a straggling or climbing rose (*crimson rambler*).

rambling /ˈræmblɪŋ/ *adj.* **1** peripatetic, wandering. **2** disconnected, desultory, incoherent. **3** (of a house, street, etc.) irregularly arranged. **4** (of a plant) straggling, climbing. □□ **ramblingly** *adv.*

rambunctious /ræmˈbʌŋkʃəs/ *adj. US colloq.* **1** uncontrollably exuberant. **2** unruly. □□ **rambunctiously** *adv.* **rambunctiousness** *n.* [19th c.: orig. unkn.]

rambutan /ræmˈbuːt(ə)n/ *n.* **1** a red plum-sized prickly fruit. **2** an East Indian tree, *Nephelium lappaceum*, that bears this. [Malay *rambūtan* f. *rambut* hair, in allusion to its spines]

RAMC *abbr.* (in the UK) Royal Army Medical Corps.

ramekin /ˈræmɪkɪn/ *n.* **1** (in full **ramekin case** or **dish**) a small dish for baking and serving an individual portion of food. **2** food served in such a dish, esp. a small quantity of cheese baked with breadcrumbs, eggs, etc. [F *ramequin*, of LG or Du. orig.]

ramie /ˈræmɪ/ *n.* **1** any of various tall East Asian plants of the genus *Boehmeria*, esp. *B. nivea*. **2** a strong fibre obtained from this, woven into cloth. [Malay *rāmī*]

ramification /͵ræmɪfɪˈkeɪʃ(ə)n/ *n.* **1** the act or an instance of ramifying; the state of being ramified. **2** a subdivision of a complex structure or process comparable to a tree's branches. [F f. *ramifier*: see RAMIFY]

ramify /ˈræmɪ͵faɪ/ *n.* (**-ies, -ied**) **1** *intr.* form branches or subdivisions or offshoots, branch out. **2** *tr.* (usu. in *passive*) cause to branch out; arrange in a branching manner. [F *ramifier* f. med.L *ramificare* f. L *ramus* branch]

ramin /ræˈmiːn/ *n.* **1** any Malaysian tree of the genus *Gonystylus*, esp. *G. bancanus*. **2** the light-coloured hardwood obtained from this tree. [Malay]

ramjet /ˈræmdʒet/ *n.* a type of jet engine in which air is drawn in and compressed by the forward motion of the engine.

rammer see RAM.

rammy /ˈræmɪ/ *n.* (*pl.* **-ies**) *Sc. sl.* a brawl, a fight (esp. between gangs); a quarrel. [perh. f. Sc. *rammle* row, uproar, var. of RAMBLE]

ramose /ˈræməʊs, ˈreɪ-/ *adj.* branched; branching. [L *ramosus* f. *ramus* branch]

ramp¹ /ræmp/ *n. & v.* —*n.* **1** a slope or inclined plane, esp. for joining two levels of ground, floor, etc. **2** movable stairs for entering or leaving an aircraft. **3** an upward bend in a stair-rail. **4** *Brit.* a transverse ridge in a road to control the speed of vehicles. —*v.* **1** *tr.* furnish or build with a ramp. **2** *intr.* **a** assume or be in a threatening posture. **b** (often foll. by *about*) storm, rage, rush. **c** *Heraldry* be rampant. **3** *intr. Archit.* (of a wall) ascend or descend to a different level. [ME (as verb in heraldic sense) f. F *rampe* f. OF *ramper* creep, crawl]

ramp² /ræmp/ *n. & v. Brit. sl.* —*n.* a swindle or racket, esp. one conducted by the levying of exorbitant prices. —*v.* **1** *intr.* engage in a ramp. **2** *tr.* subject (a person etc.) to a ramp. [16th c.: orig. unkn.]

rampage /ræmˈpeɪdʒ/ *v. & n.* —*v.intr.* **1** (often foll. by *about*) rush wildly or violently about. **2** rage, storm. —*n.* /often ˈræm-/ wild or violent behaviour. □ **on the rampage** rampaging. □□ **rampageous** *adj.* **rampager** *n.* [18th c., perh. f. RAMP¹]

rampant /ˈræmpənt/ *adj.* **1** (placed after noun) *Heraldry* (of an animal) standing on its left hind foot with its forepaws in the air (*lion rampant*). **2** unchecked, flourishing excessively (*rampant violence*). **3** violent or extravagant in action or opinion (*rampant theorists*). **4** rank, luxuriant. □□ **rampancy** *n.* **rampantly** *adv.* [ME f. OF, part. of *ramper*: see RAMP¹]

rampart /ˈræmpɑːt/ *n. & v.* —*n.* **1 a** a defensive wall with a broad top and usu. a stone parapet. **b** a walkway on top of such a wall. **2** a defence or protection. —*v.tr.* fortify or protect with or as with a rampart. [F *rempart, rempar* f. *remparer* fortify f. *emparer* take possession of, ult. f. L *ante* before + *parare* prepare]

rampion /ˈræmpɪən/ *n.* **1** a bellflower, *Campanula rapunculus*, with white tuberous roots used as a salad. **2** any of various plants of the genus *Phyteuma*, with clusters of hornlike buds and flowers. [ult. f. med.L *rapuncium, rapontium*, prob. f. L *rapum* RAPE²]

ramrod /ˈræmrɒd/ *n.* **1** a rod for ramming down the charge of a muzzle-loading firearm. **2** a thing that is very straight or rigid.

ramshackle /ˈræm͵ʃæk(ə)l/ *adj.* (usu. of a house or

vehicle) tumbledown, rickety. [earlier *ramshackled* past part. of obs. *ransackle* RANSACK]

ramsons /'ræms(ə)nz/ *n.* (usu. treated as *sing.*) **1 a** a broad-leaved garlic, *Allium ursinum*, with elongate pungent-smelling bulbous roots. **2** the root of this, eaten as a relish. [OE *hramsan* pl. of *hramsa* wild garlic, later taken as sing.]

RAN *abbr.* Royal Australian Navy.

ran *past* of RUN.

ranch /rɑːntʃ/ *n. & v.* —*n.* **1 a** a cattle-breeding establishment esp. in the US and Canada. **b** a farm where other animals are bred (*mink ranch*). **2** *US* a single-storey or split-level house. —*v.intr.* farm on a ranch. [Sp. *rancho* group of persons eating together]

rancher /'rɑːntʃə(r)/ *n.* **1** a person who farms on a ranch. **2** *US* a modern single-storey house.

ranchero /rɑːn'tʃeərəʊ/ *n.* (*pl.* **-os**) a person who farms or works on a ranch, esp. in Mexico. [Sp. (as RANCH)]

rancid /'rænsɪd/ *adj.* smelling or tasting like rank stale fat. □□ **rancidity** /-'sɪdɪtɪ/ *n.* **rancidness** *n.* [L *rancidus* stinking]

rancour /'ræŋkə(r)/ *n.* (*US* **rancor**) inveterate bitterness, malignant hate, spitefulness. □□ **rancorous** *adj.* **rancorously** *adv.* [ME f. OF f. LL *rancor -oris* (as RANCID)]

rand[1] /rænd, rɑːnt/ *n.* **1** the chief monetary unit of South Africa and some neighbouring countries. **2** *S.Afr.* a ridge of high ground on either side of a river. [Afrik., = edge, rel. to RAND[2]: sense 1 f. *the Rand*, gold-field district near Johannesburg]

rand[2] /rænd/ *n.* a levelling-strip of leather between the heel and sides of a shoe or boot. [OE f. Gmc]

R & B *abbr.* (also **R. & B.**) rhythm and blues.

R & D *abbr.* (also **R. & D.**) research and development.

random /'rændəm/ *adj.* **1** made, done, etc., without method or conscious choice (*random selection*). **2** *Statistics* **a** with equal chances for each item. **b** given by a random process. **3** (of masonry) with stones of irregular size and shape. □ **at random** without aim or purpose or principle. **random-access** *Computing* (of a memory or file) having all parts directly accessible, so that it need not read sequentially. **random error** *Statistics* an error in measurement caused by factors which vary from one measurement to another. □□ **randomize** *v.tr.* (also **-ise**) **randomization** /-'zeɪʃ(ə)n/ *n.* **randomly** *adv.* **randomness** *n.* [ME f. OF *randon* great speed f. *randir* gallop]

R and R *abbr.* (also **R. and R.**) **1** rescue and resuscitation. **2** rest and recreation. **3** rock and roll.

randy /'rændɪ/ *adj.* (**randier, randiest**) **1** lustful; eager for sexual gratification. **2** *Sc.* loud-tongued, boisterous, lusty. □□ **randily** *adv.* **randiness** *n.* [perh. f. obs. *rand* f. obs. Du. *randen*, *ranten* RANT]

ranee /'rɑːnɪ/ *n.* (also **rani**) *hist.* a raja's wife or widow; a Hindu queen. [Hindi *rānī* = Skr. *rājnī* fem. of *rājan* king]

rang *past* of RING[2].

rangatira /ˌræŋgə'tiːrə/ *n. NZ* a Maori chief or noble. [Maori]

range /reɪndʒ/ *n. & v.* —*n.* **1 a** the region between limits of variation, esp. as representing a scope of effective operation (*a voice of astonishing range; the whole range of politics*). **b** such limits. **c** a limited scale or series (*the range of the thermometer readings is about 10 degrees*). **2** the area included in or concerned with something. **3 a** the distance attainable by a gun or projectile (*the enemy are out of range*). **b** the distance between a gun or projectile and its objective. **4** a row, series, line, or tier, esp. of mountains or buildings. **5 a** an open or enclosed area with targets for shooting. **b** a testing-ground for military equipment. **6 a** a fireplace with ovens and hotplates for cooking. **b** *US* an electric or gas cooker. **7** the area over which a thing, esp. a plant or animal, is distributed (*gives the ranges of all species*). **8** the distance that can be covered by a vehicle or

aircraft without refuelling. **9** the distance between a camera and the subject to be photographed. **10** the extent of time covered by a forecast etc. **11 a** a large area of open land for grazing or hunting. **b** a tract over which one wanders. **12** lie, direction (*the range of the strata is east and west*). —*v.* **1** *intr.* **a** reach; lie spread out; extend; be found or occur over a specified district; vary between limits (*ages ranging from twenty to sixty*). **b** run in a line (*ranges north and south*). **2** *tr.* (usu. in *passive* or *refl.*) place or arrange in a row or ranks or in a specified situation or order or company (*ranged their troops; ranged themselves with the majority party; trees ranged in ascending order of height*). **3** *intr.* rove, wander (*ranged through the woods; his thoughts range over past, present, and future*). **4** *tr.* traverse in all directions (*ranging the woods*). **5** *Printing* **a** *tr.* make (type) lie flush at the ends of successive lines. **b** *intr.* (of type) lie flush. **6** *intr.* **a** (often foll. by *with*) be level. **b** (foll. by *with*, *among*) rank; find one's right place (*ranges with the great writers*). **7** *intr.* **a** (of a gun) send a projectile over a specified distance (*ranges over a mile*). **b** (of a projectile) cover a specified distance. **c** obtain the range of a target by adjustment after firing past it or short of it. □ **ranging-pole** (or **-rod**) *Surveying* a pole or rod for setting a straight line. [ME f. OF *range* row, rank f. *ranger* f. *rang* RANK[1]]

rangé /rɑ̃'ʒeɪ/ *adj.* (*fem.* **rangée**) domesticated, orderly, settled. [F]

rangefinder /'reɪndʒˌfaɪndə(r)/ *n.* an instrument for estimating the distance of an object, esp. one to be shot at or photographed.

ranger /'reɪndʒə(r)/ *n.* **1** a keeper of a royal or national park, or of a forest. **2** a member of a body of armed men, esp.: **a** a mounted soldier. **b** *US* a commando. **3** (**Ranger**) *Brit.* a senior Guide. **4** a wanderer. □□ **rangership** *n.*

rangy /'reɪndʒɪ/ *adj.* (**rangier, rangiest**) (of a person) tall and slim.

rani var. of RANEE.

rank[1] /ræŋk/ *n. & v.* —*n.* **1 a** a position in a hierarchy, a grade of advancement. **b** a distinct social class, a grade of dignity or achievement (*people of all ranks; in the top rank of performers*). **c** high social position (*persons of rank*). **d** a place in a scale. **2** a row or line. **3** a single line of soldiers drawn up abreast. **4** *Brit.* a place where taxis stand to await customers. **5** order, array. **6** *Chess* a row of squares across the board (cf. FILE[2]). —*v.* **1** *intr.* have rank or place (*ranks next to the king*). **2** *tr.* classify, give a certain grade to. **3** *tr.* arrange (esp. soldiers) in a rank or ranks. **4** *US* **a** *tr.* take precedence of (a person) in respect to rank. **b** *intr.* have the senior position among the members of a hierarchy etc. □ **break rank** fail to remain in line. **close ranks** maintain solidarity. **keep rank** remain in line. **other ranks** soldiers other than commissioned officers. **rank and fashion** high society. **rank and file** ordinary undistinguished people (orig. = *the ranks*). **the ranks** the common soldiers, i.e. privates and corporals. **rise from the ranks 1** (of a private or a non-commissioned officer) receive a commission. **2** (of a self-made man or woman) advance by one's own exertions. [OF *ranc*, *renc* f. Gmc, rel. to RING[1]]

rank[2] /ræŋk/ *adj.* **1** too luxuriant, coarse; choked with or apt to produce weeds or excessive foliage. **2 a** foul-smelling, offensive. **b** loathsome, indecent, corrupt. **3** flagrant, virulent, gross, complete, unmistakable, strongly marked (*rank outsider*). □□ **rankly** *adv.* **rankness** *n.* [OE *ranc* f. Gmc]

ranker /'ræŋkə(r)/ *n.* **1** a soldier in the ranks. **2** a commissioned officer who has been in the ranks.

ranking /'ræŋkɪŋ/ *n. & adj.* —*n.* ordering by rank; classification. —*adj.* *US* having a high rank or position.

rankle /'ræŋk(ə)l/ *v.intr.* **1** (of envy, disappointment, etc., or their cause) cause persistent annoyance or resentment. **2** *archaic* (of a wound, sore, etc.) fester, continue to be painful. [ME (in sense 2) f. OF *rancler* f. *rancle*, *draoncle* festering sore f. med.L *dranculus*, *dracunculus* dimin. of *draco* serpent]

ransack /ˈrænsæk/ *v.tr.* **1** pillage or plunder (a house, country, etc.). **2** thoroughly search (a place, a receptacle, a person's pockets, one's conscience, etc.). □□ **ransacker** *n.* [ME f. ON *rannsaka* f. *rann* house + *-saka* f. *sœkja* seek]

ransom /ˈrænsəm/ *n. & v.* —*n.* **1** a sum of money or other payment demanded or paid for the release of a prisoner. **2** the liberation of a prisoner in return for this. —*v.tr.* **1** buy the freedom or restoration of; redeem. **2** hold to ransom. **3** release for a ransom. □□ **ransomer** *n.* (in sense 1 of *v.*). [ME f. OF *ransoun(er)* f. L *redemptio -onis* REDEMPTION]

rant /rænt/ *v. & n.* —*v.* **1** *intr.* use bombastic language. **2** *tr. & intr.* declaim, recite theatrically. **3** *tr. & intr.* preach noisily. —*n.* **1** a piece of ranting, a tirade. **2** empty turgid talk. □□ **ranter** *n.* **rantingly** *n.* [Du. *ranten* rave]

ranunculaceous /rəˌnʌŋkjuˈleɪʃəs/ *adj.* of or relating to the family Ranunculaceae of flowering plants, including clematis and delphiniums.

ranunculus /rəˈnæŋkjʊləs/ *n.* (*pl.* **ranunculuses** or **ranunculi** /-ˌlaɪ/) any plant of the genus *Ranunculus*, usu. having bowl-shaped flowers with many stamens and carpels, including buttercups and crowfoots. [L, orig. dimin. of *rana* frog]

RAOC *abbr.* (in the UK) Royal Army Ordnance Corps.

rap¹ /ræp/ *n. & v.* —*n.* **1** a smart slight blow. **2** a knock, a sharp tapping sound. **3** *sl.* blame, censure, or punishment. **4** *sl.* a conversation. **5 a** a rhyming monologue recited rhythmically to prerecorded music. **b** (in full **rap music**) a style of rock music with a pronounced beat and words recited rather than sung. —*v.* (**rapped**, **rapping**) **1** *tr.* strike smartly. **2** *intr.* knock; make a sharp tapping sound (*rapped on the table*). **3** *tr.* criticize adversely. **4** *intr. sl.* talk. □ **beat the rap** *US* escape punishment. **rap on** (or **over**) **the knuckles** a reprimand or reproof. **rap out 1** utter (an oath, order, pun, etc.) abruptly or on the spur of the moment. **2** *Spiritualism* express (a message or word) by raps. **take the rap** suffer the consequences. □□ **rapper** *n.* [ME, prob. imit.]

rap² /ræp/ *n.* a small amount, the least bit (*don't care a rap*). [Ir. *ropaire* Irish counterfeit coin]

rapacious /rəˈpeɪʃəs/ *adj.* grasping, extortionate, predatory. □□ **rapaciously** *adv.* **rapaciousness** *n.* **rapacity** /rəˈpæsɪtɪ/ *n.* [L *rapax -acis* f. *rapere* snatch]

RAPC *abbr.* (in the UK) Royal Army Pay Corps.

rape¹ /reɪp/ *n. & v.* —*n.* **1 a** the act of forcing a woman to have sexual intercourse against her will. **b** forcible sodomy. **2** (often foll. by *of*) violent assault, forcible interference, violation. **3** *poet.* carrying off (esp. of a woman) by force. **4** an instance of rape. —*v.tr.* **1** commit rape on (a person, usu. a woman). **2** violate, assault, pillage. **3** *poet.* take by force. [ME f. AF *rap(er)* f. L *rapere* seize]

rape² /reɪp/ *n.* a plant, *Brassica napus*, grown as food for sheep and for its seed, from which oil is made. Also called COLZA, COLE. □ **rape-cake** rape-seed pressed into a flat shape after the extraction of oil and used as manure or cattle food. **rape-oil** an oil made from rape-seed and used as a lubricant and in foodstuffs. [ME f. L *rapum*, *rapa* turnip]

rape³ /reɪp/ *n. hist.* (in the UK) any of the six ancient divisions of Sussex. [OE, var. of *rāp* ROPE, with ref. to the fencing-off of land]

rape⁴ /reɪp/ *n.* **1** the refuse of grapes after winemaking, used in making vinegar. **2** a vessel used in vinegar-making. [F *râpe*, med.L *raspa*]

raphia var. of RAFFIA.

raphide /ˈreɪfaɪd/ *n.* a needle-shaped crystal of an irritant substance such as oxalic acid formed in a plant. [back-form. f. *raphides* pl. of *raphis* f. Gk *rhaphis -idos* needle]

rapid /ˈræpɪd/ *adj. & n.* —*adj.* (**rapider**, **rapidest**) **1** quick, swift. **2** acting or completed in a short time. **3** (of a slope) descending steeply. **4** *Photog.* fast. —*n.* (usu. in *pl.*) a steep descent in a river-bed, with a swift current. □ **rapid eye-movement** a type of jerky movement of the eyes during periods of dreaming. **rapid-fire** (*attrib.*) fired, asked, etc., in quick succession. **rapid transit** (*attrib.*) denoting high-speed urban transport of passengers. □□ **rapidity** /rəˈpɪdɪtɪ/ *n.* **rapidly** *adv.* **rapidness** *n.* [L *rapidus* f. *rapere* seize]

rapier /ˈreɪpɪə(r)/ *n.* a light slender sword used for thrusting. [prob. f. Du. *rapier* or LG *rappir*, f. F *rapière*, of unkn. orig.]

rapine /ˈræpaɪn, -pɪn/ *n. rhet.* plundering, robbery. [ME f. OF or f. L *rapina* f. *rapere* seize]

rapist /ˈreɪpɪst/ *n.* a person who commits rape.

rapparee /ˌræpəˈriː/ *n. hist.* a 17th-c. Irish irregular soldier or freebooter. [Ir. *rapaire* short pike]

rappee /ræˈpiː/ *n.* a coarse kind of snuff. [F (*tabac*) *râpé* rasped (tobacco)]

rappel /ræˈpel/ *n. & v.intr.* (**rappelled**, **rappelling**; *US* **rappeled**, **rappeling**) = ABSEIL. [F, = recall, f. *rappeler* (as RE-, APPEAL)]

rapport /ræˈpɔː(r)/ *n.* **1** relationship or communication, esp. when useful and harmonious (*in rapport with*; *establish a rapport*). **2** *Spiritualism* communication through a medium. [F f. *rapporter* (as RE-, AP-, *porter* f. L *portare* carry)]

rapporteur /ˌræpɔːˈtɜː(r)/ *n.* a person who prepares an account of the proceedings of a committee etc. for a higher body. [F (as RAPPORT)]

rapprochement /ræˈprɒʃmɑ̃/ *n.* the resumption of harmonious relations, esp. between States. [F f. *rapprocher* (as RE-, APPROACH)]

rapscallion /ræpˈskæljən/ *n. archaic* or *joc.* a rascal, scamp, or rogue. [earlier *rascallion*, perh. f. RASCAL]

rapt /ræpt/ *adj.* **1** fully absorbed or intent, enraptured (*listen with rapt attention*). **2** carried away with feeling or lofty thought. **3** carried away bodily. □□ **raptly** *adv.* **raptness** *n.* [ME f. L *raptus* past part. of *rapere* seize]

raptor /ˈræptə(r)/ *n.* any bird of prey, e.g. an owl, falcon, etc. [L, = ravisher, plunderer f. *rapere* rapt-seize]

raptorial /ræpˈtɔːrɪəl/ *adj. & n.* —*adj.* (of a bird or animal) adapted for seizing prey; predatory. —*n.* **1** = RAPTOR. **2** a predatory animal. [L *raptor*: see RAPTOR]

rapture /ˈræptʃə(r)/ *n.* **1 a** ecstatic delight, mental transport. **b** (in *pl.*) great pleasure or enthusiasm or the expression of it. **2** *archaic* the act of transporting a person from one place to another. □ **go into** (or **be in**) **raptures** be enthusiastic; talk enthusiastically. □□ **rapturous** *adj.* **rapturously** *adv.* **rapturousness** *n.* [obs. F *rapture* or med.L *raptura* (as RAPT)]

rara avis /ˌreərə ˈeɪvɪs, ˌrɑːrə ˈævɪs/ *n.* (*pl.* *rarae aves* /-riː -viːz/) a rarity; a kind of person or thing rarely encountered. [L, = rare bird]

rare¹ /reə(r)/ *adj.* (**rarer**, **rarest**) **1** seldom done or found or occurring, uncommon, unusual, few and far between. **2** exceptionally good (*had a rare time*). **3** of less than the usual density, with only loosely packed substance (*the rare atmosphere of the mountain tops*). □ **rare bird** = RARA AVIS. **rare earth 1** a lanthanide element. **2** an oxide of such an element. **rare gas** = noble gas. □□ **rareness** *n.* [ME f. L *rarus*]

rare² /reə(r)/ *adj.* (**rarer**, **rarest**) (of meat) underdone. [var. of obs. *rear* half-cooked (of eggs), f. OE *hrēr*]

rarebit /ˈreəbɪt/ *n.* = *Welsh rabbit*. [RARE¹ + BIT¹]

raree-show /ˈreəriːˌʃəʊ/ *n.* **1** a show or spectacle. **2** a show carried about in a box; a peep-show. [app. = *rare show* as pronounced by Savoyard showmen]

rarefy /ˈreərɪˌfaɪ/ *v.* (**-ies**, **-ied**) **1** *tr. & intr.* make or become less dense or solid (*rarefied air*). **2** *tr.* purify or refine (a person's nature etc.). **3** *tr.* make (an idea etc.) subtle. □□ **rarefaction** /-ˈfækʃ(ə)n/ *n.*

rarefactive /-'fæktɪv/ *adj.* **rarefication** /-fɪ'keɪʃ(ə)n/ *n.* [ME f. OF *rarefier* or med.L *rarificare* f. L *rarefacere* f. *rarus* rare + *facere* make]

rarely /'reəlɪ/ *adv.* **1** seldom; not often. **2** in an unusual degree; exceptionally. **3** exceptionally well.

raring /'reərɪŋ/ *adj.* (foll. by *to* + infin.) *colloq.* enthusiastic, eager (*raring to go*). [part. of rare, dial. var. of ROAR or REAR²]

rarity /'reərɪtɪ/ *n.* (*pl.* **-ies**) **1** rareness. **2** an uncommon thing, esp. one valued for being rare. [F *rareté* or L *raritas* (as RARE¹)]

rascal /'rɑːsk(ə)l/ *n.* often *joc.* a dishonest or mischievous person, esp. a child. □□ **rascaldom** *n.* **rascalism** *n.* **rascality** /-'skælɪtɪ/ *n.* (*pl.* **-ies**). **rascally** *adj.* [ME f. OF *rascaille* rabble, prob. ult. f. L *radere ras-* scrape]

rase var. of RAZE.

rash¹ /ræʃ/ *adj.* reckless, impetuous, hasty; acting or done without due consideration. □□ **rashly** *adv.* **rashness** *n.* [ME, prob. f. OE *ræsc* (unrecorded) f. Gmc]

rash² /ræʃ/ *n.* **1** an eruption of the skin in spots or patches. **2** (usu. foll. by *of*) a sudden widespread phenomenon, esp. of something unwelcome (*a rash of strikes*). [18th c.: prob. rel. to OF *ra(s)che* eruptive sores. = It. *raschia* itch]

rasher /'ræʃə(r)/ *n.* a thin slice of bacon or ham. [16th c.: orig. unkn.]

rasp /rɑːsp/ *n.* & *v.* —*n.* a coarse kind of file having separate teeth. —*v.* **1** *tr.* **a** scrape with a rasp. **b** scrape roughly. **c** (foll. by *off*, *away*) remove by scraping. **2 a** *intr.* make a grating sound. **b** *tr.* say gratingly or hoarsely. **3** *tr.* grate upon (a person or a person's feelings), irritate. □□ **raspingly** *adv.* **raspy** *adj.* [ME f. OF *raspe(r)* ult. f. WG]

raspberry /'rɑːzbərɪ/ *n.* (*pl.* **-ies**) **1 a** a bramble, *Rubus idaeus*, having usu. red berries consisting of numerous drupels on a conical receptacle. **b** this berry. **2** any of various red colours. **3** *colloq.* **a** a sound made with the lips expressing dislike, derision, or disapproval (orig. *raspberry tart*, rhyming sl. = *fart*). **b** a show of strong disapproval (*got a raspberry from the audience*). □ **raspberry-cane** a raspberry plant. **raspberry vinegar** a kind of syrup made from raspberries. [16th-c. *rasp* (now dial.) f. obs. *raspis*, of unkn. orig., + BERRY]

rasper /'rɑːspə(r)/ *n.* **1** a person or thing that rasps. **2** *Hunting* a high difficult fence.

Rasta /'ræstə/ *n.* & *adj.* = RASTAFARIAN. [abbr.]

Rastafarian /ˌræstə'feərɪən/ *n.* & *adj.* —*n.* a member of a sect of Jamaican origin regarding Blacks as a chosen people and the former Emperor Haile Selassie of Ethiopia (d. 1975, entitled *Ras Tafari*) as God. —*adj.* of or relating to this sect. □□ **Rastafarianism** *n.*

raster /'ræstə(r)/ *n.* a pattern of scanning lines for a cathode-ray tube picture. [G, = screen, f. L *rastrum* rake f. *radere ras-* scrape]

rat /ræt/ *n.* & *v.* —*n.* **1 a** any of several rodents of the genus *Rattus* (*brown rat*). **b** any similar rodent (*muskrat*; *water-rat*). **2** a deserter from a party, cause, difficult situation, etc.; a turncoat (from the superstition that rats desert a sinking ship). **3** *colloq.* an unpleasant person. **4** a worker who refuses to join a strike, or who blacklegs. **5** (in *pl.*) *sl.* an exclamation of contempt, annoyance, etc. —*v.intr.* (**ratted, ratting**) **1** (of a person or dog) hunt or kill rats. **2** *colloq.* desert a cause, party, etc. **3** (foll. by *on*) **a** betray; let down. **b** inform on. □ **rat-catcher** a person who rids buildings of rats etc. **rat kangaroo** *Austral.* any of various small ratlike marsupials of the family Potoroidae, having kangaroo-like hind limbs for jumping. **rat race** a fiercely competitive struggle for position, power, etc. **rat's tail** a thing shaped like a rat's tail, e.g. a tapering cylindrical file. **rat-tail** **1** the grenadier fish. **2** a horse with a hairless tail. **3** such a tail. **rat-tail** (or **-tailed**) **spoon** a spoon with a tail-like moulding from the handle to the back of the bowl. [OE *ræt* & OF *rat*]

rata /'rɑːtə/ *n.* any large tree of the genus *Metrosideros*, esp. *M. robusta* of New Zealand, with crimson flowers and hard red wood. [Maori]

ratable var. of RATEABLE.

ratafia /ˌrætə'fiːə/ *n.* **1** a liqueur flavoured with almonds or kernels of peach, apricot, or cherry. **2** a kind of biscuit similarly flavoured. [F, perh. rel. to TAFIA]

ratan var. of RATTAN.

rataplan /ˌrætə'plæn/ *n.* & *v.* —*n.* a drumming sound. —*v.* (**rataplanned, rataplanning**) **1** *tr.* play (a tune) on or as on a drum. **2** *intr.* make a rataplan. [F: imit.]

ratatat (also **rat-a-tat**) var. of RAT-TAT.

ratatouille /ˌrætə'tuːɪ, -'twiː/ *n.* a vegetable dish made of stewed onions, courgettes, tomatoes, aubergines, and peppers. [F dial.]

ratbag /'rætbæg/ *n.* *sl.* an unpleasant or disgusting person.

ratch /rætʃ/ *n.* **1** a ratchet. **2** a ratchet-wheel. [perh. f. G *Ratsche*: cf. RATCHET]

ratchet /'rætʃɪt/ *n.* & *v.* —*n.* **1** a set of teeth on the edge of a bar or wheel in which a device engages to ensure motion in one direction only. **2** (in full **ratchet-wheel**) a wheel with a rim so toothed. —*v.* (**ratcheted, ratcheting**) **1** *tr.* **a** provide with a ratchet. **b** make into a ratchet. **2** *tr.* & *intr.* move as under the control of a ratchet. [F *rochet* blunt lance-head, bobbin, ratchet, etc., prob. ult. f. Gmc]

rate¹ /reɪt/ *n.* & *v.* —*n.* **1** a stated numerical proportion between two sets of things (the second usu. expressed as unity), esp. as a measure of amount or degree (*moving at a rate of 50 miles per hour*) or as the basis of calculating an amount or value (*rate of taxation*). **2** a fixed or appropriate charge or cost or value; a measure of this (*postal rates*; *the rate for the job*). **3** rapidity of movement or change (*travelling at a great rate*; *prices increasing at a dreadful rate*). **4** class or rank (*first-rate*). **5** *Brit.* **a** an assessment levied by local authorities at so much per pound of the assessed value of buildings and land owned or leased. **b** (in *pl.*) the amount payable by this. —*v.* **1** *tr.* **a** estimate the worth or value of (*I do not rate him very highly*). **b** assign a fixed value to (a coin or metal) in relation to a monetary standard. **c** assign a value to (work, the power of a machine, etc.). **2** *tr.* consider; regard as (*I rate them among my benefactors*). **3** *intr.* (foll. by *as*) rank or be rated. **4** *tr.* *Brit.* **a** subject to the payment of a local rate. **b** value for the purpose of assessing rates. **5** *tr.* be worthy of, deserve. **6** *tr.* *Naut.* place in a specified class (cf. RATING¹). □ **at any rate** in any case, whatever happens. **at this** (or **that**) **rate** if this example is typical or this assumption is true. **rate-capping** *Brit.* the imposition of an upper limit on the rate leviable by a local authority. [ME f. OF f. med.L *rata* f. L *pro rata parte* or *portione* according to the proportional share f. *ratus* past part. of *rēri* reckon]

rate² /reɪt/ *v.tr.* scold angrily. [ME: orig. unkn.]

rate³ var. of RET.

rateable /'reɪtəb(ə)l/ *adj.* (also **ratable**) **1** *Brit.* liable to payment of rates. **2** able to be rated or estimated. □ **rateable value** the value at which a house etc. is assessed for payment of rates. □□ **rateability** /-'bɪlɪtɪ/ *n.* **rateably** *adv.*

ratel /'reɪt(ə)l, 'rɑː-/ *n.* an African and Indian nocturnal flesh-eating burrowing mammal, *Mellivora capensis*. Also called *honey-badger*. [Afrik., of unkn. orig.]

ratepayer /'reɪtˌpeɪə(r)/ *n.* *Brit.* a person liable to pay rates.

rathe /reɪð/ *adj.* *poet.* coming, blooming, etc., early in the year or day. □ **rathe-ripe** **1** ripening early. **2** precocious. [OE *hræth*, *hræd* f. Gmc]

rather /'rɑːðə(r)/ *adv.* **1** (often foll. by *than*) by preference; for choice (*would rather not go*; *would rather stay than go*). **2** (usu. foll. by *than*) more truly; as a more likely alternative (*is stupid rather than* *honest*). **3** more precisely (*a book, or rather, a pamphlet*). **4** slightly; to some extent; somewhat (*became rather drunk; I rather think you know him*). **5** /rɑːˈɔ̃ː(r)/ *Brit.* (as an emphatic response) indeed, assuredly (*Did you like it?—Rather!*). □**had rather** would rather. [ME f. OE *hrathor*, compar. of *hræthe* (adv.) f. *hræth* (adj.): see RATHE]

rathskeller /ˈrɑːtsˌkelə(r)/ *n.* *US* a beer-saloon or restaurant in a basement. [G, = (restaurant in) town-hall cellar]

ratify /ˈrætɪˌfaɪ/ *v.tr.* (**-ies, -ied**) confirm or accept (an agreement made in one's name) by formal consent, signature, etc. □□**ratifiable** *adj.* **ratification** /-fɪˈkeɪʃ(ə)n/ *n.* **ratifier** *n.* [ME f. OF *ratifier* f. med.L *ratificare* (as RATE[1])]

rating[1] /ˈreɪtɪŋ/ *n.* **1** the act or an instance of placing in a rank or class or assigning a value to. **2** the estimated standing of a person as regards credit etc. **3** *Naut.* **a** *Brit.* a non-commissioned sailor. **b** a person's position or class on a ship's books. **4** *Brit.* an amount fixed as a local rate. **5** the relative popularity of a broadcast programme as determined by the estimated size of the audience. **6** *Naut.* any of the classes into which racing yachts are distributed by tonnage.

rating[2] /ˈreɪtɪŋ/ *n.* an angry reprimand.

ratio /ˈreɪʃɪəʊ/ *n.* (*pl.* **-os**) the quantitative relation between two similar magnitudes determined by the number of times one contains the other integrally or fractionally (*in the ratio of three to two; the ratios 1:5 and 20:100 are the same*). [L (as RATE[1])]

ratiocinate /ˌrætɪˈɒsɪˌneɪt, ˌræʃɪ-/ *v.intr.* *literary* go through logical processes, reason, esp. using syllogisms. □□**ratiocination** /-ˈneɪʃ(ə)n/ *n.* **ratiocinative** /-nətɪv/ *adj.* **ratiocinator** *n.* [L *ratiocinari* (as RATIO)]

ration /ˈræʃ(ə)n/ *n.* & *v.* —*n.* **1** a fixed official allowance of food, clothing, etc., in a time of shortage. **2** (foll. by *of*) a single portion of provisions, fuel, clothing, etc. **3** (usu. in *pl.*) a fixed daily allowance of food, esp. in the armed forces (and formerly of forage for animals). **4** (in *pl.*) provisions. —*v.tr.* **1** limit (persons or provisions) to a fixed ration. **2** (usu. foll. by *out*) share out (food etc.) in fixed quantities. □**given out with the rations** *Mil. sl.* awarded without regard to merit. **ration book** (or **card**) a document entitling the holder to a ration. [F f. It. *razione* or Sp. *ración* f. L *ratio -onis* reckoning, RATIO]

rational /ˈræʃən(ə)l/ *adj.* **1** of or based on reasoning or reason. **2** sensible, sane, moderate; not foolish or absurd or extreme. **3** endowed with reason, reasoning. **4** rejecting what is unreasonable or cannot be tested by reason in religion or custom. **5** *Math.* (of a quantity or ratio) expressible as a ratio of whole numbers. □**rational dress** *hist.* a style of dress adopted by some women in the late nineteenth century, including bloomers or knickerbockers. **rational horizon** see HORIZON 1c. □□**rationality** /-ˈnælɪtɪ/ *n.* **rationally** *adv.* [ME f. L *rationalis* (as RATION)]

rationale /ˌræʃəˈnɑːl/ *n.* **1** (often foll. by *of*) the fundamental reason or logical basis of anything. **2** a reasoned exposition; a statement of reasons. [mod.L, neut. of L *rationalis*: see RATIONAL]

rationalism /ˈræʃənəˌlɪz(ə)m/ *n.* **1** *Philos.* the theory that reason is the foundation of certainty in knowledge (opp. EMPIRICISM (see EMPIRIC), SENSATIONALISM). **2** *Theol.* the practice of treating reason as the ultimate authority in religion. **3** a belief in reason rather than religion as a guiding principle in life. □□**rationalist** *n.* **rationalistic** /-ˈlɪstɪk/ *adj.* **rationalistically** /-ˈlɪstɪkəlɪ/ *adv.*

rationalize /ˈræʃənəˌlaɪz/ *v.* (also **-ise**) **1 a** *tr.* offer or subconsciously adopt a rational but specious explanation of (one's behaviour or attitude). **b** *intr.* explain one's behaviour or attitude in this way. **2** *tr.* make logical and consistent. **3** *tr.* make (a business etc.) more efficient by reorganizing it to reduce or

eliminate waste of labour, time, or materials. **4** *tr.* (often foll. by *away*) explain or explain away rationally. **5** *tr.* *Math.* clear of surds. **6** *intr.* be or act as a rationalist. □□**rationalization** /-ˈzeɪʃ(ə)n/ *n.* **rationalizer** *n.*

ratite /ˈrætaɪt/ *adj.* & *n.* —*adj.* (of a bird) having a keelless breastbone, and unable to fly (opp. CARINATE). —*n.* a flightless bird, e.g. an ostrich, emu, cassowary, etc. [L *ratis* raft]

ratline /ˈrætlɪn/ *n.* (also **ratlin**) (usu. in *pl.*) any of the small lines fastened across a sailing-ship's shrouds like ladder-rungs. [ME: orig. unkn.]

ratoon /rəˈtuːn/ *n.* & *v.* —*n.* a new shoot springing from a root of sugar cane etc. after cropping. —*v.intr.* send up ratoons. [Sp. *retoño* sprout]

ratsbane /ˈrætsbeɪn/ *n.* anything poisonous to rats, esp. a plant.

rattan /rəˈtæn/ *n.* (also **ratan**) **1** any East Indian climbing palm of the genus *Calamus* etc. with long thin jointed pliable stems. **2** a piece of rattan stem used as a walking stick etc. [earlier *rot(t)ang* f. Malay *rōtan* prob. f. *raut* pare]

rat-tat /rætˈtæt/ *n.* (also **rat-tat-tat** /ˌrættætˈtæt/, **ratatat, rat-a-tat** /ˌrætəˈtæt/) a rapping sound, esp. of a knocker. [imit.]

ratter /ˈrætə(r)/ *n.* **1** a dog or other animal that hunts rats. **2** *sl.* a person who betrays a cause, party, friend, etc.

rattle /ˈræt(ə)l/ *v.* & *n.* —*v.* **1 a** *intr.* give out a rapid succession of short sharp hard sounds. **b** *tr.* make (a chair, window, crockery, etc.) do this. **c** *intr.* cause such sounds by shaking something (*rattled at the door*). **2 a** *intr.* move with a rattling noise. **b** *intr.* drive a vehicle or ride or run briskly. **c** *tr.* cause to move quickly (*the bill was rattled through Parliament*). **3 a** *tr.* (usu. foll. by *off*) say or recite rapidly. **b** *intr.* (usu. foll. by *on*) talk in a lively thoughtless way. **4** *tr.* *colloq.* disconcert, alarm, fluster, make nervous, frighten. —*n.* **1** a rattling sound. **2** an instrument or plaything made to rattle esp. in order to amuse babies or to give an alarm. **3** the set of horny rings in a rattlesnake's tail. **4** a plant with seeds that rattle in their cases when ripe (*red rattle*; *yellow rattle*). **5** uproar, bustle, noisy gaiety, racket. **6 a** a noisy flow of words. **b** empty chatter, trivial talk. **7** *archaic* a lively or thoughtless incessant talker. □**rattle the sabre** threaten war. □□**rattly** *adj.* [ME, prob. f. MDu. & LG *ratelen* (imit.)]

rattlebox /ˈræt(ə)lˌbɒks/ *n.* **1** a rattle consisting of a box with objects inside. **2** a rickety old vehicle etc.

rattler /ˈrætlə(r)/ *n.* **1** a thing that rattles, esp. an old or rickety vehicle. **2** *colloq.* a rattlesnake. **3** *sl.* a remarkably good specimen of anything.

rattlesnake /ˈræt(ə)lˌsneɪk/ *n.* any of various poisonous American snakes of the family Viperidae, esp. of the genus *Crotalus* or *Sistrurus*, with a rattling structure of horny rings in its tail.

rattletrap /ˈræt(ə)lˌtræp/ *n.* & *adj.* *colloq.* —*n.* a rickety old vehicle etc. —*adj.* rickety.

rattling /ˈrætlɪŋ/ *adj.* & *adv.* —*adj.* **1** that rattles. **2** brisk, vigorous (*a rattling pace*). —*adv.* remarkably (*a rattling good story*).

ratty /ˈrætɪ/ *adj.* (**rattier, rattiest**) **1** relating to or infested with rats. **2** *colloq.* irritable or angry. **3** *colloq.* wretched, nasty. □□**rattily** *adv.* **rattiness** *n.*

raucous /ˈrɔːkəs/ *adj.* harsh-sounding, loud and hoarse. □□**raucously** *adv.* **raucousness** *n.* [L *raucus*]

raunchy /ˈrɔːntʃɪ/ *adj.* (**raunchier, raunchiest**) *colloq.* **1** coarse, earthy, boisterous; sexually provocative. **2** esp. *US* slovenly, grubby. □□**raunchily** *adv.* **raunchiness** *n.* [20th c.: orig. unkn.]

ravage /ˈrævɪdʒ/ *v.* & *n.* —*v.tr.* & *intr.* devastate, plunder. —*n.* **1** the act or an instance of ravaging; devastation, damage. **2** (usu. in *pl.*; foll. by *of*) destructive effect (*survived the ravages of winter*). □□**ravager** *n.* [F *ravage(r)* alt. f. *ravine* rush of water]

rave[1] /reɪv/ v. & n. —v. **1** intr. talk wildly or furiously in or as in delirium. **2** intr. (usu. foll. by *about*, *of*, *over*) speak with rapturous admiration; go into raptures. **3** tr. bring into a specified state by raving (*raved himself hoarse*). **4** tr. utter with ravings (*raved their grief*). **5** intr. (of the sea, wind, etc.) howl, roar. **6** tr. & intr. colloq. enjoy oneself freely (esp. *rave it up*). —n. **1** (usu. *attrib*.) colloq. a highly enthusiastic review of a film, play, etc. (*a rave review*). **2** sl. an infatuation. **3** (also **rave-up**) colloq. a lively party. **4** the sound of the wind etc. raving. [ME, prob. f. ONF *raver*, rel. to (M)LG *reven* be senseless, rave]

rave[2] /reɪv/ n. **1** a rail of a cart. **2** (in *pl*.) a permanent or removable framework added to the sides of a cart to increase its capacity. [var. of dial. *rathe* (15th c., of unkn. orig.)]

ravel /ˈræv(ə)l/ v. & n. —v. (**ravelled**, **ravelling**; US **raveled**, **raveling**) **1** tr. & intr. entangle or become entangled or knotted. **2** tr. confuse or complicate (a question or problem). **3** intr. fray out. **4** tr. (often foll. by *out*) disentangle, unravel, distinguish the separate threads or subdivisions of. —n. **1** a tangle or knot. **2** a complication. **3** a frayed or loose end. [prob. f. Du. *ravelen* tangle, fray out, unweave]

ravelin /ˈrævlɪn/ n. hist. an outwork of fortifications, with two faces forming a salient angle. [F f. obs. It. *ravellino*, of unkn. orig.]

ravelling /ˈrævəlɪŋ/ n. a thread from fabric which is frayed or unravelled.

raven[1] /ˈreɪv(ə)n/ n. & adj. —n. a large glossy blue-black crow, *Corvus corax*, feeding chiefly on carrion etc., having a hoarse cry. —adj. glossy black (*raven tresses*). [OE *hræfn* f. Gmc]

raven[2] /ˈræv(ə)n/ v. **1** intr. **a** plunder. **b** (foll. by *after*) seek prey or booty. **c** (foll. by *about*) go plundering. **d** prowl for prey (*ravening beast*). **2 a** tr. devour voraciously. **b** intr. (usu. foll. by *for*) have a ravenous appetite. **c** intr. (often foll. by *on*) feed voraciously. [OF *raviner* ravage ult. f. L *rapina* RAPINE]

ravenous /ˈrævənəs/ adj. **1** very hungry, famished. **2** (of hunger, eagerness, etc., or of an animal) voracious. **3** rapacious. ☐☐ **ravenously** adv. **ravenousness** n. [ME f. OF *ravineus* (as RAVEN[2])]

raver /ˈreɪvə(r)/ n. **1** colloq. an uninhibited pleasure-loving person. **2** a person who raves; a madman or madwoman.

ravin /ˈrævɪn/ n. poet. or rhet. **1** robbery, plundering. **2** the seizing and devouring of prey. **3** prey. ☐ **beast of ravin** a beast of prey. [ME f. OF *ravine* f. L *rapina* RAPINE]

ravine /rəˈviːn/ n. a deep narrow gorge or cleft. ☐☐ **ravined** adj. [F (as RAVIN)]

raving /ˈreɪvɪŋ/ n., adj., & adv. —n. (usu. in *pl*.) wild or delirious talk. —adj. delirious, frenzied. —adj. & adv. colloq. as an intensive (*a raving beauty*; *raving mad*). ☐☐ **ravingly** adv.

ravioli /ˌrævɪˈəʊlɪ/ n. small pasta envelopes containing minced meat etc. [It.]

ravish /ˈrævɪʃ/ v.tr. **1** commit rape on (a woman). **2** enrapture; fill with delight. **3** archaic **a** carry off (a person or thing) by force. **b** (of death, circumstances, etc.) take from life or from sight. ☐☐ **ravisher** n. **ravishment** n. [ME f. OF *ravir* ult. f. L *rapere* seize]

ravishing /ˈrævɪʃɪŋ/ adj. entrancing, delightful. ☐☐ **ravishingly** adv.

raw /rɔː/ adj. & n. —adj. **1** (of food) uncooked. **2** in the natural state; not processed or manufactured (*raw sewage*). **3** (of alcoholic spirit) undiluted. **4** (of statistics etc.) not analysed or processed. **5** (of a person) inexperienced, untrained; new to an activity (*raw recruits*). **6 a** stripped of skin; having the flesh exposed. **b** sensitive to the touch from having the flesh exposed. **7** (of the atmosphere, day, etc.) chilly and damp. **8** crude in artistic quality; lacking finish. **9** (of the edge of cloth) without hem or selvage. **10** (of silk) as reeled from cocoons. **11** (of grain) unmalted. —n. a raw place on a person's or horse's body.

☐ **come the raw prawn** Austral. sl. attempt to deceive. **in the raw** **1** in its natural state without mitigation (*life in the raw*). **2** naked. **raw-boned** gaunt and bony. **raw deal** harsh or unfair treatment. **raw material** that from which the process of manufacture makes products. **raw sienna** a brownish-yellow ferruginous earth used as a pigment. **raw umber** umber in its natural state, dark yellow in colour. **touch on the raw** upset (a person) on a sensitive matter. ☐☐ **rawish** adj. **rawly** adv. **rawness** n. [OE *hrēaw* f. Gmc]

rawhide /ˈrɔːhaɪd/ n. **1** untanned hide. **2** a rope or whip of this.

Rawlplug /ˈrɔːlplʌg/ n. propr. a thin cylindrical plug for holding a screw or nail in masonry. [*Rawlings*, name of the engineers who introduced it]

ray[1] /reɪ/ n. & v. —n. **1** a single line or narrow beam of light from a small or distant source. **2** a straight line in which radiation travels to a given point. **3** (in *pl*.) radiation of a specified type (*gamma rays*; *X-rays*). **4** a trace or beginning of an enlightening or cheering influence (*a ray of hope*). **5 a** any of a set of radiating lines or parts of things. **b** any of a set of straight lines passing through one point. **6** the marginal portion of a composite flower, e.g. a daisy. **7 a** a radial division of a starfish. **b** each of a set of bones etc. supporting a fish's fin. —v. **1** intr. (foll. by *forth*, *out*) (of light, thought, emotion, etc.) issue in or as if in rays. **2** intr. & tr. radiate. ☐ **ray gun** (esp. in science fiction) a gun causing injury or damage by the emission of rays. ☐☐ **rayed** adj. **rayless** adj. **raylet** n. [ME f. OF *rai* f. L *radius*: see RADIUS]

ray[2] /reɪ/ n. a large cartilaginous fish of the order Batoidea, with a broad flat body, winglike pectoral fins and a long slender tail, used as food. [ME f. OF *raie* f. L *raia*]

ray[3] /reɪ/ n. (also **re**) Mus. **1** (in tonic sol-fa) the second note of a major scale. **2** the note D in the fixed-doh system. [ME *re* f. L *resonare*: see GAMUT]

rayon /ˈreɪɒn/ n. any of various textile fibres or fabrics made from cellulose. [arbitrary f. RAY[1]]

raze /reɪz/ v.tr. (also **rase**) **1** completely destroy; tear down (esp. *raze to the ground*). **2** erase; scratch out (esp. in abstract senses). [ME *rase* = wound slightly f. OF *raser* shave close ult. f. L *radere* *ras-* scrape]

razor /ˈreɪzə(r)/ n. & v. —n. an instrument with a sharp blade used in cutting hair esp. from the skin. —v.tr. **1** use a razor on. **2** shave; cut down close. ☐ **razor-back** an animal with a sharp ridged back, esp. a rorqual. **razor-bill** an auk, *Alca torda*, with a sharp-edged bill. **razor-blade** a blade used in a razor, esp. a flat piece of metal with a sharp edge or edges used in a safety razor. **razor-cut** a haircut made with a razor. **razor-** (or **razor's**) **edge** **1** a keen edge. **2** a sharp mountain-ridge. **3** a critical situation (*found themselves on a razor-edge*). **4** a sharp line of division. **razor-fish** (or **-shell**) any of various bivalve molluscs of the family Solenidae, with a shell like the handle of a cutthroat razor. [ME f. OF *rasor* (as RAZE)]

razz /ræz/ n. & v. US sl. —n. = RASPBERRY 3. —v.tr. tease, ridicule. [*razzberry*, corrupt. of RASPBERRY]

razzle-dazzle /ˈræzəlˌdæz(ə)l/ n. (also **razzle**) sl. **1 a** glamorous excitement; bustle. **b** a spree. **2** extravagant publicity. [redupl. of DAZZLE]

razzmatazz /ˌræzməˈtæz/ n. (also **razzamatazz** /ˌræzəmə-/) colloq. **1** = RAZZLE-DAZZLE. **2** insincere actions; humbug. [prob. alt. f. RAZZLE-DAZZLE]

Rb symb. Chem. the element rubidium.

RC abbr. **1** Roman Catholic. **2** Red Cross. **3** reinforced concrete.

RCA abbr. **1** (in the UK) Royal College of Art. **2** (in the US) Radio Corporation of America.

RCAF abbr. Royal Canadian Air Force.

RCM abbr. (in the UK) Royal College of Music.

RCMP abbr. Royal Canadian Mounted Police.

RCN abbr. **1** (in the UK) Royal College of Nursing. **2** Royal Canadian Navy.

RCP abbr. (in the UK) Royal College of Physicians.

RCS abbr. (in the UK): **1** Royal College of Scientists. **2** Royal College of Surgeons. **3** Royal Corps of Signals.

RCVS abbr. (in the UK) Royal College of Veterinary Surgeons.

RD abbr. **1** refer to drawer. **2** (in the UK) Royal Naval Reserve Decoration.

Rd. abbr. Road (in names).

RDC abbr. Brit. hist. Rural District Council.

RDF abbr. radio direction-finder.

RE abbr. **1** (in the UK) Royal Engineers. **2** religious education.

Re symb. Chem. the element rhenium.

re[1] /reɪ, riː/ prep. **1** in the matter of (as the first word in a heading, esp. of a legal document). **2** colloq. about, concerning. [L, ablat. of res thing]

re[2] var. of RAY[3].

re- /riː, rɪ, re/ prefix **1** attachable to almost any verb or its derivative, meaning: **a** once more; afresh, anew (readjust; renumber). **b** back; with return to a previous state (reassemble; reverse). ¶ A hyphen is normally used when the word begins with e (re-enact), or to distinguish the compound from a more familiar one-word form (re-form = form again). **2** (also **red-** before a vowel, as in redolent) in verbs and verbal derivatives denoting: **a** in return; mutually (react; resemble). **b** opposition (repel; resist). **c** behind or after (relic; remain). **d** retirement or secrecy (recluse; reticence). **e** off, away, down (recede; relegate; repress). **f** frequentative or intensive force (redouble; refine; resplendent). **g** negative force (recant; reveal). [L re-, red-, again, back, etc.]

reabsorb /ˌriːəbˈsɔːb, -ˈzɔːb/ v.tr. absorb again. □□ **reabsorption** n.

reaccept /ˌriːəkˈsept/ v.tr. accept again. □□ **reacceptance** n.

reaccustom /ˌriːəˈkʌstəm/ v.tr. accustom again.

reach /riːtʃ/ v. & n. —v. **1** intr. & tr. (often foll. by out) stretch out; extend. **2** intr. stretch out a limb, the hand, etc.; make a reaching motion or effort. **3** intr. (often foll. by for) make a motion or effort to touch or get hold of, or to attain (reached for his pipe). **4** tr. get as far as; arrive at (reached Lincoln at lunch-time; your letter reached me today). **5** tr. get to or attain (a specified point) on a scale (the temperature reached 90°; the number of applications reached 100). **6** intr. (foll. by to) attain to; be adequate for (my income will not reach to it). **7** tr. succeed in achieving; attain (have reached agreement). **8** tr. make contact with the hand etc., or by telephone etc. (was out all day and could not be reached). **9** tr. succeed in influencing or having the required effect on (could not manage to reach their audience). **10** tr. hand, pass (reach me that book). **11** tr. take with an outstretched hand. **12** intr. Naut. sail with the wind abeam or abaft the beam. —n. **1** the extent to which a hand etc. can be reached out, influence exerted, motion carried out, or mental powers used. **2** an act of reaching out. **3** a continuous extent, esp. a stretch of river between two bends, or the part of a canal between locks. **4** Naut. a distance traversed in reaching. □**out of reach** not able to be reached or attained. **reach-me-down** ready-made. □□ **reachable** adj. **reacher** n. [OE ræcan f. WG]

reacquaint /ˌriːəˈkweɪnt/ v.tr. & refl. (usu. foll. by with) make (a person or oneself) acquainted again. □□ **reacquaintance** n.

reacquire /ˌriːəˈkwaɪə(r)/ v.tr. acquire anew. □□ **reacquisition** /-ˌækwɪˈzɪʃ(ə)n/ n.

react /rɪˈækt/ v. **1** intr. (foll. by to) respond to a stimulus; undergo a change or show behaviour due to some influence (how did they react to the news?). **2** intr. (often foll. by against) be actuated by repulsion to; tend in a reverse or contrary direction. **3** intr. (often foll. by upon) produce a reciprocal or responsive effect; act upon the agent (they react upon each other). **4** intr. (foll. by with) Chem. & Physics (of a substance or particle) be the cause of activity or interaction with another (nitrous oxide reacts with the metal). **5** tr. (foll. by with) Chem. cause (a substance) to react with another. **6** intr. Mil. make a counter-attack. **7** intr. Stock Exch. (of shares) fall after rising. [RE- + ACT or med.L reagere react- (as RE-, L agere do, act)]

re-act /riːˈækt/ v.tr. act (a part) again.

reactance /rɪˈækt(ə)ns/ n. Electr. a component of impedance in an AC circuit, due to capacitance or inductance or both.

reactant /rɪˈækt(ə)nt/ n. Chem. a substance that takes part in, and undergoes change during a reaction.

reaction /rɪˈækʃ(ə)n/ n. **1** the act or an instance of reacting; a responsive or reciprocal action. **2 a** a responsive feeling (what was your reaction to the news?). **b** an immediate or first impression. **3** the occurrence of a (physical or emotional) condition after a period of its opposite. **4** a bodily response to an external stimulus, e.g. a drug. **5** a tendency to oppose change or to advocate return to a former system, esp. in politics. **6** the interaction of substances undergoing chemical change. **7** propulsion by emitting a jet of particles etc. in the direction opposite to that of the intended motion. □□ **reactionist** n. & adj. [REACT + -ION or med.L reactio (as RE-, ACTION)]

reactionary /rɪˈækʃənərɪ/ adj. & n. —adj. tending to oppose (esp. political) change and advocate return to a former system. —n. (pl. -ies) a reactionary person.

reactivate /rɪˈæktɪˌveɪt/ v.tr. restore to a state of activity; bring into action again. □□ **reactivation** /-ˈveɪʃ(ə)n/ n.

reactive /rɪˈæktɪv/ adj. **1** showing reaction. **2** of or relating to reactance. □□ **reactivity** /-ˈtɪvɪtɪ/ n.

reactor /rɪˈæktə(r)/ n. **1** a person or thing that reacts. **2** (in full **nuclear reactor**) an apparatus or structure in which a controlled nuclear chain reaction releases energy. **3** Electr. a component used to provide reactance, esp. an inductor. **4** an apparatus for the chemical reaction of substances. **5** Med. a person who has a reaction to a drug etc.

read /riːd/ v. & n. —v. (past and past part. **read** /red/) **1** tr. (also absol.) reproduce mentally or (often foll. by aloud, out, off, etc.) vocally the written or printed words of (a book, author, etc.) by following the symbols with the eyes or fingers. **2** tr. convert or be able to convert into the intended words or meaning (written or other symbols or the things expressed in this way). **3** tr. interpret mentally. **4** tr. deduce or declare an (esp. accurate) interpretation of (read the expression on my face). **5** tr. (often foll. by that +clause) find (a thing) recorded or stated in print etc. (I read somewhere that you are leaving). **6** tr. interpret (a statement or action) in a certain sense (my silence is not to be read as consent). **7** tr. (often foll. by into) assume as intended or deducible from a writer's words; find (implications) (you read too much into my letter). **8** tr. bring into a specified state by reading (read myself to sleep). **9** tr. (of a meter or other recording instrument) show (a specified figure etc.) (the thermometer reads 20°). **10** intr. convey meaning in a specified manner when read (it reads persuasively). **11** intr. sound or affect a hearer or reader as specified when read (the book reads like a parody). **12 a** tr. study by reading (esp. a subject at university). **b** intr. carry out a course of study by reading (is reading for the Bar). **13** tr. (as **read** /red/ adj.) versed in a subject (esp. literature) by reading (a well-read person; was widely read in law). **14** tr. **a** (of a computer) copy or transfer (data). **b** (foll. by in, out) enter or extract (data) in an electronic storage device. **15** tr. **a** understand or interpret (a person) by hearing words or seeing signs, gestures, etc. **b** interpret (cards, a person's hand, etc.) as a fortune-teller. **c** interpret (the sky) as an astrologer or meteorologist. **16** tr. Printing check the correctness of and emend (a proof). **17** tr. (of an editor or text) give as the word or words probably used or intended by an author. —*n.* **1** a spell of reading. **2** *colloq.* a book etc. as regards its readability (*is a really good read*). □**read between the lines** look for or find hidden meaning (in a document etc.). **read-in** the entry of data in an electronic storage device. **read a person like a book** understand a person's motives etc. **read-only memory** *Computing* a memory read at high speed but not capable of being changed by program instructions. **read out 1** read aloud. **2** *US* expel from a political party etc. **read-out** information retrieved from a computer. **read up** make a special study of (a subject). **read-write** *Computing* capable of reading existing data and accepting alterations or further input (cf. *read-only memory*). [OE *rǣdan* advise, consider, discern f. Gmc]

readable /ˈriːdəb(ə)l/ *adj.* **1** able to be read; legible. **2** interesting or pleasant to read. □□ **readability** /-ˈbɪlɪtɪ/ *n.* **readableness** *n.* **readably** *adv.*

readapt /ˌriːəˈdæpt/ *v.intr.* & *tr.* become or cause to become adapted anew. □□ **readaptation** /riːˌædæpˈteɪʃ(ə)n/ *n.*

readdress /ˌriːəˈdres/ *v.tr.* **1** change the address of (a letter or parcel). **2** address (a problem etc.) anew. **3** speak or write to anew.

reader /ˈriːdə(r)/ *n.* **1** a person who reads or is reading. **2** a book of extracts for learning, esp. a language. **3** a device for producing an image that can be read from microfilm etc. **4** *Brit.* a university lecturer of the highest grade below professor. **5** a publisher's employee who reports on submitted manuscripts. **6** a printer's proof-corrector. **7** a person appointed to read aloud, esp. parts of a service in a church. **8** a person entitled to use a particular library. [OE (as READ)]

readership /ˈriːdəʃɪp/ *n.* **1** the readers of a newspaper etc. **2** the number or extent of these.

readily /ˈredɪlɪ/ *adv.* **1** without showing reluctance; willingly. **2** without difficulty.

reading /ˈriːdɪŋ/ *n.* **1 a** the act or an instance of reading or perusing (*the reading of the will*). **b** matter to be read (*have plenty of reading with me*). **c** the specified quality of this (*it made exciting reading*). **2** (in *comb.*) used for reading (*reading-lamp*; *reading-room*). **3** literary knowledge (*a person of wide reading*). **4** an entertainment at which a play, poems, etc., are read (*poetry reading*). **5** a figure etc. shown by a meter or other recording instrument. **6** an interpretation or view taken (*what is your reading of the facts?*). **7** an interpretation made (of drama, music, etc.). **8** each of the successive occasions on which a bill must be presented to a legislature for acceptance (see also *first reading*, *second reading*, *third reading*). **9** the version of a text, or the particular wording, conjectured or given by an editor etc. □**reading age** reading ability expressed as the age for which the same ability is calculated as average (*has a reading age of eight*). [OE (as READ)]

readjust /ˌriːəˈdʒʌst/ *v.tr.* adjust again or to a former state. □□ **readjustment** *n.*

readmit /ˌriːədˈmɪt/ *v.tr.* (**readmitted**, **readmitting**) admit again. □□ **readmission** *n.*

readopt /ˌriːəˈdɒpt/ *v.tr.* adopt again. □□ **readoption** *n.*

ready /ˈredɪ/ *adj.*, *adv.*, *n.*, & *v.* —*adj.* (**readier**, **readiest**) (usu. *predic.*) **1** with preparations complete (*dinner is ready*). **2** in a fit state (*are you ready to go?*). **3** willing, inclined, or resolved (*he is always ready to complain*; *I am ready for anything*). **4** within reach; easily secured (*a ready source of income*). **5** fit for immediate use (*was ready to hand*). **6** immediate, unqualified (*found ready acceptance*). **7** prompt, quick, facile (*is always ready with excuses*; *has a ready wit*). **8** (foll. by *to* + infin.) about to do something (*a bud just ready to burst*). **9** provided beforehand. —*adv.* **1** beforehand. **2** so as not to require doing when the time comes for use (*the cases are ready packed*). —*n.* (*pl.* -**ies**) *sl.* **1** (prec. by *the*) =

ready money. **2** (in *pl.*) bank notes. —*v.tr.* (-**ies**, -**ied**) make ready; prepare. □**at the ready** ready for action. **make ready** prepare. **ready-made** (or -**to-wear**) (esp. of clothes) made in a standard size, not to measure. **ready-mix** (or -**mixed**) (of concrete, paint, food, etc.) having some or all of the constituents already mixed together. **ready money 1** actual coin or notes. **2** payment on the spot. **ready reckoner** a book or table listing standard numerical calculations as used esp. in commerce. **ready, steady** (or **get set**), **go** the usual formula for starting a race. □□ **readiness** *n.* [ME *rædi(g)*, *re(a)di*, f. OE *rǣde* f. Gmc]

reaffirm /ˌriːəˈfɜːm/ *v.tr.* affirm again. □□ **reaffirmation** /-ˌæfəˈmeɪʃ(ə)n/ *n.*

reafforest /ˌriːəˈfɒrɪst/ *v.tr.* replant (former forest land) with trees. □□ **reafforestation** /-ˈsteɪʃ(ə)n/ *n.*

reagency /riːˈeɪdʒənsɪ/ *n.* reactive power or operation.

reagent /riːˈeɪdʒ(ə)nt/ *n. Chem.* **1** a substance used to cause a reaction, esp. to detect another substance. **2** a reactive substance or force. [RE- + AGENT: cf. REACT]

real[1] /rɪəl/ *adj.* & *adv.* —*adj.* **1** actually existing as a thing or occurring in fact. **2** genuine; rightly so called; not artificial or merely apparent. **3** *Law* consisting of or relating to immovable property such as land or houses (*real estate*) (cf. *personal property*). **4** appraised by purchasing power; adjusted for changes in the value of money (*real value*; *income in real terms*). **5** *Philos.* having an absolute and necessary and not merely contingent existence. **6** *Math.* (of a quantity) having no imaginary part (see IMAGINARY 2). **7** *Optics* (of an image etc.) such that light actually passes through it. —*adv. Sc.* & *US colloq.* really, very. □**for real** *colloq.* as a serious or actual concern; in earnest. **real ale** beer regarded as brewed in a traditional way, with secondary fermentation in the cask. **real life** that lived by actual people, as distinct from fiction, drama, etc. **real live** (*attrib.*) often *joc.* actual; not pretended or simulated (*a real live burglar*). **the real McCoy** see McCOY. **real money** current coin or notes; cash. **real tennis** the original form of tennis played on an indoor court. **the real thing** (of an object or emotion) genuine, not inferior. **real time** the actual time during which a process or event occurs. **real-time** (*attrib.*) *Computing* (of a system) in which the response time is of the order of milliseconds, e.g. in an airline booking system. □□ **realness** *n.* [AF = OF *reel*, LL *realis* f. L *res* thing]

real[2] /reɪˈɑːl/ *n. hist.* a former coin and monetary unit of various Spanish-speaking countries. [Sp., noun use of *real* (adj.) (as ROYAL)]

realgar /rɪˈælɡə(r)/ *n.* a mineral of arsenic sulphide used as a pigment and in fireworks. [ME f. med.L f. Arab. *rahj al-gār* dust of the cave]

realign /ˌriːəˈlaɪn/ *v.tr.* **1** align again. **2** regroup in politics etc. □□ **realignment** *n.*

realism /ˈriːəˌlɪz(ə)m/ *n.* **1** the practice of regarding things in their true nature and dealing with them as they are. **2** fidelity to nature in representation; the showing of life etc. as it is in fact. **3** *Philos.* **a** the doctrine that universals or abstract concepts have an objective existence (opp. NOMINALISM). **b** the belief that matter as an object of perception has real existence. □□ **realist** *n.*

realistic /rɪəˈlɪstɪk/ *adj.* **1** regarding things as they are; following a policy of realism. **2** based on facts rather than ideals. □□ **realistically** *adv.*

reality /rɪˈælɪtɪ/ *n.* (*pl.* -**ies**) **1** what is real or existent or underlies appearances. **2** (foll. by *of*) the real nature of (a thing). **3** real existence; the state of being real. **4** resemblance to an original (*the model was impressive in its reality*). □**in reality** in fact. [med.L *realitas* or F *réalité* (as REAL[1])]

realize /ˈrɪəlaɪz/ *v.tr.* (also -**ise**) **1** (often foll. by *that* + clause) be fully aware of; conceive as real. **2** understand clearly. **3** present as real; make realistic;

give apparent reality to (*the story was powerfully realized on stage*). **4** convert into actuality; achieve (*realized a childhood dream*). **5 a** convert into money. **b** acquire (profit). **c** be sold for (a specified price). **6** *Mus.* reconstruct (a part) in full from a figured bass. □□ **realizable** *adj.* **realizability** /-'bɪlɪtɪ/ *n.* **realization** /-'zeɪʃ(ə)n/ *n.* **realizer** *n.*

reallocate /riː'æləˌkeɪt/ *v.tr.* allocate again or differently. □□ **reallocation** /-'keɪʃ(ə)n/ *n.*

reallot /ˌriːə'lɒt/ *v.tr.* (**reallotted, reallotting**) allot again or differently. □□ **reallotment** *n.*

really /'rɪəlɪ/ *adv.* **1** in reality; in fact. **2** positively, assuredly (*really useful*). **3** (as a strong affirmative) indeed, I assure you. **4** an expression of mild protest or surprise. **5** (in *interrog.*) (expressing disbelief) is that so? (*They're musicians.—Really?*).

realm /relm/ *n.* **1** *formal* esp. *Law* a kingdom. **2** a sphere or domain (*the realm of imagination*). [ME f. OF *realme, reaume*, f. L *regimen -minis* (see REGIMEN): infl. by OF *reiel* ROYAL]

realpolitik /reɪˌɑːlpɒli'tiːk/ *n.* politics based on realities and material needs, rather than on morals or ideals. [G]

realtor /'riːəltə(r)/ *n.* US a real-estate agent, esp. (**Realtor**) a member of the National Association of Realtors.

realty /'riːəltɪ/ *n. Law* real estate (opp. PERSONALTY).

ream[1] /riːm/ *n.* **1** twenty quires or 500 (formerly 480) sheets of paper (or a larger number, to allow for waste). **2** (in *pl.*) a large quantity of paper or writing (*wrote reams about it*). [ME *rēm, rīm* f. OF *raime* etc., ult. f. Arab. *rīzma* bundle]

ream[2] /riːm/ *v.tr.* **1** widen (a hole in metal etc.) with a borer. **2** turn over the edge of (a cartridge-case etc.). **3** *Naut.* open (a seam) for caulking. **4** US squeeze the juice from (fruit). □□ **reamer** *n.* [19th c.: orig. uncert.]

reanimate /riː'ænɪˌmeɪt/ *v.tr.* **1** restore to life. **2** restore to activity or liveliness. □□ **reanimation** /-'meɪʃ(ə)n/ *n.*

reap /riːp/ *v.tr.* **1** cut or gather (a crop, esp. grain) as a harvest. **2** harvest the crop of (a field etc.). **3** receive as the consequence of one's own or others' actions. [OE *ripan, reopan*, of unkn. orig.]

reaper /'riːpə(r)/ *n.* **1** a person who reaps. **2** a machine for reaping. □ **the Reaper** (or **grim Reaper**) death personified.

reappear /ˌriːə'pɪə(r)/ *v.intr.* appear again or as previously. □□ **reappearance** *n.*

reapply /ˌriːə'plaɪ/ *v.tr.* & *intr.* (**-ies, -ied**) apply again, esp. submit a further application (for a position etc.). □□ **reapplication** /ˌriːæplɪ'keɪʃ(ə)n/ *n.*

reappoint /ˌriːə'pɔɪnt/ *v.tr.* appoint again to a position previously held. □□ **reappointment** *n.*

reapportion /ˌriːə'pɔːʃ(ə)n/ *v.tr.* apportion again or differently. □□ **reapportionment** *n.*

reappraise /ˌriːə'preɪz/ *v.tr.* appraise or assess again. □□ **reappraisal** *n.*

rear[1] /rɪə(r)/ *n.* & *adj.* —*n.* **1** the back part of anything. **2** the space behind, or position at the back of, anything (*a large house with a terrace at the rear*). **3** the hindmost part of an army or fleet. **4** *colloq.* the buttocks. —*adj.* at the back. □ **bring up the rear** come last. **in the rear** behind; at the back. **rear admiral** a naval officer ranking below vice admiral. **rear commodore** a yacht-club officer below vice commodore. **rear-lamp** (or **-light**) a usu. red light at the rear of a vehicle. **rear sight** the sight nearest to the stock on a firearm. **rear-view mirror** a mirror fixed inside the windscreen of a motor vehicle enabling the driver to see traffic etc. behind. **take in the rear** *Mil.* attack from behind. [prob. f. (*in the*) REARWARD or REARGUARD]

rear[2] /rɪə(r)/ *v.* **1** *tr.* **a** bring up and educate (children). **b** breed and care for (animals). **c** cultivate (crops). **2** *intr.* (of a horse etc.) raise itself on its hind legs. **3** *tr.* **a** set upright. **b** build. **c** hold upwards (*rear one's*

head). **4** *intr.* extend to a great height. □□ **rearer** *n.* [OE *rǣran* f. Gmc]

rearguard /'rɪəgɑːd/ *n.* **1** a body of troops detached to protect the rear, esp. in retreats. **2** a defensive or conservative element in an organization etc. □ **rearguard action 1** *Mil.* an engagement undertaken by a rearguard. **2** a defensive stand in argument etc., esp. when losing. [OF *rereguarde* (as RETRO-, GUARD)]

rearm /riː'ɑːm/ *v.tr.* (also *absol.*) arm again, esp. with improved weapons. □□ **rearmament** *n.*

rearmost /'rɪəməʊst/ *adj.* furthest back.

rearrange /ˌriːə'reɪndʒ/ *v.tr.* arrange again in a different way. □□ **rearrangement** *n.*

rearrest /ˌriːə'rest/ *v.* & *n.* —*v.tr.* arrest again. —*n.* an instance of rearresting or being rearrested.

rearward /'rɪəwəd/ *n., adj.,* & *adv.* —*n.* rear, esp. in prepositional phrases (*to the rearward of; in the rearward*). —*adj.* to the rear. —*adv.* (also **rearwards**) towards the rear. [AF *rerewarde* = REARGUARD]

reascend /ˌriːə'send/ *v.tr.* & *intr.* ascend again or to a former position. □□ **reascension** *n.*

reason /'riːz(ə)n/ *n.* & *v.* —*n.* **1** a motive, cause, or justification (*has good reasons for doing this*; *there is no reason to be angry*). **2** a fact adduced or serving as this (*I can give you my reasons*). **3** the intellectual faculty by which conclusions are drawn from premisses. **4** sanity (*has lost his reason*). **5** *Logic* a premiss of a syllogism, esp. a minor premiss when given after the conclusion. **6** a faculty transcending the understanding and providing a priori principles; intuition. **7** sense; sensible conduct; what is right or practical or practicable; moderation. —*v.* **1** *intr.* form or try to reach conclusions by connected thought. **2** *intr.* (foll. by *with*) use an argument (with a person) by way of persuasion. **3** *tr.* (foll. by *that* + clause) conclude or assert in argument. **4** *tr.* (foll. by *why, whether, what* + clause) discuss; ask oneself. **5** *tr.* (foll. by *into, out of*) persuade or move by argument (*I reasoned them out of their fears*). **6** *tr.* (foll. by *out*) think or work out (consequences etc.). **7** *tr.* (often as **reasoned** *adj.*) express in logical or argumentative form. **8** *tr.* embody reason in (an amendment etc.). □ **by reason of** owing to. **in** (or **within**) **reason** within the bounds of sense or moderation. **it stands to reason** (often foll. by *that* + clause) it is evident or logical. **listen to reason** be persuaded to act sensibly. **see reason** acknowledge the force of an argument. **with reason** justifiably. □□ **reasoner** *n.* **reasoning** *n.* **reasonless** *adj.* [ME f. OF *reisun, res(o)un, raisoner*, ult. f. L *ratio -onis* f. *rēri* rat-consider]

reasonable /'riːzənəb(ə)l/ *adj.* **1** having sound judgement; moderate; ready to listen to reason. **2** in accordance with reason; not absurd. **3 a** within the limits of reason; not greatly less or more than might be expected. **b** inexpensive; not extortionate. **c** tolerable, fair. **4** *archaic* endowed with the faculty of reason. □□ **reasonableness** *n.* **reasonably** *adv.* [ME f. OF *raisonable* (as REASON) after L *rationabilis*]

reassemble /ˌriːə'semb(ə)l/ *v.intr.* & *tr.* assemble again or into a former state. □□ **reassembly** *n.*

reassert /ˌriːə'sɜːt/ *v.tr.* assert again. □□ **reassertion** *n.*

reassess /ˌriːə'ses/ *v.tr.* assess again, esp. differently. □□ **reassessment** *n.*

reassign /ˌriːə'saɪn/ *v.tr.* assign again or differently. □□ **reassignment** *n.*

reassume /ˌriːə'sjuːm/ *v.tr.* take on oneself or undertake again. □□ **reassumption** /-'sʌmpʃ(ə)n/ *n.*

reassure /ˌriːə'ʃʊə(r)/ *v.tr.* **1** restore confidence to; dispel the apprehensions of. **2** confirm in an opinion or impression. □□ **reassurance** *n.* **reassurer** *n.* **reassuring** *adj.* **reassuringly** *adv.*

reattach /ˌriːə'tætʃ/ *v.tr.* attach again or in a former position. □□ **reattachment** *n.*

reattain /ˌriːəˈteɪn/ v.tr. attain again. □□ **reattainment** n.

reattempt /ˌriːəˈtempt/ v.tr. attempt again, esp. after failure.

Réaumur /ˈreɪəʊˌmjʊə(r)/ adj. expressed in or related to the scale of temperature at which water freezes at 0° and boils at 80° under standard conditions. □ **Réaumur scale** this scale. [R. de Réaumur, Fr. physicist d. 1757]

reave /riːv/ v. (past and past part. **reft** /reft/) archaic **1** tr. **a** (foll. by of) forcibly deprive of. **b** (foll. by away, from) take by force or carry off. **2** intr. make raids; plunder; = REIVE. [OE rēafian f. Gmc: cf. ROB]

reawaken /ˌriːəˈweɪkən/ v.tr. & intr. awaken again.

rebarbative /rɪˈbɑːbətɪv/ adj. literary repellent, unattractive. [F rébarbatif -ive f. barbe beard]

rebate[1] /ˈriːbeɪt/ n. & v. —n. **1** a partial refund of money paid. **2** a deduction from a sum to be paid; a discount. —v.tr. pay back as a rebate. □□ **rebatable** adj. **rebater** n. [earlier = diminish: ME f. OF rabattre (as RE-, ABATE)]

rebate[2] /ˈriːbeɪt/ n. & v.tr. = RABBET. [respelling of RABBET, after REBATE[1]]

rebec /ˈriːbek/ n. (also **rebeck**) Mus. a medieval usu. three-stringed instrument played with a bow. [F rebec var. of OF rebebe rubebe f. Arab. rabāb]

rebel n., adj., & v. —n. /ˈreb(ə)l/ **1** a person who fights against, resists, or refuses allegiance to, the established government. **2** a person or thing that resists authority or control. —adj. /ˈreb(ə)l/ (attrib.) **1** rebellious. **2** of or concerning rebels. **3** in rebellion. —v.intr. /rɪˈbel/ (**rebelled**, **rebelling**; US **rebeled**, **rebeling**) (usu. foll. by against) **1** act as a rebel; revolt. **2** feel or display repugnance. [ME f. OF rebelle, rebeller f. L rebellis (as RE-, bellum war)]

rebellion /rɪˈbeljən/ n. open resistance to authority, esp. organized armed resistance to an established government. [ME f. OF f. L rebellio -onis (as REBEL)]

rebellious /rɪˈbeljəs/ adj. **1** tending to rebel, insubordinate. **2** in rebellion. **3** defying lawful authority. **4** (of a thing) unmanageable, refractory. □□ **rebelliously** adv. **rebelliousness** n. [ME f. REBELLION + -OUS or f. earlier rebellous + -IOUS]

rebid /ˈriːbɪd/ v. & n. —v. /also riːˈbɪd/ (**rebidding**; past and past part. **rebid**) Cards **1** intr. bid again. **2** tr. bid (a suit) again at a higher level. —n. **1** the act of rebidding. **2** a bid made in this way.

rebind /riːˈbaɪnd/ v.tr. (past and past part. **rebound**) bind (esp. a book) again or differently.

rebirth /riːˈbɜːθ, ˈriː-/ n. **1** a new incarnation. **2** spiritual enlightenment. **3** a revival (the rebirth of learning). □□ **reborn** /riːˈbɔːn/ adj.

reboot /riːˈbuːt/ v.tr. (often absol.) Computing boot up (a system) again.

rebore v. & n. —v.tr. /riːˈbɔː(r)/ make a new boring in, esp. widen the bore of (the cylinder in an internal-combustion engine). —n. /ˈriːbɔː(r)/ **1** the process of doing this. **2** a rebored engine.

rebound[1] v. & n. —v.intr. /rɪˈbaʊnd/ **1** spring back after action or impact. **2** (foll. by upon) (of an action) have an adverse effect upon (the doer). —n. /ˈriːbaʊnd/ **1** the act or an instance of rebounding; recoil. **2** a reaction after a strong emotion. □ **on the rebound** while still recovering from an emotional shock, esp. rejection by a lover. □□ **rebounder** n. [ME f. OF rebonder, rebondir (as RE-, BOUND[1])]

rebound[2] /riːˈbaʊnd/ past and past part. of REBIND.

rebroadcast /riːˈbrɔːdkɑːst/ v. & n. —v.tr. (past **rebroadcast** or **rebroadcasted**; past part. **rebroadcast**) broadcast again. —n. a repeat broadcast.

rebuff /rɪˈbʌf/ n. & v. —n. **1** a rejection of one who makes advances, proffers help or sympathy, shows interest or curiosity, makes a request, etc. **2** a repulse; a snub. —v.tr. give a rebuff to. [obs. F rebuffe(r) f. It. ribuffo, ribuffare, rabbuffo, rabbuffare (as RE-, buffo puff)]

rebuild /riːˈbɪld/ v.tr. (past and past part. **rebuilt**) build again or differently.

rebuke /rɪˈbjuːk/ v. & n. —v.tr. reprove sharply; subject to protest or censure. —n. **1** the act of rebuking. **2** the process of being rebuked. **3** a reproof. □□ **rebuker** n. **rebukingly** adv. [ME f. AF & ONF rebuker (as RE-, OF buchier beat, orig. cut down wood f. busche log)]

rebury /riːˈberɪ/ v.tr. (**-ies**, **-ied**) bury again. □□ **reburial** n.

rebus /ˈriːbəs/ n. **1** an enigmatic representation of a word (esp. a name), by pictures etc. suggesting its parts. **2** Heraldry a device suggesting the name of its bearer. [F rébus f. L rebus, ablat. pl. of res thing]

rebut /rɪˈbʌt/ v.tr. (**rebutted**, **rebutting**) **1** refute or disprove (evidence or a charge). **2** force or turn back; check. □□ **rebutment** n. **rebuttable** adj. **rebuttal** n. [ME f. AF rebuter, OF rebo(u)ter (as RE-, BUTT[1])]

rebutter /rɪˈbʌtə(r)/ n. **1** a refutation. **2** Law a defendant's reply to the plaintiff's surrejoinder. [AF rebuter (as REBUT)]

recalcitrant /rɪˈkælsɪtrənt/ adj. & n. —adj. **1** obstinately disobedient. **2** objecting to restraint. —n. a recalcitrant person. □□ **recalcitrance** n. **recalcitrantly** adv. [L recalcitrare (as RE-, calcitrare kick out with the heels f. calx calcis heel)]

recalculate /riːˈkælkjʊˌleɪt/ v.tr. calculate again. □□ **recalculation** /-ˈleɪʃ(ə)n/ n.

recalesce /ˌriːkəˈles/ v.intr. grow hot again (esp. of iron allowed to cool from white heat, whose temperature rises at a certain point for a short time). □□ **recalescence** n. [L recalescere (as RE-, calescere grow hot)]

recall /rɪˈkɔːl/ v. & n. —v.tr. **1** summon to return from a place or from a different occupation, inattention, a digression, etc. **2** recollect, remember. **3** bring back to memory; serve as a reminder of. **4** revoke or annul (an action or decision). **5** cancel or suspend the appointment of (an official sent overseas etc.). **6** revive, resuscitate. **7** take back (a gift). —n. /also ˈriːkɔl/ **1** the act or an instance of recalling, esp. a summons to come back. **2** the act of remembering. **3** the ability to remember. **4** the possibility of recalling, esp. in the sense of revoking (beyond recall). **5** US removal of an elected official from office. □□ **recallable** adj.

recant /rɪˈkænt/ v. **1** tr. withdraw and renounce (a former belief or statement) as erroneous or heretical. **2** intr. disavow a former opinion, esp. with a public confession of error. □□ **recantation** /ˌriːkænˈteɪʃ(ə)n/ n. **recanter** n. [L recantare revoke (as RE-, cantare sing, chant)]

recap /ˈriːkæp/ v. & n. colloq. —v.tr. & intr. (**recapped**, **recapping**) recapitulate. —n. recapitulation. [abbr.]

recapitalize /riːˈkæpɪtəˌlaɪz/ v.tr. (also **-ise**) capitalize (shares etc.) again. □□ **recapitalization** /-ˈzeɪʃ(ə)n/ n.

recapitulate /ˌriːkəˈpɪtjʊˌleɪt/ v.tr. **1** go briefly through again; summarize. **2** go over the main points or headings of. □□ **recapitulative** /-lətɪv/ adj. **recapitulatory** /-lətərɪ/ adj. [L recapitulare (as RE-, capitulum CHAPTER)]

recapitulation /ˌriːkəˌpɪtjʊˈleɪʃ(ə)n/ n. **1** the act or an instance of recapitulating. **2** Biol. the reappearance in embryos of successive type-forms in the evolutionary line of development. **3** Mus. part of a movement, esp. in sonata form, in which themes from the exposition are restated. [ME f. OF recapitulation or LL recapitulatio (as RECAPITULATE)]

recapture /riːˈkæptʃə(r)/ v. & n. —v.tr. **1** capture again; recover by capture. **2** re-experience (a past emotion etc.). —n. the act or an instance of recapturing.

recast /riːˈkɑːst/ v. & n. —v.tr. (past and past part. **recast**) **1** put into a new form. **2** improve the arrangement of. **3** change the cast of (a play etc.). —

b but d dog f few g get h he j yes k cat l leg m man n no p pen r red s sit t top v voice

n. **1** the act or an instance of recasting. **2** a recast form.

recce /'rekɪ/ *n.* & *v. colloq.* —*n.* a reconnaisance. —*v.tr.* & *intr.* (**recced, recceing**) reconnoitre. [abbr.]

recd. *abbr.* received.

recede /rɪ'siːd/ *v.intr.* **1** go or shrink back or further off. **2** be left at an increasing distance by an observer's motion. **3** slope backwards (*a receding chin*). **4** decline in force or value. **5** (foll. by *from*) withdraw from (an engagement, opinion, etc.). **6** (of a man's hair) cease to grow at the front, sides, etc. [ME f. L *recedere* (as RE-, *cedere cess-* go)]

re-cede /riː'siːd/ *v.tr.* cede back to a former owner.

receipt /rɪ'siːt/ *n.* & *v.* —*n.* **1** the act or an instance of receiving or being received into one's possession (*will pay on receipt of the goods*). **2** a written acknowledgement of this, esp. of the payment of money. **3** (usu. in *pl.*) an amount of money etc. received. **4** *archaic* a recipe. —*v.tr.* place a written or printed receipt on (a bill). [ME *receit(e)* f. AF & ONF *receite*, OF *reçoite, recete* f. med.L *recepta* fem. past part. of L *recipere* RECEIVE: -*p*- inserted after L]

receive /rɪ'siːv/ *v.tr.* **1** take or accept (something offered or given) into one's hands or possession. **2** acquire; be provided with or given (*have received no news*; *will receive a small fee*). **3** accept delivery of (something sent). **4** have conferred or inflicted on one (*received many honours*; *received a heavy blow on the head*). **5 a** stand the force or weight of. **b** bear up against; encounter with opposition. **6** consent to hear (a confession or oath) or consider (a petition). **7** (also *absol.*) accept or have dealings with (stolen property knowing of the theft). **8** admit; consent or prove able to hold; provide accommodation for (*received many visitors*). **9** (of a receptacle) be able to hold (a specified amount or contents). **10** greet or welcome, esp. in a specified manner (*how did they receive your offer?*). **11** entertain as a guest etc. **12** admit to membership of a society, organization, etc. **13** be marked more or less permanently with (an impression etc.). **14** convert (broadcast signals) into sound or pictures. **15** *Tennis* be the player to whom the server serves (the ball). **16** (often as **received** *adj.*) give credit to; accept as authoritative or true (*received opinion*). **17** eat or drink (the Eucharistic bread and wine). □**be at** (or **on**) **the receiving end** *colloq.* bear the brunt of something unpleasant. **received pronunciation** (or **Received Standard**) the form of spoken English based on educated speech in southern England. **receiving-order** *Brit.* an order of a court authorizing a receiver (see RECEIVER 3) to act. □□ **receivable** *adj.* [ME f. OF *receivre, reçoivre* f. L *recipere recept-* (as RE-, *capere* take)]

receiver /rɪ'siːvə(r)/ *n.* **1** a person or thing that receives. **2** the part of a machine or instrument that receives sound, signals, etc. (esp. the part of a telephone that contains the earpiece). **3** (in full **official receiver**) a person appointed by a court to administer the property of a bankrupt or insane person, or property under litigation. **4** a radio or television receiving apparatus. **5** a person who receives stolen goods. **6** *Chem.* a vessel for collecting the products of distillation, chromatography, etc.

receivership /rɪ'siːvəʃɪp/ *n.* **1** the office of official receiver. **2** the state of being dealt with by a receiver (esp. *in receivership*).

recension /rɪ'senʃ(ə)n/ *n.* **1** the revision of a text. **2** a particular form or version of a text resulting from such revision. [L *recensio* f. *recensēre* revise (as RE-, *censēre* review)]

recent /'riːs(ə)nt/ *adj.* & *n.* —*adj.* **1** not long past; that happened, appeared, began to exist, or existed lately. **2** not long established; lately begun; modern. **3** (**Recent**) *Geol.* = HOLOCENE. —*n. Geol.* = HOLOCENE. □□ **recency** *n.* **recently** *adv.* **recentness** *n.* [L *recens recentis* or F *récent*]

receptacle /rɪ'septək(ə)l/ *n.* **1** a containing vessel,

place, or space. **2** *Bot.* **a** the common base of floral organs. **b** the part of a leaf or thallus in some algae where the reproductive organs are situated. [ME f. OF *receptacle* or L *receptaculum* (as RECEPTION)]

reception /rɪ'sepʃ(ə)n/ *n.* **1** the act or an instance of receiving or the process of being received, esp. of a person into a place or group. **2** the manner in which a person or thing is received (*got a cool reception*). **3** a social occasion for receiving guests, esp. after a wedding. **4** a formal or ceremonious welcome. **5** a place where guests or clients etc. report on arrival at a hotel, office, etc. **6 a** the receiving of broadcast signals. **b** the quality of this (*we have excellent reception*). □**reception order** an order authorizing the entry of a patient into a mental hospital. **reception room** a room available or suitable for receiving company or visitors. [ME f. OF *reception* or L *receptio* (as RECEIVE)]

receptionist /rɪ'sepʃənɪst/ *n.* a person employed in a hotel, office, etc., to receive guests, clients, etc.

receptive /rɪ'septɪv/ *adj.* **1** able or quick to receive impressions or ideas. **2** concerned with receiving stimuli etc. □□ **receptively** *adv.* **receptiveness** *n.* **receptivity** /ˌriːsep'tɪvɪtɪ/ *n.* [F *réceptif -ive* or med.L *receptivus* (as RECEPTION)]

receptor /rɪ'septə(r)/ *n.* (often *attrib.*). *Biol.* **1** an organ able to respond to an external stimulus such as light, heat, or a drug, and transmit a signal to a sensory nerve. **2** a region of a cell, tissue, etc., that responds to a molecule or other substance. [OF *receptour* or L *receptor* (as RECEPTIVE)]

recess /rɪ'ses, 'riːses/ *n.* & *v.* —*n.* **1** a space set back in a wall; a niche. **2** (often in *pl.*) a remote or secret place (*the innermost recesses*). **3** a temporary cessation from work, esp. of Parliament, or *US* of a lawcourt or during a school day. **4** *Anat.* a fold or indentation in an organ. **5** *Geog.* a receding part of a mountain chain etc. —*v.* **1** *tr.* make a recess in. **2** *tr.* place in a recess; set back. **3** *US* **a** *intr.* take a recess; adjourn. **b** *tr.* order a temporary cessation from the work of (a court etc.). [L *recessus* (as RECEDE)]

recession /rɪ'seʃ(ə)n/ *n.* **1** a temporary decline in economic activity or prosperity. **2** a receding or withdrawal from a place or point. **3** a receding part of an object; a recess. □□ **recessionary** *adj.* [L *recessio* (as RECESS)]

recessional /rɪ'seʃən(ə)l/ *adj.* & *n.* —*adj.* sung while the clergy and choir withdraw after a service. —*n.* a recessional hymn.

recessive /rɪ'sesɪv/ *adj.* **1** tending to recede. **2** *Phonet.* (of an accent) falling near the beginning of a word. **3** *Genetics* (of an inherited characteristic) appearing in offspring only when not masked by a dominant characteristic inherited from one parent. □□ **recessively** *adv.* **recessiveness** *n.* [RECESS after *excessive*]

recharge *v.* & *n.* —*v.tr.* /riː'tʃɑːdʒ/ **1** charge again. **2** reload. —*n.* /'riːtʃɑːdʒ/ **1** a renewed charge. **2** material etc. used for this. □□ **rechargeable** /riː'tʃɑːdʒəb(ə)l/ *adj.*

réchauffé /reɪ'ʃəʊfeɪ/ *n.* **1** a warmed-up dish. **2** a rehash. [F past part. of *réchauffer* (as RE-, CHAFE)]

recheck *v.* & *n.* —*v.tr.* & *intr.* /riː'tʃek/ check again. —*n.* /'riːtʃek/ a second or further check or inspection.

recherché /rə'ʃeəʃeɪ/ *adj.* **1** carefully sought out; rare or exotic. **2** far-fetched, obscure. [F, past part. of *rechercher* (as RE-, *chercher* seek)]

rechristen /riː'krɪs(ə)n/ *v.tr.* **1** christen again. **2** give a new name to.

recidivist /rɪ'sɪdɪvɪst/ *n.* a person who relapses into crime. □□ **recidivism** *n.* **recidivistic** /-'vɪstɪk/ *adj.* [F *récidiviste* f. *récidiver* f. med.L *recidivare* f. L *recidivus* f. *recidere* (as RE-, *cadere* fall)]

recipe /'resɪpɪ/ *n.* **1** a statement of the ingredients and procedure required for preparing cooked food. **2** an expedient; a device for achieving something. **3** a medical prescription. [2nd sing. imper. (as used in prescriptions) of L *recipere* take, RECEIVE]

recipient /rɪˈsɪpɪənt/ *n. & adj.* —*n.* a person who receives something. —*adj.* **1** receiving. **2** receptive. ▫▫**recipiency** *n.* [F *récipient* f. It. *recipiente* or L *recipiens* f. *recipere* RECEIVE]

reciprocal /rɪˈsɪprək(ə)l/ *adj. & n.* —*adj.* **1** in return (*offered a reciprocal greeting*). **2** mutual (*their feelings are reciprocal*). **3** *Gram.* (of a pronoun) expressing mutual action or relation (as in *each other*). **4** inversely correspondent; complementary (*natural kindness matched by a reciprocal severity*). —*n. Math.* an expression or function so related to another that their product is unity (½ *is the reciprocal of 2*). ▫▫ **reciprocality** /-ˈkælɪtɪ/ *n.* **reciprocally** *adv.* [L *reciprocus* ult. f. *re-* back + *pro* forward]

reciprocate /rɪˈsɪprəˌkeɪt/ *v.* **1** *tr.* return or requite (affection etc.). **2** *intr.* (foll. by *with*) offer or give something in return (*reciprocated with an invitation to lunch*). **3** *tr.* give and receive mutually; interchange. **4 a** *intr.* (of a part of a machine) move backwards and forwards. **b** *tr.* cause to do this. ▫**reciprocating engine** an engine using a piston or pistons moving up and down in cylinders. ▫▫ **reciprocation** /-ˈkeɪʃ(ə)n/ *n.* **reciprocator** *n.* [L *reciprocare reciprocat-* (as RECIPROCAL)]

reciprocity /ˌresɪˈprɒsɪtɪ/ *n.* **1** the condition of being reciprocal. **2** mutual action. **3** give and take, esp. the interchange of privileges between countries and organizations. [F *réciprocité* f. *réciproque* f. L *reciprocus* (as RECIPROCAL)]

recirculate /riːˈsɜːkjʊˌleɪt/ *v.tr. & intr.* circulate again, esp. make available for reuse. ▫▫ **recirculation** /-ˈleɪʃ(ə)n/ *n.*

recital /rɪˈsaɪt(ə)l/ *n.* **1** the act or an instance of reciting or being recited. **2** the performance of a programme of music by a solo instrumentalist or singer or by a small group. **3** (foll. by *of*) a detailed account of (connected things or facts); a narrative. **4** *Law* the part of a legal document that states the facts. ▫▫ **recitalist** *n.*

recitation /ˌresɪˈteɪʃ(ə)n/ *n.* **1** the act or an instance of reciting. **2** a thing recited. [OF *recitation* or L *recitatio* (as RECITE)]

recitative /ˌresɪtəˈtiːv/ *n.* **1** musical declamation of the kind usual in the narrative and dialogue parts of opera and oratorio. **2** the words or part given in this form. [It. *recitativo* (as RECITE)]

recite /rɪˈsaɪt/ *v.* **1** *tr.* repeat aloud or declaim (a poem or passage) from memory, esp. before an audience. **2** *intr.* give a recitation. **3** *tr.* mention in order; enumerate. ▫▫ **reciter** *n.* [ME f. OF *reciter* or L *recitare* (as RE-, CITE)]

reck /rek/ *v. archaic or poet.* (only in *neg.* or *interrog.*) **1** *tr.* (foll. by *of*) pay heed to; take account of; care about. **2** *tr.* pay heed to. **3** *intr.* (usu. with *it* as subject) be of importance (*it recks little*). [OE *reccan*, rel. to OHG *ruohhen*]

reckless /ˈreklɪs/ *adj.* disregarding the consequences or danger etc.; lacking caution; rash. ▫▫ **recklessly** *adv.* **recklessness** *n.* [OE *recceléas* (as RECK)]

reckon /ˈrekən/ *v.* **1** *tr.* count or compute by calculation. **2** *tr.* (foll. by *in*) count in or include in computation. **3** *tr.* (often foll. by *as* or *to be*) consider or regard (*reckon him wise*; *reckon them to be beyond hope*). **4** *tr.* **a** (foll. by *that* + clause) conclude after calculation; be of the considered opinion. **b** *colloq.* (foll. by *to* + infin.) expect (*reckons to finish by Friday*). **5** *intr.* make calculations; add up an account or sum. **6** *intr.* (foll. by *on*, *upon*) rely on, count on, or base plans on. **7** *intr.* (foll. by *with*) **a** take into account. **b** settle accounts with. ▫**reckon up 1** count up; find the total of. **2** settle accounts. **to be reckoned with** of considerable importance; not to be ignored. [OE (*ge*)*recenian* f. WG]

reckoner /ˈrekənə(r)/ *n.* = *ready reckoner.*

reckoning /ˈrekənɪŋ/ *n.* **1** the act or an instance of counting or calculating. **2** a consideration or opinion. **3 a** the settlement of an account. **b** an account. ▫**day

of reckoning** the time when something must be atoned for or avenged.

reclaim /rɪˈkleɪm/ *v. & n.* —*v.tr.* **1** seek the return of (one's property). **2** claim in return or as a rebate etc. **3** bring under cultivation, esp. from a state of being under water. **4 a** win back or away from vice or error or a waste condition; reform. **b** tame, civilize. —*n.* the act or an instance of reclaiming; the process of being reclaimed. ▫▫ **reclaimable** *adj.* **reclaimer** *n.* **reclamation** /ˌrekləˈmeɪʃ(ə)n/ *n.* [ME f. OF *reclamer reclaim-* f. L *reclamare* cry out against (as RE-, *clamare* shout)]

reclassify /riːˈklæsɪˌfaɪ/ *v.tr.* (**-ies**, **-ied**) classify again or differently. ▫▫ **reclassification** /-fɪˈkeɪʃ(ə)n/ *n.*

reclinate /ˈreklɪˌneɪt/ *adj. Bot.* bending downwards. [L *reclinatus*, past part. of *reclinare* (as RECLINE)]

recline /rɪˈklaɪn/ *v.* **1** *intr.* assume or be in a horizontal or leaning position, esp. in resting. **2** *tr.* cause to recline or move from the vertical. ▫▫ **reclinable** *adj.* [ME f. OE *recliner* or L *reclinare* bend back, recline (as RE-, *clinare* bend)]

recliner /rɪˈklaɪnə(r)/ *n.* **1** a comfortable chair for reclining in. **2** a person who reclines.

reclothe /riːˈkləʊð/ *v.tr.* clothe again or differently.

recluse /rɪˈkluːs/ *n. & adj.* —*n.* a person given to or living in seclusion or isolation, esp. as a religious discipline; a hermit. —*adj.* favouring seclusion; solitary. ▫▫ **reclusion** /rɪˈkluːʒ(ə)n/ *n.* **reclusive** *adj.* [ME f. OF *reclus recluse* past part. of *reclure* f. L *recludere reclus-* (as RE-, *claudere* shut)]

recognition /ˌrekəgˈnɪʃ(ə)n/ *n.* the act or an instance of recognizing or being recognized. ▫▫ **recognitory** /rɪˈkɒgnɪtərɪ/ *adj.* [L *recognitio* (as RECOGNIZE)]

recognizance /rɪˈkɒgnɪz(ə)ns/ *n.* **1** a bond by which a person undertakes before a court or magistrate to observe some condition, e.g. to appear when summoned. **2** a sum pledged as surety for this. [ME f. OF *recon(n)issance* (as RE-, COGNIZANCE)]

recognizant /rɪˈkɒgnɪz(ə)nt/ *adj.* (usu. foll. by *of*) **1** showing recognition (of a favour etc.). **2** conscious or showing consciousness (of something).

recognize /ˈrekəgˌnaɪz/ *v.tr.* (also **-ise**) **1** identify (a person or thing) as already known; know again. **2** realize or discover the nature of. **3** (foll. by *that*) realize or admit. **4** acknowledge the existence, validity, character, or claims of. **5** show appreciation of; reward. **6** (foll. by *as*, *for*) treat or acknowledge. **7** (of a chairperson etc.) allow (a person) to speak in a debate etc. ▫▫ **recognizable** *n.* **recognizability** /-əˈbɪlɪtɪ/ *n.* **recognizably** *adv.* **recognizer** *n.* [OF *recon(n)iss-* stem of *reconnaistre* f. L *recognoscere recognit-* (as RE-, *cognoscere* learn)]

recoil /rɪˈkɔɪl/ *v. & n.* —*v.intr.* **1** suddenly move or spring back in fear, horror, or disgust. **2** shrink mentally in this way. **3** rebound after an impact. **4** (foll. by *on*, *upon*) have an adverse reactive effect on (the originator). **5** (of a gun) be driven backwards by its discharge. **6** retreat under an enemy's attack. **7** *Physics* (of an atom etc.) move backwards by the conservation of momentum on emission of a particle. —*n.* /also ˈriːkɔɪl/ **1** the act or an instance of recoiling. **2** the sensation of recoiling. [ME f. OF *reculer* (as RE-, L *culus* buttocks)]

recollect /ˌrekəˈlekt/ *v.tr.* **1** remember. **2** succeed in remembering; call to mind. [L *recolligere recollect-* (as RE-, COLLECT¹)]

re-collect /ˌriːkəˈlekt/ *v.tr.* **1** collect again. **2** (*refl.*) recover control of (oneself).

recollection /ˌrekəˈlekʃ(ə)n/ *n.* **1** the act or power of recollecting. **2** a thing recollected. **3 a** a person's memory (*to the best of my recollection*). **b** the time over which memory extends (*happened within my recollection*). ▫▫ **recollective** *adj.* [F *recollection* or med.L *recollectio* (as RECOLLECT)]

recolonize /riːˈkɒləˌnaɪz/ *v.tr.* (also **-ise**) colonize again. ▫▫ **recolonization** /-ˈzeɪʃ(ə)n/ *n.*

recolour /riːˈkʌlə(r)/ *v.tr.* colour again or differently.

recombinant /riːˈkɒmbɪnənt/ *adj. & n. Biol.* —*adj.*

(of a gene etc.) formed by recombination. —n. a recombinant organism or cell. ▫**recombinant DNA** DNA that has been recombined using constituents from different sources.

recombination /ˌriːˌkɒmbɪˈneɪʃ(ə)n/ n. Biol. the rearrangement, esp. by crossing over in chromosomes, of nucleic acid molecules forming a new sequence of the constituent nucleotides.

recombine /ˌriːkəmˈbaɪn/ v.tr. & intr. combine again or differently.

recommence /ˌriːkəˈmens/ v.tr. & intr. begin again. ▫▫ **recommencement** n.

recommend /ˌrekəˈmend/ v.tr. **1** suggest as fit for some purpose or use. **2** (often foll. by that + clause or to + infin.) advise as a course of action etc. (I recommend that you stay where you are). **3** (of qualities, conduct, etc.) make acceptable or desirable. **4** (foll. by to) commend or entrust (to a person or a person's care). ▫▫ **recommendable** adj. **recommendation** /-ˈdeɪʃ(ə)n/ n. **recommendatory** /-dətərɪ/ adj. **recommender** n. [ME (in sense 4) f. med.L recommendare (as RE-, COMMEND)]

recommit /ˌriːkəˈmɪt/ v.tr. (**recommitted**, **recommitting**) **1** commit again. **2** return (a bill etc.) to a committee for further consideration. ▫▫ **recommitment** n. **recommittal** n.

recompense /ˈrekəmˌpens/ v. & n. —v.tr. **1** make amends to (a person) or for (a loss etc.). **2** requite; reward or punish (a person or action). —n. **1** a reward; requital. **2** retribution; satisfaction given for an injury. [ME f. OF recompense(r) f. LL recompensare (as RE-, COMPENSATE)]

recompose /ˌriːkəmˈpəʊz/ v.tr. compose again or differently.

reconcile /ˈrekənˌsaɪl/ v.tr. **1** make friendly again after an estrangement. **2** (usu. in refl. or passive; foll. by to) make acquiescent or contentedly submissive to (something disagreeable or unwelcome) (was reconciled to failure). **3** settle (a quarrel etc.). **4 a** harmonize; make compatible. **b** show the compatibility of by argument or in practice (cannot reconcile your views with the facts). ▫▫ **reconcilable** adj. **reconcilability** /-əˈbɪlɪtɪ/ n. **reconcilement** n. **reconciler** n. **reconciliation** /-ˌsɪlɪˈeɪʃ(ə)n/ n. **reconciliatory** /-kənˈsɪlɪətərɪ/ adj. [ME f. OF reconcilier or L reconciliare (as RE-, conciliare CONCILIATE)]

recondite /ˈrekənˌdaɪt, rɪˈkɒn-/ adj. **1** (of a subject or knowledge) abstruse; out of the way; little known. **2** (of an author or style) dealing in abstruse knowledge or allusions; obscure. ▫▫ **reconditely** adv. **reconditeness** n. [L reconditus (as RE-, conditus past part. of condere hide)]

recondition /ˌriːkənˈdɪʃ(ə)n/ v.tr. **1** overhaul, refit, renovate. **2** make usable again. ▫▫ **reconditioner** n.

reconfigure /ˌriːkənˈfɪɡə(r)/ v.tr. configure again or differently. ▫▫ **reconfiguration** /-ɡəˈreɪʃ(ə)n/ n.

reconfirm /ˌriːkənˈfɜːm/ v.tr. confirm, establish, or ratify anew. ▫▫ **reconfirmation** /-kɒnfəˈmeɪʃ(ə)n/ n.

reconnaissance /rɪˈkɒnɪs(ə)ns/ n. **1** a survey of a region, esp. a military examination to locate an enemy or ascertain strategic features. **2** a preliminary survey or inspection. [F (earlier -oissance) f. stem of reconnaître (as RECONNOITRE)]

reconnect /ˌriːkəˈnekt/ v.tr. connect again. ▫▫ **reconnection** n.

reconnoitre /ˌrekəˈnɔɪtə(r)/ v. & n. (US **reconnoiter**) —v. **1** tr. make a reconnaissance of (an area, enemy position, etc.). **2** intr. make a reconnaissance. —n. a reconnaissance. [obs. F reconnoître f. L recognoscere RECOGNIZE]

reconquer /riːˈkɒŋkə(r)/ v.tr. conquer again. ▫▫ **reconquest** n.

reconsider /ˌriːkənˈsɪdə(r)/ v.tr. & intr. consider again, esp. for a possible change of decision. ▫▫ **reconsideration** /-ˈreɪʃ(ə)n/ n.

reconsign /ˌriːkənˈsaɪn/ v.tr. consign again or differently. ▫▫ **reconsignment** n.

reconsolidate /ˌriːkənˈsɒlɪˌdeɪt/ v.tr. & intr. consolidate again. ▫▫ **reconsolidation** /-ˈdeɪʃ(ə)n/ n.

reconstitute /riːˈkɒnstɪˌtjuːt/ v. & tr. **1** build up again from parts; reconstruct. **2** reorganize. **3** restore the previous constitution of (dried food etc.) by adding water. ▫▫ **reconstitution** /-ˈtjuːʃ(ə)n/ n.

reconstruct /ˌriːkənˈstrʌkt/ v.tr. **1** build or form again. **2 a** form a mental or visual impression of (past events) by assembling the evidence for them. **b** re-enact (a crime). **3** reorganize. ▫▫ **reconstructable** adj. (also **reconstructible**). **reconstruction** n. **reconstructive** adj. **reconstructor** n.

reconvene /ˌriːkənˈviːn/ v.tr. & intr. convene again, esp. of a meeting etc.) after a pause in proceedings.

reconvert /ˌriːkənˈvɜːt/ v.tr. convert back to a former state. ▫▫ **reconversion** n.

record n. & v. —n. /ˈrekɔːd/ **1 a** a piece of evidence or information constituting an (esp. official) account of something that has occurred, been said, etc. **b** a document preserving this. **2** the state of being set down or preserved in writing or some other permanent form (is a matter of record). **3 a** (in full **gramophone record**) a thin plastic disc carrying recorded sound in grooves on each surface, for reproduction by a record-player. **b** a trace made on this or some other medium, e.g. magnetic tape. **4 a** an official report of the proceedings and judgement in a court of justice. **b** a copy of the pleadings etc. constituting a case to be decided by a court (see also court of record). **5 a** the facts known about a person's past (has an honourable record of service). **b** a list of a person's previous criminal convictions. **6** the best performance (esp. in sport) or most remarkable event of its kind on record (often attrib.: a record attempt). **7** an object serving as a memorial of a person or thing; a portrait. **8** Computing a number of related items of information which are handled as a unit. —v.tr. /rɪˈkɔːd/ **1** set down in writing or some other permanent form for later reference, esp. as an official record. **2** convert (sound, a broadcast, etc.) into permanent form for later reproduction. **3** establish or constitute a historical or other record of. ▫**break** (or **beat**) **the record** outdo all previous performances etc. **for the record** as an official statement etc. **go on record** state one's opinion or judgement openly or officially, so that it is recorded. **have a record** be known as a criminal. **a matter of record** a thing established as a fact by being recorded. **off the record** as an unofficial or confidential statement etc. **on record** officially recorded; publicly known. **put** (or **get** or **set** etc.) **the record straight** correct a misapprehension. **recorded delivery** a Post Office service in which the dispatch and receipt of a letter or parcel are recorded. **recording angel** an angel that supposedly registers each person's good and bad actions. **record-player** an apparatus for reproducing sound from gramophone records. ▫▫ **recordable** adj. [ME f. OF record remembrance, recorder record, f. L recordari remember (as RE-, cor cordis heart)]

recorder /rɪˈkɔːdə(r)/ n. **1** an apparatus for recording, esp. a tape recorder. **2 a** a keeper of records. **b** a person who makes an official record. **3** Brit. **a** a barrister or solicitor of at least ten years' standing, appointed to serve as a part-time judge. **b** hist. a judge in certain courts. **4** Mus. a woodwind instrument like a flute but blown through the end and having a more hollow tone. ▫▫ **recordership** n. (in sense 3). [ME f. AF recordour, OF recordeur & f. RECORD (in obs. sense 'practise a tune')]

recording /rɪˈkɔːdɪŋ/ n. **1** the process by which audio or video signals are recorded for later reproduction. **2** material or a programme recorded.

recordist /rɪˈkɔːdɪst/ n. a person who records sound.

recount /rɪˈkaʊnt/ v.tr. **1** narrate. **2** tell in detail. [ONF & AF reconter (as RE-, COUNT[1])]

re-count v. & n. —v. /riːˈkaʊnt/ tr. count again. —n. /ˈriːkaʊnt/ a re-counting, esp. of votes in an election.

recoup /rɪˈkuːp/ v.tr. **1** recover or regain (a loss). **2** compensate or reimburse for a loss. **3** Law deduct or keep back (part of a sum due). □recoup oneself recover a loss. □□recoupable adj. recoupment n. [F recouper (as RE-, couper cut)]

recourse /rɪˈkɔːs/ n. **1** resorting to a possible source of help. **2** a person or thing resorted to. □have recourse to turn to (a person or thing) for help. without recourse a formula used by the endorser of a bill etc. to disclaim responsibility for payment. [ME f. OF recours f. L recursus (as RE-, COURSE)]

recover /rɪˈkʌvə(r)/ v. & n. —v. **1** tr. regain possession or use or control of, reclaim. **2** intr. return to health or consciousness or to a normal state or position (have recovered from my illness; the country never recovered from the war). **3** tr. obtain or secure (compensation etc.) by legal process. **4** tr. retrieve or make up for (a loss, setback, etc.). **5** refl. regain composure or consciousness or control of one's limbs. **6** tr. retrieve (reusable substances) from industrial waste. —n. the recovery of a normal position in fencing etc. □□recoverable adj. recoverability /-ˈbɪlɪtɪ/ n. recoverer n. [ME f. AF recoverer, OF recoverer f. L recuperare RECUPERATE]

re-cover /riːˈkʌvə(r)/ v.tr. **1** cover again. **2** provide a (chair etc.) with a new cover.

recovery /rɪˈkʌvərɪ/ n. (pl. -ies) **1** the act or an instance of recovering; the process of being recovered. **2** Golf a stroke bringing the ball out of a bunker etc. [ME f. AF recoverie, OF reco(u)vree (as RECOVER)]

recreant /ˈrekrɪənt/ adj. & n. literary —adj. **1** craven, cowardly. **2** apostate. —n. **1** a coward. **2** an apostate. □□recreancy n. recreantly adv. [ME f. OF, part. of recroire f. med.L (se) recredere yield in trial by combat (as RE-, credere entrust)]

re-create /ˌriːkrɪˈeɪt/ v.tr. create over again. □□ re-creation n.

recreation /ˌrekrɪˈeɪʃ(ə)n/ n. **1** the process or means of refreshing or entertaining oneself. **2** a pleasurable activity. □recreation-ground public land for games etc. □□recreational adj. recreationally adv. recreative /ˈrekrɪˌeɪtɪv/ adj. [ME f. OF f. L recreatio -onis f. recreare create again, renew]

recriminate /rɪˈkrɪmɪˌneɪt/ v.intr. make mutual or counter accusations. □□recrimination /-ˈneɪʃ(ə)n/ n. recriminative /-nətɪv/ adj. recriminatory /-nətərɪ/ adj. [med.L recriminare (as RE-, criminare accuse f. crimen CRIME)]

recross /riːˈkrɒs/ v.tr. & intr. cross or pass over again.

recrudesce /ˌriːkruːˈdes, ˌrek-/ v.intr. (of a disease or difficulty etc.) break out again, esp. after a dormant period. □□recrudescence n. recrudescent adj. [back-form. f. recrudescent, -ence f. L recrudescere (as RE-, crudus raw)]

recruit /rɪˈkruːt/ n. & v. —n. **1** a serviceman or servicewoman newly enlisted and not yet fully trained. **2** a new member of a society or organization. **3** a beginner. —v. **1** tr. enlist (a person) as a recruit. **2** tr. form (an army etc.) by enlisting recruits. **3** intr. get or seek recruits. **4** tr. replenish or reinvigorate (numbers, strength, etc.). □□recruitable adj. recruiter n. recruitment n. [earlier = reinforcement, f. obs. F dial. recrute ult. f. F recroître increase again f. L recrescere]

recrystallize /riːˈkrɪstəˌlaɪz/ v.tr. & intr. (also -ise) crystallize again. □□recrystallization /-ˈzeɪʃ(ə)n/ n.

recta pl. of RECTUM.

rectal /ˈrekt(ə)l/ adj. of or by means of the rectum. □□rectally adv.

rectangle /ˈrekˌtæŋg(ə)l/ n. a plane figure with four straight sides and four right angles, esp. one with the adjacent sides unequal. [F rectangle or med.L rectangulum f. LL rectiangulum f. L rectus straight + angulus ANGLE¹]

rectangular /rekˈtæŋgʊlə(r)/ adj. **1 a** shaped like a rectangle. **b** having the base or sides or section shaped like a rectangle. **2 a** placed at right angles. **b** having parts or lines placed at right angles. □rectangular coordinates coordinates measured along axes at right angles. rectangular hyperbola a hyperbola with rectangular asymptotes. □□ rectangularity /-ˈlærɪtɪ/ n. rectangularly adv.

recti pl. of RECTUS.

rectifier /ˈrektɪˌfaɪə(r)/ n. **1** a person or thing that rectifies. **2** Electr. an electrical device that allows a current to flow preferentially in one direction by converting an alternating current into a direct one.

rectify /ˈrektɪˌfaɪ/ v.tr. (-ies, -ied) **1** adjust or make right; correct, amend. **2** purify or refine, esp. by repeated distillation. **3** find a straight line equal in length to (a curve). **4** convert (alternating current) to direct current. □□rectifiable adj. rectification /-fɪˈkeɪʃ(ə)n/ n. [ME f. OF rectifier f. med.L rectificare f. L rectus right]

rectilinear /ˌrektɪˈlɪnɪə(r)/ adj. (also rectilineal /-nɪəl/) **1** bounded or characterized by straight lines. **2** in or forming a straight line. □□rectilinearity /-ˈærɪtɪ/ n. rectilinearly adv. [LL rectilineus f. L rectus straight + linea LINE¹]

rectitude /ˈrektɪˌtjuːd/ n. **1** moral uprightness. **2** righteousness. **3** correctness. [ME f. OF rectitude or LL rectitudo f. L rectus right]

recto /ˈrektəʊ/ n. (pl. -os) **1** the right-hand page of an open book. **2** the front of a printed leaf of paper or manuscript (opp. VERSO). [L recto (folio) on the right (leaf)]

rector /ˈrektə(r)/ n. **1** (in the Church of England) the incumbent of a parish where all tithes formerly passed to the incumbent (cf. VICAR). **2** RC Ch. a priest in charge of a church or religious institution. **3 a** the head of some schools, universities, and colleges. **b** (in Scotland) an elected representative of students on a university's governing body. □□rectorate /-rət/ n. rectorial /-ˈtɔːrɪəl/ adj. rectorship n. [ME f. OF rectour or L rector ruler f. regere rect- rule]

rectory /ˈrektərɪ/ n. (pl. -ies) **1** a rector's house. **2** (in the Church of England) a rector's benefice. [AF & OF rectorie or med.L rectoria (as RECTOR)]

rectrix /ˈrektrɪks/ n. (pl. rectrices /-rɪˌsiːz/) a bird's strong tail-feather directing flight. [L, fem. of rector ruler: see RECTOR]

rectum /ˈrektəm/ n. (pl. rectums or recta /-tə/) the final section of the large intestine, terminating at the anus. [L rectum (intestinum) straight (intestine)]

rectus /ˈrektəs/ n. (pl. recti /-taɪ/) Anat. a straight muscle. [L, = straight]

recumbent /rɪˈkʌmbənt/ adj. lying down; reclining. □□recumbency n. recumbently adv. [L recumbere recline (as RE-, cumbere lie)]

recuperate /rɪˈkuːpəˌreɪt/ v. **1** intr. recover from illness, exhaustion, loss, etc. **2** tr. regain (health, something lost, etc.). □□recuperable adj. recuperation /-ˈreɪʃ(ə)n/ n. recuperative /-rətɪv/ adj. recuperator n. [L recuperare recuperat- recover]

recur /rɪˈkɜː(r)/ v.intr. (recurred, recurring) **1** occur again; be repeated. **2** (of a thought, idea, etc.) come back to one's mind. **3** (foll. by to) go back in thought or speech. □recurring decimal a decimal fraction in which the same figures are repeated indefinitely. [L recurrere recurs- (as RE-, currere run)]

recurrent /rɪˈkʌrənt/ adj. **1** recurring; happening repeatedly. **2** (of a nerve, vein, branch, etc.) turning back so as to reverse direction. □□recurrence n. recurrently adv.

recursion /rɪˈkɜːʃ(ə)n/ n. **1** the act or an instance of returning. **2** Math. the repeated application of a procedure or definition to a previous result to obtain a series of values. □recursion formula Math. an expression giving successive terms of a series etc. □□recursive adj. [LL recursio (as RECUR)]

recurve /rɪˈkɜːv/ v.tr. & intr. bend backwards. □□ recurvate /-vət/ adj. recurvature n. [L recurvare recurvat- (as RE-, curvare bend)]

recusant /ˈrekjʊz(ə)nt/ n. & adj. —n. a person who

refuses submission to an authority or compliance with a regulation, esp. *hist.* one who refused to attend services of the Church of England. *—adj.* of or being a recusant. □□ **recusance** *n.* **recusancy** *n.* [L *recusare* refuse]

recycle /riːˈsaɪk(ə)l/ *v.tr.* return (material) to a previous stage of a cyclic process, esp. convert (waste) to reusable material. □□ **recyclable** *adj.*

red /red/ *adj. & n.* *—adj.* **1** of or near the colour seen at the least-refracted end of the visible spectrum, of shades ranging from that of blood to pink or deep orange. **2** flushed in the face with shame, anger, etc. **3** (of the eyes) bloodshot or red-rimmed with weeping. **4** (of the hair) reddish-brown, orange, tawny. **5** involving or having to do with bloodshed, burning, violence, or revolution. **6** *colloq.* communist or socialist. **7 (Red)** Russian, Soviet (*the Red Army*). **8** (of wine) made from dark grapes and coloured by their skins. *—n.* **1** a red colour or pigment. **2** red clothes or material (*dressed in red*). **3** *colloq.* a communist or socialist. **4 a** a red ball, piece, etc., in a game or sport. **b** the player using such pieces. **5** the debit side of an account (*in the red*). **6** a red light. □**red admiral** a butterfly, *Vanessa atalanta*, with red bands on each pair of wings. **red bark** a red kind of cinchona. **red biddy** *colloq.* a mixture of cheap wine and methylated spirits. **red-blooded** virile, vigorous. **red-bloodedness** vigour, spirit. **red card** *Football* a card shown by the referee to a player being sent off the field. **red carpet** privileged treatment of an eminent visitor. **red cedar** an American juniper, *Juniperus virginiana*. **red cell** (or **corpuscle**) an erythrocyte. **red cent** *US* the smallest (orig. copper) coin; a trivial sum. **Red Crescent** an organization like the Red Cross in Muslim countries. **red cross 1** St George's cross, the national emblem of England. **2** the Christian side in the crusades. **Red Cross 1** an international organization (originally medical) bringing relief to victims of war or natural disaster. **2** the emblem of this organization. **red deer** a deer, *Cervus elaphus*, with a rich red-brown summer coat turning dull-brown in winter. **red duster** *Brit. colloq.* = *red ensign*. **red dwarf** an old relatively cool star. **red ensign** see ENSIGN. **red-eye 1** = RUDD. **2** *US sl.* cheap whisky. **red-faced** embarrassed, ashamed. **red flag 1** the symbol of socialist revolution. **2** a warning of danger. **red fox** a native British fox, *Vulpes vulpes*, having a characteristic deep red or fawn coat. **red giant** a relatively cool giant star. **red grouse** a subspecies of the willow grouse, native to Britain and familiar as a game-bird. **Red Guard** *hist.* a member of a militant youth movement in China (1966–76). **red gum 1** a teething-rash in children. **2 a** a reddish resin. **b** any of various kinds of eucalyptus yielding this. **red-handed** in or just after the act of committing a crime, doing wrong, etc. **red hat 1** a cardinal's hat. **2** the symbol of a cardinal's office. **red-headed 1** (of a person) having red hair. **2** (of birds etc.) having a red head. **red heat 1** the temperature or state of something so hot as to emit red light. **2** great excitement. **red herring 1** dried smoked herring. **2** a misleading clue or distraction (so called from the practice of using the scent of red herring in training hounds). **red-hot 1** heated until red. **2** highly exciting. **3** (of news) fresh; completely new. **4** intensely excited. **5** enraged. **red-hot poker** any plant of the genus *Kniphofia*, with spikes of usually red or yellow flowers. **Red Indian** *offens.* an American Indian. **red lead** a red form of lead oxide used as a pigment. **red-letter day** a day that is pleasantly noteworthy or memorable (orig. a festival marked in red on the calendar). **red light 1** a signal to stop on a road, railway, etc. **2** a warning or refusal. **red-light district** a district containing many brothels. **red man** = *Red Indian*. **red meat** meat that is red when raw (e.g. beef or lamb). **red mullet** a marine fish, *Mullus surmuletus*, valued as food.

red pepper 1 cayenne pepper. **2** the ripe fruit of the capsicum plant, *Capsicum annuum*. **red rag** something that excites a person's rage (so called because red is supposed to provoke bulls). **red rattle** a pink-flowered marsh plant, *Pedicularis palustris*. **red roan** see ROAN[1]. **red rose** the emblem of Lancashire or the Lancastrians. **red shift** the displacement of the spectrum to longer wavelengths in the light coming from distant galaxies etc. in recession. **red spider** any of various mites of the family Tetranychidae infesting hothouse plants esp. vines. **red squirrel** a native British squirrel, *Sciurus vulgaris*, with reddish fur. **Red Star** the emblem of some Communist countries. **red tape** excessive bureaucracy or adherence to formalities esp. in public business. **red-water 1** a bacterial disease of calves, a symptom of which is the passing of reddish urine. **2** a mass of water made red by pigmented plankton, esp. *Gonyanlax tamarensis*. □□ **reddish** *adj.* **reddy** *adj.* **redly** *adv.* **redness** *n.* [OE *rēad* f. Gmc]

redact /rɪˈdækt/ *v.tr.* put into literary form; edit for publication. □□ **redactor** *n.* [L *redigere redact-* (as RE-, *agere* bring)]

redaction /rɪˈdækʃ(ə)n/ *n.* **1** preparation for publication. **2** revision, editing, rearrangement. **3** a new edition. □□ **redactional** *adj.* [F *rédaction* f. LL *redactio* (as REDACT)]

redan /rɪˈdæn/ *n.* a fieldwork with two faces forming a salient angle. [F f. *redent* notching (as RE-, *dent* tooth)]

redbreast /ˈredbrest/ *n. colloq.* a robin.

redbrick /ˈredbrɪk/ *adj.* esp. *Brit.* (of a university) founded relatively recently.

redbud /ˈredbʌd/ *n.* any American tree of the genus *Cercis*, with pale pink flowers.

redcap /ˈredkæp/ *n.* **1** *Brit.* a member of the military police. **2** *US* a railway porter.

redcoat /ˈredkəʊt/ *n. hist.* a British soldier (so called from the scarlet uniform of most regiments).

redcurrant /ˈred,kʌrənt/ *n.* **1** a widely cultivated shrub, *Ribes rubrum*. **2** a small red edible berry of this plant.

redd /red/ *v.tr.* (*past* and *past part.* **redd**) *dial.* **1** clear up. **2** arrange, tidy, compose, settle. [ME: cf. MLG, MDu. *redden*]

redden /ˈred(ə)n/ *v.tr. & intr.* make or become red.

reddle /ˈred(ə)l/ *n.* red ochre; ruddle. [var. of RUDDLE]

rede /riːd/ *n. & v. archaic* *—n.* advice, counsel. *—v.tr.* **1** advise. **2** read (a riddle or dream). [OE *rǣd* f. Gmc, rel. to READ (of which the verb is a ME var. retained for archaic senses)]

redecorate /riːˈdekəreɪt/ *v.tr.* decorate again or differently. □□ **redecoration** /-ˈreɪʃ(ə)n/ *n.*

redeem /rɪˈdiːm/ *v.tr.* **1** buy back; recover by expenditure of effort or by a stipulated payment. **2** make a single payment to discharge (a regular charge or obligation). **3** convert (tokens or bonds etc.) into goods or cash. **4** (of God or Christ) deliver from sin and damnation. **5** make up for; be a compensating factor in (*has one redeeming feature*). **6** (foll. by *from*) save from (a defect). **7** *refl.* save (oneself) from blame. **8** purchase the freedom of (a person). **9** save (a person's life) by ransom. **10** save or rescue or reclaim. **11** fulfil (a promise). □□ **redeemable** *adj.* [ME f. OF *redimer* or L *redimere redempt-* (as RE-, *emere* buy)]

redeemer /rɪˈdiːmə(r)/ *n.* a person who redeems. □**the Redeemer** Christ.

redefine /ˌriːdɪˈfaɪn/ *v.tr.* define again or differently. □□ **redefinition** /-defɪˈnɪʃ(ə)n/ *n.*

redemption /rɪˈdempʃ(ə)n/ *n.* **1** the act or an instance of redeeming; the process of being redeemed. **2** man's deliverance from sin and damnation. **3** a thing that redeems. □□ **redemptive** *adj.* [ME f. OF f. L *redemptio* (as REDEEM)]

redeploy /ˌriːdɪˈplɔɪ/ *v.tr.* send (troops, workers, etc.) to a new place or task. □□ **redeployment** *n.*

redesign /ˌriːdɪˈzaɪn/ *v.tr.* design again or differently.

redetermine /ˌriːdɪˈtɜːmɪn/ v.tr. determine again or differently. □□ **redetermination** /-ˈneɪʃ(ə)n/ n.

redevelop /ˌriːdɪˈveləp/ v.tr. develop anew (esp. an urban area, with new buildings). □□ **redeveloper** n. **redevelopment** n.

redfish /ˈredfɪʃ/ n. **1** a male salmon in the spawning season. **2** a rose-fish.

redhead /ˈredhed/ n. a person with red hair.

redial /riːˈdaɪəl/ v.tr. & intr. (**redialled**, **redialling**; US **redialed**, **redialing**) dial again.

redid past of REDO.

rediffusion /ˌriːdɪˈfjuːʒ(ə)n/ n. the relaying of broadcast programmes esp. by cable from a central receiver.

redingote /ˈredɪŋɡəʊt/ n. a woman's long coat with a cutaway front or a contrasting piece on the front. [F f. E riding-coat]

redintegrate /rɪˈdɪntɪˌɡreɪt/ v.tr. **1** restore to wholeness or unity. **2** renew or re-establish in a united or perfect state. □□ **redintegration** /-ˈɡreɪʃ(ə)n/ n. **redintegrative** adj. [ME f. L redintegrare (as RE-, INTEGRATE)]

redirect /ˌriːdaɪˈrekt, -dɪˈrekt/ v.tr. direct again, esp. change the address of (a letter). □□ **redirection** n.

rediscover /ˌriːdɪˈskʌvə(r)/ v.tr. discover again. □□ **rediscovery** n. (pl. -ies).

redissolve /ˌriːdɪˈzɒlv/ v.tr. & intr. dissolve again. □□ **redissolution** /-ˌdɪsəˈluːʃ(ə)n/ n.

redistribute /ˌriːdɪˈstrɪˌbjuːt, disp. riːˈdɪs-/ v.tr. distribute again or differently. □□ **redistribution** /-ˈbjuː(ʃ)ə)n/ n. **redistributive** /-ˈtrɪbjʊtɪv/ adj.

redivide /ˌriːdɪˈvaɪd/ v.tr. divide again or differently. □□ **redivision** /-ˈvɪʒ(ə)n/ n.

redivivus /ˌredrɪˈviːvəs/ adj. (placed after noun) come back to life. [L (as RE-, vivus living)]

redneck /ˈrednek/ n. US often derog. a working-class White in the southern US, esp. a politically conservative one.

redo /riːˈduː/ v.tr. (3rd sing. present **redoes**; past **redid**; past part. **redone**) **1** do again or differently. **2** redecorate.

redolent /ˈredələnt/ adj. **1** (foll. by of, with) strongly reminiscent or suggestive or mentally associated. **2** fragrant. **3** having a strong smell; odorous. □□ **redolence** n. **redolently** adv. [ME f. OF redolent or L redolēre (as RE-, olēre smell)]

redouble /riːˈdʌb(ə)l/ v. & n. —v. **1** tr. & intr. make or grow greater or more intense or numerous; intensify, increase. **2** intr. Bridge double again a bid already doubled by an opponent. —n. Bridge the redoubling of a bid. [F redoubler (as RE-, DOUBLE)]

redoubt /rɪˈdaʊt/ n. Mil. an outwork or fieldwork usu. square or polygonal and without flanking defences. [F redoute f. obs. It. ridotta f. med.L reductus refuge f. past part. of L reducere withdraw (see REDUCE): -b- after DOUBT (cf. REDOUBTABLE)]

redoubtable /rɪˈdaʊtəb(ə)l/ adj. formidable, esp. as an opponent. □□ **redoubtably** adv. [ME f. OF redoutable f. redouter fear (as RE-, DOUBT)]

redound /rɪˈdaʊnd/ v.intr. **1** (foll. by to) (of an action etc.) make a great contribution to (one's credit or advantage etc.). **2** (foll. by upon, on) come as the final result to; come back or recoil upon. [ME, orig. = overflow, f. OF redonder f. L redundare surge (as RE-, unda wave)]

redox /ˈredɒks, ˈriː-/ n. Chem. (often attrib.) oxidation and reduction. [reduction + oxidation]

redpoll /ˈredpəʊl/ n. a finch, Acanthis flammea, with a red forehead, similar to a linnet.

redraft /riːˈdrɑːft/ v.tr. draft (a writing or document) again.

redraw /riːˈdrɔː/ v.tr. (past **redrew**; past part. **redrawn**) draw again or differently.

redress /rɪˈdres/ v. & n. —v.tr. **1** remedy or rectify (a wrong or grievance etc.). **2** readjust; set straight again. —n. **1** reparation for a wrong. **2** (foll. by of) the act or process of redressing (a grievance etc.). □ **redress the balance** restore equality. □□

redressable adj. **redressal** n. **redresser** n. (also **redressor**). [ME f. OF redresse(r), redrecier (as RE-, DRESS)]

re-dress /riːˈdres/ v.tr. & intr. dress again or differently.

redshank /ˈredʃæŋk/ n. either of two sandpipers, Tringa totanus and T. erythropus, with bright-red legs.

redskin /ˈredskɪn/ n. colloq. offens. an American Indian.

redstart /ˈredstɑːt/ n. **1** any European red-tailed songbird of the genus Phoenicurus. **2** any of various similar American warblers of the family Parulidae. [RED + OE steort tail]

reduce /rɪˈdjuːs/ v. **1** tr. & intr. make or become smaller or less. **2** tr. (foll. by to) bring by force or necessity (to some undesirable state or action) (reduced them to tears; were reduced to begging). **3** tr. convert to another (esp. simpler) form (reduced it to a powder). **4** tr. convert (a fraction) to the form with the lowest terms. **5** tr. (foll. by to) bring or simplify or adapt by classification or analysis (the dispute may be reduced to three issues). **6** tr. make lower in status or rank. **7** tr. lower the price of. **8** intr. lessen one's weight or size. **9** tr. weaken (is in a very reduced state). **10** tr. impoverish. **11** tr. subdue; bring back to obedience. **12** intr. & tr. Chem. **a** combine or cause to combine with hydrogen. **b** undergo or cause to undergo addition of electrons. **13** tr. Chem. convert (oxide etc.) to metal. **14** tr. **a** (in surgery) restore (a dislocated etc. part) to its proper position. **b** remedy (a dislocation etc.) in this way. **15** tr. Photog. make (a negative or print) less dense. **16** tr. Cookery boil off excess liquid from. □ **reduced circumstances** poverty after relative prosperity. **reduce to the ranks** demote (an NCO) to the rank of private. **reducing agent** Chem. a substance that brings about reduction by oxidation and losing electrons. □□ **reducer** n. **reducible** adj. **reducibility** /-ˈbɪlɪti/ n. [ME in sense 'restore to original or proper position', f. L reducere reduct- (as RE-, ducere bring)]

reductio ad absurdum /rɪˌdʌktɪəʊ æd æbˈzɜːdəm/ n. a method of proving the falsity of a premiss by showing that the logical consequence is absurd; an instance of this. [L, = reduction to the absurd]

reduction /rɪˈdʌkʃ(ə)n/ n. **1** the act or an instance of reducing; the process of being reduced. **2** an amount by which prices etc. are reduced. **3** a reduced copy of a picture etc. **4** an arrangement of an orchestral score for piano etc. □□ **reductive** adj. [ME f. OF reduction or L reductio (as REDUCE)]

reductionism /rɪˈdʌkʃəˌnɪz(ə)m/ n. **1** the tendency to or principle of analysing complex things into simple constituents. **2** often derog. the doctrine that a system can be fully understood in terms of its isolated parts, or an idea in terms of simple concepts. □□ **reductionist** n. **reductionistic** /-ˈnɪstɪk/ adj.

redundant /rɪˈdʌnd(ə)nt/ adj. **1** superfluous; not needed. **2** that can be omitted without any loss of significance. **3** (of a person) no longer needed at work and therefore unemployed. **4** Engin. & Computing (of a component) not needed but included in case of failure in another component. □□ **redundancy** n. (pl. -ies). **redundantly** adv. [L redundare redundant- (as REDOUND)]

reduplicate /rɪˈdjuːplɪˌkeɪt/ v.tr. **1** make double. **2** repeat. **3** repeat (a letter or syllable or word) exactly or with a slight change (e.g. hurly-burly, see-saw). □□ **reduplication** /-ˈkeɪʃ(ə)n/ n. **reduplicative** /-kətɪv/ adj. [LL reduplicare (as RE-, DUPLICATE)]

redwing /ˈredwɪŋ/ n. a thrush, Turdus iliacus, with red underwings showing in flight.

redwood /ˈredwʊd/ n. **1** an exceptionally large Californian conifer, Sequoia sempervirens, yielding red wood. **2** any tree yielding red wood.

reebok /ˈriːbɒk/ n. (also **rhebok**) a small S. African antelope, Pelea capreolus, with sharp horns. [Du., = roebuck]

re-echo /ˌriːˈekəʊ/ v.intr. & tr. (-oes, -oed) **1** echo. **2** echo repeatedly; resound.

reed[1] /riːd/ n. & v. —n. **1 a** any of various water or marsh plants with a firm stem, esp. of the genus *Phragmites*. **b** a tall straight stalk of this. **2** (collect.) reeds growing in a mass or used as material esp. for thatching. **3** Brit. wheat-straw prepared for thatching. **4** a pipe of reed or straw. **5 a** the vibrating part of the mouthpiece of some wind instruments, e.g. the oboe and clarinet, made of reed or other material and producing the sound. **b** (esp. in pl.) a reed instrument. **6** a weaver's comblike implement for separating the threads of the warp and correctly positioning the weft. **7** (in pl.) a set of semicylindrical adjacent mouldings like reeds laid together. —v.tr. **1** thatch with reed. **2** make (straw) into reed. **3** fit (a musical instrument) with a reed. **4** decorate with a moulding of reeds. □**reed bunting** a small brown bird, *Emberiza schoeniclus*, frequenting reed-beds. **reed-mace** a tall reedlike water-plant, *Typha latifolia*, with straplike leaves and a head of numerous tiny red-brown flowers. **reed-organ** a harmonium etc. with the sound produced by metal reeds. **reed-pipe 1** a wind instrument with sound produced by a reed. **2** an organ-pipe with a reed. **reed-stop** a reeded organ-stop. **reed-warbler** any bird of the genus *Acrocephalus*, esp. *A. scirpaceus*, frequenting reed-beds. [OE *hrēod* f. WG]

reed[2] /riːd/ n. the fourth stomach of a ruminant; the abomasum. [OE *rēada*]

reedbuck /ˈriːdbʌk/ n. an antelope, *Redunca redunca*, native to W. Africa.

reeded /ˈriːdɪd/ adj. Mus. (of an instrument) having a vibrating reed.

reeding /ˈriːdɪŋ/ n. Archit. a small semicylindrical moulding or ornamentation (cf. REED[1] n. 7).

re-edit /riːˈedɪt/ v.tr. (-edited, -editing) edit again or differently. □□**re-edition** /-ˈdɪʃ(ə)n/ n.

reedling /ˈriːdlɪŋ/ n. a bearded tit. [REED[1]]

re-educate /riːˈedjʊkeɪt/ v.tr. educate again, esp. to change a person's views or beliefs. □□**re-education** /-ˈkeɪʃ(ə)n/ n.

reedy /ˈriːdɪ/ adj. (**reedier, reediest**) **1** full of reeds. **2** like a reed, esp. in weakness or slenderness. **3** (of a voice) like a reed instrument in tone; not full. □□ **reediness** n.

reef[1] /riːf/ n. **1** a ridge of rock or coral etc. at or near the surface of the sea. **2 a** a lode of ore. **b** the bedrock surrounding this. [earlier *riff(e)* f. MDu., MLG *rif*, *ref*, f. ON *rif* RIB]

reef[2] /riːf/ n. & v. Naut. —n. each of several strips across a sail, for taking it in or rolling it up to reduce the surface area in a high wind. —v.tr. **1** take in a reef or reefs of (a sail). **2** shorten (a topmast or a bowsprit). □**reefing-jacket** a thick close-fitting double-breasted jacket. **reef-knot** a double knot made symmetrically to hold securely and cast off easily. **reef-point** each of several short pieces of rope attached to a sail to secure it when reefed. [ME *riff*, *refe* f. Du. *reef*, *rif* f. ON *rif* RIB, in the same sense: cf. REEF[1]]

reefer /ˈriːfə(r)/ n. **1** sl. a marijuana cigarette. **2** = *reefing-jacket* (see REEF[2]). **3 a** a person who reefs. **b** colloq. a midshipman. [REEF[2] (in sense 1, = a thing rolled) + -ER[1]]

reek /riːk/ v. & n. —v.intr. (often foll. by *of*) **1** smell strongly and unpleasantly. **2** have unpleasant or suspicious associations (*this reeks of corruption*). **3** give off smoke or fumes. —n. **1** a foul or stale smell. **2** esp. Sc. smoke. **3** vapour; a visible exhalation (esp. from a chimney). □□**reeky** adj. [OE *rēocan* (v.), *rēc* (n.), f. Gmc]

reel /riːl/ n. & v. —n. **1** a cylindrical device on which thread, silk, yarn, paper, film, wire, etc., are wound. **2** a quantity of thread etc. wound on a reel. **3** a device for winding and unwinding a line as required, esp. in fishing. **4** a revolving part in various machines. **5 a** a lively folk or Scottish dance, of two or more couples facing each other. **b** a piece of music

for this. —v. **1** tr. wind (thread, a fishing-line, etc.) on a reel. **2** tr. (foll. by *in*, *up*) draw (fish etc.) in or up by the use of a reel. **3** intr. stand or walk or run unsteadily. **4** intr. be shaken mentally or physically. **5** intr. rock from side to side, or swing violently. **6** intr. dance a reel. □**reel off** say or recite very rapidly and without apparent effort. □□ **reeler** n. [OE *hrēol*, of unkn. orig.]

re-elect /ˌriːɪˈlekt/ v.tr. elect again, esp. to a further term of office. □□ **re-election** /-ɪˈlekʃ(ə)n/ n. **re-eligible** /-ˈelɪdʒɪb(ə)l/ adj.

re-embark /ˌriːɪmˈbɑːk/ v.intr. & tr. go or put on board ship again. □□**re-embarkation** /-ˈkeɪʃ(ə)n/ n.

re-emerge /ˌriːɪˈmɜːdʒ/ v.intr. emerge again; come back out. □□**re-emergence** n. **re-emergent** adj.

re-emphasize /riːˈemfəsaɪz/ v.tr. place renewed emphasis on. □□**re-emphasis** /-ˈemfəsɪs/ n.

re-employ /ˌriːɪmˈplɔɪ/ v.tr. employ again. □□ **re-employment** n.

re-enact /ˌriːɪˈnækt/ v.tr. act out (a past event). □□ **re-enactment** n.

re-enlist /ˌriːɪnˈlɪst/ v.intr. enlist again, esp. in the armed services. □□**re-enlister** n.

re-enter /riːˈentə(r)/ v.tr. & intr. enter again; go back in. □□**re-entrance** /-ˈentrəns/ n.

re-entrant /riːˈentrənt/ adj. & n. —adj. **1** esp. *Fortification* (of an angle) pointing inwards (opp. SALIENT). **2** Geom. reflex. —n. a re-entrant angle.

re-entry /riːˈentrɪ/ n. (pl. **-ies**) **1** the act of entering again, esp. (of a spacecraft, missile, etc.) re-entering the earth's atmosphere. **2** Law an act of retaking or repossession.

re-equip /ˌriːɪˈkwɪp/ v.tr. & intr. (**-equipped**, **-equipping**) provide or be provided with new equipment.

re-erect /ˌriːɪˈrekt/ v.tr. erect again.

re-establish /ˌriːɪˈstæblɪʃ/ v.tr. establish again or anew. □□**re-establishment** n.

re-evaluate /ˌriːɪˈvæljʊeɪt/ v.tr. evaluate again or differently. □□**re-evaluation** /-ˈeɪʃ(ə)n/ n.

reeve[1] /riːv/ n. **1** hist. **a** the chief magistrate of a town or district. **b** an official supervising a landowner's estate. **c** any of various minor local officials. **2** Can. the president of a village or town council. [OE (ge)*rēfa*, *girǣfa*]

reeve[2] /riːv/ v.tr. (past **rove** /rəʊv/ or **reeved**) Naut. **1** (usu. foll. by *through*) thread (a rope or rod etc.) through a ring or other aperture. **2** pass a rope through (a block etc.). **3** fasten (a rope or block) in this way. [prob. f. Du. *rēven* REEF[2]]

reeve[3] /riːv/ n. a female ruff (see RUFF[1]). [17th c.: orig. unkn.]

re-examine /ˌriːɪgˈzæmɪn/ v.tr. examine again or further (esp. a witness after cross-examination). □□ **re-examination** /-ˈneɪʃ(ə)n/ n.

re-export v. & n. —v.tr. /ˌriːɪkˈspɔːt/ export again (esp. imported goods after further processing or manufacture). —n. /riːˈekspɔːt/ **1** the process of re-exporting. **2** something re-exported. □□ **re-exportation** /-ˈteɪʃ(ə)n/ n. **re-exporter** /ˌriːɪkˈspɔːtə(r)/ n.

ref /ref/ n. colloq. a referee in sports. [abbr.]

ref. abbr. **1** reference. **2** refer to.

reface /riːˈfeɪs/ v.tr. put a new facing on (a building).

refashion /riːˈfæʃ(ə)n/ v.tr. fashion again or differently.

refection /rɪˈfekʃ(ə)n/ n. literary **1** refreshment by food or drink (*we took refection*). **2** a light meal. [ME f. OF f. L *refectio -onis* f. *reficere* (as REFECTORY)]

refectory /rɪˈfektərɪ, ˈrefɪktərɪ/ n. (pl. **-ies**) a room used for communal meals, esp. in a monastery or college. □**refectory table** a long narrow table. [LL *refectorium* f. L *reficere* refresh (as RE-, *facere* make)]

refer /rɪˈfɜː(r)/ v. (**referred, referring**) (usu. foll. by *to*) **1** tr. trace or ascribe (to a person or thing as a cause or source) (*referred their success to their popularity*). **2** tr. consider as belonging (to a certain date or place or class). **3** tr. send on or direct (a person, or a question for decision) (*the matter was referred to arbitration; referred him to her previous answer*). **4** *intr.* make an appeal or have recourse to (some authority or source of information) (*referred to his notes*). **5** *tr.* send (a person) to a medical specialist etc. **6** *tr.* (foll. by *back to*) send (a proposal etc.) back to (a lower body, court, etc.). **7** *intr.* (foll. by *to*) (of a person speaking) make an allusion or direct the hearer's attention (*decided not to refer to our other problems*). **8** *intr.* (foll. by *to*) (of a statement etc.) have a particular relation; be directed (*this paragraph refers to the events of last year*). **9** *tr.* (foll. by *to*) interpret (a statement) as being directed to (a particular context etc.). **10** *tr.* fail (a candidate in an examination). □**referred pain** pain felt in a part of the body other than its actual source. **refer to drawer** a banker's note suspending payment of a cheque. □□ **referable** /rɪˈfɜːrəb(ə)l, ˈrefər-/ *adj.* **referrer** *n.* [ME f. OF *referer* f. L *referre* carry back (as RE-, *ferre* bring)]

referee /ˌrefəˈriː/ *n. & v.* —*n.* **1** an umpire esp. in football or boxing. **2** a person whose opinion or judgement is sought in some connection, or who is referred to for a decision in a dispute etc. **3** a person willing to testify to the character of an applicant for employment etc. —*v.* (**referees, refereed**) **1** *intr.* act as referee. **2** *tr.* be the referee of (a game etc.).

reference /ˈrefərəns/ *n. & v.* —*n.* **1** the referring of a matter for decision or settlement or consideration to some authority. **2** the scope given to this authority. **3** (foll. by *to*) **a** a relation or respect or correspondence (*success seems to have little reference to merit*). **b** an allusion (*made no reference to our problems*). **c** a direction to a book etc. (or a passage in it) where information may be found. **d** a book or passage so cited. **4 a** the act of looking up a passage etc. or looking in a book for information. **b** the act of referring to a person etc. for information. **5 a** a written testimonial supporting an applicant for employment etc. **b** a person giving this. —*v.tr.* provide (a book etc.) with references to authorities. □**reference book** a book intended to be consulted for information on individual matters rather than read continuously. **reference library** a library in which the books are for consultation not loan. **with** (or **in**) **reference to** regarding; as regards; about. **without reference to** not taking account of. □□ **referential** /-ˈrenʃ(ə)l/ *adj.*

referendum /ˌrefəˈrendəm/ *n.* (*pl.* **referendums** or **referenda** /-də/) **1** the process of referring a political question to the electorate for a direct decision by general vote. **2** a vote taken by referendum. [L, gerund or neut. gerundive of *referre*: see REFER]

referent /ˈrefərənt/ *n.* the idea or thing that a word etc. symbolizes. [L *referens* (as REFERENDUM)]

referral /rɪˈfɜːr(ə)l/ *n.* the referring of an individual to an expert or specialist for advice, esp. the directing of a patient by a GP to a medical specialist.

refill *v. & n.* —*v.tr.* /riːˈfɪl/ **1** fill again. **2** provide a new filling for. —*n.* /ˈriːfɪl/ **1** a new filling. **2** the material for this. □□ **refillable** /-ˈfɪləb(ə)l/ *adj.*

refine /rɪˈfaɪn/ *v.* **1** *tr.* free from impurities or defects; purify, clarify. **2** *tr. & intr.* make or become more polished or elegant or cultured. **3** *tr. & intr.* make or become more subtle or delicate in thought, feelings, etc. □□ **refinable** *adj.* [RE- + FINE¹ *v.*]

refined /rɪˈfaɪnd/ *adj.* characterized by polish or elegance or subtlety.

refinement /rɪˈfaɪnmənt/ *n.* **1** the act of refining or the process of being refined. **2** fineness of feeling or taste. **3** polish or elegance in behaviour or manner. **4** an added development or improvement (*a car with several refinements*). **5** a piece of subtle reasoning. **6** a fine distinction. **7** a subtle or ingenious example or display (*all the refinements of reasoning*). [REFINE + -MENT, after F *raffinement*]

refiner /rɪˈfaɪnə(r)/ *n.* a person or firm whose business is to refine crude oil, metal, sugar, etc.

refinery /rɪˈfaɪnəri/ *n.* (*pl.* **-ies**) a place where oil etc. is refined.

refit *v. & n.* —*v.tr. & intr.* /riːˈfɪt/ (**refitted, refitting**) make or become fit or serviceable again (esp. of a ship undergoing renewal and repairs). —*n.* /ˈriːfɪt/ the act or an instance of refitting; the process of being refitted. □□ **refitment** *n.*

reflag /riːˈflæg/ *v.tr.* (**reflagged, reflagging**) change the national registration of (a ship).

reflate /riːˈfleɪt/ *v.tr.* cause reflation of (a currency or economy etc.). [RE- after *inflate, deflate*]

reflation /riːˈfleɪʃ(ə)n/ *n.* the inflation of a financial system to restore its previous condition after deflation. [RE- after *inflation, deflation*]

reflect /rɪˈflekt/ *v.* **1** *tr.* **a** (of a surface or body) throw back (heat, light, sound, etc.). **b** cause to rebound (*reflected light*). **2** *tr.* (of a mirror) show an image of; reproduce to the eye or mind. **3** *tr.* correspond in appearance or effect to; have as a cause or source (*their behaviour reflects a wish to succeed*). **4** *tr.* **a** (of an action, result, etc.) show or bring (credit, discredit, etc.). **b** (*absol.*; usu. foll. by *on, upon*) bring discredit on. **5 a** *intr.* (often foll. by *on, upon*) meditate on; think about. **b** *tr.* (foll. by *that, how,* etc. + clause) consider; remind oneself. **6** *intr.* (usu. foll. by *upon, on*) make disparaging remarks. □**reflecting telescope** = REFLECTOR. [ME f. OF *reflecter* or L *reflectere* (as RE-, *flectere flex-* bend)]

reflection /rɪˈflekʃ(ə)n/ *n.* (also **reflexion**) **1** the act or an instance of reflecting; the process of being reflected. **2 a** a reflected light, heat, or colour. **b** a reflected image. **3** reconsideration (*on reflection*). **4** (often foll. by *on*) discredit or a thing bringing discredit. **5** (often foll. by *on, upon*) an idea arising in the mind; a comment or apophthegm. □**angle of reflection** *Physics* the angle made by a reflected ray with a perpendicular to the reflecting surface. □□ **reflectional** *adj.* [ME f. OF *reflexion* or LL *reflexio* (as REFLECT), with assim. to *reflect*]

reflective /rɪˈflektɪv/ *adj.* **1** (of a surface etc.) giving a reflection or image. **2** (of mental faculties) concerned in reflection or thought. **3** (of a person or mood etc.) thoughtful; given to meditation. □□ **reflectively** *adv.* **reflectiveness** *n.*

reflector /rɪˈflektə(r)/ *n.* **1** a piece of glass or metal etc. for reflecting light in a required direction, e.g. a red one on the back of a motor vehicle or bicycle. **2 a** a telescope etc. using a mirror to produce images. **b** the mirror itself.

reflet /rəˈfleɪ/ *n.* lustre or iridescence, esp. on pottery. [F f. It. *riflesso* reflection, REFLEX]

reflex /ˈriːfleks/ *adj. & n.* —*adj.* **1** (of an action) independent of the will, as an automatic response to the stimulation of a nerve (e.g. a sneeze). **2** (of an angle) exceeding 180°. **3** bent backwards. **4** (of light) reflected. **5** (of a thought etc.) introspective; directed back upon itself or its own operations. **6** (of an effect or influence) reactive; coming back upon its author or source. —*n.* **1** a reflex action. **2** a sign or secondary manifestation (*law is a reflex of public opinion*). **3** reflected light or a reflected image. **4** a word formed by development from an earlier stage of a language. □**reflex arc** *Anat.* the sequence of nerves involved in a reflex action. **reflex camera** a camera with a ground-glass focusing screen on which the image is formed by a combination of lens and mirror, enabling the scene to be correctly composed and focused. □□ **reflexly** *adv.* [L *reflexus* (as REFLECT)]

reflexible /rɪˈfleksɪb(ə)l/ *adj.* capable of being reflected. □□ **reflexibility** /-ˈbɪlɪti/ *n.*

reflexion *Brit.* var. of REFLECTION.

reflexive /rɪˈfleksɪv/ *adj. & n. Gram.* —*adj.* **1** (of a word or form) referring back to the subject of a sentence (esp. of a pronoun, e.g. *myself*). **2** (of a verb) having a reflexive pronoun as its object (as in *to wash oneself*). —*n.* a reflexive word or form, esp. a pronoun. □□ **reflexively** *adv.* **reflexiveness** *n.* **reflexivity** /-ˈsɪvɪti/ *n.*

reflexology /ˌriːflekˈsɒlədʒɪ/ n. **1** a system of massage through reflex points on the feet, hands, and head, used to relieve tension and treat illness. **2** Psychol. the scientific study of reflexes. □□ **reflexologist** n.

refloat /riːˈfləʊt/ v.tr. set (a stranded ship) afloat again.

refluent /ˈrefluənt/ adj. flowing back (refluent tide). □□ **refluence** n. [ME f. L refluere (as RE-, fluere flow)]

reflux /ˈriːflʌks/ n. & v. —n. **1** a backward flow. **2** Chem. a method of boiling a liquid so that any vapour is liquefied and returned to the boiler. —v.tr. & intr. Chem. boil or be boiled under reflux.

refocus /riːˈfəʊkəs/ v.tr. (**refocused, refocusing** or **refocussed, refocussing**) adjust the focus of (esp. a lens).

reforest /riːˈfɒrɪst/ v.tr. = REAFFOREST. □□ **reforestation** /-ˈsteɪʃ(ə)n/ n.

reforge /riːˈfɔːdʒ/ v.tr. forge again or differently.

reform /rɪˈfɔːm/ v. & n. —v. **1** tr. & intr. make or become better by the removal of faults and errors. **2** tr. abolish or cure (an abuse or malpractice). **3** tr. US correct (a legal document). **4** tr. Chem. convert (a straight-chain hydrocarbon) by catalytic reaction to a branched-chain form for use as petrol. —n. **1** the removal of faults or abuses, esp. of a moral or political or social kind. **2** an improvement made or suggested. □ **Reformed Church** a Church that has accepted the principles of the Reformation, esp. a Calvinist Church (as distinct from Lutheran). **Reform Judaism** a simplified and rationalized form of Judaism. **reform school** an institution to which young offenders are sent to be reformed. □□ **reformable** adj. [ME f. OF reformer or L reformare (as RE-, FORM)]

re-form /riːˈfɔːm/ v.tr. & intr. form again. □□ **re-formation** /-ˈmeɪʃ(ə)n/ n.

reformat /riːˈfɔːmæt/ v.tr. (**reformatted, reformatting**) format anew.

reformation /ˌrefəˈmeɪʃ(ə)n/ n. the act of reforming or process of being reformed, esp. a radical change for the better in political or religious or social affairs. □ **the Reformation** hist. a 16th-c. movement for the reform of abuses in the Roman Church ending in the establishment of the Reformed and Protestant Churches. □□ **Reformational** adj. [ME f. OF reformation or L reformatio (as REFORM)]

re-formation /ˌriːfɔːˈmeɪʃ(ə)n/ n. the process or an instance of forming or being formed again.

reformative /rɪˈfɔːmətɪv/ adj. tending or intended to produce reform. [OF reformatif -ive or med.L reformativus (as REFORM)]

reformatory /rɪˈfɔːmətərɪ/ n. & adj. —n. (pl. -ies) US & hist. = reform school. —adj. reformative.

reformer /rɪˈfɔːmə(r)/ n. a person who advocates or brings about (esp. political or social) reform.

reformism /rɪˈfɔːmɪz(ə)m/ n. a policy of reform rather than abolition or revolution. □□ **reformist** n.

reformulate /riːˈfɔːmjʊˌleɪt/ v.tr. formulate again or differently. □□ **reformulation** /-ˈleɪʃ(ə)n/ n.

refract /rɪˈfrækt/ v.tr. **1** (of water, air, glass, etc.) deflect (a ray of light etc.) at a certain angle when it enters obliquely from another medium. **2** determine the refractive condition of (the eye). [L refringere refract- (as RE-, frangere break)]

refraction /rɪˈfrækʃ(ə)n/ n. the process by which or the extent to which light is refracted. □ **angle of refraction** the angle made by a refracted ray with the perpendicular to the refracting surface. [F réfraction or LL refractio (as REFRACT)]

refractive /rɪˈfræktɪv/ adj. of or involving refraction. □ **refractive index** the ratio of the velocity of light in a vacuum to its velocity in a specified medium.

refractometer /ˌriːfrækˈtɒmɪtə(r)/ n. an instrument for measuring a refractive index. □□ **refractometric** /-təˈmetrɪk/ adj. **refractometry** n.

refractor /rɪˈfræktə(r)/ n. **1** a refracting medium or lens. **2** a telescope using a lens to produce an image.

refractory /rɪˈfræktərɪ/ adj. & n. —adj. **1** stubborn,

unmanageable, rebellious. **2 a** (of a wound, disease, etc.) not yielding to treatment. **b** (of a person etc.) resistant to infection. **3** (of a substance) hard to fuse or work. —n. (pl. -ies) a substance especially resistant to heat, corrosion, etc. □□ **refractorily** adv. **refractoriness** n. [alt. of obs. refractary f. L refractarius (as REFRACT)]

refrain[1] /rɪˈfreɪn/ v.intr. (foll. by from) avoid doing (an action) (refrain from smoking). □□ **refrainment** n. [ME f. OF refrener f. L refrenare (as RE-, frenum bridle)]

refrain[2] /rɪˈfreɪn/ n. **1** a recurring phrase or number of lines, esp. at the ends of stanzas. **2** the music accompanying this. [ME f. OF refrain (earlier refrait) ult. f. L refringere (as RE-, frangere break), because the refrain 'broke' the sequence]

refrangible /rɪˈfrændʒɪb(ə)l/ adj. that can be refracted. □□ **refrangibility** /-ˈbɪlɪtɪ/ n. [mod.L refrangibilis f. refrangere = L refringere: see REFRACT]

refreeze /riːˈfriːz/ v.tr. & intr. (past **refroze**; past part. **refrozen**) freeze again.

refresh /rɪˈfreʃ/ v.tr. **1 a** (of food, rest, amusement, etc.) give fresh spirit or vigour to. **b** (esp. refl.) revive with food, rest, etc. (refreshed myself with a short sleep). **2** revive or stimulate (the memory), esp. by consulting the source of one's information. **3** make cool. [ME f. OF refreschi(e)r f. fres fresche FRESH]

refresher /rɪˈfreʃə(r)/ n. **1** something that refreshes, esp. a drink. **2** Law an extra fee payable to counsel in a prolonged case. □ **refresher course** a course reviewing or updating previous studies.

refreshing /rɪˈfreʃɪŋ/ adj. **1** serving to refresh. **2** welcome or stimulating because sincere or untypical (refreshing innocence). □□ **refreshingly** adv.

refreshment /rɪˈfreʃmənt/ n. **1** the act of refreshing or the process of being refreshed in mind or body. **2** (usu. in pl.) food or drink that refreshes. **3** something that refreshes or stimulates the mind. [ME f. OF refreschement (as REFRESH)]

refrigerant /rɪˈfrɪdʒərənt/ n. & adj. —n. **1** a substance used for refrigeration. **2** Med. a substance that cools or allays fever. —adj. cooling. [F réfrigérant or L refrigerant- (as REFRIGERATE)]

refrigerate /rɪˈfrɪdʒəˌreɪt/ v. **1** tr. & intr. make or become cool or cold. **2** tr. subject (food etc.) to cold in order to freeze or preserve it. □□ **refrigeration** /-ˈreɪʃ(ə)n/ n. **refrigerative** /-rətɪv/ adj. [L refrigerare (as RE-, frigus frigoris cold)]

refrigerator /rɪˈfrɪdʒəˌreɪtə(r)/ n. a cabinet or room in which food etc. is kept cold.

refrigeratory /rɪˈfrɪdʒərətərɪ/ adj. & n. —adj. serving to cool. —n. (pl. -ies) hist. a cold-water vessel attached to a still for condensing vapour. [mod.L refrigeratorium (n.), L refrigeratorius (adj.) (as REFRIGERATE)]

refringent /rɪˈfrɪndʒ(ə)nt/ adj. Physics refracting. □□ **refringence** n. **refringency** n. [L refringere: see REFRACT]

refroze past of REFREEZE.

refrozen past part. of REFREEZE.

reft past part. of REAVE.

refuel /riːˈfjuːəl/ v. (**refuelled, refuelling**; US **refueled, refueling**) **1** intr. replenish a fuel supply. **2** tr. supply with more fuel.

refuge /ˈrefjuːdʒ/ n. **1** a shelter from pursuit or danger or trouble. **2** a person or place etc. offering this. **3** a person, thing, or course resorted to in difficulties. **4** a traffic island. [ME f. OF f. L refugium (as RE-, fugere flee)]

refugee /ˌrefjʊˈdʒiː/ n. a person taking refuge, esp. in a foreign country from war or persecution or natural disaster. [F réfugié past part. of (se) réfugier (as REFUGE)]

refulgent /rɪˈfʌldʒ(ə)nt/ adj. literary shining; gloriously bright. □□ **refulgence** n. **refulgently** adv. [L refulgēre (as RE-, fulgēre shine)]

refund v. & n. —v. /rɪˈfʌnd/ tr. (also absol.) **1** pay back (money or expenses). **2** reimburse (a person).

—*n.* /'ri:fʌnd/ **1** an act of refunding. **2** a sum refunded; a repayment. □□ **refundable** /rɪ'fʌndəb(ə)l/ *adj.*

refunder /rɪ'fʌndə(r)/ *n.* [ME in sense 'pour back', f. OF *refonder* or L *refundere* (as RE-, *fundere* pour), later assoc. with FUND]

re-fund /ri:'fʌnd/ *v.tr.* fund (a debt etc.) again.

refurbish /ri:'fɜ:bɪʃ/ *v.tr.* **1** brighten up. **2** restore and redecorate. □□ **refurbishment** *n.*

refurnish /ri:'fɜ:nɪʃ/ *v.tr.* furnish again or differently.

refusal /rɪ'fju:z(ə)l/ *n.* **1** the act or an instance of refusing; the state of being refused. **2** (in full **first refusal**) the right or privilege of deciding to take or leave a thing before it is offered to others.

refuse[1] /rɪ'fju:z/ *v.* **1** *tr.* withhold acceptance of or consent to (*refuse an offer; refuse orders*). **2** *tr.* (often foll. by *to* + infin.) indicate unwillingness (*I refuse to go; the car refuses to start; I refuse!*). **3** *tr.* (often with double object) not grant (a request) made by (a person) (*refused me a day off; I could not refuse them*). **4** *tr.* (also *absol.*) (of a horse) be unwilling to jump (a fence etc.). □□ **refusable** *adj.* **refuser** *n.* [ME f. OF *refuser* prob. ult. f. L *recusare* (see RECUSANT) after *refutare* REFUTE]

refuse[2] /'refju:s/ *n.* items rejected as worthless; waste. [ME, perh. f. OF *refusé* past part. (as REFUSE)]

re-fuse /ri:'fju:z/ *v.tr.* fuse again; provide with a new fuse.

refusenik /rɪ'fju:znɪk/ *n.* a Jew in the Soviet Union who has been refused permission to emigrate to Israel. [REFUSE[1] + -NIK]

refute /rɪ'fju:t/ *v.tr.* **1** prove the falsity or error of (a statement etc. or the person advancing it). **2** rebut or repel by argument. **3** *disp.* deny or contradict (without argument). ¶ Often confused in this sense with *repudiate*. □□ **refutable** *adj.* **refutal** *n.* **refutation** /,refju'teɪʃ(ə)n/ *n.* **refuter** *n.* [L *refutare* (as RE-: cf. CONFUTE)]

reg /redʒ/ *n. colloq.* = *registration mark.* [abbr.]

regain /rɪ'geɪn/ *v.tr.* obtain possession or use of after loss (*regain consciousness*). [F *regagner* (as RE-, GAIN)]

regal /'ri:g(ə)l/ *adj.* **1** royal; of or by a monarch or monarchs. **2** fit for a monarch; magnificent. □□ **regally** *adv.* [ME f. OF *regal* or L *regalis* f. *rex regis* king]

regale /rɪ'geɪl/ *v.tr.* **1** entertain lavishly with feasting. **2** (foll. by *with*) entertain or divert with (talk etc.). **3** (of beauty, flowers, etc.) give delight to. □□ **regalement** *n.* [F *régaler* f. *gale* pleasure]

regalia /rɪ'geɪlɪə/ *n.pl.* **1** the insignia of royalty used at coronations. **2** the insignia of an order or of civic dignity. [med.L, = royal privileges, f. L neut. pl. of *regalis* REGAL]

regalism /'ri:gə,lɪz(ə)m/ *n.* the doctrine of a sovereign's ecclesiastical supremacy.

regality /rɪ'gælɪtɪ/ *n.* (*pl.* -ies) **1** the state of being a king or queen. **2** an attribute of sovereign power. **3** a royal privilege. [ME f. OF *regalité* or med.L *regalitas* (as REGAL)]

regard /rɪ'gɑ:d/ *v.* & *n.* —*v.tr.* **1** gaze on steadily (usu. in a specified way) (*regarded them suspiciously*). **2** give heed to; take into account; let one's course be affected by. **3** look upon or contemplate mentally in a specified way (*I regard them kindly; I regard it as an insult*). **4** (of a thing) have relation to; have some connection with. —*n.* **1** a gaze; a steady or significant look. **2** (foll. by *to, for*) attention or care. **3** (foll. by *for*) esteem; kindly feeling; respectful opinion. **4** a respect; a point attended to (*in this regard*). **5** (in *pl.*) an expression of friendliness in a letter etc.; compliments (*sent my best regards*). □ **as regards** about, concerning; in respect of. **in** (or **with**) **regard to** as concerns; in respect of. [ME f. OF *regard* f. *regarder* (as RE-, *garder* GUARD)]

regardant /rɪ'gɑ:d(ə)nt/ *adj. Heraldry* looking backwards. [AF & OF (as REGARD)]

regardful /rɪ'gɑ:dfʊl/ *adj.* (foll. by *of*) mindful of; paying attention to.

regarding /rɪ'gɑ:dɪŋ/ *prep.* about, concerning; in respect of.

regardless /rɪ'gɑ:dlɪs/ *adj.* & *adv.* —*adj.* (foll. by *of*) without regard or consideration for (*regardless of the expense*). —*adv.* without paying attention (*carried on regardless*). □□ **regardlessly** *adv.* **regardlessness** *n.*

regather /rɪ'gæðə(r)/ *v.tr.* & *intr.* **1** gather or collect again. **2** meet again.

regatta /rɪ'gætə/ *n.* a sporting event consisting of a series of boat or yacht races. [It. (Venetian)]

regd. *abbr.* registered.

regelate /,ri:dʒ'leɪt, 'redʒ-/ *v.intr.* freeze again (esp. of pieces of ice etc. frozen together after temporary thawing of the surfaces). □□ **regelation** /-'leɪʃ(ə)n/ *n.* [RE- + L *gelare* freeze]

regency /'ri:dʒənsɪ/ *n.* (*pl.* -ies) **1** the office of regent. **2** a commission acting as regent. **3 a** the period of office of a regent or regency commission. **b** (**Regency**) a particular period of a regency, esp. (in Britain) from 1811 to 1820, and (in France) from 1715 to 1723 (often *attrib.*: *Regency costume*). [ME f. med.L *regentia* (as REGENT)]

regenerate *v.* & *adj.* —*v.* /rɪ'dʒenə,reɪt/ **1** *tr.* & *intr.* bring or come into renewed existence; generate again. **2** *tr.* improve the moral condition of. **3** *tr.* impart new, more vigorous, and spiritually greater life to (a person or institution etc.). **4** *intr.* reform oneself. **5** *tr.* invest with a new and higher spiritual nature. **6** *intr.* & *tr. Biol.* regrow or cause (new tissue) to regrow to replace lost or injured tissue. **7** *tr.* & *intr. Chem.* restore or be restored to an initial state of reaction or process. —*adj.* /rɪ'dʒenərət/ **1** spiritually born again. **2** reformed. □□ **regeneration** /-'reɪʃ(ə)n/ *n.* **regenerative** /-rətɪv/ *adj.* **regeneratively** /-rə,tɪvlɪ/ *adv.* **regenerator** *n.* [L *regenerare* (as RE-, GENERATE)]

regent /'ri:dʒ(ə)nt/ *n.* & *adj.* —*n.* **1** a person appointed to administer a State because the monarch is a minor or is absent or incapacitated. **2** *US* a member of the governing body of a State university. —*adj.* (placed after noun) acting as regent (*Prince Regent*). □ **regent-bird** an Australian bower bird, *Sericulus chrysocephalus.* [ME f. OF *regent* or L *regere* rule]

regerminate /ri:'dʒɜ:mɪ,neɪt/ *v.tr.* & *intr.* germinate again. □□ **regermination** /-'neɪʃ(ə)n/ *n.*

reggae /'regeɪ/ *n.* a W. Indian style of music with a strongly accented subsidiary beat. [W.Ind.]

regicide /'redʒɪ,saɪd/ *n.* **1** a person who kills or takes part in killing a king. **2** the act of killing a king. □□ **regicidal** /-'saɪd(ə)l/ *adj.* [L *rex regis* king + -CIDE]

regild /ri:'gɪld/ *v.tr.* gild again, esp. to renew faded or worn gilding.

regime /reɪ'ʒi:m/ *n.* (also **régime**) **1 a** a method or system of government. **b** *derog.* a particular government. **2** a prevailing order or system of things. **3** the conditions under which a scientific or industrial process occurs. [F *régime* (as REGIMEN)]

regimen /'redʒɪ,men/ *n.* **1** esp. *Med.* a prescribed course of exercise, way of life, and diet. **2** *archaic* a system of government. [L f. *regere* rule]

regiment *n.* & *v.* —*n.* /'redʒɪmənt/ **1 a** a permanent unit of an army usu. commanded by a colonel and divided into several companies or troops or batteries and often into two battalions. **b** an operational unit of artillery etc. **2** (usu. foll. by *of*) a large array or number. **3** *archaic* rule, government. —*v.tr.* /'redʒɪ,ment/ **1** organize (esp. oppressively) in groups or according to a system. **2** form into a regiment or regiments. □□ **regimentation** /-'teɪʃ(ə)n/ *n.* [ME (in sense 3) f. OF f. LL *regimentum* (as REGIMEN)]

regimental /,redʒɪ'ment(ə)l/ *adj.* & *n.* —*adj.* of or relating to a regiment. —*n.* (in *pl.*) military uniform, esp. of a particular regiment. □□ **regimentally** *adv.*

Regina /rɪ'dʒaɪnə/ *n.* the reigning queen (following a name or in the titles of lawsuits, e.g. *Regina v. Jones* the Crown versus Jones). [L, = queen f. *rex regis* king]

æ **cat** ɑ: **arm** e **bed** ɜ: **her** ɪ **sit** i: **see** ɒ **hot** ɔ: **saw** ʌ **run** ʊ **put** u: **too** ə **ago** aɪ **my**

region /'ri:dʒ(ə)n/ n. **1** an area of land, or division of the earth's surface, having definable boundaries or characteristics (*a mountainous region; the region between London and the coast*). **2** an administrative district esp. in Scotland. **3** a part of the body round or near some organ etc. (*the lumbar region*). **4 a** sphere or realm (*the region of metaphysics*). **5 a** a separate part of the world or universe. **b** a layer of the atmosphere or the sea according to its height or depth. □**in the region of** approximately. □□ **regional** *adj.* **regionalism** *n.* **regionalist** *n.* & *adj.* **regionalize** *v.tr.* (also **-ise**). **regionally** *adv.* [ME f. OF f. L *regio -onis* direction, district f. *regere* direct]

régisseur /,reɪʒɪ'sɜ:(r)/ n. the director of a theatrical production, esp. a ballet. [F *régisseur* stage-manager]

register /'redʒɪstə(r)/ n. & v. —n. **1** an official list e.g. of births, marriages, and deaths, of shipping, of professionally qualified persons, or of qualified voters in a constituency. **2** a book in which items are recorded for reference. **3** a device recording speed, force, etc. **4** (in electronic devices) a location in a store of data, used for a specific purpose and with quick access time. **5 a** the compass of a voice or instrument. **b** a part of this compass (*lower register*). **6** an adjustable plate for widening or narrowing an opening and regulating a draught, esp. in a fire-grate. **7 a** a set of organ pipes. **b** a sliding device controlling this. **8** = *cash register* (see CASH[1]). **9** *Linguistics* each of several forms of a language (colloquial, formal, literary, etc.) usually used in particular circumstances. **10** *Printing* the exact correspondence of the position of printed matter on the two sides of a leaf. **11** *Printing* & *Photog.* the correspondence of the position of colour-components in a printed positive. —v. **1** *tr.* set down (a name, fact, etc.) formally; record in writing. **2** *tr.* make a mental note of; notice. **3** *tr.* enter or cause to be entered in a particular register. **4** *tr.* entrust (a letter etc.) to a post office for transmission by registered post. **5** *intr.* & *refl.* put one's name on a register, esp. as an eligible voter or as a guest in a register kept by a hotel etc. **6** *tr.* (of an instrument) record automatically; indicate. **7 a** *tr.* express (an emotion) facially or by gesture (*registered surprise*). **b** *intr.* (of an emotion) show in a person's face or gestures. **8** *intr.* make an impression on a person's mind (*did not register at all*). **9** *intr.* & *tr.* *Printing* correspond or cause to correspond exactly in position. □**registered nurse** a nurse with a State certificate of competence. **registered post** a postal procedure with special precautions for safety and for compensation in case of loss. **register office** *Brit.* a State office where civil marriages are conducted and births, marriages, and deaths are recorded with the issue of certificates. ¶ The name in official use, and generally preferred to *registry office*. □□ **registrable** *adj.* [ME & OF *registre*, *registre* or med.L *regestrum*, *registrum*, alt. of *regestum* f. LL *regesta* things recorded (as RE-, L *gerere gest-* carry)]

registrar /,redʒɪs'trɑː(r), 'redʒ-/ n. **1** an official responsible for keeping a register or official records. **2** the chief administrative officer in a university. **3** a middle-ranking hospital doctor undergoing training as a specialist. **4** (in the UK) the judicial and administrative officer of the High Court etc. □**Registrar General** a government official responsible for holding a population census. □□ **registrarship** n. [med.L *registrarius* f. *registrum* REGISTER]

registrary /'redʒɪstrəri/ n. (pl. **-ies**) the registrar of Cambridge University.

registration /,redʒɪ'streɪʃ(ə)n/ n. the act or an instance of registering; the process of being registered. □**registration mark** (or **number**) a combination of letters and figures identifying a motor vehicle etc. [obs. F *régistration* or med.L *registratio* (as REGISTRAR)]

registry /'redʒɪstri/ n. (pl. **-ies**) **1** a place or office

where registers or records are kept. **2** registration. □**registry office** = *register office*. [obs. *registery* f. med.L *registerium* (as REGISTER)]

Regius professor /'ri:dʒɪəs/ n. *Brit.* the holder of a chair founded by a sovereign (esp. one at Oxford or Cambridge instituted by Henry VIII) or filled by Crown appointment. [L, = royal, f. *rex regis* king]

reglaze /ri:'gleɪz/ v.tr. glaze (a window etc.) again.

reglet /'reglɪt/ n. **1** *Archit.* a narrow strip separating mouldings. **2** *Printing* a thin strip of wood or metal separating type. [F *réglet* dimin. of *règle*]

regnal /'regn(ə)l/ adj. of a reign. □**regnal year** a year reckoned from the date or anniversary of a sovereign's accession. [AL *regnalis* (as REIGN)]

regnant /'regnənt/ adj. **1** reigning (*Queen regnant*). **2** (of things, qualities, etc.) predominant, prevalent. [L *regnare* REIGN]

regolith /'regəlɪθ/ n. *Geol.* unconsolidated solid material covering the bedrock of a planet. [erron. f. Gk *rhēgos* rug, blanket + -LITH]

regorge /rɪ'gɔːdʒ/ v. **1** *tr.* bring up or expel again after swallowing. **2** *intr.* gush or flow back from a pit, channel, etc. [F *regorger* or RE- + GORGE]

regrade /ri:'greɪd/ v.tr. grade again or differently.

regress v. & n. —v. /rɪ'gres/ **1** *intr.* move backwards, esp. (in abstract senses) return to a former state. **2** *intr.* & *tr.* *Psychol.* return or cause to return mentally to a former stage of life, esp. through hypnosis or mental illness. —n. /'ri:gres/ **1** the act or an instance of going back. **2** reasoning from effect to cause. [ME (as n.) f. L *regressus* f. *regredi regress-* (as RE-, *gradi* step)]

regression /rɪ'greʃ(ə)n/ n. **1** a backward movement, esp. a return to a former state. **2** a relapse or reversion. **3** *Psychol.* a return to an earlier stage of development, esp. through hypnosis or mental illness. **4** *Statistics* a measure of the relation between the mean value of one variable (e.g. output) and corresponding values of other variables (e.g. time and cost). [L *regressio* (as REGRESS)]

regressive /rɪ'gresɪv/ adj. **1** regressing; characterized by regression. **2** (of a tax) proportionally greater on lower incomes. □□ **regressively** adv. **regressiveness** n.

regret /rɪ'gret/ v. & n. —v.tr. (**regretted**, **regretting**) (often foll. by *that* + clause) **1** feel or express sorrow or repentance or distress over (an action or loss etc.) (*I regret that I forgot; regretted your absence*). **2** (often foll. by *to* + infin. or *that* + clause) acknowledge with sorrow or remorse (*I regret to say that you are wrong; regretted he would not be attending*). —n. **1** a feeling of sorrow, repentance, disappointment, etc., over an action or loss etc. **2** (often in *pl.*) an (esp. polite or formal) expression of disappointment or sorrow at an occurrence, inability to comply, etc. (*refused with many regrets; heard with regret of her death*). □**give** (or **send**) **one's regrets** formally decline an invitation. [ME f. OF *regreter* bewail]

regretful /rɪ'gretfʊl/ adj. feeling or showing regret. □□ **regretfully** adv. **regretfulness** n.

regrettable /rɪ'gretəb(ə)l/ adj. (of events or conduct) undesirable, unwelcome; deserving censure. □□ **regrettably** adv.

regroup /ri:'gru:p/ v.tr. & intr. group or arrange again or differently. □□ **regroupment** n.

regrow /ri:'grəʊ/ v.intr. & tr. grow again, esp. after an interval. □□ **regrowth** n.

Regt. *abbr.* Regiment.

regulable /'regjʊləb(ə)l/ adj. able to be regulated.

regular /'regjʊlə(r)/ adj. & n. —adj. **1** conforming to a rule or principle; systematic. **2** (of a structure or arrangement) harmonious, symmetrical (*regular features*). **3** acting or done or recurring uniformly or calculably in time or manner; habitual, constant, orderly. **4** conforming to a standard of etiquette or procedure; correct; according to convention. **5** properly constituted or qualified; not defective or amateur; pursuing an occupation as one's main pursuit (*cooks as well as a regular cook*; *has no regular profession*). **6** *Gram.* (of a noun, verb, etc.) following the normal type of inflection. **7** *colloq.* complete, thorough, absolute (*a regular hero*). **8** *Geom.* **a** (of a figure) having all sides and all angles equal. **b** (of a solid) bounded by a number of equal figures. **9** *Eccl.* (placed before or after noun) **a** bound by religious rule. **b** belonging to a religious or monastic order (*canon regular*). **10** (of forces or troops etc.) relating to or constituting a permanent professional body (*regular soldiers*; *regular police force*). **11** (of a person) defecating or menstruating at predictable times. **12** *Bot.* (of a flower) having radial symmetry. —*n.* **1** a regular soldier. **2** *colloq.* a regular customer, visitor, etc. **3** *Eccl.* one of the regular clergy. **4** *colloq.* a person permanently employed. □ **keep regular hours** do the same thing, esp. going to bed and getting up, at the same time each day. □□ **regularity** /-'lærɪtɪ/ *n.* **regularize** *v.tr.* (also **-ise**). **regularization** /-'zeɪʃ(ə)n/ *n.* **regularly** *adv.* [ME *reguler*, *regular* f. OF *reguler* f. L *regularis* f. *regula* RULE]

regulate /'regjʊˌleɪt/ *v.tr.* **1** control by rule. **2** subject to restrictions. **3** adapt to requirements. **4** alter the speed of (a machine or clock) so that it may work accurately. □□ **regulative** /-lətɪv/ *adj.* **regulator** *n.* **regulatory** /-lətərɪ/ *adj.* [LL *regulare regulat-* f. L *regula* RULE]

regulation /ˌregjʊ'leɪʃ(ə)n/ *n.* **1** the act or an instance of regulating; the process of being regulated. **2** a prescribed rule; an authoritative direction. **3** (*attrib.*) **a** in accordance with regulations; of the correct type etc. (*the regulation speed*; *a regulation tie*). **b** *colloq.* usual (*the regulation soup*).

regulo /'regjʊˌləʊ/ *n.* (usu. foll. by a numeral) each of the numbers of a scale denoting temperature in a gas oven (*cook at regulo 6*). [*Regulo*, propr. term for a thermostatic gas oven control]

regulus /'regjʊləs/ *n.* (*pl.* **reguluses** or **reguli** /-ˌlaɪ/) *Chem.* **1** the purer or metallic part of a mineral that separates by sinking on reduction. **2** an impure metallic product formed during the smelting of various ores. □□ **reguline** /-ˌlaɪn/ *adj.* [L, dimin. of *rex regis* king: orig. of a metallic form of antimony, so called because of its readiness to combine with gold]

regurgitate /rɪ'gɜːdʒɪˌteɪt/ *v.* **1** *tr.* bring (swallowed food) up again to the mouth. **2** *tr.* cast or pour out again (*required by the exam to regurgitate facts*). **3** *intr.* be brought up again; gush back. □□ **regurgitation** /-'teɪʃ(ə)n/ *n.* [med.L *regurgitare* (as RE-, L *gurges gurgitis* whirlpool)]

rehab /'riːhæb/ *n. colloq.* rehabilitation. [abbr.]

rehabilitate /ˌriːhə'bɪlɪˌteɪt/ *v.tr.* **1** restore to effectiveness or normal life by training etc., esp. after imprisonment or illness. **2** restore to former privileges or reputation or a proper condition. □□ **rehabilitation** /-'teɪʃ(ə)n/ *n.* **rehabilitative** /-lətɪv/ *adj.* [med.L *rehabilitare* (as RE-, HABILITATE)]

rehandle /riː'hænd(ə)l/ *v.tr.* **1** handle again. **2** give a new form or arrangement to.

rehang /riː'hæŋ/ *v.tr.* (*past* and *past part.* **rehung**) hang (esp. a picture or a curtain) again or differently.

rehash *v.* & *n.* —*v.tr.* /riː'hæʃ/ put (old material) into a new form without significant change or improvement. —*n.* /'riːhæʃ/ **1** material rehashed. **2** the act or an instance of rehashing.

rehear /riː'hɪə(r)/ *v.tr.* (*past* and *past part.* **reheard** /riː'hɜːd/) hear again.

rehearsal /rɪ'hɜːs(ə)l/ *n.* **1** the act or an instance of rehearsing. **2** a trial performance or practice of a play, recital, etc.

rehearse /rɪ'hɜːs/ *v.* **1** *tr.* practise (a play, recital, etc.) for later public performance. **2** *intr.* hold a rehearsal. **3** *tr.* train (a person) by rehearsal. **4** *tr.* recite or say over. **5** *tr.* give a list of; enumerate. **rehearser** *n.* [ME f. AF *rehearser*, OF *reherc(i)er*,

perh. formed as RE- + *hercer* to harrow f. *herse* harrow: see HEARSE]

reheat *v.* & *n.* —*v.tr.* /riː'hiːt/ heat again. —*n.* /'riːhiːt/ the process of using the hot exhaust to burn extra fuel in a jet engine and produce extra power. □□ **reheater** /-'hiːtə(r)/ *n.*

reheel /riː'hiːl/ *v.tr.* fit (a shoe etc.) with a new heel.

rehoboam /ˌriːhə'bəʊəm/ *n.* a wine bottle of about six times the standard size. [*Rehoboam* King of Israel (1 Kings 11–14)]

rehouse /riː'haʊz/ *v.tr.* provide with new housing.

rehung *past* and *past part.* of REHANG.

rehydrate /ˌriːhaɪ'dreɪt/ *v.* **1** *intr.* absorb water again after dehydration. **2** *tr.* add water to (esp. food) again to restore to a palatable state. □□ **rehydratable** *adj.* **rehydration** /-'dreɪʃ(ə)n/ *n.*

Reich /raɪx/ *n.* the former German State, esp. the Third Reich. □ **First Reich** the Holy Roman Empire, 962–1806. **Second Reich** the German Empire 1871–1918. **Third Reich** the Nazi regime, 1933–45. ¶ Only *Third Reich* is normal historical terminology. [G, = empire]

Reichstag /'raɪxstɑːg/ *n. hist.* **1** the main legislature of the German State under the Second and Third Reichs. **2** the building in which this met. [G]

reify /'riːɪˌfaɪ/ *v.tr.* (**-ies**, **-ied**) convert (a person, abstraction, etc.) into a thing; materialize. □□ **reification** /-fɪ'keɪʃ(ə)n/ *n.* **reificatory** /-fɪ'keɪtərɪ/ *adj.* [L *res* thing + -FY]

reign /reɪn/ *v.* & *n.* —*v.intr.* **1** hold royal office; be king or queen. **2** prevail; hold sway (*confusion reigns*). **3** (as **reigning** *adj.*) (of a winner, champion, etc.) currently holding the title etc. —*n.* **1** sovereignty, rule. **2** the period during which a sovereign rules. [ME f. OF *reigne* kingdom f. L *regnare* f. *rex regis* king]

reignite /ˌriːɪg'naɪt/ *v.tr.* & *intr.* ignite again.

Reilly var. of RILEY.

reimburse /ˌriːɪm'bɜːs/ *v.tr.* **1** repay (a person who has expended money). **2** repay (a person's expenses). □□ **reimbursable** *adj.* **reimbursement** *n.* **reimburser** *n.* [RE- + obs. *imburse* put in a purse f. med.L *imbursare* (as IM-, PURSE)]

reimport *v.* & *n.* —*v.tr.* /ˌriːɪm'pɔːt/ import (goods processed from exported materials). —*n.* /riː'ɪmpɔːt/ **1** the act or an instance of reimporting. **2** a reimported item. □□ **reimportation** /-'teɪʃ(ə)n/ *n.*

reimpose /ˌriːɪm'pəʊz/ *v.tr.* impose again, esp. after a lapse. □□ **reimposition** /-pə'zɪʃ(ə)n/ *n.*

rein /reɪn/ *n.* & *v.* —*n.* (in *sing.* or *pl.*) **1** a long narrow strap with each end attached to the bit, used to guide or check a horse etc. in riding or driving. **2** a similar device used to restrain a young child. **3** a means of control. —*v.tr.* **1** check or manage with reins. **2** (foll. by *up*, *back*) pull up or back with reins. **3** (foll. by *in*) hold in as with reins; restrain. **4** govern, restrain, control. □ **draw rein 1** stop one's horse. **2** pull up. **3** abandon an effort. **give free rein to** remove constraints from; allow full scope to. **keep a tight rein on** allow little freedom to. □□ **reinless** *adj.* [ME f. OF *rene*, *reigne*, earlier *resne*, ult. f. L *retinēre* RETAIN]

reincarnation /ˌriːɪnkɑː'neɪʃ(ə)n/ *n.* (in some beliefs) the rebirth of a soul in a new body. □□ **reincarnate** /-'kɑːneɪt/ *v.tr.* **reincarnate** /-'kɑːnət/ *adj.*

reincorporate /ˌriːɪn'kɔːpəˌreɪt/ *v.tr.* incorporate afresh. □□ **reincorporation** /-'reɪʃ(ə)n/ *n.*

reindeer /'reɪndɪə(r)/ *n.* (*pl.* same or **reindeers**) a subarctic deer, *Rangifer tarandus*, of which both sexes have large antlers, used domestically for drawing sledges and as a source of milk, flesh, and hide. □ **reindeer moss** an arctic lichen, *Cladonia rangiferina*, with short branched stems growing in clumps. [ME f. ON *hreindȳri* f. *hreinn* reindeer + *dȳr* DEER]

reinfect /ˌriːɪn'fekt/ *v.tr.* infect again. □□ **reinfection** /ˌriːɪn'fekʃ(ə)n/ *n.*

reinforce /ˌriːɪn'fɔːs/ *v.tr.* strengthen or support, esp.

with additional personnel or material or by an increase of numbers or quantity or size etc. □ **reinforced concrete** concrete with metal bars or wire etc. embedded to increase its tensile strength. □□ **reinforcer** n. [earlier *renforce* f. F *renforcer*]

reinforcement /ˌriːɪnˈfɔːsmənt/ n. **1** the act or an instance of reinforcing; the process of being reinforced. **2** a thing that reinforces. **3** (in *pl.*) reinforcing personnel or equipment etc.

reinsert /ˌriːɪnˈsɜːt/ v.tr. insert again. □□ **reinsertion** /-ˈsɜːʃ(ə)n/ n.

reinstate /ˌriːɪnˈsteɪt/ v.tr. **1** replace in a former position. **2** restore (a person etc.) to former privileges. □□ **reinstatement** n.

reinsure /ˌriːɪnˈʃʊə(r)/ v.tr. & intr. insure again (esp. of an insurer securing himself by transferring some or all of the risk to another insurer). □□ **reinsurance** n. **reinsurer** n.

reintegrate /riːˈɪntɪˌgreɪt/ v.tr. **1** = REDINTEGRATE. **2** integrate back into society. □□ **reintegration** /-ˈgreɪʃ(ə)n/ n.

reinter /ˌriːɪnˈtɜː(r)/ v.tr. inter (a corpse) again. □□ **reinterment** n.

reinterpret /ˌriːɪnˈtɜːprɪt/ v.tr. (**reinterpreted, reinterpreting**) interpret again or differently. □□ **reinterpretation** /-ˈteɪʃ(ə)n/ n.

reintroduce /ˌriːɪntrəˈdjuːs/ v.tr. introduce again. □□ **reintroduction** /-ˈdʌkʃ(ə)n/ n.

reinvest /ˌriːɪnˈvest/ v.tr. invest again (esp. money in other property etc.). □□ **reinvestment** n.

reinvigorate /ˌriːɪnˈvɪgəˌreɪt/ v.tr. impart fresh vigour to. □□ **reinvigoration** /-ˈreɪʃ(ə)n/ n.

reissue /riːˈɪʃuː, -sjuː/ v. & n. —v.tr. (**reissues, reissued, reissuing**) issue again or in a different form. —n. a new issue, esp. of a previously published book.

reiterate /riːˈɪtəˌreɪt/ v.tr. say or do again or repeatedly. □□ **reiteration** /-ˈreɪʃ(ə)n/ n. **reiterative** /-rətɪv/ adj. [L *reiterare* (as RE-, ITERATE)]

reive /riːv/ v.intr. esp. Sc. make raids; plunder. □□ **reiver** n. [var. of REAVE]

reject v. & n. —v.tr. /rɪˈdʒekt/ **1** put aside or send back as not to be used or done or complied with etc. **2** refuse to accept or believe in. **3** rebuff or snub (a person). **4** (of a body or digestive system) cast up again; vomit, evacuate. **5** Med. show an immune response to (a transplanted organ or tissue) so that it fails to survive. —n. /ˈriːdʒekt/ a thing or person rejected as unfit or below standard. □□ **rejectable** /rɪˈdʒektəb(ə)l/ adj. **rejecter** /rɪˈdʒektə(r)/ n. (also **rejector**). **rejection** /rɪˈdʒekʃ(ə)n/ n. **rejective** adj. [ME f. L *rejicere reject-* (as RE-, *jacere* throw)]

rejig /riːˈdʒɪg/ v.tr. (**rejigged, rejigging**) **1** re-equip (a factory etc.) for a new kind of work. **2** rearrange.

rejoice /rɪˈdʒɔɪs/ v. **1** intr. feel great joy. **2** intr. (foll. by *that* + clause or *to* + infin.) be glad. **3** intr. (foll. by *in, at*) take delight. **4** intr. celebrate some event. **5** tr. cause joy to. □□ **rejoicer** n. **rejoicingly** adv. [ME f. OF *rejoir rejoiss-* (as RE-, JOY)]

rejoin¹ /riːˈdʒɔɪn/ v. **1** tr. & intr. join together again; reunite. **2** tr. join (a companion etc.) again.

rejoin² /rɪˈdʒɔɪn/ v. **1** tr. say in answer, retort. **2** intr. Law reply to a charge or pleading in a lawsuit. [ME f. OF *rejoindre rejoign-* (as RE-, JOIN)]

rejoinder /rɪˈdʒɔɪndə(r)/ n. **1** what is said in reply. **2** a retort. **3** Law a reply by rejoining. [AF *rejoinder* (unrecorded: as REJOIN²)]

rejuvenate /rɪˈdʒuːvɪˌneɪt/ v.tr. make young or as if young again. □□ **rejuvenation** /-ˈneɪʃ(ə)n/ n. **rejuvenator** n. [RE- + L *juvenis* young]

rejuvenesce /rɪˌdʒuːvɪˈnes/ v. **1** intr. become young again. **2** Biol. **a** intr. (of cells) gain fresh vitality. **b** tr. impart fresh vitality to (cells). □□ **rejuvenescent** adj. **rejuvenescence** n. [LL *rejuvenescere* (as RE-, L *juvenis* young)]

rekindle /riːˈkɪnd(ə)l/ v.tr. & intr. kindle again.

-rel /r(ə)l/ suffix with diminutive or derogatory force (*cockerel; scoundrel*). [from or after OF *-erel(le)*]

relabel /riːˈleɪb(ə)l/ v.tr. (**relabelled, relabelling;** US **relabeled, relabeling**) label (esp. a commodity) again or differently.

relapse /rɪˈlæps/ v. & n. —v.intr. (usu. foll. by *into*) fall back or sink again (into a worse state after an improvement). —n. /also ˈriː-/ the act or an instance of relapsing, esp. a deterioration in a patient's condition after a partial recovery. □ **relapsing fever** a bacterial infectious disease with recurrent periods of fever. □□ **relapser** n. [L *relabi relaps-* (as RE-, *labi* slip)]

relate /rɪˈleɪt/ v. **1** tr. narrate or recount (incidents, a story, etc.). **2** tr. (in *passive*; often foll. by *to*) be connected by blood or marriage. **3** tr. (usu. foll. by *to, with*) bring into relation (with one another); establish a connection between (*cannot relate your opinion to my own experience*). **4** intr. (foll. by *to*) have reference to; concern (*see only what relates to themselves*). **5** intr. (foll. by *to*) bring oneself into relation to; associate with. □□ **relatable** adj. [L *referre relat-* bring back: see REFER]

related /rɪˈleɪtɪd/ adj. connected, esp. by blood or marriage. □□ **relatedness** n.

relater /rɪˈleɪtə(r)/ n. (also **relator**) a person who relates something, esp. a story; a narrator.

relation /rɪˈleɪʃ(ə)n/ n. **1 a** what one person or thing has to do with another. **b** the way in which one person stands or is related to another. **c** the existence or effect of a connection, correspondence, contrast, or feeling prevailing between persons or things, esp. when qualified in some way (*bears no relation to the facts; enjoyed good relations for many years*). **2 a** relative; a kinsman or kinswoman. **3** (in *pl.*) **a** (foll. by *with*) dealings (with others). **b** sexual intercourse. **4** = RELATIONSHIP. **5 a** narration (*his relation of the events*). **b** a narrative. **6** Law the laying of information. □ **in relation to** as regards. [ME f. OF *relation* or L *relatio* (as RELATE)]

relational /rɪˈleɪʃən(ə)l/ adj. **1** of, belonging to, or characterized by relation. **2** having relation. □ **relational database** Computing a database structured to recognize the relation of stored items of information.

relationship /rɪˈleɪʃənʃɪp/ n. **1** the fact or state of being related. **2** colloq. **a** a connection or association (*enjoyed a good working relationship*). **b** an emotional (esp. sexual) association between two people. **3** a condition or character due to being related. **4** kinship.

relative /ˈrelətɪv/ adj. & n. —adj. **1** considered or having significance in relation to something else (*relative velocity*). **2** (foll. by *to*) having existence only as perceived or considered by (*beauty is relative to the eye of the beholder*). **3** (foll. by *to*) proportioned to (something else) (*growth is relative to input*). **4** implying comparison or contextual relation ('*heat*' is a relative word). **5** comparative; compared one with another (*their relative advantages*). **6** having mutual relations; corresponding in some way; related to each other. **7** (foll. by *to*) having reference or relating (*the facts relative to the issue*). **8** involving a different but corresponding idea (*the concepts of husband and wife are relative to each other*). **9** Gram. **a** (of a word, esp. a pronoun) referring to an expressed or implied antecedent and attaching a subordinate clause to it, e.g. *which, who*. **b** (of a clause) attached to an antecedent by a relative word. **10** Mus. (of major and minor keys) having the same key signature. **11** (of a service rank) corresponding in grade to another in a different service. **12** pertinent, relevant; related to the subject (*need more relative proof*). —n. **1** a person connected by blood or marriage. **2** a species related to another by common origin (*the apes, man's closest relatives*). **3** Gram. a relative word, esp. a pronoun. **4** Philos. a relative thing or term. □ **relative atomic mass** the ratio of the average mass of one atom of an element to one twelfth of the mass of an atom of carbon-12: also called *atomic weight*. **relative density** Chem. the ratio of the density of a substance to the density of a standard, usu. water for a liquid or solid, and air for a gas. **relative molecular mass** the ratio of the average mass of one molecule of an element or compound to one twelfth of the mass of an atom of carbon-12: also called *molecular weight*. □□ **relatival** /-ˈtaɪv(ə)l/ *adj.* (in sense 3 of *n.*). **relatively** *adv.* **relativeness** *n.* [ME f. OF *relatif -ive* or LL *relativus* having reference or relation (as RELATE)]

relativism /ˈrelətɪˌvɪz(ə)m/ *n.* the doctrine that knowledge is relative, not absolute. □□ **relativist** *n.*

relativistic /ˌrelətɪˈvɪstɪk/ *adj. Physics* (of phenomena etc.) accurately described only by the theory of relativity. □□ **relativistically** *adv.*

relativity /ˌreləˈtɪvɪtɪ/ *n.* **1** the fact or state of being relative. **2** *Physics* **a** (**special theory of relativity**) a theory based on the principle that all motion is relative and that light has constant velocity, regarding space-time as a four-dimensional continuum, and modifying previous conceptions of geometry. **b** (**general theory of relativity**) a theory extending this to gravitation and accelerated motion.

relator /rɪˈleɪtə(r)/ *n.* **1** var. of RELATER. **2** *Law* a person who makes a relation (see RELATION 6). [L (as RELATE)]

relax /rɪˈlæks/ *v.* **1** *tr. & intr.* make or become less stiff or rigid or tense. **2** *tr. & intr.* make or become less formal or strict (*rules were relaxed*). **3** *tr.* reduce or abate (one's attention, efforts, etc.). **4** *intr.* cease work or effort. **5** *tr.* (as **relaxed** *adj.*) at ease; unperturbed. □□ **relaxedly** *adv.* **relaxedness** *n.* **relaxer** *n.* [ME f. L *relaxare* (as RE-, LAX)]

relaxant /rɪˈlæks(ə)nt/ *n. & adj.* —*n.* a drug etc. that relaxes and reduces tension. —*adj.* causing relaxation.

relaxation /ˌriːlækˈseɪʃ(ə)n/ *n.* **1** the act of relaxing or state of being relaxed. **2** recreation or rest, esp. after a period of work. **3** a partial remission or relaxing of a penalty, duty, etc. **4** a lessening of severity, precision, etc. **5** *Physics* the restoration of equilibrium following disturbance. [L *relaxatio* (as RELAX)]

relay /ˈriːleɪ/ *n. & v.* —*n.* **1** a fresh set of people or horses substituted for tired ones. **2** a gang of workers, supply of material, etc., deployed on the same basis (*operated in relays*). **3** = *relay race*. **4** a device activating changes in an electric circuit etc. in response to other changes affecting itself. **5 a** a device to receive, reinforce, and transmit a telegraph message, broadcast programme, etc. **b** a relayed message or transmission. —*v.tr.* /ˈriːleɪ, rɪˈleɪ/ **1** receive (a message, broadcast, etc.) and transmit it to others. **2 a** arrange in relays. **b** provide with or replace by relays. □**relay race** a race between teams of which each member in turn covers part of the distance. [ME f. OF *relai* (n.), *relayer* (v.) (as RE-, *laier* ult. f. L *laxare*): cf. RELAX]

re-lay /riːˈleɪ/ *v.tr.* (*past* and *past part.* **re-laid**) lay again or differently.

relearn /riːˈlɜːn/ *v.tr.* learn again.

release /rɪˈliːs/ *v. & n.* —*v.tr.* **1** (often foll. by *from*) set free; liberate, unfasten. **2** allow to move from a fixed position. **3 a** make (information, a recording, etc.) publicly or generally available. **b** issue (a film etc.) for general exhibition. **4** *Law* **a** remit (a debt). **b** surrender (a right). **c** make over (property or money) to another. —*n.* **1** deliverance or liberation from a restriction, duty, or difficulty. **2** a handle or catch that releases part of a mechanism. **3** a document or item of information made available for publication (*press release*). **4 a** a film or record etc. that is released. **b** the act or an instance of releasing or the process of being released in this way. **5** *Law* **a** the act of releasing (property, money, or a right) to another. **b** a document effecting this. □□ **releasable** *adj.* **releasee** /-ˈsiː/ *n.* (in sense 4 of *v.*). **releaser** *n.* **releasor** *n.* (in sense 4 of *v.*). [ME f. OF *reles* (n.), *relesser* (v.), *relais(i)er* f. L *relaxare*: see RELAX]

relegate /ˈrelɪˌgeɪt/ *v.tr.* **1** consign or dismiss to an inferior or less important position; demote. **2** transfer (a sports team) to a lower division of a league etc. **3** banish or send into exile. **4** (foll. by *to*) **a** transfer (a matter) for decision or implementation. **b** refer (a person) for information. □□ **relegable** *adj.* **relegation** /-ˈgeɪʃ(ə)n/ *n.* [L *relegare relegat-* (as RE-, *legare* send)]

relent /rɪˈlent/ *v.intr.* **1** abandon a harsh intention. **2** yield to compassion. **3** relax one's severity; become less stern. [ME f. med.L *relentare* (unrecorded), formed as RE- + L *lentāre* bend f. *lentus* flexible]

relentless /rɪˈlentlɪs/ *adj.* **1** unrelenting; insistent and uncompromising. **2** continuous; oppressively constant (*the pressure was relentless*). □□ **relentlessly** *adv.* **relentlessness** *n.*

re-let /riːˈlet/ *v.tr.* (-**letting**; *past* and *past part.* -**let**) let (a property) for a further period or to a new tenant.

relevant /ˈrelɪv(ə)nt/ *adj.* (often foll. by *to*) bearing on or having reference to the matter in hand. □□ **relevance** *n.* **relevancy** *n.* **relevantly** *adv.* [med.L *relevans*, part. of L *relevare* RELIEVE]

reliable /rɪˈlaɪəb(ə)l/ *adj.* **1** that may be relied on. **2** of sound and consistent character or quality. □□ **reliability** /-ˈbɪlɪtɪ/ *n.* **reliableness** *n.* **reliably** *adv.*

reliance /rɪˈlaɪəns/ *n.* **1** (foll. by *in, on*) trust, confidence (*put full reliance in you*). **2** a thing relied upon. □□ **reliant** *adj.*

relic /ˈrelɪk/ *n.* **1** an object interesting because of its age or association. **2** a part of a deceased holy person's body or belongings kept as an object of reverence. **3** a surviving custom or belief etc. from a past age. **4** a memento or souvenir. **5** (in *pl.*) what has survived destruction or wasting or use. **6** (in *pl.*) the dead body or remains of a person. [ME *relike, relique*, etc. f. OF *relique* f. L *reliquiae*: see RELIQUIAE]

relict /ˈrelɪkt/ *n.* **1 a** a geological or other object surviving in its primitive form. **b** an animal or plant known to have existed in the same form in previous geological ages. **2** (foll. by *of*) *archaic* a widow. [L *relinquere relict-* leave behind (as RE-, *linquere* leave): sense 2 f. OF *relicte* f. L *relicta*]

relief /rɪˈliːf/ *n.* **1 a** the alleviation of or deliverance from pain, distress, anxiety, etc. **b** the feeling accompanying such deliverance. **2** a feature etc. that diversifies monotony or relaxes tension. **3** assistance (esp. financial) given to those in special need or difficulty (*rent relief*). **4 a** the replacing of a person or persons on duty by another or others. **b** a person or persons replacing others in this way. **5** (usu. *attrib.*) a thing supplementing another in some service, esp. an extra vehicle providing public transport at peak times. **6 a** a method of moulding or carving or stamping in which the design stands out from the surface, with projections proportioned and more (**high relief**) or less (**low relief**) closely approximating to those of the objects depicted (cf. ROUND *n.* 9). **b** a piece of sculpture in relief. **c** a representation of relief given by an arrangement of line or colour or shading. **7** vividness, distinctness (*brings the facts out in sharp relief*). **8** (foll. by *of*) the reinforcement (esp. the raising of a siege) of a place. **9** esp. *Law* the redress of a hardship or grievance. □**relief map 1** a map indicating hills and valleys by shading etc. rather than by contour lines alone. **2** a map-model showing elevations and depressions, usu. on an exaggerated relative scale. **relief printing** = LETTERPRESS 2. **relief road** a road taking traffic around a congested (esp. urban) area. [ME f AF *relef*, OF *relief* (in sense 6 F *relief* f. It. *rilievo*) f. *relever*: see RELIEVE]

relieve /rɪˈliːv/ *v.tr.* **1** bring or provide aid or assistance to. **2** alleviate or reduce (pain, suffering, etc.). **3** mitigate the tedium or monotony of. **4** bring military support for (a besieged place). **5** release (a person) from a duty by acting as or providing a substitute. **6** (foll. by *of*) take (a burden or responsibility) away from (a person). **7** bring into relief; cause to appear solid or detached. □**relieve one's feelings** use strong language or vigorous behaviour when annoyed. **relieve oneself** urinate or defecate. □□ **relievable** adj. **reliever** n. [ME f. OF relever f. L relevare (as RE-, levis light)]

relieved /rɪˈliːvd/ predic.adj. freed from anxiety or distress (am very relieved to hear it). □□ **relievedly** adv.

relievo /rɪˈliːvəʊ/ n. (also **rilievo** /riːˈljeɪvəʊ/) (pl. -os) = RELIEF 6. [It. rilievo RELIEF 6]

relight /riːˈlaɪt/ v.tr. light (a fire etc.) again.

religio- /rɪˈlɪɡɪəʊ, rɪˈlɪdʒɪəʊ/ comb. form 1 religion. 2 religious.

religion /rɪˈlɪdʒ(ə)n/ n. 1 the belief in a superhuman controlling power, esp. in a personal God or gods entitled to obedience and worship. 2 the expression of this in worship. 3 a particular system of faith and worship. 4 life under monastic vows (the way of religion). 5 a thing that one is devoted to (football is their religion). □**freedom of religion** the right to follow whatever religion one chooses. □□ **religionless** adj. [ME f. AF religiun, OF religion f. L religio -onis obligation, bond, reverence]

religionism /rɪˈlɪdʒə,nɪz(ə)m/ n. excessive religious zeal. □□ **religionist** n.

religiose /rɪˈlɪdʒɪəʊs/ adj. excessively religious. [L religiosus (as RELIGIOUS)]

religiosity /rɪ,lɪdʒɪˈɒsɪtɪ/ n. the condition of being religious or religiose. [ME f. L religiositas (as RELIGIOUS)]

religious /rɪˈlɪdʒəs/ adj. & n. —adj. 1 devoted to religion; pious, devout. 2 of or concerned with religion. 3 of or belonging to a monastic order. 4 scrupulous, conscientious (a religious attention to detail). —n. (pl. same) a person bound by monastic vows. □□ **religiously** adv. **religiousness** n. [ME f. AF religius, OF religious f. L religiosus (as RELIGION)]

reline /riːˈlaɪn/ v.tr. renew the lining of (a garment etc.).

relinquish /rɪˈlɪŋkwɪʃ/ v.tr. 1 surrender or resign a right or possession. 2 give up or cease from (a habit, plan, belief, etc.). 3 relax hold of (an object held). □□ **relinquishment** n. [ME f. OF relinquir f. L relinquere (as RE-, linquere leave)]

reliquary /ˈrelɪkwərɪ/ n. (pl. -ies) esp. Relig. a receptacle for relics. [F reliquaire (as RELIC)]

reliquiae /rɪˈlɪkwɪ,iː/ n.pl. 1 remains. 2 Geol. fossil remains of animals or plants. [L f. reliquus remaining, formed as RE- + linquere liq- leave]

relish /ˈrelɪʃ/ n. & v. —n. 1 (often foll. by for) a great liking or enjoyment. b keen or pleasurable longing (had no relish for travelling). 2 a an appetizing flavour. b an attractive quality (fishing loses its relish in winter). 3 a condiment eaten with plainer food to add flavour, esp. a piquant sauce, pickle, etc. 4 (foll. by of) a distinctive taste or tinge. —v.tr. 1 a get pleasure out of; enjoy greatly. b look forward to, anticipate with pleasure (did not relish what lay before her). 2 add relish to. □□ **relishable** adj. [alt. (with assim. to -ISH²)· of obs. reles f. OF reles, relais remainder f. relaisser: see RELEASE]

relive /riːˈlɪv/ v.tr. live (an experience etc.) over again, esp. in the imagination.

reload /riːˈləʊd/ v.tr. (also absol.) load (esp. a gun) again.

relocate /,riːləʊˈkeɪt/ v. 1 tr. locate in a new place. 2 tr. & intr. move to a new place (esp. to live or work). □□ **relocation** /-ˈkeɪʃən/ n.

reluctant /rɪˈlʌkt(ə)nt/ adj. (often foll. by to + infin.) unwilling or disinclined (most reluctant to agree). □□ **reluctance** n. **reluctantly** adv. [L reluctari (as RE-, luctari struggle)]

rely /rɪˈlaɪ/ v.intr. (-ies, -ied) (foll. by on, upon) 1 depend on with confidence or assurance (am relying on your judgement). 2 be dependent on (relies on her for everything). [ME (earlier senses 'rally, be a vassal

of') f. OF relier bind together f. L religare (as RE-, ligare bind)]

REM abbr. rapid eye-movement.

rem /rem/ n. (pl. same) a unit of effective absorbed dose of ionizing radiation in human tissue, equivalent to one roentgen of X-rays. [roentgen equivalent man]

remade past and past part. of REMAKE.

remain /rɪˈmeɪn/ v.intr. 1 be left over after others or other parts have been removed or used or dealt with. 2 be in the same place or condition during further time; continue to exist or stay; be left behind (remained at home; it will remain cold). 3 (foll. by compl.) continue to be (remained calm; remains President). [ME f. OF remain- stressed stem of remanoir or f. OF remaindre ult. f. L remanēre (as RE-, manēre stay)]

remainder /rɪˈmeɪndə(r)/ n. & v. —n. 1 a part remaining or left over. 2 remaining persons or things. 3 a number left after division or subtraction. 4 the copies of a book left unsold when demand has fallen. 5 Law an interest in an estate that becomes effective in possession only when a prior interest (devised at the same time) ends. —v.tr. dispose of (a remainder of books) at a reduced price. [ME (in sense 5) f. AF, = OF remaindre: see REMAIN]

remains /rɪˈmeɪnz/ n.pl. 1 what remains after other parts have been removed or used etc. 2 relics of antiquity, esp. of buildings (Roman remains). 3 a person's body after death. 4 an author's (esp. unpublished) works left after death.

remake v. & n. —v.tr. /riːˈmeɪk/ (past and past part. **remade**) make again or differently. —n. /ˈriːmeɪk/ a thing that has been remade, esp. a cinema film.

reman /riːˈmæn/ v.tr. (**remanned**, **remanning**) 1 equip (a fleet etc.) with new personnel. 2 make courageous again.

remand /rɪˈmɑːnd/ v. & n. —v.tr. return (a prisoner) to custody, esp. to allow further inquiries to be made. —n. a recommittal to custody. □**on remand** in custody pending trial. **remand centre** (in the UK) an institution to which accused persons are remanded pending trial. [ME f. LL remandare (as RE-, mandare commit)]

remanent /ˈremənənt/ adj. 1 remaining, residual. 2 (of magnetism) remaining after the magnetizing field has been removed. □□ **remanence** n. [ME f. L remanēre REMAIN]

remark /rɪˈmɑːk/ v. & n. —v. 1 tr. (often foll. by that + clause) a say by way of comment. b take notice of; regard with attention. 2 intr. (usu. foll. by on, upon) make a comment. —n. 1 a written or spoken comment; anything said. 2 a the act of noticing or observing (worthy of remark). b the act of commenting (let it pass without remark). [F remarque, remarquer (as RE-, MARK¹)]

remarkable /rɪˈmɑːkəb(ə)l/ adj. 1 worth notice; exceptional. 2 striking, conspicuous. □□ **remarkableness** n. **remarkably** adv. [F remarquable (as REMARK)]

remarry /riːˈmærɪ/ v.intr. & tr. (-ies, -ied) marry again. □□ **remarriage** n.

remaster /riːˈmɑːstə(r)/ v.tr. make a new master of (a recording), esp. to improve the sound quality.

rematch /ˈriːmætʃ/ n. a return match or game.

REME /ˈriːmiː/ abbr. (in the UK) Royal Electrical and Mechanical Engineers.

remeasure /riːˈmeʒə(r)/ v.tr. measure again. □□ **remeasurement** n.

remedial /rɪˈmiːdɪəl/ adj. 1 affording or intended as a remedy (remedial therapy). 2 (of teaching) for slow or backward children. □□ **remedially** adv. [LL remedialis f. L remedium (as REMEDY)]

remedy /ˈremɪdɪ/ n. & v. —n. (pl. -ies) (often foll. by for, against) 1 a medicine or treatment (for a disease etc.). 2 a means of counteracting or removing anything undesirable. 3 redress; legal or other reparation. 4 the margin within which coins as minted may differ from the standard fineness and weight. —*v.tr.* (-ies, -ied) rectify; make good. □□

remediable /rɪ'miːdɪəb(ə)l/ *adj.* [ME f. AF *remedie*, OF *remede* or L *remedium* (as RE-, *medēri* heal)]

remember /rɪ'membə(r)/ *v.tr.* **1** keep in the memory; not forget. **2 a** (also *absol.*) bring back into one's thoughts, call to mind (knowledge or experience etc.). **b** (often foll. by *to* + infin. or *that* + clause) have in mind (a duty, commitment, etc.) (*will you remember to lock the door?*). **3** think of or acknowledge (a person) in some connection, esp. in making a gift etc. **4** (foll. by *to*) convey greetings from (one person) to (another) (*remember me to your mother*). **5** mention (in prayer). □**remember oneself** recover one's manners or intentions after a lapse. □□ **rememberer** *n.* [ME f. OF *remembrer* f. LL *rememorari* (as RE-, L *memor* mindful)]

remembrance /rɪ'membrəns/ *n.* **1** the act of remembering or process of being remembered. **2** a memory or recollection. **3** a keepsake or souvenir. **4** (in *pl.*) greetings conveyed through a third person. □**Remembrance Day 1** = *Remembrance Sunday*. **2** *hist.* Armistice Day. **Remembrance Sunday** (in the UK) the Sunday nearest 11 Nov., when those who were killed in the wars of 1914–18 and 1939–45 are commemorated. [ME f. OF (as REMEMBER)]

remex /'riːmeks/ *n.* (*pl.* **remiges** /'remɪ,dʒiːz/) a primary or secondary feather in a bird's wing. [L, = rower, f. *remus* oar]

remind /rɪ'maɪnd/ *v.tr.* **1** (foll. by *of*) cause (a person) to remember or think of. **2** (foll. by *to* + infin. or *that* + clause) cause (a person) to remember (a commitment etc.) (*remind them to pay their subscriptions*).

reminder /rɪ'maɪndə(r)/ *n.* **1** a thing that reminds, esp. a letter or bill. **2** (often foll. by *of*) a memento or souvenir.

remindful /rɪ'maɪndfʊl/ *adj.* (often foll. by *of*) acting as a reminder; reviving the memory.

reminisce /,remɪ'nɪs/ *v.intr.* indulge in reminiscence. □□ **reminiscer** *n.* [back-form. f. REMINISCENCE]

reminiscence /,remɪ'nɪs(ə)ns/ *n.* **1** the act of remembering things past; the recovery of knowledge by mental effort. **2 a** a past fact or experience that is remembered. **b** the process of narrating this. **3** (in *pl.*) a collection in literary form of incidents and experiences that a person remembers. **4** *Philos.* (esp. in Platonism) the theory of the recovery of things known to the soul in previous existences. **5** a characteristic of one thing reminding or suggestive of another. □□ **reminiscential** /-'senʃ(ə)l/ *adj.* [LL *reminiscentia* f. L *reminisci* remember]

reminiscent /,remɪ'nɪs(ə)nt/ *adj.* **1** (foll. by *of*) tending to remind one of or suggest. **2** concerned with reminiscence. **3** (of a person) given to reminiscing. □□ **reminiscently** *adv.*

remise /rɪ'miːz/ *v. & n.* —*v.intr.* **1** *Law* surrender or make over (a right or property). **2** *Fencing* make a remise. —*n.* *Fencing* a second thrust made after the first has failed. [F f. *remis*, *remise* past part. of *remettre* put back: cf. REMIT]

remiss /rɪ'mɪs/ *adj.* careless of duty; lax, negligent. □□ **remissly** *adv.* **remissness** *n.* [ME f. L *remissus* past part. of *remittere* slacken: see REMIT]

remissible /rɪ'mɪsɪb(ə)l/ *adj.* that may be remitted. [F *rémissible* or LL *remissibilis* (as REMIT)]

remission /rɪ'mɪʃ(ə)n/ *n.* **1** the reduction of a prison sentence on account of good behaviour. **2** the remitting of a debt or penalty etc. **3** a diminution of force, effect, or degree (esp. of disease or pain). **4** (often foll. by *of*) forgiveness (of sins etc.). □□ **remissive** *adj.* [ME f. OF *remission* or L *remissio* (as REMIT)]

remit *v. & n.* —*v.* /rɪ'mɪt/ (**remitted**, **remitting**) **1** *tr.* cancel or refrain from exacting or inflicting (a debt or punishment etc.). **2** *intr. & tr.* abate or slacken; cease or cease from partly or entirely. **3** *tr.*

send (money etc.) in payment. **4** *tr.* cause to be conveyed by post. **5** *tr.* **a** (foll. by *to*) refer (a matter for decision etc.) to some authority. **b** *Law* send back (a case) to a lower court. **6** *tr.* **a** (often foll. by *to*) postpone or defer. **b** (foll. by *in*, *into*) send or put back into a previous state. **7** *tr. Theol.* (usu. of God) pardon (sins etc.). —*n.* /'riːmɪt, rɪ'mɪt/ **1** the terms of reference of a committee etc. **2** an item remitted for consideration. □□ **remittable** /rɪ'mɪtəb(ə)l/ *adj.*

remittal /rɪ'mɪt(ə)l/ *n.* **remittee** /rɪmɪ'tiː/ *n.* **remitter** /rɪ'mɪtə(r)/ *n.* [ME f. L *remittere remiss-* (as RE-, *mittere* send)]

remittance /rɪ'mɪt(ə)ns/ *n.* **1** money sent, esp. by post, for goods or services or as an allowance. **2** the act of sending money. □**remittance man** *hist.* an emigrant subsisting on remittances from home.

remittent /rɪ'mɪt(ə)nt/ *adj.* (of a fever) that abates at intervals. [L *remittere* (as REMIT)]

remix *v. & n.* —*v.tr.* /riː'mɪks/ mix again. —*n.* /'riːmɪks/ a sound recording that has been remixed.

remnant /'remnənt/ *n.* **1** a small remaining quantity. **2** a piece of cloth etc. left when the greater part has been used or sold. **3** (foll. by *of*) a surviving trace (*a remnant of empire*). [ME (earlier *remenant*) f. OF *remenant* f. *remenoir* REMAIN]

remodel /riː'mɒd(ə)l/ *v.tr.* (**remodelled**, **remodelling**; US **remodeled**, **remodeling**) **1** model again or differently. **2** reconstruct.

remodify /riː'mɒdɪ,faɪ/ *v.tr.* (-ies, -ied) modify again. □□ **remodification** /-fɪ'keɪʃ(ə)n/ *n.*

remold US var. of REMOULD.

remonetize /riː'mʌnɪ,taɪz/ *v.tr.* (also -ise) restore (a metal etc.) to its former position as legal tender. □□ **remonetization** /-'zeɪʃ(ə)n/ *n.*

remonstrance /rɪ'mɒnstrəns/ *n.* **1** the act or an instance of remonstrating. **2** an expostulation or protest. [ME f. obs. F *remonstrance* or med.L *remonstrantia* (as REMONSTRATE)]

remonstrate /'remən,streɪt/ *v.* **1** *intr.* (foll. by *with*) make a protest; argue forcibly (*remonstrated with them over the delays*). **2** *tr.* (often foll. by *that* + clause) urge protestingly. □□ **remonstrant** /rɪ'mɒnstrənt/ *adj.* **remonstration** /-'streɪʃ(ə)n/ *n.* **remonstrative** /rɪ'mɒnstrətɪv/ *adj.* **remonstrator** *n.* [med.L *remonstrare* (as RE-, *monstrare* show)]

remontant /rɪ'mɒnt(ə)nt/ *adj. & n.* —*adj.* blooming more than once a year. —*n.* a remontant rose. [F *remonter* REMOUNT]

remora /'remərə/ *n. Zool.* any of various marine fish of the family Echeneidae, which attach themselves by modified sucker-like fins to other fish and to ships. [L, = hindrance (as RE-, *mora* delay, from the former belief that the fish slowed ships down)]

remorse /rɪ'mɔːs/ *n.* **1** deep regret for a wrong committed. **2** compunction; a compassionate reluctance to inflict pain (esp. in *without remorse*). [ME f. OF *remors* f. med.L *remorsus* f. L *remordēre remors-* vex (as RE-, *mordēre* bite)]

remorseful /rɪ'mɔːsfʊl/ *adj.* filled with repentance. □□ **remorsefully** *adv.*

remorseless /rɪ'mɔːslɪs/ *adj.* without compassion or compunction. □□ **remorselessly** *adv.* **remorselessness** *n.*

remortgage /riː'mɔːgɪdʒ/ *v. & n.* —*v.tr.* (also *absol.*) mortgage again; revise the terms of an existing mortgage on (a property). —*n.* a different or altered mortgage.

remote /rɪ'məʊt/ *adj.* (**remoter**, **remotest**) **1** far away in place or time. **2** out of the way; situated away from the main centres of population, society, etc. **3** distantly related (*a remote ancestor*). **4** slight, faint (esp. in *not the remotest chance, idea*, etc.). **5** (of a person) aloof; not friendly. **6** (foll. by *from*) widely different; separate by nature (*ideas remote from the subject*). □**remote control** control of a machine or apparatus from a distance by means of signals transmitted from a radio or electronic device. **remote-controlled** (of a machine etc.) controlled at a distance. □□ **remotely** *adv.* **remoteness** *n.* [ME f. L *remotus* (as REMOVE)]

remould *v. & n.* (*US* **remold**) —*v.tr.* /riːˈməʊld/ **1** mould again; refashion. **2** re-form the tread of (a tyre). —*n.* /ˈriːməʊld/ a remoulded tyre.

remount *v. & n.* —*v.* /riːˈmaʊnt/ **1 a** *tr.* mount (a horse etc.) again. **b** *intr.* get on horseback again. **2** *tr.* get on to or ascend (a ladder, hill, etc.) again. **3** *tr.* provide (a person) with a fresh horse etc. **4** *tr.* put (a picture) on a fresh mount. —*n.* /ˈriːmaʊnt/ **1** a fresh horse for a rider. **2** a supply of fresh horses for a regiment.

removal /rɪˈmuːv(ə)l/ *n.* **1** the act or an instance of removing; the process of being removed. **2** the transfer of furniture and other contents on moving house.

remove /rɪˈmuːv/ *v. & n.* —*v.* **1** *tr.* take off or away from the place or position occupied (*remove the top carefully*). **2** *tr.* **a** move or take to another place; change the situation of (*will you remove the tea things?*). **b** get rid of; eliminate (*will remove all doubts*). **3** *tr.* cause to be no longer present or available; take away (*all privileges were removed*). **4** *tr.* (often foll. by *from*) dismiss (from office). **5** *tr. colloq.* kill, assassinate. **6** *tr.* (in *passive*; foll. by *from*) distant or remote in condition (*the country is not far removed from anarchy*). **7** *tr.* (as **removed** *adj.*) (esp. of cousins) separated by a specified number of steps of descent (*a first cousin twice removed* = a grandchild of a first cousin). **8** *formal* **a** *intr.* (usu. foll. by *from, to*) change one's home or place of residence. **b** *tr.* conduct the removal of. —*n.* **1** a degree or remoteness; a distance. **2** a stage in a gradation; a degree (*is several removes from what I expected*). **3** *Brit.* a form or division in some schools. □□ **removable** *adj.* **removability** /-ˈbɪlɪtɪ/ *n.* **remover** *n.* (esp. in sense 8b of *v.*). [ME f. OF *removeir* f. L *removēre remot-* (as RE-, *movēre* move)]

remunerate /rɪˈmjuːnəˌreɪt/ *v.tr.* **1** reward; pay for services rendered. **2** serve as or provide recompense for (toil etc.) or to (a person). □□ **remuneration** /-ˈreɪʃ(ə)n/ *n.* **remunerative** /-rətɪv/ *adj.* **remuneratory** /-rətərɪ/ *adj.* [L *remunerari* (as RE-, *munus muneris* gift)]

Renaissance /rɪˈneɪs(ə)ns, rəˈn-, -sɑ̃s/ *n.* **1** the revival of art and literature under the influence of classical models in the 14th–16th c. **2** the period of this. **3** the culture and style of art, architecture, etc. developed during this era. **4** (**renaissance**) any similar revival. [F *renaissance* (as RE-, F *naissance* birth f. L *nascentia* or F *naitre naiss-* be born f. Rmc: cf. NASCENT)]

renal /ˈriːn(ə)l/ *adj.* of or concerning the kidneys. [F *rénal* f. LL *renalis* f. L *renes* kidneys]

rename /riːˈneɪm/ *v.tr.* name again; give a new name to.

renascence /rɪˈnæs(ə)ns/ *n.* **1** rebirth; renewal. **2** = RENAISSANCE. [RENASCENT]

renascent /rɪˈnæs(ə)nt/ *adj.* springing up anew; being reborn. [L *renasci* (as RE-, *nasci* be born)]

rencontre /rɛnˈkɒntə(r)/ *n. archaic* = RENCOUNTER. [F (as RENCOUNTER)]

rencounter /rɛnˈkaʊntə(r)/ *n. & v.* —*n.* **1** an encounter; a chance meeting. **2** a battle, skirmish, or duel. —*v.tr.* encounter; meet by chance. [F *rencontre(r)* (as RE-, ENCOUNTER)]

rend /rɛnd/ *v.* (*past* and *past part.* **rent** /rɛnt/) *archaic* or *rhet.* **1** *tr.* (foll. by *off, from, away*, etc.; also *absol.*) tear or wrench forcibly. **2** *tr. & intr.* split or divide in pieces or into factions (*a country rent by civil war*). **3** *tr.* cause emotional pain to (the heart etc.). □**rend the air** sound piercingly. **rend one's garments** (or **hair**) display extreme grief or rage. [OE *rendan*, rel. to MLG *rende*]

render /ˈrɛndə(r)/ *v.tr.* **1** cause to be or become; make (*rendered us helpless*). **2** give or pay (money, service, etc.), esp. in return or as a thing due (*render thanks; rendered good for evil*). **3** (often foll. by *to*) **a** give (assistance) (*rendered aid to the injured man*). **b** show (obedience etc.). **c** do (a service etc.). **4** submit; send in; present (an account, reason, etc.). **5 a** represent or portray artistically, musically, etc. **b** act (a role); represent (a character, idea, etc.) (*the dramatist's conception was well rendered*). **c** *Mus.* perform; execute. **6** translate (*rendered the poem into French*). **7** (often foll. by *down*) melt down (fat etc.) esp. to clarify; extract by melting. **8** cover (stone or brick) with a coat of plaster. **9** *archaic* **a** give back; hand over; deliver, give up, surrender (*render to Caesar the things that are Caesar's*). **b** show (obedience). □**render-set** *v.tr.* (-**setting**; *past* and *past part.* -**set**) plaster (a wall etc.) with two coats. —*n.* a plastering of two coats. —*adj.* of two coats. □□ **renderer** *n.* [ME f. OF *rendre* ult. f. L *reddere reddit-* (as RE-, *dare* give)]

rendering /ˈrɛndərɪŋ/ *n.* **1 a** the act or an instance of performing music, drama, etc.; an interpretation or performance (*an excellent rendering of the part*). **b** a translation. **2 a** the act or an instance of plastering stone, brick, etc. **b** this coating. **3** the act or an instance of giving, yielding, or surrendering.

rendezvous /ˈrɒndɪˌvuː, -deɪˌvuː/ *n. & v.* —*n.* (*pl.* same /-ˌvuːz/) **1** an agreed or regular meeting-place. **2** a meeting by arrangement. **3** a place appointed for assembling troops, ships, etc. —*v.intr.* (**rendezvouses** /-ˌvuːz/; **rendezvoused** /-ˌvuːd/; **rendezvousing** /-ˌvuːɪŋ/) meet at a rendezvous. [F *rendez-vous* present yourselves f. *rendre*: see RENDER]

rendition /rɛnˈdɪʃ(ə)n/ *n.* (often foll. by *of*) **1** an interpretation or rendering of a dramatic role, piece of music, etc. **2** a visual representation. [obs. F f. *rendre* RENDER]

renegade /ˈrɛnɪˌgeɪd/ *n. & v.* —*n.* **1** a person who deserts a party or principles. **2** an apostate; a person who abandons one religion for another. —*v.intr.* be a renegade. [Sp. *renegado* f. med.L *renegatus* (as RE-, L *negare* deny)]

renegado /ˌrɛnɪˈgeɪdəʊ/ *n.* (*pl.* -**oes**) *archaic* = RENEGADE. [Sp. (as RENEGADE)]

renege /rɪˈniːg, -ˈneg, -ˈneɪg/ *v.* (also **renegue**) **1** *intr.* **a** go back on one's word; change one's mind; recant. **b** (foll. by *on*) go back on (a promise or undertaking or contract). **2** *tr.* deny, renounce, abandon (a person, faith, etc.). **3** *intr. Cards* revoke. □□ **reneger** *n.* **reneguer** *n.* [med.L *renegare* (as RE-, L *negare* deny)]

renegotiate /ˌriːnɪˈgəʊʃɪˌeɪt/ *v.tr.* (also *absol.*) negotiate again or on different terms. □□ **renegotiable** *adj.* **renegotiation** /-ˈeɪʃ(ə)n/ *n.*

renew /rɪˈnjuː/ *v.tr.* **1** revive; regenerate; make new again; restore to the original state. **2** reinforce; resupply; replace. **3** repeat or re-establish; resume after an interruption (*renewed our acquaintance; a renewed attack*). **4** get, begin, make, say, give, etc. anew. **5** (also *absol.*) grant or be granted a continuation of or continued validity of (a licence, subscription, lease, etc.). **6** recover (one's youth, strength, etc.). □□ **renewable** *adj.* **renewability** /-əˈbɪlɪtɪ/ *n.* **renewal** *n.* **renewer** *n.*

reniform /ˈriːnɪˌfɔːm/ *adj.* esp. *Med.* kidney-shaped. [L *ren* kidney + -FORM]

rennet /ˈrɛnɪt/ *n.* **1** curdled milk found in the stomach of an unweaned calf, used in curdling milk for cheese, junket, etc. **2** a preparation made from the stomach-membrane of a calf or from certain fungi, used for the same purpose. [ME, prob. f. an OE form *rynet* (unrecorded), rel. to RUN]

rennin /ˈrɛnɪn/ *n. Biochem.* an enzyme secreted into the stomach of unweaned mammals causing the clotting of milk. [RENNET + -IN]

renominate /riːˈnɒmɪˌneɪt/ *v.tr.* nominate for a further term of office. □□ **renomination** /-ˈneɪʃ(ə)n/ *n.*

renounce /rɪˈnaʊns/ *v.* **1** *tr.* consent formally to abandon; surrender; give up (a claim, right, possession, etc.). **2** *tr.* repudiate; refuse to recognize any longer (*renouncing their father's authority*). **3** *tr.* **a** decline further association or disclaim relationship with (*renounced my former friends*). **b** withdraw from; discontinue; forsake. **4** *intr. Law* refuse or resign a right or position esp. as an heir or trustee. **5** *intr. Cards* follow with a card of another suit when having no card of the suit led (cf. REVOKE). □**renounce the world** abandon society or material affairs. □□ **renounceable** *adj.* **renouncement** *n.* **renouncer** *n.* [ME f. OF *renoncer* f. L *renuntiare* (as RE-, *nuntiare* announce)]

renovate /ˈrenəˌveɪt/ *v.tr.* **1** restore to good condition; repair. **2** make new again. □□ **renovation** /-ˈveɪʃ(ə)n/ *n.* **renovative** *adj.* **renovator** *n.* [L *renovare* (as RE-, *novus* new)]

renown /rɪˈnaʊn/ *n.* fame; high distinction; celebrity (*a city of great renown*). [ME f. AF *ren(o)un*, OF *renon*, *renom* f. *renomer* make famous (as RE-, L *nominare* NOMINATE)]

renowned /rɪˈnaʊnd/ *adj.* famous; celebrated.

rent[1] /rent/ *n. & v.* — *n.* **1** a tenant's periodical payment to an owner or landlord for the use of land or premises. **2** payment for the use of a service, equipment, etc. — *v.* **1** *tr.* (often foll. by *from*) take, occupy, or use at a rent (*rented a cottage from the local farmer*). **2** *tr.* (often foll. by *out*) let or hire (a thing) for rent. **3** *intr.* (foll. by *at*) be let or hired out at a specified rate (*the land rents at £100 per month*). □**for rent** *US* available to be rented. **rent-a-** (in *comb.*) often *joc.* denoting availability for hire (*rent-a-van*; *rent-a-crowd*). **rent-boy** a young male prostitute. **rent-free** with exemption from rent. **rent-roll** the register of a landlord's lands etc. with the rents due from them; the sum of one's income from rent. [ME f. OF *rente* f. Rmc (as RENDER)]

rent[2] /rent/ *n.* **1** a large tear in a garment etc. **2** an opening in clouds etc. **3** a cleft, fissure, or gorge. [obs. *rent* var. of REND]

rent[3] *past* and *past part.* of REND.

rentable /ˈrentəb(ə)l/ *adj.* **1** available or suitable for renting. **2** giving an adequate ratio of profit to capital. □□ **rentability** /-ˈbɪlɪtɪ/ *n.*

rental /ˈrent(ə)l/ *n.* **1** the amount paid or received as rent. **2** the act of renting. **3** an income from rents. **4** *US* a rented house etc. □**rental library** *US* a library which rents books for a fee. [ME f. AF *rental* or AL *rentale* (as RENT[1])]

renter /ˈrentə(r)/ *n.* **1** a person who rents. **2** *Cinematog.* (in the UK) a person who distributes cinema films. **3** *sl.* a male prostitute.

rentier /ˈrɑ̃tɪˌeɪ/ *n.* a person living on dividends from property, investments, etc. [F f. *rente* dividend]

renumber /riːˈnʌmbə(r)/ *v.tr.* change the number or numbers given or allocated to.

renunciation /rɪˌnʌnsɪˈeɪʃ(ə)n/ *n.* **1** the act or an instance of renouncing or giving up. **2** self-denial. **3** a document expressing renunciation. □□ **renunciant** /rɪˈnʌnsɪənt/ *n. & adj.* **renunciative** /rɪˈnʌnsɪətɪv/ *adj.* **renunciatory** /rɪˈnʌnʃətərɪ/ *adj.* [ME f. OF *renonciation* or LL *renuntiatio* (as RENOUNCE)]

renvoi /rɑ̃ˈvwʌ/ *n. Law* the act or an instance of referring a case, dispute, etc. to a different jurisdiction. [F f. *renvoyer* send back]

reoccupy /riːˈɒkjʊˌpaɪ/ *v.tr.* (-**ies**, -**ied**) occupy again. □□ **reoccupation** /-ˈpeɪʃ(ə)n/ *n.*

reoccur /ˌriːəˈkɜː(r)/ *v.intr.* (**reoccurred**, **reoccurring**) occur again or habitually. □□ **reoccurrence** /-ˈkʌrəns/ *n.*

reopen /riːˈəʊpən/ *v.tr. & intr.* open again.

reorder /riːˈɔːdə(r)/ *v. & n.* — *v.tr.* order again. — *n.* a renewed or repeated order for goods.

reorganize /riːˈɔːgəˌnaɪz/ *v.tr.* (also -**ise**) organize differently. □□ **reorganization** /-ˈzeɪʃ(ə)n/ *n.* **reorganizer** *n.*

reorient /riːˈɔːrɪˌent, -ˈɒrɪˌent/ *v.tr.* **1** give a new direction to (ideas etc.); redirect (a thing). **2** help (a person) find his or her bearings again. **3** change the outlook of (a person). **4** (refl., often foll. by *to*) adjust oneself to or come to terms with something.

reorientate /riːˈɔːrɪənˌteɪt/ *v.tr.* = REORIENT. □□ **reorientation** /-ˈteɪʃ(ə)n/ *n.*

Rep. *abbr. US* **1** a Representative in Congress. **2** a Republican.

rep[1] /rep/ *n. colloq.* a representative, esp. a commercial traveller. [abbr.]

rep[2] /rep/ *n. colloq.* **1** repertory. **2** a repertory theatre or company. [abbr.]

rep[3] /rep/ *n.* (also **repp**) a textile fabric with a corded surface, used in curtains and upholstery. [F *reps*, of unkn. orig.]

rep[4] /rep/ *n. US sl.* reputation. [abbr.]

repack /riːˈpæk/ *v.tr.* pack again.

repackage /riːˈpækɪdʒ/ *v.tr.* **1** package again or differently. **2** present in a new form. □□ **repackaging** *n.*

repaginate /riːˈpædʒɪˌneɪt/ *v.tr.* paginate again; renumber the pages of. □□ **repagination** /-ˈneɪʃ(ə)n/ *n.*

repaid *past* and *past part.* of REPAY.

repaint *v. & n.* — *v.tr.* /riːˈpeɪnt/ **1** paint again or differently. **2** restore the paint or colouring of. — *n.* /ˈriːpeɪnt/ **1** the act of repainting. **2** a repainted thing, esp. a golf ball.

repair[1] /rɪˈpeə(r)/ *v. & n.* — *v.tr.* **1** restore to good condition after damage or wear. **2** renovate or mend by replacing or fixing parts or by compensating for loss or exhaustion. **3** set right or make amends for (loss, wrong, error, etc.). — *n.* **1** the act or an instance of restoring to sound condition (*in need of repair*; *closed during repair*). **2** the result of this (*the repair is hardly visible*). **3** good or relative condition for working or using (*must be kept in repair*; *in good repair*). □□ **repairable** *adj.* **repairer** *n.* [ME f. OF *reparer* f. L *reparare* (as RE-, *parare* make ready)]

repair[2] /rɪˈpeə(r)/ *v. & n.* — *v.intr.* (foll. by *to*) resort; have recourse; go often or in great numbers for a specific purpose (*repaired to Spain*). — *n. archaic* **1** resort (*have repair to*). **2** a place of frequent resort. **3** popularity (*a place of great repair*). [ME f. OF *repaire(r)* f. LL *repatriare* REPATRIATE)]

repairman /rɪˈpeəmən/ *n.* (*pl.* -**men**) a man who repairs machinery etc.

repand /rɪˈpænd/ *adj. Bot.* with an undulating margin; wavy. [L *repandus* (as RE-, *pandus* bent)]

repaper /riːˈpeɪpə(r)/ *v.tr.* paper (a wall etc.) again.

reparable /ˈrepərəb(ə)l/ *adj.* (of a loss etc.) that can be made good. □□ **reparability** /-ˈbɪlɪtɪ/ *n.* **reparably** *adv.* [F f. L *reparabilis* (as REPAIR[1])]

reparation /ˌrepəˈreɪʃ(ə)n/ *n.* **1** the act or an instance of making amends. **2 a** compensation. **b** (esp. in *pl.*) compensation for war damage paid by the defeated State. **3** the act or an instance of repairing or being repaired. □□ **reparative** /ˈrepərətɪv, rɪˈpærətɪv/ *adj.* [ME f. OF f. LL *reparatio -onis* (as REPAIR)]

repartee /ˌrepɑːˈtiː/ *n.* **1** the practice or faculty of making witty retorts; sharpness or wit in quick reply. **2 a** a witty retort. **b** witty retorts collectively. [F *repartie* fem. past part. of *repartir* start again, reply promptly (as RE-, *partir* PART)]

repartition /ˌriːpɑːˈtɪʃ(ə)n/ *v.tr.* partition again.

repass /riːˈpɑːs/ *v.tr. & intr.* pass again, esp. on the way back. [ME f. OF *repasser*]

repast /rɪˈpɑːst/ *n. formal* **1** a meal, esp. of a specified kind (*a light repast*). **2** food and drink supplied for or eaten at a meal. [ME f. OF *repaistre* f. LL *repascere* *repast-* feed]

repat /ˈriːpæt, riːˈpæt/ *n. colloq.* **1** a repatriate. **2** repatriation. [abbr.]

repatriate /riːˈpætrɪˌeɪt/ *v. & n.* — *v.* **1** *tr.* restore (a person) to his or her native land. **2** *intr.* return to one's own native land. — *n.* a person who has been repatriated. □□ **repatriation** /-ˈeɪʃ(ə)n/ *n.* [LL *repatriare* (as RE-, L *patria* native land)]

repay /riːˈpeɪ/ *v.* (*past* and *past part.* **repaid**) **1** *tr.* pay back (money). **2** *tr.* return (a blow, visit, etc.). **3** *tr.* make repayment to (a person). **4** *tr.* make return for; requite (a service, action, etc.) (*must repay their kindness*; *the book repays close study*). **5** *tr.* (often foll. by *for*) give in recompense. **6** *intr.* make repayment. □□ **repayable** *adj.* **repayment** *n.* [OF *repaier* (as RE-, PAY¹)]

repeal /rɪ'piːl/ *v. & n.* —*v.tr.* revoke, rescind, or annul (a law, act of parliament, etc.). —*n.* the act or an instance of repealing. □□ **repealable** *adj.* [ME f. AF *repeler*, OF *rapeler* (as RE-, APPEAL)]

repeat /rɪ'piːt/ *v. & n.* —*v.* **1** *tr.* say or do over again. **2** *tr.* recite, rehearse, report, or reproduce (something from memory) (*repeated a poem*). **3** *tr.* imitate (an action etc.). **4** *intr.* recur; appear again, perhaps several times (*a repeating pattern*). **5** *tr.* used for emphasis (*am not, repeat not, going*). **6** *intr.* (of food) be tasted intermittently for some time after being swallowed as a result of belching or indigestion. **7** *intr.* (of a watch etc.) strike the last quarter etc. over again when required. **8** *intr.* (of a firearm) fire several shots without reloading. **9** *intr.* *US* illegally vote more than once in an election. —*n.* **1 a** the act or an instance of repeating. **b** a thing repeated (often *attrib.: repeat prescription*). **2** a repeated broadcast. **3** *Mus.* **a** a passage intended to be repeated. **b** a mark indicating this. **4** a pattern repeated in wallpaper etc. **5** *Commerce* **a** a consignment similar to a previous one. **b** an order given for this; a reorder. □ **repeating decimal** a recurring decimal. **repeat itself** recur in the same form. **repeat oneself** say or do the same thing over again. □□ **repeatable** *adj.* **repeatability** /-'bɪlɪtɪ/ *n.* **repeatedly** *adv.* [ME f. OF *repeter* f. L *repetere* (as RE-, *petere* seek)]

repeater /rɪ'piːtə(r)/ *n.* **1** a person or thing that repeats. **2** a firearm which fires several shots without reloading. **3** a watch or clock which repeats its strike when required. **4** a device for the automatic re-transmission or amplification of an electrically transmitted message. **5** a signal lamp indicating the state of another that is invisible.

repêchage /,repɪ'ʃɑːʒ/ *n.* (in rowing etc.) an extra contest in which the runners-up in the eliminating heats compete for a place in the final. [F *repêcher* fish out, rescue]

repel /rɪ'pel/ *v.tr.* (**repelled**, **repelling**) **1** drive back; ward off; repulse. **2** refuse admission or approach or acceptance to (*repel an assailant*). **3** be repulsive or distasteful to. □□ **repeller** *n.* [ME f. L *repellere* (as RE-, *pellere puls-* drive)]

repellent /rɪ'pelənt/ *adj. & n.* —*adj.* **1** that repels. **2** disgusting, repulsive. —*n.* a substance that repels esp. insects etc. □□ **repellence** *n.* **repellency** *n.* **repellently** *adv.* [L *repellere* (as REPEL)]

repent¹ /rɪ'pent/ *v.* **1** *intr.* (often foll. by *of*) feel deep sorrow about one's actions etc. **2** *tr.* (also *absol.*) wish one had not done, regret (one's wrong, omission, etc.); resolve not to continue a wrongdoing etc.). **3** *refl.* (often foll. by *of*) *archaic* feel regret or penitence about (*now I repent me*). □□ **repentance** *n.* **repentant** *adj.* **repenter** *n.* [ME f. OF *repentir* (as RE-, *pentir* ult. f. L *paenitēre*)]

repent² /'riːpənt/ *adj. Bot.* creeping, esp. growing along the ground or just under the surface. [L *repere* creep]

repeople /riː'piːp(ə)l/ *v.tr.* people again; increase the population of.

repercussion /,riːpə'kʌʃ(ə)n/ *n.* **1** (often foll. by *of*) an indirect effect or reaction following an event or action (*consider the repercussions of moving*). **2** the recoil after impact. **3** an echo or reverberation. □□ **repercussive** /-'kʌsɪv/ *adj.* [ME f. OF *repercussion* or L *repercussio* (as RE-, PERCUSSION)]

repertoire /'repə,twɑː(r)/ *n.* **1** a stock of pieces etc. that a company or a performer knows or is prepared to give. **2** a stock of regularly performed pieces, regularly used techniques, etc. (*went through his repertoire of excuses*). [F *répertoire* f. LL (as REPERTORY)]

repertory /'repətərɪ/ *n.* (*pl.* **-ies**) **1** = REPERTOIRE. **2** the theatrical performance of various plays for short periods by one company. **3 a** a repertory company. **b** repertory theatres regarded collectively. **4** a store

or collection, esp. of information, instances, etc. □ **repertory company** a theatrical company that performs plays from a repertoire. [LL *repertorium* f. L *reperire repert-* find]

repetend /'repɪ,tend/ *n.* **1** the recurring figures of a decimal. **2** the recurring word or phrase; a refrain. [L *repetendum* (as REPEAT)]

répétiteur /re,petɪ'tɜː(r)/ *n.* **1** a tutor or coach of musicians, esp. opera singers. **2** a person who supervises ballet rehearsals etc. [F]

repetition /,repɪ'tɪʃ(ə)n/ *n.* **1 a** the act or an instance of repeating or being repeated. **b** the thing repeated. **2** a copy or replica. **3** a piece to be learned by heart. **4** the ability of a musical instrument to repeat a note quickly. □□ **repetitional** *adj.* **repetitionary** *adj.* [F *répétition* or L *repetitio* (as REPEAT)]

repetitious /,repɪ'tɪʃəs/ *adj.* characterized by repetition, esp. when unnecessary or tiresome. □□ **repetitiously** *adv.* **repetitiousness** *n.*

repetitive /rɪ'petɪtɪv/ *adj.* = REPETITIOUS. □□ **repetitively** *adv.* **repetitiveness** *n.*

rephrase /riː'freɪz/ *v.tr.* express in an alternative way.

repine /rɪ'paɪn/ *v.intr.* (often foll. by *at*, *against*) fret; be discontented. [RE- + PINE², after *repent*]

repique /rɪ'piːk/ *n. & v.* —*n.* (in piquet) the winning of 30 points on cards alone before beginning to play. —*v.* (**repiques**, **repiqued**, **repiquing**) **1** *intr.* score repique. **2** *tr.* score repique against (another person). [F *repic* (as RE-, PIQUE²)]

replace /rɪ'pleɪs/ *v.tr.* **1** put back in place. **2** take the place of; succeed; be substituted for. **3** find or provide a substitute for. **4** (often foll. by *with*, *by*) fill up the place of. **5** (in *passive*, often foll. by *by*) be succeeded or have one's place filled by another; be superseded. □□ **replaceable** *adj.* **replacer** *n.*

replacement /rɪ'pleɪsmənt/ *n.* **1** the act or an instance of replacing or being replaced. **2** a person or thing that takes the place of another.

replan /riː'plæn/ *v.tr.* (**replanned**, **replanning**) plan again or differently.

replant /riː'plɑːnt/ *v.tr.* **1** transfer (a plant etc.) to a larger pot, a new site, etc. **2** plant (ground) again; provide with new plants.

replay *v. & n.* —*v.tr.* /riː'pleɪ/ play (a match, recording, etc.) again. —*n.* /'riːpleɪ/ the act or an instance of replaying a match, a recording, or a recorded incident in a game etc.

replenish /rɪ'plenɪʃ/ *v.tr.* **1** (often foll. by *with*) fill up again. **2** renew (a supply etc.). **3** (as **replenished** *adj.*) filled; fully stored or stocked; full. □□ **replenisher** *n.* **replenishment** *n.* [ME f. OF *replenir* (as RE-, *plenir* f. *plein* full f. L *plenus*)]

replete /rɪ'pliːt/ *adj.* (often foll. by *with*) **1** filled or well-supplied with. **2** stuffed; gorged; sated. □□ **repleteness** *n.* **repletion** *n.* [ME f. OF *replet replete* or L *repletus* past part. of *replēre* (as RE-, *plēre plet-* fill)]

replevin /rɪ'plevɪn/ *n. Law* **1** the provisional restoration or recovery of distrained goods pending the outcome of trial and judgement. **2** a writ granting this. **3** the action arising from this process. [ME f. AF f. OF *replevir* (as REPLEVY)]

replevy /rɪ'plevɪ/ *v.tr.* (**-ies**, **-ied**) *Law* recover by replevin. [OF *replevir* recover f. Gmc]

replica /'replɪkə/ *n.* **1** a duplicate of a work made by the original artist. **2** a facsimile, an exact copy. **3** a copy or model, esp. on a smaller scale. [It. f. *replicare* REPLY]

replicate *v., adj., & n.* —*v.tr.* /'replɪ,keɪt/ **1** repeat (an experiment etc.). **2** make a replica of. **3** fold back. —*adj.* /'replɪkət/ *Bot.* folded back on itself. —*n.* /'replɪkət/ *Mus.* a tone one more octaves above or below the given tone. □□ **replicable** /'replɪkəb(ə)l/ *adj.* (in sense 1 of *v.*). **replicability** /,replɪkə'bɪlɪtɪ/ *n.* (in sense 1 of *v.*). **replicative** /'replɪkətɪv/ *adj.* [L *replicare* (as RE-, *plicare* fold)]

replication /,replɪ'keɪʃ(ə)n/ *n.* **1** a reply or response, esp. a reply to an answer. **2** *Law* the plaintiff's reply to the defendant's plea. **3 a** the act or an instance of copying. **b** a copy. **c** the process by which genetic material or a living organism gives rise to a copy of itself. [ME f. OF *replicacion* f. L *replicatio -onis* (as REPLICATE)]

reply /rɪˈplaɪ/ *v. & n.* —*v.* (-**ies**, -**ied**) **1** *intr.* (often foll. by *to*) make an answer, respond in word or action. **2** *tr.* say in answer (*he replied, 'Please yourself'*). —*n.* (*pl.* -**ies**) **1** the act of replying (*what did they say in reply?*). **2** what is replied; a response. **3** *Law* = REPLICATION. □**reply coupon** a coupon exchangeable for stamps in any country for prepaying the reply to a letter. **reply paid 1** *hist.* (of a telegram) with the cost of a reply prepaid by the sender. **2** (of an envelope etc.) for which the addressee undertakes to pay postage. □□ **replier** *n.* [ME f. OF *replier* f. L (as REPLICATE)]

repoint /riːˈpɔɪnt/ *v.tr.* point (esp. brickwork) again.
repolish /riːˈpɒlɪʃ/ *v.tr.* polish again.
repopulate /riːˈpɒpjʊˌleɪt/ *v.tr.* populate again or increase the population of. □□**repopulation** /-ˈleɪʃ(ə)n/ *n.*

report /rɪˈpɔːt/ *v. & n.* —*v.* **1** *tr.* **a** bring back or give an account of. **b** state as fact or news, narrate or describe or repeat, esp. as an eyewitness or hearer etc. **c** relate as spoken by another. **2** *tr.* make an official or formal statement about. **3** *tr.* (often foll. by *to*) name or specify (an offender or offence) (*shall report you for insubordination; reported them to the police*). **4** *intr.* (often foll. by *to*) present oneself to a person as having returned or arrived (*report to the manager on arrival*). **5** *tr.* (also *absol.*) take down word for word or summarize or write a description of for publication. **6** *intr.* make or draw up or send in a report. **7** *intr.* (often foll. by *to*) be responsible (to a superior, supervisor, etc.) (*reports directly to the managing director*). **8** *tr. Parl.* (of a committee chairman) announce that the committee has dealt with (a bill). **9** *intr.* (often foll. by *of*) give a report to convey that one is well, badly, etc. impressed (*reports well of the prospects*). —*n.* **1** an account given or opinion formally expressed after investigation or consideration. **2** a description, summary, or reproduction of a scene or speech or law case, esp. for newspaper publication or broadcast. **3** common talk; rumour. **4** the way a person or thing is spoken of (*I hear a good report of you*). **5** a periodical statement on (esp. a school pupil's) work, conduct, etc. **6** the sound of an explosion. □**report back** deliver a report to the person, organization, etc. for whom one acts etc. **reported speech** the speaker's words with the changes of person, tense, etc. usual in reports, e.g. *he said that he would go* (opp. *direct speech*). **report progress** state what has been done so far. **report stage** (in the UK) the debate on a bill in the House of Commons or House of Lords after it is reported. □□ **reportable** *adj.* **reportedly** *adv.* [ME f. OF *reporter* f. L *reportare* (as RE-, *portare* bring)]

reportage /ˌrepɔːˈtɑːʒ/ *n.* **1** the describing of events, esp. the reporting of news etc. for the press and for broadcasting. **2** the typical style of this. **3** factual presentation in a book etc. [REPORT, after F]

reporter /rɪˈpɔːtə(r)/ *n.* **1** a person employed to report news etc. for newspapers or broadcasts. **2** a person who reports.

reportorial /ˌrɪpɔːˈtɔːrɪəl/ *adj.* US of newspaper reporters. □□ **reportorially** *adv.* [REPORTER, after *editorial*]

repose¹ /rɪˈpəʊz/ *n. & v.* —*n.* **1** the cessation of activity or excitement or toil. **2** sleep. **3** a peaceful or quiescent state; stillness; tranquillity. **4** *Art* a restful effect; harmonious combination. **5** composure or ease of manner. —*v.* **1** *intr. & refl.* lie down in rest (*reposed on a sofa*). **2** *tr.* (often foll. by *on*) lay (one's head etc.) to rest (on a pillow etc.). **3** *intr.* (often foll. by *in, on*) lie, be lying or laid, esp. in sleep or death. **4** *tr.* give rest to; refresh with rest. **5** *intr.* (foll. by *on,*

upon) be supported or based on. **6** *intr.* (foll. by *on*) (of memory etc.) dwell on. □□ **reposal** *n.* **reposeful** *adj.* **reposefully** *adv.* **reposefulness** *n.* [ME f. OF *repos(er)* f. LL *repausare* (as RE-, *pausare* PAUSE)]

repose² /rɪˈpəʊz/ *v.tr.* (foll. by *in*) place (trust etc.) in. □□ **reposal** *n.* [RE- + POSE¹ after L *reponere reposit-*]

reposition /ˌriːpəˈzɪʃ(ə)n/ *v.* **1** *tr.* move or place in a different position. **2** *intr.* adjust or alter one's position.

repository /rɪˈpɒzɪtərɪ/ *n.* (*pl.* -**ies**) **1** a place where things are stored or may be found, esp. a warehouse or museum. **2** a receptacle. **3** (often foll. by *of*) **a** a book, person, etc. regarded as a store of information etc. **b** the recipient of confidences or secrets. [obs. F *repositoire* or L *repositorium* (as REPOSE²)]

repossess /ˌriːpəˈzes/ *v.tr.* regain possession of (esp. property or goods on which repayment of a debt is in arrears). □□ **repossession** *n.* **repossessor** *n.*

repot /riːˈpɒt/ *v.tr.* (**repotted, repotting**) put (a plant) in another, esp. larger, pot.

repoussé /rəˈpuːseɪ/ *adj. & n.* —*adj.* hammered into relief from the reverse side. —*n.* ornamental metalwork fashioned in this way. [F, past part. of *repousser* (as RE-, *pousser* PUSH)]

repp var. of REP³.

repped /rept/ *adj.* having a surface like rep.

repr. *abbr.* **1** represent, represented, etc. **2** reprint, reprinted.

reprehend /ˌreprɪˈhend/ *v.tr.* rebuke; blame; find fault with. □□ **reprehension** *n.* [ME f. L *reprehendere* (as RE-, *prehendere* seize)]

reprehensible /ˌreprɪˈhensɪb(ə)l/ *adj.* deserving censure or rebuke; blameworthy. □□ **reprehensibility** /-ˈbɪlɪtɪ/ *n.* **reprehensibly** *adv.* [LL *reprehensibilis* (as REPREHEND)]

represent /ˌreprɪˈzent/ *v.tr.* **1** stand for or correspond to (*the comment does not represent all our views*). **2** (often in *passive*) be a specimen or example of; exemplify (*all types of people were represented in the audience*). **3** act as an embodiment of; symbolize (*the sovereign represents the majesty of the State; numbers are represented by letters*). **4** call up in the mind by description or portrayal or imagination; place a likeness of before the mind or senses. **5** serve or be meant as a likeness of. **6 a** state by way of expostulation or persuasion (*represented the rashness of it*). **b** (foll. by *to*) try to bring (the facts influencing conduct) home to (*represented the risks to his client*). **7** (often foll. by *as, to be*) describe or depict as; declare or make out (*represented them as martyrs; not what you represent it to be*). **8** (foll. by *that* + clause) allege. **9** show, or play the part of, on stage. **10** fill the place of; be a substitute or deputy for; be entitled to act or speak for (*the Queen was represented by the Princess of Wales*). **11** be elected as a member of Parliament, a legislature, etc. by (*represents a rural constituency*). □□ **representable** *adj.* **representability** /-ˈbɪlɪtɪ/ *n.* [ME f. OF *representer* or f. L *repraesentare* (as RE-, PRESENT²)]

representation /ˌreprɪzenˈteɪʃ(ə)n/ *n.* **1** the act or an instance of representing or being represented. **2** a thing (esp. a painting etc.) that represents another. **3** (esp. in *pl.*) a statement made by way of allegation or to convey opinion. [ME f. OF *representation* or L *repraesentatio* (as REPRESENT)]

representational /ˌreprɪzenˈteɪʃən(ə)l/ *adj.* of representation. □**representational art** art seeking to portray the physical appearance of a subject. □□ **representationalism** *n.* **representationalist** *adj. & n.*

representationism /ˌreprɪzenˈteɪʃəˌnɪz(ə)m/ *n.* the doctrine that perceived objects are only a representation of real external objects. □□ **representationist** *n.*

representative /ˌreprɪˈzentətɪv/ *adj. & n.* —*adj.* **1** typical of a class or category. **2** containing typical specimens of all or many classes (*a representative sample*). **3 a** consisting of elected deputies etc. **b**

based on the representation of a nation etc. by such deputies (*representative government*). **4** (foll. by *of*) serving as a portrayal or symbol of (*representative of their attitude to work*). **5** that presents or can present ideas to the mind (*imagination is a representative faculty*). —*n.* **1** (foll. by *of*) a sample, specimen, or typical embodiment or analogue of. **2 a** the agent of a person or society. **b** a commercial traveller. **3** a delegate; a substitute. **4** a deputy in a representative assembly. **5** (of art) representational. □□ **representatively** *adv.* **representativeness** *n.* [ME f. OF *representatif -ive* or med.L *repraesentativus* (as REPRESENT)]

repress /rɪ'pres/ *v.tr.* **1 a** check; restrain; keep under; quell. **b** suppress; prevent from sounding, rioting, or bursting out. **2** *Psychol.* actively exclude (an unwelcome thought) from conscious awareness. **3** (usu. as **repressed** *adj.*) subject (a person) to the suppression of his or her thoughts or impulses. □□ **represser** *n.* **repressible** *adj.* **repression** /-'preʃ(ə)n/ *n.* **repressive** *adj.* **repressively** *adv.* **repressiveness** *n.* **repressor** *n.* [ME f. L *reprimere* (as RE-, *premere* PRESS[1])]

reprice /ri:'praɪs/ *v.tr.* price again or differently. □□

reprieve /rɪ'pri:v/ *v. & n.* —*v.tr.* **1** remit, commute, or postpone the execution of (a condemned person). **2** give respite to. —*n.* **1 a** the act or an instance of reprieving or being reprieved. **b** a warrant for this. **2** respite; a respite or temporary escape. [ME as past part. *repryed* f. AF & OF *repris* past part. of *reprendre* (as RE-, *prendre* f. L *prehendere* take): 16th-c. -*v*- unexpl.]

reprimand /'reprɪ,mɑːnd/ *n. & v.* —*n.* (often foll. by *for*) an official or sharp rebuke (for a fault etc.). —*v.tr.* administer this to. [F *réprimande(r)* f. Sp. *reprimenda* f. L *reprimenda* neut. pl. gerundive of *reprimere* REPRESS]

reprint *v. & n.* —*v.tr.* /ri:'prɪnt/ print again. —*n.* /'ri:prɪnt/ **1** the act or an instance of reprinting a book etc. **2** the book etc. reprinted. **3** the quantity reprinted. □□ **reprinter** *n.*

reprisal /rɪ'praɪz(ə)l/ *n.* **1** an act of retaliation. **2** *hist.* the forcible seizure of a foreign subject or his or her goods as an act of retaliation. [ME (in sense 2) f. AF *reprisaille* f. med.L *reprisalia* f. *repraehensalia* (as REPREHEND)]

reprise /rɪ'pri:z/ *n.* **1** a repeated passage in music. **2** a repeated item in a musical programme. [F, fem. past part. of *reprendre* (see REPRIEVE)]

repro /'ri:prəʊ/ *n.* (*pl.* -**os**) (often *attrib.*) a reproduction or copy. [abbr.]

reproach /rɪ'prəʊtʃ/ *v. & n.* —*v.tr.* **1** express disapproval to (a person) for a fault etc. **2** scold; rebuke; censure. **3** *archaic* rebuke (an offence). —*n.* **1** a rebuke or censure (*heaped reproaches on them*). **2** (often foll. by *to*) a thing that brings disgrace or discredit (*their behaviour is a reproach to us all*). **3** a disgraced or discredited state (*live in reproach and ignominy*). **4** (in *pl.*) *RC Ch.* a set of antiphons and responses for Good Friday representing the reproaches of Christ to his people. □**above** (or **beyond**) **reproach** perfect. □□ **reproachable** *adj.* **reproacher** *n.* **reproachingly** *adv.* [ME f. OF *reproche(r)* f. Rmc (as RE-, L *prope* near)]

reproachful /rɪ'prəʊtʃfʊl/ *adj.* full of or expressing reproach. □□ **reproachfully** *adv.* **reproachfulness** *n.*

reprobate /'reprə,beɪt/ *n., adj., & v.* —*n.* **1** an unprincipled person; a person of highly immoral character. **2** a person who is condemned by God. —*adj.* **1** immoral. **2** hardened in sin. —*v.tr.* **1** express or feel disapproval of; censure. **2** (of God) condemn; exclude from salvation. □□ **reprobation** /-'beɪʃ(ə)n/ *n.* [ME f. L *reprobare reprobat-* disapprove (as RE-, *probare* approve)]

reprocess /ri:'prəʊses/ *v.tr.* process again or differently.

reproduce /,ri:prə'dju:s/ *v.* **1** *tr.* produce a copy or

representation of. **2** *tr.* cause to be seen or heard etc. again (*tried to reproduce the sound exactly*). **3** *intr.* produce further members of the same species by natural means. **4** *refl.* produce offspring (*reproduced itself several times*). **5** *intr.* give a specified quality or result when copied (*reproduces badly in black and white*). **6** *tr. Biol.* form afresh (a lost part etc. of the body). □□ **reproducer** *n.* **reproducible** *adj.* **reproducibility** /-'bɪlɪtɪ/ *n.* **reproducibly** *adv.*

reproduction /,ri:prə'dʌkʃ(ə)n/ *n.* **1** the act or an instance of reproducing. **2** a copy of a work of art, esp. a print or photograph of a painting. **3** (*attrib.*) (of furniture etc.) made in imitation of a certain style or of an earlier period. □□ **reproductive** *adj.* **reproductively** *adv.* **reproductiveness** *n.*

reprogram /ri:'prəʊgræm/ *v.tr.* (also **reprogramme** (**reprogrammed**, **reprogramming**; US **reprogramed**, **reprograming**) program (esp. a computer) again or differently. □□ **reprogramable** *adj.* (also **reprogrammable**).

reprography /rɪ'prɒgrəfɪ/ *n.* the science and practice of copying documents by photography, xerography, etc. □□ **reprographer** *n.* **reprographic** /,ri:prə'græfɪk/ *adj.* **reprographically** /,ri:prə'græfɪkəlɪ/ *adv.* [REPRODUCE + -GRAPHY]

reproof[1] /rɪ'pru:f/ *n.* **1** blame (*a glance of reproof*). **2** a rebuke; words expressing blame. [ME f. OF *reprove* f. *reprover* REPROVE]

reproof[2] /ri:'pru:f/ *v.tr.* **1** render (a coat etc.) waterproof again. **2** make a fresh proof of (printed matter etc.).

reprove /rɪ'pru:v/ *v.tr.* rebuke (a person, a person's conduct, etc.). □□ **reprovable** *adj.* **reprover** *n.* **reprovingly** *adv.* [ME f. OF *reprover* f. LL *reprobare* disapprove: see REPROBATE]

reptant /'rept(ə)nt/ *adj.* (of a plant or animal) creeping. [L *reptare reptant-* frequent. of *repere* crawl]

reptile /'reptaɪl/ *n. & adj.* —*n.* **1** any cold-blooded scaly animal of the class Reptilia, including snakes, lizards, crocodiles, turtles, tortoises, etc. **2** a mean, grovelling, or repulsive person. —*adj.* **1** (of an animal) creeping. **2** mean, grovelling. □□ **reptilian** /-'tɪlɪən/ *adj. & n.* [ME f. LL *reptilis* f. L *repere rept-* crawl]

republic /rɪ'pʌblɪk/ *n.* **1** a State in which supreme power is held by the people or their elected representatives or by an elected or nominated president, not by a monarch etc. **2** a society with equality between its members (*the literary republic*). □ **Republic Day** the day on which the foundation of a republic is commemorated; in India 26 January. [F *république* f. L *respublica* f. *res* concern + *publicus* PUBLIC]

republican /rɪ'pʌblɪkən/ *adj. & n.* —*adj.* **1** of or constituted as a republic. **2** characteristic of a republic. **3** advocating or supporting republican government. —*n.* **1** a person advocating or supporting republican government. **2** (**Republican**) (in the US) a member or supporter of the Republican Party. **3** an advocate of a united Ireland. □ **Republican Party** one of the two main US political parties, favouring only a moderate degree of central power (cf. *Democratic Party*). □□ **republicanism** *n.*

republish /ri:'pʌblɪʃ/ *v.tr.* (also *absol.*) publish again or in a new edition etc. □□ **republication** /-'keɪʃ(ə)n/ *n.*

repudiate /rɪ'pju:dɪ,eɪt/ *v.tr.* **1 a** disown; disavow; reject. **b** refuse dealings with. **c** deny. **2** refuse to recognize or obey (authority or a treaty). **3** refuse to discharge (an obligation or debt). **4** (esp. of the ancients or non-Christians) divorce (one's wife). □□ **repudiable** *adj.* **repudiation** /-'eɪʃ(ə)n/ *n.* **repudiator** *n.* [L *repudiare* f. *repudium* divorce]

repugnance /rɪ'pʌgnəns/ *n.* (also **repugnancy**) **1** (usu. foll. by *to, against*) antipathy; aversion. **2** (usu. foll. by *of, between, to, with*) inconsistency or incompatibility of ideas, statements, etc. [ME (in sense 2) f. F *répugnance* or L *repugnantia* f. *repugnare* oppose (as RE-, *pugnare* fight)]

repugnant /rɪˈpʌgnənt/ *adj.* **1** (often foll. by *to*) extremely distasteful. **2** (often foll. by *to*) contradictory. **3** (often foll. by *with*) incompatible. **4** *poet.* refractory; resisting. □□ **repugnantly** *adv.* [ME f. F *répugnant* or L (as REPUGNANCE)]

repulse /rɪˈpʌls/ *v. & n.* —*v.tr.* **1** drive back (an attack or attacking enemy) by force of arms. **2 a** rebuff (friendly advances or their maker). **b** refuse (a request or offer or its maker). **3** be repulsive to, repel. **4** foil in controversy. —*n.* **1** the act or an instance of repulsing or being repulsed. **2** a rebuff. [L *repellere repuls-* drive back (as REPEL)]

repulsion /rɪˈpʌlʃ(ə)n/ *n.* **1** aversion; disgust. **2** esp. *Physics* the force by which bodies tend to repel each other or increase their mutual distance (opp. ATTRACTION). [LL *repulsio* (as REPEL)]

repulsive /rɪˈpʌlsɪv/ *adj.* **1** causing aversion or loathing; loathsome, disgusting. **2** *Physics* exerting repulsion. **3** *archaic* (of behaviour etc.) cold, unsympathetic. □□ **repulsively** *adv.* **repulsiveness** *n.* [F *répulsif -ive* or f. REPULSE]

repurchase /riːˈpɜːtʃɪs/ *v. & n.* —*v.tr.* purchase again. —*n.* the act or an instance of purchasing again.

repurify /riːˈpjʊərɪfaɪ/ *v.tr.* (-ies, -ied) purify again. □□ **repurification** /-frˈkeɪʃ(ə)n/ *n.*

reputable /ˈrepjʊtəb(ə)l/ *adj.* of good repute; respectable. □□ **reputably** *adv.* [obs. F or f. med.L *reputabilis* (as REPUTE)]

reputation /ˌrepjʊˈteɪʃ(ə)n/ *n.* **1** what is generally said or believed about a person's or thing's character or standing (*has a reputation for dishonesty*). **2** the state of being well thought of; distinction; respectability (*have my reputation to think of*). **3** (foll. by *of*, *for* + verbal noun) credit or discredit (*has the reputation of driving hard bargains*). [ME f. L *reputatio* (as REPUTE)]

repute /rɪˈpjuːt/ *n. & v.* —*n.* reputation (*known by repute*). —*v.tr.* **1** (as **reputed** *adj.*) (often foll. by *to* + infin.) be generally considered or reckoned (*is reputed to be the best*). **2** (as **reputed** *adj.*) passing as being, but probably not being (*his reputed father*). □□ **reputedly** *adv.* [ME f. OF *reputer* or L *reputare* (as RE-, *putare* think)]

request /rɪˈkwest/ *n. & v.* —*n.* **1** the act or an instance of asking for something; a petition (*came at his request*). **2** a thing asked for. **3** the state of being sought after; demand (*in great request*). **4** a letter etc. asking for a particular record etc. to be played on a radio programme, often with a personal message. —*v.tr.* **1** ask to be given or allowed or favoured with (*request a hearing*; *requests your presence*). **2** (foll. by *to* + infin.) ask a person to do something (*requested her to answer*). **3** (foll. by *that* + clause) ask that. □ **by** (or **on**) **request** in response to an expressed wish. **request programme** a programme composed of items requested by the audience. **request stop** a bus-stop at which a bus stops only on a passenger's request. □□ **requester** *n.* [ME f. OF *requeste(r)* ult. f. L *requaerere* (as REQUIRE)]

requiem /ˈrekwɪˌem/ *n.* **1** (**Requiem**) (also *attrib.*) *chiefly RC Ch.* a mass for the repose of the souls of the dead. **2** *Mus.* the musical setting for this. [ME f. accus. of L *requies* rest, the initial word of the mass]

requiescat /ˌrekwɪˈeskæt/ *n.* a wish or prayer for the repose of a dead person. [L, = may he or she rest (in peace)]

require /rɪˈkwaɪə(r)/ *v.tr.* **1** need; depend on for success or fulfilment (*the work requires much patience*). **2** lay down as an imperative (*did all that was required by law*). **3** command; instruct (a person etc.). **4** order; insist on (an action or measure). **5** (often foll. by *of*, *from*, or *that* + clause) demand (of or from a person) as a right. **6** wish to have (*is there anything else you require?*). □□ **requirer** *n.*

requirement *n.* [ME f. OF *requere* ult. f. L *requirere* (as RE-, *quaerere* seek)]

requisite /ˈrekwɪzɪt/ *adj. & n.* —*adj.* required by circumstances; necessary to success etc. —*n.* (often foll. by *for*) a thing needed (for some purpose). □□ **requisitely** *adv.* [ME f. L *requisitus* past part. (as REQUIRE)]

requisition /ˌrekwɪˈzɪʃ(ə)n/ *n. & v.* —*n.* **1** an official order laying claim to the use of property or materials. **2** a formal written demand that some duty should be performed. **3** being called or put into service. —*v.tr.* demand the use or supply of, esp. by requisition order. □ **under** (or **in**) **requisition** being used or applied. □□ **requisitioner** *n.* **requisitionist** *n.* [F *réquisition* or L *requisitio* (as REQUIRE)]

requite /rɪˈkwaɪt/ *v.tr.* **1** make return for (a service). **2** (often foll. by *with*) reward or avenge (a favour or injury). **3** (often foll. by *for*) make return to (a person). **4** (often foll. by *for*, *with*) repay with good or evil (*requite like for like*; *requite hate with love*). □□ **requital** *n.* [RE- + *quite* var. of QUIT]

reran *past* of RERUN.

reread /riːˈriːd/ *v. & n.* —*v.tr.* (*past* and *past part.* **reread** /-ˈred/) read again. —*n.* an instance of reading again. □□ **re-readable** *adj.*

reredos /ˈrɪədɒs/ *n. Eccl.* an ornamental screen covering the wall at the back of an altar. [ME f. AF f. OF *areredos* f. *arere* behind + *dos* back: cf. ARREARS]

re-release /ˌriːrɪˈliːs/ *v. & n.* —*v.tr.* release (a record, film, etc.) again. —*n.* a re-released record, film, etc.

re-route /riːˈruːt/ *v.tr.* (-**routeing**) send or carry by a different route.

rerun /riːˈrʌn/ *v. & n.* —*v.tr.* (**rerunning**; *past* **reran**; *past part.* **rerun**) run (a race, film, etc.) again. —*n.* /ˈriːrʌn/ **1** the act or an instance of rerunning. **2** a film etc. shown again.

resale /riːˈseɪl/ *n.* the sale of a thing previously bought. □ **resale price maintenance** a manufacturer's practice of setting a minimum resale price for goods. □□ **resalable** *adj.*

resat *past* and *past part.* of RESIT.

reschedule /riːˈʃedjuːl, -ˈskedʒʊəl/ *v.tr.* alter the schedule of; replan.

rescind /rɪˈsɪnd/ *v.tr.* abrogate, revoke, cancel. □□ **rescindable** *adj.* **rescindment** *n.* **rescission** /-ˈsɪʒ(ə)n/ *n.* [L *rescindere resciss-* (as RE-, *scindere* cut)]

rescript /ˈriːskrɪpt/ *n.* **1** a Roman emperor's written reply to an appeal for guidance, esp. on a legal point. **2** *RC Ch.* the Pope's decision on a question of doctrine or papal law. **3** an official edict or announcement. **4 a** the act or an instance of rewriting. **b** the thing rewritten. [L *rescriptum*, neut. past part. of *rescribere rescript-* (as RE-, *scribere* write)]

rescue /ˈreskjuː/ *v. & n.* —*v.tr.* (**rescues, rescued, rescuing**) **1** (often foll. by *from*) save or set free or bring away from attack, custody, danger, or harm. **2** *Law* **a** unlawfully liberate (a person). **b** forcibly recover (property). —*n.* the act or an instance of rescuing or being rescued; deliverance. □ **rescue bid** *Bridge* a bid made to get one's partner out of a difficult situation. □□ **rescuable** *adj.* **rescuer** *n.* [ME *rescowe* f. OF *rescoure* f. Rmc, formed as RE- + L *excutere* (as EX-¹, *quatere* shake)]

reseal /riːˈsiːl/ *v.tr.* seal again. □□ **resealable** *adj.*

research /rɪˈsɜːtʃ, *disp.* ˈriːsɜːtʃ/ *n. & v.* —*n.* **1 a** the systematic investigation into and study of materials, sources, etc., in order to establish facts and reach new conclusions. **b** (usu. in *pl.*) an endeavour to discover new or collate old facts etc. by the scientific study of a subject or by a course of critical investigation. **2** (*attrib.*) engaged in or intended for research (*research assistant*). —*v.* **1** *tr.* do research into or for. **2** *intr.* make researches. □ **research and development** (in industry etc.) work directed towards the innovation, introduction, and improvement of products and processes. □□

researchable *adj.* **researcher** *n.* [obs. F *recerche* (as RE-, SEARCH)]

reseat /riːˈsiːt/ *v.tr.* **1** (also *refl.*) seat (oneself, a person, etc.) again. **2** provide with a fresh seat or seats.

resect /rɪˈsekt/ *v.tr. Surgery* **1** cut out part of (a lung etc.). **2** pare down (bone, cartilage, etc.). □□ **resection** *n.* **resectional** *adj.* **resectionist** *n.* [L *resecare resect-* (as RE-, *secare* cut)]

reseda /ˈresɪdə/ *n.* **1** any plant of the genus *Reseda*, with sweet-scented flowers, e.g. a mignonette. **2** /also ˈrez-/ the pale green colour of mignonette flowers. [L, perh. f. imper. of *resedare* assuage, with ref. to its supposed curative powers]

reselect /ˌriːsɪˈlekt/ *v.tr.* select again or differently. □□ **reselection** *n.*

resell /riːˈsel/ *v.tr.* (*past* and *past part.* **resold**) sell (an object etc.) after buying it.

resemblance /rɪˈzembləns/ *n.* (often foll. by *to*, *between*, *of*) a likeness or similarity. □□ **resemblant** *adj.* [ME f. AF (as RESEMBLE)]

resemble /rɪˈzemb(ə)l/ *v.tr.* be like; have a similarity to, or features in common with, or the same appearance as. □□ **resembler** *n.* [ME f. OF *resembler* (as RE-, *sembler* f. L *similare* f. *similis* like)]

resent /rɪˈzent/ *v.tr.* show or feel indignation at; be aggrieved by (a circumstance, action, or person) (*we resent being patronized*). [obs. F *resentir* (as RE-, *sentire* feel)]

resentful /rɪˈzentfʊl/ *adj.* feeling resentment. □□ **resentfully** *adv.* **resentfulness** *n.*

resentment /rɪˈzentmənt/ *n.* (often foll. by *at*, *of*) indignant or bitter feelings; anger. [It. *risentimento* or F *ressentiment* (as RESENT)]

reserpine /rɪˈsɜːpiːn/ *n.* an alkaloid obtained from plants of the genus *Rauwolfia*, used as a tranquillizer and in the treatment of hypertension. [G *Reserpin* f. mod.L Rauwolfia (f. L. *Rauwolf*, Ger. botanist d. 1596) *serpentina*]

reservation /ˌrezəˈveɪʃ(ə)n/ *n.* **1** the act or an instance of reserving or being reserved. **2** a booking (of a room, berth, seat, etc.). **3** the thing booked, e.g. a room in a hotel. **4** an express or tacit limitation or exception to an agreement etc. (*had reservations about the plan*). **5** *Brit.* a strip of land between the carriageways of a road. **6** an area of land reserved for occupation by American Indians, African Blacks, or Australian Aboriginals, etc. **7 a** a right or interest retained in an estate being conveyed. **b** the clause reserving this. **8** *Eccl.* **a** the practice of retaining for some purpose a portion of the Eucharistic elements (esp. the bread) after celebration. **b** *RC Ch.* the power of absolution reserved to a superior. **c** *RC Ch.* the right reserved to the Pope of nomination to a vacant benefice. [ME f. OF *reservation* or LL *reservatio* (as RESERVE)]

reserve /rɪˈzɜːv/ *v. & n.* —*v.tr.* **1** postpone, put aside, keep back for a later occasion or special use. **2** order to be specially retained or allocated for a particular person or at a particular time. **3** retain or secure, esp. by formal or legal stipulation (*reserve the right to*). **4** postpone delivery of (judgement etc.) (*reserved my comments until the end*). —*n.* **1** a thing reserved for future use; an extra stock or amount (*a great reserve of strength; huge energy reserves*). **2** a limitation, qualification, or exception attached to something (*accept your offer without reserve*). **3 a** self-restraint; reticence; lack of cordiality (*difficult to overcome his reserve*). **b** (in artistic or literary expression) absence from exaggeration or ill-proportioned effects. **4** a company's profit added to capital. **5** (in *sing.* or *pl.*) assets kept readily available as cash or at a central bank, or as gold or foreign exchange (*reserve currency*). **6** (in *sing.* or *pl.*) **a** troops withheld from action to reinforce or protect others. **b** forces in addition to the regular army, navy, airforce, etc., but available in an emergency. **7** a member of the military reserve. **8** an extra player

chosen to be a possible substitute in a team. **9** a place reserved for special use, esp. as a habitat for a native tribe or for wildlife (*game reserve*; *nature reserve*). **10** the intentional suppression of the truth (*exercised a certain amount of reserve*). **11** (in the decoration of ceramics or textiles) an area which still has the original colour of the material or the colour of the background. □**in reserve** unused and available if required. **reserve grade** *Austral.* a second-grade team. **reserve price** the lowest acceptable price stipulated for an item sold at an auction. **with all** (or **all proper**) **reserve** without endorsing. □□ **reservable** *adj.* **reserver** *n.* [ME f. OF *reserver* f. L *reservare* keep)]

re-serve /riːˈsɜːv/ *v.tr. & intr.* serve again.

reserved /rɪˈzɜːvd/ *adj.* **1** reticent; slow to reveal emotion or opinions; uncommunicative. **2 a** set apart, destined for some use or fate. **b** (often foll. by *for*, *to*) left by fate for; falling first or only to. □**reserved occupation** an occupation from which a person will not be taken for military service. □□ **reservedly** /-vɪdlɪ/ *adv.* **reservedness** *n.*

reservist /rɪˈzɜːvɪst/ *n.* a member of the reserve forces.

reservoir /ˈrezəˌvwɑː(r)/ *n.* **1** a large natural or artificial lake used as a source of water supply. **2 a** any natural or artificial receptacle esp. for or of fluid. **b** a place where fluid etc. collects. **3** a part of a machine etc. holding fluid. **4** (usu. foll. by *of*) a reserve or supply esp. of information. [F *réservoir* f. *réserver* RESERVE]

reset /riːˈset/ *v.tr.* (**resetting**; *past* and *past part.* **reset**) set (a broken bone, gems, a mechanical device, etc.) again or differently. □□ **resettable** *adj.* **resettability** /-ˈbɪlɪtɪ/ *n.*

resettle /riːˈset(ə)l/ *v.tr. & intr.* settle again. □□ **resettlement** *n.*

reshape /riːˈʃeɪp/ *v.tr.* shape or form again or differently.

reshuffle /riːˈʃʌf(ə)l/ *v. & n.* —*v.tr.* **1** shuffle (cards) again. **2** interchange the posts of (government ministers etc.). —*n.* the act or an instance of reshuffling.

reside /rɪˈzaɪd/ *v.intr.* **1** (often foll. by *at*, *in*, *abroad*, etc.) (of a person) have one's home, dwell permanently. **2** (of power, a right, etc.) rest or be vested in. **3** (of an incumbent official) be in residence. **4** (foll. by *in*) (of a quality) be present or inherent in. [ME, prob. back-form. f. RESIDENT infl. by F *résider* or L *residēre* (as RE-, *sedēre* sit)]

residence /ˈrezɪd(ə)ns/ *n.* **1** the act or an instance of residing. **2 a** the place where a person resides; an abode. **b** a mansion; the official house of a government minister etc. **c** a house, esp. one of considerable pretension (*returned to their London residence*). □**in residence** dwelling at a specified place, esp. for the performance of duties or work. [ME f. OF *residence* or med.L *residentia* f. L *residēre*: see RESIDE]

residency /ˈrezɪdənsɪ/ *n.* (*pl.* **-ies**) **1** = RESIDENCE 1, 2a. **2** *US* a period of specialized medical training; the position of a resident. **3** *hist.* the official residence of the Governor-General's representative or other government agent at an Indian native court; the territory supervised by this official. **4** a musician's regular engagement at a club etc. **5** a group or organization of intelligence agents in a foreign country.

resident /ˈrezɪd(ə)nt/ *n. & adj.* —*n.* **1** (often foll. by *of*) **a** a permanent inhabitant (of a town or neighbourhood). **b** a bird belonging to a species that does not migrate. **2** a guest in a hotel etc. staying overnight. **3** *hist.* a British government agent in any semi-independent State, esp. the Governor-General's agent at an Indian native court. **4** *US* a medical graduate engaged in specialized practice under supervision in a hospital. **5** an intelligence agent in a foreign country. —*adj.* **1** residing; in residence. **2 a** having quarters on the premises of one's work etc.

(*resident housekeeper*; *resident doctor*). **b** working regularly in a particular place. **3** located in; inherent (*powers of feeling are resident in the nerves*). **4** (of birds etc.) non-migratory. □□ **residentship** *n.* (in sense 3 of *n.*). [ME f. OF *resident* or L: see RESIDE]

residential /ˌrezɪ'denʃ(ə)l/ *adj.* **1** suitable for or occupied by private houses (*residential area*). **2** used as a residence (*residential hotel*). **3** based on or connected with residence (*the residential qualification for voters; a residential course of study*). □□ **residentially** *adv.*

residentiary /ˌrezɪ'denʃəri/ *adj. & n.* —*adj.* of, subject to, or requiring, official residence. —*n.* (*pl.* -**ies**) an ecclesiastic who must officially reside in a place. [med.L *residentiarius* (as RESIDENCE)]

residua *pl.* of RESIDUUM.

residual /rɪ'zɪdjʊəl/ *adj. & n.* —*adj.* **1** remaining, left as a residue or residuum. **2** *Math.* resulting from subtraction. **3** (in calculation) still unaccounted for or not eliminated. —*n.* **1** a quantity left over or *Math.* resulting from subtraction. **2** an error in calculation not accounted for or eliminated. □□ **residually** *adv.*

residuary /rɪ'zɪdjʊəri/ *adj.* **1** of the residue of an estate (*residuary bequest*). **2** of or being a residuum; residual; still remaining.

residue /'rezɪˌdju/ *n.* **1** what is left over or remains; a remainder; the rest. **2** *Law* what remains of an estate after the payment of charges, debts, and bequests. **3** esp. *Chem.* a residuum. [ME f. OF *residu* f. L *residuum*: see RESIDUUM]

residuum /rɪ'zɪdjʊəm/ *n.* (*pl.* **residua** /-djʊə/) **1** *Chem.* a substance left after combustion or evaporation. **2** a remainder or residue. [L, neut. of *residuus* remaining f. *residēre*: see RESIDE]

resign /rɪ'zaɪn/ *v.* **1** *intr.* **a** (often foll. by *from*) give up office, one's employment, etc. (*resigned from the Home Office*). **b** (often foll. by *as*) retire (*resigned as chief executive*). **2** *tr.* (often foll. by *to, into*) relinquish; surrender; hand over (a right, charge, task, etc.). **3** *tr.* give up (hope etc.). **4** *refl.* (usu. foll. by *to*) **a** reconcile (oneself, one's mind, etc.) to the inevitable (*have resigned myself to the idea*). **b** surrender (oneself to another's guidance). **5** *intr.* *Chess* etc. discontinue play and admit defeat. □□ **resigner** *n.* [ME f. OF *resigner* f. L *resignare* unseal, cancel (as RE-, *signare* sign, seal)]

re-sign /riː'saɪn/ *v.tr. & intr.* sign again.

resignation /ˌrezɪg'neɪʃ(ə)n/ *n.* **1** the act or an instance of resigning, esp. from one's job or office. **2** the document etc. conveying this intention. **3** the state of being resigned; the uncomplaining endurance of a sorrow or difficulty. [ME f. OF f. med.L *resignatio* (as RESIGN)]

resigned /rɪ'zaɪnd/ *adj.* (often foll. by *to*) having resigned oneself; submissive, acquiescent. □□ **resignedly** /-nɪdlɪ/ *adv.* **resignedness** *n.*

resile /rɪ'zaɪl/ *v.intr.* **1** (of something stretched or compressed) recoil to resume a former size and shape; spring back. **2** have or show resilience or recuperative power. **3** (usu. foll. by *from*) withdraw from a course of action. [obs. F *resilir* or L *resilire* (as RE-, *salire* jump)]

resilient /rɪ'zɪlɪənt/ *adj.* **1** (of a substance etc.) recoiling; springing back; resuming its original shape after bending, stretching, compression, etc. **2** (of a person) readily recovering from shock, depression, etc.; buoyant. □□ **resilience** *n.* **resiliency** *n.* **resiliently** *adv.* [L *resiliens resilient-* (as RESILE)]

resin /'rezɪn/ *n. & v.* —*n.* **1** an adhesive inflammable substance insoluble in water, secreted by some plants, and often extracted by incision, esp. from fir and pine (cf. GUM¹). **2** (in full **synthetic resin**) a solid or liquid organic compound made by polymerization etc. and used in plastics etc. —*v.tr.* (**resined, resining**) rub or treat with resin. □□ **resinate** /-nət/ *n.* **resinate** /-ˌneɪt/ *v.tr.* **resinoid** *adj. & n.* **resinous** *adj.* [ME *resyn, rosyn* f. L *resina* & med.L *rosina, rosinum*]

resist /rɪ'zɪst/ *v. & n.* —*v.* **1** *tr.* withstand the action or effect of; repel. **2** *tr.* stop the course or progress of; prevent from reaching, penetrating, etc. **3** *tr.* abstain from (pleasure, temptation, etc.). **4** *tr.* strive against; try to impede; refuse to comply with (*resist arrest*). **5** *intr.* offer opposition; refuse to comply. —*n.* a protective coating of a resistant substance, applied esp. to parts of calico that are not to take dye or to parts of pottery that are not to take glaze or lustre. □**cannot** (or **could not** etc.) **resist 1** (foll. by verbal noun) feel obliged or strongly inclined to (*cannot resist teasing me about it*). **2** is certain to be amused, attracted, etc., by (*can't resist children's clothes*). □□ **resistant** *adj.* **resister** *n.* **resistible** *adj.* **resistibility** /-'bɪlɪtɪ/ *n.* [ME f. OF *resister* or L *resistere* (as RE-, *sistere* stop, redupl. of *stare* stand)]

resistance /rɪ'zɪst(ə)ns/ *n.* **1** the act or an instance of resisting; refusal to comply. **2** the power of resisting (*showed resistance to wear and tear*). **3** *Biol.* the ability to withstand adverse conditions. **4** the impeding, slowing, or stopping effect exerted by one material thing on another. **5** *Physics* **a** the property of hindering the conduction of electricity, heat, etc. **b** the measure of this in a body. ¶ Symb.: **R. 6** a resistor. **7** (in full **resistance movement**) a secret organization resisting authority, esp. in an occupied country. [ME f. F *résistance, résistence* f. LL *resistentia* (as RESIST)]

resistive /rɪ'zɪstɪv/ *adj.* **1** able to resist. **2** *Electr.* of or concerning resistance.

resistivity /ˌrɪzɪs'tɪvɪtɪ/ *n.* *Electr.* a measure of the resisting power of a specified material to the flow of an electric current.

resistless /rɪ'zɪstlɪs/ *adj.* *archaic poet.* **1** irresistible; relentless. **2** unresisting. □□ **resistlessly** *adv.*

resistor /rɪ'zɪstə(r)/ *n.* *Electr.* a device having resistance to the passage of an electrical current.

resit *v. & n.* —*v.tr.* /riː'sɪt/ (**resitting**; *past* and *past part.* **resat**) sit (an examination) again after failing. —*n.* /'riːsɪt/ **1** the act or an instance of resitting an examination. **2** an examination held specifically to enable candidates to resit.

re-site /riː'saɪt/ *v.tr.* place on another site; relocate.

resold *past* and *past part.* of RESELL.

resoluble /rɪ'zɒljʊb(ə)l/ *adj.* **1** that can be resolved. **2** (foll. by *into*) analysable. [F *résoluble* or L *resolubilis* (as RESOLVE, after *soluble*)]

re-soluble /riː'sɒljʊb(ə)l/ *adj.* that can be dissolved again.

resolute /'rezəˌluːt, -ˌljuːt/ *adj.* (of a person or a person's mind or action) determined; decided; firm of purpose; not vacillating. □□ **resolutely** *adv.* **resoluteness** *n.* [L *resolutus* past part. of *resolvere* (see RESOLVE)]

resolution /ˌrezə'luːʃ(ə)n, -'ljuːʃ(ə)n/ *n.* **1** a resolute temper or character; boldness and firmness of purpose. **2** a thing resolved on; an intention (*New Year's resolutions*). **3 a** a formal expression of opinion or intention by a legislative body or public meeting. **b** the formulation of this (*passed a resolution*). **4** (usu. foll. by *of*) the act or an instance of solving doubt or a problem or question (*towards a resolution of the difficulty*). **5 a** a separation into components; decomposition. **b** the replacing of a single force etc. by two or more jointly equivalent to it. **6** (foll. by *into*) analysis; conversion into another form. **7** *Mus.* the act or an instance of causing discord to pass into concord. **8** *Physics* etc. the smallest interval measurable by a scientific instrument; the resolving power. **9** *Med.* the disappearance of inflammation etc. without suppuration. **10** *Prosody* the substitution of two short syllables for one long. [ME f. L *resolutio* (as RESOLVE)]

resolutive /'rezəˌluːtɪv, -ˌljuːtɪv/ *adj.* *Med.* having the power or ability to dissolve. □**resolutive condition**

Law a condition whose fulfilment terminates a contract etc. [med.L *resolutivus* (as RESOLVE)]

resolve /rɪˈzɒlv/ *v.* & *n.* —*v.* **1** *intr.* make up one's mind; decide firmly (*resolve to do better*). **2** *tr.* (of circumstances etc.) cause (a person) to do this (*events resolved him to leave*). **3** *tr.* (foll. by *that* + clause) (of an assembly or meeting) pass a resolution by vote (*the committee resolved that immediate action should be taken*). **4** *intr.* & *tr.* (often foll. by *into*) separate or cause to separate into constituent parts; disintegrate; analyse; dissolve. **5** *tr.* (of optical or photographic equipment) separate or distinguish between closely adjacent objects. **6** *tr.* & *intr.* (foll. by *into*) convert or be converted. **7** *tr.* & *intr.* (foll. by *into*) reduce by mental analysis into. **8** *tr.* solve; explain; clear up; settle (doubt, argument, etc.). **9** *tr.* & *intr. Mus.* convert or be converted into concord. **10** *tr. Med.* remove (inflammation etc.) without suppuration. **11** *tr. Prosody* replace (a long syllable) by two short syllables. **12** *tr. Mech.* replace (a force etc.) by two or more jointly equivalent to it. —*n.* **1 a** a firm mental decision or intention; a resolution (*made a resolve not to go*). **b** *US* a formal resolution by a legislative body or public meeting. **2** resoluteness; steadfastness. □**resolving power** an instrument's ability to distinguish very small or very close objects. □□**resolvable** *adj.* **resolvability** /-ˈbɪlɪtɪ/ *n.* **resolver** *n.* [ME f. L *resolvere resolut-* (as RE-, SOLVE)]

resolved /rɪˈzɒlvd/ *adj.* resolute, determined. □□ **resolvedly** /-ˈvɪdlɪ/ *adv.* **resolvedness** *n.*

resolvent /rɪˈzɒlv(ə)nt/ *adj.* & *n.* esp. *Med.* —*adj.* (of a drug, application, substance, etc.) effecting the resolution of a tumour etc. —*n.* such a drug etc.

resonance /ˈrezənəns/ *n.* **1** the reinforcement or prolongation of sound by reflection or synchronous vibration. **2** *Mech.* a condition in which an object or system is subjected to an oscillating force having a frequency close to its own natural frequency. **3** *Chem.* the property of a molecule having a structure best represented by two or more forms rather than a single structural formula. **4** *Physics* a short-lived elementary particle that is an excited state of a more stable particle. [OF f. L *resonantia* echo (as RESONANT)]

resonant /ˈrezənənt/ *adj.* **1** (of sound) echoing, resounding; continuing to sound; reinforced or prolonged by reflection or synchronous vibration. **2** (of a body, room, etc.) tending to reinforce or prolong sounds esp. by synchronous vibration. **3** (often foll. by *with*) (of a place) resounding. **4** of or relating to resonance. □□ **resonantly** *adv.* [F *résonnant* or L *resonare resonant-* (as RE-, *sonare* sound)]

resonate /ˈrezəneɪt/ *v.intr.* produce or show resonance; resound. [L *resonare resonat-* (as RESONANT)]

resonator /ˈrezəneɪtə(r)/ *n. Mus.* **1** an instrument responding to a single note and used for detecting it in combinations. **2** an appliance for giving resonance to sound or other vibrations.

resorb /rɪˈsɔːb/ *v.tr.* absorb again. □□ **resorbence** *n.* **resorbent** *n.* [L *resorbēre resorpt-* (as RE-, *sorbēre* absorb)]

resorcin /rɪˈzɔːsɪn/ *n.* = RESORCINOL. [RESIN + ORCIN]

resorcinol /rɪˈzɔːsɪˌnɒl/ *n. Chem.* a crystalline organic compound usu. made by synthesis and used in the production of dyes, drugs, resins, etc.

resorption /rɪˈzɔːpʃ(ə)n/ *n.* **1** the act or an instance of resorbing; the state of being resorbed. **2** the absorption of tissue within the body. □□ **resorptive** /-tɪv/ *adj.* [RESORB after *absorption*]

resort /rɪˈzɔːt/ *n.* & *v.* —*n.* **1** a place frequented esp. for holidays or for a specified purpose or quality (*seaside resort; health resort*). **2 a** a thing to which one has recourse; an expedient or measure (*a taxi was our best resort*). **b** (foll. by *to*) recourse; use of (*without resort to violence*). **3** a tendency to frequent or be frequented (*places of great resort*). —*v.intr.* **1** (foll. by *to*) turn to as an expedient (*resorted to threats*). **2** (foll. by *to*) go often or in large numbers

to. □**in the** (or **as a**) **last resort** when all else has failed. □□ **resorter** *n.* [ME f. OF *resortir* (as RE-, *sortir* come or go out)]

re-sort /riːˈsɔːt/ *v.tr.* sort again or differently.

resound /rɪˈzaʊnd/ *v.* **1** *intr.* (often foll. by *with*) (of a place) ring or echo (*the hall resounded with laughter*). **2** *intr.* (of a voice, instrument, sound, etc.) produce echoes; go on sounding; fill the place with sound. **3** *intr.* **a** (of fame, a reputation, etc.) be much talked of. **b** (foll. by *through*) produce a sensation (*the call resounded through Europe*). **4** *tr.* (often foll. by *of*) proclaim or repeat loudly (the praises) of a person or thing (*resounded the praises of Greece*). **5** *tr.* (of a place) re-echo (a sound). [ME f. RE- + SOUND¹ *v.*, after OF *resoner* or L *resonare*: see RESONANT]

resounding /rɪˈzaʊndɪŋ/ *adj.* **1** in senses of RESOUND. **2** unmistakable; emphatic (*was a resounding success*). □□ **resoundingly** *adv.*

resource /rɪˈsɔːs, -ˈzɔːs/ *n.* **1** an expedient or device (*escape was their only resource*). **2** (usu. in *pl.*) **a** the means available to achieve an end, fulfil a function, etc. **b** a stock or supply that can be drawn on. **c** *US* available assets. **3** (in *pl.*) a country's collective wealth or means of defence. **4** a leisure occupation (*reading is a great resource*). **5 a** a skill in devising expedients (*a person of great resource*). **b** practical ingenuity; quick wit (*full of resource*). **6** *archaic* the possibility of aid (*lost without resource*). □**one's own resources** one's own abilities, ingenuity, etc. □□ **resourceful** *adj.* **resourcefully** *adv.* **resourcefulness** *n.* **resourceless** *adj.* **resourcelessness** *n.* [F *ressource*, *ressourse*, fem. past part. of OF dial. *resourdre* (as RE-, L *surgere* rise)]

respect /rɪˈspekt/ *n.* & *v.* —*n.* **1** deferential esteem felt or shown towards a person or quality. **2 a** (foll. by *of, for*) heed or regard. **b** (foll. by *to*) attention to or consideration of (*without respect to the results*). **3** an aspect, detail, particular, etc. (*correct except in this one respect*). **4** reference, relation (*a morality that has no respect to religion*). **5** (in *pl.*) a person's polite messages or attentions (*give my respects to your mother*). —*v.tr.* **1** regard with deference, esteem, or honour. **2 a** avoid interfering with, harming, degrading, insulting, injuring, or interrupting. **b** treat with consideration. **c** refrain from offending, corrupting, or tempting (a person, a person's feelings, etc.). □**in respect of** as concerns; with reference to. **in respect that** because. **with** (or **with all due**) **respect** a mollifying formula preceding an expression of disagreement with another's views. □□ **respecter** *n.* [ME f. OF *respect* or L *respectus* f. *respicere* (as RE-, *specere* look at) or f. *respectare* frequent. of *respicere*]

respectability /rɪˌspektəˈbɪlɪtɪ/ *n.* **1** the state of being respectable. **2** those who are respectable.

respectable /rɪˈspektəb(ə)l/ *adj.* **1** deserving respect. **2 a** of fair social standing. **b** having the qualities necessary for such standing. **3** honest and decent in conduct etc. **4** of some merit or importance. **5** tolerable, passable, fairly good or competent (*a respectable try*). **6** (of activities, clothes, etc.) presentable; befitting a respectable person. **7** reasonably good in condition or appearance. **8** appreciable in number, size, amount, etc. **9** primly conventional. □□ **respectably** *adv.*

respectful /rɪˈspektfʊl/ *adj.* showing deference (*stood at a respectful distance*). □□ **respectfully** *adv.* **respectfulness** *n.*

respecting /rɪˈspektɪŋ/ *prep.* with reference or regard to; concerning.

respective /rɪˈspektɪv/ *adj.* concerning or appropriate to each of several individually; proper to each (*go to your respective places*). [F *respectif -ive* f. med.L *respectivus* (as RESPECT)]

respectively /rɪˈspektɪvlɪ/ *adv.* for each separately or in turn, and in the order mentioned (*she and I gave £10 and £1 respectively*).

---

w *we*   z *zoo*   ʃ *she*   ʒ *decision*   θ *thin*   ð *this*   ŋ *ring*   x *loch*   tʃ *chip*   dʒ *jar*   (*see over for vowels*)

respell /riːˈspel/ v.tr. (past and past part. **respelt** or **respelled**) spell again or differently, esp. phonetically.

respirable /ˈrespərəb(ə)l, rɪˈspaɪrəb(ə)l/ adj. (of air, gas, etc.) able or fit to be breathed. [F respirable or LL respirabilis (as RESPIRE)]

respirate /ˈrespɪˌreɪt/ v.tr. subject to artificial respiration. [back-form. f. RESPIRATION]

respiration /ˌrespɪˈreɪʃ(ə)n/ n. **1 a** the act or an instance of breathing. **b** a single inspiration or expiration; a breath. **2** Biol. in living organisms, the process involving the release of energy and carbon dioxide from the oxidation of complex organic substances. [ME f. F respiration or L respiratio (as RESPIRE)]

respirator /ˈrespɪˌreɪtə(r)/ n. **1** an apparatus worn over the face to prevent poison gas, cold air, dust particles, etc., from being inhaled. **2** Med. an apparatus for maintaining artificial respiration.

respire /rɪˈspaɪə(r)/ v. **1** intr. breathe air. **2** intr. inhale and exhale air. **3** intr. (of a plant) carry out respiration. **4** tr. breathe (air etc.). **5** intr. breathe again; take a breath. **6** intr. get rest or respite; recover hope or spirit. □□ **respiratory** /rɪˈspɪrətəri, ˈrespəˌreɪtəri/ adj. [ME f. OF respirer or f. L respirare (as RE-, spirare breathe)]

respite /ˈrespaɪt, -pɪt/ n. & v. —n. **1** an interval of rest or relief. **2** a delay permitted before the discharge of an obligation or the suffering of a penalty. —v.tr. **1** grant respite to; reprieve (a condemned person). **2** postpone the execution or exaction of (a sentence, obligation, etc.). **3** give temporary relief from (pain or care) or to (a sufferer). [ME f. OF respit f. L respectus RESPECT]

resplendent /rɪˈsplend(ə)nt/ adj. brilliant, dazzlingly or gloriously bright. □□ **resplendence** n. **resplendency** n. **resplendently** adv. [ME f. L resplendēre (as RE-, splendēre glitter)]

respond /rɪˈspɒnd/ v. & n. —v. **1** intr. answer, give a reply. **2** intr. act or behave in an answering or corresponding manner. **3** intr. (usu. foll. by to) show sensitiveness to by behaviour or change (does not respond to kindness). **4** intr. (of a congregation) make answers to a priest etc. **5** intr. Bridge make a bid on the basis of a partner's preceding bid. **6** tr. say (something) in answer. —n. **1** Archit. a half-pillar or half-pier attached to a wall to support an arch, esp. at the end of an arcade. **2** Eccl. a responsory; a response to a versicle. □□ **respondence** n. **respondency** n. **responder** n. [ME f. OF respondre answer ult. f. L respondēre respons- answer (as RE-, spondēre pledge)]

respondent /rɪˈspɒnd(ə)nt/ n. & adj. —n. **1** a defendant, esp. in an appeal or divorce case. **2** a person who makes an answer or defends an argument etc. —adj. **1** making answer. **2** (foll. by to) responsive. **3** in the position of defendant.

response /rɪˈspɒns/ n. **1** an answer given in word or act; a reply. **2** a feeling, movement, change, etc., caused by a stimulus or influence. **3** (often in pl.) Eccl. any part of the liturgy said or sung in answer to the priest; a responsory. **4** Bridge a bid made in responding. [ME f. OF respons(e) or L responsum neut. past part. of respondēre RESPOND]

responsibility /rɪˌspɒnsɪˈbɪlɪti/ n. (pl. -ies) **1 a** (often foll. by for, of) the state or fact of being responsible (refuses all responsibility for it; will take the responsibility of doing it). **b** authority; the ability to act independently and make decisions (a job with more responsibility). **2** the person or thing for which one is responsible (the food is my responsibility). □ on **one's own responsibility** without authorization.

responsible /rɪˈspɒnsɪb(ə)l/ adj. **1** (often foll. by to, for) liable to be called to account (to a person or for a thing). **2** morally accountable for one's actions; capable of rational conduct. **3** of good credit, position, or repute; respectable; evidently trustworthy. **4** (often foll. by for) being the primary

cause (a short circuit was responsible for the power failure). **5** (of a ruler or government) not autocratic. **6** involving responsibility (a responsible job). □□ **responsibleness** n. **responsibly** adv. [obs. F f. L responsēre: see RESPOND]

responsive /rɪˈspɒnsɪv/ adj. **1** (often foll. by to) responding readily (to some influence). **2** sympathetic; impressionable. **3 a** answering. **b** by way of answer. **4** (of a liturgy etc.) using responses. □□ **responsively** adv. **responsiveness** n. [F responsif -ive or LL responsivus (as RESPOND)]

responsory /rɪˈspɒnsəri/ n. (pl. -ies) an anthem said or sung by a soloist and choir after a lesson. [ME f. LL responsorium (as RESPOND)]

respray v. & n. —v.tr. /riːˈspreɪ/ spray again (esp. to change the colour of the paint on a vehicle). —n. /ˈriːspreɪ/ the act or an instance of respraying.

rest[1] /rest/ v. & n. —v. **1** intr. cease, abstain, or be relieved from exertion, action, movement, or employment; be tranquil. **2** intr. be still or asleep, esp. to refresh oneself or recover strength. **3** tr. give relief or repose to; allow to rest (a chair to rest my legs). **4** intr. (foll. by on, upon, against) lie on; be supported by; be spread out on; be propped against. **5** intr. (foll. by on, upon) depend, be based, or rely on. **6** intr. (foll. by on, upon) (of a look) alight or be steadily directed on. **7** tr. (foll. by on, upon) place for support or foundation. **8** intr. (of a problem or subject) be left without further investigation or discussion (let the matter rest). **9** intr. **a** lie in death. **b** (foll. by in) lie buried in (a churchyard etc.). **10** tr. (as **rested** adj.) refreshed or reinvigorated by resting. **11** intr. US conclude the calling of witnesses in a law case (the prosecution rests). **12** intr. (of land) lie fallow. **13** intr. (foll. by in) repose trust in (am content to rest in God). —n. **1** repose or sleep, esp. in bed at night (get a good night's rest). **2** freedom from or the cessation of exertion, worry, activity, etc. (give the subject a rest). **3** a period of resting (take a 15-minute rest). **4** a support or prop for holding or steadying something. **5** Mus. **a** an interval of silence of a specified duration. **b** the sign denoting this. **6** a place of resting or abiding, esp. a lodging place or shelter provided for sailors, cabmen, etc. **7** a pause in elocution. **8** a caesura in verse. □ **at rest** not moving; not agitated or troubled; dead. **be resting** Brit. euphem. (of an actor) be out of work. **rest-baulk** a ridge left unploughed between furrows. **rest one's case** conclude one's argument etc. **rest-cure** a rest usu. of some weeks as a medical treatment. **rest-day 1** a day spent in rest. **2** = day of rest. **rest** (or **God rest**) **his** (or **her**) **soul** may God grant his (or her) soul repose. **rest-home** a place where old or frail people can be cared for. **rest-house** Ind. a house for travellers to rest in. **resting-place** a place provided or used for resting. **rest mass** Physics the mass of a body when at rest. **rest on one's laurels** see LAUREL. **rest on one's oars** see OAR. **rest room** esp. US a public lavatory in a factory, shop, etc. **rest up** US rest oneself thoroughly. **set at rest** settle or relieve (a question, a person's mind, etc.). □□ **rester** n. [OE ræst, rest (n.), ræstan, restan (v.)]

rest[2] /rest/ n. & v. —n. (prec. by the) **1** the remaining part or parts; the others; the remainder of some quantity or number (finish what you can and leave the rest). **2** Brit. Econ. the reserve fund, esp. of the Bank of England. **3** hist. a rally in tennis. —v.intr. **1** remain in a specified state (rest assured). **2** (foll. by with) be left in the hands or charge of (the final arrangements rest with you). □ **and all the rest** (or **the rest of it**) and all else that might be mentioned; etcetera. **for the rest** as regards anything else. [ME f. OF reste rester f. L restare (as RE-, stare stand)]

restart v. & n. —v.tr. & intr. /riːˈstɑːt/ begin again. —n. /ˈriːstɑːt/ a new beginning.

restate /riːˈsteɪt/ v.tr. express again or differently, esp. more clearly or convincingly. □□ **restatement** n.

restaurant /'restə,rɒnt, -,rɔ̃/ n. public premises where meals or refreshments may be had. □**restaurant car** Brit. a dining-car on a train. [F f. restaurer RESTORE]

restaurateur /,restərə'tɜː(r)/ n. a restaurant-keeper. [F (as RESTAURANT)]

restful /'restfʊl/ adj. **1** favourable to quiet or repose. **2** free from disturbing influences. **3** soothing. □□ **restfully** adv. **restfulness** n.

rest-harrow /'rest,hærəʊ/ n. any tough-rooted plant of the genus Ononis, native to Europe and the Mediterranean. [obs. rest (v.) = ARREST (in sense 'stop') + HARROW]

restitution /,restɪ'tjuːʃ(ə)n/ n. **1** (often foll. by of) the act or an instance of restoring a thing to its proper owner. **2** reparation for an injury (esp. make restitution). **3** esp. Theol. the restoration of a thing to its original state. **4** the resumption of an original shape or position because of elasticity. □□ **restitutive** /'restɪ,tjuːtɪv/ adj. [ME f. OF restitution or L restitutio f. restituere restitut- restore (as RE-, statuere establish)]

restive /'restɪv/ adj. **1** fidgety; restless. **2** (of a horse) refusing to advance, stubbornly standing still or moving backwards or sideways; jibbing; refractory. **3** (of a person) unmanageable; rejecting control. □□ **restively** adv. **restiveness** n. [ME f. OF restif -ive f. Rmc (as REST[2])]

restless /'restlɪs/ adj. **1** finding or affording no rest. **2** uneasy; agitated. **3** constantly in motion, fidgeting, etc. □□ **restlessly** adv. **restlessness** n. [OE restlēas (as REST, -LESS)]

restock /riː'stɒk/ v.tr. (also absol.) stock again or differently.

restoration /,restə'reɪʃ(ə)n/ n. **1** the act or an instance of restoring or being restored. **2** a model or drawing representing the supposed original form of an extinct animal, ruined building, etc. **3 a** the re-establishment of a monarch etc. **b** the period of this. **4** (**Restoration**) hist. **a** (prec. by the) the re-establishment of Charles II as king of England in 1660. **b** (often attrib.) the literary period following this (Restoration comedy). [17th-c. alt. (after RESTORE) of restauration, ME f. OF restauration or LL restauratio (as RESTORE)]

restorative /rɪ'stɒrətɪv/ adj. & n. —adj. tending to restore health or strength. —n. a restorative medicine, food, etc. (needs a restorative). □□ **restoratively** adv. [ME var. of obs. restaurative f. OF restauratif -ive (as RESTORE)]

restore /rɪ'stɔː(r)/ v.tr. **1** bring back or attempt to bring back to the original state by rebuilding, repairing, repainting, emending, etc. **2** bring back to health etc.; cure. **3** give back to the original owner etc.; make restitution of. **4** reinstate; bring back to dignity or right. **5** replace; put back; bring back to a former condition. **6** make a representation of the supposed original state of (a ruin, extinct animal, etc.). **7** reinstate by conjecture (missing words in a text, missing pieces, etc.). □□ **restorable** adj. **restorer** n. [ME f. OF restorer f. L restaurare]

restrain /rɪ'streɪn/ v.tr. **1** (often refl., usu. foll. by from) check or hold in; keep in check or under control or within bounds. **2** repress; keep down. **3** confine; imprison. □□ **restrainable** adj. **restrainer** n. [ME f. OF restrei(g)n- stem of restreindre f. L restringere restrict- (as RE-, stringere tie)]

re-strain /riː'streɪn/ v.tr. strain again.

restrainedly /rɪ'streɪnɪdlɪ/ adv. with self-restraint.

restraint /rɪ'streɪnt/ n. **1** the act or an instance of restraining or being restrained. **2** a stoppage; a check; a controlling agency or influence. **3 a** self-control; avoidance of excess or exaggeration. **b** austerity of literary expression. **4** reserve of manner. **5** confinement, esp. because of insanity. **6** something which restrains or holds in check. □**in restraint of** in order to restrain. **restraint of trade** action seeking to interfere with free-market conditions.

[ME f. OF restreinte fem. past part. of restreindre: see RESTRAIN]

restrict /rɪ'strɪkt/ v.tr. (often foll. by to, within) **1** confine, bound, limit (restricted parking; restricted them to five days a week). **2** subject to limitation. **3** withhold from general circulation or disclosure. □**restricted area 1** Brit. an area in which there is a special speed limit for vehicles. **2** US an area which military personnel are not allowed to enter. □□ **restrictedly** adv. **restrictedness** n. [L restringere: see RESTRAIN]

restriction /rɪ'strɪkʃ(ə)n/ n. **1** the act or an instance of restricting; the state of being restricted. **2** a thing that restricts. **3** a limitation placed on action. □□ **restrictionist** adj. & n. [ME f. OF restriction or L restrictio (as RESTRICT)]

restrictive /rɪ'strɪktɪv/ adj. imposing restrictions. □**restrictive clause** Gram. a relative clause, usu. without surrounding commas. **restrictive practice** Brit. an agreement to limit competition or output in industry. □□ **restrictively** adv. **restrictiveness** n. [ME f. OF restrictif -ive or med.L restrictivus (as RESTRICT)]

restring /riː'strɪŋ/ v.tr. (past and past part. **restrung**) **1** fit (a musical instrument) with new strings. **2** thread (beads etc.) on a new string.

restructure /riː'strʌktʃə(r)/ v.tr. give a new structure to; rebuild; rearrange.

restudy /riː'stʌdɪ/ v.tr. (-ies, -ied) study again.

restyle /riː'staɪl/ v.tr. **1** reshape; remake in a new style. **2** give a new designation to (a person or thing).

result /rɪ'zʌlt/ n. & v. —n. **1** a consequence, issue, or outcome of something. **2** a satisfactory outcome; a favourable result (gets results). **3** a quantity, formula, etc., obtained by calculation. **4** (in pl.) a list of scores or winners etc. in an examination or sporting event. —v.intr. **1** (often foll. by from) arise as the actual consequence or follow as a logical consequence (from conditions, causes, etc.). **2** (often foll. by in) have a specified end or outcome (resulted in a large profit). □**without result** in vain; fruitless. □□ **resultful** adj. **resultless** adj. [ME f. med.L resultare f. L (as RE-, saltare frequent. of salire jump)]

resultant /rɪ'zʌlt(ə)nt/ adj. & n. —adj. resulting, esp. as the total outcome of more or less opposed forces. —n. Math. a force etc. equivalent to two or more acting in different directions at the same point.

resume /rɪ'zjuːm/ v. & n. —v. **1** tr. & intr. begin again or continue after an interruption. **2** tr. & intr. begin to speak, work, or use again; recommence. **3** tr. get back; take back; recover; reoccupy (resume one's seat). —n. = RÉSUMÉ. □□ **resumable** adj. [ME f. OF resumer or L resumere resumpt- (as RE-, sumere take)]

résumé /'rezjʊ,meɪ/ n. **1** a summary. **2** US a curriculum vitae. [F past part. of résumer (as RESUME)]

resumption /rɪ'zʌmpʃ(ə)n/ n. the act or an instance of resuming (ready for the resumption of negotiations). □□ **resumptive** adj. [ME f. OF resumption or LL resumptio (as RESUME)]

resupinate /rɪ'sjuːpɪnət/ adj. (of a leaf etc.) upside down. [L resupinatus past part. of resupinare bend back: see SUPINE]

resurface /riː'sɜːfɪs/ v. **1** tr. lay a new surface on (a road etc.). **2** intr. rise or arise again; turn up again.

resurgent /rɪ'sɜːdʒ(ə)nt/ adj. **1** rising or arising again. **2** tending to rise again. □□ **resurgence** n. [L resurgere resurrect- (as RE-, surgere rise)]

resurrect /,rezə'rekt/ v. **1** tr. colloq. revive the practice, use, or memory of. **2** tr. take from the grave; exhume. **3** tr. dig up. **4** tr. & intr. raise or rise from the dead. [back-form. f. RESURRECTION]

resurrection /,rezə'rekʃ(ə)n/ n. **1** the act or an instance of rising from the dead. **2** (**Resurrection**) **a** Christ's rising from the dead. **b** the rising of the dead at the Last Judgement. **3** a revival after disuse, inactivity, or decay. **4** exhumation. **5** the unearthing of a lost or forgotten thing; restoration to vogue or memory. □**resurrection plant** any of various plants, including clubmosses of the genus *Selaginella* and the Rose of Jericho, unfolding when moistened after being dried. □□ **resurrectional** *adj.* [ME f. OF f. LL *resurrectio -onis* (as RESURGENT)]

resurvey *v.* & *n.* —*v.tr.* /ˌriːsɜːˈveɪ/ survey again; reconsider. —*n.* /riːˈsɜːveɪ/ the act or an instance of resurveying.

resuscitate /rɪˈsʌsɪˌteɪt/ *v.tr.* & *intr.* **1** revive from unconsciousness or apparent death. **2** return or restore to vogue, vigour, or vividness. □□ **resuscitation** /-ˈteɪʃ(ə)n/ *n.* **resuscitative** *adj.* **resuscitator** *n.* [L *resuscitare* (as RE-, *suscitare* raise)]

ret /ret/ *v.* (also **rate** /reɪt/) (**retted, retting**) **1** *tr.* soften (flax, hemp, etc.) by soaking or by exposure to moisture. **2** *intr.* (often as **retted** *adj.*) (of hay etc.) be spoilt by wet or rot. [ME, rel. to ROT]

ret. *abbr.* retired; returned.

retable /rɪˈteɪb(ə)l/ *n.* **1** a frame enclosing decorated panels above the back of an altar. **2** a shelf. [F *rétable, retable* f. Sp. *retablo* f. med.L *retrotabulum* rear table (as RETRO-, TABLE)]

retail /ˈriːteɪl/ *n., adj., adv.,* & *v.* —*n.* the sale of goods in relatively small quantities to the public, and usu. not for resale (cf. WHOLESALE). —*adj.* & *adv.* by retail; at a retail price (*do you buy wholesale or retail?*). —*v.* /also rɪˈteɪl/ **1** *tr.* sell (goods) in retail trade. **2** *intr.* (often foll. by *at, of*) (of goods) be sold in this way (esp. for a specified price) (*retails at £4.95*). **3** *tr.* recount; relate details of. □**retail price index** an index of the variation in the prices of retail goods. □□ **retailer** *n.* [ME f. OF *retaille* a piece cut off f. *retaillier* (as RE-, TAIL²)]

retain /rɪˈteɪn/ *v.tr.* **1 a** keep possession of; not lose; continue to have, practise, or recognize. **b** not abolish, discard, or alter. **2** keep in one's memory. **3** keep in place; hold fixed. **4** secure the services of (a person, esp. a barrister) with a preliminary payment. □**retaining fee** a fee paid to secure a person, service, etc. **retaining wall** a wall supporting and confining a mass of earth or water. □□ **retainable** *adj.* **retainability** /-ˈbɪlɪtɪ/ *n.* **retainment** *n.* [ME f. AF *retei(g)n-* f. stem of OF *retenir* ult. f. L *retinēre retent-* (as RE-, *tenēre* hold)]

retainer /rɪˈteɪnə(r)/ *n.* **1** a person or thing that retains. **2** *Law* a fee for retaining a barrister etc. **3 a** *hist.* a dependant or follower of a person of rank. **b** *joc.* an old and faithful friend or servant (esp. *old retainer*). **4** *Brit.* a reduced rent paid to retain accommodation during a period of non-occupancy.

retake *v.* & *n.* —*v.tr.* /riːˈteɪk/ (*past* **retook**; *past part.* **retaken**) **1** take again. **2** recapture. —*n.* /ˈriːteɪk/ **1 a** the act or an instance of retaking. **b** a thing retaken, e.g. an examination. **2 a** the act or an instance of filming a scene or recording music etc. again. **b** the scene or recording obtained in this way.

retaliate /rɪˈtælɪˌeɪt/ *v.* **1** *intr.* repay an injury, insult, etc., in kind; attack in return; make reprisals. **2** *tr.* **a** (usu. foll. by *upon*) cast (an accusation) back upon a person. **b** repay (an injury or insult) in kind. □□ **retaliation** /-ˈeɪʃ(ə)n/ *n.* **retaliative** /-ˈtælɪətɪv/ *adj.* **retaliator** *n.* **retaliatory** /-ˈtælɪətərɪ/ *adj.* [L *retaliare* (as RE-, *talis* such)]

retard /rɪˈtɑːd/ *v.* & *n.* —*v.tr.* **1** make slow or late. **2** delay the progress, development, arrival, or accomplishment of. —*n.* retardation. □**in retard** delayed, in the rear. □□ **retardant** *adj.* & *n.* **retardation** /ˌriːtɑːˈdeɪʃ(ə)n/ *n.* **retardative** *adj.* **retardatory** *adj.* **retarder** *n.* **retardment** *n.* [F *retarder* f. L *retardare* (as RE-, *tardus* slow)]

retardate /rɪˈtɑːdeɪt/ *adj.* & *n. US* —*adj.* mentally retarded. —*n.* a mentally retarded person. [L *retardare:* see RETARD]

retarded /rɪˈtɑːdɪd/ *adj.* backward in mental or physical development.

retch /retʃ, riːtʃ/ *v.* & *n.* —*v.intr.* make a motion of vomiting esp. involuntarily and without effect. —*n.*

such a motion or the sound of it. [var. of (now dial.) *reach* f. OE *hrǣcan* spit, ON *hrækja* f. Gmc, of imit. orig.]

retd. *abbr.* **1** retired. **2** returned.

rete /ˈriːtɪ/ *n.* (*pl.* **retia** /-tɪə, -ʃɪə/) *Anat.* an elaborate network or plexus of blood vessels and nerve cells. [L *rete* net]

reteach /riːˈtiːtʃ/ *v.tr.* (*past* and *past part.* **retaught**) teach again or differently.

retell /riːˈtel/ *v.tr.* (*past* and *past part.* **retold**) tell again or in a different version.

retention /rɪˈtenʃ(ə)n/ *n.* **1 a** the act or an instance of retaining; the state of being retained. **b** the ability to retain things experienced or learned; memory. **2** *Med.* the failure to evacuate urine or another secretion. [ME f. OF *retention* or L *retentio* (as RETAIN)]

retentive /rɪˈtentɪv/ *adj.* **1** (often foll. by *of*) tending to retain (moisture etc.). **2** (of memory or a person) not forgetful. **3** *Surgery* (of a ligature etc.) serving to keep something in place. □□ **retentively** *adv.* **retentiveness** *n.* [ME f. OF *retentif -ive* or med.L *retentivus* (as RETAIN)]

retexture /riːˈtekstʃə(r)/ *v.tr.* treat (material, a garment, etc.) so as to restore its original texture.

rethink *v.* & *n.* —*v.tr.* /riːˈθɪŋk/ (*past* and *past part.* **rethought**) think about (something) again, esp. with a view to making changes. —*n.* /ˈriːθɪŋk/ a reassessment; a period of rethinking.

retia *pl.* of RETE.

retiarius /ˌretɪˈɑːrɪəs/ *n.* (*pl.* **retiarii** /-rɪˌaɪ/) a Roman gladiator using a net to trap his opponent. [L f. *rete* net]

reticence /ˈretɪs(ə)ns/ *n.* **1** the avoidance of saying all one knows or feels, or of saying more than is necessary; reserve in speech. **2** a disposition to silence; taciturnity. **3** the act or an instance of holding back some fact. **4** abstinence from overemphasis in art. □□ **reticent** *adj.* **reticently** *adv.* [L *reticentia* f. *reticēre* (as RE-, *tacēre* be silent)]

reticle /ˈretɪk(ə)l/ *n.* a network of fine threads or lines in the focal plane of an optical instrument to help accurate observation. [L *reticulum:* see RETICULUM]

reticula *pl.* of RETICULUM.

reticulate *v.* & *adj.* —*v.tr.* & *intr.* /rɪˈtɪkjʊˌleɪt/ **1** divide or be divided in fact or appearance into a network. **2** arrange or be arranged in small squares or with intersecting lines. —*adj.* /rɪˈtɪkjʊlət/ reticulated. □□ **reticulately** /rɪˈtɪkjʊlətlɪ/ *adv.* **reticulation** /-ˈleɪʃ(ə)n/ *n.* [L *reticulatus* reticulated (as RETICULUM)]

reticule /ˈretɪˌkjuːl/ *n.* **1** = RETICLE. **2** usu. *hist.* a woman's netted or other bag, esp. with a drawstring, carried or worn to serve the purpose of a pocket. [F *réticule* f. L (as RETICULUM)]

reticulum /rɪˈtɪkjʊləm/ *n.* (*pl.* **reticula** /-lə/) **1** a netlike structure; a fine network, esp. of membranes etc. in living organisms. **2** a ruminant's second stomach. □□ **reticular** *adj.* **reticulose** *adj.* [L, dimin. of *rete* net]

retie /riːˈtaɪ/ *v.tr.* (**retying**) tie again.

retiform /ˈriːtɪˌfɔːm/ *adj.* netlike, reticulated. [L *rete* net + -FORM]

retina /ˈretɪnə/ *n.* (*pl.* **retinas, retinae** /-ˌniː/) a layer at the back of the eyeball sensitive to light, and triggering nerve impulses via the optic nerve to the brain where the visual image is formed. □□ **retinal** *adj.* [ME f. med.L f. L *rete* net]

retinitis /ˌretɪˈnaɪtɪs/ *n.* inflammation of the retina.

retinol /ˈretɪˌnɒl/ *n.* a vitamin found in green and yellow vegetables, egg-yolk, and fish-liver oil, essential for growth and vision in dim light. Also called *vitamin A.* [RETINA + -OL¹]

retinue /ˈretɪˌnjuː/ *n.* a body of attendants accompanying an important person. [ME f. OF *retenue* fem. past part. of *retenir* RETAIN]

retiral /rɪˈtaɪər(ə)l/ *n.* esp. *Sc.* retirement from office etc.

retire /rɪ'taɪə(r)/ v. **1 a** intr. leave office or employment, esp. because of age (*retire from the army*; *retire on a pension*). **b** tr. cause (a person) to retire from work. **2** intr. withdraw; go away; retreat. **3** intr. seek seclusion or shelter. **4** intr. go to bed. **5** tr. withdraw (troops). **6** intr. & tr. Cricket (of a batsman) voluntarily end or be compelled to suspend one's innings (*retired hurt*). **7** tr. Econ. withdraw (a bill or note) from circulation or currency. □**retire from the world** become a recluse. **retire into oneself** become uncommunicative or unsociable. **retiring age** the age at which most people normally retire from work. □□ **retirer** n. [F retirer (as RE-, tirer draw)]

retired /rɪ'taɪəd/ adj. **1 a** having retired from employment (*a retired teacher*). **b** relating to a retired person (*received retired pay*). **2** withdrawn from society or observation; secluded (*lives a retired life*). □□ **retiredness** n.

retirement /rɪ'taɪəmənt/ n. **1 a** the act or an instance of retiring. **b** the condition of having retired. **2 a** seclusion or privacy. **b** a secluded place. □ **retirement pension** Brit. a pension paid by the State to retired people above a certain age.

retiring /rɪ'taɪərɪŋ/ adj. shy; fond of seclusion. □□ **retiringly** adv.

retold past and past part. of RETELL.

retook past of RETAKE.

retool /riː'tuːl/ v.tr. equip (a factory etc.) with new tools.

retort[1] /rɪ'tɔːt/ n. & v. —n. **1** an incisive or witty or angry reply. **2** the turning of a charge or argument against its originator. **3** a piece of retaliation. —v. **1 a** tr. say by way of a retort. **b** intr. make a retort. **2** tr. repay (an insult or attack) in kind. **3** tr. (often foll. by on, upon) return (mischief, a charge, sarcasm, etc.) to its originator. **4** tr. (often foll. by against) make (an argument) tell against its user. **5** tr. (as **retorted** adj.) recurved; twisted or bent backwards. [L retorquēre retort- (as RE-, torquēre twist)]

retort[2] /rɪ'tɔːt/ n. & v. —n. **1** a vessel usu. of glass with a long recurved neck used in distilling liquids. **2** a vessel for heating mercury for purification, coal to generate gas, or iron and carbon to make steel. —v.tr. purify (mercury) by heating in a retort. [F retorte f. med.L retorta fem. past part. of retorquēre: see RETORT[1]]

retortion /rɪ'tɔːʃ(ə)n/ n. **1** the act or an instance of bending back; the condition of being bent back. **2** retaliation by a State on the subjects of another. [RETORT[1], perh. after contortion]

retouch /riː'tʌtʃ/ v. & n. —v.tr. improve or repair (a composition, picture, photographic negative or print, etc.) by fresh touches or alterations. —n. the act or an instance of retouching. □□ **retoucher** n. [prob. f. F retoucher (as RE-, TOUCH)]

retrace /rɪ'treɪs/ v.tr. **1** go back over (one's steps etc.). **2** trace back to a source or beginning. **3** recall the course of in one's memory. [F retracer (as RE-, TRACE[1])]

retract /rɪ'trækt/ v. **1** tr. (also absol.) withdraw or revoke (a statement or undertaking). **2 a** tr. & intr. (esp. with ref. to part of the body) draw or be drawn back or in. **b** tr. draw (an undercarriage etc.) into the body of an aircraft. □□ **retractable** adj. **retraction** n. **retractive** adj. [L retrahere or (in sense 1) retractare (as RE-, trahere tract- draw)]

retractile /rɪ'træktaɪl/ adj. capable of being retracted. □□ **retractility** /-'tɪlɪtɪ/ n. [RETRACT, after contractile]

retractor /rɪ'træktə(r)/ n. **1** a muscle used for retracting. **2** a device for retracting.

retrain /riː'treɪn/ v.tr. & intr. train again or further, esp. for new work.

retral /'riː'trəl/ adj. Biol. hinder, posterior; at the back. [RETRO- + -AL]

retranslate /ˌriː'trænz'leɪt, -s'leɪt, ˌriː'trɑː'n-/ v.tr. translate again, esp. back into the original language. □□ **retranslation** n.

retransmit /ˌriː'trænz'mɪt, -s'mɪt, ˌriː'trɑː'n-/ v.tr. (**retransmitted, retransmitting**) transmit (esp. radio signals or broadcast programmes) back again or to a further distance. □□ **retransmission** /-'mɪʃ(ə)n/ n.

retread v. & n. —v.tr. /riː'tred/ (past retrod; past part. retrodden or (in sense 2) retreaded) **1** tread (a path etc.) again. **2** put a fresh tread on (a tyre). —n. /'riː'tred/ a retreaded tyre.

retreat /rɪ'triːt/ v. & n. —v. **1 a** intr. (esp. of military forces) go back, retire; relinquish a position. **b** tr. cause to retreat; move back. **2** intr. (esp. of features) recede; slope back. —n. **1 a** the act or an instance of retreating. **b** Mil. a signal for this. **2** withdrawal into privacy or security. **3** a place of shelter or seclusion. **4** a period of seclusion for prayer and meditation. **5** Mil. a bugle-call at sunset. **6** a place for the reception of the elderly or others in need of care. [ME f. OF retret (n.), retraiter (v.) f. L retrahere: see RETRACT]

retrench /rɪ'trentʃ/ v. **1 a** tr. reduce the amount of (costs). **b** intr. cut down expenses; introduce economies. **2** tr. shorten or abridge. □□ **retrenchment** n. [obs. F retrencher (as RE-, TRENCH)]

retrial /riː'traɪəl/ n. a second or further (judicial) trial.

retribution /ˌretrɪ'bjuːʃ(ə)n/ n. requital usu. for evil done; vengeance. □□ **retributive** /rɪ'trɪbjʊtɪv/ adj. **retributory** /rɪ'trɪbjʊtərɪ/ adj. [ME f. LL retributio (as RE-, tribuere tribut- assign)]

retrieve /rɪ'triːv/ v. & n. —v.tr. **1 a** regain possession of. **b** recover by investigation or effort of memory. **2 a** restore to knowledge or recall to mind. **b** obtain (information stored in a computer etc.). **3** (of a dog) find and bring in (killed or wounded game etc.). **4** (foll. by from) recover or rescue (esp. from a bad state). **5** restore to a flourishing state; revive. **6** repair or set right (a loss or error etc.) (*managed to retrieve the situation*). —n. the possibility of recovery (*beyond retrieve*). □□ **retrievable** adj. **retrieval** n. [ME f. OF retroeve- stressed stem of retrover (as RE-, trover find)]

retriever /rɪ'triːvə(r)/ n. **1 a** a dog of a breed used for retrieving game. **b** this breed. **2** a person who retrieves something.

retro- /'retrəʊ/ comb. form **1** denoting action back or in return (retroact; retroflex). **2** Anat. & Med. denoting location behind. [L retro backwards]

retroact /ˌretrəʊ'ækt/ v.intr. **1** operate in a backward direction. **2** have a retrospective effect. **3** react. □□ **retroaction** n.

retroactive /ˌretrəʊ'æktɪv/ adj. (esp. of legislation) having retrospective effect. □□ **retroactively** adv. **retroactivity** /-'tɪvɪtɪ/ n.

retrocede /ˌretrəʊ'siːd/ v. **1** intr. move back; recede. **2** tr. cede back again. □□ **retrocedence** n. **retrocedent** adj. **retrocession** /-'seʃ(ə)n/ n. **retrocessive** /-'sesɪv/ adj. [L retrocedere (as RETRO-, cedere cessgo)]

retrochoir /'retrəʊˌkwaɪə(r)/ n. the part of a cathedral or large church behind the high altar. [med.L retrochorus (as RETRO-, CHOIR)]

retrod past of RETREAD.

retrodden past part. of RETREAD.

retrofit /'retrəʊfɪt/ v.tr. (-fitted, -fitting) modify (machinery, vehicles, etc.) to incorporate changes and developments introduced after manufacture. [RETROACTIVE + REFIT]

retroflex /'retrəfleks/ adj. (also **retroflexed**) **1** Anat., Med., & Bot. turned backwards. **2** Phonet. = CACUMINAL. □□ **retroflexion** /-'flekʃ(ə)n/ n. [L retroflectere retroflex- (as RETRO-, flectere bend)]

retrogradation /ˌretrəʊɡrə'deɪʃ(ə)n/ n. Astron. **1** the apparent backward motion of a planet in the zodiac. **2** the apparent motion of a celestial body from east to west. **3** backward movement of the lunar nodes on the ecliptic. [LL retrogradatio (as RETRO-, GRADATION)]

retrograde /'retrəˌɡreɪd/ adj., n., & v. —adj. **1**

directed backwards; retreating. **2** reverting esp. to an inferior state; declining. **3** inverse, reversed (*in retrograde order*). **4** *Astron.* in or showing retrogradation. —*n.* a degenerate person. —*v.intr.* **1** move backwards; recede, retire. **2** decline, revert. **3** *Astron.* show retrogradation. ▫▫ **retrogradely** *adv.* [ME f. L *retrogradus* (as RETRO-, *gradus* step, *gradi* walk)]

retrogress /ˌretrəˈgres/ *v.intr.* **1** go back; move backwards. **2** deteriorate. ▫▫ **retrogressive** *adj.* [RETRO-, after PROGRESS *v.*]

retrogression /ˌretrəˈgreʃ(ə)n/ *n.* **1** backward or reversed movement. **2** a return to a less advanced state; a reversal of development; a decline or deterioration. **3** *Astron.* = RETROGRADATION. ▫▫ **retrogressive** /-sɪv/ *adj.* [RETRO-, after *progression*]

retroject /ˈretrəʊˌdʒekt/ *v.tr.* throw back (usu. opp. PROJECT). [RETRO-, after PROJECT *v.*]

retro-rocket /ˈretrəʊˌrɒkɪt/ *n.* an auxiliary rocket for slowing down a spacecraft etc., e.g. when re-entering the earth's atmosphere.

retrorse /rɪˈtrɔːs/ *adj. Biol.* turned back or down. ▫▫ **retrorsely** *adv.* [L *retrorsus* = *retroversus* (as RETRO-, *versus* past part. of *vertere* turn)]

retrospect /ˈretrəˌspekt/ *n.* **1** (foll. by *to*) regard or reference to precedent or authority, or to previous conditions. **2** a survey of past time or events. ▫ **in retrospect** when looked back on. [RETRO-, after PROSPECT *n.*]

retrospection /ˌretrəˈspekʃ(ə)n/ *n.* **1** the action of looking back esp. into the past. **2** an indulgence or engagement in retrospect. [prob. f. *retrospect* (v.) (as RETROSPECT)]

retrospective /ˌretrəˈspektɪv/ *adj. & n.* —*adj.* **1** looking back on or dealing with the past. **2** (of an exhibition, recital, etc.) showing an artist's development over his or her lifetime. **3** (of a statute etc.) applying to the past as well as the future; retroactive. **4** (of a view) lying to the rear. —*n.* a retrospective exhibition, recital, etc. ▫▫ **retrospectively** *adv.*

retrosternal /ˌretrəʊˈstɜːn(ə)l/ *adj. Anat. & Med.* behind the breastbone.

retroussé /rəˈtruːseɪ/ *adj.* (of the nose) turned up at the tip. [F, past part. of *retrousser* tuck up (as RE-, TRUSS)]

retrovert /ˈretrəʊˌvɜːt/ *v.tr.* **1** turn backwards. **2** *Med.* (as **retroverted** *adj.*) (of the womb) having a backward inclination. ▫▫ **retroversion** /-ˈvɜːʃ(ə)n/ *n.* [LL *retrovertere* (as RETRO-, *vertere* vers- turn)]

retrovirus /ˈretrəʊˌvaɪərəs/ *n. Biol.* any of a group of RNA viruses which form DNA during the replication of their RNA. [mod.L f. initial letters of *reverse transcriptase* + VIRUS]

retry /riːˈtraɪ/ *v.tr.* (-ies, -ied) try (a defendant or lawsuit) a second or further time. ▫▫ **retrial** *n.*

retsina /retˈsiːnə/ *n.* a Greek white wine flavoured with resin. [mod. Gk]

retune /riːˈtjuːn/ *v.tr.* **1** tune (a musical instrument) again or differently. **2** tune (a radio etc.) to a different frequency.

returf /riːˈtɜːf/ *v.tr.* provide with new turf.

return /rɪˈtɜːn/ *v. & n.* —*v.* **1** *intr.* come or go back. **2** *tr.* bring or put or send back to the person or place etc. where originally belonging or obtained (*returned the fish to the river*; *have you returned my scissors?*). **3** *tr.* pay back or reciprocate; give in response (*decided not to return the compliment*). **4** *tr.* yield (a profit). **5** *tr.* say in reply; retort. **6** *tr.* (in cricket or tennis etc.) hit or send (the ball) back after receiving it. **7** *tr.* state or mention or describe officially, esp. in answer to a writ or formal demand. **8** *tr.* (of an electorate) elect as an MP, government, etc. **9** *tr. Cards* **a** lead (a suit) previously led or bid by a partner. **b** lead (a suit or card) after taking a trick. **10** *tr. Archit.* continue (a wall etc.) in a changed direction, esp. at right angles. —*n.* **1** the act or an instance of coming or going back. **2 a** the act or an instance of giving or

sending or putting or paying back. **b** a thing given or sent back. **3** (in full **return ticket**) esp. *Brit.* a ticket for a journey to a place and back to the starting-point. **4** (in *sing.* or *pl.*) **a** the proceeds or profit of an undertaking. **b** the acquisition of these. **5** a formal report or statement compiled or submitted by order (*an income-tax return*). **6** (in full **return match** or **game**) a second match etc. between the same opponents. **7** *Electr.* a conductor bringing a current back to its source. **8** *Brit.* a sheriff's report on a writ. **9** esp. *Brit.* **a** a person's election as an MP etc. **b** a returning officer's announcement of this. **10** *Archit.* a part receding from the line of the front, e.g. the side of a house or of a window-opening. ▫ **by return (of post)** by the next available post in the return direction. **in return** as an exchange or reciprocal action. **many happy returns (of the day)** a greeting on a birthday. **return crease** *Cricket* each of two lines joining the popping-crease and bowling-crease at right angles to the bowling-crease and extending beyond it. **returning officer** *Brit.* an official conducting an election in a constituency and announcing the results. **return thanks** express thanks esp. in a grace at meals or in response to a toast or condolence. ▫▫ **returnable** *adj.* **returner** *n.* **returnless** *adj.* [ME f. OF *returner* (as RE-, TURN)]

returnee /rɪtɜːˈniː/ *n.* a person who returns home from abroad, esp. after war service.

retuse /rɪˈtjuːs/ *adj.* esp. *Bot.* having a broad end with a central depression. [L *retundere retus-* (as RE-, *tundere* beat)]

retying *pres. part.* of RETIE.

retype /riːˈtaɪp/ *v.tr.* type again, esp. to correct errors.

reunify /riːˈjuːnɪˌfaɪ/ *v.tr.* (-ies, -ied) restore (esp. separated territories) to a political unity. ▫▫ **reunification** /-fɪˈkeɪʃ(ə)n/ *n.*

reunion /riːˈjuːnjən, -nɪən/ *n.* **1 a** the act or an instance of reuniting. **b** the condition of being reunited. **2** a social gathering esp. of people formerly associated. [F *réunion* or AL *reunio* f. L *reunire* unite (as RE-, UNION)]

reunite /ˌriːjuːˈnaɪt/ *v.tr. & intr.* bring or come back together.

reupholster /ˌriːʌpˈhəʊlstə(r)/ *v.tr.* upholster anew. ▫▫ **reupholstery** *n.*

reuse *v. & n.* —*v.tr.* /riːˈjuːz/ use again or more than once. —*n.* /riːˈjuːs/ a second or further use. ▫▫ **reusable** /-ˈjuːzəb(ə)l/ *adj.*

reutilize /riːˈjuːtɪˌlaɪz/ *v.tr.* (also **-ise**) utilize again or for a different purpose. ▫▫ **reutilization** /-ˈzeɪʃ(ə)n/ *n.*

Rev. *abbr.* **1** Reverend. **2** Revelation (New Testament).

rev /rev/ *n. & v. colloq.* —*n.* (in *pl.*) the number of revolutions of an engine per minute (*running at 3,000 revs*). —*v.* (**revved**, **revving**) **1** *intr.* (of an engine) revolve; turn over. **2** *tr.* (also *absol.*; often foll. by *up*) cause (an engine) to run quickly. ▫ **rev counter** = *revolution counter*. [abbr.]

revaccinate /riːˈvæksɪˌneɪt/ *v.tr.* vaccinate again. ▫▫ **revaccination** /-ˈneɪʃ(ə)n/ *n.*

revalue /riːˈvæljuː/ *v.tr.* (**revalues**, **revalued**, **revaluing**) *Econ.* give a different value to, esp. give a higher value to, (a currency) in relation to other currencies or gold (opp. DEVALUE). ▫▫ **revaluation** /-ˈeɪʃ(ə)n/ *n.*

revamp /riːˈvæmp/ *v.tr.* **1** renovate, revise, improve. **2** patch up. [RE- + VAMP¹]

revanchism /rɪˈvæntʃɪz(ə)m/ *n. Polit.* a policy of seeking to retaliate, esp. to recover lost territory. ▫▫ **revanchist** *n. & adj.* [F *revanche* (as REVENGE)]

revarnish /riːˈvɑːnɪʃ/ *v.tr.* varnish again.

Revd *abbr.* Reverend.

reveal¹ /rɪˈviːl/ *v.tr.* **1** display or show; allow to appear. **2** (often as **revealing** *adj.*) disclose, divulge, betray (*revealed his plans*; *a revealing remark*). **3** *tr.* (in *refl.* or *passive*) come to sight or knowledge. **4** *Relig.* (esp. of God) make known by inspiration or supernatural means. □**revealed religion** a religion based on revelation (opp. *natural religion*). □□ **revealable** adj. **revealer** n. **revealingly** adv. [ME f. OF *reveler* or L *revelare* (as RE-, *velum* veil)]

reveal[2] /rɪˈviːl/ n. an internal side surface of an opening or recess, esp. of a doorway or window-aperture. [obs. *revale* (v.) lower f. OF *revaler* f. *avaler* (as RE-, VAIL)]

reveille /rɪˈvælɪ, rɪˈvelɪ/ n. a military waking-signal sounded in the morning on a bugle or drums etc. [F *réveillez* imper. pl. of *réveiller* awaken (as RE-, *veiller* f. L *vigilare* keep watch)]

revel /ˈrev(ə)l/ v. & n. —v. (**revelled, revelling**; US **reveled, reveling**) **1** intr. have a good time; be extravagantly festive. **2** intr. (foll. by *in*) take keen delight in. **3** tr. (foll. by *away*) throw away (money or time) in revelry. —n. (in *sing.* or *pl.*) the act or an instance of revelling. □□ **reveller** n. **revelry** n. (pl. **-ies**). [ME f. OF *reveler* riot f. L *rebellare* REBEL v.]

revelation /ˌrevəˈleɪʃ(ə)n/ n. **1 a** the act or an instance of revealing, esp. the supposed disclosure of knowledge to humankind by a divine or supernatural agency. **b** knowledge disclosed in this way. **2 a** striking disclosure (*it was a revelation to me*). **3** (**Revelation** or *colloq.* **Revelations**) (in full **the Revelation of St John the Divine**) the last book of the New Testament, describing visions of heaven. □□ **revelational** adj. [ME f. OF *revelation* or LL *revelatio* (as REVEAL[1])]

revelationist /ˌrevəˈleɪʃənɪst/ n. a believer in divine revelation.

revelatory /ˌrevəˈleɪtərɪ/ adj. serving to reveal, esp. something significant. [L *revelare*: see REVEAL[1]]

revenant /ˈrevənənt/ n. a person who has returned, esp. supposedly from the dead. [F, pres. part. of *revenir*: see REVENUE]

revenge /rɪˈvendʒ/ n. & v. —n. **1** retaliation for an offence or injury. **2** an act of retaliation. **3** the desire for this; a vindictive feeling. **4** (in games) a chance to win after an earlier defeat. —v. **1** tr. (in *refl.* or *passive*; often foll. by *on, upon*) inflict retaliation for an offence. **2** tr. take revenge for (an offence). **3** tr. avenge (a person). **4** intr. take vengeance. □□ **revenger** n. [ME f. OF *revenger, revencher* f. LL *revindicare* (as RE-, *vindicare* lay claim to)]

revengeful /rɪˈvendʒfʊl/ adj. eager for revenge. □□ **revengefully** adv. **revengefulness** n.

revenue /ˈrevəˌnjuː/ n. **1 a** income, esp. of a large amount, from any source. **b** (in *pl.*) items constituting this. **2** a State's annual income from which public expenses are met. **3** the department of the civil service collecting this. □**revenue tax** a tax imposed to raise revenue, rather than to affect trade. [ME f. OF *revenu(e)* past part. of *revenir* f. L *revenire* return (as RE-, *venire* come)]

reverb /rɪˈvɜːb, ˈriːvɜːb/ n. Mus. colloq. **1** reverberation. **2** a device to produce this. [abbr.]

reverberate /rɪˈvɜːbəˌreɪt/ v. **1 a** intr. (of sound, light, or heat) be returned or echoed or reflected repeatedly. **b** tr. return (a sound etc.) in this way. **2** intr. (of a story, rumour, etc.) be heard much or repeatedly. □**reverberating furnace** a furnace constructed to throw heat back on to the substance exposed to it. □□ **reverberant** adj. **reverberantly** adv. **reverberation** /-ˈreɪʃ(ə)n/ n. **reverberative** /-rətɪv/ adj. **reverberator** n. **reverberatory** /-rətərɪ/ adj. [L *reverberare* (as RE-, *verberare* lash f. *verbera* (pl.) scourge)]

revere /rɪˈvɪə(r)/ v.tr. hold in deep and usu. affectionate or religious respect; venerate. [F *révérer* or L *reverēri* (as RE-, *verēri* fear)]

reverence /ˈrevərəns/ n. & v. —n. **1 a** the act of revering or the state of being revered (*hold in reverence; feel reverence for*). **b** the capacity for revering (*lacks reverence*). **2** archaic a gesture showing that one reveres; a bow or curtsy. **3** (**Reverence**) a title used of or to some members of the clergy.

—v.tr. regard or treat with reverence. [ME f. OF f. L *reverentia* (as REVERE)]

reverend /ˈrevərənd/ adj. & n. —adj. (esp. as the title of a clergyman) deserving reverence. —n. colloq. a clergyman. □**Most Reverend** the title of an archbishop or an Irish Roman Catholic bishop. **Reverend Mother** the title of the Mother Superior of a convent. **Right Reverend** the title of a bishop. **Very Reverend** the title of a dean etc. [ME f. OF *reverend* or L *reverendus* gerundive of *reverēri*: see REVERE]

reverent /ˈrevərənt/ adj. feeling or showing reverence. □□ **reverently** adv. [ME f. L *reverens* (as REVERE)]

reverential /ˌrevəˈrenʃ(ə)l/ n. of the nature of, due to, or characterized by reverence. □□ **reverentially** adv. [med.L *reverentialis* (as REVERE)]

reverie /ˈrevərɪ/ n. **1** a fit of abstracted musing (*was lost in a reverie*). **2** archaic a fantastic notion or theory; a delusion. **3** Mus. an instrumental piece suggesting a dreamy or musing state. [obs. F *resverie* f. OF *reverie* rejoicing, revelry f. *rever* be delirious, of unkn. orig.]

revers /rɪˈvɪə(r)/ n. (pl. same /-ˈvɪəz/) **1** the turned-back edge of a garment revealing the under-surface. **2** the material on this surface. [F, = REVERSE]

reverse /rɪˈvɜːs/ v., adj., & n. —v. **1** tr. turn the other way round or up or inside out. **2** tr. change to the opposite character or effect (*reversed the decision*). **3** intr. & tr. travel or cause to travel backwards. **4** tr. make (an engine etc.) work in a contrary direction. **5** tr. revoke or annul (a decree, act, etc.). **6** intr. (of a dancer, esp. in a waltz) revolve in the opposite direction. —adj. **1** placed or turned in an opposite direction or position. **2** opposite or contrary in character or order; inverted. —n. **1** the opposite or contrary (*the reverse is the case; is the reverse of the truth*). **2** the contrary of the usual manner. **3** an occurrence of misfortune; a disaster, esp. a defeat in battle (*suffered a reverse*). **4** reverse gear or motion. **5** the reverse side of something. **6 a** the side of a coin or medal etc. bearing the secondary design. **b** this design (cf. OBVERSE). **7** the verso of a leaf. □**reverse arms** hold a rifle with the butt upwards. **reverse the charges** Brit. make the recipient of a telephone call responsible for payment. **reverse gear** a gear used to make a vehicle etc. travel backwards. **reversing light** a white light at the rear of a vehicle operated when the vehicle is in reverse gear. **reverse Polish notation** see *Polish notation*. **reverse strata** Geol. a fault in which the overlying side of a mass of rock is displaced upward in relation to the underlying side. □□ **reversal** n. **reversely** adv. **reverser** n. **reversible** adj. **reversibility** /-ˈbɪlɪtɪ/ n. **reversibly** adv. [ME f. OF *revers* (n.), *reverser* (v.), f. L *revertere revers-* (as RE-, *vertere* turn)]

reversion /rɪˈvɜːʃ(ə)n/ n. **1 a** the legal right (esp. of the original owner, or his or her heirs) to possess or succeed to property on the death of the present possessor. **b** property to which a person has such a right. **2** Biol. a return to ancestral type. **3** a return to a previous state, habit, etc. **4** a sum payable on a person's death, esp. by way of life insurance. □□ **reversional** adj. **reversionary** adj. [ME f. OF *reversion* or L *reversio* (as REVERSE)]

revert /rɪˈvɜːt/ v. **1** intr. (foll. by *to*) return to a former state, practice, opinion, etc. **2** intr. (of property, an office, etc.) return by reversion. **3** intr. fall back into a wild state. **4** tr. turn (one's eyes or steps) back. □□ **reverter** n. (in sense 2). [ME f. OF *revertir* or L *revertere* (as REVERSE)]

revertible /rɪˈvɜːtɪb(ə)l/ adj. (of property) subject to reversion.

revet /rɪˈvet/ v.tr. (**revetted, revetting**) face (a rampart, wall, etc.) with masonry, esp. in fortification. [F *revêtir* f. OF *revestir* f. LL *revestire* (as RE-, *vestire* clothe f. *vestis*)]

revetment /rɪˈvetmənt/ n. a retaining wall or facing. [F *revêtement* (as REVET)]

review /rɪˈvjuː/ n. & v. —n. 1 a general survey or assessment of a subject or thing. 2 a retrospect or survey of the past. 3 revision or reconsideration (*is under review*). 4 a display and formal inspection of troops etc. 5 a published account or criticism of a book, play, etc. 6 a periodical publication with critical articles on current events, the arts, etc. 7 a second view. —v.tr. 1 survey or look back on. 2 reconsider or revise. 3 hold a review of (troops etc.). 4 write a review of (a book, play, etc.). 5 view again. □**court of review** a court before which sentences etc. come for revision. □□ **reviewable** adj. **reviewal** n. **reviewer** n. [obs. F *reveue* f. *revoir* (as RE-, *voir* see)]

revile /rɪˈvaɪl/ v. 1 tr. abuse; criticize abusively. 2 intr. talk abusively; rail. □□ **revilement** n. **reviler** n. **reviling** n. [ME f. OF *reviler* (as RE-, VILE)]

revise /rɪˈvaɪz/ v. & n. —v.tr. 1 examine or re-examine and improve or amend (esp. written or printed matter). 2 consider and alter (an opinion etc.). 3 (also *absol.*) *Brit.* read again (work learnt or done) to improve one's knowledge, esp. for an examination. —n. *Printing* a proof-sheet including corrections made in an earlier proof. □**Revised Standard Version** a revision in 1946–52 of the Authorized Version of the Bible. **Revised Version** a revision in 1881–5 of the Authorized Version of the Bible. □□ **revisable** adj. **revisal** n. **reviser** n. **revisory** adj. [F *réviser* look at, or L *revisere* (as RE-, *visere* intensive of *vidēre* vis- see)]

revision /rɪˈvɪʒ(ə)n/ n. 1 the act or an instance of revising; the process of being revised. 2 a revised edition or form. □□ **revisionary** adj. [OF *revision* or LL *revisio* (as REVISE)]

revisionism /rɪˈvɪʒəˌnɪz(ə)m/ n. often *derog.* a policy of revision or modification, esp. of Marxism on evolutionary socialist (rather than revolutionary) or pluralist principles. □□ **revisionist** n. & adj.

revisit /riːˈvɪzɪt/ v.tr. (**revisited, revisiting**) visit again.

revitalize /riːˈvaɪtəˌlaɪz/ v.tr. (also **-ise**) imbue with new life and vitality. □□ **revitalization** /-ˈzeɪʃ(ə)n/ n.

revival /rɪˈvaɪv(ə)l/ n. 1 the act or an instance of reviving; the process of being revived. 2 a new production of an old play etc. 3 a revived use of an old practice, custom, etc. 4 a a reawakening of religious fervour. b a series of evangelistic meetings to promote this. 5 restoration to bodily or mental vigour or to life or consciousness.

revivalism /rɪˈvaɪvəˌlɪz(ə)m/ n. belief in or the promotion of a revival, esp. of religious fervour. □□ **revivalist** n. **revivalistic** /-ˈlɪstɪk/ adj.

revive /rɪˈvaɪv/ v.intr. & tr. 1 come or bring back to consciousness or life or strength. 2 come or bring back to existence, use, notice, etc. □□ **revivable** adj. [ME f. OF *revivre* or LL *revivere* (as RE-, L *vivere* live)]

reviver /rɪˈvaɪvə(r)/ n. 1 a person or thing that revives. 2 *colloq.* a stimulating drink. 3 a preparation used for restoring faded colours etc.

revivify /rɪˈvɪvɪˌfaɪ/ v.tr. (**-ies, -ied**) restore to animation, activity, vigour, or life. □□ **revivification** /-fɪˈkeɪʃ(ə)n/ n. [F *revivifier* or LL *revivificare* (as RE-, VIVIFY)]

revoke /rɪˈvəʊk/ v. & n. —v. 1 tr. rescind, withdraw, or cancel (a decree or promise etc.). 2 intr. *Cards* fail to follow suit when able to do so. —n. *Cards* the act of revoking. □□ **revocable** /ˈrevəkəb(ə)l/ adj. **revocability** /ˌrevəkəˈbɪlɪtɪ/ n. **revocation** /ˌrevəˈkeɪʃ(ə)n/ n. **revocatory** /ˈrevəkətərɪ/ adj. **revoker** n. [ME f. OF *revoquer* or L *revocare* (as RE-, *vocare* call)]

revolt /rɪˈvəʊlt/ v. & n. —v. 1 intr. a rise in rebellion against authority. b (as **revolted** adj.) having revolted. 2 a tr. (often in *passive*) affect with strong disgust; nauseate (*was revolted by the thought of it*). b intr. (often foll. by *at, against*) feel strong disgust.

—n. 1 an act of rebelling. 2 a state of insurrection (*in revolt*). 3 a sense of loathing. 4 a mood of protest or defiance. [F *révolter* f. It. *rivoltare* ult. f. L *revolvere* (as REVOLVE)]

revolting /rɪˈvəʊltɪŋ/ adj. disgusting, horrible. □□ **revoltingly** adv.

revolute /ˈrevəˌluːt/ adj. *Bot.* etc. having a rolled-back edge. [L *revolutus* past part. of *revolvere*: see REVOLVE]

revolution /ˌrevəˈluːʃ(ə)n/ n. 1 a the forcible overthrow of a government or social order, in favour of a new system. b (in Marxism) the replacement of one ruling class by another; the class struggle which is expected to lead to political change and the triumph of communism. 2 any fundamental change or reversal of conditions. 3 the act or an instance of revolving. 4 a motion in orbit or a circular course or round an axis or centre; rotation. b the single completion of an orbit or rotation. c the time taken for this. 5 a cyclic recurrence. □**revolution counter** a device for indicating the number or rate of revolutions of an engine etc. □□ **revolutionism** n. **revolutionist** n. [ME f. OF *revolution* or LL *revolutio* (as REVOLVE)]

revolutionary /ˌrevəˈluːʃənərɪ/ adj. & n. —adj. 1 involving great and often violent change. 2 of or causing political revolution. 3 (**Revolutionary**) of or relating to a particular revolution, esp. the War of American Independence. —n. (pl. **-ies**) an instigator or supporter of political revolution.

revolutionize /ˌrevəˈluːʃəˌnaɪz/ v.tr. (also **-ise**) introduce fundamental change to.

revolve /rɪˈvɒlv/ v. 1 intr. & tr. turn or cause to turn round, esp. on an axis; rotate. 2 intr. move in a circular orbit. 3 tr. ponder (a problem etc.) in the mind. □**revolving credit** credit that is automatically renewed as debts are paid off. **revolving door** a door with usu. four partitions turning round a central axis. □□ **revolvable** adj. [ME f. L *revolvere* (as RE-, *volvere* roll)]

revolver /rɪˈvɒlvə(r)/ n. a pistol with revolving chambers enabling several shots to be fired without reloading.

revue /rɪˈvjuː/ n. a theatrical entertainment of a series of short usu. satirical sketches and songs. [F, = REVIEW n.]

revulsion /rɪˈvʌlʃ(ə)n/ n. 1 abhorrence; a sense of loathing. 2 a sudden violent change of feeling. 3 a sudden reaction in taste, fortune, trade, etc. 4 *Med.* counterirritation; the treatment of one disordered organ etc. by acting upon another. [F *revulsion* or L *revulsio* (as RE-, *vellere vuls-* pull)]

revulsive /rɪˈvʌlsɪv/ adj. & n. *Med.* —adj. producing revulsion. —n. a revulsive substance.

reward /rɪˈwɔːd/ n. & v. 1 a a return or recompense for service or merit. b requital for good or evil; retribution. 2 a sum offered for the detection of a criminal, the restoration of lost property, etc. —v.tr. give a reward to (a person) or for (a service etc.). □□ **rewardless** adj. [ME f. AF, ONF *reward* = OF *reguard* REGARD]

rewarding /rɪˈwɔːdɪŋ/ adj. (of an activity etc.) well worth doing; providing satisfaction. □□ **rewardingly** adv.

rewarewa /ˈreɪwəˈreɪwə/ n. a tall red-flowered tree, *Knightia excelsa*, of New Zealand. [Maori]

rewash /riːˈwɒʃ/ v.tr. wash again.

reweigh /riːˈweɪ/ v.tr. weigh again.

rewind /riːˈwaɪnd/ v.tr. (*past* and *past part.* **rewound**) wind (a film or tape etc.) back to the beginning. □□ **rewinder** n.

rewire /riːˈwaɪə(r)/ v.tr. provide (a building etc.) with new wiring. □□ **rewirable** adj.

reword /riːˈwɜːd/ v.tr. change the wording of.

rewound *past* and *past part.* of REWIND.

rewrap /riːˈræp/ v.tr. (**rewrapped, rewrapping**) wrap again or differently.

rewrite v. & n. —v.tr. /riːˈraɪt/ (*past* **rewrote;** *past part.* **rewritten**) write again or differently. —n.

/'riːraɪt/ **1** the act or an instance of rewriting. **2** a thing rewritten.

Rex /reks/ *n.* the reigning king (following a name or in the titles of lawsuits, e.g. *Rex v. Jones* the Crown versus Jones). [L]

Rexine /'reksiːn/ *n. propr.* an artificial leather used in upholstery, bookbinding, etc. [20th c.: orig. unkn.]

Reynard /'renɑːd, 'reɪ-/ *n.* a fox (esp. as a proper name in stories). [ME f. OF *Renart* name of a fox in the *Roman de Renart*]

Reynolds number /'renəldz/ *n. Physics* a quantity indicating the degree of turbulence of flow past an obstacle etc. [O. *Reynolds*, Engl. physicist d. 1912]

Rf *symb. Chem.* the element rutherfordium.

r.f. *abbr.* radio frequency.

RFA *abbr.* (in the UK) Royal Fleet Auxiliary.

RFC *abbr.* **1** Rugby Football Club. **2** *hist.* Royal Flying Corps.

RGS *abbr.* Royal Geographical Society.

Rh[1] *symb. Chem.* the element rhodium.

Rh[2] *abbr.* **1** Rhesus. **2** Rhesus factor.

r.h. *abbr.* right hand.

RHA *abbr.* (in the UK) Royal Horse Artillery.

rhabdomancy /'ræbdə,mænsɪ/ *n.* the use of a divining-rod, esp. for discovering subterranean water or mineral ore. [Gk *rhabdomanteia* f. *rhabdos* rod: see -MANCY]

Rhadamanthine /,rædə'mænθaɪn/ *adj.* stern and incorruptible in judgement. [*Rhadamanthus* f. L f. Gk *Rhadamanthos*, name of a judge in the underworld]

Rhaeto-Romance /,riːtəʊrəʊ'mæns/ *adj. & n.* (also **Rhaeto-Romanic** /-'mænɪk/) —*adj.* of or in any of the Romance dialects of SE Switzerland and Tyrol, esp. Romansh and Ladin. —*n.* any of these dialects. [L *Rhaetus* of Rhaetia in the Alps + ROMANIC]

rhapsode /'ræpsəʊd/ *n.* a reciter of epic poems, esp. of Homer in ancient Greece. [Gk *rhapsōidos* f. *rhaptō* stitch + *ōidē* song, ODE]

rhapsodist /'ræpsədɪst/ *n.* **1** a person who rhapsodizes. **2** = RHAPSODE.

rhapsodize /'ræpsə,daɪz/ *v.intr.* (also **-ise**) talk or write rhapsodies.

rhapsody /'ræpsədɪ/ *n.* (*pl.* **-ies**) **1** an enthusiastic or extravagant utterance or composition. **2** *Mus.* a piece of music in one extended movement, usu. emotional in character. **3** *Gk Antiq.* an epic poem, or part of it, of a length for one recitation. □□ **rhapsodic** /ræp'sɒdɪk/ *adj.* **rhapsodical** /ræp'sɒdɪk(ə)l/ *adj.* (in senses 1, 2). [L *rhapsodia* f. Gk *rhapsōidia* (as RHAPSODE)]

rhatany /'rætənɪ/ *n.* (*pl.* **-ies**) **1** either of two American shrubs, *Krameria trianda* and *K. argentea*, having an astringent root when dried. **2** the root of either of these. [mod.L *rhatania* f. Port. *ratanha*, Sp. *ratania*, f. Quechua *rataña*]

rhea /'riːə/ *n.* any of several S. American flightless birds of the family Rheidae, like but smaller than an ostrich. [mod.L genus name f. L f. Gk *Rhea* mother of Zeus]

rhebok var. of REEBOK.

Rhenish /'riːnɪʃ, 'ren-/ *adj. & n.* —*adj.* of the Rhine and the regions adjoining it. —*n.* wine from this area. [ME *rynis, rynisch* etc., f. AF *reneis*, OF *r(a)inois* f. L *Rhenanus* f. *Rhenus* Rhine]

rhenium /'riːnɪəm/ *n. Chem.* a rare metallic element of the manganese group, occurring naturally in molybdenum ores and used in the manufacture of superconducting alloys. ¶ Symb.: **Re**. [mod.L f. L *Rhenus* Rhine]

rheology /riːˈɒlədʒɪ/ *n.* the science dealing with the flow and deformation of matter. □□ **rheological** /-ə'lɒdʒɪk(ə)l/ *adj.* **rheologist** *n.* [Gk *rheos* stream + -LOGY]

rheostat /'riːə,stæt/ *n. Electr.* an instrument used to control a current by varying the resistance. □□ **rheostatic** /-'stætɪk/ *adj.* [Gk *rheos* stream + -STAT]

rhesus /'riːsəs/ *n.* (in full **rhesus monkey**) a small catarrhine monkey, *Macaca mulatta*, common in N.

India. □**rhesus baby** an infant with a haemolytic disorder caused by the incompatibility of its own rhesus-positive blood with its mother's rhesus-negative blood. **rhesus factor** an antigen occurring on the red blood cells of most humans and some other primates (as in the rhesus monkey, in which it was first observed). **rhesus negative** lacking the rhesus factor. **rhesus positive** having the rhesus factor. [mod.L, arbitrary use of L *Rhesus* f. Gk *Rhēsos*, mythical King of Thrace]

rhetor /'riːtə(r)/ *n.* **1** an ancient Greek or Roman teacher or professor of rhetoric. **2** usu. *derog.* an orator. [ME f. LL *rethor* f. L *rhetor* f. Gk *rhētōr*]

rhetoric /'retərɪk/ *n.* **1** the art of effective or persuasive speaking or writing. **2** language designed to persuade or impress (often with an implication of insincerity or exaggeration etc.). [ME f. OF *rethorique* f. L *rhetorica, -ice* f. Gk *rhētorikē (tekhnē)* (art) of rhetoric (as RHETOR)]

rhetorical /rɪ'tɒrɪk(ə)l/ *adj.* **1** expressed with a view to persuasive or impressive effect; artificial or extravagant in language. **2** of the nature of rhetoric. **3 a** of or relating to the art of rhetoric. **b** given to rhetoric; oratorical. □**rhetorical question** a question asked not for information but to produce an effect, e.g. *who cares?* for *nobody cares*. □□ **rhetorically** *adv.* [ME f. L *rhetoricus* f. Gk *rhētorikos* (as RHETOR)]

rhetorician /,retə'rɪʃ(ə)n/ *n.* **1** an orator. **2** a teacher of rhetoric. **3** a rhetorical speaker or writer. [ME f. OF *rethoricien* (as RHETORICAL)]

rheum /ruːm/ *n.* a watery discharge from a mucous membrane, esp. of the eyes or nose. [ME f. OF *reume* ult. f. Gk *rheuma -atos* stream f. *rheō* flow]

rheumatic /ruːˈmætɪk/ *adj. & n.* —*adj.* **1** of, relating to, or suffering from rheumatism. **2** producing or produced by rheumatism. —*n.* a person suffering from rheumatism. □**rheumatic fever** a non-infectious fever with inflammation and pain in the joints. □□ **rheumatically** *adv.* **rheumaticky** *adj. colloq.* [ME f. OF *reumatique* or L *rheumaticus* f. Gk *rheumatikos* (as RHEUM)]

rheumatics /ruːˈmætɪks/ *n.pl.* (treated as *sing.*; often prec. by *the*) *colloq.* rheumatism.

rheumatism /'ruːmə,tɪz(ə)m/ *n.* any disease marked by inflammation and pain in the joints, muscles, or fibrous tissue, esp. rheumatoid arthritis. [F *rhumatisme* or L *rheumatismus* f. Gk *rheumatismos* f. *rheumatizō* f. *rheuma* stream]

rheumatoid /'ruːmə,tɔɪd/ *adj.* having the character of rheumatism. □**rheumatoid arthritis** a chronic progressive disease causing inflammation and stiffening of the joints.

rheumatology /,ruːmə'tɒlədʒɪ/ *n.* the study of rheumatic diseases. □□ **rheumatological** /-tə'lɒdʒ-ɪk(ə)l/ *adj.* **rheumatologist** *n.*

RHG *abbr.* (in the UK) Royal Horse Guards.

rhinal /'raɪn(ə)l/ *adj. Anat.* of a nostril or the nose. [Gk *rhis rhin-*: see RHINO-]

rhinestone /'raɪnstəʊn/ *n.* an imitation diamond. [*Rhine*, river and region in Germany + STONE]

rhinitis /raɪ'naɪtɪs/ *n.* inflammation of the mucous membrane of the nose. [Gk *rhis rhinos* nose]

rhino[1] /'raɪnəʊ/ *n.* (*pl.* same or **-os**) *colloq.* a rhinoceros. [abbr.]

rhino[2] /'raɪnəʊ/ *n. Brit. sl.* money. [17th c.: orig. unkn.]

rhino- /'raɪnəʊ/ *comb. form Anat.* the nose. [Gk *rhis rhinos* nostril, nose]

rhinoceros /raɪ'nɒsərəs/ *n.* (*pl.* same or **rhinoceroses**) any of various large thick-skinned plant-eating ungulates of the family Rhinocerotidae of Africa and S. Asia, with one horn or in some cases two horns on the nose and plated or folded skin. □**rhinoceros bird** = *ox-pecker*. **rhinoceros horn** a mass of keratinized fibres, reputed to have medicinal or aphrodisiac powers. □□ **rhinocerotic** /raɪ,nɒsə-

'rɒtɪk/ *adj.* [ME f. L f. Gk *rhinokerōs* (as RHINO-, *keras* horn)]

rhinopharyngeal /ˌraɪnəʊfəˈrɪndʒɪəl/ *adj.* of or relating to the nose and pharynx.

rhinoplasty /ˈraɪnəʊˌplæstɪ/ *n.* plastic surgery of the nose. ▭▭ **rhinoplastic** *adj.*

rhizo- /ˈraɪzəʊ/ *comb. form Bot.* a root. [Gk *rhiza* root]

rhizocarp /ˈraɪzəʊˌkɑːp/ *n.* a plant with a perennial root but stems that wither. [RHIZO- + Gk *karpos* fruit]

rhizoid /ˈraɪzɔɪd/ *adj. & n. Bot.* —*adj.* rootlike. —*n.* a root-hair or filament in mosses, ferns, etc.

rhizome /ˈraɪzəʊm/ *n.* an underground rootlike stem bearing both roots and shoots. [Gk *rhizōma* f. *rhizoō* take root (as RHIZO-)]

rhizopod /ˈraɪzəʊˌpɒd/ *n.* any protozoa of the class Rhizopodea, forming rootlike pseudopodia.

rho /rəʊ/ *n.* the seventeenth letter of the Greek alphabet (*P*, ρ). [Gk]

rhodamine /ˈrəʊdəmɪn/ *n. Chem.* any of various red synthetic dyes used to colour textiles. [RHODO- + AMINE]

Rhode Island Red /rəʊd/ *n.* an orig. American breed of reddish-black domestic fowl.

Rhodes Scholarship /rəʊdz/ *n.* any of several scholarships awarded annually and tenable at Oxford University by students from certain Commonwealth countries, South Africa, the United States, and W. Germany. ▭▭ **Rhodes Scholar** *n.* [Cecil *Rhodes*, Brit. statesman d. 1902, who founded them]

rhodium /ˈrəʊdɪəm/ *n. Chem.* a hard white metallic element of the platinum group, occurring naturally in platinum ores and used in making alloys and plating jewellery. ¶ Symb.: **Rh.** [Gk *rhodon* rose (from the colour of the solution of its salts)]

rhodo- /ˈrəʊdəʊ/ *comb. form* esp. *Mineral. & Chem.* rose-coloured. [Gk *rhodon* rose]

rhodochrosite /ˌrəʊdəʊˈkrəʊsaɪt/ *n.* a mineral form of manganese carbonate occurring in rose-red crystals. [Gk *rhodokhrous* rose-coloured]

rhododendron /ˌrəʊdəˈdendrən/ *n.* any evergreen shrub of the genus Rhododendron, with large clusters of trumpet-shaped flowers. [L, = oleander, f. Gk (as RHODO-, *dendron* tree)]

rhodopsin /rəʊˈdɒpsɪn/ *n.* = *visual purple.* [Gk *rhodon* rose + *opsis* sight]

rhodora /rəˈdɔːrə/ *n.* a N. American pink-flowered shrub, Rhodora canadense. [mod.L f. L plant-name f. Gk *rhodon* rose]

rhomb /rɒm/ *n.* = RHOMBUS. ▭▭ **rhombic** *adj.* [F *rhombe* or L *rhombus*]

rhombi *pl.* of RHOMBUS.

rhombohedron /ˌrɒmbəˈhiːdrən/ *n.* (*pl.* **-hedrons** or **-hedra** /-drə/) **1** a solid bounded by six equal rhombuses. **2** a crystal in this form. ▭▭ **rhombohedral** *adj.* [RHOMBUS, after *polyhedron* etc.]

rhomboid /ˈrɒmbɔɪd/ *adj. & n.* —*adj.* (also **rhomboidal** /-ˈbɔɪd(ə)l/) having or nearly having the shape of a rhombus. —*n.* a quadrilateral of which only the opposite sides and angles are equal. [F *rhomboïde* or LL *rhomboides* f. Gk *rhomboeidēs* (as RHOMB)]

rhomboideus /rɒmˈbɔɪdɪəs/ *n.* (*pl.* **rhomboidei** /-dɪˌaɪ/) *Anat.* a muscle connecting the shoulder-blade to the vertebrae. [mod.L *rhomboideus* RHOMBOID]

rhombus /ˈrɒmbəs/ *n.* (*pl.* **rhombuses** or **rhombi** /-baɪ/) *Geom.* a parallelogram with oblique angles and equal sides. [L f. Gk *rhombos*]

RHS *abbr.* **1** Royal Historical Society. **2** Royal Horticultural Society. **3** Royal Humane Society.

rhubarb /ˈruːbɑːb/ *n.* **1 a** any of various plants of the genus *Rheum*, esp. *R. rhaponticum*, producing long fleshy dark-red leaf-stalks used cooked as food. **b** the leaf-stalks of this. **2 a** a root of a Chinese and Tibetan plant of the genus *Rheum*. **b** a purgative made from this. **3 a** *colloq.* a murmurous conversation or noise,

esp. the repetition of the word 'rhubarb' by crowd actors. **b** *sl.* nonsense; worthless stuff. **4** *US sl.* a heated dispute. [ME f. OF *r(e)ubarbe*, shortening of med.L *r(h)eubarbarum*, alt. (by assoc. with Gk *rhēon* rhubarb) of *rhabarbarum* foreign 'rha', ult. f. Gk *rha* + *barbaros* foreign]

rhumb /rʌm/ *n. Naut.* **1** any of the 32 points of the compass. **2** the angle between two successive compass-points. **3** (in full **rhumb-line**) **a** a line cutting all meridians at the same angle. **b** the line followed by a ship sailing in a fixed direction. [F *rumb* prob. f. Du. *ruim* room, assoc. with L *rhombus*: see RHOMBUS]

rhumba var. of RUMBA.

rhyme /raɪm/ *n. & v.* —*n.* **1** identity of sound between words or the endings of words, esp. in verse. **2** (in *sing.* or *pl.*) verse having rhymes. **3 a** the use of rhyme. **b** a poem having rhymes. **4** a word providing a rhyme. —*v.* **1** *intr.* **a** (of words or lines) produce a rhyme. **b** (foll. by *with*) act as a rhyme (with another). **2** *intr.* make or write rhymes; versify. **3** *tr.* put or make (a story etc.) into rhyme. **4** *tr.* (foll. by *with*) treat (a word) as rhyming with another. ▭ **rhyming slang** slang that replaces words by rhyming words or phrases, e.g. *stairs* by *apples and pears*, often with the rhyming element omitted (as in TITFER). **without rhyme or reason** lacking discernible sense or logic. ▭▭ **rhymeless** *adj.* **rhymer** *n.* **rhymist** *n.* [ME *rime* f. OF *rime* f. med.L *rithmus, rythmus* f. L f. Gk *rhuthmos* RHYTHM]

rhymester /ˈraɪmstə(r)/ *n.* a writer of (esp. simple) rhymes.

rhyolite /ˈraɪəˌlaɪt/ *n.* a fine-grained volcanic rock of granitic composition. [G *Rhyolit* f. Gk *rhuax* lava-stream + *lithos* stone]

rhythm /ˈrɪð(ə)m/ *n.* **1** a measured flow of words and phrases in verse or prose determined by various relations of long and short or accented and unaccented syllables. **2** the aspect of musical composition concerned with periodical accent and the duration of notes. **3** *Physiol.* movement with a regular succession of strong and weak elements. **4** a regularly recurring sequence of events. **5** *Art* a harmonious correlation of parts. ▭ **rhythm and blues** popular music with a blues theme and a strong rhythm. **rhythm method** birth control by avoiding sexual intercourse when ovulation is likely to occur. **rhythm section** the part of a dance band or jazz band mainly supplying rhythm, usu. consisting of piano, bass, and drums. ▭▭ **rhythmless** *adj.* [F *rhythme* or L *rhythmus* f. Gk *rhuthmos*, rel. to *rhēo* flow]

rhythmic /ˈrɪðmɪk/ *adj.* (also **rhythmical**) **1** relating to or characterized by rhythm. **2** regularly occurring. ▭▭ **rhythmically** *adv.* [F *rhythmique* or L *rhythmicus* (as RHYTHM)]

rhythmicity /rɪðˈmɪsɪtɪ/ *n.* **1** rhythmical quality or character. **2** the capacity for maintaining a rhythm.

RI *abbr.* **1** King and Emperor. **2** Queen and Empress. **3** *US* Rhode Island (also in official postal use). **4** Royal Institute or Institution. [sense 1 f. L *rex et imperator*: sense 2 f. L *regina et imperatrix*]

ria /ˈrɪə/ *n. Geog.* a long narrow inlet formed by the partial submergence of a river valley. [Sp. *ría* estuary]

rial /ˈriːɑːl/ *n.* (also **riyal**) the monetary unit of Iran, equal to 100 dinars. [Pers. f. Arab. *riyal* f. Sp. *real* ROYAL]

rib /rɪb/ *n. & v.* —*n.* **1** each of the curved bones articulated in pairs to the spine and protecting the thoracic cavity and its organs. **2** a joint of meat from this part of an animal. **3** a ridge or long raised piece often of stronger or thicker material across a surface or through a structure serving to support or strengthen it. **4** any of a ship's transverse curved timbers forming the framework of the hull. **5** *Knitting* a combination of plain and purl stitches producing a ribbed somewhat elastic fabric. **6** each of the hinged

RIBA 1035 ride

rods supporting the fabric of an umbrella. **7** a vein of a leaf or an insect's wing. **8** *Aeron.* a structural member in an aerofoil. —*v.tr.* (**ribbed, ribbing**) **1** provide with ribs; act as the ribs of. **2** *colloq.* make fun of; tease. **3** mark with ridges. **4** plough with spaces between the furrows. □□ **ribless** *adj.* [OE *rib, ribb* f. Gmc]

RIBA *abbr.* Royal Institute of British Architects.

ribald /ˈrɪb(ə)ld/ *adj. & n.* —*adj.* (of language or its user) coarsely or disrespectfully humorous; scurrilous. —*n.* a user of ribald language. [ME (earlier sense 'low-born retainer') f. OF *ribau(l)d* f. *riber* pursue licentious pleasures f. Gmc]

ribaldry /ˈrɪbəldrɪ/ *n.* ribald talk or behaviour.

riband /ˈrɪbənd/ *n.* a ribbon. [ME f. OF *riban*, prob. f. a Gmc compound of BAND¹]

ribbed /rɪbd/ *adj.* having ribs or riblike markings.

ribbing /ˈrɪbɪŋ/ *n.* **1** ribs or a riblike structure. **2** *colloq.* the act or an instance of teasing.

ribbon /ˈrɪbən/ *n.* **1 a** a narrow strip or band of fabric, used esp. for trimming or decoration. **b** material in this form. **2** a ribbon of a special colour etc. worn to indicate some honour or membership of a sports team etc. **3** a long narrow strip of anything, e.g. impregnated material forming the inking agent in a typewriter. **4** (in *pl.*) ragged strips (*torn to ribbons*). □**ribbon development** the building of houses along a main road, usu. one leading out of a town or village. **ribbon worm** a nemertean. □□ **ribboned** *adj.* [var. of RIBAND]

ribbonfish /ˈrɪbənfɪʃ/ *n.* any of various long slender flat fishes of the family Trachypteridae.

ribcage /ˈrɪbkeɪdʒ/ *n.* the wall of bones formed by the ribs round the chest.

riboflavin /ˌraɪbəʊˈfleɪvɪn/ *n.* (also **riboflavine** /-viːn/) a vitamin of the B complex, found in liver, milk, and eggs, essential for energy production. Also called *vitamin B₂*. [RIBOSE + L *flavus* yellow]

ribonucleic acid /ˌraɪbənjuːˈkliːɪk/ *n.* a nucleic acid yielding ribose on hydrolysis, present in living cells, esp. in ribosomes where it is involved in protein synthesis. ¶ Abbr.: **RNA**. [RIBOSE + NUCLEIC ACID]

ribose /ˈraɪbəʊs/ *n.* a sugar found in many nucleosides and in several vitamins and enzymes. [G, alt. f. *Arabinose* a related sugar]

ribosome /ˈraɪbə‚səʊm/ *n. Biochem.* each of the minute particles consisting of RNA and associated proteins found in the cytoplasm of living cells, concerned with the synthesis of proteins. □□ **ribosomal** *adj.* [RIBONUCLEIC (ACID) + -SOME³]

ribwort /ˈrɪbwɜːt/ *n.* a kind of plantain (see PLANTAIN¹) with long narrow ribbed leaves.

rice /raɪs/ *n. & v.* *n.* **1** a swamp grass, *Oryza sativa*, cultivated in marshes, esp. in Asia. **2** the grains of this, used as cereal food. —*v.tr. US* sieve (cooked potatoes etc.) into thin strings. □**rice-bowl** an area producing much rice. **rice-paper** edible paper made from the pith of an oriental tree and used for painting and in cookery. □□ **ricer** *n.* [ME *rys* f. OF *ris* f. It. *riso*, ult. f. Gk *oruza*, of oriental orig.]

ricercar /ˌriːʃeəˈkɑː(r)/ *n.* (also **ricercare** /-ˈkɑːre/) an elaborate contrapuntal instrumental composition in fugal or canonic style, esp. of the 16th–18th c. [It., = seek out]

rich /rɪtʃ/ *adj.* **1** having much wealth. **2** (often foll. by *in, with*) splendid, costly, elaborate (*rich tapestries*; *rich with lace*). **3** valuable (*rich offerings*). **4** copious, abundant, ample (*a rich harvest*; *a rich supply of ideas*). **5** (often foll. by *in, with*) (of soil or a region etc.) abounding in natural resources or means of production; fertile (*rich in nutrients*; *rich with vines*). **6** (of food or diet) containing much fat or spice etc. **7** (of the mixture in an internal-combustion engine) containing a high proportion of fuel. **8** (of colour or sound or smell) mellow and deep, strong and full. **9 a** (of an incident or assertion etc.) highly amusing or ludicrous; outrageous. **b** (of humour) earthy. □□ **richen** *v.intr. & tr.* **richness** *n.* [OE *rīce* f. Gmc f.

Celt., rel. to L *rex* king: reinforced in ME f. OF *riche* rich, powerful, of Gmc orig.]

riches /ˈrɪtʃɪz/ *n.pl.* abundant means; valuable possessions. [ME *richesse* f. OF *richeise* f. *riche* RICH, taken as pl.]

richly /ˈrɪtʃlɪ/ *adv.* **1** in a rich way. **2** fully, thoroughly (*richly deserves success*).

Richter scale /ˈrɪktə/ *n.* a scale of 0 to 10 for representing the strength of an earthquake. [C. F. *Richter*, Amer. seismologist d. 1985]

ricin /ˈrɪsɪn/ *n.* a toxic substance obtained from castor oil beans and causing gastroenteritis, jaundice, and heart failure. [mod.L *ricinus communis* castor oil]

rick¹ /rɪk/ *n. & v.* —*n.* a stack of hay, corn, etc., built into a regular shape and usu. thatched. —*v.tr.* form into a rick or ricks. [OE *hrēac*, of unkn. orig.]

rick² /rɪk/ *n. & v.* (also **wrick**) —*n.* a slight sprain or strain. —*v.tr.* sprain or strain slightly. [ME *wricke* f. MLG *wricken* move about, sprain]

rickets /ˈrɪkɪts/ *n.* (treated as *sing.* or *pl.*) a disease of children with softening of the bones (esp. the spine) and bow-legs, caused by a deficiency of vitamin D. [17th c.: orig. uncert., but assoc. by medical writers with Gk *rhakhitis* RACHITIS]

rickettsia /rɪˈketsɪə/ *n.* a parasitic micro-organism of the genus *Rickettsia* causing typhus and other febrile diseases. □□ **rickettsial** *adj.* [mod.L f. H. T. *Ricketts*, Amer. pathologist d. 1910]

rickety /ˈrɪkɪtɪ/ *adj.* **1 a** insecure or shaky in construction; likely to collapse. **b** feeble. **2 a** suffering from rickets. **b** resembling or of the nature of rickets. □□ **ricketiness** *n.* [RICKETS + -Y¹]

rickey /ˈrɪkɪ/ *n.* (*pl.* **-eys**) a drink of spirit (esp. gin), lime-juice, etc. [20th c.: prob. f. the surname *Rickey*]

rickrack var. of RICRAC.

rickshaw /ˈrɪkʃɔː/ *n.* (also **ricksha** /-ʃə/) a light two-wheeled hooded vehicle drawn by one or more persons. [abbr. of *jinricksha*, *jinrikshaw* f. Jap. *jin-rikisha* f. *jin* person + *riki* power + *sha* vehicle]

ricochet /ˈrɪkəˌʃeɪ, -ˌʃet/ *n. & v.* —*n.* **1** the action of a projectile, esp. a shell or bullet, in rebounding off a surface. **2** a hit made after this. —*v.intr.* (**ricocheted** /-ˌʃeɪd/; **ricocheting** /-ˌʃeɪɪŋ/ or **ricochetted** /-ˌʃetɪd/; **ricochetting** /-ˌʃetɪŋ/) (of a projectile) rebound one or more times from a surface. [F, of unkn. orig.]

ricotta /rɪˈkɒtə/ *n.* a soft Italian cheese. [It., = recooked, f. L *recoquere* (as RE-, *coquere* cook)]

ricrac /ˈrɪkræk/ *n.* (also **rickrack**) a zigzag braided trimming for garments. [redupl. of RACK¹]

RICS *abbr.* Royal Institution of Chartered Surveyors.

rictus /ˈrɪktəs/ *n. Anat. & Zool.* the expanse or gape of a mouth or beak. □□ **rictal** *adj.* [L, = open mouth f. *ringi rict-* to gape]

rid /rɪd/ *v.tr.* (**ridding**; *past* and *past part.* **rid** or *archaic* **ridded**) (foll. by *of*) make (a person or place) free of something unwanted. □**be** (or **get**) **rid of** be freed or relieved of (something unwanted); dispose of. [ME, earlier = 'clear (land etc.)' f. ON *rythja*]

riddance /ˈrɪd(ə)ns/ *n.* the act of getting rid of something. □**good riddance** welcome relief from an unwanted person or thing.

ridden *past part.* of RIDE.

riddle¹ /ˈrɪd(ə)l/ *n. & v.* —*n.* **1** a question or statement testing ingenuity in divining its answer or meaning. **2** a puzzling fact or thing or person. —*v.* **1** *intr.* speak in or propound riddles. **2** *tr.* solve or explain (a riddle). □□ **riddler** *n.* [OE *rædels, rædelse* opinion, riddle, rel. to READ]

riddle² /ˈrɪd(ə)l/ *v. & n.* —*v.tr.* (usu. foll. by *with*) **1** make many holes in, esp. with gunshot. **2** (in *passive*) fill; spread through; permeate (*was riddled with errors*). **3** pass through a riddle. —*n.* a coarse sieve. [OE *hriddel*, earlier *hrīder*: cf. *hrīdrian* sift]

riddling /ˈrɪdlɪŋ/ *adj.* expressed in riddles; puzzling. □□ **riddlingly** *adv.*

ride /raɪd/ *v. & n.* —*v.* (*past* **rode** /rəʊd/; *past part.* **ridden** /ˈrɪd(ə)n/) **1** *tr.* travel or be carried on (a

---

aʊ *how* eɪ *day* əʊ *no* eə *hair* ɪə *near* ɔɪ *boy* ʊə *poor* aɪə *fire* aʊə *sour* (*see over for consonants*)

bicycle etc.) or esp. *US* in (a vehicle). **2** *intr.* (often foll. by *on*, *in*) travel or be conveyed (on a bicycle or in a vehicle). **3** *tr.* sit on and control or be carried by (a horse etc.). **4** *intr.* (often foll. by *on*) be carried (on a horse etc.). **5** *tr.* be carried or supported by (*the ship rides the waves*). **6** *tr.* a traverse on horseback etc., ride over or through (*ride 50 miles*; *rode the prairie*). **b** compete or take part in on horseback etc. (*rode a good race*). **7** *intr.* **a** lie at anchor; float buoyantly. **b** (of the moon) seem to float. **8** *intr.* (foll. by *in*, *on*) rest in or on while moving. **9** *tr.* yield to (a blow) so as to reduce its impact. **10** *tr.* give a ride to; cause to ride (*rode the child on his back*). **11** *tr.* (of a rider) cause (a horse etc.) to move forward (*rode their horses at the fence*). **12** *tr.* **a** (in *passive*; foll. by *by*, *with*) be oppressed or dominated by; be infested with (*was ridden with guilt*). **b** (as **ridden** *adj.*) infested or afflicted (usu. in *comb.*: *a rat-ridden cellar*). **13** *intr.* (of a thing normally level or even) project or overlap. **14** *tr.* mount (a female) in copulation. **15** *tr. US* annoy or seek to annoy. —*n.* **1** an act or period of travel in a vehicle. **2** a spell of riding on a horse, bicycle, person's back, etc. **3** a path (esp. through woods) for riding on. **4** the quality of sensations when riding (*gives a bumpy ride*). □**let a thing ride** leave it alone; let it take its natural course. **ride again** reappear, esp. unexpectedly and reinvigorated. **ride down** overtake or trample on horseback. **ride for a fall** act recklessly risking defeat or failure. **ride herd on** see HERD. **ride high** be elated or successful. **ride out** come safely through (a storm etc., or a danger or difficulty). **ride roughshod over** see ROUGHSHOD. **ride to hounds** see HOUND. **ride up** (of a garment, carpet, etc.) work or move out of its proper position. **take for a ride** *colloq.* hoax or deceive. □□ **ridable** *adj.* [OE *rīdan*]

rider /ˈraɪdə(r)/ *n.* **1** a person who rides (esp. a horse). **2 a** an additional clause amending or supplementing a document. **b** *Brit. Parl.* an addition or amendment to a bill at its third reading. **c** a corollary. **d** *Brit.* a recommendation etc. added to a judicial verdict. **3** *Math.* a problem arising as a corollary of a theorem etc. **4** a piece in a machine etc. that surmounts or bridges or works on or over others. **5** (in *pl.*) an additional set of timbers or iron plates strengthening a ship's frame. □□ **riderless** *adj.* [OE *rīdere* (as RIDE)]

ridge /rɪdʒ/ *n. & v.* —*n.* **1** the line of the junction of two surfaces sloping upwards towards each other (*the ridge of a roof*). **2** a long narrow hilltop, mountain range, or watershed. **3** any narrow elevation across a surface. **4** *Meteorol.* an elongated region of high barometric pressure. **5** *Agriculture* a raised strip of arable land, usu. one of a set separated by furrows. **6** *Hort.* a raised hotbed for melons etc. —*v.* **1** *tr.* mark with ridges. **2** *tr. Agriculture* break up (land) into ridges. **3** *tr. Hort.* plant (cucumbers etc.) in ridges. **4** *tr. & intr.* gather into ridges. □**ridge-piece** (or **-tree**) a beam along the ridge of a roof. **ridge-pole 1** the horizontal pole of a long tent. **2** = *ridge-piece.* **ridge-tile** a tile used in making a roof-ridge. □□ **ridgy** *adj.* [OE *hrycg* f. Gmc]

ridgeway /ˈrɪdʒweɪ/ *n.* a road or track along a ridge.

ridicule /ˈrɪdɪˌkjuːl/ *n. & v.* —*n.* subjection to derision or mockery. —*v.tr.* make fun of; subject to ridicule; laugh at. [F or f. L *ridiculum* neut. of *ridiculus* laughable f. *ridēre* laugh]

ridiculous /rɪˈdɪkjʊləs/ *adj.* **1** deserving or inviting ridicule. **2** unreasonable, absurd. □□ **ridiculously** *adv.* **ridiculousness** *n.* [L *ridiculosus* (as RIDICULE)]

riding[1] /ˈraɪdɪŋ/ *n.* **1** in senses of RIDE *v.* **2** the practice or skill of riders of horses. **3** = RIDE *n.* 3. □**riding-light** (or **-lamp**) a light shown by a ship at anchor. **riding-school** an establishment teaching skills in horsemanship.

riding[2] /ˈraɪdɪŋ/ *n.* **1** each of three former administrative divisions (**East Riding, North Riding, West Riding**) of Yorkshire. **2** an electoral division of Canada. [OE *thriding* (unrecorded) f. ON *thrithjungr*

third part f. *thrithi* THIRD: *th-* was lost owing to the preceding *-t* or *-th* of *east* etc.]

Riesling /ˈriːzlɪŋ, -slɪŋ/ *n.* **1** a kind of dry white wine produced in Germany, Austria, and elsewhere. **2** the variety of grape from which this is produced. [G]

rife /raɪf/ *predic.adj.* **1** of common occurrence; widespread. **2** (foll. by *with*) abounding in; teeming with. □□ **rifeness** *n.* [OE *rȳfe* prob. f. ON *rífr* acceptable f. *reifa* enrich, *reifr* cheerful]

riff /rɪf/ *n. & v.* —*n.* a short repeated phrase in jazz etc. —*v.intr.* play riffs. [20th c.: abbr. of RIFFLE *n.*]

riffle /ˈrɪf(ə)l/ *v. & n.* —*v.* **1** *tr.* **a** turn (pages) in quick succession. **b** shuffle (playing-cards) esp. by flexing and combining the two halves of a pack. **2** *intr.* (often foll. by *through*) leaf quickly (through pages). —*n.* **1** the act or an instance of riffling. **2** (in gold-washing) a groove or slat set in a trough or sluice to catch gold particles. **3** *US* **a** a shallow part of a stream where the water flows brokenly. **b** a patch of waves or ripples on water. [perh. var. of RUFFLE]

riff-raff /ˈrɪfræf/ *n.* (often prec. by *the*) rabble; disreputable or undesirable persons. [ME *riff and raff* f. OF *rif et raf*]

rifle[1] /ˈraɪf(ə)l/ *n. & v.* —*n.* **1** a gun with a long rifled barrel, esp. one fired from shoulder-level. **2** (in *pl.*) riflemen. —*v.tr.* make spiral grooves in (a gun or its barrel or bore) to make a bullet spin. □**rifle bird** any dark green Australian bird of paradise of the genus *Ptiloris.* **rifle-range** a place for rifle-practice. **rifle-shot 1** the distance coverable by a shot from a rifle. **2** a shot fired with a rifle. [OF *rifler* graze, scratch f. Gmc]

rifle[2] /ˈraɪf(ə)l/ *v.tr.* & (foll. by *through*) *intr.* **1** search and rob, esp. of all that can be found. **2** carry off as booty. [ME f. OF *rifler* graze, scratch, plunder f. ODu. *riffelen*]

rifleman /ˈraɪf(ə)lmən/ *n.* (*pl.* **-men**) **1** a soldier armed with a rifle. **2** a small yellow and green New Zealand bird, *Acanthisitta chloris.*

rifling /ˈraɪflɪŋ/ *n.* the arrangement of grooves on the inside of a gun's barrel.

rift /rɪft/ *n. & v.* —*n.* **1 a** a crack or split in an object. **b** an opening in a cloud etc. **2** a cleft or fissure in earth or rock. **3** a disagreement; a breach in friendly relations. —*v.tr.* tear or burst apart. □**rift-valley** a steep-sided valley formed by subsidence of the earth's crust between nearly parallel faults. □□ **riftless** *adj.* **rifty** *adj.* [ME, of Scand. orig.]

rig[1] /rɪg/ *v. & n.* —*v.tr.* (**rigged, rigging**) **1 a** provide (a sailing ship) with sails, rigging, etc. **b** prepare ready for sailing. **2** (often foll. by *out*, *up*) fit with clothes or other equipment. **3** (foll. by *up*) set up hastily or as a makeshift. **4** assemble and adjust the parts of (an aircraft). —*n.* **1** the arrangement of masts, sails, rigging, etc., of a sailing ship. **2** equipment for a special purpose, e.g. a radio transmitter. **3** = *oil rig.* **4** a person's or thing's look as determined by clothing, equipment, etc., esp. uniform. □**in full rig** *colloq.* smartly or ceremonially dressed. **rig-out** *Brit. colloq.* an outfit of clothes. □□ **rigged** *adj.* (also in *comb.*). [ME, perh. of Scand. orig.: cf. Norw. *rigga* bind or wrap up]

rig[2] /rɪg/ *v. & n.* —*v.tr.* (**rigged, rigging**) manage or conduct fraudulently (*they rigged the election*). —*n.* **1** a trick or dodge. **2** a way of swindling. □**rig the market** cause an artificial rise or fall in prices. □□ **rigger** *n.* [19th c.: orig. unkn.]

rigadoon /ˌrɪɡəˈduːn/ *n.* **1** a lively dance in duple or quadruple time for two persons. **2** the music for this. [F *rigodon*, *rigaudon*, perh. f. its inventor *Rigaud*]

rigger /ˈrɪɡə(r)/ *n.* **1** a person who rigs or who arranges rigging. **2** (of a rowing-boat) = OUTRIGGER 5a. **3** a ship rigged in a specified way. **4** a worker on an oil rig.

rigging /ˈrɪɡɪŋ/ *n.* **1** a ship's spars, ropes, etc., supporting and controlling the sails. **2** the ropes and

b *but* d *dog* f *few* g *get* h *he* j *yes* k *cat* l *leg* m *man* n *no* p *pen* r *red* s *sit* t *top* v *voice*

wires supporting the structure of an airship or biplane.

right /raɪt/ *adj.*, *n.*, *v.*, *adv.*, & *int.* —*adj.* **1** (of conduct etc.) just, morally or socially correct (*it is only right to tell you*; *I want to do the right thing*). **2** true, correct; not mistaken (*the right time*; *you were right about the weather*). **3** less wrong or not wrong (*which is the right way to town?*). **4** more or most suitable or preferable (*the right person for the job*; *along the right lines*). **5** in a sound or normal condition; physically or mentally healthy; satisfactory (*the engine doesn't sound right*). **6 a** on or towards the side of the human body which corresponds to the position of east if one regards oneself as facing north. **b** on or towards that part of an object which is analogous to a person's right side or (with opposite sense) which is nearer to a spectator's right hand. **7** (of a side of fabric etc.) meant for display or use (*turn it right side up*). **8** *colloq.* or *archaic* real; properly so called (*made a right mess of it*; *a right royal welcome*). —*n.* **1** that which is morally or socially correct or just; fair treatment (often in *pl.*: *the rights and wrongs of the case*). **2** (often foll. by *to*, or *to* + *infin.*) a justification or fair claim (*has no right to speak like that*). **3** a thing one may legally or morally claim; the state of being entitled to a privilege or immunity or authority to act (*a right of reply*; *human rights*). **4** the right-hand part or region or direction. **5** *Boxing* **a** the right hand. **b** a blow with this. **6** (often **Right**) *Polit.* **a** a group or section favouring conservatism (orig. the more conservative section of a continental legislature, seated on the president's right). **b** such conservatives collectively. **7** the side of a stage which is to the right of a person facing the audience. **8** (esp. in marching) the right foot. **9** the right wing of an army. —*v.tr.* **1** (often *refl.*) restore to a proper or straight or vertical position. **2 a** correct (mistakes etc.); set in order. **b** avenge (a wrong or a wronged person); make reparation for or to. **c** vindicate, justify, rehabilitate. —*adv.* **1** straight (*go right on*). **2** *colloq.* immediately; without delay (*I'll be right back*; *do it right now*). **3 a** (foll. by *to*, *round*, *through*, etc.) all the way (*sank right to the bottom*; *ran right round the block*). **b** (foll. by *off*, *out*, etc.) completely (*came right off its hinges*; *am right out of butter*). **4** exactly, quite (*right in the middle*). **5** justly, properly, correctly, truly, satisfactorily (*did not act right*; *not holding it right*; *if I remember right*). **6** on or to the right side. **7** *archaic* very; to the full (*am right glad to hear it*; *dined right royally*). —*int. colloq.* expressing agreement or assent. □ **as right as rain** perfectly sound and healthy. **at right angles** placed to form a right angle. **by right** (or **rights**) if right were done. **do right by** act dutifully towards (a person). **in one's own right** through one's own position or effort etc. **in the right** having justice or truth on one's side. **in one's right mind** sane; competent to think and act. **of** (or **as of**) **right** having legal or moral etc. entitlement. **on the right side of 1** in the favour of (a person etc.). **2** somewhat less than (a specified age). **put** (or **set**) **right 1** restore to order, health, etc. **2** correct the mistaken impression etc. of (a person). **put** (or **set**) **to rights** make correct or well ordered. **right about** (or **about-turn** or **about-face**) **1** a right turn continued to face the rear. **2** a reversal of policy. **3** a hasty retreat. **right and left** (or **right, left, and centre**) on all sides. **right angle** an angle of 90°, made by lines meeting with equal angles on either side. **right-angled 1** containing or making a right angle. **2** involving right angles, not oblique. **right arm** one's most reliable helper. **right ascension** see ASCENSION. **right away** (or **off**) immediately. **right bank** the bank of a river on the right facing downstream. **right bower** see BOWER³. **right field** *Baseball* the part of the outfield to the right of the batter as he faces the pitcher. **right hand 1** =

right-hand man. **2** the most important position next to a person (*stand at God's right hand*). **right-hand** *adj.* **1** on or towards the right side of a person or thing (*right-hand drive*). **2** done with the right hand (*right-hand blow*). **3** (of a screw) = RIGHT-HANDED 4b. **right-hand man** an indispensable or chief assistant. **Right Honourable** *Brit.* a title given to certain high officials, e.g. Privy Counsellors. **right-minded** (or **-thinking**) having sound views and principles. **right of search** *Naut.* see SEARCH. **right of way 1** a right established by usage to pass over another's ground. **2** a path subject to such a right. **3** the right of one vehicle to proceed before another. **right oh!** (or **ho!**) = RIGHTO. **right on!** *colloq.* an expression of strong approval or encouragement. **a right one** *Brit. colloq.* a silly or foolish person. **Right Reverend** see REVEREND. **right sphere** *Astron.* see SPHERE. **right turn** a turn that brings one's front to face as one's right side did before. **right whale** any large-headed whale of the family Balaenidae, rich in whalebone and easily captured. **right wing 1** the right side of a football etc. team on the field. **2** the conservative section of a political party or system. **right-wing** *adj.* conservative or reactionary. **right-winger** a person on the right wing. **right you are!** *colloq.* an exclamation of assent. **she's** (or **she'll be**) **right** *Austral. colloq.* that will be all right. **too right** *sl.* an expression of agreement. **within one's rights** not exceeding one's authority or entitlement. □□ **rightable** *adj.* **righter** *n.* **rightish** *adj.* **rightless** *adj.* **rightlessness** *n.* **rightness** *n.* [OE *riht* (adj.), *rihtan* (v.), *rihte* (adv.)]

righten /ˈraɪt(ə)n/ *v.tr.* make right or correct.

righteous /ˈraɪtʃəs/ *adj.* (of a person or conduct) morally right; virtuous, law-abiding. □□ **righteously** *adv.* **righteousness** *n.* [OE *rihtwīs* (as RIGHT *n.* + -WISE or RIGHT *adj.* + WISE²),· assim. to *bounteous* etc.]

rightful /ˈraɪtfʊl/ *adj.* **1 a** (of a person) legitimately entitled to (a position etc.) (*the rightful heir*). **b** (of status or property etc.) that one is entitled to. **2** (of an action etc.) equitable, fair. □□ **rightfully** *adv.* **rightfulness** *n.* [OE *rihtful* (as RIGHT *n.*)]

right-handed /raɪtˈhændɪd/ *adj.* **1** using the right hand by preference as more serviceable than the left. **2** (of a tool etc.) made to be used with the right hand. **3** (of a blow) struck with the right hand. **4 a** turning to the right; towards the right. **b** (of a screw) advanced by turning to the right (clockwise). □□ **right-handedly** *adv.* **right-handedness** *n.*

right-hander /raɪtˈhændə(r)/ *n.* **1** a right-handed person. **2** a right-handed blow.

rightism /ˈraɪtɪz(ə)m/ *n. Polit.* the principles or policy of the right. □□ **rightist** *n.* & *adj.*

rightly /ˈraɪtlɪ/ *adv.* justly, properly, correctly, justifiably.

rightmost /ˈraɪtməʊst/ *adj.* furthest to the right.

righto /ˈraɪtəʊ, raɪˈtəʊ/ *intr. Brit. colloq.* expressing agreement or assent.

rightward /ˈraɪtwəd/ *adv.* & *adj.* —*adv.* (also **rightwards** /-wədz/) towards the right. —*adj.* going towards or facing the right.

rigid /ˈrɪdʒɪd/ *adj.* **1** not flexible; that cannot be bent (*a rigid frame*). **2** (of a person, conduct, etc.) inflexible, unbending, strict, harsh, punctilious (*a rigid disciplinarian*; *rigid economy*). □□ **rigidity** /-ˈdʒɪdɪtɪ/ *n.* **rigidly** *adv.* **rigidness** *n.* [F *rigide* or L *rigidus* f. *rigēre* be stiff]

rigidify /rɪˈdʒɪdɪˌfaɪ/ *v.tr.* & *intr.* (-ies, -ied) make or become rigid.

rigmarole /ˈrɪɡməˌrəʊl/ *n.* **1** a lengthy and complicated procedure. **2 a** a rambling or meaningless account or tale. **b** such talk. [orig. *ragman roll* = a catalogue, of unkn. orig.]

rigor¹ /ˈrɪɡə(r), ˈraɪɡɔː(r)/ *n. Med.* **1** a sudden feeling of cold with shivering accompanied by a rise in temperature, preceding a fever etc. **2** rigidity of the body caused by shock or poisoning etc. [ME f. L f. *rigēre* be stiff]

rigor[2] *US* var. of RIGOUR.

rigor mortis /ˌrɪgə ˈmɔːtɪs/ *n.* stiffening of the body after death. [L, = stiffness of death]

rigorous /ˈrɪgərəs/ *adj.* **1** characterized by or showing rigour; strict, severe. **2** strictly exact or accurate. **3** (of the weather) cold, severe. □□ **rigorously** *adv.* **rigorousness** *n.* [OF *rigorous* or LL *rigorosus* (as RIGOR[1])]

rigour /ˈrɪgə(r)/ *n.* (*US* **rigor**) **1 a** severity, strictness, harshness. **b** (in *pl.*) harsh measures or conditions. **2** logical exactitude. **3** strict enforcement of rules etc. (*the utmost rigour of the law*). **4** austerity of life; puritanical discipline. [ME f. OF *rigour* f. L *rigor* (as RIGOR[1])]

Rig-Veda /rɪgˈveɪdə, -ˈviːdə/ *n.* the oldest and principal of the Hindu Vedas (see VEDA). [Skr. *ṛigvēda* f. *ṛic* praise + *vēda* VEDA]

rile /raɪl/ *v.tr.* **1** *colloq.* anger, irritate. **2** *US* make (water) turbulent or muddy. [var. of ROIL]

Riley /ˈraɪlɪ/ *n.* (also **Reilly**) □ **the life of Riley** *colloq.* a carefree existence. [20th c.: orig. unkn.]

rilievo var. of RELIEVO.

rill /rɪl/ *n.* **1** a small stream. **2** a shallow channel cut in the surface of soil or rocks by running water. **3** var. of RILLE. [LG *ril, rille*]

rille /rɪl/ *n.* (also **rill**) *Astron.* a cleft or narrow valley on the moon's surface. [G (as RILL)]

rim /rɪm/ *n. & v.* —*n.* **1 a** a raised edge or border. **b** a margin or verge, esp. of something circular. **2** the part of a pair of spectacles surrounding the lenses. **3** the outer edge of a wheel, on which the tyre is fitted. **4** a boundary line (*the rim of the horizon*). —*v.tr.* (**rimmed, rimming**) **1 a** provide with a rim. **b** be a rim for or to. **2** edge, border. □ **rim-brake** a brake acting on the rim of a wheel. □□ **rimless** *adj.* **rimmed** *adj.* (also in *comb.*). [OE *rima* edge: cf. ON *rimi* ridge (the only known cognate)]

rime[1] /raɪm/ *n. & v.* —*n.* **1** frost, esp. formed from cloud or fog. **2** *poet.* hoar-frost. —*v.tr.* cover with rime. [OE *hrīm*]

rime[2] *archaic* var. of RHYME.

rimose /ˈraɪməʊz/ *adj.* (also **rimous** /-məs/) esp. *Bot.* full of chinks or fissures. [L *rimosus* f. *rima* chink]

rimu /ˈriːmuː/ *n.* *NZ* a softwood tree, *Dacrydium cupressinum*, native to New Zealand. [Maori]

rimy /ˈraɪmɪ/ *adj.* (**rimier, rimiest**) frosty; covered with frost.

rind /raɪnd/ *n. & v.* —*n.* **1** the tough outer layer or covering of fruit and vegetables, cheese, bacon, etc. **2** the bark of a tree or plant. —*v.tr.* strip the bark from. □□ **rinded** *adj.* (also in *comb.*). **rindless** *adj.* [OE *rind(e)*]

rinderpest /ˈrɪndəˌpest/ *n.* a virulent infectious disease of ruminants (esp. cattle). [G f. *Rinder* cattle + *Pest* PEST]

ring[1] /rɪŋ/ *n. & v.* —*n.* **1** a circular band, usu. of precious metal, worn on a finger as an ornament or a token of marriage or betrothal. **2** a circular band of any material. **3** the rim of a cylindrical or circular object, or a line or band round it. **4** a mark or part having the form of a circular band (*had rings round his eyes; smoke rings*). **5** = annual ring. **6 a** an enclosure for a circus performance, betting at races, the showing of cattle, etc. **b** (prec. by *the*) bookmakers collectively. **c** a roped enclosure for boxing or wrestling. **7 a** a group of people or things arranged in a circle. **b** such an arrangement. **8** a combination of traders, bookmakers, spies, politicians, etc. acting together usu. illicitly for the control of operations or profit. **9** a circular or spiral course. **10** = gas ring. **11** *Astron.* **a** a thin band or disc of particles etc. round a planet. **b** a halo round the moon. **12** *Archaeol.* a circular prehistoric earthwork usu. of a bank and ditch. **13** *Chem.* a group of atoms each bonded to two others in a closed sequence. **14** *Math.* a set of

elements with two binary operations, addition and multiplication, the second being distributive over the first and associative. —*v.tr.* **1** make or draw a circle round. **2** (often foll. by *round, about, in*) encircle or hem in (game or cattle) **3** put a ring on (a bird etc.) or through the nose of (a pig, bull, etc.). **4** cut (fruit, vegetables, etc.) into rings. □ **ring-binder** a loose-leaf binder with ring-shaped clasps that can be opened to pass through holes in the paper. **ring circuit** an electrical circuit serving a number of power points with one fuse in the supply to the circuit. **ring-dove 1** the woodpigeon. **2** the collared dove. **ringed plover** either of two small plovers, *Charadrius hiaticula* and *C. dubius*. **ring finger** the finger next to the little finger, esp. of the left hand, on which the wedding ring is usu. worn. **ring main 1** an electrical supply serving a series of consumers and returning to the original source, so that each consumer has an alternative path in the event of a failure. **2** = ring circuit. **ring-neck** any of various ring-necked birds esp. a type of pheasant, *Phasianus colchicus*, with a white neck-ring. **ring-necked** *Zool.* having a band or bands of colour round the neck. **ring ouzel** a thrush, *Turdus torquatus*, with a white crescent across its breast. **ring-pull** (of a tin) having a ring for pulling to break its seal. **ring road** a bypass encircling a town. **ring-tailed 1** (of monkeys, lemurs, racoons, etc.) having a tail ringed in alternate colours. **2** with the tail curled at the end. **run** (or **make**) **rings round** *colloq.* outclass or outwit (another person). □□ **ringed** *adj.* (also in *comb.*). **ringless** *adj.* [OE *hring* f. Gmc]

ring[2] /rɪŋ/ *v. & n.* —*v.* (*past* **rang** /ræŋ/; *past part.* **rung** /rʌŋ/) **1** *intr.* (often foll. by *out* etc.) give a clear resonant or vibrating sound of or as of a bell (*a shot rang out; a ringing laugh; the telephone rang*). **2** *tr.* **a** make (esp. a bell) ring. **b** (*absol.*) call for service or attention by ringing a bell (*you rang, madam?*). **3** *tr.* (also *absol.*; often foll. by *up*) *Brit.* call by telephone (*will ring you on Monday; did you ring?*). **4** *intr.* (usu. foll. by *with, to*) (of a place) resound or be permeated with a sound, or an attribute, e.g. fame (*the theatre rang with applause*). **5** *intr.* (of the ears) be filled with a sensation of ringing. **6** *tr.* **a** sound (a peal etc.) on bells. **b** (of a bell) sound (the hour etc.). **7** *tr.* (foll. by *in, out*) usher in or out with bell-ringing (*ring in the May; rang out the Old Year*). **8** *intr.* (of sentiments etc.) convey a specified impression (*words rang hollow*). —*n.* **1** a ringing sound or tone. **2 a** the act of ringing a bell. **b** the sound caused by this. **3** *colloq.* a telephone call (*give me a ring*). **4** a specified feeling conveyed by an utterance (*had a melancholy ring*). **5** a set of esp. church bells. □ **ring back** make a return telephone call to (a person who has telephoned earlier). **ring a bell** see BELL[1]. **ring the changes (on)** see CHANGE. **ring down** (or **up**) **the curtain 1** cause the curtain to be lowered or raised. **2** (foll. by *on*) mark the end or the beginning of (an enterprise etc.). **ring in 1** report or make contact by telephone. **2** *Austral. & NZ sl.* substitute fraudulently. **ring in one's ears** (or **heart** etc.) linger in the memory. **ringing tone** a sound heard by a telephone caller when the number dialled is being rung. **ring off** *Brit.* end a telephone call by replacing the receiver. **ring true** (or **false**) convey an impression of truth or falsehood. **ring up 1** *Brit.* call by telephone. **2** record (an amount etc.) on a cash register. □□ **ringed** *adj.* (also in *comb.*). **ringer** *n.* **ringing** *adj.* **ringingly** *adv.* [OE *hringan*]

ringbark /ˈrɪŋbɑːk/ *v.tr.* cut a ring in the bark of (a tree) to kill it or retard its growth and thereby improve fruit production.

ringbolt /ˈrɪŋbɒlt/ *n.* a bolt with a ring attached for fitting a rope to etc.

ringer /ˈrɪŋə(r)/ *n. sl.* **1 a** esp. *US* an athlete or horse entered in a competition by fraudulent means, esp. as a substitute. **b** a person's double, esp. an imposter. **2** *Austral.* **a** the fastest shearer in a shed. **b** a stockman or station hand. **3** a person who rings, esp. a bell-ringer. □**be a ringer** (or **dead ringer**) **for** resemble (a person) exactly. [RING² + -ER¹]

ringhals /ˈrɪŋhæls/ n. a large venomous snake, *Hemachatus hemachatus*, of Southern Africa, with a white ring or two across the neck. [Afrik. *rinkhals* f. *ring* RING¹ + *hals* neck]

ringleader /ˈrɪŋˌliːdə(r)/ n. a leading instigator in an illicit or illegal activity.

ringlet /ˈrɪŋlɪt/ n. **1** a curly lock of hair, esp. a long one. **2** a butterfly, *Aphantopus hyperantus*, with spots on its wings. □□ **ringleted** adj. **ringlety** adj.

ringmaster /ˈrɪŋˌmɑːstə(r)/ n. the person directing a circus performance.

ringside /ˈrɪŋsaɪd/ n. the area immediately beside a boxing ring or circus ring etc. (often *attrib.: a ringside seat; a ringside view*). □□ **ringsider** n.

ringster /ˈrɪŋstə(r)/ n. a person who participates in a political or commercial ring (see RING¹ n. 8).

ringtail /ˈrɪŋteɪl/ n. **1** a ring-tailed opossum, lemur, or phalanger. **2** a golden eagle up to its third year. **3** a female hen-harrier.

ringworm /ˈrɪŋwɜːm/ n. any of various fungous infections of the skin causing circular inflamed patches, esp. on a child's scalp.

rink /rɪŋk/ n. **1** an area of natural or artificial ice for skating or the game of curling etc. **2** an enclosed area for roller-skating. **3** a building containing either of these. **4** *Bowls* a strip of the green used for playing a match. **5** a team in bowls or curling. [ME (orig. Sc.), = jousting-ground: perh. orig. f. OF *renc* RANK¹]

rinse /rɪns/ v. & n. —v.tr. (often foll. by *through*, *out*) **1** wash with clean water. **2** apply liquid to. **3** wash lightly. **4** put (clothes etc.) through clean water to remove soap or detergent. **5** (foll. by *out*, *away*) clear (impurities) by rinsing. —n. **1** the act or an instance of rinsing (*give it a rinse*). **2** a solution for cleansing the mouth. **3** a dye for the temporary tinting of hair (*a blue rinse*). □□ **rinser** n. [ME f. OF *rincer*, *raincier*, of unkn. orig.]

riot /ˈraɪət/ n. & v. —n. **1 a** a disturbance of the peace by a crowd; an occurrence of public disorder. **b** (*attrib.*) involved in suppressing riots (*riot police*; *riot shield*). **2** uncontrolled revelry; noisy behaviour. **3** (foll. by *of*) a lavish display or enjoyment (*a riot of emotion; a riot of colour and sound*). **4** *colloq.* a very amusing thing or person. —v.intr. **1** make or engage in a riot. **2** live wantonly; revel. □**read the Riot Act** put a firm stop to insubordination etc.; give a severe warning (from the name of a former act partly read out to disperse rioters). **run riot 1** throw off all restraint. **2** (of plants) grow or spread uncontrolled. □□ **rioter** n. **riotless** adj. [ME f. OF *riote*, *rioter*, *rihoter*, of unkn. orig.]

riotous /ˈraɪətəs/ adj. **1** marked by or involving rioting. **2** characterized by wanton conduct. **3** wildly profuse. □□ **riotously** adv. **riotousness** n. [ME f. OF (as RIOT)]

RIP *abbr.* may he or she or they rest in peace. [L *requiescat* (pl. *requiescant*) *in pace*]

rip¹ /rɪp/ v. & n. —v.tr. & intr. (**ripped**, **ripping**) **1** *tr.* tear or cut (a thing) quickly or forcibly away or apart (*ripped out the lining; ripped the book up*). **2** *tr.* **a** make (a hole etc.) by ripping. **b** make a long tear or cut in. **3** *intr.* come violently apart; split. **4** *intr.* rush along. —n. **1** a long tear or cut. **2** an act of ripping. □**let rip** *colloq.* **1** act or proceed without restraint. **2** speak violently. **3** not check the speed of or interfere with (a person or thing). **rip-cord** a cord for releasing a parachute from its pack. **rip into** attack (a person) verbally. **rip off** *colloq.* defraud, steal. **rip-off** n. *colloq.* **1** a fraud or swindle. **2** financial exploitation. [ME: orig. unkn.]

rip² /rɪp/ n. a stretch of rough water in the sea or in a river, caused by the meeting of currents. □**rip current** (or **tide**) **1** a strong surface current from the shore. **2** a state of conflicting psychological forces. [18th c.: perh. rel. to RIP¹]

rip³ /rɪp/ n. **1** a dissolute person. **2** a rascal. **3** a worthless horse. [perh. f. *rep*, abbr. of REPROBATE]

riparian /raɪˈpeərɪən/ adj. & n. esp. *Law* —adj. of or on a river-bank (*riparian rights*). —n. an owner of property on a river-bank. [L *riparius* f. *ripa* bank]

ripe /raɪp/ adj. **1** (of grain, fruit, cheese, etc.) ready to be reaped or picked or eaten. **2** mature; fully developed (*ripe in judgement; a ripe beauty*). **3** (of a person's age) advanced. **4** (often foll. by *for*) fit or ready (*when the time is ripe; land ripe for development*). **5** (of the complexion etc.) red and full like ripe fruit. □□ **ripely** adv. **ripeness** n. [OE *rīpe* f. WG]

ripen /ˈraɪpən/ v.tr. & intr. make or become ripe.

ripieno /rɪˈpjeɪnəʊ/ n. (pl. **-os** or **ripieni** /-nɪ/) *Mus.* a body of accompanying instruments in baroque concerto music. [It. (as RE-, *pieno* full)]

riposte /rɪˈpɒst/ n. & v. —n. **1** a quick sharp reply or retort. **2** a quick return thrust in fencing. —v.intr. deliver a riposte. [F *ri(s)poste*, *ri(s)poster* f. It. *risposta* RESPONSE]

ripper /ˈrɪpə(r)/ n. **1** a person or thing that rips. **2** a murderer who rips the victims' bodies.

ripping /ˈrɪpɪŋ/ adj. *Brit. archaic colloq.* very enjoyable (*a ripping good yarn*). □□ **rippingly** adv.

ripple¹ /ˈrɪp(ə)l/ n. & v. —n. **1** a ruffling of the water's surface, a small wave or series of waves. **2** a gentle lively sound that rises and falls, e.g. of laughter or applause. **3** a wavy appearance in hair, material, etc. **4** *Electr.* a slight variation in the strength of a current etc. **5** ice-cream with added syrup giving a coloured ripple effect (*raspberry ripple*). **6** *US* a riffle in a stream. —v. **1** a *intr.* form ripples; flow in ripples. **b** *tr.* cause to do this. **2** *intr.* show or sound like ripples. □**ripple mark** a ridge or ridged surface left on sand, mud, or rock by the action of water or wind. □□ **ripplet** n. **ripply** adj. [17th c.: orig. unkn.]

ripple² /ˈrɪp(ə)l/ n. & v. —n. a toothed implement used to remove seeds from flax. —v.tr. treat with a ripple. [corresp. to MDu. & MLG *repel(en)*, OHG *riffila*, *rifilōn*]

riprap /ˈrɪpræp/ n. *US* a collection of loose stone as a foundation for a structure. [redupl. of RAP¹]

rip-roaring /ˈrɪpˌrɔːrɪŋ/ adj. **1** wildly noisy or boisterous. **2** excellent, first-rate. □□ **rip-roaringly** adv.

ripsaw /ˈrɪpsɔː/ n. a coarse saw for sawing wood along the grain.

ripsnorter /ˈrɪpˌsnɔːtə(r)/ n. *colloq.* an energetic, remarkable, or excellent person or thing. □□ **ripsnorting** adj. **ripsnortingly** adv.

rise /raɪz/ v. & n. —v.intr. (past **rose** /rəʊz/; past part. **risen** /ˈrɪz(ə)n/) **1** move from a lower position to a higher one; come or go up. **2** grow, project, expand, and incline upwards; become higher. **3** (of the sun, moon, or stars) appear above the horizon. **4 a** get up from lying or sitting or kneeling (*rose to their feet; rose from the table*). **b** get out of bed, esp. in the morning (*do you rise early?*). **5** recover a standing or vertical position; become erect (*rose to my full height*). **6** (of a meeting etc.) cease to sit for business; adjourn (*Parliament rises next week; the court will rise*). **7** reach a higher position or level or amount (*the flood has risen; prices are rising*). **8** develop greater intensity, strength, volume, or pitch (*the colour rose in her cheeks; the wind is rising; their voices rose with excitement*). **9** make progress; reach a higher social position (*rose from the ranks*). **10 a** come to the surface of liquid (*bubbles rose from the bottom; waited for the fish to rise*). **b** (of a person) react to provocation (*rise to the bait*). **11** become or be visible above the surroundings etc., stand prominently (*mountains rose to our right*). **12 a** (of buildings etc.) undergo construction from the foundations (*office blocks were rising all around*). **b** (of a tree etc.) grow to a (usu. specified) height. **13** come to life again (*rise from the ashes; risen from the dead*). **14** (of dough) swell by the action of yeast etc. **15** (often foll. by *up*) cease to be quiet or submissive; rebel (*rise in arms*). **16** originate; have as its source (*the river rises in the* *mountains*). **17** (of wind) start to blow. **18** (of a person's spirits) become cheerful. **19** (of a barometer) show a higher atmospheric pressure. **20** (of a horse) rear (*rose on its hind legs*). **21** (of a bump, blister, etc.) form. **22** (of the stomach) show nausea. —*n.* **1** an act or manner or amount of rising. **2** an upward slope or hill or movement (*a rise in the road; the house stood on a rise; the rise and fall of the waves*). **3** an increase in sound or pitch. **4 a** an increase in amount, extent, etc. (*a rise in unemployment*). **b** *Brit.* an increase in salary, wages, etc. **5** an increase in status or power. **6** social, commercial, or political advancement; upward progress. **7** the movement of fish to the surface. **8** origin. **9 a** the vertical height of a step, arch, incline, etc. **b** = RISER 2. □**get** (or **take**) **a rise out of** *colloq.* provoke an emotional reaction from (a person), esp. by teasing. **on the rise** on the increase. **rise above 1** be superior to (petty feelings etc.). **2** show dignity or strength in the face of (difficulty, poor conditions, etc.). **rise and shine** (usu. as *imper.*) *colloq.* get out of bed smartly; wake up. **rise in the world** attain a higher social position. **rise to** develop powers equal to (an occasion). **rise with the sun** (or **lark**) get up early in the morning. [OE *rīsan* f. Gmc]

riser /'raɪzə(r)/ *n.* **1** a person who rises esp. from bed (*an early riser*). **2** a vertical section between the treads of a staircase. **3** a vertical pipe for the flow of liquid or gas.

rishi /'rɪʃɪ/ *n.* (*pl.* **rishis**) a Hindu sage or saint. [Skr. *ṛiṣi*]

risible /'rɪzɪb(ə)l/ *adj.* **1** laughable, ludicrous. **2** inclined to laugh. **3** *Anat.* relating to laughter (*risible nerves*). □□**risibility** /-'bɪlɪtɪ/ *n.* **risibly** *adv.* [LL *risibilis* f. L *rīdēre ris-* laugh]

rising /'raɪzɪŋ/ *adj.* & *n.* —*adj.* **1** going up; getting higher. **2** increasing (*rising costs*). **3** advancing to maturity or high standing (*the rising generation; a rising young lawyer*). **4** approaching a specified age (*the rising fives*). **5** (of ground) sloping upwards. —*n.* a revolt or insurrection. □**rising damp** moisture absorbed from the ground into a wall.

risk /rɪsk/ *n.* & *v.* —*n.* **1** a chance or possibility of danger, loss, injury, or other adverse consequences (*a health risk; a risk of fire*). **2** a person or thing causing a risk or regarded in relation to risk (*is a poor risk*). —*v.tr.* **1** expose to risk. **2** accept the chance of (*could not risk getting wet*). **3** venture on. □**at risk** exposed to danger. **at one's (own) risk** accepting responsibility, agreeing to make no claims. **at the risk of** with the possibility of (an adverse consequence). **put at risk** expose to danger. **risk capital** money put up for speculative business investment. **risk one's neck** put one's own life in danger. **run a** (or **the**) **risk** (often foll. by *of*) expose oneself to danger or loss etc. **take** (or **run**) **a risk** chance the possibility of danger etc. [F *risque, risquer* f. It. *risco* danger, *riscare* run into danger]

risky /'rɪskɪ/ *adj.* (**riskier, riskiest**) **1** involving risk. **2** = RISQUÉ. □□**riskily** *adv.* **riskiness** *n.*

Risorgimento /rɪˌsɔːdʒɪ'mentəʊ/ *n. hist.* a movement for the unification and independence of Italy (achieved in 1870). [It., = resurrection]

risotto /rɪ'zɒtəʊ/ *n.* (*pl.* **-os**) an Italian dish of rice cooked in stock with meat, onions, etc. [It.]

risqué /'rɪskeɪ, -'keɪ/ *adj.* (of a story etc.) slightly indecent or liable to shock. [F, past part. of *risquer* RISK]

rissole /'rɪsəʊl/ *n.* a compressed mixture of meat and spices, coated in breadcrumbs and fried. [F f. OF *ruissole, roussole* ult. f. LL *russeolus* reddish f. L *russus* red]

rit. /rɪt/ *abbr. Mus.* ritardando.

ritardando /ˌrɪtɑː'dændəʊ/ *adv.* & *n. Mus.* (*pl.* **-os** or **ritardandi** /-dɪ/) = RALLENTANDO. [It.]

rite /raɪt/ *n.* **1** a religious or solemn observance or act (*burial rites*). **2** an action or procedure required or usual in this. **3** a body of customary observances characteristic of a Church or a part of it (*the Latin rite*). □**rite of passage** (often in *pl.*) a ritual or event marking a stage of a person's advance through life, e.g. marriage. □□**riteless** *adj.* [ME f. OF *rit, rite* or L *ritus* (esp. religious) usage]

ritenuto /ˌrɪtə'nuːtəʊ/ *adv.* & *n. Mus.* —*adv.* with immediate reduction of speed. —*n.* (*pl.* **-os** or **ritenuti** /-tɪ/) a passage played in this way. [It.]

ritornello /ˌrɪtɔː'neləʊ/ *n. Mus.* (*pl.* **-os** or **ritornelli** /-lɪ/) a short instrumental refrain, interlude, etc., in a vocal work. [It., dimin. of *ritorno* RETURN]

ritual /'rɪtjʊəl/ *n.* & *adj.* —*n.* **1** a prescribed order of performing rites. **2** a procedure regularly followed. —*adj.* of or done as a ritual or rites (*ritual murder*). □□**ritualize** *v.tr.* & *intr.* (also **-ise**). **ritualization** /-'zeɪʃ(ə)n/ *n.* (also **-isation**). **ritually** *adv.* [L *ritualis* (as RITE)]

ritualism /'rɪtjʊəˌlɪz(ə)m/ *n.* the regular or excessive practice of ritual. □□**ritualist** *n.* **ritualistic** /-'lɪstɪk/ *adj.* **ritualistically** /-'lɪstɪkəlɪ/ *adv.*

ritzy /'rɪtzɪ/ *adj.* (**ritzier, ritziest**) *colloq.* **1** high-class, luxurious. **2** ostentatiously smart. □□**ritzily** *adv.* **ritziness** *n.* [*Ritz*, the name of luxury hotels f. C. *Ritz*, Swiss hotel-owner d. 1918]

rival /'raɪv(ə)l/ *n.* & *v.* —*n.* **1** a person competing with another for the same objective. **2** a person or thing that equals another in quality. **3** (*attrib.*) being a rival or rivals (*a rival firm*). —*v.tr.* (**rivalled, rivalling**; *US* **rivaled, rivaling**) **1** be the rival of or comparable to. **2** seem or claim to be as good as. [L *rivalis*, orig. = using the same stream, f. *rivus* stream]

rivalry /'raɪvəlrɪ/ *n.* (*pl.* **-ies**) the state or an instance of being rivals; competition.

rive /raɪv/ *v.* (*past* **rived**; *past part.* **riven** /'rɪv(ə)n/) *archaic* or *poet.* **1** *tr.* split or tear apart violently. **2 a** *tr.* split (wood or stone). **b** *intr.* be split. [ME f. ON *rífa*]

river /'rɪvə(r)/ *n.* **1** a copious natural stream of water flowing in a channel to the sea or a lake etc. **2** a copious flow (*a river of lava; rivers of blood*). **3** (*attrib.*) (in the names of animals, plants, etc.) living in or associated with the river. □**river blindness** a tropical disease of the skin caused by a parasitic worm, the larvae of which can migrate into the eye and cause blindness. **river capture** the diversion of the upper headwaters of a mountain stream into a more powerful one. **sell down the river** *colloq.* betray or let down. □□**rivered** *adj.* (also in *comb.*). **riverless** *adj.* [ME f. AF *river, rivere*, OF *riviere* river or river-bank ult. f. L *riparius* f. *ripa* bank]

riverine /'rɪvəˌraɪn/ *adj.* of or on a river or river-bank; riparian.

riverside /'rɪvəˌsaɪd/ *n.* the ground along a river-bank.

rivet /'rɪvɪt/ *n.* & *v.* —*n.* a nail or bolt for holding together metal plates etc., its headless end being beaten out or pressed down when in place. —*v.tr.* (**riveted, riveting**) **1 a** join or fasten with rivets. **b** beat out or press down the end of (a nail or bolt). **c** fix; make immovable. **2 a** (foll. by *on, upon*) direct intently (one's eyes or attention etc.). **b** (esp. as **riveting** *adj.*) engross (a person or the attention). □□**riveter** *n.* [ME f. OF f. *river* clench, of unkn. orig.]

riviera /ˌrɪvɪ'eərə/ *n.* a coastal region with a sub-tropical climate, vegetation, etc., esp. that of SE France and NW Italy. [It., = sea-shore]

rivière /riːv'jeə(r), 'rɪvɪˌeə(r)/ *n.* a gem necklace, esp. of more than one string. [F, = RIVER]

rivulet /'rɪvjʊlɪt/ *n.* a small stream. [obs. *riveret* f. F, dimin. of *rivière* RIVER, perh. after It. *rivoletto* dimin. of *rivolo* dimin. of *rivo* f. L *rivus* stream]

riyal var. of RIAL.

RL *abbr.* Rugby League.

rly. *abbr.* railway.

RM *abbr.* **1** (in the UK) Royal Marines. **2** Resident Magistrate. **3** (in the UK) Royal Mail.

rm. *abbr.* room.

RMA *abbr.* Royal Military Academy.

r.m.s. *abbr. Math.* root-mean-square.

RN *abbr.* **1** (in the UK) Royal Navy. **2** (in the UK) Registered Nurse.

Rn *symb. Chem.* the element radon.

RNA *abbr.* ribonucleic acid.

RNAS *abbr.* (in the UK) Royal Naval Air Service (or Station).

RNLI *abbr.* (in the UK) Royal National Lifeboat Institution.

RNZAF *abbr.* Royal New Zealand Air Force.

RNZN *abbr.* Royal New Zealand Navy.

roach¹ /rəʊtʃ/ *n.* (*pl.* same) a small freshwater fish, esp. *Rutilus rutilus*, allied to the carp. [ME f. OF *roc(h)e*, of unkn. orig.]

roach² /rəʊtʃ/ *n.* **1** *US colloq.* a cockroach. **2** *sl.* the butt of a marijuana cigarette. [abbr.]

roach³ /rəʊtʃ/ *n. Naut.* an upward curve in the foot of a square sail. [18th c.: orig. unkn.]

road¹ /rəʊd/ *n.* **1 a** a path or way with a specially prepared surface, used by vehicles, pedestrians, etc. **b** the part of this used by vehicles (*don't step in the road*). **2** one's way or route (*our road took us through unexplored territory*). **3** an underground passage in a mine. **4** *US* a railway. **5** (usu. in *pl.*) a partly sheltered piece of water near the shore in which ships can ride at anchor. □**by road** using transport along roads. **get out of the** (or **my** etc.) **road** *colloq.* cease to obstruct a person. **in the** (or **my** etc.) **road** *colloq.* obstructing a person or thing. **one for the road** *colloq.* a final (esp. alcoholic) drink before departure. **on the road** travelling, esp. as a firm's representative, itinerant performer, or vagrant. **road fund** *Brit. hist.* a fund for the construction and maintenance of roads and bridges. **road fund licence** *Brit.* a disc displayed on a vehicle certifying payment of road tax. **road-hog** *colloq.* a reckless or inconsiderate road-user, esp. a motorist. **road-holding** the capacity of a moving vehicle to remain stable when cornering at high speeds etc. **road-house** an inn or club on a major road. **road hump** = *sleeping policeman* (see SLEEP). **road-manager** the organizer and supervisor of a musicians' tour. **road-map** a map showing the roads of a country or area. **road-metal** broken stone used in road-making or for railway ballast. **road sense** a person's capacity for safe behaviour on the road, esp. in traffic. **road show 1 a** a performance given by a touring company, esp. a group of pop musicians. **b** a company giving such performances. **2** a radio or television programme done on location. **road sign** a sign giving information or instructions to road users. **road tax** a periodic tax payable on road vehicles. **road test** a test of the performance of a vehicle on the road. **road-test** *v.tr.* test (a vehicle) on the road. **the road to** the way of getting to or achieving (*the road to London; the road to ruin*). **road train** a large lorry pulling one or more trailers. **rule of the road** the custom or law regulating which side of the road is to be taken by vehicles (also riders or ships) meeting or passing each other. **take the road** set out. □□ **roadless** *adj.* [OE rād f. rīdan RIDE]

road² /rəʊd/ *v.tr.* (also *absol.*) (of a dog) follow up (a game-bird) by the scent of its trail. [19th c.: orig. unkn.]

roadbed /'rəʊdbed/ *n.* **1** the foundation structure of a railway. **2** the material laid down to form a road. **3** *US* the part of a road on which vehicles travel.

roadblock /'rəʊdblɒk/ *n.* a barrier or barricade on a road, esp. one set up by the authorities to stop and examine traffic.

roadie /'rəʊdɪ/ *n. colloq.* an assistant employed by a touring band of musicians to erect and maintain equipment.

roadman /'rəʊdmən/ *n.* (*pl.* -men) a man employed to repair or maintain roads.

roadroller /'rəʊd,rəʊlə(r)/ *n.* a motor vehicle with a heavy roller, used in road-making.

roadrunner /'rəʊd,rʌnə(r)/ *n.* a bird of Mexican and US deserts, *Geococcyx californianus*, related to the cuckoo, and a poor flier but fast runner.

roadside /'rəʊdsaɪd/ *n.* the strip of land beside a road.

roadstead /'rəʊdsted/ *n.* = ROAD¹ 5. [ROAD¹ + *stead* in obs. sense 'place']

roadster /'rəʊdstə(r)/ *n.* **1** an open car without rear seats. **2** a horse or bicycle for use on the road.

roadway /'rəʊdweɪ/ *n.* **1** a road. **2** = ROAD¹ 1b. **3** the part of a bridge or railway used for traffic.

roadwork /'rəʊdwɜːk/ *n.* **1** (in *pl.*) the construction or repair of roads, or other work involving digging up a road surface. **2** athletic exercise or training involving running on roads.

roadworthy /'rəʊd,wɜːðɪ/ *adj.* **1** fit to be used on the road. **2** (of a person) fit to travel. □□ **roadworthiness** *n.*

roam /rəʊm/ *v. & n.* —*v.* **1** *intr.* ramble, wander. **2** *tr.* travel unsystematically over, through, or about. —*n.* an act of roaming; a ramble. □□ **roamer** *n.* [ME: orig. unkn.]

roan¹ /rəʊn/ *adj. & n.* —*adj.* (of an animal, esp. a horse or cow) having a coat of which the prevailing colour is thickly interspersed with hairs of another colour, esp. bay or sorrel or chestnut mixed with white or grey. —*n.* a roan animal. □**blue roan** *adj.* black mixed with white. —*n.* a blue roan animal. **red roan** *adj.* bay mixed with white or grey. —*n.* a red roan animal. **strawberry roan** *adj.* chestnut mixed with white or grey. —*n.* a strawberry roan animal. [OF, of unkn. orig.]

roan² /rəʊn/ *n.* soft sheepskin leather used in book-binding as a substitute for morocco. [ME, perh. f. *Roan*, old name of *Rouen* in N. France]

roar /rɔː(r)/ *n. & v.* —*n.* **1** a loud deep hoarse sound, as made by a lion, a person in pain or rage or excitement, thunder, a loud engine, etc. **2** a loud laugh. —*v.* **1** *intr.* **a** utter or make a roar. **b** utter loud laughter. **c** (of a horse) make a loud noise in breathing as a symptom of disease. **2** *intr.* travel in a vehicle at high speed, esp. with the engine roaring. **3** *tr.* (often foll. by *out*) say, sing, or utter (words, an oath, etc.) in a loud tone. □□ **roarer** *n.* [OE *rārian*, of imit. orig.]

roaring /'rɔːrɪŋ/ *adj.* in senses of ROAR *v.* □**roaring drunk** very drunk and noisy. **roaring forties** stormy ocean tracts between lat. 40° and 50° S. **roaring trade** (or **business**) very brisk trade or business. **roaring twenties** the decade of the 1920s (with ref. to its postwar buoyancy). □□ **roaringly** *adv.*

roast /rəʊst/ *v., adj., & n.* —*v.* **1** *tr.* **a** cook (food, esp. meat) in an oven or by exposure to open heat. **b** heat (coffee beans) before grinding. **2** *tr.* heat (the ore of metal) in a furnace. **3** *tr.* **a** expose (a torture victim) to fire or great heat. **b** *tr. & refl.* expose (oneself or part of oneself) to warmth. **4** *tr.* criticize severely, denounce. **5** *intr.* undergo roasting. —*attrib.adj.* (of meat or a potato, chestnut, etc.) roasted. —*n.* **1 a** roast meat. **b** a dish of this. **c** a piece of meat for roasting. **2** the process of roasting. **3** *US* a party where roasted food is eaten. [ME f. OF *rost*, *rostir*, f. Gmc]

roaster /'rəʊstə(r)/ *n.* **1** a person or thing that roasts. **2 a** an oven or dish for roasting food in. **b** an ore-roasting furnace. **c** a coffee-roasting apparatus. **3** something fit for roasting, e.g. a fowl, a potato, etc.

roasting /'rəʊstɪŋ/ *adj. & n.* —*adj.* very hot. —*n.* **1** in senses of ROAST *v.* **2** a severe criticism or denunciation.

rob /rɒb/ *v.tr.* (**robbed**, **robbing**) (often foll. by *of*) **1** take unlawfully from, esp. by force or threat of force (*robbed the safe; robbed her of her jewels*). **2** deprive of what is due or normal (*was robbed of my sleep*). **3** (*absol.*) commit robbery. □**rob Peter to pay Paul** take away from one to give to another, discharge one debt by incurring another. [ME f. OF rob(b)er f. Gmc: cf. REAVE]

robber /'rɒbə(r)/ n. a person who commits robbery. ▫**robber baron 1** a plundering feudal lord. **2** an unscrupulous plutocrat. [ME f. AF & OF (as ROB)]

robbery /'rɒbərɪ/ n. (pl. -ies) **1 a** the act or process of robbing, esp. with force or threat of force. **b** an instance of this. **2** excessive financial demand or cost (set us back £20—it was sheer robbery). [ME f. OF roberie (as ROB)]

robe /rəub/ n. & v. —n. **1** a long loose outer garment. **2** esp. US a dressing-gown. **3** a baby's outer garment esp. at a christening. **4** (often in pl.) a long outer garment worn as an indication of the wearer's rank, office, profession, etc.; a gown or vestment. **5** US a blanket or wrap of fur. —v. **1** tr. clothe (a person) in a robe; dress. **2** intr. put on one's robes or vestments. [ME f. OF f. Gmc (as ROB, orig. sense 'booty')]

robin /'rɒbɪn/ n. **1** (also **robin redbreast**) a small brown European bird, Erithacus rubecula, the adult of which has a red throat and breast. **2** US a red-breasted thrush, Turdus migratorius. **3** a bird similar in appearance etc. to either of these. ▫**Robin Hood** (with ref. to the legend of the medieval forest outlaw) a person who acts illegally or unfavourably towards the rich for the benefit of the poor. [ME f. OF, familiar var. of the name Robert]

robinia /rə'bɪnɪə/ n. any N. American tree or shrub of the genus Robinia, e.g. a locust tree or false acacia. [mod.L, f. J. Robin, 17th-c. French gardener]

roborant /'rəubərənt, 'rɒb-/ adj. & n. Med. —adj. strengthening. —n. a strengthening drug. [L roborare f. robur -oris strength]

robot /'rəubɒt/ n. **1** a machine with a human appearance or functioning like a human. **2** a machine capable of carrying out a complex series of actions automatically. **3** a person who works mechanically and efficiently but insensitively. **4** S.Afr. an automatic traffic-signal. ▫▫**robotic** /-'bɒtɪk/ adj. **robotize** v.tr. (also **-ise**). [Czech (in K. Čapek's play R.U.R. (Rossum's Universal Robots) 1920), f. robota forced labour]

robotics /rəu'bɒtɪks/ n.pl. the study of robots; the art or science of their design and operation.

robust /rəu'bʌst/ adj. (**robuster**, **robustest**) **1** (of a person, animal, or thing) strong and sturdy, esp. in physique or construction. **2** (of exercise, discipline, etc.) vigorous, requiring strength. **3** (of intellect or mental attitude) straightforward, not given to nor confused by subtleties. **4** (of a statement, reply, etc.) bold, firm, unyielding. **5** (of wine etc.) full-bodied. ▫▫**robustly** adv. **robustness** n. [F robuste or L robustus firm and hard f. robus, robur oak, strength]

ROC abbr. (in the UK) Royal Observer Corps.

roc /rɒk/ n. a gigantic bird of Eastern legend. [Sp. rocho ult. f. Arab ruḵ]

rocaille /rəu'kaɪ/ n. **1** an 18th-c. style of ornamentation based on rock and shell motifs. **2** a rococo style. [F f. roc (as ROCK¹)]

rocambole /'rɒkəm,bəul/ n. an alliaceous plant, Allium scorodoprasum, with a garlic-like bulb used for seasoning. [F f. G Rockenbolle]

roche moutonnée /,rɒʃ mu:'tɒneɪ/ n. Geol. a small bare outcrop of rock shaped by glacial erosion. [F, = fleecy rock]

rochet /'rɒtʃɪt/ n. a vestment resembling a surplice, used chiefly by bishops and abbots. [ME f. OF, dimin. f. Gmc]

rock¹ /rɒk/ n. **1 a** the hard material of the earth's crust, exposed on the surface or underlying the soil. **b** a similar material on other planets. **2** Geol. any natural material, hard or soft (e.g. clay), consisting of one or more minerals. **3 a** a mass of rock projecting and forming a hill, cliff, reef, etc. **b** (**the Rock**) Gibraltar. **4** a large detached stone. **5** US a stone of any size. **6** a firm and dependable support or protection. **7** a source of danger or destruction. **8** Brit. a hard usu. cylindrical stick of confectionery

made from sugar with flavouring esp. of peppermint. **9** (in pl.) US sl. money. **10** sl. a precious stone, esp. a diamond. **11** sl. a solid form of cocaine. **12** (in pl.) coarse sl. the testicles. ▫**get one's rocks off** coarse sl. **1** achieve sexual satisfaction. **2** obtain enjoyment. **on the rocks** colloq. **1** short of money. **2** broken down. **3** (of a drink) served undiluted with ice-cubes. **rock-bed** a base of rock or a rocky bottom. **rock-bottom** adj. (of prices etc.) the very lowest. —n. the very lowest level. **rock-bound** (of a coast) rocky and inaccessible. **rock-cake** a small currant cake with a hard rough surface. **rock-candy** US = sense 8 of n. **rock cress** = ARABIS. **rock-crystal** transparent colourless quartz usu. in hexagonal prisms. **rock-dove** a wild dove, Columba livia, frequenting rocks, supposed ancestor of the domestic pigeon. **rock-face** a vertical surface of natural rock. **rock-fish** a rock-frequenting goby, bass, wrasse, catfish, etc. **rock-garden** an artifical mound or bank of earth and stones planted with rock-plants etc.; a garden in which rockeries are the chief feature. **rock-pigeon** = rock-dove. **rock-pipit** a species of pipit, Anthus spinoletta, frequenting rocky shores. **rock-plant** any plant growing on or among rocks. **rock python** any large snake of the family Boidae, esp. the African python Python sebae. **rock-rabbit** any of several species of hyrax. **rock rose** any plant of the genus Cistus, Helianthemum, etc., with rose-like flowers. **rock-salmon 1** any of several fishes, esp. Brit. (as a commercial name) the catfish and dogfish. **2** US an amberjack. **rock-salt** common salt as a solid mineral. **rock-wool** inorganic material made into matted fibre esp. for insulation or soundproofing. ▫▫**rockless** adj. **rocklet** n. **rocklike** adj. [ME f. OF ro(c)que, roche, med.L rocca, of unkn. orig.]

rock² /rɒk/ v. & n. —v. **1** tr. move gently to and fro in or as if in a cradle; set or maintain such motion (rock him to sleep; the ship was rocked by the waves). **2** intr. be or continue in such motion (sat rocking in his chair; the ship was rocking on the waves). **3 a** intr. sway from side to side; shake, oscillate, reel (the house rocks). **b** tr. cause to do this (an earthquake rocked the house). **4** tr. distress, perturb. **5** intr. dance to or play rock music. —n. **1** a rocking movement (gave the chair a rock). **2** a spell of rocking (had a rock in his chair). **3 a** = rock and roll. **b** any of a variety of types of modern popular music with a rocking or swinging beat, derived from rock and roll. ▫**rock and** (or **rock 'n'**) **roll** a type of popular dance-music originating in the 1950s, characterized by a heavy beat and simple melodies, often with a blues element. **rock and** (or **rock 'n'**) **roller** a devotee of rock and roll. **rock the boat** colloq. disturb the equilibrium of a situation. **rocking-chair** a chair mounted on rockers or springs for gently rocking in. **rocking-horse** a model of a horse on rockers or springs for a child to rock on. **rocking-stone** a poised boulder easily rocked. **rock-shaft** a shaft that oscillates about an axis without making complete revolutions. [OE roccian, prob. f. Gmc]

rockabilly /'rɒkə,bɪlɪ/ n. a type of popular music combining elements of rock and roll and hill-billy music. [blend of rock and roll and hill-billy]

rockburst /'rɒkbɜːst/ n. a sudden rupture or collapse of highly stressed rock in a mine.

rocker /'rɒkə(r)/ n. **1** a person or thing that rocks. **2** a curved bar or similar support, on which something can rock. **3** a rocking-chair. **4** Brit. a young devotee of rock music, characteristically associated with leather clothing and motor cycles. **5** a skate with a highly curved blade. **6** a switch constructed on a pivot mechanism operating between the 'on' and 'off' positions. **7** any rocking device forming part of a mechanism. ▫**off one's rocker** sl. crazy.

rockery /'rɒkərɪ/ n. (pl. -ies) a heaped arrangement

of rough stones with soil between them for growing rock-plants on.

rocket[1] /'rɒkɪt/ *n. & v.* —*n.* **1** a cylindrical projectile that can be propelled to a great height or distance by combustion of its contents, used esp. as a firework or signal. **2** an engine using a similar principle but not dependent on air intake for its operation. **3** a rocket-propelled missile, spacecraft, etc. **4** *Brit. sl.* a severe reprimand. —*v.* (**rocketed, rocketing**) **1** *tr.* bombard with rockets. **2** *intr.* **a** move rapidly upwards or away. **b** increase rapidly (*prices rocketed*). [F *roquette* f. It. *rochetto* dimin. of *rocca* ROCK[2],· with ref. to its cylindrical shape]

rocket[2] /'rɒkɪt/ *n.* **1** (also **sweet rocket**) any of various fast-growing plants, esp. of the genus *Hesperis* or *Sisymbrium*. **2** a cruciferous annual plant, *Eruca sativa*, grown for salad. □**wall-rocket** a yellow-flowered weed, *Diplotaxis muralis*, emitting a foul smell when crushed. **yellow rocket** winter cress. [F *roquette* f. It. *rochetta, ruchetta* dimin. of *ruca* f. L *eruca* downy-stemmed plant]

rocketeer /ˌrɒkɪ'tɪə(r)/ *n.* **1** a discharger of rockets. **2** a rocket expert or enthusiast.

rocketry /'rɒkɪtrɪ/ *n.* the science or practice of rocket propulsion.

rockfall /'rɒkfɔːl/ *n.* **1** a descent of loose rocks. **2** a mass of fallen rock.

rockhopper /'rɒk,hɒpə(r)/ *n.* a small penguin, *Eudyptes crestatus*, of the Antarctic and New Zealand, with a crest of feathers on the forehead.

rockling /'rɒklɪŋ/ *n.* any of various small marine fish of the cod family, esp. of the genus *Ciliata* and *Rhinomenus*, found in pools among rocks.

rocky[1] /'rɒkɪ/ *adj. & n.* —*adj.* (**rockier, rockiest**) **1** of or like rock. **2** full of or abounding in rock or rocks (*a rocky shore*). —*n.* (**the Rockies**) the Rocky Mountains in western N. America. □□**rockiness** *n.*

rocky[2] /'rɒkɪ/ *adj.* (**rockier, rockiest**) *colloq.* unsteady, tottering. □□**rockily** *adv.* **rockiness** *n.* [ROCK[2]]

rococo /rə'kəʊkəʊ/ *adj. & n.* —*adj.* **1** of a late baroque style of decoration prevalent in 18th-c. continental Europe, with asymmetrical patterns involving scroll-work, shell motifs, etc. **2** (of literature, music, architecture, and the decorative arts) highly ornamented, florid. —*n.* the rococo style. [F, joc. alt. f. ROCAILLE]

rod /rɒd/ *n.* **1** a slender straight bar esp. of wood or metal. **2** this as a symbol of office. **3 a** a stick or bundle of twigs used in caning or flogging. **b** (prec. by *the*) the use of this. **4 a** = *fishing-rod.* **b** an angler using a rod. **5 a** a slender straight round stick growing as a shoot on a tree. **b** this when cut. **6** (as a measure) a perch or square perch (see PERCH[1]). **7** *US sl.* = *hot rod.* **8** *US sl.* a pistol or revolver. **9** *Anat.* any of numerous rod-shaped structures in the eye, detecting dim light. □**make a rod for one's own back** act in a way that will bring one trouble later. □□**rodless** *adj.* **rodlet** *n.* **rodlike** *adj.* [OE *rodd*, prob. rel. to ON *rudda* club]

rode[1] *past of* RIDE.

rode[2] /rəʊd/ *v.intr.* **1** (of wildfowl) fly landwards in the evening. **2** (of woodcock) fly in the evening during the breeding season. [18th c.: orig. unkn.]

rodent /'rəʊd(ə)nt/ *n. & adj.* —*n.* any mammal of the order Rodentia with strong incisors and no canine teeth, e.g. rat, mouse, squirrel, beaver, porcupine. —*adj.* **1** of the order Rodentia. **2** gnawing (esp. *Med.* of slow-growing ulcers). □**rodent officer** *Brit.* an official dealing with rodent pests. □□**rodential** /-'denʃ(ə)l/ *adj.* [L *rodere ros-* gnaw]

rodenticide /rə'dentɪˌsaɪd/ *n.* a poison used to kill rodents.

rodeo /'rəʊdɪəʊ, rə'deɪəʊ/ *n.* (*pl.* **-os**) **1** an exhibition or entertainment involving cowboys' skills in handling animals. **2** an exhibition of other skills, e.g. in motor cycling. **3 a** a round-up of cattle on a ranch for branding etc. **b** an enclosure for this. [Sp. f. *rodear* go round ult. f. L *rotare* ROTATE[1]]

rodham /'rɒdəm/ *n.* a raised bank in the Fen district of E. Anglia, formed on the bed of a dry river-course. [20th c.: orig. uncert.]

rodomontade /ˌrɒdəmɒn'teɪd/ *n., adj., & v.* —*n.* **1** boastful or bragging talk or behaviour. **2** an instance of this. —*adj.* boastful or bragging. —*v.intr.* brag, talk boastfully. [F f. obs. It. *rodomontada* f. F *rodomont* & It. *rodomonte* f. the name of a boastful character in the *Orlando* epics]

roe[1] /rəʊ/ *n.* **1** (also **hard roe**) the mass of eggs in a female fish's ovary. **2** (also **soft roe**) the milt of a male fish. □**roe-stone** oolite. □□**roed** *adj.* (also in *comb.*). [ME *row*(*e*), *rough*, f. MLG, MDu. *roge*(*n*), OHG *rogo, rogan*, ON *hrogn*]

roe[2] /rəʊ/ *n.* (*pl.* same or **roes**) (also **roe-deer**) a small European and Asian deer, *Capreolus capreolus*. [OE *rā*(*ha*)]

roebuck /'rəʊbʌk/ *n.* a male roe.

roentgen /'rʌntjən/ *n.* a unit of ionizing radiation, the amount producing one electrostatic unit of positive or negative ionic charge in one cubic centimetre of air under standard conditions. □**roentgen rays** X-rays. [W. C. *Röntgen*, Ger. physicist d. 1923, discoverer of X-rays]

roentgenography /ˌrʌntjə'nɒgrəfɪ/ *n.* photography using X-rays.

roentgenology /ˌrʌntjə'nɒlədʒɪ/ *n.* = RADIOLOGY.

rogation /rəʊ'geɪʃ(ə)n/ *n.* (usu. in *pl.*) *Eccl.* a solemn supplication consisting of the litany of the saints chanted on the three days before Ascension day. □**Rogation Days** the three days before Ascension Day. **Rogation Sunday** the Sunday preceding these. □□**rogational** *adj.* [ME f. L *rogatio* f. *rogare* ask]

roger /'rɒdʒə(r)/ *int. & v.* —*int.* **1** your message has been received and understood (used in radio communication etc.). **2** *sl.* I agree. —*v. coarse sl.* **1** *intr.* have sexual intercourse. **2** *tr.* have sexual intercourse with (a woman). [the name *Roger*, code for *R*]

rogue /rəʊg/ *n. & v.* —*n.* **1** a dishonest or unprincipled person. **2** *joc.* a mischievous person, esp. a child. **3** (usu. *attrib.*) **a** a wild animal driven away or living apart from the herd and of fierce temper (*rogue elephant*). **b** a stray, irresponsible, or undisciplined person or thing (*rogue trader*). **4** an inferior or defective specimen among many acceptable ones. —*v.tr.* remove rogues (sense 4 of *n.*) from. □**rogues' gallery** a collection of photographs of known criminals etc., used for identification of suspects. [16th-c. cant word: orig. unkn.]

roguery /'rəʊgərɪ/ *n.* (*pl.* **-ies**) conduct or an action characteristic of rogues.

roguish /'rəʊgɪʃ/ *adj.* **1** playfully mischievous. **2** characteristic of rogues. □□**roguishly** *adv.* **roguishness** *n.*

roil /rɔɪl/ *v.tr.* **1** make (a liquid) turbid by agitating it. **2** *US* = RILE 1. [perh. f. OF *ruiler* mix mortar f. LL *regulare* regulate]

roister /'rɔɪstə(r)/ *v.intr.* (esp. as **roistering** *adj.*) revel noisily; be uproarious. □□**roisterer** *n.* **roistering** *n.* **roisterous** *adj.* (obs. *roister* roisterer f. F *rustre* ruffian var. of *ruste* f. L *rusticus* RUSTIC]

Roland /'rəʊlənd/ *n.* □**a Roland for an Oliver 1** an effective retort. **2** a well-balanced combat or exchange. [name of the legendary nephew of Charlemagne celebrated with his comrade Oliver in the *Chanson de Roland*]

role /rəʊl/ *n.* (also **rôle**) **1** an actor's part in a play, film, etc. **2** a person's or thing's characteristic or expected function (*the role of the tape recorder in language-learning*). □**role model** a person looked to by others as an example in a particular role. **role-playing** an exercise in which participants act the part of another character, used in psychotherapy, language-teaching, etc. [F *rôle* and obs. F *roule, rolle,* = ROLL *n.*]

roll /rəʊl/ v. & n. —v. **1 a** intr. move or go in some direction by turning over and over on an axis (the ball rolled under the table; a barrel started rolling). **b** tr. cause to do this (rolled the barrel into the cellar). **2** tr. make revolve between two surfaces (rolled the clay between his palms). **3 a** intr. (foll. by along, by, etc.) move or advance on or (of time etc.) as if on wheels etc. (the bus rolled past; the pram rolled off the pavement; the years rolled by). **b** tr. cause to do this (rolled the tea trolley into the kitchen). **c** intr. (of a person) be conveyed in a vehicle (the farmer rolled by on his tractor). **4 a** tr. turn over and over on itself to form a more or less cylindrical or spherical shape (rolled a newspaper). **b** tr. make by forming material into a cylinder or ball (rolled a cigarette; rolled a huge snowball). **c** tr. accumulate into a mass (rolled the dough into a ball). **d** tr. (foll. by into) make a specified shape of itself (the hedgehog rolled into a ball). **5** tr. flatten or form by passing a roller etc. over or by passing between rollers (roll the lawn; roll pastry; roll thin foil). **6** intr. & tr. change or cause to change direction by rotatory movement (his eyes rolled; he rolled his eyes). **7** intr. **a** wallow, turn about in a fluid or a loose medium (the dog rolled in the dust). **b** (of a horse etc.) lie on its back and kick about, esp. in an attempt to dislodge its rider. **8** intr. **a** (of a moving ship, aircraft, or vehicle) sway to and fro on an axis parallel to the direction of motion. **b** walk with an unsteady swaying gait (they rolled out of the pub). **9 a** intr. undulate, show or go with an undulating surface or motion (rolling hills; rolling mist; the waves roll in). **b** tr. carry or propel with such motion (the river rolls its waters to the sea). **10 a** intr. (of machinery) start functioning or moving (the cameras rolled; the train began to roll). **b** tr. cause (machinery) to do this. **11** intr. & tr. sound or utter with a vibratory or trilling effect (words rolled off his tongue; thunder rolled in the distance; he rolls his rs). **12** US sl. **a** tr. overturn (a car etc.). **b** intr. (of a car etc.) overturn. **13** tr. US throw (dice). **14** tr. sl. rob (esp. a helpless victim). —n. **1** a rolling motion or gait; undulation (the roll of the hills). **2 a** a spell of rolling (a roll in the mud). **b** a gymnastic exercise in which the body is rolled into a tucked position and turned in a forward or backward circle. **c** (esp. a **roll in the hay**) colloq. an act of sexual intercourse or erotic fondling. **3** the continuous rhythmic sound of thunder or a drum. **4** Aeron. a complete revolution of an aircraft about its longitudinal axis. **5 a** a cylinder formed by turning flexible material over and over on itself without folding (a roll of carpet; a roll of wallpaper). **b** a filled cake or pastry of similar form (fig roll; sausage roll). **6 a** a small portion of bread individually baked. **b** this with a specified filling (ham roll). **7** a more or less cylindrical or semicylindrical straight or curved mass of something (rolls of fat; a roll of hair). **8 a** an official list or register (the electoral roll). **b** the total numbers on this (the schools' rolls have fallen). **c** a document, esp. an official record, in scroll form. **9** a cylinder or roller, esp. to shape metal in a rolling-mill. **10** Archit. **a** a moulding of convex section. **b** a spiral scroll of an Ionic capital. **11** US & Austral. money, esp. as banknotes rolled together. □ **be rolling** colloq. be very rich. **be rolling in** colloq. have plenty of (esp. money). **on a roll** US sl. experiencing a bout of success or progress; engaged in a period of intense activity. **roll back** US cause (esp. prices) to decrease. **roll-back** n. a reduction (esp. in price). **roll bar** an overhead metal bar strengthening the frame of a vehicle (esp. in racing) and protecting the occupants if the vehicle overturns. **roll-call** a process of calling out a list of names to establish who is present. **rolled gold** gold in the form of a thin coating applied to a baser metal by rolling. **rolled into one** combined in one person or thing. **rolled oats** oats that have been husked and crushed. **roll in** arrive in great numbers or quantity. **rolling barrage** = creeping barrage.

rolling drunk swaying or staggering from drunkenness. **rolling-mill** a machine or factory for rolling metal into shape. **rolling-pin** a cylinder for rolling out pastry, dough, etc. **rolling-stock 1** the locomotives, carriages, or other vehicles, used on a railway. **2** US the road vehicles of a company. **rolling stone** a person who is unwilling to settle for long in one place. **rolling strike** industrial action through a series of limited strikes by consecutive groups. **roll-neck** (of a garment) having a high loosely turned-over neck. **roll of honour** a list of those honoured, esp. the dead in war. **roll on** v.tr. **1** put on or apply by rolling. **2** (in imper.) colloq. (of a time, in eager expectation) come quickly (roll on Friday!). **roll-on** (attrib.) (of deodorant etc.) applied by means of a rotating ball in the neck of the container. —n. a light elastic corset. **roll-on roll-off** (of a ship, a method of transport, etc.) in which vehicles are driven directly on at the start of the voyage and off at the end of it. **roll over 1** send (a person) sprawling or rolling. **2** Econ. finance the repayment of (maturing stock etc.) by an issue of new stock. **roll-over** n. **1** Econ. the extension or transfer of a debt or other financial relationship. **2** colloq. the overturning of a vehicle etc. **roll-top desk** a desk with a flexible cover sliding in curved grooves. **roll up 1** colloq. arrive in a vehicle; appear on the scene. **2** make into or form a roll. **3** Mil. drive the flank of (an enemy line) back and round so that the line is shortened or surrounded. **roll-up** (or **roll-your-own**) n. a hand-rolled cigarette. **roll up one's sleeves** see SLEEVE. **strike off the rolls** debar (esp. a solicitor) from practising after dishonesty etc. □□ **rollable** adj. [ME f. OF rol(l)er, rouler, ro(u)lle f. L rotulus dimin. of rota wheel]

rollaway /'rəʊləˌweɪ/ adj. US (of a bed etc.) that can be removed on wheels or castors.

roller /'rəʊlə(r)/ n. **1 a** a hard revolving cylinder for smoothing the ground, spreading ink or paint, crushing or stamping, rolling up cloth on, hanging a towel on, etc., used alone or as a rotating part of a machine. **b** a cylinder for diminishing friction when moving a heavy object. **2** a small cylinder on which hair is rolled for setting. **3** a long swelling wave. **4** (also **roller bandage**) a long surgical bandage rolled up for convenient application. **5** a kind of tumbler-pigeon. **6 a** any brilliantly plumaged bird of the family Coraciidae, with characteristic tumbling display-flight. **b** a breed of canary with a trilling song. □ **roller bearing** a bearing like a ball-bearing but with small cylinders instead of balls. **roller-coaster** n. a switchback at a fair etc. —adj. that goes up and down, or changes, suddenly and repeatedly. —v.intr. (or **roller-coast**) go up and down or change in this way. **roller-skate** see SKATE[1]. **roller-skater** a person who roller-skates. **roller towel** a towel with the ends joined, hung on a roller.

rollerball /'rəʊləˌbɔːl/ n. a ball-point pen using thinner ink than other ball-points.

rollick /'rɒlɪk/ v. & n. —v.intr. (esp. as **rollicking** adj.) be jovial or exuberant, indulge in high spirits, revel. —n. **1** exuberant gaiety. **2** a spree or escapade. [19th-c., prob. dial.: perh. f. ROMP + FROLIC]

rollmop /'rəʊlmɒp/ n. a rolled uncooked pickled herring fillet. [G Rollmops]

roly-poly /ˌrəʊlɪ'pəʊlɪ/ n. & adj. —n. (pl. **-ies**) **1** (also **roly-poly pudding**) a pudding made of a strip of suet pastry covered with jam etc., formed into a roll, and boiled or baked. **2** US a tumbler toy. **3** Austral. a bushy plant, esp. Salsola kali, that breaks off and is rolled by the wind. —adj. (usu. of a child) podgy, plump. [prob. formed on ROLL]

ROM /rɒm/ n. Computing read-only memory. [abbr.]

Rom /rɒm/ n. (pl. **Roma** /'rɒmə/) a male gypsy. [Romany, = man, husband]

Rom. abbr. Romans (New Testament).

rom. abbr. roman (type).

Romaic /rəʊ'meɪɪk/ n. & adj. —n. the vernacular

language of modern Greece. —*adj.* of or relating to this language. [Gk *Rhōmaikos* Roman (used esp. of the Eastern Empire)]

romaine /rə'meɪn/ *n. US* a cos lettuce. [F, fem. of *romain* (as ROMAN)]

romaji /'rəʊmədʒɪ/ *n.* a system of Romanized spelling used to transliterate Japanese. [Jap.]

Roman /'rəʊmən/ *adj. & n.* —*adj.* **1 a** of ancient Rome or its territory or people. **b** *archaic* of its language. **2** of medieval or modern Rome. **3** of papal Rome, esp. = ROMAN CATHOLIC. **4** of a kind ascribed to the early Romans (*Roman honesty*; *Roman virtue*). **5** surviving from a period of Roman rule (*Roman road*). **6** (**roman**) (of type) of a plain upright kind used in ordinary print. **7** (of the alphabet etc.) based on the ancient Roman system with letters A–Z. —*n.* **1 a** a citizen of the ancient Roman Republic or Empire. **b** a soldier of the Roman Empire. **2** a citizen of modern Rome. **3** = ROMAN CATHOLIC. **4** (**roman**) roman type. **5** (in *pl.*) the Christians of ancient Rome. □**Holy Roman Empire** the Western part of the Roman Empire as revived by Charlemagne in 800. **Roman candle** a firework discharging a series of flaming coloured balls and sparks. **Roman Empire** *hist.* that established by Augustus in 27 BC and divided by Theodosius in AD 395 into the Western or Latin and Eastern or Greek Empire. **Roman holiday** enjoyment derived from others' discomfiture. **Roman law** the law-code developed by the ancient Romans and forming the basis of many modern codes. **Roman nose** one with a high bridge; an aquiline nose. **roman numeral** any of the Roman letters representing numbers: I = 1, V = 5, X = 10, L = 50, C = 100, D = 500, M = 1000. [ME f. OF *Romain* (n. & adj.) f. L *Romanus* f. *Roma* Rome]

roman-à-clef /rəʊmaːnaːˈkleɪ/ *n.* (*pl.* **romans-à-clef** *pronunc.* same) a novel in which real persons or events appear with invented names. [F, = novel with a key]

Roman Catholic *adj. & n.* —*adj.* of the part of the Christian Church acknowledging the Pope as its head. —*n.* a member of this Church. □□ **Roman Catholicism** *n.* [17th-c. transl. L (*Ecclesia*) *Romana Catholica* (*et Apostolica*), app. orig. as a conciliatory term: see ROMAN, CATHOLIC]

romance /rə'mæns/ *n., adj., & v.* —*n.* / also *disp.* 'rəʊ-/ **1** an atmosphere or tendency characterized by a sense of remoteness from or idealization of everyday life. **2 a** a prevailing sense of wonder or mystery surrounding the mutual attraction in a love affair. **b** sentimental or idealized love. **c** a love affair. **3 a** a literary genre with romantic love or highly imaginative unrealistic episodes forming the central theme. **b** a work of this genre. **4** a medieval tale, usu. in verse, of some hero of chivalry, of the kind common in the Romance languages. **5 a** exaggeration or picturesque falsehood. **b** an instance of this. **6** (**Romance**) the languages descended from Latin regarded collectively. **7** *Mus.* a short informal piece. —*adj.* (**Romance**) of any of the languages descended from Latin (French, Italian, Spanish, etc.). —*v.* **1** *intr.* exaggerate or distort the truth, esp. fantastically. **2** *tr.* court, woo. [ME f. OF *romanz, -ans, -ance,* ult. f. L *Romanicus* ROMANIC]

romancer /rə'mænsə(r)/ *n.* **1** a writer of romances, esp. in the medieval period. **2** a liar who resorts to fantasy.

Romanesque /ˌrəʊmə'nesk/ *n. & adj.* —*n.* a style of architecture prevalent in Europe *c.*900–1200, with massive vaulting and round arches (cf. NORMAN). —*adj.* of the Romanesque style of architecture. [F f. *roman* ROMANCE]

roman-fleuve /ˌrəʊmãˈflɜːv/ *n.* (*pl.* **romans-fleuves** *pronunc.* same) **1** a novel featuring the leisurely description of the lives of members of a family etc. **2** a sequence of self-contained novels. [F, = river novel]

Romanian /rəʊ'meɪnɪən/ *n. & adj.* (also **Rumanian** /ruː-/) —*n.* **1 a** a native or national of Romania in E.

Europe. **b** a person of Romanian descent. **2** the language of Romania. —*adj.* of or relating to Romania or its people or language.

Romanic /rəʊ'mænɪk/ *n. & adj.* —*n.* = ROMANCE *n.* 6. —*adj.* **1 a** of or relating to Romance. **b** Romance-speaking. **2** descended from the ancient Romans or inheriting aspects of their social or political life. [L *Romanicus* (as ROMAN)]

Romanism /'rəʊmə,nɪz(ə)m/ *n.* Roman Catholicism.

Romanist /'rəʊmənɪst/ *n.* **1** a student of Roman history or law or of the Romance languages. **2 a** a supporter of Roman Catholicism. **b** a Roman Catholic. [mod.L *Romanista* (as ROMAN)]

romanize /'rəʊmə,naɪz/ *v.tr.* (also **-ise**) **1** make Roman or Roman Catholic in character. **2** put into the Roman alphabet or into roman type. □□ **romanization** /-'zeɪʃ(ə)n/ *n.*

Romano /rəʊ'maːnəʊ/ *n.* a strong-tasting hard cheese, orig. made in Italy. [It., = ROMAN]

Romano- /rəʊ'maːnəʊ/ *comb. form* Roman; Roman and (*Romano-British*).

Romansh /rəʊ'mænʃ, -'maːnʃ/ *n. & adj.* (also **Rumansh** /ruː-/) —*n.* the Rhaeto-Romanic dialects, esp. as spoken in the Swiss canton of Grisons. —*adj.* of these dialects. [Romansh *Ruman(t)sch, Roman(t)sch* f. med.L *romanice* (adv.) (as ROMANCE)]

romantic /rəʊ'mæntɪk/ *adj. & n.* —*adj.* **1** of, characterized by, or suggestive of an idealized, sentimental, or fantastic view of reality; remote from experience (*a romantic picture*; *a romantic setting*). **2** inclined towards or suggestive of romance in love (*a romantic woman*; *a romantic evening*; *romantic words*). **3** (of a person) imaginative, visionary, idealistic. **4 a** (of style in art, music, etc.) concerned more with feeling and emotion than with form and aesthetic qualities; preferring grandeur or picturesqueness to finish and proportion. **b** (also **Romantic**) of or relating to the 18th-19th-c. romantic movement or style in the European arts. **5** (of a project etc.) unpractical, fantastic. —*n.* **1** a romantic person. **2** a romanticist. □□ **romantically** *adv.* [*romant* tale of chivalry etc. f. OF f. *romanz* ROMANCE]

romanticism /rəʊ'mæntɪ,sɪz(ə)m/ *n.* (also **Romanticism**) adherence to a romantic style in art, music, etc.

romanticist /rəʊ'mæntɪsɪst/ *n.* (also **Romanticist**) a writer or artist of the romantic school.

romanticize /rəʊ'mæntɪ,saɪz/ *v.* (also **-ise**) **1** *tr.* **a** make or render romantic or unreal (*a romanticized account of war*). **b** describe or portray in a romantic fashion. **2** *intr.* indulge in romantic thoughts or actions. □□ **romanticization** /-'zeɪʃ(ə)n/ *n.*

Romany /'rɒmənɪ, 'rəʊ-/ *n. & adj.* —*n.* (*pl.* **-ies**) **1 a** Gypsy. **2** the Indo-European language of the Gypsies. —*adj.* **1** of or concerning Gypsies. **2** of the Romany language. [Romany *Romani* fem. and pl. of *Romano* (adj.) (ROM)]

Romeo /'rəʊmɪəʊ/ *n.* (*pl.* **-os**) a passionate male lover or seducer. [the hero of Shakesp. *Romeo and Juliet*]

Romish /'rəʊmɪʃ/ *adj.* usu. *derog.* Roman Catholic.

romneya /'rɒmnɪə/ *n.* any shrub of the genus *Romneya,* bearing poppy-like flowers. [T. *Romney* Robinson, Brit. astronomer d. 1882]

romp /rɒmp/ *v. & n.* —*v.intr.* **1** play about roughly and energetically. **2** (foll. by *along, past,* etc.) *colloq.* proceed without effort. —*n.* a spell of romping or boisterous play. □**romp in** (or **home**) *colloq.* finish as the easy winner. □□ **rompingly** *adv.* **rompy** *adj.* (**rompier, rompiest**). [perh. var. of RAMP¹]

romper /'rɒmpə(r)/ *n.* (usu. in *pl.*) (also **romper suit**) a young child's one-piece garment covering legs and trunk.

rondavel /rɒn'daːvel/ *n. S.Afr.* **1** a round tribal hut usu. with a thatched conical roof. **2** a similar building, esp. as a holiday cottage, or as an outbuilding on a farm etc. [Afrik. *rondawel*]

ronde /rɒnd/ *n.* **1** a dance in which the dancers move in a circle. **2** a course of talk, activity, etc. [F, fem. of *rond* ROUND *adj.*]

rondeau /'rɒndəʊ/ *n.* (*pl.* **rondeaux** *pronunc.* same or /-əʊz/) a poem of ten or thirteen lines with only two rhymes throughout and with the opening words used twice as a refrain. [F, earlier *rondel*: see RONDEL]

rondel /'rɒnd(ə)l/ *n.* a rondeau, esp. one of special form. [ME f. OF f. *rond* ROUND: cf. ROUNDEL]

rondo /'rɒndəʊ/ *n.* (*pl.* **-os**) *Mus.* a form with a recurring leading theme, often found in the final movement of a sonata or concerto etc. [It. f. F *rondeau*: see RONDEAU]

rone /rəʊn/ *n. Sc.* a gutter for carrying off rain from a roof.

ronin /'rəʊnɪn/ *n. hist.* (in feudal Japan) a lordless wandering samurai; an outlaw. [Jap.]

röntgen etc. var. of ROENTGEN etc.

roo /ruː/ *n.* (also **'roo**) *Austral. colloq.* a kangaroo. [abbr.]

rood /ruːd/ *n.* **1** a crucifix, esp. one raised on a screen or beam at the entrance to the chancel. **2** a quarter of an acre. □**rood-loft** a gallery on top of a rood-screen. **rood-screen** a wooden or stone carved screen separating nave and chancel. [OE *rōd*]

roof /ruːf/ *n. & v.* —*n.* (*pl.* **roofs** or *disp.* **rooves** /ruːvz/) **1 a** the upper covering of a building, usu. supported by its walls. **b** the top of a covered vehicle. **c** the top inner surface of an oven, refrigerator, etc. **2** the overhead rock in a cave or mine etc. **3** the branches or the sky etc. overhead. **4** (of prices etc.) the upper limit or ceiling. —*v.tr.* **1** (often foll. by *in*, *over*) cover with or as with a roof. **2** be the roof of. □**go through the roof** *colloq.* (of prices etc.) reach extreme or unexpected heights. **hit** (or **go through** or **raise**) **the roof** *colloq.* become very angry. **roof-garden** a garden on the flat roof of a building. **roof of the mouth** the palate. **a roof over one's head** somewhere to live. **roof-rack** a framework for carrying luggage etc. on the roof of a vehicle. **roof-tree** the ridge-piece of a roof. **under one roof** in the same building. **under a person's roof** in a person's house (esp. with ref. to hospitality). □□ **roofed** *adj.* (also in *comb.*). **roofless** *adj.* [OE *hrōf*]

roofage /'ruːfɪdʒ/ *n.* the expanse of a roof or roofs.

roofer /'ruːfə(r)/ *n.* a person who constructs or repairs roofs.

roofing /'ruːfɪŋ/ *n.* **1** material for constructing a roof. **2** the process of constructing a roof or roofs.

roofscape /'ruːfskeɪp/ *n.* a scene or view of roofs.

rooftop /'ruːftɒp/ *n.* **1** the outer surface of a roof. **2** (esp. in *pl.*) the level of a roof.

rooibos /'rɔɪbɒs/ *n. S.Afr.* **1** an evergreen shrub of the genus *Aspalathus*, with leaves used to make tea. **2** a shrub or small tree, *Combretum apiculatum*, with spikes of scented yellow flowers. [Afrik., = red bush]

rooinek /'rɔɪnek/ *n. S.Afr. sl. offens.* a British or English-speaking South African. [Afrik., = red-neck]

rook[1] /rʊk/ *n. & v.* —*n.* **1** a black European and Asiatic bird, *Corvus frugilegus*, of the crow family, nesting in colonies in tree-tops. **2** a sharper, esp. at dice or cards; a person who lives off inexperienced gamblers etc. —*v.tr.* **1** charge (a customer) extortionately. **2** win money from (a person) at cards etc. esp. by swindling. [OE *hrōc*]

rook[2] /rʊk/ *n.* a chess piece with its top in the shape of a battlement. [ME f. OF *roc(k)* ult. f. Arab. *rukk*, orig. sense uncert.]

rookery /'rʊkərɪ/ *n.* (*pl.* **-ies**) **1 a** a colony of rooks. **b** a clump of trees having rooks' nests. **2** a colony of sea birds (esp. penguins) or seals.

rookie /'rʊkɪ/ *n. sl.* **1** a new recruit, esp. in the army or police. **2** *US* a new member of a sports team. [corrupt. of *recruit*, after ROOK[1]]

room /ruːm, rʊm/ *n. & v.* —*n.* **1** a space that is or might be occupied by something; capaciousness or ability to accommodate contents (*it takes up too much room*; *there is plenty of room*; *we have no room here for idlers*). **b** space in or on (*houseroom*; *shelf-room*).

2 a a part of a building enclosed by walls or partitions, floor and ceiling. **b** (in *pl.*) a set of these occupied by a person or family; apartments or lodgings. **c** persons present in a room (*the room fell silent*). **3** (in *comb.*) a room or area for a specified purpose (*auction-room*). **4** (foll. by *for*, or *to* + infin.) opportunity or scope (*room to improve things*; *no room for dispute*). —*v.intr. US* have a room or rooms; lodge, board. □**make room** (often foll. by *for*) clear a space (for a person or thing) by removal of others; make way, yield place. **not** (or **no**) **room to swing a cat** a very confined space. **rooming-house** a lodging house. **room-mate** a person occupying the same room as another. **room service** (in a hotel etc.) service of food or drink taken to a guest's room. □□ **-roomed** *adj.* (in *comb.*). **roomful** *n.* (*pl.* **-fuls**). [OE *rūm* f. Gmc]

roomer /'ruːmə(r), 'rʊmə(r)/ *n. US* a lodger occupying a room or rooms without board.

roomette /ruː'met, rʊ-/ *n. US* **1** a private single compartment in a sleeping-car. **2** a small bedroom for letting.

roomie /'ruːmɪ/ *n. US colloq.* a room-mate.

roomy /'ruːmɪ/ *adj.* (**roomier**, **roomiest**) having much room, spacious. □□ **roomily** *adv.* **roominess** *n.*

roost[1] /ruːst/ *n. & v.* —*n.* **1** a branch or other support on which a bird perches, esp. a place where birds regularly settle to sleep. **2** a place offering temporary sleeping-accommodation. —*v.* **1** *intr.* **a** (of a bird) settle for rest or sleep. **b** (of a person) stay for the night. **2** *tr.* provide with a sleeping-place. □**come home to roost** (of a scheme etc.) recoil unfavourably upon the originator. [OE *hrōst*]

roost[2] /ruːst/ *n.* a tidal race in the Orkneys and Shetlands. [ON *röst*]

rooster /'ruːstə(r)/ *n.* esp. *US* a domestic cock.

root[1] /ruːt/ *n. & v.* —*n.* **1 a** the part of a plant normally below the ground, attaching it to the earth and conveying nourishment to it from the soil. **b** (in *pl.*) such a part divided into branches or fibres. **c** the corresponding organ of an epiphyte; the part attaching ivy to its support. **d** the permanent underground stock of a plant. **e** any small plant with a root for transplanting. **2** any plant, e.g. a turnip or carrot, with an edible root. **b** such a root. **3** (in *pl.*) the sources of or reasons for one's long-standing emotional attachment to a place, community, etc. **4 a** the embedded part of a bodily organ or structure, e.g. hair, tooth, nail, etc. **b** the part of a thing attaching it to a greater or more fundamental whole. **c** (in *pl.*) the base of a mountain etc. **5 a** the basic cause, source, or origin (*love of money is the root of all evil*; *has its roots in the distant past*). **b** (*attrib.*) (of an idea etc.) from which the rest originated. **6** the basis of something, its means of continuance or growth (*has its root(s) in selfishness*; *has no root in the nature of things*). **7** the essential substance or nature of something (*get to the root of things*). **8** *Math.* **a** a number or quantity that when multiplied by itself a usu. specified number of times gives a specified number or quantity (*the cube root of eight is two*). **b** a square root. **c** a value of an unknown quantity satisfying a given equation. **9** *Philol.* any ultimate unanalysable element of language; a basis, not necessarily surviving as a word in itself, on which words are made by the addition of prefixes or suffixes or by other modification. **10** *Mus.* the fundamental note of a chord. **11** *Bibl.* a scion, an offshoot (*there shall be a root of Jesse*). **12** *Austral. & NZ coarse sl.* **a** an act of sexual intercourse. **b** a (female) sexual partner. —*v.* **1 a** *intr.* take root or grow roots. **b** *tr.* cause to do this (*take care to root them firmly*). **2** *tr.* **a** fix firmly; establish (*fear rooted him to the spot*). **b** (as **rooted** *adj.*) firmly established (*her affection was deeply rooted*; *rooted objection to*). **3** *tr.* (usu. foll. by *out*, *up*) drag or dig up by the roots. **4** *tr. Austral. coarse sl.* **a** have sexual intercourse with (a woman). **b** exhaust, frustrate. □**pull up by the roots 1** uproot. **2** eradicate, destroy. **put down roots 1** begin to draw nourishment from the soil. **2** become settled or established. **root and branch** thorough(ly), radical(ly). **root beer** *US* an effervescent drink made from an extract of roots. **root-mean-square** *Math.* the square root of the arithmetic mean of the squares of a set of values. **root out** find and get rid of. **root sign** *Math.* = *radical sign.* **strike at the root** (or **roots**) **of** set about destroying. **strike** (or **take**) **root 1** begin to grow and draw nourishment from the soil. **2** become fixed or established. □□**rootage** *n.* **rootedness** *n.* **rootless** *adj.* **rootlet** *n.* **rootlike** *adj.* **rooty** *adj.* [OE *rōt* f. ON *rót*, rel. to WORT & L *radix*: see RADIX]

root² /ruːt/ *v.* **1 a** *intr.* (of an animal, esp. a pig) turn up the ground with the snout, beak, etc., in search of food. **b** *tr.* (foll. by *up*) turn up (the ground) by rooting. **2 a** *intr.* (foll. by *around*, *in*, etc.) rummage. **b** *tr.* (foll. by *out* or *up*) find or extract by rummaging. **3** *intr.* (foll. by *for*) *US sl.* encourage by applause or support. □□**rooter** *n.* (in sense 3). [earlier *wroot* f. OE *wrōtan* & ON *róta*: rel. to OE *wrōt* snout]

rootle /ˈruːt(ə)l/ *v.intr.* & *tr. Brit.* = ROOT² 1, 2. [ROOT²]

rootstock /ˈruːtstɒk/ *n.* **1** a rhizome. **2** a plant into which a graft is inserted. **3** a primary form from which offshoots have arisen.

rooves see ROOF.

rope /rəʊp/ *n.* & *v.* —*n.* **1 a** stout cord made by twisting together strands of hemp, sisal, flax, cotton, nylon, wire, or similar material. **b** a piece of this. **c** *US* a lasso. **2** (foll. by *of*) a quantity of onions, ova, or pearls strung together. **3** (in *pl.*, prec. by *the*) **a** the conditions in some sphere of action (*know the ropes; show a person the ropes*). **b** the ropes enclosing a boxing- or wrestling-ring or cricket ground. **4** (prec. by *the*) **a** a halter for hanging a person. **b** execution by hanging. —*v.* **1** *tr.* fasten, secure, or catch with rope. **2** *tr.* (usu. foll. by *off*, *in*) enclose (a space) with rope. **3** *Mountaineering* **a** *tr.* connect (a party) with a rope; attach (a person) to a rope. **b** (*absol.*) put on a rope. **c** *intr.* (foll. by *down*, *up*) climb down or up using a rope. □**give a person plenty of rope** (or **enough rope to hang himself** or **herself**) give a person enough freedom of action to bring about his or her own downfall. **on the rope** *Mountaineering* roped together. **on the ropes 1** *Boxing* forced against the ropes by the opponent's attack. **2** near defeat. **rope in** persuade to take part. **rope into** persuade to take part in (*was roped into doing the washing-up*). **rope-ladder** two long ropes connected by short crosspieces, used as a ladder. **rope-moulding** a moulding cut spirally in imitation of rope-strands. **rope of sand** delusive security. **rope's end** *hist.* a short piece of rope used to flog (formerly, esp. a sailor) with. **rope-walk** a long piece of ground where ropes are made. **rope-walker** a performer on a tightrope. **rope-walking** the action of performing on a tightrope. **rope-yard** a rope-making establishment. **rope-yarn 1** material obtained by unpicking rope-strands, or used for making them. **2** a piece of this. **3** a mere trifle. [OE *rāp* f. Gmc]

ropeable /ˈrəʊpəb(ə)l/ *adj.* (also **ropable**) **1** capable of being roped. **2** *Austral.* & *NZ sl.* angry.

ropemanship /ˈrəʊpmənʃɪp/ *n.* skill in rope-walking or climbing with ropes.

ropeway /ˈrəʊpweɪ/ *n.* a cable railway.

roping /ˈrəʊpɪŋ/ *n.* a set or arrangement of ropes.

ropy /ˈrəʊpɪ/ *adj.* (also **ropey**) (**ropier**, **ropiest**) **1** *Brit. colloq.* poor in quality. **2** (of wine, bread, etc.) forming viscous or gelatinous threads. **3** like a rope. □□**ropily** *adv.* **ropiness** *n.*

roque /rəʊk/ *n. US* croquet played on a hard court surrounded by a bank. [alt. form of ROQUET]

Roquefort /ˈrɒkfɔː(r)/ *n. propr.* **1** a soft blue cheese made from ewes' milk. **2** a salad-dressing made of this. [*Roquefort* in S. France]

roquet /ˈrəʊkeɪ, -kɪ/ *v.* & *n. Croquet* —*v.* (**roqueted,**

roqueting) **1** *tr.* **a** cause one's ball to strike (another ball). **b** (of a ball) strike (another). **2** *intr.* strike another ball thus. —*n.* an instance of roqueting. [app. arbitr. f. CROQUET *v.*, orig. used in the same sense]

ro-ro /ˈrəʊrəʊ/ *adj.* roll-on roll-off. [abbr.]

rorqual /ˈrɔːkw(ə)l/ *n.* any of various whales of the family Balaenopteridae esp. *Balaenoptera musculus*, having a dorsal fin. Also called *fin-back*, *fin whale*. [F f. Norw. *røyrkval* f. OIcel. *reythr* the specific name + *hvalr* WHALE¹]

Rorschach test /ˈrɔːʃɑːk/ *n. Psychol.* a type of personality test in which a standard set of ink-blots is presented one by one to the subject, who is asked to describe what they suggest or resemble. [H. *Rorschach*, Swiss psychiatrist d. 1922]

rort /rɔːt/ *n. Austral. sl.* **1** a trick, a fraud; a dishonest practice. **2** a wild party. [back-form. f. RORTY]

rorty /ˈrɔːtɪ/ *adj.* (**rortier**, **rortiest**) *Brit. sl.* **1** splendid; boisterous, rowdy (*had a rorty time*). **2** coarse, earthy. [19th c.: orig. unkn.]

rosace /ˈrəʊzeɪs/ *n.* **1** a rose-window. **2** a rose-shaped ornament or design. [F f. L *rosaceus*: see ROSACEOUS]

rosaceous /rəʊˈzeɪʃəs/ *adj. Bot.* of the large plant family Rosaceae, which includes the rose. [L *rosaceus* f. *rosa* rose]

rosaline /ˈrəʊzəˌliːn/ *n.* a variety of fine needlepoint or pillow lace. [prob. F]

rosaniline /rəʊˈzænɪˌliːn, -lɪn, -ˌlaɪn/ *n.* **1 a** an organic base derived from aniline. **b** a red dye obtained from this. **2** fuchsine. [ROSE¹ + ANILINE]

rosarian /rəˈzeərɪən/ *n.* a person who cultivates roses, esp. professionally. [L *rosarium* ROSARY]

rosarium /rəˈzeərɪəm/ *n.* a rose-garden. [L (as ROSARY)]

rosary /ˈrəʊzərɪ/ *n.* (*pl.* **-ies**) **1** *RC Ch.* **a** a form of devotion in which five (or fifteen) decades of Hail Marys are repeated, each decade preceded by an Our Father and followed by a Glory Be. **b** a string of 55 (or 165) beads for keeping count in this. **c** a book containing this devotion. **2** a similar form of bead-string used in other religions. **3** a rose-garden or rose-bed. [ME f. L *rosarium* rose-garden, neut. of *rosarius* (as ROSE¹)]

roscoe /ˈrɒskəʊ/ *n. US sl.* a gun, esp. a pistol or revolver. [the name *Roscoe*]

rose¹ /rəʊz/ *n.*, *adj.*, & *v.* —*n.* **1** any prickly bush or shrub of the genus *Rosa*, bearing usu. fragrant flowers generally of a red, pink, yellow, or white colour. **2** this flower. **3** any flowering plant resembling this (*Christmas rose; rock rose*). **4 a** a light crimson colour, pink. **b** (usu. in *pl.*) a rosy complexion (*roses in her cheeks*). **5 a** a representation of the flower in heraldry or decoration (esp. as the national emblem of England). **b** a rose-shaped design, e.g. on a compass card or on the sound-hole of a lute etc. **6** the sprinkling-nozzle of a watering-can or hose. **7** a circular mounting on a ceiling through which the wiring of an electric light passes. **8 a** a rose diamond. **b** a rose-window. **9** (in *pl.*) used in various phrases to express favourable circumstances, ease, success, etc. (*roses all the way; everything's roses*). **10** an excellent person or thing, esp. a beautiful woman (*English rose; rose between two thorns; not the rose but near it*). —*adj.* = *rose-coloured* 1. —*v.tr.* (esp. as **rosed** *adj.*) make (one's face, a snow-slope, etc.) rosy. □**rose-apple 1** a tropical tree of the genus *Eugenia*, cultivated for its foliage and fragrant fruit. **2** this fruit. **rose-bush** a rose plant. **rose-chafer** a green or copper-coloured beetle, *Cetonia aurata*, frequenting roses. **rose-colour** the colour of a pale red rose, warm pink. **rose-coloured 1** of rose-colour. **2** optimistic, sanguine, cheerful (*takes rose-coloured views*). **rose comb** a flat fleshy comb of a fowl. **rose-cut** cut as a rose diamond. **rose diamond** a hemispherical diamond with the curved part cut in triangular facets. **rose-engine** an appendage to a lathe for engraving curved patterns. **rose-fish** a bright red food fish, *Sebastes marinus*, of the N. Atlantic. **rose geranium** a pink-flowered sweet-scented pelargonium, *Pelargonium graveolus*. **rose-hip** = HIP². **rose-leaf** (*pl.* -leaves) **1** a petal of a rose. **2** a leaf of a rose. **rose madder** a pale pink pigment. **rose-mallow** = HIBISCUS. **rose nail** a nail with a head shaped like a rose diamond. **rose of Jericho** a resurrection plant, *Anastatica hierochuntica*. **rose of Sharon 1** a species of hypericum, *Hypericum calycinum*, with dense foliage and golden-yellow flowers: also called AARON'S BEARD. **2** *Bibl.* a flowering plant of unknown identity. **rose-pink** = *rose-colour*, *rose-coloured*. **rose-point** a point lace with a design of roses. **rose-red** *adj.* red like a rose, rose-coloured. — *n.* this colour. **rose-root** a yellow-flowered plant, *Rhodiola rosea*, with roots smelling like a rose when dried or bruised. **rose-tinted** = *rose-coloured*. **rose-tree** a rose plant, esp. a standard rose. **rose-water** perfume made from roses. **rose-window** a circular window, usu. with roselike or spokelike tracery. **see through rose-coloured** (or **-tinted**) **spectacles** regard (circumstances etc.) with unfounded favour or optimism. **under the rose** in confidence; under pledge of secrecy. **Wars of the Roses** *hist.* the 15th-c. civil wars between Yorkists with a white rose as an emblem and Lancastrians with a red rose. □□ **roseless** *adj.* **roselike** *adj.* [ME f. OE *rōse* f. L *rosa*]

rose² *past of* RISE.

rosé /ˈrəʊzeɪ/ *n.* any light pink wine, coloured by only brief contact with red grape-skins. [F, = pink]

roseate /ˈrəʊzɪət/ *adj.* **1** = *rose-coloured* (see ROSE¹). **2** having a partly pink plumage (*roseate spoonbill*; *roseate tern*). [L *roseus* rosy (as ROSE¹)]

rosebay /ˈrəʊzbeɪ/ *n.* an oleander, rhododendron, or willow-herb.

rosebowl /ˈrəʊzbəʊl/ *n.* a bowl for displaying cut roses.

rosebud /ˈrəʊzbʌd/ *n.* **1** a bud of a rose. **2** a pretty young woman.

rosella /rəˈzelə/ *n.* **1** any brightly coloured Australian parakeet of the genus *Platycercus*. **2** *Austral.* an easily-shorn sheep. [corrupt. of *Rosehill*, NSW, where the bird was first found]

rosemaling /ˈrəʊzəˌmɑːlɪŋ, -ˌmɔːlɪŋ/ *n.* the art of painting wooden furniture etc. with flower motifs. [Norw., = rose painting]

rosemary /ˈrəʊzmərɪ/ *n.* an evergreen fragrant shrub, *Rosmarinus officinalis*, with leaves used as a culinary herb, in perfumery, etc., and taken as an emblem of remembrance. [ME, earlier *rosmarine* ult. f. L *ros marinus* f. *ros* dew + *marinus* MARINE, with assim. to ROSE¹ and *Mary* name of the Virgin]

roseola /rəʊˈziːələ/ *n.* **1** a rosy rash in measles and similar diseases. **2** a mild febrile disease of infants. □□ **roseolar** *adj.* **roseolous** *adj.* [mod. var. of RUBEOLA f. L *roseus* rose-coloured]

rosery /ˈrəʊzərɪ/ *n.* (*pl.* -ies) a rose-garden.

Rosetta stone /rəʊˈzetə/ *n.* a key to previously unattainable understanding. [a stone found near *Rosetta* in Egypt, with a trilingual inscription of the 2nd c. BC in Egyptian hieroglyphs, demotic, and Greek, important in the decipherment of hieroglyphs]

rosette /rəʊˈzet/ *n.* **1** a rose-shaped ornament made usu. of ribbon and worn esp. as a supporter's badge, or as an award or the symbol of an award in a competition, esp. by a prizewinning animal. **2** *Archit.* **a** a carved or moulded ornament resembling or representing a rose. **b** a rose-window. **3** an object or symbol or arrangement of parts resembling a rose. **4** *Biol.* **a** a roselike cluster of parts. **b** markings resembling a rose. **5** a rose diamond. □□ **rosetted** *adj.* [F dimin. of *rose* ROSE¹]

rosewood /ˈrəʊzwʊd/ *n.* any of several fragrant close-grained woods used in making furniture.

Rosh Hashana /rɒʃ ˌhɑːʃəˈnɑː, rəʊʃ həˈʃəʊnəʊ/ *n.*

(also **Rosh Hashanah**) the Jewish New Year. [Heb., = beginning (lit. 'head') of the year]

Roshi /ˈrəʊʃɪ/ *n.* (*pl.* **Roshis**) the spiritual leader of a community of Zen Buddhist monks. [Jap.]

Rosicrucian /ˌrəʊzɪˈkruːʃ(ə)n/ *n.* & *adj.* — *n.* **1** *hist.* a member of a 17th–18th-c. society devoted to the study of metaphysical and mystical lore (said to have been founded in 1484 by Christian Rosenkreuz). **2** a member of any of several later organizations deriving from this. — *adj.* of or relating to the Rosicrucians. □□ **Rosicrucianism** *n.* [mod.L *rosa crucis* (or *crux*), as Latinization of G *Rosenkreuz*]

rosin /ˈrɒzɪn/ *n.* & *v.* — *n.* resin, esp. the solid residue after distillation of oil of turpentine from crude turpentine. — *v.tr.* (**rosined, rosining**) **1** rub (esp. the bow of a violin etc.) with rosin. **2** smear or seal up with rosin. □□ **rosiny** *adj.* [ME, alt. f. RESIN]

rosolio /rəˈzəʊlɪəʊ/ *n.* (also **rosoglio**) (*pl.* -os) a sweet cordial of spirits, sugar, and flavouring. [It., f. mod.L *ros solis* dew of the sun]

RoSPA /ˈrɒspə/ *abbr.* (in the UK) Royal Society for the Prevention of Accidents.

roster /ˈrɒstə(r), ˈrəʊstə(r)/ *n.* & *v.* — *n.* a list or plan showing turns of duty or leave for individuals or groups esp. of a military force. — *v.tr.* place on a roster. [Du. *rooster* list, orig. gridiron f. *roosten* ROAST, with ref. to its parallel lines]

rostra *pl. of* ROSTRUM.

rostral /ˈrɒstr(ə)l/ *adj.* **1** *Zool.* & *Bot.* of or on the rostrum. **2** *Anat.* **a** nearer the hypophysial area in the early embryo. **b** nearer the region of the nose and mouth in post-embryonic life. **3** (of a column etc.) adorned with the beaks of ancient war-galleys or with representations of these. □□ **rostrally** *adv.*

rostrated /rɒˈstreɪtɪd/ *adj.* **1** *Zool.* & *Bot.* having or ending in a rostrum. **2** = ROSTRAL 3. [L *rostratus* (as ROSTRUM)]

rostrum /ˈrɒstrəm/ *n.* (*pl.* **rostra** /-strə/ or **rostrums**) **1 a** a platform for public speaking. **b** a conductor's platform facing the orchestra. **c** a similar platform for other purposes, e.g. for supporting a film or television camera. **2** *Zool.* & *Bot.* a beak, stiff snout, or beaklike part, esp. of an insect or arachnid. **3** *Rom. Antiq.* the beak of a war-galley. □□ (all in sense 2) **rostrate** /-strət/ *adj.* **rostriferous** /-ˈstrɪfərəs/ *adj.* **rostriform** *adj.* [L, = beak f. *rodere ros-* gnaw: orig. *rostra* (pl., in sense 1a) in the Roman forum adorned with beaks of captured galleys]

rosy /ˈrəʊzɪ/ *adj.* (**rosier, rosiest**) **1** coloured like a pink or red rose (esp. of the complexion as indicating good health, of a blush, wine, the sky, light, etc.). **2** optimistic, hopeful, cheerful (*a rosy future*; *a rosy attitude to life*). □□ **rosily** *adv.* **rosiness** *n.*

rot /rɒt/ *v.*, *n.*, & *int.* — *v.* (**rotted, rotting**) **1** *intr.* **a** (of animal or vegetable matter) lose its original form by the chemical action of bacteria, fungi, etc.; decay. **b** (foll. by *off*, *away*) crumble or drop from a stem etc. through decomposition. **2** *intr.* **a** (of society, institutions, etc.) gradually perish from lack of vigour or use. **b** (of a prisoner etc.) waste away (*left to rot in prison*); (of a person) languish. **3** *tr.* cause to rot, make rotten. **4** *tr. Brit. sl.* tease, abuse, denigrate. **5** *intr. Brit. sl.* joke. — *n.* **1** the process or state of rotting. **2** *sl.* nonsense; an absurd or foolish statement, argument, or proposal. **3** a sudden series of (usu. unaccountable) failures; a rapid decline in standards etc. (*a rot set in*; *we must try to stop the rot*). **4** (often prec. by *the*) a virulent liver-disease of sheep. — *int.* expressing incredulity or ridicule. □ **rot-gut** *sl.* cheap harmful alcoholic liquor. [OE *rotian* (v.): (n.) ME, perh. f. Scand.: cf. Icel., Norw. *rot*]

rota /ˈrəʊtə/ *n.* **1** esp. *Brit.* a list of persons acting, or duties to be done, in rotation; a roster. **2** (**Rota**) *RC Ch.* the supreme ecclesiastical and secular court. [L, = wheel]

Rotarian /rəʊˈteərɪən/ *n.* & *adj.* — *n.* a member of Rotary. — *adj.* of Rotary. [ROTARY + -AN]

rotary /ˈrəʊtərɪ/ *adj. & n.* —*adj.* acting by rotation (*rotary drill*; *rotary pump*). —*n.* (*pl.* **-ies**) **1** a rotary machine. **2** *US* a traffic roundabout. **3** (**Rotary**) (in full **Rotary International**) a worldwide charitable society of businessmen, orig. named from members entertaining in rotation. □**Rotary club** a local branch of Rotary. **rotary-wing** (of an aircraft) deriving lift from rotary aerofoils. [med.L *rotarius* (as ROTA)]

rotate¹ /rəʊˈteɪt/ *v.* **1** *intr. & tr.* move round an axis or centre, revolve. **2** *a tr.* take or arrange in rotation. **b** *intr.* act or take place in rotation (*the chairmanship will rotate*). □□**rotatable** *adj.* **rotative** /ˈrəʊtətɪv/ *adj.* **rotatory** /ˈrəʊtətərɪ, -ˈteɪtərə/ *adj.* [L *rotare* f. *rota* wheel]

rotate² /ˈrəʊteɪt/ *adj. Bot.* wheel-shaped. [formed as ROTA]

rotation /rəʊˈteɪʃ(ə)n/ *n.* **1** the act or an instance of rotating or being rotated. **2** a recurrence; a recurrent series or period; a regular succession of various members of a group in office etc. **3** a system of growing different crops in regular order to avoid exhausting the soil. □□**rotational** *adj.* **rotationally** *adv.* [L *rotatio*]

rotator /rəʊˈteɪtə(r)/ *n.* **1** a machine or device for causing something to rotate. **2** *Anat.* a muscle that rotates a limb etc. **3** a revolving apparatus or part. [L (as ROTATE¹)]

Rotavator /ˈrəʊtəˌveɪtə(r)/ *n.* (also **Rotovator**) *propr.* a machine with a rotating blade for breaking up or tilling the soil. □□**rotavate** *v.tr.* [ROTARY + CULTIVATOR]

rote /rəʊt/ *n.* (usu. prec. by *by*) mechanical or habitual repetition (with ref. to acquiring knowledge). [ME: orig. unkn.]

rotenone /ˈrəʊtəˌnəʊn/ *n.* a toxic crystalline substance obtained from the roots of derris and other plants, used as an insecticide. [Jap. *rotenon* f. *roten* derris]

rotifer /ˈrəʊtɪfə(r)/ *n.* any minute aquatic animal of the phylum Rotifera, with rotatory organs used in swimming and feeding. [mod.L *rotiferus* f. L *rota* wheel + *-fer* bearing]

rotisserie /rəʊˈtɪsərɪ/ *n.* **1** a restaurant etc. where meat is roasted or barbecued. **2** a cooking appliance with a rotating spit for roasting and barbecuing meat. [F *rôtisserie* (as ROAST)]

rotogravure /ˌrəʊtəɡrəˈvjʊə(r)/ *n.* **1** a printing system using a rotary press with intaglio cylinders, usu. running at high speed. **2** a sheet etc. printed with this system. [G *Rotogravur* (name of a company) assim. to PHOTOGRAVURE]

rotor /ˈrəʊtə(r)/ *n.* **1** a rotary part of a machine, esp. in the distributor of an internal-combustion engine. **2** a set of radiating aerofoils round a hub on a helicopter, providing lift when rotated. [irreg. for ROTATOR]

Rotovator var. of ROTAVATOR.

rotten /ˈrɒt(ə)n/ *adj.* (**rottener**, **rottenest**) **1** rotting or rotted; falling to pieces or liable to break or tear from age or use. **2** morally, socially, or politically corrupt. **3** *sl.* disagreeable, unpleasant (*had a rotten time*). **b** (of a plan etc.) ill-advised, unsatisfactory (*a rotten idea*). **c** disagreeably ill (*feel rotten today*). □**rotten borough** *hist.* (before 1832) an English borough able to elect an MP though having very few voters. **rotten-stone** decomposed siliceous limestone used as a powder for polishing metals. □□**rottenly** *adv.* **rottenness** *n.* [ME f. ON *rotinn*, rel. to ROT, RET]

rotter /ˈrɒtə(r)/ *n.* esp. *Brit. sl.* an objectionable, unpleasant, or reprehensible person. [ROT]

Rottweiler /ˈrɒtˌvaɪlə(r), -ˌwaɪlə(r)/ *n.* **1** a dog of a tall black-and-tan breed. **2** this breed. [G f. *Rottweil* in SW Germany]

rotund /rəʊˈtʌnd/ *adj.* **1 a** circular, round. **b** (of a person) large and plump, podgy. **2** (of speech, literary style, etc.) sonorous, grandiloquent. □□**rotundity** *n.* **rotundly** *adv.* [L *rotundus* f. *rotare* ROTATE¹]

rotunda /rəʊˈtʌndə/ *n.* **1** a building with a circular ground-plan, esp. one with a dome. **2** a circular hall or room. [earlier *rotonda* f. It. *rotonda* (*camera*) round (chamber), fem. of *rotondo* round (as ROTUND)]

rouble /ˈruːb(ə)l/ *n.* (also **ruble**) the chief monetary unit of the USSR. [F f. Russ. *rubl'*]

roué /ˈruːeɪ/ *n.* a debauchee, esp. an elderly one; a rake. [F, past part. of *rouer* break on wheel, = one deserving this]

rouge /ruːʒ/ *n. & v.* —*n.* **1** a red powder or cream used for colouring the cheeks. **2** powdered ferric oxide etc. as a polishing agent esp. for metal. —*v.* **1** *tr.* colour with rouge. **2** *intr.* **a** apply rouge to one's cheeks. **b** become red, blush. □**rouge-et-noir** /ˌruːʒˈnwɑː(r)/ a gambling game using a table with red and black marks, on which players place stakes. [F, = red, f. L *rubeus*, rel. to RED]

rough /rʌf/ *adj., adv., n., & v.* —*adj.* **1 a** having an uneven or irregular surface, not smooth or level or polished. **b** *Tennis* applied to the side of a racket from which the twisted gut projects. **2** (of ground, country, etc.) having many bumps, obstacles, etc. **3 a** hairy, shaggy. **b** (of cloth) coarse in texture. **4 a** (of a person or behaviour) not mild or quiet or gentle; boisterous, unrestrained (*rough manners*; *rough play*). **b** (of language etc.) coarse, indelicate. **c** (of wine etc.) sharp or harsh in taste. **5** (of the sea, weather, etc.) violent, stormy. **6** disorderly, riotous (*a rough part of town*). **7** harsh, insensitive, inconsiderate (*rough words*; *rough treatment*). **8 a** unpleasant, severe, demanding (*had a rough time*). **b** unfortunate, unreasonable, undeserved (*had rough luck*). **c** (foll. by *on*) hard or unfair towards. **9** lacking finish, elaboration, comfort, etc. (*rough lodgings*; *a rough welcome*). **10** incomplete, rudimentary (*a rough attempt*; *a rough makeshift*). **11 a** inexact, approximate, preliminary (*a rough estimate*; *a rough sketch*). **b** (of stationery etc.) for use in writing rough notes etc. **12** *colloq.* **a** ill, unwell (*am feeling rough*). **b** depressed, dejected. —*adv.* in a rough manner (*the land should be ploughed rough*; *play rough*). —*n.* **1** (usu. prec. by *the*) a hard part or aspect of life; hardship (*take the rough with the smooth*). **2** rough ground (*over rough and smooth*). **3** a rough or violent person (*met a bunch of roughs*). **4** *Golf* rough ground off the fairway between tee and green. **5** an unfinished or provisional or natural state (*have written it in rough*; *shaped from the rough*). **6** (prec. by *the*) the general way or tendency (*is true in the rough*). —*v.tr.* **1** (foll. by *up*) ruffle (feathers, hair, etc.) by rubbing against the grain. **2 a** (foll. by *out*) shape or plan roughly. **b** (foll. by *in*) sketch roughly. **3** give the first shaping to (a gun, lens, etc.). □**rough-and-ready** rough or crude but effective; not elaborate or over-particular. **rough-and-tumble** *adj.* irregular, scrambling, disorderly. —*n.* a haphazard fight; a scuffle. **rough breathing** see BREATHING. **rough coat** a first coat of plaster applied to a surface. **rough copy 1** a first or original draft. **2** a copy of a picture etc. showing only the essential features. **rough deal** hard or unfair treatment. **rough diamond 1** an uncut diamond. **2** a person of good nature but rough manners. **rough-dry** (**-dries**, **-dried**) dry (clothes) without ironing. **the rough edge** (or **side**) **of one's tongue** severe or harsh words. **rough-handle** treat or handle roughly. **rough-hew** (*past part.* **-hewed** or **-hewn**) shape out roughly; give crude form to. **rough-hewn** uncouth, unrefined. **rough house** *sl.* a disturbance or row; boisterous play. **rough-house** *v. sl.* **1** *tr.* handle (a person) roughly. **2** *intr.* make a disturbance; act violently. **rough it** do without basic comforts. **rough justice 1** treatment that is approximately fair. **2** treatment that is not at all fair. **rough passage 1** a crossing over rough sea. **2** a difficult time or experience. **rough ride** a difficult time or experience. **rough-rider** a person who breaks in or can ride unbroken horses. **rough stuff** *colloq.* boisterous or violent behaviour. **rough tongue** a habit of rudeness in speaking. **rough trade** *sl.* a tough or sadistic element among male homosexuals. **rough up** *sl.* treat (a person) with violence; attack violently. **rough work** **1** preliminary or provisional work. **2** *colloq.* violence. **3** a task requiring the use of force. **sleep rough** sleep outdoors, or not in a proper bed. □□ **roughness** *n.* [OE *rūh* f. WG]

roughage /ˈrʌfɪdʒ/ *n.* **1** coarse material with a high fibre content, the part of food which stimulates digestion. **2** coarse fodder. [ROUGH + -AGE 3]

roughcast /ˈrʌfkɑːst/ *n.*, *adj.*, & *v.* —*n.* plaster of lime and gravel, used on outside walls. —*adj.* **1** (of a wall etc.) coated with roughcast. **2** (of a plan etc.) roughly formed, preliminary. —*v.tr.* (*past* and *past part.* -**cast**) **1** coat (a wall) with roughcast. **2** prepare (a plan, essay, etc.) in outline.

roughen /ˈrʌf(ə)n/ *v.tr.* & *intr.* make or become rough.

roughie /ˈrʌfɪ/ *n. dial. sl.* **1** a rough; a hooligan. **2** *Austral.* **a** an outsider. **b** an unfair or unreasonable act.

roughish /ˈrʌfɪʃ/ *adj.* somewhat rough.

roughly /ˈrʌflɪ/ *adv.* **1** in a rough manner. **2** approximately (*roughly 20 people attended*). □ **roughly speaking** in an approximate sense (*it is, roughly speaking, a square*).

roughneck /ˈrʌfnek/ *n. colloq.* **1** a rough or rowdy person. **2** a worker on an oil rig.

roughshod /ˈrʌfʃɒd/ *adj.* (of a horse) having shoes with nail-heads projecting to prevent slipping. □ **ride roughshod over** treat inconsiderately or arrogantly.

roughy /ˈrʌfɪ/ *n.* (*pl.* -**ies**) *Austral.* & *NZ* a fish, *Arripis georgianus*, of the perch family. [perh. f. ROUGH]

roulade /ruːˈlɑːd/ *n.* **1** a dish cooked or served in the shape of a roll, esp. a rolled piece of meat or sponge with a filling. **2** a florid passage of runs etc. in solo vocal music, usu. sung to one syllable. [F f. *rouler* to roll]

rouleau /ˈruːləʊ/ *n.* (*pl.* **rouleaux** or **rouleaus** /-əʊz/) **1** a cylindrical packet of coins. **2** a coil or roll of ribbon etc., esp. as trimming. [F f. *rôle* ROLL *n.*]

roulette /ruːˈlet/ *n.* **1** a gambling game using a table in which a ball is dropped on to a revolving wheel with numbered compartments, players betting on the number at which the ball comes to rest. **2** *Math.* a curve generated by a point on a curve rolling on another. **3 a** a revolving toothed wheel used in engraving. **b** a similar wheel for making perforations between postage stamps in a sheet. □□ **rouletted** *adj.* (in sense 3b). [F, dimin. of *rouelle* f. LL *rotella* dimin. of L *rota* wheel]

round /raʊnd/ *adj.*, *n.*, *adv.*, *prep.*, & *v.* —*adj.* **1** shaped like or approximately like a circle, sphere, or cylinder; having a convex or circular outline or surface; curved, not angular. **2** done with or involving circular motion. **3 a** entire, continuous, complete (*a round dozen*); fully expressed or developed; all together, not broken or defective or scanty. **b** (of a sum of money) considerable. **4** genuine, candid, outspoken; (of a statement etc.) categorical, unmistakable. **5** (usu. *attrib.*) (of a number) expressed for convenience or as an estimate in fewer significant numerals or with a fraction removed (*spent £297.32, or in round figures £300*). **6 a** (of a style) flowing. **b** (of a voice) not harsh. **7** *Phonet.* (of a vowel) pronounced with rounded lips. —*n.* **1** a round object or form. **2 a** a revolving motion, a circular or recurring course (*the earth in its yearly round*). **b** a regular recurring series of activities or functions (*one's daily round; a continuous round of pleasure*). **c** a recurring succession or series of meetings for discussion etc. (*a new round of talks on disarmament*).

3 a a fixed route on which things are regularly delivered (*milk round*). **b** a route or sequence by which people or things are regularly supervised or inspected (*a watchman's round; a doctor's rounds*). **4** an allowance of something distributed or measured out, esp.: **a** a single provision of drinks etc. to each member of a group. **b** ammunition to fire one shot; the act of firing this. **5 a** a slice across a loaf of bread. **b** a sandwich made from whole slices of bread. **c** a thick disc of beef cut from the haunch as a joint. **6** each of a set or series, a sequence of actions by each member of a group in turn, esp. **a** one spell of play in a game etc. **b** one stage in a competition. **7** *Golf* the playing of all the holes in a course once. **8** *Archery* a fixed number of arrows shot from a fixed distance. **9** (**the round**) a form of sculpture in which the figure stands clear of any ground (cf. RELIEF 6a). **10** *Mus.* a canon for three or more unaccompanied voices singing at the same pitch or in octaves. **11** (in *pl.*) *Mil.* **a** a watch that goes round inspecting sentries. **b** a circuit made by this. **12** a rung of a ladder. **13** (foll. by *of*) the circumference, bounds, or extent of (*in all the round of Nature*). —*adv.* **1** with circular motion (*wheels go round*). **2** with return to the starting-point or an earlier state (*summer soon comes round*). **3 a** with rotation, or change to an opposite position (*he turned round to look*). **b** with change to an opposite opinion etc. (*they were angry but I soon won them round*). **4** to, at, or affecting all or many points of a circumference or an area or the members of a company etc. (*tea was then handed round; may I look round?*). **5** in every direction from a centre or within a radius (*spread destruction round; everyone for a mile round*). **6** by a circuitous way (*will you jump over or go round?; go a long way round*). **7 a** to a person's house etc. (*ask him round; will be round soon*). **b** to a more prominent or convenient position (*brought the car round*). **8** measuring a (specified distance) in girth. —*prep.* **1** so as to encircle or enclose (*tour round the world; has a blanket round him*). **2** at or to points on the circumference of (*sat round the table*). **3** with successive visits to (*hawks them round the cafés*). **4** in various directions from or with regard to (*towns round Birmingham; shells bursting round them*). **5** having as an axis of revolution or as a central point (*turns round its centre of gravity; write a book round an event*). **6 a** so as to double or pass in a curved course (*go round the corner*). **b** having passed in this way (*be round the corner*). **c** in the position that would result from this (*find them round the corner*). **7** so as to come close from various sides but not into contact. —*v.* **1 a** *tr.* give a round shape to. **b** *intr.* assume a round shape. **2** *tr.* double or pass round (a corner, cape, etc.). **3** *tr.* express (a number) in a less exact but more convenient form (also foll. by *down* when the number is decreased and *up* when it is increased). **4** *tr.* pronounce (a vowel) with rounded lips. □ **go the round** (or **rounds**) (of news etc.) be passed on from person to person. **in the round 1** with all features shown; all things considered. **2** *Theatr.* with the audience round at least three sides of the stage. **3** (of sculpture) with all sides shown; not in relief. **make the round of** go round. **make** (or **go**) **one's rounds** take a customary route for inspection etc. **round about 1** in a ring (about); all round; on all sides (of). **2** with a change to an opposite position. **3** approximately (*cost round about £50*). **round and round** several times round. **round-arm** *Cricket* (of bowling) with the arm swung horizontally. **round the bend** see BEND¹. **round brackets** brackets of the form (). **round dance 1** a dance in which couples move in circles round the ballroom. **2** a dance in which the dancers form one large circle. **round down** see sense 3 of *v.* **round off** (or **out**) **1** bring to a complete or symmetrical or well-ordered state. **2** smooth out; blunt the corners or angles of. **round on a person** make a sudden verbal attack on or unexpected retort to a person. **round out** = *round off* 1. **round peg in a square hole** = *square peg in a round hole* (see PEG). **round robin** 1 a petition esp. with signatures written in a circle to conceal the order of writing. 2 *US* a tournament in which each competitor plays in turn against every other. **round-shouldered** with shoulders bent forward so that the back is rounded. **Round Table** (in allusion to that at which King Arthur and his knights sat so that none should have precedence) 1 an international charitable association which holds discussions, debates, etc., and undertakes community service. 2 (**round table**) an assembly for discussion, esp. at a conference (often *attrib.: round-table talks*). **round trip** a trip to one or more places and back again (esp. by a circular route). **round the twist** see TWIST. **round up** collect or bring together, esp. by going round (see also sense 3 of *v.*). **round-up** *n.* 1 a systematic rounding up of people or things. 2 a summary; a résumé of facts or events. □□ **roundish** *adj.* **roundness** *n.* [ME f. OF *ro(u)nd-* stem of *ro(o)nt*, *reont* f. L *rotundus* ROTUND]

roundabout /ˈraʊndəˌbaʊt/ *n. & adj.* —*n.* 1 *Brit.* a road junction at which traffic moves in one direction round a central island. 2 *Brit.* **a** a large revolving device in a playground, for children to ride on. **b** = MERRY-GO-ROUND 1. —*adj.* circuitous, circumlocutory, indirect.

roundel /ˈraʊnd(ə)l/ *n.* 1 a small disc, esp. a decorative medallion. 2 a circular identifying mark painted on military aircraft, esp. the red, white, and blue of the RAF. 3 a poem of eleven lines in three stanzas. [ME f. OF *rondel(le)* (as ROUND)]

roundelay /ˈraʊndɪˌleɪ/ *n.* a short simple song with a refrain. [F *rondelet* (as RONDEL), with assim. to LAY³ or *virelay*]

rounder /ˈraʊndə(r)/ *n.* 1 (in *pl.*; treated as *sing.*) a game with a bat and ball in which players after hitting the ball run through a round of bases. 2 a complete round of a player through all the bases as a unit of scoring in rounders.

Roundhead /ˈraʊndhed/ *n. hist.* a member of the Parliamentary party in the English Civil War. [f. their custom of wearing the hair cut short]

roundhouse /ˈraʊndhaʊs/ *n.* 1 a circular repairshed for railway locomotives, built round a turntable. 2 *sl.* a blow given with a wide sweep of the arm. **b** *US Baseball* a pitch made with a sweeping sidearm motion. 3 *hist.* a prison; a place of detention. 4 *Naut.* a cabin or set of cabins on the after part of the quarterdeck, esp. on a sailing-ship.

roundly /ˈraʊndlɪ/ *adv.* 1 bluntly, in plain language, severely (*was roundly criticized; told them roundly that he refused*). 2 in a thoroughgoing manner (*go roundly to work*). 3 in a circular way (*swells out roundly*).

roundsman /ˈraʊndzmən/ *n.* (*pl.* -**men**) 1 *Brit.* a tradesman's employee going round delivering and taking orders. 2 *US* a police officer in charge of a patrol. 3 *Austral.* a journalist covering a specified subject (*political roundsman*).

roundworm /ˈraʊndwɜːm/ *n.* a worm, esp. a nematode, with a rounded body.

roup¹ /raʊp/ *n. & v. Sc. & N.Engl.* —*n.* an auction. —*v.tr.* sell by auction. [ME 'to shout', of Scand. orig.]

roup² /ruːp/ *n.* an infectious poultry-disease, esp. of the respiratory tract. □□ **roupy** *adj.* [16th c.: orig. unkn.]

rouse /raʊz/ *v.* 1 **a** *tr.* (often foll. by *from, out of*) bring out of sleep, wake. **b** *intr.* (often foll. by *up*) cease to sleep, wake up. 2 (often foll. by *up*) **a** *tr.* stir up, make active or excited, startle out of inactivity or confidence or carelessness (*roused them from their complacency; was roused to protest*). **b** *intr.* become active. 3 *tr.* provoke to anger (*is terrible when roused*). 4 *tr.* evoke (feelings). 5 *tr.* (usu. foll. by *in, out, up*) *Naut.* haul vigorously. 6 *tr.* startle (game) from a lair or cover. 7 *tr.* stir (liquid, esp. beer while

brewing). □ **rouse oneself** overcome one's indolence. □□ **rousable** *adj.* **rouser** *n.* [orig. as a hawking and hunting term, so prob. f. AF: orig. unkn.]

rouseabout /ˈraʊzəˌbaʊt/ *n. Austral. & NZ* an unskilled labourer or odd jobber, esp. on a farm.

rousing /ˈraʊzɪŋ/ *adj.* 1 exciting, stirring (*a rousing cheer; a rousing song*). 2 (of a fire) blazing strongly. □□ **rousingly** *adv.*

roust /raʊst/ *v.tr.* 1 (often foll. by *up, out*) **a** rouse, stir up. **b** root out. 2 *US sl.* jostle, harass, rough up. □ **roust around** rummage. [perh. alt. of ROUSE]

roustabout /ˈraʊstəˌbaʊt/ *n.* 1 a labourer on an oil rig. 2 an unskilled or casual labourer. 3 *US* a dock labourer or deck hand. 4 *Austral.* = ROUSEABOUT.

rout¹ /raʊt/ *n. & v.* —*n.* 1 a disorderly retreat of defeated troops. 2 **a** an assemblage or company esp. of revellers or rioters. **b** *Law* an assemblage of three or more persons who have made a move towards committing an illegal act. 3 riot, tumult, disturbance, clamour, fuss. 4 *Brit. archaic* a large evening party or reception. —*v.tr.* put to rout. □ **put to rout** put to flight, defeat utterly. [ME f. AF *rute*, OF *route* ult. f. L *ruptus* broken]

rout² /raʊt/ *v.* 1 *intr. & tr.* = ROOT². 2 *tr.* cut a groove, or any pattern not extending to the edges, in (a wooden or metal surface). □ **rout out** force or fetch out of bed or from a house or hiding-place. [var. of ROOT²]

route /ruːt, *Mil.* also raʊt/ *n. & v.* —*n.* 1 a way or course taken (esp. regularly) in getting from a starting-point to a destination. 2 *US* a round travelled in delivering, selling, or collecting goods. 3 *Mil. archaic* marching orders. —*v.tr.* (**routeing**) send or forward or direct to be sent by a particular route. □ **route man** *US* = ROUNDSMAN 1. **route march** a training-march for troops. [ME f. OF *r(o)ute* road ult. f. L *ruptus* broken]

router /ˈraʊtə(r)/ *n.* a type of plane with two handles used in routing.

routine /ruːˈtiːn/ *n., adj., & v.* —*n.* 1 a regular course or procedure, an unvarying performance of certain acts. 2 a set sequence in a performance, esp. a dance, comedy act, etc. 3 *Computing* a sequence of instructions for performing a task. —*adj.* 1 performed as part of a routine (*routine duties*). 2 of a customary or standard kind. —*v.tr.* organize according to a routine. □□ **routinely** *adv.* [F (as ROUTE)]

routinism /ruːˈtiːnɪz(ə)m/ *n.* the prevalence of routine. □□ **routinist** *n. & adj.*

routinize /ruːˈtiːnaɪz/ *v.tr.* (also -**ise**) subject to a routine; make into a matter of routine. □□ **routinization** /-ˈzeɪʃ(ə)n/ *n.*

roux /ruː/ *n.* (*pl.* same) a mixture of fat (esp. butter) and flour used in making sauces etc. [F, = browned (butter): see RUSSET]

rove¹ /rəʊv/ *v. & n.* —*v.* 1 *intr.* wander without a settled destination, roam, ramble. 2 *intr.* (of eyes) look in changing directions. 3 *tr.* wander over or through. —*n.* an act of roving (*on the rove*). □ **rove-beetle** any long-bodied beetle of the family Staphylinidae, usu. found in decaying animal and vegetable matter. **roving commission** authority given to a person or persons conducting an inquiry to travel as may be necessary. **roving eye** a tendency to ogle or towards infidelity. [ME, orig. a term in archery = shoot at a casual mark with the range not determined, perh. f. dial. *rave* stray, prob. of Scand. orig.]

rove² *past of* REEVE².

rove³ /rəʊv/ *n. & v.* —*n.* a sliver of cotton, wool, etc., drawn out and slightly twisted. —*v.tr.* form into roves. [18th c.: orig. unkn.]

rove⁴ /rəʊv/ *n.* a small metal plate or ring for a rivet to pass through and be clenched over, esp. in boat-building. [ON *ró*, with excrescent *v*]

rover¹ /ˈrəʊvə(r)/ *n.* 1 a roving person; a wanderer. 2 *Croquet* **a** a ball that has passed all the hoops but not pegged out. **b** a player whose ball is a rover. **3** *Archery* **a** a mark chosen at undetermined range. **b** a mark for long-distance shooting. **4** (**Rover**) *Brit.* a senior Scout. ¶ Now called *Venture Scout*.

rover² /ˈrəʊvə(r)/ *n.* a sea robber, a pirate. [ME f. MLG, MDu. *rōver* f. *rōven* rob, rel. to REAVE]

rover³ /ˈrəʊvə(r)/ *n.* a person or machine that makes roves of fibre.

row¹ /rəʊ/ *n.* **1** a number of persons or things in a more or less straight line. **2** a line of seats across a theatre etc. (*in the front row*). **3** a street with a continuous line of houses along one or each side. **4** a line of plants in a field or garden. **5** a horizontal line of entries in a table etc. □**a hard row to hoe** a difficult task. **in a row 1** forming a row. **2** *colloq.* in succession (*two Sundays in a row*). **row-house** *US* a terrace house. [ME *raw, row,* f. OE f. Gmc]

row² /rəʊ/ *v. & n.* —*v.* **1** *tr.* propel (a boat) with oars. **2** *tr.* convey (a passenger) in a boat in this way. **3** *intr.* propel a boat in this way. **4** *tr.* make (a stroke) or achieve (a rate of striking) in rowing. **5** *tr.* compete in (a race) by rowing. **6** *tr.* row a race with. —*n.* **1** a spell of rowing. **2** an excursion in a rowing-boat. □**row-boat** *US* = *rowing-boat.* **row down** overtake in a rowing, esp. bumping, race. **rowing-boat** *Brit.* a small boat propelled by oars. **rowing-machine** a device for exercising the muscles used in rowing. **row out** exhaust by rowing (*the crew were completely rowed out at the finish*). **row over** complete the course of a boat race with little effort, owing to the absence or inferiority of competitors. □□**rower** *n.* [OE *rōwan* f. Gmc, rel. to RUDDER, L *remus* oar]

row³ /raʊ/ *n. & v. colloq.* —*n.* **1** a loud noise or commotion. **2** a fierce quarrel or dispute. **3 a** a severe reprimand. **b** the condition of being reprimanded (*shall get into a row*). —*v.* **1** *intr.* make or engage in a row. **2** *tr.* reprimand. □**make** (or **kick up**) **a row 1** raise a noise. **2** make a vigorous protest. [18th-c. sl.: orig. unkn.]

rowan /ˈrəʊən, ˈraʊ-/ *n.* (in full **rowan-tree**) **1** *Sc. & N.Engl.* the mountain ash. **2** *US* a similar tree, *Sorbus americana,* native to America. **3** (in full **rowan-berry**) the scarlet berry of either of these trees. [Scand., corresp. to Norw. *rogn, raun,* Icel. *reynir*]

rowdy /ˈraʊdɪ/ *adj. & n.* —*adj.* (**rowdier, rowdiest**) noisy and disorderly. —*n.* (*pl.* -**ies**) a rowdy person. □□**rowdily** *adv.* **rowdiness** *n.* **rowdyism** *n.* [19th-c. US, orig. = lawless backwoodsman: orig. unkn.]

rowel /ˈraʊəl/ *n. & v.* —*n.* **1** a spiked revolving disc at the end of a spur. **2** a circular piece of leather etc. with a hole in the centre inserted between a horse's skin and flesh to discharge an exudate. —*v.tr.* (**rowelled, rowelling;** *US* **roweled, roweling**) **1** urge with a rowel. **2** insert a rowel in. [ME f. OF *roel(e)* f. LL *rotella* dimin. of L *rota* wheel]

rowen /ˈraʊən/ *n.* (in *sing.* or *pl.*) *US* a second growth of grass, an aftermath. [ME f. OF *regain* (as GAIN)]

rowlock /ˈrɒlək, ˈrʌlək/ *n.* a device on a boat's gunwale, esp. a pair of thole-pins, serving as a fulcrum for an oar and keeping it in place. [alt. of earlier OARLOCK, after ROW²]

Rowton house /ˈraʊt(ə)n/ *n. Brit. hist.* a type of lodging-house for poor men, providing better conditions than a common lodging-house. [Lord *Rowton,* English social reformer d. 1903]

royal /ˈrɔɪəl/ *adj. & n.* —*adj.* **1** of or suited to or worthy of a king or queen. **2** in the service or under the patronage of a king or queen. **3** belonging to the king or queen (*the royal hands; the royal anger*). **4** of the family of a king or queen. **5** kingly, majestic, stately, splendid. **6** on a great scale, of exceptional size or quality, first-rate (*gave us royal entertainment; in royal spirits; had a royal time*). —*n.* **1** *colloq.* a member of the royal family. **2** a royal sail or mast. **3** a royal stag. **4** a size of paper, about 620 × 500 mm (25 × 20 in.). **5** (**the Royals**) the Royal Marines. □**Royal Air Force** the British air force. **royal**

assent see ASSENT. **royal blue** *Brit.* a deep vivid blue. **Royal British Legion** a national association of ex-members of the armed forces, founded in 1921. **royal burgh** *hist.* (in Scotland) a burgh holding a charter from the Crown. **Royal Commission** see COMMISSION. **royal duke** see DUKE. **Royal Engineers** the engineering branch of the British army. **royal family** the family to which a sovereign belongs. **royal fern** a fern, *Osmunda regalis,* with huge spreading fronds. **royal flush** see FLUSH³. **royal icing** a hard white icing made from icing sugar and egg-whites. **Royal Institution** a British society founded in 1799 for the diffusion of scientific knowledge. **royal jelly** a substance secreted by honey-bee workers and fed by them to future queen bees. **Royal Marine** a British marine (see MARINE *n.* 2). **royal mast** a mast above a topgallant mast. **Royal Navy** the British navy. **royal oak** a sprig of oak worn on 29 May to commemorate the restoration of Charles II (1660), who hid in an oak after the battle of Worcester (1651). **royal plural** the first person plural 'we' used by a single person. **royal road to** way of attaining without trouble. **royal sail** a sail above a topgallant sail. **Royal Society** (in full **Royal Society of London**) a society founded in 1662 to promote scientific discussion. **royal stag** a stag with a head of 12 or more points. **royal standard** a banner bearing royal heraldic arms. **royal tennis** real tennis. **Royal Victorian Chain** (in the UK) an order founded by Edward VII in 1902 and conferred by the sovereign on special occasions. **Royal Victorian Order** (in the UK) an order founded by Queen Victoria in 1896 and conferred usu. for great service rendered to the sovereign. **royal warrant** a warrant authorizing a tradesperson to supply goods to a specified royal person. □□**royally** *adv.* [ME f. OF *roial* f. L *regalis* REGAL]

royalist /ˈrɔɪəlɪst/ *n.* **1 a** a supporter of monarchy. **b** *hist.* a supporter of the royal side in the English Civil War. **2** *US* a reactionary, esp. a reactionary business tycoon. □□**royalism** *n.*

royalty /ˈrɔɪəltɪ/ *n.* (*pl.* -**ies**) **1** the office or dignity or power of a king or queen, sovereignty. **2 a** royal persons. **b** member of a royal family. **3** a sum paid to a patentee for the use of a patent or to an author etc. for each copy of a book etc. sold or for each public performance of a work. **4 a** a royal right (now esp. over minerals) granted by the sovereign to an individual or corporation. **b** a payment made by a producer of minerals, oil, or natural gas to the owner of the site or of the mineral rights over it. [ME f. OF *roialté* (as ROYAL)]

rozzer /ˈrɒzə(r)/ *n. Brit. sl.* a policeman. [19th c.: orig. unkn.]

RP *abbr.* received pronunciation.

RPI *abbr.* retail price index.

r.p.m. *abbr.* **1** revolutions per minute. **2** resale price maintenance.

RPO *abbr.* Royal Philharmonic Orchestra.

RR *abbr. US* **1** railroad. **2** rural route.

RS *abbr.* **1** (in the UK) Royal Society. **2** *US* Received Standard. **3** (in the UK) Royal Scots.

Rs. *abbr.* rupee(s).

RSA *abbr.* **1** (in the UK) Royal Society of Arts. **2** Royal Scottish Academy; Royal Scottish Academician.

RSC *abbr.* **1** (in the UK) Royal Shakespeare Company. **2** (in the UK) Royal Society of Chemistry.

RSFSR *abbr.* Russian Soviet Federative Socialist Republic.

RSJ *abbr.* rolled steel joist.

RSM *abbr.* Regimental Sergeant-Major.

RSPB *abbr.* (in the UK) Royal Society for the Protection of Birds.

RSPCA *abbr.* (in the UK) Royal Society for the Prevention of Cruelty to Animals.

RSV *abbr.* Revised Standard Version (of the Bible).

RSVP *abbr.* (in an invitation etc.) please answer. [F *répondez s'il vous plaît*]

RT *abbr.* **1** radio telegraphy. **2** radio telephony.

rt. *abbr.* right.

Rt. Hon. *abbr. Brit.* Right Honourable.

Rt. Revd. *abbr.* (also **Rt. Rev.**) Right Reverend.

RU *abbr.* Rugby Union.

Ru *symb. Chem.* the element ruthenium.

rub¹ /rʌb/ *v. & n.* —*v.* (**rubbed, rubbing**) **1** *tr.* move one's hand or another object with firm pressure over the surface of. **2** *tr.* (usu. foll. by *against, in, on, over*) apply (one's hand etc.) in this way. **3** *tr.* clean or polish or make dry or bare by rubbing. **4** *tr.* (often foll. by *over*) apply (polish, ointment, etc.) by rubbing. **5** *tr.* (foll. by *in, into, through*) use rubbing to make (a substance) go into or through something. **6** *tr.* (often foll. by *together*) move or slide (objects) against each other. **7** *intr.* (foll. by *against, on*) move with contact or friction. **8** *tr.* chafe or make sore by rubbing. **9** *intr.* (of cloth, skin, etc.) become frayed or worn or sore or bare with friction. **10** *tr.* reproduce the design of (a sepulchral brass or a stone) by rubbing paper laid on it with heelball or coloured chalk etc. **11** *tr.* (foll. by *to*) reduce to powder etc. by rubbing. **12** *intr. Bowls* (of a bowl) be slowed or diverted by the unevenness of the ground. —*n.* **1** a spell or an instance of rubbing (*give it a rub*). **2 a** an impediment or difficulty (*there's the rub*). **b** *Bowls* an inequality of the ground impeding or diverting a bowl; the diversion or hindering of a bowl by this. □**rub along** *colloq.* cope or manage without undue difficulty. **rub down** dry or smooth or clean by rubbing. **rub-down** *n.* an instance of rubbing down. **rub elbows with** *US* = *rub shoulders with*. **rub one's hands** rub one's hands together usu. in sign of keen satisfaction, or for warmth. **rub it in** (or **rub a person's nose in it**) emphasize or repeat an embarrassing fact etc. **rub noses** rub one's nose against another's in greeting. **rub off 1** (usu. foll. by *on*) be transferred by contact, be transmitted (*some of his attitudes have rubbed off on me*). **2** remove by rubbing. **rub of** (or **on**) **the green** *Golf* an accidental interference with the course or position of a ball. **rub on** *colloq.* = *rub along*. **rub out 1** erase with a rubber. **2** esp. *US sl.* kill, eliminate. **rub shoulders with** associate or come into contact with (another person). **rub up 1** polish (a tarnished object). **2** brush up (a subject or one's memory). **3** mix (pigment etc.) into paste by rubbing. **rub-up** *n.* the act or an instance of rubbing up. **rub up the wrong way** irritate or repel as by stroking a cat against the lie of its fur. [ME *rubben*, perh. f. LG *rubben*, of unkn. orig.]

rub² /rʌb/ *n.* = RUBBER². [abbr.]

rubato /ruːˈbɑːtəʊ/ *adj. & n. Mus.* —*n.* (*pl.* **-os** or **rubati** /-tiː/) the temporary disregarding of strict tempo. —*adj.* performed with a flexible tempo. [It., = robbed]

rubber¹ /ˈrʌbə(r)/ *n.* **1** a tough elastic polymeric substance made from the latex of plants or synthetically. **2** esp. *Brit.* a piece of this or another substance for erasing pencil or ink marks. **3** *colloq.* a condom. **4** (in *pl.*) *US* galoshes. **5** a person who rubs; a masseur or masseuse. **6 a** an implement used for rubbing. **b** part of a machine operating by rubbing. □**rubber band** a loop of rubber for holding papers etc. together. **rubber plant 1** an evergreen plant, *Ficus elastica*, with dark-green shiny leaves, often cultivated as a house-plant. **2** (also **rubber tree**) any of various tropical trees yielding latex, esp. *Hevea brasiliensis*. **rubber solution** a liquid drying to a rubber-like material, used esp. as an adhesive in mending rubber articles. **rubber stamp 1** a device for inking and imprinting on a surface. **2 a** a person who mechanically copies or agrees to others' actions. **b** an indication of such agreement. **rubber-stamp** *v.tr.* approve automatically without proper consideration. □□**rubbery** *adj.* **rubberiness**

n. [RUB¹ + -ER¹, from its early use to rub out pencil marks]

rubber² /ˈrʌbə(r)/ *n.* **1** a match of three or five successive games between the same sides or persons at whist, bridge, cricket, lawn tennis, etc. **2** (prec. by *the*) **a** the act of winning two games in a rubber. **b** a third game when each side has won one. [orig. unkn.: used as a term in bowls from *c.*1600]

rubberize /ˈrʌbəˌraɪz/ *v.tr.* (also **-ise**) treat or coat with rubber.

rubberneck /ˈrʌbəˌnek/ *n. & v. colloq.* —*n.* a person who stares inquisitively or stupidly. —*v.intr.* act in this way.

rubbing /ˈrʌbɪŋ/ *n.* **1** in senses of RUB¹ *v.* **2** an impression or copy made by rubbing (see RUB¹ *v.* 10).

rubbish /ˈrʌbɪʃ/ *n. & v.* —*n.* esp. *Brit.* **1** waste material; debris, refuse, litter. **2** worthless material or articles; trash. **3** (often as *int.*) absurd ideas or suggestions; nonsense. —*v.tr. colloq.* **1** criticize severely. **2** reject as worthless. □□**rubbishy** *adj.* [ME f. AF *rubbous* etc., perh. f. RUBBLE]

rubble /ˈrʌb(ə)l/ *n.* **1** waste or rough fragments of stone or brick etc. **2** pieces of undressed stone used, esp. as filling-in, for walls. **3** *Geol.* loose angular stones etc. as the covering of some rocks. **4** water-worn stones. □□**rubbly** *adj.* [ME *robyl, rubel*, of uncert. orig.: cf. OF *robe* spoils]

rube /ruːb/ *n. US colloq.* a country bumpkin. [abbr. of the name *Reuben*]

rubefy /ˈruːbɪˌfaɪ/ *v.tr.* (also **rubify**) (**-ies, -ied**) **1** make red. **2** *Med.* (of a counterirritant) stimulate (the skin etc.) to redness. □□**rubefacient** /-ˈfeɪʃ(ə)nt/ *adj. & n.* **rubefaction** /ˌruːbɪˈfækʃ(ə)n/ *n.* [ME f. OF *rubifier, rubefier* f. med.L *rubificare* f. L *rubefacere* f. *rubeus* red]

rubella /ruːˈbelə/ *n. Med.* an acute infectious virus disease with a red rash; German measles. [mod.L, neut. pl. of L *rubellus* reddish]

rubellite /ˈruːbəˌlaɪt/ *n.* a red variety of tourmaline. [L *rubellus* reddish]

rubeola /ruːˈbiːələ/ *n. Med.* measles. [med.L f. L *rubeus* red]

Rubicon /ˈruːbɪˌkɒn/ *n.* **1** a boundary which once crossed betokens irrevocable commitment; a point of no return. **2** (**rubicon**) the act of winning a game in piquet before an opponent has scored 100. [the ancient name of a stream forming the boundary of Julius Caesar's province and crossed by him in 49 BC as the start of a war with Pompey]

rubicund /ˈruːbɪˌkʌnd/ *adj.* (of a face, complexion, or person in these respects) ruddy, high-coloured. □□**rubicundity** /-ˈkʌndɪtɪ/ *n.* [F *rubicond* or L *rubicundus* f. *rubēre* be red]

rubidium /ruːˈbɪdɪəm/ *n. Chem.* a soft silvery element occurring naturally in various minerals and as the radioactive isotope rubidium-87. ¶ Symb.: **Rb**. [L *rubidus* red (with ref. to its spectral lines)]

rubify var. of RUBEFY.

rubiginous /ruːˈbɪdʒɪnəs/ *adj. formal* rust-coloured. [L *rubigo- inis* rust]

Rubik's cube /ˈruːbɪks/ *n.* a puzzle in which the aim is to restore the faces of a composite cube to single colours by rotating layers of constituent smaller cubes. [E. *Rubik*, its Hung. inventor]

ruble var. of ROUBLE.

rubric /ˈruːbrɪk/ *n.* **1** a direction for the conduct of divine service inserted in a liturgical book. **2** a heading or passage in red or special lettering. **3** explanatory words. **4** an established custom. □□ **rubrical** *adj.* [ME f. OF *rubrique, rubrice* or L *rubrica* (*terra*) red (earth or ochre) as writing-material, rel. to *rubeus* red]

rubricate /ˈruːbrɪˌkeɪt/ *v.tr.* **1** mark with red; print or write in red. **2** provide with rubrics. □□ **rubrication** /-ˈkeɪʃ(ə)n/ *n.* **rubricator** *n.* [L *rubricare* f. *rubrica*: see RUBRIC]

ruby /ˈruːbɪ/ *n., adj., & v.* —*n.* (*pl.* **-ies**) **1** a rare precious stone consisting of corundum with a colour varying from deep crimson or purple to pale rose. **2** a glowing purple-tinged red colour. —*adj.* of this colour. —*v.tr.* (-ies, -ied) dye or tinge ruby-colour. □**ruby glass** glass coloured with oxides of copper, iron, lead, tin, etc. **ruby-tail** a wasp, *Chrysis ignita*, with a ruby-coloured hinder part. **ruby wedding** the fortieth anniversary of a wedding. [ME f. OF *rubi* f. med.L *rubinus* (*lapis*) red (stone), rel. to L *rubeus* red]

RUC *abbr.* Royal Ulster Constabulary.

ruche /ruːʃ/ *n.* a frill or gathering of lace etc. as a trimming. □□**ruched** *adj.* **ruching** *n.* [F f. med.L *rusca* tree-bark, of Celt. orig.]

ruck[1] /rʌk/ *n.* **1** (prec. by *the*) the main body of competitors not likely to overtake the leaders. **2** an undistinguished crowd of persons or things. **3** *Rugby Football* a loose scrum with the ball on the ground. **4** *Austral. Rules* a group of three mobile players. [ME, = stack of fuel, heap, rick: app. Scand., = Norw. *ruka* in the same senses]

ruck[2] /rʌk/ *v. & n.* —*v.tr. & intr.* (often foll. by *up*) make or become creased or wrinkled. —*n.* a crease or wrinkle. [ON *hrukka*]

ruckle /ˈrʌk(ə)l/ *v. & n. Brit.* = RUCK[2].

rucksack /ˈrʌksæk, ˈrʊk-/ *n.* a bag slung by straps from both shoulders and resting on the back. [G f. *rucken* dial. var. of *Rücken* back + *Sack* SACK[1]]

ruckus /ˈrʌkəs/ *n. esp. US* a row or commotion. [cf. RUCTION, RUMPUS]

ruction /ˈrʌkʃ(ə)n/ *n. colloq.* **1** a disturbance or tumult. **2** (in *pl.*) unpleasant arguments or reactions. [19th c.: orig. unkn.]

rudaceous /ruːˈdeɪʃəs/ *adj.* (of rock) composed of fragments of relatively large size. [L *rudus* rubble]

rudbeckia /rʌdˈbekɪə/ *n.* a composite garden plant of the genus *Rudbeckia*, native to N. America. [mod.L f. O. *Rudbeck*, Sw. botanist d. 1740]

rudd /rʌd/ *n.* (*pl.* same) a freshwater fish, *Scardinius erythrophthalmus*, resembling a roach and having red fins. [app. rel. to *rud* red colour f. OE *rudu*, rel. to RED]

rudder /ˈrʌdə(r)/ *n.* **1 a** a flat piece hinged vertically to the stern of a ship for steering. **b** a vertical aerofoil pivoted from the tailplane of an aircraft, for controlling its horizontal movement. **2** a guiding principle etc. □□**rudderless** *adj.* [OE *rōther* f. WG *rōthra-* f. the stem of ROW[2]]

ruddle /ˈrʌd(ə)l/ *n. & v.* —*n.* a red ochre, esp. of a kind used for marking sheep. —*v.tr.* mark or colour with or as with ruddle. [rel. to obs. *rud*: see RUDD]

ruddock /ˈrʌdək/ *n. dial.* the robin redbreast. [OE *rudduc* (as RUDDLE)]

ruddy /ˈrʌdɪ/ *adj. & v.* —*adj.* (**ruddier, ruddiest**) **1 a** (of a person or complexion) freshly or healthily red. **b** (of health, youth, etc.) marked by this. **2** reddish. **3** *Brit. colloq.* bloody, damnable. —*v.tr. & intr.* (-ies, -ied) make or grow ruddy. □□**ruddily** *adv.* **ruddiness** *n.* [OE *rudig* (as RUDD)]

rude /ruːd/ *adj.* **1** (of a person, remark, etc.) impolite or offensive. **2** roughly made or done; lacking subtlety or accuracy (*a rude plough*). **3** primitive or uneducated (*rude chaos; rude simplicity*). **4** abrupt, sudden, startling, violent (*a rude awakening; a rude reminder*). **5** *colloq.* indecent, lewd (*a rude joke*). **6** vigorous or hearty (*rude health*). □**be rude to** speak impolitely to; insult. □□**rudely** *adv.* **rudeness** *n.* **rudery** *n.* **rudish** *adj.* [ME f. OF f. L *rudis* unwrought]

ruderal /ˈruːdər(ə)l/ *adj. & n.* —*adj.* (of a plant) growing on or in rubbish or rubble. —*n.* a ruderal plant. [mod.L *ruderalis* f. L *rudera* pl. of *rudus* rubble]

rudiment /ˈruːdɪmənt/ *n.* **1** (in *pl.*) the elements or first principles of a subject. **2** (in *pl.*) an imperfect beginning of something undeveloped or yet to develop. **3** a part or organ imperfectly developed as being vestigial or having no function (e.g. the breast in males). [F *rudiment* or L *rudimentum* (as RUDE, after *elementum* ELEMENT)]

rudimentary /ˌruːdɪˈmentərɪ/ *adj.* **1** involving basic principles; fundamental. **2** incompletely developed; vestigial. □□**rudimentarily** /-ˈmentərɪlɪ/ *adv.* **rudimentariness** /-ˈmentərɪnɪs/ *n.*

rue[1] /ruː/ *v. & n.* —*v.tr.* (**rues, rued, rueing** or **ruing**) repent of; bitterly feel the consequences of; wish to be undone or non-existent (esp. *rue the day*). —*n. archaic* **1** repentance; dejection at some occurrence. **2** compassion or pity. [OE *hrēow, hrēowan*]

rue[2] /ruː/ *n.* a perennial evergreen shrub, *Ruta graveolens*, with bitter strong-scented leaves formerly used in medicine. [ME f. OF f. L *ruta* f. Gk *rhutē*]

rueful /ˈruːfʊl/ *adj.* expressing sorrow, genuine or humorously affected. □□**ruefully** *adv.* **ruefulness** *n.* [ME, f. RUE[1]]

rufescent /ruːˈfes(ə)nt/ *adj. Zool.* etc. reddish. □□ **rufescence** *n.* [L *rufescere* f. *rufus* reddish]

ruff[1] /rʌf/ *n.* **1** a projecting starched frill worn round the neck esp. in the 16th c. **2** a projecting or conspicuously coloured ring of feathers or hair round a bird's or animal's neck. **3** a domestic pigeon like a jacobin. **4** (*fem.* **reeve** /riːv/) a wading bird, *Philomachus pugnax*, of which the male has a ruff and ear-tufts in the breeding season. □□**rufflike** *adj.* [perh. f. *ruff* = ROUGH]

ruff[2] /rʌf/ *n.* (also **ruffe**) any of various fish, esp. a perch-like freshwater fish, *Gymnocephalus cernua*, found in European lakes and rivers. [ME, prob. f. ROUGH]

ruff[3] /rʌf/ *v. & n.* —*v.intr. & tr.* trump at cards. —*n.* an act of ruffing. [orig. the name of a card-game: f. OF *roffle, rouffle*, = It. *ronfa* (perh. alt. of *trionfo* TRUMP[1])]

ruffian /ˈrʌfɪən/ *n.* a violent lawless person. □□ **ruffianism** *n.* **ruffianly** *adv.* [F *ruf(f)ian* f. It. *ruffiano*, perh. f. dial. *rofia* scurf]

ruffle /ˈrʌf(ə)l/ *v. & n.* —*v.* **1** *tr.* disturb the smoothness or tranquillity of. **2** *tr.* upset the calmness of (a person). **3** *tr.* gather (lace etc.) into a ruffle. **4** *tr.* (often foll. by *up*) (of a bird) erect (its feathers) in anger, display, etc. **5** *intr.* undergo ruffling. **6** *intr.* lose smoothness or calmness. —*n.* **1** an ornamental gathered or goffered frill of lace etc. worn at the opening of a garment esp. round the wrist, breast, or neck. **2** perturbation, bustle. **3** a rippling effect on water. **4** the ruff of a bird etc. (see RUFF[1] 2). **5** *Mil.* a vibrating drum-beat. [ME: orig. unkn.]

rufous /ˈruːfəs/ *adj.* (esp. of animals) reddish-brown. [L *rufus* red, reddish]

rug /rʌg/ *n.* **1** a floor-mat of shaggy material or thick pile. **2** a thick woollen coverlet or wrap. □**pull the rug from under** deprive of support; weaken, unsettle. [prob. f. Scand.: cf. Norw. dial. *rugga* coverlet, Sw. *rugg* ruffled hair: rel. to RAG[1]]

Rugby /ˈrʌgbɪ/ *n.* (in full **Rugby football**) a team game played with an oval ball that may be kicked, carried, and passed from hand to hand. □**Rugby League** partly professional Rugby football with teams of 13. **Rugby Union** amateur Rugby football with teams of 15. [*Rugby* School in S. England, where it was first played]

rugged /ˈrʌgɪd/ *adj.* **1** (of ground or terrain) having a rough uneven surface. **2** (of features) strongly marked; irregular in outline. **3 a** unpolished; lacking gentleness or refinement (*rugged grandeur*). **b** harsh in sound. **c** austere, unbending (*rugged honesty*). **d** involving hardship (*a rugged life*). **4** (esp. of a machine) robust, sturdy. □□**ruggedly** *adv.* **ruggedness** *n.* [ME, prob. f. Scand.: cf. RUG, and Sw. *rugga*, roughen]

rugger /ˈrʌgə(r)/ *n. Brit. colloq.* Rugby football.

rugose /ˈruːgəʊs, -gəʊz/ *adj.* esp. *Biol.* wrinkled, corrugated. □□**rugosely** *adv.* **rugosity** /-ˈgɒsɪtɪ/ *n.* [L *rugosus* f. *ruga* wrinkle]

ruin /ˈruːɪn/ n. & v. —n. **1** a destroyed or wrecked state. **2** a person's or thing's downfall or elimination (*the ruin of my hopes*). **3 a** the complete loss of one's property or position (*bring to ruin*). **b** a person who has suffered ruin. **4** (in *sing.* or *pl.*) the remains of a building etc. that has suffered ruin (*an old ruin*; *ancient ruins*). **5** a cause of ruin (*will be the ruin of us*). —v. **1** tr. **a** bring to ruin (*your extravagance has ruined me*). **b** utterly impair or wreck (*the rain ruined my hat*). **2** tr. (esp. as **ruined** adj.) reduce to ruins. **3** intr. poet. fall headlong or with a crash. □**in ruins 1** in a state of ruin. **2** completely wrecked (*their hopes were in ruins*). [ME f. OF *ruine* f. L *ruina* f. *ruere* fall]

ruination /ˌruːɪˈneɪʃ(ə)n/ n. **1** the act of bringing to ruin. **2** the act of ruining or the state of being ruined. [obs. *ruinate* (as RUIN)]

ruinous /ˈruːɪnəs/ adj. **1** bringing ruin; disastrous (*at ruinous expense*). **2** in ruins; dilapidated. □□ **ruinously** adv. **ruinousness** n. [ME f. L *ruinosus* (as RUIN)]

rule /ruːl/ n. & v. —n. **1** a principle to which an action conforms or is required to conform. **2** a prevailing custom or standard; the normal state of things. **3** government or dominion (*under British rule*; *the rule of law*). **4** a graduated straight measure used in carpentry etc.; a ruler. **5** *Printing* **a** a thin strip of metal for separating headings, columns, etc. **b** a thin line or dash. **6** a code of discipline of a religious order. **7** *Law* an order made by a judge or court with reference to a particular case only. **8** (**Rules**) *Austral.* = Australian Rules. —v. **1** tr. exercise decisive influence over; keep under control. **2** tr. & (foll. by *over*) intr. have sovereign control of (*rules over a vast kingdom*). **3** tr. (often foll. by *that* + clause) pronounce authoritatively (*was ruled out of order*). **4** tr. **a** make parallel lines across (paper). **b** make (a straight line) with a ruler etc. **5** intr. (of prices or goods etc. in regard to price or quality etc.) have a specified general level; be for the most part (*the market ruled high*). **6** tr. (in *passive*; foll. by *by*) consent to follow (advice etc.); be guided by. □ **as a rule** usually; more often than not. **by rule** in a regulation manner; mechanically. **rule of the road** see ROAD¹. **rule of three** a method of finding a number in the same ratio to one given as exists between two others given. **rule of thumb** a rule for general guidance, based on experience or practice rather than theory. **rule out** exclude; pronounce irrelevant or ineligible. **rule the roost** (or **roast**) be in control. **run the rule over** examine cursorily for correctness or adequacy. □□ **ruleless** adj. [ME f. OF *reule*, *reuler* f. LL *regulare* f. L *regula* straight stick]

ruler /ˈruːlə(r)/ n. **1** a person exercising government or dominion. **2** a straight usu. graduated strip or cylinder of wood, metal, etc., used to draw lines or measure distance. □□ **rulership** n.

ruling /ˈruːlɪŋ/ n. & adj. —n. an authoritative decision or announcement. —adj. prevailing; currently in force (*ruling prices*). □ **ruling passion** a motive that habitually directs one's actions.

rum¹ /rʌm/ n. **1** a spirit distilled from sugar-cane residues or molasses. **2** *US* intoxicating liquor. □ **rum baba** see BABA. [17th c.: perh. abbr. of contemporary forms *rumbullion*, *rumbustion*, of unkn. orig.]

rum² /rʌm/ adj. *Brit. colloq.* **1** odd, strange, queer. **2** difficult, dangerous. □ **rum go** (or **start**) *colloq.* a surprising occurrence or unforeseen turn of affairs. □□ **rumly** adv. **rumness** n. [16th-c. cant, orig. = fine, spirited, perh. var. of ROM]

Rumanian var. of ROMANIAN.

Rumansh var. of ROMANSH.

rumba /ˈrʌmbə/ n. & v. (also **rhumba**) —n. **1** a Cuban Negro dance. **2 a** a ballroom dance imitative of this. **b** the music for it. —v.tr. (**rumbas**, **rumbaed** /-bəd/ or **rumba'd**, **rumbaing** /-bəɪŋ/) dance the rumba. [Amer. Sp.]

rumble /ˈrʌmb(ə)l/ v. & n. —v. **1** intr. make a continuous deep resonant sound as of distant thunder. **2** intr. (foll. by *along*, *by*, *past*, etc.) (of a person or vehicle) move with a rumbling noise. **3** tr. (often foll. by *out*) utter or say with a rumbling sound. **4** tr. *Brit. sl.* find out about (esp. something illicit). —n. **1** a rumbling sound. **2** *US sl.* a street-fight between gangs. □ **rumble seat** *US* an uncovered folding seat in the rear of a motor car. □□ **rumbler** n. [ME *romble*, prob. f. MDu. *rommelen*, *rummelen* (imit.)]

rumbustious /rʌmˈbʌstʃəs/ adj. *colloq.* boisterous, noisy, uproarious. □□ **rumbustiously** adv. **rumbustiousness** n. [prob. var. of *robustious* boisterous, ROBUST]

rumen /ˈruːmen/ n. (pl. **rumens** or **rumina** /-mɪnə/) the first stomach of a ruminant, in which food, esp. cellulose, is partly digested by bacteria. [L *rumen ruminis* throat]

ruminant /ˈruːmɪnənt/ n. & adj. —n. an animal that chews the cud regurgitated from its rumen. —adj. **1** of or belonging to ruminants. **2** contemplative; given to or engaged in meditation. [L *ruminari ruminant-* (as RUMEN)]

ruminate /ˈruːmɪˌneɪt/ v. **1** tr. & (foll. by *over*, *on*, etc.) intr. meditate, ponder. **2** intr. (of ruminants) chew the cud. □□ **rumination** /-ˈneɪʃ(ə)n/ n. **ruminative** /-nətɪv/ adj. **ruminatively** /-nətɪvlɪ/ adv. **ruminator** n.

rummage /ˈrʌmɪdʒ/ v. & n. —v. **1** tr. & (foll. by *in*, *through*, *among*) intr. search, esp. untidily and unsystematically. **2** tr. (foll. by *out*, *up*) find among other things. **3** tr. (foll. by *about*) disarrange; make untidy in searching. —n. **1** an instance of rummaging. **2** things found by rummaging; a miscellaneous accumulation. □ **rummage sale** esp. *US* a jumble sale. □□ **rummager** n. [earlier as noun in obs. sense 'arranging of casks etc. in a hold': OF *arrumage* f. *arrumer* stow (as AD-, *run* ship's hold f. MDu. *ruim* ROOM)]

rummer /ˈrʌmə(r)/ n. a large drinking-glass. [rel. to Du. *roemer*, LG *römer* f. *roemen* praise, boast]

rummy¹ /ˈrʌmɪ/ n. a card-game played usu. with two packs, in which the players try to form sets and sequences of cards. [20th c.: orig. unkn.]

rummy² /ˈrʌmɪ/ adj. *Brit. colloq.* = RUM².

rumour /ˈruːmə(r)/ n. & v. (*US* **rumor**) —n. **1** general talk or hearsay of doubtful accuracy. **2** (often foll. by *of*, or *that* + clause) a current but unverified statement or assertion (*heard a rumour that you are leaving*). —v.tr. (usu. in *passive*) report by way of rumour (*it is rumoured that you are leaving*; *you are rumoured to be leaving*). [ME f. OF *rumur*, *rumor* f. L *rumor -oris* noise]

rump /rʌmp/ n. **1** the hind part of a mammal, esp. the buttocks. **2 a** a small or contemptible remnant of a parliament or similar body. **b** (**the Rump**) *hist.* the remnant of the English Long Parliament 1648–53 or after its restoration in 1659. □ **rump steak** a cut of beef from the rump. □□ **rumpless** adj. [ME, prob. f. Scand.]

rumple /ˈrʌmp(ə)l/ v.tr. & intr. make or become creased or ruffled. □□ **rumply** adj. [obs. *rumple* (n.) f. MDu. *rompel* f. *rompe* wrinkle]

rumpus /ˈrʌmpəs/ n. *colloq.* a disturbance, brawl, row, or uproar. □ **rumpus room** *US* a room in the basement of a house for games and play. [18th c.: prob. fanciful]

run /rʌn/ v. & n. —v. (**running**; past **ran** /ræn/; past part. **run**) **1** intr. go with quick steps on alternate feet, never having both or all feet on the ground at the same time. **2** intr. flee, abscond. **3** intr. go or travel hurriedly, briefly, etc. **4** intr. **a** advance by or as by rolling or on wheels, or smoothly or easily. **b** be in action or operation (*left the engine running*). **5** intr. be current or operative; have duration (*the lease runs for 99 years*). **6** intr. (of a bus, train, etc.) travel or be travelling on its route (*the train is running late*). **7** intr. (of a play, exhibition, etc.) be staged or presented (*is now running at the Apollo*). **8** intr.

extend; have a course or order or tendency (*the road runs by the coast*; *prices are running high*). **9 a** *intr.* compete in a race. **b** *intr.* finish a race in a specified position. **c** *tr.* compete in (a race). **10** *intr.* (often foll. by *for*) seek election (*ran for president*). **11 a** *intr.* (of a liquid etc. or its container) flow or be wet; drip. **b** *tr.* flow with. **12** *tr.* **a** cause (water etc.) to flow. **b** fill (a bath) with water. **13** *intr.* spread rapidly or beyond the proper place (*ink ran over the table*; *a shiver ran down my spine*). **14** *intr. Cricket* (of a batsman) run from one wicket to the other in scoring a run. **15** *tr.* traverse or make one's way through or over (a course, race, or distance). **16** *tr.* perform (an errand). **17** *tr.* publish (an article etc.) in a newspaper or magazine. **18 a** *tr.* cause (a machine or vehicle etc.) to operate. **b** *intr.* (of a mechanism or component etc.) move or work freely. **19** *tr.* direct or manage (a business etc.). **20** *tr.* own and use (a vehicle) regularly. **21** *tr.* take (a person) for a journey in a vehicle (*shall I run you to the shops?*). **22** *tr.* cause to run or go in a specified way (*ran the car into a tree*). **23** *tr.* enter (a horse etc.) for a race. **24** *tr.* smuggle (guns etc.). **25** *tr.* chase or hunt. **26** *tr.* allow (an account) to accumulate for a time before paying. **27** *intr. Naut.* (of a ship etc.) go straight and fast. **28** *intr.* (of salmon) go up river from the sea. **29** *intr.* (of a colour in a fabric) spread from the dyed parts. **30 a** *intr.* (of a thought, the eye, the memory, etc.) pass in a transitory or cursory way (*ideas ran through my mind*). **b** *tr.* cause (one's eye) to look cursorily (*ran my eye down the page*). **31** *intr.* (of hosiery) ladder. **32** *intr.* (of a candle) gutter. **33** *intr.* (of an orifice, esp. the eyes or nose) exude liquid matter. **34** *tr.* sew (fabric) loosely or hastily with running stitches. **35** *tr.* turn (cattle etc.) out to graze. —*n.* **1** an act or spell of running. **2** a short trip or excursion, esp. for pleasure. **3** a distance travelled. **4** a general tendency of development or movement. **5** a rapid motion. **6** a regular route. **7** a continuous or long stretch or spell or course (*a metre's run of wiring*; *had a run of bad luck*). **8** (often foll. by *on*) **a** a high general demand (for a commodity, currency, etc.) (*a run on the dollar*). **b** a sudden demand for repayment by a large number of customers of (a bank). **9** a quantity produced in one period of production (*a print run*). **10** a general or average type or class (*not typical of the general run*). **11 a** *Cricket* a point scored by the batsmen each running to the other's wicket, or an equivalent point awarded for some other reason. **b** *Baseball* a point scored usu. by the batter returning to the plate after touching the other bases. **12** (foll. by *of*) free use of or access to (*had the run of the house*). **13 a** an animal's regular track. **b** an enclosure for fowls. **c** a range of pasture. **14** a ladder in hosiery. **15** *Mus.* a rapid scale passage. **16** a class or line of goods. **17** a batch or drove of animals born or reared together. **18** a shoal of fish in motion. **19** a trough for water to run in. **20** *US* a small stream or brook. **21 a** a single journey, esp. by an aircraft. **b** (of an aircraft) a flight on a straight and even course at a constant speed before or while dropping bombs. **c** an offensive military operation. ◻at **a** (or **the**) **run** running. on **the run 1** escaping, running away. **2** hurrying about from place to place. **run about 1** bustle; hurry from one person or place to another. **2** (esp. of children) play or wander without restraint. **run across 1** happen to meet. **2** (foll. by *to*) make a brief journey or a flying visit (to a place). **run after 1** pursue with attentions; seek the society of. **2** give much time to (a pursuit etc.). **3** pursue at a run. **run against** happen to meet. **run along** *colloq.* depart. **run around 1** *Brit.* take from place to place by car etc. **2** deceive or evade repeatedly. **3** (often foll. by *with*) *sl.* engage in sexual relations (esp. casually or illicitly). **run-around** *n.* (esp. in phr. **give a person the run-around**) deceit or evasion. **run at** attack by charging or rushing. **run away 1** get away by running; flee, abscond. **2** elope. **3** (of a horse) bolt.

run away with 1 carry off (a person, stolen property, etc.). **2** win (a prize) easily. **3** accept (a notion) hastily. **4** (of expense etc.) consume (money etc.). **5** (of a horse) bolt with (a rider, a carriage or its occupants). **run a blockade** see BLOCKADE. **run down 1** knock down or collide with. **2** reduce the strength or numbers of (resources). **3** (of an unwound clock etc.) stop. **4** (of a person or a person's health) become feeble from overwork or underfeeding. **5** discover after a search. **6** disparage. **run-down** *n.* **1 a** reduction in numbers. **2** a detailed analysis. —*adj.* **1** decayed after prosperity. **2** enfeebled through overwork etc. **run dry** cease to flow, be exhausted. **run for it** seek safety by fleeing. **a run** (or **a good run**) **for one's money 1** vigorous competition. **2** pleasure derived from an activity. **run foul of** collide or become entangled with (another vessel etc.). **run the gauntlet** see GAUNTLET[2]. **run a person hard** (or **close**) press a person severely in a race or competition, or in comparative merit. **run high 1** (of the sea) have a strong current with a high tide. **2** (of feelings) be strong. **run in 1** run (a new engine or vehicle) carefully in the early stages. **2** *colloq.* arrest. **3** (of a combatant) rush to close quarters. **4** incur (a debt). **run-in** *n.* **1** the approach to an action or event. **2** a quarrel. **run in the family** (of a trait) be common in the members of a family. **run into 1** collide with. **2** encounter. **3** reach as many as (a specified figure). **4** fall into (a practice, absurdity, etc.). **5** be continuous or coalesce with. **run into the ground** *colloq.* bring (a person) to exhaustion etc. **run it fine** see FINE[1]. **run its course** follow its natural progress; be left to itself. **run low** (or **short**) become depleted, have too little (*our tea ran short*; *we ran short of tea*). **run off 1** flee. **2** produce (copies etc.) on a machine. **3** decide (a race or other contest) after a series of heats or in the event of a tie. **4** flow or cause to flow away. **5** write or recite fluently. **6** digress suddenly. **run-off** *n.* **1** an additional competition, election, race, etc., after a tie. **2** an amount of rainfall that is carried off an area by streams and rivers. **3** *NZ* a separate area of land where young animals etc. are kept. **run off one's feet** very busy. **run-of-the-mill** ordinary, undistinguished. **run on 1** (of written characters) be joined together. **2** continue in operation. **3** elapse. **4** speak volubly. **5** talk incessantly. **6** *Printing* continue on the same line as the preceding matter. **run out 1** come to an end; become used up. **2** (foll. by *of*) exhaust one's stock of. **3** put down the wicket of (a batsman who is running). **4** escape from a containing vessel. **5** (of rope) pass out; be paid out. **6** jut out. **7** come out of a contest in a specified position etc. or complete a required score etc. (*they ran out worthy winners*). **8** complete (a race). **9** advance (a gun etc.) so as to project. **10** exhaust oneself by running. **run-out** *n.* the dismissal of a batsman by being run out. **run out on** *colloq.* desert (a person). **run over 1** overflow. **2** study or repeat quickly. **3** (of a vehicle or its driver) pass over, knock down or crush. **4** touch (the notes of a piano etc.) in quick succession. **5** (often foll. by *to*) go quickly by a brief journey or for a flying visit. **run ragged** exhaust (a person). **run rings round** see RING[1]. **run riot** see RIOT. **run a** (or **the**) **risk** see RISK. **run the show** *colloq.* dominate in an undertaking etc. **run a temperature** be feverish. **run through 1** examine or rehearse briefly. **2** peruse. **3** deal successively with. **4** consume (an estate etc.) by reckless or quick spending. **5** traverse. **6** pervade. **7** pierce with a sword etc. **8** draw a line through (written words). **run-through** *n.* **1** a rehearsal. **2** a brief survey. **run to 1** have the money or ability for. **2** reach (an amount or number). **3** (of a person) show a tendency to (*runs to fat*). **4 a** be enough for (some expense or undertaking). **b** have the resources or capacity for. **5** fall into (ruin). **run to earth 1** *Hunting* chase to its lair. **2** discover after a long search. **run to meet**

---

b *but* d *dog* f *few* g *get* h *he* j *yes* k *cat* l *leg* m *man* n *no* p *pen* r *red* s *sit* t *top* v *voice*

anticipate (one's troubles etc.). **run to seed** see SEED. **run up 1** accumulate (a debt etc.) quickly. **2** build or make hurriedly. **3** raise (a flag). **4** grow quickly. **5** rise in price. **6** (foll. by *to*) amount to. **7** force (a rival bidder) to bid higher. **8** add up (a column of figures). **9** (foll. by *to*) go quickly by a brief journey or for a flying visit. **run-up** *n.* **1** (often foll. by *to*) the period preceding an important event. **2** *Golf* a low approach shot. **run up against** meet with (a difficulty or difficulties). **run upon** (of a person's thoughts etc.) be engrossed by; dwell upon. **run wild** grow or stray unchecked or undisciplined or untrained. □□ **runnable** *adj.* [OE *rinnan*]

runabout /ˈrʌnəˌbaʊt/ *n.* a light car or aircraft.

runaway /ˈrʌnəˌweɪ/ *n.* **1** a fugitive. **2** an animal or vehicle that is running out of control. **3** (*attrib.*) **a** that is running away or out of control (*runaway inflation; had a runaway success*). **b** done or performed after running away (*a runaway wedding*).

runcible spoon /ˈrʌnsɪb(ə)l/ *n.* a fork curved like a spoon, with three broad prongs, one edged. [nonsense word used by E. Lear, Engl. humorist d. 1888, perh. after *rouncival* large pea]

runcinate /ˈrʌnsɪnət/ *adj. Bot.* (of a leaf) saw-toothed, with lobes pointing towards the base. [mod.L *runcinatus* f. L *runcina* PLANE² (formerly taken to mean saw)]

rune /ruːn/ *n.* **1** any of the letters of the earliest Germanic alphabet used by Scandinavians and Anglo-Saxons from about the 3rd c. and formed by modifying Roman or Greek characters to suit carving. **2** a similar mark of mysterious or magic significance. **3** a Finnish poem or a division of it. □ **rune-staff 1** a magic wand inscribed with runes. **2** a runic calendar. □□ **runic** *adj.* [ON *rún* (only in pl. *rúnar*) magic sign, rel. to OE *rún*]

rung¹ /rʌŋ/ *n.* **1** each of the horizontal supports of a ladder. **2** a strengthening crosspiece in the structure of a chair etc. □□ **runged** *adj.* **rungless** *adj.* [OE *hrung*]

rung² *past part.* of RING².

runlet /ˈrʌnlɪt/ *n.* a small stream.

runnel /ˈrʌn(ə)l/ *n.* **1** a brook or rill. **2** a gutter. [later form (assim. to RUN) of *rinel* f. OE *rynel* (as RUN)]

runner /ˈrʌnə(r)/ *n.* **1** a person who runs, esp. in a race. **2 a** a creeping plant-stem that can take root. **b** a twining plant. **3** a rod or groove or blade on which a thing slides. **4** a sliding ring on a rod etc. **5 a** messenger, scout, collector, or agent for a bank etc.; a tout. **6** *hist.* **a** police officer. **7** a running bird. **8 a** a smuggler. **b** = *blockade-runner.* **9** a revolving millstone. **10** *Naut.* a rope in a single block with one end round a tackle-block and the other having a hook. **11** (in full **runner bean**) *Brit.* a twining bean plant, *Phaseolus multiflorus*, with red flowers and long green seed pods. Also called *scarlet runner.* **12** each of the long pieces on the underside of a sledge etc. that forms the contact in sliding. **13** a roller for moving a heavy article. **14** a long narrow ornamental cloth or rug. □ **do a runner** *sl.* leave hastily; flee. **runner-up** (*pl.* **runners-up** or **runner-ups**) the competitor or team taking second place.

running /ˈrʌnɪŋ/ *n.* & *adj.* —*n.* **1** the action of runners in a race etc. **2** the way a race etc. proceeds. —*adj.* **1** continuing on an essentially continuous basis though changing in detail (*a running battle*). **2** consecutive; one after another (*three days running*). **3** done with a run (*a running jump*). □ **in** (or **out of**) **the running** (of a competitor) with a good (or poor) chance of winning. **make** (or **take up**) **the running** take the lead; set the pace. **running account** a current account. **running-board** a footboard on either side of a vehicle. **running commentary** an oral description of events as they occur. **running fire** successive shots from a line of troops etc. **running gear** the moving or running parts of a machine, esp. the wheels and suspension of a vehicle. **running hand** writing in which the pen etc. is not

lifted after each letter. **running head** (or **headline**) a heading printed at the top of a number of consecutive pages of a book etc. **running knot** a knot that slips along the rope etc. and changes the size of a noose. **running light 1** = *navigation light.* **2** each of a small set of lights on a motor vehicle that remain illuminated while the vehicle is running. **running mate** *US* **1** a candidate for a secondary position in an election. **2** a horse entered in a race in order to set the pace for another horse from the same stable which is intended to win. **running repairs** minor or temporary repairs etc. to machinery while in use. **running rope** a rope that is freely movable through a pulley etc. **running sore** a suppurating sore. **running stitch 1** a line of small non-overlapping stitches for gathering etc. **2** one of these stitches. **running water** water flowing in a stream or from a tap etc. **take a running jump** (esp. as *int.*) *sl.* go away.

runny /ˈrʌnɪ/ *adj.* (**runnier, runniest**) **1** tending to run or flow. **2** excessively fluid.

runt /rʌnt/ *n.* **1** a small pig, esp. the smallest in a litter. **2** a weakling; an undersized person. **3** a large domestic pigeon. **4** a small ox or cow, esp. of various Scottish Highland or Welsh breeds. □□ **runty** *adj.* [16th c.: orig. unkn.]

runway /ˈrʌnweɪ/ *n.* **1** a specially prepared surface along which aircraft take off and land. **2** a trail to an animals' watering-place. **3** an incline down which logs are slid. **4** a raised gangway in a theatre, fashion display, etc.

rupee /ruːˈpiː/ *n.* the chief monetary unit of India, Pakistan, Sri Lanka, Nepal, Mauritius, and the Seychelles. [Hind. *rūpiyah* f. Skr. *rūpya* wrought silver]

rupiah /ruːˈpiːə/ *n.* the chief monetary unit of Indonesia. [as RUPEE]

rupture /ˈrʌptʃə(r)/ *n.* & *v.* —*n.* **1** the act or an instance of breaking; a breach. **2** a breach of harmonious relations; a disagreement and parting. **3** *Med.* an abdominal hernia. —*v.* **1** *tr.* break or burst (a cell or membrane etc.). **2** *tr.* sever (a connection). **3** *intr.* undergo a rupture. **4** *tr. & intr.* affect with or suffer a hernia. □□ **rupturable** *adj.* [ME f. OF *rupture* or L *ruptura* f. *rumpere rupt-* break]

rural /ˈrʊər(ə)l/ *adj.* in, of, or suggesting the country (opp. URBAN); pastoral or agricultural (*in rural seclusion; a rural constituency*). □ **rural dean** see DEAN¹. **rural district** *Brit. hist.* a group of country parishes governed by an elected council. □□ **ruralism** *n.* **ruralist** *n.* **rurality** /-ˈrælɪtɪ/ *n.* **ruralize** *v.* (also **-ise**). **ruralization** /-laɪˈzeɪʃ(ə)n/ *n.* **rurally** *adv.* [ME f. OF *rural* or LL *ruralis* f. *rus ruris* the country]

Ruritanian /ˌrʊərɪˈteɪnɪən/ *adj.* relating to or characteristic of romantic adventure or its setting. [*Ruritania*, an imaginary setting in SE Europe in the novels of Anthony Hope (d. 1933)]

rusa /ˈruːsə/ *n.* any of various E. Indian deer of the genus *Cervus*, esp. a sambur. [mod.L f. Malay]

ruse /ruːz/ *n.* a stratagem or trick. [ME f. OF f. *ruser* drive back, perh. ult. f. L *rursus* backwards: cf. RUSH¹]

rush¹ /rʌʃ/ *v.* & *n.* —*v.* **1** *intr.* go, move, or act precipitately or with great speed. **2** *tr.* move or transport with great haste (*was rushed to hospital*). **3** *intr.* (foll. by *at*) **a** move suddenly and quickly towards. **b** begin impetuously. **4** *tr.* perform or deal with hurriedly (*don't rush your dinner; the bill was rushed through Parliament*). **5** *tr.* force (a person) to act hastily. **6** *tr.* attack or capture by sudden assault. **7** *tr. sl.* overcharge (a customer). **8** *tr. US* pay attentions to (a person) with a view to securing acceptance of a proposal. **9** *tr.* pass (an obstacle) with a rapid dash. **10** *intr.* flow, fall, spread, or roll impetuously or fast (*felt the blood rush to my face; the river rushes past*). —*n.* **1** an act of rushing; a violent advance or attack. **2** a period of great activity. **3** (*attrib.*) done with great haste or speed (*a rush job*). **4** a sudden migration of large numbers. **5** (foll. by *on, for*) a sudden strong demand for a commodity. **6** (in *pl.*) *colloq.* the first prints of a film after a period of shooting. **7** *Football* **a** a combined dash by several players with the ball. **b** *US* the act of carrying the ball. □**rush one's fences** act with undue haste. **rush hour** a time each day when traffic is at its heaviest. □□**rusher** *n.* **rushingly** *adv.* [ME f. AF *russher*, = OF *ruser, russer*: see RUSE]

rush² /rʌʃ/ *n.* **1 a** any marsh or waterside plant of the family Juncaceae, with naked slender tapering pith-filled stems (properly leaves) formerly used for strewing floors and still used for making chair-bottoms and plaiting baskets etc. **b** a stem of this. **c** (*collect.*) rushes as a material. **2** *archaic* a thing of no value (*not worth a rush*). □**rush candle** a candle made by dipping the pith of a rush in tallow. □□ **rushlike** *adv.* **rushy** *adj.* [OE *rysc, rysce*, corresp. to MLG, MHG *rusch*]

rushlight /rʌʃlaɪt/ *n.* a rush candle.

rusk /rʌsk/ *n.* a slice of bread rebaked usu. as a light biscuit, esp. as food for babies. [Sp. or Port. *rosca* twist, coil, roll of bread]

russet /rʌsɪt/ *adj. & n.* —*adj.* **1** reddish-brown. **2** *archaic* rustic, homely, simple. —*n.* **1** a reddish-brown colour. **2** a kind of rough-skinned russet-coloured apple. **3** *hist.* a coarse homespun reddish-brown or grey cloth used for simple clothing. □□**russety** *adj.* [ME f. AF f. OF *rosset, rousset*, dimin. of *roux* red f. Prov. *ros*, It. *rosso* f. L *russus* red]

Russia leather /rʌʃə/ *n.* a durable bookbinding leather from skins impregnated with birch-bark oil. [*Russia* in E. Europe]

Russian /rʌʃ(ə)n/ *n. & adj.* —*n.* **1 a** a native or national of Russia or the Soviet Union. **b** a person of Russian descent. **2** the language of Russia and the official language of the Soviet Union. —*adj.* **1** of or relating to Russia. **2** of or in Russian. □**Russian boot** a boot that loosely encloses the calf. **Russian olive** = OLEASTER. **Russian roulette 1** an act of daring in which one (usu. with others in turn) squeezes the trigger of a revolver held to one's head with one chamber loaded, having first spun the chamber. **2** a potentially dangerous enterprise. **Russian salad** a salad of mixed diced vegetables with mayonnaise. □□**Russianize** *v.tr.* (also **-ise**). **Russianization** /-naɪˈzeɪʃ(ə)n/ *n.* **Russianness** *n.* [med.L *Russianus*]

Russify /rʌsɪfaɪ/ *v.tr.* (**-ies, -ied**) make Russian in character. □□**Russification** /-fɪˈkeɪʃ(ə)n/ *n.*

Russki /rʌskɪ/ *n.* (also **Russky**) (*pl.* **Russkis** or **-ies**) often *offens.* a Russian or Soviet. [RUSSIAN after Russ. surnames ending in *-ski*]

Russo- /rʌsəʊ/ *comb. form* Russian; Russian and.

Russophile /rʌsəʊfaɪl/ *n.* a person who is fond of Russia or the Russians.

rust /rʌst/ *n. & v.* —*n.* **1 a** a reddish or yellowish-brown coating formed on iron or steel by oxidation, esp. as a result of moisture. **b** a similar coating on other metals. **2 a** any of various plant-diseases with rust-coloured spots caused by fungi of the order Uredinales. **b** the fungus causing this. **3** an impaired state due to disuse or inactivity. —*v.* **1** *tr. & intr.* affect or be affected with rust; undergo oxidation. **2** *intr.* (of bracken etc.) become rust-coloured. **3** *intr.* (of a plant) be attacked by rust. **4** *intr.* lose quality or efficiency by disuse or inactivity. □□**rustless** *adj.* [OE *rūst* f. Gmc]

rustic /rʌstɪk/ *adj. & n.* —*adj.* **1** having the characteristics of or associations with the country or country life. **2** unsophisticated, simple, unrefined. **3** of rude or country workmanship. **4** made of untrimmed branches or rough timber (*a rustic bench*). **5** (of lettering) freely formed. **6** *Archit.* with

rough-hewn or roughened surface or with sunk joints. **7** *archaic* rural. —*n.* a person from or living in the country, esp. a simple unsophisticated one. □□**rustically** *adv.* **rusticity** /-ˈtɪsɪtɪ/ *n.* [ME f. L *rusticus* f. *rus* the country]

rusticate /rʌstɪˌkeɪt/ *v.* **1** *tr.* send down (a student) temporarily from university. **2** *intr.* retire to or live in the country. **3** *tr.* make rural. **4** *tr.* mark (masonry) with sunk joints or a roughened surface. □□ **rustication** /-ˈkeɪʃ(ə)n/ *n.* [L *rusticari* live in the country (as RUSTIC)]

rustle /rʌs(ə)l/ *v. & n.* —*v.* **1** *intr. & tr.* make or cause to make a gentle sound as of dry leaves blown in a breeze. **2** *intr.* (often foll. by *along* etc.) move with a rustling sound. **3** *tr.* (also *absol.*) steal (cattle or horses). **4** *intr.* *US colloq.* hustle. —*n.* a rustling sound or movement. □**rustle up** *colloq.* produce quickly when needed. □□ **rustler** *n.* (esp. in sense 3 of v.). [ME *rustel* etc. (imit.): cf. obs. Flem. *ruysselen*, Du. *ritselen*]

rustproof /rʌstpruːf/ *adj. & v.* —*adj.* (of a metal) not susceptible to corrosion by rust. —*v.tr.* make rustproof.

rustre /rʌstə(r)/ *n.* *Heraldry* a lozenge with a round hole. [F]

rusty /rʌstɪ/ *adj.* (**rustier, rustiest**) **1** rusted or affected by rust. **2** stiff with age or disuse. **3** (of knowledge etc.) faded or impaired by neglect (*my French is a bit rusty*). **4** rust-coloured. **5** (of black clothes) discoloured by age. **6 a** of antiquated appearance. **b** antiquated or behind the times. **7** (of a voice) croaking or creaking. □□**rustily** *adv.* **rustiness** *n.* [OE *rūstig* (as RUST)]

rut¹ /rʌt/ *n. & v.* —*n.* **1** a deep track made by the passage of wheels. **2** an established (esp. tedious) mode of practice or procedure. —*v.tr.* (**rutted, rutting**) mark with ruts. □**in a rut** following a fixed (esp. tedious or dreary) pattern of behaviour that is difficult to change. □□**rutty** *adj.* [prob. f. OF *rote* (as ROUTE)]

rut² /rʌt/ *n. & v.* —*n.* the periodic sexual excitement of a male deer, goat, ram, etc. —*v.intr.* (**rutted, rutting**) be affected with rut. □□**ruttish** *adj.* [ME f. OF *rut, ruit* f. L *rugitus* f. *rugire* roar]

rutabaga /ˌruːtəˈbɑːgə/ *n.* a swede. [Sw. dial. *rotabagge*]

ruthenium /ruːˈθiːnɪəm/ *n.* *Chem.* a rare hard white metallic transition element, occurring naturally in platinum ores, and used as a chemical catalyst and in certain alloys. ¶ Symb.: **Ru.** [med.L *Ruthenia* Russia (from its discovery in ores from the Urals)]

rutherfordium /ˌrʌðəˈfɔːdɪəm/ *n.* *Chem.* an artificially made transuranic metallic element produced by bombarding an isotope of Californium. ¶ Symb.: **Rf.** Also called KURCHATOVIUM. [E. *Rutherford*, Engl. physicist d. 1937]

ruthless /ruːθlɪs/ *adj.* having no pity or compassion. □□**ruthlessly** *adv.* **ruthlessness** *n.* [ME, f. *ruth* compassion f. RUE¹]

rutile /ruːtaɪl/ *n.* a mineral form of titanium dioxide. [F *rutile* or G *Rutil* f. L *rutilus* reddish]

RV *abbr.* Revised Version (of the Bible).

Ry. *abbr.* Railway.

-ry /rɪ/ *suffix* = -ERY (*infantry; rivalry*). [shortened f. -ERY, or by analogy]

rye /raɪ/ *n.* **1 a** a cereal plant, *Secale cereale*, with spikes bearing florets which yield wheatlike grains. **b** the grain of this used for bread and fodder. **2** (in full **rye whisky**) whisky distilled from fermented rye. [OE *ryge* f. Gmc]

ryegrass /raɪgrɑːs/ *n.* any forage or lawn grass of the genus *Lolium*, esp. *L. perenne*. [obs. *ray-grass*, of unkn. orig.]

ryokan /rɪˈəʊkən/ *n.* a traditional Japanese inn. [Jap.]

ryot /raɪət/ *n.* an Indian peasant. [Urdu *raˈīyat* f. Arab. *raˈīya* flock, subjects f. *raˈā* to pasture]

æ *cat* ɑː *arm* e *bed* ɜː *her* ɪ *sit* iː *see* ɒ *hot* ɔː *saw* ʌ *run* ʊ *put* uː *too* ə *ago* aɪ *my*

S

S¹ /es/ n. (also **s**) (pl. **Ss** or **S's** /'esɪz/) **1** the nineteenth letter of the alphabet. **2** an S-shaped object or curve.

S² abbr. (also **S.**) **1** Saint. **2** siemens. **3** Society. **4** South, Southern.

S³ symb. Chem. the element sulphur.

s. abbr. **1** second(s). **2** shilling(s). **3** singular. **4** son. **5** succeeded. [sense 2 orig. f. L solidus: see SOLIDUS]

's /s; z after a vowel sound or voiced consonant/ abbr. **1** is, has (he's; it's; John's; Charles's). **2** us (let's). **3** colloq. does (what's he say?).

-s¹ /s; z after a vowel sound or voiced consonant, e.g. ways, bags/ suffix denoting the plurals of nouns (cf. -ES¹). [OE -as pl. ending]

-s² /s; z after a vowel sound or voiced consonant, e.g. ties, begs/ suffix forming the 3rd person sing. present of verbs (cf. -ES²). [OE dial., prob. f. OE 2nd person sing. present ending -es, -as]

-s³ /s; z after a vowel sound or voiced consonant, e.g. besides/ suffix **1** forming adverbs (afterwards; besides). **2** forming possessive pronouns (hers; ours). [formed as -'s¹]

-s⁴ /s; z after a vowel sound or voiced consonant/ suffix forming nicknames or pet names (Fats; ducks). [after -s¹]

-s' /s; z after a vowel sound or voiced consonant/ suffix denoting the possessive case of plural nouns and sometimes of singular nouns ending in s (the boys' shoes; Charles' book). [as -'s¹]

's- /s, z/ prefix archaic (esp. in oaths) God's ('sblood; 'struth). [abbr.]

-'s¹ /s; z after a vowel sound or voiced consonant/ suffix denoting the possessive case of singular nouns and of plural nouns not ending in -s (John's book; the book's cover; the children's shoes). [OE genit. sing. ending]

-'s² /s; z after a vowel sound or voiced consonant/ suffix denoting the plural of a letter or symbol (S's; 8's). [as -s¹]

SA abbr. **1** Salvation Army. **2** sex appeal. **3 a** South Africa. **b** South America. **c** South Australia. **4** hist. Sturmabteilung (the paramilitary force of the Nazi party).

sabadilla /ˌsæbə'dɪlə/ n. **1** a Mexican plant, Schoeno-caulon officinale, with seeds yielding veratrine. **2** a preparation of these seeds, used in medicine and agriculture. [Sp. cebadilla dimin. of cebada barley]

Sabaoth /'sæbɑːˌɒθ, sæ'bɑːɒθ/ n.pl. Bibl. heavenly hosts (see HOST¹ 2) (Lord of Sabaoth). [ME f. LL f. Gk Sabaōth f. Heb. ṣᵉbāōṯ pl. of ṣābā host (of heaven)]

Sabbatarian /ˌsæbə'teərɪən/ n. & adj. —n. **1** a strict sabbath-keeping Jew. **2** a Christian who favours observing Sunday strictly as the sabbath. **3** a Christian who observes Saturday as the sabbath. —adj. relating to or holding the tenets of Sabbatarians. □□ **Sabbatarianism** n. [LL sabbatarius f. L sabbatum: see SABBATH]

sabbath /'sæbəθ/ n. **1** (in full **sabbath day**) a day of rest and religious observance kept by Christians on Sunday, Jews on Saturday, and Muslims on Friday. **2** a period of rest. **3** (in full **witches' sabbath**) a supposed general midnight meeting of witches with the Devil. [OE sabat, L sabbatum, & OF sabbat, f. Gk sabbaton f. Heb. šabbāṯ f. šāḇaṯ to rest]

sabbatical /sə'bætɪk(ə)l/ adj. & n. —adj. **1** of or appropriate to the sabbath. **2** (of leave) granted at intervals to a university teacher for study or travel, orig. every seventh year. —n. a period of sabbatical leave. □ **sabbatical year 1** Bibl. every seventh year, prescribed by the Mosaic law to be observed as a 'sabbath', during which the land was allowed to rest.

2 a year's sabbatical leave. □□ **sabbatically** adv. [LL sabbaticus f. Gk sabbatikos of the sabbath]

saber US var. of SABRE.

Sabian /'seɪbɪən/ adj. & n. —adj. of a sect classed in the Koran with Muslims, Jews, and Christians, as believers in the true God. —n. a member of this sect. [Arab. ṣābī']

sabicu /'sæbɪˌkuː/ n. **1** a W. Indian tree, Lysiloma latisiliqua, grown for timber. **2** the mahogany-like wood of this tree. [Cuban Sp. sabicú]

Sabine /'sæbaɪn/ adj. & n. —adj. of or relating to a people of the central Apennines in ancient Italy. —n. a member of this people. [L Sabinus]

Sabin vaccine /'seɪbɪn/ n. an oral vaccine giving immunity against poliomyelitis. [A. B. Sabin, US virologist b. 1906]

sable¹ /'seɪb(ə)l/ n. **1 a** a small brown-furred flesh-eating mammal, Martes zibellina, of N. Europe and parts of N. Asia, related to the marten. **b** its skin or fur. **2** a fine paintbrush made of sable fur. [ME f. OF f. med.L sabelum f. Slav.]

sable² /'seɪb(ə)l/ n. & adj. —n. **1** esp. poet. black. **2** (in pl.) mourning garments. **3** (in full **sable antelope**) a large stout-horned African antelope, Hippotragus niger, the males of which are mostly black in old age. —adj. **1** (usu. placed after noun) Heraldry black. **2** esp. poet. dark, gloomy. □□ **sabled** adj. **sably** adv. [ME f. OF (in Heraldry): gen. taken to be identical with SABLE¹, although sable fur is dark brown]

sabot /'sæbəʊt, 'sæbəʊ/ n. **1** a kind of simple shoe hollowed out from a block of wood. **2** a wooden-soled shoe. **3** Austral. a small snub-nosed yacht. □□ **saboted** /'sæbəʊd/ adj. [F, blend of savate shoe + botte boot]

sabotage /'sæbəˌtɑːʒ/ n. & v. —n. deliberate damage to productive capacity, esp. as a political act. —v.tr. **1** commit sabotage on. **2** destroy, spoil; make useless (sabotaged my plans). [F f. saboter make a noise with sabots, bungle, wilfully destroy: see SABOT]

saboteur /ˌsæbə'tɜː(r)/ n. a person who commits sabotage. [F]

sabra /'sæbrə/ n. a Jew born in Israel. [mod. Heb. sābrāh opuntia fruit]

sabre /'seɪbə(r)/ n. & v. (US **saber**) —n. **1** a cavalry sword with a curved blade. **2** a cavalry soldier and horse. **3** a light fencing-sword with a tapering blade. —v.tr. cut down or wound with a sabre. □ **sabre-bill** any S. American bird of the genus Campylorhamphus with a long curved bill. **sabre-cut 1** a blow with a sabre. **2** a wound made or a scar left by this. **sabre-rattling** a display or threat of military force. **sabre-toothed** designating any of various extinct mammals having long sabre-shaped upper canines. **sabre-wing** a S. American humming-bird, Campylopterus falcatus, with curved wings. [F, earlier sable f. G Sabel, Säbel, Schabel f. Pol. szabla or Magyar szablya]

sabretache /'sæbəˌtæʃ/ n. a flat satchel on long straps worn by some cavalry officers from the left of the waist-belt. [F f. G Säbeltasche (as SABRE, Tasche pocket)]

sabreur /sæ'brɜː(r)/ n. a user of the sabre, esp. a cavalryman. [F f. sabrer SABRE v.]

SAC abbr. (in the UK) Senior Aircraftman.

sac /sæk/ n. **1** a baglike cavity, enclosed by a membrane, in an animal or plant. **2** the distended membrane surrounding a hernia, cyst, tumour, etc. [F sac or L saccus SACK¹]

saccade /sæ'kɑːd/ n. a brief rapid movement of the

eye between fixation points. ▫▫ **saccadic** /sə'kædɪk/ adj. [F, = violent pull, f. OF *saquer, sachier* pull]

saccate /'sækeɪt/ adj. *Bot.* **1** dilated into a bag. **2** contained in a sac.

saccharide /'sækə,raɪd/ n. *Chem.* = SUGAR 2. [mod.L *saccharum* sugar + -IDE]

saccharimeter /,sækə'rɪmɪtə(r)/ n. any instrument, esp. a polarimeter, for measuring the sugar content of a solution. [F *saccharimètre* (as SACCHARIDE)]

saccharin /'sækərɪn/ n. a very sweet substance used as a non-fattening substitute for sugar. [G (as SACCHARIDE) + -IN]

saccharine /'sækə,riːn/ adj. **1** sugary. **2** of, containing, or like sugar. **3** unpleasantly over-polite, sentimental, etc.

saccharo- /'sækərəʊ/ comb. form sugar; sugar and. [Gk *sakkharon* sugar]

saccharogenic /,sækərəʊ'dʒenɪk/ adj. producing sugar.

saccharometer /,sækə'rɒmɪtə(r)/ n. any instrument, esp. a hydrometer, for measuring the sugar content of a solution.

saccharose /'sækə,rəʊs, -,rəʊz/ n. sucrose. [mod.L *saccharum* sugar + -OSE²]

sacciform /'sæksɪ,fɔːm/ adj. sac-shaped. [L *saccus* sac + -FORM]

saccule /'sækjuːl/ n. a small sac or cyst. ▫▫ **saccular** adj. [L *sacculus* (as SAC)]

sacerdotal /,sækə'dəʊt(ə)l/ adj. **1** of priests or the priestly office; priestly. **2** (of a doctrine etc.) ascribing sacrificial functions and supernatural powers to ordained priests; claiming excessive authority for the priesthood. ▫▫ **sacerdotalism** n. **sacerdotalist** n. **sacerdotally** adv. [ME f. OF *sacerdotal* or L *sacerdotalis* f. *sacerdos -dotis* priest]

sachem /'seɪtʃəm/ n. **1** the supreme chief of some American Indian tribes. **2** *US* a political leader. [Narraganset, = SAGAMORE]

sachet /'sæʃeɪ/ n. **1** a small bag or packet containing a small portion of a substance, esp. shampoo. **2** a small perfumed bag. **3 a** dry perfume for laying among clothes etc. **b** a packet of this. [F, dimin. of *sac* f. L *saccus*]

sack¹ /sæk/ n. & v. —n. **1 a** a large strong bag, usu. made of hessian, paper, or plastic, for storing or conveying goods. **b** (usu. foll. by *of*) this with its contents (*a sack of potatoes*). **c** a quantity contained in a sack. **2** (prec. by *the*) *colloq.* dismissal from employment. **3** (prec. by *the*) *US sl.* bed. **4 a** a woman's short loose dress with a sacklike appearance. **b** *archaic* or *hist.* a woman's loose gown, or a silk train attached to the shoulders of this. **5** a man's or woman's loose-hanging coat not shaped to the back. —v.tr. **1** put into a sack or sacks. **2** *colloq.* dismiss from employment. ▫▫ **sack race** a race between competitors in sacks up to the waist or neck. ▫▫ **sackful** n. (*pl.* -**fuls**). **sacklike** adj. [OE *sacc* f. L *saccus* f. Gk *sakkos*, of Semitic orig.]

sack² /sæk/ v. & n. —v.tr. **1** plunder and destroy (a captured town etc.). **2** steal valuables from (a place). —n. the sacking of a captured place. [orig. as noun, f. F *sac* in phr. *mettre à sac* put to sack, f. It. *sacco* SACK¹]

sack³ /sæk/ n. *hist.* a white wine formerly imported into Britain from Spain and the Canaries (*sherry sack*). [16th-c. *wyne seck*, f. F *vin sec* dry wine]

sackbut /'sækbʌt/ n. an early form of trombone. [F *saquebute*, earlier *saqueboute* hook for pulling a man off a horse f. *saquer* pull, *boute* (as BUTT¹)]

sackcloth /'sækklɒθ/ n. **1** a coarse fabric of flax or hemp. **2** clothing made of this, formerly worn as a penance or in mourning (esp. *sackcloth and ashes*).

sacking /'sækɪŋ/ n. material for making sacks; sackcloth.

sacra *pl.* of SACRUM.

sacral /'seɪkr(ə)l/ adj. **1** *Anat.* of or relating to the sacrum. **2** *Anthropol.* of or for sacred rites. [E or L *sacrum*: see SACRUM]

sacrament /'sækrəmənt/ n. **1** a religious ceremony or act of the Christian Churches regarded as an outward and visible sign of inward and spiritual grace: applied by the Eastern, pre-Reformation Western, and Roman Catholic Churches to the seven rites of baptism, confirmation, the Eucharist, penance, extreme unction, ordination, and matrimony, but restricted by most Protestants to baptism and the Eucharist. **2** a thing of mysterious and sacred significance; a sacred influence, symbol, etc. **3** (also **Blessed** or **Holy Sacrament**) (prec. by *the*) **a** the Eucharist. **b** the consecrated elements, esp. the bread or Host. **4** an oath or solemn engagement taken. [ME f. OF *sacrement* f. L *sacramentum* solemn oath etc. f. *sacrare* hallow f. *sacer* SACRED, used in Christian L as transl. of Gk *mustērion* MYSTERY¹]

sacramental /,sækrə'ment(ə)l/ adj. & n. —adj. **1** of or of the nature of a sacrament or the sacrament. **2** (of a doctrine etc.) attaching great importance to the sacraments. —n. an observance analogous to but not reckoned among the sacraments, e.g. the use of holy water or the sign of the cross. ▫▫ **sacramentalism** n. **sacramentalist** n. **sacramentality** /-'tælɪtɪ/ n. **sacramentally** adv. [ME f. F *sacramental* or LL *sacramentalis* (as SACRAMENT)]

sacrarium /sə'kreərɪəm/ n. (*pl.* **sacraria** /-rɪə/) **1** the sanctuary of a church. **2** *RC Ch.* a piscina. **3** *Rom. Antiq.* a shrine; the room (in a house) containing the penates. [L f. *sacer sacri* holy]

sacred /'seɪkrɪd/ adj. **1 a** (often foll. by *to*) exclusively dedicated or appropriated (to a god or to some religious purpose). **b** made holy by religious association. **c** connected with religion; used for a religious purpose (*sacred music*). **2 a** safeguarded or required by religion, reverence, or tradition. **b** sacrosanct. **3** (of writings etc.) embodying the laws or doctrines of a religion. ▫**Sacred College** *RC Ch.* the body of cardinals. **sacred cow** *colloq.* an idea or institution unreasonably held to be above criticism (with ref. to the Hindus' respect for the cow as a holy animal). **Sacred Heart** *RC Ch.* the heart of Christ as an object of devotion. **sacred number** a number associated with religious symbolism, e.g. 7. ▫▫ **sacredly** adv. **sacredness** n. [ME, past part. of obs. *sacre* consecrate f. OF *sacrer* f. L *sacrare* f. *sacer sacri* holy]

sacrifice /'sækrɪ,faɪs/ n. & v. —n. **1 a** the act of giving up something valued for the sake of something else more important or worthy. **b** a thing given up in this way. **c** the loss entailed in this. **2 a** the slaughter of an animal or person or the surrender of a possession as an offering to a deity. **b** an animal, person, or thing offered in this way. **3** an act of prayer, thanksgiving, or penitence as propitiation. **4** *Theol.* **a** Christ's offering of himself in the Crucifixion. **b** the Eucharist as either a propitiatory offering of the body and blood of Christ or an act of thanksgiving. **5** (in games) a loss incurred deliberately to avoid a greater loss or to obtain a compensating advantage. —v. **1** tr. give up (a thing) as a sacrifice. **2** tr. (foll. by *to*) devote or give over to. **3** tr. (also *absol.*) offer or kill as a sacrifice. ▫▫ **sacrificial** /-'fɪʃ(ə)l/ adj. **sacrificially** /-'fɪʃəlɪ/ adv. [ME f. OF f. L *sacrificium*: cf. *sacrificus* (as SACRED)]

sacrilege /'sækrɪlɪdʒ/ n. the violation or misuse of what is regarded as sacred. ▫▫ **sacrilegious** /-'lɪdʒəs/ adj. **sacrilegiously** /-'lɪdʒəslɪ/ adv. [ME f. OF f. L *sacrilegium* f. *sacrilegus* stealer of sacred things, f. *sacer sacri* sacred + *legere* take possession of]

sacring /'seɪkrɪŋ/ n. *archaic* **1** the consecration of the Eucharistic elements. **2** the ordination and consecration of a bishop, sovereign, etc. ▫**sacring bell** a bell rung at the elevation of the elements in the Eucharist. [ME f. obs. *sacre*: see SACRED]

sacristan /'sækrɪst(ə)n/ n. **1** a person in charge of a sacristy and its contents. **2** *archaic* the sexton of a parish church. [ME f. med.L *sacristanus* (as SACRED)]

sacristy /'sækrɪstɪ/ n. (pl. **-ies**) a room in a church, where the vestments, sacred vessels, etc., are kept and the celebrant can prepare for a service. [F sacristie or It. sacrestia or med.L sacristia (as SACRED)]

sacro- /'seɪkrəʊ/ comb. form denoting the sacrum (sacro-iliac).

sacrosanct /'sækrəʊ,sæŋkt/ adj. (of a person, place, law, etc.) most sacred; inviolable. □□ **sacrosanctity** /-'sæŋktɪtɪ/ n. [L sacrosanctus f. sacro ablat. of sacrum sacred rite (see SACRED) + sanctus (as SAINT)]

sacrum /'seɪkrəm/ n. (pl. **sacra** /-krə/ or **sacrums**) Anat. a triangular bone formed from fused vertebrae and situated between the two hip-bones of the pelvis. [L os sacrum transl. Gk hieron osteon sacred bone (from its sacrificial use)]

SACW abbr. (in the UK) Senior Aircraftwoman.

SAD abbr. seasonal affective disorder.

sad /sæd/ adj. (**sadder**, **saddest**) **1** unhappy; feeling sorrow or regret. **2** causing or suggesting sorrow (a sad story). **3** regrettable. **4** shameful, deplorable (is in a sad state). **5** (of a colour) dull, neutral-tinted. **6** (of dough etc.) heavy, having failed to rise. □ **sad-iron** a solid flat-iron. **sad sack** US colloq. a very inept person. □□ **saddish** adj. **sadly** adv. **sadness** n. [OE sæd f. Gmc, rel. to L satis]

sadden /'sæd(ə)n/ v.tr. & intr. make or become sad.

saddle /'sæd(ə)l/ n. & v. —n. **1** a seat of leather etc., usu. raised at the front and rear, fastened on a horse etc. for riding. **2** a seat for the rider of a bicycle etc. **3** a joint of meat consisting of the two loins. **4** a ridge rising to a summit at each end. **5** the part of a draught-horse's harness to which the shafts are attached. **6** a part of an animal's back resembling a saddle in shape or marking. **7** the rear part of a male fowl's back. **8** a support for a cable or wire on top of a suspension-bridge, pier, or telegraph-pole. **9** a fireclay bar for supporting ceramic ware in a kiln. —v.tr. **1** put a saddle on (a horse etc.). **2** a (foll. by with) burden (a person) with a task, responsibility, etc. **b** (foll. by on, upon) impose (a burden) on a person. **3** (of a trainer) enter (a horse) for a race. □ **in the saddle 1** mounted. **2** in office or control. **saddle-bag 1** each of a pair of bags laid across a horse etc. behind the saddle. **2** a bag attached behind the saddle of a bicycle or motor cycle. **saddle-bow** the arched front or rear of a saddle. **saddle-cloth** a cloth laid on a horse's back under the saddle. **saddle-horse** a horse for riding. **saddle-sore** chafed by riding on a saddle. **saddle stitch** a stitch of thread or a wire staple passed through the centre of a magazine or booklet. **saddle-tree 1** the frame of a saddle. **2** a tulip-tree (with saddle-shaped leaves). □□ **saddleless** adj. [OE sadol, sadul f. Gmc]

saddleback /'sæd(ə)l,bæk/ n. **1** Archit. a tower-roof with two opposite gables. **2** a hill with a concave upper outline. **3** a black pig with a white stripe across the back. **4** any of various birds with a saddle-like marking esp. a New Zealand bird, Philesturnus carunculatus. □□ **saddlebacked** adj.

saddler /'sædlə(r)/ n. a maker of or dealer in saddles and other equipment for horses.

saddlery /'sædlərɪ/ n. (pl. **-ies**) **1** the saddles and other equipment of a saddler. **2** a saddler's business or premises.

Sadducee /'sædjʊ,siː/ n. a member of a Jewish sect or party of the time of Christ that denied the resurrection of the dead, the existence of spirits, and the obligation of the traditional oral law (cf. PHARISEE, ESSENE). □□ **Sadducean** /-'siːən/ adj. [OE sadducēas f. LL Sadducaeus f. Gk Saddoukaios f. Heb. ṣᵉdûḳî, prob. = descendant of Zadok (2 Sam. 8: 17)]

sadhu /'saːduː/ n. (in India) a holy man, sage, or ascetic. [Skr., = holy man]

sadism /'seɪdɪz(ə)m/ n. **1** a form of sexual perversion characterized by the enjoyment of inflicting pain or suffering on others (cf. MASOCHISM). **2** colloq. the enjoyment of cruelty to others. □□ **sadist** n. **sadistic**

/sə'dɪstɪk/ adj. **sadistically** /sə'dɪstɪkəlɪ/ adv. [F sadisme f. Count or 'Marquis' de Sade, Fr. writer d. 1814]

sado-masochism /,seɪdəʊ'mæsə,kɪz(ə)m/ n. the combination of sadism and masochism in one person. □□ **sado-masochist** n. **sado-masochistic** /-'kɪstɪk/ adj.

s.a.e. abbr. stamped addressed envelope.

safari /sə'faːrɪ/ n. (pl. **safaris**) **1** a hunting or scientific expedition, esp. in E. Africa (go on safari). **2** a sightseeing trip to see African animals in their natural habitat. □ **safari park** an enclosed area where lions etc. are kept in relatively open spaces for public viewing from vehicles driven through. **safari suit** a lightweight suit usu. with short sleeves and four pleated pockets in the jacket. [Swahili f. Arab. safara to travel]

safe /seɪf/ adj. & n. —adj. **1 a** free of danger or injury. **b** (often foll. by from) out of or not exposed to danger (safe from their enemies). **2** affording security or not involving danger or risk (put it in a safe place). **3** reliable, certain; that can be reckoned on (a safe catch; a safe method; is safe to win). **4** prevented from escaping or doing harm (have got him safe). **5** (also **safe and sound**) uninjured; with no harm done. **6** cautious and unenterprising; consistently moderate. —n. **1** a strong lockable cabinet etc. for valuables. **2** = meat safe. □ **on the safe side** with a margin of security against risks. **safe bet** a bet that is certain to succeed. **safe-breaker** (or **-blower** or **-cracker**) a person who breaks open and robs safes. **safe conduct 1** a privilege of immunity from arrest or harm, esp. on a particular occasion. **2** a document securing this. **safe deposit** a building containing strongrooms and safes let separately. **safe house** a place of refuge or rendezvous for spies etc. **safe keeping** preservation in a safe place. **safe light** Photog. a filtered light for use in a darkroom. **safe period** the time during and near the menstrual period when conception is least likely. **safe seat** a seat in Parliament etc. that is usually won with a large margin by a particular party. **safe sex** sexual activity in which precautions are taken to reduce the risk of spreading sexually transmitted diseases, esp. Aids. □□ **safely** adv. **safeness** n. [ME f. AF saf, OF sauf f. L salvus uninjured: (n.) orig. save f. SAVE[1]]

safeguard /'seɪfgaːd/ n. & v. —n. **1** a proviso, stipulation, quality, or circumstance, that tends to prevent something undesirable. **2** a safe conduct. —v.tr. guard or protect (rights etc.) by a precaution or stipulation. [ME f. AF salve garde, OF sauve garde (as SAFE, GUARD)]

safety /'seɪftɪ/ n. (pl. **-ies**) **1** the condition of being safe; freedom from danger or risks. **2** (attrib.) **a** designating any of various devices for preventing injury from machinery (safety bar; safety lock). **b** designating items of protective clothing (safety helmet). □ **safety-belt 1** = seat-belt. **2** a belt or strap securing a person to prevent injury. **safety-catch** a contrivance for locking a gun-trigger or preventing the accidental operation of machinery. **safety curtain** a fireproof curtain that can be lowered to cut off the auditorium in a theatre from the stage. **safety factor** (or **factor of safety**) **1** the ratio of a material's strength to an expected strain. **2** a margin of security against risks. **safety film** a cinematographic film on a slow-burning or non-flammable base. **safety first** a motto advising caution. **safety fuse 1** a fuse (see FUSE[2]) containing a slow-burning composition for firing detonators from a distance. **2** Electr. a protective fuse (see FUSE[1]). **safety glass** glass that will not splinter when broken. **safety harness** a system of belts or restraints to hold a person to prevent falling or injury. **safety lamp** a miner's lamp so protected as not to ignite firedamp. **safety match** a match igniting only on a specially prepared surface. **safety net** a net placed to catch an acrobat etc. in case of a fall. **safety pin** a pin with a point that is bent back to the head and is held in a guard when closed. **safety razor** a razor with a guard to reduce the risk of cutting the skin. **safety-valve 1** (in a steam boiler) a valve opening automatically to relieve excessive pressure. **2** a means of giving harmless vent to excitement etc. **safety zone** US an area of a road marked off for pedestrians etc. to wait safely. [ME *sauvete* f. OF *sauveté* f. med.L *salvitas -tatis* f. L *salvus* (as SAFE)]

safflower /'sæflaʊə(r)/ *n.* **1 a** a thistle-like plant, *Carthamus tinctorius*, yielding a red dye. **b** its dried petals. **2** a dye made from these, used in rouge etc. [Du. *saffloer* or G *Safflor* f. OF *saffleur* f. obs. It. *saffiore*, of unkn. orig.]

saffron /'sæfrən/ *n. & adj.* —*n.* **1** an orange flavouring and food colouring made from the dried stigmas of the crocus, *Crocus sativus*. **2** the colour of this. **3** = *meadow saffron*. —*adj.* saffron-coloured. □□ **saffrony** *adj.* [ME f. OF *safran* f. Arab. *za'farān*]

safranine /'sæfrə,ni:n/ *n.* (also **safranin** /-nɪn/) any of a large group of mainly red dyes used in biological staining etc. [F *safranine* (as SAFFRON): orig. of dye from saffron]

sag /sæg/ *v. & n.* —*v.intr.* (**sagged, sagging**) **1** sink or subside under weight or pressure, esp. unevenly. **2** have a downward bulge or curve in the middle. **3** fall in price. **4** (of a ship) drift from its course, esp. to leeward. —*n.* **1 a** the amount that a rope etc. sags. **b** the distance from the middle of its curve to a straight line between its supports. **2** a sinking condition; subsidence. **3** a fall in price. **4** *Naut.* a tendency to leeward. □□ **saggy** *adj.* [ME f. MLG *sacken*, Du. *zakken* subside]

saga /'sɑ:gə/ *n.* **1** a long story of heroic achievement, esp. a medieval Icelandic or Norwegian prose narrative. **2** a series of connected books giving the history of a family etc. **3** a long involved story. [ON, = narrative, rel. to SAW[3]]

sagacious /sə'geɪʃ(ə)s/ *adj.* **1** mentally penetrating; gifted with discernment; having practical wisdom. **2** acute-minded, shrewd. **3** (of a saying, plan, etc.) showing wisdom. **4** (of an animal) exceptionally intelligent; seeming to reason or deliberate. □□ **sagaciously** *adv.* **sagacity** /sə'gæsɪtɪ/ *n.* [L *sagax sagacis*]

sagamore /'sægə,mɔ:(r)/ *n.* = SACHEM 1. [Penobscot *sagamo*]

sage[1] /seɪdʒ/ *n.* **1** an aromatic herb, *Salvia officinalis*, with dull greyish-green leaves. **2** its leaves used in cookery. □ **sage and onion** (or **onions**) a stuffing used with poultry, pork, etc. **sage Derby** (or **cheese**) a cheese made with an infusion of sage which flavours and mottles it. **sage-green** the colour of sage-leaves. **sage tea** a medicinal infusion of sage-leaves. □□ **sagy** *adj.* [ME f. OF *sauge* f. L *salvia* healing plant f. *salvus* safe]

sage[2] /seɪdʒ/ *n. & adj.* —*n.* **1** often *iron.* a profoundly wise man. **2** any of the ancients traditionally regarded as the wisest of their time. —*adj.* **1** profoundly wise, esp. from experience. **2** of or indicating profound wisdom. **3** often *iron.* wise-looking; solemn-faced. □□ **sagely** *adv.* **sageness** *n.* **sageship** *n.* [ME f. OF ult. f. L *sapere* be wise]

sagebrush /'seɪdʒbrʌʃ/ *n.* **1** a growth of shrubby aromatic plants of the genus *Artemisia*, esp. *A. tridentata*, found in some semi-arid regions of western N. America. **2** this plant.

saggar /'sægə(r)/ *n.* (also **sagger**) a protective fireclay box enclosing ceramic ware while it is being fired. [prob. contr. of SAFEGUARD]

sagittal /'sædʒɪt(ə)l/ *adj. Anat.* **1** of or relating to the suture between the parietal bones of the skull. **2** in the same plane as this, or in a parallel plane. [F f. med.L *sagittalis* f. *sagitta* arrow]

Sagittarius /,sædʒɪ'teərɪəs/ *n.* **1** a constellation, traditionally regarded as contained in the figure of an archer. **2 a** the ninth sign of the zodiac (the Archer). **b** a person born when the sun is in this sign. □□ **Sagittarian** *adj. & n.* [ME f. L, = archer, f. *sagitta* arrow]

sagittate /'sædʒɪ,teɪt/ *adj. Bot. & Zool.* shaped like an arrowhead.

sago /'seɪgəʊ/ *n.* (*pl.* **-os**) **1** a kind of starch, made from the powdered pith of the sago palm and used in puddings etc. **2** (in full **sago palm**) any of several tropical palms and cycads, esp. *Cycas circinalis* and *Metroxylon sagu*, from which sago is made. [Malay *sāgū* (orig. through Port.)]

saguaro /sæ'gwɑ:rəʊ/ *n.* (also **sahuaro** /sæ'wɑ:rəʊ/) (*pl.* **-os**) a giant cactus, *Carnegiea gigantea*, of the SW United States and Mexico. [Mex. Sp.]

sahib /sɑ:b, 'sɑ:hɪb/ *n.* **1** *hist.* (in India) a form of address, often placed after the name, to European men. **2** *colloq.* a gentleman (*pukka sahib*). [Urdu f. Arab. *ṣāḥīb* friend, lord]

said *past* and *past part.* of SAY[1].

saiga /'saɪgə, 'seɪ-/ *n.* an antelope, *Saiga tatarica*, of the Asian steppes. [Russ.]

sail /seɪl/ *n. & v.* —*n.* **1** a piece of material (orig. canvas, now usu. nylon etc.) extended on rigging to catch the wind and propel a boat or ship. **2** a ship's sails collectively. **3 a** a voyage or excursion in a sailing-ship. **b** a voyage of specified duration. **4** a ship, esp. as discerned from its sails. **5** (*collect.*) ships in a squadron or company (*a fleet of twenty sail*). **6** (in *pl.*) *Naut.* **a** *sl.* a maker or repairer of sails. **b** *hist.* a chief petty officer in charge of rigging. **7** a wind-catching apparatus, usu. a set of boards, attached to the arm of a windmill. **8 a** the dorsal fin of a sailfish. **b** the tentacle of a nautilus. **c** the float of a Portuguese man-of-war. —*v.* **1** *intr.* travel on water by the use of sails or engine-power. **2** *tr.* **a** navigate (a ship etc.). **b** travel on (a sea). **3** *tr.* set (a toy boat) afloat. **4** *intr.* glide or move smoothly or in a stately manner. **5** *intr.* (often foll. by *through*) *colloq.* succeed easily (*sailed through the exams*). □ **sail-arm** the arm of a windmill. **sail close to** (or **near**) **the wind 1** sail as nearly against the wind as possible. **2** come close to indecency or dishonesty; risk overstepping the mark. **sail-fluke** = MEGRIM[2]. **sailing-boat** (or **-ship** or **-vessel**) a vessel driven by sails. **sailing-master** an officer navigating a ship, esp. *Brit.* a yacht. **sailing orders** instructions to a captain regarding departure, destination, etc. **sail into** *colloq.* attack physically or verbally with force. **take in sail 1** furl the sail or sails of a vessel. **2** moderate one's ambitions. **under sail** with sails set. □□ **sailable** *adj.* **sailed** *adj.* (also in *comb.*). **sailless** *adj.* [OE *segel* f. Gmc]

sailboard /'seɪlbɔ:d/ *n.* a board with a mast and sail, used in windsurfing. □□ **sailboarder** *n.* **sailboarding** *n.*

sailboat /'seɪlbəʊt/ *n.* US a boat driven by sails.

sailcloth /'seɪlklɒθ/ *n.* **1** canvas for sails. **2** a canvas-like dress material.

sailer /'seɪlə(r)/ *n.* a ship of specified sailing-power (*a good sailer*).

sailfish /'seɪlfɪʃ/ *n.* **1** any fish of the genus *Istiophorus*, with a large dorsal fin. **2** a basking shark.

sailor /'seɪlə(r)/ *n.* **1** a seaman or mariner, esp. one below the rank of officer. **2** a person considered as liable or not liable to seasickness (*a good sailor*). □ **sailor hat 1** a straw hat with a straight narrow brim and flat top. **2** a hat with a turned-up brim in imitation of a sailor's, worn by women and children. □□ **sailoring** *n.* **sailorless** *adj.* **sailorly** *adj.* [var. of SAILER]

sailplane /'seɪlpleɪn/ *n.* a glider designed for sustained flight.

sainfoin /'seɪnfɔɪn, 'sæn-/ *n.* a leguminous plant, *Onobrychis viciifolia*, grown for fodder and having pink flowers. [obs. F *saintfoin* f. mod.L *sanum foenum* wholesome hay (because of its medicinal properties)]

saint /seɪnt, before a name usu. sənt/ *n. & v.* —*n.* (*abbr.* **St** or **S**; *pl.* **Sts** or **SS**) **1** a holy or (in some Churches) a canonized person regarded as having a place in heaven. **2** (**Saint** or **St**) the title of a saint or archbishop, hence the name of a church etc. (*St Paul's*) or (often with the loss of the apostrophe) the name of a town etc. (*St Andrews*; *St Albans*). **3** a very virtuous person; a person of great real or affected holiness (*would try the patience of a saint*). **4** a member of the company of heaven (*with all the angels and saints*). **5** (*Bibl.*, *archaic*, and used by Puritans, Mormons, etc.) one of God's chosen people; a member of the Christian Church or one's own branch of it. —*v.tr.* **1** canonize; admit to the calendar of saints. **2** call or regard as a saint. **3** (as **sainted** *adj.*) sacred; of a saintly life; worthy to be regarded as a saint. □**my sainted aunt** see AUNT. **saint's day** a Church festival in memory of a saint. □□ **saintdom** *n.* **sainthood** *n.* **saintlike** *adj.* **saintling** *n.* **saintship** *n.* [ME f. OF *seint*, *saint* f. L *sanctus* holy, past part. of *sancire* consecrate]

St Andrew's cross /'ændruːz/ *n.* an X-shaped cross.

St Anthony cross /'æntənɪ/ *n.* (also **St Anthony's cross** /'æntənɪz/) a T-shaped cross.

St Anthony's fire /'æntənɪz/ *n.* erysipelas or ergotism.

St Bernard /'bɜːnəd/ *n.* (in full **St Bernard dog**) **1** a very large dog of a breed orig. kept to rescue travellers by the monks of the Hospice on the Great St Bernard pass in the Alps. **2** this breed.

St Elmo's fire /'elməʊz/ *n.* a corposant.

St George's cross /'dʒɔːdʒɪz/ *n.* a +-shaped cross, red on a white background.

St John's wort /dʒɒnz/ *n.* any yellow-flowered plant of the genus *Hypericum*, esp. *H. androsaemum*.

St Leger /'ledʒə(r)/ *n.* a horse-race at Doncaster in England for three-year-olds. [f. the founder's name]

St Luke's summer /luːks/ *n. Brit.* a period of fine weather expected about 18 Oct.

saintly /'seɪntlɪ/ *adj.* (**saintlier**, **saintliest**) very holy or virtuous. □□ **saintliness** *n.*

St Martin's summer /'mɑːtɪnz/ *n. Brit.* a period of fine weather expected about 11 Nov.

saintpaulia /sənt'pɔːlɪə/ *n.* any plant of the genus *Saintpaulia*, esp. the African violet. [Baron W. von *Saint Paul*, Ger. soldier d. 1910, its discoverer]

St Vitus's dance /'vaɪtəsɪz/ *n.* = *Sydenham's chorea* (see CHOREA).

saith /seθ/ *archaic 3rd sing. present* of SAY[1].

saithe /seɪθ/ *n. Sc.* a codlike fish, *Pollachius virens*, with skin that soils fingers like wet coal. Also called COALFISH, COLEY, POLLACK. [ON *seithr*]

sake[1] /seɪk/ *n.* (esp. **for the sake of** or **for one's sake**) **1** out of consideration for; in the interest of; because of; owing to (*for my own sake as well as yours*). **2** in order to please, honour, get, or keep (*for the sake of uniformity*). □**for Christ's** (or **God's** or **goodness'** or **Heaven's** or **Pete's** etc.) **sake** an expression of urgency, impatience, supplication, anger, etc. **for old times' sake** in memory of former times. [OE *sacu* contention, charge, fault, sake f. Gmc]

sake[2] /'sɑːkɪ/ *n.* a Japanese alcoholic drink made from rice. [Jap.]

saker /'seɪkə(r)/ *n.* **1** a large falcon, *Falco cherrug*, used in hawking, esp. the larger female bird. **2** *hist.* an old form of cannon. [ME f. OF *sacre* (in both senses), f. Arab. *ṣaḳr*]

saki /'sɑːkɪ/ *n.* (*pl.* **sakis**) any monkey of the genus *Pithecia* or *Chiropotes*, native to S. America, having coarse fur and a long non-prehensile tail. [F f. Tupi *çahy*]

Sakta /'ʃɑːktə/ *n.* a member of a Hindu sect worshipping the Sakti. [Skr. *śākta* relating to power or to the SAKTI]

Sakti /'ʃæktɪ/ *n.* (also **sakti**) (in Hinduism) the female principle, esp. when personified as the wife of a god. [Skr. *śakti* power, divine energy]

sal /sɑːl/ *n.* a N. Indian tree, *Shorea robusta*, yielding teaklike timber and dammar resin. [Hindi *sāl*]

salaam /sə'lɑːm/ *n. & v.* —*n.* **1** the oriental salutation

'Peace'. **2** an Indian obeisance, with or without the salutation, consisting of a low bow of the head and body with the right palm on the forehead. **3** (in *pl.*) respectful compliments. —*v.* **1** *tr.* make a salaam to (a person). **2** *intr.* make a salaam. [Arab. *salām*]

salable var. of SALEABLE.

salacious /sə'leɪʃəs/ *adj.* **1** lustful; lecherous. **2** (of writings, pictures, talk, etc.) tending to cause sexual desire. □□ **salaciously** *adv.* **salaciousness** *n.* **salacity** /sə'læsɪtɪ/ *n.* [L *salax salacis* f. *salire* leap]

salad /'sæləd/ *n.* **1** a cold dish of various mixtures of raw or cooked vegetables or herbs, usu. seasoned with oil, vinegar, etc. **2** a vegetable or herb suitable for eating raw. □**salad cream** creamy salad-dressing. **salad days** a period of youthful inexperience. **salad-dressing** a mixture of oil, vinegar, etc., used with salad. [ME f. OF *salade* f. Prov. *salada* ult. f. L *sal* salt]

salade var. of SALLET.

salamander /'sæləˌmændə(r)/ *n.* **1** *Zool.* any tailed newtlike amphibian of the order Urodela, esp. the genus *Salamandra*, once thought able to endure fire. **2** a mythical lizard-like creature credited with this property. **3** *US* = GOPHER[1]. **4** an elemental spirit living in fire. **5** a red-hot iron used for lighting pipes, gunpowder, etc. **6** a metal plate heated and placed over food to brown it. □□ **salamandrian** /-'mændrɪən/ *adj.* **salamandrine** /-'mændrɪn/ *adj.* **salamandroid** /-'mændrɔɪd/ *adj. & n.* (in sense 1). [ME f. OF *salamandre* f. L *salamandra* f. Gk *salamandra*]

salami /sə'lɑːmɪ/ *n.* (*pl.* **salamis**) a highly-seasoned orig. Italian sausage often flavoured with garlic. [It., pl. of *salame*, f. LL *salare* (unrecorded) to salt]

sal ammoniac /ˌsæl ə'məʊnɪˌæk/ *n.* ammonium chloride, a white crystalline salt. [L *sal ammoniacus* 'salt of Ammon', associated with the Roman temple of Ammon in N. Africa]

salariat /sə'leərɪət/ *n.* the salaried class. [F f. *salaire* (see SALARY), after *prolétariat*]

salary /'sælərɪ/ *n. & v.* —*n.* (*pl.* **-ies**) a fixed regular payment, usu. monthly or quarterly, made by an employer to an employee, esp. a professional or white-collar worker (cf. WAGE *n.* 1). —*v.tr.* (**-ies, -ied**) (usu. as **salaried** *adj.*) pay a salary to. [ME f. AF *salarie*, OF *salaire* f. L *salarium* orig. soldier's salt-money f. *sal* salt]

sale /seɪl/ *n.* **1** the exchange of a commodity for money etc.; an act or instance of selling. **2** the amount sold (*the sales were enormous*). **3** the rapid disposal of goods at reduced prices for a period esp. at the end of a season etc. **4 a** an event at which goods are sold. **b** a public auction. □**on** (or **for**) **sale** offered for purchase. **sale of work** an event where goods made by parishioners etc. are sold for charity. **sale or return** an arrangement by which a purchaser takes a quantity of surplus goods with the right of returning surplus goods without payment. **sale-ring** a circle of buyers at an auction. **sales clerk** *US* a salesman or saleswoman in a shop. **sales department** etc. the section of a firm concerned with selling as opposed to manufacturing or dispatching goods. **sales engineer** a salesperson with technical knowledge of the goods and their market. **sales resistance** the opposition or apathy of a prospective customer etc. to be overcome by salesmanship. **sales talk** persuasive talk to promote the sale of goods or the acceptance of an idea etc. **sales tax** a tax on sales or on the receipts from sales. [OE *sala* f. ON]

saleable /'seɪləb(ə)l/ *adj.* (also **salable**) fit to be sold; finding purchasers. □□ **saleability** /-'bɪlɪtɪ/ *n.*

salep /'sæləp/ *n.* a starchy preparation of the dried tubers of various orchids, used in cookery and formerly medicinally. [F f. Turk. *sālep* f. Arab. (*ḳuṣa-'l-*) *ta'lab* fox, fox's testicles]

saleratus /ˌsælə'reɪtəs/ *n. US* an ingredient of baking powder consisting mainly of potassium or sodium bicarbonate. [mod.L *sal aeratus* aerated salt]

saleroom /'seɪlruːm, -rum/ n. esp. *Brit.* a room in which items are sold at auction.

salesgirl /'seɪlzgɜːl/ n. a saleswoman.

Salesian /sə'liːʒ(ə)n/ n. & adj. —n. a member of an educational religious order within the RC Church. —adj. of or relating to this order. [St François de Sales, Fr. RC bishop d. 1622]

saleslady /'seɪlz,leɪdɪ/ n. (pl. -ies) a saleswoman.

salesman /'seɪlzmən/ n. (pl. -men; fem. **saleswoman**, pl. -women) 1 a person employed to sell goods in a shop, or as an agent between the producer and retailer. 2 *US* a commercial traveller.

salesmanship /'seɪlzmənʃɪp/ n. 1 skill in selling. 2 the techniques used in selling.

salesperson /'seɪlz,pɜːs(ə)n/ n. a salesman or saleswoman (used as a neutral alternative).

salesroom /'seɪlzruːm, -rum/ n. *US* = SALEROOM.

Salian /'seɪlɪən/ adj. & n. —adj. of or relating to the Salii, a 4th-c. Frankish people living near the River Ijssel, from which the Merovingians were descended. —n. a member of this people. [LL *Salii*]

Salic /'sælɪk, 'seɪ-/ adj. = SALIAN. □**Salic law** *hist.* 1 a law excluding females from dynastic succession, esp. as the alleged fundamental law of the French monarchy. 2 a Frankish law-book extant in Merovingian and Carolingian times. [F *Salique* or med.L *Salicus* f. *Salii* (as SALIAN)]

salicet /'sælɪsɪt/ n. an organ stop like a salicional but one octave higher. [as SALICIONAL]

salicin /'sælɪsɪn/ n. (also **salicine** /-,siːn/) a bitter crystalline glucoside with analgesic properties, obtained from poplar and willow bark. [F *salicine* f. L *salix -icis* willow]

salicional /sə'lɪʃən(ə)l/ n. an organ stop with a soft reedy tone like that of a willow-pipe. [G f. L *salix* as SALICIN]

salicylic acid /,sælɪ'sɪlɪk/ n. a bitter chemical used as a fungicide and in the manufacture of aspirin and dyestuffs. □□ **salicylate** /sə'lɪsɪ,leɪt/ n. [*salicyl* its radical f. F *salicyle* (as SALICIN)]

salient /'seɪlɪənt/ adj. & n. —adj. 1 jutting out; prominent; conspicuous, most noticeable. 2 (of an angle, esp. in fortification) pointing outwards (opp. RE-ENTRANT). 3 *Heraldry* (of a lion etc.) standing on its hind legs with the forepaws raised. 4 *archaic* **a** leaping or dancing. **b** (of water etc.) jetting forth. —n. a salient angle or part of a work in fortification; an outward bulge in a line of military attack or defence. □**salient point** *archaic* the initial stage, origin, or first beginning. □□ **salience** n. **saliency** n. **saliently** adv. [L *salire* leap]

salientian /,seɪlɪ'enʃ(ə)n/ adj. & n. = ANURAN. [mod.L *Salientia* (as SALIENT)]

saliferous /sə'lɪfərəs/ adj. *Geol.* (of rock etc.) containing much salt. [L *sal* salt + -FEROUS]

salina /sə'laɪnə/ n. a salt lake. [Sp. f. med.L, = salt pit (as SALINE)]

saline /'seɪlaɪn/ adj. & n. —adj. 1 (of natural waters, springs, etc.) impregnated with or containing salt or salts. 2 (of food or drink etc.) tasting of salt. 3 of chemical salts. 4 of the nature of a salt. 5 (of medicine) containing a salt or salts of alkaline metals or magnesium. —n. 1 a salt lake, spring, marsh, etc. 2 a salt-pan or salt-works. 3 a saline substance, esp. a medicine. 4 a solution of salt in water. □□ **salinity** /sə'lɪnɪtɪ/ n. **salinization** /,sælɪnaɪ'zeɪʃ(ə)n/ n. **salinometer** /,sælɪ'nɒmɪtə(r)/ n. [ME f. L *sal* salt]

saliva /sə'laɪvə/ n. liquid secreted into the mouth by glands to provide moisture and facilitate chewing and swallowing. □**saliva test** a scientific test requiring a saliva sample. □□ **salivary** /sə'laɪ-, 'sælɪ-/ adj. [ME f. L]

salivate /'sælɪ,veɪt/ v. 1 *intr.* secrete or discharge saliva esp. in excess or in greedy anticipation. 2 *tr.* produce an unusual secretion of saliva in (a person) usu. with mercury. □□ **salivation** /,sælɪ'veɪʃ(ə)n/ n. [L *salivare* (as SALIVA)]

Salk vaccine /sɔːlk/ n. a vaccine developed against polio. [J. E. *Salk*, Amer. scientist b. 1914]

sallee /'sælɪ/ n. (also **sally**) (pl. -ees or -ies) *Austral.* any of several eucalypts and acacias resembling the willow. [Aboriginal]

sallet /'sælɪt/ n. (also **salade** /sə'lɑːd/) *hist.* a light helmet with an outward-curving rear part. [F *salade* ult. f. L *caelare* engrave f. *caelum* chisel]

sallow[1] /'sæləʊ/ adj. & n. —adj. (**sallower**, **sallowest**) (of the skin or complexion, or of a person) of a sickly yellow or pale brown. —v.tr. & intr. make or become sallow. □□ **sallowish** adj. **sallowness** n. [OE *salo* dusky f. Gmc]

sallow[2] /'sæləʊ/ n. 1 a willow-tree, esp. one of a low-growing or shrubby kind. 2 the wood or a shoot of this. □□ **sallowy** adj. [OE *salh salg-* f. Gmc, rel. to OHG *salaha*, ON *selja*, L *salix*]

Sally /'sælɪ/ n. (pl. -ies) *colloq.* 1 (usu. prec. by *the*) the Salvation Army. 2 a member of this. [abbr.]

sally[1] /'sælɪ/ n. & v. (pl. -ies) —n. 1 a sudden charge from a fortification upon its besiegers; a sortie. 2 a going forth; an excursion. 3 a witticism; a piece of banter; a lively remark esp. by way of attack upon a person or thing or of a diversion in argument. 4 a sudden start into activity; an outburst. 5 *archaic* an escapade. —v.intr. (-ies, -ied) 1 (usu. foll. by *out*, *forth*) go for a walk, set out on a journey etc. 2 (usu. foll. by *out*) make a military sally. 3 *archaic* issue or come out suddenly. □**sally-port** an opening in a fortification for making a sally from. [F *saillie* fem. past part. of *saillir* issue f. OF *salir* f. L *salire* leap]

sally[2] /'sælɪ/ n. (pl. -ies) 1 the part of a bell-rope prepared with inwoven wool for holding. 2 **a** the first movement of a bell when set for ringing. **b** the bell's position when set. □**sally-hole** the hole through which the bell-rope passes. [perh. f. SALLY[1] in sense 'leaping motion']

sally[3] var. of SALLEE.

Sally Lunn /,sælɪ 'lʌn/ n. *Brit.* a sweet light teacake, properly served hot. [perh. f. the name of a woman selling them at Bath *c.*1800]

salmagundi /,sælmə'gʌndɪ/ n. (pl. **salmagundis**) 1 a dish of chopped meat, anchovies, eggs, onions, etc., and seasoning. 2 a general mixture; a miscellaneous collection of articles, subjects, qualities, etc. [F *salmigondis* of unkn. orig.]

salmanazar /,sælmə'neɪzə(r)/ n. a wine bottle of about 12 times the standard size. [*Shalmaneser* king of Assyria (2 Kings 17–18)]

salmi /'sælmɪ/ n. (pl. **salmis**) a ragout or casserole esp. of partly roasted game-birds. [F, abbr. formed as SALMAGUNDI]

salmon /'sæmən/ n. & adj. —n. (pl. same or (esp. of types) **salmons**) 1 any anadromous fish of the family Salmonidae, esp. of the genus *Salmo*, much prized for its (often smoked) pink flesh. 2 *Austral.* & *NZ* the barramundi or a similar fish. —adj. salmon-pink. □**salmon-ladder** (or -**leap**) a series of steps or other arrangement incorporated in a dam to allow salmon to pass upstream. **salmon-pink** the colour of salmon flesh. **salmon trout** a large silver-coloured trout, *Salmo trutta*. □□ **salmonoid** adj. & n. (in sense 1). **salmony** adj. [ME f. AF *sa(u)moun*, OF *saumon* f. L *salmo -onis*]

salmonella /,sælmə'nelə/ n. (pl. **salmonellae** /-liː/) 1 any bacterium of the genus *Salmonella*, esp. any of various serotypes causing food poisoning. 2 food poisoning caused by infection with salmonellae. □□ **salmonellosis** /-'ləʊsɪs/ n. [mod.L f. D. E. *Salmon*, Amer. veterinary surgeon d. 1914]

salon /'sælɒn, -lɔ̃/ n. 1 the reception room of a large, esp. French or continental, house. 2 a room or establishment where a hairdresser, beautician, etc., conducts trade. 3 *hist.* a meeting of eminent people in the reception room of a (esp. Parisian) lady of fashion. 4 (**Salon**) an annual exhibition in Paris of the work of living artists. □**salon music** light music for the drawing-room etc. [F: see SALOON]

saloon /sə'luːn/ n. **1 a** a large room or hall, esp. in a hotel or public building. **b** a public room or gallery for a specified purpose (*billiard-saloon; shooting-saloon*). **2** (in full **saloon car**) a motor car with a closed body and no partition behind the driver. **3** a public room on a ship. **4** *US* a drinking-bar. **5** (in full **saloon bar**) *Brit.* the more comfortable bar in a public house. **6** (in full **saloon car**) *Brit.* a luxurious railway carriage serving as a lounge etc. □**saloon deck** a deck for passengers using the saloon. **saloon-keeper** *US* a publican or bartender. **saloon pistol** (or **rifle**) a pistol or rifle adapted for short-range practice in a shooting-saloon. [F *salon* f. It. *salone* augment. of *sala* hall]

Salopian /sə'ləʊpɪən/ n. & adj. —n. a native or inhabitant of Shropshire. —adj. of or relating to Shropshire. [AF *Salopesberia* f. ME f. OE *Scrobbesbyrig* Shrewsbury]

salpiglossis /ˌsælpɪ'ɡlɒsɪs/ n. any solanaceous plant of the genus *Salpiglossis*, cultivated for its funnel-shaped flowers. [mod.L, irreg. f. Gk *salpigx* trumpet + *glōssa* tongue]

salping- /'sælpɪŋ/ comb. form Med. denoting the Fallopian tubes. [Gk *salpigx salpiggos*, lit. 'trumpet']

salpingectomy /ˌsælpɪŋ'dʒektəmɪ/ n. (pl. **-ies**) Med. the surgical removal of the Fallopian tubes.

salpingitis /ˌsælpɪn'dʒaɪtɪs/ n. Med. inflammation of the Fallopian tubes.

salsa /'sælsə/ n. **1** a kind of dance music of Latin American origin, incorporating jazz and rock elements. **2** a dance performed to this music. [Sp. (as SAUCE)]

salsify /'sælsɪfɪ, -ˌfaɪ/ n. (pl. **-ies**) **1** a European plant, *Tragopogon porrifolius*, with long cylindrical fleshy roots. **2** this root used as a vegetable. □**black salsify** scorzonera. [F *salsifis* f. obs. It. *salsefica*, of unkn. orig.]

SALT /sɔːlt, sɒlt/ abbr. Strategic Arms Limitation Talks (or Treaty).

salt /sɔːlt, sɒlt/ n., adj., & v. —n. **1** (also **common salt**) sodium chloride; the substance that gives sea water its characteristic taste, got in crystalline form by mining from strata consisting of it or by the evaporation of sea water, and used for seasoning or preserving food, or for other purposes. **2** a chemical compound formed from the reaction of an acid with a base, with all or part of the hydrogen of the acid replaced by a metal or metal-like radical. **3** sting; piquancy; pungency; wit (*added salt to the conversation*). **4** (in *sing.* or *pl.*) **a** a substance resembling salt in taste, form, etc. (*bath salts; Epsom salts; smelling-salts*). **b** (esp. in *pl.*) this type of substance used as a laxative. **5** a marsh, esp. one flooded by the tide, often used as a pasture or for collecting water for salt-making. **6** (also **old salt**) an experienced sailor. **7** (in *pl.*) an exceptional rush of sea water up river. —adj. **1** impregnated with, containing, or tasting of salt; cured or preserved or seasoned with salt. **2** (of a plant) growing in the sea or in salt marshes. **3** (of tears etc.) bitter. **4** (of wit) pungent. —v.tr. **1** cure or preserve with salt or brine. **2** season with salt. **3** make (a narrative etc.) piquant. **4** sprinkle (the ground etc.) with salt esp. in order to melt snow etc. **5** treat with a solution of salt or mixture of salts. **6** (as **salted** adj.) (of a horse or person) hardened or proof against diseases etc. caused by the climate or by special conditions. □**eat salt with** be a guest of. **in salt** sprinkled with salt or immersed in brine as a preservative. **not made of salt** not disconcerted by wet weather. **put salt on the tail of** capture (with ref. to jocular directions given to children for catching a bird). **salt an account** *sl.* set an extremely high or low price for articles. **salt-and-pepper** (of materials etc. and esp. of hair) with light and dark colours mixed together. **salt away** (or **down**) *sl.* put money etc. by. **salt the books** *sl.* show receipts as larger than they really have been. **salt-cat** a mass of salt mixed with gravel, urine, etc., to attract pigeons and keep them at home. **salt dome** a mass of salt forced up into sedimentary rocks. **salt fish** *W.Ind.* preserved cod. **salt-glaze** a hard stoneware glaze produced by throwing salt into a hot kiln containing the ware. **salt-grass** *US* grass growing in salt meadows or in alkaline regions. **salt horse** *Naut. sl.* **1** salt beef. **2** a naval officer with general duties. **salt lake** a lake of salt water. **salt-lick 1** a place where animals go to lick salt from the ground. **2** this salt. **salt-marsh** = sense 5 of n. **salt meadow** a meadow subject to flooding with salt water. **salt a mine** *sl.* introduce extraneous ore, material, etc., to make the source seem rich. **the salt of the earth** a person or people of great worthiness, reliability, honesty, etc.; those whose qualities are a model for the rest (Matt. 5:13). **salt-pan** a vessel, or a depression near the sea, used for getting salt by evaporation. **salt-shaker** *US* a container of salt for sprinkling on food. **salt-spoon** a small spoon usu. with a short handle and a roundish deep bowl for taking table salt. **salt water 1** sea water. **2** *sl.* tears. **salt-water** adj. of or living in the sea. **salt-well** a bored well yielding brine. **salt-works** a place where salt is produced. **take with a pinch** (or **grain**) **of salt** regard as exaggerated; be incredulous about; believe only part of. **worth one's salt** efficient, capable. □□ **saltish** adj. **saltless** adj. **saltly** adv. **saltness** n. [OE *s(e)alt s(e)altan*, OS, ON, Goth. *salt*, OHG *salz* f. Gmc]

saltarello /ˌsæltə'reləʊ/ n. (pl. **-os** or **saltarelli** /-lɪ/) an Italian and Spanish dance for one couple, with sudden skips. [It. *salterello*, Sp. *saltarelo*, rel. to It. *saltare* and Sp. *saltar* leap, dance f. L *saltare* (as SALTATION)]

saltation /sæl'teɪʃ(ə)n/ n. **1** the act or an instance of leaping or dancing; a jump. **2** a sudden transition or movement. □□ **saltatory** /'sæltətərɪ/ adj. **saltatorial** /ˌsæltə'tɔːrɪəl/ adj. [L *saltatio* f. *saltare* frequent. of *salire salt-* leap]

saltbush /'sɔːltbʊʃ, 'sɒlt-/ n. = ORACHE.

salt-cellar /'sɔːltˌselə(r), 'sɒlt-/ n. **1** a vessel holding salt for table use. **2** *colloq.* an unusually deep hollow above the collar-bone, esp. found in women. [SALT + obs. *saler* f. AF f. OF *salier* salt-box f. L (as SALARY), assim. to CELLAR]

salter /'sɔːltə(r), 'sɒl-/ n. **1** a manufacturer or dealer in salt. **2** a workman at a salt-works. **3** a person who salts fish etc. **4** = *dry-salter*. [OE *sealtere* (as SALT)]

saltern /'sɔːlt(ə)n, 'sɒlt-/ n. **1** a salt-works. **2** a set of pools for the natural evaporation of sea water. [OE *sealtærn* (as SALT, *ærn* building)]

saltigrade /'sæltɪˌɡreɪd/ adj. & n. Zool. —adj. (of arthropods) moving by leaping or jumping. —n. a saltigrade arthropod, e.g. a spider, sand-hopper, etc. [mod.L *Saltigradae* f. L *saltus* leap f. *salire salt-* + *-gradus* walking]

salting /'sɔːltɪŋ, 'sɒl-/ n. **1** in senses of SALT v. **2** (esp. in *pl.*) Geol. a salt marsh; a marsh overflowed by the sea.

saltire /'sɔːlˌtaɪə(r)/ n. Heraldry an ordinary formed by a bend and a bend sinister crossing like a St Andrew's cross. □**in saltire** arranged in this way. □□ **saltirewise** adv. [ME f. OF *sau(l)toir* etc. stirrup-cord, stile, saltire, f. med.L *saltatorium* (as SALTATION)]

saltpetre /ˌsɒlt'piːtə(r), ˌsɔːlt-/ n. (*US* **saltpeter**) potassium nitrate, a white crystalline salty substance used in preserving meat and as a constituent of gunpowder. [ME f. OF *salpetre* f. med.L *salpetra* prob. for *sal petrae* (unrecorded) salt of rock (i.e. found as an incrustation): assim. to SALT]

saltus /'sæltəs/ n. *literary* a sudden transition; a breach of continuity. [L, = leap]

saltwort /'sɔːltwɜːt, 'sɒlt-/ n. any plant of the genus *Salsola*; glasswort.

salty /'sɔːltɪ, 'sɒl-/ adj. (**saltier, saltiest**) tasting of, containing, or preserved with salt. □□ **saltiness** n.

salubrious /sə'luːbrɪəs, sə'ljuː-/ adj. **1** health-giving;

healthy. **2** (of surroundings etc.) pleasant; agreeable. □□ **salubriously** *adv.* **salubriousness** *n.* **salubrity** *n.* [L *salubris* f. *salus* health]

saluki /sə'lu:kɪ/ *n.* (*pl.* **salukis**) **1** a tall swift slender dog of a silky-coated breed with large ears and a fringed tail and feet. **2** this breed. [Arab. *salūḳī*]

salutary /'sæljutərɪ/ *adj.* **1** producing good effects; beneficial. **2** *archaic* health-giving. [ME f. F *salutaire* or L *salutaris* f. *salus -utis* health]

salutation /ˌsælju:'teɪʃ(ə)n/ *n.* **1** a sign or expression of greeting or recognition of another's arrival or departure. **2** words spoken or written to enquire about another's health or well-being. □□ **salutational** *adj.* [ME f. OF *salutation* or L *salutatio* (as SALUTE)]

salutatory /sə'lju:tətərɪ, sə'lu:-/ *adj. & n.* —*adj.* of salutation. —*n.* (*pl.* -**ies**) *US* an oration, esp. as given by a member of a graduating class, often the second-ranking member. □□ **salutatorian** /-'tɔ:rɪən/ *n.* (in sense of n.). [L *salutatorius* (as SALUTE)]

salute /sə'lu:t, -'lju:t/ *n. & v.* —*n.* **1** a gesture of respect, homage, or courteous recognition, esp. made to or by a person when arriving or departing. **2 a** *Mil. & Naut.* a prescribed or specified movement of the hand or of weapons or flags as a sign of respect or recognition. **b** (prec. by *the*) the attitude taken by an individual soldier, sailor, policeman, etc., in saluting. **3** the discharge of a gun or guns as a formal or ceremonial sign of respect or celebration. **4** *Fencing* the formal performance of certain guards etc. by fencers before engaging. —*v.* **1 a** *tr.* make a salute to. **b** *intr.* (often foll. by *to*) perform a salute. **2** *tr.* greet; make a salutation to. **3** *tr.* (foll. by *with*) receive or greet with (a smile etc.). **4** *tr. archaic* hail as (king etc.). □**take the salute 1** (of the highest officer present) acknowledge it by gesture as meant for him. **2** receive ceremonial salutes by members of a procession. □□ **saluter** *n.* [ME f. L *salutare* f. *salus -utis* health]

salvage /'sælvɪdʒ/ *n. & v.* —*n.* **1** the rescue of a ship, its cargo, or other property, from loss at sea, destruction by fire, etc. **2** the property etc. saved in this way. **3 a** the saving and utilization of waste paper, scrap material, etc. **b** the materials salvaged. **4** payment made or due to a person who has saved a ship or its cargo. —*v.tr.* **1** save from a wreck, fire, etc. **2** retrieve or preserve (something favourable) in adverse circumstances (*tried to salvage some dignity*). □□ **salvageable** *adj.* **salvager** *n.* [F f. med.L *salvagium* f. L *salvare* SAVE[1]]

salvation /sæl'veɪʃ(ə)n/ *n.* **1** the act of saving or being saved; preservation from loss, calamity, etc. **2** deliverance from sin and its consequences and admission to heaven, brought about by Christ. **3** a religious conversion. **4** a person or thing that saves (*was the salvation of*). □**Salvation Army** a world-wide evangelical organization on quasi-military lines for the revival of Christianity and helping the poor. □□ **salvationism** *n.* **salvationist** *n.* (both nouns esp. with ref. to the Salvation Army). [ME f. OF *sauvacion, salvacion,* f. eccl.L *salvatio -onis* f. *salvare* SAVE[1], transl. Gk *sōtēria*]

salve[1] /sælv, sɑ:v/ *n. & v.* —*n.* **1** a healing ointment. **2** (often foll. by *for*) a thing that is soothing or consoling for wounded feelings, an uneasy conscience, etc. **3** *archaic* a thing that explains away a discrepancy or palliates a fault. —*v.tr.* **1** soothe (pride, self-love, conscience, etc.). **2** *archaic* anoint (a wound etc.). **3** *archaic* smooth over, make good, vindicate, harmonize, etc. [OE *s(e)alf(e), s(e)alfian* f. Gmc; senses 1 and 3 of v. partly f. L *salvare* SAVE[1]]

salve[2] /sælv/ *v.tr.* **1** save (a ship or its cargo) from loss at sea. **2** save (property) from fire. □□ **salvable** *adj.* [back-form. f. SALVAGE]

salver /'sælvə(r)/ *n.* a tray usu. of gold, silver, brass, or electroplate, on which drinks, letters, etc., are offered. [F *salve* tray for presenting food to the king

f. Sp. *salva* assaying of food f. *salvar* SAVE: assoc. with *platter*]

Salve Regina /ˌsælveɪ rə'dʒi:nə/ *n.* **1** a Roman Catholic hymn or prayer said or sung after compline and after the Divine Office from Trinity Sunday to Advent. **2** the music for this. [f. the opening words *salve regina* hail (holy) queen]

salvia /'sælvɪə/ *n.* any plant of the genus *Salvia*, esp. *S. splendens* with red or blue flowers. [L, = SAGE[1]]

Salvo /'sælvəʊ/ *n.* (*pl.* -**os**) *Austral. sl.* a member of the Salvation Army. [abbr.]

salvo[1] /'sælvəʊ/ *n.* (*pl.* -**oes** or -**os**) **1** the simultaneous firing of artillery or other guns esp. as a salute, or in a sea-fight. **2** a number of bombs released from aircraft at the same moment. **3** a round or volley of applause. [earlier *salve* f. F f. It. *salva* salutation (as SAVE[1])]

salvo[2] /'sælvəʊ/ *n.* (*pl.* -**os**) **1** a saving clause; a reservation (*with an express salvo of their rights*). **2** a tacit reservation. **3** a quibbling evasion; a bad excuse. **4** an expedient for saving reputation or soothing pride or conscience. [L, ablat. of *salvus* SAFE as used in *salvo jure* without prejudice to the rights of (a person)]

sal volatile /ˌsæl vɒ'lætɪlɪ/ *n.* ammonium carbonate, esp. in the form of a flavoured solution in alcohol used as smelling-salts. [mod.L, = volatile salt]

salvor /'sælvə(r)/ *n.* a person or ship making or assisting in salvage. [SALVE[2]]

SAM *abbr.* surface-to-air missile.

Sam. *abbr.* Samuel (Old Testament).

samadhi /sə'mɑ:dɪ/ *n. Buddhism & Hinduism* **1** a state of concentration induced by meditation. **2** a state into which a perfected holy man is said to pass at his apparent death. [Skr. *samādhi* contemplation]

samara /'sæmərə, sə'mɑ:-/ *n. Bot.* a winged seed from the sycamore, ash, etc. [mod.L f. L, = elm-seed]

Samaritan /sə'mærɪt(ə)n/ *n. & adj.* —*n.* **1** (in full **good Samaritan**) a charitable or helpful person (with ref. to Luke 10:33 etc.). **2** a member of an organization which counsels people in distress by telephone or face to face. **3** a native of Samaria in West Jordan. **4** the language of this people. **5** an adherent of the Samaritan religious system, accepting only the Samaritan Pentateuch. —*adj.* of Samaria or the Samaritans. □**Samaritan Pentateuch** a recension used by Samaritans of which the MSS are in archaic characters. □□ **Samaritanism** *n.* [LL *Samaritanus* f. Gk *Samareitēs* f. *Samareia* Samaria]

samarium /sə'meərɪəm/ *n. Chem.* a soft silvery metallic element of the lanthanide series, occurring naturally in monazite etc. and used in making ferromagnetic alloys. ¶ Symb.: **Sm**. [*samarskite* the mineral in which its spectrum was first observed, f. *Samarski* name of a 19th-c. Russ. official]

samba /'sæmbə/ *n. & v.* —*n.* **1** a Brazilian dance of African origin. **2** a ballroom dance imitative of this. **3** the music for this. —*v.intr.* (**sambas, sambaed** /-bəd/ or **samba'd, sambaing** /-bəɪŋ/) dance the samba. [Port., of Afr. orig.]

sambar /'sæmbə(r)/ *n.* (also **samba, sambhar**) either of two large deer, *Cervus unicolor* or *C. equinus*, native to S. Asia. [Hindi *sā(m)bar*]

Sambo /'sæmbəʊ/ *n.* (*pl.* -**os** or -**oes**) **1** *sl. offens.* a Black person. **2** (**sambo**) *hist.* a person of mixed race esp. of Negro and Indian or Negro and European blood. [Sp. *zambo* perh. = *zambo* bandy-legged; sense 1 perh. a different word f. Foulah *sambo* uncle]

Sam Browne /sæm 'braʊn/ *n.* (in full **Sam Browne belt**) an army officer's belt and the strap supporting it. [Sir *Samuel J. Browne*, Brit. military commander d. 1901]

same /seɪm/ *adj., pron., & adv.* —*adj.* **1** (often prec. by *the*) identical; not different; unchanged (*everyone was looking in the same direction*; *the same car was used in another crime*; *saying the same thing over and over*). **2** unvarying, uniform, monotonous (*the* *same old story*). **3** (usu. prec. by *this*, *these*, *that*, *those*) (of a person or thing) previously alluded to; just mentioned; aforesaid (*this same man was later my husband*). —*pron.* (prec. by *the*) **1** the same person or thing (*the others asked for the same*). **2** *Law* or *archaic* the person or thing just mentioned (*detected the youth breaking in and apprehended the same*). —*adv.* (usu. prec. by *the*) similarly; in the same way (*we all feel the same*; *I want to go, the same as you do*). □**all** (or **just**) **the same 1** emphatically the same. **2** in spite of changed conditions, adverse circumstances, etc. (*but you should offer, all the same*). **at the same time 1** simultaneously. **2** notwithstanding; in spite of circumstances etc. **be all** (or **just**) **the same to** an expression of indifference or impartiality (*it's all the same to me what we do*). **by the same token** see TOKEN. **same here** *colloq.* the same applies to me. **the same to you!** may you do, have, find, etc., the same thing; likewise. **the very same** emphatically the same. □□**sameness** *n.* [ME f. ON *sami*, *sama*, with Gmc cognates]

samey /ˈseɪmɪ/ *adj.* (**samier**, **samiest**) *colloq.* lacking in variety; monotonous. □□**sameyness** *n.*

samfu /ˈsæmfuː/ *n.* a suit consisting of a jacket and trousers, worn by Chinese women and sometimes men. [Cantonese]

Samhain /saʊn, ˈsaʊɪn/ *n. Brit.* 1 Nov., celebrated by the Celts as a festival marking the beginning of winter. [Ir. *Samhain*]

Samian /ˈseɪmɪən/ *n. & adj.* —*n.* a native or inhabitant of Samos, an island in the Aegean sea. —*adj.* of Samos. □**Samian ware** fine red pottery from various parts of the Roman Empire, esp. Gaulish types often found on Roman sites in Britain. [L *Samius* f. Gk *Samios* Samos]

samisen /ˈsæmɪsɪn/ *n.* a long three-stringed Japanese guitar, played with a plectrum. [Jap. f. Chin. *san-hsien* f. *san* three + *hsien* string]

samite /ˈsæmaɪt, ˈseɪ-/ *n. hist.* a rich medieval dress-fabric of silk occas. interwoven with gold. [ME f. OF *samit* f. med.L *examitum* f. med. Gk *hexamiton* f. Gk *hexa-* six + *mitos* thread]

samizdat /ˈsæmɪzˌdæt, -ˈdæt/ *n.* a system of clandestine publication of banned literature in the USSR. [Russ., = self-publishing house]

Samnite /ˈsæmnaɪt/ *n. & adj.* —*n.* **1** a member of a people of ancient Italy often at war with republican Rome. **2** the language of this people. —*adj.* of this people or their language. [ME f. L *Samnites* (pl.), rel. to *Sabinus* SABINE]

Samoan /səˈməʊən/ *n. & adj.* —*n.* **1** a native of Samoa, a group of islands in the Pacific. **2** the language of this people. —*adj.* of or relating to Samoa or its people or language. [*Samoa*]

samosa /səˈməʊsə/ *n.* a triangular pastry fried in ghee or oil, containing spiced vegetables or meat. [Hind.]

samovar /ˈsæməˌvɑː(r)/ *n.* a Russian urn for making tea, with an internal heating tube to keep water at boiling-point. [Russ., = self-boiler]

Samoyed /ˈsæməˌjed/ *n.* **1** a member of a people of northern Siberia. **2** the language of this people. **3** (also **samoyed**) **a** a dog of a white Arctic breed. **b** this breed. [Russ. *samoed*]

Samoyedic /ˌsæməˈjedɪk/ *n. & adj.* —*n.* the language of the Samoyeds. —*adj.* of or relating to the Samoyeds.

samp /sæmp/ *n. US* **1** coarsely-ground maize. **2** porridge made of this. [Algonquin *nasamp* softened by water]

sampan /ˈsæmpæn/ *n.* a small boat usu. with a stern-oar or stern-oars, used in the Far East. [Chin. *san-ban* f. *san* three + *ban* board]

samphire /ˈsæmˌfaɪə(r)/ *n.* **1** an umbelliferous maritime rock plant, *Crithmum maritimum*, with aromatic fleshy leaves used in pickles. **2** the glasswort. [earlier *samp(i)ere* f. F (*herbe de*) *Saint Pierre* St Peter('s herb)]

sample /ˈsɑːmp(ə)l/ *n. & v.* —*n.* **1** a small part or quantity intended to show what the whole is like. **2** a small amount of fabric, food, or other commodity, esp. given to a prospective customer. **3** a specimen, esp. one taken for scientific testing or analysis. **4** an illustrative or typical example. —*v.tr.* **1** take or give samples of. **2** try the qualities of. **3** get a representative experience of. □**sample bag** *Austral.* an (orig. free) bag of advertisers' samples. [ME f. AF *assample*, OF *essample* EXAMPLE]

sampler¹ /ˈsɑːmplə(r)/ *n.* a piece of embroidery worked in various stitches as a specimen of proficiency (often displayed on a wall etc.). [OF *essamplaire* (as EXEMPLAR)]

sampler² /ˈsɑːmplə(r)/ *n.* **1** a person who samples. **2** *US* a collection of representative items etc.

samsara /səmˈsɑːrə/ *n. Ind. Philos.* the endless cycle of death and rebirth to which life in the material world is bound. □□**samsaric** *adj.* [Skr. *saṃsāra* a wandering through]

samskara /sənˈskɑːrə/ *n. Ind. Philos.* **1** a purificatory ceremony or rite marking an event in one's life. **2** a mental impression, instinct, or memory. [Skr. *samskāra* a making perfect, preparation]

Samson /ˈsæms(ə)n/ *n.* a person of great strength or resembling Samson in some respect. □**Samson-** (or **Samson's-**) **post 1** a strong pillar passing through the hold of a ship or between decks. **2** a post in a whaleboat to which a harpoon rope is attached. [LL f. Gk *Sampsōn* f. Heb. *šimšôn* (Judg. 13-16)]

samurai /ˈsæmʊˌraɪ, -jʊˌraɪ/ *n.* (*pl.* same) **1** a Japanese army officer. **2** *hist.* a military retainer of the daimios; a member of a military caste in Japan. [Jap.]

san /sæn/ *n.* = SANATORIUM 2. [abbr.]

sanative /ˈsænətɪv/ *adj.* **1** healing; curative. **2** of or tending to physical or moral health. [ME f. OF *sanatif* or LL *sanativus* f. L *sanare* cure]

sanatorium /ˌsænəˈtɔːrɪəm/ *n.* (*pl.* **sanatoriums** or **sanatoria** /-rɪə/) **1** an establishment for the treatment of invalids, esp. of convalescents and the chronically sick. **2** *Brit.* a room or building for sick people in a school etc. [mod.L (as SANATIVE)]

sanctify /ˈsæŋktɪˌfaɪ/ *v.tr.* (**-ies**, **-ied**) **1** consecrate; set apart or observe as holy. **2** purify or free from sin. **3** make legitimate or binding by religious sanction; justify; give the colour of morality or innocence to. **4** make productive of or conducive to holiness. □□**sanctification** /-fɪˈkeɪʃ(ə)n/ *n.* **sanctifier** *n.* [ME f. OF *saintifier* f. eccl.L *sanctificare* f. L *sanctus* holy]

sanctimonious /ˌsæŋktɪˈməʊnɪəs/ *adj.* making a show of sanctity or piety. □□**sanctimoniously** *adv.* **sanctimoniousness** *n.* **sanctimony** /ˈsæŋktɪmənɪ/ *n.* [L *sanctimonia* sanctity (as SAINT)]

sanction /ˈsæŋkʃ(ə)n/ *n. & v.* —*n.* **1** approval or encouragement given to an action etc. by custom or tradition; express permission. **2** confirmation or ratification of a law etc. **3 a** a penalty for disobeying a law or rule, or a reward for obeying it. **b** a clause containing this. **4** *Ethics* a consideration operating to enforce obedience to any rule of conduct. **5** (esp. in *pl.*) military or esp. economic action by a State to coerce another to conform to an international agreement or norms of conduct. **6** *Law hist.* a law or decree. —*v.tr.* **1** authorize, countenance, or agree to (an action etc.). **2** ratify; attach a penalty or reward to; make binding. □□**sanctionable** *adj.* [F f. L *sanctio -onis* f. *sancire sanct-* make sacred]

sanctitude /ˈsæŋktɪˌtjuːd/ *n. archaic* saintliness. [ME f. L *sanctitudo* (as SAINT)]

sanctity /ˈsæŋktɪtɪ/ *n.* (*pl.* **-ies**) **1** holiness of life; saintliness. **2** sacredness; the state of being hallowed. **3** inviolability. **4** (in *pl.*) sacred obligations, feelings, etc. [ME f. OF *sain(c)tité* or L *sanctitas* (as SAINT)]

sanctuary /ˈsæŋktjʊərɪ/ *n.* (*pl.* **-ies**) **1** a holy place; a church, temple, etc. **2 a** the inmost recess or holiest part of a temple etc. **b** the part of the chancel containing the high altar. **3** a place where birds, wild

aʊ how eɪ day əʊ no eə hair ɪə near ɔɪ boy ʊə poor aɪə fire aʊə sour (*see over for consonants*)

animals, etc., are bred and protected. **4** a place of refuge, esp. for political refugees. **5 a** immunity from arrest. **b** the right to offer this. **6** *hist.* a sacred place where a fugitive from the law or a debtor was secured by medieval Church law against arrest or violence. □**take sanctuary** resort to a place of refuge. [ME f. AF *sanctuarie*, OF *sanctuaire* f. L *sanctuarium* (as SAINT)]

sanctum /'sæŋktəm/ *n.* (*pl.* **sanctums**) **1** a holy place. **2** *colloq.* a person's private room, study, or den. □**sanctum sanctorum** /sæŋk'tɔːrəm/ **1** the holy of holies in the Jewish temple. **2** = sense 2 of n. **3** an inner retreat. **4** an esoteric doctrine etc. [L, neut. of *sanctus* holy, past part. of *sancire* consecrate: *sanctorum* genit. pl. in transl. of Heb. *ḳ̇ōdeš haḳḳ̇dāšim* holy of holies]

sanctus /'sæŋktəs/ *n.* (also **Sanctus**) **1** the prayer or hymn beginning 'Holy, holy, holy' said or sung at the end of the Eucharistic preface. **2** the music for this. □**sanctus bell** a handbell or the bell in the turret at the junction of the nave and the chancel, rung at the sanctus or at the elevation of the Eucharist. [ME f. L, = holy]

sand /sænd/ *n. & v.* —*n.* **1** a loose granular substance resulting from the wearing down of esp. siliceous rocks and found on the seashore, river-beds, deserts, etc. **2** (in *pl.*) grains of sand. **3** (in *pl.*) an expanse or tracts of sand. **4** a light yellow-brown colour like that of sand. **5** (in *pl.*) a sandbank. **6** *US colloq.* firmness of purpose; grit. —*v.tr.* **1** smooth or polish with sandpaper or sand. **2** sprinkle or overlay with, or bury under, sand. **3** adulterate (sugar etc.) with sand. □**sand bar** a sandbank at the mouth of a river or *US* on the coast. **sand-bath** a vessel of heated sand to provide uniform heating. **sand-bed** a stratum of sand. **sand-cloud** driving sand in a simoom. **sand-crack 1** a fissure in a horse's hoof. **2** a crack in the human foot from walking on hot sand. **3** a crack in brick due to imperfect mixing. **sand dollar** *US* any of various round flat sea urchins, esp. of the order Clypeasteroida. **sand-dune** (or **-hill**) a mound or ridge of sand formed by the wind. **sand eel** any eel-like fish of the family Ammodytidae or Hypotychidae: also called LAUNCE. **sand-flea** a chigoe or sand-hopper. **sand-glass** = HOURGLASS. **sand-groper** *Austral.* **1** a gold-rush pioneer. **2** *joc.* a Western Australian. **sand-hill** a dune. **sand-hopper** any of various small jumping crustaceans of the order Amphipoda, burrowing on the seashore. **sand-martin** a swallow-like bird, *Riparia riparia*, nesting in the side of a sandy bank etc. **the sands are running out** the allotted time is nearly at an end. **sand-shoe** a shoe with a canvas, rubber, hemp, etc., sole for use on sand. **sand-skipper** = *sand-hopper*. **sand-yacht** a boat on wheels propelled along a beach by wind. □□**sander** *n.* **sandlike** *adj.* [OE *sand* f. Gmc]

sandal[1] /'sænd(ə)l/ *n. & v.* —*n.* **1** a light shoe with an openwork upper or no upper, attached to the foot usu. by straps. **2** a strap for fastening a low shoe, passing over the instep or around the ankle. —*v.tr.* (**sandalled, sandalling;** *US* **sandaled, sandaling**) **1** (esp. as **sandalled** *adj.*) put sandals on (a person, his feet). **2** fasten or provide (a shoe) with a sandal. [ME f. L *sandalium* f. Gk *sandalion* dimin. of *sandalon* wooden shoe, prob. of Asiatic orig.]

sandal[2] /'sænd(ə)l/ *n.* = SANDALWOOD. □**sandal-tree** any tree yielding sandalwood, esp. the white sandalwood, *Santalum album*, of India. [ME f. med.L *sandalum*, ult. f. Skr. *candana*]

sandalwood /'sænd(ə)l,wʊd/ *n.* **1** the scented wood of a sandal-tree. **2** a perfume derived from this. □**red sandalwood** the red wood from either of two SE Asian trees, *Adenanthera pavonina* and *Pterocarpus santalinus*, used as timber and to produce a red dye. **sandalwood oil** a yellow aromatic oil made from the sandal-tree.

sandarac /'sændə,ræk/ *n.* (also **sandarach**) **1** the gummy resin of a N. African conifer, *Tetraclinis articulata*, used in making varnish. **2** = REALGAR. [L *sandaraca* f. Gk *sandarakē*, of Asiatic orig.]

sandbag /'sændbæg/ *n. & v.* —*n.* a bag filled with sand for use: **1** (in fortification) for making temporary defences or for the protection of a building etc. against blast and splinters or floodwaters. **2** as ballast esp. for a boat or balloon. **3** as a weapon to inflict a heavy blow without leaving a mark. **4** to stop a draught from a window or door. —*v.tr.* (**-bagged, -bagging**) **1** barricade or defend. **2** place sandbags against (a window, chink, etc.). **3** fell with a blow from a sandbag. **4** *US* coerce by harsh means. □□**sandbagger** *n.*

sandbank /'sændbæŋk/ *n.* a deposit of sand forming a shallow place in the sea or a river.

sandblast /'sændblɑːst/ *v. & n.* —*v.tr.* roughen, treat, or clean with a jet of sand driven by compressed air or steam. —*n.* this jet. □□**sandblaster** *n.*

sandbox /'sændbɒks/ *n.* **1** *Railways* a box of sand on a locomotive for sprinkling slippery rails. **2** *Golf* a container for sand used in teeing. **3** a sandpit enclosed in a box. **4** *hist.* a device for sprinkling sand to dry ink.

sandboy /'sændbɔɪ/ *n.* □**happy as a sandboy** extremely happy or carefree. [prob. = a boy hawking sand for sale]

sandcastle /'sænd,kɑːs(ə)l/ *n.* a shape like a castle made in sand, usu. by a child on the seashore.

sanderling /'sændəlɪŋ/ *n.* a small wading bird, *Calidris alba*, of the sandpiper family. [perh. f. an OE form *sandyrthling* (unrecorded, as SAND + *yrthling* ploughman, also the name of a bird)]

sanders /'sændəz/ *n.* (also **saunders** /'sɔː-/) sandalwood, esp. red sandalwood. [ME f. OF *sandre* var. of *sandle* SANDAL[2]]

sandfly /'sændflaɪ/ *n.* (*pl.* **-ies**) **1** any midge of the genus *Simulium*. **2** any biting fly of the genus *Phlebotomus* transmitting the viral disease leishmaniasis.

sandhi /'sændi/ *n. Gram.* the process whereby the form of a word changes as a result of its position in an utterance (e.g. the change from *a* to *an* before a vowel). [Skr. *saṃdhi* putting together]

sandhog /'sændhɒg/ *n. US* a person who works underwater laying foundations, constructing tunnels, etc.

sandiver /'sændɪvə(r)/ *n.* liquid scum formed in glass-making. [ME app. f. F *suin de verre* exhalation of glass f. *suer* to sweat]

sandlot /'sændlɒt/ *n. US* a piece of unoccupied sandy land used for children's games.

sandman /'sændmæn/ *n.* the personification of tiredness causing children's eyes to smart towards bedtime.

sandpaper /'sænd,peɪpə(r)/ *n.* paper with sand or another abrasive stuck to it for smoothing or polishing.

sandpiper /'sænd,paɪpə(r)/ *n.* any of various wading birds of the family Scolopacidae, frequenting moorland and coastal areas.

sandpit /'sændpɪt/ *n.* a hollow partly filled with sand, usu. for children to play in.

sandsoap /'sændsəʊp/ *n.* heavy-duty gritty soap.

sandstock /'sændstɒk/ *n.* brick made with sand dusted on the surface.

sandstone /'sændstəʊn/ *n.* **1** any clastic rock containing particles visible to the naked eye. **2** a sedimentary rock of consolidated sand commonly red, yellow, brown, grey, or white.

sandstorm /'sændstɔːm/ *n.* a desert storm of wind with clouds of sand.

sandwich /'sænwɪdʒ, -wɪtʃ/ *n. & v.* —*n.* **1** two or more slices of usu. buttered bread with a filling of meat, cheese, etc., between them. **2** a cake of two or more layers with jam or cream between (*bake a sponge sandwich*). —*v.tr.* **1** put (a thing, statement, etc.) between two of another character. **2** squeeze in between others (*sat sandwiched in the middle*). □**sandwich-board** one of two advertisement boards carried by a sandwich-man. **sandwich course** a course of training with alternate periods of practical experience and theoretical instruction. **sandwich-man** (*pl.* **-men**) a man who walks the streets with sandwich-boards hanging before and behind. [4th Earl of *Sandwich*, Engl. nobleman d. 1792, said to have eaten food in this form so as not to leave the gaming-table]

sandwort /ˈsændwɜːt/ *n.* any low-growing plant of the genus *Arenaria*, usu. bearing small white flowers.

sandy /ˈsændɪ/ *adj.* (**sandier**, **sandiest**) **1** having the texture of sand. **2** having much sand. **3 a** (of hair) yellowish-red. **b** (of a person) having sandy hair. □**sandy blight** *Austral.* conjunctivitis with sandlike grains in the eye. □□**sandiness** *n.* **sandyish** *adj.* [OE *sandig* (as SAND)]

sane /seɪn/ *adj.* **1** of sound mind; not mad. **2** (of views etc.) moderate; sensible. □□**sanely** *adv.* **saneness** *n.* [L *sanus* healthy]

sang *past* of SING.

sangar /ˈsæŋɡə(r)/ *n.* (also **sanga** /ˈsæŋɡə/) a stone breastwork round a hollow. [Pashto *sangar*]

sangaree /ˌsæŋɡəˈriː/ *n.* a cold drink of wine diluted and spiced. [Sp. *sangría* SANGRIA]

sang-froid /sɑ̃ˈfrwɑː/ *n.* composure, coolness, etc., in danger or under agitating circumstances. [F, = cold blood]

sangrail /sæŋˈɡreɪl/ *n.* = GRAIL. [ME f. OF *saint graal* (as SAINT, GRAIL)]

sangria /sæŋˈɡriːə/ *n.* a Spanish drink of red wine with lemonade, fruit, etc. [Sp., = bleeding: cf. SANGAREE]

sanguinary /ˈsæŋɡwɪnərɪ/ *adj.* **1** accompanied by or delighting in bloodshed. **2** bloody; bloodthirsty. **3** (of laws) inflicting death freely. □□**sanguinarily** *adv.* **sanguinariness** *n.* [L *sanguinarius* f. *sanguis -inis* blood]

sanguine /ˈsæŋɡwɪn/ *adj.* & *n.* —*adj.* **1** optimistic; confident. **2** (of the complexion) florid; bright; ruddy. **3** *hist.* of a ruddy complexion with a courageous and hopeful amorous disposition. **4** *hist.* of the temperament in which blood predominates over the other humours. **5** *Heraldry* or *literary* blood red. **6** *archaic* bloody; bloodthirsty. —*n.* **1** a blood-red colour. **2** a crayon of chalk coloured red or flesh with iron oxide. □□**sanguinely** *adv.* **sanguineness** *n.* (both in sense 1 of *n.*). [ME f. OF *sanguin -ine* blood-red f. L *sanguineus* (as SANGUINARY)]

sanguineous /sæŋˈɡwɪnɪəs/ *adj.* **1** sanguinary. **2** *Med.* of or relating to blood. **3** blood-red. **4** full-blooded; plethoric. [L *sanguineus* (as SANGUINE)]

Sanhedrin /ˈsænɪdrɪn/ *n.* (also **Sanhedrim** /-rɪm/) the highest court of justice and the supreme council in ancient Jerusalem with 71 members. [late Heb. *sanhedrin* f. Gk *sunedrion* (as SYN-, *hedra* seat)]

sanicle /ˈsænɪk(ə)l/ *n.* any umbelliferous plant of the genus *Sanicula*, esp. *S. europaea*, formerly believed to have healing properties. [ME ult. f. med.L *sanicula* perh. f. L *sanus* healthy]

sanify /ˈsænɪfaɪ/ *v.tr.* (**-ies**, **-ied**) make healthy; improve the sanitary state of. [L *sanus* healthy]

sanitarium /ˌsænɪˈteərɪəm/ *n.* (*pl.* **sanitariums** or **sanitaria** /-rɪə/) *US* = SANATORIUM. [pseudo-L f. L *sanitas* health]

sanitary /ˈsænɪtərɪ/ *adj.* **1** of the conditions that affect health, esp. with regard to dirt and infection. **2** hygienic; free from or designed to kill germs, infection, etc. □**sanitary engineer** a person dealing with systems needed to maintain public health. **sanitary towel** (*US* **napkin**) an absorbent pad used during menstruation. **sanitary ware** porcelain for lavatories etc. □□**sanitarian** /-ˈteərɪən/ *n.* & *adj.* **sanitarily** *adv.* **sanitariness** *n.* [F *sanitaire* f. L *sanitas*: see SANITY]

sanitation /ˌsænɪˈteɪʃ(ə)n/ *n.* **1** sanitary conditions. **2** the maintenance or improving of these. **3** the

disposal of sewage and refuse from houses etc. □□ **sanitate** /ˈsænɪteɪt/ *v.tr.* & *intr.* **sanitationist** *n.* [irreg. f. SANITARY]

sanitize /ˈsænɪtaɪz/ *v.tr.* (also **-ise**) **1** make sanitary; disinfect. **2** *US colloq.* render (information etc.) more acceptable by removing improper or disturbing material. □□ **sanitizer** *n.*

sanity /ˈsænɪtɪ/ *n.* **1 a** the state of being sane. **b** mental health. **2** the tendency to avoid extreme views. [ME f. L *sanitas* (as SANE)]

sank *past* of SINK.

sannyasi /sʌnˈjɑːsɪ/ *n.* (also **sanyasi**) (*pl.* same) a Hindu religious mendicant. [Hindi & Urdu *sannyāsī* f. Skr. *saṃnyāsin* laying aside f. *saṃ* together, *ni* down, *as* throw]

sans /sænz, sɑ̃/ *prep.* archaic or joc. without. [ME f. OF *san(z)*, *sen(s)* ult. f. L *sine*, infl. by L *absentia* in the absence of]

sansculotte /ˌsænzkjʊˈlɒt, ˌsɑːkjʊ-/ *n.* **1** *hist.* a lower-class Parisian republican in the French Revolution. **2** an extreme republican or revolutionary. □□ **sansculottism** *n.* [F, lit. = without knee-breeches]

sanserif /sænˈserɪf/ *n.* & *adj.* (also **sans-serif**) *Printing* —*n.* a form of type without serifs. —*adj.* without serifs. [app. f. SANS + SERIF]

Sanskrit /ˈsænskrɪt/ *n.* & *adj.* —*n.* the ancient and sacred language of the Hindus in India. —*adj.* of or in this language. □□ **Sanskritic** /-ˈskrɪtɪk/ *adj.* **Sanskritist** *n.* [Skr. *saṃskṛta* composed, elaborated, f. *saṃ* together, *kṛ* make, *-ta* past part. ending]

Santa Claus /ˈsæntə ˌklɔːz/ *n.* (also *colloq.* **Santa**) a person said to bring children presents on the night before Christmas. [orig. US f. Du. dial. *Sante Klaas* St Nicholas]

santolina /ˌsæntəˈliːnə/ *n.* any aromatic shrub of the genus *Santolina*, with finely divided leaves and small usu. yellow flowers. [mod.L, var. of SANTONICA]

santonica /sænˈtɒnɪkə/ *n.* **1** a shrubby wormwood plant, *Artemisia cina*, yielding santonin. **2** the dried flower-heads of this used as an anthelmintic. [L f. *Santones* an Aquitanian tribe]

santonin /ˈsæntənɪn/ *n.* a toxic drug extracted from santonica and other plants of the genus *Artemisia*, used as an anthelmintic. [SANTONICA + -IN]

sanyasi var. of SANNYASI.

sap[1] /sæp/ *n.* & *v.* —*n.* **1** the vital juice circulating in plants. **2** vigour; vitality. **3** = SAPWOOD. **4** *US sl.* a bludgeon (orig. one made from a sapling). —*v.tr.* (**sapped**, **sapping**) **1** drain or dry (wood) of sap. **2** exhaust the vigour of (*my energy had been sapped by disappointment*). **3** remove the sapwood from (a log). **4** *US sl.* hit with a sap. □**sap-green** *n.* **1** the pigment made from buckthorn berries. **2** the colour of this. —*adj.* of this colour. □□ **sapful** *adj.* **sapless** *adj.* [OE *sæp* prob. f. Gmc]

sap[2] /sæp/ *n.* & *v.* —*n.* **1** a tunnel or trench to conceal assailants' approach to a fortified place; a covered siege-trench. **2** an insidious or slow undermining of a belief, resolution, etc. —*v.* (**sapped**, **sapping**) **1** *intr.* **a** dig a sap or saps. **b** approach by a sap. **2** *tr.* undermine; make insecure by removing the foundations. **3** *tr.* destroy insidiously. [ult. f. It. *zappa* spade, spadework, in part through F *sappe* sap(p)er, prob. of Arab. orig.]

sap[3] /sæp/ *n. sl.* a foolish person. [abbr. of *sapskull* f. SAP[1] = sapwood + SKULL]

sapanwood var. of SAPPANWOOD.

sapele /səˈpiːlɪ/ *n.* **1** any of several large W. African hardwood trees of the genus *Entandrophragma*. **2** the reddish-brown mahogany-like timber of these trees. [W. Afr. name]

sapid /ˈsæpɪd/ *adj. literary* **1** having (esp. an agreeable) flavour; savoury; palatable; not insipid. **2** *literary* (of talk, writing, etc.) not vapid or uninteresting. □□ **sapidity** /səˈpɪdɪtɪ/ *n.* [L *sapidus* f. *sapere* taste]

sapient /ˈseɪpɪənt/ *adj. literary* **1** wise. **2** aping wisdom; of fancied sagacity. □□ **sapience** *n.*

sapiently adv. [ME f. OF sapient or L part. stem of sapere be wise]

sapiential /ˌseɪpɪˈenʃ(ə)l, ˌsæ-/ adj. literary of or relating to wisdom. [ME f. F sapiential or eccl.L sapientialis f. L sapientia wisdom]

sapling /ˈsæplɪŋ/ n. 1 a young tree. 2 a youth. 3 a greyhound in its first year.

sapodilla /ˌsæpəˈdɪlə/ n. a large evergreen tropical American tree, Manilkara zapota, with edible fruit and durable wood, and sap from which chicle is obtained. □ **sapodilla plum** the fruit of this tree. [Sp. zapotillo dimin. of zapote f. Aztec tzápotl]

saponaceous /ˌsæpəˈneɪʃəs/ adj. 1 of, like, or containing soap; soapy. 2 joc. unctuous; flattering. [mod.L saponaceus f. L sapo -onis soap]

saponify /səˈpɒnɪˌfaɪ/ v. (-ies, -ied) 1 tr. turn (fat or oil) into soap by reaction with an alkali. 2 convert (an ester) to an acid and alcohol. 3 intr. become saponified. □□ **saponifiable** adj. **saponification** /-fɪˈkeɪʃ(ə)n/ n. [F saponifier (as SAPONACEOUS)]

saponin /ˈsæpənɪn/ n. any of a group of plant glycosides, esp. those derived from the bark of the tree Quillaja saponaria, that foam when shaken with water and are used in detergents and fire extinguishers. [F saponine f. L sapo -onis soap]

sapor /ˈseɪpɔː(r)/ n. 1 a quality perceptible by taste, e.g. sweetness. 2 the distinctive taste of a substance. 3 the sensation of taste. [ME f. L sapere taste]

sappanwood /ˈsæpənˌwʊd/ n. (also **sapanwood**) the heartwood of an E. Indian tree, Caesalpinia sappan, formerly used as a source of red dye. [Du. sapan f. Malay sapang, of S. Indian orig.]

sapper /ˈsæpə(r)/ n. 1 a person who digs saps. 2 Brit. a soldier of the Royal Engineers (esp. as the official term for a private).

Sapphic /ˈsæfɪk/ adj. & n. —adj. 1 of or relating to Sappho, poetess of Lesbos c.600 BC, or her poetry. 2 lesbian. —n. (in pl.) (**sapphics**) verse in a metre associated with Sappho. [F sa(p)phique f. L Sapphicus f. Gk Sapphikos f. Sapphō]

sapphire /ˈsæfaɪə(r)/ n. & adj. —n. 1 a transparent blue precious stone consisting of corundum. 2 a precious transparent corundum of any colour. 3 the bright blue of a sapphire. 4 a humming-bird with bright blue colouring. —adj. of sapphire blue. □ **sapphire wedding** a 45th wedding anniversary. □□ **sapphirine** /ˈsæfɪˌraɪn/ adj. [ME f. OF safir f. L sapphirus f. Gk sappheiros prob. = lapis lazuli]

sappy /ˈsæpɪ/ adj. (**sappier**, **sappiest**) 1 full of sap. 2 young and vigorous. □□ **sappily** adv. **sappiness** n.

sapro- /ˈsæprəʊ/ comb. form Biol. rotten, putrefying. [Gk sapros putrid]

saprogenic /ˌsæprəˈdʒenɪk/ adj. causing or produced by putrefaction.

saprophagous /sæˈprɒfəgəs/ adj. feeding on decaying matter.

saprophile /ˈsæprəˌfaɪl/ n. a bacterium inhabiting putrid matter. □□ **saprophilous** /-ˈprɒfɪləs/ adj.

saprophyte /ˈsæprəˌfaɪt/ n. any plant or micro-organism living on dead or decayed organic matter. □□ **saprophytic** /-ˈfɪtɪk/ adj.

sapwood /ˈsæpwʊd/ n. the soft outer layers of recently formed wood between the heartwood and the bark.

saraband /ˈsærəˌbænd/ n. 1 a stately old Spanish dance. 2 music for this or in its rhythm, usu. in triple time often with a long note on the second beat of the bar. [F sarabande f. Sp. & It. zarabanda]

Saracen /ˈsærəs(ə)n/ n. & adj. hist. —n. 1 an Arab or Muslim at the time of the Crusades. 2 a nomad of the Syrian and Arabian desert. —adj. of the Saracens. □ **Saracen corn** Brit. archaic buckwheat. **Saracen's head** the head of a Saracen or Turk as a heraldic charge or inn-sign. □□ **Saracenic** /ˌsærəˈsenɪk/ adj. [ME f. OF sar(r)azin, sar(r)acin f. LL Saracenus f. late Gk Sarakēnos perh. f. Arab. šarḳī eastern]

sarangi /səˈræŋgɪ/ n. (pl. **sarangis**) an Indian

stringed instrument played with a bow. [Hindi sārangī]

sarape var. of SERAPE.

sarcasm /ˈsɑːˌkæz(ə)m/ n. 1 a bitter or wounding remark. 2 a taunt, esp. one ironically worded. 3 language consisting of such remarks. 4 the faculty of using this. □□ **sarcastic** /sɑːˈkæstɪk/ adj. **sarcastically** /sɑːˈkæstɪkəlɪ/ adv. [F sarcasme or f. LL sarcasmus f. late Gk sarkasmos f. Gk sarkazō tear flesh, in late Gk gnash the teeth, speak bitterly f. sarx sarkos flesh]

sarcenet var. of SARSENET.

sarcoma /sɑːˈkəʊmə/ n. (pl. **sarcomas** or **sarcomata** /-mətə/) a malignant tumour of connective or other non-epithelial tissue. □□ **sarcomatosis** /-ˈtəʊsɪs/ n. **sarcomatous** adj. [mod.L f. Gk sarkōma f. sarkoō become fleshy f. sarx sarkos flesh]

sarcophagus /sɑːˈkɒfəgəs/ n. (pl. **sarcophagi** /-ˌgaɪ, -ˌdʒaɪ/) a stone coffin, esp. one adorned with a sculpture or inscription. [L f. Gk sarkophagos flesh-consuming (as SARCOMA, -phagos -eating)]

sarcoplasm /ˈsɑːkəˌplæz(ə)m/ n. Anat. the cytoplasm in which muscle fibrils are embedded. [Gk sarx sarkos flesh + PLASMA]

sarcous /ˈsɑːkəs/ adj. consisting of flesh or muscle. [Gk sarx sarkos flesh]

sard /sɑːd/ n. a yellow or orange-red cornelian. [ME f. F sarde or L sarda = LL sardius f. Gk sardios prob. f. Sardō Sardinia]

sardelle /sɑːˈdel/ n. any of several fish resembling the sardine. [It. sardella dimin. of sarda f. L (as SARDINE[1])]

sardine[1] /sɑːˈdiːn/ n. a young pilchard or similar young or small herring-like marine fish. □ **like sardines** crowded close together (as sardines are in tins). [ME f. OF sardine = It. sardina f. L f. sarda f. Gk, perh. f. Sardō Sardinia]

sardine[2] /ˈsɑːdaɪn/ n. a precious stone mentioned in Rev. 4:3. [ME f. LL sardinus f. Gk sardinos var. of sardios SARD]

sardius /ˈsɑːdɪəs/ n. Bibl. etc. a precious stone. [ME f. LL f. Gk sardios sard]

sardonic /sɑːˈdɒnɪk/ adj. 1 grimly jocular. 2 (of laughter etc.) bitterly mocking or cynical. □□ **sardonically** adv. **sardonicism** /-ˌsɪz(ə)m/ n. [F sardonique, earlier sardonien f. L sardonius f. Gk sardonios of Sardinia, alt. of sardanios Homeric epithet of bitter or scornful laughter]

sardonyx /ˈsɑːdənɪks/ n. onyx in which white layers alternate with sard. [ME f. L f. Gk sardonux (prob. as SARD, ONYX)]

saree var. of SARI.

sargasso /sɑːˈgæsəʊ/ n. (also **sargassum**) (pl. **-os** or **-oes** or **sargassa**) any seaweed of the genus Sargassum, with berry-like air-vessels, found floating in island-like masses, esp. in the Sargasso Sea of the N. Atlantic. Also called GULFWEED. [Port. sargaço, of unkn. orig.]

sarge /sɑːdʒ/ n. sl. sergeant. [abbr.]

sari /ˈsɑːrɪ/ n. (also **saree**) (pl. **saris** or **sarees**) a length of cotton or silk draped round the body, traditionally worn as a main garment by Indian women. [Hindi sāṛ(h)ī]

sark /sɑːk/ n. Sc. & N.Engl. a shirt or chemise. [ME serk f. ON serkr f. Gmc]

sarking /ˈsɑːkɪŋ/ n. boarding between the rafters and the roof. [SARK + -ING[1]]

sarky /ˈsɑːkɪ/ adj. (**sarkier**, **sarkiest**) Brit. sl. sarcastic. □□ **sarkily** adv. **sarkiness** n. [abbr.]

sarmentose /ˈsɑːmənˌtəʊs/ adj. (also **sarmentous** /-ˈmentəs/) Bot. having long thin trailing shoots. [L sarmentosus f. sarmenta (pl.) twigs, brushwood, f. sarpere to prune]

sarnie /ˈsɑːnɪ/ n. Brit. colloq. a sandwich. [abbr.]

sarong /səˈrɒŋ/ n. 1 a Malay and Javanese garment consisting of a long strip of (often striped) cloth worn by both sexes tucked round the waist or under the armpits. **2** a woman's garment resembling this. [Malay, lit. 'sheath']

saros /'saːrɒs/ n. *Astron.* a period of about 18 years between repetitions of eclipses. [Gk f. Babylonian *šār(u)* 3,600 (years)]

sarrusophone /sə'ruːsəˌfəʊn/ n. a metal wind instrument played with a double reed like an oboe. [*Sarrus*, 19th-c. Fr. inventor]

sarsaparilla /ˌsɑːsəpə'rɪlə/ n. **1** a preparation of the dried roots of various plants, esp. smilax, used to flavour some drinks and medicines and formerly as a tonic. **2** any of the plants yielding this. [Sp. *zarzaparilla* f. *zarza* bramble, prob. + dimin. of *parra* vine]

sarsen /'sɑːs(ə)n/ n. *Geol.* a sandstone boulder carried by ice during a glacial period. [prob. var. of SARACEN]

sarsenet /'sɑːsənɪt/ n. (also **sarcenet**) a fine soft silk material used esp. for linings. [ME f. AF *sarzinett* perh. dimin. of *sarzin* SARACEN after OF *drap sarrasinois* Saracen cloth]

sartorial /sɑː'tɔːrɪəl/ adj. **1** of a tailor or tailoring. **2** of men's clothes. □□ **sartorially** adv. [L *sartor* tailor f. *sarcire sart-* patch]

sartorius /sɑː'tɔːrɪəs/ n. *Anat.* the long narrow muscle running across the front of each thigh. [mod.L f. L *sartor* tailor (the muscle being used in adopting a tailor's cross-legged posture)]

Sarum use /'seərəm/ n. *Eccl.* the order of divine service used in the diocese of Salisbury before the Reformation. [med.L *Sarum* Salisbury, perh. f. L *Sarisburia*]

SAS abbr. (in the UK) Special Air Service.

s.a.s.e. abbr. *US* self-addressed stamped envelope.

sash[1] /sæʃ/ n. a long strip or loop of cloth etc. worn over one shoulder usu. as part of a uniform or insignia, or worn round the waist, usu. by a woman or child. □□ **sashed** adj. [earlier *shash* f. Arab. *šāš* muslin, turban]

sash[2] /sæʃ/ n. **1** a frame holding the glass in a sash-window and usu. made to slide up and down in the grooves of a window aperture. **2** the glazed sliding light of a glasshouse or garden frame. □ **sash-cord** a strong cord attaching the sash-weights to a sash. **sash-tool** a glazier's or painter's brush for work on sash-windows. **sash-weight** a weight attached to each end of a sash to balance it at any height. **sash-window** a window with one or two sashes of which one or each can be slid vertically over the other to make an opening. □□ **sashed** adj. [*sashes* corrupt. of CHASSIS, mistaken for pl.]

sashay /'sæʃeɪ/ v.intr. esp. *US colloq.* walk or move ostentatiously, casually, or diagonally. [corrupt. of CHASSÉ]

sashimi /'sæʃɪmɪ/ n. a Japanese dish of garnished raw fish in thin slices. [Jap.]

sasin /'sæsɪn/ n. = BLACKBUCK. [Nepali]

sasine /'seɪsɪn/ n. *Sc. Law* **1** the possession of feudal property. **2** an act or document granting this. [var. of SEISIN]

Sask. abbr. Saskatchewan.

sasquatch /'sæskwætʃ/ n. a supposed yeti-like animal of NW America. [Amer. Ind.]

sass /sæs/ n. & v. *US colloq.* —n. impudence, cheek. —v.tr. be impudent to, cheek. [var. of SAUCE]

sassaby /'sæsəbɪ/ n. (pl. **-ies**) a S. African antelope, *Damaliscus lunatus*, similar to the hartebeest. [Tswana *tsessébe, -ábi*]

sassafras /'sæsəˌfræs/ n. **1** a small tree, *Sassafras albidum*, native to N. America, with aromatic leaves and bark. **2** a preparation of oil extracted from the leaves, or from its bark, used medicinally or in perfumery. [Sp. *sasafrás* or Port. *sassafraz*, of unkn. orig.]

Sassanian /sæ'seɪnɪən/ n. & adj. (also **Sassanid** /'sæsənɪd/) —n. a member of a Persian dynasty ruling 211-651. —adj. of or relating to this dynasty. [*Sasan*, founder of the dynasty]

Sassenach /'sæsəˌnæx, -ˌnæk/ n. & adj. *Sc. & Ir.* usu. derog. —n. an English person. —adj. English. [Gael. *Sasunnoch*, Ir. *Sasanach* f. L *Saxones* Saxons]

sassy /'sæsɪ/ adj. (**sassier, sassiest**) esp. *US colloq.* = SAUCY. □□ **sassily** adv. **sassiness** n. [var. of SAUCY]

sastrugi /sæ'struːgɪ/ n.pl. wavelike irregularities on the surface of hard polar snow, caused by winds. [Russ. *zastrugi* small ridges]

Sat. abbr. Saturday.

sat past and past part. of SIT.

Satan /'seɪt(ə)n/ n. the Devil; Lucifer. [OE f. LL f. Gk f. Heb. *śāṭān* lit. 'adversary' f. *śaṭan* oppose, plot against]

satanic /sə'tænɪk/ adj. **1** of, like, or befitting Satan. **2** diabolical, hellish. □□ **satanically** adv.

Satanism /'seɪtəˌnɪz(ə)m/ n. **1** the worship of Satan, with a travesty of Christian forms. **2** the pursuit of evil for its own sake. **3** deliberate wickedness. □□ **Satanist** n. **Satanize** v.tr. (also **-ise**).

Satanology /ˌseɪtə'nɒlədʒɪ/ n. **1** beliefs concerning the Devil. **2** a history or collection of these.

satay /'sæteɪ/ n. (also **satai, saté**) an Indonesian and Malaysian dish consisting of small pieces of meat grilled on a skewer and usu. served with spiced sauce. [Malayan *satai sate*, Indonesian *sate*]

SATB abbr. *Mus.* soprano, alto, tenor, and bass (as a combination of voices).

satchel /'sætʃ(ə)l/ n. a small bag usu. of leather and hung from the shoulder with a strap, for carrying books etc. esp. to and from school. [ME f. OF *sachel* f. L *saccellus* (as SACK[1])]

sate /seɪt/ v.tr. **1** gratify (desire, a desirous person) to the full. **2** cloy, surfeit, weary with over-abundance (*sated with pleasure*). □□ **sateless** adj. poet. [prob. f. dial. *sade*, OE *sadian* (as SAD), assim. to SATIATE]

sateen /sæ'tiːn/ n. cotton fabric woven like satin with a glossy surface. [*satin* after *velveteen*]

satellite /'sætəˌlaɪt/ n. & adj. —n. **1** a celestial body orbiting the earth or another planet. **2** an artificial body placed in orbit round the earth or another planet. **3** a follower; a hanger-on. **4** an underling; a member of an important person's staff or retinue. **5** (in full **satellite State**) a small country etc. nominally independent but controlled by or dependent on another. —adj. **1** transmitted by satellite (*satellite communications; satellite television*). **2** esp. *Computing* secondary; dependent; minor (*networks of small satellite computers*). □ **satellite dish** a concave dish-shaped aerial for receiving broadcasting signals transmitted by satellite. **satellite town** a small town economically or otherwise dependent on a nearby larger town. □□ **satellitic** /-'lɪtɪk/ adj. **satellitism** n. [F *satellite* or L *satelles satellitis* attendant]

sati var. of SUTTEE.

satiate /'seɪʃɪˌeɪt/ adj. & v. —adj. archaic satiated. —v.tr. = SATE. □□ **satiable** /-ʃəb(ə)l/ adj. archaic. **satiation** /-'eɪʃ(ə)n/ n. [L *satiatus* past part. of *satiare* f. *satis* enough]

satiety /sə'taɪɪtɪ/ n. **1** the state of being glutted or satiated. **2** the feeling of having too much of something. **3** (foll. by *of*) a cloyed dislike of. □ **to satiety** to an extent beyond what is desired. [obs. F *societé* f. L *satietas -tatis* f. *satis* enough]

satin /'sætɪn/ n., adj., & v. —n. a fabric of silk or various man-made fibres, with a glossy surface on one side produced by a twill weave with the weft-threads almost hidden. —adj. smooth as satin. —v.tr. (**satined, satining**) give a glossy surface to (paper). □ **satin finish 1** a polish given to silver etc. with a metallic brush. **2** any effect resembling satin in texture produced on materials in various ways. **satin paper** fine glossy writing paper. **satin spar** a fibrous variety of gypsum. **satin stitch** a long straight embroidery stitch, giving the appearance of satin. **satin white** a white pigment of calcium sulphate and alumina. □□ **satinized** adj. (also **-ised**). **satiny** adj. [ME f. OF f. Arab. *zaytūnī* of *Tseutung* in China]

satinette /ˌsætɪ'net/ n. (also **satinet**) a satin-like fabric made partly or wholly of cotton or synthetic fibre.

satinflower /ˈsætɪnˌflaʊə(r)/ n. **1** any plant of the genus *Clarkia*, with pink or lavender flowers. **2** = HONESTY 3.

satinwood /ˈsætɪnˌwʊd/ n. **1 a** (in full **Ceylon satinwood**) a tree, *Chlororylon swietenia*, native to central and southern India and Ceylon. **b** (in full **West Indian satinwood**) a tree, *Fagara flava*, native to the West Indies, Bermuda, the Bahamas, and southern Florida. **2** the yellow glossy timber of either of these trees.

satire /ˈsætaɪə(r)/ n. **1** the use of ridicule, irony, sarcasm, etc., to expose folly or vice or to lampoon an individual. **2** a work or composition in prose or verse using satire. **3** this branch of literature. **4** a thing that brings ridicule upon something else. **5** *Rom. Antiq.* a poetic medley, esp. a poem ridiculing prevalent vices or follies. [F *satire* or L *satira* later form of *satura* medley]

satiric /səˈtɪrɪk/ adj. **1** of satire or satires. **2** containing satire (*wrote a satiric review*). **3** writing satire (*a satiric poet*). [F *satirique* or LL *satiricus* (as SATIRE)]

satirical /səˈtɪrɪk(ə)l/ adj. **1** = SATIRIC. **2** given to the use of satire in speech or writing or to cynical observation of others; sarcastic; humorously critical. □□ **satirically** adv.

satirist /ˈsætərɪst/ n. **1** a writer of satires. **2** a satirical person.

satirize /ˈsætɪˌraɪz/ v.tr. (also **-ise**) **1** assail or ridicule with satire. **2** write a satire upon. **3** describe satirically. □□ **satirization** /-ˈzeɪʃ(ə)n/ n. [F *satiriser* (as SATIRE)]

satisfaction /ˌsætɪsˈfækʃ(ə)n/ n. **1** the act or an instance of satisfying; the state of being satisfied (*heard this with great satisfaction*). **2** a thing that satisfies desire or gratifies feeling (*is a great satisfaction to me*). **3** a thing that settles an obligation or pays a debt. **4 a** (foll. by *for*) atonement; compensation (*demanded satisfaction*). **b** *Theol.* Christ's atonement for the sins of mankind. □ **to one's satisfaction** so that one is satisfied. [ME f. OF f. L *satisfactio -onis* (as SATISFY)]

satisfactory /ˌsætɪsˈfæktərɪ/ adj. **1** adequate; causing or giving satisfaction (*was a satisfactory pupil*). **2** satisfying expectations or needs; leaving no room for complaint (*a satisfactory result*). □□ **satisfactorily** adv. **satisfactoriness** n. [F *satisfactoire* or med.L *satisfactorius* (as SATISFY)]

satisfy /ˈsætɪsˌfaɪ/ v. (**-ies**, **-ied**) **1** tr. **a** meet the expectations or desires of; comply with (a demand). **b** be accepted by (a person, his taste) as adequate; be equal to (a preconception etc.). **2** tr. put an end to (an appetite or want) by supplying what was required. **3** tr. rid (a person) of an appetite or want in a similar way. **4** intr. give satisfaction; leave nothing to be desired. **5** tr. pay (a debt or creditor). **6** tr. adequately meet, fulfil, or comply with (conditions, obligations, etc.) (*has satisfied all the legal conditions*). **7** tr. (often foll. by *of, that*) provide with adequate information or proof, convince (*satisfied the others that they were right; satisfy the court of their innocence*). **8** tr. *Math.* (of a quantity) make (an equation) true. **9** tr. (in *passive*) **a** (foll. by *with*) contented or pleased with. **b** (foll. by *to*) demand no more than or consider it enough to do. □ **satisfy the examiners** reach the standard required to pass an examination. **satisfy oneself** (often foll. by *that* + clause) be certain in one's own mind. □□ **satisfiable** adj. **satisfiability** /-əˈbɪlɪtɪ/ n. **satisfiedly** adv. **satisfying** adj. **satisfyingly** adv. [ME f. OF *satisfier* f. L *satisfacere satisfact-* f. *satis* enough]

satori /səˈtɔːrɪ/ n. *Buddhism* sudden enlightenment. [Jap.]

satrap /ˈsætræp/ n. **1** a provincial governor in the ancient Persian empire. **2** a subordinate ruler, colonial governor, etc. [ME f. OF *satrape* or L *satrapa*

f. Gk *satrapēs* f. OPers. *xšathra-pāvan* country-protector]

satrapy /ˈsætrəpɪ/ n. (pl. **-ies**) a province ruled over by a satrap.

satsuma /ˈsætsʊmə/ n. **1** (also sæt'su:mə) a variety of tangerine orig. grown in Japan. **2** (**Satsuma**) (in full **Satsuma ware**) cream-coloured Japanese pottery. [*Satsuma* a province in Japan]

saturate /ˈsætʃəˌreɪt, -tjʊˌreɪt/ v.tr. **1** fill with moisture; soak thoroughly. **2** (often foll. by *with*) fill to capacity. **3** cause (a substance, solution, vapour, metal, or air) to absorb, hold, or combine with the greatest possible amount of another substance, or of moisture, magnetism, electricity, etc. **4** cause (a substance) to combine with the maximum amount of another substance. **5** supply (a market) beyond the point at which the demand for a product is satisfied. **6** (foll. by *with, in*) imbue with or steep in (learning, tradition, prejudice, etc.). **7** overwhelm (enemy defences, a target area, etc.) by concentrated bombing. **8** (as **saturated** adj.) **a** (of colour) full; rich; free from an admixture of white. **b** (of fat molecules) containing the greatest number of hydrogen atoms. □□ **saturate** /-rət/ adj. *literary*. **saturable** /-rəb(ə)l/ adj. **saturant** /-rənt/ n. & adj. [L *saturare* f. *satur* full]

saturation /ˌsætʃəˈreɪʃ(ə)n, -tjʊˈreɪʃ(ə)n/ n. the act or an instance of saturating; the state of being saturated. □ **saturation point** the stage beyond which no more can be absorbed or accepted.

Saturday /ˈsætəˌdeɪ, -dɪ/ n. & adv. —n. the seventh day of the week, following Friday. —adv. *colloq.* **1** on Saturday. **2** (**Saturdays**) on Saturdays; each Saturday. [OE *Sætern(es) dæg* transl. of L *Saturni dies* day of Saturn]

Saturn /ˈsætə(r)n/ n. **1 a** the sixth planet from the sun, with a system of broad flat rings circling it, and the most distant of the five planets known in the ancient world. **b** *Astrol.* Saturn as a supposed astrological influence on those born under its sign, characterized by coldness and gloominess. **2** *Alchemy* the metal lead. □□ **Saturnian** /səˈtɜːnɪən/ adj. [L *Saturnus*, Roman god of agriculture, identified with Kronos, father of Zeus, perh. f. Etruscan]

saturnalia /ˌsætəˈneɪlɪə/ n. (pl. same or **saturnalias**) **1** (usu. **Saturnalia**) *Rom.Hist.* the festival of Saturn in December, characterized by unrestrained merry-making for all, the predecessor of Christmas. **2** (as *sing.* or *pl.*) a scene of wild revelry or tumult; an orgy. □□ **saturnalian** adj. [L, neut. pl. of *Saturnalis* (as SATURN)]

saturnic /səˈtɜːnɪk/ adj. *Med.* affected with lead-poisoning. □□ **saturnism** /ˈsætəˌnɪz(ə)m/ [SATURN 2]

saturniid /səˈtɜːnɪɪd/ n. any large moth of the family Saturniidae, including emperor moths. [mod.L]

saturnine /ˈsætəˌnaɪn/ adj. **1 a** of a sluggish gloomy temperament. **b** (of looks etc.) dark and brooding. **2** *archaic* of the metal lead. **b** *Med.* of or affected by lead-poisoning. □□ **saturninely** adv. [ME f. OF *saturnin* f. med.L *Saturninus* (as SATURN)]

satyagraha /sʌtˈjɑːɡrəˌhɑː/ n. *Ind.* **1** *hist.* a policy of passive resistance to British rule advocated by Gandhi. **2** passive resistance as a policy. [Skr. f. *satya* truth + *āgraha* obstinacy]

satyr /ˈsætə(r)/ n. **1** (in Greek mythology) one of a class of Greek woodland gods with a horse's ears and tail, or (in Roman representations) with a goat's ears, tail, legs, and budding horns. **2** a lustful or sensual man. **3** = SATYRID. [ME f. OF *satyre* or L *satyrus* f. Gk *saturos*]

satyriasis /ˌsætɪˈraɪəsɪs/ n. *Med.* excessive sexual desire in men. [LL f. Gk *saturiasis* (as SATYR)]

satyric /səˈtɪrɪk/ adj. (in Greek mythology) of or relating to satyrs. □ **satyric drama** a kind of ancient Greek comic play with a chorus of satyrs. [L *satyricus* f. Gk *saturikos* (as SATYR)]

satyrid /səˈtɪrɪd/ n. any butterfly of the family

b *but* d *dog* f *few* g *get* h *he* j *yes* k *cat* l *leg* m *man* n *no* p *pen* r *red* s *sit* t *top* v *voice*

Satyridae, with distinctive eyelike markings on the wings. [mod.L *Satyridae* f. the genus-name *Satyrus* (as SATYR)]

sauce /sɔːs/ *n. & v.* —*n.* **1** any of various liquid or semi-solid preparations taken as a relish with food; the liquid constituent of a dish (*mint sauce*; *tomato sauce*; *chicken in a lemon sauce*). **2** something adding piquancy or excitement. **3** *colloq.* impudence, impertinence, cheek. **4** *US* stewed fruit etc. eaten as dessert or used as a garnish. —*v.tr.* **1** *colloq.* be impudent to; cheek. **2** *archaic* **a** season with sauce or condiments. **b** add excitement to. □ **sauce-boat** a kind of jug or dish used for serving sauces etc. **sauce for the goose** what is appropriate in one case (by implication appropriate in others). □□ **sauceless** *adj.* [ME f. OF ult. f. L *salsus* f. *salere sals-* to salt f. *sal* salt]

saucepan /ˈsɔːspən/ *n.* a usu. metal cooking pan, usu. round with a lid and a long handle at the side, used for boiling, stewing, etc., on top of a cooker. □□ **saucepanful** *n.* (*pl.* **-fuls**).

saucer /ˈsɔːsə(r)/ *n.* **1** a shallow circular dish used for standing a cup on and to catch drips. **2** any similar dish used to stand a plant pot etc. on. □□ **saucerful** *n.* (*pl.* **-fuls**). **saucerless** *adj.* [ME, = condiment-dish, f. OF *saussier(e)* sauce-boat, prob. f. LL *salsarium* (as SAUCE)]

saucy /ˈsɔːsɪ/ *adj.* (**saucier**, **sauciest**) **1** impudent, cheeky. **2** *colloq.* smart-looking (*a saucy hat*). **3** *colloq.* smutty, suggestive. □□ **saucily** *adv.* **sauciness** *n.* [earlier sense 'savoury', f. SAUCE]

Saudi /ˈsaʊdɪ/ *n. & adj.* (also **Saudi Arabian**) —*n.* (*pl.* **Saudis**) **1 a** a native or national of Saudi Arabia. **b** a person of Saudi descent. **2** a member of the dynasty founded by King Saud. —*adj.* of or relating to Saudi Arabia or the Saudi dynasty. [A. Ibn-*Saud*, Arab. king d. 1953]

sauerkraut /ˈsaʊəkraʊt/ *n.* a German dish of chopped pickled cabbage. [G f. *sauer* SOUR + *Kraut* vegetable]

sauger /ˈsɔːgə(r)/ *n.* *US* a small American pike-perch. [19th c.: orig. unkn.]

sauna /ˈsɔːnə/ *n.* **1** a Finnish-style steam bath. **2** a building used for this. [Finn.]

saunders var. of SANDERS.

saunter /ˈsɔːntə(r)/ *v. & n.* —*v.intr.* **1** walk slowly; amble, stroll. **2** proceed without hurry or effort. —*n.* **1** a leisurely ramble. **2** a slow gait. □□ **saunterer** *n.* [ME, = muse: orig. unkn.]

saurian /ˈsɔːrɪən/ *adj.* of or like a lizard. [mod.L *Sauria* f. Gk *saura* lizard]

sauropod /ˈsɔːrəʊ,pɒd/ *n.* any of a group of plant-eating dinosaurs with a long neck and tail, and four thick limbs. [Gk *saura* lizard + *pous pod-* foot]

saury /ˈsɔːrɪ/ *n.* (*pl.* **-ies**) a long-beaked marine fish, *Scomberesox saurus*, of temperate waters. [perh. f. LL f. Gk *sauros* horse-mackerel]

sausage /ˈsɒsɪdʒ/ *n.* **1 a** minced pork, beef, or other meat seasoned and often mixed with other ingredients, encased in cylindrical form in a skin, for cooking and eating hot or cold. **b** a length of this. **2** a sausage-shaped object. □ **not a sausage** *colloq.* nothing at all. **sausage dog** *Brit. colloq.* a dachshund. **sausage machine 1** a sausage-making machine. **2** a relentlessly uniform process. **sausage meat** minced meat used in sausages or as a stuffing etc. **sausage roll** *Brit.* sausage meat enclosed in a pastry roll and baked. [ME f. ONF *saussiche* f. med.L *salsicia* f. L *salsus*: see SAUCE]

sauté /ˈsəʊteɪ/ *adj., n., & v.* —*adj.* (esp. of potatoes etc.) quickly fried in a little hot fat. —*n.* food cooked in this way. —*v.tr.* (**sautéd** or **sautéed**) cook in this way. [F, past part. of *sauter* jump]

Sauternes /səʊˈtɜːn/ *n.* a sweet white wine from Sauternes in the Bordeaux region of France.

savage /ˈsævɪdʒ/ *adj., n., & v.* —*adj.* **1** fierce; cruel (*savage persecution*; *a savage blow*). **2** wild; primitive (*savage tribes*; *a savage animal*). **3** *archaic* (of scenery

etc.) uncultivated (*a savage scene*). **4** *colloq.* angry; bad-tempered (*in a savage mood*). **5** *Heraldry* (of the human figure) naked. —*n.* **1** *Anthropol. derog.* a member of a primitive tribe. **2** a cruel or barbarous person. —*v.tr.* **1** (esp. of a dog, wolf, etc.) attack and bite or trample. **2** (of a critic etc.) attack fiercely. □□ **savagedom** *n.* **savagely** *adv.* **savageness** *n.* **savagery** *n.* (*pl.* **-ies**). [ME f. OF *sauvage* wild f. L *silvaticus* f. *silva* a wood]

savannah /səˈvænə/ *n.* (also **savanna**) a grassy plain in tropical and subtropical regions, with few or no trees. [Sp. *zavana* perh. of Carib orig.]

savant /ˈsæv(ə)nt, sæˈvɑː/ *n.* (*fem.* **savante** /ˈsæv(ə)nt or sæˈvɑːt/) a learned person, esp. a distinguished scientist etc. [F, part. of *savoir* know (as SAPIENT)]

savate /səˈvɑːt/ *n.* a form of boxing in which feet and fists are used. [F, orig. a kind of shoe: cf. SABOT]

save[1] /seɪv/ *v. & n.* —*v.* **1** *tr.* (often foll. by *from*) rescue, preserve, protect, or deliver from danger, harm, discredit, etc. (*saved my life*; *saved me from drowning*). **2** *tr.* (often foll. by *up*) keep for future use; reserve; refrain from spending (*saved up £150 for a new bike*; *likes to save plastic bags*). **3** *tr.* (often *refl.*) **a** relieve (another person or oneself) from spending (money, time, trouble, etc.); prevent exposure to (annoyance etc.) (*saved myself £50*; *a word processor saves time*). **b** obviate the need or likelihood of (*soaking saves scrubbing*). **4** *tr.* preserve from damnation; convert (*saved her soul*). **5** *tr. & refl.* husband or preserve (one's strength, health, etc.) (*saving himself for the last lap*; *save your energy*). **6** *intr.* (often foll. by *up*) save money for future use. **7** *tr.* **a** avoid losing (a game, match, etc.). **b** prevent an opponent from scoring (a goal etc.). **c** stop (a ball etc.) from entering the goal. —*n.* **1** *Football* etc. the act of preventing an opponent's scoring etc. **2** *Bridge* a sacrifice-bid to prevent unnecessary losses. □ **save-all 1** a device to prevent waste. **2** *hist.* a pan with a spike for burning up candle-ends. **save appearances** present a prosperous, respectable, etc. appearance. **save-as-you-earn** *Brit.* a method of saving by regular deduction from earnings at source. **save one's breath** not waste time speaking to no effect. **save a person's face** see FACE. **save the situation** (or **day**) find or provide a solution to difficulty or disaster. **save one's skin** (or **neck** or **bacon**) avoid loss, injury, or death; escape from danger. **save the tide** get in or out (of port etc.) while it lasts. **save the trouble** avoid useless or pointless effort. □□ **savable** *adj.* (also **saveable**). [ME f. AF *sa(u)ver*, OF *salver*, *sauver* f. LL *salvare* f. L *salvus* SAFE]

save[2] /seɪv/ *prep. & conj. archaic* or *poet.* —*prep.* except; but (*all save him*). —*conj.* (often foll. by *for*) unless; but; except (*happy save for one want*; *is well save that he has a cold*). [ME f. OF *sauf sauve* f. L *salvo, salva*, ablat. sing. of *salvus* SAFE]

saveloy /ˈsævə,lɔɪ/ *n.* a seasoned red pork sausage, dried and smoked, and sold ready to eat. [corrupt. of F *cervelas*, *-at*, f. It. *cervellata* (*cervello* brain)]

saver /ˈseɪvə(r)/ *n.* **1** a person who saves esp. money. **2** (often in *comb.*) a device for economical use (of time etc.) (*found the short cut a time-saver*). **3** *Racing sl.* a hedging bet.

savin /ˈsævɪn/ *n.* (also **savine**) **1** a bushy juniper, *Juniperus sabina*, usu. spreading horizontally, and yielding oil formerly used in the treatment of amenorrhoea. **2** *US* = red cedar. [OE f. OF *savine* f. L *sabina* (*herba*) Sabine (herb)]

saving /ˈseɪvɪŋ/ *adj., n., & prep.* —*adj.* (often in *comb.*) making economical use of (*labour-saving*). —*n.* **1** anything that is saved. **2** an economy (*a saving in expenses*). **3** (usu. in *pl.*) money saved. —*prep.* **1** with the exception of; except (*all saving that one*). **2** without offence to (*saving your presence*). □ **saving clause** *Law* a clause containing a stipulation of exemption etc. **saving grace 1** the redeeming grace of God. **2** a redeeming quality or

w *we* z *zoo* ʃ *she* ʒ *decision* θ *thin* ð *this* ŋ *ring* x *loch* tʃ *chip* dʒ *jar* (*see over for vowels*)

characteristic. **savings account** a deposit account. **savings bank** a bank receiving small deposits at interest and returning the profits to the depositors. **savings certificate** *Brit.* an interest-bearing document issued by the Government for the benefit of savers. [ME f. SAVE[1]: prep. prob. f. SAVE[2] after *touching*]

saviour /'seɪvjə(r)/ *n.* (*US* **savior**) **1** a person who saves or delivers from danger, destruction, etc. (*the saviour of the nation*). **2** (**Saviour**) (prec. by *the*, *our*) Christ. [ME f. OF *sauvëour* f. eccl.L *salvator -oris* (transl. Gk *sōtēr*) f. LL *salvare* SAVE[1]]

savoir faire /ˌsævwɑː 'feə(r)/ *n.* the ability to act suitably in any situation; tact. [F, = know how to do]

savor *US* var. of SAVOUR.

savory[1] /'seɪvərɪ/ *n.* (*pl.* **-ies**) any herb of the genus *Satureia*, esp. *S. hortensis* and *S. montana*, used esp. in cookery. [ME *saverey*, perh. f. OE *sætherie* f. L *satureia*]

savory[2] *US* var. of SAVOURY.

savour /'seɪvə(r)/ *n. & v.* (*US* **savor**) —*n.* **1** a characteristic taste, flavour, relish, etc. **2** a quality suggestive of or containing a small amount of another. **3** *archaic* a characteristic smell. —*v.* **1** *tr.* **a** appreciate and enjoy the taste of (food). **b** enjoy or appreciate (an experience etc.). **2** *intr.* (foll. by *of*) **a** suggest by taste, smell, etc. (*savours of mushrooms*). **b** imply or suggest a specified quality (*savours of impertinence*). □□ **savourless** *adj.* [ME f. OF f. L *sapor -oris* f. *sapere* to taste]

savoury /'seɪvərɪ/ *adj. & n.* (*US* **savory**) —*adj.* **1** having an appetizing taste or smell. **2** (of food) salty or piquant, not sweet (*a savoury omelette*). **3** pleasant; acceptable. —*n.* (*pl.* **-ies**) *Brit.* a savoury dish served as an appetizer or at the end of dinner. □□ **savourily** *adv.* **savouriness** *n.* [ME f. OF *savouré* past part. (as SAVOUR)]

savoy /sə'vɔɪ/ *n.* a hardy variety of cabbage with wrinkled leaves. [*Savoy* in SE France]

Savoyard /sə'vɔɪɑːd, ˌsævɔɪ'ɑːd/ *n. & adj.* —*n.* a native of Savoy in SE France. —*adj.* of or relating to Savoy or its people etc. [F f. *Savoie* Savoy]

savvy /'sævɪ/ *v., n., & adj. sl.* —*v.intr. & tr.* (**-ies**, **-ied**) know. —*n.* knowingness; shrewdness; understanding. —*adj.* (**savvier**, **savviest**) *US* knowing; wise. [orig. Black & Pidgin E after Sp. *sabe usted* you know]

saw[1] /sɔː/ *n. & v.* —*n.* **1 a** a hand tool having a toothed blade used to cut esp. wood with a to-and-fro movement. **b** any of several mechanical power-driven devices with a toothed rotating disk or moving band, for cutting. **2** *Zool.* etc. a serrated organ or part. —*v.* (*past part.* **sawn** /sɔːn/ or **sawed**) **1** *tr.* **a** cut (wood etc.) with a saw. **b** make (boards etc.) with a saw. **2** *intr.* use a saw. **3 a** *intr.* move to and fro with a motion as of a saw or person sawing (*sawing away on his violin*). **b** *tr.* divide (the air etc.) with gesticulations. □**saw-doctor** a machine for making the teeth of a saw. **saw-edged** with a jagged edge like a saw. **saw-frame** a frame in which a saw-blade is held taut. **saw-gate** = *saw-frame*. **saw-gin** = *cotton-gin*. **saw-horse** a rack supporting wood for sawing. **sawn-off** (*US* **sawed-off**) **1** (of a gun) having part of the barrel sawn off to make it easier to handle and give a wider field of fire. **2** *colloq.* (of a person) short. **saw-pit** a pit in which the lower of two men working a pit-saw stands. **saw-set** a tool for wrenching saw-teeth in alternate directions to allow the saw to work freely. **saw-wort** a composite plant, *Serratula tinctoria*, yielding a yellow dye from its serrated leaves. □□ **sawlike** *adj.* [OE *saga* f. Gmc]

saw[2] *past* of SEE[1].

saw[3] /sɔː/ *n.* a proverb; a maxim (*that's just an old saw*). [OE *sagu* f. Gmc, rel. to SAY: cf. SAGA]

sawbill /'sɔːbɪl/ *n.* a merganser.

sawbones /'sɔːbəʊnz/ *n. sl.* a doctor or surgeon.

sawbuck /'sɔːbʌk/ *n. US* **1** a saw-horse. **2** *sl.* a $10 note.

sawdust /'sɔːdʌst/ *n.* powdery particles of wood produced in sawing.

sawfish /'sɔːfɪʃ/ *n.* any large marine fish of the family Pristidae, with a toothed flat snout used as a weapon.

sawfly /'sɔːflaɪ/ *n.* (*pl.* **-flies**) any insect of the superfamily Tenthredinidae, with a serrated ovipositor, the larvae of which are injurious to plants.

sawmill /'sɔːmɪl/ *n.* a factory in which wood is sawn mechanically into planks or boards.

sawn *past part.* of SAW[1].

sawtooth /'sɔːtuːθ/ *adj.* **1** (also **sawtoothed** /-tuːθt/) (esp. of a roof, wave, etc.) shaped like the teeth of a saw with one steep and one slanting side. **2** (of a wave-form) showing a slow linear rise and rapid linear fall.

sawyer /'sɔːjə(r)/ *n.* **1** a person who saws timber professionally. **2** *US* an uprooted tree held fast by one end in a river. **3** *NZ* a large wingless horned grasshopper whose grubs bore in wood. [ME, earlier *sawer*, f. SAW[1]]

sax[1] /sæks/ *n. colloq.* **1** a saxophone. **2** a saxophone-player. □□ **saxist** *n.* [abbr.]

sax[2] /sæks/ *n.* (also **zax** /zæks/) a slater's chopper, with a point for making nail-holes. [OE *seax* knife f. Gmc]

saxatile /'sæksətaɪl/ *adj.* living or growing on or among rocks. [F *saxatile* or L *saxatilis* f. *saxum* rock]

saxboard /'sæksbɔːd/ *n.* the uppermost strake of an open boat. [SAX[2] + BOARD]

saxe /sæks/ *n.* (in full **saxe blue**) (often *attrib.*) a lightish blue colour with a greyish tinge. [F, = Saxony, the source of a dye of this colour]

saxhorn /'sækshɔːn/ *n.* any of a series of different-sized brass wind instruments with valves and a funnel-shaped mouthpiece, used mainly in military and brass bands. [*Sax*, name of its Belgian inventors, + HORN]

saxicoline /sæk'sɪkəˌlaɪn/ *adj.* (also **saxicolous**) *Biol.* = SAXATILE. [mod.L *saxicolus* f. *saxum* rock + *colere* inhabit]

saxifrage /'sæksɪˌfreɪdʒ/ *n.* any plant of the genus *Saxifraga*, growing on rocky or stony ground and usu. bearing small white, yellow, or red flowers. [ME f. OF *saxifrage* or LL *saxifraga* (*herba*) f. L *saxum* rock + *frangere* break]

Saxon /'sæks(ə)n/ *n. & adj.* —*n.* **1** *hist.* **a** a member of the Germanic people that conquered parts of England in 5th–6th c. **b** (usu. **Old Saxon**) the language of the Saxons. **2** = ANGLO-SAXON. **3** a native of modern Saxony in Germany. **4** the Germanic (as opposed to Latin or Romance) elements of English. —*adj.* **1** *hist.* of or concerning the Saxons. **2** belonging to or originating from the Saxon language or Old English. **3** of or concerning modern Saxony or Saxons. □**Saxon architecture** the form of Romanesque architecture preceding the Norman in England. **Saxon blue** a solution of indigo in sulphuric acid as a dye. □□ **Saxondom** *n.* **Saxonism** *n.* **Saxonist** *n.* **Saxonize** /-ˌnaɪz/ *v.tr. & intr.* (also **-ise**). [ME f. OF f. LL *Saxo -onis* f. Gk *Saxones* (pl.) f. WG: cf. OE *Seaxan*, *Seaxe* (pl.)]

saxony /'sæksənɪ/ *n.* **1** a fine kind of wool. **2** cloth made from this. [*Saxony* in Germany f. LL *Saxonia* (as SAXON)]

saxophone /'sæksəˌfəʊn/ *n.* **1** a keyed brass reed instrument in several sizes and registers, used esp. in jazz and dance music. **2** a saxophone-player. □□ **saxophonic** /-'fɒnɪk/ *adj.* **saxophonist** /-'sɒfənɪst, -səˌfəʊnɪst/ *n.* [*Sax* (as SAXHORN) + -PHONE]

say /seɪ/ *v. & n.* —*v.* (*3rd sing. present* **says** /sez/; *past and past part.* **said** /sed/) **1** *tr.* (often foll. by *that* + clause) **a** utter (specified words) in a speaking voice; remark (*said 'Damn!'*; *said that he was satisfied*). **b** put into words; express (*that was well said*; *cannot say what I feel*). **2** *tr.* (often foll. by *that* +

clause) **a** state; promise or prophesy (*says that there will be war*). **b** have specified wording; indicate (*says here that he was killed*; *the clock says ten to six*). **3** *tr.* (in *passive*; usu. foll. by *to* + infin.) be asserted or described (*is said to be 93 years old*). **4** *tr.* (foll. by *to* + infin.) *colloq.* tell a person to do something (*he said to bring the car*). **5** *tr.* convey (information) (*spoke for an hour but said little*). **6** *tr.* put forward as an argument or excuse (*much to be said in favour of it*; *what have you to say for yourself?*). **7** *tr.* (often *absol.*) form and give an opinion or decision as to (*who did it I cannot say*; *do say which you prefer*). **8** *tr.* select, assume, or take as an example or (a specified number etc.) as near enough (*shall we say this one?*; *paid, say, £20*). **9** *tr.* **a** speak the words of (prayers, Mass, a grace, etc.). **b** repeat (a lesson etc.); recite (*can't say his tables*). **10** *tr.* Art etc. convey (inner meaning or intention) (*what is the director saying in this film?*). **11** *intr.* **a** speak; talk. **b** (in *imper.*) *poet.* tell me (*what is your name, say!*). **12** *tr.* (**the said**) *Law* or *joc.* the previously mentioned (*the said witness*). **13** *intr.* (as *int.*) *US* an exclamation of surprise, to attract attention, etc. —*n.* **1 a** an opportunity for stating one's opinion etc. (*let him have his say*). **b** a stated opinion. **2 a** share in a decision (*had no say in the matter*). □**how say you?** *Law* how do you find? (addressed to the jury requesting its verdict). **I etc. cannot** (or **could not**) **say** I etc. do not know. **I'll say** *colloq.* yes indeed. **I say!** *Brit.* an exclamation expressing surprise, drawing attention, etc. **it is said** the rumour is that. **not to say** and indeed; or possibly even (*his language was rude not to say offensive*). **said he** (or **I** etc.) *colloq.* or *poet.* he etc. said. **say for oneself** say by way of conversation, oratory, etc. **say much** (or **something**) **for** indicate the high quality of. **say no** refuse or disagree. **say out** express fully or candidly. **says I** (or **he** etc.) *colloq.* I, he, etc., said (used in reporting conversation). **say-so 1** the power of decision. **2** mere assertion (*cannot proceed merely on his say-so*). **say something** make a short speech. **says you!** *colloq.* I disagree. **say when** *colloq.* indicate when enough drink or food has been given. **say the word 1** indicate that you agree or give permission. **2** give the order etc. **say yes** agree. **that is to say 1** in other words, more explicitly. **2** or at least. **they say** it is rumoured. **to say nothing of** = *not to mention* (see MENTION). **what do** (or **would**) **you say to?** would you like? **when all is said and done** after all, in the long run. **you can say that again!** (or **you said it!**) *colloq.* I agree emphatically. **you don't say so** *colloq.* an expression of amazement or disbelief. □□**sayable** *adj.* **sayer** *n.* [OE *secgan* f. Gmc]

SAYE *abbr. Brit.* save-as-you-earn.

saying /'seɪɪŋ/ *n.* **1** the act or an instance of saying. **2** a maxim, proverb, adage, etc. □**as the saying goes** (or **is**) an expression used in introducing a proverb, cliché, etc. **go without saying** be too well known or obvious to need mention. **there is no saying** it is impossible to know.

Sb *symb. Chem.* the element antimony. [L *stibium*]

SBN *abbr.* Standard Book Number (cf. ISBN).

S. by E. *abbr.* South by East.

S. by W. *abbr.* South by West.

SC *abbr.* **1** *US* South Carolina (also in official postal use). **2** special constable.

Sc *symb. Chem.* the element scandium.

sc. *abbr.* scilicet.

s.c. *abbr.* small capitals.

scab /skæb/ *n. & v.* —*n.* **1** a dry rough crust formed over a cut, sore, etc. in healing. **2** (often *attrib.*) *colloq. derog.* a person who refuses to strike or join a trade union, or who tries to break a strike by working; a blackleg. **3** the mange or a similar skin disease esp. in animals. **4** a fungous plant-disease causing scablike roughness. **5** a dislikeable person. —*v.intr.* (**scabbed, scabbing**) **1** act as a scab. **2** (of a

wound etc.) form a scab; heal over. □□**scabbed** *adj.* **scabby** *adj.* (**scabbier, scabbiest**). **scabbiness** *n.* **scablike** *adj.* [ME f. ON *skabbr* (unrecorded), corresp. to OE *sceabb*]

scabbard /'skæbəd/ *n.* **1** *hist.* a sheath for a sword, bayonet, etc. **2** *US* a sheath for a revolver etc. □**scabbard-fish** any of various silvery-white marine fish shaped like a sword-scabbard, esp. *Lepidopus caudatus*. [ME *sca(u)berc* etc. f. AF prob. f. Frank.]

scabies /'skeɪbiːz/ *n.* a contagious skin disease causing severe itching (cf. ITCH). [ME f. L f. *scabere* scratch]

scabious /'skeɪbɪəs/ *n. & adj.* —*n.* any plant of the genus *Scabiosa*, *Knautia*, etc., with pink, white, or esp. blue pincushion-shaped flowers. —*adj.* affected with mange; scabby. [ME f. med.L *scabiosa* (*herba*) formerly regarded as a cure for skin disease: see SCABIES]

scabrous /'skeɪbrəs/ *adj.* **1** having a rough surface; bearing short stiff hairs, scales, etc.; scurfy. **2** (of a subject, situation, etc.) requiring tactful treatment; hard to handle with decency. **3 a** indecent, salacious. **b** behaving licentiously. □□**scabrously** *adv.* **scabrousness** *n.* [F *scabreux* or LL *scabrosus* f. L *scaber* rough]

scad /skæd/ *n.* any fish of the family Carangidae native to tropical and subtropical seas, usu. having an elongated body and very large spiky scales. [17th c.: orig. unkn.]

scads /skædz/ *n.pl. US colloq.* large quantities. [19th c.: orig. unkn.]

scaffold /'skæfəʊld, -f(ə)ld/ *n. & v.* —*n.* **1 a** *hist.* a raised wooden platform used for the execution of criminals. **b** a similar platform used for drying tobacco etc. **2** = SCAFFOLDING. **3** (prec. by *the*) death by execution. —*v.tr.* attach scaffolding to (a building). □□**scaffolder** *n.* [ME f. AF f. OF (*e*)*schaffaut*, earlier *escadafaut*: cf. CATAFALQUE]

scaffolding /'skæfəʊldɪŋ, -fəldɪŋ/ *n.* **1 a** a temporary structure formed of poles, planks, etc., erected by workmen and used by them while building or repairing a house etc. **b** materials used for this. **2** a temporary conceptual framework used for constructing theories etc.

scagliola /skæˈljəʊlə/ *n.* imitation stone or plaster mixed with glue. [It. *scagliuola* dimin. of *scaglia* SCALE¹]

scalable /'skeɪləb(ə)l/ *adj.* capable of being scaled or climbed. □□**scalability** /-'bɪlɪtɪ/ *n.*

scalar /'skeɪlə(r)/ *adj. & n.* Math. & Physics —*adj.* (of a quantity) having only magnitude, not direction. —*n.* a scalar quantity (cf. VECTOR). [L *scalaris* f. *scala* ladder; see SCALE³]

scalawag var. of SCALLYWAG.

scald¹ /skɔːld, skɒld/ *v. & n.* —*v.tr.* **1** burn (the skin etc.) with hot liquid or steam. **2** heat (esp. milk) to near boiling-point. **3** (usu. foll. by *out*) clean (a pan etc.) by rinsing with boiling water. **4** treat (poultry etc.) with boiling water to remove feathers etc. —*n.* **1** a burn etc. caused by scalding. **2** a skin disease caused esp. by air pollution etc. affecting the fruits of some plants. □**like a scalded cat** moving unusually fast. **scalded cream** a dessert made from milk scalded and allowed to stand. **scalding tears** hot bitter tears of grief etc. □□**scalder** *n.* [ME f. AF, ONF *escalder*, OF *eschalder* f. LL *excaldare* (as EX-¹, L *calidus* hot)]

scald² var. of SKALD.

scale¹ /skeɪl/ *n. & v.* —*n.* **1** each of the small thin bony or horny overlapping plates protecting the skin of fish and reptiles. **2** something resembling a fish-scale, esp.: **a** a pod or husk. **b** a flake of skin; a scab. **c** a rudimentary leaf, feather, or bract. **d** each of the structures covering the wings of butterflies and moths. **e** *Bot.* a layer of a bulb. **3 a** a flake formed on the surface of rusty iron. **b** a thick white deposit formed in a kettle, boiler, etc. by the action of heat on water. **4** plaque formed on teeth. —*v.* **1** *tr.*

remove scale or scales from (fish, nuts, iron, etc.). **2** *tr.* remove plaque from (teeth) by scraping. **3** *intr.* **a** (of skin, metal, etc.) form, come off in, or drop, scales. **b** (usu. foll. by *off*) (of scales) come off. □**scale-armour** *hist.* armour formed of metal scales attached to leather etc. **scale-board** very thin wood used for the back of a mirror, picture, etc. **scale-bug** = *scale insect.* **scale-fern** any of various spleenworts, esp. *Asplenium ceterach.* **scale insect** any of various insects, esp. of the family Coccidae, clinging to plants and secreting a shieldlike scale as covering. **scale-leaf** a modified leaf resembling a scale. **scale-moss** a type of liverwort with scalelike leaves. **scales fall from a person's eyes** a person is no longer deceived (cf. Acts 9:18). **scale-winged** lepidopterous. **scale-work** an overlapping arrangement. □□ **scaled** *adj.* (also in *comb.*). **scaleless** /ˈskeɪllɪs/ *adj.* **scaler** *n.* [ME f. OF *escale* f. Gmc, rel. to SCALE²]

scale² /skeɪl/ *n. & v.* —*n.* **1 a** (often in *pl.*) a weighing machine or device (*bathroom scales*). **b** (also **scale-pan**) each of the dishes on a simple scale balance. **2** (**the Scales**) the zodiacal sign or constellation Libra. —*v.tr.* (of something weighed) show (a specified weight) in the scales. □**pair of scales** a simple balance. **throw into the scale** cause to be a factor in a contest, debate, etc. **tip** (or **turn**) **the scales 1** (usu. foll. by *at*) outweigh the opposite scale-pan (at a specified weight); weigh. **2** (of a motive, circumstance, etc.) be decisive. [ME f. ON *skál* bowl f. Gmc]

scale³ /skeɪl/ *n. & v.* —*n.* **1** a series of degrees; a graded classification system (*pay fees according to a prescribed scale; high on the social scale; seven points on the Richter scale*). Geog. & Archit. **2 a** (often *attrib.*) Geog. & Archit. a ratio of size in a map, model, picture, etc. (*on a scale of one centimetre to the kilometre; a scale model*). **b** relative dimensions or degree (*generosity on a grand scale*). **3** *Mus.* an arrangement of all the notes in any system of music in ascending or descending order (*chromatic scale; major scale*). **4 a** a set of marks on a line used in measuring, reducing, enlarging, etc. **b** a rule determining the distances between these. **c** a piece of metal, apparatus, etc. on which these are marked. **5** (in full **scale of notation**) *Math.* the ratio between units in a numerical system (*decimal scale*). —*v.* **1** *tr.* **a** (also *absol.*) climb a wall, height, etc. esp. with a ladder. **b** climb (the social scale, heights of ambition, etc.). **2** *tr.* represent in proportional dimensions; reduce to a common scale. **3** *intr.* (of quantities etc.) have a common scale; be commensurable. □**economies of scale** proportionate savings gained by using larger quantities. **in scale** (of drawing etc.) in proportion to the surroundings etc. **play** (or **sing**) **scales** *Mus.* perform the notes of a scale as an exercise for the fingers or voice. **scale down** make smaller in proportion; reduce in size. **scale up** make larger in proportion; increase in size. **scaling-ladder** *hist.* a ladder used to climb esp. fortress walls, esp. to break a siege. **to scale** with a uniform reduction or enlargement. □□ **scaler** *n.* [(n.) ME (= ladder): (v.) ME f. OF *escaler* or med.L *scalare* f. L *scala* f. *scandere* climb]

scalene /ˈskeɪliːn/ *adj. & n.* —*adj.* (esp. of a triangle) having sides unequal in length. —*n.* **1** (in full **scalene muscle**) = SCALENUS. **2** a scalene triangle. □**scalene cone** (or **cylinder**) a cone (or cylinder) with the axis not perpendicular to the base. [LL *scalenus* f. Gk *skalēnos* unequal, rel. to *skolios* bent]

scalenus /skəˈliːnəs/ *n.* (*pl.* **scaleni** /-naɪ/) any of several muscles extending from the neck to the first and second ribs. [mod.L: see SCALENE]

scallawag var. of SCALLYWAG.

scallion /ˈskæljən/ *n.* a shallot or spring onion; any long-necked onion with a small bulb. [ME f. AF *scal(o)un* = OF *escalo(i)gne* ult. f. L *Ascalonia* (*caepa*) (onion) of *Ascalon* in anc. Palestine]

scallop /ˈskæləp, ˈskɒl-/ *n. & v.* (also **scollop** /ˈskɒl-/) **1** any of various bivalve molluscs of the family Pectinidae, esp. of the genus *Chlamys* or *Pecten*, much prized as food. **2** (in full **scallop shell**) **a** a single valve from the shell of a scallop, with grooves and ridges radiating from the middle of the hinge and edged with small rounded lobes, often used for cooking or serving food. **b** *hist.* a representation of this shell worn as a pilgrim's badge. **3** (in *pl.*) an ornamental edging cut in material in imitation of a scallop-edge. **4** a small pan or dish shaped like a scallop shell and used for baking or serving food. —*v.tr.* (**scalloped**, **scalloping**) **1** cook in a scallop. **2** ornament (an edge or material) with scallops or scalloping. □□ **scalloper** *n.* **scalloping** *n.* (in sense 3 of *n.*). [ME f. OF *escalope* prob. f. Gmc]

scallywag /ˈskælɪˌwæg/ *n.* (also **scalawag**, **scallawag** /ˈskælə-/) a scamp; a rascal. [19th-c. US sl.: orig. unkn.]

scalp /skælp/ *n. & v.* —*n.* **1** the skin covering the top of the head, with the hair etc. attached. **2 a** *hist.* the scalp of an enemy cut or torn away as a trophy by an American Indian. **b** a trophy or symbol of triumph, conquest, etc. **3** *Sc.* a bare rock projecting above water etc. —*v.tr.* **1** *hist.* take the scalp of (an enemy). **2** criticize savagely. **3** *US* defeat; humiliate. **4** *US colloq.* resell (shares, tickets, etc.) at a high or quick profit. □□ **scalpless** *adj.* [ME, prob. of Scand. orig.]

scalpel /ˈskælp(ə)l/ *n.* a surgeon's small sharp knife shaped for holding like a pen. [F *scalpel* or L *scalpellum* dimin. of *scalprum* chisel f. *scalpere* scratch]

scalper /ˈskælpə(r)/ *n.* **1** a person or thing that scalps (esp. in sense 4 of *v.*). **2** (also **scauper**, **scorper** /ˈskɔːpə(r)/) an engraver's tool for hollowing out woodcut or linocut designs. [SCALP + -ER¹: sense 2 also f. L *scalper* cutting tool f. *scalpere* carve]

scaly /ˈskeɪlɪ/ *adj.* (**scalier**, **scaliest**) covered in or having many scales or flakes. □□ **scaliness** *n.*

scam /skæm/ *n. US sl.* **1** a trick or swindle; a fraud. **2** a story or rumour. [20th c.: orig. unkn.]

scammony /ˈskæmənɪ/ *n.* (*pl.* **-ies**) an Asian plant, *Convolvulus scammonia*, bearing white or pink flowers, the dried roots of which are used as a purgative. [ME f. OF *scamonee, escamonie* or L *scammonia* f. Gk *skammōnia*]

scamp¹ /skæmp/ *n. colloq.* a rascal; a rogue. □□ **scampish** *adj.* [*scamp* rob on highway, prob. f. MDu. *schampen* decamp f. OF *esc(h)amper* (as EX-¹, L *campus* field)]

scamp² /skæmp/ *v.tr.* do (work etc.) in a perfunctory or inadequate way. [perh. formed as SCAMP¹: cf. SKIMP]

scamper /ˈskæmpə(r)/ *v. & n.* —*v.intr.* (usu. foll. by *about*, *through*) run and skip impulsively or playfully. —*n.* the act or an instance of scampering. [prob. formed as SCAMP¹]

scampi /ˈskæmpɪ/ *n.pl.* **1** large prawns. **2** (often treated as *sing.*) a dish of these, usu. fried. [It.]

scan /skæn/ *v. & n.* —*v.* (**scanned**, **scanning**) **1** *tr.* look at intently or quickly (*scanned the horizon; rapidly scanned the speech for errors*). **2** *intr.* (of a verse etc.) be metrically correct; be capable of being recited etc. metrically (*this line doesn't scan*). **3** *tr.* **a** examine all parts of (a surface etc.) to detect radioactivity etc. **b** cause (a particular region) to be traversed by a radar etc. beam. **4** *tr.* resolve (a picture) into its elements of light and shade in a prearranged pattern for the purposes esp. of television transmission. **5** *tr.* test the metre of (a line of verse etc.) by reading with the emphasis on its rhythm, or by examining the number of feet etc. **6** *tr.* **a** make a scan of (the body or part of it). **b** examine (a patient etc.) with a scanner. —*n.* **1** the act or an instance of scanning. **2** an image obtained by scanning or with a scanner. □□ **scannable** *adj.* [ME f. L *scandere* climb: in LL = scan verses (from the raising of one's foot in marking rhythm)]

scandal /'skænd(ə)l/ *n.* **1 a** a thing or a person causing general public outrage or indignation. **b** the outrage etc. so caused, esp. as a subject of common talk. **c** malicious gossip or backbiting. **2** *Law* a public affront, esp. an irrelevant abusive statement in court. □**scandal sheet** *derog.* a newspaper etc. giving prominence to esp. malicious gossip. □□ **scandalous** *adj.* **scandalously** *adv.* **scandalousness** *n.* [ME f. OF *scandale* f. eccl.L *scandalum* f. Gk *skandalon* snare, stumbling-block]

scandalize /'skændə,laɪz/ *v.tr.* (also **-ise**) offend the moral feelings, sensibilities, etc. of; shock. [ME in sense 'make a scandal of' f. F *scandaliser* or eccl.L *scandalizo* f. Gk *skandalizō* (as SCANDAL)]

scandalmonger /'skænd(ə)l,mʌŋgə(r)/ *n.* a person who spreads malicious scandal.

Scandinavian /,skændɪ'neɪvɪən/ *n. & adj.* —*n.* **1 a** a native or inhabitant of Scandinavia (Denmark, Norway, Sweden, and Iceland). **b** a person of Scandinavian descent. **2** the family of languages of Scandinavia. —*adj.* of or relating to Scandinavia or its people or languages. [L *Scandinavia*]

scandium /'skændɪəm/ *n. Chem.* a rare soft silver-white metallic element occurring naturally in lanthanide ores. ¶ Symb.: **Sc**. [mod.L f. *Scandia* Scandinavia (source of the minerals containing it)]

scannable see SCAN.

scanner /'skænə(r)/ *n.* **1** a device for scanning or systematically examining all the parts of something. **2** a machine for measuring the intensity of radiation, ultrasound reflections, etc., from the body as a diagnostic aid. **3** a person who scans or examines critically. **4** a person who scans verse.

scansion /'skænʃ(ə)n/ *n.* **1** the metrical scanning of verse. **2** the way a verse etc. scans. [L *scansio* (LL of metre) f. *scandere* scans- climb]

scant /skænt/ *adj. & v.* —*adj.* barely sufficient; deficient (*with scant regard for the truth*; *scant of breath*). —*v.tr. archaic* provide (a supply, material, a person, etc.) grudgingly; skimp; stint. □□ **scantly** *adv.* **scantness** *n.* [ME f. ON *skamt* neut. of *skammr* short]

scantling /'skæntlɪŋ/ *n.* **1 a** a timber beam of small cross-section. **b** a size to which a stone or timber is to be cut. **2** a set of standard dimensions for parts of a structure, esp. in shipbuilding. **3** (usu. foll. by *of*) *archaic* **a** a specimen or sample. **b** one's necessary supply; a modicum or small amount. [alt. after -LING¹ f. obs. *scantlon* f. OF *escantillon* sample]

scanty /'skæntɪ/ *adj.* (**scantier, scantiest**) **1** of small extent or amount. **2** barely sufficient. □□ **scantily** *adv.* **scantiness** *n.* [obs. *scant* scanty supply f. ON *skamt* neut. adj.: see SCANT]

scape /skeɪp/ *n.* **1** a long flower-stalk coming directly from the root. **2** the base of an insect's antenna. [L *scapus* f. Gk *skapos*, rel. to SCEPTRE]

-scape /skeɪp/ *comb. form* forming nouns denoting a view or a representation of a view (*moonscape*; *seascape*). [after LANDSCAPE]

scapegoat /'skeɪpgəʊt/ *n. & v.* —*n.* **1** a person bearing the blame for the sins, shortcomings, etc. of others, esp. as an expedient. **2** *Bibl.* a goat sent into the wilderness after the Jewish chief priest had symbolically laid the sins of the people upon it (Lev. 16). —*v.tr.* make a scapegoat of. □□ **scapegoater** *n.* [*scape* (archaic, = escape) + GOAT, = the goat that escapes]

scapegrace /'skeɪpgreɪs/ *n.* a rascal; a scamp, esp. a young person or child. [*scape* (as SCAPEGOAT) + GRACE = one who escapes the grace of God]

scaphoid /'skæfɔɪd/ *adj. & n. Anat.* = NAVICULAR. [mod.L *scaphoides* f. Gk *skaphoeidēs* f. *skaphos* boat]

scapula /'skæpjʊlə/ *n.* (*pl.* **scapulae** /-,liː/ or **scapulas**) the shoulder-blade. [LL, sing. of L *scapulae*]

scapular /'skæpjʊlə(r)/ *adj. & n.* —*adj.* of or relating to the shoulder or shoulder-blade. —*n.* **1 a** a monastic short cloak covering the shoulders. **b** a symbol of affiliation to an ecclesiastical order, consisting of two strips of cloth hanging down the breast and back and joined across the shoulders. **2** a bandage for or over the shoulders. **3** a scapular feather. □**scapular feather** a feather growing near the insertion of the wing. [(adj.) f. SCAPULA: (n.) f. LL *scapulare* (as SCAPULA)]

scapulary /'skæpjʊlərɪ/ *n.* (*pl.* **-ies**) **1** = SCAPULAR *n.* 1. **2** = SCAPULAR *n.* 3. [ME f. OF *eschapeloyre* f. med.L *scapelorium, scapularium* (as SCAPULA)]

scar¹ /skɑː(r)/ *n. & v.* —*n.* **1 a** usu. permanent mark on the skin left after the healing of a wound, burn, or sore. **2** the lasting effect of grief etc. on a person's character or disposition. **3** a mark left by damage etc. (*the table bore many scars*). **4** a mark left on the stem etc. of a plant by the fall of a leaf etc. —*v.* (**scarred, scarring**) **1** *tr.* (esp. as **scarred** *adj.*) mark with a scar or scars (*was scarred for life*). **2** *intr.* heal over; form a scar. **3** *tr.* form a scar on. □□ **scarless** *adj.* [ME f. OF *eschar(r)e* f. LL *eschara* f. Gk *eskhara* scab]

scar² /skɑː(r)/ *n.* (also **scaur** /skɔː(r)/) a steep craggy outcrop of a mountain or cliff. [ME f. ON *sker* low reef in the sea]

scarab /'skærəb/ *n.* **1 a** the sacred dung-beetle of ancient Egypt. **b** = SCARABAEID. **2** an ancient Egyptian gem cut in the form of a beetle and engraved with symbols on its flat side, used as a signet etc. [L *scarabaeus* f. Gk *skarabeios*]

scarabaeid /,skærə'biːɪd/ *n.* any beetle of the family Scarabaeidae, including the dung-beetle, cockchafer, etc. [mod.L *Scarabaeidae* (as SCARAB)]

scaramouch /'skærə,maʊtʃ/ *n. archaic* a boastful coward; a braggart. [It. *Scaramuccia* stock character in Italian farce f. *scaramuccia* = SKIRMISH, infl. by F form *Scaramouche*]

scarce /skeəs/ *adj. & adv.* —*adj.* **1** (usu. *predic.*) (esp. of food, money, etc.) insufficient for the demand; scanty. **2** hard to find; rare. —*adv. archaic or literary* scarcely. □**make oneself scarce** *colloq.* keep out of the way; surreptitiously disappear. □□ **scarceness** *n.* [ME f. AF & ONF (*e*)*scars*, OF *eschars* f. L *excerpere*: see EXCERPT]

scarcely /'skeəslɪ/ *adv.* **1** hardly; barely; only just (*I scarcely know him*). **2** surely not (*he can scarcely have said so*). **3** a mild or apologetic or ironical substitute for 'not' (*I scarcely expected to be insulted*).

scarcity /'skeəsɪtɪ/ *n.* (*pl.* **-ies**) (often foll. by *of*) a lack or inadequacy, esp. of food.

scare /skeə(r)/ *v. & n.* —*v.* **1** *tr.* frighten, esp. suddenly (*his expression scared us*). **2** *tr.* (as **scared** *adj.*) (usu. foll. by *of*, or *to* + infin.) frightened; terrified (*scared of his own shadow*). **3** *tr.* (usu. foll. by *away*, *off*, *up*, etc.) drive away by frightening. **4** *intr.* become scared (*they don't scare easily*). —*n.* **1** a sudden attack of fright (*gave me a scare*). **2** a general, esp. baseless, fear of war, invasion, epidemic, etc. (*a measles scare*). **3** a financial panic causing share-selling etc. □**scaredy-cat** /'skeədɪ,kæt/ *colloq.* a timid person. **scare-heading** (or **-head**) a shockingly sensational newspaper headline. **scare up** (or **out**) esp. *US* **1** frighten (game etc.) out of cover. **2** *colloq.* manage to find; discover (*see if we can scare up a meal*). □□ **scarer** *n.* [ME *skerre* f. ON *skirra* frighten f. *skjarr* timid]

scarecrow /'skeə,krəʊ/ *n.* **1** a human figure dressed in old clothes and set up in a field to scare birds away. **2** *colloq.* a badly-dressed, grotesque-looking, or very thin person. **3** *archaic* an object of baseless fear.

scaremonger /'skeə,mʌŋgə(r)/ *n.* a person who spreads frightening reports or rumours. □□ **scaremongering** *n.*

scarf¹ /skɑːf/ *n.* (*pl.* **scarves** /skɑːvz/ or **scarfs**) a square, triangular, or esp. long narrow strip of material worn round the neck, over the shoulders, or tied round the head (of a woman), for warmth or ornament. □**scarf-pin** (or **-ring**) *Brit.* an ornamental device for fastening a scarf. **scarf-skin** the outermost layer of the skin constantly scaling off, esp. that at the base of the nails. **scarf-wise** worn diagonally across the body from shoulder to hip. □□ **scarfed** *adj.* [prob. alt. of *scarp* (infl. by SCARF²)· f. ONF *escarpe* = OF *escherpe* sash]

scarf² /skɑːf/ *v. & n.* —*v.tr.* join the ends of (pieces of esp. timber, metal, or leather) by bevelling or notching them to fit and then bolting, brazing, or sewing them together; cut the blubber of (a whale). —*n.* **1** a joint made by scarfing. **2** a cut on a whale made by scarfing. [ME (earlier as noun) prob. f. OF *escarf* (unrecorded) perh. f. ON]

scarifier /'skærɪˌfaɪə(r), 'skeə-/ *n.* **1** a thing or person that scarifies. **2** a machine with prongs for loosening soil without turning it. **3** a spiked road-breaking machine.

scarify¹ /'skærɪˌfaɪ, 'skeə-/ *v.tr.* (**-ies, -ied**) **1 a** make superficial incisions in. **b** cut off skin from. **2** hurt by severe criticism etc. **3** loosen (soil) with a scarifier. □□ **scarification** /-frˈkeɪʃ(ə)n/ *n.* [ME f. F *scarifier* f. LL *scarificare* f. L *scarifare* f. Gk *skariphaomai* f. *skariphos* stylus]

scarify² /'skeərɪˌfaɪ/ *v.tr. & intr.* (**-ies, -ied**) *colloq.* scare; terrify.

scarious /'skeəriəs/ *adj.* (of a part of a plant etc.) having a dry membranous appearance; thin and brittle. [F *scarieux* or mod.L *scariosus*]

scarlatina /ˌskɑːləˈtiːnə/ *n.* = *scarlet fever*. [mod.L f. It. *scarlattina* (*febbre* fever) dimin. of *scarlatto* SCARLET]

scarlet /'skɑːlɪt/ *n. & adj.* —*n.* **1** a brilliant red colour tinged with orange. **2** clothes or material of this colour (*dressed in scarlet*). —*adj.* of a scarlet colour. □ **scarlet fever** an infectious bacterial fever, affecting esp. children, with a scarlet rash. **scarlet hat** *RC Ch.* a cardinal's hat as a symbol of rank. **scarlet pimpernel** a small annual wild plant, *Anagallis arvensis*, with small esp. scarlet flowers closing in rainy or cloudy weather: also called *poor man's weather-glass*. **scarlet rash** = ROSEOLA 1. **scarlet runner 1** a runner bean. **2** a scarlet-flowered climber bearing this bean. **scarlet woman** *derog.* a notoriously promiscuous woman, a prostitute. [ME f. OF *escarlate*: ult. orig. unkn.]

scaroid /'skærɔɪd, 'skeə-/ *n. & adj.* —*n.* any colourful marine fish of the family Scaridae, native to tropical and temperate seas, including the scarus. —*adj.* of or relating to this family.

scarp /skɑːp/ *n. & v.* —*n.* **1** the inner wall or slope of a ditch in a fortification (cf. COUNTERSCARP). **2** a steep slope. —*v.tr.* **1** make (a slope) perpendicular or steep. **2** provide (a ditch) with a steep scarp and counterscarp. **3** (as **scarped** *adj.*) (of a hillside etc.) steep; precipitous. [It. *scarpa*]

scarper /'skɑːpə(r)/ *v.intr. Brit. sl.* run away; escape. [prob. f. It. *scappare* escape, infl. by rhyming sl. *Scapa Flow* = go]

scarus /'skeərəs/ *n.* any fish of the genus *Scarus*, with brightly coloured scales, and teeth fused to form a parrot-like beak used for eating coral. Also called *parrot-fish*. [L f. Gk *skaros*]

scarves *pl.* of SCARF¹.

scary /'skeərɪ/ *adj.* (**scarier, scariest**) *colloq.* scaring, frightening. □□ **scarily** *adv.*

scat¹ /skæt/ *v. & int. colloq.* —*v.intr.* (**scatted, scatting**) depart quickly. —*int.* go! [perh. abbr. of SCATTER]

scat² /skæt/ *n. & v.* —*n.* improvised jazz singing using sounds imitating instruments, instead of words. —*v.intr.* (**scatted, scatting**) sing scat. [prob. imit.]

scathe /skeɪð/ *v. & n.* —*v.tr.* **1** *poet.* injure esp. by blasting or withering. **2** (as **scathing** *adj.*) witheringly scornful (*scathing sarcasm*). **3** (with *neg.*) do the least harm to (*shall not be scathed*) (cf. UNSCATHED). —*n.* (usu. with *neg.*) *archaic* harm; injury (*without scathe*). □□ **scatheless** *predic.adj.*

scathingly *adv.* [(v.) ME f. ON *skatha* = OE *sceathian*: (n.) OE f. ON *skathi* = OE *sceatha* malefactor, injury, f. Gmc]

scatology /skæˈtɒlədʒɪ/ *n.* **1 a** a morbid interest in excrement. **b** a preoccupation with obscene literature, esp. that concerned with the excretory functions. **c** such literature. **2** the study of fossilized dung. **3** the study of excrement for esp. diagnosis. □□ **scatological** /-təˈlɒdʒɪk(ə)l/ *adj.* [Gk *skōr skatos* dung + -LOGY]

scatophagous /skæˈtɒfəgəs/ *adj.* feeding on dung. [as SCATOLOGY + Gk *-phagos* -eating]

scatter /'skætə(r)/ *v. & n.* —*v.* **1** *tr.* **a** throw here and there; strew (*scattered gravel on the road*). **b** cover by scattering (*scattered the road with gravel*). **2** *tr. & intr.* **a** move or cause to move in flight etc.; disperse (*scattered to safety at the sound*). **b** disperse or cause (hopes, clouds, etc.) to disperse. **3** *tr.* (as **scattered** *adj.*) not clustered together; wide apart; sporadic (*scattered villages*). **4** *tr. Physics* deflect or diffuse (light, particles, etc.). **5 a** *intr.* (of esp. a shotgun) fire a charge of shot diffusely. **b** *tr.* fire (a charge) in this way. —*n.* **1** the act or an instance of scattering. **2** a small amount scattered. **3** the extent of distribution of esp. shot. □ **scatter cushions** (or **rugs**, etc.) cushions, rugs, etc., placed here and there for effect. **scatter-shot** *n. & adj. US* firing at random. □□ **scatterer** *n.* [ME, prob. var. of SHATTER]

scatterbrain /'skætəˌbreɪn/ *n.* a person given to silly or disorganized thought with lack of concentration. □□ **scatterbrained** *adj.*

scatty /'skætɪ/ *adj.* (**scattier, scattiest**) *Brit. colloq.* scatterbrained; disorganized. □□ **scattily** *adv.* **scattiness** *n.* [abbr.]

scaup /skɔːp/ *n.* any diving duck of the genus *Aythya*. [*scaup* Sc. var. of *scalp* mussel-bed, which it frequents]

scauper var. of SCALPER 2.

scaur var. of SCAR².

scavenge /'skævɪndʒ/ *v.* **1** *tr. & intr.* (usu. foll. by *for*) search for and collect (discarded items). **2** *tr.* remove unwanted products from (an internal-combustion engine cylinder etc.). [back-form. f. SCAVENGER]

scavenger /'skævɪndʒə(r)/ *n.* **1** a person who seeks and collects discarded items. **2** an animal, esp. a beetle, feeding on carrion, refuse, etc. **3** *Brit. archaic* a person employed to clean the streets etc. □□ **scavengery** *n.* [ME *scavager* f. AF *scawager* f. *scawage* f. ONF *escauwer* inspect f. Flem. *scauwen*, rel. to SHOW: for *-n-* cf. MESSENGER]

scazon /'skeɪz(ə)n, 'skæz-/ *n. Prosody* a Greek or Latin metre of limping character, esp. a trimeter of two iambuses and a spondee or trochee. [L f. Gk *skazōn* f. *skazō* limp]

Sc.D. *abbr.* Doctor of Science. [L *scientiae doctor*]

SCE *abbr.* Scottish Certificate of Education.

scena /'ʃeɪnɑː/ *n. Mus.* **1** a scene or part of an opera. **2** an elaborate dramatic solo usu. including recitative. [It. f. L: see SCENE]

scenario /sɪˈnɑːrɪəʊ, -ˈneərɪəʊ/ *n.* (*pl.* **-os**) **1** an outline of the plot of a play, film, opera, etc., with details of the scenes, situations, etc. **2** a postulated sequence of future events. □□ **scenarist** *n.* (in sense 1). [It. (as SCENA)]

scend /send/ *n. & v. Naut.* —*n.* **1** the impulse given by a wave or waves (*scend of the sea*). **2** a plunge of a vessel. —*v.intr.* (of a vessel) plunge or pitch owing to the impulse of a wave. [alt. f. SEND or DESCEND]

scene /siːn/ *n.* **1** a place in which events in real life, drama, or fiction occur; the locality of an event etc. (*the scene was set in India; the scene of the disaster*). **2 a** an incident in real life, fiction, etc. (*distressing scenes occurred*). **b** a description or representation of an incident etc. (*scenes of clerical life*). **3** a public incident displaying emotion, temper, etc., esp. when embarrassing to others (*made a scene in the restaurant*). **4 a** a continuous portion of a play in a fixed setting and usu. without a change of personnel; a subdivision of an act. **b** a similar section of a film, book, etc. **5 a** any of the pieces of scenery used in a play. **b** these collectively. **6 a** a landscape or a view (*a desolate scene*). **7** *colloq.* **a** an area of action or interest (*not my scene*). **b** a way of life; a milieu (*well-known on the jazz scene*). **8** *archaic* the stage of a theatre. □**behind the scenes 1** *Theatr.* among the actors, scenery, etc. offstage. **2** not known to the public; secret. **behind-the-scenes** (*attrib.*) secret, using secret information (*a behind-the-scenes investigation*). **change of scene** a variety of surroundings esp. through travel. **come on the scene** arrive. **quit the scene** die; leave. **scene-dock** a space for storing scenery near the stage. **scene-shifter** a person who moves scenery in a theatre. **scene-shifting** this activity. **set the scene 1** describe the location of events. **2** give preliminary information. [L *scena* f. Gk *skēnē* tent, stage]

scenery /ˈsiːnəri/ n. **1** the general appearance of the natural features of a landscape, esp. when picturesque. **2** *Theatr.* the painted representations of landscape, rooms, etc., used as the background in a play etc. □**change of scenery** = *change of scene* (see SCENE). [earlier *scenary* f. It. SCENARIO: assim. to -ERY]

scenic /ˈsiːnɪk/ adj. **1 a** picturesque; impressive or beautiful (*took the scenic route*). **b** of or concerning natural scenery (*flatness is the main scenic feature*). **2** (of a picture etc.) representing an incident. **3** *Theatr.* of or on the stage (*scenic performances*). □**scenic railway 1** a miniature railway running through artificial scenery at funfairs etc. **2** = *big dipper* 1. □□**scenically** adv. [L *scenicus* f. Gk *skēnikos* of the stage (as SCENE)]

scent /sent/ n. & v. —n. **1** a distinctive, esp. pleasant, smell (*the scent of hay*). **2 a** a scent trail left by an animal perceptible to hounds etc. **b** clues etc. that can be followed like a scent trail (*lost the scent in Paris*). **c** the power of detecting or distinguishing smells etc. or of discovering things (*some dogs have little scent; the scent for talent*). **3** *Brit.* = PERFUME 2. **4** a trail laid in a paper-chase. —v. **1** tr. **a** discern by scent (*the dog scented game*). **b** sense the presence of (*scent treachery*). **2** tr. make fragrant or foul-smelling. **3** tr. (as **scented** adj.) having esp. a pleasant smell (*scented soap*). **4** intr. exercise the sense of smell (*goes scenting about*). **5** tr. apply the sense of smell to (*scented the air*). □**false scent 1** a scent trail laid to deceive. **2** false clues etc. intended to deflect pursuers. **on the scent** having a clue. **put** (or **throw**) **off the scent** deceive by false clues etc. **scent-bag** a bag of aniseed etc. used to lay a trail in drag-hunting. **scent-gland** (or **-organ**) a gland in some animals secreting musk, civet, etc. **scent out** discover by smelling or searching. □□**scentless** adj. [ME *sent* f. OF *sentir* perceive, smell, f. L *sentire*; *-c-* (17th c.) unexpl.]

scepsis /ˈskɛpsɪs/ n. (*US* **skepsis**) **1** philosophic doubt. **2** sceptical philosophy. [Gk *skepsis* inquiry, doubt f. *skeptomai* consider]

scepter *US* var. of SCEPTRE.

sceptic /ˈskɛptɪk/ n. & adj. (*US* **skeptic**) —n. **1** a person inclined to doubt all accepted opinions; a cynic. **2** a person who doubts the truth of Christianity and other religions. **3** *hist.* a person who accepts the philosophy of Pyrrhonism. —adj. = SCEPTICAL. □□**scepticism** /-ˌsɪz(ə)m/ n. [F *sceptique* or L *scepticus* f. Gk *skeptikos* (as SCEPSIS)]

sceptical /ˈskɛptɪk(ə)l/ adj. (*US* **skeptical**) **1** inclined to question the truth or soundness of accepted ideas, facts, etc.; critical; incredulous. **2** *Philos.* of or accepting the philosophy of Pyrrhonism, denying the possibility of knowledge. □□**sceptically** adv.

sceptre /ˈsɛptə(r)/ n. (*US* **scepter**) **1** a staff borne esp. at a coronation as a symbol of sovereignty. **2** royal or imperial authority. □□**sceptred** adj. [ME f.

OF (*s*)*ceptre* f. L *sceptrum* f. Gk *skēptron* f. *skēptō* lean on]

sch. *abbr.* **1** scholar. **2** school. **3** schooner.

schadenfreude /ˈʃɑːdənˌfrɔɪdə/ n. the malicious enjoyment of another's misfortunes. [G f. *Schaden* harm + *Freude* joy]

schappe /ˈʃæpə/ n. fabric or yarn made from waste silk. [G, = waste silk]

schedule /ˈʃɛdjuːl, ˈskɛ-/ n. & v. —n. **1 a** a list or plan of intended events, times, etc. **b** a plan of work (*not on my schedule for next week*). **2** a list of rates or prices. **3** *US* a timetable. **4** a tabulated inventory etc. esp. as an appendix to a document. —v.tr. **1** include in a schedule. **2** make a schedule of. **3** *Brit.* include (a building) in a list for preservation or protection. □**according to schedule** (or **on schedule**) as planned; on time. **behind schedule** behind time. **scheduled flight** (or **service** etc.) a public flight, service, etc., according to a regular timetable. **scheduled territories** *hist.* = *sterling area*. □□ **scheduler** n. [ME f. OF *cedule* f. LL *schedula* slip of paper, dimin. of *scheda* f. Gk *schedē* papyrus-leaf]

scheelite /ˈʃiːlaɪt/ n. *Mineral.* calcium tungstate in its mineral crystalline form. [K. W. *Scheele*, Sw. chemist d. 1786]

schema /ˈskiːmə/ n. (*pl.* **schemata** /-mətə/ or **schemas**) **1** a synopsis, outline, or diagram. **2** a proposed arrangement. **3** *Logic* a syllogistic figure. **4** (in Kantian philosophy) a conception of what is common to all members of a class; a general type or essential form. [Gk *schēma -atos* form, figure]

schematic /skɪˈmætɪk, skiː-/ adj. & n. —adj. **1** of or concerning a scheme or schema. **2** representing objects by symbols etc. —n. a schematic diagram, esp. of an electronic circuit. □□**schematically** adv.

schematism /ˈskiːməˌtɪz(ə)m/ n. a schematic arrangement or presentation. [mod.L *schematismus* f. Gk *schēmatismos* (as SCHEMATIZE)]

schematize /ˈskiːməˌtaɪz/ v.tr. (also **-ise**) **1** put in a schematic form; arrange. **2** represent by a scheme or schema. □□**schematization** /-ˈzeɪʃ(ə)n/ n.

scheme /skiːm/ n. & v. —n. **1 a** a systematic plan or arrangement for work, action, etc. **b** a proposed or operational systematic arrangement (*a colour scheme*). **2** an artful or deceitful plot. **3** a timetable, outline, syllabus, etc. —v. **1** intr. (often foll. by *for*, or *to* + infin.) plan esp. secretly or deceitfully; intrigue. **2** tr. plan to bring about, esp. artfully or deceitfully (*schemed their downfall*). □□**schemer** n. [L *schema* f. Gk (as SCHEMA)]

scheming /ˈskiːmɪŋ/ adj. & n. —adj. artful, cunning, or deceitful. —n. plots; intrigues. □□**schemingly** adv.

schemozzle var. of SHEMOZZLE.

scherzando /skeəˈtsændəʊ/ adv., adj., & n. *Mus.* —adv. & adj. in a playful manner. —n. (*pl.* **scherzandos** or **scherzandi** /-dɪ/) a passage played in this way. [It., gerund of *scherzare* to jest (as SCHERZO)]

scherzo /ˈskeəˌtsəʊ/ n. (*pl.* **-os**) *Mus.* a vigorous, light, or playful composition, usu. as a movement in a symphony, sonata, etc. [It., lit. 'jest']

schilling /ˈʃɪlɪŋ/ n. **1** the chief monetary unit of Austria. **2** a coin equal to the value of one schilling. [G (as SHILLING)]

schipperke /ˈʃɪpəkɪ, ˈʃɪp-/ n. **1** a small black tailless dog of a breed with a ruff of fur round its neck. **2** this breed. [Du. dial., = little boatman, f. its use as a watchdog on barges]

schism /ˈsɪz(ə)m, ˈskɪ-/ n. **1 a** the division of a group into opposing sections or parties. **b** any of the sections so formed. **2 a** the separation of a Church into two Churches or the secession of a group owing to doctrinal, disciplinary, etc., differences. **b** the offence of causing or promoting such a separation. [ME f. OF *s(c)isme* f. eccl.L *schisma* f. Gk *skhisma -atos* cleft f. *skhizō* to split]

schismatic /sɪzˈmætɪk, skɪz-/ adj. & n. (also

schismatical) —*adj.* inclining to, concerning, or guilty of, schism. —*n.* **1** a holder of schismatic opinions. **2** a member of a schismatic faction or a seceded branch of a Church. □□ **schismatically** *adv.* [ME f. OF *scismatique* f. eccl.L *schismaticus* f. eccl.Gk *skhismatikos* (as SCHISM)]

schist /ʃɪst/ *n.* a foliated metamorphic rock composed of layers of different minerals and splitting into thin irregular plates. □□ **schistose** *adj.* [F *schiste* f. L *schistos* f. Gk *skhistos* split (as SCHISM)]

schistosome /ˈʃɪstəˌsəʊm/ *n.* = BILHARZIA 1. [Gk *skhistos* divided (as SCHISM) + *sōma* body]

schistosomiasis /ˌʃɪstəsəˈmaɪəsɪs/ *n.* = BILHARZIASIS. [mod.L *Schistosoma* (the genus-name, as SCHISTOSOME)]

schizanthus /skɪˈzænθəs/ *n.* any plant of the genus *Schizanthus*, with showy flowers in various colours, and finely-divided leaves. [mod.L f. Gk *skhizō* to split + *anthos* flower]

schizo /ˈskɪtsəʊ/ *adj.* & *n.* *colloq.* —*adj.* schizophrenic. —*n.* (*pl.* **-os**) a schizophrenic. [abbr.]

schizocarp /ˈskɪzəˌkɑːp/ *n.* *Bot.* any of a group of dry fruits that split into single-seeded parts when ripe. □□ **schizocarpic** /-ˈkɑːpɪk/ *adj.* **schizocarpous** /-ˈkɑːpəs/ *adj.* [Gk *skhizō* to split + *karpos* fruit]

schizoid /ˈskɪtsɔɪd/ *adj.* & *n.* —*adj.* (of a person or personality etc.) tending to or resembling schizophrenia or a schizophrenic, but usu. without delusions. —*n.* a schizoid person.

schizomycete /ˌskɪtsəˈmaɪsiːt/ *n.* a former name for a bacterium. [Gk *skhizō* to split + *mukēs -ētos* mushroom]

schizophrenia /ˌskɪtsəˈfriːnɪə/ *n.* a mental disease marked by a breakdown in the relation between thoughts, feelings, and actions, frequently accompanied by delusions and retreat from social life. □□ **schizophrenic** /-ˈfrenɪk, -ˈfriːnɪk/ *adj.* & *n.* [mod.L f. Gk *skhizō* to split + *phrēn* mind]

schizothymia /ˌskɪtsəʊˈθaɪmɪə, ˌskɪz-/ *n.* *Psychol.* an introvert condition with a tendency to schizophrenia. □□ **schizothymic** *adj.* [mod.L (as SCHIZOPHRENIA + Gk *thumos* temper)]

schlemiel /ʃləˈmiːl/ *n.* *US colloq.* a foolish or unlucky person. [Yiddish *shlumiel*]

schlep /ʃlep/ *v.* & *n.* (also **schlepp**) *colloq.* —*v.* (**schlepped, schlepping**) **1** *tr.* carry, drag. **2** *intr.* go or work tediously or effortfully. —*n.* esp. *US* trouble or hard work. [Yiddish *shlepn* f. G *schleppen* drag]

schlieren /ˈʃlɪərən/ *n.* **1** a visually discernible area or stratum of different density in a transparent medium. **2** *Geol.* an irregular streak of mineral in igneous rock. [G, pl. of *Schliere* streak]

schlock /ʃlɒk/ *n.* *US colloq.* inferior goods; trash. [Yiddish *shlak* a blow]

schmaltz /ʃmɔːlts, ʃmælts/ *n.* esp. *US colloq.* sentimentality, esp. in music, drama, etc. □□ **schmaltzy** *adj.* (**schmaltzier, schmaltziest**). [Yiddish f. G *Schmalz* dripping, lard]

schmuck /ʃmʌk/ *n.* esp. *US sl.* a foolish or contemptible person. [Yiddish]

schnapps /ʃnæps/ *n.* any of various spirits drunk in N. Europe. [G, = dram of liquor f. LG & Du. *snaps* mouthful (as SNAP)]

schnauzer /ˈʃnaʊtsə(r), ˈʃnaʊzə(r)/ *n.* **1** a dog of a German breed with a close wiry coat and heavy whiskers round the muzzle. **2** this breed. [G f. *Schnauze* muzzle, SNOUT]

schnitzel /ˈʃnɪtz(ə)l/ *n.* an escalope of veal. □ **Wiener** (or **Vienna**) **schnitzel** a breaded, fried, and garnished schnitzel. [G, = slice]

schnorkel var. of SNORKEL.

schnorrer /ˈʃnɔːrə(r)/ *n.* esp. *US sl.* a beggar or scrounger; a layabout. [Yiddish f. G *Schnurrer*]

scholar /ˈskɒlə(r)/ *n.* **1** a learned person, esp. in language, literature, etc.; an academic. **2** the holder of a scholarship. **3 a** a person with specified academic ability (*is a poor scholar*). **b** a person who learns (*am a scholar of life*). **4** *archaic colloq.* a person able to

read and write. **5** *archaic* a schoolboy or schoolgirl. □ **scholar's mate** see MATE². □□ **scholarly** *adv.* **scholarliness** *n.* [ME f. OE *scol(i)ere* & OF *escol(i)er* f. LL *scholaris* f. L *schola* SCHOOL¹]

scholarship /ˈskɒləʃɪp/ *n.* **1 a** academic achievement; learning of a high level. **b** the methods and standards characteristic of a good scholar (*shows great scholarship*). **2** payment from the funds of a school, university, local government, etc., to maintain a student in full-time education, awarded on the basis of scholarly achievement.

scholastic /skəˈlæstɪk/ *adj.* & *n.* —*adj.* **1** of or concerning universities, schools, education, teachers, etc. **2** pedantic; formal (*shows scholastic precision*). **3** *Philos. hist.* of, resembling, or concerning the schoolmen, esp. in dealing with logical subtleties. —*n.* **1** a student. **2** *Philos. hist.* a schoolman. **3** a theologian of scholastic tendencies. **4** *RC Ch.* a member of any of several religious orders, who is between the novitiate and the priesthood. □□ **scholastically** *adv.* **scholasticism** /-ˌsɪz(ə)m/ *n.* [L *scholasticus* f. Gk *skholastikos* studious f. *skholazō* be at leisure, formed as SCHOOL]

scholiast /ˈskəʊlɪˌæst/ *n.* *hist.* an ancient or medieval scholar, esp. a grammarian, who annotated ancient literary texts. □□ **scholiastic** /-ˈæstɪk/ *adj.* [med.Gk *skholiastēs* f. *skholiazō* write scholia: see SCHOLIUM]

scholium /ˈskəʊlɪəm/ *n.* (*pl.* **scholia** /-lɪə/) a marginal note or explanatory comment, esp. by an ancient grammarian on a classical text. [mod.L f. Gk *skholion* f. *skholē* disputation: see SCHOOL]

school¹ /skuːl/ *n.* & *v.* —*n.* **1 a** an institution for educating or giving instruction, esp. *Brit.* for children under 19 years, or *US* for any level of instruction including college or university. **b** (*attrib.*) associated with or for use in school (*a school bag; school dinners*). **2 a** the buildings used by such an institution. **b** the pupils, staff, etc. of a school. **c** the time during which teaching is done, or the teaching itself (*no school today*). **3 a** a branch of study with separate examinations at a university; a department or faculty (*the history school*). **b** *Brit.* the hall in which university examinations are held. **c** (in *pl.*) *Brit.* such examinations. **4 a** the disciples, imitators, or followers of a philosopher, artist, etc. (*the school of Epicurus*). **b** a group of artists etc. whose works share distinctive characteristics. **c** a group of people sharing a cause, principle, method, etc. (*school of thought*). **5** *Brit.* a group of gamblers or of persons drinking together (*a poker school*). **6** *colloq.* instructive or disciplinary circumstances, occupation, etc. (*the school of adversity; learnt in a hard school*). **7** *hist.* a medieval lecture-room. **8** *Mus.* (usu. foll. by *of*) a handbook or book of instruction (*school of counterpoint*). **9** (in *pl.*; prec. by *the*) *hist.* medieval universities, their teachers, disputations, etc. —*v.tr.* **1** send to school; provide for the education of. **2** (often foll. by *to*) discipline; train; control. **3** (as **schooled** *adj.*) (foll. by *in*) educated or trained (*schooled in humility*). □ **at** (*US* **in**) **school** attending lessons etc. **go to school 1** begin one's education. **2** attend lessons. **leave school** finish one's education. **of the old school** according to former and esp. better tradition (*a gentleman of the old school*). **school age** the age-range in which children normally attend school. **school board** *US* or *hist.* a board or authority for local education. **school-days** the time of being at school, esp. in retrospect. **school-inspector** a government official reporting on the efficiency, teaching standards, etc. of schools. **school-leaver** *Brit.* a child leaving school esp. at the minimum specified age. **school-leaving age** the minimum age at which a schoolchild may leave school. **school-ma'm** (or **-marm**) *US colloq.* a schoolmistress. **school-marmish** *colloq.* prim and fussy. **school-ship** a training-ship. **school-time 1** lesson-time at school or at home. **2** school-days. **school year** = academic year. [ME f. OE *scōl, scolu,*

& f. OF *escole* ult. f. L *schola* school f. Gk *skholē* leisure, disputation, philosophy, lecture-place]

school² /skuːl/ *n.* & *v.* —*n.* (often foll. by *of*) a shoal of fish, porpoises, whales, etc. —*v.intr.* form schools. [ME f. MLG, MDu. *schōle* f. WG]

schoolable /'skuːləb(ə)l/ *adj.* liable by age etc. to compulsory education.

schoolboy /'skuːlbɔɪ/ *n.* a boy attending school.

schoolchild /'skuːltʃaɪld/ *n.* a child attending school.

schoolfellow /'skuːlˌfeləʊ/ *n.* a past or esp. present member of the same school.

schoolgirl /'skuːlgɜːl/ *n.* a girl attending school.

schoolhouse /'skuːlhaʊs/ *n. Brit.* **1** a building used as a school, esp. in a village. **2** a dwelling-house adjoining a school.

schoolie /'skuːlɪ/ *n. Austral. sl.* & *dial.* a schoolteacher.

schooling /'skuːlɪŋ/ *n.* **1** education, esp. at school. **2** training or discipline, esp. of an animal.

schoolman /'skuːlmən/ *n. (pl.* -men) **1** *hist.* a teacher in a medieval European university. **2** *RC Ch. hist.* a theologian seeking to deal with religious doctrines by the rules of Aristotelian logic. **3** *US* a male teacher.

schoolmaster /'skuːlˌmɑːstə(r)/ *n.* a head or assistant male teacher. □□ **schoolmasterly** *adj.*

schoolmastering /'skuːlˌmɑːstərɪŋ/ *n.* teaching as a profession.

schoolmate /'skuːlmeɪt/ *n.* = SCHOOLFELLOW.

schoolmistress /'skuːlˌmɪstrɪs/ *n.* a head or assistant female teacher.

schoolmistressy /'skuːlˌmɪstrɪsɪ/ *adj. colloq.* prim and fussy.

schoolroom /'skuːlruːm, -rʊm/ *n.* a room used for lessons in a school or esp. in a private house.

schoolteacher /'skuːlˌtiːtʃə(r)/ *n.* a person who teaches in a school. □□ **schoolteaching** *n.*

schooner /'skuːnə(r)/ *n.* **1** a fore-and-aft rigged ship with two or more masts, the foremast being smaller than the other masts. **2 a** *Brit.* a measure or glass for esp. sherry. **b** *US* & *Austral.* a tall beer-glass. **3** *US hist.* = *prairie schooner.* [18th c.: orig. uncert.]

schorl /ʃɔːl/ *n.* black tourmaline. [G *Schörl*]

schottische /ʃɒ'tiːʃ/ *n.* **1** a kind of slow polka. **2** the music for this. [G *der schottische Tanz* the Scottish dance]

Schottky effect /'ʃɒtkɪ/ *n. Electronics* the increase in thermionic emission from a solid surface due to the presence of an external electric field. [W. *Schottky*, Ger. physicist d. 1976]

Schrödinger equation /'ʃrəʊdɪŋə(r)/ *n. Physics* a differential equation used in quantum mechanics for the wave function of a particle. [E. *Schrödinger*, Austrian physicist d. 1961]

schuss /ʃʊs/ *n.* & *v.* —*n.* a straight downhill run on skis. —*v.intr.* make a schuss. [G, lit. 'shot']

schwa /ʃwɑː, ʃvɑː/ *n.* (also **sheva** /ʃə'vɑː/) *Phonet.* **1** the indistinct unstressed vowel sound as in *a* moment ago. **2** the symbol /ə/ representing this in the International Phonetic Alphabet. [G f. Heb. *šᵉwā*, app. f. *šaw'* emptiness]

sciagraphy /skaɪ'ægrəfɪ/ *n.* (also **skiagraphy**) the art of shading in drawing etc. □□ **sciagram** /'skaɪəˌgræm/ *n.* **sciagraph** /'skaɪəˌgrɑːf/ *n.* & *v.tr.* **sciagraphic** /ˌskaɪə'græfɪk/ *adj.* [F *sciagraphie* f. L *sciagraphia* f. Gk *skiagraphia* f. *skia* shadow]

sciamachy /saɪ'æməkɪ/ *n.* (also **skiamachy** /skaɪ-/) *formal* **1** fighting with shadows. **2** imaginary or futile combat. [Gk *skiamakhia* (as SCIAGRAPHY, *-makhia* -fighting)]

sciatic /saɪ'ætɪk/ *adj.* **1** of the hip. **2** of or affecting the sciatic nerve. **3** suffering from or liable to sciatica. □ **sciatic nerve** the largest nerve in the human body, running from the pelvis to the thigh. □□ **sciatically** *adv.* [F *sciatique* f. LL *sciaticus* f. L *ischiadicus* f. Gk *iskhiadikos* subject to sciatica f. *iskhion* hip-joint]

sciatica /saɪ'ætɪkə/ *n.* neuralgia of the hip and thigh;

a pain in the sciatic nerve. [ME f. LL *sciatica (passio)* fem. of *sciaticus*: see SCIATIC]

science /'saɪəns/ *n.* **1** a branch of knowledge conducted on objective principles involving the systematized observation of and experiment with phenomena, esp. concerned with the material and functions of the physical universe (see also *natural science*). **2 a** systematic and formulated knowledge, esp. of a specified type or on a specified subject (*political science*). **b** the pursuit or principles of this. **3** an organized body of knowledge on a subject (*the science of philology*). **4** skilful technique rather than strength or natural ability. **5** *archaic* knowledge of any kind. □ **science fiction** fiction based on imagined future scientific discoveries or environmental changes, frequently dealing with space travel, life on other planets, etc. **science park** an area devoted to scientific research or the development of science-based industries. [ME f. OF f. L *scientia* f. *scire* know]

scienter /saɪ'entə(r)/ *adv. Law* intentionally; knowingly. [L f. *scire* know]

sciential /saɪ'enʃ(ə)l/ *adj.* concerning or having knowledge. [LL *scientialis* (as SCIENCE)]

scientific /ˌsaɪən'tɪfɪk/ *adj.* **1 a** (of an investigation etc.) according to rules laid down in exact science for performing observations and testing the soundness of conclusions. **b** systematic, accurate. **2** used in, engaged in, or relating to (esp. natural) science (*scientific discoveries*; *scientific terminology*). **3** assisted by expert knowledge. □□ **scientifically** *adv.* [F *scientifique* or LL *scientificus* (as SCIENCE)]

scientism /'saɪənˌtɪz(ə)m/ *n.* **1 a** a method or doctrine regarded as characteristic of scientists. **b** the use or practice of this. **2** often *derog.* an excessive belief in or application of scientific method. □□ **scientistic** /-'tɪstɪk/ *adj.*

scientist /'saɪəntɪst/ *n.* **1** a person with expert knowledge of a (usu. physical or natural) science. **2** a person using scientific methods.

scientology /ˌsaɪən'tɒlədʒɪ/ *n.* a religious system based on self-improvement and promotion through grades of esp. self-knowledge. □□ **scientologist** *n.* [L *scientia* knowledge + -LOGY]

sci-fi /'saɪfaɪ, saɪ'faɪ/ *n.* (often *attrib.*) *colloq.* science fiction. [abbr.: cf. HI-FI]

scilicet /'saɪlɪˌset, 'skiːlɪˌket/ *adv.* to wit; that is to say; namely (introducing a word to be supplied or an explanation of an ambiguity). [ME f. L, = *scire licet* one is permitted to know]

scilla /'sɪlə/ *n.* any liliaceous plant of the genus *Scilla*, related to the bluebell, usu. bearing small blue star-shaped or bell-shaped flowers and having long glossy straplike leaves. [L f. Gk *skilla*]

Scillonian /sɪ'ləʊnɪən/ *adj.* & *n.* —*adj.* of or relating to the Scilly Isles off the coast of Cornwall. —*n.* a native of the Scilly Isles. [*Scilly*, perh. after *Devonian*]

scimitar /'sɪmɪtə(r)/ *n.* an oriental curved sword usu. broadening towards the point. [F *cimeterre*, It. *scimitarra*, etc., of unkn. orig.]

scintigram /'sɪntɪˌgræm/ *n.* an image of an internal part of the body, produced by scintigraphy.

scintigraphy /sɪn'tɪgrəfɪ/ *n.* the use of a radioisotope and a scintillation counter to get an image or record of a bodily organ etc. [SCINTILLATION + -GRAPHY]

scintilla /sɪn'tɪlə/ *n.* **1** a trace. **2** a spark. [L]

scintillate /'sɪntɪˌleɪt/ *v.intr.* **1** (esp. as **scintillating** *adj.*) talk cleverly or wittily; be brilliant. **2** sparkle; twinkle; emit sparks. **3** *Physics* fluoresce momentarily when struck by a charged particle etc. □□ **scintillant** *adj.* **scintillatingly** *adv.* [L *scintillare* (as SCINTILLA)]

scintillation /ˌsɪntɪ'leɪʃ(ə)n/ *n.* **1** the process or state of scintillating. **2** the twinkling of a star. **3** a flash produced in a material by an ionizing particle etc. □ **scintillation counter** a device for detecting and recording scintillation.

scintiscan /'sɪntɪˌskæn/ *n.* an image or other record showing the distribution of radioactive traces in parts of the body, used in the detection and diagnosis of various diseases. [SCINTILLATION + SCAN]

sciolist /'saɪəlɪst/ n. a superficial pretender to knowledge. □□ **sciolism** /-'lɪz(ə)m/ n. **sciolistic** /-'lɪstɪk/ adj. [LL sciolus smatterer f. L scire know]

scion /'saɪən/ n. 1 (US cion) a shoot of a plant etc., esp. one cut for grafting or planting. 2 a descendant; a younger member of (esp. a noble) family. [ME f. OF ciun, cion, sion shoot, twig, of unkn. orig.]

scire facias /ˌsaɪərɪ 'feɪʃɪˌæs/ n. Law a writ to enforce or annul a judgement, patent, etc. [L, = let (him) know]

scirocco var. of SIROCCO.

scirrhus /'sɪrəs, 'skɪ-/ n. (pl. **scirrhi** /-raɪ/) a carcinoma which is hard to the touch. □□ **scirrhoid** adj. **scirrhosity** /sɪ'rɒsɪtɪ/ n. **scirrhous** adj. [mod.L f. Gk skir(r)os f. skiros hard]

scissel /'skɪs(ə)l/ n. waste clippings etc. of metal produced during coin manufacture. [F cisaille f. cisailler clip with shears]

scissile /'sɪsaɪl/ adj. able to be cut or divided. [L scissilis f. scindere sciss- cut]

scission /'sɪʃ(ə)n/ n. 1 the act or an instance of cutting; the state of being cut. 2 a division or split. [ME f. OF scission or LL scissio (as SCISSILE)]

scissor /'sɪzə(r)/ v.tr. 1 (usu. foll. by off, up, into, etc.) cut with scissors. 2 (usu. foll. by out) clip out (a newspaper article etc.)

scissors /'sɪzəz/ n.pl. 1 (also **pair of scissors** sing.) an instrument for cutting fabric, paper, hair, etc., having two pivoted blades with finger and thumb holes in the handles, operating by closing on the material to be cut. 2 (treated as sing.) **a** a method of high-jumping with a forward and backward movement of the legs. **b** a hold in wrestling in which the opponent's body or esp. head is gripped between the legs. □ **scissor-bill** = SKIMMER 4. **scissor-bird** (or **-tail**) a fork-tailed flycatcher, Tyrannus forficatus. **scissors and paste** a method of compiling a book, article, etc., from extracts from others or without independent research. □□ **scissorwise** adv. [ME sisoures f. OF cisoires f. LL cisoria pl. of cisorium cutting instrument (as CHISEL): assoc. with L scindere sciss-cut]

sciurine /'saɪjʊˌraɪn/ adj. 1 of or relating to the family Sciuridae, including squirrels and chipmunks. 2 squirrel-like. □□ **sciuroid** adj. [L sciurus f. Gk skiouros squirrel f. skia shadow + oura tail]

sclera /'sklɪərə/ n. the white of the eye; a white membrane coating the eyeball. □□ **scleral** adj. **scleritis** /sklɪə'raɪtɪs/ n. **sclerotomy** /-'rɒtəmɪ/ n. (pl. **-ies**). [mod.L f. fem. of Gk sklēros hard]

sclerenchyma /sklɪə'reŋkɪmə/ n. the woody tissue found in a plant, formed from lignified cells and usu. providing support. [mod.L f. Gk sklēros hard + egkhuma infusion, after parenchyma]

scleroid /'sklɪəˌrɔɪd/ adj. Bot. & Zool. having a hard texture; hardened. [Gk sklēros hard]

scleroma /sklɪə'rəʊmə/ n. (pl. **scleromata** /-mətə/) an abnormal patch of hardened skin or mucous membrane. [mod.L f. Gk sklērōma (as SCLEROSIS)]

sclerometer /sklɪə'rɒmɪtə(r)/ n. an instrument for determining the hardness of materials. [Gk sklēros hard + -METER]

sclerophyll /'sklɪərəfɪl/ n. any woody plant with leathery leaves retaining water. □□ **sclerophyllous** /-'rɒfɪləs/ adj. [Gk sklēros hard + phullon leaf]

scleroprotein /ˌsklɪərəʊ'prəʊtiːn/ n. Biochem. any insoluble structural protein. [Gk sklēros hard + PROTEIN]

sclerosed /'sklɪəˌrəʊst, -ˌrəʊzd/ adj. affected by sclerosis.

sclerosis /sklɪə'rəʊsɪs/ n. 1 an abnormal hardening of body tissue (see also ARTERIOSCLEROSIS, ATHEROSCLEROSIS). 2 (in full **multiple** or **disseminated sclerosis**) a chronic and progressive disease of the nervous system resulting in symptoms including paralysis and speech defects. 3 Bot. the hardening of

a cell-wall with lignified matter. [ME f. med.L f. Gk sklērōsis f. sklēroō harden]

sclerotic /sklɪə'rɒtɪk/ adj. & n. —adj. 1 of or having sclerosis. 2 of or relating to the sclera. —n. = SCLERA. □□ **sclerotitis** /-rə'taɪtɪs/ n. [med.L sclerotica (as SCLEROSIS)]

sclerous /'sklɪərəs/ adj. Physiol. hardened; bony. [Gk sklēros hard]

SCM abbr. (in the UK) 1 State Certified Midwife. 2 Student Christian Movement.

scoff¹ /skɒf/ v. & n. —v.intr. (usu. foll. by at) speak derisively, esp. of serious subjects; mock; be scornful. —n. 1 mocking words; a taunt. 2 an object of ridicule. □□ **scoffer** n. **scoffingly** adv. [perh. f. Scand.: cf. early mod. Da. skuf, skof jest, mockery]

scoff² /skɒf/ v. & n. colloq. —v.tr. & intr. eat greedily. —n. food; a meal. [(n.) f. Afrik. schoff repr. Du. schoft quarter of a day (hence, meal): (v.) orig. var. of dial. scaff, assoc. with the noun]

scold /skəʊld/ v. & n. —v. 1 tr. rebuke (esp. a child, employee, or inferior). 2 intr. find fault noisily; complain; rail. —n. archaic a nagging or grumbling woman. □□ **scolder** n. **scolding** n. [ME (earlier as noun), prob. f. ON skáld SKALD]

scolex /'skəʊleks/ n. (pl. **scoleces** /-'liːsiːz/ or **scolices** /-lɪˌsiːz/) the head of a larval or adult tapeworm. [mod.L f. Gk skōlēx worm]

scoliosis /ˌskɒlɪ'əʊsɪs/ n. an abnormal lateral curvature of the spine. □□ **scoliotic** /-'ɒtɪk/ adj. [mod.L f. Gk f. skolios bent]

scollop var. of SCALLOP.

scolopendrium /ˌskɒlə'pendrɪəm/ n. any of various ferns, esp. hart's tongue. [mod.L f. Gk skolopendrion f. skolopendra millipede (because of the supposed resemblance)]

scomber /'skɒmbə(r)/ n. any marine fish of the family Scombridae, including mackerels, tunas, and bonitos. □□ **scombrid** n. **scombroid** adj. & n. [L f. Gk skombros]

sconce¹ /skɒns/ n. 1 a flat candlestick with a handle. 2 a bracket candlestick to hang on a wall. [ME f. OF esconse lantern or med.L sconsa f. L absconsa fem. past part. of abscondere hide: see ABSCOND]

sconce² /skɒns/ n. 1 a small fort or earthwork usu. defending a ford, pass, etc. 2 archaic a shelter or screen. [Du. schans brushwood f. MHG schanze]

scone /skɒn, skəʊn/ n. a small sweet or savoury cake of flour, fat, and milk, baked quickly in an oven. [orig. Sc., perh. f. MDu. schoon(broot), MLG schon(brot) fine (bread)]

scoop /skuːp/ n. & v. —n. 1 any of various objects resembling a spoon, esp.: **a** a short-handled deep shovel used for transferring grain, sugar, coal, coins, etc. **b** a large long-handled ladle used for transferring liquids. **c** the excavating part of a digging-machine etc. **d** Med. a long-handled spoonlike instrument used for scraping parts of the body etc. **e** an instrument used for serving portions of mashed potato, ice-cream, etc. 2 a quantity taken up by a scoop. 3 a movement of or resembling scooping. 4 a piece of news published by a newspaper etc. in advance of its rivals. 5 a large profit made quickly or by anticipating one's competitors. 6 Mus. a singer's exaggerated portamento. 7 a scooped-out hollow etc. —v.tr. 1 (usu. foll. by out) hollow out with or as if with a scoop. 2 (usu. foll. by up) lift with or as if with a scoop. 3 forestall (a rival newspaper, reporter, etc.) with a scoop. 4 secure (a large profit etc.) esp. suddenly. □ **scoop-neck** the rounded low-cut neck of a garment. **scoop-net** a net used for sweeping a river bottom, or for catching bait. □□ **scooper** n. **scoopful** n. (pl. **-fuls**). [ME f. MDu., MLG schōpe bucket etc., rel. to SHAPE]

scoot /skuːt/ v. & n. colloq. —v.intr. run or dart away, esp. quickly. —n. the act or an instance of scooting. [19th-c. US (earlier scout): orig. unkn.]

scooter /'skuːtə(r)/ n. & v. —n. 1 a child's toy consisting of a footboard mounted on two wheels and a long steering-handle, propelled by resting one foot on the footboard and pushing the other against the ground. **2** (in full **motor scooter**) a light two-wheeled open motor vehicle with a shieldlike protective front. **3** *US* a sailboat able to travel on both water and ice. —*v.intr.* travel or ride on a scooter. □□ **scooterist** *n.*

scopa /'skəʊpə/ *n.* (*pl.* **scopae** /-piː/) a small brushlike tuft of hairs, esp. on the leg of a bee for collecting pollen. [sing. of L *scopae* = twigs, broom]

scope[1] /skəʊp/ *n.* **1 a** the extent to which it is possible to range; the opportunity for action etc. (*this is beyond the scope of our research*). **b** the sweep or reach of mental activity, observation, or outlook (*an intellect limited in its scope*). **2** *Naut.* the length of cable extended when a ship rides at anchor. **3** *archaic* a purpose, end, or intention. [It. *scopo* aim f. Gk *skopos* target f. *skeptomai* look at]

scope[2] /skəʊp/ *n. colloq.* a telescope, microscope, or other device ending in -*scope*. [abbr.]

-scope /skəʊp/ *comb. form* forming nouns denoting: **1** a device looked at or through (*kaleidoscope; telescope*). **2** an instrument for observing or showing (*gyroscope; oscilloscope*). □□ **-scopic** /'skɒpɪk/ *comb. form* forming adjectives. [from or after mod.L -*scopium* f. Gk *skopeō* look at]

scopolamine /skə'pɒləmɪn, -ˌmiːn/ *n.* = HYOSCINE. [*Scopolia* genus-name of the plants yielding it, f. G. A. *Scopoli*, It. naturalist d. 1788 + AMINE]

scopula /'skɒpjʊlə/ *n.* (*pl.* **scopulae** /-ˌliː/) any of various small brushlike structures, esp. on the legs of spiders. [LL, dimin. of L *scopa*: see SCOPA]

-scopy /skəpɪ/ *comb. form* indicating viewing or observation, usu. with an instrument ending in -*scope* (*microscopy*).

scorbutic /skɔː'bjuːtɪk/ *adj. & n.* —*adj.* relating to, resembling, or affected with scurvy. —*n.* a person affected with scurvy. □□ **scorbutically** *adv.* [mod.L *scorbuticus* f. med.L *scorbutus* scurvy, perh. f. MLG *schorbūk* f. *schoren* break + *būk* belly]

scorch /skɔːtʃ/ *v. & n.* —*v.* **1** *tr.* **a** burn the surface of with flame or heat so as to discolour, parch, injure, or hurt. **b** affect with the sensation of burning. **2** *intr.* become discoloured etc. with heat. **3** *tr.* (as **scorching** *adj.*) *colloq.* **a** (of the weather) very hot. **b** (of criticism etc.) stringent; harsh. **4** *intr. colloq.* (of a motorist etc.) go at excessive speed. —*n.* **1** a mark made by scorching. **2** *colloq.* a spell of fast driving etc. □ **scorched earth policy** the burning of crops etc. and the removing or destroying of anything that might be of use to an enemy force occupying a country. □□ **scorchingly** *adv.* [ME, perh. rel. to *skorkle* in the same sense]

scorcher /'skɔːtʃə(r)/ *n.* **1** a person or thing that scorches. **2** *colloq.* **a** a very hot day. **b** a fine specimen.

score /skɔː(r)/ *n. & v.* —*n.* **1 a** the number of points, goals, runs, etc., made by a player, side, etc., in some games. **b** the total number of points etc. at the end of a game (*the score was five-nil*). **c** the act of gaining esp. a goal (*a superb score there!*). **2** (*pl.* same or **scores**) twenty or a set of twenty. **3** (in *pl.*) a great many (*scores of people arrived*). **4 a** a reason or motive (*rejected on the score of absurdity*). **b** topic; subject (*no worries on that score*). **5** *Mus.* **a** a usu. printed copy of a composition showing all the vocal and instrumental parts arranged one below the other. **b** the music composed for a film or play, esp. for a musical. **6** *colloq.* **a** a piece of good fortune. **b** the act or an instance of scoring off another person. **7** *colloq.* the state of affairs; the present situation (*asked what the score was*). **8** a notch, line, etc. cut or scratched into a surface. **9 a** an amount due for payment. **b** a running account kept by marks against a customer's name. **10** *Naut.* a groove in a block or dead-eye to hold a rope. —*v.* **1** *tr.* **a** win or gain (a goal, run, points, etc., or success etc.) (*scored a century*). **b** count for a score of (points in a game etc.) (*a bull's-eye scores most points*). **c** allot a score

to (a competitor etc.). **d** make a record of (a point etc.). **2** *intr.* **a** make a score in a game (*failed to score*). **b** keep the tally of points, runs, etc. in a game. **3** *tr.* mark with notches, incisions, lines, etc.; slash; furrow (*scored his name on the desk*). **4** *intr.* secure an advantage by luck, cunning, etc. (*that is where he scores*). **5** *tr. Mus.* **a** orchestrate (a piece of music). **b** (usu. foll. by *for*) arrange for an instrument or instruments. **c** write the music for (a film, musical, etc.). **d** write out in a score. **6** *tr.* (usu. foll. by *up*) mark (a total owed etc.) in a score (see sense 9b of *n.*). **b** (usu. foll. by *against, to*) enter (an item of debt to a customer). **7** *intr. sl.* **a** obtain drugs illegally. **b** (of a man) make a sexual conquest. **8** *tr.* (usu. foll. by *against, to*) mentally record (an offence etc.). **9** *tr. US* criticize (a person) severely. □ **keep score** (or **the score**) register the score as it is made. **know the score** *colloq.* be aware of the essential facts. **on the score of** for the reason that; because of. **on that score** so far as that is concerned. **score-book** (or **-card** or **-sheet**) a book etc. prepared for entering esp. cricket scores in. **score draw** a draw in football in which goals are scored. **score off** (or **score points off**) *colloq.* humiliate, esp. verbally in repartee etc. **score out** draw a line through (words etc.). **score under** underline. □□ **scorer** *n.* **scoring** *n. Mus.* [(n.) f. OE: sense 5 f. the line or bar drawn through all staves: (v.) partly f. ON *skora* f. ON *skor* notch, tally, twenty, f. Gmc: see SHEAR]

scoreboard /'skɔːbɔːd/ *n.* a large board for publicly displaying the score in a game or match.

scoria /'skɔːrɪə/ *n.* (*pl.* **scoriae** /-rɪˌiː/) **1** cellular lava, or fragments of it. **2** the slag or dross of metals. □□ **scoriaceous** /-'eɪʃəs/ *adj.* [L f. Gk *skōria* refuse f. *skōr* dung]

scorify /'skɔːrɪˌfaɪ/ *v.tr.* (-**ies**, -**ied**) **1** reduce to dross. **2** assay (precious metal) by treating a portion of its ore fused with lead and borax. □□ **scorification** /-fɪ'keɪʃ(ə)n/ *n.* **scorifier** *n.*

scorn /skɔːn/ *n. & v.* —*n.* **1** disdain, contempt, derision. **2** an object of contempt etc. (*the scorn of all onlookers*). —*v.tr.* **1** hold in contempt or disdain. **2** (often foll. by *to* + infin.) abstain from or refuse to do as unworthy (*scorns lying; scorns to lie*). □ **think scorn of** despise. □□ **scorner** *n.* [ME f. OF *es-c(h)arn(ir)* ult. f. Gmc: cf. OS *skern* MOCKERY]

scornful /'skɔːnfʊl/ *adj.* (often foll. by *of*) full of scorn; contemptuous. □□ **scornfully** *adv.* **scornfulness** *n.*

scorper var. of SCALPER 2.

Scorpio /'skɔːpɪəʊ/ *n.* (*pl.* -**os**) **1** a constellation, traditionally regarded as contained in the figure of a scorpion. **2 a** the eighth sign of the zodiac (the Scorpion). **b** a person born when the sun is in this sign. □□ **Scorpian** *adj. & n.* [ME f. L (as SCORPION)]

scorpioid /'skɔːpɪˌɔɪd/ *adj. & n.* —*adj.* **1** *Zool.* of, relating to, or resembling a scorpion; of the scorpion order. **2** *Bot.* (of an inflorescence) curled up at the end, and uncurling as the flowers develop. —*n.* this type of inflorescence. [Gk *skorpioeidēs* (as SCORPIO)]

scorpion /'skɔːpɪən/ *n.* **1** an arachnid of the order Scorpionida, with lobster-like pincers and a jointed tail that can be bent over to inflict a poisoned sting on prey held in its pincers. **2** (in full **false scorpion**) a similar arachnid of the order Pseudoscorpionida, smaller and without a tail. **3** (**the Scorpion**) the zodiacal sign or constellation Scorpio. **4** *Bibl.* a whip with metal points (1 Kings 12:11). □ **scorpion fish** any of various marine fish of the family Scorpaenidae, with venomous spines on the head and gills. **scorpion fly** any insect of the order Mecoptera, esp. of the family Panorpidae, the males of which have a swollen abdomen curved upwards like a scorpion's sting. **scorpion grass** = *forget-me-not*. [ME f. OF f. L *scorpio -onis* f. *scorpius* f. Gk *skorpios*]

scorzonera /ˌskɔːzə'nɪərə/ *n.* **1** a composite plant, *Scorzonera hispanica*, with long tapering purple-brown roots. **2** the root used as a vegetable. [It. f. *scorzone* venomous snake ult f. med.L *curtio*]

Scot /skɒt/ *n.* **1 a** a native of Scotland. **b** a person of Scottish descent. **2** *hist.* a member of a Gaelic people that migrated from Ireland to Scotland around the 6th c. [OE *Scottas* (pl.) f. LL *Scottus*]

scot /skɒt/ *n. hist.* a payment corresponding to a modern tax, rate, etc. □**pay scot and lot** share the financial burdens of a borough etc. (and so be allowed to vote). **scot-free** unharmed; unpunished; safe. [ME f. ON *skot* & f. OF *escot*, of Gmc orig.: cf. SHOT¹]

Scotch /skɒtʃ/ *adj.* & *n.* —*adj.* var. of SCOTTISH or SCOTS. —*n.* **1** var. of SCOTTISH or SCOTS. **2** Scotch whisky. □**Scotch broth** a soup made from beef or mutton with pearl barley etc. **Scotch cap** = BONNET *n.* 1b. **Scotch catch** *Mus.* a short note on the beat followed by a long one. **Scotch egg** a hard-boiled egg enclosed in sausage meat and fried. **Scotch fir** (or **pine**) a pine tree, *Pinus sylvestris*, native to Europe and Asia. **Scotch kale** a variety of kale with purplish leaves. **Scotch mist 1** a thick drizzly mist common in the Highlands. **2** a retort made to a person implying that he or she has imagined or failed to understand something. **Scotch pebble** agate, jasper, cairngorm, etc., found in Scotland. **Scotch pine** = *Scotch fir.* **Scotch snap** = *Scotch catch.* **Scotch terrier 1** a small terrier of a rough-haired short-legged breed. **2** this breed. **Scotch whisky** whisky distilled in Scotland, esp. from malted barley. ¶ *Scots* or *Scottish* is generally preferred in Scotland, except in the special compounds given above. [contr. of SCOTTISH]

scotch¹ /skɒtʃ/ *v.* & *n.* —*v.tr.* **1** put an end to; frustrate (*injury scotched his attempt*). **2** *archaic* a wound without killing; slightly disable. **b** make incisions in; score. —*n.* **1** *archaic* a slash. **2** a line on the ground for hopscotch. [ME: orig. unkn.]

scotch² /skɒtʃ/ *n.* & *v.* —*n.* a wedge or block placed against a wheel etc. to prevent its slipping. —*v.tr.* hold back (a wheel, barrel, etc.) with a scotch. [17th c.: perh. = *scatch* stilt f. OF *escache*]

Scotchman /'skɒtʃmən/ *n.* (*pl.* **-men**) *fem.* **Scotchwoman**, *pl.* **-women**) = SCOTSMAN. ¶ *Scotsman* etc. are generally preferred in Scotland.

scoter /'skəʊtə(r)/ *n.* (*pl.* same or **scoters**) a large marine duck of the genus *Melanitta*. [17th c.: orig. unkn.]

scotia /'skəʊʃə/ *n.* a concave moulding, esp. at the base of a column. [L f. Gk *skotia* f. *skotos* darkness, with ref. to the shadow produced]

Scoticism var. of SCOTTICISM.

Scoticize var. of SCOTTICIZE.

Scotland Yard /ˌskɒtlənd 'jɑːd/ *n.* **1** the headquarters of the London Metropolitan Police. **2** its Criminal Investigation Department. [*Great and New Scotland Yard*, streets where it was successively situated until 1967]

scotoma /skɒ'təʊmə/ *n.* (*pl.* **scotomata** /-mətə/) a partial loss of vision or blind spot in an otherwise normal visual field. [LL f. Gk *skotōma* f. *skotoō* darken f. *skotos* darkness]

Scots /skɒts/ *adj.* & *n.* esp. *Sc.* —*adj.* **1** = SCOTTISH *adj.* **2** in the dialect, accent, etc., of (esp. Lowlands) Scotland. —*n.* **1** = SCOTTISH *n.* **2** the form of English spoken in (esp. Lowlands) Scotland. [ME orig. *Scottis*, north. var. of SCOTTISH]

Scotsman /'skɒtsmən/ *n.* (*pl.* **-men**) *fem.* **Scotswoman**, *pl.* **-women**) **1** a native of Scotland. **2** a person of Scottish descent.

Scotticism /'skɒtɪˌsɪz(ə)m/ *n.* (also **Scoticism**) a Scottish phrase, word, or idiom. [LL *Scot(t)icus*]

Scotticize /'skɒtɪˌsaɪz/ *v.* (also **Scoticize, -ise**) **1** *tr.* imbue with or model on Scottish ways etc. **2** *intr.* imitate the Scottish in idiom or habits.

Scottie /'skɒtɪ/ *n. colloq.* **1** (also **Scottie dog**) a Scotch terrier. **2** a Scot.

Scottish /'skɒtɪʃ/ *adj.* & *n.* —*adj.* of or relating to Scotland or its inhabitants. —*n.* (prec. by *the*; treated as *pl.*) the people of Scotland (see also SCOTS). □□ **Scottishness** *n.*

scoundrel /'skaʊndr(ə)l/ *n.* an unscrupulous villain; a rogue. □□ **scoundreldom** *n.* **scoundrelism** *n.* **scoundrelly** *adj.* [16th c.: orig. unkn.]

scour¹ /'skaʊə(r)/ *v.* & *n.* —*v.tr.* **1 a** cleanse or brighten by rubbing, esp. with soap, chemicals, sand, etc. **b** (usu. foll. by *away, off*, etc.) clear (rust, stains, reputation, etc.) by rubbing, hard work, etc. (*scoured the slur from his name*). **2** (of water, or a person with water) clear out (a pipe, channel, etc.) by flushing through. **3** *hist.* purge (the bowels) drastically. —*n.* **1** the act or an instance of scouring; the state of being scoured, esp. by a swift water current (*the scour of the tide*). **2** diarrhoea in cattle. **3** a substance used for scouring. □**scouring-rush** any of various horsetail plants with a rough siliceous coating used for polishing wood etc. □□ **scourer** *n.* [ME f. MDu., MLG *schūren* f. F *escurer* f. LL *excurare* clean (off) (as EX-¹, CURE)]

scour² /'skaʊə(r)/ *v.* **1** *tr.* hasten over (an area etc.) searching thoroughly (*scoured the streets for him; scoured the pages of the newspaper*). **2** *intr.* range hastily esp. in search or pursuit. [ME: orig. unkn.]

scourge /skɜːdʒ/ *n.* & *v.* —*n.* **1** a whip used for punishment, esp. of people. **2** a person or thing seen as punishing, esp. on a large scale (*the scourge of famine; Genghis Khan, the scourge of Asia*). —*v.tr.* **1** whip. **2** punish; afflict; oppress. □□ **scourger** *n.* [ME f. OF *escorge* (n.), *escorgier* (v.) (ult. as EX-¹,· L *corrigia* thong, whip)]

Scouse /skaʊs/ *n.* & *adj. colloq.* —*n.* **1** the dialect of Liverpool. **2** (also **Scouser** /'skaʊsə(r)/) a native of Liverpool. **3** (**scouse**) = LOBSCOUSE. —*adj.* of or relating to Liverpool. [abbr. of LOBSCOUSE]

scout¹ /skaʊt/ *n.* & *v.* —*n.* **1** a person, esp. a soldier, sent out to get information about the enemy's position, strength, etc. **2** the act of seeking (esp. military) information (*on the scout*). **3** = talent-scout. **4** (**Scout**) a member of the Scout Association, a boys' association intended to develop character esp. by open-air activities. **5** a college servant, esp. at Oxford University. **6** *colloq.* a person; a fellow. **7** a ship or aircraft designed for reconnoitring, esp. a small fast aircraft. —*v.* **1** *intr.* act as a scout. **2** *intr.* (foll. by *about, around*) make a search. **3** *tr.* (often foll. by *out*) *colloq.* explore to get information about (territory etc.). □**Queen's** (or **King's**) **Scout** a Scout who has reached the highest standard of proficiency. □□ **scouter** *n.* **scouting** *n.* [ME f. OF *escouter* listen, earlier *ascolter* ult. f. L *auscultare*]

scout² /skaʊt/ *v.tr.* reject (an idea etc.) with scorn. [Scand.: cf. ON *skúta, skúti* taunt]

Scouter /'skaʊtə(r)/ *n.* an adult member of the Scout Association.

Scoutmaster /'skaʊtˌmɑːstə(r)/ *n.* a person in charge of a group of Scouts.

scow /skaʊ/ *n.* esp. *US* a flat-bottomed boat used as a lighter etc. [Du. *schouw* ferry-boat]

scowl /skaʊl/ *n.* & *v.* —*n.* a severe frown producing a sullen, bad-tempered, or threatening look on a person's face. —*v.intr.* make a scowl. □□ **scowler** *n.* [ME, prob. f. Scand.: cf. Da. *skule* look down or sidelong]

SCPS *abbr.* (in the UK) Society of Civil and Public Servants.

SCR *abbr. Brit.* Senior Common (or Combination) Room.

scr. *abbr.* scruple(s) (of weight).

scrabble /'skræb(ə)l/ *v.* & *n.* —*v.intr.* (often foll. by *about, at*) scratch or grope to find or collect or hold on to something. —*n.* **1** an act of scrabbling. **2** (**Scrabble**) *propr.* a game in which players build up words from letter-blocks on a board. [MDu. *schrabbelen* frequent. of *schrabben* SCRAPE]

scrag /skræg/ *n.* & *v.* —*n.* **1** (also **scrag-end**) the inferior end of a neck of mutton. **2** a skinny person or animal. **3** *colloq.* a person's neck. —*v.tr.* (**scragged, scragging**) *sl.* **1** strangle, hang. **2** seize roughly by the neck. **3** handle roughly; beat up. [perh. alt. f. dial. *crag* neck, rel. to MDu. *crāghe*, MLG *krage*]

scraggly /'skræglɪ/ *adj.* sparse and irregular.

scraggy /'skrægɪ/ *adj.* (**scraggier, scraggiest**) thin and bony. □□ **scraggily** *adv.* **scragginess** *n.*

scram /skræm/ *v.intr.* (**scrammed, scramming**) (esp. in *imper.*) *colloq.* go away. [20th c.: perh. f. SCRAMBLE]

scramble /'skræmb(ə)l/ *v. & n.* —*v.* **1** *intr.* make one's way over rough ground, rocks, etc., by clambering, crawling, etc. **2** *intr.* (foll. by *for, at*) struggle with competitors (for a thing or share of it). **3** *intr.* move with difficulty, hastily, or anxiously. **4** *tr.* a mix together indiscriminately. **b** jumble or muddle. **5** *tr.* cook (eggs) by heating them when broken and well mixed with butter, milk, etc. **6** *tr.* change the speech frequency of (a broadcast transmission or telephone conversation) so as to make it unintelligible without a corresponding decoding device. **7** *intr.* move hastily. **8** *tr. colloq.* execute (an action etc.) awkwardly and inefficiently. **9** *intr.* (of fighter aircraft or their pilots) take off quickly in an emergency or for action. —*n.* **1** an act of scrambling. **2** a difficult climb or walk. **3** (foll. by *for*) an eager struggle or competition. **4** *Brit.* a motor-cycle race over rough ground. **5** an emergency take-off by fighter aircraft. □**scrambled egg** *colloq.* gold braid on a military officer's cap. [16th c. (imit.): cf. dial. synonyms *scamble, cramble*]

scrambler /'skræmblə(r)/ *n.* a device for scrambling telephone conversations.

scran /skræn/ *n. sl.* **1** food, eatables. **2** remains of food. □**bad scran** *Ir.* bad luck. [18th c.: orig. unkn.]

scrap[1] /skræp/ *n. & v.* —*n.* **1** a small detached piece; a fragment or remnant. **2** rubbish or waste material. **3** an extract or cutting from something written or printed. **4** discarded metal for reprocessing (often *attrib.*: *scrap metal*). **5** (with *neg.*) the smallest piece or amount (*not a scrap of food left*). **6** (in *pl.*) **a** odds and ends. **b** bits of uneaten food. **7** (in *sing* or *pl.*) a residuum of melted fat or of fish with the oil expressed. —*v.tr.* (**scrapped, scrapping**) discard as useless. □**scrap heap 1** a pile of scrap materials. **2** a state of uselessness. **scrap merchant** a dealer in scrap. [ME f. ON *skrap*, rel. to *skrapa* SCRAPE]

scrap[2] /skræp/ *n. & v. colloq.* —*n.* a fight or rough quarrel, esp. a spontaneous one. —*v.tr.* (**scrapped, scrapping**) (often foll. by *with*) have a scrap. □□ **scrapper** *n.* [perh. f. SCRAPE]

scrapbook /'skræpbʊk/ *n.* a book of blank pages for sticking cuttings, drawings, etc., in.

scrape /skreɪp/ *v. & n.* —*v.* **1** *tr.* **a** move a hard or sharp edge across (a surface), esp. to make something smooth. **b** apply (a hard or sharp edge) in this way. **2** *tr.* (foll. by *away, off,* etc.) remove (a stain, projection, etc.) by scraping. **3** *tr.* **a** rub (a surface) harshly against another. **b** scratch or damage by scraping. **4** *tr.* make (a hollow) by scraping. **5 a** *tr.* draw or move with a sound of, or resembling, scraping. **b** *intr.* emit or produce such a sound. **c** *tr.* produce such a sound from. **6** *intr.* (often foll. by *along, by, through,* etc.) move or pass along while almost touching close or surrounding features, obstacles, etc. (*the car scraped through the narrow lane*). **7** *tr.* just manage to achieve (a living, an examination pass, etc.). **8** *intr.* (often foll. by *by, through*) **a** barely manage. **b** pass an examination etc. with difficulty. **9** *tr.* (foll. by *together, up*) contrive to bring or provide; amass with difficulty. **10** *intr.* be economical. **11** *intr.* draw back a foot in making a clumsy bow. **12** *tr.* clear (a ship's bottom) of barnacles etc. **13** *tr.* completely clear (a plate) of food. **14** *tr.* (foll. by *back*) draw (the hair) tightly back off the forehead. —*n.* **1** the act or sound of scraping. **2** a scraped place (on the skin etc.). **3** a thinly applied layer of butter etc. on bread. **4** the scraping of a foot in bowing. **5** *colloq.* an awkward predicament, esp. resulting from an escapade. □**scrape acquaintance with** contrive to get to know

(a person). **scrape the barrel** *colloq.* be reduced to one's last resources. [ME f. ON *skrapa* or MDu. *schrapen*]

scraper /'skreɪpə(r)/ *n.* a device used for scraping, esp. for removing dirt etc. from a surface.

scraperboard /'skreɪpəbɔːd/ *n. Brit.* cardboard or board with a blackened surface which can be scraped off for making white-line drawings.

scrapie /'skreɪpɪ/ *n.* a viral disease of sheep involving the central nervous system and characterized by lack of coordination causing affected animals to rub against trees etc. for support.

scraping /'skreɪpɪŋ/ *n.* **1** in senses of SCRAPE *v.* & *n.* **2** (esp. in *pl.*) a fragment produced by this.

scrappy /'skræpɪ/ *adj.* (**scrappier, scrappiest**) **1** consisting of scraps. **2** incomplete; carelessly arranged or put together. □□ **scrappily** *adv.* **scrappiness** *n.*

scrapyard /'skræpjɑːd/ *n.* a place where (esp. metal) scrap is collected.

scratch /skrætʃ/ *v., n.,* & *adj.* —*v.* **1** *tr.* score or mark the surface of with a sharp or pointed object. **2** *tr.* **a** make a long narrow superficial wound in (the skin). **b** cause (a person or part of the body) to be scratched (*scratched himself on the table*). **3** *tr.* (also *absol.*) scrape without marking, esp. with the hand to relieve itching (*stood there scratching*). **4** *tr.* make or form by scratching. **5** *tr.* scribble; write hurriedly or awkwardly (*scratched a quick reply; scratched a large A*). **6** *tr.* (foll. by *together, up,* etc.) obtain (a thing) by scratching or with difficulty. **7** *tr.* (foll. by *out, off, through*) cancel or strike (out) with a pencil etc. **8** *tr.* (also *absol.*) withdraw (a competitor, candidate, etc.) from a race or competition. **9** *intr.* (often foll. by *about, around,* etc.) **a** scratch the ground etc. in search. **b** look around haphazardly (*they were scratching about for evidence*). —*n.* **1** a mark or wound made by scratching. **2** a sound of scratching. **3** a spell of scratching oneself. **4** *colloq.* a superficial wound. **5** a line from which competitors in a race (esp. those not receiving a handicap) start. **6** (in *pl.*) a disease of horses in which the pastern appears scratched. **7** *sl.* money. —*attrib.adj.* **1** collected by chance. **2** collected or made from whatever is available; heterogeneous (*a scratch crew*). **3** with no handicap given (*a scratch race*). □**from scratch 1** from the beginning. **2** without help or advantage. **scratch along** make a living etc. with difficulty. **scratch one's head** be perplexed. **scratch my back and I will scratch yours 1** do me a favour and I will return it. **2** used in reference to mutual aid or flattery. **scratch pad 1** esp. *US* a pad of paper for scribbling. **2** *Computing* a small fast memory for the temporary storage of data. **scratch the surface** deal with a matter only superficially. **up to scratch** up to the required standard. □□ **scratcher** *n.* [ME, prob. f. synonymous ME *scrat* & *cratch*, both of uncert. orig.: cf. MLG *kratsen*, OHG *krazzōn*]

scratchy /'skrætʃɪ/ *adj.* (**scratchier, scratchiest**) **1** tending to make scratches or a scratching noise. **2** (esp. of a garment) tending to cause itchiness. **3** (of a drawing etc.) done in scratches or carelessly. □□ **scratchily** *adv.* **scratchiness** *n.*

scrawl /skrɔːl/ *v. & n.* —*v.* **1** *tr.* & *intr.* write in a hurried untidy way. **2** *tr.* (foll. by *out*) cross out by scrawling over. —*n.* **1** a piece of hurried writing. **2** a scrawled note. □□ **scrawly** *adj.* [perh. f. obs. *scrawl* sprawl, alt. of CRAWL]

scrawny /'skrɔːnɪ/ *adj.* (**scrawnier, scrawniest**) lean, scraggy. □□ **scrawniness** *n.* [var. of dial. *scranny*: cf. archaic *scrannel* (of sound) weak, feeble]

scream /skriːm/ *n. & v.* —*n.* **1** a loud high-pitched piercing cry expressing fear, pain, extreme fright, etc. **2** the act of emitting a scream. **3** *colloq.* an irresistibly funny occurrence or person. —*v.* **1** *intr.* emit a scream. **2** *tr.* speak or sing (words etc.) in a screaming tone. **3** *intr.* make or move with a shrill sound like a scream. **4** *intr.* laugh uncontrollably. **5** *intr.* be blatantly obvious or conspicuous. **6** *intr. colloq.* turn informer. [OE or MDu.]

screamer /'skriːmə(r)/ *n.* **1** a person or thing that screams. **2** any S. American goose-like bird of the family Anhimidae, frequenting marshland and having a characteristic shrill cry. **3** *colloq.* a tale that raises screams of laughter. **4** *US colloq.* a sensational headline.

scree /skriː/ *n.* (in *sing.* or *pl.*) **1** small loose stones. **2** a mountain slope covered with these. [prob. backform. f. *screes* (pl.) ult. f. ON *skritha* landslip, rel. to *skrítha* glide]

screech /skriːtʃ/ *n. & v.* —*n.* a harsh high-pitched scream. —*v.tr. & intr.* utter with or make a screech. ▫**screech-owl** any owl that screeches instead of hooting, esp. a barn-owl or a small American owl, *Otus asio.* ▫▫**screecher** *n.* **screechy** *adj.* (**screechier, screechiest**). [16th-c. var. of ME *scritch* (imit.)]

screed /skriːd/ *n.* **1** a long usu. tiresome piece of writing or speech. **2 a** a strip of plaster or other material placed on a surface as a guide to thickness. **b** a levelled layer of material (e.g. cement) applied to a floor or other surface. [ME, prob. var. of SHRED]

screen /skriːn/ *n. & v.* —*n.* **1** a fixed or movable upright partition for separating, concealing, or sheltering from draughts or excessive heat or light. **2 a** a thing used as a shelter, esp. from observation. **3 a** a measure adopted for concealment. **b** the protection afforded by this (*under the screen of night*). **4 a** a blank usu. white or silver surface on which a photographic image is projected. **b** (prec. by *the*) the cinema industry. **5** the surface of a cathode-ray tube or similar electronic device, esp. of a television, VDU, etc., on which images appear. **6** = *sight-screen.* **7** = WINDSCREEN. **8** a frame with fine wire netting to keep out flies, mosquitoes, etc. **9** *Physics* a body intercepting light, heat, electric or magnetic induction, etc., in a physical apparatus. **10** *Photog.* a piece of ground glass in a camera for focusing. **11** a large sieve or riddle, esp. for sorting grain, coal, etc., into sizes. **12** a system of checking for the presence or absence of a disease, ability, attribute, etc. **13** *Printing* a transparent finely-ruled plate or film used in half-tone reproduction. **14** *Mil.* a body of troops, ships, etc., detached to warn of the presence of an enemy force. —*v.tr.* **1** (often foll. by *from*) **a** afford shelter to; hide partly or completely. **b** protect from detection, censure, etc. **2** (foll. by *off*) shut off or hide behind a screen. **3 a** show (a film etc.) on a screen. **b** broadcast (a television programme). **4** prevent from causing, or protect from, electrical interference. **5 a** test (a person or group) for the presence or absence of a disease. **b** check on (a person) for the presence or absence of a quality, esp. reliability or loyalty. **6** pass (grain, coal, etc.) through a screen. ▫**screen printing** a process like stencilling with ink forced through a prepared sheet of fine material (orig. silk). **screen test** an audition for a part in a cinema film. ▫▫**screenable** *adj.* **screener** *n.* [ME f. ONF *escren, escran:* cf. OHG *skrank* barrier]

screenings /'skriːnɪŋz/ *n.pl.* refuse separated by sifting.

screenplay /'skriːnpleɪ/ *n.* the script of a film, with acting instructions, scene directions, etc.

screenwriter /'skriːn,raɪtə(r)/ *n.* a person who writes a screenplay.

screw /skruː/ *n. & v.* —*n.* **1** a thin cylinder or cone with a spiral ridge or thread running round the outside (**male screw**) or the inside (**female screw**). **2** (in full **wood-screw**) a metal male screw with a slotted head and a sharp point for fastening things, esp. in carpentry, by being rotated to form a thread in wood etc. **3** (in full **screw-bolt**) a metal male screw with a blunt end on which a nut is threaded to bolt things together. **4** a wooden or metal straight screw used to exert pressure. **5** (in *sing.* or *pl.*) an

instrument of torture acting in this way. **6** (in full **screw-propeller**) a form of propeller with twisted blades acting like a screw on the water or air. **7** one turn of a screw. **8** (foll. by *of*) *Brit.* a small twisted-up paper (of tobacco etc.). **9** *Brit.* (in billiards etc.) an oblique curling motion of the ball. **10** *sl.* a prison warder. **11** *Brit. sl.* an amount of salary or wages. **12** *coarse sl.* **a** an act of sexual intercourse. **b** a partner in this. ¶ Usually considered a taboo use. **13** *sl.* a mean or miserly person. **14** *sl.* a worn-out horse. —*v.* **1** *tr.* fasten or tighten with a screw or screws. **2** *tr.* turn (a screw). **3** *intr.* twist or turn round like a screw. **4** *intr.* (of a ball etc.) swerve. **5** *tr.* **a** put psychological etc. pressure on to achieve an end. **b** oppress. **6** *tr.* (foll. by *out of*) extort (consent, money, etc.) from (a person). **7** *tr.* (also *absol.*) *coarse sl.* have sexual intercourse with. ¶ Usually considered a taboo use. **8** *intr.* (of a rolling ball, or of a person etc.) take a curling course; swerve. **9** *intr.* (often foll. by *up*) make tenser or more efficient. ▫**have one's head screwed on the right way** *colloq.* have common sense. **have a screw loose** *colloq.* be slightly crazy. **put the screws on** *colloq.* exert pressure, esp. to extort or intimidate. **screw cap** = *screw top.* **screw-coupling** a female screw with threads at both ends for joining lengths of pipes or rods. **screw eye** a screw with a loop for passing cord etc. through instead of a slotted head. **screw gear** an endless screw with a cog-wheel or pinion. **screw hook** a hook to hang things on, with a screw point for fastening it. **screw-jack** a vehicle jack (see JACK¹) worked by a screw device. **screw pine** any plant of the genus *Pandanus*, with its leaves arranged spirally and resembling those of a pineapple. **screw-plate** a steel plate with threaded holes for making male screws. **screw-tap** a tool for making female screws. **screw top** (also (with hyphen) *attrib.*) a cap or lid that can be screwed on to a bottle, jar, etc. **screw up 1** contract or contort (one's face etc.). **2** contract and crush into a tight mass (a piece of paper etc.). **3** summon up (one's courage etc.). **4** *sl.* **a** bungle or mismanage. **b** spoil or ruin (an event, opportunity, etc.). **screw-up** *n. sl.* a bungle, muddle, or mess. **screw valve** a stopcock opened and shut by a screw. ▫▫**screwable** *adj.* **screwer** *n.* [ME f. OF *escroue* female screw, nut, f. L *scrofa* sow]

screwball /'skruːbɔːl/ *n. & adj. US sl.* —*n.* a crazy or eccentric person. —*adj.* crazy.

screwdriver /'skruː,draɪvə(r)/ *n.* a tool with a shaped tip to fit into the head of a screw to turn it.

screwed /skruːd/ *adj.* **1** twisted. **2** *sl.* **a** ruined; rendered ineffective. **b** drunk.

screwy /'skruːɪ/ *adj.* (**screwier, screwiest**) *sl.* **1** crazy or eccentric. **2** absurd. ▫▫**screwiness** *n.*

scribble¹ /'skrɪb(ə)l/ *v. & n.* —*v.* **1** *tr. & intr.* write carelessly or hurriedly. **2** *intr.* often *derog.* be an author or writer. **3** *intr. & tr.* draw carelessly or meaninglessly. —*n.* **1** a scrawl. **2** a hasty note etc. **3** careless handwriting. ▫▫**scribbler** *n.* **scribbly** *adj.* [ME f. med.L *scribillare* dimin. of L *scribere* write]

scribble² /'skrɪb(ə)l/ *v.tr.* card (wool, cotton, etc.) coarsely. [prob. f. LG: cf. LG *schrubbeln* (in the same sense), frequent. f. LG *schrubben*: see SCRUB¹]

scribe /skraɪb/ *n. & v.* —*n.* **1** a person who writes out documents, esp. an ancient or medieval copyist of manuscripts. **2** *Bibl.* an ancient Jewish record-keeper or professional theologian and jurist. **3** (in full **scribe-awl**) a pointed instrument for making marks on wood, bricks, etc., to guide a saw, or in sign-writing. **4** *US colloq.* a writer, esp. a journalist. —*v.tr.* mark (wood etc.) with a scribe (see sense 3 of *n.*). ▫▫**scribal** *adj.* **scriber** *n.* [(n.) ME f. L *scriba* f. *scribere* write: (v.) perh. f. DESCRIBE]

scrim /skrɪm/ *n.* open-weave fabric for lining or upholstery etc. [18th c.: orig. unkn.]

scrimmage /'skrɪmɪdʒ/ *n. & v.* —*n.* **1** a rough or confused struggle; a brawl. **2** *Amer. Football* a sequence of play beginning with the placing of the ball on the ground with its longest axis at right angles to the goal-line. —*v*. **1** *intr*. engage in a scrimmage. **2** *tr*. *Amer. Football* put (the ball) into a scrimmage. □□ **scrimmager** *n*. [var. of SKIRMISH]

scrimp /skrɪmp/ *v*. **1** *intr*. be sparing or parsimonious. **2** *tr*. use sparingly. □□ **scrimpy** *adj*. [18th c., orig. Sc.: perh. rel. to SHRIMP]

scrimshank /ˈskrɪmʃæŋk/ *v.intr. Brit. sl*. esp. *Mil*. shirk duty. □□ **scrimshanker** *n*. [19th c.: orig. unkn.]

scrimshaw /ˈskrɪmʃɔː/ *v. & n*. —*v.tr*. (also *absol*.) adorn (shells, ivory, etc.) with carved or coloured designs (as sailors' pastime at sea). —*n*. work or a piece of work of this kind. [19th c.: perh. f. a surname]

scrip /skrɪp/ *n*. **1** a provisional certificate of money subscribed to a bank or company etc. entitling the holder to a formal certificate and dividends. **2** (*collect*.) such certificates. **3** an extra share or shares instead of a dividend. [abbr. of *subscription receipt*]

script /skrɪpt/ *n. & v*. —*n*. **1** handwriting as distinct from print; written characters. **2** type imitating handwriting. **3** an alphabet or system of writing (*the Russian script*). **4** the text of a play, film, or broadcast. **5** an examinee's set of written answers. **6** *Law* an original document as distinct from a copy. —*v.tr*. write a script for (a film etc.). [ME, = thing written, f. OF escri(p)t f. L *scriptum*, neut. past part. of *scribere* write]

scriptorium /ˌskrɪpˈtɔːrɪəm/ *n*. (*pl*. **scriptoria** /-rɪə/ or **scriptoriums**) a room set apart for writing, esp. in a monastery. □□ **scriptorial** *adj*. [med.L (as SCRIPT)]

scriptural /ˈskrɪptʃər(ə)l, -tʃʊər(ə)l/ *adj*. **1** of or relating to a scripture, esp. the Bible. **2** having the authority of a scripture. □□ **scripturally** *adv*. [LL *scripturalis* f. L *scriptura*: see SCRIPTURE]

scripture /ˈskrɪptʃə(r)/ *n*. **1** sacred writings. **2** (**Scripture** or **the Scriptures**) **a** the Bible as a collection of sacred writings in Christianity. **b** the sacred writings of any other religion. [ME f. L *scriptura* (as SCRIPT)]

scriptwriter /ˈskrɪptˌraɪtə(r)/ *n*. a person who writes a script for a film, broadcast, etc. □□ **scriptwriting** *n*.

scrivener /ˈskrɪvənə(r)/ *n. hist*. **1** a copyist or drafter of documents. **2** a notary. **3** a broker. **4** a moneylender. [ME f. obs. *scrivein* f. OF *escrivein* ult. f. L (as SCRIBE)]

scrobiculate /skrəˈbɪkjʊlət/ *adj. Bot. & Zool*. pitted, furrowed. [f. L *scrobiculus* f. *scrobis* trench]

scrod /skrɒd/ *n. US* a young cod or haddock, esp. as food. [19th c.: perh. rel. to SHRED]

scrofula /ˈskrɒfjʊlə/ *n. archaic* a disease with glandular swellings, prob. a form of tuberculosis. Also called *king's evil*. □□ **scrofulous** *adj*. [ME f. med.L (sing.) f. LL *scrofulae* (pl.) scrofulous swelling, dimin. of L *scrofa* a sow]

scroll /skrəʊl/ *n. & v*. —*n*. **1** a roll of parchment or paper esp. with writing on it. **2** a book in the ancient roll form. **3** an ornamental design or carving imitating a roll of parchment. —*v*. **1** *tr*. (often foll. by *down, up*) move a (display on a VDU screen) in order to view new material. **2** *tr*. inscribe in or like a scroll. **3** *intr*. curl up like paper. □ **scroll saw** a saw for cutting along curved lines in ornamental work. [ME *scrowle* alt. f. *rowle* ROLL, perh. after *scrow* (in the same sense), formed as ESCROW]

scrolled /skrəʊld/ *adj*. having a scroll ornament.

scrollwork /ˈskrəʊlwɜːk/ *n*. decoration of spiral lines, esp. as cut by a scroll saw.

Scrooge /skruːdʒ/ *n*. a mean or miserly person. [a character in Dickens's *Christmas Carol*]

scrotum /ˈskrəʊtəm/ *n*. (*pl*. **scrota** /-tə/ or **scrotums**) a pouch of skin containing the testicles. □□ **scrotal** *adj*. **scrotitis** /-ˈtaɪtɪs/ *n*. [L]

scrounge /skraʊndʒ/ *v. & n. colloq*. —*v*. **1** *tr*. (also *absol*.) obtain (things) illicitly or by cadging. **2** *intr*. search about to find something at no cost. —*n*. an act of scrounging. □ **on the scrounge** engaged in

scrounging. □□ **scrounger** *n*. [var. of dial. *scrunge* steal]

scrub[1] /skrʌb/ *v. & n*. —*v*. (**scrubbed, scrubbing**) **1** *tr*. rub hard so as to clean, esp. with a hard brush. **2** *intr*. use a brush in this way. **3** *intr*. (often foll. by *up*) (of a surgeon etc.) thoroughly clean the hands and arms by scrubbing, before operating. **4** *tr*. *colloq*. scrap or cancel (a plan, order, etc.). **5** *tr*. use water to remove impurities from (gas etc.). —*n*. the act or an instance of scrubbing; the process of being scrubbed. □ **scrubbing-brush** (*US* **scrub-brush**) a hard brush for scrubbing floors. **scrub round** *colloq*. circumvent, avoid. [ME prob. f. MLG, MDu. *schrobben*, *schrubben*]

scrub[2] /skrʌb/ *n*. **1 a** vegetation consisting mainly of brushwood or stunted forest growth. **b** an area of land covered with this. **2** (of livestock) of inferior breed or physique (often *attrib*.: *scrub horse*). **3 a** small or dwarf variety (often *attrib*.: *scrub pine*). **4** *US Sport colloq*. a team or player not of the first class. □ **scrub turkey** a megapode. **scrub typhus** a rickettsial disease of the W. Pacific transmitted by mites. □□ **scrubby** *adj*. [ME, var. of SHRUB[1]]

scrubber /ˈskrʌbə(r)/ *n*. **1** an apparatus using water or a solution for purifying gases etc. **2** *sl. derog*. a sexually promiscuous woman.

scruff[1] /skrʌf/ *n*. the back of the neck as used to grasp and lift or drag an animal or person by (esp. *scruff of the neck*). [alt. of *scuff*, perh. f. ON *skoft* hair]

scruff[2] /skrʌf/ *n. colloq*. an untidy or scruffy person. [orig. = SCURF, later 'worthless thing', or back-form. f. SCRUFFY]

scruffy /ˈskrʌfɪ/ *adj*. (**scruffier, scruffiest**) *colloq*. shabby, slovenly, untidy. □□ **scruffily** *adv*. **scruffiness** *n*. [*scruff* var. of SCURF + -Y[1]]

scrum /skrʌm/ *n*. **1** *Rugby Football* an arrangement of the forwards of each team in two opposing groups, each with arms interlocked and heads down, with the ball thrown in between them to restart play. **2** *colloq*. a milling crowd. □ **scrum-half** a half-back who puts the ball into the scrum. [abbr. of SCRUMMAGE]

scrummage /ˈskrʌmɪdʒ/ *n. Rugby Football* = SCRUM 1. [as SCRIMMAGE]

scrump /skrʌmp/ *v.tr. Brit. colloq*. steal (fruit) from an orchard or garden. [cf. SCRUMPY]

scrumple /ˈskrʌmp(ə)l/ *v.tr*. crumple, wrinkle. [var. of CRUMPLE]

scrumptious /ˈskrʌmpʃəs/ *adj. colloq*. **1** delicious. **2** pleasing, delightful. □□ **scrumptiously** *adv*. **scrumptiousness** *n*. [19th c.: orig. unkn.]

scrumpy /ˈskrʌmpɪ/ *n. Brit. colloq*. rough cider, esp. as made in the West Country of England. [dial. *scrump* small apple]

scrunch /skrʌntʃ/ *v. & n*. —*v.tr. & intr*. **1** (usu. foll. by *up*) make or become crushed or crumpled. **2** make or cause to make a crunching sound. —*n*. the act or an instance of scrunching. [var. of CRUNCH]

scruple /ˈskruːp(ə)l/ *n. & v*. —*n*. **1** (in *sing*. or *pl*.) **a** regard to the morality or propriety of an action. **b** a feeling of doubt or hesitation caused by this. **2** *Brit. hist*. an apothecaries' weight of 20 grains. **3** *archaic* a very small quantity. —*v.intr*. **1** (foll. by *to* + infin.; usu. with *neg*.) be reluctant because of scruples (*did not scruple to stop their allowance*). **2** feel or be influenced by scruples. [F *scrupule* or L *scrupulus* f. *scrupus* rough pebble, anxiety]

scrupulous /ˈskruːpjʊləs/ *adj*. **1** conscientious or thorough even in small matters. **2** careful to avoid doing wrong. **3** punctilious; over-attentive to details. □□ **scrupulosity** /-ˈlɒsɪtɪ/ *n*. **scrupulously** *adv*. **scrupulousness** *n*. [ME f. F *scrupuleux* or L *scrupulosus* (as SCRUPLE)]

scrutineer /ˌskruːtɪˈnɪə(r)/ *n*. a person who scrutinizes or examines something, esp. the conduct and result of a ballot.

scrutinize /ˈskruːtɪnaɪz/ *v.tr*. (also **-ise**) look closely at; examine with close scrutiny. □□ **scrutinizer** *n*.

scrutiny /'skru:tɪnɪ/ n. (pl. -ies) 1 a critical gaze. 2 a close investigation or examination of details. 3 an official examination of ballot-papers to check their validity or accuracy of counting. [ME f. L *scrutinium* f. *scrutari* search f. *scruta* rubbish: orig. of rag-collectors]

scry /skraɪ/ v.intr. (-ies, -ied) divine by crystal-gazing. □□ **scryer** n. [shortening f. DESCRY]

scuba /'sku:bə, 'skju:-/ n. (pl. **scubas**) an aqualung. [acronym f. self-contained underwater breathing apparatus]

scuba-diving /'sku:bə,daɪvɪŋ, 'skju:-/ n. swimming underwater using a scuba, esp. as a sport. □□ **scuba-dive** v.intr. **scuba-diver** n.

scud /skʌd/ v. & n. —v.intr. (**scudded, scudding**) 1 fly or run straight, fast, and lightly; skim along. 2 *Naut.* run before the wind. —n. 1 a spell of scudding. 2 a scudding motion. 3 vapoury driving clouds. 4 a driving shower; a gust. 5 wind-blown spray. [perh. alt. of SCUT, as if to race like a hare]

scuff /skʌf/ v. & n. —v. 1 tr. graze or brush against. 2 tr. mark or wear down (shoes) in this way. 3 intr. walk with dragging feet; shuffle. —n. a mark of scuffing. [imit.]

scuffle /'skʌf(ə)l/ n. & v. —n. a confused struggle or disorderly fight at close quarters. —v.intr. engage in a scuffle. [prob. f. Scand.: cf. Sw. *skuffa* to push, rel. to SHOVE]

sculduggery var. of SKULDUGGERY.

scull /skʌl/ n. & v. —n. 1 either of a pair of small oars used by a single rower. 2 an oar placed over the stern of a boat to propel it, usu. by a twisting motion. 3 (in pl.) a race between boats with single pairs of oars. —v.tr. propel (a boat) with sculls. [ME: orig. unkn.]

sculler /'skʌlə(r)/ n. 1 a user of sculls. 2 a boat intended for sculling.

scullery /'skʌlərɪ/ n. (pl. -ies) a small kitchen or room at the back of a house for washing dishes etc. [ME f. AF *squillerie*, OF *escuelerie* f. *escuele* dish f. L *scutella* salver dimin. of *scutra* wooden platter]

scullion /'skʌljən/ n. archaic 1 a cook's boy. 2 a person who washes dishes etc. [ME: orig. unkn.]

sculpin /'skʌlpɪn/ n. any of numerous fish of the family Cottidae, native to non-tropical regions, having large spiny heads. [perh. f. obs. *scorpene* f. L *scorpaena* f. Gk *skorpaina* a fish]

sculpt /skʌlpt/ v.tr. & intr. (also **sculp**) sculpture. [F *sculpter* f. *sculpteur* SCULPTOR: now regarded as an abbr.]

sculptor /'skʌlptə(r)/ n. (fem. **sculptress** /-trɪs/) an artist who makes sculptures. [L (as SCULPTURE)]

sculpture /'skʌlptʃə(r)/ n. & v. —n. 1 the art of making forms, often representational, in the round or in relief by chiselling stone, carving wood, modelling clay, casting metal, etc. 2 a work or works of sculpture. 3 *Zool.* & *Bot.* raised or sunken markings on a shell etc. —v. 1 tr. represent in or adorn with sculpture. 2 intr. practise sculpture. □□ **sculptural** adj. **sculpturally** adv. **sculpturesque** adj. [ME f. L *sculptura* f. *sculpere sculpt-* carve]

scum /skʌm/ n. & v. —n. 1 a layer of dirt, froth, or impurities etc. forming at the top of liquid, esp. in boiling or fermentation. 2 (foll. by *of*) the most worthless part of something. 3 colloq. a worthless person or group. —v. (**scummed, scumming**) 1 tr. remove scum from; skim. 2 tr. be or form a scum on. 3 intr. (of a liquid) develop scum. □□ **scummy** adj. (**scummier, scummiest**) adj. [ME f. MLG, MDu. *schūm*, OHG *scūm* f. Gmc]

scumble /'skʌmb(ə)l/ v. & n. —v.tr. 1 modify (a painting) by applying a thin opaque coat of paint to give a softer or duller effect. 2 modify (a drawing) similarly with light pencilling etc. —n. 1 material used in scumbling. 2 the effect produced by scumbling. [perh. frequent. of SCUM v.tr.]

scuncheon /'skʌntʃ(ə)n/ n. the inside face of a

---

door-jamb, window-frame, etc. [ME f. OF *escoinson* (as EX-[1], COIN)]

scunge /skʌndʒ/ n. Austral. & NZ colloq. 1 dirt, scum. 2 a dirty or disagreeable person. □□ **scungy** adj. (**scungier, scungiest**). [perh. f. E dial. *scrunge* steal: cf. SCROUNGE]

scunner /'skʌnə(r)/ v. & n. Sc. —v.intr. feel disgust or nausea. —n. 1 a strong dislike (esp. *take a scunner at* or *against*). 2 an object of loathing. [14th c.: orig. uncert.]

scup /skʌp/ n. an E. American fish, *Stenostomus chrysops*, a kind of porgy. [Narraganset *mishcup* thick-scaled f. *mishe* large + *cuppi* scale]

scupper[1] /'skʌpə(r)/ n. a hole in a ship's side to carry off water from the deck. [ME (perh. f. AF) f. OF *escopir* f. Rmc *skuppire* (unrecorded) to spit: orig. imit.]

scupper[2] /'skʌpə(r)/ v.tr. Brit. sl. 1 sink (a ship or its crew). 2 defeat or ruin (a plan etc.). 3 kill. [19th c.: orig. unkn.]

scurf /skɜːf/ n. 1 flakes on the surface of the skin, cast off as fresh skin develops below, esp. those of the head; dandruff. 2 any scaly matter on a surface. □□ **scurfy** adj. [OE, prob. f. ON & earlier OE *sceorf*, rel. to *sceorfan* gnaw, *sceorfian* cut to shreds]

scurrilous /'skʌrɪləs/ adj. 1 (of a person or language) grossly or indecently abusive. 2 given to or expressed with low humour. □□ **scurrility** /-'rɪlɪtɪ/ n. (pl. -ies). **scurrilously** adv. **scurrilousness** n. [F *scurrile* or L *scurrilus* f. *scurra* buffoon]

scurry /'skʌrɪ/ v. & n. —v.intr. (-ies, -ied) run or move hurriedly, esp. with short quick steps; scamper. —n. (pl. -ies) 1 the act or sound of scurrying. 2 bustle, haste. 3 a flurry of rain or snow. [abbr. of *hurry-scurry* redupl. of HURRY]

scurvy /'skɜːvɪ/ n. & adj. —n. a disease caused by a deficiency of vitamin C, characterized by swollen bleeding gums and the opening of previously healed wounds, esp. formerly affecting sailors. —adj. (**scurvier, scurviest**) paltry, low, mean, dishonourable, contemptible. □ **scurvy grass** any cress-like seaside plant of the genus *Cochlearia*, orig. taken as a cure for scurvy. □□ **scurvied** adj. **scurvily** adv. [SCURF + -Y[1]: noun sense by assoc. with F *scorbut* (cf. SCORBUTIC)]

scut /skʌt/ n. a short tail, esp. of a hare, rabbit, or deer. [ME: orig. unkn.: cf. obs. *scut* short, shorten]

scuta pl. of SCUTUM.

scutage /'skju:tɪdʒ/ n. hist. money paid by a feudal landowner instead of personal service. [ME f. med.L *scutagium* f. L *scutum* shield]

scutch /skʌtʃ/ v.tr. dress (fibrous material, esp. retted flax) by beating. □□ **scutcher** n. [OF *escouche*, *escoucher* (dial.), *escousser*, ult. f. L *excutere excuss-* (as EX-[1], *quatere* shake)]

scutcheon /'skʌtʃ(ə)n/ n. 1 = ESCUTCHEON. 2 an ornamented brass etc. plate round or over a keyhole. 3 a plate for a name or inscription. [ME f. ESCUTCHEON]

scute /skju:t/ n. Zool. etc. = SCUTUM. [L (as SCUTUM)]

scutellum /skju'teləm/ n. (pl. **scutella** /-lə/) Bot. & Zool. a scale, plate, or any shieldlike formation on a plant, insect, bird, etc., esp. one of the horny scales on a bird's foot. □□ **scutellate** /'skju:tələt/ adj. **scutellation** /,skju:tə'leɪʃ(ə)n/ n. [mod.L dimin. of L *scutum* shield]

scutter /'skʌtə(r)/ v. & n. —v.intr. colloq. scurry. —n. the act or an instance of scuttering. [perh. alt. of SCUTTLE[2]]

scuttle[1] /'skʌt(ə)l/ n. 1 a receptacle for carrying and holding a small supply of coal. 2 Brit. the part of a motor-car body between the windscreen and the bonnet. [ME f. ON *skutill*, OHG *scuzzila* f. L *scutella* dish]

scuttle[2] /'skʌt(ə)l/ v. & n. —v.intr. 1 scurry; hurry along. 2 run away; flee from danger or difficulty. —n. 1 a hurried gait. 2 a precipitate flight or departure. [cf. dial. *scuddle* frequent. of SCUD]

scuttle[3] /'skʌt(ə)l/ n. & v. —n. a hole with a lid in a

---

b *but* d *dog* f *few* g *get* h *he* j *yes* k *cat* l *leg* m *man* n *no* p *pen* r *red* s *sit* t *top* v *voice*

ship's deck or side. —*v.tr.* let water into (a ship) to sink it, esp. by opening the seacocks. [ME, perh. f. obs. F *escoutille* f. Sp. *escotilla* hatchway dimin. of *escota* cutting out cloth]

scuttlebutt /'skʌt(ə)l,bʌt/ *n.* **1** a water-butt on the deck of a ship, for drinking from. **2** *colloq.* rumour, gossip.

scutum /'skju:təm/ *n.* (*pl.* **scuta** /-tə/) each of the shieldlike plates or scales forming the bony covering of a crocodile, sturgeon, turtle, armadillo, etc. □□ **scutal** *adj.* **scutate** *adj.* [L, = oblong shield]

Scylla and Charybdis /,sɪlə ənd kə'rɪbdɪs/ *n.pl.* two dangers such that avoidance of one increases the risk from the other. [the names of a sea-monster and whirlpool in Gk mythology]

scyphozoan /,saɪfə'zəʊən/ *n. & adj.* —*n.* any marine jellyfish of the class Scyphozoa, with tentacles bearing stinging cells. —*adj.* of or relating to this class. [as SCYPHUS + Gk *zōion* animal]

scyphus /'saɪfəs/ *n.* (*pl.* **scyphi** /-faɪ/) **1** *Gk Antiq.* a footless drinking-cup with two handles below the level of the rim. **2** *Bot.* a cup-shaped part as in a narcissus flower or in lichens. □□ **scyphose** *adj.* [mod.L f. Gk *skuphos*]

scythe /saɪð/ *n. & v.* —*n.* a mowing and reaping implement with a long curved blade swung over the ground by a long pole with two short handles projecting from it. —*v.tr.* cut with a scythe. [OE *sīthe* f. Gmc]

Scythian /'sɪðɪən/ *adj. & n.* —*adj.* of or relating to ancient Scythia, a region north of the Black Sea. —*n.* **1** an inhabitant of Scythia. **2** the language of this region. [L *Scythia* f. Gk *Skuthia* Scythia]

SD *abbr.* *US* South Dakota (in official postal use).

S.Dak. *abbr.* South Dakota.

SDI *abbr.* strategic defence initiative.

SDLP *abbr.* (in N. Ireland) Social Democratic and Labour Party.

SDP *abbr.* (in the UK) Social Democratic Party.

SDR *abbr.* special drawing right (from the International Monetary Fund).

SE *abbr.* **1** south-east. **2** south-eastern.

Se *symb. Chem.* the element selenium.

se- /sə, sɪ/ *prefix* apart, without (*seclude*; *secure*). [L f. OL *se* (prep. & adv.)]

sea /si:/ *n.* **1** the expanse of salt water that covers most of the earth's surface and surrounds its land masses. **2** any part of this as opposed to land or fresh water. **3** a particular (usu. named) tract of salt water partly or wholly enclosed by land (*the North Sea; the Dead Sea*). **4** a large inland lake (*the Sea of Galilee*). **5** the waves of the sea, esp. with reference to their local motion or state (*a choppy sea*). **6** (foll. by *of*) a vast quantity or expanse (*a sea of troubles; a sea of faces*). **7** (*attrib.*) living or used in, on, or near the sea (often prefixed to the name of a marine animal, plant, etc., having a superficial resemblance to what it is named after) (*sea lettuce*). □ **at sea 1** in a ship on the sea. **2** (also **all at sea**) perplexed, confused. **by sea** in a ship or ships. **go to sea** become a sailor. **on the sea 1** in a ship at sea. **2** situated on the coast. **put** (or **put out**) **to sea** leave land or port. **sea anchor** a device such as a heavy bag dragged in the water to retard the drifting of a ship. **sea anemone** any of various coelenterates of the order Actiniaria having a polypoid body bearing a ring of tentacles around the mouth. **sea-angel** an angel-fish. **sea bass** any of various marine fishes like the bass, esp. *Centropristis striatus*. **sea bird** a bird frequenting the sea or the land near the sea. **sea bream** = PORGY. **sea breeze** a breeze blowing towards the land from the sea, esp. during the day (cf. *land breeze*). **sea buckthorn** a maritime shrub, *Hippophaë rhamnoides*, with orange berries. **sea change** a notable or unexpected transformation (with ref. to Shakesp. *Tempest* I. ii. 403). **sea-chest** a sailor's storage-chest. **sea coal** *archaic* mineral coal, as distinct from charcoal etc. **sea cow 1** a sirenian. **2**

a walrus. **sea cucumber** a holothurian, esp. a *bêche-de-mer*. **sea dog** an old or experienced sailor. **sea eagle** any fish-eating eagle esp. of the genus *Haliaëtus*. **sea-ear** = ORMER. **sea elephant** any large seal of the genus *Mirounga*, the male of which has a proboscis: also called *elephant seal*. **sea fan** any colonial coral of the order Gorgonacea supported by a fanlike horny skeleton. **sea front** the part of a coastal town directly facing the sea. **sea-girt** *literary* surrounded by sea. **sea gooseberry** any marine animal of the phylum Ctenophora, with an ovoid body bearing numerous cilia. **sea-green** bluish-green (as of the sea). **sea hare** any of various marine molluscs of the order Anaspidea, having an internal shell and long extensions from its foot. **sea holly** a spiny-leaved blue-flowered evergreen plant, *Eryngium maritimum*. **sea horse 1** any of various small upright marine fish of the family Syngnathidae, esp. *Hippocampus hippocampus*, having a body suggestive of the head and neck of a horse. **2** a mythical creature with a horse's head and fish's tail. **sea-island cotton** a fine-quality long-stapled cotton grown on islands off the southern US. **sea lavender** any maritime plant of the genus *Limonium*, with small brightly-coloured funnel-shaped flowers. **sea legs** the ability to keep one's balance and avoid seasickness when at sea. **sea level** the mean level of the sea's surface, used in reckoning the height of hills etc. and as a barometric standard. **sea lily** any of various sessile echinoderms, esp. of the class Crinoidea, with long jointed stalks and feather-like arms for trapping food. **sea lion** any large, eared seal of the Pacific, esp. of the genus *Zalophus* or *Otaria*. **sea loch** = LOCH 2. **Sea Lord** (in the UK) a naval member of the Admiralty Board. **sea mile** = *nautical mile*. **sea mouse** any iridescent marine annelid of the genus *Aphrodite*. **sea onion** = SQUILL 2. **sea otter** a Pacific otter, *Enhydra lutris*, using a stone balanced on its abdomen to crack bivalve molluscs. **sea pink** a maritime plant, *Armeria maritima*, with bright pink flowers: also called THRIFT. **sea purse** the egg-case of a skate or shark. **sea room** clear space at sea for a ship to turn or manœuvre in. **sea salt** salt produced by evaporating sea water. **Sea Scout** a member of the maritime branch of the Scout Association. **sea serpent** (or **snake**) **1** a snake of the family Hydrophidae, living in the sea. **2** an enormous legendary serpent-like sea monster. **sea shell** the shell of a salt-water mollusc. **sea snail 1** a small slimy fish of the family Liparididae, with a ventral sucker. **2** any spiral-shelled mollusc, e.g. a whelk. **sea squirt** any marine tunicate of the class Ascidiacea, consisting of a bag-like structure with apertures for the flow of water. **sea trout** = *salmon trout*. **sea urchin** a small marine echinoderm of the class Echinoidea, with a spherical or flattened spiny shell. **sea wall** a wall or embankment erected to prevent encroachment by the sea. **sea water** water in or taken from the sea. [OE *sæ* f. Gmc]

seabed /'si:bed/ *n.* the ground under the sea; the ocean floor.

seaboard /'si:bɔ:d/ *n.* **1** the seashore or coastal region. **2** the line of a coast.

seaborne /'si:bɔ:n/ *adj.* transported by sea.

seacock /'si:kɒk/ *n.* a valve below a ship's water-line for letting water in or out.

seafarer /'si:,feərə(r)/ *n.* **1** a sailor. **2** a traveller by sea.

seafaring /'si:,feərɪŋ/ *adj. & n.* travelling by sea, esp. regularly.

seafood /'si:fu:d/ *n.* edible sea fish or shellfish.

seagoing /'si:,gəʊɪŋ/ *adj.* **1** (of ships) fit for crossing the sea. **2** (of a person) seafaring.

seagull /'si:gʌl/ *n.* = GULL[1].

seakale /'si:keɪl/ *n.* a cruciferous maritime plant, *Crambe maritima*, having coarsely-toothed leaves and used as a vegetable. □ **seakale beet** = CHARD.

seal[1] /siːl/ n. & v. —n. **1** a piece of wax, lead, paper, etc., with a stamped design, attached to a document as a guarantee of authenticity. **2** a similar material attached to a receptacle, envelope, etc., affording security by having to be broken to allow access to the contents. **3** an engraved piece of metal, gemstone, etc., for stamping a design on a seal. **4 a** a substance or device used to close an aperture or act as a fastening. **b** an amount of water standing in the trap of a drain to prevent foul air from rising. **5** an act or gesture or event regarded as a confirmation or guarantee. **6** a significant or prophetic mark (has the seal of death in his face). **7** a decorative adhesive stamp. **8** esp. Eccl. a vow of secrecy; an obligation to silence. —v.tr. **1** close securely or hermetically. **2** stamp or fasten with a seal. **3** fix a seal to. **4** certify as correct with a seal or stamp. **5** (often foll. by up) confine or fasten securely. **6** settle or decide (their fate is sealed). **7** (foll. by off) put barriers round (an area) to prevent entry and exit, esp. as a security measure. **8** apply a non-porous coating to (a surface) to make it impervious. □**Great Seal** (in the UK) the seal in the charge of the Lord Chancellor or Lord Keeper used in sealing important State papers. **one's lips are sealed** one is obliged to keep a secret. **sealed-beam** (attrib.) designating a vehicle headlamp with a sealed unit consisting of the light source, reflector, and lens. **sealed book** see BOOK. **sealed orders** orders for procedure not to be opened before a specified time. **sealing-wax** a mixture of shellac and rosin with turpentine and pigment, softened by heating and used to make seals. **seal ring** a finger ring with a seal. **seals of office** (in the UK) those held during tenure esp. by the Lord Chancellor or a Secretary of State. **set one's seal to** (or on) authorize or confirm. □□**sealable** adj. [ME f. AF seal, OF seel f. L sigillum dimin. of signum SIGN]

seal[2] /siːl/ n. & v. —n. any fish-eating amphibious sea mammal of the family Phocidae or Otariidae, with flippers and webbed feet. —v.intr. hunt for seals. [OE seolh seol- f. Gmc]

sealant /ˈsiːlənt/ n. material for sealing, esp. to make something airtight or watertight.

sealer /ˈsiːlə(r)/ n. a ship or person engaged in hunting seals.

sealery /ˈsiːləri/ n. (pl. -ies) a place for hunting seals.

sealskin /ˈsiːlskɪn/ n. **1** the skin or prepared fur of a seal. **2** (often attrib.) a garment made from this.

Sealyham /ˈsiːliəm/ n. (in full **Sealyham terrier**) **1** a terrier of a wire-haired short-legged breed. **2** this breed. [Sealyham in S. Wales]

seam /siːm/ n. & v. —n. **1** a line where two edges join, esp. of two pieces of cloth etc. turned back and stitched together, or of boards fitted edge to edge. **2** a fissure between parallel edges. **3** a wrinkle or scar. **4** a stratum of coal etc. —v.tr. **1** join with a seam. **2** (esp. as **seamed** adj.) mark or score with or as with a seam. □**bursting at the seams** full to overflowing. **seam bowler** Cricket a bowler who makes the ball deviate by bouncing off its seam. □□**seamer** n. **seamless** adj. [OE seam f. Gmc]

seaman /ˈsiːmən/ n. (pl. -**men**) **1** a sailor, esp. one below the rank of officer. **2** a person regarded in terms of skill in navigation (a poor seaman). □□ **seamanlike** adj. **seamanly** adj. [OE sæman (as SEA, MAN)]

seamanship /ˈsiːmənʃɪp/ n. skill in managing a ship or boat.

seamstress /ˈsemstrɪs/ n. (also **sempstress**) a woman who sews, esp. professionally; a needle-woman. [OE sēamestre fem. f. sēamere tailor, formed as SEAM + -STER + -ESS[1]]

seamy /ˈsiːmi/ adj. (**seamier**, **seamiest**) **1** marked with or showing seams. **2** unpleasant, disreputable (esp. the seamy side). □□**seaminess** n.

Seanad /ˈʃænəð/ n. the upper House of Parliament in the Republic of Ireland. [Ir., = senate]

seance /ˈseɪɑ̃s/ n. (also **séance**) a meeting at which

spiritualists attempt to make contact with the dead. [F séance f. OF seoir f. L sedēre sit]

seaplane /ˈsiːpleɪn/ n. an aircraft designed to take off from and land and float on water.

seaport /ˈsiːpɔːt/ n. a town with a harbour for seagoing ships.

SEAQ abbr. Stock Exchange Automated Quotations (computerized access to share information).

seaquake /ˈsiːkweɪk/ n. an earthquake under the sea.

sear /sɪə(r)/ v. & adj. —v.tr. **1 a** scorch, esp. with a hot iron; cauterize, brand. **b** (as **searing** adj.) scorching, burning (searing pain). **2** cause pain or great anguish to. **3** brown (meat) quickly at a high temperature so that it will retain its juices in cooking. **4** make (one's conscience, feelings, etc.) callous. **5** archaic blast, wither. —adj. (also **sere**) literary (esp. of a plant etc.) withered, dried up. [OE sēar (adj.), sēarian (v.), f. Gmc]

search /sɜːtʃ/ v. & n. —v. **1** tr. look through or go over thoroughly to find something. **2** tr. examine or feel over (a person) to find anything concealed. **3** tr. **a** probe or penetrate into. **b** examine or question (one's mind, conscience, etc.) thoroughly. **4** intr. (often foll. by for) make a search or investigation. **5** intr. (as **searching** adj.) (of an examination) thorough; leaving no loopholes. **6** tr. (foll. by out) look probingly for; seek out. —n. **1** an act of searching. **2** an investigation. □**in search of** trying to find. **right of search** a belligerent's right to stop a neutral vessel and search it for prohibited goods. **search me!** colloq. I do not know. **search-party** a group of people organized to look for a lost person or thing. **search warrant** an official authorization to enter and search a building. □□**searchable** adj. **searcher** n. **searchingly** adv. [ME f. AF sercher, OF cerchier f. LL circare go round (as CIRCUS)]

searchlight /ˈsɜːtʃlaɪt/ n. **1** a powerful outdoor electric light with a concentrated beam that can be turned in any direction. **2** the light or beam from this.

seascape /ˈsiːskeɪp/ n. a picture or view of the sea.

seashore /ˈsiːʃɔː(r)/ n. **1** land close to or bordering on the sea. **2** Law the area between high and low water marks.

seasick /ˈsiːsɪk/ adj. suffering from sickness or nausea from the motion of a ship at sea. □□ **seasickness** n.

seaside /ˈsiːsaɪd/ n. the sea-coast, esp. as a holiday resort.

season /ˈsiːz(ə)n/ n. & v. —n. **1** each of the four divisions of the year (spring, summer, autumn, and winter) associated with a type of weather and a stage of vegetation. **2** a time of year characterized by climatic or other features (the dry season). **3 a** the time of year when a plant is mature or flowering etc. **b** the time of year when an animal breeds or is hunted. **4** a proper or suitable time. **5** a time when something is plentiful or active or in vogue. **6** (usu. prec. by the) = high season. **7** the time of year regularly devoted to an activity (the football season). **8** the time of year dedicated to social life generally (went up to London for the season). **9** a period of indefinite or varying length. **10** Brit. colloq. = season ticket. —v. **1** tr. flavour (food) with salt, herbs, etc. **2** tr. enhance with wit, excitement, etc. **3** tr. temper or moderate. **4** tr. & intr. **a** make or become suitable or in the desired condition, esp. by exposure to the air or weather; mature. **b** make or become experienced or accustomed (seasoned soldiers). □**in season 1** (of foodstuff) available in plenty and in good condition. **2** (of an animal) on heat. **3** timely. **season ticket** a ticket entitling the holder to any number of journeys, admittances, etc., in a given period. □□ **seasoner** n. [ME f. OF seson f. L satio -onis (in Rmc sense 'seed-time') f. serere sat- sow]

seasonable /ˈsiːzənəb(ə)l/ adj. **1** suitable to or usual in the season. **2** opportune. **3** meeting the needs of the occasion. □□ **seasonableness** *n.* **seasonably** *adv.*

seasonal /'si:zən(ə)l/ *adj.* of, depending on, or varying with the season. □ **seasonal affective disorder** a depressive state associated with late autumn and winter and thought to be caused by a lack of light. □□ **seasonality** /-'nælɪtɪ/ *n.* **seasonally** *adv.*

seasoning /'si:zənɪŋ/ *n.* condiments added to food.

seat /si:t/ *n. & v.* —*n.* **1** a thing made or used for sitting on; a chair, stool, saddle, etc. **2** the buttocks. **3** the part of the trousers etc. covering the buttocks. **4** the part of a chair etc. on which the sitter's weight directly rests. **5** a place for one person in a theatre, vehicle, etc. **6** the occupation of a seat. **7** esp. *Brit.* **a** the right to occupy a seat, esp. as a Member of the House of Commons. **b** a member's constituency. **8** the part of a machine that supports or guides another part. **9** a site or location of something specified (*a seat of learning*; *the seat of the emotions*). **10** a country mansion, esp. with large grounds. **11** the manner of sitting on a horse etc. —*v.tr.* **1** cause to sit. **2 a** provide sitting accommodation for (*the cinema seats 500*). **b** provide with seats. **3** (as **seated** *adj.*) sitting. **4** put or fit in position. □ **be seated** sit down. **by the seat of one's pants** *colloq.* by instinct rather than logic or knowledge. **seat-belt** a belt securing a person in the seat of a car or aircraft. **take a** (or **one's**) **seat** sit down. □□ **seatless** *adj.* [ME f. ON *sæti* (= OE *gesete* f. Gmc)]

-seater /'si:tə(r)/ *n.* (in *comb.*) having a specified number of seats (*a 16-seater bus*).

seating /'si:tɪŋ/ *n.* **1** seats collectively. **2** sitting accommodation.

SEATO /'si:təʊ/ *abbr.* South-East Asia Treaty Organization.

seaward /'si:wəd/ *adv., adj., & n.* —*adv.* (also **seawards**) towards the sea. —*adj.* going or facing towards the sea. —*n.* such a direction or position.

seaway /'si:weɪ/ *n.* **1** an inland waterway open to seagoing ships. **2** a ship's progress. **3** a ship's path across the sea.

seaweed /'si:wi:d/ *n.* any of various algae growing in the sea or on the rocks on a shore.

seaworthy /'si:wɜːðɪ/ *adj.* (esp. of a ship) fit to put to sea. □□ **seaworthiness** *n.*

sebaceous /sɪ'beɪʃəs/ *adj.* fatty; of or relating to tallow or fat. □ **sebaceous gland** (or **follicle** or **duct**) a gland etc. secreting or conveying oily matter to lubricate the skin and hair. [L *sebaceus* f. *sebum* tallow]

seborrhoea /ˌsebə'rɪə/ *n.* (*US* **seborrhea**) excessive discharge of sebum from the sebaceous glands. □□ **seborrhoeic** *adj.* [SEBUM after *gonorrhoea* etc.]

sebum /'si:bəm/ *n.* the oily secretion of the sebaceous glands. [mod.L f. L *sebum* grease]

Sec. *abbr.* secretary.

sec /sek/ *adj.* (of wine) dry. [F f. L *siccus*]

sec[1] *abbr.* secant.

sec[2] /sek/ *n. colloq.* (in phrases) a second (of time). [abbr.]

sec. *abbr.* second(s).

secant /'si:kənt, 'se-/ *adj. & n. Math.* —*adj.* cutting (*secant line*). —*n.* **1** a line cutting a curve at one or more points. **2** the ratio of the hypotenuse to the shorter side adjacent to an acute angle (in a right-angled triangle). ¶ Abbr.: **sec.** [F *sécant(e)* f. L *secare secant-* cut]

secateurs /ˌsekə'tɜːz/ *n.pl.* esp. *Brit.* a pair of pruning clippers for use with one hand. [F *sécateur* cutter, irreg. f. L *secare* cut]

secco /'sekəʊ/ *n.* the technique of painting on dry plaster with pigments mixed in water. [It., = dry, f. L *siccus*]

secede /sɪ'si:d/ *v.intr.* (usu. foll. by *from*) withdraw formally from membership of a political federation or a religious body. □□ **seceder** *n.* [L *secedere secess-* (as SE-, *cedere* go)]

secession /sɪ'seʃ(ə)n/ *n.* **1** the act or an instance of

seceding. **2** (**Secession**) *hist.* the withdrawal of eleven southern States from the US Union in 1860, leading to the Civil War. □□ **secessional** *adj.* **secessionism** *n.* **secessionist** *n.* [F *sécession* or L *secessio* (as SECEDE)]

seclude /sɪ'klu:d/ *v.tr.* (also *refl.*) **1** keep (a person or place) retired or away from company. **2** (esp. as **secluded** *adj.*) hide or screen from view. [ME f. L *secludere seclus-* (as SE-, *claudere* shut)]

seclusion /sɪ'klu:ʒ(ə)n/ *n.* **1** a secluded state; retirement, privacy. **2** a secluded place. □□ **seclusionist** *n.* **seclusive** /-sɪv/ *adj.* [med.L *seclusio* (as SECLUDE)]

second[1] /'sekənd/ *n., adj., & v.* —*n.* **1** the position in a sequence corresponding to that of the number 2 in the sequence 1-2. **2** something occupying this position. **3** the second person etc. in a race or competition. **4** *Mus.* **a** an interval or chord spanning two consecutive notes in the diatonic scale (e.g. C to D). **b** a note separated from another by this interval. **5** = *second gear.* **6** another person or thing in addition to one previously mentioned or considered (*the policeman was then joined by a second*). **7** (in *pl.*) **a** goods of a second or inferior quality. **b** coarse flour, or bread made from it. **8** (in *pl.*) *colloq.* **a** a second helping of food at a meal. **b** the second course of a meal. **9** an attendant assisting a combatant in a duel, boxing-match, etc. **10 a** a place in the second class of an examination. **b** a person having this. —*adj.* **1** that is the second; next after first. **2** additional, further; other besides one previously mentioned or considered (*ate a second cake*). **3** subordinate in position or importance etc.; inferior. **4** *Mus.* performing a lower or subordinate part (*second violins*). **5** such as to be comparable to; closely reminiscent of (*a second Callas*). —*v.tr.* **1** supplement, support; back up. **2** formally support or endorse (a nomination or resolution etc., or its proposer). □ **at second hand** by hearsay, not direct observation etc. **in the second place** as a second consideration etc. **second advent** a supposed return of Christ to earth. **second ballot** a deciding ballot between candidates coming first (without an absolute majority) and second in a previous ballot. **second-best** *adj.* next after best. —*n.* a less adequate or desirable alternative. **second cause** *Logic* a cause that is itself caused. **second chamber** the upper house of a bicameral parliament. **second class** the second-best group or category, esp. of hotel or train accommodation or (in the UK) of postal services. **second-class** *adj.* **1** of or belonging to the second class. **2** inferior in quality, status, etc. (*second-class citizens*). —*adv.* by second-class post, train, etc. (*travelled second-class*). **second coming** *Theol.* the second advent of Christ on earth. **second cousin** see COUSIN. **second-degree** *Med.* denoting burns that cause blistering but not permanent scars. **second fiddle** see FIDDLE. **second floor 1** *Brit.* the floor two levels above the ground floor. **2** *US* the floor above the ground floor. **second gear** the second (and next to lowest) in a sequence of gears. **second-generation** denoting the offspring of a first generation, esp. of immigrants. **second-guess** *colloq.* **1** anticipate or predict by guesswork. **2** judge or criticize with hindsight. **second honeymoon** a holiday like a honeymoon, taken by a couple after some years of marriage. **second in command** the officer next in rank to the commanding or chief officer. **second lieutenant** an army officer next below lieutenant or *US* first lieutenant. **second name** a surname. **second nature** (often foll. by *to*) an acquired tendency that has become instinctive (*is second nature to him*). **second officer** an assistant mate on a merchant ship. **second person** *Gram.* see PERSON. **second-rate** of mediocre quality; inferior. **second-rater** a person or thing that is second-rate. **second reading** a second presentation of a bill to a legislative assembly, in the UK to approve its general principles and in the US to debate committee reports.

second self a close friend or associate. **second sight** the supposed power of being able to perceive future or distant events. **second-sighted** having the gift of second sight. **second string** an alternative course of action, means of livelihood, etc., invoked if the main one is unsuccessful. **second teeth** the teeth that replace the milk teeth in a mammal. **second thoughts** a new opinion or resolution reached after further consideration. **second to none** surpassed by no other. **second wind 1** recovery of the power of normal breathing during exercise after initial breathlessness. **2** renewed energy to continue an effort. □□ **seconder** n. (esp. in sense 2 of v.). [ME f. OF f. L secundus f. sequi follow]

second² /'sekənd/ n. **1** a sixtieth of a minute of time or angular distance. ¶ Symb.: ″. **2** the SI unit of time, based on the natural periodicity of the caesium atom. ¶ Abbr.: **s**. **3** colloq. a very short time (wait a second). □**second hand** an extra hand in some watches and clocks, recording seconds. [F f. med.L secunda (minuta) secondary (minute)]

second³ /sɪ'kɒnd/ v.tr. Brit. transfer (a military officer or other official or worker) temporarily to other employment or to another position. □□ **secondment** n. [F en second in the second rank (of officers)]

secondary /'sekəndərɪ/ adj. & n. —adj. **1** coming after or next below what is primary. **2** derived from or depending on or supplementing what is primary. **3** (of education, a school, etc.) for those who have had primary education, usu. from 11 to 18 years. **4** Electr. **a** (of a cell or battery) having a reversible chemical reaction and therefore able to store energy. **b** denoting a device using electromagnetic induction, esp. a transformer. —n. (pl. -ies) **1** a secondary thing. **2** a secondary device or current. □**secondary colour** the result of mixing two primary colours. **secondary feather** a feather growing from the second joint of a bird's wing. **secondary picketing** the picketing of premises of a firm not otherwise involved in the dispute in question. **secondary planet** a satellite of a planet (cf. primary planet). **secondary sexual characteristics** those distinctive of one sex but not directly related to reproduction. □□ **secondarily** adv. **secondariness** n. [ME f. L secundarius (as SECOND¹)]

seconde /sə'kɔ̃d/ n. Fencing the second of eight parrying positions. [F, fem. of second SECOND¹]

second-hand /ˌsekənd'hænd/ adj. & adv. —adj. /also 'sek-/ **1 a** (of goods) having had a previous owner; not new. **b** (of a shop etc.) where such goods can be bought. **2** (of information etc.) accepted on another's authority and not from original investigation. —adv. **1** on a second-hand basis. **2** at second hand; not directly.

secondly /'sekəndlɪ/ adv. **1** furthermore; in the second place. **2** as a second item.

secondo /sɪ'kɒndəʊ/ n. (pl. **secondi** /-dɪ/) Mus. the second or lower part in a duet etc. [It.]

secrecy /'si:krɪsɪ/ n. **1** the keeping of secrets as a fact, habit, or faculty. **2** a state in which all information is withheld (was done in great secrecy). □**sworn to secrecy** having promised to keep a secret. [ME f. secretie f. obs. secre (adj.) or SECRET adj.]

secret /'si:krɪt/ adj. & n. —adj. **1** kept or meant to be kept private, unknown, or hidden from all or all but a few. **2** acting or operating secretly. **3** fond of, prone to, or able to preserve secrecy. **4** (of a place) hidden, completely secluded. —n. **1** a thing kept or meant to be kept secret. **2** a thing known only to a few. **3** a mystery. **4** a valid but not commonly known or recognized method of achieving or maintaining something (what's their secret?; correct breathing is the secret of good health). **5** RC Ch. a prayer concluding the offertory of the mass. □**in secret** secretly. **in** (or **in on**) **the secret** among the number of those who know it. **keep a secret** not reveal it. **secret agent** a spy acting for a country. **secret ballot** a

ballot in which votes are cast in secret. **secret police** a police force operating in secret for political purposes. **secret service** a government department concerned with espionage. **secret society** a society whose members are sworn to secrecy about it. □□ **secretly** adv. [ME f. OF f. L secretus (adj.) separate, set apart f. secernere secret- (as SE-, cernere sift)]

secretaire /ˌsekrɪ'teə(r)/ n. an escritoire. [F (as SECRETARY)]

secretariat /ˌsekrə'teərɪət/ n. **1** a permanent administrative office or department, esp. a governmental one. **2** its members or premises. **3** the office of secretary. [F secrétariat f. med.L secretariatus (as SECRETARY)]

secretary /'sekrɪtərɪ, 'sekrətrɪ/ n. (pl. -ies) **1** a person employed by an individual or in an office etc. to assist with correspondence, keep records, make appointments, etc. **2** an official appointed by a society etc. to conduct its correspondence, keep its records, etc. **3** (in the UK) the principal assistant of a government minister, ambassador, etc. □**secretary bird** a long-legged snake-eating African bird, Sagittarius serpentarius, with a crest likened to a quill pen stuck over a writer's ear. **Secretary-General** the principal administrator of an organization. **Secretary of State 1** (in the UK) the head of a major government department. **2** (in the US) the chief government official responsible for foreign affairs. □□ **secretarial** /-'teərɪəl/ adj. **secretaryship** n. [ME f. LL secretarius (as SECRET)]

secrete¹ /sɪ'kri:t/ v.tr. Biol. (of a cell, organ, etc.) produce by secretion. □□ **secretor** n. **secretory** adj. [back-form. f. SECRETION]

secrete² /sɪ'kri:t/ v.tr. conceal; put into hiding. [obs. secret (v.) f. SECRET]

secretion /sɪ'kri:ʃ(ə)n/ n. **1** Biol. **a** a process by which substances are produced and discharged from a cell for a function in the organism or for excretion. **b** the secreted substance. **2** the act or an instance of concealing (the secretion of stolen goods). [F sécrétion or L secretio separation (as SECRET)]

secretive /'si:krɪtɪv/ adj. inclined to make or keep secrets; uncommunicative. □□ **secretively** adv. **secretiveness** n. [back-form. f. secretiveness after F secrétivité (as SECRET)]

sect /sekt/ n. **1 a** a body of people subscribing to religious doctrines usu. different from those of an established Church from which they have separated. **b** usu. derog. a nonconformist or other Church. **c** a party or faction in a religious body. **d** a religious denomination. **2** the followers of a particular philosopher or philosophy, or school of thought in politics etc. [ME f. OF secte or L secta f. the stem of sequi secut- follow]

sect. abbr. section.

sectarian /sek'teərɪən/ adj. & n. —adj. **1** of or concerning a sect. **2** bigoted or narrow-minded in following the doctrines of one's sect. —n. **1** a member of a sect. **2** a bigot. □□ **sectarianism** n. **sectarianize** v.tr. (also -ise). [SECTARY]

sectary /'sektərɪ/ n. (pl. -ies) a member of a religious or political sect. [med.L sectarius adherent (as SECT)]

section /'sekʃ(ə)n/ n. & v. —n. **1** a part cut off or separated from something. **2** each of the parts into which a thing is divided (actually or conceptually) or divisible or out of which a structure can be fitted together. **3** a distinct group or subdivision of a larger body of people (the wind section of an orchestra). **4** a subdivision of a book, document, statute, etc. **5** US **a** an area of land. **b** one square mile of land. **c** a particular district of a town (residential section). **6** a subdivision of an army platoon. **7** esp. Surgery a separation by cutting. **8** Biol. a thin slice of tissue etc., cut off for microscopic examination. **9 a** the cutting of a solid by or along a plane. **b** the resulting figure or the area of this. **10** a representation of the internal structure of something as if cut across along a vertical or horizontal plane. **11** Biol. a group, esp.

b but d dog f few g get h he j yes k cat l leg m man n no p pen r red s sit t top v voice

a subgenus. —*v.tr.* **1** arrange in or divide into sections. **2** *Brit.* cause (a person) to be compulsorily committed to a psychiatric hospital in accordance with a section of a mental health act. **3** *Biol.* cut into thin slices for microscopic examination. □ **section-mark** the sign (§) used as a reference mark to indicate the start of a section of a book etc. [F *section* or L *sectio* f. *secare sect-* cut]

sectional /'sekʃən(ə)l/ *adj.* **1** relating to a section, esp. of a community. **b** partisan. **2** made in sections. **3** local rather than general. □□ **sectionalism** *n.* **sectionalist** *n. & adj.* **sectionalize** *v.tr.* (also **-ise**). **sectionally** *adv.*

sector /'sektə(r)/ *n.* **1** a distinct part or branch of an enterprise, or of society, the economy, etc. **2** *Mil.* a subdivision of an area for military operations, controlled by one commander or headquarters. **3** the plane figure enclosed by two radii of a circle, ellipse, etc., and the arc between them. **4** a mathematical instrument consisting of two arms hinged at one end and marked with sines, tangents, etc., for making diagrams etc. □□ **sectoral** *adj.* [LL, techn. use of L *sector* cutter (as SECTION)]

sectorial /sek'tɔːrɪəl/ *adj.* **1** of or like a sector or sectors. **2** = CARNASSIAL.

secular /'sekjʊlə(r)/ *adj. & n.* —*adj.* **1** concerned with the affairs of this world; not spiritual or sacred. **2** (of education etc.) not concerned with religion or religious belief. **3 a** not ecclesiastical or monastic. **b** (of clergy) not bound by a religious rule. **4** occurring once in an age or century. **5** lasting for or occurring over an indefinitely long time. —*n.* a secular priest. □ **secular variation** *Astron.* variation compensated over a long period of time. □□ **secularism** *n.* **secularist** *n.* **secularity** /-'lærɪtɪ/ *n.* **secularize** *v.tr.* (also **-ise**). **secularization** /-'zeɪʃ(ə)n/ *n.* **secularly** *adv.* [ME (in senses 1–3 f. OF *seculer*) f. L *saecularis* f. *saeculum* generation, age]

secund /sɪ'kʌnd/ *adj. Bot.* arranged on one side only (as the flowers of lily of the valley). □□ **secundly** *adv.* [L *secundus* (as SECOND)]

secure /sɪ'kjʊə(r)/ *adj. & v.* —*adj.* **1** untroubled by danger or fear. **2** safe against attack: impregnable. **3** reliable; certain not to fail (*the pain is secure*). **4** fixed or fastened so as not to give way or get loose or be lost (*made the door secure*). **5 a** (foll. by *of*) certain to achieve (*secure of victory*). **b** (foll. by *against, from*) safe, protected (*secure against attack*). —*v.tr.* **1** make secure or safe; fortify. **2** fasten, close, or confine securely. **3** succeed in obtaining or achieving (*have secured front seats*). **4** guarantee against loss (*a loan secured by property*). **5** compress (a blood-vessel) to prevent bleeding. □ **secure arms** *Mil.* hold a rifle with the muzzle downward and the lock in the armpit to guard it from rain. □□ **securable** *adj.* **securely** *adv.* **securement** *n.* [L *securus* (as SE-, *cura* care)]

security /sɪ'kjʊərɪtɪ/ *n.* (*pl.* **-ies**) **1** a secure condition or feeling. **2** a thing that guards or guarantees. **3 a** the safety of a State, company, etc., against espionage, theft, or other danger. **b** an organization for ensuring this. **4** a thing deposited or pledged as a guarantee of the fulfilment of an undertaking or the payment of a loan, to be forfeited in case of default. **5** (often in *pl.*) a certificate attesting credit or the ownership of stock, bonds, etc. □ **on security of** using as a guarantee. **security blanket 1** an official sanction on information in the interest of security. **2** a blanket or other familiar object given as a comfort to a child. **Security Council** a permanent body of the United Nations seeking to maintain peace and security. **security guard** a person employed to protect the security of buildings, vehicles, etc. **security risk** a person whose presence may threaten security. [ME f. OF *securité* or L *securitas* (as SECURE)]

sedan /sɪ'dæn/ *n.* **1** (in full **sedan chair**) an enclosed chair for conveying one person, carried between horizontal poles by two porters, common in the 17th–18th c. **2** *US* an enclosed motor car for four or more

people. [perh. alt. f. It. dial., ult. f. L *sella* saddle f. *sedēre* sit]

sedate[1] /sɪ'deɪt/ *adj.* tranquil and dignified; equable, serious. □□ **sedately** *adv.* **sedateness** *n.* [L *sedatus* past part. of *sedare* settle f. *sedēre* sit]

sedate[2] /sɪ'deɪt/ *v.tr.* put under sedation. [back-form. f. SEDATION]

sedation /sɪ'deɪʃ(ə)n/ *n.* a state of rest or sleep esp. produced by a sedative drug. [F *sédation* or L *sedatio* (as SEDATE[1])]

sedative /'sedətɪv/ *n. & adj.* —*n.* a drug, influence, etc., that tends to calm or soothe. —*adj.* calming, soothing; inducing sleep. [ME f. OF *sedatif* or med.L *sedativus* (as SEDATE[1])]

sedentary /'sedəntərɪ/ *adj.* **1** sitting (*a sedentary posture*). **2** (of work etc.) characterized by much sitting and little physical exercise. **3** (of a person) spending much time seated. **4** *Zool.* not migratory, free-swimming, etc. □□ **sedentarily** *adv.* **sedentariness** *n.* [F *sédentaire* or L *sedentarius* f. *sedēre* sit]

Seder /'seɪdə(r)/ *n.* the ritual for the first night or first two nights of the Passover. [Heb. *sēḏer* order]

sederunt /sɪ'deərənt/ *n. Sc.* a sitting of an ecclesiastical assembly or other body. [L, = (the following persons) sat f. *sedēre* sit]

sedge /sedʒ/ *n.* **1** any grasslike plant of the genus *Carex* with triangular stems, usu. growing in wet areas. **2** an expanse of this plant. □ **sedge-warbler** (or **-wren**) a small warbler, *Acrocephalus schoenobaenus*, that breeds in sedge. □□ **sedgy** *adj.* [OE *secg* f. Gmc]

sedile /sɪ'daɪlɪ/ *n.* (*pl.* **sedilia** /-'dɪlɪə/) (usu. in *pl.*) *Eccl.* each of usu. three stone seats for priests in the south wall of a chancel, often canopied and decorated. [L, = seat f. *sedēre* sit]

sediment /'sedɪmənt/ *n.* **1** matter that settles to the bottom of a liquid; dregs. **2** *Geol.* matter that is carried by water or wind and deposited on the surface of the land, and may in time become consolidated into rock. □□ **sedimentary** /-'mentərɪ/ *adj.* **sedimentation** /-'teɪʃ(ə)n/ *n.* [F *sédiment* or L *sedimentum* (as SEDILE)]

sedition /sɪ'dɪʃ(ə)n/ *n.* **1** conduct or speech inciting to rebellion or a breach of public order. **2** agitation against the authority of a State. □□ **seditious** *adj.* **seditiously** *adv.* [ME f. OF *sedition* or L *seditio* f. *sed-* = SE- + *ire* it- go]

seduce /sɪ'djuːs/ *v.tr.* **1** tempt or entice into sexual activity or into wrongdoing. **2** coax or lead astray; tempt (*seduced by the smell of coffee*). □□ **seducer** *n.* **seducible** *adj.* [L *seducere seduct-* (as SE-, *ducere* lead)]

seduction /sɪ'dʌkʃ(ə)n/ *n.* **1** the act or an instance of seducing; the process of being seduced. **2** something that tempts or allures. [F *séduction* or L *seductio* (as SEDUCE)]

seductive /sɪ'dʌktɪv/ *adj.* tending to seduce; alluring, enticing. □□ **seductively** *adv.* **seductiveness** *n.* [SEDUCTION after *inductive* etc.]

seductress /sɪ'dʌktrɪs/ *n.* a female seducer. [obs. *seductor* male seducer (as SEDUCE)]

sedulous /'sedjʊləs/ *adj.* **1** persevering, diligent, assiduous. **2** (of an action etc.) deliberately and consciously continued; painstaking. □□ **sedulity** /sɪ'djuːlɪtɪ/ *n.* **sedulously** *adv.* **sedulousness** *n.* [L *sedulus* zealous]

sedum /'siːdəm/ *n.* any plant of the genus *Sedum*, with fleshy leaves and star-shaped yellow, pink, or white flowers, e.g. stonecrop. [L, = houseleek]

see[1] /siː/ *v.* (*past* **saw** /sɔː/; *past part.* **seen** /siːn/) **1** *tr.* discern by use of the eyes; observe; look at (*can you see that spider?; saw him fall over*). **2** *intr.* have or use the power of discerning objects with the eyes (*sees best at night*). **3** *tr.* discern mentally; understand (*I see what you mean; could not see the joke*). **4** *tr.* watch; be a spectator of (a film, game, etc.). **5** *tr.* ascertain or establish by inquiry or research or reflection (*I will see if the door is open*). **6** *tr.* consider; deduce from observation (*I see that you are a brave man*). **7** *tr.* contemplate; foresee mentally (*we saw that no good would come of it*; *can see myself doing this job indefinitely*). **8** *tr.* look at for information (usu. in *imper.* as a direction in or to a book: *see page 15*). **9** *tr.* meet or be near and recognize (*I saw your mother in town*). **10** *tr.* **a** meet socially (*sees her sister most weeks*). **b** meet regularly as a boyfriend or girlfriend; court (*is still seeing that tall man*). **11** *tr.* give an interview to (*the doctor will see you now*). **12** *tr.* visit to consult (*went to see the doctor*). **13** *tr.* find out or learn, esp. from a visual source (*I see the match has been cancelled*). **14** *intr.* reflect; consider further; wait until one knows more (*we shall have to see*). **15** *tr.* interpret or have an opinion of (*I see things differently now*). **16** *tr.* experience; have presented to one's attention (*I never thought I would see this day*). **17** *tr.* recognize as acceptable; foresee (*do you see your daughter marrying this man?*). **18** *tr.* observe without interfering (*stood by and saw them squander my money*). **19** *tr.* find attractive (*can't think what she sees in him*). **20** *intr.* (usu. foll. by *to*, or *that* + infin.) make provision for; ensure; attend to (*shall see to your request immediately*; *see that he gets home safely*) (cf. *see to it*). **21** *tr.* escort or conduct (to a place etc.) (*saw them home*). **22** *tr.* be a witness of (an event etc.) (*see the New Year in*). **23** *tr.* supervise (an action etc.) (*will stay and see the doors locked*). **24** *tr.* **a** (in gambling, esp. poker) equal (a bet). **b** equal the bet of (a player), esp. to see the player's cards. □**as far as I can see** to the best of my understanding or belief. **as I see it** in my opinion. **do you see?** do you understand? **has seen better days** has declined from former prosperity, good condition, etc. **I'll be seeing you** *colloq.* an expression on parting. **I see** I understand (referring to an explanation etc.). **let me see** an appeal for time to think before speaking etc. **see about** attend to. **see after** 1 take care of. 2 = *see about*. **see the back of** *colloq.* be rid of (an unwanted person or thing). **see a person damned first** *colloq.* refuse categorically and with hostility to do what a person wants. **see eye to eye** see EYE. **see fit** see FIT¹. **see here!** = *look here*. **see into** investigate. **see life** gain experience of the world, often by enjoying oneself. **see the light** 1 realize one's mistakes etc. 2 suddenly see the way to proceed. 3 undergo religious conversion. **see the light of day** (usu. with *neg.*) come into existence. **see off** 1 be present at the departure of (a person) (*saw them off at Heathrow*). 2 *colloq.* ward off, get the better of (*managed to see off an investigation into their working methods*). **see out** 1 accompany out of a building etc. 2 finish (a project etc.) completely. 3 remain awake, alive, etc., until the end of (a period). 4 last longer than; outlive. **see over** inspect; tour and examine. **see reason** see REASON. **see red** become suddenly enraged. **see a person right** make sure that a person is rewarded, safe, etc. **see service** see SERVICE. **see stars** *colloq.* see lights before one's eyes as a result of a blow on the head. **see things** have hallucinations or false imaginings. **see through** 1 not be deceived by; detect the true nature of. 2 penetrate visually. **see-through** *adj.* (esp. of clothing) translucent. **see a person through** support a person during a difficult time. **see a thing through** persist with it until it is completed. **see to** it (foll. by *that* + clause) ensure (*see to it that I am not disturbed*) (cf. sense 20 of *v.*). **see one's way clear to** feel able or entitled to. **see the world** see WORLD. **see you** (or **see you later**) *colloq.* an expression on parting. **we shall see** 1 let us await the outcome. 2 a formula for declining to act at once. **will see about it** a formula for declining to act at once. **you see** 1 you understand. 2 you will understand when I explain. □□**seeable** *adj.* [OE *sēon* f. Gmc]

see² /siː/ *n.* 1 the area under the authority of a bishop or archbishop, a diocese (*the see of Norwich*). 2 the

office or jurisdiction of a bishop or archbishop (*fill a vacant see*). □**See of Rome** the papacy, the Holy See. [ME f. AF *se(d)* ult. f. L *sedes* seat f. *sedēre* sit]

seed /siːd/ *n.* & *v.* —*n.* 1 a a flowering plant's unit of reproduction (esp. in the form of grain) capable of developing into another such plant. **b** seeds collectively, esp. as collected for sowing (*is full of seed*; *to be kept for seed*). 2 a semen. **b** milt. 3 (foll. by *of*) prime cause, beginning, germ (*seeds of doubt*). 4 *archaic* offspring, progeny, descendants (*the seed of Abraham*). 5 *Sport* a seeded player. 6 a small seedlike container for the application of radium etc. 7 a seed crystal. —*v.* 1 *tr.* **a** place seeds in. **b** sprinkle with or as with seed. 2 *intr.* sow seeds. 3 *intr.* produce or drop seed. 4 *tr.* remove seeds from (fruit etc.). 5 *tr.* place a crystal or crystalline substance in (a solution etc.) to cause crystallization or condensation (esp. in a cloud to produce rain). 6 *tr.* *Sport* **a** assign to (a strong competitor in a knockout competition) a position in an ordered list so that strong competitors do not meet each other in early rounds (*is seeded seventh*). **b** arrange (the order of play) in this way. 7 *intr.* go to seed. □**go** (or **run**) **to seed** 1 cease flowering as seed develops. 2 become degenerate, unkempt, ineffective, etc. **raise up seed** *archaic* beget children. **seed-bed** 1 a bed of fine soil in which to sow seeds. 2 a place of development. **seed-cake** cake containing whole seeds esp. of caraway as flavouring. **seed-coat** the outer integument of a seed. **seed-corn** 1 good quality corn kept for seed. 2 assets reused for future profit or benefit. **seed crystal** a crystal used to initiate crystallization. **seed-eater** a bird (esp. a finch) living mainly on seeds. **seed-fish** a fish that is ready to spawn. **seed-leaf** a cotyledon. **seed-lip** a basket for seed in sowing by hand. **seed money** money allocated to initiate a project. **seed-pearl** a very small pearl. **seed-plot** a place of development. **seed-potato** a potato kept for seed. **seed-time** the sowing season. **seed-vessel** a pericarp. □□**seedless** *adj.* [OE *sǣd* f. Gmc, rel. to sow¹]

seeder /ˈsiːdə(r)/ *n.* 1 a person or thing that seeds. 2 a machine for sowing seed, esp. a drill. 3 an apparatus for seeding raisins etc. 4 *Brit.* a spawning fish.

seedling /ˈsiːdlɪŋ/ *n.* a young plant, esp. one raised from seed and not from a cutting etc.

seedsman /ˈsiːdzmən/ *n.* (*pl.* **-men**) a dealer in seeds.

seedy /ˈsiːdɪ/ *adj.* (**seedier, seediest**) 1 full of seed. 2 going to seed. 3 shabby-looking, in worn clothes. 4 *colloq.* unwell. □□**seedily** *adv.* **seediness** *n.*

seeing /ˈsiːɪŋ/ *conj.* & *n.* —*conj.* (usu. foll. by *that* + clause) considering that, inasmuch as, because (*seeing that you do not know it yourself*). —*n.* *Astron.* the quality of observed images as determined by atmospheric conditions.

seek /siːk/ *v.* (*past* and *past part.* **sought** /sɔːt/) 1 a *tr.* make a search or inquiry for. **b** *intr.* (foll. by *for*, *after*) make a search or inquiry. 2 *tr.* a try or want to find or get. **b** ask for; request (*sought help from him*; *seeks my aid*). 3 *tr.* (foll. by *to* + infin.) endeavour or try. 4 *tr.* make for or resort to (a place or person, for advice, health, etc.) (*sought his bed*; *sought a fortune-teller*; *sought the shore*). 5 *tr.* *archaic* aim at, attempt. 6 *intr.* (foll. by *to*) *archaic* resort. □**seek dead** an order to a retriever to find killed game. **seek out** 1 search for and find. 2 single out for companionship, etc. **sought-after** much in demand; generally desired or courted. **to seek** (or **much to seek** or **far to seek**) deficient, lacking, or not yet found (*the reason is not far to seek*; *an efficient leader is yet to seek*). □□**seeker** *n.* (also in *comb.*). [OE *sēcan* f. Gmc]

seel /siːl/ *v.tr.* *archaic* close (a person's eyes). [obs. *sile* f. F *ciller*, *siller*, or med.L *ciliare* f. L *cilium* eyelid]

seem /siːm/ *v.intr.* 1 give the impression or sensation of being (*seems ridiculous*; *seems certain to win*). 2 (foll. by *to* + infin.) appear or be perceived or ascertained (*he seems to be breathing*; *they seem to have left*). □**can't seem to** *colloq.* seem unable to. **do not seem to** *colloq.* somehow do not (*I do not seem to like him*). **it seems** (or **would seem**) (often foll. by *that* + clause) it appears to be true or the fact (in a hesitant, guarded, or ironical statement). [ME f. ON *sœma* honour f. *sœmr* fitting]

seeming[1] /ˈsiːmɪŋ/ *adj.* **1** apparent but perhaps not real (*with seeming sincerity*). **2** apparent only; ostensible (*the seeming and the real*; *seemingvirtuous*). □□**seemingly** *adv.*

seeming[2] /ˈsiːmɪŋ/ *n. literary* **1** appearance, aspect. **2** deceptive appearance.

seemly /ˈsiːmlɪ/ *adj.* (**seemlier**, **seemliest**) conforming to propriety or good taste; decorous, suitable. □□**seemliness** *n.* [ME f. ON *sœmiligr* (as SEEM)]

seen *past part.* of SEE[1].

seep /siːp/ *v. & n.* —*v.intr.* ooze out; percolate slowly. —*n.* US a place where petroleum etc. oozes slowly out of the ground. [perh. dial. form of OE *sipian* to soak]

seepage /ˈsiːpɪdʒ/ *n.* **1** the act of seeping. **2** the quantity that seeps out.

seer[1] /ˈsiːə(r), sɪə(r)/ *n.* **1** a person who sees. **2** a prophet; a person who sees visions; a person of supposed supernatural insight esp. as regards the future. [ME f. SEE[1]]

seer[2] /sɪə(r)/ *n.* an Indian (varying) measure of weight (about one kilogram) or liquid measure (about one litre). [Hindi *ser*]

seersucker /ˈsɪəˌsʌkə(r)/ *n.* material of linen, cotton, etc., with a puckered surface. [Pers. *šir o šakar*, lit. 'milk and sugar']

see-saw /ˈsiːsɔː/ *n.*, *v.*, *adj.*, & *adv.* —*n.* **1 a** a device consisting of a long plank balanced on a central support for children to sit on at each end and move up and down by pushing the ground with their feet. **b** a game played on this. **2** an up-and-down or to-and-fro motion. **3** a contest in which the advantage repeatedly changes from one side to the other. —*v.intr.* **1** play on a see-saw. **2** move up and down as on a see-saw. **3** vacillate in policy, emotion, etc. —*adj. & adv.* with up-and-down or backward-and-forward motion (*see-saw motion*). □**go see-saw** vacillate or alternate. [redupl. of SAW[1]]

seethe /siːð/ *v.* **1** *intr.* boil, bubble over. **2** *intr.* be very agitated, esp. with anger (*seething with discontent*; *I was seething inwardly*). **3** *tr. & intr. archaic* cook by boiling. □□**seethingly** *adv.* [OE *sēothan* f. Gmc]

segment /ˈsegmənt/ *n. & v.* —*n.* **1** each of several parts into which a thing is or can be divided or marked off. **2** *Geom.* a part of a figure cut off by a line or plane intersecting it, esp.: **a** the part of a circle enclosed between an arc and a chord. **b** the part of a line included between two points. **c** the part of a sphere cut off by any plane not passing through the centre. **3** the smallest distinct part of a spoken utterance. **4** *Zool.* each of the longitudinal sections of the body of certain animals (e.g. worms). —*v.* /usu. -ˈment/ **1** *intr. & tr.* divide into segments. **2** *intr. Biol.* (of a cell) undergo cleavage or divide into many cells. □□**segmental** /-ˈment(ə)l/ *adj.* **segmentalize** /-ˈmentəˌlaɪz/ *v.tr.* (also **-ise**). **segmentalization** /-ˌmentəlaɪˈzeɪʃ(ə)n/ *n.* **segmentally** /-ˈmentəlɪ/ *adv.* **segmentary** *adj.* **segmentation** /-ˈteɪʃ(ə)n/ *n.* [L *segmentum* f. *secare* cut]

sego /ˈsiːgəʊ/ *n.* (*pl.* **-os**) (in full **sego lily**) a N. American plant, *Calochortus nuttallii*, with green and white bell-shaped flowers. [Paiute]

segregate[1] /ˈsegrɪˌgeɪt/ *v.* **1** *tr.* put apart from the rest; isolate. **2** *tr.* enforce racial segregation on (persons) or in (a community etc.). **3** *intr.* separate from a mass and collect together. **4** *intr. Biol.* (of alleles) separate into dominant and recessive groups.

□□**segregable** /-gəb(ə)l/ *adj.* **segregative** *adj.* [L *segregare* (as SE-, *grex gregis* flock)]

segregate[2] /ˈsegrɪgət/ *adj.* **1** *Zool.* simple or solitary, not compound. **2** *archaic* set apart, separate. [L *segregatus* past part. (as SEGREGATE[1])]

segregation /ˌsegrɪˈgeɪʃ(ə)n/ *n.* **1** enforced separation of racial groups in a community etc. **2** the act or an instance of segregating; the state of being segregated. □□**segregational** *adj.* **segregationist** *n. & adj.* [LL *segregatio* (as SEGREGATE[1])]

segue /ˈsegweɪ/ *v. & n. esp. Mus.* —*v.intr.* (**segues**, **segued**, **seguing**) (usu. foll. by *into*) go on without a pause. —*n.* an uninterrupted transition from one song or melody to another. [It., = follows]

seguidilla /ˌsegɪˈdriljə/ *n.* **1** a Spanish dance in triple time. **2** the music for this. [Sp. f. *seguida* following f. *seguir* follow]

Sehnsucht /ˈzeɪnzuːxt/ *n.* yearning, wistful longing. [G]

sei /seɪ/ *n.* a small rorqual, *Balaenoptera borealis*. [Norw. *sejhval* sei whale]

seicento /seɪˈtʃentəʊ/ *n.* the style of Italian art and literature of the 17th c. □□**seicentist** *n.* **seicentoist** *n.* [It., = 600, used with ref. to the years 1600-99]

seiche /seɪʃ/ *n.* a fluctuation in the water-level of a lake etc., usu. caused by changes in barometric pressure. [Swiss F]

Seidlitz powder /ˈsedlɪts/ *n.* (US **Seidlitz powders**) a laxative medicine of two powders mixed separately with water and then poured together to effervesce. [named with ref. to the mineral water of *Seidlitz* in Bohemia]

seif /siːf, seɪf/ *n.* (in full **seif dune**) a sand-dune in the form of a long narrow ridge. [Arab. *saif* sword (from its shape)]

seigneur /seɪˈnjɜː(r)/ *n.* (also **seignior** /ˈseɪnjə(r)/) a feudal lord; the lord of a manor. □**grand seigneur** /grɑ̃/ a person of high rank or noble presence. □□**seigneurial** *adj.* **seigniorial** /-ˈnjɔːrɪəl/ *adj.* [ME f. OF *seigneur*, *seignor* f. L SENIOR]

seigniorage /ˈseɪnjərɪdʒ/ *n.* (also **seignorage**) **1 a** a profit made by issuing currency, esp. by issuing coins rated above their intrinsic value. **b** *hist.* the Crown's right to a percentage on bullion brought to a mint for coining. **2** *hist.* something claimed by a sovereign or feudal superior as a prerogative. [ME f. OF *seignorage*, *seigneurage* (as SEIGNEUR)]

seigniory /ˈseɪnjərɪ/ *n.* (*pl.* **-ies**) **1** lordship, sovereign authority. **2** (also **seigneury**) a seigneur's domain. [ME f. OF *seignorie* (as SEIGNEUR)]

seine /seɪn/ *n. & v.* —*n.* (also **seine-net**) a fishing-net for encircling fish, with floats at the top and weights at the bottom edge, and usu. hauled ashore. —*v.intr. & tr.* fish or catch with a seine. □□**seiner** *n.* [ME f. OF *saïne*, & OE *segne* f. WG f. L *sagena* f. Gk *sagēnē*]

seise var. of SEIZE 9.

seisin /ˈsiːzɪn/ *n.* (also **seizin**) *Law* **1** possession of land by freehold. **2** the act of taking such possession. **3** what is so held. [ME f. AF *sesine*, OF *seisine*, *saisine* (as SEIZE)]

seismic /ˈsaɪzmɪk/ *adj.* of or relating to an earthquake or earthquakes. □□**seismal** *adj.* **seismical** *adj.* **seismically** *adv.* [Gk *seismos* earthquake f. *seiō* shake]

seismo- /ˈsaɪzməʊ/ *comb. form* earthquake. [Gk *seismos*]

seismogram /ˈsaɪzməˌgræm/ *n.* a record given by a seismograph.

seismograph /ˈsaɪzməˌgrɑːf/ *n.* an instrument that records the force, direction, etc., of earthquakes. □□**seismographic** /-ˈgræfɪk/ *adj.* **seismographical** /-ˈgræfɪk(ə)l/ *adj.*

seismology /saɪzˈmɒlədʒɪ/ *n.* the scientific study and recording of earthquakes and related phenomena. □□**seismological** /-məˈlɒdʒɪk(ə)l/ *adj.* **seismologically** /-məˈlɒdʒɪkəlɪ/ *adv.* **seismologist** *n.*

seize /siːz/ *v.* **1** *tr.* take hold of forcibly or suddenly.

2 *tr.* take possession of forcibly (*seized the fortress*; *seized power*). **3** *tr.* take possession of (contraband goods, documents, etc.) by warrant or legal right, confiscate, impound. **4** *tr.* affect suddenly (*panic seized us*; *was seized by apoplexy*; *was seized with remorse*). **5** *tr.* take advantage of (an opportunity). **6** *tr.* comprehend quickly or clearly. **7** *intr.* (usu. foll. by *on*, *upon*) **a** take hold forcibly or suddenly. **b** take advantage eagerly (*seized on a pretext*). **8** *intr.* (usu. foll. by *up*) (of a moving part in a machine) become stuck or jammed from undue heat, friction, etc. **9** *tr.* (also **seise**) (usu. foll. by *of*) *Law* put in possession of. **10** *tr. Naut.* fasten or attach by binding with turns of yarn etc. □**seized** (or **seised**) **of 1** possessing legally. **2** aware or informed of. □□ **seizable** *adj.* **seizer** *n.* [ME f. OF *seizir*, *saisir* give seisin f. Frank. f. L *sacire* f. Gmc]

seizin var. of SEISIN.

seizing /ˈsiːzɪŋ/ *n. Naut.* a cord or cords used for seizing (see SEIZE 10).

seizure /ˈsiːʒə(r)/ *n.* **1** the act or an instance of seizing; the state of being seized. **2** a sudden attack of apoplexy etc., a stroke.

sejant /ˈsiːdʒ(ə)nt/ *adj.* (placed after noun) *Heraldry* (of an animal) sitting upright on its haunches. [properly *seiant* f. OF var. of *seant* sitting f. *seoir* f. L *sedēre* sit]

Sekt /zekt/ *n.* a German sparkling white wine. [G]

selachian /sɪˈleɪkɪən/ *n. & adj.* —*n.* any fish of the subclass Selachii, including sharks and dogfish. —*adj.* of or relating to this subclass. [mod.L *Selachii* f. Gk *selakhos* shark]

seladang /səˈlɑːdæŋ/ *n.* a Malayan gaur. [Malay]

selah /ˈsiːlə/ *int.* often used at the end of a verse in Psalms and Habakkuk, supposed to be a musical direction. [Heb. *se·lāh*]

seldom /ˈseldəm/ *adv. & adj.* —*adv.* rarely, not often. —*adj.* rare, uncommon. [OE *seldan* f. Gmc]

select /sɪˈlekt/ *v. & adj.* —*v.tr.* choose, esp. as the best or most suitable. —*adj.* **1** chosen for excellence or suitability; choice. **2** (of a society etc.) exclusive, cautious in admitting members. □**select committee** see COMMITTEE. □□ **selectable** *adj.* **selectness** *n.* [L *seligere select-* (as SE-, *legere* choose)]

selectee /sɪlekˈtiː/ *n. US* a conscript.

selection /sɪˈlekʃ(ə)n/ *n.* **1** the act or an instance of selecting; the state of being selected. **2** a selected person or thing. **3** things from which a choice may be made. **4** *Biol.* the process in which environmental and genetic influences determine which types of organism thrive better than others, regarded as a factor in evolution. □□ **selectional** *adj.* **selectionally** *adv.* [L *selectio* (as SELECT)]

selective /sɪˈlektɪv/ *adj.* **1** using or characterized by selection. **2** able to select, esp. (of a radio receiver) able to respond to a chosen frequency without interference from others. □**selective service** *US hist.* service in the armed forces under conscription. □□ **selectively** *adv.* **selectiveness** *n.* **selectivity** /ˌsɪlekˈtɪvɪtɪ, ˌsel-, ˌsiːl-/ *n.*

selector /sɪˈlektə(r)/ *n.* **1** a person who selects, esp. one who selects a representative team in a sport. **2** a device that selects, esp. a device in a vehicle that selects the required gear.

selenite /ˈselɪˌnaɪt/ *n.* a form of gypsum occurring as transparent crystals or thin plates. □□ **selenitic** /-ˈnɪtɪk/ *adj.* [L *selenites* f. Gk *selēnītēs lithos* moon-stone f. *selēnē* moon]

selenium /sɪˈliːnɪəm/ *n. Chem.* a non-metallic element occurring naturally in various metallic sulphide ores and characterized by the variation of its electrical resistivity with intensity of illumination. ¶ Symb.: **Se.** □**selenium cell** a piece of this used as a photoelectric device. □□ **selenate** /ˈselɪˌneɪt/ *n.* **selenic** /sɪˈliːnɪk/ *adj.* **selenious** *adj.* [mod.L f. Gk *selēnē* moon + -IUM]

seleno- /sɪˈliːnəʊ/ *comb. form* moon. [Gk *selēnē* moon]

selenography /ˌsiːlɪˈnɒɡrəfɪ/ *n.* the study or mapping of the moon. □□ **selenographer** *n.* **selenographic** /-nəˈɡræfɪk/ *adj.*

selenology /ˌsiːlɪˈnɒlədʒɪ/ *n.* the scientific study of the moon. □□ **selenologist** *n.*

self /self/ *n. & adj.* —*n.* (*pl.* **selves** /selvz/) **1** a person's or thing's own individuality or essence (*showed his true self*). **2** a person or thing as the object of introspection or reflexive action (*the consciousness of self*). **3 a** one's own interests or pleasure (*cares for nothing but self*). **b** concentration on these (*self is a bad guide to happiness*). **4** *Commerce* or *colloq.* myself, yourself, himself, etc. (*cheque drawn to self*; *ticket admitting self and friend*). **5** used in phrases equivalent to *myself*, *yourself*, *himself*, etc. (*his very self*; *your good selves*). **6** (*pl.* **selfs**) a flower of uniform colour, or of the natural wild colour. —*adj.* **1** of the same colour as the rest or throughout. **2** (of a flower) of the natural wild colour. **3** (of colour) uniform, the same throughout. □**one's better self** one's nobler impulses. **one's former** (or **old**) **self** oneself as one formerly was. [OE f. Gmc]

self- /self/ *comb. form* expressing reflexive action: **1** of or directed towards oneself or itself (*self-respect*; *self-cleaning*). **2** by oneself or itself, esp. without external agency (*self-evident*). **3** on, in, for, or relating to oneself or itself (*self-confident*; *self-confident*).

self-abandon /ˌselfəˈbænd(ə)n/ *n.* (also **self-abandonment**) the abandonment of oneself, esp. to passion or an impulse. □□ **self-abandoned** *adj.*

self-abasement /ˌselfəˈbeɪsmənt/ *n.* the abasement of oneself; self-humiliation; cringing.

self-abhorrence /ˌselfəbˈhɒrəns/ *n.* the abhorrence of oneself; self-hatred.

self-abnegation /ˌselfˌæbnɪˈɡeɪʃ(ə)n/ *n.* the abnegation of oneself, one's interests, needs, etc.; self-sacrifice.

self-absorption /ˌselfəbˈzɔːpʃ(ə)n/ *n.* **1** absorption in oneself. **2** *Physics* the absorption, by a body, of radiation emitted within it. □□ **self-absorbed** /-ˈzɔːbd/ *adj.*

self-abuse /ˌselfəˈbjuːs/ *n.* **1** the reviling or abuse of oneself. **2** *archaic* masturbation.

self-accusation /ˌselfˌækjuːˈzeɪʃ(ə)n/ *n.* the accusing of oneself. □□ **self-accusatory** /-əˈkjuːzətərɪ/ *adj.*

self-acting /selfˈæktɪŋ/ *adj.* acting without external influence or control; automatic. □□ **self-action** /-ˈækʃ(ə)n/ *n.* **self-activity** /-ækˈtɪvɪtɪ/ *n.*

self-addressed /ˌselfəˈdrest/ *adj.* (of an envelope etc.) having one's own address on for return communication.

self-adhesive /ˌselfədˈhiːsɪv/ *adj.* (of an envelope, label, etc.) adhesive, esp. without being moistened.

self-adjusting /ˌselfəˈdʒʌstɪŋ/ *adj.* (of machinery etc.) adjusting itself. □□ **self-adjustment** *n.*

self-admiration /selfˌædməˈreɪʃ(ə)n/ *n.* the admiration of oneself; pride; conceit.

self-advancement /ˌselfədˈvɑːnsmənt/ *n.* the advancement of oneself.

self-advertisement /ˌselfədˈvɜːtɪsmənt/ *n.* the advertising or promotion of oneself. □□ **self-advertiser** /-ˈædvəˌtaɪzə(r)/ *n.*

self-affirmation /selfˌæfəˈmeɪʃ(ə)n/ *n. Psychol.* the recognition and assertion of the existence of the conscious self.

self-aggrandizement /ˌselfəˈɡrændɪzmənt/ *n.* the act or process of enriching oneself or making oneself powerful. □□ **self-aggrandizing** /-ˈɡrændaɪzɪŋ/ *adj.*

self-analysis /ˌselfəˈnæləsɪs/ *n. Psychol.* the analysis of oneself, one's motives, character, etc. □□ **self-analysing** /-ˈænəˌlaɪzɪŋ/ *adj.*

self-appointed /ˌselfəˈpɔɪntɪd/ *adj.* designated so by oneself, not authorized by another (*a self-appointed guardian*).

self-appreciation /ˌselfəˌpriːʃɪˈeɪʃ(ə)n/ *n.* a good opinion of oneself; conceit.

self-approbation /selfˌæprəˈbeɪʃ(ə)n/ *n.* = SELF-APPROBATION.

self-approval /ˌselfəˈpruːv(ə)l/ *n.* = SELF-APPRECIATION.

self-assertion /ˌselfəˈsɜːʃ(ə)n/ *n.* the aggressive promotion of oneself, one's views, etc. □□ **self-asserting** *adj.* **self-assertive** *adj.* **self-assertiveness** *n.*

self-assurance /ˌselfəˈʃʊərəns/ *n.* confidence in one's own abilities etc. □□ **self-assured** *adj.* **self-assuredly** *adv.*

self-aware /ˌselfəˈweə(r)/ *adj.* conscious of one's character, feelings, motives, etc. □□ **self-awareness** *n.*

self-begotten /ˌselfbɪˈɡɒt(ə)n/ *adj.* produced by oneself or itself; not made externally.

self-betrayal /ˌselfbɪˈtreɪəl/ *n.* **1** the betrayal of oneself. **2** the inadvertent revelation of one's true thoughts etc.

self-binder /selfˈbaɪndə(r)/ *n.* a reaping machine with an automatic mechanism for binding the sheaves.

self-born /selfˈbɔːn/ *adj.* produced by itself or oneself; not made externally.

self-catering /selfˈkeɪtərɪŋ/ *adj.* (esp. of a holiday or holiday premises) providing rented accommodation with cooking facilities but without food.

self-censorship /selfˈsensəʃɪp/ *n.* the censoring of oneself.

self-centred /selfˈsentəd/ *adj.* preoccupied with one's own personality or affairs. □□ **self-centredly** *adv.* **self-centredness** *n.*

self-certification /ˌselfˌsɜːtɪfɪˈkeɪʃ(ə)n/ *n.* the practice by which an employee declares in writing that an absence from work was due to illness.

self-cleaning /selfˈkliːnɪŋ/ *adj.* (esp. of an oven) cleaning itself when heated etc.

self-closing /selfˈkləʊzɪŋ/ *adj.* (of a door etc.) closing automatically.

self-cocking /selfˈkɒkɪŋ/ *adj.* (of a gun) with the hammer raised by the trigger, not by hand.

self-collected /ˌselfkəˈlektɪd/ *adj.* composed, serene, self-assured.

self-coloured /selfˈkʌləd/ *adj.* **1 a** having the same colour throughout (*buttons and belt are self-coloured*). **b** (of material) natural; undyed. **2 a** (of a flower) of uniform colour. **b** having its colour unchanged by cultivation or hybridization.

self-command /selfkəˈmaːnd/ *n.* = SELF-CONTROL.

self-communion /ˌselfkəˈmjuːnɪən/ *n.* meditation upon one's own character, conduct, etc.

self-conceit /selfkənˈsiːt/ *n.* = SELF-SATISFACTION. □□ **self-conceited** *adj.*

self-condemnation /ˌselfˌkɒndemˈneɪʃ(ə)n/ *n.* **1** the blaming of oneself. **2** the inadvertent revelation of one's own sin, crime, etc. □□ **self-condemned** /-kənˈdemd/ *adj.*

self-confessed /ˌselfkənˈfest/ *adj.* openly admitting oneself to be (*a self-confessed thief*).

self-confidence /selfˈkɒnfɪd(ə)ns/ *n.* = SELF-ASSURANCE. □□ **self-confident** *adj.* **self-confidently** *adv.*

self-congratulation /ˌselfkənˌɡrætjʊˈleɪʃ(ə)n/ *n.* = SELF-SATISFACTION. □□ **self-congratulatory** /-kənˈɡrætʊlətəri/ *adj.*

self-conquest /selfˈkɒŋkwest/ *n.* the overcoming of one's worst characteristics etc.

self-conscious /selfˈkɒnʃəs/ *adj.* **1** socially inept through embarrassment or shyness. **2** *Philos.* having knowledge of one's own existence; self-contemplating. □□ **self-consciously** *adv.* **self-consciousness** *n.*

self-consistent /ˌselfkənˈsɪst(ə)nt/ *adj.* (of parts of the same whole etc.) consistent; not conflicting. □□ **self-consistency** *n.*

self-constituted /selfˈkɒnstɪˌtjuːtɪd/ *adj.* (of a person, group, etc.) assuming a function without authorization or right; self-appointed.

self-contained /selfkənˈteɪnd/ *adj.* **1** (of a person) uncommunicative; independent. **2** *Brit.* (esp. of

living-accommodation) complete in itself. □□ **self-containment** *n.*

self-contempt /ˌselfkənˈtempt/ *n.* contempt for oneself. □□ **self-contemptuous** *adj.*

self-content /ˌselfkənˈtent/ *n.* satisfaction with oneself, one's life, achievements, etc. □□ **self-contented** *adj.*

self-contradiction /selfˌkɒntrəˈdɪkʃ(ə)n/ *n.* internal inconsistency. □□ **self-contradictory** *adj.*

self-control /ˌselfkənˈtrəʊl/ *n.* the power of controlling one's external reactions, emotions, etc. □□ **self-controlled** *adj.*

self-convicted /ˌselfkənˈvɪktɪd/ *adj.* = SELF-CONDEMNED (see SELF-CONDEMNATION).

self-correcting /ˌselfkəˈrektɪŋ/ *adj.* correcting itself without external help.

self-created /ˌselfkrɪˈeɪtɪd/ *adj.* created by oneself or itself. □□ **self-creation** /-ˈeɪʃ(ə)n/ *n.*

self-critical /selfˈkrɪtɪk(ə)l/ *adj.* critical of oneself, one's abilities, etc. □□ **self-criticism** /-ˌsɪz(ə)m/ *n.*

self-deception /ˌselfdɪˈsepʃ(ə)n/ *n.* deceiving oneself esp. concerning one's true feelings etc. □□ **self-deceit** /-dɪˈsiːt/ *n.* **self-deceiver** /-dɪˈsiːvə(r)/ *n.* **self-deceiving** /-dɪˈsiːvɪŋ/ *adj.* **self-deceptive** *adj.*

self-defeating /ˌselfdɪˈfiːtɪŋ/ *adj.* (of an attempt, action, etc.) doomed to failure because of internal inconsistencies etc.

self-defence /ˌselfdɪˈfens/ *n.* **1** an aggressive act, speech, etc., intended as defence (*had to hit him in self-defence*). **2** (usu. **the noble art of self-defence**) boxing. □□ **self-defensive** *adj.*

self-delight /ˌselfdɪˈlaɪt/ *n.* delight in oneself or one's existence.

self-delusion /ˌselfdɪˈluːʒ(ə)n, -ˈljuːʒ(ə)n/ *n.* the act or an instance of deluding oneself.

self-denial /ˌselfdɪˈnaɪəl/ *n.* = SELF-ABNEGATION. □ **self-denying ordinance** *hist.* a resolution of the Long Parliament 1645 depriving Members of Parliament of civil and military office. □□ **self-denying** *adj.*

self-dependence /ˌselfdɪˈpend(ə)ns/ *adj.* dependence only on oneself or itself; independence. □□ **self-dependent** *adj.*

self-deprecation /selfˌdeprɪˈkeɪʃ(ə)n/ *n.* the act of disparaging or belittling oneself. □□ **self-deprecating** /-ˈdeprɪˌkeɪtɪŋ/ *adj.* **self-deprecatingly** /-ˈdeprɪˌkeɪtɪŋli/ *adv.*

self-despair /ˌselfdɪˈspeə(r)/ *n.* despair with oneself.

self-destroying /ˌselfdɪˈstrɔɪɪŋ/ *adj.* destroying oneself or itself.

self-destruct /ˌselfdɪˈstrʌkt/ *v.* & *adj.* esp. *US* —*v.intr.* (of a spacecraft, bomb, etc.) explode or disintegrate automatically, esp. when pre-set to do so. —*attrib.adj.* enabling a thing to self-destruct (*a self-destruct device*).

self-destruction /ˌselfdɪˈstrʌkʃ(ə)n/ *n.* **1** the process or an act of destroying oneself or itself. **2** esp. *US* the process or an act of self-destructing. □□ **self-destructive** *adj.* **self-destructively** *adv.*

self-determination /ˌselfdɪˌtɜːmɪˈneɪʃ(ə)n/ *n.* **1 a** nation's right to determine its own allegiance, government, etc. **2** the ability to act with free will, as opposed to fatalism etc. □□ **self-determined** /-ˈtɜːmɪnd/ *adj.* **self-determining** /-ˈtɜːmɪnɪŋ/ *adj.*

self-development /ˌselfdɪˈveləpmənt/ *n.* the development of oneself, one's abilities, etc.

self-devotion /ˌselfdɪˈvəʊʃ(ə)n/ *n.* the devotion of oneself to a person or cause.

self-discipline /selfˈdɪsɪplɪn/ *n.* the act of or ability to apply oneself, control one's feelings, etc.; self-control. □□ **self-disciplined** *adj.*

self-discovery /ˌselfdɪˈskʌvəri/ *n.* the process of acquiring insight into oneself, one's character, desires, etc.

self-disgust /ˌselfdɪsˈɡʌst/ *n.* disgust with oneself.

self-doubt /selfˈdaʊt/ *n.* lack of confidence in oneself, one's abilities, etc.

self-drive /self'draɪv/ adj. (of a hired vehicle) driven by the hirer.

self-educated /self'edju:ˌkeɪtɪd/ adj. educated by oneself by reading etc., without formal instruction. □□ **self-education** /-'keɪʃ(ə)n/ n.

self-effacing /ˌselfɪ'feɪsɪŋ/ adj. retiring; modest; timid. □□ **self-effacement** n. **self-effacingly** adv.

self-elective /ˌselfɪ'lektɪv/ adj. (of a committee etc.) proceeding esp. by co-opting members etc.

self-employed /ˌselfɪm'plɔɪd/ adj. working for oneself, as a freelance or owner of a business etc.; not employed by an employer. □□ **self-employment** n.

self-esteem /ˌselfɪ'sti:m/ n. a good opinion of oneself.

self-evident /self'evɪd(ə)nt/ adj. obvious; without the need of evidence or further explanation. □□ **self-evidence** n. **self-evidently** adv.

self-examination /ˌselfɪgˌzæmɪ'neɪʃ(ə)n/ n. **1** the study of one's own conduct, reasons, etc. **2** the examining of one's body for signs of illness etc.

self-executing /self'eksɪˌkju:tɪŋ/ adj. Law (of a law, legal clause, etc.) not needing legislation etc. to be enforced; automatic.

self-existent /ˌselfɪg'zɪst(ə)nt/ adj. existing without prior cause; independent.

self-explanatory /ˌselfɪk'splænətərɪ/ adj. easily understood; not needing explanation.

self-expression /ˌselfɪk'spreʃ(ə)n/ n. the expression of one's feelings, thoughts, etc., esp. in writing, painting, music, etc. □□ **self-expressive** adj.

self-faced /self'feɪst/ adj. (of stone) unhewn; undressed.

self-feeder /self'fi:də(r)/ n. **1** a furnace, machine, etc., that renews its own fuel or material automatically. **2** a device for supplying food to farm animals automatically. □□ **self-feeding** adj.

self-fertile /self'fɜ:taɪl/ adj. (of a plant etc.) self-fertilizing. □□ **self-fertility** /-'tɪlɪtɪ/ n.

self-fertilization /self,fɜ:tɪlaɪ'zeɪʃ(ə)n/ n. the fertilization of plants by their own pollen, not from others. □□ **self-fertilized** /-'fɜ:tɪˌlaɪzd/ adj. **self-fertilizing** /-'fɜ:tɪˌlaɪzɪŋ/ adj.

self-financing /self'faɪnænsɪŋ/ adj. that finances itself, esp. (of a project or undertaking) that pays for its own implementation or continuation. □□ **self-finance** v.tr.

self-flattery /self'flætərɪ/ n. = SELF-APPRECIATION. □□ **self-flattering** adj.

self-forgetful /ˌselffə'getful/ adj. unselfish. □□ **self-forgetfulness** n.

self-fulfilling /ˌselfful'fɪlɪŋ/ adj. (of a prophecy, forecast, etc.) bound to come true as a result of actions brought about by its being made.

self-fulfilment /ˌselfful'fɪlmənt/ n. (US -**fulfillment**) the fulfilment of one's own hopes and ambitions.

self-generating /self'dʒenəˌreɪtɪŋ/ adj. generated by itself or oneself, not externally.

self-glorification /self,glɔːrɪfɪ'keɪʃ(ə)n/ n. the proclamation of oneself, one's abilities, etc.; self-satisfaction.

self-government /self'gʌvənmənt/ n. **1** (esp. of a former colony etc.) government by its own people. **2** = SELF-CONTROL. □□ **self-governed** adj. **self-governing** adj.

self-hate /self'heɪt/ n. = SELF-HATRED.

self-hatred /self'heɪtrɪd/ n. hatred of oneself, esp. of one's actual self when contrasted with one's imagined self.

self-heal /self'hi:l/ n. any of several plants, esp. *Prunella vulgaris*, believed to have healing properties.

self-help /self'help/ n. **1** the theory that individuals should provide for their own support and improvement in society. **2** the act or faculty of providing for or improving oneself.

selfhood /'selfhʊd/ n. personality, separate and conscious existence.

self-image /self'ɪmɪdʒ/ n. one's own idea or picture of oneself, esp. in relation to others.

self-importance /ˌselfɪm'pɔ:t(ə)ns/ n. a high opinion of oneself; pompousness. □□ **self-important** adj. **self-importantly** adv.

self-imposed /ˌselfɪm'pəʊzd/ adj. (of a task or condition etc.) imposed on and by oneself, not externally (*self-imposed exile*).

self-improvement /ˌselfɪm'pru:vmənt/ n. the improvement of one's own position or disposition by one's own efforts.

self-induced /ˌselfɪn'dju:st/ adj. **1** induced by oneself or itself. **2** *Electr.* produced by self-induction.

self-inductance /ˌselfɪn'dʌkt(ə)ns/ n. *Electr.* the property of an electric circuit that causes an electromotive force to be generated in it by a change in the current flowing through it (cf. *mutual inductance*).

self-induction /ˌselfɪn'dʌkʃ(ə)n/ n. *Electr.* the production of an electromotive force in a circuit when the current in that circuit is varied. □□ **self-inductive** adj.

self-indulgent /ˌselfɪn'dʌldʒ(ə)nt/ adj. indulging or tending to indulge oneself in pleasure, idleness, etc. □□ **self-indulgence** n. **self-indulgently** adv.

self-inflicted /ˌselfɪn'flɪktɪd/ adj. (esp. of a wound, damage, etc.) inflicted by and on oneself, not externally.

self-interest /self'ɪntrəst, -trɪst/ n. one's personal interest or advantage. □□ **self-interested** adj.

selfish /'selfɪʃ/ adj. **1** deficient in consideration for others; concerned chiefly with one's own personal profit or pleasure; actuated by self-interest. **2** (of a motive etc.) appealing to self-interest. □□ **selfishly** adv. **selfishness** n.

self-justification /self,dʒʌstɪfɪ'keɪʃ(ə)n/ n. the justification or excusing of oneself, one's actions, etc.

self-knowledge /self'nɒlɪdʒ/ n. the understanding of oneself, one's motives, etc.

selfless /'selflɪs/ adj. disregarding oneself or one's own interests; unselfish. □□ **selflessly** adv. **selflessness** n.

self-loading /self'ləʊdɪŋ/ adj. (esp. of a gun) loading itself. □□ **self-loader** n.

self-locking /self'lɒkɪŋ/ adj. locking itself.

self-love /self'lʌv/ n. **1** selfishness; self-indulgence. **2** *Philos.* regard for one's own well-being and happiness.

self-made /self'meɪd/ adj. **1** successful or rich by one's own effort. **2** made by oneself.

self-mastery /self'mɑ:stərɪ/ n. = SELF-CONTROL.

selfmate /'selfmeɪt/ n. *Chess* checkmate in which a player forces the opponent to achieve checkmate.

self-mocking /self'mɒkɪŋ/ adj. mocking oneself or itself.

self-motion /self'məʊʃ(ə)n/ n. motion caused by oneself or itself, not externally. □□ **self-moving** /-'mu:vɪŋ/ adj.

self-motivated /self'məʊtɪˌveɪtɪd/ adj. acting on one's own initiative without external pressure. □□ **self-motivation** /-'veɪʃ(ə)n/ n.

self-murder /self'mɜ:də(r)/ n. = SUICIDE. □□ **self-murderer** n.

self-neglect /ˌselfnɪ'glekt/ n. neglect of oneself.

selfness /'selfnɪs/ n. **1** individuality, personality, essence. **2** selfishness or self-regard.

self-opinionated /ˌselfə'pɪnjəˌneɪtɪd/ adj. **1** stubbornly adhering to one's own opinions. **2** arrogant. □□ **self-opinion** n.

self-perpetuating /ˌselfpə'petju:ˌeɪtɪŋ/ adj. perpetuating itself or oneself without external agency. □□ **self-perpetuation** /-'eɪʃ(ə)n/ n.

self-pity /self'pɪtɪ/ n. extreme sorrow for one's own troubles etc. □□ **self-pitying** adj. **self-pityingly** adv.

self-pollination /self,pɒlɪ'neɪʃ(ə)n/ n. the pollination of a flower by pollen from the same plant. □□ **self-pollinated** adj. **self-pollinating** adj. **self-pollinator** n.

self-portrait /ˌselfˈpɔːtrɪt/ n. a portrait or description of an artist, writer, etc., by himself or herself.

self-possessed /ˌselfpəˈzest/ adj. habitually exercising self-control; composed. □□ **self-possession** /-ˈzeʃ(ə)n/ n.

self-praise /selfˈpreɪz/ n. boasting; self-glorification.

self-preservation /ˌselfprezəˈveɪʃ(ə)n/ n. 1 the preservation of one's own life, safety, etc. 2 this as a basic instinct of human beings and animals.

self-proclaimed /ˌselfprəˈkleɪmd/ adj. proclaimed by oneself or itself to be such.

self-propagating /ˌselfˈprɒpəˌgeɪtɪŋ/ adj. (esp. of a plant) able to propagate itself.

self-propelled /ˌselfprəˈpeld/ adj. (esp. of a motor vehicle etc.) moving or able to move without external propulsion. □□ **self-propelling** adj.

self-protection /ˌselfprəˈtekʃ(ə)n/ n. protecting oneself or itself. □□ **self-protective** adj.

self-raising /selfˈreɪzɪŋ/ adj. Brit. (of flour) having a raising agent already added.

self-realization /ˌselfˌrɪəlaɪˈzeɪʃ(ə)n/ n. 1 the development of one's faculties, abilities, etc. 2 this as an ethical principle.

self-recording /ˌselfrɪˈkɔːdɪŋ/ adj. (of a scientific instrument etc.) automatically recording its measurements.

self-regard /ˌselfrɪˈgɑːd/ n. 1 a proper regard for oneself. 2 a selfishness. b conceit.

self-registering /selfˈredʒɪstərɪŋ/ adj. (of a scientific instrument etc.) automatically registering its measurements.

self-regulating /selfˈregjʊˌleɪtɪŋ/ adj. regulating oneself or itself without intervention. □□ **self-regulation** /-ˈleɪʃ(ə)n/ n. **self-regulatory** /-lətəri/ adj.

self-reliance /ˌselfrɪˈlaɪəns/ n. reliance on one's own resources etc.; independence. □□ **self-reliant** adj. **self-reliantly** adv.

self-renewal /ˌselfrɪˈnjuːəl/ n. the act or process of renewing oneself or itself.

self-renunciation /ˌselfrɪˌnʌnsɪˈeɪʃ(ə)n/ n. 1 = SELF-SACRIFICE. 2 unselfishness.

self-reproach /ˌselfrɪˈprəʊtʃ/ n. reproach or blame directed at oneself. □□ **self-reproachful** adj.

self-respect /ˌselfrɪˈspekt/ n. respect for oneself, a feeling that one is behaving with honour, dignity, etc. □□ **self-respecting** adj.

self-restraint /ˌselfrɪˈstreɪnt/ n. = SELF-CONTROL. □□ **self-restrained** adj.

self-revealing /ˌselfrɪˈviːlɪŋ/ adj. revealing one's character, motives, etc., esp. inadvertently. □□ **self-revelation** /-ˌrevəˈleɪʃ(ə)n/ n.

self-righteous /selfˈraɪtʃəs/ adj. excessively conscious of or insistent on one's rectitude, correctness, etc. □□ **self-righteously** adv. **self-righteousness** n.

self-righting /selfˈraɪtɪŋ/ adj. (of a boat) righting itself when capsized.

self-rising /selfˈraɪzɪŋ/ adj. US = SELF-RAISING.

self-rule /selfˈruːl/ n. = SELF-GOVERNMENT 1.

self-sacrifice /selfˈsækrɪˌfaɪs/ n. the negation of one's own interests, wishes, etc., in favour of those of others. □□ **self-sacrificing** adj.

selfsame /ˈselfseɪm/ attrib.adj. (prec. by the) the very same (the selfsame village).

self-satisfaction /ˌselfˌsætɪsˈfækʃ(ə)n/ n. excessive and unwarranted satisfaction with oneself, one's achievements, etc.; complacency. □□ **self-satisfied** /-ˈsætɪsˌfaɪd/ adj. **self-satisfiedly** /-ˈsætɪsˌfaɪdli/ adv.

self-sealing /selfˈsiːlɪŋ/ adj. 1 (of a pneumatic tyre, fuel tank, etc.) automatically able to seal small punctures. 2 (of an envelope) self-adhesive.

self-seeking /ˈselfˌsiːkɪŋ/ adj. & n. seeking one's own welfare before that of others. □□ **self-seeker** n.

self-selection /ˌselfsɪˈlekʃ(ə)n/ n. the act of selecting oneself or itself. □□ **self-selecting** adj.

self-service /selfˈsɜːvɪs/ adj. & n. —adj. (often attrib.) 1 (of a shop, restaurant, garage, etc.) where customers serve themselves and pay at a checkout counter etc. 2 (of a machine) serving goods after the insertion of coins. —n. colloq. a self-service store, garage, etc.

self-serving /selfˈsɜːvɪŋ/ adj. = SELF-SEEKING.

self-slaughter /selfˈslɔːtə(r)/ n. = SUICIDE.

self-sown /selfˈsəʊn/ adj. grown from seed scattered naturally.

self-starter /selfˈstɑːtə(r)/ n. 1 an electric appliance for starting a motor vehicle engine without the use of a crank. 2 an ambitious person who needs no external motivation.

self-sterile /selfˈsteraɪl/ adj. Biol. not being self-fertile. □□ **self-sterility** /-stəˈrɪlɪti/ n.

self-styled /selfˈstaɪld/ adj. called so by oneself; would-be; pretended (a self-styled artist).

self-sufficient /ˌselfsəˈfɪʃ(ə)nt/ adj. 1 a needing nothing; independent. b (of a person, nation, etc.) able to supply one's needs for a commodity, esp. food, from one's own resources. 2 content with one's own opinion; arrogant. □□ **self-sufficiency** n. **self-sufficiently** adv. **self-sufficing** /-səˈfaɪsɪŋ/ adj.

self-suggestion /ˌselfsəˈdʒestʃ(ə)n/ n. = AUTO-SUGGESTION.

self-supporting /ˌselfsəˈpɔːtɪŋ/ adj. 1 capable of maintaining oneself or itself financially. 2 staying up or standing without external aid. □□ **self-support** n.

self-surrender /ˌselfsəˈrendə(r)/ n. the surrender of oneself or one's will etc. to an influence, emotion, or other person.

self-sustaining /ˌselfsəˈsteɪnɪŋ/ adj. sustaining oneself or itself. □□ **self-sustained** adj.

self-taught /selfˈtɔːt/ adj. educated or trained by oneself, not externally.

self-torture /selfˈtɔːtʃə(r)/ n. the inflicting of pain, esp. mental, on oneself.

self-willed /selfˈwɪld/ adj. obstinately pursuing one's own wishes. □□ **self-will** n.

self-winding /selfˈwaɪndɪŋ/ adj. (of a watch etc.) having an automatic winding apparatus.

self-worth /selfˈwɜːθ/ n. = SELF-ESTEEM.

Seljuk /ˈseldʒʊk/ n. & adj. —n. a member of any of the Turkish dynasties (11th–13th c.) of central and western Asia preceding Ottoman rule. —adj. of or relating to the Seljuks. □□ **Seljukian** /-ˈdʒuːkɪən/ adj. & n. [Turk. seljūq (name of their reputed ancestor)]

sell /sel/ v. & n. —v. (past and past part. **sold** /səʊld/) 1 tr. make over or dispose of in exchange for money. 2 tr. keep a stock of for sale or be a dealer in (do you sell candles?). 3 intr. (of goods) be purchased (will never sell; these are selling well). 4 intr. (foll. by at, for) have a specified price (sells at £5). 5 tr. betray for money or other reward (sell one's country). 6 tr. offer dishonourably for money or other consideration; make a matter of corrupt bargaining (sell justice; sell oneself; sell one's honour). 7 tr. a advertise or publish the merits of. b give (a person) information on the value of something, inspire with a desire to buy or acquire or agree to something. 8 tr. cause to be sold (the author's name alone will sell many copies). 9 tr. sl. disappoint by not keeping an engagement etc., by failing in some way, or by trickery (sold again!). —n. colloq. 1 a manner of selling (soft sell). 2 a deception or disappointment. □**sell-by** date the latest recommended date of sale marked on the packaging of esp. perishable food. **sell down the river** see RIVER. **sell** the (or a) **dummy** see DUMMY. **selling-point** an advantageous feature. **selling-race** a horse-race after which the winning horse must be auctioned. **sell one's life dear** (or **dearly**) do great injury before being killed. **sell off** sell the remainder of (goods) at reduced prices. **sell out 1 a** sell all one's stock-in-trade, one's shares in a company, etc. **b** sell (all or some of one's stock, shares, etc.). **2 a** betray. **b** be treacherous or disloyal. **sell-out** n. 1 a commercial success, esp. the selling of all tickets for a show. 2 a betrayal. **sell the pass** see PASS². **sell a pup** see PUP. **sell short** disparage, underestimate. **sell up** *Brit.* **1** sell one's business, house, etc. **2** sell the goods of (a debtor). **sold on** *colloq.* enthusiastic about. □□ **sellable** *adj.* [OE *sellan* f. Gmc]

seller /'selə(r)/ *n.* **1** a person who sells. **2** a commodity that sells well or badly. □**seller's** (or **sellers'**) **market** an economic position in which goods are scarce and expensive.

Sellotape /'selə,teɪp/ *n.* & *v.* —*n. propr.* adhesive usu. transparent cellulose or plastic tape. —*v.tr.* (**sellotape**) fix with Sellotape. [CELLULOSE + TAPE]

seltzer /'seltsə(r)/ *n.* (in full **seltzer water**) **1** medicinal mineral water from Nieder-Selters in Germany. **2** an artificial substitute for this; soda water. [G *Selterser* (adj.) f. *Selters*]

selvage /'selvɪdʒ/ *n.* (also **selvedge**) **1 a** an edging that prevents cloth from unravelling (either an edge along the warp or a specially woven edging). **b** a border of different material or finish intended to be removed or hidden. **2** *Geol.* an alteration zone at the edge of a rock mass. **3** the edge-plate of a lock with an opening for the bolt. [ME f. SELF + EDGE, after Du. *selfegghe*]

selves *pl.* of SELF.

semanteme /sɪ'mænti:m/ *n. Linguistics* a fundamental element expressing an image or idea. [F *sémantème* (as SEMANTIC)]

semantic /sɪ'mæntɪk/ *adj.* relating to meaning in language; relating to the connotations of words. □□ **semantically** *adv.* [F *sémantique* f. Gk *sēmantikos* significant f. *sēmainō* signify f. *sēma* sign]

semantics /sɪ'mæntɪks/ *n.pl.* (usu. treated as *sing.*) the branch of linguistics concerned with meaning. □□ **semantician** /-'tɪʃ(ə)n/ *n.* **semanticist** /-tɪsɪst/ *n.*

semaphore /'semə,fɔː(r)/ *n.* & *v.* —*n.* **1** *Mil.* etc. a system of sending messages by holding the arms or two flags in certain positions according to an alphabetic code. **2** a signalling apparatus consisting of a post with a movable arm or arms, lanterns, etc., for use (esp. on railways) by day or night. —*v.intr.* & *tr.* signal or send by semaphore. □□ **semaphoric** /-'fɒrɪk/ *adj.* **semaphorically** /-'fɒrɪkəlɪ/ *adv.* [F *sémaphore*, irreg. f. Gk *sēma* sign + *-phoros* -PHORE]

semasiology /sɪ,meɪsɪ'ɒlədʒɪ/ *n.* semantics. □□ **semasiological** /-ə'lɒdʒɪk(ə)l/ *adj.* [G *Semasiologie* f. Gk *sēmasia* meaning f. *sēmainō* signify]

sematic /sɪ'mætɪk/ *adj. Zool.* (of colouring, markings, etc.) significant; serving to warn off enemies or attract attention. [Gk *sēma sēmatos* sign]

semblable /'semblab(ə)l/ *n.* & *adj.* —*n.* a counterpart or equal. —*adj. archaic* having the semblance of something, seeming. [ME f. OF (as SEMBLANCE)]

semblance /'sembləns/ *n.* **1** the outward or superficial appearance of something (*put on a semblance of anger*). **2** resemblance. [ME f. OF f. *sembler* f. L *similare, simulare* SIMULATE]

semé /'semɪ, 'semeɪ/ *adj.* (also **semée**) *Heraldry* covered with small bearings of indefinite number (e.g. stars, fleurs-de-lis) arranged all over the field. [F, past part. of *semer* to sow]

semeiology var. of SEMIOLOGY.

semeiotics var. of SEMIOTICS.

sememe /'semi:m, 'si:m-/ *n. Linguistics* the unit of meaning carried by a morpheme. [as SEMANTIC]

semen /'si:mən/ *n.* the reproductive fluid of male animals, containing spermatozoa in suspension. [ME f. L *semen seminis* seed f. *serere* to sow]

semester /sɪ'mestə(r)/ *n.* a half-year course or term in (esp. German and US) universities. [G f. L *semestris* six-monthly (f. *sex* six + *mensis* month]

semi /'semɪ/ *n.* (*pl.* **semis**) *colloq.* **1** *Brit.* a semi-detached house. **2** *US* a semi-trailer. [abbr.]

semi- /'semɪ/ *prefix* **1** half (*semicircle*). **2** partly; in some degree or particular (*semi-official; semi-detached*). **3** almost (*a semi-smile*). **4** occurring or appearing twice in a specified period (*semi-annual*). [F, It., etc. or L, corresp. to Gk HEMI-, Skr. *sāmi*]

semi-annual /,semɪ'ænjʊəl/ *adj.* occurring, published, etc., twice a year. □□ **semi-annually** *adv.*

semi-automatic /,semɪ,ɔːtə'mætɪk/ *adj.* **1** partially automatic. **2** (of a firearm) having a mechanism for continuous loading but not for continuous firing.

semi-basement /,semɪ'beɪsmənt/ *n.* a storey partly below ground level.

semi-bold /,semɪ'bəʊld/ *adj. Printing* printed in a type darker than normal but not as dark as bold.

semibreve /'semɪ,bri:v/ *n. Mus.* the longest note now in common use, having the time value of two minims or four crochets, and represented by a ring with no stem. Also called *whole note*.

semicircle /'semɪ,sɜːk(ə)l/ *n.* **1** half of a circle or of its circumference. **2** a set of objects ranged in, or an object forming, a semicircle. [L *semicirculus* (as SEMI-, CIRCLE)]

semicircular /,semɪ'sɜːkjʊlə(r)/ *adj.* **1** forming or shaped like a semicircle. **2** arranged as or in a semicircle. □**semicircular canal** one of three fluid-filled channels in the ear giving information to the brain to help maintain balance. [LL *semicircularis* (as SEMICIRCLE)]

semi-civilized /,semɪ'sɪvɪ,laɪzd/ *adj.* partially civilized.

semicolon /,semɪ'kəʊlən, -lɒn/ *n.* a punctuation mark (;) of intermediate value between a comma and full stop.

semiconducting /,semɪkən'dʌktɪŋ/ *adj.* having the properties of a semiconductor.

semiconductor /,semɪkən'dʌktə(r)/ *n.* a solid substance that is a non-conductor when pure or at a low temperature but has a conductivity between that of insulators and that of most metals when containing a suitable impurity or at a higher temperature and is used in integrated circuits, transistors, diodes, etc.

semi-conscious /,semɪ'kɒnʃəs/ *adj.* partly or imperfectly conscious.

semicylinder /,semɪ'sɪlɪndə(r)/ *n.* half of a cylinder cut longitudinally. □□ **semicylindrical** /-'lɪndrɪk(ə)l/ *adj.*

semidemisemiquaver /'semɪ,demɪ,semɪ,kweɪvə(r)/ *n. Mus.* = HEMIDEMISEMIQUAVER. [SEMI- + DEMISEMIQUAVER]

semi-deponent /,semɪdɪ'pəʊnənt/ *adj. Gram.* (of a Latin verb) having active forms in present tenses and passive forms with active sense in perfect tenses.

semi-detached /,semɪdɪ'tætʃt/ *adj.* & *n.* —*adj.* (of a house) joined to another by a party-wall on one side only. —*n.* a semi-detached house.

semidiameter /,semɪdaɪ'æmɪtə(r)/ *n.* half of a diameter. [LL (as SEMI-, DIAMETER)]

semi-documentary /,semɪ,dɒkjʊ'mentərɪ/ *adj.* & *n.* —*adj.* (of a film) having a factual background and a fictitious story. —*n.* (*pl.* **-ies**) a semi-documentary film.

semi-dome /'semɪ,dəʊm/ *n.* **1** a half-dome formed by vertical section. **2** a part of a structure more or less resembling a dome.

semi-double /,semɪ'dʌb(ə)l/ *adj.* (of a flower) intermediate between single and double in having only the outer stamens converted to petals.

semifinal /,semɪ'faɪn(ə)l/ *n.* a match or round immediately preceding the final.

semifinalist /,semɪ'faɪnəlɪst/ *n.* a competitor in a semifinal.

semi-finished /,semɪ'fɪnɪʃt/ *adj.* prepared for the final stage of manufacture.

semi-fitted /,semɪ'fɪtɪd/ *adj.* (of a garment) shaped to the body but not closely fitted.

semifluid /,semɪ'flu:ɪd/ *adj.* & *n.* —*adj.* of a consistency between solid and liquid. —*n.* a semifluid substance.

semi-infinite /,semɪ'ɪnfɪnɪt/ *adj. Math.* limited in one direction and stretching to infinity in the other.

semi-invalid /,semɪ'ɪnvə,li:d, -lɪd/ *n.* a person somewhat enfeebled or partially disabled.

semi-liquid /,semɪ'lɪkwɪd/ *adj.* & *n.* = SEMIFLUID.

semi-lunar /ˌsemɪˈluːnə(r)/ adj. shaped like a half moon or crescent. □**semi-lunar bone** a bone of this shape in the carpus. **semi-lunar cartilage** a cartilage of this shape in the knee. **semi-lunar valve** a valve of this shape in the heart. [mod.L semilunaris (as SEMI-, LUNAR)]

semi-metal /ˌsemɪˈmet(ə)l/ n. a substance with some of the properties of metals. [mod.L semimetallum (as SEMI-, METAL)]

semi-monthly /ˌsemɪˈmʌnθlɪ/ adj. & adv. —adj. occurring, published, etc., twice a month. —adv. twice a month.

seminal /ˈsemɪn(ə)l/ adj. **1** of or relating to seed, semen, or reproduction. **2** germinal. **3** rudimentary, undeveloped. **4** (of ideas etc.) providing the basis for future development. □**seminal fluid** semen. □□ **seminally** adv. [ME f. OF seminal or L seminalis (as SEMEN)]

seminar /ˈsemɪnɑː(r)/ n. **1** a small class at a university etc. for discussion and research. **2** a short intensive course of study. **3** a conference of specialists. [G (as SEMINARY)]

seminary /ˈsemɪnərɪ/ n. (pl. -ies) **1** a training-college for priests, rabbis, etc. **2** a place of education or development. □□ **seminarist** n. [ME f. L seminarium seed-plot, neut. of seminarius (adj.) (as SEMEN)]

seminiferous /ˌsemɪˈnɪfərəs/ adj. **1** bearing seed. **2** conveying semen. [L semin- f. SEMEN f. -FEROUS]

semi-official /ˌsemɪəˈfɪʃ(ə)l/ adj. **1** partly official; rather less than official. **2** (of communications to newspapers etc.) made by an official with the stipulation that the source should not be revealed. □□ **semi-officially** adv.

semiology /ˌsiːmɪˈɒlədʒɪ, ˌsem-/ n. (also **semeiology**) = SEMIOTICS. □□ **semiological** /-əˈlɒdʒɪk(ə)l/ adj. **semiologist** n. [Gk sēmeion sign f. sēma mark]

semi-opaque /ˌsemɪəʊˈpeɪk/ adj. not fully transparent.

semiotics /ˌsiːmɪˈɒtɪks, ˌsem-/ n. (also **semeiotics**) **1** the study of signs and symbols in various fields, esp. language. **2** Med. symptomatology. □□ **semiotic** adj. **semiotical** adj. **semiotically** adv. **semiotician** /-ˈtɪʃ(ə)n/ n. [Gk sēmeiōtikos of signs (as SEMIOLOGY)]

semi-permanent /ˌsemɪˈpɜːmənənt/ adj. rather less than permanent.

semi-permeable /ˌsemɪˈpɜːmɪəb(ə)l/ adj. (of a membrane etc.) allowing small molecules, but not large ones, to pass through.

semi-plume /ˈsemɪˌpluːm/ n. a feather with a firm stem but a downy web.

semiprecious /ˌsemɪˈpreʃəs/ adj. (of a gem) less valuable than a precious stone.

semi-pro /ˌsemɪˈprəʊ/ adj. & n. (pl. -os) US colloq. = SEMI-PROFESSIONAL.

semi-professional /ˌsemɪprəˈfeʃ(ə)n(ə)l/ adj. & n. —adj. **1** receiving payment for an activity but not relying on it for a living. **2** involving semi-professionals. —n. a semi-professional musician, sportsman, etc.

semiquaver /ˈsemɪˌkweɪvə(r)/ n. Mus. a note having the time value of half a quaver and represented by a large dot with a two-hooked stem. Also called sixteenth note.

semi-rigid /ˌsemɪˈrɪdʒɪd/ adj. (of an airship) having a stiffened keel attached to a flexible gas container.

semi-skilled /ˌsemɪˈskɪld/ adj. (of work or a worker) having or needing some training but less than for a skilled worker.

semi-smile /ˈsemɪˌsmaɪl/ n. an expression that is not quite a smile.

semi-solid /ˌsemɪˈsɒlɪd/ adj. viscous, semifluid.

semi-sweet /ˈsemɪˌswiːt/ adj. (of biscuits etc.) slightly sweetened.

semi-synthetic /ˌsemɪsɪnˈθetɪk/ adj. Chem. (of a substance) that is prepared synthetically but derives from a naturally occurring material.

Semite /ˈsiːmaɪt, ˈsem-/ n. a member of any of the peoples supposed to be descended from Shem, son of Noah (Gen. 10:21 ff.), including esp. the Jews, Arabs, Assyrians, and Phoenicians. □□ **Semitism** /ˈsemɪˌtɪz(ə)m/ n. **Semitist** /ˈsemɪtɪst/ n. **Semitize** /ˈsemɪˌtaɪz/ v.tr. (also -ise). **Semitization** /ˌsemɪtaɪˈzeɪʃ(ə)n/ n. [mod.L Semita f. LL f. Gk Sēm Shem]

Semitic /sɪˈmɪtɪk/ adj. **1** of or relating to the Semites, esp. the Jews. **2** of or relating to the languages of the family including Hebrew and Arabic. [mod.L Semiticus (as SEMITE)]

semitone /ˈsemɪˌtəʊn/ n. Mus. the smallest interval used in classical European music; half a tone.

semi-trailer /ˌsemɪˈtreɪlə(r)/ n. a trailer having wheels at the back but supported at the front by a towing vehicle.

semi-transparent /ˌsemɪtrænsˈpærənt, ˌsemɪtrɑːn-, -ˈpeərənt/ adj. partially or imperfectly transparent.

semi-tropics /ˌsemɪˈtrɒpɪks/ n.pl. = SUBTROPICS. □□ **semi-tropical** adj.

semi-vowel /ˈsemɪˌvaʊəl/ n. **1** a sound intermediate between a vowel and a consonant (e.g. w, y). **2** a letter representing this. [after L semivocalis]

semi-weekly /ˌsemɪˈwiːklɪ/ adj. & adv. —adj. occurring, published, etc., twice a week. —adv. twice a week.

semmit /ˈsemɪt/ n. Sc. an undershirt. [ME: orig. unkn.]

semolina /ˌseməˈliːnə/ n. **1** the hard grains left after the milling of flour, used in puddings etc. and in pasta. **2** a pudding etc. made of this. [It. semolino dimin. of semola bran f. L simila flour]

sempiternal /ˌsempɪˈtɜːn(ə)l/ adj. rhet. eternal, everlasting. □□ **sempiternally** adv. **sempiternity** n. [ME f. OF sempiternel f. LL sempiternalis f. L sempiternus f. semper always + aeternus eternal]

semplice /ˈsemplɪˌtʃeɪ, -tʃɪ/ adv. Mus. in a simple style of performance. [It., = SIMPLE]

sempre /ˈsempreɪ, -rɪ/ adv. Mus. throughout, always (sempre forte). [It.]

sempstress var. of SEAMSTRESS.

SEN abbr. (in the UK) State Enrolled Nurse.

Sen. abbr. **1** Senior. **2** US a Senator. **b** Senate.

senarius /sɪˈneərɪəs/ n. (pl. **senarii** /-ɪˌaɪ/) Prosody a verse of six feet, esp. an iambic trimeter. [L: see SENARY]

senary /ˈsiːnərɪ, ˈsen-/ adj. of six, by sixes. [L senarius f. seni distrib. of sex six]

senate /ˈsenɪt/ n. **1** a legislative body, esp. the upper and smaller assembly in the US, France, and other countries, in the States of the US, etc. **2** the governing body of a university or (in the US) a college. **3** Rom.Hist. the State council of the republic and empire sharing legislative power with the popular assemblies, administration with the magistrates, and judicial power with the knights. [ME f. OF senat f. L senatus f. senex old man]

senator /ˈsenətə(r)/ n. **1** a member of a senate. **2** (in Scotland) a Lord of Session. □□ **senatorial** /-ˈtɔːrɪəl/ adj. **senatorship** n. [ME f. OF senateur f. L senator -oris (as SENATE)]

send /send/ v. (past and past part. **sent** /sent/) **1** tr. **a** order or cause to go or be conveyed (send a message to headquarters; sent me a book; sends goods all over the world). **b** propel; cause to move (send a bullet; sent him flying). **c** cause to go or become (send into raptures; send to sleep). **d** dismiss with or without force (sent her away; sent him about his business). **2** intr. send a message or letter (he sent to warn me). **3** tr. (of God, providence, etc.) grant or bestow or inflict; bring about; cause to be (send rain; send a judgement; send her victorious!). **4** tr. sl. affect emotionally, put into ecstasy. □**send away for** send an order to a dealer for (goods). **send down** Brit. **1** rusticate or expel from a university. **2** sentence to imprisonment. **3** Cricket bowl (a ball or an over). **send for 1** summon. **2** order by post. **send in 1** cause to go in. **2** submit (an entry etc.) for a competition etc. **send off 1** get (a letter, parcel, etc.)

dispatched. **2** attend the departure of (a person) as a sign of respect etc. **3** *Sport* (of a referee) order (a player) to leave the field and take no further part in the game. **send-off** *n.* a demonstration of goodwill etc. at the departure of a person, the start of a project, etc. **send off for** = *send away for*. **send on** transmit to a further destination or in advance of one's own arrival. **send a person to Coventry** see COVENTRY. **send up 1** cause to go up. **2** transmit to a higher authority. **3** *Brit. colloq.* satirize or ridicule, esp. by mimicking. **4** *US* sentence to imprisonment. **send-up** *n. Brit. colloq.* a satire or parody. **send word** send information. □□ **sendable** *adj.* **sender** *n.* [OE *sendan* f. Gmc]

sendal /ˈsend(ə)l/ *n. hist.* **1** a thin rich silk material. **2** a garment of this. [ME f. OF *cendal*, ult. f. Gk *sindōn*]

senecio /sɪˈniːʃɪəʊ/ *n.* any composite plant of the genus *Senecio*, including many cultivated species as well as groundsel and ragwort. [L *senecio* old man, groundsel, with ref. to the hairy fruits]

senesce /sɪˈnes/ *v.intr.* grow old. □□ **senescence** *n.* **senescent** *adj.* [L *senescere* f. *senex* old]

seneschal /ˈsenɪʃ(ə)l/ *n.* **1** the steward or major-domo of a medieval great house. **2** a judge in Sark. [ME f. OF f. med.L *seniscalus* f. Gmc, = old servant]

senhor /seɪnˈjɔː(r)/ *n.* a title used of or to a Portuguese or Brazilian man. [Port. f. L *senior*: see SENIOR]

senhora /seɪnˈjɔːrə/ *n.* a title used of or to a Portuguese woman or a Brazilian married woman. [Port., fem. of SENHOR]

senhorita /ˌseɪnjəˈriːtə/ *n.* a title used of or to a Brazilian unmarried woman. [Port., dimin. of SENHORA]

senile /ˈsiːnaɪl/ *adj. & n.* —*adj.* **1** of or characteristic of old age (*senile apathy*; *senile decay*). **2** having the weaknesses or diseases of old age. —*n.* a senile person. □□ **senility** /sɪˈnɪlɪtɪ/ *n.* [F *sénile* or L *senilis* f. *senex* old man]

senior /ˈsiːnɪə(r)/ *adj. & n.* —*adj.* **1** (often foll. by *to*) more or most advanced in age or standing. **2** of high or highest position. **3** (placed after a person's name) senior to another of the same name. **4** (of a school) having pupils in an older age-range (esp. over 11). **5** *US* of the final year at a university, high school, etc. —*n.* **1** a person of advanced age or comparatively long service etc. **2** one's elder, or one's superior in length of service, membership, etc. (*is my senior*). **3** a senior student. □ **senior citizen** an elderly person, esp. an old-age pensioner. **senior college** *US* a college in which the last two years' work for a bachelor's degree is done. **senior common** (or **combination**) **room** *Brit.* a room for use by senior members of a college. **senior nursing officer** the person in charge of nursing services in a hospital. **senior officer** an officer to whom a junior is responsible. **senior partner** the head of a firm. **senior service** *Brit.* the Royal Navy as opposed to the Army. **senior tutor** *Brit.* a college tutor in charge of the teaching arrangements. □□ **seniority** /ˌsiːnɪˈɒrɪtɪ/ *n.* [ME f. L, = older, older man, compar. of *senex senis* old man, old]

senna /ˈsenə/ *n.* **1** a cassia tree. **2** a laxative prepared from the dried pods of this. [med.L *sena* f. Arab. *sanā*]

sennet[1] /ˈsenɪt/ *n. hist.* a signal call on a trumpet or cornet (in the stage directions of Elizabethan plays). [perh. var. of SIGNET]

sennet[2] var. of SINNET.

sennight /ˈsenaɪt/ *n. archaic* a week. [OE *seofon nihta* seven nights]

sennit /ˈsenɪt/ *n.* **1** *hist.* plaited straw, palm leaves, etc., used for making hats. **2** = SINNET. [var. of SINNET]

señor /senˈjɔː(r)/ *n.* (*pl.* **señores** /-rez/) a title used of or to a Spanish-speaking man. [Sp. f. L *senior*: see SENIOR]

señora /senˈjɔːrə/ *n.* a title used of or to a Spanish-speaking married woman. [Sp., fem. of SEÑOR]

señorita /ˌsenjəˈriːtə/ *n.* a title used of or to a Spanish-speaking unmarried woman. [Sp., dimin. of SEÑORA]

Senr. *abbr.* Senior.

sensate /ˈsenseɪt/ *adj.* perceived by the senses. [LL *sensatus* having senses (as SENSE)]

sensation /senˈseɪʃ(ə)n/ *n.* **1** the consciousness of perceiving or seeming to perceive some state or condition of one's body or its parts or senses or of one's mind or its emotions; an instance of such consciousness (*lost all sensation in my left arm*; *had a sensation of giddiness*; *a sensation of pride*; *in search of a new sensation*). **2 a** a stirring of emotions or intense interest esp. among a large group of people (*the news caused a sensation*). **b** a person, event, etc., causing such interest. **3** the sensational use of literary etc. material. [med.L *sensatio* f. L *sensus* SENSE]

sensational /senˈseɪʃən(ə)l/ *adj.* **1** causing or intended to cause great public excitement etc. **2** of or causing sensation. □□ **sensationally** *adv.*

sensationalism /senˈseɪʃənəˌlɪz(ə)m/ *n.* **1** the use of or interest in the sensational in literature, political agitation, etc. **2** *Philos.* the theory that ideas are derived solely from sensation (opp. RATIONALISM). □□ **sensationalist** *n. & adj.* **sensationalistic** /-ˈlɪstɪk/ *adj.*

sense /sens/ *n. & v.* —*n.* **1 a** any of the special bodily faculties by which sensation is roused (*has keen senses*; *has a dull sense of smell*). **b** sensitiveness of all or any of these. **2** the ability to perceive or feel or to be conscious of the presence or properties of things. **3** (foll. by *of*) consciousness (*sense of having done well*; *sense of one's own importance*). **4** (often foll. by *of*) **a** quick or accurate appreciation, understanding, or instinct regarding a specified matter (*sense of the ridiculous*; *road sense*; *the moral sense*). **b** the habit of basing one's conduct on such instinct. **5** practical wisdom or judgement, common sense; conformity to these (*has plenty of sense*; *what is the sense of talking like that?*; *has more sense than to do that*). **6 a** a meaning; the way in which a word etc. is to be understood (*the sense of the word is clear*; *I mean that in the literal sense*). **b** intelligibility or coherence or possession of a meaning. **7** the prevailing opinion among a number of people. **8** (in *pl.*) a person's sanity or normal state of mind. **9** *Math.* etc. **a** a direction of movement. **b** that which distinguishes a pair of entities which differ only in that each is the reverse of the other. —*v.tr.* **1** perceive by a sense or senses. **2** be vaguely aware of. **3** realize. **4** (of a machine etc.) detect. **5** *US* understand. □ **bring a person to his** or **her senses 1** cure a person of folly. **2** restore a person to consciousness. **come to one's senses 1** regain consciousness. **2** become sensible after acting foolishly. **the five senses** sight, hearing, smell, taste, and touch. **in a** (or **one**) **sense** if the statement is understood in a particular way (*what you say is true in a sense*). **in one's senses** sane. **make sense** be intelligible or practicable. **make sense of** show or find the meaning of. **man of sense** a sagacious man. **out of one's senses** in or into a state of madness (*is out of her senses*; *frightened him out of his senses*). **sense-datum** (*pl.* **-data**) *Philos.* an element of experience received through the senses. **sense of direction** the ability to know without guidance the direction in which one is or should be moving. **sense of humour** see HUMOUR. **sense-organ** a bodily organ conveying external stimuli to the sensory system. **take leave of one's senses** go mad. **take the sense of the meeting** ascertain the prevailing opinion. **under a sense of wrong** feeling wronged. [ME f. L *sensus* faculty of feeling, thought, meaning, f. *sentire sens-* feel]

senseless /ˈsenslɪs/ *adj.* **1** unconscious. **2** wildly foolish. **3** without meaning or purpose. **4** incapable of sensation. □□ **senselessly** adv. **senselessness** n.

sensibility /ˌsensɪˈbɪlɪtɪ/ n. (pl. **-ies**) **1** capacity to feel (little finger lost its sensibility). **2 a** openness to emotional impressions, susceptibility, sensitiveness (sensibility to kindness). **b** an exceptional or excessive degree of this (sense and sensibility). **3** (in pl.) a tendency to feel offended etc. [ME f. LL sensibilitas (as SENSIBLE)]

sensible /ˈsensɪb(ə)l/ adj. **1** having or showing wisdom or common sense; reasonable, judicious (a sensible person; a sensible compromise). **2 a** perceptible by the senses (sensible phenomena). **b** great enough to be perceived; appreciable (a sensible difference). **3** (of clothing etc.) practical and functional. **4** (foll. by of) aware; not unmindful (was sensible of his peril). □ **sensible horizon** see HORIZON 1b. □□ **sensibleness** n. **sensibly** adv. [ME f. OF sensible or L sensibilis (as SENSE)]

sensitive /ˈsensɪtɪv/ adj. & n. —adj. **1** (often foll. by to) very open to or acutely affected by external stimuli or mental impressions; having sensibility. **2** (of a person) easily offended or emotionally hurt. **3** (often foll. by to) (of an instrument etc.) responsive to or recording slight changes. **4** (often foll. by to) **a** (of photographic materials) prepared so as to respond (esp. rapidly) to the action of light. **b** (of any material) readily affected by or responsive to external action. **5** (of a topic etc.) subject to restriction of discussion to prevent embarrassment, ensure security, etc. **6** (of a market) liable to quick changes of price. —n. a person who is sensitive (esp. to supposed occult influences). □ **sensitive plant 1** a plant whose leaves curve downwards and leaflets fold together when touched, esp. mimosa. **2** a sensitive person. □□ **sensitively** adv. **sensitiveness** n. [ME, = sensory, f. OF sensitif -ive or med.L sensitivus, irreg. f. L sentire sens- feel]

sensitivity /ˌsensɪˈtɪvɪtɪ/ n. the quality or degree of being sensitive.

sensitize /ˈsensɪˌtaɪz/ v.tr. (also **-ise**) **1** make sensitive. **2** Photog. make sensitive to light. **3** make (an organism etc.) abnormally sensitive to a foreign substance. □□ **sensitization** /-ˈzeɪʃ(ə)n/ n. **sensitizer** n.

sensitometer /ˌsensɪˈtɒmɪtə(r)/ n. Photog. a device for measuring sensitivity to light.

sensor /ˈsensə(r)/ n. a device giving a signal for the detection or measurement of a physical property to which it responds. [SENSORY, after MOTOR]

sensorium /senˈsɔːrɪəm/ n. (pl. **sensoria** /-rɪə/ or **sensoriums**) **1** the seat of sensation, the brain, brain and spinal cord, or grey matter of these. **2** Biol. the whole sensory apparatus including the nerve-system. □□ **sensorial** adj. **sensorially** adv. [LL f. L sentire sens- feel]

sensory /ˈsensərɪ/ adj. of sensation or the senses. □□ **sensorily** adv. [as SENSORIUM]

sensual /ˈsensjʊəl, ˈsenʃʊəl/ adj. **1 a** of or depending on the senses only and not on the intellect or spirit; carnal, fleshly (sensual pleasures). **b** given to the pursuit of sensual pleasures or the gratification of the appetites; self-indulgent sexually or in regard to food and drink; voluptuous, licentious. **c** indicative of a sensual nature (sensual lips). **2** of sense or sensation, sensory. **3** Philos. of, according to, or holding the doctrine of, sensationalism. □□ **sensualism** n. **sensualist** n. **sensualize** v.tr. (also **-ise**). **sensually** adv. [ME f. LL sensualis (as SENSE)]

sensuality /ˌsensjʊˈælɪtɪ, ˌsenʃʊ-/ n. gratification of the senses, self-indulgence. [ME f. F sensualité f. LL sensualitas (as SENSUAL)]

sensum /ˈsensəm/ n. (pl. **sensa** /-sə/) Philos. a sense-datum. [mod.L, neut. past part. of L sentire feel]

sensuous /ˈsensjʊəs/ adj. of or derived from or affecting the senses, esp. aesthetically rather than

sensually. □□ **sensuously** adv. **sensuousness** n. [L sensus sense]

sent past and past part. of SEND.

sentence /ˈsent(ə)ns/ n. & v. —n. **1 a** a set of words complete in itself as the expression of a thought, containing or implying a subject and predicate, and conveying a statement, question, exclamation, or command. **b** a piece of writing or speech between two full stops or equivalent pauses, often including several grammatical sentences (e.g. I went; he came). **2 a** a decision of a lawcourt, esp. the punishment allotted to a person convicted in a criminal trial. **b** the declaration of this. **c** Logic a series of signs or symbols expressing a proposition in an artificial or logical language. —v.tr. **1** declare the sentence of (a convicted criminal etc.). **2** (foll. by to) declare (such a person) to be condemned to a specified punishment. □ **under sentence of** having been condemned to (under sentence of death). [ME f. OF f. L sententia opinion f. sentire be of opinion]

sentential /senˈtenʃ(ə)l/ adj. Gram. & Logic of a sentence. [L sententialis (as SENTENCE)]

sententious /senˈtenʃəs/ adj. **1** (of a person) fond of pompous moralizing. **2** (of a style) affectedly formal. **3** aphoristic, pithy, given to the use of maxims, affecting a concise impressive style. □□ **sententiously** adv. **sententiousness** n. [L sententiosus (as SENTENCE)]

sentient /ˈsenʃ(ə)nt/ adj. having the power of perception by the senses. □□ **sentience** n. **sentiency** n. **sentiently** adv. [L sentire feel]

sentiment /ˈsentɪmənt/ n. **1** a mental feeling (the sentiment of pity). **2 a** the sum of what one feels on some subject. **b** a verbal expression of this. **3** the expression of a view or desire esp. as formulated for a toast (concluded his speech with a sentiment). **4** an opinion as distinguished from the words meant to convey it (the sentiment is good though the words are injudicious). **5** a view or tendency based on or coloured with emotion (animated by noble sentiments). **6** such views collectively, esp. as an influence (sentiment unchecked by reason is a bad guide). **7** the tendency to be swayed by feeling rather than by reason. **8 a** mawkish tenderness. **b** the display of this. **9** an emotional feeling conveyed in literature or art. [ME f. OF sentement f. med.L sentimentum f. L sentire feel]

sentimental /ˌsentɪˈment(ə)l/ adj. **1** of or characterized by sentiment. **2** showing or affected by emotion rather than reason. **3** appealing to sentiment. □ **sentimental value** the value of a thing to a particular person because of its associations. □□ **sentimentalism** n. **sentimentalist** n. **sentimentality** /-ˈtælɪtɪ/ n. **sentimentalize** v.intr. & tr. (also **-ise**). **sentimentalization** /-laɪˈzeɪʃ(ə)n/ n. **sentimentally** adv.

sentinel /ˈsentɪn(ə)l/ n. & v. —n. a sentry or lookout. —v.tr. (**sentinelled, sentinelling**; US **sentineled, sentineling**) **1** station sentinels at or in. **2** poet. keep guard over or in. [F sentinelle f. It. sentinella, of unkn. orig.]

sentry /ˈsentrɪ/ n. (pl. **-ies**) a soldier etc. stationed to keep guard. □ **sentry-box** a wooden cabin intended to shelter a standing sentry. **sentry-go** the duty of pacing up and down as a sentry. [perh. f. obs. centrinel, var. of SENTINEL]

sepal /ˈsep(ə)l, ˈsiː-/ n. Bot. each of the divisions or leaves of the calyx. [F sépale, mod.L sepalum, perh. formed as SEPARATE + PETAL]

separable /ˈsepərəb(ə)l/ adj. **1** able to be separated. **2** Gram. (of a prefix, or a verb in respect of a prefix) written as a separate word in some collocations. □□ **separability** /-ˈbɪlɪtɪ/ n. **separableness** n. **separably** adv. [F séparable or L separabilis (as SEPARATE)]

separate adj., n., & v. —adj. /ˈsepərət/ (often foll. by from) forming a unit that is or may be regarded as apart or by itself; physically disconnected, distinct, or individual (*living in separate rooms*; *the two questions are essentially separate*). —*n.* /'sepərət/ **1** (in *pl.*) separate articles of clothing suitable for wearing together in various combinations. **2** an offprint. —*v.* /'sepə‚reɪt/ **1** *tr.* make separate, sever, disunite. **2** *tr.* prevent union or contact of. **3** *intr.* go different ways, disperse. **4** *intr.* cease to live together as a married couple. **5** *intr.* (foll. by *from*) secede. **6** *tr.* **a** divide or sort (milk, ore, fruit, light, etc.) into constituent parts or sizes. **b** (often foll. by *out*) extract or remove (an ingredient, waste product, etc.) by such a process for use or rejection. **7** *tr.* US discharge, dismiss. □□ **separately** *adv.* **separateness** *n.* **separative** /-rətɪv/ *adj.* **separatory** /-rətərɪ/ *adj.* [L *separare separat-* (as SE-, *parare* make ready)]

separation /‚sepə'reɪʃ(ə)n/ *n.* **1** the act or an instance of separating; the state of being separated. **2** (in full **judicial separation** or **legal separation**) an arrangement by which a husband and wife remain married but live apart. **3** any of three or more monochrome reproductions of a coloured picture which can combine to reproduce the full colour of the original. □ **separation order** an order of court for judicial separation. [ME f. OF f. L *separatio -onis* (as SEPARATE)]

separatist /'sepərətɪst/ *n.* a person who favours separation, esp. for political or ecclesiastical independence (opp. UNIONIST 2). □□ **separatism** *n.*

separator /'sepə‚reɪtə(r)/ *n.* a machine for separating, e.g. cream from milk.

Sephardi /sɪ'fɑːdɪ/ *n.* (*pl.* **Sephardim** /-dɪm/) a Jew of Spanish or Portuguese descent (cf. ASHKENAZI). □□ **Sephardic** *adj.* [LHeb., f. sᵉ*p̄āraḏ*, a country mentioned in Obad. 20 and taken to be Spain]

sepia /'siːpɪə/ *n.* **1** a dark reddish-brown colour. **2 a** a brown pigment prepared from a black fluid secreted by cuttlefish, used in monochrome drawing and in water-colours. **b** a brown tint used in photography. **3** a drawing done in sepia. **4** the fluid secreted by cuttlefish. [L f. Gk *sēpia* cuttlefish]

sepoy /'siːpɔɪ/ *n. hist.* a native Indian soldier under European, esp. British, discipline. [Urdu & Pers. *sipāhī* soldier f. *sipāh* army]

seppuku /se'puːkuː/ *n.* hara-kiri. [Jap.]

sepsis /'sepsɪs/ *n.* **1** the state of being septic. **2** blood-poisoning. [mod.L f. Gk *sēpsis* f. *sēpō* make rotten]

Sept. *abbr.* **1** September. **2** Septuagint.

sept /sept/ *n.* a clan, esp. in Ireland. [prob. alt. of SECT]

sept- var. of SEPTI-.

septa *pl.* of SEPTUM.

septal[1] /'sept(ə)l/ *adj.* **1** of a septum or septa. **2** *Archaeol.* (of a stone or slab) separating compartments in a burial chamber. [SEPTUM]

septal[2] /'sept(ə)l/ *adj.* of a sept or septs.

septate /'septeɪt/ *adj. Bot., Zool.,* & *Anat.* having a septum or septa; partitioned. □□ **septation** /-'teɪʃ(ə)n/ *n.*

septcentenary /‚septsen'tiːnərɪ/ *n.* & *adj.* —*n.* (*pl.* -ies) **1** a seven-hundredth anniversary. **2** a festival marking this. —*adj.* of or concerning a septcentenary.

September /sep'tembə(r)/ *n.* the ninth month of the year. [ME f. L *September* f. *septem* seven: orig. the seventh month of the Roman year]

septenarius /‚septɪ'neərɪəs/ *n.* (*pl.* **septenarii** /-rɪ‚aɪ/) *Prosody* a verse of seven feet, esp. a trochaic or iambic tetrameter catalectic. [L f. *septeni* distributive of *septem* seven]

septenary /sep'tiːnərɪ, 'septɪn-/ *adj.* & *n.* —*adj.* of seven, by sevens, on the basis of seven. —*n.* (*pl.* -ies) **1** a group or set of seven (esp. years). **2** a septenarius. [L *septenarius* (as SEPTENARIUS)]

septenate /'septɪ‚neɪt/ *adj. Bot.* **1** growing in sevens. **2** having seven divisions. [L *septeni* (as SEPTENARIUS)]

septennial /sep'tenɪəl/ *adj.* **1** lasting for seven years.

2 recurring every seven years. [LL *septennis* f. L *septem* seven + *annus* year]

septennium /sep'tenɪəm/ *n.* (*pl.* **septenniums** or **septennia** /-nɪə/) a period of seven years.

septet /sep'tet/ *n.* (also **septette**) **1** *Mus.* **a** a composition for seven performers. **b** the performers of such a composition. **2** any group of seven. [G *Septett* f. L *septem* seven]

septfoil /'setfɔɪl/ *n.* **1** a seven-lobed ornamental figure. **2** *archaic* tormentil. [LL *septifolium* after CINQUEFOIL, TREFOIL]

septi- /'septɪ/ *comb. form* (also **sept-** before a vowel) seven. [L f. *septem* seven]

septic /'septɪk/ *adj.* contaminated with bacteria from a festering wound etc., putrefying. □ **septic tank** a tank in which the organic matter in sewage is disintegrated through bacterial activity. □□ **septically** *adv.* **septicity** /-'tɪsɪtɪ/ *n.* [L *septicus* f. Gk *sēptikos* f. *sēpō* make rotten]

septicaemia /‚septɪ'siːmɪə/ *n.* (US **septicemia**) blood-poisoning. □□ **septicaemic** *adj.* [mod.L f. Gk *sēptikos* + *haima* blood]

septillion /sep'tɪljən/ *n.* (*pl.* same) a thousand raised to the eighth (or formerly, esp. *Brit.*, the fourteenth) power (10²⁴ and 10⁴² respectively). [F f. *sept* seven, after *billion* etc.]

septimal /'septɪm(ə)l/ *adj.* of the number seven. [L *septimus* seventh f. *septem* seven]

septime /'septiːm/ *n. Fencing* the seventh of the eight parrying positions. [L *septimus* (as SEPTIMAL)]

septivalent /sep'tɪvələnt/ *adj.* (also **septavalent**) *Chem.* having a valency of seven.

septuagenarian /‚septjuədʒɪ'neərɪən/ *n.* & *adj.* —*n.* a person from 70 to 79 years old. —*adj.* of this age. [L *septuagenarius* f. *septuageni* distributive of *septuaginta* seventy]

Septuagesima /‚septjuə'dʒesɪmə/ *n.* (in full **Septuagesima Sunday**) the Sunday before Sexagesima. [ME f. L, = seventieth (day), formed as SEPTUAGINT, perh. after QUINQUAGESIMA or with ref. to the period of 70 days from Septuagesima to the Saturday after Easter]

Septuagint /'septjuə‚dʒɪnt/ *n.* a Greek version of the Old Testament including the Apocrypha, said to have been made about 270 BC by seventy-two translators. [L *septuaginta* seventy]

septum /'septəm/ *n.* (*pl.* **septa** /-tə/) *Anat., Bot.,* & *Zool.* a partition such as that between the nostrils or the chambers of a poppy-fruit or of a shell. [L *s(a)eptum* f. *saepire saept-* enclose f. *saepes* hedge]

septuple /'septjʊp(ə)l/ *adj., n.,* & *v.* —*adj.* **1** sevenfold, having seven parts. **2** being seven times as many or as much. —*n.* a sevenfold number or amount. —*v.tr.* & *intr.* multiply by seven. [LL *septuplus* f. L *septem* seven]

septuplet /'sep‚tjʊplɪt, sep'tjuː'plɪt/ *n.* **1** one of seven children born at one birth. **2** *Mus.* a group of seven notes to be played in the time of four or six. [as SEPTUPLE, after TRIPLET etc.]

sepulchral /sɪ'pʌlkr(ə)l/ *adj.* **1** of a tomb or interment (*sepulchral mound*; *sepulchral customs*). **2** suggestive of the tomb, funereal, gloomy, dismal (*sepulchral look*). □□ **sepulchrally** *adv.* [F *sépulchral* or L *sepulchralis* (as SEPULCHRE)]

sepulchre /'sepəlkə(r)/ *n.* & *v.* (US **sepulcher**) —*n.* a tomb esp. cut in rock or built of stone or brick, a burial vault or cave. —*v.tr.* **1** lay in a sepulchre. **2** serve as a sepulchre for. □ **the Holy Sepulchre** the tomb in which Christ was laid. **whited sepulchre** a hypocrite (with ref. to Matt. 23:27). [ME f. OF f. L *sepulc(h)rum* f. *sepelire sepult-* bury]

sepulture /'sepəltʃə(r)/ *n. literary* the act or an instance of burying or putting in the grave. [ME f. OF f. L *sepultura* (as SEPULCHRE)]

seq. *abbr.* (*pl.* **seqq.**) the following. [L *sequens* etc.]

sequacious /sɪ'kweɪʃəs/ *adj.* **1** (of reasoning or a reasoner) not inconsequent, coherent. **2** *archaic* inclined to follow, lacking independence or originality, servile. □□ **sequaciously** *adv.* **sequacity** /sɪˈkwæsɪtɪ/ *n.* [L *sequax* f. *sequi* follow]

sequel /ˈsiːkw(ə)l/ *n.* **1** what follows (esp. as a result). **2** a novel, film, etc., that continues the story of an earlier one. □**in the sequel** as things developed afterwards. [ME f. OF *sequelle* or L *sequel(l)a* f. *sequi* follow]

sequela /sɪˈkwiːlə/ *n.* (*pl.* **sequelae** /-liː/) *Med.* (esp. in *pl.*) a morbid condition or symptom following a disease. [L f. *sequi* follow]

sequence /ˈsiːkwəns/ *n. & v.* —*n.* **1** succession, coming after or next. **2** order of succession (*shall follow the sequence of events; give the facts in historical sequence*). **3** a set of things belonging next to one another on some principle of order; a series without gaps. **4** a part of a film dealing with one scene or topic. **5** a set of poems on one theme. **6** a set of three or more playing-cards next to one another in value. **7** *Mus.* repetition of a phrase or melody at a higher or lower pitch. **8** *Eccl.* a hymn said or sung after the Gradual or Alleluia that precedes the Gospel. **9** succession without implication of causality (opp. CONSEQUENCE). —*v.tr.* **1** arrange in a definite order. **2** *Biochem.* ascertain the sequence of monomers in (esp. a polypeptide or nucleic acid). □**sequence of tenses** *Gram.* the dependence of the tense of a subordinate verb on the tense of the principal verb, according to certain rules (e.g. *I think you are, thought you were, wrong*). □□ **sequencer** *n.* [ME f. LL *sequentia* f. L *sequens* pres. part. of *sequi* follow]

sequent /ˈsiːkwənt/ *adj.* **1** following as a sequence or consequence. **2** consecutive. □□ **sequently** *adv.* [OF *sequent* or L *sequens* (as SEQUENCE)]

sequential /sɪˈkwenʃ(ə)l/ *adj.* forming a sequence or consequence or sequela. □□ **sequentiality** /-ʃɪˈælɪtɪ/ *n.* **sequentially** *adv.* [SEQUENCE, after CONSEQUENTIAL]

sequester /sɪˈkwestə(r)/ *v.tr.* **1** (esp. as **sequestered** *adj.*) seclude, isolate, set apart (*sequester oneself from the world; a sequestered life; a sequestered cottage*). **2** = SEQUESTRATE. **3** *Chem.* bind (a metal ion) so that it cannot react. [ME f. OF *sequestrer* or LL *sequestrare* commit for safe keeping f. L *sequester* trustee]

sequestrate /sɪˈkwestreɪt, ˈsiːkwɪ-/ *v.tr.* **1** confiscate, appropriate. **2** *Law* take temporary possession of (a debtor's estate etc.). **3** *Eccl.* apply (the income of a benefice) to clearing the incumbent's debts or accumulating a fund for the next incumbent. □□ **sequestrable** *adj.* **sequestration** /ˌsiːkwɪˈstreɪʃ(ə)n/ *n.* **sequestrator** /ˈsiːkwɪˌstreɪtə(r)/ *n.* [LL *sequestrare* (as SEQUESTER)]

sequestrum /sɪˈkwestrəm/ *n.* (*pl.* **sequestra** /-trə/) a piece of dead bone or other tissue detached from the surrounding parts. □□ **sequestral** *adj.* **sequestrotomy** /ˌsiːkwɪsˈtrɒtəmɪ/ *n.* (*pl.* **-ies**) [mod.L, neut. of L *sequester* standing apart]

sequin /ˈsiːkwɪn/ *n.* **1** a circular spangle for attaching to clothing as an ornament. **2** *hist.* a Venetian gold coin. □□ **sequinned** *adj.* (also **sequined**). [F f. It. *zecchino* f. *zecca* a mint f. Arab. *sikka* a die]

sequoia /sɪˈkwɔɪə/ *n.* a Californian evergreen coniferous tree, *Sequoia sempervirens*, of very great height. [mod.L genus-name, f. *Sequoiah*, the name of a Cherokee]

sera *pl.* of SERUM.

serac /seˈræk/ *n.* one of the tower-shaped masses into which a glacier is divided at steep points by crevasses crossing it. [Swiss F *sérac*, orig. the name of a compact white cheese]

seraglio /seˈrɑːlɪəʊ, sɪ-/ *n.* (*pl.* **-os**) **1** a harem. **2** *hist.* a Turkish palace, esp. that of the Sultan with government offices etc. at Constantinople. [It. *serraglio* f. Turk. f. Pers. *sarāy* palace: cf. SERAI]

serai /seˈraɪ, seˈrɑːɪ/ *n.* a caravanserai. [Turk. f. Pers. (as SERAGLIO)]

serang /səˈræŋ/ *n.* Anglo-Ind. a native head of a Lascar crew. [Hindi f. Pers. *sarhang* commander]

serape /seˈrɑːpeɪ/ *n.* (also **sarape** /sæ-/, **zarape** /zæ-/) a shawl or blanket worn as a cloak by Spanish Americans. [Mexican Sp.]

seraph /ˈserəf/ *n.* (*pl.* **seraphim** /-fɪm/ or **seraphs**) an angelic being, one of the highest order of the ninefold celestial hierarchy gifted esp. with love and associated with light, ardour, and purity. [back-form. f. *seraphim* (cf. CHERUB) (pl.) f. LL f. Gk *seraphim* f. Heb. *śĕrāpīm*]

seraphic /səˈræfɪk/ *adj.* **1** of or like the seraphim. **2** ecstatically adoring, fervent, or serene. □□ **seraphically** *adv.* [med.L *seraphicus* f. LL (as SERAPH)]

seraskier /ˌserəˈskɪə(r)/ *n.* *hist.* the Turkish Commander-in-Chief and minister of war. [Turk. f. Pers. *sar'askar* head of army]

Serb /sɜːb/ *n. & adj.* —*n.* **1** a native of Serbia in Yugoslavia. **2** a person of Serbian descent. —*adj.* = SERBIAN. [Serbian *Srb*]

Serbian /ˈsɜːbɪən/ *n. & adj.* —*n.* **1** the dialect of the Serbs (cf. SERBO-CROAT). **2** = SERB. —*adj.* of or relating to the Serbs or their dialect.

Serbo- /ˈsɜːbəʊ/ *comb. form* Serbian.

Serbo-Croat /ˌsɜːbəʊˈkrəʊæt/ *n. & adj.* (also **Serbo-Croatian** /-krəʊˈeɪʃ(ə)n/) —*n.* the main official language of Yugoslavia, combining Serbian and Croatian dialects. —*adj.* of or relating to this language.

SERC *abbr.* (in the UK) Science and Engineering Research Council.

sere¹ /sɪə(r)/ *n.* a catch of a gunlock holding the hammer at half or full cock. [prob. f. OF *serre* lock, bolt, grasp, f. *serrer* (see SERRIED)]

sere² var. of SEAR *adj.*

sere³ /sɪə(r)/ *n.* *Ecol.* a sequence of animal or plant communities. [L *serere* join in a SERIES]

serein /səˈræ̃/ *n.* a fine rain falling in tropical climates from a cloudless sky. [F f. OF *serain* ult. f. L *serum* evening f. *serus* late]

serenade /ˌserəˈneɪd/ *n. & v.* —*n.* **1** a piece of music sung or played at night, esp. by a lover under his lady's window, or suitable for this. **2** = SERENATA. —*v.tr.* sing or play a serenade to. □□ **serenader** *n.* [F *sérénade* f. It. *serenata* f. *sereno* SERENE]

serenata /ˌserəˈnɑːtə/ *n.* *Mus.* **1** a cantata with a pastoral subject. **2** a simple form of suite for orchestra or wind band. [It. (as SERENADE)]

serendipity /ˌserənˈdɪpɪtɪ/ *n.* the faculty of making happy and unexpected discoveries by accident. □□ **serendipitous** *adj.* **serendipitously** *adv.* [coined by Horace Walpole (1754) after *The Three Princes of Serendip* (Sri Lanka), a fairy-tale]

serene /sɪˈriːn, səˈriːn/ *adj. & n.* —*adj.* (**serener, serenest**) **1 a** (of the sky, the air, etc.) clear and calm. **b** (of the sea etc.) unruffled. **2** placid, tranquil, unperturbed. —*n.* *poet.* a serene expanse of sky, sea, etc. □**all serene** *Brit. sl.* all right. **Serene Highness** a title used in addressing and referring to members of some European royal families (*His Serene Highness; Their Serene Highnesses; Your Serene Highness*). □□ **serenely** *adv.* **sereneness** *n.* [L *serenus*]

serenity /sɪˈrenɪtɪ, sə'r-/ *n.* (*pl.* **-ies**) **1** tranquillity, being serene. **2** (**Serenity**) a title used in addressing and referring to a reigning prince or similar dignitary (*your Serenity*). [F *sérénité* or L *serenitas* (as SERENE)]

serf /sɜːf/ *n.* **1** *hist.* a labourer not allowed to leave the land on which he worked, a villein. **2** an oppressed person, a drudge. □□ **serfage** *n.* **serfdom** *n.* **serfhood** *n.* [OF f. L *servus* slave]

serge /sɜːdʒ/ *n.* a durable twilled worsted etc. fabric. [ME f. OF *sarge, serge* ult. f. L *serica* (*lana*): see SILK]

sergeant /ˈsɑːdʒ(ə)nt/ *n.* **1** a non-commissioned Army or Air Force officer next below warrant officer. **2** a police officer ranking below (*Brit.*) inspector or (*US*) captain. □**company sergeant-major** *Mil.* the highest non-commissioned officer of a company. **Sergeant Baker** *Austral.* a large brightly-coloured marine fish, *Aulopus purpurissatus*. **sergeant-fish**

a marine fish, *Rachycentron canadum*, with lateral stripes suggesting a chevron. **sergeant-major** *Mil.* **1** (in full **regimental sergeant-major**) *Brit.* a warrant-officer assisting the adjutant of a regiment or battalion. **2** *US* the highest-ranking non-commissioned officer. □□**sergeancy** *n.* (*pl.* **-ies**). **sergeantship** *n.* [ME f. OF *sergent* f. L *serviens -entis* servant f. *servire* SERVE]

Sergt. *abbr.* Sergeant.

serial /ˈsɪərɪəl/ *n. & adj.* —*n.* **1** a story, play, or film which is published, broadcast, or shown in regular instalments. **2** a periodical. —*adj.* **1** of or in or forming a series. **2** (of a story etc.) in the form of a serial. **3** *Mus.* using transformations of a fixed series of notes (see SERIES). **4** (of a publication) appearing in successive parts published usu. at regular intervals, periodical. □**serial killer** a person who murders continuously with no apparent motive. **serial number** a number showing the position of an item in a series. **serial rights** the right to publish a story or book as a serial. □□**seriality** /-ɪˈælɪtɪ/ *n.* **serially** *adv.* [SERIES + -AL]

serialist /ˈsɪərɪəlɪst/ *n.* a composer or advocate of serial music. □□**serialism** *n.*

serialize /ˈsɪərɪəˌlaɪz/ *v.tr.* (also **-ise**) **1** publish or produce in instalments. **2** arrange in a series. **3** *Mus.* compose according to a serial technique. □□ **serialization** /-ˈzeɪʃ(ə)n/ *n.*

seriate *adj. & v.* —*adj.* /ˈsɪərɪɪt/ in the form of a series; in orderly sequence. —*v.tr.* /ˈsɪərɪˌeɪt/ arrange in a seriate manner. □□**seriation** /-ˈeɪʃ(ə)n/ *n.*

seriatim /ˌsɪərɪˈeɪtɪm, ˌser-/ *adv.* point by point; taking one subject etc. after another in regular order (*consider seriatim*). [med.L f. L *series*, after LITERATIM etc.]

Seric /ˈsɪərɪk/ *adj. archaic* Chinese. [L *sericus*; see SILK]

sericeous /sɪˈrɪʃəs/ *adj.* Bot. & Zool. covered with silky hairs. [LL *sericeus* silken]

sericulture /ˈserɪˌkʌltʃ(ə)r/ *n.* **1** silkworm-breeding. **2** the production of raw silk. □□**sericultural** /-ˈkʌltʃər(ə)l/ *adj.* **sericulturist** /-ˈkʌltʃərɪst/ *n.* [F *sériciculture* f. LL *sericum*: see SILK, CULTURE]

seriema /ˌserɪˈiːmə/ *n.* (also **cariama** /ˌkærɪˈɑːmə/) *Zool.* any S. American bird of the family Cariamidae, having a long neck and legs and a crest above the bill. [mod.L f. Tupi *siriema* etc. crested]

series /ˈsɪəriːz, -rɪz/ *n.* (*pl.* same) **1** a number of things of which each is similar to the preceding or in which each successive pair are similarly related; a sequence, succession, order, row, or set. **2** a set of successive games between the same teams. **3** a set of programmes with the same actors etc. or on related subjects but each complete in itself. **4** a set of lectures by the same speaker or on the same subject. **5 a** a set of successive issues of a periodical, of articles on one subject or by one writer, etc., esp. when numbered separately from a preceding or following set (*second series*). **b** a set of independent books in a common format or under a common title or supervised by a common general editor. **6** *Philately* a set of stamps, coins, etc., of different denominations but issued at one time, in one reign, etc. **7** *Geol.* **a** a set of strata with a common characteristic. **b** the rocks deposited during a specific epoch. **8** *Mus.* an arrangement of the twelve notes of the chromatic scale as a basis for serial music. **9** *Electr.* **a** a set of circuits or components arranged so that the current passes through each successively. **b** a set of batteries etc. having the positive electrode of each connected with the negative electrode of the next. **10** *Chem.* a set of elements with common properties or of compounds related in composition or structure. **11** *Math.* a set of quantities constituting a progression or having the several values determined by a common relation. □**arithmetical** (or **geometrical**) **series** a series in arithmetical (or geometrical) progression. **in series 1** in ordered succession. **2** *Electr.* (of a set

of circuits or components) arranged so that the current passes through each successively. [L, = row, chain f. *serere* join, connect]

serif /ˈserɪf/ *n.* a slight projection finishing off a stroke of a letter as in T contrasted with T (cf. SANSERIF). □□**seriffed** *adj.* [perh. f. Du. *schreef* dash, line f. Gmc]

serigraphy /səˈrɪgrəfɪ/ *n.* the art or process of printing designs by means of a silk screen. □□ **serigraph** /ˈserɪˌgrɑːf/ *n.* **serigrapher** *n.* [irreg. f. L *sericum* SILK]

serin /ˈserɪn/ *n.* any small yellow Mediterranean finch of the genus *Serinus*, esp. the wild canary *S. serinus.* [F, of uncert. orig.]

serinette /ˌserɪˈnet/ *n.* an instrument for teaching cage-birds to sing. [F (as SERIN)]

seringa /səˈrɪŋgə/ *n.* **1** = SYRINGA. **2** any of various rubber-trees of the genus *Hevea*, native to Brazil. [F (as SYRINGA)]

serio-comic /ˌsɪərɪəʊˈkɒmɪk/ *adj.* combining the serious and the comic, jocular in intention but simulating seriousness or vice versa. □□**serio-comically** *adv.*

serious /ˈsɪərɪəs/ *adj.* **1** thoughtful, earnest, sober, sedate, responsible, not reckless or given to trifling (*has a serious air; a serious young person*). **2** important, demanding consideration (*this is a serious matter*). **3** not slight or negligible (*a serious injury; a serious offence*). **4** sincere, in earnest, not ironical or joking (*are you serious?*). **5** (of music and literature) not merely for amusement (opp. LIGHT² 5a). **6** not perfunctory (*serious thought*). **7** not to be trifled with (*a serious opponent*). **8** concerned with religion or ethics (*serious subjects*). □□**seriousness** *n.* [ME f. OF *serieux* or LL *seriosus* f. L *serius*]

seriously /ˈsɪərɪəslɪ/ *adv.* **1** in a serious manner (esp. introducing a sentence, implying that irony etc. is now to cease). **2** to a serious extent.

serjeant /ˈsɑːdʒ(ə)nt/ *n.* **1** (in full **serjeant-at-law**, *pl.* **serjeants-at-law**) *hist.* a barrister of the highest rank. **2** *Brit.* (in official lists) a sergeant in the Army. □**Common Serjeant** *Brit.* a circuit judge of the Central Criminal Court with duties in the City of London. **serjeant-at-arms** (*pl.* **serjeants-at-arms**) an official of a court or city or parliament, with ceremonial duties. □□**serjeantship** *n.* [var. of SERGEANT]

sermon /ˈsɜːmən/ *n.* **1** a spoken or written discourse on a religious or moral subject, esp. a discourse based on a text or passage of Scripture and delivered in a service by way of religious instruction or exhortation. **2** a piece of admonition or reproof, a lecture. **3** a moral reflection suggested by natural objects etc. (*sermons in stones*). □**Sermon on the Mount** the discourse of Christ recorded in Matt. 5-7. [ME f. AF *sermun*, OF *sermon* f. L *sermo -onis* discourse, talk]

sermonette /ˌsɜːməˈnet/ *n.* a short sermon.

sermonize /ˈsɜːməˌnaɪz/ *v.* (also **-ise**) **1** *tr.* deliver a moral lecture to. **2** *intr.* deliver a moral lecture. □□ **sermonizer** *n.*

serology /sɪəˈrɒlədʒɪ/ *n.* the scientific study of blood sera and their effects. □□**serological** /-rəˈlɒdʒɪk(ə)l/ *adj.* **serologist** *n.*

serosa /səˈrəʊsə/ *n.* a serous membrane. [mod.L, fem. of med.L *serosus* SEROUS]

serotine /ˈserətɪn/ *n.* a chestnut-coloured European bat, *Eptesicus serotinus.* [F *sérotine* f. L *serotinus* late, of the evening, f. *serus* late]

serotonin /ˌsɪərəˈtəʊnɪn/ *n. Biol.* a compound present in blood serum, which constricts the blood vessels and acts as a neurotransmitter. [SERUM + TONIC + -IN]

serous /ˈsɪərəs/ *adj.* of or like or producing serum; watery. □**serous gland** (or **membrane**) a gland or membrane with a serous secretion. □□**serosity** /-ˈrɒsɪtɪ/ *n.* [F *séreux* or med.L *serosus* (as SERUM)]

serpent /ˈsɜːpənt/ *n.* **1** usu. *literary.* **a** a snake, esp.

of a large kind. **b** a scaly limbless reptile. **2** a sly or treacherous person, esp. one who exploits a position of trust to betray it. **3** *Mus.* an old bass wind instrument made from leather-covered wood, roughly in the form of an S. **4 (the Serpent)** *Bibl.* Satan (see Gen. 3, Rev. 20). [ME f. OF f. L *serpens -entis* part. of *serpere* creep]

serpentine /ˈsɜːpənˌtaɪn/ *adj., n.,* & *v.* —*adj.* **1** of or like a serpent. **2** coiling, tortuous, sinuous, meandering, writhing (*the serpentine windings of the stream*). **3** cunning, subtle, treacherous. —*n.* **1** a soft rock mainly of hydrated magnesium silicate, usu. dark green and sometimes mottled or spotted like a serpent's skin, taking a high polish and used as a decorative material. **2** *Skating* a figure of three circles in a line. —*v.intr.* move sinuously, meander. □**serpentine verse** a metrical line beginning and ending with the same word. [ME f. OF *serpentin* f. LL *serpentinus* (as SERPENT)]

serpiginous /sɜːˈpɪdʒɪnəs/ *adj.* (of a skin-disease etc.) creeping from one part to another. [med.L *serpigo -ginis* ringworm f. L *serpere* creep]

SERPS /sɜːps/ *abbr.* (in the UK) State earnings-related pension scheme.

serpula /ˈsɜːpjʊlə/ *n.* (*pl.* **serpulae** /-liː/) any of various marine worms of the family Serpulidae, living in intricately twisted shell-like tubes. [LL, = small serpent, f. L *serpere* creep]

serra /ˈserə/ *n.* (*pl.* **serrae** /-riː/) a serrated organ, structure, or edge. [L, = saw]

serradilla /ˌserəˈdɪlə/ *n.* (*pl.* **serradillae** /-liː/) a clover, *Ornithopus sativus*, grown as fodder. [Port., dimin. of *serrado* serrated]

serran /ˈserən/ *n.* any marine fish of the family Serranidae. [mod.L *serranus* f. L *serra* saw]

serrate *v.* & *adj.* —*v.tr.* /seˈreɪt/ (usu. as **serrated** *adj.*) provide with a sawlike edge. —*adj.* /ˈserɪt/ esp. *Anat., Bot.,* & *Zool.* notched like a saw. □□ **serration** *n.* [LL *serrare serrat-* f. L *serra* saw]

serried /ˈserɪd/ *adj.* (of ranks of soldiers, rows of trees, etc.) pressed together; without gaps; close. [past part. of *serry* press close prob. f. F *serré* past part. of *serrer* close ult. f. L *sera* lock, or past part. of obs. *serr* f. OF *serrer*]

serrulate /ˈserʊˌleɪt/ *adj.* esp. *Anat., Bot.,* & *Zool.* finely serrate; with a series of small notches. □□ **serrulation** /-ˈleɪʃ(ə)n/ *n.* [mod.L *serrulatus* f. L *serrula* dimin. of *serra* saw]

serum /ˈsɪərəm/ *n.* (*pl.* **sera** /-rə/ or **serums**) **1 a** an amber-coloured liquid that separates from a clot when blood coagulates. **b** whey. **2** *Med.* blood serum (usu. from a non-human mammal) as an antitoxin or therapeutic agent, esp. in inoculation. **3** a watery fluid in animal bodies. □**serum sickness** a reaction to an injection of serum, characterized by skin eruption, fever, etc. [L, = whey]

serval /ˈsɜːv(ə)l/ *n.* a tawny black-spotted long-legged African cat, *Felis serval*. [F f. Port. *cerval* deerlike f. *cervo* deer f. L *cervus*]

servant /ˈsɜːv(ə)nt/ *n.* **1** a person who has undertaken (usu. in return for stipulated pay) to carry out the orders of an individual or corporate employer, esp. a person employed in a house on domestic duties or as a personal attendant. **2** a devoted follower, a person willing to serve another (*a servant of Jesus Christ*). □**your humble servant** *Brit. archaic* a formula preceding a signature or expressing ironical courtesy. **your obedient servant** *Brit.* a formula preceding a signature, now used only in certain formal letters. [ME f. OF (as SERVE)]

serve /sɜːv/ *v.* & *n.* —*v.* **1** *tr.* do a service for (a person, community, etc.). **2** *tr.* (also *absol.*) be a servant to. **3** *intr.* carry out duties (*served on six committees*). **4** *intr.* **a** (foll. by *in*) be employed in (an organization, esp. the armed forces, or a place, esp. a foreign country) (*served in the air force*). **b** be a member of the armed forces. **5 a** *tr.* be useful to or serviceable for; meet the needs of; do what is required

for (*serve a purpose; one packet serves him for a week*). **b** *intr.* meet requirements; perform a function (*a sofa serving as a bed*). **c** *intr.* (foll. by *to* + infin.) avail, suffice (*his attempt served only to postpone the inevitable; it serves to show the folly of such action*). **6** *tr.* go through a due period of (office, apprenticeship, a prison sentence, etc.). **7** *tr.* set out or present (food) for those about to eat it (*asparagus served with butter; dinner was then served*). **8** *intr.* (in full **serve at table**) act as a waiter. **9** *tr.* **a** attend to (a customer in a shop). **b** (foll. by *with*) supply with (goods) (*was serving a customer with apples; served the town with gas*). **10** *tr.* treat or act towards (a person) in a specified way (*has served me shamefully; you may serve me as you will*). **11** *tr.* **a** (often foll. by *on*) deliver (a writ etc.) to the person concerned in a legally formal manner (*served a warrant on him*). **b** (foll. by *with*) deliver a writ etc. to (a person) in this way (*served her with a summons*). **12** *tr. Tennis* etc. **a** (also *absol.*) deliver (a ball etc.) to begin or resume play. **b** produce (a fault etc.) by doing this. **13** *tr. Mil.* keep (a gun, battery, etc.) firing. **14** *tr.* (of an animal, esp. a stallion etc. hired for the purpose) copulate with (a female). **15** *tr.* distribute (*served the ammunition out; served the rations round*). **16** *tr.* render obedience to (a deity etc.). **17** *Eccl.* **a** *intr.* act as a server. **b** *tr.* act as a server at (a service). **18** *intr.* (of a tide) be suitable for a ship to leave harbour etc. **19** *tr. Naut.* bind (a rope etc.) with thin cord to strengthen it. **20** *tr.* play (a trick etc.) on. —*n.* **1** *Tennis* etc. **a** the act or an instance of serving. **b** a manner of serving. **c** a person's turn to serve. **2** *Austral. sl.* a reprimand. □**it will serve** it will be adequate. **serve one's needs** (or **need**) be adequate. **serve out** retaliate on. **serve the purpose of** take the place of, be used as. **serve a person right** be a person's deserved punishment or misfortune. **serve one's time 1** hold office for the normal period. **2** (also **serve time**) undergo imprisonment, apprenticeship, etc. **serve one's** (or **the**) **turn** be adequate. **serve up** offer for acceptance. [ME f. OF *servir* f. L *servire* f. *servus* slave]

server /ˈsɜːvə(r)/ *n.* **1** a person who serves. **2** *Eccl.* a person assisting the celebrant at a service, esp. the Eucharist.

servery /ˈsɜːvərɪ/ *n.* (*pl.* **-ies**) a room from which meals etc. are served and in which utensils are kept.

service¹ /ˈsɜːvɪs/ *n.* & *v.* —*n.* **1** the act of helping or doing work for another or for a community etc. **2** work done in this way. **3** assistance or benefit given to someone. **4** the provision or system of supplying a public need, e.g. transport, or (often in *pl.*) the supply of water, gas, electricity, telephone, etc. **5 a** the fact or status of being a servant. **b** employment or a position as a servant. **6** a state or period of employment doing work for an individual or organization (*resigned after 15 years' service*). **7 a** a public or Crown department or organization employing officials working for the State (*civil service; secret service*). **b** employment in this. **8** (in *pl.*) the armed forces. **9** (*attrib.*) of the kind issued to the armed forces (*a service revolver*). **10 a** a ceremony of worship according to prescribed forms. **b** a form of liturgy for this. **11** the provision of what is necessary for the installation and maintenance of a machine etc. or operation. **b** a periodic routine maintenance of a motor vehicle etc. **12** assistance or advice given to customers after the sale of goods. **13 a** the act or process of serving food, drinks, etc. **b** an extra charge nominally made for this. **14** a set of dishes, plates, etc., used for serving meals (*a dinner service*). **15** *Tennis* etc. **a** the act or an instance of serving. **b** a person's turn to serve. **c** the manner or quality of serving. **d** (in full **service game**) a game in which a particular player serves. —*v.tr.* **1** provide service or services for, esp. maintain. **2** maintain or repair (a car, machine, etc.). **3** pay interest on (a debt). **4** supply with a service. □**at a person's**

service ready to serve or assist a person. **be of service** be available to assist. **in service 1** employed as a servant. **2** available for use. **on active service** serving in the armed forces in wartime. **out of service** not available for use. **see service 1** have experience of service, esp. in the armed forces. **2** (of a thing) be much used. **service area 1** an area beside a major road for the supply of petrol, refreshments, etc. **2** the area served by a broadcasting station. **service-book** a book of authorized forms of worship of a Church. **service bus** (or **car**) *Austral. & NZ* a motor coach. **service charge** an additional charge for service in a restaurant, hotel, etc. **service dress** ordinary military etc. uniform. **service flat** a flat in which domestic service and sometimes meals are provided by the management. **service industry** one providing services not goods. **service line** (in tennis etc.) a line marking the limit of the area into which the ball must be served. **service road** a road parallel to a main road, serving houses, shops, etc. **service station** an establishment beside a road selling petrol and oil etc. to motorists and often able to carry out maintenance. **take service with** become a servant to. [ME f. OF *service* or L *servitium* f. *servus* slave]

service[2] /ˈsɜːvɪs/ *n.* (in full **service tree**) a European tree of the genus *Sorbus*, esp. *S. domestica* with toothed leaves, cream-coloured flowers, and small round or pear-shaped fruit eaten when overripe. □**service-berry 1** the fruit of the service tree. **2 a** any American shrub of the genus *Amelanchier*. **b** the edible fruit of this. [earlier *serves*, pl. of obs. *serve* f. OE *syrfe* f. Gmc *surbhjōn* ult. f. L *sorbus*]

serviceable /ˈsɜːvɪsəb(ə)l/ *adj.* **1** useful or usable. **2** able to render service. **3** durable; capable of withstanding difficult conditions. **4** suited for ordinary use rather than ornament. □□**serviceability** /-ˈbɪlɪtɪ/ *n.* **serviceableness** *n.* **serviceably** *adv.* [ME f. OF *servisable* (as SERVICE[1])]

serviceman /ˈsɜːvɪsmən/ *n.* (*pl.* **-men**) **1** a man serving in the armed forces. **2** a man providing service or maintenance.

servicewoman /ˈsɜːvɪsˌwʊmən/ *n.* (*pl.* **-women**) a woman serving in the armed forces.

serviette /ˌsɜːvɪˈet/ *n.* esp. *Brit.* a napkin for use at table. [ME f. OF f. *servir* SERVE]

servile /ˈsɜːvaɪl/ *adj.* **1** of or being or like a slave or slaves. **2** slavish, fawning; completely dependent. □□ **servilely** *adv.* **servility** /-ˈvɪlɪtɪ/ *n.* [ME f. L *servilis* f. *servus* slave]

serving /ˈsɜːvɪŋ/ *n.* a quantity of food served to one person.

servitor /ˈsɜːvɪt(ə)r/ *n.* **1** *archaic* **a** a servant. **b** an attendant. **2** *hist.* an Oxford undergraduate performing menial duties in exchange for assistance from college funds. □□**servitorship** *n.* [ME f. OF f. LL (as SERVE)]

servitude /ˈsɜːvɪˌtjuːd/ *n.* **1** slavery. **2** subjection (esp. involuntary); bondage. **3** *Law* the subjection of property to an easement. [ME f. OF f. L *servitudo -inis* f. *servus* slave]

servo /ˈsɜːvəʊ/ *n.* (*pl.* **-os**) **1** (in full **servo-mechanism**) a powered mechanism producing motion or forces at a higher level of energy than the input level, e.g. in the brakes and steering of large motor vehicles, esp. where feedback is employed to make the control automatic. **2** (in full **servo-motor**) the motive element in a servomechanism. **3** (in *comb.*) of or involving a servomechanism (*servo-assisted*). [L *servus* slave]

sesame /ˈsesəmɪ/ *n. Bot.* **1** an E. Indian herbaceous plant, *Sesamum indicum*, with seeds used as food and yielding an edible oil. **2** its seeds. □**open sesame** a means of acquiring or achieving what is normally unattainable (from the magic words used in the *Arabian Nights' Entertainments*). [L *sesamum* f. Gk *sēsamon, sēsamē*]

sesamoid /ˈsesəˌmɔɪd/ *adj. & n.* —*adj.* shaped like a sesame seed; nodular (esp. of small independent bones developed in tendons passing over an angular structure such as the kneecap and the navicular bone). —*n.* a sesamoid bone.

sesqui- /ˈseskwɪ/ *comb. form* **1** denoting one and a half. **2** *Chem.* (of a compound) in which there are three equivalents of a named element or radical to two others. [L (as SEMI-, -*que* and)]

sesquicentenary /ˌseskwɪsenˈtiːnərɪ/ *n.* (*pl.* **-ies**) a one-hundred-and-fiftieth anniversary.

sesquicentennial /ˌseskwɪsenˈtenɪəl/ *n. & adj.* —*n.* = SESQUICENTENARY. —*adj.* of or relating to a sesquicentennial.

sess var. of CESS[1].

sessile /ˈsesaɪl/ *adj.* **1** *Bot. & Zool.* (of a flower, leaf, eye, etc.) attached directly by its base without a stalk or peduncle. **2** fixed in one position; immobile. □**sessile oak** = DURMAST. [L *sessilis* f. *sedēre* sess-sit]

session /ˈseʃ(ə)n/ *n.* **1** the process of assembly of a deliberative or judicial body to conduct its business. **2** a single meeting for this purpose. **3** a period during which such meetings are regularly held. **4 a** an academic year. **b** the period during which a school etc. has classes. **5** a period devoted to an activity (*poker session; recording session*). **6** the governing body of a Presbyterian Church. □**in session** assembled for business; not on vacation. **petty sessions 1** a meeting of two or more magistrates for the summary trial of certain offences. **2** = *quarter sessions*. □□**sessional** *adj.* [ME f. OF *session* or L *sessio -onis* (as SESSILE)]

sesterce /ˈsestɜːs/ *n.* (also **sestertius** /seˈstɜːʃəs/) (*pl.* **sesterces** /ˈsestəˌsiːz/ or **sestertii** /-ˈstɜːʃɪɪ/) an ancient Roman coin and monetary unit equal to one quarter of a denarius. [L *sestertius* (*nummus* coin) = 2½ f. *semis* half + *tertius* third]

sestet /sesˈtet/ *n.* **1** the last six lines of a sonnet. **2** a sextet. [It. *sestetto* f. *sesto* f. L *sextus* a sixth]

sestina /sesˈtiːnə/ *n.* a form of rhymed or unrhymed poem with six stanzas of six lines and a final triplet, all stanzas having the same six words at the line-ends in six different sequences. [It. (as SESTET)]

set[1] /set/ *v.* (**setting**; *past* and *past part.* **set**) **1** *tr.* put, lay, or stand (a thing) in a certain position or location (*set it on the table; set it upright*). **2** *tr.* (foll. by *to*) apply (one thing) to (another) (*set pen to paper*). **3** *tr.* a fix ready or in position. **b** dispose suitably for use, action, or display. **4** *tr.* **a** adjust the hands of (a clock or watch) to show the right time. **b** adjust (an alarm clock) to sound at the required time. **5** *tr.* **a** fix, arrange, or mount. **b** insert (a jewel) in a ring, framework, etc. **6** *tr.* make (a device) ready to operate. **7** *tr.* lay (a table) for a meal. **8** *tr.* arrange (the hair) while damp so that it dries in the required style. **9** *tr.* (foll. by *with*) ornament or provide (a surface, esp. a precious item) (*gold set with gems*). **10** *tr.* bring by placing or arranging or other means into a specified state; cause to be (*set things in motion; set it on fire*). **11** *intr. & tr.* harden or solidify (*the jelly is set; the cement has set*). **12** *intr.* (of the sun, moon, etc.) appear to move towards and below the earth's horizon (as the earth rotates). **13** *tr.* represent (a story, play, scene, etc.) as happening in a certain time or place. **14** *tr.* **a** (foll. by *to* + infin.) cause or instruct (a person) to perform a specified activity (*set them to work*). **b** (foll. by pres. part.) start (a person or thing) doing something (*set him chatting; set the ball rolling*). **15** *tr.* present or impose as work to be done or a matter to be dealt with (*set them an essay*). **16** *tr.* exhibit as a type or model (*set a good example*). **17** *tr.* initiate; take the lead in (*set the fashion; set the pace*). **18** *tr.* establish (a record etc.). **19** *tr.* determine or decide (*the itinerary is set*). **20** *tr.* appoint or establish (*set them in authority*). **21** *tr.* join, attach, or fasten. **22** *tr.* **a** put parts of (a broken or dislocated bone, limb, etc.) into the correct position for healing. **b** deal with (a fracture or dislocation) in this way. **23**

tr. (in full **set to music**) provide (words etc.) with music for singing. **24** *tr.* (often foll. by *up*) *Printing* **a** arrange or produce (type or film etc.) as required. **b** arrange the type or film etc. for (a book etc.). **25** *intr.* (of a tide, current, etc.) have a certain motion or direction. **26** *intr.* (of a face) assume a hard expression. **27** *tr.* **a** cause (a hen) to sit on eggs. **b** place (eggs) for a hen to sit on. **28** *tr.* put (a seed, plant, etc.) in the ground to grow. **29** *tr.* give the teeth of (a saw) an alternate outward inclination. **30** *tr.* esp. *US* start (a fire). **31** *intr.* (of eyes etc.) become motionless. **32** *intr.* feel or show a certain tendency (*opinion is setting against it*). **33** *intr.* **a** (of blossom) form into fruit. **b** (of fruit) develop from blossom. **c** (of a tree) develop fruit. **34** *intr.* (in full **set to partner**) (of a dancer) take a position facing one's partner. **35** *intr.* (of a hunting dog) take a rigid attitude indicating the presence of game. **36** *intr.* *dial.* or *sl.* sit. □**set about 1** begin or take steps towards. **2** *colloq.* attack. **set (a person or thing) against (another) 1** consider or reckon (a thing) as a counterpoise or compensation for. **2** cause to oppose. **set apart** separate, reserve, differentiate. **set aside** see ASIDE. **set back 1** place further back in place or time. **2** impede or reverse the progress of. **3** *colloq.* cost (a person) a specified amount. **set-back** *n.* **1** a reversal or arrest of progress. **2** a relapse. **set by** *archaic* save for future use. **set down 1** record in writing. **2** allow to alight from a vehicle. **3** (foll. by *to*) attribute to. **4** (foll. by *as*) explain or describe to oneself as. **set eyes on** see EYE. **set one's face against** see FACE. **set foot on** (or **in**) see FOOT. **set forth 1** begin a journey. **2** make known; expound. **set forward** begin to advance. **set free** release. **set one's hand to** see HAND. **set one's heart** (or **hopes**) **on** want or hope for eagerly. **set in 1** (of weather, a condition, etc.) begin (and seem likely to continue), become established. **2** insert (esp. a sleeve etc. into a garment). **set little by** consider to be of little value. **set a person's mind at rest** see MIND. **set much by** consider to be of much value. **set off 1** begin a journey. **2** detonate (a bomb etc.). **3** initiate, stimulate. **4** cause (a person) to start laughing, talking, etc. **5** serve as an adornment or foil to; enhance. **6** (foll. by *against*) use as a compensating item. **set-off** *n.* **1** a thing set off against another. **2** a thing of which the amount or effect may be deducted from that of another or opposite tendency. **3** a counterpoise. **4** a counter-claim. **5** a thing that embellishes; an adornment to something. **6** *Printing* = OFFSET 7. **set on** (or **upon**) **1** attack violently. **2** cause or urge to attack. **set out 1** begin a journey. **2** (foll. by *to* + infin.) aim or intend. **3** demonstrate, arrange, or exhibit. **4** mark out. **5** declare. **set sail 1** hoist the sails. **2** begin a voyage. **set the scene** see SCENE. **set store by** (or **on**) see STORE. **set one's teeth 1** clench them. **2** summon one's resolve. **set to** begin doing something vigorously, esp. fighting, arguing, or eating. **set-to** *n.* (*pl.* **-tos**) *colloq.* a fight or argument. **set up 1** place in position or view. **2** organize or start (a business etc.). **3** establish in some capacity. **4** supply the needs of. **5** begin making (a loud sound). **6** cause or make arrangements for (a condition or situation). **7** prepare (a task etc. for another). **8** restore or enhance the health of (a person). **9** establish (a record). **10** propound (a theory). **11** *colloq.* put (a person) in a dangerous or vulnerable position. **set-up** *n.* **1** an arrangement or organization. **2** the manner or structure or position of this. **set oneself up as** make pretensions to being. [OE *settan* f. Gmc]

set² /set/ *n.* **1** a number of things or persons that belong together or resemble one another or are usually found together. **2** a collection or group. **3** a section of society consorting together or having similar interests etc. **4** a collection of implements, vessels, etc., regarded collectively and needed for a specified purpose (*cricket set; teaset; a set of teeth*). **5** a piece of electric or electronic apparatus, esp. a

radio or television receiver. **6** (in tennis etc.) a group of games counting as a unit towards a match for the player or side that wins a defined number or proportion of the games. **7** *Math.* & *Logic* a collection of distinct entities, individually specified or satisfying specified conditions, forming a unit. **8** a group of pupils or students having the same average ability. **9 a** a slip, shoot, bulb, etc., for planting. **b** a young fruit just set. **10 a** a habitual posture or conformation; the way the head etc. is carried or a dress etc. flows. **b** (also **dead set**) a setter's pointing in the presence of game. **11** the way, drift, or tendency (of a current, public opinion, state of mind, etc.) (*the set of public feeling is against it*). **12** the way in which a machine, device, etc., is set or adjusted. **13** esp. *Austral.* & *NZ colloq.* a grudge. **14 a** the alternate outward deflection of the teeth of a saw. **b** the amount of this. **15** the last coat of plaster on a wall. **16** *Printing* **a** the amount of spacing in type controlling the distance between letters. **b** the width of a piece of type. **17** a warp or bend or displacement caused by continued pressure or a continued position. **18** a setting, including stage furniture etc., for a play or film etc. **19** a sequence of songs or pieces performed in jazz or popular music. **20** the setting of the hair when damp. **21** (also **sett**) a badger's burrow. **22** (also **sett**) a granite paving-block. **23** a predisposition or expectation influencing a response. **24** a number of people making up a square dance. □**make a dead set at 1** make a determined attack on. **2** seek to win the affections of. **set point** *Tennis* etc. **1** the state of a game when one side needs only one more point to win the set. **2** this point. **set theory** the branch of mathematics concerned with the manipulation of sets. [sense 1 (and related senses) f. OF *sette* f. L *secta* SECT: other senses f. SET¹]

set³ /set/ *adj.* **1** in senses of SET¹. **2** prescribed or determined in advance. **3** fixed, unchanging, unmoving. **4** (of a phrase or speech etc.) having invariable or predetermined wording; not extempore. **5** prepared for action. **6** (foll. by *on*, *upon*) determined to acquire or achieve etc. **7** (of a book etc.) specified for reading in preparation for an examination. **8** (of a meal) served according to a fixed menu. □**set fair** (of the weather) without a sign of breaking. **set phrase** an invariable or usual arrangement of words. **set piece 1** a formal or elaborate arrangement, esp. in art or literature. **2** fireworks arranged on scaffolding etc. **set screw** a screw for adjusting or clamping parts of a machine. **set scrum** *Rugby Football* a scrum ordered by the referee. **set square** a right-angled triangular plate for drawing lines, esp. at 90°, 45°, 60°, or 30°. [past part. of SET¹]

seta /ˈsiːtə/ *n.* (*pl.* **setae** /-tiː/) *Bot.* & *Zool.* stiff hair; bristle. □□ **setaceous** /-ˈteɪʃəs/ *adj.* [L, = bristle]

setiferous /sɪˈtɪfərəs/ *adj.* (also **setigerous** /sɪˈtɪdʒərəs/) having bristles. [L *seta* bristle, *setiger* bristly + -FEROUS, -GEROUS]

seton /ˈsiːt(ə)n/ *n.* *Surgery* a skein of cotton etc. passed below the skin and left with the ends protruding to promote drainage etc. [ME f. med.L *seto*, *seta* silk, app. f. L *seta* bristle]

setose /ˈsiːtəʊz/ *adj.* *Biol.* bristly. [L *seta* bristle]

Setswana var. of TSWANA (and the preferred form for the language).

sett var. of SET² 21, 22.

settee /seˈtiː/ *n.* a seat (usu. upholstered), with a back and usu. arms, for more than one person. [18th c.: perh. a fanciful var. of SETTLE²]

setter /ˈsetə(r)/ *n.* **1 a** a dog of a large long-haired breed trained to stand rigid when scenting game (see SET¹ 35). **b** this breed. **2** a person or thing that sets.

setting /ˈsetɪŋ/ *n.* **1** the position or manner in which a thing is set. **2** the immediate surroundings (of a house etc.). **3** the surroundings of any object regarded as its framework; the environment of a thing. **4** the place and time, scenery, etc., of a story, drama, etc.

5 a frame in which a jewel is set. **6** the music to which words of a poem, song, etc., are set. **7** a set of cutlery and other accessories for one person at a table. **8** the way in which or level at which a machine is set to operate. □**setting lotion** lotion used to prepare the hair for being set.

settle¹ /'set(ə)l/ v. **1** tr. & intr. (often foll. by *down*) establish or become established in a more or less permanent abode or way of life. **2** intr. & tr. (often foll. by *down*) **a** cease or cause to cease from wandering, disturbance, movement, etc. **b** adopt a regular or secure style of life. **c** (foll. by *to*) apply oneself (to work, an activity, a way of life, etc.) (*settled down to writing letters*). **3 a** intr. sit or come down to stay for some time. **b** tr. cause to do this. **4** tr. & intr. bring to or attain fixity, certainty, composure, or quietness. **5** tr. determine or decide or agree upon (*shall we settle a date?*). **6** tr. **a** resolve (a dispute etc.). **b** deal with (a matter) finally. **7** tr. terminate (a lawsuit) by mutual agreement. **8** intr. **a** (foll. by *for*) accept or agree to (esp. an alternative not one's first choice). **b** (foll. by *on*) decide on. **9** tr. (also *absol.*) pay (a debt, an account, etc.). **10** intr. (as **settled** adj.) not likely to change for a time (*settled weather*). **11** tr. **a** aid the digestion of (food). **b** remedy the disordered state of (nerves, the stomach, etc.). **12** tr. **a** colonize. **b** establish colonists in. **13** intr. subside; fall to the bottom or on to a surface (*the foundations have settled*; *wait till the sediment settles*; *the dust will settle*). **14** intr. (of a ship) begin to sink. **15** tr. get rid of the obstruction of (a person) by argument or conflict or killing. □**settle one's affairs** make any necessary arrangements (e.g. write a will) when death is near. **settle a person's hash** see HASH¹. **settle in** become established in a place. **settle up 1** (also *absol.*) pay (an account, debt, etc.). **2** finally arrange (a matter). **settle with 1** pay all or part of an amount due to (a creditor). **2** get revenge on. **settling day** the fortnightly pay-day on the Stock Exchange. □□ **settleable** adj. [OE *setlan* (as SETTLE²)· f. Gmc]

settle² /'set(ə)l/ n. a bench with a high back and arms and often with a box fitted below the seat. [OE *setl* place to sit f. Gmc]

settlement /'setəlmənt/ n. **1** the act or an instance of settling; the process of being settled. **2 a** the colonization of a region. **b** a place or area occupied by settlers. **c** a small village. **3 a** a political or financial etc. agreement. **b** an arrangement ending a dispute. **4 a** the terms on which property is given to a person. **b** a deed stating these. **c** the amount of property given. **d** = *marriage settlement*. **5** the process of settling an account. **6** subsidence of a wall, house, soil, etc.

settler /'setlə(r)/ n. a person who goes to settle in a new country or place; an early colonist.

settlor /'setlə(r)/ n. *Law* a person who makes a settlement esp. of a property.

seven /'sev(ə)n/ n. & adj. —n. **1** one more than six, or three less than ten; the sum of four units and three units. **2** a symbol for this (7, vii, VII). **3** a size etc. denoted by seven. **4** a set or team of seven individuals. **5** the time of seven o'clock (*is it seven yet?*). **6** a card with seven pips. —adj. that amount to seven. □**the seven deadly sins** the sins of pride, covetousness, lust, anger, gluttony, envy, and sloth. **the seven seas** the oceans of the world: the Arctic, Antarctic, N. Pacific, S. Pacific, N. Atlantic, S. Atlantic, and Indian Oceans. **the seven wonders of the world** see WONDER. **seven year itch** a supposed tendency to infidelity after seven years of marriage. [OE *seofon* f. Gmc]

sevenfold /'sevən,fəʊld/ adj. & adv. **1** seven times as much or as many. **2** consisting of seven parts.

seventeen /,sevən'ti:n/ n. & adj. —n. **1** one more than sixteen, or seven more than ten. **2** a symbol for this (17, xvii, XVII). **3** a size etc. denoted by seventeen.

—adj. that amount to seventeen. □□ **seventeenth** adj. & n. [OE *seofontīene*]

seventh /'sev(ə)nθ/ n. & adj. —n. **1** the position in a sequence corresponding to the number 7 in the sequence 1-7. **2** something occupying this position. **3** one of seven equal parts of a thing. **4** *Mus.* **a** an interval or chord spanning seven consecutive notes in the diatonic scale (e.g. C to B). **b** a note separated from another by this interval. —adj. that is the seventh. □**in seventh heaven** see HEAVEN. **Seventh-Day Adventists** a staunchly protestant branch of the Adventists with beliefs based rigidly on faith and the Scriptures and the imminent return of Christ to earth, and observing the sabbath on Saturday. □□ **seventhly** adv.

seventy /'sevntɪ/ n. & adj. —n. (pl. **-ies**) **1** the product of seven and ten. **2** a symbol for this (70, lxx, LXX). **3** (in *pl.*) the numbers from 70 to 79, esp. the years of a century or of a person's life. —adj. that amount to seventy. □**seventy-first, -second**, etc. the ordinal numbers between seventieth and eightieth. **seventy-one, -two**, etc. the cardinal numbers between seventy and eighty. □□ **seventieth** adj. & n. **seventyfold** adj. & adv. [OE *-seofontig*]

sever /'sevə(r)/ v. **1** tr. & intr. (often foll. by *from*) divide, break, or make separate, esp. by cutting. **2** tr. & intr. break off or away; separate, part, divide (*severed our friendship*). **3** tr. end the employment contract of (a person). □□ **severable** adj. [ME f. AF *severer*, OF *sevrer* ult. f. L *separare* SEPARATE *v.*]

several /'sevr(ə)l/ adj. & n. —adj. & n. more than two but not many. —adj. **1** separate or respective; distinct (*all went their several ways*). **2** *Law* applied or regarded separately (opp. JOINT). □□ **severally** adv. [ME f. AF f. AL *separalis* f. L *separ* SEPARATE adj.]

severalty /'sevrəltɪ/ n. **1** separateness. **2** the individual or unshared tenure of an estate etc. (esp. *in severalty*). [ME f. AF *severalte* (as SEVERAL)]

severance /'sevərəns/ n. **1** the act or an instance of severing. **2** a severed state. □**severance pay** an amount paid to an employee on the early termination of a contract.

severe /sɪ'vɪə(r)/ adj. **1** rigorous, strict, and harsh in attitude or treatment (*a severe critic*; *severe discipline*). **2** serious, critical (*a severe shortage*). **3** vehement or forceful (*a severe storm*). **4** extreme (in an unpleasant quality) (*a severe winter*; *severe cold*). **5** arduous or exacting; making great demands on energy, skill, etc. (*severe competition*). **6** unadorned; plain in style (*severe dress*). □□ **severely** adv. **severity** /-'verɪtɪ/ n. [F *sévère* or L *severus*]

severy /'sevərɪ/ n. (pl. **-ies**) *Archit.* a space or compartment in a vaulted ceiling. [ME f. OF *civoire* (as CIBORIUM)]

Seville orange /'sevɪl/ n. a bitter orange used for marmalade. [*Seville* in Spain]

Sèvres /'seɪvr/ n. fine porcelain, often with elaborate decoration, made at Sèvres in the suburbs of Paris.

sew /səʊ/ v.tr. (past part. **sewn** /səʊn/ or **sewed**) **1** (also *absol.*) fasten, join, etc., by making stitches with a needle and thread or a sewing-machine. **2** make (a garment etc.) by sewing. **3** (often foll. by *on, in*, etc.) attach by sewing (*shall I sew on your buttons?*). □**sew up 1** join or enclose by sewing. **2** *colloq.* (esp. in *passive*) satisfactorily arrange or finish dealing with (a project etc.). **3** esp. *US* obtain exclusive use of. [OE *si(o)wan*]

sewage /'su:ɪdʒ, 'sju:-/ n. waste matter, esp. excremental, conveyed in sewers. □**sewage farm** (or **works**) a place where sewage is treated, esp. to produce manure.

sewen var. of SEWIN.

sewer /'su:ə(r), 'sju:-/ n. a conduit, usu. underground, for carrying off drainage water and sewage. □**sewer rat** the common brown rat. [ME f. AF *sever(e)*, ONF *se(u)wiere* channel to carry off the overflow from a fishpond, ult. f. L *ex-* out of + *aqua* water]

sewerage /'suːərɪdʒ, 'sjuː-/ n. a system of or drainage by sewers.

sewin /'sjuːɪn/ n. (also **sewen**) a salmon trout of Welsh etc. rivers. [16th c.: orig. unkn.]

sewing /'səʊɪŋ/ n. a piece of material or work to be sewn.

sewing-machine /'səʊɪŋməˌʃiːn/ n. a machine for sewing or stitching.

sewn past part. of SEW.

sex /seks/ n., adj., & v. —n. **1** either of the main divisions (male and female) into which living things are placed on the basis of their reproductive functions. **2** the fact of belonging to one of these. **3** males or females collectively. **4** sexual instincts, desires, etc., or their manifestation. **5** colloq. sexual intercourse. —adj. **1** of or relating to sex (sex education). **2** arising from a difference or consciousness of sex (sex antagonism; sex urge). —v.tr. **1** determine the sex of. **2** (as **sexed** adj.) **a** having a sexual appetite (highly sexed). **b** having sexual characteristics. □**sex act** (usu. prec. by the) the (or an) act of sexual intercourse. **sex appeal** sexual attractiveness. **sex change** an apparent change of sex by surgical means and hormone treatment. **sex chromosome** a chromosome concerned in determining the sex of an organism, which in most animals are of two kinds, the X-chromosome and the Y-chromosome. **sex hormone** a hormone affecting sexual development or behaviour. **sex kitten** colloq. a young woman who asserts her sex appeal. **sex life** a person's activity related to sexual instincts. **sex-linked** Genetics carried on or by a sex chromosome. **sex maniac** colloq. a person needing or seeking excessive gratification of the sexual instincts. **sex object** a person regarded mainly in terms of sexual attractiveness. **sex-starved** lacking sexual gratification. **sex symbol** a person widely noted for sex appeal. □□**sexer** n. [ME f. OF sexe or L sexus]

sexagenarian /ˌseksədʒɪ'neərɪən/ n. & adj. —n. a person from 60 to 69 years old. —adj. of this age. [L sexagenarius f. sexageni distrib. of sexaginta sixty]

Sexagesima /ˌseksə'dʒesɪmə/ n. the Sunday before Quinquagesima. [ME f. eccl.L, = sixtieth (day), prob. named loosely as preceding QUINQUAGESIMA]

sexagesimal /ˌseksə'dʒesɪm(ə)l/ adj. & n. —adj. **1** of sixtieths. **2** of sixty. **3** reckoning or reckoned by sixtieths. —n. (in full **sexagesimal fraction**) a fraction with a denominator equal to a power of 60 as in the divisions of the degree and hour. □□**sexagesimally** adv. [L sexagesimus (as SEXAGESIMA)]

sexcentenary /ˌseksen'tiːnərɪ/ n. & adj. —n. (pl. -ies) **1** a six-hundredth anniversary. **2** a celebration of this. —adj. **1** of or relating to a sexcentenary. **2** occurring every six hundred years.

sexennial /sek'senɪəl/ adj. **1** lasting six years. **2** recurring every six years. [SEXI- + L annus year]

sexfoil /'seksfɔɪl/ n. a six-lobed ornamental figure. [SEXI-, after CINQUEFOIL, TREFOIL]

sexi- /'seksɪ/ comb. form (also **sex-** before a vowel) six. [L sex six]

sexism /'seksɪz(ə)m/ n. prejudice or discrimination, esp. against women, on the grounds of sex. □□**sexist** adj. & n.

sexivalent /'seksɪˌveɪlənt/ adj. (also **sexvalent**) Chem. having a valency of six.

sexless /'sekslɪs/ adj. **1** Biol. neither male nor female. **2** lacking in sexual desire or attractiveness. □□**sexlessly** adv. **sexlessness** n.

sexology /sek'sɒlədʒɪ/ n. the study of sexual life or relationships, esp. in human beings. □□**sexological** /-ə'lɒdʒɪk(ə)l/ adj. **sexologist** n.

sexpartite /seks'pɑːtaɪt/ adj. divided into six parts.

sexploitation /ˌseksplɔɪ'teɪʃ(ə)n/ n. colloq. the exploitation of sex, esp. commercially.

sexpot /'sekspɒt/ n. colloq. a sexy person (esp. a woman).

sext /sekst/ n. Eccl. **1** the canonical hour of prayer appointed for the sixth daytime hour (i.e. noon). **2** the office of sext. [ME f. L sexta hora sixth hour f. sextus sixth]

sextant /'sekst(ə)nt/ n. an instrument with a graduated arc of 60° used in navigation and surveying for measuring the angular distance of objects by means of mirrors. [L sextans -ntis sixth part f. sextus sixth]

sextet /sek'stet/ n. (also **sextette**) **1** Mus. a composition for six voices or instruments. **2** the performers of such a piece. **3** any group of six. [alt. of SESTET after L sex six]

sextillion /seks'tɪljən/ n. (pl. same or **sextillions**) a thousand raised to the seventh (or formerly, esp. Brit., the twelfth) power (10^{21} and 10^{36} respectively) (cf. BILLION). □□**sextillionth** [F f. L sex six, after septillion etc.]

sexto /'sekstəʊ/ n. (pl. -os) **1** a size of book or page in which each leaf is one-sixth that of a printing-sheet. **2** a book or sheet of this size. [L sextus sixth, as QUARTO]

sextodecimo /ˌsekstəʊ'desɪməʊ/ n. (pl. -os) **1** a size of book or page in which each leaf is one-sixteenth that of a printing-sheet. **2** a book or sheet of this size. [L sextus decimus 16th (as QUARTO)]

sexton /'sekst(ə)n/ n. a person who looks after a church and churchyard, often acting as bell-ringer and gravedigger. □**sexton beetle** any beetle of the genus Necrophorus, burying carrion to serve as a nidus for its eggs. [ME segerstane etc., f. AF, OF segerstein, secrestein f. med.L sacristanus SACRISTAN]

sextuple /'seks,tjuːp(ə)l/ adj., n., & v. —adj. **1** sixfold. **2** having six parts. **3** being six times as many or much. —n. a sixfold number or amount. —v.tr. & intr. multiply by six; increase sixfold. □□**sextuply** adv. [med.L sextuplus, irreg. f. L sex six, after LL quintuplus QUINTUPLE]

sextuplet /'seks,tjuːplɪt, -'tjuːplɪt/ n. **1** each of six children born at one birth. **2** Mus. a group of six notes to be played in the time of four. [SEXTUPLE, after triplet etc.]

sexual /'seksjʊəl, -ʃʊəl/ adj. **1** of or relating to sex, or to the sexes or the relations between them. **2** Bot. (of classification) based on the distinction of sexes in plants. **3** Biol. having a sex. □**sexual intercourse** the insertion of a man's erect penis into a woman's vagina, usu. followed by the ejaculation of semen. □□**sexuality** /-'ælɪtɪ/ n. **sexually** adv. [LL sexualis (as SEX)]

sexvalent var. of SEXIVALENT.

sexy /'seksɪ/ adj. (**sexier**, **sexiest**) **1** sexually attractive or stimulating. **2** sexually aroused. **3** concerned with or engrossed in sex. □□**sexily** adv. **sexiness** n.

sez /sez/ sl. says (sez you). [phonetic repr.]

SF abbr. science fiction.

sf abbr. Mus. sforzando.

SFA abbr. Scottish Football Association.

sforzando /sfɔː'tsændəʊ/ adj., adv., & n. (also **sforzato** /-'tsɑːtəʊ/) —adj. & adv. Mus. with sudden emphasis. —n. (pl. -os or **sforzandi** /-dɪ/) **1** a note or group of notes especially emphasized. **2** an increase in emphasis and loudness. [It., verbal noun and past part. of sforzare use force]

sfumato /sfuː'mɑːtəʊ/ adj. & n. Painting —adj. with indistinct outlines. —n. the technique of allowing tones and colours to shade gradually into one another. [It., past part. of sfumare shade off f. s- = EX-¹ + fumare smoke]

sfz abbr. Mus. sforzando.

SG abbr. **1** US senior grade. **2** Law Solicitor-General. **3** specific gravity.

sgd. abbr. signed.

sgraffito /sgrɑːˈfiːtəʊ/ n. (pl. **sgraffiti** /-tɪ/) a form of decoration made by scratching through wet plaster on a wall or through slip on ceramic ware, showing a different-coloured under-surface. [It., past part. of sgraffire scratch f. s- = EX-¹ + graffio scratch]

Sgt. abbr. Sergeant.

au how eɪ day əʊ no eə hair ɪə near ɔɪ boy ʊə poor aɪə fire aʊə sour (see over for consonants)

sh *int.* calling for silence. [var. of HUSH]

sh. *abbr. Brit. hist.* shilling(s).

shabby /ˈʃæbɪ/ *adj.* (**shabbier, shabbiest**) **1** in bad repair or condition; faded and worn, dingy, dilapidated. **2** dressed in old or worn clothes. **3** of poor quality. **4** contemptible, dishonourable (*a shabby trick*). □□ **shabbily** *adv.* **shabbiness** *n.* **shabbyish** *adj.* [*shab* scab f. OE *sceabb* f. ON, rel. to SAB]

shabrack /ˈʃæbræk/ *n. hist.* a cavalry saddle-cloth. [G *Schabracke* of E. European orig.: cf. Russ. *shabrak*]

shack /ʃæk/ *n. & v.* —*n.* a roughly built hut or cabin. —*v.intr.* (foll. by *up*) *sl.* cohabit, esp. as lovers. [perh. f. Mex. *jacal*, Aztec *xacatli* wooden hut]

shackle /ˈʃæk(ə)l/ *n. & v.* —*n.* **1** a metal loop or link, closed by a bolt, to connect chains etc. **2** a fetter enclosing the ankle or wrist. **3** (usu. in *pl.*) a restraint or impediment. —*v.tr.* fetter, impede, restrain. □ **shackle-bolt 1** a bolt for closing a shackle. **2** a bolt with a shackle at its end. [OE *sc(e)acul* fetter, corresp. to LG *shäkel* link, coupling, ON *skökull* wagon-pole f. Gmc]

shad /ʃæd/ *n.* (*pl.* same or **shads**) *Zool.* any deep-bodied edible marine fish of the genus *Alosa*, spawning in fresh water. [OE *sceadd* of unkn. orig.]

shaddock /ˈʃædək/ *n. Bot.* **1** the largest citrus fruit, with a thick yellow skin and bitter pulp. Also called POMELO. **2** the tree, *Citrus grandis*, bearing these. [Capt. *Shaddock*, who introduced it to the W. Indies in the 17th c.]

shade /ʃeɪd/ *n. & v.* —*n.* **1** comparative darkness (and usu. coolness) caused by shelter from direct light and heat. **2** a place or area sheltered from the sun. **3** a darker part of a picture etc. **4** a colour, esp. with regard to its depth or as distinguished from one nearly like it. **5** comparative obscurity. **6** a slight amount (*am a shade better today*). **7** a translucent cover for a lamp etc. **8** a screen excluding or moderating light. **9** an eye-shield. **10** (in *pl.*) esp. US *colloq.* sunglasses. **11** a slightly differing variety (*all shades of opinion*). **12** *literary* **a** a ghost. **b** (in *pl.*) Hades. **13** (in *pl.*; foll. by *of*) suggesting reminiscence or unfavourable comparison (*shades of Dr Johnson!*). —*v.* **1** *tr.* screen from light. **2** *tr.* cover, moderate, or exclude the light of. **3** *tr.* darken, esp. with parallel pencil lines to represent shadow etc. **4** *intr. & tr.* (often foll. by *away, off, into*) pass or change by degrees. □ **in the shade** in comparative obscurity. □□ **shadeless** *adj.* [OE *sc(e)adu* f. Gmc]

shading /ˈʃeɪdɪŋ/ *n.* **1** the representation of light and shade, e.g. by pencilled lines, on a map or drawing. **2** the graduation of tones from light to dark to create a sense of depth.

shadoof /ʃəˈduːf/ *n.* a pole with a bucket and counterpoise used esp. in Egypt for raising water. [Egypt. Arab. *šādūf*]

shadow /ˈʃædəʊ/ *n. & v.* —*n.* **1** shade or a patch of shade. **2** a dark figure projected by a body intercepting rays of light, often regarded as an appendage. **3** an inseparable attendant or companion. **4** a person secretly following another. **5** the slightest trace (*not the shadow of a doubt*). **6** a weak or insubstantial remnant or thing (*a shadow of his former self*). **7** (*attrib.*) *Brit.* denoting members of a political party in opposition holding responsibilities parallel to those of the government (*shadow Home Secretary*; *shadow cabinet*). **8** the shaded part of a picture. **9** a substance used to colour the eyelids. **10** gloom or sadness. —*v.tr.* **1** cast a shadow over. **2** secretly follow and watch the movements of. □ **shadow-boxing** boxing against an imaginary opponent as a form of training. □□ **shadower** *n.* **shadowless** *adj.* [repr. OE *scead(u)we*, oblique case of *sceadu* SHADE]

shadowgraph /ˈʃædəʊˌɡrɑːf/ *n.* **1** an image or photograph made by means of X-rays; = RADIOGRAM 2. **2** a picture formed by a shadow cast on a lighted surface. **3** an image formed by light refracted differently by different densities of a fluid.

shadowy /ˈʃædəʊɪ/ *adj.* **1** like or having a shadow. **2** full of shadows. **3** vague, indistinct. □□ **shadowiness** *n.*

shady /ˈʃeɪdɪ/ *adj.* (**shadier, shadiest**) **1** giving shade. **2** situated in shade. **3** (of a person or behaviour) disreputable; of doubtful honesty. □□ **shadily** *adv.* **shadiness** *n.*

shaft /ʃɑːft/ *n. & v.* —*n.* **1 a** an arrow or spear. **b** the long slender stem of these. **2** a remark intended to hurt or provoke (*a shaft of malice*; *shafts of wit*). **3** (foll. by *of*) **a** a ray (of light). **b** a bolt (of lightning). **4** the stem or handle of a tool, implement, etc. **5** a column, esp. between the base and capital. **6** a long narrow space, usu. vertical, for access to a mine, a lift in a building, for ventilation, etc. **7** a long and narrow part supporting or connecting or driving a part or parts of greater thickness etc. **8** each of the pair of poles between which a horse is harnessed to a vehicle. **9** the central stem of a feather. **10** *Mech.* a large axle or revolving bar transferring force by belts or cogs. **11** *US colloq.* harsh or unfair treatment. —*v.tr. US colloq.* treat unfairly. [OE *scæft, sceaft* f. Gmc]

shafting /ˈʃɑːftɪŋ/ *n. Mech.* **1** a system of connected shafts for transmitting motion. **2** material from which shafts are cut.

shag[1] /ʃæɡ/ *n.* **1** a rough growth or mass of hair etc. **2** a coarse kind of cut tobacco. **3** a cormorant, esp. the crested cormorant, *Phalacrocorax aristotelis*. [OE *sceacga*, rel. to ON *skegg* beard, OE *sceaga* coppice]

shag[2] /ʃæɡ/ *v.tr.* (**shagged, shagging**) *coarse sl.* ¶ Usually considered a taboo word. **1** have sexual intercourse with. **2** (usu. in *passive*; often foll. by *out*) exhaust; tire out. [18th c.: orig. unkn.]

shaggy /ˈʃæɡɪ/ *adj.* (**shaggier, shaggiest**) **1** hairy, rough-haired. **2** unkempt. **3** (of the hair) coarse and abundant. **4** *Biol.* having a hairlike covering. □ **shaggy-dog story** a long rambling story amusing only by its being inconsequential. □□ **shaggily** *adv.* **shagginess** *n.*

shagreen /ʃæˈɡriːn/ *n.* **1** a kind of untanned leather with a rough granulated surface. **2** a sharkskin rough with natural papillae, used for rasping and polishing. [var. of CHAGRIN in the sense 'rough skin']

shah /ʃɑː/ *n. hist.* a title of the former monarch of Iran. □□ **shahdom** *n.* [Pers. *šāh* f. OPers. *kšāyţiya* king]

shaikh var. of SHEIKH.

shake /ʃeɪk/ *v. & n.* —*v.* (*past* **shook** /ʃʊk/; *past part.* **shaken** /ˈʃeɪkən/) **1** *tr. & intr.* move forcefully or quickly up and down or to and fro. **2 a** *intr.* tremble or vibrate markedly. **b** *tr.* cause to do this. **3** *tr.* **a** agitate or shock. **b** *colloq.* upset the composure of. **4** *tr.* weaken or impair; make less convincing or firm or courageous (*shook his confidence*). **5** *intr.* (of a voice, note, etc.) make tremulous or rapidly alternating sounds; trill (*his voice shook with emotion*). **6** *tr.* brandish; make a threatening gesture with (one's fist, a stick, etc.). **7** *intr. colloq.* shake hands (*they shook on the deal*). **8** *tr.* esp. *US colloq.* = *shake off.* —*n.* **1** the act or an instance of shaking; the process of being shaken. **2** a jerk or shock. **3** (in *pl.*; prec. by *the*) a fit of or tendency to trembling or shivering. **4** *Mus.* a trill. **5** = *milk shake.* □ **in two shakes** (**of a lamb's** or **dog's tail**) very quickly. **no great shakes** *colloq.* not very good or significant. **shake a person by the hand** = *shake hands.* **shake down 1** settle or cause to fall by shaking. **2** settle down. **3** become established; get into harmony with circumstances, surroundings, etc. **4** *US sl.* extort money from. **shake the dust off one's feet** depart indignantly or disdainfully. **shake hands** (often foll. by *with*) clasp right hands at meeting or parting, in reconciliation or congratulation, or over a concluded bargain. **shake one's head** move one's head from side to side in refusal, denial, disapproval, or

---

b *but* d *dog* f *few* g *get* h *he* j *yes* k *cat* l *leg* m *man* n *no* p *pen* r *red* s *sit* t *top* v *voice*

concern. **shake in one's shoes** tremble with apprehension. **shake a leg 1** begin dancing. **2** make a start. **shake off 1** get rid of (something unwanted). **2** manage to evade (a person who is following or pestering one). **shake out 1** empty by shaking. **2** spread or open (a sail, flag, etc.) by shaking. **shake-out** n. = *shake-up*. **shake up 1** mix (ingredients) by shaking. **2** restore to shape by shaking. **3** disturb or make uncomfortable. **4** rouse from lethargy, apathy, conventionality, etc. **shake-up** n. an upheaval or drastic reorganization. □□ **shakeable** adj. (also **shakable**). [OE *sc(e)acan* f. Gmc]

shakedown /'ʃeɪkdaʊn/ n. **1** a makeshift bed. **2** US sl. a swindle; a piece of extortion. **3** (attrib.) US colloq. denoting a voyage, flight, etc., to test a new ship or aircraft and its crew.

shaken past part. of SHAKE.

shaker /'ʃeɪkə(r)/ n. **1** a person or thing that shakes. **2** a container for shaking together the ingredients of cocktails etc. **3** (**Shaker**) a member of an American religious sect living simply, in celibate mixed communities. □□ **Shakeress** n. (in sense 3). **Shakerism** n. (in sense 3). [ME, f. SHAKE: sense 3 from religious dances]

Shakespearian /ʃeɪk'spɪərɪən/ adj. & n. (also **Shakespearean**) —adj. **1** of or relating to William Shakespeare, English dramatist d. 1616. **2** in the style of Shakespeare. —n. a student of Shakespeare's works etc.

shako /'ʃeɪkəʊ/ n. (pl. **-os**) a cylindrical peaked military hat with a plume. [F *schako* f. Magyar *csákó* (*süveg*) peaked (cap) f. *csák* peak f. G *Zacken* spike]

shakuhachi /ˌʃʌkʊ'hʌtʃɪ/ n. (pl. **shakuhachis**) a Japanese bamboo flute. [Jap. f. *shaku* a measure of length + *hachi* eight (tenths)]

shaky /'ʃeɪkɪ/ adj. (**shakier**, **shakiest**) **1** unsteady; apt to shake; trembling. **2** unsound, infirm (a *shaky hand*). **3** unreliable, wavering (a *shaky promise*; *got off to a shaky start*). □□ **shakily** adv. **shakiness** n.

shale /ʃeɪl/ n. soft finely stratified rock that splits easily, consisting of consolidated mud or clay. □ **shale oil** oil obtained from bituminous shale. □□ **shaly** adj. [prob. f. G *Schale* f. OE *sc(e)alu* rel. to ON *skál* (see SCALE²)]

shall /ʃæl, ʃ(ə)l/ v.aux. (3rd sing. present **shall**; archaic 2nd sing. present **shalt** as below; past **should** /ʃʊd, ʃəd/) (foll. by infin. without *to*, or absol.; present and past only in use) **1** (in the 1st person) expressing the future tense (I shall return soon) or (with *shall* stressed) emphatic intention (I shall have a party). **2** (in the 2nd and 3rd persons) expressing a strong assertion or command rather than a wish (cf. WILL¹) (you shall not catch me again; they shall go to the party). ¶ For the other persons in senses 1, 2 see WILL¹. **3** expressing a command or duty (thou shalt not steal; they shall obey). **4** (in 2nd-person questions) expressing an enquiry, esp. to avoid the form of a request (cf. WILL¹) (shall you go to France?). □ **shall I?** do you want me to? [OE *sceal* f. Gmc]

shallot /ʃə'lɒt/ n. an onion-like plant, *Allium ascalonicum*, with a cluster of small bulbs. [*eschalot* f. F *eschalotte* alt. of OF *eschaloigne*: see SCALLION]

shallow /'ʃæləʊ/ adj., n., & v. —adj. **1** of little depth. **2** superficial, trivial (a *shallow mind*). —n. (often in pl.) a shallow place. —v.intr. & tr. become or make shallow. □□ **shallowly** adv. **shallowness** n. [ME, prob. rel. to *schald*, OE *sceald* SHOAL²]

shalom /ʃə'lɒm/ n. & int. a Jewish salutation at meeting or parting. [Heb. *šālôm* peace]

shalt /ʃælt/ archaic 2nd person sing. of SHALL.

sham /ʃæm/ v., n., & adj. —v. (**shammed**, **shamming**) **1** intr. feign, pretend. **2** tr. **a** pretend to be. **b** simulate (is *shamming sleep*). —n. **1** imposture, pretence. **2** a person or thing pretending or pretended to be what he or she or it is not. —adj. pretended, counterfeit. □□ **shammer** n. [perh. north. dial. var. of SHAME]

shaman /'ʃæmən/ n. a witch-doctor or priest claiming

to communicate with gods etc. □□ **shamanism** n.

shamanist n. & adj. **shamanistic** /-'nɪstɪk/ adj. [G *Schamane* & Russ. *shaman* f. Tungusian *samán*]

shamateur /'ʃæmə,tɜː(r)/ n. derog. a sports player who makes money from sporting activities though classed as an amateur. □□ **shamateurism** n. [SHAM + AMATEUR]

shamble /'ʃæmb(ə)l/ v. & n. —v.intr. walk or run with a shuffling or awkward gait. —n. a shambling gait. [prob. f. dial. *shamble* (adj.) ungainly, perh. f. *shamble legs* with ref. to straddling trestles: see SHAMBLES]

shambles /'ʃæmb(ə)lz/ n.pl. (usu. treated as sing.) **1** colloq. a mess or muddle (the *room was a shambles*). **2** a butcher's slaughterhouse. **3** a scene of carnage. [pl. of *shamble* stool, stall f. OE *sc(e)amul* f. WG f. L *scamellum* dimin. of *scamnum* bench]

shambolic /ʃæm'bɒlɪk/ adj. colloq. chaotic, unorganized. [SHAMBLES, prob. after SYMBOLIC]

shame /ʃeɪm/ n. & v. —n. **1** a feeling of distress or humiliation caused by consciousness of the guilt or folly of oneself or an associate. **2** a capacity for experiencing this feeling, esp. as imposing a restraint on behaviour (has *no sense of shame*). **3** a state of disgrace, discredit, or intense regret. **4 a** a person or thing that brings disgrace etc. **b** a thing or action that is wrong or regrettable. —v.tr. **1** bring shame on; make ashamed; put to shame. **2** (foll. by *into*, *out of*) force by shame (was *shamed into confessing*). □ **for shame!** a reproof to a person for not showing shame. **put to shame** disgrace or humiliate by revealing superior qualities etc. **shame on you!** you should be ashamed. **what a shame!** how unfortunate! [OE *sc(e)amu*]

shamefaced /ʃeɪm'feɪst, 'ʃeɪm-/ adj. **1** showing shame. **2** bashful, diffident. □□ **shamefacedly** /also -sɪdlɪ/ adv. **shamefacedness** n. [16th-c. alt. of *shamefast*, by assim. to FACE]

shameful /'ʃeɪmfʊl/ adj. **1** that causes or is worthy of shame. **2** disgraceful, scandalous. □□ **shamefully** adv. **shamefulness** n. [OE *sc(e)amful* (as SHAME, -FUL)]

shameless /'ʃeɪmlɪs/ adj. **1** having or showing no sense of shame. **2** impudent. □□ **shamelessly** adv. **shamelessness** n. [OE *sc(e)amlēas* (as SHAME, -LESS)]

shammy /'ʃæmɪ/ n. (pl. **-ies**) (in full **shammy leather**) colloq. = CHAMOIS 2. [repr. corrupted pronunc.]

shampoo /ʃæm'puː/ n. & v. —n. **1** liquid or cream used to lather and wash the hair. **2** a similar substance for washing a car or carpet etc. **3** an act or instance of cleaning with shampoo. —v.tr. (**shampoos**, **shampooed**) wash with shampoo. [Hind. *chhāmpo*, imper. of *chhāmpnā* to press]

shamrock /'ʃæmrɒk/ n. any of various plants with trifoliate leaves, esp. *Trifolium repens* or *Medicago lupulina*, used as the national emblem of Ireland. [Ir. *seamróg* trefoil, dimin. of *seamar* clover + *og* young]

shamus /'ʃeɪməs/ n. US sl. a detective. [20th c.: orig. uncert.]

shandy /'ʃændɪ/ n. (pl. **-ies**) a mixture of beer with lemonade or ginger beer. [19th c.: orig. unkn.]

shanghai /ʃæŋ'haɪ/ v. & n. —v.tr. (**shanghais**, **shanghaied**, **shanghaiing**) **1** force (a person) to be a sailor on a ship by using drugs or other trickery. **2** colloq. put into detention or an awkward situation by trickery. **3** Austral. & NZ shoot with a catapult. —n. (pl. **shanghais**) Austral. & NZ a catapult. [*Shanghai* in China]

Shangri-La /ˌʃæŋgrɪ'lɑː/ n. an imaginary paradise on earth. [the name of a hidden Tibetan valley in J. Hilton's *Lost Horizon* (1933)]

shank /ʃæŋk/ n. **1 a** the leg. **b** the lower part of the leg; the leg from knee to ankle. **c** the shin-bone. **2** the lower part of an animal's foreleg, esp. as a cut of meat. **3** a shaft or stem. **4 a** the long narrow part of a tool etc. joining the handle to the working end. **b** the

w *we*   z *zoo*   ʃ *she*   ʒ *decision*   θ *thin*   ð *this*   ŋ *ring*   x *loch*   tʃ *chip*   dʒ *jar*   (see over for vowels) stem of a key, spoon, anchor, etc. **c** the straight part of a nail or fish-hook. **5** the narrow middle of the sole of a shoe. □**shanks's mare** (or **pony**) one's own legs as a means of conveyance. □□ **shanked** *adj.* (also in *comb.*). [OE *sceanca* f. WG]

shanny /'ʃænɪ/ *n.* (*pl.* **-ies**) a long-bodied olive-green European marine fish, *Blennius pholis*. [19th c.: orig. unkn.: cf. 18th-c. *shan*]

shan't /ʃɑːnt/ *contr.* shall not.

shantung /ʃænˈtʌŋ/ *n.* soft undressed Chinese silk, usu. undyed. [*Shantung*, Chinese province]

shanty[1] /'ʃæntɪ/ *n.* (*pl.* **-ies**) **1** a hut or cabin. **2** a crudely built shack. □**shanty town** a poor or depressed area of a town, consisting of shanties. [19th c., orig. N.Amer.: perh. f. Can.F *chantier*]

shanty[2] /'ʃæntɪ/ *n.* (also **chanty**) (*pl.* **-ies**) (in full **sea shanty**) a song with alternating solo and chorus, of a kind orig. sung by sailors while hauling ropes etc. [prob. F *chantez*, imper. pl. of *chanter* sing: see CHANT]

SHAPE /ʃeɪp/ *abbr.* Supreme Headquarters Allied Powers Europe.

shape /ʃeɪp/ *n.* & *v.* —*n.* **1** the total effect produced by the outlines of a thing. **2** the external form or appearance of a person or thing. **3** a specific form or guise. **4** a description or sort or way (*not on offer in any shape or form*). **5** a definite or proper arrangement (*must get our ideas into shape*). **6 a** condition, as qualified in some way (*in good shape*; *in poor shape*). **b** (when unqualified) good condition (*back in shape*). **7** a person or thing as seen, esp. indistinctly or in the imagination (*a shape emerged from the mist*). **8** a mould or pattern. **9** a jelly etc. shaped in a mould. **10** a piece of material, paper, etc., made or cut in a particular form. —*v.* **1** *tr.* give a certain shape or form to; fashion, create. **2** *tr.* (foll. by *to*) adapt or make conform. **3** *intr.* give signs of a future shape or development. **4** *tr.* frame mentally; imagine. **5** *intr.* assume or develop into a shape. **6** *tr.* direct (one's life, course, etc.). □**lick** (or **knock**) **into shape** make presentable or efficient. **shape up 1** take a (specified) form. **2** show promise; make good progress. **shape up well** be promising. □□ **shapable** *adj.* (also **shapeable**). **shaped** *adj.* (also in *comb.*). **shaper** *n.* [OE *gesceap* creation f. Gmc]

shapeless /'ʃeɪplɪs/ *adj.* lacking definite or attractive shape. □□ **shapelessly** *adv.* **shapelessness** *n.*

shapely /'ʃeɪplɪ/ *adj.* (**shapelier**, **shapeliest**) **1** well formed or proportioned. **2** of elegant or pleasing shape or appearance. □□ **shapeliness** *n.*

shard /ʃɑːd/ *n.* **1** a broken piece of pottery or glass etc. **2** = POTSHERD. **3** a fragment of volcanic rock. **4** the wing-case of a beetle. [OE *sceard*: sense 3 f. *shard-borne* (Shakesp.) = born in a shard (dial., = cow-dung), wrongly taken as 'borne on shards']

share[1] /ʃeə(r)/ *n.* & *v.* —*n.* **1** a portion that a person receives from or gives to a common amount. **2 a** a part contributed by an individual to an enterprise or commitment. **b** a part received by an individual from this (*got a large share of the credit*). **3** part-proprietorship of property held by joint owners, esp. any of the equal parts into which a company's capital is divided entitling its owner to a proportion of the profits. —*v.* **1** *tr.* get or have or give a share of. **2** *tr.* use or benefit from jointly with others. **3** *intr.* have a share; be a sharer (*shall I share with you?*). **4** *intr.* (foll. by *in*) participate. **5** *tr.* (often foll. by *out*) a divide and distribute. **b** give away part of. □**share and share alike** make an equal division. **share-farmer** *Austral.* & *NZ* a tenant farmer who receives a share of the profits from the owner. □□ **shareable** *adj.* (also **sharable**). **sharer** *n.* [ME f. OE *scearu* division, rel. to SHEAR]

share[2] /ʃeə(r)/ *n.* = PLOUGHSHARE. [OE *scear, scær* f. Gmc]

sharecropper /'ʃeəˌkrɒpə(r)/ *n.* esp. *US* a tenant farmer who gives a part of each crop as rent. □□ **sharecrop** *v.tr.* & *intr.* (**-cropped**, **-cropping**).

shareholder /'ʃeəˌhəʊldə(r)/ *n.* an owner of shares in a company.

shariah /ʃəˈriːə/ *n.* the Muslim code of religious law. [Arab.*šarīʿa*]

sharif /ʃəˈriːf/ *n.* (also **shereef**, **sherif**) **1** a descendant of Muhammad through his daughter Fatima, entitled to wear a green turban or veil. **2** a Muslim leader. [Arab. *šarīf* noble f. *šarafa* be exalted]

shark[1] /ʃɑːk/ *n.* any of various large usu. voracious marine fish with a long body and prominent dorsal fin. [16th c.: orig. unkn.]

shark[2] /ʃɑːk/ *n. colloq.* a person who unscrupulously exploits or swindles others. [16th c.: orig. perh. f. G *Schurke* worthless rogue: infl. by SHARK[1]]

sharkskin /'ʃɑːkskɪn/ *n.* **1** the skin of a shark. **2** a smooth dull-surfaced fabric.

sharp /ʃɑːp/ *adj., n., adv.,* & *v.* —*adj.* **1** having an edge or point able to cut or pierce. **2** tapering to a point or edge. **3** abrupt, steep, angular (*a sharp fall*; *a sharp turn*). **4** well-defined, clean-cut. **5 a** severe or intense (*has a sharp temper*). **b** (of food etc.) pungent, keen (*a sharp appetite*). **c** (of a frost) severe, hard. **6** (of a voice or sound) shrill and piercing. **7** (of sand etc.) composed of angular grains. **8** (of words or temper etc.) harsh or acrimonious (*had a sharp tongue*). **9** (of a person) acute; quick to perceive or comprehend. **10** quick to take advantage; artful, unscrupulous, dishonest. **11** vigorous or brisk. **12** *Mus.* **a** above the normal pitch. **b** (of a key) having a sharp or sharps in the signature. **c** (C, F, etc., **sharp**) a semitone higher than C, F, etc. **13** *colloq.* stylish or flashy with regard to dress. —*n.* **1** *Mus.* **a** a note raised a semitone above natural pitch. **b** the sign (♯) indicating this. **2** *colloq.* a swindler or cheat. **3** a fine sewing-needle. —*adv.* **1** punctually (*at nine o'clock sharp*). **2** suddenly, abruptly, promptly (*pulled up sharp*). **3** at a sharp angle. **4** *Mus.* above the true pitch (*sings sharp*). —*v.* **1** *intr. archaic* cheat or swindle at cards etc. **2** *tr. US Mus.* make sharp. □**sharp end** *colloq.* **1** the bow of a ship. **2** the scene of direct action or decision. **sharp practice** dishonest or barely honest dealings. **sharp-set 1** set with a sharp edge. **2** hungry. □□ **sharply** *adv.* **sharpness** *n.* [OE *sc(e)arp* f. Gmc]

sharpen /'ʃɑːpən/ *v.tr.* & *intr.* make or become sharp. □□ **sharpener** *n.*

sharper /'ʃɑːpə(r)/ *n.* a swindler, esp. at cards.

sharpish /'ʃɑːpɪʃ/ *adj.* & *adv. colloq.* —*adj.* fairly sharp. —*adv.* **1** fairly sharply. **2** quite quickly.

sharpshooter /'ʃɑːpˌʃuːtə(r)/ *n.* a skilled marksman. □□ **sharpshooting** *n.* & *adj.*

sharp-witted /ʃɑːpˈwɪtɪd/ *adj.* keenly perceptive or intelligent. □□ **sharp-wittedly** *adv.* **sharp-wittedness** *n.*

shashlik /'ʃæʃlɪk/ *n.* (in Asia and E. Europe) a kebab of mutton and garnishings. [Russ. *shashlyk*, ult. f. Turk. *šiš* spit, skewer: cf. SHISH KEBAB]

Shasta /'ʃæstə/ *n.* (in full **Shasta daisy**) a European plant, *Chrysanthemum maximum*, with large daisy-like flowers. [*Shasta* in California]

Shastra /'ʃɑːstrə/ *n.* Hindu sacred writings. [Hindi *śāstr*, Skr. *śāstra*]

shatter /'ʃætə(r)/ *v.* **1** *tr.* & *intr.* break suddenly in pieces. **2** *tr.* severely damage or utterly destroy (*shattered hopes*). **3** *tr.* greatly upset or discompose. **4** *tr.* (usu. as **shattered** *adj.*) exhaust. □□ **shatterer** *n.* **shattering** *adj.* **shatteringly** *adv.* **shatter-proof** *adj.* [ME, rel. to SCATTER]

shave /ʃeɪv/ *v.* & *n.* —*v.tr.* (*past part.* **shaved** or (as *adj.*) **shaven**) **1** remove (bristles or hair) from the face etc. with a razor. **2** (also *absol.*) remove bristles or hair with a razor from the face etc. of (a person) or (a part of the body). **3 a** reduce by a small amount. **b** take (a small amount) away from. **4** cut thin slices from the surface of (wood etc.) to shape it. **5** pass close to without touching; miss narrowly. —*n.* **1** an act of shaving or the process of being shaved. **2** a close approach without contact. **3** a narrow miss or escape; = *close shave* (see CLOSE¹). **4** a tool for shaving wood etc. [OE *sc(e)afan* (sense 4 of noun f. OE *sceafa*) f. Gmc]

shaveling /ˈʃeɪvlɪŋ/ *n. archaic* **1** a shaven person. **2** a monk, friar, or priest.

shaven see SHAVE.

shaver /ˈʃeɪvə(r)/ *n.* **1** a person or thing that shaves. **2** an electric razor. **3** *colloq.* a young lad.

Shavian /ˈʃeɪvɪən/ *adj. & n.* —*adj.* of or in the manner of G. B. Shaw, Irish-born dramatist d. 1950, or his ideas. —*n.* an admirer of Shaw. [*Shavius*, Latinized form of *Shaw*]

shaving /ˈʃeɪvɪŋ/ *n.* **1** a thin strip cut off the surface of wood etc. **2** (*attrib.*) used in shaving the face (*shaving-cream*).

Shavuoth /ʃəˈvuːəs, ˌʃɑːvʊˈɒt/ *n.* (also **Shavuot**) the Jewish Pentecost. [Heb. *šāḇū'ōt* = weeks, with ref. to the weeks between Passover and Pentecost]

shaw /ʃɔː/ *n. esp. Brit.* the stalks and leaves of potatoes, turnips, etc. [perh. = SHOW *n.*]

shawl /ʃɔːl/ *n.* a piece of fabric, usu. rectangular and often folded into a triangle, worn over the shoulders or head or wrapped round a baby. □**shawl collar** a rolled collar extended down the front of a garment without lapel notches. □□**shawled** *adj.* [Urdu etc. f. Pers. *šāl*, prob. f. *Shāliāt* in India]

shawm /ʃɔːm/ *n. Mus.* a medieval double-reed wind instrument with a sharp penetrating tone. [ME f. OF *chalemie, chalemel, chalemeaus* (pl.), ult. f. L *calamus* f. Gk *kalamos* reed]

shchi /ʃiː/ *n.* a Russian cabbage soup. [Russ.]

she /ʃiː/ *pron. & n.* —*pron.* (*obj.* **her**; *poss.* **her**; *pl.* **they**) **1** the woman or girl or female animal previously named or in question. **2** a thing regarded as female, e.g. a vehicle or ship. **3** *Austral. & NZ colloq.* it; the state of affairs (*she'll be right*). —*n.* **1** a female; a woman. **2** (in *comb.*) female (*she-goat*). □**she-devil** a malicious or spiteful woman. [ME *scæ, sche*, etc., f. OE fem. demonstr. pron. & adj. *sīo, sēo*, acc. *sīe*]

s/he *pron.* a written representation of 'he or she' used to indicate both sexes.

shea /ʃiː/ *n.* a W. African tree, *Vitellaria paradoxa*, bearing nuts containing a large amount of fat. □**shea-butter** a butter made from this fat. [Mandingo *si, se, sye*]

sheading /ˈʃiːdɪŋ/ *n.* each of the six administrative divisions of the Isle of Man. [SHED¹ + -ING¹]

sheaf /ʃiːf/ *n. & v.* —*n.* (*pl.* **sheaves** /ʃiːvz/) a group of things laid lengthways together and usu. tied, esp. a bundle of cornstalks tied after reaping, or a collection of papers. —*v.tr.* make into sheaves. [OE *scēaf* f. Gmc (as SHOVE)]

shealing var. of SHIELING.

shear /ʃɪə(r)/ *v. & n.* —*v.* (*past* **sheared**, *archaic* except *Austral. & NZ* **shore** /ʃɔː(r)/; *past part.* **shorn** /ʃɔːn/ or **sheared**) **1** *tr.* cut with scissors or shears etc. **2** *tr.* remove or take off by cutting. **3** *tr.* clip the wool off (a sheep etc.). **4** *tr.* (foll. by *of*) **a** strip bare. **b** deprive. **5** *tr. & intr.* (often foll. by *off*) distort or be distorted, or break, from a structural strain. —*n.* **1** *Mech. & Geol.* a strain produced by pressure in the structure of a substance, when its layers are laterally shifted in relation to each other. **2** (in *pl.*) (also **pair of shears** *sing.*) a large clipping or cutting instrument shaped like scissors for use in gardens etc. □□**shearer** *n.* [OE *sceran* f. Gmc]

shearling /ˈʃɪəlɪŋ/ *n.* **1** a sheep that has been shorn once. **2** wool from a shearling.

shearwater /ˈʃɪəˌwɔːtə(r)/ *n.* **1** any long-winged sea bird of the genus *Puffinus*, usu. flying near the surface of the water. **2** = SKIMMER 4.

sheatfish /ˈʃiːtfɪʃ/ *n.* (*pl.* same or **sheatfishes**) a large freshwater catfish, *Silurus glanis*, native to European waters. [earlier *sheath-fish*, prob. after G *Scheid*]

sheath /ʃiːθ/ *n.* (*pl.* **sheaths** /ʃiːðz, ʃiːθs/) **1** a close-fitting cover, esp. for the blade of a knife or sword. **2** a condom. **3** *Bot., Anat., & Zool.* an enclosing case or

tissue. **4** the protective covering round an electric cable. **5** a woman's close-fitting dress. □**sheath knife** a dagger-like knife carried in a sheath. □□ **sheathless** *adj.* [OE *scǣth, scēath*]

sheathe /ʃiːð/ *v.tr.* **1** put into a sheath. **2** encase; protect with a sheath. [ME f. SHEATH]

sheathing /ˈʃiːðɪŋ/ *n.* a protective casing or covering.

sheave¹ /ʃiːv/ *v.tr.* make into sheaves.

sheave² /ʃiːv/ *n.* a grooved wheel in a pulley-block etc., for a rope to run on. [ME f. OE *scife* (unrecorded) f. Gmc]

sheaves *pl.* of SHEAF.

shebang /ʃɪˈbæŋ/ *n. US sl.* **1** a matter or affair (esp. *the whole shebang*). **2** a shed or hut. [19th c.: orig. unkn.]

shebeen /ʃɪˈbiːn/ *n. esp. Ir.* an unlicensed house selling alcoholic liquor. [Anglo-Ir. *síbín* f. *séibe* mugful]

shed¹ /ʃed/ *n.* **1** a one-storeyed structure usu. of wood for storage or shelter for animals etc., or as a workshop. **2** a large roofed structure with one side open, for storing or maintaining machinery etc. **3** *Austral. & NZ* an open-sided building for shearing sheep or milking cattle. [app. var. of SHADE¹]

shed² /ʃed/ *v.tr.* (**shedding**; *past* and *past part.* **shed**) **1** let or cause to fall off (*trees shed their leaves*). **2** take off (clothes). **3** reduce (an electrical power load) by disconnection etc. **4** cause to fall or flow (*shed blood*; *shed tears*). **5** disperse, diffuse, radiate (*shed light*). □**shed light on** see LIGHT¹. [OE *sc(e)adan* f. Gmc]

she'd /ʃiːd, ʃɪd/ *contr.* **1** she had. **2** she would.

shedder /ˈʃedə(r)/ *n.* **1** a person or thing that sheds. **2** a female salmon after spawning.

shedhand /ˈʃedhænd/ *n. Austral. & NZ* an unskilled assistant in a shearing shed.

sheen /ʃiːn/ *n.* **1** a gloss or lustre on a surface. **2** radiance, brightness. □□**sheeny** *adj.* [obs. *sheen* beautiful, resplendent f. OE *scēne*: sense assim. to SHINE]

sheep /ʃiːp/ *n.* (*pl.* same) **1** any ruminant mammal of the genus *Ovis* with a thick woolly coat, esp. kept in flocks for its wool or meat, and noted for its timidity. **2** a bashful, timid, or silly person. **3** (usu. in *pl.*) **a** a member of a minister's congregation. **b** a parishioner. □**separate the sheep from the goats** divide into superior and inferior groups (cf. Matt. 25: 33). **sheep-dip** a preparation for cleansing sheep of vermin or preserving their wool. **2** the place where sheep are dipped in this. **sheep-run** an extensive sheepwalk, esp. in Australia. **sheep's-bit** a plant, *Jasione montana*, resembling a scabious. □□ **sheeplike** *adj.* [OE *scēp, scæp, scēap*]

sheepdog /ˈʃiːpdɒg/ *n.* **1** a dog trained to guard and herd sheep. **2 a** a dog of various breeds suitable for this. **b** any of these breeds.

sheepfold /ˈʃiːpfəʊld/ *n.* an enclosure for penning sheep.

sheepish /ˈʃiːpɪʃ/ *adj.* **1** bashful, shy, reticent. **2** embarrassed through shame. □□**sheepishly** *adv.* **sheepishness** *n.*

sheepshank /ˈʃiːpʃæŋk/ *n.* a knot used to shorten a rope temporarily.

sheepskin /ˈʃiːpskɪn/ *n.* **1** a garment or rug of sheep's skin with the wool on. **2** leather from a sheep's skin used in bookbinding.

sheepwalk /ˈʃiːpwɔːk/ *n. Brit.* a tract of land on which sheep are pastured.

sheer¹ /ʃɪə(r)/ *adj. & adv.* —*adj.* **1** no more or less than; mere, unqualified, absolute (*sheer luck*; *sheer determination*). **2** (of a cliff or ascent etc.) perpendicular; very steep. **3** (of a textile) very thin; diaphanous. —*adv.* **1** directly, outright. **2** perpendicularly. □□**sheerly** *adv.* **sheerness** *n.* [ME *schere* prob. f. dial. *shire* pure, clear f. OE *scīr* f. Gmc]

sheer² /ʃɪə(r)/ *v. & n.* —*v.intr.* **1** esp. *Naut.* swerve or change course. **2** (foll. by *away, off*) go away, esp. from a person or topic one dislikes or fears. —*n.*

Naut. a deviation from a course. [perh. f. MLG *scheren* = SHEAR *v.*]

sheer³ /ʃɪə(r)/ *n.* the upward slope of a ship's lines towards the bow and stern. [prob. f. SHEAR *n.*]

sheerlegs /'ʃɪəlegz/ *n.pl.* (treated as *sing.*) a hoisting apparatus made from poles joined at or near the top and separated at the bottom for masting ships, installing engines, etc. [*sheer*, var. of SHEAR *n.* + LEG]

sheet¹ /ʃiːt/ *n. & v.* —*n.* **1** a large rectangular piece of cotton or other fabric, used esp. in pairs as inner bedclothes. **2 a** a broad usu. thin flat piece of material (e.g. paper or metal). **b** (*attrib.*) made in sheets (*sheet iron*). **3** a wide continuous surface or expanse of water, ice, flame, falling rain, etc. **4** a set of unseparated postage stamps. **5** *derog.* a newspaper, esp. a disreputable one. **6** a complete piece of paper of the size in which it was made, for printing and folding as part of a book. —*v.* **1** *tr.* provide or cover with sheets. **2** *tr.* form into sheets. **3** *intr.* (of rain etc.) fall in sheets. □**sheet lightning** a lightning flash with its brightness diffused by reflection. **sheet metal** metal formed into thin sheets by rolling, hammering, etc. **sheet music** music published in cut or folded sheets, not bound. [OE *scēte, scīete* f. Gmc]

sheet² /ʃiːt/ *n.* **1** a rope or chain attached to the lower corner of a sail for securing or controlling it. **2** (in *pl.*) the space at the bow or stern of an open boat. □**flowing sheets** sheets eased for free movement in the wind. **sheet anchor 1** a second anchor for use in emergencies. **2** a person or thing depended on in the last resort. **sheet bend** a method of temporarily fastening one rope through the loop of another. [ME f. OE *scēata*, ON *skaut* (as SHEET¹)]

sheeting /'ʃiːtɪŋ/ *n.* material for making bed linen.

sheikh /ʃeɪk/ *n.* (also **shaikh, sheik**) **1** a chief or head of an Arab tribe, family, or village. **2** a Muslim leader. □□ **sheikhdom** *n.* [ult. f. Arab. *šayk* old man, sheikh, f. *šāḵa* be or grow old]

sheila /'ʃiːlə/ *n. Austral. & NZ sl.* a girl or young woman. [orig. *shaler* (of unkn. orig.): assim. to the name *Sheila*]

shekel /'ʃek(ə)l/ *n.* **1** the chief monetary unit of modern Israel. **2** *hist.* a silver coin and unit of weight used in ancient Israel and the Middle East. **3** (in *pl.*) *colloq.* money; riches. [Heb. *šeḵel* f. *šāḵal* weigh]

shelduck /'ʃeldʌk/ *n.* (*pl.* same or **shelducks**; *masc.* **sheldrake**, *pl.* same or **sheldrakes**) any bright-plumaged coastal wild duck of the genus *Tadorna*, esp. *T. tadorna.* [ME prob. f. dial. *sheld* pied, rel. to MDu. *schillede* variegated, + DRAKE]

shelf¹ /ʃelf/ *n.* (*pl.* **shelves** /ʃelvz/) **1 a** a thin flat piece of wood or metal etc. projecting from a wall, or as part of a unit, used to support books etc. **b** a flat-topped recess in a wall etc. used for supporting objects. **2 a** a projecting horizontal ledge in a cliff face etc. **b** a reef or sandbank under water. **c** = *continental shelf.* □**on the shelf 1** (of a woman) past the age when she might expect to be married. **2** (esp. of a retired person) no longer active or of use. **shelf-life** the amount of time for which a stored item of food etc. remains usable. **shelf-mark** a notation on a book showing its place in a library. **shelf-room** available space on a shelf. □□ **shelved** /ʃelvd/ *adj.* **shelfful** *n.* (*pl.* **-fuls**). **shelflike** *adj.* [ME f. (M)LG *schelf*, rel. to OE *scylfe* partition, *scylf* crag]

shelf² /ʃelf/ *n. & v. Austral. sl.* —*n.* an informer. —*v.tr.* inform upon. [20th c.: orig. uncert.]

shell /ʃel/ *n. & v.* —*n.* **1 a** the hard outer case of many marine molluscs (*cockle shell*). **b** the esp. hard but fragile outer covering of a bird's, reptile's, etc. egg. **c** the usu. hard outer case of a nut-kernel, seed, etc. **d** the carapace of a tortoise, turtle, etc. **e** the wing-case or pupa-case of many insects etc. **2 a** an explosive projectile or bomb for use in a big gun or mortar. **b** a hollow metal or paper case used as a container for fireworks, explosives, cartridges, etc.

c *US* a cartridge. **3** a mere semblance or outer form without substance. **4** any of several things resembling a shell in being an outer case, esp.: **a** a light racing-boat. **b** a hollow pastry case. **c** the metal framework of a vehicle body etc. **d** the walls of an unfinished or gutted building, ship, etc. **e** an inner or roughly-made coffin. **f** a building shaped like a conch. **g** the handguard of a sword. **5** a group of electrons with almost equal energy in an atom. —*v.* **1** *tr.* remove the shell or pod from. **2** *tr.* bombard (a town, troops, etc.) with shells. **3** *tr.* provide or cover with a shell or shells. **4** *intr.* (usu. foll. by *off*) (of metal etc.) come off in scales. **5** *intr.* (of a seed etc.) be released from a shell. □**come out of one's shell** cease to be shy; become communicative. **shell-bit** a gouge-shaped boring bit. **shell company** an unimportant firm made the subject of a take-over bid because of its status on the Stock Exchange etc. **shell egg** an egg still in its shell, not dried etc. **shell-heap** (or **-mound**) *hist.* a kitchen midden. **shell-jacket** an army officer's tight-fitting undress jacket reaching to the waist. **shell-lime** fine quality lime produced by burning sea shells. **shell-money** shells used as a medium of exchange, e.g. wampum. **shell out** (also *absol.*) *colloq.* **1** pay (money). **2** hand over (a required sum). **shell-out** *n.* **1** the act of shelling out. **2** a game of snooker etc. played by three or more people. **shell-pink** a delicate pale pink. **shell-shock** a nervous breakdown resulting from exposure to battle. **shell-shocked** suffering from shell-shock. **shell-work** ornamentation consisting of shells cemented on to wood etc. □□ **shelled** *adj.* **shell-less** *adj.* **shell-like** *adj.* **shellproof** *adj.* (in sense 2a of *n.*). **shelly** *adj.* [OE *sc(i)ell* f. Gmc: cf. SCALE¹]

she'll /ʃiːl, ʃɪl/ *contr.* she will; she shall.

shellac /ʃə'læk/ *n. & v.* —*n.* lac resin melted into thin flakes and used for making varnish (cf. LAC¹). —*v.tr.* (**shellacked, shellacking**) **1** varnish with shellac. **2** *US sl.* defeat or thrash soundly. [SHELL + LAC, transl. F *laque en écailles* lac in thin plates]

shellback /'ʃelbæk/ *n. sl.* an old sailor.

shellfish /'ʃelfɪʃ/ *n.* **1** an aquatic shelled mollusc, e.g. an oyster, winkle, etc. **2** a crustacean, e.g. a crab, shrimp, etc.

Shelta /'ʃeltə/ *n.* an ancient hybrid secret language used by Irish tinkers, gypsies, etc. [19th c.: orig. unkn.]

shelter /'ʃeltə(r)/ *n. & v.* —*n.* **1** anything serving as a shield or protection from danger, bad weather, etc. **2 a** a place of refuge provided esp. for the homeless etc. **b** *US* an animal sanctuary. **3** a shielded condition; protection (*took shelter under a tree*). —*v.* **1** *tr.* act or serve as shelter to; protect; conceal; defend (*sheltered them from the storm*; *had a sheltered upbringing*). **2** *intr. & refl.* find refuge; take cover (*sheltered under a tree*; *sheltered themselves behind the wall*). □**shelter-belt** a line of trees etc. planted to protect crops from the wind. □□ **shelterer** *n.* **shelterless** *adj.* [16th c.: perh. f. obs. *sheltron* phalanx f. OE *scieldtruma* (as SHIELD, *truma* troop)]

sheltie /'ʃeltɪ/ *n.* (also **shelty**) (*pl.* **-ies**) a Shetland pony or sheepdog. [prob. repr. ON *Hjalti* Shetlander as pronounced in Orkney]

shelve¹ /ʃelv/ *v.tr.* **1** put (books etc.) on a shelf. **2 a** abandon or defer (a plan etc.). **b** remove (a person) from active work etc. **3** fit (a cupboard etc.) with shelves. □□ **shelver** *n.* **shelving** *n.* [*shelves* pl. of SHELF]

shelve² /ʃelv/ *v.intr.* (of ground etc.) slope in a specified direction (*land shelved away to the horizon*). [perh. f. *shelvy* (adj.) having underwater reefs f. *shelve* (n.) ledge, f. SHELVE¹]

shelves *pl.* of SHELF.

shemozzle /ʃɪ'mɒz(ə)l/ *n.* (also **schemozzle**) *sl.* **1** a brawl or commotion. **2** a muddle. [Yiddish after LHeb. *šel-lō'-mazzāl* of no luck]

shenanigan /ʃɪ'nænɪgən/ *n.* (esp. in *pl.*) *colloq.* **1**

high-spirited behaviour; nonsense. **2** trickery; dubious manœuvres. [19th c.: orig. unkn.]

Sheol /ˈʃiːəʊl, -ɒl/ *n.* the Hebrew underworld abode of the dead. [Heb. *šeʾôl*]

shepherd /ˈʃepəd/ *n. & v.* —*n.* **1** (*fem.* **shepherdess** /ˈʃepədɪs/) a person employed to tend sheep, esp. at pasture. **2** a member of the clergy etc. who cares for and guides a congregation. —*v.tr.* **1 a** tend (sheep etc.) as a shepherd. **b** guide (followers etc.). **2** marshal or drive (a crowd etc.) like sheep. □**the Good Shepherd** Christ. **shepherd dog** a sheepdog. **shepherd's crook** a staff with a hook at one end used by shepherds. **shepherd's needle** a white-flowered common plant, *Scandix pecten-veneris*, with spiny fruit. **shepherd's pie** a dish of minced meat under a layer of mashed potato. **shepherd's plaid 1** a small black and white check pattern. **2** woollen cloth with this pattern. **shepherd's purse** a white-flowered hairy cornfield plant, *Capsella bursa-pastoris*, with triangular or cordate pods. [OE *scēaphierde* (as SHEEP, HERD)]

sherardize /ˈʃerəˌdaɪz/ *v.tr.* (also **-ise**) coat (iron or steel) with zinc by heating in contact with zinc dust. [*Sherard* Cowper-Coles, Engl. inventor d. 1936]

Sheraton /ˈʃerət(ə)n/ *n.* (often *attrib.*) a style of furniture introduced in England *c.*1790, with delicate and graceful forms. [T. *Sheraton*, Engl. furniture-maker d. 1806]

sherbet /ˈʃɜːbət/ *n.* **1 a** a flavoured sweet effervescent powder or drink. **b** *US* a water-ice. **2** a cooling drink of sweet diluted fruit-juices esp. in Arabic countries. **3** *Austral. joc.* beer. [Turk. *şerbet*, Pers. *šerbet* f. Arab. *šarba* drink f. *šariba* to drink: cf. SHRUB², SYRUP]

sherd /ʃɜːd/ *n.* = POTSHERD. [var. of SHARD]

shereef (also **sherif**) var. of SHARIF.

sheriff /ˈʃerɪf/ *n.* **1** *Brit.* **a** (also **High Sheriff**) the chief executive officer of the Crown in a county, administering justice etc. **b** an honorary officer elected annually in some towns. **2** *US* an elected officer in a county, responsible for keeping the peace. □**sheriff court** *Sc.* a county court. **sheriff-depute** *Sc.* the chief judge of a county or district. □□ **sheriffalty** *n.* (*pl.* **-ies**). **sheriffdom** *n.* **sheriffhood** *n.* **sheriffship** *n.* [OE *scīr-gerēfa* (as SHIRE, REEVE¹)]

Sherpa /ˈʃɜːpə/ *n.* (*pl.* same or **Sherpas**) **1** a Himalayan people living on the borders of Nepal and Tibet, and skilled in mountaineering. **2** a member of this people. [native name]

sherry /ˈʃerɪ/ *n.* (*pl.* **-ies**) **1** a fortified wine orig. from S. Spain. **2** a glass of this. □**sherry cobbler** see COBBLER 2. **sherry-glass** a small wineglass used for sherry. [earlier *sherris* f. Sp. (*vino de*) *Xeres* (now Jerez de la Frontera) in Andalusia]

she's /ʃiːz, ʃɪz/ *contr.* **1** she is. **2** she has.

Shetlander /ˈʃetləndə(r)/ *n.* a native of the Shetland Islands, NNE of the mainland of Scotland.

Shetland lace /ˈʃetlənd/ *n.* openwork woollen trimming.

Shetland pony /ˈʃetlənd/ *n.* **1** a pony of a small hardy rough-coated breed. **2** this breed.

Shetland sheepdog /ˈʃetlənd/ *n.* **1** a small dog of a collie-like breed. **2** this breed.

Shetland wool /ˈʃetlənd/ *n.* a fine loosely twisted wool from Shetland sheep.

sheva var. of SCHWA.

shew *archaic* var. of SHOW.

shewbread /ˈʃəʊbred/ *n.* twelve loaves that were displayed in a Jewish temple and renewed each sabbath.

Shiah /ˈʃiːə/ *n.* one of the two main branches of Islam, esp. in Iran, that rejects the first three Sunni Caliphs and regards Ali as Muhammad's first successor. [Arab. *šīʿa* party (of Ali, Muhammad's cousin and son-in-law)]

shiatsu /ʃɪˈætsuː/ *n.* a kind of therapy of Japanese origin, in which pressure is applied with the thumbs and palms to certain points of the body. [Jap., = finger pressure]

shibboleth /ˈʃɪbəˌleθ/ *n.* a long-standing formula, doctrine, or phrase, etc., held to be true by a party or sect (*must abandon outdated shibboleths*). [ME f. Heb. *šibbōleṭ* ear of corn, used as a test of nationality for its difficult pronunciation (Judg. 12:6)]

shicer /ˈʃaɪsə(r)/ *n. Austral.* **1** *Mining* an unproductive claim or mine. **2** *sl.* **a** a swindler, welsher, or cheat. **b** a worthless thing; a failure. [G *Scheisser* contemptible person]

shicker /ˈʃɪkə(r)/ *adj.* (also **shickered** /ˈʃɪkəd/) *Austral. & NZ sl.* drunk. [Yiddish *shiker* f. Heb. *šikkôr* f. *šākar* be drunk]

shield /ʃiːld/ *n. & v.* —*n.* **1 a** esp. *hist.* a piece of armour of esp. metal, carried on the arm or in the hand to deflect blows from the head or body. **b** a thing serving to protect (*insurance is a shield against disaster*). **2** a thing resembling a shield, esp.: **a** a trophy in the form of a shield. **b** a protective plate or screen in machinery etc. **c** a shieldlike part of an animal, esp. a shell. **d** a similar part of a plant. **e** *Geol.* a large rigid area of the earth's crust, usu. of Precambrian rock, which has been unaffected by later orogenic episodes. **f** *US* a policeman's shield-shaped badge. **3** *Heraldry* a stylized representation of a shield used for displaying a coat of arms etc. —*v.tr.* protect or screen, esp. from blame or lawful punishment. □**shield fern 1** any common fern of the genus *Polystichum*, with shield-shaped indusia. **2** = BUCKLER 2. □□ **shieldless** *adj.* [OE *sc(i)eld* f. Gmc: prob. orig. = board, rel. to SCALE¹]

shieling /ˈʃiːlɪŋ/ *n.* (also **shealing**) *Sc.* **1** a roughly constructed hut orig. esp. for pastoral use. **2** pasture for cattle. [Sc. *shiel* hut: ME, of unkn. orig.]

shier *compar.* of SHY¹.

shiest *superl.* of SHY¹.

shift /ʃɪft/ *v. & n.* —*v.* **1** *intr. & tr.* change or move or cause to change or move from one position to another. **2** *tr.* remove, esp. with effort (*washing won't shift the stains*). **3** *sl.* **a** *intr.* hurry (*we'll have to shift!*). **b** *tr.* consume (food or drink) hastily or in bulk. **c** *tr.* sell (esp. dubious goods). **4** *intr.* contrive or manage as best one can. **5** *US* **a** *tr.* change (gear) in a vehicle. **b** *intr.* change gear. **6** *intr.* (of cargo) get shaken out of place. **7** *intr. archaic* be evasive or indirect. —*n.* **1 a** the act or an instance of shifting. **b** the substitution of one thing for another; a rotation. **2 a** a relay of workers (*the night shift*). **b** the time for which they work (*an eight-hour shift*). **3 a** a device, stratagem, or expedient. **b** a dodge, trick, or evasion. **4 a** a woman's straight unwaisted dress. **b** *archaic* a loose-fitting undergarment. **5** a displacement of spectral lines (see also *red shift*). **6** (also **sound shift**) a systematic change in pronunciation as a language evolves. **7** a key on a keyboard used to switch between lower and upper case etc. **8** *Bridge* **a** a change of suit in bidding. **b** *US* a change of suit in play. **9** the positioning of successive rows of bricks so that their ends do not coincide. **10** *US* **a** a gear lever in a motor vehicle. **b** a mechanism for this. □**make shift** manage or contrive; get along somehow (*made shift without it*). **shift for oneself** rely on one's own efforts. **shift one's ground** take up a new position in an argument etc. **shift off** get rid of (responsibility etc.) to another. □□ **shiftable** *adj.* **shifter** *n.* [OE *sciftan* arrange, divide, etc., f. Gmc]

shiftless /ˈʃɪftlɪs/ *adj.* lacking resourcefulness; lazy; inefficient. □□ **shiftlessly** *adv.* **shiftlessness** *n.*

shifty /ˈʃɪftɪ/ *adj. colloq.* (**shiftier**, **shiftiest**) not straightforward; evasive; deceitful. □□ **shiftily** *adv.* **shiftiness** *n.*

shigella /ʃɪˈɡelə/ *n.* any airborne bacterium of the genus *Shigella*, some of which cause dysentery. [mod.L f. K. *Shiga*, Jap. bacteriologist d. 1957 + dimin. suffix]

shih-tzu /ˈʃiːˈtsuː/ *n.* **1** a dog of a breed with long silky erect hair and short legs. **2** this breed. [Chin. *shizi* lion]

Shiite /ˈʃiːaɪt/ *n. & adj.* —*n.* an adherent of the Shiah

branch of Islam. —*adj.* of or relating to Shiah. □□
Shiism /'ʃiːɪz(ə)m/ *n.*

shikar /ʃɪ'kɑː(r)/ *n. Ind.* hunting. [Urdu f. Pers. *šikār*]

shiksa /'ʃɪksə/ *n.* often *offens.* (used by Jews) a gentile
girl or woman. [Yiddish *shikse* f. Heb. *šiqṣā* f. *sheqeṣ*
detested thing + *-â fem. suffix*]

shill /ʃɪl/ *n. US* a person employed to decoy or entice
others into buying, gambling, etc. [prob. f. earlier
shillaber, of unkn. orig.]

shillelagh /ʃɪ'leɪlə, -lɪ/ *n.* a thick stick of blackthorn
or oak used in Ireland esp. as a weapon. [*Shillelagh*
in Co. Wicklow, Ireland]

shilling /'ʃɪlɪŋ/ *n.* **1** *hist.* a former British coin and
monetary unit worth one-twentieth of a pound or
twelve pence. **2** a monetary unit in Kenya, Tanzania,
and Uganda. □**shilling-mark** *hist.* = SOLIDUS. **take
the King's (or Queen's) shilling** *hist.* enlist as a
soldier (formerly a soldier was paid a shilling on
enlisting). [OE *scilling*, f. Gmc]

shilly-shally /'ʃɪlɪˌʃælɪ/ *v., adj., & n.* —*v.intr.* (**-ies,
-ied**) hesitate to act or choose; be undecided; vacillate. —*adj.* vacillating. —*n.* indecision; vacillation.
□□**shilly-shallyer** *n.* (also **-shallier**). [orig. *shill I,
shall I*, redupl. of *shall I?*]

shily var. of SHYLY (see SHY[1]).

shim /ʃɪm/ *n. & v.* —*n.* a thin strip of material
used in machinery etc. to make parts fit. —*v.tr.*
(**shimmed, shimming**) fit or fill up with a shim.
[18th c.: orig. unkn.]

shimmer /'ʃɪmə(r)/ *v. & n.* —*v.intr.* shine with a
tremulous or faint diffused light. —*n.* such a light. □□
shimmeringly *adv.* **shimmery** *adj.* [OE *scymrian* f.
Gmc: cf. SHINE]

shimmy /'ʃɪmɪ/ *n. & v.* —*n.* (*pl.* **-ies**) **1** *hist.* a kind
of ragtime dance in which the whole body is shaken.
2 *archaic colloq.* = CHEMISE. **3** *US* an abnormal
vibration of esp. the front wheels of a motor vehicle.
—*v.intr.* (**-ies, -ied**) **1 a** *hist.* dance a shimmy. **b**
move in a similar manner. **2** shake or vibrate
abnormally. [20th c.: orig. uncert.]

shin /ʃɪn/ *n. & v.* —*n.* **1** the front of the leg below the
knee. **2** a cut of beef from the lower foreleg. —*v.tr.*
& (usu. foll. by *up, down*) *intr.* (**shinned, shinning**)
climb quickly by clinging with the arms and legs.
□**shin-bone** = TIBIA. **shin-pad** (or **-guard**) a protective pad for the shins, worn when playing football
etc. [OE *sinu*]

shindig /'ʃɪndɪg/ *n. colloq.* **1** a festive, esp. noisy,
party. **2** = SHINDY 1. [prob. f. SHINDY]

shindy /'ʃɪndɪ/ *n.* (*pl.* **-ies**) *colloq.* **1** a brawl, disturbance, or noise (*kicked up a shindy*). **2** = SHINDIG
1. [perh. alt. of SHINTY]

shine /ʃaɪn/ *v. & n.* —*v.* (*past* and *past part.* **shone**
/ʃɒn/ or **shined**) **1** *intr.* emit or reflect light; be
bright; glow (*the lamp was shining*; *his face shone
with gratitude*). **2** *intr.* (of the sun, a star, etc.) not be
obscured by clouds etc.; be visible. **3** *tr.* cause (a
lamp etc.) to shine. **4** *tr.* (*past* and *past part.* **shined**)
make bright; polish (*shined his shoes*). **5** *intr.* be
brilliant in some respect; excel (*does not shine in
conversation*; *is a shining example*). —*n.* **1** light;
brightness, esp. reflected. **2** a high polish; lustre. **3**
US the act or an instance of shining esp. shoes.
□**shine up to** *US* seek to ingratiate oneself with.
take the shine out of 1 spoil the brilliance or
newness of. **2** throw into the shade by surpassing.
take a shine to *colloq.* take a fancy to; like. □□
shiningly *adv.* [OE *scīnan* f. Gmc]

shiner /'ʃaɪnə(r)/ *n.* **1** a thing that shines. **2** *colloq.* a
black eye. **3** *US* any of various small silvery freshwater fish, esp. of the genus *Notropis*. **4** (usu. in *pl.*)
sl. **a** *archaic* money. **b** a jewel.

shingle[1] /'ʃɪŋ(ə)l/ *n.* (in *sing.* or *pl.*) small rounded
pebbles, esp. on a sea-shore. □□**shingly** *adj.* [16th c.:
orig. uncert.]

shingle[2] /'ʃɪŋ(ə)l/ *n. & v.* —*n.* **1** a rectangular
wooden tile used on roofs, spires, or esp. walls. **2**
archaic **a** shingled hair. **b** the act of shingling hair.

3 *US* a small signboard, esp. of a doctor, lawyer, etc.
—*v.tr.* **1** roof or clad with shingles. **2** *archaic* **a** cut
(a woman's hair) very short. **b** cut the hair of (a
person or head) in this way. [ME app. f. L *scindula*,
earlier *scandula*]

shingles /'ʃɪŋg(ə)lz/ *n.pl.* (usu. treated as *sing.*) an
acute painful viral inflammation of the nerve ganglia,
with a skin eruption often forming a girdle around
the middle of the body. [ME f. med.L *cingulus* f. L
cingulum girdle f. *cingere* gird]

shinny /'ʃɪnɪ/ *v.intr.* (**-ies, -ied**) (usu. foll. by *up,
down*) *US colloq.* shin (up or down a tree etc.).

Shinto /'ʃɪntəʊ/ *n.* the official religion of Japan
incorporating the worship of ancestors and
nature-spirits. □□**Shintoism** *n.* **Shintoist** *n.* [Jap. f.
Chin. *shen dao* way of the gods]

shinty /'ʃɪntɪ/ *n.* (*pl.* **-ies**) *Brit.* **1** a game like hockey
played with a ball and curved sticks, and taller
goalposts. **2** a stick or ball used in shinty. [earlier
shinny, app. f. the cry used in the game *shin ye, shin
you, shin t' ye*, of unkn. orig.]

shiny /'ʃaɪnɪ/ *adj.* (**shinier, shiniest**) **1** having a
shine; glistening; polished; bright. **2** (of clothing, esp.
the seat of trousers etc.) having the nap worn off. □□
shinily *adv.* **shininess** *n.* [SHINE]

ship /ʃɪp/ *n. & v.* —*n.* **1 a** any large seagoing vessel
(cf. BOAT). **b** a sailing-vessel with a bowsprit and
three, four, or five square-rigged masts. **2** *US* an
aircraft. **3** a spaceship. **4** *colloq.* a boat, esp. a
racing-boat. —*v.* (**shipped, shipping**) **1** *tr.* put, take,
or send away (goods, passengers, sailors, etc.) on
board ship. **2** *tr.* **a** take in (water) over the side of a
ship, boat, etc. **b** take (oars) from the rowlocks and
lay them inside a boat. **c** fix (a rudder etc.) in
its place on a ship etc. **d** step (a mast). **3** *intr.* **a**
take ship; embark. **b** (of a sailor) take service on
a ship (*shipped for Africa*). **4** *tr.* deliver (goods) to a
forwarding agent for conveyance. □**ship-breaker** a
contractor who breaks up old ships. **ship-broker** an
agent in shipping goods and insuring ships. **ship
burial** *Archaeol.* burial in a wooden ship under a
mound. **ship-canal** a canal large enough for ships
to pass inland. **ship** (or **ship's**) **chandler** see CHAND-
LER. **ship-fever** typhus. **ship-money** *hist.* a tax
raised to provide ships for the navy in the 17th c.
ship of the desert the camel. **ship off 1** send or
transport by ship. **2** *colloq.* send (a person) away.
ship of the line *hist.* a large battleship fighting in
the front line of battle. **ship-rigged** square-rigged.
ship's articles the terms on which seamen take
service on a ship. **ship's biscuit** *hist.* a hard coarse
kind of biscuit kept and eaten on board ship. **ship's
boat** a small boat carried on board a ship. **ship's
company** a ship's crew. **ship's corporal** see
CORPORAL[1] 2. **ship a sea** be flooded by a wave. **ship's
husband** an agent appointed by the owners to see to
the provisioning of a ship in port. **ship's papers**
documents establishing the ownership, nationality,
nature of the cargo, etc., of a ship. **take ship** embark.
when a person's ship comes home (or **in**) when a
person's fortune is made. □□**shipless** *adj.* **shippable**
adj. [OE *scip, scipian* f. Gmc]

-ship /ʃɪp/ *suffix* forming nouns denoting: **1** a quality
or condition (*friendship; hardship*). **2** status, office,
or honour (*authorship; lordship*). **3** a tenure of office
(*chairmanship*). **4** a skill in a certain capacity
(*workmanship*). **5** the collective individuals of a
group (*membership*). [OE *-scipe* etc. f. Gmc]

shipboard /'ʃɪpbɔːd/ *n.* (usu. *attrib.*) used or occurring on board a ship (*a shipboard romance*). □**on
shipboard** on board ship.

shipbuilder /'ʃɪpˌbɪldə(r)/ *n.* a person, company,
etc., that constructs ships. □□**shipbuilding** *n.*

shiplap /'ʃɪplæp/ *v. & n.* —*v.tr.* fit (boards) together
for cladding etc. so that each overlaps the one below.
—*n.* such cladding.

shipload /'ʃɪpləʊd/ *n.* a quantity of goods forming a
cargo.

shipmaster /'ʃɪpˌmaːstə(r)/ n. a ship's captain.

shipmate /'ʃɪpmeɪt/ n. a fellow member of a ship's crew.

shipment /'ʃɪpmənt/ n. **1** an amount of goods shipped; a consignment. **2** the act or an instance of shipping goods etc.

shipowner /'ʃɪpˌəʊnə(r)/ n. a person owning a ship or ships or shares in ships.

shipper /'ʃɪpə(r)/ n. a person or company that sends or receives goods by ship, or *US* by land or air. [OE *scipere* (as SHIP)]

shipping /'ʃɪpɪŋ/ n. **1** the act or an instance of shipping goods etc. **2** ships, esp. the ships of a country, port, etc. □**shipping-agent** a person acting for a ship or ships at a port etc. **shipping-articles** = *ship's articles*. **shipping-bill** *Brit.* a manifest of goods shipped. **shipping-master** *Brit.* an official presiding at the signing of ship's articles, paying off of seamen, etc. **shipping-office** the office of a shipping-agent or -master.

shipshape /'ʃɪpʃeɪp/ adv. & predic.adj. in good order; trim and neat.

shipway /'ʃɪpweɪ/ n. a slope on which a ship is built and down which it slides to be launched.

shipworm /'ʃɪpwɜːm/ n. = TEREDO.

shipwreck /'ʃɪprek/ n. & v. —n. **1 a** the destruction of a ship by a storm, foundering, etc. **b** a ship so destroyed. **2** (often foll. by *of*) the destruction of hopes, dreams, etc. —v. **1** tr. inflict shipwreck on (a ship, a person's hopes, etc.). **2** intr. suffer shipwreck.

shipwright /'ʃɪpraɪt/ n. **1** a shipbuilder. **2** a ship's carpenter.

shipyard /'ʃɪpjaːd/ n. a place where ships are built, repaired, etc.

shiralee /'ʃɪrəˌliː/ n. *Austral.* a tramp's swag or bundle. [20th c.: orig. unkn.]

shire /'ʃaɪə(r)/ n. *Brit.* **1** a county. **2** (**the Shires**) **a** a group of English counties with names ending or formerly ending in *-shire*, extending NE from Hampshire and Devon. **b** the midland counties of England. **c** the fox-hunting district of mainly Leicestershire and Northants. **3** *Austral.* a rural area with its own elected council. □**shire-horse** a heavy powerful type of draught-horse bred chiefly in the midland counties of England. [OE *scīr*, OHG *scīra* care, official charge: orig. unkn.]

-shire /ʃə(r), ʃɪə(r)/ suffix forming the names of counties (*Derbyshire*; *Hampshire*).

shirk /ʃɜːk/ v. & n. —v.tr. (also absol.) shrink from; avoid; get out of (duty, work, responsibility, fighting, etc.). —n. a person who shirks. □□**shirker** n. [obs. *shirk* (n.) sponger, perh. f. G *Schurke* scoundrel]

shirr /ʃɜː(r)/ n. & v. **1** two or more rows of esp. elastic gathered threads in a garment etc. forming smocking. **2** elastic webbing. —v.tr. **1** gather (material) with parallel threads. **2** *US* bake (eggs) without shells. □□**shirring** n. [19th c.: orig. unkn.]

shirt /ʃɜːt/ n. **1** a man's upper-body garment of cotton etc., having a collar, sleeves, and esp. buttons down the front, and often worn under a jacket or sweater. **2** a similar garment worn by a woman; a blouse. **3** = NIGHTSHIRT. □**keep one's shirt on** colloq. keep one's temper. **put one's shirt on** colloq. bet all one has on; be sure of. **shirt blouse** = sense 2 of n. **shirt-dress** = SHIRTWAISTER. **shirt-front** the breast of a shirt, esp. of a stiffened evening shirt. **the shirt off one's back** colloq. one's last remaining possessions. **shirt-tail** the lower curved part of a shirt below the waist. □□**shirted** adj. **shirting** n. **shirtless** adj. [OE *scyrte*, corresp. to ON *skyrta* (cf. SKIRT) f. Gmc: cf. SHORT]

shirtsleeve /'ʃɜːtsliːv/ n. (usu. in pl.) the sleeve of a shirt. □**in shirtsleeves** wearing a shirt with no jacket etc. over it.

shirtwaist /'ʃɜːtweɪst/ n. esp. *US* a woman's blouse resembling a shirt.

shirtwaister /'ʃɜːtˌweɪstə(r)/ n. *US* a woman's dress with a bodice like a shirt. [SHIRT, WAIST]

shirty /'ʃɜːtɪ/ adj. (**shirtier, shirtiest**) colloq. angry; annoyed. □□**shirtily** adv. **shirtiness** n.

shish kebab /ˌʃɪʃ kɪˈbæb/ n. a dish of pieces of marinated meat and vegetables cooked and served on skewers. [Turk. *şiş kebabı* f. *şiş* skewer, KEBAB roast meat]

shit /ʃɪt/ v., n., & int. coarse sl. ¶ Usually considered a taboo word. —v. (**shitting**; past and past part. **shitted** or **shit**) intr. & tr. expel faeces from the body or cause (faeces etc.) to be expelled. —n. **1** faeces. **2** an act of defecating. **3** a contemptible or worthless person or thing. **4** nonsense. **5** an intoxicating drug, esp. cannabis. —int. an exclamation of disgust, anger, etc. [OE *scītan* (unrecorded) f. Gmc]

shitty /'ʃɪtɪ/ adj. (**shittier, shittiest**) coarse sl. **1** disgusting, contemptible. **2** covered with excrement.

Shiva var. of SIVA.

shivaree esp. *US* var. of CHARIVARI.

shiver[1] /'ʃɪvə(r)/ v. & n. —v.intr. **1** tremble with cold, fear, etc. **2** suffer a quick trembling movement of the body; shudder. —n. **1** a momentary shivering movement. **2** (in pl.) an attack of shivering, esp. from fear or horror (*got the shivers in the dark*). □□ **shiverer** n. **shiveringly** adv. **shivery** adj. [ME *chivere*, perh. f. *chavele* chatter (as JOWL[1])]

shiver[2] /'ʃɪvə(r)/ n. & v. —n. (esp. in pl.) each of the small pieces into which esp. glass is shattered when broken; a splinter. —v.tr. & intr. break into shivers. □**shiver my timbers** a reputed piratical curse. [ME *scifre*, rel. to OHG *scivaro* splinter f. Gmc]

shivoo /ʃɪˈvuː/ n. *Austral.* colloq. a party or celebration.

shoal[1] /ʃəʊl/ n. & v. —n. **1** a great number of fish swimming together (cf. SCHOOL[2]). **2** a multitude; a crowd (*shoals of letters*). —v.intr. (of fish) form shoals. [prob. re-adoption of MDu. *schōle* SCHOOL[2]]

shoal[2] /ʃəʊl/ n., v., & adj. —n. **1 a** an area of shallow water. **b** a submerged sandbank visible at low water. **2** (esp. in pl.) hidden danger or difficulty. —v. **1** intr. (of water) get shallower. **2** tr. (of a ship etc.) move into a shallower part of (water). —adj. archaic (of water) shallow. □□ **shoaly** adj. [OE *sceald* f. Gmc, rel. to SHALLOW]

shoat /ʃəʊt/ n. *US* a young pig, esp. newly weaned. [ME: cf. W.Flem. *schote*]

shock[1] /ʃɒk/ n. & v. —n. **1** a violent collision, impact, tremor, etc. **2** a sudden and disturbing effect on the emotions, physical reactions, etc. (*the news was a great shock*). **3** an acute state of prostration following a wound, pain, etc., esp. when much blood is lost (*died of shock*). **4** = *electric shock*. **5** a disturbance in stability causing fluctuations in an organization, monetary system, etc. —v. **1** tr. **a** affect with shock; horrify; outrage; disgust; sadden. **b** (absol.) cause shock. **2** tr. (esp. in passive) affect with an electric or pathological shock. **3** intr. experience shock (*I don't shock easily*). **4** intr. archaic collide violently. □**shock absorber** a device on a vehicle etc. for absorbing shocks, vibrations, etc. **shock-brigade** (or -workers) a body of esp. voluntary workers in the USSR engaged in an especially arduous task. **shock stall** excessive strain produced by air resistance on an aircraft approaching the speed of sound. **shock tactics 1** sudden and violent action. **2** *Mil.* a massed cavalry charge. **shock therapy** (or **treatment**) *Psychol.* a method of treating depressive patients by electric shock or drugs inducing coma and convulsions. **shock troops** troops specially trained for assault. **shock wave** a sharp change of pressure in a narrow region travelling through air etc. caused by explosion or by a body moving faster than sound. □□ **shockable** adj. **shockability** /-'bɪlɪtɪ/ n. [F *choc*, *choquer*, of unkn. orig.]

shock[2] /ʃɒk/ n. & v. —n. a group of usu. twelve corn-sheaves stood up with their heads together in a field. —v.tr. arrange (corn) in shocks. [ME, perh. repr. OE *sc(e)oc* (unrecorded)]

shock³ /ʃɒk/ *n.* an unkempt or shaggy mass of hair. [cf. obs. *shock*(*-dog*), earlier *shough*, shaggy-haired poodle]

shocker /'ʃɒkə(r)/ *n. colloq.* **1** a shocking, horrifying, unacceptable, etc. person or thing. **2** *hist.* a sordid or sensational novel etc. **3** a shock absorber.

shocking /'ʃɒkɪŋ/ *adj. & adv.* —*adj.* **1** causing indignation or disgust. **2** *colloq.* very bad (*shocking weather*). —*adv. colloq.* shockingly (*shocking bad manners*). □**shocking pink** a vibrant shade of pink. □□**shockingly** *adv.* **shockingness** *n.*

shockproof /'ʃɒkpruːf/ *adj.* resistant to the effects of (esp. physical) shock.

shod *past* and *past part.* of SHOE.

shoddy /'ʃɒdɪ/ *adj. & n.* —*adj.* (**shoddier, shoddiest**) **1** trashy; shabby; poorly made. **2** counterfeit. —*n.* (*pl.* **-ies**) **1 a** an inferior cloth made partly from the shredded fibre of old woollen cloth. **b** such fibre. **2** any thing of shoddy quality. □□ **shoddily** *adv.* **shoddiness** *n.* [19th c.: orig. dial.]

shoe /ʃuː/ *n. & v.* —*n.* **1** either of a pair of protective foot-coverings of leather, plastic, etc., having a sturdy sole and, in Britain, not reaching above the ankle. **2** a metal rim nailed to the hoof of a horse etc.; a horseshoe. **3** anything resembling a shoe in shape or use, esp.: **a** a drag for a wheel. **b** = *brake shoe* (see BRAKE¹). **c** a socket. **d** a ferrule, esp. on a sledge-runner. **e** a mast-step. **f** a box from which cards are dealt in casinos at baccarat etc. —*v.tr.* (**shoes, shoeing**; *past* and *past part.* **shod** /ʃɒd/) **1** fit (esp. a horse etc.) with a shoe or shoes. **2** protect (the end of a pole etc.) with a metal shoe. **3** (as **shod** *adj.*) (in *comb.*) having shoes etc. of a specified kind (*dry-shod*; *roughshod*). □**be in a person's shoes** be in his or her situation, difficulty, etc. **dead men's shoes** property or a position etc. coveted by a prospective successor. **if the shoe fits** *US* = *if the cap fits* (see CAP). **shoe-bill** an African stork-like bird, *Balaeniceps rex*, with a large flattened bill for catching aquatic prey. **shoe-buckle** a buckle worn as ornament or as a fastening on a shoe. **shoe-leather** leather for shoes, esp. when worn through by walking. **shoe-tree** a shaped block for keeping a shoe in shape when not worn. **where the shoe pinches** where one's difficulty or trouble is. □□**shoeless** *adj.* [OE *scōh, scōg(e)an* f. Gmc]

shoeblack /'ʃuːblæk/ *n.* a person who cleans the shoes of passers-by for payment.

shoebox /'ʃuːbɒks/ *n.* **1** a box for packing shoes. **2** a very small space or dwelling.

shoehorn /'ʃuːhɔːn/ *n.* a curved piece of horn, metal, etc., for easing the heel into a shoe.

shoelace /'ʃuːleɪs/ *n.* a cord for lacing up shoes.

shoemaker /'ʃuːˌmeɪkə(r)/ *n.* a maker of boots and shoes. □□**shoemaking** *n.*

shoeshine /'ʃuːʃaɪn/ *n.* esp. *US* a polish given to shoes.

shoestring /'ʃuːstrɪŋ/ *n.* **1** a shoelace. **2** *colloq.* a small esp. inadequate amount of money (*living on a shoestring*). **3** (*attrib.*) barely adequate; precarious (*a shoestring majority*).

shofar /'ʃəʊfə(r)/ *n.* (*pl.* **shofroth** /'ʃəʊfrəʊt/) a ram's-horn trumpet used by Jews in religious ceremonies and as an ancient battle-signal. [Heb. *šōp̄ār*, pl. *šōp̄ārōt*]

shogun /'ʃəʊgʊn/ *n. hist.* any of a succession of Japanese hereditary Commanders-in-Chief and virtual rulers before 1868. □□**shogunate** /-nət/ *n.* [Jap., = general, f. Chin. *jiang jun*]

shone *past* and *past part.* of SHINE.

shonky /'ʃɒŋkɪ/ *adj.* (**shonkier, shonkiest**) *Austral. sl.* unreliable, dishonest. [perh. E dial. *shonk* smart]

shoo /ʃuː/ *int. & v.* —*int.* an exclamation used to frighten away birds, children, etc. —*v.* (**shoos, shooed**) **1** *intr.* utter the word 'shoo!'. **2** *tr.* (usu. foll. by *away*) drive (birds etc.) away by shooing. □**shoo-in** *US* something easy or certain to succeed. [imit.]

shook¹ /ʃʊk/ *past* of SHAKE. —*predic.adj. colloq.* **1** (foll. by *up*) emotionally or physically disturbed; upset. **2** (foll. by *on*) *Austral. & NZ* keen on; enthusiastic about (*not too shook on the English climate*).

shook² /ʃʊk/ *n. US* a set of staves and headings for a cask, ready for fitting together. [18th c.: orig. unkn.]

shoot /ʃuːt/ *v., n., & int.* —*v.* (*past* and *past part.* **shot** /ʃɒt/) **1** *tr.* **a** cause (a gun, bow, etc.) to fire. **b** discharge (a bullet, arrow, etc.) from a gun, bow, etc. **c** kill or wound (a person, animal, etc.) with a bullet, arrow, etc. from a gun, bow, etc. **2** *intr.* discharge a gun etc. esp. in a specified way (*shoots well*). **3** *tr.* send out, discharge, propel, etc., esp. violently or swiftly (*shot out the contents*; *shot a glance at his neighbour*). **4** *intr.* (often foll. by *out, along, forth*, etc.) come or go swiftly or vigorously. **5** *intr.* **a** (of a plant etc.) put forth buds etc. **b** (of a bud etc.) appear. **6** *intr.* **a** hunt game etc. with a gun. **b** (usu. foll. by *over*) shoot game over an estate etc. **7** *tr.* shoot game in or on (coverts, an estate, etc.). **8** *tr.* film or photograph (a scene, film, etc.). **9** *tr.* (also *absol.*) esp. *Football* **a** score (a goal). **b** take a shot at (the goal). **10** *tr.* (of a boat) sweep swiftly down or under (a bridge, rapids, falls, etc.). **11** *tr.* move (a door-bolt) to fasten or unfasten a door etc. **12** *tr.* let (rubbish, load, etc.) fall or slide from a container, lorry, etc. **13** *intr.* **a** (usu. foll. by *through, up*, etc.) (of a pain) pass with a stabbing sensation. **b** (of part of the body) be intermittently painful. **14** *intr.* (often foll. by *out*) project abruptly (*the mountain shoots out against the sky*). **15** *tr.* (often foll. by *up*) *sl.* inject esp. oneself with (a drug). **16** *tr. US colloq.* **a** play a game of (craps, pool, etc.). **b** throw (a die or dice). **17** *tr. Golf colloq.* make (a specified score) for a round or hole. **18** *tr. colloq.* pass (traffic-lights at red). **19** *tr.* plane (the edge of a board) accurately. **20** *intr. Cricket* (of a ball) dart along the ground after pitching. —*n.* **1** the act or an instance of shooting. **2 a** a young branch or sucker. **b** the new growth of a plant. **3** *Brit.* **a** a hunting party, expedition, etc. **b** land shot over for game. **4** = CHUTE¹. **5** a rapid in a stream. —*int. colloq.* **1** a demand for a reply, information, etc. **2** *US euphem.* an exclamation of disgust, anger, etc. (see SHIT). □**shoot ahead** come quickly to the front of competitors etc. **shoot one's bolt** see BOLT¹. **shoot down 1** kill (a person) by shooting. **2** cause (an aircraft, its pilot, etc.) to crash by shooting. **3** argue effectively against (a person, argument, etc.). **shoot it out** *sl.* engage in a decisive gun-battle. **shoot a line** *sl.* talk pretentiously. **shoot one's mouth off** *sl.* talk too much or indiscreetly. **shoot-out** *colloq.* a decisive gun battle. **shoot through** *Austral. & NZ sl.* depart; escape, abscond. **shoot up 1** grow rapidly, esp. (of a person) grow taller. **2** rise suddenly. **3** terrorize (a district) by indiscriminate shooting. **4** *sl.* = sense 15 of *v.* **the whole shoot** = *the whole shooting match* (see SHOOTING). □□**shootable** *adj.* [OE *scēotan* f. Gmc: cf. SHEET¹, SHOT¹, SHUT]

shooter /'ʃuːtə(r)/ *n.* **1** a person or thing that shoots. **2 a** (in *comb.*) a gun or other device for shooting (*peashooter*; *six-shooter*). **b** *sl.* a pistol etc. **3** a player who shoots or is able to shoot a goal in football, netball, etc. **4** *Cricket* a ball that shoots. **5** a person who throws a die or dice.

shooting /'ʃuːtɪŋ/ *n. & adj.* —*n.* **1** the act or an instance of shooting. **2 a** the right of shooting over an area of land. **b** an estate etc. rented to shoot over. —*adj.* moving, growing, etc. quickly (*a shooting pain in the arm*). □**shooting-box** *Brit.* a lodge used by sportsmen in the shooting-season. **shooting-brake** (or **-break**) *Brit.* an estate car. **shooting-coat** (or **-jacket**) a coat designed to be worn when shooting game. **shooting-gallery** a place used for shooting at targets with rifles etc. **shooting-iron** esp. *US colloq.* a firearm. **shooting-range** a ground with butts for rifle practice. **shooting star** a small meteor moving rapidly and burning up on entering the earth's atmosphere. **shooting-stick** a walking-stick with a foldable seat. **shooting war** a war in which there is shooting (opp. *cold war, war of nerves* etc.). **the whole shooting match** *colloq.* everything.

shop /ʃɒp/ *n. & v.* —*n.* **1** a building, room, etc., for the retail sale of goods or services (*chemist's shop; betting-shop*). **2** a place in which manufacture or repairing is done; a workshop (*engineering-shop*). **3** a profession, trade, business, etc., esp. as a subject of conversation (*talk shop*). **4** *colloq.* an institution, establishment, place of business, etc. —*v.* (**shopped, shopping**) **1** *intr.* **a** go to a shop or shops to buy goods. **b** *US* = *window-shop.* **2** *tr.* esp. *Brit. sl.* inform against (a criminal etc.). □**all over the shop** *colloq.* **1** in disorder (*scattered all over the shop*). **2** in every place (*looked for it all over the shop*). **3** wildly (*hitting out all over the shop*). **set up shop** establish oneself in business etc. **shop around** look for the best bargain. **shop assistant** *Brit.* a person who serves customers in a shop. **shop-boy** (or **-girl**) an assistant in a shop. **shop-floor** workers in a factory etc. as distinct from management. **shop-soiled 1** (of an article) soiled or faded by display in a shop. **2** (of a person, idea, etc.) grubby; tarnished; no longer fresh or new. **shop steward** a person elected by workers in a factory etc. to represent them in dealings with management. **shop-window 1** a display window in a shop. **2** an opportunity for displaying skills, talents, etc. **shop-worn** = *shop-soiled.* □□ **shopless** *adj.* **shoppy** *adj.* [ME f. AF & OF *eschoppe* booth f. MLG *schoppe*, OHG *scopf* porch]

shopkeeper /ˈʃɒpˌkiːpə(r)/ *n.* the owner and manager of a shop. □□ **shopkeeping** *n.*

shoplifter /ˈʃɒpˌlɪftə(r)/ *n.* a person who steals goods while appearing to shop. □□ **shoplifting** *n.*

shopman /ˈʃɒpmən/ *n.* (*pl.* **-men**) **1** *Brit.* a shopkeeper or shopkeeper's assistant. **2** a workman in a repair shop.

shopper /ˈʃɒpə(r)/ *n.* **1** a person who makes purchases in a shop. **2** a shopping bag or trolley. **3** *sl.* an informer.

shopping /ˈʃɒpɪŋ/ *n.* **1** (often *attrib.*) the purchase of goods etc. (*shopping expedition*). **2** goods purchased (*put the shopping on the table*). □ **shopping centre** an area or complex of shops, with associated facilities.

shopwalker /ˈʃɒpˌwɔːkə(r)/ *n. Brit.* an attendant in a large shop who directs customers, supervises assistants, etc.

shoran /ˈʃɔːræn/ *n.* a system of aircraft navigation using the return of two radar signals by two ground stations. [*short range navigation*]

shore[1] /ʃɔː(r)/ *n.* **1** the land that adjoins the sea or a large body of water. **2** (usu. in *pl.*) a country; a sea-coast (*often visits these shores; on a distant shore*). **3** *Law* land between ordinary high and low water marks. □ **in shore** on the water near or nearer to the shore (cf. INSHORE). **on shore** ashore. **shore-based** operating from a base on shore. **shore leave** *Naut.* **1** permission to go ashore. **2** a period of time ashore. □□ **shoreless** *adj.* **shoreward** *adj. & adv.* **shorewards** *adv.* [ME f. MDu., MLG *schōre*, perh. f. the root of SHEAR]

shore[2] /ʃɔː(r)/ *v. & n.* —*v.tr.* (often foll. by *up*) support with or as if with a shore or shores; hold up. —*n.* a prop or beam set obliquely against a ship, wall, tree, etc., as a support. □□ **shoring** *n.* [ME f. MDu., MLG *schōre* prop, of unkn. orig.]

shore[3] see SHEAR.

shoreweed /ˈʃɔːwiːd/ *n.* a stoloniferous plant, *Littorella uniflora*, growing in shallow water.

shorn *past part.* of SHEAR.

short /ʃɔːt/ *adj., adv., n., & v.* —*adj.* **1 a** measuring little; not long from end to end (*a short distance*). **b** not long in duration; brief (*a short time ago; had a short life*). **c** seeming less than the stated amount (*a few short years of happiness*). **2** of small height; not tall (*a short square tower; was shorter than average*). **3 a** (usu. foll. by *of, on*) having a partial or total lack;

deficient; scanty (*short of spoons; is rather short on sense*). **b** not far-reaching; acting or being near at hand (*within short range*). **4 a** concise; brief (*kept his speech short*). **b** curt; uncivil (*was short with her*). **5** (of the memory) unable to remember distant events. **6** *Phonet. & Prosody* of a vowel or syllable: **a** having the lesser of the two recognized durations. **b** unstressed. **c** (of an English vowel) having a sound other than that called long (cf. LONG[1] *adj.* 8). **7 a** (of pastry) crumbling; not holding together. **b** (of clay) having poor plasticity. **8** esp. *Stock Exch.* **a** (of stocks, a stockbroker, crops, etc.) sold or selling when the amount is not in hand, with reliance on getting the deficit in time for delivery. **b** (of a bill of exchange) maturing at an early date. **9** *Cricket* **a** (of a ball) pitching relatively near the bowler. **b** (of a fielder or his position) relatively near the batsman. **10** (of a drink of spirits) undiluted. —*adv.* **1** before the natural or expected time or place; abruptly (*pulled up short; cut short the celebrations*). **2** rudely; uncivilly (*spoke to him short*). —*n.* **1** *colloq.* a short drink, esp. spirits. **2** a short circuit. **3** a short film. **4** *Stock Exch.* **a** a person who sells short. **b** (in *pl.*) short-dated stocks. **5** *Phonet.* **a** a short syllable or vowel. **b** a mark indicating that a vowel is short. **6** (in *pl.*) a mixture of bran and coarse flour. —*v.tr. & intr.* short-circuit. □ **be caught** (or **taken**) **short 1** be put at a disadvantage. **2** *colloq.* urgently need to urinate or defecate. **bring up** (or **pull up**) **short** check or pause abruptly. **come short** be inadequate or disappointing. **come short of** fail to reach or amount to. **for short** as a short name (*Tom for short*). **get** (or **have**) **by the short hairs** *colloq.* be in complete control of (a person). **go short** (often foll. by *of*) not have enough. **in short** to use few words; briefly. **in short order** *US* immediately. **in the short run** over a short period of time. **in short supply** scarce. **in the short term** = *in the short run.* **make short work of** accomplish, dispose of, destroy, consume, etc. quickly. **short and sweet** esp. *iron.* brief and pleasant. **short-arm** (of a blow etc.) delivered with the arm not fully extended. **short back and sides** a haircut in which the hair is cut short at the back and the sides. **short change** insufficient money given as change. **short-change** *v.tr.* rob or cheat by giving short change. **short circuit** an electric circuit through small resistance, esp. instead of the resistance of a normal circuit. **short-circuit 1** cause a short circuit or a short circuit in. **2** shorten or avoid (a journey, work, etc.) by taking a more direct route etc. **short commons** insufficient food. **short cut 1** a route shortening the distance travelled. **2** a quick way of accomplishing something. **short date** an early date for the maturing of a bill etc. **short-dated** due for early payment or redemption. **short-day** (of a plant) needing the period of light each day to fall below some limit to cause flowering. **short division** *Math.* division in which the quotient is written directly without being worked out in writing. **short drink** a strong alcoholic drink served in small measures. **short-eared owl** an owl, *Asio flammeus*, frequenting open country and hunting at dawn or dusk. **short for** an abbreviation for (*'Bob' is short for 'Robert'*). **short fuse** a quick temper. **short game** *Golf* approaching and putting. **short-handed** undermanned or understaffed. **short haul 1** the transport of goods over a short distance. **2** a short-term effort. **short head** *Racing* a distance less than the length of a horse's head. **short-head** *v.tr.* beat by a short head. **short hundredweight** see HUNDREDWEIGHT. **short list** *Brit.* a list of selected candidates from which a final choice is made. **short-list** *v.tr. Brit.* put on a short list. **short-lived** ephemeral; not long-lasting. **short mark** = BREVE 2. **short measure** less than the professed amount. **short metre** *Prosody* a hymn stanza of four lines with 6, 6, 8, and 6 syllables. **short notice** an insufficient length of warning time. **short odds** nearly equal stakes or chances in betting. **short of 1** see sense 3a of *adj.* **2** less than (*nothing short of a miracle*). **3** distant from (*two miles short of home*). **4** without going so far as; except (*did everything short of destroying it*). **short of breath** panting, short-winded. **short on** *colloq.* see sense 3a of *adj.* **short order** *US* an order in a restaurant for quickly cooked food. **short-pitched** *Cricket* (of a ball) pitching relatively near the bowler. **short-range 1** having a short range. **2** relating to a fairly immediate future time (*short-range possibilities*). **short rib** = *floating rib.* **short score** *Mus.* a score not giving all parts. **short shrift** curt or dismissive treatment. **short sight** the inability to focus except on comparatively near objects. **short-sleeved** with sleeves not reaching below the elbow. **short-staffed** having insufficient staff. **short story** a story with a fully developed theme but shorter than a novel. **short suit** a suit of less than four cards. **short temper** self-control soon or easily lost. **short-term** occurring in or relating to a short period of time. **short time** the condition of working fewer than the regular hours per day or days per week. **short title** an abbreviated form of a title of a book etc. **short ton** see TON. **short view** a consideration of the present only, not the future. **short waist 1** a high or shallow waist of a dress. **2** a short upper body. **short wave** a radio wave of frequency greater than 3 MHz. **short weight** weight less than it is alleged to be. **short whist** whist with ten or five points to a game. **short wind** quickly exhausted breathing-power. **short-winded 1** having short wind. **2** incapable of sustained effort. □□ **shortish** *adj.* **shortness** *n.* [OE *sceort* f. Gmc: cf. SHIRT, SKIRT]

shortage /ˈʃɔːtɪdʒ/ *n.* (often foll. by *of*) a deficiency; an amount lacking (*a shortage of 100 tons*).

shortbread /ˈʃɔːtbred/ *n.* a crisp rich crumbly type of biscuit made with butter, flour, and sugar.

shortcake /ˈʃɔːtkeɪk/ *n.* **1** = SHORTBREAD. **2** a cake made of short pastry and filled with fruit and cream.

shortcoming /ˈʃɔːtˌkʌmɪŋ/ *n.* failure to come up to a standard; a defect.

shortcrust /ˈʃɔːtkrʌst/ *n.* (in full **shortcrust pastry**) a type of crumbly pastry made with flour and fat.

shorten /ˈʃɔːt(ə)n/ *v.* **1** *intr.* & *tr.* become or make shorter or short; curtail. **2** *Naut.* reduce the amount of (sail spread). **3** *intr.* & *tr.* (with reference to gambling odds, prices, etc.) become or make shorter; decrease.

shortening /ˈʃɔːtənɪŋ/ *n.* fat used for making pastry, esp. for making short pastry.

shortfall /ˈʃɔːtfɔːl/ *n.* a deficit below what was expected.

shorthand /ˈʃɔːthænd/ *n.* **1** (often *attrib.*) a method of rapid writing in abbreviations and symbols esp. for taking dictation. **2** an abbreviated or symbolic mode of expression. □ **shorthand typist** *Brit.* a typist qualified to take and transcribe shorthand.

shorthorn /ˈʃɔːthɔːn/ *n.* **1** an animal of a breed of cattle with short horns. **2** this breed.

shortie var. of SHORTY.

shortly /ˈʃɔːtlɪ/ *adv.* **1** (often foll. by *before, after*) before long; soon (*will arrive shortly; arrived shortly after him*). **2** in a few words; briefly. **3** curtly. [OE *scortlice* (as SHORT, -LY²)]

shorts /ʃɔːts/ *n.pl.* **1** trousers reaching only to the knees or higher. **2** *US* underpants.

short-sighted /ʃɔːtˈsaɪtɪd, ˈʃɔːt-/ *adj.* **1** having short sight. **2** lacking imagination or foresight. □□ **short-sightedly** *adv.* **short-sightedness** *n.*

shortstop /ˈʃɔːtstɒp/ *n.* a baseball fielder near second base.

shorty /ˈʃɔːtɪ/ *n.* (also **shortie**) (*pl.* **-ies**) *colloq.* **1** a person shorter than average. **2** a short garment, esp. a nightdress or raincoat.

shot¹ /ʃɒt/ *n.* **1** the act or an instance of firing a gun, cannon, etc. (*several shots were heard*). **2** an attempt to hit by shooting or throwing etc. (*took a shot at*

him). **3 a** a single non-explosive missile for a cannon, gun, etc. **b** (*pl.* same or **shots**) a small lead pellet used in quantity in a single charge or cartridge in a shotgun. **c** (as *pl.*) these collectively. **4 a** a photograph. **b** a film sequence photographed continuously by one camera. **5 a** a stroke or a kick in a ball game. **b** *colloq.* an attempt to guess or do something (*let him have a shot at it*). **6** *colloq.* a person having a specified skill with a gun etc. (*is not a good shot*). **7** a heavy ball thrown by a shot-putter. **8** the launch of a space rocket (*a moonshot*). **9** the range, reach, or distance to or at which a thing will carry or act (*out of earshot*). **10** a remark aimed at a person. **11** *colloq.* **a** a drink of esp. spirits. **b** an injection of a drug, vaccine, etc. (*has had his shots*). □ **like a shot** *colloq.* without hesitation; willingly. **make a bad shot** guess wrong. **not a shot in one's** (or **the**) **locker 1** no money left. **2** not a chance left. **shot-blasting** the cleaning of metal etc. by the impact of a stream of shot. **shot-firer** a person who fires a blasting-charge in a mine etc. **shot in the arm** *colloq.* **1** stimulus or encouragement. **2** an alcoholic drink. **shot in the dark** a mere guess. **shot-put** an athletic contest in which a shot is thrown a great distance. **shot-putter** an athlete who puts the shot. **shot-tower** *hist.* a tower in which shot was made from molten lead poured through sieves at the top and falling into water at the bottom. □□ **shotproof** *adj.* [OE *sc(e)ot, gesc(e)ot* f. Gmc: cf. SHOOT]

shot² /ʃɒt/ *past* and *past part.* of SHOOT. —*adj.* **1** (of coloured material) woven so as to show different colours at different angles. **2** *colloq.* **a** exhausted; finished. **b** drunk. **3** (of a board-edge) accurately planed. □ **be** (or **get**) **shot of** *sl.* be (or get) rid of. **shot through** permeated or suffused. [past part. of SHOOT]

shot³ /ʃɒt/ *n.* *colloq.* a reckoning, a bill, esp. at an inn etc. (*paid his shot*). [ME, = SHOT¹: cf. OE *scēotan* shoot, pay, contribute, and SCOT]

shotgun /ˈʃɒtɡʌn/ *n.* a smooth-bore gun for firing small shot at short range. □ **shotgun marriage** (or **wedding**) *colloq.* an enforced or hurried wedding, esp. because of the bride's pregnancy.

shotten herring /ˈʃɒt(ə)n/ *n.* **1** a herring that has spawned. **2** *archaic* a weakened or dispirited person. [ME, archaic past part. of SHOOT]

should /ʃʊd, ʃəd/ *v.aux.* (*3rd sing.* **should**) *past* of SHALL, used esp.: **1** in reported speech, esp. with the reported element in the 1st person (*I said I should be home by evening*). ¶ Cf. WILL¹, WOULD, now more common in this sense, esp. to avoid implications of sense 2. **2 a** to express a duty, obligation, or likelihood; = OUGHT¹ (*I should tell you; you should have been more careful; they should have arrived by now*). **b** (in the 1st person) to express a tentative suggestion (*I should like to say something*). **3 a** expressing the conditional mood in the 1st person (cf. WOULD) (*I should have been killed if I had gone*). **b** forming a conditional protasis or indefinite clause (*if you should see him; should they arrive, tell them where to go*). **4** expressing purpose = MAY, MIGHT¹ (*in order that we should not worry*).

shoulder /ˈʃəʊldə(r)/ *n.* & *v.* —*n.* **1 a** the part of the body at which the arm, foreleg, or wing is attached. **b** (in full **shoulder joint**) the end of the upper arm joining with the collar-bone and blade-bone. **c** either of the two projections below the neck from which the arms depend. **2** the upper foreleg and shoulder blade of a pig, lamb, etc. when butchered. **3** (in *pl.*) **a** the upper part of the back and arms. **b** this part of the body regarded as capable of bearing a burden or blame, providing comfort, etc. (*needs a shoulder to cry on*). **4** a strip of land next to a metalled road (*pulled over on to the shoulder*). **5** a part of a garment covering the shoulder. **6** a part of anything resembling a shoulder in form or function, as in a bottle, mountain, tool, etc. —*v.* **1 a** *tr.* push with the shoulder; jostle. **b** *intr.* make one's way by jostling (*shouldered through the crowd*). **2** *tr.* take (a burden etc.) on one's shoulders (*shouldered the family's problems*). □**put** (or **set**) **one's shoulder to the wheel** make an effort. **shoulder arms** hold a rifle with the barrel against the shoulder and the butt in the hand. **shoulder-bag** a woman's handbag that can be hung from the shoulder. **shoulder-belt** a bandolier or other strap passing over one shoulder and under the opposite arm. **shoulder-blade** *Anat.* either of the large flat bones of the upper back; the scapula. **shoulder-high** up to or as high as the shoulders. **shoulder-holster** a gun holster worn in the armpit. **shoulder-knot** a knot of ribbon, metal, lace, etc. worn as part of a ceremonial dress. **shoulder-length** (of hair etc.) reaching to the shoulders. **shoulder loop** *US* the shoulder-strap of an army, air-force, or marines officer. **shoulder mark** *US* the shoulder-strap of a naval officer. **shoulder-note** *Printing* a marginal note at the top of a page. **shoulder-of-mutton sail** = *leg-of-mutton sail*. **shoulder-pad** a pad sewn into a garment to bulk out the shoulder. **shoulder-strap 1** a strip of fabric, leather, etc. suspending a bag or garment from the shoulder. **2** a strip of cloth from shoulder to collar on a military uniform bearing a symbol of rank etc. **3** a similar strip on a raincoat. **shoulder to shoulder 1** side by side. **2** with closed ranks or united effort. □□**shouldered** *adj.* (also in *comb.*). [OE *sculdor* f. WG]

shouldn't /ˈʃʊd(ə)nt/ *contr.* should not.

shout /ʃaʊt/ *v.* & *n.* —*v.* **1** *intr.* make a loud cry or vocal sound; speak loudly (*shouted for attention*). **2** *tr.* say or express loudly; call out (*shouted that the coast was clear*). **3** *tr.* (also *absol.*) *Austral.* & *NZ colloq.* treat (another person) to drinks etc. —*n.* **1** a loud cry expressing joy etc. or calling attention. **2** *colloq.* one's turn to order a round of drinks etc. (*your shout I think*). □**all over bar** (or **but**) **the shouting** *colloq.* the contest is virtually decided. **shout at** speak loudly to etc. **shout down** reduce to silence by shouting. **shout for** call for by shouting. **shout-up** *colloq.* a noisy argument. □□**shouter** *n.* [ME, perh. rel. to SHOOT: cf. ON *skúta* SCOUT]

shove /ʃʌv/ *v.* & *n.* —*v.* **1** *tr.* (also *absol.*) push vigorously; move by hard or rough pushing (*shoved him out of the way*). **2** *intr.* (usu. foll. by *along, past, through,* etc.) make one's way by pushing (*shoved through the crowd*). **3** *tr. colloq.* put somewhere (*shoved it in the drawer*). —*n.* an act of shoving or of prompting a person into action. □**shove-halfpenny** a form of shoveboard played with coins etc. on a table esp. in licensed premises. **shove off 1** start from the shore in a boat. **2** *sl.* depart; go away (*told him to shove off*). [OE *scūfan* f. Gmc]

shovel /ˈʃʌv(ə)l/ *n.* & *v.* —*n.* **1 a** a spadelike tool for shifting quantities of coal, earth, etc., esp. having the sides curved upwards. **b** the amount contained in a shovel; a shovelful. **2** a machine or part of a machine having a similar form or function. —*v.tr.* (**shovelled, shovelling**; *US* **shoveled, shoveling**) **1** shift or clear (coal etc.) with or as if with a shovel. **2** *colloq.* move (esp. food) in large quantities or roughly (*shovelled peas into his mouth*). □**shovel hat** a broad-brimmed hat esp. worn by some clergymen. □□**shovelful** *n.* (*pl.* **-fuls**). [OE *scofl* f. Gmc (see SHOVE)]

shovelboard /ˈʃʌv(ə)l,bɔːd/ *n.* a game played esp. on a ship's deck by pushing discs with the hand or with a long-handled shovel over a marked surface. [earlier *shoveboard* f. SHOVE + BOARD]

shovelhead /ˈʃʌv(ə)l,hed/ *n.* a shark, *Sphyrna tiburo*, like the hammerhead but smaller. Also called BONNETHEAD.

shoveller /ˈʃʌvələ(r)/ *n.* (also **shoveler**) **1** a person or thing that shovels. **2** a duck, *Anas clypeata*, with a broad shovel-like beak. [SHOVEL: sense 2 earlier *shovelard* f. -ARD, perh. after *mallard*]

show /ʃəʊ/ *v.* & *n.* —*v.* (*past part.* **shown** /ʃəʊn/ or showed) **1** *intr.* & *tr.* be, or allow or cause to be, visible; manifest; appear (*the buds are beginning to show; white shows the dirt*). **2** *tr.* (often foll. by *to*) offer, exhibit, or produce (a thing) for scrutiny etc. (*show your tickets please; showed him my poems*). **3** *tr.* **a** indicate (one's feelings) by one's behaviour etc. (*showed mercy to him*). **b** indicate (one's feelings to a person etc.) (*showed him particular favour*). **4** *intr.* (of feelings etc.) be manifest (*his dislike shows*). **5** *tr.* **a** demonstrate; point out; prove (*has shown it to be false; showed that he knew the answer*). **b** (usu. foll. by *how to* + infin.) cause (a person) to understand or be capable of doing (*showed them how to knit*). **6** *tr.* (*refl.*) exhibit oneself as being (*showed herself to be fair*). **7** *tr.* & *intr.* (with ref. to a film) be presented or cause to be presented. **8** *tr.* exhibit (a picture, animal, flower, etc.) in a show. **9** *tr.* (often foll. by *in, out, up,* etc.) conduct or lead (*showed them to their rooms*). **10** *intr.* = *show up* 3 (*waited but he didn't show*). **11** *intr. US* finish in the first three in a race. —*n.* **1** the act or an instance of showing; the state of being shown. **2 a** a spectacle, display, exhibition, etc. (*a fine show of blossom*). **b** a collection of things etc. shown for public entertainment or in competition (*dog show; flower show*). **3 a** a play etc., esp. a musical. **b** a light entertainment programme on television etc. **c** any public entertainment or performance. **4 a** an outward appearance, semblance, or display (*made a show of agreeing; a show of strength*). **b** empty appearance; mere display (*did it for show; that's all show*). **5** *colloq.* an undertaking, business, etc. (*sold the whole show*). **6** *colloq.* an opportunity of acting, defending oneself, etc. (*gave him a fair show; made a good show of it*). **7** *Med.* a discharge of blood etc. from the vagina at the onset of childbirth. □**give the show** (or **whole show**) **away** demonstrate the inadequacies or reveal the truth. **good** (or **bad** or **poor**) **show!** *colloq.* **1** that was well (or badly) done. **2** that was lucky (or unlucky). **nothing to show for** no visible result of (effort etc.). **on show** being exhibited. **show business** *colloq.* the theatrical profession. **show-card** a card used for advertising. **show one's cards** = *show one's hand*. **show cause** *Law* allege with justification. **show a clean pair of heels** *colloq.* retreat speedily; run away. **show one's colours** make one's opinion clear. **show a person the door** dismiss or eject a person. **show one's face** make an appearance; let oneself be seen. **show fight** be persistent or belligerent. **show the flag** see FLAG[1]. **show forth** *archaic* exhibit; expound. **show one's hand 1** disclose one's plans. **2** reveal one's cards. **show house** (or **flat** etc.) a furnished and decorated house (or flat etc.) on a new estate shown to prospective buyers. **show in** see sense 9 of *v.* **show a leg** *colloq.* get out of bed. **show off 1** display to advantage. **2** *colloq.* act pretentiously; display one's wealth, knowledge, etc. **show-off** *n. colloq.* a person who shows off. **show of force** proof that one is prepared to use force. **show of hands** raised hands indicating a vote for or against, usu. without being counted. **show oneself 1** be seen in public. **2** see sense 6 of *v.* **show out** see sense 9 of *v.* **show-piece 1** an item of work presented for exhibition or display. **2** an outstanding example or specimen. **show-place** a house etc. that tourists go to see. **show round** take (a person) to places of interest; act as guide for (a person) in a building etc. **show-stopper** *colloq.* a performance receiving prolonged applause. **show one's teeth** reveal one's strength; be aggressive. **show through 1** be visible although supposedly concealed. **2** (of real feelings etc.) be revealed inadvertently. **show trial** esp. *hist.* a judicial trial designed by the State to terrorize or impress the public. **show up 1** make or be conspicuous or clearly visible. **2** expose (a fraud, impostor, inferiority, etc.). **3** *colloq.* appear; be present; arrive. **4** *colloq.* embarrass or humiliate (*don't show me up by wearing

aʊ how eɪ day əʊ no eə hair ɪə near ɔɪ boy ʊə poor aɪə fire aʊə sour (*see over for consonants*)

jeans). **show the way 1** indicate what has to be done etc. by attempting it first. **2** show others which way to go etc. **show the white feather** appear cowardly (see also *white feather*). **show willing** display a willingness to help etc. **show-window** a window for exhibiting goods etc. [ME f. OE *scēawian* f. WG: cf. SHEEN]

showbiz /'ʃəʊbɪz/ *n. colloq.* = *show business*.

showboat /'ʃəʊbəʊt/ *n. US* a river steamer on which theatrical performances are given.

showcase /'ʃəʊkeɪs/ *n. & v.* —*n.* **1** a glass case used for exhibiting goods etc. **2** a place or medium for presenting (esp. attractively) to general attention. —*v.tr.* display in or as if in a showcase.

showdown /'ʃəʊdaʊn/ *n.* **1** a final test or confrontation; a decisive situation. **2** the laying down face up of the players' cards in poker.

shower /'ʃaʊə(r)/ *n. & v.* —*n.* **1** a brief fall of esp. rain, hail, sleet, or snow. **2 a** a brisk flurry of arrows, bullets, dust, stones, sparks, etc. **b** a similar flurry of gifts, letters, honours, praise, etc. **3** (in full **shower-bath**) **a** a cubicle, bath, etc. in which one stands under a spray of water. **b** the apparatus etc. used for this. **c** the act of bathing in a shower. **4** a group of particles initiated by a cosmic-ray particle in the earth's atmosphere. **5** *US* a party for giving presents to a prospective bride, etc. **6** *Brit. sl.* a contemptible or unpleasant person or group of people. —*v.* **1** *tr.* discharge (water, missiles, etc.) in a shower. **2** *intr.* use a shower-bath. **3** *tr.* (usu. foll. by *on*, *upon*) lavishly bestow (gifts etc.). **4** *intr.* descend or come in a shower (*it showered on and off all day*). □□ **showery** *adj.* [OE *scūr* f. Gmc]

showerproof /'ʃaʊə,pru:f/ *adj. & v.* —*adj.* resistant to light rain. —*v.tr.* render showerproof.

showgirl /'ʃəʊgɜ:l/ *n.* an actress who sings and dances in musicals, variety shows, etc.

showing /'ʃəʊɪŋ/ *n.* **1** the act or an instance of showing. **2** a usu. specified quality of performance (*made a poor showing*). **3** the presentation of a case; evidence (*on present showing it must be true*). [OE *scēawung* (as SHOW)]

showjumping /'ʃəʊ,dʒʌmpɪŋ/ *n.* the sport of riding horses over a course of fences and other obstacles, with penalty points for errors. □□ **showjump** *v.intr.* **showjumper** *n.*

showman /'ʃəʊmən/ *n.* (*pl.* **-men**) **1** the proprietor or manager of a circus etc. **2** a person skilled in self-advertisement or publicity. □□ **showmanship** *n.*

shown *past part.* of SHOW.

showroom /'ʃəʊru:m, -rʊm/ *n.* a room in a factory, office building, etc. used to display goods for sale.

showy /'ʃəʊɪ/ *adj.* (**showier**, **showiest**) **1** brilliant; gaudy, esp. vulgarly so. **2** striking. □□ **showily** *adv.* **showiness** *n.*

s.h.p. *abbr.* shaft horsepower.

shrank *past* of SHRINK.

shrapnel /'ʃræpn(ə)l/ *n.* **1** fragments of a bomb etc. thrown out by an explosion. **2** a shell containing bullets or pieces of metal timed to burst short of impact. [Gen. H. *Shrapnel*, Brit. soldier d. 1842, inventor of the shell]

shred /ʃred/ *n. & v.* —*n.* **1** a scrap, fragment, or strip of esp. cloth, paper, etc. **2** the least amount, remnant (*not a shred of evidence*). —*v.tr.* (**shredded**, **shredding**) tear or cut into shreds. □ **tear to shreds** completely refute (an argument etc.). [OE *scrēad* (unrecorded) piece cut off, *scrēadian* f. WG: see SHROUD]

shredder /'ʃredə(r)/ *n.* **1** a machine used to reduce documents to shreds. **2** any device used for shredding.

shrew /ʃru:/ *n.* **1** any small usu. insect-eating mouse-like mammal of the family Soricidae, with a long pointed snout. **2** a bad-tempered or scolding woman. □□ **shrewish** *adj.* (in sense 2). **shrewishly** *adv.*

shrewishness *n.* [OE *scrēawa*, *scrǣwa* shrew-mouse: cf. OHG *scrawaz* dwarf, MHG *schrawaz* etc. devil]

shrewd /ʃru:d/ *adj.* **1 a** showing astute powers of judgement; clever and judicious (*a shrewd observer*; *made a shrewd guess*). **b** (of a face etc.) shrewd-looking. **2** *archaic* **a** (of pain, cold, etc.) sharp, biting. **b** (of a blow, thrust, etc.) severe, hard. **c** mischievous; malicious. □□ **shrewdly** *adv.* **shrewdness** *n.* [ME, = malignant, f. SHREW in sense 'evil person or thing', or past part. of obs. *shrew* to curse, f. SHREW]

shriek /ʃri:k/ *v. & n.* —*v.* **1** *intr.* **a** utter a shrill screeching sound or words esp. in pain or terror. **b** (foll. by *of*) provide a clear or blatant indication of. **2** *tr.* a utter (sounds or words) by shrieking (*shrieked his name*). **b** indicate clearly or blatantly. —*n.* a high-pitched piercing cry or sound; a scream. □ **shriek out** say in shrill tones. **shriek with laughter** laugh uncontrollably. □□ **shrieker** *n.* [imit.: cf. dial. *screak*, ON *skrækja*, and SCREECH]

shrieval /'ʃri:v(ə)l/ *adj.* of or relating to a sheriff. [*shrieve* obs. var. of SHERIFF]

shrievalty /'ʃri:vəltɪ/ *n.* (*pl.* **-ies**) **1** a sheriff's office or jurisdiction. **2** the tenure of this. [as SHRIEVAL + -*alty* as in mayoralty etc.]

shrift /ʃrɪft/ *n. archaic* **1** confession to a priest. **2** confession and absolution. □ **short shrift 1** curt treatment. **2** *archaic* little time between condemnation and execution or punishment. [OE *scrift* (verbal noun) f. SHRIVE]

shrike /ʃraɪk/ *n.* any bird of the family Laniidae, with a strong hooked and toothed bill, that impales its prey of small birds and insects on thorns. Also called *butcher-bird*. [perh. rel. to OE *scric* thrush, MLG *schrīk* corncrake (imit.): cf. SHRIEK]

shrill /ʃrɪl/ *adj. & v.* —*adj.* **1** piercing and high-pitched in sound. **2** *derog.* (esp. of a protester) sharp, unrestrained, unreasoning. —*v.* **1** *intr.* (of a cry etc.) sound shrilly. **2** *tr.* (of a person etc.) utter or send out (a song, complaint, etc.) shrilly. □□ **shrilly** *adv.* **shrillness** *n.* [ME, rel. to LG *schrell* sharp in tone or taste f. Gmc]

shrimp /ʃrɪmp/ *n. & v.* —*n.* **1** (*pl.* same or **shrimps**) any of various small (esp. marine) edible crus-taceans, with ten legs, grey-green when alive and pink when boiled. **2** *colloq.* a very small slight person. —*v.intr.* go catching shrimps. □ **shrimp plant** an evergreen shrub, *Justicia brandegeana*, bearing small white flowers in clusters of pinkish-brown bracts. □□ **shrimper** *n.* [ME, prob. rel. to MLG *schrempen* wrinkle, MHG *schrimpfen* contract, and SCRIMP]

shrine /ʃraɪn/ *n. & v.* —*n.* **1** esp. *RC Ch.* **a** a chapel, church, altar, etc., sacred to a saint, holy person, relic, etc. **b** the tomb of a saint etc. **c** a casket esp. containing sacred relics; a reliquary. **d** a niche containing a holy statue etc. **2** a place associated with or containing memorabilia of a particular person, event, etc. **3** a Shinto place of worship. —*v.tr. poet.* enshrine. [OE *scrīn* f. Gmc f. L *scrinium* case for books etc.]

shrink /ʃrɪŋk/ *v. & n.* —*v.* (*past* **shrank** /ʃræŋk/; *past part.* **shrunk** /ʃrʌŋk/ or (esp. as *adj.*) **shrunken** /'ʃrʌŋkən/) **1** *tr. & intr.* make or become smaller; contract, esp. by the action of moisture, heat, or cold. **2** *intr.* (usu. foll. by *from*) **a** retire; recoil; flinch; cower (*shrank from her touch*). **b** be averse from doing (*shrinks from meeting them*). **3** (as **shrunken** *adj.*) (esp. of a face, person, etc.) having grown smaller esp. because of age, illness, etc. —*n.* **1** the act or an instance of shrinking; shrinkage. **2** *sl.* a psychiatrist (from 'head-shrinker'). □ **shrinking violet** an exaggeratedly shy person. **shrink into oneself** become withdrawn. **shrink on** slip (a metal tyre etc.) on while expanded with heat and allow to tighten. **shrink-resistant** (of textiles etc.) resistant to shrinkage when wet etc. **shrink-wrap** (-**wrapped**, -**wrapping**) enclose (an article) in (esp.

transparent) film that shrinks tightly on to it. □□
shrinkable *adj.* **shrinker** *n.* **shrinkingly** *adv.*
shrink-proof *adj.* [OE *scrincan*: cf. *skrynka* to
wrinkle]

shrinkage /ˈʃrɪŋkɪdʒ/ *n.* **1 a** the process or fact of
shrinking. **b** the degree or amount of shrinking. **2**
an allowance made for the reduction in takings due
to wastage, theft, etc.

shrive /ʃraɪv/ *v.tr.* (*past* **shrove** /ʃrəʊv/; *past part.*
shriven /ˈʃrɪv(ə)n/) *RC Ch. archaic* **1** (of a priest) hear
the confession of, assign penance to, and absolve. **2**
(*refl.*) (of a penitent) submit oneself to a priest for
confession etc. [OE *scrīfan* impose as penance, WG f.
L *scribere* write]

shrivel /ˈʃrɪv(ə)l/ *v.tr.* & *intr.* (**shrivelled**,
shrivelling or *US* **shriveled**, **shriveling**) contract
or wither into a wrinkled, folded, rolled-up, contorted, or dried-up state. [perh. f. ON: cf. Sw. dial.
skryvla to wrinkle]

shriven *past part.* of SHRIVE.

shroud /ʃraʊd/ *n.* & *v.* —*n.* **1 a** sheetlike garment
for wrapping a corpse for burial. **2** anything that
conceals like a shroud (*wrapped in a shroud of
mystery*). **3** (in *pl.*) *Naut.* a set of ropes forming part
of the standing rigging and supporting the mast or
topmast. —*v.tr.* **1** clothe (a body) for burial. **2**
cover, conceal, or disguise (*hills shrouded in mist*).
□**shroud-laid** (of a rope) having four strands laid
right-handed on a core. □□ **shroudless** *adj.* [OE *scrūd*
f. Gmc: see SHRED]

shrove *past* of SHRIVE.

Shrovetide /ˈʃrəʊvtaɪd/ *n.* Shrove Tuesday and
the two days preceding it when it was formerly
customary to be shriven. [ME *shrove* abnormally f.
SHROVE]

Shrove Tuesday /ʃrəʊv/ *n.* the day before Ash
Wednesday.

shrub[1] /ʃrʌb/ *n.* a woody plant smaller than a tree
and having a very short stem with branches near
the ground. □□ **shrubby** *adj.* [ME f. OE *scrubb*, *scrybb*
shrubbery: cf. NFris. *skrobb* brushwood, WFlem.
schrobbe vetch, Norw. *skrubba* dwarf cornel, and
SCRUB[2]]

shrub[2] /ʃrʌb/ *n.* a cordial made of sweetened fruit-
juice and spirits, esp. rum. [Arab. *šurb*, *šarāb* f.
šariba to drink: cf. SHERBET, SYRUP]

shrubbery /ˈʃrʌbərɪ/ *n.* (*pl.* **-ies**) an area planted
with shrubs.

shrug /ʃrʌg/ *v.* & *n.* —*v.* (**shrugged**, **shrugging**) **1**
intr. slightly and momentarily raise the shoulders to
express indifference, helplessness, contempt, etc. **2**
tr. **a** raise (the shoulders) in this way. **b** shrug the
shoulders to express (indifference etc.) (*shrugged his
consent*). —*n.* the act or an instance of shrugging.
□**shrug off** dismiss as unimportant etc. by or as if
by shrugging. [ME: orig. unkn.]

shrunk (also **shrunken**) *past part.* of SHRINK.

shtick /ʃtɪk/ *n. sl.* a theatrical routine, gimmick, etc.
[Yiddish f. G *Stück* piece]

shuck /ʃʌk/ *n.* & *v. US* —*n.* **1** a husk or pod. **2** the
shell of an oyster or clam. **3** (in *pl.*) *colloq.* an
expression of contempt or regret or self-deprecation
in response to praise. —*v.tr.* remove the shucks of;
shell. □□ **shucker** *n.* [17th c.: orig. unkn.]

shudder /ˈʃʌdə(r)/ *v.* & *n.* —*v.intr.* **1** shiver esp.
convulsively from fear, cold, repugnance, etc. **2** feel
strong repugnance etc. (*shudder to think what might
happen*). **3** (of a machine etc.) vibrate or quiver. —*n.*
1 the act or an instance of shuddering. **2** (in *pl.*; prec.
by *the*) *colloq.* a state of shuddering. □□
shudderingly *adv.* **shuddery** *adj.* [ME *shod(d)er* f.
MDu. *schūderen*, MLG *schōderen* f. Gmc]

shuffle /ˈʃʌf(ə)l/ *v.* & *n.* —*v.* **1** *tr.* move with a
scraping, sliding, or dragging motion (*shuffles along*;
shuffling his feet). **2** *tr.* **a** (also *absol.*) rearrange (a
pack of cards) by sliding them over each other
quickly. **b** rearrange; intermingle; confuse (*shuffled
the documents*). **3** *tr.* (usu. foll. by *on*, *off*, *into*) assume

or remove (clothes, a burden, etc.) esp. clumsily
or evasively (*shuffled on his clothes*; *shuffled off
responsibility*). **4** *intr.* **a** equivocate; prevaricate. **b**
continually shift one's position; fidget. **5** *intr.* (foll.
by *out of*) escape evasively (*shuffled out of the blame*).
—*n.* **1** a shuffling movement. **2** the act or an instance
of shuffling cards. **3** a general change of relative
positions. **4** a piece of equivocation; sharp practice.
5 a quick scraping movement of the feet in dancing
(see also *double shuffle*). □**shuffle-board** =
SHOVELBOARD. **shuffle the cards** change policy etc.
□□ **shuffler** *n.* [perh. f. LG *schuffeln* walk clumsily f.
Gmc: cf. SHOVE]

shufti /ˈʃʊftɪ/ *n.* (*pl.* **shuftis**) *Brit. colloq.* a look or
glimpse. [Arab. *šaffa* try to see]

shun /ʃʌn/ *v.tr.* (**shunned**, **shunning**) avoid; keep
clear of (*shuns human company*). [OE *scunian*, of
unkn. orig.]

shunt /ʃʌnt/ *v.* & *n.* —*v.* **1** *intr.* & *tr.* diverge or cause
(a train) to be diverted esp. on to a siding. **2** *tr. Electr.*
provide (a current) with a shunt. **3** *tr.* **a** postpone or
evade. **b** divert (a decision etc.) on to another person
etc. —*n.* **1** the act or an instance of shunting on to a
siding. **2** *Electr.* a conductor joining two points of a
circuit, through which more or less of a current may
be diverted. **3** *Surgery* an alternative path for the
circulation of the blood. **4** *sl.* a motor accident, esp.
a collision of vehicles travelling one close behind
another. □□ **shunter** *n.* [ME, perh. f. SHUN]

shush /ʃʊʃ, ʃʌʃ/ *int.* & *v.* —*int.* = HUSH *int.* —*v.* **1**
intr. **a** call for silence by saying *shush*. **b** be silent
(*they shushed at once*). **2** *tr.* make or attempt to make
silent. [imit.]

shut /ʃʌt/ *v.* (**shutting**; *past* and *past part.* **shut**) **1**
tr. **a** move (a door, window, lid, lips, etc.) into position
so as to block an aperture (*shut the lid*). **b** close or
seal (a room, window, box, eye, mouth, etc.) by
moving a door etc. (*shut the box*). **2** *intr.* become or
be capable of being closed or sealed (*the door shut
with a bang*; *the lid shuts automatically*). **3** *intr.* & *tr.*
become or make (a shop, business, etc.) closed for
trade (*the shops shut at five*; *shuts his shop at five*). **4** *tr.*
bring (a book, hand, telescope, etc.) into a folded-up or
contracted state. **5** *tr.* (usu. foll. by *in*, *out*) keep (a
person, sound, etc.) in or out of a room etc. by
shutting a door etc. (*shut out the noise*; *shut them in*).
6 *tr.* (usu. foll. by *in*) catch (a finger, dress, etc.) by
shutting something on it (*shut her finger in the door*).
7 *tr.* bar access to (a place etc.) (*this entrance is shut*).
□**be** (or **get**) **shut of** *sl.* be (or get) rid of (*were glad to
get shut of him*). **shut the door on** refuse to consider;
make impossible. **shut down 1** stop (a factory,
nuclear reactor, etc.) from operating. **2** (of a factory
etc.) stop operating. **3** push or pull (a window-sash
etc.) down into a closed position. **shut-down** *n.* the
closure of a factory etc. **shut-eye** *colloq.* sleep. **shut
one's eyes** (or **ears** or **heart** or **mind**) to pretend
not, or refuse, to see (or hear or feel sympathy for or
think about). **shut in** (of hills, houses, etc.) encircle,
prevent access etc. to or escape from (*were shut in by
the sea on three sides*) (see also sense 5). **shut off 1**
stop the flow of (water, gas, etc.) by shutting a valve.
2 separate from society etc. **shut-off** *n.* **1** something
used for stopping an operation. **2** a cessation of flow,
supply, or activity. **shut out 1** exclude (a person,
light, etc.) from a place, situation, etc. **2** screen
(landscape etc.) from view. **3** prevent (a possibility
etc.). **4** block (a painful memory etc.) from the mind.
5 *US* prevent (an opponent) from scoring (see also
sense 5). **shut-out bid** *Bridge* a pre-emptive bid.
shut to 1 close (a door etc.). **2** (of a door etc.) close
as far as it will go. **shut up 1** close all doors and
windows of (a house etc.); bolt and bar. **2** imprison
(a person). **3** close (a box etc.) securely. **4** *colloq.*
reduce to silence by rebuke etc. **5** put (a thing) away
in a box etc. **6** (esp. in *imper.*) *colloq.* stop talking.
shut up shop 1 close a business, shop, etc. **2** cease
business etc. permanently. **shut your face** (or **head**

or **mouth** or **trap**)! *sl.* an impolite request to stop talking. [OE *scyttan* f. WG: cf. SHOOT]

shutter /'ʃʌtə(r)/ *n. & v.* —*n.* **1** a person or thing that shuts. **2 a** each of a pair or set of panels fixed inside or outside a window for security or privacy or to keep the light in or out. **b** a structure of slats on rollers used for the same purpose. **3** a device that exposes the film in a photographic camera. **4** *Mus.* the blind of a swell-box in an organ used for controlling the sound-level. —*v.tr.* **1** put up the shutters of. **2** provide with shutters. □**put up the shutters 1** cease business for the day. **2** cease business etc. permanently. □□ **shutterless** *adj.*

shuttering /'ʃʌtərɪŋ/ *n.* **1** a temporary structure usu. of wood, used to hold concrete during setting. **2** material for making shutters.

shuttle /'ʃʌt(ə)l/ *n. & v.* —*n.* **1 a** a bobbin with two pointed ends used for carrying the weft-thread across between the warp-threads in weaving. **b** a bobbin carrying the lower thread in a sewing-machine. **2** a train, bus, etc., going to and fro over a short route continuously. **3** = SHUTTLECOCK. **4** = *space shuttle.* —*v.* **1** *intr. & tr.* move or cause to move to and fro like a shuttle. **2** *intr.* travel in a shuttle. □**shuttle armature** *Electr.* an armature with a single coil wound on an elongated iron bobbin. **shuttle diplomacy** negotiations conducted by a mediator who travels successively to several countries. **shuttle service** a train or bus etc. service operating to and fro over a short route. [OE *scytel* dart f. Gmc: cf. SHOOT]

shuttlecock /'ʃʌt(ə)l,kɒk/ *n.* **1** a cork with a ring of feathers, or a similar device of plastic, used instead of a ball in badminton and in battledore and shuttlecock. **2** a thing passed repeatedly back and forth. [SHUTTLE + COCK¹,· prob. f. the flying motion]

shy¹ /ʃaɪ/ *adj., v., & n.* —*adj.* (**shyer, shyest** or **shier, shiest**) **1 a** diffident or uneasy in company; timid. **b** (of an animal, bird, etc.) easily startled; timid. **2** (foll. by *of*) avoiding; chary of (*shy of his aunt*; *shy of going to meetings*). **3** (in *comb.*) showing fear of or distaste for (*gun-shy*; *work-shy*). **4** (often foll. by *of, on*) *colloq.* having lost; short of (*I'm shy three quid*; *shy of the price of admission*). —*v.intr.* (**shies, shied**) **1** (usu. foll. by *at*) (esp. of a horse) start suddenly aside (at an object, noise, etc.) in fright. **2** (usu. foll. by *away from, at*) avoid accepting or becoming involved in (a proposal etc.) in alarm. —*n.* a sudden startled movement. □□ **shyer** *n.* **shyly** *adv.* (also **shily**). **shyness** *n.* [OE *sceoh* f. Gmc]

shy² /ʃaɪ/ *v. & n.* —*v.tr.* (**shies, shied**) (also *absol.*) fling or throw (a stone etc.). —*n.* the act or an instance of shying. □**have a shy at** *colloq.* **1** try to hit with a stone etc. **2** make an attempt at. **3** jeer at. □□ **shyer** *n.* [18th c.: orig. unkn.]

Shylock /'ʃaɪlɒk/ *n.* a hard-hearted money-lender; a miser. [character in Shakesp. *Merchant of Venice*]

shyster /'ʃaɪstə(r)/ *n.* esp. *US colloq.* a person, esp. a lawyer, who uses unscrupulous methods. [19th c.: orig. uncert.]

SI *abbr.* **1** (Order of the) Star of India. **2** the international system of units of measurement (F *Système International*).

Si *symb. Chem.* the element silicon.

si /siː/ *n. Mus.* = TE. [F f. It., perh. f. the initials of *Sancte Iohannes*: see GAMUT]

sialagogue /'saɪələ,gɒg/ *n. & adj.* —*n.* a medicine inducing the flow of saliva. —*adj.* inducing such a flow. [F f. Gk *sialon* saliva + *agōgos* leading]

siamang /'saɪə,mæŋ, 'siːə,mæŋ/ *n.* a large black gibbon, *Hylobates syndactylus*, native to Sumatra and the Malay peninsula. [Malay]

Siamese /,saɪə'miːz/ *n. & adj.* —*n.* (*pl.* same) **1 a** native of Siam (now Thailand) in SE Asia. **b** the language of Siam. **2** (in full **Siamese cat**) **a** a cat of a cream-coloured short-haired breed with a brown face and ears and blue eyes. **b** this breed. —*adj.* of or concerning Siam, its people, or language.

□**Siamese twins 1** twins joined at any part of the body and sometimes sharing organs etc. **2** any closely associated pair.

sib /sɪb/ *n. & adj.* —*n.* **1** a brother or sister (cf. SIBLING). **2** a blood relative. **3** a group of people recognized by an individual as his or her kindred. —*adj.* (usu. foll. by *to*) esp. *Sc.* related; akin. [OE *sib(b)*]

Siberian /saɪ'bɪərɪən/ *n. & adj.* —*n.* **1** a native of Siberia in the northern Soviet Union. **2** a person of Siberian descent. —*adj.* of or relating to Siberia.

sibilant /'sɪbɪlənt/ *adj. & n.* —*adj.* **1** (of a letter or set of letters, as *s, sh*) sounded with a hiss. **2** hissing (*a sibilant whisper*). —*n.* a sibilant letter or letters. □□ **sibilance** *n.* **sibilancy** *n.* [L *sibilare sibilant*- hiss]

sibilate /'sɪbɪ,leɪt/ *v.tr. & intr.* pronounce with or utter a hissing sound. □□ **sibilation** /-'leɪʃ(ə)n/ *n.*

sibling /'sɪblɪŋ/ *n.* each of two or more children having one or both parents in common. [SIB + -LING¹]

sibship /'sɪbʃɪp/ *n.* **1** the state of belonging to a sib or the same sib. **2** a group of children having the same two parents.

sibyl /'sɪbɪl/ *n.* **1** any of the women in ancient times supposed to utter the oracles and prophecies of a god. **2** a prophetess, fortune-teller, or witch. [ME f. OF *Sibile* or med.L *Sibilla* f. L *Sibylla* f. Gk *Sibulla*]

sibylline /'sɪbɪ,laɪn/ *adj.* **1** of or from a sibyl. **2** oracular; prophetic. □**the Sibylline books** a collection of oracles belonging to the ancient Roman State and used for guidance by magistrates etc. [L *Sibyllinus* (as SIBYL)]

sic /sɪk/ *adv.* (usu. in brackets) used, spelt, etc., as written (confirming, or calling attention to, the form of quoted or copied words). [L, = so, thus]

siccative /'sɪkətɪv/ *n. & adj.* —*n.* a substance causing drying, esp. mixed with oil-paint etc. for quick drying. —*adj.* having such properties. [LL *siccativus* f. *siccare* to dry]

sice¹ /saɪs/ *n.* the six on dice. [ME f. OF *sis* f. L *sex* six]

sice² var. of SYCE.

Sicilian /sɪ'sɪljən, -lɪən/ *n. & adj.* —*n.* **1** a native of Sicily, an island off the S. coast of Italy. **2** a person of Sicilian descent. —*adj.* of or relating to Sicily. [L *Sicilia* Sicily]

siciliano /sɪtʃɪ'ljɑːnəʊ/ *n.* (*pl.* **-os**) (also **siciliana** /-nə/) a dance, song, or instrumental piece in 6/8 or 12/8 time, often in a minor key, and evoking a pastoral mood. [It., = Sicilian]

sick¹ /sɪk/ *adj., n., & v.* —*adj.* **1** (often in *comb.*) esp. *Brit.* vomiting or tending to vomit (*feels sick*; *has been sick*; *seasick*). **2** esp. *US* ill; affected by illness (*has been sick for a week*; *a sick man*; *sick with measles*). **3 a** (often foll. by *at*) esp. mentally perturbed; disordered (*the product of a sick mind*; *sick at heart*). **b** (often foll. by *for*, or in *comb.*) pining; longing (*sick for a sight of home*; *lovesick*). **4** (often foll. by *of*) *colloq.* **a** disgusted; surfeited (*sick of chocolates*). **b** angry, esp. because of surfeit (*am sick of being teased*). **5** *colloq.* (of humour etc.) jeering at misfortune, illness, death, etc.; morbid (*sick joke*). **6** (of a ship) needing repair (esp. of a specified kind) (*paint-sick*). —*n. Brit. colloq.* vomit. —*v.tr.* (usu. foll. by *up*) *Brit. colloq.* vomit (*sicked up his dinner*). □**go sick** report oneself as ill. **look sick** *colloq.* be unimpressive or embarrassed. **sick at** (or **to**) **one's stomach** *US* vomiting or tending to vomit. **sick-benefit** *Brit.* an allowance made by the State to a person absent from work through sickness. **sick building syndrome** a high incidence of illness in office workers, attributed to the immediate working surroundings. **sick-call 1** a visit by a doctor to a sick person etc. **2** *Mil.* a summons for sick men to attend. **sick-flag** a yellow flag indicating disease at a quarantine station or on ship. **sick headache** a migraine headache with vomiting. **sick-leave** leave of absence granted because of illness. **sick-list** a list of the sick, esp. in a regiment, ship, etc. **sick-making**

colloq. sickening. **sick nurse** = NURSE. **sick-pay** pay given to an employee etc. on sick-leave. **take sick** *colloq.* be taken ill. □□ **sickish** *adj.* [OE *sēoc* f. Gmc]

sick² /sɪk/ *v.tr.* (usu. in *imper.*) (esp. to a dog) set upon (a rat etc.). [19th c., dial. var. of SEEK]

sickbay /'sɪkbeɪ/ *n.* **1** part of a ship used as a hospital. **2** any room etc. for sick people.

sickbed /'sɪkbed/ *n.* **1** an invalid's bed. **2** the state of being an invalid.

sicken /'sɪkən/ *v.* **1** *tr.* affect with loathing or disgust. **2** *intr.* **a** (often foll. by *for*) show symptoms of illness (*is sickening for measles*). **b** (often foll. by *at*, or *to* + infin.) feel nausea or disgust (*he sickened at the sight*). **3** (as **sickening** *adj.*) **a** loathsome, disgusting. **b** *colloq.* very annoying. □□ **sickeningly** *adv.*

sickie /'sɪkɪ/ *n.* *Austral.* & *NZ colloq.* a period of sick-leave, usu. taken with insufficient medical reason.

sickle /'sɪk(ə)l/ *n.* **1** a short-handled farming tool with a semicircular blade, used for cutting corn, lopping, or trimming. **2** anything sickle-shaped, esp. the crescent moon. □ **sickle-bill** any of various curlews with a sickle-shaped bill. **sickle-cell** a sickle-shaped blood-cell, esp. as found in a type of severe hereditary anaemia. **sickle-feather** each of the long middle feathers of a cock's tail. [OE *sicol, sicel* f. L *secula* f. *secare* cut]

sickly /'sɪklɪ/ *adj.* (**sicklier, sickliest**) **1 a** of weak health; apt to be ill. **b** (of a person's complexion, look, etc.) languid, faint, or pale, suggesting sickness (*a sickly smile*). **c** (of light or colour) faint, pale, feeble. **2** causing ill health (*a sickly climate*). **3** (of a book etc.) sentimental or mawkish. **4** inducing or connected with nausea (*a sickly taste*). **5** (of a colour etc.) of an unpleasant shade inducing nausea (*a sickly green*). □□ **sickliness** *n.* [ME, prob. after ON *sjukligr* (as SICK¹)]

sickness /'sɪknɪs/ *n.* **1** the state of being ill; disease. **2** a specified disease (*sleeping sickness*). **3** vomiting or a tendency to vomit. □ **sickness benefit** (in the UK) benefit paid by the State for sickness interrupting paid employment. [OE *sēocnesse* (as SICK¹, -NESS)]

sickroom /'sɪkruːm, -rʊm/ *n.* **1** a room occupied by a sick person. **2** a room adapted for sick people.

sidalcea /sɪ'dælsɪə/ *n.* any mallow-like plant of the genus *Sidalcea*, bearing racemes of white, pink, or purple flowers. [mod.L f. *Sida* + *Alcea*, names of related genera]

side /saɪd/ *n.* & *v.* —*n.* **1 a** each of the more or less flat surfaces bounding an object (*a cube has six sides; this side up*). **b** a more or less vertical inner or outer plane or surface (*the side of a house; a mountainside*). **c** such a vertical lateral surface or plane as distinct from the top or bottom, front or back, or ends (*at the side of the house*). **2 a** the half of a person or animal that is on the right or the left, esp. of the torso (*has a pain in his right side*). **b** the left or right half or a specified part of a thing, area, building, etc. (*put the box on that side*). **c** (often in *comb.*) a position next to a person or thing (*grave-side; seaside; stood at my side*). **d** a specified direction relating to a person or thing (*on the north side of; came from all sides*). **e** half of a butchered carcass (*a side of bacon*). **3 a** either surface of a thing regarded as having two surfaces. **b** the amount of writing needed to fill one side of a sheet of paper (*write three sides*). **4** any of several aspects of a question, character, etc. (*many sides to his character; look on the bright side*). **5 a** each of two sets of opponents in war, politics, games, etc. (*the side that bats first; much to be said on both sides*). **b** a cause or philosophical position etc. regarded as being in conflict with another (*on the side of right*). **6 a** a part or region near the edge and remote from the centre (*at the side of the room*). **b** (*attrib.*) a subordinate, peripheral, or detached part (*a side-road; a side-table*). **7 a** each of the bounding lines of a plane rectilinear figure (*a hexagon has six*

sides). **b** each of two quantities stated to be equal in an equation. **8** a position nearer or farther than, or right or left of, a dividing line (*on this side of the Alps; on the other side of the road*). **9** a line of hereditary descent through the father or the mother. **10** (in full **side spin**) *Brit.* a spinning motion given to a billiard-ball etc. by hitting it on one side, not centrally. **11** *Brit. sl.* boastfulness; swagger (*has no side about him*). **12** *Brit. colloq.* a television channel (*shall we try another side?*). —*v.intr.* (usu. foll. by *with*) take part or be on the same side as a disputant etc. (*sided with his father*). □ **by the side of 1** close to. **2** compared with. **from side to side 1** right across. **2** alternately each way from a central line. **let the side down** fail one's colleagues, esp. by frustrating their efforts or embarrassing them. **on one side 1** not in the main or central position. **2** aside (*took him on one side to explain*). **on the . . . side** fairly, somewhat (qualifying an adjective: *on the high side*). **on the side 1** as a sideline; in addition to one's regular work etc. **2** secretly or illicitly. **3** *US* as a side dish. **on this side of the grave** in life. **side-arms** swords, bayonets, or pistols. **side-band** a range of frequencies near the carrier frequency of a radio wave, concerned in modulation. **side-bet** a bet between opponents, esp. in card-games, over and above the ordinary stakes. **side-bone** either of the small forked bones under the wings of poultry. **side by side** standing close together, esp. for mutual support. **side-car 1** a small car for a passenger or passengers attached to the side of a motor cycle. **2** a cocktail of orange liqueur, lemon juice, and brandy. **3** a jaunting car. **side-chapel** a chapel in the aisle or at the side of a church. **side dish** an extra dish subsidiary to the main course. **side-door 1** a door in or at the side of a building. **2** an indirect means of access. **side-drum** a small double-headed drum in a jazz or military band or in an orchestra (orig. hung at the drummer's side). **side-effect** a secondary, usu. undesirable, effect. **side-glance** a sideways or brief glance. **side-issue** a point that distracts attention from what is important. **side-note** a marginal note. **side-on** *adv.* from the side. —*adj.* **1** from or towards one side. **2** (of a collision) involving the side of a vehicle. **side-road** a minor or subsidiary road, esp. joining or diverging from a main road. **side-saddle** *n.* a saddle for a woman rider with both feet on the same side of the horse. —*adv.* sitting in this position on a horse. **side salad** a salad served as a side dish. **side-seat** a seat in a vehicle etc. in which the occupant has his back to the side of the vehicle. **side-slip** *n.* **1** a skid. **2** *Aeron.* a sideways movement instead of forward. —*v.intr.* **1** skid. **2** *Aeron.* move sideways instead of forward. **side-splitting** causing violent laughter. **side-street** a minor or subsidiary street. **side-stroke 1** a stroke towards or from a side. **2** an incidental action. **3** a swimming stroke in which the swimmer lies on his or her side. **side-swipe** *n.* **1** a glancing blow along the side. **2** incidental criticism etc. —*v.tr.* hit with or as if with a side-swipe. **side-table** a table placed at the side of a room or apart from the main table. **side-trip** a minor excursion during a voyage or trip; a detour. **side valve** a valve in a vehicle engine, operated from the side of the cylinder. **side-view 1** a view obtained sideways. **2** a profile. **side-wheeler** *US* a steamer with paddle-wheels. **side-whiskers** whiskers growing on the cheeks. **side wind 1** wind from the side. **2** an indirect agency or influence. **take sides** support one or other cause etc. □□ **sideless** *adj.* [OE *sīde* f. Gmc]

sideboard /'saɪdbɔːd/ *n.* a table or esp. a flat-topped cupboard at the side of a dining-room for supporting and containing dishes, table linen, decanters, etc.

sideboards /'saɪdbɔːdz/ *n.pl. Brit. colloq.* hair grown by a man down the sides of his face; side-whiskers.

sideburns /'saɪdbɜːnz/ *n.pl.* = SIDEBOARDS.

[*burnsides* pl. of *burnside* f. General *Burnside* d. 1881 who affected this style]

sided /'saɪdɪd/ *adj.* **1** having sides. **2** (in *comb.*) having a specified side or sides (*one-sided*). □□ **-sidedly** *adv.* **sidedness** *n.* (also in *comb.*).

sidehill /'saɪdhɪl/ *n. US* a hillside.

sidekick /'saɪdkɪk/ *n. colloq.* a close associate.

sidelight /'saɪdlaɪt/ *n.* **1** a light from the side. **2** incidental information etc. **3** *Brit.* a light at the side of the front of a motor vehicle to warn of its presence. **4** *Naut.* the red port or green starboard light on a ship under way.

sideline /'saɪdlaɪn/ *n. & v.* —*n.* **1** work etc. done in addition to one's main activity. **2** (usu. in *pl.*) **a** a line bounding the side of a hockey-pitch, tennis-court, etc. **b** the space next to these where spectators etc. sit. —*v.tr. US* remove (a player) from a team through injury, suspension, etc. □**on** (or **from**) **the sidelines** in (or from) a position removed from the main action.

sidelong /'saɪdlɒŋ/ *adj. & adv.* —*adj.* inclining to one side; oblique (*a sidelong glance*). —*adv.* obliquely (*moved sidelong*). [*sideling* (as SIDE, -LING²):· see -LONG]

sidereal /saɪˈdɪərɪəl/ *adj.* of or concerning the constellations or fixed stars. □ **sidereal clock** a clock showing sidereal time. **sidereal day** the time between successive meridional transits of a star or esp. of the first point of Aries, about four minutes shorter than the solar day. **sidereal time** time measured by the apparent diurnal motion of the stars. **sidereal year** a year longer than the solar year by 20 minutes 23 seconds because of precession. [L *sidereus* f. *sidus sideris* star]

siderite /'sɪdəˌraɪt/ *n.* **1** a mineral form of ferrous carbonate. **2** a meteorite consisting mainly of nickel and iron. [Gk *sidēros* iron]

siderostat /'sɪdərəˌstæt/ *n.* an instrument used for keeping the image of a celestial body in a fixed position. [L *sidus sideris* star, after *heliostat*]

sideshow /'saɪdʃəʊ/ *n.* **1** a minor show or attraction in an exhibition or entertainment. **2** a minor incident or issue.

sidesman /'saɪdzmən/ *n.* (*pl.* **-men**) an assistant churchwarden, who shows worshippers to their seats, takes the collection, etc.

sidestep /'saɪdstep/ *n. & v.* —*n.* a step taken sideways. —*v.tr.* (**-stepped**, **-stepping**) **1** esp. *Football* avoid (esp. a tackle) by stepping sideways. **2** evade. □□ **sidestepper** *n.*

sidetrack /'saɪdtræk/ *n. & v.* —*n.* a railway siding. —*v.tr.* **1** turn into a siding; shunt. **2 a** postpone, evade, or divert treatment or consideration. **b** divert (a person) from considering etc.

sidewalk /'saɪdwɔːk/ *n. US* a pedestrian path at the side of a road; a pavement.

sideward /'saɪdwəd/ *adj. & adv.* —*adj.* = SIDEWAYS. —*adv.* (also **sidewards** /-wədz/) = SIDEWAYS.

sideways /'saɪdweɪz/ *adv. & adj.* —*adv.* **1** to or from a side (*moved sideways*). **2** with one side facing forward (*sat sideways on the bus*). —*adj.* to or from a side (*a sideways movement*). □□ **sidewise** *adv. & adj.*

sidewinder /'saɪdˌwaɪndə(r)/ *n.* **1** a desert rattlesnake, *Crotalus cerastes*, native to N. America, moving with a lateral motion. **2** *US* a sideways blow.

siding /'saɪdɪŋ/ *n.* **1** a short track at the side of and opening on to a railway line, used for shunting trains. **2** *US* cladding material for the outside of a building.

sidle /'saɪd(ə)l/ *v. & n.* —*v.intr.* (usu. foll. by *along*, *up*) walk in a timid, furtive, stealthy, or cringing manner. —*n.* the act or an instance of sidling. [back-form. f. *sideling*, SIDELONG]

SIDS *abbr.* sudden infant death syndrome; = *cot-death* (see COT¹).

siege /siːdʒ/ *n.* **1 a** a military operation in which an attacking force seeks to compel the surrender of a fortified place by surrounding it and cutting off supplies etc. **b** a similar operation by police etc. to force the surrender of an armed person. **c** the perio during which a siege lasts. **2** a persistent attack campaign of persuasion. □**lay siege to** esp. *M* conduct the siege of. **raise the siege of** abandon cause the abandonment of an attempt to take place) by siege. **siege-gun** *hist.* a heavy gun used i sieges. **siege-train** artillery and other equipme for a siege, with vehicles etc. [ME f. OF *sege* seat *assegier* BESIEGE]

siemens /'siːmənz/ *n. Electr.* the SI unit of co ductance, equal to one reciprocal ohm. ¶ Abbr.: [W. von *Siemens*, Ger. electrical engineer, d. 1892]

sienna /sɪˈenə/ *n.* **1** a kind of ferruginous earth use as a pigment in paint. **2** its colour of yellowish-brow (**raw sienna**) or reddish-brown (**burnt sienna**). [(*terra di*) *Sienna* (earth of) Siena in Tuscany]

sierra /sɪˈerə/ *n.* a long jagged mountain chain, es in Spain or Spanish America. [Sp. f. L *serra* saw]

siesta /sɪˈestə/ *n.* an afternoon sleep or rest esp. i hot countries. [Sp. f. L *sexta* (*hora*) sixth hour]

sieve /sɪv/ *n. & v.* —*n.* a utensil having a perforate or meshed bottom for separating solids or coars material from liquids or fine particles, or for reducin a soft solid to a fine pulp. —*v.tr.* **1** put through o sift with a sieve. **2** examine (evidence etc.) to selec or separate. □**head like a sieve** *colloq.* a memor that retains little. □□ **sievelike** *adj.* [OE *sife* f. WG]

siffleur /siːˈflɜːr/ *n.* (*fem.* **siffleuse** /-ˈflɜːz/) a pr fessional whistler. [F f. *siffler* whistle]

sift /sɪft/ *v.* **1** *tr.* sieve (material) into finer an coarser parts. **2** *tr.* (usu. foll. by *from*, *out*) separat (finer or coarser parts) from material. **3** *tr.* sprinkl (esp. sugar) from a perforated container. **4** *t* examine (evidence, facts, etc.) in order to asses authenticity etc. **5** *intr.* (of snow, light, etc.) fall as from a sieve. □**sift through** examine by sifting. □□ **sifter** *n.* (also in *comb.*). [OE *siftan* f. WG]

Sig. *abbr.* Signor.

sigh /saɪ/ *v. & n.* —*v.* **1** *intr.* emit a long deep audibl breath expressive of sadness, weariness, longin relief, etc. **2** *intr.* (foll. by *for*) yearn for (a lost perso or thing). **3** *tr.* utter or express with sighs ('*Never* he sighed). **4** *intr.* (of the wind etc.) make a soun like sighing. —*n.* **1** the act or an instance of sighin **2** a sound made in sighing (*a sigh of relief*). [ME *sihe* etc., prob. back-form. f. *sihte* past of *sīhen* f. OE *sīca* **sight** /saɪt/ *n. & v.* —*n.* **1 a** the faculty of seeing wit the eyes (*lost his sight*). **b** the act or an instance o seeing; the state of being seen. **2** a thing seen; display, show, or spectacle (*not a pretty sight*; *beautiful sight*). **3** a way of looking at or considerin a thing (*in my sight he can do no wrong*). **4** a range o space within which a person etc. can see or an objec be seen (*he's out of sight*; *they are just coming int sight*). **5** (usu. in *pl.*) noteworthy features of a town area, etc. (*went to see the sights*). **6 a** a device on gun or optical instrument used for assisting th precise aim or observation. **b** the aim or observatio so gained (*got a sight of him*). **7** *colloq.* a person o thing having a ridiculous, repulsive, or dishevelle appearance (*looked a perfect sight*). **8** *colloq.* a grea quantity (*will cost a sight of money*; *is a sigh better than he was*). —*v.tr.* **1** get sight of, esp by approaching (*they sighted land*). **2** observe th presence of (esp. aircraft, animals, etc.) (*sighte buffalo*). **3** take observations of (a star etc.) with an instrument. **4 a** provide (a gun, quadrant, etc.) with sights. **b** adjust the sight of (a gun etc.). **c** aim (a gun etc.) with sights. □**at first sight** on first glimpse or impression. **at** (or **on**) **sight** as soon as a person or a thing has been seen (*plays music at sight*; *liked him on sight*). **catch** (or **lose**) **sight of** begin (or cease) to see or be aware of. **get a sight of** manage to see; glimpse. **have lost sight of** no longer know the whereabouts of. **in sight 1** visible. **2** near at hand (*salvation is in sight*). **in** (or **within**) **sight of** so as to see or be seen from. **lower one's sights** become less ambitious. **out of my sight!** go at once! **out o**

sight 1 not visible. 2 *colloq.* excellent; delightful. **out of sight out of mind** we forget the absent. **put out of sight** hide, ignore. **set one's sights on** aim at (*set her sights on a directorship*). **sight for the gods** (or **sight for sore eyes**) a welcome person or thing, esp. a visitor. **sight-glass** a transparent device for observing the interior of apparatus etc. **sighting shot** an experimental shot to guide riflemen in adjusting their sights. **sight-line** a hypothetical line from a person's eye to what is seen. **sight-read** (*past* and *past part.* **-read** /-red/) read and perform (music) at sight. **sight-reader** a person who sight-reads. **sight-screen** *Cricket* a large white screen on wheels placed near the boundary in line with the wicket to help the batsman see the ball. **sight-sing** sing (music) at sight. **sight unseen** without previous inspection. □□ **sighter** *n.* [OE (*ge*)*sihth*]

sighted /ˈsaɪtɪd/ *adj.* 1 capable of seeing; not blind. 2 (in *comb.*) having a specified kind of sight (*long-sighted*).

sightless /ˈsaɪtlɪs/ *adj.* 1 blind. 2 *poet.* invisible. □□ **sightlessly** *adv.* **sightlessness** *n.*

sightly /ˈsaɪtlɪ/ *adj.* attractive to the sight; not unsightly. □□ **sightliness** *n.*

sightseer /ˈsaɪtˌsiːə(r)/ *n.* a person who visits places of interest; a tourist. □□ **sightsee** *v.intr.* & *tr.* **sightseeing** *n.*

sightworthy /ˈsaɪtˌwɜːðɪ/ *adj.* worth seeing.

sigillate /ˈsɪdʒɪlət/ *adj.* 1 (of pottery) having impressed patterns. 2 *Bot.* having seal-like marks. [L *sigillatus* f. *sigillum* seal dimin. of *signum* sign]

siglum /ˈsɪgləm/ *n.* (*pl.* **sigla** /-lə/) a letter (esp. an initial) or other symbol used to denote a word in a book, esp. to refer to a particular text. [LL *sigla* (pl.), perh. f. *singula* neut. pl. of *singulus* single]

sigma /ˈsɪgmə/ *n.* the eighteenth letter of the Greek alphabet (Σ, σ, or, when final, ς). [L f. Gk]

sigmate /ˈsɪgmət/ *adj.* 1 sigma-shaped. 2 S-shaped.

sigmoid /ˈsɪgmɔɪd/ *adj.* & *n.* —*adj.* 1 curved like the uncial sigma (**ϲ**); crescent-shaped. 2 S-shaped. —*n.* (in full **sigmoid flexure**) *Anat.* the curved part of the intestine between the colon and the rectum. [Gk *sigmoeidēs* (as SIGMA)]

sign /saɪn/ *n.* & *v.* —*n.* 1 a a thing indicating or suggesting a quality or state etc.; a thing perceived as indicating a future state or occurrence (*violence is a sign of weakness*; *shows all the signs of decay*). b a miracle evidencing supernatural power; a portent (*did signs and wonders*). 2 a a mark, symbol, or device used to represent something or to distinguish the thing on which it is put (*marked the jar with a sign*). b a technical symbol used in algebra, music, etc. (*a minus sign*; *a repeat sign*). 3 a gesture or action used to convey information, an order, request, etc. (*gave him a sign to leave*; *conversed by signs*). 4 a publicly displayed board etc. giving information; a signboard or signpost. 5 any objective evidence of a disease, usu. specified (*Babinski's sign*). 6 a password (*advanced and gave the sign*). 7 any of the twelve divisions of the zodiac, named from the constellations formerly situated in them (*the sign of Cancer*). 8 *US* the trail of a wild animal. 9 *Math.* etc. the positiveness or negativeness of a quantity. —*v.* 1 *tr.* a (also *absol.*) write (one's name, initials, etc.) on a document etc. indicating that one has authorized it. b write one's name etc. on (a document) as authorization. 2 *intr.* & *tr.* communicate by gesture (*signed to me to come*; *signed their assent*). 3 *tr.* & *intr.* engage or be engaged by signing a contract etc. (see also *sign on*, *sign up*). 4 *tr.* mark with a sign (esp. with the sign of the cross in baptism). □**make no sign** seem unconscious; not protest. **sign and countersign** secret words etc. used as passwords. **sign away** convey (one's right, property, etc.) by signing a deed etc. **sign for** acknowledge receipt of by signing. **sign language** a system of communication by visual gestures, used esp. by the deaf. **sign of the cross** a Christian sign made in blessing or prayer, by tracing a cross from the forehead to the chest and to each shoulder, or in the air. **sign off** 1 end work, broadcasting, a letter, etc., esp. by writing or speaking one's name. 2 a end a period of employment, contract, etc. b end the period of employment or contract of (a person). 3 *Brit.* stop receiving unemployment benefit after finding work. 4 *Bridge* indicate by a conventional bid that one is seeking to end the bidding. **sign-off** *n. Bridge* such a bid. **sign of the times** a portent etc. showing a likely trend. **sign on** 1 agree to a contract, employment, etc. 2 begin work, broadcasting, etc., esp. by writing or announcing one's name. 3 employ (a person). 4 *Brit.* register as unemployed. **sign-painter** (or **-writer**) a person who paints signboards etc. **sign up** 1 engage or employ (a person). 2 enlist in the armed forces. 3 a commit (another person or oneself) by signing etc. (*signed you up for dinner*). b enrol (*signed up for evening classes*). □□ **signable** *adj.* **signer** *n.* [ME f. OF *signe*, *signer* f. L *signum*, *signare*]

signal[1] /ˈsɪgn(ə)l/ *n.* & *v.* —*n.* 1 a a usu. prearranged sign conveying information, guidance, etc. esp. at a distance (*waved as a signal to begin*). b a message made up of such signs (*signals made with flags*). 2 an immediate occasion or cause of movement, action, etc. (*the uprising was a signal for repression*). 3 *Electr.* a an electrical impulse or impulses or radio waves transmitted as a signal. b a sequence of these. 4 a light, semaphore, etc., on a railway giving instructions or warnings to train-drivers etc. 5 *Bridge* a prearranged mode of bidding or play to convey information to one's partner. —*v.* (**signalled**, **signalling**; *US* **signaled**, **signaling**) 1 *intr.* make signals. 2 *tr.* a (often foll. by *to* + *infin.*) make signals to; direct. b transmit (an order, information, etc.) by signal; announce (*signalled her agreement*; *signalled that the town had been taken*). □**signal-book** a list of signals arranged for sending esp. naval and military messages. **signal-box** *Brit.* a building beside a railway track from which signals are controlled. **signal of distress** esp. *Naut.* an appeal for help, esp. from a ship by firing guns. **signal-tower** *US* = *signal-box*. □□ **signaller** *n.* [ME f. OF f. Rmc & med.L *signale* neut. of LL *signalis* f. L *signum* SIGN]

signal[2] /ˈsɪgn(ə)l/ *adj.* remarkably good or bad; noteworthy (*a signal victory*). □□ **signally** *adv.* [F *signalé* f. It. past part. *segnalato* distinguished f. *segnale* SIGNAL[1]]

signalize /ˈsɪgnəˌlaɪz/ *v.tr.* (also **-ise**) 1 make noteworthy or remarkable. 2 lend distinction or lustre to. 3 indicate.

signalman /ˈsɪgn(ə)lmən/ *n.* (*pl.* **-men**) 1 a railway employee responsible for operating signals and points. 2 a person who displays or receives naval etc. signals.

signary /ˈsɪgnərɪ/ *n.* (*pl.* **-ies**) a list of signs constituting the syllabic or alphabetic symbols of a language. [L *signum* SIGN + -ARY[1], · after *syllabary*]

signatory /ˈsɪgnətərɪ/ *n.* & *adj.* —*n.* (*pl.* **-ies**) a party or esp. a State that has signed an agreement or esp. a treaty. —*adj.* having signed such an agreement etc. [L *signatorius* of sealing f. *signare signat-* mark]

signature /ˈsɪgnətʃə(r)/ *n.* 1 a a person's name, initials, or mark used in signing a letter, document, etc. b the act of signing a document etc. 2 *archaic* a distinctive action, characteristic, etc. 3 *Mus.* a = *key signature*. b = *time signature*. 4 *Printing* a a letter or figure placed at the foot of one or more pages of each sheet of a book as a guide for binding. b such a sheet after folding. 5 *US* directions given to a patient as part of a medical prescription. □**signature tune** esp. *Brit.* a distinctive tune used to introduce a particular programme or performer on television or radio. [med.L *signatura* (LL = marking of sheep), as SIGNATORY]

signboard /ˈsaɪnbɔːd/ *n.* a board with a name or symbol etc. displayed outside a shop or hotel etc.

signet /ˈsɪgnɪt/ n. **1** a seal used instead of or with a signature as authentication. **2** (prec. by *the*) the royal seal formerly used for special purposes in England and Scotland, and in Scotland later as the seal of the Court of Session. ▫**signet-ring** a ring with a seal set in it. [ME f. OF *signet* or med.L *signetum* (as SIGN)]

significance /sɪgˈnɪfɪkəns/ n. **1** importance; noteworthiness (*his opinion is of no significance*). **2** a concealed or real meaning (*what is the significance of his statement?*). **3** the state of being significant. **4** *Statistics* the extent to which a result deviates from a hypothesis such that the difference is due to more than errors in sampling. [OF *significance* or L *significantia* (as SIGNIFY)]

significant /sɪgˈnɪfɪkənt/ adj. **1** having a meaning; indicative. **2** having an unstated or secret meaning; suggestive (*refused it with a significant gesture*). **3** noteworthy; important; consequential (*a significant figure in history*). **4** *Statistics* of or relating to the significance in the difference between an observed and calculated result. ▫**significant figure** *Math.* a digit conveying information about a number containing it, and not a zero used simply to fill vacant space at the beginning or end. ▫▫**significantly** adv. [L *significare*: see SIGNIFY]

signification /ˌsɪgnɪfɪˈkeɪʃ(ə)n/ n. **1** the act of signifying. **2** (usu. foll. by *of*) exact meaning or sense, esp. of a word or phrase. [ME f. OF f. L *significatio -onis* (as SIGNIFY)]

significative /sɪgˈnɪfɪkətɪv/ adj. **1** (esp. of a symbol etc.) signifying. **2** having a meaning. **3** (usu. foll. by *of*) serving as a sign or evidence. [ME f. OF *significatif -ive*, or LL *significativus* (as SIGNIFY)]

signify /ˈsɪgnɪˌfaɪ/ v. (**-ies**, **-ied**) **1** *tr.* be a sign or indication of (*a yawn signifies boredom*). **2** *tr.* mean; have as its meaning (*'Dr' signifies 'doctor'*). **3** *tr.* communicate; make known (*signified their agreement*). **4** *intr.* be of importance; matter (*it signifies little*). ▫▫**signifier** n. [ME f. OF *signifier* f. L *significare* (as SIGN)]

signing /ˈsaɪnɪŋ/ n. a person who has signed a contract, esp. to join a professional sports team.

signor /ˈsiːnjɔː(r)/ n. (pl. **signori** /-ˈnjɔːriː/) **1** a title or form of address used of or to an Italian-speaking man, corresponding to Mr or sir. **2** an Italian man. [It. f. L *senior*: see SENIOR]

signora /siːnˈjɔːrə/ n. **1** a title or form of address used of or to an Italian-speaking married woman, corresponding to Mrs or madam. **2** a married Italian woman. [It., fem. of SIGNOR]

signorina /ˌsiːnjəˈriːnə/ n. **1** a title or form of address used of or to an Italian-speaking unmarried woman. **2** an Italian unmarried woman. [It., dimin. of SIGNORA]

signory /ˈsiːnjərɪ/ n. (pl. **-ies**) **1** = SEIGNIORY. **2** *hist.* the governing body of a medieval Italian republic. [ME f. OF *s(e)ignorie* (as SEIGNEUR)]

signpost /ˈsaɪnpəʊst/ n. & v. —n. **1** a post erected at a crossroads with arms indicating the direction to and sometimes also the distance from various places. **2** a means of guidance; an indication. —v.tr. **1** provide with a signpost or signposts. **2** indicate (a course of action, direction, etc.).

sika /ˈsiːkə/ n. a small forest-dwelling deer, *Cervus nippon*, native to Japan. [Jap. *shika*]

Sikh /siːk, sɪk/ n. a member of an Indian monotheistic sect founded in the 16th c. [Hindi, = disciple, f. Skr. *sishya*]

Sikhism /ˈsiːkɪz(ə)m, ˈsɪk-/ n. the religious tenets of the Sikhs.

silage /ˈsaɪlɪdʒ/ n. & v. —n. **1** storage in a silo. **2** green fodder that has been stored in a silo. —v.tr. put into a silo. [alt. of ENSILAGE after *silo*]

sild /sɪlt/ n. a small immature herring, esp. one caught in N. European seas. [Da. & Norw.]

silence /ˈsaɪləns/ n. & v. —n. **1** absence of sound. **2** abstinence from speech or noise. **3** the avoidance of mentioning a thing, betraying a secret, etc. **4** oblivion; the state of not being mentioned. —v.tr. make

silent, esp. by coercion or superior argument. ▫**silence** without speech or other sound. **reduce** (▫ put) **to silence** refute in argument. [ME f. OF f. *silentium* (as SILENT)]

silencer /ˈsaɪlənsə(r)/ n. any of various devices fo reducing the noise emitted by the exhaust of a moto vehicle, a gun, etc.

silent /ˈsaɪlənt/ adj. **1** not speaking; not uttering o making or accompanied by any sound. **2** (of a letter written but not pronounced, e.g. *b* in *doubt*. **3** (of film) without a synchronized soundtrack. **4** (of person) taciturn; speaking little. **5** saying or re cording nothing on some subject (*the records ar silent on the incident*). **6** (of spirits) unflavoure ▫**silent majority** those of moderate opinions wh rarely assert them. **silent partner** *US* = *sleepin partner* (see SLEEP). ▫▫**silently** adv. [L *silēre silen* be silent]

silenus /saɪˈliːnəs/ n. (pl. **sileni** /-naɪ/) (in Gree mythology) a bearded old man like a satyr, some times with the tail and legs of a horse. [L f. G *seilēnos*]

silex /ˈsaɪleks/ n. a kind of glass made of fuse quartz. [L (as SILICA)]

silhouette /ˌsɪluˈet/ n. & v. —n. **1** a representatio of a person or thing showing the outline only, usu done in solid black on white or cut from paper. **2** th dark shadow or outline of a person or thing agains a lighter background. —v.tr. represent or (usu. i *passive*) show in silhouette. ▫**in silhouette** seen o placed in outline. [Étienne de *Silhouette*, Fr. autho and politician d. 1767]

silica /ˈsɪlɪkə/ n. silicon dioxide, occurring as quart etc. and as a principal constituent of sandstone an other rocks. ▫**silica gel** hydrated silica in a har granular form used as a desiccant. ▫▫**siliceou** /-ˈlɪʃəs/ adj. (also **silicious**). **silicic** /-ˈlɪsɪk/ adj **silicify** /-ˈlɪsɪˌfaɪ/ v.tr. & intr. (**-ies**, **-ied** **silicification** /-sɪfɪˈkeɪʃ(ə)n/ n. [L *silex -icis* flint after *alumina* etc.]

silicate /ˈsɪlɪˌkeɪt/ n. any of the many insoluble compounds of a metal combined with silicon and oxygen, occurring widely in the rocks of the earth's crust.

silicon /ˈsɪlɪkən/ n. *Chem.* a non-metallic element occurring widely in silica and silicates, and used in the manufacture of glass. ¶ Symb.: Si. ▫**silicon chip** a silicon microchip. **silicon carbide** = CARBORUNDUM. **Silicon Valley** an area with a high concentration of electronics industries. [L *silex -icis* flint (after *carbon*, *boron*), alt. of earlier *silicium*]

silicone /ˈsɪlɪˌkəʊn/ n. any of the many polymeric organic compounds of silicon and oxygen with high resistance to cold, heat, water, and the passage of electricity.

silicosis /ˌsɪlɪˈkəʊsɪs/ n. lung fibrosis caused by the inhalation of dust containing silica. ▫▫**silicotic** /-ˈkɒtɪk/ adj.

siliqua /ˈsɪlɪkwə/ n. (also **silique** /sɪˈliːk/) (pl. **siliquae** /-kwiː/ or **siliques** /sɪˈliːks/) the long narrow seed-pod of a cruciferous plant. ▫▫**siliquose** /-ˌkwəʊs/ adj. **siliquous** /-kwəs/ adj. [L, = pod]

silk /sɪlk/ n. **1** a fine strong soft lustrous fibre produced by silkworms in making cocoons. **2** a similar fibre spun by some spiders etc. **3** thread or cloth made from silk fibre. **4** (in pl.) kinds of silk cloth or garments made from it, esp. as worn by a jockey in a horse-owner's colours. **5** *Brit. colloq.* Queen's (or King's) Counsel, as having the right to wear a silk gown. **6** (*attrib.*) made of silk (*silk blouse*). **7** the silky styles of the female maize-flower. ▫**silk cotton** kapok or a similar substance. **silk-fowl** a breed of fowl with a silky plumage. **silk-gland** a gland secreting the substance produced as silk. **silk hat** a tall cylindrical hat covered with silk plush. **silk moth** any of various large moths of the family Saturniidae, esp. *Hyalophora cecropia*. **silk-screen printing** = *screen printing*. **take silk** *Brit.* become a Queen's (or King's) Counsel. □□ **silklike** adj. [OE *sioloc, seolec* (cf. ON *silki*) f. LL *sericum* neut. of L *sericus* f. *seres* f. Gk *Sēres* an oriental people]

silken /'sɪlkən/ adj. **1** made of silk. **2** wearing silk. **3** soft or lustrous as silk. **4** (of a person's manner etc.) suave or insinuating. [OE *seolcen* (as SILK)]

silkworm /'sɪlkwɜːm/ n. the caterpillar of the moth *Bombyx mori*, which spins its cocoon of silk.

silky /'sɪlkɪ/ adj. (**silkier**, **silkiest**) **1** like silk in smoothness, softness, fineness, or lustre. **2** (of a person's manner etc.) suave, insinuating. □□ **silkily** adv. **silkiness** n.

sill /sɪl/ n. (also **cill**) **1** a shelf or slab of stone, wood, or metal at the foot of a window or doorway. **2** a horizontal timber at the bottom of a dock or lock entrance, against which the gates close. **3** *Geol.* a tabular sheet of igneous rock intruded between other rocks and parallel with their planar structure. [OE *syll, sylle*]

sillabub var. of SYLLABUB.

sillimanite /'sɪlɪmənaɪt/ n. an aluminium silicate occurring in orthorhombic crystals or fibrous masses. [B. *Silliman*, Amer. chemist d. 1864]

silly /'sɪlɪ/ adj. & n. —adj. (**sillier**, **silliest**) **1** lacking sense; foolish, imprudent, unwise. **2** weak-minded. **3** *Cricket* (of a fielder or position) very close to the batsman (*silly mid-off*). **4** *archaic* innocent, simple, helpless. —n. (pl. **-ies**) *colloq.* a foolish person. □**silly billy** *colloq.* a foolish person. **the silly season** high summer as the season when newspapers often publish trivial material for lack of important news. □□ **sillily** adv. **silliness** n. [later form of ME *sely* (dial. *seely*) happy, repr. OE *sǣlig* (recorded in *un-sǣlig* unhappy) f. Gmc]

silo /'saɪləʊ/ n. & v. —n. (pl. **-os**) **1** a pit or airtight structure in which green crops are pressed and kept for fodder, undergoing fermentation. **2** a pit or tower for the storage of grain, cement, etc. **3** an underground chamber in which a guided missile is kept ready for firing. —v.tr. (**-oes**, **-oed**) make silage of. [Sp. f. L *sirus* f. Gk *siros* corn-pit]

silt /sɪlt/ n. & v. —n. sediment deposited by water in a channel, harbour, etc. —v.tr. & intr. (often foll. by *up*) choke or be choked with silt. □□ **siltation** /-'teɪʃ(ə)n/ n. **silty** adj. [ME, perh. rel. to Da., Norw. *sylt*, OLG *sulta*, OHG *sulza* salt marsh, formed as SALT]

siltstone /'sɪltstəʊn/ n. rock of consolidated silt.

Silurian /saɪ'ljʊərɪən/ adj. & n. *Geol.* —adj. of or relating to the third period of the Palaeozoic era with evidence of the first fish and land plants, and the formation of mountains and new land areas. ¶ Cf. Appendix II. —n. this period or system. [L *Silures*, a people of ancient SE Wales]

silva var. of SYLVA.

silvan var. of SYLVAN.

silver /'sɪlvə(r)/ n., adj., & v. —n. *Chem.* **1** a greyish-white lustrous malleable ductile precious metallic element, occurring naturally as the element and in mineral form, and used chiefly with an admixture of harder metals for coin, plate, and ornaments, as a subordinate monetary medium, and in compounds for photography etc. ¶ Symb.: **Ag**. **2** the colour of silver. **3** silver or cupro-nickel coins. **4** esp. *Sc.* money. **5** silver vessels or implements, esp. cutlery. **6** household cutlery of any material. **7** = *silver medal*. —adj. **1** made wholly or chiefly of silver. **2** coloured like silver. —v. **1** tr. coat or plate with silver. **2** tr. provide (a mirror-glass) with a backing of tin amalgam etc. **3** tr. (of the moon or a white light) give a silvery appearance to. **4 a** tr. turn (the hair) grey or white. **b** intr. (of the hair) turn grey or white. □**silver age** a period regarded as inferior to a golden age, e.g. that of post-classical Latin literature in the early Imperial period. **silver band** *Brit.* a band playing silver-plated instruments. **silver birch** a common birch, *Betula alba*, with silver-coloured bark. **silver fir** any fir of the genus *Abies*, with the under-sides of its leaves coloured silver. **silver fox 1** an American red fox at a time when its fur is black with white tips. **2** its fur. **silver gilt 1** gilded silver. **2** an imitation gilding of yellow lacquer over silver leaf. **silver-grey** a lustrous grey. **silver jubilee 1** the 25th anniversary of a sovereign's accession. **2** any other 25th anniversary. **silver Latin** literary Latin of the early Imperial period. **silver-leaf** a fungal disease of fruit trees. **silver lining** a consolation or hopeful feature in misfortune. **silver medal** a medal of silver, usu. awarded as second prize. **silver nitrate** a colourless solid that is soluble in water and formerly used in photography. **silver paper 1** a fine white tissue-paper for wrapping silver. **2** aluminium or tin foil. **silver plate** vessels, spoons, etc., of copper etc. plated with silver. **silver salmon** a coho. **silver sand** a fine pure sand used in gardening. **silver screen** (usu. prec. by *the*) motion pictures collectively. **silver solder** solder containing silver. **silver spoon** a sign of future prosperity. **silver standard** a system by which the value of a currency is defined in terms of silver, for which the currency may be exchanged. **silver thaw** a glassy coating of ice formed on the ground or an exposed surface, caused by freezing rain or a sudden light frost. **silver tongue** eloquence. **silver wedding** the 25th anniversary of a wedding. **silver weed** a plant with silvery leaves, esp. a potentilla, *Potentilla anserina*, with silver-coloured leaves. [OE *seolfor* f. Gmc]

silverfish /'sɪlvəfɪʃ/ n. (pl. same or **-fishes**) **1** any small silvery wingless insect of the order Thysanura, esp. *Lepisma saccharina* in houses and other buildings. **2** a silver-coloured fish, esp. a colourless variety of goldfish.

silvern /'sɪlv(ə)n/ adj. *archaic* or *poet.* = SILVER adj. [OE *seolfren, silfren* (as SILVER)]

silverside /'sɪlvəsaɪd/ n. *Brit.* the upper side of a round of beef from the outside of the leg.

silversmith /'sɪlvəsmɪθ/ n. a worker in silver; a manufacturer of silver articles. □□ **silversmithing** n.

silverware /'sɪlvəweə(r)/ n. articles made of or coated with silver.

silvery /'sɪlvərɪ/ adj. **1** like silver in colour or appearance. **2** having a clear gentle ringing sound. **3** (of the hair) white and lustrous. □□ **silveriness** n.

silviculture /'sɪlvɪkʌltʃə(r)/ n. (also **sylviculture**) the growing and tending of trees as a branch of forestry. □□ **silvicultural** /-'kʌltʃər(ə)l/ adj. **silviculturist** /-'kʌltʃərɪst/ n. [F f. L *silva* a wood + F *culture* CULTURE]

simian /'sɪmɪən/ adj. & n. —adj. **1** of or concerning the anthropoid apes. **2** like an ape or monkey (a *simian walk*). —n. an ape or monkey. [L *simia* ape, perh. f. L *simus* f. Gk *simos* flat-nosed]

similar /'sɪmɪlə(r)/ adj. **1** like, alike. **2** (often foll. by *to*) having a resemblance. **3** of the same kind, nature, or amount. **4** *Geom.* shaped alike. □□ **similarity** /-'lærɪtɪ/ n. (pl. **-ies**). **similarly** adv. [F *similaire* or med.L *similaris* f. L *similis* like]

simile /'sɪmɪlɪ/ n. **1** a figure of speech involving the comparison of one thing with another of a different kind, as an illustration or ornament (e.g. *as brave as a lion*). **2** the use of such comparison. [ME f. L, neut. of *similis* like]

similitude /sɪ'mɪlɪtjuːd/ n. **1** the likeness, guise, or outward appearance of a thing or person. **2** a comparison or the expression of a comparison. **3** *archaic* a counterpart or facsimile. [ME f. OF *similitude* or L *similitudo* (as SIMILE)]

simmer /'sɪmə(r)/ v. & n. —v. **1** intr. & tr. be or keep bubbling or boiling gently. **2** intr. be in a state of suppressed anger or excitement. —n. a simmering condition. □**simmer down** become calm or less agitated. [alt. of ME (now dial.) *simper*, perh. imit.]

simnel cake /'sɪmn(ə)l/ n. *Brit.* a rich fruit cake, usu. with a marzipan layer and decoration, eaten esp. at Easter or during Lent. [ME f. OF *simenel*, ult. f. L *simila* or Gk *semidalis* fine flour]

simon-pure /ˌsaɪmən'pjʊə(r)/ *adj.* real, genuine. [(*the real*) *Simon Pure*, a character in Centlivre's *Bold Stroke for a Wife* (1717)]

simony /'saɪmənɪ, 'sɪm-/ *n.* the buying or selling of ecclesiastical privileges, e.g. pardons or benefices. □□ **simoniac** /-'məʊnɪˌæk/ *adj.* & *n.* **simoniacal** /-'naɪək(ə)l/ *adj.* [ME f. OF *simonie* f. LL *simonia* f. *Simon Magus* (Acts 8:18)]

simoom /sɪ'muːm/ *n.* (also **simoon** /-'muːn/) a hot dry dust-laden wind blowing at intervals esp. in the Arabian desert. [Arab. *samūm* f. *samma* to poison]

simp /sɪmp/ *n. US colloq.* a simpleton. [abbr.]

simpatico /sɪm'pætɪˌkəʊ/ *adj.* congenial, likeable. [It. & Sp. (as SYMPATHY)]

simper /'sɪmpə(r)/ *v.* & *n.* —*v.* **1** *intr.* smile in a silly or affected way. **2** *tr.* express by or with simpering. —*n.* such a smile. □□ **simperingly** *adv.* [16th c.: cf. Du. and Scand. *semper*, *simper*, G *zimp(f)er* elegant, delicate]

simple /'sɪmp(ə)l/ *adj.* & *n.* —*adj.* **1** easily understood or done; presenting no difficulty (*a simple explanation*; *a simple task*). **2** not complicated or elaborate; without luxury or sophistication. **3** not compound; consisting of or involving only one element or operation etc. **4** absolute, unqualified, straightforward (*the simple truth*; *a simple majority*). **5** foolish or ignorant; gullible, feeble-minded (*am not so simple as to agree to that*). **6** plain in appearance or manner; unsophisticated, ingenuous, artless. **7** of low rank; humble, insignificant (*simple people*). **8** *Bot.* **a** consisting of one part. **b** (of fruit) formed from one pistil. —*n. archaic* **1** a herb used medicinally. **2** a medicine made from it. □ **simple eye** an eye of an insect, having only one lens. **simple fracture** a fracture of the bone only, without a skin wound. **simple harmonic motion** see HARMONIC. **simple interest** interest payable on a capital sum only (cf. *compound interest* (see COMPOUND)). **simple interval** *Mus.* an interval of one octave or less. **simple machine** any of the basic mechanical devices for applying a force (e.g. an inclined plane, wedge, or lever). **simple sentence** a sentence with a single subject and predicate. **Simple Simon** a foolish person (from the nursery-rhyme character). **simple time** *Mus.* a time with two, three, or four beats in a bar. □□ **simpleness** *n.* [ME f. OF f. L *simplus*]

simple-minded /ˌsɪmp(ə)l'maɪndɪd/ *adj.* **1** natural, unsophisticated. **2** feeble-minded. □□ **simple-mindedly** *adv.* **simple-mindedness** *n.*

simpleton /'sɪmp(ə)lt(ə)n/ *n.* a foolish, gullible, or halfwitted person. [SIMPLE after surnames f. place-names in *-ton*]

simplex /'sɪmpleks/ *adj.* & *n.* —*adj.* **1** simple; not compounded. **2** *Computing* (of a circuit) allowing transmission of signals in one direction only. —*n.* a simple or uncompounded thing, esp. a word. [L, = single, var. of *simplus* simple]

simplicity /sɪm'plɪsɪtɪ/ *n.* the fact or condition of being simple. □ **be simplicity itself** be extremely easy. [OF *simplicité* or L *simplicitas* (as SIMPLEX)]

simplify /'sɪmplɪˌfaɪ/ *v.tr.* (**-ies**, **-ied**) make simple; make easy or easier to do or understand. □□ **simplification** /-fɪ'keɪʃ(ə)n/ *n.* [F *simplifier* f. med.L *simplificare* (as SIMPLE)]

simplism /'sɪmplɪz(ə)m/ *n.* **1** affected simplicity. **2** the unjustifiable simplification of a problem etc.

simplistic /sɪm'plɪstɪk/ *adj.* **1** excessively or affectedly simple. **2** oversimplified so as to conceal or distort difficulties. □□ **simplistically** *adv.*

simply /'sɪmplɪ/ *adv.* **1** in a simple manner. **2** absolutely; without doubt (*simply astonishing*). **3** merely (*was simply trying to please*).

simulacrum /ˌsɪmjʊ'leɪkrəm/ *n.* (*pl.* **simulacra** /-krə/) **1** an image of something. **2 a** a shadowy likeness; a deceptive substitute. **b** mere pretence. [L (as SIMULATE)]

simulate /'sɪmjʊˌleɪt/ *v.tr.* **1 a** pretend to have or feel (an attribute or feeling). **b** pretend to be. **2** imitate or counterfeit. **3 a** imitate the conditions of (a situation etc.), e.g. for training. **b** produce a computer model of (a process). **4** (as **simulated** *adj.*) made to resemble the real thing but not genuinely such (*simulated fur*). **5** (of a word) take or have an altered form suggested by (a word wrongly taken to be its source, e.g. *amuck*). □□ **simulation** /-'leɪʃ(ə)n/ *n.* **simulative** /-lətɪv/ *adj.* [L *simulare* f. *similis* like]

simulator /'sɪmjʊˌleɪtə(r)/ *n.* **1** a person or thing that simulates. **2** a device designed to simulate the operations of a complex system, used esp. in training.

simulcast /'sɪməlˌkɑːst/ *n.* simultaneous transmission of the same programme on radio and television. [SIMULTANEOUS + BROADCAST]

simultaneous /ˌsɪməl'teɪnɪəs/ *adj.* (often foll. by *with*) occurring or operating at the same time. □ **simultaneous equations** equations involving two or more unknowns and having the same values in each equation. □□ **simultaneity** /-tə'neɪɪtɪ/ *n.* **simultaneously** *adv.* **simultaneousness** *n.* [med.L *simultaneus* f. L *simul* at the same time, prob. after *instantaneus* etc.]

simurg /sɪ'mɜːg/ *n.* a monstrous bird of Persian myth, with the power of reasoning and speech. [Pers. *sīmurg* f. Pahlavi *sīn* eagle + *murg* bird]

sin[1] /sɪn/ *n.* & *v.* —*n.* **1 a** the breaking of divine or moral law, esp. by a conscious act. **b** such an act. **2** an offence against good taste or propriety etc. —*v.* (**sinned**, **sinning**) **1** *intr.* commit a sin. **2** *intr.* (foll. by *against*) offend. **3** *tr. archaic* commit (a sin). □ **sin** *colloq.* extremely (*ugly as sin*). **for one's sins** *joc.* as a judgement on one for something or other. **like sin** *colloq.* vehemently or forcefully. **live in sin** *colloq.* live together without being married. **sin bin** *colloq.* **1** *Ice Hockey* a penalty box. **2** a place set aside for offenders of various kinds. □□ **sinless** *adj.* **sinlessly** *adv.* **sinlessness** *n.* [OE *syn(n)*]

sin[2] /saɪn/ *abbr.* sine.

Sinaitic /ˌsaɪneɪ'ɪtɪk/ *adj.* of or relating to Mount Sinai or of the Sinai peninsula. [var. of *Sinaic* f. *Sinai* f. Heb. *sīnay*, with *t* added for euphony]

sinanthropus /sɪn'ænθrəpəs/ *n.* an apelike human of the extinct genus *Sinanthropus*. [mod.L, as SINO-Chinese (remains having been found near Peking) + Gk *anthrōpos* man]

since /sɪns/ *prep., conj.,* & *adv.* —*prep.* throughout, or at a point in, the period between (a specified time, event, etc.) and the time present or being considered (*must have happened since yesterday*; *has been going on since June*; *the greatest composer since Beethoven*). —*conj.* **1** during or in the time after (*what have you been doing since we met?*; *has not spoken since the dog died*). **2** for the reason that, because; inasmuch as (*since you are drunk I will drive you home*). **3** (*ellipt.*) as being (*a more useful, since better designed, tool*). —*adv.* **1** from that time or event until now or the time being considered (*have not seen them since*; *had been healthy ever since*; *has since been cut down*). **2** ago (*happened many years since*). [ME, reduced form of obs. *sithence* or f. dial. *sin* (f. *sithen*) f. OE *siththon*]

sincere /sɪn'sɪə(r)/ *adj.* (**sincerer, sincerest**) **1** free from pretence or deceit; the same in reality as in appearance. **2** genuine, honest, frank. □□ **sincereness** *n.* **sincerity** /-'serɪtɪ/ *n.* [L *sincerus* clean, pure]

sincerely /sɪn'sɪəlɪ/ *adv.* in a sincere manner. □ **yours sincerely** a formula for ending an informal letter.

sinciput /'sɪnsɪˌpʊt/ *n. Anat.* the front of the skull from the forehead to the crown. □□ **sincipital** /-'sɪpɪt(ə)l/ *adj.* [L f. *semi-* half + *caput* head]

sine /saɪn/ *n. Math.* **1** the trigonometric function that is equal to the ratio of the side opposite a given angle (in a right-angled triangle) to the hypotenuse. **2** a function of the line drawn from one end of an arc perpendicularly to the radius through the other. □**sine curve** (or **wave**) a curve representing periodic oscillations of constant amplitude as given by a sine function: also called SINUSOID. [L *sinus* curve, fold of a toga, used in med.L as transl. of Arab. *jayb* bosom, sine]

sinecure /'saɪnɪˌkjʊə(r), 'sɪn-/ n. a position that requires little or no work but usu. yields profit or honour. □□ **sinecurism** n. **sinecurist** n. [L *sine cura* without care]

sine die /ˌsaɪnɪ 'daɪɪ, ˌsɪneɪ 'diːeɪ/ adv. (of business adjourned indefinitely) with no appointed date. [L, = without day]

sine qua non /ˌsɪneɪ kwɑː 'nəʊn/ n. an indispensable condition or qualification. [L, = without which not]

sinew /'sɪnjuː/ n. & v. —n. **1** tough fibrous tissue uniting muscle to bone; a tendon. **2** (in *pl.*) muscles; bodily strength; wiriness. **3** (in *pl.*) that which forms the strength or framework of a plan, city, organization, etc. —v.tr. poet. serve as the sinews of; sustain; hold together. □**the sinews of war** money. □□ **sinewless** adj. **sinewy** adj. [OE *sin(e)we* f. Gmc]

sinfonia /ˌsɪnfə'nɪə, sɪn'fəʊnɪə/ n. Mus. **1** a symphony. **2** (in Baroque music) an orchestral piece used as an introduction to an opera, cantata, or suite. **3** (**Sinfonia**; usu. in names) a small symphony orchestra. [It., = SYMPHONY]

sinfonietta /ˌsɪnfə'njetə/ n. Mus. **1** a short or simple symphony. **2** (**Sinfonietta**; usu. in names) a small symphony orchestra. [It., dimin. of *sinfonia*: see SINFONIA]

sinful /'sɪnfʊl/ adj. **1** (of a person) committing sin, esp. habitually. **2** (of an act) involving or characterized by sin. □□ **sinfully** adv. **sinfulness** n. [OE *synfull* (as SIN, -FUL)]

sing /sɪŋ/ v. & n. —v. (past **sang** /sæŋ/; past part. **sung** /sʌŋ/) **1** intr. utter musical sounds with the voice, esp. words with a set tune. **2** tr. utter or produce by singing (*sing another song*). **3** intr. (of the wind, a kettle, etc.) make inarticulate melodious or humming, buzzing, or whistling sounds. **4** intr. (of the ears) be affected as with a buzzing sound. **5** intr. sl. turn informer; confess. **6** intr. archaic compose poetry. **7** tr. & (foll. by *of*) intr. celebrate in verse. **8** tr. (foll. by *in*, *out*) usher (esp. the new or old year) in or out with singing. **9** tr. bring to a specified state by singing (*sang the child to sleep*). —n. **1** an act or spell of singing. **2** US a meeting for amateur singing. □**sing-along** a tune etc. to which one can sing in accompaniment. **singing hinny** see HINNY². **singing saw** = *musical saw*. **sing out** call out loudly; shout. **sing the praises of** see PRAISE. **sing up** sing more loudly. □□ **singable** adj. **singer** n. **singingly** adv. [OE *singan* f. Gmc]

sing. abbr. singular.

singe /sɪndʒ/ v. & n. —v. (**singeing**) **1** tr. & intr. burn superficially or lightly. **2** tr. burn the bristles or down off (the carcass of a pig or fowl) to prepare it for cooking. **3** tr. burn off the tips of (the hair) in hairdressing. —n. a superficial burn. □**singe one's wings** suffer some harm esp. in a risky attempt. [OE *sencgan* f. WG]

Singh /sɪŋ/ n. **1** a title adopted by the warrior castes of N. India. **2** a surname adopted by male Sikhs. [Hind. *siṅgh* f. Skr. *siṅhá* lion]

Singhalese var. of SINHALESE.

single /'sɪŋg(ə)l/ adj., n., & v. —adj. **1** one only, not double or multiple. **2** united or undivided. **3 a** designed or suitable for one person (*single room*). **b** used or done by one person etc. or one set or pair. **4** one by itself; not one of several (*a single tree*). **5** regarded separately (*every single thing*). **6** not married. **7** Brit. (of a ticket) valid for an outward journey only, not for the return. **8** (with *neg.* or *interrog.*) even one; not to speak of more (*did not see a single person*). **9** (of a flower) having only one circle of petals. **10** lonely, unaided. **11** archaic free from duplicity, sincere, consistent, guileless, ingenuous.

—n. **1** a single thing, or item in a series. **2** Brit. a single ticket. **3** a short pop record with one piece of music etc. on each side. **4** Cricket a hit for one run. **5** (usu. *in pl.*) a game with one player on each side. **6** an unmarried person (*young singles*). **7** sl. US a one-dollar note. —v.tr. (foll. by *out*) choose as an example or as distinguishable or to serve some purpose. □**single acrostic** see ACROSTIC. **single-acting** (of an engine etc.) having pressure applied only to one side of the piston. **single-breasted** (of a coat etc.) having only one set of buttons and buttonholes, not overlapping. **single combat** a duel. **single cream** thin cream with a relatively low fat-content. **single cut** (of a file) with grooves cut in one direction only, not crossing. **single-decker** esp. Brit. a bus having only one deck. **single entry** a system of bookkeeping in which each transaction is entered in one account only. **single file** a line of people or things arranged one behind another. **single-handed** adv. **1** without help from another. **2** with one hand. —adj. **1** done etc. single-handed. **2** for one hand. **single-handedly** in a single-handed way. **single-lens reflex** denoting a reflex camera in which a single lens serves the film and the viewfinder. **single-line** with movement of traffic in only one direction at a time. **single parent** a person bringing up a child or children without a partner. **singles bar** a bar for single people seeking company. **single-seater** a vehicle with one seat. **single stick 1** a basket-hilted stick of about a sword's length. **2** one-handed fencing with this. **single-tree** US = SWINGLETREE. □□ **singleness** n. **singly** adv. [ME f. OF f. L *singulus*, rel. to *simplus* SIMPLE]

single-minded /ˌsɪŋg(ə)l'maɪndɪd/ adj. having or intent on only one purpose. □□ **single-mindedly** adv. **single-mindedness** n.

singlet /'sɪŋglɪt/ n. **1** Brit. a garment worn under or instead of a shirt; a vest. **2** a single unresolvable line in a spectrum. [SINGLE + -ET¹,· after *doublet*, the garment being unlined]

singleton /'sɪŋg(ə)lt(ə)n/ n. **1** one card only of a suit, esp. as dealt to a player. **2 a** a single person or thing. **b** an only child. **3** a single child or animal born, not a twin etc. [SINGLE, after *simpleton*]

singsong /'sɪŋsɒŋ/ adj., n., & v. —adj. uttered with a monotonous rhythm or cadence. —n. **1** a singsong manner. **2** Brit. an informal gathering for singing. —v.intr. & tr. (past and past part. **singsonged**) speak or recite in a singsong manner.

singular /'sɪŋgjʊlə(r)/ adj. & n. —adj. **1** unique; much beyond the average; extraordinary. **2** eccentric or strange. **3** Gram. (of a word or form) denoting or referring to a single person or thing. **4** Math. possessing unique properties. **5** single, individual. —n. Gram. **1** a singular word or form. **2** the singular number. □□ **singularly** adv. [ME f. OF *singuler* f. L *singularis* (as SINGLE)]

singularity /ˌsɪŋgjʊ'lærɪtɪ/ n. (pl. -ies) **1** the state or condition of being singular. **2** an odd trait or peculiarity. **3** Physics & Math. a point at which a function takes an infinite value, esp. in space-time when matter is infinitely dense. [ME f. OF *singularité* f. LL *singularitas* (as SINGULAR)]

singularize /'sɪŋgjʊləˌraɪz/ v.tr. (also -**ise**) **1** distinguish, individualize. **2** make singular. □□ **singularization** /-'zeɪʃ(ə)n/ n.

sinh /ʃaɪn, saɪ'neɪtʃ/ abbr. Math. hyperbolic sine. [*sine* + *hyperbolic*]

Sinhalese /ˌsɪnhə'liːz, ˌsɪnə'liːz/ n. & adj. (also **Singhalese** /ˌsɪŋg-/) —n. (pl. same) **1** a member of a people originally from N. India and now forming the majority of the population of Sri Lanka. **2** an Indic language spoken by this people. —adj. of or relating to this people or language. [Skr. *siṅhalam* Sri Lanka (Ceylon) + -ESE]

sinister /'sɪnɪstə(r)/ adj. **1** suggestive of evil; looking malignant or villainous. **2** wicked or criminal (*a sinister motive*). **3** of evil omen. **4** Heraldry of or on the left-hand side of a shield etc. (i.e. to the observer's right). **5** *archaic* left-hand. □□ **sinisterly** *adv.* **sinisterness** *n.* [ME f. OF *sinistre* or L *sinister* left]

sinistral /'sɪnɪstr(ə)l/ *adj. & n.* —*adj.* **1** left-handed. **2** of or on the left. **3** (of a flat-fish) with the left side uppermost. **4** (of a spiral shell) with whorls rising to the left and not (as usually) to the right. □□ **sinistrality** /-'trælɪtɪ/ *n.* **sinistrally** *adv.*

sinistrorse /'sɪnɪˌstrɔːs/ *adj.* rising towards the left, esp. of the spiral stem of a plant. [L *sinistrorsus* f. *sinister* left + *vorsus* past part. of *vertere* turn]

sink /sɪŋk/ *v. & n.* —*v.* (*past* **sank** /sæŋk/ or **sunk** /sʌŋk/; *past part.* **sunk** or **sunken**) **1** *intr.* fall or come slowly downwards. **2** *intr.* disappear below the horizon (*the sun is sinking*). **3** *intr.* **a** go or penetrate below the surface esp. of a liquid. **b** (of a ship) go to the bottom of the sea etc. **4** *intr.* settle down comfortably (*sank into a chair*). **5** *intr.* **a** gradually lose strength or value or quality etc.; decline (*my heart sank*). **b** (of the voice) descend in pitch or volume. **c** (of a sick person) approach death. **6** *tr.* send (a ship) to the bottom of the sea etc. **7** *tr.* cause or allow to sink or penetrate (*sank its teeth into my leg*). **8** *tr.* cause the failure of (a plan etc.) or the discomfiture of (a person). **9** *tr.* dig (a well) or bore (a shaft). **10** *tr.* engrave (a die) or inlay (a design). **11** *tr.* **a** invest (money) (*sunk a large sum into the business*). **b** lose (money) by investment. **12** *tr.* **a** cause (a ball) to enter a pocket in billiards, a hole at golf, etc. **b** achieve this by (a stroke). **13** *tr.* overlook or forget; keep in the background (*sank their differences*). **14** *intr.* (of a price etc.) become lower. **15** *intr.* (of a storm or river) subside. **16** *intr.* (of ground) slope down, or reach a lower level by subsidence. **17** *intr.* (foll. by *on*, *upon*) (of darkness) descend (on a place). **18** *tr.* lower the level of. **19** *tr.* (usu. in *passive*; foll. by *in*) absorb; hold the attention of (*be sunk in thought*). —*n.* **1** a fixed basin with a water-supply and outflow pipe. **2** a place where foul liquid collects. **3** a place of vice or corruption. **4** a pool or marsh in which a river's water disappears by evaporation or percolation. **5** *Physics* a body or process used to absorb or dissipate heat. **6** (in full **sink-hole**) *Geol.* a cavity in limestone etc. into which a stream etc. disappears. □ **sink in 1** penetrate or make its way in. **2** become gradually comprehended (*paused to let the words sink in*). **sinking feeling** a bodily sensation caused by hunger or apprehension. **sinking fund** money set aside for the gradual repayment of a debt. **sink or swim** even at the risk of complete failure (*determined to try, sink or swim*). **sunk fence** a fence formed by, or along the bottom of, a ditch. □□ **sinkable** *adj.* **sinkage** *n.* [OE *sincan* f. Gmc]

sinker /'sɪŋkə(r)/ *n.* **1** a weight used to sink a fishing-line or sounding-line. **2** *US* a doughnut.

sinner /'sɪnə(r)/ *n.* a person who sins, esp. habitually.

sinnet /'sɪnɪt/ *n.* (also **sennit**) *Naut.* braided cordage made in flat or round or square form from 3 to 9 cords. [17th c.: orig. unkn.]

Sinn Fein /ʃɪn 'feɪn/ *n.* a political movement and party seeking a united republican Ireland, now linked to the IRA. □□ **Sinn Feiner** *n.* [Ir. *sinn féin* we ourselves]

Sino- /'saɪnəʊ/ *comb. form* Chinese; Chinese and (*Sino-American*). [Gk *Sinai* the Chinese]

sinologue /'saɪnəˌlɒg, 'sɪ-/ *n.* an expert in sinology. [F, formed as SINO- + Gk *-logos* speaking]

sinology /saɪ'nɒlədʒɪ, sɪ-/ *n.* the study of Chinese language, history, customs, etc. □□ **sinological** /-nə'lɒdʒɪk(ə)l/ *adj.* **sinologist** *n.*

sinter /'sɪntə(r)/ *n. & v.* —*n.* **1** a siliceous or calcareous rock formed by deposition from springs. **2** a substance formed by sintering. —*v.intr. & tr.* coalesce or cause to coalesce from powder into solid by heating. [G, = E *sinder* CINDER]

sinuate /'sɪnjʊət/ *adj.* esp. *Bot.* wavy-edged; with distinct inward and outward bends along the edge. [L *sinuatus* past part. of *sinuare* bend]

sinuosity /ˌsɪnjʊ'ɒsɪtɪ/ *n.* (*pl.* **-ies**) **1** the state of being sinuous. **2** a bend, esp. in a stream or road. [F *sinuosité* or med.L *sinuositas* (as SINUOUS)]

sinuous /'sɪnjʊəs/ *adj.* with many curves; tortuous, undulating. □□ **sinuously** *adv.* **sinuousness** *n.* [F *sinueux* or L *sinuosus* (as SINUS)]

sinus /'saɪnəs/ *n.* **1** a cavity of bone or tissue, esp. in the skull connecting with the nostrils. **2** *Med.* a fistula esp. to a deep abscess. **3** *Bot.* the curve between the lobes of a leaf. [L, = bosom, recess]

sinusitis /ˌsaɪnə'saɪtɪs/ *n.* inflammation of a nasal sinus.

sinusoid /'saɪnəˌsɔɪd/ *n.* **1** a curve having the form of a sine wave. **2** a small irregular-shaped blood-vessel, esp. found in the liver. □□ **sinusoidal** /-'sɔɪd(ə)l/ *adj.* [F *sinusoïde* f. L *sinus*: see SINUS]

Sion var. of ZION.

-sion /ʃ(ə)n, ʒ(ə)n/ *suffix* forming nouns (see -ION) from Latin participial stems in *-s-* (*mansion*; *mission*; *persuasion*).

Sioux /suː/ *n. & adj.* —*n.* (*pl.* same) **1** a member of a group of N. American Indian peoples. **2** the language of this group. —*adj.* of or relating to this people or language. □□ **Siouan** /'suːən/ *adj. & n.* [F f. a native name]

sip /sɪp/ *v. & n.* —*v.tr. & intr.* (**sipped**, **sipping**) drink in one or more small amounts or by spoonfuls. —*n.* **1** a small mouthful of liquid (*a sip of brandy*). **2** the act of taking this. □□ **sipper** *n.* [ME: perh. a modification of SUP¹]

sipe /saɪp/ *n.* a groove or channel in the tread of a tyre to improve its grip. [dial. *sipe* to ooze f. OE *sīpian*, MLG *sīpen*, of unkn. orig.]

siphon /'saɪf(ə)n/ *n. & v.* (also **syphon**) —*n.* **1** a pipe or tube shaped like an inverted V or U with unequal legs to convey a liquid from a container to a lower level by atmospheric pressure. **2** (in full **siphon-bottle**) an aerated-water bottle from which liquid is forced out through a tube by the pressure of gas. **3** *Zool.* **a** a canal or conduit esp. in cephalopods. **b** the sucking-tube of some insects etc. —*v.tr. & intr.* (often foll. by *off*) **1** conduct or flow through a siphon. **2** divert or set aside (funds etc.). □□ **siphonage** *n.* **siphonal** *adj.* **siphonic** /-'fɒnɪk/ *adj.* [F *siphon* or L *sipho -onis* f. Gk *siphōn* pipe]

siphonophore /saɪ'fɒnəˌfɔː(r)/ *n.* any usu. translucent marine hydrozoan of the order Siphonophora, e.g. the Portuguese man-of-war. [Gk *siphōno-* (as SIPHON, -PHORE)]

sippet /'sɪpɪt/ *n.* **1** a small piece of bread etc. soaked in liquid. **2** a piece of toast or fried bread as a garnish. **3** a fragment. [app. dimin. of SOP]

sir /sɜː(r)/ *n.* **1** a polite or respectful form of address or mode of reference to a man. **2** (**Sir**) a titular prefix to the forename of a knight or baronet. [ME, reduced form of SIRE]

sirdar /'sɜːdɑː(r)/ *n. Ind.* etc. **1** a person of high political or military rank. **2** a Sikh. [Urdu *sardār* f. Pers. *sar* head + *dār* possessor]

sire /'saɪə(r)/ *n. & v.* —*n.* **1** the male parent of an animal, esp. a stallion kept for breeding. **2** *archaic* a respectful form of address, now esp. to a king. **3** *archaic poet.* a father or male ancestor. —*v.tr.* (esp. of a stallion) beget. [ME f. OF ult. f. L *senior*: see SENIOR]

siren /'saɪərən/ *n.* **1 a** a device for making a loud prolonged signal or warning sound, esp. by revolving a perforated disc over a jet of compressed air or steam. **b** the sound made by this. **2** (in Greek mythology) each of a number of women or winged creatures whose singing lured unwary sailors on to rocks. **3** a sweet singer. **4 a** a dangerously fascinating woman; a temptress. **b** a tempting pursuit etc. **5** (*attrib.*) irresistibly tempting. **6** an eel-shaped tailed amphibian of the family Sirenidae. □ **siren suit** a one-piece garment for the whole body, easily put on or taken off, orig. for use in air-raid shelters. [ME f. OF *sereine*, *sirene* f. LL *Sirena* fem. f. L f. Gk *Seirēn*]

sirenian /saɪˈriːnɪən/ *adj. & n.* —*adj.* of the order Sirenia of large aquatic plant-eating mammals, e.g. the manatee and dugong. —*n.* any mammal of this order. [mod.L *Sirenia* (as SIREN)]

sirgang /ˈsɜːgæŋ/ *n.* an Asian magpie, *Kitta chinensis*, having mainly green plumage with red wings. [a name in the E. Indies]

sirloin /ˈsɜːlɔɪn/ *n.* the upper and choicer part of a loin of beef. [OF (as SUR¹-, LOIN)]

sirocco /sɪˈrɒkəʊ/ *n.* (also **scirocco**) (*pl.* **-os**) **1** a Saharan simoom reaching the northern shores of the Mediterranean. **2** a warm sultry rainy wind in S. Europe. [F f. It. *scirocco*, ult. f. Arab. *Šarūḳ* east wind]

sirrah /ˈsɪrə/ *n. archaic* = SIR (as a form of address). [prob. f. ME *sïrë* SIR]

sirree /sɪˈriː/ *int. US colloq.* as an emphatic, esp. after *yes* or *no*. [SIR + emphatic suffix]

sirup *US* var. of SYRUP.

SIS *abbr.* Secret Intelligence Service.

sis /sɪs/ *n. colloq.* a sister. [abbr.]

sisal /ˈsaɪs(ə)l/ *n.* **1** a Mexican plant, *Agave sisalana*, with large fleshy leaves. **2** the fibre made from this plant, used for cordage, ropes, etc. [*Sisal*, the port of Yucatan, Mexico]

siskin /ˈsɪskɪn/ *n.* a dark-streaked yellowish-green songbird, *Carduelis spinus*, allied to the goldfinch. [MDu. *siseken* dimin., rel. to MLG *sīsek*, MHG *zīse*, *zīsec*, of Slav. origin]

sissy /ˈsɪsɪ/ *n. & adj.* (also **cissy**) *colloq.* —*n.* (*pl.* **-ies**) an effeminate or cowardly person. —*adj.* (**sissier, sissiest**) effeminate; cowardly. □□ **sissified** *adj.* **sissiness** *n.* **sissyish** *adj.* [SIS + -Y²]

sister /ˈsɪstə(r)/ *n.* **1** a woman or girl in relation to sons and other daughters of her parents. **2 a** (often as a form of address) a close female friend or associate. **b** a female fellow member of a trade union, class, sect, or the human race. **3** a senior female nurse. **4** a member of a female religious order. **5** (*attrib.*) of the same type or design or origin etc. (*sister ship*; *prose, the younger sister of verse*). □ **sister german** see GERMAN. **sister-in-law** (*pl.* **sisters-in-law**) **1** the sister of one's wife or husband. **2** the wife of one's brother. **3** the wife of one's brother-in-law. **Sister of Mercy** a member of an educational or charitable order of women, esp. that founded in Dublin in 1827. **sister uterine** see UTERINE. □□ **sisterless** *adj.* **sisterly** *adj.* **sisterliness** *n.* [ME *sister* (f. ON), *suster* etc. (repr. OE *sweoster* f. Gmc)]

sisterhood /ˈsɪstəˌhʊd/ *n.* **1 a** the relationship between sisters. **b** sisterly friendliness; companionship; mutual support. **2 a** a society or association of women, esp. when bound by monastic vows or devoting themselves to religious or charitable work or the feminist cause. **b** its members collectively.

Sistine /ˈsɪstiːn, ˈsɪstaɪn/ *adj.* of any of the Popes called Sixtus, esp. Sixtus IV. □ **Sistine Chapel** a chapel in the Vatican, with frescoes by Michelangelo and other painters. [It. *Sistino* f. *Sisto* Sixtus]

sistrum /ˈsɪstrəm/ *n.* (*pl.* **sistra** /-trə/) a jingling metal instrument used by the ancient Egyptians esp. in the worship of Isis. [ME f. L f. Gk *seistron* f. *seiō* shake]

Sisyphean /ˌsɪsɪˈfiːən/ *adj.* (of toil) endless and fruitless like that of Sisyphus in Greek mythology (whose task in Hades was to push uphill a stone that at once rolled down again).

sit /sɪt/ *v. & n.* —*v.* (**sitting**; *past* and *past part.* **sat** /sæt/) **1** *intr.* adopt or be in a position in which the body is supported more or less upright by the buttocks resting on the ground or a raised seat etc., with the thighs usu. horizontal. **2** *tr.* cause to sit; place in a sitting position. **3** *intr.* **a** (of a bird) perch. **b** (of an animal) rest with the hind legs bent and the body close to the ground. **4** *intr.* (of a bird) remain on its nest to hatch its eggs. **5** *intr.* **a** be engaged in an occupation in which the sitting position is usual.

b (of a committee, legislative body, etc.) be engaged in business. **c** (of an individual) be entitled to hold some office or position (*sat as a magistrate*). **6** *intr.* (usu. foll. by *for*) pose in a sitting position (for a portrait). **7** *intr.* (foll. by *for*) be a Member of Parliament for (a constituency). **8** *tr.* & (foll. by *for*) *intr. Brit.* be a candidate for (an examination). **9** *intr.* be in a more or less permanent position or condition (esp. of inactivity or being out of use or out of place). **10** *intr.* (of clothes etc.) fit or hang in a certain way. **11** *tr.* keep or have one's seat on (a horse etc.). **12** *intr.* act as a babysitter. **13** *intr.* (often foll. by *before*) (of an army) take a position outside a city etc. to besiege it. —*n.* the way a dress etc. sits on a person. □ **be sitting pretty** be comfortably or advantageously placed. **make a person sit up** *colloq.* surprise or interest a person. **sit at a person's feet** be a person's pupil. **sit at home** be inactive. **sit back** relax one's efforts. **sit by** look on without interfering. **sit down 1** sit after standing. **2** cause to sit. **3** (foll. by *under*) submit tamely to (an insult etc.). **sit-down** *adj.* (of a meal) eaten sitting at a table. **sit-down strike** a strike in which workers refuse to leave their place of work. **sit heavy on the stomach** take a long time to be digested. **sit in 1** occupy a place as a protest. **2** (foll. by *for*) take the place of. **3** (foll. by *on*) be present as a guest or observer at (a meeting etc.). **sit-in** *n.* a protest involving sitting in. **sit in judgement** assume the right of judging others; be censorious. **sit loosely on** not be very binding. **sit on 1** be a member of (a committee etc.). **2** hold a session or inquiry concerning. **3** *colloq.* delay action about (*the government has been sitting on the report*). **4** *colloq.* repress or rebuke or snub (*felt rather sat on*). **sit on the fence** see FENCE. **sit on one's hands 1** take no action. **2** refuse to applaud. **sit out 1** take no part in (a dance etc.). **2** stay till the end of (esp. an ordeal). **3** sit outdoors. **4** outstay (other visitors). **sit tight** *colloq.* **1** remain firmly in one's place. **2** not be shaken off or move away or yield to distractions. **sit up 1** rise from a lying to a sitting position. **2** sit firmly upright. **3** go to bed later than the usual time. **4** *colloq.* become interested or aroused etc. **sit-up** *n.* a physical exercise in which a person sits up without raising the legs from the ground. **sit up and take notice** *colloq.* have one's interest aroused, esp. suddenly. **sit-upon** *colloq.* the buttocks. **sit well** have a good seat in riding. **sit well on** suit or fit. [OE *sittan* f. Gmc]

sitar /ˈsɪtɑː(r), sɪˈtɑː(r)/ *n.* a long-necked Indian lute with movable frets. □□ **sitarist** /sɪˈtɑːrɪst/ *n.* [Hindi *sitār*]

sitcom /ˈsɪtkɒm/ *n. colloq.* a situation comedy. [abbr.]

site /saɪt/ *n. & v.* **1** the ground chosen or used for a town or building. **2** a place where some activity is or has been conducted (*camping site*; *launching site*). —*v.tr.* **1** locate or place. **2** provide with a site. [ME f. AF *site* or L *situs* local position]

Sitka /ˈsɪtkə/ *n.* (in full **Sitka spruce**) a fast-growing spruce, *Picea sitchensis*, native to N. America and yielding timber. [*Sitka* in Alaska]

sitrep /ˈsɪtrep/ *n.* a report on the current military situation in an area. [*situation report*]

sits vac /sɪts ˈvæk/ *abbr.* situations vacant.

sitter /ˈsɪtə(r)/ *n.* **1** a person who sits, esp. for a portrait. **2** = BABYSITTER (see BABYSIT). **3** *colloq.* **a** an easy catch or shot. **b** an easy task. **4** a sitting hen.

sitting /ˈsɪtɪŋ/ *n. & adj.* —*n.* **1** a continuous period of being seated, esp. engaged in an activity (*finished the book in one sitting*). **2** a time during which an assembly is engaged in business. **3** a session in which a meal is served (*dinner will be served in two sittings*). **4** *Brit. Law* = TERM 5c. **5** a clutch of eggs. —*adj.* **1** having sat down. **2** (of an animal or bird) not running or flying. **3** (of a hen) engaged in hatching. □ **sitting duck** (or **target**) *colloq.* a vulnerable person or thing. **sitting pretty** see PRETTY. **sitting-room 1** a room in a house for relaxed sitting in. **2** space enough to accommodate seated persons. **sitting tenant** a tenant already in occupation of premises.

situate v. & adj. —v.tr. /'sɪtjʊˌeɪt/ (usu. in *passive*) **1** put in a certain position or circumstances (*is situated at the top of a hill; how are you situated at the moment?*). **2** establish or indicate the place of; put in a context. —adj. /'sɪtjʊət/ *Law* or *archaic* situated. [med.L *situare situat-* f. L *situs* site]

situation /ˌsɪtjʊ'eɪʃ(ə)n/ n. **1** a place and its surroundings (*the house stands in a fine situation*). **2** a set of circumstances; a position in which one finds oneself; a state of affairs (*came out of a difficult situation with credit*). **3** an employee's position or job. **4** a critical point or complication in a drama. □**situation comedy** a comedy in which the humour derives from the situations the characters are placed in. **situations vacant** (or **wanted**) headings of lists of employment offered and sought. □□**situational** adj. [ME f. F *situation* or med.L *situatio* (as SITUATE)]

sitz-bath /'sɪtsbɑːθ/ n. a hip-bath. [partial transl. of G *Sitzbad* f. *sitzen* sit + *Bad* bath]

Siva /'siːvə, 'ʃiːvə/ n. (also **Shiva** /'ʃiːvə/) a Hindu deity associated with the powers of reproduction and dissolution, regarded by some as the supreme being and by others as a member of the triad. □□**Sivaism** n. **Sivaite** n. & adj. [Skr. *Śiva*, lit. the auspicious one]

six /sɪks/ n. & adj. —n. **1** one more than five, or four less than ten; the product of two units and three units. **2** a symbol for this (6, vi, VI). **3** a size etc. denoted by six. **4** a set or team of six individuals. **5** *Cricket* a hit scoring six runs by clearing the boundary without bouncing. **6** the time of six o'clock (*is it six yet?*). **7** a card etc. with six pips. —adj. that amount to six. □**at sixes and sevens** in confusion or disagreement. **knock for six** *colloq.* utterly surprise or overcome (a person). **the Six Counties** the counties of N. Ireland. **six-gun** = *six-shooter*. **six of one and half a dozen of the other** a situation of little real difference between the alternatives. **six-shooter** a revolver with six chambers. [OE *siex* etc. f. Gmc]

sixain /'sɪkseɪn/ n. a six-line stanza. [F f. *six* six]

sixer /'sɪksə(r)/ n. **1** the leader of a group of six Brownies or Cubs. **2** *Cricket* a hit for six runs.

sixfold /'sɪksfəʊld/ adj. & adv. **1** six times as much or as many. **2** consisting of six parts.

sixpence /'sɪkspəns/ n. *Brit.* **1** the sum of six pence, esp. before decimalization. **2** *hist.* a coin worth six old pence (2½p).

sixpenny /'sɪkspənɪ/ adj. *Brit.* costing or worth six pence, esp. before decimalization.

sixte /sɪkst/ n. *Fencing* the sixth of the eight parrying positions.

sixteen /ˌsɪks'tiːn, 'sɪks-/ n. & adj. —n. **1** one more than fifteen, or six more than ten. **2** a symbol for this (16, xvi, XVI). **3** a size etc. denoted by sixteen. —adj. that amount to sixteen. □**sixteenth note** esp. *US Mus.* = SEMIQUAVER. □□**sixteenth** adj. & n. [OE *sixtiene* (as SIX, -TEEN)]

sixteenmo /sɪks'tiːnməʊ/ n. (pl. **-os**) sextodecimo. [English reading of the symbol 16mo]

sixth /sɪksθ/ n. & adj. —n. **1** the position in a sequence corresponding to that of the number 6 in the sequence 1-6. **2** something occupying this position. **3** any of six equal parts of a thing. **4** *Mus.* **a** an interval or chord spanning six consecutive notes in the diatonic scale (e.g. C to A). **b** a note separated from another by this interval. —adj. that is the sixth. □**sixth form** *Brit.* a form in a secondary school for pupils over 16. **sixth-form college** *Brit.* a college for pupils over 16. **sixth-former** a pupil in the sixth form. **sixth sense 1** a supposed faculty giving intuitive or extrasensory knowledge. **2** such knowledge. □□**sixthly** adv. [SIX]

Sixtine /'sɪkstiːn, -taɪn/ adj. = SISTINE. [mod.L *Sixtinus* f. *Sixtus*]

sixty /'sɪkstɪ/ n. & adj. —n. (pl. **-ies**) **1** the product of six and ten. **2** a symbol for this (60, lx, LX). **3** (in pl.) the numbers from 60 to 69, esp. the years of a century or of a person's life. **4** a set of sixty persons or things. —adj. that amount to sixty. □**sixty-first, -second**, etc. the ordinal numbers between sixtieth and seventieth. **sixty-fourmo** /ˌsɪkstɪ'fɔːməʊ/ (pl. **-os**) **1** a size of book in which each leaf is one-sixty-fourth of a printing-sheet. **2** a book of this size (after DUO-DECIMO etc.). **sixty-fourth note** esp. *US Mus.* = HEMIDEMISEMIQUAVER. **sixty-four thousand** (or **sixty-four**) **dollar question** a difficult and crucial question (from the top prize in a broadcast quiz show). **sixty-one, -two**, etc. the cardinal numbers between sixty and seventy. □□**sixtieth** adj. & n. **sixtyfold** adj. & adv. [OE *siextig* (as SIX, -TY²)]

sizable var. of SIZEABLE.

sizar /'saɪzə(r)/ n. a student at Cambridge or at Trinity College, Dublin, paying reduced fees and formerly having certain menial duties. □□**sizarship** n. [SIZE¹ = ration]

size¹ /saɪz/ n. & v. —n. **1** the relative bigness or extent of a thing, dimensions, magnitude (*is of vast size; size matters less than quality*). **2** each of the classes, usu. numbered, into which things otherwise similar, esp. garments, are divided according to size (*is made in several sizes; takes size 7 in gloves; is three sizes too big*). —v.tr. sort or group in sizes or according to size. □**of a size** having the same size. **of some size** fairly large. **the size of** as big as. **the size of it** *colloq.* a true account of the matter (*that is the size of it*). **size-stick** a shoemaker's measure for taking the length of a foot. **size up 1** estimate the size of. **2** *colloq.* form a judgement of. **what size?** how big? □□**sized** adj. (also in comb.). **sizer** n. [ME f. OF *sise* f. *assise* ASSIZE, or f. ASSIZE]

size² /saɪz/ n. & v. —n. a gelatinous solution used in glazing paper, stiffening textiles, preparing plastered walls for decoration, etc. —v.tr. glaze or stiffen or treat with size. [ME, perh. = SIZE¹]

sizeable /'saɪzəb(ə)l/ adj. (also **sizable**) large or fairly large. □□**sizeably** adv.

sizzle /'sɪz(ə)l/ v. & n. —v.intr. **1** make a sputtering or hissing sound as of frying. **2** *colloq.* be in a state of great heat or excitement or marked effectiveness. —n. **1** a sizzling sound. **2** *colloq.* a state of great heat or excitement. □□**sizzler** n. **sizzling** adj. & adv. (*sizzling hot*). [imit.]

SJ abbr. Society of Jesus.

SJAA abbr. (in the UK) St John Ambulance Association.

SJAB abbr. (in the UK) St John Ambulance Brigade.

sjambok /'ʃæmbɒk/ n. & v. —n. (in S. Africa) a rhinoceros-hide whip. —v.tr. flog with a sjambok. [Afrik. f. Malay *samboq*, *chambok* f. Urdu *chābuk*]

SJC abbr. (in the US) Supreme Judicial Court.

skald /skɔːld, skɒld/ n. (also **scald**) (in ancient Scandinavia) a composer and reciter of poems honouring heroes and their deeds. □□**skaldic** adj. [ON *skáld*, of unkn. orig.]

skat /skɑːt/ n. a three-handed card-game with bidding. [G f. It. *scarto* a discard f. *scartare* discard]

skate¹ /skeɪt/ n. & v. —n. **1** each of a pair of steel blades (or of boots with blades attached) for gliding on ice. **2** (in full **roller skate**) each of a pair of metal frames with small wheels, fitted to shoes for riding on a hard surface. **3** a device on which a heavy object moves. —v. **1 a** intr. move on skates. **b** tr. perform (a specified figure) on skates. **2** intr. (foll. by over) refer fleetingly to, disregard. □**get one's skates on** *Brit. sl.* make haste. **skate on thin ice** *colloq.* behave rashly, risk danger, esp. by dealing with a subject needing tactful treatment. **skating-rink** a piece of ice artificially made, or a floor used, for skating. □□ **skater** n. [orig. *scates* (pl.) f. Du. *schaats* (sing.) f. ONF *escace*, OF *eschasse* stilt]

skate² /skeɪt/ n. (pl. same or **skates**) any cartilaginous marine fish of the family Rajidae, esp.

Raja batis, a large flat rhomboidal fish used as food. [ME f. ON *skata*]

skate[3] /skeɪt/ *n. sl.* a contemptible, mean, or dishonest person (esp. *cheap skate*). [19th c.: orig. uncert.]

skateboard /ˈskeɪtbɔːd/ *n. & v.* —*n.* a short narrow board on roller-skate wheels for riding on while standing. —*v.intr.* ride on a skateboard. □□ **skateboarder** *n.*

skean /skiːn, ˈskiːən/ *n. hist.* a Gaelic dagger formerly used in Ireland and Scotland. □**skean-dhu** /-ˈduː/ *n.* a dagger worn in the stocking as part of Highland costume. [Gael. *sgian* knife, *dubh* black]

sked /sked/ *n. & v. colloq.* —*n.* = SCHEDULE. —*v.tr.* (**skedded, skedding**) = SCHEDULE. [abbr.]

skedaddle /skɪˈdæd(ə)l/ *v. & n. colloq.* —*v.intr.* run away, depart quickly, flee. —*n.* a hurried departure or flight. [19th c.: orig. unkn.]

skeet /skiːt/ *n.* a shooting sport in which a clay target is thrown from a trap to simulate the flight of a bird. [ON *skjóta* SHOOT]

skeeter[1] /ˈskiːtə(r)/ *n. US & Austral. sl.* a mosquito. [abbr.]

skeeter[2] var. of SKITTER.

skeg /skeg/ *n.* **1** a fin underneath the rear of a surfboard. **2** the after part of a vessel's keel or a projection from it. [ON *skeg* beard, perh. via Du. *scheg(ge)*]

skein /skeɪn/ *n.* **1** a loosely-coiled bundle of yarn or thread. **2** a flock of wild geese etc. in flight. **3** a tangle or confusion. [ME f. OF *escaigne*, of unkn. orig.]

skeleton /ˈskelɪt(ə)n/ *n.* **1 a** a hard internal or external framework of bones, cartilage, shell, woody fibre, etc., supporting or containing the body of an animal or plant. **b** the dried bones of a human being or other animal fastened together in the same relative positions as in life. **2** the supporting framework or structure or essential part of a thing. **3** a very thin or emaciated person or animal. **4** the remaining part of anything after its life or usefulness is gone. **5** an outline sketch, an epitome or abstract. **6** (*attrib.*) having only the essential or minimum number of persons, parts, etc. (*skeleton plan; skeleton staff*). □**skeleton at the feast** something that spoils one's pleasure; an intrusive worry. **skeleton in the cupboard** (*US* **closet**) a discreditable or embarrassing fact kept secret. **skeleton key** a key designed to fit many locks by having the interior of the bit hollowed. □□ **skeletal** *adj.* **skeletally** *adv.* **skeletonize** *v.tr.* (also **-ise**). [mod.L f. Gk, neut. of *skeletos* dried-up f. *skellō* dry up]

skep /skep/ *n.* **1 a** a wooden or wicker basket of any of various forms. **b** the quantity contained in this. **2** a straw or wicker beehive. [ME f. ON *skeppa*]

skepsis *US* var. of SCEPSIS.

skeptic *US* var. of SCEPTIC.

skeptical *US* var. of SCEPTICAL.

skerrick /ˈskerɪk/ *n.* (usu. with *neg.*) *US & Austral. colloq.* the smallest bit (*not a skerrick left*). [N.Engl. dial.; orig. uncert.]

skerry /ˈskerɪ/ *n.* (pl. **-ies**) *Sc.* a reef or rocky island. [Orkney dial. f. ON *sker*: cf. SCAR[2]]

sketch /sketʃ/ *n. & v.* —*n.* **1** a rough, slight, merely outlined, or unfinished drawing or painting, often made to assist in making a more finished picture. **2** a brief account without many details conveying a general idea of something, a rough draft or general outline. **3** a very short play, usu. humorous and limited to one scene. **4** a short descriptive piece of writing. **5** a musical composition of a single movement. **6** *colloq.* a comical person or thing. —*v.* **1** *tr.* make or give a sketch of. **2** *intr.* draw sketches esp. of landscape (*went out sketching*). **3** *tr.* (often foll. by *in, out*) indicate briefly or in outline. □**sketch-book** (or **-block**) a pad of drawing-paper for doing sketches on. **sketch-map** a roughly-drawn map with few details. □□ **sketcher** *n.* [Du. *schets* or

G *Skizze* f. It. *schizzo* f. *schizzare* make a sketch ult. f. Gk *skhēdios* extempore]

sketchy /ˈsketʃɪ/ *adj.* (**sketchier, sketchiest**) **1** giving only a slight or rough outline, like a sketch. **2** *colloq.* unsubstantial or imperfect esp. through haste. □□ **sketchily** *adv.* **sketchiness** *n.*

skeuomorph /ˈskjuːəʊˌmɔːf/ *n.* **1** an object or feature copying the design of a similar artefact in another material. **2** an ornamental design resulting from the nature of the material used or the method of working it. □□ **skeuomorphic** /-ˈmɔːfɪk/ *adj.* [Gk *skeuos* vessel, implement + *morphē* form]

skew /skjuː/ *adj., n., & v.* —*adj.* **1** oblique, slanting, set askew. **2** *Math.* **a** lying in three dimensions (*skew curve*). **b** (of lines) not coplanar. **c** (of a statistical distribution) not symmetrical. —*n.* **1** a slant. **2** *Statistics* skewness. —*v.* **1** *tr.* make skew. **2** *tr.* distort. **3** *intr.* move obliquely. **4** *intr.* twist. □**on the skew** askew. **skew arch** (or **bridge**) an arch (or bridge) with the line of the arch not at right angles to the abutment. **skew chisel** a chisel with an oblique edge. **skew-eyed** *Brit.* squinting. **skew gear** a gear consisting of two cog-wheels having non-parallel, non-intersecting axes. **skew-whiff** /skjuːˈwɪf/ *Brit. colloq.* askew. □□ **skewness** *n.* [ONF *eskiu(w)er* (v.) = OF *eschuer*: see ESCHEW]

skewback /ˈskjuːbæk/ *n.* the sloping face of the abutment on which an extremity of an arch rests.

skewbald /ˈskjuːbɔːld/ *adj. & n.* —*adj.* (of an animal) with irregular patches of white and another colour (properly not black) (cf. PIEBALD). —*n.* a skewbald animal, esp. a horse. [ME *skued* (orig. uncert.), after PIEBALD]

skewer /ˈskjuːə(r)/ *n. & v.* —*n.* a long pin designed for holding meat compactly together while cooking. —*v.tr.* fasten together or pierce with or as with a skewer. [17th c., var. of dial. *skiver*: orig. unkn.]

ski /skiː/ *n. & v.* —*n.* (*pl.* **skis** or **ski**) **1** each of a pair of long narrow pieces of wood etc., usu. pointed and turned up at the front, fastened under the feet for travelling over snow. **2** a similar device under a vehicle or aircraft. **3** = WATER-SKI. **4** (*attrib.*) for wear when skiing (*ski boots*). —*v.* (**skis, ski'd** or **skied** /skiːd/; **skiing**) **1** *intr.* travel on skis. **2** *tr.* ski at (a place). □**ski-bob** *n.* a machine like a bicycle with skis instead of wheels. —*v.intr.* (**-bobbed, -bobbing**) ride a ski-bob. **ski-bobber** a person who ski-bobs. **ski-jump 1** a steep slope levelling off before a sharp drop to allow a skier to leap through the air. **2** a jump made from this. **ski-jumper** a person who takes part in ski-jumping. **ski-jumping** the sport of leaping off a ski-jump with marks awarded for style and distance attained. **ski-lift** a device for carrying skiers up a slope, usu. on seats hung from an overhead cable. **ski-plane** an aeroplane having its undercarriage fitted with skis for landing on snow or ice. **ski-run** a slope prepared for skiing. □□ **skiable** *adj.* [Norw. f. ON *skíth* billet, snow-shoe]

skiagraphy var. of SCIAGRAPHY.

skiamachy var. of SCIAMACHY.

skid /skɪd/ *v. & n.* —*v.* (**skidded, skidding**) **1** *intr.* (of a vehicle, a wheel, or a driver) slide on slippery ground, esp. sideways or obliquely. **2** *tr.* cause (a vehicle etc.) to skid. **3** *intr.* slip, slide. **4** *intr. colloq.* fail or decline or err. **5** *tr.* support or move or protect or check with a skid. —*n.* **1** the act or an instance of skidding. **2** a piece of wood etc. serving as a support, ship's fender, inclined plane, etc. **3** a braking device, esp. a wooden or metal shoe preventing a wheel from revolving or used as a drag. **4** a runner beneath an aircraft for use when landing. □**hit the skids** *colloq.* enter a rapid decline or deterioration. **on the skids** *colloq.* **1** about to be discarded or defeated. **2** ready for launching. **put the skids under** *colloq.* **1** hasten the downfall or failure of. **2** cause to hasten. **skid-lid** *sl.* a crash-helmet. **skid-pan** *Brit.* **1** a slippery surface prepared for vehicle-drivers to practise control of skidding. **2** a braking device. **skid road** *US* **1** a road for hauling logs along. **2** a part of a town frequented by loggers or vagrants. **skid row** *US* a part of a town frequented by vagrants, alcoholics, etc. [17th c.: orig. unkn.]

skiddoo /skɪ'duː/ *v.intr.* (also **skidoo**) (**-oos, -ooed**) *US sl.* go away; depart. [perh. f. SKEDADDLE]

skier[1] /'skiːə(r)/ *n.* a person who skis.

skier[2] var. of SKYER.

skiff /skɪf/ *n.* a light rowing-boat or sculling-boat. [F *esquif* f. It. *schifo*, rel. to SHIP]

skiffle /'skɪf(ə)l/ *n.* a kind of folk music played by a small group, mainly with a rhythmic accompaniment to a singing guitarist etc. [perh. imit.]

ski-joring /'skiːˌdʒɔːrɪŋ, ʃiːˈjɜːrɪŋ/ *n.* a winter sport in which a skier is towed by a horse or vehicle. □□ **ski-jorer** *n.* [Norw. *skikjøring* (as SKI, *kjøre* drive)]

skilful /'skɪlfʊl/ *adj.* (*US* **skillful**) (often foll. by *at, in*) having or showing skill; practised, expert, adroit, ingenious. □□ **skilfully** *adv.* **skilfulness** *n.*

skill /skɪl/ *n.* (often foll. by *in*) expertness, practised ability, facility in an action; dexterity or tact. □□ **skill-less** *adj.* (*archaic* **skilless**). [ME f. ON *skil* distinction]

skilled /skɪld/ *adj.* **1** (often foll. by *in*) having or showing skill; skilful. **2** (of a worker) highly trained or experienced. **3** (of work) requiring skill or special training.

skillet /'skɪlɪt/ *n.* **1** *Brit.* a small metal cooking-pot with a long handle and usu. legs. **2** *US* a frying-pan. [ME, perh. f. OF *escuelete* dimin. of *escuele* platter f. LL *scutella*]

skillful *US* var. of SKILFUL.

skilly /'skɪlɪ/ *n. Brit.* **1** a thin broth or soup or gruel (usu. of oatmeal and water flavoured with meat). **2** an insipid beverage; tea or coffee. [abbr. f. *skilligalee*, prob. fanciful]

skim /skɪm/ *v. & n.* —*v.* (**skimmed, skimming**) **1** *tr.* **a** take scum or cream or a floating layer from the surface of (a liquid). **b** take (cream etc.) from the surface of a liquid. **2** *tr.* **a** keep touching lightly or nearly touching (a surface) in passing over. **b** deal with or treat (a subject) superficially. **3** *intr.* **a** (often foll. by *over, along*) go lightly over a surface, glide along in the air. **b** (foll. by *over*) = sense 2b of *v.* **4** *a tr.* read superficially, look over cursorily, gather the salient facts contained in. **b** *intr.* (usu. foll. by *through*) read or look over cursorily. **5** *tr. US sl.* conceal or divert (income) to avoid paying tax. —*n.* **1** the act or an instance of skimming. **2** a thin covering on a liquid (*skim of ice*). □ **skim the cream off** take the best part of. **skim** (or **skimmed**) **milk** milk from which the cream has been skimmed. [ME, back-form. f. SKIMMER]

skimmer /'skɪmə(r)/ *n.* **1** a device for skimming liquids. **2** a person who skims. **3** a flat hat, esp. a broad-brimmed straw hat. **4** any long-winged marine bird of the genus *Rynchops* that feeds by skimming over water with its knifelike lower mandible immersed. **5** a hydroplane, hydrofoil, hovercraft, or other vessel that has little or no displacement at speed. **6** *US* a sheath-like dress. [ME f. OF *escumoir* f. *escumer* f. *escume* SCUM]

skimmia /'skɪmɪə/ *n.* any evergreen shrub of the genus *Skimmia*, native to E. Asia, with red berries. [mod.L f. Jap.]

skimp /skɪmp/ *v., adj., & n.* —*v.* **1** *tr.* (often foll. by *in*) supply (a person etc.) meagrely with food, money, etc. **2** *tr.* use a meagre or insufficient amount of, stint (material, expenses, etc.). **3** *intr.* be parsimonious. —*adj.* scanty. —*n. colloq.* a small or scanty thing, esp. a skimpy garment. [18th c.: orig. unkn.: cf. SCRIMP]

skimpy /'skɪmpɪ/ *adj.* (**skimpier, skimpiest**) meagre; not ample or sufficient. □□ **skimpily** *adv.* **skimpiness** *n.*

skin /skɪn/ *n. & v.* —*n.* **1** the flexible continuous covering of a human or other animal body. **2 a** the

skin of a flayed animal with or without the hair etc. **b** a material prepared from skins esp. of smaller animals (opp. HIDE²). **3** a person's skin with reference to its colour or complexion (*has a fair skin*). **4** an outer layer or covering, esp. the coating of a plant, fruit, or sausage. **5** a film like skin on the surface of a liquid etc. **6** a container for liquid, made of an animal's whole skin. **7 a** the planking or plating of a ship or boat, inside or outside the ribs. **b** the outer covering of any craft or vehicle, esp. an aircraft or spacecraft. **8** *Brit. sl.* a skinhead. **9** *US Cards* a game in which each player has one card which he bets will not be the first to be matched by a card dealt from the pack. **10** = *gold-beater's skin*. **11** a duplicating stencil. —*v.* (**skinned, skinning**) **1** *tr.* remove the skin from. **2** (often foll. by *over*) *a tr.* cover (a sore etc.) with or as with skin. **b** *intr.* (of a wound etc.) become covered with new skin. **3** *tr. sl.* fleece or swindle. □ **be skin and bone** be very thin. **by** (or **with**) **the skin of one's teeth** by a very narrow margin. **change one's skin** undergo an impossible change of character etc. **get under a person's skin** *colloq.* interest or annoy a person intensely. **have a thick** (or **thin**) **skin** be insensitive (or sensitive) to criticism etc. **no skin off one's nose** *colloq.* a matter of indifference or even benefit to one. **skin-deep** (of a wound, or of an emotion, an impression, beauty, etc.) superficial, not deep or lasting. **skin-diver** a person who swims underwater without a diving-suit, usu. in deep water with an aqualung and flippers. **skin-diving** such swimming. **skin effect** *Electr.* the tendency of a high-frequency alternating current to flow through the outer layer only of a conductor. **skin-flick** *sl.* an explicitly pornographic film. **skin-food** a cosmetic intended to improve the condition of the skin. **skin friction** friction at the surface of a solid and a fluid in relative motion. **skin game** *US sl.* a swindling game. **skin-graft 1** the surgical transplanting of skin. **2** a piece of skin transferred in this way. **skin test** a test to determine whether an immune reaction is elicited when a substance is applied to or injected into the skin. **skin-tight** (of a garment) very close-fitting. **to the skin** through all one's clothing (*soaked to the skin*). **with a whole skin** unwounded. □□ **skinless** *adj.* **skin-like** *adj.* **skinned** *adj.* (also in *comb.*). [OE *scin(n)* f. ON *skinn*]

skinflint /'skɪnflɪnt/ *n.* a miserly person.

skinful /'skɪnfʊl/ *n.* (*pl.* **-fuls**) *colloq.* enough alcoholic liquor to make one drunk.

skinhead /'skɪnhed/ *n.* **1** *Brit.* a youth with close-cropped hair, esp. one of an aggressive gang. **2** *US* recruit in the Marines.

skink /skɪŋk/ *n.* any small lizard of the family Scincidae. [F *scinc* or L *scincus* f. Gk *skigkos*]

skinner /'skɪnə(r)/ *n.* **1** a person who skins animals or prepares skins. **2** a dealer in skins, a furrier. **3** *Austral. Racing sl.* a result very profitable to bookmakers.

skinny /'skɪnɪ/ *adj.* (**skinnier, skinniest**) **1** thin or emaciated. **2** (of clothing) tight-fitting. **3** made of or like skin. □ **skinny-dipping** esp. *US colloq.* bathing in the nude. □□ **skinniness** *n.*

skint /skɪnt/ *adj. Brit. sl.* having no money left. [= *skinned*, past part. of SKIN]

skip[1] /skɪp/ *v. & n.* —*v.* (**skipped, skipping**) **1** *intr.* **a** move along lightly, esp. by taking two steps with each foot in turn. **b** jump lightly from the ground, esp. so as to clear a skipping-rope. **c** jump about, gambol, caper, frisk. **2** *intr.* (often foll. by *from, off, to*) move quickly from one point, subject, or occupation to another; be desultory. **3** (also *absol.*) *tr.* omit in dealing with a series or in reading (*skip every tenth row; always skips the small print*). **4** *tr. colloq.* not participate in. **5** *tr. colloq.* depart quickly from; leave hurriedly. **6** *intr.* (often foll. by *out, off*) *colloq.* make off, disappear. **7** *tr.* make (a stone) ricochet on the surface of water. —*n.* **1** a skipping movement or action. **2** *Computing* the action of passing over part of a sequence of data or instructions. **3** *US colloq.* a person who defaults or absconds. □**skip it** *sl.* **1** abandon a topic etc. **2** make off, disappear. **skipping-rope** (*US* **skip-rope**) a length of rope revolved over the head and under the feet while jumping as a game or exercise. **skip zone** the annular region round a broadcasting station where neither direct nor reflected waves are received. [ME, prob. f. Scand.]

skip² /skɪp/ *n.* **1** a large container for builders' refuse etc. **2** a cage, bucket, etc., in which men or materials are lowered and raised in mines and quarries. **3** = SKEP. [var. of SKEP]

skip³ /skɪp/ *n. & v.* —*n.* the captain or director of a side at bowls or curling. —*v.tr.* (**skipped**, **skipping**) be the skip of. [abbr. of SKIPPER¹]

skipjack /ˈskɪpdʒæk/ *n.* **1** (in full **skipjack tuna**) a small striped Pacific tuna, *Katsuwonus pelamus*, used as food. **2** a click beetle. **3** a kind of sailing-boat used off the East coast of the US. [SKIP¹ + JACK¹]

skipper¹ /ˈskɪpə(r)/ *n. & v.* —*n.* **1** a sea captain, esp. the master of a small trading or fishing vessel. **2** the captain of an aircraft. **3** the captain of a side in games. —*v.tr.* act as captain of. [ME f. MDu., MLG *schipper* f. *schip* SHIP]

skipper² /ˈskɪpə(r)/ *n.* **1** a person who skips. **2** any brown thick-bodied butterfly of the family Hesperiidae.

skippet /ˈskɪpɪt/ *n.* a small round wooden box to enclose and protect a seal attached to a document. [ME: orig. unkn.]

skirl /skɜːl/ *n. & v.* —*n.* the shrill sound characteristic of bagpipes. —*v.intr.* make a skirl. [prob. Scand.: ult. imit.]

skirmish /ˈskɜːmɪʃ/ *n. & v.* —*n.* **1** a piece of irregular or unpremeditated fighting esp. between small or outlying parts of armies or fleets, a slight engagement. **2** a short argument or contest of wit etc. —*v.intr.* engage in a skirmish. □□**skirmisher** *n.* [ME f. OF *eskirmir*, *escremir* f. Frank.]

skirr /skɜː(r)/ *v.intr.* move rapidly esp. with a whirring sound. [perh. rel. to SCOUR¹ or SCOUR²]

skirret /ˈskɪrɪt/ *n.* a perennial umbelliferous plant, *Sium sisarum*, formerly cultivated in Europe for its edible root. [ME *skirwhit(e)*, perh. formed as SHEER¹, WHITE]

skirt /skɜːt/ *n. & v.* —*n.* **1** a woman's outer garment hanging from the waist. **2** the part of a coat etc. that hangs below the waist. **3** a hanging part round the base of a hovercraft. **4** (in *sing.* or *pl.*) an edge, border, or extreme part. **5** (also **bit of skirt**) *sl. offens.* a woman regarded as an object of sexual desire. **6** (in full **skirt of beef** etc.) **a** the diaphragm and other membranes as food. **b** *Brit.* a cut of meat from the lower flank. **7** a flap of a saddle. **8** a surface that conceals or protects the wheels or underside of a vehicle or aircraft. —*v.* **1** *tr.* go along or round or past the edge of. **2** *tr.* be situated along. **3** *tr.* avoid dealing with (an issue etc.). **4** *intr.* (foll. by *along*) go along the coast, a wall, etc. □**skirt-dance** a dance with graceful manipulation of a full skirt. □□**skirted** *adj.* (also in *comb.*). **skirtless** *adj.* [ME f. ON *skyrta* shirt, corresp. to OE *scyrte*: see SHIRT]

skirting /ˈskɜːtɪŋ/ *n.* (in full **skirting-board**) *Brit.* a narrow board etc. along the bottom of the wall of a room.

skit¹ /skɪt/ *n.* (often foll. by *on*) a light, usu. short, piece of satire or burlesque. [rel. to *skit* move lightly and rapidly, perh. f. ON (cf. *skjóta* SHOOT)]

skit² /skɪt/ *n. colloq.* **1** a large number, a crowd. **2** (in *pl.*) heaps, lots. [20th c.: cf. SCADS]

skite /skaɪt/ *v. & n.* —*v.intr.* *Austral. & NZ colloq.* boast, brag. —*n.* **1** *Austral. & NZ colloq.* **a** a boaster. **b** boasting; boastfulness. **2** *Sc.* a drinking-bout; a spree (*on the skite*). [Sc. & N.Engl. dial., = a person regarded with contempt: cf. BLATHERSKITE]

skitter /ˈskɪtə(r)/ *v.intr.* (also **skeeter** /ˈskiːtə(r)/) **1**

a (usu. foll. by *along*, *across*) move lightly or hastily. **b** (usu. foll. by *about*, *off*) hurry about, dart off. **2** fish by drawing bait jerkily across the surface of the water. [app. frequent. of dial. *skite*, perh. formed as SKIT¹]

skittery /ˈskɪtərɪ/ *adj.* skittish, restless.

skittish /ˈskɪtɪʃ/ *adj.* **1** lively, playful. **2** (of a horse etc.) nervous, inclined to shy, fidgety. □□**skittishly** *adv.* **skittishness** *n.* [ME, perh. formed as SKIT¹]

skittle /ˈskɪt(ə)l/ *n. & v.* —*n.* **1** a pin used in the game of skittles. **2** (in *pl.*; usu. treated as *sing.*) **a** a game like ninepins played with usu. nine wooden pins set up at the end of an alley to be bowled down usu. with wooden balls or a wooden disc. **b** (in full **table skittles**) a game played with similar pins set up on a board to be knocked down by swinging a suspended ball. **c** *colloq.* chess not played seriously. —*v.tr.* (often foll. by *out*) *Cricket* get (batsmen) out in rapid succession. [17th c. (also *kittle-pins*): orig. unkn.]

skive /skaɪv/ *v. & n.* —*v.* **1** *tr.* split or pare (hides, leather, etc.). **2** *intr. Brit. sl.* **a** evade a duty, shirk. **b** (often foll. by *off*) avoid work by absenting oneself, play truant. —*n.* *sl.* **1** an instance of shirking. **2** an easy option. □□**skiver** *n.* [ON *skífa*, rel. to ME *schīve* slice]

skivvy /ˈskɪvɪ/ *n.* (*pl.* **-ies**) **1** *Brit. colloq. derog.* a female domestic servant. **2** *US* **a** thin high-necked long-sleeved garment. **b** (in *pl.*) underwear of vest and underpants. [20th c.: orig. unkn.]

skol /skɒl, skəʊl/ *n.* (also **skoal**) used as a toast in drinking. [Da. *skaal*, Sw. *skål*, f. ON *skál* bowl]

skua /ˈskjuːə/ *n.* any large predatory sea bird of the family Stercorariidae which pursues other birds and makes them disgorge the fish they have caught. [mod.L f. Faroese *skúgvur*, ON *skúfr*]

skulduggery /skʌlˈdʌgərɪ/ *n.* (also **sculduggery**, **skullduggery**) trickery; unscrupulous behaviour. [earlier *sculduddery*, orig. Sc. = unchastity (18th c.: orig. unkn.)]

skulk /skʌlk/ *v. & n.* —*v.intr.* **1** move stealthily, lurk, or keep oneself concealed, esp. in a cowardly or sinister way. **2** stay or sneak away in time of danger. **3** shirk duty. —*n.* **1** a person who skulks. **2** a company of foxes. □□**skulker** *n.* [ME f. Scand.: cf. Norw. *skulka* lurk, Da. *skulke*, Sw. *skolka* shirk]

skull /skʌl/ *n.* **1** the bony case of the brain of a vertebrate. **2 a** the part of the skeleton corresponding to the head. **b** this with the skin and soft internal parts removed. **c** a representation of this. **3** the head as the seat of intelligence. □**out of one's skull** *sl.* out of one's mind, crazy. **skull and crossbones** a representation of a skull with two thigh-bones crossed below it as an emblem of piracy or death. **skull session** *US sl.* a discussion or conference. □□ **skulled** *adj.* (also in *comb.*). [ME *scolle*: orig. unkn.]

skullcap /ˈskʌlkæp/ *n.* **1** a small close-fitting peakless cap. **2** the top part of the skull. **3** any plant of the genus *Scutellaria*, with helmet-shaped bilabiate flowers.

skunk /skʌŋk/ *n. & v.* —*n.* **1 a** any of various cat-sized flesh-eating mammals of the family Mustelidae, esp. *Mephitis mephitis* having a distinctive black and white striped fur and able to emit a powerful stench from a liquid secreted by its anal glands as a defence. **b** its fur. **2** *colloq.* a thoroughly contemptible person. —*v.tr.* **1** *US sl.* defeat. **2** fail to pay (a bill etc.). □**skunk-bear** *US* a wolverine. **skunk-cabbage** *US* a herbaceous plant, *Lysichiton americanum*, with an offensive-smelling spathe. [Amer. Ind. *segankw*, *segongw*]

sky /skaɪ/ *n. & v.* —*n.* (*pl.* **skies**) (in *sing.* or *pl.*) **1** the region of the atmosphere and outer space seen from the earth. **2** the weather or climate evidenced by this. —*v.tr.* (**skies**, **skied**) **1** *Cricket* etc. hit (a ball) high into the air. **2** hang (a picture) high on a wall. □**sky-blue** *adj. & n.* a bright clear blue. **sky-blue pink** an imaginary colour. **sky-clad** *sl.*

naked (esp. in witchcraft). **sky cloth** *Theatr.* a backcloth painted or coloured to represent the sky. **sky-high** *adv.* & *adj.* as if reaching the sky, very high. **the sky is the limit** there is practically no limit. **sky pilot** *sl.* a clergyman. **sky-rocket** *n.* a rocket exploding high in the air. —*v.intr.* (**-rocketed**, **-rocketing**) (esp. of prices etc.) rise very steeply or rapidly. **sky-shouting** the sending of messages from an aircraft to the ground by means of a loudspeaker. **sky-sign** an advertisement on the roof of a building. **sky wave** a radio wave reflected from the ionosphere. **sky-writing** legible smoke-trails made by an aeroplane esp. for advertising. **to the skies** very highly; without reserve (*praised to the skies*). **under the open sky** out of doors. □□ **skyey** *adj.* **skyless** *adj.* [ME *ski(es)* cloud(s) f. ON *ský*]

skydiving /ˈskaɪˌdaɪvɪŋ/ *n.* the sport of performing acrobatic manœuvres under free fall with a parachute. □□ **skydive** *v.intr.* **skydiver** *n.*

skyer /ˈskaɪə(r)/ *n.* (also **skier**) *Cricket* a high hit.

Skye terrier /skaɪ/ *n.* a small long-bodied short-legged long-haired slate or fawn coloured variety of Scotch terrier. [*Skye*, an island of the Inner Hebrides]

skyjack /ˈskaɪdʒæk/ *v.* & *n. sl.* —*v.tr.* hijack (an aircraft). —*n.* an act of skyjacking. □□ **skyjacker** *n.* [SKY + HIJACK]

skylark /ˈskaɪlɑːk/ *n.* & *v.* —*n.* a lark, *Alauda arvensis* of Eurasia and N. Africa, that sings while hovering in flight. —*v.intr.* play tricks or practical jokes, indulge in horseplay, frolic. [SKY + LARK¹: (v.) with pun on LARK¹, LARK²]

skylight /ˈskaɪlaɪt/ *n.* a window set in the plane of a roof or ceiling.

skyline /ˈskaɪlaɪn/ *n.* the outline of hills, buildings, etc., defined against the sky; the visible horizon.

skysail /ˈskaɪseɪl, -s(ə)l/ *n.* a light sail above the royal in a square-rigged ship.

skyscape /ˈskaɪskeɪp/ *n.* **1** a picture chiefly representing the sky. **2** a view of the sky.

skyscraper /ˈskaɪˌskreɪpə(r)/ *n.* a very tall building of many storeys.

skyward /ˈskaɪwəd/ *adv.* & *adj.* —*adv.* (also **skywards**) towards the sky. —*adj.* moving skyward.

skywatch /ˈskaɪwɒtʃ/ *n.* the activity of watching the sky for aircraft etc.

skyway /ˈskaɪweɪ/ *n.* **1** a route used by aircraft. **2** the sky as a medium of transport.

slab /slæb/ *n.* & *v.* —*n.* **1** a flat broad fairly thick usu. square or rectangular piece of solid material, esp. stone. **2** a large flat piece of cake, chocolate, etc. **3** (of timber) an outer piece sawn from a log. **4** *Brit.* a mortuary table. —*v.tr.* (**slabbed**, **slabbing**) remove slabs from (a log or tree) to prepare it for sawing into planks. [ME: orig. unkn.]

slack¹ /slæk/ *adj.*, *n.*, *v.*, & *adv.* —*adj.* **1** (of rope etc.) not taut. **2** inactive or sluggish. **3** negligent or remiss. **4** (of tide etc.) neither ebbing nor flowing. **5** (of trade or business or a market) with little happening. **6** loose. **7** *Phonet.* lax. **8** relaxed, languid. —*n.* **1** the slack part of a rope (*haul in the slack*). **2** a slack time in trade etc. **3** *colloq.* a spell of inactivity or laziness. **4** (in *pl.*) full-length loosely-cut trousers for informal wear. —*v.* **1 a** *tr.* & *intr.* slacken. **b** *tr.* loosen (rope etc.). **2** *intr. colloq.* take a rest, be lazy. **3** *tr.* slake (lime). —*adv.* **1** slackly. **2** slowly or insufficiently (*dry slack*; *bake slack*). □ **slack hand** lack of full control in riding or governing. **slack lime** slaked lime. **slack off 1** loosen. **2** lose or cause to lose vigour. **slack rein** = *slack hand*. **slack suit** *US* casual clothes of slacks and a jacket or shirt. **slack up** reduce the speed of a train etc. before stopping. **slack water** a time near the turn of the tide, esp. at low tide. **take up the slack** use up a surplus or make up a deficiency; avoid an undesirable lull. □□ **slackly** *adv.* **slackness** *n.* [OE *slæc* f. Gmc]

slack² /slæk/ *n.* coal-dust or small pieces of coal. [ME prob. f. LG or Du.]

slacken /ˈslækən/ *v.tr.* & *intr.* make or become slack. □ **slacken off** = *slack off* (see SLACK¹).

slacker /ˈslækə(r)/ *n.* a shirker; an indolent person.

slag /slæg/ *n.* & *v.* —*n.* **1** vitreous refuse left after ore has been smelted, dross separated in a fused state in the reduction of ore, clinkers. **2** volcanic scoria. **3** *sl. derog.* **a** a prostitute or promiscuous woman. **b** a worthless or insignificant person. —*v.* (**slagged**, **slagging**) **1** *intr.* **a** form slag. **b** cohere into a mass like slag. **2** *tr.* (often foll. by *off*) *sl.* criticize, insult. □ **slag-heap** a hill of refuse from a mine etc. **slag-wool** = *mineral wool*. □□ **slaggy** *adj.* (**slaggier**, **slaggiest**). [MLG *slagge*, perh. f. *slagen* strike, with ref. to fragments formed by hammering]

slain *past part.* of SLAY¹.

slainte /ˈslɑːntʃə/ *int.* a Gaelic toast: good health! [Gael. *sláinte*, lit. 'health']

slake /sleɪk/ *v.tr.* **1** assuage or satisfy (thirst, revenge, etc.). **2** disintegrate (quicklime) by chemical combination with water. [OE *slacian* f. *slæc* SLACK¹]

slalom /ˈslɑːləm/ *n.* **1** a ski-race down a zigzag course defined by artificial obstacles. **2** an obstacle race in canoes or cars or on skateboards or water-skis. [Norw., lit. 'sloping track']

slam¹ /slæm/ *v.* & *n.* —*v.* (**slammed**, **slamming**) **1** *tr.* & *intr.* shut forcefully and loudly. **2** *tr.* put down (an object) with a similar sound. **3** *intr.* move violently (*he slammed out of the room*). **4** *tr.* & *intr.* put or come into sudden action (*slam the brakes on*). **5** *tr. sl.* criticize severely. **6** *tr. sl.* hit. **7** *tr. sl.* gain an easy victory over. —*n.* **1** a sound of or as of a slammed door. **2** the shutting of a door etc. with a loud bang. **3** (usu. prec. by *the*) *US sl.* prison. [prob. f. Scand.: cf. ON *slam(b)ra*]

slam² /slæm/ *n. Cards* the winning of every trick in a game. □ **grand slam 1** *Bridge* the winning of 13 tricks. **2** the winning of all of a group of championships or matches in a sport. **small** (or **little**) **slam** *Bridge* the winning of 12 tricks. [orig. name of a card-game: perh. f. obs. *slampant* trickery]

slambang /slæmˈbæŋ/ *adv.* & *adj.* —*adv.* with the sound of a slam. —*adj. colloq.* impressive, exciting, or energetic.

slammer /ˈslæmə(r)/ *n.* (usu. prec. by *the*) *sl.* prison.

slander /ˈslɑːndə(r)/ *n.* & *v.* —*n.* **1** a malicious, false, and injurious statement spoken about a person. **2** the uttering of such statements; calumny. **3** *Law* false oral defamation (cf. LIBEL). —*v.tr.* utter slander about; defame falsely. □□ **slanderer** *n.* **slanderous** *adj.* **slanderously** *adv.* [ME *sclaundre* f. AF *esclaundre*, OF *esclandre* alt. f. *escandle* f. LL *scandalum*: see SCANDAL]

slang /slæŋ/ *n.* & *v.* —*n.* words, phrases, and uses that are regarded as very informal and are often restricted to special contexts or are peculiar to a specified profession, class, etc. (*racing slang*; *schoolboy slang*). —*v.* **1** *tr.* use abusive language to. **2** *intr.* use such language. □ **slanging-match** a prolonged exchange of insults. [18th-c. cant: orig. unkn.]

slangy /ˈslæŋɪ/ *adj.* (**slangier**, **slangiest**) **1** of the character of slang. **2** fond of using slang. □□ **slangily** *adv.* **slanginess** *n.*

slant /slɑːnt/ *v.*, *n.*, & *adj.* —*v.* **1** *intr.* slope; diverge from a line; lie or go obliquely to a vertical or horizontal line. **2** *tr.* cause to do this. **3** *tr.* (often as **slanted** *adj.*) present (information) from a particular angle esp. in a biased or unfair way. —*n.* **1** a slope; an oblique position. **2** a way of regarding a thing; a point of view, esp. a biased one. —*adj.* sloping, oblique. □ **on a** (or **the**) **slant** aslant. **slant-eyed** having slanting eyes. **slant height** the height of a cone from the vertex to the periphery of the base. [aphetic form of ASLANT: (v.) rel. to ME *slent* f. ON *sletta* dash, throw]

slantwise /ˈslɑːntwaɪz/ *adv.* aslant.

slap /slæp/ *n.*, *v.*, & *adv.* —*v.* (**slapped**, **slapping**) **1** *tr.* & *intr.* strike with the palm of the hand or a flat object, or so as to make a similar noise. **2** *tr.* lay forcefully (*slapped the money on the table*; *slapped a writ on the offender*). **3** *tr.* put hastily or carelessly (*slap some paint on the walls*). **4** *tr.* (often foll. by *down*) *colloq.* reprimand or snub. —*n.* **1** a blow with the palm of the hand or a flat object. **2** a slapping sound. —*adv.* **1** with the suddenness or effectiveness or true aim of a blow, suddenly, fully, directly (*ran slap into him*; *hit me slap in the eye*). **2** = slap-bang. □**slap and tickle** *Brit. colloq.* light-hearted amorous amusement. **slap-bang** violently, noisily, headlong. **slap-happy** *colloq.* **1** cheerfully casual or flippant. **2** punch-drunk. **slap in the face** a rebuff or affront. **slap on the back** *n.* congratulations. —*v.tr.* congratulate. **slap-up** esp. *Brit. colloq.* excellent, lavish; done regardless of expense (*slap-up meal*). [LG *slapp* (imit.)]

slapdash /ˈslæpdæʃ/ *adj. & adv.* —*adj.* hasty and careless. —*adv.* in a slapdash manner.

slapjack /ˈslæpdʒæk/ *n. US* a kind of pancake cooked on a griddle. [SLAP + JACK¹]

slapstick /ˈslæpstɪk/ *n.* **1** boisterous knockabout comedy. **2** a flexible divided lath used by a clown. [SLAP + STICK¹]

slash /slæʃ/ *v. & n.* —*v.* **1** *intr.* make a sweeping or random cut or cuts with a knife, sword, whip, etc. **2** *tr.* make such a cut or cuts at. **3** *tr.* make a long narrow gash or gashes in. **4** *tr.* reduce (prices etc.) drastically. **5** *tr.* censure vigorously. **6** *tr.* make (one's way) by slashing. **7** *tr.* **a** lash (a person etc.) with a whip. **b** crack (a whip). —*n.* **1 a** a slashing cut or stroke. **b** a wound or slit made by this. **2** an oblique stroke; a solidus. **3** *Brit. sl.* an act of urinating. **4** *US* debris resulting from the felling or destruction of trees. □**slash-and-burn** (of cultivation) in which vegetation is cut down, allowed to dry, and then burned off before seeds are planted. □□**slasher** *n.* [ME perh. f. OF *esclachier* break in pieces]

slashed /slæʃt/ *adj.* (of a sleeve etc.) having slits to show a lining or puffing of other material.

slashing /ˈslæʃɪŋ/ *adj.* vigorously incisive or effective.

slat /slæt/ *n.* a thin narrow piece of wood or plastic or metal, esp. used in an overlapping series as in a fence or Venetian blind. [ME *s(c)lat* f. OF *esclat* splinter etc. f. *esclater* split f. Rmc]

slate /sleɪt/ *n., v., & adj.* —*n.* **1** a fine-grained grey, green, or bluish-purple metamorphic rock easily split into flat smooth plates. **2** a piece of such a plate used as roofing-material. **3** a piece of such a plate used for writing on, usu. framed in wood. **4** the colour of slate. **5** *US* a list of nominees for office etc. —*v.tr.* **1** cover with slates esp. as roofing. **2** *Brit. colloq.* criticize severely; scold. **3** *US* make arrangements for (an event etc.). **4** *US* propose or nominate for office etc. —*adj.* made of slate. □**on the slate** *Brit.* recorded as a debt to be paid. **slate-blue** (or **-black**) a shade of blue (or black) occurring in slate. **slate-colour** a dark bluish or greenish grey. **slate-coloured** of this colour. **slate-grey** a shade of grey occurring in slate. **slate-pencil** a small rod of soft slate used for writing on slate. **wipe the slate clean** forgive or cancel the record of past offences. □□**slating** *n.* **slaty** *adj.* [ME *s(c)late* f. OF *esclate*, fem. form of *esclat* SLAT]

slater /ˈsleɪtə(r)/ *n.* **1** a person who slates roofs etc. **2** a woodlouse or similar crustacean.

slather /ˈslæðə(r)/ *n. & v.* —*n.* **1** (usu. in *pl.*) *US colloq.* a large amount. **2** (often **open slather**) *Austral. & NZ sl.* unrestricted scope for action. —*v.tr. US colloq.* **1** spread thickly. **2** squander. [19th c.: orig. unkn.]

slatted /ˈslætɪd/ *adj.* having slats.

slattern /ˈslæt(ə)n/ *n.* a slovenly woman. □□ **slatternly** *adj.* **slatternliness** *n.* [17th c.: rel. to *slattering* slovenly, f. dial. *slatter* to spill, slop, waste, frequent. of *slat* strike]

slaughter /ˈslɔːtə(r)/ *n. & v.* —*n.* **1** the killing of an animal or animals for food. **2** the killing of many persons or animals at once or continuously; carnage, massacre. —*v.tr.* **1** kill (people) in a ruthless manner or on a great scale. **2** kill for food, butcher. **3** *colloq.* defeat utterly. □□ **slaughterer** *n.* **slaughterous** *adj.* [ME *slahter* ult. f. ON *slátr* butcher's meat, rel. to SLAY¹]

slaughterhouse /ˈslɔːtəˌhaʊs/ *n.* **1** a place for the slaughter of animals as food. **2** a place of carnage.

Slav /slɑːv/ *n. & adj.* —*n.* a member of a group of peoples in Central and Eastern Europe speaking Slavonic languages. —*adj.* **1** of or relating to the Slavs. **2** Slavonic. □□ **Slavism** *n.* [ME *Sclave* f. med.L *Sclavus*, late Gk *Sklabos*, & f. med.L *Slavus*]

slave /sleɪv/ *n. & v.* —*n.* **1** a person who is the legal property of another or others and is bound to absolute obedience, a human chattel. **2** a drudge, a person working very hard. **3** (foll. by *of, to*) a helpless victim of some dominating influence (*slave of fashion*; *slave to duty*). **4** a machine, or part of one, directly controlled by another. —*v.* **1** *intr.* (often foll. by *at, over*) work very hard. **2** *tr.* (foll. by *to*) subject (a device) to control by another. □**slave-bangle** a bangle of gold, glass, etc., worn by a woman usu. above the elbow. **slave-born** born in slavery, born of slave parents. **slave-bracelet** = *slave-bangle*. **slave-drive** (*past* **-drove**; *past part.* **-driven**) work (a person) hard, esp. excessively. **slave-driver 1** an overseer of slaves at work. **2** a person who works others hard. **slave labour** forced labour. **slave ship** *hist.* a ship transporting slaves, esp. from Africa. **Slave State** *hist.* any of the southern States of the US in which slavery was legal before the Civil War. **slave-trade** *hist.* the procuring, transporting, and selling of human beings, esp. African Blacks, as slaves. **slave-trader** *hist.* a person engaged in the slave-trade. [ME f. OF *esclave* = med.L *sclavus*, *sclava* Slav (captive): see SLAV]

slaver¹ /ˈsleɪvə(r)/ *n. hist.* a ship or person engaged in the slave-trade.

slaver² /ˈslævə(r)/ *n. & v.* —*n.* **1** saliva running from the mouth. **2 a** fulsome or servile flattery. **b** drivel, nonsense. —*v.intr.* **1** let saliva run from the mouth, dribble. **2** (foll. by *over*) show excessive sentimentality over, or desire for. [ME prob. f. LG or Du.: cf. SLOBBER]

slavery /ˈsleɪvərɪ/ *n.* **1** the condition of a slave. **2** exhausting labour; drudgery. **3** the custom of having slaves.

slavey /ˈsleɪvɪ/ *n.* (*pl.* **-eys**) *colloq.* a maidservant, esp. a hard-worked one.

Slavic /ˈslɑːvɪk/ *adj. & n.* = SLAVONIC.

slavish /ˈsleɪvɪʃ/ *adj.* **1** of, like, or as of slaves. **2** showing no attempt at originality or development. **3** abject, servile, base. □□ **slavishly** *adv.* **slavishness** *n.*

Slavonic /sləˈvɒnɪk/ *adj. & n.* —*adj.* **1** of or relating to the group of Indo-European languages including Russian, Polish, and Czech. **2** of or relating to the Slavs. —*n.* the Slavonic language-group. □**Old Church Slavonic** the earliest written Slavonic language, surviving as a liturgical language in the Orthodox Church. [med.L *S(c)lavonicus* f. *S(c)lavonia* country of Slavs f. *Sclavus* SLAV]

slaw /slɔː/ *n.* coleslaw. [Du. *sla*, shortened f. *salade* SALAD]

slay¹ /sleɪ/ *v.tr.* (*past* **slew** /sluː/; *past part.* **slain** /sleɪn/) **1** *literary* or *joc.* kill. **2** *sl.* overwhelm with delight; convulse with laughter. □□ **slayer** *n.* [OE *slēan* f. Gmc]

slay² var. of SLEY.

SLBM *abbr.* submarine-launched ballistic missile.

SLD *abbr.* (in the UK) Social and Liberal Democrats. ¶ In 1989 officially replaced by *Liberal Democrats*.

sleaze /sliːz/ *n. & v. colloq.* —*n.* **1** sleaziness. **2** a person of low moral standards. —*v.intr.* move in a sleazy fashion. [back-form. f. SLEAZY]

sleazy /ˈsliːzɪ/ *adj.* (**sleazier, sleaziest**) **1** squalid, tawdry. **2** slatternly. **3** (of textiles etc.) flimsy. □□ **sleazily** adv. **sleaziness** n. [17th c.: orig. unkn.]

sled /sled/ n. & v. US —n. a sledge. —v.intr. (**sledded**, **sledding**) ride on a sledge. [MLG *sledde*, rel. to SLIDE]

sledge[1] /sledʒ/ n. & v. —n. **1** a vehicle with runners for conveying loads or passengers esp. over snow, drawn by horses, dogs, or reindeer or pushed or pulled by one or more persons. **2** a toboggan. —v.intr. & tr. travel or convey by sledge. [MDu. *sleedse*, rel. to SLED]

sledge[2] /sledʒ/ n. = SLEDGEHAMMER.

sledgehammer /ˈsledʒˌhæmə(r)/ n. **1** a large heavy hammer used to break stone etc. **2** (attrib.) heavy or powerful (a *sledgehammer blow*). [OE *slecg*, rel. to SLAY[1]]

sleek /sliːk/ adj. & v. —adj. **1** (of hair, fur, or skin, or an animal or person with such hair etc.) smooth and glossy. **2** looking well-fed and comfortable. **3** ingratiating. **4** (of a thing) smooth and polished. —v.tr. make sleek, esp. by stroking or pressing down. □□ **sleekly** adv. **sleekness** n. **sleeky** adj. [later var. of SLICK]

sleep /sliːp/ n. & v. —n. **1** a condition of body and mind such as that which normally recurs for several hours every night, in which the nervous system is inactive, the eyes closed, the postural muscles relaxed, and consciousness practically suspended. **2** a period of sleep (*shall try to get a sleep*). **3** a state like sleep, such as rest, quiet, negligence, or death. **4** the prolonged inert condition of hibernating animals. **5** a substance found in the corners of the eyes after sleep. —v. (*past* and *past part.* **slept** /slept/) **1** intr. **a** be in a state of sleep. **b** fall asleep. **2** intr. (foll. by *at*, *in*, etc.) spend the night. **3** tr. provide sleeping accommodation for (*the house sleeps six*). **4** intr. (foll. by *with*, *together*) have sexual intercourse, esp. in bed. **5** intr. (foll. by *on*, *over*) not decide (a question) until the next day. **6** intr. (foll. by *through*) fail to be woken by. **7** intr. be inactive or dormant. **8** intr. be dead; lie in the grave. **9** tr. **a** (foll. by *off*) remedy by sleeping (*slept off his hangover*). **b** (foll. by *away*) spend in sleeping (*sleep the hours away*). **10** intr. (of a top) spin so steadily as to seem motionless. □**get to sleep** manage to fall asleep. **go to sleep 1** enter a state of sleep. **2** (of a limb) become numbed by pressure. **in one's sleep** while asleep. **last sleep** death. **let sleeping dogs lie** avoid stirring up trouble. **put to sleep 1** anaesthetize. **2** kill (an animal) painlessly. **sleep around** colloq. be sexually promiscuous. **sleep in 1** remain asleep later than usual in the morning. **2** sleep by night at one's place of work. **sleeping-bag** a lined or padded bag to sleep in esp. when camping etc. **Sleeping Beauty** a fairy-tale heroine who slept for 100 years. **sleeping-car** (or **-carriage**) a railway coach provided with beds or berths. **sleeping-draught** a drink to induce sleep. **sleeping partner** a partner not sharing in the actual work of a firm. **sleeping-pill** a pill to induce sleep. **sleeping policeman** a ramp etc. in the road intended to cause traffic to reduce speed. **sleeping sickness** any of several tropical diseases with extreme lethargy caused by a trypanosome transmitted by a tsetse-fly bite. **sleeping-suit** a child's one-piece night-garment. **sleep-learning** learning by hearing while asleep. **sleep like a log** (or **top**) sleep soundly. **the sleep of the just** sound sleep. **sleep out** sleep by night out of doors, or not at one's place of work. **sleep-out** n. Austral. & NZ a veranda, porch, or outbuilding providing sleeping accommodation. [OE *slēp*, *slæp* (n.), *slēpan*, *slæpan* (v.) f. Gmc]

sleeper /ˈsliːpə(r)/ n. **1** a person or animal that sleeps. **2** Brit. a wooden or concrete beam laid horizontally as a support, esp. for railway track. **3 a** a sleeping-car. **b** a berth in this. **4** Brit. a ring worn in a pierced ear to keep the hole from closing. **5** a thing that is suddenly successful after being undistinguished. **6** a

sleeping-suit. **7** a spy or saboteur etc. who remains inactive while establishing a secure position.

sleepless /ˈsliːplɪs/ adj. **1** characterized by lack of sleep (a *sleepless night*). **2** unable to sleep. **3** continually active or moving. □□ **sleeplessly** adv. **sleeplessness** n.

sleepwalk /ˈsliːpwɔːk/ v.intr. walk or perform other actions while asleep. □□ **sleepwalker** n.

sleepy /ˈsliːpɪ/ adj. (**sleepier**, **sleepiest**) **1** drowsy; ready for sleep; about to fall asleep. **2** lacking activity or bustle (a *sleepy little town*). **3** habitually indolent, unobservant, etc. □**sleepy sickness** encephalitis lethargica, an infection of the brain with drowsiness and sometimes a coma. □□ **sleepily** adv. **sleepiness** n.

sleepyhead /ˈsliːpɪˌhed/ n. (esp. as a form of address) a sleepy or inattentive person.

sleet /sliːt/ n. & v. —n. **1** a mixture of snow and rain falling together. **2** hail or snow melting as it falls. **3** US a thin coating of ice. —v.intr. (prec. by *it* as subject) sleet falls (*it is sleeting*; *if it sleets*). □□ **sleety** adj. [ME prob. f. OE: rel. to MLG *slōten* (pl.) hail, MHG *slōz(e)* f. Gmc]

sleeve /sliːv/ n. **1** the part of a garment that wholly or partly covers an arm. **2** the cover of a gramophone record. **3** a tube enclosing a rod or smaller tube. **4 a** a wind-sock. **b** a drogue towed by an aircraft. □**roll up one's sleeves** prepare to fight or work. **sleeve-board** a small ironing-board for pressing sleeves. **sleeve-coupling** a tube for connecting shafts or pipes. **sleeve-link** a cuff-link. **sleeve-note** a descriptive note on a record-sleeve. **sleeve-nut** a long nut with right-hand and left-hand screw-threads for drawing together pipes or shafts conversely threaded. **sleeve-valve** a valve in the form of a cylinder with a sliding movement. **up one's sleeve** concealed but ready for use, in reserve. □□ **sleeved** adj. (also in comb.). **sleeveless** adj. [OE *slēfe*, *slīefe*, *slȳf*]

sleeving /ˈsliːvɪŋ/ n. tubular covering for electric cable etc.

sleigh /sleɪ/ n. & v. —n. a sledge, esp. one for riding on. —v.intr. travel on a sleigh. □**sleigh-bell** any of a number of tinkling bells attached to the harness of a sleigh-horse etc. [orig. US, f. Du. *slee*, rel. to SLED]

sleight /slaɪt/ n. archaic **1** a deceptive trick or device or movement. **2** dexterity. **3** cunning. □**sleight of hand 1** dexterity esp. in conjuring or fencing. **2** a display of dexterity, esp. a conjuring trick. [ME *sleghth* f. ON *slœgth* f. *slœgr* SLY]

slender /ˈslendə(r)/ adj. (**slenderer**, **slenderest**) **1 a** of small girth or breadth (a *slender pillar*). **b** gracefully thin (a *slender waist*). **2** relatively small or scanty; slight, meagre, inadequate (*slender hopes*; *slender resources*). □**slender loris** see LORIS. □□ **slenderly** adv. **slenderness** n. [ME: orig. unkn.]

slenderize /ˈslendəˌraɪz/ v. (also **-ise**) **1** tr. **a** make (a thing) slender. **b** make (one's figure) appear slender. **2** intr. make oneself slender; slim.

slept past and past part. of SLEEP.

sleuth /sluːθ/ n. & v. colloq. —n. a detective. —v. **1** intr. act as a detective. **2** tr. investigate. □**sleuth-hound 1** a bloodhound. **2** colloq. a detective, an investigator. [orig. in *sleuth-hound*: ME f. *sleuth* f. ON *slóth* track, trail: cf. SLOT[2]]

slew[1] /sluː/ v. & n. (also **slue**) —v.tr. & intr. (often foll. by *round*) turn or swing forcibly or with effort out of the forward or ordinary position. —n. such a change of position. [18th-c. Naut.: orig. unkn.]

slew[2] past of SLAY[1].

slew[3] /sluː/ n. esp. US colloq. a large number or quantity. [Ir. *sluagh*]

sley /sleɪ/ n. (also **slay**) a weaver's reed. [OE *slege*, rel. to SLAY[1]]

slice /slaɪs/ n. & v. —n. **1** a thin broad piece or wedge cut off or out esp. from meat or bread or a cake, pie, or large fruit. **2** a share; a part taken or allotted or gained (a *slice of territory*; a *slice of the* profits). **3** an implement with a broad flat blade for serving fish etc. or for scraping or chipping. **4** *Golf & Lawn Tennis* a slicing stroke. —*v.* **1** *tr.* (often foll. by *up*) cut into slices. **2** *tr.* (foll. by *off*) cut (a piece) off. **3** *intr.* (foll. by *into*, *through*) cut with or like a knife. **4** (also *absol.*) a *Golf* strike (the ball) so that it deviates away from the striker. **b** (in other sports) propel (the ball) forward at an angle. **5** *tr.* go through (air etc.) with a cutting motion. □**slice of life** a realistic representation of everyday experience. □□ **sliceable** *adj.* **slicer** *n.* (also in *comb.*). [ME f. OF *esclice*, *esclicier* splinter f. Frank. *slītjan*, rel. to SLIT]

slick /slɪk/ *adj.*, *n.*, & *v.* —*adj.* *colloq.* **1 a** (of a person or action) skilful or efficient; dextrous (*gave a slick performance*). **b** superficially or pretentiously smooth and dextrous. **c** glib. **2 a** sleek, smooth. **b** slippery. —*n.* **1** a smooth patch of oil etc., esp. on the sea. **2** *Motor Racing* a smooth tyre. **3** *US* a glossy magazine. **4** *US sl.* a slick person. —*v.tr. colloq.* **1** make sleek or smart. **2** (usu. foll. by *down*) flatten (one's hair etc.). □□ **slickly** *adv.* **slickness** *n.* [ME *slike(n)*, prob. f. OE: cf. SLEEK]

slicker /'slɪkə(r)/ *n.* *US* **1** *colloq.* **a** a plausible rogue. **b** a smart and sophisticated city-dweller (cf. *city slicker*). **2** a raincoat of smooth material.

slide /slaɪd/ *v.* & *n.* —*v.* (*past* and *past part.* **slid** /slɪd/) **1 a** *intr.* move along a smooth surface with continuous contact on the same part of the thing moving (cf. ROLL). **b** *tr.* cause to do this (*slide the drawer into place*). **2** *intr.* move quietly; glide; go smoothly along. **3** *intr.* pass gradually or imperceptibly. **4** *intr.* glide over ice on one or both feet without skates (under gravity or with momentum got by running). **5** *intr.* (foll. by *over*) barely touch upon (a delicate subject etc.). **6** *intr.* & *tr.* (often foll. by *into*) move or cause to move quietly or unobtrusively (*slid his hand into mine*). **7** *intr.* take its own course (*let it slide*). —*n.* **1 a** the act or an instance of sliding. **b** a rapid decline. **2** an inclined plane down which children, goods, etc., slide; a chute. **3 a** a track made by or for sliding, esp. on ice. **b** a slope prepared with snow or ice for tobogganing. **4** a part of a machine or instrument that slides, esp. a slide-valve. **5 a** a thing slid into place, esp. a piece of glass holding an object for a microscope. **b** a mounted transparency usu. placed in a projector for viewing on a screen. **6** *Brit.* = *hair-slide*. **7** a part or parts of a machine on or between which a sliding part works. □**let things slide** be negligent; allow deterioration. **slide fastener** *US* a zip-fastener. **slide-rule** a ruler with a sliding central strip, graduated logarithmically for making rapid calculations, esp. multiplication and division. **slide-valve** a sliding piece that opens and closes an aperture by sliding across it. **sliding door** a door drawn across an aperture on a slide, not turning on hinges. **sliding keel** *Naut.* a centreboard. **sliding roof** a part of a roof (esp. in a motor car) made able to slide and so form an aperture. **sliding scale** a scale of fees, taxes, wages, etc., that varies as a whole in accordance with variation of some standard. **sliding seat** a seat able to slide to and fro on runners etc., esp. in a racing-boat to adjust the length of a stroke. □□ **slidable** *adj.* **slidably** *adv.* **slider** *n.* [OE *slīdan*]

slideway /'slaɪdweɪ/ *n.* = SLIDE *n.* 7.

slight /slaɪt/ *adj.*, *v.*, & *n.* —*adj.* **1 a** inconsiderable; of little significance (*has a slight cold*; *the damage is very slight*). **b** barely perceptible (*a slight smell of gas*). **c** not much or great or thorough, inadequate, scanty (*a conclusion based on very slight observation*; *paid him slight attention*). **2** slender, frail-looking (*saw a slight figure approaching*; *supported by a slight framework*). **3** (in *superl.*, with *neg.* or *interrog.*) any whatever (*paid not the slightest attention*). —*v.tr.* **1** treat or speak of (a person etc.) as not worth attention, fail in courtesy or respect towards; markedly neglect. **2** *hist.* make militarily useless, raze (a fortification etc.). —*n.* a marked piece of

neglect, a failure to show due respect. □**not in the slightest** not at all. **put a slight upon** = sense 1 of *v.* □□ **slightingly** *adv.* **slightish** *adj.* **slightly** *adv.* **slightness** *n.* [ME *slyght*, *sleght* f. ON *sléttr* level, smooth f. Gmc]

slily var. of SLYLY (see SLY).

slim /slɪm/ *adj.*, *v.*, & *n.* —*adj.* (**slimmer, slimmest**) **1 a** of small girth or thickness, of long narrow shape. **b** gracefully thin, slenderly built. **c** not fat or overweight. **2** small, insufficient (*a slim chance of success*). **3** clever, artful, crafty, unscrupulous. —*v.* (**slimmed, slimming**) **1** *intr.* make oneself slimmer by dieting, exercise, etc. **2** *tr.* make slim or slimmer. —*n.* a course of slimming. □□ **slimly** *adv.* **slimmer** *n.* **slimming** *n.* & *adj.* **slimmish** *adj.* **slimness** *n.* [LG or Du. f. Gmc]

slime /slaɪm/ *n.* & *v.* —*n.* thick slippery mud or a substance of similar consistency, e.g. liquid bitumen or a mucus exuded by fish etc. —*v.tr.* cover with slime. □**slime mould** a spore-bearing microorganism secreting slime. [OE *slīm* f. Gmc, rel. to L *limus* mud, Gk *limnē* marsh]

slimline /'slɪmlaɪn/ *adj.* of slender design.

slimy /'slaɪmɪ/ *adj.* (**slimier, slimiest**) **1** of the consistency of slime. **2** covered, smeared with, or full of slime. **3** disgustingly dishonest, meek, or flattering. **4** slippery, hard to hold. □□ **slimily** *adv.* **sliminess** *n.*

sling[1] /slɪŋ/ *n.* & *v.* —*n.* **1 a** a strap, belt, etc., used to support or raise a hanging weight, e.g. a rifle, a ship's boat, or goods being transferred. **2** a bandage looped round the neck to support an injured arm. **3** a strap or string used with the hand to give impetus to a small missile, esp. a stone. **4** *Austral. sl.* a tip or bribe. —*v.tr.* (*past* and *past part.* **slung** /slʌŋ/) **1** (also *absol.*) hurl (a stone etc.) from a sling. **2** *colloq.* throw. **3** suspend with a sling, allow to swing suspended, arrange so as to be supported from above, hoist or transfer with a sling. □**sling-back 1** a shoe held in place by a strap above the heel. **2** (in full **sling-back chair**) a chair with a fabric seat suspended from a rigid frame. **sling-bag** a bag with a long strap which may be hung from the shoulder. **sling one's hook** see HOOK. **sling off at** *Austral.* & *NZ sl.* disparage; mock; make fun of. **slung shot** a metal ball attached by a thong etc. to the wrist and used esp. by criminals as a weapon. [ME, prob. f. ON *slyngva* (v.)]

sling[2] /slɪŋ/ *n.* a sweetened drink of spirits (esp. gin) and water. [18th c.: orig. unkn.]

slinger /'slɪŋə(r)/ *n.* a person who slings, esp. the user of a sling.

slingshot /'slɪŋʃɒt/ *n.* *US* a catapult.

slink[1] /slɪŋk/ *v.intr.* (*past* and *past part.* **slunk** /slʌŋk/) (often foll. by *off*, *away*, *by*) move in a stealthy or guilty or sneaking manner. [OE *slincan* crawl]

slink[2] /slɪŋk/ *v.* & *n.* —*v.tr.* (also *absol.*) (of an animal) produce (young) prematurely. —*n.* **1** an animal, esp. a calf, so born. **2** its flesh. [app. f. SLINK[1]]

slinky /'slɪŋkɪ/ *adj.* (**slinkier, slinkiest**) **1** stealthy. **2** (of a garment) close-fitting and flowing, sinuous. **3** gracefully slender. □□ **slinkily** *adv.* **slinkiness** *n.*

slip[1] /slɪp/ *v.* & *n.* —*v.* (**slipped, slipping**) **1** *intr.* slide unintentionally esp. for a short distance; lose one's footing or balance or place by unintended sliding. **2** *intr.* go or move with a sliding motion (*as the door closes the catch slips into place*; *slipped into her nightdress*). **3** *intr.* escape restraint or capture by being slippery or hard to hold or by not being grasped (*the eel slipped through his fingers*). **4** *intr.* make one's or its way unobserved or quietly or quickly (*just slip across to the baker's*; *errors will slip in*). **5** *intr.* **a** make a careless or casual mistake. **b** fall below the normal standard, deteriorate, lapse. **6** *tr.* insert or transfer stealthily or casually or with a sliding motion (*slipped a coin into his hand*; *slipped the papers into his pocket*). **7** *tr.* **a** release from restraint (*slipped the greyhounds from the leash*). **b** detach (an anchor) from a ship. **c** *Brit*. detach (a carriage) from a moving train. **d** release (the clutch of a motor vehicle) for a moment. **e** (of an animal) produce (young) prematurely. **8** *tr*. move (a stitch) to the other needle without knitting it. **9** *tr*. (foll. by *on*, *off*) pull (a garment) hastily on or off. **10** *tr*. escape from; give the slip to (*the dog slipped its collar*; *point slipped my mind*). —*n*. **1** the act or an instance of slipping. **2** an accidental or slight error. **3** a loose covering or garment, esp. a petticoat or pillowcase. **4 a** a reduction in the movement of a pulley etc. due to slipping of the belt. **b** a reduction in the distance travelled by a ship or aircraft arising from the nature of the medium in which its propeller revolves. **5** (in *sing*. or *pl*.) **a** an artificial slope of stone etc. on which boats are landed. **b** an inclined structure on which ships are built or repaired. **6** *Cricket* **a** a fielder stationed for balls glancing off the bat to the off side. **b** (in *sing*. or *pl*.) the position of such a fielder (*caught in the slips*; *caught at slip*). **7** a leash to slip dogs. □**give a person the slip** escape from or evade him or her. **let slip 1** release accidentally or deliberately, esp. from a leash. **2** miss (an opportunity). **3** utter inadvertently. **let slip the dogs of war** *poet*. open hostilities. **let slip through one's fingers 1** lose hold of. **2** miss the opportunity of having. **slip away** depart without leave-taking etc. **slip-carriage** *Brit*. a railway carriage on an express for detaching at a station where the rest of the train does not stop. **slip-case** a close-fitting case for a book. **slip-coach** *Brit*. = *slip-carriage*. **slip-cover 1 a** a calico etc. cover for furniture out of use. **b** *US* = *loose cover*. **2** a jacket or slip-case for a book. **slip form** a mould in which a structure of uniform cross-section is cast by filling it with concrete and continually moving and refilling it. **slip-hook** a hook with a contrivance for releasing it readily when necessary. **slip-knot 1** a knot that can be undone by a pull. **2** a running knot. **slip off** depart without leave-taking etc. **slip of the pen** (or **tongue**) a small mistake in which something is written (or said) unintentionally. **slip-on** *adj*. (of shoes or clothes) that can be easily slipped on and off. —*n*. a slip-on shoe or garment. **slip-over** (of a garment) to be slipped on over the head. **slipped disc** a disc between vertebrae that has become displaced and causes lumbar pain. **slip-ring** a ring for sliding contact in a dynamo or electric motor. **slip-road** *Brit*. a road for entering or leaving a motorway etc. **slip-rope** *Naut*. a rope with both ends on board so that casting loose either end frees the ship from her moorings. **slip sheet** *Printing* a sheet of paper placed between newly printed sheets to prevent set-off or smudging. **slip something over on** *colloq*. outwit. **slip-stitch** *n*. **1** a loose stitch joining layers of fabric and not visible externally. **2** a stitch moved to the other needle without being knitted. —*v.tr*. sew with slip-stitch. **slip up** *colloq*. make a mistake. **slip-up** *n*. *colloq*. a mistake, a blunder. **there's many a slip 'twixt cup and lip** nothing is certain till it has happened. [ME prob. f. MLG *slippen*: cf. SLIPPERY]

slip² /slɪp/ *n*. **1 a** a small piece of paper esp. for writing on. **b** a long narrow strip of thin wood, paper, etc. **c** a printer's proof on such paper; a galley proof. **2** a cutting taken from a plant for grafting or planting, a scion. □**slip of a** small and slim (*a slip of a girl*). [ME, prob. f. MDu., MLG *slippe* cut, strip, etc.]

slip³ /slɪp/ *n*. clay in a creamy mixture with water, used mainly for decorating earthenware. □**slip casting** the manufacture of ceramic ware by allowing slip to solidify in a mould. **slip-ware** decorated with slip. [OE *slipa*, *slyppe* slime: cf. COWSLIP]

slipover /'slɪp,əʊvə(r)/ *n*. a pullover, usu. without sleeves.

slippage /'slɪpɪdʒ/ *n*. **1** the act or an instance of slipping. **2 a** a decline, esp. in popularity or value. **b** failure to meet a deadline or fulfil a promise; delay.

slipper /'slɪpə(r)/ *n*. & *v*. —*n*. **1** a light loose comfortable indoor shoe. **2** a light slip-on shoe for dancing etc. —*v.tr*. beat or strike with a slipper. □**slipper bath** *Brit*. a bath shaped like a slipper, with a covered end. □□**slippered** *adj*.

slipperwort /'slɪpə,wɜːt/ *n*. calceolaria.

slippery /'slɪpərɪ/ *adj*. **1** difficult to hold firmly because of smoothness, wetness, sliminess, or elusive motion. **2** (of a surface) difficult to stand on, causing slips by its smoothness or muddiness. **3** unreliable, unscrupulous, shifty. **4** (of a subject) requiring tactful handling. □**slippery elm 1** the N. American red elm, *Ulmus fulva*. **2** the medicinal inner bark of this. **slippery slope** a course leading to disaster. □□ **slipperily** *adv*. **slipperiness** *n*. [prob. coined by Coverdale (1535) after Luther's *schlipfferig*, MHG *slipferig* f. *slipfern*, *slipfen* f. Gmc: partly f. *slipper* slippery (now dial.) f. OE *slipor* f. Gmc]

slippy /'slɪpɪ/ *adj*. (**slippier**, **slippiest**) *colloq*. slippery. □**look** (or **be**) **slippy** *Brit*. look sharp; make haste. □□ **slippiness** *n*.

slipshod /'slɪpʃɒd/ *adj*. **1** (of speech or writing, a speaker or writer, a method of work, etc.) careless, unsystematic; loose in arrangement. **2** slovenly. **3** having shoes down at heel.

slipstream /'slɪpstriːm/ *n*. & *v*. —*n*. **1** a current of air or water driven back by a revolving propeller or a moving vehicle. **2** an assisting force regarded as drawing something along with or behind something else. —*v.tr*. **1** follow closely behind (another vehicle). **2** pass after travelling in another's slipstream.

slipway /'slɪpweɪ/ *n*. a slip for building ships or landing boats.

slit /slɪt/ *n*. & *v*. —*n*. **1** a long straight narrow incision. **2** a long narrow opening comparable to a cut. —*v.tr*. (**slitting**; *past* and *past part*. **slit**) **1** make a slit in; cut or tear lengthwise. **2** cut into strips. □**slit-eyed** having long narrow eyes. **slit-pocket** a pocket with a vertical opening giving access to the pocket or to a garment beneath. **slit trench** a narrow trench for a soldier or a weapon. □□ **slitter** *n*. [ME *slitte*, rel. to OE *slītan*, f. Gmc]

slither /'slɪðə(r)/ *v*. & *n*. —*v.intr*. slide unsteadily; go with an irregular slipping motion. —*n*. an instance of slithering. □□ **slithery** *adj*. [ME var. of *slidder* (now dial.) f. *slid(e)rian* frequent. f. *slid-*, weak grade of *slīdan* SLIDE]

slitty /'slɪtɪ/ *adj*. (**slittier**, **slittiest**) (of the eyes) long and narrow.

sliver /'slɪvə(r), 'slaɪvə(r)/ *n*. & *v*. —*n*. **1** a long thin piece cut or split off. **2** a piece of wood torn from a tree or from timber. **3** a splinter, esp. from an exploded shell. **4** a strip of loose textile fibres after carding. —*v.tr*. & *intr*. **1** break off as a sliver. **2** break up into slivers. **3** form into slivers. [ME, rel. to *slive* cleave (now dial.) f. Gmc]

slivovitz /'slɪvəvɪts/ *n*. a plum brandy made esp. in Yugoslavia and Romania. [Serbo-Croat *šljivovica* f. *šljiva* plum]

Sloane /sləʊn/ *n*. (in full **Sloane Ranger**) *Brit*. *sl*. a fashionable and conventional upper-class young person, esp. living in London. □□ **Sloaney** *adj*. [*Sloane* Square, London + Lone *Ranger*, a cowboy hero]

slob /slɒb/ *n*. **1** *colloq*. a stupid, careless, coarse, or fat person. **2** *Ir*. muddy land. □□ **slobbish** *adj*. [Ir. *slab* mud f. E *slab* ooze, sludge, prob. f. Scand.]

slobber /'slɒbə(r)/ *v*. & *n*. —*v.intr*. **1** slaver. **2** (foll. by *over*) show excessive sentiment. —*n*. saliva running from the mouth; slaver. □□ **slobbery** *adj*. [ME, = Du. *slobbern*, of imit. orig.]

sloe /sləʊ/ *n*. **1** = BLACKTHORN. **2** its small bluish-black fruit with a sharp sour taste. □**sloe-eyed 1** having eyes of this colour. **2** slant-eyed. **sloe-gin** a liqueur of sloes steeped in gin. [OE *slā(h)* f. Gmc]

slog /slɒg/ *v*. & *n*. —*v*. (**slogged**, **slogging**) **1** *intr*. &

tr. hit hard and usu. wildly esp. in boxing or at cricket. **2** *intr.* (often foll. by *away, on*) walk or work doggedly. —*n.* **1** a hard random hit. **2 a** a hard steady work. **b** a spell of this. ▫▫ **slogger** *n.* [19th c.: orig. unkn.: cf. SLUG²]

slogan /ˈsləʊgən/ *n.* **1** a short catchy phrase used in advertising etc. **2** a party cry; a watchword or motto. **3** *hist.* a Scottish Highland war-cry. [Gael. *sluagh-ghairm* f. *sluagh* army + *gairm* shout]

sloop /sluːp/ *n.* **1** a small one-masted fore-and-aft-rigged vessel with mainsail and jib. **2** (in full **sloop of war**) *Brit. hist.* a small warship with guns on the upper deck only. ▫ **sloop-rigged** rigged like a sloop. [Du. *sloep(e)*, of unkn. orig.]

sloosh /sluːʃ/ *n.* & *v. colloq.* —*n.* a pouring or pouring sound of water. —*v.intr.* **1** flow with a rush. **2** make a heavy splashing or rushing noise. [imit.]

sloot /sluːt/ *n.* (also **sluit**) *S.Afr.* a deep gully formed by heavy rain. [Afrik. f. Du. *sloot* ditch]

slop¹ /slɒp/ *v.* & *n.* —*v.* (**slopped, slopping**) **1** (often foll. by *over*) **a** *intr.* spill or flow over the edge of a vessel. **b** *tr.* allow to do this. **2** *tr.* make (the floor, clothes, etc.) wet or messy by slopping, spill or splash liquid on. **3** *intr.* (usu. foll. by *over*) gush; be effusive or maudlin. —*n.* **1** a quantity of liquid spilled or splashed. **2** weakly sentimental language. **3** (in *pl.*) waste liquid, esp. dirty water or the waste contents of kitchen, bedroom, or prison vessels. **4** (in *sing.* or *pl.*) unappetizing weak liquid food. **5** *Naut.* a choppy sea. ▫ **slop about** move about in a slovenly manner. **slop-basin** *Brit.* a basin for the dregs of cups at table. **slop out** carry slops out (in prison etc.). **slop-pail** a pail for removing bedroom or kitchen slops. [earlier sense 'slush', prob. rel. to *slyppe*: cf. COWSLIP]

slop² /slɒp/ *n.* **1** a workman's loose outer garment. **2** (in *pl.*) ready-made or cheap clothing. **3** (in *pl.*) clothes and bedding supplied to sailors in the navy. **4** (in *pl.*) *archaic* wide baggy trousers esp. as worn by sailors. [ME: cf. OE *oferslop* surplice f. Gmc]

slope /sləʊp/ *n.* & *v.* —*n.* **1** an inclined position or direction; a state in which one end or side is at a higher level than another; a position in a line neither parallel nor perpendicular to level ground or to a line serving as a standard. **2** a piece of rising or falling ground. **3 a** a difference in level between the two ends or sides of a thing (*a slope of 5 metres*). **b** the rate at which this increases with distance etc. **4** a place for skiing on the side of a hill or mountain. **5** (prec. by *the*) the position of a rifle when sloped. —*v.* **1** *intr.* have or take a slope; slant esp. up or down; lie or tend obliquely, esp. to ground level. **2** *tr.* place or arrange or make in or at a slope. ▫ **slope arms** place one's rifle in a sloping position against one's shoulder. **slope off** *sl.* go away, esp. to evade work etc. [shortening of ASLOPE]

sloppy /ˈslɒpɪ/ *adj.* (**sloppier, sloppiest**) **1 a** (of the ground) wet with rain; full of puddles. **b** (of food etc.) watery and disagreeable. **c** (of a floor, table, etc.) wet with slops, having water etc. spilt on it. **2** unsystematic, careless, not thorough. **3** (of a garment) ill-fitting or untidy. **4** (of sentiment or talk) weakly emotional, maudlin. **5** *colloq.* (of the sea) choppy. ▫▫ **sloppily** *adv.* **sloppiness** *n.*

slosh /slɒʃ/ *v.* & *n.* —*v.* **1** *intr.* (often foll. by *about*) splash or flounder about, move with a splashing sound. **2** *tr. Brit. sl.* hit esp. heavily. **3** *tr. colloq.* **a** pour (liquid) clumsily. **b** pour liquid on. —*n.* **1** slush. **2 a** an instance of splashing. **b** the sound of this. **3** *Brit. sl.* a heavy blow. **4** a quantity of liquid. [var. of SLUSH]

sloshed /slɒʃt/ *adj. Brit. sl.* drunk.

sloshy /ˈslɒʃɪ/ *adj.* (**sloshier, sloshiest**) **1** slushy. **2** sloppy, sentimental.

slot¹ /slɒt/ *n.* & *v.* —*n.* **1 a** a slit or other aperture in a machine etc. for something (esp. a coin) to be inserted. **2** a slit, groove, channel, or long aperture into which something fits or in which something

works. **3** an allotted place in an arrangement or scheme, esp. in a broadcasting schedule. —*v.* (**slotted, slotting**) **1** *tr.* & *intr.* place or be placed into or as if into a slot. **2** *tr.* provide with a slot or slots. ▫ **slot-machine** a machine worked by the insertion of a coin, esp.: **1** one for automatic retail of small articles. **2** one allowing a spell of play at a pin-table etc. **3** *US* = *fruit machine.* [ME, = hollow of the breast, f. OF *esclot*, of unkn. orig.]

slot² /slɒt/ *n.* **1** the track of a deer etc. esp. as shown by footprints. **2** a deer's foot. [OF *esclot* hoof-print of a horse, prob. f. ON *slóth* trail: cf. SLEUTH]

sloth /sləʊθ/ *n.* **1** laziness or indolence; reluctance to make an effort. **2** any slow-moving nocturnal mammal of the family Bradypodidae or Megalonychidae of S. America, having long limbs and hooked claws for hanging upside down from branches of trees. ▫ **sloth bear** a large-lipped black shaggy bear, *Melursus ursinus*, of India. [ME f. SLOW + -TH²]

slothful /ˈsləʊθfʊl/ *adj.* lazy; characterized by sloth. ▫▫ **slothfully** *adv.* **slothfulness** *n.*

slouch /slaʊtʃ/ *v.* & *n.* —*v.* **1** *intr.* stand or move or sit in a drooping ungainly fashion. **2** *tr.* bend one side of the brim of (a hat) downwards (opp. COCK¹). **3** *intr.* droop, hang down loosely. —*n.* **1** a slouching posture or movement, a stoop. **2** a downward bend of a hat-brim (opp. COCK¹). **3** *sl.* an incompetent or slovenly worker or operator or performance. ▫ **slouch hat** a hat with a wide flexible brim. ▫▫ **slouchy** *adj.* (**slouchier, slouchiest**). [16th c.: orig. unkn.]

slough¹ /slaʊ/ *n.* a swamp; a miry place; a quagmire. ▫ **Slough of Despond** a state of hopeless depression (with ref. to Bunyan's *Pilgrim's Progress*). ▫▫ **sloughy** *adj.* [OE *slōh, slō(g)*]

slough² /slʌf/ *n.* & *v.* —*n.* **1** a part that an animal casts or moults, esp. a snake's cast skin. **2** dead tissue that drops off from living flesh etc. **3** a habit etc. that has been abandoned. —*v.* **1** *tr.* cast off as a slough. **2** *intr.* (often foll. by *off*) drop off as a slough. **3** *intr.* cast off a slough. **4** *intr.* (often foll. by *away, down*) (of soil, rock, etc.) collapse or slide into a hole or depression. ▫▫ **sloughy** *adj.* [ME, perh. rel. to LG *slu(we)* husk]

Slovak /ˈsləʊvæk/ *n.* & *adj.* —*n.* **1** a member of a Slavonic people inhabiting Slovakia in Czechoslovakia. **2** the language of this people, one of the two official languages of Czechoslovakia. —*adj.* of or relating to this people or language. [Slovak etc. *Slovák*, rel. to SLOVENE]

sloven /ˈslʌv(ə)n/ *n.* a person who is habitually untidy or careless. [ME perh. f. Flem. *sloef* dirty or Du. *slof* careless]

Slovene /ˈsləʊviːn, sləˈviːn/ (also **Slovenian** /-ˈviːnɪən/) *n.* & *adj.* —*n.* **1** a member of a Slavonic people in Slovenia in Yugoslavia. **2** the language of this people. —*adj.* of or relating to Slovenia or its people or language. [G *Slovene* f. Styrian etc. *Slovenec* f. OSlav. *Slov-*, perh. rel. to *slovo* word]

slovenly /ˈslʌvənlɪ/ *adj.* & *adv.* —*adj.* careless and untidy; unmethodical. —*adv.* in a slovenly manner. ▫▫ **slovenliness** *n.*

slow /sləʊ/ *adj., adv.,* & *v.* —*adj.* **1 a** taking a relatively long time to do a thing or cover a distance (also foll. by *of: slow of speech*). **b** not quick; acting or moving or done without speed. **2** gradual; obtained over a length of time (*slow growth*). **3** not producing, allowing, or conducive to speed (*in the slow lane*). **4** (of a clock etc.) showing a time earlier than is the case. **5** (of a person) not understanding readily; not learning easily. **6** dull; uninteresting; tedious. **7** slack or sluggish (*business is slow*). **8** (of a fire or oven) giving little heat. **9** *Photog.* **a** (of a film) needing long exposure. **b** (of a lens) having a small aperture. **10 a** reluctant; tardy (*not slow to defend himself*). **b** not hasty or easily moved (*slow to take offence*). **11** (of a cricket-pitch, tennis-court, putting-green, etc.) on which the ball bounces or runs slowly. —*adv.* **1** at a slow pace; slowly. **2** (in *comb.*) (*slow-moving traffic*). —*v.* (usu. foll. by *down, up*) **1** *intr.* & *tr.* reduce one's speed or the speed of (a vehicle etc.). **2** *intr.* reduce one's pace of life; live or work less intensely. □**slow and sure** of the attitude that haste is risky. **slow but sure** achieving the required result eventually. **slow-down** the action of slowing down; a go-slow. **slow handclap** slow clapping by an audience as a sign of displeasure or boredom. **slow loris** see LORIS. **slow march** the marching time adopted by troops in a funeral procession etc. **slow-match** a slow-burning match for lighting explosives etc. **slow motion 1** the operation or speed of a film using slower projection or more rapid exposure so that actions etc. appear much slower than usual. **2** the simulation of this in real action. **slow neutron** a neutron with low kinetic energy esp. after moderation (cf. *fast neutron* (see FAST[1])). **slow poison** a poison eventually causing death by repeated doses. **slow puncture** a puncture causing only slow deflation of the tyre. **slow reactor** *Physics* a nuclear reactor using mainly slow neutrons (cf. *fast reactor* (see FAST[1])). **slow virus** a progressive disease caused by a virus or virus-like organism that multiplies slowly in the host organism and has a long incubation period, such as scrapie or BSE. □□ **slowish** *adj.* **slowly** *adv.* **slowness** *n.* [OE *slāw* f. Gmc]

slowcoach /'sləʊkəʊtʃ/ *n. Brit.* **1** a slow or lazy person. **2** a dull-witted person. **3** a person behind the times in opinions etc.

slowpoke /'sləʊpəʊk/ *n. US* = SLOWCOACH.

slow-worm /'sləʊwɜːm/ *n.* a small European legless lizard, *Anguis fragilis*, giving birth to live young. Also called BLINDWORM. [OE *slā-wyrm*: first element of uncert. orig., assim. to SLOW]

SLR *abbr.* **1** *Photog.* single-lens reflex. **2** self-loading rifle.

slub[1] /slʌb/ *n.* & *adj.* —*n.* **1** a lump or thick place in yarn or thread. **2** fabric woven from thread etc. with slubs. —*adj.* (of material etc.) with an irregular appearance caused by uneven thickness of the warp. [19th c.: orig. unkn.]

slub[2] /slʌb/ *n.* & *v.* —*n.* wool slightly twisted in preparation for spinning. —*v.tr.* (**slubbed, slubbing**) twist (wool) in this way. [18th c.: orig. unkn.]

sludge /slʌdʒ/ *n.* **1** thick greasy mud. **2** muddy or slushy sediment. **3** sewage. **4** *Mech.* an accumulation of dirty oil, esp. in the sump of an internal-combustion engine. **5** *Geol.* sea-ice newly formed in small pieces. **6** (usu. *attrib.*) a muddy colour (*sludge green*). □□ **sludgy** *adj.* [cf. SLUSH]

slue var. of SLEW[1].

slug[1] /slʌg/ *n.* **1** a small shell-less mollusc of the class Gastropoda often destructive to plants. **2 a** a bullet esp. of irregular shape. **b** a missile for an airgun. **3** *Printing* **a** a metal bar used in spacing. **b** a line of type in Linotype printing. **4** esp. *US* a tot of liquor. **5** a unit of mass, given an acceleration of 1 foot per second per second by a force of 1 lb. **6** a roundish lump of metal. [ME *slugg(e)* sluggard, prob. f. Scand.]

slug[2] /slʌg/ *v.* & *n. US* —*v.tr.* (**slugged, slugging**) strike with a hard blow. —*n.* a hard blow. □**slug it out 1** fight it out. **2** endure; stick it out. □□ **slugger** *n.* [19th c.: orig. unkn.]

slugabed /'slʌgəˌbed/ *n. archaic* a lazy person who lies late in bed. [*slug* (v.) (see SLUGGARD) + ABED]

sluggard /'slʌgəd/ *n.* a lazy sluggish person. □□ **sluggardly** *adv.* **sluggardliness** *n.* [ME f. *slug* (v.) be slothful (prob. f. Scand.: cf. SLUG[1])· + -ARD]

sluggish /'slʌgɪʃ/ *adj.* inert; inactive; slow-moving; torpid; indolent (*a sluggish circulation; a sluggish stream*). □□ **sluggishly** *adv.* **sluggishness** *n.* [ME f. SLUG[1] or *slug* (v.): see SLUGGARD]

sluice /sluːs/ *n.* & *v.* —*n.* **1** (also **sluice-gate, sluice-valve**) a sliding gate or other contrivance for controlling the volume or flow of water. **2** (also

sluice-way) an artificial water-channel esp. for washing ore. **3** a place for rinsing. **4** the act or an instance of rinsing. **5** the water above or below or issuing through a floodgate. —*v.* **1** *tr.* provide or wash with a sluice or sluices. **2** *tr.* rinse, pour or throw water freely upon. **3** *tr.* (foll. by *out, away*) wash out or away with a flow of water. **4** *tr.* flood with water from a sluice. **5** *intr.* (of water) rush out from a sluice, or as if from a sluice. [ME f. OF *escluse* ult. f. L *excludere* EXCLUDE]

sluit var. of SLOOT.

slum /slʌm/ *n.* & *v.* —*n.* **1** an overcrowded and squalid back street, district, etc., usu. in a city and inhabited by very poor people. **2** a house or building unfit for human habitation. —*v.intr.* (**slummed, slumming**) **1** live in slumlike conditions. **2** go about the slums through curiosity, to examine the condition of the inhabitants, or for charitable purposes. □**slum clearance** the demolition of slums and rehousing of their inhabitants. **slum it** *colloq.* put up with conditions less comfortable than usual. □□ **slummy** *adj.* (**slummier, slummiest**). **slumminess** *n.* [19th c.: orig. cant]

slumber /'slʌmbə(r)/ *v.* & *n. poet. rhet.* —*v.intr.* **1** sleep, esp. in a specified manner. **2** be idle, drowsy, or inactive. —*n.* a sleep, esp. of a specified kind (*fell into a fitful slumber*). □**slumber away** spend (time) in slumber. **slumber-wear** nightclothes. □□ **slumberer** *n.* **slumberous** *adj.* **slumbrous** *adj.* [ME *slūmere* etc. f. *slūmen* (v.) or *slūme* (n.) f. OE *slūma: -b-* as in *number*]

slump /slʌmp/ *n.* & *v.* —*n.* **1** a sudden severe or prolonged fall in prices or values of commodities or securities. **2** a sharp or sudden decline in trade or business usu. bringing widespread unemployment. **3** a lessening of interest or commitment in a subject or undertaking. —*v.intr.* **1** undergo a slump; fail; fall in price. **2** sit or fall heavily or limply (*slumped into a chair*). **3** lean or subside. [17th c., orig. 'sink in a bog': imit.]

slung *past* and *past part.* of SLING[1].

slunk *past* and *past part.* of SLINK[1].

slur /slɜː(r)/ *v.* & *n.* —*v.* (**slurred, slurring**) **1** *tr.* & *intr.* pronounce or write indistinctly so that the sounds or letters run into one another. **2** *tr. Mus.* **a** perform (a group of two or more notes) legato. **b** mark (notes) with a slur. **3** *tr. archaic* or *US* put a slur on (a person or a person's character); make insinuations against. **4** *tr.* (usu. foll. by *over*) pass over (a fact, fault, etc.) lightly; conceal or minimize. —*n.* **1** an imputation of wrongdoing; blame; stigma (*a slur on my reputation*). **2** the act or an instance of slurring in pronunciation, singing, or writing. **3** *Mus.* a curved line to show that two or more notes are to be sung to one syllable or played or sung legato. [17th c.: orig. unkn.]

slurp /slɜːp/ *v.* & *n.* —*v.tr.* eat or drink noisily. —*n.* the sound of this; a slurping gulp. [Du. *slurpen, slorpen*]

slurry /'slʌrɪ/ *n.* (*pl.* **-ies**) **1** a semi-liquid mixture of fine particles and water; thin mud. **2** thin liquid cement. **3** a fluid form of manure. **4** a residue of water and particles of coal left at pit-head washing plants. [ME, rel. to dial. *slur* thin mud]

slush /slʌʃ/ *n.* **1** watery mud or thawing snow. **2** silly sentiment. □**slush fund** reserve funding esp. as used for political bribery. [17th c., also *sludge* and *slutch*: orig. unkn.]

slushy /'slʌʃɪ/ *adj.* (**slushier, slushiest**) like slush; watery. □□ **slushiness** *n.*

slut /slʌt/ *n. derog.* a slovenly woman; a slattern; a hussy. □□ **sluttish** *adj.* **sluttishness** *n.* [ME: orig. unkn.]

sly /slaɪ/ *adj.* (**slyer, slyest**) **1** cunning; crafty; wily. **2 a** (of a person) practising secrecy or stealth. **b** (of an action etc.) done etc. in secret. **3** hypocritical; ironical. **4** knowing; arch; bantering; insinuating. **5** *Austral.* & *NZ sl.* (esp. of liquor) illicit. □**on the sly**

privately; covertly; without publicity (*smuggled some through on the sly*). **sly dog** *colloq.* a person who is discreet about mistakes or pleasures. □□ **slyly** *adv.* (also **slily**). **slyness** *n.* [ME *sleh* etc. f. ON *slœgr* cunning, orig. 'able to strike' f. *slóg-* past stem of *slá* strike: cf. SLEIGHT]

slyboots /ˈslaɪbuːts/ *n. colloq.* a sly person.

slype /slaɪp/ *n.* a covered way or passage between a cathedral etc. transept and the chapter house or deanery. [perh. = *slipe* a long narrow piece of ground, = SLIP² 1]

SM *abbr.* **1** sadomasochism. **2** Sergeant-Major.

Sm *symb. Chem.* the element samarium.

smack¹ /smæk/ *n., v.,* & *adv.* —*n.* **1** a sharp slap or blow esp. with the palm of the hand or a flat object. **2** a hard hit at cricket etc. **3** a loud kiss (*gave her a hearty smack*). **4** a loud sharp sound (*heard the smack as it hit the floor*). —*v.* **1** *tr.* strike with the open hand etc. **2** *tr.* part (one's lips) noisily in eager anticipation or enjoyment of food or another delight. **3** *tr.* crack (a whip). **4** *tr.* & *intr.* move, hit, etc., with a smack. —*adv. colloq.* **1** with a smack. **2** suddenly; directly; violently (*landed smack on my desk*). **3** exactly (*hit it smack in the centre*). □ **have a smack at** *colloq.* make an attempt, attack, etc., at. **a smack in the eye** (or **face**) *colloq.* a rebuff; a setback. [MDu. *smack(en)* of imit. orig.]

smack² /smæk/ *v.* & *n.* (foll. by *of*) —*v.intr.* **1** have a flavour of; taste of (*smacked of garlic*). **2** suggest the presence or effects of (*it smacks of nepotism*). —*n.* **1** a flavour; a taste that suggests the presence of something. **2** (in a person's character etc.) a barely discernible quality (*just a smack of superciliousness*). **3** (in food etc.) a very small amount (*add a smack of ginger*). [OE *smæc*]

smack³ /smæk/ *n.* a single-masted sailing-boat for coasting or fishing. [Du. *smak* f. earlier *smacke*; orig. unkn.]

smack⁴ /smæk/ *n. sl.* a hard drug, esp. heroin, sold or used illegally. [prob. alt. of Yiddish *schmeck* sniff]

smacker /ˈsmækə(r)/ *n. sl.* **1** a loud kiss. **2** a resounding blow. **3 a** *Brit.* £1. **b** *US* $1.

small /smɔːl/ *adj., n.,* & *adv.* —*adj.* **1** not large or big. **2** slender; thin. **3** not great in importance, amount, number, strength, or power. **4** not much; trifling (*a small token; paid small attention*). **5** insignificant; unimportant (*a small matter; from small beginnings*). **6** consisting of small particles (*small gravel; small shot*). **7** doing something on a small scale (*a small farmer*). **8** socially undistinguished; poor or humble. **9** petty; mean; ungenerous; paltry (*a small spiteful nature*). **10** young; not fully grown or developed (*a small child*). —*n.* **1** the slenderest part of something (esp. *small of the back*). **2** (in *pl.*) *Brit. colloq.* small items of laundry, esp. underwear. —*adv.* into small pieces (*chop it small*). □ **feel** (or **look**) **small** be humiliated; appear mean or humiliated. **in a small way** unambitiously; on a small scale. **no small** considerable; a good deal of (*no small excitement about it*). **small arms** portable firearms, esp. rifles, pistols, light machine-guns, sub-machine-guns, etc. **small beer 1** a trifling matter; something unimportant. **2** weak beer. **small-bore** (of a firearm) with a narrow bore, in international and Olympic shooting use. .22 inch calibre (5.6 millimetre bore). **small capital** a capital letter which is of the same dimensions as the lower-case letters in the same typeface minus ascenders and descenders, as THIS. **small change 1** money in the form of coins as opposed to notes. **2** trivial remarks. **small circle** see CIRCLE. **small claims court** *Brit.* a local tribunal in which claims for small amounts can be heard and decided quickly and cheaply without legal representation. **small craft** a general term for small boats and fishing vessels. **small fry 1** young children or the young of various species. **2** small or insignificant things or people. **small hours** the early hours of the morning after

midnight. **small intestine** see INTESTINE. **small letter** (in printed material) a lower-case letter. **small mercy** a minor concession, benefit, etc. (*be grateful for small mercies*). **small potatoes** an insignificant person or thing. **small print 1** printed matter in small type. **2** inconspicuous and usu. unfavourable limitations etc. in a contract. **small profits and quick returns** the policy of a cheap shop etc. relying on large trade. **small-scale** made or occurring in small amounts or to a lesser degree. **small slam** see SLAM². **small-sword** a light tapering thrusting-sword, esp. *hist.* for duelling. **small talk** light social conversation. **small-time** *colloq.* unimportant or petty. **small-timer** *colloq.* a small-time operator; an insignificant person. **small-town** relating to or characteristic of a small town; unsophisticated; provincial. **small wonder** not very surprising. □□ **smallish** *adj.* **smallness** *n.* [OE *smæl* f. Gmc]

smallgoods /ˈsmɔːlɡʊdz/ *n. Austral.* delicatessen meats.

smallholder /ˈsmɔːlˌhəʊldə(r)/ *n. Brit.* a person who farms a smallholding.

smallholding /ˈsmɔːlˌhəʊldɪŋ/ *n. Brit.* an agricultural holding smaller than a farm.

small-minded /smɔːlˈmaɪndɪd/ *adj.* petty; of rigid opinions or narrow outlook. □□ **small-mindedly** *adv.* **small-mindedness** *n.*

smallpox /ˈsmɔːlpɒks/ *n. hist.* an acute contagious viral disease, with fever and pustules, usu. leaving permanent scars.

smalt /smɒlt, smɔːlt/ *n.* **1** glass coloured blue with cobalt. **2** a pigment made by pulverizing this. [F f. It. *smalto* f. Gmc, rel. to SMELT¹]

smarm /smɑːm/ *v.tr. colloq.* **1** (often foll. by *down*) smooth, plaster down (hair etc.) usu. with cream or oil. **2** flatter fulsomely. [orig. dial. (also *smalm*), of uncert. orig.]

smarmy /ˈsmɑːmɪ/ *adj.* (**smarmier**, **smarmiest**) *colloq.* ingratiating; flattering; obsequious. □□ **smarmily** *adv.* **smarminess** *n.*

smart /smɑːt/ *adj., v., n.,* & *adv.* —*adj.* **1 a** clever; ingenious; quickwitted (*a smart talker; gave a smart answer*). **b** keen in bargaining; quick to take advantage. **c** (of transactions etc.) unscrupulous to the point of dishonesty. **2** well-groomed; neat; bright and fresh in appearance (*a smart suit*). **3** in good repair; showing bright colours, new paint, etc. (*a smart red bicycle*). **4** stylish; fashionable; prominent in society (*in all the smart restaurants; the smart set*). **5** quick; brisk (*set a smart pace*). **6** painfully severe; sharp; vigorous (*a smart blow*). —*v.intr.* **1** (of a person or a part of the body) feel or give acute pain or distress (*my eye smarts; smarting from the insult*). **2** (of an insult, grievance, etc.) rankle. **3** (foll. by *for*) suffer the consequences of (*you will smart for this*). —*n.* a bodily or mental sharp pain; a stinging sensation. —*adv.* smartly; in a smart manner. □ **look smart** make haste. **smart-arse** (or **-ass**) = SMART ALEC. **smart-money 1** money paid or exacted as a penalty or compensation. **2** money invested by persons with expert knowledge. □□ **smartingly** *adv.* **smartish** *adj.* & *adv.* **smartly** *adv.* **smartness** *n.* [OE *smeart*, *smeortan*]

smart alec /ˈælɪk/ *n.* (also **aleck**, **alick**) *colloq.* a person displaying ostentatious or smug cleverness. □□ **smart-alecky** *adj.* [SMART + *Alec*, dimin. of the name *Alexander*]

smarten /ˈsmɑːt(ə)n/ *v.tr.* & *intr.* (usu. foll. by *up*) make or become smart or smarter.

smarty /ˈsmɑːtɪ/ *n.* (*pl.* -**ies**) *colloq.* **1** a know-all; a smart alec. **2** a smartly-dressed person; a member of a smart set. □ **smarty-boots** (or **-pants**) = SMARTY 1. [SMART]

smash /smæʃ/ *v., n.,* & *adv.* —*v.* **1** *tr.* & *intr.* (often foll. by *up*) **a** break into pieces; shatter. **b** bring or come to sudden or complete destruction, defeat, or disaster. **2** *tr.* (foll. by *into, through*) (of a vehicle etc.) move with great force and impact. **3** *tr.* & *intr.*

(foll. by *in*) break in with a crushing blow (*smashed in the window*). **4** *tr*. (in tennis, squash, etc.) hit (a ball etc.) with great force, esp. downwards (*smashed it back over the net*). **5** *intr*. (of a business etc.) go bankrupt, come to grief. **6** *tr*. (as **smashed** *adj*.) *sl*. intoxicated. —*n*. **1** the act or an instance of smashing; a violent fall, collision, or disaster. **2** the sound of this. **3** (in full **smash hit**) a very successful play, song, performer, etc. **4** a stroke in tennis, squash, etc., in which the ball is hit esp. downwards with great force. **5** a violent blow with a fist etc. **6** bankruptcy; a series of commercial failures. **7** a mixture of spirits (usu. brandy) with flavoured water and ice. —*adv*. with a smash (*fell smash on the floor*). □**go to smash** be ruined etc. **smash-and-grab** (of a robbery etc.) in which the thief smashes a shop-window and seizes goods. **smash-up** a violent collision; a complete smash. [18th c., prob. imit. after *smack*, *smite* and *bash*, *mash*, etc.]

smasher /'smæʃə(r)/ *n*. **1** *colloq*. a very beautiful or pleasing person or thing. **2** a person or thing that smashes.

smashing /'smæʃɪŋ/ *adj*. *colloq*. superlative; excellent; wonderful; beautiful. □□ **smashingly** *adv*.

smatter /'smætə(r)/ *n*. (also **smattering**) a slight superficial knowledge of a language or subject. □□ **smatterer** *n*. [ME *smatter* talk ignorantly, prate: orig. unkn.]

smear /smɪə(r)/ *v*. & *n*. —*v.tr*. **1** daub or mark with a greasy or sticky substance or with something that stains. **2** blot; smudge; obscure the outline of (writing, artwork, etc.). **3** defame the character of; slander; attempt to or succeed in discrediting (a person or his name) publicly. —*n*. **1** the act or an instance of smearing. **2** *Med*. **a** material smeared on a microscopic slide etc. for examination. **b** a specimen of this. □**smear test** = *cervical smear*. □□ **smearer** *n*. **smeary** *adj*. [OE *smierwan* f. Gmc]

smegma /'smegmə/ *n*. a sebaceous secretion in the folds of the skin, esp. of the foreskin. □□ **smegmatic** /-'mætɪk/ *adj*. [L f. Gk *smēgma -atos* detergent f. *smēkhō* cleanse]

smell /smel/ *n*. & *v*. —*n*. **1** the faculty of perceiving odours or scents (*has a fine sense of smell*). **2** the quality in substances that is perceived by this (*the smell of thyme*; *this rose has no smell*). **3** an unpleasant odour. **4** the act of inhaling to ascertain smell. —*v*. (*past* and *past part*. **smelt** /smelt/ or **smelled**) **1** *tr*. perceive the smell of; examine by smell (*thought I could smell gas*). **2** *intr*. emit odour. **3** *intr*. seem by smell to be (*this milk smells sour*). **4** *intr*. (foll. by *of*) **a** be redolent of (*smells of fish*). **b** be suggestive of (*smells of dishonesty*). **5** *intr*. stink; be rank. **6** *tr*. perceive as if by smell; detect, discern, suspect (*smell a bargain*; *smell blood*). **7** *intr*. have or use a sense of smell. **8** *intr*. (foll. by *about*) sniff or search about. **9** *intr*. (foll. by *at*) inhale the smell of. □**smelling-bottle** a small bottle of smelling-salts. **smelling-salts** ammonium carbonate mixed with scent to be sniffed as a restorative in faintness etc. **smell out 1** detect by smell; find out by investigation. **2** (of a dog etc.) hunt out by smell. **smell a rat** begin to suspect trickery etc. □□ **smellable** *adj*. **smeller** *n*. **smell-less** *adj*. [ME *smel*(*le*), prob. f. OE]

smelly /'smelɪ/ *adj*. (**smellier**, **smelliest**) having a strong or unpleasant smell. □□ **smelliness** *n*.

smelt[1] /smelt/ *v.tr*. **1** extract metal from (ore) by melting. **2** extract (metal) from ore by melting. □□ **smelter** *n*. **smeltery** *n*. (*pl*. **-ies**). [MDu., MLG *smelten*, rel. to MELT]

smelt[2] *past* and *past part*. of SMELL.

smelt[3] /smelt/ *n*. (*pl*. same or **smelts**) any small green and silver fish of the genus *Osmerus* etc. allied to salmon and used as food. [OE, of uncert. orig.: cf. SMOLT]

smew /smju:/ *n*. a small merganser, *Mergus albellus*. [17th c., rel. to *smeath*, *smee* = smew, widgeon, etc.]

smidgen /'smɪdʒ(ə)n/ *n*. (also **smidgin** /-dʒɪn/)

colloq. a small bit or amount. [perh. f. *smitch* in the same sense: cf. dial. *smitch* wood-smoke]

smilax /'smaɪlæks/ *n*. **1** any climbing shrub of the genus *Smilax*, the roots of some species of which yield sarsaparilla. **2** a climbing kind of asparagus, *Asparagus medeoloides*, used decoratively by florists. [L f. Gk, = bindweed]

smile /smaɪl/ *v*. & *n*. —*v*. **1** *intr*. relax the features into a pleased or kind or gently sceptical expression or a forced imitation of these, usu. with the lips parted and the corners of the mouth turned up. **2** *tr*. express by smiling (*smiled their consent*). **3** *tr*. give (a smile) of a specified kind (*smiled a sardonic smile*). **4** *intr*. (foll. by *on*, *upon*) adopt a favourable attitude towards; encourage (*fortune smiled on me*). **5** *intr*. have a bright or favourable aspect (*the smiling countryside*). **6** *tr*. (foll. by *away*) drive (a person's anger etc.) away (*smiled their tears away*). **7** *intr*. (foll. by *at*) a ridicule or show indifference to (*smiled at my feeble attempts*). **b** favour; smile on. **8** *tr*. (foll. by *into*, *out of*) bring (a person) into or out of a specified mood etc. by smiling (*smiled them into agreement*). —*n*. **1** the act or an instance of smiling. **2** a smiling expression or aspect. □**come up smiling** *colloq*. recover from adversity and cheerfully face what is to come. □□ **smileless** *adj*. **smiler** *n*. **smiley** *adj*. **smilingly** *adv*. [ME perh. f. Scand., rel. to SMIRK: cf. OHG *smīlenter*]

smirch /smɜːtʃ/ *v*. & *n*. —*v.tr*. mark, soil, or smear (a thing, a person's reputation, etc.). —*n*. **1** a spot or stain. **2** a blot (on one's character etc.). [ME: orig. unkn.]

smirk /smɜːk/ *n*. & *v*. —*n*. an affected, conceited, or silly smile. —*v.intr*. put on or wear a smirk. □□ **smirker** *n*. **smirkingly** *adv*. **smirky** *adj*. **smirkily** *adv*. [OE *sme*(*a*)*rcian*]

smit /smɪt/ *archaic past part*. of SMITE.

smite /smaɪt/ *v*. & *n*. —*v*. (*past* **smote** /sməʊt/; *past part*. **smitten** /'smɪt(ə)n/) *archaic* or *literary* **1** *tr*. strike or hit. **2** *tr*. chastise; defeat. **3** *tr*. (in *passive*) **a** have a sudden strong effect on (*was smitten by his conscience*). **b** infatuate, fascinate (*was smitten by her beauty*). **4** *intr*. (foll. by *on*, *upon*) come forcibly or abruptly upon. —*n*. a blow or stroke. □□ **smiter** *n*. [OE *smītan* smear f. Gmc]

smith /smɪθ/ *n*. & *v*. —*n*. **1** (esp. in *comb*.) a worker in metal (*goldsmith*; *tinsmith*). **2** a person who forges iron; a blacksmith. **3** a craftsman (*wordsmith*). —*v.tr*. make or treat by forging. [OE f. Gmc]

smithereens /ˌsmɪðə'riːnz/ *n.pl*. (also **smithers** /'smɪðəz/) small fragments (*smash into smithereens*). [19th c.: orig. unkn.]

smithery /'smɪðərɪ/ *n*. (*pl*. **-ies**) **1** a smith's work. **2** (esp. in naval dockyards) a smithy.

smithy /'smɪðɪ/ *n*. (*pl*. **-ies**) a blacksmith's workshop; a forge. [ME f. ON *smithja*]

smitten *past part*. of SMITE.

smock /smɒk/ *n*. & *v*. —*n*. **1** a loose shirtlike garment with the upper part closely gathered in smocking. **2** (also **smock-frock**) a loose overall, esp. *hist*. a field-labourer's outer linen garment. —*v.tr*. adorn with smocking. [OE *smoc*, prob. rel. to OE *smūgan* creep, ON *smjúga* put on a garment]

smocking /'smɒkɪŋ/ *n*. an ornamental effect on cloth made by gathering the material tightly into pleats, often with stitches in a honeycomb pattern.

smog /smɒg/ *n*. fog intensified by smoke. □□ **smoggy** *adj*. (**smoggier**, **smoggiest**). [portmanteau word]

smoke /sməʊk/ *n*. & *v*. —*n*. **1** a visible suspension of carbon etc. in air, emitted from a burning substance. **2** an act or period of smoking tobacco (*had a quiet smoke*). **3** *colloq*. a cigarette or cigar (*got a smoke?*). **4** (**the Smoke**) *Brit*. & *Austral*. *colloq*. a big city, esp. London. —*v*. **1** *intr*. **a** emit smoke or visible vapour (*smoking ruins*). **b** (of a lamp etc.) burn badly with the emission of smoke. **c** (of a chimney or fire) discharge smoke into the room. **2 a** *intr*. inhale and exhale the smoke of a cigarette or cigar or pipe. **b**

intr. do this habitually. **c** *tr.* use (a cigarette etc.) in this way. **3** *tr.* darken or preserve by the action of smoke (*smoked salmon*). **4** *tr.* spoil the taste of in cooking. **5** *tr.* **a** rid of insects etc. by the action of smoke. **b** subdue (insects, esp. bees) in this way. **6** *tr. archaic* make fun of. **7** *tr.* bring (oneself) into a specified state by smoking. □**go up in smoke** *colloq.* **1** be destroyed by fire. **2** (of a plan etc.) come to nothing. **no smoke without fire** rumours are not entirely baseless. **smoke-ball 1** a puff-ball. **2** a projectile filled with material emitting dense smoke, used to conceal military operations etc. **smoke bomb** a bomb that emits dense smoke on exploding. **smoke-bush** = *smoke-plant*. **smoked glass** glass darkened with smoke. **smoke-dried** cured in smoke. **smoke-ho** *Austral. & NZ colloq.* = SMOKO. **smoke out 1** drive out by means of smoke. **2** drive out of hiding or secrecy etc. **smoke-plant** (or **-tree**) any ornamental shrub of the genus *Cotinus*, with feathery smokelike fruit-stalks. **smoke-ring** smoke from a cigarette etc. exhaled in the shape of a ring. **smoke-room** *Brit.* = SMOKING-ROOM. **smoke-stone** cairngorm. **smoke-tunnel** a form of wind-tunnel using smoke filaments to show the motion of air. □□ **smokable** *adj.* (also **smokeable**). [OE *smoca* f. weak grade of the stem of *smēocan* emit smoke]

smokeless /ˈsməʊklɪs/ *adj.* having or producing no smoke. □**smokeless zone** a district in which it is illegal to create smoke and where only smokeless fuel may be used.

smoker /ˈsməʊkə(r)/ *n.* **1** a person or thing that smokes, esp. a person who habitually smokes tobacco. **2** a compartment on a train, in which smoking is allowed. **3** esp. *US* an informal social gathering of men. □**smoker's cough** an ailment caused by excessive smoking.

smokescreen /ˈsməʊkskriːn/ *n.* **1** a cloud of smoke diffused to conceal (esp. military) operations. **2** a device or ruse for disguising one's activities.

smokestack /ˈsməʊkstæk/ *n.* **1** a chimney or funnel for discharging the smoke of a locomotive or steamer. **2** a tall chimney.

smoking-jacket /ˈsməʊkɪŋˌdʒækɪt/ *n.* an ornamental jacket formerly worn by men while smoking.

smoking-room /ˈsməʊkɪŋˌruːm, -ˌrʊm/ *n.* a room in a hotel or house, kept for smoking in.

smoko /ˈsməʊkəʊ/ *n.* (*pl.* **-os**) *Austral. & NZ colloq.* **1** a stoppage of work for a rest and a smoke. **2** a tea break.

smoky /ˈsməʊkɪ/ *adj.* (**smokier, smokiest**) **1** emitting, veiled or filled with, or obscured by, smoke (*smoky fire; smoky room*). **2** stained with or coloured like smoke (*smoky glass*). **3** having the taste or flavour of smoked food (*smoky bacon*). □□ **smokily** *adv.* **smokiness** *n.*

smolder *US* var. of SMOULDER.

smolt /sməʊlt/ *n.* a young salmon migrating to the sea for the first time. [ME (orig. Sc. & N.Engl.): orig. unkn.]

smooch /smuːtʃ/ *n. & v. colloq.* —*n.* **1** *Brit.* a period of slow dancing close together. **2** a spell of kissing and caressing. —*v.intr.* engage in a smooch. □□ **smoocher** *n.* **smoochy** *adj.* (**smoochier, smoochiest**). [dial. *smouch* imit.]

smoodge /smuːdʒ/ *v.intr.* (also **smooge**) *Austral. & NZ* **1** behave in a fawning or ingratiating manner. **2** behave amorously. [prob. var. of dial. *smudge* kiss, sidle up to, beg in a sneaking way]

smooth /smuːð/ *adj., v., n., & adv.* —*adj.* **1** having a relatively even and regular surface; free from perceptible projections, lumps, indentations, and roughness. **2** not wrinkled, pitted, scored, or hairy (*smooth skin*). **3** that can be traversed without check. **4** (of liquids) of even consistency; without lumps (*mix to a smooth paste*). **5** (of the sea etc.) without waves or undulations. **6** (of a journey, passage, progress, etc.) untroubled by difficulties or adverse conditions.

7 having an easy flow or correct rhythm (*smooth breathing; a smooth metre*). **8 a** not harsh in sound or taste. **b** (of wine etc.) not astringent. **9** (of a person, his or her manner, etc.) suave, conciliatory, flattering, unruffled, or polite (*a smooth talker; he's very smooth*). **10** (of movement etc.) not suddenly varying; not jerky. —*v.* **1** *tr. & intr.* (often foll. by *out, down*) make or become smooth. **2** (often foll. by *out, down, over, away*) **a** *tr.* reduce or get rid of (differences, faults, difficulties, etc.) in fact or appearance. **b** *intr.* (of difficulties etc.) diminish, become less obtrusive (*it will all smooth over*). **3** *tr.* modify (a graph, curve, etc.) so as to lessen irregularities. **4** *tr.* free from impediments or discomfort (*smooth the way; smooth the declining years*). —*n.* **1** a smoothing touch or stroke (*gave his hair a smooth*). **2** the easy part of life (*take the rough with the smooth*). —*adv.* smoothly (*the course of true love never did run smooth*). □**in smooth water** having passed obstacles or difficulties. **smooth-bore** a gun with an unrifled barrel. **smooth-faced** hypocritically friendly. **smoothing-iron** *hist.* a flat-iron. **smoothing-plane** a small plane for finishing the planing of wood. **smooth muscle** a muscle without striations, usu. occurring in hollow organs and performing involuntary functions. **smooth talk** *colloq.* bland specious language. **smooth-talk** *v.tr.* address or persuade with this. **smooth-tongued** insincerely flattering. □□ **smoothable** *adj.* **smoother** *n.* **smoothish** *adj.* **smoothly** *adv.* **smoothness** *n.* [OE *smōth*]

smoothie /ˈsmuːðɪ/ *n. colloq.* a person who is smooth (see SMOOTH *adj.* 9). [SMOOTH]

smorgasbord /ˈsmɔːɡəsˌbɔːd/ *n.* open sandwiches served with delicacies as hors d'œuvres or a buffet. [Sw. f. *smör* butter + *gås* goose, lump of butter + *bord* table]

smorzando /smɔːˈtsændəʊ/ *adj., adv., & n. Mus.* —*adj. & adv.* dying away. —*n.* (*pl.* **-os** or **smorzandi** /-dɪ/) a smorzando passage. [It., gerund of *smorzare* extinguish]

smote *past of* SMITE.

smother /ˈsmʌðə(r)/ *v. & n.* —*v.* **1** *tr.* suffocate; stifle; kill by stopping the breath of or excluding air from. **2** *tr.* (foll. by *with*) overwhelm with (kisses, gifts, kindness, etc.) (*smothered with affection*). **3** *tr.* (foll. by *in, with*) cover entirely in or with (*chicken smothered in mayonnaise*). **4** *tr.* extinguish or deaden (a fire or flame) by covering it or heaping it with ashes etc. **5** *intr.* **a** die of suffocation. **b** have difficulty breathing. **6** *tr.* (often foll. by *up*) suppress or conceal; keep from notice or publicity. **7** *tr. US* defeat rapidly or utterly. —*n.* **1** a cloud of dust or smoke. **2** obscurity caused by this. □**smothered mate** *Chess* checkmate in which the king, having no vacant square to move to, is checkmated by a knight. [ME *smorther* f. the stem of OE *smorian* suffocate]

smothery /ˈsmʌðərɪ/ *adj.* tending to smother; stifling.

smoulder /ˈsməʊldə(r)/ *v. & n.* (*US* **smolder**) —*v.intr.* **1** burn slowly with smoke but without a flame; slowly burn internally or invisibly. **2** (of emotions etc.) exist in a suppressed or concealed state. **3** (of a person) show silent or suppressed anger, hatred, etc. —*n.* a smouldering or slow-burning fire. [ME, rel. to LG *smöln*, MDu. *smölen*]

smriti /ˈsmrɪtɪ/ *n.* Hindu traditional teachings on religion etc. [Skr. *smṛti* remembrance]

smudge[1] /smʌdʒ/ *n. & v.* —*n.* **1** a blurred or smeared line or mark; a blot; a smear of dirt. **2** a stain or blot on a person's character etc. —*v.* **1** *tr.* make a smudge on. **2** *intr.* become smeared or blurred (*smudges easily*). **3** *tr.* smear or blur the lines of (writing, drawing, etc.) (*smudge the outline*). **4** *tr.* defile, sully, stain, or disgrace (a person's name, character, etc.). □□ **smudgeless** *adj.* [ME: orig. unkn.]

smudge[2] /smʌdʒ/ *n. US* an outdoor fire with dense smoke made to keep off insects, protect plants against frost, etc. □**smudge-pot** a container holding burning material that produces a smudge. [*smudge* (v.) cure (herring) by smoking (16th c.: orig. unkn.)]

smudgy /ˈsmʌdʒɪ/ *adj.* (**smudgier, smudgiest**) **1** smudged. **2** likely to produce smudges. □□**smudgily** *adv.* **smudginess** *n.*

smug /smʌg/ *adj.* (**smugger, smuggest**) self-satisfied; complacent. □□**smugly** *adv.* **smugness** *n.* [16th c., orig. 'neat' f. LG *smuk* pretty]

smuggle /ˈsmʌg(ə)l/ *v.tr.* **1** (also *absol.*) import or export (goods) illegally esp. without payment of customs duties. **2** (foll. by *in, out*) convey secretly. **3** (foll. by *away*) put into concealment. □□**smuggler** *n.* **smuggling** *n.* [17th c. (also *smuckle*) f. LG *smukkeln smuggelen*]

smut /smʌt/ *n. & v.* —*n.* **1** a small flake of soot etc. **2** a spot or smudge made by this. **3** obscene or lascivious talk, pictures, or stories. **4 a** a fungous disease of cereals in which parts of the ear change to black powder. **b** any fungus of the order Ustilaginales causing this. —*v.* (**smutted, smutting**) **1** *tr.* mark with smuts. **2** *tr.* infect (a plant) with smut. **3** *intr.* (of a plant) contract smut. □**smut-ball** *Agriculture* grain affected by smut. **smut-mill** a machine for freeing grain from smut. □□**smutty** *adj.* (**smuttier, smuttiest**) (esp. in sense 3 of *n.*). **smuttily** *adv.* **smuttiness** *n.* [rel. to LG *smutt*, MHG *smutz(en)* etc.: cf. OE *smitt(ian)* smear, and SMUDGE[1]]

Sn *symb. Chem.* the element tin.

snack /snæk/ *n. & v.* —*n.* **1** a light, casual, or hurried meal. **2** a small amount of food eaten between meals. **3** *Austral. sl.* something easy to accomplish. —*v.intr.* eat a snack. □**snack bar** a place where snacks are sold. [ME, orig. a snap or bite, f. MDu. *snac(k)* f. *snacken* (v.), var. of *snappen*]

snaffle /ˈsnæf(ə)l/ *n. & v.* —*n.* (in full **snaffle-bit**) a simple bridle-bit without a curb and usu. with a single rein. —*v.tr.* **1** put a snaffle on. **2** *colloq.* steal; seize; appropriate. [prob. f. LG or Du.: cf. MLG, MDu. *snavel* beak, mouth]

snafu /snæˈfuː/ *adj. & n. sl.* —*adj.* in utter confusion or chaos. —*n.* this state. [acronym for 'situation normal: all *f*ouled (or *f*ucked) *u*p']

snag[1] /snæg/ *n. & v.* —*n.* **1** an unexpected or hidden obstacle or drawback. **2** a jagged or projecting point or broken stump. **3** a tear in material etc. **4** a short tine of an antler. —*v.tr.* (**snagged, snagging**) **1** catch or tear on a snag. **2** clear (land, a waterway, a tree-trunk, etc.) of snags. **3** *US* catch or obtain by quick action. □□**snagged** *adj.* **snaggy** *adj.* [prob. f. Scand.: cf. Norw. dial. *snag(e)* sharp point]

snag[2] /snæg/ *n.* (usu. in *pl.*) *Austral. sl.* a sausage. [20th c.: orig. unkn.]

snaggle-tooth /ˈsnæg(ə)l/ *n.* (*pl.* **snaggle-teeth**) an irregular or projecting tooth. □□**snaggle-toothed** *adj.* [SNAG[1] + -LE[2]]

snail /sneɪl/ *n.* any slow-moving gastropod mollusc with a spiral shell able to enclose the whole body. □**snail's pace** a very slow movement. □□**snail-like** *adj.* [OE *snæg(e)l* f. Gmc]

snake /sneɪk/ *n. & v.* —*n.* **1 a** any long limbless reptile of the suborder Ophidia, including boas, pythons, and poisonous forms such as cobras and vipers. **b** a limbless lizard or amphibian. **2** (also **snake in the grass**) a treacherous person or secret enemy. **3** (prec. by *the*) a system of interconnected exchange rates for the EEC currencies. —*v.intr.* move or twist like a snake. □**snake bird** a fish-eating bird, *Anhinga anhinga*, with a long slender neck. **snake-charmer** a person appearing to make snakes move by music etc. **snake-pit 1** a pit containing snakes. **2** a scene of vicious behaviour. **snakes and ladders** a game with counters moved along a board with advances up 'ladders' or returns down 'snakes' depicted on the board. **snake's head** a bulbous plant, *Fritillaria meleagris*, with bell-shaped pendent flowers. □□**snakelike** *adj.* [OE *snaca*]

snakeroot /ˈsneɪkruːt/ *n.* any of various N. American plants, esp. *Cimicifuga racemosa*, with roots reputed to contain an antidote to snake's poison.

snaky /ˈsneɪkɪ/ *adj.* **1** of or like a snake. **2** winding; sinuous. **3** showing coldness, ingratitude, venom, or guile. **4 a** infested with snakes. **b** (esp. of the hair of the Furies) composed of snakes. **5** *Austral. sl.* angry; irritable. □□**snakily** *adv.* **snakiness** *n.*

snap /snæp/ *v., n., adv., & adj.* —*v.* (**snapped, snapping**) **1** *intr. & tr.* break suddenly or with a snap. **2** *intr. & tr.* emit or cause to emit a sudden sharp sound or crack. **3** *intr. & tr.* open or close with a snapping sound (*the bag snapped shut*). **4 a** *intr.* (often foll. by *at*) speak irritably or spitefully (to a person) (*did not mean to snap at you*). **b** *tr.* say irritably or spitefully. **5** *intr.* (often foll. by *at*) (esp. of a dog etc.) make a sudden audible bite. **6** *tr. & intr.* move quickly (*snap into action*). **7** *tr.* take a snapshot of. **8** *tr. Amer. Football* put (the ball) into play on the ground by a quick backward movement. —*n.* **1** an act or sound of snapping. **2** a crisp biscuit or cake (*brandy snap; ginger snap*). **3** a snapshot. **4** (in full **cold snap**) a sudden brief spell of cold weather. **5** *Brit.* **a** a card-game in which players call 'snap' when two similar cards are exposed. **b** (as *int.*) on noticing the (often unexpected) similarity of two things. **6** crispness of style; fresh vigour or liveliness in action; zest; dash; spring. **7** *US sl.* an easy task (*it was a snap*). —*adv.* with the sound of a snap (*heard it go snap*). —*adj.* done or taken on the spur of the moment, unexpectedly, or without notice (*snap decision*). □**snap at** accept (bait, a chance, etc.) eagerly (see also senses 4a and 5 of *v.*). **snap bean** *US* a bean grown for its pods which are broken into pieces and eaten. **snap-bolt** (or **-lock**) a bolt etc. which locks automatically when a door or window closes. **snap-brim** (of a hat) with a brim that can be turned up and down at opposite sides. **snap-fastener** = *press-stud* (see PRESS[1]). **snap one's fingers 1** make an audible fillip, esp. in rhythm to music etc. **2** (often foll. by *at*) defy; show contempt for. **snap-hook** (or **-link**) a hook or link with a spring allowing the entrance but barring the escape of a cord, link, etc. **snap off** break off or bite off. **snap off a person's head** address a person angrily or rudely. **snap out** say irritably. **snap out of** *sl.* get rid of (a mood, habit, etc.) by a sudden effort. **snapping turtle** any large American freshwater turtle of the family Chelydridae which seizes prey with a snap of its jaws. **snap up 1** accept (an offer, a bargain) quickly or eagerly. **2** pick up or catch hastily or smartly. **3** interrupt (another person) before he or she has finished speaking. □□**snappable** *adj.* **snappingly** *adv.* [prob. f. MDu. or MLG *snappen*, partly imit.]

snapdragon /ˈsnæpˌdragən/ *n.* a plant, *Antirrhinum majus*, with a bag-shaped flower like a dragon's mouth.

snapper /ˈsnæpə(r)/ *n.* **1** a person or thing that snaps. **2** any of several fish of the family Lutjanidae, used as food. **3** a snapping turtle. **4** *US* a cracker (as a toy).

snappish /ˈsnæpɪʃ/ *adj.* **1** (of a person's manner or a remark) curt; ill-tempered; sharp. **2** (of a dog etc.) inclined to snap. □□**snappishly** *adv.* **snappishness** *n.*

snappy /ˈsnæpɪ/ *adj.* (**snappier, snappiest**) *colloq.* **1** brisk, full of zest. **2** neat and elegant (*a snappy dresser*). **3** snappish. □**make it snappy** be quick about it. □□**snappily** *adv.* **snappiness** *n.*

snapshot /ˈsnæpʃɒt/ *n.* a casual photograph taken quickly with a small hand-camera.

snare /sneə(r)/ *n. & v.* —*n.* **1** a trap for catching birds or animals, esp. with a noose of wire or cord. **2** a thing that acts as a temptation. **3** a device for tempting an enemy etc. to expose himself or herself to danger, failure, loss, capture, defeat, etc. **4** (in *sing.* or *pl.*) *Mus.* twisted strings of gut, hide, or wire stretched across the lower head of a side-drum to produce a rattling sound. **5** (in full **snare drum**) a drum fitted with snares. **6** *Surgery* a wire loop for extracting polyps etc. —*v.tr.* **1** catch (a bird etc.) in a snare. **2** ensnare; lure or trap (a person) with a snare. □□ **snarer** *n.* (also in *comb.*). [OE *sneare* f. ON *snara*: senses 4 & 5 prob. f. MLG or MDu.]

snark /snɑːk/ *n.* a fabulous animal, orig. the subject of a nonsense poem. [*The Hunting of the Snark* (1876) by Lewis Carroll]

snarl¹ /snɑːl/ *v. & n.* —*v.* **1** *intr.* (of a dog) make an angry growl with bared teeth. **2** *intr.* (of a person) speak cynically; make bad-tempered complaints or criticisms. **3** *tr.* (often foll. by *out*) **a** utter in a snarling tone. **b** express (discontent etc.) by snarling. —*n.* the act or sound of snarling. □□ **snarler** *n.* **snarlingly** *adv.* **snarly** *adj.* (**snarlier**, **snarliest**). [earlier *snar* f. (M)LG, MHG *snarren*]

snarl² /snɑːl/ *v. & n.* —*v.* **1** *tr.* (often foll. by *up*) twist; entangle; confuse and hamper the movement of (traffic etc.). **2** *intr.* (often foll. by *up*) become entangled, congested, or confused. **3** *tr.* adorn the exterior of (a narrow metal vessel) with raised work. —*n.* a knot or tangle. □**snarling iron** an implement used for snarling metal. **snarl-up** *colloq.* a traffic jam; a muddle; a mistake. [ME f. *snare* (n. & v.): sense 3 perh. f. noun in dial. sense 'knot in wood']

snatch /snætʃ/ *v. & n.* —*v.tr.* **1** seize quickly, eagerly, or unexpectedly, esp. with outstretched hands. **2** steal (a wallet, handbag, etc.). **3** secure with difficulty (*snatched an hour's rest*). **4** (foll. by *away, from*) take away or from esp. suddenly (*snatched away my hand*). **5** (foll. by *from*) rescue narrowly (*snatched from the jaws of death*). **6** (foll. by *at*) **a** try to seize by stretching or grasping suddenly. **b** take (an offer etc.) eagerly. —*n.* **1** an act of snatching (*made a snatch at it*). **2** a fragment of a song or talk etc. (*caught a snatch of their conversation*). **3** *US sl.* a kidnapping. **4** (in weight-lifting) the rapid raising of a weight from the floor to above the head. **5** a short spell of activity etc. □**in** (or **by**) **snatches** in fits and starts. □□ **snatcher** *n.* (esp. in sense 3 of *n.*). **snatchy** *adj.* [ME *snecchen*, *sna(c)che*, perh. rel. to SNACK]

snavel /ˈsnæv(ə)l/ *v.tr.* (also **snavle**, **snavvle**) *Austral. sl.* catch; take; steal. [E dial. (as SNAFFLE)]

snazzy /ˈsnæzɪ/ *adj.* (**snazzier**, **snazziest**) *sl.* smart or attractive esp. in an ostentatious way. □□ **snazzily** *adv.* **snazziness** *n.* [20th c.: orig. unkn.]

sneak /sniːk/ *v., n., & adj.* —*v.* **1** *intr.* & *tr.* (foll. by *in, out, past, away,* etc.) go or convey furtively; slink. **2** *tr. sl.* steal unobserved; make off with. **3** *intr. Brit. school sl.* tell tales; turn informer. **4** *intr.* (as **sneaking** *adj.*) **a** furtive; undisclosed (*have a sneaking affection for him*). **b** persistent in one's mind; nagging (*a sneaking feeling that it is not right*). —*n.* **1** a mean-spirited cowardly underhand person. **2** *Brit. school sl.* a tale-tale. —*adj.* acting or done without warning; secret (*a sneak attack*). □**sneak-thief** a thief who steals without breaking in; a pickpocket. □□ **sneakingly** *adv.* [16th c., prob. dial.: perh. rel. to ME *snike*, OE *snīcan* creep]

sneaker /ˈsniːkə(r)/ *n. sl.* each of a pair of soft-soled canvas etc. shoes.

sneaky /ˈsniːkɪ/ *adj.* (**sneakier**, **sneakiest**) given to or characterized by sneaking; furtive, mean. □□ **sneakily** *adv.* **sneakiness** *n.*

sneck /snek/ *n. & v. Sc. & N.Engl.* —*n.* a latch. —*v.tr.* latch (a door etc.); close or fasten with a sneck. [ME, rel. to SNATCH]

sneer /snɪə(r)/ *n. & v.* —*n.* a derisive smile or remark. —*v.* **1** *intr.* (often foll. by *at*) smile derisively. **2** *tr.* say sneeringly. **3** *intr.* (often foll. by *at*) speak derisively esp. covertly or ironically (*sneered at his attempts*). □□ **sneerer** *n.* **sneeringly** *adv.* [16th c.: orig. unkn.]

sneeze /sniːz/ *n. & v.* —*n.* **1** a sudden involuntary expulsion of air from the nose and mouth caused by irritation of the nostrils. **2** the sound of this. —*v.intr.* make a sneeze. □**not to be sneezed at** *colloq.* not contemptible; considerable; notable. □□

sneezer *n.* **sneezy** *adj.* [ME *snese*, app. alt. of obs. *fnese* f. OE *-fnēsan*, ON *fnýsa* & replacing earlier and less expressive *nese*]

sneezewort /ˈsniːzwɜːt/ *n.* a kind of yarrow, *Achillea ptarmica*, whose dried leaves are used to induce sneezing.

Snell's law /snelz/ *n. Physics* the law that the ratio of the sines of the angles of incidence and refraction of a wave are constant when it passes between two given media. [W. *Snell*, Du. mathematician d. 1626]

snib /snɪb/ *v. & n. Sc. & Ir.* —*v.tr.* (**snibbed**, **snibbing**) bolt, fasten, or lock (a door etc.). —*n.* a lock, catch, or fastening for a door or window. [19th c.: orig. uncert.]

snick /snɪk/ *v. & n.* —*v.tr.* **1** cut a small notch in. **2** make a small incision in. **3** *Cricket* deflect (the ball) slightly with the bat. —*n.* **1** a small notch or cut. **2** *Cricket* a slight deflection of the ball by the bat. [18th c.: prob. f. *snick-a-snee* fight with knives]

snicker /ˈsnɪkə(r)/ *v. & n.* —*v.intr.* **1** = SNIGGER *v.* **2** whinny, neigh. —*n.* **1** = SNIGGER *n.* **2** a whinny, a neigh. □□ **snickeringly** *adv.* [imit.]

snide /snaɪd/ *adj. & n.* —*adj.* **1** sneering; slyly derogatory; insinuating. **2** counterfeit; bogus. **3** *US* mean; underhand. —*n.* a snide person or remark. □□ **snidely** *adv.* **snideness** *n.* [19th-c. colloq.: orig. unkn.]

sniff /snɪf/ *v. & n.* —*v.* **1** *intr.* draw up air audibly through the nose to stop it running or to detect a smell or as an expression of contempt. **2** *tr.* (often foll. by *up*) draw in (a scent, drug, liquid, or air) through the nose. **3** *tr.* draw in the scent of (food, drink, flowers, etc.) through the nose. —*n.* **1** an act or sound of sniffing. **2** the amount of air etc. sniffed up. □**sniff at** **1** try the smell of; show interest in. **2** show contempt for or discontent with. **sniff out** detect; discover by investigation. □□ **sniffingly** *adv.* [ME, imit.]

sniffer /ˈsnɪfə(r)/ *n.* **1** a person who sniffs, esp. one who sniffs a drug or toxic substances (often in *comb.*: *glue-sniffer*). **2** *sl.* the nose. **3** *colloq.* any device for detecting gas, radiation, etc. □**sniffer-dog** *colloq.* a dog trained to sniff out drugs or explosives.

sniffle /ˈsnɪf(ə)l/ *v. & n.* —*v.intr.* sniff slightly or repeatedly. —*n.* **1** the act of sniffling. **2** (in *sing.* or *pl.*) a cold in the head causing a running nose and sniffling. □□ **sniffler** *n.* **sniffly** *adj.* [imit.: cf. SNIVEL]

sniffy /ˈsnɪfɪ/ *adj. colloq.* (**sniffier**, **sniffiest**) **1** inclined to sniff. **2** disdainful; contemptuous. □□ **sniffily** *adv.* **sniffiness** *n.*

snifter /ˈsnɪftə(r)/ *n.* **1** *sl.* a small drink of alcohol. **2** *US* a balloon glass for brandy. □**snifter-valve** a valve in a steam engine to allow air in or out. [dial. *snift* sniff, perh. f. Scand.: imit.]

snig /snɪg/ *v.tr.* (**snigged**, **snigging**) *Austral. & NZ* drag with a jerk. □**snigging chain** a chain used to move logs. [E dial.]

snigger /ˈsnɪgə(r)/ *n. & v.* —*n.* a half-suppressed secretive laugh. —*v.intr.* utter such a laugh. □□ **sniggerer** *n.* **sniggeringly** *adv.* [var. of SNICKER]

sniggle /ˈsnɪg(ə)l/ *v.intr.* fish (for eels) by pushing bait into a hole. [ME *snig* small eel, of unkn. orig.]

snip /snɪp/ *v. & n.* —*v.tr.* (**snipped**, **snipping**) (also *absol.*) cut (cloth, a hole, etc.) with scissors or shears, esp. in small quick strokes. —*n.* **1** an act of snipping. **2** a piece of material etc. snipped off. **3** *sl.* **a** something easily achieved. **b** *Brit.* a bargain; something cheaply acquired. **4** (in *pl.*) hand-shears for metal cutting. □**snip at** make snipping strokes at. □□ **snipping** *n.* [LG & Du. *snippen* imit.]

snipe /snaɪp/ *n. & v.* —*n.* (*pl.* same or **snipes**) any of various wading birds, esp. of the genus *Gallinago*, with a long straight bill and frequenting marshes. —*v.* **1** *intr.* fire shots from hiding run. at long range. **2** *tr.* kill by sniping. **3** *intr.* (foll. by *at*) make a sly critical attack. **4** *intr.* go snipe-shooting. □**snipe eel** any eel of the family Nemichthyidae, having a long slender snout. **snipe fish** any marine fish of the family Macrorhamphosidae, with a long slender snout. □□ **sniper** *n*. [ME, prob. f. Scand.: cf. Icel. *mýrisnípa*, & MDu., MLG *snippe*, OHG *snepfa*]

snippet /'snɪpɪt/ *n*. **1** a small piece cut off. **2** (usu. in *pl*.; often foll. by *of*) **a** a scrap or fragment of information, knowledge, etc. **b** a short extract from a book, newspaper, etc. □□ **snippety** *adj*.

snippy /'snɪpɪ/ *adj*. (**snippier**, **snippiest**) *colloq*. fault-finding, snappish, sharp. □□ **snippily** *adv*. **snippiness** *n*.

snit /snɪt/ *n*. *US* a rage; a sulk (esp. *in a snit*). [20th c.: orig. unkn.]

snitch /snɪtʃ/ *v*. & *n*. —*v*. *sl*. **1** *tr*. steal. **2** *intr*. (often foll. by *on*) inform on a person. —*n*. an informer. [17th c.: orig. unkn.]

snivel /'snɪv(ə)l/ *v*. & *n*. —*v*.*intr*. (**snivelled**, **snivelling**; *US* **sniveled**, **sniveling**) **1** weep with sniffling. **2** run at the nose; make a repeated sniffing sound. **3** show weak or tearful sentiment. —*n*. **1** running mucus. **2** hypocritical talk; cant. □□ **sniveller** *n*. **snivelling** *adj*. **snivellingly** *adv*. [ME f. OE *snyflan* (unrecorded) f. *snofl* mucus: cf. SNUFFLE]

snob /snɒb/ *n*. **1 a** a person with an exaggerated respect for social position or wealth and who despises socially inferior connections. **b** (*attrib*.) related to or characteristic of this attitude. **2** a person who behaves with servility to social superiors. **3** a person who despises others whose (usu. specified) tastes or attainments are considered inferior (*an intellectual snob; a wine snob*). □□ **snobbery** *n*. (*pl*. **-ies**). **snobbish** *adj*. **snobbishly** *adv*. **snobbishness** *n*. **snobby** *adj*. (**snobbier**, **snobbiest**). [18th c. (now dial.) 'cobbler': orig. unkn.]

snoek /snuːk/ *n*. *S.Afr.* a barracouta. [Afrik. f. Du., = PIKE[1], f. MLG *snōk*, prob. rel. to SNACK]

snog /snɒg/ *v*. & *n*. *Brit*. *sl*. —*v*.*intr*. (**snogged**, **snogging**) engage in kissing and caressing. —*n*. a spell of snogging. [20th c.: orig. unkn.]

snood /snuːd/ *n*. **1** an ornamental hairnet usu. worn at the back of the head. **2** a ring of woollen etc. material worn as a hood. **3** a short line attaching a hook to a main line in sea fishing. **4** *hist*. a ribbon or band worn by unmarried women in Scotland to confine their hair. [OE *snōd*]

snook[1] /snuːk/ *n*. *sl*. a contemptuous gesture with the thumb to the nose and the fingers spread out. □**cock a snook** (often foll. by *at*) **1** make this gesture. **2** register one's contempt (for a person, establishment, etc.). [19th c.: orig. unkn.]

snook[2] /snuːk/ *n*. a marine fish, *Centropomus undecimalis*, used as food. [Du. *snoek*: see SNOEK]

snooker /'snuːkə(r)/ *n*. & *v*. —*n*. **1** a game played with cues on a rectangular baize-covered table in which the players use a cue-ball (white) to pocket the other balls (15 red and 6 coloured) in a set order. **2** a position in this game in which a direct shot at a permitted ball is impossible. —*v*.*tr*. **1** (also *refl*.) subject (oneself or another player) to a snooker. **2** (esp. as **snookered** *adj*.) *sl*. defeat; thwart. [19th c.: orig. unkn.]

snoop /snuːp/ *v*. & *n*. *colloq*. —*v*.*intr*. **1** pry into matters one need not be concerned with. **2** (often foll. by *about*, *around*) investigate in order to find out transgressions of the law etc. —*n*. **1** an act of snooping. **2** a person who snoops; a detective. □□ **snooper** *n*. **snoopy** *adj*. [Du. *snœpen* eat on the sly]

snooperscope /'snuːpə,skəʊp/ *n*. *US* a device which converts infrared radiation into a visible image, esp. used for seeing in the dark.

snoot /snuːt/ *n*. *sl*. the nose. [var. of SNOUT]

snooty /'snuːtɪ/ *adj*. (**snootier**, **snootiest**) *colloq*. supercilious; conceited. □□ **snootily** *adv*. **snootiness** *n*. [20th c.: orig. unkn.]

snooze /snuːz/ *n*. & *v*. *colloq*. —*n*. a short sleep, esp. in the daytime. —*v*.*intr*. take a snooze. □□ **snoozer** *n*. **snoozy** *adj*. (**snoozier**, **snooziest**). [18th-c. *sl*.: orig. unkn.]

snore /snɔː(r)/ *n*. & *v*. —*n*. a snorting or grunting

sound in breathing during sleep. —*v*.*intr*. make this sound. □**snore away** pass (time) sleeping or snoring. □□ **snorer** *n*. **snoringly** *adv*. [ME, prob. imit.: cf. SNORT]

snorkel /'snɔːk(ə)l/ *n*. & *v*. (also **schnorkel** /'ʃnɔː-/) —*n*. **1** a breathing-tube for an underwater swimmer. **2** a device for supplying air to a submerged submarine. —*v*.*intr*. (**snorkelled**, **snorkelling**; *US* **snorkeled**, **snorkeling**) use a snorkel. □□ **snorkeller** *n*. [G *Schnorchel*]

snort /snɔːt/ *n*. & *v*. —*n*. **1** an explosive sound made by the sudden forcing of breath through the nose, esp. expressing indignation or incredulity. **2** a similar sound made by an engine etc. **3** *colloq*. a small drink of liquor. **4** an inhaled dose of a (usu. illegal) powdered drug. —*v*. **1** *intr*. make a snort. **2** *intr*. (of an engine etc.) make a sound resembling this. **3** *tr*. (also *absol*.) *sl*. inhale (a usu. illegal narcotic drug, esp. cocaine or heroin). **4** *tr*. express (defiance etc.) by snorting. □**snort out** express (words, emotions, etc.) by snorting. [ME, prob. imit.: cf. SNORE]

snorter /'snɔːtə(r)/ *n*. *colloq*. **1** something very impressive or difficult. **2** something vigorous or violent.

snot /snɒt/ *n*. *sl*. **1** nasal mucus. **2** a term of contempt for a person. □**snot-rag** a handkerchief. [prob. f. MDu., MLG *snotte*, MHG *snuz*, rel. to SNOUT]

snotty /'snɒtɪ/ *adj*. (**snottier**, **snottiest**) *sl*. **1** running or foul with nasal mucus. **2** contemptible. **3** supercilious, conceited. □□ **snottily** *adv*. **snottiness** *n*.

snout /snaʊt/ *n*. **1** the projecting nose and mouth of an animal. **2** *derog*. a person's nose. **3** the pointed front of a thing; a nozzle. **4** *Brit*. *sl*. tobacco or a cigarette. □**snout-beetle** a weevil. □□ **snouted** *adj*. (also in *comb*.). **snoutlike** *adj*. **snouty** *adj*. [ME f. MDu., MLG *snūt*]

snow /snəʊ/ *n*. & *v*. —*n*. **1** atmospheric vapour frozen into ice crystals and falling to earth in light white flakes. **2** a fall of this, or a layer of it on the ground. **3** a thing resembling snow in whiteness or texture etc. **4** a mass of flickering white spots on a television or radar screen, caused by interference or a poor signal. **5** *sl*. cocaine. **6** a dessert or other dish resembling snow. **7** frozen carbon dioxide. —*v*. **1** *intr*. (prec. by *it* as subject) snow falls (*it is snowing*; *if it snows*). **2** *tr*. (foll. by *in*, *over*, *up*, etc.) confine or block with large quantities of snow. **3** *tr*. & *intr*. sprinkle or scatter or fall as or like snow. **4** *intr*. come in large numbers or quantities. **5** *tr*. *US sl*. deceive or charm with plausible words. □**be snowed under** be overwhelmed, esp. with work. **snow-blind** temporarily blinded by the glare of light reflected by large expanses of snow. **snow-blindness** this blindness. **snow-blink** the reflection in the sky of snow or ice fields. **snow boot** an overboot of rubber and cloth. **snow-broth** melted or melting snow. **snow bunting** a mainly white finch, *Plectrophenax nivalis*. **snow goose** a white Arctic goose, *Anser caerulescens*, with black-tipped wings. **snow-ice** opaque white ice formed from melted snow. **snow leopard** = OUNCE[2]. **snow owl** = *snowy owl*. **snow partridge** a mainly white partridge, *Lerwa lerwa*. **snow-slip** an avalanche. **snow-white** pure white. □□ **snowless** *adj*. **snowlike** *adj*. [OE *snāw* f. Gmc]

snowball /'snəʊbɔːl/ *n*. & *v*. —*n*. **1** snow pressed together into a ball, esp. for throwing in play. **2** anything that grows or increases rapidly like a snowball rolled on snow. —*v*. **1** *intr*. & *tr*. throw or pelt with snowballs. **2** *intr*. increase rapidly. □**snowball-tree** a guelder rose.

snowberry /'snəʊbərɪ/ *n*. (*pl*. **-ies**) any shrub of the genus *Symphoricarpos*, with white berries.

snowblower /'snəʊ,bləʊə(r)/ *n*. a machine that clears snow by blowing it to the side of the road etc.

snowbound /'snəʊbaʊnd/ *adj*. prevented by snow from going out or travelling.

snowcap /'snəʊkæp/ *n*. **1** the tip of a mountain when covered with snow. **2** a white-crowned humming-bird, *Microchera albocoronata*, native to Central America. □□ **snowcapped** *adj*.

snowdrift /'snəʊdrɪft/ *n*. a bank of snow heaped up by the action of the wind.

snowdrop /'snəʊdrɒp/ *n*. a bulbous plant, *Galanthus nivalis*, with white drooping flowers in the early spring.

snowfall /'snəʊfɔːl/ *n*. **1** a fall of snow. **2** *Meteorol*. the amount of snow that falls on one occasion or on a given area within a given time.

snowfield /'snəʊfiːld/ *n*. a permanent wide expanse of snow in mountainous or polar regions.

snowflake /'snəʊfleɪk/ *n*. **1** each of the small collections of crystals in which snow falls. **2 a** any bulbous plant of the genus *Leucojum*, with snowdrop-like flowers. **b** the white flower of this plant.

snowline /'snəʊlaɪn/ *n*. the level above which snow never melts entirely.

snowman /'snəʊmæn/ *n*. (*pl*. **-men**) a figure resembling a man, made of compressed snow.

snowmobile /'snəʊməˌbiːl/ *n*. a motor vehicle, esp. with runners or Caterpillar tracks, for travelling over snow.

snowplough /'snəʊplaʊ/ *n*. (*US* **snowplow**) a device, or a vehicle equipped with one, for clearing roads of thick snow.

snowshoe /'snəʊʃuː/ *n*. & *v*. —*n*. a flat device like a racket attached to a boot for walking on snow without sinking in. —*v.intr*. travel on snowshoes. □□ **snowshoer** *n*.

snowstorm /'snəʊstɔːm/ *n*. a heavy fall of snow, esp. with a high wind.

snowy /'snəʊɪ/ *adj*. (**snowier**, **snowiest**) **1** of or like snow. **2** (of the weather etc.) with much snow. □ **snowy owl** a large white owl, *Nyctea scandiaca*, native to the Arctic. □□ **snowily** *adv*. **snowiness** *n*.

SNP *abbr*. Scottish National Party.

Snr. *abbr*. Senior.

snub /snʌb/ *v*., *n*., & *adj*. —*v.tr*. (**snubbed**, **snubbing**) **1** rebuff or humiliate with sharp words or a marked lack of cordiality. **2** check the movement of (a boat, horse, etc.) esp. by a rope wound round a post etc. —*n*. an act of snubbing; a rebuff. —*adj*. short and blunt in shape. □ **snub nose** a short turned-up nose. **snub-nosed** having a snub nose. □□ **snubber** *n*. **snubbingly** *adv*. [ME f. ON *snubba* chide, check the growth of]

snuff[1] /snʌf/ *n*. & *v*. —*n*. the charred part of a candle-wick. —*v.tr*. trim the snuff from (a candle). □ **snuff it** *Brit. sl*. die. **snuff out 1** extinguish by snuffing. **2** kill; put an end to. [ME *snoffe*, *snuffe*: orig. unkn.]

snuff[2] /snʌf/ *n*. & *v*. —*n*. powdered tobacco or medicine taken by sniffing it up the nostrils. —*v.intr*. take snuff. □ **snuff-coloured** dark yellowish-brown. **up to snuff** *colloq*. **1** *Brit*. knowing; not easily deceived. **2** up to standard. [Du. *snuf* (*tabak* tobacco) f. MDu. *snuffen* snuffle]

snuffbox /'snʌfbɒks/ *n*. a small usu. ornamental box for holding snuff.

snuffer /'snʌfə(r)/ *n*. **1** a small hollow cone with a handle used to extinguish a candle. **2** (in *pl*.) an implement like scissors used to extinguish a candle or trim its wick.

snuffle /'snʌf(ə)l/ *v*. & *n*. —*v*. **1** *intr*. make sniffing sounds. **2 a** *intr*. speak nasally, whiningly, or like one with a cold. **b** *tr*. (often foll. by *out*) say in this way. **3** *intr*. breathe noisily as through a partially blocked nose. **4** *intr*. sniff. —*n*. **1** a snuffling sound or tone. **2** (in *pl*.) a partial blockage of the nose causing snuffling. **3** a sniff. □□ **snuffler** *n*. **snuffly** *adj*. [prob. f. LG & Du. *snuffelen* (as SNUFF[2]): cf. SNIVEL]

snuffy[1] /'snʌfɪ/ *adj*. (**snuffier**, **snuffiest**) **1** annoyed. **2** irritable. **3** supercilious or contemptuous. [SNUFF[1] + -Y[1]]

snuffy[2] /'snʌfɪ/ *adj*. like snuff in colour or substance. [SNUFF[2] + -Y[2]]

snug /snʌg/ *adj*. & *n*. —*adj*. (**snugger**, **snuggest**) **1 a** cosy, comfortable, sheltered; well enclosed or placed or arranged. **b** cosily protected from the weather or cold. **2** (of an income etc.) allowing comfort and comparative ease. —*n*. *Brit*. a small room in a pub or inn. □□ **snugly** *adv*. **snugness** *n*. [16th c. (orig. Naut.): prob. of LG or Du. orig.]

snuggery /'snʌgərɪ/ *n*. (*pl*. **-ies**) **1** a snug place, esp. a person's private room or den. **2** *Brit*. = SNUG *n*.

snuggle /'snʌg(ə)l/ *v.intr*. & *tr*. (usu. foll. by *down*, *up*, *together*) settle or draw into a warm comfortable position. [SNUG + -LE[4]]

So. *abbr*. South.

so[1] /səʊ/ *adv*. & *conj*. —*adv*. **1** (often foll. by *that* + clause) to such an extent, or to the extent implied (*why are you so angry?*; *do stop complaining so*; *they were so pleased that they gave us a bonus*). **2** (with *neg*.; often foll. by *as* + clause) to the extent to which . . . is or does etc., or to the extent implied (*was not so late as I expected*; *am not so eager as you*). ¶ In positive constructions *as . . . as . . .* is used: see AS[1]. **3** (foll. by *that* or *as* + clause) to the degree or in the manner implied (*so expensive that few can afford it*; *so small as to be invisible*; *am not so foolish as to agree to that*). **4** (adding emphasis) to that extent; in that or a similar manner (*I want to leave and so does she*; *you said it was good, and so it is*). **5** to a great or notable degree (*I am so glad*). **6** (with verbs of state) in the way described (*am not very fond of it but may become so*). **7** (with verb of saying or thinking etc.) as previously mentioned or described (*I think so*; *so he said*; *so I should hope*). —*conj*. (often foll. by *that* + clause) **1** with the result that (*there was none left, so we had to go without*). **2** in order that (*came home early so that I could see you*). **3** and then; as the next step (*so then the car broke down*; *and so to bed*). **4 a** (introducing a question) then; after that (*so what did you tell them?*). **b** (*absol*.) = *so what?* □ **and so on** (or **forth**) **1** and others of the same kind. **2** and in other similar ways. **so as** (foll. by *to* + infin.) in order to (*did it so as to get it finished*). **so be it** an expression of acceptance or resignation. **so-called** commonly designated or known as, often incorrectly. **so far** see FAR. **so far as** see FAR. **so far so good** see FAR. **so long!** *colloq*. goodbye till we meet again. **so long as** see LONG[1]. **so much 1** a certain amount (of). **2** a great deal of (*is so much nonsense*). **3** (with *neg*.) **a** less than; to a lesser extent (*not so much forgotten as ignored*). **b** not even (*didn't give me so much as a penny*). **so much for** that is all that need be done or said about. **so so** *adj*. (usu. *predic*.) indifferent; not very good. —*adv*. indifferently; only moderately well. **so to say** (or **speak**) an expression of reserve or apology for an exaggeration or neologism etc. **so what?** *colloq*. why should that be considered significant? [OE *swā* etc.]

so[2] var. of SOH.

-so /səʊ/ *comb. form* = -SOEVER.

soak /səʊk/ *v*. & *n*. —*v*. **1** *tr*. & *intr*. make or become thoroughly wet through saturation with or in liquid. **2** *tr*. (of rain etc.) drench. **3** *tr*. (foll. by *in*, *up*) absorb (liquid). **b** acquire (knowledge etc.) copiously. **4** *refl*. (often foll. by *in*) steep (oneself) in a subject of study etc. **5** *intr*. (foll. by *in*, *into*, *through*) (of liquid) make its way or penetrate by saturation. **6** *tr*. *colloq*. extract money from by an extortionate charge, taxation, etc. (*soak the rich*). **7** *intr*. *colloq*. drink persistently, booze. **8** *tr*. (as **soaked** *adj*.) very drunk. —*n*. **1** the act of soaking or the state of being soaked. **2** a drinking-bout. **3** *colloq*. a hard drinker. □□ **soakage** *n*. **soaker** *n*. **soaking** *n*. & *adj*. [OE *socian* rel. to *soc* sucking at the breast, *sūcan* SUCK]

soakaway /'səʊkəˌweɪ/ *n*. an arrangement for disposing of waste water by letting it percolate through the soil.

so-and-so /'səʊənd,səʊ/ *n*. (*pl*. **so-and-so's**) **1** a particular person or thing not needing to be specified (*told me to do so-and-so*). **2** *colloq.* a person disliked or regarded with disfavour (*the so-and-so left me behind*).

soap /səʊp/ *n. & v.* —*n.* **1** a cleansing agent that is a compound of fatty acid with soda or potash or (**insoluble soap**) with another metallic oxide, of which the soluble kinds when rubbed in water yield a lather used in washing. **2** *colloq.* = *soap opera.* —*v.tr.* **1** apply soap to. **2** scrub or rub with soap. □ **soap flakes** soap in the form of thin flakes, for washing clothes etc. **soap opera** a broadcast drama, usu. serialized in many episodes, dealing with sentimental domestic themes (so called because orig. sponsored in the US by soap manufacturers). **soap powder** powdered soap esp. with additives. □□ **soapless** *adj.* **soaplike** *adj.* [OE *sāpe* f. WG]

soapbark /ˈsəʊpbɑːk/ *n.* an American tree, *Quillaja saponaria*, with bark yielding saponin.

soapberry /ˈsəʊpˌberɪ/ *n.* (*pl.* **-ies**) any of various tropical American shrubs, esp. of the genus *Sapindus*, with fruits yielding saponin.

soapbox /ˈsəʊpbɒks/ *n.* **1** a box for holding soap. **2** a makeshift stand for a public speaker.

soapstone /ˈsəʊpstəʊn/ *n.* steatite.

soapsuds /ˈsəʊpsʌdz/ *n.pl.* = SUDS 1.

soapwort /ˈsəʊpwɜːt/ *n.* a European plant, *Saponaria officinalis*, with pink or white flowers and leaves yielding a soapy substance.

soapy /ˈsəʊpɪ/ *adj.* (**soapier, soapiest**) **1** of or like soap. **2** containing or smeared with soap. **3** (of a person or manner) unctuous or flattering. □□ **soapily** *adv.* **soapiness** *n.*

soar /sɔː(r)/ *v.intr.* **1** fly or rise high. **2** reach a high level or standard (*prices soared*). **3** maintain height in the air without flapping the wings or using power. □□ **soarer** *n.* **soaringly** *adv.* [ME f. OF *essorer* ult. f. L (as EX-1, *aura* breeze)]

sob /sɒb/ *v. & n.* —*v.* (**sobbed, sobbing**) **1** *intr.* draw breath in convulsive gasps usu. with weeping under mental distress or physical exhaustion. **2** *tr.* (usu. foll. by *out*) utter with sobs. **3** *tr.* bring (oneself) to a specified state by sobbing (*sobbed themselves to sleep*). —*n.* a convulsive drawing of breath, esp. in weeping. □ **sob story** a story or explanation appealing mainly to the emotions. **sob-stuff** *colloq.* sentimental talk or writing. □□ **sobber** *n.* **sobbingly** *adv.* [ME *sobbe* (prob. imit.)]

sober /ˈsəʊbə(r)/ *adj. & n.* —*adj.* (**soberer, soberest**) **1** not affected by alcohol. **2** not given to excessive drinking of alcohol. **3** moderate, well-balanced, tranquil, sedate. **4** not fanciful or exaggerated (*the sober truth*). **5** (of a colour etc.) quiet and inconspicuous. —*v.tr. & intr.* (often foll. by *down, up*) make or become sober or less wild, reckless, enthusiastic, visionary, etc. (*a sobering thought*). □ **as sober as a judge** completely sober. □□ **soberingly** *adv.* **soberly** *adv.* [ME f. OF *sobre* f. L *sobrius*]

sobriety /səˈbraɪɪtɪ/ *n.* the state of being sober. [ME f. OF *sobrieté* or L *sobrietas* (as SOBER)]

sobriquet /ˈsəʊbrɪˌkeɪ/ *n.* (also **soubriquet** /ˈsuː-/) **1** a nickname. **2** an assumed name. [F, orig. = 'tap under the chin']

Soc. *abbr.* **1** Socialist. **2** Society.

socage /ˈsɒkɪdʒ/ *n.* (also **soccage**) a feudal tenure of land involving payment of rent or other non-military service to a superior. [ME f. AF *socage* f. *soc* f. OE *sōcn* SOKE]

soccer /ˈsɒkə(r)/ *n.* Association football. [Assoc. + -ER3]

sociable /ˈsəʊʃəb(ə)l/ *adj. & n.* —*adj.* **1** fitted for or liking the society of other people; ready and willing to talk and act with others. **2** (of a person's manner or behaviour etc.) friendly. **3** (of a meeting etc.) marked by friendliness, not stiff or formal. —*n.* **1** an open carriage with facing side seats. **2** an S-shaped couch for two occupants partly facing each other. **3** *US* a social. □□ **sociability** /-ˈbɪlɪtɪ/ *n.* **sociableness**

n. **sociably** *adv.* [F *sociable* or L *sociabilis* f. *sociare* to unite f. *socius* companion]

social /ˈsəʊʃ(ə)l/ *adj. & n.* —*adj.* **1** of or relating to society or its organization. **2** concerned with the mutual relations of human beings or of classes of human beings. **3** living in organized communities; unfitted for a solitary life (*man is a social animal*). **4** needing companionship; gregarious, interdependent. **b** cooperative; practising the division of labour. **5** existing only as a member of a compound organism. **6 a** (of insects) living together in organized communities. **b** (of birds) nesting near each other in communities. **7** (of plants) growing thickly together and monopolizing the ground they grow on. —*n.* a social gathering, esp. one organized by a club, congregation, etc. □ **social anthropology** the comparative study of peoples through their culture and kinship systems. **social climber** *derog.* a person anxious to gain a higher social status. **social contract** (or **compact**) an agreement to cooperate for social benefits, e.g. by sacrificing some individual freedom for State protection. **social credit** the economic theory that the profits of industry should be distributed to the general public. **social democracy** a socialist system achieved by democratic means. **social democrat** a person who advocates social democracy. **social order** the network of human relationships in society. **social realism** the expression of social or political views in art. **social science a** the scientific study of human society and social relationships. **b** a branch of this (e.g. politics or economics). **social scientist** a student of or expert in the social sciences. **social secretary** a person who makes arrangements for the social activities of a person or organization. **social security** State assistance to those lacking in economic security and welfare, e.g. the aged and the unemployed. **social service** philanthropic activity. **social services** services provided by the State for the community, esp. education, health, and housing. **social war** *hist.* a war fought between allies. **social work** work of benefit to those in need of help or welfare, esp. done by specially trained personnel. **social worker** a person trained to do social work. □□ **sociality** /ˌsəʊʃɪˈælɪtɪ/ *n.* **socially** *adv.* [F *social* or L *socialis* allied f. *socius* friend]

socialism /ˈsəʊʃəˌlɪz(ə)m/ *n.* **1** a political and economic theory of social organization which advocates that the community as a whole should own and control the means of production, distribution, and exchange. **2** policy or practice based on this theory. □□ **socialist** *n. & adj.* **socialistic** /-ˈlɪstɪk/ *adj.* **socialistically** /-ˈlɪstɪkəlɪ/ *adv.* [F *socialisme* (as SOCIAL)]

socialite /ˈsəʊʃəˌlaɪt/ *n.* a person prominent in fashionable society.

socialize /ˈsəʊʃəˌlaɪz/ *v.* (also **-ise**) **1** *intr.* act in a sociable manner. **2** *tr.* make social. **3** *tr.* organize on socialistic principles. □ **socialized medicine** *US* the provision of medical services for all from public funds. □□ **socialization** /-ˈzeɪʃ(ə)n/ *n.*

society /səˈsaɪətɪ/ *n.* (*pl.* **-ies**) **1** the sum of human conditions and activity regarded as a whole functioning interdependently. **2** a social community (*all societies must have firm laws*). **3 a** a social mode of life. **b** the customs and organization of an ordered community. **4** *Ecol.* a plant community. **5 a** the socially advantaged or prominent members of a community (*society would not approve*). **b** this, or a part of it, qualified in some way (*is not done in polite society*). **6** participation in hospitality; other people's homes or company (*avoids society*). **7** companionship, company (*avoids the society of such people*). **8** an association of persons united by a common aim or interest or principle (*formed a music society*). □ **Society of Friends** see QUAKER. **Society of Jesus** see JESUIT. □□ **societal** *adj.* (esp. in sense 1).

æ *cat* ɑː *arm* e *bed* ɜː *her* ɪ *sit* iː *see* ɒ *hot* ɔː *saw* ʌ *run* ʊ *put* uː *too* ə *ago* aɪ *my*

societally *adv.* [F *société* f. L *societas -tatis* f. *socius* companion]

socio- /'səʊsɪəʊ, -ʃɪəʊ/ *comb. form* **1** of society (and). **2** of or relating to sociology (and). [L *socius* companion]

sociobiology /ˌsəʊsɪəʊbaɪ'ɒlədʒɪ, ˌsəʊʃɪəʊ-/ *n.* the scientific study of the biological aspects of social behaviour. □□ **sociobiological** /-ˌbaɪə'lɒdʒɪk(ə)l/ *adj.* **sociobiologically** /-ˌbaɪə'lɒdʒɪkəlɪ/ *adv.* **sociobiologist** *n.*

sociocultural /ˌsəʊsɪəʊ'kʌltʃər(ə)l, ˌsəʊʃɪəʊ-/ *adj.* combining social and cultural factors. □□ **socioculturally** *adv.*

socio-economic /ˌsəʊsɪəʊˌiːkə'nɒmɪk, ˌsəʊʃɪəʊ-/ *adj.* relating to or concerned with the interaction of social and economic factors. □□ **socio-economically** *adv.*

sociolinguistic /ˌsəʊsɪəʊlɪŋ'gwɪstɪk, ˌsəʊʃɪəʊ-/ *adj.* relating to or concerned with language in its social aspects. □□ **sociolinguist** *n.* **sociolinguistically** *adv.*

sociolinguistics /ˌsəʊsɪəʊlɪŋ'gwɪstɪks, ˌsəʊʃɪəʊ-/ *n.* the study of language in relation to social factors.

sociology /ˌsəʊsɪ'ɒlədʒɪ, ˌsəʊʃɪ-/ *n.* **1** the study of the development, structure, and functioning of human society. **2** the study of social problems. □□ **sociological** /-ə'lɒdʒɪk(ə)l/ *adj.* **sociologically** /-ə'lɒdʒɪkəlɪ/ *adv.* **sociologist** *n.* [F *sociologie* (as SOCIO-, -LOGY)]

sociometry /ˌsəʊsɪ'ɒmɪtrɪ, ˌsəʊʃɪ-/ *n.* the study of relationships within a group of people. □□ **sociometric** /-ə'metrɪk/ *adj.* **sociometrically** /-ə'metrɪkəlɪ/ *adv.* **sociometrist** *n.*

sock¹ /sɒk/ *n.* (*pl.* **socks** or *informal & Commerce* **sox** /sɒks/) **1** a short knitted covering for the foot, usu. not reaching the knee. **2** a removable inner sole put into a shoe for warmth etc. **3** an ancient Greek or Roman comic actor's light shoe. **4** comic drama. □**pull one's socks up** *Brit. colloq.* make an effort to improve. **put a sock in it** *Brit. sl.* be quiet. [OE *socc* f. L *soccus* comic actor's shoe, light low-heeled slipper, f. Gk *sukkhos*]

sock² /sɒk/ *v. & n. colloq.* —*v.tr.* hit (esp. a person) forcefully. —*n.* **1** a hard blow. **2** *US* the power to deliver a blow. □**sock it to** attack or address (a person) vigorously. [*c*.1700 (cant): orig. unkn.]

socket /'sɒkɪt/ *n. & v.* —*n.* **1** a natural or artificial hollow for something to fit into or stand firm or revolve in. **2** *Electr.* a device receiving a plug, light-bulb, etc., to make a connection. **3** *Golf* the part of an iron club into which the shaft is fitted. —*v.tr.* (**socketed, socketing**) **1** place in or fit with a socket. **2** *Golf* hit (a ball) with the socket of a club. [ME f. AF, dimin. of OF *soc* ploughshare, prob. of Celt. orig.]

sockeye /'sɒkaɪ/ *n.* a blue-backed salmon of Alaska etc., *Oncorhynchus nerka.* [Salish *sukai* fish of fishes]

socle /'səʊk(ə)l/ *n. Archit.* a plain low block or plinth serving as a support for a column, urn, statue, etc., or as the foundation of a wall. [F f. It. *zoccolo* orig. 'wooden shoe' f. L *socculus* f. *soccus* SOCK¹]

Socratic /sə'krætɪk/ *adj. & n.* —*adj.* of or relating to the Greek philosopher Socrates (d. 399 BC) or his philosophy, esp. the method associated with him of seeking the truth by a series of questions and answers. —*n.* a follower of Socrates. □**Socratic irony** a pose of ignorance assumed in order to entice others into making statements that can then be challenged. □□ **Socratically** *adv.* [L *Socraticus* f. Gk *Sōkratikos* f. *Sōkratēs*]

sod¹ /sɒd/ *n. & v.* —*n.* **1** turf or a piece of turf. **2** the surface of the ground. —*v.tr.* (**sodded, sodding**) cover (the ground) with sods. □**under the sod** in the grave. [ME f. MDu., MLG *sode*, of unkn. orig.]

sod² /sɒd/ *n. & v. esp. Brit. coarse sl.* ¶ Often considered a taboo word. —*n.* **1** an unpleasant or awkward person or thing. **2** a person of a specified kind; a fellow (*the lucky sod*). —*v.tr.* (**sodded, sodding**) **1** (often *absol.* or as *int.*) an exclamation of annoyance (*sod them, I don't care!*). **2** (as **sodding**

adj.) a general term of contempt. □**sod off** go away. **Sod's Law** = MURPHY'S LAW. [abbr. of SODOMITE]

soda /'səʊdə/ *n.* **1** any of various compounds of sodium in common use, e.g. washing soda, caustic soda. **2** (in full **soda water**) water made effervescent by impregnation with carbon dioxide under pressure and used alone or with spirits etc. as a drink (orig. made with sodium bicarbonate). **3** esp. *US* a sweet effervescent drink. □**soda bread** bread leavened with baking-soda. **soda fountain 1** a device supplying soda water. **2** a shop or counter equipped with this. **soda lime** a mixture of calcium oxide and sodium hydroxide. [med.L, perh. f. *sodanum* glasswort (used as a remedy for headaches) f. *soda* headache f. Arab. *ṣudā*ʿ f. *ṣadaʿa* split]

sodality /səʊ'dælɪtɪ/ *n.* (*pl.* **-ies**) a confraternity or association, esp. a Roman Catholic religious guild or brotherhood. [F *sodalité* or L *sodalitas* f. *sodalis* comrade]

sodden /'sɒd(ə)n/ *adj. & v.* —*adj.* **1** saturated with liquid; soaked through. **2** rendered stupid or dull etc. with drunkenness. **3** (of bread etc.) doughy; heavy and moist. —*v.intr. & tr.* become or make sodden. □□ **soddenly** *adv.* **soddenness** *n.* [archaic past part. of SEETHE]

sodium /'səʊdɪəm/ *n. Chem.* a soft silver-white reactive metallic element, occurring naturally in soda, salt, etc., that is important in industry and is an essential element in living organisms. ¶ Symb.: **Na.** □**sodium bicarbonate** a white soluble powder used in the manufacture of fire extinguishers and effervescent drinks. **sodium carbonate** a white powder with many commercial applications including the manufacture of soap and glass. **sodium chloride** a colourless crystalline compound occurring naturally in sea water and halite; common salt. **sodium hydroxide** a deliquescent compound which is strongly alkaline and used in the manufacture of salt and pepper: also called *caustic soda.* **sodium nitrate** a white powdery compound used mainly in the manufacture of fertilizers. **sodium-vapour lamp** (or **sodium lamp**) a lamp using an electrical discharge in sodium vapour and giving a yellow light. □□ **sodic** *adj.* [SODA + -IUM]

Sodom /'sɒdəm/ *n.* a wicked or depraved place. [*Sodom* in ancient Palestine, destroyed for its wickedness (Gen. 18–19)]

sodomite /'sɒdəmaɪt/ *n.* a person who practises sodomy. [ME f. OF f. LL *Sodomita* f. Gk *Sodomitēs* inhabitant of Sodom f. *Sodoma* Sodom]

sodomy /'sɒdəmɪ/ *n.* = BUGGERY. □□ **sodomize** *v.tr.* (also **-ise**). [ME f. med.L *sodomia* f. LL *peccatum Sodomiticum* sin of Sodom: see SODOM]

soever /səʊ'evə(r)/ *adv. literary* of any kind; to any extent (*how great soever it may be*).

-soever /səʊ'evə(r)/ *comb. form* (added to relative pronouns, adverbs, and adjectives) of any kind; to any extent (*whatsoever; howsoever*).

sofa /'səʊfə/ *n.* a long upholstered seat with a back and arms, for two or more people. □**sofa bed** a sofa that can be converted into a temporary bed. [F, ult. f. Arab. *ṣuffa*]

soffit /'sɒfɪt/ *n.* the under-surface of an architrave, arch, balcony, etc. [F *soffite* or It. *soffitta*, *-itto* ult. f. L *suffixus* (as SUFFIX)]

S. of S. *abbr.* Song of Songs (Old Testament).

soft /sɒft/ *adj., adv., & n.* —*adj.* **1** (of a substance, material, etc.) lacking hardness or firmness; yielding to pressure; easily cut. **2** (of cloth etc.) having a smooth surface or texture; not rough or coarse. **3** (of air etc.) mellow, mild, balmy; not noticeably cold or hot. **4** (of water) free from mineral salts and therefore good for lathering. **5** (of a light or colour etc.) not brilliant or glaring. **6** (of a voice or sounds) gentle and pleasing. **7** *Phonet.* **a** (of a consonant) sibilant or palatal (as *c* in *ice*, *g* in *age*). **b** voiced or unaspirated. **8** (of an outline etc.) not sharply defined. **9** (of an action or manner etc.) gentle, conciliatory, complimentary, amorous. **10** (of the heart or feelings etc.) compassionate, sympathetic. **11** (of a person's character or attitude etc.) feeble, lenient, silly, sentimental. **12** *colloq.* (of a job etc.) easy. **13** (of drugs) mild; not likely to cause addiction. **14** (of radiation) having little penetrating power. **15** (also **soft-core**) (of pornography) suggestive or erotic but not explicit. **16** *Stock Exch.* (of currency, prices, etc.) likely to fall in value. **17** *Polit.* moderate; willing to compromise (*the soft left*). **18** peaceful (*soft slumbers*). **19** *Brit.* (of the weather etc.) rainy or moist or thawing. —*adv.* softly (*play soft*). —*n.* a silly weak person. □**be soft on** *colloq.* **1** be lenient towards. **2** be infatuated with. **have a soft spot for** be fond of or affectionate towards (a person). **soft answer** a good-tempered answer to abuse or an accusation. **soft-boiled** (of an egg) lightly boiled with the yolk soft or liquid. **soft-centred** (of a person) soft-hearted, sentimental. **soft coal** bituminous coal. **soft detergent** a biodegradable detergent. **soft drink** a non-alcoholic drink. **soft focus** *Photog.* the slight deliberate blurring of a picture. **soft fruit** *Brit.* small stoneless fruit (strawberry, currant, etc.). **soft furnishings** *Brit.* curtains, rugs, etc. **soft goods** *Brit.* textiles. **soft-headed** feeble-minded. **soft-headedness** feeble-mindedness. **soft-land** make a soft landing. **soft landing** a landing by a spacecraft without its suffering major damage. **soft option** the easier alternative. **soft palate** the rear part of the palate. **soft-paste** denoting an 'artificial' porcelain containing glassy materials and fired at a comparatively low temperature. **soft pedal** a pedal on a piano that makes the tone softer. **soft-pedal** *v.tr.* & (often foll. by *on*) *intr.* (**-pedalled, -pedalling**; *US* **-pedaled, -pedaling**) **1** refrain from emphasizing; be restrained (about). **2** play with the soft pedal down. **soft roe** see ROE[1]. **soft sell** restrained or subtly persuasive salesmanship. **soft-sell** *v.tr.* (*past* and *past part.* **-sold**) sell by this method. **soft soap 1** a semifluid soap made with potash. **2** *colloq.* persuasive flattery. **soft-soap** *v.tr. colloq.* persuade (a person) with flattery. **soft-spoken** speaking with a gentle voice. **soft sugar** granulated or powdered sugar. **soft tack** bread or other good food (opp. *hard tack*). **soft tissues** tissues of the body that are not bony or cartilaginous. **soft touch** *colloq.* a gullible person, esp. over money. **soft wicket** a wicket with moist or sodden turf. □□**softish** *adj.* **softness** *n.* [OE *sōfte* agreeable, earlier *sēfte* f. WG]

softa /'sɒftə/ *n.* a Muslim student of sacred law and theology. [Turk. f. Pers. *sūkta* burnt, afire]

softball /'sɒftbɔːl/ *n.* **1** a ball like a baseball but softer and larger. **2** a modified form of baseball using this.

soften /'sɒf(ə)n/ *v.* **1** *tr.* & *intr.* make or become soft or softer. **2** *tr.* (often foll. by *up*) **a** reduce the strength of (defences) by bombing or some other preliminary attack. **b** reduce the resistance of (a person). □**softening of the brain** a morbid degeneration of the brain, esp. in old age. □□**softener** *n.*

soft-hearted /sɒft'hɑːtɪd/ *adj.* tender, compassionate; easily moved. □□**soft-heartedness** *n.*

softie /'sɒftɪ/ *n.* (also **softy**) *colloq.* a weak or silly or soft-hearted person.

softly /'sɒftlɪ/ *adv.* in a soft, gentle, or quiet manner. □**softly softly** (of an approach or strategy) cautious; discreet and cunning.

software /'sɒftweə(r)/ *n.* the programs and other operating information used by a computer (opp. HARDWARE 3).

softwood /'sɒftwʊd/ *n.* the wood of pine, spruce, or other conifers, easily sawn.

softy var. of SOFTIE.

SOGAT /'sɒʊgæt/ *abbr.* (in the UK) Society of Graphical and Allied Trades. ¶ From 1982 officially called SOGAT 82.

soggy /'sɒgɪ/ *adj.* (**soggier, soggiest**) sodden, saturated, dank. □□**soggily** *adv.* **sogginess** *n.* [dial. *sog* a swamp]

soh /səʊ/ *n.* (also **so, sol** /sɒl/) *Mus.* **1** (in tonic sol-fa) the fifth note of a major scale. **2** the note G in the fixed-doh system. [*sol* f. ME *sol* f. L *solve*: see GAMUT]

soi-disant /,swa:di:'zɑ̃/ *adj.* self-styled or pretended. [F f. *soi* oneself + *disant* saying]

soigné /'swa:njeɪ/ *adj.* (*fem.* **soignée** *pronunc.* same) carefully finished or arranged; well-groomed. [past part. of F *soigner* take care of f. *soin* care]

soil[1] /sɔɪl/ *n.* **1** the upper layer of earth in which plants grow, consisting of disintegrated rock usu. with an admixture of organic remains (*alluvial soil*; *rich soil*). **2** ground belonging to a nation; territory (*on British soil*). □**soil mechanics** the study of the properties of soil as affecting its use in civil engineering. **soil science** pedology. □□**soilless** *adj.* **soily** *adj.* [ME f. AF, perh. f. L *solium* seat, taken in sense of L *solum* ground]

soil[2] /sɔɪl/ *v.* & *n.* —*v.tr.* **1** make dirty; smear or stain with dirt (*soiled linen*). **2** tarnish, defile; bring discredit to (*would not soil my hands with it*). —*n.* **1** a dirty mark; a stain, smear, or defilement. **2** filth; refuse matter. □**soil pipe** the discharge-pipe of a lavatory. [ME f. OF *suiller, soiller*, etc., ult. f. L *sucula* dimin. of *sus* pig]

soil[3] /sɔɪl/ *v.tr.* feed (cattle) on fresh-cut green fodder (orig. for purging). [perh. f. SOIL[2]]

soirée /'swa:reɪ/ *n.* an evening party, usu. in a private house, for conversation or music. [F f. *soir* evening]

soixante-neuf /,swa:sɑ̃'nɜ:f/ *n. sl.* sexual activity between two people involving mutual oral stimulation of the genitals. [F, = sixty-nine, from the position of the couple]

sojourn /'sɒdʒ(ə)n, -dʒɜ:n, 'sʌ-/ *n.* & *v.* —*n.* a temporary stay. —*v.intr.* stay temporarily. □□ **sojourner** *n.* [ME f. OF *sojorn* etc. f. LL SUB- + *diurnum* day]

soke /səʊk/ *n. Brit. hist.* **1** a right of local jurisdiction. **2** a district under a particular jurisdiction and administration. [ME f. AL *sōca* f. OE *sōcn* prosecution f. Gmc]

Sol /sɒl/ *n.* (in Roman mythology) the sun, esp. as a personification. [ME f. L]

sol[1] var. of SOH.

sol[2] /sɒl/ *n. Chem.* a liquid suspension of a colloid. [abbr. of SOLUTION]

sola[1] /'səʊlə/ *n.* a pithy-stemmed E. Indian swamp plant, *Aeschynomene indica.* □**sola topi** an Indian sun-helmet made from its pith. [Urdu & Bengali *solā*, Hindi *sholā*]

sola[2] *fem.* of SOLUS.

solace /'sɒləs/ *n.* & *v.* —*n.* comfort in distress, disappointment, or tedium. —*v.tr.* give solace to. □**solace oneself with** find compensation or relief in. [ME f. OF *solas* f. L *solatium* f. *solari* CONSOLE[1]]

solan /'səʊlən/ *n.* (in full **solan goose**) a gannet, *Sula bassana.* [prob. f. ON *súla* gannet + *önd, and-* duck]

solanaceous /,sɒlə'neɪʃəs/ *adj.* of or relating to the plant family Solanaceae, including potatoes, nightshades, and tobacco. [mod.L *solanaceae* f. L *sōlānum* nightshade]

solar /'səʊlə(r)/ *adj.* & *n.* —*adj.* of, relating to, or reckoned by the sun (*solar eclipse*; *solar time*). —*n.* **1** a solarium. **2** an upper chamber in a medieval house. □**solar battery** (or **cell**) a device converting solar radiation into electricity. **solar constant** the quantity of heat reaching the earth from the sun. **solar day** the interval between successive meridian transits of the sun at a place. **solar month** one-twelfth of the solar year. **solar myth** a tale explained as symbolizing solar phenomena. **solar panel** a panel designed to absorb the sun's rays as a source of energy for operating electricity or heating. **solar plexus** a complex of radiating nerves at the pit of the stomach. **solar system** the sun and the celestial bodies whose motion it governs. **solar wind** the continuous flow of charged particles from the sun. **solar year** the time taken for the earth to travel once round the sun, equal to 365 days, 5 hours, 48 minutes, and 46 seconds. [ME f. L *solaris* f. *sol* sun]

solarium /sə'leəriəm/ *n.* (*pl.* **solaria** /-riə/) a room equipped with sun-lamps or fitted with extensive areas of glass for exposure to the sun. [L, = sundial, sunning-place (as SOLAR)]

solarize /'səʊlə,raɪz/ *v.intr.* & *tr.* (also **-ise**) *Photog.* undergo or cause to undergo change in the relative darkness of parts of an image by long exposure. □□ **solarization** /-'zeɪʃ(ə)n/ *n.*

solatium /sə'leɪʃɪəm/ *n.* (*pl.* **solatia** /-ʃɪə/) a thing given as a compensation or consolation. [L, = SOLACE]

sold *past* and *past part.* of SELL.

soldanella /,sɒldə'nelə/ *n.* any dwarf Alpine plant of the genus *Soldanella*, having bell-shaped flowers with fringed petals. [mod.L f. It.]

solder /'səʊldə/, 'sɒ-/ *n.* & *v.* —*n.* **1** a fusible alloy used to join less fusible metals or wires etc. **2** a cementing or joining agency. —*v.tr.* join with solder. □ **soldering iron** a tool used for applying solder. □□ **solderable** *n.* **solderer** *n.* [ME f. OF *soudure* f. *souder* f. L *solidare* fasten f. *solidus* SOLID]

soldier /'səʊldʒə(r)/ *n.* & *v.* —*n.* **1** a person serving in or having served in an army. **2** (in full **common soldier**) a private or NCO in an army. **3** a military commander of specified ability (*a great soldier*). **4** (in full **soldier ant**) a wingless ant or termite with a large head and jaws for fighting in defence of its colony. **5** (in full **soldier beetle**) a reddish-coloured beetle, *Rhagonycha fulva*, with flesh-eating larvae. —*v.intr.* serve as a soldier (*was off soldiering*). □ **soldier of Christ** an active or proselytizing Christian. **soldier of fortune** an adventurous person ready to take service under any State or person; a mercenary. **soldier on** *colloq.* persevere doggedly. □□ **soldierly** *adj.* **soldiering** *n.* [ME *souder* etc. f. OF *soudier*, *soldier* f. *soulde* (soldier's) pay f. L *solidus*: see SOLIDUS]

soldiery /'səʊldʒərɪ/ *n.* (*pl.* **-ies**) **1** soldiers, esp. of a specified character. **2** a group of soldiers.

sole[1] /səʊl/ *n.* & *v.* —*n.* **1** the under-surface of the foot. **2** the part of a shoe, sock, etc., corresponding to this (esp. excluding the heel). **3** the lower surface or base of an implement, e.g. a plough, golf-club head, etc. **4** the floor of a ship's cabin. —*v.tr.* provide (a shoe etc.) with a sole. □ **sole-plate** the bedplate of an engine etc. □□ **-soled** *adj.* (in *comb.*). [OF ult. f. L *solea* sandal, sill: cf. OE unrecorded *solu* or *sola* f. *solum* bottom, pavement, sole]

sole[2] /səʊl/ *n.* any flatfish of the family Soleidae, esp. *Solea solea* used as food. [ME f. OF f. Prov. *sola* ult. f. L *solea* (as SOLE[1], named from its shape)]

sole[3] /səʊl/ *adj.* **1** (*attrib.*) one and only; single, exclusive (*the sole reason*; *has the sole right*). **2** *archaic* or *Law* (esp. of a woman) unmarried. **3** *archaic* alone, unaccompanied. □□ **solely** *adv.* [ME f. OF *soule* f. L *sola* fem. of *solus* alone]

solecism /'sɒlɪ,sɪz(ə)m/ *n.* **1** a mistake of grammar or idiom; a blunder in the manner of speaking or writing. **2** a piece of bad manners or incorrect behaviour. □□ **solecist** *n.* **solecistic** /-'sɪstɪk/ *adj.* [F *solécisme* or L *soloecismus* f. Gk *soloikismos* f. *soloikos* speaking incorrectly]

solemn /'sɒləm/ *adj.* **1** serious and dignified (*a solemn occasion*). **2** formal; accompanied by ceremony (*a solemn oath*). **3** mysteriously impressive. **4** (of a person) serious or cheerless in manner (*looks rather solemn*). **5** full of importance; weighty (*a solemn warning*). **6** grave, sober, deliberate; slow in movement or action (*a solemn promise*; *solemn music*). □ **solemn mass** = *high mass* (see MASS[2]). □□ **solemnly** *adv.* **solemnness** *n.* [ME f. OF *solemne* f. L *sol(l)emnis* customary, celebrated at a fixed date f. *sollus* entire]

solemnity /sə'lemnɪtɪ/ *n.* (*pl.* **-ies**) **1** the state of

being solemn; a solemn character or feeling; solemn behaviour. **2** a rite or celebration; a piece of ceremony. [ME f. OF *solem(p)nité* f. L *sollemnitas -tatis* (as SOLEMN)]

solemnize /'sɒləm,naɪz/ *v.tr.* (also **-ise**) **1** duly perform (a ceremony esp. of marriage). **2** celebrate (a festival etc.). **3** make solemn. □□ **solemnization** /-'zeɪʃ(ə)n/ *n.* [ME f. OF *solem(p)niser* f. med.L *solemnizare* (as SOLEMN)]

solen /'səʊlən/ *n.* any razor-shell of the genus *Solen*. [L f. Gk *sōlēn* tube, shellfish]

solenoid /'səʊlə,nɔɪd, 'sɒl-/ *n.* a cylindrical coil of wire acting as a magnet when carrying electric current. □□ **solenoidal** /-'nɔɪd(ə)l/ *adj.* [F *solénoïde* (as SOLEN)]

sol-fa /'sɒlfɑː/ *n.* & *v.* —*n.* = SOLMIZATION; (cf. *tonic sol-fa*). —*v.tr.* (**-fas**, **-faed**) sing (a tune) with sol-fa syllables. [SOL[1] + FA]

solfatara /,sɒlfə'tɑːrə/ *n.* a volcanic vent emitting only sulphurous and other vapours. [name of a volcano near Naples, f. It. *solfo* sulphur]

solfeggio /sɒl'fedʒɪəʊ/ *n.* (*pl.* **solfeggi** /-dʒiː/) *Mus.* **1** an exercise in singing using sol-fa syllables. **2** solmization. [It. (as SOL-FA)]

soli *pl.* of SOLO.

solicit /sə'lɪsɪt/ *v.* (**solicited**, **soliciting**) **1** *tr.* & (foll. by *for*) *intr.* ask repeatedly or earnestly for or seek or invite (business etc.). **2** *tr.* (often foll. by *for*) make a request or petition to (a person). **3** *tr.* accost (a person) and offer one's services as a prostitute. □□ **solicitation** /-'teɪʃ(ə)n/ *n.* [ME f. OF *solliciter* f. L *sollicitare* agitate f. *sollicitus* anxious f. *sollus* entire + *citus* past part., = set in motion]

solicitor /sə'lɪsɪtə(r)/ *n.* **1** *Brit.* a member of the legal profession qualified to deal with conveyancing, draw up wills, etc., and to advise clients and instruct barristers. **2** a person who solicits. **3** *US* a canvasser. **4** *US* the chief law officer of a city etc. □ **Solicitor-General 1** (in the UK) the Crown law officer below the Attorney General or (in Scotland) below the Lord Advocate. **2** (in the US) the law officer below the Attorney General. [ME f. OF *solliciteur* (as SOLICIT)]

solicitous /sə'lɪsɪtəs/ *adj.* **1** (often foll. by *of*, *about*, etc.) showing interest or concern. **2** (foll. by *to* + infin.) eager, anxious. □□ **solicitously** *adv.* **solicitousness** *n.* [L *sollicitus* (as SOLICIT)]

solicitude /sə'lɪsɪ,tjuːd/ *n.* **1** the state of being solicitous; solicitous behaviour. **2** anxiety or concern. [ME f. OF *sollicitude* f. L *sollicitudo* (as SOLICITOUS)]

solid /'sɒlɪd/ *adj.* & *n.* —*adj.* (**solider**, **solidest**) **1** firm and stable in shape; not liquid or fluid (*solid food*; *water becomes solid at 0°C*). **2** of such material throughout, not hollow or containing cavities (*a solid sphere*). **3** of the same substance throughout (*solid silver*). **4** of strong material or construction or build, not flimsy or slender etc. **5 a** having three dimensions. **b** concerned with solids (*solid geometry*). **6 a** sound and reliable; genuine (*solid arguments*). **b** staunch and dependable (*a solid Tory*). **7** sound but without any special flair etc. (*a solid piece of work*). **8** financially sound. **9** (of time) uninterrupted, continuous (*spend four solid hours on it*). **10 a** unanimous, undivided (*support has been pretty solid so far*). **b** (foll. by *for*) united in favour of. **11** (of printing) without spaces between the lines etc. **12** (of a tyre) without a central air space. **13** (foll. by *with*) *US colloq.* on good terms. **14** *Austral.* & *NZ colloq.* severe, unreasonable. —*n.* **1** a solid substance or body. **2** (in *pl.*) solid food. **3** *Geom.* a body or magnitude having three dimensions. □ **solid angle** an angle formed by planes etc. meeting at a point. **solid colour** colour covering the whole of an object, without a pattern etc. **solid-drawn** (of a tube etc.) pressed or drawn out from a solid bar of metal. **solid solution** solid material containing one substance uniformly distributed in another. **solid state** the state of matter that retains its boundaries without support. **solid-state** *adj.* using the electronic properties of solids (e.g. a semiconductor) to replace those of valves. □□ **solidly** *adv.* **solidness** *n.* [ME f. OF *solide* f. L *solidus*, rel. to *salvus* safe, *sollus* entire]

solidarity /ˌsɒlɪˈdærɪtɪ/ *n.* **1** unity or agreement of feeling or action, esp. among individuals with a common interest. **2** mutual dependence. [F *solidarité* f. *solidaire* f. *solide* SOLID]

solidi *pl.* of SOLIDUS.

solidify /səˈlɪdɪˌfaɪ/ *v.tr.* & *intr.* (**-ies**, **-ied**) make or become solid. □□ **solidification** /-fɪˈkeɪʃ(ə)n/ *n.* **solidifier** *n.*

solidity /səˈlɪdɪtɪ/ *n.* the state of being solid; firmness.

solidus /ˈsɒlɪdəs/ *n.* (*pl.* **solidi** /-ˌdaɪ/) **1** an oblique stroke (/) used in writing fractions (3/4), to separate other figures and letters, or to denote alternatives (*and/or*) and ratios (*miles/day*). **2** (in full **solidus curve**) a curve in a graph of the temperature and composition of a mixture, below which the substance is entirely solid. **3** *hist.* a gold coin of the later Roman Empire. [ME (in sense 3) f. L: see SOLID]

solifluction /ˌsɒʊlɪˈflʌkʃ(ə)n, ˌsɒl-/ *n.* the gradual movement of wet soil etc. down a slope. [L *solum* soil + L *fluctio* flowing f. *fluere fluct-* flow]

soliloquy /səˈlɪləkwɪ/ *n.* (*pl.* **-ies**) **1** the act of talking when alone or regardless of any hearers, esp. in drama. **2** part of a play involving this. □□ **soliloquist** *n.* **soliloquize** *v.intr.* (also **-ise**). [LL *soliloquium* f. L *solus* alone + *loqui* speak]

soliped /ˈsɒlɪˌped/ *adj.* & *n.* —*adj.* (of an animal) solid-hoofed. —*n.* a solid-hoofed animal. [F *solipède* or mod.L *solipes -pedis* f. L *solidipes* f. *solidus* solid + *pes* foot]

solipsism /ˈsɒlɪpˌsɪz(ə)m/ *n.* *Philos.* the view that the self is all that exists or can be known. □□ **solipsist** *n.* **solipsistic** /-ˈsɪstɪk/ *adj.* **solipsistically** /-ˈsɪstɪkəlɪ/ *adv.* [L *solus* alone + *ipse* self]

solitaire /ˈsɒlɪˌteə(r)/ *n.* **1** a diamond or other gem set by itself. **2** a ring having a single gem. **3** a game for one player played by removing pegs etc. one at a time from a board by jumping others over them until only one is left. **4** *US* = PATIENCE 4. **5** any of various extinct dodo-like flightless birds of the family Raphidae. **6** any American thrush of the genus *Myadestes*. [F f. L *solitarius* (as SOLITARY)]

solitary /ˈsɒlɪtərɪ/ *adj.* & *n.* —*adj.* **1** living alone; not gregarious; without companions; lonely (*a solitary existence*). **2** (of a place) secluded or unfrequented. **3** single or sole (*a solitary instance*). **4** (of an insect) not living in communities. **5** *Bot.* growing singly, not in a cluster. —*n.* (*pl.* **-ies**) **1** a recluse or anchorite. **2** *colloq.* = **solitary confinement**. □ **solitary confinement** isolation of a prisoner in a separate cell as a punishment. □□ **solitarily** *adv.* **solitariness** *n.* [ME f. L *solitarius* f. *solus* alone]

solitude /ˈsɒlɪˌtjuːd/ *n.* **1** the state of being solitary. **2** a lonely place. [ME f. OF *solitude* or L *solitudo* f. *solus* alone]

solmization /ˌsɒlmɪˈzeɪʃ(ə)n/ *n.* *Mus.* a system of associating each note of a scale with a particular syllable, now usu. *doh ray me fah soh lah te*, with doh as C in the fixed-doh system and as the keynote in the movable-doh or tonic sol-fa system. □□ **solmizate** /ˈsɒlmɪˌzeɪt/ *v.intr.* & *tr.* [F *solmisation* (as SOL¹, MI)]

solo /ˈsəʊləʊ/ *n.*, *v.*, & *adv.* —*n.* (*pl.* **-os**) **1** (*pl.* **-os** or **soli** /-liː/) **a** a vocal or instrumental piece or passage, or a dance, performed by one person with or without accompaniment. **b** (*attrib.*) performed or performing as a solo (*solo passage; solo violin*). **2 a** an unaccompanied flight by a pilot in an aircraft. **b** anything done by one person unaccompanied. **c** (*attrib.*) unaccompanied, alone. **3** (in full **solo whist**) **a** a card-game like whist in which one player may oppose the others. **b** a declaration or the act of playing to win five tricks at this. —*v.* (**-oes**, **-oed**) **1** *intr.* perform a solo, esp. a solo flight. **2** *tr.* perform or achieve as a solo. —*adv.* unaccompanied, alone (*flew solo for the first time*). □ **solo stop** an organ

stop especially suitable for imitating a solo performance on another instrument. [It. f. L *solus* alone]

soloist /ˈsəʊləʊɪst/ *n.* a performer of a solo, esp. in music.

Solomon /ˈsɒləmən/ *n.* a very wise person. □ **Solomon's seal 1** a figure like the Star of David. **2** any liliaceous plant of the genus *Polygonatum*, with arching stems and drooping green and white flowers. □□ **Solomonic** /ˌsɒləˈmɒnɪk/ *adj.* [*Solomon*, king of Israel in the 10th c. BC, famed for his wisdom]

solstice /ˈsɒlstɪs/ *n.* **1** either of the times when the sun is furthest from the equator. **2** the point in its ecliptic reached by the sun at a solstice. □ **summer solstice** the time at which the sun is furthest north from the equator, about 21 June in the northern hemisphere. **winter solstice** the time at which the sun is furthest south from the equator, about 22 Dec. in the northern hemisphere. □□ **solstitial** /sɒlˈstɪʃ(ə)l/ *adj.* [ME f. OF f. L *solstitium* f. *sol* sun + *sistere stit-* make stand]

solubilize /ˈsɒljʊbɪˌlaɪz/ *v.tr.* (also **-ise**) make soluble or more soluble. □□ **solubilization** /-ˈzeɪʃ(ə)n/ *n.*

soluble /ˈsɒljʊb(ə)l/ *adj.* **1** that can be dissolved, esp. in water. **2** that can be solved. □ **soluble glass** = *water-glass*. □□ **solubility** /-ˈbɪlɪtɪ/ *n.* [ME f. OF f. LL *solubilis* (as SOLVE)]

solus /ˈsəʊləs/ *predic.adj.* (*fem.* **sola** /-lə/) (esp. in a stage direction) alone, unaccompanied. [L]

solute /ˈsɒljuːt/ *n.* a dissolved substance. [L *solutum*, neut. of *solutus*: see SOLVE]

solution /səˈluːʃ(ə)n, -ˈljuːʃ(ə)n/ *n.* **1** the act or a means of solving a problem or difficulty. **2 a** the conversion of a solid or gas into a liquid by mixture with a liquid solvent. **b** the state resulting from this (*held in solution*). **3** the act of dissolving or the state of being dissolved. **4** the act of separating or breaking. **5** = *rubber solution* (see RUBBER¹). □ **solution set** *Math.* the set of all the solutions of an equation or condition. [ME f. OF f. L *solutio -onis* (as SOLVE)]

Solutrean /səˈluːtrɪən/ *n.* & *adj.* (also **Solutrian**) —*n.* the palaeolithic period in Europe following the Aurignacian and preceding the Magdalenian. —*n.* the culture of this period. [*Solutré* in E. France, where remains of it were found]

solvate /ˈsɒlveɪt/ *v.intr.* & *tr.* enter or cause to enter combination with a solvent. □□ **solvation** /-ˈveɪʃ(ə)n/ *n.*

solve /sɒlv/ *v.tr.* find an answer to, or an action or course that removes or effectively deals with (a problem or difficulty). □□ **solvable** *adj.* **solver** *n.* [ME, = loosen, f. L *solvere solut-* unfasten, release]

solvent /ˈsɒlv(ə)nt/ *adj.* & *n.* —*adj.* **1** able to dissolve or form a solution with something. **2** having enough money to meet one's liabilities. —*n.* **1** a solvent liquid etc. **2** a dissolving or weakening agent. □□ **solvency** *n.* (in sense 2).

Som. *abbr.* Somerset.

soma¹ /ˈsəʊmə/ *n.* **1** the body as distinct from the soul. **2** the body of an organism as distinct from its reproductive cells. [Gk *sōma -atos* body]

soma² /ˈsəʊmə/ *n.* **1** an intoxicating drink used in Vedic ritual. **2** a plant yielding this. [Skr. *sōma*]

Somali /səˈmɑːlɪ/ *n.* & *adj.* —*n.* **1** (*pl.* same or **Somalis**) a member of a Hamitic Muslim people of Somalia in NE Africa. **2** the Cushitic language of this people. —*adj.* of or relating to this people or language. □□ **Somalian** *adj.* [native name]

somatic /səˈmætɪk/ *adj.* of or relating to the body, esp. as distinct from the mind. □ **somatic cell** any cell of a living organism except the reproductive cells. □□ **somatically** *adv.* [Gk *sōmatikos* (as SOMA¹)]

somato- /ˈsəʊmətəʊ/ *comb. form* the human body. [Gk *sōma -atos* body]

somatogenic /ˌsəʊmətəʊˈdʒenɪk/ *adj.* originating in the body.

somatology /ˌsəʊməˈtɒlədʒɪ/ *n.* the science of living bodies physically considered.

somatotonic /ˌsəʊmətəʊˈtɒnɪk/ *adj.* like a meso-morph in temperament, with predominantly phys-ical interests.

somatotrophin /ˌsəʊmətəʊˈtrəʊfɪn/ *n.* a growth hor-mone secreted by the pituitary gland. [as SOMATO-, TROPHIC]

somatotype /ˈsəʊmətəʊˌtaɪp/ *n.* physique expressed in relation to various extreme types.

sombre /ˈsɒmbə(r)/ *adj.* (also *US* **somber**) **1** dark, gloomy (*a sombre sky*). **2** oppressively solemn or sober. **3** dismal, foreboding (*a sombre prospect*). □□ **sombrely** *adv.* **sombreness** *n.* [F *sombre* f. OF *sombre* (n.) ult. f. L SUB- + *umbra* shade]

sombrero /sɒmˈbreərəʊ/ *n.* (*pl.* **-os**) a broad-brimmed felt or straw hat worn esp. in Mexico and the south-west US. [Sp. f. *sombra* shade (as SOMBRE)]

some /sʌm/ *adj., pron.,* & *adv.* —*adj.* **1** an unspecified amount or number of (*some water; some apples; some of them*). **2** that is unknown or unnamed (*will return some day; some fool has locked the door; to some extent*). **3** denoting an approximate number (*waited some twenty minutes*). **4** a considerable amount or number of (*went to some trouble*). **5** (usu. stressed) **a** at least a small amount of (*do have some con-sideration*). **b** such to a certain extent (*that is some help*). **c** *colloq.* notably such (*I call that some story*). —*pron.* some people or things, some number or amount (*I have some already; would you like some more?*). —*adv. colloq.* to some extent (*we talked some; do it some more*). □ **and then some** *sl.* and plenty more than that. **some few** see FEW. [OE *sum* f. Gmc]

-some[1] /səm/ *suffix* forming adjectives meaning: **1** adapted to; productive of (*cuddlesome; fearsome*). **2** characterized by being (*fulsome; lithesome*). **3** apt to (*tiresome; meddlesome*). [OE *-sum*]

-some[2] /səm/ *suffix* forming nouns from numerals, meaning 'a group of (so many)' (*foursome*). [OE *sum* SOME, used after numerals in genit. pl.]

-some[3] /səʊm/ *comb. form* denoting a portion of a body, esp. of a cell (*chromosome; ribosome*). [Gk *sōma* body]

somebody /ˈsʌmbədɪ/ *pron.* & *n.* —*pron.* some person. —*n.* (*pl.* **-ies**) a person of importance (*is really somebody now*).

someday /ˈsʌmdeɪ/ *adv.* at some time in the future.

somehow /ˈsʌmhaʊ/ *adv.* **1** for some reason or other (*somehow I never liked them*). **2** in some unspecified or unknown way (*he somehow dropped behind*). **3** no matter how (*must get it finished somehow*).

someone /ˈsʌmwʌn/ *n.* & *pron.* = SOMEBODY.

someplace /ˈsʌmpleɪs/ *adv. US colloq.* = SOME-WHERE.

somersault /ˈsʌməˌsɒlt/ *n.* & *v.* (also **summersault**) —*n.* an acrobatic movement in which a person turns head over heels in the air or on the ground and lands on the feet. —*v.intr.* perform a somersault. [OF *sombresault* alt. f. *sobresault* ult. f. L *supra* above + *saltus* leap f. *salire* to leap]

something /ˈsʌmθɪŋ/ *n., pron.,* & *adv.* —*n.* & *pron.* **1 a** some unspecified or unknown thing (*have some-thing to tell you; something has happened*). **b** (in full **something or other**) as a substitute for an unknown or forgotten description (*a student of something or other*). **2** a known or understood but unexpressed quantity, quality, or extent (*there is something about it I do not like; is something of a fool*). **3** *colloq.* an important or notable person or thing (*the party was quite something*). —*adv. archaic* in some degree. □ **or something** or some unspecified alternative possibility (*must have run away or something*). **see something of** encounter (a person) briefly or occasionally. **something else 1** something different. **2** *colloq.* something exceptional. **something like 1** an amount in the region of (*left something like a million pounds*). **2** somewhat like (*shaped something like a cigar*). **3** *colloq.* impressive; a fine specimen of. **something of** to some extent; in some sense (*is* something of an expert*). [OE *sum thing* (as SOME, THING)]

sometime /ˈsʌmtaɪm/ *adv.* & *adj.* —*adv.* **1** at some unspecified time. **2** formerly. —*adj.* former (*the sometime mayor*).

sometimes /ˈsʌmtaɪmz/ *adv.* at some times; occasionally.

somewhat /ˈsʌmwɒt/ *adv., n.,* & *pron.* —*adv.* to some extent (*behaviour that was somewhat strange; answered somewhat hastily*). —*n.* & *pron. archaic* something (*loses somewhat of its force*). □ **more than somewhat** *colloq.* very (*was more than somewhat perplexed*).

somewhen /ˈsʌmwen/ *adv. colloq.* at some time.

somewhere /ˈsʌmweə(r)/ *adv.* & *pron.* —*adv.* in or to some place. —*pron.* some unspecified place. □ **get somewhere** *colloq.* achieve success. **somewhere about** approximately.

somite /ˈsəʊmaɪt/ *n.* each body-division of a meta-merically segmented animal. □□ **somitic** /səʊˈmɪtɪk/ *adj.* [Gk *sōma* body + -ITE[1]]

sommelier /ˈsɒməˌljeɪ/ *n.* a wine waiter. [F, = butler, f. *somme* pack (as SUMPTER)]

somnambulism /sɒmˈnæmbjʊˌlɪz(ə)m/ *n.* **1** sleep-walking. **2** a condition of the brain inducing this. □□ **somnambulant** *adj.* **somnambulantly** *adv.* **somnambulist** *n.* **somnambulistic** /-ˈlɪstɪk/ *adj.* **somnambulistically** /-ˈlɪstɪkəlɪ/ *adv.* [L *somnus* sleep + *ambulare* walk]

somniferous /sɒmˈnɪfərəs/ *adj.* inducing sleep; sop-orific. [L *somnifer* f. *somnium* dream]

somnolent /ˈsɒmnələnt/ *adj.* **1** sleepy, drowsy. **2** inducing drowsiness. **3** *Med.* in a state between sleeping and waking. □□ **somnolence** *n.* **somnolency** *n.* **somnolently** *adv.* [ME f. OF *sompnolent* or L *somnolentus* f. *somnus* sleep]

son /sʌn/ *n.* **1** a boy or man in relation to either or both of his parents. **2 a** a male descendant. **b** (foll. by *of*) a male member of a family, nation, etc. **3** a person regarded as inheriting an occupation, quality, etc., or associated with a particular attribute (*sons of freedom; sons of the soil*). **4** (in full **my son**) a form of address esp. to a boy. **5** (**the Son**) (in Christian belief) the second person of the Trinity. □ **son-in-law** (*pl.* **sons-in-law**) the husband of one's daughter. **son of a bitch** *sl.* a general term of contempt. **son of a gun** *colloq.* a jocular or affectionate form of address or reference. □□ **sonless** *adj.* **sonship** *n.* [OE *sunu* f. Gmc]

sonant /ˈsəʊnənt/ *adj.* & *n. Phonet.* —*adj.* (of a sound) voiced and syllabic. —*n.* a voiced sound, esp. other than a vowel and capable of forming a syllable, e.g. *l, m, n, ng, r*. □□ **sonancy** *n.* [L *sonare sonant-* sound]

sonar /ˈsəʊnɑː(r)/ *n.* **1** a system for the underwater detection of objects by reflected or emitted sound. **2** an apparatus for this. [*sound* navigation and ranging, after *radar*]

sonata /səˈnɑːtə/ *n.* a composition for one instrument or two (one usu. being a piano accompaniment), usu. in several movements with one (esp. the first) or more in sonata form. □ **sonata form** a type of composition in three sections (exposition, de-velopment, and recapitulation) in which two themes (or subjects) are explored according to set key relationships. [It., = sounded (orig. as distinct from sung): fem. past part. of *sonare* sound]

sonatina /ˌsɒnəˈtiːnə/ *n.* a simple or short sonata. [It., dimin. of SONATA]

sonde /sɒnd/ *n.* a device sent up to obtain information about atmospheric conditions, esp. = RADIOSONDE. [F, = sounding(-line)]

sone /səʊn/ *n.* a unit of subjective loudness, equal to 40 phons. [L *sonus* sound]

son et lumière /ˌsɒneɪˈluːmjeə(r)/ *n.* an entertainment by night at a historic monument, building, etc., using lighting effects and recorded sound to give a dramatic narrative of its history. [F, = sound and light]

song /sɒŋ/ n. **1** a short poem or other set of words set to music or meant to be sung. **2** singing or vocal music (*burst into song*). **3** a musical composition suggestive of a song. **4** the musical cry of some birds. **5** a short poem in rhymed stanzas. **6** *archaic* poetry or verse. □**for a song** *colloq.* very cheaply. **on song** *Brit. colloq.* performing exceptionally well. **song and dance** *colloq.* a fuss or commotion. **song cycle** a set of musically linked songs on a romantic theme. **Song of Songs** (or **of Solomon**) a poetic Old Testament book traditionally attributed to Solomon. **song sparrow** a N. American sparrow, *Melospiza melodia*, with a characteristic musical song. **song thrush** a thrush, *Turdus philomelos*, of Europe and W. Asia, with a song partly mimicked from other birds. □□ **songless** *adj.* [OE *sang* f. Gmc (as SING)]

songbird /'sɒŋbɜːd/ n. a bird with a musical call.

songbook /'sɒŋbʊk/ n. a collection of songs with music.

songsmith /'sɒŋsmɪθ/ n. a writer of songs.

songster /'sɒŋstə(r)/ n. (*fem.* **songstress**) /-strɪs/ **1** a singer, esp. a fluent and skilful one. **2** a songbird. **3** a poet. **4** *US* a songbook. [OE *sangestre* (as SONG, -STER)]

songwriter /'sɒŋ,raɪtə(r)/ n. a writer of songs or the music for them.

sonic /'sɒnɪk/ *adj.* of or relating to or using sound or sound waves. □**sonic bang** (or **boom**) a loud explosive noise caused by the shock wave from an aircraft when it passes the speed of sound. **sonic barrier** = *sound barrier* (see SOUND[1]). **sonic mine** a mine exploded by the sound of a passing ship. □□ **sonically** *adv.* [L *sonus* sound]

sonnet /'sɒnɪt/ n. & v. —n. a poem of 14 lines (usu. pentameters) using any of a number of formal rhyme schemes, in English usu. having ten syllables per line. —v. (**sonneted, sonneting**) **1** *intr.* write sonnets. **2** *tr.* address sonnets to. [F *sonnet* or It. *sonetto* dimin. of *suono* SOUND[1]]

sonneteer /,sɒnɪ'tɪə(r)/ n. usu. *derog.* a writer of sonnets.

sonny /'sʌnɪ/ n. *colloq.* a familiar form of address to a young boy.

sonobuoy /'səʊnə,bɔɪ/ n. a buoy for detecting underwater sounds and transmitting them by radio. [L *sonus* sound + BUOY]

sonometer /sə'nɒmɪtə(r)/ n. **1** an instrument for measuring the vibration frequency of a string etc. **2** an audiometer. [L *sonus* sound + -METER]

sonorous /'sɒnərəs, sə'nɔːrəs/ *adj.* **1** having a loud, full, or deep sound; resonant. **2** (of a speech, style, etc.) imposing, grand. □□ **sonority** /sə'nɒrɪtɪ/ n. **sonorously** *adv.* **sonorousness** n. [L *sonorus* f. *sonor* sound]

sonsy /'sɒnsɪ/ *adj.* (also **sonsie**) (**sonsier, sonsiest**) *Sc.* **1** plump, buxom. **2** of a cheerful disposition. **3** bringing good fortune. [ult. f. Ir. & Gael. *sonas* good fortune f. *sona* fortunate]

sook /sʊk/ n. *Austral. & NZ sl.* **1** *derog.* a timid bashful person; a coward or sissy. **2** a hand-reared calf. [E dial. *suck*, call-word for a calf]

sool /suːl/ *v.tr. Austral. & NZ sl.* **1** (of a dog) attack or worry (an animal). **2** (often foll. by *on*) urge or goad. □□ **sooler** n. [var. of 17th-c. (now dial.) *sowl* seize roughly, of unkn. orig.]

soon /suːn/ *adv.* **1** after no long interval of time (*shall soon know the result*). **2** relatively early (*must you go so soon?*). **3** (prec. by *how*) early (with relative rather than distinctive sense) (*how soon will it be ready?*). **4** readily or willingly (in expressing choice or preference: *which would you sooner do?*; *would as soon stay behind*). □**as** (or **so**) **soon as** (implying a causal or temporal connection) at the moment that; not later than; as early as (*came as soon as I heard about it*; *disappears as soon as it's time to pay*). **no sooner . . . than** at the very moment that (*we no sooner arrived than the rain stopped*). **sooner or later** at

some future time; eventually. □□ **soonish** *adv.* [OE *sōna* f. WG]

soot /sʊt/ n. & v. —n. a black carbonaceous substance rising in fine flakes in the smoke of wood, coal, oil, etc., and deposited on the sides of a chimney etc. —v.tr. cover with soot. [OE *sōt* f. Gmc]

sooth /suːθ/ n. *archaic* truth, fact. □**in sooth** really, truly. [OE *sōth* (orig. adj., = true) f. Gmc]

soothe /suːð/ *v.tr.* **1** calm (a person or feelings). **2** soften or mitigate (pain). **3** *archaic* flatter or humour. □□ **soother** n. **soothing** *adj.* **soothingly** *adv.* [OE *sōthian* verify f. *sōth* true: see SOOTH]

soothsayer /'suːθ,seɪə(r)/ n. a diviner or seer. [ME, = one who says the truth: see SOOTH]

sooty /'sʊtɪ/ *adj.* (**sootier, sootiest**) **1** covered with or full of soot. **2** (esp. of an animal or bird) black or brownish-black. □**sooty albatross** an albatross, *Diomedia chrysostoma*, with grey-brown plumage. □□ **sootily** *adv.* **sootiness** n.

sop /sɒp/ n. & v. —n. **1** a piece of bread etc. dipped in gravy etc. **2** a thing given or done to pacify or bribe. —v. (**sopped, sopping**) **1** *intr.* be drenched (*came home sopping*; *sopping wet clothes*). **2** *tr.* (foll. by *up*) absorb (liquid) in a towel etc. **3** *tr.* wet thoroughly; soak. [OE *sopp*, corresp. to MLG *soppe*, OHG *sopfa* bread and milk, prob. f. a weak grade of the base of OE *sūpan*: see SUP[1]]

sophism /'sɒfɪz(ə)m/ n. a false argument, esp. one intended to deceive. [ME f. OF *sophime* f. L f. Gk *sophisma* clever device f. *sophizomai* become wise f. *sophos* wise]

sophist /'sɒfɪst/ n. **1** one who reasons with clever but fallacious arguments. **2** *Gk Antiq.* a paid teacher of philosophy and rhetoric, esp. one associated with moral scepticism and specious reasoning. □□ **sophistic** /-'fɪstɪk/ *adj.* **sophistical** /sə'fɪstɪk(ə)l/ *adj.* **sophistically** /sə'fɪstɪkəlɪ/ *adv.* [L *sophistes* f. Gk *sophistēs* f. *sophizomai*: see SOPHISM]

sophisticate v., *adj.*, & n. —v. /sə'fɪstɪ,keɪt/ **1** *tr.* make (a person etc.) educated, cultured, or refined. **2** *tr.* make (equipment or techniques etc.) highly developed or complex. **3** *tr.* **a** involve (a subject) in sophistry. **b** mislead (a person) by sophistry. **4** *tr.* deprive (a person or thing) of its natural simplicity, make artificial by worldly experience etc. **5** *tr.* tamper with (a text etc.) for purposes of argument etc. **6** *tr.* adulterate (wine etc.). **7** *intr.* use sophistry. —*adj.* /sə'fɪstɪkət/ sophisticated. —n. /sə'fɪstɪkət/ a sophisticated person. □□ **sophistication** /-'keɪʃ(ə)n/ n. [med.L *sophisticare* tamper with f. *sophisticus* (as SOPHISM)]

sophisticated /sə'fɪstɪ,keɪtɪd/ *adj.* **1** (of a person) educated and refined; discriminating in taste and judgement. **2** (of a thing, idea, etc.) highly developed and complex. □□ **sophisticatedly** *adv.*

sophistry /'sɒfɪstrɪ/ n. (*pl.* **-ies**) **1** the use of sophisms. **2** a sophism.

sophomore /'sɒfə,mɔː(r)/ n. *US* a second-year university or high-school student. □□ **sophomoric** /-'mɒrɪk/ *adj.* [earlier *sophumer* f. *sophum*, obs. var. of SOPHISM]

Sophy /'səʊfɪ/ n. (*pl.* **-ies**) *hist.* a ruler of Persia in the 16th–17th c. [Pers. *ṣafī* surname of the dynasty, f. Arab. *ṣafī-ud-dīn* pure of religion, title of the founder's ancestor]

soporific /,sɒpə'rɪfɪk/ *adj.* & n. —*adj.* tending to produce sleep. —n. a soporific drug or influence. □□ **soporiferous** *adj.* **soporifically** *adv.* [L *sopor* sleep + -FIC]

sopping /'sɒpɪŋ/ *adj.* (also **sopping wet**) soaked with liquid; wet through. [pres. part. of SOP v.]

soppy /'sɒpɪ/ *adj.* (**soppier, soppiest**) **1** *Brit. colloq.* **a** silly or foolish in a feeble or self-indulgent way. **b** mawkishly sentimental. **2** *Brit. colloq.* (foll. by *on*) foolishly infatuated with. **3** soaked with water. □□ **soppily** *adv.* **soppiness** n. [SOP + -Y[1]]

sopranino /ˌsɒprəˈniːnəʊ/ n. (pl. -os) Mus. an instrument higher than soprano, esp. a recorder or saxophone. [It., dimin. of SOPRANO]

soprano /səˈprɑːnəʊ/ n. (pl. -os or soprani /-nɪ/) 1 a the highest singing-voice. b a female or boy singer with this voice. c a part written for it. 2 a an instrument of a high or the highest pitch in its family. b its player. □soprano-clef an obsolete clef placing middle C on the lowest line of the staff. [It. f. sopra above f. L supra]

sora /ˈsɔːrə/ n. (in full **sora rail**) a bird, Porzana carolina, frequenting the marshes of N. and S. Carolina etc. in the autumn and used as food. [prob. a native name]

sorb /sɔːb/ n. 1 = service tree (see SERVICE²). 2 (in full **sorb-apple**) its fruit. [F sorbe or L sorbus service tree, sorbum service-berry]

sorbefacient /ˌsɔːbɪˈfeɪʃ(ə)nt/ adj. & n. Med. —adj. causing absorption. —n. a sorbefacient drug etc. [L sorbēre suck in + -FACIENT]

sorbet /ˈsɔːbeɪ, -bɪt/ n. 1 a water-ice. 2 sherbet. [F f. It. sorbetto f. Turk. şerbet f. Arab. šarba to drink: cf. SHERBET]

Sorbo /ˈsɔːbəʊ/ n. Brit. propr. (in full **Sorbo rubber**) a spongy rubber. [ABSORB + -O]

sorcerer /ˈsɔːsərə(r)/ n. (fem. **sorceress** /-rɪs/) a person who claims to use magic powers; a magician or wizard. □□**sorcerous** adj. **sorcery** n. (pl. -ies). [obs. sorcer f. OF sorcier ult. f. L sors sortis lot]

sordid /ˈsɔːdɪd/ adj. 1 dirty or squalid. 2 ignoble, mean, or mercenary. 3 mean or niggardly. 4 dull-coloured. □□**sordidly** adv. **sordidness** n. [F sordide or L sordidus f. sordēre be dirty]

sordino /sɔːˈdiːnəʊ/ n. (pl. **sordini** /-nɪ/) Mus. a mute for a bowed or wind instrument. [It. f. sordo mute f. L surdus]

sore /sɔː(r)/ adj., n., & adv. —adj. 1 (of a part of the body) painful from injury or disease (has a sore arm). 2 (of a person) suffering pain. 3 (often foll. by about, at) aggrieved or vexed. 4 archaic grievous or severe (in sore need). —n. 1 a sore place on the body. 2 a source of distress or annoyance (reopen old sores). —adv. archaic grievously, severely. □**sore point** a subject causing distress or annoyance. **sore throat** an inflammation of the lining membrane at the back of the mouth etc. □□**soreness** n. [OE sār (n. & adj.), sāre (adv.), f. Gmc]

sorehead /ˈsɔːhed/ n. US a touchy or disgruntled person.

sorel /ˈsɒr(ə)l/ n. Brit. a male fallow deer in its third year. [var. of SORREL²]

sorely /ˈsɔːlɪ/ adv. 1 extremely, badly (am sorely tempted; sorely in need of repair). 2 severely (am sorely vexed). [OE sārlīce (as SORE, -LY²)]

sorghum /ˈsɔːgəm/ n. any tropical cereal grass of the genus Sorghum, e.g. durra. [mod.L f. It. sorgo, perh. f. unrecorded Rmc syricum (gramen) Syrian (grass)]

sori pl. of SORUS.

soroptimist /səˈrɒptɪmɪst/ n. a member of an international association of clubs for professional and business women. [L soror sister + OPTIMIST (as OPTIMISM)]

sorority /səˈrɒrɪtɪ/ n. (pl. -ies) US a female students' society in a university or college. [med.L sororitas or L soror sister, after fraternity]

sorosis /səˈrəʊsɪs/ n. (pl. **soroses** /-siːz/) Bot. a fleshy compound fruit, e.g. a pineapple or mulberry. [mod.L f. Gk sōros heap]

sorption /ˈsɔːpʃ(ə)n/ n. absorption or adsorption happening jointly or separately. [back-form. f. absorption, adsorption]

sorrel¹ /ˈsɒr(ə)l/ n. any acid-leaved herb of the genus Rumex, used in salads and for flavouring. [ME f. OF surele, sorele f. Gmc]

sorrel² /ˈsɒr(ə)l/ adj. & n. —adj. of a light reddish-brown colour. —n. 1 this colour. 2 a sorrel animal, esp. a horse. 3 Brit. a sorrel. [ME f. OF sorel f. sor yellowish f. Frank.]

sorrow /ˈsɒrəʊ/ n. & v. —n. 1 mental distress caused by loss or disappointment etc. 2 a cause of sorrow. 3 lamentation. —v.intr. 1 feel sorrow. 2 mourn. □□ **sorrower** n. **sorrowing** adj. [OE sorh, sorg]

sorrowful /ˈsɒrəʊfʊl/ adj. 1 feeling or showing sorrow. 2 distressing, lamentable. □□ **sorrowfully** adv. **sorrowfulness** n. [OE sorhful (as SORROW, -FUL)]

sorry /ˈsɒrɪ/ adj. (**sorrier**, **sorriest**) 1 (predic.) pained or regretful or penitent (were sorry for what they had done; am sorry that you have to go). 2 (predic.; foll. by for) feeling pity or sympathy for (a person). 3 as an expression of apology. 4 wretched; in a poor state (a sorry sight). □**sorry for oneself** dejected. □□**sorrily** adv. **sorriness** n. [OE sārig f. WG (as SORE, -Y²)]

sort /sɔːt/ n. & v. —n. 1 a group of things etc. with common attributes; a class or kind. 2 (foll. by of) roughly of the kind specified (is some sort of doctor). 3 colloq. a person of a specified character or kind (a good sort). 4 Printing a letter or piece in a fount of type. 5 Computing the arrangement of data in a prescribed sequence. 6 archaic a manner or way. —v.tr. (often foll. by out, over) arrange systematically or according to type, class, etc. □**after a sort** after a fashion. **in some sort** to a certain extent. **of a sort** (or **of sorts**) colloq. not fully deserving the name (a holiday of sorts). **out of sorts** 1 slightly unwell. 2 in low spirits; irritable. **sort of** colloq. as it were; to some extent (I sort of expected it). **sort out** 1 separate into sorts. 2 select (things of one or more sorts) from a miscellaneous group. 3 disentangle or put into order. 4 resolve (a problem or difficulty). 5 colloq. deal with or reprimand (a person). □□**sortable** adj. **sorter** n. **sorting** n. [ME f. OF sorte ult. f. L sors sortis lot, condition]

sortie /ˈsɔːtɪ/ n. & v. —n. 1 a sally, esp. from a besieged garrison. 2 an operational flight by a single military aircraft. —v.intr. (**sorties**, **sortied**, **sortieing**) make a sortie; sally. [F, fem. past part. of sortir go out]

sortilege /ˈsɔːtɪlɪdʒ/ n. divination by lots. [ME f. OF f. med.L sortilegium sorcery f. L sortilegus sorcerer (as SORT, legere choose)]

sorus /ˈsɔːrəs/ n. (pl. **sori** /-raɪ/) Bot. a heap or cluster, esp. of spore-cases on the under-surface of a fern-leaf, or in a fungus or lichen. [mod.L f. Gk sōros heap]

SOS /ˌesəʊˈes/ n. (pl. **SOSs**) 1 an international code-signal of extreme distress, used esp. by ships at sea. 2 an urgent appeal for help. 3 Brit. a message broadcast to an untraceable person in an emergency. [chosen as being easily transmitted and recognized in Morse code]

sostenuto /ˌsɒstəˈnuːtəʊ/ adv., adj., & n. Mus. —adv. & adj. in a sustained or prolonged manner. —n. (pl. -os) a passage to be played in this way. [It., past part. of sostenere SUSTAIN]

sot /sɒt/ n. & v. —n. a habitual drunkard. —v.intr. (**sotted**, **sotting**) tipple. □□ **sottish** adj. [OE sott & OF sot foolish, f. med.L sottus, of unkn. orig.]

soteriology /sɒˌtɪərɪˈɒlədʒɪ/ n. Theol. the doctrine of salvation. [Gk sōtēria salvation + -LOGY]

Sothic /ˈsəʊθɪk/ adj. of or relating to the dog-star, esp. with ref. to the ancient Egyptian year fixed by its heliacal rising. [Gk Sōthis f. the Egypt. name of the dog-star]

sotto voce /ˌsɒtəʊ ˈvəʊtʃɪ/ adv. in an undertone or aside. [It. sotto under f. L subtus + voce voice]

sou /suː/ n. 1 hist. a former French coin of low value. 2 (usu. with neg.) colloq. a very small amount of money (hasn't a sou). [F, orig. pl. sous f. OF sout f. L SOLIDUS]

soubrette /suːˈbret/ n. 1 a pert maidservant or similar female character in a comedy. 2 an actress taking this part. [F f. Prov. soubreto fem. of soubret coy f. sobrar f. L superare be above]

soubriquet var. of SOBRIQUET.

souchong /ˈsuːʃɒŋ/ n. a fine black kind of China tea. [Chin. *xiao* small + *zhong* sort]

souffle /ˈsuːf(ə)l/ n. *Med.* a low murmur heard in the auscultation of various organs etc. [F f. *souffler* blow f. L *sufflare*]

soufflé /ˈsuːfleɪ/ n. & adj. —n. **1** a light spongy dish usu. made with flavoured egg yolks added to stiffly beaten whites of eggs and baked (*cheese soufflé*). **2** any of various light sweet or savoury dishes made with beaten egg whites. —adj. **1** light and frothy or spongy (*omelette soufflé*). **2** (of ceramics) decorated with small spots. [F past part. (as SOUFFLE)]

sough /saʊ, sʌf/ v. & n. —v.intr. make a moaning, whistling, or rushing sound as of the wind in trees etc. —n. this sound. [OE *swōgan* resound]

sought *past* and *past part.* of SEEK.

souk /suːk/ n. (also **suk, sukh, suq**) a market-place in Muslim countries. [Arab. *sūk*]

soul /səʊl/ n. **1** the spiritual or immaterial part of a human being, often regarded as immortal. **2** the moral or emotional or intellectual nature of a person or animal. **3** the personification or pattern of something (*the very soul of discretion*). **4** an individual (*not a soul in sight*). **5 a** a person regarded with familiarity or pity etc. (*the poor soul was utterly confused*). **b** a person regarded as embodying moral or intellectual qualities (*left that to meaner souls*). **6** a person regarded as the animating or essential part of something (*the life and soul of the party*). **7** emotional or intellectual energy or intensity, esp. as revealed in a work of art (*pictures that lack soul*). **8** Black American culture or music etc. □ **soul-destroying** (of an activity etc.) deadeningly monotonous. **soul food** the traditional food of American Blacks. **soul mate** a person ideally suited to another. **soul music** a kind of music incorporating elements of rhythm and blues and gospel music, popularized by American Blacks. **the soul of honour** a person incapable of dishonourable conduct. **soul-searching** n. the examination of one's emotions and motives. —adj. characterized by this. **upon my soul** an exclamation of surprise. □□ **-souled** adj. (in *comb.*). [OE *sāwol, sāwel, sāwl*, f. Gmc]

soulful /ˈsəʊlfʊl/ adj. **1** having or expressing or evoking deep feeling. **2** *colloq.* over-emotional. □□ **soulfully** adv. **soulfulness** n.

soulless /ˈsəʊllɪs/ adj. **1** lacking sensitivity or noble qualities. **2** having no soul. **3** undistinguished or uninteresting. □□ **soullessly** adv. **soullessness** n.

sound[1] /saʊnd/ n. & v. —n. **1** a sensation caused in the ear by the vibration of the surrounding air or other medium. **2 a** vibrations causing this sensation. **b** similar vibrations whether audible or not. **3** what is or may be heard. **4** an idea or impression conveyed by words (*don't like the sound of that*). **5** mere words (*sound and fury*). **6** (in full **musical sound**) sound produced by continuous and regular vibrations (opp. NOISE n. 3). **7** any of a series of articulate utterances (*vowel and consonant sounds*). **8** music, speech, etc., accompanying a film or other visual presentation. **9** (often *attrib.*) broadcasting by radio as distinct from television. —v. **1** intr. & tr. emit or cause to emit sound. **2** tr. utter or pronounce (*sound a note of alarm*). **3** intr. convey an impression when heard (*you sound worried*). **4** tr. give an audible signal for (an alarm etc.). **5** tr. test (the lungs etc.) by noting the sound produced. **6** tr. cause to resound; make known (*sound their praises*). □ **sound barrier** the high resistance of air to objects moving at speeds near that of sound. **sound effect** a sound other than speech or music made artificially for use in a play, film, etc. **sound engineer** an engineer dealing with acoustics etc. **sound-hole** an aperture in the belly of some stringed instruments. **sound off** talk loudly or express one's opinions forcefully. **sound-post** a small prop between the belly and back of some stringed instruments. **sound shift** see SHIFT n. 6.

sound spectrograph an instrument for analysing sound into its frequency components. **sound wave** a wave of compression and rarefaction, by which sound is propagated in an elastic medium, e.g. air. □□ **soundless** adj. **soundlessly** adv. **soundlessness** n. [ME f. AF *soun*, OF *son* (n.), AF *suner*, OF *soner* (v.) f. L *sonus*]

sound[2] /saʊnd/ adj. & adv. —adj. **1** healthy; not diseased or injured. **2** (of an opinion or policy etc.) correct, orthodox, well-founded, judicious. **3** financially secure (*a sound investment*). **4** undisturbed (*a sound sleeper*). **5** severe, hard (*a sound blow*). —adv. soundly (*sound asleep*). □□ **soundly** adv. **soundness** n. [ME *sund, isund* f. OE *gesund* f. WG]

sound[3] /saʊnd/ v. & n. —v.tr. & intr. **1** tr. test the depth or quality of the bottom of (the sea or a river etc.). **2** tr. (often foll. by *out*) inquire (esp. cautiously or discreetly) into the opinions or feelings of (a person). **3** tr. find the depth of water in (a ship's hold). **4** tr. get records of temperature, humidity, pressure, etc. from (the upper atmosphere). **5** tr. examine (a person's bladder etc.) with a probe. **6** intr. (of a whale or fish) dive to the bottom. —n. a surgeon's probe. □□ **sounder** n. [ME f. OF *sonder* ult. f. L SUB- + *unda* wave]

sound[4] /saʊnd/ n. **1 a** a narrow passage of water connecting two seas or a sea with a lake etc. **b** an arm of the sea. **2** a fish's swim-bladder. [OE *sund*, = ON *sund* swimming, strait, f. Gmc (as SWIM)]

soundboard /ˈsaʊndbɔːd/ n. a thin sheet of wood over which the strings of a piano etc. pass to increase the sound produced.

soundbox /ˈsaʊndbɒks/ n. the hollow chamber providing resonance and forming the body of a stringed musical instrument.

sounding[1] /ˈsaʊndɪŋ/ n. **1 a** the action or process of measuring the depth of water, now usu. by means of echo. **b** an instance of this (*took a sounding*). **2** (in *pl.*) **a** a region close to the shore of the right depth for sounding. **b** *Naut.* measurements taken by sounding. **c** cautious investigation (*made soundings as to his suitability*). **3 a** the determination of any physical property at a depth in the sea or at a height in the atmosphere. **b** an instance of this. □ **sounding-balloon** a balloon used to obtain information about the upper atmosphere. **sounding-line** a line used in sounding the depth of water. **sounding-rod** a rod used in finding the depth of water in a ship's hold (see SOUND[3]).

sounding[2] /ˈsaʊndɪŋ/ adj. **1** giving forth (esp. loud or resonant) sound (*sounding brass*). **2** emptily boastful, resonant, or imposing (*sounding promises*).

sounding-board /ˈsaʊndɪŋbɔːd/ n. **1** a canopy over a pulpit etc. to direct sound towards the congregation. **2** = SOUNDBOARD. **3 a** a means of causing opinions etc. to be more widely known (*used his students as a sounding-board*). **b** a person etc. used as a trial audience.

soundproof /ˈsaʊndpruːf/ adj. & v. —adj. impervious to sound. —v.tr. make soundproof.

soundtrack /ˈsaʊndtræk/ n. **1** the recorded sound element of a film. **2** this recorded on the edge of a film in optical or magnetic form.

soup /suːp/ n. & v. —n. **1** a usu. savoury liquid dish made by boiling meat, fish, or vegetables etc. in stock or water. **2** *US sl.* nitroglycerine or gelignite, esp. for safe-breaking. **3** *sl.* the chemicals in which film is developed. **4** *colloq.* fog; thick cloud. —v.tr. (usu. foll. by *up*) *colloq.* **1** increase the power and efficiency of (an engine). **2** increase the impact or power of (writing, music, etc.). □ **in the soup** *colloq.* in difficulties. **soup and fish** *colloq.* evening dress. **soup-kitchen** a place dispensing soup etc. to the poor. **soup-plate** a deep wide-rimmed plate for serving soup. **soup-spoon** a large round-bowled spoon for drinking soup. [F *soupe* sop, broth, f. LL *suppa* f. Gmc: cf. SOP, SUP[1]]

æ cat ɑ: *arm* e bed ɜ: *her* ɪ sit i: *see* ɒ hot ɔ: *saw* ʌ run ʊ put u: *too* ə ago aɪ my

soupçon /'suːpsɔ̃/ n. a very small quantity; a dash. [F f. OF sou(s)peçon f. med.L suspectio -onis: see SUSPICION]

soupy /'suːpɪ/ adj. (**soupier, soupiest**) **1** of or resembling soup. **2** colloq. sentimental; mawkish. □□ **soupily** adv. **soupiness** n.

sour /'saʊə(r)/ adj., n., & v. —adj. **1** having an acid taste like lemon or vinegar, esp. because of unripeness (sour apples). **2 a** (of food, esp. milk or bread) bad because of fermentation. **b** smelling or tasting rancid or unpleasant. **3** (of a person, temper, etc.) harsh; morose; bitter. **4** (of a thing) unpleasant; distasteful. **5** (of the soil) deficient in lime and usually dank. —n. **1** US a drink with lemon- or lime-juice (whisky sour). **2** an acid solution used in bleaching etc. —v.tr. & intr. make or become sour (soured the cream; soured by misfortune). □**go** (or **turn**) **sour 1** (of food etc.) become sour. **2** turn out badly (the job went sour on him). **3** lose one's keenness. **sour cream** cream deliberately fermented by adding bacteria. **sour grapes** resentful disparagement of something one cannot personally acquire. **sour mash** US a brewing- or distilling-mash made acid to promote fermentation. □□ **sourish** adj. **sourly** adv. **sourness** n. [OE sūr f. Gmc]

source /sɔːs/ n. & v. —n. **1** a spring or fountain-head from which a stream issues (the sources of the Nile). **2** a place, person, or thing from which something originates (the source of all our troubles). **3** a person or document etc. providing evidence (reliable sources of information; historical source material). **4 a** a body emitting radiation etc. **b** Physics a place from which a fluid or current flows. **c** Electronics a part of a transistor from which carriers flow into the inter-electrode channel. —v.tr. obtain (esp. components) from a specified source. □**at source** at the point of origin or issue. **source-criticism** the evaluation of different, esp. successive, literary or historical sources. [ME f. OF sors, sourse, past part. of sourdre rise f. L surgere]

sourcebook /'sɔːsbʊk/ n. a collection of documentary sources for the study of a subject.

sourdough /'saʊə,dəʊ/ n. US **1** fermenting dough, esp. that left over from a previous baking, used as leaven. **2** an old-timer in Alaska etc. [dial., = leaven, in allusion to piece of sour dough for raising bread baked in winter]

sourpuss /'saʊə,pʊs/ n. colloq. a sour-tempered person. [SOUR + PUSS = face]

soursop /'saʊə,sɒp/ n. **1** a W. Indian evergreen tree, Annona muricata. **2** the large succulent fruit of this tree.

sous- /suː(z)/ prefix (in words adopted from French) subordinate, under (sous-chef). [F]

sousaphone /'suːzə,fəʊn/ n. a large brass bass wind instrument encircling the player's body. □□ **sousaphonist** n. [J. P. Sousa, Amer. bandmaster d. 1932, after saxophone]

souse /saʊs/ v. & n. —v. **1** tr. put (gherkins, fish, etc.) in pickle. **2** tr. & intr. plunge into liquid. **3** tr. (as **soused** adj.) colloq. drunk. **4** tr. (usu. foll. by in) soak (a thing) in liquid. **5** tr. (usu. foll. by over) throw (liquid) over a thing. —n. **1 a** pickle made with salt. **b** US food, esp. a pig's head etc., in pickle. **2** a dip, plunge, or drenching in water. **3** colloq. **a** a drinking-bout. **b** a drunkard. [ME f. OF sous, souz pickle f. OS sultia, OHG sulza brine f. Gmc: cf. SALT]

soutache /suːˈtæʃ/ n. a narrow flat ornamental braid used to trim garments. [F f. Magyar sujtás]

soutane /suːˈtɑːn/ n. RC Ch. a cassock worn by a priest. [F f. It. sottana f. sotto under f. L subtus]

souteneur /ˌsuːtəˈnɜː(r)/ n. a pimp. [F, = protector]

souter /'suːtə(r)/ n. Sc. & N.Engl. a shoemaker; a cobbler. [OE sūtere f. L sutor f. suere sut- sew]

souterrain /'suːtə,reɪn/ n. esp. Archaeol. an underground chamber or passage. [F f. sous under + terre earth]

south /saʊθ/ n., adj., adv., & v. —n. **1** the point of

the horizon 90° clockwise from east. **2** the compass point corresponding to this. **3** the direction in which this lies. **4** (usu. **the South**) **a** the part of the world or a country or a town lying to the south. **b** the Southern States of the US. **5** Bridge a player occupying the position designated 'south'. —adj. **1** towards, at, near, or facing the south (a south wall; south country). **2** coming from the south (south wind). —adv. **1** towards, at, or near the south (they travelled south). **2** (foll. by of) further south than. —v.intr. **1** move towards the south. **2** (of a celestial body) cross the meridian. □**South African** adj. of or relating to the republic of South Africa. —n. **1** a native or national of South Africa. **2** a person of South African descent. **South American** adj. of or relating to South America. —n. a native or citizen of South America. **south by east** (or **west**) between south and south-south-east (or south-south-west). **south-east** n. **1** the point of the horizon midway between south and east. **2** the compass point corresponding to this. **3** the direction in which this lies. —adj. of, towards, or coming from the south-east. —adv. towards, at, or near the south-east. **South-East** the part of a country or town lying to the south-east. **south-easterly** adj. & adv. = south-east. **south-eastern** lying on the south-east side. **south pole** see POLE². **South Sea** the southern Pacific Ocean. **South Sea Bubble** hist. a scheme for trading in the southern hemisphere to repay the British national debt, which started and collapsed in 1720. **south-south-east** the point or direction midway between south and south-east. **south-south-west** the point or direction midway between south and south-west. **south-west** n. **1** the point of the horizon midway between south and west. **2** the compass point corresponding to this. **3** the direction in which this lies. —adj. of, towards, or coming from the south-west. —adv. towards, at, or near the south-west. **South-West** the part of a country or town lying to the south-west. **south-westerly** adj. & adv. = south-west. **south-western** lying on the south-west side. **south wind** a wind blowing from the south. **to the south** (often foll. by of) in a southerly direction. [OE sūth]

southbound /'saʊθbaʊnd/ adj. travelling or leading southwards.

Southdown /'saʊθdaʊn/ n. **1** a sheep of a breed raised esp. for mutton, orig. on the South Downs of Hampshire and Sussex. **2** this breed.

southeaster /saʊθˈiːstə(r)/ n. a south-east wind.

souther /'saʊθə(r)/ n. a south wind.

southerly /'sʌðəlɪ/ adj., adv., & n. —adj. & adv. **1** in a southern position or direction. **2** (of a wind) blowing from the south. —n. (pl. -**ies**) a southerly wind.

southern /'sʌð(ə)n/ adj. esp. Geog. **1** of or in the south; inhabiting the south. **2** lying or directed towards the south (at the southern end). □**Southern Cross** a southern constellation in the shape of a cross. **Southern hemisphere** the half of the earth below the equator. **southern lights** the aurora australis. **Southern States** the States in the south, esp. the south-east, of the US. □□ **southernmost** adj. [OE sūtherne (as SOUTH, -ERN)]

southerner /'sʌðənə(r)/ n. a native or inhabitant of the south.

southernwood /'sʌð(ə)nwʊd/ n. a bushy kind of wormwood, Artemisia abrotanum.

southing /'saʊθɪŋ/ n. **1** a southern movement. **2** Naut. the distance travelled or measured southward. **3** Astron. the angular distance of a star etc. south of the celestial equator.

southpaw /'saʊθpɔː/ n. & adj. colloq. —n. a left-handed person, esp. in boxing. —adj. left-handed.

southward /'saʊθwəd/ adj., adv., & n. —adj. & adv. (also **southwards**) towards the south. —n. a southward direction or region.

southwester /saʊθˈwestə(r)/ n. a south-west wind.

souvenir /ˌsuːvəˈnɪə(r)/ n. & v. —n. (often foll. by of) a memento of an occasion, place, etc. —*v.tr. sl.* take as a 'souvenir'; pilfer, steal. [F f. *souvenir* remember f. L *subvenire* occur to the mind (as SUB-, *venire* come)]

souvlaki /suːˈvlɑːkɪ/ *n.* (*pl.* **souvlakia** /-kɪə/) a Greek dish of pieces of meat grilled on a skewer. [mod. Gk]

sou'wester /saʊˈwestə(r)/ *n.* **1** = SOUTHWESTER. **2** a waterproof hat with a broad flap covering the neck.

sov. /sɒv/ *abbr. Brit.* sovereign.

sovereign /ˈsɒvrɪn/ *n. & adj.* —*n.* **1** a supreme ruler, esp. a monarch. **2** *Brit. hist.* a gold coin nominally worth £1. —*adj.* **1 a** supreme (*sovereign power*). **b** unmitigated (*sovereign contempt*). **2** excellent; effective (*a sovereign remedy*). **3** possessing sovereign power (*a sovereign State*). **4** royal (*our sovereign lord*). ▫**the sovereign good** the greatest good, esp. for a State, its people, etc. **sovereign pontiff** see PONTIFF. ▫▫**sovereignly** *adv.* **sovereignty** *n.* (*pl.* **-ies**). [ME f. OF *so(u)verain* f. L: *-g-* by assoc. with *reign*]

soviet /ˈsəʊvɪət, ˈsɒ-/ *n. & adj.* —*n.* **1** an elected local, district, or national council in the USSR. **2** (**Soviet**) a citizen of the USSR. **3** *hist.* a revolutionary council of workers, peasants, etc. before 1917. —*adj.* (usu. **Soviet**) of or concerning the Soviet Union. ▫▫ **Sovietize** *v.tr.* (also **-ise**). **Sovietization** /-taɪˈzeɪʃ(ə)n/ *n.* [Russ. *sovet* council]

sovietologist /ˌsəʊvɪəˈtɒlədʒɪst, ˌsɒ-/ *n.* a person who studies the Soviet Union.

sow[1] /səʊ/ *v.tr.* (*past* **sowed** /səʊd/; *past part.* **sown** /səʊn/ or **sowed**) **1** (also *absol.*) **a** scatter (seed) on or in the earth. **b** (often foll. by *with*) plant (a field etc.) with seed. **2** initiate; arouse (*sowed doubt in her mind*). **3** (foll. by *with*) cover thickly with. ▫**sow the seed** (or **seeds**) of first give rise to; implant (an idea etc.). ▫▫ **sower** *n.* **sowing** *n.* [OE *sāwan* f. Gmc]

sow[2] /saʊ/ *n.* **1 a** a female adult pig, esp. after farrowing. **b** a female guinea-pig. **c** the female of some other species. **2 a** the main trough through which molten iron runs into side-channels to form pigs. **b** a large block of iron so formed. **3** (in full **sow bug**) esp. *US* a woodlouse. [OE *sugu*]

sowback /ˈsaʊbæk/ *n.* a low ridge of sand etc.

sowbread /ˈsaʊbred/ *n.* a tuberous plant, *Cyclamen hederifolium*, with solitary nodding flowers.

sown *past part.* of SOW[1].

sowthistle /ˈsaʊˌθɪs(ə)l/ *n.* any plant of the genus *Sonchus* with thistle-like leaves and milky juice.

sox *informal* or *Commerce pl.* of SOCK[1].

soy /sɔɪ/ *n.* (also **soya** /ˈsɔɪjə/) **1** (also **soy sauce**) a sauce made in Japan and China from pickled soya beans. **2** (in full **soy bean**) = *soya bean*. [Jap. *shō-yu* f. Chin. *shi-you* f. *shi* salted beans + *you* oil]

soya /ˈsɔɪə/ *n.* (in full **soya bean**) **1 a** a leguminous plant, *Glycine soja*, orig. of SE Asia, cultivated for the edible oil and flour it yields, and used as a replacement for animal protein in certain foods. **b** the seed of this. **2** (also **soya sauce**) = SOY 1. [Du. *soja* f. Malay *soi* (as SOY)]

sozzled /ˈsɒz(ə)ld/ *adj. colloq.* very drunk. [past part. of dial. *sozzle* mix sloppily (prob. imit.)]

SP *abbr.* starting price.

spa /spɑː/ *n.* **1** a curative mineral spring. **2** a place or resort with this. [*Spa* in Belgium]

space /speɪs/ *n. & v.* —*n.* **1 a** a continuous unlimited area or expanse which may or may not contain objects etc. **b** an interval between one, two, or three-dimensional points or objects (*a space of 10 metres*). **c** an empty area; room (*clear a space in the corner*; *occupies too much space*). **d** a large unoccupied region (*the wide open spaces*). **3** = *outer space*. **4** an interval of time (*in the space of an hour*). **5** the amount of paper used in writing etc. (*hadn't the space to discuss it*). **6 a** a blank between printed, typed, or written words, etc. **b** a piece of metal providing this. **7** *Mus.* each of the blanks between the lines of a staff. —*v.tr.* **1** set or arrange at intervals. **2** put spaces between (esp. words, letters,

lines, etc. in printing, typing, or writing). **3** (as **spaced** *adj.*) (often foll. by *out*) *sl.* in a state of euphoria, esp. from taking drugs. ▫**space age** the era when space travel has become possible. **space-bar** a long key in a typewriter for making a space between words etc. **space flight 1** a journey through space. **2** = *space travel*. **space out** put more or wider spaces or intervals between. **space probe** = PROBE *n.* 4. **space rocket** a rocket used to launch a spacecraft. **space-saving** occupying little space. **space shuttle** a rocket for repeated use esp. between the earth and a space station. **space station** an artificial satellite used as a base for operations in space. **space-time** (or **space-time continuum**) the fusion of the concepts of space and time, esp. as a four-dimensional continuum. **space travel** travel through outer space. **space traveller** a traveller in outer space; an astronaut. **space vehicle** = SPACECRAFT. **space walk** any physical activity by an astronaut in space outside a spacecraft. ▫▫ **spacer** *n.* **spacing** *n.* (esp. in sense 2 of *v.*). [ME f. OF *espace* f. L *spatium*]

spacecraft /ˈspeɪskrɑːft/ *n.* a vehicle used for travelling in space.

spaceman /ˈspeɪsmæn/ *n.* (*pl.* **-men**; *fem.* **spacewoman**, *pl.* **-women**) = *space traveller*.

spaceship /ˈspeɪsʃɪp/ *n.* a spacecraft, esp. one controlled by its crew.

spacesuit /ˈspeɪssjuːt, -suːt/ *n.* a garment designed to allow an astronaut to survive in space.

spacial var. of SPATIAL.

spacious /ˈspeɪʃəs/ *adj.* having ample space; covering a large area; roomy. ▫▫ **spaciously** *adv.* **spaciousness** *n.* [ME f. OF *spacios* or L *spatiosus* (as SPACE)]

spade[1] /speɪd/ *n. & v.* —*n.* **1** a tool used for digging or cutting the ground etc., with a sharp-edged metal blade and a long handle. **2** a tool of a similar shape for various purposes, e.g. for removing the blubber from a whale. **3** anything resembling a spade. —*v.tr.* dig over (ground) with a spade. ▫**call a spade a spade** speak plainly or bluntly. **spade beard** an oblong-shaped beard. **spade foot** a square spadelike enlargement at the end of a chair-leg. ▫▫ **spadeful** *n.* (*pl.* **-fuls**). [OE *spadu, spada*]

spade[2] /speɪd/ *n.* **1 a** a playing-card of a suit denoted by black inverted heart-shaped figures with small stalks. **b** (in *pl.*) this suit. **2** *sl. offens.* a Black. ▫**in spades** *sl.* to a high degree, with great force. **spade guinea** *hist.* a guinea of George III's reign with a spade-shaped shield on the reverse. [It. *spade* pl. of *spada* sword f. L *spatha* f. Gk *spathē*, rel. to SPADE[1]: assoc. with the shape of a pointed spade]

spadework /ˈspeɪdwɜːk/ *n.* hard or routine preparatory work.

spadille /spəˈdɪl/ *n.* **1** the ace of spades in ombre and quadrille. **2** the highest trump, esp. the ace of spades. [F f. Sp. *espadilla* dimin. of *espada* sword (as SPADE[2])]

spadix /ˈspeɪdɪks/ *n.* (*pl.* **spadices** /-ˌsiːz/) *Bot.* a spike of flowers closely arranged round a fleshy axis and usu. enclosed in a spathe. ▫▫ **spadiceous** /-ˈdɪʃəs/ *adj.* [L f. Gk, = palm-branch]

spae /speɪ/ *v.intr. & tr. Sc.* foretell; prophesy. [ME f. ON *spá*]

spaewife /ˈspeɪwaɪf/ *n. Sc.* a female fortune-teller or witch.

spaghetti /spəˈgetɪ/ *n.* pasta made in solid strings, between macaroni and vermicelli in thickness. ▫**spaghetti Bolognese** /ˌbɒləˈneɪz/ spaghetti served with a sauce of minced beef, tomato, onion, etc. **spaghetti junction** a multi-level road junction, esp. on a motorway. **spaghetti western** a western film made cheaply in Italy. [It., pl. of dimin. of *spago* string: *Bolognese* It., = of Bologna]

spahi /ˈspɑːhiː/ *n. hist.* **1** a member of the Turkish irregular cavalry. **2** a member of the Algerian cavalry in French service. [Turk. *sipāhī* formed as SEPOY]

spake /speɪk/ *archaic past* of SPEAK.

spall /spɔːl/ n. & v. —n. a splinter or chip, esp. of rock. —v.intr. & tr. break up or cause (ore) to break up in preparation for sorting. [ME (also *spale*): orig. unkn.]

spallation /spɔːˈleɪʃ(ə)n/ n. *Physics* the breakup of a bombarded nucleus into several parts.

spalpeen /spælˈpiːn/ n. *Ir.* **1** a rascal; a villain. **2** a youngster. [Ir. *spailpín*, of unkn. orig.]

Spam /spæm/ n. *propr.* a tinned meat product made mainly from ham. [*spiced ham*]

span[1] /spæn/ n. & v. —n. **1** the full extent from end to end in space or time (*the span of a bridge*; *the whole span of history*). **2** each arch or part of a bridge between piers or supports. **3** the maximum lateral extent of an aeroplane, its wing, a bird's wing, etc. **4 a** the maximum distance between the tips of the thumb and little finger. **b** this as a measurement, equal to 9 inches. **5** a short distance or time (*our life is but a span*). —v. (**spanned, spanning**) **1** tr. **a** (of a bridge, arch, etc.) stretch from side to side of; extend across (*the bridge spanned the river*). **b** (of a builder etc.) bridge (a river etc.). **2** tr. extend across (space or a period of time etc.). **3** tr. measure or cover the extent of (a thing) with one's hand with the fingers stretched (*spanned a tenth on the piano*). **4** intr. *US* move in distinct stretches like the span-worm. □**span roof** a roof with two inclined sides (opp. PENTHOUSE 2, *lean-to* (see LEAN[1])). **span-worm** *US* the caterpillar of the geometer moth. [OE *span(n)* or OF *espan*]

span[2] /spæn/ n. **1** *Naut.* a rope with both ends fastened to take purchase in a loop. **2** *US* a matched pair of horses, mules, etc. **3** *S.Afr.* a team of two or more pairs of oxen. [LG & Du. *span* f. *spannen* unite]

span[3] see SPICK AND SPAN.

span[4] /spæn/ *archaic past* of SPIN.

spandrel /ˈspændrɪl/ n. *Archit.* **1** the almost triangular space between one side of the outer curve of an arch, a wall, and the ceiling or framework. **2** the space between the shoulders of adjoining arches and the ceiling or moulding above. □**spandrel wall** a wall built on the curve of an arch, filling in the spandrel. [perh. f. AF *spaund(e)re*, or f. *espaundre* EXPAND]

spang /spæŋ/ adv. *US colloq.* exactly; completely (*spang in the middle*). [20th c.: orig. unkn.]

spangle /ˈspæŋg(ə)l/ n. & v. —n. **1** a small thin piece of glittering material esp. used in quantity to ornament a dress etc.; a sequin. **2** a small sparkling object. **3** (in full **spangle gall**) a spongy excrescence on oak-leaves. —v.tr. (esp. as **spangled** adj.) cover with or as with spangles (*star-spangled*; *spangled costume*). □□**spangly** /-ŋglɪ/ adj. [ME f. *spang* f. MDu. *spange*, OHG *spanga*, ON *spöng* brooch f. Gmc]

Spaniard /ˈspænjəd/ n. **1 a** a native or national of Spain in southern Europe. **b** a person of Spanish descent. **2** *NZ* a spear grass. [ME f. OF *Espaignart* f. *Espaigne* Spain]

spaniel /ˈspænj(ə)l/ n. **1 a** a dog of any of various breeds with a long silky coat and drooping ears. **b** any of these breeds. **2** an obsequious or fawning person. [ME f. OF *espaigneul* Spanish (dog) f. Rmc *Hispaniolus* (unrecorded) f. *Hispania* Spain]

Spanish /ˈspænɪʃ/ adj. & n. —adj. of or relating to Spain or its people or language. —n. **1** the language of Spain and Spanish America. **2** (prec. by *the*; treated as *pl.*) the people of Spain. □**Spanish America** those parts of America orig. settled by Spaniards, including Central and South America and part of the West Indies. **Spanish Armada** *hist.* the Spanish war fleet sent against England in 1588. **Spanish bayonet** a yucca, *Yucca aloifolia*, with stiff sharp-pointed leaves. **Spanish chestnut** = CHESTNUT n. 1b. **Spanish fly** a bright green beetle, *Lytta vesicatoria*, formerly dried and used for raising blisters, as a supposed aphrodisiac, etc. **Spanish goat** a goat, *Capra pyrenaica*, inhabiting the Pyrenees. **Spanish guitar** the standard six-stringed acoustic guitar, used esp. for classical and folk music. **Spanish mackerel** any of various large mackerels, esp. *Scomber colias* or *S. maculatus*. **Spanish Main** *hist.* the NE coast of South America between the Orinoco river and Panama, and adjoining parts of the Caribbean Sea. **Spanish omelette** an omelette containing chopped vegetables and often not folded. **Spanish onion** a large mild-flavoured onion. **Spanish windlass** the use of a stick as a lever for tightening ropes etc. [ME f. *Spain*, with shortening of the first element]

spank /spæŋk/ v. & n. —v. **1** tr. slap esp. on the buttocks with the open hand, a slipper, etc. **2** intr. (of a horse etc.) move briskly, esp. between a trot and a gallop. —n. a slap esp. with the open hand on the buttocks. [perh. imit.]

spanker /ˈspæŋkə(r)/ n. **1** a person or thing that spanks. **2** *Naut.* a fore-and-aft sail set on the after side of the mizen-mast. **3** a fast horse. **4** *colloq.* a person or thing of notable size or quality.

spanking /ˈspæŋkɪŋ/ adj., adv., & n. —adj. **1** (esp. of a horse) moving quickly; lively; brisk (*at a spanking trot*). **2** *colloq.* striking; excellent. —adv. *colloq.* very, exceedingly (*spanking clean*). —n. the act or an instance of slapping, esp. on the buttocks as a punishment for children.

spanner /ˈspænə(r)/ n. **1** *Brit.* an instrument for turning or gripping a nut on a screw etc. (cf. WRENCH). **2** the cross-brace of a bridge etc. □**a spanner in the works** *Brit. colloq.* a drawback or impediment. [G *spannen* draw tight: see SPAN[2]]

spar[1] /spɑː(r)/ n. **1** a stout pole esp. used for the mast, yard, etc. of a ship. **2** the main longitudinal beam of an aeroplane wing. □**spar-buoy** a buoy made of a spar with one end moored so that the other stands up. **spar-deck** the light upper deck of a vessel. [ME *sparre*, *sperre* f. OF *esparre* or ON *sperra* or direct f. Gmc: cf. MDu., MLG *sparre*, OS, OHG *sparro*]

spar[2] /spɑː(r)/ v. & n. —v.intr. (**sparred, sparring**) **1** (often foll. by *at*) make the motions of boxing without landing heavy blows. **2** engage in argument (*they are always sparring*). **3** (of a gamecock) fight with the feet or spurs. —n. **1 a** a sparring motion. **b** a boxing-match. **2** a cock-fight. **3** an argument or dispute. □**sparring partner** **1** a boxer employed to engage in sparring with another as training. **2** a person with whom one enjoys arguing. [ME f. OE *sperran*, *spyrran*, of unkn. orig.: cf. ON *sperrask* kick out]

spar[3] /spɑː(r)/ n. any crystalline, easily cleavable and non-lustrous mineral, e.g. calcite or fluorspar. □□**sparry** adj. [MLG, rel. to OE *spæren* of plaster, *spærstân* gypsum]

sparable /ˈspærəb(ə)l/ n. a headless nail used for the soles and heels of shoes. [contr. of *sparrow-bill*, also used in this sense]

sparaxis /spəˈræksɪs/ n. any S. African iridaceous plant of the genus *Sparaxis*, with showy flowers and jagged spathes. [mod.L f. Gk, = laceration, f. *sparassō* tear]

spare /speə(r)/ adj., n., & v. —adj. **1 a** not required for ordinary use; extra (*have no spare cash*; *spare time*). **b** reserved for emergency or occasional use (*slept in the spare room*). **2** lean; thin. **3** scanty; frugal; not copious (*a spare diet*; *a spare prose style*). **4** *colloq.* not wanted or used by others (*a spare seat in the front row*). —n. **1** *Brit.* a spare part; a duplicate. **2** *Bowling* the knocking-down of all the pins with the first two balls. —v. **1** tr. afford to give or do without; dispense with (*cannot spare him just now*; *can spare you a couple*). **2** tr. **a** abstain from killing, hurting, wounding, etc. (*spared his feelings*; *spared her life*). **b** abstain from inflicting or causing; relieve from (*spare me this talk*; *spare my blushes*). **3** tr. be frugal or grudging of (*no expense spared*). **4** intr. *archaic* be frugal. □**go spare** *colloq.* **1** *Brit.* become extremely angry or distraught. **2** be unwanted by others. **not**

spare oneself exert one's utmost efforts. **spare part** a duplicate part to replace a lost or damaged part of a machine etc. **spare tyre 1** an extra tyre carried in a motor vehicle for emergencies. **2** *Brit. colloq.* a roll of fat round the waist. **to spare** left over; additional (*an hour to spare*). □□ **sparely** *adv.* **spareness** *n.* **sparer** *n.* [OE *spær*, *sparian* f. Gmc]

spare-rib /speə'rɪb/ *n.* closely-trimmed ribs of esp. pork. [prob. f. MLG *ribbesper*, by transposition and assoc. with SPARE]

sparge /spɑːdʒ/ *v.tr.* moisten by sprinkling, esp. in brewing. □□ **sparger** *n.* [app. f. L *spargere* sprinkle]

sparing /'speərɪŋ/ *adj.* **1** inclined to save; economical. **2** restrained; limited. □□ **sparingly** *adv.* **sparingness** *n.*

spark[1] /spɑːk/ *n. & v.* —*n.* **1 a** a fiery particle thrown off from a fire, or alight in ashes, or produced by a flint, match, etc. **2** (often foll. by *of*) a particle of a quality etc. (*not a spark of life*; *a spark of interest*). **3** *Electr.* **a** a light produced by a sudden disruptive discharge through the air etc. **b** such a discharge serving to ignite the explosive mixture in an internal-combustion engine. **4 a** a flash of wit etc. **b** anything causing interest, excitement, etc. **c** (also **bright spark**) a witty or lively person. **5** a small bright object or point, e.g. in a gem. **6** (**Sparks**) a nickname for a radio operator or an electrician. —*v.* **1** *intr.* emit sparks of fire or electricity. **2** *tr.* (often foll. by *off*) stir into activity; initiate (a process) suddenly. **3** *intr. Electr.* produce sparks at the point where a circuit is interrupted. □ **spark chamber** an apparatus designed to show ionizing particles. **spark-gap** the space between electric terminals where sparks occur. **sparking-plug** *Brit.* = *spark-plug*. **spark-plug** a device for firing the explosive mixture in an internal-combustion engine. □□ **sparkless** *adj.* **sparky** *adj.* [ME f. OE *spærca*, *spearca*]

spark[2] /spɑːk/ *n. & v.* —*n.* **1** a lively young fellow. **2** a gallant, a beau. —*v.intr.* play the gallant. □□ **sparkish** *adj.* [prob. a fig. use of SPARK[1]]

sparkle /'spɑːk(ə)l/ *v. & n.* —*v.intr.* **1 a** emit or seem to emit sparks; glitter; glisten (*her eyes sparkled*). **b** be witty; scintillate (*sparkling repartee*). **2** (of wine etc.) effervesce (cf. STILL[1] *adj.* 4). —*n.* a gleam, spark. □□ **sparkly** *adj.* [ME f. SPARK[1] + -LE[4]]

sparkler /'spɑːklə(r)/ *n.* **1** a person or thing that sparkles. **2** a hand-held sparkling firework. **3** *colloq.* a diamond or other gem.

sparling /'spɑːlɪŋ/ *n.* a European smelt, *Osmerus eperlanus.* [ME f. OF *esperlinge*, of Gmc orig.]

sparoid /'spæərɔɪd/ *n. & adj.* —*n.* any marine fish of the family Sparidae, e.g. a porgy. —*adj.* of or concerning the Sparidae. [mod.L *Sparoides* f. L *sparus* f. Gk *sparos* sea-bream]

sparrow /'spærəʊ/ *n.* **1** any small brownish-grey bird of the genus *Passer*, esp. the house sparrow and tree sparrow. **2** any of various birds of similar appearance such as the hedge sparrow. □ **sparrow-grass** *dial.* or *colloq.* asparagus. [OE *spearwa* f. Gmc]

sparrowhawk /'spærəʊˌhɔːk/ *n.* a small hawk, *Accipiter nisus,* preying on small birds.

sparse /spɑːs/ *adj.* thinly dispersed or scattered; not dense (*sparse population*; *sparse greying hair*). □□ **sparsely** *adv.* **sparseness** *n.* **sparsity** *n.* [L *sparsus* past part. of *spargere* scatter]

Spartan /'spɑːt(ə)n/ *adj. & n.* —*adj.* **1** of or relating to Sparta in ancient Greece. **2 a** possessing the qualities of courage, endurance, stern frugality, etc., associated with Sparta. **b** (of a regime, conditions, etc.) lacking comfort; austere. —*n.* a citizen of Sparta. [ME f. L *Spartanus* f. *Sparta* f. Gk *Sparta, -tē*]

spartina /spɑː'tiːnə/ *n.* any grass of the genus *Spartina,* with rhizomatous roots and growing in wet or marshy ground. [Gk *spartinē* rope]

spasm /'spæz(ə)m/ *n.* **1** a sudden involuntary muscular contraction. **2** a sudden convulsive movement or emotion etc. (*a spasm of coughing*). **3** (usu. foll. by *of*) *colloq.* a brief spell of an activity. [ME f. OF *spasme* or L *spasmus* f. Gk *spasmos, spasma* f. *spaō* pull]

spasmodic /spæz'mɒdɪk/ *adj.* **1** of, caused by, or subject to, a spasm or spasms (*a spasmodic jerk*; *spasmodic asthma*). **2** occurring or done by fits and starts (*spasmodic efforts*). □□ **spasmodically** *adv.* [mod.L *spasmodicus* f. Gk *spasmōdēs* (as SPASM)]

spastic /'spæstɪk/ *adj. & n.* —*adj.* **1** *Med.* suffering from cerebral palsy with spasm of the muscles. **2** *offens.* weak, feeble, incompetent. **3** spasmodic. —*n. Med.* a spastic person. □□ **spastically** *adv.* **spasticity** /-'tɪsɪtɪ/ *n.* [L *spasticus* f. Gk *spastikos* pulling f. *spaō* pull]

spat[1] *past* and *past part.* of SPIT.

spat[2] /spæt/ *n.* **1** (usu. in *pl.*) *hist.* a short cloth gaiter protecting the shoe from mud etc. **2** a cover for an aircraft wheel. [abbr. of SPATTERDASH]

spat[3] /spæt/ *n. & v. US colloq.* —*n.* **1** a petty quarrel. **2** a slight amount. —*v.intr.* (**spatted, spatting**) quarrel pettily. [prob. imit.]

spat[4] /spæt/ *n. & v.* —*n.* the spawn of shellfish, esp. the oyster. —*v.* (**spatted, spatting**) **1** *intr.* (of an oyster) spawn. **2** *tr.* shed (spawn). [AF, of unkn. orig.]

spatchcock /'spætʃkɒk/ *n. & v.* —*n.* a chicken or esp. game bird split open and grilled. —*v.tr.* **1** treat (poultry) in this way. **2** *colloq.* insert or interpolate (a phrase, sentence, story, etc.) esp. incongruously. [orig. in Ir. use, expl. by Grose (1785) as f. *dispatch-cock,* but cf. SPITCHCOCK]

spate /speɪt/ *n.* **1** a river-flood (*the river is in spate*). **2** a large or excessive amount (*a spate of enquiries*). [ME, Sc. & N.Engl.: orig. unkn.]

spathe /speɪð/ *n. Bot.* a large bract or pair of bracts enveloping a spadix or flower-cluster. □□ **spathaceous** /spə'ðeɪʃəs/ *adj.* [L f. Gk *spathē* broad blade etc.]

spathic /'spæθɪk/ *adj.* (of a mineral) like spar (see SPAR[3]), esp. in cleavage. □ **spathic iron ore** = SIDERITE. □□ **spathose** *adj.* [*spath* spar f. G *Spath*]

spatial /'speɪʃ(ə)l/ *adj.* (also **spacial**) of or concerning space (*spatial extent*). □□ **spatiality** /-ʃɪ'ælɪtɪ/ *n.* **spatialize** *v.tr.* (also **-ise**). **spatially** *adv.* [L *spatium* space]

spatio-temporal /ˌspeɪʃɪəʊ'tempər(ə)l/ *adj. Physics & Philos.* belonging to both space and time or to space-time. □□ **spatio-temporally** *adv.* [formed as SPATIAL + TEMPORAL]

spatter /'spætə(r)/ *v. & n.* —*v.* **1** *tr.* **a** (often foll. by *with*) splash (a person etc.) (*spattered him with mud*). **b** scatter or splash (liquid, mud, etc.) here and there. **2** *intr.* (of rain etc.) fall here and there (*glass spattered down*). **3** *tr.* slander (a person's honour etc.). —*n.* **1** (usu. foll. by *of*) a splash (*a spatter of mud*). **2** a quick pattering sound. [frequent. f. base as in Du., LG *spatten* burst, spout]

spatterdash /'spætəˌdæʃ/ *n.* **1** (usu. in *pl.*) *hist.* a cloth or other legging to protect the stockings etc. from mud etc. **2** *US* = ROUGHCAST.

spatula /'spætjʊlə/ *n.* **1** a broad-bladed knife-like implement used for spreading, stirring, mixing (paints), etc. **2** a doctor's instrument for pressing the tongue down or to one side. [L, var. of *spathula,* dimin. of *spatha* SPATHE]

spatulate /'spætjʊlət/ *adj.* **1** spatula-shaped. **2** (esp. of a leaf) having a broad rounded end. [SPATULA]

spavin /'spævɪn/ *n. Vet.* a disease of a horse's hock with a hard bony tumour or excrescence. □ **blood** (or **bog**) **spavin** a distension of the joint by effusion of lymph or fluid. **bone spavin** a deposit of bony substance uniting the bones. □□ **spavined** *adj.* [ME f. OF *espavin,* var. of *esparvain* f. Gmc]

spawn /spɔːn/ *v. & n.* —*v.* **1 a** *tr.* (also *absol.*) (of a fish, frog, mollusc, or crustacean) produce (eggs). **b**

intr. be produced as eggs or young. **2** *tr. derog.* (of people) produce (offspring). **3** *tr.* produce or generate, esp. in large numbers. —*n.* **1** the eggs of fish, frogs, etc. **2** *derog.* human or other offspring. **3** a white fibrous matter from which fungi are produced; mycelium. □□ **spawner** *n.* [ME f. AF *espaundre* shed roe, OF *espandre* EXPAND]

spay /speɪ/ *v.tr.* sterilize (a female animal) by removing the ovaries. [ME f. AF *espeier*, OF *espeer* cut with a sword f. *espee* sword f. L *spatha*: see SPATHE]

SPCK *abbr.* Society for Promoting Christian Knowledge.

speak /spiːk/ *v.* (*past* **spoke** /spəʊk/; *past part.* **spoken** /ˈspəʊkən/) **1** *intr.* make articulate verbal utterances in an ordinary (not singing) voice. **2** *tr.* **a** utter (words). **b** make known or communicate (one's opinion, the truth, etc.) in this way (*never speaks sense*). **3** *intr.* **a** (foll. by *to, with*) hold a conversation (*spoke to him for an hour*; *spoke with them about their work*). **b** (foll. by *of*) mention in writing etc. (*speaks of it in his novel*). **c** (foll. by *for*) articulate the feelings of (another person etc.) in speech or writing (*speaks for our generation*). **4** *intr.* (foll. by *to*) **a** address; converse with (a person etc.). **b** speak in confirmation of or with reference to (*spoke to the resolution*; *can speak to his innocence*). **c** *colloq.* reprove (*spoke to them about their lateness*). **5** *intr.* make a speech before an audience etc. (*spoke for an hour on the topic*; *has a good speaking voice*). **6** *tr.* use or be able to use (a specified language) (*cannot speak French*). **7** *intr.* (of a gun, a musical instrument, etc.) make a sound. **8** *intr.* (usu. foll. by *to*) *poet.* communicate feeling etc., affect, touch (*the sunset spoke to her*). **9** *intr.* (of a hound) bark. **10** *tr.* hail and hold communication with (a ship). **11** *tr. archaic* **a** (of conduct etc.) show (a person) to be (*his conduct speaks him generous*). **b** be evidence of (*the loud laugh speaks the vacant mind*). □**not** (or **nothing**) **to speak of** not (or nothing) worth mentioning; practically not (or nothing). **speak for itself** need no supporting evidence. **speak for oneself 1** give one's own opinions. **2** not presume to speak for others. **speak one's mind** speak bluntly or frankly. **speak out** speak loudly or freely, give one's opinion. **speak up** = *speak out.* **speak volumes** (of a fact etc.) be very significant. **speak volumes** (or **well** etc.) **for 1** be abundant evidence of. **2** place in a favourable light. □□ **speakable** *adj.* [OE *sprecan*, later *specan*]

speakeasy /ˈspiːkˌiːzɪ/ *n.* (*pl.* **-ies**) *US hist. sl.* an illicit liquor shop or drinking club during Prohibition.

speaker /ˈspiːkə(r)/ *n.* **1** a person who speaks, esp. in public. **2** a person who speaks a specified language (esp. in *comb.*: *a French-speaker*). **3** (**Speaker**) the presiding officer in a legislative assembly, esp. the House of Commons. **4** = LOUDSPEAKER. □□ **speakership** *n.*

speaking /ˈspiːkɪŋ/ *n. & adj.* —*n.* the act or an instance of uttering words etc. —*adj.* **1** that speaks; capable of articulate speech. **2** (of a portrait) lifelike; true to its subject (*a speaking likeness*). **3** (in *comb.*) speaking or capable of speaking a specified foreign language (*French-speaking*). **4** with a reference or from a point of view specified (*roughly speaking*; *professionally speaking*). □**on speaking terms** (foll. by *with*) **1** slightly acquainted. **2** on friendly terms. **speaking acquaintance 1** a person one knows slightly. **2** this degree of familiarity. **speaking clock** *Brit.* a telephone service giving the correct time in words. **speaking-trumpet** *hist.* an instrument for making the voice carry. **speaking-tube** a tube for conveying the voice from one room, building, etc., to another.

spear /spɪə(r)/ *n. & v.* —*n.* **1** a thrusting or throwing weapon with a pointed usu. steel tip and a long shaft. **2** a similar barbed instrument used for catching fish etc. **3** *archaic* a spearman. **4** a pointed stem of asparagus etc. —*v.tr.* pierce or strike with or as if

with a spear (*speared an olive*). □**spear gun** a gun used to propel a spear in underwater fishing. **spear side** the male side of a family. [OE *spere*]

spearhead /ˈspɪəhed/ *n. & v.* —*n.* **1** the point of a spear. **2** an individual or group chosen to lead a thrust or attack. —*v.tr.* act as the spearhead of (an attack etc.).

spearman /ˈspɪəmən/ *n.* (*pl.* **-men**) *archaic* a person, esp. a soldier, who uses a spear.

spearmint /ˈspɪəmɪnt/ *n.* a common garden mint, *Mentha spicata*, used in cookery and to flavour chewing-gum.

spearwort /ˈspɪəwɜːt/ *n.* an aquatic plant, *Ranunculus lingua*, with thick hollow stems, long narrow spear-shaped leaves, and yellow flowers.

spec[1] /spek/ *n. colloq.* a commercial speculation or venture. □**on spec** in the hope of success; as a gamble, on the off chance. [abbr. of SPECULATION]

spec[2] /spek/ *n. colloq.* a detailed working description; a specification. [abbr. of SPECIFICATION]

special /ˈspeʃ(ə)l/ *adj. & n.* —*adj.* **1 a** particularly good; exceptional; out of the ordinary (*bought them a special present*; *took special trouble*). **b** peculiar; specific; not general (*lacks the special qualities required*; *the word has a special sense*). **2** for a particular purpose (*sent on a special assignment*). **3** in which a person specializes (*statistics is his special field*). **4** denoting education for children with particular needs, e.g. the handicapped. —*n.* a special person or thing, e.g. a special constable, train, examination, edition of a newspaper, dish on a menu, etc. □**special area** *Brit.* a district for which special economic provision is made in legislation. **Special Branch** (in the UK) a police department dealing with political security. **special case 1** a written statement of fact presented by litigants to a court. **2** an exceptional or unusual case. **special constable** *Brit.* a policeman sworn in to assist in times of emergency etc. **special correspondent** a journalist writing for a newspaper on special events or a special area of interest. **special delivery** a delivery of mail in advance of the regular delivery. **special drawing rights** the right to purchase extra foreign currency from the International Monetary Fund. **special edition** an extra edition of a newspaper including later news than the ordinary edition. **special effects** scenic illusions created by props and camera-work. **special intention** see INTENTION. **special jury** a jury with members of a particular social standing (cf. *common jury*). **special licence** *Brit.* a marriage licence allowing immediate marriage without banns, or at an unusual time or place. **special pleading 1** *Law* pleading with reference to new facts in a case. **2** a specious or unfair argument favouring the speaker's point of view. **special verdict** *Law* a verdict stating the facts as proved but leaving the court to draw conclusions from them. □□ **specially** *adv.* **specialness** *n.* [ME f. OF *especial* ESPECIAL or L *specialis* (as SPECIES)]

specialist /ˈspeʃəlɪst/ *n.* (usu. foll. by *in*) **1** a person who is trained in a particular branch of a profession, esp. medicine (*a specialist in dermatology*). **2** a person who specially or exclusively studies a subject or a particular branch of a subject. □□ **specialism** /-ˌlɪz(ə)m/ *n.* **specialistic** /-ˈlɪstɪk/ *adj.*

speciality /ˌspeʃɪˈælɪtɪ/ *n.* (*pl.* **-ies**) **1** a special pursuit, product, operation, etc., to which a company or a person gives special attention. **2** a special feature, characteristic, or skill. [ME f. OF *especialité* or LL *specialitas* (as SPECIAL)]

specialize /ˈspeʃəlaɪz/ *v.* (also **-ise**) **1** *intr.* (often foll. by *in*) **a** be or become a specialist (*specializes in optics*). **b** devote oneself to an area of interest, skill, etc. (*specializes in insulting people*). **2** *Biol.* **a** *tr.* (esp. in *passive*) adapt or set apart (an organ etc.) for a particular purpose. **b** *intr.* (of an organ etc.) become adapted etc. in this way. **3** *tr.* make specific or individual. **4** *tr.* modify or limit (an idea, statement, etc.). □□ **specialization** /-'zeɪʃ(ə)n/ *n.* [F *spécialiser* (as SPECIAL)]

specialty /'speʃəltɪ/ *n.* (*pl.* -ies) **1** esp. *US* = SPECI-ALITY. **2** *Law* an instrument under seal; a sealed contract. [ME f. OF (*e*)*specialté* (as SPECIAL)]

speciation /ˌspiːsɪ'eɪʃən, ˌspiːʃ-/ *n. Biol.* the formation of a new species in the course of evolution.

specie /'spiːʃiː, -ʃɪ/ *n.* coin money as opposed to paper money. [L, ablat. of SPECIES in phrase *in specie*]

species /'spiːʃiːz, 'spiːsɪz, 'spiːs-/ *n.* (*pl.* same) **1** a class of things having some common characteristics. **2** *Biol.* a category in the system of classification of living organisms consisting of similar individuals capable of exchanging genes or interbreeding. **3** a kind or sort. **4** *Logic* a group subordinate to a genus and containing individuals agreeing in some common attribute(s) and called by a common name. **5** *Law* a form or shape given to materials. **6** *Eccl.* the visible form of each of the elements of consecrated bread and wine in the Eucharist. [L, = appearance, kind, beauty, f. *specere* look]

specific /spɪ'sɪfɪk/ *adj. & n.* —*adj.* **1** clearly defined; definite (*has no specific name; told me so in specific terms*). **2** relating to a particular subject; peculiar (*a style specific to that*). **3** a of or concerning a species (*the specific name for a plant*). **b** possessing, or concerned with, the properties that characterize a species (*the specific forms of animals*). **4** (of a duty or a tax) assessed by quantity or amount, not by the value of goods. —*n.* **1** *archaic* a specific medicine or remedy. **2** a specific aspect or factor (*shall we discuss specifics?*). □ **specific cause** the cause of a particular form of a disease. **specific difference** a factor that differentiates a species. **specific disease** a disease caused by one identifiable agent. **specific gravity** = *relative density*. **specific heat capacity** the heat required to raise the temperature of the unit mass of a given substance by a given amount (usu. one degree). **specific medicine** a medicine having a distinct effect in curing a certain disease. **specific performance** *Law* the performance of a contractual duty, as ordered in cases where damages would not be adequate remedy. □□ **specifically** *adv.* **specificity** /-'fɪsɪtɪ/ *n.* **specificness** *n.* [LL *specificus* (as SPECIES)]

specification /ˌspesɪfɪ'keɪʃ(ə)n/ *n.* **1** the act or an instance of specifying; the state of being specified. **2** (esp. in *pl.*) a detailed description of the construction, workmanship, materials, etc., of work done or to be done, prepared by an architect, engineer, etc. **3** a description by an applicant for a patent of the construction and use of his invention. **4** *Law* the conversion of materials into a new product not held to be the property of the owner of the materials. [med.L *specificatio* (as SPECIFY)]

specify /'spesɪfaɪ/ *v.tr.* (-ies, -ied) **1** (also *absol.*) name or mention expressly (*specified the type he needed*). **2** (usu. foll. by *that* + clause) name as a condition (*specified that he must be paid at once*). **3** include in specifications (*a French window was not specified*). □□ **specifiable** *adj.* **specifier** *n.* [ME f. OF *specifier* or LL *specificare* (as SPECIFIC)]

specimen /'spesɪmən/ *n.* **1** an individual or part taken as an example of a class or whole, esp. when used for investigation or scientific examination (*specimens of copper ore; a specimen of your handwriting*). **2** *Med.* a sample of urine for testing. **3** *colloq.* usu. *derog.* a person of a specified sort. [L f. *specere* look]

speciology /ˌspiːsɪ'ɒlədʒɪ/ *n.* the scientific study of species or of their origin etc. □□ **speciological** /-ə'lɒdʒɪk(ə)l/ *adj.*

specious /'spiːʃəs/ *adj.* **1** superficially plausible but actually wrong (*a specious argument*). **2** misleadingly attractive in appearance. □□ **speciosity** /-ʃɪ'ɒsɪtɪ/ *n.* **speciously** *adv.* **speciousness** *n.* [ME, = beautiful, f. L *speciosus* (as SPECIES)]

speck /spek/ *n. & v.* —*n.* **1** a small spot, dot, or stain. **2** (foll. by *of*) a particle (*speck of dirt*). **3** a rotten spot in fruit. —*v.tr.* (esp. as **specked** *adj.*) marked with specks. □□ **speckless** *adj.* [OE *specca*: cf. SPECKLE]

speckle /'spek(ə)l/ *n. & v.* —*n.* a small spot, mark, or stain, esp. in quantity on the skin, a bird's egg, etc. —*v.tr.* (esp. as **speckled** *adj.*) mark with speckles or patches. [ME f. MDu. *spekkel*]

specs /speks/ *n.pl. colloq.* a pair of spectacles. [abbr.]

spectacle /'spektək(ə)l/ *n.* **1** a public show, ceremony, etc. **2** anything attracting public attention (*a charming spectacle; a disgusting spectacle*). □ **make a spectacle of oneself** make oneself an object of ridicule. [ME f. OF f. L *spectaculum* f. *spectare* frequent. of *specere* look]

spectacled /'spektək(ə)ld/ *adj.* **1** wearing spectacles. **2** (of an animal) having facial markings resembling spectacles. □ **spectacled bear** a S. American bear, *Tremarctos ornatus.* **spectacled cobra** the Indian cobra.

spectacles /'spektək(ə)lz/ *n.pl.* (also **pair of spectacles** *sing.*) a pair of lenses in a frame resting on the nose and ears, used to correct defective eyesight or protect the eyes.

spectacular /spek'tækjʊlə(r)/ *adj. & n.* —*adj.* **1** of or like a public show; striking, amazing, lavish. **2** strikingly large or obvious (*a spectacular increase in output*). —*n.* an event intended to be spectacular, esp. a musical film or play. □□ **spectacularly** *adv.* [SPECTACLE, after *oracular* etc.]

spectate /spek'teɪt/ *v.intr.* be a spectator, esp. at a sporting event. [back-form. f. SPECTATOR]

spectator /spek'teɪtə(r)/ *n.* a person who looks on at a show, game, incident, etc. □ **spectator sport** a sport attracting spectators rather than participants. □□ **spectatorial** /-tə'tɔːrɪəl/ *adj.* [F *spectateur* or L *spectator* f. *spectare:* see SPECTACLE]

spectra *pl.* of SPECTRUM.

spectral /'spektr(ə)l/ *adj.* **1** a of or relating to spectres or ghosts. **b** ghostlike. **2** of or concerning spectra or the spectrum (*spectral colours; spectral analysis*). □□ **spectrally** *adv.*

spectre /'spektə(r)/ *n.* (*US* **specter**) **1** a ghost. **2** a haunting presentiment or preoccupation (*the spectre of war*). **3** (in *comb.*) used in the names of some animals because of their thinness, transparency, etc. (*spectre-bat; spectre-crab*). □ **Spectre of the Brocken** a huge shadowy image of the observer projected on mists about a mountain-top (observed on the Brocken in Germany). [F *spectre* or L *spectrum:* see SPECTRUM]

spectro- /'spektrəʊ/ *comb. form* a spectrum.

spectrochemistry /ˌspektrəʊ'kemɪstrɪ/ *n.* chemistry based on the study of the spectra of substances.

spectrogram /'spektrəʊˌgræm/ *n.* a record obtained with a spectrograph.

spectrograph /'spektrəʊˌgrɑːf/ *n.* an apparatus for photographing or otherwise recording spectra. □□ **spectrographic** /-'græfɪk/ *adj.* **spectrographically** /-'græfɪkəlɪ/ *adv.* **spectrography** /spek'trɒgrəfɪ/ *n.*

spectroheliograph /ˌspektrəʊ'hiːlɪəˌgrɑːf/ *n.* an instrument for taking photographs of the sun in the light of one wavelength only.

spectrohelioscope /ˌspektrəʊ'hiːlɪəˌskəʊp/ *n.* a device similar to a spectroheliograph, for visual observation.

spectrometer /spek'trɒmɪtə(r)/ *n.* an instrument used for the measurement of observed spectra. □□ **spectrometric** /ˌspektrə'metrɪk/ *adj.* **spectrometry** *n.* [G *Spektrometer* or F *spectromètre* (as SPECTRO-, -METER)]

spectrophotometer /ˌspektrəʊfəʊ'tɒmɪtə(r)/ *n.* an instrument for measuring and recording the intensity of light in various parts of the spectrum. □□ **spectrophotometric** /-tə'metrɪk/ *adj.* **spectrophotometry** *n.*

spectroscope /'spektrəˌskəʊp/ *n.* an instrument for producing and recording spectra for examination.

b *but* d *dog* f *few* g *get* h *he* j *yes* k *cat* l *leg* m *man* n *no* p *pen* r *red* s *sit* t *top* v *voice*

□□ **spectroscopic** /-'skɒpɪk/ *adj.* **spectroscopical**
/-'skɒpɪk(ə)l/ *adj.* **spectroscopist** /-'trɒskəpɪst/ *n.*
spectroscopy /-'trɒskəpɪ/ *n.* [G *Spektroskop* or F
spectroscope (as SPECTRO-, -SCOPE)]

spectrum /'spektrəm/ *n.* (*pl.* **spectra** /-trə/) **1** the
band of colours, as seen in a rainbow etc., arranged
in a progressive series according to their refrangibility or wavelength. **2** the entire range of
wavelengths of electromagnetic radiation. **3 a** an
image or distribution of parts of electromagnetic
radiation arranged in a progressive series according
to wavelength. **b** this as characteristic of a body or
substance when emitting or absorbing radiation. **4** a
similar image or distribution of energy, mass, etc.,
arranged according to frequency, charge, etc. **5** the
entire range or a wide range of anything arranged
by degree or quality etc. **6** (in full **ocular spectrum**)
an after-image. □**spectrum** (or **spectral**) **analysis**
chemical analysis by means of a spectroscope. [L, =
image, apparition f. *specere* look]

specula *pl.* of SPECULUM.

specular /'spekjʊlə(r)/ *adj.* **1** of or having the nature
of a speculum. **2** reflecting. □**specular iron ore**
lustrous haematite. [L *specularis* (as SPECULUM)]

speculate /'spekjʊ,leɪt/ *v.* **1** *intr.* (usu. foll. by
on, upon, about) form a theory or conjecture, esp.
without a firm factual basis; meditate (*speculated on
their prospects*). **2** *tr.* (foll. by *that, how*, etc. + clause)
conjecture, consider (*speculated how he might achieve
it*). **3** *intr.* **a** invest in stocks etc. in the hope of gain
but with the possibility of loss. **b** gamble recklessly.
□□ **speculator** *n.* [L *speculari* spy out, observe f.
specula watch-tower f. *specere* look]

speculation /,spekjʊ'leɪʃ(ə)n/ *n.* **1** the act or an
instance of speculating; a theory or conjecture (*made
no speculation as to her age; is given to speculation*).
2 a speculative investment or enterprise (*bought
it as a speculation*). **b** the practice of business
speculating. **3** a game in which trump cards are
bought or sold. [ME f. OF *speculation* or LL *speculatio*
(as SPECULATE)]

speculative /'spekjʊlətɪv/ *adj.* **1** of, based on, engaged in, or inclined to speculation. **2** (of a business
investment) involving the risk of loss (*a speculative
builder*). □□ **speculatively** *adv.* **speculativeness** *n.*
[ME f. OF *speculatif -ive* or LL *speculativus* (as
SPECULATE)]

speculum /'spekjʊləm/ *n.* (*pl.* **specula** /-lə/) **1**
Surgery an instrument for dilating the cavities of
the human body for inspection. **2** a mirror, usu. of
polished metal, esp. in a reflecting telescope. **3**
Ornithol. a lustrous coloured area on the wing of
some birds, esp. ducks. □**speculum-metal** an alloy
of copper and tin used as a mirror, esp. in a telescope.
[L, = mirror, f. *specere* look]

sped *past* and *past part.* of SPEED.

speech /spiːtʃ/ *n.* **1** the faculty or act of speaking. **2** a
formal public address. **3** a manner of speaking (*a
man of blunt speech*). **4** a remark (*after this speech he
was silent*). **5** the language of a nation, region, group,
etc. **6** *Mus.* the act of sounding in an organ-pipe etc.
□**the Queen's** (or **King's**) **Speech** a statement
including the Government's proposed measures read
by the sovereign at the opening of Parliament.
speech day *Brit.* an annual prize-giving day in many
schools, usu. marked by speeches etc. **speech-
reading** lip-reading. **speech therapist** a person who
practises speech therapy. **speech therapy** treatment
to improve defective speech. **speech-writer** a person
employed to write speeches for a politician etc. to
deliver. □□ **speechful** *adj.* [OE *sprǽc*, later *spēc* f.
WG, rel. to SPEAK]

speechify /'spiːtʃɪ,faɪ/ *v.intr.* (**-ies, -ied**) *joc.* or *derog.*
make esp. boring or long speeches. □□
speechification /-fɪ'keɪʃ(ə)n/ *n.* **speechifier** *n.*

speechless /'spiːtʃlɪs/ *adj.* **1** temporarily unable to
speak because of emotion etc. (*speechless with rage*).

2 dumb. □□ **speechlessly** *adv.* **speechlessness** *n.*
[OE *spǽclēas* (as SPEECH, -LESS)]

speed /spiːd/ *n.* & *v.* —*n.* **1** rapidity of movement
(*with all speed; at full speed*). **2** a rate of progress or
motion over a distance in time (*attains a high speed*).
3 a a gear appropriate to a range of speeds of a
bicycle. **b** *US* or *archaic* such a gear in a motor
vehicle. **4** *Photog.* **a** the sensitivity of film to light. **b**
the light-gathering power of a lens. **c** the duration
of an exposure. **5** *sl.* an amphetamine drug, esp.
methamphetamine. **6** *archaic* success, prosperity
(*send me good speed*). —*v.* (*past* and *past part.* **sped**
/sped/) **1** *intr.* go fast (*sped down the street*). **2** (*past*
and *past part.* **speeded**) **a** *intr.* (of a motorist etc.)
travel at an illegal or dangerous speed. **b** *tr.* regulate
the speed of (an engine etc.). **c** *tr.* cause (an engine
etc.) to go at a fixed speed. **3** *tr.* send fast or on its
way (*speed an arrow from the bow*). **4** *intr.* & *tr.*
archaic be or make prosperous or successful (*how
have you sped?; God speed you!*). □**at speed** moving
quickly. **speed bump** (or **hump**) a transverse ridge
in the road to control the speed of vehicles. **speed
limit** the maximum speed at which a road vehicle
may legally be driven in a particular area etc. **speed
merchant** *colloq.* a motorist who enjoys driving fast.
speed up move or work at greater speed. **speed-up**
n. an increase in the speed or rate of working. □□
speeder *n.* [OE *spēd, spēdan* f. Gmc]

speedball /'spiːdbɔːl/ *n. sl.* a mixture of cocaine with
heroin or morphine.

speedboat /'spiːdbəʊt/ *n.* a motor boat designed for
high speed.

speedo /'spiːdəʊ/ *n.* (*pl.* **-os**) *colloq.* = SPEEDOMETER.
[abbr.]

speedometer /spiː'dɒmɪtə(r)/ *n.* an instrument on a
motor vehicle etc. indicating its speed to the driver.
[SPEED + -METER[1]]

speedway /'spiːdweɪ/ *n.* **1 a** motor-cycle racing. **b** a
stadium or track used for this. **2** *US* a road or track
used for fast motor traffic.

speedwell /'spiːdwel/ *n.* any small herb of the genus
Veronica, with a creeping or ascending stem and tiny
blue or pink flowers. [app. f. SPEED + WELL[1]]

speedy /'spiːdɪ/ *adj.* (**speedier, speediest**) **1** moving
quickly; rapid. **2** done without delay; prompt (*a
speedy answer*). □□ **speedily** *adv.* **speediness** *n.*

speiss /spaɪs/ *n.* a compound of arsenic, iron, etc.,
formed in smelting certain lead ores. [G *Speise* food,
amalgam]

speleology /,spiːlɪ'ɒlədʒɪ, ,spe-/ *n.* **1** the scientific
study of caves. **2** the exploration of caves. □□
speleological /-ə'lɒdʒɪk(ə)l/ *adj.* **speleologist** *n.* [F
spéléologie f. L *spelaeum* f. Gk *spēlaion* cave]

spell[1] /spel/ *v.tr.* (*past* and *past part.* **spelt** or **spelled**)
1 (also *absol.*) write or name the letters that form (a
word etc.) in correct sequence (*spell 'exaggerate'*;
cannot spell properly). **2 a** (of letters) make up or
form (a word etc.). **b** (of circumstances, a scheme,
etc.) result in; involve (*spell ruin*). □**spell out** (or
over) **1** make out (words, writing, etc.) letter by
letter. **2** explain in detail (*spelled out what the change
would mean*). □□ **spellable** *adj.* [ME f. OF *espel(l)er*,
f. Frank. (as SPELL[2])]

spell[2] /spel/ *n.* **1** a form of words used as a magical
charm or incantation. **2** an attraction or fascination
exercised by a person, activity, quality, etc. □**under
a spell** mastered by or as if by a spell. [OE *spel(l)* f.
Gmc]

spell[3] /spel/ *n.* & *v.* —*n.* **1** a short or fairly short
period (*a cold spell in April*). **2** a turn of work (*did a
spell of woodwork*). **3** *Austral.* a period of rest from
work. —*v.* **1** *tr.* relieve or take the place of (a
person) in work etc. **b** allow to rest briefly. **2** *intr.*
Austral. take a brief rest. [earlier as verb: later form
of dial. *spele* take place of f. OE *spelian*, of unkn.
orig.]

spell[4] /spel/ *n.* a splinter of wood etc. [perh. f. obs.
speld]

spellbind /'spelbaind/ *tr.* (*past* and *past part.* **spellbound**) **1** bind with or as if with a spell; entrance. **2** (as **spellbound** *adj.*) entranced, fascinated, esp. by a speaker, activity, quality, etc. □□ **spellbinder** *n.* **spellbindingly** *adv.*

speller /'spelə(r)/ *n.* **1** a person who spells esp. in a specified way (*is a poor speller*). **2** a book on spelling.

spellican var. of SPILLIKIN.

spelling /'spelɪŋ/ *n.* **1** the process or activity of writing or naming the letters of a word etc. **2** the way a word is spelled. **3** the ability to spell (*his spelling is weak*). □ **spelling-bee** a spelling competition.

spelt[1] *past* and *past part.* of SPELL[1].

spelt[2] /spelt/ *n.* a species of wheat, *Triticum aestivum*. [OE f. OS *spelta* (OHG *spelza*), ME f. MLG, MDu. *spelte*]

spelter /'speltə(r)/ *n.* impure zinc, esp. for commercial purposes. [corresp. to OF *espeautre*, MDu. *speauter*, G *Spialter*, rel. to PEWTER]

spelunker /spɪ'lʌŋkə(r)/ *n. US* a person who explores caves, esp. as a hobby. □□ **spelunking** *n.* [obs. *spelunk* cave f. L *spelunca*]

spence /spens/ *n. archaic* a buttery or larder. [ME f. OF *despense* f. L *dispensa* fem. past part. of *dispendere*: see DISPENSE]

spencer[1] /'spensə(r)/ *n.* **1** a short close-fitting jacket. **2** a woman's thin usu. woollen under-bodice worn for extra warmth in winter. [prob. f. the 2nd Earl *Spencer*, Engl. politician d. 1834]

spencer[2] /'spensə(r)/ *n. Naut.* a trysail. [perh. f. K. *Spencer* (early 19th c.)]

spend /spend/ *v.tr.* (*past* and *past part.* **spent** /spent/) **1** (usu. foll. by *on*) **a** (also *absol.*) pay out (money) in making a purchase etc. (*spent £5 on a new pen*). **b** pay out (money) for a particular person's benefit or for the improvement of a thing (*had to spend £200 on the car*). **2 a** use or consume (time or energy) (*shall spend no more effort; how do you spend your Sundays?*). **b** (also *refl.*) use up; exhaust; wear out (*their ammunition was all spent; his anger was soon spent; spent herself campaigning for justice*). **3** *tr.* (as **spent** *adj.*) having lost its original force or strength; exhausted (*the storm is spent; spent bullets*). □ **spending money** pocket money. **spend a penny** *Brit. colloq.* urinate or defecate (from the coin-operated locks of public lavatories). □□ **spendable** *adj.* **spender** *n.* [OE *spendan* f. L *expendere* (see EXPEND): in ME perh. also f. obs. *dispend* f. OF *despendre* expend f. L *dispendere*: see DISPENSE]

spendthrift /'spendθrɪft/ *n.* & *adj.* —*n.* an extravagant person; a prodigal. —*adj.* extravagant; prodigal.

Spenserian /spen'sɪərɪən/ *adj.* of, relating to, or in the style of Edmund Spenser, Engl. poet d. 1599. □ **Spenserian stanza** the stanza used by Spenser in the *Faerie Queene*, with eight iambic pentameters and an alexandrine, rhyming ababbcbcc. [E. *Spenser*]

spent *past* and *past part.* of SPEND.

sperm /spɜːm/ *n.* (*pl.* same or **sperms**) **1** = SPERMATOZOON. **2** the male reproductive fluid containing spermatozoa; semen. **3** = *sperm whale*. **4** = SPERMACETI. **5** = *sperm oil*. □ **sperm bank** a supply of semen stored for use in artificial insemination. **sperm count** the number of spermatozoa in one ejaculation or a measured amount of semen. **sperm oil** an oil obtained from the head of a sperm whale, and used as a lubricant. **sperm whale** a large whale, *Physeter macrocephalus*, hunted for the spermaceti and sperm oil contained in its bulbous head, and for the ambergris found in its intestines: also called CACHALOT. [ME f. LL *sperma* f. Gk *sperma -atos* seed f. *speirō* sow: in *sperm whale* an abbr. of SPERMACETI]

spermaceti /ˌspɜːmə'setɪ/ *n.* a white waxy substance produced by the sperm whale to aid buoyancy, and used in the manufacture of candles, ointments, etc. □□ **spermacetic** *adj.* [ME f. med.L f. LL *sperma*

sperm + *ceti* genit. of *cetus* f. Gk *kētos* whale, from the belief that it was whale-spawn]

spermary /'spɜːmərɪ/ *n.* (*pl.* **-ies**) an organ in which human or animal sperms are generated. [mod.L *spermarium* (as SPERM)]

spermatic /spɜː'mætɪk/ *adj.* of or relating to a sperm or spermary. □ **spermatic cord** a bundle of nerves, ducts, and blood vessels passing to the testicles. [LL *spermaticus* f. Gk *spermatikos* (as SPERM)]

spermatid /'spɜːmətɪd/ *n. Biol.* an immature male sex cell formed from a spermatocyte, which may develop into a spermatozoon. □□ **spermatidal** /-'taɪd(ə)l/ *adj.*

spermato- /'spɜːmətəʊ/ *comb. form Biol.* a sperm or seed.

spermatocyte /'spɜːmətəʊˌsaɪt/ *n.* a cell produced from a spermatogonium and which may divide by meiosis into spermatids.

spermatogenesis /ˌspɜːmətəʊ'dʒenɪsɪs/ *n.* the production or development of mature spermatozoa. □□ **spermatogenetic** /-dʒɪ'netɪk/ *adj.*

spermatogonium /ˌspɜːmətəʊ'gəʊnɪəm/ *n.* (*pl.* **spermatogonia** /-nɪə/) a cell produced at an early stage in the formation of spermatozoa, from which spermatocytes develop. [SPERM + mod.L *gonium* f. Gk *gonos* offspring, seed]

spermatophore /'spɜːmətəʊˌfɔː(r)/ *n.* an albuminous capsule containing spermatozoa found in various invertebrates. □□ **spermatophoric** /-'fɒrɪk/ *adj.*

spermatophyte /'spɜːmətəʊˌfaɪt/ *n.* any seed-bearing plant.

spermatozoid /ˌspɜːmətəʊ'zəʊɪd/ *n.* the mature motile male sex cell of some plants.

spermatozoon /ˌspɜːmətəʊ'zəʊɒn/ *n.* (*pl.* **spermatozoa** /-'zəʊə/) the mature motile sex cell in animals. □□ **spermatozoal** *adj.* **spermatozoan** *adj.* **spermatozoic** *adj.* [SPERM + Gk *zōion* animal]

spermicide /'spɜːmɪˌsaɪd/ *n.* a substance able to kill spermatozoa. □□ **spermicidal** /-'saɪd(ə)l/ *adj.*

spermo- /'spɜːməʊ/ *comb. form* = SPERMATO-.

spew /spjuː/ *v.* (also **spue**) **1** *tr.* & *intr.* vomit. **2** (often foll. by *out*) **a** *tr.* expel (contents) rapidly and forcibly. **b** *intr.* (of contents) be expelled in this way. □□ **spewer** *n.* [OE *spīwan, spēowan* f. Gmc]

sp. gr. *abbr.* specific gravity.

sphagnum /'sfægnəm/ *n.* (*pl.* **sphagna** /-nə/) (in full **sphagnum moss**) any moss of the genus *Sphagnum*, growing in bogs and peat, and used as packing esp. for plants, as fertilizer, etc. [mod.L f. Gk *sphagnos* a moss]

sphalerite /'sfælərˌaɪt/ *n.* = BLENDE. [Gk *sphaleros* deceptive: cf. BLENDE]

spheno- /'sfiːnəʊ/ *comb. form Anat.* the sphenoid bone. [Gk f. *sphēn* wedge]

sphenoid /'sfiːnɔɪd/ *adj.* & *n.* —*adj.* **1** wedge-shaped. **2** of or relating to the sphenoid bone. —*n.* (in full **sphenoid bone**) a large compound bone forming the base of the cranium behind the eyes. □□ **sphenoidal** /-'nɔɪd(ə)l/ *adj.* [mod.L *sphenoides* f. Gk *sphēnoeidēs* f. *sphēn* wedge]

sphere /sfɪə(r)/ *n.* & *v.* —*n.* **1** a solid figure, or its surface, with every point on its surface equidistant from its centre. **2** an object having this shape; a ball or globe. **3 a** any celestial body. **b** a globe representing the earth. **c** *poet.* the heavens; the sky. **d** the sky perceived as a vault upon or in which celestial bodies are represented as lying. **e** *hist.* each of a series of revolving concentrically arranged spherical shells in which celestial bodies were formerly thought to be set in a fixed relationship. **4 a** a field of action, influence, or existence (*have done much within their own sphere*). **b** a (usu. specified) stratum of society or social class (*moves in quite another sphere*). —*v.tr. archaic* or *poet.* **1** enclose in or as in a sphere. **2** form into a sphere. □ **music** (or **harmony**) **of the spheres** the natural harmonic tones supposedly produced by the movement of the celestial spheres (see sense 3e of *n.*) or the bodies fixed in them.

æ *cat* ɑː *arm* e *bed* ɜː *her* ɪ *sit* iː *see* ɒ *hot* ɔː *saw* ʌ *run* ʊ *put* uː *too* ə *ago* aɪ *my*

oblique (or **parallel** or **right**) **sphere** the sphere of the apparent heavens at a place where there is an oblique, zero, or right angle between the equator and the horizon. **sphere of influence** the claimed or recognized area of a State's interests, an individual's control, etc. □□ **spheral** *adj.* [ME *sper(e)* f. OF *espere* f. LL *sphera*, L f. Gk *sphaira* ball]

-sphere /ˈsfɪə(r)/ *comb. form* **1** having the form of a sphere (*bathysphere*). **2** a region round the earth (*atmosphere*).

spheric /ˈsfɪərɪk/ *adj.* = SPHERICAL. □□ **sphericity** /-ˈrɪsɪtɪ/ *n.*

spherical /ˈsferɪk(ə)l/ *adj.* **1** shaped like a sphere; globular. **2 a** of or relating to the properties of spheres (*spherical geometry*). **b** formed inside or on the surface of a sphere (*spherical triangle*). □ **spherical aberration** a loss of definition in the image produced by a spherically curved mirror or lens. **spherical angle** an angle formed by the intersection of two great circles of a sphere. □□ **spherically** *adv.* [LL *sphaericus* f. Gk *sphairikos* (as SPHERE)]

spheroid /ˈsfɪərɔɪd/ *n.* **1** a spherelike but not perfectly spherical body. **2** a solid generated by a half-revolution of an ellipse about its major axis (**prolate spheroid**) or minor axis (**oblate spheroid**). □□ **spheroidal** /sfɪəˈrɔɪd(ə)l/ *adj.* **spheroidicity** /-ˈdɪsɪtɪ/ *n.*

spherometer /sfɪəˈrɒmɪtə(r)/ *n.* an instrument for finding the radius of a sphere and for the exact measurement of the thickness of small bodies. [F *sphéromètre* (as SPHERE, -METER)]

spherule /ˈsferuːl/ *n.* a small sphere. □□ **spherular** *adj.* [LL *sphaerula* dimin. of L *sphaera* (as SPHERE)]

spherulite /ˈsferəlaɪt/ *n.* a vitreous globule as a constituent of volcanic rocks. □□ **spherulitic** /-ˈlɪtɪk/ *adj.*

sphincter /ˈsfɪŋktə(r)/ *n. Anat.* a ring of muscle surrounding and serving to guard or close an opening or tube, esp. the anus. □□ **sphincteral** *adj.* **sphinctered** *adj.* **sphincterial** /-ˈtɪərɪəl/ *adj.* **sphincteric** /-ˈterɪk/ *adj.* [L f. Gk *sphigktēr* f. *sphiggō* bind tight]

sphingid /ˈsfɪŋɡɪd/ *n.* any hawk moth of the family Sphingidae. [as SPHINX + -ID³]

sphinx /sfɪŋks/ *n.* **1** (**Sphinx**) (in Greek mythology) the winged monster of Thebes, having a woman's head and a lion's body, whose riddle Oedipus guessed and who consequently killed herself. **2** *Antiq.* **a** any of several ancient Egyptian stone figures having a lion's body and a human or animal head. **b** (**the Sphinx**) the huge sphinx near the Pyramids at Giza. **3** an enigmatic or inscrutable person. **4 a** a hawk moth. **b** a species of baboon, *Papio sphinx*. [L f. Gk *Sphigx*, app. f. *sphiggō* draw tight]

sphragistics /sfrəˈdʒɪstɪks/ *n.pl.* (also treated as *sing.*) the study of engraved seals. [F *sphragistique* (n. & adj.) f. Gk *sphragistikos* f. *sphragis* seal]

sphygmo- /ˈsfɪɡməʊ/ *comb. form Physiol.* a pulse or pulsation. [Gk *sphugmo-* f. *sphugmos* pulse f. *sphuzō* to throb]

sphygmogram /ˈsfɪɡməʊˌɡræm/ *n.* a record produced by a sphygmograph.

sphygmograph /ˈsfɪɡməʊˌɡrɑːf/ *n.* an instrument for showing the character of a pulse in a series of curves. □□ **sphygmographic** /-ˈɡræfɪk/ *adj.* **sphygmographically** /-ˈɡræfɪkəlɪ/ *adv.* **sphygmography** /-ˈmɒɡrəfɪ/ *n.*

sphygmology /sfɪɡˈmɒlədʒɪ/ *n.* the scientific study of the pulse. □□ **sphygmological** /-məˈlɒdʒɪk(ə)l/ *adj.*

sphygmomanometer /ˌsfɪɡməʊməˈnɒmɪtə(r)/ *n.* an instrument for measuring blood pressure. □□ **sphygmomanometric** /-nəˈmetrɪk/ *adj.*

spica /ˈspaɪkə/ *n.* **1** *Bot.* a spike or spikelike form. **2** *Surgery* a spiral bandage with reversed turns, suggesting an ear of corn. □□ **spicate** /-keɪt/ *adj.* **spicated** /-ˈkeɪtɪd/ *adj.* [L, = spike, ear of corn, rel. to *spina* SPINE: in sense 2 after Gk *stakhus*]

spiccato /spɪˈkɑːtəʊ/ *n., adj.,* & *adv. Mus.* —*n.* (*pl.* **-os**) **1** a style of staccato playing on stringed instruments involving bouncing the bow on the strings. **2** a passage in this style. —*adj.* performed or to be performed in this style. —*adv.* in this style. [It., = detailed, distinct]

spice /spaɪs/ *n.* & *v.* —*n.* **1** an aromatic or pungent vegetable substance used to flavour food, e.g. cloves, pepper, or mace. **2** spices collectively (*a dealer in spice*). **3 a** an interesting or piquant quality. **b** (foll. by *of*) a slight flavour or suggestion (*a spice of malice*). —*v.tr.* **1** flavour with spice. **2** add an interesting or piquant quality to (*a book spiced with humour*). [ME f. OF *espice(r)* f. L *species* specific kind: in LL pl. = merchandise]

spicebush /ˈspaɪsbʊʃ/ *n.* any aromatic shrub of the genus *Lindera* or *Calycanthus*, native to America.

spick and span /ˌspɪk ənd ˈspæn/ *adj.* **1** smart and new. **2** neat and clean. [16th-c. *spick and span new*, emphatic extension of ME *span new* f. ON *spán-nýr* f. *spánn* chip + *nýr* new]

spicknel /ˈspɪkn(ə)l/ *n.* = BALDMONEY. [var. of SPIGNEL]

spicule /ˈspɪkjuːl/ *n.* **1** any small sharp-pointed body. **2** *Zool.* a small hard calcareous or siliceous body, esp. in the framework of a sponge. **3** *Bot.* a small or secondary spike. **4** *Astron.* a spikelike prominence, esp. one appearing as a jet of gas in the sun's corona. □□ **spicular** *adj.* **spiculate** /-lət/ *adj.* [mod.L *spicula*, *spiculum*, dimins. of SPICA]

spicy /ˈspaɪsɪ/ *adj.* (**spicier, spiciest**) **1** of, flavoured with, or fragrant with spice. **2** piquant, pungent; sensational or improper (*a spicy story*). □□ **spicily** *adv.* **spiciness** *n.*

spider /ˈspaɪdə(r)/ *n.* & *v.* —*n.* **1 a** any eight-legged arthropod of the order Araneae with a round unsegmented body, many of which spin webs for the capture of insects as food. **b** any of various similar or related arachnids, e.g. a red spider. **2** any object comparable to a spider, esp. as having numerous or prominent legs or radiating spokes. **3** *Brit.* a radiating series of elastic ties used to hold a load in place on a vehicle etc. —*v.intr.* **1** move in a scuttling manner suggestive of a spider (*fingers spidered across the map*). **2** cause to move or appear in this way. **3** (as **spidering** *adj.*) spiderlike in form, manner, or movement (*spidering streets*). □ **spider crab** any of various crabs of the family Majidae with a pear-shaped body and long thin legs. **spider monkey** any S. American monkey of the genus *Ateles*, with long limbs and a prehensile tail. **spider plant** any of various house plants with long narrow striped leaves. □□ **spiderish** *adj.* [OE *spīthra* (as SPIN)]

spiderman /ˈspaɪdəˌmæn/ *n.* (*pl.* **-men**) *Brit. colloq.* a person who works at great heights in building construction.

spiderwort /ˈspaɪdəˌwɜːt/ *n.* any plant of the genus *Tradescantia*, esp. *T. virginiana*, having flowers with long hairy stamens.

spidery /ˈspaɪdərɪ/ *adj.* elongated and thin (*spidery handwriting*).

spiegeleisen /ˈspiːɡ(ə)lˌaɪz(ə)n/ *n.* an alloy of iron and manganese, used in steel-making. [G f. *Spiegel* mirror + *Eisen* iron]

spiel /ʃpiːl/ *n.* & *v. sl.* —*n.* a glib speech or story, esp. a salesman's patter. —*v.* **1** *intr.* speak glibly; hold forth. **2** *tr.* reel off (patter etc.). [G, = play, game]

spieler /ˈʃpiːlə(r)/ *n. sl.* **1** esp. *US* a person who spiels. **2** *Austral.* a gambler; a swindler. [G (as SPIEL)]

spiffing /ˈspɪfɪŋ/ *adj. archaic sl.* **1** excellent. **2** smart, handsome. [19th c.: orig. unkn.]

spiffy /ˈspɪfɪ/ *adj.* (**spiffier, spiffiest**) esp. *US sl.* = SPIFFING. □□ **spiffily** *adv.*

spiflicate /ˈspɪflɪˌkeɪt/ *v.tr.* (also **spifflicate**) esp. *joc.* **1** destroy. **2** beat (in a fight etc.). [18th c.: fanciful]

spignel /ˈspɪɡn(ə)l/ *n.* = BALDMONEY. [perh. f. ME *spigurnel* plant-name, f. med.L *spigurnellus*, of unkn. orig.]

spigot /ˈspɪgət/ n. **1** a small peg or plug, esp. for insertion into the vent-hole of a cask. **2 a** US a tap. **b** a device for controlling the flow of liquid in a tap. **3** the plain end of a pipe-section fitting into the socket of the next one. [ME, perh. f. Prov. *espigou(n)* f. L *spiculum* dimin. of *spicum* = SPICA]

spike[1] /spaɪk/ n. & v. —n. **1 a** a sharp point. **b** a pointed piece of metal, esp. the top of an iron railing etc. **2 a** any of several metal points set into the sole of a running-shoe to prevent slipping. **b** (in pl.) a pair of running-shoes with spikes. **3 a** a pointed metal rod standing on a base and used for filing news items etc. esp. when rejected for publication. **b** a similar spike used for bills etc. **4** a large stout nail esp. as used for railways. **5** sl. a hypodermic needle. **6** Brit. sl. a doss-house. **7** Electronics a pulse of very short duration in which a rapid increase in voltage is followed by a rapid decrease. —v.tr. **1 a** fasten or provide with spikes. **b** fix on or pierce with spikes. **2** (of a newspaper editor etc.) reject (a story) by filing it on a spike. **3** colloq. **a** lace (a drink) with alcohol, a drug, etc. **b** contaminate (a substance) with something added. **4** make useless, put an end to, thwart (an idea etc.). **5** hist. plug up the vent of (a gun) with a spike. □**spike a person's guns** spoil his or her plans. **spike heel** a high tapering heel of a shoe. [ME perh. f. MLG, MDu. *spiker*, rel. to SPOKE[1]]

spike[2] /spaɪk/ n. Bot. **1** a flower-cluster formed of many flower-heads attached closely on a long stem. **2** a separate sprig of any plant in which flowers form a spikelike cluster. □□ **spikelet** n. [ME, = ear of corn, f. L SPICA]

spikenard /ˈspaɪknɑːd/ n. **1** Bot. an Indian plant, *Nardostachys grandiflora*. **2** hist. a costly perfumed ointment made from this. [ME ult. f. med.L *spica nardi* (as SPIKE[2], NARD) after Gk *nardostakhus*]

spiky[1] /ˈspaɪkɪ/ adj. (**spikier, spikiest**) **1** like a spike; having many spikes. **2** colloq. easily offended; prickly. □□ **spikily** adv. **spikiness** n.

spiky[2] /ˈspaɪkɪ/ adj. Bot. having spikes or ears.

spile /spaɪl/ n. & v. —n. **1 a** a wooden peg or spigot. **2** a large timber or pile for driving into the ground. **3** US a small spout for tapping the sap from a sugar-maple etc. —v.tr. make a spile-hole in (a cask etc.) in order to draw off liquid. [MDu., MLG, = wooden peg etc.: in sense 'pile' app. alt. of PILE[2]]

spill[1] /spɪl/ v. & n. —v. (past and past part. **spilt** or **spilled**) **1** intr. & tr. fall or run or cause (a liquid, powder, etc.) to fall or run out of a vessel, esp. unintentionally. **2 a** tr. & intr. throw (a person etc.) from a vehicle, saddle, etc. **b** intr. (esp. of a crowd) tumble out quickly from a place etc. (*the fans spilled into the street*). **3** tr. sl. disclose (information etc.). **4** tr. Naut. **a** empty (a sail) of wind. **b** lose (wind) from a sail. —n. **1 a** the act or an instance of spilling or being spilt. **b** a quantity spilt. **2** a tumble or fall, esp. from a horse etc. (*had a nasty spill*). **3** Austral. the vacating of all or several posts of a parliamentary party to allow reorganization. □**spill the beans** colloq. divulge information etc., esp. unintentionally or indiscreetly. **spill blood** be guilty of bloodshed. **spill the blood of** kill or injure (a person). **spill over 1** overflow. **2** (of a surplus population) be forced to move (cf. OVERSPILL). □□ **spillage** /-ɪdʒ/ n. **spiller** n. [OE *spillan* kill, rel. to OE *spildan* destroy: orig. unkn.]

spill[2] /spɪl/ n. a thin strip of wood, folded or twisted paper, etc., used for lighting a fire, candles, a pipe, etc. [ME, rel. to SPILE]

spillikin /ˈspɪlɪkɪn/ n. (also **spellican** /ˈspelɪkən/) **1** a splinter of wood, bone, etc. **2** (in pl.) a game in which a heap of spillikins is to be removed one at a time without moving the others. [SPILL[2] + -KIN]

spillover /ˈspɪlˌəʊvə(r)/ n. **1 a** the process or an instance of spilling over. **b** a thing that spills over. **2** a consequence, repercussion, or by-product.

spillway /ˈspɪlweɪ/ n. a passage for surplus water from a dam.

spilt past and past part. of SPILL[1].

spilth /spɪlθ/ n. **1** material that is spilled. **2** the act or an instance of spilling. **3** an excess or surplus.

spin /spɪn/ v. & n. —v. (**spinning**; past and past part. **spun** /spʌn/) **1** intr. **a** turn or cause (a person or thing) to turn or whirl round quickly. **2** tr. (also absol.) **a** draw out and twist (wool, cotton, etc.) into threads. **b** make (yarn) in this way. **c** make a similar type of thread from (a synthetic substance etc.). **3** tr. (of a spider, silkworm, etc.) make (a web, gossamer, a cocoon, etc.) by extruding a fine viscous thread. **4** tr. tell or write (a story, essay, article, etc.) (*spins a good tale*). **5** tr. impart spin to (a ball). **6** intr. (of a person's head etc.) be dizzy through excitement, astonishment, etc. **7** tr. shape (metal) on a mould in a lathe etc. **8** intr. esp. Cricket (of a ball) move through the air with spin. **9** tr. (as **spun** adj.) converted into threads (*spun glass*; *spun gold*; *spun sugar*). **10** tr. fish in (a stream, pool, etc.) with a spinner. **11** tr. toss (a coin). **12** tr. = spin-dry. —n. **1** a spinning motion; a whirl. **2** an aircraft's diving descent combined with rotation. **3 a** a revolving motion through the air, esp. in a rifle bullet or in a billiard, tennis, or table tennis ball struck aslant. **b** Cricket a twisting motion given to the ball in bowling. **4** colloq. a brief drive in a motor vehicle, aeroplane, etc., esp. for pleasure. **5** Physics the intrinsic angular momentum of an elementary particle. **6** Austral. & NZ sl. a piece of good or bad luck. □**spin bowler** Cricket an expert at bowling with spin. **spin-drier** a machine for drying wet clothes etc. centrifugally in a revolving drum. **spin-dry** (**-dries, -dried**) dry (clothes etc.) in this way. **spin off** throw off by centrifugal force in spinning. **spin-off** n. an incidental result or results esp. as a side benefit from industrial technology. **spin out 1** prolong (a discussion etc.). **2** make (a story, money, etc.) last as long as possible. **3** spend or consume (time, one's life, etc.), by discussion or in an occupation etc.). **4** Cricket dismiss (a batsman or side) by spin bowling. **spin a yarn** orig. Naut. tell a story. **spun silk** a cheap material made of short-fibred and waste silk. **spun yarn** Naut. a line formed of rope-yarns twisted together. [OE *spinnan*]

spina bifida /ˌspaɪnə ˈbɪfɪdə/ n. a congenital defect of the spine, in which part of the spinal cord and its meninges are exposed through a gap in the backbone. [mod.L (as SPINE, BIFID)]

spinach /ˈspɪnɪdʒ, -ɪtʃ/ n. **1** a green garden vegetable, *Spinacia oleracea*, with succulent leaves. **2** the leaves of this plant used as food. □**spinach beet** a variety of beetroot cultivated for its edible leaves. □□ **spinaceous** /-ˈneɪʃəs/ adj. **spinachy** adj. [prob. MDu. *spinaetse*, *spinag(i)e*, f. OF *espinage*, *espinache* f. med.L *spinac(h)ia* etc. f. Arab. *'isfānāḵ* f. Pers. *ispānāḵ*: perh. assim. to L *spina* SPINE, with ref. to its prickly seeds]

spinal /ˈspaɪn(ə)l/ adj. of or relating to the spine (*spinal curvature*; *spinal disease*). □**spinal canal** a cavity through the vertebrae containing the spinal cord. **spinal column** the spine. **spinal cord** a cylindrical structure of the central nervous system enclosed in the spine, connecting all parts of the body with the brain. □□ **spinally** adv. [LL *spinalis* (as SPINE)]

spindle /ˈspɪnd(ə)l/ n. & v. —n. **1 a** a pin in a spinning-wheel used for twisting and winding the thread. **b** a small bar with tapered ends used for the same purpose in hand-spinning. **c** a pin bearing the bobbin of a spinning-machine. **2** a pin or axis that revolves or on which something revolves. **3** a turned piece of wood used as a banister, chair leg, etc. **4** Biol. a spindle-shaped mass of microtubules formed when a cell divides. **5** a varying measure of length for yarn. **6** a slender person or thing. —v.intr. have, or grow into, a long slender form. □**spindle berry** the fruit of the spindle tree. **spindle-shanked** having long thin legs.

spindle-shanks a person with such legs.
spindle-shaped having a circular cross-section and tapering towards each end. **spindle side** = *distaff side*. **spindle tree** any shrub or small tree of the genus *Euonymus*, esp. *E. europaeus* with greenish-white flowers, pink or red berries, and hard wood used for spindles. [OE *spinel* (as SPIN)]

spindly /'spɪndlɪ/ *adj.* (**spindlier, spindliest**) long or tall and thin; thin and weak.

spindrift /'spɪndrɪft/ *n.* spray blown along the surface of the sea. [Sc. var. of *spoondrift* f. *spoon* run before wind or sea + DRIFT]

spine /spaɪn/ *n.* **1** a series of vertebrae extending from the skull to the small of the back, enclosing the spinal cord and providing support for the thorax and abdomen; the backbone. **2** *Zool. & Bot.* any hard pointed process or structure. **3** a sharp ridge or projection, esp. of a mountain range or slope. **4** a central feature, main support, or source of strength. **5** the part of a book's jacket or cover that encloses the page-fastening part and usu. faces outwards on a shelf. □**spine-chiller** a frightening story, film, etc. **spine-chilling** (esp. of a story etc.) frightening. □□ **spined** *adj.* [ME f. OF *espine* or L *spina* thorn, backbone]

spinel /spɪ'nel/ *n.* **1** any of a group of hard crystalline minerals of various colours, consisting chiefly of oxides of magnesium and aluminium. **2** any substance of similar composition or properties. □**spinel ruby** a deep-red variety of spinel used as a gem. [F *spinelle* f. It. *spinella*, dimin. of *spina*: see SPINE]

spineless /'spaɪnlɪs/ *adj.* **1 a** having no spine; invertebrate. **b** (of a fish) having no fin-spines. **2** (of a person) lacking energy or resolution; weak and purposeless. □□ **spinelessly** *adv.* **spinelessness** *n.*

spinet /spɪ'net, 'spɪnɪt/ *n. Mus. hist.* a small harpsichord with oblique strings. [obs. F *espinette* f. It. *spinetta* virginal, spinet, dimin. of *spina* thorn etc. (as SPINE), with ref. to the plucked strings]

spinifex /'spɪnɪˌfeks/ *n.* any Australian grass of the genus *Spinifex*, with coarse, spiny leaves. [mod.L f. L *spina* SPINE + *-fex* maker f. *facere* make]

spinnaker /'spɪnəkə(r)/ *n.* a large triangular sail carried opposite the mainsail of a racing-yacht running before the wind. [fanciful f. *Sphinx*, name of yacht first using it, perh. after *spanker*]

spinner /'spɪnə(r)/ *n.* **1** a person or thing that spins. **2** *Cricket* **a** a spin bowler. **b** a spun ball. **3** a spin-drier. **4 a** a real or artificial fly for esp. trout-fishing. **b** revolving bait. **5** a manufacturer or merchant engaged in (esp. cotton-) spinning. **6** = SPINNERET. **7** *archaic* a spider.

spinneret /'spɪnəˌret/ *n.* **1** the spinning-organ in a spider, silkworm, etc. **2** a device for forming filaments of synthetic fibre.

spinney /'spɪnɪ/ *n.* (*pl.* **-eys**) *Brit.* a small wood; a thicket. [OF *espinei* f. L *spinetum* thicket f. *spina* thorn]

spinning /'spɪnɪŋ/ *n.* the act or an instance of spinning. □**spinning-jenny** *hist.* a machine for spinning with more than one spindle at a time. **spinning-machine** a machine that spins fibres continuously. **spinning-top** = TOP². **spinning-wheel** a household machine for spinning yarn or thread with a spindle driven by a wheel attached to a crank or treadle.

spinose /'spaɪnəʊs/ *adj.* (also **spinous** /-nəs/) *Bot.* (of a plant) having many spines.

Spinozism /spɪ'nəʊzɪz(ə)m/ *n. Philos.* the doctrine of Spinoza that there is one infinite substance of which extension and thought are attributes and human beings are changing forms. □□ **Spinozist** *n.* **Spinozistic** /-'zɪstɪk/ *adj.* [B. de *Spinoza*, Du. philosopher d. 1677]

spinster /'spɪnstə(r)/ *n.* **1** an unmarried woman. **2** a woman, esp. elderly, thought unlikely to marry. □□ **spinsterhood** *n.* **spinsterish** *adj.* **spinsterishness** *n.* [ME, orig. = woman who spins]

spinthariscope /spɪn'θærɪˌskəʊp/ *n.* an instrument with a fluorescent screen showing the incidence of alpha particles by flashes. [irreg. f. Gk *spintharis* spark + -SCOPE]

spinule /'spɪnjuːl/ *n. Bot. & Zool.* a small spine. □□ **spinulose** *adj.* **spinulous** *adj.* [L *spinula* dimin. of *spina* SPINE]

spiny /'spaɪnɪ/ *adj.* (**spinier, spiniest**) **1** full of spines; prickly. **2** perplexing, troublesome, thorny. □**spiny anteater** = ECHIDNA. **spiny lobster** any of various large edible crustaceans of the family Palinuridae, esp. *Palinuris vulgaris*, with a spiny shell and no large anterior claws. □□ **spininess** *n.*

spiracle /'spaɪərək(ə)l/ *n.* (also **spiraculum** /ˌspaɪə'rækjʊləm/) (*pl.* **spiracles** or **spiracula** /-lə/) an external respiratory opening in insects, whales, and some fish. □□ **spiracular** /-'rækjʊlə(r)/ *adj.* [L *spiraculum* f. *spirare* breathe]

spiraea /ˌspaɪə'riːə/ *n.* (*US* **spirea**) any rosaceous shrub of the genus *Spiraea*, with clusters of small white or pink flowers. [L f. Gk *speiraia* f. *speira* coil]

spiral /'spaɪər(ə)l/ *adj., n., & v.* —*adj.* **1** winding about a centre in an enlarging or decreasing continuous circular motion, either on a flat plane or rising in a cone; coiled. **2** winding continuously along or as if along a cylinder, like the thread of a screw. —*n.* **1** a plane or three-dimensional spiral curve. **2** a spiral spring. **3** a spiral formation in a shell etc. **4** a spiral galaxy. **5** a progressive rise or fall of prices, wages, etc., each responding to an upward or downward stimulus provided by the other (*a spiral of rising prices and wages*). —*v.* (**spiralled, spiralling**; *US* **spiraled, spiraling**) **1** *intr.* move in a spiral course, esp. upwards or downwards. **2** *tr.* make spiral. **3** *intr.* esp. *Econ.* (of prices, wages, etc.) rise or fall, esp. rapidly (cf. sense 5 of *n.*). □**spiral balance** a device for measuring weight by the torsion of a spiral spring. **spiral galaxy** a galaxy in which the matter is concentrated mainly in one or more spiral arms. **spiral staircase** a staircase rising in a spiral round a central axis. □□ **spirality** /-'rælɪtɪ/ *n.* **spirally** *adv.* [F *spiral* or med.L *spiralis* (as SPIRE²)]

spirant /'spaɪərənt/ *adj. & n. Phonet.* —*adj.* (of a consonant) uttered with a continuous expulsion of breath, esp. fricative. —*n.* such a consonant. [L *spirare spirant-* breathe]

spire¹ /'spaɪə(r)/ *n. & v.* —*n.* **1** a tapering cone- or pyramid-shaped structure built esp. on a church tower (cf. STEEPLE). **2** the continuation of a tree trunk above the point where branching begins. **3** any tapering thing, e.g. the spike of a flower. —*v.tr.* provide with a spire. □□ **spiry** /'spaɪrɪ/ *adj.* [OE *spīr*]

spire² /'spaɪə(r)/ *n.* **1 a** a spiral; a coil. **b** a single twist of this. **2** the upper part of a spiral shell. [F f. L *spira* f. Gk *speira* coil]

spirea *US* var. of SPIRAEA.

spirillum /ˌspaɪə'rɪləm/ *n.* (*pl.* **spirilla** /-lə/) **1** any bacterium of the genus *Spirillum*, characterized by a rigid spiral structure. **2** any bacterium with a similar shape. [mod.L, irreg. dimin. of L *spira* SPIRE²]

spirit /'spɪrɪt/ *n. & v.* —*n.* **1 a** the vital animating essence of a person or animal (*was sadly broken in spirit*). **b** the intelligent non-physical part of a person; the soul. **2 a** a rational or intelligent being without a material body. **b** a supernatural being such as a ghost, fairy, etc. (*haunted by spirits*). **3** a prevailing mental or moral condition or attitude; a mood; a tendency (*public spirit; took it in the wrong spirit*). **4 a** (usu. in *pl.*) strong distilled liquor, e.g. brandy, whisky, gin, rum. **b** a distilled volatile liquid (*wood spirit*). **c** purified alcohol (*methylated spirit*). **d** a solution of a volatile principle in alcohol; a tincture (*spirit of ammonia*). **5 a** a person's mental or moral nature or qualities, usu. specified (*has an unbending spirit*). **b** a person viewed as possessing these (*is an ardent spirit*). **c** (in full **high spirit**) courage, energy, vivacity, dash (*played with spirit; infused him with spirit*). **6** the real meaning as opposed to lip service or verbal expression (*the spirit of the law*). **7** *archaic* an immaterial principle thought to govern vital phenomena (*animal spirits*). —*v.tr.* (**spirited**, **spiriting**) (usu. foll. by *away*, *off*, etc.) convey rapidly and secretly by or as if by spirits. □**in** (or **in the**) **spirit** inwardly (*shall be with you in spirit*). **spirit duplicator** a duplicator using an alcoholic solution to reproduce copies from a master sheet. **spirit gum** a quick-drying solution of gum used esp. for attaching false hair. **spirit-lamp** a lamp burning methylated or other volatile spirits instead of oil. **spirit-level** a bent glass tube nearly filled with alcohol used to test horizontality by the position of an air-bubble. **the spirit moves a person** he or she feels inclined (to do something) (orig. in Quaker use). **spirit** (or **spirits**) **of wine** *archaic* purified alcohol. **spirits of salt** *archaic* hydrochloric acid. **spirit up** animate or cheer (a person). [ME f. AF (*e*)*spirit*, OF *esp*(*e*)*rit*, f. L *spiritus* breath, spirit f. *spirare* breathe]

spirited /ˈspɪrɪtɪd/ *adj.* **1** full of spirit; animated, lively, brisk, or courageous (*a spirited attack*; *a spirited translation*). **2** having a spirit or spirits of a specified kind (*high-spirited*; *mean-spirited*). □□ **spiritedly** *adv.* **spiritedness** *n.*

spiritless /ˈspɪrɪtlɪs/ *adj.* lacking courage, vigour, or vivacity. □□ **spiritlessly** *adv.* **spiritlessness** *n.*

spiritual /ˈspɪrɪtjʊəl/ *adj. & n.* —*adj.* **1** of or concerning the spirit as opposed to matter. **2** concerned with sacred or religious things; holy; divine; inspired (*the spiritual life*; *spiritual songs*). **3** (of the mind etc.) refined, sensitive; not concerned with the material. **4** (of a relationship etc.) concerned with the soul or spirit etc., not with external reality (*his spiritual home*). —*n.* = *Negro spiritual.* □**spiritual courts** ecclesiastical courts. □□ **spirituality** /-ˈælɪtɪ/ *n.* **spiritually** *adv.* **spiritualness** *n.* [ME f. OF *spirituel* f. L *spiritualis* (as SPIRIT)]

spiritualism /ˈspɪrɪtjʊə.lɪz(ə)m/ *n.* **1 a** the belief that the spirits of the dead can communicate with the living, esp. through mediums. **b** the practice of this. **2** *Philos.* the doctrine that the spirit exists as distinct from matter, or that spirit is the only reality (cf. MATERIALISM). □□ **spiritualist** *n.* **spiritualistic** /-ˈlɪstɪk/ *adj.*

spiritualize /ˈspɪrɪtjʊə.laɪz/ *v.tr.* (also **-ise**) **1** make (a person or a person's character, thoughts, etc.) spiritual; elevate. **2** attach a spiritual as opposed to a literal meaning to. □□ **spiritualization** /-ˈzeɪʃ(ə)n/ *n.*

spirituel /ˌspɪrɪtjʊˈel/ *adj.* (also **spirituelle**) (of the mind) refined and yet spirited; witty. [F *spirituel*, fem. *-elle* (as SPIRITUAL)]

spirituous /ˈspɪrɪtjʊəs/ *adj.* **1** containing much alcohol. **2** distilled, as whisky, rum, etc. (*spirituous liquor*). □□ **spirituousness** *n.* [L *spiritus* spirit, or F *spiritueux*]

spiro-¹ /ˈspaɪərəʊ/ *comb. form* a coil. [L *spira*, Gk *speira* coil]

spiro-² /ˈspaɪərəʊ/ *comb. form* breath. [irreg. f. L *spirare* breathe]

spirochaete /ˈspaɪərəʊˌkiːt/ *n.* (US **spirochete**) any of various flexible spiral-shaped bacteria. [SPIRO-¹ + Gk *khaitē* long hair]

spirograph /ˈspaɪərəˌɡrɑːf/ *n.* an instrument for recording breathing movements. □□ **spirographic** /-ˈɡræfɪk/ *adj.* **spirographically** /-ˈɡræfɪkəlɪ/ *adv.*

spirogyra /ˌspaɪərəʊˈdʒaɪərə/ *n.* any freshwater alga of the genus *Spirogyra*, with cells containing spiral bands of chlorophyll. [mod.L f. SPIRO-¹ + Gk *guros gura* round]

spirometer /spaɪˈrɒmɪtə(r)/ *n.* an instrument for measuring the air capacity of the lungs.

spirt var. of SPURT.

spit¹ /spɪt/ *v. & n.* —*v.* (**spitting**; *past* and *past part.* **spat** /spæt/ or **spit**) **1** *intr.* **a** eject saliva from the mouth. **b** do this as a sign of hatred or contempt (*spat at him*). **2** *tr.* (usu. foll. by *out*) **a** eject (saliva, blood, food, etc.) from the mouth (*spat the meat out*).

b utter (oaths, threats, etc.) vehemently ('*Damn you!*' *he spat*). **3** *intr.* (of a fire, pen, pan, etc.) send out sparks, ink, hot fat, etc. **4** *intr.* (of rain) fall lightly (*it's only spitting*). **5** *intr.* (esp. of a cat) make a spitting or hissing noise in anger or hostility. —*n.* **1** spittle. **2** the act or an instance of spitting. **3** the foamy liquid secretion of some insects used to protect their young. □**the spit** (or **very spit**) **of** *colloq.* the exact double of (cf. *spitting image*). **spit and polish 1** the cleaning and polishing duties of a soldier etc. **2** exaggerated neatness and smartness. **spit chips** *Austral. sl.* **1** feel extreme thirst. **2** be angry or frustrated. **spit it out** *colloq.* say what is on one's mind. **spitting cobra** the African black-necked cobra, *Naja nigricollis*, that ejects venom by spitting, not striking. **spitting distance** a very short distance. **spitting image** (foll. by *of*) *colloq.* the exact double of (another person or thing). □□ **spitter** *n.* [OE *spittan*, of imit. orig.: cf. SPEW]

spit² /spɪt/ *n. & v.* —*n.* **1** a slender rod on which meat is skewered before being roasted on a fire etc.; a skewer. **2 a** a small point of land projecting into the sea. **b** a long narrow underwater bank. —*v.tr.* (**spitted**, **spitting**) **1** thrust a spit through (meat etc.). **2** pierce or transfix with a sword etc. □**spit-roast** cook on a spit. □□ **spitty** *adj.* [OE *spitu* f. WG]

spit³ /spɪt/ *n.* (*pl.* same or **spits**) a spade-depth of earth (*dig it two spit deep*). [MDu. & MLG, = OE *spittan* dig with spade, prob. rel. to SPIT²]

spitball /ˈspɪtbɔːl/ *n. & v.* —*n.* US **1** a ball of chewed paper etc. used as a missile. **2** a baseball moistened by the pitcher to impart spin. —*v.intr.* throw out suggestions for discussion. □□ **spitballer** *n.*

spitchcock /ˈspɪtʃkɒk/ *n. & v.* —*n.* an eel split and broiled. —*v.tr.* prepare (an eel, fish, bird, etc.) in this way. [16th c.: orig. unkn.: cf. SPATCHCOCK]

spite /spaɪt/ *n. & v.* —*n.* **1** ill will, malice towards a person (*did it from spite*). **2** a grudge. —*v.tr.* thwart, mortify, annoy (*does it to spite me*). □**in spite of** notwithstanding. **in spite of oneself** etc. though one would rather have done otherwise. [ME f. OF *despit* DESPITE]

spiteful /ˈspaɪtfʊl/ *adj.* motivated by spite; malevolent. □□ **spitefully** *adv.* **spitefulness** *n.*

spitfire /ˈspɪtfaɪə(r)/ *n.* a person of fiery temper.

spittle /ˈspɪt(ə)l/ *n.* saliva, esp. as ejected from the mouth. □□ **spittly** *adj.* [alt. of ME (now dial.) *spattle* = OE *spātl* f. *spǣtan* to spit, after SPIT¹]

spittoon /spɪˈtuːn/ *n.* a metal or earthenware pot with esp. a funnel-shaped top, used for spitting into.

spitz /spɪts/ *n.* **1** a small type of dog with a pointed muzzle, esp. a Pomeranian. **2** this breed. [G *Spitz* (*hund*) f. *spitz* pointed + *Hund* dog]

spiv /spɪv/ *n. Brit. colloq.* a man, often characterized by flashy dress, who makes a living by illicit or unscrupulous dealings. □□ **spivvish** *adj.* **spivvy** *adj.* [20th c.: orig. unkn.]

splanchnic /ˈsplæŋknɪk/ *adj.* of or relating to the viscera; intestinal. [mod.L *splanchnicus* f. Gk *splagkhnikos* f. *splagkhna* entrails]

splash /splæʃ/ *v. & n.* —*v.* **1** *intr. & tr.* spatter or cause (liquid) to spatter in small drops. **2** *tr.* cause (a person) to be spattered with liquid etc. (*splashed them with mud*). **3** *intr.* **a** (of a person) cause liquid to spatter (*was splashing about in the bath*). **b** (usu. foll. by *across*, *along*, etc.) move while spattering liquid etc. (*splashed across the carpet in his boots*). **c** step, fall, or plunge etc. into a liquid etc. so as to cause a splash (*splashed into the sea*). **4** *tr.* display (news) prominently. **5** *tr.* decorate with scattered colour. **6** *tr.* spend (money) ostentatiously. —*n.* **1** the act or an instance of splashing. **2 a** a quantity of liquid splashed. **b** the resulting noise (*heard a splash*). **3** a spot of dirt etc. splashed on to a thing. **4** a prominent news feature etc. **5** a daub or patch of colour, esp. on an animal's coat. **6** *Brit. colloq.* a small quantity of liquid, esp. of soda water etc. to dilute spirits. □**make a splash** attract much attention, esp. by extravagance. **splash out** *colloq.* spend money freely. □□ **splashy** *adj.* (**splashier**, **splashiest**). [alt. of PLASH¹]

splashback /ˈsplæʃbæk/ *n.* a panel behind a sink etc. to protect the wall from splashes.

splashdown /ˈsplæʃdaʊn/ *n.* the alighting of a spacecraft on the sea.

splat¹ /splæt/ *n.* a flat piece of thin wood in the centre of a chair-back. [*splat* (v.) split up, rel. to SPLIT]

splat² /splæt/ *n., adv., & v. colloq.* —*n.* a sharp cracking or slapping sound (*hit the wall with a splat*). —*adv.* with a splat (*fell splat on his head*). —*v.intr. & tr.* (**splatted, splatting**) fall or hit with a splat. [abbr. of SPLATTER]

splatter /ˈsplætə(r)/ *v. & n.* —*v.tr. & intr.* **1** splash esp. with a continuous noisy action. **2** *US* spatter. —*n.* a noisy splashing sound. [imit.]

splay /spleɪ/ *v., n., & adj.* —*v.* **1** *tr.* (usu. foll. by *out*) spread (the elbows, feet, etc.) out. **2** *intr.* (of an aperture or its sides) diverge in shape or position. **3** *tr.* construct (a window, doorway, aperture, etc.) so that it diverges or is wider at one side of the wall than the other. —*n.* a surface making an oblique angle with another, e.g. the splayed side of a window or embrasure. —*adj.* **1** wide and flat. **2** turned outward. **splay-foot** a broad flat foot turned outward. **splay-footed** having such feet. [ME f. DISPLAY]

spleen /spliːn/ *n.* **1** an abdominal organ involved in maintaining the proper condition of blood in most vertebrates. **2** lowness of spirits; moroseness, ill temper, spite (from the earlier belief that the spleen was the seat of such feelings) (*a fit of spleen*; *vented their spleen*). □□ **spleenful** *adj.* **spleeny** *adj.* [ME f. OF *esplen* f. L *splen* f. Gk *splēn*]

spleenwort /ˈspliːnwɜːt/ *n.* any fern of the genus *Asplenium*, formerly used as a remedy for disorders of the spleen.

splen- /spliːn/ *comb. form Anat.* the spleen. [Gk (as SPLEEN)]

splendent /ˈsplend(ə)nt/ *adj. formal* **1** shining; lustrous. **2** illustrious. [ME f. L *splendēre* to shine]

splendid /ˈsplendɪd/ *adj.* **1** magnificent, gorgeous, brilliant, sumptuous (*a splendid palace*; *a splendid achievement*). **2** dignified; impressive (*splendid isolation*). **3** excellent; fine (*a splendid chance*). □□ **splendidly** *adv.* **splendidness** *n.* [F *splendide* or L *splendidus* (as SPLENDENT)]

splendiferous /splenˈdɪfərəs/ *adj. colloq.* or *joc.* splendid. □□ **splendiferously** *adv.* **splendiferousness** *n.* [irreg. f. SPLENDOUR]

splendour /ˈsplendə(r)/ *n.* (*US* **splendor**) **1** great or dazzling brightness. **2** magnificence; grandeur. [ME f. AF *splendeur* or L *splendor* (as SPLENDENT)]

splenectomy /spliːˈnektəmɪ/ *n.* (*pl.* **-ies**) the surgical excision of the spleen.

splenetic /splɪˈnetɪk/ *adj. & n.* —*adj.* **1** ill-tempered; peevish. **2** of or concerning the spleen. —*n.* a splenetic person. □□ **splenetically** *adv.* [LL *spleneticus* (as SPLEEN)]

splenic /ˈspliːnɪk, ˈsplen-/ *adj.* of or in the spleen. □ **splenic fever** anthrax. □□ **splenoid** /ˈspliːnɔɪd/ *adj.* [F *splénique* or L *splenicus* f. Gk *splēnikos* (as SPLEEN)]

splenitis /splɪˈnaɪtɪs/ *n.* inflammation of the spleen.

splenius /ˈspliːnɪəs/ *n.* (*pl.* **splenii** /-nɪˌaɪ/) *Anat.* either section of muscle on each side of the neck and back serving to draw back the head. □□ **splenial** *adj.* [mod.L f. Gk *splēnion* bandage]

splenology /spliːˈnɒlədʒɪ/ *n.* the scientific study of the spleen.

splenomegaly /ˌspliːnəˈmegəlɪ/ *n.* a pathological enlargement of the spleen. [SPLEN- + *megaly* (as MEGALO-)]

splenotomy /spliːˈnɒtəmɪ/ *n.* (*pl.* **-ies**) a surgical incision into or dissection of the spleen.

splice /splaɪs/ *v. & n.* —*v.tr.* **1** join the ends of (ropes) by interweaving strands. **2** join (pieces of timber, magnetic tape, film, etc.) in an overlapping position.

3 (esp. as **spliced** *adj.*) *colloq.* join in marriage. —*n.* a joint consisting of two ropes, pieces of wood, film, etc., made by splicing, e.g. the handle and blade of a cricket bat. □ **splice the main brace** *Naut. hist.* issue an extra tot of rum. □□ **splicer** *n.* [prob. f. MDu. *splissen*, of uncert. orig.]

spliff /splɪf/ *n.* (also **splif**) *sl.* a cannabis cigarette. [20th c.: orig. unkn.]

spline /splaɪn/ *n. & v.* —*n.* **1** a rectangular key fitting into grooves in the hub and shaft of a wheel and allowing longitudinal play. **2** a slat. **3** a flexible wood or rubber strip used esp. in drawing large curves. —*v.tr.* fit with a spline (sense 1). [orig. E. Anglian dial., perh. rel. to SPLINTER]

splint /splɪnt/ *n. & v.* —*n.* **1 a** a strip of rigid material used for holding a broken bone etc. when set. **b** a rigid or flexible strip of esp. wood used in basketwork etc. **2** a tumour or bony excrescence on the inside of a horse's leg. **3** a thin strip of wood etc. used to light a fire, pipe, etc. **4** = *splint-bone*. —*v.tr.* secure (a broken limb etc.) with a splint or splints. □ **splint-bone 1** either of two small bones in a horse's foreleg lying behind and close to the cannon-bone. **2** the human fibula. **splint-coal** hard bituminous laminated coal burning with great heat. [ME *splent(e)* f. MDu. *splinte* or MLG *splinte*, *splente* metal plate or pin, rel. to SPLINTER]

splinter /ˈsplɪntə(r)/ *v. & n.* —*v.tr. & intr.* break into fragments. —*n.* a small thin sharp-edged piece broken off from wood, stone, etc. □ **splinter-bar** *Brit.* a crossbar in a vehicle to which traces are attached; a swingletree. **splinter group** (or **party**) a group or party that has broken away from a larger one. **splinter-proof** proof against splinters e.g. from bursting shells or bombs. □□ **splintery** *adj.* [ME f. MDu. (= LG) *splinter*, *splenter*, rel. to SPLINT]

split /splɪt/ *v. & n.* —*v.* (**splitting**; *past* and *past part.* **split**) **1** *intr. & tr.* **a** break or cause to break forcibly into parts, esp. with the grain or into halves. **b** (often foll. by *up*) divide into parts (*split into groups*; *split up the money equally*). **2** *tr. & intr.* (often foll. by *off*, *away*) remove or be removed by breaking, separating, or dividing (*split the top off the bottle*; *split away from the main group*). **3** *intr. & tr.* **a** (usu. foll. by *up*, *on*, *over*, etc.) separate esp. through discord (*split up after ten years*; *they were split on the question of picketing*). **b** (foll. by *with*) quarrel or cease association with (another person etc.). **4** *tr.* cause the fission of (an atom). **5** *intr. & tr. sl.* leave, esp. suddenly. **6** *intr.* (usu. foll. by *on*) *colloq.* betray secrets; inform (*split on them to the police*). **7** *intr.* **a** (as **splitting** *adj.*) (esp. of a headache) very painful; acute. **b** (of the head) suffer great pain from a headache, noise, etc. **8** *intr.* (of a ship) be wrecked. **9** *tr. US colloq.* dilute (whisky etc.) with water. —*n.* **1** the act or an instance of splitting; the state of being split. **2** a fissure, vent, crack, cleft, etc. **3** a separation into parties; a schism. **4** (in *pl.*) *Brit.* the athletic feat of leaping in the air or sitting down with the legs at right angles to the body in front and behind, or at the sides with the trunk facing forwards. **5** a split osier etc. used for parts of basketwork. **6** each strip of steel, cane, etc., of the reed in a loom. **7** a single thickness of split hide. **8** the turning up of two cards of equal value in faro, so that the stakes are divided. **9 a** half a bottle of mineral water. **b** half a glass of liquor. **10** *colloq.* a division of money, esp. the proceeds of crime. □ **split the difference** take the average of two proposed amounts. **split gear** (or **pulley** or **wheel**) a gear etc. made in halves for removal from a shaft. **split hairs** make small and insignificant distinctions. **split infinitive** a phrase consisting of an infinitive with an adverb etc. inserted between *to* and the verb, e.g. *seems to really like it*. **split-level** (of a building) having a room or rooms a fraction of a storey higher than other parts. **split mind** = SCHIZOPHRENIA. **split pea** a pea dried and split in half for cooking. **split personality** the alteration or dissociation of personality occurring in some mental illnesses, esp. schizophrenia and hysteria. **split pin** a metal cotter passed through a hole and held by the pressing back of the two ends. **split ring** a small steel ring with two spiral turns, such as a key-ring. **split-screen** a screen on which two or more separate images are displayed. **split second** a very brief moment of time. **split shift** a shift comprising two or more separate periods of duty. **split shot** (or **stroke**) *Croquet* a stroke driving two touching balls in different directions. **split one's sides** be convulsed with laughter. **split the ticket** (or **one's vote**) *US* vote for candidates of more than one party. **split the vote** *Brit.* (of a candidate or minority party) attract votes from another so that both are defeated by a third. □□ **splitter** *n*. [orig. Naut. f. MDu. *splitten*, rel. to *spletten*, *splīten*, MHG *splīzen*]

splodge /splɒdʒ/ *n. & v. colloq.* —*n.* a daub, blot, or smear. —*v.tr.* make a large, esp. irregular, spot or patch on. □□ **splodgy** *adj.* [imit., or alt. of SPLOTCH]

splosh /splɒʃ/ *v. & n. colloq.* —*v.tr. & intr.* move with a splashing sound. —*n.* **1** a splashing sound. **2** a splash of water etc. **3** *sl.* money. [imit.]

splotch /splɒtʃ/ *n. & v.tr.* = SPLODGE. □□ **splotchy** *adj.* [perh. f. SPOT + obs. *plotch* BLOTCH]

splurge /splɜːdʒ/ *n. & v. colloq.* —*n.* **1** an ostentatious display or effort. **2** an instance of sudden great extravagance. —*v.intr.* **1** (usu. foll. by *on*) spend effort or esp. large sums of money (*splurged on new furniture*). **2** splash heavily. [19th-c. US: prob. imit.]

splutter /ˈsplʌtə(r)/ *v. & n.* —*v.* **1** *intr.* **a** speak in a hurried, vehement, or choking manner. **b** emit particles from the mouth, sparks, hot oil, etc., with spitting sounds. **2** *tr.* **a** speak or utter (words, threats, a language, etc.) rapidly or incoherently. **b** emit (food, sparks, hot oil, etc.) with a spitting sound. —*n.* spluttering speech. □□ **splutterer** *n.* **splutteringly** *adv.* [SPUTTER by assoc. with *splash*]

Spode /spəʊd/ *n.* a type of fine pottery or porcelain. [J. *Spode*, Engl. maker of china d. 1827]

spoil /spɔɪl/ *v. & n.* —*v.* (*past* and *past part.* **spoilt** or **spoiled**) **1** *tr.* **a** damage; diminish the value of (*was spoilt by the rain; will spoil all the fun*). **b** reduce a person's enjoyment etc. of (*the news spoiled his dinner*). **2** *tr.* injure the character of (esp. a child, pet, etc.) by excessive indulgence. **3** *intr.* **a** (of food) go bad, decay; become unfit for eating. **b** (usu. in *neg.*) (of a joke, secret, etc.) become stale through long keeping. **4** *tr.* render (a ballot paper) invalid by improper marking. **5** *tr.* (foll. by *of*) *archaic* or *literary* plunder or deprive (a person of a thing) by force or stealth (*spoiled him of all his possessions*). —*n.* **1** (usu. in *pl.*) **a** plunder taken from an enemy in war, or seized by force. **b** esp. *joc.* profit or advantages gained by succeeding to public office, high position, etc. **2** earth etc. thrown up in excavating, dredging, etc. □ **be spoiling for** aggressively seek (a fight etc.). **spoils system** *US* the practice of giving public office to the adherents of a successful party. **spoilt for choice** having so many choices that it is difficult to choose. [ME f. OF *espoillier*, *espoille* f. L *spoliare* f. *spolium* spoil, plunder, or f. DESPOIL]

spoilage /ˈspɔɪlɪdʒ/ *n.* **1** paper spoilt in printing. **2** the spoiling of food etc. by decay.

spoiler /ˈspɔɪlə(r)/ *n.* **1** a person or thing that spoils. **2 a** a device on an aircraft to retard its speed by interrupting the air flow. **b** a similar device on a vehicle to improve its road-holding at speed.

spoilsman /ˈspɔɪlzmən/ *n.* (*pl.* -**men**) *US* esp. *Polit.* **1** an advocate of the spoils system. **2** a person who seeks to profit by it.

spoilsport /ˈspɔɪlspɔːt/ *n.* a person who spoils others' pleasure or enjoyment.

spoilt *past* and *past part.* of SPOIL.

spoke¹ /spəʊk/ *n. & v.* —*n.* **1** each of the bars running from the hub to the rim of a wheel. **2** a rung

of a ladder. **3** each radial handle of the wheel of a ship etc. —*v.tr.* **1** provide with spokes. **2** obstruct (a wheel etc.) by thrusting a spoke in. □ **put a spoke in a person's wheel** *Brit.* thwart or hinder a person. **spoke-bone** the radius of the forearm. □□ **spokewise** *adv.* [OE *spāca* f. WG]

spoke² *past* of SPEAK.

spoken /ˈspəʊkən/ *past part.* of SPEAK. —*adj.* (in *comb.*) speaking in a specified way (*smooth-spoken; well-spoken*). □ **spoken for** claimed, requisitioned (*this seat is spoken for*).

spokeshave /ˈspəʊkʃeɪv/ *n.* a blade set between two handles, used for shaping spokes and other esp. curved work where an ordinary plane is not suitable.

spokesman /ˈspəʊksmən/ *n.* (*pl.* -**men**; *fem.* **spokeswoman**, *pl.* -**women**) **1** a person who speaks on behalf of others, esp. in the course of public relations. **2** a person deputed to express the views of a group etc. [irreg. f. SPOKE² after *craftsman* etc.]

spokesperson /ˈspəʊks,pɜːs(ə)n/ *n.* (*pl.* -**persons** or -**people**) a spokesman or spokeswoman.

spoliation /,spəʊlɪˈeɪʃ(ə)n/ *n.* **1 a** plunder or pillage, esp. of neutral vessels in war. **b** extortion. **2** *Eccl.* the taking of the fruits of a benefice under a pretended title etc. **3** *Law* the destruction, mutilation, or alteration, of a document to prevent its being used as evidence. □□ **spoliator** /ˈspəʊ-/ *n.* **spoliatory** /ˈspəʊlɪətərɪ/ *adj.* [ME f. L *spoliatio* (as SPOIL)]

spondaic /spɒnˈdeɪɪk/ *adj.* **1** of or concerning spondees. **2** (of a hexameter) having a spondee as a fifth foot. [F *spondaïque* or LL *spondaicus* = LL *spondiacus* f. Gk *spondeiakos* (as SPONDEE)]

spondee /ˈspɒndiː/ *n. Prosody* a foot consisting of two long (or stressed) syllables. [ME f. OF *spondee* or L *spondeus* f. Gk *spondeios* (*pous* foot) f. *spondē* libation, as being characteristic of music accompanying libations]

spondulicks /spɒnˈdjuːlɪks/ *n.pl. sl.* money. [19th c.: orig. unkn.]

spondylitis /,spɒndɪˈlaɪtɪs/ *n.* inflammation of the vertebrae. [L *spondylus* vertebra f. Gk *spondulos* + -ITIS]

sponge /spʌndʒ/ *n. & v.* —*n.* **1** any aquatic animal of the phylum Porifera, with pores in its body wall and a rigid internal skeleton. **2 a** the skeleton of a sponge, esp. the soft light elastic absorbent kind used in bathing, cleansing surfaces, etc. **b** a piece of porous rubber or plastic etc. used similarly. **3** a thing of spongelike absorbency or consistency, e.g. a sponge pudding, cake, porous metal, etc. (*lemon sponge*). **4** = SPONGER. **5** *colloq.* a person who drinks heavily. **6** cleansing with or as with a sponge (*had a quick sponge this morning*). —*v.* **1** *tr.* wipe or cleanse with a sponge. **2** *tr.* (also *absol.*; often foll. by *down, over*) sluice water over (the body, a car, etc.). **3** *tr.* (often foll. by *out, away*, etc.) wipe off or efface (writing, a memory, etc.) with or as with a sponge. **4** *tr.* (often foll. by *up*) absorb with or as with a sponge. **5** *intr.* (often foll. by *on, off*) live as a parasite; be meanly dependent upon (another person). **6** *tr.* obtain (drink etc.) by sponging. **7** *intr.* gather sponges. **8** *tr.* apply paint with a sponge to (walls, furniture, etc.). □ **sponge bag** a waterproof bag for toilet articles. **sponge cake** a very light cake with a spongelike consistency. **sponge cloth 1** soft, lightly-woven cloth with a slightly wrinkled surface. **2** a thin spongy material used for cleaning. **sponge pudding** *Brit.* a steamed or baked pudding of fat, flour, and eggs with a usu. specified flavour. **sponge rubber** liquid rubber latex processed into a spongelike substance. **sponge tree** a spiny tropical acacia, *Acacia farnesiana*, with globose heads of fragrant yellow flowers yielding a perfume: also called OPOPANAX. □□ **spongeable** *adj.* **spongelike** *adj.* **spongiform** *adj.* (esp. in senses 1, 2). [OE f. L *spongia* f. Gk *spoggia, spoggos*]

sponger /ˈspʌndʒə(r)/ *n.* a person who contrives to live at another's expense.

spongy /'spʌndʒɪ/ adj. (**spongier, spongiest**) **1** like a sponge, esp. in being porous, compressible, elastic, or absorbent. **2** (of metal) finely divided and loosely coherent. □□ **spongily** adv. **sponginess** n.

sponsion /'spɒnʃ(ə)n/ n. **1** being a surety for another. **2** a pledge or promise made on behalf of the State by an agent not authorized to do so. [L sponsio f. spondēre spons- promise solemnly]

sponson /'spɒns(ə)n/ n. **1** a projection from the side of a warship or tank to enable a gun to be trained forward and aft. **2** a short subsidiary wing to stabilize a seaplane. **3** a triangular platform supporting the wheel on a paddle-steamer. [19th c.: orig. unkn.]

sponsor /'spɒnsə(r)/ n. & v. —n. **1** a person who supports an activity done for charity by pledging money in advance. **2 a** a person or organization that promotes or supports an artistic or sporting activity etc. **b** esp. US a business organization that promotes a broadcast programme in return for advertising time. **3** an organization lending support to an election candidate. **4** a person who introduces a proposal for legislation. **5** a godparent at baptism or esp. RC Ch. a person who presents a candidate for confirmation. **6** a person who makes himself or herself responsible for another. —v.tr. be a sponsor for. □□ **sponsorial** /spɒn'sɔːrɪəl/ adj. **sponsorship** n. [L (as SPONSION)]

spontaneous /spɒn'teɪnɪəs/ adj. **1** acting or done or occurring without external cause. **2** voluntary, without external incitement (made a spontaneous offer of his services). **3** Biol. (of structural changes in plants and muscular activity esp. in young animals) instinctive, automatic, prompted by no motive. **4** (of bodily movement, literary style, etc.) gracefully natural and unconstrained. **5** (of sudden movement etc.) involuntary, not due to conscious volition. **6** growing naturally without cultivation. □**spontaneous combustion** the ignition of a mineral or vegetable substance (e.g. a heap of rags soaked with oil, a mass of wet coal) from heat engendered within itself, usu. by rapid oxidation. **spontaneous generation** the supposed production of living from non-living matter as inferred from the appearance of life (due in fact to bacteria etc.) in some infusions; abiogenesis. **spontaneous suggestion** suggestion from association of ideas without conscious volition. □□ **spontaneity** /ˌspɒntə'niːɪtɪ, -'neɪɪtɪ/ n. **spontaneously** adv. **spontaneousness** n. [LL spontaneus f. sponte of one's own accord]

spoof /spuːf/ n. & v. colloq. —n. **1** a parody. **2** a hoax or swindle. —v.tr. **1** parody. **2** hoax, swindle. □□ **spoofer** n. **spoofery** n. [invented by A. Roberts, English comedian d. 1933]

spook /spuːk/ n. & v. —n. **1** colloq. a ghost. **2** US sl. a spy. —v. US sl. **1** tr. frighten, unnerve, alarm. **2** intr. take fright, become alarmed. [Du., = MLG spōk, of unkn. orig.]

spooky /'spuːkɪ/ adj. (**spookier, spookiest**) **1** colloq. ghostly, eerie. **2** US sl. nervous; easily frightened. **3** US sl. of spies or espionage. □□ **spookily** adv. **spookiness** n.

spool /spuːl/ n. & v. —n. **1 a** a reel for winding magnetic tape, photographic film, etc., on. **b** a reel for winding yarn or US thread on. **c** a quantity of tape, yarn, etc., wound on a spool. **2** the revolving cylinder of an angler's reel. —v.tr. wind on a spool. [ME f. OF espole or f. MLG spōle, MDu. spoele, OHG spuolo, of unkn. orig.]

spoon /spuːn/ n. & v. —n. **1 a** a utensil consisting of an oval or round bowl and a handle for conveying food (esp. liquid) to the mouth, for stirring, etc. **b** a spoonful, esp. of sugar. **c** (in pl.) Mus. a pair of spoons held in the hand and beaten together rhythmically. **2** a spoon-shaped thing, esp.: **a** (in full **spoon-bait**) a bright revolving piece of metal used as a lure in fishing. **b** an oar with a broad curved blade. **c** a wooden-headed golf club. **3** colloq. **a** a silly or demonstratively fond lover. **b** a simpleton. —v. **1** tr. (often foll. by up, out) take (liquid etc.) with a

spoon. **2** tr. hit (a ball) feebly upwards. **3** colloq. **a** intr. behave in an amorous way, esp. foolishly. **b** tr. archaic woo in a silly or sentimental way. **4** intr. fish with a spoon-bait. □**born with a silver spoon in one's mouth** born in affluence. **spoon-bread** US soft maize bread. □□ **spooner** n. **spoonful** n. (pl. **-fuls**). [OE spōn chip of wood f. Gmc]

spoonbill /'spuːnbɪl/ n. **1** any large wading bird of the subfamily Plataleidae, having a bill with a very broad flat tip. **2** a shoveller duck.

spoonerism /'spuːnəˌrɪz(ə)m/ n. a transposition, usu. accidental, of the initial letters etc. of two or more words, e.g. you have hissed the mystery lectures. [Revd W. A. Spooner, English scholar d. 1930, reputed to make such errors in speaking]

spoonfeed /'spuːnfiːd/ v.tr. (past and past part. **-fed**) **1** feed (a baby etc.) with a spoon. **2** provide help, information, etc., to (a person) without requiring any effort on the recipient's part. **3** artificially encourage (an industry) by subsidies or import duties.

spoony /'spuːnɪ/ adj. & n. colloq. archaic —adj. (**spoonier, spooniest**) **1** (often foll. by on) sentimental, amorous. **2** foolish, silly. —n. (pl. **-ies**) a simpleton. □□ **spoonily** adv. **spooniness** n.

spoor /spʊə(r)/ n. & v. —n. the track or scent of an animal. —v.tr. & intr. follow by the spoor. □□ **spoorer** n. [Afrik. f. MDu. spo(o)r f. Gmc]

sporadic /spə'rædɪk/ adj. occurring only here and there or occasionally, separate, scattered. □□ **sporadically** adv. [med.L sporadicus f. Gk sporadikos f. sporas -ados scattered: cf. speirō to sow]

sporangium /spə'rændʒɪəm/ n. (pl. **sporangia** /-dʒɪə/) Bot. a receptacle in which spores are found. □□ **sporangial** adj. [mod.L f. Gk spora SPORE + aggeion vessel]

spore /spɔː(r)/ n. **1** a specialized reproductive cell of many plants and micro-organisms. **2** these collectively. [mod.L spora f. Gk spora sowing, seed f. speirō sow]

sporo- /'spɔːrəʊ/ comb. form Biol. a spore. [Gk spora (as SPORE)]

sporogenesis /ˌspɔːrə'dʒenɪsɪs/ n. the process of spore formation.

sporogenous /spə'rɒdʒɪnəs/ adj. producing spores.

sporophyte /'spɔːrəˌfaɪt/ n. a spore-producing form of plant with alternating sexual and asexual generations. □□ **sporophytic** /-'fɪtɪk/ adj. **sporophytically** /-'fɪtɪkəlɪ/ adv.

sporran /'spɒrən/ n. a pouch, usu. of leather or sealskin covered with fur etc., worn by a Highlander in front of the kilt. [Gael. sporan f. med.L bursa PURSE]

sport /spɔːt/ n. & v. —n. **1 a** a game or competitive activity, esp. an outdoor one involving physical exertion, e.g. cricket, football, racing, hunting. **b** such activities collectively (the world of sport). **2** (in pl.) Brit. **a** a meeting for competing in sports, esp. athletics (school sports). **b** athletics. **3** amusement, diversion, fun. **4** colloq. **a** a fair or generous person. **b** a person behaving in a specified way, esp. regarding games, rules, etc. (a bad sport at tennis). **c** Austral. a form of address, esp. between males. **d** US a playboy. **5** Biol. an animal or plant deviating suddenly or strikingly from the normal type. **6** a plaything or butt (was the sport of Fortune). —v. **1** intr. divert oneself, take part in a pastime. **2** tr. wear, exhibit, or produce, esp. ostentatiously (sported a gold tie-pin). **3** intr. Biol. become or produce a sport. □**have good sport** be successful in shooting, fishing, etc. **in sport** jestingly. **make sport of** make fun of, ridicule. **the sport of kings** horse-racing (less often war, hunting, or surfing). **sports car** an open, low-built fast car. **sports coat** (or **jacket**) a man's jacket for informal wear. **sports writer** a person who writes (esp. as a journalist) on sports. □□ **sporter** n. [ME f. DISPORT]

sporting /'spɔːtɪŋ/ adj. **1** interested in sport (a sporting man). **2** sportsmanlike, generous (a sporting *offer*). **3** concerned in sport (*a sporting dog; sporting news*). □**a sporting chance** some possibility of success. **sporting house** *US* a brothel. □□ **sportingly** *adv.*

sportive /ˈspɔːtɪv/ *adj.* playful. □□ **sportively** *adv.* **sportiveness** *n.*

sportscast /ˈspɔːtskɑːst/ *n. US* a broadcast of a sports event or information about sport. □□ **sportscaster** *n.*

sportsman /ˈspɔːtsmən/ *n.* (*pl.* **-men**; *fem.* **sportswoman**, *pl.* **-women**) **1** a person who takes part in much sport, esp. professionally. **2** a person who behaves fairly and generously. □□ **sportsmanlike** *adj.* **sportsmanly** *adj.* **sportsmanship** *n.*

sporty /ˈspɔːtɪ/ *adj.* (**sportier**, **sportiest**) *colloq.* **1** fond of sport. **2** rakish, showy. □□ **sportily** *adv.* **sportiness** *n.*

sporule /ˈspɔːruːl/ *n.* a small spore or a single spore. □□ **sporular** *adj.* [F *sporule* or mod.L *sporula* (as SPORE)]

spot /spɒt/ *n. & v.* —*n.* **1 a** a small part of the surface of a thing distinguished by colour, texture, etc., usu. round or less elongated than a streak or stripe (*a blue tie with pink spots*). **b** a small mark or stain. **c** a pimple. **d** a small circle or other shape used in various numbers to distinguish faces of dice, playing-cards in a suit, etc. **e** a moral blemish or stain (*without a spot on his reputation*). **2 a** a particular place; a definite locality (*dropped it on this precise spot; the spot where William III landed*). **b** a place used for a particular activity (often in *comb.*: *nightspot*). **c** (*prec. by the*) *Football* the place from which a penalty kick is taken. **3** a particular part of one's body or aspect of one's character. **4 a** *colloq.* one's esp. regular position in an organization, programme of events, etc. **b** a place or position in a performance or show (*did the spot before the interval*). **5** *Brit.* **a** *colloq.* a small quantity of anything (*a spot of lunch; a spot of trouble*). **b** a drop (*a spot of rain*). **c** *colloq.* a drink. **6** = SPOTLIGHT. **7** (usu. *attrib.*) money paid or goods delivered immediately after a sale (*spot cash; spot silver*). **8** *Billiards* etc. **a** a small round black patch to mark the position where a ball is placed at certain times. **b** (in full **spot-ball**) the white ball distinguished from the other by two black spots. —*v.* (**spotted**, **spotting**) **1** *tr.* **a** *colloq.* single out beforehand (the winner of a race etc.). **b** *colloq.* recognize the identity, nationality, etc., of (*spotted him at once as the murderer*). **c** watch for and take note of (trains, talent, etc.). **d** *colloq.* catch sight of. **e** *Mil.* locate (an enemy's position), esp. from the air. **2 a** *tr. & intr.* mark or become marked with spots. **b** *tr.* stain, soil (a person's character etc.). **3** *intr.* make spots, rain slightly (*it was spotting with rain*). **4** *tr.* *Billiards* place (a ball) on a spot. □**in a spot** (or **in a tight** etc. **spot**) *colloq.* in difficulty. **on the spot 1** at the scene of an action or event. **2** *colloq.* in a position such that response or action is required. **3** without delay or change of place, then and there. **4** (of a person) wide awake, equal to the situation, in good form at a game etc. **put on the spot** *US sl.* decide to murder. **running on the spot** raising the feet alternately as in running but without moving forwards or backwards. **spot check** a test made on the spot or on a randomly-selected subject. **spot height 1** the altitude of a point. **2** a figure on a map showing this. **spot on** *Brit. colloq. adj.* precise; on target. —*adv.* precisely. **spot weld** a weld made in spot welding. **spot-weld** *v.tr.* join by spot welding. **spot welder** a person or device that spot-welds. **spot welding** welding two surfaces together in a series of discrete points. [ME, perh. f. MDu. *spotte*, LG *spot*, ON *spotti* small piece]

spotless /ˈspɒtlɪs/ *adj.* immaculate; absolutely clean or pure. □□ **spotlessly** *adv.* **spotlessness** *n.*

spotlight /ˈspɒtlaɪt/ *n. & v.* —*n.* **1** a beam of light directed on a small area, esp. on a particular part of

a theatre stage or of the road in front of a vehicle. **2** a lamp projecting this. **3** full attention or publicity. —*v.tr.* (*past* and *past part.* **-lighted** or **-lit**) **1** direct a spotlight on. **2** make conspicuous, draw attention to.

spotted /ˈspɒtɪd/ *adj.* marked or decorated with spots. □**spotted dick** (or **dog**) **1** *Brit.* a suet pudding containing currants. **2** a Dalmatian dog. **spotted fever 1** cerebrospinal meningitis. **2** typhus. □□ **spottedness** *n.*

spotter /ˈspɒtə(r)/ *n.* **1** (often in *comb.*) a person who spots people or things (*train-spotter*). **2** an aviator or aircraft employed in locating enemy positions etc.

spotty /ˈspɒtɪ/ *adj.* (**spottier**, **spottiest**) **1** marked with spots. **2** patchy, irregular. □□ **spottily** *adv.* **spottiness** *n.*

spouse /spauz, spaus/ *n.* a husband or wife. [ME *spūs(e)* f. OF *sp(o)us* (masc.), *sp(o)use* (fem.), vars. of *espous(e)* f. L *sponsus sponsa* past part. of *spondēre* betroth]

spout /spaut/ *n. & v.* —*n.* **1 a** a projecting tube or lip through which a liquid etc. is poured from a teapot, kettle, jug, etc., or issues from a fountain, pump, etc. **b** a sloping trough down which a thing may be shot into a receptacle. **c** *hist.* a lift serving a pawnbroker's storeroom. **2** a jet or column of liquid, grain, etc. **3** (in full **spout-hole**) a whale's blow-hole. —*v.tr. & intr.* **1** discharge or issue forcibly in a jet. **2** utter (verses etc.) or speak in a declamatory manner, speechify. □**up the spout** *sl.* **1** useless, ruined, hopeless. **2** pawned. **3** pregnant. □□ **spouter** *n.* **spoutless** *adj.* [ME f. MDu. *spouten*, orig. imit.]

SPQR *abbr.* **1** *hist.* the Senate and people of Rome. **2** small profits and quick returns. [sense 1 f. L *Senatus Populusque Romanus*]

Spr. *abbr.* (in the UK) Sapper.

sprag /spræg/ *n.* **1** a thick piece of wood or similar device used as a brake. **2** a support-prop in a coal mine. [19th c.: orig. unkn.]

sprain /spreɪn/ *v. & n.* —*v.tr.* wrench (an ankle, wrist, etc.) violently so as to cause pain and swelling but not dislocation. —*n.* **1** such a wrench. **2** the resulting inflammation and swelling. [17th c.: orig. unkn.]

sprang *past* of SPRING.

sprat /spræt/ *n. & v.* —*n.* **1** a small European herring-like fish, *Sprattus sprattus*, much used as food. **2** a similar fish, e.g. a sand eel or a young herring. —*v.intr.* (**spratted**, **spratting**) fish for sprats. □**a sprat to catch a mackerel** a small risk to gain much. □□ **spratter** *n.* **spratting** *n.* [OE *sprot*]

sprauncy /ˈsprɔːnsɪ/ *adj.* (**sprauncier**, **spraunciest**) *Brit. sl.* smart or showy. [20th c.: perh. rel. to dial. *sprouncey* cheerful]

sprawl /sprɔːl/ *v. & n.* —*v.* **1 a** *intr.* sit or lie or fall with limbs flung out or in an ungainly way. **b** *tr.* spread (one's limbs) in this way. **2** *intr.* (of handwriting, a plant, a town, etc.) be of irregular or straggling form. —*n.* **1** a sprawling movement or attitude. **2** a straggling group or mass. **3** the straggling expansion of an urban or industrial area. □□ **sprawlingly** *adv.* [OE *spreawlian*]

spray[1] /spreɪ/ *n. & v.* —*n.* **1** water or other liquid flying in small drops from the force of the wind, the dashing of waves, or the action of an atomizer etc. **2** a liquid preparation to be applied in this form with an atomizer etc., esp. for medical purposes. **3** an instrument or apparatus for such application. —*v.tr.* (also *absol.*) **1** throw (liquid) in the form of spray. **2** sprinkle (an object) with small drops or particles, esp. (a plant) with an insecticide. **3** (*absol.*) (of a tom-cat) mark its environment with the smell of its urine, as an attraction to females. □**spray-dry** (**-dries**, **-dried**) dry (milk etc.) by spraying into hot air etc. **spray-gun** a gunlike device for spraying paint etc. **spray-paint** paint (a surface) by means of a spray. □□ **sprayable** *adj.* **sprayer** *n.* [earlier *spry*, perh. rel. to MDu. *spra(e)yen*, MHG *spræjen* sprinkle]

spray[2] /spreɪ/ *n.* **1** a sprig of flowers or leaves, or a branch of a tree with branchlets or flowers, esp. a slender or graceful one. **2** an ornament in a similar form (*a spray of diamonds*). □□ **sprayey** /'spreɪɪ/ *adj.* [ME f. OE *spræg* (unrecorded)]

spread /spred/ *v. & n.* —*v.* (*past* and *past part.* **spread**) **1** *tr.* (often foll. by *out*) **a** open or extend the surface of. **b** cause to cover a larger surface (*spread butter on bread*). **c** display to the eye or the mind (*the view was spread out before us*). **2** *intr.* (often foll. by *out*) have a wide or specified or increasing extent (*on every side spread a vast desert; spreading trees*). **3** *intr. & tr.* become or make widely known, felt, etc. (*rumours are spreading; spread a little happiness*). **4** *tr.* cover the surface of (*spread the wall with paint; a meadow spread with daisies*). **b** lay (a table). —*n.* **1** the act or an instance of spreading. **2** capability of expanding (*has a large spread*). **3** diffusion (*spread of learning*). **4** breadth, compass (*arches of equal spread*). **5** an aircraft's wing-span. **6** increased bodily girth (*middle-aged spread*). **7** the difference between two rates, prices, etc. **8** *colloq.* an elaborate meal. **9** a sweet or savoury paste for spreading on bread etc. **10** a bedspread. **11** printed matter spread across two facing pages or across more than one column. **12** *US* a ranch with extensive land. □ **spread eagle 1** a representation of an eagle with legs and wings extended as an emblem. **2** *hist.* a person secured with arms and legs spread out, esp. to be flogged. **spread-eagle** *v.tr.* (usu. as **spread-eagled** *adj.*) **1** place (a person) in this position. **2** defeat utterly. **3** spread out. —*adj.* *US* bombastic, esp. noisily patriotic. **spread oneself** be lavish or discursive. **spread one's wings** see WING. □□ **spreadable** *adj.* **spreader** *n.* [OE -*sprǣdan* f. WG]

spreadsheet /'spredʃiːt/ *n.* a computer program allowing manipulation and flexible retrieval of esp. tabulated numerical data.

Sprechgesang /'ʃprexgəˌzɑːŋ/ *n. Mus.* a style of dramatic vocalization between speech and song. [G, lit. 'speech song']

spree /spriː/ *n. & v. colloq.* —*n.* **1** a lively extravagant outing (*shopping spree*). **2** a bout of fun or drinking etc. —*v.intr.* (**sprees, spreed**) have a spree. □ **on the spree** engaged in a spree. [19th c.: orig. unkn.]

sprig[1] /sprɪg/ *n. & v.* —*n.* **1** a small branch or shoot. **2** an ornament resembling this, esp. on fabric. **3** usu. *derog.* a youth or young man (*a sprig of the nobility*). —*v.tr.* (**sprigged, sprigging**) **1** ornament with sprigs (*a dress of sprigged muslin*). **2** (usu. as **sprigging** *n.*) decorate (ceramic ware) with ornaments in applied relief. □□ **spriggy** *adj.* [ME f. or rel. to LG *sprick*]

sprig[2] /sprɪg/ *n.* a small tapering headless tack. [ME: orig. unkn.]

sprightly /'spraɪtlɪ/ *adj.* (**sprightlier, sprightliest**) vivacious, lively, brisk. □□ **sprightliness** *n.* [*spright* var. of SPRITE + -LY[1]]

spring /sprɪŋ/ *v. & n.* —*v.* (*past* **sprang** /spræŋ/ or *US* **sprung** /sprʌŋ/; *past part.* **sprung**) **1** *intr.* jump; move rapidly or suddenly (*sprang from his seat; sprang through the gap; spring to their assistance*). **2** *intr.* move rapidly as from a constrained position or by the action of a spring (*the branch sprang back; the door sprang to*). **3** *intr.* (usu. foll. by *from*) originate or arise (*springs from an old family; their actions spring from a false conviction*). **4** *intr.* (usu. foll. by *up*) come into being; appear, esp. suddenly (*a breeze sprang up; the belief has sprung up*). **5** *tr.* cause to act suddenly, esp. by means of a spring (*spring a trap*). **6** *tr.* (often foll. by *on*) produce or develop or make known suddenly or unexpectedly (*has sprung a new theory; loves to spring surprises*). **7** *tr. sl.* contrive the escape or release of. **8** *tr.* rouse (game) from earth or covert. **9 a** *intr.* become warped or split. **b** *tr.* split, crack (wood or a wooden implement). **10** *tr.* (usu. as **sprung** *adj.*) provide (a motor vehicle etc.) with springs. **11 a** *tr. colloq.* spend (money). **b** *intr.* (usu. foll. by *for*) *US & Austral. sl.*

pay for a treat. **12** *tr.* cause (a mine) to explode. —*n.* **1** a jump (*took a spring; rose with a spring*). **2** a backward movement from a constrained position; a recoil, e.g. of a bow. **3** elasticity; ability to spring back strongly (*a mattress with plenty of spring*). **4** a resilient device usu. of bent or coiled metal used esp. to drive clockwork or for cushioning in furniture or vehicles. **5 a** the season in which vegetation begins to appear, the first season of the year, in the N. hemisphere from March to May and in the S. hemisphere from September to November. **b** *Astron.* the period from the vernal equinox to the summer solstice. **c** (often foll. by *of*) the early stage of life etc. **d** = *spring tide*. **6** a place where water, oil, etc., wells up from the earth; the basin or flow so formed (*hot springs; mineral springs*). **7** the motive for or origin of an action, custom, etc. (*the springs of human action*). **8** *sl.* an escape or release from prison. **9** the upward curve of a beam etc. from a horizontal line. **10** the splitting or yielding of a plank etc. under strain. □ **spring balance** a balance that measures weight by the tension of a spring. **spring bed** a bed with a spring mattress. **spring chicken 1** a young fowl for eating (orig. available only in spring). **2** (esp. with *neg.*) a young person (*she's no spring chicken*). **spring-clean** *n.* a thorough cleaning of a house or room, esp. in spring. —*v.tr.* clean (a house or room) in this way. **spring fever** a restless or lethargic feeling sometimes associated with spring. **spring greens** the leaves of young cabbage plants. **spring a leak** develop a leak (orig. *Naut.*, from timbers springing out of position). **spring-loaded** containing a compressed or stretched spring pressing one part against another. **spring mattress** a mattress containing or consisting of springs. **spring onion** an onion taken from the ground before the bulb has formed, and eaten raw in salad. **spring roll** a Chinese snack consisting of a pancake filled with vegetables etc. and fried. **spring tide** a tide just after new and full moon when there is the greatest difference between high and low water. **spring water** water from a spring, as opposed to river or rain water. **sprung rhythm** a poetic metre approximating to speech, each foot having one stressed syllable followed by a varying number of unstressed. □□ **springless** *adj.* **springlet** *n.* **springlike** *adj.* [OE *springan* f. Gmc]

springboard /'sprɪŋbɔːd/ *n.* **1** a springy board giving impetus in leaping, diving, etc. **2** a source of impetus in any activity. **3** *US & Austral.* a platform inserted in the side of a tree, on which a lumberjack stands to chop at some height from the ground.

springbok /'sprɪŋbɒk/ *n.* **1** a southern African gazelle, *Antidorcas marsupialis*, with the ability to run with high springing jumps. **2** (**Springbok**) a South African, esp. one who has played for South Africa in international sporting competitions. [Afrik. f. Du. *springen* SPRING + *bok* antelope]

springe /sprɪndʒ/ *n.* a noose or snare for catching small game. [ME, rel. to obs. *sprenge*, and SPRING]

springer /'sprɪŋə(r)/ *n.* **1** a person or thing that springs. **2 a** a small spaniel of a breed used to spring game. **b** this breed. **3** *Archit.* **a** the part of an arch where the curve begins. **b** the lowest stone of this. **c** the bottom stone of the coping of a gable. **d** a rib of a groined roof or vault. **4** a springbok.

springtail /'sprɪŋteɪl/ *n.* any wingless insect of the order Collembola, leaping by means of a springlike caudal part.

springtide /'sprɪŋtaɪd/ *n. poet.* = SPRINGTIME.

springtime /'sprɪŋtaɪm/ *n.* **1** the season of spring. **2** a time compared to this.

springy /'sprɪŋɪ/ *adj.* (**springier, springiest**) **1** springing back quickly when squeezed or stretched, elastic. **2** (of movements) as of a springy substance. □□ **springily** *adv.* **springiness** *n.*

sprinkle /'sprɪŋk(ə)l/ *v. & n.* —*v.tr.* **1** scatter (liquid, ashes, crumbs, etc.) in small drops or particles. **2**

(often foll. by *with*) subject (the ground or an object) to sprinkling with liquid etc. **3** (of liquid etc.) fall on in this way. **4** distribute in small amounts. —*n.* (usu. foll. by *of*) **1** a light shower. **2** = SPRINKLING. [ME, perh. f. MDu. *sprenkelen*]

sprinkler /'sprɪŋklə(r)/ *n.* a person or thing that sprinkles, esp. a device for sprinkling water on a lawn or to extinguish fires.

sprinkling /'sprɪŋklɪŋ/ *n.* (usu. foll. by *of*) a small thinly distributed number or amount.

sprint /sprɪnt/ *v. & n.* —*v.* **1** *intr.* run a short distance at full speed. **2** *tr.* run (a specified distance) in this way. —*n.* **1** such a run. **2** a similar short spell of maximum effort in cycling, swimming, motor racing, etc. □□ **sprinter** *n.* [ON *sprinta* (unrecorded), of unkn. orig.]

sprit /sprɪt/ *n.* a small spar reaching diagonally from the mast to the upper outer corner of the sail. [OE *sprēot* pole, rel. to SPROUT]

sprite /spraɪt/ *n.* an elf, fairy, or goblin. [ME f. *sprit* var. of SPIRIT]

spritsail /'sprɪts(ə)l, -seɪl/ *n.* **1** a sail extended by a sprit. **2** *hist.* a sail extended by a yard set under the bowsprit.

spritz /sprɪts/ *v. & n. US* —*v.tr.* sprinkle, squirt, or spray. —*n.* the act or an instance of spritzing. [G *spritzen* to squirt]

spritzer /'sprɪtsə(r)/ *n.* a mixture of wine and soda water. [G *Spritzer* a splash]

sprocket /'sprɒkɪt/ *n.* **1** each of several teeth on a wheel engaging with links of a chain, e.g. on a bicycle, or with holes in film or tape or paper. **2** (also **sprocket-wheel**) a wheel with sprockets. [16th c.: orig. unkn.]

sprog /sprɒg/ *n. sl.* a child; a baby. [orig. services' sl., = new recruit: perh. f. obs. *sprag* lively young man]

sprout /spraʊt/ *v. & n.* —*v.* **1** *tr.* put forth, produce (shoots, hair, etc.) (*has sprouted a moustache*). **2** *intr.* begin to grow, put forth shoots. **3** *intr.* spring up, grow to a height. —*n.* **1** a shoot of a plant. **2** = BRUSSELS SPROUT. [OE *sprūtan* (unrecorded) f. WG]

spruce[1] /spruːs/ *adj. & v.* —*adj.* neat in dress and appearance; trim, smart. —*v. tr. & intr.* (usu. *refl.*; usu. foll. by *up*) make or become smart. □□ **sprucely** *adv.* **spruceness** *n.* [perh. f. SPRUCE[2] in obs. sense 'Prussian', in the collocation *spruce* (*leather*) *jerkin*]

spruce[2] /spruːs/ *n.* any coniferous tree of the genus *Picea*, with dense foliage growing in a distinctive conical shape. **2** the wood of this tree used as timber. □ **spruce beer** a fermented beverage using spruce twigs and needles as flavouring. [alt. of obs. *Pruce* Prussia: cf. PRUSSIAN]

spruce[3] /spruːs/ *v. Brit. sl.* **1** *tr.* deceive. **2** *intr.* lie, practise deception. **3** *intr.* evade a duty, malinger. □□ **sprucer** *n.* [20th c.: orig. unkn.]

sprue[1] /spruː/ *n.* **1** a channel through which metal or plastic is poured into a mould. **2** a piece of metal or plastic which has filled a sprue and solidified there. [19th c.: orig. unkn.]

sprue[2] /spruː/ *n.* a tropical disease with ulceration of the mucous membrane of the mouth and chronic enteritis. [Du. *spruw* THRUSH[2]; cf. Flem. *spruwen* sprinkle]

spruik /spruːk/ *v.intr. Austral. & NZ sl.* speak in public, esp. as a showman. □□ **spruiker** *n.* [20th c.: orig. unkn.]

spruit /spreɪt/ *n. S.Afr.* a small watercourse, usu. dry except during the rainy season. [Du., rel. to SPROUT]

sprung see SPRING.

spry /spraɪ/ *adj.* (**spryer, spryest**) active, lively. □□ **spryly** *adv.* **spryness** *n.* [18th c., dial. & US: orig. unkn.]

spud /spʌd/ *n. & v.* —*n.* **1** *sl.* a potato. **2** a small narrow spade for cutting the roots of weeds etc. —*v.tr.* (**spudded, spudding**) **1** (foll. by *up, out*) remove (weeds) with a spud. **2** (also *absol.*; often foll.

by *in*) make the initial drilling for (an oil well). □ **spud-bashing** *Brit. sl.* a lengthy spell of peeling potatoes. [ME: orig. unkn.]

spue var. of SPEW.

spumante /spuːˈmæntɪ/ *n.* an Italian sparkling white wine (cf. ASTI). [It., = 'sparkling']

spume /spjuːm/ *n. & v.intr.* froth, foam. □□ **spumous** *adj.* **spumy** *adj.* (**spumier, spumiest**). [ME f. OF (*e*)*spume* or L *spuma*]

spumoni /spuːˈməʊnɪ/ *n. US* a kind of ice-cream dessert. [It. *spumone* f. *spuma* SPUME]

spun *past* and *past part.* of SPIN.

spunk /spʌŋk/ *n.* **1** touchwood. **2** *colloq.* courage, mettle, spirit. **3** *coarse sl.* semen. ¶ Usually considered a taboo use. [16th c.: orig. unkn.: cf. PUNK]

spunky /'spʌŋkɪ/ *adj.* (**spunkier, spunkiest**) *colloq.* brave, spirited. □□ **spunkily** *adv.*

spur /spɜː(r)/ *n. & v.* —*n.* **1** a device with a small spike or a spiked wheel worn on a rider's heel for urging a horse forward. **2** a stimulus or incentive. **3** a spur-shaped thing, esp.: **a** a projection from a mountain or mountain range. **b** a branch road or railway. **c** a hard projection on a cock's leg. **d** a steel point fastened to the leg of a gamecock. **e** a climbing-iron. **f** a small support for ceramic ware in a kiln. **4** *Bot.* **a** a slender hollow projection from part of a flower. **b** a short fruit-bearing shoot. —*v.* (**spurred, spurring**) **1** *tr.* prick (a horse) with spurs. **2** *tr.* **a** (often foll. by *on*) incite (a person) (*spurred him on to greater efforts*; *spurred her to try again*). **b** stimulate (interest etc.). **3** *intr.* (often foll. by *on, forward*) ride a horse hard. **4** *tr.* (esp. as **spurred** *adj.*) provide (a person, boots, a gamecock) with spurs. □ **on the spur of the moment** on a momentary impulse; impromptu. **put** (or **set**) **spurs to** **1** spur (a horse). **2** stimulate (resolution etc.). **spur-gear** = *spur-wheel.* **spur royal** *hist.* a 15-shilling coin of James I bearing a spurlike sun with rays. **spur-wheel** a cog-wheel with radial teeth. □□ **spurless** *adj.* [OE *spora, spura* f. Gmc, rel. to SPURN]

spurge /spɜːdʒ/ *n.* any plant of the genus *Euphorbia*, exuding an acrid milky juice once used medicinally as a purgative. □ **spurge laurel** any shrub of the genus *Daphne*, esp. *D. laureola*, with small yellow flowers. [ME f. OF *espurge* f. *espurgier* f. L *expurgare* (as EX-[1], PURGE)]

spurious /'spjʊərɪəs/ *adj.* **1** not genuine, not being what it purports to be, not proceeding from the pretended source (*a spurious excuse*). **2** having an outward similarity of form or function only. **3** (of offspring) illegitimate. □□ **spuriously** *adv.* **spuriousness** *n.* [L *spurius* false]

spurn /spɜːn/ *v. & n.* —*v.tr.* **1** reject with disdain; treat with contempt. **2** repel or thrust back with one's foot. —*n.* an act of spurning. □□ **spurner** *n.* [OE *spurnan, spornan*, rel. to SPUR]

spurrier /'spʌrɪə(r)/ *n.* a spur-maker.

spurry /'spʌrɪ/ *n.* (also **spurrey**) (*pl.* **-ies** or **-eys**) a slender plant of the genus *Spergula*, esp. the corn-spurry, a white-flowered weed in cornfields etc. [Du. *spurrie*, prob. rel. to med.L *spergula*]

spurt /spɜːt/ *v. & n.* —*v.* **1** (also **spirt**) **a** *intr.* gush out in a jet or stream. **b** *tr.* cause (liquid etc.) to do this. **2** *intr.* make a sudden effort. —*n.* **1** (also **spirt**) a sudden gushing out, a jet. **2** a short sudden effort or increase of pace esp. in racing. [16th c.: orig. unkn.]

sputnik /'spʊtnɪk, 'spʌt-/ *n.* each of a series of Russian artificial satellites launched from 1957. [Russ., = fellow-traveller]

sputter /'spʌtə(r)/ *v. & n.* —*v.* **1** *intr.* emit spitting sounds, esp. when being heated. **2** *intr.* (often foll. by *at*) speak in a hurried or vehement fashion. **3** *tr.* emit with a spitting sound. **4** *tr.* speak or utter (words, threats, a language, etc.) rapidly or incoherently. **5** *tr. Physics* deposit (metal) by using fast ions etc. to eject particles of it from a target. —*n.* a sputtering sound, esp. sputtering speech. □□ **sputterer** *n.* [Du. *sputteren* (imit.)]

sputum /'spju:təm/ *n.* (*pl.* **sputa** /-tə/) **1** saliva, spittle. **2** a mixture of saliva and mucus expectorated from the respiratory tract, usu. a sign of disease. [L, neut. past part. of *spuere* spit]

spy /spaɪ/ *n.* & *v.* —*n.* (*pl.* **spies**) **1** a person who secretly collects and reports information on the activities, movements, etc., of an enemy, competitor, etc. **2** a person who keeps watch on others, esp. furtively. —*v.* (**spies, spied**) **1** *tr.* discern or make out, esp. by careful observation (*spied a house in the distance*). **2** *intr.* (often foll. by *on*) act as a spy, keep a close and secret watch. **3** *intr.* (often foll. by *into*) pry. □**I spy** a children's game of guessing a visible object from the initial letter of its name. **spy-master** *colloq.* the head of an organization of spies. **spy out** explore or discover, esp. secretly. [ME f. OF *espie* espying, *espier* espy f. Gmc]

spyglass /'spaɪɡlɑ:s/ *n.* a small telescope.

spyhole /'spaɪhəʊl/ *n.* a peep-hole.

sq. *abbr.* square.

Sqn. Ldr. *abbr.* Squadron Leader.

squab /skwɒb/ *n.* & *adj.* —*n.* **1** a short fat person. **2** a young esp. unfledged pigeon or other bird. **3 a** a stuffed cushion. **b** *Brit.* the padded back or side of a car-seat. **4** a sofa or ottoman. —*adj.* short and fat, squat. □**squab-chick** an unfledged bird. **squab pie** **1** pigeon pie. **2** a pie of mutton, pork, onions, and apples. [17th c.: orig. unkn.: cf. obs. *quab* shapeless thing, Sw. dial. *sqvabba* fat woman]

squabble /'skwɒb(ə)l/ *n.* & *v.* —*n.* a petty or noisy quarrel. —*v.intr.* engage in a squabble. □□ **squabbler** *n.* [prob. imit.: cf. Sw. dial. *sqvabbel* a dispute]

squabby /'skwɒbɪ/ *adj.* (**squabbier, squabbiest**) short and fat; squat.

squad /skwɒd/ *n.* **1** a small group of people sharing a task etc. **2** *Mil.* a small number of men assembled for drill etc. **3** *Sport* a group of players forming a team. **4 a** (often in *comb.*) a specialized unit within a police force (*drug squad*). **b** = *flying squad.* **5** a group or class of people of a specified kind (*the awkward squad*). □**squad car** a police car having a radio link with headquarters. [F *escouade* var. of *escadre* f. It. *squadra* SQUARE]

squaddie /'skwɒdɪ/ *n.* (also **squaddy**) (*pl.* **-ies**) *Brit. Mil. sl.* **1** a recruit. **2** a private.

squadron /'skwɒdrən/ *n.* **1** an organized body of persons. **2** a principal division of a cavalry regiment or armoured formation, consisting of two troops. **3** a detachment of warships employed on a particular duty. **4** a unit of the Royal Air Force with 10 to 18 aircraft. □**Squadron Leader** the commander of a squadron of the Royal Air Force, the officer next below Wing Commander. [It. *squadrone* (as SQUAD)]

squail /skweɪl/ *n.* **1** (in *pl.*) a game with small wooden discs propelled across a table or board. **2** each of these discs. □**squail-board** a board used in squails. [19th c.: orig. unkn.: cf. dial. *kayles* skittles]

squalid /'skwɒlɪd/ *adj.* **1** filthy, repulsively dirty. **2** mean or poor in appearance. **3** wretched, sordid. □□ **squalidity** *n.* /-'lɪdɪtɪ/ **squalidly** *adv.* **squalidness** *n.* [L *squalidus* f. *squalēre* be rough or dirty]

squall /skwɔ:l/ *n.* & *v.* —*n.* **1** a sudden or violent gust or storm of wind, esp. with rain or snow or sleet. **2** a discordant cry; a scream (esp. of a baby). **3** (esp. in *pl.*) trouble, difficulty. —*v.* **1** *intr.* utter a squall; scream, cry out violently as in fear or pain. **2** *tr.* utter in a screaming or discordant voice. □□ **squally** *adj.* [prob. f. SQUEAL after BAWL]

squalor /'skwɒlə(r)/ *n.* the state of being filthy or squalid. [L, as SQUALID]

squama /'skweɪmə/ *n.* (*pl.* **squamae** /-mi:/) **1** a scale on an animal or plant. **2** a thin scalelike plate of bone. **3** a scalelike feather. □□ **squamate** /-meɪt/ *adj.* **squamose** *adj.* **squamous** *adj.* **squamule** *n.* [L *squama*]

squander /'skwɒndə(r)/ *v.tr.* **1** spend (money, time, etc.) wastefully. **2** dissipate (a fortune etc.) wastefully. □□ **squanderer** *n.* [16th c.: orig. unkn.]

square /skweə(r)/ *n., adj., adv.,* & *v.* —*n.* **1** an equilateral rectangle. **2 a** an object of this shape or approximately this shape. **b** a small square area on a game-board. **c** a square scarf. **d** an academic cap with a stiff square top; a mortarboard. **3 a** an open (usu. four-sided) area surrounded by buildings, esp. one planted with trees etc. and surrounded by houses. **b** an open area at the meeting of streets. **c** *Cricket* a closer-cut area at the centre of a ground, any strip of which may be prepared as a wicket. **d** an area within barracks etc. for drill. **e** *US* a block of buildings bounded by four streets. **4** the product of a number multiplied by itself (*81 is the square of 9*). **5** an L-shaped or T-shaped instrument for obtaining or testing right angles. **6** *sl.* a conventional or old-fashioned person, one ignorant of or opposed to current trends. **7** a square arrangement of letters, figures, etc. **8** a body of infantry drawn up in rectangular form. **9** a unit of 100 sq. ft. as a measure of flooring etc. **10** *US* a square meal (*three squares a day*). —*adj.* **1** having the shape of a square. **2** having or in the form of a right angle (*table with square corners*). **3** angular and not round; of square section (*has a square jaw*). **4** designating a unit of measure equal to the area of a square whose side is one of the unit specified (*square metre*). **5** (often foll. by *with*) a level, parallel. **b** on a proper footing; even, quits. **6 a** (usu. foll. by *to*) at right angles. **b** *Cricket* on a line through the stumps at right angles to the wicket. **7** having the breadth more nearly equal to the length or height than is usual (*a man of square frame*). **8** properly arranged; in good order, settled (*get things square*). **9** (also **all square**) **a** not in debt, with no money owed. **b** having equal scores, esp. *Golf* having won the same number of holes as one's opponent. **c** (of scores) equal. **10** fair and honest (*his dealings are not always quite square*). **11** uncompromising, direct, thorough (*was met with a square refusal*). **12** *sl.* conventional or old-fashioned, unsophisticated, conservative (cf. sense 6 of *n.*). **13** *Mus.* (of rhythm) simple, straightforward. —*adv.* **1** squarely (*sat square on his seat*). **2** fairly, honestly (*play square*). —*v.* **1** *tr.* make square or rectangular, give a rectangular cross-section to (timber etc.). **2** *tr.* multiply (a number) by itself (*3 squared is 9*). **3** *tr.* & *intr.* (usu. foll. by *to, with*) adjust; make or be suitable or consistent; reconcile (*the results do not square with your conclusions*). **4** *tr.* mark out in squares. **5** *tr.* settle or pay (a bill etc.). **6** *tr.* place (one's shoulders etc.) squarely facing forwards. **7** *tr. colloq.* **a** pay or bribe. **b** secure the acquiescence etc. of (a person) in this way. **8** *tr.* (also *absol.*) make the scores of (a match etc.) all square. **9** *intr.* assume the attitude of a boxer. **10** *tr. Naut.* **a** lay (yards) at right angles with the keel making them at the same time horizontal. **b** get (dead-eyes) horizontal. **c** get (ratlines) horizontal and parallel to one another. □**back to square one** *colloq.* back to the starting-point with no progress made. **get square with** pay or compound with (a creditor). **on the square** *adj.* **1** *colloq.* honest, fair. **2** having membership of the Freemasons. —*adv.* *colloq.* honestly, fairly (*can be trusted to act on the square*). **out of square** not at right angles. **perfect square** = *square number*. **square accounts with** see ACCOUNT. **square away** *US* tidy up. **square-bashing** *Brit. Mil. sl.* drill on a barrack-square. **square brackets** brackets of the form [ ]. **square-built** of comparatively broad shape. **square the circle 1** construct a square equal in area to a given circle (a problem incapable of a purely geometrical solution). **2** do what is impossible. **square dance** a dance with usu. four couples facing inwards from four sides. **square deal** a fair bargain, fair treatment. **squared paper** paper marked out in squares, esp. for plotting graphs. **square-eyed** *joc.*

w *we* z *zoo* ʃ *she* ʒ decision θ *thin* ð *this* ŋ *ring* x *loch* tʃ *chip* dʒ *jar* (*see over for vowels*)

affected by or given to excessive viewing of television.
square leg *Cricket* **1** the fielding position at some distance on the batsman's leg side and nearly opposite the stumps. **2** a fielder in this position. **square meal** a substantial and satisfying meal. **square measure** measure expressed in square units. **square number** the square of an integer e.g. 1, 4, 9, 16. **square off 1** *US* assume the attitude of a boxer. **2** *Austral.* placate or conciliate. **3** mark out in squares. **square peg in a round hole** see PEG. **square piano** an early type of piano, small and oblong in shape. **square-rigged** with the principal sails at right angles to the length of the ship and extended by horizontal yards slung to the mast by the middle (opp. *fore-and-aft rigged*). **square root** the number that multiplied by itself gives a specified number (*3 is the square root of 9*). **square sail** a four-cornered sail extended on a yard slung to the mast by the middle. **square-shouldered** with broad and not sloping shoulders (cf. *round-shouldered*). **square-toed 1** (of shoes or boots) having square toes. **2** wearing such shoes or boots. **3** formal, prim. **square up** settle an account etc. **square up to 1** move towards (a person) in a fighting attitude. **2** face and tackle (a difficulty etc.) resolutely. **square wave** *Physics* a wave with periodic sudden alternations between only two values of quantity. □□ **squarely** *adv.* **squareness** *n.* **squarer** *n.* **squarish** *adj.* [ME f. OF *esquare*, *esquarré*, *esquarrer*, ult. f. EX-¹ + L *quadra* square]

squarial /ˈskweərɪəl/ *n.* a square satellite dish. [SQUARE + AERIAL]

squarrose /ˈskwɒrəʊs/ *adj. Bot. & Zool.* rough with scalelike projections. [L *squarrosus* scurfy, scabby]

squash¹ /skwɒʃ/ *v. & n.* —*v.* **1** *tr.* crush or squeeze flat or into pulp. **2** *intr.* (often foll. by *into*) make one's way by squeezing. **3** *tr.* pack tight, crowd. **4** *tr.* **a** silence (a person) with a crushing retort etc. **b** dismiss (a proposal etc.). **c** quash (a rebellion). —*n.* **1** a crowd; a crowded assembly. **2** a sound of or as of something being squashed, or of a soft body falling. **3** *Brit.* a concentrated drink made of crushed fruit etc., diluted with water. **4** (in full **squash rackets**) a game played with rackets and a small fairly soft ball against the walls of a closed court. **5** a squashed thing or mass. □ **squash tennis** *US* a game similar to squash, played with a lawn-tennis ball. □□ **squashy** *adj.* (**squashier, squashiest**). **squashily** *adv.* **squashiness** *n.* [alt. of QUASH]

squash² /skwɒʃ/ *n.* (*pl.* same or **squashes**) **1** any of various trailing plants of the genus *Cucurbita*, esp. *C. maxima*, *C. moschata*, and *C. pepo*, having pumpkin-like fruits. **2** the fruit of these cooked and eaten as a vegetable. [obs. (*i*)*squoutersquash* f. Narraganset *asquutasquash* f. *asq* uncooked + *squash* green]

squat /skwɒt/ *v., adj., & n.* —*v.* (**squatted, squatting**) **1** *intr.* **a** crouch with the hams resting on the backs of the heels. **b** sit on the ground etc. with the knees drawn up and the heels close to or touching the hams. **2** *tr.* put (a person) into a squatting position. **3** *intr. colloq.* sit down. **4** **a** *intr.* act as a squatter. **b** *tr.* occupy (a building) as a squatter. **5** *intr.* (of an animal) crouch close to the ground. —*adj.* (**squatter, squattest**) **1** (of a person etc.) short and thick, dumpy. **2** in a squatting posture. —*n.* **1** a squatting posture. **2 a** a place occupied by a squatter or squatters. **b** being a squatter. □□ **squatly** *adv.* **squatness** *n.* [ME f. OF *esquatir* flatten f. *es*-EX-¹ + *quatir* press down, crouch ult. f. L *coactus* past part. of *cogere* compel: see COGENT]

squatter /ˈskwɒtə(r)/ *n.* **1** a person who takes unauthorized possession of unoccupied premises. **2** *Austral.* **a** a sheep-farmer esp. on a large scale. **b** *hist.* a person who gets the right of pasturage from the government on easy terms. **3** a person who settles on new esp. public land without title. **4** a person who squats.

squaw /skwɔː/ *n.* a N. American Indian woman or wife. □ **squaw-man** a White married to a squaw. **squaw winter** (in N. America) a brief wintry spell before an Indian Summer. [Narraganset *squaws*, Massachusetts *squaw* woman]

squawk /skwɔːk/ *n. & v.* —*n.* **1** a loud harsh cry esp. of a bird. **2** a complaint. —*v.intr.* utter a squawk. □ **squawk-box** *colloq.* a loudspeaker or intercom. □□ **squawker** *n.* [imit.]

squeak /skwiːk/ *n. & v.* —*n.* **1 a** a short shrill cry as of a mouse. **b** a slight high-pitched sound as of an unoiled hinge. **2** (also **narrow squeak**) a narrow escape, a success barely attained. —*v.* **1** *intr.* make a squeak. **2** *tr.* utter (words) shrilly. **3** *intr.* (foll. by *by, through*) *colloq.* pass narrowly. **4** *intr. sl.* turn informer. [ME, imit.: cf. SQUEAL, SHRIEK, and Sw. *skväka* croak]

squeaker /ˈskwiːkə(r)/ *n.* **1** a person or thing that squeaks. **2** a young bird, esp. a pigeon.

squeaky /ˈskwiːkɪ/ *adj.* (**squeakier, squeakiest**) making a squeaking sound. □ **squeaky clean 1** completely clean. **2** above criticism; beyond reproach. □□ **squeakily** *adv.* **squeakiness** *n.*

squeal /skwiːl/ *n. & v.* —*n.* a prolonged shrill sound, esp. a cry of a child or a pig. —*v.* **1** *intr.* make a squeal. **2** *tr.* utter (words) with a squeal. **3** *intr. sl.* turn informer. **4** *intr. sl.* protest loudly or excitedly. □□ **squealer** *n.* [ME, imit.]

squeamish /ˈskwiːmɪʃ/ *adj.* **1** easily nauseated or disgusted. **2** fastidious or overscrupulous in questions of propriety, honesty, etc. □□ **squeamishly** *adv.* **squeamishness** *n.* [ME var. of *squeamous* (now dial.), f. AF *escoymos*, of unkn. orig.]

squeegee /ˈskwiːdʒiː/ *n. & v.* —*n.* **1** a rubber-edged implement set on a long handle and used for cleaning windows, etc. **2** a small similar instrument or roller used in photography. —*v.tr.* (**squeegees, squeegeed**) treat with a squeegee. [*squeege*, strengthened form of SQUEEZE]

squeeze /skwiːz/ *v. & n.* —*v.* **1** *tr.* **a** exert pressure on from opposite or all sides, esp. in order to extract moisture or reduce size. **b** compress with one's hand or between two bodies. **c** reduce the size of or alter the shape of by squeezing. **2** *tr.* (often foll. by *out*) extract (moisture) by squeezing. **3 a** *tr.* force (a person or thing) into or through a small or narrow space. **b** *intr.* make one's way by squeezing. **c** *tr.* make (one's way) by squeezing. **4** *tr.* **a** harass by exactions; extort money etc. from. **b** constrain; bring pressure to bear on. **c** (usu. foll. by *out of*) obtain (money etc.) by extortion, entreaty, etc. **d** *Bridge* subject (a player) to a squeeze. **5** *tr.* press (a person's hand) with one's own as a sign of sympathy, affection, etc. **6** *tr.* (often foll. by *out*) produce with effort (*squeezed out a tear*). —*n.* **1** an instance of squeezing; the state of being squeezed. **2** *Brit.* a close embrace. **3** a crowd or crowded state; a crush. **4** a small quantity produced by squeezing (*a squeeze of lemon*). **5** a sum of money extorted or exacted, esp. an illicit commission. **6** *Econ.* a restriction on borrowing, investment, etc., in a financial crisis. **7** an impression of a coin etc. taken by pressing damp paper, wax, etc., against it. **8** (in full **squeeze play**) **a** *Bridge* leading winning cards until an opponent is forced to discard an important card. **b** *Baseball* hitting a ball short to the infield to enable a runner on third base to start for home as soon as the ball is pitched. □ **put the squeeze on** *colloq.* coerce or pressure (a person). **squeeze bottle** a flexible container whose contents are extracted by squeezing it. **squeeze-box** *sl.* an accordion or concertina. □□ **squeezable** *adj.* **squeezer** *n.* [earlier *squise*, intensive of obs. *queise*, of unkn. orig.]

squelch /skwɛltʃ/ *v. & n.* —*v.* **1** *intr.* **a** make a sucking sound as of treading in thick mud. **b** move with a squelching sound. **2** *tr.* **a** disconcert, silence. **b** stamp on, crush flat, put an end to. —*n.* an instance of squelching. □□ **squelcher** *n.* **squelchy** *adj.* [imit.]

æ *cat* ɑː *arm* e *bed* ɜː *her* ɪ *sit* iː *see* ɒ *hot* ɔː *saw* ʌ *run* ʊ *put* uː *too* ə *ago* aɪ *my*

squib /skwɪb/ n. & v. —n. **1** a small firework burning with a hissing sound and usu. with a final explosion. **2** a short satirical composition, a lampoon. —v. (**squibbed, squibbing**) **1** tr. US Football kick (the ball) a comparatively short distance on a kick-off; execute (a kick) in this way. **2** archaic **a** intr. write lampoons. **b** tr. lampoon. [16th c.: orig. unkn.: perh. imit.]

squid /skwɪd/ n. & v. —n. **1** any of various ten-armed cephalopods, esp. of the genus Loligo, used as bait or food. **2** artificial bait for fish imitating a squid in form. —v.intr. (**squidded, squidding**) fish with squid as bait. [17th c.: orig. unkn.]

squidgy /ˈskwɪdʒɪ/ adj. (**squidgier, squidgiest**) colloq. squashy, soggy. [imit.]

squiffed /skwɪft/ adj. sl. = SQUIFFY.

squiffy /ˈskwɪfɪ/ adj. (**squiffier, squiffiest**) esp. Brit. sl. slightly drunk. [19th c.: orig. unkn.]

squiggle /ˈskwɪg(ə)l/ n. & v. —n. a short curly line, esp. in handwriting or doodling. —v. **1** tr. write in a squiggly manner; scrawl. **2** intr. wriggle, squirm. □□ **squiggly** adj. [imit.]

squill /skwɪl/ n. **1** any bulbous plant of the genus Scilla, esp. S. autumnalis. **2** a seashore plant, Urginea maritima, having bulbs used in diuretic and purgative preparations. Also called sea onion. **3** any crustacean of the genus Squilla. [ME f. L squilla, scilla f. Gk skilla]

squinch /skwɪntʃ/ n. a straight or arched structure across an interior angle of a square tower to carry a superstructure, e.g. a dome. [var. of obs. scunch, abbr. of SCUNCHEON]

squint /skwɪnt/ v., n., & adj. —v. **1** intr. have the eyes turned in different directions, have a squint. **2** intr. (often foll. by at) look obliquely or with half-closed eyes. **3** tr. close (one's eyes) quickly, hold (one's eyes) half-shut. —n. **1** = STRABISMUS. **2** a stealthy or sidelong glance. **3** colloq. a glance or look (had a squint at it). **4** an oblique opening through the wall of a church affording a view of the altar. **5** a leaning or inclination towards a particular object or aim. —adj. **1** squinting. **2** looking different ways. □ **squint-eyed 1** squinting. **2** malignant, ill-willed. □□ **squinter** n. **squinty** adj. [ASQUINT: (adj.) perh. f. squint-eyed f. obs. squint (adv.) f. ASQUINT]

squire /ˈskwaɪə(r)/ n. & v. —n. **1** a country gentleman, esp. the chief landowner in a country district. **2** hist. a knight's attendant. **3** Brit. colloq. a jocular form of address to a man. **4** US a magistrate or lawyer. **5** Austral. a young snapper fish. —v.tr. (of a man) attend upon or escort (a woman). □□ **squiredom** n. **squirehood** n. **squirelet** n. **squireling** n. **squirely** adj. **squireship** n. [ME f. OF esquier ESQUIRE]

squirearch /ˈskwaɪərɑːk/ n. a member of the squirearchy. □□ **squirearchical** /-ˈrɑːkɪk(ə)l/ adj. (also **squirarchical**). [back-form. f. SQUIREARCHY, after MONARCH]

squirearchy /ˈskwaɪərɑːkɪ/ n. (also **squirarchy**) (pl. -ies) landowners collectively, esp. as a class having political or social influence; a class or body of squires. [SQUIRE, after HIERARCHY etc.]

squireen /ˌskwaɪəˈriːn/ n. Brit. the owner of a small landed property esp. in Ireland.

squirl /skwɜːl/ n. colloq. a flourish or twirl, esp. in handwriting. [perh. f. SQUIGGLE + TWIRL or WHIRL]

squirm /skwɜːm/ v. & n. —v.intr. **1** wriggle, writhe. **2** show or feel embarrassment or discomfiture. —n. a squirming movement. □□ **squirmer** n. **squirmy** adj. (**squirmier, squirmiest**). [imit., prob. assoc. with WORM]

squirrel /ˈskwɪr(ə)l/ n. & v. —n. **1** any rodent of the family Sciuridae, e.g. the red squirrel, grey squirrel, etc., often of arboreal habits, with a bushy tail arching over its back, and pointed ears. **2** the fur of this animal. **3** a person who hoards objects, food, etc. —v. (**squirrelled, squirrelling**; US **squirreled, squirreling**) **1** tr. (often foll. by away) hoard (objects,

food, time, etc.) (squirrelled it away in the cupboard). **2** intr. (often foll. by around) bustle about. □ **squirrel cage 1** a small cage containing a revolving cylinder like a treadmill, on which a captive squirrel may exercise. **2** a form of rotor used in small electric motors, resembling the cylinder of a squirrel cage. **3** a monotonous or repetitive way of life. **squirrel** (or **squirrel-tail**) **grass** a grass, Hordeum jubatum, with bushy spikelets. **squirrel-monkey** a small yellow-haired monkey, Saimiri sciureus, native to S. America. [ME f. AF esquirel, OF esquireul, ult. f. L sciurus f. Gk skiouros f. skia shade + oura tail]

squirrelly /ˈskwɪrəlɪ/ adj. **1** like a squirrel. **2 a** inclined to bustle about. **b** (of a person) unpredictable, nervous, demented.

squirt /skwɜːt/ v. & n. —v. **1** tr. eject (liquid or powder) in a jet as from a syringe. **2** intr. (of liquid or powder) be discharged in this way. **3** tr. splash with liquid or powder ejected by squirting. —n. **1 a** a jet of water etc. **b** a small quantity produced by squirting. **2 a** a syringe. **b** (in full **squirt-gun**) a kind of toy syringe. **3** colloq. an insignificant but presumptuous person. □□ **squirter** n. [ME, imit.]

squish /skwɪʃ/ n. & v. —n. a slight squelching sound. —v. **1** intr. move with a squish. **2** tr. colloq. squash, squeeze. □□ **squishy** adj. (**squishier, squishiest**). [imit.]

squit /skwɪt/ n. Brit. **1** sl. a small or insignificant person. **2** dial. nonsense. [cf. dial. squirt insignificant person, and squit to squirt]

squitch /skwɪtʃ/ n. couch grass. [alt. f. QUITCH]

squiz /skwɪz/ n. Austral. & NZ sl. a look or glance. [prob. f. QUIZ²]

Sr symb. Chem. the element strontium.

Sr. abbr. **1** Senior. **2** Señor. **3** Signor. **4** Eccl. Sister.

sr abbr. steradian(s).

SRC abbr. (in the UK) Science Research Council.

Sri Lankan /ʃriː ˈlæŋkən, ʃrɪˈlæŋkən, srɪ-/ n. & adj. —n. **1** a native or national of Sri Lanka (formerly Ceylon), an island in the Indian Ocean. **2** a person of Sri Lankan descent. —adj. of or relating to Sri Lanka or its people.

SRN abbr. (in the UK) State Registered Nurse.

SRO abbr. standing room only.

SS abbr. **1** Saints. **2** steamship. **3** hist. Nazi special police force. [sense 3 f. G Schutz-Staffel]

SSAFA abbr. (in the UK) Soldiers', Sailors', and Airmen's Families Association.

SSC abbr. (in Scotland) Solicitor to the Supreme Court.

SSE abbr. south-south-east.

SSP abbr. (in the UK) statutory sick pay.

SSRC abbr. (in the UK) Social Science Research Council.

SSSI abbr. (in the UK) Site of Special Scientific Interest.

SST abbr. supersonic transport.

SSW abbr. south-south-west.

St abbr. **1** Saint. **2** stokes.

St. abbr. Street.

st. abbr. **1** stone (in weight). **2** Cricket stumped by.

-st var. of -EST².

Sta. abbr. Station.

stab /stæb/ v. & n. —v. (**stabbed, stabbing**) **1** tr. pierce or wound with a (usu. short) pointed tool or weapon e.g. a knife or dagger. **2** intr. (often foll. by at) aim a blow with such a weapon. **3** intr. cause a sensation like being stabbed (stabbing pain). **4** tr. hurt or distress (a person, feelings, conscience, etc.). **5** intr. (foll. by at) aim a blow at a person's reputation, etc. —n. **1 a** an instance of stabbing. **b** a blow or thrust with a knife etc. **2** a wound made in this way. **3** a blow or pain inflicted on a person's feelings. **4** colloq. an attempt, a try. □ **stab in the back** n. a treacherous or slanderous attack. —v.tr. slander or betray. □□ **stabber** n. [ME: cf. dial. stob in sense 1 of v.]

Stabat Mater /ˌstɑːbæt ˈmɑːtə(r)/ n. **1** a Latin hymn

on the suffering of the Virgin Mary at the Crucifixion. **2** a musical setting for this. [the opening words, L *Stabat mater dolorosa* 'Stood the mother, full of grief']

stabile /'sterbail, -bɪl/ *n.* a rigid, free-standing abstract sculpture or structure of wire, sheet metal, etc. [L *stabilis* STABLE¹, after MOBILE]

stability /stə'bɪlɪtɪ/ *n.* the quality or state of being stable. [ME f. OF *stableté* f. L *stabilitas* f. *stabilis* STABLE¹]

stabilize /'sterbɪˌlaɪz/ *v.tr. & intr.* (also **-ise**) make or become stable. □□ **stabilization** /-'zeɪʃ(ə)n/ *n.*

stabilizer /'sterbɪˌlaɪzə(r)/ *n.* (also **-iser**) a device or substance used to keep something stable, esp.: **1** a gyroscope device to prevent rolling of a ship. **2** *US* the horizontal tailplane of an aircraft. **3** (in *pl.*) a pair of small wheels fitted to the rear wheel of a child's bicycle.

stable¹ /'sterb(ə)l/ *adj.* (**stabler**, **stablest**) **1** firmly fixed or established; not easily adjusted, destroyed, or altered (*a stable structure*; *a stable government*). **2** firm, resolute; not wavering or fickle (*a stable and steadfast friend*). **3** *Chem.* (of a compound) not readily decomposing. **4** *Physics* (of an isotope) not subject to radioactive decay. □ **stable equilibrium** a state in which a body when disturbed tends to return to equilibrium. □□ **stableness** *n.* **stably** *adv.* [ME f. AF *stable*, OF *estable* f. L *stabilis* f. *stare* stand]

stable² /'sterb(ə)l/ *n. & v.* —*n.* **1** a building set apart and adapted for keeping horses. **2** an establishment where racehorses are kept and trained. **3** the racehorses of a particular stable. **4** persons, products, etc., having a common origin or affiliation. **5** such an origin or affiliation. —*v.tr.* put or keep (a horse) in a stable. □ **stable-boy** a boy employed in a stable. **stable-companion** (or **-mate**) **1** a horse of the same stable. **2** a member of the same organization. **stable-girl** a girl employed in a stable. **stable-lad** a person employed in a stable. □□ **stableful** *n.* (*pl.* **-fuls**). [ME f. OF *estable* f. L *stabulum* f. *stare* stand]

stableman /'sterb(ə)lmən/ *n.* (*pl.* **-men**) a person employed in a stable.

stabling /'sterblɪŋ/ *n.* accommodation for horses.

stablish /'stæblɪʃ/ *v.tr. archaic* fix firmly; establish; set up. [var. of ESTABLISH]

staccato /stə'kɑːtəʊ/ *adv., adj., & n. esp. Mus.* —*adv. & adj.* with each sound or note sharply detached or separated from the others (cf. LEGATO, TENUTO). —*n.* (*pl.* **-os**) **1** a staccato passage in music etc. **2** staccato delivery or presentation. □ **staccato mark** a dot or stroke above or below a note, indicating that it is to be played staccato. [It., past part. of *staccare* = *distaccare* DETACH]

stack /stæk/ *n. & v.* —*n.* **1** a pile or heap, esp. in orderly arrangement. **2** a circular or rectangular pile of hay, straw, etc., or of grain in sheaf, often with a sloping thatched top, a rick. **3** *colloq.* a large quantity (*a stack of work*; *has stacks of money*). **4 a** = *chimney-stack*. **b** = SMOKESTACK. **c** a tall factory chimney. **5** a stacked group of aircraft. **6** (also **stack-room**) a part of a library where books are compactly stored, esp. one to which the public does not have direct access. **7** *Brit.* a high detached rock esp. off the coast of Scotland and the Orkneys. **8** a pyramidal group of rifles, a pile. **9** *Computing* a set of storage locations which store data in such a way that the most recently stored item is the first to be retrieved. **10** *Brit.* a measure for a pile of wood of 108 cu. ft. (30.1 cubic metres). —*v.tr.* **1** pile in a stack or stacks. **2 a** arrange (cards) secretly for cheating. **b** manipulate (circumstances etc.) to one's advantage. **3** cause (aircraft) to fly round the same point at different levels while waiting to land at an airport. □ **stack arms** *hist.* = *pile arms.* **stack up** *US colloq.* present oneself, measure up. **stack-yard** an enclosure for stacks of hay, straw, etc. □□ **stackable** *adj.* **stacker** *n.* [ME f. ON *stakkr* haystack f. Gmc]

stacte /'stæktɪ/ *n.* a sweet spice used by the ancient Jews in making incense. [ME f. L f. Gk *staktē* f. *stazō* drip]

staddle /'stæd(ə)l/ *n.* a platform or framework supporting a rick etc. □ **staddle-stone** a stone supporting a staddle or rick etc. [OE *stathol* base f. Gmc, rel. to STAND]

stadium /'sterdɪəm/ *n.* (*pl.* **stadiums**) **1** an athletic or sports ground with tiers of seats for spectators. **2** (*pl.* **stadiums** or **stadia** /-dɪə/) *Antiq.* **a** a course for a foot-race or chariot-race. **b** a measure of length, about 185 metres. **3** a stage or period of development etc. [ME f. L f. Gk *stadion*]

stadtholder /'stɑːdˌhəʊldə(r), 'stɑːt-, 'stæ-/ *n.* (also **stadholder**) *hist.* **1** the chief magistrate of the United Provinces of the Netherlands. **2** the viceroy or governor of a province or town in the Netherlands. □□ **stadtholdership** *n.* [Du. *stadhouder* deputy f. *stad* STEAD + *houder* HOLDER, after med.L LOCUM TENENS]

staff¹ /stɑːf/ *n. & v.* —*n.* **1 a** a stick or pole for use in walking or climbing or as a weapon. **b** a stick or pole as a sign of office or authority. **c** a person or thing that supports or sustains. **d** a flagstaff. **e** *Surveying* a rod for measuring distances, heights, etc. **f** a token given to an engine-driver on a single-track railway as authority to proceed over a given section of line. **g** a spindle in a watch. **2 a** a body of persons employed in a business etc. (*editorial staff of a newspaper*). **b** those in authority within an organization, esp. the teachers in a school. **c** *Mil.* etc. a body of officers assisting an officer in high command and concerned with an army, regiment, fleet, or air force as a whole (*general staff*). **d** (usu. **Staff**) *Mil.* = *staff sergeant.* **3** (*pl.* **staffs** or **staves** /stervz/) *Mus.* a set of usu. five parallel lines on any one or between any adjacent two of which a note is placed to indicate its pitch. —*v.tr.* provide (an institution etc.) with staff. □ **staff college** *Brit. Mil.* etc. a college at which officers are trained for staff duties. **staff notation** *Mus.* notation by means of a staff, esp. as distinct from tonic sol-fa. **staff nurse** *Brit.* a nurse ranking just below a sister. **staff officer** *Mil.* an officer serving on the staff of an army etc. **staff sergeant 1** *Brit.* the senior sergeant of a non-infantry company. **2** *US* a non-commissioned officer ranking just above sergeant. □□ **staffed** *adj.* (also in *comb.*). [OE *stæf* f. Gmc]

staff² /stɑːf/ *n.* a mixture of plaster of Paris, cement, etc., as a temporary building-material. [19th c.: orig. unkn.]

staffage /stə'fɑːʒ/ *n.* accessory items in a painting, esp. figures or animals in a landscape picture. [G f. *staffieren* decorate, perh. f. OF *estoffer*: see STUFF]

staffer /'stɑːfə(r)/ *n. US* a member of a staff, esp. of a newspaper.

Staffs. *abbr.* Staffordshire.

stag /stæg/ *n. & v.* —*n.* **1** an adult male deer, esp. one with a set of antlers. **2** *Brit. Stock Exch.* a person who applies for shares of a new issue with a view to selling at once for a profit. **3** a man who attends a social gathering unaccompanied by a woman. —*v.tr.* (**stagged**, **stagging**) *Brit. Stock Exch.* deal in (shares) as a stag. □ **stag beetle** any beetle of the family Lucanidae, the male of which has large branched mandibles resembling a stag's antlers. **stag-** (or **stag's-**) **horn 1** the horn of a stag, used to make knife-handles, snuff-boxes, etc. **2** any of various ferns, esp. of the genus *Platycerium*, having fronds like antlers. **stag-night** (or **-party**) an all-male celebration, esp. in honour of a man about to marry. [ME f. OF *stacga*, *stagga* (unrecorded): cf. *docga* dog, *frogga* frog, etc., and ON *staggr*, *staggi* male bird]

stage /steɪdʒ/ *n. & v.* —*n.* **1** a point or period in a process or development (*reached a critical stage*; *is in the larval stage*). **2 a** a raised floor or platform, esp. one on which plays etc. are performed before an audience. **b** (prec. by *the*) the acting or theatrical profession, dramatic art or literature, the drama. **c** the scene of action (*the stage of politics*). **d** =

landing-stage. **3 a** a regular stopping-place on a route. **b** the distance between two stopping-places. **c** *Brit.* = *fare-stage*. **4** *Astronaut.* a section of a rocket with a separate engine, jettisoned when its propellant is exhausted. **5** *Geol.* a range of strata forming a subdivision of a series. **6** *Electronics* a single amplifying transistor or valve with the associated equipment. **7** the surface on which an object is placed for inspection through a microscope. —*v.tr.* **1** present (a play etc.) on stage. **2** arrange the occurrence of (*staged a demonstration*; *staged a comeback*). □**go on the stage** become an actor. **hold the stage** dominate a conversation etc. **stage direction** an instruction in the text of a play as to the movement, position, tone, etc., of an actor, or sound effects etc. **stage door** an actors' and workmen's entrance from the street to a theatre behind the stage. **stage effect 1** an effect produced in acting or on the stage. **2** an artificial or theatrical effect produced in real life. **stage fright** nervousness on facing an audience esp. for the first time. **stage-hand** a person handling scenery etc. during a performance on stage. **stage left** (or **right**) on the left (or right) side of the stage, facing the audience. **stage-manage 1** be the stage-manager of. **2** arrange and control for effect. **stage-management** the job or craft of a stage-manager. **stage-manager** the person responsible for lighting and other mechanical arrangements for a play etc. **stage name** a name assumed for professional purposes by an actor. **stage play** a play performed on stage rather than broadcast etc. **stage rights** exclusive rights to perform a particular play. **stage-struck** filled with an inordinate desire to go on the stage. **stage whisper 1** an aside. **2** a loud whisper meant to be heard by others than the person addressed. □□ **stageable** *adj.* **stageability** /-dʒə'bɪlɪtɪ/ *n.* **stager** *n.* [ME f. OF *estage* dwelling ult. f. L *stare* stand]

stagecoach /'steɪdʒkəʊtʃ/ *n. hist.* a large closed horse-drawn coach running regularly by stages between two places.

stagecraft /'steɪdʒkrɑːft/ *n.* skill or experience in writing or staging plays.

stagey var. of STAGY.

stagflation /stæg'fleɪʃ(ə)n/ *n. Econ.* a state of inflation without a corresponding increase of demand and employment. [STAGNATION (as STAGNATE) + INFLATION]

stagger /'stægə(r)/ *v. & n.* —*v.* **1 a** *intr.* walk unsteadily, totter. **b** *tr.* cause to totter (*was staggered by the blow*). **2 a** *tr.* shock, confuse; cause to hesitate or waver (*the question staggered them*; *they were staggered at the suggestion*). **b** *intr.* hesitate; waver in purpose. **3** *tr.* arrange (events, hours of work, etc.) so that they do not coincide. **4** *tr.* arrange (objects) so that they are not in line, esp.: **a** arrange (a road-crossing) so that the side-roads are not in line. **b** set (the spokes of a wheel) to incline alternately to right and left. —*n.* **1** a tottering movement. **2** (in *pl.*) **a** a disease of the brain and spinal cord esp. in horses and cattle, causing staggering. **b** giddiness. **3** an overhanging or slantwise or zigzag arrangement of like parts in a structure etc. □□ **staggerer** *n.* [alt. of ME *stacker* (now dial.) f. ON *stakra* frequent. of *staka* push, stagger]

staggering /'stægərɪŋ/ *adj.* **1** astonishing, bewildering. **2** that staggers. □□ **staggeringly** *adv.*

staghound /'stæghaʊnd/ *n.* **1** any large dog of a breed used for hunting deer by sight or scent. **2** this breed.

staging /'steɪdʒɪŋ/ *n.* **1** the presentation of a play etc. **2 a** a platform or support or scaffolding, esp. temporary. **b** shelves for plants in a greenhouse. □**staging area** an intermediate assembly point for troops in transit. **staging post** a regular stopping-place, esp. on an air route.

stagnant /'stægnənt/ *adj.* **1** (of liquid) motionless, having no current. **2** (of life, action, the mind,

business, a person) showing no activity, dull, sluggish. □□ **stagnancy** *n.* **stagnantly** *adv.* [L *stagnare stagnant-* f. *stagnum* pool]

stagnate /stæg'neɪt/ *v.intr.* be or become stagnant. □□ **stagnation** *n.*

stagy /'steɪdʒɪ/ *adj.* (also **stagey**) (**stagier**, **stagiest**) theatrical, artificial, exaggerated. □□ **stagily** *adv.* **staginess** *n.*

staid /steɪd/ *adj.* of quiet and steady character; sedate. □□ **staidly** *adv.* **staidness** *n.* [= *stayed*, past part. of STAY[1]]

stain /steɪn/ *v. & n.* —*v.* **1** *tr. & intr.* discolour or be discoloured by the action of liquid sinking in. **2** *tr.* sully, blemish, spoil, damage (a reputation, character, etc.). **3** *tr.* colour (wood, glass, etc.) by a process other than painting or covering the surface. **4** *tr.* impregnate (a specimen) for microscopic examination with colouring matter that makes the structure visible by being deposited in some parts more than in others. **5** *tr.* print colours on (wallpaper). —*n.* **1** a discoloration, a spot or mark caused esp. by contact with foreign matter and not easily removed (*a cloth covered with tea-stains*). **2 a** a blot or blemish. **b** damage to a reputation etc. (*a stain on one's character*). **3** a substance used in staining. □**stained glass** dyed or coloured glass, esp. in a lead framework in a window (also (with hyphen) *attrib.*: *stained-glass window*). □□ **stainable** *adj.* **stainer** *n.* [ME f. *distain* f. OF *desteindre desteign-* (as DIS-, TINGE)]

stainless /'steɪnlɪs/ *adj.* **1** (esp. of a reputation) without stains. **2** not liable to stain. □**stainless steel** chrome steel not liable to rust or tarnish under ordinary conditions.

stair /steə(r)/ *n.* **1** each of a set of fixed indoor steps (*on the top stair but one*). **2** (usu. in *pl.*) a set of indoor steps (*passed him on the stairs*; *down a winding stair*). **3** (in *pl.*) a landing-stage. □**stair-rod** a rod for securing a carpet in the angle between two steps. [OE *stæger* f. Gmc]

staircase /'steəkeɪs/ *n.* **1** a flight of stairs and the supporting structure. **2** a part of a building containing a staircase.

stairhead /'steəhed/ *n.* a level space at the top of stairs.

stairway /'steəweɪ/ *n.* **1** a flight of stairs, a staircase. **2** the way up this.

stairwell /'steəwel/ *n.* the shaft in which a staircase is built.

staithe /steɪð/ *n. Brit.* a wharf, esp. a waterside coal depot equipped for loading vessels. [ME f. ON *stöth* landing-stage f. Gmc, rel. to STAND]

stake[1] /steɪk/ *n. & v.* —*n.* **1** a stout stick or post sharpened at one end and driven into the ground as a support, boundary mark, etc. **2** *hist.* **a** the post to which a person was tied to be burnt alive. **b** (prec. by *the*) death by burning as a punishment (*was condemned to the stake*). **3** a long vertical rod in basket-making. **4** a metalworker's small anvil fixed on a bench by a pointed prop. —*v.tr.* **1** fasten, secure, or support with a stake or stakes. **2** (foll. by *off, out*) mark off (an area) with stakes. **3** state or establish (a claim). □**pull** (or **pull up**) **stakes** depart; go to live elsewhere. **stake-boat** a boat anchored to mark the course for a boat race etc. **stake-body** (*pl.* **-ies**) *US* a body for a lorry etc. having a flat open platform with removable posts along the sides. **stake-net** a fishing-net hung on stakes. **stake out** *colloq.* **1** place under surveillance. **2** place (a person) to maintain surveillance. **stake-out** *n.* esp. *US colloq.* a period of surveillance. [OE *staca* f. WG, rel. to STICK[2]]

stake[2] /steɪk/ *n. & v.* —*n.* **1** a sum of money etc. wagered on an event, esp. deposited with a stakeholder. **2** (often foll. by *in*) an interest or concern, esp. financial. **3** (in *pl.*) **a** money offered as a prize esp. in a horse-race. **b** such a race (*maiden stakes*; *trial stakes*). —*v.tr.* **1** a wager (*staked £5 on the next race*). **b** risk (*staked everything on convincing* him). **2** *US colloq.* give financial or other support to. □**at stake 1** risked, to be won or lost (*life itself is at stake*). **2** at issue, in question. □□ **staker** *n.* [16th c.: perh. f. STAKE¹]

stakeholder /ˈsteɪkˌhəʊldə(r)/ *n.* an independent party with whom each of those who make a wager deposits the money etc. wagered.

Stakhanovite /stəˈkɑːnəˌvaɪt/ *n.* a worker (esp. in the USSR) who increases his output to an exceptional extent, and so gains special awards. □□ **Stakhanovism** /-ˌvɪz(ə)m/ *n.* **Stakhanovist** /-vɪst/ *n.* [A. G. *Stakhanov*, Russian coal-miner d. 1977]

stalactite /ˈstæləkˌtaɪt, stəˈlæk-/ *n.* a deposit of calcium carbonate having the shape of a large icicle, formed by the trickling of water from the roof of a cave, cliff overhang, etc. □□ **stalactic** /-ˈlæktɪk/ *adj.* **stalactiform** /-ˈlæktɪˌfɔːm/ *adj.* **stalactitic** /-ˈtɪtɪk/ *adj.* [mod.L *stalactites* f. Gk *stalaktos* dripping f. *stalassō* drip]

Stalag /ˈstælæg/ *n. hist.* a German prison camp, esp. for non-commissioned officers and privates. [G f. *Stamm* base, main stock, *Lager* camp]

stalagmite /ˈstæləgˌmaɪt/ *n.* a deposit of calcium carbonate formed by the dripping of water into the shape of a large inverted icicle rising from the floor of a cave etc., often uniting with a stalactite. □□ **stalagmitic** /-ˈmɪtɪk/ *adj.* [mod.L *stalagmites* f. Gk *stalagma* a drop f. *stalassō* (as STALACTITE)]

stale¹ /steɪl/ *adj. & v.* —*adj.* (**staler, stalest**) **1 a** not fresh, not quite new (*stale bread is best for toast*). **b** musty, insipid, or otherwise the worse for age or use. **2** trite or unoriginal (*a stale joke; stale news*). **3** (of an athlete or other performer) having ability impaired by excessive exertion or practice. **4** *Law* (esp. of a claim) having been left dormant for an unreasonably long time. —*v.tr. & intr.* make or become stale. □□ **stalely** *adv.* **staleness** *n.* [ME, prob. f. AF & OF f. *estaler* halt: cf. STALL¹]

stale² /steɪl/ *n. & v.* —*n.* the urine of horses and cattle. —*v.intr.* (esp. of horses and cattle) urinate. [ME, perh. f. OF *estaler* adopt a position (cf. STALE¹)]

stalemate /ˈsteɪlmeɪt/ *n. & v.* —*n.* **1** *Chess* a position counting as a draw, in which a player is not in check but cannot move except into check. **2** a deadlock or drawn contest. —*v.tr.* **1** *Chess* bring (a player) to a stalemate. **2** bring to a standstill. [obs. *stale* (f. AF *estale* f. *estaler* be placed: cf. STALL¹) + MATE²]

Stalinism /ˈstɑːlɪˌnɪz(ə)m/ *n.* **1** the policies followed by Stalin in the government of the USSR, esp. centralization, totalitarianism, and the pursuit of socialism. **2** any rigid centralized authoritarian form of socialism. □□ **Stalinist** *n.* [J. V. *Stalin* (Dzhugashvili), Soviet statesman d. 1953]

stalk¹ /stɔːk/ *n.* **1** the main stem of a herbaceous plant. **2** the slender attachment or support of a leaf, flower, fruit, etc. **3** a similar support for an organ etc. in an animal. **4** a slender support or linking shaft in a machine, object, etc., e.g. the stem of a wineglass. **5** the tall chimney of a factory etc. □**stalk-eyed** (of crabs, snails, etc.) having the eyes mounted on stalks. □□ **stalked** *adj.* (also in *comb.*). **stalkless** *adj.* **stalklet** *n.* **stalklike** *adj.* **stalky** *adj.* [ME *stalke*, prob. dimin. of (now dial.) *stale* rung of a ladder, long handle, f. OE *stalu*]

stalk² /stɔːk/ *v. & n.* —*v.* **1 a** *tr.* pursue or approach (game or an enemy) stealthily. **b** *intr.* steal up to game under cover. **2** *intr.* stride, walk in a stately or haughty manner. —*n.* **1** the stalking of game. **2** an imposing gait. □**stalking-horse 1** a horse behind which a hunter is concealed. **2** a pretext concealing one's real intentions or actions. □□ **stalker** *n.* (also in *comb.*). [OE f. Gmc, rel. to STEAL]

stall¹ /stɔːl/ *n. & v.* —*n.* **1 a** a trader's stand or booth in a market etc., or out of doors. **b** a compartment in a building for the sale of goods. **c** a table in this on which goods are exposed. **2 a** a stable or cowhouse. **b** a compartment for one animal in this. **3 a** a fixed seat in the choir or chancel of a church, more or less

enclosed at the back and sides and often canopied, esp. one appropriated to a clergyman (*canon's stall; dean's stall*). **b** the office or dignity of a canon etc. **4** (usu. in *pl.*) *Brit.* each of a set of seats in a theatre, usu. on the ground floor. **5 a** a compartment for one person in a shower-bath, lavatory, etc. **b** a compartment for one horse at the start of a race. **6 a** the stalling of an engine or aircraft. **b** the condition resulting from this. **7** a receptacle for one object (*finger-stall*). —*v.* **1 a** *intr.* (of a motor vehicle or its engine) stop because of an overload on the engine or an inadequate supply of fuel to it. **b** *intr.* (of an aircraft or its pilot) reach a condition where the speed is too low to allow effective operation of the controls. **c** *tr.* cause (an engine or vehicle or aircraft) to stall. **2** *tr.* **a** put or keep (cattle etc.) in a stall or stalls esp. for fattening (*a stalled ox*). **b** furnish (a stable etc.) with stalls. **3** *intr.* **a** (of a horse or cart) stick fast as in mud or snow. **b** *US* be snowbound. □**stall-feed** fatten (cattle) in a stall. [OE *steall* f. Gmc, rel. to STAND: partly f. OF *estal* f. Frank.]

stall² /stɔːl/ *v. & n.* —*v.* **1** *intr.* play for time when being questioned etc. **2** *tr.* delay, obstruct, block. —*n.* an instance of stalling. □**stall off** evade or deceive. [*stall* pickpocket's confederate, orig. 'decoy' f. AF *estal(e)*, prob. rel. to STALL¹]

stallage /ˈstɔːlɪdʒ/ *n. Brit.* **1** space for a stall or stalls in a market etc. **2** the rent for such a stall. **3** the right to erect such a stall. [ME f. OF *estalage* f. *estal* STALL¹]

stallholder /ˈstɔːlˌhəʊldə(r)/ *n.* a person in charge of a stall at a market etc.

stallion /ˈstæljən/ *n.* an uncastrated adult male horse, esp. one kept for breeding. [ME f. OF *estalon* ult. f. a Gmc root rel. to STALL¹]

stalwart /ˈstɔːlwət/ *adj. & n.* —*adj.* **1** strongly built, sturdy. **2** courageous, resolute, determined (*stalwart supporters*). —*n.* a stalwart person, esp. a loyal uncompromising partisan. □□ **stalwartly** *adv.* **stalwartness** *n.* [Sc. var. of obs. *stalworth* f. OE *stǣlwierthe* f. *stǣl* place, WORTH]

stamen /ˈsteɪmən/ *n.* the male fertilizing organ of a flowering plant, including the anther containing pollen. □□ **staminiferous** /ˌstæmɪˈnɪfərəs/ *adj.* [L *stamen staminis* warp in an upright loom, thread]

stamina /ˈstæmɪnə/ *n.* the ability to endure prolonged physical or mental strain; staying power, power of endurance. [L, pl. of STAMEN in sense 'warp, threads spun by the Fates']

staminate /ˈstæmɪnət/ *adj.* (of a plant) having stamens, esp. stamens but not pistils.

stammer /ˈstæmə(r)/ *v. & n.* —*v.* **1** *intr.* speak (habitually, or on occasion from embarrassment etc.) with halting articulation, esp. with pauses or rapid repetitions of the same syllable. **2** *tr.* (often foll. by *out*) utter (words) in this way (*stammered out an excuse*). —*n.* **1** a tendency to stammer. **2** an instance of stammering. □□ **stammerer** *n.* **stammeringly** *adv.* [OE *stamerian* f. WG]

stamp /stæmp/ *v. & n.* —*v.* **1 a** *tr.* bring down (one's foot) heavily on the ground etc. **b** *tr.* crush, flatten, or bring into a specified state in this way (*stamped down the earth round the plant*). **c** *intr.* bring down one's foot heavily; walk with heavy steps. **2** *tr.* **a** impress (a pattern, mark, etc.) on metal, paper, butter, etc., with a die or similar instrument of metal, wood, rubber, etc. **b** impress (a surface) with a pattern etc. in this way. **3** *tr.* affix a postage or other stamp to (an envelope or document). **4** *tr.* assign a specific character to; characterize; mark out (*stamps the story an invention*). **5** *tr.* crush or pulverize (ore etc.). —*n.* **1** an instrument for stamping a pattern or mark. **2 a** a mark or pattern made by this. **b** the impression of an official mark required to be made for revenue purposes on deeds, bills of exchange, etc., as evidence of payment of tax. **3** a small adhesive piece of paper indicating that a price, fee, or tax has been paid, esp. a postage stamp. **4** a mark impressed on or label etc. affixed to a commodity as evidence of quality etc. **5 a** a heavy downward blow with the foot. **b** the sound of this. **6 a** a characteristic mark or impress (*bears the stamp of genius*). **b** character, kind (*avoid people of that stamp*). **7** the block that crushes ore in a stamp-mill. □**Stamp Act** an act concerned with stamp-duty, esp. that imposing the duty on the American colonies in 1765 and repealed in 1766. **stamp-collecting** the collecting of postage stamps as objects of interest or value. **stamp-collector** a person engaged in stamp-collecting. **stamp-duty** a duty imposed on certain kinds of legal document. **stamp-hinge** see HINGE. **stamping-ground** a favourite haunt or place of action. **stamp-machine** a coin-operated machine for selling postage stamps. **stamp-mill** a mill for crushing ore etc. **stamp-office** an office for the issue of government stamps and the receipt of stamp-duty etc. **stamp on 1** impress (an idea etc.) on (the memory etc.). **2** suppress. **stamp out 1** produce by cutting out with a die etc. **2** put an end to, crush, destroy. **stamp-paper 1** paper with the government revenue stamp. **2** the gummed marginal paper of a sheet of postage stamps. □□**stamper** *n.* [prob. f. OE *stampian* (v.) (unrecorded) f. Gmc: infl. by OF *estamper* (v.) and F *estampe* (n.) also f. Gmc]

stampede /stæm'piːd/ *n. & v.* —*n.* **1** a sudden flight and scattering of a number of horses, cattle, etc. **2** a sudden flight or hurried movement of people due to interest or panic. **3** *US* the spontaneous response of many persons to a common impulse. —*v.* **1** *intr.* take part in a stampede. **2** *tr.* cause to do this. **3** *tr.* cause to act hurriedly or unreasoningly. □□ **stampeder** *n.* [Sp. *estampida* crash, uproar, ult. f. Gmc, rel. to STAMP]

stance /stɑːns, stæns/ *n.* **1** an attitude or position of the body esp. when hitting a ball etc. **2** a standpoint; an attitude of mind. **3** *Sc.* a site for a market, taxi rank, etc. [F f. It. *stanza*: see STANZA]

stanch[1] /stɑːntʃ, stɔːntʃ/ *v.tr.* (also **staunch**) **1** restrain the flow of (esp. blood). **2** restrain the flow from (esp. a wound). [ME f. OF *estanchier* f. Rmc]

stanch[2] var. of STAUNCH[1].

stanchion /'stɑːnʃ(ə)n/ *n. & v.* —*n.* **1** a post or pillar, an upright support, a vertical strut. **2** an upright bar, pair of bars, or frame, for confining cattle in a stall. —*v.tr.* **1** supply with a stanchion. **2** fasten (cattle) to a stanchion. [ME f. AF *stanchon*, OF *estanchon* f. *estance* prob. ult. f. L *stare* stand]

stand /stænd/ *v. & n.* —*v.* (*past* and *past part.* **stood** /stʊd/) **1** *intr.* have or take or maintain an upright position, esp. on the feet or a base. **2** *intr.* be situated or located (*here once stood a village*). **3** *intr.* be of a specified height (*stands six foot three*). **4** *intr.* be in a specified condition (*stands accused; the thermometer stood at 90°; the matter stands as follows; stood in awe of them*). **5** *tr.* place or set in an upright or specified position (*stood it against the wall*). **6** *intr.* **a** move to and remain in a specified position (*stand aside*). **b** take a specified attitude (*stand aloof*). **7** *intr.* maintain a position; avoid falling or moving or being moved (*the house will stand for another century; stood for hours arguing*). **8** *intr.* assume a stationary position; cease to move (*now stand still*). **9** *intr.* remain valid or unaltered; hold good (*the former conditions must stand*). **10** *intr. Naut.* hold a specified course (*stand in for the shore; you are standing into danger*). **11** *tr.* endure without yielding or complaining; tolerate (*cannot stand the pain; how can you stand him?*). **12** *tr.* provide for another or others at one's own expense (*stood him a drink*). **13** *intr.* (often foll. by *for*) *Brit.* be a candidate (for an office, legislature, or constituency) (*stood for Parliament; stood for Finchley*). **14** *intr.* act in a specified capacity (*stood proxy*). **15** *tr.* undergo (trial). **16** *intr. Cricket* act as umpire. **17** *intr.* (of a dog) point, set. **18** *intr.* (in full **stand at stud**) (of a stallion) be available for breeding. —*n.* **1** a cessation

from motion or progress, a stoppage (*was brought to a stand*). **2 a** a halt made, or a stationary condition assumed, for the purpose of resistance. **b** resistance to attack or compulsion (esp. *make a stand*). **c** *Cricket* a prolonged period at the wicket by two batsmen. **3 a** a position taken up (*took his stand near the door*). **b** an attitude adopted. **4 a** a rack, set of shelves, table, etc., on or in which things may be placed (*music stand; hatstand*). **5 a** a small open-fronted structure for a trader outdoors or in a market etc. **b** a structure occupied by a participating organization at an exhibition. **6** a standing-place for vehicles (*cab-stand*). **7 a** a raised structure for persons to sit or stand on. **b** *US* a witness-box (*take the stand*). **8** *Theatr.* etc. each halt made on a tour to give one or more performances. **9** a group of growing plants (*stand of trees; stand of clover*). □**as it stands 1** in its present condition, unaltered. **2** in the present circumstances. **be at a stand** *archaic* be unable to proceed, be in perplexity. **it stands to reason** see REASON. **stand alone** be unequalled. **stand and deliver!** *hist.* a highwayman's order to hand over valuables etc. **stand at bay** see BAY[5]. **stand back 1** withdraw; take up a position further from the front. **2** withdraw psychologically in order to take an objective view. **stand by 1** stand nearby; look on without interfering (*will not stand by and see him ill-treated*). **2** uphold, support, side with (a person). **3** adhere to, abide by (terms or promises). **4** *Naut.* stand ready to take hold of or operate (an anchor etc.). **stand-by** *n.* (*pl.* **-bys**) **1** a person or thing ready if needed in an emergency etc. **2** readiness for duty (*on stand-by*). —*adj.* **1** ready for immediate use. **2** (of air travel) not booked in advance but allocated on the basis of earliest availability. **stand camera** a camera for use on a tripod, not hand-held. **stand a chance** see CHANCE. **stand corrected** accept correction. **stand down 1** withdraw (a person) or retire from a team, witness-box, or similar position. **2** *Brit.* cease to be a candidate etc. **3** *Brit. Mil.* go off duty. **stand easy!** see EASY. **stand for 1** represent, signify, imply ('*US* stands for 'United States'; *democracy stands for a great deal more than that*). **2** (often with *neg.*) *colloq.* endure, tolerate, acquiesce in. **3** espouse the cause of. **stand one's ground** maintain one's position, not yield. **stand high** be high in status, price, etc. **stand in** (usu. foll. by *for*) deputize; act in place of another. **stand-in** *n.* a deputy or substitute, esp. for an actor when the latter's acting ability is not needed. **stand in the breach** see BREACH. **stand in good stead** see STEAD. **stand in with** be in league with. **stand of arms** *Brit. Mil.* a complete set of weapons for one man. **stand of colours** *Brit. Mil.* a regiment's flags. **stand off 1** move or keep away, keep one's distance. **2** *Brit.* temporarily dispense with the services of (an employee). **stand-off** *n.* **1** *US* a deadlock. **2** = *stand-off half*. **stand-off half** *Rugby Football* a halfback who forms a link between the scrum-half and the three-quarters. **stand on 1** insist on, observe scrupulously (*stand on ceremony; stand on one's dignity*). **2** *Naut.* continue on the same course. **stand on me** *sl.* rely on me; believe me. **stand on one's own feet** (or **legs**) be self-reliant or independent. **stand out 1** be prominent or conspicuous or outstanding. **2** (usu. foll. by *against, for*) hold out; persist in opposition or support or endurance. **stand over 1** stand close to (a person) to watch, control, threaten, etc. **2** be postponed, be left for later settlement etc. **stand pat** see PAT[2]. **stand to 1** *Mil.* stand ready for an attack (esp. before dawn or after dark). **2** abide by, adhere to (terms or promises). **3** be likely or certain to (*stands to lose everything*). **4** uphold, support, or side with (a person). **stand treat** bear the expense of entertainment etc. **stand up 1 a** rise to one's feet from a sitting or other position. **b** come to or remain in or place in a standing position. **2** (of an argument etc.) be valid. **3** *colloq.* fail to keep an appointment with. **stand-up** *attrib.adj.* **1** (of a meal) eaten standing. **2** (of a fight) violent, thorough, or fair and square. **3** (of a collar) upright, not turned down. **4** (of a comedian) performing by standing before an audience and telling jokes. **stand up for** support, side with, maintain (a person or cause). **stand upon** = *stand on*. **stand up to 1** meet or face (an opponent) courageously. **2** be resistant to the harmful effects of (wear, use, etc.). **stand well** (usu. foll. by *with*) be on good terms or in good repute. **take one's stand on** base one's argument etc. on, rely on. □□ **stander** *n*. [OE *standan* f. Gmc]

standalone /ˈstændəˈləʊn/ *adj*. (of a computer) operating independently of a network or other system.

standard /ˈstændəd/ *n. & adj.* —*n.* **1** an object or quality or measure serving as a basis or example or principle to which others conform or should conform or by which the accuracy or quality of others is judged (*by present-day standards*). **2 a** the degree of excellence etc. required for a particular purpose (*not up to standard*). **b** average quality (*of a low standard*). **3** the ordinary procedure, or quality or design of a product, without added or novel features. **4** a distinctive flag, esp. the flag of a cavalry regiment as distinct from the *colours* of an infantry regiment. **5 a** an upright support. **b** an upright water or gas pipe. **6 a** a tree or shrub that stands alone without support. **b** a shrub grafted on an upright stem and trained in tree form (*standard rose*). **7** a document specifying nationally or internationally agreed properties for manufactured goods etc. (*British Standard*). **8** a thing recognized as a model for imitation etc. **9** a tune or song of established popularity. **10 a** a system by which the value of a currency is defined in terms of gold or silver or both. **b** the prescribed proportion of the weight of fine metal in gold or silver coins. **11** a measure for timber, equivalent to 165 cu. ft. (4.7 cubic metres). **12** *Brit. hist.* a grade of classification in elementary schools. —*adj.* **1** serving or used as a standard (*a standard size*). **2** of a normal or prescribed quality or size etc. **3** having recognized and permanent value; authoritative (*the standard book on the subject*). **4** (of language) conforming to established educated usage (*Standard English*). □ **multiple standard** a standard of value obtained by averaging the prices of a number of products. **raise a standard** take up arms; rally support (*raised the standard of revolt*). **standard-bearer 1** a soldier who carries a standard. **2** a prominent leader in a cause. **standard deviation** see DEVIATION. **standard lamp** *Brit.* a lamp set on a tall upright with its base standing on the floor. **standard of living** the degree of material comfort available to a person or class or community. **standard time** a uniform time for places in approximately the same longitude, established in a country or region by law or custom. [ME f. AF *estaundart*, OF *estendart* f. *estendre*, as EXTEND: in senses 5 and 6 of *n.* affected by association with STAND]

Standardbred /ˈstændədˌbred/ *n.* US **1** a horse of a breed able to attain a specified speed, developed esp. for trotting. **2** this breed.

standardize /ˈstændəˌdaɪz/ *v.tr.* (also -ise) **1** cause to conform to a standard. **2** determine the properties of by comparison with a standard. □□ **standardizable** *adj.* **standardization** /-ˈzeɪʃ(ə)n/ *n.* **standardizer** *n.*

standee /stænˈdiː/ *n. colloq.* a person who stands, esp. when all seats are occupied.

standing /ˈstændɪŋ/ *n. & adj.* —*n.* **1** esteem or repute, esp. high; status, position (*people of high standing; is of no standing*). **2** duration (*a dispute of long standing*). **3** length of service, membership, etc. —*adj.* **1** that stands, upright. **2 a** established, permanent (*a standing rule*). **b** not made, raised, etc., for the occasion (*a standing army*). **3** (of a jump, start, race, etc.) performed from rest or from a standing position. **4** (of water) stagnant. **5** (of corn) unreaped. **6** (of a stallion) that stands at stud. **7**

Printing (formerly, of type) not yet distributed after use. □ **all standing 1** *Naut.* without time to lower the sails. **2** taken by surprise. **in good standing** fully paid-up as a member etc. **leave a person standing** make far more rapid progress than he or she. **standing committee** see COMMITTEE. **standing joke** an object of permanent ridicule. **standing order** an instruction to a banker to make regular payments, or to a newsagent etc. for a regular supply of a periodical etc. **standing orders** the rules governing the manner in which all business shall be conducted in a parliament, council, society, etc. **standing ovation** a rousing ovation conferred by an audience risen from their seats. **standing rigging** rigging which is fixed in position. **standing-room** space to stand in. **standing wave** *Physics* the vibration of a system in which some particular points remain fixed while others between them vibrate with the maximum amplitude (cf. *travelling wave*).

standoffish /stændˈɒfɪʃ/ *adj.* cold or distant in manner. □□ **standoffishly** *adv.* **standoffishness** *n.*

standout /ˈstændaʊt/ *n.* US a remarkable person or thing.

standpipe /ˈstændpaɪp/ *n.* a vertical pipe extending from a water supply, esp. one connecting a temporary tap to the mains.

standpoint /ˈstændpɔɪnt/ *n.* **1** the position from which a thing is viewed. **2** a mental attitude.

standstill /ˈstændstɪl/ *n.* a stoppage; an inability to proceed.

stanhope /ˈstænhəʊp/ *n.* a light open carriage for one with two or four wheels. [Fitzroy *Stanhope*, Engl. clergyman d. 1864, for whom the first one was made]

staniel /ˈstænj(ə)l/ *n.* a kestrel. [OE *stāngella* 'stoneyeller' f. *stān* stone + *gellan* yell]

stank past of STINK.

stannary /ˈstænərɪ/ *n.* (*pl.* -ies) *Brit.* **1** a tin-mine. **2** (usu. in *pl.*) a tin-mining district in Cornwall and Devon. □ **stannary court** a legal body for the regulation of tin-miners in the stannaries. [med.L *stannaria* (pl.) f. LL *stannum* tin]

stannic /ˈstænɪk/ *adj. Chem.* of or relating to tetravalent tin (*stannic acid; stannic chloride*). [LL *stannum* tin]

stannous /ˈstænəs/ *adj. Chem.* of or relating to bivalent tin (*stannous salts; stannous chloride*).

stanza /ˈstænzə/ *n.* **1** the basic metrical unit in a poem or verse consisting of a recurring group of lines (often four lines and usu. not more than twelve) which may or may not rhyme. **2** a group of four lines in some Greek and Latin metres. □□ **stanza'd** *adj.* (also **stanzaed**) (also in *comb.*). **stanzaic** /-ˈzeɪɪk/ *adj.* [It., = standing-place, chamber, stanza, ult. f. L *stare* stand]

stapelia /stəˈpiːlɪə/ *n.* any S. African plant of the genus *Stapelia*, with flowers having an unpleasant smell. [mod.L f. J. B. von *Stapel*, Du. botanist d. 1636]

stapes /ˈsteɪpiːz/ *n.* (*pl.* same) a small stirrup-shaped bone in the ear of a mammal. [mod.L f. med.L *stapes* stirrup]

staphylococcus /ˌstæfɪləˈkɒkəs/ *n.* (*pl.* **staphylococci** /-kaɪ/) any bacterium of the genus *Staphylococcus*, occurring in grapelike clusters, and sometimes causing pus formation usu. in the skin and mucous membranes of animals. □□ **staphylococcal** *adj.* [mod.L f. Gk *staphulē* bunch of grapes + *kokkos* berry]

staple¹ /ˈsteɪp(ə)l/ *n. & v.* —*n.* a U-shaped metal bar or piece of wire with pointed ends for driving into, securing, or fastening together various materials or for driving through and clenching papers, netting, electric wire, etc. —*v.tr.* provide or fasten with a staple. □ **staple gun** a hand-held device for driving in staples. □□ **stapler** *n.* [OE *stapol* f. Gmc]

staple² /ˈsteɪp(ə)l/ *n., adj., & v.* —*n.* **1** the principal or an important article of commerce (*the staples of British Industry*). **2** the chief element or a main component, e.g. of a diet. **3** a raw material. **4** the fibre of cotton or wool etc. as determining its quality (*cotton of fine staple*). —*adj.* **1** main or principal (*staple commodities*). **2** important as a product or an export. —*v.tr.* sort or classify (wool etc.) according to fibre. [ME f. OF *estaple* market f. MLG, MDu. *stapel* market (as STAPLE[1])]

star /stɑː(r)/ *n. & v.* —*n.* **1** a celestial body appearing as a luminous point in the night sky. **2** (in full **fixed star**) such a body so far from the earth as to appear motionless (cf. PLANET, COMET). **3** a large naturally luminous gaseous body such as the sun is. **4** a celestial body regarded as influencing a person's fortunes etc. (*born under a lucky star*). **5** a thing resembling a star in shape or appearance. **6** a star-shaped mark, esp. a white mark on a horse's forehead. **7** a figure or object with radiating points esp. as the insignia of an order, as a decoration or mark of rank, or showing a category of excellence (*a five-star hotel; was awarded a gold star*). **8 a** a famous or brilliant person; the principal or most prominent performer in a play, film, etc. (*the star of the show*). **b** (*attrib.*) outstanding; particularly brilliant (*star pupil*). **9** (in full **star connection**) *Electr.* a Y-shaped arrangement of three-phase windings. **10** = *star prisoner*. —*v.* (**starred**, **starring**) **1 a** *tr.* (of a film etc.) feature as a principal performer. **b** *intr.* (of a performer) be featured in a film etc. **2** (esp. as **starred** *adj.*) **a** mark, set, or adorn with a star or stars. **b** put an asterisk or star beside (a name, an item in a list, etc.). □**my stars!** *colloq.* an expression of surprise. **star-apple** an edible purple apple-like fruit (with a starlike cross-section) of a tropical evergreen tree, *Chrysophyllum cainito*. **Star Chamber** *Brit. Law* **1** *hist.* a court of civil and criminal jurisdiction noted for its arbitrary procedure, and abolished in 1640. **2** any arbitrary or oppressive tribunal. **star-crossed** *archaic* ill-fated. **star fruit** = CARAMBOLA. **star-gaze 1** gaze at or study the stars. **2** gaze intently. **star-gazer 1** *colloq.* usu. *derog.* or *joc.* an astronomer or astrologer. **2** *Austral. sl.* a horse that turns its head when galloping. **star of Bethlehem** any of various plants with starlike flowers esp. *Ornithogalum umbellatum* with white star-shaped flowers striped with green on the outside (see Matt. 2:9). **Star of David** a figure consisting of two interlaced equilateral triangles used as a Jewish and Israeli symbol. **star prisoner** *Brit. sl.* a convict serving a first prison sentence. **star route** *US* a postal delivery route served by private contractors. **Stars and Bars** the flag of the Confederate States of the US. **Stars and Stripes** the national flag of the US. **star sapphire** a cabochon sapphire reflecting a star-like image due to its regular internal structure. **star shell** an explosive projectile designed to burst in the air and light up the enemy's position. **star-spangled** (esp. of the US national flag) covered or glittering with stars. **star stream** a systematic drift of stars. **star-studded** containing or covered with many stars, esp. featuring many famous performers. **star turn** the principal item in an entertainment or performance. **Star Wars** *colloq.* the strategic defence initiative. □□ **stardom** *n.* **starless** *adj.* **starlike** *adj.* [OE *steorra* f. Gmc]

starboard /ˈstɑːbəd/ *n. & v. Naut. & Aeron.* —*n.* the right-hand side (looking forward) of a ship, boat, or aircraft (cf. PORT[3]). —*v.tr.* (also *absol.*) turn (the helm) to starboard. □**starboard tack** see TACK[1] 4. **starboard watch** see WATCH *n.* 3b. [OE *stēorbord* = rudder side (see STEER, BOARD), early Teutonic ships being steered with a paddle over the right side]

starch /stɑːtʃ/ *n. & v.* —*n.* **1** an odourless tasteless polysaccharide occurring widely in plants and obtained chiefly from cereals and potatoes, forming an important constituent of the human diet. **2** a preparation of this for stiffening fabric before ironing. **3** stiffness of manner; formality. —*v.tr.* stiffen (clothing) with starch. □**starch-reduced** (esp. of food) containing less than the normal proportion of

starch. □□ **starcher** *n.* [earlier as verb: ME *sterche* f. OE *stercan* (unrecorded) stiffen f. Gmc: cf. STARK]

starchy /ˈstɑːtʃɪ/ *adj.* (**starchier**, **starchiest**) **1 a** of or like starch. **b** containing much starch. **2** (of a person) precise, prim. □□**starchily** *adv.* **starchiness** *n.*

stardust /ˈstɑːdʌst/ *n.* **1** a twinkling mass. **2** a romantic mystical look or sensation. **3** a multitude of stars looking like dust.

stare /steə(r)/ *v. & n.* —*v.* **1** *intr.* (usu. foll. by *at*) look fixedly with eyes open, esp. as the result of curiosity, surprise, bewilderment, admiration, horror, etc. (*sat staring at the door; stared in amazement*). **2** *intr.* (of eyes) be wide open and fixed. **3** *intr.* be unpleasantly prominent or striking. **4** *tr.* (foll. by *into*) reduce (a person) to a specified condition by staring (*stared me into silence*). —*n.* a staring gaze. □**stare down** (or **out**) outstare. **stare a person in the face** be evident or imminent. □□ **starer** *n.* [OE *starian* f. Gmc]

starfish /ˈstɑːfɪʃ/ *n.* an echinoderm of the class Asteroidea with five or more radiating arms.

stark /stɑːk/ *adj. & adv.* —*adj.* **1** desolate, bare (*a stark landscape*). **2** sharply evident (*in stark contrast*). **3** downright, sheer (*stark madness*). **4** completely naked. **5** *archaic* strong, stiff, rigid. —*adv.* completely, wholly (*stark mad; stark naked*). □□ **starkly** *adv.* **starkness** *n.* [OE *stearc* f. Gmc: stark naked f. earlier *start-naked* f. obs. *start* tail: cf. REDSTART]

Stark effect /stɑːk/ *n. Physics* the splitting of a spectrum line into several components by the application of an electric field. [J. *Stark*, Ger. physicist d. 1957]

starkers /ˈstɑːkəz/ *adj. Brit. sl.* stark naked.

starlet /ˈstɑːlɪt/ *n.* **1** a promising young performer, esp. a woman. **2** a little star.

starlight /ˈstɑːlaɪt/ *n.* **1** the light of the stars (*walked home by starlight*). **2** (*attrib.*) = STARLIT (*a starlight night*).

starling[1] /ˈstɑːlɪŋ/ *n.* **1** a small gregarious partly migratory bird, *Sturnus vulgaris*, with blackish-brown speckled lustrous plumage, chiefly inhabiting cultivated areas. **2** any similar bird of the family Sturnidae. [OE *stærlinc* f. *stær* starling f. Gmc: cf. -LING[1]]

starling[2] /ˈstɑːlɪŋ/ *n.* piles built around or upstream of a bridge or pier to protect it from floating rubbish etc. [perh. corrupt. of (now dial.) *staddling* STADDLE]

starlit /ˈstɑːlɪt/ *adj.* **1** lighted by stars. **2** with stars visible.

starry /ˈstɑːrɪ/ *adj.* (**starrier**, **starriest**) **1** covered with stars. **2** resembling a star. □**starry-eyed** *colloq.* **1** visionary; enthusiastic but impractical. **2** euphoric. □□ **starrily** *adv.* **starriness** *n.*

START /stɑːt/ *abbr.* Strategic Arms Reduction Treaty (or Talks).

start /stɑːt/ *v. & n.* —*v.* **1** *tr. & intr.* begin; commence (*started work; started crying; started to shout; the play starts at eight*). **2** *tr.* set (proceedings, an event, etc.) in motion (*start the meeting; started a fire*). **3** *intr.* (often foll. by *on*) make a beginning (*started on a new project*). **4** *intr.* (often foll. by *after, for*) set oneself in motion or action ('*wait!*' *he shouted, and started after her*). **5** *intr.* set out; begin a journey etc. (*we start at 6 a.m.*). **6** (often foll. by *up*) **a** *intr.* (of a machine) begin operating (*the car wouldn't start*). **b** *tr.* cause (a machine etc.) to begin operating (*tried to start the engine*). **7** *tr.* a cause or enable (a person) to make a beginning (with something) (*started me in business with £10,000*). **b** (foll. by pres. part.) cause (a person) to begin (doing something) (*the smoke started me coughing*). **c** *Brit. colloq.* complain or be critical (*don't you start*). **8** *tr.* (often foll. by *up*) found or establish; originate. **9** *intr.* (foll. by *at, with*) have as the first of a series of items, e.g. in a meal (*we started with soup*). **10** *tr.* give a signal to (competitors) to start in a race. **11** *intr.* (often foll. by *up, from*, etc.)

make a sudden movement from surprise, pain, etc. (*started at the sound of my voice*). **12** *intr.* (foll. by *out*, *up*, *from*, etc.) spring out, up, etc. (*started up from the chair*). **13** *tr.* conceive (a baby). **14** *tr.* rouse (game etc.) from its lair. **15 a** *intr.* (of timbers etc.) spring from their proper position; give way. **b** *tr.* cause or experience (timbers etc.) to do this. **16** *intr.* (foll. by *out*, *to*, etc.) (of a thing) move or appear suddenly (*tears started to his eyes*). **17** *intr.* (foll. by *from*) (of eyes, usu. with exaggeration) burst forward (from their sockets etc.). **18** *tr.* pour out (liquor) from a cask. —*n.* **1** a beginning of an event, action, journey, etc. (*missed the start*; *an early start to-morrow*; *made a fresh start*). **2** the place from which a race etc. begins. **3** an advantage given at the beginning of a race etc. (*a 15-second start*). **4** an advantageous initial position in life, business, etc. (*a good start in life*). **5** a sudden movement of surprise, pain, etc. (*you gave me a start*). **6** an intermittent or spasmodic effort or movement (esp. *in* or *by fits and starts*). **7** *colloq.* a surprising occurrence (*a queer start*; *a rum start*). □**for a start** *colloq.* as a beginning; in the first place. **get the start of** gain an advantage over. **start a hare** see HARE. **start in** *colloq.* **1** begin. **2** (foll. by *on*) *US* make a beginning on. **start off 1** begin; commence (*started off on a lengthy monologue*). **2** begin to move (*it's time we started off*). **start out 1** begin a journey. **2** *colloq.* (foll. by *to* + infin.) proceed as intending (to do something). **start over** *US* begin again. **start school** attend school for the first time. **start something** *colloq.* cause trouble. **start up** arise; occur. **to start with 1** in the first place; before anything else is considered (*should never have been there to start with*). **2** at the beginning (*had six members to start with*). [OE (orig. in sense 11) f. Gmc]

starter /'sta:tə(r)/ *n.* **1** a person or thing that starts. **2** an esp. automatic device for starting the engine of a motor vehicle etc. **3** a person giving the signal for the start of a race. **4** a horse or competitor starting in a race (*a list of probable starters*). **5** the first course of a meal. **6** the initial action etc. □**for starters** *sl.* to start with. **under starter's orders** (of racehorses etc.) in a position to start a race and awaiting the starting-signal.

starting /'sta:tɪŋ/ *n.* in senses of START *v.* □**starting-block** a shaped rigid block for bracing the feet of a runner at the start of a race. **starting-gate** a movable barrier for securing a fair start in horse-races. **starting-handle** *Brit. Mech.* a crank for starting a motor engine. **starting pistol** a pistol used to give the signal for the start of a race. **starting-point** the point from which a journey, process, argument, etc. begins. **starting post** the post from which competitors start in a race. **starting price** the odds ruling at the start of a horse-race. **starting stall** a compartment for one horse at the start of a race.

startle /'sta:t(ə)l/ *v.tr.* give a shock or surprise to; cause (a person etc.) to start with surprise or sudden alarm. □□ **startler** *n.* [OE *steartlian* (as START, -LE⁴)]

startling /'sta:tlɪŋ/ *adj.* **1** surprising. **2** alarming (*startling news*). □□ **startlingly** *adv.*

starve /sta:v/ *v.* **1** *intr.* die of hunger; suffer from malnutrition. **2** *tr.* cause to die of hunger or suffer from lack of food. **3** *intr.* suffer from extreme poverty. **4** *intr. colloq.* feel very hungry (*I'm starving*). **5** *intr.* **a** suffer from mental or spiritual want. **b** (foll. by *for*) feel a strong craving for (sympathy, amusement, knowledge, etc.). **6** *tr.* **a** (foll. by *of*) deprive of; keep scantily supplied with (*starved of affection*). **b** cause to suffer from mental or spiritual want. **7** *tr.* **a** (foll. by *into*) compel by starving (*starved into submission*). **b** (foll. by *out*) compel to surrender etc. by starving (*starved them out*). **8** *intr. archaic* or *dial.* perish with or suffer from cold. □□ **starvation** /-'veɪʃ(ə)n/ *n.* [OE *steorfan* die]

starveling /'sta:vlɪŋ/ *n.* & *adj. archaic* —*n.* a starving or ill-fed person or animal. —*adj.* **1** starving. **2** meagre.

starwort /'sta:wɜ:t/ *n.* a plant of the genus *Stellaria* with star-like flowers.

stash /stæʃ/ *v.* & *n. colloq.* —*v.tr.* (often foll. by *away*) **1** conceal; put in a safe or hidden place. **2** hoard, stow, store. —*n.* **1** a hiding-place or hide-out. **2** a thing hidden; a cache. [18th c.: orig. unkn.]

stasis /'steɪsɪs, 'stæsɪs/ *n.* (*pl.* **stases** /-si:z/) **1** inactivity; stagnation; a state of equilibrium. **2** a stoppage of circulation of any of the body fluids. [mod.L f. Gk f. *sta-* STAND]

-stasis /'stæsɪs, 'steɪsɪs/ *comb. form* (*pl.* **-stases** /-si:z/) *Physiol.* forming nouns denoting a slowing or stopping (*haemostasis*). □□ **-static** *comb. form* forming adjectives.

-stat /stæt/ *comb. form* forming nouns with ref. to keeping fixed or stationary (*rheostat*). [Gk *statos* stationary]

state /steɪt/ *n.* & *v.* —*n.* **1** the existing condition or position of a person or thing (*in a bad state of repair*; *in a precarious state of health*). **2** *colloq.* **a** an excited, anxious, or agitated mental condition (esp. *in a state*). **b** an untidy condition. **3** (usu. **State**) **a** an organized political community under one government; a commonwealth; a nation. **b** such a community forming part of a federal republic, esp. the United States of America. **4** (usu. **State**) (*attrib.*) **a** of, for, or concerned with the State (*State documents*). **b** reserved for or done on occasions of ceremony (*State apartments*; *State visit*). **c** involving ceremony (*State opening of Parliament*). **5** (usu. **State**) civil government (*Church and State*; *Secretary of State*). **6** pomp, rank, dignity (*as befits their state*). **7** (**the States**) the legislative body in Jersey, Guernsey, and Alderney. **8** *Bibliog.* one of two or more variant forms of a single edition of a book. **9 a** an etched or engraved plate at a particular stage of its progress. **b** an impression taken from this. —*v.tr.* **1** express, esp. fully or clearly, in speech or writing (*have stated my opinion*; *must state full particulars*). **2** fix, specify (*at stated intervals*). **3** *Law* specify the facts of (a case) for consideration. **4** *Mus.* play (a theme etc.) so as to make it known to the listener. □**in state** with all due ceremony. **of State** concerning politics or government. **State capitalism** a system of State control and use of capital. **State Department** (in the US) the department of foreign affairs. **State-house** *US* the building where the legislature of a State meets. **State house** *NZ* a private house built at the government's expense. **state of the art 1** the current stage of development of a practical or technological subject. **2** (usu. **state-of-the-art**) (*attrib.*) using the latest techniques or equipment (*state-of-the-art weaponry*). **state of grace** the condition of being free from grave sin. **state of life** rank and occupation. **state of things** (or **affairs** or **play**) the circumstances; the current situation. **state of war** the situation when war has been declared or is in progress. **State prisoner** see PRISONER. **State school** a school managed and funded by the public authorities. **State's evidence** see EVIDENCE. **States General** *hist.* the legislative body in the Netherlands, and in France before 1789. **State socialism** a system of State control of industries and services. **States' rights** *US* the rights and powers not assumed by the United States but reserved to its individual States. **State trial** prosecution by the State. **State university** *US* a university managed by the public authorities of a State. □□ **statable** *adj.* **statedly** *adv.* **statehood** *n.* [ME: partly f. ESTATE, partly f. L STATUS]

statecraft /'steɪtkrɑ:ft/ *n.* the art of conducting affairs of state.

stateless /'steɪtlɪs/ *adj.* **1** (of a person) having no nationality or citizenship. **2** without a State. □□ **statelessness** *n.*

stately /'steɪtlɪ/ *adj.* (**statelier**, **stateliest**) dignified;

imposing; grand. □**stately home** *Brit.* a large magnificent house, esp. one open to the public. □□ **stateliness** *n.*

statement /'steɪtmənt/ *n.* **1** the act or an instance of stating or being stated; expression in words. **2** a thing stated; a declaration (*that statement is unfounded*). **3** a formal account of facts, esp. to the police or in a court of law (*make a statement*). **4** a record of transactions in a bank account etc. **5** a formal notification of the amount due to a tradesman etc.

stater /'steɪtə(r)/ *n.* an ancient Greek gold or silver coin. [ME f. LL f. Gk *statēr*]

stateroom /'steɪtruːm, -rʊm/ *n.* **1** a state apartment in a palace, hotel, etc. **2** a private compartment in a passenger ship or *US* train.

Stateside /'steɪtsaɪd/ *adj. US colloq.* of, in, or towards the United States.

statesman /'steɪtsmən/ *n.* (*pl.* **-men**; *fem.* **stateswoman**, *pl.* **-women**) **1** a person skilled in affairs of State, esp. one taking an active part in politics. **2** a distinguished and capable politician. □□ **statesmanlike** *adj.* **statesmanly** *adj.* **statesmanship** *n.* [= *state's man* after F *homme d'état*]

statewide /'steɪtwaɪd/ *adj. US* so as to include or cover a whole State.

static /'stætɪk/ *adj. & n.* —*adj.* **1** stationary; not acting or changing; passive. **2** *Physics* **a** concerned with bodies at rest or forces in equilibrium (opp. DYNAMIC). **b** acting as weight but not moving (*static pressure*). **c** of statics. —*n.* **1** static electricity. **2** atmospherics. □**static electricity** electricity not flowing as a current. **static line** a length of cord attached to an aircraft etc. which releases a parachute without the use of a ripcord. [mod.L *staticus* f. Gk *statikos* f. *sta-* stand]

statical /'stætɪk(ə)l/ *adj.* = STATIC. □□ **statically** *adv.*

statice /'statɪsɪ/ *n.* **1** sea lavender. **2** sea pink. [L f. Gk, fem. of *statikos* STATIC (with ref. to stanching of blood)]

statics /'stætɪks/ *n.pl.* (usu. treated as *sing.*) **1** the science of bodies at rest or of forces in equilibrium (opp. DYNAMICS). **2** = STATIC. [STATIC *n.* in the same senses + -ICS]

station /'steɪʃ(ə)n/ *n. & v.* —*n.* **1 a** a regular stopping place on a railway line, with a platform and usu. administrative buildings. **b** these buildings (see also *bus station*, *coach station*). **2** a place or building etc. where a person or thing stands or is placed, esp. habitually or for a definite purpose. **3 a** a designated point or establishment where a particular service or activity is based or organized (*police station*; *polling station*). **b** *US* a subsidiary post office. **4** an establishment involved in radio or television broadcasting. **5 a** a military or naval base esp. *hist.* in India. **b** the inhabitants of this. **6** position in life; rank or status (*ideas above your station*). **7** *Austral. & NZ* a large sheep or cattle farm. **8** *Bot.* a particular place where an unusual species etc. grows. —*v.tr.* **1** assign a station to. **2** put in position. □**station-bill** *Naut.* a list showing the prescribed stations of a ship's crew for various drills or in an emergency. **station break** *US* a pause between broadcast programmes for an announcement of the identity of the station transmitting them. **station hand** *Austral.* a worker on a large sheep or cattle farm. **station house** *US* a police station. **station-keeping** the maintenance of one's proper relative position in a moving body of ships etc. **station of the cross** *RC Ch.* **a** each of a series of usu. 14 images or pictures representing the events in Christ's passion before which devotions are performed in some churches. **b** each of these devotions. **station pointer** *Naut.* a ship's navigational instrument, often a three-armed protractor, for fixing one's place on a chart from the angle in the horizontal plane between two land- or sea-marks. **station sergeant** *Brit.* the sergeant in charge of a police station. **station-wagon** an estate car. [ME, = standing, f. OF f. L *statio -onis* f. *stare* stand]

stationary /'steɪʃənərɪ/ *adj.* **1** remaining in one place, not moving (*hit a stationary car*). **2** not meant to be moved; not portable (*stationary troops*; *stationary engine*). **3** not changing in magnitude, number, quality, efficiency, etc. (*stationary temperature*). **4** (of a planet) having no apparent motion in longitude. □**stationary air** air remaining in the lungs during ordinary respiration. **stationary bicycle** a fixed exercise-machine resembling a bicycle. **stationary point** *Math.* a point on a curve where the gradient is zero. **stationary wave** = *standing wave.* □□ **stationariness** *n.* [ME f. L *stationarius* (as STATION)]

stationer /'steɪʃənə(r)/ *n.* a person who sells writing materials etc. □**Stationers' Hall** *Brit.* the hall of the Stationers' Company in London, at which a book was formerly registered for purposes of copyright. [ME, = bookseller (as STATIONARY in med.L sense 'shopkeeper', esp. bookseller, as opposed to pedlar)]

stationery /'steɪʃənərɪ/ *n.* writing materials etc. sold by a stationer. □**Stationery Office** (in the UK) the Government's publishing house which also provides stationery for Government offices.

stationmaster /'steɪʃ(ə)n,mɑːstə(r)/ *n.* the official in charge of a railway station.

statism /'steɪtɪz(ə)m/ *n.* centralized State administration and control of social and economic affairs.

statist /'steɪtɪst, 'stætɪst/ *n.* **1** a statistician. **2** a supporter of statism. [orig. 'politician' f. It. *statista* (as STATE)]

statistic /stə'tɪstɪk/ *n. & adj.* —*n.* a statistical fact or item. —*adj.* = STATISTICAL. [G *statistisch*, *Statistik* f. *Statist* (as STATIST)]

statistical /stə'tɪstɪk(ə)l/ *adj.* of or relating to statistics. □**statistical physics** physics as it is concerned with large numbers of particles to which statistics can be applied. **statistical significance** = SIGNIFICANCE 4. □□ **statistically** *adv.*

statistics /stə'tɪstɪks/ *n.pl.* (usu. treated as *sing.*) **1** the science of collecting and analysing numerical data, esp. in or for large quantities, and usu. inferring proportions in a whole from proportions in a representative sample. **2** any systematic collection or presentation of such facts. □□ **statistician** /,stætɪ'stɪʃ(ə)n/ *n.*

stator /'steɪtə(r)/ *n. Electr.* the stationary part of a machine, esp. of an electric motor or generator. [STATIONARY, after ROTOR]

statoscope /'stætə,skəʊp/ *n.* an aneroid barometer used to show minute variations of pressure, esp. to indicate the altitude of an aircraft. [Gk *statos* fixed f. *sta-* stand + -SCOPE]

statuary /'stætjʊərɪ/ *adj. & n.* —*adj.* of or for statues (*statuary art*). —*n.* (*pl.* -ies) **1** statues collectively. **2** the art of making statues. **3** a sculptor. □**statuary marble** fine-grained white marble. [L *statuarius* (as STATUE)]

statue /'stætjuː, 'stætʃuː/ *n.* a sculptured, cast, carved, or moulded figure of a person or animal, esp. life-size or larger (cf. STATUETTE). □□ **statued** *adj.* [ME f. OF f. L *statua* f. *stare* stand]

statuesque /,stætjʊ'esk, ,stætʃʊ'esk/ *adj.* like, or having the dignity or beauty of a statue. □□ **statuesquely** *adv.* **statuesqueness** *n.* [STATUE + -ESQUE, after *picturesque*]

statuette /,stætjʊ'et, ,stætʃʊ'et/ *n.* a small statue; a statue less than life-size. [F, dimin. of *statue*]

stature /'stætʃə(r)/ *n.* **1** the height of a (esp. human) body. **2** a degree of eminence, social standing, or advancement (*recruit someone of his stature*). □□ **statured** *adj.* (also in *comb.*). [ME f. OF f. L *statura* f. *stare stat-* stand]

status /'steɪtəs/ *n.* **1** rank, social position, relation to others, relative importance (*not sure of their status in the hierarchy*). **2** a superior social etc. position (*considering your status in the business*). **3** *Law* a person's legal standing which determines his or her rights and duties, e.g. citizen, alien, commoner, civilian, etc. **4** the position of affairs (*let me know if the status changes*). □**status symbol** a possession etc. taken to indicate a person's high status. [L, = standing f. *stare* stand]

status quo /ˌsteɪtəs ˈkwəʊ/ *n.* the existing state of affairs. [L, = the state in which]

statutable /ˈstætjʊtəb(ə)l/ *adj.* = STATUTORY, esp. in amount or value. □□ **statutably** *adv.*

statute /ˈstætjuːt/ *n.* **1** a written law passed by a legislative body, e.g. an Act of Parliament. **2** a rule of a corporation, founder, etc., intended to be permanent (*against the University Statutes*). **3** divine law (*kept thy statutes*). □**statute-barred** (of a case etc.) no longer legally enforceable by reason of the lapse of time. **statute-book 1** a book or books containing the statute law. **2** the body of a country's statutes. **statute law 1** (*collect.*) the body of principles and rules of law laid down in statutes as distinct from rules formulated in practical application (cf. *common law, case-law* (see CASE[1])). **2** a statute. **statute mile** see MILE 1. **statute-roll 1** the rolls in the Public Records Office containing the statutes of the Parliament of England. **2** = *statute-book*. **statutes at large** the statutes as originally enacted, regardless of later modifications. [ME f. OF *statut* f. LL *statutum* neut. past part. of L *statuere* set up f. *status*: see STATUS]

statutory /ˈstatjʊtərɪ/ *adj.* required, permitted, or enacted by statute (*statutory minimum*; *statutory provisions*). □**statutory rape** *US* the act of sexual intercourse with a minor. □□ **statutorily** *adv.*

staunch[1] /stɔːntʃ, stɑːntʃ/ *adj.* (also **stanch**) **1** trustworthy, loyal (*my staunch friend and supporter*). **2** (of a ship, joint, etc.) strong, watertight, airtight, etc. □□ **staunchly** *adv.* **staunchness** *n.* [ME f. OF *estanche* fem. of *estanc* f. Rmc: see STANCH[1]]

staunch[2] var. of STANCH[1].

stave /steɪv/ *n. & v.* —*n.* **1** each of the curved pieces of wood forming the sides of a cask, pail, etc. **2** = STAFF[1] *n.* 3. **3** a stanza or verse. **4** the rung of a ladder. —*v.tr.* (*past* and *past part.* **stove** /stəʊv/ or **staved**) **1** break a hole in. **2** crush or knock out of shape. **3** fit or furnish (a cask etc.) with staves. □**stave in** crush by forcing inwards. **stave off** avert or defer (danger or misfortune). **stave rhyme** alliteration, esp. in old Germanic poetry. [ME, backform. f. *staves*, pl. of STAFF[1]]

staves pl. of STAFF[1] *n.* 3.

stavesacre /ˈsteɪvzˌeɪkə(r)/ *n.* a larkspur, *Delphinium staphisagria*, yielding seeds used as poison for vermin. [ME f. L *staphisagria* f. Gk *staphis agria* wild raisin]

stay[1] /steɪ/ *v. & n.* —*v.* **1** *intr.* continue to be in the same place or condition; not depart or change (*stay here until I come back*). **2** *intr.* **a** (often foll. by *at, in, with*) have temporary residence as a visitor etc. (*stayed with them for Christmas*). **b** *Sc. & S.Afr.* dwell permanently. **3** *archaic* or *literary* **a** *tr.* stop or check (progress, the inroads of a disease, etc.). **b** *intr.* (esp. in *imper.*) pause in movement, action, speech, etc. (*Stay! You forget one thing*). **4** *tr.* postpone (judgement, decision, etc.). **5** *tr.* assuage (hunger etc.) esp. for a short time. **6 a** *intr.* show endurance. **b** *tr.* show endurance to the end of (a race etc.). **7** *tr.* (often foll. by *up*) *literary* support, prop up (as or with a buttress etc.). **8** *intr.* (foll. by *for, to*) wait long enough to share or join in an activity etc. (*stay to supper*; *stay for the film*). —*n.* **1 a** the act or an instance of staying or dwelling in one place. **b** the duration of this (*just a ten-minute stay*; *a long stay in London*). **2** a suspension or postponement of a sentence, judgement, etc. (*was granted a stay of execution*). **3** *archaic* or *literary* a check or restraint (*will endure no stay*; *a stay upon his activity*). **4** endurance, staying power. **5** a prop or support. **6** (in

pl.) *hist.* a corset esp. with whalebone etc. stiffening, and laced. □**has come** (or **is here**) **to stay** *colloq.* must be regarded as permanent. **stay-at-home** *adj.* remaining habitually at home. —*n.* a person who does this. **stay-bar** (or **-rod**) a support used in building or in machinery. **stay the course** pursue a course of action or endure a struggle etc. to the end. **stay one's hand** see HAND. **stay in** remain indoors or at home, esp. in school after hours as a punishment. **staying power** endurance, stamina. **stay-in strike** = *sit-down strike*. **stay the night** remain until the next day. **stay put** *colloq.* remain where it is placed or where one is. **stay up** not go to bed (until late at night). □□ **stayer** *n.* [AF *estai-* stem of OF *ester* f. L *stare* stand: sense 5 f. OF *estaye(r)* prop, formed as STAY[2]]

stay[2] /steɪ/ *n. & v.* —*n.* **1** *Naut.* a rope or guy supporting a mast, spar, flagstaff, etc. **2** a tie-piece in an aircraft etc. —*v.tr.* **1** support (a mast etc.) by stays. **2** put (a ship) on another tack. □**be in stays** (of a sailing ship) be head to the wind while tacking. **miss stays** fail to be in stays. [OE *stæg* be firm, f. Gmc]

staysail /ˈsteɪseɪl, ˈsteɪs(ə)l/ *n.* a triangular fore-and-aft sail extended on a stay.

STD *abbr.* **1** subscriber trunk dialling. **2** Doctor of Sacred Theology. [sense 2 f. L *Sanctae Theologiae Doctor*]

stead /sted/ *n.* □**in a person's** or **thing's stead** as a substitute; instead of him or her or it. **stand a person in good stead** be advantageous or serviceable to him or her. [OE *stede* f. Gmc]

steadfast /ˈstedfɑːst, ˈstedfəst/ *adj.* constant, firm, unwavering. □□ **steadfastly** *adv.* **steadfastness** *n.* [OE *stedefæst* (as STEAD, FAST[1])]

steading /ˈstedɪŋ/ *n.* *Brit.* a farmstead.

steady /ˈstedɪ/ *adj., v., adv., int., & n.* —*adj.* (**steadier, steadiest**) **1** firmly fixed or supported or standing or balanced; not tottering, rocking, or wavering. **2** done or operating or happening in a uniform and regular manner (*a steady pace*; *a steady increase*). **3 a** constant in mind or conduct; not changeable. **b** persistent. **4** (of a person) serious and dependable in behaviour; of industrious and temperate habits; safe; cautious. **5** regular, established (*a steady girlfriend*). **6** accurately directed; not faltering (*a steady hand*; *a steady eye*). **7** (of a ship) on course and upright. —*v.tr. & intr.* (**-ies, -ied**) make or become steady (*steady the boat*). —*adv.* steadily (*hold it steady*). —*int.* as a command or warning to take care. —*n.* (*pl.* **-ies**) *colloq.* a regular boyfriend or girlfriend. □**go steady** (often foll. by *with*) *colloq.* have as a regular boyfriend or girlfriend. **steady down** become steady. **steady-going** staid; sober. **steady on!** a call to take care. **steady state** an unvarying condition, esp. in a physical process, e.g. of the universe having no beginning and no end. □□ **steadier** *n.* **steadily** *adv.* **steadiness** *n.* [STEAD = place, + -Y[1]]

steak /steɪk/ *n.* **1** a thick slice of meat (esp. beef) or fish, often cut for grilling, frying, etc. **2** beef cut for stewing or braising. □**steak-house** a restaurant specializing in serving beefsteaks. **steak-knife** a knife with a serrated steel blade for eating steak. [ME f. ON *steik* rel. to *steikja* roast on spit, *stikna* be roasted]

steal /stiːl/ *v. & n.* —*v.* (*past* **stole** /stəʊl/; *past part.* **stolen** /ˈstəʊlən/) **1** *tr.* (also *absol.*) **a** take (another person's property) illegally. **b** take (property etc.) without right or permission, esp. in secret with the intention of not returning it. **2** *tr.* obtain surreptitiously or by surprise (*stole a kiss*). **3** *tr.* **a** gain insidiously or artfully. **b** (often foll. by *away*) win or get possession of (a person's affections etc.), esp. insidiously (*stole her heart away*). **4** *intr.* (foll. by *in, out, away, up, etc.*) **a** move, esp. silently or stealthily (*stole out of the room*). **b** (of a sound etc.) become gradually perceptible. **5** *tr.* **a** (in various sports) gain (a run, the ball, etc.) surreptitiously or by luck. **b** *Baseball* reach (a base) by deceiving the fielders. —*n.* **1** *US colloq.* the act or an instance of stealing or theft. **2** *colloq.* an unexpectedly easy task or good bargain. □**steal a march on** get an advantage over by surreptitious means; anticipate. **steal the show** outshine other performers, esp. unexpectedly. **steal a person's thunder** use another person's words, ideas, etc., without permission and without giving credit. □□**stealer** *n.* (also in *comb.*). [OE *stelan* f. Gmc]

stealth /stelθ/ *n.* secrecy, a secret procedure. □**by stealth** surreptitiously. [ME f. OE (as STEAL, -TH²)]

stealthy /'stelθɪ/ *adj.* (**stealthier, stealthiest**) **1** (of an action) done with stealth; proceeding imperceptibly. **2** (of a person or thing) moving with stealth. □□**stealthily** *adv.* **stealthiness** *n.*

steam /stiːm/ *n.* & *v.* —*n.* **1 a** the gas into which water is changed by boiling, used as a source of power by virtue of its expansion of volume. **b** a mist of liquid particles of water produced by the condensation of this gas. **2** any similar vapour. **3 a** energy or power provided by a steam engine or other machine. **b** *colloq.* power or energy generally. —*v.* **1** *tr.* **a** cook (food) in steam. **b** soften or make pliable (timber etc.) or otherwise treat with steam. **2** *intr.* give off steam or other vapour, esp. visibly. **3** *intr.* **a** move under steam power (*the ship steamed down the river*). **b** (foll. by *ahead, away*, etc.) *colloq.* proceed or travel fast or with vigour. **4** *tr.* & *intr.* (usu. foll. by *up*) **a** cover or become covered with condensed steam. **b** (as **steamed up** *adj.*) *colloq.* angry or excited. **5** *tr.* (foll. by *open* etc.) apply steam to the gum of (a sealed envelope) to get it open. □**get up steam** **1** generate enough power to work a steam engine. **2** work oneself into an energetic or angry state. **let off steam** relieve one's pent up feelings or energy. **run out of steam** lose one's impetus or energy. **steam age** the era when trains were drawn by steam locomotives. **steam bath** a room etc. filled with steam for bathing in. **steam boiler** a vessel (in a steam engine etc.) in which water is boiled to generate steam. **steam engine 1** an engine which uses the expansion or rapid condensation of steam to generate power. **2** a locomotive powered by this. **steam gauge** a pressure gauge attached to a steam boiler. **steam hammer** a forging-hammer powered by steam. **steam-heat** the warmth given out by steam-heated radiators etc. **steam iron** an electric iron that emits steam from its flat surface, to improve its pressing action. **steam-jacket** a casing for steam round a cylinder, for heating its contents. **steam organ** a fairground pipe-organ driven by a steam engine and played by means of a keyboard or a system of punched cards. **steam power** the force of steam applied to machinery etc. **steam shovel** an excavator powered by steam. **steam-tight** impervious to steam. **steam train** a train driven by a steam engine. **steam tug** a steamer for towing ships etc. **steam turbine** a turbine in which a high-velocity jet of steam rotates a bladed disc or drum. **under one's own steam** without assistance; unaided. [OE *stēam* f. Gmc]

steamboat /'stiːmbəʊt/ *n.* a boat propelled by a steam engine.

steamer /'stiːmə(r)/ *n.* **1** a person or thing that steams. **2** a vessel propelled by steam, esp. a ship. **3** a vessel in which things are steamed, esp. cooked by steam. □**steamer rug** *US* a travelling-rug.

steamroller /'stiːmˌrəʊlə(r)/ *n.* & *v.* —*n.* **1** a heavy slow-moving vehicle with a roller, used to flatten new-made roads. **2** a crushing power or force. —*v.tr.* **1** crush forcibly or indiscriminately. **2** (foll. by *through*) force (a measure etc.) through a legislature by overriding opposition.

steamship /'stiːmʃɪp/ *n.* a ship propelled by a steam engine.

steamy /'stiːmɪ/ *adj.* (**steamier, steamiest**) **1** like

or full of steam. **2** *colloq.* erotic, salacious. □□**steamily** *adv.* **steaminess** *n.*

stearic /'stɪərɪk/ *adj.* derived from stearin. □**stearic acid** a solid saturated fatty acid obtained from animal or vegetable fats. □□**stearate** /-ˌreɪt/ *n.* [F *stéarique* f. Gk *stear steatos* tallow]

stearin /'stɪərɪn/ *n.* **1** a glyceryl ester of stearic acid, esp. in the form of a white crystalline constituent of tallow etc. **2** a mixture of fatty acids used in candle-making. [F *stéarine* f. Gk *stear steatos* tallow]

steatite /'stɪətaɪt/ *n.* a soapstone or other impure form of talc. □□**steatitic** /-'tɪtɪk/ *adj.* [L *steatitis* f. Gk *steatītēs* f. *stear steatos* tallow]

steatopygia /ˌstɪətəʊ'pɪdʒɪə/ *n.* an excess of fat on the buttocks. □□**steatopygous** /-'paɪɡəs, -'tɒpɪɡəs/ *adj.* [mod.L (as STEATITE + Gk *pugē* rump)]

steed /stiːd/ *n.* *archaic* or *poet.* a horse, esp. a fast powerful one. [OE *stēda* stallion, rel. to STUD²]

steel /stiːl/ *n., adj.,* & *v.* —*n.* **1** any of various alloys of iron and carbon with other elements increasing strength and malleability, much used for making tools, weapons, etc., and capable of being tempered to many different degrees of hardness. **2** hardness of character; strength, firmness (*nerves of steel*). **3 a a** rod of steel, usu. roughened and tapering, on which knives are sharpened. **b** a strip of steel for expanding a skirt or stiffening a corset. **4** (not in *pl.*) *literary* a sword, lance, etc. (*foemen worthy of their steel*). —*adj.* **1** made of steel. **2** like or having the characteristics of steel. —*v.tr.* & *refl.* harden or make resolute (*steeled myself for a shock*). □**cold steel** cutting or thrusting weapons. **pressed steel** steel moulded under pressure. **steel band** a group of usu. W. Indian musicians with percussion instruments made from oil drums. **steel-clad** wearing armour. **steel engraving** the process of engraving on or an impression taken from a steel-coated copper plate. **steel wool** an abrasive substance consisting of a mass of fine steel shavings. [OE *style, stēli* f. Gmc, rel. to STAY²]

steelhead /'stiːlhed/ *n.* a large N. American rainbow trout.

steelwork /'stiːlwɜːk/ *n.* articles of steel.

steelworks /'stiːlwɜːks/ *n.pl.* (usu. treated as *sing.*) a place where steel is manufactured. □□**steelworker** *n.*

steely /'stiːlɪ/ *adj.* (**steelier, steeliest**) **1** of, or hard as, steel. **2** inflexibly severe; cold; ruthless (*steely composure; steely-eyed glance*). □□**steeliness** *n.*

steelyard /'stiːljɑːd/ *n.* a kind of balance with a short arm to take the item to be weighed and a long graduated arm along which a weight is moved until it balances.

steenbok /'steɪnbɒk, 'stiːn-/ *n.* an African dwarf-antelope, *Raphicerus campestris*. [Du. f. *steen* STONE + *bok* BUCK¹]

steep¹ /stiːp/ *adj.* & *n.* —*adj.* **1** sloping sharply; almost perpendicular (*a steep hill; steep stairs*). **2** (of a rise or fall) rapid (*a steep drop in share prices*). **3** (*predic.*) *colloq.* **a** (of a demand, price, etc.) exorbitant; unreasonable (esp. *a bit steep*). **b** (of a story etc.) exaggerated; incredible. —*n.* a steep slope; a precipice. □□**steepen** *v.intr.* & *tr.* **steepish** *adj.* **steeply** *adv.* **steepness** *n.* [OE *stēap* f. WG, rel. to STOOP¹]

steep² /stiːp/ *v.* & *n.* —*v.tr.* soak or bathe in liquid. —*n.* **1** the act or process of steeping. **2** the liquid for steeping. □**steep in 1** pervade or imbue with (*steeped in misery*). **2** make deeply acquainted with (a subject etc.) (*steeped in the classics*). [ME f. OE f. Gmc (as STOUP)]

steeple /'stiːp(ə)l/ *n.* a tall tower, esp. one surmounted by a spire, above the roof of a church. □**steeple-crowned** (of a hat) with a tall pointed crown. □□**steepled** *adj.* [OE *stēpel stȳpel* f. Gmc (as STEEP¹)]

steeplechase /'stiːp(ə)lˌtʃeɪs/ *n.* **1** a horse-race (orig. with a steeple as the goal) across the countryside or on a racecourse with ditches, hedges, etc., to jump.

2 a cross-country foot-race. □□ **steeplechaser** n.
steeplechasing n.
steeplejack /'sti:p(ə)l,dʒæk/ n. a person who climbs
tall chimneys, steeples, etc., to do repairs etc.
steer[1] /stɪə(r)/ v. & n. —v. **1** tr. **a** guide (a vehicle,
aircraft, etc.) by a wheel etc. **b** guide (a vessel) by a
rudder or helm. **2** intr. guide a vessel or vehicle in a
specified direction (tried to steer left). **3** tr. direct
(one's course). **4** intr. direct one's course in a specified
direction (steered for the railway station). **5** tr. guide
the movement or trend of (steered them into the
garden; steered the conversation away from that
subject). —n. US steering; guidance. □ **steer clear**
of take care to avoid. **steering-column** the shaft or
column which connects the steering-wheel, handlebars, etc. of a vehicle to the rest of the steering-gear.
steering committee a committee deciding the order
of dealing with business, or priorities and the general
course of operations. **steering-wheel** a wheel by
which a vehicle etc. is steered. □□ **steerable** adj.
steerer n. **steering** n. (esp. in senses 1, 2 of v.). [OE
stieran f. Gmc]
steer[2] /stɪə(r)/ n. a young male bovine animal, esp.
one castrated and raised for beef. [OE stēor f. Gmc]
steerage /'stɪərɪdʒ/ n. **1** the act of steering. **2** the
effect of the helm on a ship. **3** archaic the part of a
ship allotted to passengers travelling at the cheapest
rate. **4** hist. (in a warship) quarters assigned to
midshipmen etc. just forward of the wardroom.
□ **steerage-way** the amount of headway required by
a vessel to enable her to be controlled by the helm.
steersman /'stɪəzmən/ n. (pl. **-men**) a person who
steers a vessel.
steeve[1] /sti:v/ n. & v. Naut. —n. the angle of the
bowsprit in relation to the horizontal. —v. **1** intr. (of
a bowsprit) make an angle with the horizontal. **2** tr.
cause (the bowsprit) to do this. [17th c.: orig. unkn.]
steeve[2] /sti:v/ n. & v. Naut. —n. a long spar used in
stowing cargo. —v.tr. stow with a steeve. [ME f. OF
estiver or Sp. estivar f. L stipare pack tight]
stegosaurus /,stegə'sɔ:rəs/ n. any of a group of
plant-eating dinosaurs with a double row of large
bony plates along the spine. [mod. L f. Gk stegē
covering + sauros lizard]
stein /staɪn/ n. a large earthenware mug, esp. for
beer. [G, lit. 'stone']
steinbock /'staɪnbɒk/ n. **1** an ibex native to the
Alps. **2** = STEENBOK. [G f. Stein STONE + Bock BUCK[1]]
stela /'sti:lə/ n. (pl. **stelae** /-li:/) Archaeol. an upright
slab or pillar usu. with an inscription and sculpture,
esp. as a gravestone. [L f. Gk (as STELE)]
stele /'sti:l, 'sti:lɪ/ n. **1** Bot. the axial cylinder of
vascular tissue in the stem and roots of most plants.
2 Archaeol. = STELA. □□ **stelar** adj. [Gk stēlē standing
block]
stellar /'stelə(r)/ adj. of or relating to a star or stars.
□□ **stelliform** adj. [LL stellaris f. L stella star]
stellate /'steleɪt/ adj. (also **stellated** /ste'leɪtɪd/) **1**
arranged like a star; radiating. **2** Bot. (of leaves)
surrounding the stem in a whorl. [L stellatus f. stella
star]
stellular /'steljʊlə(r)/ adj. shaped like, or set with,
small stars. [L stellula dimin. of L stella star]
stem[1] /stem/ n. & v. —n. **1** the main body or stalk of a
plant or shrub, usu. rising into light, but occasionally
subterranean. **2** the stalk supporting a fruit, flower,
or leaf, and attaching it to a larger branch, twig, or
stalk. **3** a stem-shaped part of an object: **a** the slender
part of a wineglass between the body and the foot. **b**
the tube of a tobacco-pipe. **c** a vertical stroke in a
letter or musical note. **d** the winding-shaft of a watch.
4 Gram. the root or main part of a noun, verb, etc.,
to which inflections are added; the part that appears
unchanged throughout the cases and derivatives of
a noun, persons of a tense, etc. **5** Naut. the main
upright timber or metal piece at the bow of a ship to
which the ship's sides are joined at the fore end
(from stem to stern). **6** a line of ancestry, branch of a

family, etc. (descended from an ancient stem). **7** (in
full **drill stem**) a rotating rod, cylinder, etc., used in
drilling. —v. (**stemmed, stemming**) **1** intr. (foll. by
from) spring or originate from (stems from a desire to
win). **2** tr. remove the stem or stems from (fruit,
tobacco, etc.). **3** tr. (of a vessel etc.) hold its own or
make headway against (the tide etc.). □ **stem cell**
Biol. an undifferentiated cell from which specialized
cells develop. **stem stitch** an embroidery stitch used
for narrow stems etc. **stem-winder** US a watch
wound by turning a head on the end of a stem rather
than by a key. □□ **stemless** adj. **stemlet** n. **stemlike**
adj. **stemmed** adj. (also in comb.). [OE stemn, stefn
f. Gmc, rel. to STAND]
stem[2] /stem/ v. & n. —v. (**stemmed, stemming**) **1**
tr. check or stop. **2** tr. dam up (a stream etc.). **3** intr.
slide the tail of one ski or both skis outwards usu. in
order to turn or slow down. —n. an act of stemming
on skis. □ **stem-turn** a turn on skis made by stemming with one ski. [ON stemma f. Gmc: cf. STAMMER]
stemma /'stemə/ n. (pl. **stemmata** /'stemətə/) **1** a
family tree; a pedigree. **2** the line of descent e.g. of
variant texts of a work. **3** Zool. a simple eye; a facet
of a compound eye. [L f. Gk stemma wreath f. stephō
wreathe]
stemple /'stemp(ə)l/ n. each of several crossbars in
a mineshaft serving as supports or steps. [17th c.:
orig. uncert.: cf. MHG stempfel]
stemware /'stemweə(r)/ n. US glasses with stems.
stench /stentʃ/ n. an offensive or foul smell. □ **stench**
trap a trap in a sewer etc. to prevent the upward
passage of gas. [OE stenc smell f. Gmc, rel. to STINK]
stencil /'stensɪl/ n. & v. —n. **1** (in full **stencil-plate**)
a thin sheet of plastic, metal, card, etc., in which
a pattern or lettering is cut, used to produce a
corresponding pattern on the surface beneath it by
applying ink, paint, etc. **2** the pattern, lettering, etc.,
produced by a stencil-plate. **3** a waxed sheet etc. from
which a stencil is made by means of a typewriter.
—v.tr. (**stencilled, stencilling;** US **stenciled,**
stenciling) **1** (often foll. by on) produce (a pattern)
with a stencil. **2** decorate or mark (a surface) in this
way. [ME f. OF estanceler sparkle, cover with stars,
f. estencele spark ult. f. L scintilla]
Sten gun /sten/ n. a type of lightweight sub-
machine-gun. [S and T (the initials of the inventors'
surnames, Shepherd and Turpin) + -en after BREN]
steno /'stenəʊ/ n. (pl. **-os**) US colloq. a stenographer.
[abbr.]
stenography /ste'nɒgrəfɪ/ n. shorthand or the art
of writing this. □□ **stenographer** n. **stenographic**
/-nə'græfɪk/ adj. [Gk stenos narrow + -GRAPHY]
stenosis /stɪ'nəʊsɪs/ n. Med. the abnormal narrowing
of a passage in the body. □□ **stenotic** /-'nɒtɪk/ adj.
[mod.L f. Gk stenōsis narrowing f. stenoō make
narrow f. stenos narrow]
stenotype /'stenə,taɪp/ n. **1** a machine like a typewriter for recording speech in syllables or phonemes.
2 a symbol or the symbols used in this process. □□
stenotypist n. [STENOGRAPHY + TYPE]
Stentor /'stentə(r)/ n. (also **stentor**) a person with a
powerful voice. □□ **stentorian** /-'tɔ:rɪən/ adj. [Gk
Stentōr, herald in the Trojan War (Homer, Iliad v.
785)]
step /step/ n. & v. —n. **1 a** the complete movement
of one leg in walking or running (took a step forward).
b the distance covered by this. **2** a unit of movement
in dancing. **3** a measure taken, esp. one of several in
a course of action (took steps to prevent it; considered
it a wise step). **4 a** a surface on which a foot is placed
on ascending or descending a stair or tread. **b** a
block of stone or other platform before a door, altar,
etc. **c** the rung of a ladder. **d** a notch cut for a foot in
ice-climbing. **e** a platform etc. in a vehicle provided
for stepping up or down. **5** a short distance (only a
step from my door). **6** the sound or mark made by a
foot in walking etc. (heard a step on the stairs). **7** the
manner of walking etc. as seen or heard (know her

by her step). **8 a** a degree in the scale of promotion, advancement, or precedence. **b** one of a series of fixed points on a payscale etc. **9 a** stepping (or not stepping) in time with others or music (esp. *in* or *out of step*). **b** the state of conforming to what others are doing (*refuses to keep step with the team*). **10** (in *pl.*) (also **pair of steps** *sing.*) = STEPLADDER. **11** esp. *US Mus.* a melodic interval of one degree of the scale, i.e. a tone or semitone. **12** *Naut.* a block, socket, or platform supporting a mast. —*v.* (**stepped, stepping**) **1** *intr.* lift and set down one's foot or alternate feet in walking. **2** *intr.* come or go in a specified direction by stepping. **3** *intr.* make progress in a specified way (*stepped into a new job*). **4** *tr.* (foll. by *off*, *out*) measure (distance) by stepping. **5** *tr.* perform (a dance). **6** *tr. Naut.* set up (a mast) in a step. □**in a person's steps** following a person's example. **mind** (or **watch**) **one's step** be careful. **step by step** gradually; cautiously; by stages or degrees. **step-cut** (of a gem) cut in straight facets round the centre. **step down 1** resign from a position etc. **2** *Electr.* decrease (voltage) by using a transformer. **step in 1** enter a room, house, etc. **2 a** intervene to help or hinder. **b** act as a substitute for an indisposed colleague etc. **step-in** *attrib.adj.* (of a garment) put on by being stepped into without unfastening. —*n.* such a garment. **step it** dance. **step on it** (or **on the gas** etc.) *colloq.* **1** accelerate a motor vehicle. **2** hurry up. **step out 1** leave a room, house, etc. **2** be active socially. **3** take large steps. **stepping-stone 1** a raised stone, usu. one of a set in a stream, muddy place, etc., to help in crossing. **2** a means or stage of progress to an end. **step this way** a deferential formula meaning 'follow me'. **step up 1** increase, intensify (*must step up production*). **2** *Electr.* increase (voltage) using a transformer. **turn one's steps** go in a specified direction. □□**steplike** *adj.* **stepped** *adj.* **stepwise** *adv. & adj.* [OE *stæpe, stepe* (n.), *stæppan, steppan* (v.), f. Gmc]

step- /step/ *comb. form* denoting a relationship like the one specified but resulting from a parent's remarriage. [OE *stēop-* orphan-]

stepbrother /'step,brʌðə(r)/ *n.* a son of a step-parent by a marriage other than with one's father or mother.

stepchild /'steptʃaɪld/ *n.* a child of one's husband or wife by a previous marriage. [OE *stēopcīld* (as STEP-, CHILD)]

stepdaughter /'step,dɔːtə(r)/ *n.* a female stepchild. [OE *stēopdohtor* (as STEP-, DAUGHTER)]

stepfather /'step,fɑːðə(r)/ *n.* a male step-parent. [OE *stēopfæder* (as STEP-, FATHER)]

stephanotis /,stefə'nəʊtɪs/ *n.* any climbing tropical plant of the genus *Stephanotis*, cultivated for its fragrant waxy usu. white flowers. [mod.L f. Gk, = fit for a wreath f. *stephanos* wreath]

stepladder /'step,lædə(r)/ *n.* a short ladder with flat steps and a folding prop, used without being leant against a surface.

stepmother /'step,mʌðə(r)/ *n.* a female step-parent. [OE *stēopmōdor* (as STEP-, MOTHER)]

step-parent /'step,peərənt/ *n.* a mother's or father's later husband or wife.

steppe /step/ *n.* a level grassy unforested plain, esp. in SE Europe and Siberia. [Russ *step'*]

stepsister /'step,sɪstə(r)/ *n.* a daughter of a step-parent by a marriage other than with one's father or mother.

stepson /'stepsʌn/ *n.* a male stepchild. [OE *stēopsunu* (as STEP-, SON)]

-ster /stə(r)/ *suffix* denoting a person engaged in or associated with a particular activity or thing (*brewster; gangster; youngster*). [OE *-estre* etc. f. Gmc]

steradian /stə'reɪdɪən/ *n.* the SI unit of solid angle, equal to the angle at the centre of a sphere subtended by a part of the surface equal in area to the square of the radius. ¶ Abbr.: **sr**. [Gk *stereos* solid + RADIAN]

stercoraceous /,stɜːkə'reɪʃ(ə)s/ *adj.* **1** consisting of

or resembling dung or faeces. **2** living in dung. [L *stercus -oris* dung]

stere /stɪə(r)/ *n.* a unit of volume equal to one cubic metre. [F *stère* f. Gk *stereos* solid]

stereo /'sterɪəʊ, 'stɪə-/ *n. & adj.* —*n.* (*pl.* -os) **1 a** a stereophonic record-player, tape recorder, etc. **b** = STEREOPHONY (see STEREOPHONIC). **2** = STEREOSCOPE. —*adj.* **1** = STEREOPHONIC. **2** = STEREOSCOPIC (see STEREOSCOPE). [abbr.]

stereo- /'sterɪəʊ, 'stɪə-/ *comb. form* solid; having three dimensions. [Gk *stereos* solid]

stereobate /'sterɪəbeɪt/ *n. Archit.* a solid mass of masonry as a foundation for a building. [F *stéréobate* f. L *stereobata* f. Gk *stereobatēs* (as STEREO-, *bainō* walk)]

stereochemistry /,sterɪəʊ'kemɪstrɪ, ,stɪə-/ *n.* the branch of chemistry dealing with the three-dimensional arrangement of atoms in molecules.

stereography /sterɪ'ɒɡrəfɪ/ *n.* the art of depicting solid bodies in a plane.

stereoisomer /,sterɪəʊ'aɪsəmə(r)/ *n. Chem.* any of two or more compounds differing only in their spatial arrangement of atoms.

stereometry /,sterɪ'ɒmɪtrɪ/ *n.* the measurement of solid bodies.

stereophonic /,sterɪəʊ'fɒnɪk, ,stɪə-/ *adj.* (of sound reproduction) using two or more channels so that the sound has the effect of being distributed and of coming from more than one source. □□ **stereophonically** *adv.* **stereophony** /-'ɒfənɪ/ *n.*

stereoscope /'sterɪə,skəʊp, 'stɪə-/ *n.* a device by which two photographs of the same object taken at slightly different angles are viewed together, giving an impression of depth and solidity as in ordinary human vision. □□ **stereoscopic** /-'skɒpɪk/ *adj.* **stereoscopically** /-'skɒpɪkəlɪ/ *adv.* **stereoscopy** /-'ɒskəpɪ/ *n.*

stereotype /'sterɪəʊ,taɪp, 'stɪə-/ *n. & v.* —*n.* **1 a** a person or thing that conforms to an unjustifiably fixed, usu. standardized, mental picture. **b** such an impression or attitude. **2** a printing-plate cast from a mould of composed type. —*v.tr.* **1** (esp. as **stereotyped** *adj.*) formalize, standardize; cause to conform to a type. **2 a** print from a stereotype. **b** make a stereotype of. □□ **stereotypic** /-'tɪpɪk/ *adj.* **stereotypical** /-'tɪpɪk(ə)l/ *adj.* **stereotypically** /-'tɪpɪkəlɪ/ *adv.* **stereotypy** *n.* [F *stéréotype* (adj.) (as STEREO-, TYPE)]

steric /'stɪərɪk/ *adj. Chem.* relating to the spatial arrangement of atoms in a molecule. □**steric hindrance** the inhibiting of a chemical reaction by the obstruction of reacting atoms. [irreg. f. Gk *stereos* solid]

sterile /'steraɪl/ *adj.* **1** not able to produce crop or fruit or (of an animal) young; barren. **2** unfruitful, unproductive (*sterile discussions*). **3** free from living micro-organisms etc. **4** lacking originality or emotive force; mentally barren. □□ **sterilely** *adv.* **sterility** /stə'rɪlɪtɪ/ *n.* [F *stérile* or L *sterilis*]

sterilize /'sterɪ,laɪz/ *v.tr.* (also **-ise**) **1** make sterile. **2** deprive of the power of reproduction. □□ **sterilizable** *adj.* **sterilization** /-'zeɪʃ(ə)n/ *n.* **sterilizer** *n.*

sterlet /'stɜːlɪt/ *n.* a small sturgeon, *Acipenser ruthenus*, found in the Caspian Sea area and yielding fine caviare. [Russ. *sterlyad'*]

sterling /'stɜːlɪŋ/ *adj. & n.* —*adj.* **1** of or in British money (*pound sterling*). **2** (of a coin or precious metal) genuine; of standard value or purity. **3** (of a person or qualities etc.) of solid worth; genuine, reliable (*sterling work*). —*n.* British money (*paid in sterling*). □**sterling area** a group of countries with currencies tied to British sterling and holding reserves mainly in sterling. **sterling silver** silver of 92¼% purity. □□ **sterlingness** *n.* [prob. f. late OE *steorling* (unrecorded) f. *steorra* star + -LING[1] (because some early Norman pennies bore a small star): recorded earlier in OF *esterlin*]

stern[1] /stɜːn/ *adj.* severe, grim, strict; enforcing

discipline or submission (*a stern expression*; *stern treatment*). □**the sterner sex** men. □□**sternly** *adv.*
sternness *n.* [OE *styrne*, prob. f. a Gmc root = be rigid]

stern² /stɜːn/ *n.* **1** the rear part of a ship or boat. **2** any rear part. □**stern foremost** moving backwards. **stern on** with the stern presented. **stern-post** the central upright support at the stern, usu. bearing the rudder. □□**sterned** *adj.* (also in *comb.*). **sternmost** *adj.* **sternward** *adj.* & *adv.* **sternwards** *adv.* [ME prob. f. ON *stjórn* steering f. *stýra* STEER¹]

sternal /ˈstɜːn(ə)l/ *adj.* of or relating to the sternum. □**sternal rib** = *true rib*.

sternum /ˈstɜːnəm/ *n.* (*pl.* **sternums** or **sterna** /-nə/) the breastbone. [mod.L f. Gk *sternon* chest]

sternutation /ˌstɜːnjuːˈteɪʃ(ə)n/ *n.* *Med.* or *joc.* a sneeze or attack of sneezing. [L *sternutatio* f. *sternutare* frequent. of *sternuere* sneeze]

sternutator /ˈstɜːnjʊˌteɪtə(r)/ *n.* a substance, esp. poison gas, that causes nasal irritation, violent coughing, etc. □□**sternutatory** /-ˈnjuːtətərɪ/ *adj.* & *n.* (*pl.* **-ies**).

sternway /ˈstɜːnweɪ/ *n.* *Naut.* a backward motion or impetus of a ship.

steroid /ˈstɪərɔɪd, ˈste-/ *n.* *Biochem.* any of a group of organic compounds with a characteristic structure of four rings of carbon atoms, including many hormones, alkaloids, and vitamins. □□**steroidal** /-ˈrɔɪd(ə)l/ *adj.* [STEROL + -OID]

sterol /ˈsterɒl/ *n.* *Chem.* any of a group of naturally occurring steroid alcohols. [CHOLESTEROL, ERGO-STEROL, etc.]

stertorous /ˈstɜːtərəs/ *adj.* (of breathing etc.) heavy; sounding like snoring. □□**stertorously** *adv.* **stertorousness** *n.* [*stertor*, mod.L f. L *stertere* snore]

stet /stet/ *v.* (**stetted**, **stetting**) **1** *intr.* (usu. as an instruction written on a proof-sheet etc.) ignore or cancel the correction or alteration; let the original form stand. **2** *tr.* write 'stet' against; cancel the correction of. [L, = let it stand, f. *stare* stand]

stethoscope /ˈsteθəˌskəʊp/ *n.* an instrument used in listening to the action of the heart, lungs, etc., usu. consisting of a circular piece placed against the chest, with tubes leading to earpieces. □□**stethoscopic** /-ˈskɒpɪk/ *adj.* **stethoscopically** /-ˈskɒpɪkəlɪ/ *adv.* **stethoscopist** /-ˈθɒskəpɪst/ *n.* **stethoscopy** /-ˈθɒskəpɪ/ *n.* [F *stéthoscope* f. Gk *stēthos* breast: see -SCOPE]

stetson /ˈstets(ə)n/ *n.* a slouch hat with a very wide brim and a high crown. [J. B. *Stetson*, Amer. hat-maker d. 1906]

stevedore /ˈstiːvəˌdɔː(r)/ *n.* a person employed in loading and unloading ships. [Sp. *estivador* f. *estivar* stow a cargo f. L *stipare*: see STEEVE²]

stevengraph /ˈstiːv(ə)nˌɡrɑːf/ *n.* a colourful woven silk picture. [T. *Stevens*, Engl. weaver d. 1888, whose firm made them]

stew¹ /stjuː/ *v.* & *n.* —*v.* **1** *tr.* & *intr.* cook by long simmering in a closed vessel with liquid. **2** *intr. colloq.* be oppressed by heat or humidity, esp. in a confined space. **3** *intr. colloq.* **a** suffer prolonged embarrassment, anxiety, etc. **b** (foll. by *over*) fret or be anxious. **4** *tr.* make (tea) bitter or strong with prolonged brewing. **5** *tr.* (as **stewed** *adj.*) *colloq.* drunk. **6** *intr.* (often foll. by *over*) *colloq.* study hard. —*n.* **1** a dish of stewed meat etc. **2** *colloq.* an agitated or angry state (*be in a stew*). **3** *archaic* a hot bath. **b** (in *pl.*) a brothel. □**stew in one's own juice** be left to suffer the consequences of one's own actions. [ME f. OF *estuve*, *estuver* prob. ult. f. EX-¹ + Gk *tuphos* smoke, steam]

stew² /stjuː/ *n.* *Brit.* **1** an artificial oyster-bed. **2** a pond or large tank for keeping fish for eating. [ME f. F *estui* f. *estoier* confine ult. f. L *studium*: see STUDY]

steward /ˈstjuːəd/ *n.* & *v.* **1** a passengers' attendant on a ship or aircraft or train. **2** an official appointed to keep order or supervise arrangements at a meeting or show or demonstration etc. **3** = *shop steward*. **4** a

person responsible for supplies of food etc. for a college or club etc. **5** a person employed to manage another's property. **6** *Brit.* the title of several officers of State or the royal household (*Lord High Steward*). —*v.tr.* act as a steward of (*will steward the meeting*). □□**stewardship** *n.* [OE *stīweard* f. *stig* prob. = house, hall + *weard* WARD]

stewardess /ˌstjuːəˈdes, ˈstjuːədɪs/ *n.* a female steward, esp. on a ship or aircraft.

stg. *abbr.* sterling.

Sth. *abbr.* South.

sthenic /ˈsθenɪk/ *adj.* *Med.* (of a disease etc.) with a morbid increase of vital action esp. of the heart and arteries. [Gk *sthenos* strength, after *asthenic*]

stick¹ /stɪk/ *n.* **1 a** a short slender branch or length of wood broken or cut from a tree. **b** this trimmed for use as a support or weapon. **2** a thin rod or spike of wood etc. for a particular purpose (*cocktail stick*). **3 a** an implement used to propel the ball in hockey or polo etc. **b** (in *pl.*) the raising of the stick above the shoulder in hockey. **4** a gear lever. **5** a conductor's baton. **6 a** a slender piece of a thing, e.g. celery, dynamite, deodorant, etc. **b** a number of bombs or paratroops released rapidly from aircraft. **7** (often prec. by *the*) punishment, esp. by beating. **8** *colloq.* adverse criticism; censure, reproof (*took a lot of stick*). **9** *colloq.* a piece of wood as part of a house or furniture (*a few sticks of furniture*). **10** *colloq.* a person, esp. one who is dull or unsociable (*a funny old stick*). **11** (in *pl.*; prec. by *the*) *colloq.* remote rural areas. **12** (in *pl.*) *Austral. sl.* goalposts. **13** *Naut. sl.* a mast or spar. □**stick insect** any usu. wingless female insect of the family Phasmidae with a twiglike body. **up sticks** *colloq.* go to live elsewhere. □□**stickless** *adj.* **sticklike** *adj.* [OE *sticca* f. WG]

stick² /stɪk/ *v.* (*past* and *past part.* **stuck** /stʌk/) **1** *tr.* (foll. by *in*, *into*, *through*) insert or thrust (a thing or its point) (*stuck a finger in my eye*; *stick a pin through it*). **2** *tr.* insert a pointed thing into; stab. **3** *tr.* & *intr.* (foll. by *in*, *into*, *on*, etc.) **a** fix or be fixed on a pointed thing. **b** fix or be fixed by or as by a pointed end. **4** *tr.* & *intr.* fix or become or remain fixed by or as by adhesive etc. (*stick a label on it*; *the label won't stick*). **5** *intr.* endure; make a continued impression (*the scene stuck in my mind*; *the name stuck*). **6** *intr.* lose or be deprived of the power of motion or action through adhesion or jamming or other impediment. **7** *colloq.* **a** *tr.* put in a specified position or place, esp. quickly or haphazardly (*stick them down anywhere*). **b** *intr.* remain in a place (*stuck indoors*). **8** *colloq.* **a** *intr.* (of an accusation etc.) be convincing or regarded as valid (*could not make the charges stick*). **b** *tr.* (foll. by *on*) place the blame for (a thing) on (a person). **9** *tr. colloq.* endure, tolerate (*could not stick it any longer*). **10** *tr.* (foll. by *at*) *colloq.* persevere with. □**be stuck for** be at a loss for or in need of. **be stuck on** *colloq.* be infatuated with. **be stuck with** *colloq.* be unable to get rid of or escape from; be permanently involved with. **get stuck in** (or **into**) *sl.* begin in earnest. **stick around** *colloq.* linger; remain at the same place. **stick at it** *colloq.* persevere. **stick at nothing** allow nothing, esp. no scruples, to deter one. **stick by** (or **with** or **to**) stay loyal or close to. **stick 'em up!** *colloq.* hands up! **stick fast** adhere or become firmly fixed or trapped in a position or place. **stick in one's gizzard** see GIZZARD. **sticking-plaster** an adhesive plaster for wounds etc. **sticking-point** the limit of progress, agreement, etc. **stick-in-the-mud** *colloq.* an unprogressive or old-fashioned person. **stick in one's throat** be against one's principles. **stick it on** *sl.* **1** make high charges. **2** tell an exaggerated story. **stick it out** *colloq.* put up with or persevere with a burden etc. to the end. **stick one's neck** (or **chin**) **out** expose oneself to censure etc. by acting or speaking boldly. **stick out** protrude or cause to protrude or project (*stuck his tongue out*; *stick out your chest*).

stick out for persist in demanding. **stick out a mile** (or **like a sore thumb**) *colloq.* be very obvious or incongruous. **stick pigs** engage in pigsticking. **stick to 1** remain close to or fixed on or to. **2** remain faithful to. **3** keep to (a subject etc.) (*stick to the point*). **stick to a person's fingers** *colloq.* (of money) be embezzled by a person. **stick together** *colloq.* remain united or mutually loyal. **stick to one's guns** see GUN. **stick to it** persevere. **stick to one's last** see LAST[3]. **stick up 1** be or make erect or protruding upwards. **2** fasten to an upright surface. **3** *colloq.* rob or threaten with a gun. **stick-up** *colloq.* an armed robbery. **stick up for** support or defend or champion (a person or cause). **stick up to** be assertive in the face of; offer resistance to. **stick with** *colloq.* remain in touch with or faithful to. **stuck-up** *colloq.* affectedly superior and aloof, snobbish. □□ **stickability** /-kə'bɪlɪtɪ/ *n.* [OE *stician* f. Gmc]

sticker /'stɪkə(r)/ *n.* **1** an adhesive label or notice etc. **2** a person or thing that sticks. **3** a persistent person.

stickleback /'stɪk(ə)l,bæk/ *n.* any small fish of the family Gasterosteidae, esp. *Gasterosteus aculeatus*, with sharp spines along the back. [ME f. OE *sticel* thorn, sting + *bæc* BACK]

stickler /'stɪklə(r)/ *n.* (foll. by *for*) a person who insists on something (*a stickler for accuracy*). [obs. *stickle* be umpire, ME *stightle* control, frequent. of *stight* f. OE *stiht(i)an* set in order]

stickpin /'stɪkpɪn/ *n. US* an ornamental tie-pin.

stickweed /'stɪkwiːd/ *n. US* = RAGWEED 2.

sticky /'stɪkɪ/ *adj.* (**stickier, stickiest**) **1** tending or intended to stick or adhere. **2** glutinous, viscous. **3** (of the weather) humid. **4** *colloq.* awkward or uncooperative; intransigent (*was very sticky about giving me leave*). **5** *colloq.* difficult, awkward (*a sticky problem*). **6** *colloq.* very unpleasant or painful (*came to a sticky end*). □ **sticky wicket 1** Cricket a pitch that has been drying after rain and is difficult for the batsman. **2** *colloq.* difficult or awkward circumstances. □□ **stickily** *adv.* **stickiness** *n.*

stickybeak /'stɪkɪ,biːk/ *n. & v. Austral. & NZ sl.* —*n.* an inquisitive person. —*v.intr.* pry.

stiff /stɪf/ *adj. & n.* —*adj.* **1** rigid; not flexible. **2** hard to bend or move or turn etc.; not working freely. **3** hard to cope with; needing strength or effort (*a stiff test; a stiff climb*). **4** severe or strong (*a stiff breeze; a stiff penalty*). **5** (of a person or manner) formal, constrained; lacking spontaneity. **6** (of a muscle or limb etc., or a person affected by these) aching when used, owing to previous exertion, injury, etc. **7** (of an alcoholic or medicinal drink) strong. **8** (*predic.*) *colloq.* to an extreme degree (*bored stiff; scared stiff*). **9** (foll. by *with*) *colloq.* abounding in (*a place stiff with tourists*). —*n. sl.* **1** a corpse. **2** a foolish or useless person (*you big stiff*). □ **stiff neck** a rheumatic condition in which the head cannot be turned without pain. **stiff-necked** obstinate or haughty. **stiff upper lip** firmness, fortitude. □□ **stiffish** *adj.* **stiffly** *adv.* **stiffness** *n.* [OE *stif* f. Gmc]

stiffen /'stɪf(ə)n/ *v.tr. & intr.* make or become stiff. □□ **stiffener** *n.* **stiffening** *n.*

stifle[1] /'staɪf(ə)l/ *v.* **1** *tr.* smother, suppress (*stifled a yawn*). **2** *intr. & tr.* experience or cause to experience constraint of breathing (*stifling heat*). **3** *tr.* kill by suffocating. □□ **stifler** /-flə(r)/ *n.* **stiflingly** *adv.* [perh. alt. of ME *stuffe, stuffle* f. OF *estouffer*]

stifle[2] /'staɪf(ə)l/ *n.* (in full **stifle-joint**) a joint in the legs of horses, dogs, etc., equivalent to the knee in humans. □ **stifle-bone** the bone in front of this joint. [ME: orig. unkn.]

stigma /'stɪgmə/ *n.* (*pl.* **stigmas** or esp. in sense 4 **stigmata** /-mətə, -'mɑːtə/) **1** a mark or sign of disgrace or discredit. **2** (foll. by *of*) a distinguishing mark or characteristic. **3** the part of a pistil that receives the pollen in pollination. **4** (in *pl.*) *Eccl.* (in Christian belief) marks corresponding to those left on Christ's

body by the Crucifixion, said to have been impressed on the bodies of St Francis of Assisi and others. **5** a mark or spot on the skin or on a butterfly-wing. **6** *Med.* a visible sign or characteristic of a disease. **7** an insect's spiracle. [L f. Gk *stigma -atos* a mark made by a pointed instrument, a brand, a dot: rel. to STICK[1]]

stigmatic /stɪg'mætɪk/ *adj. & n.* —*adj.* **1** of or relating to a stigma or stigmas. **2** = ANASTIGMATIC. —*n. Eccl.* a person bearing stigmata. □□ **stigmatically** *adv.*

stigmatist /'stɪgmətɪst/ *n. Eccl.* = STIGMATIC *n.*

stigmatize /'stɪgmə,taɪz/ *v.tr.* (also **-ise**) **1** (often foll. by *as*) describe as unworthy or disgraceful. **2** *Eccl.* produce stigmata on. □□ **stigmatization** /-'zeɪʃ(ə)n/ *n.* [F *stigmatiser* or med.L *stigmatizo* f. Gk *stigmatizō* (as STIGMA)]

stilb /stɪlb/ *n.* a unit of luminance equal to one candela per square centimetre. [F f. Gk *stilbō* glitter]

stilbene /'stɪlbiːn/ *n. Chem.* an aromatic hydrocarbon forming phosphorescent crystals. [as STILB + -ENE]

stilboestrol /stɪl'biːstrɒl/ *n.* (*US* **stilbestrol**) a powerful synthetic oestrogen derived from stilbene. [STILBENE + OESTRUS]

stile[1] /staɪl/ *n.* an arrangement of steps allowing people but not animals to climb over a fence or wall. [OE *stigel* f. a Gmc root *stig-* (unrecorded) climb]

stile[2] /staɪl/ *n.* a vertical piece in the frame of a panelled door, wainscot, etc. (cf. RAIL[1] *n.* 5). [prob. f. Du. *stijl* pillar, doorpost]

stiletto /stɪ'letəʊ/ *n.* (*pl.* **-os**) **1** a short dagger with a thick blade. **2** a pointed instrument for making eyelets etc. **3** (in full **stiletto heel**) **a** a long tapering heel of a shoe. **b** a shoe with such a heel. [It., dimin. of *stilo* dagger (as STYLUS)]

still[1] /stɪl/ *adj., n., adv., & v.* —*adj.* **1** not or hardly moving. **2** with little or no sound; calm and tranquil (*a still evening*). **3** (of sounds) hushed, stilled. **4** (of a drink) not effervescing. —*n.* **1** deep silence (*in the still of the night*). **2** an ordinary static photograph (as opposed to a motion picture), esp. a single shot from a cinema film. —*adv.* **1** without moving (*stand still*). **2** even now or at a particular time (*they still did not understand; why are you still here?*). **3** nevertheless; all the same. **4** (with *compar.* etc.) even, yet, increasingly (*still greater efforts; still another explanation*). —*v.tr. & intr.* make or become still; quieten. □ **still and all** *colloq.* nevertheless. **still life** (*pl.* **still lifes**) **1** a painting or drawing of inanimate objects such as fruit or flowers. **2** this genre of painting. **still waters run deep** a quiet manner conceals depths of feeling or knowledge or cunning. □□ **stillness** *n.* [OE *stille* (adj. & adv.), *stillan* (v.), f. WG]

still[2] /stɪl/ *n.* an apparatus for distilling spirituous liquors etc. □ **still-room** *Brit.* **1** a room for distilling. **2** a housekeeper's storeroom in a large house. [obs. *still* (v.), ME f. DISTILL]

stillage /'stɪlɪdʒ/ *n.* a bench, frame, etc., for keeping articles off the floor while draining, drying, waiting to be packed, etc. [app. f. Du. *stellagie* scaffold f. *stellen* to place + F *-age*]

stillbirth /'stɪlbɜːθ/ *n.* the birth of a dead child.

stillborn /'stɪlbɔːn/ *adj.* **1** (of a child) born dead. **2** (of an idea, plan, etc.) abortive; not able to succeed.

Stillson /'stɪls(ə)n/ *n.* (in full **Stillson wrench**) a large wrench with jaws that tighten as pressure is increased. [D. C. *Stillson*, its inventor d. 1899]

stilly /'stɪlɪ/ *adv. & adj.* —*adv.* in a still manner. —*adj. poet.* still, quiet. [(adv.) OE *stillīce*: (adj.) f. STILL[1]]

stilt /stɪlt/ *n.* **1** either of a pair of poles with supports for the feet enabling the user to walk at a distance above the ground. **2** each of a set of piles or posts supporting a building etc. **3 a** any wading bird of the genus *Himantopus* with long legs. **b** (in *comb.*) denoting a long-legged kind of bird (*stilt-petrel*). **4** a three-legged support for ceramic ware in a kiln. □ **on**

stilts 1 supported by stilts. **2** bombastic, stilted. □□ **stiltless** adj. [ME & LG stilte f. Gmc]

stilted /'stɪltɪd/ adj. **1** (of a literary style etc.) stiff and unnatural; bombastic. **2** standing on stilts. **3** Archit. (of an arch) with pieces of upright masonry between the imposts and the springers. □□ **stiltedly** adv. **stiltedness** n.

Stilton /'stɪlt(ə)n/ n. propr. a kind of strong rich cheese, often with blue veins, orig. made in Stilton in S. England.

stimulant /'stɪmjʊlənt/ adj. & n. —adj. that stimulates, esp. bodily or mental activity. —n. **1** a stimulant substance, esp. a drug or alcoholic drink. **2** a stimulating influence. [L stimulare stimulant- urge, goad]

stimulate /'stɪmjʊ‚leɪt/ v.tr. **1** apply or act as a stimulus to. **2** animate, excite, arouse. **3** be a stimulant to. □□ **stimulating** adj. **stimulatingly** adv. **stimulation** /-'leɪʃ(ə)n/ n. **stimulative** /-lətɪv/ adj. **stimulator** n.

stimulus /'stɪmjʊləs/ n. (pl. **stimuli** /-‚laɪ/) **1** a thing that rouses to activity or energy. **2** a stimulating or rousing effect. **3** a thing that evokes a specific functional reaction in an organ or tissue. [L, = goad, spur, incentive]

stimy var. of STYMIE.

sting /stɪŋ/ n. & v. —n. **1** a sharp often poisonous wounding organ of an insect, snake, nettle, etc. **2 a** the act of inflicting a wound with this. **b** the wound itself or the pain caused by it. **3** a wounding or painful quality or effect (the sting of hunger; stings of remorse). **4** pungency, sharpness, vigour (a sting in the voice). **5** sl. a swindle or robbery. —v. (past and past part. **stung** /stʌŋ/) **1 a** tr. wound or pierce with a sting. **b** intr. be able to sting; have a sting. **2** intr. & tr. feel or cause to feel a tingling physical or sharp mental pain. **3** tr. (foll. by into) incite by a strong or painful mental effect (was stung into replying). **4** tr. sl. swindle or charge exorbitantly. □ **stinging-nettle** a nettle, Urtica dioica, having stinging hairs. **sting in the tail** unexpected pain or difficulty at the end. □□ **stingingly** adv. **stingless** adj. **stinglike** adj. [OE sting (n.), stingan (v.), f. Gmc]

stingaree /'stɪŋgə‚riː, ‚stɪŋgə'riː/ n. US & Austral. = STINGRAY.

stinger /'stɪŋə(r)/ n. **1** a stinging insect, snake, nettle, etc. **2** a sharp painful blow.

stingray /'stɪŋreɪ/ n. any of various broad flat-fish esp. of the family Dasyatidae, having a long pois- onous serrated spine at the base of its tail.

stingy /'stɪndʒɪ/ adj. (**stingier**, **stingiest**) niggardly, mean. □□ **stingily** adv. **stinginess** n. [perh. f. dial. stinge STING]

stink /stɪŋk/ v. & n. —v. (past **stank** /stæŋk/ or **stunk** /stʌŋk/; past part. **stunk**) **1** intr. emit a strong offensive smell. **2** tr. (often foll. by out) fill (a place) with a stink. **3** tr. (foll. by out etc.) drive (a person) out etc. by a stink. **4** intr. colloq. be or seem very unpleasant, contemptible, or scandalous. **5** intr. (foll. by of) colloq. have plenty of (esp. money). —n. **1** a strong or offensive smell; a stench. **2** colloq. a row or fuss (the affair caused quite a stink). □ **like stink** colloq. intensely; extremely hard or fast etc. (working like stink). **stink bomb** a device emitting a stink when exploded. [OE stincan sit. f. WG: cf. STENCH]

stinker /'stɪŋkə(r)/ n. **1** a person or thing that stinks. **2** sl. an objectionable person or thing. **3** sl. **a** a difficult task. **b** a letter etc. conveying strong disapproval.

stinkhorn /'stɪŋkhɔːn/ n. any foul-smelling fungus of the order Phallales.

stinking /'stɪŋkɪŋ/ adj. & adv. —adj. **1** that stinks. **2** sl. very objectionable. —adv. sl. extremely and usu. objectionably (stinking rich). □ **stinking badger** a teledu. □□ **stinkingly** adv.

stinko /'stɪŋkəʊ/ adj. sl. drunk.

stinkpot /'stɪŋkpɒt/ n. sl. **1** a term of contempt for a

person. **2** a vehicle or boat that emits foul exhaust fumes.

stinkweed /'stɪŋkwiːd/ n. = wall-rocket (see ROCKET²).

stinkwood /'stɪŋkwʊd/ n. an African tree, Ocotea bullata, with foul-smelling timber.

stint /stɪnt/ v. & n. —v.tr. **1** supply (food or aid etc.) in a niggardly amount or grudgingly. **2** (often refl.) supply (a person etc.) in this way. —n. **1** a limitation of supply or effort (without stint). **2** a fixed or allotted amount of work (do one's stint). **3** a small sandpiper, esp. a dunlin. □□ **stinter** n. **stintless** adj. [OE styntan to blunt, dull, f. Gmc, rel. to STUNT¹]

stipe /staɪp/ n. Bot. & Zool. a stalk or stem, esp. the support of a carpel, the stalk of a frond, the stem of a fungus, or an eye-stalk. □□ **stipiform** adj. **stipitate** /'stɪpɪ‚teɪt/ adj. **stipitiform** /stɪ'pɪtɪ‚fɔːm/ adj. [F f. L stipes: see STIPES]

stipel /'staɪp(ə)l/ n. Bot. a secondary stipule at the base of the leaflets of a compound leaf. □□ **stipellate** /-‚leɪt/ adj. [F stipelle f. mod.L stipella dimin. (as STIPULE)]

stipend /'staɪpend/ n. a fixed regular allowance or salary, esp. paid to a clergyman. [ME f. OF stipend(i)e or L stipendium f. stips wages + pendere to pay]

stipendiary /staɪ'pendjərɪ, stɪ-/ adj. & n. —adj. **1** receiving a stipend. **2** working for pay, not volun- tarily. —n. (pl. **-ies**) a person receiving a stipend. □ **stipendiary magistrate** a paid professional ma- gistrate. [L stipendiarius (as STIPEND)]

stipes /'staɪpiːz/ n. (pl. **stipites** /'stɪpɪ‚tiːz/) = STIPE. [L, = log, tree-trunk]

stipple /'stɪp(ə)l/ v. & n. —v. **1** tr. & intr. draw or paint or engrave etc. with dots instead of lines. **2** tr. roughen the surface of (paint, cement, etc.). —n. **1** the process or technique of stippling. **2** the effect of stippling. □□ **stippler** n. **stippling** n. [Du. stippelen frequent. of stippen to prick f. stip point]

stipulate¹ /'stɪpjʊ‚leɪt/ v.tr. **1** demand or specify as part of a bargain or agreement. **2** (foll. by for) mention or insist upon as an essential condition. **3** (as **stipulated** adj.) laid down in the terms of an agreement. □□ **stipulation** /-'leɪʃ(ə)n/ n. **stipulator** n. [L stipulari]

stipulate² /'stɪpjʊlət/ adj. Bot. having stipules. [L stipula (as STIPULE)]

stipule /'stɪpjuːl/ n. a small leaflike appendage to a leaf, usu. at the base of a leaf-stem. □□ **stipular** adj. [F stipule or L stipula straw]

stir¹ /stɜː(r)/ v. & n. —v. (**stirred**, **stirring**) **1** tr. move a spoon or other implement round and round in (a liquid etc.) to mix the ingredients or constituents. **2 a** tr. cause to move or be disturbed, esp. slightly (a breeze stirred the lake). **b** intr. be or begin to be in motion (not a creature was stirring). **c** refl. rouse (oneself), esp. from a lethargic state. **3** intr. rise from sleep (is still not stirring). **4** intr. (foll. by out of) leave; go out of (esp. one's house). **5** tr. arouse or inspire or excite (the emotions etc., or a person as regards these) (was stirred to anger; it stirred the imagination). —n. **1** an act of stirring (give it a good stir). **2** commotion or excitement; public attention (caused quite a stir). **3** the slightest movement (not a stir). □ **not stir a finger** make no effort to help. **stir the blood** inspire enthusiasm etc. **stir in** mix (an added ingredient) with a substance by stirring. **stir one's stumps** colloq. **1** begin to move. **2** become active. **stir up 1** mix thoroughly by stirring. **2** incite (trouble etc.) (loved stirring things up). **3** stimulate, excite, arouse (stirred up their curiosity). □□ **stirless** adj. **stirrer** n. [OE styrian f. Gmc]

stir² /stɜː(r)/ n. sl. a prison (esp. in stir). □ **stir-crazy** deranged from long imprisonment. [19th c.: orig. unkn.]

stir-fry /'stɜːfraɪ/ v.tr. (**-ies**, **-ied**) fry rapidly while stirring and tossing.

stirk /stɜːk/ n. Brit. dial. a yearling bullock or heifer. [OE stirc, perh. dimin. of stēor STEER²: see -OCK]

stirps /stɜːps/ n. (pl. **stirpes** /-piːz/) **1** Biol. a classificatory group. **2** Law **a** a branch of a family. **b** its progenitor. [L, = stock]

stirrer /'stɜːrə(r)/ n. **1** a thing or a person that stirs. **2** colloq. a troublemaker; an agitator.

stirring /'stɜːrɪŋ/ adj. **1** stimulating, exciting, rousing. **2** actively occupied (lead a stirring life). □□ **stirringly** adv. [OE styrende (as STIR¹)]

stirrup /'stɪrəp/ n. **1** each of a pair of devices attached to each side of a horse's saddle, in the form of a loop with a flat base to support the rider's foot. **2** (attrib.) having the shape of a stirrup. **3** (in full **stirrup bone**) = STAPES. □ **stirrup-cup** a cup of wine etc. offered to a person about to depart, orig. on horseback. **stirrup-iron** the metal loop of a stirrup. **stirrup-leather** (or **-strap**) the strap attaching a stirrup to a saddle. **stirrup-pump** a hand-operated water-pump with a foot-rest, used to extinguish small fires. [OE stigrāp f. stigan climb (as STILE¹)· + ROPE]

stitch /stɪtʃ/ n. & v. —n. **1 a** (in sewing or knitting or crocheting etc.) a single pass of a needle or the thread or loop etc. resulting from this. **b** a particular method of sewing or knitting etc. (am learning a new stitch). **2** (usu. in pl.) Surgery each of the loops of material used in sewing up a wound. **3** the least bit of clothing (hadn't a stitch on). **4** an acute pain in the side of the body induced by running etc. —v.tr. **1** sew; make stitches (in). **2** join or close with stitches. □ **in stitches** colloq. laughing uncontrollably. **a stitch in time** a timely remedy. **stitch up 1** join or mend by sewing or stitching. **2** sl. betray or cheat. □□ **stitcher** n. **stitchery** n. **stitchless** adj. [OE stice f. Gmc, rel. to STICK²]

stitchwort /'stɪtʃwɜːt/ n. any plant of the genus Stellaria, esp. S. media with an erect stem and white starry flowers, once thought to cure a stitch in the side.

stiver /'staɪvə(r)/ n. the smallest quantity or amount (don't care a stiver). [Du. stuiver a small coin, prob. rel. to STUB]

stoa /'stəʊə/ n. (pl. **stoas**) **1** a portico or roofed colonnade in ancient Greek architecture. **2** (the **Stoa**) the Stoic school of philosophy. [Gk: cf. STOIC]

stoat /stəʊt/ n. a flesh-eating mammal, Mustela erminea, of the weasel family, having brown fur in the summer turning mainly white in the winter. Also called ERMINE. [ME: orig. unkn.]

stochastic /stə'kæstɪk/ adj. **1** determined by a random distribution of probabilities. **2** (of a process) characterized by a sequence of random variables. **3** governed by the laws of probability. □□ **stochastically** adv. [Gk stokhastikos f. stokhazomai aim at, guess f. stokhos aim]

stock /stɒk/ n., adj., & v. —n. **1 a** a store of goods etc. ready for sale or distribution etc. **2** a supply or quantity of anything for use (lay in winter stocks of fuel; a great stock of information). **3** equipment or raw material for manufacture or trade etc. (rolling-stock; paper stock). **4 a** farm animals or equipment. **b** = FATSTOCK. **5 a** the capital of a business company. **b** shares in this. **6** one's reputation or popularity (his stock is rising). **7 a** money lent to a government at fixed interest. **b** the right to receive such interest. **8** a line of ancestry; family origins (comes of Cornish stock). **9** liquid made by stewing bones, vegetables, fish, etc., as a basis for soup, gravy, sauce, etc. **10** any of various fragrant-flowered cruciferous plants of the genus Matthiola or Malcolmia (orig. stock-gillyflower, so-called because it had a stronger stem than the clove gillyflower). **11** a plant into which a graft is inserted. **12** the main trunk of a tree etc. **13** (in pl.) hist. a timber frame with holes for the feet and occas. the hands and head, in which offenders were locked as a public punishment. **14** US **a** = stock company. **b** the repertory of this. **15 a** a base or support or handle for an implement or machine. **b** the crossbar of an anchor. **16** the butt of a rifle etc. **17 a** = HEADSTOCK. **b** = TAILSTOCK. **18** (in pl.) the

supports for a ship during building. **19** a band of material worn round the neck esp. in horse-riding or below a clerical collar. **20** hard solid brick pressed in a mould. —adj. **1** kept in stock and so regularly available (stock sizes). **2** perpetually repeated; hackneyed, conventional (a stock answer). —v.tr. **1** have or keep (goods) in stock. **2 a** provide (a shop or a farm etc.) with goods, equipment, or livestock. **b** fill with items needed (shelves well-stocked with books). **3** fit (a gun etc.) with a stock. □ **in stock** available immediately for sale etc. **on the stocks** in construction or preparation. **out of stock** not immediately available for sale. **stock-book** a book showing amounts of goods acquired and disposed of. **stock-car 1** a specially strengthened production car for use in racing in which collision occurs. **2** US a railway truck for transporting livestock. **stock company** US a repertory company performing mainly at a particular theatre. **stock dove** a European wild pigeon, Columba oenas, with a shorter tail and squarer head than a wood pigeon and breeding in tree-trunks. **Stock Exchange 1** a place where stocks and shares are bought and sold. **2** the dealers working there. **stock-in-trade 1** all the requisites of a trade or profession. **2** a ready supply of characteristic phrases, attitudes, etc. **stock market 1** = Stock Exchange. **2** transactions on this. **stock-still** motionless. **stock up 1** provide with or get stocks or supplies. **2** (foll. by with) get in or gather a stock of (food, fuel, etc.). **take stock 1** make an inventory of one's stock. **2** (often foll. by of) make a review or estimate of (a situation etc.). **3** (foll. by in) concern oneself with. □□ **stocker** n. **stockless** adj. [OE stoc, stocc f. Gmc]

stockade /stɒ'keɪd/ n. & v. —n. a line or enclosure of upright stakes. —v.tr. fortify with a stockade. [obs. F estocade, alt. of estacade f. Sp. estacada: rel. to STAKE¹]

stockbreeder /'stɒk,briːdə(r)/ n. a farmer who raises livestock. □□ **stockbreeding** n.

stockbroker /'stɒk,brəʊkə(r)/ n. = BROKER 2. □ **stockbroker belt** Brit. an affluent residential area, esp. near a business centre such as London. □□ **stockbrokerage** n. **stockbroking** n.

stockfish /'stɒkfɪʃ/ n. cod or a similar fish split and dried in the open air without salt.

stockholder /'stɒk,həʊldə(r)/ n. an owner of stocks or shares. □□ **stockholding** n.

stockinet /stɒkɪ'net/ n. (also **stockinette**) an elastic knitted material. [prob. f. stocking-net]

stocking /'stɒkɪŋ/ n. **1 a** either of a pair of long separate coverings for the legs and feet, usu. close-woven in wool or nylon and worn esp. by women and girls. **b** esp. US = SOCK¹. **2** any close-fitting garment resembling a stocking (bodystocking). **3** a differently-coloured, usu. white, lower part of the leg of a horse etc. □ **in one's stocking** (or **stockinged**) **feet** without shoes (esp. while being measured). **stocking cap** a knitted usu. conical cap. **stocking-filler** Brit. a small present suitable for a Christmas stocking. **stocking-stitch** Knitting a stitch of alternate rows of plain and purl, making an even pattern. □□ **stockinged** adj. (also in comb.). **stockingless** adj. [STOCK in (now dial.) sense 'stocking' + -ING¹]

stockist /'stɒkɪst/ n. Brit. a dealer who stocks goods of a particular type for sale.

stockjobber /'stɒk,dʒɒbə(r)/ n. **1** Brit. = JOBBER 1. **2** US = JOBBER 2b. □□ **stockjobbing** n.

stocklist /'stɒklɪst/ n. Brit. a regular publication stating a dealer's stock of goods with current prices etc.

stockman /'stɒkmən/ n. (pl. **-men**) **1 a** Austral. a man in charge of livestock. **b** US an owner of livestock. **2** US a person in charge of a stock of goods in a warehouse etc.

stockpile /'stɒkpaɪl/ n. & v. —n. an accumulated stock of goods, materials, weapons, etc., held in reserve. —*v.tr.* accumulate a stockpile of. □□ **stockpiler** *n.*

stockpot /'stɒkpɒt/ *n.* a pot for cooking stock for soup etc.

stockroom /'stɒkru:m, -rʊm/ *n.* a room for storing goods in stock.

stocktaking /'stɒk,teɪkɪŋ/ *n.* **1** the process of making an inventory of stock in a shop etc. **2** a review of one's position and resources.

stocky /'stɒkɪ/ *adj.* (**stockier**, **stockiest**) (of a person, plant, or animal) short and strongly built; thickset. □□ **stockily** *adv.* **stockiness** *n.*

stockyard /'stɒkjɑːd/ *n.* an enclosure with pens etc. for sorting or temporary keeping of cattle.

stodge /stɒdʒ/ *n.* & *v. colloq.* —*n.* **1** food esp. of a thick heavy kind. **2** an unimaginative person or idea. —*v.tr.* stuff with food etc. [earlier as verb: imit., after *stuff* and *podge*]

stodgy /'stɒdʒɪ/ *adj.* (**stodgier**, **stodgiest**) **1** (of food) heavy and indigestible. **2** dull and uninteresting. **3** (of a literary style etc.) turgid and dull. □□ **stodgily** *adv.* **stodginess** *n.*

stoep /stuːp/ *n. S.Afr.* a terraced veranda in front of a house. [Du., rel. to STEP]

stogy /'stəʊgɪ/ *n.* (also **stogie**) (*pl.* **-ies**) *US* **1** a long narrow roughly-made cigar. **2** a rough heavy boot. [orig. *stoga*, short for *Conestoga* in Pennsylvania]

Stoic /'stəʊɪk/ *n.* & *adj.* —*n.* **1** a member of the ancient Greek school of philosophy founded at Athens by Zeno *c.*308 BC, which sought virtue as the greatest good and taught control of one's feelings and passions. **2** (**stoic**) a stoical person. —*adj.* **1** of or like the Stoics. **2** (**stoic**) = STOICAL. [ME f. L *stoicus* f. Gk *stōikos* f. STOA (with ref. to Zeno's teaching in the *Stoa Poikilē* or Painted Porch at Athens)]

stoical /'stəʊɪk(ə)l/ *adj.* having or showing great self-control in adversity. □□ **stoically** *adv.*

stoichiometry /,stɔɪkɪ'ɒmɪtrɪ/ *n.* (also **stoichometry** /stɔɪ'kɒmɪtrɪ/) *Chem.* **1** the fixed, usu. rational numerical relationship between the relative quantities of substances in a reaction or compound. **2** the determination or measurement of these quantities. □□ **stoichiometric** /-kɪə'metrɪk/ *adj.* [Gk *stoikheion* element + -METRY]

Stoicism /'stəʊɪ,sɪz(ə)m/ *n.* **1** the philosophy of the Stoics. **2** (**stoicism**) a stoical attitude.

stoke /stəʊk/ *v.* (often foll. by *up*) **1 a** *tr.* feed and tend (a fire or furnace etc.). **b** *intr.* act as a stoker. **2** *intr. colloq.* consume food, esp. steadily and in large quantities. [back-form. f. STOKER]

stokehold /'stəʊkhəʊld/ *n.* a compartment in a steamship, containing its boilers and furnace.

stokehole /'stəʊkhəʊl/ *n.* a space for stokers in front of a furnace.

stoker /'stəʊkə(r)/ *n.* a person who tends to the furnace on a steamship. [Du. f. *stoken* stoke f. MDu. *stoken* push, rel. to STICK[1]]

stokes /stəʊks/ *n.* (*pl.* same) the cgs unit of kinematic viscosity, corresponding to a dynamic viscosity of 1 poise and a density of 1 gram per cubic centimetre, equivalent to 10^{-4} square metres per second. [Sir G. G. Stokes, Brit. physicist d. 1903]

STOL *abbr. Aeron.* short take-off and landing.

stole[1] /stəʊl/ *n.* **1** a woman's long garment like a scarf, worn over the shoulders. **2** a strip of silk etc. worn similarly as a vestment by a priest. [OE *stol, stole* (orig. a long robe) f. L *stola* f. Gk *stolē* equipment, clothing]

stole[2] *past* of STEAL.

stolen *past part.* of STEAL.

stolid /'stɒlɪd/ *adj.* **1** lacking or concealing emotion or animation. **2** not easily excited or moved. □□ **stolidity** /-'lɪdɪtɪ/ *n.* **stolidly** *adv.* **stolidness** *n.* [obs. F *stolide* or L *stolidus*]

stolon /'stəʊlɒn/ *n.* **1** *Bot.* a horizontal stem or branch that takes root at points along its length, forming new plants. **2** *Zool.* a branched stemlike structure in some invertebrates such as corals. □□ **stolonate**

/-ˌneɪt/ *adj.* **stoloniferous** /-'nɪfərəs/ *adj.* [L *stolo -onis*]

stoma /'stəʊmə/ *n.* (*pl.* **stomas** or **stomata** /-mətə/) **1** *Bot.* a minute pore in the epidermis of a leaf. **2 a** *Zool.* a small mouthlike opening in some lower animals. **b** *Surgery* a similar artificial orifice made in the stomach. □□ **stomal** *adj.* [mod.L f. Gk *stoma -atos* mouth]

stomach /'stʌmək/ *n.* & *v.* —*n.* **1 a** the internal organ in which the first part of digestion occurs, being in man a pear-shaped enlargement of the alimentary canal linking the oesophagus to the small intestine. **b** any of several such organs in animals, esp. ruminants, in which there are four (cf. RUMEN, RETICULUM, OMASUM, ABOMASUM). **2 a** the belly, abdomen, or lower front of the body (*pit of the stomach*). **b** a protuberant belly (*what a stomach he has got!*). **3** (usu. foll. by *for*) **a** an appetite (for food). **b** liking, readiness, or inclination (for controversy, conflict, danger, or an undertaking) (*had no stomach for the fight*). —*v.tr.* **1** find sufficiently palatable to swallow or keep down. **2** submit to or endure (an affront etc.) (usu. with *neg.*: *cannot stomach it*). □**muscular stomach** any organ that grinds or squeezes to aid digestion, such as a gizzard. **on an empty stomach** not having eaten recently. **on a full stomach** soon after a large meal. **stomach-ache** a pain in the belly or bowels. **stomach-pump** a syringe for forcing liquid etc. into or out of the stomach. **stomach-tube** a tube introduced into the stomach via the gullet for cleansing or emptying it. **stomach upset** (or **upset stomach**) a temporary slight disorder of the digestive system. □□ **stomachful** *n.* (*pl.* **-fuls**). **stomachless** *adj.* [ME *stomak* f. OF *stomaque, estomac* f. L *stomachus* f. Gk *stomakhos* gullet f. *stoma* mouth]

stomacher /'stʌməkə(r)/ *n. hist.* **1** a pointed front-piece of a woman's dress covering the breast and pit of the stomach, often jewelled or embroidered. **2** an ornament worn on the front of a bodice. [ME, prob. f. OF *estomacher* (as STOMACH)]

stomachic /stə'mækɪk/ *adj.* & *n.* —*adj.* **1** of or relating to the stomach. **2** promoting the appetite or assisting digestion. —*n.* a medicine or stimulant for the stomach. [F *stomachique* or L *stomachicus* f. Gk *stomakhikos* (as STOMACH)]

stomata *pl.* of STOMA.

stomatitis /,stəʊmə'taɪtɪs/ *n. Med.* inflammation of the mucous membrane of the mouth.

stomatology /,stəʊmə'tɒlədʒɪ/ *n.* the scientific study of the mouth or its diseases. □□ **stomatological** /-tə'lɒdʒɪk(ə)l/ *adj.* **stomatologist** *n.*

stomp /stɒmp/ *v.* & *n.* —*v.intr.* tread or stamp heavily. —*n.* a lively jazz dance with heavy stamping. □□ **stomper** *n.* [US dial. var. of STAMP]

stone /stəʊn/ *n.* & *v.* —*n.* **1 a** a solid non-metallic mineral matter, of which rock is made. **b** a piece of this, esp. a small piece. **2** *Building* **a** = LIMESTONE (*Portland stone*). **b** = SANDSTONE (*Bath stone*). **3** *Mineral.* = *precious stone.* **4** a stony meteorite, an aerolite. **5** (often in *comb.*) a piece of stone of a definite shape or for a particular purpose (*tombstone; stepping-stone*). **6 a** a thing resembling stone in hardness or form, e.g. the hard case of the kernel in some fruits. **b** *Med.* (often in *pl.*) a hard morbid concretion in the body esp. in the kidney or gall-bladder (*gallstones*). **7** (*pl.* same) *Brit.* a unit of weight equal to 14 lb. (6.35 kg). **8** (*attrib.*) **a** made of stone. **b** of the colour of stone. —*v.tr.* **1** pelt with stones. **2** remove the stones from (fruit). **3** face or pave etc. with stone. □**cast** (or **throw**) **stones** (or **the first stone**) make aspersions on a person's character etc. **leave no stone unturned** try all possible means. **Stone Age** a prehistoric period when weapons and tools were made of stone. **stone-coal** anthracite. **stone-cold** completely cold. **stone-cold sober** completely sober. **stone the crows** *Brit. sl.* an exclamation of surprise or disgust. **stone curlew**

b *but* d *dog* f *few* g *get* h *he* j *yes* k *cat* l *leg* m *man* n *no* p *pen* r *red* s *sit* t *top* v *voice*

any mottled brown and grey wader of the family Burhinidae, esp. *Burhinus oedicnemus*, inhabiting esp. stony open country. **stone-dead** completely dead. **stone-deaf** completely deaf. **stone-fruit** a fruit with flesh or pulp enclosing a stone. **stone parsley** an umbelliferous hedge-plant, *Sison amomum*, with aromatic seeds. **stone pine** a S. European pine-tree, *Pinus pinea*, with branches at the top spreading like an umbrella. **stone-pit** a quarry. **a stone's throw** a short distance. □□ **stoned** *adj.* (also in *comb.*). **stoneless** *adj.* **stoner** *n.* [OE *stān* f. Gmc]

stonechat /ˈstəʊntʃæt/ *n.* any small brown bird of the thrush family with black and white markings, esp. *Saxicola torquata* with a call like stones being knocked together.

stonecrop /ˈstəʊnkrɒp/ *n.* any succulent plant of the genus *Sedum*, usu. having yellow or white flowers and growing amongst rocks or in walls.

stonecutter /ˈstəʊnˌkʌtə(r)/ *n.* a person or machine that cuts or carves stone.

stoned /stəʊnd/ *adj. sl.* under the influence of alcohol or drugs.

stonefish /ˈstəʊnfɪʃ/ *n.* (*pl.* same) a venomous tropical fish, *Synanceia verrucosa*, with poison glands underlying its erect dorsal spines. Also called DEVILFISH.

stonefly /ˈstəʊnflaɪ/ *n.* (*pl.* **-flies**) any insect of the order Plecoptera, with aquatic larvae found under stones.

stoneground /ˈstəʊngraʊnd/ *adj.* (of flour) ground with millstones.

stonehatch /ˈstəʊnhætʃ/ *n.* a ringed plover.

stonemason /ˈstəʊnˌmeɪs(ə)n/ *n.* a person who cuts, prepares, and builds with stone. □□ **stonemasonry** *n.*

stonewall /ˈstəʊnwɔːl/ *v.* **1** *tr.* & *intr.* obstruct (discussion or investigation) or be obstructive with evasive answers or denials etc. **2** *intr.* *Cricket* bat with excessive caution. □□ **stonewaller** *n.* **stonewalling** *n.*

stoneware /ˈstəʊnweə(r)/ *n.* ceramic ware which is impermeable and partly vitrified but opaque.

stonewashed /ˈstəʊnwɒʃd/ *adj.* (of a garment or fabric, esp. denim) washed with abrasives to produce a worn or faded appearance.

stoneweed /ˈstəʊnwiːd/ *n.* = GROMWELL.

stonework /ˈstəʊnwɜːk/ *n.* **1** masonry. **2** the parts of a building made of stone. □□ **stoneworker** *n.*

stonewort /ˈstəʊnwɜːt/ *n.* **1** = *stone parsley*. **2** any plant of the genus *Chara*, with a calcareous deposit on the stem.

stonkered /ˈstɒŋkəd/ *adj. Austral. & NZ sl.* utterly defeated or exhausted. [20th c.: orig. unkn.]

stony /ˈstəʊnɪ/ *adj.* (**stonier**, **stoniest**) **1** full of or covered with stones (*stony soil*; *a stony road*). **2 a** hard, rigid. **b** cold, unfeeling, uncompromising (*a stony stare*; *a stony silence*). □ **stony-broke** *Brit. sl.* entirely without money. **stony-hearted** unfeeling, obdurate. □□ **stonily** *adv.* **stoniness** *n.* [OE *stānig* (as STONE)]

stood *past* and *past part.* of STAND.

stooge /stuːdʒ/ *n.* & *v. colloq.* —*n.* **1** a butt or foil, esp. for a comedian. **2** an assistant or subordinate, esp. for routine or unpleasant work. **3** a compliant person; a puppet. —*v.intr.* **1** (foll. by *for*) act as a stooge for. **2** (foll. by *about*, *around*, etc.) move about aimlessly. [20th c.: orig. unkn.]

stook /stuːk, stʊk/ *n.* & *v.* —*n.* a group of sheaves of grain stood on end in a field. —*v.tr.* arrange in stooks. [ME *stouk*, from or rel. to MLG *stūke*]

stool /stuːl/ *n.* & *v.* —*n.* **1** a seat without a back or arms, usu. for one person and consisting of a wooden slab on three or four short legs. **2 a** = FOOTSTOOL. **b** a low bench for kneeling on. **3** (usu. in *pl.*) = FAECES. **4** the root or stump of a tree or plant from which the shoots spring. **5** *US* a decoy-bird in hunting. —*v.intr.* (of a plant) throw up shoots from the root.

□ **fall between two stools** fail from vacillation between two courses etc. **stool-pigeon 1** a person acting as a decoy (orig. a decoy of a pigeon fixed to a stool). **2** a police informer. [OE *stōl* f. Gmc, rel. to STAND]

stoolball /ˈstuːlbɔːl/ *n.* a team-game played in the UK, with a bat and ball and pairs of batters scoring runs between bases.

stoolie /ˈstuːlɪ/ *n. US sl.* a person acting as a stool-pigeon.

stoop¹ /stuːp/ *v.* & *n.* —*v.* **1** *tr.* bend (one's head or body) forwards and downwards. **2** *intr.* carry one's head and shoulders bowed forward. **3** *intr.* (foll. by *to* + infin.) deign or condescend. **4** *intr.* (foll. by *to*) descend or lower oneself to (some conduct) (*has stooped to crime*). **5** *intr.* (of a hawk etc.) swoop on its prey. —*n.* **1** a stooping posture. **2** the downward swoop of a hawk etc. [OE *stūpian* f. Gmc, rel. to STEEP¹]

stoop² /stuːp/ *n. US* a porch or small veranda or set of steps in front of a house. [Du. *stoep*: see STOEP]

stoop³ var. of STOUP.

stop /stɒp/ *v.* & *n.* —*v.* (**stopped**, **stopping**) **1** *tr.* **a** put an end to (motion etc.); completely check the progress or motion or operation of. **b** effectively hinder or prevent (*stopped them playing so loudly*). **c** discontinue (an action or sequence of actions) (*stopped playing*; *stopped my visits*). **2** *intr.* come to an end; cease (*supplies suddenly stopped*). **3** *intr.* cease from motion or speaking or action; make a halt or pause (*the car stopped at the lights*; *he stopped in the middle of a sentence*; *my watch has stopped*). **4** *tr.* cause to cease action; defeat. **5** *tr. sl.* receive (a blow etc.). **6** *intr.* remain; stay for a short time. **7** *tr.* (often foll. by *up*) block or close up (a hole or leak etc.). **8** *tr.* not permit or supply as usual; discontinue or withhold (*shall stop their wages*). **9** *tr.* (in full **stop payment of** or **on**) instruct a bank to withhold payment on (a cheque). **10** *tr. Brit.* put a filling in (a tooth). **11** *tr.* obtain the required pitch from (the string of a violin etc.) by pressing at the appropriate point with the finger. **12** *tr.* plug the upper end of (an organ-pipe), giving a note an octave lower. **13** *tr. Bridge* be able to prevent opponents from taking all the tricks in (a suit). **14** *tr.* make (a sound) inaudible. **15** *tr. Boxing* **a** parry (a blow). **b** knock out (an opponent). **16** *tr. Hort.* pinch back (a plant). **17** *tr. Brit.* make (a clock, factory, etc.) cease working. **18** *tr. Brit.* provide with punctuation. **19** *tr. Naut.* make fast; stopper (a cable etc.). —*n.* **1** the act or an instance of stopping; the state of being stopped (*put a stop to*; *the vehicle was brought to a stop*). **2** a place designated for a bus or train etc. to stop. **3** a punctuation mark, esp. = *full stop* (see FULL¹). **4** a device for stopping motion at a particular point. **5** a change of pitch effected by stopping a string. **6 a** (in an organ) a row of pipes of one character. **b** a knob etc. operating these. **7** a manner of speech adopted to produce a particular effect. **8** *Optics & Photog.* = DIAPHRAGM 3. **9 a** the effective diameter of a lens. **b** a device for reducing this. **c** a unit of change of relative aperture or exposure (with a reduction of one stop equivalent to halving it). **10** (of sound) = PLOSIVE. **11** (in telegrams etc.) a full stop (see FULL¹). **12** *Bridge* a card or cards stopping a suit. **13** *Naut.* a small line used as a lashing. □ **put a stop to** cause to end, esp. abruptly. **stop at nothing** be ruthless. **stop by** (also *absol.*) call at (a place). **stop dead** (or **short**) cease abruptly. **stop down** *Photog.* reduce the aperture of (a lens) with a diaphragm. **stop-drill** a drill with a shoulder limiting the depth of penetration. **stop one's ears 1** put one's fingers in one's ears to avoid hearing. **2** refuse to listen. **stop a gap** serve to meet a temporary need. **stop-go 1** alternate stopping and restarting of progress. **2** *Brit.* the alternate restriction and stimulation of economic demand. **stop-knob** a knob controlling an organ stop. **stop lamp** a light on the rear of a vehicle showing when the brakes are applied. **stop light 1** a red traffic-light. **2** = *stop lamp*. **stop a person's mouth** induce a person by bribery or other means to keep silence about something. **stop off** (or **over**) break one's journey. **stop out 1** stay out. **2** cover (part of an area) to prevent printing, etching, etc. **stop payment** declare oneself insolvent. **stop press** *Brit.* **1** (often *attrib.*) late news inserted in a newspaper after printing has begun. **2** a column in a newspaper reserved for this. **stop valve** a valve closing a pipe against the passage of liquid. **stop-volley** (esp. in lawn tennis) a checked volley close to the net, dropping the ball dead on the other side. **with all the stops out** exerting extreme effort. □□ **stopless** *adj.* **stoppable** *adj.* [ME f. OE *-stoppian* f. LL *stuppare* STUFF: see ESTOP]

stopbank /'stɒpbæŋk/ *n. Austral.* & *NZ* an embankment built to prevent river-flooding.

stopcock /'stɒpkɒk/ *n.* an externally operated valve regulating the flow of a liquid or gas through a pipe etc.

stope /stəʊp/ *n.* a steplike part of a mine where ore etc. is being extracted. [app. rel. to STEP *n.*]

stopgap /'stɒpgæp/ *n.* (often *attrib.*) a temporary substitute.

stopoff /'stɒpɒf/ *n.* a break in one's journey.

stopover /'stɒp,əʊvə(r)/ *n.* = STOPOFF.

stoppage /'stɒpɪdʒ/ *n.* **1** the condition of being blocked or stopped. **2** a stopping (of pay). **3** a stopping or interruption of work in a factory etc.

stopper /'stɒpə(r)/ *n.* & *v.* —*n.* **1** a plug for closing a bottle etc. **2** a person or thing that stops something. **3** *Naut.* a rope or clamp etc. for checking and holding a rope cable or chain cable. —*v.tr.* close or secure with a stopper. □ **put a stopper on 1** put an end to (a thing). **2** keep (a person) quiet.

stopping /'stɒpɪŋ/ *n. Brit.* a filling for a tooth.

stopple /'stɒp(ə)l/ *n.* & *v.* —*n.* a stopper or plug. —*v.tr.* close with a stopple. [ME: partly f. STOP + -LE[1], partly f. ESTOPPEL]

stopwatch /'stɒpwɒtʃ/ *n.* a watch with a mechanism for recording elapsed time, used to time races etc.

storage /'stɔːrɪdʒ/ *n.* **1 a** the storing of goods etc. **b** a particular method of storing or the space available for it. **2** the cost of storing. **3** the electronic retention of data in a computer etc. □ **storage battery** (or **cell**) a battery (or cell) for storing electricity. **storage heater** *Brit.* an electric heater accumulating heat outside peak hours for later release.

storax /'stɔːræks/ *n.* **1 a** a fragrant resin, obtained from the tree *Styrax officinalis* and formerly used in perfume. **b** this tree. **2** (in full **Levant** or **liquid storax**) a balsam obtained from the tree *Liquidambar orientalis*. [L f. Gk, var. of STYRAX]

store /stɔː(r)/ *n.* & *v.* —*n.* **1** a quantity of something kept available for use (*a store of wine*; *a store of wit*). **2** (in *pl.*) **a** articles for a particular purpose accumulated for use (*naval stores*). **b** a supply of these or the place where they are kept. **3 a** = *department store* **b** esp. *US* any retail outlet or shop. **c** (often in *pl.*) a shop selling basic necessities (*general stores*). **4** a warehouse for the temporary keeping of furniture etc. **5** a device in a computer for storing retrievable data; a memory. —*v.tr.* **1** put (furniture etc.) in store. **2** (often foll. by *up*, *away*) accumulate (stores, energy, electricity, etc.) for future use. **3** stock or provide with something useful (*a mind stored with facts*). **4** (of a receptacle) have storage capacity for. **5** enter or retain (data) for retrieval. □ **in store 1** kept in readiness. **2** coming in the future. **3** (foll. by *for*) destined or intended. **set** (or **lay** or **put**) **store by** (or **on**) consider important or valuable. □□ **storable** *adj.* **storer** *n.* [ME f. obs. *astore* (n. & v.) f. OF *estore*, *estorer* f. L *instaurare* renew: cf. RESTORE]

storefront /'stɔːfrʌnt/ *n.* esp. *US* **1** the side of a shop facing the street. **2** a room at the front of a shop.

storehouse /'stɔːhaʊs/ *n.* a place where things are stored.

storekeeper /'stɔː,kiːpə(r)/ *n.* **1** a storeman. **2** *US* a shopkeeper.

storeman /'stɔːmən/ *n.* (*pl.* -**men**) a person responsible for stored goods.

storeroom /'stɔːruːm, -rʊm/ *n.* a room in which items are stored.

storey /'stɔːrɪ/ *n.* (also **story**) (*pl.* -**eys** or -**ies**) **1** any of the parts into which a building is divided horizontally; the whole of the rooms etc. having a continuous floor (*a third-storey window*; *a house of five storeys*). **2** a thing forming a horizontal division. □□ -**storeyed** (in *comb.*) (also -**storied**). [ME f. AL *historia* HISTORY (perh. orig. meaning a tier of painted windows or sculpture)]

storiated /'stɔːrɪ,eɪtɪd/ *adj.* decorated with historical, legendary, or emblematic designs. □□ **storiation** /-'eɪʃ(ə)n/ *n.* [shortening of HISTORIATED]

storied /'stɔːrɪd/ *adj. literary* celebrated in or associated with stories or legends.

stork /stɔːk/ *n.* **1** any long-legged large wading bird of the family Ciconiidae, esp. *Ciconia ciconia* with white plumage, black wing-tips, a long reddish beak, and red feet, nesting esp. on tall buildings. **2** this bird as the pretended bringer of babies. □ **stork's-bill** a plant of the genus *Pelargonium* or *Erodium*. [OE *storc*, prob. rel. to STARK (from its rigid posture)]

storm /stɔːm/ *n.* & *v.* —*n.* **1** a violent disturbance of the atmosphere with strong winds and usu. with thunder and rain or snow etc. **2** *Meteorol.* a wind intermediate between gale and hurricane, esp. (on the Beaufort scale) of 55-72 m.p.h. **3** a violent disturbance of the established order in human affairs. **4** (foll. by *of*) **a** a violent shower of missiles or blows. **b** an outbreak of applause, indignation, hisses, etc. (*they were greeted by a storm of abuse*). **5 a** a direct assault by troops on a fortified place. **b** the capture of a place by such an assault. —*v.* **1** *intr.* (often foll. by *at*, *away*) talk violently, rage, bluster. **2** *intr.* (usu. foll. by *in*, *out of*, etc.) move violently or angrily (*stormed out of the meeting*). **3** *tr.* attack or capture by storm. **4** *intr.* (of wind, rain, etc.) rage; be violent. □ **storm-bird** = *storm petrel*. **storm centre 1** the point to which the wind blows spirally inward in a cyclonic storm. **2** a subject etc. upon which agitation or disturbance is concentrated. **storm cloud 1** a heavy rain-cloud. **2** a threatening state of affairs. **storm-cock** a mistle-thrush. **storm-collar** a high coat-collar that can be turned up and fastened. **storm cone** *Brit.* a tarred-canvas cone hoisted as a warning of high wind, upright for the north and inverted for the south. **storm-door** an additional outer door for protection in bad weather or winter. **storm-finch** *Brit.* = *storm petrel*. **storm-glass** a sealed tube containing a solution of which the clarity is thought to change when storms approach. **storming-party** a detachment of troops ordered to begin an assault. **storm in a teacup** *Brit.* great excitement over a trivial matter. **storm-lantern** *Brit.* a hurricane lamp. **storm petrel 1** a small petrel, *Hydrobates pelagicus*, of the North Atlantic, with black and white plumage. **2** a person causing unrest. **storm-sail** a sail of smaller size and stouter canvas than the corresponding one used in ordinary weather. **storm-signal** a device warning of an approaching storm. **storm trooper 1** *hist.* a member of the Nazi political militia. **2** a member of the shock troops. **storm troops 1** = *shock troops* (see SHOCK[1]). **2** *hist.* the Nazi political militia. **storm window** an additional outer sash-window used like a storm-door. **take by storm 1** capture by direct assault. **2** rapidly captivate (a person, audience, etc.). □□ **stormless** *adj.* **stormproof** *adj.* [OE f. Gmc]

stormbound /'stɔːmbaʊnd/ *adj.* prevented by storms from leaving port or continuing a voyage.

stormy /'stɔːmɪ/ *adj.* (**stormier**, **stormiest**) **1** of or affected by storms. **2** (of a wind etc.) violent, raging, vehement. **3** full of feeling or outbursts; lively, boisterous (*a stormy meeting*). □**stormy petrel** = *storm petrel*. □□**stormily** *adv.* **storminess** *n.*

story[1] /'stɔːrɪ/ *n.* (*pl.* **-ies**) **1** an account of imaginary or past events; a narrative, tale, or anecdote. **2** the past course of the life of a person or institution etc. (*my story is a strange one*). **3** (in full **story-line**) the narrative or plot of a novel or play etc. **4** facts or experiences that deserve narration. **5** *colloq.* a fib or lie. **6** a narrative or descriptive item of news. □**the old** (or **same old**) **story** the familiar or predictable course of events. **story-book 1** a book of stories for children. **2** (*attrib.*) unreal, romantic (*a story-book ending*). **the story goes** it is said. **to cut** (or **make**) **a long story short** a formula excusing the omission of details. [ME *storie* f. AF *estorie* (OF *estoire*) f. L *historia* (as HISTORY)]

story[2] var. of STOREY.

storyboard /'stɔːrɪ,bɔːd/ *n.* a displayed sequence of pictures etc. outlining the plan of a film, television advertisement, etc.

storyteller /'stɔːrɪ,telə(r)/ *n.* **1** a person who tells stories. **2** *colloq.* a liar. □□**storytelling** *n.* & *adj.*

stoup /stuːp/ *n.* (also **stoop**) **1** a holy-water basin. **2** *archaic* a flagon, beaker, or drinking-vessel. [ME f. ON *staup* (= OE *stēap*) f. Gmc, rel. to STEEP[2]]

stoush /staʊʃ/ *v.* & *n.* *Austral.* & *NZ sl.* —*v.tr.* **1** hit; fight with. **2** attack verbally. —*n.* a fight; a beating. [19th c.: orig. uncert.]

stout /staʊt/ *adj.* & *n.* —*adj.* **1** rather fat; corpulent; bulky. **2** of considerable thickness or strength (*a stout stick*). **3** brave, resolute, vigorous (*a stout fellow*; *put up stout resistance*). —*n.* a strong dark beer brewed with roasted malt or barley. □**a stout heart** courage, resolve. **stout-hearted** courageous. **stout-heartedly** courageously. **stout-heartedness** courage. □□**stoutish** *adj.* **stoutly** *adv.* **stoutness** *n.* [ME f. AF & dial. OF *stout* f. WG, perh. rel. to STILT]

stove[1] /stəʊv/ *n.* & *v.* —*n.* **1** a closed apparatus burning fuel or electricity for heating or cooking. **2** *Brit. Hort.* a hothouse with artificial heat. —*v.tr. Brit.* force or raise (plants) in a stove. □**stove-enamel** a heatproof enamel produced by the treatment of enamelled objects in a stove. **stove-pipe** a pipe conducting smoke and gases from a stove to a chimney. **stove-pipe hat** *colloq.* a tall silk hat. [ME = sweating-room, f. MDu., MLG *stove*, OHG *stuba* f. Gmc, perh. rel. to STEW[1]]

stove[2] past and past part. of STAVE *v.*

stow /stəʊ/ *v.tr.* **1** pack (goods etc.) tidily and compactly. **2** *Naut.* place (a cargo or provisions) in its proper place and order. **3** fill (a receptacle) with articles compactly arranged. **4** (usu. in *imper.*) *sl.* abstain or cease from (*stow the noise!*). □**stow away 1** place (a thing) where it will not cause an obstruction. **2** be a stowaway on a ship etc. [ME, f. BESTOW: in Naut. use perh. infl. by Du. *stouwen*]

stowage /'stəʊɪdʒ/ *n.* **1** the act or an instance of stowing. **2** a place for this.

stowaway /'stəʊə,weɪ/ *n.* a person who hides on board a ship or aircraft etc. to get free passage.

STP *abbr.* **1** Professor of Sacred Theology. **2** standard temperature and pressure.

str. *abbr.* **1** strait. **2** stroke (of an oar).

strabismus /strə'bɪzməs/ *n. Med.* the abnormal condition of one or both eyes not correctly aligned in direction; a squint. □□**strabismal** *adj.* **strabismic** *adj.* [mod.L f. Gk *strabismos* f. *strabizō* squint f. *strabos* squinting]

Strad /stræd/ *n. colloq.* a Stradivarius. [abbr.]

straddle /'stræd(ə)l/ *v.* & *n.* —*v.* **1** *tr.* **a** sit or stand across (a thing) with the legs wide apart. **b** be situated across or on both sides of (*the town straddles the border*). **2** *intr.* **a** sit or stand in this way. **b** (of the legs) be wide apart. **3** *tr.* part (one's legs) widely. **4** *tr.* drop shots or bombs short of and beyond (a target). **5** *tr.* vacillate between two policies etc. regarding (an issue). —*n.* **1** the act or an instance of straddling. **2** *Stock Exch.* an option giving the holder

the right of either calling for or delivering stock at a fixed price. □□**straddler** *n.* [alt. of *striddle*, back-form. f. *striddlings* astride f. *strid-* = STRIDE]

Stradivarius /,strædɪ'veərɪəs/ *n.* a violin or other stringed instrument made by Antonio Stradivari of Cremona (d. 1737) or his followers. [Latinized f. *Stradivari*]

strafe /strɑːf, streɪf/ *v.* & *n.* —*v.tr.* **1** bombard; harass with gunfire. **2** reprimand. **3** abuse. **4** thrash. —*n.* an act of strafing. [joc. adaptation of G catchword (1914) *Gott strafe England* may God punish England]

straggle /'stræg(ə)l/ *v.* & *n.* —*v.intr.* **1** lack or lose compactness or tidiness. **2** be or become dispersed or sporadic. **3** trail behind others in a march or race etc. **4** (of a plant, beard, etc.) grow long and loose. —*n.* a body or group of straggling or scattered persons or things. □□**straggler** *n.* **straggly** *adj.* (**stragglier**, **straggliest**). [ME, perh. rel. to dial. *strake* go, rel. to STRETCH]

straight /streɪt/ *adj.*, *n.*, & *adv.* —*adj.* **1 a** extending uniformly in the same direction; without a curve or bend etc. **b** *Geom.* (of a line) lying on the shortest path between any two of its points. **2** successive, uninterrupted (*three straight wins*). **3** in proper order or place or condition; duly arranged; level, symmetrical (*is the picture straight?*; *put things straight*). **4** honest, candid; not evasive (*a straight answer*). **5** (of thinking etc.) logical, unemotional. **6** (of drama etc.) serious as opposed to popular or comic; employing the conventional techniques of its art form. **7 a** unmodified. **b** (of a drink) undiluted. **8** *colloq.* (of music) classical. **9** *colloq.* **a** (of a person etc.) conventional or respectable. **b** heterosexual. **10** (of an arch) flat-topped. **11** (of a person's back) not bowed. **12** (of the hair) not curly or wavy. **13** (of a knee) not bent. **14** (of the legs) not bandy or knock-kneed. **15** (of a garment) not flared. **16** coming direct from its source. **17** (of an aim, look, blow, or course) going direct to the mark. —*n.* **1** the straight part of something, esp. the concluding stretch of a racecourse. **2** a straight condition. **3** a sequence of five cards in poker. **4** *colloq.* a conventional person; a heterosexual. —*adv.* **1** in a straight line; direct; without deviation or hesitation or circumlocution (*came straight from Paris*; *I told them straight*). **2** in the right direction, with a good aim (*shoot straight*). **3** correctly (*can't see straight*). **4** *archaic* at once or immediately. □**go straight** live an honest life after being a criminal. **the straight and narrow** morally correct behaviour. **straight angle** an angle of 180°. **straight away** at once; immediately. **straight-bred** not cross-bred. **straight-cut** (of tobacco) cut length-wise into long silky fibres. **straight-edge** a bar with one edge accurately straight, used for testing. **straight-eight 1** an internal-combustion engine with eight cylinders in line. **2** a vehicle having this. **straight eye** the ability to detect deviation from the straight. **straight face** an intentionally ex-pressionless face, esp. avoiding a smile though amused. **straight-faced** having a straight face. **straight fight** *Brit. Polit.* a direct contest between two candidates. **straight flush** see FLUSH[3]. **straight from the shoulder 1** (of a blow) well delivered. **2** (of a verbal attack) frank or direct. **straight man** a comedian's stooge. **straight off** *colloq.* without hesitation, deliberation, etc. (*cannot tell you straight off*). **straight-out** *US* **1** uncompromising. **2** straightforward, genuine. **straight razor** *US* a cut-throat razor. □□**straightly** *adv.* **straightness** *n.* [ME, past part. of STRETCH]

straightaway /'streɪtə,weɪ/ *adj.* *US* **1** (of a course etc.) straight. **2** straightforward.

straighten /'streɪt(ə)n/ *v.tr.* & *intr.* **1** (often foll. by *out*) make or become straight. **2** (foll. by *up*) stand erect after bending. □□**straightener** *n.*

straightforward /streɪt'fɔːwəd/ *adj.* **1** honest or frank. **2** (of a task etc.) uncomplicated. □□ **straightforwardly** *adv.* **straightforwardness** *n.*

straightway /ˈstreɪtweɪ/ adv. archaic = straight away.

strain[1] /streɪn/ v. & n. —v. **1** tr. & intr. stretch tightly; make or become taut or tense. **2** tr. exercise (oneself, one's senses, a thing, etc.) intensely or excessively, press to extremes. **3 a** intr. make an intensive effort. **b** intr. (foll. by after) strive intensely for (straining after perfection). **4** intr. (foll. by at) tug, pull (the dog strained at the leash). **5** intr. hold out with difficulty under pressure (straining under the load). **6** tr. **a** distort from the true intention or meaning. **b** apply (authority, laws, etc.) beyond their province or in violation of their true intention. **7** tr. overtask or injure by overuse or excessive demands (strain a muscle; strained their loyalty). **8 a** tr. clear (a liquid) of solid matter by passing it through a sieve etc. **b** tr. (foll. by out) filter (solids) out from a liquid. **c** intr. (of a liquid) percolate. **9** tr. hug or squeeze tightly. **10** tr. use (one's ears, eyes, voice, etc.) to the best of one's power. —n. **1 a** the act or an instance of straining. **b** the force exerted in this. **2** an injury caused by straining a muscle etc. **3 a** severe demand on physical strength or resources. **b** the exertion needed to meet this (is suffering from strain). **4** (in sing. or pl.) a snatch or spell of music or poetry. **5** a tone or tendency in speech or writing (more in the same strain). **6** Physics **a** the condition of a body subjected to stress; molecular displacement. **b** a quantity measuring this, equal to the amount of deformation usu. divided by the original dimension. □**at strain** (or **full strain**) exerted to the utmost. **strain every nerve** make every possible effort. **strain oneself 1** injure oneself by effort. **2** make undue efforts. □□**strainable** adj. [ME f. OF estreindre estreign- f. L stringere strict- draw tight]

strain[2] /streɪn/ n. **1** a breed or stock of animals, plants, etc. **2** a moral tendency as part of a person's character (a strain of aggression). [ME, = progeny, f. OE strēon (recorded in gestrēonan beget), rel. to L struere build]

strained /streɪnd/ adj. **1** constrained, forced, artificial. **2** (of a relationship) mutually distrustful or tense. **3** (of an interpretation) involving an unreasonable assumption; far-fetched, laboured.

strainer /ˈstreɪnə(r)/ n. a device for straining liquids, vegetables, etc.

strait /streɪt/ n. & adj. —n. **1** (in sing. or pl.) a narrow passage of water connecting two seas or large bodies of water. **2** (usu. in pl.) difficulty, trouble, or distress (usu. in dire or desperate straits). —adj. archaic **1** narrow, limited; confined or confining. **2** strict or rigorous. □**strait-laced** severely virtuous; morally scrupulous; puritanical. □□**straitly** adv. **straitness** n. [ME streit f. OF estreit tight, narrow f. L strictus STRICT]

straiten /ˈstreɪt(ə)n/ v. **1** tr. restrict in range or scope. **2** tr. (as **straitened** adj.) of or marked by poverty. **3** tr. & intr. archaic make or become narrow.

strait-jacket /ˈstreɪtˌdʒækɪt/ n. & v. —n. **1** a strong garment with long arms for confining the arms of a violent prisoner, mental patient, etc. **2** restrictive measures. —v.tr. (**-jacketed**, **-jacketing**) **1** restrain with a strait-jacket. **2** severely restrict.

strake /streɪk/ n. **1** a continuous line of planking or plates from the stem to the stern of a ship. **2** a section of the iron rim of a wheel. [ME: prob. rel. to OE streccan STRETCH]

stramonium /strəˈməʊnɪəm/ n. **1** datura. **2** the dried leaves of this plant used in the treatment of asthma. [mod.L, perh. f. Tartar turman horse-medicine]

strand[1] /strænd/ v. & n. —v. **1** tr. & intr. run aground. **2** tr. (as **stranded** adj.) in difficulties, esp. without money or means of transport. —n. rhet. or poet. the margin of a sea, lake, or river, esp. the foreshore. [OE]

strand[2] /strænd/ n. & v. —n. **1** each of the threads or wires twisted round each other to make a rope or cable. **2 a** a single thread or strip of fibre. **b** a constituent filament. **3** a lock of hair. **4** an element or strain in any composite whole. —v.tr. **1** break a strand in (a rope). **2** arrange in strands. [ME: orig. unkn.]

strange /streɪndʒ/ adj. **1** unusual, peculiar, surprising, eccentric, novel. **2 a** (often foll. by to) unfamiliar, alien, foreign (lost in a strange land). **b** not one's own (strange gods). **3** (foll. by to) unaccustomed. **4** not at ease; out of one's element (felt strange in such company). □**feel strange** be unwell. **strange particle** Physics an elementary particle classified as having a non-zero value for strangeness. **strange to say** it is surprising or unusual (that). □□**strangely** adv. [ME f. OF estrange f. L extraneus EXTRANEOUS]

strangeness /ˈstreɪndʒnɪs/ n. **1** the state or fact of being strange or unfamiliar etc. **2** Physics a property of certain elementary particles that is conserved in strong interactions.

stranger /ˈstreɪndʒə(r)/ n. **1** a person who does not know or is not known in a particular place or company. **2** (often foll. by to) a person one does not know (was a complete stranger to me). **3** (foll. by to) a person entirely unaccustomed to (a feeling, experience, etc.) (no stranger to controversy). **4** a floating tea-leaf etc. held to foretell the arrival of a visitor. **5** Parl. a person who is not a member or official of the House of Commons. [ME f. OF estrangier ult. f. L (as STRANGE)]

strangle /ˈstræŋɡ(ə)l/ v.tr. **1** squeeze the windpipe or neck of, esp. so as to kill. **2** hamper or suppress (a movement, impulse, cry, etc.). □□**strangler** n. [ME f. OF estrangler f. L strangulare f. Gk straggalaō f. straggalē halter: cf. straggos twisted]

stranglehold /ˈstræŋɡ(ə)lˌhəʊld/ n. **1** a wrestling hold that throttles an opponent. **2** a deadly grip. **3** complete and exclusive control.

strangles /ˈstræŋɡ(ə)lz/ n.pl. (usu. treated as sing.) an infectious streptococcal fever, esp. affecting the respiratory tract, in a horse, ass, etc. [pl. of strangle (n.) f. STRANGLE]

strangulate /ˈstræŋɡjʊˌleɪt/ v.tr. Surgery **1** prevent circulation through (a vein, intestine, etc.) by compression. **2** remove (a tumour etc.) by binding with a cord. □**strangulated hernia** Med. a hernia in which the protruding part is constricted, preventing circulation. [L strangulare strangulat- (as STRANGLE)]

strangulation /ˌstræŋɡjʊˈleɪʃ(ə)n/ n. **1** the act of strangling or the state of being strangled. **2** the act of strangulating. [L strangulatio (as STRANGULATE)]

strangury /ˈstræŋɡjʊrɪ/ n. a condition in which urine is passed painfully and in drops. □□**strangurious** /-ˈgjʊərɪəs/ adj. [ME f. L stranguria f. Gk straggouria f. stragx -ggos drop squeezed out + ouron urine]

strap /stræp/ n. & v. —n. **1** a strip of leather or other flexible material, often with a buckle or other fastening for holding things together etc. **2** a thing like this for keeping a garment in place. **3** a loop for grasping to steady oneself in a moving vehicle. **4 a** a strip of metal used to secure or connect. **b** a leaf of a hinge. **5** Bot. a tongue-shaped part in a floret. **6** (prec. by the) punishment by beating with a strap. —v.tr. (**strapped**, **strapping**) **1** (often foll. by down, up, etc.) secure or bind with a strap. **2** beat with a strap. **3** (esp. as **strapped** adj.) colloq. subject to a shortage. **4** (often foll. by up) close (a wound) or bind (a part) with adhesive plaster. □**strap-work** ornamentation imitating plaited straps. □□**strapper** n. **strappy** adj. [dial. form of STROP]

straphanger /ˈstræpˌhæŋɡə(r)/ n. sl. a standing passenger in a bus or train. □□**straphang** v.intr.

strapless /ˈstræplɪs/ adj. (of a garment) without straps, esp. shoulder-straps.

strappado /strəˈpɑːdəʊ/ n. (pl. **-os**) hist. a form of torture in which the victim is secured to a rope and made to fall from a height almost to the ground then stopped with a jerk; an application of this; the instrument used. [F (*e*)*strapade* f. It. *strappata* f. *strappare* snatch]

strapping /'stræpɪŋ/ *adj.* (esp. of a person) large and sturdy.

strata *pl.* of STRATUM.

stratagem /'strætədʒəm/ *n.* **1** a cunning plan or scheme, esp. for deceiving an enemy. **2** trickery. [ME f. F *stratagème* f. L *stratagema* f. Gk *stratēgēma* f. *stratēgeō* be a general (*stratēgos*) f. *stratos* army + *agō* lead]

stratal see STRATUM.

strategic /strə'ti:dʒɪk/ *adj.* **1** of or serving the ends of strategy (*strategic considerations*). **2** (of materials) essential in fighting a war. **3** (of bombing or weapons) done or for use against an enemy's home territory as a longer-term military objective (opp. TACTICAL). □**strategic defence initiative** a projected US system of defence against nuclear weapons using satellites. □□ **strategical** *adj.* **strategically** *adv.* **strategics** *n.pl.* (usu. treated as *sing.*). [F *stratégique* f. Gk *stratēgikos* (as STRATAGEM)]

strategy /'strætɪdʒɪ/ *n.* (*pl.* -**ies**) **1** the art of war. **2 a** the management of an army or armies in a campaign. **b** the art of moving troops, ships, aircraft, etc. into favourable positions (cf. TACTICS). **c** an instance of this or a plan formed according to it. **3** a plan of action or policy in business or politics etc. (*economic strategy*). □□ **strategist** *n.* [F *stratégie* f. Gk *stratēgia* generalship f. *stratēgos*: see STRATAGEM]

strath /stræθ/ *n. Sc.* a broad mountain valley. [Gael. *srath*]

strathspey /stræθ'speɪ/ *n.* **1** a slow Scottish dance. **2** the music for this. [*Strathspey*, valley of the river Spey]

strati *pl.* of STRATUS.

straticulate /strə'tɪkjʊlət/ *adj. Geol.* (of rock-formations) arranged in thin strata. [STRATUM, after *vermiculate* etc.]

stratify /'strætɪˌfaɪ/ *v.tr.* (-**ies**, -**ied**) **1** (esp. as **stratified** *adj.*) arrange in strata. **2** construct in layers, social grades, etc. □□ **stratification** /-fɪ'keɪʃ(ə)n/ *n.* [F *stratifier* (as STRATUM)]

stratigraphy /strə'tɪgrəfɪ/ *n. Geol. & Archaeol.* **1** the order and relative position of strata. **2** the study of this as a means of historical interpretation. □□ **stratigraphic** /ˌstrætɪ'græfɪk/ *adj.* **stratigraphical** /ˌstrætɪ'græfɪk(ə)l/ *adj.* [STRATUM + -GRAPHY]

strato- /'strætəʊ/ *comb. form* stratus.

stratocirrus /ˌstrætəʊ'sɪrəs/ *n.* clouds combining stratus and cirrus features.

stratocracy /strə'tɒkrəsɪ/ *n.* (*pl.* -**ies**) **1** a military government. **2** domination by soldiers. [Gk *stratos* army + -CRACY]

stratocumulus /ˌstrætəʊ'kju:mjʊləs/ *n.* clouds combining cumulus and stratus features.

stratopause /'strætəʊˌpɔ:z/ *n.* the interface between the stratosphere and the ionosphere.

stratosphere /'strætəˌsfɪə(r)/ *n.* a layer of atmospheric air above the troposphere extending to about 50 km above the earth's surface, in which the lower part changes little in temperature and the upper part increases in temperature with height (cf. IONOSPHERE). □□ **stratospheric** /-'sferɪk/ *adj.* [STRATUM + SPHERE after *atmosphere*]

stratum /'strɑ:təm, 'streɪ-/ *n.* (*pl.* **strata** /-tə/) **1** esp. *Geol.* a layer or set of successive layers of any deposited substance. **2** an atmospheric layer. **3** a layer of tissue etc. **4 a** a social grade, class, etc. (*the various strata of society*). **b** *Statistics* each of the groups into which a population is divided in stratified sampling. □□ **stratal** *adj.* [L, = something spread or laid down, neut. past part. of *sternere* strew]

stratus /'streɪtəs, 'strɑː-/ *n.* (*pl.* **strati** /-taɪ/) a continuous horizontal sheet of cloud. [L, past part. of *sternere*: see STRATUM]

straw /strɔː/ *n.* **1** dry cut stalks of grain for use as fodder or as material for thatching, packing, making hats, etc. **2** a single stalk or piece of straw. **3** a thin

hollow paper or plastic tube for sucking drink from a glass etc. **4** an insignificant thing (*not worth a straw*). **5** the pale yellow colour of straw. **6** a straw hat. □**catch** (or **grasp**) **at a straw** resort to an utterly inadequate expedient in desperation, like a person drowning. **straw boss** *US* an assistant foreman. **straw-colour** pale yellow. **straw-coloured** of pale yellow. **straw in the wind** a slight hint of future developments. **straw vote** (or **poll**) an unofficial ballot as a test of opinion. **straw-worm** a caddis-worm. □□ **strawy** *adj.* [OE *strēaw* f. Gmc, rel. to STREW]

strawberry /'strɔːbərɪ/ *n.* (*pl.* -**ies**) **1 a** any plant of the genus *Fragaria*, esp. any of various cultivated varieties, with white flowers, trifoliate leaves, and runners. **b** the pulpy red edible fruit of this, having a seed-studded surface. **2** a deep pinkish-red colour. □**strawberry blonde 1** pinkish-blonde hair. **2** a woman with such hair. **strawberry mark** a soft reddish birthmark. **strawberry pear 1** a W. Indian cactaceous plant, *Hylocereus undatus*. **2** the fruit of this. **strawberry roan** see ROAN[1]. **strawberry-tree** an evergreen tree, *Arbutus unedo*, bearing strawberry-like fruit. [OE *strēa(w)berige*, *strēowberige* (as STRAW, BERRY): reason for the name unkn.]

strawboard /'strɔːbɔːd/ *n.* a coarse cardboard made of straw pulp.

stray /streɪ/ *v., n., & adj.* —*v.intr.* **1** wander from the right place; become separated from one's companions etc.; go astray. **2** deviate morally. **3** (as **strayed** *adj.*) that has gone astray. —*n.* **1** a person or thing that has strayed, esp. a domestic animal. **2** (esp. in *pl.*) electrical phenomena interfering with radio reception. —*adj.* **1** strayed or lost. **2** isolated; found or occurring occasionally (*a stray customer or two*; *hit by a stray bullet*). **3** *Physics* wasted or unwanted (*eliminate stray magnetic fields*). □□ **strayer** *n.* [ME f. AF & OF *estrayer* (v.), AF *strey* (n. & adj.) f. OF *estraié* (as ASTRAY)]

streak /striːk/ *n. & v.* —*n.* **1** a long thin usu. irregular line or band, esp. distinguished by colour (*black with red streaks*; *a streak of light above the horizon*). **2** a strain or element in a person's character (*has a streak of mischief*). **3** a spell or series (*a winning streak*). **4** a line of bacteria etc. placed on a culture medium. —*v.* **1** *tr.* mark with streaks. **2** *intr.* move very rapidly. **3** *intr. colloq.* run naked in a public place as a stunt. □**streak of lightning** a sudden prominent flash of lightning. □□ **streaker** *n.* **streaking** *n.* [OE *strica* pen-stroke f. Gmc: rel. to STRIKE]

streaky /'striːkɪ/ *adj.* (**streakier**, **streakiest**) **1** full of streaks. **2** (of bacon) with alternate streaks of fat and lean. □□ **streakily** *adv.* **streakiness** *n.*

stream /striːm/ *n. & v.* —*n.* **1** a flowing body of water, esp. a small river. **2 a** the flow of a fluid or of a mass of people (*a stream of lava*). **b** (in *sing.* or *pl.*) a large quantity of something that flows or moves along. **3** a current or direction in which things are moving or tending (*against the stream*). **4** *Brit.* a group of schoolchildren taught together as being of similar ability for a given age. —*v.* **1** *intr.* flow or move as a stream. **2** *intr.* run with liquid (*my eyes were streaming*). **3** *intr.* (of a banner or hair etc.) float or wave in the wind. **4** *tr.* emit a stream of (blood etc.). **5** *tr. Brit.* arrange (schoolchildren) in streams. □**go with the stream** do as others do. **on stream** (of a factory etc.) in operation. **stream-anchor** an anchor intermediate in size between a bower and a kedge, esp. for use in warping. **stream of consciousness 1** *Psychol.* a person's thoughts and conscious reactions to events perceived as a continuous flow. **2** a literary style depicting events in such a flow in the mind of a character. □□ **streamless** *adj.* **streamlet** *n.* [OE *strēam* f. Gmc]

streamer /'striːmə(r)/ *n.* **1** a long narrow flag. **2** a long narrow strip of ribbon or paper, esp. in a coil that unrolls when thrown. **3** a banner headline. **4** (in *pl.*) the aurora borealis or australis.

streamline /ˈstriːmlaɪn/ *v. & n.* —*v.tr.* **1** give (a vehicle etc.) the form which presents the least resistance to motion. **2** make (an organization, process, etc.) simple or more efficient or better organized. —*n.* **1** the natural course of water or air currents. **2** (often *attrib.*) the shape of an aircraft, car, etc., calculated to cause the least resistance to motion.

street /striːt/ *n.* **1 a** a public road in a city, town, or village. **b** this with the houses or other buildings on each side. **2** the persons who live or work on a particular street. □ **in the street 1** in the area outside the houses. **2** (of Stock Exchange business) done after closing-time. **not in the same street with** *colloq.* utterly inferior to in ability etc. **on the streets 1** living by prostitution. **2** homeless. **street Arab 1** a homeless child. **2** an urchin. **street credibility** familiarity with a fashionable urban subculture. **street cries** *Brit.* the cries of street hawkers. **street door** a main outer house-door opening on the street. **street jewellery** enamel advertising plates as collectors' items. **streets ahead** (often foll. by *of*) *colloq.* much superior (to). **street value** the value of drugs sold illicitly. **up** (or **right up**) **one's street** *colloq.* **1** within one's range of interest or knowledge. **2** to one's liking. □□ **streeted** *adj.* (also in *comb.*). **streetward** *adj. & adv.* [OE *strǣt* f. LL *strāta* (*via*) paved (way), fem. past part. of *sternere* lay down]

streetcar /ˈstriːtkɑː(r)/ *n. US* a tram.

streetwalker /ˈstriːtˌwɔːkə(r)/ *n.* a prostitute seeking customers in the street. □□ **streetwalking** *n. & adj.*

streetwise /ˈstriːtwaɪz/ *n.* esp. *US* familiar with the ways of modern urban life.

strength /streŋθ, streŋkθ/ *n.* **1** the state of being strong; the degree or respect in which a person or thing is strong. **2 a** a person or thing affording strength or support. **b** an attribute making for strength of character (*patience is your great strength*). **3** the number of persons present or available. **4** a full complement (*below strength*). □ **from strength** from a strong position. **from strength to strength** with ever-increasing success. **in strength** in large numbers. **on the strength of** relying on; on the basis of. **the strength of** the essence or main features of. □□ **strengthless** *adj.* [OE *strengthu* f. Gmc (as STRONG)]

strengthen /ˈstreŋθ(ə)n, -ŋkθ(ə)n/ *v.tr. & intr.* make or become stronger. □ **strengthen a person's hand** (or **hands**) encourage a person to vigorous action. □□ **strengthener** *n.*

strenuous /ˈstrenjʊəs/ *adj.* **1** requiring or using great effort. **2** energetic or unrelaxing. □□ **strenuously** *adv.* **strenuousness** *n.* [L *strenuus* brisk]

strep /strep/ *n. colloq.* = STREPTOCOCCUS. [abbr.]

streptococcus /ˌstreptəˈkɒkəs/ *n.* (*pl.* **streptococci** /-ˈkɒkaɪ/) any bacterium of the genus *Streptococcus*, usu. occurring in chains, some of which cause infectious diseases. □□ **streptococcal** *adj.* [Gk *streptos* twisted f. *strephō* turn + COCCUS]

streptomycin /ˌstreptəʊˈmaɪsɪn/ *n.* an antibiotic produced by the bacterium *Streptomyces griseus*, effective against many disease-producing bacteria. [Gk *streptos* (as STREPTOCOCCUS) + *mukēs* fungus]

stress /stres/ *n. & v.* —*n.* **1 a** a pressure or tension exerted on a material object. **b** a quantity measuring this. **2 a** a demand on physical or mental energy. **b** distress caused by this (*suffering from stress*). **3 a** emphasis (*the stress was on the need for success*). **b** accentuation; emphasis laid on a syllable or word. **c** an accent, esp. the principal one in a word (*the stress is on the first syllable*). **4** *Mech.* force per unit area exerted between contiguous bodies or parts of a body. —*v.tr.* **1** lay stress on; emphasize. **2** subject to mechanical or physical or mental stress. □ **lay stress on** indicate as important. **stress disease** a disease

resulting from continuous mental stress. □□ **stressless** *adj.* [ME f. DISTRESS, or partly f. OF *estresse* narrowness, oppression, ult. f. L *strictus* STRICT]

stressful /ˈstresfʊl/ *adj.* causing stress; mentally tiring (*had a stressful day*). □□ **stressfully** *adv.* **stressfulness** *n.*

stretch /stretʃ/ *v. & n.* —*v.* **1** *tr. & intr.* draw or be drawn or admit of being drawn out into greater length or size. **2** *tr. & intr.* make or become taut. **3** *tr. & intr.* place or lie at full length or spread out (*with a canopy stretched over them*). **4** *tr.* (also *absol.*) **a** extend (an arm, leg, etc.). **b** (often *refl.*) thrust out one's limbs and tighten one's muscles after being relaxed. **5** *intr.* have a specified length or extension; extend (*farmland stretches for many miles*). **6** *tr.* strain or exert extremely or excessively; exaggerate (*stretch the truth*). **7** *intr.* (as **stretched** *adj.*) lying at full length. —*n.* **1** a continuous extent or expanse or period (*a stretch of open road*). **2** the act or an instance of stretching; the state of being stretched. **3** (*attrib.*) able to stretch; elastic (*stretch fabric*). **4 a** *colloq.* a period of imprisonment. **b** a period of service. **5** *US* the straight side of a racetrack. **6** *Naut.* the distance covered on one tack. □ **at full stretch** working to capacity. **at a stretch 1** in one continuous period (*slept for two hours at a stretch*). **2** with much effort. **stretch one's legs** exercise oneself by walking. **stretch marks** marks on the skin resulting from a gain of weight, or on the abdomen after pregnancy. **stretch out 1** *tr.* extend (a hand or foot etc.). **2** *intr. & tr.* last for a longer period; prolong. **3** *tr.* make (money etc.) last for a sufficient time. **stretch a point** agree to something not normally allowed. **stretch one's wings** see WING. □□ **stretchable** *adj.* **stretchability** /-əˈbɪlɪtɪ/ *n.* **stretchy** *adj.* **stretchiness** *n.* [OE *streccan* f. WG: cf. STRAIGHT]

stretcher /ˈstretʃə(r)/ *n. & v.* —*n.* **1** a framework of two poles with canvas etc. between, for carrying sick, injured, or dead persons in a lying position. **2** a brick or stone laid with its long side along the face of a wall (cf. HEADER). **3** a board in a boat against which a rower presses the feet. **4** a rod or bar as a tie between chair-legs etc. **5** a wooden frame over which a canvas is stretched ready for painting. **6** *archaic sl.* an exaggeration or lie. —*v.tr.* (often foll. by *off*) convey (a sick or injured person) on a stretcher. □ **stretcher-bearer** a person who helps to carry a stretcher, esp. in war or at a major accident.

stretto /ˈstretəʊ/ *adv. Mus.* in quicker time. [It., = narrow]

strew /struː/ *v.tr.* (*past part.* **strewn** or **strewed**) **1** scatter or spread about over a surface. **2** (usu. foll. by *with*) spread (a surface) with scattered things. □□ **strewer** *n.* [OE *stre(o)wian*]

'strewth var. of 'STRUTH.

stria /ˈstraɪə/ *n.* (*pl.* -**ae** /-iː/) **1** *Anat., Zool., Bot.*, & *Geol.* **a** a linear mark on a surface. **b** a slight ridge, furrow, or score. **2** *Archit.* a fillet between the flutes of a column. [L]

striate *adj. & v.* —*adj.* /ˈstraɪɪt/ (also **striated** /-eɪtɪd/) *Anat., Zool., Bot.*, & *Geol.* marked with striae. —*v.tr.* /ˈstraɪeɪt/ mark with striae. □□ **striation** /straɪˈeɪʃ(ə)n/ *n.*

stricken /ˈstrɪkən/ *adj.* **1** affected or overcome with illness or misfortune etc. (*stricken with measles*; *grief-stricken*). **2** levelled with a strickle. **3** (often foll. by *from* etc.) *US Law* deleted. □ **stricken in years** *archaic* enfeebled by age. [archaic past part. of STRIKE]

strickle /ˈstrɪk(ə)l/ *n.* **1** a rod used in strike-measure. **2** a whetting tool. [OE *stricel*, rel. to STRIKE]

strict /strɪkt/ *adj.* **1** precisely limited or defined; without exception or deviation (*lives in strict seclusion*). **2** requiring complete compliance or exact performance; enforced rigidly (*gave strict orders*).

□□ **strictness** *n*. [L *strictus* past part. of *stringere* tighten]

strictly /'strɪktlɪ/ *adv*. **1** in a strict manner. **2** (also **strictly speaking**) applying words in their strict sense (*he is, strictly, an absconder*). **3** esp. *US colloq*. definitely.

stricture /'strɪktʃə(r)/ *n*. **1** (usu. in *pl*.; often foll. by *on, upon*) a critical or censorious remark. **2** *Med*. a morbid narrowing of a canal or duct in the body. □□ **strictured** *adj*. [ME f. L *strictura* (as STRICT)]

stride /straɪd/ *v*. & *n*. — *v*. (*past* **strode** /strəʊd/; *past part*. **stridden** /'strɪd(ə)n/) **1** *intr*. & *tr*. walk with long firm steps. **2** *tr*. cross with one step. **3** *tr*. bestride; straddle. — *n*. **1 a** a single long step. **b** the length of this. **2** a person's gait as determined by the length of stride. **3** (usu. in *pl*.) progress (*has made great strides*). **4** a settled rate of progress (*get into one's stride*; *be thrown out of one's stride*). **5** (in *pl*.) *sl*. trousers. **6** the distance between the feet parted either laterally or as in walking. □ **take in one's stride 1** clear (an obstacle) without changing one's gait to jump. **2** manage without difficulty. □□ **strider** *n*. [OE *strīdan*]

strident /'straɪd(ə)nt/ *adj*. loud and harsh. □□ **stridency** *n*. **stridently** *adv*. [L *stridere* *stridentcreak*]

stridulate /'strɪdjʊˌleɪt/ *v.intr*. (of insects, esp. the cicada and grasshopper) make a shrill sound by rubbing esp. the legs or wing-cases together. □□ **stridulant** *adj*. **stridulation** /-'leɪʃ(ə)n/ *n*. [F *striduler* f. L *stridulus* creaking (as STRIDENT)]

strife /straɪf/ *n*. **1** conflict; struggle between opposed persons or things. **2** *Austral. colloq*. trouble of any kind. [ME f. OF *estrif*: cf. OF *estriver* STRIVE]

strigil /'strɪdʒɪl/ *n*. **1** *Gk* & *Rom. Antiq*. a skin-scraper used by bathers after exercise. **2** a structure on the leg of an insect used to clean its antennae etc. [L *strigilis* f. *stringere* graze]

strigose /'straɪɡəʊs/ *adj*. **1** (of leaves etc.) having short stiff hairs or scales. **2** (of an insect etc.) streaked, striped, or ridged. [L *striga* swath, furrow]

strike /straɪk/ *v*. & *n*. — *v*. (*past* **struck** /strʌk/; *past part*. **struck** or *archaic* **stricken** /'strɪkən/) **1 a** *tr*. subject to an impact. **b** *tr*. deliver (a blow) or inflict a blow on. **2** *tr*. come or bring sharply into contact with (*the ship struck a rock*). **3** *tr*. propel or divert with a blow (*struck the ball into the pond*). **4** *intr*. (foll. by *at*) try to hit. **5** *tr*. penetrate or cause to penetrate (*struck terror into him*). **6** *tr*. ignite (a match) or produce (sparks etc.) by rubbing. **7** *tr*. make (a coin) by stamping. **8** *tr*. produce (a musical note) by striking. **9 a** *tr*. (also *absol*.) (of a clock) indicate (the time) by the sounding of a chime etc. **b** *intr*. (of time) be indicated in this way. **10** *tr*. **a** attack suddenly (*was struck with sudden terror*). **b** (of a disease) afflict. **11** *tr*. cause to become suddenly (*was struck dumb*). **12** *tr*. reach or achieve (*strike a balance*). **13** *tr*. agree on (a bargain). **14** *tr*. assume (an attitude) suddenly and dramatically. **15** *tr*. **a** discover or come across. **b** find (oil etc.) by drilling. **c** encounter (an unusual thing etc.). **16** come to the attention of or appear to (*it strikes me as silly*; *an idea suddenly struck me*). **17 a** *intr*. (of employees) engage in a strike; cease work as a protest. **b** *tr*. *US* act in this way against (an employer). **18 a** *tr*. lower or take down (a flag or tent etc.). **b** *intr*. signify surrender by striking a flag; surrender. **19** *intr*. take a specified direction (*struck east*). **20** *tr*. (also *absol*.) secure a hook in the mouth of (a fish) by jerking the tackle. **21** *tr*. (of a snake) wound with its fangs. **22** *intr*. (of oysters) attach themselves to a bed. **23 a** *tr*. insert (the cutting of a plant) in soil to take root. **b** *tr*. (also *absol*.) (of a plant or cutting etc.) put forth (roots). **24** *tr*. level (grain etc. or the measure) in strike-measure. **25** *tr*. **a** ascertain (a balance) by deducting credit or debit from the other. **b** arrive at (an average, state of balance) by equalizing all items. **26** compose (a jury) esp. by allowing both sides to

reject the same number. — *n*. **1** the act or an instance of striking. **2 a** the organized refusal by employees to work until some grievance is remedied. **b** a similar refusal to participate in some other expected activity. **3** a sudden find or success (*a lucky strike*). **4** an attack, esp. from the air. **5** *Baseball* a batter's unsuccessful attempt to hit a pitched ball, or another event counting equivalently against a batter. **6** the act of knocking down all the pins with the first ball in bowling. **7** horizontal direction in a geological structure. **8** a strickle. □ **on strike** taking part in an industrial etc. strike. **strike at the root** (or **roots**) **of** see ROOT[1]. **strike back 1** strike or attack in return. **2** (of a gas-burner) burn from an internal point before the gas has become mixed with air. **strike down 1** knock down. **2** bring low; afflict (*struck down by a virus*). **strike home 1** deal an effective blow. **2** have an intended effect (*my words struck home*). **strike in 1** intervene in a conversation etc. **2** (of a disease) attack the interior of the body from the surface. **strike it rich** *colloq*. find a source of abundance or success. **strike a light 1** produce a light by striking a match. **2** *Brit. sl*. an expression of surprise, disgust, etc. **strike lucky** have a lucky success. **strike-measure** measurement by passing a rod across the top of a heaped vessel to ensure that it is exactly full. **strike off 1** remove with a stroke. **2** delete (a name etc.) from a list. **3** produce (copies of a document). **strike oil 1** find petroleum by sinking a shaft. **2** attain prosperity or success. **strike out 1** hit out. **2** act vigorously. **3** delete (an item or name etc.). **4** set off or begin (*struck out eastwards*). **5** use the arms and legs in swimming. **6** forge or devise (a plan etc.). **7** *Baseball* **a** dismiss (a batter) by means of three strikes. **b** be dismissed in this way. **strike pay** an allowance paid to strikers by their trade union. **strike through** delete (a word etc.) with a stroke of one's pen. **strike up 1** start (an acquaintance, conversation, etc.) esp. casually. **2** (also *absol*.) begin playing (a tune etc.). **strike upon 1** have (an idea etc.) luckily occur to one. **2** (of light) illuminate. **strike while the iron is hot** act promptly at a good opportunity. **struck on** *colloq*. infatuated with. □□ **strikable** *adj*. [OE *strīcan* go, stroke f. WG]

strikebound /'straɪkbaʊnd/ *adj*. immobilized or closed by a strike.

strikebreaker /'straɪkˌbreɪkə(r)/ *n*. a person working or employed in place of others who are on strike. □□ **strikebreak** *v.intr*.

striker /'straɪkə(r)/ *n*. **1** a person or thing that strikes. **2** an employee on strike. **3** *Sport* the player who is to strike, or who is to be the next to strike, the ball. **4** *Football* an attacking player positioned well forward in order to score goals. **5** a device striking the primer in a gun.

striking /'straɪkɪŋ/ *adj*. & *n*. — *adj*. **1** impressive; attracting attention. **2** (of a clock) making a chime to indicate the hours etc. — *n*. the act or an instance of striking. □ **striking-circle** (in hockey) an elongated semicircle in front of the goal, from within which the ball must be hit in order to score. **striking-force** a military body ready to attack at short notice. **within striking distance** near enough to hit or achieve. □□ **strikingly** *adv*. **strikingness** *n*.

Strine /straɪn/ *n*. **1** a comic transliteration of Australian speech, e.g. *Emma Chissitt* = 'How much is it?' **2** (esp. uneducated) Australian English. [= *Australian* in Strine]

string /strɪŋ/ *n*. & *v*. — *n*. **1** twine or narrow cord. **2** a piece of this or of similar material used for tying or holding together, pulling, etc. **3** a length of catgut or wire etc. on a musical instrument, producing a note by vibration. **4 a** (in *pl*.) the stringed instruments in an orchestra etc. **b** (*attrib*.) relating to or consisting of stringed instruments (*string quartet*). **5** (in *pl*.) an awkward condition or complication (*the offer has no strings*). **6** a set of things strung together; a series or line of persons or things (*a string of beads*; *a string of oaths*). **7** a group of racehorses trained at one stable. **8** a tough piece connecting the two halves of a bean-pod etc. **9** a piece of catgut etc. interwoven with others to form the head of a tennis etc. racket. **10** = STRINGBOARD. —*v.* (*past* and *past part.* **strung** /strʌŋ/) **1** *tr.* supply with a string or strings. **2** *tr.* tie with string. **3** *tr.* thread (beads etc.) on a string. **4** *tr.* arrange in or as a string. **5** *tr.* remove the strings from (a bean). **6** *tr.* place a string ready for use on (a bow). **7** *tr. colloq.* hoax. **8** *intr.* (of glue etc.) become stringy. **9** *intr. Billiards* make the preliminary strokes that decide which player begins. □**on a string** under one's control or influence. **string along** *colloq.* **1** deceive, esp. by appearing to comply with (a person). **2** (often foll. by *with*) keep company (with). **string bass** *Mus.* a double-bass. **string bean 1** any of various beans eaten in their fibrous pods, esp. runner beans or French beans. **2** *colloq.* a tall thin person. **string-course** a raised horizontal band or course of bricks etc. on a building. **string out** extend; prolong (esp. unduly). **string-piece** a long timber supporting and connecting the parts of a framework. **string tie** a very narrow necktie. **string up 1** hang up on strings etc. **2** kill by hanging. **3** make tense. **string vest** a vest with large meshes. □□ **stringless** *adj.* **stringlike** *adj.* [OE *streng* f. Gmc: cf. STRONG]

stringboard /ˈstrɪŋbɔːd/ *n.* a supporting timber or skirting in which the ends of a staircase steps are set.

stringed /strɪŋd/ *adj.* (of musical instruments) having strings (also in *comb.*: *twelve-stringed guitar*).

stringendo /strɪnˈdʒendəʊ/ *adj.* & *adv. Mus.* with increasing speed. [It. f. *stringere* press: see STRINGENT]

stringent /ˈstrɪndʒ(ə)nt/ *adj.* **1** (of rules etc.) strict, precise; requiring exact performance; leaving no loophole or discretion. **2** (of a money market etc.) tight; hampered by scarcity; unaccommodating; hard to operate in. □□ **stringency** *n.* **stringently** *adv.* [L *stringere* draw tight]

stringer /ˈstrɪŋə(r)/ *n.* **1** a longitudinal structural member in a framework, esp. of a ship or aircraft. **2** *colloq.* a newspaper correspondent not on the regular staff. **3** = STRINGBOARD.

stringhalt /ˈstrɪŋhɒlt/ *n.* spasmodic movement of a horse's hind leg.

stringy /ˈstrɪŋɪ/ *adj.* (**stringier**, **stringiest**) **1** (of food etc.) fibrous, tough. **2** of or like string. **3** (of a person) tall, wiry, and thin. **4** (of a liquid) viscous; forming strings. □**stringy-bark** *Austral.* any of various eucalyptus trees with tough fibrous bark. □□ **stringily** *adv.* **stringiness** *n.*

strip[1] /strɪp/ *v.* & *n.* —*v.* (**stripped**, **stripping**) **1** *tr.* (often foll. by *of*) remove the clothes or covering from (a person or thing). **2** *intr.* (often foll. by *off*) undress oneself. **3** *tr.* (often foll. by *of*) deprive (a person) of property or titles. **4** *tr.* leave bare of accessories or fittings. **5** *tr.* remove bark and branches from (a tree). **6** *tr.* (often foll. by *down*) remove the accessory fittings of or take apart (a machine etc.) to inspect or adjust it. **7** *tr.* milk (a cow) to the last drop. **8** *tr.* remove the old hair from (a dog). **9** *tr.* remove the stems from (tobacco). **10** *tr.* tear the thread from (a screw). **11** *tr.* tear the teeth from (a gearwheel). **12** *tr.* remove (paint) or remove paint from (a surface) with solvent. **13** *tr.* (often foll. by *from*) pull or tear (a covering or property etc.) off (*stripped the masks from their faces*). **14** *intr.* (of a screw) lose its thread. **15** *intr.* (of a bullet) issue from a rifled gun without spin owing to a loss of surface. —*n.* **1** an act of stripping, esp. of undressing in striptease. **2** *colloq.* the identifying outfit worn by the members of a sports team while playing. □**strip club** a club at which striptease performances are given. **strip mine** *US* a mine worked by removing the material that overlies the ore etc. **strip-search** *n.* a search of a person involving the removal of all

clothes. —*v.tr.* search in this way. [ME f. OE *bestrīepan* plunder f. Gmc]

strip[2] /strɪp/ *n.* **1** a long narrow piece (*a strip of land*). **2** a narrow flat bar of iron or steel. **3** (in full **strip cartoon**) = comic strip. □**strip light** a tubular fluorescent lamp. **strip mill** a mill in which steel slabs are rolled into strips. **tear a person off a strip** *colloq.* angrily rebuke a person. [ME, from or rel. to MLG *strippe* strap, thong, prob. rel. to STRIP[1]]

stripe /straɪp/ *n.* **1** a long narrow band or strip differing in colour or texture from the surface on either side of it (*black with a red stripe*). **2** *Mil.* a chevron etc. denoting military rank. **3** *US* a category of character, opinion, etc. (*a man of that stripe*). **4** (usu. in *pl.*) *archaic* a blow with a scourge or lash. **5** (in *pl.*, treated as *sing.*) *colloq.* a tiger. [perh. back-form. f. *striped*: cf. MDu., MLG *strīpe*, MHG *strīfe*]

striped /straɪpt/ *adj.* marked with stripes (also in *comb.*: *red-striped*).

stripling /ˈstrɪplɪŋ/ *n.* a youth not yet fully grown. [ME, prob. f. STRIP[2] + -LING[1], in the sense of having a figure not yet filled out]

stripper /ˈstrɪpə(r)/ *n.* **1** a person or thing that strips something. **2** a device or solvent for removing paint etc. **3** a striptease performer.

striptease /ˈstrɪptiːz/ *n.* & *v.* —*n.* an entertainment in which the performer gradually undresses before the audience. —*v.intr.* perform a striptease. □□ **stripteaser** *n.*

stripy /ˈstraɪpɪ/ *adj.* (**stripier**, **stripiest**) striped; having many stripes.

strive /straɪv/ *v.intr.* (*past* **strove** /strəʊv/; *past part.* **striven** /ˈstrɪv(ə)n/) **1** (often foll. by *for*, or *to* + infin.) try hard, make efforts (*strive to succeed*). **2** (often foll. by *with*, *against*) struggle or contend. □□ **striver** *n.* [ME f. OF *estriver*, rel. to *estrif* STRIFE]

strobe /strəʊb/ *n. colloq.* **1** a stroboscope. **2** a stroboscopic lamp. [abbr.]

strobila /strəˈbaɪlə/ *n.* (*pl.* **strobilae** /-laɪ/) **1** a chain of proglottids in a tapeworm. **2** a sessile polyp-like form which divides horizontally to produce jellyfish larvae. [mod.L f. Gk *strobilē* twisted lint-plug f. *strephō* twist]

strobile /ˈstrəʊbaɪl/ *n.* **1** the cone of a pine etc. **2** the layered flower of the hop. [F *strobile* or LL *strobilus* f. Gk *strobilos* f. *strephō* twist]

strobilus /ˈstrəʊbɪləs/ *n.* (*pl.* **strobili** /-ˌlaɪ/) *Bot.* = STROBILE **1**. [LL (as STROBILE)]

stroboscope /ˈstrəʊbəˌskəʊp/ *n.* **1** *Physics* an instrument for determining speeds of rotation etc. by shining a bright light at intervals so that a rotating object appears stationary. **2** a lamp made to flash intermittently, esp. for this purpose. □□ **stroboscopic** /-ˈskɒpɪk/ *adj.* **stroboscopical** /-ˈskɒpɪk(ə)l/ *adj.* **stroboscopically** /-ˈskɒpɪkəlɪ/ *adv.* [Gk *strobos* whirling + -SCOPE]

strode *past* of STRIDE.

Stroganoff /ˈstrɒɡəˌnɒf/ *adj.* (of meat) cut into strips and cooked in sour-cream sauce (*beef Stroganoff*). [P. *Stroganoff*, 19th-c. Russ. diplomat]

stroke /strəʊk/ *n.* & *v.* —*n.* **1** the act or an instance of striking; a blow or hit (*with a single stroke*; *a stroke of lightning*). **2** a sudden disabling attack or loss of consciousness caused by an interruption in the flow of blood to the brain, esp. through thrombosis; apoplexy. **3 a** an action or movement esp. as one of a series. **b** the time or way in which such movements are done. **c** the slightest such action (*has not done a stroke of work*). **4** the whole of the motion (of a wing, oar, etc.) until the starting-position is regained. **5** (in rowing) the mode or action of moving the oar (*row a fast stroke*). **6** the whole motion (of a piston) in either direction. **7** *Golf* the action of hitting (or hitting at) a ball with a club, as a unit of scoring. **8** a mode of moving the arms and legs in swimming. **9** a method of striking with the bat etc. in games etc. (*played some unorthodox strokes*). **10** a specially successful or skilful effort (*a stroke of diplomacy*). **11 a** a mark made by the movement in one direction of a pen or pencil or paintbrush. **b** a similar mark printed. **12** a detail contributing to the general effect in a description. **13** the sound made by a striking clock. **14** (in full **stroke oar**) the oar or oarsman nearest the stern, setting the time of the stroke. **15** the act or a spell of stroking. —*v.tr.* **1** pass one's hand gently along the surface of (hair or fur etc.); caress lightly. **2** act as the stroke of (a boat or crew). □**at a stroke** by a single action. **finishing stroke** a *coup de grâce*; a final and fatal stroke. **off one's stroke** not performing as well as usual. **on the stroke** punctually. **on the stroke of nine** etc. with the clock about to strike nine etc. **stroke a person down** appease a person's anger. **stroke of business** a profitable transaction. **stroke of genius** an original or strikingly successful idea. **stroke of luck** (or **good luck**) an unforeseen opportune occurrence. **stroke play** *Golf* play in which the score is reckoned by counting the number of strokes taken for the round (cf. *match play* (see MATCH[1])). **stroke a person** (or **a person's hair**) **the wrong way** irritate a person. [OE *strācian* f. Gmc, rel. to STRIKE]

stroll /strəʊl/ *v. & n.* —*v.intr.* saunter or walk in a leisurely way. —*n.* a short leisurely walk (*go for a stroll*). □**strolling players** actors etc. going from place to place to give performances. [orig. of a vagrant, prob. f. G *strollen, strolchen* f. *Strolch* vagabond, of unkn. orig.]

stroller /ˈstrəʊlə(r)/ *n.* **1** a person who strolls. **2** *US* a pushchair.

stroma /ˈstrəʊmə/ *n.* (*pl.* **stromata** /-mətə/) *Biol.* **1** the framework of an organ or cell. **2** a fungous tissue containing spore-producing bodies. □□ **stromatic** /-ˈmætɪk/ *adj.* [mod.L f. LL f. Gk *strōma* coverlet]

strong /strɒŋ/ *adj. & adv.* —*adj.* (**stronger** /ˈstrɒŋɡə(r)/; **strongest** /ˈstrɒŋɡɪst/) **1** having the power of resistance; able to withstand great force or opposition; not easily damaged or overcome (*strong material; strong faith; a strong character*). **2** (of a person's constitution) able to overcome, or not liable to, disease. **3** (of a person's nerves) proof against fright, irritation, etc. **4** (of a patient) restored to health. **5** (of a market) having steadily high or rising prices. **6** capable of exerting great force or of doing much; muscular, powerful. **7** forceful or powerful in effect (*a strong wind; a strong protest*). **8** decided or firmly held (*a strong suspicion; strong views*). **9** (of an argument etc.) convincing or striking. **10** powerfully affecting the senses or emotions (*a strong light; strong acting*). **11** powerful in terms of size or numbers or quality (*a strong army*). **12** capable of doing much when united (*a strong combination*). **13** formidable; likely to succeed (*a strong candidate*). **14** (of a solution or drink etc.) containing a large proportion of a substance in water or another solvent (*strong tea*). **15** *Chem.* (of an acid or base) fully ionized into cations and anions in aqueous solution. **16** (of a group) having a specified number (*200 strong*). **17** (of a voice) loud or penetrating. **18** (of food or its flavour) pungent. **19** (of a person's breath) ill-smelling. **20** (of a literary style) vivid and terse. **21** (of a measure) drastic. **22** *Gram.* in Germanic languages: **a** (of a verb) forming inflections by change of vowel within the stem rather than by the addition of a suffix (e.g. *swim, swam*). **b** (of a noun or adjective) belonging to a declension in which the stem originally ended otherwise than in *-n* (opp. WEAK 9). —*adv.* strongly (*the tide is running strong*). □**come it strong** *colloq.* go to great lengths; use exaggeration. **going strong** *colloq.* continuing action vigorously; in good health or trim. **strong-arm** using force (*strong-arm tactics*). **strong drink** see DRINK. **strong grade** the stressed ablaut-form. **strong interaction** *Physics* interaction between certain elementary particles that is very strong but is effective only at short distances. **strong language** forceful language;

swearing. **strong meat** a doctrine or action acceptable only to vigorous or instructed minds. **strong-minded** having determination. **strong-mindedness** determination. **strong point 1** a thing at which one excels. **2** a specially fortified defensive position. **strong stomach** a stomach not easily affected by nausea. **strong suit 1** a suit at cards in which one can take tricks. **2** a thing at which one excels. □□ **strongish** *adj.* **strongly** *adv.* [OE f. Gmc: cf. STRING]

strongbox /ˈstrɒŋbɒks/ *n.* a strongly made small chest for valuables.

stronghold /ˈstrɒŋhəʊld/ *n.* **1** a fortified place. **2** a secure refuge. **3** a centre of support for a cause etc.

strongroom /ˈstrɒŋruːm, -rʊm/ *n.* a room designed to protect valuables against fire and theft.

strontia /ˈstrɒnʃə/ *n. Chem.* strontium oxide. [*strontian* native strontium carbonate f. Strontian in the Highland Region of Scotland, where it was discovered]

strontium /ˈstrɒntɪəm/ *n. Chem.* a soft silver-white metallic element occurring naturally in various minerals. ¶ Symb.: **Sr**. □**strontium-90** a radioactive isotope of strontium concentrated selectively in bones and teeth when taken into the body. **strontium oxide** a white compound used in the manufacture of fireworks. [STRONTIA + -IUM]

strop /strɒp/ *n. & v.* —*n.* **1** a device, esp. a strip of leather, for sharpening razors. **2** *Naut.* a collar of leather or spliced rope or iron used for handling cargo. —*v.tr.* (**stropped, stropping**) sharpen on or with a strop. [ME f. MDu., MLG *strop*, OHG *strupf*, WG f. L *stroppus*]

strophanthin /strəˈfænθɪn/ *n.* a white crystalline poisonous glucoside extracted from various tropical plants of the genus *Strophanthus* and used as a heart-tonic. [mod.L *strophanthus* f. Gk *strophos* twisted cord + *anthos* flower]

strophe /ˈstrəʊfɪ/ *n.* **1 a** a turn in dancing made by an ancient Greek chorus. **b** lines recited during this. **c** the first section of an ancient Greek choral ode or of one division of it. **2** a group of lines forming a section of a lyric poem. □□ **strophic** *adj.* [Gk *strophē*, lit. turning, f. *strephō* turn]

stroppy /ˈstrɒpɪ/ *adj.* (**stroppier, stroppiest**) *Brit. colloq.* bad-tempered; awkward to deal with. □□ **stroppily** *adv.* **stroppiness** *n.* [20th c.: perh. abbr. of OBSTREPEROUS]

strove *past* of STRIVE.

strow /strəʊ/ *v.tr.* (*past part.* **strown** /strəʊn/ or **strowed**) *archaic* = STREW. [var. of STREW]

struck *past* and *past part.* of STRIKE.

structural /ˈstrʌktʃər(ə)l/ *adj.* of, concerning, or having a structure. □**structural engineering** the branch of civil engineering concerned with large modern buildings etc. **structural formula** *Chem.* a formula showing the arrangement of atoms in the molecule of a compound. **structural linguistics** the study of language as a system of interrelated elements. **structural psychology** the study of the arrangement and composition of mental states and conscious experiences. **structural steel** strong mild steel in shapes suited to construction work. □□ **structurally** *adv.*

structuralism /ˈstrʌktʃərəlɪz(ə)m/ *n.* **1** the doctrine that structure rather than function is important. **2** structural linguistics. **3** structural psychology. □□ **structuralist** *n.*

structure /ˈstrʌktʃə(r)/ *n. & v.* —*n.* **1 a** a whole constructed unit, esp. a building. **b** the way in which a building etc. is constructed (*has a flimsy structure*). **2** a set of interconnecting parts of any complex thing; a framework (*the structure of a sentence; a new wages structure*). —*v.tr.* give structure to; organize; frame. □□ **structured** *adj.* (also in *comb.*). **structureless** *adj.* [ME f. OF *structure* or L *structura* f. *struere* struct- build]

strudel /ˈstruːd(ə)l/ *n.* a confection of thin pastry

rolled up round a filling and baked (*apple strudel*). [G]

struggle /ˈstrʌg(ə)l/ *v.* & *n.* —*v.intr.* **1** make forceful or violent efforts to get free of restraint or constriction. **2** (often foll. by *for*, or *to* + infin.) make violent or determined efforts under difficulties; strive hard (*struggled for supremacy*; *struggled to get the words out*). **3** (foll. by *with*, *against*) contend; fight strenuously (*struggled with the disease*; *struggled against superior numbers*). **4** (foll. by *along*, *up*, etc.) make one's way with difficulty (*struggled to my feet*). **5** (esp. as **struggling** *adj.*) have difficulty in gaining recognition or a living (*a struggling artist*). —*n.* **1** the act or a spell of struggling. **2** a hard or confused contest. **3** a determined effort under difficulties. □**the struggle for existence** (or **life**) the competition between organisms esp. as an element in natural selection, or between persons seeking a livelihood. □□ **struggler** *n.* [ME *strugle* frequent. of uncert. orig. (perh. imit.)]

strum /strʌm/ *v.* & *n.* —*v.tr.* (**strummed**, **strumming**) **1** play on (a stringed or keyboard instrument), esp. carelessly or unskilfully. **2** play (a tune etc.) in this way. —*n.* the sound made by strumming. □□ **strummer** *n.* [imit.: cf. THRUM¹]

struma /ˈstruːmə/ *n.* (*pl.* **strumae** /-miː/) **1** *Med.* **a** = SCROFULA. **b** = GOITRE. **2** *Bot.* a cushion-like swelling of an organ. □□ **strumose** *adj.* **strumous** *adj.* [L, = scrofulous tumour]

strumpet /ˈstrʌmpɪt/ *n. archaic* or *rhet.* a prostitute. [ME: orig. unkn.]

strung *past* and *past part.* of STRING.

strut /strʌt/ *n.* & *v.* —*n.* **1** a bar forming part of a framework and designed to resist compression. **2** a strutting gait. —*v.* (**strutted**, **strutting**) **1** *intr.* walk with a pompous or affected stiff erect gait. **2** *tr.* brace with a strut or struts. □□ **strutter** *n.* **struttingly** *adv.* [ME 'bulge, swell, strive', earlier *stroute* f. OE *strūtian* be rigid (?)]

'struth /struːθ/ *int.* (also **'strewth**) *colloq.* a mild oath. [*God's truth*]

struthious /ˈstruːθɪəs/ *adj.* of or like an ostrich. [L *struthio* ostrich]

strychnine /ˈstrɪkniːn/ *n.* a vegetable alkaloid obtained from plants of the genus *Strychnos* (esp. nux vomica), bitter and highly poisonous, used as a stimulant and (in small amounts) a tonic. □□ **strychnic** *adj.* [F f. L *strychnos* f. Gk *strukhnos* a kind of nightshade]

Sts *abbr.* Saints.

Stuart /ˈstjuːət/ *adj.* & *n.* —*adj.* of or relating to the royal family ruling Scotland 1371-1714 and England 1603-1649 and 1660-1714. —*n.* a member of this family.

stub /stʌb/ *n.* & *v.* —*n.* **1** the remnant of a pencil or cigarette etc. after use. **2** the counterfoil of a cheque or receipt etc. **3** a stunted tail etc. **4** the stump of a tree, tooth, etc. **5** (*attrib.*) going only part of the way through (*stub-mortise*; *stub-tenon*). —*v.tr.* (**stubbed**, **stubbing**) **1** strike (one's toe) against something. **2** (usu. foll. by *out*) extinguish (a lighted cigarette) by pressing the lighted end against something. **3** (foll. by *up*) grub up by the roots. **4** clear (land) of stubs. □**stub-axle** an axle supporting only one wheel of a pair. [OE *stub*, *stubb* f. Gmc]

stubble /ˈstʌb(ə)l/ *n.* **1** the cut stalks of cereal plants left sticking up after the harvest. **2 a** cropped hair or a cropped beard. **b** a short growth of unshaven hair. □□ **stubbled** *adj.* **stubbly** *adj.* [ME f. AF *stuble*, OF *estuble* f. L *stupla*, *stupula* var. of *stipula* straw]

stubborn /ˈstʌbən/ *adj.* **1** unreasonably obstinate. **2** unyielding, obdurate, inflexible. **3** refractory, intractable. □□ **stubbornly** *adv.* **stubbornness** *n.* [ME *stiborn*, *stoburn*, etc., of unkn. orig.]

stubby /ˈstʌbɪ/ *adj.* & *n.* —*adj.* (**stubbier**, **stubbiest**) short and thick. —*n.* (*pl.* **-ies**) *Austral. colloq.* a small squat bottle of beer. □□ **stubbily** *adv.* **stubbiness** *n.*

stucco /ˈstʌkəʊ/ *n.* & *v.* —*n.* (*pl.* **-oes**) plaster or cement used for coating wall surfaces or moulding into architectural decorations. —*v.tr.* (**-oes**, **-oed**) coat with stucco. [It., of Gmc orig.]

stuck *past* and *past part.* of STICK².

stuck-up see STICK².

stud¹ /stʌd/ *n.* & *v.* —*n.* **1** a large-headed nail, boss, or knob, projecting from a surface esp. for ornament. **2** a double button esp. for use with two buttonholes in a shirt-front. **3** a small object projecting slightly from a road-surface as a marker etc. **4** a rivet or crosspiece in each link of a chain-cable. **5 a** a post to which laths are nailed. **b** *US* the height of a room as indicated by the length of this. —*v.tr.* (**studded**, **studding**) **1** set with or as with studs. **2** (as **studded** *adj.*) (foll. by *with*) thickly set or strewn (*studded with diamonds*). **3** be scattered over or about (a surface). [OE *studu*, *stuthu* post, prop, rel. to G *stützen* to prop]

stud² /stʌd/ *n.* **1 a** a number of horses kept for breeding etc. **b** a place where these are kept. **2** (in full **stud-horse**) a stallion. **3** *colloq.* a young man (esp. one noted for sexual prowess). **4** (in full **stud poker**) a form of poker with betting after the dealing of successive rounds of cards face up. □**at stud** (of a male horse) publicly available for breeding on payment of a fee. **stud-book** a book containing the pedigrees of horses. **stud-farm** a place where horses are bred. [OE *stōd* f. Gmc: rel. to STAND]

studding /ˈstʌdɪŋ/ *n.* the woodwork of a lath-and-plaster wall.

studding-sail /ˈstʌns(ə)l/ *n.* a sail set on a small extra yard and boom beyond the leech of a square sail in light winds. [16th c.: orig. uncert.: perh. f. MLG, MDu. *stōtinge* a thrusting]

student /ˈstjuːd(ə)nt/ *n.* **1** a person who is studying, esp. at university or another place of higher education. **2** (*attrib.*) studying in order to become (*a student nurse*). **3** a person of studious habits. **4** *Brit.* a graduate recipient of a stipend from the foundation of a college, esp. a fellow of Christ Church, Oxford. □□ **studentship** *n.* [ME f. L *studēre* f. *studium* STUDY]

studio /ˈstjuːdɪəʊ/ *n.* (*pl.* **-os**) **1** the workroom of a painter or photographer etc. **2** a place where cinema films or recordings are made or where television or radio programmes are made or produced. □**studio couch** a couch that can be converted into a bed. **studio flat** a flat containing a room suitable as an artist's studio, or only one main room. [It. f. L (as STUDY)]

studious /ˈstjuːdɪəs/ *adj.* **1** devoted to or assiduous in study or reading. **2** studied, deliberate, painstaking (*with studious care*). **3** (foll. by *to* + infin. or *in* + verbal noun) showing care or attention. **4** (foll. by *of* + verbal noun) anxiously desirous. □□ **studiously** *adv.* **studiousness** *n.* [ME f. L *studiosus* (as STUDY)]

study /ˈstʌdɪ/ *n.* & *v.* —*n.* (*pl.* **-ies**) **1** the devotion of time and attention to acquiring information or knowledge, esp. from books. **2** (in *pl.*) the pursuit of academic knowledge (*continued their studies abroad*). **3** a room used for reading, writing, etc. **4** a piece of work, esp. a drawing, done for practice or as an experiment (*a study of a head*). **5** the portrayal in literature or another art form of an aspect of behaviour or character etc. **6** a musical composition designed to develop a player's skill. **7** a thing worth observing closely (*your face was a study*). **8** a thing that is or deserves to be investigated. **9** *Theatr.* **a** the act of memorizing a role. **b** a person who memorizes a role. **10** *archaic* a thing to be secured by pains or attention. —*v.* (**-ies**, **-ied**) **1** *tr.* make a study of; investigate or examine (a subject) (*study law*). **2** *intr.* (often foll. by *for*) apply oneself to study. **3** *tr.* scrutinize or earnestly contemplate (a visible object) (*studied their faces*). **4** *tr.* try to learn (the words of one's role etc.). **5** *tr.* take pains to achieve (a result) or pay regard to (a subject or principle etc.). **6** *tr.* (as **studied** *adj.*) deliberate, intentional, affected (*with studied politeness*). **7** *tr.* read (a book) attentively. **8**

tr. (foll. by *to* + infin.) *archaic* **a** be on the watch. **b** try constantly to manage. □**in a brown study** in a reverie; absorbed in one's thoughts. **make a study of** investigate carefully. **study group** a group of people meeting from time to time to study a particular subject or topic. □□**studiedly** *adv.* **studiedness** *n.* [ME f. OF *estudie* f. L *studium* zeal, study]

stuff /stʌf/ *n. & v.* —*n.* **1** the material that a thing is made of; material that may be used for some purpose. **2** a substance or things or belongings of an indeterminate kind or a quality not needing to be specified (*there's a lot of stuff about it in the newspapers*). **3** a particular knowledge or activity (*know one's stuff*). **4** woollen fabric (esp. as distinct from silk, cotton, and linen). **5** valueless matter, trash, refuse, nonsense (*take that stuff away*). **6** (prec. by *the*) **a** *colloq.* an available supply of something, esp. drink or drugs. **b** *sl.* money. —*v.* **1** *tr.* pack (a receptacle) tightly (*stuff a cushion with feathers*; *a head stuffed with weird notions*). **2** *tr.* (foll. by *in, into*) force or cram (a thing) (*stuffed the socks in the drawer*). **3** *tr.* fill out the skin of (an animal or bird etc.) with material to restore the original shape (*a stuffed owl*). **4** *tr.* fill (poultry etc.) with a savoury or sweet mixture, esp. before cooking. **5 a** *tr. & refl.* fill (a person or oneself) with food. **b** *tr. & intr.* eat greedily. **6** *tr.* push, esp. hastily or clumsily (*stuffed the note behind the cushion*). **7** *tr.* (usu. in *passive*; foll. by *up*) block up (a person's nose etc.). **8** *tr. sl.* (esp. as an expression of contemptuous dismissal) dispose of as unwanted (*you can stuff the job*). **9** *tr. US* place bogus votes in (a ballot-box). **10** *tr. coarse sl. offens.* have sexual intercourse with (a woman). □**bit of stuff** *sl. offens.* a woman regarded as an object of sexual desire. **do one's stuff** *colloq.* do what one has to. **get stuffed** *sl.* an exclamation of dismissal, contempt, etc. **stuff and nonsense** an exclamation of incredulity or ridicule. **stuffed shirt** *colloq.* a pompous person. **stuff gown** *Brit.* a gown worn by a barrister who has not taken silk. **stuff it** *sl.* an expression of rejection or disdain. **that's the stuff** *colloq.* that is what is wanted. □□**stuffer** *n.* (also in *comb.*). [ME *stoffe* f. OF *estoffe* (n.), *estoffer* (v.) equip, furnish f. Gk *stuphō* draw together]

stuffing /ˈstʌfɪŋ/ *n.* **1** padding used to stuff cushions etc. **2** a mixture used to stuff poultry etc., esp. before cooking. □**knock** (or **take**) **the stuffing out of** *colloq.* make feeble or weak; defeat. **stuffing-box** a box packed with material, to allow the working of an axle while remaining airtight.

stuffy /ˈstʌfɪ/ *adj.* (**stuffier, stuffiest**) **1** (of a room or the atmosphere in it) lacking fresh air or ventilation; close. **2** dull or uninteresting. **3** (of a person's nose etc.) stuffed up. **4** (of a person) dull and conventional. □□**stuffily** *adv.* **stuffiness** *n.*

stultify /ˈstʌltɪˌfaɪ/ *v.tr.* (**-ies, -ied**) **1** make ineffective, useless, or futile, esp. as a result of tedious routine (*stultifying boredom*). **2** cause to appear foolish or absurd. **3** negate or neutralize. □□**stultification** /-fɪˈkeɪʃ(ə)n/ *n.* **stultifier** *n.* [LL *stultificare* f. L *stultus* foolish]

stum /stʌm/ *n. & v.* —*n.* unfermented grape-juice; must. —*v.tr.* (**stummed, stumming**) **1** prevent from fermenting, or secure (wine) against further fermentation in a cask, by the use of sulphur etc. **2** renew the fermentation of (wine) by adding stum. [Du. *stommen* (v.), *stom* (adj.) dumb]

stumble /ˈstʌmb(ə)l/ *v. & n.* —*v.* **1** *intr.* lurch forward or have a partial fall from catching or striking or misplacing one's foot. **2** *intr.* (often foll. by *along*) walk with repeated stumbles. **3** *intr.* make a mistake or repeated mistakes in speaking etc. **4** *intr.* (foll. by *on, upon, across*) find or encounter by chance (*stumbled on a disused well*). —*n.* an act of stumbling. □**stumbling-block** an obstacle or circumstance causing difficulty or hesitation. □□**stumbler** *n.*

stumblingly *adv.* [ME *stumble* (with euphonic *b*) corresp. to Norw. *stumla*: rel. to STAMMER]

stumblebum /ˈstʌmb(ə)lˌbʌm/ *n. US colloq.* a clumsy or inept person.

stumer /ˈstjuːmə(r)/ *n. Brit. sl.* **1** a worthless cheque; a counterfeit coin or note. **2** a sham or fraud. **3** a failure. [19th c.: orig. unkn.]

stump /stʌmp/ *n. & v.* —*n.* **1** the projecting remnant of a cut or fallen tree. **2** the similar remnant of anything else (e.g. a branch or limb) cut off or worn down. **3** *Cricket* each of the three uprights of a wicket. **4** (in *pl.*) *joc.* the legs. **5** the stump of a tree, or other place, used by an orator to address a meeting. **6** a cylinder of rolled paper or other material with conical ends for softening pencil-marks and other uses in drawing. —*v.* **1** *tr.* (of a question etc.) be too hard for; puzzle. **2** *tr.* (as **stumped** *adj.*) at a loss; baffled. **3** *tr. Cricket* (esp. of a wicket-keeper) put (a batsman) out by touching the stumps with the ball while the batsman is out of the crease. **4** *intr.* walk stiffly or noisily as on a wooden leg. **5** *tr.* (also *absol.*) *US* traverse (a district) making political speeches. **6** *tr.* use a stump on (a drawing, line, etc.). □**on the stump** *colloq.* engaged in political speech-making or agitation. **stump up** *Brit. colloq.* pay or produce (the money required). **up a stump** *US* in difficulties. [ME *stompe* f. MDu. *stomp*, OHG *stumpf*]

stumper /ˈstʌmpə(r)/ *n. colloq.* **1** a puzzling question. **2** a wicket-keeper.

stumpy /ˈstʌmpɪ/ *adj.* (**stumpier, stumpiest**) short and thick. □□**stumpily** *adv.* **stumpiness** *n.*

stun /stʌn/ *v.tr.* (**stunned, stunning**) **1** knock senseless; stupefy. **2** bewilder or shock. **3** (of a sound) deafen temporarily. [ME f. OF *estoner* ASTONISH]

stung *past* and *past part.* of STING.

stunk *past* and *past part.* of STINK.

stunner /ˈstʌnə(r)/ *n. colloq.* a stunning person or thing.

stunning /ˈstʌnɪŋ/ *adj. colloq.* extremely impressive or attractive. □□**stunningly** *adv.*

stunsail /ˈstʌns(ə)l/ *n.* (also **stuns'l**) = STUDDING-SAIL.

stunt[1] /stʌnt/ *v.tr.* **1** retard the growth or development of. **2** dwarf, cramp. □□**stuntedness** *n.* [*stunt* foolish (now dial.), MHG *stunz*, ON *stuttr* short f. Gmc, perh. rel. to STUMP]

stunt[2] /stʌnt/ *n. & v.* —*n.* **1** something unusual done to attract attention. **2** a trick or daring manœuvre. **3** a display of concentrated energy. —*v.intr.* perform stunts, esp. aerobatics. □**stunt man** a man employed to take an actor's place in performing dangerous stunts. [orig. unkn.: first used in 19th-c. US college athletics]

stupa /ˈstuːpə/ *n.* a round usu. domed building erected as a Buddhist shrine. [Skr. *stūpa*]

stupe[1] /stjuːp/ *n. & v.* —*n.* a flannel etc. soaked in hot water, wrung out, and applied as a fomentation. —*v.tr.* treat with this. [ME f. L f. Gk *stupē* tow]

stupe[2] /stjuːp/ *n. sl.* a fool or stupid person.

stupefy /ˈstjuːpɪˌfaɪ/ *v.tr.* (**-ies, -ied**) **1** make stupid or insensible (*stupefied with drink*). **2** stun with astonishment (*the news was stupefying*). □□ **stupefacient** /-ˈfeɪʃ(ə)nt/ *adj.* & *n.* **stupefaction** /-ˈfækʃ(ə)n/ *n.* **stupefactive** *adj.* **stupefier** *n.* **stupefying** *adj.* **stupefyingly** *adv.* [F *stupéfier* f. L *stupefacere* f. *stupēre* be amazed]

stupendous /stjuːˈpendəs/ *adj.* amazing or prodigious, esp. in terms of size or degree (*a stupendous achievement*). □□**stupendously** *adv.* **stupendousness** *n.* [L *stupendus* gerundive of *stupēre* be amazed at]

stupid /ˈstjuːpɪd/ *adj.* (**stupider, stupidest**) *adj.* & *n.* —*adj.* **1** unintelligent, slow-witted, foolish (*a stupid fellow*). **2** typical of stupid persons (*put it in a stupid place*). **3** uninteresting or boring. **4** in a state of stupor or lethargy. **5** obtuse; lacking in sensibility. —*n. colloq.* a stupid person. □□**stupidity** /-ˈpɪdɪtɪ/ *n.*

(*pl.* **-ies**). **stupidly** *adv.* [F *stupide* or L *stupidus* (as STUPENDOUS)]

stupor /ˈstjuːpə(r)/ *n.* a dazed, torpid, or helplessly amazed state. □□ **stuporous** *adj.* [ME f. L (as STUPENDOUS)]

sturdy /ˈstɜːdɪ/ *adj. & n.* —*adj.* (**sturdier, sturdiest**) **1** robust; strongly built. **2** vigorous and determined (*sturdy resistance*). —*n.* vertigo in sheep caused by a tapeworm larva encysted in the brain. □□ **sturdied** *adj.* (in sense of *n.*). **sturdily** *adv.* **sturdiness** *n.* [ME 'reckless, violent', f. OF *esturdi, estourdi* past part. of *estourdir* stun, daze ult. f. L *ex* EX-¹ + *turdus* thrush (taken as a type of drunkenness)]

sturgeon /ˈstɜːdʒ(ə)n/ *n.* any large mailed sharklike fish of the family Acipenseridae etc. swimming up river to spawn, used as food and a source of caviare and isinglass. [ME f. AF *sturgeon*, OF *esturgeon* ult. f. Gmc]

Sturm und Drang /ˌʃtʊəm ʊnt ˈdræŋ/ *n.* a literary and artistic movement in Germany in the late 18th c., characterized by the expression of emotional unrest and strong feeling. [G, = storm and stress]

stutter /ˈstʌtə(r)/ *v. & n.* —*v.* **1** *intr.* stammer, esp. by involuntarily repeating the first consonants of words. **2** *tr.* (often foll. by *out*) utter (words) in this way. —*n.* **1** the act or habit of stuttering. **2** an instance of stuttering. □□ **stutterer** *n.* **stutteringly** *adv.* [frequent. of ME (now dial.) *stut* f. Gmc]

sty¹ /staɪ/ *n. & v.* —*n.* (*pl.* **sties**) **1** a pen or enclosure for pigs. **2** a filthy room or dwelling. **3** a place of debauchery. —*v.tr. & intr.* (**sties, stied**) lodge in a sty. [OE *stī*, prob. = *stig* hall (cf. STEWARD), f. Gmc]

sty² /staɪ/ *n.* (also **stye**) (*pl.* **sties** or **styes**) an inflamed swelling on the edge of an eyelid. [*styany* (now dial.) = *styan eye* f. OE *stīgend* sty, lit. 'riser' f. *stīgan* rise + EYE, shortened as if = *sty on eye*]

Stygian /ˈstɪdʒɪən/ *adj.* **1** (in Greek mythology) of or relating to the Styx, a river in Hades. **2** *literary* dark, gloomy, indistinct. [L *stugius* f. Gk *stugios* f. *Stux* -*ugos* Styx f. *stugnos* hateful, gloomy]

style /staɪl/ *n. & v.* —*n.* **1** a kind or sort, esp. in regard to appearance and form (*an elegant style of house*). **2** a manner of writing or speaking or performing (*written in a florid style; started off in fine style*). **3** the distinctive manner of a person or school or period, esp. in relation to painting, architecture, furniture, dress, etc. **4** the correct way of designating a person or thing. **5 a** a superior quality or manner (*do it in style*). **b** = FORM *n.* 9 (*bad style*). **6** a particular make, shape, or pattern (*in all sizes and styles*). **7** a method of reckoning dates (*old style; new style*). **8 a** an ancient writing-implement, a small rod with a pointed end for scratching letters on wax-covered tablets and a blunt end for obliterating them. **b** a thing of a similar shape esp. for engraving, tracing, etc. **9** the gnomon of a sundial. **10** *Bot.* the narrow extension of the ovary supporting the stigma. **11** (in *comb.*) = -WISE. —*v.tr.* **1** design or make etc. in a particular (esp. fashionable) style. **2** designate in a specified way. □□ **styleless** *adj.* **stylelessness** *n.* **styler** *n.* [ME f. OF *stile, style* f. L *stilus*: spelling *style* due to assoc. with Gk *stulos* column]

stylet /ˈstaɪlɪt/ *n.* **1** a slender pointed instrument; a stiletto. **2** *Med.* the stiffening wire of a catheter; a probe. [F *stilet* f. It. STILETTO]

styli *pl.* of STYLUS.

stylish /ˈstaɪlɪʃ/ *adj.* **1** fashionable; elegant. **2** having a superior quality, manner, etc. □□ **stylishly** *adv.* **stylishness** *n.*

stylist /ˈstaɪlɪst/ *n.* **1 a** a designer of fashionable styles etc. **b** a hairdresser. **2 a** a writer noted for or aspiring to good literary style. **b** (in sport or music) a person who performs with style.

stylistic /staɪˈlɪstɪk/ *adj.* of or concerning esp. literary style. □□ **stylistically** *adv.* [STYLIST + -IC, after G *stilistisch*]

stylistics /staɪˈlɪstɪks/ *n.* the study of literary style.

stylite /ˈstaɪlaɪt/ *n. Eccl. hist.* an ancient or medieval ascetic living on top of a pillar. [eccl.Gk *stulītēs* f. *stulos* pillar]

stylize /ˈstaɪlaɪz/ *v.tr.* (also **-ise**) (esp. as **stylized** *adj.*) paint, draw, etc. (a subject) in a conventional non-realistic style. □□ **stylization** /-ˈzeɪʃ(ə)n/ *n.* [STYLE + -IZE, after G *stilisieren*]

stylo /ˈstaɪləʊ/ *n.* (*pl.* **-os**) *colloq.* = STYLOGRAPH. [abbr.]

stylobate /ˈstaɪləˌbeɪt/ *n. Archit.* a continuous base supporting a row of columns. [L *stylobata* f. Gk *stulobatēs* f. *stulos* pillar, *bainō* walk]

stylograph /ˈstaɪləˌɡrɑːf/ *n.* a kind of fountain pen having a point instead of a split nib. □□ **stylographic** /-ˈɡræfɪk/ *adj.* [STYLUS + -GRAPH]

styloid /ˈstaɪlɔɪd/ *adj. & n.* —*adj.* resembling a stylus or pen. —*n.* (in full **styloid process**) a spine of bone, esp. that projecting from the base of the temporal bone. [mod.L *styloides* f. Gk *stuloeidēs* f. *stulos* pillar]

stylus /ˈstaɪləs/ *n.* (*pl.* **-li** /-laɪ/ or **-luses**) **1 a** a hard, esp. diamond or sapphire, point following a groove in a gramophone record and transmitting the recorded sound for reproduction. **b** a similar point producing such a groove when recording sound. **2** = STYLE *n.* 8, 9. [erron. spelling of L *stilus*: cf. STYLE]

stymie /ˈstaɪmɪ/ *n. & v.* (also **stimy**) —*n.* (*pl.* **-ies**) **1** *Golf* a situation where an opponent's ball lies between the player and the hole, forming a possible obstruction to play (*lay a stymie*). **2** a difficult situation. —*v.tr.* (**stymies, stymied, stymying** or **stymieing**) **1** obstruct; thwart. **2** *Golf* block (an opponent, his ball, or oneself) with a stymie. [19th c.: orig. unkn.]

styptic /ˈstɪptɪk/ *adj. & n.* —*adj.* (of a drug etc.) that checks bleeding. —*n.* a styptic drug or substance. [ME f. L *stypticus* f. Gk *stuptikos* f. *stuphō* contract]

styrax /ˈstaɪəræks/ *n.* **1** storax resin. **2** any tree or shrub of the genus *Styrax*, e.g. the storax-tree. [L f. Gk *sturax*: cf. STORAX]

styrene /ˈstaɪəriːn/ *n. Chem.* a liquid hydrocarbon easily polymerized and used in making plastics etc. [STYRAX + -ENE]

suable /ˈsuːəb(ə)l, ˈsjuː-/ *adj.* capable of being sued. □□ **suability** /-ˈbɪlɪtɪ/ *n.*

suasion /ˈsweɪʒ(ə)n/ *n.* formal persuasion as opposed to force (*moral suasion*). □□ **suasive** /ˈsweɪsɪv/ *adj.* [ME f. OF *suasion* or L *suasio* f. *suadēre suas-* urge]

suave /swɑːv/ *adj.* **1** (of a person, esp. a man) smooth; polite; sophisticated. **2** (of a wine etc.) bland, smooth. □□ **suavely** *adv.* **suaveness** *n.* **suavity** /-vɪtɪ/ *n.* (*pl.* -**ies**). [F *suave* or L *suavis* agreeable: cf. SWEET]

sub /sʌb/ *n. & v. colloq.* —*n.* **1** a submarine. **2** a subscription. **3** a substitute. **4** a sub-editor. **5** *Mil.* a subaltern. **6** *Brit.* an advance or loan against expected income. —*v.* (**subbed, subbing**) **1** *intr.* (usu. foll. by *for*) act as a substitute for a person. **2** *tr. Brit.* lend or advance (a sum) to (a person) against expected income. **3** *tr.* sub-edit. [abbr.]

sub- /sʌb, səb/ *prefix* (also **suc-** before *c*, **suf-** before *f*, **sug-** before *g*, **sup-** before *p*, **sur-** before *r*, **sus-** before *c*, *p*, *t*) **1** at or to or from a lower position (*subordinate; submerge; subtract; subsoil*). **2** secondary or inferior in rank or position (*subclass; subcommittee; sub-lieutenant; subtotal*). **3** somewhat, nearly; more or less (*subacid; subarctic; subaquatic*). **4** (forming verbs) denoting secondary action (*subdivide; sublet*). **5** denoting support (*subvention*). **6** *Chem.* (of a salt) basic (*subacetate*). [from or after L *sub-* f. *sub* under, close to, towards]

subabdominal /ˌsʌbæbˈdɒmɪn(ə)l/ *adj.* below the abdomen.

subacid /sʌbˈæsɪd/ *adj.* moderately acid or tart (*subacid fruit; a subacid remark*). □□ **subacidity** /ˌsʌbəˈsɪdɪtɪ/ *n.* [L *subacidus* (as SUB-, ACID)]

subacute /ˌsʌbəˈkjuːt/ *adj. Med.* (of a condition) between acute and chronic.

subagency /sʌbˈeɪdʒənsɪ/ *n.* (*pl.* -**ies**) a secondary or subordinate agency. □□ **subagent** *n.*

subalpine /sʌb'ælpaɪn/ *adj.* of or situated in the higher slopes of mountains just below the timberline.

subaltern /'sʌbəlt(ə)n/ *n. & adj.* —*n. Brit. Mil.* an officer below the rank of captain, esp. a second lieutenant. —*adj.* **1** of inferior rank. **2** *Logic* (of a proposition) particular, not universal. [LL *subalternus* f. *alternus* ALTERNATE *adj.*]

subantarctic /ˌsʌbænt'ɑ:ktɪk/ *adj.* of or like regions immediately north of the Antarctic Circle.

sub-aqua /sʌb'ækwə/ *adj.* of or concerning underwater swimming or diving.

subaquatic /ˌsʌbə'kwætɪk/ *adj.* **1** of more or less aquatic habits or kind. **2** underwater.

subaqueous /sʌb'eɪkwɪəs/ *adj.* **1** existing, formed, or taking place under water. **2** lacking in substance or strength; wishy-washy.

subarctic /sʌb'ɑ:ktɪk/ *adj.* of or like regions immediately south of the Arctic Circle.

subastral /sʌb'æstr(ə)l/ *adj.* terrestrial.

subatomic /ˌsʌbə'tɒmɪk/ *adj.* occurring in or smaller than an atom.

subaudition /ˌsʌbɔ:'dɪʃ(ə)n/ *n.* **1** the act of mentally supplying an omitted word or words in speech. **2** the act or process of understanding the unexpressed; reading between the lines. [LL *subauditio* f. *subaudire* understand (as SUB-, AUDITION)]

subaxillary /ˌsʌbæk'zɪlərɪ/ *adj.* **1** *Bot.* in or growing beneath the axil. **2** beneath the armpit.

sub-basement /'sʌb,beɪsmənt/ *n.* a storey below a basement.

sub-branch /'sʌbbrɑ:ntʃ/ *n.* a secondary or subordinate branch.

sub-breed /'sʌbbri:d/ *n.* a secondary or inferior breed.

subcategory /'sʌb,kætɪgərɪ/ *n.* (*pl.* **-ies**) a secondary or subordinate category. □□ **subcategorize** *v.tr.* (also **-ise**). **subcategorization** /-'zeɪʃ(ə)n/ *n.*

subcaudal /sʌb'kɔ:d(ə)l/ *adj.* of or concerning the region under the tail or the back part of the body.

subclass /'sʌbklɑ:s/ *n.* **1** a secondary or subordinate class. **2** *Biol.* a taxonomic category below a class.

sub-clause /'sʌbklɔ:z/ *n.* **1** esp. *Law* a subsidiary section of a clause. **2** *Gram.* a subordinate clause.

subclavian /sʌb'kleɪvɪən/ *adj. & n.* —*adj.* (of an artery etc.) lying or extending under the collar-bone. —*n.* such an artery. [mod.L *subclavius* (as SUB-, *clavis* key); cf. CLAVICLE]

subclinical /sʌb'klɪnɪk(ə)l/ *adj. Med.* (of a disease) not yet presenting definite symptoms.

subcommissioner /'sʌbkə,mɪʃənə(r)/ *n.* a deputy commissioner.

subcommittee /'sʌbkə,mɪtɪ/ *n.* a secondary committee.

subconical /sʌb'kɒnɪk(ə)l/ *adj.* approximately conical.

subconscious /sʌb'kɒnʃəs/ *adj. & n.* —*adj.* of or concerning the part of the mind which is not fully conscious but influences actions etc. —*n.* this part of the mind. □□ **subconsciously** *adv.* **subconsciousness** *n.*

subcontinent /'sʌb,kɒntɪnənt/ *n.* **1** a large land mass, smaller than a continent. **2** a large geographically or politically independent part of a continent. □□ **subcontinental** /-'nent(ə)l/ *adj.*

subcontract *v. & n.* —*v.* /ˌsʌbkən'trækt/ **1** *tr.* employ a firm etc. to do (work) as part of a larger project. **2** *intr.* make or carry out a subcontract. —*n.* /sʌb'kɒntrækt/ a secondary contract, esp. to supply materials, labour, etc. □□ **subcontractor** /-'træktə(r)/ *n.*

subcontrary /sʌb'kɒntrərɪ/ *adj. & n. Logic* —*adj.* (of a proposition) incapable of being false at the same time as another. —*n.* (*pl.* **-ies**) such a proposition. [LL *subcontrarius* (as SUB-, CONTRARY), transl. Gk *hupenantios*]

subcordate /sʌb'kɔ:deɪt/ *adj.* approximately heart-shaped.

subcortical /sʌb'kɔ:tɪk(ə)l/ *adj. Anat.* below the cortex.

subcostal /sʌb'kɒst(ə)l/ *adj. Anat.* below the ribs.

subcranial /sʌb'kreɪnɪəl/ *adj. Anat.* below the cranium.

subcritical /sʌb'krɪtɪk(ə)l/ *adj. Physics* of less than critical mass etc.

subculture /'sʌb,kʌltʃə(r)/ *n.* a cultural group within a larger culture, often having beliefs or interests at variance with those of the larger culture. □□ **subcultural** /-'kʌltʃər(ə)l/ *adj.*

subcutaneous /ˌsʌbkju:'teɪnɪəs/ *adj.* under the skin. □□ **subcutaneously** *adv.*

subdeacon /sʌb'di:kən/ *n. Eccl.* a minister of the order next below a deacon. □□ **subdiaconate** /-daɪ'ækə,neɪt, -daɪ'ækənət/ *n.*

subdean /sʌb'di:n/ *n.* an official ranking next below, or acting as a deputy for, a dean. □□ **subdeanery** *n.* (*pl.* **-ies**). **subdecanal** /-dɪ'keɪn(ə)l/ *adj.*

subdelirious /ˌsʌbdɪ'lɪrɪəs/ *adj.* capable of becoming delirious; mildly delirious. □□ **subdelirium** *n.*

subdivide /'sʌbdɪ,vaɪd, -'vaɪd/ *v.tr. & intr.* divide again after a first division. [ME f. L *subdividere* (as SUB-, DIVIDE)]

subdivision /'sʌbdɪ,vɪʒ(ə)n, -'vɪʒ(ə)n/ *n.* **1** the act or an instance of subdividing. **2** a secondary or subordinate division. **3** *US & Austral.* an area of land divided into plots for sale.

subdominant /sʌb'dɒmɪnənt/ *n. Mus.* the fourth note of the diatonic scale of any key.

subdue /səb'dju:/ *v.tr.* (**subdues**, **subdued**, **subduing**) **1** conquer, subjugate, or tame (an enemy, nature, one's emotions, etc.). **2** (as **subdued** *adj.*) softened; lacking in intensity; toned down (*subdued light*; *in a subdued mood*). □□ **subduable** *adj.* **subdual** *n.* [ME *sodewe* f. OF *so(u)duire* f. L *subducere* (as SUB-, *ducere* lead, bring) used with the sense of *subdere* conquer (as SUB-, *-dere* put)]

sub-editor /sʌb'edɪtə(r)/ *n.* **1** an assistant editor. **2** *Brit.* a person who edits material for printing in a book, newspaper, etc. □□ **sub-edit** *v.tr.* (**-edited**, **-editing**). **sub-editorial** /-'tɔ:rɪəl/ *adj.*

suberect /ˌsʌbɪ'rekt/ *adj.* (of an animal, plant, etc.) almost erect.

subereous /sju:'bɪərɪəs/ *adj.* (also **suberic** /sju:'berɪk/, **suberose** /'sju:bə,rəʊs/) **1** of or concerning cork. **2** corky. [L *suber* cork, cork-oak]

subfamily /'sʌb,fæmɪlɪ/ *n.* (*pl.* **-ies**) **1** *Biol.* a taxonomic category below a family. **2** any subdivision of a group.

subfloor /'sʌbflɔ:(r)/ *n.* a foundation for a floor in a building.

subform /'sʌbfɔ:m/ *n.* a subordinate or secondary form.

subfusc /'sʌbfʌsk/ *adj. & n.* —*adj. formal* dull; dusky; gloomy. —*n.* formal clothing at some universities. [L *subfuscus* f. *fuscus* dark brown]

subgenus /sʌb'dʒi:nəs/ *n.* (*pl.* **subgenera** /-'dʒenərə/) *Biol.* a taxonomic category below a genus. □□ **subgeneric** /-dʒɪ'nerɪk/ *adj.*

subglacial /sʌb'gleɪʃ(ə)l, -sɪəl/ *adj.* next to or at the bottom of a glacier.

subgroup /'sʌbgru:p/ *n. Math.* etc. a subset of a group.

subhead /'sʌbhed/ *n.* (also **subheading**) **1** a subordinate heading or title in a chapter, article, etc. **2** a subordinate division in a classification.

subhuman /sʌb'hju:mən/ *adj.* **1** (of an animal) closely related to man. **2** (of behaviour, intelligence, etc.) less than human.

subjacent /sʌb'dʒeɪs(ə)nt/ *adj.* underlying; situated below. [L *subjacēre* (as SUB-, *jacēre* lie)]

subject *n., adj., adv., & v.* —*n.* /'sʌbdʒɪkt/ **1 a** a matter, theme, etc. to be discussed, described, represented, dealt with, etc. **b** (foll. by *for*) a person, circumstance, etc., giving rise to specified feeling, action, etc. (*a subject for congratulation*). **2** a department or field of study (*his best subject is geography*). **3** *Gram.* a noun or its equivalent about which a sentence is predicated and with which the verb agrees. **4 a** any person except a monarch living under a monarchy or any other form of government (*the ruler and his subjects*). **b** any person owing obedience to another. **5** *Philos.* **a** a thinking or feeling entity; the conscious mind; the ego, esp. as opposed to anything external to the mind. **b** the central substance or core of a thing as opposed to its attributes. **6** *Mus.* a theme of a fugue or sonata; a leading phrase or motif. **7** a person of specified mental or physical tendencies (*a hysterical subject*). **8** *Logic* the part of a proposition about which a statement is made. **9** (in full **subject for dissection**) a dead body. —*adj.* /'sʌbdʒɪkt/ **1** (often foll. by *to*) owing obedience to a government, colonizing power, force, etc.; in subjection. **2** (foll. by *to*) liable, exposed, or prone to (*is subject to infection*). **3** (foll. by *to*) conditional upon; on the assumption of (*the arrangement is subject to your approval*). —*adv.* /'sʌbdʒɪkt/ (foll. by *to*) conditionally upon (*subject to your consent, I propose to try again*). —*v.tr.* /səb'dʒekt/ **1** (foll. by *to*) make liable; expose; treat (*subjected us to hours of waiting*). **2** (usu. foll. by *to*) subdue (a nation, person, etc.) to one's sway etc. □ **on the subject of** concerning, about. **subject and object** *Psychol.* the ego or self and the non-ego; consciousness and that of which it is or may be conscious. **subject catalogue** a catalogue, esp. in a library, arranged according to the subjects treated. **subject-heading** a heading in an index collecting references to a subject. **subject-matter** the matter treated of in a book, lawsuit, etc. □□ **subjection** /səb'dʒekʃ(ə)n/ *n.* **subjectless** /'sʌbdʒɪktlɪs/ *adj.* [ME *soget* etc. f. OF *suget* etc. f. L *subjectus* past part. of *subjicere* (as SUB-, *jacere* throw)]

subjective /səb'dʒektɪv/ *adj. & n.* —*adj.* **1** (of art, literature, written history, a person's views, etc.) proceeding from personal idiosyncrasy or individuality; not impartial or literal. **2** esp. *Philos.* proceeding from or belonging to the individual consciousness or perception; imaginary, partial, or distorted. **3** *Gram.* of or concerning the subject. —*n. Gram.* the subjective case. □ **subjective case** *Gram.* the nominative. □□ **subjectively** *adv.* **subjectiveness** *n.* **subjectivity** /ˌsʌbdʒek'tɪvɪtɪ/ *n.* [ME f. L *subjectivus* (as SUBJECT)]

subjectivism /səb'dʒektɪˌvɪz(ə)m/ *n. Philos.* the doctrine that knowledge is merely subjective and that there is no external or objective truth. □□ **subjectivist** *n.*

subjoin /sʌb'dʒɔɪn/ *v.tr.* add or append (an illustration, anecdote, etc.) at the end. [obs. F *subjoindre* f. L *subjungere* (as SUB-, *jungere junct-* join)]

subjoint /'sʌbdʒɔɪnt/ *n.* a secondary joint (in an insect's leg etc.).

sub judice /sʌb 'dʒuːdɪsɪ, sʊb 'juːdɪˌkeɪ/ *adj. Law* under judicial consideration and therefore prohibited from public discussion elsewhere. [L, = under a judge]

subjugate /'sʌbdʒʊˌɡeɪt/ *v.tr.* bring into subjection; subdue; vanquish. □□ **subjugable** /-ɡəb(ə)l/ *adj.* **subjugation** /-'ɡeɪʃ(ə)n/ *n.* **subjugator** *n.* [ME f. LL *subjugare* bring under the yoke (as SUB-, *jugum* yoke)]

subjunctive /səb'dʒʌŋktɪv/ *adj. & n. Gram.* —*adj.* (of a mood) denoting what is imagined or wished or possible (e.g. *if I were you, God help you, be that as it may*). —*n.* **1** the subjunctive mood. **2** a verb in this mood. □□ **subjunctively** *adv.* [F *subjonctif -ive* or LL *subjunctivus* f. L (as SUBJOIN), transl. Gk *hupotaktikos*, as being used in subjoined clauses]

subkingdom /sʌb'kɪŋdəm/ *n. Biol.* a taxonomic category below a kingdom.

sublease *n. & v.* —*n.* /'sʌbliːs/ a lease of a property by a tenant to a subtenant. —*v.tr.* /sʌb'liːs/ lease (a property) to a subtenant.

sublessee /ˌsʌble'siː/ *n.* a person who holds a sublease.

sublessor /ˌsʌble'sɔː(r)/ *n.* a person who grants a sublease.

sublet *n. & v.* —*n.* /'sʌblet/ = SUBLEASE *n.* —*v.tr.* /sʌb'let/ (-**letting**; *past* and *past part.* -**let**) = SUBLEASE *v.*

sub-lieutenant /ˌsʌblef'tenənt/ *n. Brit.* an officer ranking next below lieutenant.

sublimate *v., adj., & n.* —*v.tr.* /'sʌblɪˌmeɪt/ **1** divert the energy of (a primitive impulse, esp. sexual) into a culturally higher activity. **2** *Chem.* convert (a substance) from the solid state directly to its vapour by heat, and usu. allow to solidify again. **3** refine; purify; idealize. —*adj.* /'sʌblɪmət/ **1** *Chem.* (of a substance) sublimated. **2** purified, refined. —*n.* /'sʌblɪmət/ *Chem.* **1** a sublimated substance. **2** = *corrosive sublimate*. □□ **sublimation** /-'meɪʃ(ə)n/ *n.* [L *sublimare sublimat-* SUBLIME *v.*]

sublime /sə'blaɪm/ *adj. & v.* —*adj.* (**sublimer**, **sublimest**) **1** of the most exalted, grand, or noble kind; awe-inspiring (*sublime genius*). **2** (of indifference, impudence, etc.) arrogantly unruffled. —*v.* **1** *tr. & intr. Chem.* = SUBLIMATE *v.* 2. **2** *tr.* purify or elevate by or as if by sublimation; make sublime. **3** *intr.* become pure by or as if by sublimation. □ **Sublime Porte** see PORTE. □□ **sublimely** *adv.* **sublimity** /-'lɪmɪtɪ/ *n.* [L *sublimis* (as SUB-, second element perh. rel. to *limen* threshold, *limus* oblique)]

subliminal /səb'lɪmɪn(ə)l/ *adj. Psychol.* (of a stimulus etc.) below the threshold of sensation or consciousness. □ **subliminal advertising** the use of subliminal images in advertising on television etc. to influence the viewer at an unconscious level. **subliminal self** the part of one's personality outside conscious awareness. □□ **subliminally** *adv.* [SUB- + L *limen -inis* threshold]

sublingual /sʌb'lɪŋɡw(ə)l/ *adj.* under the tongue. [SUB- + L *lingua* tongue]

sublittoral /sʌb'lɪtər(ə)l/ *adj.* **1** (of plants, animals, deposits, etc.) living or found on the seashore just below the low-water mark. **2** of or concerning the seashore.

Sub-Lt. *abbr. Brit.* Sub-Lieutenant.

sublunary /sʌb'luːnərɪ, -'ljuːnərɪ/ *adj.* **1** beneath the moon. **2** *Astron.* **a** within the moon's orbit. **b** subject to the moon's influence. **3** of this world; earthly. [LL *sublunaris* (as SUB-, LUNAR)]

sub-machine-gun /ˌsʌbmə'ʃiːnɡʌn/ *n.* a hand-held lightweight machine-gun.

subman /'sʌbmæn/ *n.* (*pl.* -**men**) *derog.* an inferior, brutal, or stupid man.

submarginal /sʌb'mɑːdʒɪn(ə)l/ *adj.* **1** esp. *Econ.* not reaching minimum requirements. **2** (of land) that cannot be farmed profitably.

submarine /ˌsʌbmə'riːn, 'sʌb-/ *n. & adj.* —*n.* a vessel, esp. a warship, capable of operating under water and usu. equipped with torpedoes, missiles, and a periscope. —*adj.* existing, occurring, done, or used under the surface of the sea (*submarine cable*). □□ **submariner** /-'mærɪnə(r)/ *n.*

submaster /'sʌbˌmɑːstə(r)/ *n.* an assistant master or assistant headmaster in a school.

submaxillary /ˌsʌbmæk'sɪlərɪ/ *adj.* beneath the lower jaw.

submediant /sʌb'miːdɪənt/ *n. Mus.* the sixth note of the diatonic scale of any key.

submental /sʌb'ment(ə)l/ *adj.* under the chin.

submerge /səb'mɜːdʒ/ *v.* **1** *tr.* **a** place under water; flood; inundate. **b** flood or inundate with work, problems, etc. **2** *intr.* (of a submarine, its crew, a diver, etc.) dive below the surface of water. □ **the submerged tenth** the supposed fraction of the population permanently living in poverty. □□ **submergence** *n.* **submergible** *adj.* **submersion** /-'mɜːʃ(ə)n/ *n.* [L *submergere* (as SUB-, *mergere mersdip*)]

submersible /səb'mɜːsɪb(ə)l/ n. & adj. —n. a submarine operating under water for short periods. —adj. capable of being submerged. [*submerse* (v.) = SUBMERGE]

submicroscopic /sʌb,maɪkrə'skɒpɪk/ adj. too small to be seen by an ordinary microscope.

subminiature /sʌb'mɪnɪtʃə(r)/ adj. **1** of greatly reduced size. **2** (of a camera) very small and using 16-mm film.

submission /səb'mɪʃ(ə)n/ n. **1 a** the act or an instance of submitting; the state of being submitted. **b** anything that is submitted. **2** humility, meekness, obedience, submissiveness (*showed great submission of spirit*). **3** *Law* a theory etc. submitted by counsel to a judge or jury. **4** (in wrestling) the surrender of a participant yielding to the pain of a hold. [ME f. OF *submission* or L *submissio* (as SUBMIT)]

submissive /səb'mɪsɪv/ adj. **1** humble; obedient. **2** yielding to power or authority; willing to submit. ▢▢ **submissively** adv. **submissiveness** n. [SUBMISSION after *remissive* etc.]

submit /səb'mɪt/ v. (**submitted**, **submitting**) **1** (usu. foll. by *to*) **a** intr. cease resistance; give way; yield (*had to submit to defeat; will never submit*). **b** refl. surrender (oneself) to the control of another etc. **2** tr. present for consideration or decision. **3** tr. (usu. foll. by *to*) subject (a person or thing) to an operation, process, treatment, etc. (*submitted it to the flames*). **4** tr. esp. *Law* urge or represent esp. deferentially (*that, I submit, is a misrepresentation*). ▢▢ **submitter** n. [ME f. L *submittere* (as SUB-, *mittere miss-* send)]

submultiple /sʌb'mʌltɪp(ə)l/ n. & adj. —n. a number that can be divided exactly into a specified number. —adj. being such a number.

subnormal /sʌb'nɔːm(ə)l/ adj. **1** (esp. as regards intelligence) below normal. **2** less than normal. ▢▢ **subnormality** /-'mælɪtɪ/ n.

subnuclear /sʌb'njuːklɪə(r)/ adj. *Physics* occurring in or smaller than an atomic nucleus.

subocular /sʌb'ɒkjʊlə(r)/ adj. situated below or under the eyes.

suborbital /sʌb'ɔːbɪt(ə)l/ adj. **1** situated below the orbit of the eye. **2** (of a spaceship etc.) not completing a full orbit of the earth.

suborder /'sʌb,ɔːdə(r)/ n. a taxonomic category between an order and a family. ▢▢ **subordinal** /-'ɔːdɪn(ə)l/ adj.

subordinary /sʌb'ɔːdɪnərɪ/ n. (pl. **-ies**) *Heraldry* a device or bearing that is common but less so than ordinaries.

subordinate adj., n., & v. —adj. /sə'bɔːdɪnət/ (usu. foll. by *to*) of inferior importance or rank; secondary, subservient. —n. /sə'bɔːdɪnət/ a person working under another's control or orders. —v.tr. /sə'bɔːdɪneɪt/ (usu. foll. by *to*) **1** make subordinate; treat or regard as of minor importance. **2** make subservient. ▢ **subordinate clause** a clause serving as an adjective, adverb, or noun in a main sentence because of its position or a preceding conjunction. ▢▢ **subordinately** /sə'bɔːdɪnətlɪ/ adv. **subordination** /-'neɪʃ(ə)n/ n. **subordinative** /sə'bɔːdɪnətɪv/ adj. [med.L *subordinare, subordinat-* (as SUB-, L *ordinare* ordain)]

suborn /sə'bɔːn/ v.tr. induce by bribery etc. to commit perjury or any other unlawful act. ▢▢ **subornation** /,sʌbɔː'neɪʃ(ə)n/ n. **suborner** n. [L *subornare* incite secretly (as SUB-, *ornare* equip)]

suboxide /sʌb'ɒksaɪd/ n. *Chem.* an oxide containing the smallest proportion of oxygen.

subphylum /sʌb'faɪləm/ n. (pl. **subphyla** /-lə/) *Biol.* a taxonomic category below a phylum.

sub-plot /'sʌbplɒt/ n. a subordinate plot in a play etc.

subpoena /səb'piːnə, sə'piːnə/ n. & v. —n. a writ ordering a person to attend a lawcourt. —v.tr. (*past* and *past part.* **subpoenaed** or **subpoena'd**) serve a subpoena on. [ME f. L *sub poena* under penalty (the first words of the writ)]

subregion /'sʌb,riːdʒ(ə)n/ n. a division of a region, esp. with regard to natural life. ▢▢ **subregional** /-'riːdʒən(ə)l/ adj.

subreption /səb'repʃ(ə)n/ n. *formal* the obtaining of a thing by surprise or misrepresentation. [L *subreptio* purloining f. *subripere* (as SUB-, *rapere* snatch)]

subrogation /,sʌbrə'geɪʃ(ə)n/ n. *Law* the substitution of one party for another as creditor, with the transfer of rights and duties. ▢▢ **subrogate** /'sʌbrəgeɪt/ v.tr. [LL *subrogatio* f. *subrogare* choose as substitute (as SUB-, *rogare* ask)]

sub rosa /sʌb 'rəʊzə/ adj. & adv. (of communication, consultation, etc.) in secrecy or confidence. [L, lit. 'under the rose', as emblem of secrecy]

subroutine /'sʌbruː,tiːn/ n. *Computing* a routine designed to perform a frequently used operation within a program.

subscribe /səb'skraɪb/ v. **1** (usu. foll. by *to, for*) **a** tr. & intr. contribute (a specified sum) or make or promise a contribution to a fund, project, charity, etc., esp. regularly. **b** intr. enter one's name in a list of contributors to a charity etc. **c** tr. raise or guarantee raising (a sum) by so subscribing. **2** intr. (usu. foll. by *to*) express one's agreement with an opinion, resolution, etc. (*cannot subscribe to that*). **3** tr. **a** write (esp. one's name) at the foot of a document etc. (*subscribed a motto*). **b** write one's name at the foot of, sign (a document, picture, etc.). ▢**subscribe for** agree to take a copy or copies of (a book) before publication. **subscribe oneself** sign one's name as. **subscribe to** arrange to receive (a periodical etc.) regularly. [ME f. L *subscribere* (as SUB-, *scribere script-* write)]

subscriber /səb'skraɪbə(r)/ n. **1** a person who subscribes. **2** a person paying for the hire of a telephone line. ▢**subscriber trunk dialling** *Brit.* the automatic connection of trunk calls by dialling without the assistance of an operator.

subscript /'sʌbskrɪpt/ adj. & n. —adj. written or printed below the line, esp. *Math.* (of a symbol) written below and to the right of another symbol. —n. a subscript number or symbol. [L *subscriptus* (as SUBSCRIBE)]

subscription /səb'skrɪpʃ(ə)n/ n. **1 a** the act or an instance of subscribing. **b** money subscribed. **2** *Brit.* a fee for the membership of a society etc., esp. paid regularly. **3 a** an agreement to take and pay for usu. a specified number of issues of a newspaper, magazine, etc. **b** the money paid by this. **4** a signature on a document etc. **5** the offer of a reduced price to those ordering a book before publication. ▢**subscription concert** etc. each of a series of concerts etc. for which tickets are sold in advance. [ME f. L *subscriptio* (as SUBSCRIBE)]

subsection /'sʌb,sekʃ(ə)n/ n. a division of a section.

subsellium /səb'selɪəm/ n. (pl. **subsellia** /-lɪə/) = MISERICORD 1. [L f. *sella* seat]

subsequence /'sʌbsɪkwəns/ n. a subsequent incident; a consequence.

sub-sequence /'sʌb,siːkwəns/ n. a sequence forming part of a larger one.

subsequent /'sʌbsɪkwənt/ adj. (usu. foll. by *to*) following a specified event etc. in time, esp. as a consequence. ▢▢ **subsequently** adv. [ME f. OF *subsequent* or L *subsequi* (as SUB-, *sequi* follow)]

subserve /səb'sɜːv/ v.tr. serve as a means in furthering (a purpose, action, etc.). [L *subservire* (as SUB-, SERVE)]

subservient /səb'sɜːvɪənt/ adj. **1** cringing; obsequious. **2** (usu. foll. by *to*) serving as a means; instrumental. **3** (usu. foll. by *to*) subordinate. ▢▢ **subservience** n. **subserviency** n. **subserviently** adv. [L *subserviens subservient-* (as SUBSERVE)]

subset /'sʌbset/ n. **1** a secondary part of a set. **2** *Math.* a set all the elements of which are contained in another set.

subshrub /'sʌbʃrʌb/ n. a low-growing or small shrub.

subside /səb'saɪd/ v.intr. **1** cease from agitation;

become tranquil; abate (*excitement subsided*). **2** (of water, suspended matter, etc.) sink. **3** (of the ground) cave in; sink. **4** (of a building, ship, etc.) sink lower in the ground or water. **5** (of a swelling etc.) become less. **6** usu. *joc.* (of a person) sink into a sitting, kneeling, or lying posture. □□ **subsidence** /-'saɪd(ə)ns, 'sʌbsɪd(ə)ns/ *n.* [L *subsidere* (as SUB-, *sidere* settle rel. to *sedēre* sit)]

subsidiary /səb'sɪdɪərɪ/ *adj. & n.* —*adj.* **1** serving to assist or supplement; auxiliary. **2** (of a company) controlled by another. **3** (of troops): **a** paid for by subsidy. **b** hired by another nation. —*n.* (pl. -**ies**) **1** a subsidiary thing or person; an accessory. **2** a subsidiary company. □□ **subsidiarily** *adv.* **subsidiarity** /-'ærɪtɪ/ *n.* [L *subsidiarius* (as SUBSIDY)]

subsidize /'sʌbsɪˌdaɪz/ *v.tr.* (also -**ise**) **1** pay a subsidy to. **2** reduce the cost of by subsidy (*subsidized lunches*). □□ **subsidization** /-'zeɪʃ(ə)n/ *n.* **subsidizer** *n.*

subsidy /'sʌbsɪdɪ/ *n.* (pl. -**ies**) **1 a** money granted by the State or a public body etc. to keep down the price of commodities etc. (*housing subsidy*). **b** money granted to a charity or other undertaking held to be in the public interest. **c** any grant or contribution of money. **2** money paid by one State to another in return for military, naval, or other aid. **3** *hist.* **a** a parliamentary grant to the sovereign for State needs. **b** a tax levied on a particular occasion. [ME f. AF *subsidie*, OF *subside* f. L *subsidium* assistance]

subsist /səb'sɪst/ *v.* **1** *intr.* (often foll. by *on*) keep oneself alive; be kept alive (*subsists on vegetables*). **2** *intr.* remain in being; exist. **3** *intr.* (foll. by *in*) be attributable to (*its excellence subsists in its freshness*). **4** *tr. archaic* provide sustenance for. □□ **subsistent** *adj.* [L *subsistere* stand firm (as SUB-, *sistere* set, stand)]

subsistence /səb'sɪst(ə)ns/ *n.* **1** the state or an instance of subsisting. **2 a** the means of supporting life; a livelihood. **b** a minimal level of existence or the income providing this (*a bare subsistence*). □**subsistence allowance** (or **money**) esp. *Brit.* an allowance or advance on pay granted esp. as travelling expenses. **subsistence farming** farming which directly supports the farmer's household without producing a significant surplus for trade. **subsistence level** (or **wage**) a standard of living (or wage) providing only the bare necessities of life.

subsoil /'sʌbsɔɪl/ *n.* soil lying immediately under the surface soil (opp. TOPSOIL).

subsonic /sʌb'sɒnɪk/ *adj.* relating to speeds less than that of sound. □□ **subsonically** *adv.*

subspecies /'sʌbˌspiːʃiːz, -ʃiːz/ *n.* (pl. same) *Biol.* a taxonomic category below a species, usu. a fairly permanent geographically isolated variety. □□ **subspecific** /-spə'sɪfɪk/ *adj.*

substance /'sʌbst(ə)ns/ *n.* **1 a** the essential material, esp. solid, forming a thing (*the substance was transparent*). **b** a particular kind of material having uniform properties (*this substance is salt*). **2 a** reality; solidity (*ghosts have no substance*). **b** seriousness or steadiness of character (*there is no substance in him*). **3** the theme or subject of esp. a work of art, argument, etc. (*prefer the substance to the style*). **4** the real meaning or essence of a thing. **5** wealth and possessions (*a woman of substance*). **6** *Philos.* the essential nature underlying phenomena, which is subject to changes and accidents. □**in substance** generally; apart from details. [ME f. OF f. L *substantia* (as SUB-, *stare* stand)]

substandard /sʌb'stændəd/ *adj.* **1** of less than the required or normal quality or size; inferior. **2** (of language) not conforming to standard usage.

substantial /səb'stænʃ(ə)l/ *adj.* **1 a** of real importance or value (*made a substantial contribution*). **b** of large size or amount (*awarded substantial damages*). **2** of solid material or structure; stout (*a man of substantial build; a substantial house*). **3** commercially successful; wealthy. **4** essential; true in

large part (*substantial truth*). **5** having substance; real. □□ **substantiality** /-ʃɪˈælɪtɪ/ *n.* **substantially** *adv.* [ME f. OF *substantiel* or LL *substantialis* (as SUBSTANCE)]

substantialism /səb'stænʃəˌlɪz(ə)m/ *n. Philos.* the doctrine that behind phenomena there are substantial realities. □□ **substantialist** *n.*

substantialize /səb'stænʃəˌlaɪz/ *v.tr. & intr.* (also -**ise**) invest with or acquire substance or actual existence.

substantiate /səb'stænʃɪˌeɪt/ *v.tr.* prove the truth of (a charge, statement, claim, etc.); give good grounds for. □□ **substantiation** /-'eɪʃ(ə)n/ *n.* [med.L *substantiare* give substance to (as SUBSTANCE)]

substantive /'sʌbstəntɪv/ *adj. & n.* —*adj.* /also səb'stæntɪv/ **1** having separate and independent existence. **2** *Law* relating to rights and duties. **3** (of an enactment, motion, resolution, etc.) made in due form as such; not amended. **4** *Gram.* expressing existence. **5** (of a dye) not needing a mordant. **6** *Mil.* (of a rank etc.) permanent, not acting or temporary. **7** *archaic* denoting a substance. —*n. Gram.* = NOUN. □**the substantive verb** the verb 'to be'. □□ **substantival** /-'taɪv(ə)l/ *adj.* **substantively** *adv.* esp. *Gram.* [ME f. OF *substantif -ive*, or LL *substantivus* (as SUBSTANCE)]

substation /'sʌbˌsteɪʃ(ə)n/ *n.* a subordinate station, esp. one reducing the high voltage of electric power transmission to that suitable for supply to consumers.

substituent /sʌb'stɪtjʊənt/ *adj. & n. Chem.* —*adj.* (of a group of atoms) replacing another atom or group in a compound. —*n.* such a group. [L *substituere substituent-* (as SUBSTITUTE)]

substitute /'sʌbstɪˌtjuːt/ *n. & v.* —*n.* **1 a** (also *attrib.*) a person or thing acting or serving in place of another. **b** an artificial alternative to a natural substance (*butter substitute*). **2** *Sc. Law* a deputy. —*v.* **1** *intr. & tr.* (often foll. by *for*) act or cause to act as a substitute; put or serve in exchange (*substituted for her mother; substituted it for the broken one*). **2** *tr.* (usu. foll. by *by, with*) *colloq.* replace (a person or thing) with another. **3** *tr. Chem.* replace (an atom or group in a molecule) with another. □□ **substitutable** *adj.* **substitutability** /-'bɪlɪtɪ/ *n.* **substitution** /-'tjuːʃ(ə)n/ *n.* **substitutional** /-'tjuːʃən(ə)l/ *adj.* **substitutionary** /-'tjuːʃənərɪ/ *adj.* **substitutive** *adj.* [ME f. L *substitutus* past part. of *substituere* (as SUB-, *statuere* set up)]

substrate /'sʌbstreɪt/ *n.* **1** = SUBSTRATUM. **2** a surface to be painted, printed, etc., on. **3** *Biol.* **a** the substance upon which an enzyme acts. **b** the surface or material on which any particular organism grows. [Anglicized f. SUBSTRATUM]

substratum /'sʌbˌstrɑːtəm, -ˌstreɪtəm/ *n.* (pl. **substrata** /-tə/) **1** an underlying layer or substance. **2** a layer of rock or soil beneath the surface. **3** a foundation or basis (*there is a substratum of truth in it*). [mod.L, past part. of L *substernere* (as SUB-, *sternere* strew): cf. STRATUM]

substructure /'sʌbˌstrʌktʃə(r)/ *n.* an underlying or supporting structure. □□ **substructural** *adj.*

subsume /səb'sjuːm/ *v.tr.* (usu. foll. by *under*) include (an instance, idea, category, etc.) in a rule, class, category, etc. □□ **subsumable** *adj.* **subsumption** /-'sʌmpʃ(ə)n/ *n.* [med.L *subsumere* (as SUB-, *sumere sumpt-* take)]

subtenant /'sʌbˌtenənt/ *n.* a person who leases a property from a tenant. □□ **subtenancy** *n.*

subtend /sʌb'tend/ *v.tr.* **1 a** (usu. foll. by *at*) (of a line, arc, figure, etc.) form (an angle) at a particular point when its extremities are joined at that point. **b** (of an angle or chord) have bounding lines or points that meet or coincide with those of (a line or arc). **2** *Bot.* (of a bract etc.) extend under so as to embrace or enfold. [L *subtendere* (as SUB-, *tendere* stretch)]

subterfuge /'sʌbtəˌfjuːdʒ/ *n.* **1 a** an attempt to avoid blame or defeat esp. by lying or deceit. **b** a statement etc. resorted to for such a purpose. **2** this as a practice or policy. [F *subterfuge* or LL *subterfugium* f. L *subterfugere* escape secretly f. *subter* beneath + *fugere* flee]

subterminal /sʌb'tɜ:mɪn(ə)l/ *adj.* nearly at the end.

subterranean /ˌsʌbtə'reɪnɪən/ *adj.* **1** existing, occurring, or done under the earth's surface. **2** secret, underground, concealed. □□ **subterraneously** *adv.* [L *subterraneus* (as SUB-, *terra* earth)]

subtext /'sʌbtekst/ *n.* an underlying often distinct theme in a piece of writing.

subtilize /'sʌtɪˌlaɪz/ *v.* (also **-ise**) **1** *tr.* **a** make subtle. **b** elevate; refine. **2** *intr.* (usu. foll. by *upon*) argue or reason subtly. □□ **subtilization** /-'zeɪʃ(ə)n/ *n.* [F *subtiliser* or med.L *subtilizare* (as SUBTLE)]

subtitle /'sʌbˌtaɪt(ə)l/ *n. & v.* —*n.* **1** a secondary or additional title of a book etc. **2** a printed caption at the bottom of a film etc., esp. translating dialogue. —*v.tr.* provide with a subtitle or subtitles.

subtle /'sʌt(ə)l/ *adj.* (**subtler**, **subtlest**) **1** evasive or mysterious; hard to grasp (*subtle charm*; *a subtle distinction*). **2** (of scent, colour, etc.) faint, delicate, elusive (*subtle perfume*). **3 a** capable of making fine distinctions; perceptive; acute (*subtle intellect*; *subtle senses*). **b** ingenious; elaborate; clever (*a subtle device*). **4** *archaic* crafty, cunning. □□ **subtleness** *n.* **subtly** *adv.* [ME f. OF *sotil* f. L *subtilis*]

subtlety /'sʌtəltɪ/ *n.* (*pl.* **-ies**) **1** something subtle. **2** a fine distinction; an instance of hairsplitting. [ME f. OF *s(o)utilité* f. L *subtilitas -tatis* (as SUBTLE)]

subtonic /sʌb'tɒnɪk/ *n. Mus.* the note below the tonic, the seventh note of the diatonic scale of any key.

subtopia /sʌb'təʊpɪə/ *n. Brit. derog.* unsightly and sprawling suburban development. □□ **subtopian** *adj.* [SUBURB, UTOPIA]

subtotal /'sʌbˌtəʊt(ə)l/ *n.* the total of one part of a group of figures to be added.

subtract /səb'trækt/ *v.tr.* (often foll. by *from*) deduct (a part, quantity, or number) from another. □□ **subtracter** *n.* (cf. SUBTRACTOR). **subtraction** /-'trækʃ(ə)n/ *n.* **subtractive** *adj.* [L *subtrahere subtract-* (as SUB-, *trahere* draw)]

subtractor /səb'træktə(r)/ *n. Electronics* a circuit or device that produces an output dependent on the difference of two inputs.

subtrahend /'sʌbtrəˌhend/ *n. Math.* a quantity or number to be subtracted. [L *subtrahendus* gerundive of *subtrahere*: see SUBTRACT]

subtropics /sʌb'trɒpɪks/ *n.pl.* the regions adjacent to or bordering on the tropics. □□ **subtropical** *adj.*

subulate /'sʌbjʊlət/ *adj. Bot. & Zool.* slender and tapering. [L *subula* awl]

suburb /'sʌbɜ:b/ *n.* an outlying district of a city, esp. residential. [ME f. OF *suburbe* or L *suburbium* (as SUB-, *urbs urbis* city)]

suburban /sə'bɜ:bən/ *adj.* **1** of or characteristic of suburbs. **2** *derog.* provincial, uncultured, or naïve. □□ **suburbanite** *n.* **suburbanize** *v.tr.* (also **-ise**). **suburbanization** /-'zeɪʃ(ə)n/ *n.* [L *suburbanus* (as SUBURB)]

suburbia /sə'bɜ:bɪə/ *n.* often *derog.* the suburbs, their inhabitants, and their way of life.

subvention /səb'venʃ(ə)n/ *n.* a grant of money from a government etc.; a subsidy. [ME f. OF f. LL *subventio -onis* f. L *subvenire subvent-* assist (as SUB-, *venire* come)]

subversive /səb'vɜ:sɪv/ *adj. & n.* —*adj.* (of a person, organization, activity, etc.) seeking to subvert (esp. a government). —*n.* a subversive person; a revolutionary. □□ **subversion** /-'vɜ:ʃ(ə)n/ *n.* **subversively** *adv.* **subversiveness** *n.* [med.L *subversivus* (as SUBVERT)]

subvert /səb'vɜ:t/ *v.tr.* esp. *Polit.* overturn, overthrow, or upset (religion, government, the monarchy, morality, etc.). □□ **subverter** *n.* [ME f. OF *subvertir* or L *subvertere* (as SUB-, *vertere vers-* turn)]

subway /'sʌbweɪ/ *n.* **1 a** a tunnel beneath a road etc.

for pedestrians. **b** an underground passage for pipes, cables, etc. **2** esp. *US* an underground railway.

subzero /sʌb'zɪərəʊ/ *adj.* (esp. of temperature) lower than zero.

suc- /sʌk, sək/ *prefix* assim. form of SUB- before *c*.

succedaneum /ˌsʌksɪ'deɪnɪəm/ *n.* (*pl.* **succedanea** /-nɪə/) a substitute, esp. for a medicine or drug. □□ **succedaneous** *adj.* [mod.L, neut. of L *succedaneus* (as SUCCEED)]

succeed /sək'si:d/ *v.* **1** *intr.* **a** (often foll. by *in*) accomplish one's purpose; have success; prosper (*succeeded in his ambition*). **b** (of a plan etc.) be successful. **2 a** *tr.* follow in order; come next after (*night succeeded day*). **b** *intr.* (foll. by *to*) come next, be subsequent. **3** *intr.* (often foll. by *to*) come by an inheritance, office, title, or property (*succeeded to the throne*). **4** *tr.* take over an office, property, inheritance, etc. from (*succeeded his father*; *succeeded the manager*). □**nothing succeeds like success** one success leads to others. □□ **succeeder** *n.* [ME f. OF *succeder* or L *succedere* (as SUB-, *cedere cess-* go)]

succentor /sək'sentə(r)/ *n. Eccl.* a precentor's deputy in some cathedrals. □□ **succentorship** *n.* [LL f. L *succinere* (as SUB-, *canere* sing)]

succès de scandale /sʊkˌseɪ də skɔ̃'dɑ:l/ *n.* a book, play, etc. having great success because of its scandalous nature or associations. [F]

success /sək'ses/ *n.* **1** the accomplishment of an aim; a favourable outcome (*their efforts met with success*). **2** the attainment of wealth, fame, or position (*spoilt by success*). **3** a thing or person that turns out well. **4** *archaic* a usu. specified outcome of an undertaking (*ill success*). □**success story** a person's rise from poverty to wealth etc. [L *successus* (as SUCCEED)]

successful /sək'sesfʊl/ *adj.* having success; prosperous. □□ **successfully** *adv.* **successfulness** *n.*

succession /sək'seʃ(ə)n/ *n.* **1 a** the process of following in order; succeeding. **b** a series of things or people in succession. **2 a** the right of succeeding to the throne, an office, inheritance, etc. **b** the act or process of so succeeding. **c** those having such a right. **3** *Biol.* the order of development of a species or community; = SERE³. □**in quick succession** following one another at short intervals. **in succession** one after another, without intervention. **in succession to** as the successor of. **law of succession** the law regulating inheritance. **settle the succession** determine who shall succeed. **Succession State** a State resulting from the partition of a previously existing country. □□ **successional** *adj.* [ME f. OF *succession* or L *successio* (as SUCCEED)]

successive /sək'sesɪv/ *adj.* following one after another; running, consecutive. □□ **successively** *adv.* **successiveness** *n.* [ME f. med.L *successivus* (as SUCCEED)]

successor /sək'sesə(r)/ *n.* (often foll. by *to*) a person or thing that succeeds to another. [ME f. OF *successour* f. L *successor* (as SUCCEED)]

succinct /sək'sɪŋkt/ *adj.* briefly expressed; terse, concise. □□ **succinctly** *adv.* **succinctness** *n.* [ME f. L *succinctus* past part. of *succingere* tuck up (as SUB-, *cingere* gird)]

succinic acid /sʌk'sɪnɪk/ *n. Chem.* a crystalline dibasic acid derived from amber etc. □□ **succinate** /'sʌksɪˌneɪt/ *n.* [F *succinique* f. L *succinum* amber]

succor *US* var. of SUCCOUR.

succory /'sʌkərɪ/ *n.* = CHICORY 1. [alt. f. *cicoree* etc., early forms of CHICORY]

succotash /'sʌkəˌtæʃ/ *n. US* a dish of green maize and beans boiled together. [Narraganset *msiquatash*]

Succoth /sʊ'kəʊt, 'sʌkəθ/ *n.* the Jewish autumn thanksgiving festival commemorating the sheltering in the wilderness. [Heb. *sukkôt* pl. of *sukkāh* thicket, hut]

succour /'sʌkə(r)/ *n. & v.* (*US* **succor**) —*n.* **1** aid; assistance, esp. in time of need. **2** (in *pl.*) *archaic* reinforcements of troops. —*v.tr.* assist or aid (esp. a person in danger or distress). □□**succourless** *adj.* [ME f. OF *socours* f. med.L *succursus* f. L *succurrere* (as SUB-, *currere curs-* run)]

succubus /'sʌkjʊbəs/ *n.* (*pl.* **succubi** /-ˌbaɪ/) a female demon believed to have sexual intercourse with sleeping men. [LL *succuba* prostitute, med.L *succubus* f. *succubare* (as SUB-, *cubare* lie)]

succulent /'sʌkjʊlənt/ *adj.* & *n.* —*adj.* **1** juicy; palatable. **2** *colloq.* desirable. **3** *Bot.* (of a plant, its leaves, or stems) thick and fleshy. —*n.* *Bot.* a succulent plant, esp. a cactus. □□**succulence** *n.* **succulently** *adv.* [L *succulentus* f. *succus* juice]

succumb /sə'kʌm/ *v.intr.* (usu. foll. by *to*) **1** be forced to give way; be overcome (*succumbed to temptation*). **2** be overcome by death (*succumbed to his injuries*). [ME f. OF *succomber* or L *succumbere* (as SUB-, *cumbere* lie)]

succursal /sə'kɜːs(ə)l/ *adj.* *Eccl.* (of a chapel etc.) subsidiary. [F *succursale* f. med.L *succursus* (as SUCCOUR)]

such /sʌtʃ/ *adj.* & *pron.* —*adj.* **1** (often foll. by *as*) of the kind or degree in question or under consideration (*such a person*; *such people*; *people such as these*). **2** (usu. foll. by *as to* + infin. or *that* + clause) so great; in such high degree (*not such a fool as to believe them*; *had such a fright that he fainted*). **3** of a more than normal kind or degree (*we had such an enjoyable evening*; *such horrid language*). **4** of the kind or degree already indicated, or implied by the context (*there are no such things*; *such is life*). **5** *Law* or *formal* the aforesaid; of the aforesaid kind. —*pron.* **1** the thing or action in question or referred to (*such were his words*; *such was not my intention*). **2** a *Commerce* or *colloq.* the aforesaid thing or things; it, they, or them (*those without tickets should purchase such*). **b** similar things; suchlike (*brought sandwiches and such*). □**as such** as being what has been indicated or named (*a stranger is welcomed as such*; *there is no theatre as such*). **such-and-such** —*adj.* of a particular kind but not needing to be specified. —*n.* a person or thing of this kind. **such-and-such a person** someone; so-and-so. **such as 1** of a kind that; like (*a person such as we all admire*). **2** for example (*insects, such as moths and bees*). **3** those who (*such as don't need help*). **such as it is** despite its shortcomings (*you are welcome to it, such as it is*). **such a one** (usu. foll. by *as*) such a person or such a thing. **2** *archaic* some person or thing unspecified. [OE *swilc, swylc* f. Gmc: cf. LIKE¹]

suchlike /'sʌtʃlaɪk/ *adj.* & *n.* *colloq.* —*adj.* of such a kind. —*n.* things, people, etc. of such a kind.

suck /sʌk/ *v.* & *n.* —*v.* **1** *tr.* draw (a fluid) into the mouth by making a partial vacuum. **2** *tr.* (also *absol.*) **a** draw milk or other fluid from or through (the breast etc. or a container). **b** extract juice from (a fruit) by sucking. **3** *tr.* **a** draw sustenance, knowledge, or advantage from (a book etc.). **b** imbibe or gain (knowledge, advantage, etc.) as if by sucking. **4** *tr.* roll the tongue round (a sweet, teeth, one's thumb, etc.). **5** *intr.* make a sucking action or sound (*sucking at his pipe*). **6** *intr.* (of a pump etc.) make a gurgling or drawing sound. **7** *tr.* (usu. foll. by *down, in*) engulf, smother, or drown in a sucking movement. —*n.* **1** the act or an instance of sucking, esp. the breast. **2** the drawing action or sound of a whirlpool etc. **3** (often foll. by *of*) a small draught of liquor. **4** (in *pl.*; esp. as *int.*) *colloq.* **a** an expression of disappointment. **b** an expression of derision or amusement at another's discomfiture. □**give suck** *archaic* (of a mother, dam, etc.) suckle. **suck dry 1** exhaust the contents of (a bottle, the breast, etc.) by sucking. **2** exhaust (a person's sympathy, resources, etc.) as if by sucking. **suck in 1** absorb. **2** = sense 7 of *v.* **3** involve (a person) in an activity etc. esp. against his or her will. **suck up 1** (often foll. by *to*) *colloq.* behave obsequiously esp. for one's own advantage. **2** absorb. [OE *sūcan, =* L *sugere*]

sucker /'sʌkə(r)/ *n.* & *v.* —*n.* **1 a** a person or thing that sucks. **b** a sucking-pig, newborn whale, etc. **2** *sl.* **a** a gullible or easily deceived person. **b** (foll. by *for*) a person especially susceptible to. **3 a** a rubber cup etc. that adheres to a surface by suction. **b** an organ enabling an organism to cling to a surface by suction. **4** *Bot.* a shoot springing from the rooted part of a stem, from the root at a distance from the main stem, from an axil, or occasionally from a branch. **5** any of various fish that has a mouth capable of or seeming to be capable of adhering by suction. **6 a** the piston of a suction-pump. **b** a pipe through which liquid is drawn by suction. **7** *US colloq.* a lollipop. —*v.* *Bot.* **1** *tr.* remove suckers from. **2** *intr.* produce suckers.

sucking /'sʌkɪŋ/ *adj.* **1** (of a child, animal, etc.) not yet weaned. **2** *Zool.* unfledged (*sucking dove*). □**sucking-disc** an organ used for adhering to a surface. **sucking-fish** = REMORA.

suckle /'sʌk(ə)l/ *v.* **1** *tr.* **a** feed (young) from the breast or udder. **b** nourish (*suckled his talent*). **2** *intr.* feed by sucking the breast etc. □□**suckler** *n.* [ME, prob. back-form. f. SUCKLING]

suckling /'sʌklɪŋ/ *n.* an unweaned child or animal.

sucrose /'suːkrəʊz, 'sjuː-/ *n.* *Chem.* sugar, a disaccharide obtained from sugar cane, sugar beet, etc. [F *sucre* SUGAR]

suction /'sʌkʃ(ə)n/ *n.* **1** the act or an instance of sucking. **2 a** the production of a partial vacuum by the removal of air etc. in order to force in liquid etc. or procure adhesion. **b** the force produced by this process (*suction keeps the lid on*). □**suction-pump** a pump for drawing liquid through a pipe into a chamber emptied by a piston. [LL *suctio* f. L *sugere suct-* SUCK]

suctorial /sʌk'tɔːrɪəl/ *adj.* *Zool.* **1** adapted for or capable of sucking. **2** having a sucker for feeding or adhering. □□**suctorian** *n.* [mod.L *suctorius* (as SUCTION)]

Sudanese /ˌsuːdə'niːz/ *adj.* & *n.* —*adj.* of or relating to Sudan, a republic in NE Africa, or the Sudan region south of the Sahara. —*n.* (*pl.* same) **1** a native, national, or inhabitant of Sudan. **2** a person of Sudanese descent.

sudarium /sjuː'deərɪəm, suː-/ *n.* (*pl.* **sudaria** /-rɪə/) **1** a cloth for wiping the face. **2** *RC Ch.* = VERONICA 2. [L, = napkin f. *sudor* sweat]

sudatorium /ˌsjuːdə'tɔːrɪəm, ˌsuː-/ *n.* (*pl.* **sudatoria** /-rɪə/) esp. *Rom. Antiq.* **1** a hot-air or steam bath. **2** a room where such a bath is taken. [L, neut. of *sudatorius*: see SUDATORY]

sudatory /'sjuːdətərɪ, 'suː-/ *adj.* & *n.* —*adj.* promoting perspiration. —*n.* (*pl.* **-ies**) **1** a sudatory drug. **2** = SUDATORIUM. [L *sudatorius* f. *sudare* sweat]

sudd /sʌd/ *n.* floating vegetation impeding the navigation of the White Nile. [Arab., = obstruction]

sudden /'sʌd(ə)n/ *adj.* & *n.* —*adj.* occurring or done unexpectedly or without warning; abrupt, hurried, hasty (*a sudden storm*; *a sudden departure*). —*n.* *archaic* a hasty or abrupt occurrence. □**all of a sudden** unexpectedly; hurriedly; suddenly. **on a sudden** *archaic* suddenly. **sudden death** *colloq.* a decision in a tied game etc. dependent on one move, card, toss of a coin, etc. **sudden infant death syndrome** *Med.* = *cot-death* (see COT¹). □□**suddenly** *adv.* **suddenness** /-dənnɪs/ *n.* [ME f. AF *sodein, sudein*, OF *soudain* f. LL *subitanus* f. L *subitaneus* f. *subitus* sudden]

sudoriferous /ˌsjuːdə'rɪfərəs, ˌsuː-/ *adj.* (of a gland etc.) secreting sweat. [LL *sudorifer* f. L *sudor* sweat]

sudorific /ˌsjuːdə'rɪfɪk/ *adj.* & *n.* —*adj.* (of a drug) causing sweating. —*n.* a sudorific drug. [mod.L *sudorificus* f. L *sudor* sweat]

Sudra /'suːdrə/ *n.* a member of the lowest of the four great Hindu castes. [Skr. *śūdra*]

suds /sʌdz/ *n.* & *v.* —*n.pl.* **1** froth of soap and water. **2** *US colloq.* beer. —*v.* **1** *intr.* form suds. **2** *tr.* lather, cover, or wash in soapy water. □□**sudsy** *adj.* [orig.

æ *cat* ɑː *arm* e *bed* ɜː *her* ɪ *sit* iː *see* ɒ *hot* ɔː *saw* ʌ *run* ʊ *put* uː *too* ə *ago* aɪ *my*

= fen waters etc., of uncert. orig.: cf. MDu., MLG *sudde*, MDu. *sudse* marsh, bog, prob. rel. to SEETHE]

sue /su:, sju:/ *v.* (**sues**, **sued**, **suing**) **1** *tr.* (also *absol.*) *Law* institute legal proceedings against (a person). **2** *tr.* (also *absol.*) entreat (a person). **3** *intr.* (often foll. by *to*, *for*) *Law* make application to a lawcourt for redress. **4** *intr.* (often foll. by *to*, *for*) make entreaty to a person for a favour. **5** *tr.* (often foll. by *out*) make a petition in a lawcourt for and obtain (a writ, pardon, etc.). □□ **suer** *n.* [ME f. AF *suer*, *siwer*, etc. f. OF *siu-* etc. stem of *sivre* f. L *sequi* follow]

suede /sweɪd/ *n.* (often *attrib.*) **1** leather, esp. kidskin, with the flesh side rubbed to make a velvety nap. **2** (also **suede-cloth**) a woven fabric resembling suede. [F (*gants de*) *Suède* (gloves of) Sweden]

suet /'su:ɪt, 'sju:ɪt/ *n.* the hard white fat on the kidneys or loins of oxen, sheep, etc., used to make dough etc. □ **suet pudding** a pudding of suet etc., usu. boiled or steamed. □□ **suety** *adj.* [ME f. AF f. OF *seu* f. L *sebum* tallow]

suf- /sʌf, səf/ *prefix* assim. form of SUB- before *f*.

suffer /'sʌfə(r)/ *v.* **1** *intr.* undergo pain, grief, damage, etc. (*suffers acutely*; *your reputation will suffer*; *suffers from neglect*). **2** *tr.* undergo, experience, or be subjected to (pain, loss, grief, defeat, change, etc.) (*suffered banishment*). **3** *tr.* put up with; tolerate (*does not suffer fools gladly*). **4** *intr.* undergo martyrdom. **5** *intr.* (usu. foll. by *to* + infin.) *archaic* allow. □□ **sufferable** *adj.* **sufferer** *n.* **suffering** *n.* [ME f. AF *suffrir*, *soeffrir*, OF *sof(f)rir* f. L *sufferre* (as SUB-, *ferre* bear)]

sufferance /'sʌfərəns/ *n.* **1** tacit consent, abstinence from objection. **2** *archaic* submissiveness. □ **on sufferance** with toleration implied by lack of consent or objection. [ME f. AF, OF *suffraunce* f. LL *sufferentia* (as SUFFER)]

suffice /sə'faɪs/ *v.* **1** *intr.* (often foll. by *for*, or *to* + infin.) be enough or adequate (*that will suffice for our purpose*; *suffices to prove it*). **2** *tr.* meet the needs of; satisfy (*six sufficed him*). □ **suffice it to say** I shall content myself with saying. [ME f. OF *suffire* (*suffis-*) f. L *sufficere* (as SUB-, *facere* make)]

sufficiency /sə'fɪʃənsɪ/ *n.* (*pl.* **-ies**) **1** (often foll. by *of*) an adequate amount or adequate resources. **2** *archaic* being sufficient; ability; efficiency. [LL *sufficientia* (as SUFFICIENT)]

sufficient /sə'fɪʃ(ə)nt/ *adj.* **1** sufficing, adequate, enough (*is sufficient for a family*; *didn't have sufficient funds*). **2** = SELF-SUFFICIENT. **3** *archaic* competent; of adequate ability, resources, etc. □□ **sufficiently** *adv.* [ME f. OF *sufficient* or L *sufficiens* (as SUFFICE)]

suffix /'sʌfɪks/ *n.* & *v.* —*n.* **1** a verbal element added at the end of a word to form a derivative (e.g. *-ation*, *-fy*, *-ing*, *-itis*). **2** *Math.* = SUBSCRIPT. —*v.tr.* /also sə'fɪks/ append, esp. as a suffix. □□ **suffixation** /-'seɪʃ(ə)n/ *n.* [*suffixum*, *suffixus* past part. of L *suffigere* (as SUB-, *figere fix-* fasten)]

suffocate /'sʌfə,keɪt/ *v.* **1** *tr.* choke or kill by stopping breathing, esp. by pressure, fumes, etc. **2** *tr.* (often foll. by *by*, *with*) produce a choking or breathless sensation in, esp. by excitement, terror, etc. **3** *intr.* be or feel suffocated or breathless. □□ **suffocating** *adj.* **suffocatingly** *adv.* **suffocation** /-'keɪʃ(ə)n/ *n.* [L *suffocare* (as SUB-, *fauces* throat)]

Suffolk /'sʌfək/ *n.* **1** a sheep of a black-faced breed. **2** this breed. [*Suffolk* in S. England]

Suffolk punch see PUNCH⁴ 2.

suffragan /'sʌfrəgən/ *n.* (in full **suffragan bishop** or **bishop suffragan**) **1** a bishop appointed to help a diocesan bishop in the administration of a diocese. **2** a bishop in relation to his archbishop or metropolitan. □ **suffragan see** the see of a suffragan bishop. □□ **suffraganship** *n.* [ME f. AF & OF, repr. med.L *suffraganeus* assistant (bishop) f. L *suffragium* (see SUFFRAGE): orig. of a bishop summoned to vote in synod]

suffrage /'sʌfrɪdʒ/ *n.* **1 a** the right of voting in political elections (*full adult suffrage*). **b** a view

expressed by voting; a vote (*gave their suffrages for and against*). **c** opinion in support of a proposal etc. **2** (esp. in *pl.*) *Eccl.* **a** a prayer made by a priest in the liturgy. **b** a short prayer made by a congregation esp. in response to a priest. **c** *archaic* an intercessory prayer. [ME f. L *suffragium*, partly through F *suffrage*]

suffragette /,sʌfrə'dʒet/ *n. hist.* a woman seeking the right to vote through organized protest. [SUFFRAGE + -ETTE]

suffragist /'sʌfrədʒɪst/ *n.* esp. *hist.* a person who advocates the extension of the suffrage, esp. to women. □□ **suffragism** *n.*

suffuse /sə'fju:z/ *v.tr.* **1** (of colour, moisture, etc.) spread from within to colour or moisten (*a blush suffused her cheeks*). **2** cover with colour etc. □□ **suffusion** /-'fju:ʒ(ə)n/ *n.* [L *suffundere suffus-* (as SUB-, *fundere* pour)]

Sufi /'su:fɪ/ *n.* (*pl.* **Sufis**) a Muslim ascetic and mystic. □□ **Sufic** *adj.* **Sufism** *n.* [Arab. *ṣūfī*, perh. f. *ṣūf* wool (from the woollen garment worn)]

sug- /sʌg, səg/ *prefix* assim. form of SUB- before *g*.

sugar /'ʃʊgə(r)/ *n.* & *v.* —*n.* **1** a sweet crystalline substance obtained from various plants, esp. the sugar cane and sugar beet, used in cookery, confectionery, brewing, etc.; sucrose. **2** *Chem.* any of a group of soluble usu. sweet-tasting crystalline carbohydrates found esp. in plants, e.g. glucose. **3** esp. *US colloq.* darling, dear (used as a term of address). **4** sweet words; flattery. **5** anything comparable to sugar encasing a pill in reconciling a person to what is unpalatable. **6** *sl.* a narcotic drug, esp. heroin or LSD (taken on a lump of sugar). —*v.tr.* **1** sweeten with sugar. **2** make (one's words, meaning, etc.) more pleasant or welcome. **3** coat with sugar (*sugared almond*). **4** spread a sugar mixture on (a tree) to catch moths. □ **sugar beet** a beet, *Beta vulgaris*, from which sugar is extracted. **sugar-candy** see CANDY 1. **sugar cane** *Bot.* any perennial tropical grass of the genus *Saccharum*, esp. *S. officinarum*, with tall stout jointed stems from which sugar is made. **sugar-coated 1** (of food) enclosed in sugar. **2** made superficially attractive. **sugar-daddy** (*pl.* **-ies**) *sl.* an elderly man who lavishes gifts on a young woman. **sugar-gum** *Bot.* an Australian eucalyptus, *Eucalyptus cladocalyx*, with sweet foliage eaten by cattle. **sugar loaf** a conical moulded mass of sugar. **sugar-maple** any of various trees, esp. *Acer saccharum*, from the sap of which sugar is made. **sugar of lead** *Chem.* = lead acetate (see LEAD²). **sugar-pea** a variety of pea eaten whole including the pod. **sugar the pill** see PILL. **sugar soap** an alkaline compound for cleaning or removing paint. □□ **sugarless** *adj.* [ME f. OF *çukre*, *sukere* f. It. *zucchero* prob. f. med.L *saccarum* f. Arab. *sukkar*]

sugarplum /'ʃʊgə,plʌm/ *n. archaic* a small round sweet of flavoured boiled sugar.

sugary /'ʃʊgərɪ/ *adj.* **1** containing or resembling sugar. **2** excessively sweet or esp. sentimental. **3** falsely sweet or pleasant (*sugary compliments*). □□ **sugariness** *n.*

suggest /sə'dʒest/ *v.tr.* **1** (often foll. by *that* + clause) propose (a theory, plan, or hypothesis) (*suggested to them that they should wait*; *suggested a different plan*). **2 a** cause (an idea, memory, association, etc.) to present itself; evoke (*poem suggests peace*). **b** hint at (*his behaviour suggests guilt*). □ **suggest itself** (of an idea etc.) come into the mind. □□ **suggester** *n.* [L *suggerere suggest-* (as SUB-, *gerere* bring)]

suggestible /sə'dʒestɪb(ə)l/ *adj.* **1** capable of being suggested. **2** open to suggestion; easily swayed. □□ **suggestibility** /-'bɪlɪtɪ/ *n.*

suggestion /sə'dʒestʃ(ə)n/ *n.* **1** the act or an instance of suggesting; the state of being suggested. **2** a theory, plan, etc., suggested (*made a helpful suggestion*). **3** a slight trace; a hint (*a suggestion of garlic*). **4** *Psychol.* **a** the insinuation of a belief etc. into the mind. **b**

such a belief etc. [ME f. OF f. L *suggestio -onis* (as SUGGEST)]

suggestive /sə'dʒestɪv/ *adj.* **1** (usu. foll. by *of*) conveying a suggestion; evocative. **2** (esp. of a remark, joke, etc.) indecent; improper. □□ **suggestively** *adv.* **suggestiveness** *n.*

suicidal /ˌsuːɪ'saɪd(ə)l, ˌsjuː-/ *adj.* **1** inclined to commit suicide. **2** of or concerning suicide. **3** self-destructive; fatally or disastrously rash. □□ **suicidally** *adv.*

suicide /'suːɪsaɪd, 'sjuː-/ *n. & v.* —*n.* **1 a** the intentional killing of oneself. **b** a person who commits suicide. **2** a self-destructive action or course (*political suicide*). **3** (*attrib.*) *Mil.* designating a highly dangerous or deliberately suicidal operation etc. (*a suicide mission*). —*v.intr.* commit suicide. □ **suicide pact** an agreement between two or more people to commit suicide together. [mod.L *suicida, suicidium* f. L *sui* of oneself]

sui generis /ˌsjuː'aɪ 'dʒenərɪs, ˌsuːɪ 'gen-/ *adj.* of its own kind; unique. [L]

sui juris /ˌsjuː'aɪ 'dʒʊərɪs, ˌsuːɪ 'jʊə-/ *adj. Law* of age; independent. [L]

suilline /'suːɪˌlaɪn/ *adj.* of the pig family Suidae. [L *suillus* f. *sus* pig]

suint /swɪnt/ *n.* the natural grease in sheep's wool. [F f. *suer* sweat]

suit /suːt, sjuːt/ *n. & v.* —*n.* **1 a** a set of outer clothes of matching material for men, consisting usu. of a jacket, trousers, and sometimes a waistcoat. **b** a similar set of clothes for women usu. having a skirt instead of trousers. **c** (esp. in *comb.*) a set of clothes for a special occasion, occupation, etc. (*play-suit; swimsuit*). **2 a** any of the four sets (spades, hearts, diamonds, clubs) into which a pack of cards is divided. **b** a player's holding in a suit (*his strong suit was clubs*). **c** *Bridge* one of the suits as proposed trumps in bidding, frequently as opposed to no trumps. **3** (in full **suit at law**) a lawsuit (*criminal suit*). **4 a** a petition esp. to a person in authority. **b** the process of courting a woman (*paid suit to her*). **5** (usu. foll. by *of*) a set of sails, armour, etc. —*v.* **1** *tr.* go well with (a person's figure, features, character, etc.); become. **2** *tr.* (also *absol.*) meet the demands or requirements of; satisfy; agree with (*does not suit all tastes; that date will suit*). **3** *tr.* make fitting or appropriate; accommodate; adapt (*suited his style to his audience*). **4** *tr.* (as **suited** *adj.*) appropriate; well-fitted (*not suited to be an engineer*). **5** *intr.* (usu. foll. by *with*) go well with the appearance etc. of a person (*red hair suits with her complexion*). □ **suit the action to the word** carry out a promise or threat at once. **suit oneself 1** do as one chooses. **2** find something that satisfies one. [ME f. AF *siute*, OF *si(e)ute* f. fem. past part. of Rmc *sequere* (unrecorded) follow: see SUE]

suitable /'suːtəb(ə)l, 'sjuː-/ *adj.* (usu. foll. by *to, for*) well fitted for the purpose; appropriate. □□ **suitability** /-'bɪlɪtɪ/ *n.* **suitableness** *n.* **suitably** *adv.* [SUIT + -ABLE, after *agreeable*]

suitcase /'suːtkeɪs, 'sjuː-/ *n.* a usu. oblong case for carrying clothes etc., having a handle and a flat hinged lid. □□ **suitcaseful** *n.* (*pl.* -**fuls**)

suite /swiːt/ *n.* **1** a set of things belonging together, esp.: **a** a set of rooms in a hotel etc. **b** a sofa, armchairs, etc., of the same design. **2** *Mus.* **a** a set of instrumental compositions, orig. in dance style, to be played in succession. **b** a set of selected pieces from an opera, musical, etc., arranged to be played as one instrumental work. **3** a set of people in attendance; a retinue. [F (as SUIT)]

suiting /'suːtɪŋ, 'sjuː-/ *n.* cloth used for making suits.

suitor /'suːtə(r), 'sjuː-/ *n.* **1** a man seeking to marry a specified woman; a wooer. **2** a plaintiff or petitioner in a lawsuit. [ME f. AF *seutor, suitour*, etc., f. L *secutor -oris* f. *sequi secut-* follow]

suk (also **sukh**) var. of SOUK.

sukiyaki /ˌsʊkɪ'jɑːkɪ/ *n.* a Japanese dish of sliced meat simmered with vegetables and sauce. [Jap.]

sulcate /'sʌlkeɪt/ *adj.* grooved, fluted, channelled. [L *sulcatus,* past part. of *sulcare* furrow (as SULCUS)]

sulcus /'sʌlkəs/ *n.* (*pl.* **sulci** /-saɪ/) *Anat.* a groove or furrow, esp. on the surface of the brain. [L]

sulfa *US* var. of SULPHA.

sulfanilamide *US* var. of SULPHANILAMIDE.

sulfate etc. *US* var. of SULPHATE etc.

sulfur etc. *US* var. of SULPHUR etc.

sulk /sʌlk/ *v. & n.* —*v.intr.* indulge in a sulk, be sulky. —*n.* (also in *pl.*, prec. by *the*) a period of sullen esp. resentful silence (*having a sulk; got the sulks*). □□ **sulker** *n.* [perh. back-form. f. SULKY]

sulky /'sʌlkɪ/ *adj. & n.* —*adj.* (**sulkier, sulkiest**) **1** sullen, morose, or silent, esp. from resentment or ill temper. **2** sluggish. —*n.* (*pl.* -**ies**) a light two-wheeled horse-drawn vehicle for one, esp. used in trotting-races. □□ **sulkily** *adv.* **sulkiness** *n.* [perh. f. obs. *sulke* hard to dispose of]

sullage /'sʌlɪdʒ/ *n.* filth, refuse, sewage. [perh. f. AF *suillage* f. *souiller* SOIL[2]]

sullen /'sʌlən/ *adj. & n.* —*adj.* **1** morose, resentful, sulky, unforgiving, unsociable. **2 a** (of a thing) slow-moving. **b** dismal, melancholy (*a sullen sky*). —*n.* (in *pl.*, usu. prec. by *the*) *archaic* a sullen frame of mind; depression. □□ **sullenly** *adv.* **sullenness** /-ənnɪs/ *n.* [16th-c. alt. of ME *solein* f. AF f. *sol* SOLE[3]]

sully /'sʌlɪ/ *v.tr.* (-**ies, -ied**) **1** disgrace or tarnish (a person's reputation or character, a victory, etc.). **2** *poet.* dirty; soil. [perh. f. F *souiller* (as SOIL[2])]

sulpha /'sʌlfə/ *n.* (*US* **sulfa**) any drug derived from sulphanilamide (often *attrib.: sulpha drug*). [abbr.]

sulphamic acid /sʌl'fæmɪk/ *n.* (*US* **sulfamic**) a strong acid used in weed-killer, an amide of sulphuric acid. □□ **sulphamate** /'sʌlfəˌmeɪt/ *n.* [SULPHUR + AMIDE]

sulphanilamide /ˌsʌlfə'nɪləˌmaɪd/ *n.* (*US* **sulfanilamide**) a colourless sulphonamide drug with anti-bacterial properties. [*sulphanilic* (SULPHUR, ANILINE) + AMIDE]

sulphate /'sʌlfeɪt/ *n.* (*US* **sulfate**) a salt or ester of sulphuric acid. [F *sulfate* f. L *sulphur*]

sulphide /'sʌlfaɪd/ *n.* (*US* **sulfide**) *Chem.* a binary compound of sulphur.

sulphite /'sʌlfaɪt/ *n.* (*US* **sulfite**) *Chem.* a salt or ester of sulphurous acid. [F *sulfite* alt. of *sulfate* SULPHATE]

sulphonamide /sʌl'fɒnəˌmaɪd/ *n.* (*US* **sulfonamide**) a substance derived from an amide of a sulphonic acid, able to prevent the multiplication of some pathogenic bacteria. [SULPHONE + AMIDE]

sulphonate /'sʌlfəˌneɪt/ *n. & v. Chem.* —*n.* a salt or ester of sulphonic acid. —*v.tr.* convert into a sulphonate by reaction with sulphuric acid.

sulphone /'sʌlfəʊn/ *n.* (*US* **sulfone**) an organic compound containing the SO_2 group united directly to two carbon atoms. □□ **sulphonic** /-'fɒnɪk/ *adj.* [G *Sulfon* (as SULPHUR)]

sulphur /'sʌlfə(r)/ *n. & v.* (*US* **sulfur**) —*n.* **1 a** a pale-yellow non-metallic element having crystalline and amorphous forms, burning with a blue flame and a suffocating smell, and used in making gunpowder, matches, and sulphuric acid, in the vulcanizing of rubber, and in the treatment of skin diseases. ¶ Symb.: **S. b** (*attrib.*) like or containing sulphur. **2** the material of which hell-fire and lightning were believed to consist. **3** any yellow butterfly of the family Pieridae. **4** a pale greenish yellow colour. —*v.tr.* **1** treat with sulphur. **2** fumigate with sulphur. □ **sulphur candle** a candle burnt to produce sulphur dioxide for fumigating. **sulphur dioxide** a colourless pungent gas formed by burning sulphur in air and used as a food preservative. **sulphur spring** a spring impregnated with sulphur or its compounds. □□ **sulphury** *adj.* [ME f. AF *sulf(e)re,* OF *soufre* f. L *sulfur, sulp(h)ur*]

sulphurate /'sʌlfjʊˌreɪt/ *v.tr.* (*US* **sulfurate**) impregnate, fumigate, or treat with sulphur, esp.

in bleaching. □□ **sulphuration** /-'reɪʃ(ə)n/ *n.* **sulphurator** *n.*

sulphureous /sʌl'fjʊərɪəs/ *adj.* (*US* **sulfureous**) **1** of, like, or suggesting sulphur. **2** sulphur-coloured; yellow. [L *sulphureus* f. SULPHUR]

sulphuretted /ˌsʌlfjʊ'retɪd/ *adj.* (*US* **sulfureted**) *archaic* containing sulphur in combination. □ **sulphuretted hydrogen** hydrogen sulphide. [*sulphuret* sulphide f. mod.L *sulphuretum*]

sulphuric /sʌl'fjʊərɪk/ *adj.* (*US* **sulfuric**) *Chem.* containing sexivalent sulphur. □ **sulphuric acid** a dense oily colourless highly acid and corrosive fluid much used in the chemical industry. ¶ Chem. formula: H₂SO₄. [F *sulfurique* (as SULPHUR)]

sulphurize /'sʌlfjʊəˌraɪz/ *v.tr.* (also **-ise**, *US* **sulfurize**) = SULPHURATE. □□ **sulphurization** /-'zeɪʃ(ə)n/ *n.* [F *sulfuriser* (as SULPHUR)]

sulphurous /'sʌlfərəs/ *adj.* (*US* **sulfurous**) **1** relating to or suggestive of sulphur, esp. in colour. **2** *Chem.* containing quadrivalent sulphur. □ **sulphurous acid** an unstable weak acid used as a reducing and bleaching acid. [L *sulphurosus* f. SULPHUR]

sultan /'sʌlt(ə)n/ *n.* **1 a** a Muslim sovereign. **b** (**the Sultan**) *hist.* the sultan of Turkey. **2** a variety of white domestic fowl from Turkey. □□ **sultanate** /-ˌneɪt/ *n.* [F *sultan* or med.L *sultanus* f. Arab. *sulṭān* power, ruler f. *saluṭa* rule]

sultana /sʌl'tɑːnə/ *n.* **1 a** a seedless raisin used in puddings, cakes, etc. **b** the small pale yellow grape producing this. **2** the mother, wife, concubine, or daughter of a sultan. [It., fem. of *sultano* = SULTAN]

sultry /'sʌltrɪ/ *adj.* (**sultrier**, **sultriest**) **1** (of the atmosphere or the weather) hot or oppressive; close. **2** (of a person, character, etc.) passionate; sensual. □□ **sultrily** *adv.* **sultriness** *n.* [obs. *sulter* SWELTER]

sum /sʌm/ *n. & v.* —*n.* **1** the total amount resulting from the addition of two or more items, facts, ideas, feelings, etc. (*the sum of two and three is five*; *the sum of their objections is this*). **2** a particular amount of money (*paid a large sum for it*). **3 a** an arithmetical problem (*could not work out the sum*). **b** (esp. *pl.*) *colloq.* arithmetic work, esp. at an elementary level (*was good at sums*). —*v.tr.* (**summed**, **summing**) find the sum of. □ **in sum** in brief. **summing-up 1** a review of evidence and a direction given by a judge to a jury. **2** a recapitulation of the main points of an argument, case, etc. **sum total** = sense 1 of *n.* **sum up 1** (esp. of a judge) recapitulate or review the evidence in a case etc. **2** form or express an idea of the character of (a person, situation, etc.). **3** collect into or express as a total or whole. [ME f. OF *summe*, *somme* f. L *summa* main part, fem. of *summus* highest]

sumac /'suːmæk, 'ʃuː-, 'sjuː-/ *n.* (also **sumach**) **1** any shrub or tree of the genus *Rhus*, having reddish cone-shaped fruits used as a spice in cooking. **2** the dried and ground leaves of this used in tanning and dyeing. [ME f. OF *sumac* or med.L *sumac(h)* f. Arab. *summāḳ*]

Sumerian /suː'mɪərɪən, sjuː-/ *adj. & n.* —*adj.* of or relating to the early and non-Semitic element in the civilization of ancient Babylonia. —*n.* **1** a member of the early non-Semitic people of ancient Babylonia. **2** the Sumerian language. [F *sumérien* f. *Sumer* in Babylonia]

summa /'sʌmə/ *n.* (*pl.* **summae** /-miː/) a summary of what is known of a subject. [ME f. L: see SUM]

summa cum laude /ˌsʊmə kʊm 'laʊdeɪ/ *adv. & adj.* esp. *US* (of a degree, diploma, etc.) of the highest standard; with the highest distinction. [L, = with highest praise]

summarize /'sʌməˌraɪz/ *v.tr.* (also **-ise**) make or be a summary of; sum up. □□ **summarist** *n.* **summarizable** *adj.* **summarization** /-'zeɪʃ(ə)n/ *n.* **summarizer** *n.*

summary /'sʌmərɪ/ *n. & adj.* —*n.* (*pl.* **-ies**) a brief account; an abridgement. —*adj.* **1** dispensing with

needless details or formalities; brief (*a summary account*). **2** *Law* (of a trial etc.) without the customary legal formalities (*summary justice*). □ **summary conviction** a conviction made by a judge or magistrates without a jury. **summary jurisdiction** the authority of a court to use summary proceedings and arrive at a judgement. **summary offence** an offence within the scope of a summary court. □□ **summarily** *adv.* **summariness** *n.* [ME f. L *summarium* f. L *summa* SUM]

summation /sə'meɪʃ(ə)n/ *n.* **1** the finding of a total or sum; an addition. **2** a summing-up. □□ **summational** *adj.*

summer¹ /'sʌmə(r)/ *n. & v.* —*n.* **1** the warmest season of the year, in the N. hemisphere from June to August and in the S. hemisphere from December to February. **2** *Astron.* the period from the summer solstice to the autumnal equinox. **3** the hot weather typical of summer. **4** (often foll. by *of*) the mature stage of life; the height of achievement, powers, etc. **5** (esp. in *pl.*) *poet.* a year (esp. of a person's age) (*a child of ten summers*). **6** (*attrib.*) characteristic of or suitable for summer (*summer clothes*). —*v.* **1** *intr.* (usu. foll. by *at*, *in*) pass the summer. **2** *tr.* (often foll. by *at*, *in*) pasture (cattle). □ **summer-house** a light building in a garden etc. used for sitting in in fine weather. **summer lightning** sheet lightning without thunder, resulting from a distant storm. **summer pudding** *Brit.* a pudding of soft summer fruit encased in bread or sponge. **summer school** a course of lectures etc. held during the summer vacation, esp. at a university. **summer solstice** see SOLSTICE. **summer time** *Brit.* the period between March and October during which the clocks are advanced an hour (cf. SUMMERTIME). **summer-weight** (of clothes) suitable for use in summer, esp. because of their light weight. □□ **summerless** *adj.* **summerly** *adv.* **summery** *adj.* [OE *sumor*]

summer² /'sʌmə(r)/ *n.* (in full **summer-tree**) a horizontal bearing beam, esp. one supporting joists or rafters. [ME f. AF *sumer*, *somer* packhorse, beam, OF *somier* f. LL *sagmarius* f. *sagma* f. Gk *sagma* pack-saddle]

summersault var. of SOMERSAULT.

summertime /'sʌməˌtaɪm/ *n.* the season or period of summer (cf. *summer time*).

summit /'sʌmɪt/ *n.* **1** the highest point, esp. of a mountain; the apex. **2** the highest degree of power, ambition, etc. **3** (in full **summit meeting**, **talks**, etc.) a discussion, esp. on disarmament etc., between heads of government. □□ **summitless** *adj.* [ME f. OF *somet*, *som(m)ete* f. *som* top f. L *summum* neut. of *summus*]

summon /'sʌmən/ *v.tr.* **1** call upon to appear, esp. as a defendant or witness in a lawcourt. **2** (usu. foll. by *to* + infin.) call upon (*summoned her to assist*). **3** call together for a meeting or some other purpose (*summoned the members to attend*). □ **summon up** (often foll. by *to*, *for*) gather (courage, spirits, resources, etc.) (*summoned up her strength for the task*). □□ **summonable** *adj.* **summoner** *n.* [ME f. OF *somondre* f. L *summonēre* (as SUB-, *monēre* warn)]

summons /'sʌmənz/ *n. & v.* —*n.* (*pl.* **summonses**) **1** an authoritative or urgent call to attend on some occasion or do something. **2 a** a call to appear before a judge or magistrate. **b** the writ containing such a summons. —*v.tr.* esp. *Law* serve with a summons. [ME f. OF *somonce*, *sumunse* f. L *summonita* fem. past part. of *summonēre*: see SUMMON]

summum bonum /ˌsʊməm 'bʊnəm, 'bəʊ-/ *n.* the highest good, esp. as the end or determining principle in an ethical system. [L]

sumo /'suːməʊ/ *n.* (*pl.* **-os**) **1** a style of Japanese wrestling, in which a participant is defeated by touching the ground with any part of the body except the soles of the feet or by moving outside the marked area. **2** a sumo wrestler. [Jap.]

sump /sʌmp/ *n.* **1** a pit, well, hole, etc. in which

superfluous liquid collects in mines, machines, etc. **2** a cesspool. [ME, = marsh f. MDu., MLG *sump*, or (mining) G *Sumpf*, rel. to SWAMP]

sumpter /'sʌmptə(r)/ *n. archaic* **1** a packhorse. **2** any pack-animal (*sumpter-mule*). [ME f. OF *som(m)etier* f. LL f. Gk *sagma -atos* pack-saddle: cf. SUMMER²]

sumptuary /'sʌmptjʊərɪ/ *adj.* **1** regulating expenditure. **2** (of a law or edict etc.) limiting private expenditure in the interests of the State. [L *sumptuarius* f. *sumptus* cost f. *sumere sumpt*- take]

sumptuous /'sʌmptjʊəs/ *adj.* rich, lavish, costly (*a sumptuous setting*). □□ **sumptuosity** /-'ɒsɪtɪ/ *n.* **sumptuously** *adv.* **sumptuousness** *n.* [ME f. OF *somptueux* f. L *sumptuosus* (as SUMPTUARY)]

Sun. *abbr.* Sunday.

sun /sʌn/ *n. & v.* —*n.* **1 a** the star round which the earth orbits and from which it receives light and warmth. **b** any similar star in the universe with or without planets. **2** the light or warmth received from the sun (*pull down the blinds and keep out the sun*). **3** *poet.* a day or a year. **4** *poet.* a person or thing regarded as a source of glory, radiance, etc. —*v.* (**sunned, sunning**) **1** *refl.* bask in the sun. **2** *tr.* expose to the sun. **3** *intr.* sun oneself. □ **against the sun** anticlockwise. **beneath (or under) the sun** anywhere in the world. **in the sun** exposed to the sun's rays. **on which the sun never sets** (of an empire etc.) worldwide. **sun and planet** a system of gearing cog wheels. **sun-baked** dried or hardened or baked from the heat of the sun. **sun-bath** a period of exposing the body to the sun. **sun bear** a small black bear, *Helarctos malayanus*, of SE Asia, with a light-coloured mark on its chest. **sun-blind** *Brit.* a window awning. **sun-bonnet** a bonnet of cotton etc. covering the neck and shading the face, esp. for children. **sun-bow** a spectrum of colours like a rainbow produced by the sun shining on spray etc. **sun-dance** a dance of N. American Indians in honour of the sun. **sun-deck** the upper deck of a steamer. **sun-disc** a winged disc, emblematic of the sun-god. **sun-dog** = PARHELION. **sun-dress** a dress without sleeves and with a low neck. **sun-dried** dried by the sun, not by artificial heat. **sun-glasses** glasses tinted to protect the eyes from sunlight or glare. **sun-god** the sun worshipped as a deity. **sun-hat** a hat designed to protect the head from the sun. **sun-helmet** a helmet of cork etc. formerly worn by White people in the tropics. **sun in splendour** *Heraldry* the sun with rays and a human face. **one's sun is set** the time of one's prosperity is over. **sun-kissed** warmed or affected by the sun. **sun-lamp 1** a lamp giving ultraviolet rays for an artificial suntan, therapy, etc. **2** *Cinematog.* a large lamp with a parabolic reflector used in film-making. **sun lounge** a room with large windows, designed to receive sunlight. **sun parlor** *US* = **sun lounge. sun-rays 1** sunbeams. **2** ultraviolet rays used therapeutically. **sun-roof** a sliding roof on a car. **sun-stone** a cat's eye gem, esp. feldspar with embedded flecks of haematite etc. **sun-suit** a play-suit, esp. for children, suitable for sunbathing. **sun-up** esp. *US* sunrise. **sun visor** a fixed or movable shield at the top of a vehicle windscreen to shield the eyes from the sun. **take (or shoot) the sun** *Naut.* ascertain the altitude of the sun with a sextant in order to fix the latitude. **with the sun** clockwise. □□ **sunless** *adj.* **sunlessness** *n.* **sunlike** *adj.* **sunproof** *adj.* **sunward** *adv. & adj.* **sunwards** *adv.* [OE *sunne, sunna*]

sunbathe /'sʌnbeɪð/ *v.intr.* bask in the sun, esp. to tan the body. □□ **sunbather** *n.*

sunbeam /'sʌnbiːm/ *n.* a ray of sunlight.

sunbed /'sʌnbed/ *n.* **1** a lightweight, usu. folding, chair with a seat long enough to support the legs, used for sunbathing. **2** a bed for lying on under a sun-lamp.

sunbelt /'sʌnbelt/ *n.* a strip of territory receiving a high amount of sunshine, esp. the region in the southern US stretching from California to Florida.

sunbird /'sʌnbɜːd/ *n.* any small bright-plumaged Old World bird of the family Nectariniidae, resembling a humming-bird.

sunblock /'sʌnblɒk/ *n.* a cream or lotion for protecting the skin from the sun.

sunburn /'sʌnbɜːn/ *n. & v.* —*n.* tanning and inflammation of the skin caused by over-exposure to the sun. —*v.intr.* **1** suffer from sunburn. **2** (as **sunburnt** or **sunburned** *adj.*) suffering from sunburn; brown or tanned.

sunburst /'sʌnbɜːst/ *n.* **1** something resembling the sun and its rays, esp.: **a** an ornament, brooch, etc. **b** a firework. **2** the sun shining suddenly from behind clouds.

sundae /'sʌndeɪ, -dɪ/ *n.* a dish of ice-cream with fruit, nuts, syrup, etc. [perh. f. SUNDAY]

Sunday /'sʌndeɪ, -dɪ/ *n. & adv.* —*n.* **1** the first day of the week, a Christian holiday and day of worship. **2** a newspaper published on a Sunday. —*adv. colloq.* **1** on Sunday. **2** (**Sundays**) on Sunday; each Sunday. □ **Sunday best** *joc.* a person's best clothes, kept for Sunday use. **Sunday letter** = *dominical letter*. **Sunday painter** an amateur painter, esp. one with little training. **Sunday school** a school for the religious instruction of children on Sundays. [OE *sunnandæg*, transl. of L *dies solis*, Gk *hēmera hēliou* day of the sun]

sunder /'sʌndə(r)/ *v.tr. & intr. archaic* or *literary* □ **in sunder** apart. [OE *sundrian*, f. *āsundrian* etc.: *in sunder* f. ME f. *o(n)sunder* ASUNDER]

sundew /'sʌndjuː/ *n.* any small insect-consuming bog-plant of the family Droseraceae, esp. of the genus *Drosera* with hairs secreting drops of moisture.

sundial /'sʌndaɪəl/ *n.* an instrument showing the time by the shadow of a pointer cast by the sun on to a graduated disc.

sundown /'sʌndaʊn/ *n.* sunset.

sundowner /'sʌnˌdaʊnə(r)/ *n.* **1** *Austral.* a tramp who arrives at a sheep station etc. in the evening for food and shelter. **2** *Brit. colloq.* an alcoholic drink taken at sunset.

sundry /'sʌndrɪ/ *adj. & n.* —*adj.* various; several (*sundry items*). —*n.* (*pl.* **-ies**) **1** (in *pl.*) items or oddments not mentioned individually. **2** *Austral. Cricket* = EXTRA *n.* 5. [OE *syndrig* separate, rel. to SUNDER]

sunfast /'sʌnfɑːst/ *adj. US* (of dye) not subject to fading by sunlight.

sunfish /'sʌnfɪʃ/ *n.* any of various almost spherical fish, esp. a large ocean fish, *Mola mola*.

sunflower /'sʌnˌflaʊə(r)/ *n.* any very tall plant of the genus *Helianthus*, esp. *H. annus* with very large showy golden-rayed flowers, grown also for its seeds which yield an edible oil.

sung *past part.* of SING.

sunk *past* and *past part.* of SINK.

sunken /'sʌŋkən/ *adj.* **1** that has been sunk. **2** beneath the surface; submerged. **3** (of the eyes, cheeks, etc.) hollow, depressed. □ **sunken garden** a garden placed below the general level of its surroundings. [past part. of SINK]

sunlight /'sʌnlaɪt/ *n.* light from the sun.

sunlit /'sʌnlɪt/ *adj.* illuminated by sunlight.

sunn /sʌn/ *n.* (in full **sunn hemp**) an E. Indian hemplike fibre. [Urdu & Hindi *san* f. Skr. *śāṇá* hempen]

Sunna /'sʌnə/ *n.* a traditional portion of Muslim law based on Muhammad's words or acts, accepted as authoritative by many Muslims but rejected by the Shiites. [Arab., = form, way, course, rule]

Sunni /'sʌnɪ/ *n. & adj.* —*n.* (*pl.* same or **Sunnis**) **1** one of the two main branches of Islam, regarding the Sunna as equal in authority to the Koran (cf. SHIAH). **2** an adherent of this branch of Islam. —*adj.* (also **Sunnite**) of or relating to Sunni.

sunny /'sʌnɪ/ *adj.* (**sunnier, sunniest**) **1 a** bright with sunlight. **b** exposed to or warmed by the sun. **2** cheery and bright in temperament. □ **the sunny**

side 1 the side of a house, street, etc. that gets most sun. **2** the more cheerful aspect of circumstances etc. (*always looks on the sunny side*). □□ **sunnily** *adv*. **sunniness** *n*.

sunrise /'sʌnraɪz/ *n*. **1** the sun's rising at dawn. **2** the coloured sky associated with this. **3** the time at which sunrise occurs. □ **sunrise industry** any newly established industry, esp. in electronics and tele-communications, regarded as signalling prosperity.

sunset /'sʌnset/ *n*. **1** the sun's setting in the evening. **2** the coloured sky associated with this. **3** the time at which sunset occurs. **4** the declining period of life.

sunshade /'sʌnʃeɪd/ *n*. **1** a parasol. **2** an awning.

sunshine /'sʌnʃaɪn/ *n*. **1 a** the light of the sun. **b** an area lit by the sun. **2** fine weather. **3** cheerfulness; joy (*brought sunshine into her life*). **4** *Brit. colloq.* a form of address. □**sunshine roof** = *sun-roof*. □□ **sunshiny** *adj*.

sunspot /'sʌnspɒt/ *n*. one of the dark patches, changing in shape and size and lasting for varying periods, observed on the sun's surface.

sunstar /'sʌnstɑː(r)/ *n*. any starfish of the genus *Solaster*, with many rays.

sunstroke /'sʌnstrəʊk/ *n*. acute prostration or collapse from the excessive heat of the sun.

suntan /'sʌntæn/ *n. & v.* —*n*. the brownish colouring of skin caused by exposure to the sun. —*v.intr.* (**-tanned, -tanning**) colour the skin with a suntan.

suntrap /'sʌntræp/ *n*. a place sheltered from the wind and suitable for catching the sunshine.

sup¹ /sʌp/ *v. & n.* —*v.tr.* (**supped, supping**) **1** take (soup, tea, etc.) by sips or spoonfuls. **2** esp. *N.Engl. colloq.* drink (alcohol). —*n*. a sip of liquid. [OE *sūpan*]

sup² /sʌp/ *v.intr.* (usu. foll. by *off, on*) *archaic* take supper. [OF *super, soper*]

sup- /sʌp, səp/ *prefix* assim. form of SUB- before *p*.

super /'suːpə(r), 'sjuː-/ *adj. & n.* —*adj*. **1** (also **super-duper** /-'duːpə(r)/) *colloq*. (also as *int*.) exceptional; splendid. **2** *Commerce* superfine. **3** *Commerce* (of a measure) superficial, in square (not lineal or solid) measure (*120 super ft.; 120 ft. super*). —*n. colloq*. **1** *Theatr*. a supernumerary actor. **2** a superintendent. **3** superphosphate. **4** an extra, unwanted, or unimportant person; a supernumerary. **5** *Commerce* superfine cloth or manufacture. [abbr.]

super- /'suːpə(r), 'sjuː-/ *comb. form* forming nouns, adjectives, and verbs, meaning: **1** above, beyond, or over in place or time or conceptually (*superstructure; supernormal; superimpose*). **2** to a great or extreme degree (*superabundant; superhuman*). **3** extra good or large of its kind (*supertanker*). **4** of a higher kind, esp. in names of classificatory divisions (*superclass*). [from or after L *super-* f. *super* above, beyond]

superable /'suːpərəb(ə)l, 'sjuː-/ *adj*. able to be overcome. [L *superabilis* f. *superare* overcome]

superabound /ˌsuːpərə'baʊnd, ˌsjuː-/ *v.intr.* be very or too abundant. [LL *superabundare* (as SUPER-, ABOUND)]

superabundant /ˌsuːpərə'bʌnd(ə)nt, ˌsjuː-/ *adj*. abounding beyond what is normal or right. □□ **superabundance** *n*. **superabundantly** *adv*. [ME f. LL *superabundare*: see SUPERABOUND]

superadd /ˌsuːpər'æd, ˌsjuː-/ *v.tr.* add over and above. □□ **superaddition** /-ə'dɪʃ(ə)n/ *n*. [ME f. L *superaddere* (as SUPER-, ADD)]

superaltar /'suːpərˌɔːltə(r), 'sjuː-, -ˌɒltə(r)/ *n. Eccl*. a portable slab of stone consecrated for use on an unconsecrated altar etc. [ME f. med.L *superaltare* (as SUPER-, ALTAR)]

superannuate /ˌsuːpər'ænjʊˌeɪt, ˌsjuː-/ *v.tr.* **1** retire (a person) with a pension. **2** dismiss or discard as too old for use, work, etc. **3** (as **superannuated** *adj*.) too old for work or use; obsolete. □□ **superannuable** *adj*. [back-form. f. *superannuated* f. med.L *super-annuatus* f. L SUPER- + *annus* year]

superannuation /ˌsuːpərˌænjʊ'eɪʃ(ə)n, ˌsjuː-/ *n*. **1** a

pension paid to a retired person. **2** a regular payment made towards this by an employed person. **3** the process or an instance of superannuating.

superaqueous /ˌsuːpər'eɪkwɪəs, ˌsjuː-/ *adj*. above water.

superb /suː'pɜːb, sjuː-/ *adj*. **1** of the most impressive, splendid, grand, or majestic kind (*superb courage; a superb specimen*). **2** *colloq*. excellent; fine. □□ **superbly** *adv*. **superbness** *n*. [F *superbe* or L *superbus* proud]

supercalender /ˌsuːpə'kælɪndə(r), ˌsjuː-/ *v.tr.* give a highly glazed finish to (paper) by extra calendering.

supercargo /'suːpəˌkɑːgəʊ, 'sjuː-/ *n*. (*pl*. **-oes**) an officer in a merchant ship managing sales etc. of cargo. [earlier *supracargo* f. Sp. *sobrecargo* f. *sobre* over + *cargo* CARGO]

supercelestial /ˌsuːpəsɪ'lestɪəl, ˌsjuː-/ *adj*. **1** above the heavens. **2** more than heavenly. [LL *supercaelestis* (as SUPER-, CELESTIAL)]

supercharge /'suːpəˌtʃɑːdʒ, 'sjuː-/ *v.tr.* **1** (usu. foll. by *with*) charge (the atmosphere etc.) with energy, emotion, etc. **2** use a supercharger on (an internal-combustion engine).

supercharger /'suːpəˌtʃɑːdʒə(r), 'sjuː-/ *n*. a device supplying air or fuel to an internal-combustion engine at above normal pressure to increase efficiency.

superciliary /ˌsuːpə'sɪlɪərɪ, ˌsjuː-/ *adj. Anat*. of or concerning the eyebrow; over the eye. [L *supercilium* eyebrow (as SUPER-, *cilium* eyelid)]

supercilious /ˌsuːpə'sɪlɪəs, ˌsjuː-/ *adj*. assuming an air of contemptuous indifference or superiority. □□ **superciliously** *adv*. **superciliousness** *n*. [L *superciliosus* (as SUPERCILIARY)]

superclass /'suːpəˌklɑːs, 'sjuː-/ *n*. a taxonomic category between class and phylum.

supercolumnar /ˌsuːpəkə'lʌmnə(r), ˌsjuː-/ *adj. Archit*. having one order or set of columns above another. □□ **supercolumniation** /-nɪ'eɪʃ(ə)n/ *n*.

supercomputer /ˌsuːpəkəm'pjuːtə(r)/ *n*. a powerful computer capable of dealing with complex problems. □□ **supercomputing** *n*.

superconductivity /ˌsuːpəˌkɒndʌk'tɪvɪtɪ, ˌsjuː-/ *n*. *Physics* the property of zero electrical resistance in some substances at very low absolute temperatures. □□ **superconducting** /-kən'dʌktɪŋ/ *adj*. **superconductive** /-kən'dʌktɪv/ *adj*.

superconductor /ˌsuːpəkən'dʌktə(r), ˌsjuː-/ *n. Physics* a substance having superconductivity.

superconscious /ˌsuːpə'kɒnʃəs, ˌsjuː-/ *adj*. transcending human consciousness. □□ **superconsciously** *adv*. **superconsciousness** *n*.

supercool /'suːpəˌkuːl, -'kuːl, 'sjuː-/ *v. & adj.* —*v. Chem*. **1** *tr*. cool (a liquid) below its freezing-point without solidification or crystallization. **2** *intr*. (of a liquid) be cooled in this way. —*adj. sl*. very cool, relaxed, fine, etc.

supercritical /ˌsuːpə'krɪtɪk(ə)l, ˌsjuː-/ *adj. Physics* of more than critical mass etc.

super-duper var. of SUPER *adj*. 1.

superego /ˌsuːpər'iːgəʊ, -'egəʊ, ˌsjuː-/ *n*. (*pl*. **-os**) *Psychol*. the part of the mind that acts as a conscience and responds to social rules.

superelevation /ˌsuːpərˌelɪ'veɪʃ(ə)n, ˌsjuː-/ *n*. the amount by which the outer edge of a curve on a road or railway is above the inner edge.

supereminent /ˌsuːpər'emɪnənt, ˌsjuː-/ *adj*. supremely eminent, exalted, or remarkable. □□ **supereminence** *n*. **supereminently** *adv*. [L *super-eminēre* rise above (as SUPER-, EMINENT)]

supererogation /ˌsuːpərˌerə'geɪʃ(ə)n, ˌsjuː-/ *n*. the performance of more than duty requires. □**works of supererogation** *RC Ch*. actions believed to form a reserve fund of merit that can be drawn on by prayer in favour of sinners. □□ **supererogatory** /-ɪ'rɒgətərɪ/ *adj*. [LL *supererogatio* f. *supererogare* pay in addition (as SUPER-, *erogare* pay out)]

superexcellent /ˌsuːpər'eksələnt, ˌsjuː-/ *adj*. very

or supremely excellent. □□ **superexcellence** *n.*
superexcellently *adv.* [LL *superexcellens* (as SUPER-,
EXCELLENT)]
superfamily /'suːpəˌfæmɪlɪ, 'sjuː-/ *n.* (*pl.* **-ies**) a taxonomic category between family and order.
superfatted /ˌsuːpəˈfætɪd, ˌsjuː-/ *adj.* (of soap) containing extra fat.
superfecundation /ˌsuːpəˌfiːkənˈdeɪʃ(ə)n, ˌsjuː-/ *n.* =
SUPERFETATION 1.
superfetation /ˌsuːpəfiːˈteɪʃ(ə)n, ˌsjuː-/ *n.* **1** *Med.* &
Zool. a second conception during pregnancy giving
rise to embryos of different ages in the uterus. **2** *Bot.*
the fertilization of the same ovule by different kinds
of pollen. **3** the accretion of one thing on another. [F
superfétation or f. mod.L *superfetatio* f. L *superfetare*
(as SUPER-, *fetus* FOETUS)]
superficial /ˌsuːpəˈfɪʃ(ə)l, ˌsjuː-/ *adj.* **1** of or on the
surface; lacking depth (*a superficial knowledge*; *superficial wounds*). **2** swift or cursory (*a superficial
examination*). **3** apparent but not real (*a superficial
resemblance*). **4** (esp. of a person) having no depth of
character or knowledge; trivial; shallow. **5** *Commerce*
(of a measure) square (cf. SUPER *adj.* 3). □□
superficiality /-ʃɪˈælɪtɪ/ *n.* (*pl.* **-ies**). **superficially**
adv. **superficialness** *n.* [LL *superficialis* f. L (as
SUPERFICIES)]
superficies /ˌsuːpəˈfɪʃɪˌiːz, ˌsjuː-/ *n.* (*pl.* same) *Geom.* a
surface. [L (as SUPER-, *facies* face)]
superfine /'suːpəˌfaɪn, 'sjuː-/ *adj.* **1** *Commerce* of
extra quality. **2** pretending great refinement. [med.L
superfinus (as SUPER-, FINE[1])]
superfluity /ˌsuːpəˈfluːɪtɪ, ˌsjuː-/ *n.* (*pl.* **-ies**) **1** the
state of being superfluous. **2** a superfluous amount
or thing. [ME f. OF *superfluité* f. LL *superfluitas -tatis*
f. L *superfluus*: see SUPERFLUOUS]
superfluous /suːˈpɜːflʊəs, sjuː-/ *adj.* more than
enough, redundant, needless. □□ **superfluously** *adv.*
superfluousness *n.* [ME f. L *superfluus* (as SUPER-,
fluere to flow)]
supergiant /'suːpəˌdʒaɪənt, 'sjuː-/ *n.* a star of very
great luminosity and size.
superglue /'suːpəˌgluː/ *n.* any of various adhesives
with an exceptional bonding capability.
supergrass /'suːpəˌgrɑːs, 'sjuː-/ *n. colloq.* a police
informer who implicates a large number of people.
superheat /ˌsuːpəˈhiːt, ˌsjuː-/ *v.tr. Physics* **1** heat (a
liquid) above its boiling-point without vaporization.
2 heat (a vapour) above its boiling-point (*superheated
steam*). □□ **superheater** *n.*
superhet /ˌsuːpəˈhet, ˌsjuː-/ *n. colloq.* = SUPER-
HETERODYNE.
superheterodyne /ˌsuːpəˈhetərəʊˌdaɪn, ˌsjuː-/ *adj.*
& *n.* —*adj.* denoting or characteristic of a system
of radio reception in which a local variable oscillator is tuned to beat at a constant ultrasonic
frequency with carrier-wave frequencies, making
it unnecessary to vary the amplifier tuning
and securing greater selectivity. —*n.* a
superheterodyne receiver. [SUPERSONIC +
HETERODYNE]
superhighway /'suːpəˌhaɪweɪ, 'sjuː-/ *n. US* a broad
main road for fast traffic.
superhuman /ˌsuːpəˈhjuːmən, ˌsjuː-/ *adj.* **1** beyond
normal human capability. **2** higher than man. □□
superhumanly *adv.* [LL *superhumanus* (as SUPER-,
HUMAN)]
superhumeral /ˌsuːpəˈhjuːmər(ə)l, ˌsjuː-/ *n. Eccl.* a
vestment worn over the shoulders, e.g. an amice,
ephod, or pallium. [LL *superhumerale* (as SUPER-,
HUMERAL)]
superimpose /ˌsuːpərɪmˈpəʊz, ˌsjuː-/ *v.tr.* (usu. foll.
by *on*) lay (a thing) on something else. □□
superimposition /-pəˈzɪʃ(ə)n/ *n.*
superincumbent /ˌsuːpərɪnˈkʌmbənt, ˌsjuː-/ *adj.*
lying on something else.
superinduce /ˌsuːpərɪnˈdjuːs, ˌsjuː-/ *v.tr.* introduce or
induce in addition. [L *superinducere* cover over, bring
from outside (as SUPER-, INDUCE)]

superintend /ˌsuːpərɪnˈtend, ˌsjuː-/ *v.tr.* & *intr.* be
responsible for the management or arrangement of
(an activity etc.); supervise and inspect. □□
superintendence *n.* **superintendency** *n.* [eccl.L
superintendere (as SUPER-, INTEND), transl. Gk
episkopō]
superintendent /ˌsuːpərɪnˈtend(ə)nt, ˌsjuː-/ *n.* & *adj.*
—*n.* **1 a** a person who superintends. **b** a director of
an institution etc. **2 a** *Brit.* a police officer above
the rank of inspector. **b** *US* the head of a police
department. **3** *US* the caretaker of a building. —*adj.*
superintending. [eccl.L *superintendent-* part. stem of
superintendere: see SUPERINTEND]
superior /suːˈpɪərɪə(r), sjuː-, sʊ-/ *adj.* & *n.* —*adj.* **1** in
a higher position; of higher rank (*a superior officer*;
a superior court). **2 a** above the average in quality
etc. (*made of superior leather*). **b** having or showing
a high opinion of oneself; supercilious (*had a superior
air*). **3** (often foll. by *to*) **a** better or greater in some
respect (*superior to its rivals in speed*). **b** above
yielding, making concessions, paying attention, etc.
(*is superior to bribery*; *superior to temptation*). **4**
further above or out; higher, esp.: **a** *Astron.* (of a
planet) having an orbit further from the sun than
the earth's. **b** *Zool.* (of an insect's wings) folding over
others. **c** *Printing* (of figures or letters) placed above
the line. **d** *Bot.* (of the calyx) above the ovary. **e** *Bot.*
(of the ovary) above the calyx. —*n.* **1 a** person
superior to another in rank, character, etc. (*is
deferential to his superiors*; *is his superior in courage*).
2 (*fem.* **superioress** /-rɪs/) *Eccl.* the head of a
monastery or other religious institution (*Mother
Superior*; *Father Superior*). **3** *Printing* a superior
letter or figure. □ **superior numbers** esp. *Mil.* more
men etc. or their strength (*overcome by superior
numbers*). **superior persons** esp. *iron.* the better
educated or élite; prigs. □□ **superiorly** *adv.* [ME f.
OF *superior* f. L *superior -oris*, compar. of *superus*
that is above f. *super* above]
superiority /suːˌpɪərɪˈɒrɪtɪ, sjuː-, sʊ-/ *n.* the state of
being superior. □ **superiority complex** *Psychol.* an
undue conviction of one's own superiority to others.
superjacent /ˌsuːpəˈdʒeɪs(ə)nt, ˌsjuː-/ *adj.* overlying;
superincumbent. [L *superjacēre* (as SUPER-, *jacēre* lie)]
superlative /suːˈpɜːlətɪv, sjuː-/ *adj.* & *n.* —*adj.* **1** of
the highest quality or degree (*superlative wisdom*). **2**
Gram. (of an adjective or adverb) expressing the
highest or a very high degree of a quality (e.g. *bravest*, *most fiercely*) (cf. POSITIVE, COMPARATIVE). —*n.*
1 *Gram.* **a** the superlative expression or form of an
adjective or adverb. **b** a word in the superlative. **2**
something embodying excellence; the highest form
of a thing. □□ **superlatively** *adv.* **superlativeness**
n. [ME f. OF *superlatif -ive* f. LL *superlativus* f. L
superlatus (as SUPER-, *latus* past part. of *ferre* take)]
superlunary /ˌsuːpəˈluːnərɪ, ˌsjuː-, -ˈljuːnərɪ/ *adj.* **1**
situated beyond the moon. **2** belonging to a higher
world, celestial. [med.L *superlunaris* (as SUPER-,
LUNAR)]
superman /'suːpəˌmæn, 'sjuː-/ *n.* (*pl.* **-men**) **1** esp.
Philos. the ideal superior man of the future. **2** *colloq.*
a man of exceptional strength or ability. [SUPER- +
MAN, formed by G. B. Shaw after Nietzsche's G
Übermensch]
supermarket /'suːpəˌmɑːkɪt, 'sjuː-/ *n.* a large self-
service store selling foods, household goods, etc.
supermundane /ˌsuːpəˈmʌndeɪn, ˌsjuː-/ *adj.* superior
to earthly things.
supernal /suːˈpɜːn(ə)l, sjuː-/ *adj.* esp. *poet.* **1** heavenly;
divine. **2** of or concerning the sky. **3** lofty. □□
supernally *adv.* [ME f. OF *supernal* or med.L
supernalis f. L *supernus* f. *super* above]
supernatant /ˌsuːpəˈneɪt(ə)nt, ˌsjuː-/ *adj.* & *n.* esp.
Chem. —*adj.* floating on the surface of a liquid. —*n.*
a supernatant substance. [SUPER- + *natant* swimming
(as NATATION)]
supernatural /ˌsuːpəˈnætʃər(ə)l, ˌsjuː-/ *adj.* & *n.*
—*adj.* attributed to or thought to reveal some

force above the laws of nature; magical; mystical. —*n.* (prec. by *the*) supernatural, occult, or magical forces, effects, etc. □□ **supernaturalism** *n.* **supernaturalist** *n.* **supernaturalize** *v.tr.* (also **-ise**). **supernaturally** *adv.* **supernaturalness** *n.*

supernormal /ˌsuːpəˈnɔːm(ə)l, ˌsjuː-/ *adj.* beyond what is normal or natural. □□ **supernormality** /-ˈmælɪtɪ/ *n.*

supernova /ˌsuːpəˈnəʊvə, ˌsjuː-/ *n.* (*pl.* **-novae** /-viː/ or **-novas**) *Astron.* a star that suddenly increases very greatly in brightness because of an explosion ejecting most of its mass.

supernumerary /ˌsuːpəˈnjuːmərərɪ, ˌsjuː-/ *adj.* & *n.* —*adj.* **1** in excess of the normal number; extra. **2** (of a person) engaged for extra work. **3** (of an actor) appearing on stage but not speaking. —*n.* (*pl.* **-ies**) **1** an extra or unwanted person or thing. **2** a supernumerary actor. **3** a person engaged for extra work. [LL *supernumerarius* (soldier) added to a legion already complete, f. L *super numerum* beyond the number]

superorder /ˈsuːpərˌɔːdə(r), ˈsjuː-/ *n.* *Biol.* a taxonomic category between order and class. □□ **superordinal** /-ˈɔːdɪn(ə)l/ *adj.*

superordinate /ˌsuːpərˈɔːdɪnət, ˌsjuː-/ *adj.* (usu. foll. by *to*) of superior importance or rank. [SUPER-, after *subordinate*]

superphosphate /ˌsuːpəˈfɒsfeɪt, ˌsjuː-/ *n.* a fertilizer made by treating phosphate rock with sulphuric or phosphoric acid.

superphysical /ˌsuːpəˈfɪzɪk(ə)l, ˌsjuː-/ *adj.* **1** unexplainable by physical causes; supernatural. **2** beyond what is physical.

superpose /ˌsuːpəˈpəʊz, ˌsjuː-/ *v.tr.* (usu. foll. by *on*) esp. *Geom.* place (a thing or a geometric figure) on or above something else, esp. so as to coincide. □□ **superposition** /-pəˈzɪʃ(ə)n/ *n.* [F *superposer* (as SUPER-, POSE¹)]

superpower /ˈsuːpəˌpaʊə(r), ˈsjuː-/ *n.* a State of supreme power and influence, esp. the US and the USSR.

supersaturate /ˌsuːpəˈsætʃəˌreɪt, ˌsjuː-, -tjʊˌreɪt/ *v.tr.* add to (esp. a solution) beyond saturation point. □□ **supersaturation** /-ˈreɪʃ(ə)n/ *n.*

superscribe /ˈsuːpəˌskraɪb, ˈsjuː-, -ˈskraɪb/ *v.tr.* **1** write (an inscription) at the top of or on the outside of a document etc. **2** write an inscription over or on (a thing). □□ **superscription** /-ˈskrɪpʃ(ə)n/ *n.* [L *superscribere* (as SUPER-, *scribere script-* write)]

superscript /ˈsuːpəskrɪpt, ˈsjuː-/ *adj.* & *n.* —*adj.* written or printed above the line, esp. *Math.* (of a symbol) written above and to the right of another. —*n.* a superscript number or symbol. [L *superscriptus* past part. of *superscribere*: see SUPERSCRIBE]

supersede /ˌsuːpəˈsiːd, ˌsjuː-/ *v.tr.* **1 a** adopt or appoint another person or thing in place of. **b** set aside; cease to employ. **2** (of a person or thing) take the place of. □□ **supersedence** *n.* **supersedure** /-dʒə(r)/ *n.* **supersession** /-ˈseʃ(ə)n/ *n.* [OF *superseder* f. L *supersedēre* be superior to (as SUPER-, *sedēre sess-* sit)]

supersonic /ˌsuːpəˈsɒnɪk, ˌsjuː-/ *adj.* designating or having a speed greater than that of sound. □□ **supersonically** *adv.*

supersonics /ˌsuːpəˈsɒnɪks, ˌsjuː-/ *n.pl.* (treated as *sing.*) = ULTRASONICS.

superstar /ˈsuːpəstɑː(r), ˈsjuː-/ *n.* an extremely famous or renowned actor, film star, musician, etc. □□ **superstardom** *n.*

superstition /ˌsuːpəˈstɪʃ(ə)n, ˌsjuː-/ *n.* **1** credulity regarding the supernatural. **2** an irrational fear of the unknown or mysterious. **3** misdirected reverence. **4** a practice, opinion, or religion based on these tendencies. **5** a widely held but unjustified idea of the effects or nature of a thing. □□ **superstitious** *adj.* **superstitiously** *adv.* **superstitiousness** *n.* [ME f. OF *superstition* or L *superstitio* (as SUPER-, *stare stat-* stand)]

superstore /ˈsuːpəˌstɔː(r), ˈsjuː-/ *n.* a large supermarket selling a wide range of goods.

superstratum /ˈsuːpəˌstrɑːtəm, ˈsjuː-/ *n.* (*pl.* **-strata** /-tə/) an overlying stratum.

superstructure /ˈsuːpəˌstrʌktʃə(r), ˈsjuː-/ *n.* **1** the part of a building above its foundations. **2** a structure built on top of something else. **3** a concept or idea based on others. □□ **superstructural** *adj.*

supersubtle /ˌsuːpəˈsʌt(ə)l, ˌsjuː-/ *adj.* extremely or excessively subtle. □□ **supersubtlety** *n.*

supertanker /ˈsuːpəˌtæŋkə(r), ˈsjuː-/ *n.* a very large tanker ship.

supertax /ˈsuːpətæks, ˈsjuː-/ *n.* a tax on incomes above a certain level, esp. a surtax.

superterrestrial /ˌsuːpətəˈrestrɪəl, ˌsjuː-/ *adj.* **1** in or belonging to a region above the earth. **2** celestial.

supertonic /ˌsuːpəˈtɒnɪk, ˌsjuː-/ *n.* *Mus.* the note above the tonic, the second note of the diatonic scale of any key.

supervene /ˌsuːpəˈviːn, ˌsjuː-/ *v.intr.* occur as an interruption in or a change from some state. □□ **supervenient** *adj.* **supervention** /-ˈvenʃ(ə)n/ *n.* [L *supervenire supervent-* (as SUPER-, *venire* come)]

supervise /ˈsuːpəˌvaɪz, ˈsjuː-/ *v.tr.* **1** superintend, oversee the execution of (a task etc.). **2** oversee the actions or work of (a person). □□ **supervision** /-ˈvɪʒ(ə)n/ *n.* **supervisor** *n.* **supervisory** *adj.* [med.L *supervidēre supervis-* (as SUPER-, *vidēre* see)]

superwoman /ˈsuːpəˌwʊmən, ˈsjuː-/ *n.* (*pl.* **-women**) *colloq.* a woman of exceptional strength or ability.

supinate /ˈsuːpɪˌneɪt, ˈsjuː-/ *v.tr.* put (a hand or foreleg etc.) into a supine position (cf. PRONATE). □□ **supination** /-ˈneɪʃ(ə)n/ *n.* [back-form. f. *supination* f. L *supinatio* f. *supinare* f. *supinus*: see SUPINE]

supinator /ˈsuːpɪˌneɪtə(r), ˈsjuː-/ *n.* *Anat.* a muscle in the forearm effecting supination.

supine /ˈsuːpaɪn, ˈsjuː-/ *adj.* & *n.* —*adj.* **1** lying face upwards (cf. PRONE). **2** having the front or ventral part upwards; (of the hand) with the palm upwards. **3** inert, indolent; morally or mentally inactive. —*n.* a Latin verbal noun used only in the accusative and ablative cases, esp. to denote purpose (e.g. *mirabile dictu* wonderful to relate). □□ **supinely** *adv.* **supineness** *n.* [L *supinus*, rel. to *super*: (n.) f. LL *supinum* neut. (reason unkn.)]

supper /ˈsʌpə(r)/ *n.* a light evening meal. □ **sing for one's supper** do something in return for a benefit. □□ **supperless** *adj.* [ME f. OF *soper*, *super*]

supplant /səˈplɑːnt/ *v.tr.* dispossess and take the place of, esp. by underhand means. □□ **supplanter** *n.* [ME f. OF *supplanter* or L *supplantare* trip up (as SUB-, *planta* sole)]

supple /ˈsʌp(ə)l/ *adj.* & *v.* —*adj.* (**suppler, supplest**) **1** flexible, pliant; easily bent. **2** compliant; avoiding overt resistance; artfully or servilely submissive. —*v.tr.* & *intr.* make or become supple. □□ **suppleness** *n.* [ME f. OF *souple* ult. f. L *supplex supplicis* submissive]

supplejack /ˈsʌp(ə)lˌdʒæk/ *n.* any of various strong twining tropical shrubs, esp. *Berchemia scandens*. [SUPPLE + JACK¹]

supplely var. of SUPPLY².

supplement *n.* & *v.* —*n.* /ˈsʌplɪmənt/ **1** a thing or part added to remedy deficiencies (*dietary supplement*). **2** a part added to a book etc. to provide further information. **3** a separate section, esp. a colour magazine, added to a newspaper or periodical. **4** *Geom.* the amount by which an angle is less than 180° (cf. COMPLEMENT). —*v.tr.* /ˈsʌplɪmənt, ˌsʌplɪˈment/ provide a supplement for. □□ **supplemental** /-ˈment(ə)l/ *adj.* **supplementally** /-ˈmentəlɪ/ *adv.* **supplementation** /-ˈteɪʃ(ə)n/ *n.* [ME f. L *supplementum* (as SUB-, *plēre* fill)]

supplementary /ˌsʌplɪˈmentərɪ/ *adj.* forming or serving as a supplement; additional. □ **supplementary benefit** (in the UK) a weekly allowance paid by the State to those not in full-time employment and with an income below a certain level (cf. *family credit*). □□ **supplementarily** *adv.*

suppletion /sə'pliːʃ(ə)n/ *n.* the act or an instance of supplementing, esp. *Linguistics* the occurrence of unrelated forms to supply gaps in conjugation (e.g. *went* as the past of *go*). □□ **suppletive** *adj.* [ME f. OF f. med.L *suppletio -onis* (as SUPPLY¹)]

suppliant /'sʌplɪənt/ *adj. & n.* —*adj.* 1 supplicating. 2 expressing supplication. —*n.* a supplicating person. □□ **suppliantly** *adv.* [ME f. F *supplier* beseech f. L (as SUPPLICATE)]

supplicate /'sʌplɪˌkeɪt/ *v.* 1 *tr.* petition humbly to (a person) or for (a thing). 2 *intr.* (foll. by *to, for*) make a petition. □□ **supplicant** *adj. & n.* **supplication** /-'keɪʃ(ə)n/ *n.* **supplicatory** *adj.* [ME f. L *supplicare* (as SUB-, *plicare* bend)]

supply¹ /sə'plaɪ/ *v. & n.* —*v.tr.* (-ies, -ied) 1 provide or furnish (a thing needed). 2 (often foll. by *with*) provide (a person etc. with a thing needed). 3 meet or make up for (a deficiency or need etc.). 4 fill (a vacancy, place, etc.) as a substitute. —*n.* (*pl.* -ies) 1 the act or an instance of providing what is needed. 2 a stock, store, amount, etc., of something provided or obtainable (*a large supply of water*; *the gas-supply*). 3 (in *pl.*) a the collected provisions and equipment for an army, expedition, etc. b a grant of money by Parliament for the costs of government. c a money allowance to a person. 4 (often *attrib.*) a person, esp. a schoolteacher or clergyman, acting as a temporary substitute for another. 5 (*attrib.*) providing supplies or a supply (*supply officer*). □**in short supply** available in limited quantity. **on supply** (of a schoolteacher etc.) acting as a supply. **supply and demand** *Econ.* quantities available and required as factors regulating the price of commodities. **supply-side** *Econ.* denoting a policy of low taxation and other incentives to produce goods and invest. □□ **supplier** *n.* [ME f. OF *so(u)pleer* etc. f. L *supplēre* (as SUB-, *plēre* fill)]

supply² /'sʌplɪ/ *adv.* (also **supplely** /'sʌpəlɪ/) in a supple manner.

support /sə'pɔːt/ *v. & n.* —*v.tr.* 1 carry all or part of the weight of. 2 keep from falling or sinking or failing. 3 provide with a home and the necessities of life (*has a family to support*). 4 enable to last out; give strength to; encourage. 5 bear out; tend to substantiate or corroborate (a statement, charge, theory, etc.). 6 give help or countenance to, back up; second, further. 7 speak in favour of (a resolution etc.). 8 be actively interested in (a particular team or sport). 9 take a part that is secondary to (a principal actor etc.). 10 assist (a lecturer etc.) by one's presence. 11 endure, tolerate (*can no longer support the noise*). 12 maintain or represent (a part or character) adequately. 13 subscribe to the funds of (an institution). —*n.* 1 the act or an instance of supporting; the process of being supported. 2 a person or thing that supports. □**in support of** in order to support. **supporting film** (or **picture** etc.) a less important film in a cinema programme. **support price** a minimum price guaranteed to a farmer for agricultural produce and maintained by subsidy etc. □□ **supportable** *adj.* **supportability** /-tə'bɪlɪtɪ/ *n.* **supportably** *adv.* **supportingly** *adv.* **supportless** *adj.* [ME f. OF *supporter* f. L *supportare* (as SUB-, *portare* carry)]

supporter /sə'pɔːtə(r)/ *n.* 1 a person or thing that supports, esp. a person supporting a team or sport. 2 *Heraldry* the representation of an animal etc., usu. one of a pair, holding up or standing beside an escutcheon.

supportive /sə'pɔːtɪv/ *adj.* providing support or encouragement. □□ **supportively** *adv.* **supportiveness** *n.*

suppose /sə'pəʊz/ *v.tr.* (often foll. by *that* + clause) 1 assume, esp. in default of knowledge; be inclined to think (*I suppose they will return*; *what do you*

suppose he meant?). 2 take as a possibility or hypothesis (*let us suppose you are right*). 3 (in *imper.*) as a formula of proposal (*suppose we go to the party*). 4 (of a theory or result etc.) require as a condition (*design in creation supposes a creator*). 5 (in *imper.* or *pres. part.* forming a question) in the circumstances that; if (*suppose he won't let you*; *supposing we stay*). 6 (as **supposed** *adj.*) generally accepted as being so; believed (*his supposed brother*; *generally supposed to be wealthy*). 7 (in *passive*; foll. by *to* + infin.) a be expected or required (*was supposed to write to you*). b (with *neg.*) not have to; not be allowed to (*you are not supposed to go in there*). □**I suppose so** an expression of hesitant agreement. □□ **supposable** *adj.* [ME f. OF *supposer* (as SUB-, POSE¹)]

supposedly /sə'pəʊzɪdlɪ/ *adv.* as is generally supposed.

supposition /ˌsʌpə'zɪʃ(ə)n/ *n.* 1 a fact or idea etc. supposed. 2 the act or an instance of supposing. □□ **suppositional** *adj.*

suppositious /ˌsʌpə'zɪʃəs/ *adj.* hypothetical, assumed. □□ **suppositiously** *adv.* **suppositiousness** *n.* [partly f. SUPPOSITITIOUS, partly f. SUPPOSITION + -OUS]

supposititious /səˌpɒzɪ'tɪʃəs/ *adj.* spurious; substituted for the real. □□ **supposititiously** *adv.* **supposititiousness** *n.* [L *supposititius, -icius* f. *supponere supposit-* substitute (as SUB- *ponere* place)]

suppository /sə'pɒzɪtərɪ/ *n.* (*pl.* -ies) a medical preparation in the form of a cone, cylinder, etc., to be inserted into the rectum or vagina to melt. [ME f. med.L *suppositorium*, neut. of LL *suppositorius* placed underneath (as SUPPOSITITIOUS)]

suppress /sə'pres/ *v.tr.* 1 end the activity or existence of, esp. forcibly. 2 prevent (information, feelings, a reaction, etc.) from being seen, heard, or known (*tried to suppress the report*; *suppressed a yawn*). 3 a partly or wholly eliminate (electrical interference etc.). b equip (a device) to reduce such interference due to it. 4 *Psychol.* keep out of one's consciousness. □□ **suppressible** *adj.* **suppression** *n.* **suppressive** *adj.* **suppressor** *n.* [ME f. L *supprimere suppress-* (as SUB-, *premere* press)]

suppurate /'sʌpjəˌreɪt/ *v.intr.* 1 form pus. 2 fester. □□ **suppuration** /-'reɪʃ(ə)n/ *n.* **suppurative** /-rətɪv/ *adj.* [L *suppurare* (as SUB-, *purare* as PUS)]

supra /'suːprə, 'sjuː-/ *adv.* above or earlier on (in a book etc.). [L, = above]

supra- /'suːprə, 'sjuː-/ *prefix* 1 above. 2 beyond, transcending (*supranational*). [from or after L *supra-* f. *supra* above, beyond, before in time]

supramaxillary /ˌsuːprəmæk'sɪlərɪ, ˌsjuː-/ *adj.* of or relating to the upper jaw.

supramundane /ˌsuːprə'mʌndeɪn, ˌsjuː-/ *adj.* above or superior to the world.

supranational /ˌsuːprə'næʃən(ə)l, ˌsjuː-/ *adj.* transcending national limits. □□ **supranationalism** *n.* **supranationality** /-'nælɪtɪ/ *n.*

supraorbital /ˌsuːprə'ɔːbɪt(ə)l, ˌsjuː-/ *adj.* situated above the orbit of the eye.

suprarenal /ˌsuːprə'riːn(ə)l, ˌsjuː-/ *adj.* situated above the kidneys.

supremacist /suː'preməsɪst, sjuː-/ *n. & adj.* —*n.* an advocate of the supremacy of a particular group, esp. determined by race or sex. —*adj.* relating to or advocating such supremacy. □□ **supremacism** *n.*

supremacy /suː'preməsɪ, sjuː-/ *n.* (*pl.* -ies) 1 the state of being supreme. 2 the highest authority. □**Act of Supremacy** an act securing ecclesiastical supremacy to the Crown and excluding the authority of the Pope.

supreme /suː'priːm, sjuː-/ *adj. & n.* —*adj.* 1 highest in authority or rank. 2 greatest; most important. —*n.* 3 (of a penalty or sacrifice etc.) involving death. —*n.* 1 a rich cream sauce. 2 a dish served in this. □**the Supreme Being** a name for God. **Supreme Court** the highest judicial court in a State etc. **supreme pontiff** see PONTIFF. **Supreme Soviet** the governing council of the USSR or one of its constituent republics. □□ **supremely** *adv.* **supremeness** *n.* [L *supremus*, superl. of *superus* that is above f. *super* above]

suprême /suː'prɛm/ *n.* = SUPREME *n.* [F]

supremo /suː'priːməʊ, sjuː-/ *n.* (*pl.* **-os**) **1** a supreme leader or ruler. **2** a person in overall charge. [Sp., = SUPREME]

Supt. *abbr.* Superintendent.

sur-[1] /sɜː(r), sə(r)/ *prefix* = SUPER- (*surcharge*; *surrealism*). [OF]

sur-[2] /sɜː(r), sə(r)/ *prefix* assim. form of SUB- before *r*.

sura /'sʊərə/ *n.* (also **surah**) a chapter or section of the Koran. [Arab. *sūra*]

surah /'sjʊərə/ *n.* a soft twilled silk for scarves etc. [F pronunc. of *Surat* in India, where it was orig. made]

sural /'sjʊər(ə)l/ *adj.* of or relating to the calf of the leg (*sural artery*). [mod.L *suralis* f. L *sura* calf]

surcease /sɜː'siːs/ *n.* & *v. literary* —*n.* a cessation. —*v.intr.* & *tr.* cease. [ME f. OF *sursis*, *-ise* (cf. AF *sursise* omission), past part. of OF *surseoir* refrain, delay f. L (as SUPERSEDE), with assim. to CEASE]

surcharge *n.* & *v.* —*n.* /'sɜːtʃɑːdʒ/ **1** an additional charge or payment. **2** a charge made by assessors as a penalty for false returns of taxable property. **3** a mark printed on a postage stamp changing its value. **4** an additional or excessive load. **5** *Brit.* an amount in an official account not passed by the auditor and having to be refunded by the person responsible. **6** the showing of an omission in an account for which credit should have been given. —*v.tr.* /'sɜːtʃɑːdʒ, -'tʃɑːdʒ/ **1** exact a surcharge from. **2** exact (a sum) as a surcharge. **3** mark (a postage stamp) with a surcharge. **4** overload. **5** fill or saturate to excess. [ME f. OF *surcharger* (as SUR-[1], CHARGE)]

surcingle /'sɜːˌsɪŋg(ə)l/ *n.* a band round a horse's body usu. to keep a pack etc. in place. [ME f. OF *surcengle* (as SUR-[1], *cengle* girth f. L *cingula* f. *cingere* gird)]

surcoat /'sɜːkəʊt/ *n.* **1** *hist.* a loose robe worn over armour. **2** a similar sleeveless garment worn as part of the insignia of an order of knighthood. **3** *hist.* an outer coat of rich material. [ME f. OF *surcot* (as SUR-[1], *cot* coat)]

surculose /'sɜːkjʊˌləʊs/ *adj. Bot.* producing suckers. [L *surculosus* f. *surculus* twig]

surd /sɜːd/ *adj.* & *n.* —*adj.* **1** *Math.* (of a number) irrational. **2** *Phonet.* (of a sound) uttered with the breath and not the voice (e.g. *f, k, p, s, t*). —*n.* **1** *Math.* a surd number, esp. the root of an integer. **2** *Phonet.* a surd sound. [L *surdus* deaf, mute: sense 1 by mistransl. into L of Gk *alogos* irrational, speechless, through Arab. *jaḏr aṣamm* deaf root]

sure /ʃʊə(r), ʃɔː(r)/ *adj.* & *adv.* —*adj.* **1** having or seeming to have adequate reason for a belief or assertion. **2** (often foll. by *of*, or *that* + clause) convinced. **3** (foll. by *of*) having a certain prospect or confident anticipation or satisfactory knowledge of. **4** reliable or unfailing (*there is one sure way to find out*). **5** (foll. by *to* + infin.) certain. **6** undoubtedly true or truthful. —*adv. colloq.* certainly. □ **as sure as eggs is eggs** see EGG[1]. **as sure as fate** quite certain. **be sure** (in *imper.* or *infin.*; foll. by *that* + clause or *to* + infin.) take care to; not fail to (*be sure to turn the lights out*). **for sure** *colloq.* without doubt. **make sure 1** make or become certain; ensure. **2** (foll. by *of*) establish the truth or ensure the existence or happening of. **sure enough** *colloq.* **1** in fact; certainly. **2** with near certainty (*they will come sure enough*). **sure-fire** *colloq.* certain to succeed. **sure-footed** never stumbling or making a mistake. **sure-footedly** in a sure-footed way. **sure-footedness** being sure-footed. **sure thing** *int.* esp. *US colloq.* certainly. **to be sure 1** it is undeniable or admitted. **2** it must be admitted. □□ **sureness** *n.* [ME f. OF *sur sure* (earlier *sëur*) f. L *securus* SECURE]

surely /'ʃʊəlɪ/ *adv.* **1** with certainty (*the time approaches slowly but surely*). **2** as an appeal to likelihood or reason (*surely that can't be right*). **3** with safety; securely (*the goat plants its feet surely*).

surety /'ʃʊərɪtɪ, 'ʃʊətɪ/ *n.* (*pl.* **-ies**) **1** a person who takes responsibility for another's performance of an undertaking, e.g. to appear in court, or payment of a debt. **2** *archaic* a certainty. □ **of** (or **for**) **a surety** *archaic* certainly. **stand surety** become a surety, go bail. □□ **suretyship** *n.* [ME f. OF *surté*, *sëurté* f. L *securitas -tatis* SECURITY]

surf /sɜːf/ *n.* & *v.* —*n.* **1** the swell of the sea breaking on the shore or reefs. **2** the foam produced by this. —*v.intr.* go surf-riding. □ **surf-casting** fishing by casting a line into the sea from the shore. **surf-riding** the sport of being carried over the surf to the shore on a surfboard. □□ **surfer** *n.* **surfy** *adj.* [app. f. obs. *suff*, perh. assim. to *surge*: orig. applied to the Indian coast]

surface /'sɜːfɪs/ *n.* & *v.* —*n.* **1 a** the outside of a material body. **b** the area of this. **2** any of the limits terminating a solid. **3** the upper boundary of a liquid or of the ground etc. **4** the outward aspect of anything; what is apparent on a casual view or consideration (*presents a large surface to view*; *all is quiet on the surface*). **5** *Geom.* a set of points that has length and breadth but no thickness. **6** (*attrib.*) **a** of or on the surface (*surface area*). **b** superficial (*surface politeness*). —*v.* **1** *tr.* give the required surface to (a road, paper, etc.). **2** *intr.* & *tr.* rise or bring to the surface. **3** *intr.* become visible or known. **4** *intr. colloq.* become conscious; wake up. □ **come to the surface** become perceptible after having been hidden. **surface-active** (of a substance, e.g. a detergent) able to affect the wetting properties of a liquid. **surface mail** mail carried over land and by sea, and not by air. **surface noise** extraneous noise in playing a gramophone record, caused by imperfections in the grooves. **surface tension** the tension of the surface-film of a liquid, tending to minimize its surface area. □□ **surfaced** *adj.* (usu. in *comb.*). **surfacer** *n.* [F (as SUPER-[1], FACE)]

surfactant /sɜː'fækt(ə)nt/ *n.* a substance which reduces surface tension. [*surface-active*]

surfboard /'sɜːfbɔːd/ *n.* a long narrow board used in surf-riding.

surfeit /'sɜːfɪt/ *n.* & *v.* —*n.* **1** an excess esp. in eating or drinking. **2** a feeling of satiety or disgust resulting from this. —*v.* (**surfeited**, **surfeiting**) **1** *tr.* overfeed. **2** *intr.* overeat. **3** *intr.* & *tr.* (foll. by *with*) be or cause to be wearied through excess. [ME f. OF *sorfe(i)t*, *surfe(i)t* (as SUPER-, L *facere facet-* do)]

surficial /sɜː'fɪʃ(ə)l/ *adj. Geol.* of or relating to the earth's surface. □□ **surficially** *adv.* [SURFACE after *superficial*]

surge /sɜːdʒ/ *n.* & *v.* —*n.* **1** a sudden or impetuous onset (*a surge of anger*). **2** the swell of the waves at sea. **3** a heavy forward or upward motion. **4** a rapid increase in price, activity, etc. over a short period. **5** a sudden marked increase in voltage of an electric current. —*v.intr.* **1** (of waves, the sea, etc.) rise and fall or move heavily forward. **2** (of a crowd etc.) move suddenly and powerfully forwards in large numbers. **3** (of an electric current etc.) increase suddenly. **4** *Naut.* (of a rope, chain, or windlass) slip back with a jerk. □ **surge chamber** (or **tank**) a chamber designed to neutralize sudden changes of pressure in a flow of liquid. [OF *sourdre sourge-*, or *sorgir* f. Cat., f. L *surgere* rise]

surgeon /'sɜːdʒ(ə)n/ *n.* **1** a medical practitioner qualified to practise surgery. **2** a medical officer in a navy or army or military hospital. □ **surgeon fish** any tropical marine fish of the genus *Acanthurus* with movable lancet-shaped spines on each side of the tail. **surgeon general** (*pl.* **surgeons general**) *US* the head of a public health service or of an army etc. medical service. **surgeon's knot** a reef-knot with a double twist. [ME f. AF *surgien* f. OF *serurgien* (as SURGERY)]

surgery /'sɜːdʒərɪ/ *n.* (*pl.* **-ies**) **1** the branch of medicine concerned with treatment of injuries or disorders of the body by incision, manipulation or alteration of organs etc., with the hands or with instruments. **2** *Brit.* **a** a place where a doctor, dentist, etc., treats patients. **b** the occasion of this (*the doctor will see you after surgery*). **3** *Brit.* **a** a place where an MP, lawyer, or other professional person gives advice. **b** the occasion of this. [ME f. OF *surgerie* f. L *chirurgia* f. Gk *kheirourgia* handiwork, surgery f. *kheir* hand + *erg-* work]

surgical /'sɜːdʒɪk(ə)l/ *adj.* **1** of or relating to or done by surgeons or surgery. **2** resulting from surgery (*surgical fever*). **3 a** used in surgery. **b** (of a special garment etc.) worn to correct a deformity etc. □**surgical spirit** methylated spirit used in surgery for cleansing etc. □□**surgically** *adv.* [earlier *chirurgical* f. *chirurgy* f. OF *sirurgie*: see SURGEON]

suricate /'sʊərɪˌkeɪt/ *n.* a South African burrowing mongoose, *Suricata suricatta*, with grey and black stripes. [F f. S.Afr. native name]

Surinam toad /ˌsʊərɪ'næm/ *n.* = PIPA. [*Surinam* in S. America]

surly /'sɜːlɪ/ *adj.* (**surlier**, **surliest**) bad-tempered and unfriendly; churlish. □□**surlily** *adv.* **surliness** *n.* [alt. spelling of obs. *sirly* haughty f. SIR + -LY¹]

surmise /sə'maɪz/ *n.* & *v.* —*n.* a conjecture or suspicion about the existence or truth of something. —*v.* **1** *tr.* (often foll. by *that* + clause) infer doubtfully; make a surmise about. **2** *tr.* suspect the existence of. **3** *intr.* make a guess. [ME f. AF & OF fem. past part. of *surmettre* accuse f. LL *supermittere supermiss-* (as SUPER-, *mittere* send)]

surmount /sə'maʊnt/ *v.tr.* **1** overcome or get over (a difficulty or obstacle). **2** (usu. in *passive*) cap or crown (*peaks surmounted with snow*). □□ **surmountable** *adj.* [ME f. OF *surmonter* (as SUR-¹, MOUNT¹)]

surmullet /sɜː'mʌlɪt/ *n.* the red mullet. [F *surmulet* f. OF *sor* red + *mulet* MULLET]

surname /'sɜːneɪm/ *n.* & *v.* —*n.* **1** a hereditary name common to all members of a family, as distinct from a Christian or first name. **2** *archaic* an additional descriptive or allusive name attached to a person, sometimes becoming hereditary. —*v.tr.* **1** give a surname to. **2** give (a person a surname). **3** (as **surnamed** *adj.*) having as a family name. [ME, alt. of *surnoun* f. AF (as SUR-¹, NOUN name)]

surpass /sə'pɑːs/ *v.tr.* **1** outdo, be greater or better than. **2** (as **surpassing** *adj.*) pre-eminent, matchless (*of surpassing intelligence*). □□**surpassingly** *adv.* [F *surpasser* (as SUR-¹, PASS¹)]

surplice /'sɜːplɪs/ *n.* a loose white linen vestment reaching the knees, worn over a cassock by clergy and choristers at services. □□**surpliced** *adj.* [ME f. AF *surplis*, OF *sourpelis*, f. med.L *superpellicium* (as SUPER-, *pellicia* PELISSE)]

surplus /'sɜːpləs/ *n.* & *adj.* —*n.* **1** an amount left over when requirements have been met. **2 a** an excess of revenue over expenditure in a given period, esp. a financial year (opp. DEFICIT). **b** the excess value of a company's assets over the face value of its stock. —*adj.* exceeding what is needed or used. □**surplus value** *Econ.* the difference between the value of work done and wages paid. [ME f. AF *surplus*, OF *s(o)urplus* f. med.L *superplus* (as SUPER-, + *plus* more)]

surprise /sə'praɪz/ *n.* & *v.* —*n.* **1** an unexpected or astonishing event or circumstance. **2** the emotion caused by this. **3** the act of catching a person etc. unawares, or the process of being caught unawares. **4** (*attrib.*) unexpected; made or done etc. without warning (*a surprise visit*). —*v.tr.* **1** affect with surprise; turn out contrary to the expectations of (*your answer surprised me*; *I surprised her by arriving early*). **2** (usu. in *passive*; foll. by *at*) shock, scandalize

(*I am surprised at you*). **3** capture or attack by surprise. **4** come upon (a person) unawares (*surprised him taking a biscuit*). **5** (foll. by *into*) startle (a person) by surprise into an action etc. (*surprised them into consenting*). □**take by surprise** affect with surprise, esp. by an unexpected encounter or statement. □□**surprisedly** /-zɪdlɪ/ *adv.* **surprising** *adj.* **surprisingly** *adv.* **surprisingness** *n.* [OF, fem. past part. of *surprendre* (as SUR-¹, *prendre* f. L *praehendere* seize)]

surra /'sʊərə, 'sʌrə/ *n.* a febrile disease transmitted by bites of flies and affecting horses and cattle in the tropics. [Marathi]

surreal /sə'rɪəl/ *adj.* **1** having the qualities of sur-realism. **2** strange, bizarre. □□**surreality** /-'ælɪtɪ/ *n.* **surreally** *adv.* [back-form. f. SURREALISM etc.]

surrealism /sə'rɪəˌlɪz(ə)m/ *n.* a 20th-c. movement in art and literature aiming at expressing the sub-conscious mind, e.g. by the irrational juxtaposition of images. □□**surrealist** *n.* & *adj.* **surrealistic** /-'lɪstɪk/ *adj.* **surrealistically** /-'lɪstɪkəlɪ/ *adv.* [F *surréalisme* (as SUR-¹, REALISM)]

surrebutter /ˌsʌrɪ'bʌtə(r)/ *n.* *Law* the plaintiff's reply to the defendant's rebutter. [SUR-¹ + REBUTTER, after SURREJOINDER]

surrejoinder /ˌsʌrɪ'dʒɔɪndə(r)/ *n.* *Law* the plaintiff's reply to the defendant's rejoinder. [SUR-¹ + REJOINDER]

surrender /sə'rendə(r)/ *v.* & *n.* —*v.* **1** *tr.* hand over; relinquish possession of, esp. on compulsion or demand; give into another's power or control. **2** *intr.* **a** accept an enemy's demand for submission. **b** give oneself up; cease from resistance; submit. **3** *intr.* & *refl.* (foll. by *to*) give oneself over to a habit, emotion, influence, etc. **4** *tr.* give up rights under (a life-insurance policy) in return for a smaller sum re-ceived immediately. **5** *tr.* give up (a lease) before its expiry. **6** *tr.* abandon (hope etc.). —*n.* the act or an instance of surrendering. □**surrender to bail** duly appear in a lawcourt after release on bail. **surrender value** the amount payable to one who surrenders a life-insurance policy. [ME f. AF f. OF *surrendre* (as SUR-¹, RENDER)]

surreptitious /ˌsʌrəp'tɪʃəs/ *adj.* **1** covert; kept secret. **2** done by stealth; clandestine. □□**surreptitiously** *adv.* **surreptitiousness** *n.* [ME f. L *surrepticius -itius* f. *surripere surrept-* (as SUR-¹, *rapere* seize)]

surrey /'sʌrɪ/ *n.* (*pl.* **surreys**) *US* a light four-wheeled carriage with two seats facing forwards. [orig. of an adaptation of the *Surrey cart*, orig. made in *Surrey* in England]

surrogate /'sʌrəgət/ *n.* **1** a substitute, esp. for a person in a specific role or office. **2** *Brit.* a deputy, esp. of a bishop in granting marriage licences. **3** *US* a judge in charge of probate, inheritance, and guardianship. □**surrogate mother 1** a person acting the role of mother. **2** a woman who bears a child on behalf of another woman, from her own egg fertilized by the other woman's partner. □□**surrogacy** *n.* **surrogateship** *n.* [L *surrogatus* past part. of *sur-rogare* elect as a substitute (as SUR-¹, *rogare* ask)]

surround /sə'raʊnd/ *v.* & *n.* —*v.tr.* **1** come or be all round; encircle, enclose. **2** (in *passive*; foll. by *by*, *with*) have on all sides (*the house is surrounded by trees*). —*n.* **1** *Brit.* **a** a border or edging, esp. an area between the walls and carpet of a room. **b** a floor-covering for this. **2** an area or substance surrounding something. □□**surrounding** *adj.* [ME = overflow, f. AF *sur(o)under*, OF *s(o)uronder* f. LL *superundare* (as SUPER-, *undare* flow f. *unda* wave)]

surroundings /sə'raʊndɪŋz/ *n.pl.* the things in the neighbourhood of, or the conditions affecting, a person or thing.

surtax /'sɜːtæks/ *n.* & *v.* —*n.* an additional tax, esp. levied on incomes above a certain level. —*v.tr.* impose a surtax on. [F *surtaxe* (as SUR-¹, TAX)]

surtitle /'sɜːˌtaɪt(ə)l/ *n.* (esp. in opera) each of a

sequence of captions projected above the stage, translating the text being sung.

surtout /sɜːˈtuː, -ˈtuːt/ n. hist. a greatcoat or frock-coat. [F f. *sur* over + *tout* everything]

surveillance /sɜːˈveɪləns/ n. close observation, esp. of a suspected person. [F f. *surveiller* (as SUR-¹, *veiller* f. L *vigilare* keep watch)]

survey v. & n. —v.tr. /səˈveɪ/ **1** take or present a general view of. **2** examine the condition of (a building etc.). **3** determine the boundaries, extent, ownership, etc., of (a district etc.). —n. /ˈsɜːveɪ/ **1** a general view or consideration of something. **2 a** the act of surveying property. **b** the result or findings of this, esp. in a written report. **3** an inspection or investigation. **4** a map or plan made by surveying an area. **5** a department carrying out the surveying of land. [ME f. AF *survei(e)r*, OF *so(u)rveeir* (pres. stem *survey-*) f. med.L *supervidēre* (as SUPER-, *vidēre* see)]

surveyor /səˈveɪə(r)/ n. **1** a person who surveys land and buildings, esp. professionally. **2** *Brit.* an official inspector, esp. for measurement and valuation. **3** a person who carries out surveys. □□ **surveyorship** n. (esp. in sense 2). [ME f. AF & OF *surve(i)our* (as SURVEY)]

survival /səˈvaɪv(ə)l/ n. **1** the process or an instance of surviving. **2** a person, thing, or practice that has remained from a former time. □ **survival kit** emergency rations etc., esp. carried by servicemen. **survival of the fittest** the process or result of natural selection.

survive /səˈvaɪv/ v. **1** intr. continue to live or exist; be still alive or existent. **2** tr. live or exist longer than. **3** tr. remain alive after going through, or continue to exist in spite of (a danger, accident, etc.). [ME f. AF *survivre*, OF *sourvivre* f. L *supervivere* (as SUPER-, *vivere* live)]

survivor /səˈvaɪvə(r)/ n. **1** a person who survives or has survived. **2** *Law* a joint tenant who has the right to the whole estate on the other's death.

Sus. abbr. Susanna (Apocrypha).

sus var. of SUSS.

sus- /sʌs, səs/ prefix assim. form of SUB- before *c, p, t*.

susceptibility /səˌseptɪˈbɪlɪtɪ/ n. (pl. **-ies**) **1** the state of being susceptible. **2** (in pl.) a person's sensitive feelings. **3** *Physics* the ratio of magnetization to a magnetizing force.

susceptible /səˈseptɪb(ə)l/ adj. **1** impressionable, sensitive; easily moved by emotion. **2** (predic.) **a** (foll. by to) likely to be affected by; liable or vulnerable to (*susceptible to pain*). **b** (foll. by of) allowing; admitting of (*facts not susceptible of proof*). □□ **susceptibly** adv. [LL *susceptibilis* f. L *suscipere suscept-* (as SUB-, *capere* take)]

susceptive /səˈseptɪv/ adj. **1** concerned with the receiving of emotional impressions or ideas. **2** receptive. **3** = SUSCEPTIBLE. [LL *susceptivus* (as SUSCEPTIBLE)]

sushi /ˈsuːʃɪ/ n. a Japanese dish of balls of cold rice flavoured and garnished. [Jap.]

suslik /ˈsʌslɪk/ n. an E. European and Asian ground squirrel, *Citellus citellus*. [Russ.]

suspect v., n., & adj. —v.tr. /səˈspekt/ **1** have an impression of the existence or presence of (*suspects poisoning*). **2** (foll. by to be) believe tentatively, without clear ground. **3** (foll. by that + clause) be inclined to think. **4** (often foll. by of) be inclined to mentally accuse; doubt the innocence of (*suspect him of complicity*). **5** doubt the genuineness or truth of. —n. /ˈsʌspekt/ a suspected person. —adj. /ˈsʌspekt/ subject to or deserving suspicion or distrust; not sound or trustworthy. [ME f. L *suspicere suspect-* (as SUB-, *specere* look)]

suspend /səˈspend/ v.tr. **1** hang up. **2** keep inoperative or undecided for a time; defer. **3** debar temporarily from a function, office, privilege, etc. **4** (as **suspended** adj.) (of solid particles or a body in a fluid medium) sustained somewhere between top and bottom. □ **suspended animation** a temporary

cessation of the vital functions without death. **suspended sentence** a judicial sentence left unenforced subject to good behaviour during a specified period. **suspend payment** (of a company) fail to meet its financial engagements; admit insolvency. □□ **suspensible** adj. [ME f. OF *suspendre* or L *suspendere suspens-* (as SUB-, *pendere* hang)]

suspender /səˈspendə(r)/ n. **1** an attachment to hold up a stocking or sock by its top. **2** (in pl.) US a pair of braces. □ **suspender belt** a woman's undergarment with suspenders.

suspense /səˈspens/ n. **1** a state of anxious uncertainty or expectation. **2** *Law* a suspension; the temporary cessation of a right etc. □ **keep in suspense** delay informing (a person) of urgent information. **suspense account** an account in which items are entered temporarily before allocation to the right account. □□ **suspenseful** adj. [ME f. AF & OF *suspens* f. past part. of L *suspendere* SUSPEND]

suspension /səˈspenʃ(ə)n/ n. **1** the act of suspending or the condition of being suspended. **2** the means by which a vehicle is supported on its axles. **3** a substance consisting of particles suspended in a medium. **4** *Mus.* the prolongation of a note of a chord to form a discord with the following chord. □ **suspension bridge** a bridge with a roadway suspended from cables supported by structures at each end. [F *suspension* or L *suspensio* (as SUSPEND)]

suspensive /səˈspensɪv/ adj. **1** having the power or tendency to suspend or postpone. **2** causing suspense. □□ **suspensively** adv. **suspensiveness** n. [F *suspensif -ive* or med.L *suspensivus* (as SUSPEND)]

suspensory /səˈspensərɪ/ adj. (of a ligament, muscle, bandage, etc.) holding an organ etc. suspended. [F *suspensoire* (as SUSPENSION)]

suspicion /səˈspɪʃ(ə)n/ n. **1** the feeling or thought of a person who suspects. **2** the act or an instance of suspecting; the state of being suspected. **3** (foll. by of) a slight trace of. □ **above suspicion** too obviously good etc. to be suspected. **under suspicion** suspected. [ME f. AF *suspeciun* (OF *sospeçon*) f. med.L *suspectio -onis* f. L *suspicere* (as SUSPECT): assim. to F *suspicion* & L *suspicio*]

suspicious /səˈspɪʃəs/ adj. **1** prone to or feeling suspicion. **2** indicating suspicion (*a suspicious glance*). **3** inviting or justifying suspicion (*a suspicious lack of surprise*). □□ **suspiciously** adv. **suspiciousness** n. [ME f. AF & OF f. L *suspiciosus* (as SUSPICION)]

suss /sʌs/ v. & n. (also **sus**) *Brit. sl.* —v.tr. (**sussed, sussing**) **1** suspect of a crime. **2** (usu. foll. by out) **a** investigate, inspect (*go and suss out the restaurants*). **b** work out; grasp, understand, realize (*he had the market sussed*). —n. **1** a suspect. **2** a suspicion; suspicious behaviour. □ **on suss** on suspicion (of having committed a crime). [abbr. of SUSPECT, SUSPICION]

Sussex /ˈsʌsɪks/ n. **1** a speckled or red domestic fowl of an English breed. **2** this breed. [*Sussex* in S. England]

sustain /səˈsteɪn/ v.tr. **1** support, bear the weight of, esp. for a long period. **2** give strength to; encourage, support. **3** (of food) give nourishment to. **4** endure, stand; bear up against. **5** undergo or suffer (defeat or injury etc.). **6** (of a court etc.) uphold or decide in favour of (an objection etc.). **7** substantiate or corroborate (a statement or charge). **8** maintain or keep (a sound, effort, etc.) going continuously. **9** continue to represent (a part, character, etc.) adequately. □ **sustainable** adj. **sustainedly** /-nɪdlɪ/ adv. **sustainer** n. **sustainment** n. [ME f. AF *sustein-*, OF *so(u)stein-* stressed stem of *so(u)stenir* f. L *sustinēre sustent-* (as SUB-, *tenēre* hold)]

sustenance /ˈsʌstɪnəns/ n. **1 a** nourishment, food. **b** the process of nourishing. **2** a means of support; a livelihood. [ME f. AF *sustenaunce*, OF *so(u)stenance* (as SUSTAIN)]

sustentation /ˌsʌstən'teɪʃ(ə)n/ *n. formal* **1** the support of life. **2** maintenance. [ME f. OF *sustentation* or L *sustentatio* f. *sustentare* frequent. of *sustinēre* SUSTAIN]

susurration /ˌsjuːsə'reɪʃ(ə)n, ˌsuː-/ *n.* (also **susurrus** /sjuː'sʌrəs, suː-/) *literary* a sound of whispering or rustling. [ME f. LL *susurratio* f. L *susurrare*]

sutler /'sʌtlə(r)/ *n. hist.* a person following an army and selling provisions etc. to the soldiers. [obs. Du. *soeteler* f. *soetelen* befoul, perform mean duties, f. Gmc]

Sutra /'suːtrə/ *n.* **1** an aphorism or set of aphorisms in Hindu literature. **2** a narrative part of Buddhist literature. **3** Jainist scripture. [Skr. *sūtra* thread, rule, f. *siv* SEW]

suttee /sʌ'tiː, 'sʌti/ *n.* (also **sati**) (*pl.* **suttees** or **satis**) esp. *hist.* **1** the Hindu practice of a widow immolating herself on her husband's funeral pyre. **2** a widow who undergoes or has undergone this. [Hindi & Urdu f. Skr. *sati* faithful wife f. *sat* good]

suture /'suːtʃə(r)/ *n. & v.* —*n.* **1** *Surgery* **a** the joining of the edges of a wound or incision by stitching. **b** the thread or wire used for this. **2** the seamlike junction of two bones, esp. in the skull. **3** *Bot. & Zool.* a similar junction of parts. —*v.tr. Surgery* stitch up (a wound or incision) with a suture. □□ **sutural** *adj.* **sutured** *adj.* [F *suture* or L *sutura* f. *suere sut-* sew]

suzerain /'suːzərən/ *n.* **1** a feudal overlord. **2** a sovereign or State having some control over another State that is internally autonomous. □□ **suzerainty** *n.* [F, app. f. *sus* above f. L *su(r)sum* upward, after *souverain* SOVEREIGN]

s.v. *abbr.* **1** a side valve. **2** (in a reference) under the word or heading given. [sense 2 f. L *sub voce* (or *verbo*)]

svelte /svelt/ *adj.* slender, lissom, graceful. [F f. It. *svelto*]

SW *abbr.* **1** south-west. **2** south-western.

swab /swɒb/ *n. & v.* (also **swob**) —*n.* **1** a mop or other absorbent device for cleaning or mopping up. **2 a** an absorbent pad used in surgery. **b** a specimen of a possibly morbid secretion taken with a swab for examination. **3** *sl.* a term of contempt for a person. —*v.tr.* (**swabbed, swabbing**) **1** clean with a swab. **2** (foll. by *up*) absorb (moisture) with a swab. [back-form. f. *swabber* f. early mod.Du. *zwabber* f. a Gmc base = 'splash, sway']

swaddle /'swɒd(ə)l/ *v.tr.* swathe (esp. an infant) in garments or bandages etc. □ **swaddling-clothes** narrow bandages formerly wrapped round a newborn child to restrain its movements and quieten it. [ME f. SWATHE + -LE⁴]

swag /swæg/ *n. & v.* —*n.* **1** *sl.* **a** the booty carried off by burglars etc. **b** illicit gains. **2 a** an ornamental festoon of flowers etc. **b** a carved etc. representation of this. **c** drapery of similar appearance. **3** *Austral. & NZ* a traveller's or miner's bundle of personal belongings. —*v.* (**swagged, swagging**) **1** *tr.* arrange (a curtain etc.) in swags. **2** *intr.* **a** hang heavily. **b** sway from side to side. **3** *tr.* cause to sway or sag. [16th c.: prob. f. Scand.]

swage /sweɪdʒ/ *n. & v.* —*n.* **1** a die or stamp for shaping wrought iron etc. by hammering or pressure. **2** a tool for bending metal etc. —*v.tr.* shape with a swage. □ **swage-block** a block with various perforations, grooves, etc., for shaping metal. [F *s(o)uage* decorative groove, of unkn. orig.]

swagger /'swægə(r)/ *v., n., & adj.* —*v.intr.* **1** walk arrogantly or self-importantly. **2** behave arrogantly; be domineering. —*n.* **1** a swaggering gait or manner. **2** swaggering behaviour. **3** a dashing or confident air or way of doing something. **4** smartness. —*adj.* **1** *colloq.* smart or fashionable. **2** (of a coat) cut with a loose flare from the shoulders. □ **swagger stick** a short cane carried by a military officer. □□ **swaggerer** *n.* **swaggeringly** *adv.* [app. f. SWAG *v.* + -ER⁴]

swagman /'swægmæn/ *n.* (*pl.* **-men**) *Austral. & NZ* a tramp carrying a swag (see SWAG *n.* 3).

Swahili /swə'hiːlɪ, swɑː'hiːlɪ/ *n.* (*pl.* same) **1** a member of a Bantu people of Zanzibar and adjacent coasts. **2** their language, used widely as a lingua franca in E. Africa. [Arab. *sawāḥil* pl. of *sāḥil* coast]

swain /sweɪn/ *n.* **1** *archaic* a country youth. **2** *poet.* a young lover or suitor. [ME *swein* f. ON *sveinn* lad = OE *swān* swineherd, f. Gmc]

swallow¹ /'swɒləʊ/ *v. & n.* —*v.* **1** *tr.* cause or allow (food etc.) to pass down the throat. **2** *intr.* perform the muscular movement of the oesophagus required to do this. **3** *tr.* **a** accept meekly; put up with (an affront etc.). **b** accept credulously (an unlikely assertion etc.). **4** *tr.* repress; resist the expression of (a feeling etc.) (*swallow one's pride*). **5** *tr.* articulate (words etc.) indistinctly. **6** *tr.* (often foll. by *up*) engulf or absorb; exhaust; cause to disappear. —*n.* **1** the act of swallowing. **2** an amount swallowed in one action. □ **swallow-hole** *Brit.* = *sink-hole* (see SINK *n.* 6). □□ **swallowable** *adj.* **swallower** *n.* [OE *swelg* (n.), *swelgan* (v.) f. Gmc]

swallow² /'swɒləʊ/ *n.* any of various migratory swift-flying insect-eating birds of the family Hirundinidae, esp. *Hirundo rustica*, with a forked tail and long pointed wings. □ **one swallow does not make a summer** a warning against a hasty inference from one instance. **swallow-dive** a dive with the arms outspread until close to the water. **swallow-tail 1** a deeply forked tail. **2** anything resembling this shape. **3** any butterfly of the family Papilionidae with wings extended at the back to this shape. **swallow-tailed** having a swallow-tail. [OE *swealwe* f. Gmc]

swam *past of* SWIM.

swami /'swɑːmɪ/ *n.* (*pl.* **swamis**) a Hindu male religious teacher. [Hindi *swāmī* master, prince, f. Skr. *svāmin*]

swamp /swɒmp/ *n. & v.* —*n.* a piece of waterlogged ground; a bog or marsh. —*v.* **1 a** *tr.* overwhelm, flood, or soak with water. **b** *intr.* become swamped. **2** *tr.* overwhelm or make invisible etc. with an excess or large amount of something. □□ **swampy** *adj.* (**swampier, swampiest**). [17th c., = dial. *swamp* sunk (14th c.), prob. of Gmc orig.]

swan /swɒn/ *n. & v.* —*n.* **1** a large water-bird of the genus *Cygnus* etc., having a long flexible neck, webbed feet, and in most species snow-white plumage. **2** *literary* a poet. —*v.intr.* (**swanned, swanning**) (usu. foll. by *about, off,* etc.) *colloq.* move or go aimlessly or casually or with a superior air. □ **swan-dive** *US* = *swallow-dive* (see SWALLOW²). **swan-neck** a curved structure shaped like a swan's neck. **Swan of Avon** *literary* Shakespeare. **swan-upping** *Brit.* the annual taking up and marking of Thames swans. □□ **swanlike** *adj. & adv.* [OE f. Gmc]

swank /swæŋk/ *n., v., & adj. colloq.* —*n.* ostentation, swagger, bluff. —*v.intr.* behave with swank; show off. —*adj.* esp. *US* = SWANKY. [19th c.: orig. uncert.]

swankpot /'swæŋkpɒt/ *n. Brit. colloq.* a person behaving with swank.

swanky /'swæŋkɪ/ *adj.* (**swankier, swankiest**) **1** marked by swank; ostentatiously smart or showy. **2** (of a person) inclined to swank; boastful. □□ **swankily** *adv.* **swankiness** *n.*

swannery /'swɒnərɪ/ *n.* (*pl.* **-ies**) a place where swans are bred.

swansdown /'swɒnzdaʊn/ *n.* **1** the fine down of a swan, used in trimmings and esp. in powder-puffs. **2** a kind of thick cotton cloth with a soft nap on one side.

swansong /'swɒnsɒŋ/ *n.* **1** a person's last work or act before death or retirement etc. **2** a song like that fabled to be sung by a dying swan.

swap /swɒp/ *v. & n.* (also **swop**) —*v.tr. & intr.* (**swapped, swapping**) exchange or barter (one thing for another). —*n.* **1** an act of swapping. **2** a

thing suitable for swapping. **3** a thing swapped. □□
swapper n. [ME, orig. = 'hit': prob. imit.]

SWAPO /ˈswɑːpəʊ/ abbr. South West Africa People's
Organization.

Swaraj /swəˈrɑːdʒ/ n. hist. self-government or independence for India. □□ **Swarajist** n. [Skr., =
self-ruling: cf. RAJ]

sward /swɔːd/ n. literary **1** an expanse of short grass.
2 turf. □□ **swarded** adj. [OE sweard skin]

sware /sweə(r)/ archaic past of SWEAR.

swarf /swɔːf/ n. **1** fine chips or filings of stone, metal,
etc. **2** wax etc. removed in cutting a gramophone
record. [ON svarf file-dust]

swarm¹ /swɔːm/ n. & v. —n. **1** a cluster of bees
leaving the hive with the queen to establish a new
colony. **2** a large number of insects or birds moving
in a cluster. **3** a large group of people, esp. moving
over or filling a large area. **4** (in pl.; foll. by of) great
numbers. **5** a group of zoospores. —v.intr. **1** move
in or form a swarm. **2** gather or move in large
numbers. **3** (foll. by with) (of a place) be overrun,
crowded, or infested (was swarming with tourists).
[OE swearm f. Gmc]

swarm² /swɔːm/ v.intr. (foll. by up) & tr. climb (a
rope or tree etc.), esp. in a rush, by clasping or
clinging with the hands and knees etc. [16th c.: orig.
unkn.]

swart /swɔːt/ adj. archaic swarthy, dark-hued. [OE
sweart f. Gmc]

swarthy /ˈswɔːðɪ/ adj. (**swarthier**, **swarthiest**)
dark, dark-complexioned. □□ **swarthily** adv.
swarthiness n. [var. of obs. swarty (as SWART)]

swash¹ /swɒʃ/ v. & n. —v. **1** intr. (of water etc.)
wash about; make the sound of washing or rising
and falling. **2** tr. archaic strike violently. **3** intr.
archaic swagger. —n. the motion or sound of swash-
ing water. [imit.]

swash² /swɒʃ/ adj. **1** inclined obliquely. **2** (of a letter)
having a flourished stroke or strokes. □ **swash-plate**
an inclined disc revolving on an axle and giving
reciprocating motion to a part in contact with it.
[17th c.: orig. unkn.]

swashbuckler /ˈswɒʃˌbʌklə(r)/ n. a swaggering
bully or ruffian. □□ **swashbuckling** adj. & n. [SWASH¹
+ BUCKLER]

swastika /ˈswɒstɪkə/ n. **1** an ancient symbol formed
by an equal-armed cross with each arm continued at
a right angle. **2** this with clockwise continuations as
the symbol of Nazi Germany. [Skr. svastika f. svasti
well-being f. sú good + astí being]

swat /swɒt/ v. & n. —v.tr. (**swatted**, **swatting**) **1**
crush (a fly etc.) with a sharp blow. **2** hit hard and
abruptly. —n. a swatting blow. [17th c. in the sense
'sit down': N.Engl. dial. & US var. of SQUAT]

swatch /swɒtʃ/ n. **1** a sample, esp. of cloth or fabric.
2 a collection of samples. [17th c.: orig. unkn.]

swath /swɔːθ/ n. (also **swathe** /sweɪð/) (pl. **swaths**
/swɔːθs, swɔːðs/ or **swathes**) **1** a ridge of grass or corn
etc. lying after being cut. **2** a space left clear after
the passage of a mower etc. **3** a broad strip. □ **cut a
wide swath** be effective in destruction. [OE swæth,
swathu]

swathe /sweɪð/ v. & n. —v.tr. bind or enclose
in bandages or garments etc. —n. a bandage or
wrapping. [OE swathian]

swatter /ˈswɒtə(r)/ n. an implement for swatting
flies.

sway /sweɪ/ v. & n. —v. **1** intr. & tr. lean or cause to
lean unsteadily in different directions alternately. **2**
intr. oscillate irregularly; waver. **3** tr. **a** control the
motion or direction of. **b** have influence or rule over.
—n. **1** rule, influence, or government (hold sway). **2**
a swaying motion or position. □ **sway-back** an
abnormally hollowed back (esp. of a horse); lordosis.
sway-backed (esp. of a horse) having a sway-back.
[ME: cf. LG swājen be blown to and fro, Du. zwaaien
swing, wave]

swear /sweə(r)/ v. & n. —v. (past **swore** /swɔː(r)/;

past part. **sworn** /swɔːn/) **1** tr. **a** (often foll. by to +
infin. or that + clause) state or promise solemnly or
on oath. **b** take (an oath). **2** tr. colloq. say emphatically; insist (swore he had not seen it). **3** tr.
cause to take an oath (swore them to secrecy). **4** intr.
(often foll. by at) use profane or indecent language,
esp. as an expletive or from anger. **5** tr. (often foll.
by against) make a sworn affirmation of (an offence)
(swear treason against). **6** intr. (foll. by by) **a** appeal
to as a witness in taking an oath (swear by Almighty
God). **b** colloq. have or express great confidence in
(swears by yoga). **7** intr. (foll. by to; usu. in neg.)
admit the certainty of (could not swear to it). **8** intr.
(foll. by at) colloq. (of colours etc.) fail to harmonize
with. —n. a spell of swearing. □ **swear blind** colloq.
affirm emphatically. **swear in** induct into office etc.
by administering an oath. **swear off** colloq. promise
to abstain from (drink etc.). **swear-word** a profane
or indecent word, esp. uttered as an expletive. □□
swearer n. [OE swerian f. Gmc, rel. to ANSWER]

sweat /swet/ n. & v. —n. **1** moisture exuded through
the pores of the skin, esp. from heat or nervousness.
2 a state or period of sweating. **3** colloq. a state of
anxiety (was in a sweat about it). **4** colloq. **a** drudgery,
effort. **b** a laborious task or undertaking. **5** condensed
moisture on a surface. —v. (past and past part.
sweated or US **sweat**) **1** intr. exude sweat; perspire.
2 intr. be terrified, suffering, etc. **3** intr. (of a wall
etc.) exhibit surface moisture. **4** intr. drudge, toil. **5**
tr. heat (meat or vegetables) slowly in fat or water to
extract the juices. **6** tr. emit (blood, gum, etc.) like
sweat. **7** tr. make (a horse, athlete, etc.) sweat by
exercise. **8** tr. **a** cause to drudge or toil. **b** (as **sweated**
adj.) (of goods, workers, or labour) produced by
or subjected to long hours under poor conditions. **9**
tr. subject (hides or tobacco) to fermentation in
manufacturing. □ **by the sweat of one's brow** by
one's own hard work. **no sweat** colloq. there is no
need to worry. **sweat-band** a band of absorbent
material inside a hat or round a wrist etc. to soak up
sweat. **sweat blood** colloq. **1** work strenuously. **2** be
extremely anxious. **sweat gland** Anat. a spiral
tubular gland below the skin secreting sweat.
sweating-sickness an epidemic fever with sweating
prevalent in England in the 15th–16th c. **sweat it
out** colloq. endure a difficult experience to the end.
[ME swet(e), alt. (after swete v. f. OE swǣtan OHG
sweizzen roast) of swote f. OE swāt f. Gmc]

sweater /ˈswetə(r)/ n. **1** a jersey or pullover of a
kind worn before, during, or after exercise, or as
an informal garment. **2** an employer who works
employees hard in poor conditions for low pay.

sweatshirt /ˈswetʃɜːt/ n. a sleeved cotton sweater of
a kind worn by athletes before and after exercise.

sweatshop /ˈswetʃɒp/ n. a workshop where sweated
labour is used.

sweatsuit /ˈswetsuːt, -sjuːt/ n. a suit of a sweatshirt
and loose trousers, as worn by athletes etc.

sweaty /ˈswetɪ/ adj. (**sweatier**, **sweatiest**) **1** sweating; covered with sweat. **2** causing sweat. □□
sweatily adv. **sweatiness** n.

Swede /swiːd/ n. **1 a** a native or national of Sweden.
b a person of Swedish descent. **2** (**swede**) (in full
swede turnip) a large yellow-fleshed turnip, Brassica napus, orig. from Sweden. [MLG & MDu. Swēde,
prob. f. ON Svíthjóth f. Svíar Swedes + thjóth people]

Swedish /ˈswiːdɪʃ/ adj. & n. —adj. of or relating to
Sweden or its people or language. —n. the language
of Sweden.

Sweeney /ˈswiːnɪ/ n. (prec. by the) Brit. sl. the
members of a flying squad. [rhyming sl. f. Sweeney
Todd, a barber who murdered his customers]

sweep /swiːp/ v. & n. —v. (past and past part. **swept**
/swept/) **1** tr. clean or clear (a room or area etc.)
with or as with a broom. **2** intr. (often foll. by up)
clean a room etc. in this way. **3** tr. (often foll. by up)
collect or remove (dirt or litter etc.) by sweeping. **4**
tr. (foll. by aside, away, etc.) **a** push with or as with a

broom. **b** dismiss or reject abruptly (*their objections were swept aside*). **5** *tr.* (foll. by *along*, *down*, etc.) carry or drive along with force. **6** *tr.* (foll. by *off*, *away*, etc.) remove or clear forcefully. **7** *tr.* traverse swiftly or lightly (*the wind swept the hillside*). **8** *tr.* impart a sweeping motion to (*swept his hand across*). **9** *tr.* swiftly cover or affect (*a new fashion swept the country*). **10** *intr.* **a** glide swiftly; speed along with unchecked motion. **b** go majestically. **11** *intr.* (of geographical features etc.) have continuous extent. **12** *tr.* drag (a river-bottom etc.) to search for something. **13** *tr.* (of artillery etc.) include in the line of fire; cover the whole of. **14** *tr.* propel (a barge etc.) with sweeps. —*n.* **1** the act or motion or an instance of sweeping. **2** a curve in the road, a sweeping line of a hill, etc. **3** range or scope (*beyond the sweep of the human mind*). **4** = *chimney-sweep*. **5** a sortie by aircraft. **6** *colloq.* = SWEEPSTAKE. **7** a long oar worked from a barge etc. **8** the sail of a windmill. **9** a long pole mounted as a lever for raising buckets from a well. **10** *Electronics* the movement of a beam across the screen of a cathode-ray tube. □ **make a clean sweep of 1** completely abolish or expel. **2** win all the prizes etc. in (a competition etc.). **sweep away 1** abolish swiftly. **2** (usu. in *passive*) powerfully affect, esp. emotionally. **sweep the board 1** win all the money in a gambling-game. **2** win all possible prizes etc. **sweep-second hand** a second hand on a clock or watch, moving on the same dial as the other hands. **sweep under the carpet** see CARPET. **swept-back** (of an aircraft wing) fixed at an acute angle to the fuselage, inclining outwards towards the rear. **swept-up** (of hair) = UPSWEPT. **swept-wing** (of an aircraft) having swept-back wings. [ME *swepe* (earlier *swōpe*) f. OE *swāpan*]

sweepback /'swiːpbæk/ *n.* the angle at which an aircraft's wing is set back from a position at right angles to the body.

sweeper /'swiːpə(r)/ *n.* **1** a person who cleans by sweeping. **2** a device for sweeping carpets etc. **3** *Football* a defensive player positioned close to the goalkeeper.

sweeping /'swiːpɪŋ/ *adj. & n.* —*adj.* **1** wide in range or effect (*sweeping changes*). **2** taking no account of particular cases or exceptions (*a sweeping statement*). —*n.* (in *pl.*) dirt etc. collected by sweeping. □□ **sweepingly** *adv.* **sweepingness** *n.*

sweepstake /'swiːpsteɪk/ *n.* **1** a form of gambling on horse-races etc. in which all competitors' stakes are paid to the winners. **2** a race with betting of this kind. **3** a prize or prizes won in a sweepstake.

sweet /swiːt/ *adj. & n.* —*adj.* **1** having the pleasant taste characteristic of sugar. **2** smelling pleasant like roses or perfume etc.; fragrant. **3** (of sound etc.) melodious or harmonious. **4 a** not salt, sour, or bitter. **b** fresh, with flavour unimpaired by rottenness. **c** (of water) fresh and readily drinkable. **5** (of wine) having a sweet taste (opp. DRY). **6** highly gratifying or attractive. **7** amiable, pleasant (*has a sweet nature*). **8** *colloq.* (of a person or thing) pretty, charming, endearing. **9** (foll. by *on*) *colloq.* fond of; in love with. —*n.* **1** *Brit.* a small shaped piece of confectionery usu. made with sugar or sweet chocolate. **2** *Brit.* a sweet dish forming a course of a meal. **3** a sweet part of something; sweetness. **4** (in *pl.*) delights, gratification. **5** (esp. as a form of address) sweetheart etc. □ **she's sweet** *Austral. sl.* all is well. **sweet-and-sour** cooked in a sauce containing sugar and vinegar or lemon etc. **sweet basil** see BASIL. **sweet bay** = BAY². **sweet-brier** see BRIER¹. **sweet chestnut** see CHESTNUT. **sweet cicely** a white-flowered aromatic plant, *Myrrhis odorata*. **sweet corn 1** a kind of maize with kernels having a high sugar content. **2** these kernels, eaten as a vegetable when young. **sweet flag** = *sweet rush*. **sweet-gale** see GALE². **sweet pea** any climbing plant of the genus *Lathyrus*, esp. *L. odoratus* with fragrant flowers in many colours. **sweet pepper** see PEPPER. **sweet**

potato 1 a tropical climbing plant, *Ipomoea batatas*, with sweet tuberous roots used for food. **2** the root of this. **sweet rocket** see ROCKET². **sweet rush** (or **sedge**) a kind of sedge with a thick creeping aromatic rootstock used in medicine and confectionery. **sweet sultan** a sweet-scented plant, *Centaurea moschata* or *C. suaveoleus*. **sweet talk** *colloq.* flattery, blandishment. **sweet-talk** *v.tr. colloq.* flatter in order to persuade. **sweet-tempered** amiable. **sweet tooth** a liking for sweet-tasting things. **sweet violet** a sweet-scented violet, *Viola odorata*. **sweet william** a plant, *Dianthus barbatus*, with clusters of vivid fragrant flowers. □□ **sweetish** *adj.* **sweetly** *adv.* [OE *swēte* f. Gmc]

sweetbread /'swiːtbred/ *n.* the pancreas or thymus of an animal, esp. as food.

sweeten /'swiːt(ə)n/ *v.tr. & intr.* **1** make or become sweet or sweeter. **2** make agreeable or less painful. □ **sweeten the pill** see PILL. □□ **sweetening** *n.*

sweetener /'swiːtənə(r)/ *n.* **1** a substance used to sweeten food or drink. **2** *colloq.* a bribe or inducement.

sweetheart /'swiːthɑːt/ *n.* **1** a lover or darling. **2** a term of endearment (esp. as a form of address). □ **sweetheart agreement** (or **deal**) *colloq.* an industrial agreement reached privately by employers and trade unions in their own interests.

sweetie /'swiːtɪ/ *n. colloq.* **1** *Brit.* a sweet. **2** (also **sweetie-pie**) a term of endearment (esp. as a form of address).

sweeting /'swiːtɪŋ/ *n.* **1** a sweet-flavoured variety of apple. **2** *archaic* darling.

sweetmeal /'swiːtmiːl/ *n.* **1** sweetened wholemeal. **2** a sweetmeal biscuit.

sweetmeat /'swiːtmiːt/ *n.* **1** a sweet (see SWEET *n.* 1). **2** a small fancy cake.

sweetness /'swiːtnɪs/ *n.* the quality of being sweet; fragrance, melodiousness, etc. □ **sweetness and light** a display of (esp. uncharacteristic) mildness and reason.

sweetshop /'swiːtʃɒp/ *n. Brit.* a shop selling sweets as its main item.

sweetsop /'swiːtsɒp/ *n.* **1** a tropical American evergreen shrub, *Annona squamosa*. **2** the fruit of this, having a green rind and a sweet pulp.

swell /swel/ *v.*, *n.*, & *adj.* —*v.* (*past part.* **swollen** /'swəʊlən/ or **swelled**) **1** *intr.* & *tr.* grow or cause to grow bigger or louder or more intense; expand; increase in force or intensity. **2** *intr.* (often foll. by *up*) & *tr.* rise or raise up from the surrounding surface. **3** *intr.* (foll. by *out*) bulge. **4** *intr.* (of the heart as the seat of emotion) feel full of joy, pride, relief, etc. **5** *intr.* (foll. by *with*) be hardly able to restrain (pride etc.). —*n.* **1** an act or the state of swelling. **2** the heaving of the sea with waves that do not break, e.g. after a storm. **3 a** a crescendo. **b** a mechanism in an organ etc. for obtaining a crescendo or diminuendo. **4** *colloq.* a person of distinction or of dashing or fashionable appearance. **5** a protuberant part. —*adj.* **1** esp. *US colloq.* fine, splendid, excellent. **2** *colloq.* smart, fashionable. □ **swell-box** *Mus.* a box in which organ-pipes are enclosed, with a shutter for controlling the sound-level. **swelled** (or **swollen**) **head** *colloq.* conceit. **swell-organ** *Mus.* a section of an organ with pipes in a swell-box. □□ **swellish** *adj.* [OE *swellan* f. Gmc]

swelling /'swelɪŋ/ *n.* an abnormal protuberance on or in the body.

swelter /'sweltə(r)/ *v. & n.* —*v.intr.* (of the atmosphere, or a person etc. suffering from it) be uncomfortably hot. —*n.* a sweltering atmosphere or condition. □□ **swelteringly** *adv.* [base of (now dial.) *swelt* f. OE *sweltan* perish f. Gmc]

swept *past* and *past part.* of SWEEP.

swerve /swɜːv/ *v. & n.* —*v.intr. & tr.* change or cause to change direction, esp. abruptly. —*n.* **1** a swerving movement. **2** divergence from a course. □□

swerveless *adj.* **swerver** *n.* [ME, repr. OE *sweorfan* SCOUR[1]]

SWG *abbr.* standard wire gauge.

swift /swɪft/ *adj.*, *adv.*, & *n.* —*adj.* **1** quick; rapid; soon coming or passing. **2** speedy, prompt (*a swift response*; *was swift to act*). —*adv.* (archaic except in *comb.*) swiftly (*swift-moving*). —*n.* **1** any swift-flying insect-eating bird of the family Apodidae, with long wings and a superficial resemblance to a swallow. **2** a revolving frame for winding yarn etc. from. □□ **swiftly** *adv.* **swiftness** *n.* [OE, rel. to *swīfan* move in a course]

swiftie /ˈswɪftɪ/ *n. Austral. sl.* **1** a deceptive trick. **2** a person who acts or thinks quickly.

swiftlet /ˈswɪftlɪt/ *n.* a small swift of the genus *Collocalia.*

swig /swɪg/ *v.* & *n.* —*v.tr.* & *intr.* (**swigged**, **swigging**) *colloq.* drink in large draughts. —*n.* a swallow of drink, esp. a large amount. □□ **swigger** *n.* [16th c., orig. as noun in obs. sense 'liquor': orig. unkn.]

swill /swɪl/ *v.* & *n.* —*v.* **1** *tr.* (often foll. by *out*) rinse or flush; pour water over or through. **2** *tr.* & *intr.* drink greedily. —*n.* **1** an act of rinsing. **2** mainly liquid refuse as pig-food. **3** inferior liquor. □□ **swiller** *n.* [OE *swillan*, *swilian*, of unkn. orig.]

swim /swɪm/ *v.* & *n.* —*v.* (**swimming**; *past* **swam** /swæm/; *past part.* **swum** /swʌm/) **1** *intr.* propel the body through water by working the arms and legs, or (of a fish) the fins and tail. **2** *tr.* **a** traverse (a stretch of water or its distance) by swimming. **b** compete in (a race) by swimming. **c** use (a particular stroke) in swimming. **3** *intr.* float on or at the surface of a liquid (*bubbles swimming on the surface*). **4** *intr.* appear to undulate or reel or whirl. **5** *intr.* have a dizzy effect or sensation (*my head swam*). **6** *intr.* (foll. by *in*, *with*) be flooded. —*n.* **1** a spell or the act of swimming. **2** a deep pool frequented by fish in a river. □ **in the swim** involved in or acquainted with what is going on. **swim-bladder** a gas-filled sac in fishes used to maintain buoyancy. **swimming-bath** (or **-pool**) an artificial indoor or outdoor pool for swimming. **swimming-costume** *Brit.* a garment worn for swimming. □□ **swimmable** *adj.* **swimmer** *n.* [OE *swimman* f. Gmc]

swimmeret /ˈswɪmərɛt/ *n.* a swimming-foot in crustaceans.

swimmingly /ˈswɪmɪŋlɪ/ *adv.* with easy and un-obstructed progress.

swimsuit /ˈswɪmsuːt, -sjuːt/ *n.* a one-piece swimming-costume worn by women. □□ **swimsuited** *adj.*

swimwear /ˈswɪmwɛə(r)/ *n.* clothing worn for swimming.

swindle /ˈswɪnd(ə)l/ *v.* & *n.* —*v.tr.* (often foll. by *out of*) **1** cheat (a person) of money, possessions, etc. (*was swindled out of all his savings*). **2** cheat a person of (money etc.) (*swindled all his savings out of him*). —*n.* **1** an act of swindling. **2** a person or thing represented as what it is not. **3** a fraudulent scheme. □□ **swindler** *n.* [back-form. f. *swindler* f. G *Schwindler* extravagant maker of schemes, swindler, f. *schwindeln* be dizzy]

swine /swaɪn/ *n.* (*pl.* same) **1** *formal* or *US* a pig. **2** *colloq.* (*pl.* **swine** or **swines**) **a** a term of contempt or disgust for a person. **b** a very unpleasant or difficult thing. □ **swine fever** an intestinal virus disease of pigs. □□ **swinish** *adj.* (esp. in sense 2). **swinishly** *adv.* **swinishness** *n.* [OE *swīn* f. Gmc]

swineherd /ˈswaɪnhɜːd/ *n.* a person who tends pigs.

swing /swɪŋ/ *v.* & *n.* —*v.* (*past* and *past part.* **swung** /swʌŋ/) **1** *intr.* & *tr.* move or cause to move with a to-and-fro or curving motion, as of an object attached at one end and hanging free at the other. **2** *intr.* & *tr.* **a** sway. **b** hang so as to be free to sway. **c** oscillate or cause to oscillate. **3** *intr.* & *tr.* revolve or cause to revolve. **4** *intr.* move by gripping something and leaping etc. (*swung from tree to tree*). **5** *intr.* go with

a swinging gait (*swung out of the room*). **6** *intr.* (foll. by *round*) move round to the opposite direction. **7** *intr.* change from one opinion or mood to another. **8** *intr.* (foll. by *at*) attempt to hit or punch. **9 a** *intr.* (also **swing it**) play music with a swing rhythm. **b** *tr.* play (a tune) with swing. **10** *intr. colloq.* **a** be lively or up to date; enjoy oneself. **b** be promiscuous. **11** *intr. colloq.* (of a party etc.) be lively, successful, etc. **12** *tr.* have a decisive influence on (esp. voting etc.). **13** *tr. colloq.* deal with or achieve; manage. **14** *intr. colloq.* be executed by hanging. **15** *Cricket* **a** *intr.* (of the ball) deviate from a straight course in the air. **b** *tr.* cause (the ball) to do this. —*n.* **1** the act or an instance of swinging. **2** the motion of swinging. **3** the extent of swinging. **4** a swinging or smooth gait or rhythm or action. **5 a** a seat slung by ropes or chains etc. for swinging on or in. **b** a spell of swinging on this. **6** an easy but vigorous continued action. **7 a** jazz or dance music with an easy flowing rhythm. **b** the rhythmic feeling or drive of this music. **8** a discernible change in opinion, esp. the amount by which votes or points scored etc. change from one side to another. □**swing-boat** a boat-shaped swing at fairs. **swing-bridge** a bridge that can be swung to one side to allow the passage of ships. **swing-door** a door able to open in either direction and close itself when released. **swing the lead** *Brit. colloq.* malinger; shirk one's duty. **swings and roundabouts** a situation affording no eventual gain or loss (from the phr. *lose on the swings what you make on the roundabouts*). **swing shift** *US* a work shift from afternoon to late evening. **swing-wing** an aircraft wing that can move from a right-angled to a swept-back position. **swung dash** a dash (~) with alternate curves. □□ **swinger** *n.* (esp. in sense 10 of *v.*). [OE *swingan* to beat f. Gmc]

swinge /swɪndʒ/ *v.tr.* (**swingeing**) *archaic* strike hard; beat. [alt. f. ME *swenge* f. OE *swengan* shake, shatter, f. Gmc]

swingeing /ˈswɪndʒɪŋ/ *adj.* esp. *Brit.* **1** (of a blow) forcible. **2** huge or far-reaching, esp. in severity (*swingeing economies*). □□ **swingeingly** *adv.*

swinging /ˈswɪŋɪŋ/ *adj.* **1** (of gait, melody, etc.) vigorously rhythmical. **2** *colloq.* **a** lively; up to date; excellent. **b** promiscuous. □□ **swingingly** *adv.*

swingle /ˈswɪŋg(ə)l/ *n.* & *v.* —*n.* **1** a wooden instrument for beating flax and removing the woody parts from it. **2** the swinging part of a flail. —*v.tr.* clean (flax) with a swingle. [ME f. MDu. *swinghel* (as SWING, -LE[1])]

swingletree /ˈswɪŋg(ə)l,triː/ *n.* a crossbar pivoted in the middle, to which the traces are attached in a cart, plough, etc.

swingy /ˈswɪŋɪ/ *adj.* (**swingier**, **swingiest**) **1** (of music) characterized by swing (see SWING *n.* 7). **2** (of a skirt or dress) designed to swing with body movement.

swipe /swaɪp/ *v.* & *n. colloq.* —*v.* **1** *tr.* & (often foll. by *at*) *intr.* hit hard and recklessly. **2** *tr.* steal. —*n.* a reckless hard hit or attempted hit. □□ **swiper** *n.* [perh. var. of SWEEP]

swipple /ˈswɪp(ə)l/ *n.* the swingle of a flail. [ME, prob. formed as SWEEP + -LE[1]]

swirl /swɜːl/ *v.* & *n.* —*v.intr.* & *tr.* move or flow or carry along with a whirling motion. —*n.* **1** a swirling motion of or in water, air, etc. **2** the act of swirling. **3** a twist or curl, esp. as part of a pattern or design. □□ **swirly** *adj.* [ME (orig. as noun): orig. Sc., perh. of LG or Du. orig.]

swish /swɪʃ/ *v.*, *n.*, & *adj.* —*v.* **1** *tr.* swing (a scythe or stick etc.) audibly through the air, grass, etc. **2** *intr.* move with or make a swishing sound. **3** *tr.* (foll. by *off*) cut (a flower etc.) in this way. —*n.* a swishing action or sound. —*adj. colloq.* smart, fashionable. □□ **swishy** *adj.* [imit.]

Swiss /swɪs/ *adj.* & *n.* —*adj.* of or relating to Switzerland in Western Europe or its people. —*n.* (*pl.* same) **1** a native or national of Switzerland. **2** a person of Swiss descent. □**Swiss chard** = CHARD. **Swiss cheese plant** a climbing house-plant, *Monstera deliciosa*, with aerial roots and holes in the leaves (as in some Swiss cheeses). **Swiss roll** a cylindrical cake with a spiral cross-section, made from a flat piece of sponge cake spread with jam etc. and rolled up. [F *Suisse* f. MHG *Swīz*]

switch /swɪtʃ/ *n. & v.* —*n.* **1** a device for making and breaking the connection in an electric circuit. **2 a** a transfer, change-over, or deviation. **b** an exchange. **3** a slender flexible shoot cut from a tree. **4** a light tapering rod. **5** *US* a device at the junction of railway tracks for transferring a train from one track to another; = POINT *n.* 17. **6** a tress of false or detached hair tied at one end used in hairdressing. —*v.* **1** *tr.* (foll. by *on, off*) turn (an electrical device) on or off. **2** *intr.* change or transfer position, subject, etc. **3** *tr.* change or transfer. **4** *tr.* reverse the positions of; exchange (*switched chairs*). **5** *tr.* swing or snatch (a thing) suddenly (*switched it out of my hand*). **6** *tr.* beat or flick with a switch. □**switchblade** a pocket knife with the blade released by a spring. **switched-on** *colloq.* **1** up to date; aware of what is going on. **2** excited; under the influence of drugs. **switch off** *colloq.* cease to pay attention. **switch over** change or exchange. **switch-over** *n.* a change or exchange. □□**switcher** *n.* [earlier *swits*, *switz*, prob. f. LG]

switchback /ˈswɪtʃbæk/ *n.* **1** *Brit.* a railway at a fair etc., in which the train's ascents are effected by the momentum of its previous descents. **2** (often *attrib.*) a railway or road with alternate sharp ascents and descents.

switchboard /ˈswɪtʃbɔːd/ *n.* an apparatus for varying connections between electric circuits, esp. in telephony.

swither /ˈswɪðə(r)/ *v. & n.* *Sc.* —*v.intr.* hesitate; be uncertain. —*n.* doubt or uncertainty. [16th c.: orig. unkn.]

swivel /ˈswɪv(ə)l/ *n. & v.* —*n.* a coupling between two parts enabling one to revolve without turning the other. —*v.tr. & intr.* (**swivelled, swivelling**; *US* **swiveled, swiveling**) turn on or as on a swivel. □**swivel chair** a chair with a seat able to be turned horizontally. [ME f. weak grade *swif-* of OE *swīfan* sweep + -LE¹: cf. SWIFT]

swizz /swɪz/ *n.* (also **swiz**) (*pl.* **swizzes**) *Brit. colloq.* **1** something unfair or disappointing. **2** a swindle. [abbr. of SWIZZLE²]

swizzle¹ /ˈswɪz(ə)l/ *n. & v. colloq.* —*n.* a mixed alcoholic drink esp. of rum or gin and bitters made frothy. —*v.tr.* stir with a swizzle-stick. □**swizzle-stick** a stick used for frothing or flattening drinks. [19th c.: orig. unkn.]

swizzle² /ˈswɪz(ə)l/ *n. Brit. colloq.* = SWIZZ. [20th c.: prob. alt. of SWINDLE]

swob var. of SWAB.

swollen *past part.* of SWELL.

swoon /swuːn/ *v. & n. literary* —*v.intr.* faint; fall into a fainting-fit. —*n.* an occurrence of fainting. [ME *swoune* perh. back-form. f. *swogning* (n.) f. *iswogen* f. OE *geswogen* overcome]

swoop /swuːp/ *v. & n.* —*v.* **1** *intr.* (often foll. by *down*) descend rapidly like a bird of prey. **2** *intr.* (often foll. by *on*) make a sudden attack from a distance. **3** *tr.* (often foll. by *up*) *colloq.* snatch the whole of at one swoop. —*n.* a swooping or snatching movement or action. □**at** (or **in**) **one fell swoop** see FELL⁴. [perh. dial. var. of obs. *swōpe* f. OE *swāpan*: see SWEEP]

swoosh /swuʃ/ *n. & v.* —*n.* the noise of a sudden rush of liquid, air, etc. —*v.intr.* move with this noise. [imit.]

swop var. of SWAP.

sword /sɔːd/ *n.* **1** a weapon usu. of metal with a long blade and hilt with a handguard, used esp. for thrusting or striking, and often worn as part of ceremonial dress. **2** (prec. by *the*) **a** war. **b** military

power. □**put to the sword** kill, esp. in war. **sword-bearer** an official carrying the sovereign's etc. sword on a formal occasion. **sword dance** a dance in which the performers brandish swords or step about swords laid on the ground. **sword grass** a grass, *Scirpus americanus*, with swordlike leaves. **sword knot** a ribbon or tassel attached to a sword-hilt orig. for securing it to the wrist. **sword lily** = GLADIOLUS. **sword of Damocles** /ˈdæməˌkliːz/ an imminent danger (from *Damokles*, flatterer of Dionysius of Syracuse (4th c. BC) made to feast while a sword hung by a hair over him). **the sword of justice** judicial authority. **Sword of State** a sword borne before the sovereign on State occasions. **sword-swallower** a person ostensibly or actually swallowing sword blades as entertainment. □□ **swordlike** *adj.* [OE *sw(e)ord* f. Gmc]

swordbill /ˈsɔːdbɪl/ *n.* a long-billed humming-bird, *Ensifera ensifera*.

swordfish /ˈsɔːdfɪʃ/ *n.* a large marine fish, *Xiphias gladius*, with an extended swordlike upper jaw.

swordplay /ˈsɔːdpleɪ/ *n.* **1** fencing. **2** repartee; cut-and-thrust argument.

swordsman /ˈsɔːdzmən/ *n.* (*pl.* -**men**) a person of (usu. specified) skill with a sword. □□ **swordsmanship** *n.*

swordstick /ˈsɔːdstɪk/ *n.* a hollow walking-stick containing a blade that can be used as a sword.

swordtail /ˈsɔːdteɪl/ *n.* **1** a tropical fish, *Xiphophorus helleri*, with a long tail. **2** = *horseshoe crab*.

swore *past* of SWEAR.

sworn /swɔːn/ **1** *past part.* of SWEAR. **2** *adj.* bound by or as by an oath (*sworn enemies*).

swot /swɒt/ *v. & n. Brit. colloq.* —*v.* (**swotted, swotting**) **1** *intr.* study assiduously. **2** *tr.* (often foll. by *up*) study (a subject) hard or hurriedly. —*n.* **1** a person who swots. **2 a** hard study. **b** a thing that requires this. [dial. var. of SWEAT]

swum *past part.* of SWIM.

swung *past* and *past part.* of SWING.

swy /swaɪ/ *n. Austral.* two-up. [G *zwei* two]

SY *abbr.* steam yacht.

sybarite /ˈsɪbəˌraɪt/ *n. & adj.* —*n.* a person who is self-indulgent or devoted to sensuous luxury. —*adj.* fond of luxury or sensuousness. □□ **sybaritic** /-ˈrɪtɪk/ *adj.* **sybaritical** /-ˈrɪtɪk(ə)l/ *adj.* **sybaritically** /-ˈrɪtɪkəlɪ/ *adv.* **sybaritism** *n.* [orig. an inhabitant of Sybaris in S. Italy, noted for luxury, f. L *sybarita* f. Gk *subaritēs*]

sycamine /ˈsɪkəˌmaɪn, -mɪn/ *n. Bibl.* the black mulberry tree, *Morus nigra* (see Luke 17:6; in modern versions translated as 'mulberry tree'). [L *sycaminus* f. Gk *sukaminos* mulberry-tree f. Heb. *šiḳmāh* sycamore, assim. to Gk *sukon* fig]

sycamore /ˈsɪkəˌmɔː(r)/ *n.* **1** (in full **sycamore maple**) **a** a large maple, *Acer pseudoplatanus*, with winged seeds, grown for its shade and timber. **b** its wood. **2** *US* the plane-tree or its wood. **3** *Bibl.* a fig-tree, *Ficus sycomorus*, growing in Egypt, Syria, etc. [var. of SYCOMORE]

syce /saɪs/ *n.* (also **sice**) *Anglo-Ind.* a groom. [Hind. f. Arab. *sā'is*, *sāyis*]

sycomore /ˈsɪkəˌmɔː(r)/ *n. Bot.* = SYCAMORE 3. [ME f. OF *sic(h)amor* f. L *sycomorus* f. Gk *sukomoros* f. *sukon* fig + *moron* mulberry]

syconium /saɪˈkəʊnɪəm/ *n.* (*pl.* **syconia**) *Bot.* a fleshy hollow receptacle developing into a multiple fruit as in the fig. [mod.L f. Gk *sukon* fig]

sycophant /ˈsɪkəˌfænt/ *n.* a servile flatterer; a toady. □□ **sycophancy** *n.* **sycophantic** /-ˈfæntɪk/ *adj.* **sycophantically** /-ˈfæntɪkəlɪ/ *adv.* [F *sycophante* or L *sycophanta* f. Gk *sukophantēs* informer f. *sukon* fig + *phainō* show: the reason for the name is uncert., and association with informing against the illegal exportation of figs from ancient Athens (recorded by Plutarch) cannot be substantiated]

sycosis /saɪˈkəʊsɪs/ *n.* a skin-disease of the bearded

part of the face with inflammation of the hair-follicles. [mod.L f. Gk *sukōsis* f. *sukon* fig: orig. of a figlike ulcer]

syenite /'saɪə,naɪt/ *n.* a grey crystalline rock of feldspar and hornblende with or without quartz. □□ **syenitic** /-'nɪtɪk/ *adj.* [F *syénite* f. L *Syenites* (*lapis*) (stone) of *Syene* in Egypt]

syl- /sɪl/ *prefix* assim. form of SYN- before *l*.

syllabary /'sɪləbərɪ/ *n.* (*pl.* -ies) a list of characters representing syllables and (in some languages or stages of writing) serving the purpose of an alphabet. [mod.L *syllabarium* (as SYLLABLE)]

syllabi *pl.* of SYLLABUS.

syllabic /sɪ'læbɪk/ *adj.* **1** of, relating to, or based on syllables. **2** *Prosody* based on the number of syllables. **3** (of a symbol) representing a whole syllable. **4** articulated in syllables. □□ **syllabically** *adv.* **syllabicity** /-'bɪsɪtɪ/ *n.* [F *syllabique* or LL *syllabicus* f. Gk *sullabikos* (as SYLLABLE)]

syllabication /,sɪlæbɪ'keɪʃ(ə)n/ *n.* (also **syllabification**) (/-fɪ'keɪʃ(ə)n/) division into or articulation by syllables. □□ **syllabify** *v.tr.* (-ies, -ied). [med.L *syllabicatio* f. *syllabicare* f. L *syllaba*: see SYLLABLE]

syllabize /'sɪlə,baɪz/ *v.tr.* (also -ise) divide into or articulate by syllables. [med.L *syllabizare* f. Gk *sullabizō* (as SYLLABLE)]

syllable /'sɪləb(ə)l/ *n. & v.* —*n.* **1** a unit of pronunciation uttered without interruption, forming the whole or a part of a word and usu. having one vowel sound often with a consonant or consonants before or after: there are two syllables in *water* and three in *inferno.* **2** a character or characters representing a syllable. **3** (usu. with *neg.*) the least amount of speech or writing (*did not utter a syllable*). —*v.tr.* pronounce by syllables; articulate distinctly. □**in words of one syllable** expressed plainly or bluntly. □□ **syllabled** *adj.* (also in *comb.*). [ME f. AF *sillable* f. OF *sillabe* f. L *syllaba* f. Gk *sullabē* (as SYN-, *lambanō* take)]

syllabub /'sɪlə,bʌb/ *n.* (also **sillabub**) a dessert made of cream or milk flavoured, sweetened, and whipped to thicken it. [16th c.: orig. unkn.]

syllabus /'sɪləbəs/ *n.* (*pl.* **syllabuses** or **syllabi** /-,baɪ/) **1 a** the programme or outline of a course of study, teaching, etc. **b** a statement of the requirements for a particular examination. **2** *RC Ch.* a summary of points decided by papal decree regarding heretical doctrines or practices. [mod.L, orig. a misreading of L *sittybas* accus. pl. of *sittyba* f. Gk *sittuba* title-slip or label]

syllepsis /sɪ'lepsɪs/ *n.* (*pl.* **syllepses** /-siːz/) a figure of speech in which a word is applied to two others in different senses (e.g. *caught the train and a bad cold*) or to two others of which it grammatically suits one only (e.g. *neither they nor it is working*) (cf. ZEUGMA). □□ **sylleptic** *adj.* **sylleptically** *adv.* [LL f. Gk *sullēpsis* taking together f. *sullambanō*: see SYLLABLE]

syllogism /'sɪlə,dʒɪz(ə)m/ *n.* **1** a form of reasoning in which a conclusion is drawn from two given or assumed propositions (premisses): a common or middle term is present in the two premisses but not in the conclusion, which may be invalid (e.g. *all trains are long; some buses are long; therefore some buses are trains*: the common term is *long*). **2** deductive reasoning as distinct from induction. □□ **syllogistic** /-'dʒɪstɪk/ *adj.* **syllogistically** /-'dʒɪstɪkəlɪ/ *adv.* [ME f. OF *silogisme* or L *syllogismus* f. Gk *sullogismos* f. *sullogizomai* (as SYN-, *logizomai* to reason f. *logos* reason)]

syllogize /'sɪlə,dʒaɪz/ *v.* (also -ise) **1** *intr.* use syllogisms. **2** *tr.* put (facts or an argument) in the form of syllogism. [ME f. OF *sillogiser* or LL *syllogizare* f. Gk *sullogizomai* (as SYLLOGISM)]

sylph /sɪlf/ *n.* **1** an elemental spirit of the air. **2** a slender graceful woman or girl. **3** any humming-bird of the genus *Aglaiocercus* with a long forked tail. □□

sylphlike *adj.* [mod.L *sylphes,* G *Sylphen* (pl.), perh. based on L *sylvestris* of the woods + *nympha* nymph]

sylva /'sɪlvə/ *n.* (also **silva**) (*pl.* **sylvae** /-viː/ or **sylvas**) **1** the trees of a region, epoch, or environment. **2** a treatise on or a list of such trees. [L *silva* a wood]

sylvan /'sɪlv(ə)n/ *adj.* (also **silvan**) **1 a** of the woods. **b** having woods; wooded. **2** rural. [F *sylvain* (obs. *silvain*) or L *Silvanus* woodland deity f. *silva* a wood]

sylviculture var. of SILVICULTURE.

sym- /sɪm/ *prefix* assim. form of SYN- before *b, m, p*.

symbiont /'sɪmbɪənt/ *n.* an organism living in symbiosis. [Gk *sumbiōn -ountos* part. of *sumbioō* live together (as SYMBIOSIS)]

symbiosis /,sɪmbaɪ'əʊsɪs, ,sɪmbɪ-/ *n.* (*pl.* **symbioses** /-siːz/) **1 a** an interaction between two different organisms living in close physical association, usu. to the advantage of both (cf. ANTIBIOSIS). **b** an instance of this. **2 a** a mutually advantageous association or relationship between persons. **b** an instance of this. □□ **symbiotic** /-'ɒtɪk/ *adj.* **symbiotically** /-'ɒtɪkəlɪ/ *adv.* [mod.L f. Gk *sumbiōsis* a living together f. *sumbioō* live together, *sumbios* companion (as SYN-, *bios* life)]

symbol /'sɪmb(ə)l/ *n. & v.* —*n.* **1** a thing conventionally regarded as typifying, representing, or recalling something, esp. an idea or quality (*white is a symbol of purity*). **2** a mark or character taken as the conventional sign of some object, idea, function, or process, e.g. the letters standing for the chemical elements or the characters in musical notation. —*v.tr.* (**symbolled, symbolling;** *US* **symboled, symboling**) symbolize. □□ **symbology** /-'bɒlədʒɪ/ *n.* [ME f. L *symbolum* f. Gk *sumbolon* mark, token (as SYN-, *ballō* throw)]

symbolic /sɪm'bɒlɪk/ *adj.* (also **symbolical** /-'bɒlɪk(ə)l/) **1** of or serving as a symbol. **2** involving the use of symbols or symbolism. □**symbolic logic** the use of symbols to denote propositions etc. in order to assist reasoning. □□ **symbolically** *adv.* [F *symbolique* or LL *symbolicus* f. Gk *sumbolikos*]

symbolism /'sɪmbə,lɪz(ə)m/ *n.* **1 a** the use of symbols to represent ideas. **b** symbols collectively. **2** an artistic and poetic movement or style using symbols and indirect suggestion to express ideas, emotions, etc. □□ **symbolist** *n.* **symbolistic** /-'lɪstɪk/ *adj.*

symbolize /'sɪmbə,laɪz/ *v.tr.* (also -ise) **1** be a symbol of. **2** represent by means of symbols. □□ **symbolization** /-'zeɪʃ(ə)n/ *n.* [F *symboliser* f. *symbole* SYMBOL]

symmetry /'sɪmɪtrɪ/ *n.* (*pl.* -ies) **1 a** correct proportion of the parts of a thing; balance, harmony. **b** beauty resulting from this. **2 a** a structure that allows an object to be divided into parts of an equal shape and size and similar position to the point or line or plane of division. **b** the possession of such a structure. **c** approximation to such a structure. **3** the repetition of exactly similar parts facing each other or a centre. **4** *Bot.* the possession by a flower of sepals and petals and stamens and pistils in the same number or multiples of the same number. □□ **symmetric** /sɪ'metrɪk/ *adj.* **symmetrical** /-'metrɪk(ə)l/ *adj.* **symmetrically** /-'metrɪkəlɪ/ *adv.* **symmetrize** *v.tr.* (also -ise). [obs. F *symmétrie* or L *summetria* f. Gk (as SYN-, *metron* measure)]

sympathectomy /,sɪmpə'θektəmɪ/ *n.* (*pl.* -ies) the surgical removal of a sympathetic ganglion etc.

sympathetic /,sɪmpə'θetɪk/ *adj. & n.* —*adj.* **1** of, showing, or expressing sympathy. **2** due to sympathy. **3** likeable or capable of evoking sympathy. **4** (of a person) friendly and cooperative. **5** (foll. by *to*) inclined to favour (a proposal etc.) (*was most sympathetic to the idea*). **6** (of a landscape etc.) that touches the feelings by association etc. **7** (of a pain etc.) caused by a pain or injury to someone else or in another part of the body. **8** (of a sound, resonance, or string) sounding by a vibration communicated from another vibrating object. **9 a** designating the part of the nervous system consisting of nerves leaving the thoracic and lumbar regions of the spinal cord and connecting with the nerve cells in or near the viscera (see PARASYMPATHETIC). **b** (of a nerve or ganglion) belonging to this system. —*n.* **1** a sympathetic nerve. **2** the sympathetic system. □**sympathetic magic** a type of magic that seeks to achieve an effect by performing an associated action or using an associated thing. □□**sympathetically** *adv.* [SYMPATHY, after *pathetic*]

sympathize /ˈsɪmpəˌθaɪz/ *v.intr.* (also **-ise**) (often foll. by *with*) **1** feel or express sympathy; share a feeling or opinion. **2** agree with a sentiment or opinion. □□**sympathizer** *n.* [F *sympathiser* (as SYMPATHY)]

sympathy /ˈsɪmpəθɪ/ *n.* (*pl.* **-ies**) **1 a** the state of being simultaneously affected with the same feeling as another. **b** the capacity for this. **2** (often foll. by *with*) **a** the act of sharing or tendency to share (with a person etc.) in an emotion or sensation or condition of another person or thing. **b** (in *sing.* or *pl.*) compassion or commiseration; condolences. **3** (often foll. by *for*) a favourable attitude; approval. **4** (in *sing.* or *pl.*; often foll. by *with*) agreement (with a person etc.) in opinion or desire. **5** (*attrib.*) in support of another cause (*sympathy strike*). □**in sympathy** (often foll. by *with*) **1** having or showing or resulting from sympathy (with another). **2** by way of sympathetic action (*working to rule in sympathy*). [L *sympathia* f. Gk *sumpatheia* (as SYN-, *pathēs* f. *pathos* feeling)]

sympetalous /sɪmˈpetələs/ *adj. Bot.* having the petals united.

symphonic /sɪmˈfɒnɪk/ *adj.* (of music) relating to or having the form or character of a symphony. □**symphonic poem** an extended orchestral piece, usu. in one movement, on a descriptive or rhapsodic theme. □□**symphonically** *adv.*

symphonist /ˈsɪmfənɪst/ *n.* a composer of symphonies.

symphony /ˈsɪmfənɪ/ *n.* (*pl.* **-ies**) **1** an elaborate composition usu. for full orchestra, and in several movements with one or more in sonata form. **2** an interlude for orchestra alone in a large-scale vocal work. **3** = *symphony orchestra*. □**symphony orchestra** a large orchestra suitable for playing symphonies etc. [ME, = harmony of sound, f. OF *symphonie* f. L *symphonia* f. Gk *sumphōnia* (as SYN-, *-phōnos* f. *phōnē* sound)]

symphyllous /sɪmˈfɪləs/ *adj. Bot.* having the leaves united. [SYN- + Gk *phullon* leaf]

symphysis /ˈsɪmfɪsɪs/ *n.* (*pl.* **symphyses** /-ˌsiːz/) **1** the process of growing together. **2 a** a union between two bones esp. in the median plane of the body. **b** the place or line of this. □□**symphyseal** /-ˈfɪzɪəl/ *adj.* **symphysial** /-ˈfɪzɪəl/ *adj.* [mod.L f. Gk *sumphusis* (as SYN-, *phusis* growth)]

sympodium /sɪmˈpəʊdɪəm/ *n.* (*pl.* **sympodia** /-dɪə/) *Bot.* the apparent main axis or stem of a vine etc., made up of successive secondary axes. □□**sympodial** *adj.* [mod.L (as SYN-, Gk *pous podos* foot)]

symposium /sɪmˈpəʊzɪəm/ *n.* (*pl.* **symposia** /-zɪə/) **1 a** a conference or meeting to discuss a particular subject. **b** a collection of essays or papers for this purpose. **2** a philosophical or other friendly discussion. **3** a drinking-party, esp. of the ancient Greeks with conversation etc. after a banquet. [L f. Gk *sumposion* in sense 3 (as SYN-, *-potēs* drinker)]

symptom /ˈsɪmptəm/ *n.* **1** *Med.* a change in the physical or mental condition of a person, regarded as evidence of a disease (cf. SIGN 5). **2** a sign of the existence of something. [ME *synthoma* f. med.L *sinthoma*, & f. LL *symptoma* f. Gk *sumptōma -atos* chance, symptom, f. *sumpiptō* happen (as SYN-, *piptō* fall)]

symptomatic /ˌsɪmptəˈmætɪk/ *adj.* serving as a symptom. □□**symptomatically** *adv.*

symptomatology /ˌsɪmptəməˈtɒlədʒɪ/ *n.* the branch of medicine concerned with the study and interpretation of symptoms.

syn- /sɪn/ *prefix* with, together, alike. [from or after Gk *sun-* f. *sun* with]

synaeresis /sɪˈnɪərɪsɪs/ *n.* (*US* **syneresis**) (*pl.* **synaereses** /-ˌsiːz/) the contraction of two vowels into a diphthong or single vowel. [LL f. Gk *sunairesis* (as SYN-, *hairesis* f. *haireō* take)]

synaesthesia /ˌsɪniːsˈθiːzɪə/ *n.* (*US* **synesthesia**) **1** *Psychol.* the production of a mental sense-impression relating to one sense by the stimulation of another sense. **2** a sensation produced in a part of the body by stimulation of another part. □□**synaesthetic** /-ˈθetɪk/ *adj.* [mod.L f. SYN- after *anaesthesia*]

synagogue /ˈsɪnəˌgɒg/ *n.* **1** the building where a Jewish assembly or congregation meets for religious observance and instruction. **2** the assembly itself. □□**synagogal** /-ˈgɒg(ə)l/ *adj.* **synagogical** /-ˈgɒdʒɪk(ə)l/ *adj.* [ME f. OF *sinagoge* f. LL *synagoga* f. Gk *sunagōgē* meeting (as SYN-, *agō* bring)]

synallagmatic /ˌsɪnəlægˈmætɪk/ *adj.* (of a treaty or contract) imposing reciprocal obligations. [SYN- + Gk *allassō* exchange]

synapse /ˈsaɪnæps, ˈsɪn-/ *n. Anat.* a junction of two nerve-cells. [Gk *synapsis* (as SYN-, *hapsis* f. *haptō* join)]

synapsis /sɪˈnæpsɪs/ *n.* (*pl.* **synapses** /-siːz/) **1** *Anat.* = SYNAPSE. **2** *Biol.* the fusion of chromosome-pairs at the start of meiosis. □□**synaptic** /-ˈnæptɪk/ *adj.* **synaptically** /-ˈnæptɪkəlɪ/ *adv.*

synarthrosis /ˌsɪnɑːˈθrəʊsɪs/ *n.* (*pl.* **synarthroses** /-siːz/) *Anat.* an immovably fixed bone-joint, e.g. the sutures of the skull. [SYN- + Gk *arthrōsis* jointing f. *arthron* joint]

sync /sɪŋk/ *n.* & *v.* (also **synch**) *colloq.* —*n.* synchronization. —*v.tr.* & *intr.* synchronize. □**in (or out of) sync** (often foll. by *with*) according or agreeing well (or badly). [abbr.]

syncarp /ˈsɪnkɑːp/ *n.* a compound fruit from a flower with several carpels, e.g. a blackberry. [SYN- + Gk *karpos* fruit]

syncarpous /sɪnˈkɑːpəs/ *adj.* (of a flower or fruit) having the carpels united (opp. APOCARPOUS). [SYN- + Gk *karpos* fruit]

synch var. of SYNC.

synchondrosis /ˌsɪŋkɒnˈdrəʊsɪs/ *n.* (*pl.* **synchondroses** /-siːz/) *Anat.* an almost immovable bone-joint bound by a layer of cartilage, as in the spinal vertebrae. [SYN- + Gk *khondros* cartilage]

synchro- /ˈsɪŋkrəʊ/ *comb. form* synchronized, synchronous.

synchrocyclotron /ˌsɪŋkrəʊˈsaɪkləˌtrɒn/ *n.* a cyclotron able to achieve higher energies by decreasing the frequency of the accelerating electric field as the particles increase in energy and mass.

synchromesh /ˈsɪŋkrəʊˌmeʃ/ *n.* & *adj.* —*n.* a system of gear-changing, esp. in motor vehicles, in which the driving and driven gearwheels are made to revolve at the same speed during engagement by means of a set of friction clutches, thereby easing the change. —*adj.* relating to or using this system. [abbr. of *synchronized mesh*]

synchronic /sɪŋˈkrɒnɪk, sɪn-/ *adj.* describing a subject (esp. a language) as it exists at one point in time (opp. DIACHRONIC). □□**synchronically** *adv.* [LL *synchronus*: see SYNCHRONOUS]

synchronism /ˈsɪŋkrəˌnɪz(ə)m/ *n.* **1** = SYNCHRONY. **2** the process of synchronizing sound and picture in cinematography, television, etc. □□**synchronistic** /-ˈnɪstɪk/ *adj.* **synchronistically** /-ˈnɪstɪkəlɪ/ *adv.* [Gk *sugkhronismos* (as SYNCHRONOUS)]

synchronize /ˈsɪŋkrəˌnaɪz/ *v.* (also **-ise**) **1** *intr.* (often foll. by *with*) occur at the same time; be simultaneous. **2** *tr.* cause to occur at the same time. **3** *tr.* carry out the synchronism of (a film). **4** *tr.* ascertain or set forth the correspondence in the date of (events). **5 a** *tr.* cause (clocks etc.) to show a standard or uniform time. **b** *intr.* (of clocks etc.) be synchronized.

□ **synchronized swimming** a form of swimming in which participants make coordinated leg and arm movements in time to music. □□ **synchronization** /-'zeɪʃ(ə)n/ n. **synchronizer** n.

synchronous /'sɪŋkrənəs/ adj. (often foll. by with) existing or occurring at the same time. □ **synchronous motor** Electr. a motor having a speed exactly proportional to the current frequency. □□ **synchronously** adv. [LL synchronus f. Gk sugkhronos (as SYN-, khronos time)]

synchrony /'sɪŋkrəni/ n. **1** the state of being synchronic or synchronous. **2** the treatment of events etc. as being synchronous. [Gk sugkhronos: see SYNCHRONOUS]

synchrotron /'sɪŋkrə,trɒn/ n. Physics a cyclotron in which the magnetic field strength increases with the energy of the particles to keep their orbital radius constant.

syncline /'sɪŋklaɪn/ n. a rock-bed forming a trough. □□ **synclinal** /-'klaɪn(ə)l/ adj. [synclinal (as SYN-, Gk klinō lean)]

syncopate /'sɪŋkə,peɪt/ v.tr. **1** Mus. displace the beats or accents in (a passage) so that strong beats become weak and vice versa. **2** shorten (a word) by dropping interior sounds or letters, as symbology for symbolology, Gloster for Gloucester. □□ **syncopation** /-'peɪʃ(ə)n/ n. **syncopator** n. [LL syncopare swoon (as SYNCOPE)]

syncope /'sɪŋkəpi/ n. **1** Gram. the omission of interior sounds or letters in a word (see SYNCOPATE 2). **2** Med. a temporary loss of consciousness caused by a fall in blood pressure. □□ **syncopal** adj. [ME f. LL syncopē f. Gk sugkopē (as SYN-, koptō strike, cut off)]

syncretism /'sɪŋkrə,tɪz(ə)m/ n. **1** Philos. & Theol. the process or an instance of syncretizing (see SYNCRETIZE). **2** Philol. the merging of different inflectional varieties in the development of a language. □□ **syncretic** /-'krɛtɪk/ adj. **syncretist** n. **syncretistic** /-'tɪstɪk/ adj. [mod.L syncretismus f. Gk sugkrētismos f. sugkrētizō (of two parties) combine against a third f. krēs Cretan (orig. of ancient Cretan communities)]

syncretize /'sɪŋkrə,taɪz/ v.tr. (also -ise) Philos. & Theol. attempt, esp. inconsistently, to unify or reconcile differing schools of thought.

syncytium /sɪn'sɪtɪəm/ n. (pl. **syncytia** /-tɪə/) Biol. a mass of cytoplasm with several nuclei, not divided into separate cells. □□ **syncytial** adj. [formed as SYN- + -CYTE + -IUM]

syndactyl /sɪn'dæktɪl/ adj. (of an animal) having digits united as in webbed feet etc. □□ **syndactylism** n. **syndactylous** adj.

syndesis /'sɪndɪsɪs/ n. (pl. **syndeses** /-,si:z/) Biol. = SYNAPSIS 2. [mod.L f. Gk syndesis binding together f. sundeō bind together]

syndesmosis /,sɪndez'məʊsɪs/ n. the union and articulation of bones by means of ligaments. [mod.L f. Gk sundesmos binding, fastening + -OSIS]

syndetic /sɪn'dɛtɪk/ adj. Gram. of or using conjunctions. [Gk sundetikos (as SYNDESIS)]

syndic /'sɪndɪk/ n. **1** a government official in various countries. **2** Brit. a business agent of certain universities and corporations, esp. (at Cambridge University) a member of a committee of the senate. □□ **syndical** adj. [F f. LL syndicus f. Gk sundikos (as SYN-, -dikos f. dikē justice)]

syndicalism /'sɪndɪkə,lɪz(ə)m/ n. hist. a movement for transferring the ownership and control of the means of production and distribution to workers' unions. □□ **syndicalist** n. [F syndicalisme f. syndical (as SYNDIC)]

syndicate n. & v. —n. /'sɪndɪkət/ **1** a combination of individuals or commercial firms to promote some common interest. **2** an association or agency supplying material simultaneously to a number of newspapers or periodicals. **3** a group of people who combine to buy or rent property, gamble, organize crime, etc. **4** a committee of syndics. —v.tr.

/'sɪndɪ,keɪt/ **1** form into a syndicate. **2** publish (material) through a syndicate. □□ **syndication** /-'keɪʃ(ə)n/ n. [F syndicat f. med.L syndicatus f. LL syndicus: see SYNDIC]

syndrome /'sɪndrəʊm/ n. **1** a group of concurrent symptoms of a disease. **2** a characteristic combination of opinions, emotions, behaviour, etc. □□ **syndromic** /-'drɒmɪk/ adj. [mod.L f. Gk sundromē (as SYN-, dromē f. dramein to run)]

syne /saɪn/ adv., conj., & prep. Sc. since. [contr. f. ME sithen SINCE]

synecdoche /sɪ'nɛkdəkɪ/ n. a figure of speech in which a part is made to represent the whole or vice versa (e.g. new faces at the meeting; England lost by six wickets). □□ **synecdochic** /-'dɒkɪk/ adj. [ME f. L f. Gk sunekdokhē (as SYN-, ekdokhē f. ekdekhomai take up)]

synecology /,sɪnɪ'kɒlədʒɪ/ n. the ecological study of plant or animal communities. □□ **synecological** /-,i:kə'lɒdʒɪk(ə)l/ adj. **synecologist** n.

syneresis US var. of SYNAERESIS.

synergism /'sɪnə,dʒɪz(ə)m/ n. (also **synergy** /'sɪnədʒɪ/) the combined effect of drugs, organs, etc., that exceeds the sum of their individual effects. □□ **synergetic** /-'dʒɛtɪk/ adj. **synergic** /-'nɜ:dʒɪk/ adj. **synergistic** /-'dʒɪstɪk/ adj. **synergistically** /-'dʒɪstɪkəlɪ/ adv. [Gk sunergos working together (as SYN-, ergon work)]

synergist /'sɪnədʒɪst/ n. a medicine or a bodily organ (e.g. a muscle) that cooperates with another or others.

synesthesia US var. of SYNAESTHESIA.

syngamy /'sɪŋgəmɪ/ n. Biol. the fusion of gametes or nuclei in reproduction. □□ **syngamous** adj. [SYN- + Gk gamos marriage]

syngenesis /sɪn'dʒɛnəsɪs/ n. sexual reproduction from combined male and female elements.

synod /'sɪnəd/ n. **1** a Church council attended by delegated clergy and sometimes laity (see also General Synod). **2** a Presbyterian ecclesiastical court above the presbyteries and subject to the General Assembly. **3** any meeting for debate. [ME f. LL synodus f. Gk sunodos meeting (as SYN-, hodos way)]

synodic /sɪ'nɒdɪk/ adj. Astron. relating to or involving the conjunction of stars, planets, etc. □ **synodic period** the time between the successive conjunctions of a planet with the sun. [LL synodicus f. Gk sunodikos (as SYNOD)]

synodical /sɪ'nɒdɪk(ə)l/ adj. **1** (also **synodal** /'sɪnəd(ə)l/) of, relating to, or constituted as a synod. **2** = SYNODIC.

synoecious /sɪ'ni:ʃəs/ adj. Bot. having male and female organs in the same flower or receptacle. [SYN- after dioecious etc.]

synonym /'sɪnənɪm/ n. **1** a word or phrase that means exactly or nearly the same as another in the same language (e.g. shut and close). **2** a word denoting the same thing as another but suitable to a different context (e.g. serpent for snake, Hellene for Greek) or containing a different emphasis (e.g. blindworm for slow-worm). **3** a word equivalent to another in some but not all senses (e.g. ship and vessel). □□ **synonymic** /-'nɪmɪk/ adj. **synonymity** /-'nɪmɪtɪ/ n. [ME f. L synonymum f. Gk sunōnumon neut. of sunōnumos (as SYN-, onoma name): cf. ANONYMOUS]

synonymous /sɪ'nɒnɪməs/ adj. (often foll. by with) **1** having the same meaning; being a synonym (of). **2** (of a name, idea, etc.) suggestive of or associated with another (excessive drinking regarded as synonymous with violence). □□ **synonymously** adv. **synonymousness** n.

synonymy /sɪ'nɒnɪmɪ/ n. (pl. -**ies**) **1** the state of being synonymous. **2** the collocation of synonyms for emphasis (e.g. in any shape or form). **3 a** a system or collection of synonyms. **b** a treatise on synonyms. [LL synonymia f. Gk sunōnumia (as SYNONYM)]

synopsis /sɪ'nɒpsɪs/ n. (pl. **synopses** /-si:z/) **1** a summary or outline. **2** a brief general survey. □□

---

w we   z zoo   ʃ she   ʒ decision   θ thin   ð this   ŋ ring   x loch   tʃ chip   dʒ jar   (see over for vowels)

synopsize *v.tr.* (also **-ise**). [LL f. Gk (as SYN-, *opsis* seeing)]

synoptic /sɪ'nɒptɪk/ *adj.* & *n.* —*adj.* **1** of, forming, or giving a synopsis. **2** taking or affording a comprehensive mental view. **3** of the Synoptic Gospels. **4** giving a general view of weather conditions. —*n.* **1** a Synoptic Gospel. **2** the writer of a Synoptic Gospel. □**Synoptic Gospels** the Gospels of Matthew, Mark, and Luke, describing events from a similar point of view. □□**synoptical** *adj.* **synoptically** *adv.* [Gk *sunoptikos* (as SYNOPSIS)]

synoptist /sɪ'nɒptɪst/ *n.* the writer of a Synoptic Gospel.

synostosis /ˌsɪnɒ'stəʊsɪs/ *n.* the joining of bones by ankylosis etc. [SYN- + Gk *osteon* bone + -OSIS]

synovia /saɪ'nəʊvɪə, sɪn-/ *n. Physiol.* a viscous fluid lubricating joints and tendon sheaths. □**synovial membrane** a dense membrane of connective tissue secreting synovia. □□**synovial** *adj.* [mod.L, formed prob. arbitrarily by Paracelsus]

synovitis /ˌsaɪnəʊ'vaɪtɪs, sɪn-/ *n.* inflammation of the synovial membrane.

syntactic /sɪn'tæktɪk/ *adj.* of or according to syntax. □□**syntactical** *adj.* **syntactically** *adv.* [Gk *suntaktikos* (as SYNTAX)]

syntagma /sɪn'tægmə/ *n.* (*pl.* **syntagmas** or **syntagmata** /-mətə/) **1** a word or phrase forming a syntactic unit. **2** a systematic collection of statements. □□**syntagmatic** /-'mætɪk/ *adj.* **syntagmic** *adj.* [LL f. Gk *suntagma* (as SYNTAX)]

syntax /'sɪntæks/ *n.* **1** the grammatical arrangement of words, showing their connection and relation. **2** a set of rules for or an analysis of this. [F *syntaxe* or LL *syntaxis* f. Gk *suntaxis* (as SYN-, *taxis* f. *tassō* arrange)]

synth /sɪnθ/ *n. colloq.* = SYNTHESIZER.

synthesis /'sɪnθɪsɪs/ *n.* (*pl.* **syntheses** /-ˌsiːz/) **1** the process or result of building up separate elements, esp. ideas, into a connected whole, esp. into a theory or system. **2** a combination or composition. **3** *Chem.* the artificial production of compounds from their constituents as distinct from extraction from plants etc. **4** *Gram.* **a** the process of making ·compound and derivative words. **b** the tendency in a language to use inflected forms rather than groups of words, prepositions, etc. **5** the joining of divided parts in surgery. □□**synthesist** *n.* [L f. Gk *sunthesis* (as SYN-, THESIS)]

synthesize /'sɪnθɪˌsaɪz/ *v.tr.* (also **synthetize** /-ˌtaɪz/, **-ise**) **1** make a synthesis of. **2** combine into a coherent whole.

synthesizer /'sɪnθɪˌsaɪzə(r)/ *n.* an electronic musical instrument, esp. operated by a keyboard, producing a wide variety of sounds by generating and combining signals of different frequencies.

synthetic /sɪn'θetɪk/ *adj.* & *n.* —*adj.* **1** made by chemical synthesis, esp. to imitate a natural product (*synthetic rubber*). **2** (of emotions etc.) affected, insincere. **3** *Logic* (of a proposition) having truth or falsity determinable by recourse to experience (cf. ANALYTIC 3). **4** *Philol.* using combinations of simple words or elements in compounded or complex words (cf. ANALYTICAL). —*n. Chem.* a synthetic substance. □**synthetic resin** *Chem.* see RESIN *n.* 2. □□**synthetical** *adj.* **synthetically** *adv.* [F *synthétique* or mod.L *syntheticus* f. Gk *sunthetikos* f. *sunthetos* f. *suntithēmi* (as SYN-, *tithēmi* put)]

syphilis /'sɪfɪlɪs/ *n.* a contagious venereal disease progressing from infection of the genitals via the skin and mucous membrane to the bones, muscles, and brain. □□**syphilitic** /-'lɪtɪk/ *adj.* **syphilize** /-ˌlaɪz/ *v.tr.* (also **-ise**). **syphiloid** /-ˌlɔɪd/ *adj.* [mod.L f. title (*Syphilis, sive Morbus Gallicus*) of a Latin poem (1530), f. *Syphilus*, a character in it, the supposed first sufferer from the disease]

syphon var. of SIPHON.

Syriac /'sɪrɪˌæk/ *n.* & *adj.* —*n.* the language of ancient Syria, western Aramaic. —*adj.* in or relating

to this language. [L *Syriacus* f. Gk *Suriakos* f. *Suria* Syria]

Syrian /'sɪrɪən/ *n.* & *adj.* —*n.* **1** a native or national of the modern State of Syria in the Middle East; a person of Syrian descent. **2** a native or inhabitant of the region of Syria in antiquity or later. —*adj.* of or relating to the region or State of Syria.

syringa /sɪ'rɪŋgə/ *n. Bot.* **1** = *mock orange*. **2** any plant of the genus *Syringa*, esp. the lilac. [mod.L, formed as SYRINX (with ref. to the use of its stems as pipe-stems)]

syringe /sɪ'rɪndʒ, 'sɪr-/ *n.* & *v.* —*n.* **1** *Med.* **a** a tube with a nozzle and piston or bulb for sucking in and ejecting liquid in a fine stream, used in surgery. **b** (in full **hypodermic syringe**) a similar device with a hollow needle for insertion under the skin. **2** any similar device used in gardening, cooking, etc. —*v.tr.* sluice or spray (the ear, a plant, etc.) with a syringe. [ME f. med.L *syringa* (as SYRINX)]

syrinx /'sɪrɪŋks/ *n.* (*pl.* **syrinxes** or **syringes** /sɪ'rɪndʒiːz/) **1** a set of pan-pipes. **2** *Archaeol.* a narrow gallery cut in rock in an ancient Egyptian tomb. **3** the lower larynx or song-organ of birds. □□**syringeal** /sɪ'rɪndʒɪəl/ *adj.* [L *syrinx -ngis* f. Gk *surigx suriggos* pipe, channel]

Syro- /'saɪrəʊ/ *comb. form* Syrian; Syrian and (*Syro-Phoenician*). [Gk *Suro-* f. *Suros* a Syrian]

syrup /'sɪrəp/ *n.* (*US* **sirup**) **1 a** a sweet sauce made by dissolving sugar in boiling water, often used for preserving fruit etc. **b** a similar sauce of a specified flavour as a drink, medicine, etc. (*rose-hip syrup*). **2** condensed sugar-cane juice; part of this remaining uncrystallized at various stages of refining; molasses, treacle. **3** excessive sweetness of style or manner. □□**syrupy** *adj.* [ME f. OF *sirop* or med.L *siropus* f. Arab. *šarāb* beverage: cf. SHERBET, SHRUB²]

syssarcosis /ˌsɪsɑ:'kəʊsɪs/ *n.* (*pl.* **syssarcoses** /-siːz/) *Anat.* a connection between bones formed by intervening muscle. [mod.L f. Gk *sussarkōsis* (as SYN-, *sarx, sarkos* flesh)]

systaltic /sɪ'stæltɪk/ *adj.* (esp. of the heart) contracting and dilating rhythmically; pulsatory (cf. SYSTOLE, DIASTOLE). [LL *systalticus* f. Gk *sustaltikos* (as SYN-, *staltos* f. *stellō* put)]

system /'sɪstəm/ *n.* **1** a complex whole; a set of connected things or parts; an organized body of material or immaterial things. **2** a set of devices (e.g. pulleys) functioning together. **3** *Physiol.* **a** a set of organs in the body with a common structure or function (*the digestive system*). **b** the human or animal body as a whole. **4 a** method; considered principles of procedure or classification. **b** classification. **5** orderliness. **6 a** a body of theory or practice relating to or prescribing a particular form of government, religion, etc. **b** (prec. by *the*) the prevailing political or social order, esp. regarded as oppressive and intransigent. **7** a method of choosing one's procedure in gambling etc. **8** *Computing* a group of related hardware units or programs or both, esp. when dedicated to a single application. **9** one of seven general types of crystal structure. **10** a major group of geological strata (*the Devonian system*). **11** *Physics* a group of associated bodies moving under mutual gravitation etc. **12** *Mus.* the braced staves of a score. □**get a thing out of one's system** *colloq.* be rid of a preoccupation or anxiety. **systems analysis** the analysis of a complex process or operation in order to improve its efficiency, esp. by applying a computer system. □□**systemless** *adj.* [F *système* or LL *systema* f. Gk *sustēma -atos* (as SYN-, *histēmi* set up)]

systematic /ˌsɪstə'mætɪk/ *adj.* **1** methodical; done or conceived according to a plan or system. **2** regular, deliberate (*a systematic liar*). □**systematic theology** a form of theology in which the aim is to arrange religious truths in a self-consistent whole. □□ **systematically** *adv.* **systematism** /'sɪstəmə

,tɪz(ə)m/ *n.* **systematist** /'sɪstəmətɪst/ *n.* [F *systéma-tique* f. LL *systematicus* f. late Gk *sustēmatikos* (as SYSTEM)]

systematics /,sɪstə'mætɪks/ *n.pl.* (usu. treated as *sing.*) the study or a system of classification; taxonomy.

systematize /'sɪstəmə,taɪz/ *v.tr.* (also **-ise**) **1** make systematic. **2** devise a system for. □□ **systematization** /-'zeɪʃ(ə)n/ *n.* **systematizer** *n.*

systemic /sɪ'stemɪk/ *adj.* **1** *Physiol.* **a** of or concerning the whole body, not confined to a particular part (*systemic infection*). **b** (of blood circulation) other than pulmonary. **2** *Hort.* (of an insecticide, fungicide,

etc.) entering the plant via the roots or shoots and passing through the tissues. □□ **systemically** *adv.* [irreg. f. SYSTEM]

systemize /'sɪstə,maɪz/ *v.tr.* = SYSTEMATIZE. □□ **systemization** /-'zeɪʃ(ə)n/ *n.* **systemizer** *n.*

systole /'sɪstəlɪ/ *n. Physiol.* the contraction of the heart, when blood is pumped into the arteries (cf. DIASTOLE). □□ **systolic** /-'stɒlɪk/ *adj.* [LL f. Gk *sustolē* f. *sustellō* contract (as SYSTALTIC)]

syzygy /'sɪzɪdʒɪ/ *n.* (*pl.* **-ies**) **1** *Astron.* conjunction or opposition, esp. of the moon with the sun. **2** a pair of connected or correlated things. [LL *syzygia* f. Gk *suzugia* f. *suzugos* yoked, paired (as SYN-, *zugon* yoke)]

T

T¹ /tiː/ n. (also **t**) (pl. **Ts** or **T's**) **1** the twentieth letter of the alphabet. **2** a T-shaped thing (esp. *attrib.*: *T-joint*). □ **to a T** exactly; to a nicety.

T² *abbr.* **1** tera-. **2** tesla.

T³ *symb. Chem.* the isotope tritium.

t. *abbr.* **1** ton(s). **2** tonne(s).

't *pron. contr.* of IT¹ (*'tis*).

-t¹ /t/ *suffix* = -ED¹ (*crept*; *sent*).

-t² /t/ *suffix* = -EST² (*shalt*).

TA *abbr.* (in the UK) Territorial Army.

Ta *symb. Chem.* the element tantalum.

ta /taː/ *int. Brit. colloq.* thank you. [infantile form]

Taal /taːl/ n. (prec. by *the*) *hist.* an early form of Afrikaans. [Du., = language, rel. to TALE]

TAB *abbr.* **1** typhoid-paratyphoid A and B vaccine. **2** *Austral.* Totalizator Agency Board.

tab¹ /tæb/ n. & v. —n. **1 a** a small flap or strip of material attached for grasping, fastening, or hanging up, or for identification. **b** a similar object as part of a garment etc. **2** *US colloq.* a bill or price (*picked up the tab*). **3** *Brit. Mil.* a marking on the collar distinguishing a staff officer. **4 a** a stage-curtain. **b** a loop for suspending this. —v.tr. (**tabbed**, **tabbing**) provide with a tab or tabs. □ **keep tabs** (or **a tab**) **on** *colloq.* **1** keep account of. **2** have under observation or in check. [prob. f. dial.: cf. TAG¹]

tab² /tæb/ n. **1** = TABULATOR 2. **2** = TABULATOR 3. [abbr.]

tabard /'tæbəd/ n. **1** a herald's official coat emblazoned with the arms of the sovereign. **2** a woman's or girl's sleeveless jerkin. **3** *hist.* a knight's short emblazoned garment worn over armour. [ME f. OF *tabart*, of unkn. orig.]

tabaret /'tæbərɪt/ n. an upholstery fabric of alternate satin and plain stripes. [prob. f. TABBY]

tabasco /tə'bæskəʊ/ n. **1** a pungent pepper made from the fruit of *Capsicum frutescens*. **2** (**Tabasco**) *propr.* a sauce made from this used to flavour food. [*Tabasco* in Mexico]

tabbouleh /tə'buːleɪ/ n. an Arabic vegetable salad made with cracked wheat. [Arab. *tabbūla*]

tabby /'tæbɪ/ n. (pl. **-ies**) **1** (in full **tabby cat**) **a** a grey or brownish cat mottled or streaked with dark stripes. **b** any domestic cat, esp. female. **2** a kind of watered silk. **3** a plain weave. [F *tabis* (in sense 2) f. Arab. *al-'attabiya* the quarter of Baghdad where tabby was manufactured: connection of other senses uncert.]

tabernacle /'tæbə‚næk(ə)l/ n. **1** *hist.* a tent used as a sanctuary for the Ark of the Covenant by the Israelites during the Exodus. **2** *Eccl.* a canopied niche or receptacle esp. for the Eucharistic elements. **3** a place of worship in nonconformist creeds. **4** *Bibl.* a fixed or movable habitation usu. of light construction. **5** *Naut.* a socket or double post for a hinged mast that can be lowered to pass under low bridges. □ **feast of Tabernacles** = SUCCOTH. □□ **tabernacled** *adj.* [ME f. OF *tabernacle* or L *tabernaculum* tent, dimin. of *taberna* hut]

tabes /'teɪbiːz/ n. *Med.* **1** emaciation. **2** locomotor ataxy, a form of neurosyphilis. □□ **tabetic** /tə'betɪk/ *adj.* [L, = wasting away]

tabla /'tæblə, 'taː-/ n. *Ind. Mus.* a pair of small drums played with the hands. [Hind. f. Arab. *tabla* drum]

tablature /'tæblətʃə(r)/ n. *Mus.* an early form of notation indicating fingering (esp. in playing the lute), rhythm, and features other than notes. [F f. It. *tavolatura* f. *tavolare* set to music]

table /'teɪb(ə)l/ n. & v. —n. **1** a piece of furniture with a flat top and one or more legs, providing a level surface for eating, writing, or working at, playing games on, etc. **2** a flat surface serving a specified purpose (*altar table*; *bird table*). **3 a** food provided in a household (*keeps a good table*). **b** a group seated at table for dinner etc. **4 a** a set of facts or figures systematically displayed, esp. in columns (*a table of contents*). **b** matter contained in this. **c** = *multiplication table*. **5** a flat surface for working on or for machinery to operate on. **6 a** a slab of wood or stone etc. for bearing an inscription. **b** matter inscribed on this. **7** = TABLELAND. **8** *Archit.* **a** a flat usu. rectangular vertical surface. **b** a horizontal moulding, esp. a cornice. **9 a** a flat surface of a gem. **b** a cut gem with two flat faces. **10** each half or quarter of a folding board for backgammon. **11** (prec. by *the*) *Bridge* the dummy hand. —v.tr. **1** bring forward for discussion or consideration at a meeting. **2** postpone consideration of (a matter). **3** *Naut.* strengthen (a sail) with a wide hem. □ **at table** taking a meal at a table. **lay on the table 1** submit for discussion. **2** postpone indefinitely. **on the table** offered for discussion. **table knife** a knife for use at meals, esp. in eating a main course. **table licence** a licence to serve alcoholic drinks only with meals. **table linen** tablecloths, napkins, etc. **table manners** decorum or correct behaviour while eating at table. **table-mat** a mat for protecting a tabletop from hot dishes, etc. **table salt** salt that is powdered or easy to powder for use at meals. **table talk** miscellaneous informal talk at table. **table tennis** an indoor game based on lawn tennis, played with small bats and a ball bounced on a table divided by a net. **table wine** ordinary wine for drinking with a meal. **turn the tables** (often foll. by *on*) reverse one's relations (with), esp. by turning an inferior into a superior position (orig. in backgammon). **under the table** *colloq.* drunken after a meal. □□ **tableful** n. (pl. **-fuls**). **tabling** n. [ME f. OF f. L *tabula* plank, tablet, list]

tableau /'tæbləʊ/ n. (pl. **tableaux** /-ləʊz/) **1** a picturesque presentation. **2** = TABLEAU VIVANT. **3** a dramatic or effective situation suddenly brought about. □ **tableau curtains** *Theatr.* a pair of curtains drawn open by a diagonal cord. [F, = picture, dimin. of *table*: see TABLE]

tableau vivant /‚tæbləʊ 'viːvã/ n. (pl. **tableaux vivants** *pronunc.* same) *Theatr.* a silent and motionless group of people arranged to represent a scene. [F, lit. 'living picture']

tablecloth /'teɪb(ə)l‚klɒθ/ n. a cloth spread over the top of a table, esp. for meals.

table d'hôte /‚taːb(ə)l 'dəʊt/ n. a meal consisting of a set menu at a fixed price, esp. in a hotel (cf. À LA CARTE). [F, = host's table]

tableland /'teɪb(ə)l‚lænd/ n. an extensive elevated region with a level surface; a plateau.

tablespoon /'teɪb(ə)l‚spuːn/ n. **1** a large spoon for serving food. **2** an amount held by this. □□ **tablespoonful** n. (pl. **-fuls**).

tablet /'tæblɪt/ n. **1** a small measured and compressed amount of a substance, esp. of a medicine or drug. **2** a small flat piece of soap etc. **3** a flat slab of stone or wood, esp. for display or an inscription. **4** *Archit.* = TABLE 8. **5** *US* a writing-pad. [ME f. OF *tablete* f. Rmc, dimin. of L *tabula* TABLE]

tabletop /'teɪb(ə)l‚tɒp/ n. **1** the top or surface of a table. **2** (*attrib.*) that can be placed or used on a tabletop.

tableware /'teɪb(ə)l‚weə(r)/ n. dishes, plates, implements, etc., for use at meals.

tablier /'tæblɪˌeɪ/ n. hist. an apron-like part of a woman's dress. [F]

tabloid /'tæblɔɪd/ n. **1** a newspaper, usu. popular in style with bold headlines and large photographs, having pages of half size. **2** anything in a compressed or concentrated form. [orig. the propr. name of a medicine sold in tablets]

taboo /tə'buː/ n., adj., & v. (also **tabu**) —n. (pl. **taboos** or **tabus**) **1** a system or the act of setting a person or thing apart as sacred or accursed. **2** a prohibition or restriction imposed by social custom. —adj. **1** avoided or prohibited, esp. by social custom (taboo words). **2** designated as sacred and prohibited. —v.tr. (**taboos, tabooed** or **tabus, tabued**) **1** put (a thing, practice, etc.) under taboo. **2** exclude or prohibit by authority or social influence. [Tongan tabu]

tabor /'teɪbə(r)/ n. hist. a small drum, esp. one used to accompany a pipe. [ME f. OF tabour, tabur: cf. TABLA, Pers. tabīra drum]

tabouret /'tæbərɪt/ n. (US **taboret**) a low seat usu. without arms or a back. [F, = stool, dimin. as TABOR]

tabu var. of TABOO.

tabular /'tæbjʊlə(r)/ adj. **1** of or arranged in tables or lists. **2** broad and flat like a table. **3** (of a crystal) having two broad flat faces. **4** formed in thin plates. □□ **tabularly** adv. [L tabularis (as TABLE)]

tabula rasa /ˌtæbjʊlə 'rɑːzə/ n. **1** an erased tablet. **2** the human mind (esp. at birth) viewed as having no innate ideas. [L, = scraped tablet]

tabulate /'tæbjʊˌleɪt/ v.tr. arrange (figures or facts) in tabular form. □□ **tabulation** /-'leɪʃ(ə)n/ n. [LL tabulare tabulat- f. tabula table]

tabulator /'tæbjʊˌleɪtə(r)/ n. **1** a person or thing that tabulates. **2** a device on a typewriter for advancing to a sequence of set positions in tabular work. **3** Computing a machine that produces lists or tables from a data storage medium such as punched cards.

tacamahac /'tækəməˌhæk/ n. **1** a resinous gum obtained from certain tropical trees esp. of the genus Calophyllum. **2 a** the balsam poplar. **b** the resin of this. [obs. Sp. tacamahaca f. Aztec tecomahiyac]

tac-au-tac /'tækəʊˌtæk/ n. Fencing a parry combined with a riposte. [F: imit.]

tacet /'tæsɪt, 'teɪ-/ v.intr. Mus. an instruction for a particular voice or instrument to be silent. [L, = is silent]

tachism /'tæʃɪz(ə)m/ n. (also **tachisme**) a form of action painting with dabs of colour arranged randomly to evoke a subconscious feeling. [F tachisme f. tache stain]

tachistoscope /tə'kɪstəˌskəʊp/ n. an instrument for very brief measured exposure of objects to the eye. □□ **tachistoscopic** /-'skɒpɪk/ adj. [Gk takhistos swiftest + -SCOPE]

tacho /'tækəʊ/ n. (pl. **-os**) colloq. = TACHOMETER. [abbr.]

tacho- /'tækəʊ/ comb. form speed. [Gk takhos speed]

tachograph /'tækəˌɡrɑːf/ n. a device used esp. in heavy goods vehicles and coaches etc. for automatically recording speed and travel time.

tachometer /tə'kɒmɪtə(r)/ n. an instrument for measuring the rate of rotation of a shaft and hence the speed or velocity of a vehicle.

tachy- /'tækɪ/ comb. form swift. [Gk takhus swift]

tachycardia /ˌtækɪ'kɑːdɪə/ n. Med. an abnormally rapid heart rate. [TACHY- + Gk kardia heart]

tachygraphy /tə'kɪɡrəfɪ/ n. **1** stenography, esp. that of the ancient Greeks and Romans. **2** the abbreviated medieval writing of Greek and Latin. □□ **tachygrapher** n. **tachygraphic** /-'ɡræfɪk/ adj. **tachygraphical** /-'ɡræfɪk(ə)l/ adj.

tachymeter /tə'kɪmɪtə(r)/ n. **1** Surveying an instrument used to locate points rapidly. **2** a speed-indicator.

tacit /'tæsɪt/ adj. understood or implied without being stated (tacit consent). □□ **tacitly** adv. [L tacitus silent f. tacēre be silent]

taciturn /'tæsɪˌtɜːn/ adj. reserved in speech; saying little; uncommunicative. □□ **taciturnity** /-'tɜːnɪtɪ/ n. **taciturnly** adv. [F taciturne or L taciturnus (as TACIT)]

tack¹ /tæk/ n. & v. —n. **1** a small sharp broad-headed nail. **2** US a drawing-pin. **3** a long stitch used in fastening fabrics etc. lightly or temporarily together. **4 a** the direction in which a ship moves as determined by the position of its sails and regarded in terms of the direction of the wind (starboard tack). **b** a temporary change of direction in sailing to take advantage of a side wind etc. **5** a course of action or policy (try another tack). **6** Naut. **a** a rope for securing the corner of some sails. **b** the corner to which this is fastened. **7** a sticky condition of varnish etc. **8** Brit. an extraneous clause appended to a bill in Parliament. —v. **1** tr. (often foll. by down etc.) fasten with tacks. **2** tr. stitch (pieces of cloth etc.) lightly together. **3** tr. (foll. by to, on) annex (a thing). **4** intr. (often foll. by about) **a** change a ship's course by turning its head to the wind (cf. WEAR²). **b** make a series of tacks. **5** intr. change one's conduct or policy etc. **6** tr. Brit. append (a clause) to a bill. □□ **tacker** n. [ME tak etc., of uncert. orig.: cf. Bibl. tache clasp, link f. OF tache]

tack² /tæk/ n. the saddle, bridle, etc., of a horse. [shortened f. TACKLE]

tackle /'tæk(ə)l/ n. & v. —n. **1** equipment for a task or sport (fishing-tackle). **2** a mechanism, esp. of ropes, pulley-blocks, hooks, etc., for lifting weights, managing sails, etc. (block and tackle). **3** a windlass with its ropes and hooks. **4** an act of tackling in football etc. **5** Amer. Football **a** the position next to the end of the forward line. **b** the player in this position. —v.tr. **1** try to deal with (a problem or difficulty). **2** grapple with or try to overcome (an opponent). **3** enter into discussion with. **4** obstruct, intercept, or seize and stop (a player running with the ball). **5** secure by means of tackle. □ **tackle-block** a pulley over which a rope runs. **tackle-fall** a rope for applying force to the blocks of a tackle. □□ **tackler** n. **tackling** n. [ME, prob. f. MLG takel f. taken lay hold of]

tacky¹ /'tækɪ/ adj. (**tackier, tackiest**) (of glue or paint etc.) still slightly sticky after application. □□ **tackiness** n. [TACK¹ + -Y¹]

tacky² /'tækɪ/ adj. (**tackier, tackiest**) esp. US colloq. **1** showing poor taste or style. **2** tatty or seedy. □□ **tackily** adv. **tackiness** n. [19th c.: orig. unkn.]

taco /'tɑːkəʊ/ n. (pl. **-os**) a Mexican dish of meat etc. in a folded or rolled tortilla. [Mex. Sp.]

tact /tækt/ n. **1** adroitness in dealing with others or with difficulties arising from personal feeling. **2** intuitive perception of the right thing to do or say. [F f. L tactus touch, sense of touch f. tangere tact- touch]

tactful /'tæktfʊl/ adj. having or showing tact. □□ **tactfully** adv. **tactfulness** n.

tactic /'tæktɪk/ n. **1** a tactical manœuvre. **2** = TACTICS. [mod.L tactica f. Gk taktikē (tekhnē art): see TACTICS]

tactical /'tæktɪk(ə)l/ adj. **1** of, relating to, or constituting tactics (a tactical retreat). **2** (of bombing or weapons) done or for use in immediate support of military or naval operations (opp. STRATEGIC). **3** adroitly planning or planned. **4** (of voting) aimed at preventing the strongest candidate from winning by supporting the next strongest. □□ **tactically** adv. [Gk taktikos (as TACTICS)]

tactics /'tæktɪks/ n.pl. **1** (also treated as sing.) the art of disposing armed forces esp. in contact with an enemy (cf. STRATEGY). **2 a** the plans and means adopted in carrying out a scheme or achieving some end. **b** a skilful device or devices. □□ **tactician** /tæk'tɪʃ(ə)n/ n. [mod.L tactica f. Gk taktika neut.pl. f. taktos ordered f. tassō arrange]

tactile /'tæktaɪl/ adj. **1** of or connected with the sense of touch. **2** perceived by touch. **3** tangible. **4** Art (in painting) producing or concerning the effect of three-dimensional solidity. □□ **tactual** /'tæktjʊəl/ *adj.* (in senses 1, 2). **tactility** /-'tɪlɪtɪ/ *n.* [L *tactilis* f. *tangere tact-* touch]

tactless /'tæktlɪs/ *adj.* having or showing no tact. □□ **tactlessly** *adv.* **tactlessness** *n.*

tad /tæd/ *n.* US *colloq.* a small amount (often used adverbially: *a tad too salty*). [19th c.: orig. unkn.]

tadpole /'tædpəʊl/ *n.* a larva of an amphibian, esp. a frog, toad, or newt in its aquatic stage and breathing through gills. [ME *taddepolle* (as TOAD, POLL¹ from the size of its head)]

taedium vitae /ˌtiːdɪəm 'viːtaɪ, 'vaɪtiː/ *n.* weariness of life (often as a pathological state, with a tendency to suicide). [L]

taenia /'tiːnɪə/ *n.* (*US* **tenia**) (*pl.* **taeniae** /-nɪˌiː/ or **taenias**) **1** *Archit.* a fillet between a Doric architrave and frieze. **2** *Anat.* any flat ribbon-like structure, esp. the muscles of the colon. **3** any large tapeworm of the genus *Taenia*, esp. *T. saginata* and *T. soleum*, parasitic on humans. **4** *Gk Antiq.* a fillet or headband. □□ **taenioid** *adj.* [L f. Gk *tainia* ribbon]

taffeta /'tæfɪtə/ *n.* a fine lustrous silk or silklike fabric. [ME f. OF *taffetas* or med.L *taffata*, ult. f. Pers. *tāfta* past part. of *tāftan* twist]

taffrail /'tæfreɪl/ *n.* *Naut.* a rail round a ship's stern. [earlier *tafferel* f. Du. *taffereel* panel, dimin. of *tafel* (as TABLE): assim. to RAIL¹]

Taffy /'tæfɪ/ *n.* (*pl.* **-ies**) *colloq.* often *offens.* a Welshman. [supposed Welsh pronunc. of *Davy = David* (Welsh *Dafydd*)]

taffy /'tæfɪ/ *n.* (*pl.* **-ies**) *US* **1** a confection like toffee. **2** insincere flattery. [19th c.: orig. unkn.]

tafia /'tæfɪə/ *n.* *W.Ind.* rum distilled from molasses etc. [18th c.: orig. uncert.]

tag¹ /tæg/ *n. & v.* —*n.* **1** a label, esp. one for tying on an object to show its address, price, etc. **2** a metal or plastic point at the end of a lace etc. to assist insertion. **3** a loop at the back of a boot used in pulling it on. **4** *US* a licence plate of a motor vehicle. **5** a loose or ragged end of anything. **6** a ragged lock of wool on a sheep. **7** *Theatr.* a closing speech addressed to the audience. **8** a trite quotation or stock phrase. **9 a** the refrain of a song. **b** a musical phrase added to the end of a piece. **10** an animal's tail, or its tip. —*v.tr.* (**tagged, tagging**) **1** provide with a tag or tags. **2** (often foll. by *on*, *on to*) join or attach. **3** *colloq.* follow closely or trail behind. **4** *Computing* identify (an item of data) by its type for later retrieval. **5** label radioactively (see LABEL *v.* 3). **6 a** find rhymes for (verses). **b** string (rhymes) together. **7** shear away tags from (sheep). □**tag along** (often foll. by *with*) go along or accompany passively. **tag end** esp. *US* the last remnant of something. [ME: orig. unkn.]

tag² /tæg/ *n. & v.* —*n.* **1** a children's game in which one chases the rest, and anyone who is caught then becomes the pursuer. **2** *Baseball* the act of tagging a runner. —*v.tr.* (**tagged, tagging**) **1** touch in a game of tag. **2** (often foll. by *out*) put (a runner) out by touching with the ball or with the hand holding the ball. [18th c.: orig. unkn.]

Tagalog /tə'gɑːlɒg/ *n. & adj.* —*n.* **1** a member of the principal people of the Philippine Islands. **2** the language of this people. —*adj.* of or relating to this people or language. [Tagalog f. *taga* native + *ilog* river]

tagetes /tə'dʒiːtiːz/ *n.* any plant of the genus *Tagetes*, esp. any of various marigolds with bright orange or yellow flowers. [mod.L f. L *Tages* an Etruscan god]

tagliatelle /ˌtæljə'telɪ/ *n.* a form of pasta in narrow ribbons. [It.]

Tahitian /təˈhiːʃ(ə)n/ *n. & adj.* —*n.* **1** a native or national of Tahiti in the S. Pacific. **2** the language of Tahiti. —*adj.* of or relating to Tahiti or its people or language.

tahr /tɑː(r)/ *n.* any goatlike mammal of the genus *Hemitragus*, esp. *H. jemlahicus* of the Himalayas. [native name in Nepal]

tahsil /tɑːˈsiːl/ *n.* an administrative area in parts of India. [Urdu *taḥsīl* f. Arab., = collection]

t'ai chi chu'an /ˌtaɪ tʃiː 'tʃwɑːn/ *n.* (also **t'ai chi** /taɪ 'tʃiː/) a Chinese martial art and system of callisthenics consisting of sequences of very slow controlled movements. [Chin., = great ultimate boxing]

Taig /teɪg/ *n. sl. offens.* (in Northern Ireland) a Protestant name for a Catholic. [var. of *Teague*, Anglicized spelling of the Irish name *Tadhg*, a nickname for an Irishman]

taiga /'taɪgə/ *n.* coniferous forest lying between tundra and steppe, esp. in Siberia. [Russ.]

tail¹ /teɪl/ *n. & v.* **1** the hindmost part of an animal, esp. when prolonged beyond the rest of the body. **2 a** a thing like a tail in form or position, esp. something extending downwards or outwards at an extremity. **b** the rear end of anything, e.g. of a procession. **c** a long train or line of people, vehicles, etc. **3 a** the rear part of an aeroplane, with the tailplane and rudder, or of a rocket. **b** the rear part of a motor vehicle. **4** the luminous trail of particles following a comet. **5 a** the inferior or weaker part of anything, esp. in a sequence. **b** *Cricket* the end of the batting order, with the weakest batsmen. **6 a** the part of a shirt below the waist. **b** the hanging part of the back of a coat. **7** (in *pl.*) *colloq.* **a** a tailcoat. **b** evening dress including this. **8** (in *pl.*) the reverse of a coin as a choice when tossing. **9** *colloq.* a person following or shadowing another. **10** an extra strip attached to the lower end of a kite. **11** the stem of a note in music. **12** the part of a letter (e.g. *y*) below the line. **13 a** the exposed end of a slate or tile in a roof. **b** the unexposed end of a brick or stone in a wall. **14** the slender backward prolongation of a butterfly's wing. **15** a comparative calm at the end of a gale. **16** a calm stretch following rough water in a stream. —*v.* **1** *tr.* remove the stalks of (fruit). **2** *tr. &* (foll. by *after*) *intr. colloq.* shadow or follow closely. **3** *tr.* provide with a tail. **4** *tr.* dock the tail of (a lamb etc.). **5** *tr.* (often foll. by *on to*) join (one thing to another). □**on a person's tail** closely following a person. **tail back** (of traffic) form a tailback. **tail covert** any of the feathers covering the base of a bird's tail feathers. **tail-end 1** the hindmost or lowest or last part. **2** (sense 5 of the *n.*). **tail-ender** a person at the tail-end of something, esp. in cricket and athletic races. **tail in** fasten (timber) by one end into a wall etc. **tail-light** (or **-lamp**) *US* a light at the rear of a train, motor vehicle, or bicycle. **tail off** (or **away**) **1** become fewer, smaller, or slighter. **2** fall behind or away in a scattered line. **tail-off** *n.* a decline or gradual reduction, esp. in demand. **tail-race** the part of a mill-race below the water-wheel. **tail-skid** a support for the tail of an aircraft when on the ground. **tail wind** a wind blowing in the direction of travel of a vehicle or aircraft etc. **with one's tail between one's legs** in a state of dejection or humiliation. **with one's tail up** in good spirits; cheerful. □□ **tailed** *adj.* (also in *comb.*). **tailless** *adj.* [OE *tægl*, *tægel* f. Gmc]

tail² /teɪl/ *n. & adj.* *Law* —*n.* limitation of ownership, esp. of an estate limited to a person and that person's heirs. —*adj.* so limited (*estate tail; fee tail*). □**in tail** under such a limitation. [ME f. OF *taille* notch, cut, tax, f. *taillier* cut ult. f. L *talea* twig]

tailback /'teɪlbæk/ *n.* a long line of traffic extending back from an obstruction.

tailboard /'teɪlbɔːd/ *n.* a hinged or removable flap at the rear of a lorry etc.

tailcoat /'teɪlkəʊt/ *n.* a man's morning or evening coat with a long skirt divided at the back into tails and cut away in front, worn as part of formal dress.

tailgate /'teɪlgeɪt/ *n. & v.* —*n.* **1** esp. *US* **a** = TAILBOARD. **b** the tail door of an estate car or hatchback. **2** the lower end of a canal lock. —*v.* *US colloq.* **1** *intr.* drive too closely behind another

vehicle. **2** *tr.* follow (a vehicle) too closely. □□
tailgater *n.*

tailing /'teɪlɪŋ/ *n.* **1** (in *pl.*) the refuse or inferior part
of grain or ore etc. **2** the part of a beam or projecting
brick etc. embedded in a wall.

tailor /'teɪlə(r)/ *n. & v.* —*n.* a maker of clothes, esp.
one who makes men's outer garments to measure.
—*v.* **1** *tr.* make (clothes) as a tailor. **2** *tr.* make or
adapt for a special purpose. **3** *intr.* work as or be a
tailor. **4** *tr.* (esp. as **tailored** *adj.*) make clothes for
(*he was immaculately tailored*). **5** *tr.* (as **tailored**
adj.) = *tailor-made*. □**tailor-bird** any small Asian
etc. bird of the genus *Orthotomus* that stitches leaves
together to form a nest. **tailor-made** *adj.* **1** (of
clothing) made to order by a tailor. **2** made or suited
for a particular purpose (*a job tailor-made for me*).
—*n.* a tailor-made garment. **tailor's chair** a chair
without legs for sitting cross-legged like a tailor at
work. **tailor's twist** a fine strong silk thread used
by tailors. □□**tailoring** *n.* [ME & AF *taillour*, OF
tailleur cutter, formed as TAIL²]

tailored /'teɪləd/ *adj.* (of clothing) well or closely
fitted.

tailpiece /'teɪlpiːs/ *n.* **1** an appendage at the rear of
anything. **2** the final part of a thing. **3** a decoration
in a blank space at the end of a chapter etc. in a
book. **4** a piece of wood to which the strings of some
musical instruments are attached at their lower
ends.

tailpipe /'teɪlpaɪp/ *n.* the rear section of the exhaust
pipe of a motor vehicle.

tailplane /'teɪlpleɪn/ *n.* a horizontal aerofoil at the
tail of an aircraft.

tailspin /'teɪlspɪn/ *n. & v.* —*n.* **1** a spin (see SPIN *n.*
2) by an aircraft with the tail spiralling. **2** a state of
chaos or panic. —*v.intr.* (-**spinning**; *past* and *past
part.* -**spun**) perform a tailspin.

tailstock /'teɪlstɒk/ *n.* the adjustable part of a lathe
holding the fixed spindle.

taint /teɪnt/ *n. & v.* —*n.* **1** a spot or trace of decay,
infection, or some bad quality. **2** a corrupt condition
or infection. —*v.* **1** *tr.* affect with a taint. **2** *tr.* (foll.
by *with*) affect slightly. **3** *intr.* become tainted. □□
taintless *adj.* [ME, partly f. OF *teint(e)* f. L *tinctus* f.
tingere dye, partly f. ATTAINT]

taipan¹ /'taɪpæn/ *n.* the head of a foreign business in
China. [Chin.]

taipan² /'taɪpæn/ *n.* a large venomous Australian
snake, *Oxyuranus microlepidotus*. [Aboriginal]

taj /tɑːdʒ/ *n.* a tall conical cap worn by a dervish.
[Arab. *tāj*]

takahe /'tɑːkəhɪ/ *n.* = NOTORNIS. [Maori]

take /teɪk/ *v. & n.* —*v.* (**took** /tʊk/; **taken** /'teɪkən/)
1 *tr.* lay hold of; get into one's hands. **2** *tr.* acquire,
get possession of, capture, earn, or win. **3** *tr.* get
the use of by purchase or formal agreement (*take
lodgings*). **4** *tr.* (in a recipe) avail oneself of; use. **5** *tr.*
use as a means of transport (*took a taxi*). **6** *tr.*
regularly buy or subscribe to (a particular newspaper
or periodical etc.). **7** *tr.* obtain after fulfilling the
required conditions (*take a degree*). **8** *tr.* occupy (*take
a chair*). **9** *tr.* make use of (*take the next turning on
the left*). **10** *tr.* consume as food or medicine (*took
tea; took the pills*). **11** *intr.* **a** be successful or effective
(*the inoculation did not take*). **b** (of a plant, seed, etc.)
begin to grow. **12** *tr.* require or use up (*will only take
a minute; these things take time*). **13** *tr.* cause to come
or go with one; convey (*take the book home; the bus
will take you all the way*). **14** *tr.* remove; dispossess a
person of (*someone has taken my pen*). **15** *tr.* catch or
be infected with (fire or fever etc.). **16** *tr.* **a** experience
or be affected by (*take fright; take pleasure*). **b** give
play to (*take comfort*). **c** exert (*take courage; take no
notice*). **17** *tr.* find out and note (a name and address;
a person's temperature etc.) by enquiry or measurement. **18** *tr.* grasp mentally; understand (*I take
your point; I took you to mean yes*). **19** *tr.* treat or
regard in a specified way (*took the news calmly; took*

it badly). **20** *tr.* (foll. by *for*) regard as being (*do you
take me for an idiot?*). **21** *tr.* **a** accept (*take the offer*).
b submit to (*take a joke; take no nonsense; took a
risk*). **22** *tr.* choose or assume (*took a different view;
took a job; took the initiative*). **23** *tr.* derive (*takes its
name from the inventor*). **24** *tr.* (foll. by *from*) subtract
(*take 3 from 9*). **25** *tr.* execute, make, or undertake;
perform or effect (*take notes; take an oath; take a
decision; take a look*). **26** *tr.* occupy or engage oneself
in; indulge in; enjoy (*take a rest; take exercise; take a
holiday*). **27** *tr.* conduct (*took the school assembly*). **28**
tr. deal with in a certain way (*took the corner too
fast*). **29** *tr.* **a** teach or be taught (a subject). **b** be
examined in (a subject). **30** *tr.* make (a photograph)
with a camera; photograph (a person or thing). **31** *tr.*
use as an instance (*let us take Napoleon*). **32** *tr.*
Gram. have or require as part of the appropriate
construction (*this verb takes an object*). **33** *tr.* have
sexual intercourse with (a woman). **34** *tr.* (in *passive*;
foll. by *by*, *with*) be attracted or charmed by. —*n.* **1**
an amount taken or caught in one session or attempt
etc. **2** a scene or sequence of film photographed
continuously at one time. **3** esp. *US* takings, esp.
money received at a theatre for seats. **4** *Printing* the
amount of copy set up at one time. □**be taken ill**
become ill, esp. suddenly. **have what it takes** *colloq.*
have the necessary qualities etc. for success. **take
account of** see ACCOUNT. **take action** see ACTION.
take advantage of see ADVANTAGE. **take advice**
see ADVICE. **take after** resemble (esp. a parent
or ancestor). **take against** begin to dislike, esp.
impulsively. **take aim** see AIM. **take apart** **1** dismantle. **2** *colloq.* beat or defeat. **take aside** see ASIDE.
take as read accept without reading or discussing.
take away **1** remove or carry elsewhere. **2** subtract.
3 *Brit.* buy (food etc.) at a shop or restaurant for
eating elsewhere. **take-away** *Brit. attrib.adj.* (of
food) bought at a shop or restaurant for eating
elsewhere. —*n.* **1** an establishment selling this. **2**
the food itself (*let's get a take-away*). **take back** **1**
retract (a statement). **2** convey (a person or thing) to
his or her or its original position. **3** carry (a person)
in thought to a past time. **4** *Printing* transfer to the
previous line. **take the biscuit** (or **bun** or **cake**)
colloq. be the most remarkable. **take a bow** see
BOW². **take care of** see CARE. **take a chance** etc. see
CHANCE. **take down** **1** write down (spoken words). **2**
remove (a structure) by separating it into pieces. **3**
humiliate. **take effect** see EFFECT. **take for granted**
see GRANT. **take fright** see FRIGHT. **take from**
diminish; weaken; detract from. **take heart** be
encouraged. **take hold** see HOLD¹. **take-home pay**
the pay received by an employee after the deduction
of tax etc. **take ill** (*US* **sick**) *colloq.* be taken ill. **take
in** **1** receive as a lodger etc. **2** undertake (work) at
home. **3** make (a garment etc.) smaller. **4** understand
(*did you take that in?*). **5** cheat (*managed to take them
all in*). **6** include or comprise. **7** *colloq.* visit (a place)
on the way to another (*shall we take in Avebury?*). **8**
furl (a sail). **9** *Brit.* regularly buy (a newspaper etc.).
take-in *n.* a deception. **take in hand** **1** undertake;
start doing or dealing with. **2** undertake the control
or reform of (a person). **take into account** see
ACCOUNT. **take it** **1** (often foll. by *that* + clause)
assume (*I take it that you have finished*). **2** *colloq.*
endure a difficulty or hardship in a specified way
(*took it badly*). **take it easy** see EASY. **take it from
me** (or **take my word for it**) I can assure you. **take
it ill** resent it. **take it into one's head** see HEAD.
take it on one (or **oneself**) (foll. by *to* + infin.)
venture or presume. **take it or leave it** (esp. in
imper.) an expression of indifference or impatience
about another's decision after making an offer. **take
it out of** **1** exhaust the strength of. **2** have revenge
on. **take it out on** relieve one's frustration by
attacking or treating harshly. **take one's leave of**
see LEAVE². **take a lot of** (or **some**) doing be hard
to do. **take a person's name in vain** see VAIN. **take**

off 1 a remove (clothing) from one's or another's body. **b** remove or lead away. **2** deduct (part of an amount). **3** depart, esp. hastily (*took off in a fast car*). **4** *colloq.* mimic humorously. **5** jump from the ground. **6** become airborne. **7** (of a scheme, enterprise, etc.) become successful or popular. **8** have (a period) away from work. **take-off 1** the act of becoming airborne. **2** an act of mimicking. **3** a place from which one jumps. **take oneself off** go away. **take on 1** undertake (work etc.). **2** engage (an employee). **3** be willing or ready to meet (an adversary in sport, argument, etc., esp. a stronger one). **4** acquire (a new meaning etc.). **5** *colloq.* show strong emotion. **take orders** see ORDER. **take out 1** remove from within a place; extract. **2** escort on an outing. **3** get (a licence or summons etc.) issued. **4** *US* = *take away* 3. **5** *Bridge* remove (a partner or a partner's call) from a suit by bidding a different one or no trumps. **6** murder or destroy. **take a person out of** himself or herself make a person forget his or her worries. **take over 1** succeed to the management or ownership of. **2** take control. **3** *Printing* transfer to the next line. **take-over** *n.* the assumption of control (esp. of a business); the buying-out of one company by another. **take part** see PART. **take place** see PLACE. **take a person's point** see POINT. **take shape** assume a distinct form; develop into something definite. **take sides** see SIDE. **take stock** see STOCK. **take the sun** see SUN. **take that!** an exclamation accompanying a blow etc. **take one's time** not hurry. **take to 1** begin or fall into the habit of (*took to smoking*). **2** have recourse to. **3** adapt oneself to. **4** form a liking for. **take to heart** see HEART. **take to one's heels** see HEEL¹. **take to pieces** see PIECE. **take the trouble** see TROUBLE. **take up 1** become interested or engaged in (a pursuit). **2** adopt as a protégé. **3** occupy (time or space). **4** begin (residence etc.). **5** resume after an interruption. **6** interrupt or question (a speaker). **7** accept (an offer etc.). **8** shorten (a garment). **9** lift up. **10** absorb (*sponges take up water*). **11** take (a person) into a vehicle. **12** pursue (a matter etc.) further. **take a person up on** accept (a person's offer etc.). **take up with** begin to associate with. □□ **takable** *adj.* (also **takeable**). [OE *tacan* f. ON *taka*]

taker /ˈteɪkə(r)/ *n.* **1** a person who takes a bet. **2** a person who accepts an offer.

takin /ˈtɑːkɪn/ *n.* a large Tibetan horned ruminant, *Budorcas taxicolor*. [Mishmi]

taking /ˈteɪkɪŋ/ *adj.* & *n.* —*adj.* **1** attractive or captivating. **2** catching or infectious. —*n.* (in *pl.*) an amount of money taken in business. □□ **takingly** *adv.* **takingness** *n.*

tala /ˈtɑːlə/ *n.* any of the traditional rhythmic patterns of Indian music. [Skr.]

talapoin /ˈtæləˌpɔɪn/ *n.* **1** a Buddhist monk or priest. **2** a small West African monkey, *Miopithecus talapoin*. [Port. *talapão* f. Talaing *tala pói* my lord]

talaria /təˈleərɪə/ *n.pl.* (in Roman mythology) winged sandals as an attribute of Mercury, Iris, and others. [L, neut. pl. of *talaris* f. *talus* ankle]

talc /tælk/ *n.* & *v.* —*n.* **1** talcum powder. **2** any crystalline form of magnesium silicate that occurs in soft flat plates, usu. white or pale green in colour and used as a lubricator etc. —*v.tr.* (**talcked**, **talcking**) treat (a surface) with talc to lubricate or dry it. □□ **talcose** *adj.* **talcous** *adj.* **talcy** *adj.* (in sense 1). [F *talc* or med.L *talcum*, f. Arab. *ṭalḳ* f. Pers. *ṭalḳ*]

talcum /ˈtælkəm/ *n.* **1** = TALC. **2** (in full **talcum powder**) powdered talc for toilet and cosmetic use, usu. perfumed. [med.L: see TALC]

tale /teɪl/ *n.* **1** a narrative or story, esp. fictitious and imaginatively treated. **2** a report of an alleged fact, often malicious or in breach of confidence (*all sorts of tales will get about*). **3** *archaic* or *literary* a number or total (*the tale is complete*). □ **tale of a tub** an idle fiction. [OE *talu* f. Gmc: cf. TELL¹]

talebearer /ˈteɪlˌbeərə(r)/ *n.* a person who maliciously gossips or reveals secrets. □□ **talebearing** *n.* & *adj.*

talent /ˈtælənt/ *n.* **1** a special aptitude or faculty (*a talent for music; has real talent*). **2** high mental ability. **3 a** a person or persons of talent (*is a real talent; plenty of local talent*). **b** *colloq.* members of the opposite sex regarded in terms of sexual promise. **4** an ancient weight and unit of currency, esp. among the Greeks. □ **talent-scout** (or **-spotter**) a person looking for talented performers, esp. in sport and entertainment. □□ **talented** *adj.* **talentless** *adj.* [OE *talente* & OF *talent* f. L *talentum* inclination of mind f. Gk *talanton* balance, weight, sum of money]

tales /ˈteɪliːz/ *n. Law* **1** a writ for summoning jurors to supply a deficiency. **2** a list of persons who may be summoned. [ME f. L *tales* (*de circumstantibus*) such (of the bystanders), the first words of the writ]

talesman /ˈteɪliːzmən, ˈteɪlz-/ *n.* (*pl.* **-men**) *Law* a person summoned by a *tales*.

taleteller /ˈteɪlˌtelə(r)/ *n.* **1** a person who tells stories. **2** a person who spreads malicious reports.

tali *pl.* of TALUS¹.

talion /ˈtælɪən/ *n.* = LEX TALIONIS. [ME f. OF f. L *talio -onis* f. *talis* such]

talipes /ˈtælɪˌpiːz/ *n. Med.* = *club-foot*. [mod.L f. L *talus* ankle + *pes* foot]

talipot /ˈtælɪˌpɒt/ *n.* a tall S. Indian palm, *Corypha umbraculifera*, with very large fan-shaped leaves that are used as sunshades etc. [Malayalam *tālipat*, Hindi *tālpāt* f. Skr. *tālapattra* f. *tāla* palm + *pattra* leaf]

talisman /ˈtælɪzmən/ *n.* (*pl.* **talismans**) **1** an object, esp. an inscribed ring or stone, supposed to be endowed with magic powers esp. of averting evil from or bringing good luck to its holder. **2** a charm or amulet; a thing supposed capable of working wonders. □□ **talismanic** /-ˈmænɪk/ *adj.* [F & Sp. = It. *talismano*, f. med.Gk *telesmon*, Gk *telesma* completion, religious rite f. *teleō* complete f. *telos* end]

talk /tɔːk/ *v.* & *n.* —*v.* **1** *intr.* (often foll. by *to*, *with*) converse or communicate ideas by spoken words. **2** *intr.* have the power of speech. **3** *intr.* (foll. by *about*) **a** have as the subject of discussion. **b** (in *imper.*) *colloq.* as an emphatic statement (*talk about expense! It cost me £50*). **4** *tr.* express or utter in words; discuss (*you are talking nonsense; talked cricket all day*). **5** *tr.* use (a language) in speech (*is talking Spanish*). **6** *intr.* (foll. by *at*) address pompously. **7** *tr.* (usu. foll. by *into*, *out of*) bring into a specified condition etc. by talking (*talked himself hoarse; how did you talk them into it?; talked them out of the difficulty*). **8** *intr.* reveal (esp. secret) information; betray secrets. **9** *intr.* gossip (*people are beginning to talk*). **10** *intr.* have influence (*money talks*). **11** *intr.* communicate by radio. —*n.* **1** conversation or talking. **2** a particular mode of speech (*baby-talk*). **3** an informal address or lecture. **4 a** rumour or gossip (*there is talk of a merger*). **b** its theme (*their success was the talk of the town*). **5** (often in *pl.*) extended discussions or negotiations. □ **know what one is talking about** be expert or authoritative. **now you're talking** *colloq.* I like what you say, suggest, etc. **talk away 1** consume (time) in talking. **2** carry on talking (*talk away! I'm listening*). **talk back 1** reply defiantly. **2** respond on a two-way radio system. **talk big** *colloq.* talk boastfully. **talk down to** speak patronizingly or condescendingly to. **talk a person down 1** silence a person by greater loudness or persistence. **2** bring (a pilot or aircraft) to landing by radio instructions from the ground. **talk the hind leg off a donkey** talk incessantly. **talk nineteen to the dozen** see DOZEN. **talk of 1** discuss or mention. **2** (often foll. by verbal noun) express some intention of (*talked of moving to London*). **talk of the town** what is being talked about generally. **talk out** *Brit.* block the course of (a bill in Parliament) by prolonging discussion to the time of adjournment. **talk over** discuss at length. **talk a person over** (or **round**) gain agreement or compliance from a person by talking. **talk shop** talk, esp. tediously or inopportunely, about one's occupation, business, etc. **talk show** = *chat show* (see CHAT¹). **talk tall** boast. **talk through one's hat** (or **neck**) *colloq.* **1** exaggerate. **2** bluff. **3** talk wildly or nonsensically. **talk to** reprove or scold (a person). **talk to oneself** soliloquize. **talk turkey** see TURKEY. **talk up** discuss (a subject) in order to arouse interest in it. **you can't** (or **can**) **talk** *colloq.* a reproof that the person addressed is just as culpable etc. in the matter at issue. □□ **talker** *n.* [ME *talken* frequent. verb f. TALE or TELL¹]

talkathon /'tɔːkə,θɒn/ *n. colloq.* a prolonged session of talking or discussion. [TALK + MARATHON]

talkative /'tɔːkətɪv/ *adj.* fond of or given to talking. □□ **talkatively** *adv.* **talkativeness** *n.*

talkback /'tɔːkbæk/ *n.* **1** (often *attrib.*) a system of two-way communication by loudspeaker. **2** *Austral.* & *NZ* = *phone-in* (see PHONE¹).

talkie /'tɔːkɪ/ *n. esp. US colloq.* a film with a soundtrack, as distinct from a silent film. [TALK + -IE, after *movie*]

talking /'tɔːkɪŋ/ *adj.* & *n.* —*adj.* **1** that talks. **2** having the power of speech (*a talking parrot*). **3** expressive (*talking eyes*). —*n.* in senses of TALK *v.* □ **talking book** a recorded reading of a book, esp. for the blind. **talking film** (or **picture**) a film with a soundtrack. **talking head** *colloq.* a presenter etc. on television, speaking to the camera and viewed in close-up. **talking of** while we are discussing (*talking of food, what time is lunch?*). **talking-point** a topic for discussion or argument. **talking-shop** *derog.* an institution regarded as a place of argument rather than action. **talking-to** *colloq.* a reproof or reprimand (*gave them a good talking-to*).

tall /tɔːl/ *adj.* & *adv.* —*adj.* **1** of more than average height. **2** of a specified height (*looks about six feet tall*). **3** higher than the surrounding objects (*a tall building*). **4** *colloq.* extravagant or excessive (*a tall story; tall talk*). —*adv.* as if tall; proudly; in a tall or extravagant way (*sit tall*). □ **tall drink** a drink served in a tall glass. **tall hat** = *top hat* (see TOP¹). **tall order** an exorbitant or unreasonable demand. **tall ship** a sailing ship with a high mast. □□ **tallish** *adj.* **tallness** *n.* [ME, repr. OE *getæl* swift, prompt]

tallage /'tælɪdʒ/ *n. hist.* **1** a form of taxation on towns etc., abolished in the 14th c. **2** a tax on feudal dependants etc. [ME f. OF *taillage* f. *tailler* cut: see TAIL²]

tallboy /'tɔːlbɔɪ/ *n.* a tall chest of drawers sometimes in lower and upper sections or mounted on legs.

tallith /'tælɪθ/ *n.* a scarf worn by Jews esp. at prayer. [Rabbinical Heb. *ṭallīt* f. *ṭillel* to cover]

tallow /'tæləʊ/ *n.* & *v.* —*n.* the harder kinds of (esp. animal) fat melted down for use in making candles, soap, etc. —*v.tr.* grease with tallow. □ **tallow-tree** any of various trees, esp. *Sapium sebiferum* of China, yielding vegetable tallow. **vegetable tallow** a vegetable fat used as tallow. □□ **tallowish** *adj.* **tallowy** *adj.* [ME *talg, talug,* f. MLG *talg, talch,* of unkn. orig.]

tally /'tælɪ/ *n.* & *v.* —*n.* (*pl.* **-ies**) **1** the reckoning of a debt or score. **2** a total score or amount. **3 a** a mark registering a fixed number of objects delivered or received. **b** such a number as a unit. **4** *hist.* **a** a piece of wood scored across with notches for the items of an account and then split into halves, each party keeping one. **b** an account kept in this way. **5 a** a ticket or label for identification. **6** a corresponding thing, counterpart, or duplicate. —*v.* (**-ies, -ied**) (often foll. by *with*) **1** *intr.* agree or correspond. **2** *tr.* record or reckon by tally. □ **tally clerk** an official who keeps a tally of goods, esp. those loaded or unloaded in docks. **tally sheet** a paper on which a

tally is kept. **tally system** a system of sale on short credit or instalments with an account kept by tally. □□ **tallier** *n.* [ME f. AF *tallie,* AL *tallia, talia* f. L *talea:* cf. TAIL²]

tally-ho /,tælɪ'həʊ/ *int., n.,* & *v.* —*int.* a huntsman's cry to the hounds on sighting a fox. —*n.* (*pl.* **-hos**) an utterance of this. —*v.* (**-hoes, -hoed**) **1** *intr.* utter a cry of 'tally-ho'. **2** *tr.* indicate (a fox) or urge (hounds) with this cry. [cf. F *taïaut*]

tallyman /'tælɪmən/ *n.* (*pl.* **-men**) **1** a person who keeps a tally. **2** a person who sells goods on credit, esp. from door to door.

Talmud /'tælmʊd, -məd/ *n.* the body of Jewish civil and ceremonial law and legend comprising the Mishnah and the Gemara. □□ **Talmudic** /-'mʊdɪk/ *adj.* **Talmudical** /-'mʊdɪk(ə)l/ *adj.* **Talmudist** *n.* [late Heb. *talmūḏ* instruction f. Heb. *lāmaḏ* learn]

talon /'tælən/ *n.* **1** a claw, esp. of a bird of prey. **2** the cards left after the deal in a card-game. **3** the last part of a dividend-coupon sheet, entitling the holder to a new sheet on presentation. **4** the shoulder of a bolt against which the key presses in shooting it in a lock. **5** an ogee moulding. □□ **taloned** *adj.* (also in *comb.*). [ME f. OF, = heel, ult. f. L *talus:* see TALUS¹]

talus¹ /'teɪləs/ *n.* (*pl.* **tali** /-laɪ/) *Anat.* the ankle-bone supporting the tibia. Also called ASTRAGALUS. [L, = ankle, heel]

talus² /'teɪləs/ *n.* (*pl.* **taluses**) **1** the slope of a wall that tapers to the top or rests against a bank. **2** *Geol.* a sloping mass of fragments at the foot of a cliff. [F: orig. unkn.]

TAM *abbr.* television audience measurement.

tam /tæm/ *n.* a tam-o'-shanter. [abbr.]

tamable var. of TAMEABLE.

tamale /tə'mɑːlɪ/ *n.* a Mexican food of seasoned meat and maize flour steamed or baked in maize husks. [Mex. Sp. *tamal,* pl. *tamales*]

tamandua /tə'mændjuːə/ *n.* any small Central and S. American arboreal anteater of the genus *Tamandua,* with a prehensile tail used in climbing. [Port. f. Tupi *tamanduà*]

tamarack /'tæmə,ræk/ *n.* **1** an American larch, *Larix laricina.* **2** the wood from this. [Amer. Ind.]

tamarillo /,tæmə'rɪləʊ/ *n.* (*pl.* **-os**) esp. *Austral.* & *NZ* = *tree tomato.* [arbitrary marketing name: cf. Sp. *tomatillo* dimin. of *tomate* TOMATO]

tamarin /'tæmərɪn/ *n.* any S. American usu. insect-eating monkey of the genus *Saguinus,* having hairy crests and moustaches. [F f. Carib]

tamarind /'tæmərɪnd/ *n.* **1** a tropical evergreen tree, *Tamarindus indica.* **2** the fruit of this, containing an acid pulp used as food and in making drinks. [med.L *tamarindus* f. Arab. *tamr-hindī* Indian date]

tamarisk /'tæmərɪsk/ *n.* any shrub of the genus *Tamarix,* usu. with long slender branches and small pink or white flowers, that thrives by the sea. [ME f. LL *tamariscus,* L *tamarix*]

tambour /'tæmbʊə(r)/ *n.* & *v.* —*n.* **1** a drum. **2 a** a circular frame for holding fabric taut while it is being embroidered. **b** material embroidered in this way. **3** *Archit.* each of a sequence of cylindrical stones forming the shaft of a column. **4** *Archit.* the circular part of various structures. **5** *Archit.* a lobby with a ceiling and folding doors in a church porch etc. to obviate draughts. **6** a sloping buttress or projection in a fives-court etc. —*v.tr.* (also *absol.*) decorate or embroider on a tambour. [F f. *tabour* TABOR]

tamboura /tæm'bʊərə/ *n. Mus.* an Indian stringed instrument used as a drone. [Arab. *ṭanbūra*]

tambourin /'tæmbərɪn/ *n.* **1** a long narrow drum used in Provence. **2 a** a dance accompanied by a tambourin. **b** the music for this. [F, dimin. of TAMBOUR]

tambourine /,tæmbə'riːn/ *n.* a percussion instrument consisting of a hoop with a parchment stretched over one side and jingling discs in slots round the hoop. □□ **tambourinist** n. [F, dimin. of TAMBOUR]

tame /teɪm/ adj. & v. —adj. **1** (of an animal) domesticated; not wild or shy. **2** insipid; lacking spirit or interest; dull (*tame acquiescence*). **3** (of a person) amenable and available. **4** US **a** (of land) cultivated. **b** (of a plant) produced by cultivation. —v.tr. **1** make tame; domesticate; break in. **2** subdue, curb, humble; break the spirit of. □□ **tamely** adv. **tameness** n. **tamer** n. (also in comb.). [OE tam f. Gmc]

tameable /ˈteɪməb(ə)l/ adj. (also **tamable**) capable of being tamed. □□ **tameability** /-ˈbɪlɪtɪ/ n. **tameableness** n.

Tamil /ˈtæmɪl/ n. & adj. —n. **1** a member of a Dravidian people inhabiting South India and Sri Lanka. **2** the language of this people. —adj. of this people or their language. □□ **Tamilian** /-ˈmɪlɪən/ adj. [native name *Tamiḷ*, rel. to DRAVIDIAN]

Tammany /ˈtæmənɪ/ n. (also **Tammany Hall**) US **1** a corrupt political organization or group. **2** corrupt political activities. □□ **Tammanyism** n. [orig. the name of a benevolent society in New York with headquarters at Tammany Hall, which later became the headquarters of the Democratic Party in New York]

tammy /ˈtæmɪ/ n. (pl. **-ies**) = TAM-O'-SHANTER.

tam-o'-shanter /ˌtæməˈʃæntə(r)/ n. a round woollen or cloth cap of Scottish origin fitting closely round the brows but large and full above. [the hero of Burns's *Tam o' Shanter*]

tamp /tæmp/ v.tr. **1** pack (a blast-hole) full of clay etc. to get the full force of an explosion. **2** ram down (road material etc.). □□ **tamper** n. **tamping** n. (in sense 1). [perh. back-form. f. F *tampin* (var. of TAMPION, taken as = *tamping*]

tamper /ˈtæmpə(r)/ v.intr. (foll. by with) **1** meddle with or make unauthorized changes in. **2** exert a secret or corrupt influence upon; bribe. □□ **tamperer** n. **tamper-proof** adj. [var. of TEMPER]

tampion /ˈtæmpɪən/ n. (also **tompion** /ˈtɒm-/) **1** a wooden stopper for the muzzle of a gun. **2** a plug e.g. for the top of an organ-pipe. [ME f. F *tampon*, nasalized var. of *tapon*, rel. to TAP¹]

tampon /ˈtæmpɒn/ n. & v. —n. a plug of soft material used to stop a wound or absorb secretions, esp. one inserted into the vagina. —v.tr. (**tamponed**, **tamponing**) plug with a tampon. [F: see TAMPION]

tamponade /ˌtæmpəˈneɪd/ n. compression of the heart by an accumulation of fluid in the pericardial sac.

tamponage /ˈtæmpənɪdʒ/ n. = TAMPONADE.

tam-tam /ˈtæmtæm/ n. a large metal gong. [Hindi: see TOM-TOM]

tan¹ /tæn/ n., adj., & v. —n. **1** a brown skin colour resulting from exposure to ultraviolet light. **2** a yellowish-brown colour. **3** bark, esp. of oak, bruised and used to tan hides. **4** (in full **spent tan**) tan from which the tannic acid has been extracted, used for covering roads etc. —adj. yellowish-brown. —v. (**tanned**, **tanning**) **1** tr. & intr. make or become brown by exposure to ultraviolet light. **2** tr. convert (raw hide) into leather by soaking in a liquid containing tannic acid or by the use of mineral salts etc. **3** tr. sl. beat, thrash. □□ **tannable** adj. **tanning** n. **tannish** adj. [OE *tannian*, prob. f. med.L *tanare*, *tannare*, perh. f. Celtic]

tan² /tæn/ abbr. tangent.

tanager /ˈtænədʒə(r)/ n. any small American bird of the subfamily Thraupinae, the male usu. having brightly-coloured plumage. [mod.L *tanagra* f. Tupi *tangara*]

tanbark /ˈtænbɑːk/ n. the bark of oak and other trees, used to obtain tannin.

tandem /ˈtændəm/ n. & adv. —n. **1** a bicycle or tricycle with two or more seats one behind another. **2** a group of two persons or machines etc. with one behind or following the other. **3** a carriage driven tandem. —adv. with two or more horses harnessed one behind another (*drive tandem*). □**in tandem** one behind another. [L, = at length (of time), used punningly]

tandoor /ˈtænduə(r)/ n. a clay oven. [Hind.]

tandoori /tænˈduərɪ/ n. food cooked over charcoal in a tandoor (often *attrib.: tandoori chicken*). [Hind.]

Tang /tæŋ/ n. **1** a dynasty ruling China 618–c.906. **2** (*attrib.*) designating art and artefacts of this period. [Chin. *táng*]

tang¹ /tæŋ/ n. **1** a strong taste or flavour or smell. **2** a characteristic quality. **3** the projection on the blade of a tool, esp. a knife, by which the blade is held firm in the handle. [ME f. ON *tange* point, tang of a knife]

tang² /tæŋ/ v. & n. —v.tr. & intr. ring, clang; sound loudly. —n. a tanging sound. [imit.]

tanga /ˈtæŋgə/ n. a skimpy bikini of small panels connected with strings. [Port.]

tangelo /ˈtændʒəˌləʊ/ n. (pl. **-os**) a hybrid of the tangerine and grapefruit. [TANGERINE + POMELO]

tangent /ˈtændʒ(ə)nt/ n. & adj. —n. **1** a straight line, curve, or surface that meets another curve or curved surface at a point, but if extended does not intersect it at that point. **2** the ratio of the sides opposite and adjacent to an angle in a right-angled triangle. —adj. **1** (of a line or surface) that is a tangent. **2** touching. □**at a tangent** diverging from a previous course of action or thought etc. (*go off at a tangent*). **tangent galvanometer** a galvanometer with a coil through which the current to be measured is passed, its strength being proportional to the tangent of the angle of deflection. □□ **tangency** n. [L *tangere tangent-* touch]

tangential /tænˈdʒenʃ(ə)l/ adj. **1** of or along a tangent. **2** divergent. **3** peripheral. □□ **tangentially** adv.

tangerine /ˈtændʒəˌriːn/ n. **1** a small sweet orange-coloured citrus fruit with a thin skin; a mandarin. **2** a deep orange-yellow colour. [*Tangier* in Morocco]

tangible /ˈtændʒɪb(ə)l/ adj. **1** perceptible by touch. **2** definite; clearly intelligible; not elusive or visionary (*tangible proof*). □□ **tangibility** /-ˈbɪlɪtɪ/ n. **tangibleness** n. **tangibly** /-blɪ/ adv. [F *tangible* or LL *tangibilis* f. *tangere* touch]

tangle¹ /ˈtæŋg(ə)l/ v. & n. —v. **1 a** tr. intertwine (threads or hairs etc.) in a confused mass; entangle. **b** intr. become tangled. **2** intr. (foll. by with) colloq. become involved (esp. in conflict or argument) with (*don't tangle with me*). **3** tr. complicate (*a tangled affair*). —n. **1** a confused mass of intertwined threads etc. **2** a confused or complicated state (*be in a tangle*; *a love tangle*). [ME var. of obs. *tagle*, of uncert. orig.]

tangle² /ˈtæŋg(ə)l/ n. any of various seaweeds, esp. of the genus *Laminaria* or *Fucus*. [prob. f. Norw. *taangel* f. ON *thöngull*]

tangly /ˈtæŋglɪ/ adj. (**tanglier**, **tangliest**) tangled.

tango¹ /ˈtæŋgəʊ/ n. & v. —n. (pl. **-os**) **1** a slow S. American ballroom dance. **2** the music for this. —v.intr. (**-oes**, **-oed**) dance the tango. [Amer. Sp.]

tango² /ˈtæŋgəʊ/ n. a tangerine colour. [abbr. after TANGO¹]

tangram /ˈtæŋgræm/ n. a Chinese puzzle square cut into seven pieces to be combined into various figures. [19th c.: orig. unkn.]

tangy /ˈtæŋɪ/ adj. (**tangier**, **tangiest**) having a strong usu. spicy tang. □□ **tanginess** n.

tanh /θæn, tænʃ, tænˈeɪtʃ/ abbr. hyperbolic tangent.

tanist /ˈtænɪst/ n. hist. the heir apparent to a Celtic chief, usu. his most vigorous adult relation, chosen by election. □□ **tanistry** n. [Ir. & Gael. *tánaiste* heir]

tank /tæŋk/ n. & v. —n. **1** a large receptacle or storage chamber usu. for liquid or gas. **2** a heavy armoured fighting vehicle carrying guns and moving on a tracked carriage. **3** a container for the fuel supply in a motor vehicle. **4** the part of a locomotive tender containing water for the boiler. **5 a** Ind. & Austral. a reservoir. **b** dial. esp. US a pond. —v. (usu. foll. by up) esp. Brit. **1** tr. fill the tank of (a vehicle etc.) with fuel. **2** *intr.* & *colloq. tr.* (in *passive*) drink heavily; become drunk. □**tank engine** a railway engine carrying fuel and water receptacles in its own frame, not in a tender. **tank-farming** the practice of growing plants in tanks of water without soil. **tank top** a sleeveless, close-fitting upper garment with a scoop-neck. □□**tankful** *n.* (*pl.* **-fuls**). **tankless** *adj.* [Gujurati *tānkh* etc., perh. f. Skr. *tadāga* pond]

tanka /'tæŋkə/ *n.* a Japanese poem in five lines and thirty-one syllables giving a complete picture of an event or mood. [Jap.]

tankage /'tæŋkɪdʒ/ *n.* **1 a** storage in tanks. **b** a charge made for this. **2** the cubic content of a tank. **3** a kind of fertilizer obtained from refuse bones etc.

tankard /'tæŋkəd/ *n.* **1** a tall mug with a handle and sometimes a hinged lid, esp. of silver or pewter for beer. **2** the contents of or an amount held by a tankard (*drank a tankard of ale*). [ME: orig. unkn.: cf. MDu. *tanckaert*]

tanker /'tæŋkə(r)/ *n.* a ship, aircraft, or road vehicle for carrying liquids, esp. mineral oils, in bulk.

tanner[1] /'tænə(r)/ *n.* a person who tans hides.

tanner[2] /'tænə(r)/ *n. Brit. hist. sl.* a sixpence. [19th c.: orig. unkn.]

tannery /'tænərɪ/ *n.* (*pl.* **-ies**) a place where hides are tanned.

tannic /'tænɪk/ *adj.* of or produced from tan. □**tannic acid** a complex natural organic compound of a yellowish colour used as a mordant and astringent. □□**tannate** /-neɪt/ *n.* [F *tannique* (as TANNIN)]

tannin /'tænɪn/ *n.* any of a group of complex organic compounds found in certain tree-barks and oak-galls, used in leather production and ink manufacture. [F *tanin* (as TAN[1], -IN)]

tannish see TAN[1].

Tannoy /'tænɔɪ/ *n. propr.* a type of public-address system. [20th c.: orig. uncert.]

tanrec var. of TENREC.

tansy /'tænzɪ/ *n.* (*pl.* **-ies**) any plant of the genus *Tanacetum*, esp. *T. vulgare* with yellow button-like flowers and aromatic leaves, formerly used in medicines and cookery. [ME f. OF *tanesie* f. med.L *athanasia* immortality f. Gk]

tantalite /'tæntəˌlaɪt/ *n.* a rare dense black mineral, the principal source of the element tantalum. [G & Sw. *tantalit* (as TANTALUM)]

tantalize /'tæntəˌlaɪz/ *v.tr.* (also **-ise**) **1** torment or tease by the sight or promise of what is unobtainable. **2** raise and then dash the hopes of; torment with disappointment. □□ **tantalization** /-'zeɪʃ(ə)n/ *n.* **tantalizer** *n.* **tantalizingly** *adv.* [Gk *Tantalos* mythical king of Phrygia condemned to stand in water that receded when he tried to drink it and under branches that drew back when he tried to pick the fruit]

tantalum /'tæntələm/ *n. Chem.* a rare hard white metallic element occurring naturally in tantalite, resistant to heat and the action of acids, and used in surgery and for electronic components. ¶ Symb.: **Ta**. □□ **tantalic** *adj.* [formed as TANTALUS with ref. to its non-absorbent quality]

tantalus /'tæntələs/ *n.* **1** a stand in which spirit-decanters may be locked up but visible. **2** a wood ibis, *Mycteria americana*. [see TANTALIZE]

tantamount /'tæntəˌmaʊnt/ *predic.adj.* (foll. by *to*) equivalent to (*was tantamount to a denial*). [f. obs. verb f. It. *tanto montare* amount to so much]

tantivy /tæn'tɪvɪ/ *n.* & *adj. archaic* —*n.* (*pl.* **-ies**) **1** a hunting cry. **2** a swift movement; a gallop or rush. —*adj.* swift. [17th c.: perh. an imit. of hoof-beats]

tant mieux /tɑ̃ 'mjɜː/ *int.* so much the better. [F]

tant pis /tɑ̃ 'piː/ *int.* so much the worse. [F]

tantra /'tæntrə/ *n.* any of a class of Hindu or Buddhist mystical and magical writings. □□ **tantric** *adj.* **tantrism** *n.* **tantrist** *n.* [Skr., = loom, groundwork, doctrine f. *tan* stretch]

tantrum /'tæntrəm/ *n.* an outburst of bad temper or petulance (*threw a tantrum*). [18th c.: orig. unkn.]

Taoiseach /'tiːʃəx/ *n.* the Prime Minister of the Irish Republic. [Ir., = chief, leader]

Taoism /'taʊɪz(ə)m, 'taːəʊ-/ *n.* a Chinese philosophy based on the writings of Laoze (*c*.500 BC), advocating humility and religious piety. □□ **Taoist** /-ɪst/ *n.* **Taoistic** /-'ɪstɪk/ *adj.* [Chin. *dao* (right) way]

tap[1] /tæp/ *n.* & *v.* —*n.* **1** a device by which a flow of liquid or gas from a pipe or vessel can be controlled. **2** an act of tapping a telephone etc. **3** *Brit.* a taproom. **4** an instrument for cutting the thread of a female screw. —*v.tr.* (**tapped**, **tapping**) **1 a** provide (a cask) with a tap. **b** let out (a liquid) by means of, or as if by means of, a tap. **2** draw sap from (a tree) by cutting into it. **3 a** obtain information or supplies or resources from. **b** establish communication or trade with. **4** connect a listening device to (a telephone or telegraph line etc.) to listen to a call or transmission. **5** cut a female screw-thread in. □**on tap 1** ready to be drawn off by tap. **2** *colloq.* ready for immediate use; freely available. **tap root** a tapering root growing vertically downwards. **tap water** water from a piped supply. □□ **tapless** *adj.* **tappable** *adj.* [OE *tæppian* (v.), *tæppa* (n.) f. Gmc]

tap[2] /tæp/ *v.* & *n.* —*v.* (**tapped**, **tapping**) **1** *intr.* (foll. by *at*, *on*) strike a gentle but audible blow. **2** *tr.* strike lightly (*tapped me on the shoulder*). **3** *tr.* (foll. by *against* etc.) cause (a thing) to strike lightly (*tapped a stick against the window*). **4** *intr.* = TAP-DANCE *v.* (*can you tap?*). —*n.* **1 a** a light blow; a rap. **b** the sound of this (*heard a tap at the door*). **2 a** = TAP-DANCE *n.* (*goes to tap classes*). **b** a piece of metal attached to the toe and heel of a tap-dancer's shoe to make the tapping sound. **3** (in *pl.*, usu. treated as *sing.*) *US* **a** a bugle call for lights to be put out in army quarters. **b** a similar signal at a military funeral. □□ **tapper** *n.* [ME *tappe* (imit.), perh. through F *taper*]

tapa /'taːpə/ *n.* **1** the bark of a paper-mulberry tree. **2** cloth made from this, used in the Pacific islands. [Polynesian]

tap-dance /'tæpdaːns/ *n.* & *v.* —*n.* a form of display dance performed wearing shoes fitted with metal taps, with rhythmical tapping of the toes and heels. —*v.intr.* perform a tap-dance. □□ **tap-dancer** *n.* **tap-dancing** *n.*

tape /teɪp/ *n.* & *v.* —*n.* **1** a narrow strip of woven material for tying up, fastening, etc. **2 a** a strip of material stretched across the finishing line of a race. **b** a similar strip for marking off an area or forming a notional barrier. **3** (in full **adhesive tape**) a strip of opaque or transparent paper or plastic etc., esp. coated with adhesive for fastening, sticking, masking, insulating, etc. **4 a** = *magnetic tape*. **b** a tape recording or tape cassette. **5** = *tape-measure*. —*v.tr.* **1 a** tie up or join etc. with tape. **b** apply tape to. **2** (foll. by *off*) seal or mark off an area or thing with tape. **3** record on magnetic tape. **4** measure with tape. □**breast the tape** win a race. **have** (or **get**) **a person** or **thing taped** *Brit. colloq.* understand a person or thing fully. **on tape** recorded on magnetic tape. **tape deck** a platform with capstans for using magnetic tape. **tape machine** a machine for receiving and recording telegraph messages. **tape-measure** a strip of tape or thin flexible metal marked for measuring lengths. **tape-record** record (sounds) on magnetic tape. **tape recorder** apparatus for recording sounds on magnetic tape and afterwards reproducing them. **tape recording** a recording on magnetic tape. □□ **tapeable** *adj.* (esp. in sense 3 of *v.*). **tapeless** *adj.* **tapelike** *adj.* [OE *tæppa*, *tæppe*, of unkn. orig.]

taper /'teɪpə(r)/ *n.* & *v.* —*n.* **1** a wick coated with wax etc. for conveying a flame. **2** a slender candle. —*v.* (often foll. by *off*) **1** *intr.* & *tr.* diminish or reduce in thickness towards one end. **2** *tr.* & *intr.* make or become gradually less. [OE *tapur, -or, -er* wax candle, f. L PAPYRUS, whose pith was used for candle-wicks]

tapestry /'tæpɪstrɪ/ n. (pl. **-ies**) **1 a** a thick textile fabric in which coloured weft threads are woven to form pictures or designs. **b** embroidery imitating this, usu. in wools on canvas. **c** a piece of such embroidery. **2** events or circumstances etc. compared with a tapestry in being intricate, interwoven, etc. (*life's rich tapestry*). □□ **tapestried** adj. [ME, alt. f. *tapissery* f. OF *tapisserie* f. *tapissier* tapestry-worker or *tapisser* to carpet, f. *tapis*: see TAPIS]

tapetum /tə'piːtəm/ n. a light-reflecting part of the choroid membrane in the eyes of certain mammals, e.g. cats. [LL f. L *tapete* carpet]

tapeworm /'teɪpwɜːm/ n. any flatworm of the class Cestoda, with a body like segmented tape, living as a parasite in the intestines.

tapioca /ˌtæpɪ'əʊkə/ n. a starchy substance in hard white grains obtained from cassava and used for puddings etc. [Tupi-Guarani *tipioca* f. *tipi* dregs + *og, ok* squeeze out]

tapir /'teɪpə(r), -pɪə(r)/ n. any nocturnal hoofed mammal of the genus *Tapirus*, native to Central and S. America and Malaysia, having a short flexible protruding snout used for feeding on vegetation. □□ **tapiroid** adj. & n. [Tupi *tapira*]

tapis /'tæpiː/ n. a covering or tapestry. □ **on the tapis** (of a subject) under consideration or discussion. [ME, a kind of cloth, f. OF *tapiz* f. LL *tapetium* f. Gk *tapētion* dimin. of *tapēs tapētos* tapestry]

tapotement /tə'pəʊtmənt/ n. Med. rapid and repeated striking of the body as massage treatment. [F f. *tapoter* tap]

tapper see TAP[2].

tappet /'tæpɪt/ n. a lever or projecting part used in machinery to give intermittent motion, often in conjunction with a cam. [app. f. TAP[2] + -ET[1]]

taproom /'tæpruːm, -rʊm/ n. a room in which alcoholic drinks are available on tap.

tapster /'tæpstə(r)/ n. a person who draws and serves alcoholic drinks at a bar. [OE *tæppestre* orig. fem. (as TAP[1], -STER)]

tapu /'tɑːpuː/ n. & adj. NZ = TABOO. [Maori]

tar[1] /tɑː(r)/ n. & v. — n. **1** a dark thick inflammable liquid distilled from wood or coal etc. and used as a preservative of wood and iron, in making roads, as an antiseptic, etc. **2** a similar substance formed in the combustion of tobacco etc. — v.tr. (**tarred**, **tarring**) cover with tar. □ **tar and feather** smear with tar and then cover with feathers as a punishment. **tar-brush** a brush for applying tar. **tarred with the same brush** having the same faults. [OE *te(o)ru* f. Gmc, rel. to TREE]

tar[2] /tɑː(r)/ n. colloq. a sailor. [abbr. of TARPAULIN]

taradiddle /'tærəˌdɪd(ə)l/ n. (also **tarradiddle**) colloq. **1** a petty lie. **2** pretentious nonsense. [18th c.: cf. DIDDLE]

taramasalata /ˌtærəməsə'lɑːtə/ n. (also **tarama** /'tærəmə/) a pinkish pâté made from the roe of mullet or other fish with olive oil, seasoning, etc. [mod.Gk *taramas* roe (f. Turk. *tarama*) + *salata* SALAD]

tarantass /ˌtærən'tæs/ n. a springless four-wheeled Russian vehicle. [Russ. *tarantas*]

tarantella /ˌtærən'telə/ n. (also **tarantelle** /-'tel/) **1** a rapid whirling S. Italian dance. **2** the music for this. [It., f. *Taranto* in Italy (because the dance was once thought to be a cure for a tarantula bite): cf. TARANTULA]

tarantism /'tærənˌtɪz(ə)m/ n. hist. dancing mania, esp. that originating in S. Italy among those who had (actually or supposedly) been bitten by a tarantula. [mod.L *tarantismus*, It. *tarantismo* f. *Taranto* in S. Italy f. L *Tarentum*]

tarantula /tə'ræntjʊlə/ n. **1** any large hairy tropical spider of the family Theraphosidae. **2** a large black S. European spider, *Lycosa tarentula*, whose bite was formerly held to cause tarantism. [med.L f. It. *tarantola* (as TARANTISM)]

taraxacum /tə'ræksəkəm/ n. **1** any composite plant of the genus *Taraxacum*, including the dandelion. **2** a tonic etc. prepared from the dried roots of this. [med.L f. Arab. *ṭarakšaḵūk* f. Pers. *talḵ* bitter + *chakūk* purslane]

tarboosh /tɑː'buːʃ/ n. a cap like a fez, sometimes worn as part of a turban. [Egypt. Arab. *ṭarbūš*, ult. f. Pers. *sar-būš* head-cover]

Tardenoisian /ˌtɑːdɪ'nɔɪzɪən/ n. & adj. Archaeol. — n. a mesolithic culture using small flint implements. — adj. of or relating to this culture. [*Tardenois* in NE France, where remains of it were found]

tardigrade /'tɑːdɪˌɡreɪd/ n. & adj. — n. any minute freshwater animal of the phylum Tardigrada, having a short plump body and four pairs of short legs. Also called *water bear*. — adj. of or relating to this phylum. [F *tardigrade* f. L *tardigradus* f. *tardus* slow + *gradi* walk]

tardy /'tɑːdɪ/ adj. (**tardier**, **tardiest**) **1** slow to act or come or happen. **2** delaying or delayed beyond the right or expected time. □□ **tardily** adv. **tardiness** n. [F *tardif, tardive* ult. f. L *tardus* slow]

tare[1] /teə(r)/ n. **1** vetch, esp. as corn-weed or fodder. **2** (in pl.) Bibl. an injurious corn-weed (Matt. 13:24-30). [ME: orig. unkn.]

tare[2] /teə(r)/ n. **1** an allowance made for the weight of the packing or wrapping around goods. **2** the weight of a motor vehicle without its fuel or load. □ **tare and tret** the arithmetical rule for computing a tare. [ME f. F, = deficiency, tare, f. med.L *tara* f. Arab. *ṭarḥa* what is rejected f. *ṭaraḥa* reject]

targe /tɑːdʒ/ n. archaic = TARGET n. 5. [ME f. OF]

target /'tɑːɡɪt/ n. & v. — n. **1** a mark or point fired or aimed at, esp. a round or rectangular object marked with concentric circles. **2** a person or thing aimed at, or exposed to gunfire etc. (*they were an easy target*). **3** (also attrib.) an objective or result aimed at (*our export targets*; *target date*). **4** a person or thing against whom criticism, abuse, etc., is or may be directed. **5** archaic a shield or buckler, esp. a small round one. — v.tr. (**targeted**, **targeting**) **1** identify or single out (a person or thing) as an object of attention or attack. **2** aim or direct (*missiles targeted on major cities*; *should target our efforts where needed*). □□ **targetable** adj. [ME, dimin. of ME and OF *targe* shield]

tariff /'tærɪf/ n. & v. — n. **1** a table of fixed charges (a *hotel tariff*). **2 a** a duty on a particular class of imports or exports. **b** a list of duties or customs to be paid. **3** standard charges agreed between insurers etc. — v.tr. subject (goods) to a tariff. [F *tarif* f. It. *tariffa* f. Turk. *tarife* f. Arab. *ta'rīf(a)* f. *'arrafa* notify]

tarlatan /'tɑːlət(ə)n/ n. a thin stiff open-weave muslin. [F *tarlatane*, prob. of Ind. orig.]

Tarmac /'tɑːmæk/ n. & v. — n. propr. **1** = TARMACADAM. **2** a surface made of this, e.g. a runway. — v.tr. (**tarmac**) (**tarmacked**, **tarmacking**) apply tarmacadam to. [abbr.]

tarmacadam /ˌtɑːmə'kædəm/ n. a material of stone or slag bound with tar, used in paving roads etc. [TAR[1] + MACADAM]

tarn /tɑːn/ n. a small mountain lake. [ME *terne, tarne* f. ON]

tarnish /'tɑːnɪʃ/ v. & n. — v. **1** tr. lessen or destroy the lustre of (metal etc.). **2** tr. impair (one's reputation etc.). **3** intr. (of metal etc.) lose lustre. — n. **1 a** a loss of lustre. **b** a film of colour formed on an exposed surface of a mineral or metal. **2** a blemish; a stain. □□ **tarnishable** adj. [F *ternir* f. *terne* dark]

taro /'tɑːrəʊ/ n. (pl. **-os**) a tropical aroid plant, *Colocasia esculenta*, with tuberous roots used as food. Also called EDDO. [Polynesian]

tarot /'tærəʊ/ n. **1** (in sing. or pl.) **a** any of several games played with a pack of cards having five suits, the last of which is a set of permanent trumps. **b** a similar pack used in fortune-telling. **2 a** any of the trump cards. **b** any of the cards from a fortune-telling pack. [F *tarot*, It. *tarocchi*, of unkn. orig.]

tarp /tɑːp/ n. US & Austral. colloq. tarpaulin. [abbr.]

tarpan /'tɑːpæn/ n. an extinct N. European primitive wild horse. [Kirghiz Tartar]

tarpaulin /tɑːˈpɔːlɪn/ n. 1 heavy-duty waterproof cloth esp. of tarred canvas. 2 a sheet or covering of this. 3 a a sailor's tarred or oilskin hat. b archaic a sailor. [prob. f. TAR¹ + PALL¹ + -ING¹]

tarpon /'tɑːpɒn/ n. 1 a large silvery fish, Tarpon atlanticus, common in the tropical Atlantic. 2 a similar fish, Megalops cyprinoides, of the Pacific ocean. [Du. tarpoen, of unkn. orig.]

tarradiddle var. of TARADIDDLE.

tarragon /'tærəgən/ n. a bushy herb, Artemisia dracunculus, with leaves used to flavour salads, stuffings, vinegar, etc. [= med.L tarchon f. med. Gk tarkhōn, perh. through Arab. f. Gk drakōn dragon]

tarras var. of TRASS.

tarry¹ /'tɑːrɪ/ adj. (tarrier, tarriest) of or like or smeared with tar. □□ **tarriness** n.

tarry² /'tærɪ/ v.intr. (-ies, -ied) archaic or literary 1 defer coming or going. 2 linger, stay, wait. 3 be tardy. □□ **tarrier** n. [ME: orig. uncert.]

tarsal /'tɑːs(ə)l/ adj. & n. —adj. of or relating to the bones in the ankle. —n. a tarsal bone. [TARSUS + -AL]

tarsi pl. of TARSUS.

tarsi- /'tɑːsɪ/ comb. form (also **tarso-** /'tɑːsəʊ/) tarsus.

tarsia /'tɑːsɪə/ n. = INTARSIA. [It.]

tarsier /'tɑːsɪə(r)/ n. any small large-eyed arboreal nocturnal primate of the genus Tarsius, native to Borneo, the Philippines, etc., with a long tail and long hind legs used for leaping from tree to tree. [F (as TARSUS), from the structure of its foot]

tarso- comb. form var. of TARSI-.

tarsus /'tɑːsəs/ n. (pl. **tarsi** /-saɪ/) 1 a the group of bones forming the ankle and upper foot. b the shank of a bird's leg. c the terminal segment of a limb in insects. 2 the fibrous connective tissue of the eyelid. [mod.L f. Gk tarsos flat of the foot, rim of the eyelid]

tart¹ /tɑːt/ n. 1 an open pastry case containing jam etc. 2 esp. Brit. a pie with a fruit or sweet filling. □□ **tartlet** n. [ME f. OF tarte = med.L tarta, of unkn. orig.]

tart² /tɑːt/ n. & v. —n. sl. 1 a prostitute; a promiscuous woman. 2 sl. offens. a girl or woman. —v. (foll. by up) esp. Brit. colloq. 1 tr. (usu. refl.) smarten (oneself or a thing) up, esp. flashily or gaudily. 2 intr. dress up gaudily. [prob. abbr. of SWEETHEART]

tart³ /tɑːt/ adj. 1 sharp or acid in taste. 2 (of a remark etc.) cutting, bitter. □□ **tartly** adv. **tartness** n. [OE teart, of unkn. orig.]

tartan¹ /'tɑːt(ə)n/ n. 1 a pattern of coloured stripes crossing at right angles, esp. the distinctive plaid worn by the Scottish Highlanders to denote their clan. 2 woollen cloth woven in this pattern (often attrib.: a tartan scarf). [perh. f. OF tertaine, tiretaine]

tartan² /'tɑːt(ə)n/ n. a lateen-sailed single-masted ship used in the Mediterranean. [F tartane f. It. tartana, perh. f. Arab. ṭarīda]

Tartar /'tɑːtə(r)/ n. & adj. (also **Tatar** except in sense 2 of n.) —n. 1 a a member of a group of Central Asian peoples including Mongols and Turks. b the Turkic language of these peoples. 2 (**tartar**) a violent-tempered or intractable person. —adj. 1 of or relating to the Tartars. 2 of or relating to Central Asia east of the Caspian Sea. □ **tartar sauce** a sauce of mayonnaise and chopped gherkins, capers, etc. □□ **Tartarian** /-'teərɪən/ adj. [ME tartre f. OF Tartare or med.L Tartarus]

tartar /'tɑːtə(r)/ n. 1 a hard deposit of saliva, calcium phosphate, etc., that forms on the teeth. 2 a deposit of acid potassium tartrate that forms a hard crust on the inside of a cask during the fermentation of wine. □ **tartar emetic** potassium antimony tartrate used as a mordant and in medicine (formerly as an emetic). □□ **tartarize** v.tr. (also **-ise**). [ME f. med.L f. med.Gk tartaron]

tartare /tɑːˈtɑː(r)/ adj. (in full **sauce tartare**) = tartar sauce (see TARTAR). [F, = tartar]

tartaric /tɑːˈtærɪk/ adj. Chem. of or produced from tartar. □ **tartaric acid** a natural carboxylic acid found esp. in unripe grapes, used in baking powders and as a food additive. [F tartarique f. med.L tartarum: see TARTAR]

Tartarus /'tɑːtərəs/ n. (in Greek mythology): 1 an abyss below Hades where the Titans were confined. 2 a place of punishment in Hades. □□ **Tartarean** /-'teərɪən/ adj. [L f. Gk Tartaros]

tartrate /'tɑːtreɪt/ n. Chem. any salt or ester of tartaric acid. [F (as TARTAR, -ATE¹)]

tartrazine /'tɑːtrəziːn/ n. Chem. a brilliant yellow dye derived from tartaric acid and used to colour food, drugs, and cosmetics. [as TARTAR + AZO- + -INE⁴]

tarty /'tɑːtɪ/ adj. colloq. (tartier, tartiest) (esp. of a woman) vulgar, gaudy; promiscuous. □□ **tartily** adv. **tartiness** n. [TART² + -Y¹]

Tarzan /'tɑːz(ə)n/ n. a man of great agility and powerful physique. [name of the hero of stories by E. R. Burroughs, Amer. writer d. 1950]

Tas. abbr. Tasmania.

Tashi lama /'tæʃɪ ˌlɑːmə/ n. = PANCHEN LAMA.

task /tɑːsk/ n. & v. —n. a piece of work to be done or undertaken. —v.tr. 1 make great demands on (a person's powers etc.). 2 assign a task to. □ **take to task** rebuke, scold. **task force** (or **group**) 1 Mil. an armed force organized for a special operation. 2 a unit specially organized for a task. [ME f. ONF tasque = OF tasche f. med.L tasca, perh. f. taxa f. L taxare TAX]

taskmaster /'tɑːskˌmɑːstə(r)/ n. (fem. **taskmistress** /-ˌmɪstrɪs/) a person who imposes a task or burden, esp. regularly or severely.

Tasmanian /tæzˈmeɪnɪən/ n. & adj. —n. 1 a native of Tasmania, an island State of Australia. 2 a person of Tasmanian descent. —adj. of or relating to Tasmania. □ **Tasmanian devil** a bearlike nocturnal flesh-eating marsupial, Sarcophilus harrisii, now found only in Tasmania. [Tasmania f. A. J. Tasman, Du. navigator d. 1659, who discovered the island]

Tass /tæs/ n. the official news agency of the Soviet Union. [the initials of Russ. Telegrafnoe agentstvo Sovetskogo Soyuza Telegraphic Agency of the Soviet Union]

tass /tæs/ n. Sc. 1 a cup or small goblet. 2 a small draught of brandy etc. [ME f. OF tasse cup f. Arab. ṭāsa basin f. Pers. tast]

tassel¹ /'tæs(ə)l/ n. & v. —n. 1 a tuft of loosely hanging threads or cords etc. attached for decoration to a cushion, scarf, cap, etc. 2 a tassel-like head of some plants, esp. a flower-head with prominent stamens at the top of a maize stalk. —v. (**tasselled**, **tasselling**; US **tasseled**, **tasseling**) 1 tr. provide with a tassel or tassels. 2 intr. US (of maize etc.) form tassels. [ME f. OF tas(s)el clasp, of unkn. orig.]

tassel² /'tæs(ə)l/ n. (also **torsel** /'tɔː-/) a small piece of stone, wood, etc., supporting the end of a beam or joist. [OF ult. f. L taxillus small die, and tessella: see TESSELLATE]

tassie /'tæsɪ/ n. Sc. a small cup.

taste /teɪst/ n. & v. —n. 1 a the sensation characteristic of a soluble substance caused in the mouth and throat by contact with that substance (disliked the taste of garlic). b the faculty of perceiving this sensation (was bitter to the taste). 2 a small portion of food or drink taken as a sample. 3 a slight experience (a taste of success). 4 (often foll. by for) a liking or predilection (has expensive tastes; is not to my taste). 5 aesthetic discernment in art, literature, conduct, etc., esp. of a specified kind (a person of taste; dresses in poor taste). —v. 1 tr. sample or test the flavour of (food etc.) by taking it into the mouth. 2 tr. (also absol.) perceive the flavour of (could taste the lemon; cannot taste with a cold). 3 tr. (esp. with neg.) eat or drink a small portion of (had not tasted *food for days*). **4** *tr.* have experience of (*had never tasted failure*). **5** *intr.* (often foll. by *of*) have a specified flavour (*tastes bitter; tastes of onions*). □**a bad** (or **bitter** etc.) **taste** *colloq.* a strong feeling of regret or unease. **taste blood** see BLOOD. **taste bud** any of the cells or nerve-endings on the surface of the tongue by which things are tasted. **to taste** in the amount needed for a pleasing result (*add salt and pepper to taste*). □□ **tasteable** *adj.* [ME, = touch, taste, f. OF *tast, taster* touch, try, taste, ult. perh. f. L *tangere* touch + *gustare* taste]

tasteful /ˈteɪstfʊl/ *adj.* having, or done in, good taste. □□ **tastefully** *adv.* **tastefulness** *n.*

tasteless /ˈteɪstlɪs/ *adj.* **1** lacking flavour. **2** having, or done in, bad taste. □□ **tastelessly** *adv.* **tastelessness** *n.*

taster /ˈteɪstə(r)/ *n.* **1** a person employed to test food or drink by tasting it, esp. for quality or *hist.* to detect poisoning. **2** a small cup used by a wine-taster. **3** an instrument for extracting a small sample from within a cheese. [ME f. AF *tastour*, OF *tasteur* f. *taster*: see TASTE]

tasting /ˈteɪstɪŋ/ *n.* a gathering at which food or drink (esp. wine) is tasted and evaluated.

tasty /ˈteɪstɪ/ *adj.* (**tastier, tastiest**) (of food) pleasing in flavour; appetizing. □□ **tastily** *adv.* **tastiness** *n.*

tat[1] /tæt/ *n. colloq.* **1 a** tatty or tasteless clothes; worthless goods. **b** rubbish, junk. **2** a shabby person. [back-form. f. TATTY]

tat[2] /tæt/ *v.* (**tatted, tatting**) **1** *intr.* do tatting. **2** *tr.* make by tatting. [19th c.: orig. unkn.]

tat[3] see TIT[2].

ta-ta /tæˈtɑː/ *int. Brit. colloq.* goodbye (said esp. to or by a child). [19th c.: orig. unkn.]

Tatar var. of TARTAR.

tater /ˈteɪtə(r)/ *n.* (also **tatie** /-tɪ/, **tato** /-təʊ/) *sl.* = POTATO. [abbr.]

tatler *archaic* var. of TATTLER 1.

tatter /ˈtætə(r)/ *n.* (usu. in *pl.*) a rag; an irregularly torn piece of cloth or paper etc. □**in tatters** *colloq.* (of a negotiation, argument, etc.) ruined, demolished. □□ **tattery** *adj.* [ME f. ON *tötrar* rags: cf. Icel. *töturr*]

tattered /ˈtætəd/ *adj.* in tatters.

tattersall /ˈtætəˌsɔːl/ *n.* (in full **tattersall check**) a fabric with a pattern of coloured lines forming squares like a tartan. [R. *Tattersall*, Engl. horseman d. 1795: from the traditional design of horse blankets]

tatting /ˈtætɪŋ/ *n.* **1** a kind of knotted lace made by hand with a small shuttle and used for trimming etc. **2** the process of making this. [19th c.: orig. unkn.]

tattle /ˈtæt(ə)l/ *v. & n.* —*v.* **1** *intr.* prattle, chatter; gossip idly. **2** *tr.* utter (words) idly. —*n.* gossip; idle or trivial talk. □**tattle-tale** *US* a tell-tale, esp. a child. [ME f. MFlem. *tatelen, tateren* (imit.)]

tattler /ˈtætlə(r)/ *n.* a prattler; a gossip.

tattoo[1] /təˈtuː/ *n.* **1** an evening drum or bugle signal recalling soldiers to their quarters. **2** an elaboration of this with music and marching, presented as an entertainment. **3** a rhythmic tapping or drumming. [17th-c. *tap-too* f. Du. *taptoe*, lit. 'close the tap' (of the cask)]

tattoo[2] /təˈtuː, tæ-/ *v. & n.* —*v.tr.* (**tattoos, tattooed**) **1** mark (the skin) with an indelible design by puncturing it and inserting pigment. **2** make (a design) in this way. —*n.* a design made by tattooing. □□ **tattooer** *n.* **tattooist** *n.* [Polynesian]

tatty /ˈtætɪ/ *adj.* (**tattier, tattiest**) *colloq.* **1** tattered; worn and shabby. **2** inferior. **3** tawdry. □□ **tattily** *adv.* **tattiness** *n.* [orig. Sc., = shaggy, app. rel. to OE *tættec* rag, TATTER]

tau /tau, tɔː/ *n.* the nineteenth letter of the Greek alphabet (*T*, *τ*). □**tau cross** a T-shaped cross. **tau particle** *Physics* an unstable, heavy, and charged elementary particle of the lepton class. [ME f. Gk]

taught *past* and *past part.* of TEACH.

taunt /tɔːnt/ *n. & v.* —*n.* a thing said in order to anger or wound a person. —*v.tr.* **1** assail with taunts. **2** reproach (a person) contemptuously. □□ **taunter**

n. **tauntingly** *adv.* [16th c., in phr. *taunt for taunt* f. F *tant pour tant* tit for tat, hence a smart rejoinder]

taupe /təʊp/ *n.* a grey with a tinge of another colour, usu. brown. [F, = MOLE[1]]

taurine /ˈtɔːriːn, -raɪn/ *adj.* of or like a bull; bullish. [L *taurinus* f. *taurus* bull]

tauromachy /tɔːˈrɒməkɪ/ *n.* (*pl.* -**ies**) *archaic* **1** a bullfight. **2** bullfighting. [Gk *tauromakhia* f. *tauros* bull + *makhē* fight]

Taurus /ˈtɔːrəs/ *n.* **1** a constellation. **2 a** the second sign of the zodiac (the Bull). **b** a person born when the sun is in this sign. □□ **Taurean** *adj. & n.* [ME f. L, = bull]

taut /tɔːt/ *adj.* **1** (of a rope, muscles, etc.) tight; not slack. **2** (of nerves) tense. **3** (of a ship etc.) in good order or condition. □□ **tauten** *v.tr. & intr.* **tautly** *adv.* **tautness** *n.* [ME *touht, togt,* perh. = TOUGH, infl. by *tog-* past part. stem of obs. *tee* (OE *tēon*) pull]

tauto- /ˈtɔːtəʊ/ *comb. form* the same. [Gk, f. *tauto, to auto* the same]

tautog /tɔːˈtɒg/ *n.* a fish, *Tautoga onitis*, found off the Atlantic coast of N. America, used as food. [Narraganset *tautauog* (pl.)]

tautology /tɔːˈtɒlədʒɪ/ *n.* (*pl.* -**ies**) **1** the saying of the same thing twice over in different words, esp. as a fault of style (e.g. *arrived one after the other in succession*). **2** a statement that is necessarily true. □□ **tautologic** /-təˈlɒdʒɪk/ *adj.* **tautological** /-təˈlɒdʒɪk(ə)l/ *adj.* **tautologically** /-təˈlɒdʒɪkəlɪ/ *adv.* **tautologist** *n.* **tautologize** /-ˌdʒaɪz/ *v.intr.* (also -**ise**). **tautologous** /-ləgəs/ *adj.* [LL *tautologia* f. Gk (as TAUTO-, -LOGY)]

tautomer /ˈtɔːtəˌmɜː(r)/ *n. Chem.* a substance that exists as two mutually convertible isomers in equilibrium. □□ **tautomeric** /-ˈmerɪk/ *adj.* **tautomerism** /-ˈtɒməˌrɪz(ə)m/ *n.* [TAUTO- + -MER]

tautophony /tɔːˈtɒfənɪ/ *n.* repetition of the same sound. [TAUTO- + Gk *phōnē* sound]

tavern /ˈtæv(ə)n/ *n. literary* an inn or public house. [ME f. OF *taverne* f. L *taberna* hut, tavern]

taverna /təˈvɜːnə/ *n.* a Greek eating house. [mod. Gk (as TAVERN)]

TAVR *abbr.* (in the UK) Territorial and Army Volunteer Reserve. ¶ The name in use 1967–79: now **TA**.

taw[1] /tɔː/ *v.tr.* make (hide) into leather without the use of tannin, esp. by soaking in a solution of alum and salt. □□ **tawer** *n.* [OE *tawian* f. Gmc]

taw[2] /tɔː/ *n.* **1** a large marble. **2** a game of marbles. **3** a line from which players throw marbles. [18th c.: orig. unkn.]

tawdry /ˈtɔːdrɪ/ *adj. & n.* —*adj.* (**tawdrier, tawdriest**) **1** showy but worthless. **2** overornamented, gaudy, vulgar. —*n.* cheap or gaudy finery. □□ **tawdrily** *adv.* **tawdriness** *n.* [earlier as noun: short for *tawdry lace*, orig. *St Audrey's lace* f. *Audrey = Etheldrida*, patron saint of Ely]

tawny /ˈtɔːnɪ/ *adj.* (**tawnier, tawniest**) of an orange- or yellow-brown colour. □**tawny eagle** a brownish African or Asian eagle, *Aquila rapax*. **tawny owl** a reddish-brown European owl, *Strix aluco*. □□ **tawniness** *n.* [ME f. AF *tauné*, OF *tané* f. *tan* TAN[1]]

taws /tɔːz/ *n.* (also **tawse**) *Sc. hist.* a thong with a slit end formerly used in schools for punishing children. [app. pl. of obs. *taw* tawed leather, f. TAW[1]]

tax /tæks/ *n. & v.* —*n.* **1** a contribution to State revenue compulsorily levied on individuals, property, or businesses (often foll. by *on*: *a tax on luxury goods*). **2** (usu. foll. by *on, upon*) a strain or heavy demand; an oppressive or burdensome obligation. —*v.tr.* **1** impose a tax on (persons or goods etc.). **2** deduct tax from (income etc.). **3** make heavy demands on (a person's powers or resources etc.) (*you really tax my patience*). **4** (foll. by *with*) confront (a person) with a wrongdoing etc. **5** call to account. **6** *Law* examine and assess (costs etc.). □**tax avoidance** the arrangement of financial affairs to minimize payment of tax. **tax-deductible** (of expenditure) that may be paid out of income before the deduction of income tax. **tax disc** *Brit.* a paper disc displayed on the windscreen of a motor vehicle, certifying payment of excise duty. **tax evasion** the illegal non-payment or underpayment of income tax. **tax-free** exempt from taxes. **tax haven** a country etc. where income tax is low. **tax return** a declaration of income for taxation purposes. **tax shelter** a means of organizing business affairs to minimize payment of tax. **tax year** see *financial year.* □□ **taxable** *adj.* **taxer** *n.* **taxless** *adj.* [ME f. OF *taxer* f. L *taxare* censure, charge, compute, perh. f. Gk *tassō* fix]

taxa *pl.* of TAXON.

taxation /tækˈseɪʃ(ə)n/ *n.* the imposition or payment of tax. [ME f. AF *taxacioun*, OF *taxation* f. L *taxatio -onis* f. *taxare*: see TAX]

taxi /ˈtæksɪ/ *n. & v.* —*n.* (*pl.* **taxis**) **1** (in full **taxi-cab**) a motor car licensed to ply for hire and usu. fitted with a taximeter. **2** a boat etc. similarly used. —*v.* (**taxis, taxied, taxiing** or **taxying**) **1 a** *intr.* (of an aircraft or pilot) move along the ground under the machine's own power before take-off or after landing. **b** *tr.* cause (an aircraft) to taxi. **2** *intr. & tr.* go or convey in a taxi. □ **taxi dancer** a dancing partner available for hire. **taxi-driver** a driver of a taxi. **taxi rank** (*US* **stand**) a place where taxis wait to be hired. [abbr. of *taximeter cab*]

taxidermy /ˈtæksɪˌdɜːmɪ/ *n.* the art of preparing, stuffing, and mounting the skins of animals with lifelike effect. □□ **taxidermal** /-ˈdɜːm(ə)l/ *adj.* **taxidermic** /-ˈdɜːmɪk/ *adj.* **taxidermist** *n.* [Gk *taxis* arrangement + *derma* skin]

taximeter /ˈtæksɪˌmiːtə(r)/ *n.* an automatic device fitted to a taxi, recording the distance travelled and the fare payable. [F *taximètre* f. *taxe* tariff, TAX + -METER]

taxis /ˈtæksɪs/ *n.* **1** *Surgery* the restoration of displaced bones or organs by manual pressure. **2** *Biol.* the movement of a cell or organism in response to an external stimulus. **3** *Gram.* order or arrangement of words. [Gk f. *tassō* arrange]

taxman /ˈtæksmæn/ *n. colloq.* (*pl.* **-men**) an inspector or collector of taxes.

taxon /ˈtæks(ə)n/ *n.* (*pl.* **taxa** /ˈtæksə/) any taxonomic group. [back-form. f. TAXONOMY]

taxonomy /tækˈsɒnəmɪ/ *n.* **1** the science of the classification of living and extinct organisms. **2** the practice of this. □□ **taxonomic** /-səˈnɒmɪk/ *adj.* **taxonomical** /-səˈnɒmɪk(ə)l/ *adj.* **taxonomically** /-səˈnɒmɪkəlɪ/ *adv.* **taxonomist** *n.* [F *taxonomie* (as TAXIS, Gk *-nomia* distribution)]

taxpayer /ˈtæksˌpeɪə(r)/ *n.* a person who pays taxes.

tayberry /ˈteɪbərɪ/ *n.* (*pl.* **-ies**) a dark red soft fruit produced by crossing the blackberry and raspberry. [*Tay* in Scotland (where introduced in 1977)]

tazza /ˈtɑːtsə/ *n.* a saucer-shaped cup, esp. one mounted on a foot. [It.]

TB *abbr.* **1 a** tubercle bacillus. **b** tuberculosis. **2** torpedo boat.

Tb *symb. Chem.* the element terbium.

T-bone /ˈtiːbəʊn/ *n.* a T-shaped bone, esp. in steak from the thin end of a loin.

tbsp. *abbr.* tablespoonful.

Tc *symb. Chem.* the element technetium.

TCD *abbr.* Trinity College, Dublin.

TCP *abbr. propr.* a disinfectant and germicide. [*tri*-chlorophenylmethyliodasalicyl]

TD *abbr.* **1** (in the UK) Territorial (Officer's) Decoration. **2** *Ir.* Teachta Dála, Member of the Dáil.

Te *symb. Chem.* the element tellurium.

te /tiː/ *n.* (also **ti**) **1** (in tonic sol-fa) the seventh note of a major scale. **2** the note B in the fixed-doh system. [earlier *si*: F f. It., perh. f. *Sancte Iohannes*: see GAMUT]

tea /tiː/ *n. & v.* —*n.* **1 a** (in full **tea plant**) an evergreen shrub or small tree, *Camellia sinensis*, of India, China, etc. **b** its dried leaves. **2** a drink made by infusing tea-leaves in boiling water. **3** a similar

drink made from the leaves of other plants or from another substance (*camomile tea; beef tea*). **4 a** a light afternoon meal consisting of tea, bread, cakes, etc. **b** *Brit.* a cooked evening meal. —*v.* (**teaed** or **tea'd** /tiːd/) **1** *intr.* take tea. **2** *tr.* give tea to (a person). □ **tea and sympathy** *colloq.* hospitable behaviour towards a troubled person. **tea bag** a small perforated bag of tea for infusion. **tea-ball** esp. *US* a ball of perforated metal to hold tea for infusion. **tea-bread** light or sweet bread for eating at tea. **tea break** *Brit.* a pause in work etc. to drink tea. **tea caddy** a container for tea. **tea ceremony** an elaborate Japanese ritual of serving and drinking tea, as an expression of Zen Buddhist philosophy. **tea chest** a light metal-lined wooden box in which tea is transported. **tea cloth** = *tea towel.* **tea cosy** a cover to keep a teapot warm. **tea dance** an afternoon tea with dancing. **tea garden** a garden in which afternoon tea is served to the public. **tea lady** a woman employed to make tea in offices etc. **tea-leaf 1** a dried leaf of tea, used to make a drink of tea. **2** (esp. in *pl.*) these after infusion or as dregs. **3** *rhyming sl.* a thief. **tea party** a party at teatime. **tea-planter** a proprietor or cultivator of a tea plantation. **tea rose** a hybrid shrub, *Rosa odorata*, with a scent resembling that of tea. **tea towel** a towel for drying washed crockery etc. **tea-tree** *Austral. & NZ* an aromatic evergreen flowering shrub, *Leptospermum scoparium*, the manuka. **tea trolley** (*US* **wagon**) a small wheeled trolley from which tea is served. [17th-c. *tay, tey*, prob. f. Du. *tee* f. Chin. (Amoy dial.) *te*, = Mandarin dial. *cha*]

teacake /ˈtiːkeɪk/ *n. Brit.* a light yeast-based usu. sweet bun eaten at tea, often toasted.

teach /tiːtʃ/ *v.tr.* (*past and past part.* **taught** /tɔːt/) **1 a** give systematic information to (a person) or about (a subject or skill). **b** (*absol.*) practise this professionally. **c** enable (a person) to do something by instruction and training (*taught me to swim; taught me how to dance*). **2** advocate as a moral etc. principle (*my parents taught me tolerance*). **3** (foll. by *to* + infin.) **a** induce (a person) by example or punishment to do or not to do a thing (*that will teach you to sit still; that will teach you not to laugh*). **b** *colloq.* make (a person) disinclined to do a thing (*I will teach you to interfere*). □ **teach-in 1** an informal lecture and discussion on a subject of public interest. **2** a series of these. **teach a person a lesson** see LESSON. **teach school** *US* be a teacher in a school. [OE *tæcan* f. a Gmc root = 'show']

teachable /ˈtiːtʃəb(ə)l/ *adj.* **1** apt at learning. **2** (of a subject) that can be taught. □□ **teachability** /-ˈbɪlɪtɪ/ *n.* **teachableness** *n.*

teacher /ˈtiːtʃə(r)/ *n.* a person who teaches, esp. in a school. □□ **teacherly** *adj.*

teaching /ˈtiːtʃɪŋ/ *n.* **1** the profession of a teacher. **2** (often in *pl.*) what is taught; a doctrine. □ **teaching hospital** a hospital where medical students are taught. **teaching machine** any of various devices for giving instruction according to a programme measuring pupils' responses.

teacup /ˈtiːkʌp/ *n.* **1** a cup from which tea is drunk. **2** an amount held by this, about 150 ml. □□ **teacupful** *n.* (*pl.* **-fuls**).

teak /tiːk/ *n.* **1** a large deciduous tree, *Tectona grandis*, native to India and SE Asia. **2** its hard durable timber, much used in shipbuilding and furniture. [Port. *teca* f. Malayalam *tēkka*]

teal /tiːl/ *n.* (*pl.* same) **1** any of various small freshwater ducks of the genus *Anas*, esp. *A. crecca*. **2** a dark greenish-blue colour. [rel. to MDu. *tēling*, of unkn. orig.]

team /tiːm/ *n. & v.* —*n.* **1** a set of players forming one side in a game (*a cricket team*). **2** two or more persons working together. **3 a** a set of draught animals. **b** one animal or more in harness with a vehicle. —*v.* **1** *intr. & tr.* (usu. foll. by *up*) join in a team or in common action (*decided to team up with* *them*). **2** *tr.* harness (horses etc.) in a team. **3** *tr.* (foll. by *with*) match or coordinate (clothes). □ **team-mate** a fellow-member of a team or group. **team spirit** willingness to act as a member of a group rather than as an individual. **team-teaching** teaching by a team of teachers working together. [OE *tēam* offspring f. a Gmc root = 'pull', rel. to TOW¹]

teamster /ˈtiːmstə(r)/ *n.* **1** *US* a lorry-driver. **2** a driver of a team of animals.

teamwork /ˈtiːmwɜːk/ *n.* the combined action of a team, group, etc., esp. when effective and efficient.

teapot /ˈtiːpɒt/ *n.* a pot with a handle, spout, and lid, in which tea is brewed and from which it is poured.

teapoy /ˈtiːpɔɪ/ *n.* a small three- or four-legged table esp. for tea. [Hindi *tīn*, *tir-* three + Pers. *pāī* foot: sense and spelling infl. by TEA]

tear¹ /teə(r)/ *v. & n. — v.* (*past* **tore** /tɔː(r)/; *past part.* **torn** /tɔːn/) **1** *tr.* (often foll. by *up*) pull apart or to pieces with some force (*tear it in half*; *tore up the letter*). **2** *tr.* **a** make a hole or rent in by tearing (*have torn my coat*). **b** make (a hole or rent). **3** *tr.* (foll. by *away*, *off*, etc.) pull violently or with some force (*tore the book away from me*; *tore off the cover*; *tore a page out*; *tore down the notice*). **4** *tr.* violently disrupt or divide (*the country was torn by civil war*; *torn by conflicting emotions*). **5** *intr. colloq.* go or travel hurriedly or impetuously (*tore across the road*). **6** *intr.* undergo tearing (*the curtain tore down the middle*). **7** *intr.* (foll. by *at* etc.) pull violently or with some force. *— n.* **1** a hole or other damage caused by tearing. **2** a torn part of cloth etc. □ **be torn between** have difficulty in choosing between. **tear apart 1** search (a place) exhaustively. **2** criticize forcefully. **tear one's hair out** behave with extreme desperation or anger. **tear into 1** attack verbally; reprimand. **2** make a vigorous start on (an activity). **tear oneself away** leave despite a strong desire to stay. **tear sheet** a page that can be removed from a newspaper or magazine etc. for use separately. **tear to shreds** *colloq.* refute or criticize thoroughly. **that's torn it** *Brit. colloq.* that has spoiled things, caused a problem, etc. □□ **tearable** *adj.* **tearer** *n.* [OE *teran* f. Gmc]

tear² /tɪə(r)/ *n.* **1** a drop of clear salty liquid secreted by glands, that serves to moisten and wash the eye and is shed from it in grief or other strong emotions. **2** a tearlike thing; a drop. □ **in tears** crying; shedding tears. **tear-drop** a single tear. **tear-duct** a drain for carrying tears to the eye or from the eye to the nose. **tear-gas** gas that disables by causing severe irritation to the eyes. **tear-jerker** *colloq.* a story, film, etc., calculated to evoke sadness or sympathy. **without tears** presented so as to be learned or done easily. □□ **tearless** *adj.* [OE *tēar*]

tearaway /ˈteərəweɪ/ *n. Brit.* **1** an impetuous or reckless young person. **2** a hooligan.

tearful /ˈtɪəfʊl/ *adj.* **1** crying or inclined to cry. **2** causing or accompanied with tears; sad (*a tearful event*). □□ **tearfully** *adv.* **tearfulness** *n.*

tearing /ˈteərɪŋ/ *adj.* extreme, overwhelming, violent (*in a tearing hurry*).

tearless /ˈtɪəlɪs/ *adj.* not shedding tears. □□ **tearlessly** *adv.* **tearlessness** *n.*

tearoom /ˈtiːruːm, -rʊm/ *n.* a small restaurant or café where tea is served.

tease /tiːz/ *v. & n. — v.tr.* (also *absol.*) **1 a** make fun of (a person or animal) playfully or unkindly or annoyingly. **b** tempt or allure, esp. sexually, while refusing to satisfy the desire aroused. **2** pick (wool, hair, etc.) into separate fibres. **3** dress (cloth) esp. with teasels. *— n.* **1** *colloq.* a person fond of teasing. **2** an instance of teasing (*it was only a tease*). □ **tease out** separate by disentangling. □□ **teasingly** *adv.* [OE *tǣsan* f. WG]

teasel /ˈtiːz(ə)l/ *n. & v.* (also **teazel**, **teazle**) *— n.* **1** any plant of the genus *Dipsacus*, with large prickly heads that are dried and used to raise the nap on woven cloth. **2** a device used as a substitute for teasels. *—v.tr.* dress (cloth) with teasels. □□ **teaseler** *n.* [OE *tǣs(e)l*, = OHG *zeisala* (as TEASE)]

teaser /ˈtiːzə(r)/ *n.* **1** *colloq.* a hard question or task. **2** a teasing person. **3** esp. *US* a short introductory advertisement etc.

teaset /ˈtiːset/ *n.* a set of crockery for serving tea.

teashop /ˈtiːʃɒp/ *n.* esp. *Brit.* = TEAROOM.

teaspoon /ˈtiːspuːn/ *n.* **1** a small spoon for stirring tea. **2** an amount held by this. □□ **teaspoonful** *n.* (*pl.* **-fuls**).

teat /tiːt/ *n.* **1** a mammary nipple, esp. of an animal. **2** a thing resembling this, esp. a device of rubber etc. for sucking milk from a bottle. [ME f. OF *tete*, prob. of Gmc orig., replacing TIT³]

teatime /ˈtiːtaɪm/ *n.* the time in the afternoon when tea is served.

teazel (also **teazle**) var. of TEASEL.

tec /tek/ *n. colloq.* a detective. [abbr.]

tech /tek/ *n.* (also **tec**) *colloq.* a technical college. [abbr.]

technetium /tekˈniːʃ(ə)m/ *n. Chem.* an artificially produced radioactive metallic element occurring in the fission products of uranium. ¶ Symb.: **Tc**. [mod.L f. Gk *tekhnētos* artificial f. *tekhnē* art]

technic /ˈteknɪk/ *n.* **1** (usu. in *pl.*) **a** technology. **b** technical terms, details, methods, etc. **2** technique. □□ **technicist** /-sɪst/ *n.* [L *technicus* f. Gk *tekhnikos* f. *tekhnē* art]

technical /ˈteknɪk(ə)l/ *adj.* **1** of or involving or concerned with the mechanical arts and applied sciences (*technical college*; *a technical education*). **2** of or relating to a particular subject or craft etc. or its techniques (*technical terms*; *technical merit*). **3** (of a book or discourse etc.) using technical language; requiring special knowledge to be understood. **4** due to mechanical failure (*a technical hitch*). **5** legally such; such in strict interpretation (*technical assault*; *lost on a technical point*). □ **technical hitch** a temporary breakdown or problem in machinery etc. **technical knockout** *Boxing* a termination of a fight by the referee on the grounds of a contestant's inability to continue, the opponent being declared the winner. □□ **technically** *adv.* **technicalness** *n.*

technicality /ˌteknɪˈkælɪtɪ/ *n.* (*pl.* **-ies**) **1** the state of being technical. **2** a technical expression. **3** a technical point or detail (*was acquitted on a technicality*).

technician /tekˈnɪʃ(ə)n/ *n.* **1** an expert in the practical application of a science. **2** a person skilled in the technique of an art or craft. **3** a person employed to look after technical equipment and do practical work in a laboratory etc.

Technicolor /ˈteknɪˌkʌlə(r)/ *n.* (often *attrib.*) **1** *propr.* a process of colour cinematography using synchronized monochrome films, each of a different colour, to produce a colour print. **2** (usu. **technicolor**) *colloq.* **a** vivid colour. **b** artificial brilliance. □□ **technicolored** *adj.* [TECHNICAL + COLOR]

technique /tekˈniːk/ *n.* **1** mechanical skill in an art. **2** a means of achieving one's purpose, esp. skilfully. **3** a manner of artistic execution in music, painting, etc. [F (as TECHNIC)]

technocracy /tekˈnɒkrəsɪ/ *n.* (*pl.* **-ies**) **1** the government or control of society or industry by technical experts. **2** an instance or application of this. [Gk *tekhnē* art + -CRACY]

technocrat /ˈteknəkræt/ *n.* an exponent or advocate of technocracy. □□ **technocratic** /-ˈkrætɪk/ *adj.* **technocratically** /-ˈkrætɪkəlɪ/ *adv.*

technological /ˌteknəˈlɒdʒɪk(ə)l/ *adj.* of or using technology. □□ **technologically** *adv.*

technology /tekˈnɒlədʒɪ/ *n.* (*pl.* **-ies**) **1** the study or use of the mechanical arts and applied sciences. **2** these subjects collectively. □□ **technologist** *n.* [Gk *tekhnologia* systematic treatment f. *tekhnē* art]

techy var. of TETCHY.

tectonic /tekˈtɒnɪk/ *adj.* **1** of or relating to building or construction. **2** *Geol.* relating to the deformation of the earth's crust or to the structural changes caused by this (see *plate tectonics*). □□ **tectonically** *adv.* [LL *tectonicus* f. Gk *tektonikos* f. *tektōn -onos* carpenter]

tectonics /tek'tɒnɪks/ *n.pl.* (usu. treated as *sing.*) **1** *Archit.* the art and process of producing practical and aesthetically pleasing buildings. **2** *Geol.* the study of large-scale structural features (cf. *plate tectonics*).

tectorial /tek'tɔ:rɪəl/ *adj. Anat.* **1** forming a covering. **2** (in full **tectorial membrane**) the membrane covering the organ of Corti (see CORTI) in the inner ear. [L *tectorium* a cover (as TECTRIX)]

tectrix /'tektrɪks/ *n.* (*pl.* **tectrices** /-,si:z, -'traɪsi:z/) = COVERT *n.* [mod.L f. L *tegere tect-* cover]

Ted /ted/ *n.* (also **ted**) *Brit. colloq.* a Teddy boy. [abbr.]

ted /ted/ *v.tr.* (**tedded, tedding**) turn over and spread out (grass, hay, or straw) to dry or for a bedding etc. □□ **tedder** *n.* [ME f. ON *tethja* spread manure f. *tad* dung, *toddi* small piece]

teddy /'tedɪ/ *n.* (also **Teddy**) (*pl.* **-ies**) (in full **teddy bear**) a soft toy bear. [*Teddy*, pet-name of *Theodore* Roosevelt, US president d. 1919, famous as a bear-hunter]

Teddy boy /'tedɪ/ *n. Brit. colloq.* **1** a youth, esp. of the 1950s, affecting an Edwardian style of dress and appearance. **2** a young rowdy male. [*Teddy*, pet-form of *Edward*]

Te Deum /ti: 'di:əm, teɪ 'deɪəm/ **1 a** a hymn beginning *Te Deum laudamus*, 'We praise Thee, O God'. **b** the music for this. **2** an expression of thanksgiving or exultation. [L]

tedious /'ti:dɪəs/ *adj.* tiresomely long; wearisome. □□ **tediously** *adv.* **tediousness** *n.* [ME f. OF *tedieus* or LL *taediosus* (as TEDIUM)]

tedium /'ti:dɪəm/ *n.* the state of being tedious; boredom. [L *taedium* f. *taedēre* to weary]

tee¹ /ti:/ *n.* = T¹. [phonet. spelling]

tee² /ti:/ *n. & v.* —*n.* **1** *Golf* **a** a cleared space from which a golf ball is struck at the beginning of play for each hole. **b** a small support of wood or plastic from which a ball is struck at a tee. **2** a mark aimed at in bowls, quoits, curling, etc. —*v.tr.* (**tees, teed**) (often foll. by *up*) *Golf* place (a ball) on a tee ready to strike it. □ **tee off 1** *Golf* play a ball from a tee. **2** *colloq.* start, begin. [earlier (17th-c.) *teaz*, of unkn. orig.: in sense 2 perh. = TEE¹]

tee-hee /ti:'hi:/ *n. & v.* (also **te-hee**) —*n.* **1** a titter. **2** a restrained or contemptuous laugh. —*v.intr.* (**tee-hees, tee-heed**) titter or laugh in this way. [imit.]

teem¹ /ti:m/ *v.intr.* **1** be abundant (*fish teem in these waters*). **2** (foll. by *with*) be full of or swarming with (*teeming with fish; teeming with ideas*). [OE *tēman* etc. give birth to f. Gmc, rel. to TEAM]

teem² /ti:m/ *v.intr.* (often foll. by *down*) (of water etc.) flow copiously; pour (*it was teeming with rain*). [ME *tēmen* f. ON *tœma* f. *tómr* (adj.) empty]

teen /ti:n/ *adj. & n.* —*adj.* = TEENAGE. —*n.* = TEENAGER. [abbr. of TEENAGE, TEENAGER]

-teen /ti:n/ *suffix* forming the names of numerals from 13 to 19. [OE inflected form of TEN]

teenage /'ti:neɪdʒ/ *adj.* relating to or characteristic of teenagers. □□ **teenaged** *adj.*

teenager /'ti:n,eɪdʒə(r)/ *n.* a person from 13 to 19 years of age.

teens /ti:nz/ *n.pl.* the years of one's age from 13 to 19 (*in one's teens*).

teensy /'ti:nzɪ/ *adj.* (**teensier, teensiest**) *colloq.* = TEENY. □ **teensy-weensy** = *teeny-weeny*.

teeny /'ti:nɪ/ *adj.* (**teenier, teeniest**) *colloq.* tiny. □ **teeny-weeny** very tiny. [var. of TINY]

teeny-bopper /'ti:nɪ,bɒpə(r)/ *n. colloq.* a young teenager, usu. a girl, who keenly follows the latest fashions in clothes, pop music, etc.

teepee var. of TEPEE.

teeshirt var. of T-SHIRT.

teeter /'ti:tə(r)/ *v.intr.* **1** totter; stand or move unsteadily. **2** hesitate; be indecisive. □ **teeter on the brink** (or **edge**) be in imminent danger (of disaster etc.). [var. of dial. *titter*]

teeth *pl.* of TOOTH.

teethe /ti:ð/ *v.intr.* grow or cut teeth, esp. milk teeth. □ **teething-ring** a small ring for an infant to bite on while teething. **teething troubles** initial difficulties in an enterprise etc., regarded as temporary. □□ **teething** *n.*

teetotal /ti:'təʊt(ə)l/ *adj.* advocating or characterized by total abstinence from alcoholic drink. □□ **teetotalism** *n.* [redupl. of TOTAL]

teetotaller /ti:'təʊtələ(r)/ *n.* (*US* **teetotaler**) a person advocating or practising abstinence from alcoholic drink.

teetotum /ti:'təʊtəm/ *n.* **1** a spinning-top with four sides lettered to determine whether the spinner has won or lost. **2** any top spun with the fingers. [*T* (the letter on one side) + L *totum* the whole (stakes), for which *T* stood]

teff /tef/ *n.* an African cereal, *Eragrostis tef*. [Amharic *ṭēf*]

TEFL /'tef(ə)l/ *abbr.* teaching of English as a foreign language.

Teflon /'teflɒn/ *n. propr.* polytetrafluoroethylene, esp. used as a non-stick coating for kitchen utensils. [*te*tra- + *f*luor- + *-on*]

teg /teg/ *n.* a sheep in its second year. [ME *tegge* (recorded in place-names), repr. OE (unrecorded) *tegga* ewe]

tegular /'tegjʊlə(r)/ *adj.* **1** of or like tiles. **2** arranged like tiles. □□ **tegularly** *adv.* [L *tegula* tile f. *tegere* cover]

tegument /'tegjʊmənt/ *n.* the natural covering of an animal's body or part of its body. □□ **tegumental** /-'ment(ə)l/ *adj.* **tegumentary** /-'mentərɪ/ *adj.* [L *tegumentum* f. *tegere* cover]

te-hee var. of TEE-HEE.

tektite /'tektaɪt/ *n. Geol.* a small roundish glassy body of unknown origin occurring in various parts of the earth. [G *Tektit* f. Gk *tēktos* molten f. *tēkō* melt]

Tel. *abbr.* **1** Telephone. **2 a** Telegraph. **b** Telegraphic.

telaesthesia /,telɪs'θi:zɪə/ *n.* (*US* **telesthesia**) *Psychol.* the supposed perception of distant occurrences or objects otherwise than by the recognized senses. □□ **telaesthetic** /-'θetɪk/ *adj.* [mod.L, formed as TELE- + Gk *aisthēsis* perception]

telamon /'teləməʊn/ *n.* (*pl.* **telamones** /-'məʊni:z/) *Archit.* a male figure used as a pillar to support an entablature. [L *telamones* f. Gk *telamōnes* pl. of *Telamōn*, name of a mythical hero]

tele- /'telɪ/ *comb. form* **1** at or to a distance (*telekinesis*). **2** forming names of instruments for operating over long distances (*telescope*). **3** television (*telecast*). **4** done by means of the telephone (*telesales*). [Gk *tēle* f. *tēle* far off: sense 3 f. TELEVISION: sense 4 f. TELEPHONE]

tele-ad /'telɪ,æd/ *n.* an advertisement placed in a newspaper etc. by telephone.

telecamera /'telɪ,kæmrə, -mərə/ *n.* **1** a television camera. **2** a telephotographic camera.

telecast /'telɪ,kɑ:st/ *n. & v.* —*n.* a television broadcast. —*v.tr.* transmit by television. □□ **telecaster** *n.* [TELE- + BROADCAST]

telecine /'telɪ,sɪnɪ/ *n.* **1** the broadcasting of cinema film on television. **2** equipment for doing this. [TELE- + CINE]

telecommunication /,telɪkə,mju:nɪ'keɪʃ(ə)n/ *n.* **1** communication over a distance by cable, telegraph, telephone, or broadcasting. **2** (usu. in *pl.*) the branch of technology concerned with this. [F *télécommunication* (as TELE-, COMMUNICATION)]

teleconference /,telɪ'kɒnfərəns/ *n.* a conference with participants in different locations linked by telecommunication devices. □□ **teleconferencing** *n.*

teledu /'telɪ,du:/ *n.* a badger, *Mydaus javanensis*, of

Java and Sumatra, that secretes a foul-smelling liquid when attacked. [Jav.]

telefacsimile /ˌtelɪfækˈsɪmɪlɪ/ n. facsimile transmission (see FACSIMILE n. 2).

telefax /ˈtelɪˌfæks/ n. = TELEFACSIMILE. [abbr.]

telefilm /ˈtelɪfɪlm/ n. = TELECINE.

telegenic /ˌtelɪˈdʒenɪk/ adj. having an appearance or manner that looks pleasing on television. [TELE- VISION + -genic in PHOTOGENIC]

telegony /tɪˈlegənɪ/ n. Biol. the supposed influence of a previous sire on the offspring of a dam with other sires. □□ **telegonic** /ˌtelɪˈgɒnɪk/ adj. [TELE- + Gk -gonia begetting]

telegram /ˈtelɪˌgræm/ n. a message sent by telegraph and then usu. delivered in written form. ¶ In UK official use since 1981 only for international messages. [TELE- + -GRAM, after TELEGRAPH]

telegraph /ˈtelɪˌgrɑːf, -ˌgræf/ n. & v. —n. **1 a** a system of or device for transmitting messages or signals to a distance esp. by making and breaking an electrical connection. **b** (attrib.) used in this system (telegraph pole; telegraph wire). **2** (in full **telegraph board**) a board displaying scores or other information at a match, race meeting, etc. —v. **1** tr. send a message by telegraph to. **2** tr. send by telegraph. **3** tr. give an advance indication of. **4** intr. make signals (telegraphed to me to come up). □**telegraph key** a device for making and breaking the electric circuit of a telegraph system. **telegraph plant** an E. Indian plant, Desmodium gyrans, whose leaves have a spontaneous jerking motion. □□ **telegrapher** /ˈtelɪˌgrɑːfə(r), tɪˈlegrəfə(r)/ n. [F télégraphe (as TELE-, -GRAPH)]

telegraphese /ˌtelɪgrəˈfiːz/ n. colloq. or joc. an abbreviated style usual in telegrams.

telegraphic /ˌtelɪˈgræfɪk/ adj. **1** of or by telegraphs or telegrams. **2** economically worded. □**telegraphic address** an abbreviated or other registered address for use in telegrams. □□ **telegraphically** adv.

telegraphist /tɪˈlegrəfɪst/ n. a person skilled or employed in telegraphy.

telegraphy /tɪˈlegrəfɪ/ n. the science or practice of using or constructing communication systems for the reproduction of information.

Telegu var. of TELUGU.

telekinesis /ˌtelɪkaɪˈniːsɪs, -kɪˈniːsɪs/ n. Psychol. movement of objects at a distance supposedly by paranormal means. □□ **telekinetic** /-ˈnetɪk/ adj. [mod.L (as TELE-, Gk kinēsis motion f. kineō move)]

telemark /ˈtelɪˌmɑːk/ n. & v. Skiing —n. a swing turn with one ski advanced and the knee bent, used to change direction or stop short. —v.intr. perform this turn. [Telemark in Norway]

telemarketing /ˈtelɪˌmɑːkɪtɪŋ/ n. the marketing of goods etc. by means of usu. unsolicited telephone calls. □□ **telemarketer** n.

telemessage /ˈtelɪˌmesɪdʒ/ n. a message sent by telephone or telex and delivered in written form. ¶ In UK official use since 1981 for inland messages, replacing telegram.

telemeter /ˈtelɪˌmiːtə(r), tɪˈlemɪtə(r)/ n. & v. —n. an apparatus for recording the readings of an instrument and transmitting them by radio. —v. **1** intr. record readings in this way. **2** tr. transmit (readings etc.) to a distant receiving set or station. □□ **telemetric** /-ˈmetrɪk/ adj. **telemetry** /tɪˈlemətrɪ/ n.

teleology /ˌtelɪˈɒlədʒɪ, ˌtiː-/ n. (pl. -ies) Philos. **1** the explanation of phenomena by the purpose they serve rather than by postulated causes. **2** Theol. the doctrine of design and purpose in the material world. □□ **teleologic** /-əˈlɒdʒɪk/ adj. **teleological** /-əˈlɒdʒɪk(ə)l/ adj. **teleologically** /-əˈlɒdʒɪkəlɪ/ adv. **teleologism** n. **teleologist** n. [mod.L teleologia f. Gk telos teleos end + -LOGY]

teleost /ˈtelɪˌɒst/ n. any fish of the subclass Teleostei of bony fish, including eels, plaice, salmon, etc. [Gk teleo- complete + osteon bone]

telepath /ˈtelɪˌpæθ/ n. a telepathic person. [back-form. f. TELEPATHY]

telepathy /tɪˈlepəθɪ/ n. the supposed communication of thoughts or ideas otherwise than by the known senses. □□ **telepathic** /ˌtelɪˈpæθɪk/ adj. **telepathically** /ˌtelɪˈpæθɪkəlɪ/ adv. **telepathist** n. **telepathize** v.tr. & intr. (also -ise).

telephone /ˈtelɪˌfəʊn/ n. & v. —n. **1** an apparatus for transmitting speech (esp. speech) to a distance by wire or cord or radio, esp. by converting acoustic vibrations to electrical signals. **2** a transmitting and receiving instrument used in this. **3** a system of communication using a network of telephones. —v. **1** tr. speak to (a person) by telephone. **2** tr. send (a message) by telephone. **3** intr. make a telephone call. □**on the telephone 1** having a telephone. **2** by use of or using the telephone. **over the telephone** by use of or using the telephone. **telephone book** = telephone directory. **telephone box** Brit. = telephone booth. **telephone booth** (or **kiosk**) a public booth or enclosure from which telephone calls can be made. **telephone call** = CALL n. 4. **telephone directory** a book listing telephone subscribers and numbers in a particular area. **telephone exchange** = EXCHANGE n. 3. **telephone number** a number assigned to a particular telephone and used in making connections to it. **telephone operator** esp. US an operator in a telephone exchange. □□ **telephoner** n. **telephonic** /-ˈfɒnɪk/ adj. **telephonically** /-ˈfɒnɪkəlɪ/ adv.

telephonist /tɪˈlefənɪst/ n. Brit. an operator in a telephone exchange or at a switchboard.

telephony /tɪˈlefənɪ/ n. the use or a system of telephones.

telephoto /ˌtelɪˈfəʊtəʊ/ n. (pl. **-os**) (in full **telephoto lens**) a lens used in telephotography.

telephotographic /ˌtelɪˌfəʊtəˈgræfɪk/ adj. of or for or using telephotography. □□ **telephotographically** adv.

telephotography /ˌtelɪfəˈtɒgrəfɪ/ n. the photographing of distant objects with a system of lenses giving a large image.

teleport /ˈtelɪˌpɔːt/ v.tr. Psychol. move by telekinesis. □□ **teleportation** /-ˈteɪʃ(ə)n/ n. [TELE- + PORT⁴ 3]

teleprinter /ˈtelɪˌprɪntə(r)/ n. a device for transmitting telegraph messages as they are keyed, and for printing messages received.

teleprompter /ˈtelɪˌprɒmptə(r)/ n. a device beside a television or cinema camera that slowly unrolls a speaker's script out of sight of the audience (cf. AUTOCUE).

telerecord /ˈtelɪrɪˌkɔːd/ v.tr. record for television broadcasting.

telerecording /ˈtelɪrɪˌkɔːdɪŋ/ n. a recorded television broadcast.

telesales /ˈtelɪˌseɪlz/ n.pl. selling by means of the telephone.

telescope /ˈtelɪˌskəʊp/ n. & v. —n. **1** an optical instrument using lenses or mirrors or both to make distant objects appear nearer and larger. **2** = radio telescope. —v. **1** tr. press or drive (sections of a tube, colliding vehicles, etc.) together so that one slides into another like the sections of a folding telescope. **2** intr. close or be driven or be capable of closing in this way. **3** tr. compress so as to occupy less space or time. [It. telescopio or mod.L telescopium (as TELE-, -SCOPE)]

telescopic /ˌtelɪˈskɒpɪk/ adj. **1 a** of, relating to, or made with a telescope (telescopic observations). **b** visible only through a telescope (telescopic stars). **2** (esp. of a lens) able to focus on and magnify distant objects. **3** consisting of sections that telescope. □**telescopic sight** a telescope used for sighting on a rifle etc. □□ **telescopically** adv.

telesoftware /ˌtelɪˈsɒftweə(r)/ n. software transmitted or broadcast to receiving terminals.

telesthesia US var. of TELAESTHESIA.

æ cat ɑ: arm e bed ɜ: her ɪ sit iː see ɒ hot ɔ: saw ʌ run ʊ put uː too ə ago aɪ my

Teletex /'telɪˌteks/ *n. propr.* an electronic text transmission system.

teletext /'telɪˌtekst/ *n.* a news and information service, in the form of text and graphics, from a computer source transmitted to televisions with appropriate receivers (cf. CEEFAX, ORACLE).

telethon /'telɪˌθɒn/ *n.* esp. *US* an exceptionally long television programme, esp. to raise money for a charity. [TELE- + -*thon* in MARATHON]

Teletype /'telɪˌtaɪp/ *n. & v.* — *n. propr.* a kind of teleprinter. — *v.* (**teletype**) **1** *intr.* operate a teleprinter. **2** *tr.* send by means of a teleprinter.

teletypewriter /ˌtelɪ'taɪpˌraɪtə(r)/ *n.* esp. *US* = TELEPRINTER.

televiewer /'telɪˌvjuːə(r)/ *v.tr.* a person who watches television. □□ **televiewing** *adj.*

televise /'telɪˌvaɪz/ *v.tr.* transmit by television. □□ **televisable** *adj.* [back-form. f. TELEVISION]

television /'telɪˌvɪʒ(ə)n, -'vɪʒ(ə)n/ *n.* **1** a system for reproducing on a screen visual images transmitted (usu. with sound) by radio signals. **2** (in full **television set**) a device with a screen for receiving these signals. **3** television broadcasting generally.

televisual /ˌtelɪ'vɪʒʊəl, -'vɪzjʊəl/ *adj.* relating to or suitable for television. □□ **televisually** *adv.*

telex /'teleks/ *n. & v.* (also **Telex**) — *n.* an international system of telegraphy with printed messages transmitted and received by teleprinters using the public telecommunications network. — *v.tr.* send or communicate with by telex. [TELEPRINTER + EXCHANGE]

tell¹ /tel/ *v.* (*past* and *past part.* **told** /təʊld/) **1** *tr.* relate or narrate in speech or writing; give an account of (*tell me a story*). **2** *tr.* make known; express in words; divulge (*tell me your name; tell me what you want*). **3** *tr.* reveal or signify to (a person) (*your face tells me everything*). **4** *tr.* **a** utter (*don't tell lies*). **b** warn (*I told you so*). **5** *intr.* **a** (often foll. by *of, about*) divulge information or a description; reveal a secret (*I told of the plan; promise you won't tell*). **b** (foll. by *on*) *colloq.* inform against (a person). **6** *tr.* (foll. by *to* + infin.) give (a person) a direction or order (*tell them to wait; do as you are told*). **7** *tr.* assure (*it's true, I tell you*). **8** *tr.* explain in writing; instruct (*this book tells you how to cook*). **9** *tr.* decide, determine, distinguish (*cannot tell which button to press; how do you tell one from the other?*). **10** *intr.* **a** (often foll. by *on*) produce a noticeable effect (*every disappointment tells; the strain was beginning to tell on me*). **b** reveal the truth (*time will tell*). **c** have an influence (*the evidence tells against you*). **11** *tr.* (often *absol.*) count (votes) at a meeting, election, etc. □ **as far as one can tell** judging from the available information. **tell apart** distinguish between (usu. with *neg.* or *interrog.*: *could not tell them apart*). **tell me another** *colloq.* an expression of incredulity. **tell off 1** *colloq.* reprimand, scold. **2** count off or detach for duty. **tell a tale** (or **its own tale**) be significant or revealing. **tell tales** report a discreditable fact about another. **tell that to the marines** see MARINE. **tell the time** determine the time from the face of a clock or watch. **there is no telling** it is impossible to know (*there's no telling what may happen*). **you're telling me** *colloq.* I agree wholeheartedly. □□ **tellable** *adj.* [OE *tellan* f. Gmc, rel. to TALE]

tell² /tel/ *n. Archaeol.* an artificial mound in the Middle East etc. formed by the accumulated remains of ancient settlements. [Arab. *tall* hillock]

teller /'telə(r)/ *n.* **1** a person employed to receive and pay out money in a bank etc. **2** a person who counts (votes). **3** a person who tells esp. stories (*a teller of tales*). □□ **tellership** *n.*

telling /'telɪŋ/ *adj.* **1** having a marked effect; striking. **2** significant. □□ **tellingly** *adv.*

telling-off /ˌtelɪŋ'ɒf/ *n.* (*pl.* **tellings-off**) *colloq.* a reproof or reprimand.

tell-tale /'telteɪl/ *n.* **1** a person who reveals (esp.

discreditable) information about another's private affairs or behaviour. **2** (*attrib.*) that reveals or betrays (*a tell-tale smile*). **3** a device for automatic monitoring or registering of a process etc.

tellurian /te'ljʊərɪən/ *adj. & n.* — *adj.* of or inhabiting the earth. — *n.* an inhabitant of the earth. [L *tellus -uris* earth]

telluric /te'ljʊərɪk/ *adj.* **1** of the earth as a planet. **2** of the soil. **3** *Chem.* of tellurium, esp. in its higher valency. □□ **tellurate** /-rət/ *n.* [L *tellus -uris* earth: sense 3 f. TELLURIUM]

tellurium /te'ljʊərɪəm/ *n. Chem.* a rare brittle lustrous silver-white element occurring naturally in ores of gold and silver, used in semiconductors. ¶ Symb.: **Te**. □□ **telluride** /'teljʊəˌraɪd/ *n.* **tellurite** /'teljʊəˌraɪt/ *n.* **tellurous** *adj.* [L *tellus -uris* earth, prob. named in contrast to *uranium*]

telly /'telɪ/ *n.* (*pl.* **-ies**) esp. *Brit. colloq.* **1** television. **2** a television set. [abbr.]

telpher /'telfə(r)/ *n.* a system for transporting goods etc. by electrically driven trucks or cable-cars. □□ **telpherage** *n.* [TELE- + -PHORE]

telson /'tels(ə)n/ *n.* the last segment in the abdomen of Crustacea etc. [Gk, = limit]

Telugu /'teləˌguː/ *n.* (also **Telegu**) (*pl.* same or **Telegus**) **1** a member of a Dravidian people in SE India. **2** the language of this people. [Telugu]

temerarious /ˌteməˈreərɪəs/ *adj. literary* reckless, rash. [L *temerarius* f. *temere* rashly]

temerity /tɪ'merɪtɪ/ *n.* **1** rashness. **2** audacity, impudence. [L *temeritas* f. *temere* rashly]

temp /temp/ *n. & v. colloq.* — *n.* a temporary employee, esp. a secretary. — *v.intr.* work as a temp. [abbr.]

temp.¹ /temp/ *abbr.* temperature.

temp.² /temp/ *abbr.* in the time of (*temp. Henry I*). [L *tempore* ablat. of *tempus* time]

temper /'tempə(r)/ *n. & v.* — *n.* **1** habitual or temporary disposition of mind esp. as regards composure (*a person of a placid temper*). **2** irritation or anger (*in a fit of temper*). **3** a tendency to have fits of anger (*have a temper*). **4** composure or calmness (*keep one's temper; lose one's temper*). **5** the condition of metal as regards hardness and elasticity. — *v.tr.* **1** bring (metal or clay) to a proper hardness or consistency. **2** (foll. by *with*) moderate or mitigate (*temper justice with mercy*). **3** tune or modulate (a piano etc.) so as to distance intervals correctly. □ **in a bad temper** angry, peevish. **in a good temper** in an amiable mood. **out of temper** angry, peevish. **show temper** be petulant. □□ **temperable** *adj.* **temperative** /-ətɪv/ *adj.* **tempered** *adj.* **temperedly** *adv.* **temperer** *n.* [OE *temprian* (v.) f. L *temperare* mingle: infl. by OF *temprer, tremper*]

tempera /'tempərə/ *n.* a method of painting using an emulsion e.g. of pigment with egg, esp. in fine art on canvas. [It.: cf. DISTEMPER¹]

temperament /'tempərəmənt/ *n.* **1** a person's distinct nature and character, esp. as determined by physical constitution and permanently affecting behaviour (*a nervous temperament; the artistic temperament*). **2** a creative or spirited personality (*was full of temperament*). **3 a** an adjustment of intervals in tuning a piano etc. so as to fit the scale for use in all keys. **b** (**equal temperament**) an adjustment in which the 12 semitones are at equal intervals. [ME f. L *temperamentum* (as TEMPER)]

temperamental /ˌtemprə'ment(ə)l/ *adj.* **1** of or having temperament. **2 a** (of a person) liable to erratic or moody behaviour. **b** (of a thing, e.g. a machine) working unpredictably; unreliable. □□ **temperamentally** *adv.*

temperance /'tempərəns/ *n.* **1** moderation or self-restraint esp. in eating and drinking. **2 a** total or partial abstinence from alcoholic drink. **b** (*attrib.*) advocating or concerned with abstinence. [ME f. AF *temperaunce* f. L *temperantia* (as TEMPER)]

aʊ how eɪ day əʊ no eə hair ɪə near ɔɪ boy ʊə poor aɪə fire aʊə sour (*see over for consonants*)

temperate /ˈtempərət/ *adj.* **1** avoiding excess; self-restrained. **2** moderate. **3** (of a region or climate) characterized by mild temperatures. **4** abstemious. □**temperate zone** the belt of the earth between the frigid and the torrid zones. □□ **temperately** *adv.* **temperateness** *n.* [ME f. L *temperatus* past part. of *temperare*: see TEMPER]

temperature /ˈtemprɪtʃə(r)/ *n.* **1** the degree or intensity of heat of a body in relation to others, esp. as shown by a thermometer or perceived by touch etc. **2** *Med.* the degree of internal heat of the body. **3** *colloq.* a body temperature above the normal (*have a temperature*). **4** the degree of excitement in a discussion etc. □**take a person's temperature** ascertain a person's body temperature, esp. as a diagnostic aid. **temperature-humidity index** a quantity giving the measure of discomfort due to the combined effects of the temperature and humidity of the air. [F *température* or L *temperatura* (as TEMPER)]

-tempered /ˈtempəd/ *comb. form* having a specified temper or disposition (*bad-tempered*; *hot-tempered*). □□**-temperedly** *adv.* **-temperedness** *n.*

tempest /ˈtempɪst/ *n.* **1** a violent windy storm. **2** violent agitation or tumult. [ME f. OF *tempest(e)* ult. f. L *tempestas* season, storm, f. *tempus* time]

tempestuous /temˈpestjʊəs/ *adj.* **1** stormy. **2** (of a person, emotion, etc.) turbulent, violent, passionate. □□ **tempestuously** *adv.* **tempestuousness** *n.* [LL *tempestuosus* (as TEMPEST)]

tempi *pl.* of TEMPO.

Templar /ˈtemplə(r)/ *n.* **1** a lawyer or law student with chambers in the Temple, London. **2** (in full **Knight Templar**) *hist.* a member of a religious and military order for the protection of pilgrims to the Holy Land, suppressed in 1312. [ME f. AF *templer*, OF *templier*, med.L *templarius* (as TEMPLE¹)]

template /ˈtemplɪt, -pleɪt/ *n.* (also **templet**) **1 a** a pattern or gauge, usu. a piece of thin board or metal plate, used as a guide in cutting or drilling metal, stone, wood, etc. **b** a flat card or plastic pattern esp. for cutting cloth for patchwork etc. **2** a timber or plate used to distribute the weight in a wall or under a beam etc. **3** *Biochem.* the molecular pattern governing the assembly of a protein etc. [orig. *templet*: prob. f. TEMPLE³ + -ET¹, alt. after *plate*]

temple¹ /ˈtemp(ə)l/ *n.* **1** a building devoted to the worship, or regarded as the dwelling-place, of a god or gods or other objects of religious reverence. **2** *hist.* any of three successive religious buildings of the Jews in Jerusalem. **3** *US* a synagogue. **4** a place of Christian public worship, esp. a Protestant church in France. **5** a place in which God is regarded as residing, esp. a Christian's person or body. □**temple block** a percussion instrument consisting of a hollow block of wood which is struck with a stick. [OE *temp(e)l*, reinforced in ME by OF *temple*, f. L *templum* open or consecrated space]

temple² /ˈtemp(ə)l/ *n.* the flat part of either side of the head between the forehead and the ear. [ME f. OF ult. f. L *tempora* pl. of *tempus*]

temple³ /ˈtemp(ə)l/ *n.* a device in a loom for keeping the cloth stretched. [ME f. OF, orig. the same word as TEMPLE²]

templet var. of TEMPLATE.

tempo /ˈtempəʊ/ *n.* (*pl.* -os or **tempi** /-piː/) **1** *Mus.* the speed at which music is or should be played, esp. as characteristic (*waltz tempo*). **2** the rate of motion or activity (*the tempo of the war is quickening*). [It. f. L *tempus* time]

temporal /ˈtempər(ə)l/ *adj.* **1** of worldly as opposed to spiritual affairs; of this life; secular. **2** of or relating to time. **3** *Gram.* relating to or denoting time or tense (*temporal conjunction*). **4** of the temples of the head (*temporal artery*; *temporal bone*). □**temporal power** the power of an ecclesiastic, esp. the Pope, in temporal matters. □□ **temporally** *adv.* [ME f. OF *temporel* or f. L *temporalis* f. *tempus -oris* time]

temporality /ˌtempəˈrælɪtɪ/ *n.* (*pl.* -ies) **1** temporariness. **2** (usu. in *pl.*) a secular possession, esp. the properties and revenues of a religious corporation or an ecclesiastic. [ME f. LL *temporalitas* (as TEMPORAL)]

temporary /ˈtempərərɪ/ *adj.* & *n.* —*adj.* lasting or meant to last only for a limited time (*temporary buildings*; *temporary relief*). —*n.* (*pl.* -ies) a person employed temporarily (cf. TEMP). □□ **temporarily** *adv.* **temporariness** *n.* [L *temporarius* f. *tempus -oris* time]

temporize /ˈtempəraɪz/ *v.intr.* (also -ise) **1** avoid committing oneself so as to gain time; employ delaying tactics. **2** comply temporarily with the requirements of the occasion, adopt a time-serving policy. □□ **temporization** /-ˈzeɪʃ(ə)n/ *n.* **temporizer** *n.* [F *temporiser* bide one's time f. med. L *temporizare* delay f. *tempus -oris* time]

tempt /tempt/ *v.tr.* **1** entice or incite (a person) to do a wrong or forbidden thing (*tempted him to steal it*). **2** allure, attract. **3** risk provoking (esp. an abstract force or power) (*would be tempting fate to try it*). **4** *archaic* make trial of; try the resolution of (*God did tempt Abraham*). □**be tempted to** be strongly disposed to (*I am tempted to question this*). □□ **temptable** *adj.* **temptability** /-ˈbɪlɪtɪ/ *n.* [ME f. OF *tenter*, *tempter* test f. L *temptare* handle, test, try]

temptation /tempˈteɪʃ(ə)n/ *n.* **1 a** the act or an instance of tempting; the state of being tempted; incitement esp. to wrongdoing. **b** (the Temptation) the tempting of Christ by the Devil (see Matt. 4). **2** an attractive thing or course of action. **3** *archaic* putting to the test. [ME f. OF *tentacion*, *temptacion* f. L *temptatio -onis* (as TEMPT)]

tempter /ˈtemptə(r)/ *n.* (*fem.* **temptress** /-trɪs/) **1** a person who tempts. **2** (the Tempter) the Devil. [ME f. OF *tempteur* f. eccl.L *temptator -oris* (as TEMPT)]

tempting /ˈtemptɪŋ/ *adj.* **1** attractive, inviting. **2** enticing to evil. □□ **temptingly** *adv.*

tempura /ˈtempʊərə/ *n.* a Japanese dish of fish, shellfish, or vegetables, fried in batter. [Jap.]

ten /ten/ *n.* & *adj.* —*n.* **1** one more than nine. **2** a symbol for this (10, x, X). **3** a size etc. denoted by ten. **4** the time of ten o'clock (*is it ten yet?*). **5** a card with ten pips. **6** a set of ten. —*adj.* **1** that amount to ten. **2** (as a round number) several (*ten times as easy*). □**the Ten Commandments** see COMMANDMENT. **ten-gallon hat** a cowboy's large broad-brimmed hat. **ten-week stock** a variety of stock, *Matthiola incana*, said to bloom ten weeks after the sowing of the seed. [OE *tīen*, *tēn* f. Gmc]

ten. *abbr.* tenuto.

tenable /ˈtenəb(ə)l/ *adj.* **1** that can be maintained or defended against attack or objection (*a tenable position*; *a tenable theory*). **2** (foll. by *for*, *by*) (of an office etc.) that can be held for (a specified period) or by (a specified class of person). □□ **tenability** /-ˈbɪlɪtɪ/ *n.* **tenableness** *n.* [F f. *tenir* hold f. L *tenēre*]

tenace /ˈtenəs/ *n.* **1** two cards, one ranking next above, and the other next below, a card held by an opponent. **2** the holding of such cards. [F f. Sp. *tenaza*, lit. 'pincers']

tenacious /tɪˈneɪʃəs/ *adj.* **1** (often foll. by *of*) keeping a firm hold of property, principles, life, etc.; not readily relinquishing. **2** (of memory) retentive. **3** holding fast. **4** strongly cohesive. **5** persistent, resolute. **6** adhesive, sticky. □□ **tenaciously** *adv.* **tenaciousness** *n.* **tenacity** /tɪˈnæsɪtɪ/ *n.* [L *tenax -acis* f. *tenēre* hold]

tenaculum /tɪˈnækjʊləm/ *n.* (*pl.* **tenacula** /-lə/) a surgeon's sharp hook for picking up arteries etc. [L, = holding instrument, f. *tenēre* hold]

tenancy /ˈtenənsɪ/ *n.* (*pl.* -ies) **1** the status of a tenant; possession as a tenant. **2** the duration or period of this.

tenant /ˈtenənt/ *n.* & *v.* —*n.* **1** a person who rents land or property from a landlord. **2** (often foll. by *of*) the occupant of a place. **3** *Law* a person holding real property by private ownership. —*v.tr.* occupy as a tenant. □**tenant farmer** a person who farms rented land. **tenant right** *Brit.* the right of a tenant to continue a tenancy at the termination of the lease. □□**tenantable** *adj.* **tenantless** *adj.* [ME f. OF, pres. part. of *tenir* hold f. L *tenēre*]

tenantry /'tenəntrɪ/ *n.* the tenants of an estate etc.

tench /tentʃ/ *n.* (*pl.* same) a European freshwater fish, *Tinca tinca*, of the carp family. [ME f. OF *tenche* f. LL *tinca*]

tend[1] /tend/ *v.intr.* **1** (usu. foll. by *to*) be apt or inclined (*tends to lose his temper*). **2** serve, conduce. **3** be moving; be directed; hold a course (*tends in our direction*; *tends downwards*; *tends to the same conclusion*). [ME f. OF *tendre* stretch f. L *tendere* tens- or *tent*-]

tend[2] /tend/ *v.* **1** *tr.* take care of, look after (a person esp. an invalid, animals esp. sheep, a machine). **2** *intr.* (foll. by *on*, *upon*) wait on. **3** *intr.* (foll. by *to*) esp. *US* give attention to. □□**tendance** *n. archaic.* [ME f. ATTEND]

tendency /'tendənsɪ/ *n.* (*pl.* -**ies**) **1** (often foll. by *to*, *towards*) a leaning or inclination, a way of tending. **2** a group within a larger political party or movement. [med.L *tendentia* (as TEND[1])]

tendentious /ten'denʃəs/ *adj. derog.* (of writing etc.) calculated to promote a particular cause or viewpoint; having an underlying purpose. □□ **tendentiously** *adv.* **tendentiousness** *n.* [as TEND-ENCY + -OUS]

tender[1] /'tendə(r)/ *adj.* (**tenderer**, **tenderest**) **1** easily cut or chewed, not tough (*tender steak*). **2** easily touched or wounded, susceptible to pain or grief (*a tender heart*; *a tender conscience*). **3** easily hurt, sensitive (*tender skin*; *a tender place*). **4** delicate, fragile (*a tender reputation*). **5** loving, affectionate, fond (*tender parents*; *wrote tender verses*). **6** requiring tact or careful handling, ticklish (*a tender subject*). **7** (of age) early, immature (*of tender years*). **8** (usu. foll. by *of*) solicitous, concerned (*tender of his honour*). □**tender-eyed 1** having gentle eyes. **2** weak-eyed. **tender-hearted** having a tender heart, easily moved by pity etc. **tender-heartedness** being tender-hearted. **tender mercies** *iron.* attention or treatment which is not in the best interests of its recipient. **tender spot** a subject on which a person is touchy. □□ **tenderly** *adv.* **tenderness** *n.* [ME f. OF *tendre* f. L *tener*]

tender[2] /'tendə(r)/ *v. & n.* —*v.* **1** *tr.* **a** offer, present (one's services, apologies, resignation, etc.). **b** offer (money etc.) as payment. **2** *intr.* (often foll. by *for*) make a tender for the supply of a thing or the execution of work. —*n.* an offer, esp. an offer in writing to execute work or supply goods at a fixed price. □**plea of tender** *Law* a plea that the defendant has always been ready to satisfy the plaintiff's claim and now brings the sum into court. **put out to tender** seek tenders in respect of (work etc.). □□ **tenderer** *n.* [OF *tendre*: see TEND[1]]

tender[3] /'tendə(r)/ *n.* **1** a person who looks after people or things. **2** a vessel attending a larger one to supply stores, convey passengers or orders, etc. **3** a special truck closely coupled to a steam locomotive to carry fuel, water, etc. [ME f. TEND[2] or f. ATTENDER (as ATTEND)]

tenderfoot /'tendəfʊt/ *n.* a newcomer or novice, esp. in the bush or in the Scouts or Guides.

tenderize /'tendəraɪz/ *v.tr.* (also -**ise**) make tender, esp. make (meat) tender by beating etc. □□ **tenderizer** *n.*

tenderloin /'tendəlɔɪn/ *n.* **1 a** *Brit.* the middle part of a pork loin. **b** *US* the undercut of a sirloin. **2** *US sl.* a district of a city where vice and corruption are prominent.

tendon /'tend(ə)n/ *n.* **1** a cord or strand of strong tissue attaching a muscle to a bone etc. **2** (in a quadruped) = HAMSTRING. □□ **tendinitis** /,tendɪ'naɪtɪs/ *n.* **tendinous** /-dɪnəs/ *adj.* [F *tendon* or med.L *tendo -dinis* f. Gk *tenōn* sinew f. *teinō* stretch]

tendril /'tendrɪl/ *n.* **1** each of the slender leafless shoots by which some climbing plants cling for support. **2** a slender curl of hair etc. [prob. f. obs. F *tendrillon* dimin. of obs. *tendron* young shoot ult. f. L *tener* TENDER[1]]

Tenebrae /'tenə,breɪ/ *n.pl.* **1** *RC Ch. hist.* matins and lauds for the last three days of Holy Week, at which candles are successively extinguished. **2** this office set to music. [L, = darkness]

tenebrous /'tenɪbrəs/ *adj. literary* dark, gloomy. [ME f. OF *tenebrus* f. L *tenebrosus* (as TENEBRAE)]

tenement /'tenɪmənt/ *n.* **1** a room or a set of rooms forming a separate residence within a house or block of flats. **2** *US & Sc.* a house divided into and let in tenements. **3** a dwelling-place. **4 a** a piece of land held by an owner. **b** *Law* any kind of permanent property, e.g. lands or rents, held from a superior. □**tenement-house** *US & Sc.* = sense 2. □□ **tenemental** /-'ment(ə)l/ *adj.* **tenementary** /-'mentərɪ/ *adj.* [ME f. OF f. med.L *tenementum* f. *tenēre* hold]

tenesmus /tɪ'nezməs/ *n. Med.* a continual inclination to evacuate the bowels or bladder accompanied by painful straining. [med.L f. Gk *teinesmos* straining f. *teinō* stretch]

tenet /'tenɪt, 'tiːnet/ *n.* a doctrine, dogma, or principle held by a group or person. [L, = he etc. holds f. *tenēre* hold]

tenfold /'tenfəʊld/ *adj. & adv.* **1** ten times as much or as many. **2** consisting of ten parts.

tenia *US* var. of TAENIA.

Tenn. *abbr.* Tennessee.

tenné /'tenɪ/ *n. &* (usu. placed after noun) *adj.* (also **tenny**) *Heraldry* orange-brown. [obs. F, var. of *tanné* TAWNY]

tenner /'tenə(r)/ *n. colloq.* a ten-pound or ten-dollar note. [TEN]

tennis /'tenɪs/ *n.* either of two games (lawn tennis and real tennis) in which two or four players strike a ball with rackets over a net stretched across a court. □**tennis-ball** a ball used in playing tennis. **tennis-court** a court used in playing tennis. **tennis elbow** a sprain caused by or as by playing tennis. **tennis-racket** a racket used in playing tennis. **tennis shoe** a light canvas or leather soft-soled shoe suitable for tennis or general casual wear. [ME *tenetz, tenes*, etc., app. f. OF *tenez* 'take, receive', called by the server to an opponent, imper. of *tenir* take]

tenno /'tenəʊ/ *n.* (*pl.* -**os**) the Emperor of Japan viewed as a divinity. [Jap.]

tenny var. of TENNÉ.

Tennysonian /,tenɪ'səʊnɪən/ *adj.* relating to or in the style of Alfred (Lord) Tennyson, Engl. poet d. 1892.

tenon /'tenən/ *n. & v.* —*n.* a projecting piece of wood made for insertion into a corresponding cavity (esp. a mortise) in another piece. —*v.tr.* **1** cut as a tenon. **2** join by means of a tenon. □**tenon-saw** a small saw with a strong brass or steel back for fine work. □□ **tenoner** *n.* [ME f. F f. *tenir* hold f. L *tenēre*]

tenor /'tenə(r)/ *n.* **1 a** a singing-voice between baritone and alto or counter-tenor, the highest of the ordinary adult male range. **b** a singer with this voice. **c** a part written for it. **2 a** an instrument, esp. a viola, recorder, or saxophone, of which the range is roughly that of a tenor voice. **b** (in full **tenor bell**) the largest bell of a peal or set. **3** (usu. foll. by *of*) the general purport or drift of a document or speech. **4** (usu. foll. by *of*) a settled or prevailing course or direction, esp. the course of a person's life or habits. **5** *Law* **a** the actual wording of a document. **b** an exact copy. **6** the subject to which a metaphor refers (opp. VEHICLE 4). □**tenor clef** *Mus.* a clef placing middle C on the second highest line of the staff. [ME f. AF *tenur*, OF *tenour* f. L *tenor -oris* f. *tenēre* hold]

---

w *we* z *zoo* ʃ *she* ʒ *decision* θ *thin* ð *this* ŋ *ring* x *loch* tʃ *chip* dʒ *jar* (*see over for vowels*)

tenosynovitis /ˌtenəʊˌsaɪnəʊˈvaɪtɪs/ *n.* inflammation and swelling of a tendon, usu. in the wrist, often caused by repetitive movements such as typing. [Gk *tenōn* tendon + SYNOVITIS]

tenotomy /təˈnɒtəmɪ/ *n.* (*pl.* -**ies**) the surgical cutting of a tendon, esp. as a remedy for a club-foot. [F *ténotomie*, irreg. f. Gk *tenōn* -*ontos* tendon]

tenpin /ˈtenpɪn/ *n.* **1** a pin used in tenpin bowling. **2** (in *pl.*) *US* = *tenpin bowling.* □**tenpin bowling** a game developed from ninepins in which ten pins are set up at the end of an alley and bowled down with hard rubber balls.

tenrec /ˈtenrek/ *n.* (also **tanrec** /ˈtæn-/) any hedgehog-like tailless insect-eating mammal of the family Tenrecidae, esp. *Tenrec ecaudatus* native to Madagascar. [F *tanrec*, f. Malagasy *tàndraka*]

tense[1] /tens/ *adj.* & *v.* —*adj.* **1** stretched tight, strained (*tense cord*; *tense muscle*; *tense nerves*; *tense emotion*). **2** causing tenseness (*a tense moment*). **3** *Phonet.* pronounced with the vocal muscles tense. —*v.tr.* & *intr.* make or become tense. □**tense up** become tense. □□**tensely** *adv.* **tenseness** *n.* **tensity** *n.* [L *tensus* past part. of *tendere* stretch]

tense[2] /tens/ *n. Gram.* **1** a form taken by a verb to indicate the time (also the continuance or completeness) of the action etc. (*present tense*; *imperfect tense*). **2** a set of such forms for the various persons and numbers. □□**tenseless** *adj.* [ME f. OF *tens* f. L *tempus* time]

tensile /ˈtensaɪl/ *adj.* **1** of or relating to tension. **2** capable of being drawn out or stretched. □**tensile strength** resistance to breaking under tension. □□ **tensility** /tenˈsɪlɪtɪ/ *n.* [med.L *tensilis* (as TENSE[1])]

tensimeter /tenˈsɪmɪtə(r)/ *n.* **1** an instrument for measuring vapour pressure. **2** a manometer. [TENSION + -METER]

tension /ˈtenʃ(ə)n/ *n.* & *v.* —*n.* **1** the act or an instance of stretching; the state of being stretched; tenseness. **2** mental strain or excitement. **3** a strained (political, social, etc.) state or relationship. **4** *Mech.* the stress by which a bar, cord, etc. is pulled when it is part of a system in equilibrium or motion. **5** electromagnetic force (*high tension*; *low tension*). —*v.tr.* subject to tension. □□**tensional** *adj.* **tensionally** *adv.* **tensionless** *adj.* [F *tension* or L *tensio* (as TEND[1])]

tenson /ˈtens(ə)n/ *n.* (also **tenzon** /ˈtiːnz(ə)n/) **1** a contest in verse-making between troubadours. **2** a piece of verse composed for this. [F *tenson*, = Prov. *tenso* (as TENSION)]

tensor /ˈtensə(r)/ *n.* **1** *Anat.* a muscle that tightens or stretches a part. **2** *Math.* a generalized form of vector involving an arbitrary number of indices. □□ **tensorial** /-ˈsɔːrɪəl/ *adj.* [mod.L (as TEND[1])]

tent[1] /tent/ *n.* & *v.* —*n.* **1** a portable shelter or dwelling of canvas, cloth, etc., supported by a pole or poles and stretched by cords attached to pegs driven into the ground. **2** *Med.* a tentlike enclosure for control of the air supply to a patient. —*v.* **1** *tr.* cover with or as with a tent. **2** *intr.* **a** encamp in a tent. **b** dwell temporarily. □**tent-bed** a bed with a tentlike canopy, or for a patient in a tent. **tent coat** (or **dress**) a coat (or dress) cut very full. **tent-fly** (*pl.* -**flies**) **1** a flap at the entrance to a tent. **2** a piece of canvas stretched over the ridge-pole of a tent leaving an open space but keeping off sun and rain. **tent-peg** any of the pegs to which the cords of a tent are attached. **tent-pegging** a sport in which a rider tries at full gallop to carry off on the point of a lance a tent-peg fixed in the ground. **tent-stitch 1** a series of parallel diagonal stitches. **2** such a stitch. [ME f. OF *tente* ult. f. L *tendere* stretch: *tent-stitch* may be f. another word]

tent[2] /tent/ *n.* a deep-red sweet wine chiefly from Spain, used esp. as sacramental wine. [Sp. *tinto* deep-coloured f. L *tinctus* past part.: see TINGE]

tent[3] /tent/ *n. Surgery* a piece (esp. a roll) of lint, linen, etc., inserted into a wound or natural opening

to keep it open. [ME f. OF *tente* f. *tenter* probe (as TEMPT)]

tentacle /ˈtentək(ə)l/ *n.* **1** a long slender flexible appendage of an (esp. invertebrate) animal, used for feeling, grasping, or moving. **2** a thing used like a tentacle as a feeler etc. **3** *Bot.* a sensitive hair or filament. □□**tentacled** *adj.* (also in *comb.*). **tentacular** /-ˈtækjʊlə(r)/ *adj.* **tentaculate** /-ˈtækjʊlət/ *adj.* [mod.L *tentaculum* f. L *tentare* = *temptare* (see TEMPT) + -*culum* -CULE]

tentative /ˈtentətɪv/ *adj.* & *n.* —*adj.* **1** done by way of trial, experimental. **2** hesitant, not definite (*tentative suggestion*; *tentative acceptance*). —*n.* an experimental proposal or theory. □□**tentatively** *adv.* **tentativeness** *n.* [med.L *tentativus* (as TENTACLE)]

tenter[1] /ˈtentə(r)/ *n.* **1** a machine for stretching cloth to dry in shape. **2** = TENTERHOOK. [ME ult. f. med.L *tentorium* (as TEND[1])]

tenter[2] /ˈtentə(r)/ *n. Brit.* **1** a person in charge of something, esp. of machinery in a factory. **2** a workman's unskilled assistant. [*tent* (now Sc.) pay attention, perh. f. *tent* attention f. INTENT or obs. *attent* (as ATTEND)]

tenterhook /ˈtentəˌhʊk/ *n.* any of the hooks to which cloth is fastened on a tenter. □**on tenterhooks** in a state of suspense or mental agitation due to uncertainty.

tenth /tenθ/ *n.* & *adj.* —*n.* **1** the position in a sequence corresponding to the number 10 in the sequence 1–10. **2** something occupying this position. **3** one of ten equal parts of a thing. **4** *Mus.* **a** an interval or chord spanning an octave and a third in the diatonic scale. **b** a note separated from another by this interval. —*adj.* that is the tenth. □**tenth-rate** of extremely poor quality. □□**tenthly** *adv.* [ME *tenthe*, alt. of OE *teogotha*]

tenuis /ˈtenjʊɪs/ *n.* (*pl.* **tenues** /-jʊˌiːz/) *Phonet.* a voiceless stop, e.g. *k*, *p*, *t*. [L, = thin, transl. Gk *psilos* smooth]

tenuity /tɪˈnjuːɪtɪ/ *n.* **1** slenderness. **2** (of a fluid, esp. air) rarity, thinness. [L *tenuitas* (as TENUIS)]

tenuous /ˈtenjʊəs/ *adj.* **1** slight, of little substance (*tenuous connection*). **2** (of a distinction etc.) oversubtle. **3** thin, slender, small. **4** rarefied. □□ **tenuously** *adv.* **tenuousness** *n.* [L *tenuis*]

tenure /ˈtenjə(r)/ *n.* **1** a condition, or form of right or title, under which (esp. real) property is held. **2** (often foll. by *of*) **a** the holding or possession of an office or property. **b** the period of this (*during his tenure of office*). **3** guaranteed permanent employment, esp. as a teacher or lecturer after a probationary period. [ME f. OF f. *tenir* hold f. L *tenēre*]

tenured /ˈtenjəd/ *adj.* **1** (of an official position) carrying a guarantee of permanent employment. **2** (of a teacher, lecturer, etc.) having guaranteed tenure of office.

tenurial /tenˈjʊərɪəl/ *adj.* of the tenure of land. □□ **tenurially** *adv.* [med.L *tenūra* TENURE]

tenuto /təˈnuːtəʊ/ *adv.*, *adj.*, & *n. Mus.* —*adv.* & *adj.* (of a note etc.) sustained, given its full time-value (cf. LEGATO, STACCATO). —*n.* (*pl.* -**os**) a note or chord played tenuto. [It., = held]

tenzon var. of TENSON.

teocalli /ˌtiːəˈkælɪ/ *n.* (*pl.* **teocallis**) a temple of the Aztecs or other Mexican peoples, usu. on a truncated pyramid. [Nahuatl f. *teotl* god + *calli* house]

tepee /ˈtiːpiː/ *n.* (also **teepee**) a N. American Indian's conical tent, made of skins, cloth, or canvas on a frame of poles. [Sioux or Dakota Indian *tipī*]

tephra /ˈtefrə/ *n.* fragmented rock etc. ejected by a volcanic eruption. [Gk, = ash]

tepid /ˈtepɪd/ *adj.* **1** slightly warm. **2** unenthusiastic. □□**tepidity** /tɪˈpɪdɪtɪ/ *n.* **tepidly** *adv.* **tepidness** *n.* [L *tepidus* f. *tepēre* be lukewarm]

tequila /teˈkiːlə/ *n.* a Mexican liquor made from an agave. [*Tequila* in Mexico]

ter- /tɜː(r)/ *comb. form* three; threefold (*tercentenary*; *tervalent*). [L *ter* thrice]

tera- /'terə/ *comb. form* denoting a factor of 10¹². [Gk *teras* monster]

terai /təˈraɪ/ *n.* (in full **terai hat**) a wide-brimmed felt hat, often with a double crown, worn by travellers etc. in subtropical regions. [*Terai*, belt of marshy jungle between Himalayan foothills and plains, f. Hindi *tarāī* moist (land)]

terametre /'terə,miːtə(r)/ *n.* a unit of length equal to 10¹² metres.

teraph /'teraf/ *n.* (*pl.* **teraphim**, also used as *sing.*) a small image as a domestic deity or oracle of the ancient Hebrews. [ME f. LL *theraphim*, Gk *theraphin* f. Heb. *t̯erāp̯im*]

terato- /'teratəʊ/ *comb. form* monster. [Gk *teras -atos* monster]

teratogen /tə'rætədʒ(ə)n/ *n. Med.* an agent or factor causing malformation of an embryo. □□ **teratogenic** /,terətə'dʒenɪk/ *adj.* **teratogeny** /,terə'tɒdʒənɪ/ *n.*

teratology /,terə'tɒlədʒɪ/ *n.* **1** *Biol.* the scientific study of animal or vegetable monstrosities. **2** mythology relating to fantastic creatures, monsters, etc. □□ **teratological** /-tə'lɒdʒɪk(ə)l/ *adj.* **teratologist** *n.*

teratoma /,terə'təʊmə/ *n. Med.* a tumour of heterogeneous tissues, esp. of the gonads.

terbium /'tɜːbɪəm/ *n. Chem.* a silvery metallic element of the lanthanide series. ¶ Symb.: **Tb**. [mod.L f. *Ytterby* in Sweden]

terce /tɜːs/ *n. Eccl.* **1** the office of the canonical hour of prayer appointed for the third daytime hour (i.e. 9 a.m.). **2** this hour. [var. of TIERCE]

tercel /'tɜːs(ə)l/ *n.* (also **tiercel** /'tɪəs(ə)l/) *Falconry* the male of the hawk, esp. a peregrine or goshawk. [ME f. OF *tercel*, ult. a dimin. of L *tertius* third, perh. from a belief that the third egg of a clutch produced a male bird, or that the male was one-third smaller than the female]

tercentenary /,tɜːsen'tiːnərɪ, -'tenərɪ, tɜː'sentɪnərɪ/ *n.* & *adj.* —*n.* (*pl.* -ies) **1** a three-hundredth anniversary. **2** a celebration of this. —*adj.* of this anniversary.

tercentennial /,tɜːsen'tenɪəl/ *adj.* & *n.* —*adj.* **1** occurring every three hundred years. **2** lasting three hundred years. —*n.* a tercentenary.

tercet /'tɜːsɪt/ *n.* (also **tiercet** /'tɪə-/) *Prosody* a set or group of three lines rhyming or connected by rhyme with an adjacent triplet. [F f. It. *terzetto* dimin. of *terzo* third f. L *tertius*]

terebene /'terɪ,biːn/ *n.* a mixture of terpenes prepared by treating oil of turpentine with sulphuric acid, used as an expectorant etc. [TEREBINTH + -ENE]

terebinth /'terɪbɪnθ/ *n.* a small Southern European tree, *Pistacia terebinthus*, yielding turpentine. [ME f. OF *terebinte* or L *terebinthus* f. Gk *terebinthos*]

terebinthine /,terɪ'bɪnθaɪn/ *adj.* **1** of the terebinth. **2** of turpentine. [L *terebinthinus* f. Gk *terebinthinos* (as TEREBINTH)]

teredo /tə'riːdəʊ/ *n.* (*pl.* -os) any bivalve mollusc of the genus *Teredo*, esp. *T. navalis*, that bores into wooden ships etc. Also called SHIPWORM. [L f. Gk *terēdōn* f. *teirō* rub hard, wear away, bore]

terete /tə'riːt/ *adj. Biol.* smooth and rounded; cylindrical. [L *teres -etis*]

tergal /'tɜːg(ə)l/ *adj.* of or relating to the back; dorsal. [L *tergum* back]

tergiversate /'tɜːdʒɪ,vɜːseɪt/ *v.intr.* **1** be apostate; change one's party or principles. **2** equivocate; make conflicting or evasive statements. **3** turn one's back on something. □□ **tergiversation** /-'seɪʃ(ə)n/ *n.* **tergiversator** *n.* [L *tergiversari* turn one's back f. *tergum* back + *vertere* vers- turn]

-teria /'tɪərɪə/ *suffix* denoting self-service establishments (*washeteria*). [after CAFETERIA]

term /tɜːm/ *n.* & *v.* —*n.* **1** a word used to express a definite concept, esp. in a particular branch of study etc. (*a technical term*). **2** (in *pl.*) language used; mode of expression (*answered in no uncertain terms*). **3** (in *pl.*) a relation or footing (*we are on familiar terms*). **4**

(in *pl.*) **a** conditions or stipulations (*cannot accept your terms*; *do it on your own terms*). **b** charge or price (*his terms are £20 a lesson*). **5 a** a limited period of some state or activity (*for a term of five years*). **b** a period over which operations are conducted or results contemplated (*in the short term*). **c** a period of some weeks, alternating with holiday or vacation, during which instruction is given in a school, college, or university, or *Brit.* during which a lawcourt holds sessions. **d** a period of imprisonment. **e** a period of tenure. **6** *Logic* a word or words that may be the subject or predicate of a proposition. **7** *Math.* **a** each of the two quantities in a ratio. **b** each quantity in a series. **c** a part of an expression joined to the rest by + or − (e.g. *a*, *b*, *c* in *a* + *b* − *c*). **8** the completion of a normal length of pregnancy. **9** an appointed day, esp. a Scottish quarter day. **10** (in full *Brit.* **term of years** or *US* **term for years**) *Law* an interest in land for a fixed period. **11** = TERMINUS 6. **12** *archaic* a boundary or limit, esp. of time. —*v.tr.* denominate, call; assign a term to (*the music termed classical*). □ **bring to terms** cause to accept conditions. **come to terms** yield, give way. **come to terms with 1** reconcile oneself to (a difficulty etc.). **2** conclude an agreement with. **in set terms** in definite terms. **in terms** explicitly. **in terms of** in the language peculiar to, using as a basis of expression or thought. **make terms** conclude an agreement. **on terms** on terms of friendship or equality. **term paper** *US* an essay or dissertation representative of the work done during a term. **terms of reference** *Brit.* points referred to an individual or body of persons for decision or report; the scope of an inquiry etc.; a definition of this. **terms of trade** *Brit.* the ratio between prices paid for imports and those received for exports. □□ **termless** *adj.* **termly** *adj.* & *adv.* [ME f. OF *terme* f. L TERMINUS]

termagant /'tɜːməgənt/ *n.* & *adj.* —*n.* **1** an overbearing or brawling woman; a virago or shrew. **2** (**Termagant**) *hist.* an imaginary deity of violent and turbulent character, often appearing in morality plays. —*adj.* violent, turbulent, shrewish. [ME *Tervagant* f. OF *Tervagan* f. It. *Trivigante*]

terminable /'tɜːmɪnəb(ə)l/ *adj.* **1** that may be terminated. **2** coming to an end after a certain time (*terminable annuity*). □□ **terminableness** *n.*

terminal /'tɜːmɪn(ə)l/ *adj.* & *n.* —*adj.* **1 a** (of a disease) ending in death, fatal. **b** (of a patient) in the last stage of a fatal disease. **c** (of a morbid condition) forming the last stage of a fatal disease. **d** *colloq.* ruinous, disastrous, very great (*terminal laziness*). **2** of or forming a limit or terminus (*terminal station*). **3 a** *Zool.* etc. ending a series (*terminal joints*). **b** *Bot.* borne at the end of a stem etc. **4** of or done etc. each term (*terminal accounts*; *terminal examinations*). —*n.* **1** a terminating thing; an extremity. **2** a terminus for trains or long-distance buses. **3** a departure and arrival building for air passengers. **4** a point of connection for closing an electric circuit. **5** an apparatus for transmission of messages between a user and a computer, communications system, etc. **6** (in full **terminal figure**) = TERMINUS 6. **7** an installation where oil is stored at the end of a pipeline or at a port. **8** a patient suffering from a terminal illness. □ **terminal velocity** a velocity of a falling body such that the resistance of the air etc. prevents further increase of speed under gravity. □□ **terminally** *adv.* [L *terminalis* (as TERMINUS)]

terminate /'tɜːmɪ,neɪt/ *v.* **1** *tr.* & *intr.* bring or come to an end. **2** *intr.* (foll. by *in*) (of a word) end in (a specified letter or syllable etc.). **3** *tr.* end (a pregnancy) before term by artificial means. **4** *tr.* bound, limit. [L *terminare* (as TERMINUS)]

termination /,tɜːmɪ'neɪʃ(ə)n/ *n.* **1** the act or an instance of terminating; the state of being terminated. **2** *Med.* an induced abortion. **3** an ending or result of a specified kind (*a happy termination*). **4** a word's final syllable or letters or letter esp. as

aʊ *how* eɪ *day* əʊ *no* eə *hair* ɪə *near* ɔɪ *boy* ʊə *poor* aɪə *fire* aʊə *sour* (*see over for consonants*)

an element in inflection or derivation. □**put a termination to** (or **bring to a termination**) make an end of. □□**terminational** *adj.* [ME f. OF *termination* or L *terminatio* (as TERMINATE)]

terminator /ˈtɜːmɪˌneɪtə(r)/ *n.* **1** a person or thing that terminates. **2** the dividing line between the light and dark part of a planetary body.

terminer see OYER AND TERMINER.

termini *pl.* of TERMINUS.

terminism /ˈtɜːmɪˌnɪz(ə)m/ *n.* **1** the doctrine that everyone has a limited time for repentance. **2** = NOMINALISM. □□**terminist** *n.* [L]

terminological /ˌtɜːmɪnəˈlɒdʒɪk(ə)l/ *adj.* of terminology. □**terminological inexactitude** *joc.* a lie. □□**terminologically** *adv.*

terminology /ˌtɜːmɪˈnɒlədʒɪ/ *n.* (*pl.* **-ies**) **1** the system of terms used in a particular subject. **2** the science of the proper use of terms. □□**terminologist** *n.* [G *Terminologie* f. med.L TERMINUS term]

terminus /ˈtɜːmɪnəs/ *n.* (*pl.* **termini** /-ˌnaɪ/ or **terminuses**) **1** a station at the end of a railway or bus route. **2** a point at the end of a pipeline etc. **3** a final point, a goal. **4** a starting-point. **5** *Math.* the end-point of a vector etc. **6** *Archit.* a figure of a human bust or an animal ending in a square pillar from which it appears to spring, orig. as a boundary-marker. □**terminus ad quem** /æd ˈkwem/ the finishing-point of an argument, policy, period, etc. **terminus ante quem** /ˌæntɪ ˈkwem/ the finishing-point of a period. **terminus a quo** /ɑː ˈkwəʊ/ the starting-point of an argument, policy, period, etc. **terminus post quem** /pəʊst ˈkwem/ the starting-point of a period. [L, = end, limit, boundary]

termitary /ˈtɜːmɪtərɪ/ *n.* (*pl.* **-ies**) a nest of termites, usu. a large mound of earth.

termite /ˈtɜːmaɪt/ *n.* a small antlike social insect of the order Isoptera, chiefly tropical and destructive to timber. [LL *termes -mitis*, alt. of L *tarmes* after *terere* rub]

termor /ˈtɜːmə(r)/ *n.* *Law* a person who holds lands etc. for a term of years, or for life. [ME f. AF *termer* (as TERM)]

tern¹ /tɜːn/ *n.* any marine bird of the subfamily Sterninae, like a gull but usu. smaller and with a long forked tail. [of Scand. orig.: cf. Da. *terne*, Sw. *tärna* f. ON *therna*]

tern² /tɜːn/ *n.* **1** a set of three, esp. three lottery numbers that when drawn together win a large prize. **2** such a prize. [F *terne* f. L *terni* three each]

ternary /ˈtɜːnərɪ/ *adj.* **1** composed of three parts. **2** *Math.* using three as a base (*ternary scale*). □**ternary form** *Mus.* the form of a movement in which the first subject is repeated after an interposed second subject in a related key. [ME f. L *ternarius* f. *terni* three each]

ternate /ˈtɜːneɪt/ *adj.* **1** arranged in threes. **2** *Bot.* (of a leaf): **a** having three leaflets. **b** whorled in threes. □□**ternately** *adv.* [mod.L *ternatus* (as TERNARY)]

terne /tɜːn/ *n.* (in full **terne-plate**) inferior tin-plate alloyed with much lead. [prob. f. F *terne* dull: cf. TARNISH]

terotechnology /ˌterəʊtekˈnɒlədʒɪ, ˌtɪə-/ *n.* the branch of technology and engineering concerned with the installation and maintenance of equipment. [Gk *tēreō* take care of + TECHNOLOGY]

terpene /ˈtɜːpiːn/ *n.* *Chem.* any of a large group of unsaturated cyclic hydrocarbons found in the essential oils of plants, esp. conifers and oranges. [*terpentin* obs. var. of TURPENTINE]

Terpsichorean /ˌtɜːpsɪkəˈriːən/ *adj.* of or relating to dancing. [*Terpsichore* Muse of dancing]

terra alba /ˌterə ˈælbə/ *n.* a white mineral, esp. pipeclay or pulverized gypsum. [L, = white earth]

terrace /ˈterəs, -rɪs/ *n. & v.* —*n.* **1** each of a series of flat areas formed on a slope and used for cultivation. **2** a level paved area next to a house. **3 a** a row of houses on a raised level or along the top or face of a slope. **b** a row of houses built in one block of uniform

style. **4** a flight of wide shallow steps as for spectators at a sports ground. **5** *Geol.* a raised beach, or a similar formation beside a river etc. —*v.tr.* form into or provide with a terrace or terraces. □**terraced house** *Brit.* = *terrace house.* **terraced roof** a flat roof esp. of an Indian or Eastern house. **terrace house** *Brit.* any of a row of houses joined by party-walls. [OF ult. f. L *terra* earth]

terracotta /ˌterəˈkɒtə/ *n.* **1 a** unglazed usu. brownish-red earthenware used chiefly as an ornamental building-material and in modelling. **b** a statuette of this. **2** its colour. [It. *terra cotta* baked earth]

terra firma /ˌterə ˈfɜːmə/ *n.* dry land, firm ground. [L, = firm land]

terrain /teˈreɪn, tə-/ *n.* a tract of land as regarded by the physical geographer or the military tactician. [F, ult. f. L *terrenum* neut. of *terrenus* TERRENE]

terra incognita /ˌterə ɪŋˈkɒgnɪtə, ˌɪnkɒɡˈniːtə/ *n.* an unknown or unexplored region. [L, = unknown land]

terramara /ˌterəˈmɑːrə/ *n.* (*pl.* **terramare** /-reɪ/) = TERRAMARE. [It. dial.: see TERRAMARE]

terramare /ˌterəˈmɑːrɪ, -ˈmeə(r)/ *n.* **1** an ammoniacal earthy deposit found in mounds in prehistoric lake-dwellings or settlements esp. in Italy. **2** such a dwelling or settlement. [F f. It. dial. *terra mara* f. *marna* marl]

terrapin /ˈterəpɪn/ *n.* **1** any of various N. American edible freshwater turtles of the family Emydidae. **2** (**Terrapin**) *propr.* a type of prefabricated one-storey building. [Algonquian]

terrarium /teˈreərɪəm/ *n.* (*pl.* **terrariums** or **terraria** /-rɪə/) **1** a vivarium for small land animals. **2** a sealed transparent globe etc. containing growing plants. [mod.L f. L *terra* earth, after AQUARIUM]

terra sigillata /ˌterə ˌsɪdʒɪˈleɪtə/ *n.* **1** astringent clay from Lemnos or Samos. **2** Samian ware. [med.L, = sealed earth]

terrazzo /teˈrætsəʊ/ *n.* (*pl.* **-os**) a flooring-material of stone chips set in concrete and given a smooth surface. [It., = terrace]

terrene /teˈriːn/ *adj.* **1** of the earth; earthy, worldly. **2** of earth, earthy. **3** of dry land; terrestrial. [ME f. AF f. L *terrenus* f. *terra* earth]

terreplein /ˈteəpleɪn/ *n.* a level space where a battery of guns is mounted. [orig. a sloping bank behind a rampart f. F *terre-plein* f. It. *terrapieno* f. *terrapienare* fill with earth f. *terra* earth + *pieno* f. L *plenus* full]

terrestrial /təˈrestrɪəl, tɪ-/ *adj. & n.* —*adj.* **1** of or on or relating to the earth; earthly. **2 a** of or on dry land. **b** *Zool.* living on or in the ground (opp. AQUATIC, ARBOREAL, AERIAL). **c** *Bot.* growing in the soil (opp. AQUATIC, EPIPHYTIC). **3** *Astron.* (of a planet) similar in size or composition to the earth. **4** of this world, worldly (*terrestrial sins; terrestrial interests*). —*n.* an inhabitant of the earth. □**a terrestrial globe** a globe representing the earth. **the terrestrial globe** the earth. **terrestrial magnetism** the magnetic properties of the earth as a whole. **terrestrial telescope** a telescope giving an erect image for observation of terrestrial objects. □□**terrestrially** *adv.* [ME f. L *terrestris* f. *terra* earth]

terret /ˈterɪt/ *n.* (also **territ**) each of the loops or rings on a harness-pad for the driving-reins to pass through. [ME, var. of *toret* (now dial.) f. OF *to(u)ret* dimin. of TOUR]

terre-verte /teəˈveət/ *n.* a soft green earth used as a pigment. [F, = green earth]

terrible /ˈterɪb(ə)l/ *adj.* **1** *colloq.* very great or bad (*a terrible bore*). **2** *colloq.* very incompetent (*terrible at tennis*). **3** causing terror; fit to cause terror; awful, dreadful, formidable. □□**terribleness** *n.* [ME f. F f. L *terribilis* f. *terrēre* frighten]

terribly /ˈterɪblɪ/ *adv.* **1** *colloq.* very, extremely (*he was terribly nice about it*). **2** in a terrible manner.

terricolous /teˈrɪkələs/ *adj.* living on or in the earth.

b *but* d *dog* f *few* g *get* h *he* j *yes* k *cat* l *leg* m *man* n *no* p *pen* r *red* s *sit* t *top* v *voice*

[L *terricola* earth-dweller f. *terra* earth + *colere* inhabit]

terrier[1] /'terɪə(r)/ *n.* **1 a** a small dog of various breeds originally used for turning out foxes etc. from their earths. **b** any of these breeds. **2** an eager or tenacious person or animal. **3 (Terrier)** *Brit. colloq.* a member of the Territorial Army etc. [ME f. OF (*chien*) *terrier* f. med.L *terrarius* f. L *terra* earth]

terrier[2] /'terɪə(r)/ *n. hist.* **1** a book recording the site, boundaries, etc., of the land of private persons or corporations. **2** a rent-roll. **3** a collection of acknowledgements of vassals or tenants of a lordship. [ME f. OF *terrier* (adj.) = med.L *terrarius liber* (as TERRIER[1])]

terrific /tə'rɪfɪk/ *adj.* **1** *colloq.* **a** of great size or intensity. **b** excellent (*did a terrific job*). **c** excessive (*making a terrific noise*). **2** causing terror. □□ **terrifically** *adv.* [L *terrificus* f. *terrēre* frighten]

terrify /'terɪfaɪ/ *v.tr.* (**-ies, -ied**) fill with terror; frighten severely (*terrified them into submission*; *is terrified of dogs*). □□ **terrifier** *n.* **terrifyingly** *adv.* [L *terrificare* (as TERRIFIC)]

terrigenous /te'rɪdʒɪnəs/ *adj.* produced by the earth or the land (*terrigenous deposits*). [L *terrigenus* earth-born]

terrine /tə'riːn/ *n.* **1** pâté or similar food. **2** an earthenware vessel, *esp.* one in which such food is cooked or sold. [orig. form of TUREEN]

territ var. of TERRET.

territorial /ˌterɪ'tɔːrɪəl/ *adj. & n.* —*adj.* **1** of territory (*territorial possessions*). **2** limited to a district (*the right was strictly territorial*). **3** (of a person or animal etc.) tending to defend an area of territory. **4** (usu. **Territorial**) of any of the Territories of the US or Canada. —*n.* (**Territorial**) (in the UK) a member of the Territorial Army. □ **Territorial Army** (in the UK) a volunteer force locally organized to provide a reserve of trained and disciplined manpower for use in an emergency (known as *Territorial and Army Volunteer Reserve* 1967–79). **territorial waters** the waters under the jurisdiction of a State, esp. the part of the sea within a stated distance of the shore (traditionally three miles from low-water mark). □□ **territoriality** /-'ælɪtɪ/ *n.* **territorialize** *v.tr.* (also **-ise**). **territorialization** /-laɪ'zeɪʃ(ə)n/ *n.* **territorially** *adv.* [LL *territorialis* (as TERRITORY)]

territory /'terɪtərɪ, -trɪ/ *n.* (*pl.* **-ies**) **1** the extent of the land under the jurisdiction of a ruler, State, city, etc. **2** (**Territory**) an organized division of a country, esp. one not yet admitted to the full rights of a State. **3** a sphere of action or thought; a province. **4** the area over which a commercial traveller or goods-distributor operates. **5** *Zool.* an area defended by an animal or animals against others of the same species. **6** an area defended by a team or player in a game. **7** a large tract of land. [ME f. L *territorium* f. *terra* land]

terror /'terə(r)/ *n.* **1** extreme fear. **2 a** a person or thing that causes terror. **b** (also **holy terror**) *colloq.* a formidable person; a troublesome person or thing (*the twins are little terrors*). **3** the use of organized intimidation; terrorism. □ **reign of terror** a period of remorseless repression or bloodshed, esp. a period of the French Revolution 1793–4. **terror-stricken** (or **-struck**) affected with terror. [ME f. OF *terrour* f. L *terror -oris* f. *terrēre* frighten]

terrorist /'terərɪst/ *n.* a person who uses or favours violent and intimidating methods of coercing a government or community. □□ **terrorism** *n.* **terroristic** /-'rɪstɪk/ *adj.* **terroristically** /-'rɪstɪkəlɪ/ *adv.* [F *terroriste* (as TERROR)]

terrorize /'terə,raɪz/ *v.tr.* (also **-ise**) **1** fill with terror. **2** use terrorism against. □□ **terrorization** /-'zeɪʃ(ə)n/ *n.* **terrorizer** *n.*

terry /'terɪ/ *n. & adj.* —*n.* (*pl.* **-ies**) a pile fabric with the loops uncut, used esp. for towels. —*adj.* of this fabric. [18th c.: orig. unkn.]

terse /tɜːs/ *adj.* (**terser, tersest**) **1** (of language)

brief, concise, to the point. **2** curt, abrupt. □□ **tersely** *adv.* **terseness** *n.* [L *tersus* past part. of *tergēre* wipe, polish]

tertian /'tɜːʃ(ə)n/ *adj.* (of a fever) recurring every third day by inclusive counting. [ME (*fever*) *tersiane* f. L (*febris*) *tertiana* (as TERTIARY)]

tertiary /'tɜːʃərɪ/ *adj. & n.* —*adj.* **1** third in order or rank etc. **2** (**Tertiary**) *Geol.* of or relating to the first period in the Cenozoic era with evidence of the development of mammals and flowering plants (cf. PALAEOCENE, EOCENE, OLIGOCENE, MIOCENE, PLIOCENE). ¶ Cf. Appendix II. —*n.* **1** *Geol.* this period or system. **2** a member of the third order of a monastic body. □ **tertiary education** education, esp. in a college or university, that follows secondary education. [L *tertiarius* f. *tertius* third]

tertium quid /ˌtɜːʃɪəm 'kwɪd, ˌtɜːtjəm/ *n.* a third something, esp. intermediate between mind and matter or between opposite things. [L, app. transl. Gk *triton ti*]

tervalent /'tɜːvələnt, -'veɪlənt/ *adj. Chem.* having a valency of three. [TER- + *valent-* part. stem (as VALENCE[1])]

Terylene /'terɪ,liːn/ *n. propr.* a synthetic polyester used as a textile fibre. [*terephthalic* acid (f. *terebic* f. TEREBINTH + PHTHALIC ACID) + ETHYLENE]

terza rima /ˌteətsə 'riːmə/ *n. Prosody* an arrangement of (esp. iambic pentameter) triplets rhyming *aba bcb cdc* etc. as in Dante's *Divina Commedia*. [It., = third rhyme]

terzetto /teət'setəʊ, ˌtɜːt-/ *n.* (*pl.* **-os** or **terzetti** /-tɪ:/) *Mus.* a vocal or instrumental trio. [It.: see TERCET]

TESL /'tes(ə)l/ *abbr.* teaching of English as a second language.

tesla /'teslə/ *n.* the SI unit of magnetic flux density. □ **Tesla coil** a form of induction coil for producing high-frequency alternating currents. [N. *Tesla*, Croatian-born Amer. scientist d. 1943]

TESOL /'tesɒl/ *abbr.* teaching of English to speakers of other languages.

tessellate /'tesə,leɪt/ *v.tr.* **1** make from tesserae. **2** *Math.* cover (a plane surface) by repeated use of a single shape. [L *tessellare* f. *tessella* dimin. of TESSERA]

tessellated /'tesə,leɪtɪd/ *adj.* **1** of or resembling mosaic. **2** *Bot. & Zool.* regularly chequered. [L *tessellatus* or It. *tessellato* (as TESSELLATE)]

tessellation /ˌtesə'leɪʃ(ə)n/ *n.* **1** the act or an instance of tessellating; the state of being tessellated. **2** an arrangement of polygons without gaps or overlapping, esp. in a repeated pattern.

tessera /'tesərə/ *n.* (*pl.* **tesserae** /-,riː/) **1** a small square block used in mosaic. **2** *Gk & Rom. Antiq.* a small square of bone etc. used as a token, ticket, etc. □□ **tesseral** *adj.* [L f. Gk, neut. of *tesseres*, *tessares* four]

tessitura /ˌtesɪ'tʊərə/ *n. Mus.* the range within which most tones of a voice-part fall. [It., = TEXTURE]

test[1] /test/ *n. & v.* —*n.* **1** a critical examination or trial of a person's or thing's qualities. **2** the means of so examining; a standard for comparison or trial; circumstances suitable for this (*success is not a fair test*). **3** a minor examination, esp. in school (*spelling test*). **4** *colloq.* a test match. **5** a ground of admission or rejection (*is excluded by our test*). **6** *Chem.* a reagent or a procedure employed to reveal the presence of another in a compound. **7** *Brit.* a movable hearth in a reverberating furnace with a cupel used in separating gold or silver from lead. —*v.tr.* **1** put to the test; make trial of (a person or thing or quality). **2** try severely; tax a person's powers of endurance etc. **3** *Chem.* examine by means of a reagent. **4** *Brit.* refine or assay (metal). □ **put to the test** cause to undergo a test. **Test Act** *hist.* **1** an act in force 1672–1828, requiring all persons before holding office in Britain to take oaths of supremacy and allegiance or an equivalent test. **2** an act of 1871 relaxing conditions for university degrees. **test bed**

equipment for testing aircraft engines before acceptance for general use. **test card** a still television picture transmitted outside normal programme hours and designed for use in judging the quality and position of the image. **test case** *Law* a case setting a precedent for other cases involving the same question of law. **test drive** a drive taken to determine the qualities of a motor vehicle with a view to its regular use. **test-drive** *v.tr.* (*past* **-drove**; *past part.* **-driven**) drive (a vehicle) for this purpose. **test flight** a flight during which the performance of an aircraft is tested. **test-fly** *v.tr.* (**-flies**; *past* **-flew**; *past part.* **-flown**) fly (an aircraft) for this purpose. **test match** a cricket or Rugby match between teams of certain countries, usu. each of a series in a tour. **test meal** a meal of specified quantity and composition, eaten to assist tests of gastric secretion. **test out** put (a theory etc.) to a practical test. **test paper 1** a minor examination paper. **2** *Chem.* a paper impregnated with a substance changing colour under known conditions. **test pilot** a pilot who test-flies aircraft. **test-tube** a thin glass tube closed at one end used for chemical tests etc. **test-tube baby** *colloq.* a baby conceived by *in vitro* fertilization. □□ **testable** *adj.* **testability** /-ə'bɪlɪtɪ/ *n.* **testee** /tes'ti:/ *n.* [ME f. OF f. L *testu*(*m*) earthen pot, collateral form of *testa* TEST²]

test² /test/ *n.* the shell of some invertebrates, esp. foraminiferars and tunicates. [L *testa* tile, jug, shell, etc.: cf. TEST¹]

testa /'testə/ *n.* (*pl.* **testae** /-ti:/) *Bot.* a seed-coat. [L (as TEST²)]

testaceous /te'steɪʃəs/ *adj.* **1** *Biol.* having a hard continuous outer covering. **2** *Bot.* & *Zool.* of a brick-red colour. [L *testaceus* (as TEST²)]

testament /'testəmənt/ *n.* **1** a will (esp. *last will and testament*). **2** (usu. foll. by *to*) evidence, proof (*is testament to his loyalty*). **3** *Bibl.* **a** a covenant or dispensation. **b** (**Testament**) a division of the Christian Bible (see *Old Testament, New Testament*). **c** (**Testament**) a copy of the New Testament. [ME f. L *testamentum* will (as TESTATE): in early Christian L rendering Gk *diathēkē* covenant]

testamentary /ˌtestə'mentərɪ/ *adj.* of or by or in a will. [L *testamentarius* (as TESTAMENT)]

testate /'testeɪt/ *adj.* & *n.* —*adj.* having left a valid will at death. —*n.* a testate person. □□ **testacy** *n.* (*pl.* **-ies**). [L *testatus* past part. of *testari* testify, make a will, f. *testis* witness]

testator /te'steɪtə(r)/ *n.* (*fem.* **testatrix** /te'steɪtrɪks/) a person who has made a will, esp. one who dies testate. [ME f. AF *testatour* f. L *testator* (as TESTATE)]

tester¹ /'testə(r)/ *n.* **1** a person or thing that tests. **2** a sample of a cosmetic etc., allowing customers to try it before purchase.

tester² /'testə(r)/ *n.* a canopy, esp. over a four-poster bed. [ME f. med.L *testerium, testrum, testura*, ult. f. L *testa* tile]

testes *pl.* of TESTIS.

testicle /'testɪk(ə)l/ *n.* a male organ that produces spermatozoa etc., esp. one of a pair enclosed in the scrotum behind the penis of a man and most mammals. □□ **testicular** /-'stɪkjʊlə(r)/ *adj.* [ME f. L *testiculus* dimin. of *testis* witness (of virility)]

testiculate /te'stɪkjʊlət/ *adj.* **1** having or shaped like testicles. **2** *Bot.* (esp. of an orchid) having pairs of tubers so shaped. [LL *testiculatus* (as TESTICLE)]

testify /'testɪˌfaɪ/ *v.* (**-ies, -ied**) **1** *intr.* (of a person or thing) bear witness (*testified to the facts*). **2** *intr. Law* give evidence. **3** *tr.* affirm or declare (*testified his regret; testified that she had been present*). **4** *tr.* (of a thing) be evidence of, evince. □□ **testifier** *n.* [ME f. L *testificari* f. *testis* witness]

testimonial /ˌtestɪ'məʊnɪəl/ *n.* **1** a certificate of character, conduct, or qualifications. **2** a gift presented to a person (esp. in public) as a mark of esteem, in acknowledgement of services, etc. [ME f.

OF *testimoignal* (adj.) f. *tesmoin* or LL *testimonialis* (as TESTIMONY)]

testimony /'testɪmənɪ/ *n.* (*pl.* **-ies**) **1** *Law* an oral or written statement under oath or affirmation. **2** declaration or statement of fact. **3** evidence, demonstration (*called him in testimony; produce testimony*). **4** *Bibl.* the Ten Commandments. **5** *archaic* a solemn protest or confession. [ME f. L *testimonium* f. *testis* witness]

testis /'testɪs/ *n.* (*pl.* **testes** /-ti:z/) *Anat.* & *Zool.* a testicle. [L, = witness: cf. TESTICLE]

testosterone /te'stɒstəˌrəʊn/ *n.* a steroid androgen formed in the testicles. [TESTIS + STEROL + -ONE]

testudinal /te'stju:dɪn(ə)l/ *adj.* of or shaped like a tortoise. [as TESTUDO]

testudo /te'stju:dəʊ, te'stu:-/ *n.* (*pl.* **-os** or **testudines** /-dɪˌniːz/) *Rom.Hist.* **1** a screen formed by a body of troops in close array with overlapping shields. **2** a movable screen to protect besieging troops. [L *testudo -dinis*, lit. 'tortoise' (as TEST²)]

testy /'testɪ/ *adj.* (**testier, testiest**) irritable, touchy. □□ **testily** *adv.* **testiness** *n.* [ME f. AF *testif* f. OF *teste* head (as TEST²)]

tetanic /tɪ'tænɪk/ *adj.* of or such as occurs in tetanus. □□ **tetanically** *adv.* [L *tetanicus* f. Gk *tetanikos* (as TETANUS)]

tetanus /'tetənəs/ *n.* **1** a bacterial disease affecting the nervous system and marked by tonic spasm of the voluntary muscles. **2** *Physiol.* the prolonged contraction of a muscle caused by rapidly repeated stimuli. □□ **tetanize** *v.tr.* (also **-ise**). **tetanoid** *adj.* [ME f. L f. Gk *tetanos* muscular spasm f. *teinō* stretch]

tetany /'tetənɪ/ *n.* a disease with intermittent muscular spasms caused by malfunction of the parathyroid glands and a consequent deficiency of calcium. [F *tétanie* (as TETANUS)]

tetchy /'tetʃɪ/ *adj.* (also **techy**) (**-ier, -iest**) peevish, irritable. □□ **tetchily** *adv.* **tetchiness** *n.* [prob. f. *tecche, tache* blemish, fault f. OF *teche, tache*]

tête-à-tête /ˌteɪtɑː'teɪt/ *n., adv.,* & *adj.* —*n.* **1** a private conversation or interview usu. between two persons. **2** an S-shaped sofa for two people to sit face to face. —*adv.* together in private (*dined tête-à-tête*). —*adj.* **1** private, confidential. **2** concerning only two persons. [F, lit. 'head-to-head']

tête-bêche /teɪt'beʃ/ *adj.* (of a postage stamp) printed upside down or sideways relative to another. [F f. *tête* head + *béchevet* double bed-head]

tether /'teðə(r)/ *n.* & *v.* —*n.* **1** a rope etc. by which an animal is tied to confine it to the spot. **2** the extent of one's knowledge, authority, etc.; scope, limit. —*v.tr.* tie (an animal) with a tether. □ **at the end of one's tether** having reached the limit of one's patience, resources, abilities, etc. [ME f. ON *tjóthr* f. Gmc]

tetra- /'tetrə/ *comb. form* (also **tetr-** before a vowel) **1** four (*tetrapod*). **2** *Chem.* (forming names of compounds) containing four atoms or groups of a specified kind (*tetroxide*). [Gk f. *tettares* four]

tetrachord /'tetrəˌkɔːd/ *n. Mus.* **1** a scale-pattern of four notes, the interval between the first and last being a perfect fourth. **2** a musical instrument with four strings.

tetracyclic /ˌtetrə'sɪklɪk/ *adj.* **1** *Bot.* having four circles or whorls. **2** *Chem.* (of a compound) having a molecular structure of four fused hydrocarbon rings.

tetracycline /ˌtetrə'saɪkliːn/ *n.* an antibiotic with a molecule of four rings. [TETRACYCLIC + -INE⁴]

tetrad /'tetræd/ *n.* a group of four. **2** the number four. [Gk *tetras -ados* (as TETRA-)]

tetradactyl /ˌtetrə'dæktɪl/ *n. Zool.* an animal with four toes on each foot. □□ **tetradactylous** *adj.*

tetraethyl lead /ˌtetrə'iːθaɪl/ *n.* a liquid added to petrol as an antiknock agent.

tetragon /'tetrəˌgɒn/ *n.* a plane figure with four angles and four sides. [Gk *tetragōnon* quadrangle (as TETRA-, -GON)]

tetragonal /tɪ'trægən(ə)l/ *adj.* **1** of or like a tetragon.

æ *cat* ɑː *arm* e *bed* ɜː *her* ɪ *sit* iː *see* ɒ *hot* ɔː *saw* ʌ *run* ʊ *put* uː *too* ə *ago* aɪ *my*

2 *Crystallog*. (of a crystal) having three axes at right angles, two of them equal. □□ **tetragonally** *adv*.

tetragram /ˈtetrəˌgræm/ *n*. a word of four letters.

Tetragrammaton /ˌtetrəˈgræməˌtɒn/ *n*. the Hebrew name of God written in four letters, articulated as *Yahweh* etc. [Gk (as TETRA-, *gramma*, *-atos* letter)]

tetragynous /tɪˈtrædʒɪnəs/ *adj*. *Bot*. having four pistils.

tetrahedron /ˌtetrəˈhiːdrən, -ˈhedrən/ *n*. (*pl*. **tetrahedra** /-drə/ or **tetrahedrons**) a four-sided solid; a triangular pyramid. □□ **tetrahedral** *adj*. [late Gk *tetraedron* neut. of *tetraedros* four-sided (as TETRA-, -HEDRON)]

tetralogy /tɪˈtrælədʒɪ/ *n*. (*pl*. **-ies**) **1** a group of four related literary or operatic works. **2** *Gk Antiq*. a trilogy of tragedies with a satyric drama.

tetramerous /tɪˈtræmərəs/ *adj*. having four parts.

tetrameter /tɪˈtræmɪtə(r)/ *n*. *Prosody* a verse of four measures. [LL *tetrametrus* f. Gk *tetrametros* (as TETRA-, *metron* measure)]

tetrandrous /tɪˈtrændrəs/ *adj*. *Bot*. having four stamens.

tetraplegia /ˌtetrəˈpliːdʒɪə, -dʒə/ *n*. *Med*. = QUADRIPLEGIA. □□ **tetraplegic** *adj*. & *n*. [mod.L (as TETRA-, Gk *plēgē* blow, strike)]

tetraploid /ˈtetrəˌplɔɪd/ *adj*. & *n*. *Biol*. —*adj*. (of an organism or cell) having four times the haploid set of chromosomes. —*n*. a tetraploid organism or cell.

tetrapod /ˈtetrəˌpɒd/ *n*. **1** *Zool*. an animal with four feet. **2** a structure supported by four feet radiating from a centre. □□ **tetrapodous** /tɪˈtræpədəs/ *adj*. [mod.L *tetrapodus* f. Gk *tetrapous* (as TETRA-, *pous podos* foot)]

tetrapterous /tɪˈtræptərəs/ *adj*. *Zool*. having four wings. [mod.L *tetrapterus* f. Gk *tetrapteros* (as TETRA-, *pteron* wing)]

tetrarch /ˈtetrɑːk/ *n*. **1** *Rom.Hist*. **a** the governor of a fourth part of a country or province. **b** a subordinate ruler. **2** one of four joint rulers. □□ **tetrarchate** /-ˌkeɪt/ *n*. **tetrarchical** /-ˈrɑːkɪk(ə)l/ *adj*. **tetrarchy** *n*. (*pl*. **-ies**). [ME f. LL *tetrarcha* f. L *tetrarches* f. Gk *tetrarkhēs* (as TETRA-, *arkhō* rule)]

tetrastich /ˈtetrəstɪk/ *n*. *Prosody* a group of four lines of verse. [L *tetrastichon* f. Gk (as TETRA-, *stikhon* line)]

tetrastyle /ˈtetrəˌstaɪl/ *n*. & *adj*. —*n*. a building with four pillars esp. forming a portico in front or supporting a ceiling. —*adj*. (of a building) built in this way. [L *tetrastylos* f. Gk *tetrastulos* (as TETRA-, STYLE)]

tetrasyllable /ˈtetrəˌsɪləb(ə)l/ *n*. a word of four syllables. □□ **tetrasyllabic** /-ˈlæbɪk/ *adj*.

tetrathlon /teˈtræθlən/ *n*. a contest comprising four events, esp. riding, shooting, swimming, and running. [TETRA- + Gk *athlon* contest, after PENTATHLON]

tetratomic /ˌtetrəˈtɒmɪk/ *adj*. *Chem*. having four atoms (of a specified kind) in the molecule.

tetravalent /ˌtetrəˈveɪlənt/ *adj*. *Chem*. having a valency of four; quadrivalent.

tetrode /ˈtetrəʊd/ *n*. a thermionic valve having four electrodes. [TETRA- + Gk *hodos* way]

tetter /ˈtetə(r)/ *n*. *archaic* or *dial*. a pustular skin-eruption, e.g. eczema. [OE *teter*: cf. OHG *zittaroh*, G dial. *Zitteroch*, Skr. *dadru*]

Teut. *abbr*. Teutonic.

Teuto- /ˈtjuːtəʊ/ *comb. form* = TEUTON.

Teuton /ˈtjuːt(ə)n/ *n*. **1** a member of a Teutonic nation, esp. a German. **2** *hist*. a member of a N. European tribe which attacked the Roman republic *c*.110 BC. [L *Teutones, Teutoni*, f. an IE base meaning 'people' or 'country']

Teutonic /tjuːˈtɒnɪk/ *adj*. & *n*. —*adj*. **1** relating to or characteristic of the Germanic peoples or their languages. **2** German. —*n*. the early language usu. called Germanic. □□ **Teutonicism** /-ˌsɪz(ə)m/ *n*. [F *teutonique* f. L *Teutonicus* (as TEUTON)]

Tex. *abbr*. Texas.

Texan /ˈteks(ə)n/ *n*. & *adj*. —*n*. a native of Texas in the US. —*adj*. of or relating to Texas.

text /tekst/ *n*. **1** the main body of a book as distinct from notes, appendices, pictures, etc. **2** the original words of an author or document, esp. as distinct from a paraphrase of or commentary on them. **3** a passage quoted from Scripture, esp. as the subject of a sermon. **4** a subject or theme. **5** (in *pl*.) books prescribed for study. **6** *US* a textbook. **7** (in full **text-hand**) a fine large kind of handwriting esp. for manuscripts. □ **text editor** *Computing* a system or program allowing the user to enter and edit text. **text processing** *Computing* the manipulation of text, esp. transforming it from one format to another. □□ **textless** *adj*. [ME f. ONF *tixte, texte* f. L *textus* tissue, literary style (in med.L = Gospel) f. L *texere text-* weave]

textbook /ˈtekstbʊk/ *n*. & *adj*. —*n*. a book for use in studying, esp. a standard account of a subject. —*attrib.adj*. **1** exemplary, accurate (cf. COPYBOOK). **2** instructively typical. □□ **textbookish** *adj*.

textile /ˈtekstaɪl/ *n*. & *adj*. —*n*. **1** any woven material. **2** any cloth. —*adj*. **1** of weaving or cloth (*textile industry*). **2** woven (*textile fabrics*). **3** suitable for weaving (*textile materials*). [L *textilis* (as TEXT)]

textual /ˈtekstjʊəl/ *adj*. of, in, or concerning a text (*textual errors*). □ **textual criticism** the process of attempting to ascertain the correct reading of a text. □□ **textually** *adv*. [ME f. med.L *textualis* (as TEXT)]

textualist /ˈtekstjʊəlɪst/ *n*. a person who adheres strictly to the letter of the text. □□ **textualism** *n*.

texture /ˈtekstʃə(r)/ *n*. & *v*. —*n*. **1** the feel or appearance of a surface or substance. **2** the arrangement of threads etc. in textile fabric. **3** the arrangement of small constituent parts. **4** *Art* the representation of the structure and detail of objects. **5** *Mus*. the quality of sound formed by combining parts. **6** the quality of a piece of writing, esp. with reference to imagery, alliteration, etc. **7** quality or style resulting from composition (*the texture of her life*). —*v.tr*. (usu. as **textured** *adj*.) provide with a texture. □□ **textural** *adj*. **texturally** *adv*. **textureless** *adj*. [ME f. L *textura* weaving (as TEXT)]

texturize /ˈtekstʃəˌraɪz/ *v.tr*. (also **-ise**) (usu. as **texturized** *adj*.) impart a particular texture to (fabrics or food).

TG *abbr*. transformational grammar.

TGWU *abbr*. (in the UK) Transport and General Workers' Union.

Th *symb*. *Chem*. the element thorium.

Th. *abbr*. Thursday.

-th¹ /θ/ *suffix* (also **-eth** /ɪθ/) forming ordinal and fractional numbers from *four* onwards (*fourth*; *thirtieth*). [OE *-tha, -the, -otha, -othe*]

-th² /θ/ *suffix* forming nouns denoting an action or process: **1** from verbs (*birth*; *growth*). **2** from adjectives (*breadth*; *filth*; *length*). [OE *-thu, -tho, -th*]

-th³ var. of -ETH².

Thai /taɪ/ *n*. & *adj*. —*n*. (*pl*. same or **Thais**) **1 a** a native or national of Thailand in SE Asia; a member of the largest ethnic group in Thailand. **b** a person of Thai descent. **2** the language of Thailand. —*adj*. of or relating to Thailand or its people or language. [Thai, = free]

thalamus /ˈθæləməs/ *n*. (*pl*. **thalami** /-ˌmaɪ/) **1** *Anat*. either of two masses of grey matter in the forebrain, serving as relay stations for sensory tracts. **2** *Bot*. the receptacle of a flower. **3** *Gk Antiq*. an inner room or women's apartment. □□ **thalamic** /θəˈlæmɪk, ˈθæləmɪk/ *adj*. (in senses 1 and 2). [L f. Gk *thalamos*]

thalassic /θəˈlæsɪk/ *adj*. of the sea or seas, esp. small or inland seas. [F *thalassique* f. Gk *thalassa* sea]

thaler /ˈtɑːlə(r)/ *n*. *hist*. a German silver coin. [G *T(h)aler*: see DOLLAR]

thalidomide /θəˈlɪdəˌmaɪd/ *n*. a drug formerly used as a sedative but found in 1961 to cause foetal malformation when taken by a mother early in pregnancy. □ **thalidomide baby** (or **child**) a baby or child born deformed from the effects of thalidomide. [ph*thali*midoglutari*mide*]

thalli *pl.* of THALLUS.

thallium /'θælɪəm/ *n. Chem.* a rare soft white metallic element, occurring naturally in zinc blende and some iron ores. □□**thallic** *adj.* **thallous** *adj.* [formed as THALLUS, from the green line in its spectrum]

thallophyte /'θælə,faɪt/ *n. Bot.* a plant having a thallus, e.g. alga, fungus, or lichen. [mod.L *Thallophyta* (as THALLUS) + -PHYTE]

thallus /'θæləs/ *n.* (*pl.* **thalli** /-laɪ/) a plant-body without vascular tissue and not differentiated into root, stem, and leaves. □□**thalloid** *adj.* [L f. Gk *thallos* green shoot f. *thallō* bloom]

thalweg /'tɑ:lveg/ *n.* **1** *Geog.* a line where opposite slopes meet at the bottom of a valley, river, or lake. **2** *Law* a boundary between States along the centre of a river etc. [G f. *Thal* valley + *Weg* way]

than /ðən, ðæn/ *conj.* **1** introducing the second element in a comparison (*you are older than he is*; *you are older than he*). ¶ It is also possible to say *you are older than him*, with *than* treated as a preposition, esp. in less formal contexts. **2** introducing the second element in a statement of difference (*anyone other than me*). [OE *thanne* etc., orig. the same word as THEN]

thanage /'θeɪnɪdʒ/ *n. hist.* **1** the rank of thane. **2** the land granted to a thane. [ME f. AF *thanage* (as THANE)]

thanatology /ˌθænə'tɒlədʒɪ/ *n.* the scientific study of death and its associated phenomena and practices. [Gk *thanatos* death + -LOGY]

thane /θeɪn/ *n. hist.* **1** a man who held land from an English king or other superior by military service, ranking between ordinary freemen and hereditary nobles. **2** a man who held land from a Scottish king and ranked with an earl's son; the chief of a clan. □□ **thanedom** *n.* [OE *theg(e)n* servant, soldier f. Gmc]

thank /θæŋk/ *v. & n.* —*v.tr.* **1** express gratitude to (*thanked him for the present*). **2** hold responsible (*you can thank yourself for that*). —*n.* (in *pl.*) **1** gratitude (*expressed his heartfelt thanks*). **2** an expression of gratitude (*give thanks to Heaven*). **3** (as a formula) thank you (*thanks for your help*; *thanks very much*). □**give thanks** say grace at a meal. **I will thank you** a polite formula, now usu. *iron.* implying reproach (*I will thank you to go away*). **no** (or **small**) **thanks to** despite. **thank goodness** (or **God** or **heavens** etc.) **1** *colloq.* an expression of relief or pleasure. **2** an expression of pious gratitude. **thank-offering** an offering made as an act of thanksgiving. **thanks to** as the (good or bad) result of (*thanks to my foresight*; *thanks to your obstinacy*). **thank you** a polite formula acknowledging a gift or service or an offer accepted or refused. **thank-you** *n. colloq.* an instance of expressing thanks. [OE *thancian*, *thanc* f. Gmc, rel. to THINK]

thankful /'θæŋkfʊl/ *adj.* **1** grateful, pleased. **2** (of words or acts) expressive of thanks. □□ **thankfulness** *n.* [OE *thancful* (as THANK, -FUL)]

thankfully /'θæŋkfʊlɪ/ *adv.* **1** in a thankful manner. **2** *disp.* let us be thankful; fortunately (*thankfully, nobody was hurt*). [OE *thancfullice* (as THANKFUL, -LY²)]

thankless /'θæŋklɪs/ *adj.* **1** not expressing or feeling gratitude. **2** (of a task etc.) giving no pleasure or profit. **3** not deserving thanks. □□ **thanklessly** *adv.* **thanklessness** *n.*

thanksgiving /'θæŋks,gɪvɪŋ, -'gɪvɪŋ/ *n.* **1 a** the expression of gratitude, esp. to God. **b** a form of words for this. **2** (**Thanksgiving** or **Thanksgiving Day**) a national holiday for giving thanks to God, the fourth Thursday in November in the US, usu. the second Monday in October in Canada. □**General Thanksgiving** a form of thanksgiving in the Book of Common Prayer or the Alternative Service Book.

thar var. of TAHR.

that /ðæt/ *pron., adj., adv., & conj.* —*demons.pron.* (*pl.* **those** /ðəʊz/) **1** the person or thing indicated, named, or understood, esp. when observed by the speaker or when familiar to the person addressed (*I heard that*; *who is that in the garden?*; *I knew all that before*; *that is not fair*). **2** (contrasted with *this*) the further or less immediate or obvious etc. of two (*this bag is much heavier than that*). **3** the action, behaviour, or circumstances just observed or mentioned (*don't do that again*). **4** *Brit.* (on the telephone etc.) the person spoken to (*who is that?*). **5** *colloq.* referring to a strong feeling just mentioned ('*Are you glad?*' '*I am that*'). **6** (esp. in relative constructions) the one, the person, etc., described or specified in some way (*those who have cars can take the luggage*; *those unfit for use*; *a table like that described above*). **7** /ðət/ (*pl.* **that**) used instead of *which* or *whom* to introduce a defining clause, esp. one essential to identification (*the book that you sent me*; *there is nothing here that matters*). ¶ As a relative *that* usually specifies, whereas *who* or *which* need not: compare *the book that you sent me is lost* with *the book, which I gave you, is lost.* —*demons.adj.* (*pl.* **those** /ðəʊz/) **1** designating the person or thing indicated, named, understood, etc. (cf. sense 1 of *pron.*) (*look at that dog*; *what was that noise?*; *things were easier in those days*). **2** contrasted with *this* (cf. sense 2 of *pron.*) (*this bag is heavier than that one*). **3** expressing strong feeling (*shall not easily forget that day*). —*adv.* **1** to such a degree; so (*have done that much*; *will go that far*). **2** *Brit. colloq.* very (*not that good*). /ðət/ at which, on which, etc. (*at the speed that he was going he could not stop*; *the day that I first met her*). ¶ Often omitted in this sense: *the day I first met her.* —*conj.* /ðət/ except when stressed/ introducing a subordinate clause indicating: **1** a statement or hypothesis (*they say that he is better*; *there is no doubt that he meant it*; *the result was that the handle fell off*). **2** a purpose (*we live that we may eat*). **3** a result (*am so sleepy that I cannot keep my eyes open*). **4** a reason or clause (*it is rather that he lacks the time*). **5** a wish (*Oh, that summer were here!*). ¶ Often omitted in senses 1, 3: *they say he is better.* □**all that** very (*not all that good*). **and all that** (or **and that** *colloq.*) and all or various things associated with or similar to what has been mentioned; and so forth. **like that 1** of that kind (*is fond of books like that*). **2** in that manner, as you are doing, as he has been doing, etc. (*wish they would not talk like that*). **3** *colloq.* without effort (*did the job like that*). **4** of that character (*he would not accept any payment—he is like that*). **that is** (or **that is to say**) a formula introducing or following an explanation of a preceding word or words. **that's** *colloq.* you are (by virtue of present or future obedience etc.) (*that's a good boy*). **that's more like it** an acknowledgement of improvement. **that's right** an expression of approval or *colloq.* assent. **that's that** a formula concluding a narrative or discussion or indicating completion of a task. **that there** *sl.* = sense 1 of *adj.* **that will do** no more is needed or desirable. [OE *thæt*, nom. & acc. sing. neut. of demons. pron. & adj. *se*, *sēo*, *thæt* f. Gmc; *those* f. OE *thās* pl. of *thes* THIS]

thatch /θætʃ/ *n. & v.* —*n.* **1** a roof-covering of straw, reeds, palm-leaves, or similar material. **2** *colloq.* the hair of the head. —*v.tr.* (also *absol.*) cover (a roof or a building) with thatch. □□**thatcher** *n.* [n. late collateral form of *thack* (now dial.) f. OE *thæc*, after v. f. OE *theccan* f. Gmc, assim. to *thack*]

thaumatrope /'θɔ:mə,trəʊp/ *n. hist.* **1** a disc or card with two different pictures on its two sides, which combine into one by the persistence of visual impressions when the disc is rapidly rotated. **2** a zoetrope. [irreg. f. Gk *thauma* marvel + -*tropos* -turning]

thaumaturge /'θɔ:mə,tɜ:dʒ/ *n.* a worker of miracles; a wonder-worker. □□ **thaumaturgic** /-'tɜ:dʒɪk/ *adj.* **thaumaturgical** /-'tɜ:dʒɪk(ə)l/ *adj.* **thaumaturgist**

n. **thaumaturgy** *n.* [med.L *thaumaturgus* f. Gk *thaumatourgos* (adj.) f. *thauma -matos* marvel + *-ergos* -working]

thaw /θɔː/ *v. & n.* —*v.* **1** *intr.* (often foll. by *out*) (of ice or snow or a frozen thing) pass into a liquid or unfrozen state. **2** *intr.* (usu. prec. by *it* as subject) (of the weather) become warm enough to melt ice etc. (*it began to thaw*). **3** *intr.* become warm enough to lose numbness etc. **4** *intr.* become less cold or stiff in manner; become genial. **5** *tr.* (often foll. by *out*) cause to thaw. **6** *tr.* make cordial or animated. —*n.* **1** the act or an instance of thawing. **2** the warmth of weather that thaws (*a thaw has set in*). **3** *Polit.* a relaxation of control or restriction. □□ **thawless** *adj.* [OE *thawian* f. WG; orig. unkn.]

the /before a vowel ðɪ, before a consonant ðə, when stressed ðiː/ *adj. & adv.* —*adj.* (called the definite article) **1** denoting one or more persons or things already mentioned, under discussion, implied, or familiar (*gave the man a wave; shall let the matter drop; hurt myself in the arm; went to the theatre*). **2** serving to describe as unique (*the Queen; the Thames*). **3 a** (foll. by defining adj.) which is, who are, etc. (*ignored the embarrassed Mr Smith; Edward the Seventh*). **b** (foll. by adj. used *absol.*) denoting a class described (*from the sublime to the ridiculous*). **4** best known or best entitled to the name (with *the* stressed: *no relation to the Kipling; this is the book on this subject*). **5** used to indicate a following defining clause or phrase (*the book that you borrowed; the best I can do for you; the bottom of a well*). **6 a** used to indicate that a singular noun represents a species, class, etc. (*the cat loves comfort; has the novel a future?; plays the harp well*). **b** used with a noun which figuratively represents an occupation, pursuit, etc. (*went on the stage; too fond of the bottle*). **c** (foll. by the name of a unit) a, per (*5p in the pound; £5 the square metre; allow 8 minutes to the mile*). **d** *colloq.* or *archaic* designating a disease, affliction, etc. (*the measles; the toothache; the blues*). **7** (foll. by a unit of time) the present, the current (*man of the moment; questions of the day; book of the month*). **8** *Brit. colloq.* my, our (*the dog; the fridge*). **9** used before the surname of the chief of a Scottish or Irish clan (*the Macnab*). **10** *dial.* (esp. in Wales) used with a noun characterizing the occupation of the person whose name precedes (*Jones the Bread*). —*adv.* (preceding comparatives in expressions of proportional variation) in or by that (or such a) degree; on that account (*the more the merrier; the more he gets the more he wants*). □ **all the** in the full degree to be expected (*that makes it all the worse*). **so much the** (tautologically) so much, in that degree (*so much the worse for him*). [(adj.) OE, replacing *se, sēo, þæt* (= THAT), f. Gmc: (adv.) f. OE *thȳ, thē,* instrumental case]

theandric /θiːˈændrɪk/ *adj.* of the union, or by the joint agency, of the divine and human natures in Christ. [eccl.Gk *theandrikos* f. *theos* god + *anēr andros* man]

theanthropic /ˌθiːənˈθrɒpɪk/ *adj.* **1** both divine and human. **2** tending to embody deity in human form. [eccl.Gk *theanthrōpos* god-man f. *theos* god + *anthrōpos* human being]

thearchy /ˈθiːɑːkɪ/ *n.* (*pl.* **-ies**) **1** government by a god or gods. **2** a system or order of gods (*the Olympian thearchy*). [eccl.Gk *thearkhia* godhead f. *theos* god + *-arkhō* f. *arkhō* rule]

theatre /ˈθɪətə(r)/ *n.* (*US* **theater**) **1 a** a building or outdoor area for dramatic performances. **b** a cinema. **2 a** the writing and production of plays. **b** effective material for the stage (*makes good theatre*). **3** a room or hall for lectures etc. with seats in tiers. **4** *Brit.* an operating theatre. **5 a** a scene or field of action (*the theatre of war*). **b** (*attrib.*) designating weapons intermediate between tactical and strategic (*theatre nuclear missiles*). **6** a natural land-formation in a gradually rising part-circle like ancient Greek and Roman theatres. □ **theatre-goer** a frequenter of theatres. **theatre-going** frequenting theatres. **theatre-in-the-round** a dramatic performance on a stage surrounded by spectators. **theatre sister** a nurse supervising the nursing team in an operating theatre. [ME f. OF *t(h)eatre* or f. L *theatrum* f. Gk *theatron* f. *theaomai* behold]

theatric /θɪˈætrɪk/ *adj. & n.* —*adj.* = THEATRICAL. —*n.* (in *pl.*) theatrical actions.

theatrical /θɪˈætrɪk(ə)l/ *adj. & n.* —*adj.* **1** of or for the theatre; of acting or actors. **2** (of a manner, speech, gesture, or person) calculated for effect; showy, artificial, affected. —*n.* (in *pl.*) **1** dramatic performances (*amateur theatricals*). **2** theatrical actions. □□ **theatricalism** *n.* **theatricality** /-ˈkælɪtɪ/ *n.* **theatricalize** *v.tr.* (also **-ise**). **theatricalization** /-laɪˈzeɪʃ(ə)n/ *n.* **theatrically** *adv.* [LL *theatricus* f. Gk *theatrikos* f. *theatron* THEATRE]

Theban /ˈθiːbən/ *adj. & n.* —*adj.* of or relating to Thebes in ancient Egypt or ancient Greece. —*n.* a native or inhabitant of Thebes. [ME f. L *Thebanus* f. *Thebae* Thebes f. Gk *Thēbai*]

theca /ˈθiːkə/ *n.* (*pl.* **thecae** /-siː/) **1** *Bot.* a part of a plant serving as a receptacle. **2** *Zool.* a case or sheath enclosing an organ or organism. □□ **thecate** *adj.* [L f. Gk *thēkē* case]

thé dansant /ˌteɪ dɑ̃ˈsɑ̃/ *n.* = tea dance. [F]

thee /ðiː/ *pron.* objective case of THOU[1]. [OE]

theft /θeft/ *n.* **1** the act or an instance of stealing. **2** *Law* dishonest appropriation of another's property with intent to deprive him or her of it permanently. [OE *thīefth, thēofth,* later *thēoft,* f. Gmc (as THIEF)]

thegn /θeɪn/ *n. hist.* an English thane. [OE: see THANE]

theine /ˈθiːɪn, ˈθiːiːn/ *n.* = CAFFEINE. [mod.L *thea* tea + -INE[4]]

their /ðeə(r)/ *poss.pron.* (*attrib.*) **1** of or belonging to them or themselves (*their house; their own business*). **2** (**Their**) (in titles) that they are (*Their Majesties*). **3** *disp.* as a third person sing. indefinite meaning 'his or her' (*has anyone lost their purse?*). [ME f. ON *their(r)a* of them, genit. pl. of *sá* THE, THAT]

theirs /ðeəz/ *poss.pron.* the one or ones belonging to or associated with them (*it is theirs; theirs are over here*). □ **of theirs** of or belonging to them (*a friend of theirs*). [ME f. THEIR]

theism /ˈθiːɪz(ə)m/ *n.* belief in the existence of gods or a god, esp. a God supernaturally revealed to man (cf. DEISM) and sustaining a personal relation to his creatures. □□ **theist** *n.* **theistic** /-ˈɪstɪk/ *adj.* **theistical** /-ˈɪstɪk(ə)l/ *adj.* **theistically** /-ˈɪstɪkəlɪ/ *adv.* [Gk *theos* god + -ISM]

them /ð(ə)m, or, when stressed, ðem/ *pron. & adj.* —*pron.* **1** objective case of THEY (*I saw them*). **2** *colloq.* they (*it's them again; is older than them*). **3** *archaic* themselves (*they fell and hurt them*). —*adj. sl.* or *dial.* those (*them bones*). [ME *theim* f. ON: see THEY]

thematic /θɪˈmætɪk/ *adj.* **1** of or relating to subjects or topics (*thematic philately; the arrangement of the anthology is thematic*). **2** *Mus.* of melodic subjects (*thematic treatment*). **3** *Gram.* **a** of or belonging to a theme (*thematic vowel; thematic form*). **b** (of a form of a verb) having a thematic vowel. □ **thematic catalogue** *Mus.* a catalogue giving the opening themes of works as well as their names and other details. □□ **thematically** *adv.* [Gk *thematikos* (as THEME)]

theme /θiːm/ *n.* **1** a subject or topic on which a person speaks, writes, or thinks. **2** *Mus.* a prominent or frequently recurring melody or group of notes in a composition. **3** *US* a school exercise, esp. an essay, on a given subject. **4** *Gram.* the stem of a noun or verb; the part to which inflections are added, esp. composed of the root and an added vowel. **5** *hist.* any of the 29 provinces in the Byzantine empire. □ **theme park** an amusement park organized round a unifying idea. **theme song** (or **tune**) **1** a recurrent melody in a musical play or film. **2** a signature tune. [ME *teme* ult. f. Gk *thema -matos* f. *tithēmi* set, place]

themselves /ðəm'selvz/ *pron.* **1 a** *emphat. form* of THEY or THEM. **b** *refl. form* of THEM; (cf. HERSELF). **2** in their normal state of body or mind (*are quite themselves again*). □**be themselves** act in their normal, unconstrained manner.

then /ðen/ *adv., adj., & n.* —*adv.* **1** at that time; at the time in question (*was then too busy; then comes the trouble; the then existing laws*). **2 a** next, afterwards; after that (*then he told me to come in*). **b** and also (*then, there are the children to consider*). **c** after all (*it is a problem, but then that is what we are here for*). **3 a** in that case; therefore; it follows that (*then you should have said so*). **b** if what you say is true (*but then why did you take it?*). **c** (implying grudging or impatient concession) if you must have it so (*all right then, have it your own way*). **d** used parenthetically to resume a narrative etc. (*the policeman, then, knocked on the door*). —*adj.* that or who was such at the time in question (*the then Duke*). —*n.* that time (*until then*). □**then and there** immediately and on the spot. [OE *thanne, thonne,* etc., f. Gmc, rel. to THAT, THE]

thenar /'θiːnə(r)/ *n. Anat.* the ball of muscle at the base of the thumb. [earlier = palm of the hand: mod.L f. Gk]

thence /ðens/ *adv.* (also **from thence**) *archaic* or *literary* **1** from that place or source. **2** for that reason. [ME *thannes, thennes* f. *thanne, thenne* f. OE *thanon(e)* etc. f. WG]

thenceforth /ðens'fɔːθ/ *adv.* (also **from thenceforth**) *archaic* or *literary* from that time onward.

thenceforward /ðens'fɔːwəd/ *adv. archaic* or *literary* thenceforth.

theo- /'θiːəʊ/ *comb. form* God or gods. [Gk f. *theos* god]

theobromine /θiə'brəʊmɪn, -miːn/ *n.* a bitter white alkaloid obtained from cacao seeds, related to caffeine. [*Theobroma* cacao genus: mod.L f. Gk *theos* god + *brōma* food, + -INE⁴]

theocentric /θiə'sentrɪk/ *adj.* having God as its centre.

theocracy /θɪ'ɒkrəsɪ/ *n.* (*pl.* **-ies**) **1** a form of government by God or a god directly or through a priestly order etc. **2** (**the Theocracy**) the Jewish commonwealth from Moses to the monarchy. □□ **theocrat** /'θiːəˌkræt/ *n.* **theocratic** /θiə'krætɪk/ *adj.* **theocratically** /θiə'krætɪkəlɪ/ *adv.*

theocrasy /'θiːəˌkreɪsɪ, θɪ'ɒkrəsɪ/ *n.* **1** the mingling of deities into one personality. **2** the union of the soul with God through contemplation (among Neoplatonists etc.). [THEO- + Gk *krasis* mingling]

theodicy /θɪ'ɒdɪsɪ/ *n.* (*pl.* **-ies**) **1** the vindication of divine providence in view of the existence of evil. **2** an instance of this. □□ **theodicean** /-'siːən/ *adj.* [THEO- + Gk *dikē* justice]

theodolite /θɪ'ɒdəˌlaɪt/ *n.* a surveying-instrument for measuring horizontal and vertical angles with a rotating telescope. □□ **theodolitic** /-'lɪtɪk/ *adj.* [16th c. *theodelitus,* of unkn. orig.]

theogony /θɪ'ɒgənɪ/ *n.* (*pl.* **-ies**) **1** the genealogy of the gods. **2** an account of this. [THEO- + Gk *-gonia* begetting]

theologian /θiə'ləʊdʒɪən, -dʒ(ə)n/ *n.* a person trained in theology. [ME f. OF *theologien* (as THEOLOGY)]

theological /θiə'lɒdʒɪk(ə)l/ *adj.* of theology. □**theological virtues** faith, hope, and charity. □□ **theologically** *adv.* [med.L *theologicalis* f. L *theologicus* f. Gk *theologikos* (as THEOLOGY)]

theology /θɪ'ɒlədʒɪ/ *n.* (*pl.* **-ies**) **1 a** the study of theistic (esp. Christian) religion. **b** a system of theistic (esp. Christian) religion. **c** the rational analysis of a religious faith. **2** a system of theoretical principles, esp. an impractical or rigid ideology. □□ **theologist** *n.* **theologize** *v.tr. & intr.* (also **-ise**). [ME f. OF *theologie* f. L *theologia* f. Gk (as THEO-, -LOGY)]

theomachy /θɪ'ɒməkɪ/ *n.* (*pl.* **-ies**) strife among or against the gods. [THEO- + Gk *makhē* fight]

theophany /θɪ'ɒfənɪ/ *n.* (*pl.* **-ies**) a visible manifestation of God or a god to man.

theophoric /θiə'fɒrɪk/ *adj.* bearing the name of a god.

theophylline /θiə'fɪlɪn, -liːn/ *n.* an alkaloid similar to theobromine, found in tea-leaves. [irreg. f. mod.L *thea* tea + Gk *phullon* leaf + -INE⁴]

theorbo /θɪ'ɔːbəʊ/ *n.* (*pl.* **-os**) a two-necked musical instrument of the lute class much used in the seventeenth century. □□ **theorbist** *n.* [It. *tiorba,* of unkn. orig.]

theorem /'θiərəm/ *n.* esp. *Math.* **1** a general proposition not self-evident but proved by a chain of reasoning; a truth established by means of accepted truths (cf. PROBLEM). **2** a rule in algebra etc., esp. one expressed by symbols or formulae (*binomial theorem*). □□ **theorematic** /-'mætɪk/ *adj.* [F *théorème* or LL *theorema* f. Gk *theōrēma* speculation, proposition f. *theōreō* look at]

theoretic /θiə'retɪk/ *adj. & n.* —*adj.* = THEORETICAL. —*n.* (in *sing.* or *pl.*) the theoretical part of a science etc. [LL *theoreticus* f. Gk *theōrētikos* (as THEORY)]

theoretical /θiə'retɪk(ə)l/ *adj.* **1** concerned with knowledge but not with its practical application. **2** based on theory rather than experience or practice. □□ **theoretically** *adv.*

theoretician /ˌθiərɪ'tɪʃ(ə)n/ *n.* a person concerned with the theoretical aspects of a subject.

theorist /'θiərɪst/ *n.* a holder or inventor of a theory or theories.

theorize /'θiəraɪz/ *v.intr.* (also **-ise**) evolve or indulge in theories. □□ **theorizer** *n.*

theory /'θiərɪ/ *n.* (*pl.* **-ies**) **1** a supposition or system of ideas explaining something, esp. one based on general principles independent of the particular things to be explained (opp. HYPOTHESIS) (*atomic theory; theory of evolution*). **2** a speculative (esp. fanciful) view (*one of my pet theories*). **3** the sphere of abstract knowledge or speculative thought (*this is all very well in theory, but how will it work in practice?*). **4** the exposition of the principles of a science etc. (*the theory of music*). **5** *Math.* a collection of propositions to illustrate the principles of a subject (*probability theory; theory of equations*). [LL *theoria* f. Gk *theōria* f. *theōros* spectator f. *theōreō* look at]

theosophy /θɪ'ɒsəfɪ/ *n.* (*pl.* **-ies**) any of various philosophies professing to achieve a knowledge of God by spiritual ecstasy, direct intuition, or special individual relations, esp. a modern movement following Hindu and Buddhist teachings and seeking universal brotherhood. □□ **theosopher** *n.* **theosophic** /θiə'sɒfɪk/ *adj.* **theosophical** /θiə'sɒfɪk(ə)l/ *adj.* **theosophically** /θiə'sɒfɪkəlɪ/ *adv.* **theosophist** *n.* [med.L *theosophia* f. late Gk *theosophia* f. *theosophos* wise concerning God (as THEO-, *sophos* wise)]

therapeutic /ˌθerə'pjuːtɪk/ *adj.* **1** of, for, or contributing to the cure of disease. **2** contributing to general, esp. mental, well-being (*finds walking therapeutic*). □□ **therapeutical** *adj.* **therapeutically** *adv.* **therapeutist** *n.* [attrib. use of *therapeutic,* orig. form of THERAPEUTICS]

therapeutics /ˌθerə'pjuːtɪks/ *n.pl.* (usu. treated as *sing.*) the branch of medicine concerned with the treatment of disease and the action of remedial agents. [F *thérapeutique* or LL *therapeutica* (pl.) f. Gk *therapeutika* neut. pl. of *therapeutikos* f. *therapeuō* wait on, cure]

therapy /'θerəpɪ/ *n.* (*pl.* **-ies**) **1** the treatment of physical or mental disorders, other than by surgery. **2** a particular type of such treatment. □□ **therapist** *n.* [mod.L *therapia* f. Gk *therapeia* healing]

Theravada /ˌθerə'vɑːdə/ *n.* a more conservative form of Buddhism, practised in Burma (now Myanmar), Thailand, etc. [Pali *theravāda* f. *thera* elder, old + *vāda* speech, doctrine]

there /ðeə(r)/ adv., n., & int. —adv. 1 in, at, or to that place or position (lived there for some years; goes there every day). 2 at that point (in speech, performance, writing, etc.) (there he stopped). 3 in that respect (I agree with you there). 4 used for emphasis in calling attention (you there!; there goes the bell). 5 used to indicate the fact or existence of something (there is a house on the corner). —n. that place (lives somewhere near there). —int. 1 expressing confirmation, triumph, dismay, etc. (there! what did I tell you?). 2 used to soothe a child etc. (there, there, never mind). □have been there before sl. know all about it. so there colloq. that is my final decision (whether you like it or not). there and then immediately and on the spot. there it is 1 that is the trouble. 2 nothing can be done about it. there's colloq. you are (by virtue of present or future obedience etc.) (there's a dear). there you are (or go) colloq. 1 this is what you wanted etc. 2 expressing confirmation, triumph, resignation, etc. [OE thǣr, thēr f. Gmc, rel. to THAT, THE]

thereabouts /ˈðeərəˌbauts, -ˈbauts/ adv. (also **thereabout**) 1 near that place (ought to be somewhere thereabouts). 2 near that number, quantity, etc. (two litres or thereabouts).

thereafter /ðeərˈɑːftə(r)/ adv. formal after that.

thereanent /ˌðeərəˈnent/ adv. Sc. about that matter.

thereat /ðeərˈæt/ adv. archaic 1 at that place. 2 on that account. 3 after that.

thereby /ðeəˈbaɪ, ˈðeə-/ adv. by that means, as a result of that. □thereby hangs a tale much could be said about that.

therefor /ðeəˈfɔː(r)/ adv. archaic for that object or purpose.

therefore /ˈðeəfɔː(r)/ adv. for that reason; accordingly, consequently.

therefrom /ðeəˈfrɒm/ adv. archaic from that or it.

therein /ðeərˈɪn/ adv. formal 1 in that place etc. 2 in that respect.

thereinafter /ˌðeərɪnˈɑːftə(r)/ adv. formal later in the same document etc.

thereinbefore /ðeərˌɪnbɪˈfɔː(r)/ adv. formal earlier in the same document etc.

thereinto /ðeərˈɪntu/ adv. archaic into that place.

thereof /ðeərˈɒv/ adv. formal of that or it.

thereon /ðeərˈɒn/ adv. archaic on that or it (of motion or position).

thereout /ðeərˈaut/ adv. archaic out of that, from that source.

therethrough /ðeəˈθruː/ adv. archaic through that.

thereto /ðeəˈtuː/ adv. formal 1 to that or it. 2 in addition, to boot.

theretofore /ˌðeətuˈfɔː(r)/ adv. formal before that time.

thereunto /ðeərˈʌntu/ adv. archaic to that or it.

thereupon /ˌðeərəˈpɒn/ adv. 1 in consequence of that. 2 soon or immediately after that. 3 archaic upon that (of motion or position).

therewith /ðeəˈwɪð/ adv. archaic 1 with that. 2 soon or immediately after that.

therewithal /ˌðeəwɪˈðɔːl/ adv. archaic in addition, besides.

theriac /ˈθɪərɪˌæk/ n. archaic an antidote to the bites of poisonous animals, esp. snakes. [L theriaca f. Gk thēriakē antidote, fem. of thēriakos f. thēr wild beast]

therianthropic /ˌθɪərɪænˈθrɒpɪk/ adj. of or worshipping beings represented in combined human and animal forms. [Gk thērion dimin. of thēr wild beast + anthrōpos human being]

theriomorphic /ˌθɪərɪəˈmɔːfɪk/ adj. (esp. of a deity) having an animal form. [as THERIANTHROPIC + Gk morphē form]

therm /θɜːm/ n. a unit of heat, esp. as the statutory unit of gas supplied in the UK equivalent to 100,000 British thermal units or 1.055×10^8 joules. [Gk thermē heat]

thermae /ˈθɜːmiː/ n.pl. Gk & Rom. Antiq. public baths. [L f. Gk thermai (pl.) (as THERM)]

thermal /ˈθɜːm(ə)l/ adj. & n. —adj. 1 of, for, or producing heat. 2 promoting the retention of heat (thermal underwear). —n. a rising current of heated air (used by gliders, balloons, and birds to gain height). □British thermal unit the amount of heat needed to raise 1 lb. of water at maximum density through one degree Fahrenheit, equivalent to 1.055 × 10³ joules. thermal capacity the number of heat units needed to raise the temperature of a body by one degree. thermal neutron a neutron in thermal equilibrium with its surroundings. thermal reactor a nuclear reactor using thermal neutrons. thermal springs springs of naturally hot water. thermal unit a unit for measuring heat. □□ thermalize v.tr. & intr. (also -ise). thermalization /-laɪˈzeɪʃ(ə)n/ n. thermally adv. [F (as THERM)]

thermic /ˈθɜːmɪk/ adj. of or relating to heat.

thermidor see LOBSTER.

thermion /ˈθɜːmɪˌɒn/ n. an ion or electron emitted by a substance at high temperature. [THERMO- + ION]

thermionic /ˌθɜːmɪˈɒnɪk/ adj. of or relating to electrons emitted from a substance at very high temperature. □thermionic emission the emission of electrons from a heated source. thermionic valve (US tube) a device giving a flow of thermionic electrons in one direction, used esp. in the rectification of a current and in radio reception.

thermionics /ˌθɜːmɪˈɒnɪks/ n.pl. (treated as sing.) the branch of science and technology concerned with thermionic emission.

thermistor /θɜːˈmɪstə(r)/ n. Electr. a resistor whose resistance is greatly reduced by heating, used for measurement and control. [thermal resistor]

thermite /ˈθɜːmaɪt/ n. (also **thermit** /-mɪt/) a mixture of finely powdered aluminium and iron oxide that produces a very high temperature on combustion (used in welding and for incendiary bombs). [G Thermit (as THERMO-, -ITE¹)]

thermo- /ˈθɜːməʊ/ comb. form denoting heat. [Gk f. thermos hot, thermē heat]

thermochemistry /ˌθɜːməʊˈkemɪstrɪ/ n. the branch of chemistry dealing with the quantities of heat evolved or absorbed during chemical reactions. □□ thermochemical adj.

thermocouple /ˈθɜːməʊˌkʌp(ə)l/ n. a pair of different metals in contact at a point, generating a thermoelectric voltage that can serve as a measure of temperature at this point relative to their other parts.

thermodynamics /ˌθɜːməʊdaɪˈnæmɪks/ n.pl. (usu. treated as sing.) the science of the relations between heat and other (mechanical, electrical, etc.) forms of energy. □□ thermodynamic adj. thermodynamical adj. thermodynamically adv. thermodynamicist /-sɪst/ n.

thermoelectric /ˌθɜːməʊɪˈlektrɪk/ adj. producing electricity by a difference of temperatures. □□ thermoelectrically adv. thermoelectricity /-ˌɪlekˈtrɪsɪtɪ/ n.

thermogenesis /ˌθɜːməʊˈdʒenɪsɪs/ n. the production of heat, esp. in a human or animal body.

thermogram /ˈθɜːməˌgræm/ n. a record made by a thermograph.

thermograph /ˈθɜːməˌɡrɑːf/ n. 1 an instrument that gives a continuous record of temperature. 2 an apparatus used to obtain an image produced by infrared radiation from a human or animal body. □□ thermographic /-ˈgræfɪk/ adj.

thermography /θɜːˈmɒɡrəfɪ/ n. Med. the taking or use of infrared thermograms, esp. to detect tumours.

thermolabile /ˌθɜːməʊˈleɪbaɪl, -bɪl/ adj. (of a substance) unstable when heated.

thermoluminescence /ˌθɜːməʊˌluːmɪˈnes(ə)ns/ n. the property of becoming luminescent when pretreated and subjected to high temperatures, used as a means of dating ancient artefacts. □□ **thermoluminescent** adj.

thermolysis /θɜːˈmɒlɪsɪs/ n. decomposition by the action of heat. □□ **thermolytic** /-ˈlɪtɪk/ adj.

thermometer /θəˈmɒmɪtə(r)/ n. an instrument for measuring temperature, esp. a graduated glass tube with a small bore containing mercury or alcohol which expands when heated. □□ **thermometric** /ˌθɜːməˈmetrɪk/ adj. **thermometrical** /ˌθɜːmə ˈmetrɪk(ə)l/ adj. **thermometry** n. [F thermomètre or mod.L thermometrum (as THERMO-, -METER)]

thermonuclear /ˌθɜːməʊˈnjuːklɪə(r)/ adj. 1 relating to or using nuclear reactions that occur only at very high temperatures. 2 relating to or characterized by weapons using thermonuclear reactions.

thermophile /ˈθɜːməʊˌfaɪl/ n. & adj. (also **thermophil** /-fɪl/) —n. a bacterium etc. growing optimally at high temperatures. —adj. of or being a thermophile. □□ **thermophilic** /-ˈfɪlɪk/ adj.

thermopile /ˈθɜːməʊˌpaɪl/ n. a set of thermocouples esp. arranged for measuring small quantities of radiant heat.

thermoplastic /ˌθɜːməʊˈplæstɪk/ adj. & n. —adj. (of a substance) that becomes plastic on heating and hardens on cooling, and is able to repeat these processes. —n. a thermoplastic substance.

Thermos /ˈθɜːmɒs/ n. (in full **Thermos flask**) propr. a vacuum flask. [Gk (as THERMO-)]

thermosetting /ˌθɜːməʊˈsetɪŋ/ adj. (of plastics) setting permanently when heated. □□ **thermoset** /ˈθɜː-/ adj.

thermosphere /ˈθɜːməˌsfɪə(r)/ n. the region of the atmosphere beyond the mesosphere.

thermostable /ˌθɜːməʊˈsteɪb(ə)l/ adj. (of a substance) stable when heated.

thermostat /ˈθɜːməˌstæt/ n. a device that automatically regulates temperature, or that activates a device when the temperature reaches a certain point. □□ **thermostatic** /-ˈstætɪk/ adj. **thermostatically** /-ˈstætɪkəlɪ/ adv. [THERMO- + Gk statos standing]

thermotaxis /ˌθɜːməʊˈtæksɪs/ n. 1 the regulation of heat or temperature esp. in warm-blooded animals. 2 movement or stimulation in a living organism caused by heat. □□ **thermotactic** adj. **thermotaxic** adj.

thermotropism /θɜːˈmɒtrəˌpɪz(ə)m/ n. the growing or bending of a plant towards or away from a source of heat. □□ **thermotropic** /ˌθɜːməʊˈtrɒpɪk/ adj.

thesaurus /θɪˈsɔːrəs/ n. (pl. **thesauri** /-raɪ/ or **thesauruses**) 1 a a collection of concepts or words arranged according to sense. b US a book of synonyms and antonyms. 2 a dictionary or encyclopaedia. [L f. Gk thēsauros treasure]

these pl. of THIS.

thesis /ˈθiːsɪs/ n. (pl. **theses** /-siːz/) 1 a proposition to be maintained or proved. 2 a dissertation, esp. by a candidate for a degree. 3 /ˈθiːsɪs, ˈθesɪs/ an unstressed syllable or part of a metrical foot in Greek or Latin verse (opp. ARSIS). [ME f. LL f. Gk, = putting, placing, a proposition etc. f. the- root of tithēmi place]

Thespian /ˈθespɪən/ adj. & n. —adj. of or relating to tragedy or drama. —n. an actor or actress. [Gk Thespis the traditional originator of Greek tragedy]

Thess. abbr. Thessalonians (New Testament).

theta /ˈθiːtə/ n. the eighth letter of the Greek alphabet (Θ, θ). [Gk]

theurgy /ˈθiːɜːdʒɪ/ n. 1 a supernatural or divine agency esp. in human affairs. b the art of securing this. 2 the magical science of the Neoplatonists. □□ **theurgic** /-ˈɜːdʒɪk/ adj. **theurgical** /-ˈɜːdʒɪk(ə)l/ adj. **theurgist** n. [LL theurgia f. Gk theourgia f. theos god + -ergos working]

thew /θjuː/ n. (often in pl.) literary 1 muscular strength. 2 mental or moral vigour. [OE thēaw usage, conduct, of unkn. orig.]

they /ðeɪ/ pron. (obj. **them**; poss. **their, theirs**) 1 the people, animals, or things previously named or in question (pl. of HE, SHE, IT[1]). 2 people in general

(they say we are wrong). 3 those in authority (they have raised the fees). 4 disp. as a third person sing. indefinite pronoun meaning 'he or she' (anyone can come if they want to). [ME thei, obj. theim, f. ON their nom. pl. masc., theim dat. pl. of sá THE that]

they'd /ðeɪd/ contr. 1 they had. 2 they would.

they'll /ðeɪl, ðel/ contr. 1 they will. 2 they shall.

they're /ðeɪ(r), ˈðeɪə(r)/ contr. they are.

they've /ðeɪv/ contr. they have.

THI abbr. temperature-humidity index.

thiamine /ˈθaɪəmɪn, -ˌmiːn/ n. (also **thiamin**) a vitamin of the B complex, found in unrefined cereals, beans, and liver, a deficiency of which causes beriberi. Also called vitamin B_1, or ANEURIN. [THIO- + amin from VITAMIN]

thick /θɪk/ adj., n., & adv. —adj. 1 a of great or specified extent between opposite surfaces (a thick wall; a wall two metres thick). b of large diameter (a thick rope). 2 a (of a line etc.) broad; not fine. b (of script or type, etc.) consisting of thick lines. 3 a arranged closely; crowded together; dense. b numerous (fell thick as peas). 4 (usu. foll. by with) densely covered or filled (air thick with snow). 5 a firm in consistency; containing much solid matter; viscous (a thick paste; thick soup). b made of thick material (a thick coat). 6 muddy, cloudy; impenetrable by sight (thick darkness). 7 colloq. (of a person) stupid, dull. 8 (of a voice) indistinct. 9 colloq. intimate or very friendly (esp. thick as thieves). —n. a thick part of anything. —adv. thickly (snow was falling thick; blows rained down thick and fast). □ a bit thick Brit. colloq. unreasonable or intolerable. in the thick of 1 at the busiest part of. 2 heavily occupied with. thick ear Brit. sl. the external ear swollen as a result of a blow (esp. give a person a thick ear). thick-skinned not sensitive to reproach or criticism. thick-skulled (or -witted) stupid, dull; slow to learn. through thick and thin under all conditions; in spite of all difficulties. □□ **thickish** adj. **thickly** adv. [OE thicce (adj. & adv.) f. Gmc]

thicken /ˈθɪkən/ v. 1 tr. & intr. make or become thick or thicker. 2 intr. become more complicated (the plot thickens). □□ **thickener** n.

thickening /ˈθɪkənɪŋ/ n. 1 the process of becoming thick or thicker. 2 a substance used to thicken liquid. 3 a thickened part.

thicket /ˈθɪkɪt/ n. a tangle of shrubs or trees. [OE thiccet (as THICK, -ET[1])]

thickhead /ˈθɪkhed/ n. 1 colloq. a stupid person; a blockhead. 2 Austral. any bird of the genus Pachycephala; a whistler. □□ **thickheaded** /-ˈhedɪd/ adj. **thickheadedness** /-ˈhedɪdnɪs/ n.

thickness /ˈθɪknɪs/ n. 1 the state of being thick. 2 the extent to which a thing is thick. 3 a layer of material of a certain thickness (three thicknesses of cardboard). 4 a part that is thick or lies between opposite surfaces (steps cut in the thickness of the wall). [OE thicness (as THICK, -NESS)]

thickset /ˈθɪkˈset/ adj. & n. —adj. 1 heavily or solidly built. 2 set or growing close together. —n. a thicket.

thief /θiːf/ n. (pl. **thieves** /θiːvz/) a person who steals esp. secretly and without violence. [OE thēof f. Gmc]

thieve /θiːv/ v. 1 intr. be a thief. 2 tr. steal (a thing). [OE thēofian (as THIEF)]

thievery /ˈθiːvərɪ/ n. the act or practice of stealing.

thieves pl. of THIEF.

thievish /ˈθiːvɪʃ/ adj. given to stealing. □□ **thievishly** adv. **thievishness** n.

thigh /θaɪ/ n. 1 the part of the human leg between the hip and the knee. 2 a corresponding part in other animals. □ **thigh-bone** = FEMUR. □□ **-thighed** adj. (in comb.). [OE thēh, thēoh, thīoh, OHG dioh, ON thjó f. Gmc]

thill /θɪl/ n. a shaft of a cart or carriage, esp. one of a pair. [ME: orig. unkn.]

thill-horse /ˈθɪlhɔːs/ n. (also **thiller** /ˈθɪlə(r)/) a horse put between thills.

thimble /ˈθɪmb(ə)l/ n. 1 a metal or plastic cap, usu.

with a closed end, worn to protect the finger and push the needle in sewing. **2** *Mech.* a short metal tube or ferrule etc. **3** *Naut.* a metal ring concave on the outside and fitting in a loop of spliced rope to prevent chafing. [OE *thȳmel* (as THUMB, -LE¹)]

thimbleful /ˈθɪmb(ə)lfʊl/ *n.* (*pl.* **-fuls**) a small quantity, esp. of liquid to drink.

thimblerig /ˈθɪmb(ə)lrɪg/ *n.* a game often involving sleight of hand, in which three inverted thimbles or cups are moved about, contestants having to spot which is the one with a pea or other object beneath. □□ **thimblerigger** *n.* [THIMBLE + RIG² in sense 'trick, dodge']

thin /θɪn/ *adj.*, *adv.*, & *v.* —*adj.* (**thinner**, **thinnest**) **1** having the opposite surfaces close together; of small thickness or diameter. **2 a** (of a line) narrow or fine. **b** (of a script or type etc.) consisting of thin lines. **3** made of thin material (*a thin dress*). **4** lean; not plump. **5 a** not dense or copious (*thin hair*; *a thin haze*). **b** not full or closely packed (*a thin audience*). **6** of slight consistency (*a thin paste*). **7** weak; lacking an important ingredient (*thin blood*; *a thin voice*). **8** (of an excuse, argument, disguise, etc.) flimsy or transparent. —*adv.* thinly (*cut the bread very thin*). —*v.* (**thinned**, **thinning**) **1** *tr.* & *intr.* make or become thin or thinner. **2** *tr.* & *intr.* (often foll. by *out*) reduce; make or become less dense or crowded or numerous. **3** *tr.* (often foll. by *out*) remove some of a crop of (seedlings, saplings, etc.) or some young fruit from (a vine or tree) to improve the growth of the rest. □ **have a thin time** *colloq.* have a wretched or uncomfortable time. **on thin ice** see ICE. **thin air** a state of invisibility or non-existence (*vanished into thin air*). **thin end of the wedge** see WEDGE¹. **thin on the ground** see GROUND¹. **thin on top** balding. **thin-skinned** sensitive to reproach or criticism; easily upset. □□ **thinly** *adv.* **thinness** *n.* **thinnish** *adj.* [OE *thynne* f. Gmc]

thine /ðaɪn/ *poss.pron. archaic* or *dial.* **1** (*predic.* or *absol.*) of or belonging to thee. **2** (*attrib.* before a vowel) = THY. [OE *thīn* f. Gmc]

thing /θɪŋ/ *n.* **1** a material or non-material entity, idea, action, etc., that is or may be thought about or perceived. **2** an inanimate material object (*take that thing away*). **3** an unspecified object or item (*have a few things to buy*). **4** an act, idea, or utterance (*a silly thing to do*). **5** an event (*an unfortunate thing to happen*). **6** a quality (*patience is a useful thing*). **7** (with ref. to a person) expressing pity, contempt, or affection (*poor thing!*; *a dear old thing*). **8** a specimen or type of something (*the latest thing in hats*). **9** *colloq.* one's special interest or concern (*not my thing at all*). **10** *colloq.* something remarkable (*now there's a thing!*). **11** (prec. by *the*) *colloq.* **a** what is conventionally proper or fashionable. **b** what is needed or required (*your suggestion was just the thing*). **c** what is to be considered (*the thing is, shall we go or not?*). **d** what is important (*the thing about them is their reliability*). **12** (in *pl.*) personal belongings or clothing (*where have I left my things?*). **13** (in *pl.*) equipment (*painting things*). **14** (in *pl.*) affairs in general (*not in the nature of things*). **15** (in *pl.*) circumstances or conditions (*things look good*). **16** (in *pl.* with a following adjective) describable (*all things Greek*). **17** (in *pl.*) *Law* property. □ **do one's own thing** *colloq.* pursue one's own interests or inclinations. **do things to** *colloq.* affect remarkably. **have a thing about** *colloq.* be obsessed or prejudiced about. **make a thing of** *colloq.* **1** regard as essential. **2** cause a fuss about. **one** (or **just one**) **of those things** *colloq.* something unavoidable or to be accepted. [OE f. Gmc]

thingummy /ˈθɪŋəmɪ/ *n.* (*pl.* **-ies**) (also **thingamy**, **thingumabob** /-məˌbɒb/, **thingumajig** /-məˌdʒɪg/) *colloq.* a person or thing whose name one has forgotten or does not know or does not wish to mention. [THING + meaningless suffix]

thingy /ˈθɪŋɪ/ *n.* (*pl.* **-ies**) = THINGUMMY.

think /θɪŋk/ *v.* & *n.* —*v.* (*past* and *past part.* **thought** /θɔːt/) **1** *tr.* (foll. by *that* + clause) be of the opinion (*we think that they will come*). **2** *tr.* (foll. by *that* + clause or *to* + infin.) judge or consider (*is thought to be a fraud*). **3** *intr.* exercise the mind positively with one's ideas etc. (*let me think for a moment*). **4** *tr.* (foll. by *of* or *about*) **a** consider; be or become mentally aware of (*think of you constantly*). **b** form or entertain the idea of; imagine to oneself (*couldn't think of such a thing*). **c** choose mentally; hit upon (*think of a number*). **5** *tr.* have a half-formed intention (*I think I'll stay*). **6** *tr.* form a conception of (*cannot think how you do it*). **7** *tr.* reduce to a specified condition by thinking (*cannot think away a toothache*). **8** *tr.* recognize the presence or existence of (*the child thought no harm*). **9** *tr.* (foll. by *to* + infin.) intend or expect (*thinks to deceive us*). **10** *tr.* (foll. by *to* + infin.) remember (*did not think to lock the door*). —*n. colloq.* an act of thinking (*must have a think about that*). □ **think again** revise one's plans or opinions. **think aloud** utter one's thoughts as soon as they occur. **think back to** recall (a past event or time). **think better of** change one's mind about (an intention) after reconsideration. **think big** see BIG. **think fit** see FIT¹. **think for oneself** have an independent mind or attitude. **think little** (or **nothing**) **of** consider to be insignificant or unremarkable. **think much** (or **highly**) **of** have a high opinion of. **think on** (or **upon**) *archaic* think of or about. **think out 1** consider carefully. **2** produce (an idea etc.) by thinking. **think over** reflect upon in order to reach a decision. **think through** reflect fully upon (a problem etc.). **think twice** use careful consideration, avoid hasty action, etc. **think up** *colloq.* devise; produce by thought. □□ **thinkable** *adj.* [OE *thencan thōhte gethōht* f. Gmc]

thinker /ˈθɪŋkə(r)/ *n.* **1** a person who thinks, esp. in a specified way (*an original thinker*). **2** a person with a skilled or powerful mind.

thinking /ˈθɪŋkɪŋ/ *adj.* & *n.* —*adj.* using thought or rational judgement. —*n.* **1** opinion or judgement. **2** (in *pl.*) thoughts; courses of thought. □ **put on one's thinking cap** *colloq.* meditate on a problem.

think-tank /ˈθɪŋktæŋk/ *n.* a body of experts providing advice and ideas on specific national and commercial problems.

thinner /ˈθɪnə(r)/ *n.* a volatile liquid used to dilute paint etc.

thio- /ˈθaɪəʊ/ *comb. form* sulphur, esp. replacing oxygen in compounds (*thio-acid*). [Gk *theion* sulphur]

thiol /ˈθaɪɒl/ *n. Chem.* any organic compound containing an alcohol-like group but with sulphur in place of oxygen. [THIO- + -OL¹]

thiosulphate /ˌθaɪəʊˈsʌlfeɪt/ *n.* a sulphate in which one oxygen atom is replaced by sulphur.

thiourea /ˌθaɪəʊˈjʊərɪə/ *n.* a crystalline compound used in photography and the manufacture of synthetic resins.

third /θɜːd/ *n.* & *adj.* —*n.* **1** the position in a sequence corresponding to that of the number 3 in the sequence 1–3. **2** something occupying this position. **3** each of three equal parts of a thing. **4** = *third gear*. **5** *Mus.* **a** an interval or chord spanning three consecutive notes in the diatonic scale (e.g. C to E). **b** a note separated from another by this interval. **6 a** a place in the third class in an examination. **b** a person having this. —*adj.* that is the third. □ **third-best** *adj.* of third quality. —*n.* a thing in this category. **third class** the third-best group or category, esp. of hotel and train accommodation. **third-class** *adj.* **1** belonging to or travelling by the third class. **2** of poor quality; inferior. —*adv.* by the third class (*travels third-class*). **third degree** long and severe questioning esp. by police to obtain information or a confession. **third-degree** *Med.* denoting burns of the most severe kind, affecting lower layers of tissue. **third eye 1** *Hinduism* & *Buddhism* the 'eye of insight' in the forehead of an image of a deity, esp. the god Siva. **2**

the faculty of intuitive insight. **third force** a political group or party acting as a check on conflict between two opposing parties. **third gear** the third (and often next to highest) in a sequence of gears. **third man 1** a fielder positioned near the boundary behind the slips. **2** this position. **third part** each of three equal parts into which a thing is or might be divided. **third party 1** another party besides the two principals. **2** a bystander etc. **third-party** *adj.* (of insurance) covering damage or injury suffered by a person other than the insured. **third person 1** = *third party*. **2** *Gram.* see PERSON. **third-rate** inferior; very poor in quality. **third reading** a third presentation of a bill to a legislative assembly, in the UK to debate committee reports and in the US to consider it for the last time. **Third Reich** see REICH. **Third World** (usu. prec. by *the*) the developing countries of Asia, Africa, and Latin America. □□ **thirdly** *adv.* [OE *third(d)a, thridda* f. Gmc]

thirst /θɜːst/ *n. & v.* —*n.* **1** a physical need to drink liquid, or the feeling of discomfort caused by this. **2** a strong desire or craving (*a thirst for power*). —*v.intr.* (often foll. by *for* or *after*) **1** feel thirst. **2** have a strong desire. [OE *thurst, thyrstan* f. WG]

thirsty /ˈθɜːstɪ/ *adj.* (**thirstier, thirstiest**) **1** feeling thirst. **2** (of land, a season, etc.) dry or parched. **3** (often foll. by *for* or *after*) eager. **4** *colloq.* causing thirst (*thirsty work*). □□ **thirstily** *adv.* **thirstiness** *n.* [OE *thurstig, thyrstig* (as THIRST, -Y¹)]

thirteen /θɜːˈtiːn, ˈθɜː-/ *n. & adj.* —*n.* **1** one more than twelve, or three more than ten. **2** a symbol for this (13, xiii, XIII). **3** a size etc. denoted by thirteen. —*adj.* that amount to thirteen. □□ **thirteenth** *adj. & n.* [OE *thrēotīene* (as THREE, -TEEN)]

thirty /ˈθɜːtɪ/ *n. & adj.* —*n.* (*pl.* **-ies**) **1** the product of three and ten. **2** a symbol for this (30, xxx, XXX). **3** (in *pl.*) the numbers from 30 to 39, esp. the years of a century or of a person's life. —*adj.* that amount to thirty. □**thirty-first, -second**, etc. the ordinal numbers between thirtieth and fortieth. **Thirty-nine Articles** the points of doctrine assented to by those taking orders in the Church of England. **thirty-one, -two**, etc. the cardinal numbers between thirty and forty. **thirty-second note** esp. *US Mus.* = DEMI-SEMIQUAVER. **thirty-two-mo** a book with 32 leaves to the printing-sheet. □□ **thirtieth** *adj. & n.* **thirtyfold** *adj. & adv.* [OE *thrītig* (as THREE, -TY²)]

this /ðɪs/ *pron., adj., & adv.* —*demons.pron.* (*pl.* **these** /ðiːz/) **1** the person or thing close at hand or indicated or already named or understood (*can you see this?; this is my cousin*). **2** (contrasted with *that*) the person or thing nearer to hand or more immediately in mind. **3** the action, behaviour, or circumstances under consideration (*this won't do at all; what do you think of this?*). **4** (on the telephone): **a** *Brit.* the person speaking. **b** *US* the person spoken to. —*demons.adj.* (*pl.* **these** /ðiːz/) **1** designating the person or thing close at hand etc. (cf. senses 1, 2 of *pron.*). **2** (of time): **a** the present or current (*am busy all this week*). **b** relating to today (*this morning*). **c** just past or to come (*have been asking for it these three weeks*). **3** *colloq.* (in narrative) designating a person or thing previously unspecified (*then up came this policeman*). —*adv.* to this degree or extent (*knew him when he was this high; did not reach this far*). □**this and that** *colloq.* various unspecified examples of things (esp. trivial). **this here** *sl.* this particular (person or thing). **this much** the amount or extent about to be stated (*I know this much, that he was not there*). **this world** mortal life. [OE, neut. of *thes*]

thistle /ˈθɪs(ə)l/ *n.* **1** any of various prickly composite herbaceous plants of the genus *Cirsium, Carlina*, or *Carduus* etc., usu. with globular heads of purple flowers. **2** this as the Scottish national emblem. [OE *thistel* f. Gmc]

thistledown /ˈθɪs(ə)l,daʊn/ *n.* a light fluffy stuff attached to thistle-seeds and blown about in the wind.

thistly /ˈθɪslɪ/ *adj.* overgrown with thistles.

thither /ˈðɪðə(r)/ *adv.* archaic or *formal* to or towards that place. [OE *thider*, alt. (after HITHER) of *thæder*]

thixotropy /θɪkˈsɒtrəpɪ/ *n.* the property of becoming temporarily liquid when shaken or stirred etc., and returning to a gel on standing. □□ **thixotropic** /ˌθɪksə-ˈtrɒpɪk/ *adj.* [Gk *thixis* touching + *tropē* turning]

tho' var. of THOUGH.

thole¹ /θəʊl/ *n.* (in full **thole-pin**) **1** a pin in the gunwale of a boat as the fulcrum for an oar. **2** each of two such pins forming a rowlock. [OE *thol* fir-tree, peg]

thole² /θəʊl/ *v.tr. Sc.* or *archaic* **1** undergo or suffer (pain, grief, etc.). **2** permit or admit of. [OE *tholian* f. Gmc]

tholos /ˈθɒlɒs/ *n.* (*pl.* **tholoi** /-lɔɪ/) *Gk Antiq.* a dome-shaped tomb, esp. of the Mycenaean period. [Gk]

Thomism /ˈtəʊmɪz(ə)m/ *n.* the doctrine of Thomas Aquinas, Italian scholastic philosopher and theologian d. 1274, or of his followers. □□ **Thomist** *n.* **Thomistic** /-ˈmɪstɪk/ *adj.* **Thomistical** /-ˈmɪstɪk(ə)l/ *adj.*

thong /θɒŋ/ *n. & v.* —*n.* **1** a narrow strip of hide or leather used as the lash of a whip, as a halter or rein, etc. **2** *Austral., NZ, & US* = FLIP-FLOP. —*v.tr.* **1** provide with a thong. **2** strike with a thong. [OE *thwang, thwong* f. Gmc]

thorax /ˈθɔːræks/ *n.* (*pl.* **thoraces** /ˈθɔːrə,siːz/ or **thoraxes**) **1** *Anat. & Zool.* the part of the trunk between the neck and the abdomen. **2** *Gk Antiq.* a breastplate or cuirass. □□ **thoracal** /ˈθɔːrək(ə)l/ *adj.* **thoracic** /θɒˈræsɪk/ *adj.* [L f. Gk *thōrax -akos*]

thoria /ˈθɔːrɪə/ *n.* the oxide of thorium.

thorium /ˈθɔːrɪəm/ *n. Chem.* a radioactive metallic element occurring naturally in monazite, the oxide of which is used in gas-mantles. ¶ Symb.: **Th**. [*Thor*, Scand. god of thunder]

thorn /θɔːn/ *n.* **1** a stiff sharp-pointed projection on a plant. **2** a thorn-bearing shrub or tree. **3** the name of an Old English and Icelandic runic letter, = th. □**on thorns** continuously uneasy esp. in fear of being detected. **thorn-apple 1** a poisonous plant of the nightshade family, *Datura stramonium*. **2** the prickly fruit of this. **a thorn in one's flesh** (or **side**) a constant annoyance. □□ **thornless** *adj.* **thornproof** *adj.* [OE f. Gmc]

thornback /ˈθɔːnbæk/ *n.* a ray, *Raja clavata*, with spines on the back and tail.

thornbill /ˈθɔːnbɪl/ *n.* **1** any Australian warbler of the genus *Acanthiza*. **2** any of various South American humming-birds, esp. of the genus *Chalcostigma*.

thorntail /ˈθɔːnteɪl/ *n.* any S. American hummingbird of the genus *Popelairia*.

thorny /ˈθɔːnɪ/ *adj.* (**thornier, thorniest**) **1** having many thorns. **2** (of a subject) hard to handle without offence; problematic. □□ **thornily** *adv.* **thorniness** *n.*

thorough /ˈθʌrə/ *adj.* **1** complete and unqualified; not superficial (*needs a thorough change*). **2** acting or done with great care and completeness (*the report is most thorough*). **3** absolute (*a thorough nuisance*). □**thorough bass** a bass part for a keyboard player with numerals and symbols below to indicate the harmony. **thorough-paced 1** (of a horse) trained to all paces. **2** complete or unqualified. □□ **thoroughly** *adv.* **thoroughness** *n.* [orig. as adv. and prep. in the senses of *through*, f. OE *thuruh* var. of *thurh* THROUGH]

thoroughbred /ˈθʌrə,bred/ *adj. & n.* —*adj.* **1** of pure breed. **2** high-spirited. —*n.* **1** a thoroughbred animal, esp. a horse. **2** (**Thoroughbred**) **a** a breed of racehorses originating from English mares and Arab stallions. **b** a horse of this breed.

thoroughfare /ˈθʌrə,feə(r)/ *n.* a road or path open at both ends, esp. for traffic.

thoroughgoing /ˈθʌrə,gəʊɪŋ, -ˈgəʊɪŋ/ *adj.* **1** uncompromising; not superficial. **2** (usu. *attrib.*) extreme; out and out.

thorp /θɔːp/ *n.* (also **thorpe**) *archaic* a village or hamlet. ¶ Now usually only in place-names. [OE *thorp, throp*, f. Gmc]

Thos. *abbr.* Thomas.

those *pl.* of THAT.

thou[1] /ðaʊ/ *pron.* (*obj.* **thee** /ðiː/; *poss.* **thy** or **thine**; *pl.* **ye** or **you**) second person singular pronoun, now replaced by *you* except in some formal, liturgical, dialect, and poetic uses. [OE *thu* f. Gmc]

thou[2] /ðaʊ/ *n.* (*pl.* same or **thous**) *colloq.* **1** a thousand. **2** one thousandth. [abbr.]

though /ðəʊ/ *conj.* & *adv.* (also **tho'**) —*conj.* **1** despite the fact that (*though it was early we went to bed; though annoyed, I agreed*). **2** (introducing a possibility) even if (*ask him though he may refuse; would not attend though the Queen herself were there*). **3** and yet; nevertheless (*she read on, though not to the very end*). **4** in spite of being (*ready though unwilling*). —*adv. colloq.* however; all the same (*I wish you had told me, though*). [ME *thoh* etc. f. ON *thó* etc., corresp. to OE *théah*, f. Gmc]

thought[1] /θɔːt/ *n.* **1** the process or power of thinking; the faculty of reason. **2** a way of thinking characteristic of or associated with a particular time, people, group, etc. (*medieval European thought*). **3** sober reflection or consideration (*gave it much thought*). **4** an idea or piece of reasoning produced by thinking (*many good thoughts came out of the discussion*). **5** (foll. by *of* + verbal noun or *to* + infin.) a partly formed intention or hope (*gave up all thoughts of winning; had no thought to go*). **6** (usu. in *pl.*) what one is thinking; one's opinion (*have you any thoughts on this?*). **7** the subject of one's thinking (*my one thought was to get away*). **8** (prec. by *a*) somewhat (*seems to me a thought arrogant*). □**give thought to** consider; think about. **in thought** thinking, meditating. **take thought** consider matters. **thought-provoking** stimulating serious thought. **thought-reader** a person supposedly able to perceive another's thoughts. **thought-reading** the supposed perception of what another is thinking. **thought transference** telepathy. **thought-wave** an undulation of the supposed medium of thought transference. □□ **-thoughted** *adj.* (in *comb.*). [OE *thōht* (as THINK)]

thought[2] *past* and *past part.* of THINK.

thoughtful /ˈθɔːtfʊl/ *adj.* **1** engaged in or given to meditation. **2** (of a book, writer, remark, etc.) giving signs of serious thought. **3** (often foll. by *of*) (of a person or conduct) considerate; not haphazard or unfeeling. □□ **thoughtfully** *adv.* **thoughtfulness** *n.*

thoughtless /ˈθɔːtlɪs/ *adj.* **1** careless of consequences or of others' feelings. **2** due to lack of thought. □□ **thoughtlessly** *adv.* **thoughtlessness** *n.*

thousand /ˈθaʊz(ə)nd/ *n.* & *adj.* —*n.* (*pl.* **thousands** or (in sense 1) **thousand**) (in *sing.* prec. by *a* or *one*) **1** the product of a hundred and ten. **2** a symbol for this (1,000, m, M). **3** a set of a thousand things. **4** (in *sing.* or *pl.*) *colloq.* a large number. —*adj.* that amount to a thousand. □□ **thousandfold** *adj.* & *adv.* **thousandth** *adj.* & *n.* [OE *thūsend* f. Gmc]

thrall /θrɔːl/ *n. literary* **1** (often foll. by *of*, *to*) a slave (of a person, or a power or influence). **2** bondage; a state of slavery or servitude (*in thrall*). □□ **thraldom** *n.* (also **thralldom**). [OE *thrǽl* f. ON *thrǽll*, perh. f. a Gmc root = run]

thrash /θræʃ/ *v.* & *n.* —*v.* **1** *tr.* beat severely, esp. with a stick or whip. **2** *tr.* defeat thoroughly in a contest. **3** *intr.* (of a paddle wheel, branch, etc.) act like a flail; deliver repeated blows. **4** *intr.* (foll. by *about*, *around*) move or fling the limbs about violently or in panic. **5** *intr.* (of a ship) keep striking the waves; make way against the wind or tide (*thrash to windward*). **6** *tr.* = THRESH 1. —*n.* **1** an act of thrashing. **2** *colloq.* a party, esp. a lavish one. □**thrash out** discuss to a conclusion. □□ **thrashing** *n.* [OE *therscan*, later *threscan*, f. Gmc]

thrasher[1] /ˈθræʃə(r)/ *n.* **1** a person or thing that thrashes. **2** = THRESHER.

thrasher[2] /ˈθræʃə(r)/ *n.* any of various long-tailed N. American thrushlike birds of the family Mimidae. [perh. f. E dial. *thrusher* = THRUSH[1]]

thrawn /θrɔːn/ *adj. Sc.* **1** perverse or ill-tempered. **2** misshapen, crooked. [Sc. form of *thrown* in obs. senses]

thread /θred/ *n.* & *v.* —*n.* **1 a** a spun-out filament of cotton, silk, or glass etc.; yarn. **b** a length of this. **2** a thin cord of twisted yarns used esp. in sewing and weaving. **3** anything regarded as threadlike with reference to its continuity or connectedness (*the thread of life; lost the thread of his argument*). **4** the spiral ridge of a screw. **5** (in *pl.*) *sl.* clothes. **6** a thin seam or vein of ore. —*v.tr.* **1** pass a thread through the eye of (a needle). **2** put (beads) on a thread. **3** arrange (material in a strip form, e.g. film or magnetic tape) in the proper position on equipment. **4** make (one's way) carefully through a crowded place, over a difficult route, etc. **5** streak (hair etc.) as with threads. **6** form a screw-thread on. □**hang by a thread** be in a precarious state, position, etc. **thread mark** a mark in the form of a thin line made in banknote paper with highly coloured silk fibres to prevent photographic counterfeiting. □□ **threader** *n.* **threadlike** *adj.* [OE *thrǽd* f. Gmc]

threadbare /ˈθredbeə(r)/ *adj.* **1** (of cloth) so worn that the nap is lost and the thread visible. **2** (of a person) wearing such clothes. **3 a** hackneyed. **b** feeble or insubstantial (*a threadbare excuse*).

threadfin /ˈθredfɪn/ *n.* any small tropical fish of the family Polynemidae, with long streamers from its pectoral fins.

threadworm /ˈθredwɜːm/ *n.* any of various esp. parasitic threadlike nematode worms, e.g. the pinworm.

thready /ˈθredɪ/ *adj.* (**threadier**, **threadiest**) **1** of or like a thread. **2** (of a person's pulse) scarcely perceptible.

threat /θret/ *n.* **1 a** a declaration of an intention to punish or hurt. **b** *Law* a menace of bodily hurt or injury, such as may restrain a person's freedom of action. **2** an indication of something undesirable coming (*the threat of war*). **3** a person or thing as a likely cause of harm etc. [OE *thrēat* affliction etc. f. Gmc]

threaten /ˈθret(ə)n/ *v.tr.* **1** make a threat or threats against. **2** be a sign or indication of (something undesirable). **3** (foll. by *to* + infin.) announce one's intention to do an undesirable or unexpected thing (*threatened to resign*). **4** (also *absol.*) give warning of the infliction of (harm etc.) (*the clouds were threatening rain*). □□ **threatener** *n.* **threateningly** *adv.* [OE *thrēatnian* (as THREAT)]

three /θriː/ *n.* & *adj.* —*n.* **1 a** one more than two, or seven less than ten. **b** a symbol for this (3, iii, III). **2** a size etc. denoted by three. **3** the time of three o'clock. **4** a set of three. **5** a card with three pips. —*adj.* that amount to three. □**three-card trick** a game in which bets are made on which is the queen among three cards lying face downwards. **three cheers** see CHEER. **three-colour process** a process of reproducing natural colours by combining photographic images in the three primary colours. **three-cornered 1** triangular. **2** (of a contest etc.) between three parties as individuals. **three-decker 1** a warship with three gun-decks. **2** a novel in three volumes. **3** a sandwich with three slices of bread. **three-dimensional** having or appearing to have length, breadth, and depth. **three-handed 1** having or using three hands. **2** involving three players. **three-legged race** a running-race between pairs, one member of each pair having the left leg tied to the right leg of the other. **three-line whip** a written notice, underlined three times to denote urgency, to members of a political party to attend a parliamentary vote. **three parts** three quarters. **three-phase** see PHASE. **three-piece** consisting of three items (esp. of a suit of clothes or a suite of furniture). **three-ply** *adj.* of three strands, webs, or thicknesses. —*n.* **1** three-ply wool. **2** three-ply wood made by gluing together three layers with the grain in different directions. **three-point landing** *Aeron.* the landing of an aircraft on the two main wheels and the tail wheel or skid simultaneously. **three-point turn** a method of turning a vehicle round in a narrow space by moving forwards, backwards, and forwards again in a sequence of arcs. **three-quarter** *n.* (also **three-quarter back**) *Rugby Football* any of three or four players just behind the half-backs. —*adj.* **1** consisting of three-fourths of something. **2** (of a portrait) going down to the hips or showing three-fourths of the face (between full face and profile). **three-quarters** three parts out of four. **three-ring circus** esp. *US* **1** a circus with three rings for simultaneous performances. **2** an extravagant display. **the three Rs** reading, writing, and arithmetic, regarded as the fundamentals of learning. **three-way** involving three ways or participants. **three-wheeler** a vehicle with three wheels. [OE *thrī* f. Gmc]

threefold /ˈθriːfəʊld/ *adj. & adv.* **1** three times as much or as many. **2** consisting of three parts.

threepence /ˈθrepəns, ˈθrʊpəns/ *n. Brit.* the sum of three pence, esp. before decimalization.

threepenny /ˈθrepəni, ˈθrʊpəni/ *adj. Brit.* costing three pence, esp. before decimalization. □ **threepenny bit** *hist.* a former coin worth three old pence.

threescore /ˈθriːskɔː(r)/ *n. archaic* sixty.

threesome /ˈθriːsəm/ *n.* **1** a group of three persons. **2** a game etc. for three, esp. *Golf* of one against two.

thremmatology /ˌθremaˈtɒlədʒi/ *n.* the science of breeding animals and plants. [Gk *thremma -matos* nursling + -LOGY]

threnody /ˈθrenədi/ *n.* (also **threnode** /ˈθrenəʊd/) (*pl.* **-ies** or **threnodes**) **1** a lamentation, esp. on a person's death. **2** a song of lamentation. □□ **threnodial** /-ˈnəʊdɪəl/ *adj.* **threnodic** /-ˈnɒdɪk/ *adj.* **threnodist** /ˈθrenədɪst/ *n.* [Gk *thrēnōidia* f. *thrēnos* wailing + *ōidē* ODE]

threonine /ˈθriːəˌniːn, -nɪn/ *n. Biochem.* an amino acid, considered essential for growth. [*threose* (name of a tetrose sugar) ult. f. Gk *eruthros* red + -INE⁴]

thresh /θreʃ/ *v.* **1** *tr.* beat out or separate grain from (corn etc.). **2** *intr.* = THRASH *v.* 4. **3** *tr.* (foll. by *over*) analyse (a problem etc.) in search of a solution. □ **threshing-floor** a hard level floor for threshing esp. with flails. **threshing-machine** a power-driven machine for separating the grain from the straw or husk. **thresh out** = *thrash out.* [var. of THRASH]

thresher /ˈθreʃə(r)/ *n.* **1** a person or machine that threshes. **2** a shark, *Alopias vulpinus*, with a long upper lobe to its tail, that it can lash about.

threshold /ˈθreʃəʊld, -həʊld/ *n.* **1** a strip of wood or stone forming the bottom of a doorway and crossed in entering a house or room etc. **2** a point of entry or beginning (*on the threshold of a new century*). **3** *Physiol. & Psychol.* a limit below which a stimulus causes no reaction (*pain threshold*). **4** *Physics* a limit below which no reaction occurs, esp. a minimum dose of radiation producing a specified effect. **5** (often *attrib.*) a step in a scale of wages or taxation, usu. operative in specified conditions. [OE *therscold, threscold*, etc., rel. to THRASH in the sense 'tread']

threw *past* of THROW.

thrice /θraɪs/ *adv. archaic* or *literary* **1** three times. **2** (esp. in *comb.*) highly (*thrice-blessed*). [ME *thries* f. *thrie* (adv.) f. OE *thrīwa, thrīga* (as THREE, -S°)]

thrift /θrɪft/ *n.* **1** frugality; economical management. **2** a plant of the genus *Armeria*, esp. the sea pink. □ **thrift shop** (or **store**) a shop selling second-hand items usu. for charity. [ME f. ON (as THRIVE)]

thriftless /ˈθrɪftlɪs/ *adj.* wasteful, improvident. □□ **thriftlessly** *adv.* **thriftlessness** *n.*

thrifty /ˈθrɪfti/ *adj.* (**thriftier, thriftiest**) **1** economical, frugal. **2** thriving, prosperous. □□ **thriftily** *adv.* **thriftiness** *n.*

thrill /θrɪl/ *n. & v.* —*n.* **1** a wave or nervous tremor of emotion or sensation (*a thrill of joy; a thrill of re-*

cognition). **2** a throb or pulsation. **3** *Med.* a vibratory movement or resonance heard in auscultation. —*v.* **1** *intr. & tr.* feel or cause to feel a thrill (*thrilled to the sound; a voice that thrilled millions*). **2** *intr.* quiver or throb with or as with emotion. **3** *intr.* (foll. by *through, over, along*) (of an emotion etc.) pass with a thrill through etc. (*fear thrilled through my veins*). □□ **thrilling** *adj.* **thrillingly** *adv.* [*thirl* (now dial.) f. OE *thyrlian* pierce f. *thȳrel* hole f. *thurh* THROUGH]

thriller /ˈθrɪlə(r)/ *n.* an exciting or sensational story or play etc., esp. one involving crime or espionage.

thrips /θrɪps/ *n.* (*pl.* same) any insect of the order Thysanoptera, esp. a pest injurious to plants. [L f. Gk, = woodworm]

thrive /θraɪv/ *v.intr.* (*past* **throve** /θrəʊv/ or **thrived**; *past part.* **thriven** /ˈθrɪv(ə)n/ or **thrived**) **1** prosper or flourish. **2** grow rich. **3** (of a child, animal, or plant) grow vigorously. [ME f. ON *thrifask* refl. of *thrifa* grasp]

thro' var. of THROUGH.

throat /θrəʊt/ *n.* **1 a** the windpipe or gullet. **b** the front part of the neck containing this. **2** *literary* **a** a voice, esp. of a songbird. **b** a thing compared to a throat, esp. a narrow passage, entrance, or exit. **3** *Naut.* the forward upper corner of a fore-and-aft sail. □ **cut one's own throat** bring about one's own downfall. **ram** (or **thrust**) **down a person's throat** force (a thing) on a person's attention. □□ **-throated** *adj.* (in *comb.*). [OE *throte, throtu* f. Gmc]

throaty /ˈθrəʊti/ *adj.* (**throatier, throatiest**) **1** (of a voice) deficient in clarity; hoarsely resonant. **2** guttural; uttered in the throat. **3** having a prominent or capacious throat. □□ **throatily** *adv.* **throatiness** *n.*

throb /θrɒb/ *v. & n.* —*v.intr.* (**throbbed, throbbing**) **1** palpitate or pulsate, esp. with more than the usual force or rapidity. **2** vibrate or quiver with a persistent rhythm or with emotion. —*n.* **1** a throbbing. **2** a palpitation or (esp. violent) pulsation. [ME, app. imit.]

throe /θrəʊ/ *n.* (usu. in *pl.*) **1** a violent pang, esp. of childbirth or death. **2** anguish. □ **in the throes of** struggling with the task of. [ME *throwe* perh. f. OE *thrēa, thrawu* calamity, alt. perh. by assoc. with *woe*]

thrombi *pl.* of THROMBUS.

thrombin /ˈθrɒmbɪn/ *n.* an enzyme promoting the clotting of blood. [as THROMBUS + -IN]

thrombocyte /ˈθrɒmbəˌsaɪt/ *n.* a blood platelet, a small plate of protoplasm concerned in the coagulation of blood. [as THROMBUS + -CYTE]

thrombose /θrɒmˈbəʊz/ *v.tr. & intr.* affect with or undergo thrombosis. [back-form. f. THROMBOSIS]

thrombosis /θrɒmˈbəʊsɪs/ *n.* (*pl.* **thromboses** /-siːz/) the coagulation of the blood in a blood-vessel or organ. □□ **thrombotic** /-ˈbɒtɪk/ *adj.* [mod.L f. Gk *thrombōsis* curdling (as THROMBUS)]

thrombus /ˈθrɒmbəs/ *n.* (*pl.* **thrombi** /-baɪ/) a blood-clot formed in the vascular system and impeding the blood flow. [mod.L f. Gk *thrombos* lump, blood-clot]

throne /θrəʊn/ *n. & v.* —*n.* **1** a chair of State for a sovereign or bishop etc. **2** sovereign power (*came to the throne*). **3** (in *pl.*) the third order of the ninefold celestial hierarchy. **4** *colloq.* a lavatory seat and bowl. —*v.tr.* place on a throne. □□ **throneless** *adj.* [ME f. OF *trone* f. L *thronus* f. Gk *thronos* high seat]

throng /θrɒŋ/ *n. & v.* —*n.* **1** a crowd of people. **2** (often foll. by *of*) a multitude, esp. in a small space. —*v.* **1** *intr.* come in great numbers (*crowds thronged to the stadium*). **2** *tr.* flock into or crowd round; fill with or as with a crowd (*crowds thronged the streets*). [ME *thrang, throng*, OE *gethrang*, f. verbal stem *thring-thrang-*]

throstle /ˈθrɒs(ə)l/ *n.* **1** a song thrush. **2** (in full **throstle-frame**) a machine for continuously spinning wool or cotton etc. [OE f. Gmc: rel. to THRUSH¹]

throttle /ˈθrɒt(ə)l/ *n. & v.* —*n.* **1 a** (in full **throttle-valve**) a valve controlling the flow of fuel or steam etc. in an engine. **b** (in full **throttle-lever**) a lever or pedal operating this valve. **2** the throat, gullet, or windpipe. —*v.tr.* **1** choke or strangle. **2** prevent the utterance etc. of. **3** control (an engine or steam etc.) with a throttle. □ **throttle back (or down)** reduce the speed of (an engine or vehicle) by throttling. □□ **throttler** *n.* [ME *throtel* (v.), perh. f. THROAT + -LE⁴: (n.) perh. a dimin. of THROAT]

through /θruː/ *prep., adv.,* & *adj.* (also **thro'**, *US* **thru**) —*prep.* **1 a** from end to end or from side to side of. **b** going in one side or end and out the other of. **2** between or among (*swam through the waves*). **3** from beginning to end (*read through the letter; went through many difficulties*). **4** because of; by the agency, means, or fault of (*lost it through carelessness*). **5** *US* up to and including (*Monday through Friday*). —*adv.* **1** through a thing; from side to side, end to end, or beginning to end (*went through to the garden; would not let us through*). **2** having completed (esp. successfully) (*are through their exams*). **3** so as to be connected by telephone (*will put you through*). —*attrib.adj.* **1** (of a journey, route, etc.) done without a change of line or vehicle etc. or with one ticket. **2** (of traffic) going through a place to its destination. □ **be through** *colloq.* **1** (often foll. by *with*) have finished. **2** (often foll. by *with*) cease to have dealings. **3** have no further prospects (*is through as a politician*). **no through road** = *no thoroughfare.* **through and through 1** thoroughly, completely. **2** through again and again. [OE *thurh* f. WG]

throughout /θruːˈaʊt/ *prep.* & *adv.* —*prep.* right through; from end to end of (*throughout the town; throughout the 18th century*). —*adv.* in every part or respect (*the timber was rotten throughout*).

throughput /ˈθruːpʊt/ *n.* the amount of material put through a process, esp. in manufacturing or computing.

throughway /ˈθruːweɪ/ *n.* (also **thruway**) *US* a thoroughfare, esp. a motorway.

throve *past* of THRIVE.

throw /θrəʊ/ *v.* & *n.* —*v.tr.* (*past* **threw** /θruː/; *past part.* **thrown** /θrəʊn/) **1** propel with some force through the air or in a particular direction. **2** force violently into a specified position or state (*the ship was thrown on the rocks; threw themselves down*). **3** compel suddenly to be in a specified condition (*was thrown out of work*). **4** turn or move (part of the body) quickly or suddenly (*threw an arm out*). **5** project or cast (light, a shadow, a spell, etc.). **6 a** bring to the ground in wrestling. **b** (of a horse) unseat (its rider). **7** *colloq.* disconcert (*the question threw me for a moment*). **8** (foll. by *on, off,* etc.) put (clothes etc.) hastily on or off etc. **9 a** cause (dice) to fall on a table. **b** obtain (a specified number) by throwing dice. **10** cause to pass or extend suddenly to another state or position (*threw in the army; threw a bridge across the river*). **11** move (a switch or lever) so as to operate it. **12** a form (ceramic ware) on a potter's wheel. **b** turn (wood etc.) on a lathe. **13** have (a fit or tantrum etc.). **14** give (a party). **15** *colloq.* lose (a contest or race etc.) intentionally. **16** *Cricket* bowl (a ball) with an illegitimate sudden straightening of the elbow. **17** (of a snake) cast (its skin). **18** (of an animal) give birth to (young). **19** twist (silk etc.) into thread or yarn. **20** (often foll. by *into*) put into another form or language etc. —*n.* **1** an act of throwing. **2** the distance a thing is or may be thrown (*a record throw with the hammer*). **3** the act of being thrown in wrestling. **4** *Geol.* & *Mining* **a** a fault in strata. **b** the amount of vertical displacement caused by this. **5** a machine or device giving rapid rotary motion. **6** the movement of a crank or cam etc. **b** the extent of this. **7** the distance moved by the pointer of an instrument etc. **8** (in full **throw rug**) *US* **a** a light cover for furniture. **b** a light rug. **9** (prec. by *a*) *sl.* each; per item (*sold at £10 a throw*). □ **throw about (or around) 1** throw in various directions. **2** spend (one's money) ostentatiously. **throw away 1** discard as useless or unwanted. **2** waste or fail to make use of (an opportunity etc.). **3** discard (a card). **4** *Theatr.* speak

(lines) with deliberate underemphasis. **5** (in *passive;* often foll. by *on*) be wasted (*the advice was thrown away on him*). **throw-away** *adj.* **1** meant to be thrown away after (one) use. **2** (of lines etc.) deliberately underemphasized. —*n.* a thing to be thrown away after (one) use. **throw back 1** revert to ancestral character. **2** (usu. in *passive;* foll. by *on*) compel to rely on (*was thrown back on his savings*). **throw-back** *n.* **1** reversion to ancestral character. **2** an instance of this. **throw cold water on** see COLD. **throw down** cause to fall. **throw down the gauntlet (or glove)** issue a challenge. **throw dust in a person's eyes** mislead a person by misrepresentation or distraction. **throw good money after bad** incur further loss in a hopeless attempt to recoup a previous loss. **throw one's hand in 1** abandon one's chances in a card game, esp. poker. **2** give up; withdraw from a contest. **throw in 1** interpose (a word or remark). **2** include at no extra cost. **3** throw (a football) from the edge of the pitch where it has gone out of play. **4** *Cricket* return (the ball) from the outfield. **5** *Cards* give (a player) the lead, to the player's disadvantage. **throw-in** *n.* the throwing in of a football during play. **throw in one's lot with** see LOT. **throw in the towel** admit defeat. **throw light on** see LIGHT¹. **throw off 1** discard; contrive to get rid of. **2** write or utter in an offhand manner. **3** (of hounds or a hunt) begin hunting; make a start. **throw-off** the start in a hunt or race. **throw oneself at** seek blatantly as a spouse or sexual partner. **throw oneself into** engage vigorously in. **throw oneself on (or upon) 1** rely completely on. **2** attack. **throw open** (often foll. by *to*) **1** cause to be suddenly or widely open. **2** make accessible. **throw out 1** put out forcibly or suddenly. **2** discard as unwanted. **3** expel (a troublemaker etc.). **4** build (a wing of a house, a pier, or a projecting or prominent thing). **5** put forward tentatively. **6** reject (a proposal or bill in Parliament). **7** confuse or distract (a person speaking, thinking, or acting) from the matter in hand. **8** *Cricket* & *Baseball* put out (an opponent) by throwing the ball to the wicket or base. **throw over** desert or abandon. **throw stones** cast aspersions. **throw together 1** assemble hastily. **2** bring into casual contact. **throw up 1** abandon. **2** resign from. **3** *colloq.* vomit. **4** erect hastily. **5** bring to notice. **6** lift (a sash-window) quickly. **throw up (or in) the sponge 1** (of a boxer or his attendant) throw the sponge used between rounds into the air as a token of defeat. **2** abandon a contest; admit defeat. **throw one's weight about (or around)** *colloq.* act with unpleasant self-assertiveness. □□ **throwable** *adj.* **thrower** *n.* (also in *comb.*). [OE *thrāwan* twist, turn f. WG]

throwster /ˈθrəʊstə(r)/ *n.* a person who throws silk.

thru *US* var. of THROUGH.

thrum¹ /θrʌm/ *v.* & *n.* —*v.* (**thrummed**, **thrumming**) **1** *tr.* play (a stringed instrument) monotonously or unskilfully. **2** *intr.* (often foll. by *on*) drum idly. —*n.* **1** such playing. **2** the resulting sound. [imit.]

thrum² /θrʌm/ *n.* & *v.* —*n.* **1** the unwoven end of a warp-thread, or the whole of such ends, left when the finished web is cut away. **2** any short loose thread. —*v.tr.* (**thrummed**, **thrumming**) make of or cover with thrums. □□ **thrummer** *n.* **thrummy** *adj.* [OE f. Gmc]

thrush¹ /θrʌʃ/ *n.* any small or medium-sized songbird of the family Turdidae, esp. a song thrush or mistle thrush (see MISTLE THRUSH, *song thrush*). [OE *thrysce* f. Gmc: cf. THROSTLE]

thrush² /θrʌʃ/ *n.* **1 a** a disease, esp. of children, marked by whitish fungous vesicles in the mouth and throat. **b** a similar disease of the vagina. **2** inflammation affecting the frog of a horse's foot. [17th c.: orig. unkn.]

thrust /θrʌst/ *v.* & *n.* —*v.* (*past* and *past part.* **thrust**) **1** *tr.* push with a sudden impulse or with force (*thrust the letter into my pocket*). **2** *tr.* (foll. by *on*) impose (a thing) forcibly; enforce acceptance of (a thing) (*had it thrust on me*). **3** *intr.* (foll. by *at, through*) pierce or stab; make a sudden lunge. **4** *tr.* make (one's way) forcibly. **5** *intr.* (foll. by *through*, *past*, etc.) force oneself (*thrust past me abruptly*). —*n.* **1** a sudden or forcible push or lunge. **2** the propulsive force developed by a jet or rocket engine. **3** a strong attempt to penetrate an enemy's line or territory. **4** a remark aimed at a person. **5** the stress between the parts of an arch etc. **6** (often foll. by *of*) the chief theme or gist of remarks etc. **7** an attack with the point of a weapon. **8** (in full **thrust fault**) *Geol.* a low-angle reverse fault, with older strata displaced horizontally over newer. □**thrust-block** a casting or frame carrying or containing the bearings on which the collars of a propeller shaft press. **thrust oneself** (or **one's nose**) **in** obtrude, interfere. **thrust stage** a stage extending into the audience. [ME *thruste* etc. f. ON *thrýsta*]

thruster /ˈθrʌstə(r)/ *n.* **1** a person or thing that thrusts. **2** a small rocket engine used to provide extra or correcting thrust on a spacecraft.

thruway *US* var. of THROUGHWAY.

thud /θʌd/ *n. & v.* —*n.* a low dull sound as of a blow on a non-resonant surface. —*v.intr.* (**thudded**, **thudding**) make or fall with a thud. □□**thuddingly** *adv.* [prob. f. OE *thyddan* thrust]

thug /θʌg/ *n.* **1** a vicious or brutal ruffian. **2** (**Thug**) *hist.* a member of a religious organization of robbers and assassins in India. □□**thuggery** *n.* **thuggish** *adj.* **thuggishly** *adv.* **thuggishness** *n.* [Hindi & Marathi *ṭhag* swindler]

thuggee /θʌˈgiː/ *n. hist.* murder practised by the Thugs. □□**thuggism** *n.* [Hindi *ṭhagī* (as THUG)]

thuja /ˈθuːjə/ *n.* (also **thuya**) any evergreen coniferous tree of the genus *Thuja*, with small leaves closely pressed to the branches; arbor vitae. [mod.L f. Gk *thuia*, an Afr. tree]

thulium /ˈθjuːlɪəm/ *n. Chem.* a soft metallic element of the lanthanide series, occurring naturally in apatite. ¶ Symb.: **Tm**. [mod.L f. L *Thule* name of a region in the remote north]

thumb /θʌm/ *n. & v.* —*n.* **1 a** a short thick terminal projection on the human hand, set lower and apart from the other four and opposable to them. **b** a digit of other animals corresponding to this. **2** part of a glove etc. for a thumb. —*v.* **1** *tr.* wear or soil (pages etc.) with a thumb (*a well-thumbed book*). **2** *intr.* turn over pages with or as with a thumb (*thumbed through the directory*). **3** *tr.* request or obtain (a lift in a passing vehicle) by signalling with a raised thumb. **4** *tr.* use the thumb in a gesture. □**be all thumbs** be clumsy with one's hands. **thumb index** *n.* a set of lettered grooves cut down the side of a diary, dictionary, etc. for easy reference. —*v.tr.* provide (a book etc.) with these. **thumb one's nose** = *cock a snook* (see SNOOK[1]). **thumb-nut** a nut shaped for turning with the thumb and forefinger. **thumbs down** an indication of rejection or failure. **thumbs up** an indication of satisfaction or approval. **under a person's thumb** completely dominated by a person. □□**thumbed** *adj.* (also in *comb.*). **thumbless** *adj.* [OE *thūma* f. a WG root = swell]

thumbnail /ˈθʌmneɪl/ *n.* **1** the nail of a thumb. **2** (*attrib.*) denoting conciseness (*a thumbnail sketch*).

thumbprint /ˈθʌmprɪnt/ *n.* an impression of a thumb esp. as used for identification.

thumbscrew /ˈθʌmskruː/ *n.* **1** an instrument of torture for crushing the thumbs. **2** a screw with a flattened head for turning with the thumb and forefinger.

thumbtack /ˈθʌmtæk/ *n.* esp. *US* a drawing-pin.

thump /θʌmp/ *v. & n.* —*v.* **1** *tr.* beat or strike heavily esp. with the fist (*threatened to thump me*). **2** *intr.* throb or pulsate strongly (*my heart was thumping*). **3** *intr.* (foll. by *at*, *on*, etc.) deliver blows, esp. to attract attention (*thumped on the door*). **4** *tr.* (often foll. by *out*) play (a tune on a piano etc.) with a heavy touch. **5** *intr.* tread heavily. —*n.* **1** a heavy blow. **2** the sound of this. □□**thumper** *n.* [imit.]

thumping /ˈθʌmpɪŋ/ *adj. colloq.* big, prominent (*a thumping majority*; *a thumping lie*).

thunder /ˈθʌndə(r)/ *n. & v.* —*n.* **1** a loud rumbling or crashing noise heard after a lightning flash and due to the expansion of rapidly heated air. **2** a resounding loud deep noise (*thunders of applause*). **3** strong censure or denunciation. —*v.* **1** *intr.* (prec. by *it* as subject) thunder sounds (*it is thundering*; *if it thunders*). **2** *intr.* make or proceed with a noise suggestive of thunder (*the applause thundered in my ears*; *the traffic thundered past*). **3** *tr.* utter or communicate (approval, disapproval, etc.) loudly or impressively. **4** *intr.* (foll. by *against* etc.) **a** make violent threats etc. against. **b** criticize violently. □**steal a person's thunder** spoil the effect of another's idea, action, etc. by expressing or doing it first. **thunder-box** *colloq.* a primitive lavatory. □□**thunderer** *n.* **thunderless** *adj.* **thundery** *adj.* [OE *thunor* f. Gmc]

thunderbolt /ˈθʌndəbəʊlt/ *n.* **1 a** a flash of lightning with a simultaneous crash of thunder. **b** a stone etc. imagined to be a destructive bolt. **2** a sudden or unexpected occurrence or item of news. **3** a supposed bolt or shaft as a destructive agent, esp. as an attribute of a god.

thunderclap /ˈθʌndəklæp/ *n.* **1** a crash of thunder. **2** something startling or unexpected.

thundercloud /ˈθʌndəklaʊd/ *n.* a cumulus cloud with a tall diffuse top, charged with electricity and producing thunder and lightning.

thunderhead /ˈθʌndəhed/ *n.* esp. *US* a rounded cumulus cloud projecting upwards and heralding thunder.

thundering /ˈθʌndərɪŋ/ *adj. colloq.* very big or great (*a thundering nuisance*). □□**thunderingly** *adv.*

thunderous /ˈθʌndərəs/ *adj.* **1** like thunder. **2** very loud. □□**thunderously** *adv.* **thunderousness** *n.*

thunderstorm /ˈθʌndəstɔːm/ *n.* a storm with thunder and lightning and usu. heavy rain or hail.

thunderstruck /ˈθʌndəstrʌk/ *adj.* amazed; overwhelmingly surprised or startled.

Thur. *abbr.* Thursday.

thurible /ˈθjʊərɪb(ə)l/ *n.* a censer. [ME f. OF *thurible* or L *t(h)uribulum* f. *thus thur-* incense (as THURIFER)]

thurifer /ˈθjʊərɪfə(r)/ *n.* an acolyte carrying a censer. [LL f. *thus thuris* incense f. Gk *thuos* sacrifice + *-fer* -bearing]

Thurs. *abbr.* Thursday.

Thursday /ˈθɜːzdeɪ, -dɪ/ *n. & adv.* —*n.* the fifth day of the week, following Wednesday. —*adv. colloq.* **1** on Thursday. **2** (**Thursdays**) on Thursdays; each Thursday. [OE *thunresdæg*, *thur(e)sdæg*, day of thunder, representing LL *Jovis dies* day of Jupiter]

thus /ðʌs/ *adv. formal* **1 a** in this way. **b** as indicated. **2 a** accordingly. **b** as a result or inference. **3** to this extent; so (*thus far*; *thus much*). [OE (= OS *thus*), of unkn. orig.]

thuya var. of THUJA.

thwack /θwæk/ *v. & n.* —*v.tr.* hit with a heavy blow; whack. —*n.* a heavy blow. [imit.]

thwaite /θweɪt/ *n. Brit. dial.* a piece of wild land made arable. ¶ Now usually only in place-names. [ON *thveit(i)* paddock, rel. to OE *thwītan* to cut]

thwart /θwɔːt/ *v., n., prep., & adv.* —*v.tr.* frustrate or foil (a person or purpose etc.). —*n.* a rower's seat placed across a boat. —*prep. & adv. archaic* across, athwart. [ME *thwert* (adv.) f. ON *thvert* neut. of *thverr* transverse = OE *thwe(o)rh* f. Gmc]

thy /ðaɪ/ *poss.pron.* (*attrib.*) (also **thine** /ðaɪn/ before a vowel) of or belonging to thee: now replaced by *your* except in some formal, liturgical, dialect, and poetic uses. [ME *thī*, reduced f. *thīn* THINE]

thyme /taɪm/ *n.* any herb or shrub of the genus *Thymus* with aromatic leaves, esp. *T. vulgare* grown for culinary use. □□**thymy** *adj.* [ME f. OF *thym* f. *thymum* f. Gk *thumon* f. *thuō* burn a sacrifice]

thymi *pl.* of THYMUS.

thymine /ˈθaɪmiːn/ n. Biochem. a pyrimidine derivative found in all living tissue as a component base of DNA. [thymic (as THYMUS) + -INE⁴]

thymol /ˈθaɪmɒl/ n. Chem. a white crystalline phenol obtained from oil of thyme and used as an antiseptic. [as THYME + -OL¹]

thymus /ˈθaɪməs/ n. (pl. **thymi** /-maɪ/) (in full **thymus gland**) Anat. a lymphoid organ situated in the neck of vertebrates (in humans becoming much smaller at the approach of puberty) producing lymphocytes for the immune response. [mod.L f. Gk thumos]

thyristor /θaɪˈrɪstə(r)/ n. Electronics a semiconductor rectifier in which the current between two electrodes is controlled by a signal applied to a third electrode. [Gk thura gate + TRANSISTOR]

thyro- /ˈθaɪrəʊ/ comb. form (also **thyreo-** /-rɪəʊ/) thyroid.

thyroid /ˈθaɪrɔɪd/ n. & adj. —n. (in full **thyroid gland**) 1 a large ductless gland in the neck of vertebrates secreting a hormone which regulates growth and development through the rate of metabolism. 2 an extract prepared from the thyroid gland of animals and used in treating goitre and cretinism etc. —adj. Anat. & Zool. 1 connected with the thyroid cartilage (thyroid artery). 2 shield-shaped. □**thyroid cartilage** a large cartilage of the larynx, the projection of which in man forms the Adam's apple. [obs.F thyroide or mod.L thyroides, irreg. f. Gk thureoeidēs f. thureos oblong shield]

thyroxine /θaɪˈrɒksɪn/ n. the main hormone produced by the thyroid gland, involved in controlling the rate of metabolic processes. [THYROID + OX- + -INE⁴]

thyrsus /ˈθɜːsəs/ n. (pl. **thyrsi** /-saɪ/) 1 Gk & Rom. Antiq. a staff tipped with an ornament like a pine-cone, an attribute of Bacchus. 2 Bot. an inflorescence as in lilac, with the primary axis racemose and the secondary axis cymose. [L f. Gk thyrsos]

thyself /ðaɪˈself/ pron. archaic emphat. & refl. form of THOU¹, THEE.

Ti symb. Chem. the element titanium.

ti¹ /tiː/ n. any woody liliaceous plant of the genus Cordyline, esp. C. terminalis with edible roots. [Tahitian, Maori, etc.]

ti² var. of TE.

tiara /tɪˈɑːrə/ n. 1 a jewelled ornamental band worn on the front of a woman's hair. 2 a three-crowned diadem worn by a pope. 3 hist. a turban worn by ancient Persian kings. □□ **tiaraed** adj. (also **tiara'd**). [L f. Gk, of unkn. orig.]

Tibetan /tɪˈbet(ə)n/ n. & adj. —n. 1 **a** a native of Tibet in SW China. **b** a person of Tibetan descent. 2 the language of Tibet. —adj. of or relating to Tibet or its language.

tibia /ˈtɪbɪə/ n. (pl. **tibiae** /-bɪˌiː/) 1 Anat. the inner and usu. larger of two bones extending from the knee to the ankle. 2 the tibiotarsus of a bird. 3 the fourth segment of the leg in insects. □□ **tibial** adj. [L, = shin-bone]

tibiotarsus /ˌtɪbɪəʊˈtɑːsəs/ n. (pl. **tibiotarsi** /-saɪ/) the bone in a bird corresponding to the tibia fused at the lower end with some bones of the tarsus. [TIBIA + TARSUS]

tic /tɪk/ n. a habitual spasmodic contraction of the muscles esp. of the face. □**tic douloureux** /ˌduːləˈruː, -ˈrɜː/ trigeminal neuralgia. [F f. It. ticchio: douloureux F, = painful]

tice /taɪs/ n. 1 Cricket = YORKER. 2 Croquet a stroke tempting an opponent to aim at one's ball. [tice (now dial.), = ENTICE]

tick¹ /tɪk/ n. & v. —n. 1 a slight recurring click esp. that of a watch or clock. 2 esp. Brit. colloq. a moment; an instant. 3 a mark (√) to denote correctness, check items in a list, etc. —v. 1 intr. **a** (of a clock etc.) make ticks. **b** (foll. by away) (of time etc.) pass. 2 intr. (of a mechanism) work, function (take it apart to see how it ticks). 3 tr. **a** mark (a written answer etc.) with a tick. **b** (often foll. by off) mark (an item in a list etc.) with a

tick in checking. □**in two ticks** Brit. colloq. in a very short time. **tick off** colloq. reprimand. **tick over 1** (of an engine etc.) idle. **2** (of a person, project, etc.) be working or functioning at a basic or minimum level. **tick-tack** (or **tic-tac**) Brit. a kind of manual semaphore signalling used by racecourse bookmakers to exchange information. **tick-tack-toe** US noughts and crosses. **tick-tock** the ticking of a large clock etc. **what makes a person tick** colloq. a person's motivation. □□ **tickless** adj. [ME: cf. Du. tik, LG tikk touch, tick]

tick² /tɪk/ n. 1 any of various arachnids of the order Acarina, parasitic on the skin of dogs and cattle etc. 2 any of various insects of the family Hippoboscidae, parasitic on sheep and birds etc. 3 colloq. an unpleasant or despicable person. □**tick-bird** = ox-pecker. **tick fever** a bacterial or rickettsial fever transmitted by the bite of a tick. [OE ticca (recorded as ticia); ME teke, tyke: cf. MDu., MLG tēke, OHG zēcho]

tick³ /tɪk/ n. colloq. credit (buy goods on tick). [app. an abbr. of TICKET in phr. on the ticket]

tick⁴ /tɪk/ n. 1 the cover of a mattress or pillow. 2 = TICKING. [ME tikke, tēke f. WG f. L theca f. Gk thēkē case]

ticker /ˈtɪkə(r)/ n. colloq. 1 the heart. 2 a watch. 3 US a tape machine. □**ticker-tape 1** a paper strip from a tape machine. 2 this or similar material thrown from windows etc. to greet a celebrity.

ticket /ˈtɪkɪt/ n. & v. —n. 1 a written or printed piece of paper or card entitling the holder to enter a place, participate in an event, travel by public transport, use a public amenity, etc. 2 an official notification of a traffic offence etc. (parking ticket). 3 Brit. a certificate of discharge from the army. 4 a certificate of qualification as a ship's master, pilot, etc. 5 a label attached to a thing and giving its price or other details. 6 esp. US **a** a list of candidates put forward by one group esp. a political party. **b** the principles of a party. 7 (prec. by the) colloq. what is correct or needed. —v.tr. (**ticketed**, **ticketing**) attach a ticket to. □**have tickets on oneself** Austral. colloq. be conceited. **ticket-day** Brit. Stock Exch. the day before settling day, when the names of actual purchasers are handed to stockbrokers. **ticket office** an office or kiosk where tickets are sold for transport, entertainment, etc. **ticket-of-leave man** Brit. hist. a prisoner or convict who had served part of his time and was granted certain concessions, esp. leave. □□ **ticketed** adj. **ticketless** adj. [obs.F étiquet f. OF estiquet(te) f. estiquier, estechier fix f. MDu. steken]

tickety-boo /ˌtɪkətɪˈbuː/ adj. Brit. colloq. all right; in order. [20th c.: orig. uncert.]

ticking /ˈtɪkɪŋ/ n. a stout usu. striped material used to cover mattresses etc. [TICK⁴ + -ING¹]

tickle /ˈtɪk(ə)l/ v. & n. —v. 1 a tr. apply light touches or strokes to (a person or part of a person's body) so as to excite the nerves and usu. produce laughter and spasmodic movement. **b** intr. feel this sensation (my foot tickles). 2 tr. excite agreeably; amuse or divert (a person, a sense of humour, vanity, etc.) (was highly tickled at the idea; this will tickle your fancy). 3 tr. catch (a trout etc.) by rubbing it so that it moves backwards into the hand. —n. 1 an act of tickling. 2 a tickling sensation. □**tickled pink** (or **to death**) colloq. extremely amused or pleased. □□ **tickler** n. **tickly** adj. [ME, prob. frequent. of TICK¹]

ticklish /ˈtɪklɪʃ/ adj. 1 sensitive to tickling. 2 (of a matter or person to be dealt with) difficult; requiring careful handling. □□ **ticklishly** adv. **ticklishness** n.

tic-tac var. of tick-tack (see TICK¹).

tidal /ˈtaɪd(ə)l/ adj. relating to, like, or affected by tides (tidal basin; tidal river). □**tidal bore** a large wave or bore caused by constriction of the spring tide as it enters a long narrow shallow inlet. **tidal flow** the regulated movement of traffic in opposite directions on the same stretch of road at different times of the day. **tidal wave 1** Geog. an exceptionally large ocean wave esp. one caused by an underwater earthquake or volcanic eruption. **2** a widespread manifestation of feeling etc. □□ **tidally** adv.

tidbit US var. of TITBIT.

tiddledy-wink US var. of TIDDLY-WINK.

tiddler /'tɪdlə(r)/ n. Brit. colloq. **1** a small fish, esp. a stickleback or minnow. **2** an unusually small thing or person. [perh. rel. to TIDDLY² and tittlebat, a childish form of stickleback]

tiddly¹ /'tɪdlɪ/ adj. (**tiddlier, tiddliest**) esp. Brit. colloq. slightly drunk. [19th c., earlier = a drink: orig. unkn.]

tiddly² /'tɪdlɪ/ adj. (**tiddlier, tiddliest**) Brit. colloq. little.

tiddly-wink /'tɪdlɪwɪŋk/ n. (US **tiddledy-** /'tɪdəldɪ-/) **1** a counter flicked with another into a cup etc. **2** (in pl.) this game. [19th c.: perh. rel. to TIDDLY¹]

tide /taɪd/ n. & v. —n. **1 a** the periodic rise and fall of the sea due to the attraction of the moon and sun (see EBB n. 1, FLOOD n. 3). **b** the water as affected by this. **2** a time or season (usu. in comb.: Whitsuntide). **3** a marked trend of opinion, fortune, or events. —v.intr. drift with the tide, esp. work in or out of harbour with the help of the tide. □ **tide-mill** a mill with a water-wheel driven by the tide. **tide over** enable or help (a person) to deal with an awkward situation, difficult period, etc. (the money will tide me over until Friday). **tide-rip** (or **-rips**) rough water caused by opposing tides. **work double tides** work twice the normal time, or extra hard. □□ **tideless** adj. [OE tīd f. Gmc, rel. to TIME]

tideland /'taɪdlænd/ n. US land that is submerged at high tide.

tidemark /'taɪdmɑːk/ n. **1** a mark made by the tide at high water. **2** esp. Brit. **a** a mark left round a bath at the level of the water in it. **b** a line on a person's body marking the extent to which it has been washed.

tidetable /'taɪd,teɪb(ə)l/ n. a table indicating the times of high and low tides at a place.

tidewaiter /'taɪd,weɪtə(r)/ n. hist. a customs officer who boarded ships on their arrival to enforce the customs regulations.

tidewater /'taɪd,wɔːtə(r)/ n. **1** water brought by or affected by tides. **2** (attrib.) US affected by tides (tidewater region).

tidewave /'taɪdweɪv/ n. an undulation of water passing round the earth and causing high and low tides.

tideway /'taɪdweɪ/ n. **1** a channel in which a tide runs, esp. the tidal part of a river. **2** the ebb or flow in a tidal channel.

tidings /'taɪdɪŋz/ n. (as sing. or pl.) literary news, information. [OE tīdung, prob. f. ON títhindi events f. títhr occurring]

tidy /'taɪdɪ/ adj., n., & v. —adj. (**tidier, tidiest**) **1** neat, orderly; methodically arranged. **2** (of a person) methodically inclined. **3** colloq. considerable (it cost a tidy sum). —n. (pl. **-ies**) **1** a receptacle for holding small objects or waste scraps, esp. in a kitchen sink. **2** an act or spell of tidying. **3** esp. US a detachable ornamental cover for a chair-back etc. —v.tr. (**-ies, -ied**) (also absol.; often foll. by up) put in good order; make (oneself, a room, etc.) tidy. □□ **tidily** adv. **tidiness** n. [ME, = timely etc., f. TIDE + -Y¹]

tie /taɪ/ v. & n. —v. (**tying**) **1** tr. attach or fasten with string or cord etc. (tie the dog to the gate; tie his hands together; tied on a label). **2** tr. **a** form (a string, ribbon, shoelace, necktie, etc.) into a knot or bow. **b** form (a knot or bow) in this way. **3** tr. restrict or limit (a person) as to conditions, occupation, place, etc. (is tied to his family). **4** intr. (often foll. by with) achieve the same score or place as another competitor (they tied at ten games each; tied with her for first place). **5** tr. hold (rafters etc.) together by a crosspiece etc. **6** tr. Mus. **a** unite (written notes) by a tie. **b** perform (two notes) as one unbroken note. —n. **1** a cord or chain etc. used for fastening. **2** a strip of material worn round the collar and tied in a knot at the front with the ends hanging down. **3** a thing that unites or restricts persons; a bond or obligation (family ties; ties of friendship; children

are a real tie). **4** a draw, dead heat, or equality of score among competitors. **5** Brit. a match between any pair from a group of competing players or teams. **6** (also **tie-beam** etc.) a rod or beam holding parts of a structure together. **7** Mus. a curved line above or below two notes of the same pitch indicating that they are to be played for the combined duration of their time values. **8** US a railway sleeper. **9** US a shoe tied with a lace. □ **fit to be tied** colloq. very angry. **tie-break** (or **-breaker**) a means of deciding a winner from competitors who have tied. **tie-dye** (or **tie and dye**) a method of producing dyed patterns by tying string etc. to protect parts of the fabric from the dye. **tie in** (foll. by with) bring into or have a close association or agreement. **tie-in** n. **1** a connection or association. **2** (often attrib.) esp. US a form of sale or advertising that offers or requires more than a single purchase. **3** the joint promotion of related commodities etc. (e.g. a book and a film). **tie-line** a transmission line connecting parts of a system, esp. a telephone line connecting two private branch exchanges. **tie-pin** (or **-clip**) an ornamental pin or clip for holding a tie in place. **tie up 1** bind or fasten securely with cord etc. **2** invest or reserve (capital etc.) so that it is not immediately available for use. **3** moor (a boat). **4** secure (an animal). **5** obstruct; prevent from acting freely. **6** secure or complete (an undertaking etc.). **7** (often foll. by with) = **tie in. 8** (usu. in passive) fully occupy (a person). □□ **tieless** adj. [OE tīgan, tēgan (v.), tēah, tēg (n.) f. Gmc]

tied /taɪd/ adj. Brit. **1** (of a house) occupied subject to the tenant's working for its owner. **2** (of a public house etc.) bound to supply the products of a particular brewery only.

tier /tɪə(r)/ n. **1** a row or rank or unit of a structure, as one of several placed one above another (tiers of seats). **2** Naut. **a** a circle of coiled cable. **b** a place for a coiled cable. □□ **tiered** adj. (also in comb.). [earlier tire f. F f. tirer draw, elongate f. Rmc]

tierce /tɪəs/ n. **1** Eccl. = TERCE. **2** Mus. an interval of two octaves and a major third. **3** a sequence of three cards. **4** Fencing **a** the third of eight parrying positions. **b** the corresponding thrust. **5** archaic **a** a former wine-measure of one-third of a pipe. **b** a cask containing a certain quantity (varying with the goods) esp. of provisions. [ME f. OF t(i)erce f. L tertia fem. of tertius third]

tierced /tɪəst/ adj. Heraldry divided into three parts of different tinctures.

tiercel var. of TERCEL.

tiercet var. of TERCET.

tiff /tɪf/ n. **1** a slight or petty quarrel. **2** a fit of peevishness. [18th c.: orig. unkn.]

tiffany /'tɪfənɪ/ n. (pl. **-ies**) thin gauze muslin. [orig. dress worn on Twelfth Night, f. OF tifanie f. eccl.L theophania f. Gk theophaneia Epiphany]

tiffin /'tɪfɪn/ n. & v. Ind. —n. a light meal, esp. lunch. —v.intr. (**tiffined, tiffining**) take lunch etc. [app. f. tiffing sipping]

tig /tɪg/ n. = TAG². [var. of TICK¹]

tiger /'taɪgə(r)/ n. **1** a large Asian flesh-eating feline, Panthera tigris, having a yellow-brown coat with black stripes. **2** a fierce, energetic, or formidable person. □ **tiger beetle** any flesh-eating beetle of the family Cicindelidae, with spotted or striped wing-covers. **tiger-cat 1** any moderate-sized feline resembling the tiger, e.g. the ocelot, serval, or margay. **2** Austral. any of various flesh-eating marsupials of the genus Dasyurus, including the Tasmanian devil. **tiger-eye** (or **tiger's-eye**) **1** a yellow-brown striped gem of brilliant lustre. **2** US a pottery-glaze of similar appearance. **tiger lily** a tall garden lily, Lilium tigrinum, with flowers of dull orange spotted with black or purple. **tiger moth** any moth of the family Arctiidae, esp. Arctia caja, having richly spotted and streaked wings suggesting a tiger's skin. **tiger-wood** a striped or streaked wood used for cabinet-making. □□

tigerish *adj.* **tigerishly** *adv.* [ME f. OF *tigre* f. L *tigris* f. Gk *tigris*]

tight /taɪt/ *adj., n., & adv.* —*adj.* **1** closely held, drawn, fastened, fitting, etc. (*a tight hold; a tight skirt*). **2** closely and firmly put together (*a tight joint*). **3** (of clothes etc.) too closely fitting (*my shoes are rather tight*). **4** impermeable, impervious, esp. (in *comb.*) to a specified thing (*watertight*). **5** tense; stretched so as to leave no slack (*a tight bowstring*). **6** *colloq.* drunk. **7** *colloq.* (of a person) mean, stingy. **8 a** (of money or materials) not easily obtainable. **b** (of a money market) in which money is tight. **9 a** (of precautions, a programme, etc.) stringent, demanding. **b** presenting difficulties (*a tight situation*). **10** produced by or requiring great exertion or pressure (*a tight squeeze*). **11** (of control etc.) strictly imposed. —*adv.* tightly (*hold tight!*). □**tight corner** (or **place** or **spot**) a difficult situation. **tight-fisted** stingy. **tight-fitting** (of a garment) fitting (often too) close to the body. **tight-lipped** with or as with the lips compressed to restrain emotion or speech. □□**tightly** *adv.* **tightness** *n.* [prob. alt. of *thight* f. ON *théttr* watertight, of close texture]

tighten /ˈtaɪt(ə)n/ *v.tr. & intr.* make or become tight or tighter. □**tighten one's belt** see BELT.

tightrope /ˈtaɪtrəʊp/ *n.* a rope stretched tightly high above the ground, on which acrobats perform.

tights /taɪts/ *n.pl.* **1** a thin close-fitting wool or nylon etc. garment covering the legs and the lower part of the torso, worn by women in place of stockings. **2** a similar garment worn by a dancer, acrobat, etc.

tigon /ˈtaɪɡən/ *n.* the offspring of a tiger and a lioness (cf. LIGER). [portmanteau word f. TIGER + LION]

tigress /ˈtaɪɡrɪs/ *n.* **1** a female tiger. **2** a fierce or passionate woman.

tike var. of TYKE.

tiki /ˈtɪkɪ/ *n.* (*pl.* **tikis**) *NZ* a large wooden or small ornamental greenstone image representing a human figure. [Maori]

tilbury /ˈtɪlbəri/ *n.* (*pl.* **-ies**) *hist.* a light open two-wheeled carriage. [after the inventor's name]

tilde /ˈtɪldə/ *n.* a mark (˜), put over a letter, e.g. over a Spanish *n* when pronounced *ny* (as in *señor*) or a Portuguese *a* or *o* when nasalized (as in *São Paulo*). [Sp., ult. f. L *titulus* TITLE]

tile /taɪl/ *n. & v.* —*n.* **1** a thin slab of concrete or baked clay etc. used in series for covering a roof or pavement etc. **2** a similar slab of glazed pottery, cork, linoleum, etc., for covering a floor, wall, etc. **3** a thin flat piece used in a game (esp. mah-jong). —*v.tr.* cover with tiles. □**on the tiles** *colloq.* having a spree. [OE *tigule, -ele,* f. L *tegula*]

tiler /ˈtaɪlə(r)/ *n.* **1** a person who makes or lays tiles. **2** the doorkeeper of a Freemasons' lodge.

tiling /ˈtaɪlɪŋ/ *n.* **1** the process of fixing tiles. **2** an area of tiles.

till[1] /tɪl/ *prep. & conj.* —*prep.* **1** up to or as late as (*wait till six o'clock; did not return till night*). **2** up to the time of (*faithful till death; waited till the end*). —*conj.* **1** up to the time when (*wait till I return*). **2** so long that (*laughed till I cried*). ¶ *Until* is more usual when beginning a sentence. [OE & ON *til* to, rel. to TILL[3]]

till[2] /tɪl/ *n.* a drawer for money in a shop or bank etc., esp. with a device recording the amount of each purchase. [ME: orig. unkn.]

till[3] /tɪl/ *v.tr.* prepare and cultivate (land) for crops. □□ **tillable** *adj.* **tiller** *n.* [OE *tilian* strive for, cultivate, f. Gmc]

till[4] /tɪl/ *n.* stiff clay containing boulders, sand, etc. deposited by melting glaciers and ice-sheets. [17th c. (Sc.): orig. unkn.]

tillage /ˈtɪlɪdʒ/ *n.* **1** the preparation of land for crop-bearing. **2** tilled land.

tiller[1] /ˈtɪlə(r)/ *n.* a horizontal bar fitted to the head of a boat's rudder to turn it in steering. [ME f. AF *telier* weaver's beam f. med.L *telarium* f. L *tela* web]

tiller[2] /ˈtɪlə(r)/ *n. & v.* —*n.* **1** a shoot of a plant springing from the bottom of the original stalk. **2** a sapling. **3** a sucker. —*v.intr.* put forth tillers. [app. repr. OE *telgor* extended f. *telga* bough]

tilt /tɪlt/ *v. & n.* —*v.* **1** *intr. & tr.* assume or cause to assume a sloping position; heel over. **2** *intr.* (foll. by *at*) strike, thrust, or run at, with a weapon, esp. in jousting. **3** *intr.* (foll. by *with*) engage in a contest. **4** *tr.* forge or work (steel etc.) with a tilt-hammer. —*n.* **1** the act or an instance of tilting. **2** a sloping position. **3** (of medieval knights etc.) the act of charging with a lance against an opponent or at a mark, done for exercise or as a sport. **4** an encounter between opponents; an attack esp. with argument or satire (*have a tilt at*). **5** = *tilt-hammer*. □**full** (or **at full**) **tilt 1** at full speed. **2** with full force. **tilt-hammer** a heavy pivoted hammer used in forging. **tilt-yard** *hist.* a place where tilts (see sense 3 of *n.*) took place. □□ **tilter** *n.* [ME *tilte* perh. f. an OE form rel. to *tealt* unsteady f. Gmc: weapon senses of unkn. orig.]

tilth /tɪlθ/ *n.* **1** tillage, cultivation. **2** the condition of tilled soil (*in good tilth*). [OE *tilth(e)* (as TILL[3])]

Tim. *abbr.* Timothy (New Testament).

timbal /ˈtɪmb(ə)l/ *n. archaic* a kettledrum. [F *timbale*, earlier *tamballe* f. Sp. *atabal* f. Arab. *aṭ-ṭabl* the drum]

timbale /tãˈbɑːl/ *n.* a drum-shaped dish of minced meat or fish in a pastry shell. [F: see TIMBAL]

timber /ˈtɪmbə(r)/ *n.* **1** wood prepared for building, carpentry, etc. **2** a piece of wood or beam, esp. as the rib of a vessel. **3** large standing trees suitable for timber; woods or forest. **4** (esp. as *int.*) a warning cry that a tree is about to fall. □**timber hitch** a knot used in attaching a rope to a log or spar. **timber wolf** a type of large N. American grey wolf. □□ **timbering** *n.* [OE, = building, f. Gmc]

timbered /ˈtɪmbəd/ *adj.* **1** (esp. of a building) made wholly or partly of timber. **2** (of country) wooded.

timberland /ˈtɪmbəˌlænd/ *n. US* land covered with forest yielding timber.

timberline /ˈtɪmbəˌlaɪn/ *n.* (on a mountain) the line or level above which no trees grow.

timbre /ˈtæmbə(r), ˈtæbrə/ *n.* the distinctive character of a musical sound or voice apart from its pitch and intensity. [F f. Rmc f. med.Gk *timbanon* f. Gk *tumpanon* drum]

timbrel /ˈtɪmbr(ə)l/ *n. archaic* a tambourine or similar instrument. [dimin. of ME *timbre* f. OF (as TIMBRE, -LE[2])]

Timbuctoo /ˌtɪmbʌkˈtuː/ *n.* any distant or remote place. [*Timbuktu* in W. Africa]

time /taɪm/ *n. & v.* —*n.* **1** the indefinite continued progress of existence, events, etc., in past, present, and future regarded as a whole. **2 a** the progress of this as affecting persons or things (*stood the test of time*). **b** (**Time**) (in full **Father Time**) the personification of time, esp. as an old man with a scythe and hourglass. **3** a more or less definite portion of time belonging to particular events or circumstances (*the time of the Plague; prehistoric times; the scientists of the time*). **4** an allotted, available, or measurable portion of time; the period of time at one's disposal (*am wasting my time; had no time to visit; how much time do you need?*). **5** a point of time esp. in hours and minutes (*the time is 7.30; what time is it?*). **6** (prec. by *a*) an indefinite period (*waited for a time*). **7** time or an amount of time as reckoned by a conventional standard (*the time allowed is one hour; ran the mile in record time; eight o'clock New York time*). **8 a** an occasion (*last time I saw you*). **b** an event or occasion qualified in some way (*had a good time*). **9** a moment or definite portion of time destined or suitable for a purpose etc. (*now is the time to act; shall we fix a time?*). **10** (in *pl.*) expressing multiplication (*is four times as old; five times six is thirty*). **11** a lifetime (*will last my time*). **12** (in *sing.* or *pl.*) **a** the conditions of life or of a period (*hard times; times have changed*). **b** (prec. by *the*) the present age, or that being considered. **13** *colloq.* a prison sentence (*is doing time*). **14** an apprenticeship (*served his time*).

15 a period of gestation. **16** the date or expected date of childbirth (*is near her time*) or of death (*my time is drawing near*). **17** measured time spent in work (*put them on short time*). **18 a** any of several rhythmic patterns of music (*in waltz time*). **b** the duration of a note as indicated by a crotchet, minim, etc. **19** *Brit.* the moment at which the opening hours of a public house end. —*v.tr.* **1** choose the time or occasion for (*time your remarks carefully*). **2** do at a chosen or correct time. **3** arrange the time of arrival of. **4** ascertain the time taken by (a process or activity, or a person doing it). **5** regulate the duration or interval of; set times for (*trains are timed to arrive every hour*). □**against time** with utmost speed, so as to finish by a specified time (*working against time*). **ahead of time** earlier than expected. **ahead of one's time** having ideas too enlightened or advanced to be accepted by one's contemporaries. **all the time 1** during the whole of the time referred to (often despite some contrary expectation etc.) (*we never noticed, but he was there all the time*). **2** constantly (*nags all the time*). **3** at all times (*leaves a light on all the time*). **at one time 1** in or during a known but unspecified past period. **2** simultaneously (*ran three businesses at one time*). **at the same time 1** simultaneously; at a time that is the same for all. **2** nevertheless (*at the same time, I do not want to offend you*). **at a time** separately in the specified groups or numbers (*came three at a time*). **at times** occasionally, intermittently. **before time** (usu. prec. by *not*) before the due or expected time. **before one's time** prematurely (*old before his time*). **for the time being** for the present; until some other arrangement is made. **half the time** *colloq.* as often as not. **have no time for 1** be unable or unwilling to spend time on. **2** dislike. **have the time 1** be able to spend the time needed. **2** know from a watch etc. what time it is. **have a time of it** undergo trouble or difficulty. **in no (or less than no) time 1** very soon. **2** very quickly. **in one's own good time** at a time and a rate decided by oneself. **in one's own time** outside working hours. **in time 1** not late, punctual (*was in time to catch the bus*). **2** eventually (*in time you may agree*). **3** in accordance with a given rhythm or tempo, esp. of music. **in one's time** at or during some previous period of one's life (*in his time he was a great hurdler*). **keep good (or bad) time 1** (of a clock etc.) record time accurately (or inaccurately). **2** be habitually punctual (or not punctual). **keep time** move or sing etc. in time. **know the time of day** be well informed. **lose no time** (often foll. by *in* + verbal noun) act immediately (*lost no time in cashing the cheque*). **not before time** not too soon; timely. **no time** *colloq.* a very short interval (*it was no time before they came*). **out of time** unseasonable; unseasonably. **pass the time of day** *colloq.* exchange a greeting or casual remarks. **time after time 1** repeatedly, on many occasions. **2** in many instances. **time and (or time and time) again** on many occasions. **time and a half** a rate of payment for work at one and a half times the normal rate. **time-and-motion** (usu. *attrib.*) concerned with measuring the efficiency of industrial and other operations. **time bomb** a bomb designed to explode at a pre-set time. **time capsule** a box etc. containing objects typical of the present time, buried for discovery in the future. **time clock 1** a clock with a device for recording workers' hours of work. **2** a switch mechanism activated at pre-set times by a built-in clock. **time-consuming** using much or too much time. **time exposure** the exposure of photographic film for longer than the maximum normal shutter setting. **time factor** the passage of time as a limitation on what can be achieved. **time-fuse** a fuse calculated to burn for or explode at a given time. **time-honoured** esteemed by tradition or through custom. **time immemorial** (or **out of mind**) a longer time than anyone can remember or trace. **time-lag** an interval of time between an event, a

cause, etc. and its effect. **time-lapse** (of photography) using frames taken at long intervals to photograph a slow process, and shown continuously as if at normal speed. **time-limit** the limit of time within which a task must be done. **the time of day** the hour by the clock. **time off** time for rest or recreation etc. **the time of one's life** a period or occasion of exceptional enjoyment. **time out** esp. *US* **1** a brief intermission in a game etc. **2** = *time off.* **time-scale** the time allowed for or taken by a sequence of events in relation to a broader period of time. **time-served** having completed a period of apprenticeship or training. **time-server** a person who changes his or her views to suit the prevailing circumstances, fashion, etc. **time-share** a share in a property under a time-sharing scheme. **time-sharing 1** the operation of a computer system by several users for different operations at one time. **2** the use of a holiday home at agreed different times by several joint owners. **time sheet** a sheet of paper for recording hours of work etc. **time signal** an audible (esp. broadcast) signal or announcement of the exact time of day. **time signature** *Mus.* an indication of tempo following a clef, expressed as a fraction with the numerator giving the number of beats in each bar and the denominator giving the duration of each beat. **time switch** a switch acting automatically at a pre-set time. **time warp** an imaginary distortion of space in relation to time, whereby persons or objects of one age can be moved to another. **time was there was a time** (*time was when I could do that*). **time-work** work paid for by the time it takes. **time-worn** impaired by age. **time zone** a range of longitudes where a common standard time is used. [OE *tīma* f. Gmc]

timekeeper /ˈtaɪmˌkiːpə(r)/ *n.* **1** a person who records time, esp. of workers or in a game. **2 a** a watch or clock as regards accuracy (*a good timekeeper*). **b** a person as regards punctuality. □□ **timekeeping** *n.*

timeless /ˈtaɪmlɪs/ *adj.* not affected by the passage of time; eternal. □□ **timelessly** *adv.* **timelessness** *n.*

timely /ˈtaɪmlɪ/ *adj.* (**timelier, timeliest**) opportune; coming at the right time. □□ **timeliness** *n.*

timepiece /ˈtaɪmpiːs/ *n.* an instrument, such as a clock or watch, for measuring time.

timer /ˈtaɪmə(r)/ *n.* **1** a person or device that measures or records time taken. **2** an automatic mechanism for activating a device etc. at a pre-set time.

timetable /ˈtaɪmˌteɪb(ə)l/ *n. & v.* —*n.* a list of times at which events are scheduled to take place, esp. the arrival and departure of buses or trains etc., or a sequence of lessons in a school or college. —*v.tr.* include in or arrange to a timetable; schedule.

timid /ˈtɪmɪd/ *adj.* (**timider, timidest**) easily frightened; apprehensive, shy. □□ **timidity** /-ˈmɪdɪtɪ/ *n.* **timidly** *adv.* **timidness** *n.* [F *timide* or L *timidus* f. *timēre* fear]

timing /ˈtaɪmɪŋ/ *n.* **1** the way an action or process is timed, esp. in relation to others. **2** the regulation of the opening and closing of valves in an internal-combustion engine.

timocracy /tɪˈmɒkrəsɪ/ *n.* (*pl.* -**ies**) **1** a form of government in which possession of property is required in order to hold office. **2** a form of government in which rulers are motivated by love of honour. □□ **timocratic** /-əˈkrætɪk/ *adj.* [OF *timocracie* f. med.L *timocratia* f. Gk *timokratia* f. *timē* honour, worth + *kratia* -CRACY]

timorous /ˈtɪmərəs/ *adj.* **1** timid; easily alarmed. **2** frightened. □□ **timorously** *adv.* **timorousness** *n.* [ME f. OF *temoreus* f. med.L *timorosus* f. L *timor* f. *timēre* fear]

timothy /ˈtɪməθɪ/ *n.* (in full **timothy grass**) a fodder grass, *Phleum pratense*. [*Timothy* Hanson, who introduced it in Carolina *c.*1720]

timpani /'tɪmpənɪ/ *n.pl.* (also **tympani**) kettle-drums. □□ **timpanist** *n.* [It., pl. of *timpano* = TYM-PANUM]

tin /tɪn/ *n. & v.* —*n.* **1** *Chem.* a silvery-white malleable metallic element resisting corrosion, occurring naturally in cassiterite and other ores, and used esp. in alloys and for plating thin iron or steel sheets to form tin plate. ¶ Symb.: **Sn. 2 a** a vessel or container made of tin or tinned iron. **b** *Brit.* an airtight sealed container made of tin plate or aluminium for preserving food. **3** = *tin plate.* **4** *Brit. sl.* money. —*v.tr.* (**tinned, tinning**) **1** seal (food) in an airtight tin for preservation. **2** cover or coat with tin. □ **put the tin lid on** see LID. **tin can** a tin container (see sense 2 of *n.*), esp. an empty one. **tin foil** foil made of tin, aluminium, or tin alloy, used for wrapping food for cooking or storing. **tin-glaze** a glaze made white and opaque by the addition of tin oxide. **tin god 1** an object of unjustified veneration. **2** a self-important person. **tin hat** *colloq.* a military steel helmet. **tin Lizzie** *colloq.* an old or decrepit car. **tin-opener** a tool for opening tins. **tin-pan alley** the world of composers and publishers of popular music. **tin plate** sheet iron or sheet steel coated with tin. **tin-plate** *v.tr.* coat with tin. **tin soldier** a toy soldier made of metal. **tin-tack** an iron tack. **tin whistle** = *penny whistle.* [OE f. Gmc]

tinamou /'tɪnəˌmuː/ *n.* any South American bird of the family Tinamidae, resembling a grouse but related to the rhea. [F f. Galibi *tinamu*]

tinctorial /tɪŋk'tɔːrɪəl/ *adj.* **1** of or relating to colour or dyeing. **2** producing colour. [L *tinctorius* f. *tinctor* dyer: see TINGE]

tincture /'tɪŋktjə(r), -tʃə(r)/ *n. & v.* —*n.* (often foll. by *of*) **1** a slight flavour or trace. **2** a tinge (of a colour). **3** a medicinal solution (of a drug) in alcohol (*tincture of quinine*). **4** *Heraldry* an inclusive term for the metals, colours, and furs used in coats of arms. **5** *colloq.* an alcoholic drink. —*v.tr.* **1** colour slightly; tinge, flavour. **2** (often foll. by *with*) affect slightly (with a quality). [ME f. L *tinctura* dyeing (as TINGE)]

tinder /'tɪndə(r)/ *n.* a dry substance such as wood that readily catches fire from a spark. □ **tinder-box** *hist.* a box containing tinder, flint, and steel, formerly used for kindling fires. □□ **tindery** *adj.* [OE *tynder, tyndre* f. Gmc]

tine /taɪn/ *n.* a prong or tooth or point of a fork, comb, antler, etc. □□ **tined** *adj.* (also in *comb.*). [OE *tind*]

tinea /'tɪnɪə/ *n. Med.* ringworm. [L, = moth, worm]

ting /tɪŋ/ *n. & v.* —*n.* a tinkling sound as of a bell. —*v.intr. & tr.* emit or cause to emit this sound. [imit.]

tinge /tɪndʒ/ *v. & n.* —*v.tr.* (also **tingeing**) (often foll. by *with*; often in *passive*) **1** colour slightly (*is tinged with red*). **2** affect slightly (*regret tinged with satisfaction*). —*n.* **1** a tendency towards or trace of some colour. **2** a slight admixture of a feeling or quality. [ME f. L *tingere tinct-* dye, stain]

tingle /'tɪŋg(ə)l/ *v. & n.* —*v.* **1** *intr.* **a** feel a slight prickling, stinging, or throbbing sensation. **b** cause this (*the reply tingled in my ears*). **2** *tr.* make (the ear etc.) tingle. —*n.* a tingling sensation. [ME, perh. var. of TINKLE]

tingly /'tɪŋglɪ/ *adj.* (**tinglier, tingliest**) causing or characterized by tingling.

tinhorn /'tɪnhɔːn/ *n. & adj. US sl.* —*n.* a pretentious but unimpressive person. —*adj.* cheap, pretentious.

tinker /'tɪŋkə(r)/ *n. & v.* —*n.* **1** an itinerant mender of kettles and pans etc. **2** *Sc. & Ir.* a gypsy. **3** *colloq.* a mischievous person or animal. **4** a spell of tinkering. **5** a rough-and-ready worker. —*v.* **1** *intr.* (foll. by *at, with*) work in an amateurish or desultory way, esp. to adjust or mend machinery etc. **2 a** *intr.* work as a tinker. **b** *tr.* repair (pots and pans). □□ **tinkerer** *n.* [ME: orig. unkn.]

tinkle /'tɪŋk(ə)l/ *v. & n.* —*v.* **1** *intr. & tr.* make or cause to make a succession of short light ringing

sounds. **2** *intr. colloq.* urinate. —*n.* **1** a tinkling sound. **2** *Brit. colloq.* a telephone call (*will give you a tinkle on Monday*). **3** *colloq.* an act of urinating. [ME f. obs. *tink* to chink (imit.)]

tinner /'tɪnə(r)/ *n.* **1** a tin-miner. **2** a tinsmith.

tinnitus /tɪ'naɪtəs/ *n. Med.* a ringing in the ears. [L f. *tinnire tinnit-* ring, tinkle, of imit. orig.]

tinny /'tɪnɪ/ *adj. & n.* —*adj.* (**tinnier, tinniest**) **1** of or like tin. **2** (of a metal object) flimsy, insubstantial. **3 a** sounding like struck tin. **b** (of reproduced sound) thin and metallic, lacking low frequencies. **4** *Austral. sl.* lucky. —*n.* (also **tinnie**) (*pl.* **-ies**) *Austral. sl.* a can of beer. □□ **tinnily** *adv.* **tinniness** *n.*

tinpot /'tɪnpɒt/ *adj. Brit.* cheap, inferior.

tinsel /'tɪns(ə)l/ *n. & v.* —*n.* **1** glittering metallic strips, threads, etc., used as decoration to give a sparkling effect. **2** a fabric adorned with tinsel. **3** superficial brilliance or splendour. **4** (*attrib.*) showy, gaudy, flashy. —*v.tr.* (**tinselled, tinselling**) adorn with or as with tinsel. □□ **tinselled** *adj.* **tinselly** *adj.* [OF *estincele* spark f. L *scintilla*]

tinsmith /'tɪnsmɪθ/ *n.* a worker in tin and tin plate.

tinsnips /'tɪnsnɪps/ *n.* a pair of clippers for cutting sheet metal.

tinstone /'tɪnstəʊn/ *n. Geol.* = CASSITERITE.

tint /tɪnt/ *n. & v.* —*n.* **1** a variety of a colour, esp. one made lighter by adding white. **2** a tendency towards or admixture of a different colour (*red with a blue tint*). **3** a faint colour spread over a surface, esp. as a background for printing on. **4** a set of parallel engraved lines to give uniform shading. —*v.tr.* apply a tint to; colour. □□ **tinter** *n.* [alt. of earlier *tinct* f. L *tinctus* dyeing (as TINGE), perh. infl. by It. *tinto*]

tintinnabulation /ˌtɪntɪˌnæbjʊ'leɪʃ(ə)n/ *n.* a ringing or tinkling of bells. [as L *tintinnabulum* tinkling bell f. *tintinnare* redupl. form of *tinnire* ring]

tinware /'tɪnweə(r)/ *n.* articles made of tin or tin plate.

tiny /'taɪnɪ/ *adj.* (**tinier, tiniest**) very small or slight. □□ **tinily** *adv.* **tininess** *n.* [obs. *tine, tyne* (adj. & n.) small, a little: ME, of unkn. orig.]

-tion /ʃ(ə)n/ *suffix* forming nouns of action, condition, etc. (see -ION, -ATION, -ITION, -UTION). [from or after F *-tion* or L *-tio -tionis*]

tip[1] /tɪp/ *n. & v.* —*n.* **1** an extremity or end, esp. of a small or tapering thing (*tips of the fingers*). **2** a small piece or part attached to the end of a thing, e.g. a ferrule on a stick. **3** a leaf-bud of tea. —*v.tr.* (**tipped, tipping**) **1** provide with a tip. **2** *tr.* (foll. by *in*) attach (a loose sheet) to a page at the inside edge. □ **on the tip of one's tongue** about to be said, esp. after difficulty in recalling to mind. **the tip of the iceberg** a small evident part of something much larger or more significant. □□ **tipless** *adj.* **tippy** *adj.* (in sense 3). [ME f. ON *typpi* (n.), *typpa* (v.), *typptr* tipped f. Gmc (rel. to TOP[1]): prob. reinforced by MDu. & MLG *tip*]

tip[2] /tɪp/ *v. & n.* —*v.* (**tipped, tipping**) **1 a** *intr.* lean or slant. **b** *tr.* cause to do this. **2** *tr.* (foll. by *into* etc.) **a** overturn or cause to overbalance (*was tipped into the pond*). **b** discharge the contents of (a container etc.) in this way. —*n.* **1 a** a slight push or tilt. **b** a light stroke, esp. in baseball. **2** *Brit.* a place where material (esp. refuse) is tipped. □ **tip the balance** make the critical difference. **tip the scales** see SCALE[2]. **tip-up** able to be tipped, e.g. of a seat in a theatre to allow passage past. [17th c.: orig. uncert.]

tip[3] /tɪp/ *v. & n.* —*v.* (**tipped, tipping**) (often foll. by *over, up*) **1** *tr.* make a small present of money to, esp. for a service given (*have you tipped the porter?*). **2** *tr.* name as the likely winner of a race or contest etc. **3** *tr.* strike or touch lightly. **4** *tr. sl.* give, hand, pass (esp. in *tip the wink* below). —*n.* **1** a small money present, esp. for a service given. **2** a piece of private or special information, esp. regarding betting or investment. **3** a small or casual piece of advice. □ **tip off 1** give (a person) a hint or piece of special information or warning, esp. discreetly or confidentially. **2** *Basketball* start play by throwing the ball up between two opponents. **tip-off** a hint or warning etc. given discreetly or confidentially. **tip a person the wink** give a person private information. □□ **tipper** *n*. [ME: orig. uncert.]

tipcat /ˈtɪpkæt/ *n*. **1** a game with a short piece of wood tapering at the ends and struck with a stick. **2** this piece of wood.

tipper /ˈtɪpə(r)/ *n*. (often *attrib*.) a road haulage vehicle that tips at the back to discharge its load.

tippet /ˈtɪpɪt/ *n*. **1** a covering of fur etc. for the shoulders formerly worn by women. **2** a similar garment worn as part of some official costumes, esp. by the clergy. **3** *hist*. a long narrow strip of cloth as part of or an attachment to a hood etc. [ME, prob. f. TIP¹]

tipple /ˈtɪp(ə)l/ *v*. & *n*. —*v*. **1** *intr*. drink intoxicating liquor habitually. **2** *tr*. drink (liquor) repeatedly in small amounts. —*n*. *colloq*. a drink, esp. a strong one. □□ **tippler** *n*. [ME, back-form. f. *tippler*, of unkn. orig.]

tipstaff /ˈtɪpstɑːf/ *n*. **1** a sheriff's officer. **2** a metal-tipped staff carried as a symbol of office. [contr. of *tipped staff*, i.e. tipped with metal]

tipster /ˈtɪpstə(r)/ *n*. a person who gives tips, esp. about betting at horse-races.

tipsy /ˈtɪpsɪ/ *adj*. (**tipsier**, **tipsiest**) **1** slightly intoxicated. **2** caused by or showing intoxication (*a tipsy leer*). □ **tipsy-cake** *Brit*. a sponge cake soaked in wine or spirits and served with custard. □□ **tipsily** *adv*. **tipsiness** *n*. [prob. f. TIP² = inclined to lean, unsteady: for *-sy* cf. FLIMSY, TRICKSY]

tiptoe /ˈtɪptəʊ/ *n*., *v*., & *adv*. —*n*. the tips of the toes. —*v.intr*. (**tiptoes**, **tiptoed**, **tiptoeing**) walk on tiptoe, or very stealthily. —*adv*. (also **on tiptoe**) with the heels off the ground and the weight on the balls of the feet.

tiptop /ˈtɪptɒp/ *adj*., *adv*., & *n*. *colloq*. —*adj*. & *adv*. highest in excellence; very best. —*n*. the highest point of excellence.

TIR *abbr*. international road transport (esp. with ref. to EEC regulations). [F, = *transport international routier*]

tirade /taɪˈreɪd, tɪ-/ *n*. a long vehement denunciation or declamation. [F, = long speech, f. It. *tirata* volley f. *tirare* pull f. Rmc]

tirailleur /ˌtiːraːˈjɜː(r), ˌtɪrɑːˈlɜː(r)/ *n*. **1** a sharpshooter. **2** a skirmisher. [F f. *tirailler* shoot independently f. *tirer* shoot, draw, f. Rmc]

tire¹ /ˈtaɪə(r)/ *v*. **1** *tr*. & *intr*. make or grow weary. **2** *tr*. exhaust the patience or interest of; bore. **3** *tr*. (in *passive*; foll. by *of*) have had enough of; be fed up with (*was tired of arguing*). [OE *tēorian*, of unkn. orig.]

tire² /ˈtaɪə(r)/ *n*. **1** a band of metal placed round the rim of a wheel to strengthen it. **2** *US* var. of TYRE. [ME, perh. = archaic *tire* head-dress]

tired /ˈtaɪəd/ *adj*. **1** weary, exhausted; ready for sleep. **2** (of an idea etc.) hackneyed. □□ **tiredly** *adv*. **tiredness** *n*.

tireless /ˈtaɪəlɪs/ *adj*. having inexhaustible energy. □□ **tirelessly** *adv*. **tirelessness** *n*.

tiresome /ˈtaɪəsəm/ *adj*. **1** wearisome, tedious. **2** *colloq*. annoying (*how tiresome of you!*). □□ **tiresomely** *adv*. **tiresomeness** *n*.

tiro /ˈtaɪərəʊ/ *n*. (also **tyro**) (*pl*. **-os**) a beginner or novice. [L *tiro*, med.L *tyro* recruit]

'tis /tɪz/ *archaic* it is. [contr.]

tisane /tɪˈzæn/ *n*. an infusion of dried herbs etc. [F: see PTISAN]

tissue /ˈtɪʃuː, ˈtɪsjuː/ *n*. **1** any of the coherent collections of specialized cells of which animals or plants are made (*muscular tissue*; *nervous tissue*). **2** = *tissue-paper*. **3** a disposable piece of thin soft absorbent paper for wiping, drying, etc. **4** fine woven esp. gauzy fabric. **5** (foll. by *of*) a connected series (*a tissue of lies*). □ **tissue-paper** thin soft unsized paper for wrapping or protecting fragile or delicate articles. [ME f. OF *tissu* rich material, past part. of *tistre* f. L *texere* weave]

Tit. *abbr*. Titus (New Testament).

tit¹ /tɪt/ *n*. any of various small birds esp. of the family Paridae. [prob. f. Scand.]

tit² /tɪt/ *n*. □ **tit for tat** /tæt/ blow for blow; retaliation. [= earlier *tip* (TIP²)· *for tap*]

tit³ /tɪt/ *n*. **1** *colloq*. a nipple. **2** *coarse sl*. a woman's breast. ¶ Usually considered a taboo word in sense 2. [OE: cf. MLG *titte*]

tit⁴ /tɪt/ *n*. *coarse sl*. a term of contempt for a person. [20th c.: perh. f. TIT³]

Titan /ˈtaɪt(ə)n/ *n*. **1** (often **titan**) a person of very great strength, intellect, or importance. **2** (in Greek mythology) a member of a family of early gigantic gods, the offspring of Heaven and Earth. [ME f. L f. Gk]

titanic¹ /taɪˈtænɪk/ *adj*. **1** of or like the Titans. **2** gigantic, colossal. □□ **titanically** *adv*. [Gk *titanikos* (as TITAN)]

titanic² /taɪˈtænɪk, tɪ-/ *adj*. *Chem*. of titanium, esp. in quadrivalent form. □□ **titanate** /ˈtaɪtəˌneɪt, ˈtɪ-/ *n*.

titanium /taɪˈteɪnɪəm, tɪ-/ *n*. *Chem*. a grey metallic element occurring naturally in many clays etc., and used to make strong light alloys that are resistant to corrosion. ¶ Symb.: **Ti**. □ **titanium dioxide** (or **oxide**) a white oxide occurring naturally and used as a white pigment. [Gk (as TITAN) + -IUM, after *uranium*]

titbit /ˈtɪtbɪt/ *n*. (*US* **tidbit** /ˈtɪd-/) **1** a dainty morsel. **2** a piquant item of news etc. [perh. f. dial. *tid* tender + BIT¹]

titch /tɪtʃ/ *n*. (also **tich**) *colloq*. a small person. [*Tich*, stage name of Harry Relph (d. 1928), Engl. music-hall comedian]

titchy /ˈtɪtʃɪ/ *adj*. (**titchier**, **titchiest**) *colloq*. very small.

titer *US* var. of TITRE.

titfer /ˈtɪtfə(r)/ *n*. *Brit*. *sl*. a hat. [abbr. of *tit for tat*, rhyming sl.]

tithe /taɪð/ *n*. & *v*. —*n*. **1** one tenth of the annual produce of land or labour, formerly taken as a tax for the support of the Church and clergy. **2** a tenth part. —*v*. **1** *tr*. subject to tithes. **2** *intr*. pay tithes. □ **tithe barn** a barn built to hold tithes paid in kind. □□ **tithable** *adj*. [OE *teogotha* tenth]

tithing /ˈtaɪðɪŋ/ *n*. **1** the practice of taking or paying a tithe. **2** *hist*. **a** ten householders living near together and collectively responsible for each other's behaviour. **b** the area occupied by them. [OE *tīgething* (as TITHE, -ING¹)]

titi /ˈtiːtiː/ *n*. (*pl*. **titis**) any South American monkey of the genus *Callicebus*. [Tupi]

Titian /ˈtɪʃ(ə)n/ *adj*. (in full **Titian red**) (of hair) bright golden auburn. [name of *Tiziano* Vecelli, It. painter d. 1576]

titillate /ˈtɪtɪˌleɪt/ *v.tr*. **1** excite pleasantly. **2** tickle. □□ **titillatingly** *adv*. **titillation** /-ˈleɪʃ(ə)n/ *n*. [L *titillare titillat-*]

titivate /ˈtɪtɪˌveɪt/ *v.tr*. (also **tittivate**) *colloq*. **1** adorn, smarten. **2** (often *refl*.) put the finishing touches to. □□ **titivation** /-ˈveɪʃ(ə)n/ *n*. [earlier *tidivate*, perh. f. TIDY after *cultivate*]

titlark /ˈtɪtlɑːk/ *n*. a pipit, esp. the meadow pipit.

title /ˈtaɪt(ə)l/ *n*. & *v*. —*n*. **1** the name of a book, work of art, piece of music, etc. **2** the heading of a chapter, poem, document, etc. **3 a** the contents of the title-page of a book. **b** a book regarded in terms of its title (*published 20 new titles*). **4** a caption or credit in a film, broadcast, etc. **5** a form of nomenclature indicating a person's status (e.g. *professor*, *queen*) or used as a form of address or reference (e.g. *Lord*, *Mr*, *Your Grace*). **6** a championship in sport. **7** *Law* **a** the right to ownership of property with or without possession. **b** the facts constituting this. **c** (foll. by *to*) a just or recognized claim. **8** *Eccl*. **a** a fixed sphere of work and source of income as a condition for ordination. **b** a parish church in Rome under a cardinal. —*v.tr.* give a title to. □**title-deed** a legal instrument as evidence of a right, esp. to property. **title-page** a page at the beginning of a book giving the title and particulars of authorship etc. **title role** the part in a play etc. that gives it its name (e.g. *Othello*). [ME f. OF f. L *titulus* placard, title]

titled /'taɪt(ə)ld/ *adj.* having a title of nobility or rank.

titling[1] /'taɪtlɪŋ/ *n.* the impressing of a title in gold leaf etc. on the cover of a book.

titling[2] /'taɪtlɪŋ/ *n.* **1** a titlark. **2** a titmouse.

titmouse /'tɪtmaʊs/ *n.* (*pl.* **titmice** /-maɪs/) any of various small tits, esp. of the genus *Parus*. [ME *titmōse* f. TIT[1] + OE *māse* titmouse, assim. to MOUSE]

titrate /'taɪtreɪt, 'tɪ-/ *v.tr. Chem.* ascertain the amount of a constituent in (a solution) by measuring the volume of a known concentration of reagent required to complete the reaction. □□ **titratable** *adj.* **titration** /-'treɪʃ(ə)n/ *n.*

titre /'taɪtə(r)/ *n.* (*US* **titer**) *Chem.* the strength of a solution or the quantity of a constituent as determined by titration. [F, = TITRE]

titter /'tɪtə(r)/ *v. & n.* —*v.intr.* laugh in a furtive or restrained way; giggle. —*n.* a furtive or restrained laugh. □□ **titterer** *n.* **titteringly** *adv.* [imit.]

tittivate var. of TITIVATE.

tittle /'tɪt(ə)l/ *n.* **1** a small written or printed stroke or dot. **2** a particle; a whit (esp. in *not one jot or tittle*). [ME f. L (as TITLE)]

tittlebat /'tɪt(ə)l,bæt/ *n. Brit.* a stickleback. [fanciful var.]

tittle-tattle /'tɪt(ə)l,tæt(ə)l/ *n. & v.* —*n.* petty gossip. —*v.intr.* gossip, chatter. [redupl. of TATTLE]

tittup /'tɪtəp/ *v. & n.* —*v.intr.* (**tittuped, tittuping** or **tittupped, tittupping**) go about friskily or jerkily; bob up and down; canter. —*n.* such a gait or movement. [perh. imit. of hoof-beats]

titty /'tɪtɪ/ *n.* (*pl.* **-ies**) *sl.* = TIT[3] (esp. as a child's term).

titubation /,tɪtjʊ'beɪʃ(ə)n/ *n. Med.* unsteadiness esp. as caused by nervous disease. [L *titubatio* f. *titubare* totter]

titular /'tɪtjʊlə(r)/ *adj. & n.* —*adj.* **1** of or relating to a title (*the book's titular hero*). **2** existing, or being what is specified, in name or title only (*titular ruler*; *titular sovereignty*). —*n.* **1** the holder of an office etc. esp. a benefice, without the corresponding functions or obligations. **2** a titular saint. □**titular bishop** a bishop, esp. in a non-Christian country, with a see named after a Christian see no longer in existence. **titular saint** the patron saint of a particular church. □□ **titularly** *adv.* [F *titulaire* or mod.L *titularis* f. *titulus* TITLE]

tizzy /'tɪzɪ/ *n.* (*pl.* **-ies**) (also **tizz, tiz**) *colloq.* a state of nervous agitation (*in a tizzy*). [20th c.: orig. unkn.]

T-junction /'tiː,dʒʌŋkʃ(ə)n/ *n.* a road junction at which one road joins another at right angles without crossing it.

TKO *abbr. Boxing* technical knockout.

Tl *symb. Chem.* the element thallium.

TLC *abbr. colloq.* tender loving care.

TLS *abbr. Times Literary Supplement.*

TM *abbr.* Transcendental Meditation.

Tm *symb. Chem.* the element thulium.

tmesis /'tmiːsɪs/ *n.* (*pl.* **tmeses** /-siːz/) *Gram.* the separation of parts of a compound word by an intervening word or words (esp. in *colloq.* speech, e.g. *can't find it any-blooming-where*). [Gk *tmēsis* cutting f. *temnō* cut]

TN *abbr. US* Tennessee (in official postal use).

tn *abbr.* **1** *US* ton(s). **2** town.

TNT *abbr.* trinitrotoluene, a high explosive formed from toluene by substitution of three hydrogen atoms with nitro groups.

to /tə, *before a vowel* tʊ, *emphat.* tuː/ *prep. & adv.* —*prep.* **1** introducing a noun: **a** expressing what is

reached, approached, or touched (*fell to the ground*; *went to Paris*; *put her face to the window*; *five minutes to six*). **b** expressing what is aimed at: often introducing the indirect object of a verb (*throw it to me*; *explained the problem to them*). **c** as far as; up to (*went on to the end*; *have to stay from Tuesday to Friday*). **d** to the extent of (*were all drunk to a man*; *was starved to death*). **e** expressing what is followed (*according to instructions*; *made to order*). **f** expressing what is considered or affected (*am used to that*; *that is nothing to me*). **g** expressing what is caused or produced (*turn to stone*; *tear to shreds*). **h** expressing what is compared (*nothing to what it once was*; *comparable to any other*; *equal to the occasion*; *won by three goals to two*). **i** expressing what is increased (*add it to mine*). **j** expressing what is involved or composed as specified (*there is nothing to it*; *more to him than meets the eye*). **k** expressing the substance of a debit entry in accounting (*to four chairs, sixty pounds*). **l** *archaic* for; by way of (*took her to wife*). **2** introducing the infinitive: **a** as a verbal noun (*to get there is the priority*). **b** expressing purpose, consequence, or cause (*we eat to live*; *left him to starve*; *am sorry to hear that*). **c** as a substitute for *to* + infinitive (*wanted to come but was unable to*). —*adv.* **1** in the normal or required position or condition (*come to*; *heave to*). **2** (of a door) in a nearly closed position. □**to and fro 1** backwards and forwards. **2** repeatedly between the same points. [OE *tō* (adv. & prep.) f. WG]

toad /təʊd/ *n.* **1** any froglike amphibian of the family Bufonidae, esp. of the genus *Bufo*, breeding in water but living chiefly on land. **2** any of various similar amphibians including the Surinam toad. **3** a repulsive or detestable person. □**toad-eater** *archaic* a toady. **toad-in-the-hole** *Brit.* sausages or other meat baked in batter. □□ **toadish** *adj.* [OE *tādige, tādde, tāda*, of unkn. orig.]

toadfish /'təʊdfɪʃ/ *n.* any marine fish of the family Batrachoididae, with a large head and wide mouth, making grunting noises by vibrating the walls of its swim-bladder.

toadflax /'təʊdflæks/ *n.* **1** any plant of the genus *Linaria* or *Chaenorrhinum*, with flaxlike leaves and spurred yellow or purple flowers. **2** a related plant, *Cymbalaria muralis*, with lilac flowers and ivy-shaped leaves.

toadstone /'təʊdstəʊn/ *n.* a stone, sometimes precious, supposed to resemble or to have been formed in the body of a toad, formerly used as an amulet etc.

toadstool /'təʊdstuːl/ *n.* the spore-bearing structure of various fungi, usu. poisonous, with a round top and slender stalk.

toady /'təʊdɪ/ *n. & v.* —*n.* (*pl.* **-ies**) a sycophant; an obsequious hanger-on. —*v.tr.* & (foll. by *to*) *intr.* (**-ies, -ied**) behave servilely to; fawn upon. □□ **toadyish** *adj.* **toadyism** *n.* [contr. of *toad-eater*, a charlatan's attendant who ate toads (regarded as poisonous)]

toast /təʊst/ *n. & v.* —*n.* **1** bread in slices browned on both sides by radiant heat. **2 a** a person (orig. esp. a woman) or thing in whose honour a company is requested to drink. **b** a call to drink or an instance of drinking in this way. —*v.* **1** *tr.* cook or brown (bread, a teacake, cheese, etc.) by radiant heat. **2** *intr.* (of bread etc.) become brown in this way. **3** *tr.* warm (one's feet, oneself, etc.) at a fire etc. **4** *tr.* drink to the health or in honour of (a person or thing). □**have a person on toast** *colloq.* be in a position to deal with a person as one wishes. **toasting-fork** a long-handled fork for making toast before a fire. **toast rack** a rack for holding slices of toast at table. [ME (orig. as verb) f. OF *toster* roast, ult. f. L *torrēre tost-* parch: sense 2 of the noun reflects the notion that a woman's name flavours the drink as spiced toast would]

toaster /'təʊstə(r)/ n. an electrical device for making toast.

toastmaster /'təʊst,mɑːstə(r)/ n. (fem. **toastmistress** /-,mɪstrɪs/) an official responsible for announcing toasts at a public occasion.

tobacco /tə'bækəʊ/ n. (pl. **-os**) **1** (in full **tobacco-plant**) any plant of the genus Nicotiana, of American origin, with narcotic leaves used for smoking, chewing, or snuff. **2** its leaves, esp. as prepared for smoking. □**tobacco mosaic virus** a virus that causes mosaic disease in tobacco, much used in biochemical research. **tobacco-pipe** see PIPE n. 2. **tobacco-stopper** an instrument for pressing down the tobacco in a pipe. [Sp. tabaco, of Amer. Ind. orig.]

tobacconist /tə'bækənɪst/ n. a retail dealer in tobacco and cigarettes etc.

toboggan /tə'bɒgən/ n. & v. —n. a long light narrow sledge for sliding downhill esp. over compacted snow or ice. —v.intr. ride on a toboggan. □□ **tobogganer** n. **tobogganing** n. **tobogganist** n. [Can. F tabaganne f. Algonquian]

toby jug /'təʊbɪ/ n. a jug or mug for ale etc., usu. in the form of a stout old man wearing a three-cornered hat. [familiar form of the name Tobias]

toccata /tə'kɑːtə/ n. a musical composition for a keyboard instrument designed to exhibit the performer's touch and technique. [It., fem. past part. of toccare touch]

Toc H /tɒk'eɪtʃ/ n. Brit. a society, orig. of ex-servicemen and -women, founded after the war of 1914–18 for promoting Christian fellowship and social service. [toc (former telegraphy code for T) + H, for Talbot House, a soldier's club established in Belgium in 1915]

Tocharian /tə'keərɪən/ n. & adj. —n. **1** an extinct Indo-European language of a central Asian people in the first millennium AD. **2** a member of the people speaking this language. —adj. of or in this language. [F tocharien f. L Tochari f. Gk Tokharoi a Scythian tribe]

tocopherol /,təʊkəʊ'fɪərɒl/ n. any of several closely related vitamins, found in wheat-germ oil, egg yolk, and leafy vegetables, and important in the stabilization of cell membranes etc. Also called vitamin E. [Gk tokos offspring + pherō bear + -OL[1]]

tocsin /'tɒksɪn/ n. an alarm bell or signal. [F f. OF touquesain, toquassen f. Prov. tocasenh f. tocar TOUCH + senh signal-bell]

tod /tɒd/ n. Brit. sl. □**on one's tod** alone; on one's own. [20th c.: perh. f. rhyming sl. on one's Tod Sloan (name of a jockey)]

today /tə'deɪ/ adv. & n. —adv. **1** on or in the course of this present day (shall we go today?). **2** nowadays, in modern times. —n. **1** this present day (today is my birthday). **2** modern times. □**today week** (or **fortnight** etc.) a week (or fortnight etc.) from today. [OE tō dæg on (this) day (as TO, DAY)]

toddle /'tɒd(ə)l/ v. & n. —v.intr. **1** walk with short unsteady steps like those of a small child. **2** colloq. **a** (often foll. by round, to, etc.) take a casual or leisurely walk. **b** (usu. foll. by off) depart. —n. **1** a toddling walk. **2** colloq. a stroll or short walk. [16th-c. todle (Sc. & N.Engl.), of unkn. orig.]

toddler /'tɒdlə(r)/ n. a child who is just beginning to walk. □□ **toddlerhood** n.

toddy /'tɒdɪ/ n. (pl. **-ies**) **1** a drink of spirits with hot water and sugar or spices. **2** the sap of some kinds of palm, fermented to produce arrack. [Hind. tārī f. tār palm f. Skr. tāla palmyra]

to-do /tə'duː/ n. a commotion or fuss. [to do as in what's to do (= to be done)]

tody /'təʊdɪ/ n. (pl. **-ies**) any small insect-eating West Indian bird of the genus Todus, related to the kingfisher. [F todier f. L todus, a small bird]

toe /təʊ/ n. & v. —n. **1** any of the five terminal projections of the foot. **2** the corresponding part of an animal. **3** the part of an item of footwear that covers the toes. **4** the lower end or tip of an implement etc. **5** Archit. a projection from the foot of a buttress etc. to give stability. —v. (**toes**, **toed**, **toeing**) **1** tr. touch (a starting-line etc.) with the toes before starting a race. **2** tr. **a** mend the toe of (a sock etc.). **b** provide with a toe. **3** intr. (foll. by in, out) **a** walk with the toes pointed in (or out). **b** (of a pair of wheels) converge (or diverge) slightly at the front. **4** tr. Golf strike (the ball) with a part of the club too near the toe. □**on one's toes** alert, eager. **toe-clip** a clip on a bicycle-pedal to prevent the foot from slipping. **toe-hold 1** a small foothold. **2** a small beginning or advantage. **toe the line** conform to a general policy or principle, esp. unwillingly or under pressure. **turn up one's toes** colloq. die. □□ **toed** adj. (also in comb.). **toeless** adj. [OE tā f. Gmc]

toecap /'təʊkæp/ n. the (usu. strengthened) outer covering of the toe of a boot or shoe.

toenail /'təʊneɪl/ n. **1** the nail at the tip of each toe. **2** a nail driven obliquely through the end of a board etc.

toerag /'təʊræg/ n. Brit. sl. a term of contempt for a person. [earlier = tramp, vagrant, f. the rag wrapped round the foot in place of a sock]

toey /'təʊɪ/ adj. Austral. sl. restless, nervous, touchy.

toff /tɒf/ n. & v. Brit. sl. —n. a distinguished or well-dressed person; a dandy. —v.tr. (foll. by up) dress up smartly. [perh. a perversion of tuft = titled undergraduate (from the gold tassel formerly worn on the cap)]

toffee /'tɒfɪ/ n. (also **toffy**) (pl. **toffees** or **toffies**) **1** a kind of firm or hard sweet softening when sucked or chewed, made by boiling sugar, butter, etc. **2** Brit. a small piece of this. □**for toffee** sl. (prec. by can't etc.) (denoting incompetence) at all (they couldn't sing for toffee). **toffee-apple** an apple with a thin coating of toffee. **toffee-nosed** esp. Brit. sl. snobbish, pretentious. [earlier TAFFY]

toft /tɒft/ n. Brit. **1** a homestead. **2** land once occupied by this. [OE f. ON topt]

tofu /'təʊfuː/ n. (esp. in China and Japan) a curd made from mashed soya beans. [Jap. tōfu f. Chin., = rotten beans]

tog[1] /tɒg/ n. & v. colloq. —n. (usu. in pl.) an item of clothing. —v.tr. & intr. (**togged**, **togging**) (foll. by out, up) dress, esp. elaborately. [app. abbr. of 16th-c. cant togeman(s), togman, f. F toge or L toga: see TOGA]

tog[2] /tɒg/ n. a unit of thermal resistance used to express the insulating properties of clothes and quilts. [arbitrary, prob. f. TOG[1]]

toga /'təʊgə/ n. hist. an ancient Roman citizen's loose flowing outer garment. □□ **togaed** adj. (also **toga'd**). [L, rel. to tegere cover]

together /tə'geðə(r)/ adv. & adj. —adv. **1** in company or conjunction (walking together; built it together; were at school together). **2** simultaneously; at the same time (both shouted together). **3** one with another (were talking together). **4** into conjunction; so as to unite (tied them together; put two and two together). **5** into company or companionship (came together in friendship). **6** uninterruptedly (could talk for hours together). —adj. colloq. well organized or controlled. □**together with** as well as; and also. [OE tōgædere f. TO + gædre together: cf. GATHER]

togetherness /tə'geðənɪs/ n. **1** the condition of being together. **2** a feeling of comfort from being together.

toggery /'tɒgərɪ/ n. colloq. clothes, togs.

toggle /'tɒg(ə)l/ n. & v. —n. **1** a device for fastening (esp. a garment), consisting of a crosspiece which can pass through a hole or loop in one position but not in another. **2** a pin or other crosspiece put through the eye of a rope, a link of a chain, etc., to keep it in place. **3** a pivoted barb on a harpoon. **4** Computing a switch action that is operated the same way but with opposite effect on successive occasions. —v.tr. provide or fasten with a toggle. □**toggle joint** a device for exerting pressure along two jointed rods by applying a transverse force at the joint. **toggle switch** an electric switch with a projecting lever to be moved usu. up and down. [18th-c. Naut.: orig. unkn.]

Togolese /ˌtəʊgəˈliːz/ *adj.* & *n.* —*adj.* of or relating to Togo in W. Africa. —*n.* (*pl.* same) **1** a native or national of Togo. **2** a person of Togolese descent.

toil /tɔɪl/ *v.* & *n.* —*v.intr.* **1** work laboriously or incessantly. **2** make slow painful progress (*toiled along the path*). —*n.* prolonged or intensive labour; drudgery. □**toil-worn** worn or worn out by toil. □□ **toiler** *n.* [ME f. AF *toiler* (v.), *toil* (n.), dispute, OF *tooilier*, *tooil*, f. L *tudiculare* stir about f. *tudicula* machine for bruising olives, rel. to *tundere* beat]

toile /twɑːl/ *n.* **1** cloth esp. for garments. **2** a garment reproduced in muslin or other cheap material for fitting or for making copies. [F *toile* cloth f. L *tela* web]

toilet /ˈtɔɪlɪt/ *n.* **1** = LAVATORY. **2** the process of washing oneself, dressing, etc. (*make one's toilet*). **3** the cleansing of part of the body after an operation or at the time of childbirth. □**toilet paper** (or **tissue**) paper for cleaning oneself after excreting. **toilet roll** a roll of toilet paper. **toilet set** a set of hairbrushes, combs, etc. **toilet soap** soap for washing oneself. **toilet table** a dressing-table usu. with a mirror. **toilet-train** cause (a young child) to undergo toilet-training. **toilet-training** the training of a young child to use the lavatory. **toilet water** a dilute form of perfume used after washing. [F *toilette* cloth, wrapper, dimin. f. *toile*: see TOILE]

toiletry /ˈtɔɪlɪtrɪ/ *n.* (*pl.* **-ies**) (usu. in *pl.*) any of various articles or cosmetics used in washing, dressing, etc.

toilette /twɑːˈlet/ *n.* = TOILET 2. [F: see TOILET]

toils /tɔɪlz/ *n.pl.* a net or snare. [pl. of *toil* f. OF *toile* cloth f. L *tela* web]

toilsome /ˈtɔɪlsəm/ *adj.* involving toil; laborious. □□ **toilsomely** *adv.* **toilsomeness** *n.*

toing and froing /ˌtuːɪŋ ənd ˈfrəʊɪŋ/ *n.* constant movement to and fro; bustle; dispersed activity. [TO *adv.* + FRO + -ING[1]]

Tokay /təˈkeɪ/ *n.* **1** a sweet aromatic wine made near Tokaj in Hungary. **2** a similar wine produced elsewhere.

token /ˈtəʊkən/ *n.* & *adj.* —*n.* **1** a thing serving as a symbol, reminder, or distinctive mark of something (*as a token of affection; in token of my esteem*). **2** a thing serving as evidence of authenticity or as a guarantee. **3** a voucher exchangeable for goods (often of a specified kind), given as a gift. **4** anything used to represent something else, esp. a metal disc etc. used instead of money in coin-operated machines etc. **5** (*attrib.*) **a** nominal or perfunctory (*token effort*). **b** conducted briefly to demonstrate strength of feeling (*token resistance; token strike*). **c** serving to acknowledge a principle only (*token payment*). **d** chosen by way of tokenism to represent a particular group (*the token woman on the committee*). □**by this** (or **the same**) **token 1** similarly. **2** moreover. **token money** coins having a higher face value than their worth as metal. **token vote** a parliamentary vote of money, the stipulated amount of which is not meant to be binding. [OE *tāc(e)n* f. Gmc, rel. to TEACH]

tokenism /ˈtəʊkəˌnɪz(ə)m/ *n.* **1** esp. *Polit.* the principle or practice of granting minimum concessions, esp. to appease radical demands etc. (cf. TOKEN 5d). **2** making only a token effort.

tolbooth var. of TOLLBOOTH.

told past and past part. of TELL[1].

Toledo /təˈliːdəʊ/ *n.* (*pl.* **-os**) a fine sword or sword-blade made in Toledo in Spain.

tolerable /ˈtɒlərəb(ə)l/ *adj.* **1** able to be endured. **2** fairly good; mediocre. □□ **tolerability** /-ˈbɪlɪtɪ/ *n.* **tolerableness** *n.* **tolerably** *adv.* [ME f. OF f. L *tolerabilis* (as TOLERATE)]

tolerance /ˈtɒlərəns/ *n.* **1** a willingness or ability to tolerate; forbearance. **2** the capacity to tolerate. **3** an

allowable variation in any measurable property. **4** the ability to tolerate the effects of a drug etc. after continued use. [ME f. OF f. L *tolerantia* (as TOLERATE)]

tolerant /ˈtɒlərənt/ *adj.* **1** disposed or accustomed to tolerate others or their acts or opinions. **2** (foll. by *of*) enduring or patient. □□ **tolerantly** *adv.* [F *tolérant* f. L *tolerare* (as TOLERATE)]

tolerate /ˈtɒləˌreɪt/ *v.tr.* **1** allow the existence or occurrence of without authoritative interference. **2** leave unmolested. **3** endure or permit, esp. with forbearance. **4** sustain or endure (suffering etc.). **5** be capable of continued subjection to (a drug, radiation, etc.) without harm. **6** find or treat as endurable. □□ **tolerator** *n.* [L *tolerare* tolerat-endure]

toleration /ˌtɒləˈreɪʃ(ə)n/ *n.* the process or practice of tolerating, esp. the allowing of differences in religious opinion without discrimination. [F *tolération* f. L *toleratio* (as TOLERATE)]

toll[1] /təʊl/ *n.* **1** a charge payable for permission to pass a barrier or use a bridge or road etc. **2** the cost or damage caused by a disaster, battle, etc., or incurred in an achievement (*death toll*). **3** *US* a charge for a long distance telephone call. □**take its toll** be accompanied by loss or injury etc. **toll-bridge** a bridge at which a toll is charged. **toll-gate** a gate preventing passage until a toll is paid. **toll-house** a house at a toll-gate or -bridge, used by a toll-collector. **toll-road** a road maintained by the tolls collected on it. [OE f. med.L *toloneum* f. LL *teloneum* f. Gk *telōnion* toll-house f. *telos* tax]

toll[2] /təʊl/ *v.* & *n.* —*v.* **1 a** *intr.* (of a bell) sound with a slow uniform succession of strokes. **b** *tr.* ring (a bell) in this way. **c** *tr.* (of a bell) announce or mark (a death etc.) in this way. **2** *tr.* strike (the hour). —*n.* **1** the act of tolling. **2** a stroke of a bell. [ME, special use of (now dial.) *toll* entice, pull, f. an OE root *-tyllan* (recorded in *fortyllan* seduce)]

tollbooth /ˈtəʊlbuːð, -buːθ/ *n.* (also **tolbooth**) **1** a booth at the roadside from which tolls are collected. **2** *Sc. archaic* a town hall. **3** *Sc. archaic* a town gaol.

Toltec /ˈtɒltek/ *n.* **1** a member of an American Indian people that flourished in Mexico before the Aztecs. **2** the language of this people. □□ **Toltecan** *adj.* [Amer. Ind.]

tolu /təˈluː, ˈtəʊluː/ *n.* a fragrant brown balsam obtained from either of two South American trees, *Myroxylon balsamum* or *M. toluifera*, and used in perfumery and medicine. [Santiago de *Tolu* in Colombia]

toluene /ˈtɒljuˌiːn/ *n.* a colourless aromatic liquid hydrocarbon derivative of benzene, orig. obtained from tolu, used in the manufacture of explosives etc. Also called *methyl benzene*. □□ **toluic** *adj.* **toluol** *n.* [TOLU + -ENE]

tom /tɒm/ *n.* a male of various animals, esp. (in full **tom-cat**) a male cat. [abbr. of the name *Thomas*]

tomahawk /ˈtɒməˌhɔːk/ *n.* & *v.* —*n.* **1** a N. American Indian war-axe with a stone or iron head. **2** *Austral.* a hatchet. —*v.tr.* strike, cut, or kill with a tomahawk. [Renape *tämähãk* f. *tämäham* he etc. cuts]

tomato /təˈmɑːtəʊ/ *n.* (*pl.* **-oes**) **1** a glossy red or yellow pulpy edible fruit. **2** a solanaceous plant, *Lycopersicon esculentum*, bearing this. □□ **tomatoey** *adj.* [17th-c. *tomate*, = F or Sp. & Port., f. Mex. *tomatl*]

tomb /tuːm/ *n.* **1** a large esp. underground vault for the burial of the dead. **2** an enclosure cut in the earth or in rock to receive a dead body. **3** a sepulchral monument. **4** (prec. by *the*) the state of death. [ME *t(o)umbe* f. AF *tumbe*, OF *tombe* f. LL *tumba* f. Gk *tumbos*]

tombac /ˈtɒmbæk/ *n.* an alloy of copper and zinc used esp. as material for cheap jewellery. [F f. Malay *tambāga* copper]

tombola /tɒmˈbəʊlə/ *n.* *Brit.* a kind of lottery with tickets usu. drawn from a turning drum-shaped container, esp. at a fête or fair. [F *tombola* or It. f. *tombolare* tumble]

tombolo /'tɒmbə,ləʊ/ *n.* (*pl.* **-os**) a spit joining an island to the mainland. [It., = sand-dune]

tomboy /'tɒmbɔɪ/ *n.* a girl who behaves in a rough boyish way. □□ **tomboyish** *adj.* **tomboyishness** *n.*

tombstone /'tuːmstəʊn/ *n.* a stone standing or laid over a grave, usu. with an epitaph.

Tom Collins /tɒm 'kɒlɪnz/ *n.* an iced cocktail of gin with soda, lemon or lime juice, and sugar. [20th c.: orig. unkn.]

Tom, Dick, and Harry /,tɒm dɪk ənd 'hærɪ/ *n.* (usu. prec. by *any, every*) usu. *derog.* ordinary people taken at random.

tome /təʊm/ *n.* a large heavy book or volume. [F f. L *tomus* f. Gk *tomos* section, volume f. *temnō* cut]

-tome /təʊm/ *comb. form* forming nouns meaning: **1** an instrument for cutting (*microtome*). **2** a section or segment. [Gk *tomē* a cutting, *-tomos* -cutting, f. *temnō* cut]

tomentum /tə'mentəm/ *n.* (*pl.* **tomenta** /-tə/) **1** *Bot.* matted woolly down on stems and leaves. **2** *Anat.* the tufted inner surface of the pia mater in the brain. □□ **tomentose** /tə'mentəʊs, 'təʊ-/ *adj.* **tomentous** *adj.* [L, = cushion-stuffing]

tomfool /tɒm'fuːl/ *n.* **1** a foolish person. **2** (*attrib.*) silly, foolish (*a tomfool idea*).

tomfoolery /tɒm'fuːlərɪ/ *n.* (*pl.* **-ies**) **1** foolish behaviour; nonsense. **2** an instance of this.

Tommy /'tɒmɪ/ *n.* (*pl.* **-ies**) *colloq.* a British private soldier. [*Tommy (Thomas) Atkins*, a name used in specimens of completed official forms]

tommy-bar /'tɒmɪ,bɑː(r)/ *n.* a short bar for use with a box spanner.

tommy-gun /'tɒmɪ,gʌn/ *n.* a type of sub-machine-gun. [J. T. *Thompson*, US Army officer d. 1940, its co-inventor]

tommy-rot /'tɒmɪ,rɒt/ *n. sl.* nonsense.

tomogram /'tɒmə,græm/ *n.* a record obtained by tomography.

tomography /tə'mɒgrəfɪ/ *n.* a method of radiography displaying details in a selected plane within the body. [Gk *tomē* a cutting + -GRAPHY]

tomorrow /tə'mɒrəʊ/ *adv. & n.* —*adv.* **1** on the day after today. **2** at some future time. —*n.* **1** the day after today. **2** the near future. □**tomorrow morning** (or **afternoon** etc.) in the morning (or afternoon etc.) of tomorrow. **tomorrow week** a week from tomorrow. [TO + MORROW: cf. TODAY]

tompion var. of TAMPION.

Tom Thumb /tɒm 'θʌm/ *n.* **1** a dwarf or midget. **2** a dwarf variety of various plants. [the name of a tiny person in fairy stories]

tomtit /'tɒmtɪt/ *n.* a tit, esp. a blue tit.

tom-tom /'tɒmtɒm/ *n.* **1** a primitive drum beaten with the hands. **2** a tall drum beaten with the hands and used in jazz bands etc. [Hindi *tamtam*, imit.]

-tomy /təmɪ/ *comb. form* forming nouns denoting cutting, esp. in surgery (*laparotomy*). [Gk *-tomia* cutting f. *temnō* cut]

ton¹ /tʌn/ *n.* **1** (in full **long ton**) a unit of weight equal to 2,240 lb. avoirdupois (1016.05 kg). **2** (in full **short ton**) a unit of weight equal to 2,000 lb. avoirdupois (907.19 kg). **3** (in full **metric ton**) = TONNE. **4 a** (in full **displacement ton**) a unit of measurement of a ship's weight or volume in terms of its displacement of water with the loadline just immersed, equal to 2,240 lb. or 35 cu. ft. (0.99 cubic metres). **b** (in full **freight ton**) a unit of weight or volume of cargo, equal to a metric ton (1,000 kg) or 40 cu. ft. **5 a** (in full **gross ton**) a unit of gross internal capacity, equal to 100 cu. ft. (2.83 cubic metres). **b** (in full **net** or **register ton**) an equivalent unit of net internal capacity. **6** a unit of refrigerating power able to freeze 2,000 lb. of ice at 0°C in 24 hours. **7** a measure of capacity for various materials, esp. 40 cu. ft. of timber. **8** (usu. in *pl.*) *colloq.* a large number or amount (*tons of money*). **9** esp. *Brit. sl.* a

speed of 100 m.p.h. **b** a sum of £100. **c** a score of 100. □**ton-mile** one ton of goods carried one mile, as a unit of traffic. **ton-up** *Brit. sl. n.* a speed of 100 m.p.h. —*attrib.adj.* **1** (of a motor cyclist) achieving this, esp. habitually and recklessly (*ton-up kid*). **2** fond or capable of travelling at high speed. **weigh a ton** *colloq.* be very heavy. [orig. the same word as TUN: differentiated in the 17th c.]

ton² /tɔ̃/ *n.* **1** a prevailing mode or fashion. **2** fashionable society. [F]

tonal /'təʊn(ə)l/ *adj.* **1** of or relating to tone or tonality. **2** (of a fugue etc.) having repetitions of the subject at different pitches in the same key. □□ **tonally** *adv.* [med.L *tonalis* (as TONE)]

tonality /tə'nælɪtɪ/ *n.* (*pl.* **-ies**) **1** *Mus.* **a** the relationship between the tones of a musical scale. **b** the observance of a single tonic key as the basis of a composition. **2** the tone or colour scheme of a picture.

tondo /'tɒndəʊ/ *n.* (*pl.* **tondi** /-dɪ/) a circular painting or relief. [It., = round (plate), f. *rotondo* f. L *rotundus* round]

tone /təʊn/ *n. & v.* —*n.* **1** a musical or vocal sound, esp. with reference to its pitch, quality, and strength. **2** (often in *pl.*) modulation of the voice expressing a particular feeling or mood (*a cheerful tone; suspicious tones*). **3** a manner of expression in writing. **4** *Mus.* a a musical sound, esp. of a definite pitch and character. **b** an interval of a major second, e.g. C–D. **5 a** the general effect of colour or of light and shade in a picture. **b** the tint or shade of a colour. **6 a** the prevailing character of the morals and sentiments etc. in a group. **b** an attitude or sentiment expressed esp. in a letter etc. **7** the proper firmness of bodily organs. **8** a state of good or specified health or quality. **9** *Phonet.* **a** an accent on one syllable of a word. **b** a way of pronouncing a word to distinguish it from others of a similar sound (*Mandarin Chinese has four tones*). —*v.* **1** *tr.* give the desired tone to. **2** *tr.* modify the tone of. **3** *intr.* (often foll. by *to*) attune. **4** *intr.* (foll. by *with*) be in harmony (esp. of colour) (*does not tone with the wallpaper*). **5** *tr. Photog.* give (a monochrome picture) an altered colour in finishing by means of a chemical solution. **6** *intr.* undergo a change in colour by toning. □**tone-arm** the movable arm supporting the pick-up of a record-player. **tone control** a switch for varying the proportion of high and low frequencies in reproduced sound. **tone-deaf** unable to perceive differences of musical pitch accurately. **tone-deafness** the condition of being tone-deaf. **tone down 1** make or become softer in tone of sound or colour. **2** make (a statement etc.) less harsh or emphatic. **tone poem** = *symphonic poem.* **tone-row** = SERIES 8. **tone up 1** make or become stronger in tone of sound or colour. **2** make (a statement etc.) more emphatic. **whole-tone scale** see WHOLE. □□ **toneless** *adj.* **tonelessly** *adv.* **toner** *n.* [ME f. OF *ton* or L *tonus* f. Gk *tonos* tension, tone f. *teinō* stretch]

toneburst /'təʊnbɜːst/ *n.* an audio signal used in testing the transient response of audio components.

toneme /'təʊniːm/ *n.* a phoneme distinguished from another only by its tone. □□ **tonemic** /-'niːmɪk/ *adj.* [TONE after *phoneme*]

tong /tɒŋ/ *n.* a Chinese guild, association, or secret society. [Chin. *tang* meeting-place]

tonga /'tɒŋgə/ *n.* a light horse-drawn two-wheeled vehicle used in India. [Hindi *tāṅgā*]

tongs /tɒŋz/ *n.pl.* (also **pair of tongs** *sing.*) an instrument with two hinged or sprung arms for grasping and holding. [pl. of *tong* f. OE *tang(e)* f. Gmc]

tongue /tʌŋ/ *n. & v.* —*n.* **1** the fleshy muscular organ in the mouth used in tasting, licking, and swallowing, and (in man) for speech. **2** the tongue of an ox etc. as food. **3** the faculty of or a tendency in speech (*a sharp tongue*). **4** a particular language (*the German tongue*). **5** a thing like a tongue in shape or position, esp.: **a** a long low promontory. **b** a strip of leather etc., attached at one end only, under the laces in a shoe. **c** the clapper of a bell. **d** the pin of a buckle. **e** the projecting strip on a wooden etc. board fitting into the groove of another. **f** a vibrating slip in the reed of some musical instruments. **g** a jet of flame. —*v.* (**tongues, tongued, tonguing**) **1** *tr.* produce staccato etc. effects with (a flute etc.) by means of tonguing. **2** *intr.* use the tongue in this way. □**find** (or **lose**) **one's tongue** be able (or unable) to express oneself after a shock etc. **the gift of tongues** the power of speaking in unknown languages, regarded as one of the gifts of the Holy Spirit (Acts 2). **keep a civil tongue in one's head** avoid rudeness. **tongue-and-groove** applied to boards in which a tongue along one edge fits into a groove along the edge of the next, each board having a tongue on one edge and a groove on the other. **tongue-in-cheek** *adj.* ironic; slyly humorous. —*adv.* insincerely or ironically. **tongue-lashing** a severe scolding or reprimand. **tongue-tie** a speech impediment due to a malformation of the tongue. **tongue-tied 1** too shy or embarrassed to speak. **2** having a tongue-tie. **tongue-twister** a sequence of words difficult to pronounce quickly and correctly. **with one's tongue hanging out** eagerly or expectantly. **with one's tongue in one's cheek** insincerely or ironically. □□**tongued** *adj.* (also in *comb.*). **tongueless** *adj.* [OE *tunge* f. Gmc, rel. to L *lingua*]

tonguing /ˈtʌŋɪŋ/ *n. Mus.* the technique of playing a wind instrument using the tongue to articulate certain notes.

tonic /ˈtɒnɪk/ *n. & adj.* —*n.* **1** an invigorating medicine. **2** anything serving to invigorate. **3** = *tonic water*. **4** *Mus.* the first degree of a scale, forming the keynote of a piece (see KEYNOTE 3). —*adj.* **1** serving as a tonic; invigorating. **2** *Mus.* denoting the first degree of a scale. **3 a** producing tension, esp. of the muscles. **b** restoring normal tone to organs. □**tonic accent** an accent marked by a change of pitch within a syllable. **tonic sol-fa** *Mus.* a system of notation used esp. in teaching singing, with doh as the keynote of all major keys and lah as the keynote of all minor keys. **tonic spasm** continuous muscular contraction (cf. CLONUS). **tonic water** a carbonated mineral water containing quinine. □□**tonically** *adv.* [F *tonique* f. Gk *tonikos* (as TONE)]

tonicity /təˈnɪsɪtɪ/ *n.* **1** the state of being tonic. **2** a healthy elasticity of muscles etc.

tonight /təˈnaɪt/ *adv. & n.* —*adv.* on the present or approaching evening or night. —*n.* the evening or night of the present day. [TO + NIGHT: cf. TODAY]

tonka bean /ˈtɒŋkə/ *n.* the black fragrant seed of a South American tree, *Dipteryx odorata*, used in perfumery etc. [*tonka*, its name in Guyana, + BEAN]

tonnage /ˈtʌnɪdʒ/ *n.* **1** a ship's internal cubic capacity or freight-carrying capacity measured in tons. **2** the total carrying capacity esp. of a country's mercantile marine. **3** a charge per ton on freight or cargo. [orig. in sense 'duty on a tun of wine': OF *tonnage* f. *tonne* TUN: later f. TON¹]

tonne /tʌn/ *n.* a metric ton equal to 1,000 kg. [F: see TUN]

tonneau /ˈtɒnəʊ/ *n.* the part of a motor car occupied by the back seats, esp. in an open car. □**tonneau cover** a removable flexible cover for the passenger seats in an open car, boat, etc., when they are not in use. [F, lit. cask, tun]

tonometer /təˈnɒmɪtə(r)/ *n.* **1** a tuning-fork or other instrument for measuring the pitch of tones. **2** an instrument for measuring the pressure of fluid. [formed as TONE + -METER]

tonsil /ˈtɒns(ə)l, -sɪl/ *n.* either of two small masses of lymphoid tissue on each side of the root of the tongue. □□**tonsillar** *adj.* [F *tonsilles* or L *tonsillae* (pl.)]

tonsillectomy /ˌtɒnsɪˈlɛktəmɪ/ *n.* (*pl.* -**ies**) the surgical removal of the tonsils.

tonsillitis /ˌtɒnsɪˈlaɪtɪs/ *n.* inflammation of the tonsils.

tonsorial /tɒnˈsɔːrɪəl/ *adj.* usu. *joc.* of or relating to a hairdresser or hairdressing. [L *tonsorius* f. *tonsor* barber f. *tondēre tons-* shave]

tonsure /ˈtɒnsjə(r), ˈtɒnʃə(r)/ *n. & v.* —*n.* **1** the shaving of the crown of the head or the entire head, esp. of a person entering a priesthood or monastic order. **2** a bare patch made in this way. —*v.tr.* give a tonsure to. [ME f. OF *tonsure* or L *tonsura* (as TONSORIAL)]

tontine /tɒnˈtiːn, ˈtɒn-/ *n.* an annuity shared by subscribers to a loan, the shares increasing as subscribers die until the last survivor gets all, or until a specified date when the remaining survivors share the proceeds. [F, f. the name of Lorenzo *Tonti* of Naples, originator of tontines in France *c.*1653]

tony /ˈtəʊnɪ/ *adj.* (**tonier, toniest**) *US colloq.* having 'tone'; stylish, fashionable.

too /tuː/ *adv.* **1** to a greater extent than is desirable, permissible, or possible for a specified or understood purpose (*too colourful for my taste*; *too large to fit*). **2** *colloq.* extremely (*you're too kind*). **3** in addition (*are they coming too?*). **4** moreover (*we must consider, too, the time of year*). □**none too 1** rather less than (*feeling none too good*). **2** barely. **too bad** see BAD. **too much, too much for** see MUCH. **too right** see RIGHT. **too-too** *adj. & adv. colloq.* extreme, excessive(ly). [stressed form of TO, f. 16th-c. spelling *too*]

took *past* of TAKE.

tool /tuːl/ *n. & v.* —*n.* **1** any device or implement used to carry out mechanical functions whether manually or by a machine. **2** a thing used in an occupation or pursuit (*the tools of one's trade*; *literary tools*). **3** a person used as a mere instrument by another. **4** *coarse sl.* the penis. ¶ Usually considered a taboo use. **5 a** a distinct figure in the tooling of a book. **b** a small stamp or roller used to make this. —*v.tr.* **1** dress (stone) with a chisel. **2** impress a design on (a leather book-cover). **3** (foll. by *along*, *around*, etc.) *sl.* drive or ride, esp. in a casual or leisurely manner. **4** (often foll. by *up*) equip with tools. □**tool-box** a box or container for keeping tools in. **tool-pusher** a worker directing the drilling on an oil rig. **tool up 1** *sl.* arm oneself. **2** equip oneself. □□**tooler** *n.* [OE *tōl* f. Gmc]

tooling /ˈtuːlɪŋ/ *n.* **1** the process of dressing stone with a chisel. **2** the ornamentation of a book-cover with designs impressed by heated tools.

toolmaker /ˈtuːlˌmeɪkə(r)/ *n.* a person who makes precision tools, esp. tools used in a press. □□ **toolmaking** *n.*

toot¹ /tuːt/ *n. & v.* —*n.* **1** a short sharp sound as made by a horn, trumpet, or whistle. **2** *US sl.* cocaine or a snort (see SNORT *n.* 4) of cocaine. —*v.* **1** *tr.* sound (a horn etc.) with a short sharp sound. **2** *intr.* give out such a sound. □□ **tooter** *n.* [prob. f. MLG *tūten*, or imit.]

toot² /tuːt/ *n. Austral. sl.* a lavatory. [20th c.: orig. unkn.]

tooth /tuːθ/ *n. & v.* —*n.* (*pl.* **teeth** /tiːθ/) **1** each of a set of hard bony enamel-coated structures in the jaws of most vertebrates, used for biting and chewing. **2** a toothlike part or projection, e.g. the cog of a gearwheel, the point of a saw or comb, etc. **3** (often foll. by *for*) one's sense of taste; an appetite or liking. **4** (in *pl.*) force or effectiveness (*the penalties give the contract teeth*). —*v.* **1** *tr.* provide with teeth. **2** *intr.* (of cog-wheels) engage, interlock. □**armed to the teeth** completely and elaborately armed or equipped. **fight tooth and nail** fight very fiercely. **get one's teeth into** devote oneself seriously to. **in the teeth of 1** in spite of (opposition or difficulty etc.). **2** contrary to (instructions etc.). **3** directly against (the wind etc.). **set a person's teeth on edge** see EDGE. **tooth-billed** (of a bird) having toothlike projections on the cutting edges of the bill. **tooth-comb** =

fine-tooth comb (see FINE[1]). **tooth powder** powder for cleaning the teeth. **tooth shell** = *tusk shell*. □□
toothed *adj.* (also in *comb.*). **toothless** *adj.* **toothlike** *adj.* [OE *tōth* (pl. *tēth*) f. Gmc]

toothache /'tu:θeɪk/ *n.* a (usu. prolonged) pain in a tooth or teeth.

toothbrush /'tu:θbrʌʃ/ *n.* a brush for cleaning the teeth.

toothing /'tu:θɪŋ/ *n.* projecting bricks or stones left at the end of a wall to allow its continuation.

toothpaste /'tu:θpeɪst/ *n.* a paste for cleaning the teeth.

toothpick /'tu:θpɪk/ *n.* a small sharp instrument for removing small pieces of food lodged between the teeth.

toothsome /'tu:θsəm/ *adj.* (of food) delicious, appetizing. □□ **toothsomely** *adv.* **toothsomeness** *n.*

toothwort /'tu:θwɜːt/ *n.* a parasitic plant, *Lathraea squamaria*, with toothlike root scales.

toothy /'tu:θɪ/ *adj.* (**toothier, toothiest**) having or showing large, numerous, or prominent teeth (*a toothy grin*). □□ **toothily** *adv.*

tootle /'tu:t(ə)l/ *v.intr.* **1** toot gently or repeatedly. **2** (usu. foll. by *along, around,* etc.) *colloq.* move casually or aimlessly. □□ **tootler** *n.*

tootsy /'tʊtsɪ/ *n.* (also **tootsie**) (*pl.* **-ies**) *sl.* usu. *joc.* a foot. [E joc. dimin.: cf. FOOTSIE]

top[1] /tɒp/ *n., adj.,* & *v.* —*n.* **1** the highest point or part (*the top of the house*). **2 a** the highest rank or place (*at the top of the school*). **b** a person occupying this (*was top in maths*). **c** the upper end or head (*the top of the table*). **3** the upper surface of a thing, esp. of the ground, a table, etc. **4** the upper part of a thing, esp.: **a** a blouse, jumper, etc. for wearing with a skirt or trousers. **b** the upper part of a shoe or boot. **c** the stopper of a bottle. **d** the lid of a jar, saucepan, etc. **e** the creamy part of milk. **f** the folding roof of a car, pram, or carriage. **g** the upper edge or edges of a page or pages in a book (*gilt top*). **5** the utmost degree; height (*called at the top of his voice*). **6** (in *pl.*) *colloq.* a person or thing of the best quality (*he's tops at cricket*). **7** (esp. in *pl.*) the leaves etc. of a plant grown esp. for its root (*turnip-tops*). **8** (usu. in *pl.*) a bundle of long wool fibres prepared for spinning. **9** *Naut.* a platform round the head of the lower mast, serving to extend the topmost rigging or carry guns. **10** (in *pl.*) esp. *Bridge* the two or three highest cards of a suit. **11** *Brit.* = *top gear* (*climbed the hill in top*). **12** = TOPSPIN. —*adj.* **1** highest in position (*the top shelf*). **2** highest in degree or importance (*at top speed; the top job*). —*v.tr.* (**topped, topping**) **1** provide with a top, cap, etc. (*cake topped with icing*). **2** remove the top of (a plant, fruit, etc.), esp. to improve growth, prepare for cooking, etc. **3** be higher or better than; surpass; be at the top of (*topped the list*). **4** *sl.* **a** execute esp. by hanging, kill. **b** (*refl.*) commit suicide. **5** reach the top of (a hill etc.). **6** *Golf* **a** hit (a ball) above the centre. **b** make (a stroke) in this way. □ **at the top** (or **at the top of the tree**) in the highest rank of a profession etc. **come to the top** win distinction. **from top to toe** from head to foot; completely. **off the top of one's head** see HEAD. **on top 1** in a superior position; above. **2** on the upper part of the head (*bald on top*). **on top of 1** fully in command of. **2** in close proximity to. **3** in addition to. **on top of the world** *colloq.* exuberant. **over the top 1** over the parapet of a trench (and into battle). **2** into a final or decisive state. **3** to excess, beyond reasonable limits (*that joke was over the top*). **top-boot** esp. *hist.* a boot with a high top esp. of a different material or colour. **top brass** esp. *Mil. colloq.* the highest-ranking officers, heads of industries, etc. **top copy** the uppermost typed copy (cf. *carbon copy*). **top dog** *colloq.* a victor or master. **top drawer 1** the uppermost drawer in a chest etc. **2** *colloq.* high social position or origin. **top-dress** apply manure or fertilizer on the top of (earth) instead of ploughing it in. **top-dressing 1** this

process. **2** manure so applied. **3** a superficial show. **top-flight** in the highest rank of achievement. **top fruit** *Brit.* fruit grown on trees, not bushes. **top gear** *Brit.* the highest gear in a motor vehicle or bicycle. **top-hamper** an encumbrance on top, esp. the upper sails and rigging of a ship. **top hat** a man's tall silk hat. **top-hole** *Brit. colloq.* first-rate. **top-level** of the highest level of importance, prestige, etc. **top-notch** *colloq.* first-rate. **top-notcher** *colloq.* a first-rate person or thing. **top off** (or **up**) put an end or the finishing touch to (a thing). **top out** put the highest stone on (a building). **top one's part** esp. *Theatr.* act or discharge one's part to perfection. **top-sawyer 1** a sawyer in the upper position in a saw-pit. **2** a person who holds a superior position; a distinguished person. **top secret** of the highest secrecy. **top ten** (or **twenty** etc.) the first ten (or twenty etc.) gramophone records in the charts. **top up** esp. *Brit.* **1 a** complete (an amount or number). **b** fill up (a glass or other partly full container). **2** top up something for (a person) (*may I top you up with sherry?*). **top-up** *n.* an addition; something that serves to top up (esp. a partly full glass). □□ **topmost** *adj.* [OE *topp*]

top[2] /tɒp/ *n.* a wooden or metal toy, usu. conical, spherical, or pear-shaped, spinning on a point when set in motion by hand, string, etc. [OE, of uncert. orig.]

topaz /'təʊpæz/ *n.* **1** a transparent or translucent aluminium silicate mineral, usu. yellow, used as a gem. **2** any South American humming-bird of the genus *Topaza*. [ME f. OF *topace, topaze* f. L *topazus* f. Gk *topazos*]

topazolite /tə'pæzə,laɪt/ *n.* a yellow or green kind of garnet. [TOPAZ + -LITE]

topcoat /'tɒpkəʊt/ *n.* **1** an overcoat. **2** an outer coat of paint etc.

tope[1] /təʊp/ *v.intr. archaic* or *literary* drink alcohol to excess, esp. habitually. □□ **toper** *n.* [perh. f. obs. *top quaff*]

tope[2] /təʊp/ *n. Ind.* a grove, esp. of mangoes. [Telugu *tōpu*, Tamil *tōppu*]

tope[3] /təʊp/ *n.* = STUPA. [Punjab *tōp* f. Prakrit & Pali *thūpo* f. Skr. STUPA]

tope[4] /təʊp/ *n.* a small shark, *Galeorhinus galeus*. [perh. f. Corn.]

topee var. of TOPI.

topgallant /tɒp'gælənt, tə'gælənt/ *n. Naut.* the mast, sail, yard, or rigging immediately above the topmast and topsail.

top-heavy /tɒp'hevɪ/ *adj.* **1** disproportionately heavy at the top so as to be in danger of toppling. **2 a** (of an organization, business, etc.) having a disproportionately large number of people in senior administrative positions. **b** overcapitalized. **3** *colloq.* (of a woman) having a disproportionately large bust. □□ **top-heavily** *adv.* **top-heaviness** *n.*

Tophet /'təʊfɪt/ *n. Bibl.* hell. [name of a place in the Valley of Hinnom near Jerusalem used for idolatrous worship and later for burning refuse: f. Heb. *tōpet*]

tophus /'təʊfəs/ *n.* (*pl.* **tophi** /-faɪ/) **1** *Med.* a gouty deposit of crystalline uric acid and other substances at the surface of joints. **2** *Geol.* = TUFA. [L, name of loose porous stones]

topi /'təʊpɪ/ *n.* (also **topee**) (*pl.* **topis** or **topees**) *Anglo-Ind.* a hat, esp. a sola topi. [Hindi *ṭopī*]

topiary /'təʊpɪərɪ/ *adj.* & *n.* —*adj.* concerned with or formed by clipping shrubs, trees, etc. into ornamental shapes. —*n.* (*pl.* **-ies**) **1** topiary art. **2** an example of this. □□ **topiarian** /-pɪ'eərɪən/ *adj.* **topiarist** *n.* [F *topiaire* f. L *topiarius* landscape-gardener f. *topia opera* fancy gardening f. Gk *topia* pl. dimin. of *topos* place]

topic /'tɒpɪk/ *n.* **1** a theme for a book, discourse, essay, sermon, etc. **2** the subject of a conversation or argument. [L *topica* f. Gk (*ta*) *topika* topics, as title of a treatise by Aristotle f. *topos* a place, a commonplace]

topical /'tɒpɪk(ə)l/ *adj.* **1** dealing with the news, current affairs, etc. (*a topical song*). **2** dealing with a place; local. **3** *Med.* (of an ailment, medicine, etc.) affecting a part of the body. **4** of or concerning topics. □□ **topicality** /-'kælɪtɪ/ *n.* **topically** *adv.*

topknot /'tɒpnɒt/ *n.* a knot, tuft, crest, or bow of ribbon, worn or growing on the head.

topless /'tɒplɪs/ *adj.* **1** without or seeming to be without a top. **2 a** (of clothes) having no upper part. **b** (of a person) wearing such clothes; bare-breasted. **c** (of a place, esp. a beach) where women go topless. □□ **toplessness** *n.*

toplofty /tɒp'lɒftɪ/ *adj.* *US colloq.* haughty.

topman /'tɒpmən/ *n.* (*pl.* **-men**) **1** a top-sawyer. **2** *Naut.* a man doing duty in a top.

topmast /'tɒpmɑːst/ *n.* *Naut.* the mast next above the lower mast.

topography /tə'pɒgrəfɪ/ *n.* **1 a** a detailed description, representation on a map, etc., of the natural and artificial features of a town, district, etc. **b** such features. **2** *Anat.* the mapping of the surface of the body with reference to the parts beneath. □□ **topographer** *n.* **topographic** /-'græfɪk/ *adj.* **topographical** /-'græfɪk(ə)l/ *adj.* **topographically** /-'græfɪkəlɪ/ *adv.* [ME f. LL *topographia* f. Gk f. *topos* place]

topoi *pl.* of TOPOS.

topology /tə'pɒlədʒɪ/ *n.* *Math.* the study of geometrical properties and spatial relations unaffected by the continuous change of shape or size of figures. □□ **topological** /ˌtɒpə'lɒdʒɪk(ə)l/ *adj.* **topologically** /ˌtɒpə'lɒdʒɪkəlɪ/ *adv.* **topologist** *n.* [G *Topologie* f. Gk *topos* place]

toponym /'tɒpənɪm/ *n.* **1** a place-name. **2** a descriptive place-name, usu. derived from a topographical feature of the place. [TOPONYMY]

toponymy /tə'pɒnɪmɪ/ *n.* the study of the place-names of a region. □□ **toponymic** /-'nɪmɪk/ *adj.* [Gk *topos* place + *onoma* name]

topos /'tɒpɒs/ *n.* (*pl.* **topoi** /'tɒpɔɪ/) a stock theme in literature etc. [Gk, = commonplace]

topper /'tɒpə(r)/ *n.* **1** a thing that tops. **2** *colloq.* = *top hat* (see TOP[1]). **3** *colloq.* a good fellow; a good sort.

topping /'tɒpɪŋ/ *adj.* & *n.* —*adj.* **1** pre-eminent in position, rank, etc. **2** *Brit. archaic sl.* excellent. —*n.* anything that tops something else, esp. icing etc. on a cake.

topple /'tɒp(ə)l/ *v.intr.* & *tr.* (usu. foll. by *over*, *down*) **1** fall or cause to fall as if top-heavy. **2** totter or cause to totter and fall. [TOP[1] + -LE[4]]

topsail /'tɒpseɪl, -s(ə)l/ *n.* a square sail above the lowest fore-and-aft sail on a gaff.

topside /'tɒpsaɪd/ *n.* **1** *Brit.* the outer side of a round of beef. **2** the side of a ship above the water-line.

topsoil /'tɒpsɔɪl/ *n.* the top layer of soil (opp. SUBSOIL).

topspin /'tɒpspɪn/ *n.* a fast forward spinning motion imparted to a ball in tennis etc. by hitting it forward and upward.

topsy-turvy /ˌtɒpsɪ'tɜːvɪ/ *adv.*, *adj.*, & *n.* —*adv.* & *adj.* **1** upside down. **2** in utter confusion. —*n.* utter confusion. □□ **topsy-turvily** *adv.* **topsy-turviness** *n.* [app. f. TOP[1] + obs. *terve* overturn]

toque /təʊk/ *n.* **1** a woman's small brimless hat. **2** *hist.* a small cap or bonnet for a man or woman. [F, app. = It. *tocca*, Sp. *toca*, of unkn. orig.]

toquilla /tə'kiːjə/ *n.* **1** a palmlike tree, *Carludovica palmata*, native to S. America. **2** a fibre produced from the leaves of this. [Sp., = small gauze headdress, dimin. of *toca* toque]

tor /tɔː(r)/ *n.* a hill or rocky peak, esp. in Devon or Cornwall. [OE *torr*: cf. Gael. *tòrr* bulging hill]

Torah /'tɔːrə/ *n.* **1** (usu. prec. by *the*) **a** the Pentateuch. **b** a scroll containing this. **2** the will of God as revealed in Mosaic law. [Heb. *tōrāh* instruction]

torc var. of TORQUE 1.

torch /tɔːtʃ/ *n.* & *v.* —*n.* **1** (also **electric torch**) *Brit.* a portable battery-powered electric lamp. **2 a** a piece of wood, cloth, etc., soaked in tallow and lighted for illumination. **b** any similar lamp, e.g. an oil-lamp on a pole. **c** a source of heat, illumination, or

enlightenment (*bore aloft the torch of freedom*). **4** esp. *US* a blowlamp. **5** *US sl.* an arsonist. —*v.tr.* esp. *US sl.* set alight with a torch. □ **carry a torch for** suffer from unrequited love for. **put to the torch** destroy by burning. **torch-fishing** catching fish by torchlight at night. **torch-race** *Gk Antiq.* a festival performance of runners handing lighted torches to others in relays. **torch singer** a woman who sings torch songs. **torch song** a popular song of unrequited love. **torch-thistle** any tall cactus of the genus *Cereus*, with funnel-shaped flowers which open at night. [ME f. OF *torche* f. L *torqua* f. *torquēre* twist]

torchère /tɔː'ʃeə(r)/ *n.* a tall stand with a small table for a candlestick etc. [F (as TORCH)]

torchlight /'tɔːtʃlaɪt/ *n.* the light of a torch or torches.

torchon /'tɔːʃ(ə)n, -ʃɔ̃/ *n.* (in full **torchon lace**) coarse bobbin lace with geometrical designs. [F, = duster, dishcloth f. *torcher* wipe]

tore[1] *past* of TEAR[1].

tore[2] /tɔː(r)/ *n.* = TORUS 1, 4. [F f. L *torus*: see TORUS]

toreador /'tɒrɪəˌdɔː(r)/ *n.* a bullfighter, esp. on horseback. □ **toreador pants** close-fitting calf-length women's trousers. [Sp. f. *torear* fight bulls f. *toro* bull f. L *taurus*]

torero /tɒ'reərəʊ/ *n.* (*pl.* **-os**) a bullfighter. [Sp. f. *toro*: see TOREADOR]

toreutic /tə'ruːtɪk/ *adj.* & *n.* —*adj.* of or concerning the chasing, carving, and embossing of esp. metal. —*n.* (in *pl.*) the art or practice of this. [Gk *toreutikos* f. *toreuō* work in relief]

torgoch /'tɔːgɒx/ *n.* a kind of red-bellied char found in some Welsh lakes. [Welsh f. *tor* belly + *coch* red]

tori *pl.* of TORUS.

toric /'tɒrɪk/ *adj.* *Geom.* having the form of a torus or part of a torus.

torii /'tɔːrɪɪ/ *n.* (*pl.* same) the gateway of a Shinto shrine, with two uprights and two crosspieces. [Jap.]

torment *n.* & *v.* —*n.* /'tɔːment/ **1** severe physical or mental suffering (*was in torment*). **2** a cause of this. **3** *archaic* **a** torture. **b** an instrument of torture. —*v.tr.* /tɔː'ment/ **1** subject to torment (*tormented with worry*). **2** tease or worry excessively (*enjoyed tormenting the teacher*). □□ **tormentedly** *adv.* **tormentingly** *adv.* **tormentor** /-'mentə(r)/ *n.* [ME f. OF *torment*, *tormenter* f. L *tormentum* missile-engine f. *torquēre* to twist]

tormentil /'tɔːməntɪl/ *n.* a low-growing plant, *Potentilla erecta*, with bright yellow flowers and a highly astringent rootstock used in medicine. [ME f. OF *tormentille* f. med.L *tormentilla*, of unkn. orig.]

torn *past part.* of TEAR[1].

tornado /tɔː'neɪdəʊ/ *n.* (*pl.* **-oes**) **1** a violent storm of small extent with whirling winds, esp.: **a** in West Africa at the beginning and end of the rainy season. **b** in the US etc. over a narrow path often accompanied by a funnel-shaped cloud. **2** an outburst or volley of cheers, hisses, missiles, etc. □□ **tornadic** /-'nædɪk/ *adj.* [app. assim. of Sp. *tronada* thunderstorm (f. *tronar* to thunder) to Sp. *tornar* to turn]

toroid /'tɔːrɔɪd/ *n.* a figure of toroidal shape.

toroidal /tɔː'rɔɪd(ə)l/ *adj.* *Geom.* of or resembling a torus. □□ **toroidally** *adv.*

torose /'tɔːrəʊs/ *adj.* **1** *Bot.* (of plants, esp. their stalks) cylindrical with bulges at intervals. **2** *Zool.* knobby. [L *torosus* f. *torus*: see TORUS]

torpedo /tɔː'piːdəʊ/ *n.* & *v.* —*n.* (*pl.* **-oes**) **1 a** a cigar-shaped self-propelled underwater missile that explodes on impact with a ship. **b** (in full **aerial torpedo**) a similar device dropped from an aircraft. **2** *Zool.* an electric ray. **3** *US* an explosive device or firework. —*v.tr.* (**-oes**, **-oed**) **1** destroy or attack with a torpedo. **2** make (a policy, institution, plan, etc.) ineffective or inoperative; destroy. □ **torpedo-boat** a small fast lightly armed warship for carrying or discharging torpedoes. **torpedo-net** (or **-netting**) netting of steel wire hung round a ship to intercept

torpedoes. torpedo-tube a tube from which torpedoes are fired. □□**torpedo-like** adj. [L, = numbness, electric ray f. torpēre be numb]

torpefy /ˈtɔːpɪˌfaɪ/ v.tr. (-ies, -ied) make numb or torpid. [L torpefacere f. torpēre be numb]

torpid /ˈtɔːpɪd/ adj. **1** sluggish, inactive, dull, apathetic. **2** numb. **3** (of a hibernating animal) dormant. □□**torpidity** /-ˈpɪdɪtɪ/ n. **torpidly** adv. **torpidness** n. [L torpidus (as TORPOR)]

torpor /ˈtɔːpə(r)/ n. torpidity. □□**torporific** /-ˈrɪfɪk/ adj. [L f. torpēre be sluggish]

torquate /ˈtɔːkweɪt/ adj. Zool. (of an animal) with a ring of distinctive colour or texture of hair or plumage round the neck. [L torquatus (as TORQUE)]

torque /tɔːk/ n. **1** (also **torc**) hist. a necklace of twisted metal, esp. of the ancient Gauls and Britons. **2** Mech. the moment of a system of forces tending to cause rotation. □**torque converter** a device to transmit the correct torque from the engine to the axle in a motor vehicle. [(sense 1 F f. L torques) f. L torquēre to twist]

torr /tɔː(r)/ n. (pl. same) a unit of pressure used in measuring partial vacuums, equal to 133.32 pascals. [E. Torricelli, It. physicist d. 1647]

torrefy /ˈtɒrɪˌfaɪ/ v.tr. (-ies, -ied) **1** roast or dry (metallic ore, a drug, etc.). **2** parch or scorch with heat. □□**torrefaction** /-ˈfækʃ(ə)n/ n. [F torréfier f. L torrefacere f. torrēre scorch]

torrent /ˈtɒrənt/ n. **1** a rushing stream of water, lava, etc. **2** (in pl.) a great downpour of rain (came down in torrents). **3** (usu. foll. by of) a violent or copious flow (uttered a torrent of abuse). □□ **torrential** /təˈrenʃ(ə)l/ adj. **torrentially** /təˈrenʃəlɪ/ adv. [F f. It. torrente f. L torrens -entis scorching, boiling, roaring f. torrēre scorch]

Torricellian vacuum /ˌtɒrɪˈtʃelɪən, -ˈselɪən/ n. a vacuum formed when mercury in a long tube closed at one end is inverted with the open end in a reservoir of mercury (the principle on which a barometer is made). [Torricelli: see TORR]

torrid /ˈtɒrɪd/ adj. **1 a** (of the weather) very hot and dry. **b** (of land etc.) parched by such weather. **2** (of language or actions) emotionally charged; passionate, intense. □**torrid zone** the central belt of the earth between the Tropics of Cancer and Capricorn. □□**torridity** /-ˈrɪdɪtɪ/ n. **torridly** adv. **torridness** n. [F torride or L torridus f. torrēre parch]

torse /tɔːs/ n. Heraldry a wreath. [obs. F torse, torce wreath ult. f. L torta fem. past part. (as TORT)]

torsel var. of TASSEL².

torsion /ˈtɔːʃ(ə)n/ n. **1** twisting, esp. of one end of a body while the other is held fixed. **2** Math. the extent to which a curve departs from being planar. **3** Bot. the state of being twisted into a spiral. **4** Med. the twisting of the cut end of an artery after surgery etc. to impede bleeding. □**torsion balance** an instrument for measuring very weak forces by their effect upon a system of fine twisted wire. **torsion bar** a bar forming part of a vehicle suspension, twisting in response to the motion of the wheels, and absorbing their vertical movement. **torsion pendulum** a pendulum working by rotation rather than by swinging. □□**torsional** adj. **torsionally** adv. **torsionless** adj. [ME f. OF f. LL torsio -onis f. L tortio (as TORT)]

torsk /tɔːsk/ n. a fish of the cod family, Brosmius brosme, abundant in northern waters and often dried for food. [Norw. to(r)sk f. ON tho(r)skr prob. rel. to thurr dry]

torso /ˈtɔːsəʊ/ n. (pl. -os) **1** the trunk of the human body. **2** a statue of a human consisting of the trunk alone, without head or limbs. **3** an unfinished or mutilated work (esp. of art, literature, etc.). [It., = stalk, stump, torso, f. L thyrsus]

tort /tɔːt/ n. Law a breach of duty (other than under contract) leading to liability for damages. [ME f. OF f. med.L tortum wrong, neut. past part. of L torquēre tort- twist]

torte /ˈtɔːrtə/ n. (pl. **torten** /ˈtɔːt(ə)n/ or **tortes**) an elaborate sweet cake or tart. [G]

tortfeasor /ˈtɔːtˌfiːzə(r)/ n. Law a person guilty of tort. [OF tort-fesor, tort-faiseur, etc. f. tort wrong, -fesor, faiseur doer]

torticollis /ˌtɔːtɪˈkɒlɪs/ n. Med. a rheumatic etc. disease of the muscles of the neck, causing twisting and stiffness. [mod.L f. L tortus crooked + collum neck]

tortilla /tɔːˈtiːjə, -ˈtiːljə/ n. a thin flat orig. Mexican maize cake eaten hot or cold with or without a filling. [Sp. dimin. of torta cake f. LL]

tortious /ˈtɔːʃəs/ adj. Law constituting a tort; wrongful. □□**tortiously** adv. [AF torcious f. torcion extortion f. LL tortio torture: see TORSION]

tortoise /ˈtɔːtəs/ n. **1** any slow-moving land or freshwater reptile of the family Testudinidae, encased in a scaly or leathery domed shell, and having a retractile head and elephantine legs. **2** Rom. Antiq. = TESTUDO. □□**tortoise-like** adj. & adv. [ME tortuce, OF tortue, f. med.L tortuca, of uncert. orig.]

tortoiseshell /ˈtɔːtəsˌʃel/ n. & adj. —n. **1** the yellowish-brown mottled or clouded outer shell of some turtles, used for decorative hair-combs, jewellery, etc. **2 a** = tortoiseshell cat. **b** = tortoiseshell butterfly. —adj. having the colouring or appearance of tortoiseshell. □**tortoiseshell butterfly** any of various butterflies, esp. of the genus Aglais or Nymphalis, with wings mottled like tortoiseshell. **tortoiseshell cat** a domestic cat with markings resembling tortoiseshell.

tortrix /ˈtɔːtrɪks/ n. any moth of the family Tortricidae, esp. Tortrix viridana, the larvae of which live inside rolled leaves. [mod.L, fem. of L tortor twister: see TORT]

tortuous /ˈtɔːtjʊəs/ adj. **1** full of twists and turns (followed a tortuous route). **2** devious, circuitous, crooked (has a tortuous mind). □□**tortuosity** /-ˈɒsɪtɪ/ n. (pl. -ies). **tortuously** adv. **tortuousness** n. [ME f. OF f. L tortuosus f. tortus a twist (as TORT)]

torture /ˈtɔːtʃə(r)/ n. & v. —n. **1** the infliction of severe bodily pain esp. as a punishment or a means of persuasion. **2** severe physical or mental suffering (the torture of defeat). —v.tr. **1** subject to torture (tortured by guilt). **2** force out of a natural position or state; deform; pervert. □□**torturable** adj. **torturer** n. **torturous** adj. **torturously** adv. [F f. LL tortura twisting (as TORT)]

torula /ˈtɒruːlə/ n. (pl. **torulae** /-ˌliː/) **1** a yeast, Candida utilis, used medicinally as a food additive. **2** any yeast-like fungus of the genus Torula, growing on dead vegetation. [mod.L, dimin. of torus: see TORUS]

torus /ˈtɔːrəs/ n. (pl. **tori** /-raɪ/) **1** Archit. a large convex bun-shaped moulding esp. as the lowest part of the base of a column. **2** Bot. the receptacle of a flower. **3** Anat. a smooth ridge of bone or muscle. **4** Geom. a surface or solid formed by rotating a closed curve, esp. a circle, about a line in its plane but not intersecting it. [L, = swelling, bulge, cushion, etc.]

Tory /ˈtɔːrɪ/ n. & adj. —n. (pl. -ies) **1** colloq. = CONSERVATIVE n. 2. **2** hist. a member of the party that opposed the exclusion of James II and later supported the established religious and political order and gave rise to the Conservative party (opp. WHIG). **3** US hist. a loyal colonist during the American Revolution. —adj. colloq. = CONSERVATIVE adj. 3. □□**Toryism** n. [orig. = Irish outlaw, prob. f. Ir. f. tóir pursue]

tosh /tɒʃ/ n. colloq. rubbish, nonsense. [19th c.: orig. unkn.]

toss /tɒs/ v. & n. —v. **1** tr. throw up (a ball etc.) esp. with the hand. **2** tr. & intr. roll about, throw, or be thrown, restlessly or from side to side (the ship tossed on the ocean; was tossing and turning all night; tossed her head angrily). **3** tr. (usu. foll. by to, away, aside, out, etc.) throw (a thing) lightly or carelessly (tossed the letter away). **4** tr. **a** throw (a coin) into the air to decide a choice etc. by the side on which it lands. **b**

(also *absol.*; often foll. by *for*) settle a question or dispute with (a person) in this way (*tossed him for the armchair*; *tossed for it*). **5** *tr.* **a** (of a bull etc.) throw (a person etc.) up with the horns. **b** (of a horse etc.) throw (a rider) off its back. **6** *tr.* coat (food) with dressing etc. by shaking. **7** *tr.* bandy about in debate; discuss (*tossed the question back and forth*). —*n.* **1** the act or an instance of tossing (a coin, the head, etc.). **2** *Brit.* a fall, esp. from a horse. □**toss one's head** throw it back esp. in anger, impatience, etc. **tossing the caber** the Scottish sport of throwing a tree-trunk. **toss oars** raise oars to an upright position in salute. **toss off 1** drink off at a draught. **2** dispatch (work) rapidly or without effort (*tossed off an omelette*). **3** *Brit. coarse sl.* masturbate. ¶ Usually considered a taboo use in sense 3. **toss a pancake** throw it up so that it flips on to the other side in the frying-pan. **toss up** toss a coin to decide a choice etc. **toss-up** *n.* **1** a doubtful matter; a close thing (*it's a toss-up whether he wins*). **2** the tossing of a coin. [16th c.: orig. unkn.]

tosser /ˈtɒsə(r)/ *n.* **1** *Brit. coarse sl.* an unpleasant or contemptible person. **2** a person or thing that tosses.

tot[1] /tɒt/ *n.* **1** a small child (*a tiny tot*). **2** a dram of liquor. [18th c., of dial. orig.]

tot[2] /tɒt/ *v. & n.* —*v.* (**totted, totting**) **1** *tr.* (usu. foll. by *up*) add (figures etc.). **2** *intr.* (foll. by *up*) (of items) mount up. —*n. Brit. archaic* a set of figures to be added. □**totting-up 1** the adding of separate items. **2** *Brit.* the adding of convictions for driving offences to cause disqualification. **tot up to** amount to. [abbr. of TOTAL or of L *totum* the whole]

tot[3] /tɒt/ *v. & n. Brit. sl.* —*v.intr.* (**totted, totting**) collect saleable items from refuse as an occupation. —*n.* an article collected from refuse. [19th c.: orig. unkn.]

total /ˈtəʊt(ə)l/ *adj., n., & v.* —*adj.* **1** complete, comprising the whole (*the total number of people*). **2** absolute, unqualified (*in total ignorance*; *total abstinence*). —*n.* a total number or amount. —*v.* (**totalled, totalling**; *US* **totaled, totaling**) **1** *tr.* **a** amount in number to (*they totalled 131*). **b** find the total of (things, a set of figures, etc.). **2** *intr.* (foll. by *to*, *up to*) amount to, mount up to. **3** *tr. US sl.* wreck completely. □**total abstinence** abstaining completely from alcohol. **total eclipse** an eclipse in which the whole disc (of the sun, moon, etc.) is obscured. **total internal reflection** reflection without refraction of a light-ray meeting the interface between two media at more than a certain critical angle to the normal. **total recall** the ability to remember every detail of one's experience clearly. **total war** a war in which all available weapons and resources are employed. □□ **totally** *adv.* [ME f. OF f. med.L *totalis* f. *totus* entire]

totalitarian /təʊˌtælɪˈteərɪən/ *adj. & n.* —*adj.* of or relating to a centralized dictatorial form of government requiring complete subservience to the State. —*n.* a person advocating such a system. □□ **totalitarianism** *n.*

totality /təʊˈtælɪtɪ/ *n.* **1** the complete amount or sum. **2** *Astron.* the time during which an eclipse is total.

totalizator /ˈtəʊtəlaɪˌzeɪtə(r)/ *n.* (also **totalisator**) **1** a device showing the number and amount of bets staked on a race, to facilitate the division of the total among those backing the winner. **2** a system of betting based on this.

totalize /ˈtəʊtəˌlaɪz/ *v.tr.* (also **-ise**) collect into a total; find the total of. □□ **totalization** /-ˈzeɪʃ(ə)n/ *n.*

totalizer /ˈtəʊtəˌlaɪzə(r)/ *n.* = TOTALIZATOR.

tote[1] /təʊt/ *n. sl.* **1** a totalizator. **2** a lottery. [abbr.]

tote[2] /təʊt/ *v.tr.* esp. *US colloq.* carry, convey, esp. a heavy load (*toting a gun*). □**tote bag** a woman's large bag for shopping etc. **tote box** *US* a small container for goods. □□ **toter** *n.* (also in *comb.*). [17th-c. US, prob. of dial. orig.]

totem /ˈtəʊtəm/ *n.* **1** a natural object, esp. an animal, adopted by North American Indians as an emblem of a clan or an individual. **2** an image of this. □**totem-pole 1** a pole on which totems are carved or hung. **2** a hierarchy. □□ **totemic** /-ˈtemɪk/ *adj.* **totemism** *n.* **totemist** *n.* **totemistic** /-ˈmɪstɪk/ *adj.* [Algonquian]

tother /ˈtʌðə(r)/ *adj. & pron.* (also **t'other**) *dial.* or *joc.* the other. □**tell tother from which** *joc.* tell one from the other. [ME *the tother*, for earlier *thet other* 'that other'; now understood as = *the other*]

totter /ˈtɒtə(r)/ *v. & n.* —*v.intr.* **1** stand or walk unsteadily or feebly (*tottered out of the pub*). **2 a** (of a building etc.) shake or rock as if about to collapse. **b** (of a system of government etc.) be about to fall. —*n.* an unsteady or shaky movement or gait. □□ **totterer** *n.* **tottery** *adj.* [ME f. MDu. *touteren* to swing]

toucan /ˈtuːkən/ *n.* any tropical American fruit-eating bird of the family Ramphastidae, with an immense beak and brightly coloured plumage. [Tupi *tucana*, Guarani *tucã*]

touch /tʌtʃ/ *v. & n.* —*v.* **1** *tr.* come into or be in physical contact with (another thing) at one or more points. **2** *tr.* (often foll. by *with*) bring the hand etc. into contact with (*touched her arm*). **3 a** *intr.* (of two things etc.) be in or come into contact with one another (*the balls were touching*). **b** *tr.* bring (two things) into mutual contact (*they touched hands*). **4** *tr.* rouse tender or painful feelings in (*was touched by his appeal*). **5** *tr.* strike lightly (*just touched the wall with the back bumper*). **6** *tr.* (usu. with *neg.*) **a** disturb or harm (*don't touch my things*). **b** have any dealings with (*won't touch bricklaying*). **c** consume; use up; make use of (*dare not touch alcohol*; *has not touched her breakfast*; *need not touch your savings*). **d** cope with; affect; manage (*soap won't touch this dirt*). **7** *tr.* **a** deal with (a subject) lightly or in passing (*touched the matter of their expenses*). **b** concern (*it touches you closely*). **8** *tr.* **a** reach or rise as far as, esp. momentarily (*the thermometer touched 90°*). **b** (usu. with *neg.*) approach in excellence etc. (*can't touch him for style*). **9** *tr.* affect slightly; modify (*pity touched with fear*). **10** *tr.* (as **touched** *adj.*) slightly mad. **11** *tr.* (often foll. by *in*) esp. *Art* mark lightly, put in (features etc.) with a brush, pencil, etc. **12** *tr.* **a** strike (the keys, strings, etc. of a musical instrument). **b** strike the keys or strings of (a piano etc.). **13** *tr.* (usu. foll. by *for*) *sl.* ask for and get money etc. from (a person) as a loan or gift (*touched him for £5*). **14** *tr.* injure slightly (*blossom touched by frost*). **15** *tr. Geom.* be tangent to (a curve). —*n.* **1** the act or an instance of touching, esp. with the body or hand (*felt a touch on my arm*). **2 a** the faculty of perception through physical contact, esp. with the fingers (*has no sense of touch in her right arm*). **b** the qualities of an object etc. as perceived in this way (*the soft touch of silk*). **3** a small amount; a slight trace (*a touch of salt*; *a touch of irony*). **4 a** a musician's manner of playing keys or strings. **b** the manner in which the keys or strings respond to touch. **c** an artist's or writer's style of workmanship, writing, etc. (*has a delicate touch*). **5** a distinguishing quality or trait (*a professional touch*). **6** (esp. in *pl.*) **a** a light stroke with a pen, pencil, etc. **b** a slight alteration or improvement (*speech needs a few touches*). **7** = TAG[2]. **8** (prec. by *a*) slightly (*is a touch too arrogant*). **9** *sl.* **a** the act of asking for and getting money etc. from a person. **b** a person from whom money etc. is so obtained. **10** *Football* the part of the field outside the side limits. **11** *archaic* a test with or as if with a touchstone (*put it to the touch*). □**at a touch** if touched, however lightly (*opened at a touch*). **easy touch** *sl.* a person who readily parts with money. **finishing touch** (or **touches**) the final details completing and enhancing a piece of work etc. **get** (or **put**) **in** (or **into**) **touch with** come or cause to come into communication with; contact. **in touch** (often foll. by *with*) **1** in communication (*we're still in touch after all these years*). **2** up to date, esp. regarding news etc. (*keeps in touch with events*). **3** aware, conscious, empathetic (*not in touch with her own feelings*). **keep in touch** (often foll. by *with*) **1** remain informed (*kept in touch with the latest developments*). **2** continue correspondence, a friendship, etc. **lose touch** (often foll. by *with*) **1** cease to be informed. **2** cease to correspond with or be in contact with another person. **lose one's touch** not show one's customary skill. **the Nelson touch** a masterly or sympathetic approach to a problem (from Horatio Nelson, Admiral at Trafalgar). **out of touch** (often foll. by *with*) **1** not in correspondence. **2** not up to date or modern. **3** lacking in awareness or sympathy (*out of touch with his son's beliefs*). **personal touch** a characteristic or individual approach to a situation. **soft touch** = *easy touch* (see TOUCH). **to the touch** when touched (*was cold to the touch*). **touch-and-go** uncertain regarding a result; risky (*it was touch-and-go whether we'd catch the train*). **touch at** (of a ship) call at (a port etc.). **touch bottom 1** reach the bottom of water with one's feet. **2** be at the lowest or worst point. **3** be in possession of the full facts. **touch down 1** *Rugby Football & Amer. Football* touch the ground with the ball behind one's own or the opponent's goal. **2** (of an aircraft) make contact with the ground in landing. **touch football** *US* football with touching in place of tackling. **touch-hole** a small hole in a gun for igniting the charge. **touch-in-goal** *Football* each of the four corners enclosed by continuations of the touch-lines and goal-lines. **touch-judge** *Rugby Football* a linesman. **touch-line** (in various sports) either of the lines marking the side boundaries of the pitch. **touch-mark** the maker's mark on pewter. **touch-me-not** any of various plants of the genus *Impatiens*, with ripe seed-capsules jerking open when touched. **touch-needle** a needle of gold or silver alloy of known composition used as a standard in testing other alloys on a touchstone. **touch off 1** represent exactly (in a portrait etc.). **2** explode by touching with a match etc. **3** initiate (a process) suddenly (*touched off a run on the pound*). **touch of nature 1** a natural trait. **2** *colloq.* an exhibition of human feeling with which others sympathize (from a misinterpretation of Shakesp. *Troilus and Cressida* III. iii. 169). **touch of the sun 1** a slight attack of sunstroke. **2** a little sunlight. **touch on** (or **upon**) **1** treat (a subject) briefly, refer to or mention casually. **2** verge on (*that touches on impudence*). **touch-paper** paper impregnated with nitre, for firing gunpowder, fireworks, etc. **touch the spot** *colloq.* find out or do exactly what was needed. **touch-type** type without looking at the keys. **touch-typing** this skill. **touch-typist** a person who touch-types. **touch up 1** give finishing touches to or retouch (a picture, writing, etc.). **2** *Brit. sl.* **a** caress so as to excite sexually. **b** sexually molest. **3** strike (a horse) lightly with a whip. **touch wood** touch something wooden with the hand to avert ill luck. **would not touch with a bargepole** see BARGEPOLE. □□ **touchable** *adj.* [ME f. OF *tochier, tuchier* (v.), *touche* (n.): prob. imit., imitating a knock]

touchdown /ˈtʌtʃdaʊn/ *n.* **1** the act or an instance of an aircraft making contact with the ground during landing. **2** *Rugby Football & Amer. Football* the act or an instance of touching down.

touché /tuːˈʃeɪ/ *int.* **1** the acknowledgement of a hit by a fencing-opponent. **2** the acknowledgement of a justified accusation, a witticism, or a point made in reply to one's own. [F, past part. of *toucher* TOUCH]

toucher /ˈtʌtʃə(r)/ *n.* **1** a person or thing that touches. **2** *Bowls* a wood that touches the jack.

touching /ˈtʌtʃɪŋ/ *adj. & prep.* —*adj.* moving, pathetic (*a touching incident; touching confidence*). —*prep.* literary concerning; about. □□ **touchingly** *adv.* **touchingness** *n.* [ME f. TOUCH: (prep.) f. OF *touchant* pres. part. (as TOUCH)]

touchstone /ˈtʌtʃstəʊn/ *n.* **1** a fine-grained dark

schist or jasper used for testing alloys of gold etc. by marking it with them and observing the colour of the mark. **2** a standard or criterion.

touchwood /ˈtʌtʃwʊd/ *n.* readily inflammable wood, esp. when made soft by fungi, used as tinder.

touchy /ˈtʌtʃɪ/ *adj.* (**touchier, touchiest**) apt to take offence; over-sensitive. □□ **touchily** *adv.* **touchiness** *n.* [perh. alt. of TETCHY after TOUCH]

tough /tʌf/ *adj. & n.* —*adj.* **1** hard to break, cut, tear, or chew; durable; strong. **2** (of a person) able to endure hardship; hardy. **3** unyielding, stubborn, difficult (*it was a tough job; a tough customer*). **4** *colloq.* **a** acting sternly; hard (*get tough with*). **b** (of circumstances, luck, etc.) severe, unpleasant, hard, unjust. **5** *colloq.* criminal or violent (*tough guys*). —*n.* a tough person, esp. a ruffian or criminal. □ **tough guy** *colloq.* **1** a hard unyielding person. **2** a violent aggressive person. **tough it** (or **tough it out**) *colloq.* endure or withstand difficult conditions. **tough-minded** realistic, not sentimental. **tough-mindedness** being tough-minded. □□ **toughen** *v.tr. & intr.* **toughener** *n.* **toughish** *adj.* **toughly** *adv.* **toughness** *n.* [OE *tōh*]

toughie /ˈtʌfɪ/ *n. colloq.* a tough person or problem.

toupee /ˈtuːpeɪ/ *n.* (also **toupet** /tuːˈpeɪ/) a wig or artificial hairpiece to cover a bald spot. [F *toupet* hair-tuft dimin. of OF *toup* tuft (as TOP¹)]

tour /tʊə(r)/ *n. & v.* —*n.* **1 a** a journey from place to place as a holiday. **b** an excursion, ramble, or walk (*made a tour of the garden*). **2 a** a spell of duty on military or diplomatic service. **b** the time to be spent at a particular post. **3** a series of performances, matches, etc., at different places on a route through a country etc. —*v.* **1** *intr.* (usu. foll. by *through*) make a tour (*toured through India*). **2** *tr.* make a tour of (a country etc.). □ **on tour** (esp. of a team, theatre company, etc.) touring. **touring-car** a car with room for passengers and much luggage. **tour operator** a travel agent specializing in package holidays. [ME f. OF *to(u)r* f. L *tornus* f. Gk *tornos* lathe]

touraco var. of TURACO.

tour de force /ˌtʊə də ˈfɔːs/ *n.* a feat of strength or skill. [F]

tourer /ˈtʊərə(r)/ *n.* a vehicle, esp. a car, for touring. [TOUR]

tourism /ˈtʊərɪz(ə)m/ *n.* the organization and operation of (esp. foreign) holidays, esp. as a commercial enterprise.

tourist /ˈtʊərɪst/ *n.* a person making a visit or tour as a holiday; a traveller, esp. abroad (often *attrib.*: *tourist accommodation*). □ **tourist class** the lowest class of passenger accommodation in a ship, aircraft, etc. □□ **touristic** /-ˈrɪstɪk/ *adj.* **touristically** /-ˈrɪstɪkəlɪ/ *adv.*

touristy /ˈtʊərɪstɪ/ *adj.* usu. *derog.* appealing to or visited by many tourists.

tourmaline /ˈtʊəməlɪn, -məˌliːn/ *n.* a boron aluminium silicate mineral of various colours, possessing unusual electrical properties, and used in electrical and optical instruments and as a gemstone. [F f. Sinh. *toramalli* porcelain]

tournament /ˈtʊənəmənt/ *n.* **1** any contest of skill between a number of competitors, esp. played in heats (*chess tournament; tennis tournament*). **2** a display of military exercises etc. (*Royal Tournament*). **3** *hist.* **a** a pageant in which jousting with blunted weapons took place. **b** a meeting for jousting between single knights for a prize etc. [ME f. OF *torneiement* f. *torneier* TOURNEY]

tournedos /ˈtʊənəˌdəʊ/ *n.* (*pl.* same /-ˌdəʊz/) a small round thick cut from a fillet of beef. [F]

tourney /ˈtʊənɪ/ *n. & v.* —*n.* (*pl.* **-eys**) a tournament. —*v.intr.* (**-eys, -eyed**) take part in a tournament. [ME f. OF *tornei* (n.), *torneier* (v.), ult. f. L *tornus* a turn]

tourniquet /ˈtʊənɪˌkeɪ/ *n.* a device for stopping the flow of blood through an artery by twisting a bar etc. in a ligature or bandage. [F prob. f. OF *tournicle* coat of mail, TUNICLE, infl. by *tourner* TURN]

tousle /ˈtaʊz(ə)l/ *v.tr.* **1** make (esp. the hair) untidy;

rumple. **2** handle roughly or rudely. [frequent. of (now dial.) *touse*, ME f. OE rel. to OHG *-zuson*]

tous-les-mois /ˌtuːleɪˈmwɑː/ *n.* **1** food starch obtained from tubers of a canna, *Canna indica*. **2** this plant. [F, lit. = every month, prob. corrupt. of W.Ind. *toloman*]

tout /taʊt/ *v. & n.* —*v.* **1** *intr.* (usu. foll. by *for*) solicit custom persistently; pester customers (*touting for business*). **2** *tr.* solicit the custom of (a person) or for (a thing). **3** *intr.* **a** *Brit.* spy out the movements and condition of racehorses in training. **b** *US* offer racing tips for a share of the resulting profit. —*n.* a person employed in touting. □□ **touter** *n.* [ME *tūte* look out = ME (now dial.) *toot* (OE *tōtian*) f. Gmc]

tout court /tuː ˈkʊə(r)/ *adv.* without addition; simply (*called James tout court*). [F, lit. very short]

tovarish /təˈvɑːrɪʃ/ *n.* (also **tovarich**) (in the USSR) comrade (esp. as a form of address). [Russ. *tovarishch*]

tow[1] /təʊ/ *v. & n.* —*v.tr.* **1** (of a motor vehicle, horse, or person controlling it) pull (a boat, another motor vehicle, a caravan, etc.) along by a rope, tow-bar, etc. **2** pull (a person or thing) along behind one. —*n.* the act or an instance of towing; the state of being towed. □ **have in** (or **on**) **tow 1** be towing. **2** be accompanied by and often in charge of (a person). **tow-bar** a bar for towing esp. a trailer or caravan. **tow-** (or **towing-**) **line** (or **rope**) a line etc. used in towing. **tow-** (or **towing-**) **net** a net used for dragging through water to collect specimens. **tow-** (or **towing-**) **path** a path beside a river or canal used for towing a boat by horse. □□ **towable** *adj.* **towage** /-ɪdʒ/ *n.* [OE *togian* f. Gmc, rel. to TUG]

tow[2] /təʊ/ *n.* **1** the coarse and broken part of flax or hemp prepared for spinning. **2** a loose bunch of rayon etc. strands. □ **tow-coloured** (of hair) very light. **tow-head** tow-coloured or unkempt hair. **tow-headed** having very light or unkempt hair. □□ **towy** /ˈtəʊɪ/ *adj.* [ME f. MLG *touw* f. OS *tou*, rel. to ON *tó* wool: cf. TOOL]

toward *prep. & adj.* —*prep.* /təˈwɔːd, tɔːd/ = TOWARDS. —*adj.* /ˈtəʊəd/ *archaic* **1** about to take place; in process. **2** docile, apt. **3** promising, auspicious. □□ **towardness** /ˈtəʊədnɪs/ *n.* (in sense of *adj.*).

towards /təˈwɔːdz, twɔːdz, tɔːdz/ *prep.* **1** in the direction of (*set out towards town*). **2** as regards; in relation to (*his attitude towards death*). **3** as a contribution to; for (*put this towards your expenses*). **4** near (*towards the end of our journey*). [OE *tōweard* (adj.) future (as TO, -WARD)]

towel /ˈtaʊəl/ *n. & v.* —*n.* **1 a** a piece of rough-surfaced absorbent cloth used for drying oneself or a thing after washing. **b** absorbent paper used for this. **c** a cloth used for drying plates, dishes, etc.; a tea towel. **2** *Brit.* = *sanitary towel*. —*v.* (**towelled, towelling;** *US* **toweled, toweling**) **1** *tr.* (often *refl.*) wipe or dry with a towel. **2** *intr.* wipe or dry oneself with a towel. **3** *tr. sl.* thrash. □ **towel-horse** (or **-rail**) a frame for hanging towels on. □□ **towelling** *n.* [ME f. OF *toail(l)e* f. Gmc]

tower /ˈtaʊə(r)/ *n. & v.* —*n.* **1 a** a tall esp. square or circular structure, often part of a church, castle, etc. **b** a fortress etc. comprising or including a tower. **c** a tall structure housing machinery, apparatus, operators, etc. (*cooling tower*; *control tower*). **2** a place of defence; a protection. —*v.intr.* **1** (usu. foll. by *above, high*) reach or be high or above; be superior. **2** (of a bird) soar or hover. **3** (as **towering** *adj.*) **a** high, lofty (*towering intellect*). **b** violent (*towering rage*). □ **tower block** a tall building containing offices or flats. **tower of silence** a tall open-topped structure on which Parsees place their dead. **tower of strength** a person who gives strong and reliable support. □□ **towered** /ˈtaʊəd/ *adj.* **towery** *adj.* [OE *torr*, & ME *tūr*, AF & OF *tur* etc., f. L *turris* f. Gk]

town /taʊn/ *n.* **1 a** a large urban area with a name, defined boundaries, and local government, being larger than a village and usu. not created a city. **b** any densely populated area, esp. as opposed to the country or suburbs. **c** the people of a town (*the whole town knows of it*). **2 a** *Brit.* London or the chief city or town in one's

neighbourhood (*went up to town*). **b** the central business or shopping area in a neighbourhood (*just going into town*). **3** the permanent residents of a university town as distinct from the members of the university (cf. GOWN). **4** *US* = TOWNSHIP 2. □ **go to town** *colloq.* act or work with energy or enthusiasm. **on the town** *colloq.* enjoying the entertainments, esp. the night-life, of a town; celebrating. **town clerk 1** *US & hist.* the officer of the corporation of a town in charge of records etc. **2** *Brit. hist.* the secretary and legal adviser of a town corporation until 1974. **town council** the elective governing body in a municipality. **town councillor** an elected member of this. **town crier** see CRIER. **town gas** manufactured gas for domestic and commercial use. **town hall** a building for the administration of local government, having public meeting rooms etc. **town house 1** a town residence, esp. of a person with a house in the country. **2** a terrace house, esp. of a stylish modern type. **3** a house in a planned group in a town. **4** *Brit.* a town hall. **town-major** *hist.* the chief executive officer in a garrison town or fortress. **town mayor** *Brit.* the chairman of a town council. **town meeting** *US* a meeting of the voters of a town for the transaction of public business. **town planning** the planning of the construction and growth of towns. □□ **townish** *adj.* **townless** *adj.* **townlet** *n.* **townward** *adj. & adv.* **townwards** *adv.* [OE *tūn* enclosure f. Gmc]

townee /taʊˈniː/ *n.* (also **townie** /ˈtaʊnɪ/) *derog.* a person living in a town, esp. as opposed to a countryman or (in a university town) a student etc.

townscape /ˈtaʊnskeɪp/ *n.* **1** the visual appearance of a town or towns. **2** a picture of a town.

townsfolk /ˈtaʊnzfəʊk/ *n.* the inhabitants of a particular town or towns.

township /ˈtaʊnʃɪp/ *n.* **1** *S.Afr.* **a** an urban area set aside for Black (usu. African) occupation. **b** a White urban area (esp. if new or about to be developed). **2** *US & Can.* **a** a division of a county with some corporate powers. **b** a district six miles square. **3** *Brit. hist.* **a** a community inhabiting a manor, parish, etc. **b** a manor or parish as a territorial division. **c** a small town or village forming part of a large parish. **4** *Austral. & NZ* a small town; a town-site. [OE *tūnscipe* (as TOWN, -SHIP)]

townsman /ˈtaʊnzmən/ *n.* (*pl.* **-men**; *fem.* **townswoman**, *pl.* **-women**) an inhabitant of a town; a fellow citizen.

townspeople /ˈtaʊnzˌpiːp(ə)l/ *n.pl.* the people of a town.

towy see TOW[2].

toxaemia /tɒkˈsiːmɪə/ *n.* (*US* **toxemia**) **1** blood-poisoning. **2** a condition in pregnancy characterized by increased blood pressure. □□ **toxaemic** *adj.* [as TOXI- + -AEMIA]

toxi- /ˈtɒksɪ/ *comb. form* (also **toxico-** /ˈtɒksɪˌkəʊ/, **toxo-** /ˈtɒksəʊ/) poison; poisonous, toxic.

toxic /ˈtɒksɪk/ *adj.* **1** of or relating to poison (*toxic symptoms*). **2** poisonous (*toxic gas*). **3** caused by poison (*toxic anaemia*). □□ **toxically** *adv.* **toxicity** /-ˈsɪsɪtɪ/ *n.* [med.L *toxicus* poisoned f. L *toxicum* f. Gk *toxikon* (*pharmakon*) (poison for) arrows f. *toxon* bow, *toxa* arrows]

toxicology /ˌtɒksɪˈkɒlədʒɪ/ *n.* the scientific study of poisons. □□ **toxicological** /-kəˈlɒdʒɪk(ə)l/ *adj.* **toxicologist** *n.*

toxin /ˈtɒksɪn/ *n.* a poison produced by a living organism, esp. one formed in the body and stimulating the production of antibodies. [TOXIC + -IN]

toxocara /ˌtɒksəʊˈkɑːrə/ *n.* any nematode worm of the genus *Toxocara*, parasitic in the alimentary canal of dogs and cats. □□ **toxocariasis** /-kəˈraɪəsɪs/ *n.* [TOXO- (see TOXI-) + Gk *kara* head]

toxophilite /tɒkˈsɒfɪˌlaɪt/ *n. & adj.* —*n.* a student or lover of archery. —*adj.* of or concerning archery. □□ **toxophily** *n.* [Ascham's *Toxophilus* (1545) f. Gk *toxon* bow + -*philos* -PHILE]

toy /tɔɪ/ *n. & v.* —*n.* **1 a** a plaything, esp. for a child. **b** (often *attrib.*) a model or miniature replica of a thing, esp. as a plaything (*toy gun*). **2 a** a thing, esp. a gadget or instrument, regarded as providing amusement or pleasure. **b** a task or undertaking regarded in an unserious way. **3** (usu. *attrib.*) a diminutive breed or variety of dog etc. —*v.intr.* (usu. foll. by *with*) **1** trifle, amuse oneself, esp. with a person's affections; flirt (*toyed with the idea of going to Africa*). **2 a** move a material object idly (*toyed with her necklace*). **b** nibble at food etc. unenthusiastically (*toyed with a peach*). □ **toy-box** a usu. wooden box for keeping toys in. **toy boy** *colloq.* a woman's much younger male lover. **toy soldier 1** a miniature figure of a soldier. **2** *sl.* a soldier in a peacetime army. [16th c.: earlier = dallying, fun, jest, whim, trifle: orig. unkn.]

Tpr. *abbr.* Trooper.

trabeation /ˌtreɪbɪˈeɪʃ(ə)n/ *n.* the use of beams instead of arches or vaulting in construction. □□ **trabeate** /ˈtreɪbɪət/ *adj.* [L *trabs trabis* beam]

trabecula /trəˈbekjʊlə/ *n.* (*pl.* **trabeculae** /-ˌliː/) **1** *Anat.* a supporting band or bar of connective or bony tissue, esp. dividing an organ into chambers. **2** *Bot.* a beamlike projection or process within a hollow structure. □□ **trabecular** *adj.* **trabeculate** /-lət/ *adj.* [L, dimin. of *trabs* beam]

tracasserie /trəˈkæsərɪ/ *n.* **1** a state of annoyance. **2** a fuss; a petty quarrel. [F f. *tracasser* bustle]

trace¹ /treɪs/ *v.* & *n.* —*v.tr.* **1 a** observe, discover, or find vestiges or signs of by investigation. **b** (often foll. by *along*, *through*, *to*, etc.) follow or mark the track or position of (*traced their footprints in the mud; traced the outlines of a wall*). **c** (often foll. by *back*) follow to its origins (*can trace my family to the 12th century; the report has been traced back to you*). **2** (often foll. by *over*) copy (a drawing etc.) by drawing over its lines on a superimposed piece of translucent paper, or by using carbon paper. **3** (often foll. by *out*) mark out, delineate, sketch, or write esp. laboriously (*traced out a plan of the district; traced out his vision of the future*). **4** pursue one's way along (a path etc.). —*n.* **1 a** a sign or mark or other indication of something having existed; a vestige (*no trace remains of the castle; has the traces of a vanished beauty*). **b** a very small quantity. **c** an amount of rainfall etc. too small to be measured. **2** a track or footprint left by a person or animal. **3** a track left by the moving pen of an instrument etc. **4** a line on the screen of a cathode-ray tube showing the path of a moving spot. **5** a curve's projection on or intersection with a plane etc. **6** a change in the brain caused by learning processes. □ **trace element 1** a chemical element occurring in minute amounts. **2** a chemical element required only in minute amounts by living organisms for normal growth. **trace fossil** a fossil that represents a burrow, footprint, etc., of an organism. □□ **traceable** *adj.* **traceability** /-ˈbɪlɪtɪ/ *n.* **traceless** *adj.* [ME f. OF *trace* (n.), *tracier* (v.) f. L *tractus* drawing: see TRACT¹]

trace² /treɪs/ *n.* each of the two side-straps, chains, or ropes by which a horse draws a vehicle. □ **kick over the traces** become insubordinate or reckless. **trace-horse** a horse that draws in traces or by a single trace, esp. one hitched on to help uphill etc. [ME f. OF *trais*, pl. of TRAIT]

tracer /ˈtreɪsə(r)/ *n.* **1** a person or thing that traces. **2** *Mil.* a bullet etc. that is visible in flight because of flames etc. emitted. **3** an artificially produced radioactive isotope capable of being followed through the body by the radiation it produces.

tracery /ˈtreɪsərɪ/ *n.* (*pl.* **-ies**) **1** ornamental stone openwork esp. in the upper part of a Gothic window. **2** a fine decorative pattern. **3** a natural object finely patterned. □□ **traceried** *adj.*

trachea /trəˈkiːə, ˈtreɪkɪə/ *n.* (*pl.* **tracheae** /-ˈkiːiː/) **1** the passage reinforced by rings of cartilage, through which air reaches the bronchial tubes from the larynx; the windpipe. **2** each of the air passages in the body of an insect etc. **3** any duct or vessel in a plant. □□ **tracheal** /ˈtreɪkɪəl/ *adj.* **tracheate**

/ˈtreɪkɪˌeɪt/ *adj.* [ME f. med.L, = LL *trachia* f. Gk *trakheia* (*artēria*) rough (artery), f. *trakhus* rough]

tracheo- /ˈtreɪkɪəʊ/ *comb. form.*

tracheotomy /ˌtreɪkɪˈɒtəmɪ/ *n.* (also **tracheostomy** /-ˈɒstəmɪ/) (*pl.* **-ies**) an incision made in the trachea to relieve an obstruction to breathing. □ **tracheotomy tube** a breathing-tube inserted into this incision.

trachoma /trəˈkəʊmə/ *n.* a contagious disease of the eye with inflamed granulation on the inner surface of the lids. □□ **trachomatous** /-ˈkəʊmətəs, -ˈkɒmətəs/ *adj.* [mod.L f. Gk *trakhōma* f. *trakhus* rough]

trachyte /ˈtreɪkaɪt, ˈtræk-/ *n.* a light-coloured volcanic rock rough to the touch. □□ **trachytic** /trəˈkɪtɪk/ *adj.* [F f. Gk *trakhutēs* roughness (as TRACHOMA)]

tracing /ˈtreɪsɪŋ/ *n.* **1** a copy of a drawing etc. made by tracing. **2** = TRACE¹ *n.* 3. **3** the act or an instance of tracing. □ **tracing-paper** translucent paper used for making tracings.

track¹ /træk/ *n.* & *v.* —*n.* **1 a** a mark or marks left by a person, animal, or thing in passing. **b** (in *pl.*) such marks esp. footprints. **2** a rough path, esp. one beaten by use. **3** a continuous railway line (*laid three miles of track*). **4 a** a racecourse for horses, dogs, etc. **b** a prepared course for runners etc. **5 a** a groove on a gramophone record. **b** a section of a gramophone record containing one song etc. (*this side has six tracks*). **c** a lengthwise strip of magnetic tape containing one sequence of signals. **6 a** a line of travel, passage, or motion (*followed the track of the hurricane; America followed in the same track*). **b** the path travelled by a ship, aircraft, etc. (cf. COURSE *n.* 2c). **7** a continuous band round the wheels of a tank, tractor, etc. **8** the transverse distance between a vehicle's wheels. **9** = SOUNDTRACK. **10** a line of reasoning or thought (*this track proved fruitless*). —*v.* **1** *tr.* follow the track of (an animal, person, spacecraft, etc.). **2** *tr.* make out (a course, development, etc.); trace by vestiges. **3** *intr.* (often foll. by *back*, *in*, etc.) (of a film or television camera) move in relation to the subject being filmed. **4** *intr.* (of wheels) run so that the back ones are exactly in the track of the front ones. **5** *intr.* (of a gramophone stylus) follow a groove. **6** *tr.* *US* **a** make a track with (dirt etc.) from the feet. **b** leave such a track on (a floor etc.). □ **in one's tracks** *colloq.* where one stands, there and then (*stopped him in his tracks*). **keep** (or **lose**) **track of** follow (or fail to follow) the course or development of. **make tracks** *colloq.* go or run away. **make tracks for** *colloq.* go in pursuit of or towards. **off the track** away from the subject. **on a person's track 1** in pursuit of him or her. **2** in possession of a clue to a person's conduct, plans, etc. **on the wrong side of** (or **across**) **the tracks** *colloq.* in an inferior or dubious part of town. **on the wrong** (or **right**) **track** following the wrong (or right) line of inquiry. **track down** reach or capture by tracking. **track events** running-races as opposed to jumping etc. (cf. *field events*). **tracking station** an establishment set up to track objects in the sky. **track-laying** (of a vehicle) having a caterpillar tread. **track record** a person's past performance or achievements. **track shoe** a spiked shoe worn by a runner. **track suit** a loose warm suit worn by an athlete etc. for exercising or jogging. **track system** *US* streaming in education. **track with** *Austral. sl.* associate with, court. □□ **trackage** *US* *n.* [ME f. OF *trac*, perh. f. LG or Du. *tre(c)k* draught etc.]

track² /træk/ *v.* **1** *tr.* tow (a boat) by rope etc. from a bank. **2** *intr.* travel by being towed. [app. f. Du. *trekken* to draw etc., assim. to TRACK¹]

tracker /ˈtrækə(r)/ *n.* **1** a person or thing that tracks. **2** a police dog tracking by scent. **3** a wooden connecting-rod in the mechanism of an organ. **4** = *black tracker*.

tracking /ˈtrækɪŋ/ *n.* *Electr.* the formation of a conducting path over the surface of an insulating material.

tracklayer /ˈtrækˌleɪə(r)/ n. 1 US = TRACKMAN. 2 a tractor or other vehicle equipped with continuous tracks (see TRACK¹ n. 7).

tracklement /ˈtrækəlmənt/ n. an item of food, esp. a jelly, served with meat. [20th c.: orig. unkn.]

trackless /ˈtræklɪs/ adj. 1 without a track or tracks; untrodden. 2 leaving no track or trace. 3 not running on a track. □**trackless trolley** US a trolleybus.

trackman /ˈtrækmən/ n. (pl. -men) a platelayer.

trackway /ˈtrækweɪ/ n. a beaten path; an ancient roadway.

tract¹ /trækt/ n. 1 a region or area of indefinite, esp. large, extent (pathless desert tracts). 2 Anat. an area of an organ or system (respiratory tract). 3 Brit. archaic a period of time etc. [L tractus drawing f. trahere tract- draw, pull]

tract² /trækt/ n. a short treatise in pamphlet form esp. on a religious subject. [app. abbr. of L tractatus TRACTATE]

tract³ /trækt/ n. RC Ch. & Mus. an anthem replacing the alleluia in some masses. [med.L tractus (cantus) drawn-out (song), past part. of L trahere draw]

tractable /ˈtræktəb(ə)l/ adj. 1 (of a person) easily handled; manageable; docile. 2 (of material etc.) pliant, malleable. □□**tractability** /-ˈbɪlɪtɪ/ n. **tractableness** n. **tractably** adv. [L tractabilis f. tractare handle, frequent. of trahere tract- draw]

Tractarianism /trækˈteərɪəˌnɪz(ə)m/ n. hist. = OXFORD MOVEMENT. □□**Tractarian** adj. & n. [after Tracts for the Times, published in Oxford 1833–41 and outlining the movement's principles]

tractate /ˈtrækteɪt/ n. a treatise. [L tractatus f. tractare: see TRACTABLE]

traction /ˈtrækʃ(ə)n/ n. 1 the act of drawing or pulling a thing over a surface, esp. a road or track (steam traction). 2 a a sustained pulling on a limb, muscle, etc., by means of pulleys, weights, etc. b contraction, e.g. of a muscle. 3 the grip of a tyre on a road, a wheel on a rail, etc. 4 US the public transport service. □**traction-engine** a steam or diesel engine for drawing heavy loads on roads, fields, etc. **traction-wheel** the driving-wheel of a locomotive etc. □□**tractional** adj. **tractive** /ˈtræktɪv/ adj. [F traction or med.L tractio f. L trahere tract- draw]

tractor /ˈtræktə(r)/ n. 1 a motor vehicle used for hauling esp. farm machinery, heavy loads, etc. 2 a traction-engine. [LL tractor (as TRACTION)]

trad /træd/ n. & adj. esp. Brit. colloq. —n. traditional jazz. —adj. traditional. [abbr.]

trade /treɪd/ n. & v. —n. 1 a buying and selling. b buying and selling conducted between nations etc. c business conducted for profit (esp. as distinct from a profession) (a butcher by trade). d business of a specified nature or time (Christmas trade; tourist trade). 2 a skilled handicraft esp. requiring an apprenticeship (learnt a trade; his trade is plumbing). 3 (usu. prec. by the) a the people engaged in a specific trade (the trade will never agree to it; trade enquiries only). b Brit. colloq. licensed victuallers. c colloq. the submarine service. 4 US a transaction, esp. a swap. 5 (usu. in pl.) a trade wind. —v. 1 intr. (often foll. by in, with) engage in trade; buy and sell (trades in plastic novelties; we trade with Japan). 2 tr. a exchange in commerce; barter (goods). b exchange (insults, blows, etc.). 3 intr. (usu. foll. by with, for) have a transaction with a person for a thing. 4 intr. (usu. foll. by to) carry goods to a place. □**be in trade** esp. derog. be in commerce, esp. keep a shop. **foreign trade** international trade. **Trade Board** Brit. hist. a statutory body for settling disputes etc. in certain industries. **trade book** a book published by a commercial publisher and intended for general readership. **trade cycle** Brit. recurring periods of boom and recession. **trade gap** the extent by which a country's imports exceed its exports. **trade in** (often foll. by for) exchange (esp. a used car etc.) in esp. part payment for another. **trade-in** n. a thing, esp. a car, exchanged in this way. **trade journal**

a periodical containing news etc. concerning a particular trade. **trade-last** US a compliment from a third person which is reported to the person complimented in exchange for one to the reporter. **trade mark** 1 a device, word, or words, secured by legal registration or established by use as representing a company, product, etc. 2 a distinctive characteristic etc. **trade name** 1 a name by which a thing is called in a trade. 2 a name given to a product. 3 a name under which a business trades. **trade off** exchange, esp. as a compromise. **trade-off** n. such an exchange. **trade on** take advantage of (a person's credulity, one's reputation, etc.). **trade paper** = trade journal. **trade plates** number-plates used by a car-dealer etc. on unlicensed cars. **trade price** a wholesale price charged to the dealer before goods are retailed. **trade secret** 1 a secret device or technique used esp. in a trade. 2 joc. any secret. **Trades Union Congress** Brit. the official representative body of British trade unions, meeting annually. **trade** (or **trades**) **union** an organized association of workers in a trade, group of trades, or a profession, formed to protect and further their rights and interests. **trade-** (or **trades-**) **unionism** this system of association. **trade-** (or **trades-**) **unionist** a member of a trade union. **trade wind** a wind blowing continually towards the equator and deflected westward, f. obs. blow trade = blow regularly. □□**tradable** adj. **tradeable** adj. [ME f. MLG trade track f. OS trada, OHG trata: cf. TREAD]

trader /ˈtreɪdə(r)/ n. 1 a person engaged in trade. 2 a merchant ship.

tradescantia /ˌtrædɪˈskæntɪə/ n. any usu. trailing plant of the genus Tradescantia, with large blue, white, or pink flowers. [mod.L f. J. Tradescant, Engl. naturalist d. 1638]

tradesman /ˈtreɪdzmən/ n. (pl. -men; fem. **tradeswoman**, pl. -women) a person engaged in trading or a trade, esp. a shopkeeper or skilled craftsman.

tradespeople /ˈtreɪdzˌpiːp(ə)l/ n.pl. people engaged in trade and their families.

trading /ˈtreɪdɪŋ/ n. the act of engaging in trade. □**trading estate** esp. Brit. a specially-designed industrial and commercial area. **trading post** a store etc. established in a remote or unsettled region. **trading-stamp** a stamp given to customers by some stores which is exchangeable in large numbers for various articles.

tradition /trəˈdɪʃ(ə)n/ n. 1 a a custom, opinion, or belief handed down to posterity esp. orally or by practice. b this process of handing down. 2 esp. joc. an established practice or custom (it's a tradition to complain about the weather). 3 artistic, literary, etc. principles based on experience and practice; any one of these (stage tradition; traditions of the Dutch School). 4 Theol. doctrine or a particular doctrine etc. claimed to have divine authority without documentary evidence, esp.: a the oral teaching of Christ and the Apostles. b the laws held by the Pharisees to have been delivered by God to Moses. c the words and deeds of Muhammad not in the Koran. 5 Law the formal delivery of property etc. □□**traditionary** adj. **traditionist** n. **traditionless** adj. [ME f. OF tradicion or L traditio f. tradere hand on, betray (as TRANS-, dare give)]

traditional /trəˈdɪʃən(ə)l/ adj. 1 of, based on, or obtained by tradition. 2 (of jazz) in the style of the early 20th c. □□**traditionally** adv.

traditionalism /trəˈdɪʃənəˌlɪz(ə)m/ n. 1 respect, esp. excessive, for tradition, esp. in religion. 2 a philosophical system referring all religious knowledge to divine revelation and tradition. □□ **traditionalist** n. **traditionalistic** /-ˈlɪstɪk/ adj.

traditor /ˈtrædɪtə(r)/ n. (pl. **traditors** or **traditores** /-ˈtɔːriːz/) hist. an early Christian who surrendered copies of Scripture or Church property to his or her persecutors to save his or her life. [L: see TRAITOR]

traduce /trə'djuːs/ *v.tr.* speak ill of; misrepresent. □□ **traducement** *n.* **traducer** *n.* [L *traducere* disgrace (as TRANS-, *ducere duct-* lead)]

traffic /'træfɪk/ *n. & v.* —*n.* **1** (often *attrib.*) **a** vehicles moving in a public highway, esp. of a specified kind, density, etc. (*heavy traffic on the M1*; *traffic warden*). **b** such movement in the air or at sea. **2** (usu. foll. by *in*) trade, esp. illegal (*the traffic in drugs*). **3 a** the transportation of goods, the coming and going of people or goods by road, rail, air, sea, etc. **b** the persons or goods so transported. **4** dealings or communication between people etc. (*had no traffic with them*). **5** the messages, signals, etc., transmitted through a communications system; the flow or volume of such business. —*v.* (**trafficked, trafficking**) **1** *intr.* (usu. foll. by *in*) deal in something, esp. illegally (*trafficked in narcotics*; *traffics in innuendo*). **2** *tr.* deal in; barter. □**traffic circle** *US* a roundabout. **traffic cop** esp. *US colloq.* a traffic policeman. **traffic island** a paved or grassed area in a road to divert traffic and provide a refuge for pedestrians. **traffic jam** traffic at a standstill because of roadworks, an accident, etc. **traffic-light** (or **-lights** or **-signal**) a usu. automatic signal controlling road traffic esp. at junctions by coloured lights. **traffic sign** a sign conveying information, a warning, etc., to vehicle-drivers. **traffic warden** *Brit.* a uniformed official employed to help control road traffic and esp. parking. □□**trafficker** *n.* **trafficless** *adj.* [F *traf(f)ique*, Sp. *tráfico*, It. *traffico*, of unkn. orig.]

trafficator /'træfɪˌkeɪtə(r)/ *n. Brit. hist.* a signal raised automatically to indicate a change of direction in a motor vehicle. [TRAFFIC + INDICATOR]

tragacanth /'trægəˌkænθ/ *n.* a white or reddish gum from a plant, *Astragalus gummifer*, used in pharmacy, calico-printing, etc., as a vehicle for drugs, dye, etc. [F *tragacante* f. L *tragacantha* f. Gk *tragakantha*, name of a shrub, f. *tragos* goat + *akantha* thorn]

tragedian /trə'dʒiːdɪən/ *n.* **1** a writer of tragedies. **2** an actor in tragedy. [ME f. OF *tragediane* (as TRAGEDY)]

tragedienne /trəˌdʒiːdɪ'en/ *n.* an actress in tragedy. [F fem. (as TRAGEDIAN)]

tragedy /'trædʒɪdɪ/ *n.* (*pl.* **-ies**) **1** a serious accident, crime, or natural catastrophe. **2** a sad event; a calamity (*the team's defeat is a tragedy*). **3 a** a play in verse or prose dealing with tragic events and with an unhappy ending, esp. concerning the downfall of the protagonist. **b** tragic plays as a genre (cf. COMEDY). [ME f. OF *tragedie* f. L *tragoedia* f. Gk *tragōidia* app. goat-song f. *tragos* goat + *ōidē* song]

tragic /'trædʒɪk/ *adj.* **1** (also **tragical** /-k(ə)l/) sad; calamitous; greatly distressing (*a tragic tale*). **2** of, or in the style of, tragedy (*tragic drama*; *a tragic actor*). □**tragic irony** a device, orig. in Greek tragedy, by which words carry a tragic, esp. prophetic, meaning to the audience, unknown to the character speaking. □□**tragically** *adv.* [F *tragique* f. L *tragicus* f. Gk *tragikos* f. *tragos* goat: see TRAGEDY]

tragicomedy /ˌtrædʒɪ'kɒmɪdɪ/ *n.* (*pl.* **-ies**) **1 a** a play having a mixture of comedy and tragedy. **b** plays of this kind as a genre. **2** an event etc. having tragic and comic elements. □□**tragicomic** *adj.* **tragicomically** *adv.* [F *tragicomédie* or It. *tragicomedia* f. LL *tragicomoedia* f. L *tragico-comoedia* (as TRAGIC, COMEDY)]

tragopan /'trægəˌpæn/ *n.* any Asian pheasant of the genus *Tragopan*, with erect fleshy horns on its head. [L f. Gk f. *tragos* goat + *Pan* the god Pan]

trahison des clercs /ˌtraːiːˌzɔ̃ deɪ 'kleər/ *n.* the betrayal of standards, scholarship, etc., by intellectuals. [F, title of a book by J. Benda (1927)]

trail /treɪl/ *n. & v.* —*n.* **1 a** a track left by a thing, person, etc., moving over a surface (*left a trail of wreckage*; *a slug's slimy trail*). **b** a track or scent followed in hunting, seeking, etc. (*he's on the trail*). **2** a beaten path or track, esp. through a wild region. **3** a part dragging behind a thing or person; an appendage (*a trail of smoke*; *a condensation trail*). **4** the rear end of a gun-carriage stock. —*v.* **1** *tr. & intr.* draw or be drawn along behind, esp. on the ground. **2** *intr.* (often foll. by *behind*) walk wearily; lag; straggle. **3** *tr.* follow the trail of; pursue (*trailed him to his home*). **4** *intr.* be losing in a game or other contest (*trailing by three points*). **5** *intr.* (usu. foll. by *away, off*) peter out; tail off. **6** *intr.* **a** (of a plant etc.) grow or hang over a wall, along the ground etc. **b** (of a garment etc.) hang loosely. **7** *tr.* (often *refl.*) drag (oneself, one's limbs, etc.) along wearily etc. **8** *tr.* advertise (a film, a radio or television programme, etc.) in advance by showing extracts etc. **9** *tr.* apply (slip) through a nozzle or spout to decorate ceramic ware. □**at the trail** *Mil.* with arms trailed. **trail arms** *Mil.* let a rifle etc. hang balanced in one hand and, *Brit.*, parallel to the ground. **trail bike** a light motor cycle for use in rough terrain. **trail-blazer 1** a person who marks a new track through wild country. **2** a pioneer; an innovator. **trail-blazing** *n.* the act or process of blazing a trail. —*attrib.adj.* that blazes a trail; pioneering. **trail one's coat** deliberately provoke a quarrel, fight, etc. **trailing edge 1** the rear edge of an aircraft's wing etc. **2** *Electronics* the part of a pulse in which the amplitude diminishes (opp. *leading edge* (see LEADING[1])). **trailing wheel** a wheel not given direct motive power. **trail-net** a drag-net. [ME (earlier as verb) f. OF *traillier* to tow, or f. MLG *treilen* haul f. L *tragula* drag-net]

trailer /'treɪlə(r)/ *n.* **1** a person or thing that trails. **2** a series of brief extracts from a film etc., used to advertise it in advance. **3** a vehicle towed by another, esp.: **a** the rear section of an articulated lorry. **b** an open cart. **c** a platform for transporting a boat etc. **d** *US* a caravan. **4** a trailing plant.

train /treɪn/ *v. & n.* —*v.* **1 a** *tr.* (often foll. by *to* + *infin.*) teach (a person, animal, oneself, etc.) a specified skill esp. by practice (*trained the dog to beg*; *was trained in midwifery*). **b** *intr.* undergo this process (*trained as a teacher*). **2** *tr. & intr.* bring or come into a state of physical efficiency by exercise, diet, etc.; undergo physical exercise, esp. for a specific purpose (*trained me for the high jump*; *the team trains every evening*). **3** *tr.* cause (a plant) to grow in a required shape (*trained the peach tree up the wall*). **4** (usu. as **trained** *adj.*) make (the mind, eye, etc.) sharp or discerning as a result of instruction, practice, etc. **5** *tr.* (often foll. by *on*) point or aim (a gun, camera, etc.) at an object etc. **6** *colloq.* **a** *intr.* go by train. **b** *tr.* (foll. by *it* as object) make a journey by train (*trained it to Aberdeen*). **7** *tr.* (usu. foll. by *away*) *archaic* entice, lure. —*n.* **1** a series of railway carriages or trucks drawn by an engine. **2** something dragged along behind or forming the back part of a dress, robe, etc. (*wore a dress with a long train*; *the train of the peacock*). **3** a succession or series of people, things, events, etc. (*a long train of camels*; *interrupted my train of thought*; *a train of ideas*). **4** a body of followers; a retinue (*a train of admirers*). **5** a succession of military vehicles etc., including artillery, supplies, etc. (*baggage train*). **6** a line of gunpowder etc. to fire an explosive charge. **7** a series of connected wheels or parts in machinery. □**train** properly arranged or directed. **in a person's train** following behind a person. **in the train of** as a sequel of. **train-bearer** a person employed to hold up the train of a robe etc. **train down** train with exercise or diet to lower one's weight. **train-ferry** (*pl.* **-ies**) a ship that conveys a railway train across water. **train-mile** one mile travelled by one train, as a unit of traffic. **train-spotter** a person who collects locomotive numbers as a hobby. **train-spotting** this hobby. □□**trainable** *adj.* **trainability** /-'bɪlɪtɪ/ *n.* **trainee** /-'niː/ *n.* **trainless** *adj.* [ME f. OF *trainer, trahiner,* ult. f. L *trahere* draw]

trainband /'treɪnbænd/ n. hist. any of several divisions of London citizen soldiers, esp. in the Stuart period.

trainer /'treɪnə(r)/ n. 1 a person who trains. 2 a person who trains horses, athletes, footballers, etc., as a profession. 3 an aircraft or device simulating it used to train pilots. 4 Brit. a soft running shoe of leather, canvas, etc.

training /'treɪnɪŋ/ n. the act or process of teaching or learning a skill, discipline, etc. (physical training). □**go into training** begin physical training. **in training** 1 undergoing physical training. 2 physically fit as a result of this. **out of training** 1 no longer training. 2 physically unfit. **training-college** a college or school for training esp. prospective teachers. **training-ship** a ship on which young people are taught seamanship etc.

trainman /'treɪnmæn/ n. (pl. -**men**) a railway employee working on trains.

train-oil /'treɪnɔɪl/ n. oil obtained from the blubber of a whale (esp. of a right whale). [obs. train, trane train-oil f. MLG trān, MDu. traen, app. = TEAR²]

trainsick /'treɪnsɪk/ adj. affected with nausea by the motion of a train. □□ **trainsickness** n.

traipse /treɪps/ v. & n. (also **trapes**) colloq. or dial. —v.intr. 1 tramp or trudge wearily. 2 (often foll. by about) go on errands. —n. 1 a tedious journey on foot. 2 archaic a slattern. [16th-c. trapes (v.), of unkn. orig.]

trait /treɪ, treɪt/ n. a distinguishing feature or characteristic esp. of a person. [F f. L tractus (as TRACT¹)]

traitor /'treɪtə(r)/ n. (fem. **traitress** /-trɪs/) (often foll. by to) a person who is treacherous or disloyal, esp. to his country. □□ **traitorous** adj. **traitorously** adv. [ME f. OF traït(o)ur f. L traditor -oris f. tradere: see TRADITION]

trajectory /trə'dʒɛktəri, 'trædʒɪk-/ n. (pl. -**ies**) 1 the path described by a projectile flying or an object moving under the action of given forces. 2 Geom. a curve or surface cutting a system of curves or surfaces at a constant angle. [(orig. adj.) f. med.L trajectorius f. L traicere traject- (as TRANS-, jacere throw)]

tra-la /trɑːˈlɑː/ int. an expression of joy or gaiety. [imit. of song]

tram¹ /træm/ n. 1 Brit. an electrically-powered passenger vehicle running on rails laid in a public road. 2 a four-wheeled vehicle used in coal-mines. □**tram-road** hist. a road with wooden, stone, or metal wheel-tracks. [MLG & MDu. trame balk, beam, barrow-shaft]

tram² /træm/ n. (in full **tram silk**) double silk thread used for the weft of some velvets and silks. [F trame f. L trama weft]

tramcar /'træmkɑː(r)/ n. Brit. = TRAM¹ 1.

tramlines /'træmlaɪnz/ n.pl. 1 rails for a tramcar. 2 colloq. a either pair of two sets of long parallel lines at the sides of a lawn-tennis court. b similar lines at the side or back of a badminton court. 3 inflexible principles or courses of action etc.

trammel /'træm(ə)l/ n. & v. —n. 1 (usu. in pl.) an impediment to free movement; a hindrance (the trammels of domesticity). 2 a triple drag-net for fish, which are trapped in a pocket formed when they attempt to swim through. 3 an instrument for drawing ellipses etc. with a bar sliding in upright grooves. 4 a beam-compass. 5 US a hook in a fireplace for a kettle etc. —v.tr. (**trammelled**, **trammelling**; US **trammeled**, **trammeling**) confine or hamper with or as if with trammels. [in sense 'net' ME f. OF tramail f. med.L tramaculum, tremaculum, perh. formed as TRI- + macula (MAIL²): later history uncert.]

tramontana /ˌtrɑːmɒnˈtɑːnə/ n. a cold north wind in the Adriatic. [It.: see TRAMONTANE]

tramontane /trəˈmɒnteɪn/ adj. & n. —adj. 1 situated or living on the other side of mountains, esp. the Alps as seen from Italy. 2 (from the Italian point of view) foreign; barbarous. —n. 1 a tramontane person. 2 = TRAMONTANA. [ME f. It. tramontano f. L transmontanus beyond the mountains (as TRANS-, mons montis mountain)]

tramp /træmp/ v. & n. —v. 1 intr. a walk heavily and firmly (tramping about upstairs). b go on foot, esp. a distance. 2 tr. a cross on foot, esp. wearily or reluctantly. b cover (a distance) in this way (tramped forty miles). 3 tr. (often foll. by down) tread on; trample; stamp on. 4 tr. Austral. colloq. dismiss from employment, sack. 5 intr. live as a tramp. —n. 1 an itinerant vagrant or beggar. 2 the sound of a person, or esp. people, walking, marching, etc., or of horses' hooves. 3 a journey on foot, esp. protracted. 4 a an iron plate protecting the sole of a boot used for digging. b the part of a spade that it strikes. 5 esp. US sl. derog. a promiscuous woman. 6 = ocean tramp. □□ **tramper** n. **trampish** adj. [ME trampe f. Gmc]

trample /'træmp(ə)l/ v. & n. —v.tr. 1 tread under foot. 2 press down or crush in this way. —n. the sound or act of trampling. □**trample on** 1 tread heavily on. 2 treat roughly or with contempt; disregard (a person's feelings etc.). □□ **trampler** n. [ME f. TRAMP + -LE⁴]

trampoline /'træmpə,liːn/ n. & v. —n. a strong fabric sheet connected by springs to a horizontal frame, used by gymnasts etc. for somersaults, as a springboard, etc. —v.intr. use a trampoline. □□ **trampolinist** n. [It. trampolino f. trampoli stilts]

tramway /'træmweɪ/ n. 1 = tram-road (see TRAM¹). 2 a rails for a tramcar. b a tramcar system.

trance /trɑːns/ n. & v. —n. 1 a a sleeplike or half-conscious state without response to stimuli. b a hypnotic or cataleptic state. 2 such a state as entered into by a medium. 3 a state of extreme exaltation or rapture; ecstasy. —v.tr. poet. = ENTRANCE². □□ **trancelike** adj. [ME f. OF transe f. transir depart, fall into trance f. L transire: see TRANSIT]

tranche /trɑːnʃ/ n. a portion, esp. of income, or of a block of shares. [F, = slice (as TRENCH)]

tranny /'trænɪ/ n. (pl. -**ies**) esp. Brit. colloq. a transistor radio. [abbr.]

tranquil /'træŋkwɪl/ adj. calm, serene, unruffled. □□ **tranquillity** /-'kwɪlɪtɪ/ n. **tranquilly** adv. [F tranquille or L tranquillus]

tranquillize /'træŋkwɪ,laɪz/ v.tr. (US **tranquilize**, -**ise**) make tranquil, esp. by a drug etc.

tranquillizer /'træŋkwɪ,laɪzə(r)/ n. (US **tranquilizer**, -**iser**) a drug used to diminish anxiety.

trans- /trænz, trɑːns, -nz/ prefix 1 across, beyond (transcontinental; transgress). 2 on or to the other side of (transatlantic) (opp. CIS-). 3 through (transonic). 4 into another state or place (transform; transcribe). 5 surpassing, transcending (transfinite). 6 Chem. a (of an isomer) having the same atom or group on opposite sides of a given plane in the molecule (cf. CIS- 4). b having a higher atomic number than (transuranic). [from or after L trans across]

transact /træn'zækt, trɑːn-, -'sækt/ v.tr. perform or carry through (business). □□ **transactor** n. [L transigere transact- (as TRANS-, agere do)]

transaction /træn'zækʃ(ə)n, trɑːn-, -'sækʃ(ə)n/ n. 1 a a piece of esp. commercial business done; a deal (a profitable transaction). b the management of business etc. 2 (in pl.) published reports of discussions, papers read, etc., at the meetings of a learned society. □□ **transactional** adj. **transactionally** adv. [ME f. LL transactio (as TRANSACT)]

transalpine /trænz'ælpaɪn, trɑːn-, -s'ælpaɪn/ adj. beyond the Alps, esp. from the Italian point of view. [L transalpinus (as TRANS-, alpinus ALPINE)]

transatlantic /ˌtrænzət'læntɪk, ˌtrɑːn-, -sət'læntɪk/ adj. 1 beyond the Atlantic, esp.: a Brit. American. b US European. 2 crossing the Atlantic (a transatlantic flight).

transceiver /træn'siːvə(r), trɑːn-/ n. a combined radio transmitter and receiver.

transcend /træn'send, trɑːn-/ v.tr. **1** be beyond the range or grasp of (human experience, reason, belief, etc.). **2** excel; surpass. [ME f. OF transcendre or L transcendere (as TRANS-, scandere climb)]

transcendent /træn'send(ə)nt, trɑːn-/ adj. & n. —adj. **1** excelling, surpassing (transcendent merit). **2** transcending human experience. **3** Philos. **a** higher than or not included in any of Aristotle's ten categories in scholastic philosophy. **b** not realizable in experience in Kantian philosophy. **4** (esp. of the supreme being) existing apart from, not subject to the limitations of, the material universe (opp. IMMANENT). —n. Philos. a transcendent thing. □□ **transcendence** n. **transcendency** n. **transcendently** adv.

transcendental /ˌtrænsen'dent(ə)l, ˌtrɑːn-/ adj. & n. —adj. **1** = TRANSCENDENT. **2 a** (in Kantian philosophy) presupposed in and necessary to experience; a priori. **b** (in Schelling's philosophy) explaining matter and objective things as products of the subjective mind. **c** (esp. in Emerson's philosophy) regarding the divine as the guiding principle in man. **3 a** visionary, abstract. **b** vague, obscure. **4** Math. (of a function) not capable of being produced by the algebraical operations of addition, multiplication, and involution, or the inverse operations. —n. a transcendental term, conception, etc. □ **transcendental cognition** a priori knowledge. **Transcendental Meditation** a method of detaching oneself from problems, anxiety, etc., by silent meditation and repetition of a mantra. **transcendental object** a real (unknown and unknowable) object. **transcendental unity** unity brought about by cognition. □□ **transcendentally** adv. [med.L transcendentalis (as TRANSCENDENT)]

transcendentalism /ˌtrænsen'dentəˌlɪz(ə)m, ˌtrɑːn-/ n. **1** transcendental philosophy. **2** exalted or visionary language. □□ **transcendentalist** n. **transcendentalize** v.tr. (also -ise).

transcode /trænz'kəʊd, trɑːnz-/ v.tr. & intr. convert from one form of coded representation to another.

transcontinental /ˌtrænzˌkɒntɪ'nent(ə)l, trɑːnz-, træns-, trɑːns-/ adj. & n. —adj. (of a railway etc.) extending across a continent. —n. a transcontinental railway or train. □□ **transcontinentally** adv.

transcribe /træn'skraɪb, trɑːn-/ v.tr. **1** make a copy of, esp. in writing. **2** transliterate. **3** write out (shorthand, notes, etc.) in ordinary characters or continuous prose. **4 a** record for subsequent reproduction. **b** broadcast in this form. **5** arrange (music) for a different instrument etc. □□ **transcriber** n. **transcription** /-'skrɪpʃ(ə)n/ n. **transcriptional** /-'skrɪpʃən(ə)l/ adj. **transcriptive** /-'skrɪptɪv/ adj. [L transcribere transcript- (as TRANS-, scribere write)]

transcript /'trænskrɪpt, 'trɑːn-/ n. **1** a written or recorded copy. **2** any copy. [ME f. OF transcrit f. L transcriptum neut. past part.: see TRANSCRIBE]

transducer /træns'djuːsə(r), trɑːns-, -'zdjuːsə(r)/ n. any device for converting a non-electrical signal into an electrical one e.g. pressure into voltage. [L transducere lead across (as TRANS-, ducere lead)]

transect /træn'sekt, trɑːn-, -'zekt/ v.tr. cut across or transversely. □□ **transection** n. [TRANS- + L secare sect- cut]

transept /'trænsept, 'trɑːn-/ n. **1** either arm of the part of a cross-shaped church at right angles to the nave (north transept; south transept). **2** this part as a whole. □□ **transeptal** /-'sept(ə)l/ adj. [mod.L transeptum (as TRANS-, SEPTUM)]

transexual var. of TRANSSEXUAL.

transfer v. & n. —v. /træns'fɜː(r), trɑːns-/ (**transferred, transferring**) **1** tr. (often foll. by to) **a** convey, remove, or hand over (a thing etc.) (transferred the bag from the car to the station). **b** make over the possession of (property, a ticket, rights, etc.) to a person (transferred his membership to his son). **2** tr. & intr. change or move to another

group, club, department, etc. **3** intr. change from one station, route, etc., to another on a journey. **4** tr. **a** convey (a drawing etc.) from one surface to another, esp. to a lithographic stone by means of transfer-paper. **b** remove (a picture) from one surface to another, esp. from wood or a wall to canvas. **5** tr. change (the sense of a word etc.) by extension or metaphor. —n. /'trænsfɜː(r), 'trɑːns-/ **1** the act or an instance of transferring or being transferred. **2 a** design etc. conveyed or to be conveyed from one surface to another. **b** a small usu. coloured picture or design on paper, which is transferable to another surface. **3** a football player etc. who is or is to be transferred. **4 a** the conveyance of property, a right, etc. **b** a document effecting this. **5** US a ticket allowing a journey to be continued on another route etc. □ **transfer-book** a register of transfers of property, shares, etc. **transfer company** US a company conveying passengers or luggage between stations. **transfer fee** a fee paid for the transfer of esp. a professional footballer. **transfer ink** ink used for making designs on a lithographic stone or transfer-paper. **transfer list** a list of footballers available for transfer. **transfer-paper** specially coated paper to receive the impression of transfer ink and transfer it to stone. **transfer RNA** RNA conveying an amino-acid molecule from the cytoplasm to a ribosome for use in protein synthesis etc. □□ **transferee** /-'riː/ n. **transferor** /-'fɜːrə(r)/ esp. Law n. **transferrer** /-'fɜːrə(r)/ n. [ME f. F transférer or L transferre (as TRANS-, ferre lat- bear)]

transferable /træns'fɜːrəb(ə)l, trɑːns-, 'tr-/ adj. capable of being transferred. □ **transferable vote** a vote that can be transferred to another candidate if the first choice is eliminated. □□ **transferability** /-'bɪlɪtɪ/ n.

transference /'trænsfərəns, 'trɑː-/ n. **1** the act or an instance of transferring; the state of being transferred. **2** Psychol. the redirection of childhood emotions to a new object, esp. to a psychoanalyst.

transferral /træns'fɜːr(ə)l, trɑːns-/ n. = TRANSFER n. 1.

transferrin /træns'fɜːrɪn, trɑː-/ n. a protein transporting iron in the blood of animals. [TRANS- + L ferrum iron]

transfiguration /ˌtrænsˌfɪɡjʊ'reɪʃ(ə)n, trɑː-/ n. **1 a** change of form or appearance. **2 a** Christ's appearance in radiant glory to three of his disciples (Matt. 17:2, Mark 9:2–3). **b** (**Transfiguration**) the festival of Christ's transfiguration, 6 Aug. [ME f. OF transfiguration or L transfiguratio (as TRANSFIGURE)]

transfigure /træns'fɪɡə(r), trɑː-/ v.tr. change in form or appearance, esp. so as to elevate or idealize. [ME f. OF transfigurer or L transfigurare (as TRANS-, FIGURE)]

transfinite /træns'faɪnaɪt, trɑː-/ adj. **1** beyond or surpassing the finite. **2** Math. (of a number) exceeding all finite numbers.

transfix /træns'fɪks, trɑː-/ v.tr. **1** pierce with a sharp implement or weapon. **2** root (a person) to the spot with horror or astonishment; paralyse the faculties of. □□ **transfixion** /-'fɪkʃ(ə)n/ n. [L transfigere transfix- (as TRANS-, FIX)]

transform /træns'fɔːm, trɑː-/ v. & n. —v. **1 a** tr. make a thorough or dramatic change in the form, outward appearance, character, etc., of. **b** intr. (often foll. by into, to) undergo such a change. **2** tr. Electr. change the voltage etc. of (a current). **3** tr. Math. change (a mathematical entity) by transformation. —n. /'trænsfɔːm, 'trɑːns-/ Math. & Linguistics the product of a transformation. □□ **transformable** adj.

transformative adj. [ME f. OF transformer or L transformare (as TRANS-, FORM)]

transformation /ˌtrænsfə'meɪʃ(ə)n, ˌtrɑː-/ n. **1** the act or an instance of transforming; the state of being transformed. **2** Zool. a change of form at metamorphosis, esp. of insects, amphibia, etc. **3** the induced or spontaneous change of one element into another. **4** *Math.* a change from one geometrical figure, expression, or function to another of the same value, magnitude, etc. **5** *Biol.* the modification of a eukaryotic cell from its normal state to a malignant state. **6** *Linguistics* a process, with reference to particular rules, by which one grammatical pattern of sentence structure can be converted into another, or the underlying meaning of a sentence can be converted into a statement of syntax. **7** *archaic* a woman's wig. **8** a sudden dramatic change of scene on stage. [ME f. OF *transformation* or LL *transformatio* (as TRANSFORM)]

transformational /ˌtrænsfəˈmeɪʃən(ə)l/ *adj.* relating to or involving transformation. ◻ **transformational grammar** *Linguistics* a grammar that describes a language by means of transformation (see TRANSFORMATION 6). ◻◻ **transformationally** *adv.*

transformer /trænsˈfɔːmə(r), trɑː-, -zˈfɔːmə(r)/ *n.* **1** an apparatus for reducing or increasing the voltage of an alternating current. **2** a person or thing that transforms.

transfuse /trænsˈfjuːz, trɑː-/ *v.tr.* **1** permeate (*purple dye transfused the water*; *was transfused with gratitude*). **2 a** transfer (blood) from one person or animal to another. **b** inject (liquid) into a blood-vessel to replace lost fluid. **3** cause (fluid etc.) to pass from one vessel etc. to another. ◻◻ **transfusion** /-ˈfjuːʒ(ə)n/ *n.* [ME f. L *transfundere transfus-* (as TRANS-, *fundere* pour)]

transgenic /trænsˈdʒenɪk/ *adj.* *Biol.* (of an animal or plant) having genetic material introduced from another species.

transgress /trænzˈgres, trɑː-, -sˈgres/ *v.tr.* (also *absol.*) **1** go beyond the bounds or limits set by (a commandment, law, etc.); violate; infringe. **2** *Geol.* (of the sea) to spread over (the land). ◻◻ **transgression** /-ˈgreʃ(ə)n/ *n.* **transgressive** *adj.* **transgressor** *n.* [F *transgresser* or L *transgredi transgress-* (as TRANS-, *gradi* go)]

tranship var. of TRANSSHIP.

transhumance /trænsˈhjuːməns, trɑː-/ *n.* the seasonal moving of livestock to a different region. [F f. *transhumer* f. L TRANS- + *humus* ground]

transient /ˈtrænzɪənt, ˈtrɑː-, -sɪənt/ *adj. & n.* —*adj.* **1** of short duration; momentary; passing; impermanent (*life is transient*; *of transient interest*). **2** *Mus.* serving only to connect; inessential (*a transient chord*). —*n.* **1** a temporary visitor, worker, etc. **2** *Electr.* a brief current etc. ◻◻ **transience** *n.* **transiency** *n.* **transiently** *adv.* [L *transire* (as TRANS-, *ire* go)]

transilluminate /ˌtrænzɪˈluːmɪˌneɪt, ˌtrɑː-/ *v.tr.* pass a strong light through for inspection, esp. for medical diagnosis. ◻◻ **transillumination** /-ˈneɪʃ(ə)n/ *n.*

transire /trænˈsaɪə(r)/ *n.* *Brit.* a customs permit for the passage of goods. [L *transire* go across (as TRANSIENT)]

transistor /trænˈzɪstə(r), trɑː-, -ˈsɪstə(r)/ *n.* **1** a semiconductor device with three connections, capable of amplification in addition to rectification. **2** (in full **transistor radio**) a portable radio with transistors. [portmanteau word, f. TRANSFER + RESISTOR]

transistorize /trænˈzɪstəˌraɪz, trɑː-, -ˈsɪstəˌraɪz/ *v.tr.* (also **-ise**) design or equip with, or convert to, transistors rather than valves. ◻◻ **transistorization** /-ˈzeɪʃ(ə)n/ *n.*

transit /ˈtrænzɪt, ˈtrɑː-, -sɪt/ *n. & v.* —*n.* **1** the act or process of going, conveying, or being conveyed, esp. over a distance (*transit by rail*; *made a transit of the lake*). **2** a passage or route (*the overland transit*). **3 a** the apparent passage of a celestial body across the meridian of a place. **b** such an apparent passage across the sun or a planet. **4** *US* the local conveyance of passengers on public routes. —*v.* (**transited**, **transiting**) **1** *tr.* make a transit across. **2** *intr.* make a transit. ◻ **in transit** while going or being conveyed. **transit camp** a camp for the temporary accom-

modation of soldiers, refugees, etc. **transit-circle** (or **-instrument**) an instrument for observing the transit of a celestial body across the meridian. **transit-compass** (or **-theodolite**) a surveyor's instrument for measuring a horizontal angle. **transit-duty** duty paid on goods passing through a country. **transit lounge** a lounge at an airport for passengers waiting between flights. **transit visa** a visa allowing only passage through a country. [ME f. L *transitus* f. *transire* (as TRANSIENT)]

transition /trænˈzɪʃ(ə)n, trɑː-, -ˈsɪʃ(ə)n/ *n.* **1** a passing or change from one place, state, etc., to another (*an age of transition*; *a transition from plain to hills*). **2** *Mus.* a momentary modulation. **3** *Art* a change from one style to another, esp. *Archit.* from Norman to Early English. **4** *Physics* a change in an atomic nucleus or orbital electron with emission or absorption of radiation. ◻ **transition element** *Chem.* any of a set of elements in the periodic table characterized by partly filled *d* or *f* orbitals and the ability to form coloured complexes. **transition point** *Physics* the point at which different phases of the same substance can be in equilibrium. ◻◻ **transitional** *adj.* **transitionally** *adv.* **transitionary** *adj.* [F *transition* or L *transitio* (as TRANSIT)]

transitive /ˈtrænsɪtɪv, ˈtrɑː-, -zɪtɪv/ *adj.* **1** *Gram.* (of a verb or sense of a verb) that takes a direct object (whether expressed or implied), e.g. *saw* in *saw the donkey*, *saw that she was ill* (opp. INTRANSITIVE). **2** *Logic* (of a relation) such as to be valid for any two members of a sequence if it is valid for every pair of successive members. ◻◻ **transitively** *adv.* **transitiveness** *n.* **transitivity** /-ˈtɪvɪtɪ/ *n.* [LL *transitivus* (as TRANSIT)]

transitory /ˈtrænsɪtərɪ, ˈtrɑː-, -zɪtərɪ/ *adj.* not permanent, brief, transient. ◻ **transitory action** *Law* an action that can be brought in any country irrespective of where the transaction etc. started. ◻◻ **transitorily** *adv.* **transitoriness** *n.* [ME f. AF *transitorie*, OF *transitoire* f. L *transitorius* (as TRANSIT)]

translate /trænsˈleɪt, trɑː-, -zˈleɪt/ *v.* **1** *tr.* (also *absol.*) **a** (often foll. by *into*) express the sense of (a word, sentence, speech, book, etc.) in another language. **b** do this as a profession etc. (*translates for the UN*). **2** *intr.* (of a literary work etc.) be translatable, bear translation (*does not translate well*). **3** *tr.* express (an idea, book, etc.) in another, esp. simpler, form. **4** *tr.* interpret the significance of; infer as (*translated his silence as dissent*). **5** *tr.* move or change, esp. from one person, place, or condition, to another (*was translated by joy*). **6** *intr.* (foll. by *into*) result in; be converted into; manifest itself as. **7** *tr.* *Eccl.* **a** remove (a bishop) to another see. **b** remove (a saint's relics etc.) to another place. **8** *tr.* *Bibl.* convey to heaven without death; transform. **9** *tr.* *Mech.* **a** cause (a body) to move so that all its parts travel in the same direction. **b** impart motion without rotation to. ◻◻ **translatable** *adj.* **translatability** /-ˈbɪlɪtɪ/ *n.* [ME f. L *translatus*, past part. of *transferre*: see TRANSFER]

translation /trænsˈleɪʃ(ə)n, trɑː-, -zˈleɪʃ(ə)n/ *n.* **1** the act or an instance of translating. **2** a written or spoken expression of the meaning of a word, speech, book, etc. in another language. ◻◻ **translational** *adj.* **translationally** *adv.*

translator /trænsˈleɪtə(r), trɑː-, -zˈleɪtə(r)/ *n.* **1** a person who translates from one language into another. **2** a television relay transmitter. **3** a program that translates from one (esp. programming) language into another.

transliterate /trænzˈlɪtəˌreɪt, trɑː-, -sˈlɪtəˌreɪt/ *v.tr.* represent (a word etc.) in the closest corresponding letters of a different alphabet or language. ◻◻ **transliteration** /-ˈreɪʃ(ə)n/ *n.* **transliterator** *n.* [TRANS- + L *littera* letter]

translocate /ˌtrænzləʊˈkeɪt, ˌtrɑː-, -sləʊˈkeɪt/ *v.tr.* **1** move from one place to another. **2** (usu. in *passive*)

Bot. move (substances in a plant) from one part to another. □□ **translocation** *n.*

translucent /trænz'luːs(ə)nt, trɑː-, -'ljuːs(ə)nt, -s'l-/ *adj.* **1** allowing light to pass through diffusely; semi-transparent. **2** transparent. □□ **translucence** *n.* **translucency** *n.* **translucently** *adv.* [L *trans-lucēre* (as TRANS-, *lucēre* shine)]

translunar /trænz'luːnə(r), -'ljuːnə(r), -s'l-/ *adj.* **1** lying beyond the moon. **2** of or relating to space travel or a trajectory towards the moon.

transmarine /ˌtrænzmə'riːn, ˌtrɑː-, -smə'riːn/ *adj.* situated or going beyond the sea. [L *transmarinus* f. *marinus* MARINE]

transmigrant /trænz'maɪgrənt, trɑː-, -s'maɪgrənt/ *adj. & n.* —*adj.* passing through, esp. a country on the way to another. —*n.* a migrant or alien passing through a country etc. [L *transmigrant-*, part. stem of *transmigrare* (as TRANSMIGRATE)]

transmigrate /ˌtrænzmaɪ'greɪt, ˌtrɑː-, -smaɪ'greɪt/ *v.intr.* **1** (of the soul) pass into a different body; undergo metempsychosis. **2** migrate. □□ **transmigration** /-'greɪʃ(ə)n/ *n.* **transmigrator** *n.* **transmigratory** /-'maɪgrətəri/ *adj.* [ME f. L *transmigrare* (as TRANS-, MIGRATE)]

transmission /trænz'mɪʃ(ə)n, trɑː-, -s'mɪʃ(ə)n/ *n.* **1** the act or an instance of transmitting; the state of being transmitted. **2** a broadcast radio or television programme. **3** the mechanism by which power is transmitted from an engine to the axle in a motor vehicle. □ **transmission line** a conductor or conductors carrying electricity over large distances with minimum losses. [L *transmissio* (as TRANS-, MISSION)]

transmit /trænz'mɪt, trɑː-, -s'mɪt/ *v.tr.* (**transmitted, transmitting**) **1 a** pass or hand on; transfer (*transmitted the message*; *how diseases are transmitted*). **b** communicate (ideas, emotions, etc.). **2 a** allow (heat, light, sound, electricity, etc.) to pass through; be a medium for. **b** be a medium for (ideas, emotions, etc.) (*his message transmits hope*). **3** broadcast (a radio or television programme). □□ **transmissible** /-'mɪsəb(ə)l/ *adj.* **transmissive** /-'mɪsɪv/ *adj.* **transmittable** *adj.* **transmittal** *n.* [ME f. L *transmittere* (as TRANS-, *mittere miss-* send)]

transmitter /trænz'mɪtə(r), trɑː-, -z'mɪtə(r)/ *n.* **1** a person or thing that transmits. **2** a set of equipment used to generate and transmit electromagnetic waves carrying messages, signals, etc., esp. those of radio or television. **3** = NEUROTRANSMITTER.

transmogrify /trænz'mɒgrɪˌfaɪ, trɑː-, -s'mɒgrɪˌfaɪ/ *v.tr.* (-**ies**, -**ied**) *joc.* transform, esp. in a magical or surprising manner. □□ **transmogrification** /-fɪ'keɪʃ(ə)n/ *n.* [17th c.: orig. unkn.]

transmontane /trænz'mɒnteɪn, trɑː-, -s'mɒnteɪn, -'teɪn/ *adj.* = TRAMONTANE. [L *transmontanus*: see TRAMONTANE]

transmutation /ˌtrænzmjuː'teɪʃ(ə)n, ˌtrɑː-, -smjuː-'teɪʃ(ə)n/ *n.* **1** the act or an instance of transmuting or changing into another form etc. **2** *Alchemy hist.* the supposed process of changing base metals into gold. **3** *Physics* the changing of one element into another by nuclear bombardment etc. **4** *Geom.* the changing of a figure or body into another of the same area or volume. **5** *Biol.* Lamarck's theory of the change of one species into another. □□ **transmutational** *adj.* **transmutationist** *n.* [ME f. OF *transmutation* or LL *transmutatio* (as TRANS-MUTE)]

transmute /trænz'mjuːt, trɑː-, -s'mjuːt/ *v.tr.* **1** change the form, nature, or substance of. **2** *Alchemy hist.* subject (base metals) to transmutation. □□ **transmutable** *adj.* **transmutability** /-'bɪlɪti/ *n.* **transmutative** /-tətɪv/ *adj.* **transmuter** *n.* [ME f. L *transmutare* (as TRANS-, *mutare* change)]

transnational /trænz'næʃən(ə)l, trɑː-, -s'næʃən(ə)l/ *adj.* extending beyond national boundaries.

transoceanic /trænzˌəʊʃɪ'ænɪk, trɑː-, -sˌəʊʃɪ'ænɪk/ *adj.* **1** situated beyond the ocean. **2** concerned with crossing the ocean (*transoceanic flight*).

transom /'trænsəm/ *n.* **1** a horizontal bar of wood or stone across a window or the top of a door (cf. MULLION). **2** each of several beams fixed across the stern-post of a ship. **3** a beam across a saw-pit to support a log. **4** a strengthening crossbar. **5** *US* = *transom window*. □**transom window 1** a window divided by a transom. **2** a window placed above the transom of a door or larger window; a fanlight. □□ **transomed** *adj.* [ME *traversayn, transyn, -ing*, f. OF *traversin* f. *traverse* TRAVERSE]

transonic /træn'sɒnɪk, trɑː-/ *adj.* (also **trans-sonic**) relating to speeds close to that of sound. [TRANS- + SONIC, after *supersonic* etc.]

transpacific /ˌtrænzpə'sɪfɪk, ˌtrɑː-, -spə'sɪfɪk/ *adj.* **1** beyond the Pacific. **2** crossing the Pacific.

transparence /træns'pærəns, trɑː-, -'peərəns/ *n.* = TRANSPARENCY 1.

transparency /træns'pærənsɪ, trɑː-, -'peərənsɪ/ *n.* (*pl.* -**ies**) **1** the condition of being transparent. **2** *Photog.* a positive transparent photograph on glass or in a frame to be viewed using a slide projector etc. **3** a picture, inscription, etc., made visible by a light behind it. [med.L *transparentia* (as TRANSPARENT)]

transparent /træns'pærənt, trɑː-, -'peərənt/ *adj.* **1** allowing light to pass through so that bodies can be distinctly seen (cf. TRANSLUCENT). **2 a** (of a disguise, pretext, etc.) easily seen through. **b** (of a motive, quality, etc.) easily discerned; evident; obvious. **3** (of a person etc.) easily understood; frank; open. **4** *Physics* transmitting heat or other electromagnetic rays without distortion. □□ **transparently** *adv.* **transparentness** *n.* [ME f. OF f. med.L *transparens* f. L *transparēre* shine through (as TRANS-, *parēre* appear)]

transpierce /træns'pɪəs, trɑː-/ *v.tr.* pierce through.

transpire /træn'spaɪə(r), trɑː-/ *v.* **1** *intr.* (of a secret or something unknown) leak out; come to be known. **2** *intr. disp.* **a** (prec. by *it* as subject) turn out; prove to be the case (*it transpired he knew nothing about it*). **b** occur; happen. **3** *tr. & intr.* emit (vapour, sweat, etc.), or be emitted, through the skin or lungs; perspire. **4** *intr.* (of a plant or leaf) release water vapour. □□ **transpirable** *adj.* **transpiration** /-spɪ'reɪʃ(ə)n/ *n.* **transpiratory** /-rətəri/ *adj.* [F *transpirer* or med.L *transpirare* (as TRANS-, L *spirare* breathe)]

transplant *v. & n.* —*v.tr.* /træns'plɑːnt, trɑː-/ **1 a** plant in another place (*transplanted the daffodils*). **b** move to another place (*whole nations were transplanted*). **2** *Surgery* transfer (living tissue or an organ) and implant in another part of the body or in another body. —*n.* /'trænsplɑːnt, 'trɑː-/ **1** *Surgery* **a** the transplanting of an organ or tissue. **b** such an organ etc. **2** a thing, esp. a plant, transplanted. □□ **transplantable** /-'plɑːntəb(ə)l/ *adj.* **transplantation** /-'teɪʃ(ə)n/ *n.* **transplanter** /-'plɑːntə(r)/ *n.* [ME f. LL *transplantare* (as TRANS-, PLANT)]

transponder /træn'spɒndə(r), trɑː-/ *n.* a device for receiving a radio signal and automatically transmitting a different signal. [TRANSMIT + RESPOND]

transpontine /træns'pɒntaɪn, trɑː-, -z'pɒntaɪn/ *adj.* on the other side of a bridge, esp. on the south side of the Thames. [TRANS- + L *pons pontis* bridge]

transport *v. & n.* —*v.tr.* /træns'pɔːt, trɑː-/ **1** take or carry (a person, goods, troops, baggage, etc.) from one place to another. **2** *hist.* take (a criminal) to a penal colony; deport. **3** (as **transported** *adj.*) (usu. foll. by *with*) affected with strong emotion. —*n.* /'trænspɔːt, 'trɑː-/ **1 a** a system of conveying people, goods, etc., from place to place. **b** the means of this (*our transport has arrived*). **2** a ship, aircraft, etc. used to carry soldiers, stores, etc. **3** (esp. in *pl.*) vehement emotion (*transports of joy*). **4** *hist.* a transported convict. □**transport café** *Brit.* a roadside café for (esp. commercial) drivers. [ME f. OF *transporter* or L *transportare* (as TRANS-, *portare* carry)]

æ cat ɑː *arm* e bed ɜː *her* ɪ sit iː *see* ɒ hot ɔː *saw* ʌ *run* ʊ *put* uː *too* ə *ago* aɪ *my*

transportable /træns'pɔːtəb(ə)l, trɑː-/ *adj.* **1** capable of being transported. **2** *hist.* (of an offender or an offence) punishable by transportation. □□ **transportability** /-'bɪlɪtɪ/ *n.*

transportation /ˌtrænspɔː'teɪʃ(ə)n, ˌtrɑː-/ *n.* **1** the act of conveying or the process of being conveyed. **2 a** a system of conveying. **b** esp. *US* the means of this. **3** *hist.* removal to a penal colony.

transporter /træns'pɔːtə(r), trɑː-/ *n.* **1** a person or device that transports. **2** a vehicle used to transport other vehicles or large pieces of machinery etc. by road. □ **transporter bridge** a bridge carrying vehicles etc. across water on a suspended moving platform.

transpose /træns'pəʊz, trɑː-, -z'pəʊz/ *v.tr.* **1 a** cause (two or more things) to change places. **b** change the position of (a thing) in a series. **2** change the order or position of (words or a word) in a sentence. **3** *Mus.* write or play in a different key. **4** *Algebra* transfer (a term) with a changed sign to the other side of an equation. □ **transposing instrument** *Mus.* an instrument producing notes different in pitch from the written notes. **transposing piano** etc. *Mus.* a piano etc. on which a transposition may be effected mechanically. □□ **transposable** *adj.* **transposal** *n.* **transposer** *n.* [ME, = transform f. OF *transposer* (as TRANS-, L *ponere* put)]

transposition /ˌtrænspə'zɪʃ(ə)n, ˌtrɑː-, -zpə'zɪʃ(ə)n/ *n.* the act or an instance of transposing; the state of being transposed. □□ **transpositional** *adj.* **transpositive** /-'pɒzɪtɪv/ *adj.* [F *transposition* or LL *transpositio* (as TRANS-, POSITION)]

transputer /træns'pjuːtə(r), trɑː-, -z'pjuːtə(r)/ *n.* a microprocessor with integral memory designed for parallel processing. [TRANSISTOR + COMPUTER]

transsexual /trænz'seksjʊəl, trɑː-, -ʃʊəl/ *adj.* & *n.* (also **transexual**) —*adj.* having the physical characteristics of one sex and the supposed psychological characteristics of the other. —*n.* **1** a transsexual person. **2** a person whose sex has been changed by surgery. □□ **transsexualism** *n.*

transship /træn'ʃɪp, trɑː-, trænz-/ *v.tr.* (also **tranship**) *intr.* (-**shipped**, -**shipping**) transfer from one ship or form of transport to another. □□ **transshipment** *n.*

trans-sonic var. of TRANSONIC.

transubstantiation /ˌtrænsəbˌstænʃɪ'eɪʃ(ə)n, ˌtrɑː-/ *n.* *Theol.* & *RC Ch.* the conversion of the Eucharistic elements wholly into the body and blood of Christ, only the appearance of bread and wine still remaining. [med.L (as TRANS-, SUBSTANCE)]

transude /træn'sjuːd/ *v.intr.* (of a fluid) pass through the pores or interstices of a membrane etc. □□ **transudation** /-'deɪʃ(ə)n/ *n.* **transudatory** /-dətərɪ/ *adj.* [F *transsuder* f. OF *tressuer* (as TRANS-, L *sudare* sweat)]

transuranic /ˌtrænsjʊə'rænɪk, ˌtrɑː-/ *adj.* *Chem.* (of an element) having a higher atomic number than uranium.

transversal /trænz'vɜːs(ə)l, trɑː-, -s'vɜːs(ə)l/ *adj.* & *n.* —*adj.* (of a line) cutting a system of lines. —*n.* a transversal line. □□ **transversality** /-'sælɪtɪ/ *n.* **transversally** *adv.* [ME f. med.L *transversalis* (as TRANSVERSE)]

transverse /'trænzvɜːs, 'trɑː-, -'vɜːs, -ns-/ *adj.* situated, arranged, or acting in a crosswise direction. □ **transverse magnet** a magnet with poles at the sides and not the ends. **transverse wave** *Physics* a wave in which the medium vibrates at right angles to the direction of its propagation. □□ **transversely** *adv.* [L *transvertere transvers-* turn across (as TRANS-, *vertere* turn)]

transvestism /trænz'vestɪz(ə)m, trɑː-, -s'vestɪz(ə)m/ *n.* the practice of wearing the clothes of the opposite sex, esp. as a sexual stimulus. □□ **transvestist** *n.* [G *Transvestismus* f. TRANS- + L *vestire* clothe]

transvestite /trænz'vestaɪt, trɑː-, -s'vestaɪt/ *n.* a person given to transvestism.

trap¹ /træp/ *n.* & *v.* —*n.* **1 a** an enclosure or device, often baited, for catching animals, usu. by affording a way in but not a way out. **b** a device with bait for killing vermin, esp. = MOUSETRAP. **2** a trick betraying a person into speech or an act (*is this question a trap?*). **3** an arrangement to catch an unsuspecting person, e.g. a speeding motorist. **4** a device for hurling an object such as a clay pigeon into the air to be shot at. **5** a compartment from which a greyhound is released at the start of a race. **6** a shoe-shaped wooden device with a pivoted bar that sends a ball from its heel into the air on being struck at the other end with a bat. **7 a** a curve in a downpipe etc. that fills with liquid and forms a seal against the upward passage of gases. **b** a device for preventing the passage of steam etc. **8** *Golf* a bunker. **9** a device allowing pigeons to enter but not leave a loft. **10** a two-wheeled carriage (*a pony and trap*). **11** = TRAPDOOR. **12** *sl.* the mouth (esp. *shut one's trap*). **13** (esp. in *pl.*) *colloq.* a percussion instrument esp. in a jazz band. —*v.tr.* (**trapped**, **trapping**) **1** catch (an animal) in a trap. **2** catch or catch out (a person) by means of a trick, plan, etc. **3** stop and retain in or as in a trap. **4** provide (a place) with traps. □ **trap-ball** a game played with a trap (see sense 6 of *n.*). **trap-shooter** a person who practises trap-shooting. **trap-shooting** the sport of shooting at objects released from a trap. □□ **traplike** *adj.* [OE *treppe, træppe*, rel. to MDu. *trappe*, med.L *trappa*, of uncert. orig.]

trap² /træp/ *v.tr.* (**trapped**, **trapping**) (often foll. by *out*) **1** provide with trappings. **2** adorn. [obs. *trap* (n.): ME f. OF *drap*: see DRAPE]

trap³ /træp/ *n.* (in full **trap-rock**) any dark-coloured igneous rock, fine-grained and columnar in structure, esp. basalt. [Sw. *trapp* f. *trappa* stair, f. the often stairlike appearance of its outcroppings]

trapdoor /'træpdɔː(r)/ *n.* a door or hatch in a floor, ceiling, or roof, usu. made flush with the surface. □ **trapdoor spider** any of various spiders, esp. of the family Ctenizidae, that make a hinged trapdoor at the top of their nest.

trapes var. of TRAIPSE.

trapeze /trə'piːz/ *n.* a crossbar or set of crossbars suspended by ropes used as a swing for acrobatics etc. [F *trapèze* f. LL *trapezium*: see TRAPEZIUM]

trapezium /trə'piːzɪəm/ *n.* (*pl.* **trapezia** /-zɪə/ or **trapeziums**) **1** *Brit.* a quadrilateral with only one pair of sides parallel. **2** *US* = TRAPEZOID 1. [LL f. Gk *trapezion* f. *trapeza* table]

trapezoid /'træpɪzɔɪd/ *n.* **1** *Brit.* a quadrilateral with no two sides parallel. **2** *US* = TRAPEZIUM 1. □□ **trapezoidal** *adj.* [mod.L *trapezoides* f. Gk *trapezoeidēs* f. *trapeza*]

trapper /'træpə(r)/ *n.* a person who traps wild animals esp. to obtain furs.

trappings /'træpɪŋz/ *n.pl.* **1** ornamental accessories, esp. as an indication of status (*the trappings of office*). **2** the harness of a horse esp. when ornamental. [ME (as TRAP²)]

Trappist /'træpɪst/ *n.* & *adj.* —*n.* a member of a branch of the Cistercian order founded in 1664 at La Trappe in Normandy and noted for an austere rule including a vow of silence. —*adj.* of or relating to this order. [F *trappiste* f. *La Trappe*]

traps /træps/ *n.pl. colloq.* personal belongings; baggage. [perh. contr. f. TRAPPINGS]

trash /træʃ/ *n.* & *v.* —*n.* **1** esp. *US* worthless or waste stuff; rubbish, refuse. **2** a worthless person or persons. **3** a thing of poor workmanship or material. **4** (in full **cane-trash**) *W.Ind.* the refuse of crushed sugar canes and dried stripped leaves and tops of sugar cane used as fuel. —*v.tr.* **1** esp. *US colloq.* wreck. **2** strip (sugar canes) of their outer leaves to speed up the ripening process. **3** esp. *US colloq.* expose the worthless nature of; disparage. □ **trash can** *US* a dustbin. **trash-ice** (on a sea, lake, etc.) broken ice mixed with water. [16th c.: orig. unkn.]

trashy /'træʃɪ/ adj. (**trashier, trashiest**) worthless; poorly made. □□ **trashily** adv. **trashiness** n.

trass /træs/ n. (also **tarras** /tə'ræs/) a light-coloured tuff used as cement-material. [Du. *trass*, earlier *terras, tiras* f. Rmc: cf. TERRACE]

trattoria /ˌtrætə'riːə/ n. an Italian restaurant. [It.]

trauma /'trɔːmə, 'trau-/ n. (pl. **traumata** /-mətə/ or **traumas**) **1** any physical wound or injury. **2** physical shock following this, characterized by a drop in body temperature, mental confusion, etc. **3** *Psychol.* emotional shock following a stressful event, sometimes leading to long-term neurosis. □□ **traumatize** v.tr. (also **-ise**). **traumatization** /-taɪ'zeɪʃ(ə)n/ n. [Gk *trauma traumatos* wound]

traumatic /trɔː'mætɪk, trau-/ adj. **1** of or causing trauma. **2** *colloq.* (in general use) distressing; emotionally disturbing (*a traumatic experience*). **3** of or for wounds. □□ **traumatically** adv. [LL *traumaticus* f. Gk *traumatikos* (as TRAUMA)]

traumatism /'trɔːmə,tɪz(ə)m, 'trau-/ n. **1** the action of a trauma. **2** a condition produced by this.

travail /'træveɪl/ n. & v. *literary* —n. **1** painful or laborious effort. **2** the pangs of childbirth. —v.intr. undergo a painful effort, esp. in childbirth. [ME f. OF *travail, travaillier* ult. f. med.L *trepalium* instrument of torture f. L *tres* three + *palus* stake]

travel /'træv(ə)l/ v. & n. —v.intr. & tr. (**travelled, travelling**; US **traveled, traveling**) **1** intr. go from one place to another; make a journey esp. of some length or abroad. **2** tr. **a** journey along or through (a country). **b** cover (a distance) in travelling. **3** intr. *colloq.* withstand a long journey (*wines that do not travel*). **4** intr. go from place to place as a salesman. **5** intr. move or proceed in a specified manner or at a specified rate (*light travels faster than sound*). **6** intr. *colloq.* move quickly. **7** intr. pass esp. in a deliberate or systematic manner from point to point (*the photographer's eye travelled over the scene*). **8** intr. (of a machine or part) move or operate in a specified way. **9** intr. (of deer etc.) move onwards in feeding. —n. **1** a the act of travelling, esp. in foreign countries. **b** (often in *pl.*) a spell of this (*have returned from their travels*). **2** the range, rate, or mode of motion of a part in machinery. □**travel agency** (or **bureau**) an agency that makes the necessary arrangements for travellers. **travel agent** a person or firm acting as a travel agency. **travelling crane** a crane able to move on rails, esp. along an overhead support. **travelling-rug** a rug used for warmth on a journey. **travelling wave** *Physics* a wave in which the medium moves in the direction of propagation. **travel-sick** suffering from nausea caused by motion in travelling. **travel-sickness** the condition of being travel-sick. [ME, orig. = TRAVAIL]

travelled /'træv(ə)ld/ adj. experienced in travelling (also in *comb.*: *much-travelled*).

traveller /'trævələ(r)/ n. (US **traveler**) **1** a person who travels or is travelling. **2** a travelling salesman. **3** a Gypsy. **4** *Austral.* an itinerant workman; a swagman. **5** a moving mechanism, esp. a travelling crane. □**traveller's cheque** (US **check**) a cheque for a fixed amount that may be cashed on signature, usu. internationally. **traveller's joy** a wild clematis, *Clematis vitalba*. **traveller's tale** an incredible and probably untrue story.

travelogue /'trævə,lɒg/ n. a film or illustrated lecture about travel. [TRAVEL after *monologue* etc.]

traverse /'trævəs, trə'vɜːs/ v. & n. —v. **1** tr. travel or lie across (*traversed the country; a pit traversed by a beam*). **2** tr. consider or discuss the whole extent of (a subject). **3** tr. turn (a large gun) horizontally. **4** tr. *Law* deny (an allegation) in pleading. **5** tr. thwart, frustrate, or oppose (a plan or opinion). **6** intr. (of the needle of a compass etc.) turn on or as on a pivot. **7** intr. (of a horse) walk obliquely. **8** intr. make a traverse in climbing. —n. **1** a sideways movement. **2** an act of traversing. **3** a thing, esp. part of a structure, that crosses another. **4** a gallery extending from side to side of a church or other building. **5 a** a single line of survey, usu. plotted from compass bearings and chained or paced distances between angular points. **b** a tract surveyed in this way. **6** *Naut.* a zigzag line taken by a ship because of contrary winds or currents. **7** a skier's similar movement on a slope. **8** the sideways movement of a part in a machine. **9 a** a sideways motion across a rock-face from one practicable line of ascent or descent to another. **b** a place where this is necessary. **10** *Mil.* a pair of right-angle bends in a trench to avoid enfilading fire. **11** *Law* a denial, esp. of an allegation of a matter of fact. **12** the act of turning a large gun horizontally to the required direction. □□ **traversable** adj. **traversal** n. **traverser** n. [OF *traverser* f. LL *traversare, transversare* (as TRANSVERSE)]

travertine /'trævə,tiːn/ n. a white or light-coloured calcareous rock deposited from springs. [It. *travertino, tivertino* f. L *tiburtinus* of Tibur (Tivoli) near Rome]

travesty /'trævɪstɪ/ n. & v. —n. (pl. **-ies**) a grotesque misrepresentation or imitation (*a travesty of justice*). —v.tr. (**-ies, -ied**) make or be a travesty of. [(orig. adj.) f. F *travesti* past part. of *travestir* disguise, change the clothes of, f. It. *travestire* (as TRANS-, *vestire* clothe)]

travois /trə'vɔɪ/ n. (pl. same /-'vɔɪz/) a N. American Indian vehicle of two joined poles pulled by a horse etc. for carrying a burden. [earlier *travail* f. F, perh. the same word as TRAVAIL]

trawl /trɔːl/ v. & n. —v. **1** intr. **a** fish with a trawl or seine. **b** seek a suitable candidate etc. by sifting through a large number. **2** tr. **a** catch by trawling. **b** seek a suitable candidate etc. from (a certain area or group etc.) (*trawled the schools for new trainees*). —n. **1** an act of trawling. **2** (in full **trawl-net**) a large wide-mouthed fishing-net dragged by a boat along the bottom. **3** (in full **trawl-line**) US a long sea-fishing line buoyed and supporting short lines with baited hooks. [prob. f. MDu. *traghelen* to drag (cf. *traghel* drag-net), perh. f. L *tragula*]

trawler /'trɔːlə(r)/ n. **1** a boat used for trawling. **2** a person who trawls.

tray /treɪ/ n. **1** a flat shallow vessel usu. with a raised rim for carrying dishes etc. or containing small articles, papers, etc. **2** a shallow lidless box forming a compartment of a trunk. □□ **trayful** n. (pl. **-fuls**). [OE *trīg* f. Gmc, rel. to TREE]

treacherous /'tretʃərəs/ adj. **1** guilty of or involving treachery. **2** (of the weather, ice, the memory, etc.) not to be relied on; likely to fail or give way. □□ **treacherously** adv. **treacherousness** n. [ME f. OF *trecherous* f. *trecheor* a cheat f. *trechier, trichier*: see TRICK]

treachery /'tretʃərɪ/ n. (pl. **-ies**) **1** violation of faith or trust; betrayal. **2** an instance of this.

treacle /'triːk(ə)l/ n. **1** esp. *Brit.* **a** a syrup produced in refining sugar. **b** molasses. **2** cloying sentimentality or flattery. □□ **treacly** adj. [ME *triacle* f. OF f. L *theriaca* f. Gk *thēriakē* antidote against venom, fem. of *thēriakos* (adj.) f. *thērion* wild beast]

tread /tred/ v. & n. —v. (**trod** /trɒd/; **trodden** /'trɒd(ə)n/ or **trod**) **1** intr. (often foll. by on) **a** set down one's foot; walk or step (*do not tread on the grass; trod on a snail*). **b** (of the foot) be set down. **2** tr. **a** walk on. **b** (often foll. by *down*) press or crush with the feet. **3** tr. perform (steps etc.) by walking (*trod a few paces*). **4** tr. make (a hole etc.) by treading. **5** intr. (foll. by *on*) suppress; subdue mercilessly. **6** tr. make a track with (dirt etc.) from the feet. **7** tr. (often foll. by *in, into*) press down into the ground with the feet (*trod dirt into the carpet*). **8** tr. (also *absol.*) (of a male bird) copulate with (a hen). —n. **1** a manner or sound of walking (*recognized the heavy tread*). **2** (in full **tread-board**) the top surface of a step or stair. **3** the thick moulded part of a vehicle tyre for gripping the road. **4 a** the part of a wheel that touches the ground or rail. **b** the part of a rail that the wheels touch. **5** the part of the sole of a shoe that rests on the ground. **6** (of a male bird) copulation. □**tread the boards** (or **stage**) be an actor; appear on the stage. **tread on air** see AIR. **tread on a person's toes** offend a person or encroach on a person's privileges etc. **tread out 1** stamp out (a fire etc.). **2** press out (wine or grain) with the feet. **tread water** maintain an upright position in the water by moving the feet with a walking movement and the hands with a downward circular motion. **treadwheel** a treadmill or similar appliance. □□ **treader** *n.* [OE *tredan* f. WG]

treadle /ˈtred(ə)l/ *n. & v. —n.* a lever worked by the foot and imparting motion to a machine. *—v.intr.* work a treadle. [OE *tredel* stair (as TREAD)]

treadmill /ˈtredmɪl/ *n.* **1** a device for producing motion by the weight of persons or animals stepping on movable steps on the inner surface of a revolving upright wheel. **2** monotonous routine work.

treadwheel /ˈtredwiːl/ *n.* = TREADMILL 1.

treason /ˈtriːz(ə)n/ *n.* **1** (in full **high treason**: see note below) violation by a subject of allegiance to the sovereign or to the State, esp. by attempting to kill or overthrow the sovereign or to overthrow the government. **2** (in full **petty treason**) *hist.* murder of one's master or husband, regarded as a form of treason. ¶ The crime of *petty treason* was abolished in 1828; the term *high treason*, originally distinguished from *petty treason*, now has the same meaning as *treason*. □□ **treasonous** *adj.* [ME f. AF *treisoun* etc., OF *traïson*, f. L *traditio* handing over (as TRADITION)]

treasonable /ˈtriːzənəb(ə)l/ *adj.* involving or guilty of treason. □□ **treasonably** *adv.*

treasure /ˈtreʒə(r)/ *n. & v. —n.* **1 a** precious metals or gems. **b** a hoard of these. **c** accumulated wealth. **2** a thing valued for its rarity, workmanship, associations, etc. (*art treasures*). **3** *colloq.* a much loved or highly valued person. *—v.tr.* **1** (often foll. by *up*) store up as valuable. **2** value (esp. a long-kept possession) highly. □**treasure hunt 1** a search for treasure. **2** a game in which players seek a hidden object from a series of clues. **treasure trove** *Law* treasure of unknown ownership found hidden. [ME f. OF *tresor*, ult. f. Gk *thēsauros*: see THESAURUS]

treasurer /ˈtreʒərə(r)/ *n.* **1** a person appointed to administer the funds of a society or municipality etc. **2** an officer authorized to receive and disburse public revenues. □□ **treasurership** *n.* [ME f. AF *tresorer*, OF *tresorier* f. *tresor* (see TREASURE) after LL *thesaurarius*]

treasury /ˈtreʒərɪ/ *n.* (*pl.* **-ies**) **1** a place or building where treasure is stored. **2** the funds or revenue of a State, institution, or society. **3** (**Treasury**) **a** the department managing the public revenue of a country. **b** the offices and officers of this. **c** the place where the public revenues are kept. □**Treasury bench** (in the UK) the front bench in the House of Commons occupied by the Prime Minister, Chancellor of the Exchequer, etc. **treasury bill** a bill of exchange issued by the government to raise money for temporary needs. **treasury note** *US & hist.* a note issued by the Treasury for use as currency. [ME f. OF *tresorie* (as TREASURE)]

treat /triːt/ *v. & n. —v.* **1** *tr.* act or behave towards or deal with (a person or thing) in a certain way (*treated me kindly*; *treat it as a joke*). **2** *tr.* deal with or apply a process to; act upon to obtain a particular result (*treat it with acid*). **3** *tr.* apply medical care or attention to. **4** *tr.* present or deal with (a subject) in literature or art. **5** *tr.* (often foll. by *to*) provide with food or drink or entertainment at one's own expense (*treated us to dinner*). **6** *tr.* (often foll. by *with*) negotiate terms (with a person). **7** *intr.* (often foll. by *of*) give a spoken or written exposition. *—n.* **1** an event or circumstance (esp. when unexpected or

unusual) that gives great pleasure. **2** a meal, entertainment, etc., provided by one person for the enjoyment of another or others. **3** (prec. by *a*) extremely good or well (*they looked a treat*; *has come on a treat*). □□ **treatable** *adj.* **treater** *n.* **treating** *n.* [ME f. AF *treter*, OF *traitier* f. L *tractare* handle, frequent. of *trahere tract-* draw, pull]

treatise /ˈtriːtɪs, -ɪz/ *n.* a written work dealing formally and systematically with a subject. [ME f. AF *tretis* f. OF *traitier* TREAT]

treatment /ˈtriːtmənt/ *n.* **1** a process or manner of behaving towards or dealing with a person or thing (*received rough treatment*). **2** the application of medical care or attention to a patient. **3** a manner of treating a subject in literature or art. **4** (prec. by *the*) *colloq.* the customary way of dealing with a person, situation, etc. (*got the full treatment*).

treaty /ˈtriːtɪ/ *n.* (*pl.* **-ies**) **1** a formally concluded and ratified agreement between States. **2** an agreement between individuals or parties, esp. for the purchase of property. □**treaty port** *hist.* a port that a country was bound by treaty to keep open to foreign trade. [ME f. AF *treté* f. L *tractatus* TRACTATE]

treble /ˈtreb(ə)l/ *adj., n., & v. —adj.* **1 a** threefold. **b** triple. **c** three times as much or many (*treble the amount*). **2** (of a voice) high-pitched. **3** *Mus.* = SOPRANO (esp. of an instrument or with ref. to a boy's voice). *—n.* **1** a treble quantity or thing. **2** *Darts* a hit on the narrow ring enclosed by the two middle circles of a dartboard, scoring treble. **3 a** *Mus.* = SOPRANO (esp. a boy's voice or part, or an instrument). **b** a high-pitched voice. **4** the high-frequency output of a radio, record-player, etc., corresponding to the treble in music. **5** a system of betting in which the winnings and stake from the first bet are transferred to a second and then (if successful) to a third. **6** *Sport* three victories or championships in the same game, sport, etc. *—v.* **1** *tr. & intr.* make or become three times as much or many; increase threefold; multiply by three. **2** *tr.* amount to three times as much as. □**treble chance** a method of competing in a football pool in which the chances of winning depend on the number of draws and home and away wins predicted by the competitors. **treble clef** a clef placing G above middle C on the second lowest line of the staff. **treble rhyme** a rhyme including three syllables. □□ **trebly** *adv.* (in sense 1 of *adj.*). [ME f. OF f. L *triplus* TRIPLE]

trebuchet /ˈtrebjʊˌʃet/ *n.* (also **trebucket** /ˈtrebʌkɪt, ˈtriː-/) *hist.* **1** a military machine used in siege warfare for throwing stones etc. **2** a tilting balance for accurately weighing light articles. [ME f. OF f. *trebucher* overthrow, ult. f. Frank.]

trecento /treɪˈtʃentəʊ/ *n.* the style of Italian art and literature of the 14th c. □□ **trecentist** *n.* [It., = 300 used with reference to the years 1300-99]

tree /triː/ *n. & v.* **1 a** a perennial plant with a woody self-supporting main stem or trunk when mature and usu. unbranched for some distance above the ground (cf. SHRUB¹). **b** any similar plant having a tall erect usu. single stem, e.g. palm tree. **2** a piece or frame of wood etc. for various purposes (*shoe-tree*). **3** *archaic* or *poet.* **a** a gibbet. **b** a cross, esp. the one used for Christ's crucifixion. **4** (in full **tree diagram**) *Math.* a diagram with a structure of branching connecting lines. **5** = *family tree. —v.tr.* **1** force to take refuge in a tree. **2** esp. *US* put into a difficult position. **3** stretch on a shoe-tree. □**grow on trees** (usu. with *neg.*) be plentiful. **tree agate** agate with treelike markings. **tree calf** a calf binding for books stained with a treelike design. **tree-fern** a large fern, esp. of the family Cyatheaceae, with an upright trunklike stem. **tree frog** any arboreal tailless amphibian, esp. of the family Hylidae, climbing by means of adhesive discs on its digits. **tree hopper** any insect of the family Membracidae, living in trees. **tree house** a structure in a tree for children to play in. **tree line** = TIMBERLINE. **tree of heaven** an ornamental Asian tree, *Ailanthus altissima*, with evil-smelling flowers. **tree of knowledge** the branches of knowledge as a whole. **tree of life** = ARBOR VITAE. **tree ring** a ring in a cross section of a tree, from one year's growth. **tree shrew** any small insect-eating arboreal mammal of the family Tupaiidae having a pointed nose and bushy tail. **tree sparrow 1** *Brit.* a sparrow, *Passer montanus*, inhabiting woodland areas. **2** *US* a N. American finch, *Spizella arborea*, inhabiting grassland areas. **tree surgeon** a person who treats decayed trees in order to preserve them. **tree surgery** the art or practice of such treatment. **tree toad** = *tree frog*. **tree tomato** a South American shrub, *Cyphomandra betacea*, with egg-shaped red fruit. **tree-trunk** the trunk of a tree. **up a tree** esp. *US* cornered; nonplussed. □□ **treeless** *adj.* **treelessness** *n.* **tree-like** *adj.* [OE *trēow* f. Gmc]

treecreeper /'triːˌkriːpə(r)/ *n.* any small creeping bird, esp. of the family Certhiidae, feeding on insects in the bark of trees.

treen /triːn/ *n.* (treated as *pl.*) small domestic wooden objects, esp. antiques. [*treen* (adj.) wooden f. OE *trēowen* (as TREE)]

treenail /'triːneɪl/ *n.* (also **trenail**) a hard wooden pin for securing timbers etc.

treetop /'triːtɒp/ *n.* the topmost part of a tree.

trefa /'treɪfə/ *adj.* (also **tref** /treɪf/ and other variants) not kosher. [Heb. *ṭᵊrēpāh* the flesh of an animal torn f. *ṭārap* rend]

trefoil /'trefɔɪl, 'triː-/ *n.* & *adj.* — *n.* **1** any leguminous plant of the genus *Trifolium*, with leaves of three leaflets and flowers of various colours, esp. clover. **2** any plant with similar leaves. **3** a three-lobed ornamentation, esp. in tracery windows. **4** a thing arranged in or with three lobes. — *adj.* of or concerning a three-lobed plant, window tracery, etc. □□ **trefoiled** *adj.* (also in *comb.*). [ME f. AF *trifoil* f. L *trifolium* (as TRI-, *folium* leaf)]

trek /trek/ *v.* & *n.* orig. *S.Afr.* — *v.intr.* (**trekked, trekking**) **1** travel or make one's way arduously (*trekking through the forest*). **2** esp. *hist.* migrate or journey with one's belongings by ox-wagon. **3** (of an ox) draw a vehicle or pull a load. — *n.* **1 a** a journey or walk made by trekking (*it was a trek to the nearest launderette*). **b** each stage of such a journey. **2** an organized migration of a body of persons. □□ **trekker** *n.* [S.Afr. Du. *trek* (n.), *trekken* (v.) draw, travel]

trellis /'trelɪs/ *n.* & *v.* — *n.* (in full **trellis-work**) a lattice or grating of light wooden or metal bars used esp. as a support for fruit-trees or creepers and often fastened against a wall. — *v.tr.* (**trellised, trellising**) **1** provide with a trellis. **2** support (a vine etc.) with a trellis. [ME f. OF *trelis, trelice* ult. f. L *trilix* three-ply (as TRI-, *licium* warp-thread)]

trematode /'treməˌtəʊd/ *n.* any parasitic flatworm of the class Trematoda, esp. a fluke, equipped with hooks or suckers, e.g. a liver fluke. [mod.L *Trematoda* f. Gk *trēmatōdēs* perforated f. *trēma* hole]

tremble /'tremb(ə)l/ *v.* & *n.* — *v.intr.* **1** shake involuntarily from fear, excitement, weakness, etc. **2** be in a state of extreme apprehension (*trembled at the very thought of it*). **3** move in a quivering manner (*leaves trembled in the breeze*). — *n.* **1** a trembling state or movement; a quiver (*couldn't speak without a tremble*). **2** (in *pl.*) a disease (esp. of cattle) marked by trembling. □ **all of a tremble** *colloq.* **1** trembling all over. **2** extremely agitated. □□ **trembling poplar** an aspen. □□ **tremblingly** *adv.* [ME f. OF *trembler* f. med.L *tremulare* f. L *tremulus* TREMULOUS]

trembler /'tremblə(r)/ *n.* an automatic vibrator for making and breaking an electrical circuit.

trembly /'tremblɪ/ *adj.* (**tremblier, trembliest**) *colloq.* trembling; agitated.

tremendous /trɪ'mendəs/ *adj.* **1** awe-inspiring, fearful, overpowering. **2** *colloq.* remarkable, considerable, excellent (*a tremendous explosion*; *gave a tremendous performance*). □□ **tremendously** *adv.*

tremendousness *n.* [L *tremendus*, gerundive of *tremere* tremble]

tremolo /'tremələʊ/ *n. Mus.* **1** a tremulous effect in playing stringed and keyboard instruments or singing, esp. by rapid reiteration of a note; in other instruments, by rapid alternation between two notes (cf. VIBRATO). **2** a device in an organ producing a tremulous effect. [It. (as TREMULOUS)]

tremor /'tremə(r)/ *n.* & *v.* — *n.* **1** a shaking or quivering. **2** a thrill (of fear or exultation etc.). **3** (in full **earth tremor**) a slight earthquake. — *v.intr.* undergo a tremor or tremors. [ME f. OF *tremour* & L *tremor* f. *tremere* tremble]

tremulous /'tremjʊləs/ *adj.* **1** trembling or quivering (*in a tremulous voice*). **2** (of a line etc.) drawn by a tremulous hand. **3** timid or vacillating. □□ **tremulously** *adv.* **tremulousness** *n.* [L *tremulus* f. *tremere* tremble]

trenail var. of TREENAIL.

trench /trentʃ/ *n.* & *v.* — *n.* **1** a long narrow usu. deep depression or ditch. **2** *Mil.* **a** this dug by troops to stand in and be sheltered from enemy fire. **b** (in *pl.*) a defensive system of these. **3** a long narrow deep depression in the ocean bed. — *v.* **1** *tr.* dig a trench or trenches in (the ground). **2** *tr.* turn over the earth of (a field, garden, etc.) by digging a succession of adjoining ditches. **3** *intr.* (foll. by *on*, *upon*) *archaic* **a** encroach. **b** verge or border closely. □ **trench coat 1** a soldier's lined or padded waterproof coat. **2** a loose belted raincoat. **trench fever** a highly infectious disease transmitted by lice, that infested soldiers in the trenches in the war of 1914-18. **trench mortar** a light simple mortar throwing a bomb from one's own into the enemy trenches. **trench warfare** hostilities carried on from more or less permanent trenches. [ME f. OF *trenche* (n.) *trenchier* (v.), ult. f. L *truncare* TRUNCATE]

trenchant /'trentʃ(ə)nt/ *adj.* **1** (of a style or language etc.) incisive, terse, vigorous. **2** *archaic* or *poet.* sharp, keen. □□ **trenchancy** *n.* **trenchantly** *adv.* [ME f. OF, part. of *trenchier*: see TRENCH]

trencher /'trentʃə(r)/ *n.* **1** *hist.* a wooden or earthenware platter for serving food. **2** (in full **trencher cap**) a stiff square academic cap; a mortarboard. [ME f. AF *trenchour*, OF *trencheoir* f. *trenchier*: see TRENCH]

trencherman /'trentʃəmən/ *n.* (*pl.* **-men**) a person who eats well, or in a specified manner (*a good trencherman*).

trend /trend/ *n.* & *v.* — *n.* a general direction and tendency (esp. of events, fashion, or opinion etc.). — *v.intr.* **1** bend or turn away in a specified direction. **2** be chiefly directed; have a general and continued tendency. □ **trend-setter** a person who leads the way in fashion etc. **trend-setting** establishing trends or fashions. [ME 'revolve' etc. f. OE *trendan* f. Gmc: cf. TRUNDLE]

trendy /'trendɪ/ *adj.* & *n. colloq.* — *adj.* (**trendier, trendiest**) often *derog.* fashionable; following fashionable trends. — *n.* (*pl.* **-ies**) a fashionable person. □□ **trendily** *adv.* **trendiness** *n.*

trente-et-quarante /ˌtrãteɪkə'rãt/ *n.* = *rouge-et-noir*. [F, = thirty and forty]

trepan /trɪ'pæn/ *n.* & *v.* — *n.* **1** a cylindrical saw formerly used by surgeons for removing part of the bone of the skull. **2** a borer for sinking shafts. — *v.tr.* (**trepanned, trepanning**) perforate (the skull) with a trepan. □□ **trepanation** /ˌtrepə'neɪʃ(ə)n/ *n.* **trepanning** *n.* [ME f. med.L *trepanum* f. Gk *trupanon* f. *trupaō* bore f. *trupē* hole]

trepang /trɪ'pæŋ/ *n.* = BÊCHE-DE-MER 1. [Malay *trīpang*]

trephine /trɪ'faɪn, -'fiːn/ *n.* & *v.* — *n.* an improved form of trepan with a guiding centre-pin. — *v.tr.* operate on with this. □□ **trephination** /ˌtrefɪ'neɪʃ(ə)n/ *n.* [orig. *trafine*, f. L *tres fines* three ends, app. formed after TREPAN]

trepidation /ˌtrepɪ'deɪʃ(ə)n/ *n.* **1** a feeling of fear or alarm; perturbation of the mind. **2** tremulous agitation. **3** the trembling of limbs, e.g. in paralysis. [L *trepidatio* f. *trepidare* be agitated, tremble, f. *trepidus* alarmed]

trespass /ˈtrespəs/ *v. & n.* —*v.intr.* **1** (usu. foll. by *on, upon*) make an unlawful or unwarrantable intrusion (esp. on land or property). **2** (foll. by *on*) make unwarrantable claims (*shall not trespass on your hospitality*). **3** (foll. by *against*) *literary* or *archaic* offend. —*n.* **1** *Law* a voluntary wrongful act against the person or property of another, esp. unlawful entry to a person's land or property. **2** *archaic* a sin or offence. □**trespass on a person's preserves** meddle in another person's affairs. □□ **trespasser** *n.* [ME f. OF *trespasser* pass over, trespass, *trespas* (n.), f. med.L *transpassare* (as TRANS-, PASS¹)]

tress /tres/ *n. & v.* —*n.* **1** a long lock of human (esp. female) hair. **2** (in *pl.*) a woman's or girl's head of hair. —*v.tr.* arrange (hair) in tresses. □□ **tressed** *adj.* (also in *comb.*). **tressy** *adj.* [ME f. OF *tresse*, perh. ult. f. Gk *trikha* threefold]

tressure /ˈtreʃə(r)/ *n. Heraldry* a narrow orle. [ME, orig. = hair-ribbon, f. OF *tressour* etc. (as TRESS)]

trestle /ˈtres(ə)l/ *n.* **1** a supporting structure for a table etc., consisting of two frames fixed at an angle or hinged or of a bar supported by two divergent pairs of legs. **2** (in full **trestle-table**) a table consisting of a board or boards laid on trestles or other supports. **3** (in full **trestle-work**) an open braced framework to support a bridge etc. **4** (in full **trestle-tree**) *Naut.* each of a pair of horizontal pieces on a lower mast supporting the topmast etc. [ME f. OF *trestel* ult. f. L *transtrum*]

tret /tret/ *n. hist.* an allowance of extra weight formerly made to purchasers of some goods for waste in transportation. [ME f. AF & OF, var. of *trait* draught: see TRAIT]

trevally /trɪˈvælɪ/ *n.* (*pl.* **-ies**) any Australian fish of the genus *Caranx*, used as food. [prob. alt. f. *cavally*, a kind of fish, f. Sp. *caballo* horse f. L (as CAVALRY)]

trews /truːz/ *n.pl.* esp. *Brit.* trousers, esp. close-fitting tartan trousers worn by women. [Ir. *trius*, Gael. *triubhas* (sing.): cf. TROUSERS]

trey /treɪ/ *n.* (*pl.* **treys**) the three on dice or cards. [ME f. OF *trei, treis* three f. L *tres*]

TRH *abbr.* Their Royal Highnesses.

tri- /traɪ/ *comb. form* forming nouns and adjectives meaning: **1** three or three times. **2** *Chem.* (forming the names of compounds) containing three atoms or groups of a specified kind (*triacetate*). [L & Gk f. L *tres*, Gk *treis* three]

triable /ˈtraɪəb(ə)l/ *adj.* **1** liable to a judicial trial. **2** that may be tried or attempted. [ME f. AF (as TRY)]

triacetate /traɪˈæsɪˌteɪt/ *n.* a cellulose derivative containing three acetate groups, esp. as a base for man-made fibres.

triad /ˈtraɪæd/ *n.* **1** a group of three (esp. notes in a chord). **2** the number three. **3** a Chinese secret society, usu. criminal. **4** a Welsh form of literary composition with an arrangement in groups of three. □□ **triadic** /-ˈædɪk/ *adj.* **triadically** /-ˈædɪkəlɪ/ *adv.* [F *triade* or LL *trias triad-* f. Gk *trias -ados* f. *treis* three]

triadelphous /ˌtraɪəˈdelfəs/ *adj. Bot.* having stamens united in three bundles. [TRI- + Gk *adelphos* brother]

triage /ˈtraɪɪdʒ/ *n.* **1** the act of sorting according to quality. **2** the assignment of degrees of urgency to decide the order of treatment of wounds, illnesses, etc. [F f. *trier*: cf. TRY]

trial /ˈtraɪəl/ *n.* **1** a judicial examination and determination of issues between parties by a judge with or without a jury (*stood trial for murder*). **2 a** a process or mode of testing qualities. **b** experimental treatment. **c** a test (*will give you a trial*). **3** a trying thing or experience or person, esp. hardship or trouble (*the trials of old age*). **4** a sports match to test

the ability of players eligible for selection to a team. **5** a test of individual ability on a motor cycle over rough ground or on a road. **6** any of various contests involving performance by horses, dogs, or other animals. □**on trial 1** being tried in a court of law. **2** being tested; to be chosen or retained only if suitable. **trial and error** repeated (usu. varied and unsystematic) attempts or experiments continued until successful. **trial balance** (of a ledger in double-entry bookkeeping), a comparison of the totals on either side, the inequality of which reveals errors in posting. **trial jury** = *petty jury*. **trial run** a preliminary test of a vehicle, vessel, machine, etc. [AF *trial, triel* f. *trier* TRY]

trialist /ˈtraɪəlɪst/ *n.* **1** a person who takes part in a sports trial, motor-cycle trial, etc. **2** a person involved in a judicial trial.

triandrous /traɪˈændrəs/ *adj. Bot.* having three stamens.

triangle /ˈtraɪˌæŋɡ(ə)l/ *n.* **1** a plane figure with three sides and angles. **2** any three things not in a straight line, with imaginary lines joining them. **3** an implement of this shape. **4** a musical instrument consisting of a steel rod bent into a triangle and sounded by striking it with a small steel rod. **5** a situation, esp. an emotional relationship, involving three people. **6** a right-angled triangle of wood etc. as a drawing-implement. **7** *Naut.* a device of three spars for raising weights. **8** *hist.* a frame of three halberds joined at the top to which a soldier was bound for flogging. □**triangle of forces** a triangle whose sides represent in magnitude and direction three forces in equilibrium. [ME f. OF *triangle* or L *triangulum* neut. of *triangulus* three-cornered (as TRI-, ANGLE¹)]

triangular /traɪˈæŋɡjʊlə(r)/ *adj.* **1** triangle-shaped, three-cornered. **2** (of a contest or treaty etc.) between three persons or parties. **3** (of a pyramid) having a three-sided base. □□ **triangularity** /-ˈlærɪtɪ/ *n.* **triangularly** *adv.* [LL *triangularis* (as TRIANGLE)]

triangulate *v. & adj.* —*v.tr.* /traɪˈæŋɡjʊˌleɪt/ **1** divide (an area) into triangles for surveying purposes. **2 a** measure and map (an area) by the use of triangles with a known base length and base angles. **b** determine (a height, distance, etc.) in this way. —*adj.* /traɪˈæŋɡjʊlət/ *Zool.* marked with triangles. □□ **triangulately** /-lətlɪ/ *adv.* **triangulation** /-ˈleɪʃ(ə)n/ *n.* [L *triangulatus* triangular (as TRIANGLE)]

Triassic /traɪˈæsɪk/ *adj. & n. Geol.* —*adj.* of or relating to the earliest period of the Mesozoic era with evidence of an abundance of reptiles (including the earliest dinosaurs) and the emergence of mammals. ¶ Cf. Appendix II. —*n.* this period or system. [LL *trias* (as TRIAD), because the strata are divisible into three groups]

triathlon /traɪˈæθlɒn/ *n.* an athletic contest consisting of three different events. □□ **triathlete** *n.* [TRI- after DECATHLON]

triatomic /ˌtraɪəˈtɒmɪk/ *adj. Chem.* **1** having three atoms (of a specified kind) in the molecule. **2** having three replacement atoms or radicals.

triaxial /traɪˈæksɪəl/ *adj.* having three axes.

tribade /ˈtrɪbɑːd/ *n.* a woman who takes part in a simulation of sexual intercourse with another woman. □□ **tribadism** *n.* [F *tribade* or L *tribas* f. Gk f. *tribō* rub]

tribal /ˈtraɪb(ə)l/ *adj.* of, relating to, or characteristic of a tribe or tribes. □□ **tribally** *adv.*

tribalism /ˈtraɪbəˌlɪz(ə)m/ *n.* tribal organization. □□ **tribalist** *n.* **tribalistic** /-ˈlɪstɪk/ *adj.*

tribasic /traɪˈbeɪsɪk/ *adj. Chem.* (of an acid) having three replaceable hydrogen atoms.

tribe /traɪb/ *n.* **1** a group of (esp. primitive) families or communities, linked by social, economic, religious, or blood ties, and usu. having a common culture and dialect, and a recognized leader. **2** any similar natural or political division. **3** *Rom.Hist.* each of the political divisions of the Roman people. **4** each of the 12 divisions of the Israelites. **5** usu. *derog.* a set or number of persons esp. of one profession etc. or family (*the whole tribe of actors*). **6** *Biol.* a group of organisms usu. ranking between genus and the subfamily. **7** (in *pl.*) large numbers. [ME, orig. in pl. form *tribuz*, *tribus* f. OF or L *tribus* (sing. & pl.)]

tribesman /ˈtraɪbzmən/ *n.* (*pl.* **-men**) a member of a tribe or of one's own tribe.

triblet /ˈtrɪblɪt/ *n.* a mandrel used in making tubes, rings, etc. [F *triboulet*, of unkn. orig.]

tribo- /ˈtrɪbəʊ-, ˈtraɪ-/ *comb. form* rubbing, friction. [Gk *tribos* rubbing]

triboelectricity /ˌtrɪbəʊˌɪlek'trɪsɪtɪ, ˌtraɪbəʊ-/ *n.* the generation of an electric charge by friction.

tribology /traɪ'bɒlədʒɪ/ *n.* the study of friction, wear, lubrication, and the design of bearings; the science of interacting surfaces in relative motion. □□ **tribologist** *n.*

triboluminescence /ˌtrɪbəʊˌluːmɪ'nes(ə)ns, ˌtraɪ-/ *n.* the emission of light from a substance when rubbed, scratched, etc. □□ **triboluminescent** *adj.*

tribometer /traɪ'bɒmɪtə(r)/ *n.* an instrument for measuring friction in sliding.

tribrach /ˈtraɪbræk, ˈtrɪ-/ *n. Prosody* a foot of three short or unstressed syllables. □□ **tribrachic** /-ˈbrækɪk/ *adj.* [L *tribrachys* f. Gk *tribrakhus* (as TRI-, *brakhus* short)]

tribulation /ˌtrɪbjʊ'leɪʃ(ə)n/ *n.* **1** great affliction or oppression. **2** a cause of this (*was a real tribulation to me*). [ME f. OF f. eccl.L *tribulatio -onis* f. L *tribulare* press, oppress, f. *tribulum* sledge for threshing, f. *terere trit-* rub]

tribunal /traɪ'bjuːn(ə)l, trɪ-/ *n.* **1** *Brit.* a board appointed to adjudicate in some matter, esp. one appointed by the government to investigate a matter of public concern. **2** a court of justice. **3** a seat or bench for a judge or judges. **4 a** a place of judgement. **b** judicial authority (*the tribunal of public opinion*). [F *tribunal* or L *tribunus* (as TRIBUNE²)]

tribune¹ /ˈtrɪbjuːn/ *n.* **1** a popular leader or demagogue. **2** (in full **tribune of the people**) an official in ancient Rome chosen by the people to protect their interests. **3** (in full **military tribune**) a Roman legionary officer. □□ **tribunate** /-nət/ *n.* **tribuneship** *n.* [ME f. L *tribunus*, prob. f. *tribus* tribe]

tribune² /ˈtrɪbjuːn/ *n.* **1 a** a bishop's throne in a basilica. **b** an apse containing this. **2** a dais or rostrum. **3** a raised area with seats. [F f. It. f. med.L *tribuna* TRIBUNAL]

tributary /ˈtrɪbjʊtərɪ/ *n. & adj.* —*n.* (*pl.* **-ies**) **1** a river or stream flowing into a larger river or lake. **2** *hist.* a person or State paying or subject to tribute. —*adj.* **1** (of a river etc.) that is a tributary. **2** *hist.* a paying tribute. **b** serving as tribute. □□ **tributarily** *adv.* **tributariness** *n.* [ME f. L *tributarius* (as TRIBUTE)]

tribute /ˈtrɪbjuːt/ *n.* **1** a thing said or done or given as a mark of respect or affection etc. (*paid tribute to their achievements; floral tributes*). **2** *hist.* **a** a payment made periodically by one State or ruler to another, esp. as a sign of dependence. **b** an obligation to pay this (*was laid under tribute*). **3** (foll. by *to*) an indication of (some praiseworthy quality) (*their success is a tribute to their perseverance*). **4** a proportion of ore or its equivalent paid to a miner for his work, or to the owner of a mine. [ME f. L *tributum* neut. past part. of *tribuere tribut-* assign, orig. divide between tribes (*tribus*)]

tricar /ˈtraɪkɑː(r)/ *n. Brit.* a three-wheeled motor car.

trice /traɪs/ *n.* □**in a trice** in a moment; instantly. [ME *trice* (v.) pull, haul f. MDu. *trīsen*, MLG *trīssen*, rel. to MDu. *trīse* windlass, pulley]

tricentenary /ˌtraɪsen'tiːnərɪ/ *n.* (*pl.* **-ies**) = TERCENTENARY.

triceps /ˈtraɪseps/ *adj. & n.* —*adj.* (of a muscle) having three heads or points of attachment. —*n.* any triceps muscle, esp. the large muscle at the back

of the upper arm. [L, = three-headed (as TRI-, *-ceps* f. *caput* head)]

triceratops /ˌtraɪ'serə,tɒps/ *n.* a plant-eating dinosaur with three sharp horns on the forehead and a wavy-edged collar round the neck. [mod.L f. Gk *trikeratos* three-horned + *ōps* face]

trichiasis /trɪ'kaɪəsɪs/ *n. Med.* ingrowth or introversion of the eyelashes. [LL f. Gk *trikhiasis* f. *trikhiaō* be hairy]

trichina /trɪ'kaɪnə/ *n.* (*pl.* **trichinae** /-niː/) any hairlike parasitic nematode worm of the genus *Trichinella*, esp. *T. spiralis*, the adults of which live in the small intestine, and whose larvae become encysted in the muscle tissue of humans and flesh-eating animals. □□ **trichinous** *adj.* [mod.L f. Gk *trikhinos* of hair: see TRICHO-]

trichinosis /ˌtrɪkɪ'nəʊsɪs/ *n.* a disease caused by trichinae, usu. ingested in meat, and characterized by digestive disturbance, fever, and muscular rigidity.

tricho- /ˈtrɪkəʊ/ *comb. form* hair. [Gk *thrix trikhos* hair]

trichogenous /trɪ'kɒdʒənəs/ *adj.* causing or promoting the growth of hair.

trichology /trɪ'kɒlədʒɪ, traɪ-/ *n.* the study of the structure, functions, and diseases of the hair. □□ **trichologist** *n.*

trichome /ˈtraɪkəʊm/ *n. Bot.* a hair, scale, prickle, or other outgrowth from the epidermis of a plant. [Gk *trikhōma* f. *trikhoō* cover with hair (as TRICHO-)]

trichomonad /ˌtrɪkə'mɒnæd/ *n.* any flagellate protozoan of the genus *Trichomonas*, parasitic in humans, cattle, and fowls.

trichomoniasis /ˌtrɪkəmə'naɪəsɪs/ *n.* any of various infections caused by trichomonads parasitic on the urinary tract, vagina, or digestive system.

trichopathy /trɪ'kɒpəθɪ/ *n.* the treatment of diseases of the hair. □□ **trichopathic** /ˌtrɪkə'pæθɪk/ *adj.*

trichotomy /traɪ'kɒtəmɪ/ *n.* (*pl.* **-ies**) a division (esp. sharply defined) into three categories, esp. of human nature into body, soul, and spirit. □□ **trichotomic** /-kə'tɒmɪk/ *adj.* [Gk *trikha* threefold f. *treis* three, after DICHOTOMY]

trichroic /traɪ'krəʊɪk/ *adj.* (esp. of a crystal viewed in different directions) showing three colours. □□ **trichroism** /ˈtraɪkrəʊˌɪz(ə)m/ *n.* [Gk *trikhroos* (as TRI-, *khrōs* colour)]

trichromatic /ˌtraɪkrə'mætɪk/ *adj.* **1** having or using three colours. **2** (of vision) having the normal three colour-sensations, i.e. red, green, and purple. □□ **trichromatism** /-'krəʊmə,tɪz(ə)m/ *n.*

trick /trɪk/ *n. & v.* —*n.* **1** an action or scheme undertaken to fool, outwit, or deceive. **2** an optical or other illusion (*a trick of the light*). **3** a special technique; a knack or special way of doing something. **4 a** a feat of skill or dexterity. **b** an unusual action (e.g. begging) learned by an animal. **5** a mischievous, foolish, or discreditable act; a practical joke (*a mean trick to play*). **6** a peculiar or characteristic habit or mannerism (*has a trick of repeating himself*). **7 a** the cards played in a single round of a card-game, usu. one from each player. **b** such a round. **c** a point gained as a result of this. **8** (*attrib.*) done to deceive or mystify or to create an illusion (*trick photography; trick question*). **9** *Naut.* a sailor's turn at the helm, usu. two hours. —*v.tr.* **1** deceive by a trick; outwit. **2** (often foll. by *out of*, or *into* + verbal noun) cheat; treat deceitfully so as to deprive (*were tricked into agreeing; were tricked out of their savings*). **3** (of a thing) foil or baffle; take by surprise; disappoint the calculations of. □**do the trick** *colloq.* accomplish one's purpose; achieve the required result. **how's tricks?** *colloq.* how are you? **not miss a trick** see MISS¹. **trick cyclist 1** a cyclist who performs tricks, esp. in a circus. **2** *sl.* a psychiatrist. **trick of the trade** a special usu. ingenious technique or method of achieving a result in an industry or profession etc. **trick or treat** esp. *US* a children's custom of calling at houses at Hallowe'en with the threat of pranks if they are not given a small gift. **trick out** (or **up**) dress, decorate, or deck out esp. showily. **up to one's tricks** *colloq.* misbehaving. **up to a person's tricks** aware of what a person is likely to do by way of mischief. □□ **tricker** *n.* **trickish** *adj.* **trickless** *adj.* [ME f. OF dial. *trique*, OF *triche* f. *trichier* deceive, of unkn. orig.]

trickery /'trɪkərɪ/ *n.* (*pl.* **-ies**) **1** the practice or an instance of deception. **2** the use of tricks.

trickle /'trɪk(ə)l/ *v.* & *n.* —*v.* **1** *intr.* & *tr.* flow or cause to flow in drops or a small stream (*water trickled through the crack*). **2** *tr.* come or go slowly or gradually (*information trickles out*). —*n.* a trickling flow. □ **trickle charger** an electrical charger for batteries that works at a steady slow rate from the mains. [ME *trekel, trikle*, prob. imit.]

trickster /'trɪkstə(r)/ *n.* a deceiver or rogue.

tricksy /'trɪksɪ/ *adj.* (**tricksier, tricksiest**) full of tricks; playful. □□ **tricksily** *adv.* **tricksiness** *n.* [TRICK: for -*sy* cf. FLIMSY, TIPSY]

tricky /'trɪkɪ/ *adj.* (**trickier, trickiest**) **1** difficult or intricate; requiring care and adroitness (*a tricky job*). **2** crafty or deceitful. **3** resourceful or adroit. □□ **trickily** *adv.* **trickiness** *n.*

triclinic /traɪ'klɪnɪk/ *adj.* **1** (of a mineral) having three unequal oblique axes. **2** denoting the system classifying triclinic crystalline substances. [Gk TRI- + *klinō* incline]

triclinium /traɪ'klɪnɪəm, trɪ-/ *n.* (*pl.* **triclinia** /-nɪə/) *Rom. Antiq.* **1** a dining-table with couches along three sides. **2** a room containing this. [L f. Gk *triklinion* (as TRI-, *klinē* couch)]

tricolour /'trɪkələ(r), 'traɪ,kʌlə(r)/ *n.* & *adj.* (*US* **tricolor**) —*n.* a flag of three colours, esp. the French national flag of blue, white, and red. —*adj.* (also **tricoloured**) having three colours. [F *tricolore* f. LL *tricolor* (as TRI-, COLOUR)]

tricorn /'traɪkɔːn/ *adj.* & *n.* (also **tricorne**) —*adj.* **1** having three horns. **2** (of a hat) having a brim turned up on three sides. —*n.* **1** an imaginary animal with three horns. **2** a tricorn hat. [F *tricorne* or L *tricornis* (as TRI-, *cornu* horn)]

tricot /'trɪkəʊ, 'triː-/ *n.* **1 a** a hand-knitted woollen fabric. **b** an imitation of this. **2** a ribbed woollen cloth. [F, = knitting f. *tricoter* knit, of unkn. orig.]

tricrotic /traɪ'krɒtɪk/ *adj.* (of the pulse) having a triple beat. [TRI- after DICROTIC]

tricuspid /traɪ'kʌspɪd/ *n.* & *adj.* —*n.* **1** a tooth with three cusps or points. **2** a heart-valve formed of three triangular segments. —*adj.* (of a tooth) having three cusps or points.

tricycle /'traɪsɪk(ə)l/ *n.* & *v.* —*n.* **1** a vehicle having three wheels, two on an axle at the back and one at the front, driven by pedals in the same way as a bicycle. **2** a three-wheeled motor vehicle for a disabled driver. —*v.intr.* ride on a tricycle. □□ **tricyclist** *n.*

tridactyl /traɪ'dæktɪl/ *adj.* (also **tridactylous** /-'dæktɪləs/) having three fingers or toes.

trident /'traɪd(ə)nt/ *n.* **1** a three-pronged spear, esp. as an attribute of Poseidon (Neptune) or Britannia. **2** (**Trident**) a US type of submarine-launched ballistic missile. [L *tridens trident-* (as TRI-, *dens* tooth)]

tridentate /traɪ'denteɪt/ *adj.* having three teeth or prongs. [TRI- + L *dentatus* toothed]

Tridentine /traɪ'dentaɪn, trɪ-/ *adj.* & *n.* —*adj.* of or relating to the Council of Trent, held at Trento in Italy 1545–63, esp. as the basis of Roman Catholic doctrine. —*n.* a Roman Catholic adhering to this traditional doctrine. □ **Tridentine mass** the eucharistic liturgy used by the Roman Catholic Church from 1570 to 1964. [med.L *Tridentinus* f. *Tridentum* Trent]

triduum /'trɪdjʊəm/ *n.* RC Ch. esp. *hist.* three days' prayer in preparation for a saint's day or other religious occasion. [L (as TRI-, *dies* day)]

tridymite /'trɪdɪ,maɪt/ *n.* a crystallized form of silica, occurring in cavities of volcanic rocks. [G

Tridymit f. Gk *tridumos* threefold (as TRI-, *didumos* twin), from its occurrence in groups of three crystals]

tried *past* and *past part.* of TRY.

triennial /traɪ'enɪəl/ *adj.* & *n.* —*adj.* **1** lasting three years. **2** recurring every three years. —*n.* a visitation of an Anglican diocese by its bishop every three years. □□ **triennially** *adv.* [LL *triennis* (as TRI-, L *annus* year)]

triennium /traɪ'enɪəm/ *n.* (*pl.* **trienniums** or **triennia** /-nɪə/) a period of three years. [L (as TRIENNIAL)]

trier /'traɪə(r)/ *n.* **1** a person who perseveres (*is a real trier*). **2** a tester, esp. of foodstuffs. **3** a person appointed to decide whether a challenge to a juror is well-founded.

trifacial nerve /traɪ'feɪʃ(ə)l/ *n.* = TRIGEMINAL NERVE.

trifecta /traɪ'fektə/ *n.* US, Austral., & NZ a form of betting in which the first three places in a race must be predicted in the correct order. [TRI- + PERFECTA]

trifid /'traɪfɪd/ *adj.* esp. *Biol.* partly or wholly split into three divisions or lobes. [L *trifidus* (as TRI-, *findere fid-* split)]

trifle /'traɪf(ə)l/ *n.* & *v.* —*n.* **1** a thing of slight value or importance. **2 a** a small amount esp. of money (*was sold for a trifle*). **b** (prec. by *a*) somewhat (*seems a trifle annoyed*). **3** *Brit.* a confection of sponge cake with custard, jelly, fruit, cream, etc. —*v.* **1** *intr.* talk or act frivolously. **2** *intr.* (foll. by *with*) **a** treat or deal with frivolously or derisively; flirt heartlessly with. **b** refuse to take seriously. **3** *tr.* (foll. by *away*) waste (time, energies, money, etc.) frivolously. □□ **trifler** *n.* [ME f. OF *truf(f)le* by-form of *trufe* deceit, of unkn. orig.]

trifling /'traɪflɪŋ/ *adj.* **1** unimportant, petty. **2** frivolous. □□ **triflingly** *adv.*

trifocal /traɪ'fəʊk(ə)l/ *adj.* & *n.* —*adj.* having three focuses, esp. of a lens with different focal lengths. —*n.* (in *pl.*) trifocal spectacles.

trifoliate /traɪ'fəʊlɪət/ *adj.* **1** (of a compound leaf) having three leaflets. **2** (of a plant) having such leaves.

triforium /traɪ'fɔːrɪəm/ *n.* (*pl.* **triforia** /-rɪə/) a gallery or arcade above the arches of the nave, choir, and transepts of a church. [AL, of unkn. orig.]

triform /'traɪfɔːm/ *adj.* (also **triformed**) **1** formed of three parts. **2** having three forms or bodies.

trifurcate *v.* & *adj.* —*v.tr.* & *intr.* /'traɪfə,keɪt/ divide into three branches. —*adj.* /-'fɜːkət/ divided into three branches.

trig[1] /trɪg/ *n. colloq.* trigonometry. [abbr.]

trig[2] /trɪg/ *adj.* & *v. archaic* or *dial.* —*adj.* trim or spruce. —*v.tr.* (**trigged, trigging**) make trim; smarten. [ME, = trusty, f. ON *tryggr*, rel. to TRUE]

trigamous /'trɪgəməs/ *adj.* **1 a** three times married. **b** having three wives or husbands at once. **2** *Bot.* having male, female, and hermaphrodite flowers in the same head. □□ **trigamist** *n.* **trigamy** *n.* [Gk *trigamos* (as TRI-, *gamos* marriage)]

trigeminal nerve /traɪ'dʒemɪn(ə)l/ *n. Anat.* the largest cranial nerve which divides into the ophthalmic, maxillary, and mandibular nerves. □ **trigeminal neuralgia** *Med.* neuralgia involving one or more of these branches, and often causing severe pain. [as TRIGEMINUS]

trigeminus /traɪ'dʒemɪnəs/ *n.* (*pl.* **trigemini** /-,naɪ/) the trigeminal nerve. [L, = born as a triplet (as TRI-, *geminus* born at the same birth)]

trigger /'trɪgə(r)/ *n.* & *v.* —*n.* **1** a movable device for releasing a spring or catch and so setting off a mechanism (esp. that of a gun). **2** an event, occurrence, etc., that sets off a chain reaction. —*v.tr.* **1** (often foll. by *off*) set (an action or process) in motion; initiate, precipitate. **2** fire (a gun) by the use of a trigger. □ **quick on the trigger** quick to respond. **trigger fish** any usu. tropical marine fish of the family Balistidae with a first dorsal fin-spine which can be depressed by pressing on the second.

---

w *we* z *zoo* ʃ *she* ʒ *decision* θ *thin* ð *this* ŋ *ring* x *loch* tʃ *chip* dʒ *jar* (*see over for vowels*)

trigger-happy apt to shoot without or with slight provocation. □□**triggered** *adj*. [17th-c. *tricker* f. Du. *trekker* f. *trekken* pull: cf. TREK]

triglyph /'traɪglɪf/ *n. Archit.* each of a series of tablets with three vertical grooves, alternating with metopes in a Doric frieze. □□**triglyphic** /-'glɪfɪk/ *adj*. **triglyphical** /-'glɪfɪk(ə)l/ *adj*. [L *triglyphus* f. Gk *trigluphos* (as TRI-, *gluphē* carving)]

trigon /'traɪgɒn/ *n*. **1** a triangle. **2** an ancient triangular lyre or harp. **3** the cutting region of an upper molar tooth. [L *trigonum* f. Gk *trigōnon* neuter of *trigōnos* three-cornered (as TRI-, -GON)]

trigonal /'trɪgən(ə)l/ *adj*. **1** triangular; of or relating to a triangle. **2** *Biol.* triangular in cross-section. **3** (of a crystal etc.) having an axis with threefold symmetry. □□**trigonally** *adv*. [med.L *trigonalis* (as TRIGON)]

trigonometry /ˌtrɪgə'nɒmɪtrɪ/ *n*. the branch of mathematics dealing with the relations of the sides and angles of triangles and with the relevant functions of any angles. □□**trigonometric** /-nə'metrɪk/ *adj*. **trigonometrical** /-nə'metrɪk(ə)l/ *adj*. [mod.L *trigonometria* (as TRIGON, -METRY)]

trigraph /'traɪgra:f/ *n*. (also **trigram** /-græm/) **1** a group of three letters representing one sound. **2** a figure of three lines.

trigynous /'trɪdʒɪnəs/ *adj. Bot.* having three pistils.

trihedral /traɪ'hedr(ə)l, -'hi:dr(ə)l/ *adj*. having three surfaces.

trihedron /traɪ'hedrən, -'hi:drən/ *n*. a figure of three intersecting planes.

trihydric /traɪ'haɪdrɪk/ *adj. Chem.* containing three hydroxyl groups.

trike /traɪk/ *n. & v.intr. colloq.* tricycle. [abbr.]

trilabiate /traɪ'leɪbɪət/ *adj. Bot. & Zool.* three-lipped.

trilateral /traɪ'lætər(ə)l/ *adj. & n.* —*adj.* **1** of, on, or with three sides. **2** shared by or involving three parties, countries, etc. (*trilateral negotiations*). —*n.* a figure having three sides.

trilby /'trɪlbɪ/ *n*. (*pl.* -**ies**) *Brit.* a soft felt hat with a narrow brim and indented crown. □□**trilbied** *adj*. [name of the heroine in G. du Maurier's novel *Trilby* (1894), in the stage version of which such a hat was worn]

trilinear /traɪ'lɪnɪə(r)/ *adj*. of or having three lines.

trilingual /traɪ'lɪŋgw(ə)l/ *adj*. **1** able to speak three languages, esp. fluently. **2** spoken or written in three languages. □□**trilingualism** *n*.

triliteral /traɪ'lɪtər(ə)l/ *adj*. **1** of three letters. **2** (of a Semitic language) having (most) roots with three consonants.

trilith /'traɪlɪθ/ *n*. (also **trilithon** /-lɪθ(ə)n/) a monument consisting of three stones, esp. of two uprights and a lintel. □□**trilithic** /-'lɪθɪk/ *adj*. [Gk *trilithon* (as TRI-, *lithos* stone)]

trill /trɪl/ *n. & v.* —*n.* **1** a quavering or vibratory sound, esp. a rapid alternation of sung or played notes. **2** a bird's warbling sound. **3** the pronunciation of *r* with a vibration of the tongue. —*v.* **1** *intr.* produce a trill. **2** *tr.* warble (a song) or pronounce (*r* etc.) with a trill. [It. *trillo* (n.), *trillare* (v.)]

trillion /'trɪljən/ *n*. (*pl.* same or (in sense 3) **trillions**) **1** a million million (1,000,000,000,000 or 10^{12}). **2** (formerly, esp. *Brit.*) a million million million (1,000,000,000,000,000,000 or 10^{18}). **3** (in *pl.*) *colloq.* a very large number (*trillions of times*). ¶ Senses 1-2 correspond to the change in sense of *billion*. □□**trillionth** *adj. & n.* [F *trillion* or It. *trilione* (as TRI-, MILLION), after *billion*]

trilobite /'traɪlə,baɪt/ *n*. any fossil marine arthropod of the class Trilobita of Palaeozoic times, characterized by a three-lobed body. [mod.L *Trilobites* (as TRI-, Gk *lobos* lobe)]

trilogy /'trɪlədʒɪ/ *n*. (*pl.* -**ies**) **1** a group of three related literary or operatic works. **2** *Gk Antiq.* a set of three tragedies performed as a group. [Gk *trilogia* (as TRI-, -LOGY)]

trim /trɪm/ *v., n., & adj.* —*v.* (**trimmed, trimming**)

1 *tr.* **a** set in good order. **b** make neat or of the required size or form, esp. by cutting away irregular or unwanted parts. **2** *tr.* (foll. by *off, away*) remove by cutting off (such parts). **3** *tr.* **a** (often foll. by *up*) make (a person) neat in dress and appearance. **b** ornament or decorate (esp. clothing, a hat, etc. by adding ribbons, lace, etc.). **4** *tr.* adjust the balance of (a ship or aircraft) by the arrangement of its cargo etc. **5** *tr.* arrange (sails) to suit the wind. **6** *intr.* **a** associate oneself with currently prevailing views, esp. to advance oneself. **b** hold a middle course in politics or opinion. **7** *tr. colloq.* **a** rebuke sharply. **b** thrash. **c** get the better of in a bargain etc. —*n.* **1** the state or degree of readiness or fitness (*found everything in perfect trim*). **2** ornament or decorative material. **3** dress or equipment. **4** the act of trimming a person's hair. **5** the inclination of an aircraft to the horizontal. —*adj.* **1** neat or spruce. **2** in good order; well arranged or equipped. □**in trim 1** looking smart, healthy, etc. **2** *Naut.* in good order. □□**trimly** *adv.* **trimness** *n*. [perh. f. OE *trymman, trymian* make firm, arrange: but there is no connecting evidence between OE and 1500]

trimaran /'traɪmə,ræn/ *n*. a vessel like a catamaran, with three hulls side by side. [TRI- + CATAMARAN]

trimer /'traɪmə(r)/ *n. Chem.* a polymer comprising three monomer units. □□**trimeric** /-'merɪk/ *adj.* [TRI- + -MER]

trimerous /'traɪmərəs, 'trɪ-/ *adj.* having three parts.

trimester /traɪ'mestə(r)/ *n*. a period of three months, esp. of human gestation or *US* as a university term. □□**trimestral** *adj*. **trimestrial** *adj*. [F *trimestre* f. L *trimestris* (as TRI-, -*mestris* f. *mensis* month)]

trimeter /'trɪmɪtə(r)/ *n. Prosody* a verse of three measures. □□**trimetric** /traɪ'metrɪk/ *adj.* **trimetrical** /traɪ'metrɪk(ə)l/ *adj.* [L *trimetrus* f. Gk *trimetros* (as TRI-, *metron* measure)]

trimmer /'trɪmə(r)/ *n*. **1** a person who trims articles of dress. **2** a person who trims in politics etc.; a time-server. **3** an instrument for clipping etc. **4** *Archit.* a short piece of timber across an opening (e.g. for a hearth) to carry the ends of truncated joists. **5** a small capacitor etc. used to tune a radio set. **6** *Austral. colloq.* a striking or outstanding person or thing.

trimming /'trɪmɪŋ/ *n*. **1** ornamentation or decoration, esp. for clothing. **2** (in *pl.*) *colloq.* the usual accompaniments, esp. of the main course of a meal. **3** (in *pl.*) pieces cut off in trimming.

trimorphism /traɪ'mɔ:fɪz(ə)m/ *n. Bot., Zool., & Crystallog.* existence in three distinct forms. □□**trimorphic** *adj*. **trimorphous** *adj*.

trine /traɪn/ *adj. & n.* —*adj.* **1** threefold, triple; made up of three parts. **2** *Astrol.* denoting the aspect of two heavenly bodies 120° (one-third of the zodiac) apart. —*n.* a trine aspect. □□**trinal** *adj.* [ME f. OF *trin trine* f. L *trinus* threefold f. *tres* three]

Trinitarian /ˌtrɪnɪ'teərɪən/ *n. & adj.* —*n.* a person who believes in the doctrine of the Trinity. —*adj.* of or relating to this belief. □□**Trinitarianism** *n*.

trinitrotoluene /traɪˌnaɪtrə'tɒljʊ,i:n/ *n*. (also **trinitrotoluol** /-'tɒljʊ,ɒl/) = TNT.

trinity /'trɪnɪtɪ/ *n*. (*pl.* -**ies**) **1** the state of being three. **2** a group of three. **3** (**the Trinity** or **Holy Trinity**) *Theol.* the three persons of the Christian Godhead (Father, Son, and Holy Spirit). □**Trinity Brethren** the members of Trinity House. **Trinity House** *Brit.* an association concerned with the licensing of pilots, the erection and maintenance of buoys, lighthouses, etc., in England, Wales, etc. **Trinity Sunday** the next Sunday after Whit Sunday. **Trinity term** *Brit.* the university and law term beginning after Easter. [ME f. OF *trinité* f. L *trinitas -tatis* triad (as TRINE)]

trinket /'trɪŋkɪt/ *n*. a trifling ornament, jewel, etc., esp. one worn on the person. □□**trinketry** *n*. [16th c.: orig. unkn.]

trinomial /traɪ'nəʊmɪəl/ *adj. & n.* —*adj.* consisting

of three terms. —*n.* a scientific name or algebraic expression of three terms. [TRI- after BINOMIAL]

trio /'triːəʊ/ *n.* (*pl.* -**os**) **1** a set or group of three. **2** *Mus.* **a** a composition for three performers. **b** a group of three performers. **c** the central, usu. contrastive, section of a minuet, scherzo, or march. **3** (in piquet) three aces, kings, queens, or jacks in one hand. [F & It. f. L *tres* three, after *duo*]

triode /'traɪəʊd/ *n.* **1** a thermionic valve having three electrodes. **2** a semiconductor rectifier having three connections. [TRI- + ELECTRODE]

trioecious /traɪ'iːʃ(ə)s/ *adj. Bot.* having male, female, and hermaphrodite organs each on separate plants. [TRI- + Gk *oikos* house]

triolet /'triːəlɪt, 'traɪəlɪt/ *n.* a poem of eight (usu. eight-syllabled) lines rhyming *abaaabab*, the first line recurring as the fourth and seventh and the second as the eighth. [F (as TRIO)]

trioxide /traɪ'ɒksaɪd/ *n. Chem.* an oxide containing three oxygen atoms.

trip /trɪp/ *v. & n.* —*v.intr. & tr.* (**tripped, tripping**) **1** *intr.* **a** walk or dance with quick light steps. **b** (of a rhythm etc.) run lightly. **2 a** *intr. & tr.* (often foll. by *up*) stumble or cause to stumble, esp. by catching or entangling the feet. **b** *intr. & tr.* (foll. by *up*) make or cause to make a slip or blunder. **3** *tr.* detect (a person) in a blunder. **4** *intr.* make an excursion to a place. **5** *tr.* release (part of a machine) suddenly by knocking aside a catch etc. **6 a** release and raise (an anchor) from the bottom by means of a cable. **b** turn (a yard etc.) from a horizontal to a vertical position for lowering. **7** *intr. colloq.* have a hallucinatory experience caused by a drug. —*n.* **1** a journey or excursion, esp. for pleasure. **2 a** a stumble or blunder. **b** the act of tripping or the state of being tripped up. **3** a nimble step. **4** *colloq.* a hallucinatory experience caused by a drug. **5** a contrivance for a tripping mechanism etc. □**trip-hammer** a large tilt-hammer operated by tripping. **trip-wire** a wire stretched close to the ground, operating an alarm etc. when disturbed. [ME f. OF *triper, tripper*, f. MDu. *trippen* skip, hop]

tripartite /traɪ'pɑːtaɪt/ *adj.* **1** consisting of three parts. **2** shared by or involving three parties. **3** *Bot.* (of a leaf) divided into three segments almost to the base. □□**tripartitely** *adv.* **tripartition** /-'tɪʃ(ə)n/ *n.* [ME f. L *tripartitus* (as TRI-, *partitus* past part. of *partiri* divide)]

tripe /traɪp/ *n.* **1** the first or second stomach of a ruminant, esp. an ox, as food. **2** *colloq.* nonsense, rubbish (*don't talk such tripe*). [ME f. OF, of unkn. orig.]

triphibious /traɪ'fɪbɪəs/ *adj.* (of military operations) on land, on sea, and in the air. [irreg. f. TRI- after *amphibious*]

triphthong /'trɪfθɒŋ/ *n.* **1** a union of three vowels (letters or sounds) pronounced in one syllable (as in *fire*). **2** three vowel characters representing the sound of a single vowel (as in b*eau*). □□**triphthongal** /-'θɒŋɡ(ə)l/ *adj.* [F *triphtongue* (as TRI-, DIPHTHONG)]

triplane /'traɪpleɪn/ *n.* an early type of aeroplane having three sets of wings, one above the other.

triple /'trɪp(ə)l/ *adj., n., & v.* —*adj.* **1** consisting of three usu. equal parts or things; threefold. **2** involving three parties. **3** three times as much or many (*triple the amount; triple thickness*). —*n.* **1** a threefold number or amount. **2** a set of three. **3** (in *pl.*) a peal of changes on seven bells. —*v.tr. & intr.* multiply or increase by three. □**triple crown 1** *RC Ch.* the pope's tiara. **2** the act of winning all three of a group of important events in horse-racing, rugby football, etc. **triple jump** an athletic exercise or contest comprising a hop, a step, and a jump. **triple play** *Baseball* the act of putting out three runners in a row. **triple rhyme** a rhyme including three syllables. **triple time** *Mus.* that with three beats to the bar; waltz time. □□**triply** *adv.* [OF *triple* or L *triplus* f. Gk *triplous*]

triplet /'trɪplɪt/ *n.* **1** each of three children or animals born at one birth. **2** a set of three things, esp. of equal notes played in the time of two or of verses rhyming together. [TRIPLE + -ET[1], after *doublet*]

triplex /'trɪpleks/ *adj. & n.* —*adj.* triple or threefold. —*n.* (**Triplex**) *Brit. propr.* toughened or laminated safety glass for car windows etc. [L *triplex -plicis* (as TRI-, *plic-* fold)]

triplicate *adj., n., & v.* —*adj.* /'trɪplɪkət/ **1** existing in three examples or copies. **2** having three corresponding parts. **3** tripled. —*n.* /'trɪplɪkət/ each of a set of three copies or corresponding parts. —*v.tr.* /'trɪplɪˌkeɪt/ **1** make in three copies. **2** multiply by three. □**in triplicate** consisting of three exact copies. □□**triplication** /-'keɪʃ(ə)n/ *n.* [ME f. L *triplicatus* past part. of *triplicare* (as TRIPLEX)]

triplicity /trɪ'plɪsɪtɪ/ *n.* (*pl.* -**ies**) **1** the state of being triple. **2** a group of three things. **3** *Astrol.* a set of three zodiacal signs. [ME f. LL *triplicitas* f. L TRIPLEX]

triploid /'trɪplɔɪd/ *n. & adj. Biol.* —*n.* an organism or cell having three times the haploid set of chromosomes. —*adj.* of or being a triploid. [mod.L *triploides* f. Gk (as TRIPLE)]

triploidy /'trɪplɔɪdɪ/ *n.* the condition of being triploid.

tripmeter /'trɪpˌmiːtə(r)/ *n.* a vehicle instrument that can be set to record the distance of individual journeys.

tripod /'traɪpɒd/ *n.* **1** a three-legged stand for supporting a camera etc. **2** a stool, table, or utensil resting on three feet or legs. **3** *Gk Antiq.* a bronze altar at Delphi on which a priestess sat to utter oracles. □□**tripodal** /'trɪpəd(ə)l/ *adj.* [L *tripus tripodis* f. Gk *tripous* (as TRI-, *pous podos* foot)]

tripoli /'trɪpəlɪ/ *n.* = *rotten-stone*. [F f. *Tripoli* in N. Africa or in Syria]

tripos /'traɪpɒs/ *n. Brit.* (at Cambridge University) the honours examination for the BA degree. [as TRIPOD, with ref. to the stool on which graduates sat to deliver a satirical speech at the degree ceremony]

tripper /'trɪpə(r)/ *n.* **1** *Brit.* a person who goes on a pleasure trip or excursion. **2** *colloq.* a person experiencing hallucinatory effects of a drug.

triptych /'trɪptɪk/ *n.* **1 a** a picture or relief carving on three panels, usu. hinged vertically together and often used as an altarpiece. **b** a set of three associated pictures placed in this way. **2** a set of three writing-tablets hinged or tied together. **3** a set of three artistic works. [TRI-, after DIPTYCH]

triptyque /trɪp'tiːk/ *n.* a customs permit serving as a passport for a motor vehicle. [F, as TRIPTYCH (orig. having three sections)]

triquetra /traɪ'ketrə/ *n.* (*pl.* **triquetrae** /-triː/) a symmetrical ornament of three interlaced arcs. [L, fem. of *triquetrus* three-cornered]

trireme /'traɪriːm/ *n.* an ancient Greek warship, with three files of oarsmen on each side. [F *trirème* or L *triremis* (as TRI-, *remus* oar)]

trisaccharide /traɪ'sækəˌraɪd/ *n. Chem.* a sugar consisting of three linked monosaccharides.

Trisagion /trɪ'sægɪən/ *n.* a hymn, esp. in the Eastern Churches, with a triple invocation of God as holy. [ME f. Gk, neut. of *trisagios* f. *tris* thrice + *hagios* holy]

trisect /traɪ'sekt/ *v.tr.* cut or divide into three (usu. equal) parts. □□**trisection** *n.* **trisector** *n.* [TRI- + L *secare sect-* cut]

trishaw /'traɪʃɔː/ *n.* a light three-wheeled pedalled vehicle used in the Far East. [TRI- + RICKSHAW]

triskelion /trɪ'skelɪən/ *n.* a symbolic figure of three legs or lines from a common centre. [Gk TRI- + *skelos* leg]

trismus /'trɪzməs/ *n. Med.* a variety of tetanus with tonic spasm of the jaw muscles causing the mouth to remain tightly closed. [mod.L f. Gk *trismos* = *trigmos* a scream, grinding]

triste /triːst/ *adj.* sad, melancholy, dreary. [F f. L *tristis*]

trisyllable /ˈtraɪsɪləb(ə)l, traɪ-/ *n.* a word or metrical foot of three syllables. □□ **trisyllabic** /-ˈlæbɪk/ *adj.*

tritagonist /traɪˈtægənɪst, trɪ-/ *n.* the third actor in a Greek play (cf. DEUTERAGONIST). [Gk *tritagōnistēs* (as TRITO-, *agōnistēs* actor)]

trite /traɪt/ *adj.* (of a phrase, opinion, etc.) hackneyed, worn out by constant repetition. □□ **tritely** *adv.* **triteness** *n.* [L *tritus* past part. of *terere* rub]

tritiate /ˈtrɪtɪˌeɪt/ *v.tr.* replace the ordinary hydrogen in (a substance) by tritium. □□ **tritiation** /-ˈeɪʃ(ə)n/ *n.*

tritium /ˈtrɪtɪəm/ *n. Chem.* a radioactive isotope of hydrogen with a mass about three times that of ordinary hydrogen. ¶ Symb.: **T.** [mod.L f. Gk *tritos* third]

trito- /ˈtraɪtəʊ, ˈtrɪtəʊ/ *comb. form* third. [Gk *tritos* third]

Triton /ˈtraɪt(ə)n/ *n.* **1** (in Greek mythology) a minor sea-god usu. represented as a man with a fish's tail and carrying a trident and shell-trumpet. **2** (**triton**) any marine gastropod mollusc of the family Cymatiidae, with a long conical shell. **3** (**triton**) a newt. [L f. Gk *Tritōn*]

triton /ˈtraɪt(ə)n/ *n.* a nucleus of a tritium atom, consisting of a proton and two neutrons.

tritone /ˈtraɪtəʊn/ *n. Mus.* an interval of an augmented fourth, comprising three tones.

triturate /ˈtrɪtjʊˌreɪt/ *v.tr.* **1** grind to a fine powder. **2** masticate thoroughly. □□ **triturable** *adj.* **trituration** /-ˈreɪʃ(ə)n/ *n.* **triturator** *n.* [L *triturare* thresh corn f. *tritura* rubbing (as TRITE)]

triumph /ˈtraɪəmf, -ʌmf/ *n. & v.* —*n.* **1 a** the state of being victorious or successful (*returned home in triumph*). **b** a great success or achievement. **2 a** supreme example (*a triumph of engineering*). **3** joy at success; exultation (*could see triumph in her face*). **4** the processional entry of a victorious general into ancient Rome. —*v.intr.* **1** (often foll. by *over*) gain a victory; be successful; prevail. **2** ride in triumph. **3** (often foll. by *over*) exult. [ME f. OF *triumphe* (n.), *triumpher* (v.), f. L *triump(h)us* prob. f. Gk *thriambos* hymn to Bacchus]

triumphal /traɪˈʌmf(ə)l/ *adj.* of or used in or celebrating a triumph. [ME f. OF *triumphal* or L *triumphalis* (as TRIUMPH)]

triumphant /traɪˈʌmf(ə)nt/ *adj.* **1** victorious or successful. **2** exultant. □□ **triumphantly** *adv.* [ME f. OF *triumphant* or L *triumphare* (as TRIUMPH)]

triumvir /ˈtraɪəmvɪə(r), -ˈʌmvə(r)/ *n.* (*pl.* **triumvirs** or **triumviri** /-raɪ/) **1** each of three men holding a joint office. **2** a member of a triumvirate. □□ **triumviral** *adj.* [L, orig. in pl. *triumviri*, back-form. f. *trium virorum* genit. of *tres viri* three men]

triumvirate /traɪˈʌmvɪrət/ *n.* **1** a board or ruling group of three men, esp. in ancient Rome. **2** the office of triumvir.

triune /ˈtraɪjuːn/ *adj.* three in one, esp. with ref. to the Trinity. □□ **triunity** /-ˈjuːnɪtɪ/ *n.* (*pl.* **-ies**). [TRI- + L *unus* one]

trivalent /traɪˈveɪlənt/ *adj. Chem.* having a valency of three; tervalent. □□ **trivalency** *n.*

trivet /ˈtrɪvɪt/ *n.* **1** an iron tripod or bracket for a cooking pot or kettle to stand on. **2** an iron bracket designed to hook on to bars of a grate for a similar purpose. □ **as right as a trivet** *colloq.* in a perfectly good state, esp. healthy. **trivet table** a table with three feet. [ME *trevet*, app. f. L *tripes* (as TRI-, *pes pedis* foot)]

trivia /ˈtrɪvɪə/ *n.pl.* trifles or trivialities. [mod.L, pl. of TRIVIUM, infl. by TRIVIAL]

trivial /ˈtrɪvɪəl/ *adj.* **1** of small value or importance; trifling (*raised trivial objections*). **2** (of a person) concerned only with trivial things. **3** *archaic* commonplace or humdrum (*the trivial round of daily life*). **4** *Biol. & Chem.* of a name: **a** popular; not scientific. **b** specific, as opposed to generic. **5** *Math.* giving rise to no difficulty or interest. □□ **triviality**

/-ˈælɪtɪ/ *n.* (*pl.* **-ies**). **trivially** *adv.* **trivialness** *n.* [L *trivialis* commonplace f. *trivium*: see TRIVIUM]

trivialize /ˈtrɪvɪəˌlaɪz/ *v.tr.* (also **-ise**) make trivial or apparently trivial; minimize. □□ **trivialization** /-ˈzeɪʃ(ə)n/ *n.*

trivium /ˈtrɪvɪəm/ *n. hist.* a medieval university course of grammar, rhetoric, and logic. [L, = place where three roads meet (as TRI-, *via* road)]

tri-weekly /traɪˈwiːklɪ/ *adj.* produced or occurring three times a week or every three weeks.

-trix /trɪks/ *suffix* (*pl.* **-trices** /trɪsɪz, ˈtraɪsiːz/ or **-trixes**) forming feminine agent nouns corresponding to masculine nouns in *-tor*, esp. in Law (*executrix*). [L *-trix -tricis*]

tRNA *abbr.* transfer RNA.

trocar /ˈtrəʊkɑː(r)/ *n.* an instrument used for withdrawing fluid from a body cavity, esp. in oedema etc. [F *trois-quarts*, *trocart* f. *trois* three + *carre* side, face of an instrument, after its triangular form]

trochaic /trəˈkeɪɪk/ *adj. & n. Prosody* —*adj.* of or using trochees. —*n.* (usu. in *pl.*) trochaic verse. [L *trochaicus* f. Gk *trokhaikos* (as TROCHEE)]

trochal /ˈtrəʊk(ə)l/ *adj. Zool.* wheel-shaped. □ **trochal disc** *Zool.* the retractable disc on the head of a rotifer bearing a crown of cilia, used for drawing in food or for propulsion. [Gk *trokhos* wheel]

trochanter /trəˈkæntə(r)/ *n.* **1** *Anat.* any of several bony protuberances by which muscles are attached to the upper part of the thigh-bone. **2** *Zool.* the second segment of the leg in insects. [F f. Gk *trokhantēr* f. *trekhō* run]

troche /trəʊʃ/ *n.* a small usu. circular medicated tablet or lozenge. [obs. *trochisk* f. OF *trochisque* f. LL *trochiscus* f. Gk *trokhiskos* dimin. of *trokhos* wheel]

trochee /ˈtrəʊkiː, -kɪ/ *n. Prosody* a foot consisting of one long or stressed syllable followed by one short or unstressed syllable. [L *trochaeus* f. Gk *trokhaios* (*pous*) running (foot) f. *trekhō* run]

trochlea /ˈtrɒklɪə/ *n.* (*pl.* **trochleae** /-lɪˌiː/) *Anat.* a pulley-like structure or arrangement of parts, e.g. the groove at the lower end of the humerus. □□ **trochlear** *adj.* [L, = pulley f. Gk *trokhilia*]

trochoid /ˈtrəʊkɔɪd/ *adj. & n.* —*adj.* **1** *Anat.* rotating on its own axis. **2** *Geom.* (of a curve) traced by a point on a radius of a circle rotating along a straight line or another circle. —*n.* a trochoid joint or curve. □□ **trochoidal** /-ˈkɔɪd(ə)l/ *adj.* [Gk *trokhoeidēs* wheel-like f. *trokhos* wheel]

trod *past* and *past part.* of TREAD.

trodden *past part.* of TREAD.

trog /trɒg/ *n. sl.* a term of contempt for a person; a lout or hooligan. [abbr. of TROGLODYTE]

troglodyte /ˈtrɒgləˌdaɪt/ *n.* **1** a cave-dweller, esp. of prehistoric times. **2** a hermit. **3** *derog.* a wilfully obscurantist or old-fashioned person. □□ **troglodytic** /-ˈdɪtɪk/ *adj.* **troglodytical** /-ˈdɪtɪk(ə)l/ *adj.* **troglodytism** *n.* [L *troglodyta* f. Gk *trōglodutēs* f. the name of an Ethiopian people, after *trōglē* hole]

trogon /ˈtrəʊgɒn/ *n.* any tropical bird of the family Trogonidae, with a long tail and brilliantly coloured plumage. [mod.L f. Gk *trōgōn* f. *trōgō* gnaw]

troika /ˈtrɔɪkə/ *n.* **1 a** a Russian vehicle with a team of three horses abreast. **b** this team. **2** a group of three people, esp. as an administrative council. [Russ. f. *troe* three]

troilism /ˈtrɔɪlɪz(ə)m/ *n.* sexual activity involving three participants. [perh. f. F *trois* three]

Trojan /ˈtrəʊdʒ(ə)n/ *adj. & n.* —*adj.* of or relating to ancient Troy in Asia Minor. —*n.* **1** a native or inhabitant of Troy. **2** a person who works, fights, etc. courageously (*works like a Trojan*). □ **Trojan Horse 1** a hollow wooden horse said to have been used by the Greeks to enter Troy. **2** a person or device planted to bring about an enemy's downfall. [ME f. L *Troianus* f. *Troia* Troy]

troll¹ /trəʊl/ *n.* (in Scandinavian folklore) a fabulous being, esp. a giant or dwarf dwelling in a cave. [ON & Sw. *troll*, Da. *trold*]

troll[2] /trəʊl/ v. & n. —v. **1** intr. sing out in a carefree jovial manner. **2** tr. & intr. fish by drawing bait along in the water. **3** intr. esp. Brit. walk, stroll. —n. **1** the act of trolling for fish. **2** a line or bait used in this. □□ **troller** n. [ME 'stroll, roll': cf. OF troller quest, MHG trollen stroll]

trolley /'trɒlɪ/ n. (pl. **-eys**) **1** esp. Brit. a table, stand, or basket on wheels or castors for serving food, transporting luggage or shopping, gathering purchases in a supermarket, etc. **2** esp. Brit. a low truck running on rails. **3** (in full **trolley-wheel**) a wheel attached to a pole etc. used for collecting current from an overhead electric wire to drive a vehicle. **4 a** US = trolley-car. **b** Brit. = trolley bus. □**trolley bus** Brit. an electric bus running on the road and using a trolley-wheel. **trolley-car** US an electric tram using a trolley-wheel. [of dial. orig., perh. f. TROLL[2]]

trollop /'trɒləp/ n. **1** a disreputable girl or woman. **2** a prostitute. □□ **trollopish** adj. **trollopy** adj. [17th c.: perh. rel. to TRULL]

trombone /trɒm'bəʊn/ n. **1 a** a large brass wind instrument with a sliding tube. **b** its player. **2** an organ stop with the quality of a trombone. □□ **trombonist** n. [F or It. f. It. tromba TRUMPET]

trommel /'trɒm(ə)l/ n. Mining a revolving cylindrical sieve for cleaning ore. [G, = drum]

tromometer /trə'mɒmɪtə(r)/ n. an instrument for measuring very slight earthquake shocks. [Gk tromos trembling + -METER]

trompe /trɒmp/ n. an apparatus for producing a blast in a furnace by using falling water to displace air. [F, = trumpet: see TRUMP[1]]

trompe-l'œil /trɔ̃p'lɜːɪ/ n. a still-life painting etc. designed to give an illusion of reality. [F, lit. 'deceives the eye']

-tron /trɒn/ suffix Physics forming nouns denoting: **1** an elementary particle (positron). **2** a particle accelerator. **3** a thermionic valve. [after ELECTRON]

troop /truːp/ n. & v. —n. **1** an assembled company; an assemblage of people or animals. **2** (in pl.) soldiers or armed forces. **3** a cavalry unit commanded by a captain. **4** a unit of artillery and armoured formation. **5** a grouping of three or more Scout patrols. —v. **1** intr. (foll. by in, out, off, etc.) come together or move in large numbers. **2** tr. form (a regiment) into troops. □**troop the colour** esp. Brit. transfer a flag ceremonially at a public mounting of garrison guards. **troop-ship** a ship used for transporting troops. [F troupe, back-form. f. troupeau dimin. of med.L troppus flock, prob. of Gmc orig.]

trooper /'truːpə(r)/ n. **1** a private soldier in a cavalry or armoured unit. **2** Austral. & US a mounted or motor-borne policeman. **3** a cavalry horse. **4** esp. Brit. a troop-ship. □**swear like a trooper** swear extensively or forcefully.

tropaeolum /trə'piːələm/ n. a trailing or climbing plant of the genus Tropaeolum, with trumpet-shaped yellow, orange, or red flowers. [mod.L f. L tropaeum trophy, with ref. to the likeness of the flower and leaf to a helmet and shield]

trope /trəʊp/ n. a figurative (e.g. metaphorical or ironical) use of a word. [L tropus f. Gk tropos turn, way, trope f. trepō turn]

trophic /'trɒfɪk/ adj. of or concerned with nutrition (trophic nerves). [Gk trophikos f. trophē nourishment f. trephō nourish]

-trophic /'trɒfɪk/ comb. form relating to nutrition.

tropho- /'trɒfəʊ/ comb. form nourishment. [Gk trophē: see TROPHIC]

trophoblast /'trɒfəʊˌblæst/ n. a layer of tissue on the outside of a mammalian blastula, providing nourishment to an embryo.

trophy /'trəʊfɪ/ n. (pl. **-ies**) **1** a cup or other decorative object awarded as a prize or memento of victory or success in a contest etc. **2** a memento or souvenir, e.g. a deer's antlers, taken in hunting. **3** Gk & Rom. Antiq. the weapons etc. of a defeated army set up as a memorial of victory. **4** an ornamental group of symbolic or typical objects arranged for display. □□ **trophied** adj. (also in comb.). [F trophée f. L trophaeum f. Gk tropaion f. tropē rout f. trepō turn]

tropic /'trɒpɪk/ n. & adj. —n. **1** the parallel of latitude 23° 27' north (**tropic of Cancer**) or south (**tropic of Capricorn**) of the Equator. **2** each of two corresponding circles on the celestial sphere where the sun appears to turn after reaching its greatest declination. **3** (**the Tropics**) the region between the tropics of Cancer and Capricorn. —adj. **1** = TROPICAL 1. **2** of tropism. □**tropic bird** any sea bird of the family Phaethontidae, with very long central tail-feathers. [ME f. L tropicus f. Gk tropikos f. tropē turning f. trepō turn]

-tropic /'trɒpɪk/ comb. form **1** = -TROPHIC. **2** turning towards (heliotropic).

tropical /'trɒpɪk(ə)l/ adj. **1** of, peculiar to, or suggesting the Tropics (tropical fish; tropical diseases). **2** very hot; passionate, luxuriant. **3** of or by way of a trope. □**tropical year** see YEAR 1. □□ **tropically** adv.

tropism /'trəʊpɪz(ə)m/ n. Biol. the turning of all or part of an organism in a particular direction in response to an external stimulus. [Gk tropos turning f. trepō turn]

tropology /trə'pɒlədʒɪ/ n. **1** the figurative use of words. **2** figurative interpretation, esp. of the Scriptures. □□ **tropological** /ˌtrɒpə'lɒdʒɪk(ə)l/ adj. [LL tropologia f. Gk tropologia (as TROPE)]

tropopause /'trɒpəˌpɔːz, 'trəʊ-/ n. the interface between the troposphere and the stratosphere. [TROPOSPHERE + PAUSE]

troposphere /'trɒpəˌsfɪə(r), 'trəʊ-/ n. a layer of atmospheric air extending from about 6-10 km upwards from the earth's surface, in which the temperature falls with increasing height (cf. STRATOSPHERE, IONOSPHERE). □□ **tropospheric** /-'sferɪk/ adj. [Gk tropos turning + SPHERE]

troppo[1] /'trɒpəʊ/ adv. Mus. too much (qualifying a tempo indication). □**ma non troppo** but not too much so. [It.]

troppo[2] /'trɒpəʊ/ adj. Austral. sl. mentally ill from exposure to a tropical climate.

Trot /trɒt/ n. colloq. usu. derog. a Trotskyist. [abbr.]

trot /trɒt/ v. & n. —v. (**trotted, trotting**) **1** intr. (of a person) run at a moderate pace esp. with short strides. **2** intr. (of a horse) proceed at a steady pace faster than a walk lifting each diagonal pair of legs alternately. **3** intr. colloq. walk or go. **4** tr. cause (a horse or person) to trot. **5** tr. traverse (a distance) at a trot. —n. **1** the action or exercise of trotting (proceed at a trot; went for a trot). **2** (**the trots**) sl. an attack of diarrhoea. **3** a brisk steady movement or occupation. **4** (in pl.) Austral. colloq. **a** trotting-races. **b** a meeting for these. □**on the trot** colloq. **1** continually busy (kept them on the trot). **2** in succession (five weeks on the trot). **trot out 1** cause (a horse) to trot to show his paces. **2** produce or introduce (as if) for inspection and approval, esp. tediously or repeatedly. [ME f. OF troter f. Rmc & med.L trottare, of Gmc orig.]

troth /trəʊθ/ n. archaic **1** faith, loyalty. **2** truth. □**pledge** (or **plight**) **one's troth** pledge one's word esp. in marriage or betrothal. [ME trowthe, for OE trēowth TRUTH]

Trotskyism /'trɒtskɪˌɪz(ə)m/ n. the political or economic principles of L. Trotsky, Russian politician d. 1940, esp. as urging worldwide socialist revolution. □□ **Trotskyist** n. **Trotskyite** n. derog.

trotter /'trɒtə(r)/ n. **1** a horse bred or trained for trotting. **2** (usu. in pl.) **a** an animal's foot as food (pig's trotters). **b** joc. a human foot.

trotting /'trɒtɪŋ/ n. racing for trotting horses pulling a two-wheeled vehicle and driver.

troubadour /'truːbəˌdɔː(r)/ n. **1** any of a number of French medieval lyric poets composing and singing in Provençal in the 11th-13th c. on the theme of courtly love. **2** a singer or poet. [F f. Prov. *trobador* f. *trobar* find, invent, compose in verse]

trouble /'trʌb(ə)l/ *n. & v.* —*n.* **1** difficulty or distress; vexation, affliction (*am having trouble with my car*). **2 a** inconvenience; unpleasant exertion; bother (*went to a lot of trouble*). **b** a cause of this (*the child was no trouble*). **3** a cause of annoyance or concern (*the trouble with you is that you can't say no*). **4** a faulty condition or operation (*kidney trouble*; *engine trouble*). **5 a** fighting, disturbance (*crowd trouble*; *don't want any trouble*). **b** (in *pl.*) political or social unrest, public disturbances. **6** disagreement, strife (*is having trouble at home*). —*v.* **1** *tr.* cause distress or anxiety to; disturb (*were much troubled by their debts*). **2** *intr.* be disturbed or worried (*don't trouble about it*). **3** *tr.* afflict; cause pain etc. to (*am troubled with arthritis*). **4** *tr. & intr.* (often *refl.*) subject or be subjected to inconvenience or unpleasant exertion (*sorry to trouble you*; *don't trouble yourself*; *don't trouble to explain*). □**ask** (or **look**) **for trouble** *colloq.* invite trouble or difficulty by one's actions, behaviour, etc.; behave rashly or indiscreetly. **be no trouble** cause no inconvenience etc. **go to the trouble** (or **some trouble** etc.) exert oneself to do something. **in trouble 1** involved in a matter likely to bring censure or punishment. **2** *colloq.* pregnant while unmarried. **take trouble** (or **the trouble**) exert oneself to do something. **trouble and strife** *rhyming sl.* wife. **trouble spot** a place where difficulties regularly occur. □□**troubler** *n.* [ME f. OF *truble* (n.), *trubler*, *turbler* (v.) ult. f. L *turbidus* TURBID]

troubled /'trʌb(ə)ld/ *adj.* showing, experiencing, or reflecting trouble, anxiety, etc. (*a troubled mind*; *a troubled childhood*).

troublemaker /'trʌb(ə)l,meɪkə(r)/ *n.* a person who habitually causes trouble. □□**troublemaking** *n.*

troubleshooter /'trʌb(ə)l,ʃuːtə(r)/ *n.* **1** a mediator in industrial or diplomatic etc. disputes. **2** a person who traces and corrects faults in machinery etc. □□**troubleshooting** *n.*

troublesome /'trʌb(ə)lsəm/ *adj.* **1** causing trouble. **2** vexing, annoying. □□**troublesomely** *adv.* **troublesomeness** *n.*

troublous /'trʌbləs/ *adj. archaic* or *literary* full of troubles; agitated, disturbed (*troublous times*). [ME f. OF *troubleus* (as TROUBLE)]

trough /trɒf/ *n.* **1** a long narrow open receptacle for water, animal feed, etc. **2** a channel for conveying a liquid. **3** an elongated region of low barometric pressure. **4** a hollow between two wave crests. **5** the time of lowest economic performance etc. **6** a region around the minimum on a curve of variation of a quantity. **7** a low point or depression. [OE *trog* f. Gmc]

trounce /traʊns/ *v.tr.* **1** defeat heavily. **2** beat, thrash. **3** punish severely. □□**trouncer** *n.* **trouncing** *n.* [16th c., = afflict: orig. unkn.]

troupe /truːp/ *n.* a company of actors or acrobats etc. [F, = TROOP]

trouper /'truːpə(r)/ *n.* **1** a member of a theatrical troupe. **2** a staunch colleague.

trousers /'traʊzəz/ *n.pl.* **1** an outer garment reaching from the waist usu. to the ankles, divided into two parts to cover the legs. **2** (**trouser**) (*attrib.*) designating parts of this (*trouser leg*). □□**trouser-clip** = *bicycle-clip*. **trouser suit** a woman's suit of trousers and jacket. **wear the trousers** be the dominant partner in a marriage. □□**trousered** *adj.* **trouserless** *adj.* [archaic *trouse* (sing.) f. Ir. & Gael. *triubhas* TREWS: pl. form after *drawers*]

trousseau /'truːsəʊ/ *n.* (*pl.* **trousseaus** or **trousseaux** /-səʊz/) the clothes collected by a bride for her marriage. [F, lit. bundle, dimin. of *trousse* TRUSS]

trout /traʊt/ *n.* (*pl.* same or **trouts**) **1** any of various freshwater fish of the genus *Salmo* of the northern hemisphere, valued as food. **2** a similar fish of the family Salmonidae (see also *salmon trout*). **3** *sl. derog.* a woman, esp. an old or ill-tempered one (usu. *old trout*). □□**troutlet** *n.* **troutling** *n.* **trouty** *adj.* [OE *truht* f. LL *tructa*]

trouvaille /'truːvaɪ/ *n.* a lucky find; a windfall. [F f. *trouver* find]

trouvère /truː'veə(r)/ *n.* a medieval epic poet in Northern France in the 11th–14th c. [OF *trovere* f. *trover* find: cf. TROUBADOUR]

trove /trəʊv/ *n.* = *treasure trove*. [AF *trové* f. *trover* find]

trover /'trəʊvə(r)/ *n. Law* **1** finding and keeping personal property. **2** common-law action to recover the value of personal property wrongfully taken etc. [OF *trover* find]

trow /traʊ, trəʊ/ *v.tr. archaic* think, believe. [OE *trūwian*, *trēowian*, rel. to TRUE]

trowel /'traʊəl/ *n. & v.* —*n.* **1** a small hand-held tool with a flat pointed blade, used to apply and spread mortar etc. **2** a similar tool with a curved scoop for lifting plants or earth. —*v.tr.* (**trowelled**, **trowelling**; *US* **troweled**, **troweling**) **1** apply (plaster etc.). **2** dress (a wall etc.) with a trowel. [ME f. OF *truele* f. med.L *truella* f. L *trulla* scoop, dimin. of *trua* ladle etc.]

troy /trɔɪ/ *n.* (in full **troy weight**) a system of weights used for precious metals and gems, with a pound of 12 ounces or 5,760 grains. [ME, prob. f. *Troyes* in France]

trs. *abbr.* transpose (letters or words etc.).

truant /'truːənt/ *n., adj., & v.* —*n.* **1** a child who stays away from school without leave or explanation. **2** a person missing from work etc. —*adj.* (of a person, conduct, thoughts, etc.) shirking, idle, wandering. —*v.intr.* (also **play truant**) stay away as a truant. □□**truancy** *n.* [ME f. OF, prob. ult. f. Celt.: cf. Welsh *truan*, Gael. *truaghan* wretched]

truce /truːs/ *n.* **1** a temporary agreement to cease hostilities. **2** a suspension of private feuding or bickering. □□**truceless** *adj.* [ME *trew(e)s* (pl.) f. OE *trēow*, rel. to TRUE]

truck¹ /trʌk/ *n. & v.* —*n.* **1** *Brit.* an open railway wagon for carrying freight. **2** esp. *US* a vehicle for carrying heavy goods; a lorry. **3** a vehicle for transporting troops, supplies, etc. **4** a railway bogie. **5** a wheeled stand for transporting goods. **6 a** *Naut.* a wooden disc at the top of a mast with holes for halyards. **b** a small solid wheel. —*v.* **1** *tr.* convey on or in a truck. **2** *intr. US* drive a truck. **3** *intr. US sl.* proceed; go, stroll. □□**truckage** *n.* [perh. short for TRUCKLE in sense 'wheel, pulley']

truck² /trʌk/ *n. & v.* —*n.* **1** dealings; exchange, barter. **2** small wares. **3** *US* market-garden produce (*truck farm*). **4** *colloq.* odds and ends. **5** *hist.* the payment of workers in kind. —*v.tr. & intr. archaic* barter, exchange. □**have no truck with** avoid dealing with. [ME f. OF *troquer* (unrecorded) = *trocare*, of unkn. orig.]

trucker /'trʌkə(r)/ *n.* esp. *US* **1** a long-distance lorry-driver. **2** a firm dealing in long-distance carriage of goods.

truckie /'trʌkɪ/ *n. Austral. colloq.* a lorry-driver; a trucker.

trucking /'trʌkɪŋ/ *n. US* conveyance of goods by lorry.

truckle /'trʌk(ə)l/ *n. & v.* —*n.* **1** (in full **truckle-bed**) a low bed on wheels that can be stored under a larger bed. **2** *orig. dial.* a small barrel-shaped cheese. —*v.intr.* (foll. by *to*) submit obsequiously. □□**truckler** *n.* [orig. = wheel, pulley, f. AF *trocle* f. L *trochlea* pulley]

truculent /'trʌkjʊlənt/ *adj.* **1** aggressively defiant. **2** aggressive, pugnacious. **3** fierce, savage. □□**truculence** *n.* **truculency** *n.* **truculently** *adv.* [L *truculentus* f. *trux trucis* fierce]

trudge /trʌdʒ/ *v. & n.* —*v.* **1** *intr.* go on foot esp. laboriously. **2** *tr.* traverse (a distance) in this way.

—*n.* a trudging walk. □□ **trudger** *n.* [16th c.: orig. unkn.]

trudgen /ˈtrʌdʒ(ə)n/ *n.* a swimming stroke like the crawl with a scissors movement of the legs. [J. *Trudgen*, 19th-c. English swimmer]

true /truː/ *adj., adv., & v.* —*adj.* **1** in accordance with fact or reality (*a true story*). **2** genuine; rightly or strictly so called; not spurious or counterfeit (*a true friend*; *the true heir to the throne*). **3** (often foll. by *to*) loyal or faithful (*true to one's word*). **4** (foll. by *to*) accurately conforming (to a standard or expectation etc.) (*true to form*). **5** correctly positioned or balanced; upright, level. **6** exact, accurate (*a true aim*; *a true copy*). **7** (*absol.*) (also **it is true**) certainly, admittedly (*true, it would cost more*). **8** (of a note) exactly in tune. **9** *archaic* honest, upright (*twelve good men and true*). —*adv.* **1** truly (*tell me true*). **2** accurately (*aim true*). **3** without variation (*breed true*). —*v.tr.* (**trues, trued, truing** or **trueing**) bring (a tool, wheel, frame, etc.) into the exact position or form required. □ **come true** actually happen or be the case. **out of true** (or **the true**) not in the correct or exact position. **true bill** *US & hist.* a bill of indictment endorsed by a grand jury as being sustained by evidence. **true-blue** *adj.* extremely loyal or orthodox. —*n.* such a person, esp. a Conservative. **true-born** genuine (*a true-born Englishman*). **true-bred** of a genuine or good breed. **true-hearted** faithful, loyal. **true horizon** see HORIZON 1c. **true-love** a sweetheart. **true-love** (or **-lover's**) **knot** a kind of knot with interlacing bows on each side, symbolizing true love. **true north** etc. north etc. according to the earth's axis, not magnetic north. **true rib** a rib joined directly to the breastbone. **true to form** (or **type**) being or behaving etc. as expected. **true to life** accurately representing life. □□ **trueish** *adj.* **trueness** *n.* [OE *trēowe, trȳwe,* f. the Gmc noun repr. by TRUCE]

truffle /ˈtrʌf(ə)l/ *n.* **1** any strong-smelling underground fungus of the order Tuberales, used as a culinary delicacy and found esp. in France by trained dogs or pigs. **2** a usu. round sweet made of chocolate mixture covered with cocoa etc. [prob. f. Du. *truffel* f. obs. F *truffle* ult. f. L *tubera* pl. of TUBER]

trug /trʌg/ *n. Brit.* **1** a shallow oblong garden-basket usu. of wood strips. **2** *archaic* a wooden milk-pan. [perh. a dial. var. of TROUGH]

truism /ˈtruːɪz(ə)m/ *n.* **1** an obviously true or hackneyed statement. **2** a proposition that states nothing beyond what is implied in any of its terms. □□ **truistic** /-ˈɪstɪk/ *adj.*

trull /trʌl/ *n. archaic* a prostitute. [16th c.: cf. G *Trulle,* TROLLOP]

truly /ˈtruːlɪ/ *adv.* **1** sincerely, genuinely (*am truly grateful*). **2** really, indeed (*truly, I do not know*). **3** faithfully, loyally (*served them truly*). **4** accurately, truthfully (*is not truly depicted; has been truly stated*). **5** rightly, properly (*well and truly*). [OE *trēowlice* (as TRUE, -LY²)]

trumeau /truːˈməʊ/ *n.* (*pl.* **trumeaux** /-ˈməʊz/) a section of wall or a pillar between two openings, e.g. a pillar dividing a large doorway. [F]

trump¹ /trʌmp/ *n. & v.* —*n.* **1** a playing-card of a suit ranking above the others. **2** an advantage esp. involving surprise. **3** *colloq.* **a** a helpful or admired person. **b** *Austral. & NZ* a person in authority. —*v.* **1 a** *tr.* defeat (a card or its player) with a trump. **b** *intr.* play a trump card when another suit has been led. **2** *tr. colloq.* gain a surprising advantage over (a person, proposal, etc.). □ **trump card 1** a card belonging to, or turned up to determine, a trump suit. **2** *colloq.* **a** a valuable resource. **b** a surprise move to gain an advantage. **trump up** fabricate or invent (an accusation, excuse, etc.) (*on a trumped-up charge*). **turn up trumps** *Brit. colloq.* **1** turn out better than expected. **2** be greatly successful or helpful. [corrupt. of TRIUMPH in the same (now obs.) sense]

trump² /trʌmp/ *n. archaic* a trumpet-blast. □ **the last trump** the trumpet-blast to wake the dead on Judgement Day. [ME f. OF *trompe* f. Frank.: prob. imit.]

trumpery /ˈtrʌmpərɪ/ *n. & adj.* —*n.* (*pl.* **-ies**) **1 a** worthless finery. **b** a worthless article. **2** rubbish. —*adj.* **1** showy but worthless (*trumpery jewels*). **2** delusive, shallow (*trumpery arguments*). [ME f. OF *tromperie* f. *tromper* deceive]

trumpet /ˈtrʌmpɪt/ *n. & v.* —*n.* **1 a** a tubular or conical brass instrument with a flared bell and a bright penetrating tone. **b** its player. **c** an organ stop with a quality resembling a trumpet. **2 a** the tubular corona of a daffodil etc. **b** a trumpet-shaped thing (*ear-trumpet*). **3** a sound of or like a trumpet. —*v.* (**trumpeted, trumpeting**) **1** *intr.* **a** blow a trumpet. **b** (of an enraged elephant etc.) make a loud sound as of a trumpet. **2** *tr.* proclaim loudly (a person's or thing's merit). □ **trumpet-call** an urgent summons to action. **trumpet major** the chief trumpeter of a cavalry regiment. □□ **trumpetless** *adj.* [ME f. OF *trompette* dimin. (as TRUMP²)]

trumpeter /ˈtrʌmpɪtə(r)/ *n.* **1** a person who plays or sounds a trumpet, esp. a cavalry soldier giving signals. **2** a bird making a trumpet-like sound, esp.: **a** a variety of domestic pigeon. **b** a large black S. American cranelike bird of the genus *Psophia.* □ **trumpeter swan** a large N. American wild swan, *Cygnus buccinator.*

truncal /ˈtrʌŋk(ə)l/ *adj.* of or relating to the trunk of a body or a tree.

truncate *v. & adj.* —*v.tr.* /trʌŋˈkeɪt, ˈtrʌŋ-/ **1** cut the top or the end from (a tree, a body, a piece of writing, etc.). **2** *Crystallog.* replace (an edge or an angle) by a plane. —*adj.* /ˈtrʌŋkeɪt/ *Bot. & Zool.* (of a leaf or feather etc.) ending abruptly as if cut off at the base or tip. □□ **truncately** /ˈtrʌŋkeɪtlɪ/ *adv.* **truncation** /-ˈkeɪʃ(ə)n/ *n.* [L *truncare truncat-* maim]

truncheon /ˈtrʌntʃ(ə)n/ *n.* **1** esp. *Brit.* a short club or cudgel, esp. carried by a policeman. **2** a staff or baton as a symbol of authority, esp. that of the Earl Marshal. [ME f. OF *tronchon* stump ult. f. L *truncus* trunk]

trundle /ˈtrʌnd(ə)l/ *v.tr. & intr.* roll or move heavily or noisily esp. on or as on wheels. □ **trundle-bed** = TRUCKLE¹. [var. of obs. or dial. *trendle, trindle,* f. OE *trendel* circle (as TREND)]

trunk /trʌŋk/ *n.* **1** the main stem of a tree as distinct from its branches and roots. **2** a person's or animal's body apart from the limbs and head. **3** the main part of any structure. **4** a large box with a hinged lid for transporting luggage, clothes, etc. **5** *US* the luggage compartment of a motor car. **6** an elephant's elongated prehensile nose. **7** (in *pl.*) men's close-fitting shorts worn for swimming, boxing, etc. **8** the main body of an artery, nerve, etc. **9** an enclosed shaft or conduit for cables, ventilation, etc. □ **trunk call** esp. *Brit.* a telephone call on a trunk line with charges made according to distance. **trunk line** a main line of a railway, telephone system, etc. **trunk road** esp. *Brit.* an important main road. □□ **trunkful** *n.* (*pl.* **-fuls**). **trunkless** *adj.* [ME f. OF *tronc* f. L *truncus*]

trunking /ˈtrʌŋkɪŋ/ *n.* **1** a system of shafts or conduits for cables, ventilation, etc. **2** the use or arrangement of trunk lines.

trunnion /ˈtrʌnjən/ *n.* **1** a supporting cylindrical projection on each side of a cannon or mortar. **2** a hollow gudgeon supporting a cylinder in a steam engine and giving passage to the steam. [F *trognon* core, tree-trunk, of unkn. orig.]

truss /trʌs/ *n. & v.* —*n.* **1** a framework, e.g. of rafters and struts, supporting a roof or bridge etc. **2** a surgical appliance worn to support a hernia. **3** *Brit.* a bundle of old hay (56 lb.) or new hay (60 lb.) or straw (36 lb.). **4** a compact terminal cluster of flowers or fruit. **5** a large corbel supporting a monument etc. **6** *Naut.* a heavy iron ring securing the lower yards to a mast. —*v.tr.* **1** tie up (a fowl) compactly for cooking. **2** (often foll. by *up*) tie (a person) up with the arms to the sides. **3** support (a roof or bridge etc.) with a truss or trusses. □□ **trusser** *n*. [ME f. OF *trusser* (v.), *trusse* (n.), of unkn. orig.]

trust /trʌst/ *n*. & *v*. —*n*. **1 a** a firm belief in the reliability or truth or strength etc. of a person or thing. **b** the state of being relied on. **2** a confident expectation. **3 a** a thing or person committed to one's care. **b** the resulting obligation or responsibility (*am in a position of trust*; *have fulfilled my trust*). **4** a person or thing confided in (*is our sole trust*). **5** reliance on the truth of a statement etc. without examination. **6** commercial credit (*obtained goods on trust*). **7** *Law* **a** a confidence placed in a person by making that person the nominal owner of property to be used for another's benefit. **b** the right of the latter to benefit by such property. **c** the property so held. **d** the legal relation between the holder and the property so held. **8 a** a body of trustees. **b** an organization managed by trustees. **c** an organized association of several companies for the purpose of reducing or defeating competition etc., esp. one in which all or most of the stock is transferred to a central committee and shareholders lose their voting power although remaining entitled to profits. —*v*. **1** *tr*. place trust in; believe in; rely on the character or behaviour of. **2** *tr*. (foll. by *with*) allow (a person) to have or use (a thing) from confidence in its proper use (*was reluctant to trust them with my books*). **3** *tr*. (often foll. by *that* + clause) have faith or confidence or hope that a thing will take place (*I trust you will not be late*; *I trust that she is recovering*). **4** *tr*. (foll. by *to*) consign (a thing) to (a person) with trust. **5** *tr*. (foll. by *for*) allow credit to (a customer) for (goods). **6** *intr*. (foll. by *in*) place reliance in (*we trust in you*). **7** *intr*. (foll. by *to*) place (esp. undue) reliance on (*shall have to trust to luck*). □ **in trust** *Law* held on the basis of trust (see sense 7 of *n*.). **on trust 1** on credit. **2** on the basis of trust or confidence. **take on trust** accept (an assertion, claim, etc.) without evidence or investigation. **trust company** a company formed to act as a trustee or to deal with trusts. **trust fund** a fund of money etc. held in trust. **trust territory** a territory under the trusteeship of the United Nations or of a State designated by them. □□ **trustable** *adj*. **truster** *n*. [ME *troste*, *truste* (n.) f. ON *traust* f. *traustr* strong: (v.) f. ON *treysta*, assim. to the noun]

trustee /trʌsˈtiː/ *n*. **1** *Law* a person or member of a board given control or powers of administration of property in trust with a legal obligation to administer it solely for the purposes specified. **2** a State made responsible for the government of an area. □□ **trusteeship** *n*.

trustful /ˈtrʌstfʊl/ *adj*. **1** full of trust or confidence. **2** not feeling or showing suspicion. □□ **trustfully** *adv*. **trustfulness** *n*.

trusting /ˈtrʌstɪŋ/ *adj*. having trust (esp. characteristically); trustful. □□ **trustingly** *adv*. **trustingness** *n*.

trustworthy /ˈtrʌstˌwɜːðɪ/ *adj*. deserving of trust; reliable. □□ **trustworthily** *adv*. **trustworthiness** *n*.

trusty /ˈtrʌstɪ/ *adj*. & *n*. —*adj*. (**trustier**, **trustiest**) **1** *archaic* or *joc*. trustworthy (*a trusty steed*). **2** *archaic* loyal (to a sovereign) (*my trusty subjects*). —*n*. (pl. -ies) a prisoner who is given special privileges for good behaviour. □□ **trustily** *adv*. **trustiness** *n*.

truth /truːθ/ *n*. (pl. **truths** /truːðz, truːθs/) **1** the quality or a state of being true or truthful (*doubted the truth of the statement*; *there may be some truth in it*). **2 a** what is true (*tell us the whole truth*; *the truth is that I forgot*). **b** what is accepted as true (*one of the fundamental truths*). □ **in truth** *literary* truly, really. **to tell the truth** (or **truth to tell**) to be frank. **truth drug** any of various drugs supposedly able to induce a person to tell the truth. **truth table** a list indicating the truth or falsity of various propositions in logic etc. □□ **truthless** *adj*. [OE *trīewth*, *trēowth* (as TRUE)]

truthful /ˈtruːθfʊl/ *adj*. **1** habitually speaking the truth. **2** (of a story etc.) true. **3** (of a likeness etc.) corresponding to reality. □□ **truthfully** *adv*. **truthfulness** *n*.

try /traɪ/ *v*. & *n*. —*v*. (-**ies**, -**ied**) **1** *intr*. make an effort with a view to success (often foll. by *to* + infin.; *colloq*. foll. by *and* + infin.: *tried to be on time*; *try and be early*; *I shall try hard*). ¶ Use with *and* is uncommon in the past tense and in negative contexts (except in *imper*.). **2** *tr*. make an effort to achieve (*tried my best*; *had better try something easier*). **3** *tr*. **a** test (the quality of a thing) by use or experiment. **b** test the qualities of (a person or thing) (*try it before you buy*). **4** *tr*. make severe demands on (a person, quality, etc.) (*my patience has been sorely tried*). **5** *tr*. examine the effectiveness or usefulness of for a purpose (*try cold water*; *try the off-licence*; *have you tried kicking it?*). **6** *tr*. ascertain the state of fastening of (a door, window, etc.). **7** *tr*. **a** investigate and decide (a case or issue) judicially. **b** subject (a person) to trial (*will be tried for murder*). **8** *tr*. make an experiment in order to find out (*let us try which takes longest*). **9** *intr*. (foll. by *for*) **a** apply or compete for. **b** seek to reach or attain (*am going to try for a gold medal*). **10** *tr*. (often foll. by *out*) **a** extract (oil) from fat by heating. **b** treat (fat) in this way. **11** *tr*. (often foll. by *up*) smooth (roughly-planed wood) with a plane to give an accurately flat surface. —*n*. (pl. -ies) **1** an effort to accomplish something; an attempt (*give it a try*). **2** *Rugby Football* the act of touching the ball down behind the opposing goal-line, scoring points and entitling the scoring side to a kick at goal. **3** *Amer. Football* an attempt to score an extra point in various ways after a touchdown. □ **try conclusions with** see CONCLUSION. **try a fall with** contend with. **try for size** try out or test for suitability. **try one's hand** see how skilful one is, esp. at the first attempt. **trying-plane** a plane used in trying (see sense 11 of *v*.). **try it on** *colloq*. **1** test another's patience. **2** attempt to outwit or deceive another person. **try on** put on (clothes etc.) to see if they fit or suit the wearer. **try-on** *n. Brit. colloq*. **1** an act of trying it on. **2** an attempt to fool or deceive. **try out 1** put to the test. **2** test thoroughly. **try-out** *n*. an experimental test of efficiency, popularity, etc. **try-sail** /ˈtraɪs(ə)l/ a small strong fore-and-aft sail set on the mainmast or other mast of a sailing-vessel in heavy weather. **try-square** a carpenter's square, usu. with one wooden and one metal limb. [ME, = separate, distinguish, etc., f. OF *trier* sift, of unkn. orig.]

trying /ˈtraɪɪŋ/ *adj*. annoying, vexatious; hard to endure. □□ **tryingly** *adv*.

trypanosome /ˈtrɪpənəˌsəʊm/ *n. Med*. any protozoan parasite of the genus *Trypanosoma* having a long trailing flagellum and infesting the blood etc. [Gk *trupanon* borer + -SOME[3]]

trypanosomiasis /ˌtrɪpənəsəˈmaɪəsɪs/ *n*. any of several diseases caused by a trypanosome including sleeping sickness and Chagas' disease.

trypsin /ˈtrɪpsɪn/ *n*. a digestive enzyme acting on proteins and present in the pancreatic juice. □□ **tryptic** *adj*. [Gk *tripsis* friction f. *tribō* rub (because it was first obtained by rubbing down the pancreas with glycerine)]

trypsinogen /trɪpˈsɪnədʒ(ə)n/ *n*. a substance in the pancreas from which trypsin is formed.

tryptophan /ˈtrɪptəˌfæn/ *n. Biochem*. an amino acid essential in the diet of vertebrates. [as TRYPSIN + -*phan* f. Gk *phainō* appear]

tryst /trɪst/ *n*. & *v. archaic* —*n*. **1** a time and place for a meeting, esp. of lovers. **2** such a meeting (*keep a tryst*; *break one's tryst*). —*v.intr*. (foll. by *with*) make a tryst. □□ **tryster** *n*. [ME, = obs. *trist* (= TRUST) f. OF *triste* an appointed station in hunting]

tsar /zɑː(r)/ *n*. (also **czar**) **1** *hist*. the title of the former emperor of Russia. **2** a person with great authority. □□ **tsardom** *n.* **tsarism** *n.* **tsarist** *n.* [Russ. *tsar'*, ult. f. L *Caesar*]

tsarevich /'zɑːrɪvɪtʃ/ *n.* (also **czarevich**) *hist.* the eldest son of an emperor of Russia. [Russ. *tsarevich* son of a tsar]

tsarina /zɑːˈriːnə/ *n.* (also **czarina**) *hist.* the title of the former empress of Russia. [It. & Sp. (c)*zarina* f. G *Czarin, Zarin*, fem. of *Czar, Zar*]

tsetse /'tsetsɪ, 'tetsɪ/ *n.* any fly of the genus *Glossina* native to Africa, that feeds on human and animal blood with a needle-like proboscis and transmits trypanosomiasis. [Tswana]

TSH *abbr.* **1** thryroid-stimulating hormone. **2** Their Serene Highnesses.

T-shirt /'tiːʃɜːt/ *n.* (also **teeshirt**) a short-sleeved casual top, usu. of knitted cotton and having the form of a T when spread out.

tsp. *abbr.* (*pl.* **tsps.**) teaspoonful.

T-square /'tiːskweə(r)/ *n.* a T-shaped instrument for drawing or testing right angles.

tsunami /tsuːˈnɑːmɪ/ *n.* (*pl.* **tsunamis**) a long high sea wave caused by underwater earthquakes or other disturbances. [Jap. f. *tsu* harbour + *nami* wave]

Tswana /'tswɑːnə/ *n.* (also **Setswana** /se'tswɑːnə/) **1** a southern African people living in Botswana and neighbouring areas. **2** a member of this people. **3** the Bantu language of this people. ¶ *Setswana* is now the preferred form for the language. [native name]

TT *abbr.* **1** Tourist Trophy. **2** tuberculin-tested. **3 a** teetotal. **b** teetotaller.

TU *abbr.* Trade Union.

Tu. *abbr.* Tuesday.

tuatara /ˌtuːə'tɑːrə/ *n.* a large lizard-like reptile, *Sphenodon punctatus*, unique to certain small islands of New Zealand, having a crest of soft spines extending along its back, and a third eye on top of its head. [Maori f. *tua* on the back + *tara* spine]

tub /tʌb/ *n. & v.* —*n.* **1** an open flat-bottomed usu. round container for various purposes. **2** a tub-shaped (usu. plastic) carton. **3** the amount a tub will hold. **4** *colloq.* a bath. **5 a** *colloq.* a clumsy slow boat. **b** a stout roomy boat for rowing practice. **6** (in mining) a container for conveying ore, coal, etc. —*v.* (**tubbed, tubbing**) **1** *tr. & intr.* plant, bathe, or wash in a tub. **2** *tr.* enclose in a tub. **3** *tr.* line (a mine-shaft) with a wooden or iron casing. □**tub chair** a chair with solid arms continuous with a usu. semicircular back. **tub-thumper** *colloq.* a ranting preacher or orator. **tub-thumping** *colloq.* ranting oratory. □□ **tubbable** *adj.* **tubbish** *adj.* **tubful** *n.* (*pl.* **-fuls**). [ME, prob. f. LG or Du. orig.: cf. MLG, MDu. *tubbe*]

tuba /'tjuːbə/ *n.* (*pl.* **tubas**) **1 a** a low-pitched brass wind instrument. **b** its player. **2** an organ stop with the quality of a tuba. [It. f. L, = trumpet]

tubal /'tjuːb(ə)l/ *adj. Anat.* of or relating to a tube, esp. the bronchial or Fallopian tubes.

tubby /'tʌbɪ/ *adj.* (**tubbier, tubbiest**) **1** (of a person) short and fat; tub-shaped. **2** (of a violin) dull-sounding, lacking resonance. □□ **tubbiness** *n.*

tube /tjuːb/ *n. & v.* —*n.* **1** a long hollow rigid or flexible cylinder, esp. for holding or carrying air, liquids, etc. **2** a soft metal or plastic cylinder sealed at one end and having a screw cap at the other, for holding a semi-liquid substance ready for use (*a tube of toothpaste*). **3** *Anat. & Zool.* a hollow cylindrical organ in the body (*bronchial tubes; Fallopian tubes*). **4** (often prec. by *the*) *colloq.* the London underground railway system (*went by tube*). **5 a** a cathode-ray tube esp. in a television set. **b** (prec. by *the*) esp. *US colloq.* television. **6** *US* a thermionic valve. **7** = *inner tube.* **8** the cylindrical body of a wind instrument. **9** *Austral. sl.* a can of beer. —*v.tr.* **1** equip with tubes. **2** enclose in a tube. □□ **tubeless** *adj.* (esp. in sense 7 of *n.*). **tubelike** *adj.* [F *tube* or L *tubus*]

tubectomy /tjuː'bektəmɪ/ *n.* (*pl.* **-ies**) *Surgery* removal of a Fallopian tube.

tuber /'tjuːbə(r)/ *n.* **1 a** the short thick rounded part

of a stem or rhizome, usu. found underground and covered with modified buds, e.g. in a potato. **b** the similar root of a dahlia etc. **2** *Anat.* a lump or swelling. [L, = hump, swelling]

tubercle /'tjuːbək(ə)l/ *n.* **1** a small rounded protuberance esp. on a bone. **2** a small rounded swelling on the body or in an organ, esp. a nodular lesion characteristic of tuberculosis in the lungs etc. **3** a small tuber; a wartlike growth. □**tubercle bacillus** a bacterium causing tuberculosis. □□ **tuberculate** /-'bɜːkjʊlət/ *adj.* **tuberculate** /-'bɜːkjʊləs/ *adj.* [L *tuberculum*, dimin. of *tuber*: see TUBER]

tubercular /tjʊ'bɜːkjʊlə(r)/ *adj. & n.* —*adj.* of or having tubercles or tuberculosis. —*n.* a person with tuberculosis. [f. L *tuberculum* (as TUBERCLE)]

tuberculation /tjʊˌbɜːkjʊ'leɪʃ(ə)n/ *n.* **1** the formation of tubercles. **2** a growth of tubercles. [f. L *tuberculum* (as TUBERCLE)]

tuberculin /tjʊ'bɜːkjʊlɪn/ *n.* a sterile liquid from cultures of tubercle bacillus, used in the diagnosis and treatment of tuberculosis. □**tuberculin test** a hypodermic injection of tuberculin to detect a tubercular infection. **tuberculin-tested** (of milk) from cows giving a negative response to a tuberculin test. [f. L *tuberculum* (as TUBERCLE)]

tuberculosis /tjʊˌbɜːkjʊ'ləʊsɪs/ *n.* an infectious disease caused by the bacillus *Mycobacterium tuberculosis*, characterized by tubercles, esp. in the lungs (see also *pulmonary tuberculosis*).

tuberose[1] /'tjuːbəˌrəʊs/ *adj.* **1** covered with tubers; knobby. **2** of or resembling a tuber. **3** bearing tubers. □□ **tuberosity** /-'rɒsɪtɪ/ *n.* [L *tuberosus* f. TUBER]

tuberose[2] /'tjuːbəˌrəʊz/ *n.* a plant, *Polianthes tuberosa*, native to Mexico, having heavily scented white funnel-like flowers and strap-shaped leaves. [L *tuberosa* fem. (as TUBEROSE[1])]

tuberous /'tjuːbərəs/ *adj.* = TUBEROSE[1]. □**tuberous root** a thick and fleshy root like a tuber but without buds. [F *tubéreux* or L *tuberosus* f. TUBER]

tubifex /'tjuːbɪˌfeks/ *n.* any red annelid worm of the genus *Tubifex*, found in mud at the bottom of rivers and lakes and used as food for aquarium fish. [mod.L f. L *tubus* tube + *-fex* f. *facere* make]

tubiform /'tjuːbɪˌfɔːm/ *adj.* tube-shaped.

tubing /'tjuːbɪŋ/ *n.* **1** a length of tube. **2** a quantity of tubes.

tubular /'tjuːbjʊlə(r)/ *adj.* **1** tube-shaped. **2** having or consisting of tubes. **3** (of furniture etc.) made of tubular pieces. □**tubular bells** an orchestral instrument consisting of a row of vertically suspended brass tubes that are struck with a hammer.

tubule /'tjuːbjuːl/ *n.* a small tube in a plant or an animal body. [L *tubulus*, dimin. of *tubus* tube]

tubulous /'tjuːbjʊləs/ *adj.* = TUBULAR.

TUC *abbr.* (in the UK) Trades Union Congress.

tuck /tʌk/ *v. & n.* —*v.* **1** *tr.* (often foll. by *in, up*) **a** draw, fold, or turn the outer or end parts of (cloth or clothes etc.) close together so as to be held; thrust in the edge of (a thing) so as to confine it (*tucked his shirt into his trousers; tucked the sheet under the mattress*). **b** thrust in the edges of bedclothes around (a person) (*came to tuck me in*). **2** *tr.* draw together into a small space (*tucked her legs under her; the bird tucked its head under its wing*). **3** *tr.* stow (a thing) away in a specified place or way (*tucked it in a corner; tucked it out of sight*). **4** *tr.* **a** make a stitched fold in (material, a garment, etc.). **b** shorten, tighten, or ornament with stitched folds. **5** *tr.* hit (a ball) to the desired place. —*n.* **1** a flattened usu. stitched fold in material, a garment, etc., often one of several parallel folds for shortening, tightening, or ornament. **2** *Brit. colloq.* food, esp. cakes and sweets eaten by children (also *attrib.: tuck box*). **3** *Naut.* the part of a ship's hull where the planks meet under the stern. **4** (in full **tuck position**) (in diving, gymnastics, etc.) a position with the knees bent upwards into the chest and the hands clasped round the shins. □**tuck in** *colloq.* eat food heartily. **tuck-in** *n. Brit. colloq.* a large meal. **tuck into** (or **away**) *colloq.* eat (food) heartily (*tucked into their dinner*; *could really tuck it away*). **tuck-net** (or **-seine**) a small net for taking caught fish from a larger net. **tuck shop** *Brit.* a small shop, esp. near or in a school, selling food to children. [ME *tukke, tokke,* f. MDu., MLG *tucken,* = OHG *zucchen* pull, rel. to TUG]

tucker /ˈtʌkə(r)/ *n. & v.* —*n.* **1** a person or thing that tucks. **2** *hist.* a piece of lace or linen etc. in or on a woman's bodice. **3** *Austral. colloq.* food. —*v.tr.* (esp. in *passive*; often foll. by *out*) *US colloq.* tire, exhaust. □**best bib and tucker** see BIB[1]. **tucker-bag** (or **-box**) *Austral. colloq.* a container for food.

tucket /ˈtʌkɪt/ *n. archaic* a flourish on a trumpet. [ONF *toquer* beat (a drum)]

tucking /ˈtʌkɪŋ/ *n.* a series of usu. stitched tucks in material or a garment.

-tude /tjuːd/ *suffix* forming abstract nouns (*altitude*; *attitude*; *solitude*). [from or after F *-tude* f. L *-tudo -tudinis*]

Tudor /ˈtjuːdə(r)/ *adj. & n. hist.* —*adj.* **1** of, characteristic of, or associated with the royal family of England ruling 1485-1603 or this period. **2** of or relating to the architectural style of this period, esp. with half-timbering and elaborately decorated houses. —*n.* a member of the Tudor royal family. □**Tudor rose** (in late Perpendicular decoration) a conventional five-lobed figure of a rose esp. a red rose encircling a white one. [Owen *Tudor* of Wales, grandfather of Henry VII]

Tues. *abbr.* (also **Tue.**) Tuesday.

Tuesday /ˈtjuːzdeɪ, -dɪ/ *n. & adv.* —*n.* the third day of the week, following Monday. —*adv.* **1** *colloq.* on Tuesday. **2** (**Tuesdays**) on Tuesdays; each Tuesday. [OE *Tīwesdæg* f. *Tīw* the Gmc god identified with Roman Mars]

tufa /ˈtjuːfə/ *n.* **1** a porous rock composed of calcium carbonate and formed round mineral springs. **2** = TUFF. □□**tufaceous** /-ˈfeɪʃəs/ *adj.* [It., var. of *tufo*: see TUFF]

tuff /tʌf/ *n.* rock formed by the consolidation of volcanic ash. □□**tuffaceous** /-ˈfeɪʃəs/ *adj.* [F *tuf, tuffe* f. It. *tufo* f. LL *tofus,* L TOPHUS]

tuffet /ˈtʌfɪt/ *n.* **1** = TUFT 1. **2** a low seat. [var. of TUFT]

tuft /tʌft/ *n. & v.* —*n.* **1** a bunch or collection of threads, grass, feathers, hair, etc., held or growing together at the base. **2** *Anat.* a bunch of small blood-vessels. —*v.* **1** *tr.* provide with a tuft or tufts. **2** *tr.* make depressions at regular intervals in (a mattress etc.) by passing a thread through. **3** *intr.* grow in tufts. □□**tufty** *adj.* [ME, prob. f. OF *tofe, toffe,* of unkn. orig.: for *-t* cf. GRAFT[1]]

tufted /ˈtʌftɪd/ *adj.* **1** having or growing in a tuft or tufts. **2** (of a bird) having a tuft of feathers on the head.

tug /tʌg/ *v. & n.* —*v.* (**tugged, tugging**) **1** *tr. &* (foll. by *at*) *intr.* pull hard or violently; jerk (*tugged it from my grasp*; *tugged at my sleeve*). **2** *tr.* tow (a ship etc.) by means of a tugboat. —*n.* **1** a hard, violent, or jerky pull (*gave a tug on the rope*). **2** a sudden strong emotional feeling (*felt a tug as I watched them go*). **3** a small powerful boat for towing larger boats and ships. **4** an aircraft towing a glider. **5** (of a horse's harness) a loop from a saddle supporting a shaft or trace. □**tug of love** *colloq.* a dispute over the custody of a child. **tug of war 1** a trial of strength between two sides pulling against each other on a rope. **2** a decisive or severe contest. □□**tugger** *n.* [ME *togge, tugge,* intensive f. Gmc: see TOW[1]]

tugboat /ˈtʌgbəʊt/ *n.* = TUG *n.* 3.

tui /ˈtuːɪ/ *n. NZ* a large honey-eater, *Prosthemadura novaeseelandiae,* native to New Zealand and having a long protrusible bill and glossy bluish-black plumage with two white tufts at the throat. [Maori]

tuition /tjuːˈɪʃ(ə)n/ *n.* **1** teaching or instruction, esp. if paid for (*driving tuition*; *music tuition*). **2** a fee for this. □□**tuitional** *adj.* [ME f. OF f. L *tuitio -onis* f. *tuēri tuit-* watch, guard]

tularaemia /ˌtuːləˈriːmɪə/ *n.* (*US* **tularemia**) a severe infectious disease of animals transmissible to man, caused by the bacterium *Pasteurella tularense* and characterized by ulcers at the site of infection, fever, and loss of weight. □□**tularaemic** *adj.* [mod.L f. *Tulare* County in California, where it was first observed]

tulip /ˈtjuːlɪp/ *n.* **1** any bulbous spring-flowering plant of the genus *Tulipa,* esp. one of the many cultivated forms with showy cup-shaped flowers of various colours and markings. **2** a flower of this plant. □**tulip-root** a disease of oats etc. causing the base of the stem to swell. **tulip-tree** any of various trees esp. of the genus *Liriodendron,* producing tulip-like flowers. **tulip-wood** a fine-grained pale timber produced by the N. American tree *Liriodendron tulipifera.* [orig. *tulipa*(n) f. mod.L *tulipa* f. Turk. *tul(i)band* f. Pers. *dulband* TURBAN (from the shape of the expanded flower)]

tulle /tjuːl/ *n.* a soft fine silk etc. net for veils and dresses. [*Tulle* in SW France, where it was first made]

tum /tʌm/ *n. colloq.* stomach. [abbr. of TUMMY]

tumble /ˈtʌmb(ə)l/ *v. & n.* —*v.* **1** *intr. & tr.* fall or cause to fall suddenly, clumsily, or headlong. **2** *intr.* fall rapidly in amount etc. (*prices tumbled*). **3** *intr.* (often foll. by *about, around*) roll or toss erratically or helplessly to and fro. **4** *intr.* move or rush in a headlong or blundering manner (*the children tumbled out of the car*). **5** *intr.* (often foll. by *to*) *colloq.* grasp the meaning or hidden implication of an idea, circumstance, etc. (*they quickly tumbled to our intentions*). **6** *tr.* overturn; fling or push roughly or carelessly. **7** *intr.* perform acrobatic feats, esp. somersaults. **8** *tr.* rumple or disarrange; pull about; disorder. **9** *tr.* dry (washing) in a tumble-drier. **10** *tr.* clean (castings, gemstones, etc.) in a tumbling-barrel. **11** *intr.* (of a pigeon) turn over backwards in flight. —*n.* **1** a sudden or headlong fall. **2** a somersault or other acrobatic feat. **3** an untidy or confused state. □**tumble-drier** *n.* a machine for drying washing in a heated rotating drum. **tumble-dry** *v.tr. & intr.* (**-dries, -dried**) dry in a tumble-drier. **tumbling-barrel** (or **-box** etc.) a revolving device containing an abrasive substance, in which castings, gemstones, etc., are cleaned by friction. **tumbling-bay 1** the outfall of a river, reservoir, etc. **2** a pool into which this flows. [ME *tumbel* f. MLG *tummelen,* OHG *tumalōn* frequent. of *tūmōn*: cf. OE *tumbian* dance]

tumbledown /ˈtʌmb(ə)lˌdaʊn/ *adj.* falling or fallen into ruin; dilapidated.

tumbler /ˈtʌmblə(r)/ *n.* **1** a drinking-glass with no handle or foot (formerly with a rounded bottom so as not to stand upright). **2** an acrobat, esp. one performing somersaults. **3** (in full **tumbler-drier**) = *tumble-drier.* **4 a** a pivoted piece in a lock that holds the bolt until lifted by a key. **b** a notched pivoted plate in a gunlock. **5** a kind of pigeon that turns over backwards in flight. **6** an electrical switch worked by pushing a small sprung lever. **7** a toy figure that rocks when touched. **8** = *tumbling-barrel* (see TUMBLE). □□**tumblerful** *n.* (*pl.* **-fuls**).

tumbleweed /ˈtʌmb(ə)lˌwiːd/ *n. US & Austral.* a plant, *Amaranthus albus,* that forms a globular bush that breaks off in late summer and is tumbled about by the wind.

tumbrel /ˈtʌmbr(ə)l/ *n.* (also **tumbril** /-rɪl/) *hist.* **1** an open cart in which condemned persons were conveyed to their execution, esp. to the guillotine during the French Revolution. **2** a two-wheeled covered cart for carrying tools, ammunition, etc. **3** a cart that tips to empty its load, esp. one carrying dung. [ME f. OF *tumberel, tomberel* f. *tomber* fall]

tumefy /ˈtjuːmɪˌfaɪ/ *v.* (**-ies, -ied**) **1** *intr.* swell, inflate; be inflated. **2** *tr.* cause to do this. □□**tumefacient**

/-'feɪʃ(ə)nt/ *adj.* **tumefaction** /-'fækʃ(ə)n/ *n.* [F *tu-méfier* f. L *tumefacere* f. *tumēre* swell]

tumescent /tjʊ'mes(ə)nt/ *adj.* **1** becoming tumid; swelling. **2** swelling as a response to sexual stimulation. □□ **tumescence** *n.* **tumescently** *adv.* [L *tumescere* (as TUMEFY)]

tumid /'tju:mɪd/ *adj.* **1** (of parts of the body etc.) swollen, inflated. **2** (of a style etc.) inflated, bombastic. □□ **tumidity** /-'mɪdɪtɪ/ *n.* **tumidly** *adv.* **tumidness** *n.* [L *tumidus* f. *tumēre* swell]

tummy /'tʌmɪ/ *n.* (*pl.* **-ies**) *colloq.* the stomach. □ **tummy-button** the navel. [childish pronunc. of STOMACH]

tumour /'tju:mə(r)/ *n.* (*US* **tumor**) a swelling, esp. from an abnormal growth of tissue. □□ **tumorous** *adj.* [L *tumor* f. *tumēre* swell]

tumult /'tju:mʌlt/ *n.* **1** an uproar or din, esp. of a disorderly crowd. **2** an angry demonstration by a mob; a riot; a public disturbance. **3** a conflict of emotions in the mind. [ME f. OF *tumulte* or L *tumultus*]

tumultuous /tjʊ'mʌltjʊəs/ *adj.* **1** noisily vehement; uproarious; making a tumult (*a tumultuous welcome*). **2** disorderly. **3** agitated. □□ **tumultuously** *adv.* **tumultuousness** *n.* [OF *tumultuous* or L *tumultuosus* (as TUMULT)]

tumulus /'tju:mjʊləs/ *n.* (*pl.* **tumuli** /-ˌlaɪ/) an ancient burial mound or barrow. □□ **tumular** *adj.* [L f. *tumēre* swell]

tun /tʌn/ *n. & v.* — *n.* **1** a large beer or wine cask. **2** a brewer's fermenting-vat. **3** a measure of capacity, equal to 252 wine gallons. — *v.tr.* (**tunned, tunning**) store (wine etc.) in a tun. [OE *tunne* f. med.L *tunna*, prob. of Gaulish orig.]

tuna[1] /'tju:nə/ *n.* (*pl.* same or **tunas**) **1** any marine fish of the family Scombridae native to tropical and warm waters, having a round body and pointed snout, and used for food. Also called TUNNY. **2** (in full **tuna-fish**) the flesh of the tuna or tunny, usu. tinned in oil or brine. [Amer. Sp., perh. f. Sp. *atún* tunny]

tuna[2] /'tju:nə/ *n.* **1** a prickly pear, esp. *Opuntia tuna*. **2** the fruit of this. [Sp. f. Haitian]

tundish /'tʌndɪʃ/ *n.* **1** a wooden funnel esp. in brewing. **2** an intermediate reservoir in metal-founding.

tundra /'tʌndrə/ *n.* a vast level treeless Arctic region usu. with a marshy surface and underlying permafrost. [Lappish]

tune /tju:n/ *n. & v.* — *n.* a melody with or without harmony. — *v.* **1** *tr.* put (a musical instrument) in tune. **2 a** *tr.* adjust (a radio receiver etc.) to the particular frequency of the required signals. **b** *intr.* (foll. by *in*) adjust a radio receiver to the required signal (*tuned in to Radio 2*). **3** *tr.* adjust (an engine etc.) to run smoothly and efficiently. **4** *tr.* (foll. by *to*) adjust or adapt to a required or different purpose, situation, etc. **5** *intr.* (foll. by *with*) be in harmony with. □ **in tune 1** having the correct pitch or intonation (*sings in tune*). **2** (usu. foll. by *with*) harmonizing with one's company, surroundings, etc. **out of tune 1** not having the correct pitch or intonation (*always plays out of tune*). **2** (usu. foll. by *with*) clashing with one's company etc. **to the tune of** *colloq.* to the considerable sum or amount of. **tune up 1** (of an orchestra) bring the instruments to the proper or uniform pitch. **2** begin to play or sing. **3** bring to the most efficient condition. □□ **tunable** *adj.* (also **tuneable**). [ME: unexpl. var. of TONE]

tuneful /'tju:nfʊl/ *adj.* melodious, musical. □□ **tunefully** *adv.* **tunefulness** *n.*

tuneless /'tju:nlɪs/ *adj.* **1** unmelodious, unmusical. **2** out of tune. □□ **tunelessly** *adv.* **tunelessness** *n.*

tuner /'tju:nə(r)/ *n.* **1** a person who tunes musical instruments, esp. pianos. **2** a device for tuning a radio receiver.

tung /tʌŋ/ *n.* (in full **tung-tree**) a tree, *Aleurites fordii*, native to China, bearing poisonous fruits

containing seeds that yield oil. □ **tung oil** this oil used in paints and varnishes. [Chin. *tong*]

tungsten /'tʌŋst(ə)n/ *n. Chem.* a steel-grey dense metallic element with a very high melting-point, occurring naturally in scheelite and used for the filaments of electric lamps and for alloying steel etc. ¶ Symb.: **W**. □ **tungsten carbide** a very hard black substance used in making dies and cutting tools. □□ **tungstate** /-stert/ *n.* **tungstic** *adj.* **tungstous** *adj.* [Sw. f. *tung* heavy + *sten* stone]

tunic /'tju:nɪk/ *n.* **1 a** a close-fitting short coat of police or military etc. uniform. **b** a loose, often sleeveless garment usu. reaching to about the knees, as worn in ancient Greece and Rome. **c** any of various loose, pleated dresses gathered at the waist with a belt or cord. **d** a tunicle. **2** *Zool.* the rubbery outer coat of an ascidian etc. **3** *Bot.* **a** any of the concentric layers of a bulb. **b** the tough covering of a part of this. **4** *Anat.* a membrane enclosing or lining an organ. [F *tunique* or L *tunica*]

tunica /'tju:nɪkə/ *n.* (*pl.* **tunicae** /-ˌki:/) *Bot. & Anat.* = TUNIC 3, 4. [L]

tunicate /'tju:nɪkət, -ˌkeɪt/ *n. & adj.* — *n.* any marine animal of the subphylum Urochordata having a rubbery or hard outer coat, including sea squirts. — *adj.* **1** *Zool.* of or relating to this subphylum. **2 a** *Zool.* enclosed in a tunic. **b** *Bot.* having concentric layers. [L *tunicatus* past part. of *tunicare* clothe with a tunic (as TUNICA)]

tunicle /'tju:nɪk(ə)l/ *n.* a short vestment worn by a bishop or subdeacon at the Eucharist etc. [ME f. OF *tunicle* or L *tunicula* dimin. of TUNICA]

tuning /'tju:nɪŋ/ *n.* the process or a system of putting a musical instrument in tune. □ **tuning-fork** a two-pronged steel fork that gives a particular note when struck, used in tuning. **tuning-peg** (or **pin** etc.) a peg or pin etc. attached to the strings of a stringed instrument and turned to alter their tension in tuning.

tunnel /'tʌn(ə)l/ *n. & v.* — *n.* **1** an artificial underground passage through a hill or under a road or river etc., esp. for a railway or road to pass through, or in a mine. **2** an underground passage dug by a burrowing animal. **3** a prolonged period of difficulty or suffering (esp. in metaphors, e.g. *the end of the tunnel*). **4** a tube containing a propeller shaft etc. — *v.* (**tunnelled, tunnelling;** *US* **tunneled, tunneling**) **1** *intr.* (foll. by *through, into*, etc.) make a tunnel through (a hill etc.). **2** *tr.* make (one's way) by tunnelling. **3** *intr. Physics* pass through a potential barrier. □ **tunnel diode** *Electronics* a two-terminal semiconductor diode using tunnelling electrons to perform high-speed switching operations. **tunnel-kiln** a kiln in which ceramic ware is carried on trucks along a continuously-heated passage. **tunnel-net** a fishing-net wide at the mouth and narrow at the other end. **tunnel vision 1** vision that is defective in not adequately including objects away from the centre of the field of view. **2** *colloq.* inability to grasp the wider implications of a situation. □□ **tunneller** *n.* [ME f. OF *tonel* dimin. of *tonne* TUN]

tunny /'tʌnɪ/ *n.* (*pl.* same or **-ies**) = TUNA[1]. [F *thon* f. Prov. *ton*, f. L *thunnus* f. Gk *thunnos*]

tup /tʌp/ *n. & v.* — *n.* **1** esp. *Brit.* a male sheep; a ram. **2** the striking-head of a pile-driver, etc. — *v.tr.* (**tupped, tupping**) esp. *Brit.* (of a ram) copulate with (a ewe). [ME *toje, tupe*, of unkn. orig.]

Tupamaro /ˌtu:pə'mɑːrəʊ/ *n.* (*pl.* **-os**) a Marxist urban guerilla in Uruguay. [*Tupac Amaru*, the names of two Inca leaders]

tupelo /'tju:pɪˌləʊ/ *n.* (*pl.* **-os**) **1** any of various Asian and N. American deciduous trees of the genus *Nyssa*, with colourful foliage and growing in swampy conditions. **2** the wood of this tree. [Creek f. *ito* tree + *opilwa* swamp]

Tupi /'tu:pɪ/ *n. & adj.* — *n.* (*pl.* same or **Tupis**) **1** a member of an American Indian people native to the

Amazon valley. **2** the language of this people. —*adj.* of or relating to this people or language. [native name]

tuppence /'tʌpəns/ *n. Brit.* = TWOPENCE. [phonet. spelling]

tuppenny /'tʌpənɪ/ *adj. Brit.* = TWOPENNY. [phonet. spelling]

Tupperware /'tʌpəˌweə(r)/ *n. propr.* a range of plastic containers for storing food. [*Tupper*, name of the US manufacturer, + WARE¹]

tuque /tuːk/ *n.* a Canadian stocking cap. [Can. F form of TOQUE]

turaco /'tʊərəˌkəʊ/ *n.* (also **touraco**) (*pl.* -os) any African bird of the family Musophagidae, with crimson and green plumage and a prominent crest. [F f. native W.Afr. name]

Turanian /tjʊ'reɪnɪən/ *n. & adj.* —*n.* the group of Asian languages that are neither Semitic nor Indo-European, esp. the Ural-Altaic family. —*adj.* of or relating to this group. [Pers. *Tūrān* region beyond the Oxus]

turban /'tɜːbən/ *n.* **1** a man's headdress of cotton or silk wound round a cap or the head, worn esp. by Muslims and Sikhs. **2** a woman's headdress or hat resembling this. □□ **turbaned** *adj.* [16th c. (also *tulbant* etc.), ult. f. Turk. *tülbent* f. Pers. *dulband*: cf. TULIP]

turbary /'tɜːbərɪ/ *n.* (*pl.* -ies) *Brit.* **1** the right of digging turf on common ground or on another's ground. **2** a place where turf or peat is dug. [ME f. AF *turberie*, OF *tourberie* f. *tourbe* TURF]

turbellarian /ˌtɜːbɪ'leərɪən/ *n. & adj.* —*n.* any usu. free-living flatworm of the class Turbellaria, having a ciliated surface. —*adj.* of or relating to this class. [mod.L *Turbellaria* f. L *turbella* dimin. of *turba* crowd: see TURBID]

turbid /'tɜːbɪd/ *adj.* **1** (of a liquid or colour) muddy, thick; not clear. **2** (of a style etc.) confused, disordered. □□ **turbidity** /-'bɪdɪtɪ/ *n.* **turbidly** *adv.* **turbidness** *n.* [L *turbidus* f. *turba* a crowd, a disturbance]

turbinate /'tɜːbɪnət/ *adj.* **1** shaped like a spinning-top or inverted cone. **2** (of a shell) with whorls decreasing rapidly in size. **3** *Anat.* (esp. of some nasal bones) shaped like a scroll. □□ **turbinal** *adj.* **turbination** /-'neɪʃ(ə)n/ *n.* [L *turbinatus* (as TURBINE)]

turbine /'tɜːbaɪn/ *n.* a rotary motor or engine driven by a flow of water, steam, gas, wind, etc., esp. to produce electrical power. [F f. L *turbo -binis* spinning-top, whirlwind]

turbit /'tɜːbɪt/ *n.* a breed of domestic pigeon of stout build with a neck frill and short beak. [app. f. L *turbo* top, from its figure]

turbo /'tɜːbəʊ/ *n.* (*pl.* -os) = TURBOCHARGER.

turbo- /'tɜːbəʊ/ *comb. form* turbine.

turbocharger /'tɜːbəʊˌtʃɑːdʒə(r)/ *n.* a supercharger driven by a turbine powered by the engine's exhaust gases.

turbofan /'tɜːbəʊˌfæn/ *n.* **1** a jet engine in which a turbine-driven fan provides additional thrust. **2** an aircraft powered by this.

turbojet /'tɜːbəʊˌdʒet/ *n. Aeron.* **1** a jet engine in which the jet also operates a turbine-driven compressor for the air drawn into the engine. **2** an aircraft powered by this.

turboprop /'tɜːbəʊˌprɒp/ *n. Aeron.* **1** a jet engine in which a turbine is used as in a turbojet and also to drive a propeller. **2** an aircraft powered by this.

turboshaft /'tɜːbəʊˌʃɑːft/ *n.* a gas turbine that powers a shaft for driving heavy vehicles, generators, pumps, etc.

turbosupercharger /ˌtɜːbəʊˈsuːpəˌtʃɑːdʒə(r)/ *n.* = TURBOCHARGER.

turbot /'tɜːbət/ *n.* **1** a flatfish, *Scophthalmus maximus*, having large bony tubercles on the body and head and prized as food. **2** any of various similar fishes including halibut. [ME f. OF f. OSw. *törnbut* f. *törn* thorn + *but* BUTT³]

turbulence /'tɜːbjʊləns/ *n.* **1** an irregularly fluctuating flow of air or fluid. **2** *Meteorol.* stormy conditions as a result of atmospheric disturbance. **3** a disturbance, commotion, or tumult.

turbulent /'tɜːbjʊlənt/ *adj.* **1** disturbed; in commotion. **2** (of a flow of air etc.) varying irregularly; causing disturbance. **3** tumultuous. **4** insubordinate, riotous. □□ **turbulently** *adv.* [L *turbulentus* f. *turba* crowd]

Turco /'tɜːkəʊ/ *n.* (*pl.* -os) *hist.* an Algerian soldier in the French army. [Sp., Port., & It., = TURK]

Turco- /'tɜːkəʊ/ *comb. form* (also **Turko-**) Turkish; Turkish and. [med.L (as TURK)]

Turcoman var. of TURKOMAN.

turd /tɜːd/ *n. coarse sl.* **1** a lump of excrement. **2** a term of contempt for a person. ¶ Often considered a taboo word, esp. in sense 2. [OE *tord* f. Gmc]

turdoid /'tɜːdɔɪd/ *adj.* thrushlike. [L *turdus* THRUSH¹]

tureen /tjʊə'riːn, tə-/ *n.* a deep covered dish for serving soup etc. [earlier *terrine*, *-ene* f. F *terrine* large circular earthenware dish, fem. of OF *terrin* earthen ult. f. L *terra* earth]

turf /tɜːf/ *n. & v.* —*n.* (*pl.* **turfs** or **turves**) **1 a** a layer of grass etc. with earth and matted roots as the surface of grassland. **b** a piece of this cut from the ground. **2** a slab of peat for fuel. **3** (prec. by *the*) **a** horse-racing generally. **b** a general term for racecourses. —*v.tr.* **1** cover (ground) with turf. **2** (foll. by *out*) esp. *Brit. colloq.* expel or eject (a person or thing). □ **turf accountant** *Brit.* a bookmaker. [OE f. Gmc]

turfman /'tɜːfmən/ *n.* (*pl.* -men) esp. *US* a devotee of horse-racing.

turfy /'tɜːfɪ/ *adj.* (**turfier**, **turfiest**) like turf; grassy.

turgescent /tɜː'dʒes(ə)nt/ *adj.* becoming turgid; swelling. □□ **turgescence** *n.*

turgid /'tɜːdʒɪd/ *adj.* **1** swollen, inflated, enlarged. **2** (of language) pompous, bombastic. □□ **turgidity** /-'dʒɪdɪtɪ/ *n.* **turgidly** *adv.* **turgidness** *n.* [L *turgidus* f. *turgēre* swell]

turgor /'tɜːgə(r)/ *n. Bot.* the rigidity of cells due to the absorption of water. [LL (as TURGID)]

turion /'tʊərɪən/ *n. Bot.* **1** a young shoot or sucker arising from an underground bud. **2** a bud formed by certain aquatic plants. [F f. L *turio -onis* shoot]

Turk /tɜːk/ *n.* **1 a** a native or national of Turkey in SE Europe and Asia Minor. **b** a person of Turkish descent. **2** a member of a Central Asian people from whom the Ottomans derived, speaking Turkic languages. **3** *offens.* a ferocious, wild, or unmanageable person. □ **Turk's cap** a martagon lily or other plant with turban-like flowers. **Turk's head** a turban-like ornamental knot. [ME, = F *Turc*, It. etc. *Turco*, med.L *Turcus*, Pers. & Arab. *Turk*, of unkn. orig.]

turkey /'tɜːkɪ/ *n.* (*pl.* -eys) **1** a large mainly domesticated game-bird, *Meleagris gallopavo*, orig. of N. America, having dark plumage with a green or bronze sheen, prized as food esp. on festive occasions including Christmas and, in the US, Thanksgiving. **2** the flesh of the turkey as food. **3** *US sl.* **a** a theatrical failure; a flop. **b** a stupid or inept person. □ **talk turkey** *US colloq.* talk frankly and straightforwardly; get down to business. **turkey buzzard** (or **vulture**) an American vulture, *Cathartes aura*. [16th c.: short for *turkeycock* or *turkeyhen*, orig. applied to the guinea-fowl which was imported through Turkey, and then erron. to the Amer. bird]

Turkey carpet /'tɜːkɪ/ *n.* = Turkish carpet.

turkeycock /'tɜːkɪˌkɒk/ *n.* **1** a male turkey. **2** a pompous or self-important person.

Turkey red /'tɜːkɪ/ *n.* **1** a scarlet pigment obtained from the madder or alizarin. **2** a cotton cloth dyed with this.

Turki /'tɜːkɪ/ *adj. & n.* —*adj.* of or relating to a group of Ural-Altaic languages (including Turkish) and the peoples speaking them. —*n.* the Turki group of languages. □□ **Turkic** *adj.* [Pers. *turkī* (as TURK)]

Turkish /'tɜːkɪʃ/ adj. & n. —adj. of or relating to Turkey in SE Europe and Asia Minor, or to the Turks or their language. —n. this language. □**Turkish bath** 1 a hot-air or steam bath followed by washing, massage, etc. 2 (in sing. or pl.) a building for this. **Turkish carpet** a wool carpet with a thick pile and traditional bold design. **Turkish coffee** a strong black coffee. **Turkish delight** a sweet of lumps of flavoured gelatine coated in powdered sugar. **Turkish towel** a towel made of cotton terry.

Turko- var. of TURCO-.

Turkoman /'tɜːkəʊmən/ n. (also **Turcoman**) (pl. -mans) 1 a member of any of various Turkic peoples in Turkmenistan in SW Middle Asia. 2 the language of these peoples. □**Turkoman carpet** a traditional rich-coloured carpet with a soft long nap. [Pers. Turkumān (as TURK, mānistan resemble)]

turmeric /'tɜːmərɪk/ n. 1 an E. Indian plant, Curcuma longa, of the ginger family, yielding aromatic rhizomes used as a spice and for yellow dye. 2 this powdered rhizome used as a spice esp. in curry-powder. [16th-c. forms tarmaret etc. perh. f. F terre mérite and mod.L terra merita, of unkn. orig.]

turmoil /'tɜːmɔɪl/ n. 1 violent confusion; agitation. 2 din and bustle. [16th c.: orig. unkn.]

turn /tɜːn/ v. & n. —v. 1 tr. & intr. move around a point or axis so that the point or axis remains in a central position; give a rotary motion to or receive a rotary motion (turned the wheel; the wheel turns; the key turns in the lock). 2 tr. & intr. change in position so that a different side, end, or part becomes outermost or uppermost etc.; invert or reverse or cause to be inverted or reversed (turned inside out; turned it upside down). 3 a tr. give a new direction to (turn your face this way). b intr. take a new direction (turn left here; my thoughts have often turned to you). 4 tr. aim in a certain way (turned the hose on them). 5 intr. & tr. (foll. by into) change in nature, form, or condition to (turned into a dragon; then turned him into a frog; turned the book into a play). 6 intr. (foll. by to) a apply oneself to; set about (turned to doing the ironing). b have recourse to; begin to indulge in habitually (turned to drink; turned to me for help). c go on to consider next (let us now turn to your report). 7 intr. & tr. become or cause to become (turned hostile; has turned informer; your comment turned them angry). 8 a tr. & intr. (foll. by against) make or become hostile to (has turned them against us). b intr. (foll. by on, upon) become hostile to; attack (suddenly turned on them). 9 intr. (of hair or leaves) change colour. 10 intr. (of milk) become sour. 11 intr. (of the stomach) be nauseated. 12 intr. (of the head) become giddy. 13 tr. cause (milk) to become sour, (the stomach) to be nauseated, or (the head) to become giddy. 14 tr. translate (turn it into French). 15 tr. move to the other side of; go round (turned the corner). 16 tr. pass the age or time of (he has turned 40; it has now turned 4 o'clock). 17 intr. (foll. by on) depend on; be determined by (it all turns on the weather tomorrow). 18 tr. send or put into a specified place or condition; cause to go (was turned loose; turned the water out into a basin). 19 tr. perform (a somersault etc.) with rotary motion. 20 tr. remake (a garment or, esp., a sheet) putting the worn outer side on the inside. 21 tr. make (a profit). 22 tr. divert (a bullet). 23 tr. blunt (the edge of a knife, slot of a screw-head, etc.). 24 tr. shape (an object) on a lathe. 25 tr. give an (esp. elegant) form to (turn a compliment). 26 intr. Golf begin the second half of a round. 27 tr. (esp. as **turned** adj.) Printing invert (type) to make it appear upside down (a turned comma). 28 tr. pass round (the flank etc. of an army) so as to attack it from the side or rear. 29 intr. (of the tide) change from flood to ebb or vice versa. —n. 1 the act or process or an instance of turning; rotary motion (a single turn of the handle). 2 a a changed or a change of direction or tendency (took a sudden turn to the left). b a deflection or deflected part (full of twists and turns). 3 a point at which a turning or change occurs. 4 a turning of a road. 5 a change of the tide from ebb to flow or from flow to ebb. 6 a change in the course of events. 7 a tendency or disposition (is of a mechanical turn of mind). 8 an opportunity or obligation etc. that comes successively to each of several persons etc. (your turn will come; my turn to read). 9 a short walk or ride (shall take a turn in the garden). 10 a short performance on stage or in a circus etc. 11 service of a specified kind (did me a good turn). 12 purpose (served my turn). 13 colloq. a momentary nervous shock or ill feeling (gave me quite a turn). 14 Mus. an ornament consisting of the principal note with those above and below it. 15 one round in a coil of rope etc. 16 Printing a an inverted type as a temporary substitute for a missing letter. b a letter turned wrong side up. 17 a Brit. the difference between the buying and selling price of stocks etc. b a profit made from this. □**at every turn** continually; at each new stage etc. **by turns** in rotation of individuals or groups; alternately. **in turn** in succession; one by one. **in one's turn** when one's turn or opportunity comes. **not know which way** (or where) **to turn** be completely at a loss, unsure how to act, etc. **not turn a hair** see HAIR. **on the turn** 1 changing. 2 (of milk) becoming sour. 3 at the turning-point. **out of turn** 1 at a time when it is not one's turn. 2 inappropriately; inadvisedly or tactlessly (did I speak out of turn?). **take turns** (or **take it in turns**) act or work alternately or in succession. **to a turn** (esp. cooked) to exactly the right degree etc. **turn about** move so as to face in a new direction. **turn-about** n. 1 an act of turning about. 2 an abrupt change of policy etc. **turn and turn about** alternately. **turn around** esp. US = turn round. **turn away** 1 turn to face in another direction. 2 refuse to accept; reject. 3 send away. **turn back** 1 begin or cause to retrace one's steps. 2 fold back. **turn one's back on** see BACK. **turn-bench** a watchmaker's portable lathe. **turn-buckle** a device for tightly connecting parts of a metal rod or wire. **turn-cap** a revolving chimney-top. **turn the corner** 1 pass round it into another street. 2 pass the critical point in an illness, difficulty, etc. **turn a deaf ear** see DEAF. **turn down** 1 reject (a proposal, application, etc.). 2 reduce the volume or strength of (sound, heat, etc.) by turning a knob etc. 3 fold down. 4 place downwards. **turn-down** (of a collar) turned down. **turn one's hand to** see HAND. **turn a person's head** see HEAD. **turn an honest penny** see HONEST. **turn in** 1 hand in or return. 2 achieve or register (a performance, score, etc.). 3 colloq. go to bed in the evening. 4 fold inwards. 5 incline inwards (his toes turn in). 6 colloq. abandon (a plan etc.). **turn in one's grave** see GRAVE[1]. **turn off** 1 a stop the flow or operation of (water, electricity, etc.) by means of a tap, switch, etc. b operate (a tap, switch, etc.) to achieve this. 2 a enter a side-road. b (of a side-road) lead off from another road. 3 colloq. repel; cause to lose interest (turned me right off with their complaining). 4 dismiss from employment. **turn-off** n. 1 a turning off a main road. 2 colloq. something that repels or causes a loss of interest. **turn of speed** the ability to go fast when necessary. **turn on** 1 a start the flow or operation of (water, electricity, etc.) by means of a tap, switch, etc. b operate (a tap, switch, etc.) to achieve this. 2 colloq. excite; stimulate the interest of, esp. sexually. 3 tr. & intr. colloq. intoxicate or become intoxicated with drugs. **turn-on** n. colloq. a person or thing that causes (esp. sexual) arousal. **turn on one's heel** see HEEL[1]. **turn out** 1 expel. 2 extinguish (an electric light etc.). 3 dress or equip (well turned out). 4 produce (manufactured goods etc.). 5 empty or clean out (a room etc.). 6 empty (a pocket) to see the contents. 7 colloq. get out of bed. 8 go out of doors. 8 colloq. assemble; attend a meeting etc. 9 (often foll. by to + infin. or that + clause) prove to be the case;

result (*turned out to be true*; *we shall see how things turn out*). **10** *Mil.* call (a guard) from the guardroom.
turn over 1 reverse or cause to reverse vertical position; bring the under or reverse side into view (*turn over the page*). **2** upset; fall or cause to fall over. **3 a** cause (an engine) to run. **b** (of an engine) start running. **4** consider thoroughly. **5** (foll. by *to*) transfer the care or conduct of (a person or thing) to (a person) (*shall turn it all over to my deputy*; *turned him over to the authorities*). **6** do business to the amount of (*turns over £5000 a week*). **turn over a new leaf** improve one's conduct or performance. **turn round 1** turn so as to face in a new direction. **2 a** *Commerce* unload and reload (a ship, vehicle, etc.). **b** receive, process, and send out again; cause to progress through a system. **3** adopt new opinions or policy. **turn-round** *n.* **1 a** the process of loading and unloading. **b** the process of receiving, processing, and sending out again; progress through a system. **2** the reversal of an opinion or tendency. **turn the scales** see SCALE². **turn the tables** see TABLE. **turn tail** turn one's back; run away. **turn the tide** reverse the trend of events. **turn to** set about one's work (*came home and immediately turned to*). **turn to account** see ACCOUNT. **turn turtle** see TURTLE. **turn up 1** increase the volume or strength of (sound, heat, etc.) by turning a knob etc. **2** place upwards. **3** discover or reveal. **4** be found, esp. by chance (*it turned up on a rubbish dump*). **5** happen or present itself; (of a person) put in an appearance (*a few people turned up late*). **6** *colloq.* cause to vomit (*the sight turned me up*). **7** shorten (a garment) by increasing the size of the hem. **turn-up** *n.* **1** *Brit.* the lower turned up end of a trouser leg. **2** *colloq.* an unexpected (esp. welcome) happening; a surprise. [OE *tyrnan*, *turnian* f. L *tornare* f. *tornus* lathe f. Gk *tornos* lathe, circular movement: prob. reinforced in ME f. OF *turner*, *torner*]

turncoat /ˈtɜːnkəʊt/ *n.* a person who changes sides in a conflict, dispute, etc.

turncock /ˈtɜːnkɒk/ *n.* an official employed to turn on water for the mains supply etc.

turner /ˈtɜːnə(r)/ *n.* **1** a person or thing that turns. **2** a person who works with a lathe. [ME f. OF *tornere* *-eor* f. LL *tornator* (as TURN)]

turnery /ˈtɜːnərɪ/ *n.* **1** objects made on a lathe. **2** work with a lathe.

turning /ˈtɜːnɪŋ/ *n.* **1 a** a road that branches off another. **b** a place where this occurs. **2 a** use of the lathe. **b** (in *pl.*) chips or shavings from a lathe. □**turning-circle** the smallest circle in which a vehicle can turn without reversing. **turning-point** a point at which a decisive change occurs.

turnip /ˈtɜːnɪp/ *n.* **1** a cruciferous plant, *Brassica rapa*, with a large white globular root and sprouting leaves. **2** this root used as a vegetable. **3** a large thick old-fashioned watch. □**turnip-top** the leaves of the turnip eaten as a vegetable. □□ **turnipy** *adj.* [earlier *turnep(e)* f. *neep* f. L *napus*: first element of uncert. orig.]

turnkey /ˈtɜːnkiː/ *n. & adj.* —*n.* (*pl.* **-eys**) *archaic* a gaoler. —*adj.* (of a contract etc.) providing for a supply of equipment in a state ready for operation.

turnout /ˈtɜːnaʊt/ *n.* **1** the number of people attending a meeting, voting at an election, etc. (*rain reduced the turnout*). **2** the quantity of goods produced in a given time. **3** a set or display of equipment, clothes, etc.

turnover /ˈtɜːnˌəʊvə(r)/ *n.* **1** the act or an instance of turning over. **2** the amount of money taken in a business. **3** the number of people entering and leaving employment etc. **4** a small pie or tart made by folding a piece of pastry over a filling.

turnpike /ˈtɜːnpaɪk/ *n.* **1** *hist.* a defensive frame of spikes. **2** *hist.* **a** a toll-gate. **b** a road on which a toll was collected at a toll-gate. **3** *US* a motorway on which a toll is charged.

turnsick /ˈtɜːnsɪk/ *n.* = STURDY *n.*

turnside /ˈtɜːnsaɪd/ *n.* giddiness in dogs and cattle.

turnsole /ˈtɜːnsəʊl/ *n.* any of various plants supposed to turn with the sun. [OF *tournesole* f. Prov. *tournasol* f. L *tornare* TURN + *sol* sun]

turnspit /ˈtɜːnspɪt/ *n. hist.* a person or small dog used to turn a spit.

turnstile /ˈtɜːnstaɪl/ *n.* a gate for admission or exit, with revolving arms allowing people through singly.

turnstone /ˈtɜːnstəʊn/ *n.* any wading bird of the genus *Arenaria*, related to the plover, that looks under stones for small animals to eat.

turntable /ˈtɜːnˌteɪb(ə)l/ *n.* **1** a circular revolving plate supporting a gramophone record that is being played. **2** a circular revolving platform for turning a railway locomotive or other vehicle.

turpentine /ˈtɜːpənˌtaɪn/ *n. & v.* —*n.* an oleo-resin secreted by several trees esp. of the genus *Pinus*, *Pistacia*, *Syncarpia*, or *Copaifera*, and used in various commercial preparations. —*v.tr.* apply turpentine to. □**Chian turpentine** the type of turpentine secreted by the terebinth. **oil of turpentine** a volatile pungent oil distilled from turpentine, used in mixing paints and varnishes, and in medicine. [ME f. OF *ter(e)bentine* f. L *ter(e)binthina* (*resina* resin) (as TEREBINTH)]

turpeth /ˈtɜːpɪθ/ *n.* (in full **turpeth root**) the root of an E. Indian plant, *Ipomoea turpethum*, used as a cathartic. [ME f. med.L *turbit(h)um* f. Arab. & Pers. *turbid*]

turpitude /ˈtɜːpɪˌtjuːd/ *n. formal* baseness, depravity, wickedness. [F *turpitude* or L *turpitudo* f. *turpis* disgraceful, base]

turps /tɜːps/ *n. colloq.* oil of turpentine. [abbr.]

turquoise /ˈtɜːkwɔɪz, -kwɑːz/ *n.* **1** a semiprecious stone, usu. opaque and greenish- or sky-blue, consisting of hydrated copper aluminium phosphate. **2** a greenish-blue colour. [ME *turkeis* etc. f. OF *turqueise* (later *-oise*) Turkish (stone)]

turret /ˈtʌrɪt/ *n.* **1** a small tower, usu. projecting from the wall of a building as a decorative addition. **2** a low flat usu. revolving armoured tower for a gun and gunners in a ship, aircraft, fort, or tank. **3** a rotating holder for tools in a lathe etc. □**turret lathe** = *capstan lathe*. □□ **turreted** *adj.* [ME f. OF *to(u)rete* dimin. of *to(u)r* TOWER]

turtle /ˈtɜːt(ə)l/ *n.* **1** any of various marine or freshwater reptiles of the order Chelonia, encased in a shell of bony plates, and having flippers or webbed toes used in swimming. **2** the flesh of the turtle, esp. used for soup. **3** *Computing* a directional cursor in a computer graphics system which can be instructed to move around a screen. □**turn turtle** capsize. **turtle-neck 1** a high close-fitting neck on a knitted garment. **2** *US* = *polo-neck*. [app. alt. of *tortue*: see TORTOISE]

turtle-dove /ˈtɜːt(ə)lˌdʌv/ *n.* any wild dove of the genus *Streptopelia*, esp. *S. turtur*, noted for its soft cooing and its affection for its mate and young. [archaic *turtle* (in the same sense) f. OE *turtla*, *turtle* f. L *turtur*, of imit. orig.]

turves *pl.* of TURF.

Tuscan /ˈtʌskən/ *n. & adj.* —*n.* **1** an inhabitant of Tuscany in central Italy. **2** the classical Italian language of Tuscany. —*adj.* **1** of or relating to Tuscany or the Tuscans. **2** *Archit.* denoting the least ornamented of the classical orders. □**Tuscan straw** fine yellow wheat-straw used for hats etc. [ME f. F f. L *Tuscanus* f. *Tuscus* Etruscan]

tush¹ /tʌʃ/ *int. archaic* expressing strong disapproval or scorn. [ME: imit.]

tush² /tʌʃ/ *n.* **1** a long pointed tooth, esp. a canine tooth of a horse. **2** an elephant's short tusk. [OE *tusc* TUSK]

tusk /tʌsk/ *n. & v.* —*n.* **1** a long pointed tooth, esp. protruding from a closed mouth, as in the elephant, walrus, etc. **2** a tusklike tooth or other object. —*v.tr.* gore, thrust at, or tear up with a tusk or tusks. □**tusk shell 1** any of various molluscs of the class Scaphopoda. **2** its long tubular tusk-shaped shell. □□ **tusked** adj. (also in comb.). **tusky** adj. [ME alt. of OE tux var. of tusc: cf. TUSH²]

tusker /'tʌskə(r)/ n. an elephant or wild boar with well-developed tusks.

tussah US var. of TUSSORE.

tusser var. of TUSSORE.

tussive /'tʌsɪv/ adj. of or relating to a cough. [L tussis cough]

tussle /'tʌs(ə)l/ n. & v. —n. a struggle or scuffle. —v.intr. engage in a tussle. [orig. Sc. & N.Engl., perh. dimin. of touse: see TOUSLE]

tussock /'tʌsək/ n. **1** a clump of grass etc. **2** (in full **tussock moth**) any moth of the genus Orgyia etc., with tufted larvae. □ **tussock grass** grass growing in tussocks, esp. Poa flabellata from Patagonia etc. □□ **tussocky** adj. [16th c.: perh. alt. f. dial. tusk tuft]

tussore /'tʌsɔː(r), 'tʌsə(r)/ n. (also **tusser**, US **tussah** /'tʌsə(r)/) **1** an Indian or Chinese silkworm, Antereae mylitta, yielding strong but coarse brown silk. **2** (in full **tussore-silk**) silk from this and some other silkworms. [Urdu f. Hindi tasar f. Skr. tasara shuttle]

tut var. of TUT-TUT.

tutelage /'tjuːtɪlɪdʒ/ n. **1** guardianship. **2** the state or duration of being under this. **3** instruction, tuition. [L tutela f. tuēri tuit- or tut- watch]

tutelary /'tjuːtɪlərɪ/ adj. (also **tutelar** /-tɪlə(r)/) **1 a** serving as guardian. **b** relating to a guardian (tutelary authority). **2** giving protection (tutelary saint). [LL tutelaris, L -arius f. tutela: see TUTELAGE]

tutenag /'tuːtɪˌnæg/ n. **1** zinc imported from China and the E. Indies. **2** a white alloy like German silver. [Marathi tuttināg perh. f. Skr. tuttha copper sulphate + nāga tin, lead]

tutor /'tjuːtə(r)/ n. & v. —n. **1** a private teacher, esp. in general charge of a person's education. **2** a university teacher supervising the studies or welfare of assigned undergraduates. **3** Brit. a book of instruction in a subject. —v. **1** tr. act as a tutor to. **2** intr. work as a tutor. **3** tr. restrain, discipline. **4** intr. US receive tuition. □□ **tutorage** n. **tutorship** n. [ME f. AF tutour or L tutor f. tuēri tut- watch]

tutorial /tjuːˈtɔːrɪəl/ adj. & n. —adj. of or relating to a tutor or tuition. —n. a period of individual tuition given by a tutor. □□ **tutorially** adv. [L tutorius (as TUTOR)]

tutsan /'tʌts(ə)n/ n. a species of St John's wort, Hypericum androsaemum, formerly used to heal wounds etc. [ME f. AF tutsaine all healthy]

tutti /'tʊtɪ/ adv. & n. Mus. —adv. with all voices or instruments together. —n. (pl. **tuttis**) a passage to be performed in this way. [It., pl. of tutto all]

tutti-frutti /ˌtuːtɪˈfruːtɪ/ n. (pl. **-fruttis**) a confection, esp. ice-cream, of or flavoured with mixed fruits. [It., = all fruits]

tut-tut /tʌtˈtʌt/ int., n., & v. (also **tut** /tʌt/) —int. expressing rebuke, impatience, or contempt. —n. such an exclamation. —v.intr. (**-tutted**, **-tutting**) exclaim this. [imit. of a click of the tongue against the teeth]

tutty /'tʌtɪ/ n. impure zinc oxide or carbonate used as a polishing powder. [ME f. OF tutie f. med.L tutia f. Arab. tūtiyā]

tutu¹ /'tuːtuː/ n. a ballet dancer's short skirt of stiffened projecting frills. [F]

tutu² /'tuːtuː/ n. Bot. a shrub, Coriaria arborea, native to New Zealand, bearing poisonous purplish-black berries. [Maori]

tu-whit, tu-whoo /tʊˌwɪt tʊˈwuː/ n. a representation of the cry of an owl. [imit.]

tux /tʌks/ n. US colloq. = TUXEDO.

tuxedo /tʌkˈsiːdəʊ/ n. (pl. **-os** or **-oes**) US **1** a dinner-jacket. **2** a suit of clothes including this. [after a country club at Tuxedo Park, New York]

tuyère /twiːˈjeə(r), tuː-/ n. (also **tuyere**, **twyer** /'twaɪə(r)/) a nozzle through which air is forced into a furnace etc. [F f. tuyau pipe]

TV abbr. television.

TVP abbr. propr. textured vegetable protein (in foods made from vegetable but given a meatlike texture).

twaddle /'twɒd(ə)l/ n. & v. —n. useless, senseless, or dull writing or talk. —v.intr. indulge in this. □□ **twaddler** n. [alt. of earlier twattle, alt. of TATTLE]

twain /tweɪn/ adj. & n. archaic two (usu. in twain). [OE twegen, masc. form of twā TWO]

twang /twæŋ/ n. & v. —n. **1** a strong ringing sound made by the plucked string of a musical instrument or bow. **2** the nasal quality of a voice compared to this. —v. **1** intr. & tr. emit or cause to emit this sound. **2** tr. usu. derog. play (a tune or instrument) in this way. **3** tr. utter with a nasal twang. □□ **twangy** adj. [imit.]

'twas /twɒz, twəz/ archaic it was. [contr.]

twat /twɒt/ n. coarse sl. ¶ Usually considered a taboo word. **1** the female genitals. **2** Brit. a term of contempt for a person. [17th c.: orig. unkn.]

twayblade /'tweɪbleɪd/ n. any orchid of the genus Listera etc., with green or purple flowers and a single pair of leaves. [tway var. of TWAIN + BLADE]

tweak /twiːk/ v. & n. —v.tr. **1** pinch and twist sharply; pull with a sharp jerk; twitch. **2** make fine adjustments to (a mechanism). —n. an instance of tweaking. [prob. alt. of dial. twick & TWITCH¹]

twee /twiː/ adj. (**tweer** /'twiːə(r)/; **tweest** /'twiːɪst/) Brit. usu. derog. affectedly dainty or quaint. □□ **tweely** adv. **tweeness** n. [childish pronunc. of SWEET]

tweed /twiːd/ n. **1** a rough-surfaced woollen cloth, usu. of mixed flecked colours, orig. produced in Scotland. **2** (in pl.) clothes made of tweed. [orig. a misreading of tweel, Sc. form of TWILL, infl. by assoc. with the river Tweed]

Tweedledum and Tweedledee /ˌtwiːd(ə)lˈdʌm, ˌtwiːd(ə)lˈdiː/ n. a pair of persons or things that are virtually indistinguishable. [after the stock names of rival musicians]

tweedy /'twiːdɪ/ adj. (**tweedier**, **tweediest**) **1** of or relating to tweed cloth. **2** characteristic of the country gentry, heartily informal. □□ **tweedily** adv. **tweediness** n.

'tween /twiːn/ prep. archaic = BETWEEN. □ **'tween-decks** Naut. the space between decks. [contr.]

tweet /twiːt/ n. & v. —n. the chirp of a small bird. —v.intr. make a chirping noise. [imit.]

tweeter /'twiːtə(r)/ n. a loudspeaker designed to reproduce high frequencies.

tweezers /'twiːzəz/ n.pl. a small pair of pincers for taking up small objects, plucking out hairs, etc. [extended form of tweezes (cf. pincers etc.) pl. of obs. tweeze case for small instruments, f. etweese = étuis, pl. of ÉTUI]

twelfth /twelfθ/ n. & adj. —n. **1** the position in a sequence corresponding to the number 12 in the sequence 1-12. **2** something occupying this position. **3** each of twelve equal parts of a thing. **4** Mus. **a** an interval or chord spanning an octave and a fifth in the diatonic scale. **b** a note separated from another by this interval. —adj. that is the twelfth. □ **Twelfth Day** 6 Jan., the twelfth day after Christmas, the festival of the Epiphany. **twelfth man** a reserve member of a cricket team. **Twelfth Night** the evening of 5 Jan., the eve of the Epiphany. **twelfth part** = sense 3 of n. □□ **twelfthly** adv. [OE twelfta (as TWELVE)]

twelve /twelv/ n. & adj. —n. **1** one more than eleven; the product of two units and six units. **2** a symbol for this (12, xii, XII). **3** a size etc. denoted by twelve. **4** the time denoted by twelve o'clock (is it twelve yet?). **5** (**the Twelve**) the twelve apostles. **6** (**12**) Brit. (of films) classified as suitable for persons of 12 years and over. —adj. that amount to twelve. □ **twelve-note** (or **-tone**) Mus. using the twelve chromatic notes of the octave on an equal basis without dependence on a key system. [OE *twelf*(e) f. Gmc, prob. rel. to TWO]

twelvefold /'twelvfəʊld/ *adj*. & *adv*. **1** twelve times as much or as many. **2** consisting of twelve parts.

twelvemo /'twelvməʊ/ *n*. = DUODECIMO.

twelvemonth /'twelvmʌnθ/ *n. archaic* a year; a period of twelve months.

twenty /'twentɪ/ *n*. & *adj*. —*n*. (*pl*. **-ies**) **1** the product of two and ten. **2** a symbol for this (20, xx, XX). **3** (in *pl*.) the numbers from 20 to 29, esp. the years of a century or of a person's life. **4** *colloq*. a large indefinite number (*have told you twenty times*). —*adj*. that amount to twenty. □**twenty-first**, **-second**, etc. the ordinal numbers between twentieth and thirtieth. **twenty-one**, **-two**, etc. the cardinal numbers between twenty and thirty. **twenty-twenty** (or **20/20**) **1** denoting vision of normal acuity. **2** *colloq*. denoting clear perception or hindsight. □□**twentieth** *adj*. & *n*. **twentyfold** *adj*. & *adv*. [OE *twentig* (perh. as TWO, -TY²)]

'twere /twɜː(r)/ *archaic* it were. [contr.]

twerp /twɜːp/ *n*. (also **twirp**) *sl*. a stupid or objectionable person. [20th c.: orig. unkn.]

twibill /'twaɪbɪl/ *n*. a double-bladed battleaxe. [OE f. *twi*- double + BILL³]

twice /twaɪs/ *adv*. **1** two times (esp. of multiplication); on two occasions. **2** in double degree or quantity (*twice as good*). [ME *twiges* f. OE *twige* (as TWO, -s³)]

twiddle /'twɪd(ə)l/ *v*. & *n*. —*v*. **1** *tr*. & (foll. by *with* etc.) *intr*. twirl, adjust, or play randomly or idly. **2** *intr*. move twirlingly. —*n*. **1** an act of twiddling. **2** a twirled mark or sign. □**twiddle one's thumbs 1** make them rotate round each other. **2** have nothing to do. □□**twiddler** *n*. **twiddly** *adj*. [app. imit., after *twirl*, *twist*, and *fiddle*, *piddle*]

twig¹ /twɪg/ *n*. **1** a small branch or shoot of a tree or shrub. **2** *Anat*. a small branch of an artery etc. □□ **twigged** *adj*. (also in *comb*.). **twiggy** *adj*. [OE *twigge* f. a Gmc root *twi*- (unrecorded) as in TWICE, TWO]

twig² /twɪg/ *v.tr*. (**twigged**, **twigging**) *colloq*. **1** (also *absol*.) understand; grasp the meaning or nature of. **2** perceive, observe. [18th c.: orig. unkn.]

twilight /'twaɪlaɪt/ *n*. **1** the soft glowing light from the sky when the sun is below the horizon, esp. in the evening. **2** the period of this. **3** a faint light. **4** a state of imperfect knowledge or understanding. **5** a period of decline or destruction. □**twilight sleep** *Med*. a state of partial narcosis, esp. to ease the pain of childbirth. **twilight zone 1** an urban area that is becoming dilapidated. **2** any physical or conceptual area which is undefined or intermediate. [ME f. OE *twi*- two (in uncert. sense) + LIGHT¹]

twilit /'twaɪlɪt/ *adj*. (also **twilighted** /-ˌlaɪtɪd/) dimly illuminated by or as by twilight. [past part. of *twilight* (v.) f. TWILIGHT]

twill /twɪl/ *n*. & *v*. —*n*. a fabric so woven as to have a surface of diagonal parallel ridges. —*v.tr*. (esp. as **twilled** *adj*.) weave (fabric) in this way. □□**twilled** *adj*. [N.Engl. var. of obs. *twilly*, OE *twili*, f. *twi*- double, after L *bilix* (as BI-, *licium* thread)]

'twill /twɪl/ *archaic* it will. [contr.]

twin /twɪn/ *n*., *adj*., & *v*. —*n*. **1** each of a closely related or associated pair, esp. of children or animals born at a birth. **2** the exact counterpart of a person or thing. **3** a compound crystal one part of which is in a reversed position with reference to the other. **4** (**the Twins**) the zodiacal sign or constellation Gemini. —*adj*. **1** forming, or being one of, such a pair (*twin brothers*). **2** *Bot*. growing in pairs. **3** consisting of two closely connected and similar parts. —*v*. (**twinned**, **twinning**) **1** *tr*. & *intr*. **a** join intimately together. **b** (foll. by *with*) pair. **2** *intr*. bear twins. **3** *intr*. grow as a twin crystal. **4** *intr*. & *tr*. *Brit*. link or cause (a town) to link with one in a different country, for the purposes of friendship and cultural exchange. □**twin bed** each of a pair of single beds. **twin-engined** having two engines. **twin-screw** (of a ship) having two propellers on separate shafts

with opposite twists. **twin set** esp. *Brit*. a woman's matching cardigan and jumper. **twin town** *Brit*. a town which is twinned with another. □□**twinning** *n*. [OE *twinn* double, f. *twi*- two: cf. ON *twinnr*]

twine /twaɪn/ *n*. & *v*. —*n*. **1** a strong thread or string of two or more strands of hemp or cotton etc. twisted together. **2** a coil or twist. **3** a tangle; an interlacing. —*v*. **1** *tr*. form (a string or thread etc.) by twisting strands together. **2** *tr*. form (a garland etc.) of interwoven material. **3** *tr*. (often foll. by *with*) garland (a brow etc.). **4** *intr*. (often foll. by *round*, *about*) coil or wind. **5** *intr*. & *refl*. (of a plant) grow in this way. □□**twiner** *n*. [OE *twīn*, *twigin* linen, ult. f. the stem of *twi*- two]

twinge /twɪndʒ/ *n*. & *v*. —*n*. a sharp momentary local pain or pang (*a twinge of toothache*; *a twinge of conscience*). —*v.intr*. & *tr*. experience or cause to experience a twinge. [*twinge* (v.) pinch, wring f. OE *twengan* f. Gmc]

twinkle /'twɪŋk(ə)l/ *v*. & *n*. —*v*. **1** *intr*. (of a star or light etc.) shine with rapidly intermittent gleams. **2** *intr*. (of the eyes) sparkle. **3** *intr*. (of the feet in dancing) move lightly and rapidly. **4** *tr*. emit (a light or signal) in quick gleams. **5** *tr*. blink or wink (one's eyes). —*n*. **1 a** a sparkle or gleam of the eyes. **b** a blink or wink. **2** a slight flash of light; a glimmer. **3** a short rapid movement. □**in a twinkle** (or **a twinkling** or **the twinkling of an eye**) in an instant. □□**twinkler** *n*. **twinkly** *adj*. [OE *twinclian*]

twirl /twɜːl/ *v*. & *n*. —*v.tr*. & *intr*. spin or swing or twist quickly and lightly round. —*n*. **1** a twirling motion. **2** a form made by twirling, esp. a flourish made with a pen. □□**twirler** *n*. **twirly** *adj*. [16th c.: prob. alt. (after *whirl*) of obs. *tirl* TRILL]

twirp var. of TWERP.

twist /twɪst/ *v*. & *n*. —*v*. **1 a** *tr*. change the form of by rotating one end and not the other or the two ends in opposite directions. **b** *intr*. undergo such a change; take a twisted position (*twisted round in his seat*). **c** *tr*. wrench or pull out of shape with a twisting action (*twisted my ankle*). **2** *tr*. **a** wind (strands etc.) about each other. **b** form (a rope etc.) by winding the strands. **c** (foll. by *with*, *in with*) interweave. **d** form by interweaving or twining. **3 a** *tr*. give a spiral form to (a rod, column, cord, etc.) as by rotating the ends in opposite directions. **b** *intr*. take a spiral form. **4** *tr*. (foll. by *off*) break off or separate by twisting. **5** *tr*. distort or misrepresent the meaning of (words). **6 a** *intr*. take a curved course. **b** *tr*. make (one's way) in a winding manner. **7** *tr*. *Brit*. *colloq*. cheat (*twisted me out of £20*). **8** *tr*. cause (the ball, esp. in billiards) to rotate while following a curved path. **9** *tr*. (as **twisted** *adj*.) of a person or mind) emotionally unbalanced. **10** *intr*. dance the twist. —*n*. **1** the act or an instance of twisting. **2 a** a twisted state. **b** the manner or degree in which a thing is twisted. **3** a thing formed by or as by twisting, esp. a thread or rope etc. made by winding strands together. **4** the point at which a thing twists or bends. **5** usu. *derog*. a peculiar tendency of mind or character etc. **6** an unexpected development of events, esp. in a story etc. **7** a fine strong silk thread used by tailors etc. **8** a roll of bread, tobacco, etc., in the form of a twist. **9** *Brit*. a paper packet with screwed-up ends. **10** a curled piece of lemon etc. peel to flavour a drink. **11** a spinning motion given to a ball in cricket etc. to make it take a special curve. **12 a** a twisting strain. **b** the amount of twisting of a rod etc., or the angle showing this. **c** forward motion combined with rotation about an axis. **13** *Brit*. a drink made of two ingredients mixed together. **14** *Brit*. *colloq*. a swindle. **15** (prec. by *the*) a dance with a twisting movement of the body, popular in the 1960s. □**round the twist** *Brit*. *sl*. crazy. **twist a person's arm** *colloq*. apply coercion, esp. by moral pressure. **twist round one's finger** see FINGER. □□**twistable** *adj*. **twisty** *adj*. (**twistier**, **twistiest**). [ME, rel. to TWIN, TWINE]

twister /'twɪstə(r)/ *n*. **1** *Brit*. *colloq*. a swindler; a dishonest person. **2** a twisting ball in cricket or billiards. **3** *US* a tornado, waterspout, etc.

twit[1] /twɪt/ *n.* esp. *Brit. sl.* a silly or foolish person. [orig. dial.: perh. f. TWIT[2]]

twit[2] /twɪt/ *v.tr.* (**twitted, twitting**) reproach or taunt, usu. good-humouredly. [16th-c. *twite* f. *atwite* f. OE *ætwītan* reproach with f. *æt* at + *wītan* blame]

twitch /twɪtʃ/ *v. & n.* —*v.* **1** *intr.* (of the features, muscles, limbs, etc.) move or contract spasmodically. **2** *tr.* give a short sharp pull at. —*n.* **1** a sudden involuntary contraction or movement. **2** a sudden pull or jerk. **3** *colloq.* a state of nervousness. **4** a noose and stick for controlling a horse during a veterinary operation. □□ **twitchy** *adj.* (**twitchier, twitchiest**) (in sense 3 of *n.*). [ME f. Gmc: cf. OE *twiccian*, dial. *twick*]

twitcher /ˈtwɪtʃə(r)/ *n.* **1** *colloq.* a bird-watcher who tries to get sightings of rare birds. **2** a person or thing that twitches.

twitch grass /twɪtʃ/ *n.* = COUCH[2]. [var. of QUITCH]

twite /twaɪt/ *n.* a moorland finch, *Carduelis flavirostris*, resembling the linnet. [imit. of its cry]

twitter /ˈtwɪtə(r)/ *v. & n.* —*v.* **1** *intr.* (of or like a bird) emit a succession of light tremulous sounds. **2** *tr.* utter or express in this way. —*n.* **1** the act or an instance of twittering. **2** *colloq.* a tremulously excited state. □□ **twitterer** *n.* **twittery** *adj.* [ME, imit.: cf. -ER[4]]

'twixt /twɪkst/ *prep. archaic* = BETWIXT. [contr.]

two /tuː/ *n. & adj.* —*n.* **1** one more than one; the sum of one unit and another unit. **2** a symbol for this (2, ii, II). **3** a size etc. denoted by two. **4** the time of two o'clock (*is it two yet?*). **5** a set of two. **6** a card with two pips. —*adj.* that amount to two. □ **in two** in or into two pieces. **in two shakes** (or **ticks**) see SHAKE, TICK[1]. **or two** denoting several (*a thing or two* = several things). **put two and two together** make (esp. an obvious) inference from what is known or evident. **that makes two of us** *colloq.* that is true of me also. **two-bit** *US colloq.* cheap, petty. **two-by-four** a length of timber with a rectangular cross-section 2 in. by 4 in. **two by two** (or **two and two**) in pairs. **two can play at that game** *colloq.* another person's behaviour can be copied to that person's disadvantage. **two-dimensional 1** having or appearing to have length and breadth but no depth. **2** lacking depth or substance; superficial. **two-edged** double-edged. **two-faced 1** having two faces. **2** insincere; deceitful. **two-handed 1** having, using, or requiring the use of two hands. **2** (of a card-game) for two players. **two a penny** see PENNY. **two-piece** *adj.* (of a suit etc.) consisting of two matching items. —*n.* a two-piece suit etc. **two-ply** *adj.* of two strands, webs, or thicknesses. —*n.* **1** two-ply wool. **2** two-ply wood made by gluing together two layers with the grain in different directions. **two-seater 1** a vehicle or aircraft with two seats. **2** a sofa etc. for two people. **two-sided 1** having two sides. **2** having two aspects; controversial. **two-step** a round dance with a sliding step in march or polka time. **two-stroke** esp. *Brit.* (of an internal-combustion engine) having its power cycle completed in one up-and-down movement of the piston. **two-time** *colloq.* **1** deceive or be unfaithful to (esp. a partner or lover). **2** swindle, double-cross. **two-timer** *colloq.* a person who is deceitful or unfaithful. **two-tone** having two colours or sounds. **two-up** *Austral. & NZ* a gambling game with bets placed on a showing of two heads or two tails. **two-way 1** involving two ways or participants. **2** (of a switch) permitting a current to be switched on or off from either of two points. **3** (of a radio) capable of transmitting and receiving signals. **4** (of a tap etc.) permitting fluid etc. to flow in either of two channels or directions. **5** (of traffic etc.) moving in two esp. opposite directions. **two-way mirror** a panel of glass that can be seen through from one side and is a mirror on the other. **two-wheeler** a vehicle with

two wheels. [OE *twā* (fem. & neut.), *tū* (neut.), with Gmc cognates and rel. to Skr. *dwau*, *dwe*, Gk & L *duo*]

twofold /ˈtuːfəʊld/ *adj. & adv.* **1** twice as much or as many. **2** consisting of two parts.

twopence /ˈtʌpəns/ *n. Brit.* **1** the sum of two pence, esp. before decimalization. **2** *colloq.* (esp. with *neg.*) a thing of little value (*don't care twopence*).

twopenny /ˈtʌpənɪ/ *adj. Brit.* **1** costing two pence, esp. before decimalization. **2** *colloq.* cheap, worthless. □ **twopenny-halfpenny** /ˌtʌpnɪˈheɪpnɪ/ cheap, insignificant.

twosome /ˈtuːsəm/ *n.* **1** two persons together. **2** a game, dance, etc., for two persons.

'twould /twʊd/ *archaic* it would. [contr.]

twyer var. of TUYÈRE.

TX *abbr. US* Texas (in official postal use).

-ty[1] /tɪ/ *suffix* forming nouns denoting quality or condition (*cruelty*; *plenty*). [ME *-tie, -tee, -te* f. OF *-té, -tet* f. L *-tas -tatis*: cf. -ITY]

-ty[2] /tɪ/ *suffix* denoting tens (*twenty*; *thirty*; *ninety*). [OE *-tig*]

tychism /ˈtaɪkɪz(ə)m/ *n. Philos.* the theory that chance controls the universe. [Gk *tukhē* chance]

tycoon /taɪˈkuːn/ *n.* **1** a business magnate. **2** *hist.* a title applied by foreigners to the shogun of Japan 1854–68. [Jap. *taikun* great lord]

tying *pres. part.* of TIE.

tyke /taɪk/ *n.* (also **tike**) **1** esp. *Brit.* an unpleasant or coarse man. **2** a mongrel. **3** a small child. **4** *Brit. sl.* a Yorkshireman. **5** *Austral. & NZ sl. offens.* a Roman Catholic. [ME f. ON *tík* bitch: sense 5 assim. from TAIG]

tylopod /ˈtaɪləˌpɒd/ *n. & adj. Zool.* —*n.* any animal that bears its weight on the sole-pads of the feet rather than on the hoofs, esp. the camel. —*adj.* (of an animal) bearing its weight in this way. □□ **tylopodous** /-ˈlɒpədəs/ *adj.* [Gk *tulos* knob or *tulē* callus, cushion + *pous podos* foot]

tympan /ˈtɪmpən/ *n.* **1** *Printing* an appliance in a printing-press used to equalize pressure between the platen etc. and a printing-sheet. **2** *Archit.* = TYMPANUM. [F *tympan* or L *tympanum*: see TYMPANUM]

tympana *pl.* of TYMPANUM.

tympani var. of TIMPANI.

tympanic /tɪmˈpænɪk/ *adj.* **1** *Anat.* of, relating to, or having a tympanum. **2** resembling or acting like a drumhead. □ **tympanic bone** *Anat.* the bone supporting the tympanic membrane. **tympanic membrane** *Anat.* the membrane separating the outer ear and middle ear and transmitting vibrations resulting from sound waves to the inner ear.

tympanites /ˌtɪmpəˈnaɪtiːz/ *n.* a swelling of the abdomen caused by gas in the intestine etc. □□ **tympanitic** /-ˈnɪtɪk/ *adj.* [LL f. Gk *tumpanitēs* of a drum (as TYMPANUM)]

tympanum /ˈtɪmpənəm/ *n.* (*pl.* **tympanums** or **tympana** /-nə/) **1** *Anat.* **a** the middle ear. **b** the tympanic membrane. **2** *Zool.* the membrane covering the hearing organ on the leg of an insect. **3** *Archit.* **a** a vertical triangular space forming the centre of a pediment. **b** a similar space over a door between the lintel and the arch; a carving on this space. **4** a drum-wheel etc. for raising water from a stream. [L f. Gk *tumpanon* drum f. *tuptō* strike]

Tynwald /ˈtɪnwɒld/ *n.* the parliament of the Isle of Man. [ON *thing-völlr* place of assembly f. *thing* assembly + *völlr* field]

type /taɪp/ *n. & v.* —*n.* **1 a** a class of things or persons having common characteristics. **b** a kind or sort (*would like a different type of car*). **2** a person, thing, or event serving as an illustration, symbol, or characteristic specimen of another, or of a class. **3** (in *comb.*) made of, resembling, or functioning as (*ceramic-type material*; *Cheddar-type cheese*). **4** *colloq.* a person, esp. of a specified character (*is rather a quiet type*; *is not really my type*). **5** an object, conception, or work of art serving as a model for subsequent artists. **6** *Printing* **a** a piece of metal etc. with a raised letter or character on its upper surface for use in printing. **b** a kind or size of such pieces (*printed in large type*). **c** a set or supply of these (*ran short of type*). **7** a device on either side of a medal or coin. **8** *Theol.* a foreshadowing in the Old Testament of a person or event of the Christian dispensation. **9** *Biol.* an organism having or chosen as having the essential characteristics of its group and giving its name to the next highest group. —*v.* **1** *tr.* be a type or example of. **2** *tr.* & *intr.* write with a typewriter. **3** *tr.* esp. *Biol.* & *Med.* assign to a type; classify. **4** *tr.* = TYPECAST. □**in type** *Printing* composed and ready for printing. **type-founder** a designer and maker of metal types. **type-foundry** a foundry where type is made. **type-metal** *Printing* an alloy of lead etc., used for casting printing-types. **type site** *Archaeol.* a site where objects regarded as defining the characteristics of a period etc. are found. **type specimen** *Biol.* the specimen used for naming and describing a new species. □□ **typal** *adj.* [ME f. F *type* or L *typus* f. Gk *tupos* impression, figure, type, f. *tuptō* strike]

typecast /'taɪpkɑːst/ *v.tr.* (*past* and *past part.* -**cast**) assign (an actor or actress) repeatedly to the same type of role, esp. one in character.

typeface /'taɪpfeɪs/ *n. Printing* **1** a set of types or characters in a particular design. **2** the inked part of type, or the impression made by this.

typescript /'taɪpskrɪpt/ *n.* a typewritten document.

typesetter /'taɪpˌsetə(r)/ *n. Printing* **1** a person who composes type. **2** a composing-machine. □□ **typesetting** *n.*

typewrite /'taɪpraɪt/ *v.tr.* & *intr.* (*past* -**wrote**; *past part.* -**written**) *formal* = TYPE *v.* 2.

typewriter /'taɪpˌraɪtə(r)/ *n.* a machine with keys for producing printlike characters one at a time on paper inserted round a roller.

typewritten /'taɪpˌrɪt(ə)n/ *adj.* produced with a typewriter.

typhlitis /tɪf'laɪtɪs/ *n.* inflammation of the caecum. □□ **typhlitic** /-'lɪtɪk/ *adj.* [mod.L f. Gk *tuphlon* caecum or blind gut f. *tuphlos* blind + -ITIS]

typhoid /'taɪfɔɪd/ *n.* & *adj.* —*n.* **1** (in full **typhoid fever**) an infectious bacterial fever with an eruption of red spots on the chest and abdomen and severe intestinal irritation. **2** a similar disease of animals. —*adj.* like typhus. □**typhoid condition** (or **state**) a state of depressed vitality occurring in many acute diseases. □□ **typhoidal** *adj.* [TYPHUS + -OID]

typhoon /taɪ'fuːn/ *n.* a violent hurricane in E. Asian seas. □□ **typhonic** /-'fɒnɪk/ *adj.* [partly f. Port. *tufão* f. Arab. *ṭūfān* perh. f. Gk *tuphōn* whirlwind; partly f. Chin. dial. *tai fung* big wind]

typhus /'taɪfəs/ *n.* an infectious fever caused by rickettsiae, characterized by a purple rash, headaches, fever, and usu. delirium. □□ **typhous** *adj.* [mod.L f. Gk *tuphos* smoke, stupor f. *tuphō* to smoke]

typical /'tɪpɪk(ə)l/ *adj.* **1** serving as a characteristic example; representative. **2** characteristic of or serving to distinguish a type. **3** (often foll. by *of*) conforming to expected behaviour, attitudes, etc. (*is typical of them to forget*). **4** symbolic. □□ **typicality** /-'kælɪtɪ/ *n.* **typically** *adv.* [med.L *typicalis* f. L *typicus* f. Gk *tupikos* (as TYPE)]

typify /'tɪpɪfaɪ/ *v.tr.* (-**ies**, -**ied**) **1** be a representative

example of; embody the characteristics of. **2** represent by a type or symbol; serve as a type, figure, or emblem of; symbolize. □□ **typification** /-fɪ'keɪʃ(ə)n/ *n.* **typifier** *n.* [L *typus* TYPE + -FY]

typist /'taɪpɪst/ *n.* a person who uses a typewriter, esp. professionally.

typo /'taɪpəʊ/ *n.* (*pl.* -**os**) *colloq.* **1** a typographical error. **2** a typographer. [abbr.]

typographer /taɪ'pɒɡrəfə(r)/ *n.* a person skilled in typography.

typography /taɪ'pɒɡrəfɪ/ *n.* **1** printing as an art. **2** the style and appearance of printed matter. □□ **typographic** /-pə'ɡræfɪk/ *adj.* **typographical** /-pə'ɡræfɪk(ə)l/ *adj.* **typographically** /-pə'ɡræfɪkəlɪ/ *adv.* [F *typographie* or mod.L *typographia* (as TYPE, -GRAPHY)]

typology /taɪ'pɒlədʒɪ/ *n.* the study and interpretation of (esp. biblical) types. □□ **typological** /-ə'lɒdʒɪk(ə)l/ *adj.* **typologist** *n.* [Gk *tupos* TYPE + -LOGY]

tyrannical /tɪ'rænɪk(ə)l/ *adj.* **1** acting like a tyrant; imperious, arbitrary. **2** given to or characteristic of tyranny. □□ **tyrannically** *adv.* [OF *tyrannique* f. L *tyrannicus* f. Gk *turannikos* (as TYRANT)]

tyrannicide /tɪ'rænɪˌsaɪd/ *n.* **1** the act or an instance of killing a tyrant. **2** the killer of a tyrant. □□ **tyrannicidal** /-'saɪd(ə)l/ *adj.* [F f. L *tyrannicida*, -*cidium* (as TYRANT, -CIDE)]

tyrannize /'tɪrəˌnaɪz/ *v.tr.* & (foll. by *over*) *intr.* (also -**ise**) behave like a tyrant towards; rule or treat despotically or cruelly. [F *tyranniser* (as TYRANT)]

tyrannosaurus /tɪˌrænə'sɔːrəs/ *n.* (also **tyrannosaur**) any bipedal flesh-eating dinosaur of the genus *Tyrannosaurus*, esp. *T. rex* having powerful hind legs, small clawlike front legs, and a long well-developed tail. [Gk *turannos* TYRANT, after *dinosaur*]

tyranny /'tɪrənɪ/ *n.* (*pl.* -**ies**) **1** the cruel and arbitrary use of authority. **2** a tyrannical act; tyrannical behaviour. **3** **a** rule by a tyrant. **b** a period of this. **c** a State ruled by a tyrant. □□ **tyrannous** *adj.* **tyrannously** *adv.* [ME f. OF *tyrannie* f. med.L *tyrannia* f. Gk *turannia* (as TYRANT)]

tyrant /'taɪərənt/ *n.* **1** an oppressive or cruel ruler. **2** a person exercising power arbitrarily or cruelly. **3** *Gk Hist.* an absolute ruler who seized power without the legal right. [ME *tyran*, -*ant*, f. OF *tiran*, *tyrant* f. L *tyrannus* f. Gk *turannos*]

tyre /'taɪə(r)/ *n.* (*US* **tire**) a rubber covering, usu. inflated, placed round a wheel to form a soft contact with the road. □**tyre-gauge** a portable device for measuring the air-pressure in a tyre. [var. of TIRE²]

Tyrian /'tɪrɪən/ *adj.* & *n.* —*adj.* of or relating to ancient Tyre in Phoenicia. —*n.* a native or citizen of Tyre. □**Tyrian purple** see PURPLE *n.* 2. [L *Tyrius* f. *Tyrus* Tyre]

tyro var. of TIRO.

Tyrolean /ˌtɪrə'liːən/ *adj.* of or characteristic of the Tyrol, an Alpine province of Austria. □□ **Tyrolese** *adj.* & *n.*

Tyrrhene /'tɪriːn/ *adj.* & *n.* (also **Tyrrhenian** /tɪ'riːnɪən/) *archaic* or *poet.* = ETRUSCAN. [L *Tyrrhenus*]

tzatziki /tsæt'siːkɪ/ *n.* a Greek side dish of yoghurt with cucumber. [mod. Gk]

tzigane /tsɪ'ɡɑːn/ *n.* **1** a Hungarian gypsy. **2** (*attrib.*) characteristic of the tziganes or (esp.) their music. [F f. Magyar *c(z)igány*]

U

U¹ /juː/ *n.* (also **u**) (*pl.* **Us** or **U's**) **1** the twenty-first letter of the alphabet. **2** a U-shaped object or curve (esp. in *comb.*: *U-bolt*).

U² /juː/ *adj.* esp. *Brit. colloq.* **1** upper class. **2** supposedly characteristic of the upper class. [abbr.]

U³ /uː/ *adj.* a Burmese title of respect before a man's name. [Burmese]

U⁴ *abbr.* (also **U.**) **1** *Brit.* universal (of films classified as suitable without restriction). **2** university.

U⁵ *symb. Chem.* the element uranium.

u *prefix* = MU 2 (μ).

UAE *abbr.* United Arab Emirates.

ubiety /juːˈbaɪətɪ/ *n.* the fact or condition of being in a definite place; local relation. [med.L *ubietas* f. L *ubi* where]

-ubility /juˈbɪlɪtɪ/ *suffix* forming nouns from, or corresponding to, adjectives in *-uble* (*solubility*; *volubility*). [L *-ubilitas*: cf. -ITY]

ubiquitarian /juːˌbɪkwɪˈteərɪən/ *adj. & n. Theol.* —*adj.* relating to or believing in the doctrine of the omnipresence of Christ's body. —*n.* a believer in this. □□ **ubiquitarianism** *n.* [mod.L *ubiquitarius* (as UBIQUITOUS)]

ubiquitous /juːˈbɪkwɪtəs/ *adj.* **1** present everywhere or in several places simultaneously. **2** often encountered. □□ **ubiquitously** *adv.* **ubiquitousness** *n.* **ubiquity** *n.* [mod.L *ubiquitas* f. L *ubique* everywhere f. *ubi* where]

-uble /jʊb(ə)l/ *suffix* forming adjectives meaning 'that may or must be' (see -ABLE) (*soluble*; *voluble*). [F f. L *-ubilis*]

-ubly /jʊblɪ/ *suffix* forming adverbs corresponding to adjectives in *-uble*.

U-boat /ˈjuːbəʊt/ *n. hist.* a German submarine. [G *U-boot* = *Unterseeboot* under-sea boat]

UC *abbr.* University College.

u.c. *abbr.* upper case.

UCATT *abbr.* (in the UK) Union of Construction, Allied Trades, and Technicians.

UCCA /ˈʌkə/ *abbr.* (in the UK) Universities Central Council on Admissions.

UCW *abbr.* (in the UK) Union of Communication Workers.

UDA *abbr.* Ulster Defence Association (a loyalist paramilitary organization).

udal /ˈjuːd(ə)l/ *n.* (also **odal** /ˈəʊd(ə)l/) the kind of freehold right based on uninterrupted possession prevailing in N. Europe before the feudal system and still in use in Orkney and Shetland. [ON *óthal* f. Gmc]

UDC *abbr. hist.* (in the UK) Urban District Council.

udder /ˈʌdə(r)/ *n.* the mammary gland of cattle, sheep, etc., hanging as a baglike organ with several teats. □□ **uddered** *adj.* (also in *comb.*). [OE *ūder* f. WG]

UDI *abbr.* unilateral declaration of independence.

udometer /juːˈdɒmɪtə(r)/ *n. formal* a rain-gauge. [F *udomètre* f. L *udus* damp]

UDR *abbr.* Ulster Defence Regiment.

UEFA /juːˈiːfə/ *abbr.* Union of European Football Associations.

UFO /ˈjuːfəʊ/ *n.* (also **ufo**) (*pl.* **UFOs** or **ufos**) unidentified flying object. [abbr.]

ufology /juːˈfɒlədʒɪ/ *n.* the study of UFOs. □□ **ufologist** *n.*

ugh /əx, ʌg, ʌx/ *int.* **1** expressing disgust or horror. **2** the sound of a cough or grunt. [imit.]

Ugli /ˈʌglɪ/ *n.* (*pl.* **Uglis** or **Uglies**) *propr.* a mottled green and yellow citrus fruit, a hybrid of a grapefruit and tangerine. [UGLY]

uglify /ˈʌglɪˌfaɪ/ *v.tr.* (**-ies, -ied**) make ugly. □□ **uglification** /-fɪˈkeɪʃ(ə)n/ *n.*

ugly /ˈʌglɪ/ *adj.* (**uglier, ugliest**) **1** unpleasing or repulsive to see or hear (*an ugly scar*; *spoke with an ugly snarl*). **2** unpleasantly suggestive; discreditable (*ugly rumours are about*). **3** threatening, dangerous (*the sky has an ugly look*). **4** morally repulsive; vile (*ugly vices*). □ **ugly customer** an unpleasantly formidable person. **ugly duckling** a person who turns out to be beautiful or talented etc. against all expectations (with ref. to a cygnet in a brood of ducks in a tale by Andersen). □□ **uglily** *adv.* **ugliness** *n.* [ME f. ON *uggligr* to be dreaded f. *ugga* to dread]

Ugrian /ˈuːgrɪən/ *adj. & n.* (also **Ugric** /ˈuːgrɪk/) —*adj.* of or relating to the eastern branch of Finnic peoples, esp. the Finns and Magyars. —*n.* **1** a member of this people. **2** the language of this people. [Russ. *Ugry* name of a race dwelling E. of the Urals]

UHF *abbr.* ultra-high frequency.

uh-huh /ˈʌhʌ/ *int. colloq.* expressing assent. [imit.]

uhlan /ˈuːlɑːn, ˈjuːlən/ *n. hist.* a cavalryman armed with a lance in some European armies, esp. the former German army. [F & G f. Pol. (*h*)*ulan* f. Turk. *oglan* youth, servant]

UHT *abbr.* ultra heat treated (esp. of milk, for long keeping).

Uitlander /ˈeɪtˌlɒndə(r)/ *n. S.Afr.* a foreigner or alien, esp. before the Boer War. [Afrik. f. Du. *uit* out + *land* land]

UK *abbr.* United Kingdom.

UKAEA *abbr.* United Kingdom Atomic Energy Authority.

ukase /juːˈkeɪz/ *n.* **1** an arbitrary command. **2** *hist.* an edict of the Tsarist Russian government. [Russ. *ukaz* ordinance, edict f. *ukazat'* show, decree]

Ukrainian /juːˈkreɪnɪən/ *n. & adj.* —*n.* **1** a native of the Ukraine in the USSR. **2** the language of the Ukraine. —*adj.* of or relating to the Ukraine or its people or language. [*Ukraine* f. Russ. *ukraina* frontier region f. *u* at + *krai* edge]

ukulele /ˌjuːkəˈleɪlɪ/ *n.* a small four-stringed Hawaiian (orig. Portuguese) guitar. [Hawaiian, = jumping flea]

-ular /jʊlə(r)/ *suffix* forming adjectives, sometimes corresp. to nouns in *-ule* (*pustular*) but often without diminutive force (*angular*; *granular*). □□ **-ularity** /-ˈlærɪtɪ/ *suffix* forming nouns. [from or after L *-ularis* (as -ULE, -AR¹)]

ulcer /ˈʌlsə(r)/ *n.* **1** an open sore on an external or internal surface of the body, often forming pus. **2 a** a moral blemish. **b** a corroding or corrupting influence etc. □□ **ulcered** *adj.* **ulcerous** *adj.* [ME f. L *ulcus -eris*, rel. to Gk *helkos*]

ulcerate /ˈʌlsəˌreɪt/ *v.tr. & intr.* form into or affect with an ulcer. □□ **ulcerable** *adj.* **ulceration** /-ˈreɪʃ(ə)n/ *n.* **ulcerative** /-rətɪv/ *adj.* [ME f. L *ulcerare ulcerat-* (as ULCER)]

-ule /juːl/ *suffix* forming diminutive nouns (*capsule*; *globule*). [from or after L *-ulus, -ula, -ulum*]

ulema /ˈuːlɪmə/ *n.* **1** a body of Muslim doctors of sacred law and theology. **2** a member of this. [Arab. *'ulamā* pl. of *'ālim* learned f. *'alama* know]

-ulent /jʊlənt/ *suffix* forming adjectives meaning 'abounding in, full of' (*fraudulent*; *turbulent*). □□ **-ulence** *suffix* forming nouns. [L *-ulentus*]

uliginose /juːˈlɪdʒɪˌnəʊs/ *adj.* (also **uliginous** /-nəs/) *Bot.* growing in wet or swampy places. [L *uliginosus* f. *uligo -ginis* moisture]

ullage /ˈʌlɪdʒ/ *n.* **1** the amount by which a cask etc. falls short of being full. **2** loss by evaporation or leakage. [ME f. AF *ulliage*, OF *ouillage* f. *ouiller* fill up, ult. f. L *oculus* eye, with ref. to the bung-hole]

ulna /'ʌlnə/ *n.* (*pl.* **ulnae** /-niː/) **1** the thinner and longer bone in the forearm, on the side opposite to the thumb (cf. RADIUS 3). **2** *Zool.* a corresponding bone in an animal's foreleg or a bird's wing. □□ **ulnar** *adj.* [L, rel. to Gk *ōlenē* and ELL]

ulotrichan /juːˈlɒtrɪkən/ *adj.* & *n.* —*adj.* (also **ulotrichous** /-kəs/) having tightly-curled hair, esp. denoting a human type. —*n.* a person having such hair. [mod.L *Ulotrichi* f. Gk *oulos* woolly, crisp + *thrix trikhos* hair]

-ulous /jʊləs/ *suffix* forming adjectives (*fabulous*; *populous*). [L *-ulosus, -ulus*]

ulster /'ʌlstə(r)/ *n.* a man's long loose overcoat of rough cloth. [*Ulster* in Ireland, where it was orig. sold]

Ulsterman /'ʌlstəmən/ *n.* (*pl.* **-men**; *fem.* **Ulsterwoman**; *pl.* **-women**) a native of Ulster.

ult. *abbr.* ultimo.

ulterior /ʌlˈtɪərɪə(r)/ *adj.* **1** existing in the background, or beyond what is evident or admitted; hidden, secret (esp. *ulterior motive*). **2** situated beyond. **3** more remote; not immediate; in the future. □□ **ulteriorly** *adv.* [L, = further, more distant]

ultima /'ʌltɪmə/ *n.* the last syllable of a word. [L *ultima* (*syllaba*), fem. of *ultimus* last]

ultimata *pl.* of ULTIMATUM.

ultimate /'ʌltɪmət/ *adj.* & *n.* —*adj.* **1** last, final. **2** beyond which no other exists or is possible (*the ultimate analysis*). **3** fundamental, primary, unanalysable (*ultimate truths*). **4** maximum (*ultimate tensile strength*). —*n.* **1** (prec. by *the*) the best achievable or imaginable. **2** a final or fundamental fact or principle. □□ **ultimately** *adv.* **ultimateness** *n.* [LL *ultimatus* past part. of *ultimare* come to an end]

ultima Thule /ˌʌltɪmə 'θuːliː/ *n.* a far-away unknown region. [L, = furthest Thule, a remote northern region]

ultimatum /ˌʌltɪˈmeɪtəm/ *n.* (*pl.* **ultimatums** or **ultimata** /-tə/) a final demand or statement of terms by one party, the rejection of which by another could cause a breakdown in relations, war, or an end of cooperation etc. [L neut. past part.: see ULTIMATE]

ultimo /'ʌltɪˌməʊ/ *adj.* *Commerce* of last month (*the 28th ultimo*). [L *ultimo mense* in the last month]

ultimogeniture /ˌʌltɪməʊˈdʒenɪtʃə(r)/ *n.* a system in which the youngest son has the right of inheritance (cf. PRIMOGENITURE 2). [L *ultimus* last, after PRIMOGENITURE]

ultra /'ʌltrə/ *adj.* & *n.* —*adj.* favouring extreme views or measures, esp. in religion or politics. —*n.* an extremist. [orig. as abbr. of F *ultra-royaliste*: see ULTRA-]

ultra- /'ʌltrə/ *comb. form* **1** beyond; on the other side of (opp. CIS-). **2** extreme(ly), excessive(ly) (*ultra-conservative*; *ultra-modern*). [L *ultra* beyond]

ultracentrifuge /ˌʌltrəˈsentrɪˌfjuːdʒ/ *n.* a high-speed centrifuge used to separate small particles and large molecules by their rate of sedimentation from sols.

ultra-high /ˌʌltrəˈhaɪ/ *adj.* (of a frequency) in the range 300 to 3000 megahertz.

ultraist /'ʌltraɪst/ *n.* the holder of extreme positions in politics, religion, etc. □□ **ultraism** *n.*

ultramarine /ˌʌltrəməˈriːn/ *n.* & *adj.* —*n.* **1 a** a brilliant blue pigment orig. obtained from lapis lazuli. **b** an imitation of this from powdered fired clay, sodium carbonate, sulphur, and resin. **2** the colour of this. —*adj.* **1** of this colour. **2** *archaic* situated beyond the sea. [obs. It. *oltramarino* & med.L *ultramarinus* beyond the sea (as ULTRA-, MARINE), because lapis lazuli was brought from beyond the sea]

ultramicroscope /ˌʌltrəˈmaɪkrəˌskəʊp/ *n.* an optical microscope used to reveal very small particles by means of light scattered by them.

ultramicroscopic /ˌʌltrəˌmaɪkrəˈskɒpɪk/ *adj.* **1** too

small to be seen by an ordinary optical microscope. **2** of or relating to an ultramicroscope.

ultramontane /ˌʌltrəˈmɒnteɪn/ *adj.* & *n.* —*adj.* **1** situated on the other side of the Alps from the point of view of the speaker. **2** advocating supreme papal authority in matters of faith and discipline. —*n.* **1** a person living on the other side of the Alps. **2** a person advocating supreme papal authority. [med.L *ultramontanus* (as ULTRA-, L *mons montis* mountain)]

ultramundane /ˌʌltrəˈmʌndeɪn/ *adj.* lying beyond the world or the solar system. [L *ultramundanus* (as ULTRA-, *mundanus* f. *mundus* world)]

ultrasonic /ˌʌltrəˈsɒnɪk/ *adj.* of or involving sound waves with a frequency above the upper limit of human hearing. □□ **ultrasonically** *adv.*

ultrasonics /ˌʌltrəˈsɒnɪks/ *n.pl.* (usu. treated as *sing.*) the science and application of ultrasonic waves.

ultrasound /'ʌltrəˌsaʊnd/ *n.* **1** sound having an ultrasonic frequency. **2** ultrasonic waves. □ **ultrasound cardiography** = ECHOCARDIOGRAPHY.

ultrastructure /'ʌltrəˌstrʌktʃə(r)/ *n. Biol.* fine structure not visible with an optical microscope.

ultraviolet /ˌʌltrəˈvaɪələt/ *adj. Physics* **1** having a wavelength (just) beyond the violet end of the visible spectrum. **2** of or using such radiation.

ultra vires /ˌʌltrə 'vaɪəˌriːz, ˌʊltrɑː 'viːreɪz/ *adv.* & *predic.adj.* beyond one's legal power or authority. [L]

ululate /'juːlʊˌleɪt/ *v.intr.* howl; wail; make a hooting cry. □□ **ululant** *adj.* **ululation** /-'leɪʃ(ə)n/ *n.* [L *ululare ululat-* (imit.)]

um /ʌm, əm/ *int.* expressing hesitation or a pause in speech. [imit.]

-um var. of -IUM 1.

umbel /'ʌmb(ə)l/ *n. Bot.* a flower-cluster in which stalks nearly equal in length spring from a common centre and form a flat or curved surface, as in parsley. □□ **umbellar** *adj.* **umbellate** /-bə,leɪt/ *adj.* **umbellule** /-'beljuːl/ *adj.* [obs. F *umbelle* or L *umbella* sunshade, dimin. of UMBRA]

umbellifer /ʌmˈbelɪfə(r)/ *n.* any plant of the family Umbelliferae bearing umbels, including parsley and parsnip. □□ **umbelliferous** /-bəˈlɪfərəs/ *adj.* [obs. F *umbellifère* f. L (as UMBEL, *-fer* bearing)]

umber /'ʌmbə(r)/ *n.* & *adj.* —*n.* **1** a natural pigment like ochre but darker and browner. **2** the colour of this. —*adj.* **1** of this colour. **2** dark, dusky. [F (*terre d'*)*ombre* or It. (*terra di*) *ombra* = shadow (earth), f. L UMBRA or *Umbra* fem. of *Umber* Umbrian]

umbilical /ʌmˈbɪlɪk(ə)l, ˌʌmbɪˈlaɪk(ə)l/ *adj.* **1** of, situated near, or affecting the navel. **2** centrally placed. □ **umbilical cord 1** a flexible cordlike structure attaching a fœtus to the placenta. **2** *Astronaut.* a supply cable linking a missile to its launcher, or an astronaut in space to a spacecraft. [obs. F *umbilical* or f. UMBILICUS]

umbilicate /ʌmˈbɪlɪkət/ *adj.* **1** shaped like a navel. **2** having an umbilicus.

umbilicus /ʌmˈbɪlɪkəs, ˌʌmbɪˈlaɪkəs/ *n.* (*pl.* **umbilici** /-ˌsaɪ/ or **umbilicuses**) **1** *Anat.* the navel. **2** *Bot.* & *Zool.* a navel-like formation. **3** *Geom.* a point in a surface through which all cross-sections have the same curvature. [L, rel. to Gk *omphalos* and to NAVEL]

umbles /'ʌmb(ə)lz/ *n.pl.* the edible offal of deer etc. (cf. *humble pie*). [ME var. of NUMBLES]

umbo /'ʌmbəʊ/ *n.* (*pl.* **-os** or **umbones** /-ˈbəʊniːz/) **1** the boss of a shield, esp. in the centre. **2** *Bot.* & *Zool.* a rounded knob or protuberance. □□ **umbonal** *adj.* **umbonate** /-nət/ *adj.* [L *umbo -onis*]

umbra /'ʌmbrə/ *n.* (*pl.* **umbras** or **umbrae** /-briː/) *Astron.* **1** a total shadow usu. cast on the earth by the moon during a solar eclipse. **2** the dark central part of a sunspot (cf. PENUMBRA). □□ **umbral** *adj.* [L, = shade]

umbrage /'ʌmbrɪdʒ/ *n.* **1** offence; a sense of slight or injury (esp. *give* or *take umbrage at*). **2** *archaic* **a**

shade. **b** what gives shade. [ME f. OF ult. f. L *umbraticus* f. *umbra*: see UMBRA]

umbrella /ʌmˈbrelə/ *n.* **1** a light portable device for protection against rain, strong sun, etc., consisting of a usu. circular canopy of cloth mounted by means of a collapsible metal frame on a central stick. **2** protection or patronage. **3** (often *attrib*.) a co-ordinating or unifying agency (*umbrella organization*). **4** a screen of fighter aircraft or a curtain of fire put up as a protection against enemy aircraft. **5** *Zool.* the gelatinous disc of a jellyfish etc., which it contracts and expands to move through the water. □ **umbrella bird** any S. American bird of the genus *Cephalopterus*, with a black radiating crest and long wattles. **umbrella pine 1** = *stone pine*. **2** a tall Japanese evergreen conifer, *Sciadopitys verticillata*, with leaves in umbrella-like whorls. **umbrella stand** a stand for holding closed upright umbrellas. **umbrella tree** a small magnolia, *Magnolia tripetala*, with leaves in a whorl like an umbrella. □□ **umbrellaed** /-ləd/ *adj.* **umbrella-like** *adj.* [It. *ombrella*, dimin. of *ombra* shade f. L *umbra*: see UMBRA]

Umbrian /ˈʌmbrɪən/ *adj.* & *n.* **—***adj.* of or relating to Umbria in central Italy. **—***n.* **1** the language of ancient Umbria, related to Latin. **2** an inhabitant of ancient Umbria. □ **Umbrian school** a Renaissance school of Italian painting, to which Raphael and Perugino belonged.

umbriferous /ʌmˈbrɪfərəs/ *adj. formal* providing shade. [L *umbrifer* f. *umbra* shade: see -FEROUS]

umiak /ˈuːmɪˌæk/ *n.* an Eskimo skin-and-wood open boat propelled by women with paddles. [Eskimo]

umlaut /ˈʊmlaʊt/ *n.* & *v.* **—***n.* **1** a mark (¨) used over a vowel, esp. in Germanic languages, to indicate a vowel change. **2** such a vowel change, e.g. German *Mann*, *Männer*, English *man*, *men*, due to *i*, *j*, etc. (now usu. lost or altered) in the following syllable. **—***v.tr.* modify (a form or a sound) by an umlaut. [G f. *um* about + *Laut* sound]

umpire /ˈʌmpaɪə(r)/ *n.* & *v.* **—***n.* **1** a person chosen to enforce the rules and settle disputes in various sports. **2** a person chosen to arbitrate between disputants, or to see fair play. **—***v.* **1** *intr.* (usu. foll. by *for*, *in*, etc.) act as umpire. **2** *tr.* act as umpire in (a game etc.). □□ **umpirage** /-rɪdʒ/ *n.* **umpireship** *n.* [ME, later form of *noumpere* f. OF *nonper* not equal (as NON-, PEER²): for loss of *n*- cf. ADDER]

umpteen /ʌmpˈtiːn/ *adj.* & *pron. sl.* **—***adj.* in-definitely many; a lot of. **—***pron.* indefinitely many. □□ **umpteenth** *adj.* **umpty** /ˈʌmptɪ/ *adj.* [joc. form. on -TEEN]

UN *abbr.* United Nations.

un-¹ /ʌn/ *prefix* **1** added to adjectives and participles and their derivative nouns and adverbs, meaning: **a** not: denoting the absence of a quality or state (*unusable*; *uncalled-for*; *uneducated*; *unfailing*; *un-officially*; *unhappiness*). **b** the reverse of, usu. with an implication of approval or disapproval, or with some other special connotation (*unselfish*; *un-sociable*; *unscientific*). ¶ Words formed in this way often have neutral counterparts in *non-* (see NON- 6) and counterparts in *-in* (see IN-¹), e.g. *unadvisable*. **2** (less often) added to nouns, meaning 'a lack of' (*unrest*; *untruth*). ¶ The number of words that can be formed with this prefix (and similarly with *un-²*) is potentially as large as the number of adjectives in use; consequently only a selection, being considered the most current or semantically noteworthy, can be given here. [OE f. Gmc, rel. to L *in-*]

un-² /ʌn/ *prefix* added to verbs and (less often) nouns, forming verbs denoting: **1** the reversal or cancellation of an action or state (*undress*; *unlock*; *unsettle*). **2** deprivation or separation (*unmask*). **3** release from (*unburden*; *uncage*). **4** causing to be no longer (*unman*). ¶ See the note at *un-¹*. Both *un-¹* and *un-²* can be understood in some forms in *-able*, *-ed* (especially), and *-ing*: for example, *undressed* can

mean either 'not dressed' or 'no longer dressed'. [OE *un-*, *on-* f. Gmc]

'un /ən/ *pron. colloq.* one (*that's a good 'un*). [dial. var.]

UNA *abbr.* United Nations Association.

unabashed /ˌʌnəˈbæʃt/ *adj.* not abashed. □□ **unabashedly** /-ʃɪdlɪ/ *adv.*

unabated /ˌʌnəˈbeɪtɪd/ *adj.* not abated; undiminished. □□ **unabatedly** *adv.*

unable /ʌnˈeɪb(ə)l/ *adj.* (usu. foll. by *to* + infin.) not able; lacking ability.

unabridged /ˌʌnəˈbrɪdʒd/ *adj.* (of a text etc.) complete; not abridged.

unabsorbed /ˌʌnəbˈzɔːbd, -ˈsɔːbd/ *adj.* not absorbed.

unacademic /ˌʌnækəˈdemɪk/ *adj.* **1** not academic (esp. not scholarly or theoretical). **2** (of a person) not suited to academic study.

unaccented /ˌʌnækˈsentɪd/ *adj.* not accented; not emphasized.

unacceptable /ˌʌnəkˈseptəb(ə)l/ *adj.* not acceptable. □□ **unacceptableness** *n.* **unacceptably** *adv.*

unacclaimed /ˌʌnəˈkleɪmd/ *adj.* not acclaimed.

unaccommodating /ˌʌnəˈkɒməˌdeɪtɪŋ/ *adj.* not ac-commodating; disobliging.

unaccompanied /ˌʌnəˈkʌmpənɪd/ *adj.* **1** not ac-companied. **2** *Mus.* without accompaniment.

unaccomplished /ˌʌnəˈkʌmplɪʃt, -ˈkɒmplɪʃt/ *adj.* **1** not accomplished; uncompleted. **2** lacking accomplishments.

unaccountable /ˌʌnəˈkaʊntəb(ə)l/ *adj.* **1** unable to be explained. **2** unpredictable or strange in behaviour. **3** not responsible. □□ **unaccountability** /-ˈbɪlɪtɪ/ *n.* **unaccountableness** *n.* **unaccountably** *adv.*

unaccounted /ˌʌnəˈkaʊntɪd/ *adj.* of which no ac-count is given. □ **unaccounted for** unexplained; not included in an account.

unaccustomed /ˌʌnəˈkʌstəmd/ *adj.* **1** (usu. foll. by *to*) not accustomed. **2** not customary; unusual (*his unaccustomed silence*). □□ **unaccustomedly** *adv.*

unacknowledged /ˌʌnəkˈnɒlɪdʒd/ *adj.* not acknow-ledged.

unacquainted /ˌʌnəˈkweɪntɪd/ *adj.* (usu. foll. by *with*) not acquainted.

unadaptable /ˌʌnəˈdæptəb(ə)l/ *adj.* not adaptable.

unadapted /ˌʌnəˈdæptɪd/ *adj.* not adapted.

unaddressed /ˌʌnəˈdrest/ *adj.* (esp. of a letter etc.) without an address.

unadjacent /ˌʌnəˈdʒeɪs(ə)nt/ *adj.* not adjacent.

unadopted /ˌʌnəˈdɒptɪd/ *adj.* **1** not adopted. **2** *Brit.* (of a road) not taken over for maintenance by a local authority.

unadorned /ˌʌnəˈdɔːnd/ *adj.* not adorned; plain.

unadulterated /ˌʌnəˈdʌltəˌreɪtɪd/ *adj.* **1** not adul-terated; pure; concentrated. **2** sheer, complete, utter (*unadulterated nonsense*).

unadventurous /ˌʌnədˈventʃərəs/ *adj.* not adventurous. □□ **unadventurously** *adv.*

unadvertised /ʌnˈædvəˌtaɪzd/ *adj.* not advertised.

unadvisable /ˌʌnədˈvaɪzəb(ə)l/ *adj.* **1** not open to advice. **2** (of a thing) inadvisable.

unadvised /ˌʌnədˈvaɪzd/ *adj.* **1** indiscreet; rash. **2** not having had advice. □□ **unadvisedly** /-zɪdlɪ/ *adv.* **unadvisedness** *n.*

unaffected /ˌʌnəˈfektɪd/ *adj.* **1** (usu. foll. by *by*) not affected. **2** free from affectation; genuine; sincere. □□ **unaffectedly** *adv.* **unaffectedness** *n.*

unaffiliated /ˌʌnəˈfɪlɪˌeɪtɪd/ *adj.* not affiliated.

unafraid /ˌʌnəˈfreɪd/ *adj.* not afraid.

unaided /ʌnˈeɪdɪd/ *adj.* not aided; without help.

unalienable /ʌnˈeɪlɪənəb(ə)l/ *adj. Law* = INALIEN-ABLE.

unaligned /ˌʌnəˈlaɪnd/ *adj.* **1** = NON-ALIGNED. **2** not physically aligned.

unalike /ˌʌnəˈlaɪk/ *adj.* not alike; different.

unalive /ˌʌnəˈlaɪv/ *adj.* **1** lacking in vitality. **2** (foll. by *to*) not fully susceptible or awake to.

unalleviated /ˌʌnəˈliːvɪˌeɪtɪd/ adj. not alleviated; relentless.

unallied /ˌʌnəˈlaɪd/ adj. not allied; having no allies.

unallowable /ˌʌnəˈlaʊəb(ə)l/ adj. not allowable.

unalloyed /ˌʌnəˈlɔɪd, ʌnˈæl-/ **1** not alloyed; pure. **2** complete; utter (*unalloyed joy*).

unalterable /ʌnˈɔːltərəb(ə)l, ʌnˈɒl-/ adj. not alterable. □□ **unalterableness** n. **unalterably** adv.

unaltered /ʌnˈɔːltəd, ʌnˈɒl-/ adj. not altered; remaining the same.

unamazed /ˌʌnəˈmeɪzd/ adj. not amazed.

unambiguous /ˌʌnæmˈbɪɡjʊəs/ adj. not ambiguous; clear or definite in meaning. □□ **unambiguity** /-ˈɡjuːɪtɪ/ n. **unambiguously** adv.

unambitious /ˌʌnæmˈbɪʃəs/ adj. not ambitious; without ambition. □□ **unambitiously** adv. **unambitiousness** n.

unambivalent /ˌʌnæmˈbɪvələnt/ adj. (of feelings etc.) not ambivalent; straightforward. □□ **unambivalently** adv.

un-American /ˌʌnəˈmerɪkən/ adj. **1** not in accordance with American characteristics etc. **2** contrary to the interests of the US; (in the US) treasonable. □□ **un-Americanism** n.

unamiable /ʌnˈeɪmɪəb(ə)l/ adj. not amiable.

unamplified /ʌnˈæmplɪˌfaɪd/ adj. not amplified.

unamused /ˌʌnəˈmjuːzd/ adj. not amused.

unanalysable /ʌnˈænəˌlaɪzəb(ə)l/ adj. not able to be analysed.

unanalysed /ʌnˈænəˌlaɪzd/ adj. not analysed.

unaneled /ˌʌnəˈniːld/ adj. archaic not having received extreme unction.

unanimous /juːˈnænɪməs/ adj. **1** all in agreement (*the committee was unanimous*). **2** (of an opinion, vote, etc.) held or given by general consent (*the unanimous choice*). □□ **unanimity** /-nəˈnɪmɪtɪ/ n. **unanimously** adv. **unanimousness** n. [LL *unanimis*, L *unanimus* f. *unus* one + *animus* mind]

unannounced /ˌʌnəˈnaʊnst/ adj. not announced; without warning (of arrival etc.).

unanswerable /ʌnˈɑːnsərəb(ə)l/ adj. **1** unable to be refuted (*has an unanswerable case*). **2** unable to be answered (*an unanswerable question*). □□ **unanswerableness** n. **unanswerably** adv.

unanswered /ʌnˈɑːnsəd/ adj. not answered.

unanticipated /ˌʌnænˈtɪsɪˌpeɪtɪd/ adj. not anticipated.

unapparent /ˌʌnəˈpærənt/ adj. not apparent.

unappealable /ˌʌnəˈpiːləb(ə)l/ adj. esp. *Law* not able to be appealed against.

unappealing /ˌʌnəˈpiːlɪŋ/ adj. not appealing; unattractive. □□ **unappealingly** adv.

unappeasable /ˌʌnəˈpiːzəb(ə)l/ adj. not appeasable.

unappeased /ˌʌnəˈpiːzd/ adj. not appeased.

unappetizing /ʌnˈæpɪˌtaɪzɪŋ/ adj. not appetizing. □□ **unappetizingly** adv.

unapplied /ˌʌnəˈplaɪd/ adj. not applied.

unappreciated /ˌʌnəˈpriːʃɪˌeɪtɪd/ adj. not appreciated.

unappreciative /ˌʌnəˈpriːʃətɪv/ adj. not appreciative.

unapproachable /ˌʌnəˈprəʊtʃəb(ə)l/ adj. **1** not approachable; remote, inaccessible. **2** (of a person) unfriendly. □□ **unapproachability** /-ˈbɪlɪtɪ/ n. **unapproachableness** n. **unapproachably** adv.

unappropriated /ˌʌnəˈprəʊprɪˌeɪtɪd/ adj. **1** not allocated or assigned. **2** not taken into possession by anyone.

unapproved /ˌʌnəˈpruːvd/ adj. not approved or sanctioned.

unapt /ʌnˈæpt/ adj. **1** (usu. foll. by *for*) not suitable. **2** (usu. foll. by *to* + infin.) not apt. □□ **unaptly** adv. **unaptness** n.

unarguable /ʌnˈɑːɡjʊəb(ə)l/ adj. not arguable; certain.

unarm /ʌnˈɑːm/ v.tr. deprive or free of arms or armour.

unarmed /ʌnˈɑːmd/ adj. not armed; without weapons.

unarresting /ˌʌnəˈrestɪŋ/ adj. uninteresting, dull. □□ **unarrestingly** adv.

unarticulated /ˌʌnɑːˈtɪkjʊˌleɪtɪd/ adj. not articulated or distinct.

unartistic /ˌʌnɑːˈtɪstɪk/ adj. not artistic, esp. not concerned with art. □□ **unartistically** adv.

unascertainable /ˌʌnæsəˈteɪnəb(ə)l/ adj. not ascertainable.

unascertained /ˌʌnæsəˈteɪnd/ adj. not ascertained; unknown.

unashamed /ˌʌnəˈʃeɪmd/ adj. **1** feeling no guilt, shameless. **2** blatant; bold. □□ **unashamedly** /-mɪdlɪ/ adv. **unashamedness** /-mɪdnɪs/ n.

unasked /ʌnˈɑːskt/ adj. (often foll. by *for*) not asked, requested, or invited.

unassailable /ˌʌnəˈseɪləb(ə)l/ adj. unable to be attacked or questioned; impregnable. □□ **unassailability** /-ˈbɪlɪtɪ/ n. **unassailableness** n. **unassailably** adv.

unassertive /ˌʌnəˈsɜːtɪv/ adj. (of a person) not assertive or forthcoming; reticent. □□ **unassertively** adv. **unassertiveness** n.

unassignable /ˌʌnəˈsaɪnəb(ə)l/ adj. not assignable.

unassigned /ˌʌnəˈsaɪnd/ adj. not assigned.

unassimilated /ˌʌnəˈsɪmɪˌleɪtɪd/ adj. not assimilated. □□ **unassimilable** adj.

unassisted /ˌʌnəˈsɪstɪd/ adj. not assisted.

unassuaged /ˌʌnəˈsweɪdʒd/ adj. not assuaged. □□ **unassuageable** adj.

unassuming /ˌʌnəˈsjuːmɪŋ/ adj. not pretentious or arrogant; modest. □□ **unassumingly** adv. **unassumingness** n.

unatoned /ˌʌnəˈtəʊnd/ adj. not atoned for.

unattached /ˌʌnəˈtætʃt/ adj. **1** (often foll. by *to*) not attached, esp. to a particular body, organization, etc. **2** not engaged or married.

unattackable /ˌʌnəˈtækəb(ə)l/ adj. unable to be attacked or damaged.

unattainable /ˌʌnəˈteɪnəb(ə)l/ adj. not attainable. □□ **unattainableness** n. **unattainably** adv.

unattempted /ˌʌnəˈtemptɪd/ adj. not attempted.

unattended /ˌʌnəˈtendɪd/ adj. **1** (usu. foll. by *to*) not attended. **2** (of a person, vehicle, etc.) not accompanied; alone; uncared for.

unattractive /ˌʌnəˈtræktɪv/ adj. not attractive. □□ **unattractively** adv. **unattractiveness** n.

unattributable /ˌʌnəˈtrɪbjʊtəb(ə)l/ adj. (esp. of information) that cannot or may not be attributed to a source etc. □□ **unattributably** adv.

unauthentic /ˌʌnɔːˈθentɪk/ adj. not authentic. □□ **unauthentically** adv.

unauthenticated /ˌʌnɔːˈθentɪˌkeɪtɪd/ adj. not authenticated.

unauthorized /ʌnˈɔːθəˌraɪzd/ adj. (also **unauthorised**) not authorized.

unavailable /ˌʌnəˈveɪləb(ə)l/ adj. not available. □□ **unavailability** /-ˈbɪlɪtɪ/ n. **unavailableness** n.

unavailing /ˌʌnəˈveɪlɪŋ/ adj. not availing; achieving nothing; ineffectual. □□ **unavailingly** adv.

unavoidable /ˌʌnəˈvɔɪdəb(ə)l/ adj. not avoidable; inevitable. □□ **unavoidability** /-ˈbɪlɪtɪ/ n. **unavoidableness** n. **unavoidably** adv.

unavowed /ˌʌnəˈvaʊd/ adj. not avowed.

unaware /ˌʌnəˈweə(r)/ adj. & adv. —adj. **1** (usu. foll. by *of*, or *that* + clause) not aware; ignorant (*unaware of her presence*). **2** (of a person) insensitive; unperceptive. —adv. = UNAWARES. □□ **unawareness** n.

unawares /ˌʌnəˈweəz/ adv. **1** unexpectedly (*met them unawares*). **2** inadvertently (*dropped it unawares*). [earlier *unware(s)* f. OE *unwær(es)*: see WARE[2]]

unbacked /ʌnˈbækt/ adj. **1** not supported. **2** (of a horse etc.) having no backers. **3** (of a chair, picture, etc.) having no back or backing.

unbalance /ʌnˈbæləns/ v. & n. —v.tr. **1** upset the physical or mental balance of (*unbalanced by the blow; the shock unbalanced him*). **2** (as **unbalanced**

adj.) **a** not balanced. **b** (of a mind or a person) unstable or deranged. —*n*. lack of balance; instability, esp. mental.

unbar /ʌnˈbɑː(r)/ *v.tr.* (**unbarred, unbarring**) **1** remove a bar or bars from (a gate etc.). **2** unlock, open.

unbearable /ʌnˈbeərəb(ə)l/ *adj.* not bearable. □□ **unbearableness** *n.* **unbearably** *adv.*

unbeatable /ʌnˈbiːtəb(ə)l/ *adj.* not beatable; excelling.

unbeaten /ʌnˈbiːt(ə)n/ *adj.* **1** not beaten. **2** (of a record etc.) not surpassed. **3** *Cricket* (of a player) not out.

unbeautiful /ʌnˈbjuːtɪˌfʊl/ *adj.* not beautiful; ugly. □□ **unbeautifully** *adv.*

unbecoming /ˌʌnbɪˈkʌmɪŋ/ *adj.* **1** (esp. of clothing) not flattering or suiting a person. **2** (usu. foll. by *to, for*) not fitting; indecorous or unsuitable. □□ **unbecomingly** *adv.* **unbecomingness** *n.*

unbefitting /ˌʌnbɪˈfɪtɪŋ/ *adj.* not befitting; unsuitable. □□ **unbefittingly** *adv.* **unbefittingness** *n.*

unbefriended /ˌʌnbɪˈfrendɪd/ *adj.* not befriended.

unbegotten /ˌʌnbɪˈɡɒt(ə)n/ *adj.* not begotten.

unbeholden /ˌʌnbɪˈhəʊld(ə)n/ *predic.adj.* (usu. foll. by *to*) under no obligation.

unbeknown /ˌʌnbɪˈnəʊn/ *adj.* (also **unbeknownst** /-ˈnəʊnst/) (foll. by *to*) without the knowledge of (*was there all the time unbeknown to us*). [UN-¹ + *beknown* (archaic) = KNOWN]

unbelief /ˌʌnbɪˈliːf/ *n.* lack of belief, esp. in religious matters. □□ **unbeliever** *n.* **unbelieving** *adj.* **unbelievingly** *adv.* **unbelievingness** *n.*

unbelievable /ˌʌnbɪˈliːvəb(ə)l/ *adj.* not believable; incredible. □□ **unbelievability** /-ˈbɪlɪtɪ/ *n.* **unbelievableness** *n.* **unbelievably** *adv.*

unbeloved /ˌʌnbɪˈlʌvd/ *adj.* not beloved.

unbelt /ʌnˈbelt/ *v.tr.* remove or undo the belt of (a garment etc.).

unbend /ʌnˈbend/ *v.* (*past* and *past part.* **unbent**) **1** *tr. & intr.* change from a bent position; straighten. **2** *intr.* relax from strain or severity; become affable (*likes to unbend with a glass of beer*). **3** *tr. Naut.* **a** unfasten (sails) from yards and stays. **b** cast (a cable) loose. **c** untie (a rope).

unbending /ʌnˈbendɪŋ/ *adj.* **1** not bending; inflexible. **2** firm; austere (*unbending rectitude*). **3** relaxing from strain, activity, or formality. □□ **unbendingly** *adv.* **unbendingness** *n.*

unbiased /ʌnˈbaɪəst/ *adj.* (also **unbiassed**) not biased; impartial.

unbiblical /ʌnˈbɪblɪk(ə)l/ *adj.* **1** not in or authorized by the Bible. **2** contrary to the Bible.

unbiddable /ʌnˈbɪdəb(ə)l/ *adj. Brit.* disobedient; not docile.

unbidden /ʌnˈbɪd(ə)n/ *adj.* not commanded or invited (*arrived unbidden*).

unbind /ʌnˈbaɪnd/ *v.tr.* (*past* and *past part.* **unbound**) release from bonds or binding.

unbirthday /ʌnˈbɜːθdeɪ/ *n.* (often *attrib.*) *joc.* any day but one's birthday (*an unbirthday party*).

unbleached /ʌnˈbliːtʃt/ *adj.* not bleached.

unblemished /ʌnˈblemɪʃt/ *adj.* not blemished.

unblessed /ʌnˈblest/ *adj.* (also **unblest**) not blessed.

unblinking /ʌnˈblɪŋkɪŋ/ *adj.* **1** not blinking. **2** steadfast; not hesitating. **3** stolid; cool. □□ **unblinkingly** *adv.*

unblock /ʌnˈblɒk/ *v.tr.* **1** remove an obstruction from (esp. a pipe, drain, etc.). **2** (also *absol.*) *Cards* allow the later unobstructed play of (a suit) by playing a high card.

unblown /ʌnˈbləʊn/ *adj.* **1** not blown. **2** *archaic* (of a flower) not yet in bloom.

unblushing /ʌnˈblʌʃɪŋ/ *adj.* **1** not blushing. **2** unashamed; frank. □□ **unblushingly** *adv.*

unbolt /ʌnˈbəʊlt/ *v.tr.* release (a door etc.) by drawing back the bolt.

unbolted /ʌnˈbəʊltɪd/ *adj.* **1** not bolted. **2** (of flour etc.) not sifted.

unbonnet /ʌnˈbɒnɪt/ *v.* (**unbonneted, unbonneting**) **1** *tr.* remove the bonnet from. **2** *intr. archaic* remove one's hat or bonnet esp. in respect.

unbookish /ʌnˈbʊkɪʃ/ *adj.* **1** not academic; not often inclined to read. **2** free from bookishness.

unboot /ʌnˈbuːt/ *v.intr. & tr.* remove one's boots or the boots of (a person).

unborn /ʌnˈbɔːn/ *adj.* **1** not yet born (*an unborn child*). **2** never to be brought into being (*unborn hopes*).

unbosom /ʌnˈbʊz(ə)m/ *v.tr.* **1** disclose (thoughts, secrets, etc.). **2** (*refl.*) unburden (oneself) of one's thoughts, secrets, etc.

unbothered /ʌnˈbɒðəd/ *adj.* not bothered; unconcerned.

unbound¹ /ʌnˈbaʊnd/ *adj.* **1** not bound or tied up. **2** unconstrained. **3 a** (of a book) not having a binding. **b** having paper covers. **4** (of a substance or particle) in a loose or free state.

unbound² *past* and *past part.* of UNBIND.

unbounded /ʌnˈbaʊndɪd/ *adj.* not bounded; infinite (*unbounded optimism*). □□ **unboundedly** *adv.* **unboundedness** *n.*

unbrace /ʌnˈbreɪs/ *v.tr.* **1** (also *absol.*) free from tension; relax (the nerves etc.). **2** remove a brace or braces from.

unbreachable /ʌnˈbriːtʃəb(ə)l/ *adj.* not able to be breached.

unbreakable /ʌnˈbreɪkəb(ə)l/ *adj.* not breakable.

unbreathable /ʌnˈbriːðəb(ə)l/ *adj.* not able to be breathed.

unbribable /ʌnˈbraɪbəb(ə)l/ *adj.* not bribable.

unbridgeable /ʌnˈbrɪdʒəb(ə)l/ *adj.* unable to be bridged.

unbridle /ʌnˈbraɪd(ə)l/ *v.tr.* **1** remove a bridle from (a horse). **2** remove constraints from (one's tongue, a person, etc.). **3** (as **unbridled** *adj.*) unconstrained (*unbridled insolence*).

unbroken /ʌnˈbrəʊkən/ *adj.* **1** not broken. **2** not tamed (*an unbroken horse*). **3** not interrupted (*unbroken sleep*). **4** not surpassed (*an unbroken record*). □□ **unbrokenly** *adv.* **unbrokenness** /-ənnɪs/ *n.*

unbruised /ʌnˈbruːzd/ *adj.* not bruised.

unbuckle /ʌnˈbʌk(ə)l/ *v.tr.* release the buckle of (a strap, shoe, etc.).

unbuild /ʌnˈbɪld/ *v.tr.* (*past* and *past part.* **unbuilt**) **1** demolish or destroy (a building, theory, system, etc.). **2** (as **unbuilt** *adj.*) not yet built or (of land etc.) not yet built on.

unburden /ʌnˈbɜːd(ə)n/ *v.tr.* **1** relieve of a burden. **2** (esp. *refl.*; often foll. by *to*) relieve (oneself, one's conscience, etc.) by confession etc. □□ **unburdened** *adj.*

unburied /ʌnˈberɪd/ *adj.* not buried.

unbury /ʌnˈberɪ/ *v.tr.* (**-ies, -ied**) **1** remove from the ground etc. after burial. **2** unearth (a secret etc.).

unbusinesslike /ʌnˈbɪznɪsˌlaɪk/ *adj.* not businesslike.

unbutton /ʌnˈbʌt(ə)n/ *v.tr.* **1 a** unfasten (a coat etc.) by taking the buttons out of the buttonholes. **b** unbutton the clothes of (a person). **2** (*absol.*) *colloq.* relax from tension or formality; become communicative. **3** (as **unbuttoned** *adj.*) **a** not buttoned. **b** *colloq.* communicative; informal.

uncage /ʌnˈkeɪdʒ/ *v.tr.* **1** release from a cage. **2** release from constraint; liberate.

uncalled /ʌnˈkɔːld/ *adj.* not summoned or invited. □**uncalled-for** (of an opinion, action, etc.) impertinent or unnecessary (*an uncalled-for remark*).

uncandid /ʌnˈkændɪd/ *adj.* not candid; disingenuous.

uncanny /ʌnˈkænɪ/ *adj.* (**uncannier, uncanniest**) seemingly supernatural; mysterious. □□ **uncannily** *adv.* **uncanniness** *n.* [(orig. Sc. & N.Engl.) f. UN-¹ + CANNY]

uncanonical /ˌʌnkəˈnɒnɪk(ə)l/ *adj.* not canonical. □□ **uncanonically** *adv.*

uncap /ʌnˈkæp/ *v.tr.* (**uncapped, uncapping**) **1**

remove the cap from (a jar, bottle, etc.). **2** remove a cap from (the head or another person).

uncared-for /ʌnˈkeədfɔː(r)/ adj. disregarded; neglected.

uncase /ʌnˈkeɪs/ v.tr. remove from a cover or case.

uncashed /ʌnˈkæʃt/ adj. not cashed.

uncaught /ʌnˈkɔːt/ adj. not caught.

unceasing /ʌnˈsiːsɪŋ/ adj. not ceasing; continuous (unceasing effort). □□ **unceasingly** adv.

uncensored /ʌnˈsensəd/ adj. not censored.

uncensured /ʌnˈsensjəd/ adj. not censured.

unceremonious /ˌʌnserɪˈməʊnɪəs/ adj. **1** lacking ceremony or formality. **2** abrupt; discourteous. □□ **unceremoniously** adv. **unceremoniousness** n.

uncertain /ʌnˈsɜːt(ə)n/ adj. **1** not certainly knowing or known (uncertain what it means; the result is uncertain). **2** unreliable (his aim is uncertain). **3** changeable, erratic (uncertain weather). □**in no uncertain terms** clearly and forcefully. □□ **uncertainly** adv.

uncertainty /ʌnˈsɜːtəntɪ/ n. (pl. **-ies**) **1** the fact or condition of being uncertain. **2** an uncertain matter or circumstance. □**uncertainty principle** (in full **Heisenberg uncertainty principle** after W. Heisenberg, Ger. physicist d. 1976) Physics the principle that the momentum and position of a particle cannot both be precisely determined at the same time.

uncertified /ʌnˈsɜːtɪˌfaɪd/ adj. **1** not attested as certain. **2** not guaranteed by a certificate of competence etc. **3** not certified as insane.

unchain /ʌnˈtʃeɪn/ v.tr. **1** remove the chains from. **2** release; liberate.

unchallengeable /ʌnˈtʃælɪndʒəb(ə)l/ adj. not challengeable; unassailable. □□ **unchallengeably** adv.

unchallenged /ʌnˈtʃælɪndʒd/ adj. not challenged.

unchangeable /ʌnˈtʃeɪndʒəb(ə)l/ adj. not changeable; immutable, invariable. □□ **unchangeability** /-ˈbɪlɪtɪ/ n. **unchangeableness** n. **unchangeably** adv.

unchanged /ʌnˈtʃeɪndʒd/ adj. not changed; unaltered.

unchanging /ʌnˈtʃeɪndʒɪŋ/ adj. not changing; remaining the same. □□ **unchangingly** adv. **unchangingness** n.

unchaperoned /ʌnˈʃæpəˌrəʊnd/ adj. without a chaperone.

uncharacteristic /ˌʌnkærɪktəˈrɪstɪk/ adj. not characteristic. □□ **uncharacteristically** adv.

uncharged /ʌnˈtʃɑːdʒd/ adj. not charged (esp. in senses 3, 7, 8 of CHARGE v.).

uncharitable /ʌnˈtʃærɪtəb(ə)l/ adj. censorious, severe in judgement. □□ **uncharitableness** n. **uncharitably** adv.

uncharted /ʌnˈtʃɑːtɪd/ adj. not charted, mapped, or surveyed.

unchartered /ʌnˈtʃɑːtəd/ adj. **1** not furnished with a charter; not formally privileged or constituted. **2** unauthorized; illegal.

unchaste /ʌnˈtʃeɪst/ adj. not chaste. □□ **unchastely** adv. **unchasteness** n. **unchastity** /-ˈtʃæstɪtɪ/ n.

unchecked /ʌnˈtʃekt/ adj. **1** not checked. **2** freely allowed; unrestrained (unchecked violence).

unchivalrous /ʌnˈʃɪvəlrəs/ adj. not chivalrous; rude. □□ **unchivalrously** adv.

unchosen /ʌnˈtʃəʊz(ə)n/ adj. not chosen.

unchristian /ʌnˈkrɪstjən/ adj. **1 a** contrary to Christian principles, esp. uncaring or selfish. **b** not Christian. **2** colloq. outrageous. □□ **unchristianly** adv.

unchurch /ʌnˈtʃɜːtʃ/ v.tr. **1** excommunicate. **2** deprive (a building) of its status as a church.

uncial /ˈʌnsɪəl, -ʃ(ə)l/ adj. & n. —adj. **1** of or written in majuscule writing with rounded unjoined letters found in manuscripts of the 4th–8th c., from which modern capitals are derived. **2** of or relating to an inch or an ounce. —n. **1** an uncial letter. **2** an uncial style or MS. [L uncialis f. uncia inch: sense 1 in LL

sense of unciales litterae, the orig. application of which is unclear]

unciform /ˈʌnsɪˌfɔːm/ n. = UNCINATE.

uncinate /ˈʌnsɪnət/ adj. esp. Anat. hooked; crooked. [L uncinatus f. uncinus hook]

uncircumcised /ʌnˈsɜːkəmˌsaɪzd/ adj. **1** not circumcised. **2** spiritually impure; heathen. □□ **uncircumcision** /-ˈsɪʒ(ə)n/ n.

uncivil /ʌnˈsɪvɪl/ adj. **1** ill-mannered; impolite. **2** not public-spirited. □□ **uncivilly** adv.

uncivilized /ʌnˈsɪvɪˌlaɪzd/ adj. (also **uncivilised**) **1** not civilized. **2** rough; uncultured.

unclad /ʌnˈklæd/ adj. not clad; naked.

unclaimed /ʌnˈkleɪmd/ adj. not claimed.

unclasp /ʌnˈklɑːsp/ v.tr. **1** loosen the clasp or clasps of. **2** release the grip of (a hand etc.).

unclassifiable /ʌnˈklæsɪˌfaɪəb(ə)l/ adj. not classifiable.

unclassified /ʌnˈklæsɪˌfaɪd/ adj. **1** not classified. **2** (of State information) not secret.

uncle /ˈʌŋk(ə)l/ n. **1 a** the brother of one's father or mother. **b** an aunt's husband. **2** colloq. a name given by children to a male family friend. **3** sl. esp. hist. a pawnbroker. □**Uncle Sam** colloq. the federal government or citizens of the US (will fight for Uncle Sam). **Uncle Tom** derog. a Black man considered to be servile, cringing, etc. (from the hero of H. B. Stowe's Uncle Tom's Cabin, 1852). [ME f. AF uncle, OF oncle f. LL aunculus f. L avunculus maternal uncle: see AVUNCULAR]

-uncle /ˈʌŋk(ə)l/ suffix forming nouns, usu. diminutives (carbuncle). [OF -uncle, -oncle or L -unculus, -la, a special form of -ulus -ULE]

unclean /ʌnˈkliːn/ adj. **1** not clean. **2** unchaste. **3** unfit to be eaten; ceremonially impure. **4** Bibl. (of a spirit) wicked. □□ **uncleanly** adv. **uncleanly** /-ˈklenlɪ/ adj. **uncleanliness** /-ˈklenlɪnɪs/ n. **uncleanness** n. [OE unclǣne (as UN-[1], CLEAN)]

unclear /ʌnˈklɪə(r)/ adj. **1** not clear or easy to understand; obscure, uncertain. **2** (of a person) doubtful, uncertain (I'm unclear as to what you mean). □□ **unclearly** adv. **unclearness** n.

unclench /ʌnˈklentʃ/ v. **1** tr. release (clenched hands, features, teeth, etc.). **2** intr. (of clenched hands etc.) become relaxed or open.

unclinch /ʌnˈklɪntʃ/ v.tr. & intr. release or become released from a clinch.

uncloak /ʌnˈkləʊk/ v.tr. **1** expose, reveal. **2** remove a cloak from.

unclog /ʌnˈklɒg/ v.tr. (**unclogged**, **unclogging**) unblock (a drain, pipe, etc.).

unclose /ʌnˈkləʊz/ v. **1** tr. & intr. open. **2** tr. reveal; disclose.

unclothe /ʌnˈkləʊð/ v.tr. **1** remove the clothes from. **2** strip of leaves or vegetation (trees unclothed by the wind). **3** expose, reveal. □□ **unclothed** adj.

unclouded /ʌnˈklaʊdɪd/ adj. **1** not clouded; clear; bright. **2** untroubled (unclouded serenity).

uncluttered /ʌnˈklʌtəd/ adj. not cluttered; austere, simple.

unco /ˈʌŋkəʊ/ adj., adv., & n. Sc. —adj. strange, unusual; notable. —adv. remarkably; very. —n. (pl. **-os**) **1** a stranger. **2** (in pl.) news. □**the unco guid** /gɪd/ esp. derog. the rigidly religious. [ME, var. of UNCOUTH]

uncoil /ʌnˈkɔɪl/ v.tr. & intr. unwind.

uncoloured /ʌnˈkʌləd/ adj. (US **uncolored**) **1** having no colour. **2** not influenced; impartial. **3** not exaggerated.

uncombed /ʌnˈkəʊmd/ adj. (of hair or a person) not combed.

uncome-at-able /ˌʌnkʌmˈætəb(ə)l/ adj. colloq. inaccessible; unattainable. [UN-[1] + come-at-able: see COME]

uncomely /ʌnˈkʌmlɪ/ adj. **1** improper; unseemly. **2** ugly.

uncomfortable /ʌnˈkʌmftəb(ə)l/ adj. **1** not comfortable. **2** uneasy; causing or feeling disquiet (an *uncomfortable silence*). □□ **uncomfortableness** *n.* **uncomfortably** *adv.*

uncommercial /ˌʌnkəˈmɜːʃ(ə)l/ *adj.* **1** not commercial. **2** contrary to commercial principles.

uncommitted /ˌʌnkəˈmɪtɪd/ *adj.* **1** not committed. **2** unattached to any specific political cause or group.

uncommon /ʌnˈkɒmən/ *adj.* & *adv.* —*adj.* **1** not common; unusual; remarkable. **2** remarkably great etc. (*an uncommon fear of spiders*). —*adv.* archaic uncommonly (*he was uncommon fat*). □□ **uncommonly** *adv.* **uncommonness** /-mənnɪs/ *n.*

uncommunicative /ˌʌnkəˈmjuːnɪkətɪv/ *adj.* not wanting to communicate; taciturn. □□ **uncommunicatively** *adv.* **uncommunicativeness** *n.*

uncompanionable /ˌʌnkəmˈpænjənəb(ə)l/ *adj.* unsociable.

uncompensated /ʌnˈkɒmpenˌseɪtɪd/ *adj.* not compensated.

uncompetitive /ˌʌnkəmˈpetɪtɪv/ *adj.* not competitive.

uncomplaining /ˌʌnkəmˈpleɪnɪŋ/ *adj.* not complaining; resigned. □□ **uncomplainingly** *adv.*

uncompleted /ˌʌnkəmˈpliːtɪd/ *adj.* not completed; incomplete.

uncomplicated /ʌnˈkɒmplɪˌkeɪtɪd/ *adj.* not complicated; simple; straightforward.

uncomplimentary /ˌʌnkɒmplɪˈmentərɪ/ *adj.* not complimentary; insulting.

uncompounded /ˌʌnkəmˈpaʊndɪd/ *adj.* not compounded; unmixed.

uncomprehending /ˌʌnkɒmprɪˈhendɪŋ/ *adj.* not comprehending. □□ **uncomprehendingly** *adv.* **uncomprehension** /-ˈʃ(ə)n/ *n.*

uncompromising /ʌnˈkɒmprəˌmaɪzɪŋ/ *adj.* unwilling to compromise; stubborn; unyielding. □□ **uncompromisingly** *adv.* **uncompromisingness** *n.*

unconcealed /ˌʌnkənˈsiːld/ *adj.* not concealed; obvious.

unconcern /ˌʌnkənˈsɜːn/ *n.* lack of concern; indifference; apathy. □□ **unconcerned** *adj.* **unconcernedly** /-nɪdlɪ/ *adv.*

unconcluded /ˌʌnkənˈkluːdɪd/ *adj.* not concluded.

unconditional /ˌʌnkənˈdɪʃ(ə)n(ə)l/ *adj.* not subject to conditions; complete (*unconditional surrender*). □□ **unconditionality** /-ˈnælɪtɪ/ *n.* **unconditionally** *adv.*

unconditioned /ˌʌnkənˈdɪʃ(ə)nd/ *adj.* **1** not subject to conditions or to an antecedent condition. **2** (of behaviour etc.) not determined by conditioning; natural. □ **unconditioned reflex** an instinctive response to a stimulus.

unconfined /ˌʌnkənˈfaɪnd/ *adj.* not confined; boundless.

unconfirmed /ˌʌnkənˈfɜːmd/ *adj.* not confirmed.

unconformable /ˌʌnkənˈfɔːməb(ə)l/ *adj.* **1** not conformable or conforming. **2** (of rock strata) not having the same direction of stratification. **3** *hist.* not conforming to the provisions of the Act of Uniformity. □□ **unconformableness** *n.* **unconformably** *adv.* **unconformity** *n.*

uncongenial /ˌʌnkənˈdʒiːnɪəl/ *adj.* not congenial.

unconjecturable /ˌʌnkənˈdʒektʃərəb(ə)l/ *adj.* not conjecturable.

unconnected /ˌʌnkəˈnektɪd/ *adj.* **1** not physically joined. **2** not connected or associated. **3** (of speech etc.) disconnected; not joined in order or sequence (*unconnected ideas*). **4** not related by family ties. □□ **unconnectedly** *adv.* **unconnectedness** *n.*

unconquerable /ʌnˈkɒŋkərəb(ə)l/ *adj.* not conquerable. □□ **unconquerableness** *n.* **unconquerably** *adv.*

unconquered /ʌnˈkɒŋkəd/ *adj.* not conquered or defeated.

unconscionable /ʌnˈkɒnʃənəb(ə)l/ *adj.* **1 a** having no conscience. **b** contrary to conscience. **2 a** unreasonably excessive (*an unconscionable length*

of time). **b** not right or reasonable. □□ **unconscionableness** *n.* **unconscionably** *adv.* [UN-¹ + obs. *conscionable* f. *conscions* obs. var. of CONSCIENCE]

unconscious /ʌnˈkɒnʃəs/ *adj.* & *n.* —*adj.* not conscious (*unconscious of any change*; *fell unconscious on the floor*; *an unconscious prejudice*). —*n.* that part of the mind which is inaccessible to the conscious mind but which affects behaviour, emotions, etc. (cf. *collective unconscious*). □□ **unconsciously** *adv.* **unconsciousness** *n.*

unconsecrated /ʌnˈkɒnsɪˌkreɪtɪd/ *adj.* not consecrated.

unconsenting /ˌʌnkənˈsentɪŋ/ *adj.* not consenting.

unconsidered /ˌʌnkənˈsɪdəd/ *adj.* **1** not considered; disregarded. **2** (of a response etc.) immediate; not premeditated.

unconsolable /ˌʌnkənˈsəʊləb(ə)l/ *adj.* unable to be consoled; inconsolable. □□ **unconsolably** *adv.*

unconstitutional /ˌʌnkɒnstɪˈtjuːʃ(ə)n(ə)l/ *adj.* not in accordance with the political constitution or with procedural rules. □□ **unconstitutionality** /-ˈnælɪtɪ/ *n.* **unconstitutionally** *adv.*

unconstrained /ˌʌnkənˈstreɪnd/ *adj.* not constrained or compelled. □□ **unconstrainedly** /-nɪdlɪ/ *adv.*

unconstraint /ˌʌnkənˈstreɪnt/ *n.* freedom from constraint.

unconstricted /ˌʌnkənˈstrɪktɪd/ *adj.* not constricted.

unconsumed /ˌʌnkənˈsjuːmd/ *adj.* not consumed.

unconsummated /ʌnˈkɒnsjʊˌmeɪtɪd/ *adj.* not consummated.

uncontainable /ˌʌnkənˈteɪnəb(ə)l/ *adj.* not containable.

uncontaminated /ˌʌnkənˈtæmɪˌneɪtɪd/ *adj.* not contaminated.

uncontested /ˌʌnkənˈtestɪd/ *adj.* not contested. □□ **uncontestedly** *adv.*

uncontradicted /ˌʌnkɒntrəˈdɪktɪd/ *adj.* not contradicted.

uncontrollable /ˌʌnkənˈtrəʊləb(ə)l/ *adj.* not controllable. □□ **uncontrollableness** *n.* **uncontrollably** *adv.*

uncontrolled /ˌʌnkənˈtrəʊld/ *adj.* not controlled; unrestrained, unchecked.

uncontroversial /ˌʌnkɒntrəˈvɜːʃ(ə)l/ *adj.* not controversial. □□ **uncontroversially** *adv.*

uncontroverted /ˌʌnkɒntrəˈvɜːtɪd, ʌnˈkɒn-/ *adj.* not controverted. □□ **uncontrovertible** *adj.*

unconventional /ˌʌnkənˈvenʃən(ə)l/ *adj.* not bound by convention or custom; unusual; unorthodox. □□ **unconventionalism** *n.* **unconventionality** /-ˈnælɪtɪ/ *n.* **unconventionally** *adv.*

unconverted /ˌʌnkənˈvɜːtɪd/ *adj.* not converted.

unconvinced /ˌʌnkənˈvɪnst/ *adj.* not convinced.

unconvincing /ˌʌnkənˈvɪnsɪŋ/ *adj.* not convincing. □□ **unconvincingly** *adv.*

uncooked /ʌnˈkʊkt/ *adj.* not cooked; raw.

uncool /ʌnˈkuːl/ *adj. sl.* **1** unrelaxed; unpleasant. **2** (of jazz) not cool.

uncooperative /ˌʌnkəʊˈɒpərətɪv/ *adj.* not cooperative. □□ **uncooperatively** *adv.*

uncoordinated /ˌʌnkəʊˈɔːdɪˌneɪtɪd/ *adj.* **1** not coordinated. **2** (of a person's movements etc.) clumsy.

uncopiable /ʌnˈkɒpɪəb(ə)l/ *adj.* not able to be copied.

uncord /ʌnˈkɔːd/ *v.tr.* remove the cord from.

uncork /ʌnˈkɔːk/ *v.tr.* **1** draw the cork from (a bottle). **2** allow (feelings etc.) to be released.

uncorroborated /ˌʌnkəˈrɒbəˌreɪtɪd/ *adj.* (esp. of evidence etc.) not corroborated.

uncorrupted /ˌʌnkəˈrʌptɪd/ *adj.* not corrupted.

uncountable /ʌnˈkaʊntəb(ə)l/ *adj.* **1** inestimable, immense (*uncountable wealth*). **2** *Gram.* (of a noun) that cannot form a plural or be used with the indefinite article (e.g. *happiness*). □□ **uncountability** /-ˈbɪlɪtɪ/ *n.* **uncountably** *adv.*

w *we*   z *zoo*   ʃ *she*   ʒ *decision*   θ *thin*   ð *this*   ŋ *ring*   x *loch*   tʃ *chip*   dʒ *jar*   (*see over for vowels*)

uncounted /ʌnˈkaʊntɪd/ *adj.* **1** not counted. **2** very many; innumerable.

uncouple /ʌnˈkʌp(ə)l/ *v.tr.* **1** release (wagons) from couplings. **2** release (dogs etc.) from couples. □□ **uncoupled** *adj.*

uncourtly /ʌnˈkɔːtlɪ/ *adj.* not courteous; ill-mannered.

uncouth /ʌnˈkuːθ/ *adj.* **1** (of a person, manners, appearance, etc.) lacking in ease and polish; uncultured, rough (*uncouth voices; behaviour was uncouth*). **2** *archaic* not known; desolate; wild; uncivilized (*an uncouth place*). □□ **uncouthly** *adv.* **uncouthness** *n.* [OE *uncūth* unknown (as UN-[1] + *cūth* past part. of *cunnan* know, CAN[1])]

uncovenanted /ʌnˈkʌvənəntɪd/ *adj.* **1** not bound by a covenant. **2** not promised by or based on a covenant, esp. God's covenant.

uncover /ʌnˈkʌvə(r)/ *v.* **1** *tr.* **a** remove a cover or covering from. **b** make known; disclose (*uncovered the truth at last*). **2** *intr. archaic* remove one's hat, cap, etc. **3** *tr.* (as **uncovered** *adj.*) **a** not covered by a roof, clothing, etc. **b** not wearing a hat.

uncreate /ˌʌnkrɪˈeɪt/ *v.tr. literary* annihilate.

uncreated /ˌʌnkrɪˈeɪtɪd/ *adj.* existing without having been created; not created. [UN-[1] + obs. *create* f. L *creatus* past part. of *creare*: see CREATE]

uncreative /ˌʌnkrɪˈeɪtɪv/ *adj.* not creative.

uncritical /ʌnˈkrɪtɪk(ə)l/ *adj.* **1** not critical; complacently accepting. **2** not in accordance with the principles of criticism. □□ **uncritically** *adv.*

uncropped /ʌnˈkrɒpt/ *adj.* not cropped.

uncross /ʌnˈkrɒs/ *v.tr.* **1** remove (the limbs, knives, etc.) from a crossed position. **2** (as **uncrossed** *adj.*) **a** *Brit.* (of a cheque) not crossed. **b** not thwarted or challenged. **c** not wearing a cross.

uncrown /ʌnˈkraʊn/ *v.tr.* **1** deprive (a monarch etc.) of a crown. **2** deprive (a person) of a position. **3** (as **uncrowned** *adj.*) **a** not crowned. **b** having the status but not the name of (*the uncrowned king of boxing*).

uncrushable /ʌnˈkrʌʃəb(ə)l/ *adj.* not crushable.

uncrushed /ʌnˈkrʌʃt/ *adj.* not crushed.

UNCSTD *abbr.* United Nations Conference on Science and Technology for Development.

UNCTAD *abbr.* United Nations Conference on Trade and Development.

unction /ˈʌŋkʃ(ə)n/ *n.* **1 a** the act of anointing with oil etc. as a religious rite. **b** the oil etc. so used. **2 a** soothing words or thought. **b** excessive or insincere flattery. **3 a** the act of anointing for medical purposes. **b** an ointment so used. **4 a** a fervent or sympathetic quality in words or tone caused by or causing deep emotion. **b** a pretence of this. [ME f. L *unctio* f. *ung(u)ere unct-* anoint]

unctuous /ˈʌŋktjʊəs/ *adj.* **1** (of behaviour, speech, etc.) unpleasantly flattering; oily. **2** (esp. of minerals) having a greasy or soapy feel; oily. □□ **unctuously** *adv.* **unctuousness** *n.* [ME f. med.L *unctuosus* f. L *unctus* anointing (as UNCTION)]

unculled /ʌnˈkʌld/ *adj.* not culled.

uncultivated /ʌnˈkʌltɪˌveɪtɪd/ *adj.* (esp. of land) not cultivated.

uncultured /ʌnˈkʌltʃəd/ *adj.* **1** not cultured, unrefined. **2** (of soil or plants) not cultivated.

uncurb /ʌnˈkɜːb/ *v.tr.* remove a curb or curbs from. □□ **uncurbed** *adj.*

uncured /ʌnˈkjʊəd/ *adj.* **1** not cured. **2** (of pork etc.) not salted or smoked.

uncurl /ʌnˈkɜːl/ *v.intr. & tr.* relax from a curled position, untwist.

uncurtailed /ˌʌnkəˈteɪld/ *adj.* not curtailed.

uncurtained /ʌnˈkɜːt(ə)nd/ *adj.* not curtained.

uncut /ʌnˈkʌt/ *adj.* **1** not cut. **2** (of a book) with the pages not cut open or with untrimmed margins. **3** (of a book, film, etc.) complete; uncensored. **4** (of a stone, esp. a diamond) not shaped by cutting. **5** (of fabric) having its pile-loops intact (*uncut moquette*).

undamaged /ʌnˈdæmɪdʒd/ *adj.* not damaged; intact.

undated /ʌnˈdeɪtɪd/ *adj.* not provided or marked with a date.

undaunted /ʌnˈdɔːntɪd/ *adj.* not daunted. □□ **undauntedly** *adv.* **undauntedness** *n.*

undecagon /ʌnˈdekəgən/ *n.* = HENDECAGON. [L *undecim* eleven, after *decagon*]

undeceive /ˌʌndɪˈsiːv/ *v.tr.* (often foll. by *of*) free (a person) from a misconception, deception, or error.

undecided /ˌʌndɪˈsaɪdɪd/ *adj.* **1** not settled or certain (*the question is undecided*). **2** hesitating; irresolute (*undecided about their relative merits*). □□ **undecidedly** *adv.*

undecipherable /ˌʌndɪˈsaɪfərəb(ə)l/ *adj.* not decipherable.

undeclared /ˌʌndɪˈkleəd/ *adj.* not declared.

undefeated /ˌʌndɪˈfiːtɪd/ *adj.* not defeated.

undefended /ˌʌndɪˈfendɪd/ *adj.* (esp. of a lawsuit) not defended.

undefiled /ˌʌndɪˈfaɪld/ *adj.* not defiled; pure.

undefined /ˌʌndɪˈfaɪnd/ *adj.* **1** not defined. **2** not clearly marked; vague, indefinite. □□ **undefinable** *adj.* **undefinably** *adv.*

undelivered /ˌʌndɪˈlɪvəd/ *adj.* **1** not delivered or handed over. **2** not set free or released. **3 a** (of a pregnant woman) not yet having given birth. **b** (of a child) not yet born.

undemanding /ˌʌndɪˈmɑːndɪŋ/ *adj.* not demanding; easily satisfied. □□ **undemandingness** *n.*

undemocratic /ˌʌndeməˈkrætɪk/ *adj.* not democratic. □□ **undemocratically** *adv.*

undemonstrated /ʌnˈdemənˌstreɪtɪd/ *adj.* not demonstrated.

undemonstrative /ˌʌndɪˈmɒnstrətɪv/ *adj.* not expressing feelings etc. outwardly; reserved. □□ **undemonstratively** *adv.* **undemonstrativeness** *n.*

undeniable /ˌʌndɪˈnaɪəb(ə)l/ *adj.* **1** unable to be denied or disputed; certain. **2** excellent (*was of undeniable character*). □□ **undeniableness** *n.* **undeniably** *adv.*

undenied /ˌʌndɪˈnaɪd/ *adj.* not denied.

undependable /ˌʌndɪˈpendəb(ə)l/ *adj.* not to be depended upon; unreliable.

under /ˈʌndə(r)/ *prep., adv., & adj.* —*prep.* **1 a** in or to a position lower than; below; beneath (*fell under the table; under the left eye*). **b** within, on the inside of (a surface etc.) (*wore a vest under his shirt*). **2 a** inferior to; less than (*a captain is under a major; is under 18*). **b** at or for a lower cost than (*was under £20*). **3 a** subject or liable to; controlled or bound by (*lives under oppression; under pain of death; born under Saturn; the country prospered under him*). **b** undergoing (*is under repair*). **c** classified or subsumed in (*that book goes under biology; goes under many names*). **4** at the foot of or sheltered by (*hid under the wall; under the cliff*). **5** planted with (a crop). **6** powered by (sail, steam, etc.). **7** following (another player in a card game). **8** *archaic* attested by (*esp. under one's hand and seal* = signature). —*adv.* **1** in or to a lower position or condition (*kept him under*). **2** *colloq.* in or into a state of unconsciousness (*put him under for the operation*). —*adj.* lower (*the under jaw*). □ **under age** see AGE. **under one's arm** see ARM[1]. **under arms** see ARM[2]. **under one's belt** see BELT. **under one's breath** see BREATH. **under canvas** see CANVAS. **under a cloud** see CLOUD. **under control** see CONTROL. **under the counter** see COUNTER[1]. **under cover** see COVER *n.* 4. **under fire** see FIRE. **under foot** see FOOT. **under hatches** see HATCH[1]. **under a person's nose** see NOSE. **under the rose** see ROSE[1]. **under separate cover** in another envelope. **under the sun** anywhere in the world. **under water** in and covered by water. **under way** in motion; in progress. **under the weather** see WEATHER. □□ **undermost** *adj.* [OE f. Gmc]

under- /ˈʌndə(r)/ *prefix* in senses of UNDER: **1** below, beneath (*undercarriage; underground*). **2** lower in status; subordinate (*under-secretary*). **3** insufficiently, incompletely (*undercook*; *underdeveloped*). [OE (as UNDER)]

underachieve /ˌʌndərə'tʃiːv/ *v.intr.* do less well than might be expected (esp. scholastically). □□ **underachievement** *n.* **underachiever** *n.*

underact /ˌʌndər'ækt/ *v.* **1** *tr.* act (a part etc.) with insufficient force. **2** *intr.* act a part in this way.

underarm /'ʌndərˌɑːm/ *adj.* & *adv.* **1** *Sport,* esp. *Cricket* with the arm below shoulder-level. **2** under the arm. **3** in the armpit.

underbelly /'ʌndəˌbelɪ/ *n.* (*pl.* -ies) the under surface of an animal, vehicle, etc., esp. as an area vulnerable to attack.

underbid *v.* & *n.* —*v.tr.* /ˌʌndə'bɪd/ (-bidding; *past* and *past part.* -bid) **1** make a lower bid than (a person). **2** (also *absol.*) *Bridge* etc. bid less on (one's hand) than its strength warrants. —*n.* /'ʌndəˌbɪd/ **1** such a bid. **2** the act or an instance of underbidding.

underbidder /ˌʌndə'bɪdə(r)/ *n.* **1** the person who makes the bid next below the highest. **2** *Bridge* etc. a player who underbids.

underbody /'ʌndəˌbɒdɪ/ *n.* (*pl.* -ies) the under surface of the body of an animal, vehicle, etc.

underbred /ˌʌndə'bred/ *adj.* **1** ill-bred, vulgar. **2** not of pure breeding.

underbrush /'ʌndəˌbrʌʃ/ *n.* US undergrowth in a forest.

undercarriage /'ʌndəˌkærɪdʒ/ *n.* **1** a wheeled structure beneath an aircraft, usu. retracted when not in use, to receive the impact on landing and support the aircraft on the ground etc. **2** the supporting frame of a vehicle.

undercart /'ʌndəˌkɑːt/ *n.* *Brit.* *colloq.* the undercarriage of an aircraft.

undercharge /ˌʌndə'tʃɑːdʒ/ *v.tr.* **1** charge too little for (a thing) or to (a person). **2** give less than the proper charge to (a gun, an electric battery, etc.).

underclass /'ʌndəˌklɑːs/ *n.* a subordinate social class.

underclay /'ʌndəˌkleɪ/ *n.* a clay bed under a coal seam.

undercliff /'ʌndəklɪf/ *n.* a terrace or lower cliff formed by a landslip.

underclothes /'ʌndəˌkləʊðz, -ˌkləʊz/ *n.pl.* clothes worn under others, esp. next to the skin.

underclothing /'ʌndəˌkləʊðɪŋ/ *n.* underclothes collectively.

undercoat /'ʌndəˌkəʊt/ *n.* **1 a** a preliminary layer of paint under the finishing coat. **b** the paint used for this. **2** an animal's under layer of hair or down. **3** a coat worn under another. □□ **undercoating** *n.*

undercover /ˌʌndə'kʌvə(r), 'ʌn-/ *adj.* (usu. *attrib.*) **1** surreptitious. **2** engaged in spying, esp. by working with or among those to be observed (*undercover agent*).

undercroft /ˌʌndə'krɒft/ *n.* a crypt. [ME f. UNDER- + *croft* crypt f. MDu. *crofte* cave f. med.L *crupta* for L *crypta*: see CRYPT]

undercurrent /'ʌndəˌkʌrənt/ *n.* **1** a current below the surface. **2** an underlying often contrary feeling, activity, or influence (*an undercurrent of protest*).

undercut *v.* & *n.* —*v.tr.* /ˌʌndə'kʌt/ (-cutting; *past* and *past part.* -cut) **1** sell or work at a lower price or lower wages than. **2** *Golf* strike (a ball) so as to make it rise high. **3 a** cut away the part below or under (a thing). **b** cut away material to show (a carved design etc.) in relief. **4** render unstable or less firm, undermine. —*n.* /'ʌndəˌkʌt/ **1** *Brit.* the underside of a sirloin. **2** US a notch cut in a tree-trunk to guide its fall when felled. **3** any space formed by the removal or absence of material from the lower part of something.

underdeveloped /ˌʌndədɪ'veləpt/ *adj.* **1** not fully developed; immature. **2** (of a country etc.) below its potential economic level. **3** *Photog.* not developed sufficiently to give a normal image. □□ **underdevelopment** *n.*

underdog /'ʌndəˌdɒg/ *n.* **1** a dog, or usu. a person,

losing a fight. **2** a person who is in a state of inferiority or subjection.

underdone /ˌʌndə'dʌn, 'ʌn-/ *adj.* **1** not thoroughly done. **2** (of food) lightly or insufficiently cooked.

underdress /ˌʌndə'dres/ *v.tr.* & *intr.* dress too plainly or too lightly.

underemphasis /ˌʌndər'emfəsɪs/ *n.* (*pl.* -emphases /-ˌsiːz/) an insufficient degree of emphasis. □□ **underemphasize** *v.tr.* (also -ise).

underemployed /ˌʌndərɪm'plɔɪd/ *adj.* not fully employed. □□ **underemployment** *n.*

underestimate *v.* & *n.* —*v.tr.* /ˌʌndər'estɪˌmeɪt/ form too low an estimate of. —*n.* /ˌʌndər'estɪmət/ an estimate that is too low. □□ **underestimation** /-'meɪʃ(ə)n/ *n.*

underexpose /ˌʌndərɪk'spəʊz/ *v.tr.* *Photog.* expose (film) for too short a time or with insufficient light. □□ **underexposure** *n.*

underfed /ˌʌndə'fed/ *adj.* insufficiently fed.

underfelt /'ʌndəˌfelt/ *n.* felt for laying under a carpet.

underfloor /'ʌndəˌflɔː(r)/ *attrib.adj.* situated or operating beneath the floor (*underfloor heating*).

underflow /'ʌndəˌfləʊ/ *n.* an undercurrent.

underfoot /ˌʌndə'fʊt/ *adv.* **1** under one's feet. **2** on the ground. **3** in a state of subjection. **4** so as to obstruct or inconvenience.

undergarment /'ʌndəˌgɑːmənt/ *n.* a piece of underclothing.

undergird /ˌʌndə'gɜːd/ *v.tr.* **1** make secure underneath. **2** strengthen, support.

underglaze /'ʌndəˌgleɪz/ *adj.* & *n.* —*adj.* **1** (of painting on porcelain etc.) done before the glaze is applied. **2** (of colours) used in such painting. —*n.* underglaze painting.

undergo /ˌʌndə'gəʊ/ *v.tr.* (3rd *sing. present* -goes; *past* -went; *past part.* -gone) be subjected to; suffer; endure. [OE *undergān* (as UNDER-, GO¹)]

undergrad /ˌʌndə'græd/ *n.* *colloq.* = UNDER-GRADUATE. [abbr.]

undergraduate /ˌʌndə'grædjʊət/ *n.* a student at a university who has not yet taken a first degree.

underground *adv.,* *adj.,* *n.,* & *v.* —*adv.* /ˌʌndə'graʊnd/ **1** beneath the surface of the ground. **2** in or into secrecy or hiding. —*adj.* /'ʌndəˌgraʊnd/ **1** situated underground. **2** secret, hidden, esp. working secretly to subvert a ruling power. **3** unconventional, experimental (*underground press*). —*n.* /'ʌndəˌgraʊnd/ **1** an underground railway. **2** a secret group or activity, esp. aiming to subvert the established order. —*v.tr.* /'ʌndəˌgraʊnd/ lay (cables) below ground level.

undergrowth /'ʌndəˌgrəʊθ/ *n.* a dense growth of shrubs etc., esp. under large trees.

underhand *adj.* & *adv.* —*adj.* /'ʌndəˌhænd/ **1** secret, clandestine, not above-board. **2** deceptive, crafty. **3** *Sport,* esp. *Cricket* underarm. —*adv.* /ˌʌndə'hænd/ in an underhand manner. [OE (as UNDER-, HAND)]

underhanded /ˌʌndə'hændɪd/ *adj.* & *adv.* = UNDERHAND.

underhung /'ʌndəˌhʌŋ, -'hʌŋ/ *adj.* **1** (of the lower jaw) projecting beyond the upper jaw. **2** having an underhung jaw.

underlay¹ *v.* & *n.* —*v.tr.* /ˌʌndə'leɪ/ (*past* and *past part.* -laid) lay something under (a thing) to support or raise it. —*n.* /'ʌndəˌleɪ/ a thing laid under another, esp. material laid under a carpet or mattress as protection or support. [OE *underlecgan* (as UNDER-, LAY¹)]

underlay² *past* of UNDERLIE.

underlease /'ʌndəˌliːs/ *n.* & *v.tr.* = SUBLEASE.

underlet /ˌʌndə'let/ *v.tr.* (-letting; *past* and *past part.* -let) **1** sublet. **2** let at less than the true value.

underlie /ˌʌndə'laɪ/ *v.tr.* (-lying; *past* -lay; *past part.* -lain) **1** (also *absol.*) lie or be situated under (a stratum etc.). **2** (also *absol.*) (esp. as **underlying** *adj.*) (of a principle, reason, etc.) be the basis of (a doctrine, law, conduct, etc.). **3** exist beneath the superficial aspect of. [OE *underlicgan* (as UNDER-, LIE¹)]

underline *v. & n.* —*v.tr.* /ˌʌndəˈlaɪn/ **1** draw a line under (a word etc.) to give emphasis or draw attention or indicate italic or other special type. **2** emphasize, stress. —*n.* /ˈʌndəˌlaɪn/ **1** a line drawn under a word etc. **2** a caption below an illustration.

underlinen /ˈʌndəˌlɪnɪn/ *n.* underclothes esp. of linen.

underling /ˈʌndəlɪŋ/ *n.* usu. *derog.* a subordinate.

underlying *pres. part.* of UNDERLIE.

undermanned /ˌʌndəˈmænd/ *adj.* having too few people as crew or staff.

undermentioned /ˌʌndəˈmenʃ(ə)nd, ˈʌn-/ *adj.* Brit. mentioned at a later place in a book etc.

undermine /ˌʌndəˈmaɪn/ *v.tr.* **1** injure (a person, reputation, influence, etc.) by secret or insidious means. **2** weaken, injure, or wear out (health etc.) imperceptibly or insidiously. **3** wear away the base or foundation of (*rivers undermine their banks*). **4** make a mine or excavation under. □□ **underminer** *n.* **underminingly** *adv.* [ME f. UNDER- + MINE²]

underneath /ˌʌndəˈniːθ/ *prep., adv., n., & adj.* —*prep.* **1** at or to a lower place than, below. **2** on the inside of, within. —*adv.* **1** at or to a lower place. **2** inside. —*n.* the lower surface or part. —*adj.* lower. [OE *underneothan* (as UNDER + *neothan*: cf. BENEATH)]

undernourished /ˌʌndəˈnʌrɪʃt/ *adj.* insufficiently nourished. □□ **undernourishment** *n.*

underpaid *past and past part.* of UNDERPAY.

underpants /ˈʌndəˌpænts/ *n.pl.* an undergarment, esp. men's, covering the lower part of the body and part of the legs.

under-part /ˈʌndəˌpɑːt/ *n.* **1** a lower part, esp. of an animal. **2** a subordinate part in a play etc.

underpass /ˈʌndəˌpɑːs/ *n.* **1** a road etc. passing under another. **2** a crossing of this form.

underpay /ˌʌndəˈpeɪ/ *v.tr.* (*past and past part.* **-paid**) pay too little to (a person) or for (a thing). □□ **underpayment** *n.*

underpin /ˌʌndəˈpɪn/ *v.tr.* (**-pinned, -pinning**) **1** support from below with masonry etc. **2** support, strengthen.

underplant /ˌʌndəˈplɑːnt/ *v.tr.* (usu. foll. by *with*) plant or cultivate the ground about (a tall plant) with smaller ones.

underplay /ˌʌndəˈpleɪ/ *v.* **1** *tr.* play down the importance of. **2** *intr. & tr. Theatr.* **a** perform with deliberate restraint. **b** underact.

underplot /ˈʌndəˌplɒt/ *n.* a subordinate plot in a play etc.

underpopulated /ˌʌndəˈpɒpjʊˈleɪtɪd/ *adj.* having an insufficient or very small population.

underprice /ˌʌndəˈpraɪs/ *v.tr.* price lower than what is usual or appropriate.

underprivileged /ˌʌndəˈprɪvɪlɪdʒd/ *adj.* **1** less privileged than others. **2** not enjoying the normal standard of living or rights in a society.

underproduction /ˌʌndəprəˈdʌkʃ(ə)n/ *n.* production of less than is usual or required.

underproof /ˈʌndəˌpruːf/ *adj.* containing less alcohol than proof spirit does.

underprop /ˌʌndəˈprɒp/ *v.tr.* (**-propped, -propping**) **1** support with a prop. **2** support, sustain.

underquote /ˌʌndəˈkwəʊt/ *v.tr.* **1** quote a lower price than (a person). **2** quote a lower price than others for (goods etc.).

underrate /ˌʌndəˈreɪt/ *v.tr.* have too low an opinion of.

underscore *v. & n.* —*v.tr.* /ˌʌndəˈskɔː(r)/ = UNDERLINE *v.* —*n.* /ˈʌndəˌskɔː(r)/ = UNDERLINE *n.* 1.

undersea /ˈʌndəˌsiː/ *adj.* below the sea or the surface of the sea, submarine.

underseal /ˈʌndəˌsiːl/ *v. & n.* —*v.tr.* seal the underpart of (esp. a motor vehicle against rust etc.). —*n.* a protective coating for this.

under-secretary /ˌʌndəˈsekrətərɪ/ *n.* (*pl.* **-ies**) a subordinate official, esp. a junior minister or senior civil servant.

undersell /ˌʌndəˈsel/ *v.tr.* (*past and past part.* **-sold**) **1** sell at a lower price than (another seller). **2** sell at less than the true value.

underset *v. & n.* —*v.tr.* /ˌʌndəˈset/ (**-setting**; *past and past part.* **-set**) place something under (a thing). —*n.* /ˈʌndəˌset/ *Naut.* an undercurrent.

undersexed /ˌʌndəˈsekst/ *adj.* having unusually weak sexual desires.

under-sheriff /ˈʌndəˌʃerɪf/ *n.* a deputy sheriff.

undershirt /ˈʌndəˌʃɜːt/ *n.* esp. *US* an undergarment worn under a shirt; a vest.

undershoot *v. & n.* —*v.tr.* /ˌʌndəˈʃuːt/ (*past and past part.* **-shot**) **1** (of an aircraft) land short of (a runway etc.). **2** shoot short of or below. —*n.* /ˈʌndəˌʃuːt/ the act or an instance of undershooting.

undershorts /ˈʌndəˌʃɔːts/ *n. US* short underpants; trunks.

undershot /ˈʌndəˌʃɒt/ *adj.* **1** (of a water-wheel) turned by water flowing under it. **2** = UNDERHUNG.

undershrub /ˈʌndəˌʃrʌb/ *n.* = SUBSHRUB.

underside /ˈʌndəˌsaɪd/ *n.* the lower or under side or surface.

undersigned /ˈʌndəˌsaɪnd, -ˈsaɪnd/ *adj.* whose signature is appended (*we, the undersigned, wish to state . . .*).

undersized /ˈʌndəˌsaɪzd, -ˈsaɪzd/ *adj.* of less than the usual size.

underskirt /ˈʌndəˌskɜːt/ *n.* a skirt worn under another; a petticoat.

underslung /ˈʌndəˌslʌŋ/ *adj.* **1** supported from above. **2** (of a vehicle chassis) hanging lower than the axles.

undersold *past and past part.* of UNDERSELL.

undersow /ˈʌndəˌsəʊ/ *v.tr.* (*past part.* **-sown**) **1** sow (a later-growing crop) on land already seeded with another crop. **2** (foll. by *with*) sow land already seeded with (a crop) with a later-growing crop.

underspend /ˌʌndəˈspend/ *v.* (*past and past part.* **-spent**) **1** *tr.* spend less than (a specified amount). **2** *intr. & refl.* spend too little.

understaffed /ˌʌndəˈstɑːft/ *adj.* having too few staff.

understand /ˌʌndəˈstænd/ *v.* (*past and past part.* **-stood** /-ˈstʊd/) **1** *tr.* perceive the meaning of (words, a person, a language, etc.) (*does not understand what you say; understood you perfectly; cannot understand French*). **2** *tr.* perceive the significance or explanation or cause of (*do not understand why he came; could not understand what the noise was about; do not understand the point of his remark*). **3** *tr.* be sympathetically aware of the character or nature of, know how to deal with (*quite understand your difficulty; cannot understand him at all; could never understand algebra*). **4** *tr.* **a** (often foll. by *that* + clause) infer esp. from information received, take as implied, take for granted (*I understand that it begins at noon; I understand him to be a distant relation; am I to understand that you refuse?*). **b** (*absol.*) believe or assume from knowledge or inference (*he is coming tomorrow, I understand*). **5** *tr.* supply (a word) mentally (*the verb may be either expressed or understood*). **6** *intr.* have understanding (in general or in particular). □ **understand each other 1** know each other's views or feelings. **2** be in agreement or collusion. □□ **understandable** *adj.* **understandably** *adv.* **understander** *n.* [OE *understandan* (as UNDER-, STAND)]

understanding /ˌʌndəˈstændɪŋ/ *n. & adj.* —*n.* **1 a** the ability to understand or think; intelligence. **b** the power of apprehension; the power of abstract thought. **2** an individual's perception or judgement of a situation etc. **3** an agreement; a thing agreed upon, esp. informally (*had an understanding with the rival company; consented only on this understanding*). **4** harmony in opinion or feeling (*disturbed the good understanding between them*). **5** sympathetic awareness or tolerance. —*adj.* **1** having understanding or insight or good judgement. **2** sympathetic to others' feelings. □□ **understandingly** *adv.* [OE (as UNDERSTAND)]

understate /ˌʌndəˈsteɪt/ *v.tr.* **1** express in greatly or unduly restrained terms. **2** represent as being less than it actually is. □□ **understatement** /ˌʌndəˈsteɪtmənt, ˈʌndə-/ *n.* **understater** *n.*

understeer /ˈʌndəstɪə(r)/ *n. & v.* —*n.* a tendency of a motor vehicle to turn less sharply than was intended. —*v.intr.* have such a tendency.

understood *past* and *past part.* of UNDERSTAND.

understorey /ˈʌndəˌstɔːrɪ/ *n.* (*pl.* -**eys**) **1** a layer of vegetation beneath the main canopy of a forest. **2** the plants forming this.

understudy /ˈʌndəˌstʌdɪ/ *n. & v.* esp. *Theatr.* —*n.* (*pl.* -**ies**) a person who studies another's role or duties in order to act at short notice in the absence of the other. —*v.tr.* (-**ies**, -**ied**) **1** study (a role etc.) as an understudy. **2** act as an understudy to (a person).

undersubscribed /ˌʌndəsəbˈskraɪbd/ *adj.* without sufficient subscribers, participants, etc.

undersurface /ˈʌndəˌsɜːfɪs/ *n.* the lower or under surface.

undertake /ˌʌndəˈteɪk/ *v.tr.* (*past* -**took**; *past part.* -**taken**) **1** bind oneself to perform, make oneself responsible for, engage in, enter upon (work, an enterprise, a responsibility). **2** (usu. foll. by *to* + infin.) accept an obligation, promise. **3** guarantee, affirm (*I will undertake that he has not heard a word*).

undertaker /ˈʌndəˌteɪkə(r)/ *n.* **1** a person whose business is to make arrangements for funerals. **2** /also -ˈteɪkə(r)/ a person who undertakes to do something. **3** *hist.* an influential person in 17th-century England who undertook to procure particular legislation, esp. to obtain supplies from the House of Commons if the king would grant some concession.

undertaking /ˌʌndəˈteɪkɪŋ/ *n.* **1** work etc. undertaken, an enterprise (*a serious undertaking*). **2** a pledge or promise. **3** /ˈʌn-/ the management of funerals as a profession.

undertenant /ˈʌndəˌtenənt/ *n.* a subtenant. □□ **undertenancy** *n.* (*pl.* -**ies**).

underthings /ˈʌndəθɪŋz/ *n.pl. colloq.* underclothes.

undertint /ˈʌndətɪnt/ *n.* a subdued tint.

undertone /ˈʌndəˌtəʊn/ *n.* **1** a subdued tone of sound or colour. **2** an underlying quality. **3** an undercurrent of feeling.

undertook *past* of UNDERTAKE.

undertow /ˈʌndəˌtəʊ/ *n.* a current below the surface of the sea moving in the opposite direction to the surface current.

undertrick /ˈʌndətrɪk/ *n. Bridge* a trick by which the declarer falls short of his or her contract.

undervalue /ˌʌndəˈvæljuː/ *v.tr.* (-**values**, -**valued**, -**valuing**) **1** value insufficiently. **2** underestimate. □□ **undervaluation** /-juːˈeɪʃ(ə)n/ *n.*

undervest /ˈʌndəˌvest/ *n. Brit.* an undergarment worn on the upper part of the body; a vest.

underwater /ˌʌndəˈwɔːtə(r)/ *adj. & adv.* —*adj.* situated or done under water. —*adv.* under water.

underwear /ˈʌndəˌweə(r)/ *n.* underclothes.

underweight *adj. & n.* —*adj.* /ˌʌndəˈweɪt/ weighing less than is normal or desirable. —*n.* /ˈʌndəˌweɪt/ insufficient weight.

underwent *past* of UNDERGO.

underwhelm /ˌʌndəˈwelm/ *v.tr. joc.* fail to impress. [after OVERWHELM]

underwing /ˈʌndəwɪŋ/ *n.* a wing placed under or partly covered by another.

underwood /ˈʌndəˌwʊd/ *n.* undergrowth.

underwork /ˌʌndəˈwɜːk/ *v.* **1** *tr.* impose too little work on. **2** *intr.* do too little work.

underworld /ˈʌndəˌwɜːld/ *n.* **1** the part of society comprising those who live by organized crime and immorality. **2** the mythical abode of the dead under the earth. **3** the antipodes.

underwrite /ˌʌndəˈraɪt, ˈʌn-/ *v.* (*past* -**wrote**; *past part.* -**written**) **1 a** *tr.* sign, and accept liability under (an insurance policy, esp. on shipping etc.). **b** *tr.* accept (liability) in this way. **c** *intr.* practice (marine) insurance. **2** *tr.* undertake to finance or support. **3** *tr.* engage to buy all the stock in (a company etc.) not bought by the public. **4** *tr.* write below (*the underwritten names*). □□ **underwriter** /ˈʌn-/ *n.*

undescended /ˌʌndɪˈsendɪd/ *adj. Med.* (of a testicle) remaining in the abdomen instead of descending normally into the scrotum.

undeserved /ˌʌndɪˈzɜːvd/ *adj.* not deserved (as reward or punishment). □□ **undeservedly** /-vɪdlɪ/ *adv.*

undeserving /ˌʌndɪˈzɜːvɪŋ/ *adj.* not deserving. □□ **undeservingly** *adv.*

undesigned /ˌʌndɪˈzaɪnd/ *adj.* unintentional. □□ **undesignedly** /-nɪdlɪ/ *adv.*

undesirable /ˌʌndɪˈzaɪərəb(ə)l/ *adj. & n.* —*adj.* not desirable, objectionable, unpleasant. —*n.* an undesirable person. □□ **undesirability** /-ˈbɪlɪtɪ/ *n.* **undesirableness** *n.* **undesirably** *adv.*

undesired /ˌʌndɪˈzaɪəd/ *adj.* not desired.

undesirous /ˌʌndɪˈzaɪərəs/ *adj.* not desirous.

undetectable /ˌʌndɪˈtektəb(ə)l/ *adj.* not detectable. □□ **undetectability** /-ˈbɪlɪtɪ/ *n.* **undetectably** *adv.*

undetected /ˌʌndɪˈtektɪd/ *adj.* not detected.

undetermined /ˌʌndɪˈtɜːmɪnd/ *adj.* = UNDECIDED.

undeterred /ˌʌndɪˈtɜːd/ *adj.* not deterred.

undeveloped /ˌʌndɪˈveləpt/ *adj.* not developed.

undeviating /ʌnˈdiːvɪˌeɪtɪŋ/ *adj.* not deviating; steady, constant. □□ **undeviatingly** *adv.*

undiagnosed /ʌnˈdaɪəɡˌnəʊzd, ˌʌndaɪəɡˈnəʊzd/ *adj.* not diagnosed.

undid *past* of UNDO.

undies /ˈʌndɪz/ *n.pl. colloq.* (esp. women's) underclothes. [abbr.]

undifferentiated /ˌʌndɪfəˈrenʃɪˌeɪtɪd/ *adj.* not differentiated; amorphous.

undigested /ˌʌndɪˈdʒestɪd, ˌʌndaɪ-/ *adj.* **1** not digested. **2** (esp. of information, facts, etc.) not properly arranged or considered.

undignified /ʌnˈdɪɡnɪˌfaɪd/ *adj.* lacking dignity.

undiluted /ˌʌndaɪˈljuːtɪd/ *adj.* not diluted.

undiminished /ˌʌndɪˈmɪnɪʃt/ *adj.* not diminished or lessened.

undine /ˈʌndiːn/ *n.* a female water-spirit. [mod.L *undina* (word invented by Paracelsus) f. L *unda* wave]

undiplomatic /ˌʌndɪpləˈmætɪk/ *adj.* tactless. □□ **undiplomatically** *adv.*

undischarged /ˌʌndɪsˈtʃɑːdʒd/ *adj.* (esp. of a bankrupt or a debt) not discharged.

undiscipline /ʌnˈdɪsɪplɪn/ *n.* lack of discipline.

undisciplined /ʌnˈdɪsɪplɪnd/ *adj.* lacking discipline; not disciplined.

undisclosed /ˌʌndɪsˈkləʊzd/ *adj.* not revealed or made known.

undiscoverable /ˌʌndɪsˈkʌvərəb(ə)l/ *adj.* that cannot be discovered.

undiscovered /ˌʌndɪsˈkʌvəd/ *adj.* not discovered.

undiscriminating /ˌʌndɪsˈkrɪmɪˌneɪtɪŋ/ *adj.* not showing good judgement.

undisguised /ˌʌndɪsˈɡaɪzd/ *adj.* not disguised. □□ **undisguisedly** /-zɪdlɪ/ *adv.*

undismayed /ˌʌndɪsˈmeɪd/ *adj.* not dismayed.

undisputed /ˌʌndɪsˈpjuːtɪd/ *adj.* not disputed or called in question.

undissolved /ˌʌndɪˈzɒlvd/ *adj.* not dissolved.

undistinguishable /ˌʌndɪsˈtɪŋɡwɪʃəb(ə)l/ *adj.* (often foll. by *from*) indistinguishable.

undistinguished /ˌʌndɪsˈtɪŋɡwɪʃt/ *adj.* not distinguished; mediocre.

undistributed /ˌʌndɪsˈtrɪbjuːtɪd/ *adj.* not distributed. □ **undistributed middle** *Logic* a fallacy resulting from the failure of the middle term of a syllogism to refer to all the members of a class.

undisturbed /ˌʌndɪsˈtɜːbd/ *adj.* not disturbed or interfered with.

undivided /ˌʌndɪˈvaɪdɪd/ *adj.* not divided or shared; whole, entire (*gave him my undivided attention*).

undo /ʌnˈduː/ *v.tr.* (*3rd sing. present* **-does**; *past* **-did**; *past part.* **-done**) **1 a** unfasten or untie (a coat, button, parcel, etc.). **b** unfasten the clothing of (a person). **2** annul, cancel (*cannot undo the past*). **3** ruin the prospects, reputation, or morals of. [OE *undōn* (as UN-², DO¹)]

undock /ʌnˈdɒk/ *v.tr.* **1** (also *absol.*) separate (a spacecraft) from another in space. **2** take (a ship) out of a dock.

undocumented /ʌnˈdɒkjʊˌmentɪd/ *adj.* **1** *US* not having the appropriate document. **2** not proved by or recorded in documents.

undoing /ʌnˈduːɪŋ/ *n.* **1** ruin or a cause of ruin. **2** the process of reversing what has been done. **3** the action of opening or unfastening.

undomesticated /ˌʌndəˈmestɪˌkeɪtɪd/ *adj.* not domesticated.

undone /ʌnˈdʌn/ *adj.* **1** not done; incomplete (*left the job undone*). **2** not fastened (*left the buttons undone*). **3** *archaic* ruined.

undoubtable /ʌnˈdaʊtəb(ə)l/ *adj.* that cannot be doubted; indubitable.

undoubted /ʌnˈdaʊtɪd/ *adj.* certain, not questioned, not regarded as doubtful. □□ **undoubtedly** *adv.*

undrained /ʌnˈdreɪnd/ *adj.* not drained.

undraped /ʌnˈdreɪpt/ *adj.* **1** not covered with drapery. **2** naked.

undreamed /ʌnˈdriːmd, ʌnˈdremt/ *adj.* (also **undreamt** /ʌnˈdremt/) (often foll. by *of*) not dreamed or thought of or imagined.

undress /ʌnˈdres/ *v. & n.* —*v.* **1** *intr.* take off one's clothes. **2** *tr.* take the clothes off (a person). —*n.* **1** ordinary dress as opposed to full dress or uniform. **2** casual or informal dress.

undressed /ʌnˈdrest/ *adj.* **1** not or no longer dressed; partly or wholly naked. **2** (of leather etc.) not treated. **3** (of food) not having a dressing.

undrinkable /ʌnˈdrɪŋkəb(ə)l/ *adj.* unfit for drinking.

undue /ʌnˈdjuː/ *adj.* **1** excessive, disproportionate. **2** not suitable. **3** not owed. □ **undue influence** *Law* influence by which a person is induced to act otherwise than by his or her own free will, or without adequate attention to the consequences. □□ **unduly** *adv.*

undulant /ˈʌndjʊlənt/ *adj.* moving like waves; fluctuating. □ **undulant fever** brucellosis in humans. [L *undulare* (as UNDULATE)]

undulate *v. & n.* —*v.* /ˈʌndjʊˌleɪt/ *intr. & tr.* have or cause to have a wavy motion or look. —*adj.* /ˈʌndjʊlət/ wavy, going alternately up and down or in and out (*leaves with undulate margins*). □□ **undulately** *adv.* [LL *undulatus* f. L *unda* wave]

undulation /ˌʌndjʊˈleɪʃ(ə)n/ *n.* **1** a wavy motion or form, a gentle rise and fall. **2** each wave of this. **3** a set of wavy lines.

undulatory /ˈʌndjʊlətərɪ/ *adj.* **1** undulating, wavy. **2** of or due to undulation.

undutiful /ʌnˈdjuːtɪˌfʊl/ *adj.* not dutiful. □□ **undutifully** *adv.* **undutifulness** *n.*

undyed /ʌnˈdaɪd/ *adj.* not dyed.

undying /ʌnˈdaɪɪŋ/ *adj.* **1** immortal. **2** never-ending (*undying love*). □□ **undyingly** *adv.*

unearned /ʌnˈɜːnd/ *adj.* not earned. □ **unearned income** income from interest payments etc. as opposed to salary, wages, or fees. **unearned increment** an increase in the value of property not due to the owner's labour or outlay.

unearth /ʌnˈɜːθ/ *v.tr.* **1 a** discover by searching or in the course of digging or rummaging. **b** dig out of the earth. **2** drive (a fox etc.) from its earth.

unearthly /ʌnˈɜːθlɪ/ *adj.* **1** supernatural, mysterious. **2** *colloq.* absurdly early or inconvenient (*an unearthly hour*). **3** not earthly. □□ **unearthliness** *n.*

unease /ʌnˈiːz/ *n.* lack of ease, discomfort, distress.

uneasy /ʌnˈiːzɪ/ *adj.* (**uneasier**, **uneasiest**) **1** disturbed or uncomfortable in mind or body (*passed an uneasy night*). **2** disturbing (*had an uneasy suspicion*). □□ **uneasily** *adv.* **uneasiness** *n.*

uneatable /ʌnˈiːtəb(ə)l/ *adj.* not able to be eaten, esp. because of its condition (cf. INEDIBLE).

uneaten /ʌnˈiːt(ə)n/ *adj.* not eaten; left undevoured.

uneconomic /ˌʌniːkəˈnɒmɪk, ˌʌnek-/ *adj.* not economic; incapable of being profitably operated etc. □□ **uneconomically** *adv.*

uneconomical /ˌʌniːkəˈnɒmɪk(ə)l, ˌʌnek-/ *adj.* not economical; wasteful.

unedifying /ʌnˈedɪˌfaɪɪŋ/ *adj.* not edifying, esp. uninstructive or degrading. □□ **unedifyingly** *adv.*

unedited /ʌnˈedɪtɪd/ *adj.* not edited.

uneducated /ʌnˈedjʊˌkeɪtɪd/ *adj.* not educated. □□ **uneducable** /-kəb(ə)l/ *adj.*

unelectable /ˌʌnɪˈlektəb(ə)l/ *adj.* (of a candidate, party, etc.) holding views likely to bring defeat at an election.

unembellished /ˌʌnɪmˈbelɪʃt/ *adj.* not embellished or decorated.

unemotional /ˌʌnɪˈməʊʃən(ə)l/ *adj.* not emotional; lacking emotion. □□ **unemotionally** *adv.*

unemphatic /ˌʌnɪmˈfætɪk/ *adj.* not emphatic. □□ **unemphatically** *adv.*

unemployable /ˌʌnɪmˈplɔɪəb(ə)l/ *adj. & n.* —*adj.* unfitted for paid employment. —*n.* an unemployable person. □□ **unemployability** /-ˈbɪlɪtɪ/ *n.*

unemployed /ˌʌnɪmˈplɔɪd/ *adj.* **1** not having paid employment; out of work. **2** not in use.

unemployment /ˌʌnɪmˈplɔɪmənt/ *n.* **1** the state of being unemployed. **2** the condition or extent of this in a country or region etc. (*the North has higher unemployment*). □ **unemployment benefit** a payment made by the State or (in the US) a trade union to an unemployed person.

unenclosed /ˌʌnɪnˈkləʊzd/ *adj.* not enclosed.

unencumbered /ˌʌnɪnˈkʌmbəd/ *adj.* **1** (of an estate) not having any liabilities (e.g. a mortgage) on it. **2** having no encumbrance; free.

unending /ʌnˈendɪŋ/ *adj.* having or apparently having no end. □□ **unendingly** *adv.* **unendingness** *n.*

unendowed /ˌʌnɪnˈdaʊd/ *adj.* not endowed.

unendurable /ˌʌnɪnˈdjʊərəb(ə)l/ *adj.* that cannot be endured. □□ **unendurably** *adv.*

unengaged /ˌʌnɪnˈɡeɪdʒd/ *adj.* not engaged; uncommitted.

un-English /ʌnˈɪŋɡlɪʃ/ *adj.* **1** not characteristic of the English. **2** not English.

unenjoyable /ˌʌnɪnˈdʒɔɪəb(ə)l/ *adj.* not enjoyable.

unenlightened /ˌʌnɪnˈlaɪt(ə)nd/ *adj.* not enlightened.

unenterprising /ʌnˈentəˌpraɪzɪŋ/ *adj.* not enterprising.

unenthusiastic /ˌʌnɪnˌθjuːzɪˈæstɪk, ˌʌnɪnˌθuː-/ *adj.* not enthusiastic. □□ **unenthusiastically** *adv.*

unenviable /ʌnˈenvɪəb(ə)l/ *adj.* not enviable. □□ **unenviably** *adv.*

unenvied /ʌnˈenvɪd/ *adj.* not envied.

unequal /ʌnˈiːkw(ə)l/ *adj.* **1** (often foll. by *to*) not equal. **2** of varying quality. **3** lacking equal advantage to both sides (*an unequal bargain*). □□ **unequally** *adv.*

unequalize /ʌnˈiːkwəˌlaɪz/ *v.tr.* (also **-ise**) make unequal.

unequalled /ʌnˈiːkw(ə)ld/ *adj.* superior to all others.

unequipped /ˌʌnɪˈkwɪpt/ *adj.* not equipped.

unequivocal /ˌʌnɪˈkwɪvək(ə)l/ *adj.* not ambiguous, plain, unmistakable. □□ **unequivocally** *adv.* **unequivocalness** *n.*

unerring /ʌnˈɜːrɪŋ/ *adj.* not erring, failing, or missing the mark; true, certain. □□ **unerringly** *adv.* **unerringness** *n.*

unescapable /ˌʌnɪˈskeɪpəb(ə)l/ *adj.* inescapable.

UNESCO /juːˈneskəʊ/ *abbr.* (also **Unesco**) United Nations Educational, Scientific, and Cultural Organization.

unescorted /ˌʌnɪˈskɔːtɪd/ *adj.* not escorted.

unessential /ˌʌnɪˈsenʃ(ə)l/ *adj. & n.* —*adj.* **1** not essential (cf. INESSENTIAL). **2** not of the first importance. —*n.* an unessential part or thing.

unestablished /ˌʌnɪˈstæblɪʃt/ *adj.* not established.

unethical /ʌnˈeθɪk(ə)l/ *adj.* not ethical, esp. unscrupulous in business or professional conduct. □□ **unethically** *adv.*

unevangelical /ˌʌniːvænˈdʒelɪk(ə)l/ *adj.* not evangelical.

uneven /ʌnˈiːv(ə)n/ *adj.* **1** not level or smooth. **2** not uniform or equable. **3** (of a contest) unequal. □□ **unevenly** *adv.* **unevenness** *n.* [OE *unefen* (as UN-¹, EVEN¹)]

uneventful /ˌʌnɪˈventfʊl/ *adj.* not eventful. □□ **uneventfully** *adv.* **uneventfulness** *n.*

unexamined /ˌʌnɪɡˈzæmɪnd/ *adj.* not examined.

unexampled /ˌʌnɪɡˈzɑːmp(ə)ld/ *adj.* having no precedent or parallel.

unexceptionable /ˌʌnɪkˈsepʃənəb(ə)l/ *adj.* with which no fault can be found; entirely satisfactory. □□ **unexceptionableness** *n.* **unexceptionably** *adv.*

unexceptional /ˌʌnɪkˈsepʃən(ə)l/ *adj.* not out of the ordinary; usual; normal. □□ **unexceptionally** *adv.*

unexcitable /ˌʌnɪkˈsaɪtəb(ə)l/ *adj.* not easily excited. □□ **unexcitability** /-ˈbɪlɪtɪ/ *n.*

unexciting /ˌʌnɪkˈsaɪtɪŋ/ *adj.* not exciting; dull.

unexecuted /ʌnˈeksɪˌkjuːtɪd/ *adj.* not carried out or put into effect.

unexhausted /ˌʌnɪɡˈzɔːstɪd/ *adj.* **1** not used up, expended, or brought to an end. **2** not emptied.

unexpected /ˌʌnɪkˈspektɪd/ *adj.* not expected; surprising. □□ **unexpectedly** *adv.* **unexpectedness** *n.*

unexpired /ˌʌnɪkˈspaɪəd/ *adj.* that has not yet expired.

unexplainable /ˌʌnɪkˈspleɪnəb(ə)l/ *adj.* inexplicable. □□ **unexplainably** *adv.*

unexplained /ˌʌnɪkˈspleɪnd/ *adj.* not explained.

unexploited /ˌʌnɪkˈsplɔɪtɪd/ *adj.* (of resources etc.) not exploited.

unexplored /ˌʌnɪkˈsplɔːd/ *adj.* not explored.

unexposed /ˌʌnɪkˈspəʊzd/ *adj.* not exposed.

unexpressed /ˌʌnɪkˈsprest/ *adj.* not expressed or made known (*unexpressed fears*).

unexpurgated /ʌnˈekspəˌɡeɪtɪd/ *adj.* (esp. of a text etc.) not expurgated; complete.

unfaceable /ʌnˈfeɪsəb(ə)l/ *adj.* that cannot be faced or confronted.

unfading /ʌnˈfeɪdɪŋ/ *adj.* that never fades. □□ **unfadingly** *adv.*

unfailing /ʌnˈfeɪlɪŋ/ *adj.* **1** not failing. **2** not running short. **3** constant. **4** reliable. □□ **unfailingly** *adv.* **unfailingness** *n.*

unfair /ʌnˈfeə(r)/ *adj.* **1** not equitable or honest (*obtained by unfair means*). **2** not impartial or according to the rules (*unfair play*). □□ **unfairly** *adv.* **unfairness** *n.* [OE *unfæger* (as UN-¹, FAIR¹)]

unfaithful /ʌnˈfeɪθfʊl/ *adj.* **1** not faithful, esp. adulterous. **2** not loyal. **3** treacherous. □□ **unfaithfully** *adv.* **unfaithfulness** *n.*

unfaltering /ʌnˈfɔːltərɪŋ, ʌnˈfɒl-/ *adj.* not faltering; steady, resolute. □□ **unfalteringly** *adv.*

unfamiliar /ˌʌnfəˈmɪljə(r)/ *adj.* not familiar. □□ **unfamiliarity** /-lɪˈærɪtɪ/ *n.*

unfashionable /ʌnˈfæʃənəb(ə)l/ *adj.* not fashionable. □□ **unfashionableness** *n.* **unfashionably** *adv.*

unfashioned /ʌnˈfæʃ(ə)nd/ *adj.* not made into its proper shape.

unfasten /ʌnˈfɑːs(ə)n/ *v.* **1** *tr.* & *intr.* make or become loose. **2** *tr.* open the fastening(s) of. **3** *tr.* detach.

unfastened /ʌnˈfɑːs(ə)nd/ *adj.* **1** that has not been fastened. **2** that has been loosened, opened, or detached.

unfathered /ʌnˈfɑːðəd/ *adj.* **1** having no known or acknowledged father; illegitimate. **2** of unknown origin (*unfathered rumours*).

unfatherly /ʌnˈfɑːðəlɪ/ *adj.* not befitting a father. □□ **unfatherliness** *n.*

unfathomable /ʌnˈfæðəməb(ə)l/ *adj.* incapable of

being fathomed. □□ **unfathomableness** *n.* **unfathomably** *adv.*

unfathomed /ʌnˈfæðəmd/ *adj.* **1** of unascertained depth. **2** not fully explored or known.

unfavourable /ʌnˈfeɪvərəb(ə)l/ *adj.* (US **unfavorable**) not favourable; adverse, hostile. □□ **unfavourableness** *n.* **unfavourably** *adv.*

unfavourite /ʌnˈfeɪvərɪt/ *adj.* (US **unfavorite**) *colloq.* least favourite; most disliked.

unfazed /ʌnˈfeɪzd/ *adj. colloq.* untroubled; not disconcerted.

unfeasible /ʌnˈfiːzɪb(ə)l/ *adj.* not feasible; impractical. □□ **unfeasibility** /-ˈbɪlɪtɪ/ *n.* **unfeasibly** *adv.*

unfed /ʌnˈfed/ *adj.* not fed.

unfeeling /ʌnˈfiːlɪŋ/ *adj.* **1** unsympathetic, harsh, not caring about others' feelings. **2** lacking sensation or sensitivity. □□ **unfeelingly** *adv.* **unfeelingness** *n.* [OE *unfelende* (as UN-¹, FEELING)]

unfeigned /ʌnˈfeɪnd/ *adj.* genuine, sincere. □□ **unfeignedly** *adv.*

unfelt /ʌnˈfelt/ *adj.* not felt.

unfeminine /ʌnˈfemɪnɪn/ *adj.* not in accordance with, or appropriate to, female character. □□ **unfemininity** /-ˈnɪnɪtɪ/ *n.*

unfenced /ʌnˈfenst/ *adj.* **1** not provided with fences. **2** unprotected.

unfermented /ˌʌnfəˈmentɪd/ *adj.* not fermented.

unfertilized /ʌnˈfɜːtɪˌlaɪzd/ *adj.* (also **unfertilised**) not fertilized.

unfetter /ʌnˈfetə(r)/ *v.tr.* release from fetters.

unfettered /ʌnˈfetəd/ *adj.* unrestrained, unrestricted.

unfilial /ʌnˈfɪlɪəl/ *adj.* not befitting a son or daughter. □□ **unfilially** *adv.*

unfilled /ʌnˈfɪld/ *adj.* not filled.

unfiltered /ʌnˈfɪltəd/ *adj.* **1** not filtered. **2** (of a cigarette) not provided with a filter.

unfinished /ʌnˈfɪnɪʃt/ *adj.* not finished; incomplete.

unfit /ʌnˈfɪt/ *adj.* & *v.* —*adj.* (often foll. by *for*, or *to* + infin.) not fit. —*v.tr.* (**unfitted**, **unfitting**) (usu. foll. by *for*) make unsuitable. □□ **unfitly** *adv.* **unfitness** *n.*

unfitted /ʌnˈfɪtɪd/ *adj.* **1** not fit. **2** not fitted or suited. **3** not provided with fittings.

unfitting /ʌnˈfɪtɪŋ/ *adj.* not fitting or suitable, unbecoming. □□ **unfittingly** *adv.*

unfix /ʌnˈfɪks/ *v.tr.* **1** release or loosen from a fixed state. **2** detach.

unfixed /ʌnˈfɪkst/ *adj.* not fixed.

unflagging /ʌnˈflæɡɪŋ/ *adj.* tireless, persistent. □□ **unflaggingly** *adv.*

unflappable /ʌnˈflæpəb(ə)l/ *adj. colloq.* imperturbable; remaining calm in a crisis. □□ **unflappability** /-ˈbɪlɪtɪ/ *n.* **unflappably** *adv.*

unflattering /ʌnˈflætərɪŋ/ *adj.* not flattering. □□ **unflatteringly** *adv.*

unflavoured /ʌnˈfleɪvəd/ *adj.* not flavoured.

unfledged /ʌnˈfledʒd/ *adj.* **1** (of a person) inexperienced. **2** (of a bird) not yet fledged.

unfleshed /ʌnˈfleʃt/ *adj.* **1** not covered with flesh. **2** stripped of flesh.

unflinching /ʌnˈflɪntʃɪŋ/ *adj.* not flinching. □□ **unflinchingly** *adv.*

unfocused /ʌnˈfəʊkəst/ *adj.* (also **unfocussed**) not focused.

unfold /ʌnˈfəʊld/ *v.* **1** *tr.* open the fold or folds of, spread out. **2** *tr.* reveal (thoughts etc.). **3** *intr.* become opened out. **4** *intr.* develop. □□ **unfoldment** *n.* US. [OE *unfealdan* (as UN-², FOLD¹)]

unforced /ʌnˈfɔːst/ *adj.* **1** not produced by effort; easy, natural. **2** not compelled or constrained. □□ **unforcedly** *adv.*

unfordable /ʌnˈfɔːdəb(ə)l/ *adj.* that cannot be forded.

unforeseeable /ˌʌnfɔːˈsiːəb(ə)l/ *adj.* not foreseeable.

unforeseen /ˌʌnfɔːˈsiːn/ *adj.* not foreseen.

unforetold /ˌʌnfɔːˈtəʊld/ *adj.* not foretold; unpredicted.

unforgettable /ˌʌnfəˈgetəb(ə)l/ *adj.* that cannot be forgotten; memorable, wonderful (*an unforgettable experience*). □□ **unforgettably** *adv.*

unforgivable /ˌʌnfəˈgɪvəb(ə)l/ *adj.* that cannot be forgiven. □□ **unforgivably** *adv.*

unforgiven /ˌʌnfəˈgɪv(ə)n/ *adj.* not forgiven.

unforgiving /ˌʌnfəˈgɪvɪŋ/ *adj.* not forgiving. □□ **unforgivingly** *adv.* **unforgivingness** *n.*

unforgotten /ˌʌnfəˈgɒt(ə)n/ *adj.* not forgotten.

unformed /ʌnˈfɔːmd/ *adj.* **1** not formed. **2** shapeless. **3** not developed.

unformulated /ʌnˈfɔːmjʊˌleɪtɪd/ *adj.* not formulated.

unforthcoming /ˌʌnfɔːθˈkʌmɪŋ/ *adj.* not forthcoming.

unfortified /ʌnˈfɔːtɪˌfaɪd/ *adj.* not fortified.

unfortunate /ʌnˈfɔːtjʊnət, -tʃənət/ *adj.* & *n.* —*adj.* **1** having bad fortune; unlucky. **2** unhappy. **3** regrettable. **4** disastrous. —*n.* an unfortunate person.

unfortunately /ʌnˈfɔːtjʊnətlɪ, -tʃənətlɪ/ *adv.* **1** (qualifying a whole sentence) it is unfortunate that. **2** in an unfortunate manner.

unfounded /ʌnˈfaʊndɪd/ *adj.* having no foundation (*unfounded hopes*; *unfounded rumour*). □□ **unfoundedly** *adv.* **unfoundedness** *n.*

unframed /ʌnˈfreɪmd/ *adj.* (esp. of a picture) not framed.

unfreeze /ʌnˈfriːz/ *v.* (*past* **unfroze**; *past part.* **unfrozen**) **1** *tr.* cause to thaw. **2** *intr.* thaw. **3** *tr.* remove restrictions from, make (assets, credits, etc.) realizable.

unfrequented /ˌʌnfrɪˈkwentɪd/ *adj.* not frequented.

unfriended /ʌnˈfrendɪd/ *adj.* *literary* without friends.

unfriendly /ʌnˈfrendlɪ/ *adj.* (**unfriendlier**, **unfriendliest**) not friendly. □□ **unfriendliness** *n.*

unfrock /ʌnˈfrɒk/ *v.tr.* = DEFROCK.

unfroze *past* of UNFREEZE.

unfrozen *past part.* of UNFREEZE.

unfruitful /ʌnˈfruːtfʊl/ *adj.* **1** not producing good results, unprofitable. **2** not producing fruit or crops. □□ **unfruitfully** *adv.* **unfruitfulness** *n.*

unfulfilled /ˌʌnfʊlˈfɪld/ *adj.* not fulfilled. □□ **unfulfillable** *adj.*

unfunded /ʌnˈfʌndɪd/ *adj.* (of a debt) not funded.

unfunny /ʌnˈfʌnɪ/ *adj.* (**unfunnier**, **unfunniest**) not amusing (though meant to be). □□ **unfunnily** *adv.* **unfunniness** *n.*

unfurl /ʌnˈfɜːl/ *v.* **1** *tr.* spread out (a sail, umbrella, etc.). **2** *intr.* become spread out.

unfurnished /ʌnˈfɜːnɪʃt/ *adj.* **1** (usu. foll. by *with*) not supplied. **2** without furniture.

ungainly /ʌnˈgeɪnlɪ/ *adj.* (of a person, animal, or movement) awkward, clumsy. □□ **ungainliness** *n.* [UN-¹ + obs. *gainly* graceful ult. f. ON *gegn* straight]

ungallant /ʌnˈgælənt/ *adj.* not gallant. □□ **ungallantly** *adv.*

ungenerous /ʌnˈdʒenərəs/ *adj.* not generous; mean. □□ **ungenerously** *adv.* **ungenerousness** *n.*

ungenial /ʌnˈdʒiːnɪəl/ *adj.* not genial.

ungentle /ʌnˈdʒent(ə)l/ *adj.* not gentle. □□ **ungentleness** *n.* **ungently** *adv.*

ungentlemanly /ʌnˈdʒentəlmənlɪ/ *adj.* not gentlemanly. □□ **ungentlemanliness** *n.*

unget-at-able /ˌʌngetˈætəb(ə)l/ *adj.* *colloq.* inaccessible.

ungifted /ʌnˈgɪftɪd/ *adj.* not gifted or talented.

ungird /ʌnˈgɜːd/ *v.tr.* **1** release the girdle, belt, or girth of. **2** release or take off by undoing a belt or girth.

unglazed /ʌnˈgleɪzd/ *adj.* not glazed.

ungloved /ʌnˈglʌvd/ *adj.* not wearing a glove or gloves.

ungodly /ʌnˈgɒdlɪ/ *adj.* **1** impious, wicked. **2** *colloq.* outrageous (*an ungodly hour to arrive*). □□ **ungodliness** *n.*

ungovernable /ʌnˈgʌvənəb(ə)l/ *adj.* uncontrollable, violent. □□ **ungovernability** /-ˈbɪlɪtɪ/ *n.* **ungovernably** *adv.*

ungraceful /ʌnˈgreɪsfʊl/ *adj.* not graceful. □□ **ungracefully** *adv.* **ungracefulness** *n.*

ungracious /ʌnˈgreɪʃəs/ *adj.* **1** not kindly or courteous; unkind. **2** unattractive. □□ **ungraciously** *adv.* **ungraciousness** *n.*

ungrammatical /ˌʌngrəˈmætɪk(ə)l/ *adj.* contrary to the rules of grammar. □□ **ungrammaticality** /-ˈkælɪtɪ/ *n.* **ungrammatically** *adv.* **ungrammaticalness** *n.*

ungraspable /ʌnˈgrɑːspəb(ə)l/ *adj.* that cannot be grasped or comprehended.

ungrateful /ʌnˈgreɪtfʊl/ *adj.* **1** not feeling or showing gratitude. **2** not pleasant or acceptable. □□ **ungratefully** *adv.* **ungratefulness** *n.*

ungrounded /ʌnˈgraʊndɪd/ *adj.* **1** having no basis or justification; unfounded. **2** *Electr.* not earthed. **3** (foll. by *in* a subject) not properly instructed. **4** (of an aircraft, ship, etc.) no longer grounded.

ungrudging /ʌnˈgrʌdʒɪŋ/ *adj.* not grudging. □□ **ungrudgingly** *adv.*

ungual /ˈʌŋgw(ə)l/ *adj.* of, like, or bearing a nail, hoof, or claw. [L UNGUIS]

unguard /ʌnˈgɑːd/ *v.tr.* *Cards* discard a low card that was protecting (a high card) from capture.

unguarded /ʌnˈgɑːdɪd/ *adj.* **1** incautious, thoughtless (*an unguarded remark*). **2** not guarded; without a guard. □□ **unguardedly** *adv.* **unguardedness** *n.*

unguent /ˈʌŋgwənt/ *n.* a soft substance used as ointment or for lubrication. [L *unguentum* f. *unguere* anoint]

unguessable /ʌnˈgesəb(ə)l/ *adj.* that cannot be guessed or imagined.

unguiculate /ʌŋˈgwɪkjʊlət/ *adj.* **1** *Zool.* having one or more nails or claws. **2** *Bot.* (of petals) having an unguis. [mod.L *unguiculatus* f. *unguiculus* dimin. of UNGUIS]

unguided /ʌnˈgaɪdɪd/ *adj.* not guided in a particular path or direction; left to take its own course.

unguis /ˈʌŋgwɪs/ *n.* (*pl.* **ungues** /-wiːz/) **1** *Bot.* the narrow base of a petal. **2** *Zool.* a nail or claw. [L]

ungula /ˈʌŋgjʊlə/ *n.* (*pl.* **ungulae** /-ˌliː/) a hoof or claw. [L, dimin. of UNGUIS]

ungulate /ˈʌŋgjʊlət, -ˌleɪt/ *adj.* & *n.* —*adj.* hoofed. —*n.* a hoofed mammal. [LL *ungulatus* f. UNGULA]

unhallowed /ʌnˈhæləʊd/ *adj.* **1** not consecrated. **2** not sacred; unholy, wicked.

unhampered /ʌnˈhæmpəd/ *adj.* not hampered.

unhand /ʌnˈhænd/ *v.tr.* *rhet.* or *joc.* **1** take one's hands off (a person). **2** release from one's grasp.

unhandsome /ʌnˈhænsəm/ *adj.* not handsome.

unhandy /ʌnˈhændɪ/ *adj.* **1** not easy to handle or manage; awkward. **2** not skilful in using the hands. □□ **unhandily** *adv.* **unhandiness** *n.*

unhang /ʌnˈhæŋ/ *v.tr.* (*past* and *past part.* **unhung**) take down from a hanging position.

unhappy /ʌnˈhæpɪ/ *adj.* (**unhappier**, **unhappiest**) **1** not happy, miserable. **2** unsuccessful, unfortunate. **3** causing misfortune. **4** disastrous. **5** inauspicious. □□ **unhappily** *adv.* **unhappiness** *n.*

unharbour /ʌnˈhɑːbə(r)/ *v.tr.* *Brit.* dislodge (a deer) from a covert.

unharmed /ʌnˈhɑːmd/ *adj.* not harmed.

unharmful /ʌnˈhɑːmfʊl/ *adj.* not harmful.

unharmonious /ˌʌnhɑːˈməʊnɪəs/ *adj.* not harmonious.

unharness /ʌnˈhɑːnɪs/ *v.tr.* remove a harness from.

unhasp /ʌnˈhɑːsp/ *v.tr.* free from a hasp or catch; unfasten.

unhatched /ʌnˈhætʃt/ *adj.* (of an egg etc.) not hatched.

unhealthful /ʌnˈhelθfʊl/ *adj.* harmful to health, unwholesome. □□ **unhealthfulness** *n.*

unhealthy /ʌnˈhelθɪ/ *adj.* (**unhealthier**, **unhealthiest**) **1** not in good health. **2 a** (of a place etc.) harmful to health. **b** unwholesome. **c** *sl.* dangerous to life. □□ **unhealthily** *adv.* **unhealthiness** *n.*

unheard /ʌnˈhɜːd/ adj. **1** not heard. **2** (usu. **unheard-of**) unprecedented, unknown.

unheated /ʌnˈhiːtɪd/ adj. not heated.

unheeded /ʌnˈhiːdɪd/ adj. not heeded; disregarded.

unheedful /ʌnˈhiːdfʊl/ adj. heedless; taking no notice.

unheeding /ʌnˈhiːdɪŋ/ adj. not giving heed; heedless. □□ **unheedingly** adv.

unhelpful /ʌnˈhelpfʊl/ adj. not helpful. □□ **unhelpfully** adv. **unhelpfulness** n.

unheralded /ʌnˈherəldɪd/ adj. not heralded; unannounced.

unheroic /ˌʌnhɪˈrəʊɪk/ adj. not heroic. □□ **unheroically** adv.

unhesitating /ʌnˈhezɪˌteɪtɪŋ/ adj. without hesitation. □□ **unhesitatingly** adv. **unhesitatingness** n.

unhindered /ʌnˈhɪndəd/ adj. not hindered.

unhinge /ʌnˈhɪndʒ/ v.tr. **1** take (a door etc.) off its hinges. **2** (esp. as **unhinged** adj.) unsettle or disorder (a person's mind etc.), make (a person) crazy.

unhistoric /ˌʌnhɪˈstɒrɪk/ adj. not historic or historical.

unhistorical /ˌʌnhɪˈstɒrɪk(ə)l/ adj. not historical. □□ **unhistorically** adv.

unhitch /ʌnˈhɪtʃ/ v.tr. **1** release from a hitched state. **2** unhook, unfasten.

unholy /ʌnˈhəʊlɪ/ adj. (**unholier**, **unholiest**) **1** impious, profane, wicked. **2** colloq. dreadful, outrageous (made an unholy row about it). **3** not holy. □□ **unholiness** n. [OE unhālig (as UN-[1], HOLY)]

unhonoured /ʌnˈɒnəd/ adj. not honoured.

unhook /ʌnˈhʊk/ v.tr. **1** remove from a hook or hooks. **2** unfasten by releasing a hook or hooks.

unhoped /ʌnˈhəʊpt/ adj. (foll. by for) not hoped for or expected.

unhorse /ʌnˈhɔːs/ v.tr. **1** throw or drag from a horse. **2** (of a horse) throw (a rider). **3** dislodge, overthrow.

unhouse /ʌnˈhaʊz/ v.tr. deprive of shelter; turn out of a house.

unhuman /ʌnˈhjuːmən/ adj. **1** not human. **2** superhuman. **3** inhuman, brutal.

unhung[1] /ʌnˈhʌŋ/ adj. **1** not (yet) executed by hanging. **2** not hung up (for exhibition).

unhung[2] past and past part. of UNHANG.

unhurried /ʌnˈhʌrɪd/ adj. not hurried. □□ **unhurriedly** adv.

unhurt /ʌnˈhɜːt/ adj. not hurt.

unhusk /ʌnˈhʌsk/ v.tr. remove a husk or shell from.

unhygienic /ˌʌnhaɪˈdʒiːnɪk/ adj. not hygienic. □□ **unhygienically** adv.

unhyphenated /ʌnˈhaɪfəˌneɪtɪd/ adj. not hyphenated.

uni /ˈjuːnɪ/ n. (pl. **unis**) esp. Austral. & NZ colloq. a university. [abbr.]

uni- /ˈjuːnɪ/ comb. form one; having or consisting of one. [L f. unus one]

Uniat /ˈjuːnɪˌæt, -ət/ adj. & n. (also **Uniate** /-ˌeɪt/) —adj. of or relating to any community of Christians in E. Europe or the Near East that acknowledges papal supremacy but retains its own liturgy etc. —n. a member of such a community. [Russ. uniyat f. uniya f. L unio UNION]

uniaxial /ˌjuːnɪˈæksɪəl/ adj. having a single axis. □□ **uniaxially** adv.

unicameral /ˌjuːnɪˈkæmər(ə)l/ adj. with a single legislative chamber.

UNICEF /ˈjuːnɪˌsef/ abbr. United Nations Children's (orig. International Children's Emergency) Fund.

unicellular /ˌjuːnɪˈseljʊlə(r)/ adj. (of an organism, organ, tissue, etc.) consisting of a single cell.

unicolour /ˈjuːnɪˌkʌlə(r)/ adj. (also **unicoloured**) of one colour.

unicorn /ˈjuːnɪˌkɔːn/ n. **1 a** a fabulous animal with a horse's body and a single straight horn. **b** a heraldic representation of this, with a twisted horn, a deer's feet, a goat's beard, and a lion's tail. **c** used in old translations of the Old Testament for the Hebrew reʼem, a two-horned animal, probably a wild ox. **2 a** a

pair of horses and a third horse in front. **b** an equipage with these. **3** (in full **unicorn whale** or **sea-unicorn**) the narwhal. [ME f. OF unicorne f. L unicornis f. UNI- + cornu horn, transl. Gk monocerōs]

unicuspid /ˌjuːnɪˈkʌspɪd/ adj. & n. —adj. with one cusp. —n. a unicuspid tooth.

unicycle /ˈjuːnɪˌsaɪk(ə)l/ n. a single-wheeled cycle, esp. as used by acrobats. □□ **unicyclist** n.

unidea'd /ˌʌnaɪˈdɪəd/ adj. having no ideas.

unideal /ˌʌnaɪˈdɪəl/ adj. not ideal.

unidentifiable /ˌʌnaɪˈdentɪˌfaɪəb(ə)l/ adj. unable to be identified.

unidentified /ˌʌnaɪˈdentɪˌfaɪd/ adj. not identified.

unidimensional /ˌjuːnɪdaɪˈmenʃ(ə)n(ə)l/ adj. having (only) one dimension.

unidirectional /ˌjuːnɪdɪˈrekʃ(ə)n(ə)l, ˌjuːnɪdaɪ-/ adj. having only one direction of motion, operation, etc. □□ **unidirectionality** /-ˈnælɪtɪ/ n. **unidirectionally** adv.

unification /ˌjuːnɪfɪˈkeɪʃ(ə)n/ n. the act or an instance of unifying; the state of being unified. □ **Unification Church** a religious organization founded in 1954 in Korea by Sun Myung Moon (cf. MOONIE). □□ **unificatory** adj.

uniflow /ˈjuːnɪˌfləʊ/ adj. involving flow (esp. of steam or waste gases) in one direction only.

uniform /ˈjuːnɪˌfɔːm/ adj., n., & v. —adj. **1** not changing in form or character; the same, unvarying (present a uniform appearance; all of uniform size and shape). **2** conforming to the same standard, rules, or pattern. **3** constant in the course of time (uniform acceleration). **4** (of a tax, law, etc.) not varying with time or place. —n. uniform distinctive clothing worn by members of the same body, e.g. by soldiers, police, and schoolchildren. —v.tr. **1** clothe in uniform (a uniformed officer). **2** make uniform. □□ **uniformly** adv. [F uniforme or L uniformis (as UNI-, FORM)]

uniformitarian /ˌjuːnɪfɔːmɪˈteərɪən/ adj. & n. —adj. of the theory that geological processes are always due to continuously and uniformly operating forces. —n. a holder of this theory. □□ **uniformitarianism** n.

uniformity /ˌjuːnɪˈfɔːmɪtɪ/ n. (pl. **-ies**) **1** being uniform; sameness, consistency. **2** an instance of this. □ **Act of Uniformity** hist. any of four acts (esp. that of 1662) for securing uniformity in public worship and the use of a particular Book of Common Prayer. [ME f. OF uniformité or LL uniformitas (as UNIFORM)]

unify /ˈjuːnɪˌfaɪ/ v.tr. (also absol.) (**-ies**, **-ied**) reduce to unity or uniformity. □ **unified field theory** Physics a theory that seeks to explain all the field phenomena (e.g. gravitation and electromagnetism: see FIELD n. 9) formerly treated by separate theories. □□ **unifier** n. [F unifier or LL unificare (as UNI-, -FY)]

unilateral /ˌjuːnɪˈlætər(ə)l/ adj. **1** performed by or affecting only one person or party (unilateral disarmament; unilateral declaration of independence). **2** one-sided. **3** (of the parking of vehicles) restricted to one side of the street. **4** (of leaves) all on the same side of the stem. **5** (of a line of descent) through ancestors of one sex only. □□ **unilaterally** adv.

unilateralism /ˌjuːnɪˈlætərəˌlɪz(ə)m/ n. **1** unilateral disarmament. **2** US the pursuit of a foreign policy without allies. □□ **unilateralist** n. & adj.

unilingual /ˌjuːnɪˈlɪŋgw(ə)l/ adj. of or in only one language. □□ **unilingually** adv.

uniliteral /ˌjuːnɪˈlɪtər(ə)l/ adj. consisting of one letter.

unilluminated /ˌʌnɪˈluːmɪˌneɪtɪd, ˌʌnɪˈljuː-/ adj. not illuminated.

unillustrated /ʌnˈɪləˌstreɪtɪd/ adj. (esp. of a book) without illustrations.

unilocular /ˌjuːnɪˈlɒkjʊlə(r)/ adj. Bot. & Zool. single-chambered.

unimaginable /ˌʌnɪˈmædʒɪnəb(ə)l/ adj. impossible to imagine. □□ **unimaginably** adv.

unimaginative /ˌʌnɪˈmædʒɪnətɪv/ adj. lacking imagination; stolid, dull. □□ **unimaginatively** adv. **unimaginativeness** n.

unimpaired /ˌʌnɪmˈpeəd/ adj. not impaired.

unimpassioned /ˌʌnɪmˈpæʃ(ə)nd/ adj. not impassioned.

unimpeachable /ˌʌnɪmˈpiːtʃəb(ə)l/ adj. giving no opportunity for censure; beyond reproach or question. □□ **unimpeachably** adv.

unimpeded /ˌʌnɪmˈpiːdɪd/ adj. not impeded. □□ **unimpededly** adv.

unimportance /ˌʌnɪmˈpɔːt(ə)ns/ n. lack of importance.

unimportant /ˌʌnɪmˈpɔːt(ə)nt/ adj. not important.

unimposing /ˌʌnɪmˈpəʊzɪŋ/ adj. unimpressive. □□ **unimposingly** adv.

unimpressed /ˌʌnɪmˈprest/ adj. not impressed.

unimpressionable /ˌʌnɪmˈpreʃənəb(ə)l/ adj. not impressionable.

unimpressive /ˌʌnɪmˈpresɪv/ adj. not impressive. □□ **unimpressively** adv. **unimpressiveness** n.

unimproved /ˌʌnɪmˈpruːvd/ adj. 1 not made better. 2 not made use of. 3 (of land) not used for agriculture or building; not developed.

unincorporated /ˌʌnɪnˈkɔːpəˌreɪtɪd/ adj. 1 not incorporated or united. 2 not formed into a corporation.

uninfected /ˌʌnɪnˈfektɪd/ adj. not infected.

uninflamed /ˌʌnɪnˈfleɪmd/ adj. not inflamed.

uninflammable /ˌʌnɪnˈflæməb(ə)l/ adj. not inflammable.

uninflected /ˌʌnɪnˈflektɪd/ adj. 1 Gram. (of a language) not having inflections. 2 not changing or varying. 3 not bent or deflected.

uninfluenced /ʌnˈɪnfluənst/ adj. (often foll. by by) not influenced.

uninfluential /ˌʌnɪnfluˈenʃ(ə)l/ adj. having little or no influence.

uninformative /ˌʌnɪnˈfɔːmətɪv/ adj. not informative; giving little information.

uninformed /ˌʌnɪnˈfɔːmd/ adj. 1 not informed or instructed. 2 ignorant, uneducated.

uninhabitable /ˌʌnɪnˈhæbɪtəb(ə)l/ adj. that cannot be inhabited. □□ **uninhabitableness** n.

uninhabited /ˌʌnɪnˈhæbɪtɪd/ adj. not inhabited.

uninhibited /ˌʌnɪnˈhɪbɪtɪd/ adj. not inhibited. □□ **uninhibitedly** adv. **uninhibitedness** n.

uninitiated /ˌʌnɪˈnɪʃɪˌeɪtɪd/ adj. not initiated; not admitted or instructed.

uninjured /ʌnˈɪndʒəd/ adj. not injured.

uninspired /ˌʌnɪnˈspaɪəd/ adj. 1 not inspired. 2 (of oratory etc.) commonplace.

uninspiring /ˌʌnɪnˈspaɪərɪŋ/ adj. not inspiring. □□ **uninspiringly** adv.

uninstructed /ˌʌnɪnˈstrʌktɪd/ adj. not instructed or informed.

uninsurable /ˌʌnɪnˈʃʊərəb(ə)l/ adj. that cannot be insured.

uninsured /ˌʌnɪnˈʃʊəd/ adj. not insured.

unintelligent /ˌʌnɪnˈtelɪdʒ(ə)nt/ adj. not intelligent. □□ **unintelligently** adv.

unintelligible /ˌʌnɪnˈtelɪdʒɪb(ə)l/ adj. not intelligible. □□ **unintelligibility** /-ˈbɪlɪtɪ/ n. **unintelligibleness** n. **unintelligibly** adv.

unintended /ˌʌnɪnˈtendɪd/ adj. not intended.

unintentional /ˌʌnɪnˈtenʃən(ə)l/ adj. not intentional. □□ **unintentionally** adv.

uninterested /ʌnˈɪntrəstɪd, -trɪstɪd/ adj. 1 not interested. 2 unconcerned, indifferent. □□ **uninterestedly** adv. **uninterestedness** n.

uninteresting /ʌnˈɪntrəstɪŋ, -trɪstɪŋ/ adj. not interesting. □□ **uninterestingly** adv. **uninterestingness** n.

uninterpretable /ˌʌnɪnˈtɜːprɪtəb(ə)l/ adj. that cannot be interpreted.

uninterruptable /ˌʌnɪntəˈrʌptəb(ə)l/ adj. that cannot be interrupted.

uninterrupted /ˌʌnɪntəˈrʌptɪd/ adj. not interrupted. □□ **uninterruptedly** adv. **uninterruptedness** n.

uninucleate /ˌjuːnɪˈnjuːklɪˌeɪt, -ɪət/ adj. Biol. having a single nucleus.

uninventive /ˌʌnɪnˈventɪv/ adj. not inventive. □□ **uninventively** adv. **uninventiveness** n.

uninvestigated /ˌʌnɪnˈvestɪˌɡeɪtɪd/ adj. not investigated.

uninvited /ˌʌnɪnˈvaɪtɪd/ adj. not invited. □□ **uninvitedly** adv.

uninviting /ˌʌnɪnˈvaɪtɪŋ/ adj. not inviting, unattractive, repellent. □□ **uninvitingly** adv.

uninvoked /ˌʌnɪnˈvəʊkt/ adj. not invoked.

uninvolved /ˌʌnɪnˈvɒlvd/ adj. not involved.

union /ˈjuːnjən, -nɪən/ n. 1 a the act or an instance of uniting; the state of being united. b (the Union) hist. the uniting of the English and Scottish crowns in 1603, of the English and Scottish parliaments in 1707, or of Great Britain and Ireland in 1801. 2 a a whole resulting from the combination of parts or members. b a political unit formed in this way, esp. the US, the UK, the USSR, or South Africa. 3 = trade union. 4 marriage, matrimony. 5 concord, agreement (lived together in perfect union). 6 (Union) a a general social club and debating society at some universities and colleges. b the buildings or accommodation of such a society. 7 Math. the totality of the members of two or more sets. 8 Brit. hist. a two or more parishes consolidated for the administration of the poor laws. b (in full union workhouse) a workhouse erected by this. 9 Brit. an association of independent (esp. Congregational or Baptist) churches for purposes of cooperation. 10 a part of a flag with a device emblematic of union, normally occupying the upper corner next to the staff. 11 a joint or coupling for pipes etc. 12 a fabric of mixed materials, e.g. cotton with linen or silk. □**union-bashing** Brit. colloq. active opposition to trade unions and their rights. **union catalogue** a catalogue of the combined holdings of several libraries. **union down** (of a flag) hoisted with the union below as a signal of distress. **Union Jack** (or **flag**) the national ensign of the United Kingdom formed by the union of the crosses of St George, St Andrew, and St Patrick. **union jack** (in the US) a jack consisting of the union from the national flag. **union shop** a shop, factory, trade, etc., in which employees must belong to a trade union or join one within an agreed time. **union suit** US a single undergarment for the body and legs; combinations. [ME f. OF union or eccl.L unio unity f. L unus one]

unionist /ˈjuːnjənɪst, ˈjuːnɪən-/ n. 1 a a member of a trade union. b an advocate of trade unions. 2 (usu. **Unionist**) an advocate of union, esp.: a a person opposed to the rupture of the parliamentary union between Great Britain and Northern Ireland (formerly between Great Britain and Ireland). b hist. a person who opposed secession during the American Civil War. □□ **unionism** n. **unionistic** /-ˈnɪstɪk/ adj.

unionize /ˈjuːnjəˌnaɪz, ˈjuːnɪən-/ v.tr. & intr. (also **-ise**) bring or come under trade-union organization or rules. □□ **unionization** /-ˈzeɪʃ(ə)n/ n.

un-ionized /ʌnˈaɪəˌnaɪzd/ adj. (also **-ised**) not ionized.

uniparous /juːˈnɪpərəs/ adj. 1 producing one offspring at a birth. 2 Bot. having one axis or branch.

uniped /ˈjuːnɪˌped/ n. & adj. —n. a person having only one foot or leg. —adj. one-footed, one-legged. [UNI- + pes pedis foot]

unipersonal /ˌjuːnɪˈpɜːsən(ə)l/ adj. (of the Deity) existing only as one person.

uniplanar /ˌjuːnɪˈpleɪnə(r)/ adj. lying in one plane.

unipod /ˈjuːnɪˌpɒd/ n. a one-legged support for a camera etc. [UNI-, after TRIPOD]

unipolar /ˌjuːnɪˈpəʊlə(r)/ adj. 1 (esp. of an electric or magnetic apparatus) showing only one kind of polarity. 2 Biol. (of a nerve cell etc.) having only one pole. □□ **unipolarity** /-ˈlærɪtɪ/ n.

unique /juːˈniːk, juːˈniːk/ adj. & n. —adj. 1 of which there is only one; unequalled; having no like, equal, or parallel (*his position was unique*; *this vase is considered unique*). **·2** *disp.* unusual, remarkable (*the most unique man I ever met*). **—n.** a unique thing or person. □□ **uniquely** *adv.* **uniqueness** *n.* [F f. L *unicus* f. *unus* one]

unironed /ʌnˈaɪənd/ *adj.* (esp. of clothing, linen, etc.) not ironed.

uniserial /ˌjuːnɪˈsɪərɪəl/ *adj. Bot. & Zool.* arranged in one row.

unisex /ˈjuːnɪˌseks/ *adj.* (of clothing, hairstyles, etc.) designed to be suitable for both sexes.

unisexual /ˌjuːnɪˈseksjʊəl, -kʃʊəl/ *adj.* **1 a** of one sex. **b** *Bot.* having stamens or pistils but not both. **2** unisex. □□ **unisexuality** /-ʊˈælɪtɪ/ *n.* **unisexually** *adv.*

unison /ˈjuːnɪs(ə)n/ *n. & adj.* **—n.** **1** *Mus.* **a** a coincidence in pitch of sounds or notes. **b** this regarded as an interval. **2** *Mus.* a combination of voices or instruments at the same pitch or at pitches differing by one or more octaves (*sang in unison*). **3** agreement, concord (*acted in perfect unison*). **—adj.** *Mus.* coinciding in pitch. □ **unison string** a string tuned in unison with another string and meant to be sounded with it. □□ **unisonant** /jʊˈnɪsənənt/ *adj.* **unisonous** /jʊˈnɪsənəs/ *adj.* [OF *unison* or LL *unisonus* (as UNI-, *sonus* SOUND¹)]

unissued /ʌnˈɪʃuːd, ʌnˈɪsjuːd/ *adj.* not issued.

unit /ˈjuːnɪt/ *n.* **1 a** an individual thing, person, or group regarded as single and complete, esp. for purposes of calculation. **b** each of the (smallest) separate individuals or groups into which a complex whole may be analysed (*the family as the unit of society*). **2** a quantity chosen as a standard in terms of which other quantities may be expressed (*unit of heat*; *SI unit*; *mass per unit volume*). **3** *Brit.* the smallest share in a unit trust. **4** a device with a specified function forming part of a complex mechanism. **5** a piece of furniture for fitting with others like it or made of complementary parts. **6** a group with a special function in an organization. **7** a group of buildings, wards, etc., in a hospital. **8** the number 'one'. □ **unit cell** *Crystallog.* the smallest repeating group of atoms, ions, or molecules in a crystal. **unit cost** the cost of producing one item of manufacture. **unit-holder** *Brit.* a person with a holding in a unit trust. **unit price** the price charged for each unit of goods supplied. **unit trust** *Brit.* an investment company investing combined contributions from many persons in various securities and paying them dividends in proportion to their holdings. [L *unus*, prob. after DIGIT]

Unitarian /ˌjuːnɪˈteərɪən/ *n. & adj.* **—n.** **1** a person who believes that God is not a Trinity but one person. **2** a member of a religious body maintaining this and advocating freedom from formal dogma or doctrine. **—adj.** of or relating to the Unitarians. □□ **Unitarianism** *n.* [mod.L *unitarius* f. L *unitas* UNITY]

unitary /ˈjuːnɪtərɪ/ *adj.* **1** of a unit or units. **2** marked by unity or uniformity. □□ **unitarily** *adv.* **unitarity** /-ˈtærɪtɪ/ *n.*

unite /jʊˈnaɪt, juː-/ *v.* **1** *tr. & intr.* join together; make or become one; combine. **2** *tr. & intr.* join together for a common purpose or action (*united in their struggle against injustice*). **3** *tr. & intr.* join in marriage. **4** *tr.* possess (qualities, features, etc.) in combination (*united anger with mercy*). **5** *intr. & tr.* form or cause to form a physical or chemical whole (*oil will not unite with water*). □ **United Brethren** *Eccl.* the Moravians. **United Kingdom** Great Britain and Northern Ireland (until 1922, Great Britain and Ireland). **United Nations** (orig., in 1942) those united against the Axis powers in the war of 1939–45, (later) a supranational peace-seeking organization of these and many other States. **United Provinces** *hist.* **1** the seven provinces united in 1579 and forming the basis of the republic of the Netherlands. **2** an Indian administrative division formed by the union of Agra and Oudh and called Uttar Pradesh since 1950.

United Reformed Church a Church formed in 1972 from the English Presbyterian and Congregational Churches. **United States** (in full **United States of America**) a federal republic of 50 States, mostly in N. America and including Alaska and Hawaii. □□ **unitedly** *adv.* **unitive** /ˈjuːnɪtɪv/ *adj.* **unitively** /ˈjuːnɪtɪvlɪ/ *adv.* [ME f. L *unire unit-* f. *unus* one]

unity /ˈjuːnɪtɪ/ *n.* (*pl.* **-ies**) **1** oneness; being one, single, or individual; being formed of parts that constitute a whole; due interconnection and coherence of parts (*disturbs the unity of the idea*; *the pictures lack unity*; *national unity*). **2** harmony or concord between persons etc. (*lived together in unity*). **3** a thing forming a complex whole (*a person regarded as a unity*). **4** *Math.* the number 'one', the factor that leaves unchanged the quantity on which it operates. **5** *Theatr.* each of the three dramatic principles requiring limitation of the supposed time of a drama to that occupied in acting it or to a single day (**unity of time**), use of one scene throughout (**unity of place**), and concentration on the development of a single plot (**unity of action**). [ME f. OF *unité* f. L *unitas -tatis* f. *unus* one]

Univ. *abbr.* University.

univalent *adj. & n.* **—adj.** **1** /ˌjuːnɪˈveɪlənt/ *Chem.* having a valency of one. **2** /juːˈnɪvələnt/ *Biol.* (of a chromosome) remaining unpaired during meiosis. **—n.** /juːˈnɪvələnt/ *Biol.* a univalent chromosome. [UNI- + *valent-* pres. part. stem (as VALENCE¹)]

univalve /ˈjuːnɪˌvælv/ *adj. & n. Zool.* **—adj.** having one valve. **—n.** a univalve mollusc.

universal /ˌjuːnɪˈvɜːs(ə)l/ *adj. & n.* **—adj.** **1** of, belonging to, or done etc. by all persons or things in the world or in the class concerned; applicable to all cases (*the feeling was universal*; *met with universal approval*). **2** *Logic* (of a proposition) in which something is asserted of all of a class (opp. PARTICULAR). **—n.** **1** *Logic* a universal proposition. **2** *Philos.* **a** a term or concept of general application. **b** a nature or essence signified by a general term. □ **universal agent** an agent empowered to do all that can be delegated. **universal compass** a compass with legs that may be extended for large circles. **universal coupling** (or **joint**) a coupling or joint which can transmit rotary power by a shaft at any selected angle. **universal language** an artificial language intended for use by all nations. **universal proposition** *Logic* a proposition in which the predicate is affirmed or denied of all members of a class (opp. *particular proposition*). **universal suffrage** a suffrage extending to all adults with minor exceptions. **universal time** = GREENWICH MEAN TIME. □□ **universality** /-ˈsælɪtɪ/ *n.* **universalize** *v.tr.* (also **-ise**). **universalization** /-ˈzeɪʃ(ə)n/ *n.* **universally** *adv.* [ME f. OF *universal* or L *universalis* (as UNIVERSE)]

universalist /ˌjuːnɪˈvɜːsəlɪst/ *n. Theol.* **1** a person who holds that all mankind will eventually be saved. **2** a member of an organized body of Christians who hold this. □□ **universalism** *n.* **universalistic** /-ˈlɪstɪk/ *adj.*

universe /ˈjuːnɪˌvɜːs/ *n.* **1** all existing things; the whole creation; the cosmos. **2** all mankind. **3** *Statistics & Logic* all the objects under consideration. □ **universe of discourse** *Logic* = sense 3. [F *univers* f. L *universum* neut. of *universus* combined into one, whole f. UNI- + *versus* past part. of *vertere* turn]

university /ˌjuːnɪˈvɜːsɪtɪ/ *n.* (*pl.* **-ies**) **1** an educational institution designed for instruction, examination, or both, of students in many branches of advanced learning, conferring degrees in various faculties, and often embodying colleges and similar institutions. **2** the members of this collectively. **3** a team, crew, etc., representing a university. □ **at university** studying at a university. [ME f. OF *université* f. L *universitas -tatis* the whole (world), in LL college, guild (as UNIVERSE)]

univocal /jʊˈnɪvək(ə)l, ˌjuːnɪˈvəʊk(ə)l/ *adj. & n.*

—*adj.* (of a word etc.) having only one proper meaning. —*n.* a univocal word. □□ **univocality** /ˌjuːnɪvəʊˈkælɪtɪ/ *n.* **univocally** *adv.*

unjoin /ʌnˈdʒɔɪn/ *v.tr.* detach from being joined; separate.

unjoined /ʌnˈdʒɔɪnd/ *adj.* not joined.

unjoint /ʌnˈdʒɔɪnt/ *v.tr.* **1** separate the joints of. **2** disunite.

unjust /ʌnˈdʒʌst/ *adj.* not just, contrary to justice or fairness. □□ **unjustly** *adv.* **unjustness** *n.*

unjustifiable /ʌnˈdʒʌstɪˌfaɪəb(ə)l/ *adj.* not justifiable. □□ **unjustifiably** *adv.*

unjustified /ʌnˈdʒʌstɪˌfaɪd/ *adj.* not justified.

unkempt /ʌnˈkempt/ *adj.* **1** untidy, of neglected appearance. **2** uncombed, dishevelled. □□ **unkemptly** *adv.* **unkemptness** *n.* [UN-¹ + archaic *kempt* past part. of *kemb* comb f. OE *cemban*]

unkept /ʌnˈkept/ *adj.* **1** (of a promise, law, etc.) not observed; disregarded. **2** not tended; neglected.

unkillable /ʌnˈkɪləb(ə)l/ *adj.* that cannot be killed.

unkind /ʌnˈkaɪnd/ *adj.* **1** not kind. **2** harsh, cruel. **3** unpleasant. □□ **unkindly** *adv.* **unkindness** *n.*

unking /ʌnˈkɪŋ/ *v.tr.* **1** deprive of the position of king; dethrone. **2** deprive (a country) of a king.

unkink /ʌnˈkɪŋk/ *v.* **1** *tr.* remove the kinks from; straighten. **2** *intr.* lose kinks; become straight.

unknit /ʌnˈnɪt/ *v.tr.* (**unknitted, unknitting**) separate (things joined, knotted, or interlocked).

unknot /ʌnˈnɒt/ *v.tr.* (**unknotted, unknotting**) release the knot or knots of, untie.

unknowable /ʌnˈnəʊəb(ə)l/ *adj. & n.* —*adj.* that cannot be known. —*n.* **1** an unknowable thing. **2** (**the Unknowable**) the postulated absolute or ultimate reality.

unknowing /ʌnˈnəʊɪŋ/ *adj. & n.* —*adj.* (often foll. by *of*) not knowing; ignorant, unconscious. —*n.* ignorance (*cloud of unknowing*). □□ **unknowingly** *adv.* **unknowingness** *n.*

unknown /ʌnˈnəʊn/ *adj. & n.* —*adj.* (often foll. by *to*) not known, unfamiliar (*his purpose was unknown to me*). —*n.* **1** an unknown thing or person. **2** an unknown quantity (*equation in two unknowns*). □**unknown country** see COUNTRY. **unknown quantity** a person or thing whose nature, significance, etc., cannot be determined. **Unknown Soldier** an unidentified representative member of a country's armed forces killed in war, given burial with special honours in a national memorial. **unknown to** without the knowledge of (*did it unknown to me*). **Unknown Warrior** = *Unknown Soldier.* □□ **unknownness** *n.*

unlabelled /ʌnˈleɪb(ə)ld/ *adj.* (*US* **unlabeled**) not labelled; without a label.

unlaboured /ʌnˈleɪbəd/ *adj.* (*US* **unlabored**) not laboured.

unlace /ʌnˈleɪs/ *v.tr.* **1** undo the lace or laces of. **2** unfasten or loosen in this way.

unlade /ʌnˈleɪd/ *v.tr.* **1** take the cargo out of (a ship). **2** discharge (a cargo etc.) from a ship.

unladen /ʌnˈleɪd(ə)n/ *adj.* not laden. □**unladen weight** the weight of a vehicle etc. when not loaded with goods etc.

unladylike /ʌnˈleɪdɪˌlaɪk/ *adj.* not ladylike.

unlaid¹ /ʌnˈleɪd/ *adj.* not laid.

unlaid² *past* and *past part.* of UNLAY.

unlamented /ˌʌnləˈmentɪd/ *adj.* not lamented.

unlash /ʌnˈlæʃ/ *v.tr.* unfasten (a thing lashed down etc.).

unlatch /ʌnˈlætʃ/ *v.* **1** *tr.* release the latch of. **2** *tr. & intr.* open or be opened in this way.

unlawful /ʌnˈlɔːfʊl/ *adj.* not lawful; illegal, not permissible. □□ **unlawfully** *adv.* **unlawfulness** *n.*

unlay /ʌnˈleɪ/ *v.tr.* (*past and past part.* **unlaid**) *Naut.* untwist (a rope). [UN-² + LAY¹]

unleaded /ʌnˈledɪd/ *adj.* **1** (of petrol etc.) without added lead. **2** not covered, weighted, or framed with lead. **3** *Printing* not spaced with leads.

unlearn /ʌnˈlɜːn/ *v.tr.* (*past* and *past part.*

unlearned or **unlearnt**) **1** discard from one's memory. **2** rid oneself of (a habit, false information, etc.).

unlearned¹ /ʌnˈlɜːnɪd/ *adj.* not well educated; untaught, ignorant. □□ **unlearnedly** *adv.*

unlearned² /ʌnˈlɜːnd/ *adj.* (also **unlearnt** /-ˈlɜːnt/) that has not been learnt.

unleash /ʌnˈliːʃ/ *v.tr.* **1** release from a leash or restraint. **2** set free to engage in pursuit or attack.

unleavened /ʌnˈlev(ə)nd/ *adj.* not leavened; made without yeast or other raising agent.

unless /ʌnˈles, ənˈles/ *conj.* if not; except when (*shall go unless I hear from you; always walked unless I had a bicycle*). [ON or IN + LESS, assim. to UN-¹]

unlettered /ʌnˈletəd/ *adj.* **1** illiterate. **2** not well educated.

unliberated /ʌnˈlɪbəˌreɪtɪd/ *adj.* not liberated.

unlicensed /ʌnˈlaɪs(ə)nst/ *adj.* not licensed, esp. without a licence to sell alcoholic drink.

unlighted /ʌnˈlaɪtɪd/ *adj.* **1** not provided with light. **2** not set burning.

unlike /ʌnˈlaɪk/ *adj. & prep.* —*adj.* **1** not like; different from (*is unlike both his parents*). **2** uncharacteristic of (*such behaviour is unlike him*). **3** dissimilar, different. —*prep.* differently from (*acts quite unlike anyone else*). □**unlike signs** *Math.* plus and minus. □□ **unlikeness** *n.* [perh. f. ON *úlíkr*, OE *ungelic*: see LIKE¹]

unlikeable /ʌnˈlaɪkəb(ə)l/ *adj.* (also **unlikable**) not easy to like; unpleasant.

unlikely /ʌnˈlaɪklɪ/ *adj.* (**unlikelier, unlikeliest**) **1** improbable (*unlikely tale*). **2** (foll. by *to* + infin.) not to be expected to do something (*he's unlikely to be available*). **3** unpromising (*an unlikely candidate*). □□ **unlikelihood** *n.* **unlikeliness** *n.*

unlimited /ʌnˈlɪmɪtɪd/ *adj.* without limit; unrestricted; very great in number or quantity (*has unlimited possibilities; an unlimited expanse of sea*). □□ **unlimitedly** *adv.* **unlimitedness** *n.*

unlined¹ /ʌnˈlaɪnd/ *adj.* **1** (of paper etc.) without lines. **2** (of a face etc.) without wrinkles.

unlined² /ʌnˈlaɪnd/ *adj.* (of a garment etc.) without lining.

unlink /ʌnˈlɪŋk/ *v.tr.* **1** undo the links of (a chain etc.). **2** detach or set free by undoing or unfastening a link or chain.

unliquidated /ʌnˈlɪkwɪˌdeɪtɪd/ *adj.* not liquidated.

unlisted /ʌnˈlɪstɪd/ *adj.* not included in a published list, esp. of Stock Exchange prices or of telephone numbers.

unlit /ʌnˈlɪt/ *adj.* not lit.

unlivable /ʌnˈlɪvəb(ə)l/ *adj.* that cannot be lived or lived in.

unlived-in /ʌnˈlɪvdɪn/ *adj.* **1** appearing to be uninhabited. **2** unused by the inhabitants.

unload /ʌnˈləʊd/ *v.tr.* **1** (also *absol.*) remove a load from (a vehicle etc.). **2** remove (a load) from a vehicle etc. **3** remove the charge from (a firearm etc.). **4** *colloq.* get rid of. **5** (often foll. by *on*) *colloq.* **a** divulge (information). **b** (also *absol.*) give vent to (feelings). □□ **unloader** *n.*

unlock /ʌnˈlɒk/ *v.tr.* **1 a** release the lock of (a door, box, etc.). **b** release or disclose by unlocking. **2** release thoughts, feelings, etc., from (one's mind etc.).

unlocked /ʌnˈlɒkt/ *adj.* not locked.

unlooked-for /ʌnˈlʊktfɔː(r)/ *adj.* unexpected, unforeseen.

unloose /ʌnˈluːs/ *v.tr.* (also **unloosen**) loose; set free.

unlovable /ʌnˈlʌvəb(ə)l/ *adj.* not lovable.

unloved /ʌnˈlʌvd/ *adj.* not loved.

unlovely /ʌnˈlʌvlɪ/ *adj.* not attractive; unpleasant, ugly. □□ **unloveliness** *n.*

unloving /ʌnˈlʌvɪŋ/ *adj.* not loving. □□ **unlovingly** *adv.* **unlovingness** *n.*

unlucky /ʌnˈlʌkɪ/ *adj.* (**unluckier, unluckiest**) **1**

not fortunate or successful. **2** wretched. **3** bringing bad luck. **4** ill-judged. □□ **unluckily** *adv.* **unluckiness** *n.*

unmade /ʌnˈmeɪd/ *adj.* **1** not made. **2** destroyed, annulled.

unmake /ʌnˈmeɪk/ *v.tr.* (*past* and *past part.* **unmade**) undo the making of; destroy, depose, annul.

unmalleable /ʌnˈmælɪəb(ə)l/ *adj.* not malleable.

unman /ʌnˈmæn/ *v.tr.* (**unmanned**, **unmanning**) **1** deprive of supposed manly qualities (e.g. self-control, courage); cause to weep etc., discourage. **2** deprive (a ship etc.) of men.

unmanageable /ʌnˈmænɪdʒəb(ə)l/ *adj.* not (easily) managed, manipulated, or controlled. □□ **unmanageableness** *n.* **unmanageably** *adv.*

unmanly /ʌnˈmænlɪ/ *adj.* not manly. □□ **unmanliness** *n.*

unmanned /ʌnˈmænd/ *adj.* **1** not manned. **2** overcome by emotion etc.

unmannerly /ʌnˈmænəlɪ/ *adj.* **1** without good manners. **2** (of actions, speech, etc.) showing a lack of good manners. □□ **unmannerliness** *n.*

unmarked /ʌnˈmɑːkt/ *adj.* **1** not marked. **2** not noticed.

unmarketable /ʌnˈmɑːkɪtəb(ə)l/ *adj.* not marketable.

unmarried /ʌnˈmærɪd/ *adj.* not married; single.

unmask /ʌnˈmɑːsk/ *v.* **1** *tr.* **a** remove the mask from. **b** expose the true character of. **2** *intr.* remove one's mask. □□ **unmasker** *n.*

unmatchable /ʌnˈmætʃəb(ə)l/ *adj.* that cannot be matched. □□ **unmatchably** *adv.*

unmatched /ʌnˈmætʃt/ *adj.* not matched or equalled.

unmatured /ʌnməˈtjʊəd/ *adj.* not yet matured.

unmeaning /ʌnˈmiːnɪŋ/ *adj.* having no meaning or significance; meaningless. □□ **unmeaningly** *adv.* **unmeaningness** *n.*

unmeant /ʌnˈment/ *adj.* not meant or intended.

unmeasurable /ʌnˈmeʒərəb(ə)l/ *adj.* that cannot be measured. □□ **unmeasurably** *adv.*

unmeasured /ʌnˈmeʒəd/ *adj.* **1** not measured. **2** limitless.

unmelodious /ˌʌnmɪˈləʊdɪəs/ *adj.* not melodious; discordant. □□ **unmelodiously** *adv.*

unmelted /ʌnˈmeltɪd/ *adj.* not melted.

unmemorable /ʌnˈmemərəb(ə)l/ *adj.* not memorable. □□ **unmemorably** *adv.*

unmentionable /ʌnˈmenʃənəb(ə)l/ *adj.* & *n.* —*adj.* that cannot (properly) be mentioned. —*n.* **1** (in *pl.*) *joc.* **a** undergarments. **b** *archaic* trousers. **2** a person or thing not to be mentioned. □□ **unmentionability** /-ˈbɪlɪtɪ/ *n.* **unmentionableness** *n.* **unmentionably** *adv.*

unmentioned /ʌnˈmenʃ(ə)nd/ *adj.* not mentioned.

unmerchantable /ʌnˈmɜːtʃəntəb(ə)l/ *adj.* not merchantable.

unmerciful /ʌnˈmɜːsɪfʊl/ *adj.* merciless. □□ **unmercifully** *adv.* **unmercifulness** *n.*

unmerited /ʌnˈmerɪtɪd/ *adj.* not merited.

unmet /ʌnˈmet/ *adj.* (of a quota, demand, goal, etc.) not achieved or fulfilled.

unmetalled /ʌnˈmet(ə)ld/ *adj.* *Brit.* (of a road etc.) not made with road-metal.

unmethodical /ˌʌnmɪˈθɒdɪk(ə)l/ *adj.* not methodical. □□ **unmethodically** *adv.*

unmetrical /ʌnˈmetrɪk(ə)l/ *adj.* not metrical.

unmilitary /ʌnˈmɪlɪtərɪ/ *adj.* not military.

unmindful /ʌnˈmaɪndfʊl/ *adj.* (often foll. by *of*) not mindful. □□ **unmindfully** *adv.* **unmindfulness** *n.*

unmissable /ʌnˈmɪsəb(ə)l/ *adj.* that cannot or should not be missed.

unmistakable /ˌʌnmɪˈsteɪkəb(ə)l/ *adj.* that cannot be mistaken or doubted, clear. □□ **unmistakability** /-ˈbɪlɪtɪ/ *n.* **unmistakableness** *n.* **unmistakably** *adv.*

unmistaken /ˌʌnmɪˈsteɪkən/ *adj.* not mistaken; right, correct.

unmitigated /ʌnˈmɪtɪˌɡeɪtɪd/ *adj.* **1** not mitigated or modified. **2** absolute, unqualified (*an unmitigated disaster*). □□ **unmitigatedly** *adv.*

unmixed /ʌnˈmɪkst/ *adj.* not mixed. □ **unmixed blessing** a thing having advantages and no disadvantages.

unmodified /ʌnˈmɒdɪˌfaɪd/ *adj.* not modified.

unmodulated /ʌnˈmɒdjʊˌleɪtɪd/ *adj.* not modulated.

unmolested /ˌʌnməˈlestɪd/ *adj.* not molested.

unmoor /ʌnˈmʊə(r), ʌnˈmɔː(r)/ *v.tr.* **1** (also *absol.*) release the moorings of (a vessel). **2** weigh all but one anchor of (a vessel).

unmoral /ʌnˈmɒr(ə)l/ *adj.* not concerned with morality (cf. IMMORAL). □□ **unmorality** /ˌʌnməˈrælɪtɪ/ *n.* **unmorally** *adv.*

unmotherly /ʌnˈmʌðəlɪ/ *adj.* not motherly.

unmotivated /ʌnˈməʊtɪˌveɪtɪd/ *adj.* without motivation; without a motive.

unmounted /ʌnˈmaʊntɪd/ *adj.* not mounted.

unmourned /ʌnˈmɔːnd/ *adj.* not mourned.

unmoved /ʌnˈmuːvd/ *adj.* **1** not moved. **2** not changed in one's purpose. **3** not affected by emotion. □□ **unmovable** *adj.* (also **unmoveable**).

unmown /ʌnˈməʊn/ *adj.* not mown.

unmuffle /ʌnˈmʌf(ə)l/ *v.tr.* **1** remove a muffler from (a face, bell, etc.). **2** free of something that muffles or conceals.

unmurmuring /ʌnˈmɜːmərɪŋ/ *adj.* not complaining. □□ **unmurmuringly** *adv.*

unmusical /ʌnˈmjuːzɪk(ə)l/ *adj.* **1** not pleasing to the ear. **2** unskilled in or indifferent to music. □□ **unmusicality** /-ˈkælɪtɪ/ *n.* **unmusically** *adv.* **unmusicalness** *n.*

unmutilated /ʌnˈmjuːtɪˌleɪtɪd/ *adj.* not mutilated.

unmuzzle /ʌnˈmʌz(ə)l/ *v.tr.* **1** remove a muzzle from. **2** relieve of an obligation to remain silent.

unnail /ʌnˈneɪl/ *v.tr.* unfasten by the removal of nails.

unnameable /ʌnˈneɪməb(ə)l/ *adj.* that cannot be named, esp. too bad to be named.

unnamed /ʌnˈneɪmd/ *adj.* not named.

unnatural /ʌnˈnætʃər(ə)l/ *adj.* **1** contrary to nature or the usual course of nature; not normal. **2 a** lacking natural feelings. **b** extremely cruel or wicked. **3** artificial. **4** affected. □□ **unnaturally** *adv.* **unnaturalness** *n.*

unnavigable /ʌnˈnævɪɡəb(ə)l/ *adj.* not navigable. □□ **unnavigability** /-ˈbɪlɪtɪ/ *n.*

unnecessary /ʌnˈnesəsərɪ/ *adj.* & *n.* —*adj.* **1** not necessary. **2** more than is necessary (*with unnecessary care*). —*n.* (*pl.* **-ies**) (usu. in *pl.*) an unnecessary thing. □□ **unnecessarily** *adv.* **unnecessariness** *n.*

unneeded /ʌnˈniːdɪd/ *adj.* not needed.

unneighbourly /ʌnˈneɪbəlɪ/ *adj.* not neighbourly. □□ **unneighbourliness** *n.*

unnerve /ʌnˈnɜːv/ *v.tr.* deprive of strength or resolution. □□ **unnervingly** *adv.*

unnoticeable /ʌnˈnəʊtɪsəb(ə)l/ *adj.* not easily seen or noticed. □□ **unnoticeably** *adv.*

unnoticed /ʌnˈnəʊtɪst/ *adj.* not noticed.

unnumbered /ʌnˈnʌmbəd/ *adj.* **1** not marked with a number. **2** not counted. **3** countless.

UNO /ˈjuːnəʊ/ *abbr.* United Nations Organization.

unobjectionable /ˌʌnəbˈdʒekʃənəb(ə)l/ *adj.* not objectionable; acceptable. □□ **unobjectionableness** *n.* **unobjectionably** *adv.*

unobliging /ˌʌnəˈblaɪdʒɪŋ/ *adj.* not obliging; unhelpful, uncooperative.

unobscured /ˌʌnəbˈskjʊəd/ *adj.* not obscured.

unobservable /ˌʌnəbˈzɜːvəb(ə)l/ *adj.* not observable; imperceptible.

unobservant /ˌʌnəbˈzɜːv(ə)nt/ *adj.* not observant. □□ **unobservantly** *adv.*

unobserved /ˌʌnəbˈzɜːvd/ *adj.* not observed. □□ **unobservedly** /-vɪdlɪ/ *adv.*

unobstructed /ˌʌnəbˈstrʌktɪd/ *adj.* not obstructed.

unobtainable /ˌʌnəbˈteɪnəb(ə)l/ *adj.* that cannot be obtained.

unobtrusive /ˌʌnəbˈtruːsɪv/ *adj.* not making oneself or itself noticed. □□ **unobtrusively** *adv.* **unobtrusiveness** *n.*

unoccupied /ʌnˈɒkjʊˌpaɪd/ *adj.* not occupied.

unoffending /ˌʌnəˈfendɪŋ/ *adj.* not offending; harmless, innocent. □□ **unoffended** *adj.*

unofficial /ˌʌnəˈfɪʃ(ə)l/ *adj.* **1** not officially authorized or confirmed. **2** not characteristic of officials. □ **unofficial strike** a strike not formally approved by the strikers' trade union. □□ **unofficially** *adv.*

unoiled /ʌnˈɔɪld/ *adj.* not oiled.

unopened /ʌnˈəʊpənd/ *adj.* not opened.

unopposed /ˌʌnəˈpəʊzd/ *adj.* not opposed.

unordained /ˌʌnɔːˈdeɪnd/ *adj.* not ordained.

unordinary /ʌnˈɔːdɪnərɪ/ *adj.* not ordinary.

unorganized /ʌnˈɔːgəˌnaɪzd/ *adj.* (also **-ised**) not organized (cf. DISORGANIZE).

unoriginal /ˌʌnəˈrɪdʒɪn(ə)l/ *adj.* lacking originality; derivative. □□ **unoriginality** /-ˈnælɪtɪ/ *n.* **unoriginally** *adv.*

unornamental /ˌʌnɔːnəˈment(ə)l/ *adj.* not ornamental; plain.

unornamented /ʌnˈɔːnəˌmentɪd/ *adj.* not ornamented.

unorthodox /ʌnˈɔːθəˌdɒks/ *adj.* not orthodox. □□ **unorthodoxly** *adv.* **unorthodoxy** *n.*

unostentatious /ˌʌnɒstenˈteɪʃəs/ *adj.* not ostentatious. □□ **unostentatiously** *adv.* **unostentatiousness** *n.*

unowned /ʌnˈəʊnd/ *adj.* **1** unacknowledged. **2** having no owner.

unpack /ʌnˈpæk/ *v.tr.* **1** (also *absol.*) open and remove the contents of (a package, luggage, etc.). **2** take (a thing) out from a package etc. □□ **unpacker** *n.*

unpaged /ʌnˈpeɪdʒd/ *adj.* with pages not numbered.

unpaid /ʌnˈpeɪd/ *adj.* (of a debt or a person) not paid.

unpainted /ʌnˈpeɪntɪd/ *adj.* not painted.

unpaired /ʌnˈpeəd/ *adj.* **1** not arranged in pairs. **2** not forming one of a pair.

unpalatable /ʌnˈpælətəb(ə)l/ *adj.* **1** not pleasant to taste. **2** (of an idea, suggestion, etc.) disagreeable, distasteful. □□ **unpalatability** /-ˈbɪlɪtɪ/ *n.* **unpalatableness** *n.*

unparalleled /ʌnˈpærəˌleld/ *adj.* having no parallel or equal.

unpardonable /ʌnˈpɑːdənəb(ə)l/ *adj.* that cannot be pardoned. □□ **unpardonableness** *n.* **unpardonably** *adv.*

unparliamentary /ˌʌnpɑːləˈmentərɪ/ *adj.* contrary to proper parliamentary usage. □ **unparliamentary language** oaths or abuse.

unpasteurized /ʌnˈpɑːstjəˌraɪzd, -tʃəˌraɪzd, ʌnˈpæs-/ *adj.* not pasteurized.

unpatented /ʌnˈpeɪtəntɪd, ʌnˈpæt-/ *adj.* not patented.

unpatriotic /ˌʌnpætrɪˈɒtɪk, ˌʌnpeɪt-/ *adj.* not patriotic. □□ **unpatriotically** *adv.*

unpaved /ʌnˈpeɪvd/ *adj.* not paved.

unpeeled /ʌnˈpiːld/ *adj.* not peeled.

unpeg /ʌnˈpeg/ *v.tr.* (**unpegged**, **unpegging**) **1** unfasten by the removal of pegs. **2** cease to maintain or stabilize (prices etc.).

unpeople *v.* & *n.* —*v.tr.* /ʌnˈpiːp(ə)l/ depopulate. —*n.pl.* /ˈʌnˌpiːp(ə)l/ unpersons.

unperceived /ˌʌnpəˈsiːvd/ *adj.* not perceived; unobserved.

unperceptive /ˌʌnpəˈseptɪv/ *adj.* not perceptive. □□ **unperceptively** *adv.* **unperceptiveness** *n.*

unperfected /ˌʌnpəˈfektɪd/ *adj.* not perfected.

unperforated /ʌnˈpɜːfəˌreɪtɪd/ *adj.* not perforated.

unperformed /ˌʌnpəˈfɔːmd/ *adj.* not performed.

unperfumed /ʌnˈpɜːfjuːmd/ *adj.* not perfumed.

unperson /ˈʌnˌpɜːs(ə)n/ *n.* a person whose name or existence is denied or ignored.

unpersuadable /ˌʌnpəˈsweɪdəb(ə)l/ *adj.* not able to be persuaded; obstinate.

unpersuaded /ˌʌnpəˈsweɪdɪd/ *adj.* not persuaded.

unpersuasive /ˌʌnpəˈsweɪsɪv/ *adj.* not persuasive. □□ **unpersuasively** *adv.*

unperturbed /ˌʌnpəˈtɜːbd/ *adj.* not perturbed. □□ **unperturbedly** /-bɪdlɪ/ *adv.*

unphilosophical /ˌʌnfɪləˈsɒfɪk(ə)l/ *adj.* (also **unphilosophic**) **1** not according to philosophical principles. **2** lacking philosophy. □□ **unphilosophically** *adv.*

unphysiological /ˌʌnfɪzɪəˈlɒdʒɪk(ə)l/ *adj.* (also **unphysiologic**) not in accordance with normal physiological functioning. □□ **unphysiologically** *adv.*

unpick /ʌnˈpɪk/ *v.tr.* undo the sewing of (stitches, a garment, etc.).

unpicked /ʌnˈpɪkt/ *adj.* **1** not selected. **2** (of a flower) not plucked.

unpicturesque /ˌʌnpɪktʃəˈresk/ *adj.* not picturesque.

unpin /ʌnˈpɪn/ *v.tr.* (**unpinned**, **unpinning**) **1** unfasten or detach by removing a pin or pins. **2** *Chess* release (a piece that has been pinned).

unpitied /ʌnˈpɪtɪd/ *adj.* not pitied.

unpitying /ʌnˈpɪtɪɪŋ/ *adj.* not pitying. □□ **unpityingly** *adv.*

unplaceable /ʌnˈpleɪsəb(ə)l/ *adj.* that cannot be placed or classified (*his accent was unplaceable*).

unplaced /ʌnˈpleɪst/ *adj.* not placed, esp. not placed as one of the first three finishing in a race etc.

unplanned /ʌnˈplænd/ *adj.* not planned.

unplanted /ʌnˈplɑːntɪd/ *adj.* not planted.

unplausible /ʌnˈplɔːzɪb(ə)l/ *adj.* not plausible.

unplayable /ʌnˈpleɪəb(ə)l/ *adj.* **1** *Sport* (of a ball) that cannot be struck or returned. **2** that cannot be played. □□ **unplayably** *adv.*

unpleasant /ʌnˈplez(ə)nt/ *adj.* not pleasant; displeasing; disagreeable. □□ **unpleasantly** *adv.* **unpleasantness** *n.*

unpleasing /ʌnˈpliːzɪŋ/ *adj.* not pleasing. □□ **unpleasingly** *adv.*

unploughed /ʌnˈplaʊd/ *adj.* not ploughed.

unplucked /ʌnˈplʌkt/ *adj.* not plucked.

unplug /ʌnˈplʌg/ *v.tr.* (**unplugged**, **unplugging**) **1** disconnect (an electrical device) by removing its plug from the socket. **2** unstop.

unplumbed /ʌnˈplʌmd/ *adj.* **1** not plumbed. **2** not fully explored or understood. □□ **unplumbable** *adj.*

unpoetic /ˌʌnpəʊˈetɪk/ *adj.* (also **unpoetical**) not poetic.

unpointed /ʌnˈpɔɪntɪd/ *adj.* **1** having no point or points. **2 a** not punctuated. **b** (of written Hebrew etc.) without vowel points. **3** (of masonry or brickwork) not pointed.

unpolished /ʌnˈpɒlɪʃt/ *adj.* **1** not polished; rough. **2** without refinement; crude.

unpolitic /ʌnˈpɒlɪtɪk/ *adj.* impolitic, unwise.

unpolitical /ˌʌnpəˈlɪtɪk(ə)l/ *adj.* not concerned with politics. □□ **unpolitically** *adv.*

unpolled /ʌnˈpəʊld/ *adj.* **1** not having voted at an election. **2** not included in an opinion poll.

unpolluted /ˌʌnpəˈluːtɪd/ *adj.* not polluted.

unpopular /ʌnˈpɒpjʊlə(r)/ *adj.* not popular; not liked by the public or by people in general. □□ **unpopularity** /-ˈlærɪtɪ/ *n.* **unpopularly** *adv.*

unpopulated /ʌnˈpɒpjʊˌleɪtɪd/ *adj.* not populated.

unpossessed /ˌʌnpəˈzest/ *adj.* **1** (foll. by *of*) not in possession of. **2** not possessed.

unpractical /ʌnˈpræktɪk(ə)l/ *adj.* **1** not practical. **2** (of a person) not having practical skill. □□ **unpracticality** /-ˈkælɪtɪ/ *n.* **unpractically** *adv.*

unpractised /ʌnˈpræktɪst/ *adj.* (*US* **unpracticed**) **1** not experienced or skilled. **2** not put into practice.

unprecedented /ʌnˈpresɪˌdentɪd/ *adj.* **1** having no precedent; unparalleled. **2** novel. □□ **unprecedentedly** *adv.*

unpredictable /ˌʌnprɪˈdɪktəb(ə)l/ *adj.* that cannot be predicted. □□ **unpredictability** /-ˈbɪlɪtɪ/ *n.* **unpredictableness** *n.* **unpredictably** *adv.*

unpredicted /ˌʌnprɪˈdɪktɪd/ *adj.* not predicted or foretold.

unprejudiced /ʌnˈpredʒʊdɪst/ *adj.* not prejudiced.

unpremeditated /ˌʌnprɪˈmedɪˌteɪtɪd/ *adj.* not previously thought over, not deliberately planned, unintentional. □□ **unpremeditatedly** *adv.*

unprepared /ˌʌnprɪˈpeəd/ *adj.* not prepared (in advance); not ready. □□ **unpreparedly** *adv.* **unpreparedness** *n.*

unprepossessing /ˌʌnpriːpəˈzesɪŋ/ *adj.* not prepossessing; unattractive.

unprescribed /ˌʌnprɪˈskraɪbd/ *adj.* (esp. of drugs) not prescribed.

unpresentable /ˌʌnprɪˈzentəb(ə)l/ *adj.* not presentable.

unpressed /ʌnˈprest/ *adj.* not pressed, esp. (of clothing) unironed.

unpresuming /ˌʌnprɪˈzjuːmɪŋ/ *adj.* not presuming; modest.

unpresumptuous /ˌʌnprɪˈzʌmptjʊəs/ *adj.* not presumptuous.

unpretending /ˌʌnprɪˈtendɪŋ/ *adj.* unpretentious. □□ **unpretendingly** *adv.* **unpretendingness** *n.*

unpretentious /ˌʌnprɪˈtenʃəs/ *adj.* not making a great display; simple, modest. □□ **unpretentiously** *adv.* **unpretentiousness** *n.*

unpriced /ʌnˈpraɪst/ *adj.* not having a price or prices fixed, marked, or stated.

unprimed /ʌnˈpraɪmd/ *adj.* not primed.

unprincipled /ʌnˈprɪnsɪp(ə)ld/ *adj.* lacking or not based on good moral principles. □□ **unprincipledness** *n.*

unprintable /ʌnˈprɪntəb(ə)l/ *adj.* that cannot be printed, esp. because too indecent or libellous or blasphemous. □□ **unprintably** *adv.*

unprinted /ʌnˈprɪntɪd/ *adj.* not printed.

unprivileged /ʌnˈprɪvɪlɪdʒd/ *adj.* not privileged.

unproblematic /ˌʌnprɒbləˈmætɪk/ *adj.* causing no difficulty. □□ **unproblematically** *adv.*

unproclaimed /ˌʌnprəʊˈkleɪmd/ *adj.* not proclaimed.

unprocurable /ˌʌnprəˈkjʊərəb(ə)l/ *adj.* that cannot be procured.

unproductive /ˌʌnprəˈdʌktɪv/ *adj.* not productive. □□ **unproductively** *adv.* **unproductiveness** *n.*

unprofessional /ˌʌnprəˈfeʃən(ə)l/ *adj.* **1** contrary to professional standards of behaviour etc. **2** not belonging to a profession; amateur. □□ **unprofessionally** *adv.*

unprofitable /ʌnˈprɒfɪtəb(ə)l/ *adj.* not profitable. □□ **unprofitableness** *n.* **unprofitably** *adv.*

unprogressive /ˌʌnprəˈgresɪv/ *adj.* not progressive.

unpromising /ʌnˈprɒmɪsɪŋ/ *adj.* not likely to turn out well. □□ **unpromisingly** *adv.*

unprompted /ʌnˈprɒmptɪd/ *adj.* spontaneous.

unpronounceable /ˌʌnprəˈnaʊnsəb(ə)l/ *adj.* that cannot be pronounced. □□ **unpronounceably** *adv.*

unpropitious /ˌʌnprəˈpɪʃəs/ *adj.* not propitious. □□ **unpropitiously** *adv.*

unprosperous /ʌnˈprɒspərəs/ *adj.* not prosperous. □□ **unprosperously** *adv.*

unprotected /ˌʌnprəˈtektɪd/ *adj.* not protected. □□ **unprotectedness** *n.*

unprotesting /ˌʌnprəˈtestɪŋ/ *adj.* not protesting. □□ **unprotestingly** *adv.*

unprovable /ʌnˈpruːvəb(ə)l/ *adj.* that cannot be proved. □□ **unprovability** /-ˈbɪlɪtɪ/ *n.* **unprovableness** *n.*

unproved /ʌnˈpruːvd/ *adj.* (also **unproven** /-v(ə)n/) not proved.

unprovided /ˌʌnprəˈvaɪdɪd/ *adj.* (usu. foll. by *with*) not furnished, supplied, or equipped.

unprovoked /ˌʌnprəˈvəʊkt/ *adj.* (of a person or act) without provocation.

unpublished /ʌnˈpʌblɪʃt/ *adj.* not published. □□ **unpublishable** *adj.*

unpunctual /ʌnˈpʌŋktjʊəl/ *adj.* not punctual. **unpunctuality** /-tjʊˈælɪtɪ/ *n.*

unpunctuated /ʌnˈpʌŋktjʊˌeɪtɪd/ *adj.* not punctuated.

unpunishable /ʌnˈpʌnɪʃəb(ə)l/ *adj.* that cannot be punished.

unpunished /ʌnˈpʌnɪʃt/ *adj.* not punished.

unpurified /ʌnˈpjʊərɪˌfaɪd/ *adj.* not purified.

unputdownable /ˌʌnpʊtˈdaʊnəb(ə)l/ *adj. colloq.* (of a book) so engrossing that one has to go on reading it.

unqualified /ʌnˈkwɒlɪˌfaɪd/ *adj.* **1** not competent (*unqualified to give an answer*). **2** not legally or officially qualified (*an unqualified practitioner*). **3** not modified or restricted; complete (*unqualified assent; unqualified success*).

unquenchable /ʌnˈkwentʃəb(ə)l/ *adj.* that cannot be quenched. □□ **unquenchably** *adv.*

unquenched /ʌnˈkwentʃt/ *adj.* not quenched.

unquestionable /ʌnˈkwestʃənəb(ə)l/ *adj.* that cannot be disputed or doubted. □□ **unquestionability** /-ˈbɪlɪtɪ/ *n.* **unquestionableness** *n.* **unquestionably** *adv.*

unquestioned /ʌnˈkwestʃ(ə)nd/ *adj.* **1** not disputed or doubted; definite, certain. **2** not interrogated.

unquestioning /ʌnˈkwestʃənɪŋ/ *adj.* **1** asking no questions. **2** done etc. without asking questions. □□ **unquestioningly** *adv.*

unquiet /ʌnˈkwaɪət/ *adj.* **1** restless, agitated, stirring. **2** perturbed, anxious. □□ **unquietly** *adv.* **unquietness** *n.*

unquotable /ʌnˈkwəʊtəb(ə)l/ *adj.* that cannot be quoted.

unquote /ʌnˈkwəʊt/ *v.tr.* (as *int.*) (in dictation, reading aloud, etc.) indicate the presence of closing quotation marks (cf. QUOTE *v.* 5 b).

unquoted /ʌnˈkwəʊtɪd/ *adj.* not quoted, esp. on the Stock Exchange.

unravel /ʌnˈræv(ə)l/ *v.* (**unravelled, unravelling**; *US* **unraveled, unraveling**) **1** *tr.* cause to be no longer ravelled, tangled, or intertwined. **2** *tr.* probe and solve (a mystery etc.). **3** *tr.* undo (a fabric, esp. a knitted one). **4** *intr.* become disentangled or unknitted.

unreachable /ʌnˈriːtʃəb(ə)l/ *adj.* that cannot be reached. □□ **unreachableness** *n.* **unreachably** *adv.*

unread /ʌnˈred/ *adj.* **1** (of a book etc.) not read. **2** (of a person) not well-read.

unreadable /ʌnˈriːdəb(ə)l/ *adj.* **1** too dull or too difficult to be worth reading. **2** illegible. □□ **unreadability** /-ˈbɪlɪtɪ/ *n.* **unreadably** *adv.*

unready[1] /ʌnˈredɪ/ *adj.* **1** not ready. **2** not prompt in action. □□ **unreadily** *adv.* **unreadiness** *n.*

unready[2] /ʌnˈredɪ/ *adj. archaic* lacking good advice; rash (*Ethelred the Unready*). [UN-[1] + REDE, assim. to UNREADY[1]]

unreal /ʌnˈrɪəl/ *adj.* **1** not real. **2** imaginary, illusory. **3** *US* & *Austral. sl.* incredible, amazing. □□ **unreality** /-ɪˈælɪtɪ/ *n.* **unreally** *adv.*

unrealistic /ˌʌnrɪəˈlɪstɪk/ *adj.* not realistic. □□ **unrealistically** *adv.*

unrealizable /ʌnˈrɪəlaɪzəb(ə)l/ *adj.* that cannot be realized.

unrealized /ʌnˈrɪəlaɪzd/ *adj.* not realized.

unreason /ʌnˈriːz(ə)n/ *n.* lack of reasonable thought or action. [ME, = injustice, f. UN-[1] + REASON]

unreasonable /ʌnˈriːzənəb(ə)l/ *adj.* **1** going beyond the limits of what is reasonable or equitable (*unreasonable demands*). **2** not guided by or listening to reason. □□ **unreasonableness** *n.* **unreasonably** *adv.*

unreasoned /ʌnˈriːz(ə)nd/ *adj.* not reasoned.

unreasoning /ʌnˈriːzənɪŋ/ *adj.* not reasoning. □□ **unreasoningly** *adv.*

unreceptive /ˌʌnrɪˈseptɪv/ *adj.* not receptive.

unreciprocated /ˌʌnrɪˈsɪprəˌkeɪtɪd/ *adj.* not reciprocated.

unreckoned /ʌnˈrekənd/ *adj.* not calculated or taken into account.

unreclaimed /ˌʌnrɪˈkleɪmd/ *adj.* not reclaimed.

unrecognizable /ʌnˈrekəɡˌnaɪzəb(ə)l/ *adj.* (also **-isable**) that cannot be recognized. □□ **unrecognizableness** *n.* **unrecognizably** *adv.*

unrecognized /ʌnˈrekəɡˌnaɪzd/ *adj.* (also **-ised**) not recognized.

unrecompensed /ʌnˈrekəmˌpenst/ *adj.* not recompensed.

unreconciled /ʌnˈrekənˌsaɪld/ *adj.* not reconciled.

unreconstructed /ˌʌnriːkənˈstrʌktɪd/ *adj.* **1** not reconciled or converted to the current political orthodoxy. **2** not rebuilt.

unrecorded /ˌʌnrɪˈkɔːdɪd/ *adj.* not recorded. □□ **unrecordable** *adj.*

unrectified /ʌnˈrektɪˌfaɪd/ *adj.* not rectified.

unredeemable /ˌʌnrɪˈdiːməb(ə)l/ *adj.* that cannot be redeemed. □□ **unredeemably** *adv.*

unredeemed /ˌʌnrɪˈdiːmd/ *adj.* not redeemed.

unredressed /ˌʌnrɪˈdrest/ *adj.* not redressed.

unreel /ʌnˈriːl/ *v.tr.* & *intr.* unwind from a reel.

unreeve /ʌnˈriːv/ *v.tr.* (*past* **unrove**) withdraw (a rope etc.) from being reeved.

unrefined /ˌʌnrɪˈfaɪnd/ *adj.* not refined.

unreflecting /ˌʌnrɪˈflektɪŋ/ *adj.* not thoughtful. □□ **unreflectingly** *adv.* **unreflectingness** *n.*

unreformed /ˌʌnrɪˈfɔːmd/ *adj.* not reformed.

unregarded /ˌʌnrɪˈɡɑːdɪd/ *adj.* not regarded.

unregenerate /ˌʌnrɪˈdʒenərət/ *adj.* not regenerate; obstinately wrong or bad. □□ **unregeneracy** *n.* **unregenerately** *adv.*

unregistered /ʌnˈredʒɪstəd/ *adj.* not registered.

unregulated /ʌnˈreɡjʊˌleɪtɪd/ *adj.* not regulated.

unrehearsed /ˌʌnrɪˈhɜːst/ *adj.* not rehearsed.

unrelated /ˌʌnrɪˈleɪtɪd/ *adj.* not related. □□ **unrelatedness** *n.*

unrelaxed /ˌʌnrɪˈlækst/ *adj.* not relaxed.

unrelenting /ˌʌnrɪˈlentɪŋ/ *adj.* **1** not relenting or yielding. **2** unmerciful. **3** not abating or relaxing. □□ **unrelentingly** *adv.* **unrelentingness** *n.*

unreliable /ˌʌnrɪˈlaɪəb(ə)l/ *adj.* not reliable; erratic. □□ **unreliability** /-ˈbɪlɪtɪ/ *n.* **unreliableness** *n.* **unreliably** *adv.*

unrelieved /ˌʌnrɪˈliːvd/ *adj.* **1** lacking the relief given by contrast or variation. **2** not aided or assisted. □□ **unrelievedly** *adv.*

unreligious /ˌʌnrɪˈlɪdʒəs/ *adj.* **1** not concerned with religion. **2** irreligious.

unremarkable /ˌʌnrɪˈmɑːkəb(ə)l/ *adj.* not remarkable; uninteresting. □□ **unremarkably** *adv.*

unremembered /ˌʌnrɪˈmembəd/ *adj.* not remembered; forgotten.

unremitting /ˌʌnrɪˈmɪtɪŋ/ *adj.* never relaxing or slackening; incessant. □□ **unremittingly** *adv.* **unremittingness** *n.*

unremorseful /ˌʌnrɪˈmɔːsfʊl/ *adj.* lacking remorse. □□ **unremorsefully** *adv.*

unremovable /ˌʌnrɪˈmuːvəb(ə)l/ *adj.* that cannot be removed.

unremunerative /ˌʌnrɪˈmjuːnərətɪv/ *adj.* bringing no, or not enough, profit or income. □□ **unremuneratively** *adv.* **unremunerativeness** *n.*

unrenewable /ˌʌnrɪˈnjuːəb(ə)l/ *adj.* that cannot be renewed. □□ **unrenewed** *adj.*

unrepealed /ˌʌnrɪˈpiːld/ *adj.* not repealed.

unrepeatable /ˌʌnrɪˈpiːtəb(ə)l/ *adj.* **1** that cannot be done, made, or said again. **2** too indecent to be said again. □□ **unrepeatability** /-ˈbɪlɪtɪ/ *n.*

unrepentant /ˌʌnrɪˈpent(ə)nt/ *adj.* not repentant; impenitent. □□ **unrepentantly** *adv.*

unreported /ˌʌnrɪˈpɔːtɪd/ *adj.* not reported.

unrepresentative /ˌʌnreprɪˈzentətɪv/ *adj.* not representative. □□ **unrepresentativeness** *n.*

unrepresented /ˌʌnreprɪˈzentɪd/ *adj.* not represented.

unreproved /ˌʌnrɪˈpruːvd/ *adj.* not reproved.

unrequested /ˌʌnrɪˈkwestɪd/ *adj.* not requested or asked for.

unrequited /ˌʌnrɪˈkwaɪtɪd/ *adj.* (of love etc.) not returned. □□ **unrequitedly** *adv.* **unrequitedness** *n.*

unreserve /ˌʌnrɪˈzɜːv/ *n.* lack of reserve; frankness.

unreserved /ˌʌnrɪˈzɜːvd/ *adj.* **1** not reserved (*unreserved seats*). **2** without reservations; absolute (*unreserved confidence*). **3** free from reserve (*an unreserved nature*). □□ **unreservedly** /-vɪdlɪ/ *adv.* **unreservedness** *n.*

unresisted /ˌʌnrɪˈzɪstɪd/ *adj.* not resisted. □□ **unresistedly** *adv.*

unresisting /ˌʌnrɪˈzɪstɪŋ/ *adj.* not resisting. □□ **unresistingly** *adv.* **unresistingness** *n.*

unresolvable /ˌʌnrɪˈzɒlvəb(ə)l/ *adj.* (of a problem, conflict, etc.) that cannot be resolved.

unresolved /ˌʌnrɪˈzɒlvd/ *adj.* **1 a** uncertain how to act, irresolute. **b** uncertain in opinion, undecided. **2** (of questions etc.) undetermined, undecided, unsolved. **3** not broken up or dissolved. □□ **unresolvedly** /-vɪdlɪ/ *adv.* **unresolvedness** *n.*

unresponsive /ˌʌnrɪˈspɒnsɪv/ *adj.* not responsive. □□ **unresponsively** *adv.* **unresponsiveness** *n.*

unrest /ʌnˈrest/ *n.* **1** lack of rest. **2** restlessness, disturbance, agitation.

unrested /ʌnˈrestɪd/ *adj.* not refreshed by rest.

unrestful /ʌnˈrestfʊl/ *adj.* not restful. □□ **unrestfully** *adv.*

unresting /ʌnˈrestɪŋ/ *adj.* not resting. □□ **unrestingly** *adv.*

unrestored /ˌʌnrɪˈstɔːd/ *adj.* not restored.

unrestrained /ˌʌnrɪˈstreɪnd/ *adj.* not restrained. □□ **unrestrainedly** /-nɪdlɪ/ *adv.* **unrestrainedness** *n.*

unrestricted /ˌʌnrɪˈstrɪktɪd/ *adj.* not restricted. □□ **unrestrictedly** *adv.* **unrestrictedness** *n.*

unreturned /ˌʌnrɪˈtɜːnd/ *adj.* **1** not reciprocated or responded to. **2** not having returned or been returned.

unrevealed /ˌʌnrɪˈviːld/ *adj.* not revealed; secret.

unreversed /ˌʌnrɪˈvɜːst/ *adj.* (esp. of a decision etc.) not reversed.

unrevised /ˌʌnrɪˈvaɪzd/ *adj.* not revised; in an original form.

unrevoked /ˌʌnrɪˈvəʊkt/ *adj.* not revoked or annulled; still in force.

unrewarded /ˌʌnrɪˈwɔːdɪd/ *adj.* not rewarded.

unrewarding /ˌʌnrɪˈwɔːdɪŋ/ *adj.* not rewarding or satisfying.

unrhymed /ʌnˈraɪmd/ *adj.* not rhymed.

unrhythmical /ʌnˈrɪðmɪk(ə)l/ *adj.* not rhythmical. □□ **unrhythmically** *adv.*

unridable /ʌnˈraɪdəb(ə)l/ *adj.* that cannot be ridden.

unridden /ʌnˈrɪd(ə)n/ *adj.* not ridden.

unriddle /ʌnˈrɪd(ə)l/ *v.tr.* solve or explain (a mystery etc.). □□ **unriddler** *n.*

unrig /ʌnˈrɪɡ/ *v.tr.* (**unrigged, unrigging**) **1** remove the rigging from (a ship). **2** *dial.* undress.

unrighteous /ʌnˈraɪtʃəs/ *adj.* not righteous; unjust, wicked, dishonest. □□ **unrighteously** *adv.* **unrighteousness** *n.* [OE *unrihtwīs* (as UN-[1], RIGHTEOUS)]

unrip /ʌnˈrɪp/ *v.tr.* (**unripped, unripping**) open by ripping.

unripe /ʌnˈraɪp/ *adj.* not ripe. □□ **unripeness** *n.*

unrisen /ʌnˈrɪz(ə)n/ *adj.* that has not risen.

unrivalled /ʌnˈraɪv(ə)ld/ *adj.* (*US* **unrivaled**) having no equal; peerless.

unrivet /ʌnˈrɪvɪt/ *v.tr.* (**unriveted, unriveting**) **1** undo, unfasten, or detach by the removal of rivets. **2** loosen, relax, undo, detach.

unrobe /ʌnˈrəʊb/ *v.tr.* & *intr.* **1** disrobe. **2** undress.

unroll /ʌnˈrəʊl/ *v.tr.* & *intr.* **1** open out from a rolled-up state. **2** display or be displayed in this form.

unromantic /ˌʌnrəˈmæntɪk/ *adj.* not romantic. □□ **unromantically** *adv.*

unroof /ʌnˈruːf/ *v.tr.* remove the roof of.

unroofed /ʌnˈruːft/ *adj.* not provided with a roof.

unroot /ʌnˈruːt/ *v.tr.* **1** uproot. **2** eradicate.

unrope /ʌnˈrəʊp/ *v.* **1** *tr.* detach by undoing a rope. **2** *intr.* Mountaineering detach oneself from a rope.

unrounded /ʌnˈraʊndɪd/ *adj.* not rounded.

unrove *past* of UNREEVE.

unroyal /ʌnˈrɔɪəl/ adj. not royal.

unruffled /ʌnˈrʌf(ə)ld/ adj. **1** not agitated or disturbed; calm. **2** not physically ruffled.

unruled /ʌnˈruːld/ adj. **1** not ruled or governed. **2** not having ruled lines.

unruly /ʌnˈruːlɪ/ adj. (**unrulier**, **unruliest**) not easily controlled or disciplined, disorderly. ▫▫ **unruliness** n. [ME f. UN-¹ + ruly f. RULE]

UNRWA /ˈʌnrɑː/ abbr. United Nations Relief and Works Agency.

unsaddle /ʌnˈsæd(ə)l/ v.tr. **1** remove the saddle from (a horse etc.). **2** dislodge from a saddle.

unsafe /ʌnˈseɪf/ adj. not safe. ▫▫ **unsafely** adv. **unsafeness** n.

unsaid¹ /ʌnˈsed/ adj. not said or uttered.

unsaid² past and past part. of UNSAY.

unsalaried /ʌnˈsælərɪd/ adj. not salaried.

unsaleable /ʌnˈseɪləb(ə)l/ adj. not saleable. ▫▫ **unsaleability** /-ˈbɪlɪtɪ/ n.

unsalted /ʌnˈsɔːltɪd, ʌnˈsɒl-/ adj. not salted.

unsanctified /ʌnˈsæŋktɪˌfaɪd/ adj. not sanctified.

unsanctioned /ʌnˈsæŋkʃ(ə)nd/ adj. not sanctioned.

unsanitary /ʌnˈsænɪtərɪ/ adj. not sanitary.

unsatisfactory /ˌʌnsætɪsˈfæktərɪ/ adj. not satisfactory; poor, unacceptable. ▫▫ **unsatisfactorily** adv. **unsatisfactoriness** n.

unsatisfied /ʌnˈsætɪsˌfaɪd/ adj. not satisfied. ▫▫ **unsatisfiedness** n.

unsatisfying /ʌnˈsætɪsˌfaɪɪŋ/ adj. not satisfying. ▫▫ **unsatisfyingly** adv.

unsaturated /ʌnˈsætʃəˌreɪtɪd, -tjʊˌreɪtɪd/ adj. **1** Chem. (of a compound, esp. a fat or oil) having double or triple bonds in its molecule and therefore capable of further reaction. **2** not saturated. ▫▫ **unsaturation** /-ˈreɪʃ(ə)n/ n.

unsaved /ʌnˈseɪvd/ adj. not saved.

unsavoury /ʌnˈseɪvərɪ/ adj. (US **unsavory**) **1** disagreeable to the taste, smell, or feelings; disgusting. **2** disagreeable, unpleasant (an unsavoury character). **3** morally offensive. ▫▫ **unsavourily** adv. **unsavouriness** n.

unsay /ʌnˈseɪ/ v.tr. (past and past part. **unsaid**) retract (a statement).

unsayable /ʌnˈseɪəb(ə)l/ adj. that cannot be said.

unscalable /ʌnˈskeɪləb(ə)l/ adj. that cannot be scaled.

unscarred /ʌnˈskɑːd/ adj. not scarred or damaged.

unscathed /ʌnˈskeɪðd/ adj. without suffering any injury.

unscented /ʌnˈsentɪd/ adj. not scented.

unscheduled /ʌnˈʃedjuːld/ adj. not scheduled.

unscholarly /ʌnˈskɒləlɪ/ adj. not scholarly. ▫▫ **unscholarliness** n.

unschooled /ʌnˈskuːld/ adj. **1** uneducated, untaught. **2** not sent to school. **3** untrained, undisciplined. **4** not made artificial by education.

unscientific /ˌʌnsaɪənˈtɪfɪk/ adj. **1** not in accordance with scientific principles. **2** not familiar with science. ▫▫ **unscientifically** adv.

unscramble /ʌnˈskræmb(ə)l/ v.tr. restore from a scrambled state, esp. interpret (a scrambled transmission etc.). ▫▫ **unscrambler** n.

unscreened /ʌnˈskriːnd/ adj. **1 a** (esp. of coal) not passed through a screen or sieve. **b** not investigated or checked, esp. for security or medical problems. **2** not provided with a screen. **3** not shown on a screen.

unscrew /ʌnˈskruː/ v. **1** tr. & intr. unfasten or be unfastened by turning or removing a screw or screws or by twisting like a screw. **2** tr. loosen (a screw).

unscripted /ʌnˈskrɪptɪd/ adj. (of a speech etc.) delivered without a prepared script.

unscriptural /ʌnˈskrɪptʃər(ə)l, -tʃʊər(ə)l/ adj. against or not in accordance with Scripture. ▫▫ **unscripturally** adv.

unscrupulous /ʌnˈskruːpjʊləs/ adj. having no scruples, unprincipled. ▫▫ **unscrupulously** adv. **unscrupulousness** n.

unseal /ʌnˈsiːl/ v.tr. break the seal of; open (a letter, receptacle, etc.).

unsealed /ʌnˈsiːld/ adj. not sealed.

unsearchable /ʌnˈsɜːtʃəb(ə)l/ adj. inscrutable. ▫▫ **unsearchableness** n. **unsearchably** adv.

unsearched /ʌnˈsɜːtʃt/ adj. not searched.

unseasonable /ʌnˈsiːzənəb(ə)l/ adj. **1** not appropriate to the season. **2** untimely, inopportune. ▫▫ **unseasonableness** n. **unseasonably** adv.

unseasoned /ʌnˈsiːz(ə)nd/ adj. **1** not flavoured with salt, herbs, etc. **2** (esp. of timber) not matured. **3** not habituated.

unseat /ʌnˈsiːt/ v.tr. **1** remove from a seat, esp. in an election. **2** dislodge from a seat, esp. on horseback.

unseaworthy /ʌnˈsiːˌwɜːðɪ/ adj. not seaworthy.

unsecured /ˌʌnsɪˈkjʊəd/ adj. not secured.

unseeable /ʌnˈsiːəb(ə)l/ adj. that cannot be seen.

unseeded /ʌnˈsiːdɪd/ adj. Sport (of a player) not seeded.

unseeing /ʌnˈsiːɪŋ/ adj. **1** unobservant. **2** blind. ▫▫ **unseeingly** adv.

unseemly /ʌnˈsiːmlɪ/ adj. (**unseemlier**, **unseemliest**) **1** indecent. **2** unbecoming. ▫▫ **unseemliness** n.

unseen /ʌnˈsiːn/ adj. & n. —adj. **1** not seen. **2** invisible. **3** (of a translation) to be done without preparation. —n. Brit. an unseen translation.

unsegregated /ʌnˈsegrɪˌgeɪtɪd/ adj. not segregated.

unselect /ˌʌnsɪˈlekt/ adj. not select.

unselective /ˌʌnsɪˈlektɪv/ adj. not selective.

unselfconscious /ˌʌnselfˈkɒnʃəs/ adj. not self-conscious. ▫▫ **unselfconsciously** adv. **unselfconsciousness** n.

unselfish /ʌnˈselfɪʃ/ adj. mindful of others' interests. ▫▫ **unselfishly** adv. **unselfishness** n.

unsensational /ˌʌnsenˈseɪʃən(ə)l/ adj. not sensational. ▫▫ **unsensationally** adv.

unsentimental /ˌʌnsentɪˈment(ə)l/ adj. not sentimental. ▫▫ **unsentimentality** /-ˈtælɪtɪ/ n. **unsentimentally** adv.

unseparated /ʌnˈsepəˌreɪtɪd/ adj. not separated.

unserviceable /ʌnˈsɜːvɪsəb(ə)l/ adj. not serviceable; unfit for use. ▫▫ **unserviceability** /-ˈbɪlɪtɪ/ n.

unset /ʌnˈset/ adj. not set.

unsettle /ʌnˈset(ə)l/ v. **1** tr. disturb the settled state or arrangement of; discompose. **2** tr. derange. **3** intr. become unsettled. ▫▫ **unsettlement** n.

unsettled /ʌnˈset(ə)ld/ adj. **1** not (yet) settled. **2** liable or open to change or further discussion. **3** (of a bill etc.) unpaid. ▫▫ **unsettledness** n.

unsewn /ʌnˈsəʊn/ adj. not sewn. ▫ **unsewn binding** = perfect binding.

unsex /ʌnˈseks/ v.tr. deprive (a person, esp. a woman) of the qualities of her or his sex.

unsexed /ʌnˈsekst/ adj. having no sexual characteristics.

unshackle /ʌnˈʃæk(ə)l/ v.tr. **1** release from shackles. **2** set free.

unshaded /ʌnˈʃeɪdɪd/ adj. not shaded.

unshakeable /ʌnˈʃeɪkəb(ə)l/ adj. that cannot be shaken; firm, obstinate. ▫▫ **unshakeability** /-ˈbɪlɪtɪ/ n. **unshakeably** adv.

unshaken /ʌnˈʃeɪkən/ adj. not shaken. ▫▫ **unshakenly** adv.

unshapely /ʌnˈʃeɪplɪ/ adj. not shapely. ▫▫ **unshapeliness** n.

unshared /ʌnˈʃeəd/ adj. not shared.

unsharp /ʌnˈʃɑːp/ adj. Photog. not sharp. ▫▫ **unsharpness** n.

unshaved /ʌnˈʃeɪvd/ adj. not shaved.

unshaven /ʌnˈʃeɪv(ə)n/ adj. not shaved.

unsheathe /ʌnˈʃiːð/ v.tr. remove (a knife etc.) from a sheath.

unshed /ʌnˈʃed/ adj. not shed.

unshell /ʌnˈʃel/ v.tr. (usu. as **unshelled** adj.) extract from its shell.

unsheltered /ʌnˈʃeltəd/ adj. not sheltered.

unshielded /ʌnˈʃiːldɪd/ *adj.* not shielded or protected.

unship /ʌnˈʃɪp/ *v.tr.* (**unshipped, unshipping**) 1 remove or discharge (a cargo or passenger) from a ship. 2 esp. *Naut.* remove (an object, esp. a mast or oar) from a fixed position.

unshockable /ʌnˈʃɒkəb(ə)l/ *adj.* that cannot be shocked. □□ **unshockability** /-ˈbɪlɪtɪ/ *n.* **unshockably** *adv.*

unshod /ʌnˈʃɒd/ *adj.* not wearing shoes.

unshorn /ʌnˈʃɔːn/ *adj.* not shorn.

unshrinkable /ʌnˈʃrɪŋkəb(ə)l/ *adj.* (of fabric etc.) not liable to shrink. □□ **unshrinkability** /-ˈbɪlɪtɪ/ *n.*

unshrinking /ʌnˈʃrɪŋkɪŋ/ *adj.* unhesitating, fearless. □□ **unshrinkingly** *adv.*

unsighted /ʌnˈsaɪtɪd/ *adj.* 1 not sighted or seen. 2 prevented from seeing, esp. by an obstruction.

unsightly /ʌnˈsaɪtlɪ/ *adj.* unpleasant to look at, ugly. □□ **unsightliness** *n.*

unsigned /ʌnˈsaɪnd/ *adj.* not signed.

unsinkable /ʌnˈsɪŋkəb(ə)l/ *adj.* unable to be sunk. □□ **unsinkability** /-ˈbɪlɪtɪ/ *n.*

unsized[1] /ʌnˈsaɪzd/ *adj.* 1 not made to a size. 2 not sorted by size.

unsized[2] /ʌnˈsaɪzd/ *adj.* not treated with size.

unskilful /ʌnˈskɪlfʊl/ *adj.* (*US* **unskillful**) not skilful. □□ **unskilfully** *adv.* **unskilfulness** *n.*

unskilled /ʌnˈskɪld/ *adj.* lacking or not needing special skill or training.

unskimmed /ʌnˈskɪmd/ *adj.* (of milk) not skimmed.

unslakeable /ʌnˈsleɪkəb(ə)l/ *adj.* (also **unslakable**) that cannot be slaked or quenched.

unsleeping /ʌnˈsliːpɪŋ/ *adj.* not or never sleeping. □□ **unsleepingly** *adv.*

unsliced /ʌnˈslaɪst/ *adj.* (esp. of a loaf of bread when it is bought) not having been cut into slices.

unsling /ʌnˈslɪŋ/ *v.tr.* (*past* and *past part.* **unslung**) free from being slung or suspended.

unsmiling /ʌnˈsmaɪlɪŋ/ *adj.* not smiling. □□ **unsmilingly** *adv.* **unsmilingness** *n.*

unsmoked /ʌnˈsməʊkt/ *adj.* 1 not cured by smoking (*unsmoked bacon*). 2 not consumed by smoking (*an unsmoked cigar*).

unsnarl /ʌnˈsnɑːl/ *v.tr.* disentangle. [UN-[2] + SNARL[2]]

unsociable /ʌnˈsəʊʃəb(ə)l/ *adj.* not sociable, disliking the company of others. □□ **unsociability** /-ˈbɪlɪtɪ/ *n.* **unsociableness** *n.* **unsociably** *adv.*

unsocial /ʌnˈsəʊʃ(ə)l/ *adj.* 1 not social; not suitable for, seeking, or conforming to society. 2 outside the normal working day (*unsocial hours*). 3 antisocial. □□ **unsocially** *adv.*

unsoiled /ʌnˈsɔɪld/ *adj.* not soiled or dirtied.

unsold /ʌnˈsəʊld/ *adj.* not sold.

unsolder /ʌnˈsəʊldə(r), ʌnˈsɒl-/ *v.tr.* undo the soldering of.

unsoldierly /ʌnˈsəʊldʒəlɪ/ *adj.* not soldierly.

unsolicited /ˌʌnsəˈlɪsɪtɪd/ *adj.* not asked for; given or done voluntarily. □□ **unsolicitedly** *adv.*

unsolvable /ʌnˈsɒlvəb(ə)l/ *adj.* that cannot be solved, insoluble. □□ **unsolvability** /-ˈbɪlɪtɪ/ *n.* **unsolvableness** *n.*

unsolved /ʌnˈsɒlvd/ *adj.* not solved.

unsophisticated /ˌʌnsəˈfɪstɪˌkeɪtɪd/ *adj.* 1 artless, simple, natural, ingenuous. 2 not adulterated or artificial. □□ **unsophisticatedly** *adv.* **unsophisticatedness** *n.* **unsophistication** /-ˈkeɪʃ(ə)n/ *n.*

unsorted /ʌnˈsɔːtɪd/ *adj.* not sorted.

unsought /ʌnˈsɔːt/ *adj.* 1 not searched out or sought for. 2 unasked; without being requested.

unsound /ʌnˈsaʊnd/ *adj.* 1 unhealthy, diseased. 2 rotten, weak. 3 a ill-founded, fallacious. b unorthodox, heretical. 4 unreliable. 5 wicked. □ **of unsound mind** insane. □□ **unsoundly** *adv.* **unsoundness** *n.*

unsounded[1] /ʌnˈsaʊndɪd/ *adj.* 1 not uttered or pronounced. 2 not made to sound.

unsounded[2] /ʌnˈsaʊndɪd/ *adj.* unfathomed.

unsoured /ʌnˈsaʊəd/ *adj.* not soured.

unsown /ʌnˈsəʊn/ *adj.* not sown.

unsparing /ʌnˈspeərɪŋ/ *adj.* 1 lavish, profuse. 2 merciless. □□ **unsparingly** *adv.* **unsparingness** *n.*

unspeakable /ʌnˈspiːkəb(ə)l/ *adj.* 1 that cannot be expressed in words. 2 indescribably bad or objectionable. □□ **unspeakableness** *n.* **unspeakably** *adv.*

unspecialized /ʌnˈspeʃəˌlaɪzd/ *adj.* not specialized.

unspecified /ʌnˈspesɪˌfaɪd/ *adj.* not specified.

unspectacular /ˌʌnspekˈtækjʊlə(r)/ *adj.* not spectacular; dull. □□ **unspectacularly** *adv.*

unspent /ʌnˈspent/ *adj.* 1 not expended or used. 2 not exhausted or used up.

unspilled /ʌnˈspɪld/ *adj.* not spilt.

unspilt /ʌnˈspɪlt/ *adj.* not spilt.

unspiritual /ʌnˈspɪrɪtjʊəl/ *adj.* not spiritual; earthly, worldly. □□ **unspirituality** /-ʊˈælɪtɪ/ *n.* **unspiritually** *adv.* **unspiritualness** *n.*

unspoiled /ʌnˈspɔɪld/ *adj.* 1 unspoilt. 2 not plundered.

unspoilt /ʌnˈspɔɪlt/ *adj.* not spoilt.

unspoken /ʌnˈspəʊkən/ *adj.* 1 not expressed in speech. 2 not uttered as speech.

unsporting /ʌnˈspɔːtɪŋ/ *adj.* not sportsmanlike; not fair or generous. □□ **unsportingly** *adv.* **unsportingness** *n.*

unsportsmanlike /ʌnˈspɔːtsmənˌlaɪk/ *adj.* unsporting.

unspotted /ʌnˈspɒtɪd/ *adj.* 1 a not marked with a spot or spots. b morally pure. 2 unnoticed.

unsprung /ʌnˈsprʌŋ/ *adj.* not provided with a spring or springs; not resilient.

unstable /ʌnˈsteɪb(ə)l/ *adj.* (**unstabler, unstablest**) 1 not stable. 2 changeable. 3 showing a tendency to sudden mental or emotional changes. □ **unstable equilibrium** a state in which a body when disturbed tends to move farther from equilibrium. □□ **unstableness** *n.* **unstably** *adv.*

unstained /ʌnˈsteɪnd/ *adj.* not stained.

unstamped /ʌnˈstæmpt/ *adj.* 1 not marked by stamping. 2 not having a stamp affixed.

unstarched /ʌnˈstɑːtʃt/ *adj.* not starched.

unstated /ʌnˈsteɪtɪd/ *adj.* not stated or declared.

unstatesmanlike /ʌnˈsteɪtsmənˌlaɪk/ *adj.* not statesmanlike.

unstatutable /ʌnˈstætjʊtəb(ə)l/ *adj.* contrary to a statute or statutes. □□ **unstatutably** *adv.*

unsteadfast /ʌnˈstedfɑːst/ *adj.* not steadfast.

unsteady /ʌnˈstedɪ/ *adj.* (**unsteadier, unsteadiest**) 1 not steady or firm. 2 changeable, fluctuating. 3 not uniform or regular. □□ **unsteadily** *adv.* **unsteadiness** *n.*

unstick *v. & n.* —*v.* /ʌnˈstɪk/ (*past* and *past part.* **unstuck**) 1 *tr.* separate (a thing stuck to another). 2 *Aeron. colloq.* a *intr.* take off. b *tr.* cause (an aircraft) to take off. —*n.* /ˈʌnstɪk/ *Aeron. colloq.* the moment of take-off. □ **come unstuck** *colloq.* come to grief, fail.

unstinted /ʌnˈstɪntɪd/ *adj.* not stinted. □□ **unstintedly** *adv.*

unstinting /ʌnˈstɪntɪŋ/ *adj.* ungrudging, lavish. □□ **unstintingly** *adv.*

unstirred /ʌnˈstɜːd/ *adj.* not stirred.

unstitch /ʌnˈstɪtʃ/ *v.tr.* undo the stitches of.

unstop /ʌnˈstɒp/ *v.tr.* (**unstopped, unstopping**) 1 free from obstruction. 2 remove the stopper from.

unstoppable /ʌnˈstɒpəb(ə)l/ *adj.* that cannot be stopped or prevented. □□ **unstoppability** /-ˈbɪlɪtɪ/ *n.* **unstoppably** *adv.*

unstopper /ʌnˈstɒpə(r)/ *v.tr.* remove the stopper from.

unstrained /ʌnˈstreɪnd/ *adj.* 1 not subjected to straining or stretching. 2 not injured by overuse or excessive demands. 3 not forced or produced by effort. 4 not passed through a strainer.

unstrap /ʌnˈstræp/ *v.tr.* (**unstrapped, unstrapping**) undo the strap or straps of.

unstreamed /ʌn'striːmd/ adj. Brit. (of school-children) not arranged in streams.

unstressed /ʌn'strest/ adj. 1 (of a word, syllable, etc.) not pronounced with stress. 2 not subjected to stress.

unstring /ʌn'strɪŋ/ v.tr. (past and past part. **unstrung**) 1 remove or relax the string or strings of (a bow, harp, etc.). 2 remove from a string. 3 (esp. as **unstrung** adj.) unnerve.

unstructured /ʌn'strʌktʃəd/ adj. 1 not structured. 2 informal.

unstuck past and past part. of UNSTICK.

unstudied /ʌn'stʌdɪd/ adj. easy, natural, spontaneous. □□ **unstudiedly** adv.

unstuffed /ʌn'stʌft/ adj. not stuffed.

unstuffy /ʌn'stʌfi/ adj. 1 informal, casual. 2 not stuffy.

unsubdued /ˌʌnsəb'djuːd/ adj. not subdued.

unsubjugated /ʌn'sʌbdʒʊˌgeɪtɪd/ adj. not subjugated.

unsubstantial /ˌʌnsəb'stænʃ(ə)l/ adj. having little or no solidity, reality, or factual basis. □□ **unsubstantiality** /-ʃɪ'ælɪti/ n. **unsubstantially** adv.

unsubstantiated /ˌʌnsəb'stænʃɪˌeɪtɪd/ adj. not substantiated.

unsuccess /ˌʌnsək'ses/ n. 1 lack of success; failure. 2 an instance of this.

unsuccessful /ˌʌnsək'sesfʊl/ adj. not successful. □□ **unsuccessfully** adv. **unsuccessfulness** n.

unsugared /ʌn'ʃʊgəd/ adj. not sugared.

unsuggestive /ˌʌnsə'dʒestɪv/ adj. not suggestive.

unsuitable /ʌn'suːtəb(ə)l, ʌn'sjuː-/ adj. not suitable. □□ **unsuitability** /-'bɪlɪti/ n. **unsuitableness** n. **unsuitably** adv.

unsuited /ʌn'suːtɪd, ʌn'sjuː-/ adj. 1 (usu. foll. by for) not fit for a purpose. 2 (usu. foll. by to) not adapted.

unsullied /ʌn'sʌlɪd/ adj. not sullied.

unsummoned /ʌn'sʌmənd/ adj. not summoned.

unsung /ʌn'sʌŋ/ adj. 1 not celebrated in song; unknown. 2 not sung.

unsupervised /ʌn'suːpəˌvaɪzd, ʌn'sjuː-/ adj. not supervised.

unsupportable /ˌʌnsə'pɔːtəb(ə)l/ adj. 1 that cannot be endured. 2 indefensible. □□ **unsupportably** adv.

unsupported /ˌʌnsə'pɔːtɪd/ adj. not supported. □□ **unsupportedly** adv.

unsure /ʌn'ʃʊə(r), ʌn'ʃɔː(r)/ adj. not sure. □□ **unsurely** adv. **unsureness** n.

unsurpassable /ˌʌnsə'pɑːsəb(ə)l/ adj. that cannot be surpassed. □□ **unsurpassably** adv.

unsurpassed /ˌʌnsə'pɑːst/ adj. not surpassed.

unsurprising /ˌʌnsə'praɪzɪŋ/ adj. not surprising. □□ **unsurprisingly** adv.

unsusceptible /ˌʌnsə'septɪb(ə)l/ adj. not susceptible. □□ **unsusceptibility** /-'bɪlɪti/ n.

unsuspected /ˌʌnsə'spektɪd/ adj. not suspected. □□ **unsuspectedly** adv.

unsuspecting /ˌʌnsə'spektɪŋ/ adj. not suspecting. □□ **unsuspectingly** adv. **unsuspectingness** n.

unsuspicious /ˌʌnsə'spɪʃəs/ adj. not suspicious. □□ **unsuspiciously** adv. **unsuspiciousness** n.

unsustained /ˌʌnsə'steɪnd/ adj. not sustained.

unswathe /ʌn'sweɪð/ v.tr. free from being swathed.

unswayed /ʌn'sweɪd/ adj. uninfluenced, unaffected.

unsweetened /ʌn'swiːt(ə)nd/ adj. not sweetened.

unswept /ʌn'swept/ adj. not swept.

unswerving /ʌn'swɜːvɪŋ/ adj. 1 steady, constant. 2 not turning aside. □□ **unswervingly** adv.

unsworn /ʌn'swɔːn/ adj. 1 (of a person) not subjected to or bound by an oath. 2 not confirmed by an oath.

unsymmetrical /ˌʌnsɪ'metrɪk(ə)l/ adj. not symmetrical. □□ **unsymmetrically** adv.

unsympathetic /ˌʌnsɪmpə'θetɪk/ adj. not sympathetic. □□ **unsympathetically** adv.

unsystematic /ˌʌnsɪstə'mætɪk/ adj. not systematic. □□ **unsystematically** adv.

untack /ʌn'tæk/ v.tr. detach, esp. by removing tacks.

untainted /ʌn'teɪntɪd/ adj. not tainted.

untalented /ʌn'tæləntɪd/ adj. not talented.

untameable /ʌn'teɪməb(ə)l/ adj. that cannot be tamed.

untamed /ʌn'teɪmd/ adj. not tamed, wild.

untangle /ʌn'tæŋg(ə)l/ v.tr. 1 free from a tangled state. 2 free from entanglement.

untanned /ʌn'tænd/ adj. not tanned.

untapped /ʌn'tæpt/ adj. not (yet) tapped or wired (untapped resources).

untarnished /ʌn'tɑːnɪʃt/ adj. not tarnished.

untasted /ʌn'teɪstɪd/ adj. not tasted.

untaught /ʌn'tɔːt/ adj. 1 not instructed by teaching; ignorant. 2 not acquired by teaching; natural, spontaneous.

untaxed /ʌn'tækst/ adj. not required to pay or not attracting taxes.

unteach /ʌn'tiːtʃ/ v.tr. (past and past part. **untaught**) 1 cause (a person) to forget or discard previous knowledge. 2 remove from the mind (something known or taught) by different teaching.

unteachable /ʌn'tiːtʃəb(ə)l/ adj. 1 incapable of being instructed. 2 that cannot be imparted by teaching.

untearable /ʌn'teərəb(ə)l/ adj. that cannot be torn.

untechnical /ʌn'teknɪk(ə)l/ adj. not technical. □□ **untechnically** adv.

untempered /ʌn'tempəd/ adj. (of metal etc.) not brought to the proper hardness or consistency.

untenable /ʌn'tenəb(ə)l/ adj. not tenable; that cannot be defended. □□ **untenability** /-'bɪlɪti/ n. **untenableness** n. **untenably** adv.

untended /ʌn'tendɪd/ adj. not tended; neglected.

untested /ʌn'testɪd/ adj. not tested or proved.

untether /ʌn'teðə(r)/ v.tr. release (an animal) from a tether.

untethered /ʌn'teðəd/ adj. not tethered.

unthanked /ʌn'θæŋkt/ adj. not thanked.

unthankful /ʌn'θæŋkfʊl/ adj. not thankful. □□ **unthankfully** adv. **unthankfulness** n.

unthinkable /ʌn'θɪŋkəb(ə)l/ adj. 1 that cannot be imagined or grasped by the mind. 2 colloq. highly unlikely or undesirable. □□ **unthinkability** /-'bɪlɪti/ n. **unthinkableness** n. **unthinkably** adv.

unthinking /ʌn'θɪŋkɪŋ/ adj. 1 thoughtless. 2 unintentional, inadvertent. □□ **unthinkingly** adv. **unthinkingness** n.

unthought /ʌn'θɔːt/ adj. (often foll. by of) not thought of.

unthoughtful /ʌn'θɔːtfʊl/ adj. unthinking, unmindful; thoughtless. □□ **unthoughtfully** adv. **unthoughtfulness** n.

unthread /ʌn'θred/ v.tr. 1 take the thread out of (a needle etc.). 2 find one's way out of (a maze).

unthrifty /ʌn'θrɪfti/ adj. 1 wasteful, extravagant, prodigal. 2 not thriving or flourishing. □□ **unthriftily** adv. **unthriftiness** n.

unthrone /ʌn'θrəʊn/ v.tr. dethrone.

untidy /ʌn'taɪdi/ adj. (**untidier**, **untidiest**) not neat or orderly. □□ **untidily** adv. **untidiness** n.

untie /ʌn'taɪ/ v.tr. (pres. part. **untying**) 1 undo (a knot etc.). 2 unfasten the cords etc. of (a package etc.). 3 release from bonds or attachment. [OE untīgan (as UN-², TIE)]

untied /ʌn'taɪd/ adj. not tied.

until /ən'tɪl, ʌn-/ prep. & conj. = TILL¹. ¶ Used esp. when beginning a sentence and in formal style, e.g. until you told me, I had no idea; he resided there until his decease. [orig. northern ME untill f. ON und as far as + TILL¹]

untilled /ʌn'tɪld/ adj. not tilled.

untimely /ʌn'taɪmli/ adj. & adv. —adj. 1 inopportune. 2 (of death) premature. —adv. archaic 1 inopportunely. 2 prematurely. □□ **untimeliness** n.

untinged /ʌn'tɪndʒd/ adj. not tinged.

untiring /ʌn'taɪərɪŋ/ adj. tireless. □□ **untiringly** adv.

untitled /ʌn'taɪt(ə)ld/ adj. having no title.

unto /'ʌntʊ, 'ʌntə/ prep. archaic = TO prep. (in all

uses except as the sign of the infinitive); (*do unto others*; *faithful unto death*; *take unto oneself*). [ME f. UNTIL, with TO replacing northern TILL[1]]

untold /ʌnˈtəʊld/ *adj.* **1** not told. **2** not (able to be) counted or measured (*untold misery*). [OE *untéald* (as UN-[1], TOLD)]

untouchable /ʌnˈtʌtʃəb(ə)l/ *adj. & n.* —*adj.* that may not or cannot be touched. —*n.* a member of a hereditary Hindu group held to defile members of higher castes on contact. ¶ Use of the term, and social restrictions accompanying it, were declared illegal under the Indian constitution in 1949. □□ **untouchability** /-ˈbɪlɪtɪ/ *n.* **untouchableness** *n.*

untouched /ʌnˈtʌtʃt/ *adj.* **1** not touched. **2** not affected physically, not harmed, modified, used, or tasted. **3** not affected by emotion. **4** not discussed.

untoward /ˌʌntəˈwɔːd, ʌnˈtəʊəd/ *adj.* **1** inconvenient, unlucky. **2** awkward. **3** perverse, refractory. **4** unseemly. □□ **untowardly** *adv.* **untowardness** *n.*

untraceable /ʌnˈtreɪsəb(ə)l/ *adj.* that cannot be traced. □□ **untraceably** *adv.*

untraced /ʌnˈtreɪst/ *adj.* not traced.

untrained /ʌnˈtreɪnd/ *adj.* not trained.

untrammelled /ʌnˈtræm(ə)ld/ *adj.* not trammelled, unhampered.

untransferable /ˌʌntrænsˈfɜːrəb(ə)l, ˌʌntrɑːns-, ʌnˈt-/ *adj.* not transferable.

untranslatable /ˌʌntrænsˈleɪtəb(ə)l, ˌʌntrɑːn-, -zˈleɪtəb(ə)l/ *adj.* that cannot be translated satisfactorily. □□ **untranslatability** /-ˈbɪlɪtɪ/ *n.* **untranslatably** *adv.*

untransportable /ˌʌntrænsˈpɔːtəb(ə)l, ˌʌntrɑːn-/ *adj.* that cannot be transported.

untravelled /ʌnˈtræv(ə)ld/ *adj.* (*US* **untraveled**) **1** that has not travelled. **2** that has not been travelled over or through.

untreatable /ʌnˈtriːtəb(ə)l/ *adj.* (of a disease etc.) that cannot be treated.

untreated /ʌnˈtriːtɪd/ *adj.* not treated.

untried /ʌnˈtraɪd/ *adj.* **1** not tried or tested. **2** inexperienced. **3** not yet tried by a judge.

untrodden /ʌnˈtrɒd(ə)n/ *adj.* not trodden, stepped on, or traversed.

untroubled /ʌnˈtrʌb(ə)ld/ *adj.* not troubled; calm, tranquil.

untrue /ʌnˈtruː/ *adj.* **1** not true, contrary to what is the fact. **2** (often foll. by *to*) not faithful or loyal. **3** deviating from an accepted standard. □□ **untruly** *adv.* [OE *untréowe* etc. (as UN-[1], TRUE)]

untruss /ʌnˈtrʌs/ *v.tr.* unfasten (a trussed fowl).

untrustworthy /ʌnˈtrʌstˌwɜːðɪ/ *adj.* not trustworthy. □□ **untrustworthiness** *n.*

untruth /ʌnˈtruːθ/ *n.* (*pl.* /-ˈtruːðz, -ˈtruːθs/) **1** the state of being untrue, falsehood. **2** a false statement (*told me an untruth*). [OE *untréowth* etc. (as UN-[1], TRUTH)]

untruthful /ʌnˈtruːθfʊl/ *adj.* not truthful. □□ **untruthfully** *adv.* **untruthfulness** *n.*

untuck /ʌnˈtʌk/ *v.tr.* free (bedclothes etc.) from being tucked in or up.

untunable /ʌnˈtjuːnəb(ə)l/ *adj.* (of a piano etc.) that cannot be tuned.

untuned /ʌnˈtjuːnd/ *adj.* **1** not in tune, not made tuneful. **2** (of a radio receiver etc.) not tuned to any one frequency. **3** not in harmony or concord, disordered.

untuneful /ʌnˈtjuːnfʊl/ *adj.* not tuneful. □□ **untunefully** *adv.* **untunefulness** *n.*

unturned /ʌnˈtɜːnd/ *adj.* **1** not turned over, round, away, etc. **2** not shaped by turning.

untutored /ʌnˈtjuːtəd/ *adj.* uneducated, untaught.

untwine /ʌnˈtwaɪn/ *v.tr. & intr.* untwist, unwind.

untwist /ʌnˈtwɪst/ *v.tr. & intr.* open from a twisted or spiralled state.

untying *pres. part.* of UNTIE.

unusable /ʌnˈjuːzəb(ə)l/ *adj.* not usable.

unused *adj.* **1** /ʌnˈjuːzd/ **a** not in use. **b** never having been used. **2** /ʌnˈjuːst/ (foll. by *to*) not accustomed.

unusual /ʌnˈjuːʒʊəl/ *adj.* **1** not usual. **2** exceptional, remarkable. □□ **unusually** *adv.* **unusualness** *n.*

unutterable /ʌnˈʌtərəb(ə)l/ *adj.* inexpressible; beyond description (*unutterable torment*; *an unutterable fool*). □□ **unutterableness** *n.* **unutterably** *adv.*

unuttered /ʌnˈʌtəd/ *adj.* not uttered or expressed.

unvaccinated /ʌnˈvæksɪˌneɪtɪd/ *adj.* not vaccinated.

unvalued /ʌnˈvæljuːd/ *adj.* **1** not regarded as valuable. **2** not having been valued.

unvanquished /ʌnˈvæŋkwɪʃt/ *adj.* not vanquished.

unvaried /ʌnˈveərɪd/ *adj.* not varied.

unvarnished /ʌnˈvɑːnɪʃt/ *adj.* **1** not varnished. **2** (of a statement or person) plain and straightforward (*the unvarnished truth*).

unvarying /ʌnˈveərɪɪŋ/ *adj.* not varying. □□ **unvaryingly** *adv.* **unvaryingness** *n.*

unveil /ʌnˈveɪl/ *v.* **1** *tr.* remove a veil from. **2** *tr.* remove a covering from (a statue, plaque, etc.) as part of the ceremony of the first public display. **3** *tr.* disclose, reveal, make publicly known. **4** *intr.* remove one's veil.

unventilated /ʌnˈventɪˌleɪtɪd/ *adj.* **1** not provided with a means of ventilation. **2** not discussed.

unverifiable /ʌnˈverɪˌfaɪəb(ə)l/ *adj.* that cannot be verified.

unverified /ʌnˈverɪˌfaɪd/ *adj.* not verified.

unversed /ʌnˈvɜːst/ *adj.* (usu. foll. by *in*) not experienced or skilled.

unviable /ʌnˈvaɪəb(ə)l/ *adj.* not viable. □□ **unviability** /-ˈbɪlɪtɪ/ *n.*

unviolated /ʌnˈvaɪəˌleɪtɪd/ *adj.* not violated.

unvisited /ʌnˈvɪzɪtɪd/ *adj.* not visited.

unvitiated /ʌnˈvɪʃɪˌeɪtɪd/ *adj.* not vitiated.

unvoiced /ʌnˈvɔɪst/ *adj.* **1** not spoken. **2** *Phonet.* not voiced.

unwaged /ʌnˈweɪdʒd/ *adj.* not receiving a wage; out of work.

unwanted /ʌnˈwɒntɪd/ *adj.* not wanted.

unwarlike /ʌnˈwɔːlaɪk/ *adj.* not warlike.

unwarmed /ʌnˈwɔːmd/ *adj.* not warmed.

unwarned /ʌnˈwɔːnd/ *adj.* not warned or forewarned.

unwarrantable /ʌnˈwɒrəntəb(ə)l/ *adj.* indefensible, unjustifiable. □□ **unwarrantableness** *n.* **unwarrantably** *adv.*

unwarranted /ʌnˈwɒrəntɪd/ *adj.* **1** unauthorized. **2** unjustified.

unwary /ʌnˈweərɪ/ *adj.* **1** not cautious. **2** (often foll. by *of*) not aware of possible danger etc. □□ **unwarily** *adv.* **unwariness** *n.*

unwashed /ʌnˈwɒʃt/ *adj.* **1** not washed. **2** not usually washed or clean. □ **the great unwashed** *colloq.* the rabble.

unwatched /ʌnˈwɒtʃt/ *adj.* not watched.

unwatchful /ʌnˈwɒtʃfʊl/ *adj.* not watchful.

unwatered /ʌnˈwɔːtəd/ *adj.* not watered.

unwavering /ʌnˈweɪvərɪŋ/ *adj.* not wavering. □□ **unwaveringly** *adv.*

unweaned /ʌnˈwiːnd/ *adj.* not weaned.

unwearable /ʌnˈweərəb(ə)l/ *adj.* that cannot be worn.

unwearied /ʌnˈwɪərɪd/ *adj.* **1** not wearied or tired. **2** never becoming weary, indefatigable. **3** unremitting. □□ **unweariedly** *adv.* **unweariedness** *n.*

unweary /ʌnˈwɪərɪ/ *adj.* not weary.

unwearying /ʌnˈwɪərɪɪŋ/ *adj.* **1** persistent. **2** not causing or producing weariness. □□ **unwearyingly** *adv.*

unwed /ʌnˈwed/ *adj.* unmarried.

unwedded /ʌnˈwedɪd/ *adj.* unmarried. □□ **unweddedness** *n.*

unweeded /ʌnˈwiːdɪd/ *adj.* not cleared of weeds.

unweighed /ʌnˈweɪd/ *adj.* **1** not considered; hasty. **2** (of goods) not weighed.

unwelcome /ʌnˈwelkəm/ *adj.* not welcome or acceptable. □□ **unwelcomely** *adv.* **unwelcomeness** *n.*

unwell /ʌnˈwel/ *adj.* **1** not in good health; (somewhat) ill. **2** indisposed.

unwept /ʌnˈwept/ adj. **1** not wept for. **2** (of tears) not wept.

unwetted /ʌnˈwetɪd/ adj. not wetted.

unwhipped /ʌnˈwɪpt/ adj. **1** not punished by or as by whipping. **2** Brit. not subject to a party whip.

unwholesome /ʌnˈhəʊlsəm/ adj. **1** not promoting, or detrimental to, physical or moral health. **2** unhealthy, insalubrious. **3** unhealthy-looking. □□ **unwholesomely** adv. **unwholesomeness** n.

unwieldy /ʌnˈwiːldɪ/ adj. (**unwieldier**, **unwieldiest**) cumbersome, clumsy, or hard to manage, owing to size, shape, or weight. □□ **unwieldily** adv. **unwieldiness** n. [ME f. UN-¹ + wieldy active (now dial.) f. WIELD]

unwilling /ʌnˈwɪlɪŋ/ adj. not willing or inclined; reluctant. □□ **unwillingly** adv. **unwillingness** n. [OE unwillende (as UN-¹, WILLING)]

unwind /ʌnˈwaɪnd/ v. (past and past part. **unwound**) **1 a** tr. draw out (a thing that has been wound). **b** intr. become drawn out after having been wound. **2** intr. & tr. colloq. relax.

unwinking /ʌnˈwɪŋkɪŋ/ adj. **1** not winking. **2** watchful, vigilant. □□ **unwinkingly** adv.

unwinnable /ʌnˈwɪnəb(ə)l/ adj. that cannot be won.

unwisdom /ʌnˈwɪzdəm/ n. lack of wisdom, folly, imprudence. [OE unwīsdōm (as UN-¹, WISDOM)]

unwise /ʌnˈwaɪz/ adj. **1** foolish, imprudent. **2** injudicious. □□ **unwisely** adv. [OE unwīs (as UN-¹, WISE¹)]

unwished /ʌnˈwɪʃt/ adj. (usu. foll. by for) not wished for.

unwithered /ʌnˈwɪðəd/ adj. not withered; still vigorous or fresh.

unwitnessed /ʌnˈwɪtnɪst/ adj. not witnessed.

unwitting /ʌnˈwɪtɪŋ/ adj. **1** unaware of the state of the case (an unwitting offender). **2** unintentional. □□ **unwittingly** adv. **unwittingness** n. [OE unwitende (as UN-¹, WIT²)]

unwomanly /ʌnˈwʊmənlɪ/ adj. not womanly; not befitting a woman. □□ **unwomanliness** n.

unwonted /ʌnˈwəʊntɪd/ adj. not customary or usual. □□ **unwontedly** adv. **unwontedness** n.

unwooded /ʌnˈwʊdɪd/ adj. not wooded, treeless.

unworkable /ʌnˈwɜːkəb(ə)l/ adj. not workable; impracticable. □□ **unworkability** /-ˈbɪlɪtɪ/ n. **unworkableness** n. **unworkably** adv.

unworked /ʌnˈwɜːkt/ adj. **1** not wrought into shape. **2** not exploited or turned to account.

unworkmanlike /ʌnˈwɜːkmənlaɪk/ adj. badly done or made.

unworldly /ʌnˈwɜːldlɪ/ adj. **1** spiritually-minded. **2** spiritual. □□ **unworldliness** n.

unworn /ʌnˈwɔːn/ adj. not worn or impaired by wear.

unworried /ʌnˈwʌrɪd/ adj. not worried; calm.

unworthy /ʌnˈwɜːðɪ/ adj. (**unworthier**, **unworthiest**) **1** (often foll. by of) not worthy or befitting the character of a person etc. **2** discreditable, unseemly. **3** contemptible, base. □□ **unworthily** adv. **unworthiness** n.

unwound¹ /ʌnˈwaʊnd/ adj. not wound or wound up.

unwound² past and past part. of UNWIND.

unwounded /ʌnˈwuːndɪd/ adj. not wounded, unhurt.

unwoven /ʌnˈwəʊv(ə)n/ adj. not woven.

unwrap /ʌnˈræp/ v. (**unwrapped**, **unwrapping**) **1** tr. remove the wrapping from. **2** tr. open or unfold. **3** intr. become unwrapped.

unwrinkled /ʌnˈrɪŋk(ə)ld/ adj. free from wrinkles, smooth.

unwritable /ʌnˈraɪtəb(ə)l/ adj. that cannot be written.

unwritten /ʌnˈrɪt(ə)n/ adj. **1** not written. **2** (of a law etc.) resting originally on custom or judicial decision, not on statute.

unwrought /ʌnˈrɔːt/ adj. (of metals) not hammered into shape or worked into a finished condition.

unyielding /ʌnˈjiːldɪŋ/ adj. **1** not yielding to pressure etc. **2** firm, obstinate. □□ **unyieldingly** adv. **unyieldingness** n.

unyoke /ʌnˈjəʊk/ v. **1** tr. release from a yoke. **2** intr. cease work.

unzip /ʌnˈzɪp/ v.tr. (**unzipped**, **unzipping**) unfasten the zip of.

up /ʌp/ adv., prep., adj., n., & v. —adv. **1** at, in, or towards a higher place or position (jumped up in the air; what are they doing up there?). **2** to or in a place regarded as higher, esp.: **a** northwards (up in Scotland). **b** Brit. towards a major city or a university (went up to London). **3** colloq. ahead etc. as indicated (went up front). **4 a** to or in an erect position or condition (stood it up). **b** to or in a prepared or required position (wound up the watch). **c** in or into a condition of efficiency, activity, or progress (stirred up trouble; the house is up for sale; the hunt is up). **5** Brit. in a stronger or winning position or condition (our team was three goals up; am £10 up on the transaction). **6** (of a computer) running and available for use. **7** to the place or time in question or where the speaker etc. is (a child came up to me; went straight up to the door; has been fine up till now). **8** at or to a higher price or value (our costs are up; shares are up). **9 a** completely or effectually (burn up; eat up; tear up; use up). **b** more loudly or clearly (speak up). **10** in a state of completion; denoting the end of availability, supply, etc. (time is up). **11** into a compact, accumulated, or secure state (pack up; save up; tie up). **12** out of bed (are you up yet?). **13** (of the sun etc.) having risen. **14** happening, esp. unusually or unexpectedly (something is up). **15** taught or informed (is well up in French). **16** (usu. foll. by before) appearing for trial etc. (was up before the magistrate). **17** (of a road etc.) being repaired. **18** (of a jockey) in the saddle. **19** towards the source of a river. **20** inland. **21** (of the points etc. in a game): **a** registered on the scoreboard. **b** forming the total score for the time being. **22** upstairs, esp. to bed (are you going up yet?). **23** (of a theatre-curtain) raised etc. to reveal the stage. **24** (as int.) get up. **25** (of a ship's helm) with rudder to leeward. **26** in rebellion. —prep. **1** upwards along, through, or into (climbed up the ladder). **2** from the bottom to the top of. **3** along (walked up the road). **4 a** at or in a higher part of (is situated up the street). **b** towards the source of (a river). —adj. **1** directed upwards (up stroke). **2** Brit. of travel towards a capital or centre (the up train; the up platform). **3** (of beer etc.) effervescent, frothy. —n. a spell of good fortune. —v. (**upped**, **upping**) **1** intr. colloq. start up; begin abruptly to say or do something (upped and hit him). **2** intr. (foll. by with) raise; pick up (upped with his stick). **3** tr. increase or raise, esp. abruptly (upped all their prices). □ **be all up with** be disastrous or hopeless for (a person). **on the up and up** colloq. **1** Brit. steadily improving. **2** esp. US honest(ly); on the level. **something is up** colloq. something unusual or undesirable is afoot or happening. **up against 1** close to. **2** in or into contact with. **3** colloq. confronted with (up against a problem). **up against it** colloq. in great difficulties. **up-anchor** Naut. weigh anchor. **up and about** (or **doing**) having risen from bed; active. **up-and-coming** colloq. (of a person) making good progress and likely to succeed. **up and down 1** to and fro (along). **2** in every direction. **3** colloq. in varying health or spirits. **up-and-over** (of a door) opened by being raised and pushed back into a horizontal position. **up draught** an upward draught, esp. in a chimney. **up for** available for or being considered for (office etc.). **up hill and down dale** up and down hills on an arduous journey. **up in arms** see ARM². **up-market** adj. & adv. towards or relating to the dearer or more affluent sector of the market. **up the pole** see POLE¹. **ups and downs 1** rises and falls. **2** alternate good and bad fortune. **up the spout** see SPOUT. **up stage** at or to the back of a theatre stage. **up sticks** see STICK¹. **up-stroke** a stroke made or written upwards. **up to 1** until (up to the present). **2** not more than (you can have up to

w we z zoo ʃ she ʒ decision θ thin ð this ŋ ring x loch tʃ chip dʒ jar (see over for vowels)

five). **3** less than or equal to (*sums up to £10*). **4** incumbent on (*it is up to you to say*). **5** capable of or fit for (*am not up to a long walk*). **6** occupied or busy with (*what have you been up to?*). **up to date** see DATE¹. **up to the mark** see MARK¹. **up to the minute** see MINUTE¹. **up to snuff** see SNUFF². **up to one's tricks** see TRICK. **up to a person's tricks** see TRICK. **up with** *int.* expressing support for a stated person or thing. **what's up?** *colloq.* **1** what is going on? **2** what is the matter? [OE *up(p), uppe*, rel. to OHG *ũf*]

up- /ʌp/ *prefix* in senses of UP, added: **1** as an adverb to verbs and verbal derivations, = 'upwards' (*upcurved*; *update*). **2** as a preposition to nouns forming adverbs and adjectives (*up-country*; *uphill*). **3** as an adjective to nouns (*upland*; *up-stroke*). [OE *up(p)-*, = UP]

Upanishad /uːˈpænɪˌʃæd/ *n.* each of a series of philosophical compositions concluding the exposition of the Vedas. [Skr. f. *upa* near + *ni-ṣad* sit down]

upas /ˈjuːpəs/ *n.* **1** (in full **upas-tree**) **a** a Javanese tree, *Antiaris toxicaria*, yielding a milky sap used as arrow-poison. **b** *Mythol.* a Javanese tree thought to be fatal to whatever came near it. **c** a pernicious influence, practice, etc. **2** the poisonous sap of upas and other trees. [Malay *ũpas* poison]

upbeat /ˈʌpbiːt/ *n.* & *v.* —*n.* an unaccented beat in music. —*adj.* *colloq.* optimistic or cheerful.

upbraid /ʌpˈbreɪd/ *v.tr.* (often foll. by *with*, *for*) chide or reproach (a person). □□ **upbraiding** *n.* [OE *upbrēdan* (as UP-, *brēdan* = *bregdan* BRAID in obs. sense 'brandish')]

upbringing /ˈʌpˌbrɪŋɪŋ/ *n.* the bringing up of a child; education. [obs. *upbring* to rear (as UP-, BRING)]

upcast *n.* & *v.* —*n.* /ˈʌpkɑːst/ **1** the act of casting up; an upward throw. **2** *Mining* a shaft through which air leaves a mine. **3** *Geol.* = UPTHROW. —*v.tr.* /ʌpˈkɑːst/ (*past* and *past part.* **upcast**) cast up.

upcoming /ʌpˈkʌmɪŋ/ *adj.* esp. *US* forthcoming; about to happen.

up-country /ʌpˈkʌntrɪ, ˈʌp-/ *adv.* & *adj.* inland; towards the interior of a country.

update *v.* & *n.* —*v.tr.* /ʌpˈdeɪt/ bring up to date. —*n.* /ˈʌpdeɪt/ **1** the act or an instance of updating. **2** an updated version; a set of updated information. □□ **updater** *n.*

up-end /ʌpˈend/ *v.tr.* & *intr.* set or rise up on end.

upfield /ʌpˈfiːld/ *adv.* in or to a position nearer to the opponents' end of a football etc. field.

upfold /ˈʌpfəʊld/ *n. Geol.* an anticline.

upfront /ʌpˈfrʌnt, ˈʌp-/ *adv.* & *adj.* *colloq.* —*adv.* (usu. **up front**) **1** at the front; in front. **2** (of payments) in advance. —*adj.* **1** honest, open, frank. **2** (of payments) made in advance. **3** at the front or most prominent.

upgrade *v.* & *n.* —*v.tr.* /ʌpˈgreɪd/ **1** raise in rank etc. **2** improve (equipment, machinery, etc.) esp. by replacing components. —*n.* /ˈʌpgreɪd/ **1** the act or an instance of upgrading. **2** an upgraded piece of equipment etc. □**on the upgrade 1** improving in health etc. **2** advancing, progressing. □□ **upgrader** *n.*

upgrowth /ˈʌpgrəʊθ/ *n.* the process or result of growing upwards.

upheaval /ʌpˈhiːv(ə)l/ *n.* **1** a violent or sudden change or disruption. **2** *Geol.* an upward displacement of part of the earth's crust. **3** the act or an instance of heaving up.

upheave /ʌpˈhiːv/ *v.* **1** *tr.* heave or lift up, esp. forcibly. **2** *intr.* rise up.

uphill *adv.*, *adj.*, & *n.* —*adv.* /ʌpˈhɪl/ in an ascending direction up a hill, slope, etc. —*adj.* /ˈʌphɪl/ **1** sloping up; ascending. **2** arduous, difficult (*an uphill task*). —*n.* /ˈʌphɪl/ an upward slope.

uphold /ʌpˈhəʊld/ *v.tr.* (*past* and *past part.* **upheld**) **1** confirm or maintain (a decision etc., esp. of another). **2** give support or countenance to (a person, practice, etc.). □□ **upholder** *n.*

upholster /ʌpˈhəʊlstə(r)/ *v.tr.* **1** provide (furniture) with upholstery. **2** furnish (a room etc.) with furniture, carpets, etc. □**well-upholstered** *joc.* (of a person) fat. [back-form. f. UPHOLSTERER]

upholsterer /ʌpˈhəʊlstərə(r)/ *n.* a person who upholsters furniture, esp. professionally. [obs. *upholster* (n.) f. UPHOLD (in obs. sense 'keep in repair') + -STER]

upholstery /ʌpˈhəʊlstərɪ/ *n.* **1** textile covering, padding, springs, etc., for furniture. **2** an upholsterer's work.

upkeep /ˈʌpkiːp/ *n.* **1** maintenance in good condition. **2** the cost or means of this.

upland /ˈʌplənd/ *n.* & *adj.* —*n.* the higher or inland parts of a country. —*adj.* of or relating to these parts.

uplift *v.* & *n.* —*v.tr.* /ʌpˈlɪft/ **1** raise; lift up. **2** elevate or stimulate morally or spiritually. —*n.* /ˈʌplɪft/ **1** the act or an instance of being raised. **2** *Geol.* the raising of part of the earth's surface. **3** *colloq.* a morally or spiritually elevating influence. **4** support for the bust etc. from a garment. □□ **uplifter** /-ˈlɪftə(r)/ *n.* **uplifting** /-ˈlɪftɪŋ/ *adj.* (esp. in sense 2 of *v.*).

upmost var. of UPPERMOST.

upon /əˈpɒn/ *prep.* = ON. ¶ *Upon* is sometimes more formal, and is preferred in *once upon a time* and *upon my word*, and in uses such as *row upon row of seats* and *Christmas is almost upon us*. [ME f. UP + ON *prep.*, after ON *upp á*]

upper¹ /ˈʌpə(r)/ *adj.* & *n.* —*adj.* **1** higher in place; situated above another part (*the upper atmosphere*; *the upper lip*). **2** higher in rank or dignity etc. (*the upper class*). **3** situated on higher ground (*Upper Egypt*). —*n.* the part of a boot or shoe above the sole. □**on one's uppers** *colloq.* extremely short of money. **upper case** see CASE². **upper class** the highest class of society, esp. the aristocracy. **upper-class** *adj.* of the upper class. **the upper crust** *colloq.* the aristocracy. **upper-cut** *n.* an upwards blow delivered with the arm bent. —*v.tr.* hit with an upper-cut. **the upper hand** dominance or control. **Upper House** the higher house in a legislature, esp. the House of Lords. **the upper regions 1** the sky. **2** heaven. **upper works** the part of a ship that is above the water when fully laden. [ME f. UP + -ER²]

upper² /ˈʌpə(r)/ *n. sl.* a stimulant drug, esp. an amphetamine. [UP *v.* + -ER¹]

uppermost /ˈʌpəˌməʊst/ *adj.* & *adv.* —*adj.* (also **upmost** /ˈʌpməʊst/) **1** highest in place or rank. **2** predominant. —*adv.* at or to the highest or most prominent position.

uppish /ˈʌpɪʃ/ *adj.* esp. *Brit. colloq.* self-assertive or arrogant. □□ **uppishly** *adv.* **uppishness** *n.*

uppity /ˈʌpɪtɪ/ *adj. colloq.* uppish, snobbish. [fanciful f. UP]

upraise /ʌpˈreɪz/ *v.tr.* raise to a higher level.

upright /ˈʌpraɪt/ *adj.* & *n.* —*adj.* **1** erect, vertical (*an upright posture*; *stood upright*). **2** (of a piano) with vertical strings. **3** (of a person or behaviour) righteous; strictly honourable or honest. **4** (of a picture, book, etc.) greater in height than breadth. —*n.* **1** a post or rod fixed upright esp. as a structural support. **2** an upright piano. □□ **uprightly** *adv.* **uprightness** *n.* [OE *upriht* (as UP, RIGHT)]

uprise /ʌpˈraɪz/ *v.intr.* (**uprose**, **uprisen**) rise (to a standing position, etc.).

uprising /ˈʌpˌraɪzɪŋ/ *n.* a rebellion or revolt.

uproar /ˈʌprɔː(r)/ *n.* a tumult; a violent disturbance. [Du. *oproer* f. *op* up + *roer* confusion, assoc. with ROAR]

uproarious /ʌpˈrɔːrɪəs/ *adj.* **1** very noisy. **2** provoking loud laughter. □□ **uproariously** *adv.* **uproariousness** *n.*

uproot /ʌpˈruːt/ *v.tr.* **1** pull (a plant etc.) up from the ground. **2** displace (a person) from an accustomed location. **3** eradicate, destroy. □□ **uprooter** *n.*

uprose *past* of UPRISE.

uprush /'ʌprʌʃ/ n. an upward rush, esp. *Psychol.* from the subconscious.

ups-a-daisy var. of UPSY-DAISY.

upset v., n., & adj. —v. /ʌp'set/ (**upsetting**; *past* and *past part.* **upset**) **1** tr. & intr. overturn or be overturned. **2** tr. disturb the composure or digestion of (*was very upset by the news*; *ate something that upset me*). **3** tr. disrupt. **4** tr. shorten and thicken (metal, esp. a tire) by hammering or pressure. —n. /'ʌpset/ **1** a condition of upsetting or being upset (*a stomach upset*). **2** a surprising result in a game etc. —adj. /'ʌpset/ disturbed (*an upset stomach*). □**upset price** the lowest acceptable selling price of a property in an auction etc.; a reserve price. □□ **upsetter** /-'setə(r)/ n. **upsettingly** /-'setɪŋlɪ/ adv.

upshot /'ʌpʃɒt/ n. the final or eventual outcome or conclusion.

upside down /ˌʌpsaɪd 'daʊn/ adv. & adj. —adv. **1** with the upper part where the lower part should be; in an inverted position. **2** in or into total disorder (*everything was turned upside down*). —adj. (also **upside-down** attrib.) that is positioned upside down; inverted. □**upside-down cake** a sponge cake baked with fruit in a syrup at the bottom, and inverted for serving. [ME, orig. *up so down*, perh. = 'up as if down']

upsides /ʌp'saɪdz/ adv. *Brit.* colloq. (foll. by *with*) equal with (a person) by revenge, retaliation, etc. [*upside* = top part]

upsilon /'juːpsɪˌlɒn, ʌp'saɪlən/ n. the twelfth letter of the Greek alphabet (Υ, υ). [Gk, = slender U f. *psilos* slender, with ref. to its later coincidence in sound with Gk *oi*]

upstage /ʌp'steɪdʒ/ adj., adv., & v. —adj. & adv. **1** nearer the back of a theatre stage. **2** snobbish(ly). —v.tr. **1** (of an actor) move upstage to make (another actor) face away from the audience. **2** divert attention from (a person) to oneself; outshine.

upstairs adv., adj., & n. —adv. /ʌp'steəz/ to or on an upper floor. —adj. /'ʌpsteəz/ (also **upstair**) situated upstairs. —n. /ʌp'steəz/ an upper floor.

upstanding /ʌp'stændɪŋ/ adj. **1** standing up. **2** strong and healthy. **3** honest or straightforward.

upstart /'ʌpstɑːt/ n. & adj. —n. a person who has risen suddenly to prominence, esp. one who behaves arrogantly. —adj. **1** that is an upstart. **2** of or characteristic of an upstart.

upstate /'ʌpsteɪt/ n., adj., & adv. *US* —n. part of a State remote from its large cities, esp. the northern part. —adj. of or relating to this part. —adv. in or to this part. □□ **upstater** n.

upstream /'ʌpstriːm/ adv. & adj. —adv. against the flow of a stream etc. —adj. moving upstream.

upsurge /'ʌpsɜːdʒ/ n. an upward surge; a rise (esp. in feelings etc.).

upswept /'ʌpswept/ adj. **1** (of the hair) combed to the top of the head. **2** curved or sloped upwards.

upswing /'ʌpswɪŋ/ n. an upward movement or trend.

upsy-daisy /'ʌpsɪˌdeɪzɪ/ int. (also **ups-a-daisy**) expressing encouragement to a child who is being lifted or has fallen. [earlier *up-a-daisy*: cf. LACKADAISICAL]

uptake /'ʌpteɪk/ n. **1** colloq. understanding; comprehension (esp. *quick* or *slow on the uptake*). **2** the act or an instance of taking up.

upthrow /'ʌpθrəʊ/ n. **1** the act or an instance of throwing upwards. **2** *Geol.* an upward dislocation of strata.

upthrust /'ʌpθrʌst/ n. **1** upward thrust, e.g. of a fluid on an immersed body. **2** *Geol.* = UPHEAVAL.

uptight /ʌp'taɪt, 'ʌptaɪt/ adj. colloq. **1** nervously tense or angry. **2** *US* rigidly conventional.

uptown /'ʌptaʊn/ adj., adv., & n. *US* —adj. of or in the residential part of a town or city. —adv. in or into this part. —n. this part. □□ **uptowner** n.

upturn n. & v. —n. /'ʌptɜːn/ **1** an upward trend; an improvement. **2** an upheaval. —v.tr. /ʌp'tɜːn/ turn up or upside down.

UPU abbr. Universal Postal Union.

upward /'ʌpwəd/ adv. & adj. —adv. (also **upwards**) towards what is higher, superior, larger in amount, more important, or earlier. —adj. moving, extending, pointing, or leading upward. □**upwards of** more than (*found upwards of forty specimens*). [OE *upweard(es)* (as UP, -WARD)]

upwardly /'ʌpwədlɪ/ adv. in an upward direction. □**upwardly mobile** able or aspiring to advance socially or professionally.

upwarp /'ʌpwɔːp/ n. *Geol.* a broad surface elevation; an anticline.

upwind /'ʌpwɪnd/ adj. & adv. against the direction of the wind.

ur- /uːr/ comb. form primitive, original, earliest. [G]

uracil /'jʊərəsɪl/ n. *Biochem.* a pyrimidine derivative found in living tissue as a component base of RNA. [UREA + ACETIC]

uraemia /jʊ'riːmɪə/ n. (*US* **uremia**) *Med.* a morbid condition due to the presence in the blood of urinary matter normally eliminated by the kidneys. □□ **uraemic** adj. [Gk *ouron* urine + *haima* blood]

uraeus /jʊ'riːəs/ n. the sacred serpent as an emblem of power represented on the head-dress of Egyptian divinities and sovereigns. [mod.L f. Gk *ouraios*, repr. the Egypt. word for 'cobra']

Ural-Altaic /ˌjʊər(ə)læl'teɪɪk/ n. & adj. —n. *Philol.* a family of Finno-Ugric, Turkic, Mongolian, and other agglutinative languages of N. Europe and Asia. —adj. **1** of or relating to this family of languages. **2** of or relating to the Ural and Altaic mountain ranges in the USSR and central Asia.

uranium /jʊ'reɪnɪəm/ n. *Chem.* a radioactive grey dense metallic element occurring naturally in pitchblende, and capable of nuclear fission and therefore used as a source of nuclear energy. ¶ Symb.: U. □□ **uranic** /-'rænɪk/ adj. [mod.L, f. URANUS: cf. *tellurium*]

urano-[1] /'jʊərənəʊ/ comb. form the heavens. [Gk *ouranos* heaven(s)]

urano-[2] /'jʊərənəʊ/ comb. form uranium.

uranography /ˌjʊərə'nɒgrəfɪ/ n. the branch of astronomy concerned with describing and mapping the stars, planets, etc. □□ **uranographer** n. **uranographic** /-nə'græfɪk/ adj.

Uranus /'jʊərənəs, jʊ'reɪnəs/ n. a planet discovered by Herschel in 1781, the outermost of the solar system except Neptune and Pluto. [L f. Gk *Ouranos* heaven, Uranus, in Gk Mythol. the son of Gaea (Earth) and father of Kronos (Saturn), the Titans, etc.]

urban /'ɜːbən/ adj. of, living in, or situated in a town or city (*an urban population*) (opp. RURAL). □**urban district** *Brit. hist.* a group of urban communities governed by an elected council. **urban guerrilla** a terrorist operating in an urban area. **urban renewal** slum clearance and redevelopment in a city or town. **urban sprawl** the uncontrolled expansion of urban areas. [L *urbanus* f. *urbs urbis* city]

urbane /ɜː'beɪn/ adj. courteous; suave; elegant and refined in manner. □□ **urbanely** adv. **urbaneness** n. [F *urbain* or L *urbanus*: see URBAN]

urbanism /'ɜːbəˌnɪz(ə)m/ n. **1** urban character or way of life. **2** a study of urban life. □□ **urbanist** n.

urbanite /'ɜːbəˌnaɪt/ n. a dweller in a city or town.

urbanity /ɜː'bænɪtɪ/ n. **1** an urbane quality; refinement of manner. **2** urban life. [F *urbanité* or L *urbanitas* (as URBAN)]

urbanize /'ɜːbəˌnaɪz/ v.tr. (also -**ise**) **1** make urban. **2** destroy the rural quality of (a district). □□ **urbanization** /-'zeɪʃ(ə)n/ n. [F *urbaniser* (as URBAN)]

urceolate /'ɜːsɪələt/ adj. *Bot.* having the shape of a pitcher, with a large body and small mouth. [L *urceolus* dimin. of *urceus* pitcher]

urchin /'ɜːtʃɪn/ n. **1** a mischievous child, esp. young and raggedly dressed. **2** = *sea urchin*. **3** *archaic* **a** a hedgehog. **b** a goblin. [ME *hirchon*, *urcheon* f. ONF *herichon*, OF *heriçon* ult. f. L (*h*)*ericius* hedgehog]

Urdu /'ʊəduː, 'ɜː-/ n. a language related to Hindi but with many Persian words, an official language of Pakistan and also used in India. [Hind. (*zabān i*) urdū (language of the) camp, f. Pers. *urdū* f. Turki *ordū*: see HORDE]

-ure /jə(r)/ *suffix* forming: **1** nouns of action or process (*censure; closure; seizure*). **2** nouns of result (*creature; scripture*). **3** collective nouns (*legislature; nature*). **4** nouns of function (*judicature; ligature*). [from or after OF *-ure* f. L *-ura*]

urea /'juəriə, -'ri:ə/ *n. Biochem.* a soluble colourless crystalline nitrogenous compound contained esp. in the urine of mammals. □□ **ureal** *adj.* [mod.L f. F *urée* f. Gk *ouron* urine]

uremia *US* var. of URAEMIA.

ureter /juə'ri:tə(r)/ *n.* the duct by which urine passes from the kidney to the bladder or cloaca. □□ **ureteral** *adj.* **ureteric** /ˌjuərɪ'terɪk/ *adj.* **ureteritis** /-'raɪtɪs/ *n.* [F *uretère* or mod.L *ureter* f. Gk *ourētēr* f. *oureō* urinate]

urethane /jʊ'ri:θeɪn, 'juərɪˌθeɪn/ *n. Chem.* a crystalline amide, ethyl carbamate, used in plastics and paints. [F *uréthane* (as UREA, ETHANE)]

urethra /jʊə'ri:θrə/ *n.* (*pl.* **urethrae** /-ri:/ or **urethras**) the duct by which urine is discharged from the bladder. □□ **urethral** *adj.* **urethritis** /-rɪ'θraɪtɪs/ *n.* [LL f. Gk *ourēthra* (as URETER)]

urge /ɜːdʒ/ *v.* & *n.* —*v.tr.* **1** (often foll. by *on*) drive forcibly; impel; hasten (*urged them on; urged the horses forward*). **2** (often foll. by *to* + infin. or *that* + clause) encourage or entreat earnestly or persistently (*urged them to go; urged them to action; urged that they should go*). **3** (often foll. by *on, upon*) advocate (an action or argument etc.) pressingly or emphatically (to a person) (*urged the seriousness of the problem*). **4** adduce forcefully as a reason or justification (*urged the seriousness of the problem*). **5** ply (a person etc.) hard with argument or entreaty. —*n.* **1** an urging impulse or tendency. **2** a strong desire. □□ **urger** *n.* [L *urgēre* press, drive]

urgent /'ɜːdʒ(ə)nt/ *adj.* **1** requiring immediate action or attention (*an urgent need for help*). **2** importunate; earnest and persistent in demand. □□ **urgency** *n.* **urgently** *adv.* [ME f. F (as URGE)]

URI *abbr.* upper respiratory infection.

-uria /'juəriə/ *comb. form* forming nouns denoting that a substance is (esp. excessively) present in the urine. [mod.L f. Gk *-ouria* (as URINE)]

uric /'juərɪk/ *adj.* of or relating to urine. □ **uric acid** a crystalline acid forming a constituent of urine. [F *urique* (as URINE)]

urinal /juə'raɪn(ə)l, 'juərɪn(ə)l/ *n.* **1** a sanitary fitting, usu. against a wall, for men to urinate into. **2** a place or receptacle for urination. [ME f. OF f. LL *urinal* neut. of *urinalis* (as URINE)]

urinalysis /ˌjuərɪ'nælɪsɪs/ *n.* (*pl.* **urinalyses** /-ˌsi:z/) the chemical analysis of urine esp. for diagnostic purposes.

urinary /'juərɪnərɪ/ *adj.* **1** of or relating to urine. **2** affecting or occurring in the urinary system (*urinary diseases*).

urinate /'juərɪˌneɪt/ *v.intr.* discharge urine. □□ **urination** /-'neɪʃ(ə)n/ *n.* [med.L *urinare* (as URINE)]

urine /'juərɪn/ *n.* a pale-yellow fluid secreted as waste from the blood by the kidneys, stored in the bladder, and discharged through the urethra. □□ **urinous** *adj.* [ME f. OF f. L *urina*]

urn /ɜːn/ *n.* & *v.* —*n.* **1** a vase with a foot and usu. a rounded body, esp. for storing the ashes of the cremated dead or as a vessel or measure. **2** a large vessel with a tap, in which tea or coffee etc. is made or kept hot. **3** *poet.* anything in which a dead body or its remains are preserved, e.g. a grave. —*v.tr.* enclose in an urn. □□ **urnful** *n.* (*pl.* **-fuls**). [ME f. L *urna*, rel. to *urceus* pitcher]

uro-¹ /'juərəʊ/ *comb. form* urine. [Gk *ouron* urine]

uro-² /'juərəʊ/ *comb. form* tail. [Gk *oura* tail]

urochord /'juərəʊˌkɔːd/ *n.* the notochord of a tunicate.

urodele /'juərəʊˌdiːl/ *n.* any amphibian of the order Urodela, having a tail when in the adult form, including newts and salamanders. [URO-² + Gk *dēlos* evident]

urogenital /ˌjuərə'dʒenɪt(ə)l/ *adj.* of or relating to urinary and genital products or organs.

urology /juə'rɒlədʒɪ/ *n.* the scientific study of the urinary system. □□ **urologic** /-rə'lɒdʒɪk/ *adj.* **urologist** *n.*

uropygium /ˌjuərəʊ'pɪdʒɪəm/ *n.* the rump of a bird. [med.L f. Gk *ouropugion*]

uroscopy /juə'rɒskəpɪ/ *n. Med. hist.* the examination of urine, esp. in diagnosis.

Ursa Major /ˌɜːsə 'meɪdʒə(r)/ *n.* = *the Great Bear* (see BEAR²). [L, = greater bear]

Ursa Minor /ˌɜːsə 'maɪnə(r)/ *n.* = *the Little Bear* (see BEAR²). [L, = lesser bear]

ursine /'ɜːsaɪn/ *adj.* of or like a bear. [L *ursinus* f. *ursus* bear]

Ursuline /'ɜːsjuˌlaɪn, -lɪn/ *n.* & *adj.* —*n.* a nun of an order founded by St Angela in 1535 for nursing the sick and teaching girls. —*adj.* of or relating to this order. [St *Ursula*, the founder's patron saint]

urticaria /ˌɜːtɪ'keərɪə/ *n. Med.* nettle-rash. [mod.L f. L *urtica* nettle f. *urere* burn]

urticate /'ɜːtɪˌkeɪt/ *v.tr.* sting like a nettle. □□ **urtication** /-'keɪʃ(ə)n/ *n.* [med.L *urticare* f. L *urtica*: see URTICARIA]

urus /'juərəs/ *n.* = AUROCHS. [L f. Gmc]

US *abbr.* **1** United States (of America). **2** Under-Secretary. **3** unserviceable.

us /ʌs, əs/ *pron.* **1** *objective case* of WE (*they saw us*). **2** *colloq.* = WE (*it's us again*). **3** *colloq.* = ME¹ (*give us a kiss*). [OE *ūs* f. Gmc]

USA *abbr.* **1** United States of America. **2** *US* United States Army.

usable /'ju:zəb(ə)l/ *adj.* that can be used. □□ **usability** /-'bɪlɪtɪ/ *n.* **usableness** *n.*

USAF *abbr.* United States Air Force.

usage /'ju:sɪdʒ/ *n.* **1** a manner of using or treating; treatment (*damaged by rough usage*). **2** habitual or customary practice, esp. as creating a right, obligation, or standard. [ME f. OF f. *us* USE *n.*]

usance /'ju:z(ə)ns/ *n.* the time allowed by commercial usage for the payment of foreign bills of exchange. [ME f. OF (as USE)]

USDAW /'ʌzdɔː/ *abbr.* (in the UK) Union of Shop, Distributive, and Allied Workers.

use *v.* & *n.* —*v.tr.* /ju:z/ **1** cause to act or serve for a purpose; bring into service; avail oneself of (*rarely uses the car; use your discretion*). **2** treat (a person) in a specified manner (*they used him shamefully*). **3** exploit for one's own ends (*they are just using you*). **4** (in *past* /ju:st/; foll. by *to* + infin.) did or had in the past (but no longer) as a customary practice or state (*I used to be an archaeologist; it used not* (or *did not use*) *to rain so often*). **5** (as **used** *adj.*) second-hand. **6** (as **used** /ju:st/ *predic. adj.*) (foll. by *to*) familiar by habit; accustomed (*not used to hard work*). **7** apply (a name or title etc.) to oneself. —*n.* /ju:s/ **1** the act of using or the state of being used; application to a purpose (*put it to good use; is in daily use; worn and polished with use*). **2** the right or power of using (*lost the use of my right arm*). **3 a** the ability to be used (*a torch would be of use*). **b** the purpose for which a thing can be used (*it's no use talking*). **4** custom or usage (*long use has reconciled me to it*). **5** the characteristic ritual and liturgy of a church or diocese etc. **6** *Law hist.* the benefit or profit of lands, esp. in the possession of another who holds them solely for the beneficiary. □ **could use** *colloq.* would be glad to have; would be improved by having. **have no use for 1** be unable to find a use for. **2** dislike or be impatient with. **make use of 1** employ, apply. **2** benefit from. **use and wont** established custom. **use a person's name** quote a person as an authority or reference etc. **use up 1** consume completely, use the whole of. **2** find a use for (something remaining). **3** exhaust or wear out e.g. with overwork. [ME f. OF *us, user*, ult. f. L *uti us-* use]

useful /'ju:sfʊl/ *adj.* **1 a** of use; serviceable. **b** producing or able to produce good results (*gave me* *some useful hints*). **2** *colloq*. highly creditable or efficient (*a useful performance*). □**make oneself useful** perform useful services. **useful load** the load carried by an aircraft etc. in addition to its own weight. □□ **usefully** *adv*. **usefulness** *n*.

useless /'juːslɪs/ *adj*. **1** serving no purpose; unavailing (*the contents were made useless by damp*; *protest is useless*). **2** *colloq*. feeble or ineffectual (*am useless at swimming*). □□ **uselessly** *adv*. **uselessness** *n*.

user /'juːzə(r)/ *n*. **1** a person who uses (esp. a particular commodity or service, or a computer). **2** *colloq*. a drug addict. **3** *Law* the continued use or enjoyment of a right etc. □**right of user** *Law* **1** a right to use. **2** a presumptive right arising from the user. **user-friendly** esp. *Computing* (of a machine or system) designed to be easy to use.

usher /'ʌʃə(r)/ *n*. & *v*. — *n*. **1** a person who shows people to their seats in a hall or theatre etc. **2** a doorkeeper at a court etc. **3** *Brit*. an officer walking before a person of rank. **4** *archaic* or *joc*. an assistant teacher. — *v.tr*. **1** act as usher to. **2** (usu. foll. by *in*) announce or show in etc. (*ushered us into the room*; *ushered in a new era*). □□ **ushership** *n*. [ME f. AF *usser*, OF *uissier*, var. of *huissier* f. med.L *ustiarius* for L *ostiarius* f. *ostium* door]

usherette /ˌʌʃə'ret/ *n*. a female usher esp. in a cinema.

USM *abbr*. *Stock Exch*. Unlisted Securities Market.

USN *abbr*. United States Navy.

usquebaugh /'ʌskwɪˌbɔː/ *n*. esp. *Ir*. & *Sc*. whisky. [Ir. & Sc. Gael. *uisge beatha* water of life: cf. WHISKY]

USS *abbr*. United States Ship.

USSR *abbr*. Union of Soviet Socialist Republics.

usual /'juːʒəl/ *adj*. **1** such as commonly occurs, or is observed or done; customary, habitual (*the usual formalities*; *it is usual to tip them*; *forgot my keys as usual*). **2** (prec. by *the*, *my*, etc.) *colloq*. a person's usual drink etc. □□ **usually** *adv*. **usualness** *n*. [ME f. OF *usual*, *usuel* or LL *usualis* (as USE)]

usucaption /ˌjuːzjuː'kæpʃ(ə)n/ *n*. (also **usucapion** /ˌjuːzjuː'keɪpɪən/) (in Roman and Scots law) the acquisition of a title or right to property by uninterrupted and undisputed possession for a prescribed term. [OF *usucap(t)ion* or L *usucap(t)io* f. *usucapere* acquire by prescription f. *usu* by use + *capere capt-* take]

usufruct /'juːzjuːˌfrʌkt/ *n*. & *v*. — *n*. (in Roman and Scots law) the right of enjoying the use and advantages of another's property short of the destruction or waste of its substance. — *v.tr*. hold in usufruct. □□ **usufructuary** /-'frʌktjʊərɪ/ *adj*. & *n*. [med.L *usufructus* f. L *usus* (*et*) *fructus* f. *usus* USE + *fructus* FRUIT]

usurer /'juːʒərə(r)/ *n*. a person who practises usury. [ME f. AF *usurer*, OF *usureor* f. *usure* f. L *usura*: see USURY]

usurious /jʊ'ʒʊərɪəs/ *adj*. of, involving, or practising usury. □□ **usuriously** *adv*.

usurp /jʊ'zɜːp/ *v*. **1** *tr*. seize or assume (a throne or power etc.) wrongfully. **2** *intr*. (foll. by *on*, *upon*) encroach. □□ **usurpation** /ˌjuːzə'peɪʃ(ə)n/ *n*. **usurper** *n*. [ME f. OF *usurper* f. L *usurpare* seize for use]

usury /'juːʒərɪ/ *n*. **1** the act or practice of lending money at interest, esp. *Law* at an exorbitant rate. **2** interest at this rate. □**with usury** *rhet*. or *poet*. with increased force etc. [ME f. med.L *usuria* f. L *usura* (as USE)]

UT *abbr*. **1** universal time. **2** *US* Utah (in 'official postal use).

ute /juːt/ *n*. *Austral*. & *NZ sl*. a utility truck. [abbr.]

utensil /juː'tens(ə)l/ *n*. an implement or vessel, esp. for domestic use (*cooking utensils*). [ME f. OF *utensile* f. med.L, neut. of L *utensilis* usable (as USE)]

uterine /'juːtəˌraɪn, -rɪn/ *adj*. **1** of or relating to the uterus. **2** born of the same mother but not the same father (*sister uterine*). [ME f. LL *uterinus* (as UTERUS)]

uterus /'juːtərəs/ *n*. (*pl*. **uteri** /-ˌraɪ/) the womb. □□ **uteritis** /-'raɪtɪs/ *n*. [L]

utile /'juːtaɪl/ *adj*. useful; having utility. [ME f. OF f. L *utilis* f. *uti* use]

utilitarian /ˌjuːtɪlɪ'teərɪən/ *adj*. & *n*. — *adj*. **1** designed to be useful for a purpose rather than attractive; severely practical. **2** of utilitarianism. — *n*. an adherent of utilitarianism.

utilitarianism /ˌjuːtɪlɪ'teərɪəˌnɪz(ə)m/ *n*. **1** the doctrine that actions are right if they are useful or for the benefit of a majority. **2** the doctrine that the greatest happiness of the greatest number should be the guiding principle of conduct.

utility /juː'tɪlɪtɪ/ *n*. (*pl*. **-ies**) **1** the condition of being useful or profitable. **2** a useful thing. **3** = *public utility*. **4** (*attrib*.) **a** severely practical and standardized (*utility furniture*). **b** made or serving for utility. □**utility room** a room equipped with appliances for washing, ironing, and other domestic work. **utility vehicle** (or **truck** etc.) a vehicle capable of serving various functions. [ME f. OF *utilité* f. L *utilitas -tatis* (as UTILE)]

utilize /'juːtɪˌlaɪz/ *v.tr*. (also **-ise**) make practical use of; turn to account; use effectively. □□ **utilizable** *adj*. **utilization** /-'zeɪʃ(ə)n/ *n*. **utilizer** *n*. [F *utiliser* f. It. *utilizzare* (as UTILE)]

-ution /'juːʃ(ə)n, 'uːʃ(ə)n/ *suffix* forming nouns, = -ATION (*solution*). [F f. L *-utio*]

utmost /'ʌtməʊst/ *adj*. & *n*. — *adj*. **1** furthest, extreme, or greatest (*the utmost limits*; *showed the utmost reluctance*). — *n*. (prec. by *the*) the utmost point or degree etc. □**do one's utmost** do all that one can. [OE *ūt(e)mest* (as OUT, -MOST)]

Utopia /juː'təʊpɪə/ *n*. an imagined perfect place or state of things. [title of a book (1516) by Thomas More: mod.L f. Gk *ou* not + *topos* place]

Utopian /juː'təʊpɪən/ *adj*. & *n*. (also **utopian**) — *adj*. characteristic of Utopia; idealistic. — *n*. an idealistic reformer. □□ **Utopianism** *n*.

utricle /'juːtrɪk(ə)l/ *n*. a small cell or sac in an animal or plant, esp. one in the inner ear. □□ **utricular** /juː'trɪkjʊlə(r)/ *adj*. [F *utricule* or L *utriculus* dimin. of *uter* leather bag]

utter[1] /'ʌtə(r)/ *attrib.adj*. complete, total, absolute (*utter misery*; *saw the utter absurdity of it*). □□ **utterly** *adv*. **utterness** *n*. [OE *ūtera*, *ūttra*, compar. adj. f. *ūt* OUT: cf. OUTER]

utter[2] /'ʌtə(r)/ *v.tr*. **1** emit audibly (*uttered a startled cry*). **2** express in spoken or written words. **3** *Law* put (esp. forged money) into circulation. □□ **utterable** *adj*. **utterer** *n*. [ME f. MDu. *ūteren* make known, assim. to UTTER[1]]

utterance /'ʌtərəns/ *n*. **1** the act or an instance of uttering. **2** a thing spoken. **3 a** the power of speaking. **b** a manner of speaking. **4** *Linguistics* an uninterrupted chain of spoken or written words not necessarily corresponding to a single or complete grammatical unit.

uttermost /'ʌtəˌməʊst/ *adj*. furthest, extreme.

U-turn /'juːtɜːn/ *n*. **1** the turning of a vehicle in a U-shaped course so as to face in the opposite direction. **2** a reversal of policy.

UV *abbr*. ultraviolet.

uvea /'juːvɪə/ *n*. the pigmented layer of the eye, lying beneath the outer layer. [med.L f. L *uva* grape]

uvula /'juːvjʊlə/ *n*. (*pl*. **uvulae** /-ˌliː/) **1** a fleshy extension of the soft palate hanging above the throat. **2** a similar process in the bladder or cerebellum. [ME f. LL, dimin. of L *uva* grape]

uvular /'juːvjʊlə(r)/ *adj*. & *n*. — *adj*. **1** of or relating to the uvula. **2** articulated with the back of the tongue and the uvula, as in *r* in French. — *n*. a uvular consonant.

uxorial /ʌk'sɔːrɪəl/ *adj*. of or relating to a wife.

uxoricide /ʌk'sɒrɪˌsaɪd/ *n*. **1** the killing of one's wife. **2** a person who does this. □□ **uxoricidal** /-'saɪd(ə)l/ *adj*. [L *uxor* wife + -CIDE]

uxorious /ʌk'sɔːrɪəs/ *adj*. **1** greatly or excessively fond of one's wife. **2** (of behaviour etc.) showing such fondness. □□ **uxoriously** *adv.* **uxoriousness** *n.* [L *uxoriosus* f. *uxor* wife]

Uzbek /ˈʌzbek, ˈʊz-/ *n.* (also **Uzbeg** /-beg/) **1** a member of a Turkic people living mainly in Uzbekistan in the USSR. **2** the language of this people. [Uzbek]

V

V¹ /viː/ n. (also **v**) (pl. **Vs** or **V's**) **1** the twenty-second letter of the alphabet. **2** a V-shaped thing. **3** (as a Roman numeral) five.

V² abbr. (also **V.**) volt(s).

V³ symb. Chem. the element vanadium.

v. abbr. **1** verse. **2** verso. **3** versus. **4** very. **5** vide.

VA abbr. **1** US Veterans' Administration. **2** Vicar Apostolic. **3** Vice Admiral. **4** US Virginia (in official postal use). **5** (in the UK) Order of Victoria and Albert.

Va. abbr. Virginia.

vac /væk/ n. Brit. colloq. vacation (esp. of universities). [abbr.]

vacancy /'veɪkənsɪ/ n. (pl. **-ies**) **1** the state of being vacant or empty. **2** an unoccupied post or job (there are three vacancies for typists). **3** an available room in a hotel etc. **4** emptiness of mind; idleness, listlessness.

vacant /'veɪkənt/ adj. **1** not filled or occupied; empty. **2** not mentally active; showing no interest (had a vacant stare). □**vacant possession** Brit. ownership of a house etc. with any previous occupant having moved out. □□ **vacantly** adv. [ME f. OF vacant or L vacare (as VACATE)]

vacate /və'keɪt, veɪ-/ v.tr. **1** leave vacant or cease to occupy (a house, room, etc.). **2** give up tenure of (a post etc.). **3** Law annul (a judgement or contract etc.). □□ **vacatable** adj. [L vacare vacat- be empty]

vacation /və'keɪʃ(ə)n/ n. & v. —n. **1** a fixed period of cessation from work, esp. in universities and lawcourts. **2** US a holiday. **3** the act of vacating (a house or post etc.). —v.intr. US take a holiday. □**vacation land** US an area providing attractions for holidaymakers. □□ **vacationer** n. **vacationist** n. [ME f. OF vacation or L vacatio (as VACATE)]

vaccinate /'væksɪˌneɪt/ v.tr. inoculate with a vaccine to procure immunity from a disease; immunize. □□ **vaccination** /-'neɪʃ(ə)n/ n. **vaccinator** n.

vaccine /'væksiːn/ n. & adj. —n. **1** an antigenic preparation used to stimulate the production of antibodies and procure immunity from one or several diseases. **2** hist. the cowpox virus used in vaccination against smallpox. —adj. of or relating to cowpox or vaccination. □□ **vaccinal** /-sɪn(ə)l/ adj. [L vaccinus f. vacca cow]

vaccinia /væk'sɪnɪə/ n. Med. a virus used as a vaccine against smallpox. [mod.L (as VACCINE)]

vacillate /'væsɪˌleɪt/ v.intr. **1** fluctuate in opinion or resolution. **2** move from side to side; oscillate, waver. □□ **vacillation** /-'leɪʃ(ə)n/ n. **vacillator** n. [L vacillare vacillat- sway]

vacua pl. of VACUUM.

vacuole /'vækjʊˌəʊl/ n. Biol. a tiny space within the cytoplasm of a cell containing air, fluid, food particles, etc. □□ **vacuolar** /'vækjʊələ(r)/ adj. **vacuolation** /-ˈleɪʃ(ə)n/ n. [F, dimin. of L vacuus empty]

vacuous /'vækjʊəs/ adj. **1** lacking expression (a vacuous stare). **2** unintelligent (a vacuous remark). **3** empty. □□ **vacuity** /və'kjuːɪtɪ/ n. **vacuously** adv. **vacuousness** n. [L vacuus empty (as VACATE)]

vacuum /'vækjʊəm/ n. & v. —n. (pl. **vacuums** or **vacua** /-jʊə/) **1** a space entirely devoid of matter. **2** a space or vessel from which the air has been completely or partly removed by a pump etc. **3 a** the absence of the normal or previous content of a place, environment, etc. **b** the absence of former circumstances, activities, etc. **4** (pl. **vacuums**) colloq. a vacuum cleaner. **5** a decrease of pressure below the normal atmospheric value. —v. colloq. **1** tr. clean with a vacuum cleaner. **2** intr. use a vacuum cleaner.

□**vacuum brake** a brake in which pressure is caused by the exhaustion of air. **vacuum-clean** clean with a vacuum cleaner. **vacuum cleaner** an apparatus for removing dust etc. by suction. **vacuum flask** Brit. a vessel with a double wall enclosing a vacuum so that the liquid in the inner receptacle retains its temperature. **vacuum gauge** a gauge for testing the pressure after the production of a vacuum. **vacuum-packed** sealed after the partial removal of air. **vacuum pump** a pump for producing a vacuum. **vacuum tube** a tube with a near-vacuum for the free passage of electric current. [mod.L, neut. of L vacuus empty]

VAD abbr. **1** Voluntary Aid Detachment. **2** a member of this.

vade-mecum /ˌvɑːdɪ'meɪkəm, ˌveɪdɪ'miːkəm/ n. a handbook etc. carried constantly for use. [F f. mod.L, = go with me]

vagabond /'vægəˌbɒnd/ n., adj., & v. —n. **1** a wanderer or vagrant, esp. an idle one. **2** colloq. a scamp or rascal. —adj. having no fixed habitation; wandering. —v.intr. wander about as a vagabond. □□ **vagabondage** n. [ME f. OF vagabond or L vagabundus f. vagari wander]

vagal see VAGUS.

vagary /'veɪɡərɪ/ n. (pl. **-ies**) a caprice; an eccentric idea or act (the vagaries of Fortune). □□ **vagarious** /və'ɡeərɪəs/ adj. [L vagari wander]

vagi pl. of VAGUS.

vagina /və'dʒaɪnə/ n. (pl. **vaginas** or **vaginae** /-niː/) **1** the canal between the uterus and vulva of a woman or other female mammal. **2** a sheath formed round a stem by the base of a leaf. □□ **vaginal** adj. **vaginitis** /ˌvædʒɪ'naɪtɪs/ n. [L, = sheath, scabbard]

vaginismus /ˌvædʒɪ'nɪzməs/ n. a painful spasmodic contraction of the vagina, usu. in response to pressure. [mod.L (as VAGINA)]

vagrant /'veɪɡrənt/ n. & adj. —n. **1** a person without a settled home or regular work. **2** a wanderer or vagabond. —adj. **1** wandering or roving (a vagrant musician). **2** being a vagrant. □□ **vagrancy** n. **vagrantly** adv. [ME f. AF vag(a)raunt, perh. alt. f. AF wakerant etc. by assoc. with L vagari wander]

vague /veɪɡ/ adj. **1** of uncertain or ill-defined meaning or character (gave a vague answer; has some vague idea of emigrating). **2** (of a person or mind) imprecise; inexact in thought, expression, or understanding. □□ **vaguely** adv. **vagueness** n. **vaguish** adj. [F vague or L vagus wandering, uncertain]

vagus /'veɪɡəs/ n. (pl. **vagi** /-ɡaɪ/) Anat. either of the tenth pair of cranial nerves with branches to the heart, lungs, and viscera. □□ **vagal** adj. [L: see VAGUE]

vail /veɪl/ v. archaic **1** tr. lower or doff (one's plumes, pride, crown, etc.) esp. in token of submission. **2** intr. yield; give place; remove one's hat as a sign of respect etc. [ME f. obs. avale f. OF avaler to lower f. a val down, f. val VALE¹]

vain /veɪn/ adj. **1** excessively proud or conceited, esp. about one's own attributes. **2** empty, trivial, unsubstantial (vain boasts; vain triumphs). **3** useless; followed by no good result (in the vain hope of dissuading them). □**in vain** without result or success (it was in vain that we protested). **take a person's name in vain** use it lightly or profanely. □□ **vainly** adv. **vainness** n. [ME f. OF f. L vanus empty, without substance]

vainglory /veɪn'ɡlɔːrɪ/ n. literary boastfulness; extreme vanity. □□ **vainglorious** adj. **vaingloriously**

---

adv. **vaingloriousness** n. [ME, after OF *vaine gloire*, L *vana gloria*]

vair /veə(r)/ n. **1** archaic or hist. a squirrel-fur widely used for medieval linings and trimmings. **2** *Heraldry* fur represented by small shield-shaped or bell-shaped figures usu. alternately azure and argent. [ME f. OF f. L (as VARIOUS)]

Vaishnava /ˈvaɪʃnaːvaː/ n. *Hinduism* a devotee of Vishnu. [Skr. *vaiṣṇavá*]

Vaisya /ˈvaɪsjə/ n. **1** the third of the four great Hindu castes, comprising the merchants and agriculturalists. **2** a member of this caste. [Skr. *vaiśya* peasant, labourer]

valance /ˈvæləns/ n. (also **valence**) a short curtain round the frame or canopy of a bedstead, above a window, or under a shelf. □□ **valanced** adj. [ME ult. f. OF *avaler* descend: see VAIL]

vale[1] /veɪl/ n. archaic or poet. (except in place-names) a valley (*Vale of the White Horse*). □**vale of tears** literary the world as a scene of life, trouble, etc. [ME f. OF *val* f. L *vallis*, *valles*]

vale[2] /ˈvaːleɪ/ int. & n. —int. farewell. —n. a farewell. [L, impr. of *valēre* be well or strong]

valediction /ˌvælɪˈdɪkʃ(ə)n/ n. **1** the act or an instance of bidding farewell. **2** the words used in this. [L *valedicere valedict-* (as VALE[2],· *dicere* say), after *benediction*]

valedictorian /ˌvælɪdɪkˈtɔːrɪən/ n. US a person who gives a valedictory, esp. the highest-ranking member of a graduating class.

valedictory /ˌvælɪˈdɪktərɪ/ adj. & n. —adj. serving as a farewell. —n. (pl. **-ies**) a farewell address.

valence[1] /ˈveɪləns/ n. Chem. esp. US = VALENCY. □**valence electron** an electron in the outermost shell of an atom involved in forming a chemical bond.

valence[2] var. of VALANCE.

Valenciennes /væˌlɑːnsɪˈen/ n. a rich kind of lace. [*Valenciennes* in NE France, where it was made in the 17th and 18th c.]

valency /ˈveɪlənsɪ/ n. (pl. **-ies**) *Brit. Chem.* the combining power of an atom measured by the number of hydrogen atoms it can displace or combine with. [LL *valentia* power, competence f. *valēre* be well or strong]

valentine /ˈvæləntaɪn/ n. **1** a card or gift sent, often anonymously, as a mark of love or affection on St Valentine's Day (14 Feb.). **2** a sweetheart chosen on this day. [ME f. OF *Valentin* f. L *Valentinus*, name of two saints]

valerian /vəˈlɪərɪən/ n. **1** any of various flowering plants of the family Valerianaceae. **2** the root of any of these used as a medicinal sedative. □**common valerian 1** a valerian, *Valeriana officinalis*, with pink or white flowers and a strong smell liked by cats: also called SETWALL. **2** the root of this used as a medicinal sedative. [ME f. OF *valeriane* f. med.L *valeriana* (*herba*), app. fem. of *Valerianus* of Valerius]

valeric acid /vəˈlerɪk, -ˈlɪərɪk/ n. Chem. = PENTANOIC ACID. [VALERIAN + -IC]

valet /ˈvælɪt, -leɪ/ n. & v. —n. **1** a gentleman's personal attendant who looks after his clothes etc. **2** a hotel etc. employee with similar duties. —v. (**valeted, valeting**) **1** intr. work as a valet. **2** tr. act as a valet to. **3** tr. clean or clean out (a car). [F, = OF *valet*, *vaslet*, VARLET: rel. to VASSAL]

valeta var. of VELETA.

valetudinarian /ˌvælɪˌtjuːdɪˈneərɪən/ n. & adj. —n. a person of poor health or unduly anxious about health. —adj. **1** of or being a valetudinarian. **2** of poor health. **3** seeking to recover one's health. □□ **valetudinarianism** n. [L *valetudinarius* in ill health f. *valetudo -dinis* health f. *valēre* be well]

valetudinary /ˌvælɪˈtjuːdɪnərɪ/ adj. & n. (pl. **-ies**) = VALETUDINARIAN.

valgus /ˈvælgəs/ n. a deformity involving the outward displacement of the foot or hand from the midline. [L, = knock-kneed]

Valhalla /vælˈhælə/ n. **1** (in Norse mythology) a palace in which the souls of slain heroes feasted for eternity. **2** a building used for honouring the illustrious. [mod.L f. ON *Valhöll* f. *valr* the slain + *höll* HALL]

valiant /ˈvæljənt/ adj. (of a person or conduct) brave, courageous. □□ **valiantly** adv. [ME f. AF *valiaunt*, OF *vailant* ult. f. L *valēre* be strong]

valid /ˈvælɪd/ adj. **1** (of a reason, objection, etc.) sound or defensible; well-grounded. **2 a** executed with the proper formalities (*a valid contract*). **b** legally acceptable (*a valid passport*). **c** not having reached its expiry date. □□ **validity** /vəˈlɪdɪtɪ/ n. **validly** adv. [F *valide* or L *validus* strong (as VALIANT)]

validate /ˈvælɪˌdeɪt/ v.tr. make valid; ratify, confirm. □□ **validation** /-ˈdeɪʃ(ə)n/ n. [med.L *validare* f. L (as VALID)]

valine /ˈveɪliːn/ n. Biochem. an amino acid that is an essential nutrient for vertebrates and a general constituent of proteins. [VALERIC (ACID) + -INE[4]]

valise /vəˈliːz/ n. **1** a kitbag. **2** US a small portmanteau. [F f. It. *valigia* corresp. to med.L *valisia*, of unkn. orig.]

Valium /ˈvælɪəm/ n. propr. the drug diazepam used as a tranquillizer and relaxant. [20th c.: orig. uncert.]

Valkyrie /vælˈkɪərɪ, ˈvælkɪrɪ/ n. (in Norse mythology) each of Odin's twelve handmaidens who selected heroes destined to be slain in battle. [ON *Valkyrja*, lit. 'chooser of the slain' f. *valr* the slain + (unrecorded) *kur-*, *kuz-* rel. to CHOOSE]

vallecula /vəˈlekjʊlə/ n. (pl. **valleculae** /-ˌliː/) Anat. & Bot. a groove or furrow. □□ **vallecular** adj. **valleculate** /-ˌleɪt/ adj. [LL, dimin. of L *vallis* valley]

valley /ˈvælɪ/ n. (pl. **-eys**) **1** a low area more or less enclosed by hills and usu. with a stream flowing through it. **2** any depression compared to this. **3** Archit. an internal angle formed by the intersecting planes of a roof. [ME f. AF *valey*, OF *valee* ult. f. L *vallis*, *valles*: cf. VALE[1]]

vallum /ˈvæləm/ n. Rom. Antiq. a rampart and stockade as a defence. [L, collect. f. *vallus* stake]

valonia /vəˈləʊnɪə/ n. acorn-cups of an evergreen oak, *Quercus macrolepsis*, used in tanning, dyeing, and making ink. [It. *vallonia* ult. f. Gk *balanos* acorn]

valor US var. of VALOUR.

valorize /ˈvæləˌraɪz/ v.tr. (also **-ise**) raise or fix the price of (a commodity etc.) by artificial means, esp. by government action. □□ **valorization** /-ˈzeɪʃ(ə)n/ n. [back-form. f. *valorization* f. F *valorisation* (as VALOUR)]

valour /ˈvælə(r)/ n. (US **valor**) personal courage, esp. in battle. □□ **valorous** adj. [ME f. OF f. LL *valor -oris* f. *valēre* be strong]

valse /vaːls, vɔːls/ n. a waltz. [F f. G (as WALTZ)]

valuable /ˈvæljʊəb(ə)l/ adj. & n. —adj. of great value, price, or worth (*a valuable property*; *valuable information*). —n. (usu. in pl.) a valuable thing, esp. a small article of personal property. □□ **valuably** adv.

valuation /ˌvæljʊˈeɪʃ(ə)n/ n. **1 a** an estimation (esp. by a professional valuer) of a thing's worth. **b** the worth estimated. **2** the price set on a thing. □□ **valuate** /ˈvæ-/ v.tr. esp. US.

valuator /ˈvæljʊˌeɪtə(r)/ n. a person who makes valuations; a valuer.

value /ˈvæljuː/ n. & v. —n. **1** the worth, desirability, or utility of a thing, or the qualities on which these depend (*the value of regular exercise*). **2** worth as estimated; valuation (*set a high value on my time*). **3** the amount of money or goods for which a thing can be exchanged in the open market; purchasing power. **4** the equivalent of a thing; what represents or is represented by or may be substituted for a thing (*paid them the value of their lost property*). **5** (in full **value for money**) something well worth the money spent. **6** the ability of a thing to serve a purpose or cause an effect (*news value*; *nuisance value*). **7** (in *pl.*) one's principles or standards; one's judgement of what is valuable or important in life. **8** *Mus.* the duration of the sound signified by a note. **9** *Math.* the amount denoted by an algebraic term or expression. **10** (foll. by *of*) **a** a meaning (of a word etc.). **b** the quality (of a spoken sound). **11** the relative rank or importance of a playing-card, chess-piece, etc., according to the rules of the game. **12** the relation of one part of a picture to others in respect of light and shade; the part being characterized by a particular tone. **13** *Physics & Chem.* the numerical measure of a quantity or a number denoting magnitude on some conventional scale (*the value of gravity at the equator*). —*v.tr.* (**values, valued, valuing**) **1** estimate the value of; appraise (esp. professionally) (*valued the property at £200,000*). **2** have a high or specified opinion of; attach importance to (*a valued friend*). □ **value added tax** a tax on the amount by which the value of an article has been increased at each stage of its production. **value judgement** a subjective estimate of quality etc. **value received** money or its equivalent given for a bill of exchange. [ME f. OF, fem. past part. of *valoir* be worth f. L *valēre*]

valueless /'væljʊlɪs/ *adj.* having no value. □□ **valuelessness** *n.*

valuer /'væljʊə(r)/ *n.* a person who estimates or assesses values, esp. professionally.

valuta /və'lju:tə/ *n.* **1** the value of one currency with respect to another. **2** a currency considered in this way. [It., = VALUE]

valve /vælv/ *n.* **1** a device for controlling the passage of fluid through a pipe etc., esp. an automatic device allowing movement in one direction only. **2** *Anat. & Zool.* a membranous part of an organ etc. allowing a flow of blood etc. in one direction only. **3** *Brit.* = *thermionic valve.* **4** a device to vary the effective length of the tube in a brass musical instrument. **5** each of the two shells of an oyster, mussel, etc. **6** *Bot.* each of the segments into which a capsule or dry fruit dehisces. **7** *archaic* a leaf of a folding door. □□ **valvate** /-veɪt/ *adj.* **valved** *adj.* (also in *comb.*). **valveless** *adj.* **valvule** *n.* [ME f. L *valva* leaf of a folding door]

valvular /'vælvjʊlə(r)/ *adj.* **1** having a valve or valves. **2** having the form or function of a valve. [mod.L *valvula*, dimin. of L *valva*]

valvulitis /ˌvælvjʊ'laɪtɪs/ *n.* inflammation of the valves of the heart.

vambrace /'væmbreɪs/ *n. hist.* defensive armour for the forearm. [ME f. AF *vaunt-bras*, OF *avant-bras* f. *avant* before (see AVAUNT) + *bras* arm]

vamoose /və'mu:s/ *v.intr. US* (esp. as *int.*) *sl.* depart hurriedly. [Sp. *vamos* let us go]

vamp¹ /væmp/ *n. & v.* —*n.* **1** the upper front part of a boot or shoe. **2** a patched-up article. **3** an improvised musical accompaniment. —*v.* **1** *tr.* (often foll. by *up*) repair or furbish. **2** *tr.* (foll. by *up*) make by patching or from odds and ends. **3 a** *tr. & intr.* improvise a musical accompaniment (to). **b** *tr.* improvise (a musical accompaniment). **4** *tr.* put a new vamp to (a boot or shoe). [ME f. OF *avantpié* f. *avant* before (see AVAUNT) + *pied* foot]

vamp² /væmp/ *n. & v. colloq.* —*n.* **1** an unscrupulous flirt. **2** a woman who uses sexual attraction to exploit men. —*v.* **1** *tr.* allure or exploit (a man). **2** *intr.* act as a vamp. [abbr. of VAMPIRE]

vampire /'væmpaɪə(r)/ *n.* **1** a ghost or reanimated corpse supposed to leave its grave at night to suck the blood of persons sleeping. **2** a person who preys ruthlessly on others. **3** (in full **vampire bat**) any tropical (esp. South American) bat of the family Desmodontidae, with incisors for piercing flesh and feeding on blood. **4** *Theatr.* a small spring trapdoor used for sudden disappearances. □□ **vampiric**

/-'pɪrɪk/ *adj.* [F *vampire* or G *Vampir* f. Magyar *vampir* perh. f. Turk. *uber* witch]

vampirism /'væmpaɪəˌrɪz(ə)m/ *n.* **1** belief in the existence of vampires. **2** the practices of a vampire.

vamplate /'væmpleɪt/ *n. hist.* an iron plate on a lance protecting the hand when the lance was couched. [ME f. AF *vauntplate* (as VAMBRACE, PLATE)]

van¹ /væn/ *n.* **1** a covered vehicle for conveying goods etc. **2** *Brit.* a railway carriage for luggage or for the use of the guard. **3** *Brit.* a gypsy caravan. [abbr. of CARAVAN]

van² /væn/ *n.* **1** a vanguard. **2** the forefront (*in the van of progress*). [abbr. of VANGUARD]

van³ /væn/ *n.* **1** the testing of ore quality by washing on a shovel or by machine. **2** *archaic* a winnowing fan. **3** *archaic* or *poet.* a wing. [ME, southern & western var. of FAN¹,· perh. partly f. OF *van* or L *vannus*]

van⁴ /væn/ *n. Brit. Tennis colloq.* = ADVANTAGE. [abbr.]

vanadium /və'neɪdɪəm/ *n. Chem.* a hard grey metallic transition element occurring naturally in several ores and used in small quantities for strengthening some steels. ¶ Symb.: V. □□ **vanadate** /'vænəˌdeɪt/ *n.* **vanadic** /-'nædɪk/ *adj.* **vanadous** /'vænədəs/ *adj.* [mod.L f. ON *Vanadís* name of the Scand. goddess Freyja + -IUM]

Van Allen belt /væn 'ælən/ *n.* (also **Van Allen layer**) each of two regions of intense radiation partly surrounding the earth at heights of several thousand kilometres. [J. A. *Van Allen*, US physicist b. 1914]

V. & A. *abbr.* Victoria & Albert Museum (in London).

vandal /'vænd(ə)l/ *n. & adj.* —*n.* **1** a person who wilfully or maliciously destroys or damages property. **2** (**Vandal**) a member of a Germanic people that ravaged Gaul, Spain, N. Africa, and Rome in the 4th–5th c., destroying many books and works of art. —*adj.* of or relating to the Vandals. □□ **Vandalic** /-'dælɪk/ *adj.* (in sense 2 of *n.*). [L *Vandalus* f. Gmc]

vandalism /'vændəˌlɪz(ə)m/ *n.* wilful or malicious destruction or damage to works of art or other property. □□ **vandalistic** /-'lɪstɪk/ *adj.* **vandalistically** /-'lɪstɪkəlɪ/ *adv.*

vandalize /'vændəˌlaɪz/ *v.tr.* (also **-ise**) destroy or damage wilfully or maliciously.

van de Graaff generator /ˌvæn də 'grɑ:f/ *n. Electr.* a machine devised to generate electrostatic charge by means of a vertical endless belt collecting charge from a voltage source and transferring it to a large insulated metal dome, where a high voltage is produced. [R. J. *van de Graaff*, US physicist d. 1967]

van der Waals forces /ˌvæn də 'wɑ:lz/ *n.pl. Chem.* short-range attractive forces between uncharged molecules arising from the interaction of dipole moments. [J. *van der Waals*, Dutch physicist d. 1923]

vandyke /væn'daɪk/ *n. & adj.* —*n.* **1** each of a series of large points forming a border to lace or cloth etc. **2** a cape or collar etc. with these. —*adj.* (**Vandyke**) in the style of dress, esp. with pointed borders, common in portraits by Van Dyck. □ **Vandyke beard** a neat pointed beard. **Vandyke brown** a deep rich brown. [Sir A. *Van Dyck*, Anglicized *Vandyke*, Flem. painter d. 1641]

vane /veɪn/ *n.* **1** (in full **weather-vane**) a revolving pointer mounted on a church spire or other high place to show the direction of the wind (cf. WEATHERCOCK). **2** a blade of a screw propeller or a windmill etc. **3** the sight of surveying instruments, a quadrant, etc. **4** the flat part of a bird's feather formed by the barbs. □□ **vaned** *adj.* **vaneless** *adj.* [ME, southern & western var. of obs. *fane* f. OE *fana* banner f. Gmc]

vanessa /və'nesə/ *n.* any butterfly of the genus *Vanessa*, including the red admiral and the painted lady. [mod.L]

vang /væŋ/ *n. Naut.* each of two guy-ropes running from the end of a gaff to the deck. [earlier *fang* = gripping-device: OE f. ON *fang* grasp f. Gmc]

vanguard /'vænɡɑ:d/ *n.* **1** the foremost part of an

army or fleet advancing or ready to advance. **2** the leaders of a movement or of opinion etc. [earlier *vandgard*, *(a)vantgard*, f. OF *avan(t)garde* f. *avant* before (see AVAUNT) + *garde* GUARD]

vanilla /vəˈnɪlə/ n. **1 a** any tropical climbing orchid of the genus *Vanilla*, esp. *V. planifolia*, with fragrant flowers. **b** (in full **vanilla-pod**) the fruit of these. **2 a** substance obtained from the vanilla-pod or synthesized and used to flavour ice-cream, chocolate, etc. [Sp. *vainilla* pod, dimin. of *vaina* sheath, pod, f. L VAGINA]

vanillin /vəˈnɪlɪn/ n. the fragrant principle of vanilla.

vanish /ˈvænɪʃ/ v. **1** intr. **a** disappear suddenly. **b** disappear gradually; fade away. **2** intr. cease to exist. **3** intr. Math. become zero. **4** tr. cause to disappear. □**vanishing cream** an ointment that leaves no visible trace when rubbed into the skin. **vanishing-point 1** the point at which receding parallel lines viewed in perspective appear to meet. **2** the state of complete disappearance of something. [ME f. OF *e(s)vaniss-* stem of *e(s)vanir* ult. f. L *evanescere* (as EX-[1], *vanus* empty)]

Vanitory /ˈvænɪtərɪ/ n. (pl. **-ies**) propr. = vanity unit.

vanity /ˈvænɪtɪ/ n. (pl. **-ies**) **1** conceit and desire for admiration of one's personal attainments or attractions. **2 a** futility or unsubstantiality (*the vanity of human achievement*). **b** an unreal thing. **3** ostentatious display. **4** US a dressing-table. □**vanity bag** (or **case**) a bag or case carried by a woman and containing a small mirror, make-up, etc. **Vanity Fair** the world (allegorized in Bunyan's *Pilgrim's Progress*) as a scene of vanity. **vanity unit** a unit consisting of a wash-basin set into a flat top with cupboards beneath. [ME f. OF *vanité* f. L *vanitas -tatis* (as VAIN)]

vanquish /ˈvæŋkwɪʃ/ v.tr. literary conquer or overcome. □□**vanquishable** adj. **vanquisher** n. [ME *venkus*, *-quis*, etc., f. OF *vencus* past part. and *venquis* past tenses of *veintre* f. L *vincere*: assim. to -ISH[2]]

vantage /ˈvɑːntɪdʒ/ n. **1** (also **vantage point** or **ground**) a place affording a good view or prospect. **2** Tennis = ADVANTAGE. **3** archaic an advantage or gain. [ME f. AF f. OF *avantage* ADVANTAGE]

vapid /ˈvæpɪd/ adj. insipid; lacking interest; flat, dull (*vapid moralizing*). □□**vapidity** /vəˈpɪdɪtɪ/ n. **vapidly** adv. **vapidness** n. [L *vapidus*]

vapor US var. of VAPOUR.

vaporific /ˌveɪpəˈrɪfɪk/ adj. concerned with or causing vapour or vaporization.

vaporimeter /ˌveɪpəˈrɪmɪtə(r)/ n. an instrument for measuring the amount of vapour.

vaporize /ˈveɪpəˌraɪz/ v.tr. & intr. (also **-ise**) convert or be converted into vapour. □□**vaporizable** adj. (also **vaporable**). **vaporization** /-ˈzeɪʃ(ə)n/ n.

vaporizer /ˈveɪpəˌraɪz(ə)r/ n. a device that vaporizes substances, esp. for medicinal inhalation.

vapour /ˈveɪpə(r)/ n. & v. (US **vapor**) —n. **1** moisture or another substance diffused or suspended in air, e.g. mist or smoke. **2** Physics a gaseous form of a normally liquid or solid substance (cf. GAS). **3** a medicinal agent for inhaling. **4** (in pl.) archaic a state of depression or melancholy thought to be caused by exhalations of vapour from the stomach. —v.intr. **1** rise as vapour. **2** make idle boasts or empty talk. □**vapour density** the density of a gas or vapour relative to hydrogen etc. **vapour pressure** the pressure of a vapour in contact with its liquid or solid form. **vapour trail** a trail of condensed water from an aircraft or rocket at high altitude, seen as a white streak against the sky. □□**vaporous** adj. **vaporously** adv. **vaporousness** n. **vapourer** n. **vapouring** n. **vapourish** adj. **vapoury** adj. [ME f. OF *vapour* or L *vapor* steam, heat]

var. abbr. **1** variant. **2** variety.

varactor /vəˈræktə(r)/ n. a semiconductor diode with

a capacitance dependent on the applied voltage. [*varying* re*actor*]

varec /ˈværek/ n. **1** seaweed. **2** = KELP. [F *varec(h)* f. ON: rel. to WRECK]

variable /ˈveərɪəb(ə)l/ adj. & n. —adj. **1 a** that can be varied or adapted (*a rod of variable length*; *the pressure is variable*). **b** (of a gear) designed to give varying speeds. **2** apt to vary; not constant; unsteady (*a variable mood*; *variable fortunes*). **3** Math. (of a quantity) indeterminate; able to assume different numerical values. **4** (of wind or currents) tending to change direction. **5** Astron. (of a star) periodically varying in brightness. **6** Bot. & Zool. (of a species) including individuals or groups that depart from the type. **7** Biol. (of an organism or part of it) tending to change in structure or function. —n. **1** a variable thing or quantity. **2** Math. a variable quantity. **3** Naut. a shifting wind. **b** (in pl.) the region between the NE and SE trade winds. □□**variability** /-ˈbɪlɪtɪ/ n. **variableness** n. **variably** adv. [ME f. OF f. L *variabilis* (as VARY)]

variance /ˈveərɪəns/ n. **1** difference of opinion; dispute, disagreement; lack of harmony (*at variance among ourselves*; *a theory at variance with all known facts*). **2** Law a discrepancy between statements or documents. **3** Statistics a quantity equal to the square of the standard deviation. [ME f. OF f. L *variantia* difference (as VARY)]

variant /ˈveərɪənt/ adj. & n. —adj. **1** differing in form or details from the main one (*a variant spelling*). **2** having different forms (*forty variant types of pigeon*). **3** variable or changing. —n. a variant form, spelling, type, reading, etc. [ME f. OF (as VARY)]

variate /ˈveərɪət/ n. Statistics **1** a quantity having a numerical value for each member of a group. **2** a variable quantity, esp. one whose values occur according to a frequency distribution. [past part. of L *variare* (as VARY)]

variation /ˌveərɪˈeɪʃ(ə)n/ n. **1** the act or an instance of varying. **2** departure from a former or normal condition, action, or amount, or from a standard or type (*prices are subject to variation*). **3** the extent of this. **4** a thing that varies from a type. **5** Mus. a repetition (usu. one of several) of a theme in a changed or elaborated form. **6** Astron. a deviation of a heavenly body from its mean orbit or motion. **7** Math. a change in a function etc. due to small changes in the values of constants etc. **8** Ballet a solo dance. □□**variational** adj. [ME f. OF *variation* or L *variatio* (as VARY)]

varicella /ˌværɪˈselə/ n. Med. = CHICKENPOX. [mod.L, irreg. dimin. of VARIOLA]

varices pl. of VARIX.

varicocele /ˈværɪkəˌsiːl/ n. a mass of varicose veins in the spermatic cord. [formed as VARIX + -CELE]

varicoloured /ˈveərɪˌkʌləd/ adj. (US **varicolored**) **1** variegated in colour. **2** of various or different colours. [L *varius* VARIOUS + COLOURED]

varicose /ˈværɪˌkəʊs/ adj. (esp. of the veins of the legs) affected by a condition causing them to become dilated and swollen. □□**varicosity** /-ˈkɒsɪtɪ/ n. [L *varicosus* f. VARIX]

varied /ˈveərɪd/ adj. showing variety; diverse. □□**variedly** adv.

variegate /ˈveərɪˌɡeɪt, -rɪəˌɡeɪt/ v.tr. **1** mark with irregular patches of different colours. **2** diversify in appearance, esp. in colour. **3** (as **variegated** adj.) Bot. (of plants) having leaves containing two or more colours. □□**variegation** /-ˈɡeɪʃ(ə)n/ n. [L *variegare variegat-* f. *varius* various]

varietal /vəˈraɪət(ə)l/ adj. **1** esp. Bot. & Zool. of, forming, or designating a variety. **2** (of wine) made from a single designated variety of grape. □□**varietally** adv.

varietist /vəˈraɪətɪst/ n. a person whose habits etc. differ from what is normal.

variety /vəˈraɪətɪ/ n. (pl. **-ies**) **1** diversity; absence of uniformity; many-sidedness; the condition of being various (*not enough variety in our lives*). **2** a quantity or collection of different things (*for a variety of reasons*). **3 a** a class of things different in some common qualities from the rest of a larger class to which they belong. **b** a specimen or member of such a class. **4** (foll. by *of*) a different form of a thing, quality, etc. **5** *Biol.* **a** a subspecies. **b** a cultivar. **c** an individual or group usually fertile within the species to which it belongs but differing from the species type in some qualities capable of perpetuation. **6** a mixed sequence of dances, songs, comedy acts, etc. (usu. *attrib.*: *a variety show*). □**variety store** *US* a shop selling many kinds of small items. [F *variété* or L *varietas* (as VARIOUS)]

varifocal /ˌveərɪˈfəʊk(ə)l/ *adj. & n.* —*adj.* having a focal length that can be varied, esp. of a lens that allows an infinite number of focusing distances for near, intermediate, and far vision. —*n.* (in *pl.*) varifocal spectacles.

variform /ˈveərɪfɔːm/ *adj.* having various forms. [L *varius* + -FORM]

variola /vəˈraɪələ/ *n. Med.* smallpox. □□**variolar** *adj.* **varioloid** /ˈveərɪəlɔɪd/ *adj.* **variolous** *adj.* [med.L, = pustule, pock (as VARIOUS)]

variole /ˈveərɪəʊl/ *n.* **1** a shallow pit like a smallpox mark. **2** a small spherical mass in variolite. [med.L *variola*: see VARIOLA]

variolite /ˈveərɪəlaɪt/ *n.* a rock with embedded small spherical masses causing on its surface an appearance like smallpox pustules. □□**variolitic** /-ˈlɪtɪk/ *adj.* [as VARIOLE + -ITE¹]

variometer /ˌveərɪˈɒmɪtə(r)/ *n.* **1** a device for varying the inductance in an electric circuit. **2** a device for indicating an aircraft's rate of change of altitude. [as VARIOUS + -METER]

variorum /ˌveərɪˈɔːrəm/ *adj. & n.* —*adj.* **1** (of an edition of a text) having notes by various editors or commentators. **2** (of an edition of an author's works) including variant readings. —*n.* a variorum edition. [L f. *editio cum notis variorum* edition with notes by various (commentators): genit. pl. of *varius* VARIOUS]

various /ˈveərɪəs/ *adj.* **1** different, diverse (*too various to form a group*). **2** more than one, several (*for various reasons*). □□**variously** *adv.* **variousness** *n.* [L *varius* changing, diverse]

varistor /vəˈrɪstə(r)/ *n.* a semiconductor diode with resistance dependent on the applied voltage. [*var*ying *resistor*]

varix /ˈveərɪks/ *n.* (*pl.* **varices** /ˈværɪˌsiːz/) **1** *Med.* **a** a permanent abnormal dilation of a vein or artery. **b** a vein etc. dilated in this way. **2** each of the ridges across the whorls of a univalve shell. [ME f. L *varix* -*icis*]

varlet /ˈvɑːlɪt/ *n. archaic* or *joc.* **1** a menial or rascal. **2** *hist.* a knight's attendant. □□**varletry** *n.* [ME f. OF, var. of *vaslet*: see VALET]

varmint /ˈvɑːmɪnt/ *n. US* or *dial.* a mischievous or discreditable person or animal, esp. a fox. [var. of *varmin*, VERMIN]

varna /ˈvɑːnə/ *n.* each of the four Hindu castes. [Skr., = colour, class]

varnish /ˈvɑːnɪʃ/ *n. & v.* —*n.* **1** a resinous solution used to give a hard shiny transparent coating to wood, metal, paintings, etc. **2** any other preparation for a similar purpose (*nail varnish*). **3** external appearance or display without an underlying reality. **4** artificial or natural glossiness. **5** a superficial polish of manner. —*v.tr.* **1** apply varnish to. **2** gloss over (a fact). □□**varnisher** *n.* [ME f. OF *vernis* f. med.L *veronix* fragrant resin, sandarac or med.Gk *berenikē* prob. f. *Berenice* in Cyrenaica]

varsity /ˈvɑːsɪtɪ/ *n.* (*pl.* -**ies**) **1** *Brit. colloq.* (esp. with ref. to sports) university. **2** *US* a university etc. first team in a sport. [abbr.]

varus /ˈveərəs/ *n.* a deformity involving the inward displacement of the foot or hand from the midline. [L, = bent, crooked]

varve /vɑːv/ *n.* annually deposited layers of clay and silt in a lake used to determine the chronology of glacial sediments. □□**varved** *adj.* [Sw. *varv* layer]

vary /ˈveərɪ/ *v.* (-**ies**, -**ied**) **1** *tr.* make different; modify, diversify (*seldom varies the routine*; *the style is not sufficiently varied*). **2** *intr.* **a** undergo change; become or be different (*the temperature varies from 30° to 70°*). **b** be of different kinds (*his mood varies*). **3** *intr.* (foll. by *as*) be in proportion to. □□**varyingly** *adv.* [ME f. OF *varier* or L *variare* (as VARIOUS)]

vas /væs/ *n.* (*pl.* **vasa** /ˈveɪsə/) *Anat.* a vessel or duct. □**vas deferens** /ˈdefəˌrenz/ (*pl.* **vasa deferentia** /ˌdefəˈrenʃɪə/) *Anat.* the spermatic duct from the testicle to the urethra. □□**vasal** /ˈveɪs(ə)l/ *adj.* [L, = vessel]

vascular /ˈvæskjʊlə(r)/ *adj.* of, made up of, or containing vessels for conveying blood or sap etc. (*vascular functions*; *vascular tissue*). □**vascular plant** a plant with conducting tissue. □□**vascularity** /-ˈlærɪtɪ/ *n.* **vascularize** *v.tr.* (also -**ise**). **vascularly** *adv.* [mod.L *vascularis* f. L VASCULUM]

vasculum /ˈvæskjʊləm/ *n.* (*pl.* **vascula** /-lə/) a botanist's (usu. metal) collecting-case with a lengthwise opening. [L, dimin. of VAS]

vase /vɑːz/ *n.* a vessel, usu. tall and circular, used as an ornament or container, esp. for flowers. □□**vaseful** *n.* (*pl.* -**fuls**). [F f. L VAS]

vasectomy /vəˈsektəmɪ/ *n.* (*pl.* -**ies**) the surgical removal of part of each vas deferens esp. as a means of sterilization. □□**vasectomize** *v.tr.* (also -**ise**).

Vaseline /ˈvæsɪˌliːn/ *n. & v.* —*n. propr.* a type of petroleum jelly used as an ointment, lubricant, etc. —*v.tr.* (**vaseline**) treat with Vaseline. [irreg. f. G *Wasser* + Gk *elaion* oil]

vasiform /ˈveɪzɪˌfɔːm/ *adj.* **1** duct-shaped. **2** vase-shaped. [L *vasi*- f. VAS + -FORM]

vaso- /ˈveɪzəʊ/ *comb. form* a vessel, esp. a blood-vessel (*vasoconstrictive*). [L *vas*: see VAS]

vasoactive /ˌveɪzəʊˈæktɪv/ *adj.* = VASOMOTOR.

vasoconstrictive /ˌveɪzəʊkənˈstrɪktɪv/ *adj.* causing constriction of blood-vessels.

vasodilating /ˌveɪzəʊdaɪˈleɪtɪŋ/ *adj.* causing dilatation of blood-vessels. □□**vasodilation** *n.*

vasomotor /ˈveɪzəʊˌməʊtə(r)/ *adj.* causing constriction or dilatation of blood-vessels.

vasopressin /ˌveɪzəʊˈpresɪn/ *n.* a pituitary hormone acting to reduce diuresis and increase blood pressure. Also called ANTIDIURETIC HORMONE.

vassal /ˈvæs(ə)l/ *n.* **1** *hist.* a holder of land by feudal tenure on conditions of homage and allegiance. **2** *rhet.* a humble dependant. □□**vassalage** *n.* [ME f. OF f. med.L *vassallus* retainer, of Celt. orig.: the root *vassus* corresp. to OBret. *uuas*, Welsh *gwas*, Ir. *foss*: cf. VAVASOUR]

vast /vɑːst/ *adj. & n.* —*adj.* **1** immense, huge; very great (*a vast expanse of water*; *a vast crowd*). **2** *colloq.* great, considerable (*makes a vast difference*). —*n. poet.* or *rhet.* a vast space (*the vast of heaven*). □□**vastly** *adv.* **vastness** *n.* [L *vastus* void, immense]

VAT /ˌviːeɪˈtiː, væt/ *abbr.* (in the UK) value added tax.

vat /væt/ *n. & v.* —*n.* **1** a large tank or other vessel, esp. for holding liquids or something in liquid in the process of brewing, tanning, dyeing, etc. **2** a dyeing liquor in which a textile is soaked to take up a colourless soluble dye afterwards coloured by oxidation in air. —*v.tr.* (**vatted**, **vatting**) place or treat in a vat. □□**vatful** *n.* (*pl.* -**fuls**). [ME, southern & western var. of *fat*, OE *fæt* f. Gmc]

vatic /ˈvætɪk/ *adj. formal* prophetic or inspired. [L *vates* prophet]

Vatican /ˈvætɪkən/ *n.* **1** the palace and official residence of the Pope in Rome. **2** papal government. □**Vatican City** an independent Papal State in Rome, instituted in 1929. **Vatican Council** an ecumenical council of the Roman Catholic Church, esp. that held in 1869–70 or that held in 1962–5. □□**Vaticanism** *n.* **Vaticanist** *n.* [F *Vatican* or L *Vaticanus* name of a hill in Rome]

vaticinate /væˈtɪsɪˌneɪt/ *v.tr.* & *intr. formal*

prophesy. □□ **vaticinal** *adj.* **vaticination** /-'neɪʃ(ə)n/ *n.* **vaticinator** *n.* [L *vaticinari* f. *vates* prophet]

VATman /'vætmæn/ *n.* (*pl.* **-men**) *colloq.* a customs and excise officer who administers VAT.

vaudeville /'vɔːdəvɪl, 'vəʊ-/ *n.* **1** esp. *US* variety entertainment. **2** a stage play on a trivial theme with interspersed songs. **3** a satirical or topical song with a refrain. □□ **vaudevillian** /-'vɪlɪən/ *adj.* & *n.* [F, orig. of convivial song esp. any of those composed by O. Basselin, 15th-c. poet born at *Vau de Vire* in Normandy]

Vaudois[1] /'vəʊdwɑː/ *n.* & *adj.* —*n.* (*pl.* same) **1** a native of Vaud in W. Switzerland. **2** the French dialect spoken in Vaud. —*adj.* of or relating to Vaud or its dialect. [F]

Vaudois[2] /'vəʊdwɑː/ *n.* & *adj.* —*n.* (*pl.* same) a member of the Waldenses. —*adj.* of or relating to the Waldenses. [F, repr. med.L *Valdensis*: see WALDENSES]

vault /vɔːlt, vɒlt/ *n.* & *v.* —*n.* **1 a** an arched roof. **b** a continuous arch. **c** a set or series of arches whose joints radiate from a central point or line. **2** a vaultlike covering (*the vault of heaven*). **3** an underground chamber: **a** as a place of storage (*bank vaults*). **b** as a place of interment beneath a church or in a cemetery etc. (*family vault*). **4** an act of vaulting. **5** *Anat.* the arched roof of a cavity. —*v.* *intr.* leap or spring, esp. while resting on one or both hands or with the help of a pole. **2** *tr.* spring over (a gate etc.) in this way. **3** *tr.* (esp. as **vaulted**) **a** make in the form of a vault. **b** provide with a vault or vaults. □□ **vaulter** *n.* [OF *voute, vaute,* ult. f. L *volvere* roll]

vaulting /'vɔːltɪŋ, 'vɒltɪŋ/ *n.* **1** arched work in a vaulted roof or ceiling. **2** a gymnastic or athletic exercise in which participants vault over obstacles. □ **vaulting-horse** a wooden block to be vaulted over by gymnasts.

vaunt /vɔːnt/ *v.* & *n.* *literary* —*v.* **1** *intr.* boast, brag. **2** *tr.* boast of; extol boastfully. —*n.* a boast. □□ **vaunter** *n.* **vauntingly** *adv.* [ME f. AF *vaunter,* OF *vanter* f. LL *vantare* f. L *vanus* VAIN: partly obs. *avaunt* (v.) f. *avanter* f. *a-* intensive + *vanter*]

vavasory /'vævəsərɪ/ *n.* (*pl.* **-ies**) *hist.* the estate of a vavasour. [OF *vavasorie* or med.L *vavasoria* (as VAVASOUR)]

vavasour /'vævəˌsʊə(r)/ *n.* *hist.* a vassal owing allegiance to a great lord and having other vassals under him. [ME f. OF *vavas(s)our* f. med.L *vavassor,* perh. f. *vassus vassorum* VASSAL of vassals]

VC *abbr.* **1** Victoria Cross. **2** Vice-Chairman. **3** Vice-Chancellor. **4** Vice-Consul.

VCR *abbr.* video cassette recorder.

VD *abbr.* venereal disease.

VDU *abbr.* visual display unit.

VE *abbr.* Victory in Europe (in 1945). □ **VE day** 8 May, the day marking this.

've *abbr.* (chiefly after pronouns) = HAVE (*I've; they've*).

veal /viːl/ *n.* calf's flesh as food. □□ **vealy** *adj.* [ME f. AF *ve(e)l,* OF *veiaus veel* f. L *vitellus* dimin. of *vitulus* calf]

vector /'vektə(r)/ *n.* & *v.* —*n.* **1** *Math.* & *Physics* a quantity having direction as well as magnitude, esp. as determining the position of one point in space relative to another (*radius vector*). **2** a carrier of disease. **3** a course to be taken by an aircraft. —*v.tr.* direct (an aircraft in flight) to a desired point. □□ **vectorial** /-'tɔːrɪəl/ *adj.* **vectorize** *v.tr.* (also **-ise**) (in sense 1 of *n.*). **vectorization** /-təraɪ'zeɪʃ(ə)n/ *n.* [L, = carrier, f. *vehere vect-* convey]

Veda /'veɪdə, 'viː-/ *n.* (in *sing.* or *pl.*) the most ancient Hindu scriptures, esp. four collections called Rig-Veda, Sāma-Veda, Yajur-Veda, and Atharva-Veda. [Skr. *vēda,* lit. (sacred) knowledge]

Vedanta /vɪ'dæntə, ve'dɑː-/ *n.* **1** the Upanishads. **2** the Hindu philosophy based on these, esp. in its monistic form. □□ **Vedantic** *adj.* **Vedantist** *n.* [Skr. *vedānta* (as VEDA, *anta* end)]

Vedda /'vedə/ *n.* a Sri Lankan aboriginal. [Sinh. *veddā* hunter]

vedette /vɪ'det/ *n.* a mounted sentry positioned beyond an army's outposts to observe the movements of the enemy. [F, = scout, f. It. *vedetta, veletta* f. Sp. *vela(r)* watch f. L *vigilare*]

Vedic /'veɪdɪk, 'viː-/ *adj.* & *n.* —*adj.* of or relating to the Veda or Vedas. —*n.* the language of the Vedas, an older form of Sanskrit. [F *Védique* or G *Vedisch* (as VEDA)]

vee /viː/ *n.* **1** the letter V. **2** a thing shaped like a V. [name of the letter]

veer[1] /vɪə(r)/ *v.* & *n.* —*v.intr.* **1** change direction, esp. (of the wind) clockwise (cf. BACK *v.* 5). **2** change in course, opinion, conduct, emotions, etc. **3** *Naut.* = WEAR[2]. —*n.* a change of course or direction. [F *virer* f. Rmc, perh. alt. f. L *gyrare* GYRATE]

veer[2] /vɪə(r)/ *v.tr.* *Naut.* slacken or let out (a rope, cable, etc.). [ME f. MDu. *vieren*]

veg /vedʒ/ *n.* *colloq.* a vegetable or vegetables. [abbr.]

Vega /'viːgə/ *n.* *Astron.* a brilliant blue star in the constellation of the Lyre. [Sp. or med.L *Vega* f. Arab., = the falling vulture]

vegan /'viːgən/ *n.* & *adj.* —*n.* a person who does not eat or use animal products. —*adj.* using or containing no animal products. [contr. of VEGETARIAN]

vegetable /'vedʒɪtəb(ə)l, 'vedʒtəb(ə)l/ *n.* & *adj.* —*n.* **1** *Bot.* any of various plants, esp. a herbaceous plant used wholly or partly for food, e.g. a cabbage, potato, turnip, or bean. **2** *colloq.* **a** a person who is incapable of normal intellectual activity, esp. through brain injury etc. **b** a person lacking in animation or living a monotonous life. —*adj.* **1** of, derived from, relating to, or comprising plants or plant life, esp. as distinct from animal life or mineral substances. **2** of or relating to vegetables as food. **3 a** unresponsive to stimulus (*vegetable behaviour*). **b** uneventful, monotonous (*a vegetable existence*). □ **vegetable butter** a vegetable fat with the consistency of butter. **vegetable ivory** see IVORY. **vegetable marrow** see MARROW 1. **vegetable oyster** = SALSIFY. **vegetable parchment** see PARCHMENT 2. **vegetable spaghetti 1** a variety of marrow with flesh resembling spaghetti. **2** its flesh. **vegetable sponge** = LOOFAH. **vegetable tallow** see TALLOW. **vegetable wax** an exudation of certain plants such as sumac. [ME f. OF *vegetable* or LL *vegetabilis* animating (as VEGETATE)]

vegetal /'vedʒɪt(ə)l/ *adj.* **1** of or having the nature of plants (*vegetal growth*). **2** vegetative. [med.L *vegetalis* f. L *vegetare* animate]

vegetarian /ˌvedʒɪ'teərɪən/ *n.* & *adj.* —*n.* a person who abstains from animal food, esp. that from slaughtered animals, though often not eggs and dairy products. —*adj.* excluding animal food, esp. meat (*a vegetarian diet*). □□ **vegetarianism** *n.* [irreg. f. VEGETABLE + -ARIAN]

vegetate /'vedʒɪˌteɪt/ *v.intr.* **1** live an uneventful or monotonous life. **2** grow as plants do; fulfil vegetal functions. [L *vegetare* animate f. *vegetus* f. *vegēre* be active]

vegetation /ˌvedʒɪ'teɪʃ(ə)n/ *n.* **1** plants collectively; plant life (*luxuriant vegetation; no sign of vegetation*). **2** the process of vegetating. □□ **vegetational** *adj.* [med.L *vegetatio* growth (as VEGETATE)]

vegetative /'vedʒɪtətɪv/ *adj.* **1** concerned with growth and development as distinct from sexual reproduction. **2** of or relating to vegetation or plant life. □□ **vegetatively** *adv.* **vegetativeness** *n.* [ME f. OF *vegetatif -ive* or med.L *vegetativus* (as VEGETATE)]

vegie /'vedʒɪ/ *n.* (also **veggie**) *colloq.* a vegetarian. [abbr.]

vehement /'viːəmənt/ *adj.* showing or caused by strong feeling; forceful, ardent (*a vehement protest; vehement desire*). □□ **vehemence** *n.* **vehemently** *adv.* [ME f. F *véhément* or L *vehemens -entis,* perh. f.

vemens (unrecorded) deprived of mind, assoc. with *vehere* carry]

vehicle /'viːɪk(ə)l, 'vɪək(ə)l/ *n.* **1** any conveyance for transporting people, goods, etc., esp. on land. **2** a medium for thought, feeling, or action (*the stage is the best vehicle for their talents*). **3** a liquid etc. as a medium for suspending pigments, drugs, etc. **4** the literal meaning of a word or words used metaphorically (opp. TENOR 6). □□ **vehicular** /vɪ'hɪkjʊlə(r)/ *adj.* [F *véhicule* or L *vehiculum* f. *vehere* carry]

veil /veɪl/ *n. & v.* —*n.* **1** a piece of usu. more or less transparent fabric attached to a woman's hat etc., esp. to conceal the face or protect against the sun, dust, etc. **2** a piece of linen etc. as part of a nun's head-dress, resting on the head and shoulders. **3** a curtain, esp. that separating the sanctuary in the Jewish Temple. **4** a disguise; a pretext; a thing that conceals (*under the veil of friendship; a veil of mist*). **5** *Photog.* slight fogging. **6** huskiness of the voice. **7** = VELUM. —*v.tr.* **1** cover with a veil. **2** (esp. as **veiled** *adj.*) partly conceal (*veiled threats*). □ **beyond the veil** in the unknown state of life after death. **draw a veil over** avoid discussing or calling attention to. **take the veil** become a nun. □□ **veilless** *adj.* [ME f. AF *veil(e)*, OF *voil(e)* f. L *vela* pl. of VELUM]

veiling /'veɪlɪŋ/ *n.* light fabric used for veils etc.

vein /veɪn/ *n. & v.* —*n.* **1 a** any of the tubes by which blood is conveyed to the heart (cf. ARTERY). **b** (in general use) any blood-vessel (*has royal blood in his veins*). **2** a nervure of an insect's wing. **3** a slender bundle of tissue forming a rib in the framework of a leaf. **4** a streak or stripe of a different colour in wood, marble, cheese, etc. **5** a fissure in rock filled with ore or other deposited material. **6** a source of a particular characteristic (*a rich vein of humour*). **7** a distinctive character or tendency; a cast of mind or disposition; a mood (*spoke in a sarcastic vein*). —*v.tr.* fill or cover with or as with veins. □□ **veinless** *n.* **veinlet** *n.* **veinlike** *adj.* **veiny** *adj.* (**veinier**, **veiniest**). [ME f. OF *veine* f. L *vena*]

veining /'veɪnɪŋ/ *n.* a pattern of streaks or veins.

veinstone /'veɪnstəʊn/ *n.* = GANGUE.

vela *pl.* of VELUM.

velamen /vɪ'leɪmən/ *n.* (*pl.* **velamina** /-mɪnə/) an enveloping membrane esp. of an aerial root of an orchid. [L f. *velare* cover]

velar /'viːlə(r)/ *adj.* **1** of a veil or velum. **2** *Phonet.* (of a sound) pronounced with the back of the tongue near the soft palate. [L *velaris* f. *velum*: see VELUM]

Velcro /'velkrəʊ/ *n. propr.* a fastener for clothes etc. consisting of two strips of nylon fabric, one looped and one burred, which adhere when pressed together. □□ **Velcroed** *adj.* [F *velours croché* hooked velvet]

veld /velt/ *n.* (also **veldt**) *S.Afr.* open country; grassland. [Afrik. f. Du., = FIELD]

veldskoen /'feltskuːn, 'fels-/ *n.* a strong suede or leather shoe or boot. [Afrik., = field-shoe]

veleta /və'liːtə/ *n.* (also **valeta**) a ballroom dance in triple time. [Sp., = weather-vane]

velitation /,velɪ'teɪʃ(ə)n/ *n. archaic* a slight skirmish or controversy. [L *velitatio* f. *velitari* skirmish f. *veles velitis* light-armed skirmisher]

velleity /ve'liːɪtɪ/ *n. literary* **1** a low degree of volition not conducive to action. **2** a slight wish or inclination. [med.L *velleitas* f. L *velle* to wish]

vellum /'veləm/ *n.* **1 a** fine parchment orig. from the skin of a calf. **b** a manuscript written on this. **2** smooth writing-paper imitating vellum. [ME f. OF *velin* (as VEAL)]

velocimeter /,velə'sɪmɪtə(r)/ *n.* an instrument for measuring velocity.

velocipede /vɪ'lɒsɪˌpiːd/ *n.* **1** *hist.* an early form of bicycle propelled by pressure from the rider's feet on the ground. **2** *US* a child's tricycle. □□ **velocipedist** *n.* [F *vélocipède* f. L *velox -ocis* swift + *pes pedis* foot]

velocity /vɪ'lɒsɪtɪ/ *n.* (*pl.* **-ies**) **1** the measure of the rate of movement of a usu. inanimate object in a given direction. **2** speed in a given direction. **3** (in general use) speed. □ **velocity of escape** = *escape velocity*. [F *vélocité* or L *velocitas* f. *velox -ocis* swift]

velodrome /'velə,drəʊm/ *n.* a special place or building with a track for cycle-racing. [F *vélodrome* f. *vélo* bicycle (as VELOCITY, -DROME)]

velour /və'lʊə(r)/ *n.* (also **velours**) **1** a plushlike woven fabric or felt. **2** *archaic* a hat of this felt. [F *velours* velvet f. OF *velour, velous* f. L *villosus* hairy f. *villus*: see VELVET]

velouté /və'luːteɪ/ *n.* a sauce made from a roux of butter and flour with white stock. [F, = velvety]

velum /'viːləm/ *n.* (*pl.* **vela** /-lə/) a membrane, membranous covering, or flap. [L, = sail, curtain, covering, veil]

velutinous /vɪ'luːtɪnəs/ *adj.* covered with soft fine hairs. [perh. f. It. *vellutino* f. *velluto* VELVET]

velvet /'velvɪt/ *n. & adj.* —*n.* **1** a closely woven fabric of silk, cotton, etc., with a thick short pile on one side. **2** the furry skin on a deer's growing antler. **3** anything smooth and soft like velvet. —*adj.* of, like, or soft as velvet. □ **on velvet** in an advantageous or prosperous position. **velvet glove** outward gentleness, esp. cloaking firmness or strength (cf. *iron hand*). □□ **velveted** *adj.* **velvety** *adj.* [ME f. OF *veluotte* f. *velu* velvety f. med.L *villutus* f. L *villus* tuft, down]

velveteen /,velvɪ'tiːn/ *n.* **1** a cotton fabric with a pile like velvet. **2** (in *pl.*) trousers etc. made of this.

Ven. *abbr.* Venerable (as the title of an archdeacon).

vena cava /,viːnə 'keɪvə/ *n.* (*pl.* **venae cavae** /-niː -viː/) each of usu. two veins carrying blood into the heart. [L, = hollow vein]

venal /'viːn(ə)l/ *adj.* **1** (of a person) able to be bribed or corrupted. **2** (of conduct etc.) characteristic of a venal person. □□ **venality** /-'nælɪtɪ/ *n.* **venally** *adv.* [L *venalis* f. *venum* thing for sale]

venation /vɪ'neɪʃ(ə)n/ *n.* the arrangement of veins in a leaf or an insect's wing etc., or the system of venous blood vessels in an organism. □□ **venational** *adj.* [L *vena* vein]

vend /vend/ *v.tr.* **1** offer (small wares) for sale. **2** *Law* sell. □ **vending-machine** a machine that dispenses small articles for sale when a coin or token is inserted. □□ **vender** *n.* (usu. in *comb.*). **vendible** *adj.* [F *vendre* or L *vendere* sell (as VENAL, *dare* give)]

vendace /'vendeɪs/ *n.* a small delicate fish, *Coregonus albula*, found in some British lakes. [OF *vendese, -oise* f. Gaulish]

vendee /ven'diː/ *n. Law* the buying party in a sale, esp. of property.

vendetta /ven'detə/ *n.* **1 a** a blood feud in which the family of a murdered person seeks vengeance on the murderer or the murderer's family. **b** this practice as prevalent in Corsica and Sicily. **2** a prolonged bitter quarrel. [It. f. L *vindicta*: see VINDICTIVE]

vendeuse /vɑ̃'dɜːz/ *n.* a saleswoman, esp. in a fashionable dress-shop. [F]

vendor /'vendə(r), -dɔː(r)/ *n.* **1** *Law* the seller in a sale, esp. of property. **2** = *vending-machine* (see VEND). [AF *vendour* (as VEND)]

vendue /ven'djuː/ *n. US* a public auction. [Du. *vendu(e)* f. F *vendue* sale f. *vendre* VEND]

veneer /vɪ'nɪə(r)/ *n. & v.* —*n.* **1 a** a thin covering of fine wood or other surface material applied to a coarser wood. **b** a layer in plywood. **2** (often foll. by *of*) a deceptive outward appearance of a good quality etc. —*v.tr.* **1** apply a veneer to (wood, furniture, etc.). **2** disguise (an unattractive character etc.) with a more attractive manner etc. [earlier *fineer* f. G *furni(e)ren* f. OF *fournir* FURNISH]

veneering /vɪ'nɪərɪŋ/ *n.* material used as veneer.

venepuncture /'viːnɪ,pʌŋktʃə(r)/ *n.* (also **venipuncture**) *Med.* the puncture of a vein esp. with a hypodermic needle to withdraw blood or for an intravenous injection. [L *vena* vein + PUNCTURE]

venerable /'venərəb(ə)l/ *adj.* **1** entitled to veneration on account of character, age, associations, etc. (*a venerable priest; venerable relics*). **2** as the title of an archdeacon in the Church of England. **3** *RC Ch.* as the title of a deceased person who has attained a certain degree of sanctity but has not been fully beatified or canonized. □□ **venerability** /-'bɪlɪtɪ/ *n*. **venerableness** *n*. **venerably** *adv*. [ME f. OF *venerable* or L *venerabilis* (as VENERATE)]

venerate /'venəˌreɪt/ *v.tr.* **1** regard with deep respect. **2** revere on account of sanctity etc. □□ **veneration** /-'reɪʃ(ə)n/ *n*. **venerator** *n*. [L *venerari* adore, revere]

venereal /vɪ'nɪərɪəl/ *adj.* **1** of or relating to sexual desire or intercourse. **2** relating to venereal disease. □ **venereal disease** any of various diseases contracted chiefly by sexual intercourse with a person already infected. □□ **venereally** *adv*. [ME f. L *venereus* f. *venus veneris* sexual love]

venereology /vɪˌnɪərɪ'ɒlədʒɪ/ *n*. the scientific study of venereal diseases. □□ **venereological** /-ə'lɒdʒ ɪk(ə)l/ *adj*. **venereologist** *n*.

venery[1] /'venərɪ/ *n*. archaic sexual indulgence. [med.L *veneria* (as VENEREAL)]

venery[2] /'venərɪ/ *n*. archaic hunting. [ME f. OF *venerie* f. *vener* to hunt ult. f. L *venari*]

venesection /'viːnɪˌsekʃ(ə)n/ *n*. (also **venisection**) phlebotomy. [med.L *venae sectio* cutting of a vein (as VEIN, SECTION)]

Venetian /vɪ'niːʃ(ə)n/ *n. & adj.* —*n.* **1** a native or citizen of Venice in NE Italy. **2** the Italian dialect of Venice. **3** (**venetian**) = *venetian blind*. —*adj.* of Venice. □ **venetian blind** a window-blind of adjustable horizontal slats to control the light. **Venetian glass** delicate glassware made at Murano near Venice. **Venetian red** a reddish pigment of ferric oxides. **Venetian window** a window with three separate openings, the central one being arched and highest. □□ **venetianed** *adj.* (in sense 3 of *n*.). [ME f. OF *Venicien*, assim. to med.L *Venetianus* f. *Venetia* Venice]

vengeance /'vendʒ(ə)ns/ *n*. punishment inflicted or retribution exacted for wrong to oneself or to a person etc. whose cause one supports. □ **with a vengeance** in a higher degree than was expected or desired; in the fullest sense (*punctuality with a vengeance*). [ME f. OF f. *venger* avenge f. L (as VINDICATE)]

vengeful /'vendʒfʊl/ *adj.* vindictive; seeking vengeance. □□ **vengefully** *adv.* **vengefulness** *n*. [obs. *venge* avenge (as VENGEANCE)]

venial /'viːnɪəl/ *adj.* (of a sin or fault) pardonable, excusable; not mortal. □□ **veniality** /-'ælɪtɪ/ *n*. **venially** *adv*. **venialness** *n*. [ME f. OF f. LL *venialis* f. *venia* forgiveness]

venipuncture var. of VENEPUNCTURE.

venisection var. of VENESECTION.

venison /'venɪs(ə)n, -z(ə)n/ *n*. a deer's flesh as food. [ME f. OF *veneso(u)n* f. L *venatio -onis* hunting f. *venari* to hunt]

Venite /vɪ'naɪtɪ/ *n*. **1** a canticle consisting of Psalm 95. **2** a musical setting of this. [ME f. L, = 'come ye', its first word]

Venn diagram /ven/ *n*. a diagram of usu. circular areas representing mathematical sets, the areas intersecting where they have elements in common. [J. Venn, Engl. logician d. 1923]

venom /'venəm/ *n*. **1** a poisonous fluid secreted by snakes, scorpions, etc., usu. transmitted by a bite or sting. **2** malignity; virulence of feeling, language, or conduct. □□ **venomed** *adj*. [ME f. OF *venim*, var. of *venin* ult. f. L *venenum* poison]

venomous /'venəməs/ *adj.* **1 a** containing, secreting, or injecting venom. **b** (of a snake etc.) inflicting poisonous wounds by this means. **2** (of a person etc.) virulent, spiteful, malignant. □□ **venomously** *adv.* **venomousness** *n*. [ME f. OF *venimeux* f. *venim*: see VENOM]

venose /'viːnəʊz/ *adj.* having many or very marked veins. [L *venosus* f. *vena* vein]

venous /'viːnəs/ *adj.* of, full of, or contained in veins. □□ **venosity** /vɪ'nɒsɪtɪ/ *n*. **venously** *adv*. [L *venosus* VENOSE or L *vena* vein + -OUS]

vent[1] /vent/ *n. & v.* —*n.* **1** (also **vent-hole**) a hole or opening allowing motion of air etc. out of or into a confined space. **2** an outlet; free passage or play (*gave vent to their indignation*). **3** the anus esp. of a lower animal, serving for both excretion and reproduction. **4** the venting of an otter, beaver, etc. **5** an aperture or outlet through which volcanic products are discharged at the earth's surface. **6** a touch-hole of a gun. **7** a finger-hole in a musical instrument. **8** a flue of a chimney. —*v.* **1** *tr.* **a** make a vent in (a cask etc.). **b** provide (a machine) with a vent. **2** *tr.* give vent or free expression to (*vented my anger on the cat*). **3** *intr.* (of an otter or beaver) come to the surface for breath. □ **vent one's spleen** on scold or ill-treat without cause. □□ **ventless** *adj*. [partly F *vent* f. L *ventus* wind, partly F *évent* f. *éventer* expose to air f. OF *esventer* ult. f. L *ventus* wind]

vent[2] /vent/ *n*. a slit in a garment, esp. in the lower edge of the back of a coat. [ME, var. of *fent* f. OF *fente* slip ult. f. L *findere* cleave]

ventiduct /'ventɪˌdʌkt/ *n. Archit.* an air-passage, esp. for ventilation. [L *ventus* wind + *ductus* DUCT]

ventifact /'ventɪˌfækt/ *n.* a stone shaped by wind-blown sand. [L *ventus* wind + *factum* neut. past part. of *facere* make]

ventil /'ventɪl/ *n. Mus.* **1** a valve in a wind instrument. **2** a shutter for regulating the air-flow in an organ. [G f. It. *ventile* f. med.L *ventile* sluice f. L *ventus* wind]

ventilate /'ventɪˌleɪt/ *v.tr.* **1** cause air to circulate freely in (a room etc.). **2** submit (a question, grievance, etc.) to public consideration and discussion. **3** *Med.* **a** oxygenate (the blood). **b** admit or force air into (the lungs). □□ **ventilation** /-'leɪʃ(ə)n/ *n*. **ventilative** /-'leɪtɪv/ *adj*. [L *ventilare ventilat-* blow, winnow, f. *ventus* wind]

ventilator /'ventɪˌleɪtə(r)/ *n*. **1** an appliance or aperture for ventilating a room etc. **2** *Med.* = RESPIRATOR 2.

ventral /'ventr(ə)l/ *adj.* **1** *Anat. & Zool.* of or on the abdomen (cf. DORSAL). **2** *Bot.* of the front or lower surface. □ **ventral fin** either of the ventrally placed fins on a fish. □□ **ventrally** *adv*. [obs. *venter* abdomen f. L *venter ventr-*]

ventre à terre /ˌvɑːntr ɑː 'teə(r)/ *adv.* at full speed. [F, lit. with belly to the ground]

ventricle /'ventrɪk(ə)l/ *n. Anat.* **1** a cavity in the body. **2** a hollow part of an organ, esp. in the brain or heart. □□ **ventricular** /-'trɪkjʊlə(r)/ *adj*. [ME f. L *ventriculus* dimin. of *venter* belly]

ventricose /'ventrɪˌkəʊz/ *adj.* **1** having a protruding belly. **2** *Bot.* distended, inflated. [irreg. f. VENTRICLE + -OSE[1]]

ventriloquism /ven'trɪləˌkwɪz(ə)m/ *n*. the skill of speaking or uttering sounds so that they seem to come from the speaker's dummy or a source other than the speaker. □□ **ventriloquial** /ˌventrɪ 'ləʊkwɪəl/ *adj*. **ventriloquist** *n*. **ventriloquize** *v.intr.* (also **-ise**). [ult. f. L *ventriloquus* ventriloquist f. *venter* belly + *loqui* speak]

ventriloquy /ven'trɪləkwɪ/ *n*. = VENTRILOQUISM.

venture /'ventʃə(r)/ *n. & v.* —*n.* **1 a** an undertaking of a risk. **b** a risky undertaking. **2** a commercial speculation. —*v.* **1** *intr.* dare; not be afraid (*did not venture to stop them*). **2** *intr.* (usu. foll. by *out* etc.) dare to go (out), esp. outdoors. **3** *tr.* dare to put forward (an opinion, suggestion, etc.). **4 a** *tr.* expose to risk; stake (a bet etc.). **b** *intr.* take risks. **5** *intr.* (foll. by *on, upon*) dare to engage in etc. (*ventured on a longer journey*). □ **at a venture** at random; without previous consideration. **venture capital** = *risk capital*. **Venture Scout** *Brit.* a member of the Scout Association aged between 16 and 20. [*aventure* = ADVENTURE]

venturer /'ventʃərə(r)/ *n. hist.* a person who undertakes or shares in a trading venture.

venturesome /'ventʃəsəm/ *adj.* **1** disposed to take risks. **2** risky. □□ **venturesomely** *adv.* **venturesomeness** *n.*

venturi /ven'tjʊərɪ/ *n.* (*pl.* **venturis**) a short piece of narrow tube between wider sections for measuring flow-rate or exerting suction. [G. B. *Venturi*, It. physicist d. 1822]

venue /'venjuː/ *n.* **1 a** an appointed meeting-place esp. for a sports event, meeting, concert, etc. **b** a rendezvous. **2** *Law hist.* the county or other place within which a jury must be gathered and a cause tried (orig. the neighbourhood of the crime etc.). [F, = a coming, fem. past part. of *venir* come f. L *venire*]

venule /'venjuːl/ *n. Anat.* a small vein adjoining the capillaries. [L *venula* dimin. of *vena* vein]

Venus /'viːnəs/ *n.* (*pl.* **Venuses**) **1** the planet second from the sun in the solar system. **2** *poet.* **a** a beautiful woman. **b** sexual love; amorous influences or desires. □ **Venus** (or **Venus's**) **fly-trap** a flesh-consuming plant, *Dionaea muscipula*, with leaves that close on insects etc. **Venus's comb** = *shepherd's needle* (see SHEPHERD). **Venus's looking-glass** any of various plants of the genus *Legousia* with small blue flowers. □□ **Venusian** /vɪ'njuːzɪən/ *adj. & n.* [OE f. L *Venus Veneris*, the goddess of love]

veracious /və'reɪʃəs/ *adj. formal* **1** speaking or disposed to speak the truth. **2** (of a statement etc.) true or meant to be true. □□ **veraciously** *adv.* **veraciousness** *n.* [L *verax veracis* f. *verus* true]

veracity /və'ræsɪtɪ/ *n.* **1** truthfulness, honesty. **2** accuracy (of a statement etc.). [F *veracité* or med.L *veracitas* (as VERACIOUS)]

veranda /və'rændə/ *n.* (also **verandah**) **1** a portico or external gallery, usu. with a roof, along the side of a house. **2** *Austral. & NZ* a roof over a pavement in front of a shop. [Hindi *varandā* f. Port. *varanda*]

veratrine /'verə,triːn, -ɪn/ *n.* a poisonous compound obtained from sabadilla etc., and used esp. as a local irritant in the treatment of neuralgia and rheumatism. [F *vératrine* f. L *veratrum* hellebore]

verb /vɜːb/ *n. Gram.* a word used to indicate an action, state, or occurrence, and forming the main part of the predicate of a sentence (e.g. *hear, become, happen*). [ME f. OF *verbe* or L *verbum* word, verb]

verbal /'vɜːb(ə)l/ *adj., n., & v. —adj.* **1** of or concerned with words (*made a verbal distinction*). **2** oral, not written (*gave a verbal statement*). **3** *Gram.* of or in the nature of a verb (*verbal inflections*). **4** literal (*a verbal translation*). **5** talkative, articulate. *—n.* **1** *Gram.* **a** a verbal noun. **b** a word or words functioning as a verb. **2** *sl.* a verbal statement, esp. one made to the police. **3** *sl.* an insult; abuse (*gave them the verbal*). *—v.tr.* (**verballed, verballing**) *Brit. sl.* attribute a damaging statement to (a suspect). □ **verbal noun** *Gram.* a noun formed as an inflection of a verb and partly sharing its constructions (e.g. *smoking* in *smoking is forbidden*: see -ING¹). □□ **verbally** *adv.* [ME f. F *verbal* or LL *verbalis* (as VERB)]

verbalism /'vɜːbə,lɪz(ə)m/ *n.* **1** minute attention to words: verbal criticism. **2** merely verbal expression. □□ **verbalist** *n.* **verbalistic** /-'lɪstɪk/ *adj.*

verbalize /'vɜːbə,laɪz/ *v.* (also **-ise**) **1** *tr.* express in words. **2** *intr.* be verbose. **3** *tr.* make (a noun etc.) into a verb. □□ **verbalizable** *adj.* **verbalization** /-'zeɪʃ(ə)n/ *n.* **verbalizer** *n.*

verbatim /vɜː'beɪtɪm/ *adv. & adj.* in exactly the same words; word for word (*copied it verbatim; a verbatim report*). [ME f. med.L (adv.), f. L *verbum* word: cf. LITERATIM]

verbena /vɜː'biːnə/ *n.* any plant of the genus *Verbena*, bearing clusters of fragrant flowers. [L, = sacred bough of olive etc., in med.L vervain]

verbiage /'vɜːbɪɪdʒ/ *n.* needless accumulation of words; verbosity. [F f. obs. *verbeier* chatter f. *verbe* word: see VERB]

verbose /vɜː'bəʊs/ *adj.* using or expressed in more words than are needed. □□ **verbosely** *adv.* **verboseness** *n.* **verbosity** /-'bɒsɪtɪ/ *n.* [L *verbosus* f. *verbum* word]

verboten /fɜː'bəʊt(ə)n/ *adj.* forbidden, esp. by an authority. [G]

verb. sap. /vɜːb 'sæp/ *int.* expressing the absence of the need for a further explicit statement. [abbr. of L *verbum sapienti sat est* a word is enough for the wise person]

verdant /'vɜːd(ə)nt/ *adj.* **1** (of grass etc.) green, fresh-coloured. **2** (of a field etc.) covered with green grass etc. **3** (of a person) unsophisticated, raw, green. □□ **verdancy** *n.* **verdantly** *adv.* [perh. f. OF *verdeant* part. of *verdoier* be green ult. f. L *viridis* green]

verd-antique /,vɜːdæn'tiːk/ *n.* **1** ornamental usu. green serpentine. **2** a green incrustation on ancient bronze. **3** green porphyry. [obs. F, = antique green]

verderer /'vɜːdərə(r)/ *n. Brit.* a judicial officer of royal forests. [AF (earlier *verder*), OF *verdier* ult. f. L *viridis* green]

verdict /'vɜːdɪkt/ *n.* **1** a decision on an issue of fact in a civil or criminal cause or an inquest. **2** a decision; a judgement. [ME f. AF *verdit*, OF *voirdit* f. *voir, veir* true f. L *verus* + *dit* f. L DICTUM saying]

verdigris /'vɜːdɪɡrɪs, -,ɡriːs/ *n.* **1 a** a green crystallized substance formed on copper by the action of acetic acid. **b** this used as a medicine or pigment. **2** green rust on copper or brass. [ME f. OF *verte-gres, vert de Grece* green of Greece]

verdure /'vɜːdjə(r)/ *n.* **1** green vegetation. **2** the greenness of this. **3** *poet.* freshness. □□ **verdured** *adj.* **verdurous** *adj.* [ME f. OF f. *verd* green f. L *viridis*]

verge¹ /vɜːdʒ/ *n.* **1** an edge or border. **2** an extreme limit beyond which something happens (*on the verge of tears*). **3** *Brit.* a grass edging of a road, flower-bed, etc. **4** *Archit.* an edge of tiles projecting over a gable. **5** a wand or rod carried before a bishop, dean, etc., as an emblem of office. [ME f. OF f. L *virga* rod]

verge² /vɜːdʒ/ *v.intr.* **1** incline downwards or in a specified direction (*the now verging sun; verge to a close*). **2** (foll. by *on*) border on; approach closely (*verging on the ridiculous*). [L *vergere* bend, incline]

verger /'vɜːdʒə(r)/ *n.* (also **virger**) **1** an official in a church who acts as caretaker and attendant. **2** an officer who bears the staff before a bishop etc. □□ **vergership** *n.* [ME f. AF (as VERGE¹)]

verglas /'veəɡlɑː/ *n.* a thin coating of ice or frozen rain. [F]

veridical /vɪ'rɪdɪk(ə)l/ *adj.* **1** *formal* truthful. **2** *Psychol.* (of visions etc.) coinciding with reality. □□ **veridicality** /-'kælɪtɪ/ *n.* **veridically** *adv.* [L *veridicus* f. *verus* true + *dicere* say]

veriest /'verɪɪst/ *adj.* (*superl.* of VERY). *archaic* real, extreme (*the veriest fool knows that*).

verification /,verɪfɪ'keɪʃ(ə)n/ *n.* **1** the process or an instance of establishing the truth or validity of something. **2** *Philos.* the establishment of the validity of a proposition empirically. **3** the process of verifying procedures laid down in weapons agreements.

verify /'verɪ,faɪ/ *v.tr.* (**-ies, -ied**) **1** establish the truth or correctness of by examination or demonstration (*must verify the statement; verified my figures*). **2** (of an event etc.) bear out or fulfil (a prediction or promise). **3** *Law* append an affidavit to (pleadings); support (a statement) by testimony or proofs. □□ **verifiable** *adj.* **verifiably** *adv.* **verifier** *n.* [ME f. OF *verifier* f. med.L *verificare* f. *verus* true]

verily /'verɪlɪ/ *adv. archaic* really, truly. [ME f. VERY + -LY², · after OF & AF]

verisimilitude /,verɪsɪ'mɪlɪ,tjuːd/ *n.* **1** the appearance or semblance of being true or real. **2** a statement etc. that seems true. □□ **verisimilar** /-'sɪmɪlə(r)/ *adj.* [L *verisimilitudo* f. *verisimilis* probable f. *veri* genit. of *verus* true + *similis* like]

verism /'vɪərɪz(ə)m/ *n.* realism in literature or art.

□□ **verist** *n.* **veristic** /-'rɪstɪk/ *adj.* [L *verus* or It. *vero* true + -ISM]

verismo /ve'rɪzməʊ/ *n.* (esp. of opera) realism. [It. (as VERISM)]

veritable /'verɪtəb(ə)l/ *adj.* real; rightly so called (*a veritable feast*). □□ **veritably** *adv.* [OF (as VERITY)]

verity /'verɪtɪ/ *n.* (*pl.* -ies) **1** a true statement, esp. one of fundamental import. **2** truth. **3** a really existent thing. [ME f. OF *verité*, *verté* f. L *veritas* -*tatis* f. *verus* true]

verjuice /'vɜːdʒuːs/ *n.* **1** an acid liquor obtained from crab-apples, sour grapes, etc., and formerly used in cooking and medicine. **2** bitter feelings, thoughts, etc. [ME f. OF *vertjus* f. VERT green + *jus* JUICE]

verkrampte /feə'kræmptə/ *adj.* & *n.* S.Afr. —*adj.* politically or socially conservative or reactionary, esp. as regards apartheid. —*n.* a person holding such views. [Afrik., lit. narrow, cramped]

verligte /feə'lɪxtə/ *adj.* & *n.* S.Afr. —*adj.* progressive or enlightened, esp. as regards apartheid. —*n.* a person holding such views. [Afrik., = enlightened]

vermeil /'vɜːmeɪl/ *n.* **1** silver gilt. **2** an orange-red garnet. **3** *poet.* vermilion. [ME f. OF: see VERMILION]

vermi- /'vɜːmɪ/ *comb. form* worm. [L *vermis* worm]

vermian /'vɜːmɪən/ *adj.* of worms; wormlike. [L *vermis* worm]

vermicelli /,vɜːmɪ'selɪ, -'tʃelɪ/ *n.* **1** pasta made in long slender threads. **2** shreds of chocolate used as cake decoration etc. [It., pl. of *vermicello* dimin. of *verme* f. L *vermis* worm]

vermicide /'vɜːmɪ,saɪd/ *n.* a substance that kills worms.

vermicular /və'mɪkjʊlə(r)/ *adj.* **1** like a worm in form or movement; vermiform. **2** *Med.* of or caused by intestinal worms. **3** marked with close wavy lines. [med.L *vermicularis* f. L *vermiculus* dimin. of *vermis* worm]

vermiculate /və'mɪkjʊlət/ *adj.* **1** = VERMICULAR. **2** wormeaten. [L *vermiculatus* past part. of *vermiculari* be full of worms (as VERMICULAR)]

vermiculation /və,mɪkjʊ'leɪʃ(ə)n/ *n.* **1** the state or process of being eaten or infested by or converted into worms. **2** a vermicular marking. **3** a wormeaten state. [L *vermiculatio* (as VERMICULATE)]

vermiculite /və'mɪkjʊ,laɪt/ *n.* a hydrous silicate mineral usu. resulting from alteration of mica, and expandable into sponge by heating, used as an insulation material. [as VERMICULATE + -ITE¹]

vermiform /'vɜːmɪ,fɔːm/ *adj.* worm-shaped. □ **vermiform appendix** see APPENDIX 1.

vermifuge /'vɜːmɪ,fjuːdʒ/ *adj.* & *n.* —*adj.* that expels intestinal worms. —*n.* a drug that does this.

vermilion /və'mɪljən/ *n.* & *adj.* —*n.* **1** cinnabar. **2 a** a brilliant red pigment made by grinding this or artificially. **b** the colour of this. —*adj.* of this colour. [ME f. OF *vermeillon* f. *vermeil* f. L *vermiculus* dimin. of *vermis* worm]

vermin /'vɜːmɪn/ *n.* (usu. treated as *pl.*) **1** mammals and birds injurious to game, crops, etc., e.g. foxes, rodents, and noxious insects. **2** parasitic worms or insects. **3** vile persons. □□ **verminous** *adj.* [ME f. OF *vermin*, -*ine* ult. f. L *vermis* worm]

verminate /'vɜːmɪ,neɪt/ *v.intr.* **1** breed vermin. **2** become infested with parasites. □□ **vermination** /-'neɪʃ(ə)n/ *n.* [L *verminare verminat-* f. *vermis* worm]

vermivorous /vɜː'mɪvərəs/ *adj.* feeding on worms.

vermouth /'vɜːməθ, və'muːθ/ *n.* a wine flavoured with aromatic herbs. [F *vermout* f. G *Wermut* WORMWOOD]

vernacular /və'nækjʊlə(r)/ *n.* & *adj.* —*n.* **1** the language or dialect of a particular country (*Latin gave place to the vernacular*). **2** the language of a particular clan or group. **3** homely speech. —*adj.* **1** (of language) of one's native country; not of foreign origin or of learned formation. **2** (of architecture) concerned with ordinary rather than monumental buildings. □□ **vernacularism** *n.* **vernacularity** /-'lærɪtɪ/ *n.* **vernacularize** *v.tr.* (also -ise).

vernacularly *adv.* [L *vernaculus* domestic, native f. *verna* home-born slave]

vernal /'vɜːn(ə)l/ *adj.* of, in, or appropriate to spring (*vernal equinox*; *vernal breezes*). □ **vernal grass** a sweet-scented European grass, *Anthoxanthum odoratum*, grown for hay. □□ **vernally** *adv.* [L *vernalis* f. *vernus* f. *ver* spring]

vernalization /,vɜːnəlaɪ'zeɪʃ(ə)n/ *n.* (also -isation) the cooling of seed before planting, in order to accelerate flowering. □□ **vernalize** /'vɜːnə,laɪz/ *v.tr.* (also -ise). [(transl. of Russ. *yarovizatsiya*) f. VERNAL]

vernation /vɜː'neɪʃ(ə)n/ *n.* *Bot.* the arrangement of leaves in a leaf-bud (cf. AESTIVATION). [mod.L *vernatio* f. L *vernare* bloom (as VERNAL)]

vernicle /'vɜːnɪk(ə)l/ *n.* = VERONICA 2. [ME f. OF (earlier *ver(o)nique*), f. med.L VERONICA]

vernier /'vɜːnɪə(r)/ *n.* a small movable graduated scale for obtaining fractional parts of subdivisions on a fixed main scale of a barometer, sextant, etc. □ **vernier engine** an auxiliary engine for slight changes in the motion of a space rocket etc. [P. *Vernier*, Fr. mathematician d. 1637]

veronal /'verən(ə)l/ *n. propr.* a sedative drug, a derivative of barbituric acid. [G, f. *Verona* in Italy]

veronica /və'rɒnɪkə/ *n.* **1** any plant of the genus *Veronica* or *Hebe*, esp. speedwell. **2 a** a cloth supposedly impressed with an image of Christ's face. **b** any similar picture of Christ's face. **3** *Bullfighting* the movement of a matador's cape away from a charging bull. [med.L f. the name *Veronica*: in sense 2 from the association with St Veronica]

verruca /və'ruːkə/ *n.* (*pl.* **verrucae** /-siː/ or **verrucas**) a wart or similar growth. □□ **verrucose** /'verʊ,kəʊz/ *adj.* **verrucous** /'verʊkəs/ *adj.* [L]

versant /'vɜːs(ə)nt/ *n.* **1** the extent of land sloping in one direction. **2** the general slope of land. [F f. *verser* f. L *versare* frequent. of *vertere vers-* turn]

versatile /'vɜːsə,taɪl/ *adj.* **1** turning easily or readily from one subject or occupation to another; capable of dealing with many subjects (*a versatile mind*). **2** (of a device etc.) having many uses. **3** *Bot.* & *Zool.* moving freely about or up and down on a support (*versatile antenna*). **4** *archaic* changeable, inconstant. □□ **versatilely** *adv.* **versatility** /-'tɪlɪtɪ/ *n.* [F *versatile* or L *versatilis* (as VERSANT)]

verse /vɜːs/ *n.* & *v.* —*n.* **1 a** a metrical composition in general (*wrote pages of verse*). **b** a particular type of this (*English verse*). **2 a** a metrical line in accordance with the rules of prosody. **b** a group of a definite number of such lines. **c** a stanza of a poem or song with or without refrain. **3** each of the short numbered divisions of a chapter in the Bible or other scripture. **4 a** a versicle. **b** a passage (of an anthem etc.) for solo voice. —*v.tr.* **1** express in verse. **2** (usu. *refl.*; foll. by *in*) instruct; make knowledgeable. □□ **verselet** *n.* [OE *fers* f. L *versus* a turn of the plough, a furrow, a line of writing f. *vertere vers-* turn: in ME reinforced by OF *vers* f. L *versus*]

versed¹ /vɜːst/ *adj.* (foll. by *in*) experienced or skilled in; knowledgeable about. [F *versé* or L *versatus* past part. of *versari* be engaged in (as VERSANT)]

versed² /vɜːst/ *adj. Math.* reversed. □ **versed sine** unity minus cosine. [mod.L (*sinus*) *versus* turned (sine), formed as VERSE]

verset /'vɜːsɪt/ *n. Mus.* a short prelude or interlude for organ. [F: dimin. of *vers* VERSE]

versicle /'vɜːsɪk(ə)l/ *n.* each of the short sentences in a liturgy said or sung by a priest etc. and alternating with responses. □□ **versicular** /-'sɪkjʊlə(r)/ *adj.* [ME f. OF *versicule* or L *versiculus* dimin. of *versus*: see VERSE]

versicoloured /'vɜːsɪ,kʌləd/ *adj.* **1** changing from one colour to another in different lights. **2** variegated. [L *versicolor* f. *versus* past part. of *vertere* turn + *color* colour]

versify /'vɜːsɪ,faɪ/ *v.* (-ies, -ied) **1** *tr.* turn into or express in verse. **2** *intr.* compose verses. □□

versification /-fɪˈkeɪʃ(ə)n/ *n.* **versifier** *n.* [ME f. OF *versifier* f. L *versificare* (as VERSE)]

versin /ˈvɜːsaɪn/ *n.* (also **versine**) *Math.* = *versed sine* (see VERSED[2]).

version /ˈvɜːʃ(ə)n/ *n.* **1** an account of a matter from a particular person's point of view (*told them my version of the incident*). **2** a book or work etc. in a particular edition or translation (*Authorized Version*). **3** a form or variant of a thing as performed, adapted, etc. **4** a piece of translation, esp. as a school exercise. **5** *Med.* the manual turning of a foetus in the womb to improve presentation. □□ **versional** *adj.* [F *version* or med.L *versio* f. L *vertere vers-* turn]

vers libre /veə ˈliːbrə/ *n.* irregular or unrhymed verse in which the traditional rules of prosody are disregarded. [F, = free verse]

verso /ˈvɜːsəʊ/ *n.* (*pl.* **-os**) **1 a** the left-hand page of an open book. **b** the back of a printed leaf of paper or manuscript (opp. RECTO). **2** the reverse of a coin. [L *verso (folio)* on the turned (leaf)]

verst /vɜːst/ *n.* a Russian measure of length, about 1.1 km (0.66 mile). [Russ. *versta*]

versus /ˈvɜːsəs/ *prep.* against (esp. in legal and sports use). ¶ Abbr.: **v.**, **vs.** [L, = towards, in med.L against]

vert /vɜːt/ *n.* & (usu. placed after noun) *adj.* Heraldry green. [ME f. OF f. L *viridis* green]

vertebra /ˈvɜːtɪbrə/ *n.* (*pl.* **vertebrae** /-briː/) **1** each segment of the backbone. **2** (in *pl.*) the backbone. □□ **vertebral** *adj.* [L f. *vertere* turn]

vertebrate /ˈvɜːtɪbrət, -ˌbreɪt/ *n.* & *adj.* —*n.* any animal of the subphylum Vertebrata, having a spinal column, including mammals, birds, reptiles, amphibians, and fishes. —*adj.* of or relating to the vertebrates. [L *vertebratus* jointed (as VERTEBRA)]

vertebration /ˌvɜːtɪˈbreɪʃ(ə)n/ *n.* division into vertebrae or similar segments.

vertex /ˈvɜːteks/ *n.* (*pl.* **vertices** /-tɪˌsiːz/ or **vertexes**) **1** the highest point; the top or apex. **2** *Geom.* **a** each angular point of a polygon, polyhedron, etc. **b** a meeting-point of two lines that form an angle. **c** the point at which an axis meets a curve or surface. **3** *Anat.* the crown of the head. [L *vertex -ticis* whirlpool, crown of a head, vertex, f. *vertere* turn]

vertical /ˈvɜːtɪk(ə)l/ *adj.* & *n.* —*adj.* **1** at right angles to a horizontal plane, perpendicular. **2** in a direction from top to bottom of a picture etc. **3** of or at the vertex or highest point. **4** at, or passing through, the zenith. **5** *Anat.* of or relating to the crown of the head. **6** involving all the levels in an organizational hierarchy or stages in the production of a class of goods (*vertical integration*). —*n.* a vertical line or plane. □ **out of the vertical** not vertical. **vertical angles** *Math.* each pair of opposite angles made by two intersecting lines. **vertical fin** *Zool.* a dorsal, anal, or caudal fin. **vertical plane** a plane at right angles to the horizontal. **vertical take-off** the take-off of an aircraft directly upwards. □□ **verticality** /-ˈkælɪtɪ/ *n.* **verticalize** *v.tr.* (also **-ise**). **vertically** *adv.* [F *vertical* or LL *verticalis* (as VERTEX)]

verticil /ˈvɜːtɪsɪl/ *n.* *Bot.* & *Zool.* a whorl; a set of parts arranged in a circle round an axis. □□ **verticillate** /-ˈtɪsɪlət/ *adj.* [L *verticillus* whorl of a spindle, dimin. of VERTEX]

vertiginous /vəˈtɪdʒɪnəs/ *adj.* of or causing vertigo. □□ **vertiginously** *adv.* [L *vertiginosus* (as VERTIGO)]

vertigo /ˈvɜːtɪˌɡəʊ/ *n.* a condition with a sensation of whirling and a tendency to lose balance; dizziness, giddiness. [L *vertigo -ginis* whirling f. *vertere* turn]

vertu var. of VIRTU.

vervain /ˈvɜːveɪn/ *n.* *Bot.* any of various herbaceous plants of the genus *Verbena*, esp. *V. officinalis* with small blue, white, or purple flowers. [ME f. OF *verveine* f. L VERBENA]

verve /vɜːv/ *n.* enthusiasm, vigour, spirit, esp. in artistic or literary work. [F, earlier = a form of expression, f. L *verba* words]

vervet /ˈvɜːvɪt/ *n.* a small grey African monkey, *Cercopithecus aethiops*. [F]

very /ˈverɪ/ *adv.* & *adj.* —*adv.* **1** in a high degree (*did it very easily*; *had a very bad cough*; *am very much better*). **2** in the fullest sense (foll. by *own* or superl. *adj.*: *at the very latest*; *do your very best*; *my very own room*). —*adj.* **1** real, true, actual; truly such (usu. prec. by *the*, *this*, *his*, etc. emphasizing identity, significance, or extreme degree: *the very thing we need*; *those were his very words*). **2** *archaic* real, genuine (*very God*). □ **not very 1** in a low degree. **2** far from being. **very good** (or **well**) a formula of consent or approval. **very high frequency** (of radio frequency) in the range 30–300 megahertz. **Very Reverend** the title of a dean. **the very same** see SAME. [ME f. OF *verai* ult. f. L *verus* true]

Very light /ˈverɪ, ˈvɪərɪ/ *n.* a flare projected from a pistol for signalling or temporarily illuminating the surroundings. [E. W. *Very*, Amer. inventor d. 1910]

Very pistol /ˈverɪ, ˈvɪərɪ/ *n.* a gun for firing a Very light.

vesica /ˈvesɪkə/ *n.* **1** *Anat.* & *Zool.* a bladder, esp. the urinary bladder. **2** (in full **vesica piscis** or **piscium**) *Art* a pointed oval used as an aureole in medieval sculpture and painting. □□ **vesical** *adj.* [L]

vesicate /ˈvesɪˌkeɪt/ *v.tr.* raise blisters on. □□ **vesicant** *adj.* & *n.* **vesication** /-ˈkeɪʃ(ə)n/ *n.* **vesicatory** /-ˈkeɪtərɪ/ *adj.* & *n.* [LL *vesicare vesicat-* (as VESICA)]

vesicle /ˈvesɪk(ə)l/ *n.* **1** *Anat.*, *Zool.*, & *Bot.* a small bladder, bubble, or hollow structure. **2** *Geol.* a small cavity in volcanic rock produced by gas bubbles. **3** *Med.* a blister. □□ **vesicular** /vɪˈsɪkjʊlə(r)/ *adj.* **vesiculate** /vɪˈsɪkjʊlət/ *adj.* **vesiculation** /vɪˌsɪkjʊˈleɪʃ(ə)n/ *n.* [F *vésicule* or L *vesicula* dimin. of VESICA]

vesper /ˈvespə(r)/ *n.* **1** Venus as the evening star. **2** *poet.* evening. **3** (in *pl.*) **a** the sixth of the canonical hours of prayer. **b** evensong. [L *vesper* evening (star): sense 3 partly f. OF *vespres* f. eccl.L *vesperas* f. L *vespera* evening]

vespertine /ˈvespəˌtaɪn, -tɪn/ *adj.* **1** *Bot.* (of a flower) opening in the evening. **2** *Zool.* active in the evening. **3** *Astron.* setting near the time of sunset. **4** of or occurring in the evening. [L *vespertinus* f. *vesper* evening]

vespiary /ˈvespɪərɪ/ *n.* (*pl.* **-ies**) a nest of wasps. [irreg. f. L *vespa* wasp, after *apiary*]

vespine /ˈvespaɪn/ *adj.* of or relating to wasps. [L *vespa* wasp]

vessel /ˈves(ə)l/ *n.* **1** a hollow receptacle esp. for liquid, e.g. a cask, cup, pot, bottle, or dish. **2** a ship or boat, esp. a large one. **3 a** *Anat.* a duct or canal etc. holding or conveying blood or other fluid, esp. = *blood-vessel*. **b** *Bot.* a woody duct carrying or containing sap etc. **4** *Bibl.* or *joc.* a person regarded as the recipient or exponent of a quality (*a weak vessel*). [ME f. AF *vessel(e)*, OF *vaissel(le)* f. LL *vascellum* dimin. of *vas* vessel]

vest /vest/ *n.* & *v.* —*n.* **1** an undergarment worn on the upper part of the body. **2** *US* & *Austral.* a waistcoat. **3** a usu. V-shaped piece of material to fill the opening at the neck of a woman's dress. —*v.* **1** *tr.* (esp. in *passive*; foll. by *with*) bestow or confer (powers, authority, etc.) on (a person). **2** *tr.* (foll. by *in*) confer (property or power) on (a person) with an immediate fixed right of immediate or future possession. **3** *intr.* (foll. by *in*) (of property, a right, etc.) come into the possession of (a person). **4 a** *tr.* *poet.* clothe. **b** *intr.* *Eccl.* put on vestments. □ **vested interest 1** *Law* an interest (usu. in land or money held in trust) recognized as belonging to a person. **2** a personal interest in a state of affairs, usu. with an expectation of gain. [(n.) F *veste* f. It. *veste* f. L *vestis* garment: (v.) ME, orig. past part. f. OF *vestu* f. *vestir* f. L *vestire vestit-* clothe]

vesta /ˈvestə/ *n.* *hist.* a short wooden or wax match. [*Vesta*, Roman goddess of the hearth and household]

vestal /'vest(ə)l/ *adj.* & *n.* —*adj.* **1** chaste, pure. **2** of or relating to the Roman goddess Vesta. —*n.* **1** a chaste woman, esp. a nun. **2** *Rom. Antiq.* a vestal virgin. □**vestal virgin** *Rom. Antiq.* a virgin consecrated to Vesta and vowed to chastity, who shared the charge of maintaining the sacred fire burning on the goddess's altar. [ME f. L *vestalis* (adj. & n.) (as VESTA)]

vestee /ve'sti:/ *n.* = VEST *n.* 3.

vestiary /'vestɪərɪ/ *n.* & *adj.* —*n.* (*pl.* -**ies**) **1** a vestry. **2** a robing-room; a cloakroom. —*adj.* of or relating to clothes or dress. [ME f. OF *vestiarie, vestiaire*: see VESTRY]

vestibule /'vestɪ͵bju:l/ *n.* **1 a** an antechamber, hall, or lobby next to the outer door of a building. **b** a porch of a church etc. **2** *US* an enclosed entrance to a railway-carriage. **3** *Anat.* **a** a chamber or channel communicating with others. **b** part of the mouth outside the teeth. **c** the central cavity of the labyrinth of the inner ear. □□**vestibular** /-'stɪbjʊlə(r)/ *adj.* [F *vestibule* or L *vestibulum* entrance-court]

vestige /'vestɪdʒ/ *n.* **1** a trace or piece of evidence; a sign (*vestiges of an earlier civilization*; *found no vestige of their presence*). **2** a slight amount; a particle (*without a vestige of clothing*; *showed not a vestige of decency*). **3** *Biol.* a part or organ of an organism that is reduced or functionless but was well developed in its ancestors. [F f. L *vestigium* footprint]

vestigial /ve'stɪdʒɪəl, -dʒ(ə)l/ *adj.* **1** being a vestige or trace. **2** *Biol.* (of an organ) atrophied or functionless from the process of evolution (*a vestigial wing*). □□**vestigially** *adv.*

vestiture /'vestɪtʃə(r)/ *n.* **1** *Zool.* hair, scales, etc., covering a surface. **2** *archaic* **a** clothing. **b** investiture. [ME f. med.L *vestitura* f. L *vestire*: see VEST]

vestment /'vestmənt/ *n.* **1** any of the official robes of clergy, choristers, etc., worn during divine service, esp. a chasuble. **2** a garment, esp. an official or state robe. [ME f. OF *vestiment, vestement* f. L *vestimentum* (as VEST)]

vestry /'vestrɪ/ *n.* (*pl.* -**ies**) **1** a room or building attached to a church for keeping vestments in. **2** *hist.* **a** a meeting of parishioners usu. in a vestry for parochial business. **b** a body of parishioners meeting in this way. □□**vestral** *adj.* [ME f. OF *vestiaire, vestiarie,* f. L *vestiarium* (as VEST)]

vestryman /'vestrɪmən/ *n.* (*pl.* -**men**) a member of a vestry.

vesture /'vestʃə(r)/ *n.* & *v.* —*n. poet.* **1** garments, dress. **2** a covering. —*v.tr.* clothe. [ME f. OF f. med.L *vestitura* (as VEST)]

vet[1] /vet/ *n.* & *v.* —*n. colloq.* a veterinary surgeon. —*v.tr.* (**vetted, vetting**) **1** make a careful and critical examination of (a scheme, work, candidate, etc.). **2** examine or treat (an animal). [abbr.]

vet[2] /vet/ *n. US colloq.* a veteran. [abbr.]

vetch /vetʃ/ *n.* any plant of the genus *Vicia*, esp. *V. sativa*, largely used for silage or fodder. □□**vetchy** *adj.* [ME f. AF & ONF *veche* f. L *vicia*]

vetchling /'vetʃlɪŋ/ *n.* any of various plants of the genus *Lathyrus*, related to vetch.

veteran /'vetərən/ *n.* **1** a person who has grown old in or had long experience of esp. military service or an occupation (*a war veteran*; *a veteran of the theatre*; *a veteran marksman*). **2** *US* an ex-serviceman or servicewoman. **3** (*attrib.*) of or for veterans. □**veteran car** *Brit.* a car made before 1916, or (strictly) before 1905. [F *vétéran* or L *veteranus* (adj. & n.) f. *vetus -eris* old]

veterinarian /͵vetərɪ'neərɪən/ *n. US* a veterinary surgeon. [L *veterinarius* (as VETERINARY)]

veterinary /'vetə͵rɪnərɪ/ *adj.* & *n.* —*adj.* of or for diseases and injuries of farm and domestic animals, or their treatment. —*n.* (*pl.* -**ies**) a veterinary surgeon. □**veterinary surgeon** *Brit.* a person qualified to treat diseased or injured animals. [L *veterinarius* f. *veterinae* cattle]

vetiver /'vetɪvə(r)/ *n.* = CUSCUS[1]. [F *vétiver* f. Tamil *veṭṭivēru* f. *vēr* root]

veto /'vi:təʊ/ *n.* & *v.* —*n.* (*pl.* -**oes**) **1 a** a constitutional right to reject a legislative enactment. **b** the right of a permanent member of the UN Security Council to reject a resolution. **c** such a rejection. **d** an official message conveying this. **2** a prohibition (*put one's veto on a proposal*). —*v.tr.* (-**oes**, -**oed**) **1** exercise a veto against (a measure etc.). **2** forbid authoritatively. □□**vetoer** *n.* [L, = I forbid, with ref. to its use by Roman tribunes of the people in opposing measures of the Senate]

vex /veks/ *v.tr.* **1** anger by a slight or a petty annoyance; irritate. **2** *archaic* grieve, afflict. □□**vexer** *n.* **vexing** *adj.* **vexingly** *adv.* [ME f. OF *vexer* f. L *vexare* shake, disturb]

vexation /vek'seɪʃ(ə)n/ *n.* **1** the act or an instance of vexing; the state of being vexed. **2** an annoying or distressing thing. [ME f. OF *vexation* or L *vexatio -onis* (as VEX)]

vexatious /vek'seɪʃ(ə)s/ *adj.* **1** such as to cause vexation. **2** *Law* not having sufficient grounds for action and seeking only to annoy the defendant. □□**vexatiously** *adv.* **vexatiousness** *n.*

vexed /vekst/ *adj.* **1** irritated, angered. **2** (of a problem, issue, etc.) difficult and much discussed; problematic. □□**vexedly** /'veksɪdlɪ/ *adv.*

vexillology /͵veksɪ'lɒlədʒɪ/ *n.* the study of flags. □□**vexillological** /-lə'lɒdʒɪk(ə)l/ *adj.* **vexillologist** *n.* [L *vexillum* flag + -LOGY]

vexillum /vek'sɪləm/ *n.* (*pl.* **vexilla** /-lə/) **1** *Rom. Antiq.* **a** a military standard, esp. of a maniple. **b** a body of troops under this. **2** *Bot.* the large upper petal of a papilionaceous flower. **3** *Zool.* the vane of a feather. **4** *Eccl.* **a** a flag attached to a bishop's staff. **b** a processional banner or cross. [L f. *vehere vect-* carry]

VG *abbr.* **1** very good. **2** Vicar-General.

VHF *abbr.* very high frequency.

VI *abbr.* Virgin Islands.

via /'vaɪə/ *prep.* by way of; through (*London to Rome via Paris*; *send it via your secretary*). [L, ablat. of *via* way, road]

viable /'vaɪəb(ə)l/ *adj.* **1** (of a plan etc.) feasible; practicable esp. from an economic standpoint. **2 a** (of a plant, animal, etc.) capable of living or existing in a particular climate etc. **b** (of a foetus or newborn child) capable of maintaining life. **3** (of a seed or spore) able to germinate. □□**viability** /-'bɪlɪtɪ/ *n.* **viably** *adv.* [F f. *vie* life f. L *vita*]

viaduct /'vaɪə͵dʌkt/ *n.* **1** a long bridgelike structure, esp. a series of arches, carrying a road or railway across a valley or dip in the ground. **2** such a road or railway. [L *via* way, after AQUEDUCT]

vial /'vaɪəl/ *n.* a small (usu. cylindrical glass) vessel esp. for holding liquid medicines. □□**vialful** *n.* (*pl.* -**fuls**). [ME, var. of *fiole* etc.: see PHIAL]

via media /͵vaɪə 'mi:dɪə, ͵vi:ə 'medɪə/ *n. literary* a middle way or compromise between extremes. [L]

viand /'vaɪənd/ *n. formal* **1** an article of food. **2** (in *pl.*) provisions, victuals. [ME f. OF *viande* food, ult. f. L *vivenda*, neut. pl. gerundive of *vivere* to live]

viaticum /vaɪ'ætɪkəm/ *n.* (*pl.* **viatica** /-kə/) **1** the Eucharist as given to a person near or in danger of death. **2** provisions or an official allowance of money for a journey. [L, neut. of *viaticus* f. *via* road]

vibes /vaɪbz/ *n.pl. colloq.* **1** vibrations, esp. in the sense of feelings or atmosphere communicated (*the house had bad vibes*). **2** = VIBRAPHONE. [abbr.]

vibraculum /vaɪ'brækjʊləm/ *n.* (*pl.* **vibracula** /-lə/) *Zool.* a whiplike structure of bryozoans used to bring food within reach by lashing movements. □□**vibracular** *adj.* [mod.L (as VIBRATE)]

vibrant /'vaɪbrənt/ *adj.* **1** vibrating. **2** (often foll. by *with*) (of a person or thing) thrilling, quivering (*vibrant with emotion*). **3** (of sound) resonant. □□**vibrancy** *n.* **vibrantly** *adv.* [L *vibrare*: see VIBRATE]

vibraphone /'vaɪbrəˌfəʊn/ n. a percussion instrument of tuned metal bars with motor-driven resonators and metal tubes giving a vibrato effect. □□ **vibraphonist** n. [VIBRATO + -PHONE]

vibrate /vaɪ'breɪt/ v. 1 intr. & tr. move or cause to move continuously and rapidly to and fro; oscillate. 2 intr. Physics move unceasingly to and fro, esp. rapidly. 3 intr. (of a sound) throb; continue to be heard. 4 intr. (foll. by with) quiver, thrill (vibrating with passion). 5 intr. (of a pendulum) swing to and fro. □□ **vibrative** /-rətɪv/ adj. [L vibrare vibrat-shake, swing]

vibratile /'vaɪbrəˌtaɪl/ adj. 1 capable of vibrating. 2 Biol. (of cilia etc.) used in vibratory motion. [VIBRATORY, after pulsatile etc.]

vibration /vaɪ'breɪʃ(ə)n/ n. 1 the act or an instance of vibrating; oscillation. 2 Physics (esp. rapid) motion to and fro esp. of the parts of a fluid or an elastic solid whose equilibrium has been disturbed or of an electromagnetic wave. 3 (in pl.) a a mental (esp. occult) influence. b a characteristic atmosphere or feeling in a place, regarded as communicable to people present in it. □□ **vibrational** adj. [L vibratio (as VIBRATE)]

vibrato /vɪ'brɑːtəʊ/ n. Mus. a rapid slight variation in pitch in singing or playing a stringed or wind instrument, producing a tremulous effect (cf. TREMOLO). [It., past part. of vibrare VIBRATE]

vibrator /vaɪ'breɪtə(r)/ n. 1 a device that vibrates or causes vibration, esp. an electric or other instrument used in massage or for sexual stimulation. 2 Mus. a reed in a reed-organ.

vibratory /'vaɪbrətərɪ, -'breɪtərɪ/ adj. causing vibration.

vibrissae /vaɪ'brɪsiː/ n.pl. 1 stiff coarse hairs near the mouth of most mammals (e.g. a cat's whiskers) and in the human nostrils. 2 bristle-like feathers near the mouth of insect-eating birds. [L (as VIBRATE)]

viburnum /vaɪ'bɜːnəm, vɪ-/ n. Bot. any shrub of the genus Viburnum, usu. with white flowers, e.g. the guelder rose and wayfaring-tree. [L, = wayfaring-tree]

Vic. abbr. Victoria.

vicar /'vɪkə(r)/ n. 1 a (in the Church of England) an incumbent of a parish where tithes formerly passed to a chapter or religious house or layman (cf. RECTOR). b (in an Episcopal Church) a member of the clergy deputizing for another. 2 RC Ch. a representative or deputy of a bishop. 3 (in full lay vicar or vicar choral) a cleric or choir member appointed to sing certain parts of a cathedral service. □ **vicar apostolic** RC Ch. a Roman Catholic missionary or titular bishop. **vicar-general** (pl. **vicars-general**) 1 an Anglican official assisting or representing a bishop esp. in administrative matters. 2 RC Ch. a bishop's assistant in matters of jurisdiction etc. **Vicar of Christ** the Pope. □□ **vicariate** /-'keərɪət/ n. **vicarship** n. [ME f. AF viker(e), OF vicaire f. L vicarius substitute f. vicis: see VICE³]

vicarage /'vɪkərɪdʒ/ n. the residence or benefice of a vicar.

vicarial /vɪ'keərɪəl/ adj. of or serving as a vicar.

vicarious /vɪ'keərɪəs/ adj. 1 experienced in the imagination through another person (vicarious pleasure). 2 acting or done for another (vicarious suffering). 3 deputed, delegated (vicarious authority). □□ **vicariously** adv. **vicariousness** n. [L vicarius: see VICAR]

vice¹ /vaɪs/ n. 1 a evil or grossly immoral conduct. b a particular form of this, esp. involving prostitution, drugs, etc. 2 a depravity, evil. b an evil habit; a particular form of depravity (has the vice of gluttony). 3 a defect of character or behaviour (drunkenness was not among his vices). 4 a fault or bad habit in a horse etc. □ **vice ring** a group of criminals involved in organizing illegal prostitution. **vice squad** a police department enforcing laws against prostitution, drug abuse, etc. □□ **viceless** adj. [ME f. OF f. L vitium]

vice² /vaɪs/ n. & v. —n. (US **vise**) an instrument, esp. attached to a workbench, with two movable jaws between which an object may be clamped so as to leave the hands free to work on it. —v.tr. secure in a vice. □□ **vicelike** adj. [ME, = winding stair, screw, f. OF vis f. L vitis vine]

vice³ /'vaɪsɪ/ prep. in the place of; in succession to. [L, ablat. of vix (recorded in oblique forms in vic-) change]

vice⁴ /vaɪs/ n. colloq. = VICE-PRESIDENT, VICE ADMIRAL, etc. [abbr.]

vice- /vaɪs/ comb. form forming nouns meaning: 1 acting as a substitute or deputy for (vice-president). 2 next in rank to (vice admiral). [as VICE³]

vice admiral /vaɪs'ædmər(ə)l/ n. a naval officer ranking below admiral and above rear admiral. □□ **vice-admiralty** n. (pl. -ies).

vice-chamberlain /vaɪs'tʃeɪmbəlɪn/ n. a deputy chamberlain, esp. the deputy of the Lord Chamberlain.

vice-chancellor /vaɪs'tʃɑːnsələ(r)/ n. a deputy chancellor (esp. of a British university), discharging most of the administrative duties).

vicegerent /vaɪs'dʒɛrənt/ adj. & n. —adj. exercising delegated power. —n. a vicegerent person; a deputy. □□ **vicegerency** n. (pl. -ies). [med.L vicegerens (as VICE³, L gerere carry on)]

vicennial /vaɪ'sɛnɪəl/ adj. lasting for or occurring every twenty years. [LL vicennium period of 20 years f. vicies 20 times f. viginti 20 + annus year]

vice-president /vaɪs'prɛzɪd(ə)nt/ n. an official ranking below and deputizing for a president. □□ **vice-presidency** n. (pl. -ies). **vice-presidential** /-'dɛnʃ(ə)l/ adj.

viceregal /vaɪs'riːg(ə)l/ adj. of or relating to a viceroy. □□ **viceregally** adv.

vicereine /'vaɪsreɪn/ n. 1 the wife of a viceroy. 2 a woman viceroy. [F (as VICE-, reine queen)]

viceroy /'vaɪsrɔɪ/ n. a ruler exercising authority on behalf of a sovereign in a colony, province, etc. □□ **viceroyal** /-'rɔɪəl/ adj. **viceroyalty** /-'rɔɪəltɪ/ n. **viceroyship** n. [F (as VICE-, roy king)]

vicesimal /vaɪ'sɛsɪm(ə)l/ adj. = VIGESIMAL. [L vicesimus twentieth]

vice versa /ˌvaɪsɪ 'vɜːsə/ adj. with the order of the terms or conditions changed; the other way round (could go from left to right or vice versa). [L, = the position being reversed (as VICE³, versa ablat. fem. past part. of vertere turn)]

vichyssoise /ˌviːʃiː'swɑːz/ n. a creamy soup of leeks and potatoes, usu. served chilled. [F vichyssois -oise of Vichy (in France)]

Vichy water /'viːʃɪ/ n. an effervescent mineral water from Vichy in France.

vicinage /'vɪsɪnɪdʒ/ n. 1 a neighbourhood; a surrounding district. 2 relation in terms of nearness etc. to neighbours. [ME f. OF vis(e)nage ult. f. L vicinus neighbour]

vicinal /'vɪsɪn(ə)l, -'saɪn(ə)l/ adj. 1 neighbouring, adjacent. 2 of a neighbourhood; local. [F vicinal or L vicinalis f. vicinus neighbour]

vicinity /vɪ'sɪnɪtɪ/ n. (pl. -ies) 1 a surrounding district. 2 (foll. by to) nearness or closeness of place or relationship. □**in the vicinity** (often foll. by of) near (to). [L vicinitas (as VICINAL)]

vicious /'vɪʃəs/ adj. 1 bad-tempered, spiteful (a vicious dog; vicious remarks). 2 violent, severe (a vicious attack). 3 of the nature of or addicted to vice. 4 (of language or reasoning etc.) faulty or unsound. □**vicious circle** see CIRCLE n. 11. **vicious spiral** continual harmful interaction of causes and effects, esp. as causing repeated rises in both prices and wages. □□ **viciously** adv. **viciousness** n. [ME f. OF vicious or L vitiosus f. vitium VICE¹]

vicissitude /vɪ'sɪsɪˌtjuːd, vaɪ-/ n. 1 a change of circumstances, esp. variation of fortune. 2 archaic or poet. regular change; alternation. □□

vicissitudinous /-'tjuːdɪnəs/ adj. [F vicissitude or L vicissitudo -dinis f. vicissim by turns (as VICE[3])]

victim /'vɪktɪm/ n. **1** a person injured or killed as a result of an event or circumstance (a road victim; the victims of war). **2** a person or thing injured or destroyed in pursuit of an object or in gratification of a passion etc. (the victim of their ruthless ambition). **3** a prey; a dupe (fell victim to a confidence trick). **4** a living creature sacrificed to a deity or in a religious rite. [L victima]

victimize /'vɪktɪˌmaɪz/ v.tr. (also -ise) **1** single out (a person) for punishment or unfair treatment, esp. dismissal from employment. **2** make (a person etc.) a victim. □□ **victimization** /-ˈzeɪʃ(ə)n/ n. **victimizer** n.

victor /'vɪktə(r)/ n. a winner in battle or in a contest. [ME f. AF victo(u)r or L victor f. vincere vict- conquer]

victoria /vɪkˈtɔːrɪə/ n. **1** a low light four-wheeled carriage with a collapsible top, seats for two passengers, and a raised driver's seat. **2** a gigantic S. American water lily, Victoria amazonica. **3 a** species of crowned pigeon. **b** a variety of domestic pigeon. **4** (also **victoria plum**) Brit. a large red luscious variety of plum. [Queen Victoria, d. 1901]

Victoria Cross /vɪkˈtɔːrɪə/ n. a decoration awarded for conspicuous bravery in the armed services, instituted by Queen Victoria in 1856.

Victorian /vɪkˈtɔːrɪən/ adj. & n. —adj. **1** of or characteristic of the time of Queen Victoria. **2** associated with attitudes attributed to this time, esp. of prudery and moral strictness. —n. a person, esp. a writer, of this time. □□ **Victorianism** n.

Victoriana /vɪkˌtɔːrɪˈɑːnə/ n.pl. **1** articles, esp. collectors' items, of the Victorian period. **2** attitudes characteristic of this period.

Victoria sandwich /vɪkˈtɔːrɪə/ n. (also **Victoria sponge**) a sponge cake consisting of two layers of sponge with a jam filling.

victorious /vɪkˈtɔːrɪəs/ adj. **1** having won a victory; conquering, triumphant. **2** marked by victory (victorious day). □□ **victoriously** adv. **victoriousness** n. [ME f. AF victorious, OF victorieux, f. L victoriosus (as VICTORY)]

victor ludorum /ˌvɪktə luːˈdɔːrəm/ n. the overall champion in a sports competition. [L, = victor of the games]

victory /'vɪktərɪ/ n. (pl. -ies) **1** the process of defeating an enemy in battle or war or an opponent in a contest. **2** an instance of this; a triumph. [ME f. AF victorie, OF victoire, f. L victoria (as VICTOR)]

victual /'vɪt(ə)l/ n. & v. —n. (usu. in pl.) food, provisions, esp. as prepared for use. —v. (**victualled**, **victualling**; US **victualed**, **victualing**) **1** tr. supply with victuals. **2** intr. obtain stores. **3** intr. eat victuals. □□ **victualless** adj. [ME f. OF vitaille f. LL victualia, neut. pl. of L victualis f. victus food, rel. to vivere live]

victualler /'vɪtlə(r)/ n. (US **victualer**) **1 a** a person etc. who supplies victuals. **b** (in full **licensed victualler**) Brit. a publican etc. licensed to sell alcoholic liquor. **2** a ship carrying stores for other ships. [ME f. OF vitaill(i)er, vitaillour (as VICTUAL)]

vicuña /vɪˈkjuːnə/ n. **1** a S. American mammal, Vicugna vicugna, related to the llama, with fine silky wool. **2 a** cloth made from its wool. **b** an imitation of this. [Sp. f. Quechua]

vide /'vɪdeɪ, 'viː-, 'vaɪdɪ/ v.tr. (as an instruction in a reference to a passage in a book etc.) see, consult. [L, imper. of vidēre see]

videlicet /vɪˈdeliˌset/ adv. = VIZ. [ME f. L f. vidēre see + licet it is permissible]

video /'vɪdɪəʊ/ adj., n., & v. —adj. **1** relating to the recording, reproducing, or broadcasting of visual images on magnetic tape. **2** relating to the broadcasting of television pictures. —n. (pl. -os) **1** the process of recording, reproducing, or broadcasting visual images on magnetic tape. **2** the visual element of television broadcasts. **3** colloq. = video recorder. **4** a film etc. recorded on a videotape. —v.tr. (-oes, -oed) make a video recording of. □ **video cassette** a cassette of videotape. **video frequency** a frequency in the range used for video signals in television. **video game** a game played by electronically manipulating images produced by a computer program on a television screen. **video nasty** colloq. an explicitly horrific or pornographic video film. **video** (or **video cassette**) **recorder** an apparatus for recording and playing videotapes. **video signal** a signal containing information for producing a television image. [L vidēre see, after AUDIO]

videodisc /'vɪdɪəʊˌdɪsk/ n. a metal-coated disc on which visual material is recorded for reproduction on a television screen.

videophone /'vɪdɪəʊˌfəʊn/ n. a telephone device transmitting a visual image as well as sound.

videotape /'vɪdɪəʊˌteɪp/ n. & v. —n. magnetic tape for recording television pictures and sound. —v.tr. make a recording of (broadcast material etc.) with this. □ **videotape recorder** = video recorder.

videotex /'vɪdɪəʊˌteks/ n. (also **videotext** /-ˌtekst/) any electronic information system, esp. teletext or viewdata.

vidimus /'vaɪdɪməs/ n. an inspection or certified copy of accounts etc. [L, = we have seen f. vidēre see]

vie /vaɪ/ v.intr. (**vying**) (often foll. by with) compete; strive for superiority (vied with each other for recognition). [prob. f. ME (as ENVY)]

vielle /vɪˈel/ n. a hurdy-gurdy. [F f. OF viel(l)e: see VIOL]

Vienna schnitzel see SCHNITZEL.

Viennese /vɪəˈniːz/ adj. & n. —adj. of, relating to, or associated with Vienna in Austria. —n. (pl. same) a native or citizen of Vienna.

Vietnamese /ˌvɪetnəˈmiːz/ adj. & n. —adj. of or relating to Vietnam in SE Asia. —n. (pl. same) **1** a native or national of Vietnam. **2** the language of Vietnam.

vieux jeu /vɪɜ ˈʒɜ/ adj. old-fashioned, hackneyed. [F, lit. old game]

view /vjuː/ n. & v. —n. **1** range of vision; extent of visibility (came into view; in full view of the crowd). **2 a** what is seen from a particular point; a scene or prospect (a fine view of the downs; a room with a view). **b** a picture etc. representing this. **3** an inspection by the eye or mind; a visual or mental survey. **4** an opportunity for visual inspection; a viewing (a private view of the exhibition). **5 a** an opinion (holds strong views on morality). **b** a mental attitude (took a favourable view of the matter). **c** a manner of considering a thing (took a long-term view of it). —v. **1** tr. look at; survey visually; inspect (we are going to view the house). **2** tr. examine; survey mentally (different ways of viewing a subject). **3** tr. form a mental impression or opinion of; consider (does not view the matter in the same light). **4** intr. watch television. **5** tr. see (a fox) break cover. □ **have in view 1** have as one's object. **2** bear (a circumstance) in mind in forming a judgement etc. **in view of** having regard to; considering. **on view** being shown (for observation or inspection); being exhibited. **view halloo** Hunting a shout on seeing a fox break cover. **with a view to 1** with the hope or intention of. **2** with the aim of attaining (with a view to marriage). □□ **viewable** adj. [ME f. AF v(i)ewe, OF vëue fem. past part. f. vëoir see f. L vidēre]

viewdata /'vjuːˌdeɪtə/ n. a news and information service from a computer source to which a television screen is connected by telephone link.

viewer /'vjuːə(r)/ n. **1** a person who views. **2** a person watching television. **3** a device for looking at film transparencies etc.

viewfinder /'vjuːˌfaɪndə(r)/ n. a device on a camera showing the area covered by the lens in taking a photograph.

viewing /'vjuːɪŋ/ n. **1** an opportunity or occasion to view; an exhibition. **2** the act or practice of watching television.

viewless /'vjuːlɪs/ *adj.* **1** not having or affording a view. **2** lacking opinions.

viewpoint /'vjuːpɔɪnt/ *n.* a point of view, a standpoint.

vigesimal /vɪ'dʒesɪm(ə)l, vaɪ-/ *adj.* **1** of twentieths or twenty. **2** reckoning or reckoned by twenties. □□ **vigesimally** *adv.* [L *vigesimus* f. *viginti* twenty]

vigil /'vɪdʒɪl/ *n.* **1 a** keeping awake during the time usually given to sleep, esp. to keep watch or pray (*keep vigil*). **b** a period of this. **2** *Eccl.* the eve of a festival or holy day. **3** (in *pl.*) nocturnal devotions. [ME f. OF *vigile* f. L *vigilia* f. *vigil* awake]

vigilance /'vɪdʒɪləns/ *n.* watchfulness, caution, circumspection. □ **vigilance committee** *US* a self-appointed body for the maintenance of order etc. [F *vigilance* or L *vigilantia* f. *vigilare* keep awake (as VIGIL)]

vigilant /'vɪdʒɪlənt/ *adj.* watchful against danger, difficulty, etc. □□ **vigilantly** *adv.* [L *vigilans -antis* (as VIGILANCE)]

vigilante /ˌvɪdʒɪ'læntɪ/ *n.* a member of a vigilance committee or similar body. [Sp., = vigilant]

vigneron /'viːnjəˌrɔ̃/ *n.* a vine-grower. [F f. *vigne* VINE]

vignette /viː'njet/ *n. & v.* —*n.* **1** a short descriptive essay or character sketch. **2** an illustration or decorative design, esp. on the title-page of a book, not enclosed in a definite border. **3** a photograph or portrait showing only the head and shoulders with the background gradually shaded off. —*v.tr.* **1** make a portrait of (a person) in vignette style. **2** shade off (a photograph or portrait). □□ **vignettist** *n.* [F, dimin. of *vigne* VINE]

vigor *US* var. of VIGOUR.

vigoro /'vɪgəˌrəʊ/ *n.* *Austral.* a team ball game combining elements of cricket and baseball. [app. f. VIGOROUS]

vigorous /'vɪgərəs/ *adj.* **1** strong and active; robust. **2** (of a plant) growing strongly. **3** forceful; acting or done with physical or mental vigour; energetic. **4** full of vigour; showing or requiring physical strength or activity. □□ **vigorously** *adv.* **vigorousness** *n.* [ME f. OF f. med.L *vigorosus* f. L *vigor* (as VIGOUR)]

vigour /'vɪgə(r)/ *n.* (*US* vigor) **1** active physical strength or energy. **2** a flourishing physical condition. **3** healthy growth; vitality; vital force. **4 a** mental strength or activity shown in thought or speech or in literary style. **b** forcefulness; trenchancy, animation. □□ **vigourless** *adj.* [ME f. OF *vigour* f. L *vigor -oris* f. *vigēre* be lively]

vihara /vɪ'hɑːrə/ *n.* a Buddhist temple or monastery. [Skr.]

Viking /'vaɪkɪŋ/ *n. & adj.* —*n.* any of the Scandinavian seafaring pirates and traders who raided and settled in parts of NW Europe in the 8th–11th c. —*adj.* of or relating to the Vikings or their time. [ON *víkingr*, perh. f. OE *wīcing* f. *wīc* camp]

vile /vaɪl/ *adj.* **1** disgusting. **2** morally base; depraved, shameful. **3** *colloq.* abominably bad (*vile weather*). **4** *archaic* worthless. □□ **vilely** *adv.* **vileness** *n.* [ME f. OF *vil vile* f. L *vilis* cheap, base]

vilify /'vɪlɪˌfaɪ/ *v.tr.* (-**ies**, -**ied**) defame; speak evil of. □□ **vilification** /-frˈkeɪʃ(ə)n/ *n.* **vilifier** *n.* [ME in sense 'lower in value', f. LL *vilificare* (as VILE)]

vill /vɪl/ *n.* *hist.* a feudal township. [AF f. OF *vile, ville* farm f. L (as VILLA)]

villa /'vɪlə/ *n.* **1** *Rom. Antiq.* a large country house with an estate. **2** a country residence. **3** *Brit.* a detached or semi-detached house in a residential district. **4** a rented holiday home, esp. abroad. [It. & L]

village /'vɪlɪdʒ/ *n.* **1 a** a group of houses and associated buildings, larger than a hamlet and smaller than a town, esp. in a rural area. **b** the inhabitants of a village regarded as a community. **2** *Brit.* a self-contained district or community within a town

or city, regarded as having features characteristic of village life. **3** *US* a small municipality with limited corporate powers. **4** *Austral.* a select suburban shopping centre. □□ **villager** *n.* **villagey** *adj.* [ME f. OF f. L *villa*]

villain /'vɪlən/ *n.* **1** a person guilty or capable of great wickedness. **2** *colloq.* usu. *joc.* a rascal or rogue. **3** (also **villain of the piece**) (in a play etc.) a character whose evil actions or motives are important in the plot. **4** *Brit. colloq.* a professional criminal. **5** *archaic* a rustic; a boor. [ME f. OF *vilein, vilain* ult. f. L *villa*: see VILLA]

villainous /'vɪlənəs/ *adj.* **1** characteristic of a villain; wicked. **2** *colloq.* abominably bad; vile (*villainous weather*). □□ **villainously** *adv.* **villainousness** *n.*

villainy /'vɪlənɪ/ *n.* (*pl.* -**ies**) **1** villainous behaviour. **2** a wicked act. [OF *vilenie* (as VILLAIN)]

villanelle /ˌvɪlə'nel/ *n.* a usu. pastoral or lyrical poem of 19 lines, with only two rhymes throughout, and some lines repeated. [F f. It. *villanella* fem. of *villanello* rural, dimin. of *villano* (as VILLAIN)]

-ville /vɪl/ *comb. form colloq.* forming the names of fictitious places with ref. to a particular quality etc. (*dragsville; squaresville*). [F *ville* town, as in many US town-names]

villein /'vɪlɪn/ *n. hist.* a feudal tenant entirely subject to a lord or attached to a manor. [ME, var. of VILLAIN]

villeinage /'vɪlɪnɪdʒ/ *n. hist.* the tenure or status of a villein.

villus /'vɪləs/ *n.* (*pl.* **villi** /-laɪ/) **1** *Anat.* each of the short finger-like processes on some membranes, esp. on the mucous membrane of the small intestine. **2** *Bot.* (in *pl.*) long soft hairs covering fruit, flowers, etc. □□ **villiform** *adj.* **villose** *adj.* **villosity** /-'lɒsɪtɪ/ *n.* **villous** *adj.* [L, = shaggy hair]

vim /vɪm/ *n. colloq.* vigour. [perh. f. L, accus. of *vis* energy]

vimineous /vɪ'mɪnɪəs/ *adj.* *Bot.* of or producing twigs or shoots. [L *vimineus* f. *vimen viminis* osier]

vina /'viːnə/ *n.* an Indian four-stringed musical instrument with a fretted finger-board and a gourd at each end. [Skr. & Hindi *viṇā*]

vinaceous /vaɪ'neɪʃəs/ *adj.* wine-red. [L *vinaceus* f. *vinum* wine]

vinaigrette /ˌvɪnɪ'gret/ *n.* **1** (in full **vinaigrette sauce**) a salad dressing of oil, wine vinegar, and seasoning. **2** a small ornamental bottle for holding smelling-salts. [F, dimin. of *vinaigre* VINEGAR]

vincible /'vɪnsɪb(ə)l/ *adj. literary* that can be overcome or conquered. □□ **vincibility** /-'bɪlɪtɪ/ *n.* [L *vincibilis* f. *vincere* overcome]

vinculum /'vɪŋkjʊləm/ *n.* (*pl.* **vincula** /-lə/) **1** *Algebra* a horizontal line drawn over a group of terms to show they have a common relation to what follows or precedes (e.g. $a + b \times c = ac + bc$, but $a + b \times c = a + bc$). **2** *Anat.* a ligament; a fraenum. [L, = bond, f. *vincire* bind]

vindicate /'vɪndɪˌkeɪt/ *v.tr.* **1** clear of blame or suspicion. **2** establish the existence, merits, or justice of (one's courage, conduct, assertion, etc.). **3** justify (a person, oneself, etc.) by evidence or argument. □□ **vindicable** /-kəb(ə)l/ *adj.* **vindication** /-'keɪʃ(ə)n/ *n.* **vindicative** /-kətɪv/ *adj.* **vindicator** *n.* [L *vindicare* claim, avenge f. *vindex -dicis* claimant, avenger]

vindicatory /'vɪndɪˌkeɪtərɪ/ *adj.* **1** tending to vindicate. **2** (of laws) punitive.

vindictive /vɪn'dɪktɪv/ *adj.* **1** tending to seek revenge. **2** spiteful. □ **vindictive damages** *Law* damages exceeding simple compensation and awarded to punish the defendant. □□ **vindictively** *adv.* **vindictiveness** *n.* [L *vindicta* vengeance (as VINDICATE)]

vine /vaɪn/ *n.* **1** any climbing or trailing woody-stemmed plant, esp. of the genus *Vitis*, bearing grapes. **2** a slender trailing or climbing stem. □ **vine-dresser** a person who prunes, trains, and cultivates vines. □□ **viny** *adj.* [ME f. OF *vi(g)ne* f. L *vinea* vineyard f. *vinum* wine]

vinegar /'vɪnɪgə(r)/ n. **1** a sour liquid obtained from wine, cider, etc., by fermentation and used as a condiment or for pickling. **2** sour behaviour or character. □□ **vinegarish** adj. **vinegary** adj. [ME f. OF vyn egre ult. f. L vinum wine + acer, acre sour]

vinery /'vaɪnərɪ/ n. (pl. -ies) **1** a greenhouse for grapevines. **2** a vineyard.

vineyard /'vɪnjɑːd, -jəd/ n. **1** a plantation of grape-vines, esp. for wine-making. **2** Bibl. a sphere of action or labour (see Matt. 20:1). [ME f. VINE + YARD²]

vingt-et-un /ˌvæteɪˈɜː/ n. = PONTOON¹. [F, = twenty-one]

vini- /'vɪnɪ/ comb. form wine. [L vinum]

viniculture /'vɪnɪˌkʌltʃə(r)/ n. the cultivation of grapevines. □□ **vinicultural** /-ˈkʌltʃər(ə)l/ adj. **viniculturist** /-ˈkʌltʃərɪst/ n.

vinification /ˌvɪnɪfɪˈkeɪʃ(ə)n/ n. the conversion of grape-juice etc. into wine.

vining /'vaɪnɪŋ/ n. the separation of leguminous crops from their vines and pods.

vino /'viːnəʊ/ n. sl. wine, esp. of an inferior kind. [Sp. & It., = wine]

vin ordinaire /ˌvæ ɔːdɪˈneə(r)/ n. cheap (usu. red) wine as drunk in France mixed with water. [F, = ordinary wine]

vinous /'vaɪnəs/ adj. **1** of, like, or associated with wine. **2** addicted to wine. □□ **vinosity** /-ˈnɒsɪtɪ/ n. [L vinum wine]

vin rosé /ˌvæ rəʊˈzeɪ/ n. = ROSÉ. [F]

vint¹ /vɪnt/ v.tr. make (wine). [back-form. f. VINTAGE]

vint² /vɪnt/ n. a Russian card-game like auction bridge. [Russ., = screw]

vintage /'vɪntɪdʒ/ n. & adj. —n. **1 a** a season's produce of grapes. **b** the wine made from this. **2 a** the gathering of grapes for wine-making. **b** the season of this. **3** a wine of high quality from a single identified year and district. **4 a** the year etc. when a thing was made etc. **b** a thing made etc. in a particular year etc. **5** poet. or rhet. wine. —adj. **1** of high quality, esp. from the past or characteristic of the best period of a person's work. **2** of a past season. □ **vintage car** Brit. a car made between 1917 and 1930. **vintage festival** a carnival to celebrate the beginning of the vintage. [alt. (after VINTNER) of ME vendage, vindage f. OF vendange f. L vindemia f. vinum wine + demere remove]

vintager /'vɪntɪdʒə(r)/ n. a grape-gatherer.

vintner /'vɪntnə(r)/ n. a wine-merchant. [ME f. AL vintenarius, vinetarius f. AF vineter, OF vinetier f. med.L vinetarius f. L vinetum vineyard f. vinum wine]

viny see VINE.

vinyl /'vaɪnɪl/ n. any plastic made by polymerizing a compound containing the vinyl group, esp. polyvinyl chloride. □ **vinyl group** the organic radical or group CH₂CH. [L vinum wine + -YL]

viol /'vaɪəl/ n. a medieval stringed musical instru-ment, played with a bow and held vertically on the knees or between the legs. [ME viel etc. f. OF viel(l)e, alt. of viole f. Prov. viola, viula, prob. ult. f. L vitulari be joyful: cf. FIDDLE]

viola¹ /vɪˈəʊlə/ n. **1 a** an instrument of the violin family, larger than the violin and of lower pitch. **b** a viola-player. **2** a viol. □ **viola da braccio** /də ˈbrɑːtʃəʊ/ a viol corresponding to the modern viola. **viola da gamba** /də ˈgæmbə/ a viol held between the player's legs, esp. one corresponding to the modern cello. **viola d'amore** /dæˈmɔːreɪ/ a sweet-toned tenor viol. [It. & Sp., prob. f. Prov.: see VIOL]

viola² /'vaɪələ/ n. **1** any plant of the genus Viola, including the pansy and violet. **2** a cultivated hybrid of this genus. [L, = violet]

violaceous /ˌvaɪəˈleɪʃəs/ adj. **1** of a violet colour. **2** Bot. of the violet family Violaceae. [L violaceus (as VIOLA²)]

violate /'vaɪəˌleɪt/ v.tr. **1** disregard; fail to comply with (an oath, treaty, law, etc.). **2** treat (a sanctuary etc.) profanely or with disrespect. **3** break in upon, disturb (a person's privacy etc.). **4** assault sexually; rape. □□ **violable** adj. **violation** /-ˈleɪʃ(ə)n/ n. **violator** n. [ME f. L violare treat violently]

violence /'vaɪələns/ n. **1** the quality of being violent. **2** violent conduct or treatment, outrage, injury. **3** Law **a** the unlawful exercise of physical force. **b** intimidation by the exhibition of this. □ **do violence to** act contrary to; outrage. [ME f. OF f. L violentia (as VIOLENT)]

violent /'vaɪələnt/ adj. **1** involving or using great physical force (a violent person; a violent storm; came into violent collision). **2 a** intense, vehement, passionate, furious (a violent contrast; violent dislike). **b** vivid (violent colours). **3** (of death) resulting from external force or from poison (cf. NATURAL adj. 2). **4** involving an unlawful exercise of force (laid violent hands on him). □□ **violently** adv. [ME f. OF f. L violentus]

violet /'vaɪələt/ n. & adj. —n. **1 a** any plant of the genus Viola, esp. the sweet violet, with usu. purple, blue, or white flowers. **b** any of various plants resembling the sweet violet. **2** the bluish-purple colour seen at the end of the spectrum opposite red. **3 a** a pigment of this colour. **b** clothes or material of this colour. —adj. of this colour. [ME f. OF violet(te) dimin. of viole f. L VIOLA²]

violin /ˌvaɪəˈlɪn/ n. **1** a musical instrument with four strings of treble pitch played with a bow. **2** a violin-player. □□ **violinist** n. [It. violino dimin. of VIOLA¹]

violist /'vaɪəlɪst/ n. a viol- or viola-player.

violoncello /ˌvaɪələnˈtʃeləʊ, ˌviːə-/ n. (pl. -os) formal = CELLO. □□ **violoncellist** n. [It., dimin. of VIOLONE]

violone /viːəˈləʊnɪ/ n. a double-bass viol. [It., augment. of VIOLA¹]

VIP abbr. very important person.

viper /'vaɪpə(r)/ n. **1** any venomous snake of the family Viperidae, esp. the common viper (see ADDER). **2** a malignant or treacherous person. □ **viper in one's bosom** a person who betrays those who have helped him or her. **viper's bugloss** a stiff bristly blue-flowered plant, Echium vulgare. **viper's grass** scorzonera. □□ **viperine** /-ˌraɪn/ adj. **viperish** adj. **viper-like** adj. **viperous** adj. [F vipère or L vipera f. vivus alive + parere bring forth]

virago /vɪˈrɑːgəʊ, -ˈreɪgəʊ/ n. (pl. -os) **1** a fierce or abusive woman. **2** archaic a woman of masculine strength or spirit. [OE f. L, = female warrior, f. vir man]

viral /'vaɪər(ə)l/ adj. of or caused by a virus. □□ **virally** adv.

virelay /'vɪrɪˌleɪ/ n. a short (esp. old French) lyric poem with two rhymes to a stanza variously arranged. [ME f. OF virelai]

virement /'vaɪəmənt, 'viːəmɑ̃/ n. the transfer of items from one financial account to another. [F f. virer turn: see VEER¹]

vireo /'vɪrɪəʊ/ n. (pl. -os) any small American song-bird of the family Vireonidae. [L, perh. = greenfinch]

virescence /vɪˈres(ə)ns/ n. **1** greenness. **2** Bot. abnormal greenness in petals etc. normally of some bright colour. □□ **virescent** adj. [L virescere, incept. of virere be green]

virgate¹ /'vɜːgət/ adj. Bot. & Zool. slim, straight, and erect. [L virgatus f. virga rod]

virgate² /'vɜːgət/ n. Brit. hist. a varying measure of land, esp. 30 acres. [med.L virgata (rendering OE gierd-land yard-land) f. L virga rod]

virger var. of VERGER.

Virgilian /vɜːˈdʒɪlɪən/ adj. of, or in the style of, the Roman poet Virgil (d. 19 BC). [L Vergilianus f. P. Vergilius Maro, Virgil]

virgin /'vɜːdʒɪn/ n. & adj. —n. **1** a person (esp. a woman) who has never had sexual intercourse. **2 a (the Virgin)** Christ's mother the Blessed Virgin Mary. **b** a picture or statue of the Virgin. **3 (the Virgin)** the zodiacal sign or constellation Virgo. **4** colloq. a naïve, innocent, or inexperienced person (a *political virgin).* **5** a member of any order of women under a vow to remain virgins. **6** a female insect producing eggs without impregnation. —*adj.* **1** that is a virgin. **2** of or befitting a virgin (*virgin modesty*). **3** not yet used, penetrated, or tried (*virgin soil*). **4** undefiled, spotless. **5** (of clay) not fired. **6** (of metal) made from ore by smelting. **7** (of wool) not yet, or only once, spun or woven. **8** (of an insect) producing eggs without impregnation. □**virgin birth 1** the doctrine of Christ's birth without a human father. **2** parthenogenesis. **virgin comb** a honeycomb that has been used only once for honey and never for brood. **virgin forest** a forest in its untouched natural state. **virgin honey** honey taken from a virgin comb, or drained from the comb without heat or pressure. **virgin queen** an unfertilized queen bee. **the Virgin Queen** Queen Elizabeth I of England. **virgin's bower** a clematis, *Clematis viticella*. □□ **virginhood** *n.* [ME f. AF & OF *virgine* f. L *virgo -ginis*]

virginal /'vɜːdʒɪn(ə)l/ *adj. & n.* —*adj.* that is or befits or belongs to a virgin. —*n.* (usu. in *pl.*) (in full **pair of virginals**) an early form of spinet in a box, used in the sixteenth and seventeenth centuries. □□ **virginalist** *n.* **virginally** *adv.* [ME f. OF *virginal* or L *virginalis* (as VIRGIN): name of the instrument perh. from its use by young women]

Virginia /vəˈdʒɪnɪə/ *n.* **1** tobacco from Virginia. **2** a cigarette made of this. □**Virginia creeper** a N. American vine, *Parthenocissus quinquefolia*, cultivated for ornament. **Virginia reel** *US* a country dance. **Virginia** (or **Virginian**) **stock** a cruciferous plant, *Malcolmia maritima*, with white or pink flowers. □□ **Virginian** *n. & adj.* [*Virginia* in US, orig. the first English settlement (1607), f. *Virgin Queen*]

virginity /vəˈdʒɪnɪtɪ/ *n.* the state of being a virgin. [OF *virginité* f. L *virginitas* (as VIRGIN)]

Virgo /'vɜːgəʊ/ *n.* (*pl.* **-os**) **1** a constellation, traditionally regarded as contained in the figure of a woman. **2 a** the sixth sign of the zodiac (the Virgin). **b** a person born when the sun is in this sign. □□ **Virgoan** *n. & adj.* [OE f. L, = virgin]

virgule /'vɜːgjuːl/ *n.* **1** a slanting line used to mark division of words or lines. **2** = SOLIDUS 1. [F, = comma, f. L *virgula* dimin. of *virga* rod]

viridescent /ˌvɪrɪˈdes(ə)nt/ *adj.* greenish, tending to become green. □□ **viridescence** *n.* [LL *viridescere* f. L *viridis*: see VIRIDIAN]

viridian /vɪˈrɪdɪən/ *n. & adj.* —*n.* **1** a bluish-green chromium oxide pigment. **2** the colour of this. —*adj.* bluish-green. [L *viridis* green f. *virēre* be green]

viridity /vɪˈrɪdɪtɪ/ *n. literary* greenness, verdancy. [ME f. OF *viridité* or L *viriditas* f. *viridis*: see VIRIDIAN]

virile /'vɪraɪl/ *adj.* **1** of or characteristic of a man; having masculine (esp. sexual) vigour or strength. **2** of or having procreative power. **3** of a man as distinct from a woman or child. □□ **virility** /vɪˈrɪlɪtɪ/ *n.* [ME f. F *viril* or L *virilis* f. *vir* man]

virilism /'vɪrɪˌlɪz(ə)m/ *n. Med.* the development of secondary male characteristics in a female or precociously in a male.

viroid /'vaɪəˌrɔɪd/ *n.* an infectious entity affecting plants, similar to a virus but smaller and consisting only of nucleic acid without a protein coat.

virology /vaɪˈrɒlədʒɪ/ *n.* the scientific study of viruses. □□ **virological** /-rəˈlɒdʒɪk(ə)l/ *adj.* **virologically** /-rəˈlɒdʒɪkəlɪ/ *adv.* **virologist** *n.*

virtu /vɜːˈtuː/ *n.* (also **vertu**) **1** a knowledge of or expertise in the fine arts. **2** virtuosity. □**article** (or **object**) **of virtu** an article interesting because of its workmanship, antiquity, rarity, etc. [It. *virtù* VIRTUE, virtu]

virtual /'vɜːtjʊəl/ *adj.* **1** that is such for practical purposes though not in name or according to strict definition (*is the virtual manager of the business*; *take this as a virtual promise*). **2** *Optics* relating to the points at which rays would meet if produced backwards (*virtual focus*; *virtual image*). **3** *Mech.*

relating to an infinitesimal displacement of a point in a system. **4** *Computing* not physically existing as such but made by software to appear to do so (*virtual memory*). □□ **virtuality** /-jʊˈælɪtɪ/ *n.* **virtually** *adv.* [ME f. med.L *virtualis* f. L *virtus* after LL *virtuosus*]

virtue /'vɜːtjuː, -tʃuː/ *n.* **1** moral excellence; uprightness, goodness. **2** a particular form of this (*patience is a virtue*). **3** chastity, esp. of a woman. **4** a good quality (*has the virtue of being adjustable*). **5** efficacy; inherent power (*no virtue in such drugs*). **6** an angelic being of the seventh order of the celestial hierarchy (see ORDER *n.* 19). □**by** (or **in**) **virtue of** on the strength or ground of (*got the job by virtue of his experience*). **make a virtue of necessity** derive some credit or benefit from an unwelcome obligation. □□ **virtueless** *adj.* [ME f. OF *vertu* f. L *virtus -tutis* f. *vir* man]

virtuoso /ˌvɜːtjʊˈəʊsəʊ, -zəʊ/ *n.* (*pl.* **virtuosi** /-iː/ or **-os**) **1 a** a person highly skilled in the technique of a fine art, esp. music. **b** (*attrib.*) displaying the skills of a virtuoso. **2** a person with a special knowledge of or taste for works of art or virtu. □□ **virtuosic** /-ˈɒsɪk/ *adj.* **virtuosity** /-ˈɒsɪtɪ/ *n.* **virtuosoship** *n.* [It., = learned, skilful, f. LL (as VIRTUOUS)]

virtuous /'vɜːtjʊəs, -tʃʊəs/ *adj.* **1** possessing or showing moral rectitude. **2** chaste. □**virtuous circle** a beneficial recurring cycle of cause and effect (cf. *vicious circle* (see CIRCLE *n.* 11)). □□ **virtuously** *adv.* **virtuousness** *n.* [ME f. OF *vertuous* f. LL *virtuosus* f. *virtus* VIRTUE]

virulent /'vɪrʊlənt, 'vɪrjʊ-/ *adj.* **1** strongly poisonous. **2** (of a disease) violent or malignant. **3** bitterly hostile (*virulent animosity*; *virulent abuse*). □□ **virulence** *n.* **virulently** *adv.* [ME, orig. of a poisoned wound, f. L *virulentus* (as VIRUS)]

virus /'vaɪərəs/ *n.* **1** a microscopic organism consisting mainly of nucleic acid in a protein coat, multiplying only in living cells and often causing diseases. **2** *Computing* = computer virus. **3** *archaic* a poison, a source of disease. **4** a harmful or corrupting influence. [L, = slimy liquid, poison]

Vis. *abbr.* Viscount.

visa /'viːzə/ *n. & v.* —*n.* an endorsement on a passport etc. showing that it has been found correct, esp. as allowing the holder to enter or leave a country. —*v.tr.* (**visas, visaed** /-zəd/ or **visa'd, visaing**) mark with a visa. [F f. L *visa* neut. pl. past part. of *vidēre* see]

visage /'vɪzɪdʒ/ *n. literary* a face, a countenance. □□ **visaged** *adj.* (also in *comb.*). [ME f. OF f. L *visus* sight (as VISA)]

vis-à-vis /ˌviːzɑːˈviː/ *prep., adv., & n.* —*prep.* **1** in relation to. **2** opposite to. —*adv.* facing one another. —*n.* (*pl.* same) **1** a person or thing facing another, esp. in some dances. **2** a person occupying a corresponding position in another group. **3** *US* a social partner. [F, = face to face, f. *vis* face f. L (as VISAGE)]

Visc. *abbr.* Viscount.

viscacha /vɪsˈkætʃə/ *n.* (also **vizcacha** /vɪzˈk-/) any S. American burrowing rodent of the genus *Lagidium*, having valuable fur. [Sp. f. Quechua (h)*uiscacha*]

viscera /'vɪsərə/ *n.pl.* the interior organs in the great cavities of the body (e.g. brain, heart, liver), esp. in the abdomen (e.g. the intestines). [L, pl. of *viscus*: see VISCUS]

visceral /'vɪsər(ə)l/ *adj.* **1** of the viscera. **2** relating to inward feelings rather than conscious reasoning. □**visceral nerve** a sympathetic nerve (see SYMPATHETIC *adj.* 9). □□ **viscerally** *adv.*

viscid /'vɪsɪd/ *adj.* **1** glutinous, sticky. **2** semifluid. □□ **viscidity** /vɪˈsɪdɪtɪ/ *n.* [LL *viscidus* f. L *viscum* birdlime]

viscometer /vɪsˈkɒmɪtə(r)/ *n.* an instrument for measuring the viscosity of liquids. □□ **viscometric** /ˌvɪskəˈmetrɪk/ *adj.* **viscometrically** /ˌvɪskə ˈmetrɪkəlɪ/ *adv.* **viscometry** *n.* [var. of *viscosimeter* (as VISCOSITY)]

viscose /'vɪskəʊz, -kəʊs/ *n.* **1** a form of cellulose in a highly viscous state suitable for drawing into yarn. **2** rayon made from this. [LL *viscosus* (as VISCOUS)]

viscosity /vɪˈskɒsɪtɪ/ n. (pl. **-ies**) **1** the quality or degree of being viscous. **2** *Physics* **a** (of a fluid) internal friction, the resistance to flow. **b** a quantity expressing this. □**dynamic viscosity** a quantity measuring the force needed to overcome internal friction. **kinematic viscosity** a quantity measuring the dynamic viscosity per unit density. □□ **viscosimeter** /-kəˈsɪmɪtə(r)/ n. [ME f. OF *viscosité* or med.L *viscositas* (as VISCOUS)]

viscount /ˈvaɪkaʊnt/ n. a British nobleman ranking between an earl and a baron. □□ **viscountcy** n. (pl. **-ies**) **viscountship** n. **viscounty** n. (pl. **-ies**). [ME f. AF *viscounte*, OF *vi(s)conte* f. med.L *vicecomes -mitis* (as VICE-, COUNT²)]

viscountess /ˈvaɪkaʊntɪs/ n. **1** a viscount's wife or widow. **2** a woman holding the rank of viscount in her own right.

viscous /ˈvɪskəs/ adj. **1** glutinous, sticky. **2** semifluid. **3** *Physics* having a high viscosity; not flowing freely. □□ **viscously** adv. **viscousness** n. [ME f. AF *viscous* or LL *viscosus* (as VISCID)]

viscus /ˈvɪskəs/ n. (pl. **viscera** /ˈvɪsərə/) (usu. in *pl.*) any of the soft internal organs of the body. [L]

vise *US* var. of VICE².

Vishnu /ˈvɪʃnuː/ n. a Hindu god regarded by his worshippers as the supreme deity and saviour, by others as the second member of a triad with Brahma and Siva. □□ **Vishnuism** n. **Vishnuite** n. & adj. [Skr. *Vishṇu*]

visibility /ˌvɪzɪˈbɪlɪtɪ/ n. **1** the state of being visible. **2** the range or possibility of vision as determined by the conditions of light and atmosphere (*visibility was down to 50 yards*). [F *visibilité* or LL *visibilitas* f. L *visibilis*: see VISIBLE]

visible /ˈvɪzɪb(ə)l/ adj. **1 a** that can be seen by the eye. **b** (of light) within the range of wavelengths to which the eye is sensitive. **2** that can be perceived or ascertained; apparent, open (*has no visible means of support; spoke with visible impatience*). **3** (of exports etc.) consisting of actual goods (cf. *invisible exports*). □**the Church visible** the whole body of professed Christian believers. **visible horizon** see HORIZON 1b. □□ **visibleness** n. **visibly** adv. [ME f. OF *visible* or L *visibilis* f. *vidēre vis-* see]

Visigoth /ˈvɪzɪˌgɒθ/ n. a West Goth, a member of the branch of the Goths who settled in France and Spain in the 5th c. and ruled much of Spain until 711. [LL *Visigothus*]

vision /ˈvɪʒ(ə)n/ n. & v. — n. **1** the act or faculty of seeing, sight (*has impaired his vision*). **2 a** a thing or person seen in a dream or trance. **b** a supernatural or prophetic apparition. **3** a thing or idea perceived vividly in the imagination (*the romantic visions of youth; had visions of warm sandy beaches*). **4** imaginative insight. **5** statesmanlike foresight; sagacity in planning. **6** a person etc. of unusual beauty. **7** what is seen on a television screen; television images collectively. —v.tr. see or present in or as in a vision. □**field of vision** all that comes into view when the eyes are turned in some direction. **vision-mixer** a person whose job is to switch from one image to another in television broadcasting or recording. □□ **visional** adj. **visionless** adj. [ME f. OF f. L *visio -onis* (as VISIBLE)]

visionary /ˈvɪʒənərɪ/ adj. & n. —adj. **1** given to seeing visions or to indulging in fanciful theories. **2** existing only in a vision or in the imagination. **3** not practicable. —n. (pl. **-ies**) a visionary person. □□ **visionariness** n.

visit /ˈvɪzɪt/ v. & n. —v. (**visited, visiting**) **1 a** tr. (also *absol.*) go or come to see (a person, place, etc.) as an act of friendship or ceremony, on business or for a purpose, or from interest. **b** tr. go or come to see for the purpose of official inspection, supervision, consultation, or correction. **2** tr. reside temporarily with (a person) or at (a place). **3** intr. be a visitor. **4** tr. (of a disease, calamity, etc.) come upon, attack. **5** tr. *Bibl.* **a** (foll. by *with*) punish (a person). **b** (often foll. by *upon*) inflict punishment for (a sin). **6** intr. *US* **a** (foll. by *with*) go to see (a person) esp. socially. **b** (usu. foll. by *with*) converse, chat. **7** tr. *archaic* (often foll. by *with*) comfort, bless (with salvation etc.). —n. **1 a** an act of visiting, a call on a person or at a place (*was on a visit to some friends; paid him a long visit*). **b** temporary residence with a person or at a place. **2** (foll. by *to*) an occasion of going to a doctor, dentist, etc. **3** a formal or official call for the purpose of inspection etc. **4** *US* a chat. □**right of visit** = *right of visitation* (see VISITATION). □□ **visitable** adj. [ME f. OF *visiter* or L *visitare* go to see, frequent. of *visare* view f. *vidēre vis-* see: (n.) perh. f. F *visite*]

visitant /ˈvɪzɪt(ə)nt/ n. & adj. —n. **1** a visitor, esp. a supposedly supernatural one. **2** = VISITOR 2. —adj. *archaic* or *poet.* visiting. [F *visitant* or L *visitare* (as VISIT)]

visitation /ˌvɪzɪˈteɪʃ(ə)n/ n. **1** an official visit of inspection, esp. a bishop's examination of a church in his diocese. **2** trouble or difficulty regarded as a divine punishment. **3** (**Visitation**) **a** the visit of the Virgin Mary to Elizabeth related in Luke 1:39–56. **b** the festival commemorating this on 2 July. **4** *colloq.* an unduly protracted visit or social call. **5** the boarding of a vessel belonging to another State to learn its character and purpose. □**right of visitation** the right to conduct a visitation of a vessel, not including the right of search. [ME f. OF *visitation* or LL *visitatio* (as VISIT)]

visitatorial /ˌvɪzɪtəˈtɔːrɪəl/ adj. of an official visitor or visitation. [ult. f. L *visitare* (see VISIT)]

visiting /ˈvɪzɪtɪŋ/ n. & adj. —n. paying a visit or visits. —attrib.adj. (of an academic) spending some time at another institution (*a visiting professor*). □**visiting-card** a card with a person's name etc., sent or left in lieu of a formal visit. **visiting fireman** (pl. **-men**) *US sl.* a visitor given especially cordial treatment.

visitor /ˈvɪzɪtə(r)/ n. **1** a person who visits a person or place. **2** a migratory bird present in a locality for part of the year (*winter visitor*). **3** *Brit.* (in a college etc.) an official with the right or duty of occasionally inspecting and reporting. □**visitors' book** a book in which visitors to a hotel, church, embassy, etc., write their names and addresses and sometimes remarks. [ME f. AF *visitour*, OF *visiteur* (as VISIT)]

visitorial /ˌvɪzɪˈtɔːrɪəl/ adj. of an official visitor or visitation.

visor /ˈvaɪzə(r)/ n. (also **vizor**) **1 a** a movable part of a helmet covering the face. **b** *hist.* a mask. **c** the projecting front part of a cap. **2** a shield (fixed or movable) to protect the eyes from unwanted light, esp. one at the top of a vehicle windscreen. □□ **visored** adj. **visorless** adj. [ME f. AF *viser*, OF *visiere* f. *vis* face f. L *visus*: see VISAGE]

vista /ˈvɪstə/ n. **1** a long narrow view as between rows of trees. **2** a mental view of a long succession of remembered or anticipated events (*opened up new vistas to his ambition*). □□ **vistaed** adj. [It., = view, f. *visto* seen, past part. of *vedere* see f. L *vidēre*]

visual /ˈvɪzjʊəl, ˈvɪʒ-/ adj. & n. —adj. of, concerned with, or used in seeing. —n. (usu. in *pl.*) a visual image or display, a picture. □**visual aid** a film, model, etc., as an aid to learning. **visual angle** the angle formed at the eye by rays from the extremities of an object viewed. **visual display unit** *Computing* a device displaying data as characters on a screen and usu. incorporating a keyboard. **visual field** field of vision. **visual purple** a light-sensitive pigment in the retina, rhodopsin. **visual ray** *Optics* a line extended from an object to the eye. □□ **visuality** /-ʊˈælɪtɪ/ n. **visually** adv. [ME f. LL *visualis* f. L *visus* sight f. *vidēre* see]

visualize /ˈvɪzjʊəˌlaɪz, ˈvɪʒ-/ v.tr. (also **-ise**) **1** make visible esp. to one's mind (a thing not visible to the

eye). **2** make visible to the eye. □□ **visualizable** *adj.*
visualization /-'zeɪʃ(ə)n/ *n.*

vital /'vaɪt(ə)l/ *adj. & n.* —*adj.* **1** of, concerned with, or essential to organic life (*vital functions*). **2** essential to the existence of a thing or to the matter in hand (*a vital question*; *secrecy is vital*). **3** full of life or activity. **4** affecting life. **5** fatal to life or to success etc. (*a vital error*). **6** *disp.* important. —*n.* (in *pl.*) the body's vital organs, e.g. the heart and brain. □ **vital capacity** the volume of air that can be expelled from the lungs after taking the deepest possible breath. **vital force 1** (in Bergson's philosophy) life-force. **2** any mysterious vital principle. **vital power** the power to sustain life. **vital statistics 1** the number of births, marriages, deaths, etc. **2** *colloq.* the measurements of a woman's bust, waist, and hips. □□ **vitally** *adv.* [ME f. OF f. L *vitalis* f. *vita* life]

vitalism /'vaɪtə,lɪz(ə)m/ *n. Biol.* the doctrine that life originates in a vital principle distinct from chemical and other physical forces. □□ **vitalist** *n.* **vitalistic** /-'lɪstɪk/ *adj.* [F *vitalisme* or f. VITAL]

vitality /vaɪ'tælɪtɪ/ *n.* **1** liveliness, animation. **2** the ability to sustain life, vital power. **3** (of an institution, language, etc.) the ability to endure and to perform its functions. [L *vitalitas* (as VITAL)]

vitalize /'vaɪtə,laɪz/ *v.tr.* (also **-ise**) **1** endow with life. **2** infuse with vigour. □□ **vitalization** /-'zeɪʃ(ə)n/ *n.*

vitally /'vaɪtəlɪ/ *adv.* essentially, indispensably.

vitamin /'vɪtəmɪn, 'vaɪt-/ *n.* any of a group of organic compounds essential in small amounts for many living organisms to maintain normal health and development. □ **vitamin A** = RETINOL. **vitamin B complex** (or **B vitamins**) any of a group of vitamins which, although not chemically related, are often found together in the same foods. **vitamin B₁** = THIAMINE. **vitamin B₂** = RIBOFLAVIN. **vitamin B₆** = PYRIDOXINE. **vitamin B₁₂** = CYANOCOBALAMIN. **vitamin C** = ASCORBIC ACID. **vitamin D** any of a group of vitamins found in liver and fish oils, essential for the absorption of calcium and the prevention of rickets in children and osteomalacia in adults. **vitamin D₂** = CALCIFEROL. **vitamin D₃** = CHOLECALCIFEROL. **vitamin E** = TOCOPHEROL. **vitamin K** any of a group of vitamins found mainly in green leaves and essential for the blood-clotting process. **vitamin K₁** = PHYLLOQUINONE. **vitamin K₂** = MENAQUINONE. **vitamin M** esp. *US* = FOLIC ACID. [orig. *vitamine* f. L *vita* life + AMINE, because orig. thought to contain an amino acid]

vitaminize /'vɪtəmɪ,naɪz/ *v.tr.* (also **-ise**) add vitamins to.

vitellary /vɪ'telərɪ, vaɪ-/ *adj.* of or relating to the vitellus.

vitelli *pl.* of VITELLUS.

vitellin /vɪ'telɪn, vaɪ-/ *n. Chem.* the chief protein constituent of the yolk of egg. [VITELLUS + -IN]

vitelline /vɪ'telaɪn, vaɪ-, -lɪn/ *adj.* of the vitellus. □ **vitelline membrane** the yolk-sac. [med.L *vitellinus* (as VITELLUS)]

vitellus /vɪ'teləs, vaɪ-/ *n.* (*pl.* **vitelli** /-laɪ/) **1** the yolk of an egg. **2** the contents of the ovum. [L, = yolk]

vitiate /'vɪʃɪ,eɪt/ *v.tr.* **1** impair the quality or efficiency of; corrupt, debase, contaminate. **2** make invalid or ineffectual. □□ **vitiation** /-'eɪʃ(ə)n/ *n.* **vitiator** *n.* [L *vitiare* f. *vitium* VICE¹]

viticulture /'vɪtɪ,kʌltʃə(r)/ *n.* the cultivation of grapevines; the science or study of this. □□ **viticultural** /-'kʌltʃər(ə)l/ *adj.* **viticulturist** /-'kʌltʃərɪst/ *n.* [L *vitis* vine + CULTURE]

vitreous /'vɪtrɪəs/ *adj.* **1** of, or of the nature of, glass. **2** like glass in hardness, brittleness, transparency, structure, etc. (*vitreous enamel*). □ **vitreous humour** (or **body**) *Anat.* a transparent jelly-like tissue filling the eyeball. □□ **vitreousness** *n.* [L *vitreus* f. *vitrum* glass]

vitrescent /vɪ'tres(ə)nt/ *adj.* tending to become glass. □□ **vitrescence** *n.*

vitriform /'vɪtrɪ,fɔːm/ *adj.* having the form or appearance of glass.

vitrify /'vɪtrɪ,faɪ/ *v.tr. & intr.* (**-ies**, **-ied**) convert or be converted into glass or a glasslike substance esp. by heat. □□ **vitrifaction** /-'fækʃ(ə)n/ *n.* **vitrifiable** *adj.* **vitrification** /-fɪ'keɪʃ(ə)n/ *n.* [F *vitrifier* or med.L *vitrificare* (as VITREOUS)]

vitriol /'vɪtrɪəl/ *n.* **1** sulphuric acid or a sulphate, orig. one of glassy appearance. **2** caustic or hostile speech, criticism, or feeling. □ **copper vitriol** copper sulphate. **oil of vitriol** concentrated sulphuric acid. [ME f. OF *vitriol* or med.L *vitriolum* f. L *vitrum* glass]

vitriolic /,vɪtrɪ'ɒlɪk/ *adj.* (of speech or criticism) caustic or hostile.

vitta /'vɪtə/ *n.* (*pl.* **vittae** /'vɪtiː/) **1** *Bot.* an oil-tube in the fruit of some plants. **2** *Zool.* a stripe of colour. □□ **vittate** *adj.* [L, = band, chaplet]

vituperate /vɪ'tjuːpə,reɪt, vaɪ-/ *v.tr. & intr.* revile, abuse. □□ **vituperation** /-'reɪʃ(ə)n/ *n.* **vituperative** /-rətɪv/ *adj.* **vituperator** *n.* [L *vituperare* f. *vitium* VICE¹]

viva¹ /'viːvə/ *n. & v. Brit. colloq.* —*n.* = VIVA VOCE *n.* —*v.tr.* (**vivas**, **vivaed** /-vəd/ or **viva'd**, **vivaing**) = VIVA VOCE *v.* [abbr.]

viva² /'viːvə/ *int. & n.* —*int.* long live. —*n.* a cry of this as a salute etc. [It., 3rd sing. pres. subj. of *vivere* live f. L]

vivace /vɪ'vɑːtʃɪ/ *adv. Mus.* in a lively brisk manner. [It. f. L (as VIVACIOUS)]

vivacious /vɪ'veɪʃəs/ *adj.* lively, sprightly, animated. □□ **vivaciously** *adv.* **vivaciousness** *n.* **vivacity** /vɪ'væsɪtɪ/ *n.* [L *vivax -acis* f. *vivere* live]

vivarium /vaɪ'veərɪəm, vɪ-/ *n.* (*pl.* **vivaria** /-rɪə/) a place artificially prepared for keeping animals in (nearly) their natural state. [L, = warren, fishpond, f. *vivus* living f. *vivere* live]

vivat /'vaɪvæt, 'viːvæt/ *int. & n.* = VIVA². [L, 3rd sing. pres. subj. of *vivere* live]

viva voce /,vaɪvə 'vəʊtʃɪ, 'vəʊsɪ/ *adj., adv., n., & v.* —*adj.* oral. —*adv.* orally. —*n.* an oral examination for an academic qualification. —*v.tr.* (**viva-voce**) (**-voces**, **-voceed**, **-voceing**) examine orally. [med.L, = with the living voice]

viverrid /vɪ'verɪd, vaɪ-/ *n. & adj.* —*n.* any mammal of the family Viverridae, including civets, mongooses, and genets. —*adj.* of or relating to this family. [L *viverra* ferret + -ID³]

vivers /'vaɪvəz/ *n.pl. Sc.* food, victuals. [F *vivres* f. *vivre* live f. L *vivere*]

vivid /'vɪvɪd/ *adj.* **1** (of light or colour) strong, intense, glaring (*a vivid flash of lightning*; *of a vivid green*). **2** (of a mental faculty, impression, or description) clear, lively, graphic (*has a vivid imagination*; *have a vivid recollection of the scene*). **3** (of a person) lively, vigorous. □□ **vividly** *adv.* **vividness** *n.* [L *vividus* f. *vivere* live]

vivify /'vɪvɪ,faɪ/ *v.tr.* (**-ies**, **-ied**) enliven, animate, make lively or living. □□ **vivification** /-fɪ'keɪʃ(ə)n/ *n.* [F *vivifier* f. LL *vivificare* f. L *vivus* living f. *vivere* live]

viviparous /vɪ'vɪpərəs, vaɪ-/ *adj.* **1** *Zool.* bringing forth young alive, not hatching them by means of eggs (cf. OVIPAROUS). **2** *Bot.* producing bulbs or seeds that germinate while still attached to the parent plant. □□ **viviparity** /,vɪvɪ'pærɪtɪ/ *n.* **viviparously** *adv.* **viviparousness** *n.* [L *viviparus* f. *vivus*: see VIVIFY]

vivisect /'vɪvɪ,sekt/ *v.tr.* perform vivisection on. [back-form. f. VIVISECTION]

vivisection /,vɪvɪ'sekʃ(ə)n/ *n.* **1** dissection or other painful treatment of living animals for purposes of scientific research. **2** unduly detailed or ruthless criticism. □□ **vivisectional** *adj.* **vivisectionist** *n.* **vivisector** /'vɪvɪ,sektə(r)/ *n.* [L *vivus* living (see VIVIFY), after DISSECTION (as DISSECT)]

vixen /'vɪks(ə)n/ *n.* **1** a female fox. **2** a spiteful or quarrelsome woman. □□ **vixenish** *adj.* **vixenly** *adj.* [ME *fixen* f. OE, fem. of FOX]

viz. /vɪz, or by substitution 'neɪmlɪ/ *adv.* (usu. introducing a gloss or explanation) namely; that is to say; in other words (*came to a firm conclusion, viz. that we were right*). [abbr. of VIDELICET, *z* being med.L symbol for abbr. of *-et*]

vizard /'vɪzəd/ *n.* archaic a mask or disguise. [VISOR + -ARD]

vizcacha var. of VISCACHA.

vizier /vɪ'zɪə(r), 'vɪzɪə(r)/ *n.* hist. a high official in some Muslim countries, esp. in Turkey under Ottoman rule. □□ **vizierate** /-rət/ *n.* **vizierial** /vɪ'zɪərɪəl/ *adj.* **viziership** *n.* [ult. f. Arab. *wazīr* caliph's chief counsellor]

vizor var. of VISOR.

Vlach /vlæk/ *n.* & *adj.* —*n.* a member of a people inhabiting Romania and parts of the Soviet Union. —*adj.* of or relating to this people. [Bulg. f. OSlav. *Vlachŭ* Romanian etc. f. Gmc, = foreigner]

vlei /fleɪ/ *n.* S.Afr. a hollow in which water collects during the rainy season. [Du. dial. f. Du. *vallei* valley]

V-neck /viː'nek, 'viː-/ *n.* (often *attrib.*) **1** a neck of a pullover etc. with straight sides meeting at an angle in the front to form a V. **2** a garment with this.

VO (in the UK) Royal Victorian Order.

vocable /'vəʊkəb(ə)l/ *n.* a word, esp. with reference to form rather than meaning. [F *vocable* or L *vocabulum* f. *vocare* call]

vocabulary /və'kæbjʊlərɪ/ *n.* (*pl.* **-ies**) **1** the (principal) words used in a language or a particular book or branch of science etc. or by a particular author (*scientific vocabulary; the vocabulary of Shakespeare*). **2** a list of these, arranged alphabetically with definitions or translations. **3** the range of words known to an individual (*his vocabulary is limited*). **4** a set of artistic or stylistic forms or techniques, esp. a range of set movements in ballet etc. [med.L *vocabularius, -um* (as VOCABLE)]

vocal /'vəʊk(ə)l/ *adj.* & *n.* —*adj.* **1** of or concerned with or uttered by the voice (*a vocal communication*). **2** expressing one's feelings freely in speech (*was very vocal about his rights*). **3** Phonet. voiced. **4** poet. (of trees, water, etc.) endowed with a voice or a similar faculty. **5** (of music) written for or produced by the voice with or without accompaniment (cf. INSTRUMENTAL). —*n.* **1** (in *sing.* or *pl.*) the sung part of a musical composition. **2** a musical performance with singing. □ **vocal cords** folds of the lining membrane of the larynx near the opening of the glottis, with edges vibrating in the air-stream to produce the voice. **vocal score** a musical score showing the voice parts in full. □□ **vocality** /və'kælɪtɪ/ *n.* **vocally** *adv.* [ME f. L *vocalis* (as VOICE)]

vocalic /və'kælɪk/ *adj.* of or consisting of a vowel or vowels.

vocalism /'vəʊkə,lɪz(ə)m/ *n.* **1** the use of the voice in speaking or singing. **2** a vowel sound or system.

vocalist /'vəʊkəlɪst/ *n.* a singer, esp. of jazz or popular songs.

vocalize /'vəʊkə,laɪz/ *v.* (also **-ise**) **1** *tr.* **a** form (a sound) or utter (a word) with the voice. **b** make sonant (*f is vocalized into v*). **2** *intr.* utter a vocal sound. **3** *tr.* write (Hebrew etc.) with vowel points. **4** *intr. Mus.* sing with several notes to one vowel. □□ **vocalization** /-'zeɪʃ(ə)n/ *n.* **vocalizer** *n.*

vocation /və'keɪʃ(ə)n/ *n.* **1** a strong feeling of fitness for a particular career or occupation (in religious contexts regarded as a divine call). **2 a** a person's employment, esp. regarded as requiring dedication. **b** a trade or profession. [ME f. OF *vocation* or L *vocatio* f. *vocare* call]

vocational /və'keɪʃən(ə)l/ *adj.* **1** of or relating to an occupation or employment. **2** (of education or training) directed at a particular occupation and its skills. □□ **vocationalism** *n.* **vocationalize** *v.tr.* (also **-ise**). **vocationally** *adv.*

vocative /'vɒkətɪv/ *n.* & *adj.* Gram. —*n.* the case of nouns, pronouns, and adjectives used in addressing or invoking a person or thing. —*adj.* of or in this case. [ME f. OF *vocatif -ive* or L *vocativus* f. *vocare* call]

vociferate /və'sɪfə,reɪt/ *v.* **1** *tr.* utter (words etc.) noisily. **2** *intr.* shout, bawl. □□ **vociferance** *n.* **vociferant** *adj.* & *n.* **vociferation** /-'reɪʃ(ə)n/ *n.* **vociferator** *n.* [L *vociferari* f. *vox* voice + *ferre* bear]

vociferous /və'sɪfərəs/ *adj.* **1** (of a person, speech, etc.) noisy, clamorous. **2** insistently and forcibly expressing one's views. □□ **vociferously** *adv.* **vociferousness** *n.*

vocoder /və'kəʊdə(r)/ *n.* a synthesizer that produces sounds from an analysis of speech input. [VOICE + CODE]

vodka /'vɒdkə/ *n.* an alcoholic spirit made esp. in Russia by distillation of rye etc. [Russ., dimin. of *voda* water]

voe /vəʊ/ *n.* a small bay or creek in Orkney or Shetland. [Norw. *vaag*, ON *vágr*]

vogue /vəʊg/ *n.* **1** (prec. by *the*) the prevailing fashion. **2** popular use or currency (*has had a great vogue*). □ **in vogue** in fashion, generally current. **vogue-word** a word currently fashionable. □□ **voguish** *adj.* [F f. It. *voga* rowing, fashion f. *vogare* row, go well]

voice /vɔɪs/ *n.* & *v.* —*n.* **1 a** sound formed in the larynx etc. and uttered by the mouth, esp. human utterance in speaking, shouting, singing, etc. (*heard a voice; spoke in a low voice*). **b** the ability to produce this (*has lost her voice*). **2 a** the use of the voice; utterance, esp. in spoken or written words (esp. *give voice*). **b** an opinion so expressed. **c** the right to express an opinion (*I have no voice in the matter*). **d** an agency by which an opinion is expressed. **3** Gram. a form or set of forms of a verb showing the relation of the subject to the action (*active voice; passive voice*). **4** Mus. **a** a vocal part in a composition. **b** a constituent part in a fugue. **5** Phonet. sound uttered with resonance of the vocal cords, not with mere breath. **6** (usu. in *pl.*) the supposed utterance of an invisible guiding or directing spirit. —*v.tr.* **1** give utterance to; express (*the letter voices our opinion*). **2** (esp. as **voiced** *adj.*) Phonet. utter with vibration of the vocal cords (e.g. *b, d, g, v, z*). **3** Mus. regulate the tone-quality of (organ-pipes). □ **in voice** (or **good voice**) in proper vocal condition for singing or speaking. **voice-box** the larynx. **the voice of God** the expression of God's will, wrath, etc. **voice-over** narration in a film etc. not accompanied by a picture of the speaker. **voice-print** a visual record of speech, analysed with respect to frequency, duration, and amplitude. **voice vote** US a vote taken by noting the relative strength of calls of *aye* and *no*. **with one voice** unanimously. □□ **-voiced** *adj.* **voicer** *n.* (in sense 3 of *v.*). [ME f. AF *voiz*, OF *vois* f. L *vox vocis*]

voiceful /'vɔɪsfʊl/ *adj.* poet. or rhet. **1** vocal. **2** sonorous.

voiceless /'vɔɪslɪs/ *adj.* **1** dumb, mute, speechless. **2** Phonet. uttered without vibration of the vocal cords (e.g. *f, k, p, s, t*). □□ **voicelessly** *adv.* **voicelessness** *n.*

void /vɔɪd/ *adj.*, *n.*, & *v.* —*adj.* **1 a** empty, vacant. **b** (foll. by *of*) lacking; free from (*a style void of affectation*). **2** esp. Law (of a contract, deed, promise, etc.) invalid, not binding (*null and void*). **3** useless, ineffectual. **4** (often foll. by *in*) Cards (of a hand) having no cards in a given suit. **5** (of an office) vacant (esp. *fall void*). —*n.* **1** an empty space, a vacuum (*vanished into the void; cannot fill the void made by death*). **2** an unfilled space in a wall or building. **3** (often foll. by *in*) Cards the absence of cards in a particular suit. —*v.tr.* **1** render invalid. **2** (also *absol.*) excrete. □□ **voidable** *adj.* **voidness** *n.* [ME f. OF dial. *voide*, OF *vuide, vuit*, rel. to L *vacare* VACATE: *v.* partly f. AVOID, partly f. OF *voider*]

voidance /'vɔɪd(ə)ns/ *n.* **1** Eccl. a vacancy in a

benefice. **2** the act or an instance of voiding; the state of being voided. [ME f. OF (as VOID)]

voided /ˈvɔɪdɪd/ adj. Heraldry (of a bearing) having the central area cut away so as to show the field.

voile /vɔɪl, vwɑːl/ n. a thin semi-transparent dress-material of cotton, wool, or silk. [F, = VEIL]

vol. abbr. volume.

volant /ˈvəʊlənt/ adj. **1** Zool. flying, able to fly. **2** Heraldry represented as flying. **3** literary nimble, rapid. [F f. voler f. L volare fly]

volar /ˈvəʊlə(r)/ adj. Anat. of the palm or sole. [L vola hollow of hand or foot]

volatile /ˈvɒlə,taɪl/ adj. & n. —adj. **1** evaporating rapidly (volatile salts). **2** changeable, fickle. **3** lively, light-hearted. **4** apt to break out into violence. **5** transient. —n. a volatile substance. □**volatile oil** = essential oil. □□**volatileness** n. **volatility** /-ˈtɪlɪtɪ/ n. [OF volatil or L volatilis f. volare volat- fly]

volatilize /vəˈlætɪ,laɪz/ v. (also **-ise**) **1** tr. cause to evaporate. **2** intr. evaporate. □□**volatilizable** adj. **volatilization** /-ˈzeɪʃ(ə)n/ n.

vol-au-vent /ˈvɒləʊ,vɑ̃/ n. a (usu. small) round case of puff pastry filled with meat, fish, etc., and sauce. [F, lit. 'flight in the wind']

volcanic /vɒlˈkænɪk/ adj. (also **vulcanic** /vʌl-/) of, like, or produced by a volcano. □**volcanic bomb** a mass of ejected lava usu. rounded and sometimes hollow. **volcanic glass** obsidian. □□**volcanically** adv. **volcanicity** /,vɒlkəˈnɪsɪtɪ/ n. [F volcanique f. volcan VOLCANO]

volcano /vɒlˈkeɪnəʊ/ n. (pl. **-oes**) **1** a mountain or hill having an opening or openings in the earth's crust through which lava, cinders, steam, gases, etc., are or have been expelled continuously or at intervals. **2** a state of things likely to cause a violent outburst. **b** a violent esp. suppressed feeling. [It. f. L Volcanus Vulcan, Roman god of fire]

volcanology var. of VULCANOLOGY.

vole[1] /vəʊl/ n. any small ratlike or mouselike plant-eating rodent of the family Cricetidae. [orig. vole-mouse f. Norw. f. voll field + mus mouse]

vole[2] /vəʊl/ n. archaic the winning of all tricks at cards. [F f. voler fly f. L volare]

volet /ˈvɒleɪ/ n. a panel or wing of a triptych. [F f. voler fly f. L volare]

volitant /ˈvɒlɪt(ə)nt/ adj. Zool. volant. [L volitare frequent. of volare fly]

volition /vəˈlɪʃ(ə)n/ n. **1** the exercise of the will. **2** the power of willing. □**of** (or **by**) **one's own volition** voluntarily. □□**volitional** adj. **volitionally** adv. **volitive** /ˈvɒlɪtɪv/ adj. [F volition or med.L volitio f. volo I wish]

Völkerwanderung /ˈfɜːlkə,vɑːndə,rʊŋ/ n. a migration of peoples, esp. that of Germanic and Slavic peoples into Europe from the second to the eleventh centuries. [G]

volley /ˈvɒlɪ/ n. & v. —n. (pl. **-eys**) **1 a** the simultaneous discharge of a number of weapons. **b** the bullets etc. discharged in a volley. **2** (usu. foll. by of) a noisy emission of oaths etc. in quick succession. **3** Tennis the return of a ball in play before it touches the ground. **4** Football the kicking of a ball in play before it touches the ground. **5** Cricket **a** a ball pitched right up to the batsman or the stumps without bouncing. **b** the pitching of the ball in this way. —v. (**-eys**, **-eyed**) **1** tr. (also absol.) Tennis & Football return or send (a ball) by a volley. **2** tr. & absol. discharge (bullets, abuse, etc.) in a volley. **3** intr. (of bullets etc.) fly in a volley. **4** intr. (of guns etc.) sound together. **5** intr. make a sound like a volley of artillery. □□**volleyer** n. [F volée ult. f. L volare fly]

volleyball /ˈvɒlɪ,bɔːl/ n. a game for two teams of six hitting a large ball by hand over a net.

volplane /ˈvɒlpleɪn/ n. & v. Aeron. —n. a glide. —v.intr. glide. [F vol plané f. vol flight + plané past part. of planer hover, rel. to PLANE[1]]

vols. abbr. volumes.

volt[1] /vəʊlt/ n. the SI unit of electromotive force, the difference of potential that would carry one ampere of current against one ohm resistance. ¶ Abbr.: **V**. [A. Volta, It. physicist d. 1827]

volt[2] /vɒlt, vəʊlt/ v. & n. —v.intr. Fencing make a volte. —n. var. of VOLTE. [F volter (as VOLTE)]

voltage /ˈvəʊltɪdʒ/ n. electromotive force or potential difference expressed in volts.

voltaic /vɒlˈteɪɪk/ adj. archaic of electricity from a primary battery; galvanic (voltaic battery).

voltameter /vɒlˈtæmɪtə(r)/ n. an instrument for measuring an electric charge.

volte /vɒlt, vəʊlt/ n. (also **volt**) **1** Fencing a quick movement to escape a thrust. **2** a sideways circular movement of a horse. [F f. It. volta turn, fem. past part. of volgere turn f. L volvere roll]

volte-face /vɒltˈfɑːs/ n. **1** a complete reversal of position in argument or opinion. **2** the act or an instance of turning round. [F f. It. voltafaccia, ult. f. L volvere roll + facies appearance, face]

voltmeter /ˈvəʊlt,miːtə(r)/ n. an instrument for measuring electric potential in volts.

voluble /ˈvɒljʊb(ə)l/ adj. **1** speaking or spoken vehemently, incessantly, or fluently (voluble spokesman; voluble excuses). **2** Bot. twisting round a support, twining. □□**volubility** /-ˈbɪlɪtɪ/ n. **volubleness** n. **volubly** adv. [F voluble or L volubilis f. volvere roll]

volume /ˈvɒljuːm/ n. **1 a** a set of sheets of paper, usu. printed, bound together and forming part or the whole of a work or comprising several works (issued in three volumes; a library of 12,000 volumes). **b** a scroll of papyrus etc., an ancient form of book. **2 a** solid content, bulk. **b** the space occupied by a gas or liquid. **c** (foll. by of) an amount or quantity (large volume of business). **3 a** quantity or power of sound. **b** fullness of tone. **4** (foll. by of) **a** a moving mass of water etc. **b** (usu. in pl.) a wreath or coil or rounded mass of smoke etc. □□**volumed** adj. (also in comb.). [ME f. OF volum(e) f. L volumen -minis roll f. volvere to roll]

volumetric /,vɒljʊˈmetrɪk/ adj. of or relating to measurement by volume. □□**volumetrically** adv. [VOLUME + METRIC]

voluminous /vəˈljuːmɪnəs, vəˈluː-/ adj. **1** large in volume; bulky. **2** (of drapery etc.) loose and ample. **3** consisting of many volumes. **4** (of a writer) producing many books. □□**voluminosity** /-ˈnɒsɪtɪ/ n. **voluminously** adv. **voluminousness** n. [LL voluminosus (as VOLUME)]

voluntarism /ˈvɒləntə,rɪz(ə)m/ n. **1** the principle of relying on voluntary action rather than compulsion. **2** Philos. the doctrine that the will is a fundamental or dominant factor in the individual or the universe. **3** hist. the doctrine that the Church or schools should be independent of the State and supported by voluntary contributions. □□**voluntarist** n. [irreg. f. VOLUNTARY]

voluntary /ˈvɒləntərɪ/ adj. & n. —adj. **1** done, acting, or able to act of one's own free will; not constrained or compulsory, intentional (a voluntary gift). **2** unpaid (voluntary work). **3** (of an institution) supported by voluntary contributions. **4** Brit. (of a school) built by a voluntary institution but maintained by a local education authority. **5** brought about, produced, etc., by voluntary action. **6** (of a movement, muscle, or limb) controlled by the will. **7** (of a confession by a criminal) not prompted by a promise or threat. **8** Law (of a conveyance or disposition) made without return in money or other consideration. —n. (pl. **-ies**) **1 a** an organ solo played before, during, or after a church service. **b** the music for this. **c** archaic an extempore performance esp. as a prelude to other music. **2** (in competitions) a special performance left to the performer's choice. **3** hist. a person who holds that the Church or schools should be independent of the State and supported by voluntary contributions. □**Voluntary Aid Detachment**

(in the UK) a group of organized voluntary first-aid and nursing workers. **Voluntary Service Overseas** a British organization promoting voluntary work in underdeveloped countries. □□ **voluntarily** *adv.* **voluntariness** *n.* [ME f. OF *volontaire* or L *voluntarius* f. *voluntas* will]

voluntaryism /'vɒləntərɪ,ɪz(ə)m/ *n. hist.* = VOLUNTARISM 1, 3. □□ **voluntaryist** *n.*

volunteer /ˌvɒlən'tɪə(r)/ *n. & v.* —*n.* **1** a person who voluntarily undertakes a task or enters military or other service, esp. *Mil. hist.* a member of any of the corps of voluntary soldiers formerly organized in the UK and provided with instructors, arms, etc., by the State. **2** (usu. *attrib.*) a self-sown plant. —*v.* **1** *tr.* (often foll. by *to* + infin.) undertake or offer (one's services, a remark or explanation, etc.) voluntarily. **2** *intr.* (often foll. by *for*) make a voluntary offer of one's services; be a volunteer. [F *volontaire* (as VOLUNTARY), assim. to -EER]

voluptuary /və'lʌptjʊərɪ/ *n. & adj.* —*n.* (*pl.* -ies) a person given up to luxury and sensual pleasure. —*adj.* concerned with luxury and sensual pleasure. [L *volupt(u)arius* (as VOLUPTUOUS)]

voluptuous /və'lʌptjʊəs/ *adj.* of, tending to, occupied with, or derived from, sensuous or sensual pleasure. □□ **voluptuously** *adv.* **voluptuousness** *n.* [ME f. OF *voluptueux* or L *voluptuosus* f. *voluptas* pleasure]

volute /və'lju:t/ *n. & adj.* —*n.* **1** *Archit.* a spiral scroll characteristic of Ionic capitals and also used in Corinthian and composite capitals. **2 a** any marine gastropod mollusc of the genus *Voluta*. **b** the spiral shell of this. —*adj.* esp. *Bot.* rolled up. □□ **voluted** *adj.* [F *volute* or L *voluta* fem. past part. of *volvere* roll]

volution /və'lu:ʃ(ə)n, və'lju:-/ *n.* **1** a rolling motion. **2** a spiral turn. **3** a whorl of a spiral shell. **4** *Anat.* a convolution. [as VOLUTE, after REVOLUTION etc.]

vomer /'vəʊmə(r)/ *n. Anat.* the small thin bone separating the nostrils in man and most vertebrates. [L, = ploughshare]

vomit /'vɒmɪt/ *v. & n.* —*v.tr.* (**vomited**, **vomiting**) **1** (also *absol.*) eject (matter) from the stomach through the mouth. **2** (of a volcano, chimney, etc.) eject violently, belch forth. —*n.* **1** matter vomited from the stomach. **2** *archaic* an emetic. □□ **vomiter** *n.* [ME ult. f. L *vomere vomit-* or frequent. L *vomitare*]

vomitorium /ˌvɒmɪ'tɔːrɪəm/ *n.* (*pl.* **vomitoria** /-rɪə/) *Rom. Antiq.* a vomitory. [L; see VOMITORY]

vomitory /'vɒmɪtərɪ/ *adj. & n.* —*adj.* emetic. —*n.* (*pl.* -ies) *Rom. Antiq.* each of a series of passages for entrance and exit in an amphitheatre or theatre. [L *vomitorius* (adj.), *-um* (n.) (as VOMIT)]

V-1 /vi:'wʌn/ *n. hist.* a type of German flying bomb used in the war of 1939-45. [abbr. of G *Vergeltungswaffe* reprisal weapon]

voodoo /'vu:du:/ *n. & v.* —*n.* **1** use of or belief in religious witchcraft as practised among Blacks esp. in the W. Indies. **2** a person skilled in this. **3** a voodoo spell. —*v.tr.* (**voodoos**, **voodooed**) affect by voodoo; bewitch. □□ **voodooism** *n.* **voodooist** *n.* [Dahomey *vodu*]

voracious /və'reɪʃəs/ *adj.* **1** greedy in eating, ravenous. **2** very eager in some activity (*a voracious reader*). □□ **voraciously** *adv.* **voraciousness** *n.* **voracity** /və'ræsɪtɪ/ *n.* [L *vorax* f. *vorare* devour]

-vorous /vərəs/ *comb. form* forming adjectives meaning 'feeding on' (*carnivorous*). □□ **-vora** /vərə/ *comb. form* forming names of groups. **-vore** /vɔː(r)/ *comb. form* forming names of individuals. [L *-vorus* f. *vorare* devour]

vortex /'vɔːteks/ *n.* (*pl.* **vortexes** or **vortices** /-tɪ,si:z/) **1** a mass of whirling fluid, esp. a whirlpool or whirlwind. **2** any whirling motion or mass. **3** a system, occupation, pursuit, etc., viewed as swallowing up or engrossing those who approach it (*the vortex of society*). **4** *Physics* a portion of fluid whose particles have rotatory motion. □ **vortex-ring** a vortex whose axis is a closed curve, e.g. a smoke-ring.

□□ **vortical** *adj.* **vortically** *adv.* **vorticity** /vɔː'tɪsɪtɪ/ *n.* **vorticose** *adj.* **vorticular** /vɔː'tɪkjʊlə(r)/ *adj.* [L *vortex -icis* eddy, var. of VERTEX]

vorticella /ˌvɔːtɪ'selə/ *n.* any sedentary protozoan of the family Vorticellidae, consisting of a tubular stalk with a bell-shaped ciliated opening. [mod.L, dimin. of VORTEX]

vorticist /'vɔːtɪsɪst/ *n.* **1** *Art* a painter, writer, etc., of a school influenced by futurism and using the 'vortices' of modern civilization as a basis. **2** *Metaphysics* a person regarding the universe, with Descartes, as a plenum in which motion propagates itself in circles. □□ **vorticism** *n.*

votary /'vəʊtərɪ/ *n.* (*pl.* -ies; *fem.* **votaress**) (usu. foll. by *of*) **1** a person vowed to the service of God or a god or cult. **2** a devoted follower, adherent, or advocate of a person, system, occupation, etc. □□ **votarist** *n.* [L *vot-*: see VOTE]

vote /vəʊt/ *n. & v.* —*n.* **1** a formal expression of choice or opinion by means of a ballot, show of hands, etc., concerning a choice of candidate, approval of a motion or resolution, etc. (*let us have a vote on it*; *gave my vote to the independent candidate*). **2** (usu. prec. by *the*) the right to vote, esp. in a State election. **3 a** an opinion expressed by a majority of votes. **b** *Brit.* money granted by a majority of votes. **4** the collective votes that are or may be given by or for a particular group (*will lose the Welsh vote*; *the Conservative vote increased*). **5** a ticket etc. used for recording a vote. —*v.* **1** *intr.* (often foll. by *for*, *against*, or *to* + infin.) give a vote. **2** *tr.* **a** (often foll. by *that* + clause) enact or resolve by a majority of votes. **b** grant (a sum of money) by a majority of votes. **c** cause to be in a specified position by a majority of votes (*was voted off the committee*). **3** *tr. colloq.* pronounce or declare by general consent (*was voted a failure*). **4** *tr.* (often foll. by *that* + clause) *colloq.* announce one's proposal (*I vote that we all go home*). □ **put to a** (or **the**) **vote** submit to a decision by voting. **vote down** defeat (a proposal etc.) in a vote. **vote in** elect by votes. **vote of censure** = *vote of no confidence*. **vote of confidence** (or **no confidence**) a vote showing that the majority support (or do not support) the policy of the governing body etc. **vote with one's feet** *colloq.* indicate an opinion by one's presence or absence. **voting-machine** (esp. in the US) a machine for the automatic registering of votes. **voting-paper** a paper used in voting by ballot. **voting stock** stock entitling the holder to a vote. □□ **votable** *adj.* **voteless** *adj.* [ME f. past part. stem *vot-* of L *vovēre* vow]

voter /'vəʊtə(r)/ *n.* **1** a person with the right to vote at an election. **2** a person voting.

votive /'vəʊtɪv/ *adj.* offered or consecrated in fulfilment of a vow (*votive offering*; *votive picture*). □ **votive mass** *Eccl.* a mass celebrated for a special purpose or occasion. [L *votivus* (as VOTE)]

vouch /vaʊtʃ/ *v.* **1** *intr.* (foll. by *for*) answer for, be surety for (*will vouch for the truth of this*; *can vouch for him*; *could not vouch for his honesty*). **2** *tr. archaic* cite as an authority. **3** *tr. archaic* confirm or uphold (a statement) by evidence or assertion. [ME f. OF *vo(u)cher* summon etc., ult. f. L *vocare* call]

voucher /'vaʊtʃə(r)/ *n.* **1** a document which can be exchanged for goods or services as a token of payment made or promised by the holder or another. **2** a document establishing the payment of money or the truth of accounts. **3** a person who vouches for a person, statement, etc. [AF *voucher* (as VOUCH) or f. VOUCH]

vouchsafe /vaʊtʃ'seɪf/ *v.tr. formal* **1** condescend to give or grant (*vouchsafed me no answer*). **2** (foll. by *to* + infin.) condescend. [ME f. VOUCH in sense 'warrant' + SAFE]

voussoir /'vu:swɑː(r)/ *n.* each of the wedge-shaped or tapered stones forming an arch. [OF *vossoir* etc. f. pop.L *volsorium* ult. f. L *volvere* roll]

vow /vaʊ/ *n. & v.* —*n.* **1** *Relig.* a solemn promise esp.

in the form of an oath to God or another deity or to a saint. **2** (in *pl.*) the promises by which a monk or nun is bound to poverty, chastity, and obedience. **3** a promise of fidelity (*lovers' vows*; *marriage vows*). **4** (usu. as **baptismal vows**) the promises given at baptism by the baptized person or by sponsors. —*v.tr.* **1** promise solemnly (*vowed obedience*). **2** dedicate to a deity. **3** (also *absol.*) *archaic* declare solemnly. □**under a vow** having made a vow. [ME f. AF v(o)u, OF vo(u), f. L (as VOTE): (v.) f. OF vouer, in sense 2 partly f. AVOW]

vowel /'vaʊəl/ *n.* **1** a speech-sound made with vibration of the vocal cords but without audible friction, more open than a consonant and capable of forming a syllable. **2** a letter or letters representing this, as *a, e, i, o, u, aw, ah.* □**vowel gradation** = ABLAUT. **vowel mutation** = UMLAUT 2. **vowel-point** each of a set of marks indicating vowels in Hebrew etc. □□ **vowelled** *adj.* (also in *comb.*). **vowelless** *adj.* **vowelly** *adj.* [ME f. OF *vouel, voiel* f. L *vocalis* (*littera*) VOCAL (letter)]

vowelize /'vaʊə,laɪz/ *v.tr.* (also -**ise**) insert the vowels in (shorthand, Hebrew, etc.).

vox angelica /,vɒks æn'dʒelɪkə/ *n.* an organ-stop with a soft tremulous tone. [LL, = angelic voice]

vox humana /,vɒks hjuː'mɑːnə/ *n.* an organ-stop with a tone supposed to resemble a human voice. [L, = human voice]

vox pop /vɒks 'pɒp/ *n. Broadcasting colloq.* popular opinion as represented by informal comments from members of the public; statements or interviews of this kind. [abbr. of VOX POPULI]

vox populi /,vɒks 'pɒpjʊ,liː, -,laɪ/ *n.* public opinion, the general verdict, popular belief or rumour. [L, = the people's voice]

voyage /'vɔɪɪdʒ/ *n. & v.* —*n.* **1** a journey, esp. a long one by water, air, or in space. **2** an account of this. —*v.* **1** *intr.* make a voyage. **2** *tr.* traverse, esp. by water or air. □□ **voyageable** *adj.* **voyager** *n.* [ME f. AF & OF *veiage, voiage* f. L *viaticum*]

voyageur /,vwa:ja'ʒɜː(r)/ *n.* a Canadian boatman, esp. *hist.* one employed in transporting goods and passengers between trading posts. [F, = voyager (as VOYAGE)]

voyeur /vwa:'jɜː(r)/ *n.* a person who obtains sexual gratification from observing others' sexual actions or organs. □□ **voyeurism** *n.* **voyeuristic** /-'rɪstɪk/ *adj.* **voyeuristically** /-'rɪstɪkəlɪ/ *adj.* [F f. *voir* see]

VP *abbr.* Vice-President.

VR *abbr.* **1** Queen Victoria. **2** variant reading. [sense 1 f. L *Victoria Regina*]

VS *abbr.* Veterinary Surgeon.

vs. *abbr.* versus.

V-sign /'viːsaɪn/ *n.* **1** *Brit.* a sign of the letter V made with the first two fingers pointing up and the back of the hand facing outwards, as a gesture of abuse, contempt, etc. **2** a similar sign made with the palm of the hand facing outwards, as a symbol of victory.

VSO *abbr.* Voluntary Service Overseas.

VSOP *abbr.* Very Special Old Pale (brandy).

VT *abbr. US* Vermont (in official postal use).

Vt. *abbr.* Vermont.

VTO *abbr.* vertical take-off.

VTOL /'viːtɒl/ *abbr.* vertical take-off and landing.

V-2 /viː'tuː/ *n.* a type of German rocket-powered missile used in the war of 1939-45. [abbr. of G *Vergeltungswaffe* reprisal weapon]

vug /vʌg/ *n.* a rock-cavity lined with crystals. □□ **vuggy** *adj.* **vugular** *adj.* [Corn. *vooga*]

vulcanic var. of VOLCANIC.

vulcanite /'vʌlkə,naɪt/ *n.* a hard black vulcanized rubber, ebonite. [as VULCANIZE]

vulcanize /'vʌlkə,naɪz/ *v.tr.* (also -**ise**) treat (rubber or rubberlike material) with sulphur etc. esp. at a high temperature to increase its strength. □□ **vulcanizable** *adj.* **vulcanization** /-'zeɪʃ(ə)n/ *n.* **vulcanizer** *n.* [*Vulcan*, Roman god of fire and metal-working]

vulcanology /,vʌlkə'nɒlədʒɪ/ *n.* (also **volcanology** /,vɒl-/) the scientific study of volcanoes. □□ **vulcanological** /-nə'lɒdʒɪk(ə)l/ *adj.* **vulcanologist** *n.*

vulgar /'vʌlgə(r)/ *adj.* **1 a** of or characteristic of the common people, plebeian. **b** coarse in manners; low (*vulgar expressions*; *vulgar tastes*). **2** in common use; generally prevalent (*vulgar errors*). □**vulgar fraction** a fraction expressed by numerator and denominator, not decimally. **vulgar Latin** informal Latin of classical times. **the vulgar tongue** the national or vernacular language, esp. formerly as opposed to Latin. □□ **vulgarly** *adv.* [ME f. L *vulgaris* f. *vulgus* common people]

vulgarian /vʌl'geərɪən/ *n.* a vulgar (esp. rich) person.

vulgarism /'vʌlgə,rɪz(ə)m/ *n.* **1** a word or expression in coarse or uneducated use. **2** an instance of coarse or uneducated behaviour.

vulgarity /vʌl'gærɪtɪ/ *n.* (*pl.* -**ies**) **1** the quality of being vulgar. **2** an instance of this.

vulgarize /'vʌlgə,raɪz/ *v.tr.* (also -**ise**) **1** make (a person, manners, etc.) vulgar, infect with vulgarity. **2** spoil (a scene, sentiment, etc.) by making it too common, frequented, or well known. **3** popularize. □□ **vulgarization** /-'zeɪʃ(ə)n/ *n.*

Vulgate /'vʌlgeɪt, -gət/ *n.* **1 a** the Latin version of the Bible prepared mainly by St Jerome in the late fourth century. **b** the official Roman Catholic Latin text as revised in 1592. **2** (**vulgate**) the traditionally accepted text of any author. **3** (**vulgate**) common or colloquial speech. [L *vulgata* (*editio* edition), fem. past part. of *vulgare* make public f. *vulgus*: see VULGAR]

vulnerable /'vʌlnərəb(ə)l/ *adj.* **1** that may be wounded or harmed. **2** (foll. by *to*) exposed to damage by a weapon, criticism, etc. **3** *Bridge* having won one game towards rubber and therefore liable to higher penalties. □□ **vulnerability** /-'bɪlɪtɪ/ *n.* **vulnerableness** *n.* **vulnerably** *adv.* [LL *vulnerabilis* f. L *vulnerare* to wound f. *vulnus -eris* wound]

vulnerary /'vʌlnərərɪ/ *adj. & n.* —*adj.* useful or used for the healing of wounds. —*n.* (*pl.* -**ies**) a vulnerary drug, plant, etc. [L *vulnerarius* f. *vulnus*: see VULNERABLE]

vulpine /'vʌlpaɪn/ *adj.* **1** of or like a fox. **2** crafty, cunning. [L *vulpinus* f. *vulpes* fox]

vulture /'vʌltʃə(r)/ *n.* **1** any of various large birds of prey of the family Cathartidae or Accipitridae, with the head and neck more or less bare of feathers, feeding chiefly on carrion and reputed to gather with others in anticipation of a death. **2** a rapacious person. □□ **vulturine** /-,raɪn/ *adj.* **vulturish** *adj.* **vulturous** *adj.* [ME f. AF *vultur*, OF *voltour* etc., f. L *vulturius*]

vulva /'vʌlvə/ *n.* (*pl.* **vulvas**) *Anat.* the external female genitals, esp. the external opening of the vagina. □□ **vulvar** *adj.* **vulvitis** /-'vaɪtɪs/ *n.* [L, = womb]

vv. *abbr.* **1** verses. **2** volumes.

vying *pres. part.* of VIE.

W

W¹ /ˈdʌb(ə)ljuː/ n. (also **w**) (pl. **Ws** or **W's**) the twenty-third letter of the alphabet.

W² abbr. (also **W.**) **1** watt(s). **2** West; Western. **3** women's (size). **4** Welsh.

W³ symb. Chem. the element tungsten.

w. abbr. **1** wicket(s). **2** wide(s). **3** with. **4** wife.

WA abbr. **1** Western Australia. **2** US Washington (State) (in official postal use).

Waac /wæk/ n. hist. a member of the Women's Army Auxiliary Corps (Brit. 1917–19 or US 1942–8). [initials WAAC]

Waaf /wæf/ n. Brit. hist. a member of the Women's Auxiliary Air Force (1939–48). [initials WAAF]

WAC abbr. (in the US) Women's Army Corps.

wack¹ /wæk/ n. esp. US sl. a crazy person. [prob. back-form. f. WACKY]

wack² /wæk/ n. dial. a familiar term of address. [perh. f. wacker Liverpudlian]

wacke /ˈwækə/ n. hist. a greyish-green or brownish rock resulting from the decomposition of basaltic rock. [G f. MHG wacke large stone, OHG wacko pebble]

wacko /ˈwækəʊ/ adj. & n. US sl. —adj. crazy. —n. (pl. -os or -oes) a crazy person. [WACKY + -o]

wacky /ˈwæki/ adj. & n. (also **whacky**) sl. —adj. (-ier, -iest) crazy. —n. (pl. -ies) a crazy person. □□ **wackily** adv. **wackiness** n. [orig. dial., = left-handed, f. WHACK]

wad /wɒd/ n. & v. —n. **1** a lump or bundle of soft material used esp. to keep things apart or in place or to stuff up an opening. **2** a disc of felt etc. keeping powder or shot in place in a gun. **3** a number of banknotes or documents placed together. **4** Brit. sl. a bun, sandwich, etc. **5** (in sing. or pl.) a large quantity esp. of money. —v.tr. (**wadded**, **wadding**) **1** stop up (an aperture or a gun-barrel) with a wad. **2** keep (powder etc.) in place with a wad. **3** line or stuff (a garment or coverlet) with wadding. **4** protect (a person, walls, etc.) with wadding. **5** press (cotton etc.) into a wad or wadding. [perh. rel. to Du. watten, F ouate padding, cotton wool]

wadding /ˈwɒdɪŋ/ n. **1** soft pliable material of cotton or wool etc. used to line or stuff garments, quilts, etc., or to pack fragile articles. **2** any material from which gun-wads are made.

waddle /ˈwɒd(ə)l/ v. & n. —v.intr. walk with short steps and a swaying motion, like a stout short-legged person or a bird with short legs set far apart (e.g. a duck or goose). —n. a waddling gait. □□ **waddler** n. [perh. frequent. of WADE]

waddy /ˈwɒdi/ n. (pl. -ies) **1** an Australian Aboriginal's war-club. **2** Austral. & NZ any club or stick. [Aboriginal, perh. f. WOOD]

wade /weɪd/ v. & n. —v. **1** intr. walk through water or some impeding medium e.g. snow, mud, or sand. **2** intr. make one's way with difficulty or by force. **3** intr. (foll. by through) read (a book etc.) in spite of its dullness etc. **4** intr. (foll. by into) colloq. attack (a person or task) vigorously. **5** tr. ford (a stream etc.) on foot. —n. a spell of wading. □ **wade in** colloq. make a vigorous attack or intervention. **wading bird** any long-legged water-bird that wades. □□ **wadable** adj. (also **wadeable**). [OE wadan f. Gmc, = go (through)]

wader /ˈweɪdə(r)/ n. **1 a** a person who wades. **b** a wading bird, esp. any of various birds of the order Charadriiformes. **2** (in pl.) high waterproof boots, or a waterproof garment for the legs and body, worn in fishing etc.

wadi /ˈwɒdɪ, ˈwɑːdɪ/ n. (also **wady**) (pl. **wadis** or **wadies**) a rocky watercourse in N. Africa etc., dry except in the rainy season. [Arab. wādī]

WAF abbr. (in the US) Women in the Air Force.

w.a.f. abbr. with all faults.

wafer /ˈweɪfə(r)/ n. & v. —n. **1** a very thin light crisp sweet biscuit, esp. of a kind eaten with ice-cream. **2** a thin disc of unleavened bread used in the Eucharist. **3** a disc of red paper stuck on a legal document instead of a seal. **4** Electronics a very thin slice of a semiconductor crystal used as the substrate for solid-state circuitry. **5** hist. a small disc of dried paste formerly used for fastening letters, holding papers together, etc. —v.tr. fasten or seal with a wafer. □ **wafer-thin** very thin. □□ **wafery** adj. [ME f. AF wafre, ONF waufre, OF gaufre (cf. GOFFER) f. MLG wāfel waffle: cf. WAFFLE²]

waffle¹ /ˈwɒf(ə)l/ n. & v. esp. Brit. colloq. —n. verbose but aimless or ignorant talk or writing. —v.intr. indulge in waffle. □□ **waffler** n. **waffly** adj. [orig. dial., frequent. of waff = yelp, yap (imit.)]

waffle² /ˈwɒf(ə)l/ n. esp. US a small crisp batter cake. □ **waffle-iron** a utensil, usu. of two shallow metal pans hinged together, for baking waffles. [Du. wafel, waefel f. MLG wāfel: cf. WAFER]

waft /wɒft, wɑːft/ v. & n. —v.tr. & intr. convey or travel easily as through air or over water; sweep smoothly and lightly along. —n. **1** (usu. foll. by of) a whiff or scent. **2** a transient sensation of peace, joy, etc. **3** (also **weft** /weft/) Naut. a distress signal, e.g. an ensign rolled or knotted or a garment flown in the rigging. [orig. 'convoy (ship etc.)', back-form. f. obs. waughter, wafter armed convoy-ship, f. Du. or LG wachter f. wachten to guard]

wag¹ /wæg/ v. & n. —v. (**wagged**, **wagging**) **1** tr. & intr. shake or wave rapidly or energetically to and fro. **2** intr. archaic (of the world, times, etc.) go along with varied fortune or characteristics. —n. a single wagging motion (with a wag of his tail). □ **the tail wags the dog** the less or least important member of a society, section of a party, or part of a structure has control. **tongues** (or **beards** or **chins** or **jaws**) **wag** there is talk. [ME waggen f. root of OE wagian sway]

wag² /wæg/ n. **1** a facetious person, a joker. **2** Brit. sl. a truant (play the wag). [prob. f. obs. waghalter one likely to be hanged (as WAG¹, HALTER)]

wage /weɪdʒ/ n. & v. —n. **1** (in sing. or pl.) a fixed regular payment, usu. daily or weekly, made by an employer to an employee, esp. to a manual or unskilled worker (cf. SALARY). **2** (in sing. or pl.) requital (the wages of sin is death). **3** (in pl.) Econ. the part of total production that rewards labour rather than remunerating capital. —v.tr. carry on (a war, conflict, or contest). □ **living wage** a wage that affords the means of normal subsistence. **wage-claim** = pay-claim (see PAY¹). **wage-earner** a person who works for wages. **wages council** a board of workers' and employers' representatives determining wages where there is no collective bargaining. **wage slave** a person dependent on income from labour in conditions like slavery. [ME f. AF & ONF wage, OF g(u)age, f. Gmc, rel. to GAGE¹, WED]

wager /ˈweɪdʒə(r)/ n. & v.tr. & intr. = BET. □ **wager of battle** hist. an ancient form of trial by personal combat between the parties or their champions. **wager of law** hist. a form of trial in which the defendant was required to produce witnesses who would swear to his or her innocence. [ME f. AF wageure f. wager (as WAGE)]

æ cat ɑː arm e bed ɜː her ɪ sit iː see ɒ hot ɔː saw ʌ run ʊ put uː too ə ago aɪ my

waggery /ˈwægərɪ/ n. (pl. **-ies**) **1** waggish behaviour, joking. **2** a waggish action or remark, a joke.

waggish /ˈwægɪʃ/ adj. playful, facetious. □□ **waggishly** adv. **waggishness** n.

waggle /ˈwæg(ə)l/ v. & n. colloq. —v. **1** intr. & tr. wag. **2** intr. Golf swing the club-head to and fro over the ball before playing a shot. —n. a waggling motion. [WAG¹ + -LE⁴]

waggly /ˈwæglɪ/ adj. unsteady.

Wagnerian /vɑːˈɡnɪərɪən/ adj. & n. —adj. of, relating to, or characteristic of the music dramas of Richard Wagner, German composer d. 1883, esp. with reference to their large scale. —n. an admirer of Wagner or his music.

wagon /ˈwægən/ n. (also Brit. **waggon**) **1** a four-wheeled vehicle for heavy loads, often with a removable tilt or cover. **2** Brit. a railway vehicle for goods, esp. an open truck. **3** a trolley for conveying tea etc. **4** (in full **water-wagon**) a vehicle for carrying water. **5** US a light horse-drawn vehicle. **6** colloq. a motor car, esp. an estate car. □**on the wagon** (or **water-wagon**) sl. teetotal. **wagon-roof** (or **-vault**) = barrel vault. [earlier wagon, wag(h)en, f. Du. wag(h)en, rel. to OE wægn WAIN]

wagoner /ˈwægənə(r)/ n. (also Brit. **waggoner**) the driver of a wagon. [Du. wagenaar (as WAGON)]

wagonette /ˌwægəˈnet/ n. (also Brit. **waggonette**) a four-wheeled horse-drawn pleasure vehicle, usu. open, with facing side-seats.

wagon-lit /ˌvægɒ̃ˈliː/ n. (pl. **wagons-lits** pronunc. same) a sleeping-car on a Continental railway. [F]

wagtail /ˈwægteɪl/ n. any small bird of the genus Motacilla with a long tail in frequent motion.

Wahabi /wəˈhɑːbɪ/ n. (also **Wahhabi**) (pl. **-is**) a member of a sect of Muslim puritans following strictly the original words of the Koran. [Muhammad ibn Abd-el-Wahhab, founder in the 18th c.]

wahine /wɑːˈhiːnɪ/ n. NZ a woman or wife. [Maori]

wah-wah /ˈwɑːwɑː/ n. (also **wa-wa**) Mus. an effect achieved on brass instruments by alternately applying and removing a mute and on an electric guitar by controlling the output from the amplifier with a pedal. [imit.]

waif /weɪf/ n. **1** a homeless and helpless person, esp. an abandoned child. **2** an ownerless object or animal, a thing cast up by or drifting in the sea or brought by an unknown agency. □**waifs and strays 1** homeless or neglected children. **2** odds and ends. □□ **waifish** adj. [ME f. AF waif, weif, ONF gaif, prob. of Scand. orig.]

wail /weɪl/ n. & v. —n. **1** a prolonged plaintive inarticulate loud high-pitched cry of pain, grief, etc. **2** a sound like or suggestive of this. —v. **1** intr. utter a wail. **2** intr. lament or complain persistently or bitterly. **3** intr. (of the wind etc.) make a sound like a person wailing. **4** tr. poet. or rhet. bewail; wail over. □**Wailing Wall** a high wall in Jerusalem said to stand on the site of Herod's temple, where Jews traditionally pray and lament on Fridays. □□ **wailer** n. **wailful** adj. poet. **wailingly** adv. [ME f. ON, rel. to WOE]

wain /weɪn/ n. archaic **1** a wagon. **2** (prec. by the) = CHARLES'S WAIN. [OE wæg(e)n, wæn, f. Gmc, rel. to WAY, WEIGH¹]

wainscot /ˈweɪnskət/ n. & v. —n. **1** boarding or wooden panelling on the lower part of a room-wall. **2** Brit. hist. imported oak of fine quality. —v.tr. (**wainscoted**, **wainscoting**) line with wainscot. [ME f. MLG wagenschot, app. f. wagen WAGON + schot of uncert. meaning]

wainscoting /ˈweɪnskətɪŋ/ n. **1** a wainscot. **2** material for this.

wainwright /ˈweɪnraɪt/ n. a wagon-builder.

waist /weɪst/ n. **1 a** the part of the human body below the ribs and above the hips, usu. of smaller circumference than these; the narrower middle part of the normal human figure. **b** the circumference of this. **2** a similar narrow part in the middle of a violin,

hourglass, wasp, etc. **3 a** the part of a garment encircling or covering the waist. **b** the narrow middle part of a woman's dress etc. **c** US a blouse or bodice. **4** the middle part of a ship, between the forecastle and the quarterdeck. □**waist-cloth** a loincloth.

waist-deep (or **-high**) up to the waist (waist-deep in water). □□ **waisted** adj. (also in comb.). **waistless** adj. [ME wast, perh. f. OE f. the root of WAX²]

waistband /ˈweɪstbænd/ n. a strip of cloth forming the waist of a garment.

waistcoat /ˈweɪskəʊt, ˈweɪstkəʊt, ˈweskət/ n. Brit. a close-fitting waist-length garment, without sleeves or collar but usu. buttoned, worn usu. by men over a shirt and under a jacket.

waistline /ˈweɪstlaɪn/ n. the outline or the size of a person's body at the waist.

wait /weɪt/ v. & n. —v. **1** intr. **a** defer action or departure for a specified time or until some expected event occurs (wait a minute; wait till I come; wait for a fine day). **b** be expectant or on the watch (waited to see what would happen). **c** (foll. by for) refrain from going so fast that (a person) is left behind (wait for me!). **2** tr. await (an opportunity, one's turn, etc.). **3** tr. defer (a meal etc.) until a person's arrival. **4** intr. (usu. as **waiting** n.) park a vehicle for a short time at the side of a road etc. (no waiting). **5** intr. **a** (in full **wait at** or US **on table**) act as a waiter or as a servant with similar functions. **b** act as an attendant. **6** intr. (foll. by on, upon) **a** await the convenience of. **b** serve as an attendant to. **c** pay a respectful visit to. —n. **1** a period of waiting (had a long wait for the train). **2** (usu. foll. by for) watching for an enemy; ambush (lie in wait; lay wait). **3** (in pl.) Brit. **a** archaic street singers of Christmas carols. **b** hist. official bands of musicians maintained by a city or town. □**cannot wait 1** is impatient. **2** needs to be dealt with immediately. **can wait** need not be dealt with immediately. **wait-a-bit** a plant with hooked thorns etc. that catch the clothing. **wait and see** await the progress of events. **wait for it!** colloq. **1** do not begin before the proper moment. **2** used to create an interval of suspense before saying something unexpected or amusing. **wait on** Austral., NZ, & N.Engl. be patient, wait. **wait up** (often foll. by for) not go to bed until a person arrives or an event happens. **you wait!** used to imply a threat, warning, or promise. [ME f. ONF waitier f. Gmc, rel. to WAKE¹]

waiter /ˈweɪtə(r)/ n. **1** a man who serves at table in a hotel or restaurant etc. **2** a person who waits for a time, event, or opportunity. **3** a tray or salver.

waiting /ˈweɪtɪŋ/ n. **1** in senses of WAIT v. **2 a** official attendance at court. **b** one's period of this. □**waiting game** abstention from early action in a contest etc. so as to act more effectively later. **waiting-list** a list of people waiting for a thing not immediately available. **waiting-room** a room provided for people to wait in, esp. by a doctor, dentist, etc., or at a railway or bus station.

waitress /ˈweɪtrɪs/ n. a woman who serves at table in a hotel or restaurant etc.

waive /weɪv/ v.tr. refrain from insisting on or using (a right, claim, opportunity, legitimate plea, etc.). [ME f. AF weyver, OF gaiver allow to become a WAIF, abandon]

waiver /ˈweɪvə(r)/ n. Law the act or an instance of waiving. [as WAIVE]

wake¹ /weɪk/ v. & n. —v. (past **woke** /wəʊk/ or **waked**; past part. **woken** /ˈwəʊkən/ or **waked**) **1** intr. & tr. (often foll. by up) cease or cause to cease to sleep. **2** intr. & tr. (often foll. by up) become or cause to become alert, attentive, or active (needs something to wake him up). **3** intr. (archaic except as **waking** adj. & n.) be awake (in her waking hours; waking or sleeping). **4** tr. disturb (silence or a place) with noise; make re-echo. **5** tr. evoke (an echo). **6** intr. & tr. rise or raise from the dead. —n. **1** a watch beside a corpse before burial; lamentation and (less often) merrymaking in connection with this. **2** (usu.

in *pl.*) an annual holiday in (industrial) northern England. **3** *hist.* **a** a vigil commemorating the dedication of a church. **b** a fair or merrymaking on this occasion. □**be a wake-up** (often foll. by *to*) *Austral. sl.* be alert or aware. **wake-robin 1** *Brit.* an arum, esp. the cuckoo-pint. **2** *US* any plant of the genus *Trillium*. □□ **waker** *n.* [OE *wacan* (recorded only in past *woc*), *wacian* (weak form), rel. to WATCH: sense 'vigil' perh. f. ON]

wake[2] /weɪk/ *n.* **1** the track left on the water's surface by a moving ship. **2** turbulent air left behind a moving aircraft etc. □**in the wake of** behind, following, as a result of, in imitation of. [prob. f. MLG f. ON *vǫk* hole or opening in ice]

wakeful /ˈweɪkfʊl/ *adj.* **1** unable to sleep. **2** (of a night etc.) passed with little or no sleep. **3** vigilant. □□ **wakefully** *adv.* **wakefulness** *n.*

waken /ˈweɪkən/ *v.tr.* & *intr.* make or become awake. [ON *vakna* f. Gmc, rel. to WAKE[1]]

Walachian var. of WALLACHIAN.

Waldenses /wɒlˈdensiːz/ *n.pl.* a puritan religious sect orig. in S. France, now chiefly in Italy and America, founded *c.*1170 and much persecuted. □□ **Waldensian** *adj.* & *n.* [med.L f. Peter *Waldo* of Lyons, founder]

wale /weɪl/ *n.* & *v.* —*n.* **1** = WEAL[1]. **2** a ridge on a woven fabric, e.g. corduroy. **3** *Naut.* a broad thick timber along a ship's side. **4** a specially woven strong band round a woven basket. —*v.tr.* provide or mark with wales. □**wale-knot** a knot made at the end of a rope by intertwining strands to prevent unravelling or act as a stopper. [OE *walu* stripe, ridge]

walk /wɔːk/ *v.* & *n.* —*v.* **1** *intr.* **a** (of a person or other biped) progress by lifting and setting down each foot in turn, never having both feet off the ground at once. **b** progress with similar movements (*walked on his hands*). **c** go with the gait usual except when speed is desired. **d** (of a quadruped) go with the slowest gait, always having at least two feet on the ground at once. **2** *intr.* **a** travel or go on foot. **b** take exercise in this way (*walks for two hours each day*). **3** *tr.* perambulate, traverse on foot at walking speed, tread the floor or surface of. **4** *tr.* **a** cause to walk with one. **b** accompany in walking. **c** ride or lead (a horse, dog, etc.) at walking pace. **d** take charge of (a puppy) at walk (see sense 4 of *n.*). **5** *intr.* (of a ghost) appear. **6** *intr. Cricket* leave the wicket on being out. **7** *Baseball* **a** *intr.* reach first base on balls. **b** *tr.* allow to do this. **8** *intr. archaic* live in a specified manner, conduct oneself (*walk humbly*; *walk with God*). **9** *intr. US sl.* be released from suspicion or from a charge. —*n.* **1 a** an act of walking, the ordinary human gait (*go at a walk*). **b** the slowest gait of an animal. **c** a person's manner of walking (*know him by his walk*). **2 a** taking a (usu. specified) time to walk a distance (*is only ten minutes' walk from here*; *it's quite a walk to the bus-stop*). **b** an excursion on foot, a stroll or constitutional (*go for a walk*). **c** a journey on foot completed to earn money promised for a charity etc. **3 a** a place, track, or route intended or suitable for walking; a promenade, colonnade, or footpath. **b** a person's favourite place or route for walking. **c** the round of a postman, hawker, etc. **4** a farm etc. where a hound-puppy is sent to accustom it to various surroundings. **5** the place where a gamecock is kept. **6** a part of a forest under one keeper. □**in a walk** without effort (*won in a walk*). **walk about** stroll. **walk all over** *colloq.* **1** defeat easily. **2** take advantage of. **walk away from 1** easily outdistance. **2** refuse to become involved with; fail to deal with. **3** survive (an accident etc.) without serious injury. **walk away with** *colloq.* = *walk off with*. **walk the boards** be an actor. **walk the hospitals** = *walk the wards*. **walk in** (often foll. by *on*) enter or arrive, esp. unexpectedly or easily. **walk into 1** *colloq.* encounter through unwariness (*walked into the trap*). **2** *sl. archaic* attack forcefully. **3** *sl. archaic* eat heartily. **walk it 1** make a journey on

foot, not ride. **2** *colloq.* achieve something (esp. a victory) easily. **walk Matilda** see MATILDA. **walk off 1** depart (esp. abruptly). **2** get rid of the effects of (a meal, ailment, etc.) by walking (*walked off his anger*). **walk a person off his** or **her feet** (or **legs**) exhaust a person with walking. **walk off with** *colloq.* **1** steal. **2** win easily. **walk of life** an occupation, profession, or calling. **walk-on 1** (in full **walk-on part**) = *walking-on part*. **2** the player of this. **walk on air** see AIR. **walk out 1** depart suddenly or angrily. **2** (usu. foll. by *with*) *archaic* go for walks in courtship. **walk-out** *n.* a sudden angry departure, esp. as a protest or strike. **walk out on** desert, abandon. **walk over 1** *colloq.* = *walk all over*. **2** (often *absol.*) traverse (a racecourse) without needing to hurry, because one has no opponents or only inferior ones. **walk-over** *n.* an easy victory or achievement. **walk the plank** see PLANK. **walk the streets 1** be a prostitute. **2** traverse the streets esp. in search of work etc. **walk tall** *colloq.* feel justifiable pride. **walk up!** a showman's invitation to a circus etc. **walk-up** *US adj.* (of a building) allowing access to the upper floors only by stairs. —*n.* a walk-up building. **walk up to** approach (a person) for a talk etc. **walk the wards** be a medical student. □□ **walkable** *adj.* [OE *wealcan* roll, toss, wander, f. Gmc]

walkabout /ˈwɔːkəˌbaʊt/ *n.* **1** an informal stroll among a crowd by a visiting dignitary. **2** a period of wandering in the bush by an Australian Aboriginal.

walkathon /ˈwɔːkəˌθɒn/ *n.* an organized fund-raising walk. [WALK, after MARATHON]

walker /ˈwɔːkə(r)/ *n.* **1** a person or animal that walks. **2 a** a wheeled or footed framework in which a baby can learn to walk. **b** = *walking frame*.

walkie-talkie /ˌwɔːkɪˈtɔːkɪ/ *n.* a two-way radio carried on the person, esp. by policemen etc.

walking /ˈwɔːkɪŋ/ *n.* & *adj.* in senses of WALK *v.* □**walking delegate** a trade-union official who visits members and their employers for discussions. **walking dictionary** (or **encyclopaedia**) *colloq.* a person having a wide general knowledge. **walking fern** any American evergreen fern of the genus *Camptosorus*, with fronds that root at the ends. **walking frame** a usu. tubular metal frame with rubberized ferrules, used by disabled or old people to help them walk. **walking gentleman** (or **lady**) *Theatr.* a non-speaking extra; a supernumerary. **walking leaf** = *walking fern*. **walking-on part** a non-speaking dramatic role. **walking papers** *colloq.* dismissal (*gave him his walking papers*). **walking-stick 1** a stick carried when walking, esp. for extra support. **2** *US* = *stick insect* (see STICK[1]). **walking-tour** a holiday journey on foot, esp. of several days. **walking wounded 1** (of soldiers etc.) able to walk despite injuries; not bedridden. **2** *colloq.* a person or people having esp. mental or emotional difficulties.

Walkman /ˈwɔːkmən/ *n.* (*pl.* **-mans**) *propr.* a type of personal stereo equipment.

walkway /ˈwɔːkweɪ/ *n.* a passage or path for walking along, esp.: **1** a raised passageway connecting different sections of a building. **2** a wide path in a garden etc.

wall /wɔːl/ *n.* & *v.* —*n.* **1 a** a continuous and usu. vertical structure of usu. brick or stone, having little width in proportion to its length and height and esp. enclosing, protecting, or dividing a space or supporting a roof. **b** the surface of a wall, esp. inside a room (*hung the picture on the wall*). **2** anything like a wall in appearance or effect, esp.: **a** the steep side of a mountain. **b** a protection or obstacle (*a wall of steel bayonets*; *a wall of indifference*). **c** *Anat.* the outermost layer or enclosing membrane etc. of an organ, structure, etc. **d** the outermost part of a hollow structure (*stomach wall*). **e** *Mining* rock enclosing a lode or seam. —*v.tr.* **1** (esp. as **walled** *adj.*) surround or protect with a wall (*walled garden*).

2 a (usu. foll. by *up*, *off*) block or seal (a space etc.) with a wall. **b** (foll. by *up*) enclose (a person) within a sealed space (*walled them up in the dungeon*). □**go to the wall** be defeated or pushed aside. **off the wall** *US sl.* unorthodox, unconventional. **up the wall** *colloq.* crazy or furious (*went up the wall when he heard*). **wall bar** one of a set of parallel bars, attached to the wall of a gymnasium, on which exercises are performed. **wall-barley** wild barley as a weed. **wall-board** a type of wall-covering made from wood pulp etc. **wall cress** = ARABIS. **wall-fern** an evergreen polypody, *Polypodium vulgare*, with very large leaves. **wall-fruit** fruit grown on trees trained against a wall for protection and warmth. **wall game** *Brit.* a form of football played at Eton. **wall-knot** = *wale-knot*. **wall-painting** a mural or fresco. **wall pepper** a succulent stonecrop, *Sedum acre*, with a pungent taste. **wall-plate** timber laid in or on a wall to distribute the pressure of a girder etc. **wall rocket** see ROCKET[2]. **wall rue** a small fern, *Adiantum ruta-muraria*, with leaves like rue, growing on walls and rocks. **walls have ears** it is unsafe to speak openly, as there may be eavesdroppers. **wall-to-wall 1** (of a carpet) fitted to cover a whole room etc. **2** *colloq.* profuse, ubiquitous (*wall-to-wall pop music*). □□**walling** *n.* **wall-less** *adj.* [OE f. L *vallum* rampart f. *vallus* stake]

wallaby /ˈwɒləbɪ/ *n.* (*pl.* **-ies**) **1** any of various marsupials of the family Macropodidae, smaller than kangaroos, and having large hind feet and long tails. **2** (**Wallabies**) *colloq.* the Australian international Rugby Union team. □**on the wallaby** (or **wallaby track**) *Austral.* vagrant; unemployed. [Aboriginal *wolabā*]

Wallachian /wɒˈleɪkɪən/ *adj.* & *n.* (also **Walachian**) —*adj.* of the former Principality of Wallachia, now part of Romania. —*n.* a native of Wallachia. [*Wallachia* (as VLACH)]

wallah /ˈwɒlə/ *n.* orig. *Anglo-Ind.*, now *sl.* **1** a person concerned with or in charge of a usu. specified thing, business, etc. (*asked the ticket wallah*). **2** a person doing a routine administrative job; a bureaucrat. [Hindi -*wālā* suffix = -ER[1]]

wallaroo /ˌwɒləˈruː/ *n.* a large brownish-black kangaroo, *Macropus robustus*. [Aboriginal *wolarū*]

wallet /ˈwɒlɪt/ *n.* **1** a small flat esp. leather case for holding banknotes etc. **2** *archaic* a bag for carrying food etc. on a journey, esp. as used by a pilgrim or beggar. [ME *walet*, prob. f. AF *walet* (unrecorded), perh. f. Gmc]

wall-eye /ˈwɔːlaɪ/ *n.* **1 a** an eye with a streaked or opaque white iris. **b** an eye squinting outwards. **2** an American perch, *Stizostedion vitreum*, with large prominent eyes. □□**wall-eyed** *adj.* [back-form. f. *wall-eyed*: ME f. ON *vagleygr* f. *vagl* (unrecorded: cf. Icel. *vagl* film over the eye) + *auga* EYE]

wallflower /ˈwɔːlˌflaʊə(r)/ *n.* **1 a** a fragrant spring garden-plant, *Cheiranthus cheiri*, with esp. brown, yellow, or dark-red clustered flowers. **b** any of various flowering plants of the genus *Cheiranthus* or *Erysimum*, growing wild on old walls. **2** *colloq.* a neglected or socially awkward person, esp. a woman sitting out at a dance for lack of partners.

Walloon /wɒˈluːn/ *n.* & *adj.* —*n.* **1** a member of a French-speaking people inhabiting S. and E. Belgium and neighbouring France (see also FLEMING). **2** the French dialect spoken by this people. —*adj.* of or concerning the Walloons or their language. [F *Wallon* f. med.L *Wallo -onis* f. Gmc: cf. WELSH]

wallop /ˈwɒləp/ *v.* & *n.* *sl.* —*v.tr.* (**walloped**, **walloping**) **1 a** thrash; beat. **b** hit hard. **2** (as **walloping** *adj.*) big; strapping; thumping (*a walloping profit*). —*n.* **1** a heavy blow; a thump. **2** *Brit.* beer or any alcoholic drink. □□**walloping** *n.* [earlier senses 'gallop', 'boil', f. ONF (*walop* n. f.) *waloper*, OF *galoper*: cf. GALLOP]

walloper /ˈwɒləpə(r)/ *n.* **1** a person or thing that wallops. **2** *Austral. sl.* a policeman.

wallow /ˈwɒləʊ/ *v.* & *n.* —*v.intr.* **1** (esp. of an animal) roll about in mud, sand, water, etc. **2** (usu. foll. by *in*) indulge in unrestrained sensuality, pleasure, misery, etc. (*wallows in nostalgia*). —*n.* **1** the act or an instance of wallowing. **2 a** a place used by buffalo etc. for wallowing. **b** the depression in the ground caused by this. □□**wallower** *n.* [OE *walwian* roll f. Gmc]

wallpaper /ˈwɔːlˌpeɪpə(r)/ *n.* & *v.* —*n.* **1** paper sold in rolls for pasting on to interior walls as decoration. **2** an unobtrusive background, esp. (usu. *derog.*) with ref. to sound, music, etc. —*v.tr.* (often *absol.*) decorate with wallpaper.

Wall Street /ˈwɔːl striːt/ *n.* the American financial world or money market. [street in New York City where banks, the Stock Exchange, etc. are situated]

wally /ˈwɒlɪ/ *n.* (*pl.* **-ies**) *Brit. sl.* a foolish or inept person. [orig. uncert., perh. shortened form of *Walter*]

walnut /ˈwɔːlnʌt/ *n.* **1** any tree of the genus *Juglans*, having aromatic leaves and drooping catkins. **2** the nut of this tree containing an edible kernel in two half shells shaped like boats. **3** the timber of the walnut-tree used in cabinet-making. [OE *walh-hnutu* f. Gmc NUT]

Walpurgis night /vælˈpʊəgɪs/ *n.* the eve of 1 May when witches are alleged to meet on the Brocken mountain in Germany and hold revels with the Devil. [G *Walpurgisnacht* f. *Walpurgis* genit. of *Walpurga* Engl. woman saint (8th c.) + *Nacht* NIGHT]

walrus /ˈwɔːlrəs, ˈwɒl-/ *n.* a large amphibious long-tusked arctic mammal, *Odobenus rosmarus*, related to the seal and sea lion. □**walrus moustache** a long thick drooping moustache. [prob. f. Du. *walrus, -ros*, perh. by metath. after *walvisch* 'whale-fish' f. word repr. by OE *horschwæl* 'horse-whale']

waltz /wɔːls, wɒlts, wɒ-/ *n.* & *v.* —*n.* **1** a dance in triple time performed by couples who rotate and progress round the floor. **2** the usu. flowing and melodious music for this. —*v.* **1** *intr.* dance a waltz. **2** *intr.* (often foll. by *in*, *out*, *round*, etc.) *colloq.* move lightly, casually, with deceptive ease, etc. (*waltzed in and took first prize*). **3** *tr.* move (a person) in or as if in a waltz, with ease (*was waltzed off to Paris*). □**waltz Matilda** see MATILDA. □□**waltzer** *n.* [G *Walzer* f. *walzen* revolve]

wampum /ˈwɒmpəm/ *n.* beads made from shells and strung together for use as money, decoration, or as aids to memory by N. American Indians. [Algonquin *wampumpeag* f. *wap* white + *umpe* string + *-ag* pl. suffix]

wan /wɒn/ *adj.* **1** (of a person's complexion or appearance) pale; exhausted; worn. **2** (of a star etc. or its light) partly obscured; faint. **3** *archaic* (of night, water, etc.) dark, black. □□**wanly** *adv.* **wanness** *n.* [OE *wann* dark, black, of unkn. orig.]

wand /wɒnd/ *n.* **1 a** a supposedly magic stick used in casting spells by a fairy, magician, etc. **b** a stick used by a conjurer for effect. **2** a slender rod carried or used as a marker in the ground. **3** a staff symbolizing some officials' authority. **4** *colloq.* a conductor's baton. **5** a hand-held electronic device which can be passed over a bar-code to read the data this represents. [ME prob. f. Gmc: cf. WEND, WIND[2]]

wander /ˈwɒndə(r)/ *v.* & *n.* —*v.* **1** *intr.* (often foll. by *in*, *off*, etc.) go about from place to place aimlessly. **2** *intr.* **a** (of a person, river, road, etc.) wind about; diverge; meander. **b** (of esp. a person) get lost; leave home; stray from a path etc. **3** *intr.* talk or think incoherently; be inattentive or delirious. **4** *tr.* cover while wandering (*wanders the world*). —*n.* the act or an instance of wandering (*went for a wander round the garden*). □**wandering Jew 1 a** a legendary person said to have been condemned by Christ to wander the earth until the second advent. **b** a person who never settles down. **2 a** a climbing plant, *Tradescantia albiflora*, with stemless variegated leaves. **b** a trailing plant, *Zebrina pendula*, with pink flowers. **wandering sailor** the moneywort. **wander-plug** a plug that can be fitted into any of various sockets in an electrical device. □□ **wanderer** *n.* **wandering** *n.* (esp. in *pl.*). [OE *wandrian* (as WEND)]

wanderlust /'wɒndə,lʌst, 'vændə,lʊst/ *n.* an eagerness for travelling or wandering. [G]

wanderoo /,wɒndə'ruː/ *n.* a langur, *Semnopithecus vetulus*, of Sri Lanka. [Sinh. *wanderu* monkey]

wane /weɪn/ *v. & n.* —*v.intr.* **1** (of the moon) decrease in apparent size after the full moon (cf. WAX²). **2** decrease in power, vigour, importance, brilliance, size, etc.; decline. —*n.* **1** the process of waning. **2** a defect of a plank etc. that lacks square corners. □ **on the wane** waning; declining. □□ **waney** *adj.* (in sense 2 of *n.*). [OE *wanian* lessen f. Gmc]

wangle /'wæŋg(ə)l/ *v. & n. colloq.* —*v.tr.* **1** (often *refl.*) to obtain (a favour etc.) by scheming etc. (*wangled himself a free trip*). **2** alter or fake (a report etc.) to appear more favourable. —*n.* the act or an instance of wangling. □□ **wangler** *n.* [19th-c. printers' sl.: orig. unkn.]

wank /wæŋk/ *v. & n. coarse sl.* ¶ Usually considered a taboo word. —*v.intr. & tr.* masturbate. —*n.* an act of masturbating. [20th c.: orig. unkn.]

Wankel engine /'wæŋk(ə)l, 'væŋ-/ *n.* a rotary internal-combustion engine with a continuously rotated and eccentrically pivoted nearly triangular shaft. [F. *Wankel*, Ger. engineer d. 1988]

wanker /'wæŋkə(r)/ *n. coarse sl.* ¶ Usually considered a taboo word. **1** a contemptible or ineffectual person. **2** a person who masturbates.

want /wɒnt/ *v. & n.* —*v.* **1** *tr.* **a** (often foll. by *to* + infin.) desire; wish for possession of; need (*wants a toy train; wants it done immediately; wanted to leave; wanted him to leave*). **b** need or desire (a person, esp. sexually). **c** esp. *Brit.* require to be attended to in esp. a specified way (*the garden wants weeding*). **d** (foll. by *to* + infin.) *colloq.* ought; should; need (*you want to pull yourself together; you don't want to overdo it*). **2** *intr.* (usu. foll. by *for*) lack; be deficient (*wants for nothing*). **3** *tr.* be without or fall short by (esp. a specified amount or thing) (*the drawer wants a handle*). **4** *intr.* (foll. by *in, out*) esp. *US colloq.* desire to be in, out, etc. (*wants in on the deal*). **5** *tr.* (as **wanted** *adj.*) (of a suspected criminal etc.) sought by the police. —*n.* **1** (often foll. by *of*) **a** a lack, absence, or deficiency (*could not go for want of time; shows great want of judgement*). **b** poverty; need (*living in great want; in want of necessities*). **2 a** a desire for a thing etc. (*meets a long-felt want*). **b** a thing so desired (*can supply your wants*). □ **do not want to** am unwilling to. **want ad** *US* a classified newspaper advertisement for something sought. □□ **wanter** *n.* [ME f. ON *vant* neut. of *vanr* lacking = OE *wana*, formed as WANE]

wanting /'wɒntɪŋ/ *adj.* **1** lacking (in quality or quantity); deficient; not equal to requirements (*wanting in judgement; the standard is sadly wanting*). **2** absent, not supplied or provided. □ **be found wanting** fail to meet requirements.

wanton /'wɒnt(ə)n/ *adj., n., & v.* —*adj.* **1** licentious; lewd; sexually promiscuous. **2** capricious; random; arbitrary; motiveless (*wanton destruction; wanton wind*). **3** luxuriant; unrestrained (*wanton profusion*). **4** *archaic* playful; sportive (*a wanton child*). —*n. literary* an immoral or licentious person, esp. a woman. —*v.intr. literary* **1** gambol; sport; move capriciously. **2** (foll. by *with*) behave licentiously. □□ **wantonly** *adv.* **wantonness** *n.* [ME *wantowen* (*wan*-UN-¹ + *towen* f. OE *togen* past part. of *tēon* discipline, rel. to TEAM)]

wapentake /'wɒpən,teɪk, 'wæp-/ *n. Brit. hist.* (in areas of England with a large Danish population) a division of a shire; a hundred. [OE *wǣpen(ge)tæc* f. ON *vápnatak* f. *vápn* weapon + *tak* taking f. *taka* TAKE: perh. with ref. to voting in assembly by show of weapons]

wapiti /'wɒpɪtɪ/ *n.* (*pl.* **wapitis**) a N. American deer, *Cervus canadensis*. [Cree *wapitik* white deer]

War. *abbr.* Warwickshire.

war /wɔː(r)/ *n. & v.* —*n.* **1 a** armed hostilities between esp. nations; conflict (*war broke out; war zone*). **b** a specific conflict or the period of time during which such conflict exists (*was before the war*). **c** the suspension of international law etc. during such a conflict. **2** (as **the War**) a war in progress or recently ended; the most recent major war. **3 a** hostility or contention between people, groups, etc. (*war of words*). **b** (often foll. by *on*) a sustained campaign against crime, disease, poverty, etc. —*v.intr.* (**warred**, **warring**) **1** (as **warring** *adj.*) **a** rival; fighting (*warring factions*). **b** conflicting (*warring principles*). **2** make war. □ **art of war** strategy and tactics. **at war** (often foll. by *with*) engaged in a war. **go to war** declare or begin a war. **go to the wars** *archaic* serve as a soldier. **have been in the wars** *colloq.* appear injured, bruised, unkempt, etc. **war baby** a child, esp. illegitimate, born in wartime. **war bride** a woman who marries a serviceman met during a war. **war chest** funds for a war or any other campaign. **war-cloud** a threatening international situation. **war correspondent** a correspondent reporting from a scene of war. **war crime** a crime violating the international laws of war. **war criminal** a person committing or sentenced for such crimes. **war cry 1** a phrase or name shouted to rally one's troops. **2** a party slogan etc. **war damage** damage to property etc. caused by bombing, shelling, etc. **war dance** a dance performed by primitive peoples etc. before a battle or to celebrate victory. **war department** the State office in charge of the army etc. **war-game 1** a military exercise testing or improving tactical knowledge etc. **2** a battle etc. conducted with toy soldiers. **war-gaming** the playing of war-games. **war grave** the grave of a serviceman who died on active service, esp. one in a special cemetery etc. **war loan** stock issued by the British Government to raise funds in wartime. **war memorial** a monument etc. commemorating those killed in a war. **war of attrition** a war in which each side seeks to wear out the other over a long period. **war of the elements** *poet.* storms or natural catastrophes. **War Office** *hist.* the British State department in charge of the army. **war of nerves** an attempt to wear down an opponent by psychological means. **war-plane** a military aircraft. **war poet** a poet writing on war themes, esp. of the two world wars. **Wars of the Roses** *hist.* the 15th-c. civil wars between the houses of York and Lancaster, represented by white and red roses. **war-weary** (esp. of a population) exhausted and dispirited by war. **war widow** a woman whose husband has been killed in war. **war-worn** = *war-weary*. **war zone** an area in which a war takes place. [ME *werre* f. AF, ONF var. of OF *guerre*: cf. WORSE]

waratah /'wɒrətə/ *n.* an Australian crimson-flowered shrub, *Telopea speciosissima*. [Aboriginal]

warble¹ /'wɔːb(ə)l/ *v. & n.* —*v.* **1** *intr. & tr.* sing in a gentle trilling manner. **2** *tr.* **a** speak or utter in a warbling manner. **b** express in a song or verse (*warbled his love*). —*n.* a warbled song or utterance. [ME f. ONF *werble(r)* f. Frank. *hwirbilōn* whirl, trill]

warble² /'wɔːb(ə)l/ *n.* **1** a hard lump on a horse's back caused by the galling of a saddle. **2 a** the larva of a warble fly beneath the skin of cattle etc. **b** a tumour produced by this. □ **warble fly** any of various flies of the genus *Hypoderma*, infesting the skin of cattle and horses. [16th c.: orig. uncert.]

warbler /'wɔːblə(r)/ *n.* **1** a person, bird, etc. that warbles. **2** any small insect-eating bird of the family Sylviidae or, in N. America, Parulidae, including the blackcap, whitethroat, and chiff-chaff, not always remarkable for their song.

ward /wɔːd/ *n. & v.* —*n.* **1** a separate room or division of a hospital, prison, etc. (*men's surgical ward*). **2 a**

Brit. an administrative division of a constituency, usu. electing a councillor or councillors etc. **b** esp. *US* a similar administrative division. **3 a** a minor under the care of a guardian appointed by the parents or a court. **b** (in full **ward of court**) a minor or mentally deficient person placed under the protection of a court. **4** (in *pl.*) the corresponding notches and projections in a key and a lock. **5** *archaic* **a** the act of guarding or defending a place etc. **b** the bailey of a castle. **c** a guardian's control; confinement; custody. —*v.tr. archaic* guard; protect. □**ward-heeler** *US* a party worker in elections etc. **ward off 1** parry (a blow). **2** avert (danger, poverty, etc.). [OE *weard, weardian* f. Gmc: cf. GUARD]

-ward /wəd/ *suffix* (also **-wards**) added to nouns of place or destination and to adverbs of direction and forming: **1** adverbs (usu. **-wards**) meaning 'towards the place etc.' (*moving backwards; set off homewards*). **2** adjectives (usu. **-ward**) meaning 'turned or tending towards' (*a downward look; an onward rush*). **3** (less commonly) nouns meaning 'the region towards or about' (*look to the eastward*). [from or after OE *-weard* f. a Gmc root meaning 'turn']

warden /'wɔːd(ə)n/ *n.* **1** (usu. in *comb.*) a supervising official (*churchwarden; traffic warden*). **2 a** *Brit.* a president or governor of a college, school, hospital, youth hostel, etc. **b** esp. *US* a prison governor. □□ **wardenship** *n.* [ME f. AF & ONF *wardein* var. of OF *g(u)arden* GUARDIAN]

warder /'wɔːdə(r)/ *n.* **1** *Brit.* (*fem.* **wardress**) a prison officer. **2** a guard. [ME f. AF *wardere, -our* f. ONF *warder*, OF *garder* to GUARD]

wardrobe /'wɔːdrəub/ *n.* **1** a large movable or built-in cupboard with rails, shelves, hooks, etc., for storing clothes. **2** a person's entire stock of clothes. **3** the costume department or costumes of a theatre, a film company, etc. **4** a department of a royal household in charge of clothing. □**wardrobe mistress** (or **master**) a person in charge of a theatrical or film wardrobe. **wardrobe trunk** a trunk fitted with rails, shelves, etc. for use as a travelling wardrobe. [ME f. ONF *warderobe*, OF *garderobe* (as GUARD, ROBE)]

wardroom /'wɔːdruːm, -rom/ *n.* a room in a warship for the use of commissioned officers.

-wards var. of -WARD.

wardship /'wɔːdʃɪp/ *n.* **1** a guardian's care or tutelage (*under his wardship*). **2** the condition of being a ward.

ware[1] /weə(r)/ *n.* **1** (esp. in *comb.*) things of the same kind, esp. ceramics, made usu. for sale (*chinaware; hardware*). **2** (usu. in *pl.*) **a** articles for sale (*displayed his wares*). **b** a person's skills, talents, etc. **3** ceramics etc. of a specified material, factory, or kind (*Wedgwood ware; Delft ware*). [OE *waru* f. Gmc, perh. orig. = 'object of care', rel. to WARE[3]]

ware[2] /weə(r)/ *v.tr.* (also **'ware**) (esp. in hunting) look out for; avoid (usu. in *imper.*: *ware hounds!*). [OE *warian* f. Gmc (as WARE[3]), & f. ONF *warer*]

ware[3] /weə(r)/ *predic.adj. poet.* aware. [OE *wær* f. Gmc: cf. WARD]

warehouse /'weəhaus/ *n.* & *v.* —*n.* **1** a building in which esp. retail goods are stored; a repository. **2** esp. *Brit.* a wholesale or large retail store. —*v.tr.* /also -hauz/ store (esp. furniture or bonded goods) temporarily in a repository. □□ **warehouseman** *n.* (*pl.* **-men**)

warfare /'wɔːfeə(r)/ *n.* a state of war; campaigning, engaging in war (*chemical warfare*).

warfarin /'wɔːfərɪn/ *n.* a water-soluble anticoagulant used esp. as a rat poison. [*W*isconsin *A*lumni *R*esearch *F*oundation + *-arin*, after COUMARIN]

warhead /'wɔːhed/ *n.* the explosive head of a missile, torpedo, or similar weapon.

warhorse /'wɔːhɔːs/ *n.* **1** *hist.* a knight's or trooper's powerful horse. **2** *colloq.* a veteran soldier, politician, etc.; a reliable hack.

warlike /'wɔːlaɪk/ *adj.* **1** threatening war; hostile. **2**

martial; soldierly. **3** of or for war; military (*warlike preparations*).

warlock /'wɔːlɒk/ *n. archaic* a sorcerer or wizard. [OE *wær-loga* traitor f. *wær* covenant: *loga* rel. to LIE[2]]

warlord /'wɔːlɔːd/ *n.* a military commander or commander-in-chief.

warm /wɔːm/ *adj., v.,* & *n.* —*adj.* **1** of or at a fairly or comfortably high temperature. **2** (of clothes etc.) affording warmth (*needs warm gloves*). **3 a** (of a person, action, feelings, etc.) sympathetic; cordial; friendly; loving (*a warm welcome; has a warm heart*). **b** enthusiastic; hearty (*was warm in her praise*). **4** animated, heated, excited; indignant (*the dispute grew warm*). **5** *colloq. iron.* dangerous, difficult, or hostile (*met a warm reception*). **6** *colloq.* **a** (of a participant in esp. a children's game of seeking) close to the object etc. sought. **b** near to guessing or finding out a secret. **7** (of a colour, light, etc.) reddish, pink, or yellowish, etc., suggestive of warmth. **8** *Hunting* (of a scent) fresh and strong. **9 a** (of a person's temperament) amorous; sexually demanding. **b** erotic; arousing. —*v.* **1** *tr.* **a** make warm (*fire warms the room*). **b** excite; make cheerful (*warms the heart*). **2** *intr.* **a** (often foll. by *up*) warm oneself at a fire etc. (*warmed himself up*). **b** (often foll. by *to*) become animated, enthusiastic, or sympathetic (*warmed to his subject*). —*n.* **1** the act of warming; the state of being warmed (*gave it a warm; had a nice warm by the fire*). **2** the warmth of the atmosphere etc. **3** *Brit. archaic* a warm garment, esp. an army greatcoat. □**warmed-up** (*US* **-over**) **1** (of food etc.) reheated or stale. **2** stale; second-hand. **warm front** an advancing mass of warm air. **warming-pan** *hist.* a usu. brass container for live coals with a flat body and a long handle, used for warming a bed. **warm up 1** (of an athlete, performer, etc.) prepare for a contest, performance, etc. by practising. **2** (of a room etc.) become warmer. **3** (of a person) become enthusiastic etc. **4** (of a radio, engine, etc.) reach a temperature for efficient working. **5** reheat (food). **warm-up** *n.* a period of preparatory exercise for a contest or performance. **warm work 1** work etc. that makes one warm through exertion. **2** dangerous conflict etc. □□ **warmer** *n.* (also in *comb.*). **warmish** *adj.* **warmly** *adv.* **warmness** *n.* **warmth** *n.* [OE *wearm* f. Gmc]

warm-blooded /wɔːm'blʌdɪd/ *adj.* **1** (of an organism) having warm blood; mammalian (see HOMOEOTHERM). **2** ardent, passionate. □□ **warm-bloodedness** *n.*

warm-hearted /wɔːm'hɑːtɪd/ *adj.* having a warm heart; kind, friendly. □□ **warm-heartedly** *adv.* **warm-heartedness** *n.*

warmonger /'wɔː,mʌŋgə(r)/ *n.* a person who seeks to bring about or promote war. □□ **warmongering** *n.* & *adj.*

warn /wɔːn/ *v.tr.* (also *absol.*) **a** (often foll. by *of*, or *that* + clause, or *to* + infin.) inform of danger, unknown circumstances, etc. (*warned them of the danger; warned her that she was being watched; warned him to expect a visit*). **b** (often foll. by *against*) inform (a person etc.) about a specific danger, hostile person, etc. (*warned her against trusting him*). **2** (usu. with *neg.*) admonish; tell forcefully (*has been warned not to go*). **3** give (a person) cautionary notice regarding conduct etc. (*shall not warn you again*). □**warn off 1** tell (a person) to keep away (from). **2** prohibit from attending races, esp. at a specified course. □□ **warner** *n.* [OE *war(e)nian, wearnian* ult. f. Gmc: cf. WARE[3]]

warning /'wɔːnɪŋ/ *n.* **1** in senses of WARN *v.* **2** anything that serves to warn; a hint or indication of difficulty, danger, etc. **3** *archaic* = NOTICE *n.* 3b. □**warning coloration** *Biol.* conspicuous colouring that warns a predator etc. against attacking. □□ **warningly** *adv.* [OE *war(e)nung* etc. (as WARN, -ING[1])]

warp /wɔːp/ *v.* & *n.* —*v.* **1** *tr.* & *intr.* **a** make or become bent or twisted out of shape, esp. by the action of heat, damp, etc. **b** make or become perverted, bitter, or strange (*a warped sense of humour*). **2 a** *tr.* haul (a ship) by a rope attached to a fixed point. **b** *intr.* progress in this way. **3** *tr.* fertilize by flooding with warp. **4** *tr.* (foll. by *up*) choke (a channel) with an alluvial deposit etc. **5** *tr.* arrange (threads) as a warp. —*n.* **1 a** a state of being warped, esp. of shrunken or expanded timber. **b** perversion, bitterness, etc. of the mind or character. **2** the threads stretched lengthwise in a loom to be crossed by the weft. **3** a rope used in towing or warping, or attached to a trawl-net. **4** sediment etc. left esp. on poor land by standing water. □□ **warpage** *n.* (esp. in sense 1a of *v.*). **warper** *n.* (in sense 5 of *v.*). [OE *weorpan* throw, *wearp* f. Gmc]

warpaint /'wɔːpeɪnt/ *n.* **1** paint used to adorn the body before battle, esp. by N. American Indians. **2** *colloq.* elaborate make-up.

warpath /'wɔːpɑːθ/ *n.* **1** a warlike expedition of N. American Indians. **2** *colloq.* any hostile course or attitude (*is on the warpath again*).

warragal var. of WARRIGAL.

warrant /'wɒrənt/ *n.* & *v.* —*n.* **1 a** anything that authorizes a person or an action (*have no warrant for this*). **b** a person so authorizing (*I will be your warrant*). **2 a** a written authorization, money voucher, travel document, etc. (*a dividend warrant*). **b** a written authorization allowing police to search premises, arrest a suspect, etc. **3** a document authorizing counsel to represent the principal in a lawsuit (*warrant of attorney*). **4** a certificate of service rank held by a warrant-officer. —*v.tr.* **1** serve as a warrant for; justify (*nothing can warrant his behaviour*). **2** guarantee or attest to esp. the genuineness of an article, the worth of a person, etc. □ **I** (or **I'll**) **warrant** I am certain; no doubt (*he'll be sorry, I'll warrant*). **warrant-officer** an officer ranking between commissioned officers and NCOs. □□ **warranter** *n.* **warrantor** *n.* [ME f. ONF *warant*, var. of OF *guarant*, -*and* f. Frank. *werēnd* (unrecorded) f. *giwerēn* be surety for]

warrantable /'wɒrəntəb(ə)l/ *adj.* **1** able to be warranted. **2** (of a stag) old enough to be hunted (5 or 6 years). □□ **warrantableness** *n.* **warrantably** *adv.*

warrantee /ˌwɒrən'tiː/ *n.* a person to whom a warranty is given.

warranty /'wɒrəntɪ/ *n.* (*pl.* -**ies**) **1** an undertaking as to the ownership or quality of a thing sold, hired, etc., often accepting responsibility for defects or liability for repairs needed over a specified period. **2** (usu. foll. by *for* + verbal noun) an authority or justification. **3** an undertaking by an insured person of the truth of a statement or fulfilment of a condition. [ME f. AF *warantie*, var. of *garantie* (as WARRANT)]

warren /'wɒrən/ *n.* **1 a** a network of interconnecting rabbit burrows. **b** a piece of ground occupied by this. **2** a densely populated or labyrinthine building or district. **3** *hist.* a piece of ground on which game is preserved. [ME f. AF & ONF *warenne*, OF *garenne* game-park f. Gmc]

warrigal /'wɒrɪg(ə)l/ *n.* & *adj.* (also **warragal**) *Austral.* —*n.* **1** a dingo dog. **2** an untamed horse. **3** a wild Aboriginal. —*adj.* wild, untamed. [Aboriginal]

warring /'wɔːrɪŋ/ *adj.* rival, antagonistic.

warrior /'wɒrɪə(r)/ *n.* **1** a person experienced or distinguished in fighting. **2** a fighting man, esp. of primitive peoples. **3** (*attrib.*) martial (*a warrior nation*). [ME f. ONF *werreior* etc., OF *guerreior* etc. f. *werreier, guerreier* make WAR]

warship /'wɔːʃɪp/ *n.* an armoured ship used in war.

wart /wɔːt/ *n.* **1** a small hardish roundish growth on the skin caused by a virus-induced abnormal growth of papillae and thickening of the epidermis. **2 a** protuberance on the skin of an animal, surface of a plant, etc. **3** *colloq.* an objectionable person. □ **wart-hog** an African wild pig of the genus *Phacochoerus*, with a large head and warty lumps on its

face, and large curved tusks. **warts and all** *colloq.* with no attempt to conceal blemishes or inadequacies. □□ **warty** *adj.* [OE *wearte* f. Gmc]

wartime /'wɔːtaɪm/ *n.* the period during which a war is waged.

wary /'weərɪ/ *adj.* (**warier**, **wariest**) **1** on one's guard; given to caution; circumspect. **2** (foll. by *of*) cautious, suspicious (*am wary of using lifts*). **3** showing or done with caution or suspicion (*a wary expression*). □□ **warily** *adv.* **wariness** *n.* [WARE² + -Y¹]

was *1st* & *3rd sing. past* of BE.

Wash. *abbr.* Washington.

wash /wɒʃ/ *v.* & *n.* —*v.* **1** *tr.* cleanse (oneself or a part of oneself, clothes, etc.) with liquid, esp. water. **2** *tr.* (foll. by *out, off, away*, etc.) remove a stain or dirt in this way. **3** *intr.* wash oneself or esp. one's hands and face. **4** *intr.* wash clothes etc. **5** *intr.* (of fabric or dye) bear washing without damage. **6** *intr.* (foll. by *off, out*) (of a stain etc.) be removed by washing. **7** *tr. poet.* moisten, water (*tear-washed eyes*; *a rose washed with dew*). **8** *tr.* (of a river, sea, etc.) touch (a country, coast, etc.) with its waters. **9** *tr.* (of moving liquid) carry along in a specified direction (*a wave washed him overboard*; *was washed up on the shore*). **10** *tr.* a scoop out (*the water had washed a channel*). **b** erode, denude (*sea-washed cliffs*). **11** *intr.* (foll. by *over, along*, etc.) sweep, move, or splash. **12** *tr.* sift (ore) by the action of water. **13** *tr.* a brush a thin coat of watery paint or ink over (paper in water-colour painting etc., or a wall). **b** (foll. by *with*) coat (inferior metal) with gold etc. —*n.* **1 a** the act or an instance of washing; the process of being washed (*give them a good wash*; *only needed one wash*). **b** (prec. by *the*) treatment at a laundry etc. (*sent them to the wash*). **2 a** a quantity of clothes for washing or just washed. **3** the visible or audible motion of agitated water or air, esp. due to the passage of a ship etc. or aircraft. **4 a** soil swept off by water; alluvium. **b** a sandbank exposed only at low tide. **5** kitchen slops and scraps given to pigs. **6 a** thin, weak, or inferior liquid food. **b** liquid food for animals. **7** a liquid to spread over a surface to cleanse, heal, or colour. **8** a thin coating of water-colour, wall-colouring, or metal. **9** malt etc. fermenting before distillation. **10** a lotion or cosmetic. □ **come out in the wash** *colloq.* be clarified, or (of contingent difficulties) be resolved or removed, in the course of time. **wash-and-wear** *adj.* (of a fabric or garment) easily and quickly laundered. **wash-basin** a basin for washing one's hands, face, etc. **wash one's dirty linen in public** see LINEN. **wash down 1** wash completely (esp. a large surface or object). **2** (usu. foll. by *with*) accompany or follow (food) with a drink. **washed out 1** faded by washing. **2** pale. **3** *colloq.* limp, enfeebled. **washed up** esp. *US sl.* defeated, having failed. **wash one's hands** *euphem.* go to the lavatory. **wash one's hands of** renounce responsibility for. **wash-hand stand** = WASHSTAND. **wash-house** a building where clothes are washed. **wash-leather** chamois or similar leather for washing windows etc. **wash out 1** clean the inside of (a thing) by washing. **2** clean (a garment etc.) by brief washing. **3 a** rain off (an event etc.). **b** *colloq.* cancel. **4** (of a flood, downpour, etc.) make a breach in (a road etc.). **wash-out** *n.* **1** *colloq.* a fiasco; a complete failure. **2** a breach in a road, railway track, etc., caused by flooding (see also WASHOUT). **wash up 1** *tr.* (also *absol.*) esp. *Brit.* wash (crockery and cutlery) after use. **2** *US* wash one's face and hands. **won't wash** esp. *Brit. colloq.* (of an argument etc.) will not be believed or accepted. [OE *wæscan* etc. f. Gmc, rel. to WATER]

washable /'wɒʃəb(ə)l/ *adj.* that can be washed, esp. without damage. □□ **washability** /-'bɪlɪtɪ/ *n.*

washboard /'wɒʃbɔːd/ *n.* **1** a board of ribbed wood or a sheet of corrugated zinc on which clothes are scrubbed in washing. **2** this used as a percussion instrument, played with the fingers.

washday /ˈwɒʃdeɪ/ *n.* a day on which clothes etc. are washed.

washer /ˈwɒʃə(r)/ *n.* **1 a** a person or thing that washes. **b** a washing-machine. **2** a flat ring of rubber, metal, leather, etc., inserted at a joint to tighten it and prevent leakage. **3** a similar ring placed under the head of a screw, bolt, etc., or under a nut, to disperse its pressure. **4** *Austral.* a cloth for washing the face. □**washer-up** (*pl.* **washers-up**) a person who washes up dishes etc.

washerwoman /ˈwɒʃəˌwʊmən/ *n.* (*pl.* **-women**) a woman whose occupation is washing clothes; a laundress.

washeteria /ˌwɒʃəˈtɪərɪə/ *n.* = LAUNDERETTE.

washing /ˈwɒʃɪŋ/ *n.* a quantity of clothes for washing or just washed. □**washing-machine** a machine for washing clothes and linen etc. **washing-powder** powder of soap or detergent for washing clothes. **washing-soda** sodium carbonate, used dissolved in water for washing and cleaning. **washing-up** *Brit.* **1** the process of washing dishes etc. after use. **2** used dishes etc. for washing.

washland /ˈwɒʃlænd/ *n.* land periodically flooded by a stream.

washout /ˈwɒʃaʊt/ *n.* *Geol.* a narrow river-channel that cuts into pre-existing sediments (see also *wash-out*).

washroom /ˈwɒʃruːm, -rʊm/ *n.* *US* a room with washing and toilet facilities.

washstand /ˈwɒʃstænd/ *n.* a piece of furniture to hold a basin, jug, soap, etc.

washtub /ˈwɒʃtʌb/ *n.* a tub or vessel for washing clothes etc.

washy /ˈwɒʃɪ/ *adj.* (**washier**, **washiest**) **1** (of liquid food) too watery or weak; insipid. **2** (of colour) faded-looking, thin, faint. **3** (of a style, sentiment, etc.) lacking vigour or intensity. □□ **washily** *adv.* **washiness** *n.*

wasn't /ˈwɒz(ə)nt/ *contr.* was not.

Wasp /wɒsp/ *n.* (also **WASP**) *US* usu. *derog.* a middle-class American White Protestant descended from early European settlers. □□ **Waspy** *adj.* (also **WASPy**). [*White Anglo-Saxon Protestant*]

wasp /wɒsp/ *n.* **1** a stinging often flesh-eating insect of the order Hymenoptera, esp. the common social wasp *Vespa vulgaris*, with black and yellow stripes and a very thin waist. **2** (in *comb.*) any of various insects resembling a wasp in some way (*wasp-beetle*). □**wasp-waist** a very slender waist. **wasp-waisted** having a very slender waist. □□ **wasplike** *adj.* [OE *wæfs*, *wæps*, *wæsp*, f. WG: perh. rel. to WEAVE[1] (from the weblike form of its nest)]

waspish /ˈwɒspɪʃ/ *adj.* irritable, petulant; sharp in retort. □□ **waspishly** *adv.* **waspishness** *n.*

wassail /ˈwɒseɪl, ˈwɒs(ə)l/ *n. & v. archaic* —*n.* **1** a festive occasion; a drinking-bout. **2** a kind of liquor drunk on such an occasion. —*v.intr.* make merry; celebrate with drinking etc. □**wassail-bowl** (or **-cup**) a bowl or cup from which healths were drunk, esp. on Christmas Eve and Twelfth Night. □□ **wassailer** *n.* [ME *wæs hæil* etc. f. ON *ves heill*, corresp. to OE *wes hāl* 'be in health', a form of salutation: cf. HALE[1]]

Wassermann test /ˈvɑːsəmən/ *n.* a test for syphilis using the reaction of the patient's blood serum. [A. von *Wassermann*, Ger. pathologist d. 1925]

wast /wɒst, wəst/ *archaic* or *dial. 2nd sing. past of* BE.

wastage /ˈweɪstɪdʒ/ *n.* **1** an amount wasted. **2** loss by use, wear, or leakage. **3** *Commerce* loss of employees other than by redundancy.

waste /weɪst/ *v., adj., & n.* —*v.* **1** *tr.* use to no purpose or for inadequate result or extravagantly (*waste time*). **2** *tr.* fail to use (esp. an opportunity). **3** *tr.* (often foll. by *on*) give (advice etc.), utter (words etc.), without effect. **4** *tr. & intr.* wear gradually away; make or become weak; wither. **5** *tr.* ravage, devastate. **6** *tr.* treat as wasted or valueless. **7** *intr.* be expended without useful effect. —*adj.* **1** superfluous; no longer serving a purpose. **2** (of a district etc.) not inhabited or cultivated; desolate (*waste ground*). **3** presenting no features of interest. —*n.* **1** the act or an instance of wasting; extravagant or ineffectual use of an asset, of time, etc. **2** waste material or food; refuse; useless remains or by-products. **3** a waste region; a desert etc. **4** the state of being used up; diminution by wear and tear. **5** *Law* damage to an estate caused by an act or by neglect, esp. by a life-tenant. **6** = *waste pipe*. □**go** (or **run**) **to waste** be wasted. **lay waste** ravage, devastate. **waste-basket** esp. *US* = *waste-paper basket*. **waste one's breath** see BREATH. **waste not, want not** extravagance leads to poverty. **waste paper** spoiled or valueless paper. **waste-paper basket** esp. *Brit.* a receptacle for waste paper. **waste pipe** a pipe to carry off waste material, e.g. from a sink. **waste products** useless by-products of manufacture or of an organism or organisms. **waste words** see WORD. □□ **wastable** *adj.* **wasteless** *adj.* [ME f. ONF *wast(e)*, var. of OF *g(u)ast(e)*, f. L *vastus*]

wasteful /ˈweɪstfʊl/ *adj.* **1** extravagant. **2** causing or showing waste. □□ **wastefully** *adv.* **wastefulness** *n.*

wasteland /ˈweɪstlænd/ *n.* **1** an unproductive or useless area of land. **2** a place or time considered spiritually or intellectually barren.

waster /ˈweɪstə(r)/ *n.* **1** a wasteful person. **2** *colloq.* a wastrel.

wastrel /ˈweɪstr(ə)l/ *n.* **1** a wasteful or good-for-nothing person. **2** a waif; a neglected child.

watch /wɒtʃ/ *v. & n.* —*v.* **1** *tr.* keep the eyes fixed on; look at attentively. **2** *tr.* **a** keep under observation; follow observantly. **b** monitor or consider carefully; pay attention to (*have to watch my weight*; *watched their progress with interest*). **3** *intr.* (often foll. by *for*) be in an alert state; be vigilant; take heed (*watch for the holes in the road*; *watch for an opportunity*). **4** *intr.* (foll. by *over*) look after; take care of. **5** *intr. archaic* remain awake for devotions etc. —*n.* **1** a small portable timepiece for carrying on one's person. **2** a state of alert or constant observation or attention. **3** *Naut.* **a** a four-hour spell of duty. **b** (in full **starboard** or **port watch**) each of the halves, divided according to the position of the bunks, into which a ship's crew is divided to take alternate watches. **4** *hist.* a watchman or group of watchmen, esp. patrolling the streets at night. **5** a former division of the night. **6** a period of wakefulness at night. **7** *hist.* irregular Highland troops in the 18th c. □**on the watch** waiting for an expected or feared occurrence. **set the watch** *Naut.* station sentinels etc. **watch-case** the outer metal case enclosing the works of a watch. **watch-chain** a metal chain for securing a pocket-watch. **Watch Committee** *hist.* (in the UK) the committee of a county borough council dealing with policing etc. **watch-glass 1** a glass disc covering the dial of a watch. **2** a similar disc used in a laboratory etc. to hold material for use in experiments. **watching brief** see BRIEF. **watch it** (or **oneself**) *colloq.* be careful. **watch-night 1** the last night of the year. **2** a religious service held on this night. **watch out 1** (often foll. by *for*) be on one's guard. **2** as a warning of immediate danger. **watch-spring** the mainspring of a watch. **watch one's step** proceed cautiously. **watch-strap** esp. *Brit.* a strap for fastening a watch on the wrist. **watch-tower** a tower from which observation can be kept. □□ **watchable** *adj.* **watcher** *n.* (also in *comb.*). [OE *wæcce* (n.), rel. to WAKE[1]]

watchband /ˈwɒtʃbænd/ *n. US* = *watch-strap*.

watchdog /ˈwɒtʃdɒg/ *n. & v.* —*n.* **1** a dog kept to guard property etc. **2** a person or body monitoring others' rights, behaviour, etc. —*v.tr.* (**-dogged**, **-dogging**) maintain surveillance over.

watchful /ˈwɒtʃfʊl/ *adj.* **1** accustomed to watching. **2** on the watch. **3** showing vigilance. **4** *archaic* wakeful. □□ **watchfully** *adv.* **watchfulness** *n.*

watchmaker /ˈwɒtʃˌmeɪkə(r)/ *n.* a person who makes and repairs watches and clocks. □□ **watchmaking** *n.*

watchman /ˈwɒtʃmən/ *n.* (*pl.* **-men**) **1** a man employed to look after an empty building etc. at night. **2** *archaic* or *hist.* a member of a night-watch.

watchword /ˈwɒtʃwɜːd/ *n.* **1** a phrase summarizing a guiding principle; a slogan. **2** *hist.* a military password.

water /ˈwɔːtə(r)/ *n. & v.* —*n.* **1** a colourless transparent odourless tasteless liquid compound of oxygen and hydrogen. ¶ Chem. formula: H_2O. **2** a liquid consisting chiefly of this and found in seas, lakes, and rivers, in rain, and in secretions of organisms. **3** an expanse of water; a sea, lake, river, etc. **4** (in *pl.*) part of a sea or river (*in Icelandic waters*). **5** (often as **the waters**) mineral water at a spa etc. **6** the state of a tide (*high water*). **7** a solution of a specified substance in water (*lavender-water*). **8** the quality of the transparency and brilliance of a gem, esp. a diamond. **9** *Finance* an amount of nominal capital added by watering (see sense 10 of *v.*). **10** (*attrib.*) **a** found in or near water. **b** of, for, or worked by water. **c** involving, using, or yielding water. —*v.* **1** *tr.* sprinkle or soak with water. **2** *tr.* supply (a plant) with water. **3** *tr.* give water to (an animal) to drink. **4** *intr.* (of the mouth or eyes) secrete water as saliva or tears. **5** *tr.* (as **watered** *adj.*) (of silk etc.) having irregular wavy glossy markings. **6** *tr.* adulterate (milk, beer, etc.) with water. **7** *tr.* (of a river etc.) supply (a place) with water. **8** *intr.* (of an animal) go to a pool etc. to drink. **9** *intr.* (of a ship, engine, etc., or the person in charge of it) take in a supply of water. **10** *tr.* *Finance* increase (a company's debt, or nominal capital) by the issue of new shares without a corresponding addition to assets. □ **by water** using a ship etc. for travel or transport. **cast one's bread upon the waters** see BREAD. **like water** lavishly, profusely. **like water off a duck's back** see DUCK¹. **make one's mouth water** cause one's saliva to flow, stimulate one's appetite or anticipation. **of the first water 1** (of a diamond) of the greatest brilliance and transparency. **2** of the finest quality or extreme degree. **on the water** on a ship etc. **on the water-wagon** see WAGON. **water-bag** a bag of leather, canvas, etc., for holding water. **water bailiff 1** an official enforcing fishing laws. **2** *hist.* a custom-house officer at a port. **water bear** = TARDIGRADE *n.* **water-bed** a mattress of rubber or plastic etc. filled with water. **water-biscuit** a thin crisp unsweetened biscuit made from flour and water. **water blister** a blister containing a colourless fluid, not blood or pus. **water-boatman** any aquatic bug of the family Notonectidae or Corixidae, swimming with oarlike hind legs. **water-borne 1** (of goods etc.) conveyed by or travelling on water. **2** (of a disease) communicated or propagated by contaminated water. **water-buck** any of various African antelopes of the genus *Kobus*, frequenting river-banks. **water-buffalo** the common domestic Indian buffalo, *Bubalus arnee*. **water bus** a boat carrying passengers on a regular run on a river, lake, etc. **water-butt** a barrel used to catch rainwater. **water-cannon** a device giving a powerful jet of water to disperse a crowd etc. **the Water-carrier** (or **-bearer**) the zodiacal sign or constellation Aquarius. **water chestnut 1** an aquatic plant, *Trapa natans*, bearing an edible seed. **2 a** (in full **Chinese water chestnut**) a sedge, *Eleocharis tuberosa*, with rushlike leaves arising from a corm. **b** this corm used as food. **water-clock** a clock measuring time by the flow of water. **water-closet 1** a lavatory with the means for flushing the pan with water. **2** a room containing this. **water-colour** (*US* **-color**) **1** artists' paint made of pigment to be diluted with water and not oil. **2 a**

picture painted with this. **3** the art of painting with water-colours. **water-colourist** (*US* **-colorist**) a painter in water-colours. **water-cooled** cooled by the circulation of water. **water-cooler** a tank of cooled drinking-water. **water cure** = HYDROPATHY. **water-diviner** *Brit.* a person who dowses (see DOWSE¹) for water. **water down 1** dilute with water. **2** make less vivid, forceful, or horrifying. **water gauge 1** a glass tube etc. indicating the height of water in a reservoir, boiler, etc. **2** pressure expressed in terms of a head of water. **water-glass 1** a solution of sodium or potassium silicate used for preserving eggs, as a vehicle for fresco-painting, and for hardening artificial stone. **2** a tube with a glass bottom enabling objects under water to be observed. **water-hammer** a knocking noise in a water-pipe when a tap is suddenly turned off. **water-heater** a device for heating (esp. domestic) water. **water hemlock** a poisonous plant, *Cicuta maculata*, found in marshes etc.: also called COWBANE. **water-hole** a shallow depression in which water collects (esp. in the bed of a river otherwise dry). **water hyacinth** a tropical river-weed, *Eichhornia crassipes*. **water-ice** a confection of flavoured and frozen water and sugar etc.; a sorbet. **water jump** a place where a horse in a steeplechase etc. must jump over water. **water-level 1 a** the surface of the water in a reservoir etc. **b** the height of this. **2** a level below which the ground is saturated with water. **3** a level using water to determine the horizontal. **water lily** any aquatic plant of the family Nymphaeaceae, with broad flat floating leaves and large usu. cup-shaped floating flowers. **water-line 1** the line along which the surface of water touches a ship's side (marked on a ship for use in loading). **2** a linear watermark. **water main** the main pipe in a water-supply system. **water-meadow** a meadow periodically flooded by a stream. **water melon** a large smooth green melon, *Citrullus lanatus*, with red pulp and watery juice. **water meter** a device for measuring and recording the amount of water supplied to a house etc. **water-mill** a mill worked by a water-wheel. **water-nymph** a nymph regarded as inhabiting or presiding over water. **water of crystallization** water forming an essential part of the structure of some crystals. **water of life** *rhet.* spiritual enlightenment. **water ouzel** = DIPPER 1. **water-pepper** an aquatic herb, *Polygonum hydropiper*: also called SMARTWEED. **water-pipe 1** a pipe for conveying water. **2** a hookah. **water-pistol** a toy pistol shooting a jet of water. **water plantain** any ditch-plant of the genus *Alisma*, with plantain-like leaves. **water polo** a game played by swimmers, with a ball like a football. **water-power 1** mechanical force derived from the weight or motion of water. **2** a fall in the level of a river, as a source of this force. **water purslane** a creeping plant, *Lythrum portula*, growing in damp places. **water rail** a wading bird, *Rallus aquaticus*, frequenting marshes etc. **water-rat** = *water-vole*. **water-rate** a charge made for the use of the public water-supply. **water-repellent** not easily penetrated by water. **water-scorpion** any aquatic bug of the family Nepidae, living submerged and breathing through a bristle-like tubular tail. **water-softener** an apparatus or substance for softening hard water. **water-soluble** soluble in water. **water-splash** part of a road submerged by a stream or pool. **water starwort** any plant of the genus *Callitriche*, growing in water. **water-supply** the provision and storage of water, or the amount of water stored, for the use of a town, house, etc. **water-table** = *water-level* 2. **water torture** a form of torture in which the victim is exposed to the incessant dripping of water on the head, or the sound of dripping. **water-tower** a tower with an elevated tank to give pressure for distributing water. **water under the bridge** past events accepted as past and irrevocable. **water-vole** an aquatic vole, esp.

Arvicola amphibius. **water-weed** any of various aquatic plants. **water-wheel** a wheel driven by water to work machinery, or to raise water. **water-wings** inflated floats fixed on the arms of a person learning to swim. □□ **waterer** *n.* **waterless** *adj.* [OE *wæter* f. Gmc, rel. to WET]

waterbrash /'wɔːtəˌbræʃ/ *n.* pyrosis. [WATER + BRASH³]

watercourse /'wɔːtəˌkɔːs/ *n.* **1** a brook, stream, or artificial water-channel. **2** the bed along which this flows.

watercress /'wɔːtəˌkres/ *n.* a hardy perennial cress, *Nasturtium officinale*, growing in running water, with pungent leaves used in salad.

waterfall /'wɔːtəˌfɔːl/ *n.* a stream or river flowing over a precipice or down a steep hillside.

Waterford glass /'wɔːtəfəd/ *n.* a clear colourless flint glass. [*Waterford* in Ireland]

waterfowl /'wɔːtəˌfaʊl/ *n.* (usu. collect. as *pl.*) birds frequenting water, esp. swimming game-birds.

waterfront /'wɔːtəˌfrʌnt/ *n.* the part of a town adjoining a river, lake, harbour, etc.

watergate /'wɔːtəˌɡeɪt/ *n.* **1** a floodgate. **2** a gate giving access to a river etc.

watering /'wɔːtərɪŋ/ *n.* the act or an instance of supplying water or (of an animal) obtaining water. □ **watering-can** a portable container with a long spout usu. ending in a perforated sprinkler, for watering plants. **watering-hole 1** a pool of water from which animals regularly drink; = *water-hole.* **2** *sl.* a bar. **watering-place 1** = *watering-hole.* **2** a spa or seaside resort. **3** a place where water is obtained. [OE *wæterung* (as WATER, -ING¹)]

waterlogged /'wɔːtəˌlɒɡd/ *adj.* **1** saturated with water. **2** (of a boat etc.) hardly able to float from being saturated or filled with water. **3** (of ground) made useless by being saturated with water. [*waterlog* (v.), f. WATER + LOG¹, prob. orig. = 'reduce (a ship) to the condition of a log']

Waterloo /ˌwɔːtəˈluː/ *n.* a decisive defeat or contest (*meet one's Waterloo*). [*Waterloo* in Belgium, where Napoleon was finally defeated in 1815]

waterman /'wɔːtəmən/ *n.* (*pl.* **-men**) **1** a boatman plying for hire. **2** an oarsman as regards skill in keeping the boat balanced.

watermark /'wɔːtəˌmɑːk/ *n.* & *v.* —*n.* a faint design made in some paper during manufacture, visible when held against the light, identifying the maker etc. —*v.tr.* mark with this.

waterproof /'wɔːtəˌpruːf/ *adj., n.,* & *v.* —*adj.* impervious to water. —*n.* a waterproof garment or material. —*v.tr.* make waterproof.

watershed /'wɔːtəˌʃed/ *n.* **1** a line of separation between waters flowing to different rivers, basins, or seas. **2** a turning-point in affairs. [WATER + *shed* ridge of high ground (rel. to SHED²), after G *Wasserscheide*]

waterside /'wɔːtəˌsaɪd/ *n.* the margin of a sea, lake, or river.

water-ski /'wɔːtəˌskiː/ *n.* & *v.* —*n.* (*pl.* **-skis**) each of a pair of skis for skimming the surface of the water when towed by a motor boat. —*v.intr.* (**-skis, -ski'd** or **-skied** /-skiːd/; **-skiing**) travel on water-skis. □□ **water-skier** *n.*

waterspout /'wɔːtəˌspaʊt/ *n.* a gyrating column of water and spray formed by a whirlwind between sea and cloud.

watertight /'wɔːtəˌtaɪt/ *adj.* **1** (of a joint, container, vessel, etc.) closely fastened or fitted or made so as to prevent the passage of water. **2** (of an argument etc.) unassailable.

waterway /'wɔːtəˌweɪ/ *n.* **1** a navigable channel. **2** a route for travel by water. **3** a thick plank at the outer edge of a deck along which a channel is hollowed for water to run off by.

waterworks /'wɔːtəˌwɜːks/ *n.* **1** an establishment for managing a water-supply. **2** *colloq.* the shedding of tears. **3** *Brit. colloq.* the urinary system.

watery /'wɔːtərɪ/ *adj.* **1** containing too much water. **2** too thin in consistency. **3** of or consisting of water. **4** (of the eyes) suffused or running with water. **5** (of conversation, style, etc.) vapid, uninteresting. **6** (of colour) pale. **7** (of the sun, moon, or sky) rainy-looking. □ **watery grave** the bottom of the sea as a place where a person lies drowned. □□ **wateriness** *n.* [OE *wæterig* (as WATER, -Y¹)]

watt /wɒt/ *n.* the SI unit of power, equivalent to one joule per second, corresponding to the rate of energy in an electric circuit where the potential difference is one volt and the current one ampere. ¶ Symb.: **W**. □ **watt-hour** the energy used when one watt is applied for one hour. [J. *Watt,* Sc. engineer d. 1819]

wattage /'wɒtɪdʒ/ *n.* an amount of electrical power expressed in watts.

wattle¹ /'wɒt(ə)l/ *n.* & *v.* —*n.* **1 a** interlaced rods and split rods as a material for making fences, walls, etc. **b** (in *sing.* or *pl.*) rods and twigs for this use. **2** an Australian acacia with long pliant branches, with bark used in tanning and golden flowers used as the national emblem. **3** *dial.* a wicker hurdle. —*v.tr.* **1** make of wattle. **2** enclose or fill up with wattles. □ **wattle and daub** a network of rods and twigs plastered with mud or clay as a building material. [OE *watul,* of unkn. orig.]

wattle² /'wɒt(ə)l/ *n.* **1** a loose fleshy appendage on the head or throat of a turkey or other birds. **2** = BARB *n.* 3. □□ **wattled** *adj.* [16th c.: orig. unkn.]

wattmeter /'wɒtˌmiːtə(r)/ *n.* a meter for measuring the amount of electricity in watts.

waul /wɔːl/ *v.intr.* (also **wawl**) give a loud plaintive cry like a cat. [imit.]

wave /weɪv/ *v.* & *n.* —*v.* **1 a** *intr.* (often foll. by *to*) move a hand etc. to and fro in greeting or as a signal (*waved to me across the street*). **b** *tr.* move (a hand etc.) in this way. **2 a** *intr.* show a sinuous or sweeping motion as of a flag, tree, or a cornfield in the wind; flutter, undulate. **b** *tr.* impart a waving motion to. **3** *tr.* brandish (a sword etc.) as an encouragement to followers etc. **4** *tr.* tell or direct (a person) by waving (*waved them away; waved them to follow*). **5** *tr.* express (a greeting etc.) by waving (*waved goodbye to them*). **6** *tr.* give an undulating form to (hair, drawn lines, etc.); make wavy. **7** *intr.* (of hair etc.) have such a form; be wavy. —*n.* **1** a ridge of water between two depressions. **2** a long body of water curling into an arched form and breaking on the shore. **3** a thing compared to this, e.g. a body of persons in one of successive advancing groups. **4** a gesture of waving. **5 a** the process of waving the hair. **b** an undulating form produced in the hair by waving. **6 a** a temporary occurrence or increase of a condition, emotion, or influence (*a wave of enthusiasm*). **b** a specified period of widespread weather (*heat wave*). **7** *Physics* **a** the disturbance of the particles of a fluid medium to form ridges and troughs for the propagation or direction of motion, heat, light, sound, etc., without the advance of the particles. **b** a single curve in the course of this motion (see also *standing wave, travelling wave* (see TRAVEL)). **8** *Electr.* a similar variation of an electromagnetic field in the propagation of radiation through a medium or vacuum. **9** (in *pl.*; prec. by *the*) *poet.* the sea; water. □ **make waves** *colloq.* cause trouble. **wave aside** dismiss as intrusive or irrelevant. **wave down** wave to (a vehicle or its driver) as a signal to stop. **wave equation** a differential equation expressing the properties of motion in waves. **wave-form** *Physics* a curve showing the shape of a wave at a given time. **wave-front** *Physics* a surface containing points affected in the same way by a wave at a given time. **wave function** a function satisfying a wave equation and describing the properties of a wave. **wave mechanics** a method of analysis of the behaviour esp. of atomic phenomena with particles represented by wave equations (see *quantum mechanics*). **wave number** *Physics* the number of waves in a unit distance. **wave theory** *hist.* the theory that light is propagated through the ether by a wave-motion imparted to the ether by the molecular vibrations of the radiant body. □□ **waveless** *adj.* **wavelike** *adj. & adv.* [OE *wafian* (v.) f. Gmc: (n.) also alt. of ME *wawe, wage*]

waveband /ˈweɪvbænd/ *n.* a range of (esp. radio) wavelengths between certain limits.

waveguide /ˈweɪvɡaɪd/ *n. Electr.* a metal tube etc. confining and conveying microwaves.

wavelength /ˈweɪvleŋθ, -leŋkθ/ *n.* **1** the distance between successive crests of a wave, esp. points in a sound wave or electromagnetic wave. ¶ Symb.: λ. **2** this as a distinctive feature of radio waves from a transmitter. **3** *colloq.* a particular mode or range of thinking and communicating (*we don't seem to be on the same wavelength*).

wavelet /ˈweɪvlɪt/ *n.* a small wave on water.

waver /ˈweɪvə(r)/ *v.intr.* **1** be or become unsteady; falter; begin to give way. **2** be irresolute or undecided between different courses or opinions; be shaken in resolution or belief. **3** (of a light) flicker. □□ **waverer** *n.* **waveringly** *adv.* [ME f. ON *vafra* flicker f. Gmc, rel. to WAVE]

wavy /ˈweɪvɪ/ *adj.* (**wavier, waviest**) (of a line or surface) having waves or alternate contrary curves (*wavy hair*). □□ **wavily** *adv.* **waviness** *n.*

wa-wa var. of WAH-WAH.

wawl var. of WAUL.

wax[1] /wæks/ *n. & v.* —*n.* **1** a sticky plastic yellowish substance secreted by bees as the material of honeycomb cells; beeswax. **2** a white translucent material obtained from this by bleaching and purifying and used for candles, in modelling, as a basis of polishes, and for other purposes. **3** any similar substance, e.g. earwax. **4** *colloq.* **a** a gramophone record. **b** material for the manufacture of this. **5** (*attrib.*) made of wax. —*v.tr.* **1** cover or treat with wax. **2** *colloq.* record for the gramophone. □ **be wax in a person's hands** be entirely subservient to a person. **lost wax** = CIRE PERDUE. **wax-light** a taper or candle of wax. **wax-myrtle** a tree, *Myrtus cerifera*, yielding wax and oil used for candles. **wax-painting** = ENCAUSTIC. **wax palm 1** a South American palm, *Ceroxylon alpinum*, with its stem coated in a mixture of resin and wax. **2** a carnauba. **wax paper** paper waterproofed with a layer of wax. **wax-pod** a yellow-podded bean. **wax-tree** an Asian tree, *Rhus succedanea*, having white berries which yield wax. □□ **waxer** *n.* [OE *wæx, weax* f. Gmc]

wax[2] /wæks/ *v.intr.* **1** (of the moon between new and full) have a progressively larger part of its visible surface illuminated, increasing in apparent size. **2** become larger or stronger. **3** pass into a specified state or mood (*wax lyrical*). □ **wax and wane** undergo alternate increases and decreases. [OE *weaxan* f. Gmc]

wax[3] /wæks/ *n. sl.* a fit of anger. [19th c.: orig. uncert.: perh. f. WAX[2] *wroth* etc.]

waxberry /ˈwæksbərɪ/ *n.* (*pl.* -**ies**) **1** a wax-myrtle. **2** the fruit of this.

waxbill /ˈwæksbɪl/ *n.* any of various birds esp. of the family Estrildidae, with usu. red bills resembling the colour of sealing wax.

waxcloth /ˈwæksklɒθ/ *n.* oilcloth.

waxen /ˈwæks(ə)n/ *adj.* **1** having a smooth pale translucent surface as of wax. **2** able to receive impressions like wax; plastic. **3** *archaic* made of wax.

waxwing /ˈwækswɪŋ/ *n.* any bird of the genus *Bombycilla*, with small tips like red sealing-wax to some wing-feathers.

waxwork /ˈwækswɜːk/ *n.* **1 a** an object, esp. a lifelike dummy, modelled in wax. **b** the making of waxworks. **2** (in *pl.*) an exhibition of wax dummies.

waxy[1] /ˈwæksɪ/ *adj.* (**waxier, waxiest**) resembling wax in consistency or in its surface. □□ **waxily** *adv.* **waxiness** *n.* [WAX[1] + -Y[1]]

waxy[2] /ˈwæksɪ/ *adj.* (**waxier, waxiest**) *Brit. sl.* angry, quick-tempered. [WAX[3] + -Y[1]]

way /weɪ/ *n. & adv.* —*n.* **1** a road, track, path, etc., for passing along. **2** a course or route for reaching a place, esp. the best one (*asked the way to London*). **3** a place of passage into a building, through a door, etc. (*could not find the way out*). **4 a** a method or plan for attaining an object (*that is not the way to do it*). **b** the ability to obtain one's object (*has a way with him*). **5 a** a person's desired or chosen course of action. **b** a custom or manner of behaving; a personal peculiarity (*has a way of forgetting things*; *things had a way of going badly*). **6** a specific manner of life or procedure (*soon got into the way of it*). **7** the normal course of events (*that is always the way*). **8** a travelling distance; a length traversed or to be traversed (*is a long way away*). **9 a** an unimpeded opportunity of advance. **b** a space free of obstacles. **10** a region or ground over which advance is desired or natural. **11** advance in some direction; impetus, progress (*pushed my way through*). **12** movement of a ship etc. (*gather way*; *lose way*). **13** the state of being engaged in movement from place to place; time spent in this (*met them on the way home*; *with songs to cheer the way*). **14** a specified direction (*step this way*; *which way are you going?*). **15** (in *pl.*) parts into which a thing is divided (*split it three ways*). **16** *colloq.* the scope or range of something (*want a few things in the stationery way*). **17** a person's line of occupation or business. **18** a specified condition or state (*things are in a bad way*). **19** a respect (*is useful in some ways*). **20 a** (in *pl.*) a structure of timber etc. down which a new ship is launched. **b** parallel rails etc. as a track for the movement of a machine. —*adv. colloq.* to a considerable extent; far (*you're way off the mark*). □ **across** (or **over**) **the way** opposite. **any way** = ANYWAY. **be on one's way** set off; depart. **by the way 1** incidentally; as a more or less irrelevant comment. **2** during a journey. **by way of 1** through; by means of. **2** as a substitute for or as a form of (*did it by way of apology*). **3** with the intention of (*asked by way of discovering the truth*). **come one's way** become available to one; become one's lot. **find a way** discover a means of obtaining one's object. **get** (or **have**) **one's way** (or **have it one's own way** etc.) get what one wants; ensure one's wishes are met. **give way 1 a** make concessions. **b** fail to resist; yield. **2** (often foll. by *to*) concede precedence (to). **3** (of a structure etc.) be dislodged or broken under a load; collapse. **4** (foll. by *to*) be superseded by. **5** (foll. by *to*) be overcome by (an emotion etc.). **6** (of rowers) row hard. **go out of one's way** (often foll. by *to* + infin.) make a special effort; act gratuitously or without compulsion (*went out of their way to help*). **go one's own way** act independently, esp. against contrary advice. **go one's way 1** leave, depart. **2** (of events, circumstances, etc.) be favourable to one. **go a person's way** accompany a person (*are you going my way?*). **have it both ways** see BOTH. **in its way** if regarded from a particular standpoint appropriate to it. **in no way** not at all; by no means. **in a way** in a certain respect but not altogether or completely. **in the** (or **one's**) **way** forming an obstacle or hindrance. **lead the way 1** act as guide or leader. **2** show how to do something. **look the other way 1** ignore what one should notice. **2** disregard an acquaintance etc. whom one sees. **one way and another** taking various considerations into account. **one way or another** by some means. **on the** (or **one's**) **way 1** in the course of a journey etc. **2** having progressed (*is well on the way to completion*). **3** *colloq.* (of a child) conceived but not yet born. **on the way out** *colloq.* going down in status, estimation, or favour; going out of fashion. **the other way about** (or **round**) in an inverted or reversed position or direction. **out of the way 1** no longer an obstacle or hindrance. **2** disposed of; settled. **3** (of a person) imprisoned or killed. **4** (with *neg.*) common or unremarkable (*nothing out of the way*). **5** (of a place) remote, inaccessible. **out of one's way** not on one's intended route. **put a person in the way of** give a person the opportunity of. **way back** *colloq.* long ago. **way-leave** a right of way rented to another. **the way of the Cross** a series of paintings or representations of the events in Christ's passion, esp. in a church. **way of life** the principles or habits governing all one's actions etc. **way of thinking** one's customary opinion of matters. **way of the world** conduct no worse than is customary. **way-out** *colloq.* **1** unusual, eccentric. **2** avant-garde, progressive. **3** excellent, exciting. **ways and means 1** methods of achieving something. **2** methods of raising government revenue. **way station** *US* **1** a minor station on a railway. **2** a point marking progress in a certain course of action etc. **way-worn** tired with travel. [OE *weg* f. Gmc: (adv.) f. AWAY]

-way /weɪ/ *suffix* = -WAYS.

waybill /'weɪbɪl/ *n.* a list of passengers or parcels on a vehicle.

waybread /'weɪbred/ *n. Brit. archaic* a broad-leaved plantain (see PLANTAIN¹). [OE *wegbrǣde* (as WAY, BROAD)]

wayfarer /'weɪˌfeərə(r)/ *n.* a traveller, esp. on foot.

wayfaring /'weɪˌfeərɪŋ/ *n.* travelling, esp. on foot. □**wayfaring-tree** a white-flowered European and Asian shrub, *Viburnum lantana*, common along roadsides, with berries turning from green through red to black.

waylay /weɪ'leɪ/ *v.tr.* (*past* and *past part.* **waylaid**) **1** lie in wait for. **2** stop to rob or interview. □□ **waylayer** *n.*

waymark /'weɪmɑːk/ *n.* a natural or artificial object as a guide to travellers, esp. walkers.

-ways /weɪz/ *suffix* forming adjectives and adverbs of direction or manner (*sideways*) (cf. -WISE). [WAY + -'s]

wayside /'weɪsaɪd/ *n.* **1** the side or margin of a road. **2** the land at the side of a road. □**fall by the wayside** fail to continue in an endeavour or undertaking (after Luke 8:5).

wayward /'weɪwəd/ *adj.* **1** childishly self-willed or perverse; capricious. **2** unaccountable or freakish. □□ **waywardly** *adv.* **waywardness** *n.* [ME f. obs. *awayward* turned away f. AWAY + -WARD: cf. FROWARD]

wayzgoose /'weɪzguːs/ *n.* (*pl.* **-gooses**) an annual summer dinner or outing held by a printing-house for its employees. [17th c. (earlier *waygoose*): orig. unkn.]

Wb *abbr.* weber(s).

WC *abbr.* **1** water-closet. **2** West Central.

WCC *abbr.* World Council of Churches.

W/Cdr. *abbr.* Wing Commander.

WD *abbr.* **1** War Department. **2** Works Department.

we /wiː, wɪ/ *pron.* (*obj.* **us**; *poss.* **our**, **ours**) **1** (*pl.* of I²) used by and with reference to more than one person speaking or writing, or one such person and one or more associated persons. **2** used for or by a royal person in a proclamation etc. and by a writer or editor in a formal context. **3** people in general (cf. ONE *pron.* 2). **4** *colloq.* = I² (*give us a chance*). **5** *colloq.* (often implying condescension) you (*how are we feeling today?*). [OE f. Gmc]

WEA *abbr.* (in the UK) Workers' Educational Association.

weak /wiːk/ *adj.* **1** deficient in strength, power, or number; fragile; easily broken or bent or defeated. **2** deficient in vigour; sickly, feeble (*weak health*; *a weak imagination*). **3 a** deficient in resolution; easily led (*a weak character*). **b** (of an action or features) indicating a lack of resolution (*a weak surrender*; *a weak chin*). **4** unconvincing or logically deficient (*weak evidence*; *a weak argument*). **5** (of a mixed liquid or solution) watery, thin, dilute (*weak tea*). **6** (of a style etc.) not vigorous or well-knit; diffuse,

slipshod. **7** (of a crew) short-handed. **8** (of a syllable etc.) unstressed. **9** *Gram.* in Germanic languages: **a** (of a verb) forming inflections by the addition of a suffix to the stem. **b** (of a noun or adjective) belonging to a declension in which the stem originally ended in *-n* (opp. STRONG *adj.* 22). □**weak ending** an unstressed syllable in a normally stressed place at the end of a verse-line. **the weaker sex** *derog.* women. **weak grade** *Gram.* an unstressed ablaut-form. **weak interaction** *Physics* the weakest form of interaction between elementary particles. **weak-kneed** *colloq.* lacking resolution. **weak-minded 1** mentally deficient. **2** lacking in resolution. **weak-mindedness** the state of being weak-minded. **weak moment** a time when one is unusually compliant or temptable. **weak point** (or **spot**) **1** a place where defences are assailable. **2** a flaw in an argument or character or in resistance to temptation. □□ **weakish** *adj.* [ME f. ON *veikr* f. Gmc]

weaken /'wiːkən/ *v.tr. & intr.* make or become weak or weaker. □□ **weakener** *n.*

weakfish /'wiːkfɪʃ/ *n.* (*pl.* same or **-fishes**) *US* a marine fish of the genus *Cynoscion*, used as food. [obs. Du. *weekvisch* f. *week* soft (formed as WEAK) + *visch* FISH¹]

weakling /'wiːklɪŋ/ *n.* a feeble person or animal.

weakly /'wiːklɪ/ *adv. & adj.* —*adv.* in a weak manner. —*adj.* (**weaklier, weakliest**) sickly, not robust. □□ **weakliness** *n.*

weakness /'wiːknɪs/ *n.* **1** the state or condition of being weak. **2** a weak point; a defect. **3** the inability to resist a particular temptation. **4** (foll. by *for*) a self-indulgent liking (*have a weakness for chocolate*).

weal¹ /wiːl/ *n. & v.* —*n.* a ridge raised on the flesh by a stroke of a rod or whip. —*v.tr.* mark with a weal. [var. of WALE, infl. by obs. *wheal* suppurate]

weal² /wiːl/ *n. literary* welfare, prosperity; good fortune. [OE *wela* f. WG (as WELL¹)]

Weald /wiːld/ *n.* (also **weald**) (prec. by *the*) *Brit.* a formerly wooded district including parts of Kent, Surrey, and East Sussex. □**weald-clay** beds of clay, sandstone, limestone, and ironstone, forming the top of Wealden strata, with abundant fossil remains. [OE, = *wald* WOLD]

Wealden /'wiːld(ə)n/ *adj. & n. Brit.* —*adj.* **1** of the Weald. **2** resembling the Weald geologically. —*n.* a series of Lower Cretaceous freshwater deposits above Jurassic strata and below chalk, best exemplified in the Weald.

wealth /welθ/ *n.* **1** riches; abundant possessions; opulence. **2** the state of being rich. **3** (foll. by *of*) an abundance or profusion (*a wealth of new material*). **4** *archaic* welfare or prosperity. □**wealth tax** a tax on personal capital. [ME *welthe*, f. WELL¹ or WEAL² + -TH², after *health*]

wealthy /'welθɪ/ *adj.* (**wealthier, wealthiest**) having an abundance esp. of money. □□ **wealthily** *adv.* **wealthiness** *n.*

wean¹ /wiːn/ *v.tr.* **1** accustom (an infant or other young mammal) to food other than (esp. its mother's) milk. **2** (often foll. by *from*, *away from*) disengage (from a habit etc.) by enforced discontinuance. [OE *wenian* accustom f. Gmc: cf. WONT]

wean² /wiːn/ *n. Sc.* a young child. [contr. of *wee ane* little one]

weaner /'wiːnə(r)/ *n.* a young animal recently weaned.

weanling /'wiːnlɪŋ/ *n.* a newly-weaned child etc.

weapon /'wepən/ *n.* **1** a thing designed or used or usable for inflicting bodily harm (e.g. a gun or cosh). **2** a means employed for trying to gain the advantage in a conflict (*irony is a double-edged weapon*). □□ **weaponed** *adj.* (also in *comb.*). **weaponless** *adj.* [OE *wæp(e)n* f. Gmc]

weaponry /'wepənrɪ/ *n.* weapons collectively.

wear¹ /weə(r)/ *v. & n.* —*v.* (*past* **wore** /wɔː(r)/; *past part.* **worn** /wɔːn/) **1** *tr.* have on one's person as clothing or an ornament etc. (*is wearing shorts*;

---

wears earrings). **2** *tr.* be dressed habitually in (*wears green*). **3** *tr.* exhibit or present (a facial expression or appearance) (*wore a frown; the day wore a different aspect*). **4** *tr. Brit. colloq.* (usu. with *neg.*) tolerate, accept (*they won't wear that excuse*). **5** (often foll. by *away*) **a** *tr.* injure the surface of, or partly obliterate or alter, by rubbing, stress, or use. **b** *intr.* undergo such injury or change. **6** *tr. & intr.* (foll. by *off, away*) rub or be rubbed off. **7** *tr.* make (a hole etc.) by constant rubbing or dripping etc. **8** *tr. & intr.* (often foll. by *out*) exhaust, tire or be tired. **9** *tr.* (foll. by *down*) overcome by persistence. **10** *intr.* **a** remain for a specified time in working order or a presentable state; last long. **b** (foll. by *well, badly*, etc.) endure continued use or life. **11 a** *intr.* (of time) pass, esp. tediously. **b** *tr.* pass (time) gradually away. **12** *tr.* (of a ship) fly (a flag). —*n.* **1** the act of wearing or the state of being worn (*suitable for informal wear*). **2** things worn; fashionable or suitable clothing (*sportswear; footwear*). **3** (in full **wear and tear**) damage sustained from continuous use. **4** the capacity for resisting wear and tear (*still a great deal of wear left in it*). □**in wear** being regularly worn. **wear one's heart on one's sleeve** see HEART. **wear off** lose effectiveness or intensity. **wear out 1** use or be used until no longer usable. **2** tire or be tired out. **wear thin** (of patience, excuses, etc.) begin to fail. **wear the trousers** see TROUSERS. **wear** (or **wear one's years**) **well** *colloq.* remain young-looking. □□ **wearable** *adj.* **wearability** /-'brlɪtɪ/ *n.* **wearer** *n.* **wearingly** *adv.* [OE *werian* f. Gmc]

wear² /weə(r)/ *v.* (*past* and *past part.* **wore** /wɔː(r)/) **1** *tr.* bring (a ship) about by turning its head away from the wind. **2** *intr.* (of a ship) come about in this way (cf. TACK¹ *v.* 4). [17th c.: orig. unkn.]

wearisome /'wɪərɪsəm/ *adj.* tedious; tiring by monotony or length. □□ **wearisomely** *adv.* **wearisomeness** *n.*

weary /'wɪərɪ/ *adj. & v.* —*adj.* (**wearier, weariest**) **1** unequal to or disinclined for further exertion or endurance; tired. **2** (foll. by *of*) dismayed at the continuing of; impatient of. **3** tiring or tedious. —*v.* (**-ies, -ied**) **1** *tr. & intr.* make or grow weary. **2** *intr.* esp. *Sc.* long. □□ **weariless** *adj.* **wearily** *adv.* **weariness** *n.* **wearyingly** *adv.* [OE *wērig, wǣrig* f. WG]

weasel /'wiːz(ə)l/ *n. & v.* —*n.* **1** a small reddish-brown flesh-eating mammal, *Mustela nivalis*, with a slender body, related to the stoat and ferret. **2** a stoat. **3** *colloq.* a deceitful or treacherous person. —*v.intr.* (**weaselled, weaselling**; *US* **weaseled, weaseling**) **1** esp. *US* equivocate or quibble. **2** (foll. by *on, out*) default on an obligation. □**weasel-faced** having thin sharp features. **weasel word** (usu. in *pl.*) a word that is intentionally ambiguous or misleading. □□ **weaselly** *adj.* [OE *wesle, wesule* f. WG]

weather /'weðə(r)/ *n. & v.* —*n.* **1** the state of the atmosphere at a place and time as regards heat, cloudiness, dryness, sunshine, wind, and rain etc. **2** (*attrib.*) *Naut.* windward (*on the weather side*). —*v.* **1** *tr.* expose to or affect by atmospheric changes, esp. deliberately to dry, season, etc. (*weathered timber*). **2 a** *tr.* (usu. in *passive*) discolour or partly disintegrate (rock or stones) by exposure to air. **b** *intr.* be discoloured or worn in this way. **3** *tr.* make (boards or tiles) overlap downwards to keep out rain etc. **4** *tr.* **a** come safely through (a storm). **b** survive (a difficult period etc.). **5** *tr.* (of a ship or its crew) get to the windward of (a cape etc.). □**keep a** (or **one's**) **weather eye open** be watchful. **make good** (or **bad**) **weather of it** *Naut.* (of a ship) behave well (or badly) in a storm. **make heavy weather of** *colloq.* exaggerate the difficulty or burden presented by (a problem, course of action, etc.). **under the weather** *colloq.* indisposed or out of sorts. **weather-beaten** affected by exposure to the weather. **weather-bound** unable to proceed owing to bad weather. **weather-chart** (or **-map**) a diagram showing the state of the weather over a large area. **weather forecast** an analysis of the state of the weather with an assessment of likely developments over a certain time. **weather-glass** a barometer. **weather side** the side from which the wind is blowing (opp. *lee side*). **weather station** an observation post for recording meteorological data. **weather-strip** a piece of material used to make a door or window proof against rain or wind. **weather-tiles** tiles arranged to overlap like weatherboards. **weather-vane** see VANE. **weather-worn** damaged by storms etc. [OE *weder* f. Gmc]

weatherboard /'weðə,bɔːd/ *n. & v.* —*n.* **1** a sloping board attached to the bottom of an outside door to keep out the rain etc. **2** each of a series of horizontal boards with edges overlapping to keep out the rain etc. —*v.tr.* fit or supply with weatherboards. □□ **weatherboarding** *n.* (in sense 2 of *n.*).

weathercock /'weðə,kɒk/ *n.* **1** a weather-vane (see VANE) in the form of a cock. **2** an inconstant person.

weathering /'weðərɪŋ/ *n.* **1** the action of the weather on materials etc. exposed to it. **2** exposure to adverse weather conditions (see WEATHER *v.* 1).

weatherly /'weðəlɪ/ *adj. Naut.* **1** (of a ship) making little leeway. **2** capable of keeping close to the wind. □□ **weatherliness** *n.*

weatherman /'weðə,mæn/ *n.* (*pl.* **-men**) a meteorologist, esp. one who broadcasts a weather forecast.

weatherproof /'weðə,pruːf/ *adj. & v.* —*adj.* resistant to the effects of bad weather, esp. rain. —*v.tr.* make weatherproof. □□ **weatherproofed** *adj.*

weave¹ /wiːv/ *v. & n.* —*v.* (*past* **wove** /wəʊv/; *past part.* **woven** /'wəʊv(ə)n/ or **wove**) **1** *tr.* **a** form (fabric) by interlacing long threads in two directions. **b** form (thread) into fabric in this way. **2** *intr.* **a** make fabric in this way. **b** work at a loom. **3** *tr.* make (a basket or wreath etc.) by interlacing rods or flowers etc. **4** *tr.* **a** (foll. by *into*) make (facts etc.) into a story or connected whole. **b** make (a story) in this way. —*n.* a style of weaving. [OE *wefan* f. Gmc]

weave² /wiːv/ *v.intr.* **1** move repeatedly from side to side; take an intricate course to avoid obstructions. **2** *colloq.* manœuvre an aircraft in this way; take evasive action. □**get weaving** *sl.* begin action; hurry. [prob. f. ME *weve*, var. of *waive* f. ON *veifa* WAVE]

weaver /'wiːvə(r)/ *n.* **1** a person whose occupation is weaving. **2** (in full **weaver-bird**) any tropical bird of the family Ploceidae, building elaborately woven nests. □**weaver's knot** a sheet bend (see SHEET²) used in weaving.

web /web/ *n. & v.* —*n.* **1 a** a woven fabric. **b** an amount woven in one piece. **2** a complete structure or connected series (*a web of lies*). **3** a cobweb, gossamer, or a similar product of a spinning creature. **4 a** a membrane between the toes of a swimming animal or bird. **b** the vane of a bird's feather. **5 a** a large roll of paper used in a continuous printing process. **b** an endless wire mesh on rollers, on which this is made. **6** a thin flat part connecting thicker or more solid parts in machinery etc. —*v.* (**webbed, webbing**) **1** *tr.* weave a web on. **2** *intr.* weave a web. □**web-footed** having the toes connected by webs. **web offset** offset printing on a web of paper. **web-wheel** a wheel having a plate or web instead of spokes, or with rim, spokes, and centre in one piece as in watch-wheels. **web-worm** *US* a gregarious caterpillar spinning a large web in which to sleep or to feed on enclosed foliage. □□ **webbed** *adj.* [OE *web, webb* f. Gmc]

webbing /'webɪŋ/ *n.* strong narrow closely-woven fabric used for supporting upholstery, for belts, etc.

weber /'veɪbə(r)/ *n.* the SI unit of magnetic flux, causing the electromotive force of one volt in a circuit of one turn when generated or removed in one second. ¶ Abbr.: **Wb**. [W. E. *Weber*, Ger. physicist d. 1891]

Wed. *abbr.* Wednesday.

wed /wed/ *v.tr.* & *intr.* (**wedding**; *past* and *past part.* **wedded** or **wed**) **1** usu. *formal* or *literary* **a** *tr.* & *intr.* marry. **b** *tr.* join in marriage. **2** *tr.* unite (*wed efficiency to economy*). **3** *tr.* (as **wedded** *adj.*) of or in marriage (*wedded bliss*). **4** *tr.* (as **wedded** *adj.*) (foll. by *to*) obstinately attached or devoted (to a pursuit etc.). [OE *weddian* to pledge f. Gmc]

we'd /wiːd, wɪd/ *contr.* **1** we had. **2** we should; we would.

wedding /'wedɪŋ/ *n.* a marriage ceremony (considered by itself or with the associated celebrations). □ **wedding breakfast** a meal etc. usually served between a wedding and the departure for the honeymoon. **wedding cake** a rich iced cake served at a wedding reception. **wedding day** the day or anniversary of a wedding. **wedding march** a march played at the entrance of the bride or the exit of the couple at a wedding. **wedding night** the night after a wedding (esp. with ref. to its consummation). **wedding ring** a ring worn by a married person. [OE *weddung* (as WED, -ING¹)]

wedge¹ /wedʒ/ *n.* & *v.* —*n.* **1** a piece of wood or metal etc. tapering to a sharp edge, that is driven between two objects or parts of an object to secure or separate them. **2** anything resembling a wedge (*a wedge of cheese*; *troops formed a wedge*). **3** a golf club with a wedge-shaped head. **4 a** a wedge-shaped heel. **b** a shoe with this. —*v.tr.* **1** tighten, secure, or fasten by means of a wedge (*wedged the door open*). **2** force open or apart with a wedge. **3** (foll. by *in*, *into*) pack or thrust (a thing or oneself) tightly in or into. □ **thin end of the wedge** *colloq.* an action or procedure of little importance in itself, but likely to lead to more serious developments. **wedge-shaped 1** shaped like a solid wedge. **2** V-shaped. □□ **wedgelike** *adj.* **wedgewise** *adv.* [OE *wecg* f. Gmc]

wedge² /wedʒ/ *v.tr.* Pottery prepare (clay) for use by cutting, kneading, and throwing down. [17th c.: orig. uncert.]

wedgie /'wedʒɪ/ *n. colloq.* a shoe with an extended wedge-shaped heel.

Wedgwood /'wedʒwʊd/ *n. propr.* **1** ceramic ware made by J. Wedgwood, Engl. potter d. 1795, and his successors, esp. a kind of fine stoneware usu. with a white cameo design. **2** the characteristic blue colour of this stoneware.

wedlock /'wedlɒk/ *n.* the married state. □ **born in** (or **out of**) **wedlock** born of married (or unmarried) parents. [OE *wedlāc* marriage vow f. *wed* pledge (rel. to WED) + *-lāc* suffix denoting action]

Wednesday /'wenzdeɪ, -dɪ/ *n.* & *adv.* —*n.* the fourth day of the week, following Tuesday. —*adv. colloq.* **1** on Wednesday. **2** (**Wednesdays**) on Wednesdays; each Wednesday. [ME *wednesdei*, OE *wōdnesdæg* day of (the god) Odin]

Weds. *abbr.* Wednesday.

wee¹ /wiː/ *adj.* (**weer** /'wiːə(r)/; **weest** /'wiːɪst/) **1** esp. *Sc.* little; very small. **2** *colloq.* tiny; extremely small (*a wee bit*). [orig. Sc. noun, f. north.ME *wei* (small) quantity f. Anglian *wēg*: cf. WEY]

wee² /wiː/ *n.* esp. *Brit. sl.* = WEE-WEE.

weed /wiːd/ *n.* & *v.* —*n.* **1** a wild plant growing where it is not wanted. **2** a thin weak-looking person or horse. **3** (prec. by *the*) *sl.* **a** marijuana. **b** tobacco. —*v.* **1** *tr.* **a** clear (an area) of weeds. **b** remove unwanted parts from. **2** *tr.* (foll. by *out*) **a** sort out (inferior or unwanted parts etc.) for removal. **b** rid (a quantity or company) of inferior or unwanted members etc. **3** *intr.* cut off or uproot weeds. □ **weed-grown** overgrown with weeds. **weed-killer** a substance used to destroy weeds. □□ **weeder** *n.* **weedless** *adj.* [OE *wēod*, of unkn. orig.]

weeds /wiːdʒ/ *n.pl.* (in full **widow's weeds**) *archaic* deep mourning worn by a widow. [OE *wǣd(e)* garment f. Gmc]

weedy /'wiːdɪ/ *adj.* (**weedier**, **weediest**) **1** having many weeds. **2** (esp. of a person) weak, feeble; of poor stature. □□ **weediness** *n.*

week /wiːk/ *n.* **1** a period of seven days reckoned usu. from and to midnight on Saturday–Sunday. **2** a period of seven days reckoned from any point (*would like to stay for a week*). **3** the six days between Sundays. **4 a** the five days Monday to Friday. **b** a normal amount of work done in this period (*a 35-hour week*). **5** (in *pl.*) a long time; several weeks (*have not seen you for weeks*; *did it weeks ago*). **6** (prec. by a specified day) a week after (that day) (*Tuesday week*; *tomorrow week*). [OE *wice* f. Gmc, prob. orig. = sequence]

weekday /'wiːkdeɪ/ *n.* a day other than Sunday or other than at a weekend (often *attrib.*: *a weekday afternoon*).

weekend /wiːk'end, 'wiːk-/ *n.* & *v.* —*n.* **1** Sunday and Saturday or part of Saturday. **2** this period extended slightly esp. for a holiday or visit etc. (*going away for the weekend*; *a weekend cottage*). —*v.intr.* spend a weekend (*decided to weekend in the country*).

weekender /wiːk'endə(r)/ *n.* **1** a person who spends weekends away from home. **2** *Austral. colloq.* a holiday cottage.

weeklong /'wiːklɒŋ/ *adj.* lasting for a week.

weekly /'wiːklɪ/ *adj.*, *adv.*, & *n.* —*adj.* done, produced, or occurring once a week. —*adv.* once a week; from week to week. —*n.* (*pl.* **-ies**) a weekly newspaper or periodical.

ween /wiːn/ *v.tr. archaic* be of the opinion; think, suppose. [OE *wēnan* f. Gmc]

weeny /'wiːnɪ/ *adj.* (**weenier**, **weeniest**) *colloq.* tiny. □ **weeny-bopper** a girl like a teeny-bopper but younger. [WEE¹ after *tiny*, *teeny*]

weep /wiːp/ *v.* & *n.* —*v.* (*past* and *past part.* **wept** /wept/) **1** *intr.* shed tears. **2 a** *tr.* & (foll. by *for*) *intr.* shed tears for; bewail, lament over. **b** *tr.* utter or express with tears ('*Don't go*,' *he wept*; *wept her thanks*). **3 a** *intr.* be covered with or send forth drops. **b** *intr.* & *tr.* come or send forth in drops; exude liquid (*weeping sore*). **4** *intr.* (as **weeping** *adj.*) (of a tree) having drooping branches (*weeping willow*). —*n.* a fit or spell of weeping. □ **weep out** utter with tears. □□ **weepingly** *adv.* [OE *wēpan* f. Gmc (prob. imit.)]

weeper /'wiːpə(r)/ *n.* **1** a person who weeps, esp. *hist.* a hired mourner at a funeral. **2** a small image of a mourner on a monument. **3** (in *pl.*) *hist.* **a** a man's crape hatband for funerals. **b** a widow's black crape veil or white cuffs.

weepie /'wiːpɪ/ *n.* (also **weepy**) (*pl.* **-ies**) *colloq.* a sentimental or emotional film, play, etc.

weepy /'wiːpɪ/ *adj.* (**weepier**, **weepiest**) *colloq.* inclined to weep; tearful. □□ **weepily** *adv.* **weepiness** *n.*

weever /'wiːvə(r)/ *n.* any marine fish of the genus *Trachinus*, with sharp venomous dorsal spines. [perh. f. OF *wivre*, *guivre*, serpent, dragon, f. L *vipera* VIPER]

weevil /'wiːvɪl/ *n.* **1** any destructive beetle of the family Curculionidae, with its head extended into a beak or rostrum and feeding esp. on grain. **2** any insect damaging stored grain. □□ **weevily** *adj.* [ME f. MLG *wevel* f. Gmc]

wee-wee /'wiːwiː/ *n.* & *v.* esp. *Brit. sl.* —*n.* **1** the act or an instance of urinating. **2** urine. —*v.intr.* (**-wees**, **-weed**) urinate. [20th c.: orig. unkn.]

w.e.f. *abbr.* with effect from.

weft¹ /weft/ *n.* **1 a** the threads woven across a warp to make fabric. **b** yarn for these. **c** a thing woven. **2** filling-strips in basket-weaving. [OE *weft(a)* f. Gmc: rel. to WEAVE¹]

weft² var. of WAFT *n.* 3.

Wehrmacht /'veərmɑːxt/ *n. hist.* the German armed forces, esp. the army, from 1921 to 1945. [G, = defensive force]

weigh¹ /weɪ/ *v.* **1** *tr.* find the weight of. **2** *tr.* balance in the hands to guess or as if to guess the weight of.

3 *tr.* (often foll. by *out*) **a** take a definite weight of; take a specified weight from a larger quantity. **b** distribute in exact amounts by weight. **4** *tr.* **a** estimate the relative value, importance, or desirability of; consider with a view to choice, rejection, or preference (*weighed the consequences*; *weighed the merits of the candidates*). **b** (foll. by *with*, *against*) compare (one consideration with another). **5** *tr.* be equal to (a specified weight) (*weighs three kilos*; *weighs very little*). **6** *intr.* **a** have (esp. a specified) importance; exert an influence. **b** (foll. by *with*) be regarded as important by (*the point that weighs with me*). **7** *intr.* (often foll. by *on*) be heavy or burdensome (to); be depressing (to). □**weigh anchor** see ANCHOR. **weigh down 1** bring or keep down by exerting weight. **2** be oppressive or burdensome to (*weighed down with worries*). **weigh in** (of a boxer before a contest, or a jockey after a race) be weighed. **weigh-in** *n.* the weighing of a boxer before a fight. **weighing-machine** a machine for weighing persons or large weights. **weigh into** *colloq.* attack (physically or verbally). **weigh in with** *colloq.* advance (an argument etc.) assertively or boldly. **weigh out** (of a jockey) be weighed before a race. **weigh up** *colloq.* form an estimate of; consider carefully. **weigh one's words** carefully choose the way one expresses something. □□ **weighable** *adj.* **weigher** *n.* [OE *wegan* f. Gmc, rel. to WAY]

weigh² /weɪ/ *n.* □**under weigh** *disp.* = *under way*. [18th c.: from an erron. assoc. with *weigh anchor*]

weighbridge /ˈweɪbrɪdʒ/ *n.* a weighing-machine for vehicles, usu. having a plate set into the road for vehicles to drive on to.

weight /weɪt/ *n.* & *v.* —*n.* **1** *Physics* **a** the force experienced by a body as a result of the earth's gravitation (cf. MASS¹ *n.* 8). **b** any similar force with which a body tends to a centre of attraction. **2** the heaviness of a body regarded as a property of it; its relative mass or the quantity of matter contained by it giving rise to a downward force (*is twice your weight*; *kept in position by its weight*). **3 a** the quantitative expression of a body's weight (*has a weight of three pounds*). **b** a scale of such weights (*troy weight*). **4** a body of a known weight for use in weighing. **5** a heavy body esp. used in a mechanism etc. (*a clock worked by weights*). **6** a load or burden (*a weight off my mind*). **7 a** influence, importance (*carried weight with the public*). **b** preponderance (*the weight of evidence was against them*). **8** a heavy object thrown as an athletic exercise; = SHOT¹ 7. **9** the surface density of cloth etc. as a measure of its suitability. —*v.tr.* **1 a** attach a weight to. **b** hold down with a weight or weights. **2** (foll. by *with*) impede or burden. **3** *Statistics* multiply the components of (an average) by factors to take account of their importance. **4** assign a handicap weight to (a horse). **5** treat (a fabric) with a mineral etc. to make it seem stouter. □**put on weight 1** increase one's weight. **2** get fat. **throw one's weight about** (or **around**) *colloq.* be unpleasantly self-assertive. **worth one's weight in gold** (of a person) exceedingly useful or helpful. [OE *(ge)wiht* f. Gmc: cf. WEIGH¹]

weighting /ˈweɪtɪŋ/ *n.* an extra allowance paid in special cases, esp. to allow for a higher cost of living (*London weighting*).

weightless /ˈweɪtlɪs/ *adj.* (of a body, esp. in an orbiting spacecraft etc.) not apparently acted on by gravity. □□ **weightlessly** *adv.* **weightlessness** *n.*

weightlifting /ˈweɪtˌlɪftɪŋ/ *n.* the sport or exercise of lifting a heavy weight, esp. a barbell. □□ **weightlifter** *n.*

weighty /ˈweɪtɪ/ *adj.* (**weightier**, **weightiest**) **1** weighing much; heavy. **2** momentous, important. **3** (of utterances etc.) deserving consideration; careful and serious. **4** influential, authoritative. □□ **weightily** *adv.* **weightiness** *n.*

Weimaraner /ˌwaɪməˈrɑːnə, ˌvaɪ-/ *n.* a usu. grey dog

of a variety of pointer used as a gun dog. [G, f. *Weimar* in Germany, where it was developed]

weir /wɪə(r)/ *n.* **1** a dam built across a river to raise the level of water upstream or regulate its flow. **2** an enclosure of stakes etc. set in a stream as a trap for fish. [OE *wer* f. *werian* dam up]

weird /wɪəd/ *adj.* & *n.* —*adj.* **1** uncanny, supernatural. **2** *colloq.* strange, queer, incomprehensible. **3** *archaic* connected with fate. —*n.* esp. *Sc. archaic* fate, destiny. □**the weird sisters 1** the Fates. **2** witches. □□ **weirdly** *adv.* **weirdness** *n.* [(earlier as noun) f. OE *wyrd* destiny f. Gmc]

weirdie /ˈwɪədɪ/ *n.* (also **weirdy**) (*pl.* -**ies**) *colloq.* = WEIRDO.

weirdo /ˈwɪədəʊ/ *n.* (*pl.* -**os**) *colloq.* an odd or eccentric person.

Weismannism /ˈvaɪsmənˌnɪz(ə)m/ *n.* the theory of heredity assuming continuity of germ-plasm and non-transmission of acquired characteristics. [A. *Weismann*, Ger. biologist d. 1914]

weka /ˈwekə/ *n.* any flightless New Zealand rail of the genus *Gallirallus*. [Maori: imit. of its cry]

Welch /welʃ/ var. of WELSH (now only in *Royal Welch Fusiliers*).

welch var. of WELSH.

welcome /ˈwelkəm/ *n., int., v.,* & *adj.* —*n.* the act or an instance of greeting or receiving (a person, idea, etc.) gladly; a kind or glad reception (*gave them a warm welcome*). —*int.* expressing such a greeting (*welcome!*; *welcome home!*). —*v.tr.* receive with a welcome (*welcomed them home*; *would welcome the opportunity*). —*adj.* **1** that one receives with pleasure (*a welcome guest*; *welcome news*). **2** (foll. by *to*, or *to* + infin.) **a** cordially allowed or invited; released of obligation (*you are welcome to use my car*). **b** iron. gladly given (an unwelcome task, thing, etc.) (*here's my work and you are welcome to it*). □**make welcome** receive hospitably. **outstay one's welcome** stay too long as a visitor etc. **you are welcome** there is no need for thanks. □□ **welcomely** *adv.* **welcomeness** *n.* **welcomer** *n.* **welcomingly** *adv.* [orig. OE *wilcuma* one whose coming is pleasing f. *wil-* desire, pleasure + *cuma* comer, with later change to *wel-* WELL¹ after OF *bien venu* or ON *velkominn*]

weld¹ /weld/ *v.* & *n.* —*v.tr.* **1 a** hammer or press (pieces of iron or other metal usu. heated but not melted) into one piece. **b** join by fusion with an electric arc etc. **c** form by welding into some article. **2** fashion (arguments, members of a group, etc.) into an effectual or homogeneous whole. —*n.* a welded joint. □□ **weldable** *adj.* **weldability** /-ˈbɪlɪtɪ/ *n.* **welder** *n.* [alt. of WELL² *v.* in obs. sense 'melt or weld (heated metal)', prob. infl. by past part.]

weld² /weld/ *n.* **1** a plant, *Reseda luteola*, yielding a yellow dye. **2** *hist.* this dye. [ME f. OE *w(e)alde* (unrecorded): cf. MDu. *woude*, MLG *walde*]

welfare /ˈwelfeə(r)/ *n.* **1** well-being, happiness; health and prosperity (of a person or a community etc.). **2** (**Welfare**) **a** the maintenance of persons in such a condition esp. by statutory procedure or social effort. **b** financial support given for this purpose. □**welfare state 1** a system whereby the State undertakes to protect the health and well-being of its citizens, esp. those in financial or social need, by means of grants, pensions, etc. **2** a country practising this system. **welfare work** organized effort for the welfare of the poor, disabled, etc. [ME f. WELL¹ + FARE]

welfarism /ˈwelfeəˌrɪz(ə)m/ *n.* principles characteristic of a welfare state. □□ **welfarist** *n.*

welkin /ˈwelkɪn/ *n. poet.* sky; the upper air. [OE *wolcen* cloud, sky]

well¹ /wel/ *adv., adj.,* & *int.* —*adv.* (**better, best**) **1** in a satisfactory way (*you have worked well*). **2** in the right way (*well said*; *you did well to tell me*). **3** with some talent or distinction (*plays the piano well*). **4** in a kind way (*treated me well*). **5** thoroughly, carefully (*polish it well*). **6** with heartiness or approval; favourably (*speak well of; the book was well reviewed*). **7** probably, reasonably, advisably (*you may well be right; you may well ask; we might well take the risk*). **8** to a considerable extent (*is well over forty*). **9** successfully, fortunately (*it turned out well*). **10** luckily, opportunely (*well met!*). **11** with a fortunate outcome; without disaster (*were well rid of them*). **12** profitably (*did well for themselves*). **13** comfortably, abundantly, liberally (*we live well here; the job pays well*). —*adj.* (**better, best**) **1** (usu. *predic.*) in good health (*are you well?; was not a well person*). **2** (*predic.*) **a** in a satisfactory state or position (*all is well*). **b** advisable (*it would be well to enquire*). —*int.* expressing surprise, resignation, insistence, etc., or resumption or continuation of talk, used esp. after a pause in speaking (*well I never!; well, I suppose so; well, who was it?*). □**as well 1** in addition; to an equal extent. **2** (also **just as well**) with equal reason; with no loss of advantage or need for regret (*may as well give up; it would be just as well to stop now*). **as well as** in addition to. **leave** (or **let**) **well alone** avoid needless change or disturbance. **well-acquainted** (usu. foll. by *with*) familiar. **well-adjusted 1** in a good state of adjustment. **2** *Psychol.* mentally and emotionally stable. **well-advised** (usu. foll. by *to* + infin.) (of a person) prudent (*would be well-advised to wait*). **well-affected** (often foll. by *to, towards*) favourably disposed. **well and good** expressing dispassionate acceptance of a decision etc. **well and truly** decisively, completely. **well-appointed** having all the necessary equipment. **well aware** certainly aware (*well aware of the danger*). **well away 1** having made considerable progress. **2** *colloq.* fast asleep or drunk. **well-balanced 1** sane, sensible. **2** equally matched. **well-behaved** see BEHAVE. **well-being** a state of being well, healthy, contented, etc. **well-beloved** *adj.* dearly loved. —*n.* (*pl.* same) a dearly loved person. **well-born** of noble family. **well-bred** having or showing good breeding or manners. **well-built 1** of good construction. **2** (of a person) big and strong and well-proportioned. **well-chosen** (of words etc.) carefully selected for effect. **well-conditioned** in good physical or moral condition. **well-conducted** (of a meeting etc.) properly organized and controlled. **well-connected** see CONNECTED. **well-covered** *colloq.* plump, corpulent. **well-defined** clearly indicated or determined. **well-deserved** rightfully merited or earned. **well-disposed** (often foll. by *towards*) having a good disposition or friendly feeling (for). **well done 1** (of meat etc.) thoroughly cooked. **2** (of a task etc.) performed well (also as *int.*). **well-dressed** fashionably smart. **well-earned** fully deserved. **well-endowed 1** well provided with talent etc. **2** *colloq.* sexually potent or attractive. **well-favoured** good-looking. **well-fed** having or having had plenty to eat. **well-found** = *well-appointed*. **well-founded** (of suspicions etc.) based on good evidence; having a foundation in fact or reason. **well-groomed** (of a person) with carefully tended hair, clothes, etc. **well-grounded 1** = *well-founded*. **2** having a good training in or knowledge of the groundwork of a subject. **well-heeled** *colloq.* wealthy. **well-hung** *colloq.* (of a man) having large genitals. **well-informed** having much knowledge or information about a subject. **well-intentioned** having or showing good intentions. **well-judged** opportunely, skilfully, or discreetly done. **well-kept** kept in good order or condition. **well-knit** (esp. of a person) compact; not loose-jointed or sprawling. **well-known 1** known to many. **2** known thoroughly. **well-made 1** strongly or skilfully manufactured. **2** (of a person or animal) having a good build. **well-mannered** having good manners. **well-marked** distinct; easy to detect. **well-matched** see MATCH¹. **well-meaning** (or **-meant**) well-intentioned (but ineffective or unwise). **well off 1**

having plenty of money. **2** in a fortunate situation or circumstances. **well-oiled** *colloq.* **1** drunk. **2** (of a compliment etc.) easily expressed through habitual use. **well-ordered** arranged in an orderly manner. **well-paid 1** (of a job) that pays well. **2** (of a person) amply rewarded for a job. **well-pleased** highly gratified or satisfied. **well-preserved** see PRESERVE. **well-read** knowledgeable through much reading. **well-received** welcomed; favourably received. **well-rounded 1** complete and symmetrical. **2** (of a phrase etc.) complete and well expressed. **3** (of a person) having or showing a fully developed personality, ability, etc. **well-spent** (esp. of money or time) used profitably. **well-spoken** articulate or refined in speech. **well-thought-of** having a good reputation; esteemed, respected. **well-thought-out** carefully devised. **well-thumbed** bearing marks of frequent handling. **well-timed** opportune, timely. **well-to-do** prosperous. **well-tried** often tested with good results. **well-trodden** much frequented. **well-turned 1** (of a compliment, phrase, or verse) elegantly expressed. **2** (of a leg, ankle, etc.) elegantly shaped or displayed. **well-upholstered** see UPHOLSTER. **well-wisher** a person who wishes one well. **well-woman** a woman who has undergone satisfactory gynaecological tests (often *attrib.*: *well-woman clinic*). **well-worn 1** much worn by use. **2** (of a phrase etc.) trite, hackneyed. **well worth** certainly worth (*well worth a visit; well worth visiting*). ¶ A hyphen is normally used in combinations of *well-* when used attributively, but not when used predicatively, e.g. *a well-made coat* but *the coat is well made.* □□ **wellness** *n.* [OE *wel, well* prob. f. the same stem as WILL¹]

well² /wel/ *n. & v.* —*n.* **1** a shaft sunk into the ground to obtain water, oil, etc. **2** an enclosed space like a well-shaft, e.g. in the middle of a building for stairs or a lift, or for light or ventilation. **3** (foll. by *of*) a source, esp. a copious one (*a well of information*). **4 a** a mineral spring. **b** (in *pl.*) a spa. **5** = *ink-well*. **6** *archaic* a water-spring or fountain. **7** *Brit.* a railed space for solicitors etc. in a lawcourt. **8** a depression for gravy etc. in a dish or tray, or for a mat in the floor. **9** *Physics* a region of minimum potential etc. —*v.intr.* (foll. by *out, up*) spring as from a fountain; flow copiously. □**well-head** (or **-spring**) a source. [OE *wella* (= OHG *wella* wave, ON *vella* boiling heat), *wellan* boil, melt f. Gmc]

we'll /wiːl, wɪl/ *contr.* we shall; we will.

wellies /ˈwelɪz/ *n.pl. Brit. colloq.* wellingtons. [abbr.]

wellington /ˈwelɪŋt(ə)n/ *n.* (in full **wellington boot**) *Brit.* a waterproof rubber or plastic boot usu. reaching the knee. [after the 1st Duke of *Wellington*, Brit. general and statesman d. 1852]

wellnigh /ˈwelnaɪ/ *adv. archaic* or *rhet.* almost (*wellnigh impossible*).

Welsh /welʃ/ *adj. & n.* —*adj.* of or relating to Wales or its people or language. —*n.* **1** the Celtic language of Wales. **2** (prec. by *the*; treated as *pl.*) the people of Wales. □**Welsh corgi** see CORGI. **Welsh dresser** a type of dresser with open shelves above a cupboard. **Welsh harp** a harp with three rows of strings. **Welsh onion** a species of onion, *Allium fistulosum*, forming clusters of bulbs. **Welsh rabbit** (or **rarebit** by folk etymology) a dish of melted cheese etc. on toast. [OE *Welisc, Wælisc*, etc., f. Gmc f. L *Volcae*, the name of a Celtic people]

welsh /welʃ/ *v.intr.* (also **welch** /weltʃ/) **1** (of a loser of a bet, esp. a bookmaker) decamp without paying. **2** evade an obligation. **3** (foll. by *on*) **a** fail to carry out a promise to (a person). **b** fail to honour (an obligation). □□ **welsher** *n.* [19th c.: orig. unkn.]

Welshman /ˈwelʃmən/ *n.* (*pl.* **-men**) a man who is Welsh by birth or descent.

Welshwoman /ˈwelʃˌwʊmən/ *n.* (*pl.* **-women**) a woman who is Welsh by birth or descent.

welt /welt/ *n. & v.* —*n.* **1** a leather rim sewn round the edge of a shoe-upper for the sole to be attached to. **2** = WEAL¹. **3** a ribbed or reinforced border of a garment; a trimming. **4** a heavy blow. —*v.tr.* **1** provide with a welt. **2** rain welts on; thrash. [ME *welte, walt*, of unkn. orig.]

Weltanschauung /ˌveltɑːnˈʃaʊʊŋ/ *n.* a particular philosophy or view of life; a conception of the world. [G f. *Welt* world + *Anschauung* perception]

welter¹ /ˈweltə(r)/ *v. & n.* —*v.intr.* **1** roll, wallow; be washed about. **2** (foll. by *in*) lie prostrate or be soaked or steeped in blood etc. —*n.* **1** a state of general confusion. **2** (foll. by *of*) a disorderly mixture or contrast of beliefs, policies, etc. [ME f. MDu., MLG *welteren*]

welter² /ˈweltə(r)/ *n.* **1** a heavy rider or boxer. **2** *colloq.* a heavy blow. **3** *colloq.* a big person or thing. [19th c.: orig. unkn.]

welterweight /ˈweltəˌweɪt/ *n.* **1** a weight in certain sports intermediate between lightweight and middle-weight, in the amateur boxing scale 63.5–67 kg but differing for professionals, wrestlers, and weight-lifters. **2** a sportsman of this weight. □**junior welterweight 1** a weight in professional boxing of 61.2–63.5 kg. **2** a professional boxer of this weight. **light welterweight 1** a weight in amateur boxing of 60–63.5 kg. **2** an amateur boxer of this weight.

Weltschmerz /ˈveltʃmeəts/ *n.* a feeling of pessimism; an apathetic or vaguely yearning outlook on life. [G f. *Welt* world + *Schmerz* pain]

wen¹ /wen/ *n.* **1** a benign tumour on the skin esp. of the scalp. **2** an outstandingly large or congested city. □**the great wen** London. [OE *wen, wenn*, of unkn. orig.: cf. Du. *wen*, MLG *wene*, LG *wehne* tumour, wart]

wen² /wen/ *n.* (also **wyn** /wɪn/) a runic letter in Old and Middle English, later replaced by *w*. [OE, var. of *wyn* joy (see WINSOME), used because it begins with this letter: cf. THORN 3]

wench /wentʃ/ *n. & v.* —*n.* **1** *joc.* a girl or young woman. **2** *archaic* a prostitute. —*v.intr. archaic* (of a man) consort with prostitutes. □□ **wencher** *n.* [ME *wenche, wenchel* f. OE *wencel* child: cf. OE *wancol* weak, tottering]

Wend /wend/ *n.* a member of a Slavic people of N. Germany, now inhabiting E. Saxony. □□ **Wendic** *adj.* **Wendish** *adj.* [G *Wende* f. OHG *Winida*, of unkn. orig.]

wend /wend/ *v.tr. & intr. literary* or *archaic* go. □**wend one's way** make one's way. [OE *wendan* turn f. Gmc, rel. to WIND²]

Wendy house /ˈwendɪ/ *n.* a children's small house-like tent or structure for playing in. [after the house built around *Wendy* in Barrie's *Peter Pan*]

Wensleydale /ˈwenzlɪˌdeɪl/ *n.* **1** a variety of white or blue cheese. **2 a** a sheep of a breed with long wool. **b** this breed. [*Wensleydale* in Yorkshire]

went *past* of GO¹.

wentletrap /ˈwent(ə)lˌtræp/ *n.* any marine snail of the genus *Clathrus*, with a spiral shell of many whorls. [Du. *wenteltrap* winding stair, spiral shell]

wept *past* of WEEP.

were *2nd sing. past, pl. past, and past subj.* of BE.

we're /wɪə(r)/ *contr.* we are.

weren't /wɜːnt/ *contr.* were not.

werewolf /ˈwɪəwʊlf, ˈweə-/ *n.* (also **werwolf** /ˈwɜː-/) (*pl.* **-wolves**) a mythical being who at times changes from a person to a wolf. [OE *werewulf*: first element perh. f. OE *wer* man = L *vir*]

wert *archaic 2nd sing. past* of BE.

Wesleyan /ˈwezlɪən/ *adj. & n.* —*adj.* of or relat-ing to a Protestant denomination founded by the English evangelist John Wesley (d. 1791) (cf. METHODIST). —*n.* a member of this denomination. □□ **Wesleyanism** *n.*

west /west/ *n., adj., & adv.* —*n.* **1 a** the point of the horizon where the sun sets at the equinoxes (cardinal point 90° to the left of north). **b** the compass point corresponding to this. **c** the direction in which this lies. **2** (usu. **the West**) **a** European in contrast to

Oriental civilization. **b** the non-Communist States of Europe and N. America. **c** the western part of the late Roman Empire. **d** the western part of a country, town, etc. **3** *Bridge* a player occupying the position designated 'west'. —*adj.* **1** towards, at, near, or facing west. **2** coming from the west (*west wind*). —*adv.* **1** towards, at, or near the west. **2** (foll. by *of*) further west than. □**go west** *sl.* be killed or destroyed etc. **West Bank** a region west of the River Jordan assigned to Jordan in 1948 and occupied by Israel since 1967. **West Country** the south-western coun-ties of England. **West End** the entertainment and shopping area of London to the west of the City. **West Indian 1** a native or national of any island of the West Indies. **2** a person of West Indian descent. **West Indies** the islands of Central America, in-cluding Cuba and the Bahamas. **west-north-** (or **south-**) **west** the direction or compass-point midway between west and north-west (or south-west). **West Side** *US* the western part of Manhattan. [OE f. Gmc]

westbound /ˈwestbaʊnd/ *adj.* travelling or leading westwards.

westering /ˈwestərɪŋ/ *adj.* (of the sun) nearing the west. [*wester* (v.) ME f. WEST]

westerly /ˈwestəlɪ/ *adj., adv., & n.* —*adj. & adv.* **1** in a western position or direction. **2** (of a wind) blowing from the west. —*n.* (*pl.* **-ies**) a wind blowing from the west. [*wester* (adj.) f. OE *westra* f. WEST]

western /ˈwest(ə)n/ *adj. & n.* —*adj.* **1** of or in the west; inhabiting the west. **2** lying or directed towards the west. **3** (**Western**) of or relating to the West (see WEST *n.* 2). —*n.* a film or novel about cowboys in western North America. □**Western Church** the part of Christendom that has continued to derive its authority, doctrine, and ritual from the popes in Rome. **Western hemisphere** the half of the earth containing the Americas. **Western roll** a technique of turning the body over the bar in high-jumping. □□ **westernmost** *adj.* [OE *westerne* (as WEST, -ERN)]

westerner /ˈwestənə(r)/ *n.* a native or inhabitant of the west.

westernize /ˈwestəˌnaɪz/ *v.tr.* (also **Westernize, -ise**) influence with or convert to the ideas and customs etc. of the West. □□ **westernization** /-ˈzeɪʃ(ə)n/ *n.* **westernizer** *n.*

westing /ˈwestɪŋ/ *n. Naut.* the distance travelled or the angle of longitude measured westward from either a defined north-south grid line or a meridian.

Westminster /ˈwestˌmɪnstə(r)/ *n.* the Parliament at Westminster in London.

westward /ˈwestwəd/ *adj., adv., & n.* —*adj. & adv.* (also **westwards**) towards the west. —*n.* a westward direction or region.

wet /wet/ *adj., v., & n.* —*adj.* (**wetter, wettest**) **1** soaked, covered, or dampened with water or other liquid (*a wet sponge; a wet surface; got my feet wet*). **2** (of the weather etc.) rainy (*a wet day*). **3** (of paint, ink, etc.) not yet dried. **4** used with water (*wet shampoo*). **5** *Brit. colloq.* feeble, inept. **6** *Brit. Polit. colloq.* Conservative with liberal tendencies, esp. as regarded by right-wing Conservatives. **7** *sl.* (of a country, of legislation, etc.) allowing the free sale of alcoholic drink. **8** (of a baby or young child) incontinent (*is still wet at night*). —*v.tr.* (**wetting**; *past* and *past part.* **wet** or **wetted**) **1** make wet. **2 a** urinate in or on (*wet the bed*). **b** *refl.* urinate involuntarily. —*n.* **1** moisture; liquid that wets something. **2** rainy weather; a time of rain. **3** *Brit. colloq.* a feeble or inept person. **4** *Brit. Polit. colloq.* a Conservative with liberal tendencies (see sense 6 of *adj.*). **5** *colloq.* a drink. □**wet the baby's head** *colloq.* celebrate its birth with a (usu. alcoholic) drink. **wet behind the ears** immature, inexperienced. **wet blanket** see BLANKET. **wet dock** a dock in which a ship can float. **wet dream** an erotic dream with involuntary ejaculation of semen. **wet fly** an ar-tificial fly used under water by an angler. **wet look** a shiny surface given to clothing materials.

wet-nurse n. a woman employed to suckle another's child. —v.tr. **1** act as a wet-nurse to. **2** colloq. treat as if helpless. **wet pack** the therapeutic wrapping of the body in wet cloths etc. **wet suit** a close-fitting rubber garment worn by skin-divers etc. to keep warm. **wet through** (or **to the skin**) with one's clothes soaked. **wetting agent** a substance that helps water etc. to spread or penetrate. **wet one's whistle** colloq. drink. □□ **wetly** adv. **wetness** n. **wettable** adj. **wetting** n. **wettish** adj. [OE wǣt (adj. & n.), wǣtan (v.), rel. to WATER: in ME replaced by past part. of the verb]

wetback /'wetbæk/ n. US colloq. an illegal immigrant from Mexico to the US. [WET + BACK: from the practice of swimming the Rio Grande to reach the US]

wether /'weðə(r)/ n. a castrated ram. [OE f. Gmc]

wetlands /'wetləndz/ n.pl. swamps and other damp areas of land.

we've /wi:v/ contr. we have.

wey /weɪ/ n. a former unit of weight or volume varying with different kinds of goods, e.g. 3 cwt. of cheese. [OE wǣg(e) balance, weight f. Gmc, rel. to WEIGH[1]]

w.f. abbr. Printing wrong fount.

WFTU abbr. World Federation of Trade Unions.

Wg. Cdr. abbr. Wing Commander.

whack /wæk/ v. & n. colloq. —v.tr. **1** strike or beat forcefully with a sharp blow. **2** (as **whacked** adj.) esp. Brit. tired out; exhausted. —n. **1** a sharp or resounding blow. **2** sl. a share. □ **have a whack at** sl. attempt. **out of whack** esp. US sl. out of order; malfunctioning. □□ **whacker** n. **whacking** n. [imit., or alt. of THWACK]

whacking /'wækɪŋ/ adj. & adv. colloq. —adj. very large. —adv. very (a whacking great skyscraper).

whacko /'wækəʊ/ int. sl. expressing delight or enjoyment.

whacky var. of WACKY.

whale[1] /weɪl/ n. (pl. same or **whales**) any of the larger marine mammals of the order Cetacea, having a streamlined body and horizontal tail, and breathing through a blowhole on the head. □ **a whale of a** colloq. an exceedingly good or fine etc. **whale-oil** oil from the blubber of whales. **whale shark** a large tropical whalelike shark, Rhincodon typus, feeding close to the surface. [OE hwæl]

whale[2] /weɪl/ v.tr. esp. US colloq. beat, thrash. [var. of WALE]

whaleback /'weɪlbæk/ n. anything shaped like a whale's back.

whaleboat /'weɪlbəʊt/ n. a double-bowed boat of a kind used in whaling.

whalebone /'weɪlbəʊn/ n. an elastic horny substance growing in thin parallel plates in the upper jaw of some whales, used as stiffening etc. □ **whalebone whale** a baleen whale.

whaler /'weɪlə(r)/ n. **1** a whaling ship or a seaman engaged in whaling. **2** an Australian shark of the genus Carcharhinus. **3** Austral. sl. a tramp.

whaling /'weɪlɪŋ/ n. the practice or industry of hunting and killing whales, esp. for their oil or whalebone. □ **whaling-master** the captain of a whaler.

wham /wæm/ int., n., & v. colloq. —int. expressing the sound of a forcible impact. —n. such a sound. —v. (**whammed**, **whamming**) **1** intr. make such a sound or impact. **2** tr. strike forcibly. [imit.]

whammy /'wæmɪ/ n. (pl. -ies) US colloq. an evil or unlucky influence. [20th c.: orig. unkn.]

whang /wæŋ/ v. & n. colloq. —v. **1** tr. strike heavily and loudly; whack. **2** intr. (of a drum etc.) sound under or as under a blow. —n. a whanging sound or blow. [imit.]

whangee /wæŋ'giː/ n. **1** a Chinese or Japanese bamboo of the genus Phyllostachys. **2** a cane made from this. [Chin. huang old bamboo-sprouts]

whare /'wɒrɪ/ n. a Maori hut or house. [Maori]

wharf /wɔːf/ n. & v. —n. (pl. **wharves** /wɔːvz/ or **wharfs**) a level quayside area to which a ship may be moved to load and unload. —v.tr. **1** moor (a ship) at a wharf. **2** store (goods) on a wharf. [OE hwearf]

wharfage /'wɔːfɪdʒ/ n. **1** accommodation at a wharf. **2** a fee for this.

wharfie /'wɔːfɪ/ n. Austral. & NZ colloq. a waterside worker; a wharf-labourer.

wharfinger /'wɔːfɪndʒə(r)/ n. an owner or keeper of a wharf. [prob. ult. f. WHARFAGE]

wharves pl. of WHARF.

what /wɒt/ adj., pron., & adv. —interrog.adj. **1** asking for a choice from an indefinite number or for a statement of amount, number, or kind (what books have you read?; what news have you?). **2** colloq. = WHICH interrog.adj. (what book have you chosen?). —adj. (usu. in exclam.) how great or remarkable (what luck!). —rel.adj. the or any . . . that (will give you what help I can). —pron. (corresp. to the functions of the adj.) **1** what thing or things? (what is your name?; I don't know what you mean). **2** (asking for a remark to be repeated) = what did you say? **3** asking for confirmation or agreement of something not completely understood (you did what?; what, you really mean it?). **4** how much (what you must have suffered!). **5** (as rel.pron.) that or those which; a or the or any thing which (what followed was worse; tell me what you think). —adv. to what extent (what does it matter?). □ **what about** what is the news or position or your opinion of (what about me?; what about a game of tennis?). **what-d'you-call-it** (or **what's-its-name**) a substitute for a name not recalled. **what ever** what at all or in any way (what ever do you mean?) (see also WHATEVER). **what for** colloq. **1** for what reason? **2** a severe reprimand (esp. give a person what for). **what have you** colloq. (prec. by or) anything else similar. **what if? 1** what would result etc. if. **2** what would it matter if. **what is more** and as an additional point; moreover. **what next?** colloq. what more absurd, shocking, or surprising thing is possible? **what not** (prec. by and) other similar things. **what of?** what is the news concerning? **what of it?** why should that be considered significant? **what's-his** (or **-its**) **-name** = what-d'you-call-it. **what's what** colloq. what is useful or important etc. **what with** colloq. because of (usu. several things). [OE hwæt f. Gmc]

whate'er /wɒt'eə(r)/ poet. var. of WHATEVER.

whatever /wɒt'evə(r)/ adj. & pron. **1** = WHAT (in relative uses) with the emphasis on indefiniteness (lend me whatever you can; whatever money you have). **2** though anything (we are safe whatever happens). **3** (with neg. or interrog.) at all; of any kind (there is no doubt whatever). **4** colloq. = what ever. □ **or whatever** colloq. or anything similar.

whatnot /'wɒtnɒt/ n. **1** an indefinite or trivial thing. **2** a stand with shelves for small objects.

whatso /'wɒtsəʊ/ adj. & pron. archaic = WHATEVER 1, 2. [ME, = WHAT + SO, f. OE swā hwæt swā]

whatsoe'er /ˌwɒtsəʊ'eə(r)/ poet. var. of WHATSOEVER.

whatsoever /ˌwɒtsəʊ'evə(r)/ adj. & pron. = WHATEVER 1, 2, 3.

whaup /wɔːp/ n. esp. Sc. a curlew. [imit. of its cry]

wheal var. of WEAL[1].

wheat /wiːt/ n. **1** any cereal plant of the genus Triticum, bearing dense four-sided seed-spikes. **2** its grain, used in making flour etc. □ **separate the wheat from the chaff** see CHAFF. **wheat-belt** a region where wheat is the chief agricultural product. **wheat germ** the embryo of the wheat grain, extracted as a source of vitamins. **wheat-grass** = couch grass (see COUCH[2]). [OE hwǣte f. Gmc, rel. to WHITE]

wheatear /'wiːtɪə(r)/ n. any small migratory bird of the genus Oenanthe, esp. with a white belly and rump. [app. f. wheatears (as WHITE, ARSE)]

wheaten /'wiːt(ə)n/ adj. made of wheat.

wheatmeal /'wiːtmiːl/ *n.* flour made from wheat with some of the bran and germ removed.

Wheatstone bridge /'wiːtstəʊn/ *n.* an apparatus for measuring electrical resistances by equalizing the potential at two points of a circuit. [C. *Wheatstone*, Engl. physicist d. 1875]

whee /wiː/ *int.* expressing delight or excitement. [imit.]

wheedle /'wiːd(ə)l/ *v.tr.* **1** coax by flattery or endearments. **2** (foll. by *out*) **a** get (a thing) out of a person by wheedling. **b** cheat (a person) out of a thing by wheedling. □□ **wheedler** *n.* **wheedling** *adj.* **wheedlingly** *adv.* [perh. f. G *wedeln* fawn, cringe f. *Wedel* tail]

wheel /wiːl/ *n. & v.* —*n.* **1** a circular frame or disc arranged to revolve on an axle and used to facilitate the motion of a vehicle or for various mechanical purposes. **2** a wheel-like thing (*Catherine wheel*; *potter's wheel*; *steering wheel*). **3** motion as of a wheel, esp. the movement of a line of people with one end as a pivot. **4** a machine etc. of which a wheel is an essential part. **5** (in *pl.*) *sl.* a car. **6** *US sl.* = **big wheel** 2. **7** a set of short lines concluding a stanza. —*v.* **1** *intr. & tr.* **a** turn on an axis or pivot. **b** swing round in line with one end as a pivot. **2 a** *intr.* (often foll. by *about*, *round*) change direction or face another way. **b** *tr.* cause to do this. **3** *tr.* push or pull (a wheeled thing esp. a barrow, bicycle, or pram, or its load or occupant). **4** *intr.* go in circles or curves (*seagulls wheeling overhead*). □**at the wheel 1** driving a vehicle. **2** directing a ship. **3** in control of affairs. **on wheels** (or **oiled wheels**) smoothly. **wheel and deal** engage in political or commercial scheming. **wheel-back** *adj.* (of a chair) with a back shaped like or containing the design of a wheel. **wheel-house** a steersman's shelter. **wheel-lock 1** an old kind of gunlock having a steel wheel to rub against flint etc. **2** a gun with this. **wheel of Fortune** luck. **wheel-spin** rotation of a vehicle's wheels without traction. **wheels within wheels 1** intricate machinery. **2** *colloq.* indirect or secret agencies. □□ **wheeled** *adj.* (also in *comb.*). **wheelless** *adj.* [OE *hwēol*, *hwēogol* f. Gmc]

wheelbarrow /'wiːlˌbærəʊ/ *n.* a small cart with one wheel and two shafts for carrying garden loads etc.

wheelbase /'wiːlbeɪs/ *n.* the distance between the front and rear axles of a vehicle.

wheelchair /'wiːlˌtʃeə(r)/ *n.* a chair on wheels for an invalid or disabled person.

wheeler /'wiːlə(r)/ *n.* **1** (in *comb.*) a vehicle having a specified number of wheels. **2** a wheelwright. **3** a horse harnessed next to the wheels and behind another. □**wheeler-dealer** a person who wheels and deals.

wheelie /'wiːlɪ/ *n. sl.* the stunt of riding a bicycle or motor cycle for a short distance with the front wheel off the ground.

wheelman *n.* esp. *US* **1** a driver of a wheeled vehicle. **2** a helmsman.

wheelsman /'wiːlzmən/ *n.* (*pl.* **-men**) *US* a steersman.

wheelwright /'wiːlraɪt/ *n.* a person who makes or repairs esp. wooden wheels.

wheeze /wiːz/ *v. & n.* —*v.* **1** *intr.* breathe with an audible chesty whistling sound. **2** *tr.* (often foll. by *out*) utter in this way. —*n.* **1** a sound of wheezing. **2** *colloq.* **a** *Brit.* a clever scheme. **b** an actor's interpolated joke etc. **c** a catch-phrase. □□ **wheezer** *n.* **wheezingly** *adv.* **wheezy** *adj.* (**wheezier**, **wheeziest**). **wheezily** *adv.* **wheeziness** *n.* [prob. f. ON *hvæsa* to hiss]

whelk[1] /welk/ *n.* any predatory marine gastropod mollusc of the family Buccinidae, esp. the edible kind of the genus *Baccinum*, having a spiral shell. [OE *wioloc*, *weoloc*, of unkn. orig.: perh. infl. by **whelk**[2]]

whelk[2] /welk/ *n.* a pimple. [OE *hwylca* f. *hwelian* suppurate]

whelm /welm/ *v.tr. poet.* **1** engulf, submerge. **2** crush with weight, overwhelm. [OE *hwelman* (unrecorded) = *hwylfan* overturn]

whelp /welp/ *n. & v.* —*n.* **1** a young dog; a puppy. **2** *archaic* a cub. **3** an ill-mannered child or youth. **4** (esp. in *pl.*) a projection on the barrel of a capstan or windlass. —*v.tr.* (also *absol.*) **1** bring forth (a whelp or whelps). **2** *derog.* (of a human mother) give birth to. **3** originate (an evil scheme etc.). [OE *hwelp*]

when /wen/ *adv., conj., pron., & n.* —*interrog.adv.* **1** at what time? **2** on what occasion? **3** how soon? **4** how long ago? —*rel.adv.* (prec. by *time* etc.) at or on which (*there are times when I could cry*). —*conj.* **1** at the or any time that; as soon as (*come when you like*; *come when ready*; *when I was your age*). **2** although; considering that (*why stand up when you could sit down?*). **3** after which; and then; but just then (*was nearly asleep when the bell rang*). —*pron.* what time? (*till when can you stay?*; *since when it has been better*). —*n.* time, occasion, date (*fixed the where and when*). [OE *hwanne*, *hwenne*]

whence /wens/ *adv. & conj. formal* —*adv.* from what place? (*whence did they come?*). —*conj.* **1** to the place from which (*return whence you came*). **2** (often prec. by *place* etc.) from which (*the source whence these errors arise*). **3** and thence (*whence it follows that*). ¶ Use of *from whence* (as in *the place from whence they came*), though common, is generally considered incorrect. [ME *whannes*, *whennes* f. *whanne*, *whenne* f. OE *hwanon(e)* whence, formed as **WHEN** + *-s*[3]: cf. **THENCE**]

whencesoever /ˌwenssəʊ'evə(r)/ *adv. & conj. formal* from whatever place or source.

whene'er /wen'eə(r)/ *poet.* var. of **WHENEVER**.

whenever /wen'evə(r)/ *conj. & adv.* **1** at whatever time; on whatever occasion. **2** every time that. □**or whenever** *colloq.* or at any similar time.

whensoe'er /ˌwensəʊ'eə(r)/ *poet.* var. of **WHEN-SOEVER**.

whensoever /ˌwensəʊ'evə(r)/ *conj. & adv. formal* = **WHENEVER**.

where /weə(r)/ *adv., conj., pron., & n.* —*interrog.adv.* **1** in or to what place or position? (*where is the milk?*; *where are you going?*). **2** in what direction or respect? (*where does the argument lead?*; *where does it concern us?*). **3** in what book etc.?; from whom? (*where did you read that?*; *where did you hear that?*). **4** in what situation or condition? (*where does that leave us?*). —*rel.adv.* (prec. by *place* etc.) in or to which (*places where they meet*). —*conj.* **1** in or to the or any place, direction, or respect in which (*go where you like*; *that is where you are wrong*; *delete where applicable*). **2** and there (*reached Crewe, where the car broke down*). —*pron.* what place? (*where do you come from?*; *where are you going to?*). —*n.* place; scene of something (see **WHEN** *n.*). [OE *hwǣr*, *hwār*]

whereabouts *adv. & n.* —*adv.* /ˌweərə'baʊts/ where or approximately where? (*whereabouts are they?*; *show me whereabouts to look*). —*n.* /'weərəˌbaʊts/ (as *sing.* or *pl.*) a person's or thing's location roughly defined.

whereafter /weər'ɑːftə(r)/ *conj. formal* after which.

whereas /weər'æz/ *conj.* **1** in contrast or comparison with the fact that. **2** (esp. in legal preambles) taking into consideration the fact that.

whereat /weər'æt/ *conj. archaic* **1** at which place or point. **2** for which reason.

whereby /weə'baɪ/ *conj.* by what or which means.

where'er /weər'eə(r)/ *poet.* var. of **WHEREVER**.

wherefore /'weəfɔː(r), -'fɔː(r)/ *adv. & n.* —*adv. archaic* **1** for what reason? **2** for which reason. —*n.* a reason (*the whys and wherefores*).

wherefrom /weə'frɒm/ *conj. archaic* from which, from where.

wherein /weər'ɪn/ *conj. & adv. formal* —*conj.* in what or which place or respect. —*adv.* in what place or respect?

whereof /wεər'ɒv/ conj. & adv. formal —conj. of what or which (the means whereof). —adv. of what?

whereon /wεər'ɒn/ conj. & adv. archaic —conj. on what or which. —adv. on what?

wheresoe'er /ˌwεəsəʊ'εə(r)/ poet. var. of WHERE-SOEVER.

wheresoever /ˌwεəsəʊ'εvə(r)/ conj. & adv. formal or literary = WHEREVER.

whereto /wεə'tuː/ conj. & adv. formal —conj. to what or which. —adv. to what?

whereupon /ˌwεərə'pɒn, 'wεər-/ conj. immediately after which.

wherever /wεər'εvə(r)/ adv. & conj. —adv. in or to whatever place. —conj. in every place that. □**or wherever** colloq. or in any similar place.

wherewithal /'wεəwɪˌðɔːl/ n. colloq. money etc. needed for a purpose (has not the wherewithal to do it).

wherry /'wεrɪ/ n. (pl. -ies) 1 a light rowing-boat usu. for carrying passengers. 2 a large light barge. [ME: orig. unkn.]

wherryman /'wεrɪmən/ n. (pl. -men) a man employed on a wherry.

whet /wet/ v. & n. —v.tr. (whetted, whetting) 1 sharpen (a scythe or other tool) by grinding. 2 stimulate (the appetite or a desire, interest, etc.). —n. 1 the act or an instance of whetting. 2 a small quantity stimulating one's appetite for more. □□ **whetter** n. (also in comb.). [OE hwettan f. Gmc]

whether /'wεðə(r)/ conj. introducing the first or both of alternative possibilities (I doubt whether it matters; I do not know whether they have arrived or not). □**whether or no** see NO². [OE hwæther, hwether f. Gmc]

whetstone /'wetstəʊn/ n. 1 a tapered stone used with water to sharpen curved tools, e.g. sickles, hooks (cf. OILSTONE). 2 a thing that sharpens the senses etc.

whew /hwjuː/ int. expressing surprise, consternation, or relief. [imit.: cf. PHEW]

whey /weɪ/ n. the watery liquid left when milk forms curds. □**whey-faced** pale esp. with fear. [OE hwæg, hweg f. LG]

which /wɪtʃ/ adj. & pron. —interrog.adj. asking for choice from a definite set of alternatives (which John do you mean?; say which book you prefer; which way shall we go?). —rel.adj. being the one just referred to; and this or these (ten years, during which time they admitted nothing; a word of advice, which action is within your power, will set things straight). —interrog.pron. 1 which person or persons (which of you is responsible?). 2 which thing or things (say which you prefer). —rel.pron. (poss. **of which, whose** /huːz/) 1 which thing or things, usu. introducing a clause not essential for identification (cf. THAT pron. 7) (the house, which is empty, has been damaged). 2 used in place of that after in or that (there is the house in which I was born; that which you have just seen). □**which is which** a phrase used when two or more persons or things are difficult to distinguish from each other. [OE hwilc f. Gmc]

whichever /wɪtʃ'εvə(r)/ adj. & pron. 1 any which (take whichever you like; whichever one you like). 2 no matter which (whichever one wins, they both get a prize).

whichsoever /ˌwɪtʃsəʊ'εvə(r)/ adj. & pron. archaic = WHICHEVER.

whidah var. of WHYDAH.

whiff /wɪf/ n. & v. —n. 1 a puff or breath of air, smoke, etc. (went outside for a whiff of fresh air). 2 a smell (caught the whiff of a cigar). 3 (foll. by of) a trace or suggestion of scandal etc. 4 a small cigar. 5 a minor discharge (of grapeshot etc.). 6 a light narrow outrigged sculling-boat. —v. 1 tr. & intr. blow or puff lightly. 2 intr. Brit. smell (esp. unpleasant). 3 tr. get a slight smell of. [imit.]

whiffle /'wɪf(ə)l/ v. & n. —v. 1 intr. & tr. (of the wind) blow lightly, shift about. 2 intr. be variable or evasive. 3 intr. (of a flame, leaves, etc.) flicker, flutter. 4 intr. make the sound of a light wind in breathing etc. —n. a slight movement of air. □□ **whiffler** n. [WHIFF + -LE⁴]

whiffletree /'wɪf(ə)lˌtriː/ n. US = SWINGLETREE. [var. of WHIPPLETREE]

whiffy /'wɪfɪ/ adj. colloq. (**whiffier, whiffiest**) having an unpleasant smell.

Whig /wɪg/ n. hist. 1 Polit. a member of the British reforming and constitutional party that after 1688 sought the supremacy of Parliament and was eventually succeeded in the 19th c. by the Liberal Party (opp. TORY 2). 2 a 17th-c. Scottish Presbyterian. 3 US a a supporter of the American Revolution. b a member of an American political party in the 19th c., succeeded by the Republicans. □□ **Whiggery** n. **Whiggish** adj. **Whiggism** n. [prob. a shortening of Sc. whiggamer, -more, nickname of 17th-c. Sc. rebels, f. whig to drive + MARE¹]

while /waɪl/ n., conj., v., & adv. —n. 1 a space of time, time spent in some action (a long while ago; waited a while; all this while). 2 (prec. by the) a during some other process. b poet. during the time that. 3 (prec. by a) for some time (have not seen you a while). —conj. 1 during the time that; for as long as; at the same time as (while I was away, the house was burgled; fell asleep while reading). 2 in spite of the fact that; although, whereas (while I want to believe it, I cannot). 3 N.Engl. until (wait while Monday). —v.tr. (foll. by away) pass (time etc.) in a leisurely or interesting manner. —rel.adv. (prec. by time etc.) during which (the summer while I was abroad). □**all the while** during the whole time (that). **for a long while** for a long time past. **for a while** for some time. **a good** (or **great**) **while** a considerable time. **in a while** (or **little while**) soon, shortly. **worth while** (or **one's while**) worth the time or effort spent. [OE hwil f. Gmc: (conj.) abbr. of OE thā hwīle the, ME the while that]

whiles /waɪlz/ conj. archaic = WHILE. [orig. in the adverbs somewhiles, otherwhiles]

whilom /'waɪləm/ adv. & adj. archaic —adv. formerly, once. —adj. former, erstwhile (my whilom friend). [OE hwīlum dative pl. of hwīl WHILE]

whilst /waɪlst/ adv. & conj. esp. Brit. while. [ME f. WHILES: cf. AGAINST]

whim /wɪm/ n. 1 a a sudden fancy; a caprice. b capriciousness. 2 archaic a kind of windlass for raising ore or water from a mine. [17th c.: orig. unkn.]

whimbrel /'wɪmbrɪl/ n. a small curlew, esp. Numenius phaeopus. [WHIMPER (imit.): cf. dotterel]

whimper /'wɪmpə(r)/ v. & n. —v. 1 intr. make feeble, querulous, or frightened sounds; cry and whine softly. 2 tr. utter whimperingly. —n. 1 a whimpering sound. 2 a feeble note or tone (the conference ended on a whimper). □□ **whimperer** n. **whimperingly** adv. [imit., f. dial. whimp]

whimsical /'wɪmzɪk(ə)l/ adj. 1 capricious. 2 fantastic. 3 odd or quaint; fanciful, humorous. □□ **whimsicality** /-'kælɪtɪ/ n. **whimsically** adv. **whimsicalness** n.

whimsy /'wɪmzɪ/ n. (also **whimsey**) (pl. -ies or -eys) 1 a whim; a capricious notion or fancy. 2 capricious or quaint humour. [rel. to WHIM-WHAM: cf. flimsy]

whim-wham /'wɪmwæm/ n. archaic 1 a toy or plaything. 2 = WHIM 1. [redupl.: orig. uncert.]

whin¹ /wɪn/ n. (in sing. or pl.) furze, gorse. [prob. Scand.: cf. Norw. hvine, Sw. hven]

whin² /wɪn/ n. 1 hard dark esp. basaltic rock or stone. 2 a piece of this. [ME: orig. unkn.]

whinchat /'wɪntʃæt/ n. a small brownish songbird, Saxicola rubetra. [WHIN¹ + CHAT²]

whine /waɪn/ n. & v. —n. 1 a complaining long-drawn wail as of a dog. 2 a similar shrill prolonged sound. 3 a a querulous tone. b an instance of feeble or undignified complaining. —v. 1 intr. emit or utter a whine. 2 intr. complain in a querulous tone or in a feeble or undignified way. **3** *tr.* utter in a whining tone. □□**whiner** *n.* **whiningly** *adv.* **whiny** *adj.* (**whinier, whiniest**). [OE *hwīnan*]

whinge /wɪndʒ/ *v. & n. colloq.* —*v.intr.* whine; grumble peevishly. —*n.* a whining complaint; a peevish grumbling. □□**whinger** *n.* **whingingly** *adv.* **whingy** *adj.* [OE *hwinsian* f. Gmc]

whinny /ˈwɪnɪ/ *n. & v.* —*n.* (*pl.* **-ies**) a gentle or joyful neigh. —*v.intr.* (**-ies, -ied**) give a whinny. [imit.: cf. WHINE]

whinstone /ˈwɪnstəʊn/ *n.* = WHIN².

whip /wɪp/ *n. & v.* —*n.* **1** a lash attached to a stick for urging on animals or punishing etc. **2 a** a member of a political party in Parliament appointed to control its parliamentary discipline and tactics, esp. ensuring attendance and voting in debates. **b** *Brit.* the whips' written notice requesting or requiring attendance for voting at a division etc., variously underlined according to the degree of urgency (*three-line whip*). **c** (prec. by *the*) party discipline and instructions (*asked for the Labour whip*). **3** a dessert made with whipped cream etc. **4** the action of beating cream, eggs, etc., into a froth. **5** = WHIPPER-IN. **6** a rope-and-pulley hoisting apparatus. —*v.* (**whipped, whipping**) **1** *tr.* beat or urge on with a whip. **2** *tr.* beat (cream or eggs etc.) into a froth. **3** *tr. & intr.* take or move suddenly, unexpectedly, or rapidly (*whipped away the tablecloth*; *whipped out a knife*; *whip off your coat*; *whipped behind the door*). **4** *tr. Brit. sl.* steal (*who's whipped my pen?*). **5** *tr. sl.* **a** excel. **b** defeat. **6** *tr.* bind with spirally wound twine. **7** *tr.* sew with overcast stitches. □**whip-bird** any Australian bird of the genus *Psophodes* with a cry like the crack of a whip. **whip-crane** a light derrick with tackle for hoisting. **whip-graft** *Hort.* a graft with the tongue of the scion in a slot in the stock and vice versa. **whip hand 1** a hand that holds the whip (in riding etc.). **2** (usu. prec. by *the*) the advantage or control in any situation. **whip in** bring (hounds) together. **whip on** urge into action. **whip-round** esp. *Brit. colloq.* an informal collection of money from a group of people. **whip scorpion** any arachnid of the order Uropygi, with a long slender tail-like appendage, which secretes an irritating vapour. **whip snake** any of various long slender snakes of the family Colubridae. **whip-stitch** a stitch made by whipping. **whip up 1** excite or stir up (feeling etc.). **2** summon (attendance). □□**whipless** *adj.* **whiplike** *adj.* **whipper** *n.* [ME (*h*)*wippen* (v.), prob. f. MLG & MDu. *wippen* swing, leap, dance]

whipcord /ˈwɪpkɔːd/ *n.* **1** a tightly twisted cord such as is used for making whiplashes. **2** a close-woven worsted fabric.

whiplash /ˈwɪplæʃ/ *n.* **1** the flexible end of a whip. **2** a blow with a whip. □**whiplash injury** an injury to the neck caused by a jerk of the head, esp. as in a motor accident.

whipper-in /ˌwɪpəˈrɪn/ *n.* a huntsman's assistant who manages the hounds.

whippersnapper /ˈwɪpəˌsnæpə(r)/ *n.* **1** a small child. **2** an insignificant but presumptuous or intrusive (esp. young) person. [perh. for *whipsnapper*, implying noise and unimportance]

whippet /ˈwɪpɪt/ *n.* a cross-bred dog of the greyhound type used for racing. [prob. f. obs. *whippet* move briskly, f. *whip it*]

whipping /ˈwɪpɪŋ/ *n.* **1** a beating, esp. with a whip. **2** cord wound round in binding. □**whipping-boy 1** a scapegoat. **2** *hist.* a boy educated with a young prince and punished instead of him. **whipping-cream** cream suitable for whipping. **whipping-post** *hist.* a post used for public whippings. **whipping-top** a top kept spinning by blows of a lash.

whippletree /ˈwɪp(ə)lˌtriː/ *n.* = SWINGLETREE. [app. f. WHIP + TREE]

whippoorwill /ˈwɪpʊəˌwɪl/ *n.* an American nightjar, *Caprimulgus vociferus*. [imit. of its cry]

whippy /ˈwɪpɪ/ *adj.* (**whippier, whippiest**) flexible, springy. □□**whippiness** *n.*

whipsaw /ˈwɪpsɔː/ *n. & v.* —*n.* a saw with a narrow blade held at each end by a frame. —*v.* (*past part.* **-sawn** or **-sawed**) **1** *tr.* cut with a whipsaw. **2** *US sl.* **a** *tr.* cheat by joint action on two others. **b** *intr.* be cheated in this way.

whipstock /ˈwɪpstɒk/ *n.* the handle of a whip.

whir var. of WHIRR.

whirl /wɜːl/ *v. & n.* —*v.* **1** *tr. & intr.* swing round and round; revolve rapidly. **2** *tr. & intr.* (foll. by *away*) convey or go rapidly in a vehicle etc. **3** *tr. & intr.* send or travel swiftly in an orbit or a curve. **4** *intr.* **a** (of the brain, senses, etc.) seem to spin round. **b** (of thoughts etc.) be confused; follow each other in bewildering succession. —*n.* **1** a whirling movement (*vanished in a whirl of dust*). **2** a state of intense activity (*the social whirl*). **3** a state of confusion (*my mind is in a whirl*). **4** *colloq.* an attempt (*give it a whirl*). □**whirling dervish** see DERVISH. □□**whirler** *n.* **whirlingly** *adv.* [ME: (v.) f. ON *hvirfla*: (n.) f. MLG & MDu. *wervel* spindle & ON *hvirfill* circle f. Gmc]

whirligig /ˈwɜːlɪgɪg/ *n.* **1** a spinning or whirling toy. **2** a merry-go-round. **3** a revolving motion. **4** anything regarded as hectic or constantly changing (*the whirligig of time*). **5** any freshwater beetle of the family Gyrinidae that circles about on the surface. [ME f. WHIRL + obs. *gig* whipping-top]

whirlpool /ˈwɜːlpuːl/ *n.* a powerful circular eddy in the sea etc. often causing suction to its centre.

whirlwind /ˈwɜːlwɪnd/ *n.* **1** a mass or column of air whirling rapidly round and round in a cylindrical or funnel shape over land or water. **2** a confused tumultuous process. **3** (*attrib.*) very rapid (*a whirlwind romance*). □**reap the whirlwind** suffer worse results of a bad action.

whirlybird /ˈwɜːlɪˌbɜːd/ *n. colloq.* a helicopter.

whirr /wɜː(r)/ *n. & v.* (also **whir**) —*n.* a continuous rapid buzzing or softly clicking sound as of a bird's wings or of cog-wheels in constant motion. —*v.intr.* (**whirred, whirring**) make this sound. [ME, prob. Scand.: cf. Da. *hvirre*, Norw. *kvirra*, perh. rel. to WHIRL]

whisht /hwɪʃt/ *v.* (also **whist** /hwɪst/) esp. *Sc. & Ir. dial.* **1** *intr.* (esp. as *int.*) be quiet; hush. **2** *tr.* quieten. [imit.]

whisk /wɪsk/ *v. & n.* —*v.* **1** *tr.* (foll. by *away*, *off*) **a** brush with a sweeping movement. **b** take with a sudden motion (*whisked the plate away*). **2** *tr.* whip (cream, eggs, etc.). **3** *tr. & intr.* convey or go (esp. out of sight) lightly or quickly (*whisked me off to the doctor*; *the mouse whisked into its hole*). **4** *tr.* wave or lightly brandish. —*n.* **1** a whisking action or motion. **2** a utensil for whisking eggs or cream etc. **3** a bunch of grass, twigs, bristles, etc., for removing dust or flies. [ME *wisk*, prob. Scand.: cf. ON *visk* wisp]

whisker /ˈwɪskə(r)/ *n.* **1** (usu. in *pl.*) the hair growing on a man's face, esp. on the cheek. **2** each of the bristles on the face of a cat etc. **3** *colloq.* a small distance (*within a whisker of*; *won by a whisker*). **4** a strong hairlike crystal of metal etc. □**have** (or **have grown**) **whiskers** *colloq.* (esp. of a story etc.) be very old. □□**whiskered** *adj.* **whiskery** *adj.* [WHISK + -ER¹]

whisky /ˈwɪskɪ/ *n.* (*Ir., US* **whiskey**) (*pl.* **-ies** or **-eys**) **1** a spirit distilled esp. from malted barley, other grains, or potatoes, etc. **2** a drink of this. [abbr. of obs. *whiskybae*, var. of USQUEBAUGH]

whisper /ˈwɪspə(r)/ *v. & n.* —*v.* **1 a** *intr.* speak very softly without vibration of the vocal cords. **b** *intr. & tr.* talk or say in a barely audible tone or in a secret or confidential way. **2** *intr.* speak privately or conspiratorially. **3** *intr.* (of leaves, wind, or water) rustle or murmur. —*n.* **1** whispering speech (*talking in whispers*). **2** a whispering sound. **3** a thing whispered. **4** a rumour or piece of gossip. □**it is whispered** there is a rumour. **whispering-gallery**

a gallery esp. under a dome with acoustic properties such that a whisper may be heard round its entire circumference. □□ **whisperer** *n.* **whispering** *n.* [OE *hwisprian* f. Gmc]

whist[1] /wɪst/ *n.* a card-game usu. for four players, with the winning of tricks. □ **whist drive** a social occasion with the playing of progressive whist. [earlier *whisk*, perh. f. WHISK (with ref. to whisking away the tricks): perh. assoc. with WHIST[2]]

whist[2] var. of WHISHT.

whistle /'wɪs(ə)l/ *n.* & *v.* —*n.* **1** a clear shrill sound made by forcing breath through a small hole between nearly closed lips. **2** a similar sound made by a bird, the wind, a missile, etc. **3** an instrument used to produce such a sound. —*v.* **1** *intr.* emit a whistle. **2** a *intr.* give a signal or express surprise or derision by whistling. **b** *tr.* (often foll. by *up*) summon or give a signal to (a dog etc.) by whistling. **3** *tr.* (also *absol.*) produce (a tune) by whistling. **4** *intr.* (foll. by *for*) vainly seek or desire. □ **as clean** (or **clear** or **dry**) **as a whistle** very clean or clear or dry. **blow the whistle on** *colloq.* bring (an activity) to an end; inform on (those responsible). **whistle down the wind 1** let go, abandon. **2** turn (a hawk) loose. **whistle in the dark** pretend to be unafraid. **whistle-stop 1** *US* a small unimportant town on a railway. **2** a politician's brief pause for an electioneering speech on tour. **3** (*attrib.*) with brief pauses (*a whistle-stop tour*). **whistling kettle** a kettle fitted with a whistle sounded by steam when the kettle is boiling. [OE (*h*)*wistlian* (v.), (*h*)*wistle* (n.) of imit. orig.: cf. ON *hvísla* whisper, MSw. *hvisla* whistle]

whistler /'wɪslə(r)/ *n.* **1** any bird of the genus *Pachycephala*, with a whistling cry. **2** a kind of marmot.

Whit /wɪt/ *adj.* connected with, belonging to, or following Whit Sunday (*Whit Monday*; *Whit weekend*). □ **Whit Sunday** the seventh Sunday after Easter, commemorating the descent of the Holy Spirit at Pentecost (Acts 2). [OE *Hwīta Sunnandæg*, lit. white Sunday, prob. f. the white robes of the newly-baptized at Pentecost]

whit /wɪt/ *n.* a particle; a least amount (*not a whit better*). □ **every whit** the whole; wholly. **no** (or **never a** or **not a**) **whit** not at all. [earlier *w*(*h*)*yt* app. alt. f. WIGHT in phr. *no wight* etc.]

white /waɪt/ *adj.*, *n.*, & *v.* —*adj.* **1** resembling a surface reflecting sunlight without absorbing any of the visible rays; of the colour of milk or fresh snow. **2** approaching such a colour; pale esp. in the face (*turned as white as a sheet*). **3** less dark than other things of the same kind. **4** (**White**) **a** of the human group having light-coloured skin. **b** of or relating to White people. **5** albino (*white mouse*). **6 a** (of hair) having lost its colour esp. in old age. **b** (of a person) white-haired. **7** *colloq.* innocent, untainted. **8** (in *comb.*) (of esp. animals) having some white on the body (*white-throated*). **9 a** (of a plant) having white flowers or pale-coloured fruit etc. (*white hyacinth*; *white cauliflower*). **b** (of a tree) having light-coloured bark etc. (*white ash*; *white poplar*). **10** (of wine) made from white grapes or dark grapes with the skins removed. **11** (of coffee) with milk or cream added. **12** transparent, colourless (*white glass*). **13** *hist.* counter-revolutionary or reactionary (*white guard*; *white army*). —*n.* **1** a white colour or pigment. **2 a** white clothes or material (*dressed in white*). **b** (in *pl.*) white garments as worn in cricket, tennis, etc. **3 a** (in a game or sport) a white piece, ball, etc. **b** the player using such pieces. **4** the white part or albumen round the yolk of an egg. **5** the visible part of the eyeball round the iris. **6** (**White**) a member of a light-skinned race. **7** a white butterfly. **8** a blank space in printing. —*v.tr. archaic* make white. □ **bleed white** drain (a person, country, etc.) of wealth etc. **white admiral** a butterfly, *Limenitis camilla*, with a white band across its wings. **white ant** a termite.

white cell (or **corpuscle**) a leucocyte. **white Christmas** Christmas with snow on the ground. **white coal** water as a source of power. **white-collar** (of a worker) engaged in clerical or administrative rather than manual work. **white currant** a cultivar of redcurrant with pale edible berries. **whited sepulchre** see SEPULCHRE. **white dwarf** a small very dense star. **white elephant** a useless and troublesome possession or thing. **white ensign** see ENSIGN. **white feather** a symbol of cowardice (a white feather in the tail of a game-bird being a mark of bad breeding). **white fish** fish with pale flesh, e.g. plaice, cod, etc. **white flag** a symbol of surrender or a period of truce. **White Friar** a Carmelite. **white frost** see FROST. **white goods 1** domestic linen. **2** large domestic electrical equipment. **white heat 1** the temperature at which metal emits white light. **2** a state of intense passion or activity. **white hope** a person expected to achieve much for a group, organization, etc. **white horses** white-crested waves at sea. **white-hot** at white heat. **White House** the official residence of the US President in Washington. **white lead** a mixture of lead carbonate and hydrated lead oxide used as pigment. **white lie** a harmless or trivial untruth. **white light** colourless light, e.g. ordinary daylight. **white lime** lime mixed with water as a coating for walls; whitewash. **white magic** magic used only for beneficent purposes. **white matter** the part of the brain and spinal cord consisting mainly of nerve fibres (see also *grey matter*). **white meat** poultry, veal, rabbit, and pork. **white metal** a white or silvery alloy. **white monk** a Cistercian. **white night** a sleepless night. **white noise** noise containing many frequencies with equal intensities. **white-out** a dense blizzard esp. in polar regions. **white ox-eye** = *ox-eye daisy*. **White Paper** (in the UK) a Government report giving information or proposals on an issue. **white pepper** see PEPPER. **white poplar** = ABELE. **white rose** the emblem of Yorkshire or the House of York. **White Russian** a Belorussian. **white sale** a sale of household linen. **white sauce** a sauce of flour, melted butter, and milk or cream. **White slave** a woman tricked or forced into prostitution, usu. abroad. **White slavery** traffic in White slaves. **white sock** = STOCKING 3. **white spirit** light petroleum as a solvent. **white sugar** purified sugar. **white tie** a man's white bow-tie as part of full evening dress. **white vitriol** *Chem.* zinc sulphate. **white water** a shallow or foamy stretch of water. **white wedding** a wedding at which the bride wears a formal white wedding dress. **white whale** a northern cetacean, *Delphinapterus leucas*, white when adult: also called BELUGA. □□ **whitely** *adv.* **whiteness** *n.* **whitish** *adj.* [OE *hwīt* f. Gmc]

whitebait /'waɪtbeɪt/ *n.* (*pl.* same) **1** (usu. *pl.*) the small silvery-white young of herrings and sprats esp. as food. **2** *NZ* a young inanga.

whitebeam /'waɪtbiːm/ *n.* a rosaceous tree, *Sorbus aria*, having red berries and leaves with a white downy under-side.

whiteface /'waɪtfeɪs/ *n.* the white make-up of an actor etc.

whitefish /'waɪtfɪʃ/ *n.* (*pl.* same or **-fishes**) any freshwater fish of the genus *Coregonus* etc., of the trout family, and used esp. for food.

whitefly /'waɪtflaɪ/ *n.* (*pl.* **-flies**) any small insect of the family Aleyrodidae, having wings covered with white powder and feeding on the sap of shrubs, crops, etc.

Whitehall /'waɪthɔːl/ *n.* **1** the British Government. **2** its offices or policy. [a street in London in which Government offices are situated]

whitehead /'waɪthed/ *n. colloq.* a white or white-topped skin-pustule.

whiten /'waɪt(ə)n/ *v.tr.* & *intr.* make or become white. □□ **whitener** *n.* **whitening** *n.*

whitesmith /ˈwaɪtsmɪθ/ n. **1** a worker in tin. **2** a polisher or finisher of metal goods.

whitethorn /ˈwaɪtθɔːn/ n. the hawthorn.

whitethroat /ˈwaɪtθrəʊt/ n. a warbler, *Sylvia communis*, with a white patch on the throat.

whitewash /ˈwaɪtwɒʃ/ n. & v. —n. **1** a solution of quicklime or of whiting and size for whitening walls etc. **2** a means employed to conceal mistakes or faults in order to clear a person or institution of imputations. —v.tr. **1** cover with whitewash. **2** attempt by concealment to clear the reputation of. **3** (in *passive*) (of an insolvent) get a fresh start by passage through a bankruptcy court. **4** *US* defeat (an opponent) without allowing any opposing score. □□ **whitewasher** n.

whitewood /ˈwaɪtwʊd/ n. a light-coloured wood esp. prepared for staining etc.

Whitey /ˈwaɪtɪ/ n. (pl. **-eys**) sl. offens. **1** a White person. **2** White people collectively.

whither /ˈwɪðə(r)/ adv. & conj. archaic —adv. **1** to what place, position, or state? **2** (prec. by *place* etc.) to which (*the house whither we were walking*). —conj. **1** to the or any place to which (*go whither you will*). **2** and thither (*we saw a house, whither we walked*). [OE *hwider* f. Gmc: cf. WHICH, HITHER, THITHER]

whithersoever /ˌwɪðəsəʊˈevə(r)/ adj. & conj. archaic to any place to which.

whiting[1] /ˈwaɪtɪŋ/ n. a small white-fleshed fish, *Merlangus merlangus*, used as food. [ME f. MDu. *wijting*. app. formed as WHITE + -ING[3]]

whiting[2] /ˈwaɪtɪŋ/ n. ground chalk used in whitewashing, plate-cleaning, etc.

whitleather /ˈwɪtˌleðə(r)/ n. tawed leather. [ME f. WHITE + LEATHER]

whitlow /ˈwɪtləʊ/ n. an inflammation near a fingernail or toenail. [ME *whitflaw, -flow*, app. = WHITE + FLAW[1] in the sense 'crack', but perh. of LG orig.: cf. Du. *fijt*, LG *fīt* whitlow]

Whitsun /ˈwɪts(ə)n/ n. & adj. —n. = WHITSUNTIDE. —adj. = WHIT. [ME, f. *Whitsun Day* = Whit Sunday]

Whitsuntide /ˈwɪts(ə)nˌtaɪd/ n. the weekend or week including Whit Sunday.

whittle /ˈwɪt(ə)l/ v. **1** tr. & (foll. by *at*) intr. pare (wood etc.) with repeated slicing with a knife. **2** tr. (often foll. by *away, down*) reduce by repeated subtractions. [var. of ME *thwitel* long knife f. OE *thwītan* to cut off]

whity /ˈwaɪtɪ/ adj. whitish; rather white (usu. in comb.: *whity-brown*) (cf. WHITEY).

whiz /wɪz/ n. & v. (also **whizz**) colloq. —n. **1** the sound made by the friction of a body moving through the air at great speed. **2** (also **wiz**) colloq. a person who is remarkable or skilful in some respect (*is a whiz at chess*). —v.intr. (**whizzed, whizzing**) move with or make a whiz. □ **whiz-bang** colloq. **1** a high-velocity shell from a small-calibre gun, whose passage is heard before the gun's report. **2** a jumping kind of firework. **whiz-kid** colloq. a brilliant or highly successful young person. [imit.: in sense 2 infl. by WIZARD]

WHO abbr. World Health Organization.

who /huː/ pron. (obj. **whom** /huːm/ or colloq. **who**; poss. **whose** /huːz/) **1 a** what or which person or persons? (*who called?; you know who it was; whom or who did you see?*). ¶ In the last example *whom* is correct but *who* is common in less formal contexts. **b** what sort of person or persons? (*who am I to object?*). **2** (a person) that (*anyone who wishes can come; the woman whom you met; the man who you saw*). ¶ In the last two examples *whom* is correct but *who* is common in less formal contexts. **3** and or but he, she, they, etc. (*gave it to Tom, who sold it to Jim*). **4** archaic the or any person or persons that (*whom the gods love die young*). □ **as who should say** like a person who said; as though one said. **who-does-what** (of a dispute etc.) about which group of workers should do a particular job. **who**

goes there? see GO[1]. **who's who 1** who or what each person is (*know who's who*). **2** a list or directory with facts about notable persons. [OE *hwā* f. Gmc: whom f. OE dative *hwām, hwǣm*: whose f. genit. *hwæs*]

whoa /wəʊ/ int. used as a command to stop or slow a horse etc. [var. of HO]

who'd /huːd/ contr. **1** who had. **2** who would.

whodunit /huːˈdʌnɪt/ n. (also **whodunnit**) colloq. a story or play about the detection of a crime etc., esp. murder. [= *who done* (illiterate for *did*) *it?*]

whoe'er /huːˈeə(r)/ poet. var. of WHOEVER.

whoever /huːˈevə(r)/ pron. (obj. **whomever** /huːm-/ or colloq. **whoever**; poss. **whosever** /huːz-/) **1** the or any person or persons who (*whoever comes is welcome*). **2** though anyone (*whoever else objects, I do not; whosever it is, I want it*). **3** colloq. (as an intensive) who ever; who at all (*whoever heard of such a thing?*).

whole /həʊl/ adj. & n. —adj. **1** in an uninjured, unbroken, intact, or undiminished state (*swallowed it whole; there is not a plate left whole*). **2** not less than; all there is of; entire, complete (*waited a whole year; tell the whole truth; the whole school knows*). **3** (of blood or milk etc.) with no part removed. —n. **1** a thing complete in itself. **2** all there is of a thing (*spent the whole of the summer by the sea*). **3** (foll. by *of*) all members, inhabitants, etc., of (*the whole of London knows it*). □ **as a whole** as a unity; not as separate parts. **go the whole hog** see HOG. **on the whole** taking everything relevant into account; in general (*it was, on the whole, a good report; they behaved well on the whole*). **whole cloth** cloth of full size as manufactured. **whole holiday** a whole day taken as a holiday (cf. *half holiday*). **whole-life insurance** life insurance for which premiums are payable throughout the remaining life of the person insured. **whole lot** see LOT. **whole note** esp. *US Mus.* = SEMIBREVE. **whole number** a number without fractions; an integer. **whole-tone scale** *Mus.* a scale consisting entirely of tones, with no semitones. □□ **wholeness** n. [OE *hāl* f. Gmc]

wholefood /ˈhəʊlfuːd/ n. food which has not been unnecessarily processed or refined.

wholegrain /ˈhəʊlgreɪn/ adj. made with or containing whole grains (*wholegrain bread*).

wholehearted /həʊlˈhɑːtɪd/ adj. **1** (of a person) completely devoted or committed. **2** (of an action etc.) done with all possible effort, attention, or sincerity; thorough. □□ **wholeheartedly** adv. **wholeheartedness** n.

wholemeal /ˈhəʊlmiːl/ n. (usu. *attrib.*) *Brit.* meal of wheat or other cereals with none of the bran or germ removed.

wholesale /ˈhəʊlseɪl/ n., adj., adv., & v. —n. the selling of things in large quantities to be retailed by others (cf. RETAIL). —adj. & adv. **1** by wholesale; at a wholesale price (*can get it for you wholesale*). **2** on a large scale (*wholesale destruction occurred; was handing out samples wholesale*). —v.tr. sell wholesale. □□ **wholesaler** n. [ME: orig. *by whole sale*]

wholesome /ˈhəʊlsəm/ adj. **1** promoting or indicating physical, mental, or moral health (*wholesome pursuits; a wholesome appearance*). **2** prudent (*wholesome respect*). □□ **wholesomely** adv. **wholesomeness** n. [ME, prob. f. OE (unrecorded) *hālsum* (as WHOLE, -SOME[1])]

wholewheat /ˈhəʊlwiːt/ n. (usu. *attrib.*) wheat with none of the bran or germ removed; wholemeal.

wholism var. of HOLISM.

wholly /ˈhəʊllɪ/ adv. **1** entirely; without limitation or diminution (*I am wholly at a loss*). **2** purely, exclusively (*a wholly bad example*). [ME, f. OE (unrecorded) *hāllīce* (as WHOLE, -LY[2])]

whom objective case of WHO.

whomever objective case of WHOEVER.

whomso archaic objective case of WHOSO.

whomsoever objective case of WHOSOEVER.

whoop /huːp, wuːp/ n. & v. (also **hoop**) —n. **1** a loud cry of or as of excitement etc. **2** a long rasping indrawn breath in whooping cough. —v.intr. utter a whoop. □**whooping cough** an infectious bacterial disease, esp. of children, with a series of short violent coughs followed by a whoop. **whooping swan** a swan, *Cygnus cygnus*, with a characteristic whooping sound in flight. **whoop it up** *colloq.* **1** engage in revelry. **2** *US* make a stir. [ME: imit.]

whoopee int. & n. *colloq.* —int. /wʊˈpiː/ expressing exuberant joy. —n. /ˈwʊpɪ/ exuberant enjoyment or revelry. □**make whoopee** *colloq.* rejoice noisily or hilariously. **whoopee cushion** a rubber cushion that when sat on makes a sound like the breaking of wind.

whooper /ˈhuːpə(r)/ n. a whooping swan.

whoops /wʊps/ int. *colloq.* expressing surprise or apology, esp. on making an obvious mistake. [var. of OOPS]

whoosh /wʊʃ/ v., n., & int. (also **woosh**) —v.intr. & tr. move or cause to move with a rushing sound. —n. a sudden movement accompanied by a rushing sound. —int. an exclamation imitating this. [imit.]

whop /wɒp/ v.tr. (**whopped, whopping**) *sl.* **1** thrash. **2** defeat, overcome. [ME: var. of dial. *wap*, of unkn. orig.]

whopper /ˈwɒpə(r)/ n. *sl.* **1** something big of its kind. **2** a great lie.

whopping /ˈwɒpɪŋ/ adj. *sl.* very big (*a whopping lie*; *a whopping fish*).

whore /hɔː(r)/ n. & v. —n. **1** a prostitute. **2** *derog.* a promiscuous woman. —v.intr. **1** (of a man) seek or chase after whores. **2** *archaic* (foll. by *after*) commit idolatry or iniquity. □**whore-house** a brothel. □□ **whoredom** n. **whorer** n. [OE *hōre* f. Gmc]

whoremaster /ˈhɔːˌmɑːstə(r)/ n. *archaic* = WHOREMONGER.

whoremonger /ˈhɔːˌmʌŋgə(r)/ n. *archaic* a person who has dealings with whores.

whoreson /ˈhɔːs(ə)n/ n. *archaic* **1** a disliked person. **2** (*attrib.*) (of a person or thing) vile.

whorish /ˈhɔːrɪʃ/ adj. of or like a whore. □□ **whorishly** adv. **whorishness** n.

whorl /wɔːl, wɜːl/ n. **1** a ring of leaves or other organs round a stem of a plant. **2** one turn of a spiral, esp. on a shell. **3** a complete circle in a fingerprint. **4** *archaic* a small wheel on a spindle steadying its motion. □□ **whorled** adj. [ME *wharwyl*, *whorwil*, app. var. of WHIRL: infl. by *wharve* (n.) = whorl of a spindle]

whortleberry /ˈwɜːt(ə)lˌberɪ/ n. (*pl.* **-ies**) a bilberry. [16th c.: dial. form of *hurtleberry*, ME, of unkn. orig.]

whose /huːz/ pron. & adj. —pron. of or belonging to which person (*whose is this book?*). —adj. of whom or which (*whose book is this?*; *the man, whose name was Tim*; *the house whose roof was damaged*).

whoseso *archaic* poss. of WHOSO.

whosesoever poss. of WHOSOEVER.

whosever /huːˈzevə(r)/ poss. of WHOEVER.

whoso /ˈhuːsəʊ/ pron. (*obj.* **whomso** /ˈhuːm-/; poss. **whoseso** /ˈhuːz-/) *archaic* = WHOEVER. [ME, = WHO + SO[1], f. OE *swā hwā swā*]

whosoever /ˌhuːsəʊˈevə(r)/ pron. (*obj.* **whomsoever** /ˌhuːm-/; poss. **whosesoever** /ˌhuːz-/) *archaic* = WHOEVER.

why /waɪ/ adv., int., & n. —adv. **1** for what reason or purpose (*why did you do it?*; *I do not know why you came*). **b** on what grounds (*why do you say that?*). **2** (prec. by *reason* etc.) for which (*the reasons why I did it*). —int. expressing: **1** surprised discovery or recognition (*why, it's you!*). **2** impatience (*why, of course I do!*). **3** reflection (*why, yes, I think so*). **4** objection (*why, what is wrong with it?*). —n. (*pl.* **whys**) a reason or explanation (esp. *whys and wherefores*). □**why so?** on what grounds?; for what reason or purpose? [OE *hwī, hwȳ* instr. of *hwæt* WHAT f. Gmc]

whydah /ˈwiːdə/ n. (also **whidah**) any small African weaver-bird of the genus *Vidua*, the male having mainly black plumage and tail-feathers of great length. [orig. *widow-bird*, altered f. assoc. with *Whidah* (now Ouidah) in Benin]

WI *abbr.* **1** West Indies. **2** *Brit.* Women's Institute. **3** *US* Wisconsin (in official postal use).

wich- var. of WYCH-.

wick[1] /wɪk/ n. **1** a strip or thread of fibrous or spongy material feeding a flame with fuel in a candle, lamp, etc. **2** *Surgery* a gauze strip inserted in a wound to drain it. □**dip one's wick** *coarse sl.* (of a man) have sexual intercourse. **get on a person's wick** *Brit. colloq.* annoy a person. [OE *wēoce, -wēoc* (cf. MDu. *wiecke*, MLG *wēke*), of unkn. orig.]

wick[2] /wɪk/ n. *dial.* exc. in compounds e.g. *bailiwick*, and in place-names e.g. *Hampton Wick*, *Warwick* **1** a town, hamlet, or district. **2** a dairy farm. [OE *wīc*, prob. f. Gmc f. L *vicus* street, village]

wicked /ˈwɪkɪd/ adj. (**wickeder, wickedest**) **1** sinful, iniquitous, given to or involving immorality. **2** spiteful, ill-tempered; intending or intended to give pain. **3** playfully malicious. **4** *colloq.* foul; very bad; formidable (*wicked weather*; *a wicked cough*). **5** *sl.* excellent, remarkable. □**Wicked Bible** an edition of 1631, with the misprinted commandment 'thou shalt commit adultery'. □□ **wickedly** adv. **wickedness** n. [ME f. obs. *wick* (perh. adj. use of OE *wicca* wizard) + -ED[1] as in *wretched*]

wicker /ˈwɪkə(r)/ n. plaited twigs or osiers etc. as material for chairs, baskets, mats, etc. [ME, f. E.Scand.: cf. Sw. *viker* willow, rel. to *vika* bend]

wickerwork /ˈwɪkəˌwɜːk/ n. **1** wicker. **2** things made of wicker.

wicket /ˈwɪkɪt/ n. **1** *Cricket* **a** a set of three stumps with the bails in position defended by a batsman. **b** the ground between two wickets. **c** the state of this (*a slow wicket*). **d** an instance of a batsman being got out (*bowler has taken four wickets*). **e** a pair of batsmen batting at the same time (*a third-wicket partnership*). **2** (in full **wicket-door** or **-gate**) a small door or gate esp. beside or in a larger one or closing the lower part only of a doorway. **3** *US* an aperture in a door or wall usu. closed with a sliding panel. **4** *US* a croquet hoop. □**at the wicket** *Cricket* **1** batting. **2** by the wicket-keeper (*caught at the wicket*). **keep wicket** *Cricket* be a wicket-keeper. **on a good** (or **sticky**) **wicket** *colloq.* in a favourable (or unfavourable) position. **wicket-keeper** *Cricket* the fieldsman stationed close behind a batsman's wicket. [ME f. AF & ONF *wiket*, OF *guichet*, of uncert. orig.]

wickiup /ˈwɪkiˌʌp/ n. an American Indian hut of a frame covered with grass etc. [Fox *wikiyap*]

widdershins var. of WITHERSHINS.

wide /waɪd/ adj., adv., & n. —adj. **1 a** measuring much or more than other things of the same kind across or from side to side. **b** considerable; more than is needed (*a wide margin*). **2** (following a measurement) in width (*a metre wide*). **3** extending far; embracing much; of great extent (*has a wide range*; *has wide experience*; *reached a wide public*). **4** not tight or close or restricted; loose. **5 a** free, liberal; unprejudiced (*takes wide views*). **b** not specialized; general. **6** open to the full extent (*staring with wide eyes*). **7 a** (foll. by *of*) not within a reasonable distance of. **b** at a considerable distance from a point or mark. **8** *Brit. sl.* shrewd; skilled in sharp practice (*wide boy*). **9** (in comb.) extending over the whole of (*nationwide*). —adv. **1** widely. **2** to the full extent (*wide awake*). **3** far from the target etc. (*is shooting wide*). —n. **1** *Cricket* a ball judged to pass the wicket beyond the batsman's reach and so scoring a run. **2** (prec. by *the*) the wide world. □**give a wide berth to** see BERTH. **wide-angle** (of a lens) having a short focal length and hence a field covering a wide angle. **wide awake 1** fully awake. **2** *colloq.* wary, knowing. **wide ball** *Cricket* (sense 1 of n.). **wide-eyed** surprised or naïve. **wide of the mark** see MARK[1]. **wide open** (often foll. by *to*) exposed or vulnerable (to attack etc.). **wide-ranging** covering an extensive range. **the wide world** all the world great as it is. □□**wideness** n. **widish** adj. [OE *wīd* (adj.), *wīde* (adv.) f. Gmc]

wideawake /'waɪdə,weɪk/ n. a soft felt hat with a low crown and wide brim.

widely /'waɪdlɪ/ adv. **1** to a wide extent; far apart. **2** extensively (*widely read*; *widely distributed*). **3** by many people (*it is widely thought that*). **4** considerably; to a large degree (*holds a widely different view*).

widen /'waɪd(ə)n/ v.tr. & intr. make or become wider. □□**widener** n.

widespread /'waɪdspred, -'spred/ adj. widely distributed or disseminated.

widgeon /'wɪdʒ(ə)n/ n. (also **wigeon**) a species of dabbling duck, esp. *Anas penelope* or *Anas americana*. [16th c.: orig. uncert.]

widget /'wɪdʒɪt/ n. colloq. any gadget or device. [perh. alt. of GADGET]

widow /'wɪdəʊ/ n. & v. —n. **1** a woman who has lost her husband by death and has not married again. **2** a woman whose husband is often away on a specified activity (*golf widow*). **3** extra cards dealt separately and taken by the highest bidder. **4** *Printing* the short last line of a paragraph at the top of a page or column. —v.tr. **1** make into a widow or widower. **2** (as **widowed** adj.) bereft by the death of a spouse (*my widowed mother*). **3** (foll. by *of*) deprive of. □**widow-bird** a whydah. **widow's cruse** an apparently small supply that proves or seems inexhaustible (see 1 Kgs. 17:10-16). **widow's mite** a small money contribution (see Mark 12:42). **widow's peak** a V-shaped growth of hair towards the centre of the forehead. **widow's weeds** see WEEDS. [OE *widewe*, rel. to OHG *wituwa*, Skr. *vidhávā*, L *viduus* bereft, widowed, Gk *ēitheos* unmarried man]

widower /'wɪdəʊə(r)/ n. a man who has lost his wife by death and has not married again.

widowhood /'wɪdəʊ,hʊd/ n. the state or period of being a widow.

width /wɪdθ, wɪdθ/ n. **1** measurement or distance from side to side. **2** a large extent. **3** breadth or liberality of thought, views, etc. **4** a strip of material of full width as woven. □□**widthways** adv. **widthwise** adv. [17th c. (as WIDE, -TH²) replacing *wideness*]

wield /wiːld/ v.tr. **1** hold and use (a weapon or tool). **2** exert or command (power or authority etc.). □□ **wielder** n. [OE *wealdan*, *wieldan* f. Gmc]

wieldy /'wiːldɪ/ adj. (**wieldier**, **wieldiest**) easily wielded, controlled, or handled.

Wiener schnitzel /'viːnə ʃnɪts(ə)l/ n. a veal escalope breaded, fried, and garnished. [G, = Viennese slice]

wife /waɪf/ n. (pl. **wives** /waɪvz/) **1** a married woman esp. in relation to her husband. **2** archaic a woman, esp. an old or uneducated one. **3** (in comb.) a woman engaged in a specified activity (*fishwife*; *housewife*; *midwife*). □**have** (or **take**) **to wife** archaic marry (a woman). **wife-swapping** colloq. exchanging wives for sexual relations. □□**wifehood** n. **wifeless** adj. **wifelike** adj. **wifely** adj. **wifeliness** n. **wifish** adj. [OE *wīf* woman: ult. orig. unkn.]

wig¹ /wɪg/ n. an artificial head of hair esp. to conceal baldness or as a disguise, or worn by a judge or barrister or as period dress. □□**wigged** adj. (also in comb.). **wigless** adj. [abbr. of PERIWIG: cf. WINKLE]

wig² /wɪg/ v.tr. (**wigged**, **wigging**) colloq. rebuke sharply; rate. [app. f. WIG¹ in sl. or colloq. sense 'rebuke' (19th c.)]

wigeon var. of WIDGEON.

wigging /'wɪgɪŋ/ n. colloq. a reprimand.

wiggle /'wɪg(ə)l/ v. & n. colloq. —v.intr. & tr. move or cause to move quickly from side to side etc. —n. an act of wiggling. □□ **wiggler** n. [ME f. MLG & MDu. *wiggelen*: cf. WAG¹, WAGGLE]

wiggly /'wɪglɪ/ adj. (**wigglier**, **wiggliest**) colloq. **1**

showing wiggles. **2** having small irregular undulations.

wight /waɪt/ n. archaic a person (*wretched wight*). [OE *wiht* = thing, creature, of unkn. orig.]

wigwag /'wɪgwæg/ v.intr. (**wigwagged**, **wigwagging**) colloq. **1** move lightly to and fro. **2** wave flags in this way in signalling. [redupl. f. WAG¹]

wigwam /'wɪgwæm/ n. **1** a N. American Indian's hut or tent of skins, mats, or bark on poles. **2** a similar structure for children etc. [Ojibwa *wigwaum*, Algonquin *wikiwam* their house]

wilco /'wɪlkəʊ/ int. colloq. expressing compliance or agreement, esp. acceptance of instructions received by radio. [abbr. of *will comply*]

wild /waɪld/ adj., adv., & n. —adj. **1** (of an animal or plant) in its original natural state; not domesticated or cultivated (esp. of species or varieties allied to others that are not wild). **2** not civilized; barbarous. **3** (of scenery etc.) having a conspicuously desolate appearance. **4** unrestrained, disorderly, uncontrolled (*a wild youth*; *wild hair*). **5** tempestuous, violent (*a wild night*). **6 a** intensely eager; excited, frantic (*wild with excitement*; *wild delight*). **b** (of looks, appearance, etc.) indicating distraction. **c** (foll. by *about*) colloq. enthusiastically devoted to (a person or subject). **7** colloq. infuriated, angry (*makes me wild*). **8** haphazard, ill-aimed, rash (*a wild guess*; *a wild shot*; *a wild venture*). **9** (of a horse, game-bird, etc.) shy; easily startled. **10** colloq. exciting, delightful. **11** (of a card) having any rank chosen by the player holding it (*the joker is wild*). —adv. in a wild manner (*shooting wild*). —n. **1** a wild tract. **2** a desert. □**in the wild** in an uncultivated etc. state. **in** (or **out in**) **the wilds** colloq. far from normal habitation. **run wild** grow or stray unchecked or undisciplined. **sow one's wild oats** see OAT. **wild and woolly** uncouth; lacking refinement. **wild boar** see BOAR. **wild card 1** see sense 11 of adj. **2** *Computing* a character that will match any character or sequence of characters in a file name etc. **3** *Sport* an extra player or team chosen to enter a competition at the selectors' discretion. **wild cat** any of various smallish cats, esp. the European *Felis sylvestris* (cf. WILDCAT). **wild-goose chase** a foolish or hopeless and unproductive quest. **wild horse 1** a horse not domesticated or broken in. **2** (in pl.) colloq. even the most powerful influence etc. (*wild horses would not drag the secret from me*). **wild hyacinth** = BLUEBELL 1. **wild man of the woods** colloq. an orang-utan. **wild rice** any tall grass of the genus *Zizania*, yielding edible grains. **wild silk 1** silk from wild silkworms. **2** an imitation of this from short silk fibres. **Wild West** the western US in a time of lawlessness in its early history. □□**wildish** adj. **wildly** adv. **wildness** n. [OE *wilde* f. Gmc]

wildcat /'waɪldkæt/ n. & adj. —n. **1** a hot-tempered or violent person. **2** US a bobcat (cf. *wild cat*). **3** an exploratory oil well. —adj. (attrib.) **1** esp. US reckless; financially unsound. **2** (of a strike) sudden and unofficial.

wildebeest /'wɪldə,biːst, 'vɪl-/ n. = GNU. [Afrik. (as WILD, BEAST)]

wilder /'wɪldə(r)/ v.tr. archaic **1** lead astray. **2** bewilder. [perh. based on WILDERNESS]

wilderness /'wɪldənɪs/ n. **1** a desert; an uncultivated and uninhabited region. **2** part of a garden left with an uncultivated appearance. **3** (foll. by *of*) a confused assemblage of things. □**in the wilderness** out of political office. **voice in the wilderness** an unheeded advocate of reform (see Matt. 3:3 etc.). [OE *wildēornes* f. *wild dēor* wild deer]

wildfire /'waɪld,faɪə(r)/ n. hist. **1** a combustible liquid, esp. Greek fire, formerly used in warfare. **2** = WILL-O'-THE-WISP. □**spread like wildfire** spread with great speed.

wildfowl /'waɪldfaʊl/ n. (pl. same) a game-bird, esp. an aquatic one.

wilding /'waɪldɪŋ/ n. (also **wildling** /-lɪŋ/) **1** a plant sown by natural agency, esp. a wild crab-apple. **2** the fruit of such a plant. [WILD + -ING³]

wildlife /ˈwaɪldlaɪf/ *n.* wild animals collectively.

wildwood /ˈwaɪldwʊd/ *n. poet.* uncultivated or unfrequented woodland.

wile /waɪl/ *n. & v.* —*n.* (usu. in *pl.*) a stratagem; a trick or cunning procedure. —*v.tr.* (foll. by *away*, *into*, etc.) lure or entice. [ME *wīl*, perh. f. Scand. (ON *vél* craft)]

wilful /ˈwɪlfʊl/ *adj.* (*US* **willful**) **1** (of an action or state) intentional, deliberate (*wilful murder*; *wilful neglect*; *wilful disobedience*). **2** (of a person) obstinate, headstrong. □□ **wilfully** *adv.* **wilfulness** *n.* [ME f. WILL² + -FUL]

wilga /ˈwɪlgə/ *n. Austral.* a small tree of the genus *Geijera*, with white flowers. [Aboriginal]

wiliness see WILY.

will¹ /wɪl/ *v.aux. & tr.* (*3rd sing. present* **will**; *past* **would** /wʊd/) (foll. by infin. without *to*, or *absol.*; present and past only in use) **1** (in the 2nd and 3rd persons, and often in the 1st: see SHALL) expressing the future tense in statements, commands, or questions (*you will regret this*; *they will leave at once*; *will you go to the party?*). In the 1st person) expressing a wish or intention (*I will return soon*). ¶ For the other persons in senses 1, 2, see SHALL. **3** expressing desire, consent, or inclination (*will you have a sandwich?*; *come when you will*; *the door will not open*). **4** expressing ability or capacity (*the jar will hold a kilo*). **5** expressing habitual or inevitable tendency (*accidents will happen*; *will sit there for hours*). **6** expressing probability or expectation (*that will be my wife*). □ **will do** *colloq.* expressing willingness to carry out a request. [OE *wyllan*, (unrecorded) *willan* f. Gmc: rel. to L *volo*]

will² /wɪl/ *n. & v.* —*n.* **1** the faculty by which a person decides or is regarded as deciding on and initiating action (*the mind consists of the understanding and the will*). **2** (also **will-power**) control exercised by deliberate purpose over impulse; self-control (*has a strong will*; *overcame his shyness by will-power*). **3** a deliberate or fixed desire or intention (*a will to live*). **4** energy of intention; the power of effecting one's intentions or dominating others. **5** directions (usu. written) in legal form for the disposition of one's property after death (*make one's will*). **6** disposition towards others (*good will*). **7** *archaic* what one desires or ordains (*thy will be done*). —*v.tr.* **1** have as the object of one's will; intend unconditionally (*what God wills*; *willed that we should succeed*). **2** (*absol.*) exercise will-power. **3** instigate or impel by the exercise of will-power (*you can will yourself into contentment*). **4** bequeath by the terms of a will (*shall will my money to charity*). □ **at will 1** whenever one pleases. **2** *Law* able to be evicted without notice (*tenant at will*). **have one's will** obtain what one wants. **what is your will?** what do you wish done? **where there's a will there's a way** determination will overcome any obstacle. **a will of one's own** obstinacy; wilfulness of character. **with the best will in the world** however good one's intentions. **with a will** energetically or resolutely. □□ **willed** *adj.* (also in *comb.*). **willer** *n.* **will-less** *adj.* [OE *willa* f. Gmc]

willet /ˈwɪlɪt/ *n.* (*pl.* same) a large N. American wader, *Catoptrophorus semipalmatus*. [*pill-will-willet*, imit. of its cry]

willful *US* var. of WILFUL.

willie var. of WILLY.

willies /ˈwɪlɪz/ *n.pl. colloq.* nervous discomfort (esp. *give* or *get the willies*). [19th c.: orig. unkn.]

willing /ˈwɪlɪŋ/ *adj. & n.* —*adj.* **1** ready to consent or undertake (*a willing ally*; *am willing to do it*). **2** given or done etc. by a willing person (*willing hands*; *willing help*). —*n.* cheerful intention (*show willing*). □□ **willingly** *adv.* **willingness** *n.*

will-o'-the-wisp /ˌwɪləðəˈwɪsp/ *n.* **1** a phosphorescent light seen on marshy ground, perhaps resulting from the combustion of gases. **2** an elusive person. **3** a delusive hope or plan. [orig. *Will with the wisp*: *wisp* = handful of (lighted) hay etc.]

willow /ˈwɪləʊ/ *n.* **1** a tree or shrub of the genus *Salix*, growing usu. near water in temperate climates, with small flowers borne on catkins, and pliant branches yielding osiers and timber for cricket-bats, baskets, etc. **2** a cricket-bat. □ **willow grouse** a common European grouse, *Lagopus lagopus*, with brown breeding plumage and white winter plumage. **willow-herb** any plant of the genus *Epilobium* etc., esp. one with leaves like a willow and pale purple flowers. **willow-pattern** a conventional design representing a Chinese scene, often with a willow tree, of blue on white porcelain, stoneware, or earthenware. **willow-warbler** (or **-wren**) a small woodland bird, *Phylloscopus trochilus*, with a tuneful song. [OE *welig*]

willowy /ˈwɪləʊɪ/ *adj.* **1** having or bordered by willows. **2** lithe and slender.

willy /ˈwɪlɪ/ *n.* (also **willie**) (*pl.* **-ies**) *Brit. sl.* the penis.

willy-nilly /ˌwɪlɪˈnɪlɪ/ *adv. & adj.* —*adv.* whether one likes it or not. —*adj.* existing or occurring willy-nilly. [later spelling of *will I*, *nill I* I am willing, I am unwilling]

willy-willy /ˈwɪlɪˌwɪlɪ/ *n.* (*pl.* **-ies**) *Austral.* a cyclone or dust-storm. [Aboriginal]

wilt¹ /wɪlt/ *v. & n.* —*v.* **1** *intr.* (of a plant, leaf, or flower) wither, droop. **2** *intr.* (of a person) lose one's energy, flag, tire, droop. **3** *tr.* cause to wilt. —*n.* a plant-disease causing wilting. [orig. dial.: perh. alt. f. *wilk*, *welk*, of LG or Du. orig.]

wilt² /wɪlt/ *archaic 2nd person sing.* of WILL¹.

Wilton /ˈwɪlt(ə)n/ *n.* a kind of woven carpet with a thick pile. [*Wilton* in S. England]

Wilts. /wɪlts/ *abbr.* Wiltshire.

wily /ˈwaɪlɪ/ *adj.* (**wilier**, **wiliest**) full of wiles; crafty, cunning. □□ **wilily** *adv.* **wiliness** *n.*

wimp /wɪmp/ *n. colloq.* a feeble or ineffectual person. □□ **wimpish** *adj.* **wimpishly** *adv.* **wimpishness** *n.* **wimpy** *adj.* [20th c.: orig. uncert.]

wimple /ˈwɪmp(ə)l/ *n. & v.* —*n.* a linen or silk head-dress covering the neck and the sides of the face, formerly worn by women and still worn by some nuns. —*v.tr. & intr.* arrange or fall in folds. [OE *wimpel*]

Wimpy /ˈwɪmpɪ/ *n.* (*pl.* **-ies**) *propr.* a hamburger served in a plain bun.

Wimshurst machine /ˈwɪmzhɜːst/ *n.* a device for generating an electric charge by turning glass discs in opposite directions. [J. *Wimshurst*, Engl. engineer d. 1903]

win /wɪn/ *v. & n.* —*v.* (**winning**; *past* and *past part.* **won** /wʌn/) **1** *tr.* acquire or secure as a result of a fight, contest, bet, litigation, or some other effort (*won some money*; *won my admiration*). **2** *tr.* be victorious in (a fight, game, race, etc.). **3** *intr.* **a** be the victor; win a race or contest etc. (*who won?*; *persevere, and you will win*). **b** (foll. by *through*, *free*, etc.) make one's way or become by successful effort. **4** *tr.* reach by effort (*win the summit*; *win the shore*). **5** *tr.* obtain (ore) from a mine. **6** *tr.* dry (hay etc.) by exposure to the air. —*n.* victory in a game or bet etc. □ **win the day** be victorious in battle, argument, etc. **win over** persuade, gain the support of. **win one's spurs 1** *colloq.* gain distinction or fame. **2** *hist.* gain a knighthood. **win through** (or **out**) overcome obstacles. **you can't win** *colloq.* there is no way to succeed. **you can't win them all** *colloq.* a resigned expression of consolation on failure. □□ **winnable** *adj.* [OE *winnan* toil, endure: cf. OHG *winnan*, ON *vinna*]

wince¹ /wɪns/ *n. & v.* —*n.* a start or involuntary shrinking movement showing pain or distress. —*v.intr.* give a wince. □□ **wincer** *n.* **wincingly** *adv.* [ME f. OF *guenchir* turn aside: cf. WINCH, WINK]

wince[2] /wɪns/ n. a roller for moving textile fabric through a dyeing-vat. [var. of WINCH]

wincey /'wɪnsɪ/ n. (pl. **winceys**) a strong lightweight fabric of wool and cotton or linen. [orig. Sc.: app. f. *woolsey* in LINSEY-WOOLSEY]

winceyette /ˌwɪnsɪ'et/ n. Brit. a lightweight napped flannelette used esp. for nightclothes.

winch /wɪntʃ/ n. & v. —n. **1** the crank of a wheel or axle. **2** a windlass. **3** the reel of a fishing-rod. **4** = WINCE[2]. —v.tr. lift with a winch. □□ **wincher** n. [OE *wince* f. Gmc: cf. WINCE[1]]

Winchester /'wɪntʃɪstə(r)/ n. **1** propr. a breech-loading repeating rifle. **2** (in full **Winchester disk**) Computing a hermetically sealed data-storage device with high capacity (so called because its original numerical designation corresponded to that of the rifle's calibre). [O. F. *Winchester* d. 1880, US manufacturer of the rifle]

wind[1] /wɪnd/ n. & v. —n. **1 a** air in more or less rapid natural motion, esp. from an area of high pressure to one of low pressure. **b** a current of wind blowing from a specified direction or otherwise defined (*north wind*; *contrary wind*). **2 a** breath as needed in physical exertion or in speech. **b** the power of breathing without difficulty while running or making a similar continuous effort (*let me recover my wind*). **c** a spot below the centre of the chest where a blow temporarily paralyses breathing. **3** mere empty words; meaningless rhetoric. **4** gas generated in the bowels etc. by indigestion; flatulence. **5 a** an artifically produced current of air, esp. for sounding an organ or other wind instrument. **b** air stored for use or used as a current. **c** the wind instruments of an orchestra collectively (*poor balance between wind and strings*). **6** a scent carried by the wind, indicating the presence or proximity of an animal etc. —v.tr. **1** exhaust the wind of by exertion or a blow. **2** renew the wind of by rest (*stopped to wind the horses*). **3** make breathe quickly and deeply by exercise. **4** make (a baby) bring up wind after feeding. **5** detect the presence of by a scent. **6** /waɪnd/ (past and past part. **winded** or **wound** /waʊnd/) poet. sound (a bugle or call) by blowing. □ **before the wind** helped by the wind's force. **between wind and water** at a vulnerable point. **close to** (or **near**) **the wind 1** sailing as nearly against the wind as is consistent with using its force. **2** colloq. verging on indecency or dishonesty. **get wind of 1** smell out. **2** begin to suspect; hear a rumour of. **get** (or **have**) **the wind up** colloq. be alarmed or frightened. **how** (or **which**) **way the wind blows** (or **lies**) **1** what is the state of opinion. **2** what developments are likely. **in the wind** happening or about to happen. **in the wind's eye** directly against the wind. **like the wind** swiftly. **off the wind** Naut. with the wind on the quarter. **on a wind** Naut. against a wind on either bow. **on the wind** (of a sound or scent) carried by the wind. **put the wind up** colloq. alarm or frighten. **take wind** be rumoured; become known. **take the wind out of a person's sails** frustrate a person by anticipating an action or remark etc. **to the winds** (or **four winds**) **1** in all directions. **2** into a state of abandonment or neglect. **wind and weather** exposure to the effects of the elements. **wind band** a group of wind instruments as a band or section of an orchestra. **wind-break** a row of trees or a fence or wall etc. serving to break the force of the wind. **wind-chill** the cooling effect of wind blowing on a surface. **wind-cone** = *wind-sock*. **wind-force** the force of the wind esp. as measured on the Beaufort etc. scale. **wind-gap** a dried-up former river valley through ridges or hills. **wind-gauge 1** an anemometer. **2** an apparatus attached to the sights of a gun enabling allowance to be made for the wind in shooting. **3** a device showing the amount of wind in an organ. **wind instrument** a musical instrument in which sound is produced by a current of air, esp. the breath.

wind-jammer a merchant sailing-ship. **wind machine** a device for producing a blast of air or the sound of wind. **wind** (or **winds**) **of change** a force or influence for reform. **wind-rose** a diagram of the relative frequency of wind directions at a place. **wind-row** a line of raked hay, corn-sheaves, peats, etc., for drying by the wind. **wind-sail** a canvas funnel conveying air to the lower parts of a ship. **wind shear** a variation in wind velocity at right angles to the wind's direction. **wind-sleeve** = *wind-sock*. **wind-sock** a canvas cylinder or cone on a mast to show the direction of the wind at an airfield etc. **wind-tunnel** a tunnel-like device to produce an air-stream past models of aircraft etc. for the study of wind effects on them. □□ **windless** adj. [OE f. Gmc]

wind[2] /waɪnd/ v. & n. —v. (past and past part. **wound** /waʊnd/) **1** intr. go in a circular, spiral, curved, or crooked course (*a winding staircase*; *the path winds up the hill*). **2** tr. make (one's way) by such a course (*wind your way up to bed*; *wound their way into our affections*). **3** tr. wrap closely; surround with or as with a coil (*wound the blanket round me*; *wound my arms round the child*; *wound the child in my arms*). **4 a** tr. coil; provide with a coiled thread etc. (*wind the ribbon on to the card*; *wound cotton on a reel*; *winding wool into a ball*). **b** intr. coil; (of wool etc.) coil into a ball (*the creeper winds round the pole*; *the wool wound into a ball*). **5** tr. wind up (a clock etc.). **6** tr. hoist or draw with a windlass etc. (*wound the cable-car up the mountain*). —n. **1** a bend or turn in a course. **2** a single turn when winding. □ **wind down 1** lower by winding. **2** (of a mechanism) unwind. **3** (of a person) relax. **4** draw gradually to a close. **wind-down** n. colloq. a gradual lessening of excitement or reduction of activity. **wind off** unwind (string, wool, etc.). **wind round one's finger** see FINGER. **wind up 1** coil the whole of (a piece of string etc.). **2** tighten the coiling or coiled spring of (esp. a clock etc.). **3** a colloq. increase the tension or intensity of (*wound myself up to fever pitch*). **b** irritate or provoke (a person) to the point of anger. **4** bring to a conclusion; end (*wound up his speech*). **5** Commerce **a** arrange the affairs of and dissolve (a company). **b** (of a company) cease business and go into liquidation. **6** colloq. arrive finally; end in a specified state or circumstance (*you'll wind up in prison*; *wound up owing £100*). **wind-up** n. **1** a conclusion; a finish. **2** a state of anxiety; the provocation of this. **wound up** adj. (of a person) excited or tense or angry. [OE *windan* f. Gmc, rel. to WANDER, WEND]

windage /'wɪndɪdʒ/ n. **1** the friction of air against the moving part of a machine. **2 a** the effect of the wind in deflecting a missile. **b** an allowance for this. **3** the difference between the diameter of a gun's bore and its projectile, allowing the escape of gas.

windbag /'wɪndbæg/ n. colloq. a person who talks a lot but says little of any value.

windbound /'wɪndbaʊnd/ adj. unable to sail because of contrary winds.

windbreaker /'wɪndˌbreɪkə(r)/ n. US = WINDCHEATER.

windburn /'wɪndbɜːn/ n. inflammation of the skin caused by exposure to the wind.

windcheater /'wɪndˌtʃiːtə(r)/ n. a kind of wind-resistant outer jacket with close-fitting neck, cuffs, and lower edge.

winder /'waɪndə(r)/ n. a winding mechanism esp. of a clock or watch.

windfall /'wɪndfɔːl/ n. **1** an apple or other fruit blown to the ground by the wind. **2** a piece of unexpected good fortune, esp. a legacy.

windflower /'wɪndˌflaʊə(r)/ n. an anemone.

windhover /'wɪndˌhɒvə(r)/ n. Brit. a kestrel.

winding /'waɪndɪŋ/ n. **1** in senses of WIND[2] v. **2** curved or sinuous motion or movement. **3 a** a thing that is wound round or coiled. **b** Electr. coils of wire as a conductor round an armature etc.

□ **winding-engine** a machine for hoisting. **winding-sheet** a sheet in which a corpse is wrapped for burial.

windlass /'wɪndləs/ n. & v. —n. a machine with a horizontal axle for hauling or hoisting. —v.tr. hoist or haul with a windlass. [alt. (perh. by assoc. with dial. *windle* to wind) of obs. *windas* f. OF *guindas* f. ON *vindáss* f. *vinda* WIND² + *áss* pole]

windlestraw /'wɪnd(ə)lstrɔː/ n. *archaic* an old dry stalk of grass. [OE *windelstrēaw* grass for plaiting f. *windel* basket (as WIND², -LE¹)· + *strēaw* STRAW]

windmill /'wɪndmɪl/ n. **1** a mill worked by the action of the wind on its sails. **2** esp. *Brit.* a toy consisting of a stick with curved vanes attached that revolve in a wind. □ **throw one's cap** (or **bonnet**) **over the windmill** recklessly or unconventionally. **tilt at** (or **fight**) **windmills** attack an imaginary enemy or grievance.

window /'wɪndəʊ/ n. **1 a** an opening in a wall, roof, or vehicle etc., usu. with glass in fixed, sliding, or hinged frames, to admit light or air etc. and allow the occupants to see out. **b** the glass filling this opening (*have broken the window*). **2** a space for display behind the front window of a shop. **3** an aperture in a wall etc. through which customers are served in a bank, ticket office, etc. **4** an opportunity to observe or learn. **5** an opening or transparent part in an envelope to show an address. **6** a part of a VDU display selected to show a particular category or part of the data. **7 a** an interval during which atmospheric and astronomical circumstances are suitable for the launch of a spacecraft. **b** any interval or opportunity for action. **8** strips of metal foil dispersed in the air to obstruct radar detection. **9** a range of electromagnetic wavelengths for which a medium is transparent. □ **out of the window** *colloq.* no longer taken into account. **window-box** a box placed on an outside window-sill for growing flowers. **window-cleaner** a person who is employed to clean windows. **window-dressing 1** the art of arranging a display in a shop-window etc. **2** an adroit presentation of facts etc. to give a deceptively favourable impression. **window-ledge** = *window-sill*. **window-pane** a pane of glass in a window. **window-seat 1** a seat below a window, esp. in a bay or alcove. **2** a seat next to a window in an aircraft, train, etc. **window-shop** (**-shopped**, **-shopping**) look at goods displayed in shop-windows, usu. without buying anything. **window-shopper** a person who window-shops. **window-sill** a sill below a window. **window tax** *Brit. hist.* a tax on windows or similar openings (abolished in 1851). □□ **windowed** adj. (also in *comb.*). **windowless** adj. [ME f. ON *vindauga* (as WIND¹, EYE)]

windowing /'wɪndəʊɪŋ/ n. *Computing* the selection of part of a stored image for display or enlargement.

windpipe /'wɪndpaɪp/ n. the air-passage from the throat to the lungs; the trachea.

windscreen /'wɪndskriːn/ n. *Brit.* a screen of glass at the front of a motor vehicle. □ **windscreen wiper** a device consisting of a rubber blade on an arm, moving in an arc, for keeping a windscreen clear of rain etc.

windshield /'wɪndʃiːld/ n. *US* = WINDSCREEN.

Windsor /'wɪnzə(r)/ n. (usu. *attrib.*) denoting or relating to the British Royal Family since 1917. [*Windsor* in S. England, site of the royal residence at Windsor Castle]

Windsor chair /'wɪnsə(r)/ n. a wooden dining chair with a semicircular back supported by upright rods.

windsurfing /'wɪnd,sɜːfɪŋ/ n. the sport of riding on water on a sailboard. □□ **windsurf** v.intr. **windsurfer** n.

windswept /'wɪndswept/ adj. exposed to or swept back by the wind.

windward /'wɪndwəd/ adj., adv., & n. —adj. & adv. on the side from which the wind is blowing (opp.

LEEWARD). —n. the windward region, side, or direction (*to windward*; *on the windward of*). □ **get to windward of 1** place oneself there to avoid the smell of. **2** gain an advantage over.

windy /'wɪndɪ/ adj. (**windier**, **windiest**) **1** stormy with wind (*a windy night*). **2** exposed to the wind; windswept (*a windy plain*). **3** generating or characterized by flatulence. **4** *colloq.* wordy, verbose, empty (*a windy speech*). **5** *colloq.* nervous, frightened. □□ **windily** adv. **windiness** n. [OE *windig* (as WIND¹, -Y¹)]

wine /waɪn/ n. & v. —n. **1** fermented grape-juice as an alcoholic drink. **2** a fermented drink resembling this made from other fruits etc. as specified (*elderberry wine*; *ginger wine*). **3** the dark-red colour of red wine. —v. **1** *intr.* drink wine. **2** *tr.* entertain to wine. □ **wine and dine** entertain to or have a meal with wine. **wine bar** a bar or small restaurant where wine is the main drink available. **wine bottle** a glass bottle for wine, the standard size holding 75 cl or 26⅔ fl. oz. **wine box** a square carton of wine with a dispensing tap. **wine cellar 1** a cellar for storing wine. **2** the contents of this. **wine-grower** a cultivator of grapes for wine. **wine list** a list of wines available in a restaurant etc. **wine-tasting 1** judging the quality of wine by tasting it. **2** an occasion for this. **wine vinegar** vinegar made from wine as distinct from malt. **wine waiter** a waiter responsible for serving wine. □□ **wineless** adj. [OE *wīn* f. Gmc f. L *vinum*]

wineberry /'waɪnbərɪ/ n. (*pl.* **-ies**) **1 a** a deciduous bristly shrub, *Rubus phoenicolasius*, from China and Japan, producing scarlet berries used in cookery. **b** this berry. **2** = MAKO².

winebibber /'waɪn,bɪbə(r)/ n. a tippler or drunkard. □□ **winebibbing** n. & adj. [WINE + *bib* to tipple]

wineglass /'waɪnglɑːs/ n. **1** a glass for wine, usu. with a stem and foot. **2** the contents of this, a wineglassful.

wineglassful /'waɪnglɑːs,fʊl/ n. (*pl.* **-fuls**) **1** the capacity of a wineglass, esp. of the size used for sherry, as a measure of liquid, about four tablespoons. **2** the contents of a wineglass.

winepress /'waɪnpres/ n. a press in which grapes are squeezed in making wine.

winery /'waɪnərɪ/ n. (*pl.* **-ies**) esp. *US* an establishment where wine is made.

wineskin /'waɪnskɪn/ n. a whole skin of a goat etc. sown up and used to hold wine.

wing /wɪŋ/ n. & v. —n. **1** each of the limbs or organs by which a bird, bat, or insect is able to fly. **2** a rigid horizontal winglike structure forming a supporting part of an aircraft. **3** part of a building etc. which projects or is extended in a certain direction (*lived in the north wing*). **4 a** a forward player at either end of a line in football, hockey, etc. **b** the side part of a playing-area. **5** (in *pl.*) the sides of a theatre stage out of view of the audience. **6** a section of a political party in terms of the extremity of its views. **7** a flank of a battle array (*the cavalry were massed on the left wing*). **8** *Brit.* the part of a motor vehicle covering a wheel. **9 a** an air-force unit of several squadrons or groups. **b** (in *pl.*) a pilot's badge in the RAF etc. (*get one's wings*). **10** *Anat.* & *Bot.* a lateral part or projection of an organ or structure. —v. **1** *intr.* & *tr.* travel or traverse on wings or in an aircraft (*winging through the air*; *am winging my way home*). **2** *tr.* wound in a wing or an arm. **3** *tr.* equip with wings. **4** *tr.* enable to fly; send in flight (*fear winged my steps*; *winged an arrow towards them*). □ **give** (or **lend**) **wings to** speed up (a person or a thing). **on the wing** flying or in flight. **on a wing and a prayer** with only the slightest chance of success. **spread** (or **stretch**) **one's wings** develop one's powers fully. **take under one's wing** treat as a protégé. **take wing** fly away; soar. **waiting in the wings** holding oneself in readiness. **wing-beat** one complete set of motions with a wing in flying. **wing-case** the horny cover of an insect's wing. **wing-chair** a chair with side-pieces projecting forwards at the top of a high back. **wing-collar** a man's high stiff collar with turned-down corners. **wing commander** an RAF officer next below group captain. **winged words** highly apposite or significant words. **wing-game** game-birds. **wing-nut** a nut with projections for the fingers to turn it on a screw. **wing-span** (or **-spread**) measurement right across the wings of a bird or aircraft. **wing-stroke** = *wing-beat*. **wing-tip** the outer end of an aircraft's or a bird's wing. □□ **winged** *adj.* (also in *comb.*). **wingless** *adj.* **winglet** *n.* **winglike** *adj.* [ME pl. *wenge, -en, -es* f. ON *vængir*, pl. of *vængr*]

wingding /ˈwɪŋdɪŋ/ *n. sl.* **1** esp. *US* a wild party. **2** *US* a drug addict's real or feigned seizure. [20th c.: orig. unkn.]

winger /ˈwɪŋə(r)/ *n.* **1** a player on a wing in football, hockey, etc. **2** (in *comb.*) a member of a specified political wing (*left-winger*).

wink /wɪŋk/ *v. & n.* —*v.* **1 a** *tr.* close and open (one eye or both eyes) quickly. **b** *intr.* close and open an eye. **2** *intr.* (often foll. by *at*) wink one eye as a signal of friendship or greeting or to convey a message to a person. **3** *intr.* (of a light etc.) twinkle; shine or flash intermittently. —*n.* **1** the act or an instance of winking, esp. as a signal etc. **2** *colloq.* a brief moment of sleep (*didn't sleep a wink*). □ **as easy as winking** *colloq.* very easy. **in a wink** very quickly. **wink at 1** purposely avoid seeing; pretend not to notice. **2** connive at (a wrongdoing etc.). [OE *wincian* f. Gmc: cf. WINCE¹, WINCH]

winker /ˈwɪŋkə(r)/ *n.* **1** a flashing indicator light on a motor vehicle. **2** (usu. in *pl.*) a horse's blinker.

winkle /ˈwɪŋk(ə)l/ *n. & v.* —*n.* any edible marine gastropod mollusc of the genus *Littorina*; a peri-winkle. —*v.tr.* (foll. by *out*) esp. *Brit.* extract or eject (*winkled the information out of them*). □ **winkle-picker** *sl.* a shoe with a long pointed toe. □□ **winkler** *n.* [abbr. of PERIWINKLE²: cf. WIG¹]

winner /ˈwɪnə(r)/ *n.* **1** a person, racehorse, etc. that wins. **2** *colloq.* a successful or highly promising idea, enterprise, etc. (*the new scheme seemed a winner*).

winning /ˈwɪnɪŋ/ *adj. & n.* —*adj.* **1** having or bringing victory or an advantage (*the winning entry*; *a winning stroke*). **2** attractive, persuasive (*a winning smile*; *winning ways*). —*n.* (in *pl.*) money won esp. in betting etc. □ **winning-post** a post marking the end of a race. □□ **winningly** *adv.* **winningness** *n.*

winnow /ˈwɪnəʊ/ *v.tr.* **1** blow (grain) free of chaff etc. by an air-current. **2** (foll. by *out, away, from*, etc.) get rid of (chaff etc.) from grain. **3 a** sift, separate; clear of refuse or inferior specimens. **b** sift or examine (evidence for falsehood etc.). **c** clear, sort, or weed out (rubbish etc.). **4** *poet.* a fan (the air with wings). **b** flap (wings). **c** stir (the hair etc.). □□ **winnower** *n.* (in senses 1, 2). [OE *windwian* (as WIND¹)]

wino /ˈwaɪnəʊ/ *n.* (pl. **-os**) *sl.* a habitual excessive drinker of cheap wine; an alcoholic.

winsome /ˈwɪnsəm/ *adj.* (of a person, looks, or manner) winning, attractive, engaging. □□ **winsomely** *adv.* **winsomeness** *n.* [OE *wynsum* f. *wyn* JOY + -SOME¹]

winter /ˈwɪntə(r)/ *n. & v.* —*n.* **1** the coldest season of the year, in the N. hemisphere from December to February and in the S. hemisphere from June to August. **2** *Astron.* the period from the winter solstice to the vernal equinox. **3** a bleak or lifeless period or region etc. (*nuclear winter*). **4** *poet.* a year (esp. of a person's age) (*a man of fifty winters*). **5** (*attrib.*) **a** characteristic of or suitable for winter (*winter light*; *winter clothes*). **b** (of fruit) ripening late or keeping until or during winter. **c** (of wheat or other crops) sown in autumn for harvesting the following year. —*v.* **1** *intr.* (usu. foll. by *at, in*) pass the winter (*likes to winter in the Canaries*). **2** *tr.* keep or feed (plants, cattle) during winter. □ **winter aconite** see ACONITE

2. winter cress any bitter-tasting cress of the genus *Barbarea*, esp. *B. vulgaris*. **winter garden** a garden or conservatory of plants flourishing in winter. **winter jasmine** a jasmine, *Jasminum nudiflorum*, with yellow flowers. **winter quarters** a place where soldiers spend the winter. **winter sleep** hibernation. **winter solstice** see SOLSTICE. **winter sports** sports performed on snow or ice esp. in winter (e.g. skiing and ice-skating). **winter-tide** *poet.* = WINTERTIME. □□ **winterer** *n.* **winterless** *adj.* **winterly** *adj.* [OE f. Gmc, prob. rel. to WET]

wintergreen /ˈwɪntəˌgriːn/ *n.* any of several plants esp. of the genus *Pyrola* or *Gaultheria* remaining green through the winter.

winterize /ˈwɪntəraɪz/ *v.tr.* (also **-ise**) esp. *US* adapt for operation or use in cold weather. □□ **winterization** /-ˈzeɪʃ(ə)n/ *n.*

wintertime /ˈwɪntəˌtaɪm/ *n.* the season of winter.

wintry /ˈwɪntrɪ/ *adj.* (also **wintery**) (/-tərɪ/; **wintrier**, **wintriest**) **1** characteristic of winter (*wintry weather*; *a wintry sun*; *a wintry landscape*). **2** (of a smile, greeting, etc.) lacking warmth or enthusiasm. □□ **wintrily** *adv.* **wintriness** *n.* [OE *wintrig*, or f. WINTER]

winy /ˈwaɪnɪ/ *adj.* (**winier**, **winiest**) resembling wine in taste or appearance. □□ **wininess** *n.*

wipe /waɪp/ *v. & n.* —*v.tr.* **1** clean or dry the surface of by rubbing with the hands or a cloth etc. **2** rub (a cloth) over a surface. **3** spread (a liquid etc.) over a surface by rubbing. **4** (often foll. by *away, off*, etc.) **a** clear or remove by wiping (*wiped the mess off the table*; *wipe away your tears*). **b** remove or eliminate completely (*the village was wiped off the map*). **5 a** erase (data, a recording, etc., from a magnetic medium). **b** erase data from (the medium). **6** *Austral. & NZ sl.* reject or dismiss (a person or idea). —*n.* **1** an act of wiping (*give the floor a wipe*). **2** a piece of disposable absorbent cloth, usu. treated with a cleansing agent, for wiping something clean (*antiseptic wipes*). □ **wipe down** clean (esp. a vertical surface) by wiping. **wipe a person's eye** *colloq.* get the better of a person. **wipe the floor with** *colloq.* inflict a humiliating defeat on. **wipe off** annul (a debt etc.). **wipe out 1 a** destroy, annihilate (*the whole population was wiped out*). **b** obliterate (*wiped it out of my memory*). **2** *sl.* murder. **3** clean the inside of. **4** avenge (an insult etc.). **wipe-out** *n.* **1** the obliteration of one radio signal by another. **2** an instance of destruction or annihilation. **3** *sl.* a fall from a surfboard. **wipe the slate clean** see SLATE. **wipe up 1** *Brit.* dry (dishes etc.). **2** take up (a liquid etc.) by wiping. □□ **wipeable** *adj.* [OE *wīpian*: cf. OHG *wīfan* wind round, Goth. *weipan* crown: rel. to WHIP]

wiper /ˈwaɪpə(r)/ *n.* **1** = *windscreen wiper*. **2** *Electr.* a moving contact. **3** a cam or tappet.

WIPO *abbr.* World Intellectual Property Organization.

wire /ˈwaɪə(r)/ *n. & v.* —*n.* **1 a** metal drawn out into the form of a thread or thin flexible rod. **b** a piece of this. **c** (*attrib.*) made of wire. **2** a length or quantity of wire used for fencing or to carry an electric current etc. **3** esp. *US colloq.* a telegram or cablegram. —*v.tr.* **1** provide, fasten, strengthen, etc., with wire. **2** (often foll. by *up*) *Electr.* install electrical circuits in (a building, piece of equipment, etc.). **3** esp. *US colloq.* telegraph (*wired me that they were coming*). **4** snare (an animal etc.) with wire. **5** (usu. in *passive*) *Croquet* obstruct (a ball, shot, or player) by a hoop. □ **by wire** by telegraph. **get one's wires crossed** become confused and misunderstood. **wire brush 1** a brush with tough wire bristles for cleaning hard surfaces, esp. metal. **2** a brush with wire strands brushed against cymbals to produce a soft metallic sound. **wire cloth** cloth woven from wire. **wire-cutter** a tool for cutting wire. **wire gauge 1** a gauge for measuring the diameter of wire etc. **2** a standard series of sizes in which wire etc. is made.

wire gauze a stiff gauze woven from wire. **wire grass** any of various grasses with tough wiry stems. **wire-haired** (esp. of a dog) having stiff or wiry hair. **wire mattress** a mattress supported by wires stretched in a frame. **wire netting** netting of wire twisted into meshes. **wire rope** rope made by twisting wires together as strands. **wire-tapper** a person who indulges in wire-tapping. **wire-tapping** the practice of tapping (see TAP¹ *v.* 4) a telephone or telegraph line to eavesdrop. **wire-walker** an acrobat performing feats on a wire rope. **wire wheel** a vehicle-wheel with spokes of wire. **wire wool** a mass of fine wire for cleaning. □□ **wirer** *n.* [OE *wīr*]

wiredraw /ˈwaɪədrɔː/ *v.tr.* (*past* -drew /-ˌdruː/; *past part.* -drawn /-ˌdrɔːn/) **1** draw (metal) out into wire. **2** elongate; protract unduly. **3** (esp. as **wiredrawn** *adj.*) refine or apply or press (an argument etc.) with idle or excessive subtlety.

wireless /ˈwaɪəlɪs/ *n. & adj.* —*n.* **1** esp. *Brit.* **a** (in full **wireless set**) a radio receiving set. **b** the transmission and reception of radio signals. ¶ Now old-fashioned, esp. with ref. to broadcasting, and superseded by *radio.* **2** = *wireless telegraphy.* —*adj.* lacking or not requiring wires. □**wireless telegraphy** = RADIO-TELEGRAPHY.

wireman /ˈwaɪəmən/ *n.* (*pl.* **-men**) **1** esp. *US* an installer or repairer of electric wires. **2** a journalist working for a telegraphic news agency.

wirepuller /ˈwaɪəˌpʊlə(r)/ *n.* esp. *US* a politician etc. who exerts a hidden influence. □□ **wirepulling** *n.*

wireworm /ˈwaɪəˌwɜːm/ *n.* the larva of the click beetle causing damage to crop plants.

wiring /ˈwaɪərɪŋ/ *n.* **1** a system of wires providing electrical circuits. **2** the installation of this (*came to do the wiring*).

wiry /ˈwaɪərɪ/ *adj.* (**wirier**, **wiriest**) **1** tough and flexible as wire. **2** (of a person) thin and sinewy; untiring. **3** made of wire. □□ **wirily** *adv.* **wiriness** *n.*

Wis. *abbr.* Wisconsin.

wis /wɪs/ *v.intr. archaic* know well. [orig. *I wis* = obs. *iwis* 'certainly' f. OE *gewis*, erron. taken as 'I know' and as pres. tense of *wist* (WIT²)]

Wisd. *abbr.* Wisdom of Solomon (Apocrypha).

wisdom /ˈwɪzdəm/ *n.* **1** the state of being wise. **2** experience and knowledge together with the power of applying them critically or practically. **3** sagacity, prudence; common sense. **4** wise sayings, thoughts, etc., regarded collectively. □**in his** or **her wisdom** usu. *iron.* thinking it would be best (*the committee in its wisdom decided to abandon the project*). **wisdom tooth** each of four hindmost molars not usu. cut before 20 years of age. [OE *wīsdōm* (as WISE¹, -DOM)]

wise¹ /waɪz/ *adj. & v.* —*adj.* **1 a** having experience and knowledge and judiciously applying them. **b** (of an action, behaviour, etc.) determined by or showing or in harmony with such experience and knowledge. **2** sagacious, prudent, sensible, discreet. **3** having knowledge. **4** suggestive of wisdom (*with a wise nod of the head*). **5** *US colloq.* **a** alert, crafty. **b** (often foll. by *to*) having (usu. confidential) information (about). —*v.tr. & intr.* (foll. by *up*) esp. *US colloq.* put or get wise. □**be** (or **get**) **wise to** *colloq.* become aware of. **no** (or **none the** or **not much**) **wiser** knowing no more than before. **put a person wise** (often foll. by *to*) *colloq.* inform a person (about). **wise after the event** able to understand and assess an event or circumstance after its implications have become obvious. **wise guy** *colloq.* a know-all. **wise man** a wizard, esp. one of the Magi. **wise saw** a proverbial saying. **without anyone's being the wiser** undetected. □□ **wisely** *adv.* [OE *wīs* f. Gmc: see WIT²]

wise² /waɪz/ *n. archaic* way, manner, or degree (*in solemn wise; on this wise*). □**in no wise** not at all. [OE *wīse* f. Gmc f. WIT²]

-wise /waɪz/ *suffix* forming adjectives and adverbs of manner (*crosswise; clockwise; lengthwise*) or respect (*moneywise*) (cf. -WAYS). ¶ More fanciful phrase-based combinations, such as *employment-wise* (= as regards employment), are *colloq.*, and restricted to informal contexts. [as WISE²]

wiseacre /ˈwaɪzˌeɪkə(r)/ *n.* a person who affects a wise manner. [MDu. *wijssegger* soothsayer, prob. f. OHG *wīssago*, *wīzago*, assim. to WISE¹, ACRE]

wisecrack /ˈwaɪzkræk/ *n. & v. colloq.* —*n.* a smart pithy remark. —*v.intr.* make a wisecrack. □□ **wisecracker** *n.*

wisent /ˈwiːz(ə)nt/ *n.* the European bison, *Bison bonasus.* [G: cf. BISON]

wish /wɪʃ/ *v. & n.* —*v.* **1** *intr.* (often foll. by *for*) have or express a desire or aspiration for (*wish for happiness*). **2** *tr.* (often foll. by *that* + clause, usu. with *that* omitted) have as a desire or aspiration (*I wish I could sing; I wished that I was dead*). **3** *tr.* want or demand, usu. so as to bring about what is wanted (*I wish to go; I wish you to do it; I wish it done*). **4** *tr.* express one's hopes for (*we wish you well; wish them no harm; wished us a pleasant journey*). **5** *tr.* (foll. by *on, upon*) *colloq.* foist on a person. —*n.* **1 a** a desire, request, or aspiration. **b** an expression of this. **2** a thing desired (*got my wish*). □**best** (or **good**) **wishes** hopes felt or expressed for another's happiness etc. **wish-fulfilment** a tendency for subconscious desire to be satisfied in fantasy. **wishing-well** a well into which coins are dropped and a wish is made. **the wish is father to the thought** we believe a thing because we wish it true. □□ **wisher** *n.* (in sense 4 of *v.*); (also in *comb.*). [OE *wȳscan*, OHG *wunsken* f. Gmc, ult. rel. to WEEN, WONT]

wishbone /ˈwɪʃbəʊn/ *n.* **1** a forked bone between the neck and breast of a cooked bird: when broken between two people the longer portion entitles the holder to make a wish. **2** an object of similar shape.

wishful /ˈwɪʃfʊl/ *adj.* **1** (often foll. by *to* + infin.) desiring, wishing. **2** having or expressing a wish. □**wishful thinking** belief founded on wishes rather than facts. □□ **wishfully** *adv.* **wishfulness** *n.*

wish-wash /ˈwɪʃwɒʃ/ *n.* **1** a weak or watery drink. **2** insipid talk or writing. [redupl. of WASH]

wishy-washy /ˈwɪʃɪˌwɒʃɪ/ *adj.* **1** feeble, insipid, or indecisive in quality or character. **2** (of tea, soup, etc.) weak, watery, sloppy. [redupl. of WASHY]

wisp /wɪsp/ *n.* **1** a small bundle or twist of straw etc. **2** a small separate quantity of smoke, hair, etc. **3** a small thin person etc. **4** a flock (of snipe). □□ **wispy** *adj.* (**wispier**, **wispiest**). **wispily** *adv.* **wispiness** *n.* [ME: orig. uncert.: cf. WFris. *wisp*, and WHISK]

wist *past and past part.* of WIT².

wisteria /wɪˈstɪərɪə/ *n.* (also **wistaria** /-ˈsteərɪə/) any climbing plant of the genus *Wisteria*, with hanging racemes of blue, purple, or white flowers. [C. *Wistar* (or *Wister*), Amer. anatomist d. 1818]

wistful /ˈwɪstfʊl/ *adj.* (of a person, looks, etc.) yearningly or mournfully expectant or wishful. □□ **wistfully** *adv.* **wistfulness** *n.* [app. assim. of obs. *wistly* (adv.) intently (cf. WHISHT) to *wishful*, with corresp. change of sense]

wit¹ /wɪt/ *n.* **1** (in *sing.* or *pl.*) intelligence; quick understanding (*has quick wits; a nimble wit*). **2 a** the unexpected, quick, and humorous combining or contrasting of ideas or expressions (*conversation sparkling with wit*). **b** the power of giving intellectual pleasure by this. **3** a person possessing such a power, esp. a cleverly humorous person. □**at one's wit's** (or **wits'**) **end** utterly at a loss or in despair. **have** (or **keep**) **one's wits about one** be alert or vigilant or of lively intelligence. **live by one's wits** live by ingenious or crafty expedients, without a settled occupation. **out of one's wits** mad, distracted. **set one's wits to** argue with. □□ **witted** *adj.* (in sense 1); (also in *comb.*). [OE *wit(t), gewit(t)* f. Gmc]

wit² /wɪt/ *v.tr. & intr.* (*1st & 3rd sing. present* **wot** /wɒt/; *past and past part.* **wist**) (often foll. by *of*) *archaic* know. □**to wit** that is to say; namely. [OE *witan* f. Gmc]

witch /wɪtʃ/ n. & v. —n. **1** a sorceress, esp. a woman supposed to have dealings with the devil or evil spirits. **2** an ugly old woman; a hag. **3** a fascinating girl or woman. **4** a flat-fish, *Pleuronectes cynoglossus*, resembling the lemon sole. —v.tr. *archaic* **1** bewitch. **2** fascinate, charm, lure. □ **witch-doctor** a tribal magician of primitive people. **witches' sabbath** see SABBATH 3. **witch-hunt 1** *hist.* a search for and persecution of supposed witches. **2** a campaign directed against a particular group of those holding unpopular or unorthodox views, esp. communists. **the witching hour** midnight, when witches are supposedly active (after Shakesp. *Hamlet* III. ii. 377 *the witching time of night*). □□ **witching** *adj.* **witchlike** *adj.* [OE *wicca* (masc.), *wicce* (fem.), rel. to *wiccian* (v.) practise magic arts]

witch- var. of WYCH-.

witchcraft /'wɪtʃkrɑːft/ n. the use of magic; sorcery.

witchery /'wɪtʃərɪ/ n. **1** witchcraft. **2** power exercised by beauty or eloquence or the like.

witchetty /'wɪtʃətɪ/ n. (pl. -**ies**) *Austral.* a large white larva of a beetle or moth, eaten as food by Aborigines. [Aboriginal]

witch-hazel /'wɪtʃˌheɪz(ə)l/ n. (also **wych-hazel**) **1** any American shrub of the genus *Hamamelis*, with bark yielding an astringent lotion. **2** this lotion, esp. from the leaves of *H. virginiana*.

witenagemot /ˌwɪtənəɡə'məʊt/ n. *hist.* an Anglo-Saxon national council or parliament. [OE f. *witena* genit. pl. of *wita* wise man (as WIT²) + *gemōt* meeting: cf. MOOT]

with /wɪð/ prep. expressing: **1** an instrument or means used (*cut with a knife*; *can walk with assistance*). **2** association or company (*lives with his mother*; *works with Shell*; *lamb with mint sauce*). **3** cause or origin (*shiver with fear*; *in bed with measles*). **4** possession, attribution (*the man with dark hair*; *a vase with handles*). **5** circumstances; accompanying conditions (*sleep with the window open*; *a holiday with all expenses paid*). **6** manner adopted or displayed (*behaved with dignity*; *spoke with vehemence*; *handle with care*; *won with ease*). **7** agreement or harmony (*sympathize with*; *I believe with you that it can be done*). **8** disagreement, antagonism, competition (*incompatible with*; *stop arguing with me*). **9** responsibility or care for (*the decision rests with you*; *leave the child with me*). **10** material (*made with gold*). **11** addition or supply; possession of as a material, attribute, circumstance, etc. (*fill it with water*; *threaten with dismissal*; *decorate with holly*). **12** reference or regard (*be patient with them*; *how are things with you?*; *what do you want with me?*; *there's nothing wrong with expressing one's opinion*). **13** relation or causative association (*changes with the weather*; *keeps pace with the cost of living*). **14** an accepted circumstance or consideration (*with all your faults, we like you*). □ **away** (or **in** or **out** etc.) **with** (as *int.*) take, send, or put (a person or thing) away, in, out, etc. **be with a person 1** agree with and support a person. **2** *colloq.* follow a person's meaning (*are you with me?*). **one with** part of the same whole as. **with child** (or **young**) *literary* pregnant. **with it** *colloq.* **1** up to date; conversant with modern ideas etc. **2** alert and comprehending. **with-it** *adj. colloq.* (of clothes etc.) fashionable. **with that** thereupon. [OE, prob. shortened f. a Gmc prep. corresp. to OE *wither*, OHG *widar* against]

withal /wɪ'ðɔːl/ adv. & prep. *archaic* —adv. moreover; as well; at the same time. —prep. (placed after its expressed or omitted object) with (*what shall he fill his belly withal?*). [ME f. WITH + ALL]

withdraw /wɪð'drɔː/ v. (past **withdrew** /-'druː/; past part. **withdrawn** /-'drɔːn/) **1** tr. pull or take aside or back (*withdrew my hand*). **2** tr. discontinue, cancel, retract (*withdrew my support*; *the promise was later withdrawn*). **3** tr. remove, take away (*withdrew the child from school*; *withdrew their troops*). **4** tr. take (money) out of an account. **5** intr. retire or go away;

move away or back. **6** intr. (as **withdrawn** *adj.*) abnormally shy and unsociable; mentally detached. □ **withdrawing-room** *archaic* = DRAWING-ROOM 1. □□ **withdrawer** n. [ME f. *with-* away (as WITH) + DRAW]

withdrawal /wɪð'drɔːəl/ n. **1** the act or an instance of withdrawing or being withdrawn. **2** a process of ceasing to take addictive drugs, often with an unpleasant physical reaction (*withdrawal symptoms*). **3** = *coitus interruptus*.

withe /wɪθ, wɪð, waɪð/ (also **withy** /'wɪðɪ/) (pl. **withes** or **-ies**) n. a tough flexible shoot esp. of willow or osier used for tying a bundle of wood etc. [OE *withthe*, *withig* f. Gmc, rel. to WIRE]

wither /'wɪðə(r)/ v. **1** tr. & intr. (often foll. by up) make or become dry and shrivelled (*withered flowers*). **2** tr. & intr. (often foll. by away) deprive of or lose vigour, vitality, freshness, or importance. **3** intr. decay, decline. **4** tr. **a** blight with scorn etc. **b** (as **withering** *adj.*) scornful (*a withering look*). □□ **witheringly** adv. [ME, app. var. of WEATHER differentiated for certain senses]

withers /'wɪðəz/ n.pl. the ridge between a horse's shoulder-blades. [shortening of (16th-c.) *widersome* (or *-sone*) f. *wider-*, *wither-* against (cf. WITH), as the part that resists the strain of the collar: second element obscure]

withershins /'wɪðəʃɪnz/ adv. (also **widdershins** /'wɪd-/) esp. *Sc.* **1** in a direction contrary to the sun's course (considered as unlucky). **2** anticlockwise. [MLG *weddersins* f. MHG *widdersinnes* f. *wider* against + *sin* direction]

withhold /wɪð'həʊld/ v.tr. (past and past part. **-held** /-'held/) **1** (often foll. by *from*) hold back; restrain. **2** refuse to give, grant, or allow (*withhold one's consent*; *withhold the truth*). □□ **withholder** n. [ME f. *with-* away (as WITH) + HOLD¹]

within /wɪ'ðɪn/ adv. & prep. —adv. *archaic* or *literary* **1** inside; to, at, or on the inside; internally. **2** indoors (*is anyone within?*). **3** in spirit (*make me pure within*). **4** inside the city walls (*Bishopsgate within*). —prep. **1** inside; enclosed or contained by. **2 a** not beyond or exceeding (*within one's means*). **b** not transgressing (*within the law*; *within reason*). **3** not further off than (*within three miles of a station*; *within shouting distance*; *within ten days*). □ **within doors** in or into a house. **within one's grasp** see GRASP. **within reach** (or **sight**) **of** near enough to be reached or seen. [OE *withinnan* on the inside (as WITH, *innan* (adv. & prep.) within, formed as IN)]

without /wɪ'ðaʊt/ prep. & adv. —prep. **1** not having, feeling, or showing (*came without any money*; *without hesitation*; *without any emotion*). **2** with freedom from (*without fear*; *without embarrassment*). **3** in the absence of (*cannot live without you*; *the train left without us*). **4** with neglect or avoidance of (*do not leave without telling me*). ¶ Use as a *conj.*, as in *do not leave without you tell me*, is non-standard. **5** *archaic* outside (*without the city wall*). —adv. *archaic* or *literary* **1** outside (*seen from without*). **2** out of doors (*remained shivering without*). **3** in outward appearance (*rough without but kind within*). **4** outside the city walls (*Bishopsgate without*). □ **without end** infinite, eternal. [OE *withūtan* (as WITH, *ūtan* from outside, formed as OUT)]

withstand /wɪð'stænd/ v. (past and past part. **-stood** /-'stʊd/) **1** tr. oppose, resist, hold out against (a person, force, etc.). **2** intr. make opposition; offer resistance. □□ **withstander** n. [OE *withstandan* f. *with-* against (as WITH) + STAND]

withy /'wɪðɪ/ n. (pl. **-ies**) **1** a willow of any species. **2** var. of WITHE.

witless /'wɪtlɪs/ adj. **1** lacking wits; foolish, stupid. **2** crazy. □□ **witlessly** adv. **witlessness** n. [OE *witlēas* (as WIT¹, -LESS)]

witling /'wɪtlɪŋ/ n. *archaic* usu. *derog.* a person who fancies himself or herself as a wit.

witness /'wɪtnɪs/ n. & v. —n. **1** a person present at

some event and able to give information about it (cf. EYEWITNESS). **2 a** a person giving sworn testimony. **b** a person attesting another's signature to a document. **3** (foll. by *to, of*) a person or thing whose existence, condition, etc., attests or proves something (*is a living witness to their generosity*). **4** testimony, evidence, confirmation. —*v.* **1** *tr.* be a witness of (an event etc.) (*did you witness the accident?*). **2** *tr.* be witness to the authenticity of (a document or signature). **3** *tr.* serve as evidence or an indication of. **4** *intr.* (foll. by *against, for, to*) give or serve as evidence. □ **bear witness to** (or **of**) **1** attest the truth of. **2** state one's belief in. **call to witness** appeal to for confirmation etc. **witness-box** (*US* **-stand**) an enclosure in a lawcourt from which witnesses give evidence. [OE *witnes* (as WIT¹, -NESS)]

witter /ˈwɪtə(r)/ *v.intr.* (often foll. by *on*) *colloq.* speak tediously on trivial matters. [20th c.: prob. imit.]

witticism /ˈwɪtɪˌsɪz(ə)m/ *n.* a witty remark. [coined by Dryden (1677) f. WITTY, after *criticism*]

witting /ˈwɪtɪŋ/ *adj.* **1** aware. **2** intentional. □□ **wittingly** *adv.* [ME f. WIT² + -ING²]

witty /ˈwɪtɪ/ *adj.* (**wittier, wittiest**) **1** showing verbal wit. **2** characterized by wit or humour. □□ **wittily** *adv.* **wittiness** *n.* [OE *witig, wittig* (as WIT¹, -Y¹)]

wivern var. of WYVERN.

wives *pl.* of WIFE.

wiz var. of WHIZ *n.* 2.

wizard /ˈwɪzəd/ *n.* & *adj.* —*n.* **1** a sorcerer; a magician. **2** a person of remarkable powers, a genius. **3** a conjuror. —*adj. sl.* esp. *Brit.* wonderful, excellent. □□ **wizardly** *adj.* **wizardry** *n.* [ME f. WISE¹ + -ARD]

wizened /ˈwɪz(ə)nd/ *adj.* (also **wizen**) (of a person or face etc.) shrivelled-looking. [past part. of *wizen* shrivel f. OE *wisnian* f. Gmc]

wk. *abbr.* **1** week. **2** work. **3** weak.

wks. *abbr.* weeks.

Wm. *abbr.* William.

WMO *abbr.* World Meteorological Organization.

WNW *abbr.* west-north-west.

WO *abbr.* Warrant Officer.

wo /wəʊ/ *int.* = WHOA. [var. of *who* (int.), HO]

w.o. *abbr.* walk-over.

woad /wəʊd/ *n. hist.* **1** a cruciferous plant, *Isatis tinctoria*, yielding a blue dye now superseded by indigo. **2** the dye obtained from this. [OE *wād* f. Gmc]

wobbegong /ˈwɒbɪˌɡɒŋ/ *n.* an Australian brown shark, *Orectolobus maculatus*, with buff patterned markings. [Aboriginal]

wobble /ˈwɒb(ə)l/ *v.* & *n.* —*v.* **1 a** *intr.* sway or vibrate unsteadily from side to side. **b** *tr.* cause to do this. **2** *intr.* stand or go unsteadily; stagger. **3** *intr.* waver, vacillate; act inconsistently. **4** *intr.* (of the voice or sound) quaver, pulsate. —*n.* **1** a wobbling movement. **2** an instance of vacillation or pulsation. □ **wobble-board** *Austral.* a piece of fibreboard used as a musical instrument with a low booming sound. □□ **wobbler** *n.* [earlier *wabble*, corresp. to LG *wabbeln*, ON *vafla* waver f. Gmc: cf. WAVE, WAVER, -LE⁴]

wobbly /ˈwɒblɪ/ *adj.* (**wobblier, wobbliest**) **1** wobbling or tending to wobble. **2** wavy, undulating (*a wobbly line*). **3** unsteady; weak after illness (*feeling wobbly*). **4** wavering, vacillating, insecure (*the economy was wobbly*). □ **throw a wobbly** *sl.* have a fit of nerves. □□ **wobbliness** *n.*

wodge /wɒdʒ/ *n. Brit. colloq.* a chunk or lump. [alt. of WEDGE¹]

woe /wəʊ/ *n. archaic* or *literary* **1** affliction; bitter grief; distress. **2** (in *pl.*) calamities, troubles. **3** *joc.* problems (*told me a tale of woe*). □ **woe betide** there will be unfortunate consequences for (*woe betide you if you are late*). **woe is me** an exclamation of distress. [OE *wā, wǣ* f. Gmc, a natural exclam. of lament]

woebegone /ˈwəʊbɪˌɡɒn/ *adj.* dismal-looking. [WOE + *begone* = surrounded f. OE *begān* (as BE-, GO¹)]

woeful /ˈwəʊfʊl/ *adj.* **1** sorrowful; afflicted with distress (*a woeful expression*). **2** causing sorrow or affliction. **3** very bad; wretched (*woeful ignorance*). □□ **woefully** *adv.* **woefulness** *n.*

wog¹ /wɒɡ/ *n. sl. offens.* a foreigner, esp. a non-White one. [20th c.: orig. unkn.]

wog² /wɒɡ/ *n. Austral. sl.* an illness or infection. [20th c.: orig. unkn.]

woggle /ˈwɒɡ(ə)l/ *n.* a leather etc. ring through which the ends of a Scout's neckerchief are passed at the neck. [20th c.: orig. unkn.]

wok /wɒk/ *n.* a bowl-shaped frying-pan used in esp. Chinese cookery. [Cantonese]

woke *past* of WAKE¹.

woken *past part.* of WAKE¹.

wold /wəʊld/ *n.* a piece of high open uncultivated land or moor. [OE *wald* f. Gmc, perh. rel. to WILD: cf. WEALD]

wolf /wʊlf/ *n.* & *v.* —*n.* (*pl.* **wolves** /wʊlvz/) **1** a wild flesh-eating tawny-grey mammal related to the dog, esp. *Canis lupus*, preying on sheep etc. and hunting in packs. **2** *sl.* a man given to seducing women. **3** a rapacious or greedy person. **4** *Mus.* **a** a jarring sound from some notes in a bowed instrument. **b** an out-of-tune effect when playing certain chords on old organs (before the present 'equal temperament' was in use). —*v.tr.* (often foll. by *down*) devour (food) greedily. □ **cry wolf** raise repeated false alarms (so that a genuine one is disregarded). **have** (or **hold**) **a wolf by the ears** be in a precarious position. **keep the wolf from the door** avert hunger or starvation. **lone wolf** a person who prefers to act alone. **throw to the wolves** sacrifice without compunction. **wolf-cub 1** a young wolf. **2** *Brit.* the former name for a Cub Scout. **wolf-fish** any large voracious blenny of the genus *Anarrhichas*. **wolf in sheep's clothing** a hostile person who pretends friendship. **wolf-pack** an attacking group of submarines or aircraft. **wolf's-milk** spurge. **wolf-spider** any ground-dwelling spider of the family Lycosidae, hunting instead of trapping its prey. **wolf-whistle** *n.* a sexually admiring whistle by a man to a woman. —*v.intr.* make a wolf-whistle. □□ **wolfish** *adj.* **wolfishly** *adv.* **wolflike** *adj.* & *adv.* [OE *wulf* f. Gmc]

wolfhound /ˈwʊlfhaʊnd/ *n.* a borzoi or other dog of a kind used orig. to hunt wolves.

wolfram /ˈwʊlfrəm/ *n.* **1** tungsten. **2** tungsten ore; a native tungstate of iron and manganese. [G: perh. f. *Wolf* WOLF + *Rahm* cream, or MHG *rām* dirt, soot]

wolframite /ˈwʊlfrəˌmaɪt/ *n.* = WOLFRAM 2.

wolfsbane /ˈwʊlfsbeɪn/ *n.* an aconite, esp. *Aconitum lycoctonum*.

wolfskin /ˈwʊlfskɪn/ *n.* **1** the skin of a wolf. **2** a mat, cloak, etc., made from this.

wolverine /ˈwʊlvəˌriːn/ *n.* (also **wolverene**) = GLUTTON 3. [16th-c. *wolvering*, somehow derived f. *wolv-*, stem of WOLF]

wolves *pl.* of WOLF.

woman /ˈwʊmən/ *n.* (*pl.* **women** /ˈwɪmɪn/) **1** an adult human female. **2** the female sex; any or an average woman (*how does woman differ from man?*). **3** a wife or female sexual partner. **4** (prec. by *the*) emotions or characteristics traditionally associated with women (*brought out the woman in him*). **5** a man with characteristics traditionally associated with women. **6** (*attrib.*) female (*woman driver; women friends*). **7** (as second element in *comb.*) a woman of a specified nationality, profession, skill, etc. (*Englishwoman; horsewoman*). **8** *colloq.* a female domestic help. **9** *archaic* or *hist.* a queen's etc. female attendant ranking below lady (*woman of the bedchamber*). □ **woman of the streets** a prostitute. **Women's Institute** an organization of women in rural areas to meet regularly and participate in crafts, cultural activities, etc. **women's lib** *colloq.* = *women's liberation*. **women's libber** *colloq.* a supporter of women's liberation. **women's liberation** the liberation of women from inequalities and subservient status in relation to men, and from attitudes causing these. **Women's Liberation** (or

Movement) a movement campaigning for women's liberation. **women's rights** rights that promote a position of legal and social equality of women with men. □□ **womanless** *adj.* **womanlike** *adj.* [OE *wif-mon*, *-man* (as WIFE, MAN), a formation peculiar to English, the ancient word being WIFE]

womanhood /'wʊmən,hʊd/ *n.* **1** female maturity. **2** womanly instinct. **3** womankind.

womanish /'wʊmənɪʃ/ *adj.* usu. *derog.* **1** (of a man) effeminate, unmanly. **2** suitable to or characteristic of a woman. □□ **womanishly** *adv.* **womanishness** *n.*

womanize /'wʊmə,naɪz/ *v.* (also **-ise**) **1** *intr.* chase after women; philander. **2** *tr.* make womanish. □□ **womanizer** *n.*

womankind /'wʊmən,kaɪnd/ *n.* (also **womenkind** /'wɪmɪn-/) women in general.

womanly /'wʊmənlɪ/ *adj.* (of a woman) having or showing qualities traditionally associated with women; not masculine or girlish. □□ **womanliness** *n.*

womb /wuːm/ *n.* **1** the organ of conception and gestation in a woman and other female mammals; the uterus. **2** a place of origination and development. □□ **womblike** *adj.* [OE *wamb*, *womb*]

wombat /'wɒmbæt/ *n.* any burrowing plant-eating Australian marsupial of the family Vombatidae, resembling a small bear, with short legs. [Aboriginal]

women *pl.* of WOMAN.

womenfolk /'wɪmɪn,fəʊk/ *n.* **1** women in general. **2** the women in a family.

womenkind var. of WOMANKIND.

won *past* and *past part.* of WIN.

wonder /'wʌndə(r)/ *n. & v.* — *n.* **1** an emotion excited by what is unexpected, unfamiliar, or inexplicable, esp. surprise mingled with admiration or curiosity etc. **2** a strange or remarkable person or thing, specimen, event, etc. **3** (*attrib.*) having marvellous or amazing properties etc. (*a wonder drug*). **4** a surprising thing (*it is a wonder you were not hurt*). — *v.* **1** *intr.* (often foll. by *at*, or *to* + infin.) be filled with wonder or great surprise. **2** *tr.* (foll. by *that* + clause) be surprised to find. **3** *tr.* desire or be curious to know (*I wonder what the time is*). **4** *tr.* expressing a tentative enquiry (*I wonder whether you would mind?*). □ **I shouldn't wonder** *colloq.* I think it likely. **I wonder** I very much doubt it. **no** (or **small**) **wonder** (often foll. by *that* + clause) one cannot be surprised; one might have guessed; it is natural. **the seven wonders of the world** seven buildings and monuments regarded in antiquity as specially remarkable. **wonder-struck** (or **-stricken**) reduced to silence by wonder. **wonders will never cease** an exclamation of extreme (usu. agreeable) surprise. **wonder-worker** a person who performs wonders. **work** (or **do**) **wonders 1** do miracles. **2** succeed remarkably. □□ **wonderer** *n.* [OE *wundor*, *wund-rian*, of unkn. orig.]

wonderful /'wʌndə,fʊl/ *adj.* **1** very remarkable or admirable. **2** arousing wonder. □□ **wonderfully** *adv.* **wonderfulness** *n.* [OE *wunderfull* (as WONDER, -FUL)]

wondering /'wʌndərɪŋ/ *adj.* filled with wonder; marvelling (*their wondering gaze*). □□ **wonderingly** *adv.*

wonderland /'wʌndə,lænd/ *n.* **1** a fairyland. **2** a land of surprises or marvels.

wonderment /'wʌndəmənt/ *n.* surprise, awe.

wondrous /'wʌndrəs/ *adj. & adv. poet.* — *adj.* wonderful. — *adv.* wonderfully (*wondrous kind*). □□ **wondrously** *adv.* **wondrousness** *n.* [alt. of obs. *wonders* (adj. & adv.), = genit. of WONDER (cf. -s³) after *marvellous*]

wonky /'wɒŋkɪ/ *adj.* (**wonkier, wonkiest**) *Brit. sl.* **1** crooked. **2** loose, unsteady. **3** unreliable. □□ **wonkily** *adv.* **wonkiness** *n.* [fanciful formation]

wont /wəʊnt/ *adj., n., & v.* — *predic.adj.* archaic or *literary* (foll. by *to* + infin.) accustomed (*as we were wont to say*). — *n. formal* or *joc.* what is customary, one's habit (*as is my wont*). — *v.tr. & intr.* (*3rd sing. present* **wonts** or **wont**; *past* **wont** or **wonted**) *archaic* make or become accustomed. [OE *gewunod* past part. of *gewunian* f. *wunian* dwell]

won't /wəʊnt/ *contr.* will not.

wonted /'wəʊntɪd/ *attrib.adj.* habitual, accustomed, usual.

woo /wuː/ *v.tr.* (**woos, wooed**) **1** court; seek the hand or love of (a woman). **2** try to win (fame, fortune, etc.). **3** seek the favour or support of. **4** coax or importune. □□ **wooable** *adj.* **wooer** *n.* [OE *wōgian* (intr.), *āwōgian* (tr.), of unkn. orig.]

wood /wʊd/ *n.* **1 a** a hard fibrous material that forms the main substance of the trunk or branches of a tree or shrub. **b** this cut for timber or for fuel, or for use in crafts, manufacture, etc. **2** (in *sing.* or *pl.*) growing trees densely occupying a tract of land. **3** (prec. by *the*) wooden storage, esp. a cask, for wine etc. (*poured straight from the wood*). **4** a wooden-headed golf club. **5** = BOWL² *n.* 1. □**not see the wood for the trees** fail to grasp the main issue from over-attention to details. **out of the wood** (or **woods**) out of danger or difficulty. **wood alcohol** methanol. **wood anemone** a wild spring-flowering anemone, *Anemone nemorosa.* **wood-engraver** a maker of wood-engravings. **wood-engraving 1** a relief cut on a block of wood sawn across the grain. **2** a print made from this. **3** the technique of making such reliefs and prints. **wood-fibre** fibre obtained from wood esp. as material for paper. **wood hyacinth** = BLUEBELL 1. **wood nymph** a dryad or hamadryad. **wood pulp** wood-fibre reduced chemically or mechanically to pulp as raw material for paper. **wood-screw** a metal male screw with a slotted head and sharp point. **wood sorrel** a small plant, *Oxalis acetosella*, with trifoliate leaves and white flowers streaked with purple. **wood spirit** crude methanol obtained from wood. **wood warbler 1** a European woodland bird, *Phylloscopus sibilatrix*, with a trilling song. **2** any American warbler of the family Parulidae. **wood wool** fine pine etc. shavings used as a surgical dressing or for packing. □□ **woodless** *adj.* [OE *wudu, wi(o)du* f. Gmc]

woodbind /'wʊdbaɪnd/ *n.* = WOODBINE.

woodbine /'wʊdbaɪn/ *n.* **1** wild honeysuckle. **2** *US* Virginia creeper.

woodblock /'wʊdblɒk/ *n.* a block from which wood-cuts are made.

woodchuck /'wʊdtʃʌk/ *n.* a reddish-brown and grey N. American marmot, *Marmota monax.* [Amer.Ind. name: cf. Cree *wuchak, otchock*]

woodcock /'wʊdkɒk/ *n.* (*pl.* same) any game-bird of the genus *Scolopax*, inhabiting woodland.

woodcraft /'wʊdkrɑːft/ *n.* esp. *US* **1** skill in wood-work. **2** knowledge of woodland esp. in camping, scouting, etc.

woodcut /'wʊdkʌt/ *n.* **1** a relief cut on a block of wood sawn along the grain. **2** a print made from this, esp. as an illustration in a book. **3** the technique of making such reliefs and prints.

woodcutter /'wʊd,kʌtə(r)/ *n.* **1** a person who cuts wood. **2** a maker of woodcuts.

wooded /'wʊdɪd/ *adj.* having woods or many trees.

wooden /'wʊd(ə)n/ *adj.* **1** made of wood. **2** like wood. **3 a** stiff, clumsy, or stilted; without animation or flexibility (*wooden movements; a wooden performance*). **b** expressionless (*a wooden stare*). □ **wooden-head** *colloq.* a stupid person. **wooden-headed** *colloq.* stupid. **wooden-headedness** *colloq.* stupidity. **wooden horse** = *Trojan Horse.* **wooden spoon** a booby prize (orig. a spoon given to the candidate coming last in the Cambridge mathematical tripos). □□ **woodenly** *adv.* **woodenness** *n.*

woodgrouse /'wʊdgraʊs/ *n.* = CAPERCAILLIE.

woodland /'wʊdlənd/ *n.* wooded country, woods (often *attrib.: woodland scenery*). □□ **woodlander** *n.*

woodlark /'wʊdlɑːk/ *n.* a lark, *Lullula arborea.*

woodlouse /'wʊdlaʊs/ *n.* (*pl.* **-lice** /-laɪs/) any small terrestrial isopod crustacean of the genus *Oniscus* etc. feeding on rotten wood etc. and often able to roll into a ball.

woodman /ˈwʊdmən/ *n.* (*pl.* **-men**) **1** a forester. **2** a woodcutter.

woodmouse /ˈwʊdmaʊs/ *n.* (*pl.* **-mice** /-maɪs/) a fieldmouse.

woodnote /ˈwʊdnəʊt/ *n.* (often in *pl.*) a natural or spontaneous note of a bird etc.

woodpecker /ˈwʊdˌpekə(r)/ *n.* any bird of the family Picidae that climbs and taps tree-trunks in search of insects.

woodpie /ˈwʊdpaɪ/ *n.* a greater spotted woodpecker.

woodpigeon /ˈwʊdˌpɪdʒ(ə)n/ *n.* a dove, *Columba palumbus*, having white patches like a ring round its neck. Also called *ring-dove* (see RING[1]).

woodpile /ˈwʊdpaɪl/ *n.* a pile of wood, esp. for fuel.

woodruff /ˈwʊdrʌf/ *n.* a white-flowered plant of the genus *Galium*, esp. *G. odoratum* grown for the fragrance of its whorled leaves when dried or crushed.

woodrush /ˈwʊdrʌʃ/ *n.* any grassy herbaceous plant of the genus *Luzula*.

woodshed /ˈwʊdʃed/ *n.* a shed where wood for fuel is stored. □ **something nasty in the woodshed** *colloq.* a shocking or distasteful thing kept secret.

woodsman /ˈwʊdzmən/ *n.* (*pl.* **-men**) **1** a person who lives in or is familiar with woodland. **2** a person skilled in woodcraft.

woodsy /ˈwʊdzɪ/ *adj. US* like or characteristic of woods. [irreg. f. WOOD + -Y[1]]

woodwasp /ˈwʊdwɒsp/ *n.* any sawfly of the family Siricidae, esp. *Urocerus gigas*, that hangs its nest in trees and inserts its eggs into the wood of conifers where the larvae bore damaging tunnels.

woodwind /ˈwʊdwɪnd/ *n.* (often *attrib.*) **1** (*collect.*) the wind instruments of the orchestra that were (mostly) orig. made of wood, e.g. the flute and clarinet. **2** (usu. in *pl.*) an individual instrument of this kind or its player (*the woodwinds are out of tune*).

woodwork /ˈwʊdwɜːk/ *n.* **1** the making of things in wood. **2** things made of wood, esp. the wooden parts of a building. □ **crawl** (or **come**) **out of the woodwork** *colloq.* (of something unwelcome) appear; become known. □□ **woodworker** *n.* **woodworking** *n.*

woodworm /ˈwʊdwɜːm/ *n.* **1** the wood-boring larva of the furniture beetle. **2** the damaged condition of wood affected by this.

woody /ˈwʊdɪ/ *adj.* (**woodier**, **woodiest**) **1** (of a region) wooded; abounding in woods. **2** like or of wood (*woody tissue*). □ **woody nightshade** see NIGHTSHADE. □□ **woodiness** *n.*

woodyard /ˈwʊdjɑːd/ *n.* a yard where wood is used or stored.

woof[1] /wʊf/ *n. & v.* —*n.* the gruff bark of a dog. —*v.intr.* give a woof. [imit.]

woof[2] /wuːf/ *n.* = WEFT[1]. [OE *ōwef*, alt. of *ōwebb* (after *wefan* WEAVE[1]), formed as A-[2], WEB: infl. by *warp*]

woofer /ˈwuːfə(r)/ *n.* a loudspeaker designed to reproduce low frequencies (cf. TWEETER). [WOOF[1] + -ER[1]]

wool /wʊl/ *n.* **1** fine soft wavy hair from the fleece of sheep, goats, etc. **2 a** yarn produced from this hair. **b** cloth or clothing made from it. **3** any of various wool-like substances (*steel wool*). **4** soft short under-fur or down. **5** *colloq.* a person's hair, esp. when short and curly. □ **pull the wool over a person's eyes** deceive a person. **wool-fat** lanolin. **wool-fell** *Brit.* the skin of a sheep etc. with the fleece still on. **wool-gathering** absent-mindedness; dreamy inattention. **wool-grower** a breeder of sheep for wool. **wool-oil** wool. **wool-pack 1** a fleecy cumulus cloud. **2** *hist.* a bale of wool. **wool-skin** = *wool-fell*. **wool-sorters' disease** anthrax. **wool-stapler** a person who grades wool. □□ **wool-like** *adj.* [OE *wull* f. Gmc]

woollen /ˈwʊlən/ *adj. & n.* (*US* **woolen**) —*adj.* made wholly or partly of wool, esp. from short fibres. —*n.* **1** a fabric produced from wool. **2** (in *pl.*) woollen garments. [OE *wullen* (as WOOL, -EN[2])]

woolly /ˈwʊlɪ/ *adj. & n.* —*adj.* (**woollier**, **woolliest**) **1** bearing or naturally covered with wool or wool-like hair. **2** resembling or suggesting wool (*woolly clouds*). **3** (of a sound) indistinct. **4** (of thought) vague or confused. **5** *Bot.* downy. **6** lacking in definition, luminosity, or incisiveness. —*n.* (*pl.* **-ies**) *colloq.* a woollen garment, esp. a knitted pullover. □ **woolly-bear** a large hairy caterpillar, esp. of the tiger moth. □□ **woolliness** *n.*

Woolsack /ˈwʊlsæk/ *n.* **1** (in the UK) the Lord Chancellor's wool-stuffed seat in the House of Lords. **2** the position of Lord Chancellor.

woolshed /ˈwʊlʃed/ *n. Austral. & NZ* a large shed for shearing and baling wool.

woomera /ˈwʊmərə/ *n. Austral.* **1** an Aboriginal stick for throwing a dart or spear more forcibly. **2** a club used as a missile. [Aboriginal]

woop woop /ˈwuːpwuːp/ *n. Austral. & NZ sl.* **1** a jocular name for a remote outback town or district. **2** (**Woop Woop**) an imaginary remote place. [mock Aboriginal]

woosh var. of WHOOSH.

woozy /ˈwuːzɪ/ *adj.* (**woozier**, **wooziest**) *colloq.* **1** dizzy or unsteady. **2** dazed or slightly drunk. **3** vague. □□ **woozily** *adv.* **wooziness** *n.* [19th c.: orig. unkn.]

wop /wɒp/ *n. sl. offens.* an Italian or other S. European. [20th c.: orig. uncert.: perh. f. It. *guappo* bold, showy, f. Sp. *guapo* dandy]

Worcester sauce /ˈwʊstə/ *n.* a pungent sauce first made in Worcester. [*Worcester* in S. England]

Worcs. *abbr.* Worcestershire.

word /wɜːd/ *n. & v.* —*n.* **1** a sound or combination of sounds forming a meaningful element of speech, usu. shown with a space on either side of it when written or printed, used as part (or occas. as the whole) of a sentence. **2** speech, esp. as distinct from action (*bold in word only*). **3** one's promise or assurance (*gave us their word*). **4** (in *sing.* or *pl.*) a thing said, a remark or conversation. **5** (in *pl.*) the text of a song or an actor's part. **6** (in *pl.*) angry talk (*they had words*). **7** news, intelligence; a message. **8** a command, password, or motto (*gave the word to begin*). **9** a basic unit of the expression of data in a computer. —*v.tr.* put into words; select words to express (*how shall we word that?*). □ **at a word** as soon as requested. **be as good as** (or **better than**) **one's word** fulfil (or exceed) what one has promised. **break one's word** fail to do what one has promised. **have no words for** be unable to express. **have a word** (often foll. by *with*) speak briefly (to). **in other words** expressing the same thing differently. **in so many words** explicitly or bluntly. **in a** (or **one**) **word** briefly. **keep one's word** do what one has promised. **my** (or **upon my**) **word** an exclamation of surprise or consternation. **not the word for it** not an adequate or appropriate description. **of few words** taciturn. **of one's word** reliable in keeping promises (*a woman of her word*). **on** (or **upon**) **my word** a form of asseveration. **put into words** express in speech or writing. **take a person at his** or **her word** interpret a person's words literally or exactly. **take a person's word for it** believe a person's statement without investigation etc. **too . . . for words** too . . . to be adequately described (*was too funny for words*). **waste words** talk in vain. **the Word** (or **Word of God**) the Bible. **word-blind** incapable of identifying written or printed words owing to a brain defect. **word-blindness** this condition. **word-deaf** incapable of identifying spoken words owing to a brain defect. **word-deafness** this condition. **word for word** in exactly the same or (of translation) corresponding words. **word-game** a game involving the making or selection etc. of words. **word of honour** an assurance given upon one's honour. **word of mouth** speech (only). **word order** the sequence of words in a sentence, esp. affecting meaning etc. **word-painting** a vivid description in writing. **word-perfect** knowing one's part etc. by heart. **word-picture** a piece of word-painting. **word processor** a purpose-built computer system for electronically storing text entered from a keyboard, incorporating corrections, and providing a printout. **words fail me** an expression of disbelief, dismay, etc. **word-square** a set of words of equal length written one under another to read the same down as across (e.g. *too old ode*). **a word to the wise** = VERB. SAP. ▫▫ **wordage** *n.* **wordless** *adj.* **wordlessly** *adv.* **wordlessness** *n.* [OE f. Gmc]

wordbook /ˈwɜːdbʊk/ *n.* a book with lists of words; a vocabulary or dictionary.

wording /ˈwɜːdɪŋ/ *n.* **1** a form of words used. **2** the way in which something is expressed.

wordplay /ˈwɜːdpleɪ/ *n.* use of words to witty effect, esp. by punning.

wordsmith /ˈwɜːdsmɪθ/ *n.* a skilled user or maker of words.

wordy /ˈwɜːdɪ/ *adj.* (**wordier**, **wordiest**) **1** using or expressed in many or too many words; verbose. **2** consisting of words. ▫▫ **wordily** *adv.* **wordiness** *n.* [OE *wordig* (as WORD, -Y[1])]

wore[1] *past* of WEAR[1].

wore[2] *past* and *past part.* of WEAR[2].

work /wɜːk/ *n.* & *v.* —*n.* **1** the application of mental or physical effort to a purpose; the use of energy. **2 a** a task to be undertaken. **b** the materials for this. **c** (prec. by *the*; foll. by *of*) a task occupying (no more than) a specified time (*the work of a moment*). **3** a thing done or made by work; the result of an action; an achievement; a thing made. **4** a person's employment or occupation etc., esp. as a means of earning income (*looked for work*; *is out of work*). **5 a** a literary or musical composition. **b** (in *pl.*) all such by an author or composer etc. **6** actions or experiences of a specified kind (*good work!*; *this is thirsty work*). **7 a** (in *comb.*) things or parts made of a specified material or with specified tools etc. (*ironwork*; *needlework*). **b** *archaic* needlework. **8** (in *pl.*) the operative part of a clock or machine. **9** *Physics* the exertion of force overcoming resistance or producing molecular change (*convert heat into work*). **10** (in *pl.*) *colloq.* all that is available; everything needed. **11** (in *pl.*) operations of building or repair (*road works*). **12** (in *pl.*; often treated as *sing.*) a place where manufacture is carried on. **13** (usu. in *pl.*) *Theol.* a meritorious act. **14** (usu. in *pl.* or in *comb.*) a defensive structure (*earthworks*). **15** (in *comb.*) **a** ornamentation of a specified kind (*poker-work*). **b** articles having this. —*v.* (*past* and *past part.* **worked** or (esp. as *adj.*) **wrought**) **1** *intr.* (often foll. by *at, on*) do work; be engaged in bodily or mental activity. **2** *intr.* **a** be employed in certain work (*works in industry*; *works as a secretary*). **b** (foll. by *with*) be the workmate of (a person). **3** *intr.* (often foll. by *for*) make efforts; conduct a campaign (*works for peace*). **4** *intr.* (foll. by *in*) be a craftsman (in a material). **5** *intr.* operate or function, esp. effectively (*how does this machine work?*; *your idea will not work*). **6** *intr.* (of a part of a machine) run, revolve; go through regular motions. **7** *tr.* carry on, manage, or control (*cannot work the machine*). **8** *tr.* **a** put or keep in operation or at work; cause to toil (*this mine is no longer worked*; *works the staff very hard*). **b** cultivate (land). **9** *tr.* bring about; produce as a result (*worked miracles*). **10** *tr.* knead, hammer; bring to a desired shape or consistency. **11** *tr.* do, or make by, needlework etc. **12** *tr.* & *intr.* (cause to) progress or penetrate, or make (one's way), gradually or with difficulty in a specified way (*worked our way through the crowd*; *worked the peg into the hole*). **13** *intr.* (foll. by *loose* etc.) gradually become (loose etc.) by constant movement. **14** *tr.* artificially excite (*worked themselves into a rage*). **15** *tr.* solve (a sum)

by mathematics. **16** *tr.* **a** purchase with one's labour instead of money (*work one's passage*). **b** obtain by labour the money for (one's way through university etc.). **17** *intr.* (foll. by *on, upon*) have influence. **18** *intr.* be in motion or agitated; cause agitation, ferment (*his features worked violently*; *the yeast began to work*). **19** *intr.* *Naut.* sail against the wind. □**at work** in action or engaged in work. **give a person the works 1** *colloq.* give or tell a person everything. **2** *colloq.* treat a person harshly. **3** *sl.* kill a person. **have one's work cut out** be faced with a hard task. **set to work** begin or cause to begin operations. **work away** (or **on**) continue to work. **work-basket** (or **-bag** etc.) a basket or bag etc. containing sewing materials. **work camp** a camp at which community work is done esp. by young volunteers. **work one's fingers to the bone** see BONE. **work in** find a place for. **work it** *colloq.* bring it about; achieve a desired result. **work of art** a fine picture, poem, or building etc. **work off** get rid of by work or activity. **work out 1** solve (a sum) or find out (an amount) by calculation. **2** (foll. by *at*) be calculated (*the total works out at 230*). **3** give a definite result (*this sum will not work out*). **4** have a specified result (*the plan worked out well*). **5** provide for the details of (*has worked out a scheme*). **6** accomplish or attain with difficulty (*work out one's salvation*). **7** exhaust with work (*the mine is worked out*). **8** engage in physical exercise or training. **work over 1** examine thoroughly. **2** *colloq.* treat with violence. **works council** esp. *Brit.* a group of employees representing those employed in a works etc. in discussions with their employers. **work-shy** disinclined to work. **works of supererogation** see SUPEREROGATION. **work study** a system of assessing methods of working so as to achieve the maximum output and efficiency. **work table** a table for working at, esp. with a sewing-machine. **work to rule** (esp. as a form of industrial action) follow official working rules exactly in order to reduce output and efficiency. **work-to-rule** the act or an instance of working to rule. **work up 1** bring gradually to an efficient state. **2** (foll. by *to*) advance gradually to a climax. **3** elaborate or excite by degrees. **4** mingle (ingredients) into a whole. **5** learn (a subject) by study. **work one's will** (foll. by *on, upon*) *archaic* accomplish one's purpose on (a person or thing). **work wonders** see WONDER. ▫▫ **workless** *adj.* [OE *weorc* etc. f. Gmc]

workable /ˈwɜːkəb(ə)l/ *adj.* **1** that can be worked or will work. **2** that is worth working; practicable, feasible (*a workable quarry*; *a workable scheme*). ▫▫ **workability** (/-ˈbɪlɪtɪ/) *n.* **workableness** *n.* **workably** *adv.*

workaday /ˈwɜːkəˌdeɪ/ *adj.* **1** ordinary, everyday, practical. **2** fit for, used, or seen on workdays.

workaholic /ˌwɜːkəˈhɒlɪk/ *n.* *colloq.* a person addicted to working.

workbench /ˈwɜːkbentʃ/ *n.* a bench for doing mechanical or practical work, esp. carpentry.

workbox /ˈwɜːkbɒks/ *n.* a box for holding tools, materials for sewing, etc.

workday /ˈwɜːkdeɪ/ *n.* esp. *US* a day on which work is usually done.

worker /ˈwɜːkə(r)/ *n.* **1** a person who works, esp. a manual or industrial employee. **2** a neuter or undeveloped female of various social insects, esp. a bee or ant, that does the basic work of its colony. □**worker priest** a French Roman Catholic or an Anglican priest who engages part-time in secular work.

workforce /ˈwɜːkfɔːs/ *n.* **1** the workers engaged or available in an industry etc. **2** the number of such workers.

workhorse /ˈwɜːkhɔːs/ *n.* a horse, person, or machine that performs hard work.

workhouse /ˈwɜːkhaʊs/ *n.* **1** *Brit. hist.* a public institution in which the destitute of a parish received board and lodging in return for work done. **2** *US* a house of correction for petty offenders.

working /ˈwɜːkɪŋ/ *adj. & n.* —*adj.* **1** engaged in work, esp. in manual or industrial labour. **2** functioning or able to function. —*n.* **1** the activity of work. **2** the act or manner of functioning of a thing. **3 a** a mine or quarry. **b** the part of this in which work is being or has been done (*a disused working*). □**working capital** the capital actually used in a business. **working class** the class of people who are employed for wages, esp. in manual or industrial work. **working-class** *adj.* of the working class. **working day** esp. *Brit.* **1** a workday. **2** the part of the day devoted to work. **working drawing** a drawing to scale, serving as a guide for construction or manufacture. **working hours** hours normally devoted to work. **working hypothesis** a hypothesis used as a basis for action. **working knowledge** knowledge adequate to work with. **working lunch** etc. a meal at which business is conducted. **working order** the condition in which a machine works (satisfactorily or as specified). **working-out 1** the calculation of results. **2** the elaboration of details. **working party** a group of people appointed to study a particular problem or advise on some question.

workload /ˈwɜːkləʊd/ *n.* the amount of work to be done by an individual etc.

workman /ˈwɜːkmən/ *n.* (*pl.* **-men**) **1** a man employed to do manual labour. **2** a person considered with regard to skill in a job (*a good workman*).

workmanlike /ˈwɜːkmənˌlaɪk/ *adj.* characteristic of a good workman; showing practised skill.

workmanship /ˈwɜːkmənʃɪp/ *n.* **1** the degree of skill in doing a task or of finish in the product made. **2** a thing made or created by a specified person etc.

workmate /ˈwɜːkmeɪt/ *n.* a person engaged in the same work as another.

workout /ˈwɜːkaʊt/ *n.* a session of physical exercise or training.

workpeople /ˈwɜːkˌpiːp(ə)l/ *n.pl.* people in paid employment.

workpiece /ˈwɜːkpiːs/ *n.* a thing worked on with a tool or machine.

workplace /ˈwɜːkpleɪs/ *n.* a place at which a person works; an office, factory, etc.

workroom /ˈwɜːkruːm, -rʊm/ *n.* a room for working in, esp. one equipped for a certain kind of work.

worksheet /ˈwɜːkʃiːt/ *n.* **1** a paper for recording work done or in progress. **2** a paper listing questions or activities for students etc. to work through.

workshop /ˈwɜːkʃɒp/ *n.* **1** a room or building in which goods are manufactured. **2 a** a meeting for concerted discussion or activity (*a dance workshop*). **b** the members of such a meeting.

workstation /ˈwɜːkˌsteɪʃ(ə)n/ *n.* **1** the location of a stage in a manufacturing process. **2** a computer terminal or the desk etc. where this is located.

worktop /ˈwɜːktɒp/ *n.* a flat surface for working on, esp. in a kitchen.

workwoman /ˈwɜːkˌwʊmən/ *n.* (*pl.* **-women**) a female worker or operative.

world /wɜːld/ *n.* **1 a** the earth, or a planetary body like it. **b** its countries and their inhabitants. **c** all people; the earth as known or in some particular respect. **2 a** the universe or all that exists; everything. **b** everything that exists outside oneself (*dead to the world*). **3 a** the time, state, or scene of human existence. **b** (prec. by *the*, *this*) mortal life. **4** secular interests and affairs. **5** human affairs; their course and conditions; active life (*how goes the world with you?*). **6** average, respectable, or fashionable people or their customs or opinions. **7** all that concerns or all who belong to a specified class, time, domain, or sphere of activity (*the medieval world; the world of sport*). **8** (foll. by *of*) a vast amount (*that makes a world of difference*). **9** (*attrib.*) affecting many nations, of all nations (*world politics; a world champion*). □**all the world and his wife 1** any large mixed gathering

of people. **2** all with pretensions to fashion. **bring into the world** give birth to or attend at the birth of. **carry the world before one** have rapid and complete success. **come into the world** be born. **for all the world** (foll. by *like*, *as if*) precisely (*looked for all the world as if they were real*). **get the best of both worlds** benefit from two incompatible sets of ideas, circumstances, etc. **in the world** of all; at all (used as an intensifier in questions) (*what in the world is it?*). **man** (or **woman**) **of the world** a person experienced and practical in human affairs. **the next** (or **other**) **world** a supposed life after death. **out of this world** *colloq.* extremely good etc. (*the food was out of this world*). **see the world** travel widely; gain wide experience. **think the world of** have a very high regard for. **World Bank** *colloq.* the International Bank for Reconstruction and Development, an organization administering economic aid between member nations. **world-beater** a person or thing surpassing all others. **world-class** of a quality or standard regarded as high throughout the world. **World Cup** a competition between football or other sporting teams from various countries. **world-famous** known throughout the world. **the world, the flesh, and the devil** the various kinds of temptation. **world language 1** an artificial language for international use. **2** a language spoken in many countries. **world-line** *Physics* a curve in space-time joining the positions of a particle throughout its existence. **the** (or **all the**) **world over** throughout the world. **world power** a nation having power and influence in world affairs. **the world's end** the farthest attainable point of travel. **World Series** the US championship for baseball teams. **world-shaking** of supreme importance. **the world to come** supposed life after death. **world-view** = WELTANSCHAUUNG. **world war** a war involving many important nations (*First World War* of 1914–18; *Second World War* of 1939–45). **world-weariness** being world-weary. **world-weary** weary of the world and life on it. **world without end** for ever. [OE *w(e)orold*, *world* f. a Gmc root meaning 'age': rel. to OLD]

worldling /ˈwɜːldlɪŋ/ *n.* a worldly person.

worldly /ˈwɜːldlɪ/ *adj.* (**worldlier**, **worldliest**) **1** temporal or earthly (*worldly goods*). **2** engrossed in temporal affairs, esp. the pursuit of wealth and pleasure. □**worldly-minded** intent on worldly things. **worldly wisdom** prudence as regards one's own interests. **worldly-wise** having worldly wisdom. □□**worldliness** *n.* [OE *woruldlic* (as WORLD, -LY¹)]

worldwide /ˈwɜːldwaɪd, -ˈwaɪd/ *adj. & adv.* —*adj.* affecting, occurring in, or known in all parts of the world. —*adv.* throughout the world.

worm /wɜːm/ *n. & v.* —*n.* **1** any of various types of creeping or burrowing invertebrate animals with long slender bodies and no limbs, esp. segmented in rings or parasitic in the intestines or tissues. **2** the long slender larva of an insect, esp. in fruit or wood. **3** (in *pl.*) intestinal or other internal parasites. **4** a blindworm or slow-worm. **5** a maggot supposed to eat dead bodies in the grave. **6** an insignificant or contemptible person. **7 a** the spiral part of a screw. **b** a short screw working in a worm-gear. **8** the spiral pipe of a still in which the vapour is cooled and condensed. **9** the ligament under a dog's tongue. —*v.* **1** *intr. & tr.* (often *refl.*) move with a crawling motion (*wormed through the bushes; wormed our way through the bushes*). **2** *intr. & refl.* (foll. by *into*) insinuate oneself into a person's favour, confidence, etc. **3** *tr.* (foll. by *out*) obtain (a secret etc.) by cunning persistence (*managed to worm the truth out of them*). **4** *tr.* cut the worm of (a dog's tongue). **5** *tr.* rid (a plant or dog etc.) of worms. **6** *tr. Naut.* make (a rope etc.) smooth by winding thread between the strands. □**food for worms** a dead person. **worm-cast** a convoluted mass of earth left on the surface by a burrowing earthworm. **worm-fishing** fishing with worms for bait. **worm-gear** an arrangement of a toothed wheel worked by a revolving spiral. **worm-hole** a hole left by the passage of a worm. **worm-seed 1** seed used to expel intestinal worms. **2** a plant e.g. santonica bearing this seed. **worm's-eye view** a view as seen from below or from a humble position. **worm-wheel** the wheel of a worm-gear. **a** (or **even a**) **worm will turn** the meekest will resist or retaliate if pushed too far. □□ **wormer** *n*. **wormlike** *adj*. [OE *wyrm* f. Gmc]

wormeaten /ˈwɜːmˌiːt(ə)n/ *adj*. **1 a** eaten into by worms. **b** rotten, decayed. **2** old and dilapidated.

wormwood /ˈwɜːmwʊd/ *n*. **1** any woody shrub of the genus *Artemisia*, with a bitter aromatic taste, used in the preparation of vermouth and absinthe and in medicine. **2** bitter mortification or a source of this. [ME, alt. f. obs. *wormod* f. OE *wormōd*, *wermōd*, after *worm*, *wood*: cf. VERMOUTH]

wormy /ˈwɜːmɪ/ *adj*. (**wormier**, **wormiest**) **1** full of worms. **2** wormeaten. □□ **worminess** *n*.

worn /wɔːn/ *past part*. of WEAR[1]. —*adj*. **1** damaged by use or wear. **2** looking tired and exhausted. **3** (in full **well-worn**) (of a joke etc.) stale; often heard.

worriment /ˈwʌrɪmənt/ *n*. esp. *US* **1** the act of worrying or state of being worried. **2** a cause of worry.

worrisome /ˈwʌrɪsəm/ *adj*. causing or apt to cause worry or distress. □□ **worrisomely** *adv*.

worrit /ˈwʌrɪt/ *n*. *colloq*. = WORRY. [orig. alt. in general use of WORRY]

worry /ˈwʌrɪ/ *v*. & *n*. —*v*. (**-ies**, **-ied**) **1** *intr*. give way to anxiety or unease; allow one's mind to dwell on difficulty or troubles. **2** *tr*. harass, importune; be a trouble or anxiety to. **3** *tr*. **a** (of a dog etc.) shake or pull about with the teeth. **b** attack repeatedly. **4** (as **worried** *adj*.) **a** uneasy, troubled in the mind. **b** suggesting worry (*a worried look*). —*n*. (*pl*. **-ies**) **1** a thing that causes anxiety or disturbs a person's tranquillity. **2** a disturbed state of mind; anxiety; a worried state. **3** a dog's worrying of its quarry. □**not to worry** *colloq*. there is no need to worry. **worry along** (or **through**) manage to advance by persistence in spite of obstacles. **worry beads** a string of beads manipulated with the fingers to occupy or calm oneself. **worry-guts** (or **-wart**) *colloq*. a person who habitually worries unduly. **worry oneself** (usu. in *neg*.) take needless trouble. **worry out** obtain (the solution to a problem etc.) by dogged effort. □□ **worriedly** *adv*. **worrier** *n*. **worryingly** *adv*. [OE *wyrgan* strangle f. WG]

worse /wɜːs/ *adj*., *adv*., & *n*. —*adj*. **1** more bad. **2** (*predic*.) in or into worse health or a worse condition (*is getting worse*; *is none the worse for it*). —*adv*. more badly or more ill. —*n*. **1** a worse thing or things (*you might do worse than accept*). **2** (prec. by *the*) a worse condition (*a change for the worse*). □**none the worse** (often foll. by *for*) not adversely affected (by). **or worse** or as an even worse alternative. **the worse for drink** fairly drunk. **the worse for wear 1** damaged by use. **2** injured. **worse luck** see LUCK. **worse off** in a worse (esp. financial) position. [OE *wyrsa*, *wiersa* f. Gmc]

worsen /ˈwɜːs(ə)n/ *v.tr*. & *intr*. make or become worse.

worship /ˈwɜːʃɪp/ *n*. & *v*. —*n*. **1 a** homage or reverence paid to a deity, esp. in a formal service. **b** the acts, rites, or ceremonies of worship. **2** adoration or devotion comparable to religious homage shown towards a person or principle (*the worship of wealth*; *regarded them with worship in their eyes*). **3** *archaic* worthiness, merit; recognition given or due to these; honour and respect. —*v*. (**worshipped**, **worshipping**; *US* **worshiped**, **worshiping**) **1** *tr*. adore as divine; honour with religious rites. **2** *tr*. idolize or regard with adoration (*worships the ground she walks on*). **3** *intr*. attend public worship. **4** *intr*. be full of adoration. □**Your** (or **His** or **Her**) **Worship** esp. *Brit*. a title of respect used to or of a mayor,

certain magistrates, etc. □□ **worshipper** *n*. (*US* **worshiper**). [OE *weorthscipe* (as WORTH, -SHIP)]

worshipful /ˈwɜːʃɪpfʊl/ *adj*. **1** (usu. **Worshipful**) *Brit*. a title given to justices of the peace and to certain old companies or their officers etc. **2** *archaic* entitled to honour or respect. **3** *archaic* imbued with a spirit of veneration. □□ **worshipfully** *adv*. **worshipfulness** *n*.

worst /wɜːst/ *adj*., *adv*., *n*., & *v*. —*adj*. most bad. —*adv*. most badly. —*n*. the worst part, event, circumstance, or possibility (*the worst of the storm is over*; *prepare for the worst*). —*v.tr*. get the better of; defeat, outdo. □**at its** etc. **worst** in the worst state. **at worst** (or **the worst**) in the worst possible case. **do your worst** an expression of defiance. **get** (or **have**) **the worst of it** be defeated. **if the worst comes to the worst** if the worst happens. [OE *wierresta*, *wyrresta* (adj.), *wyrst*, *wyrrest* (adv.), f. Gmc]

worsted /ˈwʊstɪd/ *n*. **1** a fine smooth yarn spun from combed long staple wool. **2** fabric made from this. [*Worste(a)d* in S. England]

wort /wɜːt/ *n*. **1** *archaic* (except in names) a plant or herb (*liverwort*; *St John's wort*). **2** the infusion of malt which after fermentation becomes beer. [OE *wyrt*: rel. to ROOT[1]]

worth /wɜːθ/ *adj*. & *n*. —*predic.adj*. (governing a noun like a preposition) **1** of a value equivalent to (*is worth £50*; *is worth very little*). **2** such as to justify or repay; deserving; bringing compensation for (*worth doing*; *not worth the trouble*). **3** possessing or having property amounting to (*is worth a million pounds*). —*n*. **1** what a person or thing is worth; the (usu. specified) merit of (*of great worth*; *persons of worth*). **2** the equivalent of money in a commodity (*ten pounds' worth of petrol*). □**for all one is worth** *colloq*. with one's utmost efforts; without reserve. **for what it is worth** without a guarantee of its truth or value. **worth it** *colloq*. worth the time or effort spent. **worth one's salt** see SALT. **worth while** (or **one's while**) see WHILE. [OE *w(e)orth*]

worthless /ˈwɜːθlɪs/ *adj*. without value or merit. □□ **worthlessly** *adv*. **worthlessness** *n*.

worthwhile /wɜːθˈwaɪl, -ˈwaɪl/ *adj*. that is worth the time or effort spent; of value or importance. □□ **worthwhileness** *n*.

worthy /ˈwɜːðɪ/ *adj*. & *n*. —*adj*. (**worthier**, **worthiest**) **1** estimable; having some moral worth; deserving respect (*lived a worthy life*). **2** (of a person) entitled to (esp. condescending) recognition (*a worthy old couple*). **3 a** (foll. by *of* or *to* + infin.) deserving (*worthy of a mention*; *worthy to be remembered*). **b** (foll. by *of*) adequate or suitable to the dignity etc. of (*in words worthy of the occasion*). —*n*. (*pl*. **-ies**) **1** a worthy person. **2** a person of some distinction. **3** *joc*. a person. □□ **worthily** *adv*. **worthiness** *n*. [ME *wurthi* etc. f. WORTH]

-worthy /ˈwɜːðɪ/ *comb. form* forming adjectives meaning: **1** deserving of (*blameworthy*; *noteworthy*). **2** suitable or fit for (*newsworthy*; *roadworthy*).

wot see WIT[2].

wotcher /ˈwɒtʃə(r)/ *int*. *Brit*. *sl*. a form of casual greeting. [corrupt. of *what cheer*]

would /wʊd, wəd/ *v.aux*. (*3rd sing*. **would**) *past* of WILL[1], used esp.: **1** (in the 2nd and 3rd persons, and often in the 1st: see SHOULD) **a** in a reported speech (*he said he would be home by evening*). **b** to express the conditional mood (*they would have been killed if they had gone*). **2** to express habitual action (*would wait for her every evening*). **3** to express a question or polite request (*would they like it?*; *would you come in, please?*). **4** to express probability (*I guess she would be over fifty by now*). **5** (foll. by *that* + clause) *literary* to express a wish (*would that you were here*). **6** to express consent (*they would not help*). □**would-be** often *derog*. desiring or aspiring to be (*a would-be politician*). [OE *wolde*, past of *wyllan*: see WILL[1]]

wouldn't /'wʊd(ə)nt/ *contr.* would not. □**I wouldn't know** *colloq.* (as is to be expected) I do not know.

wouldst /wʊdst/ *archaic 2nd sing. past of* WOULD.

Woulfe bottle /wʊlf/ *n. Chem.* a jar with more than one neck, used for passing a gas through a liquid etc. [P. *Woulfe*, Engl. chemist d. 1803]

wound[1] /wuːnd/ *n. & v.* —*n.* **1** an injury done to living tissue by a cut or blow etc., esp. beyond the cutting or piercing of the skin. **2** an injury to a person's reputation or a pain inflicted on a person's feelings. **3** *poet.* the pangs of love. —*v.tr.* inflict a wound on (*wounded soldiers*; *wounded feelings*). □□ **woundingly** *adv.* **woundless** *adj.* [OE *wund* (n.), *wundian* (v.)]

wound[2] *past* and *past part. of* WIND[2] (cf. WIND[1] *v.* 6).

woundwort /'wuːndwɜːt/ *n.* any of various plants esp. of the genus *Stachys*, formerly supposed to have healing properties.

wove[1] *past of* WEAVE[1].

wove[2] /wəʊv/ *adj.* (of paper) made on a wire-gauze mesh and so having a uniform unlined surface. [var. of *woven*, past part. of WEAVE[1]]

woven *past part. of* WEAVE[1].

wow[1] /waʊ/ *int., n., & v.* —*int.* expressing astonishment or admiration. —*n. sl.* a sensational success. —*v.tr. sl.* impress or excite greatly. [orig. Sc.: imit.]

wow[2] /waʊ/ *n.* a slow pitch-fluctuation in sound-reproduction, perceptible in long notes. [imit.]

wowser /'waʊzə(r)/ *n. Austral. sl.* **1** a puritanical fanatic. **2** a spoilsport. **3** a teetotaller. [20th c.: orig. uncert.]

WP *abbr.* word processor or processing.

w.p. *abbr.* weather permitting.

w.p.b. *abbr.* waste-paper basket.

WPC *abbr.* (in the UK) woman police constable.

w.p.m. *abbr.* words per minute.

WRAC *abbr.* (in the UK) Women's Royal Army Corps.

wrack /ræk/ *n.* **1** seaweed cast up or growing on the shore. **2** destruction. **3** a wreck or wreckage. **4** = RACK[2]. **5** = RACK[5]. [ME f. MDu. *wrak* or MLG *wra(c)k*, a parallel formation to OE *wræc*, rel. to *wrecan* WREAK: cf. WRECK, RACK[5]]

WRAF *abbr.* (in the UK) Women's Royal Air Force.

wraggle-taggle var. of RAGGLE-TAGGLE.

wraith /reɪθ/ *n.* **1** a ghost or apparition. **2** the spectral appearance of a living person supposed to portend that person's death. □□ **wraithlike** *adj.* [16th-c. Sc.: orig. unkn.]

wrangle /'ræŋg(ə)l/ *n. & v.* —*n.* a noisy argument, altercation, or dispute. —*v.* **1** *intr.* engage in a wrangle. **2** *tr. US* herd (cattle). [ME, prob. f. LG or Du.: cf. LG *wrangelen*, frequent. of *wrangen* to struggle, rel. to WRING]

wrangler /'ræŋglə(r)/ *n.* **1** a person who wrangles. **2** *US* a cowboy. **3** (at Cambridge University) a person placed in the first class of the mathematical tripos.

wrap /ræp/ *v. & n.* —*v.tr.* (**wrapped, wrapping**) **1** (often foll. by *up*) envelop in folded or soft encircling material (*wrap it up in paper*; *wrap up a parcel*). **2** (foll. by *round, about*) arrange or draw (a pliant covering) round (a person) (*wrapped the scarf closer around me*). **3** (foll. by *round*) *sl.* crash (a vehicle) into a stationary object. —*n.* **1** a shawl or scarf or other such addition to clothing; a wrapper. **2** esp. *US* material used for wrapping. □ **take the wraps off** disclose. **under wraps** in secrecy. **wrap-over** *adj.* (*attrib.*) (of a garment) having no seam at one side but wrapped around the body and fastened. —*n.* such a garment. **wrapped up in** engrossed or absorbed in. **wrap up 1** finish off, bring to completion (*wrapped up the deal in two days*). **2** put on warm clothes (*mind you wrap up well*). **3** (in *imper.*) *sl.* be quiet. [ME: orig. unkn.]

wraparound /'ræpə,raʊnd/ *adj. & n.* (also **wrapround** /'ræpraʊnd/) —*adj.* **1** (esp. of clothing)

designed to wrap round. **2** curving or extending round at the edges. —*n.* anything that wraps round.

wrappage /'ræpɪdʒ/ *n.* a wrapping or wrappings.

wrapper /'ræpə(r)/ *n.* **1** a cover for a sweet, chocolate, etc. **2** a cover enclosing a newspaper or similar packet for posting. **3** a paper cover of a book, usu. detachable. **4** a loose enveloping robe or gown. **5** a tobacco-leaf of superior quality enclosing a cigar.

wrapping /'ræpɪŋ/ *n.* (esp. in *pl.*) material used to wrap; wraps, wrappers. □ **wrapping paper** strong or decorative paper for wrapping parcels.

wrapround var. of WRAPAROUND.

wrasse /ræs/ *n.* any bright-coloured marine fish of the family Labridae with thick lips and strong teeth. [Corn. *wrach*, var. of *gwrach*, = Welsh *gwrach*, lit. 'old woman']

wrath /rɒθ, rɔːθ/ *n. literary* extreme anger. [OE *wrǣththu* f. *wrāth* WROTH]

wrathful /'rɒθfʊl/ *adj. literary* extremely angry. □□ **wrathfully** *adv.* **wrathfulness** *n.*

wrathy /'rɔːθɪ/ *adj. US* = WRATHFUL.

wreak /riːk/ *v.tr.* **1** (usu. foll. by *upon*) give play or satisfaction to; put in operation (vengeance or one's anger etc.). **2** cause (damage etc.) (*the hurricane wreaked havoc on the crops*). **3** *archaic* avenge (a wrong or wronged person). □□ **wreaker** *n.* [OE *wrecan* drive, avenge, etc., f. Gmc: cf. WRACK, WRECK, WRETCH]

wreath /riːθ/ *n.* (*pl.* **wreaths** /riːðz, riːθs/) **1** flowers or leaves fastened in a ring esp. as an ornament for a person's head or a building or for laying on a grave etc. as a mark of honour or respect. **2 a** a similar ring of soft twisted material such as silk. **b** *Heraldry* a representation of this below a crest. **3** a carved representation of a wreath. **4** (foll. by *of*) a curl or ring of smoke or cloud. **5** a light drifting mass of snow etc. [OE *writha* f. weak grade of *wrīthan* WRITHE]

wreathe /riːð/ *v.* **1** *tr.* encircle as, with, or like a wreath. **2** *tr.* (foll. by *round*) put (one's arms etc.) round (a person etc.). **3** *intr.* (of smoke etc.) move in the shape of wreaths. **4** *tr.* form (flowers, silk, etc.) into a wreath. **5** *tr.* make (a garland). [partly back-form. f. archaic *wrethen* past part. of WRITHE; partly f. WREATH]

wreck /rek/ *n. & v.* —*n.* **1** the destruction or disablement esp. of a ship. **2** a ship that has suffered a wreck (*the shores are strewn with wrecks*). **3** a greatly damaged or disabled building, thing, or person (*had become a physical and mental wreck*). **4** (foll. by *of*) a wretched remnant or disorganized set of remains. **5** *Law* goods etc. cast up by the sea. —*v.* **1** *tr.* cause the wreck of (a ship etc.). **2** *tr.* completely ruin (hopes, chances, etc.). **3** *intr.* suffer a wreck. **4** *tr.* (as **wrecked** *adj.*) involved in a shipwreck (*wrecked sailors*). **5** *intr. US* deal with wrecked vehicles etc. □ **wreck-master** an officer appointed to take charge of goods etc. cast up from a wrecked ship. [ME f. AF *wrec* etc. (cf. VAREC) f. a Gmc root meaning 'to drive': cf. WREAK]

wreckage /'rekɪdʒ/ *n.* **1** wrecked material. **2** the remnants of a wreck. **3** the action or process of wrecking.

wrecker /'rekə(r)/ *n.* **1** a person or thing that wrecks or destroys. **2** esp. *hist.* a person on the shore who tries to bring about a shipwreck in order to plunder or profit by the wreckage. **3** esp. *US* a person employed in demolition, or in recovering a wrecked ship or its contents. **4** *US* a person who breaks up damaged vehicles for spares and scrap. **5** *US* a vehicle or train used in recovering a damaged one.

Wren /ren/ *n.* (in the UK) a member of the Women's Royal Naval Service. [orig. in pl., f. abbr. WRNS]

wren /ren/ *n.* any small usu. brown short-winged songbird of the family Troglodytidae, esp. *Troglodytes troglodytes* of Europe, having an erect tail. [OE *wrenna*, rel. to OHG *wrendo, wrendilo,* Icel. *rindill*]

wrench /rentʃ/ n. & v. —n. **1** a violent twist or oblique pull or act of tearing off. **2** an adjustable tool like a spanner for gripping and turning nuts etc. **3** an instance of painful uprooting or parting (*leaving home was a great wrench*). **4** *Physics* a combination of a couple with the force along its axis. —v.tr. **1** twist or pull violently round or sideways. **2** (often foll. by *off*, *away*, etc.) pull off with a wrench. **3** distort (facts) to suit a theory etc. [(earlier as verb:) OE *wrencan* twist]

wrest /rest/ v. & n. —v.tr. **1** force or wrench away from a person's grasp. **2** (foll. by *from*) obtain by effort or with difficulty. **3** distort into accordance with one's interests or views (*wrest the law to suit themselves*). —n. *archaic* a key for tuning a harp or piano etc. □**wrest-block** (or **-plank**) the part of a piano or harpsichord holding the wrest-pins. **wrest-pin** each of the pins to which the strings of a piano or harpsichord are attached. [OE *wræstan* f. Gmc, rel. to WRIST]

wrestle /'res(ə)l/ v. & n. —n. **1** a contest in which two opponents grapple and try to throw each other to the ground esp. as an athletic sport under a code of rules. **2** a hard struggle. —v. **1** *intr.* (often foll. by *with*) take part in a wrestle. **2** *tr.* fight (a person) in a wrestle (*wrestled his opponent to the ground*). **3** *intr.* **a** (foll. by *with*, *against*) struggle, contend. **b** (foll. by *with*) do one's utmost to deal with (a task, difficulty, etc.). **4** *tr.* move with efforts as if wrestling. □□ **wrestler** n. **wrestling** n. [OE (unrecorded) *wræstlian*: cf. MLG *wrosteln*, OE *wraxlian*]

wretch /retʃ/ n. **1** an unfortunate or pitiable person. **2** (often as a playful term of depreciation) a reprehensible or contemptible person. [OE *wrecca* f. Gmc]

wretched /'retʃid/ adj. (**wretcheder**, **wretchedest**) **1** unhappy or miserable. **2** of bad quality or no merit; contemptible. **3** unsatisfactory or displeasing. □**feel wretched 1** be unwell. **2** be much embarrassed. □□ **wretchedly** adv. **wretchedness** n. [ME, irreg. f. WRETCH + -ED¹: cf. WICKED]

wrick *Brit.* var. of RICK².

wriggle /'rɪg(ə)l/ v. & n. —v. **1** *intr.* (of a worm etc.) twist or turn its body with short writhing movements. **2** *intr.* (of a person or animal) make wriggling motions. **3** *tr.* & *intr.* (foll. by *along* etc.) move or go in this way (*wriggled into the corner*; *wriggled his hand into the hole*). **4** *tr.* make (one's way) by wriggling. **5** *intr.* practise evasion. —n. an act of wriggling. □**wriggle out of** *colloq.* avoid on a contrived pretext. □□ **wriggler** n. **wriggly** adj. [ME f. MLG *wriggelen* frequent. of *wriggen*]

wright /raɪt/ n. a maker or builder (usu. in comb.: *playwright*; *shipwright*). [OE *wryhta*, *wyrhta* f. WG: cf. WORK]

wring /rɪŋ/ v. & n. —v.tr. (*past* and *past part.* **wrung** /rʌŋ/) **1 a** squeeze tightly. **b** (often foll. by *out*) squeeze and twist esp. to remove liquid. **2** twist forcibly; break by twisting. **3** distress or torture. **4** extract by squeezing. **5** (foll. by *out*, *from*) obtain by pressure or importunity; extort. —n. an act of wringing; a squeeze. □**wring a person's hand** clasp it forcibly or press it with emotion. **wring one's hands** clasp them as a gesture of great distress. **wring the neck of** kill (a chicken etc.) by twisting its neck. [OE *wringan*, rel. to WRONG]

wringer /'rɪŋə(r)/ n. a device for wringing water from washed clothes etc.

wringing /'rɪŋɪŋ/ adj. (in full **wringing wet**) so wet that water can be wrung out.

wrinkle /'rɪŋk(ə)l/ n. & v. —n. **1** a slight crease or depression in the skin such as is produced by age. **2** a similar mark in another flexible surface. **3** *colloq.* a useful tip or clever expedient. —v. **1** *tr.* make wrinkles in. **2** *intr.* form wrinkles; become marked with wrinkles. [orig. repr. OE *gewrinclod* sinuous]

wrinkly /'rɪŋklɪ/ adj. & n. —adj. (**wrinklier**, **wrinkliest**) having many wrinkles. —n. (also

wrinklie) (pl. **-ies**) *sl. offens.* an old or middle-aged person.

wrist /rɪst/ n. **1** the part connecting the hand with the forearm. **2** the corresponding part in an animal. **3** the part of a garment covering the wrist. **4 a** (in full **wrist-work**) the act or practice of working the hand without moving the arm. **b** the effect got in fencing, ball games, sleight of hand, etc., by this. **5** (in full **wrist-pin**) *Mech.* a stud projecting from a crank etc. as an attachment for a connecting-rod. □**wrist-drop** the inability to extend the hand through paralysis of the forearm muscles. **wrist-watch** a small watch worn on a strap round the wrist. [OE f. Gmc, prob. f. a root rel. to WRITHE]

wristband /'rɪstbænd/ n. a band forming or concealing the end of a shirt-sleeve; a cuff.

wristlet /'rɪstlɪt/ n. a band or ring worn on the wrist to strengthen or guard it or as an ornament, bracelet, handcuff, etc.

wristy /'rɪstɪ/ adj. (esp. of a shot in cricket, tennis, etc.) involving or characterized by movement of the wrist.

writ¹ /rɪt/ n. **1** a form of written command in the name of a sovereign, court, State, etc., to act or abstain from acting in some way. **2** a Crown document summoning a peer to Parliament or ordering the election of a member or members of Parliament. □**serve a writ on** deliver a writ to (a person). **one's writ runs** one has authority (as specified). [OE (as WRITE)]

writ² /rɪt/ *archaic past part.* of WRITE. □**writ large** in magnified or emphasized form.

write /raɪt/ v. (*past* **wrote** /rəʊt/; *past part.* **written** /'rɪt(ə)n/) **1** *intr.* mark paper or some other surface by means of a pen, pencil, etc., with symbols, letters, or words. **2** *tr.* form or mark (such symbols etc.). **3** *tr.* form or mark the symbols that represent or constitute (a word or sentence, or a document etc.). **4** *tr.* fill or complete (a sheet, cheque, etc.) with writing. **5** *tr.* put (data) into a computer store. **6** *tr.* (esp. in *passive*) indicate (a quality or condition) by one's or its appearance (*guilt was written on his face*). **7** *tr.* compose (a text, article, novel, etc.) for written or printed reproduction or publication; put into literary etc. form and set down in writing. **8** *intr.* engaged in composing a text, article, etc. (*writes for the local newspaper*). **9** *intr.* (foll. by *to*) write and send a letter (to a recipient). **10** *tr.* *US* or *colloq.* write and send a letter to (a person) (*wrote him last week*). **11** *tr.* convey (news, information, etc.) by letter (*wrote that they would arrive next Friday*). **12** *tr.* state in written or printed form (*it is written that*). **13** *tr.* cause to be recorded. **14** *tr.* underwrite (an insurance policy). **15** *tr.* (foll. by *into*, *out of*) include or exclude (a character or episode) in a story by suitable changes of the text. **16** *tr.* *archaic* describe in writing. □**nothing to write home about** *colloq.* of little interest or value. **write down 1** record or take note of in writing. **2** write as if for those considered inferior. **3** disparage in writing. **4** reduce the nominal value of (stock, goods, etc.). **write in 1** send a suggestion, query, etc., in writing to an organization, esp. a broadcasting station. **2** *US* add (an extra name) on a list of candidates when voting. **write-in** n. *US* an instance of writing in (see *write in 2*). **write off 1** write and send a letter. **2** cancel the record of (a bad debt etc.); acknowledge the loss of or failure to recover (an asset). **3** damage (a vehicle etc.) so badly that it cannot be repaired. **4** compose with facility. **write-off** n. a thing written off, esp. a vehicle too badly damaged to be repaired. **write out 1** write in full or in finished form. **2** exhaust (oneself) by writing (*have written myself out*). **write up 1** write a full account of. **2** praise in writing. **3** make entries to bring (a diary etc.) up to date. **write-up** n. *colloq.* a written or published account, a review. □□ **writable** adj. [OE *wrītan* scratch, score, write, f. Gmc: orig.

used of symbols inscribed with sharp tools on stone or wood]

writer /'raɪtə(r)/ *n.* **1** a person who writes or has written something. **2** a person who writes books; an author. **3** a clerk, esp. in the Navy or in government offices. **4** a scribe. □**writer's cramp** a muscular spasm due to excessive writing. **Writer to the Signet** a Scottish solicitor conducting cases in the Court of Session. [OE *wrītere* (as WRITE)]

writhe /raɪð/ *v. & n.* —*v.* **1** *intr.* twist or roll oneself about in or as if in acute pain. **2** *intr.* suffer severe mental discomfort or embarrassment (*writhed with shame; writhed at the thought of it*). **3** *tr.* twist (one's body etc.) about. —*n.* an act of writhing. [OE *wrīthan*, rel. to WREATHE]

writing /'raɪtɪŋ/ *n.* **1** a group or sequence of letters or symbols. **2** = HANDWRITING. **3** (usu. in *pl.*) a piece of literary work done; a book, article, etc. **4** (**Writings**) the Hagiographa. □**in writing** in written form. **writing-desk** a desk for writing at, esp. with compartments for papers etc. **the writing on the wall** an ominously significant event etc. (see Dan. 5: 5, 25-8). **writing-pad** a pad (see PAD¹ *n.* 2) of paper for writing on. **writing-paper** paper for writing (esp. letters) on.

written *past part.* of WRITE.

WRNS *abbr.* (in the UK) Women's Royal Naval Service.

wrong /rɒŋ/ *adj., adv., n., & v.* —*adj.* **1** mistaken; not true; in error (*gave a wrong answer; we were wrong to think that*). **2** unsuitable; less or least desirable (*the wrong road; a wrong decision*). **3** contrary to law or morality (*it is wrong to steal*). **4** amiss; out of order, in or into a bad or abnormal condition (*something wrong with my heart; my watch has gone wrong*). —*adv.* (usually placed last) in a wrong manner or direction; with an incorrect result (*guessed wrong; told them wrong*). —*n.* **1** what is morally wrong; a wrong action. **2** injustice; unjust action or treatment (*suffer wrong*). —*v.tr.* **1** treat unjustly; do wrong to. **2** mistakenly attribute bad motives to; discredit. □**do wrong** commit sin; transgress, offend. **do wrong to** malign or mistreat (a person). **get in wrong with** incur the dislike or disapproval of (a person). **get on the wrong side of** fall into disfavour with. **get wrong 1** misunderstand (a person, statement, etc.). **2** obtain an incorrect answer to. **get** (or **get hold of**) **the wrong end of the stick** misunderstand completely. **go down the wrong way** (of food) enter the windpipe instead of the gullet. **go wrong 1** take the wrong path. **2** stop functioning properly. **3** depart from virtuous or suitable behaviour. **in the wrong** responsible for a quarrel, mistake, or offence. **on the wrong side of 1** out of favour with (a person). **2** somewhat more than (a stated age). **wrong-foot** *colloq.* **1** (in tennis, football, etc.) play so as to catch (an opponent) off balance. **2** disconcert; catch unprepared. **wrong-headed** perverse and obstinate. **wrong-headedly** in a wrong-headed manner. **wrong-headedness** the state of being wrong-headed. **wrong side** the worse or undesired or unusable side of something, esp. fabric. **wrong side out** inside out. **wrong way round** in the opposite or reverse of the normal or desirable orientation or sequence etc. □□ **wronger** *n.* **wrongly** *adv.* **wrongness** *n.* [OE *wrang* f. ON *rangr* awry, unjust, rel. to WRING]

wrongdoer /'rɒŋ,duːə(r)/ *n.* a person who behaves immorally or illegally. □□ **wrongdoing** *n.*

wrongful /'rɒŋfʊl/ *adj.* **1** characterized by unfairness or injustice. **2** contrary to law. **3** (of a person) not entitled to the position etc. occupied. □□ **wrongfully** *adv.* **wrongfulness** *n.*

wrong'un /'rɒŋən/ *n. colloq.* a person of bad character. [contr. of *wrong one*]

wrote *past* of WRITE.

wroth /rəʊθ, rɒθ/ *predic.adj.* archaic angry. [OE *wrāth* f. Gmc]

wrought /rɔːt/ *archaic past* and *past part.* of WORK. —*adj.* (of metals) beaten out or shaped by hammering. □**wrought iron** a tough malleable form of iron suitable for forging or rolling, not cast.

wrung *past* and *past part.* of WRING.

WRVS *abbr.* (in the UK) Women's Royal Voluntary Service.

wry /raɪ/ *adj.* (**wryer, wryest** or **wrier, wriest**) **1** distorted or turned to one side. **2** (of a face or smile etc.) contorted in disgust, disappointment, or mockery. **3** (of humour) dry and mocking. □□ **wryly** *adv.* **wryness** *n.* [*wry* (v.) f. OE *wrīgian* tend, incline, in ME deviate, swerve, contort]

wryneck /'raɪnek/ *n.* **1** = TORTICOLLIS. **2** any bird of the genus *Jynx* of the woodpecker family, able to turn its head over its shoulder.

WSW *abbr.* west-south-west.

wt. *abbr.* weight.

Wu /wuː/ *n.* a dialect of Chinese spoken in the Kiangsu and Chekiang Provinces. [Chin.]

wunderkind /'vʊndəkɪnt/ *n. colloq.* a person who achieves great success while relatively young. [G f. *Wunder* wonder + *Kind* child]

wurst /vʊəst, vɜːst/ *n.* German or Austrian sausage. [G]

WV *abbr. US* West Virginia (in official postal use).

W.Va. *abbr.* West Virginia.

WW *abbr. US* World War (I, II).

WX *abbr.* women's extra-large size.

WY *abbr. US* Wyoming (in official postal use).

wych- /wɪtʃ/ *comb. form* (also **wich-, witch-**) in names of trees with pliant branches. [OE *wic(e)* app. f. a Gmc root meaning 'bend': rel. to WEAK]

wych-alder /'wɪtʃ,ɔːldə(r)/ *n.* an American plant, *Fothergilla gardenii*, with alder-like leaves.

wych-elm /'wɪtʃelm/ *n.* a species of elm, *Ulmus glabra*.

wych-hazel /'wɪtʃ,heɪz(ə)l/ *n.* **1** var. of WITCH-HAZEL. **2** = WYCH-ELM.

Wykehamist /'wɪkəmɪst/ *adj. & n.* —*adj.* of or concerning Winchester College. —*n.* a past or present member of Winchester College. [mod.L *Wykehamista* f. William of *Wykeham*, bishop of Winchester and founder of the college (d. 1404)]

wyn var. of WEN².

wynd /waɪnd/ *n. Sc.* a narrow street or alley. [ME, app. f. the stem of WIND²]

Wyo. *abbr.* Wyoming.

WYSIWYG /'wɪzɪwɪg/ *adj.* (also **wysiwyg**) *Computing* denoting the representation of text onscreen in a form exactly corresponding to its appearance on a printout. [acronym of *what you see is what you get*]

wyvern /'waɪv(ə)n/ *n.* (also **wivern**) *Heraldry* a winged two-legged dragon with a barbed tail. [ME *wyver* f. OF *wivre, guivre* f. L *vipera*: for *-n* cf. BITTERN]

X

X¹ /eks/ n. (also **x**) (pl. **Xs** or **X's**) **1** the twenty-fourth letter of the alphabet. **2** (as a Roman numeral) ten. **3** (usu. **x**) *Algebra* the first unknown quantity. **4** *Geom.* the first coordinate. **5** an unknown or unspecified number or person etc. **6** a cross-shaped symbol esp. used to indicate position (*X marks the spot*) or incorrectness or to symbolize a kiss or a vote, or as the signature of a person who cannot write.

X² *symb.* (of films) classified as suitable for adults only. ¶ Formerly used in the UK to indicate that persons under 18 would not be admitted; it was replaced in 1983 by *18*, but is still used in the US.

-x /z/ *suffix* forming the plural of many nouns in *-u* taken from French (*beaux*; *tableaux*). [F]

xanthate /ˈzænθeɪt/ n. any salt or ester of xanthic acid.

xanthic /ˈzænθɪk/ adj. yellowish. □**xanthic acid** any colourless unstable acid containing the −OCS₂H group. [Gk *xanthos* yellow]

Xanthippe /zænˈθɪpɪ/ n. (also **Xantippe** /-ˈtɪpɪ/) a shrewish or ill-tempered woman or wife. [name of Socrates' wife]

xanthoma /zænˈθəʊmə/ n. (pl. **xanthomas** or **xanthomata** /-tə/) *Med.* **1** a skin disease characterized by irregular yellow patches. **2** such a patch. [as XANTHIC + -OMA]

xanthophyll /ˈzænθəfɪl/ n. any of various oxygen-containing carotenoids associated with chlorophyll, some of which cause the yellow colour of leaves in the autumn. [as XANTHIC + Gk *phullon* leaf]

X-chromosome /ˈeksˌkrəʊməˌsəʊm/ n. a sex chromosome of which the number in female cells is twice that in male cells. [*X* as an arbitrary label + CHROMOSOME]

x.d. *abbr.* ex dividend.

Xe *symb. Chem.* the element xenon.

xebec /ˈziːbek/ n. (also **zebec**, **zebeck**) a small three-masted Mediterranean vessel with lateen and usu. some square sails. [alt. (after Sp. *xabeque*) of F *chebec* f. It. *sciabecco* f. Arab. *šabāk*]

xeno- /ˈzenəʊ/ *comb. form* **1 a** foreign. **b** a foreigner. **2** other. [Gk *xenos* strange, foreign, stranger]

xenogamy /zeˈnɒɡəmɪ/ n. *Bot.* cross-fertilization. □□ **xenogamous** adj.

xenolith /ˈzenəlɪθ/ n. *Geol.* an inclusion within an igneous rock mass, usu. derived from the immediately surrounding rock.

xenon /ˈzenɒn/ n. *Chem.* a heavy colourless odourless inert gaseous element occurring in traces in the atmosphere and used in fluorescent lamps. ¶ Symb.: **Xe**. [Gk, neut. of *xenos* strange]

xenophobe /ˈzenəˌfəʊb/ n. a person given to xenophobia.

xenophobia /ˌzenəˈfəʊbɪə/ n. a deep dislike of foreigners. □□ **xenophobic** adj.

xeranthemum /zɪəˈrænθɪməm/ n. a composite plant of the genus *Xeranthemum*, with dry everlasting composite flowers. [mod.L f. Gk *xēros* dry + *anthemon* flower]

xeric /ˈzɪərɪk/ adj. *Ecol.* having or characterized by dry conditions. [as XERO- + -IC]

xero- /ˈzɪərəʊ, ˈzerəʊ/ *comb. form* dry. [Gk *xēros* dry]

xeroderma /ˌzɪərəˈdɜːmə/ n. any of various diseases characterized by extreme dryness of the skin, esp. ichthyosis. [mod.L (as XERO-, Gk *derma* skin)]

xerograph /ˈzɪərəˌɡrɑːf, ˈze-/ n. a copy produced by xerography.

xerography /zɪəˈrɒɡrəfɪ, ze-/ n. a dry copying process in which black or coloured powder adheres to parts of a surface remaining electrically charged after exposure of the surface to light from an image of the document to be copied. □□ **xerographic** /-rəˈɡræfɪk/ adj. **xerographically** /-rəˈɡræfɪkəlɪ/ adv.

xerophilous /zɪəˈrɒfɪləs, ze-/ adj. (of a plant) adapted to extremely dry conditions.

xerophyte /ˈzɪərəˌfaɪt, ˈze-/ n. (also **xerophile** /-ˌfaɪl/) a plant able to grow in very dry conditions, e.g. in a desert.

Xerox /ˈzɪərɒks, ˈze-/ n. & v. —n. *propr.* **1** a machine for copying by xerography. **2** a copy made using this machine. —v.tr. (**xerox**) reproduce by this process. [invented f. XEROGRAPHY]

Xhosa /ˈkəʊsə, ˈkɔː-/ n. & adj. —n. **1** (pl. same or **Xhosas**) a member of a Bantu people of Cape Province, South Africa. **2** the Bantu language of this people, similar to Zulu. —adj. of or relating to this people or language. [native name]

xi /saɪ, ɡzaɪ, zaɪ/ n. the fourteenth letter of the Greek alphabet (Ξ, ξ). [Gk]

-xion /kʃ(ə)n/ *suffix* forming nouns (see -ION) from Latin participial stems in *-x-* (*fluxion*).

xiphisternum /ˌzɪfɪˈstɜːnəm/ n. *Anat.* = *xiphoid process*. [as XIPHOID + STERNUM]

xiphoid /ˈzɪfɔɪd/ adj. *Biol.* sword-shaped. □**xiphoid process** the cartilaginous process at the lower end of the sternum. [Gk *xiphoeidēs* f. *xiphos* sword]

Xmas /ˈkrɪsməs, ˈeksməs/ n. *colloq.* = CHRISTMAS. [abbr., with X for the initial chi of Gk *Khristos* Christ]

xoanon /ˈzəʊəˌnɒn/ n. (pl. **xoana** /-nə/) Gk *Antiq.* a primitive usu. wooden image of a deity supposed to have fallen from heaven. [Gk f. *xeō* carve]

X-ray /ˈeksreɪ/ n. & v. (also **x-ray**) —n. **1** (in pl.) electromagnetic radiation of short wavelength, able to pass through opaque bodies. **2** an image made by the effect of X-rays on a photographic plate, esp. showing the position of bones etc. by their greater absorption of the rays. —v.tr. photograph, examine, or treat with X-rays. □**X-ray astronomy** the branch of astronomy concerned with the X-ray emissions of celestial bodies. **X-ray crystallography** the study of crystals and their structure by means of the diffraction of X-rays by the regularly spaced atoms of a crystalline material. **X-ray tube** a device for generating X-rays by accelerating electrons to high energies and causing them to strike a metal target from which the X-rays are emitted. [transl. of G *x-Strahlen* (pl.) f. *Strahl* ray, so called because when discovered in 1895 the nature of the rays was unknown]

xylem /ˈzaɪləm/ n. *Bot.* woody tissue (cf. PHLOEM). [Gk *xulon* wood]

xylene /ˈzaɪliːn/ n. *Chem.* one of three isomeric hydrocarbons formed from benzene by the substitution of two methyl groups, obtained from wood etc. [formed as XYLEM + -ENE]

xylo- /ˈzaɪləʊ/ *comb. form* wood. [Gk *xulon* wood]

xylocarp /ˈzaɪləˌkɑːp/ n. a hard woody fruit. □□ **xylocarpous** /-ˈkɑːpəs/ adj.

xylograph /ˈzaɪləˌɡrɑːf/ n. a woodcut or wood-engraving (esp. an early one).

xylography /zaɪˈlɒɡrəfɪ/ n. **1** the (esp. early or primitive) practice of making woodcuts or wood-engravings. **2** the use of wood blocks in printing.

Xylonite /ˈzaɪləˌnaɪt/ n. *propr.* a kind of celluloid. [irreg. f. *xyloidin* (as XYLO-) + -ITE¹]

xylophagous /zaɪˈlɒfəɡəs/ adj. (of an insect or mollusc) eating, or boring into, wood.

xylophone /ˈzaɪləˌfəʊn/ n. a musical instrument of wooden or metal bars graduated in length and struck with a small wooden hammer or hammers. □□

æ *cat* ɑː *arm* e *bed* ɜː *her* ɪ *sit* iː *see* ɒ *hot* ɔː *saw* ʌ *run* ʊ *put* uː *too* ə *ago* aɪ *my*

xylophonic /-ˈfɒnɪk/ *adj.* **xylophonist** *n.* [Gk *xulon* wood + -PHONE]

xystus /ˈzɪstəs/ *n.* (*pl.* **xysti** /-taɪ/) **1** a covered portico used by athletes in ancient Greece for exercise. **2** *Rom. Antiq.* a garden walk or terrace. [L f. Gk *xustos* smooth f. *xuō* scrape]

Y

Y¹ /waɪ/ n. (also **y**) (pl. **Ys** or **Y's**) **1** the twenty-fifth letter of the alphabet. **2** (usu. **y**) *Algebra* the second unknown quantity. **3** *Geom.* the second coordinate. **4 a** a Y-shaped thing, esp. an arrangement of lines, piping, roads, etc. **b** a forked clamp or support.

Y² *abbr.* (also **Y.**) **1** yen. **2** Yeomanry. **3** *US* = YMCA, YWCA.

Y³ *symb. Chem.* the element yttrium.

y. *abbr.* year(s).

y- /ɪ/ *prefix archaic* forming past participles, collective nouns, etc. (*yclept*). [OE *ge-* f. Gmc]

-y¹ /ɪ/ *suffix* forming adjectives: **1** from nouns and adjectives, meaning: **a** full of; having the quality of (*messy*; *icy*; *horsy*). **b** addicted to (*boozy*). **2** from verbs, meaning 'inclined to', 'apt to' (*runny*; *sticky*). [from or after OE *-ig* f. Gmc]

-y² /ɪ/ *suffix* (also **-ey**, **-ie**) forming diminutive nouns, pet names, etc. (*granny*; *Sally*; *nightie*; *Mickey*). [ME (orig. Sc.)]

-y³ /ɪ/ *suffix* forming nouns denoting: **1** state, condition, or quality (*courtesy*; *orthodoxy*; *modesty*). **2** an action or its result (*colloquy*; *remedy*; *subsidy*). [from or after F *-ie* f. L *-ia*, *-ium*, Gk *-eia*, *-ia*: cf. -ACY, -ERY, -GRAPHY, and others]

yabby /ˈjæbɪ/ n. (also **yabbie**) (pl. **-ies**) *Austral.* **1** a small freshwater crayfish, esp. of the genus *Cherax*. **2** a marine prawn, *Callianassa australiensis*, often used as bait. [Aboriginal]

yacht /jɒt/ n. & v. —n. **1** a light sailing-vessel, esp. equipped for racing. **2** a larger usu. power-driven vessel equipped for cruising. **3** a light vessel for travel on sand or ice. —v.intr. race or cruise in a yacht. □ **yacht-club** a club esp. for yacht-racing. □□ **yachting** n. [early mod.Du. *jaghte* = *jaghtschip* fast pirate-ship f. *jag(h)t* chase f. *jagen* to hunt + *schip* SHIP]

yachtsman /ˈjɒtsmən/ n. (pl. **-men**; fem. **yachtswoman**, pl. **-women**) a person who sails yachts.

yack /jæk/ n. & v. (also **yackety-yack** /ˌjækətɪˈjæk/) sl. derog. —n. trivial or unduly persistent conversation. —v.intr. engage in this. [imit.]

yacka (also **yacker**) var. of YAKKA.

yaffle /ˈjæf(ə)l/ n. dial. a green woodpecker, *Picus viridus*. [imit. of its laughing cry]

yager var. of JAEGER.

yah /jɑː/ int. expressing derision or defiance. [imit.]

yahoo /jəˈhuː, jɑː-/ n. a coarse bestial person. [name of an imaginary race of brutish creatures in Swift's *Gulliver's Travels* (1726)]

Yahweh /ˈjɑːweɪ/ n. (also **Yahveh** /-veɪ/) the Hebrew name of God in the Old Testament. [Heb. *YHVH* with added vowels: see JEHOVAH]

Yahwist /ˈjɑːwɪst/ n. (also **Yahvist** /-vɪst/) the postulated author or authors of parts of the Hexateuch in which God is regularly named *Yahweh*.

yak /jæk/ n. a long-haired humped Tibetan ox, *Bos grunniens*. [Tibetan *gyag*]

yakka /ˈjækə/ n. (also **yacka**, **yacker**) *Austral. sl.* work. [Aboriginal]

Yale lock /jeɪl/ n. propr. a type of lock for doors etc. with a cylindrical barrel turned by a flat key with a serrated edge. [L. *Yale*, Amer. inventor d. 1868]

yam /jæm/ n. **1 a** any tropical or subtropical climbing plant of the genus *Dioscorea*. **b** the edible starchy tuber of this. **2** *US* a sweet potato. [Port. *inhame* or Sp. *iñame*, orig. uncert.]

yammer /ˈjæmə(r)/ n. & v. colloq. or dial. —n. **1** a lament, wail, or grumble. **2** voluble talk. —v.intr. **1** utter a yammer. **2** talk volubly. □□ **yammerer** n. [OE *geōmrian* f. *geōmor* sorrowful]

yandy /ˈjændɪ/ v. & n. *Austral.* —v.tr. (**-ies**, **-ied**) separate (grass seed) from refuse by special shaking. —n. (pl. **-ies**) a shallow dish used for this. [Aboriginal]

yang /jæŋ/ n. (in Chinese philosophy) the active male principle of the universe (cf. YIN). [Chin.]

Yank /jæŋk/ n. colloq. often derog. an inhabitant of the US; an American. [abbr.]

yank /jæŋk/ v. & n. colloq. —v.tr. pull with a jerk. —n. a sudden hard pull. [19th c.: orig. unkn.]

Yankee /ˈjæŋkɪ/ n. colloq. **1** often derog. = YANK. **2** *US* an inhabitant of New England or one of the northern States. **3** hist. a Federal soldier in the Civil War. **4** a type of bet on four or more horses to win (or be placed) in different races. **5** (attrib.) of or as of the Yankees. □ **Yankee Doodle 1** an American tune and song regarded as a national air. **2** = YANKEE. [18th c.: orig. uncert.: perh. f. Du. *Janke* dimin. of *Jan* John attested (17th c.) as a nickname]

yap /jæp/ v. & n. —v.intr. (**yapped**, **yapping**) **1** bark shrilly or fussily. **2** colloq. talk noisily, foolishly, or complainingly. —n. a sound of yapping. □□ **yapper** n. [imit.]

yapok /ˈjæpɒk/ n. = POSSUM 2. [*Oyapok*, *Oiapoque*, N. Brazilian river]

yapp /jæp/ n. Brit. a form of bookbinding with a limp leather cover projecting to fold over the edges of the leaves. [name of a London bookseller *c.*1860, for whom it was first made]

yarborough /ˈjɑːbərə/ n. a whist or bridge hand with no card above a 9. [Earl of *Yarborough* (d. 1897), said to have betted against its occurrence]

yard¹ /jɑːd/ n. **1** a unit of linear measure equal to 3 feet (0.9144 metre). **2** this length of material (*a yard and a half of cloth*). **3** a square or cubic yard esp. (in building) of sand etc. **4** a cylindrical spar tapering to each end slung across a mast for a sail to hang from. **5** (in pl.; foll. by of) colloq. a great length (*yards of spare wallpaper*). □ **by the yard** at great length. **yard-arm** the outer extremity of a ship's yard. **yard of ale** Brit. **1** a deep slender beer glass, about a yard long and holding two to three pints. **2** the contents of this. [OE *gerd* f. WG]

yard² /jɑːd/ n. & v. —n. **1** a piece of enclosed ground esp. attached to a building or used for a particular purpose. **2** *US* the garden of a house. —v.tr. put (cattle) into a stockyard. □ **the Yard** Brit. colloq. = SCOTLAND YARD. **yard-man 1** a person working in a railway-yard or timber-yard. **2** *US* a gardener or a person who does various outdoor jobs. **yard-master** the manager of a railway-yard. [OE *geard* enclosure, region, f. Gmc: cf. GARDEN]

yardage /ˈjɑːdɪdʒ/ n. **1** a number of yards of material etc. **2 a** the use of a stockyard etc. **b** payment for this.

yardbird /ˈjɑːdbɜːd/ n. *US sl.* **1** a new military recruit. **2** a convict.

yardstick /ˈjɑːdstɪk/ n. **1** a standard used for comparison. **2** a measuring rod a yard long, usu. divided into inches etc.

yarmulke /ˈjɑːmʊlkə/ n. (also **yarmulka**) a skullcap worn by Jewish men. [Yiddish]

yarn /jɑːn/ n. & v. —n. **1** any spun thread, esp. for knitting, weaving, rope-making, etc. **2** colloq. a long or rambling story or discourse. —v.intr. colloq. tell yarns. [OE *gearn*]

yarran /ˈjærən/ n. any of several Australian acacias,

esp. *Acacia homalophylla*, a small tree with scented wood used for fencing, fuel, etc. [Aboriginal]

yarrow /'jærəʊ/ n. any perennial herb of the genus *Achillea*, esp. milfoil. [OE *gearwe*, of unkn. orig.]

yashmak /'jæʃmæk/ n. a veil concealing the face except the eyes, worn by some Muslim women when in public. [Arab. *yašmak*, Turk. *yaşmak*]

yataghan /'jætəˌgæn/ n. a sword without a guard and often with a double-curved blade, used in Muslim countries. [Turk. *yātāğan*]

yaw /jɔː/ v. & n. —v.intr. (of a ship or aircraft etc.) fail to hold a straight course; fall off; go unsteadily (esp. turning from side to side). —n. the yawing of a ship etc. from its course. [16th c.: orig. unkn.]

yawl /jɔːl/ n. **1** a two-masted fore-and-aft sailing-boat with the mizen-mast stepped far aft. **2** a small kind of fishing-boat. **3** *hist.* a ship's jolly boat with four or six oars. [MLG *jolle* or Du. *jol*, of unkn. orig.: cf. JOLLY[2]]

yawn /jɔːn/ v. & n. —v. **1** *intr.* (as a reflex) open the mouth wide and inhale esp. when sleepy or bored. **2** *intr.* (of a chasm etc.) gape, be wide open. **3** *tr.* utter or say with a yawn. —n. **1** an act of yawning. **2** *colloq.* a boring or tedious idea, activity, etc. □□ **yawner** n. **yawningly** adv. [OE *ginian, geonian*]

yawp /jɔːp/ n. & v. US —n. **1** a harsh or hoarse cry. **2** foolish talk. —v.intr. utter these. □□ **yawper** n. [ME (imit.)]

yaws /jɔːz/ n.pl. (usu. treated as *sing.*) a contagious tropical skin-disease with large red swellings. [17th c.: orig. unkn.]

Yb *symb. Chem.* the element ytterbium.

Y-chromosome /'waɪˌkrəʊməˌsəʊm/ n. a sex chromosome occurring only in male cells. [*Y* as an arbitrary label + CHROMOSOME]

yclept /ɪ'klept/ adj. *archaic* or *joc.* called (by the name of). [OE *gecleopod* past part. of *cleopian* call f. Gmc]

yd. *abbr.* yard (measure).

yds. *abbr.* yards (measure).

ye[1] /jiː/ pron. *archaic* pl. of THOU[1]. □**ye gods!** *joc.* an exclamation of astonishment. [OE *ge* f. Gmc]

ye[2] /jiː/ adj. *pseudo-archaic* = THE (*ye olde tea-shoppe*). [var. spelling f. the *y*-shaped letter THORN (representing *th*) in the 14th c.]

yea /jeɪ/ adv. & n. *archaic* —adv. **1** yes. **2** indeed, nay (*ready, yea eager*). —n. the word 'yea'. □**yea and nay** shilly-shally. **yeas and nays** affirmative and negative votes. [OE *gea, ge* f. Gmc]

yeah /jeə/ adv. *colloq.* yes. □**oh yeah?** expressing incredulity. [casual pronunc. of YES]

yean /jiːn/ v.tr. & intr. *archaic* bring forth (a lamb or kid). [perh. f. OE *geēanian* (unrecorded, as Y-, *ēanian* to lamb)]

yeanling /'jiːnlɪŋ/ n. *archaic* a young lamb or kid.

year /jɪə(r), jɜː(r)/ n. **1** (also **astronomical year, equinoctial year, natural year, solar year, tropical year**) the time occupied by the earth in one revolution round the sun, 365 days, 5 hours, 48 minutes, and 46 seconds in length (cf. *sidereal year*). **2** (also **calendar year, civil year**) the period of 365 days (**common year**) or 366 days (see *leap year*) from 1 Jan. to 31 Dec., used for reckoning time in ordinary affairs. **3 a** a period of the same length as this starting at any point (*four years ago*). **b** such a period in terms of a particular activity etc. occupying its duration (*school year; tax year*). **4** (in *pl.*) age or time of life (*young for his years*). **5** (usu. in *pl.*) *colloq.* a very long time (*it took years to get served*). **6** a group of students entering college etc. in the same academic year. □**in the year of Our Lord** (foll. by the year) in a specified year AD. **of the year** chosen as outstanding in a particular year (*sportsman of the year*). **a year and a day** the period specified in some legal matters to ensure the completion of a full year. **the year dot** see DOT[1]. **year in, year out** continually over a period of years. **year-long** lasting a year or the whole year. **year of grace** the year AD.

year-round existing etc. throughout the year. [OE *gē(a)r* f. Gmc]

yearbook /'jɪəbʊk, 'jɜː-/ n. an annual publication dealing with events or aspects of the (usu. preceding) year.

yearling /'jɪəlɪŋ, 'jɜː-/ n. & adj. —n. **1** an animal between one and two years old. **2** a racehorse in the calendar year after the year of foaling. —adj. **1** a year old; having existed or been such for a year (*a yearling heifer*). **2** intended to terminate after one year (*yearling bonds*).

yearly /'jɪəlɪ, 'jɜː-/ adj. & adv. —adj. **1** done, produced, or occurring once a year. **2** of or lasting a year. —adv. once a year; from year to year. [OE *gēarlic, -lice* (as YEAR)]

yearn /jɜːn/ v.intr. **1** (usu. foll. by *for, after*, or *to* + infin.) have a strong emotional longing. **2** (usu. foll. by *to, towards*) be filled with compassion or tenderness. □□ **yearner** n. **yearning** n. & adj. **yearningly** adv. [OE *giernan* f. a Gmc root meaning 'eager']

yeast /jiːst/ n. **1** a greyish-yellow fungous substance obtained esp. from fermenting malt liquors and used as a fermenting agent, to raise bread, etc. **2** any of various unicellular fungi in which vegetative reproduction takes place by budding or fission. □□ **yeastless** adj. **yeastlike** adj. [OE *gist, giest* (unrecorded): cf. MDu. *ghist*, MHG *jist*, ON *jöstr*]

yeasty /'jiːstɪ/ adj. (**yeastier, yeastiest**) **1** frothy or tasting like yeast. **2** in a ferment. **3** working like yeast. **4** (of talk etc.) light and superficial. □□ **yeastily** adv. **yeastiness** n.

yegg /jeg/ n. US *sl.* a travelling burglar or safe-breaker. [20th c.: perh. a surname]

yell /jel/ n. & v. —n. **1** a loud sharp cry of pain, anger, fright, encouragement, delight, etc. **2** a shout. **3** US an organized cry, used esp. to support a sports team. **4** *sl.* an amusing person or thing. —v.intr. & tr. make or utter with a yell. [OE *g(i)ellan* f. Gmc]

yellow /'jeləʊ/ adj., n., & v. —adj. **1** of the colour between green and orange in the spectrum, of buttercups, lemons, egg-yolks, or gold. **2** of the colour of faded leaves, ripe wheat, etc. **3** having a yellow skin or complexion. **4** *colloq.* cowardly. **5** (of looks, feelings, etc.) jealous, envious, or suspicious. **6** (of newspapers etc.) unscrupulously sensational. —n. **1** a yellow colour or pigment. **2** yellow clothes or material (*dressed in yellow*). **3 a** a yellow ball, piece, etc., in a game or sport. **b** the player using such pieces. **4** (usu. in *comb.*) a yellow moth or butterfly. **5** (in *pl.*) jaundice of horses etc. **6** US a peach-disease with yellowed leaves. —v.tr. & intr. make or become yellow. □**yellow arsenic** = ORPIMENT. **yellow-belly 1** *colloq.* a coward. **2** any of various fish with yellow underparts. **yellow card** *Football* a card shown by the referee to a player being cautioned. **yellow fever** a tropical virus disease with fever and jaundice. **yellow flag 1** a flag displayed by a ship in quarantine. **2** an iridaceous plant, *Iris pseudacorus*, with slender sword-shaped leaves and yellow flowers. **yellow jack 1** = *yellow fever*. **2** = *yellow flag*. **yellow line** (in the UK) a line painted along the side of the road in yellow either singly or in pairs to denote parking restrictions. **yellow metal** brass of 60 parts copper and 40 parts zinc. **Yellow Pages** *propr.* a section of a telephone directory on yellow paper and listing business subscribers according to the goods or services they offer. **the yellow peril** the political or military threat regarded as emanating from Asian peoples, esp. the Chinese. **yellow rattle** a yellow-flowered plant of the genus *Rhinanthus*. **yellow rocket** see ROCKET[2]. **yellow spot** the point of acutest vision in the retina. **yellow streak** *colloq.* a trait of cowardice. □□ **yellowish** adj. **yellowly** adv. **yellowness** n. **yellowy** adj. [OE *geolu, geolo* f. WG, rel. to GOLD]

yellowback /'jeləʊˌbæk/ n. a cheap novel etc. in a yellow cover.

yellowhammer /'jeləʊ,hæmə(r)/ n. a bunting, *Emberiza citrinella*, of which the male has a yellow head, neck, and breast. [16th c.: orig. of *hammer* uncert.]

yelp /jelp/ n. & v. —n. a sharp shrill cry of or as of a dog in pain or excitement. —v.intr. utter a yelp. □□ **yelper** n. [OE *gielp(an)* boast (imit.): cf. YAWP]

yen[1] /jen/ n. (pl. same) the chief monetary unit of Japan. [Jap. f. Chin. *yuan* round, dollar]

yen[2] /jen/ n. & v. colloq. —n. a longing or yearning. —v.intr. (**yenned, yenning**) feel a longing. [Chin. dial.]

yeoman /'jəʊmən/ n. (pl. **-men**) **1** esp. *hist.* a man holding and cultivating a small landed estate. **2** *hist.* a person qualified by possessing free land of an annual value of 40 shillings to serve on juries, vote for the knight of the shire, etc. **3** *Brit.* a member of the yeomanry force. **4** *hist.* a servant in a royal or noble household. **5** (in full **yeoman of signals**) a petty officer in the Navy, concerned with visual signalling. **6** *US* a petty officer performing clerical duties on board ship. □ **Yeoman of the Guard 1** a member of the British sovereign's bodyguard. **2** (in general use) a warder in the Tower of London. **yeoman** (or **yeoman's**) **service** efficient or useful help in need. **Yeoman Usher** *Brit.* the deputy of Black Rod. □□ **yeomanly** adj. [ME *yoman, yeman*, etc., prob. f. YOUNG + MAN]

yeomanry /'jəʊmənrɪ/ n. (pl. **-ies**) **1** a body of yeomen. **2** *Brit. hist.* a volunteer cavalry force raised from the yeoman class (1794-1908).

yep /jep/ adv. & n. (also **yup** /jʌp/) *US colloq.* = YES. [corrupt.]

-yer /jə(r)/ suffix var. of -IER esp. after *w* (*bowyer; lawyer*).

yerba maté /'jɜːbə ,mæteɪ/ n. = MATÉ. [Sp., = herb maté]

yes /jes/ adv. & n. —adv. **1** equivalent to an affirmative sentence: the answer to your question is affirmative, it is as you say or as I have said, the statement etc. made is correct, the request or command will be complied with, the negative statement etc. made is not correct. **2** (in answer to a summons or address) an acknowledgement of one's presence. —n. an utterance of the word *yes*. □ **say yes** grant a request or confirm a statement. **yes?** **1** indeed? is that so? **2** what do you want? **yes and** a form for introducing a stronger phrase (*he came home drunk—yes, and was sick*). **yes and no** that is partly true and partly untrue. **yes-man** (pl. **-men**) *colloq.* a weakly acquiescent person. [OE *gēse, gīse*, prob. f. *gīa sīe* may it be (*gīa* is unrecorded)]

yester- /'jestə(r)/ comb. form *poet.* or *archaic* of yesterday; that is the last past (*yester-eve*). [OE *geostran*]

yesterday /'jestə,deɪ/ adv. & n. —adv. **1** on the day before today. **2** in the recent past. —n. **1** the day before today. **2** the recent past. □ **yesterday morning** (or **afternoon** etc.) in the morning (or afternoon etc.) of yesterday. [OE *giestran dæg* (as YESTER-, DAY)]

yesteryear /'jestə,jɪə(r)/ n. literary **1** last year. **2** the recent past.

yet /jet/ adv. & conj. —adv. **1** as late as, or until, now or then (*there is yet time; your best work yet*). **2** (with *neg.* or *interrog.*) so soon as, or by, now or then (*it is not time yet; have you finished yet?*). **3** again; in addition (*more and yet more*). **4** in the remaining time available; before all is over (*I will do it yet*). **5** (foll. by *compar.*) even (*a yet more difficult task*). **6** nevertheless; and in spite of that; but for all that (*it is strange, and yet it is true*). —conj. but at the same time; but nevertheless (*I won, yet what good has it done?*). □ **nor yet** and also not (*won't listen to me nor yet to you*). [OE *gīet(a)*, = OFris. *iēta*, of unkn. orig.]

yeti /'jetɪ/ n. = *Abominable Snowman.* [Tibetan]

yew /juː/ n. **1** any dark-leaved evergreen coniferous tree of the genus *Taxus*, having seeds enclosed in a fleshy red aril, and often planted in churchyards. **2** its wood, used formerly as a material for bows and still in cabinet-making. [OE *īw, ēow* f. Gmc]

Y-fronts /'waɪfrʌnts/ n. propr. men's or boys' briefs with a Y-shaped seam at the front.

Yggdrasil /'ɪgdrəsɪl/ n. (in Scandinavian mythology) an ash-tree whose roots and branches join heaven, earth, and hell. [ON *yg(g)drasill* f. *Yggr* Odin + *drasill* horse]

YHA abbr. (in the UK) Youth Hostels Association.

Yid /jɪd/ n. sl. offens. a Jew. [back-form. f. YIDDISH]

Yiddish /'jɪdɪʃ/ n. & adj. —n. a vernacular used by Jews in or from central and eastern Europe, orig. a German dialect with words from Hebrew and several modern languages. —adj. of or relating to this language. [G *jüdisch* Jewish]

Yiddisher /'jɪdɪʃ(ə)r/ n. & adj. —n. a person speaking Yiddish. —adj. Yiddish-speaking.

yield /jiːld/ v. & n. —v. **1** tr. (also absol.) produce or return as a fruit, profit, or result (*the land yields crops; the land yields poorly; the investment yields 15%*). **2** tr. give up; surrender, concede; comply with a demand for (*yielded the fortress; yielded themselves prisoners*). **3** intr. (often foll. by *to*) **a** surrender; make submission. **b** give consent or change one's course of action in deference to; respond as required to (*yielded to persuasion*). **4** intr. (foll. by *to*) be inferior or confess inferiority to (*I yield to none in understanding the problem*). **5** intr. (foll. by *to*) give right of way to other traffic. **6** intr. *US* allow another the right to speak in a debate etc. —n. an amount yielded or produced; an output or return. □ **yield point** *Physics* the stress beyond which a material becomes plastic. □□ **yielder** n. [OE *g(i)eldan* pay f. Gmc]

yielding /'jiːldɪŋ/ adj. **1** compliant, submissive. **2** (of a substance) able to bend; not stiff or rigid. □□ **yieldingly** adv. **yieldingness** n.

yin /jɪn/ n. (in Chinese philosophy) the passive female principle of the universe (cf. YANG). [Chin.]

yip /jɪp/ v. & n. *US* —v.intr. (**yipped, yipping**) = YELP v. —n. = YELP n. [imit.]

yippee /'jɪpiː, -'piː/ int. expressing delight or excitement. [natural excl.]

-yl /ɪl/ suffix *Chem.* forming nouns denoting a radical (*ethyl, hydroxyl; phenyl*).

ylang-ylang /'iːlæŋ,iːlæŋ/ n. (also **ilang-ilang**) **1** a Malayan tree, *Cananga odorata*, from the fragrant yellow flowers of which a perfume is distilled. **2** the perfume itself. [Tagalog *álang-ilang*]

YMCA abbr. Young Men's Christian Association.

-yne /aɪn/ suffix *Chem.* forming names of unsaturated compounds containing a triple bond (*ethyne* = acetylene).

yob /jɒb/ n. *Brit. sl.* a lout or hooligan. □□ **yobbish** adj. **yobbishly** adv. **yobbishness** n. [back sl. for BOY]

yobbo /'jɒbəʊ/ n. (pl. **-os**) *Brit. sl.* = YOB.

yod /jɒd/ n. **1** the tenth and smallest letter of the Hebrew alphabet. **2** its semivowel sound /j/. [Heb. *yōd* f. *yad* hand]

yodel /'jəʊd(ə)l/ v. & n. —v.tr. & intr. (**yodelled, yodelling;** *US* **yodeled, yodeling**) sing with melodious inarticulate sounds and frequent changes between falsetto and the normal voice in the manner of the Swiss mountain-dwellers. —n. a yodelling cry. □□ **yodeller** n. [G *jodeln*]

yoga /'jəʊgə/ n. **1** a Hindu system of philosophic meditation and asceticism designed to effect reunion with the universal spirit. **2** = HATHA YOGA. □□ **yogic** /'jəʊgɪk/ adj. [Hind. f. Skr., = union]

yogh /jɒg/ n. a Middle English letter used for certain values of *g* and *y*. [ME]

yoghurt /'jɒgət/ n. (also **yogurt**) a semi-solid sourish food prepared from milk fermented by added bacteria. [Turk. *yoğurt*]

yogi /'jəʊgɪ/ n. a person proficient in yoga. □□ **yogism** n. [Hind. f. YOGA]

yo-heave-ho /ˈjəʊhiːvˌhəʊ/ int. & n. = heave-ho.

yo-ho /jəʊˈhəʊ/ int. (also **yo-ho-ho** /ˌjəʊhəʊˈhəʊ/) 1 used to attract attention. 2 = YO-HEAVE-HO. [cf. YO-HEAVE-HO & HO]

yoicks /jɔɪks/ int. (also **hoicks** /hɔɪks/) a cry used by fox-hunters to urge on the hounds. [orig. unkn.: cf. *hyke* call to hounds, HEY¹]

yoke /jəʊk/ n. & v. —n. 1 a wooden crosspiece fastened over the necks of two oxen etc. and attached to the plough or wagon to be drawn. 2 (pl. same or **yokes**) a pair (of oxen etc.). 3 an object like a yoke in form or function, e.g. a wooden shoulder-piece for carrying a pair of pails, the top section of a dress or skirt etc. from which the rest hangs. 4 sway, dominion, or servitude, esp. when oppressive. 5 a bond or union, esp. that of marriage. 6 *Rom.Hist.* an uplifted yoke, or an arch of three spears symbolizing it, under which a defeated army was made to march. 7 *archaic* the amount of land that one yoke of oxen could plough in a day. 8 a crossbar on which a bell swings. 9 the crossbar of a rudder to whose ends ropes are fastened. 10 a bar of soft iron between the poles of an electromagnet. —v. 1 tr. put a yoke on. 2 tr. couple or unite (a pair). 3 tr. (foll. by to) link (one thing) to (another). 4 intr. match or work together. [OE *geoc* f. Gmc]

yokel /ˈjəʊk(ə)l/ n. a rustic, a country bumpkin. [perh. f. dial. *yokel* green woodpecker]

yolk¹ /jəʊk/ n. 1 the yellow internal part of an egg that nourishes the young before it hatches. 2 *Biol.* the corresponding part of any animal ovum. □**yolk-bag** (or **-sac**) a membrane enclosing the yolk of an egg. □□ **yolked** adj. (also in *comb.*). **yolkless** adj. **yolky** adj. [OE *geol(o)ca* f. *geolu* YELLOW]

yolk² /jəʊk/ n. = SUINT. [OE *eowoca* (unrecorded)]

Yom Kippur /jɒm ˈkɪpə(r)/ n. = Day of Atonement (see ATONEMENT). [Heb.]

yomp /jɒmp/ v.intr. *Brit. sl.* march with heavy equipment over difficult terrain. [20th c.: orig. unkn.]

yon /jɒn/ adj., adv., & pron. *literary & dial.* —adj. & adv. yonder. —pron. yonder person or thing. [OE *geon*]

yonder /ˈjɒndə(r)/ adv. & adj. —adv. over there; at some distance in that direction; in the place indicated by pointing etc. —adj. situated yonder. [ME: cf. OS *gendra*, Goth. *jaindrē*]

yoni /ˈjəʊnɪ/ n. a symbol of the female genitals venerated by Hindus etc. [Skr., = source, womb, female genitals]

yonks /jɒŋks/ n.pl. *sl.* a long time (*haven't seen them for yonks*). [20th c.: orig. unkn.]

yoo-hoo /ˈjuːhuː/ int. used to attract a person's attention. [natural excl.]

yore /jɔː(r)/ n. *literary* □**of yore** formerly; in or of old days. [OE *geāra*, *geāre*, etc., adv. forms of uncert. orig.]

york /jɔːk/ v.tr. *Cricket* bowl with a yorker. [back-form. f. YORKER]

yorker /ˈjɔːkə(r)/ n. *Cricket* a ball bowled so that it pitches immediately under the bat. [prob. f. *York*, as having been introduced by Yorkshire players]

Yorkist /ˈjɔːkɪst/ n. & adj. —n. *hist.* a follower of the House of York or of the White Rose party supporting it in the Wars of the Roses (cf. LANCASTRIAN). —adj. of or concerning the House of York.

Yorks. abbr. Yorkshire.

Yorkshire fog /ˈjɔːkʃə/ n. a fodder-grass, *Holcus lanatus.*

Yorkshireman /ˈjɔːkʃəmən/ n. (pl. **-men**; fem. **Yorkshirewoman**, pl. **-women**) a native of Yorkshire in N. England.

Yorkshire pudding /ˈjɔːkʃə/ n. a baked batter pudding usu. eaten with roast beef. [*Yorkshire* in N. England]

Yorkshire terrier /ˈjɔːkʃə/ n. a small long-haired blue-grey and tan kind of terrier.

Yoruba /ˈjɒrʊbə/ n. 1 a member of a Black African people inhabiting the west coast, esp. Nigeria. 2 the language of this people. [native name]

you /juː/ pron. (obj. **you**; poss. **your, yours**) 1 used with reference to the person or persons addressed or one such person and one or more associated persons. 2 (as int. with a noun) in an exclamatory statement (*you fools!*). 3 (in general statements) one, a person, anyone, or everyone (*it's bad at first, but you get used to it*). □**you-all** *US colloq.* you (usu. more than one person). **you and yours** you together with your family, property, etc. **you-know-what** (or **-who**) something or someone unspecified but understood. [OE *ēow* accus. & dative of *gē* YE¹ f. WG: supplanting *ye* because of the more frequent use of the obj. case, and *thou* and *thee* as the more courteous form]

you'd /juːd, jʊd/ contr. 1 you had. 2 you would.

you'll /juːl, jʊl, jɔːl/ contr. you will; you shall.

young /jʌŋ/ adj. & n. —adj. (**younger** /ˈjʌŋgə(r)/; **youngest** /ˈjʌŋgɪst/) 1 not far advanced in life, development, or existence; not yet old. 2 immature or inexperienced. 3 felt in or characteristic of youth (*young love*; *young ambition*). 4 representing young people (*Young Conservatives*; *Young England*). 5 distinguishing a son from his father (*young Jones*). 6 (**younger**) **a** distinguishing one person from another of the same name (*the younger Pitt*). **b** *Sc.* the heir of a landed commoner. —n. (collect.) offspring, esp. of animals before or soon after birth. □**with young** (of an animal) pregnant. **young blood** see BLOOD. **younger hand** *Cards* the second player of two. **young fustic** see FUSTIC. **young hopeful** see HOPEFUL. **young idea** the child's mind. **young lady** *colloq.* a girlfriend or sweetheart. **young man** a boyfriend or sweetheart. **young person** *Law* (in the UK) a person generally between 14 and 17 years of age. **Young Pretender** Charles Stuart (1720–80), grandson of James II and claimant to the British throne. **young thing** *archaic* or *colloq.* an indulgent term for a young person. **Young Turk** 1 a member of a revolutionary party in Turkey in 1908. 2 a young person eager for radical change to the established order. **young turk** *offens.* a violent child or youth. **young 'un** *colloq.* a youngster. **young woman** *colloq.* a girlfriend or sweetheart. □□ **youngish** adj.

youngling n. [OE *g(e)ong* f. Gmc]

youngster /ˈjʌŋstə(r)/ n. a child or young person.

younker /ˈjʌŋkə(r)/ n. *archaic* = YOUNGSTER. [MDu. *jonckher* f. *jonc* YOUNG + *hēre* lord: cf. JUNKER]

your /jɔː(r), jʊə(r)/ poss.pron. (attrib.) 1 of or belonging to you or yourself or yourselves (*your house*; *your own business*). 2 *colloq.* usu. *derog.* much talked of; well known (*none so fallible as your self-styled expert*). [OE *ēower* genit. of *gē* YE¹]

you're /jɔː(r), jʊə(r), jɔ:(r)/ contr. you are.

yours /jɔːz, jʊəz/ poss.pron. 1 the one or ones belonging to or associated with you (*it is yours*; *yours are over there*). 2 your letter (*yours of the 10th*). 3 introducing a formula ending a letter (*yours ever*; *yours truly*). □**of yours** of or belonging to you (*a friend of yours*).

yourself /jɔːˈself, jʊə-/ pron. (pl. **yourselves** /-ˈselvz/) 1 **a** emphat. form of YOU. **b** refl. form of YOU. 2 in your normal state of body or mind (*are quite yourself again*). □**be yourself** act in your normal, unconstrained manner. **how's yourself?** *sl.* how are you? (esp. after answering a similar enquiry).

youth /juːθ/ n. (pl. **youths** /juːðz/) 1 the state of being young; the period between childhood and adult age. 2 the vigour or enthusiasm, inexperience, or other characteristic of this period. 3 an early stage of development etc. 4 a young person (esp. male). 5 (pl.) young people collectively (*the youth of the country*). □**youth club** (or **centre**) a place or organization provided for young people's leisure activities. **youth hostel** a place where (esp. young) holiday-makers can put up cheaply for the night. **youth hosteller** a user of a youth hostel. [OE *geoguth* f. Gmc, rel. to YOUNG]

youthful /'juːθfʊl/ adj. **1** young, esp. in appearance or manner. **2** having the characteristics of youth (*youthful impatience*). **3** having the freshness or vigour of youth (*a youthful complexion*). □□ **youthfully** adv. **youthfulness** n.

you've /juːv, jʊv/ contr. you have.

yowl /jaʊl/ n. & v. —n. a loud wailing cry of or as of a cat or dog in pain or distress. —v.intr. utter a yowl. [imit.]

yo-yo /'jəʊjəʊ/ n. & v. —n. (pl. **yo-yos**) **1** a toy consisting of a pair of discs with a deep groove between them in which string is attached and wound, and which can be spun alternately downward and upward by its weight and momentum as the string unwinds and rewinds. **2** a thing that repeatedly falls and rises again. —v.intr. (**yo-yoes, yo-yoed**) **1** play with a yo-yo. **2** move up and down; fluctuate. [20th c.: orig. unkn.]

yr. abbr. **1** year(s). **2** younger. **3** your.

yrs. abbr. **1** years. **2** yours.

ytterbium /ɪ'tɜːbɪəm/ n. Chem. a silvery metallic element of the lanthanide series occurring naturally as various isotopes. ¶ Symb.: **Yb**. [mod.L f. *Ytterby* in Sweden]

yttrium /'ɪtrɪəm/ n. Chem. a greyish metallic element resembling the lanthanides, occurring naturally in uranium ores and used in making superconductors. ¶ Symb.: **Y**. [formed as YTTERBIUM]

yuan /juː'ɑːn/ n. (pl. same) the chief monetary unit of China. [Chin.: see YEN[1]]

yucca /'jʌkə/ n. any American white-flowered liliaceous plant of the genus *Yucca*, with swordlike leaves. [Carib]

yuck /jʌk/ int. & n. (also **yuk**) sl. —int. an expression of strong distaste or disgust. —n. something messy or repellent. [imit.]

yucky /'jʌkɪ/ adj. (also **yukky**) (**-ier, -iest**) sl. **1** messy, repellent. **2** sickly, sentimental.

Yugoslav /'juːgəˌslɑːv/ n. & adj. (also **Jugoslav**) —n. **1** a native or national of Yugoslavia. **2** a person of Yugoslav descent. —adj. of or relating to Yugoslavia or its people. □□ **Yugoslavian** adj. & n. [Austrian G *Jugoslav* f. Serb. *jugo-* f. *jug* south + SLAV]

yuk var. of YUCK.

yukky var. of YUCKY.

yule /juːl/ n. (in full **yule-tide**) archaic the Christmas festival. □ **yule-log 1** a large log burnt in the hearth on Christmas Eve. **2** a log-shaped chocolate cake eaten at Christmas. [OE *gēol(a)*: cf. ON *jól*]

yummy /'jʌmɪ/ adj. (**yummier, yummiest**) colloq. tasty, delicious. [YUM-YUM + -Y[1]]

yum-yum /jʌm'jʌm/ int. expressing pleasure from eating or the prospect of eating. [natural excl.]

yup var. of YEP.

yuppy /'jʌpɪ/ n. (pl. **-ies**) colloq., usu. derog. a young middle-class professional person working in a city. [young urban professional]

YWCA abbr. Young Women's Christian Association.

Z

Z /zed/ *n.* (also **z**) (*pl.* **Zs** or **Z's**) **1** the twenty-sixth letter of the alphabet. **2** (usu. **z**) *Algebra* the third unknown quantity. **3** *Geom.* the third coordinate. **4** *Chem.* atomic number.

zabaglione /ˌzɑːbɑːˈljəʊneɪ/ *n.* an Italian sweet of whipped and heated egg yolks, sugar, and (esp. Marsala) wine. [It.]

zaffre /ˈzæfə(r)/ *n.* (*US* **zaffer**) an impure cobalt oxide used as a blue pigment. [It. *zaffera* or F *safre*]

zag /zæg/ *n.* a sharp change of direction in a zigzag course. [ZIGZAG]

ZANU /ˈzɑːnuː/ *abbr.* Zimbabwe African National Union.

zany /ˈzeɪnɪ/ *adj.* & *n.* —*adj.* (**zanier**, **zaniest**) comically idiotic; crazily ridiculous. —*n.* **1** a buffoon or jester. **2** *hist.* an attendant clown awkwardly mimicking a chief clown in shows; a merry andrew. □□ **zanily** *adv.* **zaniness** *n.* [F *zani* or It. *zan(n)i*, Venetian form of *Gianni*, *Giovanni* John]

zap /zæp/ *v.*, *n.*, & *int. sl.* —*v.* (**zapped**, **zapping**) **1** *tr.* **a** kill or destroy; deal a sudden blow to. **b** hit forcibly (*zapped the ball over the net*). **2** *intr.* & *tr.* move quickly and vigorously. **3** *tr.* overwhelm emotionally. **4** *tr. Computing* erase or change (an item in a program). **5** *intr.* (foll. by *through*) fast-wind a videotape to skip a section. —*n.* **1** energy, vigour. **2** a strong emotional effect. —*int.* expressing the sound or impact of a bullet, ray gun, etc., or any sudden event. [imit.]

zapateado /ˌzæpətɑˈdəʊ/ *n.* (*pl.* **-os**) **1** a flamenco dance with rhythmic stamping of the feet. **2** this technique or action. [Sp. f. *zapato* shoe]

zappy /ˈzæpɪ/ *adj.* (**zappier**, **zappiest**) *colloq.* **1** lively, energetic. **2** striking.

ZAPU /ˈzɑːpuː/ *abbr.* Zimbabwe African People's Union.

zarape var. of SERAPE.

Zarathustrian var. of ZOROASTRIAN.

zariba /zəˈriːbə/ *n.* (also **zareba**) **1** a hedged or palisaded enclosure for the protection of a camp or village in the Sudan etc. **2** a restricting or confining influence. [Arab. *zarība* cattle-pen]

zarzuela /θɑːˈθweɪlə/ *n.* a Spanish traditional form of musical comedy. [Sp.: app. f. a place-name]

zax var. of SAX[2].

zeal /ziːl/ *n.* **1** earnestness or fervour in advancing a cause or rendering service. **2** hearty and persistent endeavour. [ME *zele* f. eccl.L *zelus* f. Gk *zēlos*]

zealot /ˈzelət/ *n.* **1** an uncompromising or extreme partisan; a fanatic. **2** (**Zealot**) *hist.* a member of an ancient Jewish sect aiming at a world Jewish theocracy and resisting the Romans until AD 70. □□ **zealotry** *n.* [eccl.L *zelotes* f. Gk *zēlōtēs* (as ZEAL)]

zealous /ˈzeləs/ *adj.* full of zeal; enthusiastic. □□ **zealously** *adv.* **zealousness** *n.*

zebec (also **zebeck**) var. of XEBEC.

zebra /ˈzebrə, ˈziː-/ *n.* **1** any of various African quadrupeds, esp. *Equus burchelli*, related to the ass and horse, with black and white stripes. **2** (*attrib.*) with alternate dark and pale stripes. □**zebra crossing** *Brit.* a striped street-crossing where pedestrians have precedence over vehicles. □□ **zebrine** /-braɪn/ *adj.* [It. or Port. f. Congolese]

zebu /ˈziːbuː/ *n.* a humped ox, *Bos indicus*, of India, E. Asia, and Africa. [F *zébu*, of unkn. orig.]

Zech. *abbr.* Zechariah (Old Testament).

zed /zed/ *n. Brit.* the letter Z. [F *zède* f. LL *zeta* f. Gk ZETA]

zedoary /ˈzedəʊərɪ/ *n.* an aromatic ginger-like substance made from the rootstock of E. Indian plants of the genus *Curcuma* and used in medicine, perfumery, and dyeing. [ME f. med.L *zedoarium* f. Pers. *zidwār*]

zee /ziː/ *n. US* the letter Z. [17th c.: var. of ZED]

Zeeman effect /ˈzeɪmən/ *n. Physics* the splitting of the spectrum line into several components by a magnetic field. [P. *Zeeman*, Du. physicist d. 1943]

zein /ˈziːɪn/ *n. Biochem.* the principal protein of maize. [*Zea* the generic name of maize + -IN]

Zeitgeist /ˈtsaɪtɡaɪst/ *n.* **1** the spirit of the times. **2** the trend of thought and feeling in a period. [G f. *Zeit* time + *Geist* spirit]

Zen /zen/ *n.* a form of Mahayana Buddhism emphasizing the value of meditation and intuition. □□ **Zenist** *n.* (also **Zennist**). [Jap., = meditation]

zenana /zɪˈnɑːnə/ *n.* the part of a house for the seclusion of women of high-caste families in India and Iran. [Hind. *zenāna* f. Pers. *zanāna* f. *zan* woman]

Zend /zend/ *n.* an interpretation of the Avesta, each Zend being part of the Zend-Avesta. □**Zend-Avesta** the Zoroastrian sacred writings of the Avesta or text and Zend or commentary. [Pers. *zand* interpretation]

Zener cards /ˈziːnə/ *n.* a set of 25 cards each with one of five different symbols, used in ESP research. [K. E. *Zener*, Amer. psychologist b. 1903]

zenith /ˈzenɪθ, ˈziː-/ *n.* **1** the part of the celestial sphere directly above an observer (opp. NADIR). **2** the highest point in one's fortunes; a time of great prosperity etc. □**zenith distance** an arc intercepted between a celestial body and its zenith; the complement of a body's altitude. [ME f. OF *cenit* or med.L *cenit* ult. f. Arab. *samt* (*ar-ra's*) path (over the head)]

zenithal /ˈzenɪθ(ə)l/ *adj.* of or relating to a zenith. □**zenithal projection** a projection of part of a globe on to a plane tangential to the centre of the part, showing the correct directions of all points from the centre.

zeolite /ˈziːəˌlaɪt/ *n.* each of a number of minerals consisting mainly of hydrous silicates of calcium, sodium, and aluminium, able to act as cation exchangers. □□ **zeolitic** /-ˈlɪtɪk/ *adj.* [Sw. & G *zeolit* f. Gk *zeō* boil + -LITE (from their characteristic swelling and fusing under the blowpipe)]

Zeph. *abbr.* Zephaniah (Old Testament).

zephyr /ˈzefə(r)/ *n.* **1** *literary* a mild gentle wind or breeze. **2** a fine cotton fabric. **3** an athlete's thin gauzy jersey. [F *zéphyr* or L *zephyrus* f. Gk *zephuros* (god of the) west wind]

Zeppelin /ˈzepəlɪn/ *n. hist.* a German large dirigible airship of the early 20th c., orig. for military use. [Count F. von *Zeppelin*, Ger. airman d. 1917, its first constructor]

zero /ˈzɪərəʊ/ *n.* & *v.* —*n.* (*pl.* **-os**) **1 a** the figure 0; nought. **b** no quantity or number; nil. **2** a point on the scale of an instrument from which a positive or negative quantity is reckoned. **3** (*attrib.*) having a value of zero; no, not any (*zero population growth*). **4** (in full **zero-hour**) **a** the hour at which a planned, esp. military, operation is timed to begin. **b** a crucial moment. **5** the lowest point; a nullity or nonentity. —*v.tr.* (**-oes**, **-oed**) **1** adjust (an instrument etc.) to zero point. **2** set the sights of (a gun) for firing. □**zero in on 1** take aim at. **2** focus one's attention on. **zero option** a disarmament proposal for the total removal of certain types of weapons on both sides. **zero-rated** on which no value added tax is charged. **zero-sum** (of a game, political situation, etc.) in which whatever is gained by one side is lost by the other so that the net change is always zero. [F *zéro* or It. *zero* f. OSp. f. Arab. *ṣifr* CIPHER]

zeroth /'zɪərəʊθ/ *adj.* immediately preceding what is regarded as 'first' in a series.

zest /zest/ *n.* **1** piquancy; a stimulating flavour or quality. **2 a** keen enjoyment or interest. **b** (often foll. by *for*) relish. **c** gusto (*entered into it with zest*). **3** a scraping of orange or lemon peel as flavouring. □□ **zestful** *adj.* **zestfully** *adv.* **zestfulness** *n.* **zesty** *adj.* (**zestier, zestiest**). [F *zeste* orange or lemon peel, of unkn. orig.]

zeta /'zi:tə/ *n.* the sixth letter of the Greek alphabet (Z, ζ). [Gk *zēta*]

zetetic /zɪ'tetɪk/ *adj.* proceeding by inquiry. [Gk *zētētikos* f. *zēteō* seek]

zeugma /'zju:gmə/ *n.* a figure of speech using a verb or adjective with two nouns, to one of which it is strictly applicable while the word appropriate to the other is not used (e.g. *with weeping eyes and* [sc. *grieving*] *hearts*) (cf. SYLLEPSIS). □□ **zeugmatic** /-'mætɪk/ *adj.* [L f. Gk *zeugma -atos* f. *zeugnumi* to yoke, *zugon* yoke]

zho var. of DZHO.

zibet /'zɪbɪt/ *n.* (US **zibeth**) **1** an Asian or Indian civet, *Viverra zibetha*. **2** its scent. [med.L *zibethum*: see CIVET]

zidovudine /ˌzaɪdəʊ'vju:di:n/ *n.* = AZT. [chem. name *azidothymidine*]

ziff /zɪf/ *n. Austral. sl.* a beard. [20th c.: orig. unkn.]

ziggurat /'zɪgəˌræt/ *n.* a rectangular stepped tower in ancient Mesopotamia, surmounted by a temple. [Assyr. *ziqquratu* pinnacle]

zigzag /'zɪgzæg/ *n., adj., adv.,* & *v.* —*n.* **1** a line or course having abrupt alternate right and left turns. **2** (often in *pl.*) each of these turns. —*adj.* having the form of a zigzag; alternating right and left. —*adv.* with a zigzag course. —*v.intr.* (**zigzagged, zigzagging**) move in a zigzag course. □□ **zigzaggedly** *adv.* [F f. G *zickzack*]

zilch /zɪltʃ/ *n.* esp. US *sl.* nothing. [20th c.: orig. uncert.]

zillah /'zɪlə/ *n.* an administrative district in India, containing several parganas. [Hind. *ḍilah* division]

zillion /'zɪljən/ *n. colloq.* an indefinite large number. □□ **zillionth** *adj.* & *n.* [Z (perh. = unknown quantity) + MILLION]

zinc /zɪŋk/ *n. Chem.* a white metallic element occurring naturally as zinc blende, and used as a component of brass, in galvanizing sheet iron, in electric batteries, and in printing-plates. ¶ Symb.: **Zn**. □**flowers of zinc** = *zinc oxide*. **zinc blende** see BLENDE. **zinc chloride** a white crystalline deliquescent solid used as a preservative and flux. **zinc oxide** a powder used as a white pigment and in medicinal ointments. **zinc sulphate** a white water-soluble compound used as a mordant. □□ **zinced** *adj.* [G *Zink*, of unkn. orig.]

zinco /'zɪŋkəʊ/ *n.* & *v.* —*n.* (*pl.* -**os**) = ZINCOGRAPH. —*v.tr.* & *intr.* (-**oes**, -**oed**) = ZINCOGRAPH. [abbr.]

zincograph /'zɪŋkəˌgrɑːf/ *n.* & *v.* —*n.* **1** a zinc plate with a design etched in relief on it for printing from. **2** a print taken from this. —*v.* **1** *tr.* & *intr.* etch on zinc. **2** *tr.* reproduce (a design) in this way. □□ **zincography** /-'kɒgrəfɪ/ *n.*

zincotype /'zɪŋkəˌtaɪp/ *n.* = ZINCOGRAPH.

zing /zɪŋ/ *n.* & *v. colloq.* —*n.* vigour, energy. —*v.intr.* move swiftly or with a shrill sound. □□ **zingy** *adj.* (**zingier, zingiest**). [imit.]

Zingaro /'zɪŋgəˌrəʊ/ *n.* (*pl.* **Zingari** /-ˌriː/) a gypsy. [It.]

zinger /'zɪŋə(r)/ *n.* US *sl.* an outstanding person or thing.

zinnia /'zɪnɪə/ *n.* a composite plant of the genus *Zinnia*, with showy rayed flowers of deep red and other colours. [J. G. *Zinn*, Ger. physician and botanist d. 1759]

Zion /'zaɪən/ *n.* (also **Sion** /'saɪən/) **1** the hill of Jerusalem on which the city of David was built. **2 a** the Jewish people or religion. **b** the Christian

Church. **3** (in Christian thought) the Kingdom of God in Heaven. [OE f. eccl.L *Sion* f. Heb. *ṣiyōn*]

Zionism /'zaɪəˌnɪz(ə)m/ *n.* a movement (orig.) for the reestablishment and (now) the development of a Jewish nation in what is now Israel. □□ **Zionist** *n.*

zip /zɪp/ *n.* & *v.* —*n.* **1** a light fast sound, as of a bullet passing through air. **2** energy, vigour. **3** esp. *Brit.* **a** (in full **zip-fastener**) a fastening device of two flexible strips with interlocking projections closed or opened by pulling a slide along them. **b** (*attrib.*) having a zip-fastener (*zip bag*). —*v.* (**zipped, zipping**) **1** *tr.* & *intr.* (often foll. by *up*) fasten with a zip-fastener. **2** *intr.* move with zip or at high speed. [imit.]

Zip code /zɪp/ *n.* US a system of postal codes consisting of five-digit numbers. [*zone improvement plan*]

zipper /'zɪpə(r)/ *n.* & *v.* esp. US —*n.* a zip-fastener. —*v.tr.* (often foll. by *up*) fasten with a zipper. □□ **zippered** *adj.*

zippy /'zɪpɪ/ *adj.* (**zippier, zippiest**) *colloq.* **1** bright, fresh, lively. **2** fast, speedy. □□ **zippily** *adv.* **zippiness** *n.*

zircon /'zɜːkən/ *n.* a zirconium silicate of which some translucent varieties are cut into gems (see HYACINTH 4, JARGON²). [G *Zirkon*: cf. JARGON²]

zirconium /zə'kəʊnɪəm/ *n. Chem.* a grey metallic element occurring naturally in zircon and used in various industrial applications. ¶ Symb.: **Zr**. [mod.L f. ZIRCON + -IUM]

zit /zɪt/ *n.* esp. US *sl.* a pimple. [20th c.: orig. unkn.]

zither /'zɪðə(r)/ *n.* a musical instrument consisting of a flat wooden soundbox with numerous strings stretched across it, placed horizontally and played with the fingers and a plectrum. □□ **zitherist** *n.* [G (as CITTERN)]

zizz /zɪz/ *n.* & *v. colloq.* —*n.* **1** a whizzing or buzzing sound. **2** a short sleep. —*v.intr.* **1** make a whizzing sound. **2** doze or sleep. [imit.]

zloty /'zlɒtɪ/ *n.* (*pl.* same or **zlotys**) the chief monetary unit of Poland. [Pol., lit. 'golden']

Zn *symb. Chem.* the element zinc.

zodiac /'zəʊdɪˌæk/ *n.* **1 a** a belt of the heavens limited by lines about 8° from the ecliptic on each side, including all apparent positions of the sun, moon, and planets as known to ancient astronomers, and divided into twelve equal parts (**signs of the zodiac**), each formerly containing the similarly named constellation but now by precession of the equinoxes coinciding with the constellation that bears the name of the preceding sign: Aries, Taurus, Gemini, Cancer, Leo, Virgo, Libra, Scorpio, Sagittarius, Capricorn(us), Aquarius, Pisces. **b** a diagram of these signs. **2** a complete cycle, circuit, or compass. [ME f. OF *zodiaque* f. L *zodiacus* f. Gk *zōidiakos* f. *zōidion* sculptured animal-figure, dimin. of *zōion* animal]

zodiacal /zə'daɪək(ə)l/ *adj.* of or in the zodiac. □ **zodiacal light** a luminous area of sky shaped like a tall triangle occasionally seen in the east before sunrise or in the west after sunset, esp. in the Tropics. [F (as ZODIAC)]

zoetrope /'zəʊɪˌtrəʊp/ *n. hist.* an optical toy in the form of a cylinder with a series of pictures on the inner surface which give an impression of continuous motion when viewed through slits with the cylinder rotating. [irreg. f. Gk *zōē* life + *-tropos* turning]

zoic /'zəʊɪk/ *adj.* **1** of or relating to animals. **2** *Geol.* (of rock etc.) containing fossils; with traces of animal or plant life. [prob. back-form. f. AZOIC]

Zöllner's lines /'tsɜːlnəz/ *n.* parallel lines made to appear not parallel by short oblique intersecting lines. [J. K. F. *Zöllner*, Ger. physicist d. 1882]

zollverein /'tsɒlfəˌraɪn/ *n. hist.* a customs union, esp. of German States in the 19th c. [G]

zombie /'zɒmbɪ/ *n.* **1** *colloq.* a dull or apathetic person. **2** a corpse said to be revived by witchcraft. [W.Afr. *zumbi* fetish]

zonation /zəʊ'neɪʃ(ə)n/ *n.* distribution in zones, esp.

(*Ecol.*) of plants into zones characterized by the dominant species.

zonda /'zɒndə/ *n.* a hot dusty north wind in Argentina. [Amer. Sp.]

zone /zəʊn/ *n. & v.* —*n.* **1** an area having particular features, properties, purpose, or use (*danger zone*; *erogenous zone*; *smokeless zone*). **2** any well-defined region of more or less beltlike form. **3 a** an area between two exact or approximate concentric circles. **b** a part of the surface of a sphere enclosed between two parallel planes, or of a cone or cylinder etc., between such planes cutting it perpendicularly to the axis. **4** (in full **time zone**) a range of longitudes where a common standard time is used. **5** *Geol.* etc. a range between specified limits of depth, height, etc., esp. a section of strata distinguished by characteristic fossils. **6** *Geog.* any of five divisions of the earth bounded by circles parallel to the equator (see FRIGID, TEMPERATE, TORRID). **7** an encircling band or stripe distinguishable in colour, texture, or character from the rest of the object encircled. **8** *archaic* a belt or girdle worn round the body. —*v.tr.* **1** encircle as or with a zone. **2** arrange or distribute by zones. **3** assign as or to a particular area. □□ **zonal** *adj.* **zoning** *n.* (in sense 3 of *v.*). [F *zone* or L *zona* girdle f. Gk *zōnē*]

zonk /zɒŋk/ *v. & n. sl.* —*v.* **1** *tr.* hit or strike. **2** (foll. by *out*) **a** *tr.* overcome with sleep; intoxicate. **b** *intr.* fall heavily asleep. —*n.* (often as *int.*) the sound of a blow or heavy impact. [imit.]

zoo /zu:/ *n.* a zoological garden. [abbr.]

zoo- /'zəʊə/ *comb. form* of animals or animal life. [Gk *zōio-* f. *zōion* animal]

zoogeography /ˌzəʊədʒɪ'ɒɡrəfɪ/ *n.* the branch of zoology dealing with the geographical distribution of animals. □□ **zoogeographic** /-ˌdʒiːə'ɡræfɪk/ *adj.* **zoogeographical** /-ˌdʒiːə'ɡræfɪk(ə)l/ *adj.* **zoogeographically** /-ˌdʒiːə'ɡræfɪkəlɪ/ *adv.*

zoography /zəʊ'ɒɡrəfɪ/ *n.* descriptive zoology.

zooid /'zəʊɔɪd/ *n.* **1** a more or less independent invertebrate organism arising by budding or fission. **2** a distinct member of an invertebrate colony. □□ **zooidal** /-'ɔɪd(ə)l/ *adj.* [formed as ZOO- + -OID]

zoolatry /zəʊ'ɒlətrɪ/ *n.* the worship of animals.

zoological /ˌzəʊə'lɒdʒɪk(ə)l, *disp.* ˌzu:ə-/ *adj.* of or relating to zoology. □**zoological garden** (or **gardens**) a public garden or park with a collection of animals for exhibition and study. □□ **zoologically** *adv.*

zoology /zəʊ'ɒlədʒɪ, *disp.* ˌzu:-/ *n.* the scientific study of animals, esp. with reference to their structure, physiology, classification, and distribution. □□ **zoologist** *n.* [mod.L *zoologia* (as ZOO-, -LOGY)]

zoom /zu:m/ *v. & n.* —*v.* **1** *intr.* move quickly, esp. with a buzzing sound. **2 a** *intr.* cause an aeroplane to mount at high speed and a steep angle. **b** *tr.* cause (an aeroplane) to do this. **3 a** *intr.* (of a camera) close up rapidly from a long shot to a close-up. **b** *tr.* cause (a lens or camera) to do this. —*n.* **1** an aeroplane's steep climb. **2** a zooming camera shot. □**zoom lens** a lens allowing a camera to zoom by varying the focal length. [imit.]

zoomancy /'zəʊəˌmænsɪ/ *n.* divination from the appearances or behaviour of animals.

zoomorphic /ˌzəʊə'mɔːfɪk/ *adj.* **1** dealing with or represented in animal forms. **2** having gods of animal form. □□ **zoomorphism** *n.*

zoonosis /ˌzəʊə'nəʊsɪs/ *n.* any of various diseases which can be transmitted to humans from animals. [ZOO- + Gk *nosos* disease]

zoophyte /'zəʊəˌfaɪt/ *n.* a plantlike animal, esp. a coral, sea anemone, or sponge. □□ **zoophytic** /-'fɪtɪk/ *adj.* [Gk *zōophuton* (as ZOO-, -PHYTE)]

zooplankton /ˌzəʊə'plæŋkt(ə)n/ *n.* plankton consisting of animals.

zoospore /'zəʊəˌspɔː(r)/ *n.* a spore of fungi, algae, etc. capable of motion. □□ **zoosporic** /-'spɔːrɪk/ *adj.*

zootomy /zəʊ'ɒtəmɪ/ *n.* the dissection or anatomy of animals.

zoot suit /zu:t/ *n. colloq.* a man's suit with a long loose jacket and high-waisted tapering trousers. [rhyming on SUIT]

zori /'zɒrɪ/ *n.* (*pl.* **zoris**) a Japanese straw or rubber etc. sandal. [Jap.]

zoril /'zɒrɪl/ *n.* (also **zorille**) a flesh-eating African mammal, *Ictonyx striatus*, of the skunk and the weasel family. [F *zorille* f. Sp. *zorrilla* dimin. of *zorro* fox]

Zoroastrian /ˌzɒrəʊ'æstrɪən/ *adj. & n.* (also **Zarathustrian** /ˌzærə'θʊstrɪən/) —*adj.* of or relating to Zoroaster (or Zarathustra) or the dualistic religious system taught by him or his followers in the Zend-Avesta, based on the concept of a conflict between a spirit of light and good and a spirit of darkness and evil. —*n.* a follower of Zoroaster. □□ **Zoroastrianism** *n.* [L *Zoroastres* f. Gk *Zōroastrēs* f. Avestan *Zarathustra*, Persian founder of the religion in the 6th c. BC]

Zouave /zu:'ɑ:v, zwɑ:v/ *n.* a member of a French light-infantry corps originally formed of Algerians and retaining their oriental uniform. [F f. *Zouaoua*, name of a tribe]

zounds /zaʊndz/ *int. archaic* expressing surprise or indignation. [(*God*)'s *wounds* (i.e. those of Christ on the Cross)]

ZPG *abbr.* zero population growth.

Zr *symb. Chem.* the element zirconium.

zucchetto /tsʊ'ketəʊ/ *n.* (*pl.* **-os**) a Roman Catholic ecclesiastic's skullcap, black for a priest, purple for a bishop, red for a cardinal, and white for a pope. [It. *zucchetta* dimin. of *zucca* gourd, head]

zucchini /zu:'ki:nɪ/ *n.* (*pl.* same or **zucchinis**) esp. *US & Austral.* a courgette. [It., pl. of *zucchino* dimin. of *zucca* gourd]

zugzwang /'tsʊktsvɑ:ŋ/ *n. Chess* an obligation to move in one's turn even when this must be disadvantageous. [G f. *Zug* move + *Zwang* compulsion]

Zulu /'zu:lu:/ *n. & adj.* —*n.* **1** a member of a Black South African people orig. inhabiting Zululand and Natal. **2** the language of this people. —*adj.* of or relating to this people or language. [native name]

zwieback /'zwi:bæk, 'tsvi:bɑ:k/ *n.* a kind of biscuit rusk or sweet cake toasted in slices. [G, = twice baked]

Zwinglian /'zwɪŋlɪən, 'tsvɪ-/ *n. & adj.* —*n.* a follower of the Swiss religious reformer U. Zwingli (d. 1531). —*adj.* of or relating to Zwingli or his reforms.

zwitterion /'zwɪtəˌraɪən, 'tsvɪ-/ *n.* a molecule or ion having separate positively and negatively charged groups. [G f. *Zwitter* a hybrid]

zygo- /'zaɪɡəʊ/ *comb. form* joining, pairing. [Gk *zugo-* f. *zugon* yoke]

zygodactyl /ˌzaɪɡəʊ'dæktɪl/ *adj. & n.* —*adj.* (of a bird) having two toes pointing forward and two backward. —*n.* such a bird. □□ **zygodactylous** *adj.*

zygoma /zaɪ'ɡəʊmə, zɪ-/ *n.* (*pl.* **zygomata** /-tə/) the bony arch of the cheek formed by connection of the zygomatic and temporal bones. [Gk *zugōma -atos* f. *zugon* yoke]

zygomatic /ˌzaɪɡə'mætɪk, ˌzɪ-/ *adj.* of or relating to the zygoma. □**zygomatic arch** = ZYGOMA. **zygomatic bone** the bone that forms the prominent part of the cheek.

zygomorphic /ˌzaɪɡə'mɔːfɪk/ *adj.* (also **zygomorphous** /-'mɔːfəs/) (of a flower) divisible into similar halves only by one plane of symmetry.

zygospore /'zaɪɡəˌspɔː(r)/ *n.* a thick-walled spore formed by certain fungi.

zygote /'zaɪɡəʊt/ *n. Biol.* a cell formed by the union of two gametes. □□ **zygotic** /-'ɡɒtɪk/ *adj.* **zygotically** /-'ɡɒtɪkəlɪ/ *adv.* [Gk *zugōtos* yoked f. *zugoō* to yoke]

zymase /'zaɪmeɪs/ *n.* the enzyme fraction in yeast which catalyses the alcoholic fermentation of glucose. [F f. Gk *zumē* leaven]

zymology /zaɪˈmɒlədʒɪ/ n. Chem. the scientific study of fermentation. □□ **zymological** /-məˈlɒdʒɪk(ə)l/ adj. **zymologist** n. [as ZYMASE + -LOGY]

zymosis /zaɪˈməʊsɪs, zɪ-/ n. archaic fermentation. [mod.L f. Gk zumōsis (as ZYMASE)]

zymotic /zaɪˈmɒtɪk, zɪ-/ adj. archaic of or relating to fermentation. □**zymotic disease** archaic an epi-demic, endemic, contagious, infectious, or sporadic disease regarded as caused by the multiplication of germs introduced from outside. [Gk zumōtikos (as ZYMOSIS)]

zymurgy /ˈzaɪmɜːdʒɪ/ n. the branch of applied chemistry dealing with the use of fermentation in brewing etc. [Gk zumē leaven, after metallurgy]

APPENDICES

APPENDICES

APPENDIX I
Countries of the World

(Countries are given for linguistic information on the names in use; some dependent territories are included.)

Country	Person (name in general use)	Related Adjective (in general use)
Afghanistan	Afghan	Afghan
Albania	Albanian	Albanian
Algeria	Algerian	Algerian
America see United States of America		
Andorra	Andorran	Andorran
Angola	Angolan	Angolan
Antigua and Barbuda	Antiguan, Barbudan	Antiguan, Barbudan
Argentina	Argentinian	Argentine or Argentinian
Australia	Australian	Australian
Austria	Austrian	Austrian
the Bahamas	Bahamian	Bahamian
Bahrain	Bahraini	Bahraini
Bangladesh	Bangladeshi	Bangladeshi
Barbados	Barbadian	Barbadian
Belgium	Belgian	Belgian
Belize	Belizian	Belizian
Benin	Beninese	Beninese
Bermuda (dependent territory)	Bermudan or Bermudian	Bermudan or Bermudian
Bhutan	Bhutanese	Bhutanese
Bolivia	Bolivian	Bolivian
Botswana (see also TSWANA in the dictionary)		
Brazil	Brazilian	Brazilian
Britain see Great Britain		
Brunei	Bruneian	Bruneian
Bulgaria	Bulgarian	Bulgarian
Burkina	Burkinese	Burkinese
Burma (now officially called Myanmar)	Burmese	Burmese
Burundi	Burundian	Burundian
Cambodia (also called Kampuchea)	Cambodian	Cambodian
Cameroon	Cameroonian	Cameroonian
Canada	Canadian	Canadian
Cape Verde Islands	Cape Verdean	Cape Verdean
Cayman Islands (dependent territory)	Cayman Islander	
Central African Republic		
Chad	Chadian	Chadian
Chile	Chilean	Chilean

Country	Person (name in general use)	Related Adjective (in general use)
China	Chinese	Chinese
Colombia	Colombian	Colombian
Comoros	Comoran	Comoran
Congo	Congolese	Congolese
Costa Rica	Costa Rican	Costa Rican
Cuba	Cuban	Cuban
Cyprus	Cypriot	Cypriot
Czechoslovakia	Czech *or* Czechoslovak	Czech *or* Czechoslovak
Denmark	Dane	Danish
Djibouti	Djiboutian	Djiboutian
Dominica	Dominican	Dominican
Dominican Republic	Dominican	Dominican
Ecuador	Ecuadorean	Ecuadorean
Egypt	Egyptian	Egyptian
El Salvador	Salvadorean	Salvadorean
England	Englishman, Englishwoman	English
Equatorial Guinea	Equatorial Guinean	
Ethiopia	Ethiopian	Ethiopian
Falkland Islands (*dependent territory*)	Falkland Islander	
Fiji	Fijian	Fijian
Finland	Finn	Finnish
France	Frenchman, Frenchwoman	French
Gabon	Gabonese	Gabonese
Gambia	Gambian	Gambian
German Democratic Republic (East Germany)	East German	East German
Germany, Federal Republic of (West Germany)	West German	West German
Ghana	Ghanaian	Ghanaian
Gibraltar (*dependent territory*)	Gibraltarian	Gibraltarian
Great Britain	Briton	British
Greece	Greek	Greek
Grenada	Grenadian	Grenadian
Guatemala	Guatemalan	Guatemalan
Guinea	Guinean	Guinean
Guinea-Bissau		
Guyana	Guyanese	Guyanese
Haiti	Haitian	Haitian
Holland *see* Netherlands		
Honduras	Honduran	Honduran
Hong Kong (*dependent territory*)		
Hungary	Hungarian	Hungarian

Country	Person (name in general use)	Related Adjective (in general use)
Iceland	Icelander	Icelandic
India	Indian	Indian
Indonesia	Indonesian	Indonesian
Iran	Iranian	Iranian
Iraq	Iraqi	Iraqi
Ireland, Republic of	Irishman[1], Irishwoman[1]	Irish
Israel	Israeli	Israeli
Italy	Italian	Italian
Ivory Coast		
Jamaica	Jamaican	Jamaican
Japan	Japanese	Japanese
Jordan	Jordanian	Jordanian
Kampuchea see Cambodia		
Kenya	Kenyan	Kenyan
Kiribati		Kiribati
Korea, North	North Korean	North Korean
Korea, South	South Korean	South Korean
Kuwait	Kuwaiti	Kuwaiti
Laos	Laotian	Laotian
Lebanon	Lebanese	Lebanese
Lesotho	Mosotho, pl. Basotho	
Liberia	Liberian	Liberian
Libya	Libyan	Libyan
Liechtenstein	Liechtensteiner	
Luxemburg	Luxemburger	
Madagascar	Malagasy or Madagascan	Madagascan or Malagasy
Malawi	Malawian	Malawian
Malaysia	Malaysian	Malaysian
Maldives, the	Maldivian	Maldivian
Mali	Malian	Malian
Malta	Maltese	Maltese
Mauritania	Mauritanian	Mauritanian
Mauritius	Mauritian	Mauritian
Mexico	Mexican	Mexican
Monaco	Monégasque or Monacan	Monégasque or Monacan
Mongolia	Mongolian	Mongolian
Montserrat (dependent territory)		
Morocco	Moroccan	Moroccan
Mozambique	Mozambican	Mozambican
Myanmar see Burma		
Namibia	Namibian	Namibian
Nauru	Nauruan	Nauruan
Nepal	Nepalese	Nepalese

[1] May also denote a person from Northern Ireland.

Country	Person (name in general use)	Related Adjective (in general use)
Netherlands	Dutchman *or* Dutchwoman *or* Netherlander	Dutch
New Zealand	New Zealander	
Nicaragua	Nicaraguan	Nicaraguan
Niger	Nigerien	
Nigeria	Nigerian	Nigerian
Norway	Norwegian	Norwegian
Oman	Omani	Omani
Pakistan	Pakistani	Pakistani
Panama	Panamanian	Panamanian
Papua New Guinea	Papua New Guinean *or* Papuan	Papua New Guinean *or* Papuan
Paraguay	Paraguayan	Paraguayan
Peru	Peruvian	Peruvian
Philippines	Filipino, Filipina	Filipino *or* Philippine
Pitcairn Islands (*dependent territory*)	Pitcairn Islander	
Poland	Pole	Polish
Portugal	Portuguese	Portuguese
Puerto Rico	Puerto Rican	Puerto Rican
Qatar	Qatari	Qatari
Romania	Romanian	Romanian
Russia *see* Union of Soviet Socialist Republics		
Rwanda	Rwandan	Rwandan
St Helena (*dependent territory*)	St Helenian	St Helenian
St Kitts-Nevis-Anguilla		
St Lucia	St Lucian	St Lucian
St Vincent	Vincentian	Vincentian
San Marino		
São Tomé and Principe		
Saudi Arabia	Saudi Arabian *or* Saudi	Saudi Arabian *or* Saudi
Scotland	Scot, Scotsman, Scotswoman	Scottish *or* Scots *or* Scotch (*see* SCOTCH in the dictionary)
Senegal	Senegalese	Senegalese
Seychelles	Seychellois	Seychellois
Sierra Leone	Sierra Leonean	Sierra Leonean
Singapore	Singaporean	Singaporean
Solomon Islands	Solomon Islander	
Somalia	Somali	Somali
South Africa	South African	South African
Soviet Union *see* Union of Soviet Socialist Republics		
Spain	Spaniard	Spanish

Country	Person (name in general use)	Related Adjective (in general use)
Sri Lanka	Sri Lankan	Sri Lankan
Sudan	Sudanese	Sudanese
Surinam	Surinamer or Surinamese	Surinamese
Swaziland	Swazi	Swazi
Sweden	Swede	Swedish
Switzerland	Swiss	Swiss
Syria	Syrian	Syrian
Tanzania	Tanzanian	Tanzanian
Thailand	Thai	Thai
Togo	Togolese	Togolese
Tonga	Tongan	Tongan
Trinidad and Tobago	Trinidadian and Tobagan or Tobagonian	Trinidadian and Tobagan or Tobagonian
Tunisia	Tunisian	Tunisian
Turkey	Turk	Turkish
Tuvalu	Tuvaluan	Tuvaluan
Uganda	Ugandan	Ugandan
Union of Soviet Socialist Republics or Soviet Union	Russian or Soviet	Russian or Soviet
United Arab Emirates		
United Kingdom	Briton	British
United States of America	American	American
Uruguay	Uruguayan	Uruguayan
Vanuatu		
Vatican City		Vatican
Venezuela	Venezuelan	Venezuelan
Vietnam	Vietnamese	Vietnamese
Virgin Islands	Virgin Islander	
Wales	Welshman, Welshwoman	Welsh
Western Samoa	Western Samoan	Western Samoan
Yemen Arab Republic	Yemeni	Yemeni
Yemen, People's Democratic Republic of	South Yemeni	South Yemeni
Yugoslavia	Yugoslav	Yugoslav
Zaïre	Zaïrean	Zaïrean
Zambia	Zambian	Zambian
Zimbabwe	Zimbabwean	Zimbabwean

APPENDIX II
Major Divisions of Geological Time

Era	Period	Epoch	Millions of years ago
Cenozoic	Quaternary	Holocene	0.01
		Pleistocene	2
	Tertiary	Pliocene	5
		Miocene	24
		Oligocene	38
		Eocene	55
		Palaeocene	65
Mesozoic	Cretaceous		144
	Jurassic		213
	Triassic		248
Palaeozoic	Permian		286
	Carboniferous		360
	Devonian		408
	Silurian		438
	Ordovician		505
	Cambrian		590
	Precambrian		

The Chemical Elements

(Further information can be found in the dictionary.)

element	symbol	atomic number	element	symbol	atomic number
actinium	Ac	89	hydrogen	H	1
aluminium	Al	13	indium	In	49
americium	Am	95	iodine	I	53
antimony	Sb	51	iridium	Ir	77
argon	Ar	18	iron	Fe	26
arsenic	As	33	krypton	Kr	36
astatine	At	85	kurchatovium[1]	Ku	104
barium	Ba	56	lanthanum	La	57
berkelium	Bk	97	lawrencium	Lr	103
beryllium	Be	4	lead	Pb	82
bismuth	Bi	83	lithium	Li	3
boron	B	5	lutetium	Lu	71
bromine	Br	35	magnesium	Mg	12
cadmium	Cd	48	manganese	Mn	25
caesium	Cs	55	mendelevium	Md	101
calcium	Ca	20	mercury	Hg	80
californium	Cf	98	molybdenum	Mo	42
carbon	C	6	neodymium	Nd	60
cerium	Ce	58	neon	Ne	10
chlorine	Cl	17	neptunium	Np	93
chromium	Cr	24	nickel	Ni	28
cobalt	Co	27	niobium	Nb	41
copper	Cu	29	nitrogen	N	7
curium	Cm	96	nobelium	No	102
dysprosium	Dy	66	osmium	Os	76
einsteinium	Es	99	oxygen	O	8
erbium	Er	68	palladium	Pd	46
europium	Eu	63	phosphorus	P	15
fermium	Fm	100	platinum	Pt	78
fluorine	F	9	plutonium	Pu	94
francium	Fr	87	polonium	Po	84
gadolinium	Gd	64	potassium	K	19
gallium	Ga	31	praseodymium	Pr	59
germanium	Ge	32	promethium	Pm	61
gold	Au	79	protactinium	Pa	91
hafnium	Hf	72	radium	Ra	88
hahnium[1]	Ha	105	radon	Rn	86
helium	He	2	rhenium	Re	75
holmium	Ho	67	rhodium	Rh	45

[1] Names formed systematically and without attribution are preferred by IUPAC for numbers from 104 onward, and are used exclusively for numbers from 106 onward. Names based on the atomic number are formed on the numerical roots *nil* (= 0), *un* (= 1), *bi* (= 2), etc. (e.g. *unnilquadium* = 104, *ununbium* = 112, etc.)

APPENDIX III

element	symbol	atomic number	element	symbol	atomic number
rubidium	Rb	37	terbium	Tb	65
ruthenium	Ru	44	thallium	Tl	81
rutherfordium[1]	Rf	104	thorium	Th	90
samarium	Sm	62	thulium	Tm	69
scandium	Sc	21	tin	Sn	50
selenium	Se	34	titanium	Ti	22
silicon	Si	14	tungsten	W	74
silver	Ag	47	uranium	U	92
sodium	Na	11	vanadium	V	23
strontium	Sr	38	xenon	Xe	54
sulphur	S	16	ytterbium	Yb	70
tantalum	Ta	73	yttrium	Y	39
technetium	Tc	43	zinc	Zn	30
tellurium	Te	52	zirconium	Zr	40

APPENDIX IV
Weights and Measures

1. British and American, with Approximate Metric Equivalents

Linear Measure
1 inch	= 25.4 millimetres exactly
1 foot = 12 inches	= 0.3048 metre exactly
1 yard = 3 feet	= 0.9144 metre exactly
1 (statute) mile = 1,760 yards	= 1.609 kilometres

Square Measure
1 square inch	= 6.45 sq. centimetres
1 square foot = 144 sq. in.	= 9.29 sq. decimetres
1 square yard = 9 sq. ft.	= 0.836 sq. metre
1 acre = 4,840 sq. yd.	= 0.405 hectare
1 square mile = 640 acres	= 259 hectares

Cubic Measure
1 cubic inch	= 16.4 cu. centimetres
1 cubic foot = 1,728 cu. in.	= 0.0283 cu. metre
1 cubic yard = 27 cu. ft.	= 0.765 cu. metre

Capacity Measure
BRITISH
1 pint = 20 fluid oz.	
= 34.68 cu. in.	= 0.568 litre
1 quart = 2 pints	= 1.136 litres
1 gallon = 4 quarts	= 4.546 litres
1 peck = 2 gallons	= 9.092 litres
1 bushel = 4 pecks	= 36.4 litres
1 quarter = 8 bushels	= 2.91 hectolitres

AMERICAN DRY
1 pint = 33.60 cu. in.	= 0.550 litre
1 quart = 2 pints	= 1.101 litres
1 peck = 8 quarts	= 8.81 litres
1 bushel = 4 pecks	= 35.3 litres

AMERICAN LIQUID
1 pint = 16 fluid oz.	
= 28.88 cu. in.	= 0.473 litre
1 quart = 2 pints	= 0.946 litre
1 gallon = 4 quarts	= 3.785 litres

Avoirdupois Weight
1 grain	= 0.065 gram
1 dram	= 1.772 grams
1 ounce = 16 drams	= 28.35 grams
1 pound = 16 ounces	
= 7,000 grains	= 0.4536 kilogram
1 stone = 14 pounds	= 6.35 kilograms
1 quarter = 2 stones	= 12.70 kilograms
1 hundredweight = 4 quarters	= 50.80 kilograms
1 short ton = 2,000 pounds	= 0.907 tonne
1 (long) ton = 20 hundredweight	= 1.016 tonnes

2. Metric, with Approximate British Equivalents

Linear Measure

1 millimetre	= 0.039 inch
1 centimetre = 10 mm	= 0.394 inch
1 decimetre = 10 cm	= 3.94 inches
1 metre = 10 dm	= 1.094 yards
1 decametre = 10 m	= 10.94 yards
1 hectometre = 100 m	= 109.4 yards
1 kilometre = 1,000 m	= 0.6214 mile

Square Measure

1 square centimetre	= 0.155 sq. inch
1 square metre	= 1.196 sq. yards
1 are = 100 square metres	= 119.6 sq. yards
1 hectare = 100 ares	= 2.471 acres
1 square kilometre	= 0.386 sq. mile

Cubic Measure

1 cubic centimetre	= 0.061 cu. inch
1 cubic metre	= 1.308 cu. yards

Capacity Measure

1 millilitre	= 0.002 pint (British)
1 centilitre = 10 ml	= 0.018 pint
1 decilitre = 10 cl	= 0.176 pint
1 litre = 10 dl	= 1.76 pints
1 decalitre = 10 l	= 2.20 gallons
1 hectolitre = 100 l	= 2.75 bushels
1 kilolitre = 1,000 l	= 3.44 quarters

Weight

1 milligram	= 0.015 grain
1 centigram = 10 mg	= 0.154 grain
1 decigram = 10 cg	= 1.543 grains
1 gram = 10 dg	= 15.43 grains
1 decagram = 10 g	= 5.64 drams
1 hectogram = 100 g	= 3.527 ounces
1 kilogram = 1,000 g	= 2.205 pounds
1 tonne (metric ton) = 1,000 kg	= 0.984 (long) ton

3. Temperature

Fahrenheit: water boils (under standard conditions) at 212° and freezes at 32°.
Celsius or Centigrade: water boils at 100° and freezes at 0°.
Kelvin: water boils at 373.15 K and freezes at 273.15 K.
To convert Centigrade into Fahrenheit: multiply by 9, divide by 5, and add 32.
To convert Fahrenheit into Centigrade: subtract 32, multiply by 5, and divide by 9.
To convert Centigrade into Kelvin: add 273.15.

4. The Power Notation

This expresses concisely any power of 10 (any number that is composed of factors 10), and is sometimes used in the dictionary.

$$10^2 \text{ or ten squared} = 10 \times 10 = 100$$
$$10^3 \text{ or ten cubed} = 10 \times 10 \times 10 = 1,000$$
$$10^4 = 10 \times 10 \times 10 \times 10 = 10,000$$
$$10^{10} = 1 \text{ followed by ten noughts} = 10,000,000,000$$
$$10^{-2} = 1/10^2 = 1/100$$
$$10^{-10} = 1/10^{10} = 1/10,000,000,000$$

5. The Metric Prefixes

	Abbreviations	Factors
deca	da	10
hecto	h	10^2
kilo	k	10^3
mega	M	10^6
giga	G	10^9
tera	T	10^{12}
peta	P	10^{15}
exa	E	10^{18}
deci	d	10^{-1}
centi	c	10^{-2}
milli	m	10^{-3}
micro	μ	10^{-6}
nano	n	10^{-9}
pico	p	10^{-12}
femto	f	10^{-15}
atto	a	10^{-18}

Pronunciations and derivations of these are given at their alphabetical places in the dictionary. They may be applied to any units of the metric system: hectogram (abbr. hg) = 100 grams; kilowatt (abbr. kW) = 1,000 watts; megahertz (MHz) = 1 million hertz; centimetre (cm) = $\frac{1}{100}$ metre; microvolt (μV) = one millionth of a volt; picofarad (pF) = 10^{-12} farad, and are sometimes applied to other units (megabit, microinch).

6. Chemical Notation

The symbol for a molecule shows the symbols for the elements contained in it (C = carbon, H = hydrogen, etc.), each followed by a subscript numeral denoting the number of atoms of the element in the molecule where this number is more than one. For example, the water molecule (H_2O) contains two atoms of hydrogen and one of oxygen.

APPENDIX V
Counties of the United Kingdom

(Official names with abbreviations in general use)

ENGLAND

Avon
Bedfordshire (Beds.)
Berkshire (Berks.)
Buckinghamshire (Bucks.)
Cambridgeshire (Cambs.)
Cheshire (Ches.)
Cleveland
Cornwall (Corn.)
Cumbria
Derbyshire (Derby.)
Devon
Dorset
Durham (Dur.)
East Sussex
Essex
Gloucestershire (Glos.)
Greater London
Greater Manchester
Hampshire (Hants)
Hereford & Worcester
Hertfordshire (Herts.)
Humberside
Isle of Wight (IOW)

Kent
Lancashire (Lancs.)
Leicestershire (Leics.)
Lincolnshire (Lincs.)
Merseyside
Norfolk
Northamptonshire (Northants)
Northumberland (Northumb.)
North Yorkshire
Nottinghamshire (Notts.)
Oxfordshire (Oxon.)
Shropshire
Somerset (Som.)
South Yorkshire
Staffordshire (Staffs.)
Suffolk
Surrey
Tyne and Wear
Warwickshire (War.)
West Midlands
West Sussex
West Yorkshire
Wiltshire (Wilts.)

NORTHERN IRELAND

Antrim
Armagh
Down

Fermanagh (Ferm.)
Londonderry
Tyrone

SCOTLAND

Regions
Borders
Central
Dumfries & Galloway
Fife
Grampian

Highland
Lothian
Strathclyde
Tayside

Islands Areas
Orkney
Shetland

Western Isles

WALES

Clwyd
Dyfed
Gwent
Gwynedd

Mid Glamorgan
Powys
South Glamorgan
West Glamorgan

States of the USA

(with official and official postal abbreviations)

Alabama (Ala., AL)	Montana (Mont., MT)
Alaska (Alas., AK)	Nebraska (Nebr., NB)
Arizona (Ariz., AZ)	Nevada (Nev., NV)
Arkansas (Ark., AR)	New Hampshire (NH)
California (Calif., CA)	New Jersey (NJ)
Colorado (Col., CO)	New Mexico (N. Mex., NM)
Connecticut (Conn., CT)	New York (NY)
Delaware (Del., DE)	North Carolina (NC)
Florida (Fla., FL)	North Dakota (N. Dak., ND)
Georgia (Ga., GA)	Ohio (OH)
Hawaii (HI)	Oklahoma (Okla., OK)
Idaho (ID)	Oregon (Oreg., OR)
Illinois (Ill., IL)	Pennsylvania (Pa., PA)
Indiana (Ind., IN)	Rhode Island (RI)
Iowa (Ia., IA)	South Carolina (SC)
Kansas (Kan., KS)	South Dakota (S. Dak., SD)
Kentucky (Ky., KY)	Tennessee (Tenn., TN)
Louisiana (La., LA)	Texas (Tex., TX)
Maine (Me., ME)	Utah (UT)
Maryland (Md., MD)	Vermont (Vt., VT)
Massachusetts (Mass., MA)	Virginia (Va., VA)
Michigan (Mich., MI)	Washington (Wash., WA)
Minnesota (Minn., MN)	West Virginia (W. Va., WV)
Mississippi (Miss., MS)	Wisconsin (Wis., WI)
Missouri (Mo., MO)	Wyoming (Wyo., WY)

Books of the Bible

OLD TESTAMENT

Genesis (Gen.)
Exodus (Exod.)
Leviticus (Lev.)
Numbers (Num.)
Deuteronomy (Deut.)
Joshua (Josh.)
Judges (Judg.)
Ruth
First Book of Samuel (1 Sam.)
Second Book of Samuel (2 Sam.)
First Book of Kings (1 Kgs.)
Second Book of Kings (2 Kgs.)
First Book of Chronicles (1 Chr.)
Second Book of Chronicles (2 Chr.)
Ezra
Nehemiah (Neh.)
Esther
Job
Psalms (Ps.)
Proverbs (Prov.)

Ecclesiastes (Eccles.)
Song of Songs, Song of Solomon,
    Canticles (S. of S., Cant.)
Isaiah (Isa.)
Jeremiah (Jer.)
Lamentations (Lam.)
Ezekiel (Ezek.)
Daniel (Dan.)
Hosea (Hos.)
Joel
Amos
Obadiah (Obad.)
Jonah
Micah (Mic.)
Nahum (Nah.)
Habakkuk (Hab.)
Zephaniah (Zeph.)
Haggai (Hag.)
Zechariah (Zech.)
Malachi (Mal.)

APOCRYPHA

First Book of Esdras (1 Esd.)
Second Book of Esdras (2 Esd.)
Tobit
Judith
Rest of Esther (Rest of Esth.)
Wisdom of Solomon (Wisd.)
Ecclesiasticus, Wisdom of Jesus the Son
    of Sirach (Ecclus., Sir.)

Baruch
Song of the Three Children
    (S. of III Ch.)
Susanna (Sus.)
Bel and the Dragon (Bel & Dr.)
Prayer of Manasses (Pr. of Man.)
First Book of Maccabees (1 Macc.)
Second Book of Maccabees (2 Macc.)

NEW TESTAMENT

Gospel according to St Matthew (Matt.)
Gospel according to St Mark (Mark)
Gospel according to St Luke (Luke)
Gospel according to St John (John)
Acts of the Apostles (Acts)
Epistle to the Romans (Rom.)
First Epistle to the Corinthians (1 Cor.)
Second Epistle to the Corinthians
    (2 Cor.)
Epistle to the Galatians (Gal.)
Epistle to the Ephesians (Eph.)
Epistle to the Philippians (Phil.)
Epistle to the Colossians (Col.)
First Epistle to the Thessalonians
    (1 Thess.)

Second Epistle to the Thessalonians (2
    Thess.)
First Epistle to Timothy (1 Tim.)
Second Epistle to Timothy (2 Tim.)
Epistle to Titus (Tit.)
Epistle to Philemon (Philem.)
Epistle to the Hebrews (Heb.)
Epistle of James (Jas.)
First Epistle of Peter (1 Pet.)
Second Epistle of Peter (2 Pet.)
First Epistle of John (1 John)
Second Epistle of John (2 John)
Third Epistle of John (3 John)
Epistle of Jude (Jude)
Revelation, Apocalypse (Rev., Apoc.)

APPENDIX VIII
Punctuation Marks

Punctuation is a complicated subject, and only the main principles can be discussed here. The explanations are based on practice in British English; usage in American English differs in some instances. The main headings are as follows:

1. General remarks
2. Capital letter
3. Full stop
4. Semicolon
5. Comma
6. Colon
7. Question mark
8. Exclamation mark
9. Apostrophe
10. Quotation marks
11. Brackets
12. Dash
13. Hyphen

1. General remarks

The purpose of punctuation is to mark out strings of words into manageable groups and help clarify their meaning (or in some cases to prevent a wrong meaning being deduced). The marks most commonly used to divide a piece of prose or other writing are the full stop, the semicolon, and the comma, with the strength of the dividing or separating role diminishing from the full stop to the comma. The full stop therefore marks the main division into sentences; the semicolon joins sentences (as in this sentence); and the comma (which is the most flexible in use and causes most problems) separates smaller elements with the least loss of continuity. Brackets and dashes also serve as separators— often more strikingly than commas, as in this sentence.

2. Capital letter

2.1.1 This is used for the first letter of the word beginning a sentence in most cases:

He decided not to come. Later he changed his mind.

2.1.2 A sentence or clause contained in a subordinate or parenthetic role within a larger one does not normally begin with a capital letter:

I have written several letters (there are many to be written) and hope to finish them tomorrow.

2.1.3 In the following, however, the sentence is a separate one and therefore does begin with a capital letter:

There is more than one possibility. (I have said this often before.) So we should think carefully before acting.

2.1.4 A capital letter also begins sentences that form quoted speech:

The assistant turned and replied, 'There are no more left.'

2.2 It is used in proper names (*Paris, John Smith*), names of people and languages and related adjectives (*Englishman, Austrian, French*), names of institutions and institutional groups (*the British Museum, Protestants, Conservatives*), and names of days and months (*Tuesday, March*) and related words (*Easter Sunday*). It is also used by convention in names that are trade marks (*Biro, Jacuzzi*).

2.3 It is used in titles of books, newspapers, plays, films, television programmes, etc., and in headings and captions.

2.4 It is used in designations of rank or relationship when used as titles (*King John, Aunt Mabel, Pope Gregory*), and to designate divinity (*God, the Almighty*, etc.).

2.5 Lines of verse often begin with a capital letter.

2.6 Many abbreviations consist partly or entirely of the initial letters of words in capital letters (with or without a full stop): *BBC, DoE, M.Litt.*

3. Full stop

3.1 This is used to mark the end of a sentence when it is a statement (and not a question or exclamation). In prose, sentences marked by full stops normally represent a discrete or distinct statement; more closely connected or complementary statements are joined by a semicolon (as here).

3.2.1 Full stops are used to mark many abbreviations (*Weds., Gen., p.m.*). They are often omitted in abbreviations that are familiar or very common (*Dr, Mr, Mrs*, etc.), in abbreviations that consist entirely of capital letters (*BBC, GMT*, etc.), and in acronyms that are pronounced as a word rather than a sequence of letters (*Nato, Ernie*, etc.).

3.2.2 If an abbreviation with a full stop comes at the end of a sentence, another full stop is not added when the full stop of the abbreviation is the last character:

> *They have a collection of many animals, including dogs, cats, tortoises, snakes, etc.*

but

> *They have a collection of many animals (dogs, cats, tortoises, snakes, etc.).*

3.3 A sequence of three full stops is used to mark an ellipsis or omission in a sequence of words, especially when forming an incomplete quotation. When the omission occurs at the end of a sentence, a fourth point is added as the full stop of the whole sentence:

> *He left the room, banged the door, . . . and went out.*
> *The report said: 'There are many issues to be considered, of which the chief are money, time, and personnel. . . . Let us consider personnel first.'*

3.4 A full stop is used as a decimal point (*10.5 per cent; £1.65*), and to divide hours and minutes in giving time (*6.15 p.m.*), although a colon is usual in American use (*6:15 p.m.*).

4. Semicolon

4.1.1 The main role of the semicolon is to unite sentences that are closely associated or that complement or parallel each other in some way, as in the following:

In the north of the city there is a large industrial area with little private housing; further east is the university.
To err is human; to forgive, divine.

4.1.2 It is often used as a stronger division in a sentence that already includes divisions by means of commas:

He came out of the house, which lay back from the road, and saw her at the end of the path; but instead of continuing towards her, he hid until she had gone.

4.2 It is used in a similar way in lists of names or other items, to indicate a stronger division:

I should like to thank the managing director, Stephen Jones; my secretary, Mary Cartwright; and my assistant, Kenneth Sloane.

5. Comma

5.1 Use of the comma is more difficult to describe than other punctuation marks, and there is much variation in practice. Essentially, its role is to give detail to the structure of sentences, especially longer ones, and make their meaning clear. Too many commas can be distracting; too few can make a piece of writing difficult to read or, worse, difficult to understand.

5.2.1 The comma is widely used to separate the main clauses of a compound sentence when they are not sufficiently close in meaning or content to form a continuous unpunctuated sentence, and are not distinct enough to warrant a semicolon. A conjunction such as *and, but, yet*, etc., is normally used:

The road runs through a beautiful wooded valley, and the railway line follows it closely.

5.2.2 It is considered incorrect to join the clauses of a compound sentence without a conjunction. In the following sentence, the comma should either be replaced by a semicolon, or be retained and followed by *and*:

I like swimming very much, I go to the pool every week.

5.2.3 It is also considered incorrect to separate a subject from its verb with a comma:

Those with the smallest incomes and no other means, should get most support.

5.3.1 Commas are usually inserted between adjectives coming before a noun:

An enterprising, ambitious person.
A cold, damp, badly heated room.

5.3.2 But the comma is omitted when the last adjective has a closer relation to the noun than the others:

A distinguished foreign politician.
A little old lady.

5.4 An important role of the comma is to prevent ambiguity or (momentary) misunderstanding, especially after a verb used intransitively where it might otherwise be taken to be transitive:

With the police pursuing, the people shouted loudly.

Other examples follow:

He did not want to leave, from a feeling of loyalty.
In the valley below, the houses appeared very small.
However, much as I should like to I cannot agree.
(compare *However much I should like to I cannot agree.*)

5.5.1 The comma is used in pairs to separate elements in a sentence that are not part of the main statement:

I should like you all, ladies and gentlemen, to raise your glasses.
There is no sense, as far as I can see, in this suggestion.
It appears, however, that we were wrong.

5.5.2 It is also used to separate a relative clause from its antecedent when the clause is not serving an identifying function:

The book, which was on the table, was a present.

In the above sentence, the information in the *which* clause is incidental to the main statement; without the comma, it would form an essential part of it in identifying which book is being referred to (and could be replaced by *that*):

The book which/that was on the table was a present.

5.6.1 Commas are used to separate items in a list or sequence. Usage varies as to the inclusion of a comma before *and* in the last item; the practice in this dictionary is to include it:

The following will report at 9.30 sharp: Jones, Smith, Thompson, and Williams.

5.6.2 A final comma before *and*, when used regularly and consistently, has the advantage of clarifying the grouping at a composite name occurring at the end of a list:

We shall go to Smiths, Boots, Woolworths, and Marks and Spencer.

5.7 A comma is used in numbers of four or more figures, to separate each group of three consecutive figures starting from the right (e.g. *10,135,793*).

6. Colon

6.1 The main role of the colon is to separate main clauses when there is a step forward from the first to the second, especially from introduction to main point, from general statement to example, from cause to effect, and from premiss to conclusion:

There is something I want to say: I should like you all to know how grateful I am to you.

It was not easy: to begin with I had to find the right house.
The weather was bad: so we decided to stay at home.
(In this example, a comma could be used, but the emphasis on cause and effect would be much reduced.)

6.2 It also introduces a list of items. In this use a dash should not be added:

The following will be needed: a pen, pencil, rubber, piece of paper, and ruler.

6.3 It is used to introduce, more formally and emphatically than a comma would, speech or quoted material:

I told them last week: 'Do not in any circumstances open this door.'

7. Question mark

?

7.1.1 This is used in place of the full stop to show that the preceding sentence is a question:

Do you want another piece of cake?
He really is her husband?

7.1.2 It is not used when the question is implied by indirect speech:

I asked you whether you wanted another piece of cake.

7.2 It is used (often in brackets) to express doubt or uncertainty about a word or phrase immediately following or preceding it:

Julius Caesar, born (?) 100 BC.
They were then seen boarding a bus (to London?).

8. Exclamation mark

!

This is used after an exclamatory word, phrase, or sentence expressing any of the following:

8.1 Absurdity:	*What an idea!*
8.2 Command or warning:	*Go to your room!*
	Be careful!
8.3 Contempt or disgust:	*They are revolting!*
8.4 Emotion or pain:	*I hate you!*
	That really hurts!
	Ouch!
8.5 Enthusiasm:	*I'd love to come!*
8.6 Wish or regret:	*Let me come!*
	If only I could swim!

8.7 Wonder, admiration, or surprise: *What a good idea!*
Aren't they beautiful!

9. Apostrophe ,

9.1.1 The main use is to indicate the possessive case, as in *John's book*, *the girls' mother*, etc. It comes before the *s* in singular and plural nouns not ending in *s*, as in *the boy's games* and *the women's games*. It comes after the *s* in plural nouns ending in *s*, as in *the boys' games*.

9.1.2 In singular nouns ending in *s* practice differs between (for example) *Charles'* and *Charles's*; in some cases the shorter form is preferable for reasons of sound, as in *Xerxes' fleet*.

9.1.3 It is also used to indicate a place or business, e.g. *the butcher's*. In this use it is often omitted in some names, e.g. *Smiths*, *Lloyds Bank*.

9.2 It is used to indicate a contraction, e.g. *he's*, *wouldn't*, *Bo's'un*, *o'clock*.

9.3 It is sometimes used to form a plural of individual letters or numbers, although this use is diminishing. It is helpful in *cross your t's* but unnecessary in *MPs* and *1940s*.

9.4 For its use as a quotation mark, see section 10.

10. Quotation marks ' '

10.1 The main use is to indicate direct speech and quotations. A single turned comma (') is normally used at the beginning, and a single apostrophe (') at the end of the quoted matter:

She said, 'I have something to ask you.'

10.2 The closing quotation mark should come after any punctuation mark which is part of the quoted matter, but before any mark which is not:

They shouted, 'Watch out!'.
They were described as 'an unruly bunch'.
Did I hear you say 'go away!'?

10.3 Punctuation dividing a sentence of reported speech is put inside the quotation marks:

'Go away,' he said, 'and don't ever come back.'

10.4 Quotation marks are also used of cited words and phrases:

What does 'integrated circuit' mean?

10.5 A quotation within a quotation is put in double quotation marks:

'Have you any idea,' he said, 'what "integrated circuit" means?'

11. Brackets

11.1 The types of brackets used in normal punctuation are round brackets () and square brackets [].

11.2 The main use of round brackets is to enclose explanations and extra information or comment:

He is (as he always was) a rebel.
Zimbabwe (formerly Rhodesia).
They talked about Machtpolitik *(power politics).*

11.3 They are used to give references and citations:

Thomas Carlyle (1795–1881).
A discussion of integrated circuits (see p. 38).

11.4 They are used to enclose reference letters or figures, e.g. *(1) (a).*

11.5 They are used to enclose optional words:

There are many (apparent) difficulties.
(In this example, the difficulties may or may not be only apparent.)

11.6.1 Square brackets are used less often. The main use is to enclose extra information attributable to someone (normally an editor) other than the writer of the surrounding text:

The man walked in, and his sister [Sarah] greeted him.

11.6.2 They are used in some contexts to convey special kinds of information, especially when round brackets are also used for other purposes: for example, in this dictionary they are used to give the etymologies at the end of entries.

12. Dash

12.1 A single dash is used to indicate a pause, whether a hesitation in speech or to introduce an explanation or expansion of what comes before it:

'I think you should have—told me,' he replied.
We then saw the reptiles—snakes, crocodiles, that sort of thing.

12.2 A pair of dashes is used to indicate asides and parentheses, like the use of commas as explained at 5.5.1 above, but forming a more distinct break:

People in the north are more friendly—and helpful—than those in the south.
There is nothing to be gained—unless you want a more active social life—in moving to the city.

12.3 It is sometimes used to indicate an omitted word, for example a coarse word in reported speech:

'— you all,' he said.

13. Hyphen

13.1 The hyphen has two main functions: to link words or elements of words into longer words and compounds, and to mark the division of a word at the end of a line in print or writing.

13.2.1 The use of the hyphen to connect words to form compound words is diminishing in English, especially when the elements are of one syllable as in *birdsong, eardrum*, and *playgroup*, and also in some longer formations such as *figurehead* and *nationwide*. The hyphen is used more often in routine and occasional couplings, especially when reference to the senses of the separate elements is considered important or unavoidable, as in *boiler-room*. It is often retained to avoid awkward collisions of letters, as in *breast-stroke*.

13.2.2 The hyphen serves to connect words that have a syntactic link, as in *hard-covered books* and *French-speaking people*, where the reference is to books with hard covers and people who speak French, rather than hard books with covers and French people who can speak (which would be the senses conveyed if the hyphens were omitted). It is also used to avoid more extreme kinds of ambiguity, as in *twenty-odd people*.

13.2.3 A particularly important use of the hyphen is to link compounds and phrases used attributively, as in *a well-known man* (but *the man is well known*), and *Christmas-tree lights* (but *the lights on the Christmas tree*).

13.2.4 It is also used to connect elements to form words in cases such as *re-enact* (where the collision of two *es* would be awkward), *re-form* (= to form again, to distinguish it from *reform*), and some other prefixed words such as those in *anti-, non-, over-*, and *post-*. Usage varies in this regard, and much depends on how well established and clearly recognizable the resulting formation is. When the second element is a name, a hyphen is usual (as in *anti-Darwinian*).

13.2.5 It is used to indicate a common second element in all but the last of a list, e.g. *two-, three-*, or *fourfold*.

13.3 The hyphen used to divide a word at the end of a line is a different matter, because it is not a permanent feature of the spelling. It is more common in print, where the text has to be accurately spaced and the margin justified; in handwritten and typed or word-processed material it can be avoided altogether. In print, words need to be divided carefully and consistently, taking account of the appearance and structure of the word. Detailed guidance on word-division may be found in the *Oxford Spelling Dictionary* (1986).

The Greek and Russian Alphabets

THE GREEK ALPHABET

Capital	Lower-case	English transliteration
A	α	a
B	β	b
Γ	γ	g
Δ	δ	d
E	ε	e
Z	ζ	z
H	η	ē
Θ	θ	th
I	ι	i
K	κ	k
Λ	λ	l
M	μ	m
N	ν	n
Ξ	ξ	x
O	ο	o
Π	π	p
P	ρ	r
Σ	σ, (at end of word ς)	s
T	τ	t
Y	υ	u
Φ	φ	ph
X	χ	kh
Ψ	ψ	ps
Ω	ω	ō

' (rough breathing) over vowel = prefixed h (ἁ = ha)

over rho = suffixed h (ῥ = rh)

' (smooth breathing) over vowel or rho: not transliterated

. (iota subscript) under vowel = suffixed i (ᾳ = ai)

APPENDIX IX

THE RUSSIAN ALPHABET

Capital	Lower-case	English transliteration
А	а	a
Б	б	b
В	в	v
Г	г	g
Д	д	d
Е	е	e
Ё	ё	ë
Ж	ж	zh
З	з	z
И	и	i
Й	й	ĭ
К	к	k
Л	л	l
М	м	m
Н	н	n
О	о	o
П	п	p
Р	р	r
С	с	s
Т	т	t
У	у	u
Ф	ф	f
Х	х	kh
Ц	ц	ts
Ч	ч	ch
Ш	ш	sh
Щ	щ	shch
Ъ	ъ	″ ('hard sign')
Ы	ы	y
Ь	ь	′ ('soft sign')
Э	э	é
Ю	ю	yu
Я	я	ya

Notes

Notes

Notes

Notes

Notes

Notes

Notes

Notes

Notes

Principal Abbreviations used in the Dictionary

(*continued*)

perh.	perhaps		Sp.	Spanish
Pers.	Persian		spec.	special(ly)
pers.	person(al)		Stock Exch.	Stock Exchange
Peruv.	Peruvian		subj.	subject; subjunctive
Pharm.	Pharmacy; Pharmacology		superl.	superlative
Philol.	Philology		Sw.	Swedish
Philos.	Philosophy		syll.	syllable
Phoen.	Phoenician		symb.	symbol
Phonet.	Phonetics		syn.	synonym
Photog.	Photography		techn.	technical(ly)
phr.	phrase		Telev.	Television
Phrenol.	Phrenology		Teut.	Teutonic
Physiol.	Physiology		Theatr.	Theatre, Theatrical
pl.	plural		Theol.	Theology
poet.	poetical		tr.	transitive
Pol.	Polish		transf.	in transferred sense
Polit.	Politics		transl.	translation
pop.	popular, not technical		Turk.	Turkish
Port.	Portuguese		Typog.	Typography
poss.	possessive		ult.	ultimate(ly)
prec.	preceded, preceding		uncert.	uncertain
predic.	predicate; predicative(ly)		unexpl.	unexplained
prep.	preposition		univ.	university
pres.part.	present participle		unkn.	unknown
prob.	probable, probably		US	American, in American use
pron.	pronoun		usu.	usual(ly)
pronunc.	pronunciation			
propr.	proprietary term		v.	verb
Prov.	Provençal		var.	variant(s)
Psychol.	Psychology		v.aux.	auxiliary verb
			Vet.	Veterinary
RC Ch.	Roman Catholic Church		v.intr.	intransitive verb
			voc.	vocative
redupl.	reduplicated		v.refl.	reflexive verb
ref.	reference		v.tr.	transitive verb
refl.	reflexive(ly)			
rel.	related; relative		WG	West Germanic
Relig.	Religion		W.Ind.	West Indian, of the West Indies
repr.	representing			
Rhet.	Rhetoric		Zool.	Zoology
rhet.	rhetorical(ly)			
Rmc	Romanic			
Rom.	Roman			
Russ.	Russian			
S.Afr.	South Africa, South African			
S.Amer.	South America, South American			
Sc.	Scottish			
Scand.	Scandinavia, Scandinavian			
Sci.	Science			
Shakesp.	Shakespeare			
sing.	singular			
Sinh.	Sinhalese			
Skr.	Sanskrit			
sl.	slang			
Slav.	Slavonic			
Sociol.	Sociology			